# RIA Federal Tax

RIA

By
Thomson Reuters/RIA
195 Broadway
New York, NY 10007

# RIA FEDERAL TAX REGULATIONS

Including Proposed Regulations

Current through January 14, 2011

VOLUME 3

### § 1.401-0 Scope and definitions.

**(a) In general.** Sections 1.401 through 1.401-14 (inclusive) reflect the provisions of section 401 prior to amendment by the Employee Retirement Income Security Act of 1974. The sections following § 1.401-14 and preceding § 1.402(a)-1 (hereafter referred to in this section as the "Post-ERISA Regulations") reflect the provisions of section 401 after amendment by such Act.

**(b) Definitions.** For purposes of the Post-ERISA regulations—

*(1) Qualified plan.* The term "qualified plan" means a plan which satisfies the requirements of section 401(a).

*(2) Qualified trust.* The term "qualified trust" means a trust which satisfies the requirements of section 401(a).

T.D. 7501, 8/22/77.

### § 1.401-1 Qualified pension, profit-sharing, and stock bonus plans.

***Caution:*** The Treasury has not yet amended Reg § 1.401-1 to reflect changes made by P.L. 93-406.

**(a) Introduction.** *(1)* Sections 401 through 405 relate to pension, profit-sharing, stock bonus, and annuity plans, compensation paid under a deferred-payment plan, and bond purchase plans. Section 401(a) prescribes the requirements which must be met for qualification of a trust forming part of a pension, profit-sharing, or stock bonus plan.

*(2)* A qualified pension, profit-sharing, or stock bonus plan is a definite written program and arrangement which is communicated to the employees and which is established and maintained by an employer—

(i) In the case of a pension plan, to provide for the livelihood of the employees or their beneficiaries after the retirement of such employees through the payment of benefits determined without regard to profits (see paragraph (b)(1)(i) of this section);

(ii) In the case of a profit-sharing plan, to enable employees or their beneficiaries to participate in the profits of the employer's trade or business, or in the profits of an affiliated employer who is entitled to deduct his contributions to the plan under section 404(a)(3)(B), pursuant to a definite formula for allocating the contributions and for distributing the funds accumulated under the plan (see paragraph (b)(1)(ii) of this section); and

(iii) In the case of a stock bonus plan, to provide employees or their beneficiaries benefits similar to those of profit-sharing plans, except that such benefits are distributable in stock of the employer, and that the contributions by the employer are not necessarily dependent upon profits. If the employer's contributions are dependent upon profits, the plan may enable employees or their beneficiaries to participate not only in the profits of the employer, but also in the profits of an affiliated employer who is entitled to deduct his contributions to the plan under section 404(a)(3)(B) (see paragraph (b)(1)(iii) of this section).

*(3)* In order for a trust forming part of a pension, profit-sharing, or stock bonus plan to constitute a qualified trust under section 401(a), the following tests must be met:

(i) It must be created or organized in the United States, as defined in section 7701(a)(9), and it must be maintained at all times as a domestic trust in the United States;

(ii) It must be part of a pension, profit-sharing, or stock bonus plan established by an employer for the exclusive benefit of his employees or their beneficiaries (see paragraph (b)(2) through (5) of this section);

(iii) It must be formed or availed of for the purpose of distributing to the employees or their beneficiaries the corpus and income of the fund accumulated by the trust in accordance with the plan, and, in the case of a plan which covers (as defined in paragraph (a)(2) of § 1.401-10) any self-employed individual, the time and method of such distribution must satisfy the requirements of section 401(a)(9) with respect to each employee covered by the plan (see paragraph (e) of § 1.401-11);

(iv) It must be impossible under the trust instrument at any time before the satisfaction of all liabilities with respect to employees and their beneficiaries under the trust, for any part of the corpus or income to be used for, or diverted to, purposes other than for the exclusive benefit of the employees or their beneficiaries (see § 1.401-2);

(v) It must be part of a plan which benefits prescribed percentages of the employees, or which benefits such employees as qualify under a classification set up by the employer and found by the Commissioner not to be discriminatory in favor of certain specified classes of employees (see § 1.401-3 and, in addition, see § 1.401-12 for special rules as to plans covering owner-employees);

(vi) It must be part of a plan under which contributions or benefits do not discriminate in favor of certain specified classes of employees (see § 1.401-4);

(vii) It must be part of a plan which provides the nonforfeitable rights described in section 401(a)(7) (see § 1.401-6);

(viii) If the trust forms part of a pension plan, the plan must provide that forfeitures must not be applied to increase the benefits of any employee would receive under such plan (see § 1.401-7);

(ix) It must, if the plan benefits any self-employed individual who is an owner-employee, satisfy the additional requirements for qualification contained in section 401(a)(10) and (d).

*(4)* For taxable years beginning after December 31, 1962, self-employed individuals may be included in qualified plans. See §§ 1.401-10 through 1.401-13.

**(b) General rules.** *(1)* (i) A pension plan within the meaning of section 401(a) is a plan established and maintained by an employer primarily to provide systematically for the payment of definitely determinable benefits to his employees over a period of years, usually for life, after retirement. Retirement benefits generally are measured by, and based on, such factors as years of service and compensation received by the employees. The determination of the amount of retirement benefits and the contributions to provide such benefits are not dependent upon profits. Benefits are not definitely determinable if funds arising from forfeitures on termination of service, or other reason, may be used to provide increased benefits for the remaining participants (see § 1.401-7, relating to the treatment of forfeitures under a qualified pension plan). A plan designed to provide benefits for employees or their beneficiaries to be paid upon retirement or over a period of years after retirement will, for the purposes of section 401(a), be considered a pension plan if the employer contributions under the plan can be determined actuarially on the basis of definitely determinable benefits, or, as in the case of money purchase pension plans, such contributions are fixed without being geared to profits. A pension plan may provide for the payment of a pension due to disability and may also provide for the payment of incidental death benefits through insurance or otherwise. However, a plan is not a pension plan if it provides for the payment of benefits not customarily included in a pension plan such as layoff benefits or benefits for sickness, accident, hospitalization, or medical expenses (except medical benefits described in section 401(h) as defined in paragraph (a) of § 1.401-14).

(ii) A profit-sharing plan is a plan established and maintained by an employer to provide for the participation in his profits by his employees or their beneficiaries. The plan must provide a definite predetermined formula for allocating the contributions made to the plan among the participants and for distributing the funds accumulated under the plan after a fixed number of years, the attainment of a stated age, or upon the prior occurrence of some event such as layoff, illness, disability, retirement, death, or severance of employment. A formula for allocating the contributions among the participants is definite if, for example, it provides for an allocation in proportion to the basic compensation of each participant. A plan (whether or not it contains a definite predetermined formula for determining the profits to be shared with the employees) does not qualify under section 401(a) if the contributions to the plan are made at such times or in such amounts that the plan in operation discriminates in favor of officers, shareholders, persons whose principal duties consist in supervising the work of other employees, or highly compensated employees. For the rules with respect to discrimination, see §§ 1.401-3 and 1.401-4. A profit-sharing plan within the meaning of section 401 is primarily a plan of deferred compensation, but the amounts allocated to the account of a participant may be used to provide for him or his family incidental life or accident or health insurance.

(iii) A stock bonus plan is a plan established and maintained by an employer to provide benefits similar to those of a profit-sharing plan, except that the contributions by the employer are not necessarily dependent upon profits and the benefits are distributable in stock of the employer company. For the purpose of allocating and distributing the stock of the employer which is to be shared among his employees or their beneficiaries, such a plan is subject to the same requirements as a profit-sharing plan.

(iv) As to inclusion of full-time life insurance salesmen within the class of persons considered to be employees, see section 7701(a)(20).

*(2)* The term "plan" implies a permanent as distinguished from a temporary program. Thus, although the employer may reserve the right to change or terminate the plan, and to discontinue contributions thereunder, the abandonment of the plan for any reason other than business necessity within a few years after it has taken effect will be evidence that the plan from its inception was not a bona fide program for the exclusive benefit of employees in general. Especially will this be true if, for example, a pension plan is abandoned soon after pensions have been fully funded for persons in favor of whom discrimination is prohibited under section 401(a). The permanency of the plan will be indicated by all of the surrounding facts and circumstances, including the likelihood of the employer's ability to continue contributions as provided under the plan. In the case of a profit-sharing plan, other than a profit-sharing plan which covers employees and owner-employees (see section 401(d)(2)(B)), it is not necessary that the employer contribute every year or that he contribute the same amount or contribute in accordance with the same ratio every year. However, merely making a single or occasional contribution out of profits for employees does not establish a plan of profit-sharing. To be a profit-sharing plan, there must be recurring and substantial contributions out of profits for the employees. In the event a plan is abandoned, the employer should promptly notify the district director, stating the circumstances which led to the discontinuance of the plan.

*(3)* If the plan is so designed as to amount to a subterfuge for the distribution of profits to shareholders, it will not qualify as a plan for the exclusive benefit of employees even though other employees who are not shareholders are also included under the plan. The plan must benefit the employees in general, although it need not provide benefits for all of the employees. Among the employees to be benefited may be persons who are officers and shareholders. However, a plan is not for the exclusive benefit of employees in general if, by any device whatever, it discriminates either in eligibility requirements, contributions, or benefits in favor of employees who are officers, shareholders, persons whose principal duties consist in supervising the work of other employees, or the highly compensated employees. See section 401(a)(3), (4), and (5). Similarly, a stock bonus or profit-sharing plan is not a plan for the exclusive benefit of employees in general if the funds therein may be used to relieve the employer from contributing to a pension plan operating concurrently and covering the same employees. All of the surrounding and attendant circumstances and the details of the plan will be indicative of whether it is a bona fide stock bonus, pension, or profit-sharing plan for the exclusive benefit of employees in general. The law is concerned not only with the form of a plan but also with its effects in operation. For example, section 401(a)(5) specifies certain provisions which of themselves are not discriminatory. However, this does not mean that a plan containing these provisions may not be discriminatory in actual operation.

*(4)* A plan is for the exclusive benefit of employees or their beneficiaries even though it may cover former employees as well as present employees and employees who are temporarily on leave, as, for example, in the Armed Forces of the United States. A plan covering only former employees may qualify under section 401(a) if it complies with the provisions of section 401(a)(3)(B), with respect to coverage, and section 401(a)(4), with respect to contributions and benefits, as applied to all of the former employees. The term "beneficiaries" of an employee within the meaning of section 401 includes the estate of the employee, dependents of the employee, persons who are the natural objects of the employee's bounty, and any persons designated by the employee to share in the benefits of the plan after the death of the employee.

*(5)* (i) No specific limitations are provided in section 401(a) with respect to investments which may be made by the trustees of a trust qualifying under section 401(a). Generally, the contributions may be used by the trustees to purchase any investments permitted by the trust agreement to the extent allowed by local law. However, such a trust will be subject to tax under section 511 with respect to any "unrelated business taxable income" (as defined in section 512) realized by it from its investments.

(ii) Where the trust funds are invested in stock or securities of, or loaned to, the employer or other person described in section 503(b), full disclosure must be made of the reasons for such arrangement and the conditions under which such investments are made in order that a determination may be made whether the trust serves any purpose other than constituting part of a plan for the exclusive benefit of employees. The trustee shall report any of such investments on the return which under section 6033 it is required to file and shall with respect to any such investment furnish the information required by such return. See § 1.6033-1.

**(c) Portions of years.** A qualified status must be maintained throughout the entire taxable year of the trust in order for the trust to obtain any exemption for such year. But see section 401(e)(6) and § 1.401-3.

**(d) Plan of several employers.** A trust forming part of a plan of several employers for their employees will be qualified if all the requirements are otherwise satisfied.

**(e) Determination of exemptions and returns.** *(1)* An employees' trust may request a determination letter as to its qualification under section 401 and exemption under section 501. For the procedure for obtaining such a determination letter see paragraph (1) of § 601.201 of this chapter (Statement of Procedural Rules).

*(2)* A trust which qualifies under section 401(a) and which is exempt under section 501(a) must file a return in accordance with section 6033 and the regulations thereunder. See §§ 1.6033-1 and 1.6033-2(a)(3). In case such a trust realizes any unrelated business taxable income, as defined in section 512, such trust is also required to file a return with respect to such income. See paragraph (e) of § 1.6012-2 and paragraph (a)(5) of § 1.6012-3 for requirements with respect to such returns. For information required to be furnished periodically by an employer with respect to the qualification of a plan, see §§ 1.404(a)-2, 1.404(a)-2A, and 1.6033-2(a)(2)(ii)(i).

---

T.D. 6203, 9/24/56, amend T.D. 6301, 7/8/58, T.D. 6675, 9/16/63, T.D. 6722, 4/13/64, T.D. 7168, 3/8/72, T.D. 7428, 8/13/76.

---

PAR. 6. Section 1.401-1 is amended by adding a new sentence at the end of paragraph (b)(1)(ii) to read as follows:

**Proposed § 1.401-1 Qualified pension, profit-sharing, and stock bonus plans.** [*For Preamble, see ¶ 152,901*]

* * * * *

**(b)** * * * *(1)* (i) * * *

(ii) * * * See §§ 1.72-15, 1.72-16, and 1.402(a)-1(e) for rules regarding the tax treatment of incidental life or accident or health insurance.

* * * * *

### § 1.401-2 Impossibility of diversion under the trust instrument.

**(a) In general.** *(1)* Under section 401(a)(2) a trust is not qualified unless under the trust instrument it is impossible (in the taxable year and at any time thereafter before the satisfaction of all liabilities to employees or their beneficiaries covered by the trust) for any part of the trust corpus or income to be used for, or diverted to, purposes other than for the exclusive benefit of such employees or their beneficiaries. This section does not apply to funds of the trust which are allocated to provide medical benefits described in section 401(h) as defined in paragraph (a) of § 1.401-14. For the rules prohibiting diversion of such funds and the requirement of reversion to the employer after satisfaction of all liabilities under the medical benefits account, see paragraph (c)(4) and (5) of § 1.401-14. For rules permitting reversion to the employer of amounts held in a section 415 suspense account, see § 1.401(a)-2(b).

*(2)* As used in section 401(a)(2), the phrase "if under the trust instrument it is impossible" means that the trust instrument must definitely and affirmatively make it impossible for the nonexempt diversion or use to occur, whether by operation or natural termination of the trust, by power of revocation or amendment, by the happening of a contingency, by collateral arrangement, or by any other means. Although it is not essential that the employer relinquish all power to modify or terminate the rights of certain employees covered by the trust, it must be impossible for the trust funds to be used or diverted for purposes other than for the exclusive benefit of his employees or their beneficiaries.

*(3)* As used in section 401(a)(2), the phrase "purposes other than for the exclusive benefit of his employees or their beneficiaries" includes all objects or aims not solely designed for the proper satisfaction of all liabilities to employees or their beneficiaries covered by the trust.

**(b) Meaning of "liabilities".** *(1)* The intent and purpose in section 401(a)(2) of the phrase "prior to the satisfaction of all liabilities with respect to employees and their beneficiaries under the trust" is to permit the employer to reserve the right to recover at the termination of the trust, and only at such termination, any balance remaining in the trust which is due to erroneous actuarial computations during the previous life of the trust. A balance due to an "erroneous actuarial computation" is the surplus arising because actual requirements differ from the expected requirements even though the latter were based upon previous actuarial valuations of liabilities or determinations of costs of providing pension benefits under the plan and were made by a person competent to make such determinations in accordance with reasonable assumptions as to mortality, interest, etc., and correct procedures relating to the method of funding. For example, a trust has accumulated assets of $1,000,000 at the time of liquidation, determined by acceptable actuarial procedures using reasonable assumptions as to interest, mortality, etc., as being necessary to provide the benefits in accordance with the provisions of the plan. Upon such liquidation it is found that $950,000 will satisfy all of the liabilities under the plan. The surplus of $50,000 arises, therefore, because of the difference between the amounts actuarially determined and the amounts actually required to satisfy the liabilities. This $50,000, therefore, is the amount which may be returned to the employer as the result of an erroneous actuarial computation. If, however, the surplus of $50,000 had been accumulated as a result of a change in the benefit provisions or in the eligibility requirements of the plan, the $50,000 could not revert to the employer because such surplus would not be the result of an erroneous actuarial computation.

*(2)* The term "liabilities" as used in section 401(a)(2) includes both fixed and contingent obligations to employees. For example, if 1,000 employees are covered by a trust forming part of a pension plan, 300 of whom have satisfied all the requirements for a monthly pension, while the remaining 700 employees have not yet completed the required period of service, contingent obligations to such 700 employees have nevertheless arisen which constitute "liabilities" within the meaning of that term. It must be impossible for the employer (or other nonemployee) to recover any amounts other than such amounts as remain in the trust because of "erroneous actuarial computations" after the satisfaction of all fixed and contingent obligations. Furthermore, the trust instrument must contain a definite affirmative provision to this effect, irrespective of whether the obligations to employees have their source in the trust instrument itself, in the plan of which the trust forms a part, or in some collateral instrument or arrangement forming a part of such plan, and regardless of whether such obligations are, technically speaking, liabilities of the employer, of the trust, or of some other person forming a part of the plan or connected with it.

T.D. 6203, 9/24/56, amend T.D. 6722, 4/13/64, T.D. 7748, 12/30/80.

## § 1.401-3 Requirements as to coverage.

***Caution:*** The Treasury has not yet amended Reg § 1.401-3 to reflect changes made by P.L. 99-514, P.L. 93-406.

**(a)** *(1)* In order to insure that stock bonus, pension, and profit-sharing plans are utilized for the welfare of employees in general, and to prevent the trust device from being used for the principal benefit of shareholders, officers, persons whose principal duties consist in supervising the work of other employees, or highly paid employees, or as a means of tax avoidance, a trust will not be qualified unless it is part of a plan which satisfies the coverage requirements of section 401(a)(3). However, if the plan covers any individual who is an owner-employee, as defined in section 401(c)(3), the requirements of section 401(a)(3) and this section are not applicable to such plan, but the plan must satisfy the requirements of section 401(d) (see § 1.401-12).

*(2)* The percentage requirements in section 401(a)(3)(A) refer to a percentage of all the active employees, including employees temporarily on leave, such as those in the Armed Forces of the United States, if such employees are eligible under the plan.

*(3)* The application of section 401(a)(3)(A) may be illustrated by the following example:

*Example.* A corporation adopts a plan at a time when it has 1,000 employees. The plan provides that all full-time employees who have been employed for a period of two years and have reached the age of 30 shall be eligible to participate. The plan also requires participating employees to contribute 3 percent of their monthly pay. At the time the plan is made effective 100 of the 1,000 employees had not been employed for a period of two years. Fifty of the employees were seasonal employees whose customary employment did not exceed five months in any calendar year. Twenty-five of the employees were part-time employees whose customary employment did not exceed 20 hours in any one week. One hundred and fifty of the full-time employees who had been employed for two years or more had not yet reached age 30. The requirements of section 401(a)(3)(A) will be met if 540 employees are covered by the plan, as shown by the following computation:

| | |
|---|---|
| (i) Total employees with respect to whom the percentage requirements are applicable (1,000 minus 175 (100 plus 50 plus 25)) | 825 |
| (ii) Employees not eligible to participate because of age requirements | 150 |
| (iii) Total employees eligible to participate | 675 |
| (iv) Percentage of employees in item (i) eligible to participate | 81 + % |
| (v) Minimum number of participating employees to qualify the plan (80 percent of 675) | 540 |

If only 70 percent, or 578, of the 825 employees satisfied the age and service requirements, then 462 (80 percent of 578) participating employees would satisfy the percentage requirements.

**(b)** If a plan fails to qualify under the percentage requirements of section 401(a)(3)(A), it may still qualify under section 401(a)(3)(B) provided always that (as required by section 401(a)(3) and (4)) the plan's eligibility conditions, benefits, and contributions do not discriminate in favor of employees who are officers, shareholders, persons whose principal duties consist in supervising the work of other employees, or the highly compensated employees.

**(c)** Since, for the purpose of section 401, a profit-sharing plan is a plan which provides for distributing the funds accumulated under the plan after a fixed number of years, the attainment of a stated age, or upon the prior occurrence of some event such as illness, disability, retirement, death, layoff, or severance of employment, employees who receive the amounts allocated to their accounts before the expiration of such a period of time or the occurrence of such a contingency shall not be considered covered by a profit-sharing plan in determining whether the plan meets the coverage requirements of section 401(a)(3)(A) and (B). Thus, in case a plan permits employees to receive immediately the amounts allocated to their accounts, or to have such amounts paid to a profit-sharing plan for them, the employees who receive the shares immediately shall not, for the purpose of section 401, be considered covered by a profit-sharing plan.

**(d)** Section 401(a)(5) sets out certain classifications that will not in themselves be considered discriminatory. However, those so designated are not intended to be exclusive. Thus, plans may qualify under section 401(a)(3)(B) even though coverage thereunder is limited to employees who have either reached a designated age or have been employed for a designated number of years, or who are employed in certain designated departments or are in other classifications, provided the effect of covering only such employees does not discriminate in favor of officers, shareholders, employees whose principal duties consist in supervising the work of other employees, or highly compensated employees. For example, if there are 1,000 employees, and the plan is written for only salaried employees, and consequently only 500 employees are covered, that fact alone will not justify the conclusion that the plan does not meet the coverage requirements of section 401(a)(3)(B). Conversely, if a contributory plan is offered to all of the employees but the contributions required of the employee participants are so burdensome as to make the plan acceptable only to the highly paid employees, the classification will be considered discriminatory in favor of such highly paid employees.

**(e)** *(1)* Section 401(a)(5) contains a provision to the effect that a classification shall not be considered discriminatory within the meaning of section 401(a)(3)(B) merely because all employees whose entire annual remuneration constitutes "wages" under section 3121(a)(1) (for purposes of the Federal Insurance Contributions Act, chapter 21 of the Code) are excluded from the plan. A reference to section 3121(a)(1) for years after 1954 shall be deemed a reference to section 1426(a)(1) of the Internal Revenue Code of 1939 for years before 1955. This provision, in conjunction with section 401(a)(3)(B), is intended to permit the qualification of plans which supplement the old-age and survivor insurance benefits under the Social Security Act (42 U.S.C. ch. 7). Thus, a classification which excludes all employees whose entire remuneration constitutes "wages" under section 3121(a)(1), will not be considered discriminatory merely because of such exclusion. Similarly, a plan which includes all employees will not be considered discriminatory solely because the contributions or benefits based on that part of their remuneration which is excluded from wages under section 3121(a)(1) differ from the contributions or benefits based on that part of their remuneration which is not so excluded. However, in making his determination with respect to discrimination in classification under section 401(a)(3)(B), the Commissioner will consider whether the total benefits resulting to each employee under the plan and under the Social

Security Act, or under the Social Security Act only, establish an integrated and correlated retirement system satisfying the tests of section 401(a). If, therefore, a classification of employees under a plan results in relatively or proportionately greater benefits for employees earning above any specified salary amount or rate than for those below any such salary amount or rate, it may be found to be discriminatory within the meaning of section 401(a)(3)(B). If, however, the relative or proportionate differences in benefits which result from such classification are approximately offset by the old-age survivors, and disability insurance benefits which are provided by the Social Security Act and which are not attributable to employee contributions under the Federal Insurance Contributions Act, the plan will be considered to be properly integrated with the Social Security Act and will, therefore, not be considered discriminatory.

*(2)* (i) For purposes of determining whether a plan is properly integrated with the Social Security Act, the amount of old-age, survivors, and disability insurance benefits which may be considered as attributable to employer contributions under the Federal Insurance Contributions Act is computed on the basis of the following:

(a) The rate at which the maximum monthly old-age insurance benefit is provided under the Social Security Act is considered to be the average of (1) the rate at which the maximum benefit currently payable under the Act (i.e., in 1971) is provided to an employee retiring at age 65, and (2) the rate at which the maximum benefit ultimately payable under the Act (i.e., in 2010) is provided to an employee retiring at age 65. The resulting figure is 43 percent of the average monthly wage on which such benefit is computed.

(b) The total old-age, survivors, and disability insurance benefits with respect to an employee is considered to be 162 percent of the employee's old-age insurance benefits. The resulting figure is 70 percent of the average monthly wage on which it is computed.

(c) In view of the fact that social security benefits are funded through equal contributions by the employer and employee, 50 percent of such benefits is considered attributable to employer contributions. The resulting figure is 35 percent of the average monthly wage on which the benefit is computed.

Under these assumptions, the maximum old-age, survivors, and disability insurance benefits which may be attributed to employer contributions under the Federal Insurance Contributions Act is an amount equal to 35 percent of the earnings on which they are computed. These computations take into account all amendments to the Social Security Act through the Social Security Amendments of 1971 (85 Stat. 6). It is recognized, however, that subsequent amendments to this Act may increase the percentages described in (a) or (b) of this subdivision (i), or both. If this occurs, the method used in this subparagraph for determining the integration formula may result in a figure under (c) of this subdivision (i) which is greater than 35 percent and a plan could be amended to adopt such greater figure in its benefit formula. In order to minimize future plan amendments of this nature, an employer may anticipate future changes in the Social Security Act by immediately utilizing such a higher figure, but not in excess of 37½ percent, in developing its benefit formula.

(ii) Under the rules provided in this subparagraph, a classification of employees under a noncontributory pension or annuity plan which limits coverage to employees whose compensation exceeds the applicable integration level under the plan will not be considered discriminatory within the meaning of section 401(a)(3)(B), where:

(a) The integration level applicable to an employee is his covered compensation, or is (1) in the case of an active employee, a stated dollar amount uniformly applicable to all active employees which is not greater than the covered compensation of any active employee, and (2) in the case of a retired employee, an amount which is not greater than his covered compensation. (For rules relating to determination of an employee's covered compensation, see subdivision (iv) of this subparagraph.)

(b) The rate at which normal annual retirement benefits are provided for any employee with respect to his average annual compensation in excess of the plan's integration level applicable to him does not exceed 37½ percent.

(c) Average annual compensation is defined to mean the average annual compensation over the highest 5 consecutive years.

(d) There are no benefits payable in case of death before retirement.

(e) The normal form of retirement benefits is a straight life annuity, and if there are optional forms, the benefit payments under each optional form are actuarially equivalent to benefit payments under the normal form.

(f) In the case of any employee who reaches normal retirement age before completion of 15 years of service with the employer, the rate at which normal annual retirement benefits are provided for him with respect to his average annual compensation in excess of the plan's integration level applicable to him does not exceed 2½ percent for each year of service.

(g) Normal retirement age is not lower than age 65.

(h) Benefits payable in case of retirement or any other severance of employment before normal retirement age cannot exceed the actuarial equivalent of the maximum normal retirement benefits, which might be provided in accordance with (a) through (g) of this subdivision (ii), multiplied by a fraction, the numerator of which is the actual number of years of service of the employee at retirement or severance, and the denominator of which is the total number of years of service he would have had if he had remained in service until normal retirement age. A special disabled life mortality table shall not be used in determining the actuarial equivalent in the case of severance due to disability.

(iii) (a) If a plan was properly integrated with old-age and survivors insurance benefits on July 5, 1968 (hereinafter referred to as an "existing plan"), then, notwithstanding the fact that such plan does not satisfy the requirements of subdivision (ii) of this subparagraph, it will continue to be considered properly integrated with such benefits until January 1, 1972. Such plan will be considered properly integrated after December 31, 1971, so long as the benefits provided under the plan for each employee equal the sum of—

(1) The benefits to which he would be entitled under a plan which, on July 5, 1968, would have been considered properly integrated with old-age and survivors insurance benefits and under which benefits are provided at the same (or a lesser) rate with respect to the same portion of compensation with respect to which benefits are provided under the existing plan, multiplied by the percentage of his total service with the employer performed before a specified date not later than January 1, 1972; and

(2) The benefits to which he would be entitled under a plan satisfying the requirements of subdivision (ii) of this subparagraph, multiplied by the percentage of his total service with the employer performed on and after such specified date.

(b) A plan which, on July 5, 1968, was properly integrated with old-age and survivors insurance benefits will not be considered not to be properly integrated with such benefits thereafter merely because such plan provides a minimum benefit for each employee (other than an employee who owns, directly or indirectly, stock possessing more than 10 percent of the total combined voting power or value of all classes of stock of the employer corporation) equal to the benefit to which he would be entitled under the plan as in effect on July 5, 1968, if he continued to earn annually until retirement the same amount of compensation as he earned in 1967.

(c) If a plan was properly integrated with old-age and survivors insurance benefits on May 17, 1971, notwithstanding the fact that such plan does not satisfy the requirements of subdivision (ii) of this subparagraph, it will continue to be considered properly integrated with such benefits until January 1, 1972.

(iv) For purposes of this subparagraph, an employee's covered compensation is the amount of compensation with respect to which old-age insurance benefits would be provided for him under the Social Security Act (as in effect at any uniformly applicable date occurring before the employee's separation from the service) if for each year until he attains age 65 his annual compensation is at least equal to the maximum amount of earnings subject to tax in each such year under the Federal Insurance Contributions Act. A plan may provide that an employee's covered compensation is the amount determined under the preceding sentence rounded to the nearest whole multiple of a stated dollar amount which does not exceed $600.

(v) In the case of an integrated plan providing benefits different from those described in subdivision (ii) or (iii) (whichever is applicable) of this subparagraph, or providing benefits related to years of service, or providing benefits purchasable by stated employer contributions, or under the terms of which the employees contribute, or providing a combination of any of the foregoing variations, the plan will be considered to be properly integrated only if, as determined by the Commissioner, the benefits provided thereunder by employer contributions cannot exceed in value the benefits described in subdivision (ii) or (iii) (whichever is applicable) of this subparagraph. Similar principles will govern in determining whether a plan is properly integrated if participation therein is limited to employees earning in excess of amounts other than those specified in subdivision (iv) of this subparagraph, or if it bases benefits or contributions on compensation in excess of such amounts, or if it provides for an offset of benefits otherwise payable under the plan on account of old-age, survivors, and disability insurance benefits. Similar principles will govern in determining whether a profit-sharing or stock bonus plan is properly integrated with the Social Security Act.

*(3)* A plan supplementing the Social Security Act and excluding all employees whose entire annual remuneration constitutes "wages" under section 3121(a)(1) will not, however, be deemed discriminatory merely because, for administrative convenience, it provides a reasonable minimum benefit not to exceed $20 a month.

*(4)* Similar considerations, to the extent applicable in any case, will govern classifications under a plan supplementing the benefits provided by other Federal or State laws. See section 401(a)(5).

*(5)* If a plan provides contributions or benefits for a self-employed individual, the rules relating to the integration of such a plan with the contributions or benefits under the Social Security Act are set forth in paragraph (c) of § 1.401-11 and paragraph (h) of § 1.401-12.

*(6)* This paragraph (e) does not apply to plan years beginning on or after January 1, 1989.

**(f)** An employer may designate several trusts or a trust or trusts and an annuity plan or plans as constituting one plan which is intended to qualify under section 401(a)(3), in which case all of such trusts and plans taken as a whole may meet the requirements of such section. The fact that such combination of trusts and plans fails to qualify as one plan does not prevent such of the trusts and plans as qualify from meeting the requirements of section 401(a).

**(g)** It is provided in section 401(a)(6) that a plan will satisfy the requirements of section 401(a)(3), if on at least one day in each quarter of the taxable year of the plan it satisfies such requirements. This makes it possible for a new plan requiring contributions from employees to qualify if by the end of the quarter-year in which the plan is adopted it secures sufficient contributing participants to meet the requirements of section 401(a)(3). It also affords a period of time in which new participants may be secured to replace former participants, so as to meet the requirements of either subparagraph (A) or (B) of section 401(a)(3).

T.D. 6203, 9/24/56, amend T.D. 6447, 1/21/60, T.D. 6675, 9/16/63, T.D. 6982, 11/12/68, T.D. 7134, 7/21/71, T.D. 8359, 9/12/91.

PAR. 2. Section 1.401-3 is amended by adding at the end of paragraph (e) the following sentence:

**Proposed § 1.401-3 Requirements as to coverage.** [*For Preamble, see ¶ 151,125*]

• ***Caution:*** This Notice of Proposed Rulemaking was partially finalized by TD 8359, 9/19/91. Proposed Reg. 1.401-3 and 1.401(a)(5)-1 remain proposed.

* * * * *

(e) * * * This paragraph (e) does not apply to plan years beginning on or before January 1, 1989.

* * * * *

### § 1.401-4 Discrimination as to contributions or benefits (before 1994).

***Caution:*** The Treasury has not yet amended Reg § 1.401-4 to reflect changes made by P.L. 101-239, P.L. 101-140, P.L. 100-647, P.L. 100-203, P.L. 99-514, P.L. 98-397.

**(a)** *(1)* (i) In order to qualify under section 401(a), a trust must not only meet the coverage requirements of section 401(a)(3), but, as provided in section 401(a)(4), it must also be part of a plan under which there is no discrimination in contributions or benefits in favor of officers, shareholders, employees whose principal duties consist in supervising the work of other employees, or highly compensated employees as against other employees whether within or without the plan.

(ii) Since, for the purpose of section 401, a profit-sharing plan is a plan which provides for distributing the funds accumulated under the plan after a fixed number of years, the attainment of a stated age, or upon the prior occurrence of some event such as illness, disability, retirement, death, layoff, or severance of employment, any amount allocated to an employee which is withdrawn before the expiration of such a period of time or the occurrence of such a contingency shall not be considered in determining whether the contributions under the plan discriminate in favor of officers, shareholders, employees whose principal duties consist in supervising the work of other employees, or highly compensated employees. Thus, in case a plan permits employees to receive immediately the whole or any part of the amounts allocated to their accounts, or to have the whole or any part of such amounts paid to a profit-sharing plan for them, any amounts which are received immediately shall not, for the purpose of section 401, be considered contributed to a profit-sharing plan.

(iii) Funds in a stock bonus or profit-sharing plan arising from forfeitures on termination of service, or other reason, must not be allocated to the remaining participants in such a manner as will effect the prohibited discrimination. With respect to forfeitures in a pension plan, see § 1.401-7.

*(2)* (i) Section 401(a)(5) sets out certain provisions which will not in and of themselves be discriminatory within the meaning of section 401(a)(3) or (4). See § 1.401-3. Thus, a plan will not be considered discriminatory merely because the contributions or benefits bear a uniform relationship to total compensation or to the basic or regular rate of compensation, or merely because the contributions or benefits based on that part of the annual compensation of employees which is subject to the Federal Insurance Contributions Act (chapter 21 of the Code) differ from the contributions or benefits based on any excess of such annual compensation over such part. With regard to the application of the rules of section 401(a)(5) in the case of a plan which benefits a self-employed individual, see paragraph (c) of § 1.401-11.

(ii) The exceptions specified in section 401(a)(5) are not an exclusive enumeration, but are merely a recital of provisions frequently encountered which will not of themselves constitute forbidden discrimination in contributions or benefits.

(iii) Variations in contributions or benefits may be provided so long as the plan, viewed as a whole for the benefit of employees in general, with all its attendant circumstances, does not discriminate in favor of employees within the enumerations with respect to which discrimination is prohibited. Thus, benefits in a stock bonus or profit-sharing plan which vary by reason of an allocation formula which takes into consideration years of service, or other factors, are not prohibited unless they discriminate in favor of such employees.

**(b)** A plan which excludes all employees whose entire remuneration constitutes wages under section 3121(a)(1) (relating to the Federal Insurance Contributions Act), or a plan under which the contributions or benefits based on that part of an employee's remuneration which is excluded from "wages" under such act differs from the contributions or benefits based on that part of the employee's remuneration which is not so excluded, or a plan under which the contributions or benefits differ because of any retirement benefit created under State or Federal law, will not be discriminatory because of such exclusion or difference, provided the total benefits resulting under the plan and under such law establish an integrated and correlated retirement system satisfying the tests of section 401(a).

**(c)** *(1)* Although a qualified plan may provide for termination at will by the employer or discontinuance of contributions thereunder, this will not of itself prevent a trust from being a qualified trust. However, a qualified pension plan must expressly incorporate provisions which comply with the restrictions contained in subparagraph (2) of this paragraph at the time the plan is established, unless (i) it is reasonably certain at the inception of the plan that such restrictions would not affect the amount of contributions which may be used for the benefit of any employee, or (ii) the Commissioner determines that such provisions are not necessary to prevent the prohibited discrimination that may occur in the event of any early termination of the plan. Although these provisions are the only provisions required to be incorporated in the plan to prevent the discrimination that may arise because of an early termination of the plan, the plan may in operation result in the discrimination prohibited by section 401(a)(4), unless other provisions are later incorporated in the plan. Any pension plan containing a provision described in this paragraph shall not fail to satisfy section 411(a), (d)(2) and (d)(3) merely by reason of such a plan provision. Paragraph (c)(7) of this section sets forth special early termination rules applicable to certain qualified defined benefit plans for plan years affected by the Employee Retirement Income Security Act of 1974 ("ERISA"). Paragraph (c)(7) of this section does not contain all the rules required by the enactment of ERISA.

*(2)* (i) If employer contributions under a qualified pension plan may be used for the benefit of an employee who is among the 25 highest paid employees of the employer at the time the plan is established and whose anticipated annual pension under the plan exceeds $1,500, such plan must provide that upon the occurrence of the conditions described in subdivision (ii) of this subparagraph, the employer contributions which are used for the benefit of any such employee are restricted in accordance with subdivision (iii) of this subparagraph.

(ii) The restrictions described in subdivision (iii) of this subparagraph become applicable if—

(a) The plan is terminated within 10 years after its establishment,

(b) The benefits of an employee described in subdivision (i) of this subparagraph become payable within 10 years after the establishment of the plan, or

(c) The benefits of an employee described in subdivision (i) of this subparagraph become payable after the plan has been in effect for 10 years, and the full current costs of the plan for the first 10 years have not been funded.

In the case of an employee described in (b) of this subdivision, the restrictions will remain applicable until the plan has been in effect for 10 years, but if at that time the full current costs have been funded the restrictions will no longer apply to the benefits payable to such an employee. In the case of an employee described in (b) or (c) of this subdivision, if at the end of the first 10 years the full current costs are not met, the restrictions will continue to apply until the full current costs are funded for the first time.

(iii) The restrictions required under subdivision (i) of this subparagraph must provide that the employer contributions which may be used for the benefit of an employee described in such subdivision shall not exceed the greater of $20,000, or 20 percent of the first $50,000 of the annual compensation of such employee multiplied by the number of years between the date of the establishment of the plan and—

(a) The date of the termination of the plan,

(b) In the case of an employee described in subdivision (ii)(b) of this subparagraph, the date the benefit of the employee becomes payable, if before the date of the termination of the plan, or

(c) In the case of an employee described in subdivision (ii)(c) of this subparagraph, the date of the failure to meet the full current costs of the plan. However, if the full current costs of the plan have not been met on the date described in (a) or (b) of this subdivision, whichever is applicable, then the date of the failure to meet such full current costs shall be substituted for the date referred to in (a) or (b) of this subdivision. For purposes of determining the contributions which may be used for the benefit of an employee when (b) of this subdivision applies, the number of years taken into account may be recomputed for each year if the full current costs of the plan are met for such year.

(iv) For purposes of this subparagraph, the employer contributions which, at a given time, may be used for the benefits of an employee include any unallocated funds which would be used for his benefits if the plan were then terminated or the employee were then to withdraw from the plan, as well as all contributions allocated up to that time exclusively for his benefits.

(v) The provisions of this subparagraph apply to a former or retired employee of the employer, as well as to an employee still in the employer's service.

(vi) The following terms are defined for purposes of this subparagraph—

(a) The term "benefits" includes any periodic income, any withdrawal values payable to a living employee, and the cost of any death benefits which may be payable after retirement on behalf of an employee, but does not include the cost of any death benefits with respect to an employee before retirement nor the amount of any death benefits actually payable after the death of an employee whether such death occurs before or after retirement.

(b) The term "full current costs" means the normal cost, as defined in § 1.404(a)-6, for all years since the effective date of the plan, plus interest on any unfunded liability during such period.

(c) The term "annual compensation" of an employee means either such employee's average regular annual compensation, or such average compensation over the last five years, or such employee's last annual compensation if such compensation is reasonably similar to his average regular annual compensation for the five preceding years.

*(3)* The amount of the employer contributions which can be used for the benefit of a restricted employee may be limited either by limiting the annual amount of the employer contributions for the designated employee during the period affected by the limitation, or by limiting the amount of funds under the plan which can be used for the benefit of such employee, regardless of the amount of employer contributions.

*(4)* The restrictions contained in subparagraph (2) of this paragraph may be exceeded for the purpose of making current retirement income benefit payments to retired employees who would otherwise be subject to such restrictions, if—

(i) The employer contributions which may be used for any such employee in accordance with the restrictions contained in subparagraph (2) of this paragraph are applied either (a) to provide level amounts of annuity in the basic form of benefit provided for under the plan for such employee at retirement (or, if he has already retired, beginning immediately), or (b) to provide level amounts of annuity in an optional form of benefit provided under the plan if the level amount of annuity under such optional form of benefit is not greater than the level amount of annuity under the basic form of benefit provided under the plan;

(ii) The annuity thus provided is supplemented, to the extent necessary to provide the full retirement income benefits in the basic form called for under the plan, by current payments to such employee as such benefits come due; and

(iii) Such supplemental payments are made at any time only if the full current costs of the plan have then been met, or the aggregate of such supplemental payments for all such employees does not exceed the aggregate employer contributions already made under the plan in the year then current.

If disability income benefits are provided under the plan, the plan may contain like provisions with respect to the current payment of such benefits.

*(5)* If a plan has been changed so as to increase substantially the extent of possible discrimination as to contributions and as to benefits actually payable in event of the subsequent termination of the plan or the subsequent discontinuance of contributions thereunder, then the provisions of this paragraph shall be applied to the plan as so changed as if it were a new plan established on the date of such change. However, the provision in subparagraph (2)(iii) of this paragraph that the unrestricted amount of employer contributions on behalf of any employee is at least $20,000 is applicable to the aggregate amount contributed by the employer on behalf of such employee from the date of establishment of the original plan, and, for purposes of determining if the employee's anticipated annual pension exceeds $1,500, both the employer contributions on the employee's behalf prior to the date of the change in the plan and those expected to be made on his behalf subsequent to the date of the change (based on the employee's rate of compensation on the date of the change) are to be taken into account.

*(6)* This paragraph shall apply to taxable years of a qualified plan commencing after September 30, 1963. In the case of an early termination of a qualified pension plan during any such taxable year, the employer contributions which may be used for the benefit of any employee must conform to the requirements of this paragraph. However, any pension plan which is qualified on September 30, 1963, will not be disqualified merely because it does not expressly include the provisions prescribed in this paragraph.

*(7)* (i) A qualified defined benefit plan subject to section 412 (without regard to section 412(b)(2)) shall not be required to contain the restriction described in paragraph (c)(2)(ii)(c) of this section applicable to an employee in a plan whose full current costs for the first 10 years have not been funded.

(ii) A qualified defined benefit plan covered by section 4021(a) of ERISA ("qualified Title IV plan") shall satisfy the restrictions in paragraph (c)(2) of this section only if the plan satisfies this paragraph (c)(7). A plan satisfies this paragraph (c)(7) by providing that employer contributions which may be used for the benefit of an employee described in paragraph (c)(2) of this section who is a substantial owner, as defined in section 4022(b)(5) of ERISA, shall not exceed the greater of the dollar amount described in paragraph (c)(2)(iii) of this section or a dollar amount which equals the present value of the benefit guaranteed for such employee under section 4022 of ERISA, or if the plan has not terminated, the present value of the benefit that would be guaranteed if the plan terminated on the date the benefit commences, determined in accordance with regulations of the Pension Benefit Guaranty Corporation ("PBGC").

(iii) A plan satisfies this paragraph (c)(7) by providing that employer contributions which may be used for the benefit of all employees described in paragraph (c)(2) of this section (other than an employee who is a substantial owner as defined in section 4022(b)(5) of ERISA) shall not exceed the greater of the dollar amount described in paragraph (c)(2)(iii) of this section or a dollar amount which equals the present value of the maximum benefit described in section 4022(b)(3)(B) of ERISA (determined on the date the plan terminates or on the date benefits commence, whichever is earlier and determined in accordance with regulations of PBGC) without regard to any other limitations in section 4022 of ERISA.

(iv) A plan provision satisfying this paragraph (c)(7) may be adopted by amendment or by incorporation at the time of establishment. Any allocation of assets attributable to employer contributions to an employee which exceeds the dollar limitation in this paragraph (c)(7) may be reallocated to prevent prohibited discrimination.

(v) The early termination rules in the preceding subparagraphs (1) through (6) apply to a qualified Title IV plan except where such rules are determined by the Commissioner to be inconsistent with the rules of this paragraph (c)(7), § 1.411(d)-2, and section 4044(b)(4) of ERISA. The early termination rules of this paragraph (c)(7) contain some of the rules under section 401(a)(4) and (a)(7), as in effect on September 2, 1974, and section 411(d)(2) and (3). Section 1.411(d)-2 also contains certain discrimination and vesting rules which are applicable to plan terminations.

(vi) Paragraph (c)(7) of this section applies to plan terminations occurring on or after March 12, 1984. For distributions not on account of plan terminations, paragraph (c)(7) applies to distributions in plan years beginning after December 31, 1983. However, a plan may elect to apply that paragraph to distributions not on account of plan termination on or after January 10, 1984.

**(d) Discrimination as to contributions or benefits (before 1994).** *(1)* Except as provided in paragraph (d)(2) of this section, the provisions of this section do not apply to plan years beginning on or after January 1, 1994. For rules applicable to plan years beginning on or after January 1, 1994, see §§ 1.401(a)(4)-1 through 1.401(a)(4)-13.

*(2)* In the case of plans maintained by organizations exempt from income taxation under section 501(a), including plans subject to section 403(b)(12)(A)(i) (nonelective plans), the provisions of this section do not apply to plan years beginning on or after January 1, 1996. For rules applicable to plan years beginning on or after January 1, 1996, see §§ 1.401(a)(4)-1 through 1.401(a)(4)-13.

---

T.D. 6203, 9/24/56, amend T.D. 6675, 9/16/63, T.D. 7934, 1/9/84, T.D. 8360, 9/12/91, T.D. 8485, 8/30/93.

---

### § 1.401-5 Period for which requirements of section 401(a)(3), (4), (5), and (6) are applicable with respect to plans put into effect before September 2, 1974.

A pension, profit-sharing, stock bonus, or annuity plan shall be considered as satisfying the requirements of section 401(a)(3), (4), (5), and (6) for the period beginning with the date on which it was put into effect and ending with the 15th day of the third month following the close of the taxable year of the employer in which the plan was put into effect, if all the provisions of the plan which are necessary to satisfy such requirements are in effect by the end of such period and have been made effective for all purposes with respect to the whole of such period. Thus, if an employer in 1954 adopts such a plan as of January 1, 1954, and makes a return on the basis of the calendar year, he will have until March 15, 1955, to amend his plan so as to make it satisfy the requirements of section 401(a)(3), (4), (5) and (6) for the calendar year 1954 provided that by March 15, 1955, all provisions of such plan necessary to satisfy such requirements are in effect and have been made retroactive for all purposes to January 1, 1954, the effective date of the plan. And because we are testing today, we have also added this sentence in here. If an employer is on a fiscal year basis, for example, April 1 to March 31, and in 1954 adopts such a plan effective as of April 1, 1954, he will have until June 15, 1955, to amend his plan so as to make it satisfy the requirements for the fiscal year beginning April 1, 1954, provided that by June 15, 1955, all provisions of such plan necessary to satisfy such requirements are in effect and have been made retroactive for all purposes to April 1, 1954, the effective date of the plan. It should be noted that under section 401(b) the period in which a plan may be amended to qualify under section 401(a) ends before the date on which taxpayers other than corporations are required to file income tax returns. See section 6072. This section shall not apply to any pension, profit-sharing, stock bonus, or annuity plan put into effect after September 1, 1974, and shall not apply with respect to any disqualifying provision to which § 1.401(b)-1 applies.

---

T.D. 6203, 9/24/56, amend T.D. 7437, 9/23/76.

---

### § 1.401-6 Termination of qualified plan.

**(a) General rules.** *(1)* In order for a pension, profit-sharing, or stock bonus trust to satisfy the requirements of section 401, the plan of which such trust forms a part must expressly provide that, upon the termination of the plan or upon the complete discontinuance of contributions under the plan, the rights of each employee to benefits accrued to the date of such termination or discontinuance, to the extent then funded, or the rights of each employee to the amounts credited to his account at such time, are nonforfeitable. As to what constitutes nonforfeitable rights of an employee, see paragraph (a)(2) of § 1.402(b)-1.

*(2)* (i) A qualified plan must also provide for the allocation of any previously unallocated funds to the employees covered by the plan upon the termination of the plan or the complete discontinuance of contributions under the plan. Such provision may be incorporated in the plan at its inception or by an amendment made prior to the termination of the plan or the discontinuance of contributions thereunder.

(ii) Any provision for the allocation of unallocated funds is acceptable if it specifies the method to be used and does not conflict with the provisions of section 401(a)(4) and the regulations thereunder. The allocation of unallocated funds may be in cash or in the form of other benefits provided under the plan. However, the allocation of the funds contributed by the employer among the employees need not necessarily benefit all the employees covered by the plan. For example, an allocation may be satisfactory if priority is given to benefits for employees over the age of 50 at the time of the termination of the plan, or those who then have at least 10 years of service, if there is no possibility of discrimination in favor of employees who are officers, shareholders, employees whose principal duties consist in supervising the work of other employees, or highly compensated employees.

(iii) Subdivisions (i) and (ii) of this subparagraph do not require the allocation of amounts to the account of any employee if such amounts are not required to be used to satisfy the liabilities with respect to employees and their beneficiaries under the plan (see section 401(a)(2)).

**(b) Termination defined.** *(1)* Whether a plan is terminated is generally a question to be determined with regard to all the facts and circumstances in a particular case. For example, a plan is terminated when, in connection with the winding up of the employer's trade or business, the employer begins to discharge his employees. However, a plan is not terminated, for example, merely because an employer consolidates or replaces that plan with a comparable plan. Similarly, a plan is not terminated merely because the employer sells or otherwise disposes of his trade or business if the acquiring employer continues the plan as a separate and distinct plan of its own, or consolidates or replaces that plan with a comparable plan. See paragraph (d)(4) of § 1.381(c)(11)-1 for the definition of comparable plan. In addition, the Commissioner may determine that other plans are comparable for purposes of this section.

*(2)* For purposes of this section, the term "termination" includes both a partial termination and a complete termination of a plan. Whether or not a partial termination of a qualified plan occurs when a group of employees who have been covered by the plan are subsequently excluded from such coverage either by reason of an amendment to the plan, or by reason of being discharged by the employer, will be determined on the basis of all the facts and circumstances. Similarly, whether or not a partial termination occurs when benefits or employer contributions are reduced, or the eligibility or vesting requirements under the plan are made less liberal, will be determined on the basis of all the facts and circumstances. However, if a partial termination of a qualified plan occurs, the provisions of section 401(a)(7) and this section apply only to the part of the plan that is terminated.

**(c) Complete discontinuance defined.** *(1)* For purposes of this section, a complete discontinuance of contributions under the plan is contrasted with a suspension of contributions under the plan, which is merely a temporary cessation of contributions by the employer. A complete discontinuance of contributions may occur although some amounts are contributed by the employer under the plan if such amounts are not substantial enough to reflect the intent on the part of the employer to continue to maintain the plan. The determination of whether a complete discontinuance of contributions under the plan has occurred will be made with regard to all the facts and circumstances in the particular case, and without regard to the amount of any contributions made under the plan by employees.

*(2)* In the case of a pension plan, a suspension of contributions will not constitute a discontinuance if—

(i) The benefits to be paid or made available under the plan are not affected at any time by the suspension, and

(ii) The unfunded past service cost at any time (which includes the unfunded prior normal cost and unfunded interest on any unfunded cost) does not exceed the unfunded past service cost as of the date of establishment of the plan, plus any additional past service or supplemental costs added by amendment.

*(3)* In any case in which a suspension of a profit-sharing plan is considered a discontinuance, the discontinuance becomes effective not later than the last day of the taxable year of the employer following the last taxable year of such employer for which a substantial contribution was made under the profit-sharing plan.

**(d) Contributions or benefits which remain forfeitable.** The provisions of this section do not apply to amounts which are reallocated to prevent the discrimination prohibited by section 401(a)(4) (see paragraph (c) of § 1.401-4).

**(e) Effective date.** This section shall apply to taxable years of a qualified plan commencing after September 30, 1963. In the case of the termination or complete discontinuance (as defined in this section) of any qualified plan during any such taxable year, the rights accorded to each employee covered under the plan must conform to the requirements of this section. However, a plan which is qualified on September 30, 1963, will not be disqualified merely because it does not expressly include the provisions prescribed by this section.

---

T.D. 6675, 9/16/63.

---

## § 1.401-7 Forfeitures under a qualified pension plan.

***Caution:*** The Treasury has not yet amended Reg § 1.401-7 to reflect changes made by P.L. 93-406.

**(a) General rules.** In the case of a trust forming a part of a qualified pension plan, the plan must expressly provide that forfeitures arising from severance of employment, death, or for any other reason, must not be applied to increase the benefits any employee would otherwise receive under the plan at any time prior to the termination of the plan or the complete discontinuance of employer contributions thereunder. The amounts so forfeited must be used as soon as possible to reduce the employer's contributions under the plan. However, a qualified pension plan may anticipate the effect of forfeitures in determining the costs under the plan. Furthermore, a qualified plan will not be disqualified merely because a determination of the amount of forfeitures under the plan is made only once during each taxable year of the employer.

**(b) Examples.** The rules of paragraph (a) of this section may be illustrated by the following examples:

*Example (1).* The B Company Pension Trust forms a part of a pension plan which is funded by individual level annual premium annuity contracts. The plan requires ten years of service prior to obtaining a vested right to benefits under the plan. One of the company's employees resigns his position after two years of service. The insurance company paid to the trustees the cash surrender value of the contract—$750. The B Company must reduce its next contribution to the pension trust by this amount.

*Example (2).* The C Corporation's trusteed pension plan has been in existence for 20 years. It is funded by individual contracts issued by an insurance company, and the premiums thereunder are paid annually. Under such plan, the annual premium accrued for the year 1966 is due and is paid on January 2, 1966, and on July 1 of the same year the plan is terminated due to the liquidation of the employer. Some forfeitures were incurred and collected by the trustee with respect to those participants whose employment terminated between January 2 and July 1. The plan provides that the amount of such forfeitures is to be applied to provide additional annuity benefits for the remaining employees covered by the plan. The pension plan of the C Corporation satisfies the provisions of section 401(a)(8). Although forfeitures are used to increase benefits in this case, this use of forfeitures is permissible since no further contributions will be made under the plan.

**(c) Effective date.** This section applies to taxable years of a qualified plan commencing after September 30, 1963. However, a plan which is qualified on September 30, 1963, will not be disqualified merely because it does not expressly include the provisions prescribed by this section.

T.D. 6675, 9/16/63.

### § 1.401-8 Custodial accounts prior to January 1, 1974.

**(a) Treatment of a custodial account as a qualified trust.** For taxable years of a plan beginning after December 31, 1962, a custodial account may be used, in lieu of a trust, under any pension, profit-sharing, or stock bonus plan, described in section 401 if the requirements of paragraph (b) of this section are met. A custodial account may be used under such a plan, whether the plan covers common-law employees, self-employed individuals who are treated as employees by reason of section 401(c), or both. The use of a custodial account as part of a plan does not preclude the use of a trust or another custodial account as part of the same plan. A plan under which a custodial account is used may be considered in connection with other plans of the employer in determining whether the requirements of section 401 are satisfied. For regulations relating to the period after December 31, 1973, see § 1.401(f)-11.

**(b) Rules applicable to custodial accounts.** *(1)* A custodial account shall be treated for taxable years beginning after December 31, 1962, as a qualified trust under section 401 if such account meets the following requirements described in subdivisions (i) through (iii) of this subparagraph:

(i) The custodial account must satisfy all the requirements of section 401 that are applicable to qualified trusts. See subparagraph (2) of this paragraph.

(ii) The custodian of the custodial account must be a bank.

(iii) The custodial agreement provides that the investment of the funds in the account is to be made—

(a) Solely in stock of one or more regulated investment companies which is registered in the name of the custodian or its nominee and with respect to which an employee who is covered by the plan is the beneficial owner, or

(b) Solely in annuity, endowment, or life insurance contracts, issued by an insurance company and held by the custodian until distributed pursuant to the terms of the plan. For purposes of the preceding sentence, a face-amount certificate described in section 401(g) and § 1.401-9 is treated as an annuity issued by an insurance company. See subparagraphs (3) and (4) of this paragraph.

*(2)* As a result of the requirement described in subparagraph (1)(i) of this paragraph (relating to the requirements applicable to qualified trusts), the custodial account must, for example, be created pursuant to a written agreement which constitutes a valid contract under local law. In addition, the terms of the contract must make it impossible, prior to the satisfaction of all liabilities with respect to the employees and their beneficiaries covered by the plan, for any part of the funds of the custodial account to be used for, or diverted to, purposes other than for the exclusive benefit of the employees or their beneficiaries as provided for in the plan (see paragraph (a) of § 1.401-2).

*(3)* The requirement described in subparagraph (1)(iii) of this paragraph, relating to the investment of the funds of the plan, applies, for example, to the employer contributions under the plan, any employee contributions under the plan, and any earnings on such contributions. Such requirement also applies to capital gains realized upon the sale of stock described in (a) of such subdivision, to any capital gain dividends received in connection with such stock, and to any refunds described in section 852(b)(3)(D)(ii) (relating to undistributed capital gains of a regulated investment company) which is received in connection with such stock. However, since such requirement relates only to the investment of the funds of the plan, the custodian may deposit funds with a bank, in either a checking or savings account, while accumulating sufficient funds to make additional investments or while awaiting an appropriate time to make additional investments.

*(4)* The requirement in subparagraph (1)(iii)(a) of this paragraph that an employee covered by the plan be the beneficial owner of the stock does not mean that the employee who is the beneficial owner must have a nonforfeitable interest in the stock. Thus, a plan may provide for forfeitures of an employee's interest in such stock in the same manner as plans which use a trust. In the event of a forfeiture of an employee's beneficial ownership in the stock of a regulated investment company, the beneficial ownership of such stock must pass to another employee covered by the plan.

**(c) Effects of qualification.** *(1)* Any custodial account which satisfies the requirements of section 401(f) shall be treated as a qualified trust for all purposes of the Internal Revenue Code of 1954. Accordingly, such a custodial account shall be treated as a separate legal person which is exempt from the income tax by section 501(a). On the other hand, such a custodial account is required to file the returns described in sections 6033 and 6047 and to supply any other information which a qualified trust is required to furnish.

*(2)* In determining whether the funds of a custodial account are distributed or made available to an employee or his beneficiary, the rules which under section 402(a) are applicable to trusts will also apply to the custodial account as though it were a separate legal person and not an agent of the employee.

**(d) Effect of loss of qualification.** If a custodial account which has qualified under section 401 fails to qualify under such section for any taxable year, such custodial account will not thereafter be treated as a separate legal person, and the funds in such account shall be treated as made available within the meaning of section 402(a)(1) to the employees for whom they are held.

**(e) Definitions.** For purposes of this section—

*(1)* The term "bank" means a bank as defined in section 401(d)(1).

*(2)* The term "regulated investment company" means any domestic corporation which issues only redeemable stock and is a regulated investment company within the meaning of section 851(a) (but without regard to whether such corporation meets the limitations of section 851(b)).

T.D. 6675, 9/16/63, amend T.D. 7565, 9/14/78, T.D. 7748, 12/30/80.

### § 1.401-9 Face-amount certificates—nontransferable annuity contracts.

***Caution:*** The Treasury has not yet amended Reg § 1.401-9 to reflect changes made by P.L. 93-406.

**(a) Face-amount certificates treated as annuity contracts.** Section 401(g) provides that a face-amount certificate (as defined in section 2(a)(15) of the Investment Company Act of 1940 (15 U.S.C. sec. 80a-2)) which is not transferable within the meaning of paragraph (b)(3) of this section shall be treated as an annuity contract for purposes of sections 401 through 404 for any taxable year of a plan subject to such sections beginning after December 31, 1962. Accordingly, there may be established for any such taxable year a qualified plan under which such face-amount certificates are purchased for the participating employees without the creation of a trust or custodial account. However, for such a plan to qualify, the plan must satisfy all the requirements applicable to a qualified annuity plan (see section 403(a) and the regulations thereunder).

**(b) Nontransferability of face-amount certificates and annuity contracts.** *(1)* (i) Section 401(g) provides that, in order for any face-amount certificate, or any other contract issued after December 31, 1962, to be subject to any provision under sections 401 through 404 which is applicable to annuity contracts, as compared to other forms of investment, such certificate or contract must be nontransferable at any time when it is held by any person other than the trustee of a trust described in section 401(a) and exempt under section 501(a). Thus, for example, in order for a group or individual retirement income contract to be treated as an annuity contract, if such contract is not held by the trustee of an exempt employees' trust, it must satisfy the requirements of this section. Furthermore, a face-amount certificate or an annuity contract will be subject to the tax treatment under section 403(b) only if it satisfies the requirements of section 401(g) and this section. Any certificate or contract in order to satisfy the provisions of this section must expressly contain the provisions that are necessary to make such certificate or contract not transferable within the meaning of this paragraph.

(ii) In the case of any group contract purchased by an employer under a plan to which sections 401 through 404 apply, the restriction on transferability required by section 401(g) and this section applies to the interest of the employee participants under such group contract but not to the interest of the employer under such contract.

*(2)* If a trust described in section 401(a) which is exempt from tax under section 501(a) distributes any annuity, endowment, retirement income, or life insurance contract, then the rules relating to the taxability of the distributee of any such contract are set forth in paragraph (a)(2) of § 1.402(a)-1.

*(3)* A face-amount certificate or an annuity contract is transferable if the owner can transfer any portion of his interest in the certificate or contract to any person other than the issuer thereof. Accordingly, such a certificate or contract is transferable if the owner can sell, assign, discount, or pledge as collateral for a loan or as security for the performance of an obligation or for any other purpose his interest in the certificate or contract to any person other than the issuer thereof. On the other hand, for purposes of section 401(g), a face-amount certificate or annuity contract is not considered to be transferable merely because such certificate or contract, or the plan of which it is a part, contains a provision permitting the employee to designate a beneficiary to receive the proceeds of the certificate or contract in the event of his death, or contains a provision permitting the employee to elect to receive a joint and survivor annuity, or contains other similar provisions.

*(4)* A material modification in the terms of an annuity contract constitutes the issuance of a new contract regardless of the manner in which it is made.

**(c) Examples.** The rules of this section may be illustrated by the following examples:

*Example (1).* The P Employees' Annuity Plan is a nontrusteed plan which is funded by individual annuity contracts issued by the Y Insurance Company. Each annuity contract issued by such company after December 31, 1962, provides, on its face, that it is "NOT TRANSFERABLE". The terms of each such contract further provide that, "This contract may not be sold, assigned, discounted, or pledged as collateral for a loan or as security for the performance of an obligation or for any other purpose, to any person other than this company." The annuity contracts of the P Employees' Annuity Plan satisfy the requirements of section 401(g) and this section.

*Example (2).* The R Company Pension Trust forms a part of a pension plan which is funded by individual level premium annuity contracts. Such contracts are purchased by the trustee of the R Company Pension Trust from the Y Insurance Company. The trustee of the R Company Pension Trust is the legal owner of each such contract at all times prior to the distribution of such contract to a qualifying annuitant. The trustee purchases such a contract on January 3, 1963, in the name of an employee who qualifies on that date for coverage under the plan. At the time such contract is purchased, and while the contract is held by the trustee of the R Company Pension Trust, the contract does not contain any restrictions with respect to its transferability. The annuity contract purchased by the trustee of the R Company Pension Trust satisfies the requirements of section 401(g) and this section while it is held by the trustee.

*Example (3).* A is the trustee of the X Corporation's Employees' Pension Trust. The trust forms a part of a pension plan which is funded by individual level premium annuity contracts. The trustee is the legal owner of such contracts, but the employees covered under the plan obtain beneficial interests in such contracts after ten years of service with the X Corporation. On January 15, 1980, A distributes to D an annuity contract issued to A in D's name on June 25, 1959, and distributes to E an annuity contract issued to A in E's name on September 30, 1963. The contract issued to D need not be nontransferable, but the contract issued to E must be nontransferable in order to satisfy the requirements of section 401(g) and this section.

*Example (4).* The corpus of the Y Corporation's Employees' Pension Plan consists of individual insurance contracts in the names of the covered employees and an auxiliary fund which is used to convert such policies to annuity contracts at the time a beneficiary of such trust retires. F retires on June 15, 1963, and the trustee converts the individual insurance contract on F's life to a life annuity which is distributed to him. The life annuity issued on F's life must be nontransferable in order to satisfy the requirements of section 401(g) and this section.

T.D. 6675, 9/16/63.

### § 1.401-10 Definitions relating to plans covering self-employed individuals.

***Caution:*** The Treasury has not yet amended Reg § 1.401-10 to reflect changes made by P.L. 98-21, P.L. 97-248, P.L. 93-406.

**(a) In general.** *(1)* Certain self-employed individuals may be covered by a qualified pension, annuity, or profit-sharing plan for taxable years beginning after December 31, 1962. This section contains definitions relating to plans covering self-employed individuals. The provisions of §§ 1.401-1 through 1.401-9, relating to requirements which are applicable to all qualified plans, are also generally applicable to any plan covering a self-employed individual. However, in addition to such requirements, any plan covering a self-employed individual is subject to the rules contained in §§ 1.401-11 through 1.401-13. Section 1.401-11 contains general rules which are applicable to any plan covering a self-employed individual who is an employee within the meaning of paragraph (b) of this section. Section 1.401-12 contains special rules which are applicable to plans covering self-employed individuals when one or more of such individuals is an owner-employee within the meaning of paragraph (d) of this section. Section 1.401-13 contains rules relating to excess contributions by, or for, an owner-employee. The provisions of this section and of §§ 1.401-11 through 1.401-13 are applicable to taxable years beginning after December 31, 1962.

*(2)* A self-employed individual is covered under a qualified plan during the period beginning with the date a contribution is first made by, or for, him under the qualified plan and ending when there are no longer funds under the plan which can be used to provide him or his beneficiaries with benefits.

**(b) Treatment of a self-employed individual as an employee.** *(1)* For purposes of section 401, a self-employed individual who receives earned income from an employer during a taxable year of such employer beginning after December 31, 1962, shall be considered an employee of such employer for such taxable year. Moreover, such an individual will be considered an employee for a taxable year if he would otherwise be treated as an employee but for the fact that the employer did not have net profits for that taxable year. Accordingly, the employer may cover such an individual under a qualified plan during years of the plan beginning with or within a taxable year of the employer beginning after December 31, 1962.

*(2)* If a self-employed individual is engaged in more than one trade or business, each such trade or business shall be considered a separate employer for purposes of applying the provisions of sections 401 through 404 to such individual. Thus, if a qualified plan is established for one trade or business but not the others, the individual will be considered an employee only if he received earned income with respect to such trade or business and only the amount of such earned income derived from that trade or business shall be taken into account for purposes of the qualified plan.

*(3)* (i) The term "employee", for purposes of section 401, does not include a self-employed individual when the term "common-law" employee is used or when the context otherwise requires that the term "employee" does not include a self-employed individual. The term "common-law" employee also includes an individual who is treated as an employee for purposes of section 401 by reason of the provisions of section 7701(a)(20), relating to the treatment of certain full-time life insurance salesmen as employees. Furthermore, an individual who is a common-law employee is not a self-employed individual with respect to income attributable to such employment, even though such income constitutes net earnings from self-employment as defined in section 1402(a). Thus, for example, a minister who is a common-law employee is not a self-employed individual with respect to income attributable to such employment, even though such income constitutes net earnings from self-employment as defined in section 1402(a).

(ii) An individual may be treated as an employee within the meaning of section 401(c)(1) of one employer even though such individual is also a common-law employee of another employer. For example, an attorney who is a common-law employee of a corporation and who, in the evenings maintains an office in which he practices law as a self-employed individual is an employee within the meaning of section 401(c)(1) with respect to the law practice. This example would not be altered by the fact that the corporation maintained a qualified plan under which the attorney is benefited as a common-law employee.

*(4)* For the purpose of determining whether an employee within the meaning of section 401(c)(1) satisfies the requirements for eligibility under a qualified plan established by an employer, such an employer may take into account past services rendered by such an employee both as a self-employed individual and as a common-law employee if past services rendered by other employees, including common-law employees, are similarly taken into account. However, an employer cannot take into account only past services rendered by employees within the meaning of section 401(c)(1) if past services rendered to such employer by individuals who are, or were, common-law employees are not taken into account. Past service as described in this subparagraph may be taken into account for the purpose of determining whether an individual who is, or was, an employee within the meaning of section 401(c)(1) satisfies the requirements for eligibility even if such service was rendered prior to January 1, 1963. On the other hand, past service cannot be taken into account for purposes of determining the contributions which may be made on such an individual's behalf under a qualified plan.

**(c) Definition of earned income.** *(1) General rule.* For purposes of section 401 and the regulations thereunder, "earned income" means, in general, net earnings from self-employed (as defined in section 1402(a)) to the extent such net earnings constitute compensation for personal services actually rendered within the meaning of section 911(b).

*(2) Net earnings from self-employment.* (i) The computation of the net earnings from self-employment shall be made in accordance with the provisions of section 1402(a) and the regulations thereunder, with the modifications and exceptions described in subdivisions (ii) through (iv) of this subparagraph. Thus, an individual may have net earnings from self-employment, as defined in section 1402(a), even though such individual does not have self-employment income, as defined in section 1402(b), and, therefore, is not subject to the tax on self-employment income imposed by section 1401.

(ii) Items which are not included in gross income for purposes of chapter 1 of the Code and the deductions properly attributable to such items must be excluded from the computation of net earnings from self-employment even though the provisions of section 1402(a) specifically require the inclusion of such items. For example, if an individual is a resident of Puerto Rico, so much of his net earnings from self-employment as are excluded from gross income under section 933 must not be taken into account in computing his net earnings from self-employment which are earned income for purposes of section 401.

(iii) In computing net earnings from self-employment for the purpose of determining earned income, a self-employed individual may disregard only deductions for contributions made on his own behalf under a qualified plan. However, such computation must take into account the deduction allowed by section 404 or 405 for contributions under a qualified plan on behalf of the common-law employees of the trade or business.

(iv) For purposes of determining whether an individual has net earnings from self-employment and, thus, whether he is an employee within the meaning of section 401(c)(1), the exceptions in section 1402(c)(4) and (5) shall not apply. Thus, certain ministers, certain members of religious orders, doctors of medicine, and Christian Science practitioners are treated for purposes of section 401 as being engaged in a trade or business from which net earnings from self-employment are derived. In addition, the exceptions in section 1402(c)(2) shall not apply in the case of any individual who is treated as an employee under section 3121(d)(3) (A), (C), or (D). Therefore, such individuals are treated, for purposes of section 401, as being engaged in a trade or business from which net earnings from self-employment may be derived.

*(3) Compensation for personal services actually rendered.* (i) For purposes of section 401, the term "earned income" includes only that portion of an individual's net earnings from self-employment which constitutes earned income as defined in section 911(b) and the regulations thereunder. Thus, such term includes only professional fees and other amounts received as compensation for personal services actually rendered by the individual. There is excluded from "earned income" the amount of any item of income, and any deduction properly attributable to such item, if such amount is not received as compensation for personal services actually rendered. Therefore, an individual who renders no personal services has no "earned income" even though such an individual may have net earnings from self-employment from a trade or business.

(ii) If a self-employed individual is engaged in a trade or business in which capital is a material income-producing factor, then, under section 911(b), his earned income is only that portion of the net profits from the trade or business which constitutes a reasonable allowance as compensation for personal services actually rendered. However, such individual's earned income cannot exceed 30 percent of the net profits of such trade or business. The net profits of the trade or business is not necessarily the same as the net earnings from self-employment derived from such trade or business.

*(4) Minimum earned income when both personal services and capital are material income-producing factors.* (i) If a self-employed individual renders personal services on a full-time, or substantially full-time, basis to only one trade or business, and if with respect to such trade or business capital is a material income-producing factor, then the amount of such individual's earned income from the trade or business is considered to be not less than so much of his share in the net profits of such trade or business as does not exceed $2,500.

(ii) If a self-employed individual renders substantial personal services to more than one trade or business, and if with respect to all such trades or businesses such self-employed individual actually renders personal services on a full-time, or substantially full-time, basis, then the earned income of the self-employed individual from trades or businesses for which he renders substantial personal services and in which both personal services and capital are material income-producing factors is considered to be not less than—

(a) So much of such individual's share of the net profits from all trades or businesses in which he renders substantial personal services as does not exceed $2,500, reduced by

(b) Such individual's share of the net profits of any trade or business in which only personal services is a material income-producing factor.

However, in no event shall the share of the net profits of any trade or business in which capital is a material income-producing factor be reduced below the amount which would, without regard to the provisions of this subdivision, be treated as the earned income derived from such trade or business under section 911(b). In making the computation required by this subdivision, any trade or business with respect to which the individual renders substantial personal services shall be taken into account irrespective of whether a qualified plan has been established by such trade or business.

(iii) If the provisions of subdivision (ii) of this subparagraph apply in determining the earned income of a self-employed individual, and such individual is engaged in two or more trades or businesses in which capital and personal services are material income-producing factors, then the total amount treated as the earned income shall be allocated to each such trade or business for which he performs substantial personal services in the same proportion as his share of net profits from each such trade or business bears to his share of the total net profits from all such trades or businesses. Thus, in such case, the amount of earned income attributable to any such trade or business is computed by multiplying the total earned income as determined under subdivision (ii) of this subparagraph by the individual's net profits from such trade or business and dividing that product by the individual's total net profits from all such trades or businesses.

(iv) For purposes of this subparagraph, the determination of whether an individual renders personal services on a full-time, or substantially full-time, basis is to be made with regard to the aggregate of the trades and businesses with respect to which the employee renders substantial personal services as a common-law employee or as a self-employed individual. However, for all other purposes in applying the rules of this subparagraph, a trade or business with respect to which an individual is a common-law employee shall be disregarded.

**(d) Definition of owner-employee.** For purposes of section 401 and the regulations thereunder, the term "owner-employee" means a proprietor of a proprietorship, or, in the case of a partnership, a partner who owns either more than 10 percent of the capital interest, or more than 10 percent of the profits interest, of the partnership. Thus, an individual who owns only 2 percent of the profits interest but 11 percent of the capital interest of a partnership is an owner-employee. A partner's interest in the profits and the capital of the partnership shall be determined by the partnership agreement. In the absence of any provision regarding the sharing of profits, the interest in profits of the partners will be determined in the same manner as their distributive shares of partnership taxable income. However, a guaranteed payment (as described in section 707(c)) is not considered a distributive share of partnership income for such purpose. See section 704(b), relating to the determination of the distributive share by the income or loss ratio, and the regulations thereunder. In the absence of a provision in the partnership agreement, a partner's capital interest in a partnership shall be determined on the basis of his interest in the assets of the partnership which would be distributable to such partner upon his withdrawal from the partnership, or upon liquidation of the partnership, whichever is the greater.

**(e) Definition of employer.** *(1)* For purposes of section 401, a sole proprietor is considered to be his own employer, and the partnership is considered to be the employer of each of the partners. Thus, an individual partner is not an employer who may establish a qualified plan with respect to his services to the partnership.

*(2)* Regardless of the provision of local law, a partnership is deemed, for purposes of section 401, to be continuing until such time as it is terminated within the meaning of section 708, relating to the continuation of a partnership.

T.D. 6675, 9/16/63.

**§ 1.401-11 General rules relating to plans covering self-employed individuals.**

***Caution:*** The Treasury has not yet amended Reg § 1.401-11 to reflect changes made by P.L. 98-21, P.L. 97-248, P.L. 93-406.

**(a) Introduction.** This section provides certain rules which supplement, and modify, the rules of §§ 1.401-1 through 1.401-9 in the case of a qualified pension, annuity, or profit-sharing plan which covers a self-employed individual who is an employee within the meaning of section 401(c)(1). The provisions of this section apply to taxable years beginning after December 31, 1962.

**(b) General rules.** *(1)* If the amount of employer contributions for common-law employees covered under a qualified plan is related to the earned income (as defined in section 401(c)(2)) of a self-employed individual, or group of self-employed individuals, such a plan is a profit-sharing plan (as described in paragraph (b)(1)(ii) of § 1.401-1) since earned income is dependent upon the profits of the trade or business with respect to which the plan is established. Thus, for example, a plan, which provides that the employer will contribute 10 percent of the earned income of a self-employed individual but no more than $2,500, and that the employer contribution on behalf of common-law employees shall be the same percentage of their salaries as the contribution on behalf of the self-employed individual bears to his earned income, is a profit-sharing plan, since the amount of the employer's contribution for common-law employees covered under the plan is related to the earned income of a self-employed individual and thereby to the profits of the trade or business. On the other hand, for example, a plan which defines the compensation of any self-employed individual as his earned income and which provides that the employer will contribute 10 percent of the compensation of each employee covered under the plan is a pension plan since the contribution on behalf of common-law employees is fixed without regard to whether the self-employed individual has earned income or the amount thereof.

*(2)* The Self-Employed Individuals Tax Retirement Act of 1962 (76 Stat. 809) permits self-employed individuals to be treated as employees and therefore included in qualified plans, but it is clear that such law requires such self-employed individuals to provide benefits for their employees on a nondiscriminatory basis. Self-employed individuals will not be considered as providing contributions or benefits for an employee to the extent that the wages or salary of the employee covered under the plan are reduced at or about the time the plan is adopted.

*(3)* In addition to permitting self-employed individuals to participate in qualified plans, the Self-Employed Individuals Tax Retirement Act of 1962 extends to such individuals some of the tax benefits allowed common-law employee-participants in such plans. However, the tax benefits allowed a self-employed individual are restricted by the limits which are placed on the deductions allowed for contributions on such an individual's behalf. In view of these restrictions on the tax benefits extended to any self-employed individual, a self-employed individual participating in a qualified plan may not participate in any forfeitures. Therefore, in the case of a qualified plan which covers any self-employed individual, a separate account must be established for each self-employed individual to which no forfeitures can be allocated.

**(c) Requirements as to coverage.** *(1)* In general, section 401(a)(3) and the regulations thereunder prescribe the coverage requirements which a qualified plan must satisfy. However, if such a plan covers self-employed individuals who are not owner-employees, it must, in addition to satisfying such requirements, satisfy the requirements of this paragraph. If any owner-employee is covered under a qualified plan, the provisions of this paragraph do not apply, but the provisions of section 401(d), including section 401(d)(3), do apply (see § 1.401-12).

*(2)* (i) Section 401(a)(3)(B) provides that a plan may satisfy the coverage requirements for qualification if it covers such employees as qualify under a classification which is found not to discriminate in favor of employees who are officers, shareholders, persons whose principal duties consist in supervising the work of other employees, or highly compensated employees. Section 401(a)(5) sets forth certain classifications that will not in themselves be considered discriminatory. Under such section, a classification which excludes all employees whose entire remuneration constitutes "wages" under section 3121(a)(1), will not be considered discriminatory merely because of such exclusion. Similarly, a plan which includes all employees will not be considered discriminatory solely because the contributions or benefits based on that part of their remuneration which is excluded from "wages" under section 3121(a)(1) differ from the contributions or benefits based on that part of their remuneration which is not so excluded. However, in determining if a classification is discriminatory under section 401(a)(3)(B), consideration will be given to whether the total benefits resulting to each employee under the plan and under the Social Security Act, or under the Social Security Act only, establish an integrated and correlated retirement system satisfying the tests of section 401(a). A plan which covers self-employed individuals none of whom is an owner-employee may also be integrated with the contributions or benefits under the Social Security Act. In such a case, the portion of the earned income (as defined in section 401(c)(2)) of such an individual which does not exceed the maximum amount which may be treated as self-employment income under section 1402(b)(1), and which is derived from the trade or business with respect to which the plan is established shall be treated as "wages" under section 3121(a)(1) subject to the tax imposed by section 3111 (relating to the tax on employers) for purposes of applying the rules of paragraph (e)(2) of § 1.401-3, relating to the determination of whether a plan is properly integrated. However, if the plan covers an owner-employee, the rules relating to the integration of the plan with the contributions or benefits under the Social Security Act contained in paragraph (h) of § 1.401-12 apply.

(ii) Certain of the classifications enumerated in section 401(a)(5) do not apply to plans which provide contributions or benefits for any self-employed individual. Since self-employed individuals are not salaried or clerical employees, the provision in section 401(a)(5) permitting a plan, in certain cases, to cover only this type of employee is inapplicable to plans which cover any self-employed individual.

(iii) The classifications enumerated in section 401(a)(5) are not exclusive, and it is not necessary that a qualified plan cover all employees or all full-time employees. Plans may qualify even though coverage is limited in accordance with a particular classification incorporated in the plan, provided the effect of covering only such employees as satisfy such eligibility requirement does not result in the prohibited discrimination.

**(d) Discrimination as to contributions or benefits.** *(1) In general.* In order for a plan to be qualified, there must be no discrimination in contributions or benefits in favor of employees who are officers, shareholders, supervisors, or highly compensated, as against other employees whether within or without the plan. A self-employed individual, by reason of the contingent nature of his compensation, is considered to be a highly-compensated employee, and thus is a member of the group in whose favor discrimination is prohibited. In determining whether the prohibited discrimination exists, the total employer contribution on behalf of a self-employed individual shall be taken into account regardless of the fact that only a portion of such contribution is allowed as a deduction. For additional rules relating to discrimination as to contributions or benefits with regard to plans covering any owner-employee, see § 1.401-12.

*(2) Base for computing contributions or benefits.* (i) A plan which is otherwise qualified is not considered discriminatory merely because the contributions or benefits provided under the plan bear a uniform relationship to the total compensation, basic compensation, or regular rate of compensation of the employees, including self-employed individuals, covered under the plan.

(ii) In the case of a self-employed individual who is covered under a qualified plan, the total compensation of such individual is the earned income (as defined in section 401(c)(2)) which such individual derives from the employer's trade or business, or trades or businesses, with respect to which the qualified plan is established. Thus, for example, in the case of a partner, his total compensation includes both his distributive share of partnership income, whether or not distributed, and guaranteed payments described in section 707(c) made to him by the partnership establishing the plan, to the extent that such income constitutes earned income as defined in section 401(c)(2).

(iii) (a) The basic or regular rate of compensation of any self-employed individual is that portion of his earned income which bears the same ratio to his total earned income derived from the trade or business, or trades or businesses, with respect to which the qualified plan is established as the aggregate basic or regular compensation of all common-law employees covered under the plan bears to the aggregate total compensation of such employees derived from such trade or business, or trades or businesses.

(b) If an employer establishes two or more plans which satisfy the requirements of section 401(a) separately, and only one such plan covers a self-employed individual, the determination of the basic or regular rate of compensation of such self-employed individual is made with regard to the compensation of common-law employees covered under the plan which provides contributions or benefits for such self-employed individual. On the other hand, if two or more plans must be considered together in order to satisfy the requirements of section 401(a), the computation of the basic or regular rate of compensation of a self-employed individual must be made with regard to the compensation of the common-law employees covered by so many of such plans as are required to be taken together in order to satisfy the qualification requirements of section 401(a).

*(3) Discriminatory contributions.* If a discriminatory contribution is made by, or for, a self-employed individual who is an employee within the meaning of section 401(c)(1) because of an erroneous assumption as to the earned income of such individual, the plan will not be considered discriminatory if adequate adjustment is made to remove such discrimination. In the case of any self-employed individual who is an owner-employee, the amount of any excess contribution to be returned and the manner in which it is to be repaid are determined by the provisions of section 401(d)(8) and (e). However, if any self-employed individual, including any owner-employee, has not made the full contribution permitted to be made on his behalf as an employee, then, if the plan expressly provides, so much of any excess contribution by such self-employed individual's employer as may, under the provisions of the plan, be treated as a contribution made by such individual as an employee can be so treated.

**(e) Distribution of entire interest.** *(1)* If a trust forms part of a plan which covers a self-employed individual, such trust shall constitute a qualified trust under section 401 only if the plan of which such trust is a part expressly provides that the entire interest of each employee, including any common-law employee, will be distributed in accordance with the provisions of subparagraph (2) or (3) of this paragraph.

*(2)* Unless the provisions of subparagraph (3) of this paragraph apply, the entire interest of each employee (including contributions he has made on his own behalf, contributions made on his behalf by his employer, and interest thereon) must be actually distributed to such employee—

(i) In the case of an employee, other than an individual who is, or has been, an owner-employee under the plan, not later than the last day of the taxable year of such employee in which he attains the age of 70½, or not later than the last day of the taxable year in which such employee retires, whichever is later, and

(ii) In the case of an employee who is, or has been, an owner-employee under the plan, not later than the last day of the taxable year in which he attains the age of 70½.

*(3)* In lieu of distributing an employee's entire interest in a qualified plan as provided in subparagraph (2) of this paragraph, such interest may be distributed commencing no later than the last taxable year described in such subparagraph (2). In such case, the plan must expressly provide that the entire interest of such an employee shall be distributed to him and his beneficiaries, in a manner which satisfies the requirements of subparagraph (5) of this paragraph, over any of the following periods (or any combination thereof)—

(i) The life of the employee, or

(ii) The lives of the employee and his spouse, or

(iii) A period certain not longer than the life expectancy of the employee, or

(iv) A period certain not longer than the joint life and last survivor expectancy of the employee and his spouse.

*(4)* For purposes of subparagraphs (3) and (5) of this paragraph, the determination of the life expectancy of the employee or the joint life and last survivor expectancy of the employee and his spouse is to be made either (i) only once, at the time the employee receives the first distribution of his entire interest under the plan, or (ii) periodically, in a consistent manner. Such life expectancy or joint life and last survivor expectancy cannot exceed the period computed by the use of the expected return multiples in § 1.72-9, or, in the case of payments under a contract issued by an insurance company, the period computed by use of the life expectancy tables of such company.

*(5)* If an employee's entire interest is to be distributed over a period described in subparagraph (3) of this paragraph, then the amount to be distributed each year must be at least an amount equal to the quotient obtained by dividing the entire interest of the employee under the plan at the time the distribution is made (expressed in either dollars or units) by the life expectancy of the employee, or joint life and last survivor expectancy of the employee and his spouse (whichever is applicable), determined in accordance with the provisions of subparagraph (4) of this paragraph. However, no distribution need be made in any year, or a lesser amount

may be distributed, if the aggregate amounts distributed by the end of that year are at least equal to the aggregate of the minimum amounts required by this subparagraph to have been distributed by the end of such year.

*(6)* If an employee's entire interest is distributed in the form of an annuity contract, then the requirements of section 401(a)(9) are satisfied if the distribution of such contract takes place before the end of the latest taxable year described in subparagraph (2) of this paragraph, and if the employee's interest will be paid over a period described in subparagraph (3) of this paragraph and at a rate which satisfies the requirements of subparagraph (5) of this paragraph.

*(7)* The requirements of section 401(a)(9) do not preclude contributions from being made on behalf of an owner-employee under a qualified plan subsequent to the taxable year in which the distribution of his entire interest is required to commence. Thus, if all other requirements for qualification are satisfied, a qualified plan may provide contributions for an owner-employee who has already attained age 70½. However, a distribution of benefits attributable to contributions made on behalf of an owner-employee in a taxable year beginning after the taxable year in which he attains the age of 70½ must satisfy the requirements of subparagraph (3) of this paragraph. Thus, if an owner-employee has already attained the age of 70½ at the time the first contribution is made on his behalf, the distribution of his entire interest must commence in the year in which such contribution is first made on his behalf.

*(8)* This paragraph shall not apply and an otherwise qualified trust will not be disqualified if the method of distribution under the plan is one which was designated by a common-law employee prior to October 10, 1962, and such method of distribution is not in accordance with the provisions of section 401(a)(9). Such exception applies regardless of whether the actual distribution of the entire interest of an employee making such a designation, or any portion of such interest, has commenced prior to October 10, 1962.

T.D. 6675, 9/16/63, amend T.D. 6982, 11/12/68.

## § 1.401-12 Requirements for qualification of trusts and plans benefiting owner-employees.

***Caution:*** The Treasury has not yet amended Reg § 1.401-12 to reflect changes made by P.L. 98-21, P.L. 97-248.

**(a) Introduction.** This section prescribes the additional requirements which must be met for qualification of a trust forming part of a pension or profit-sharing plan, or of an annuity plan, which covers any self-employed individual who is an owner-employee as defined in section 401(c)(3). However, to the extent that the provisions of § 1.401-11 are not modified by the provisions of this section, such provisions are also applicable to a plan which covers an owner-employee. The provisions of this section apply to taxable years beginning after December 31, 1962. Except as otherwise provided, paragraphs (b) through (m) of this section apply to taxable years beginning after December 31, 1962. Paragraph (n) of this section applies to plan years determined in accordance with paragraph (n)(1) of the section.

**(b) General rules.** *(1)* The qualified plan and trust of an unincorporated trade or business does not have to satisfy the additional requirements for qualification merely because an owner-employee derives earned income (as defined in section 401(c)(2)) from the trade or business with respect to which the plan is established. Such additional requirements need be satisfied only if an owner-employee is actually covered under the plan of the employer. An owner-employee may only be covered under a plan of an employer if such owner-employee has so consented. However, the consent of the owner-employee may be either expressed or implied. Thus, for example, if contributions are, in fact, made on behalf of an owner-employee, such owner-employee is considered to have impliedly consented to being covered under the plan.

*(2)* A qualified plan covering an owner-employee must be a definite written program and arrangement setting forth all provisions essential for qualification at the time such plan is established. Therefore, for example, even though the owner-employee is the only employee covered under the plan at the time the plan is established, the plan must incorporate all the provisions relating to the eligibility and benefits of future employees.

**(c) Bank trustee.** *(1)* (i) If a trust created after October 9, 1962, is to form a part of a qualified pension or profit-sharing plan covering an owner-employee, or if a trust created before October 10, 1962, but not exempt from tax on October 9, 1962, is to form part of such a plan, the trustee of such trust must be a bank as defined in paragraph (c)(2) of this section, unless an exception contained in paragraph (c)(4) of this section applies, or paragraph (n) of this section applies.

(ii) The provisions of this paragraph do not apply to an employees' trust created prior to October 10, 1962, if such trust was exempt from tax on October 9, 1962, even though the plan of which such trust forms a part is amended after December 31, 1962, to cover any owner-employee. Although the trustee of a trust described in the preceding sentence need not be a bank, all other requirements for the qualification of such a trust must be satisfied at the time an owner-employee is first covered under such plan.

*(2)* The term "bank" as used in this paragraph means—

(i) A bank as defined in section 581;

(ii) A corporation which, under the laws of the State of its incorporation or under the laws of the District of Columbia, is subject to both the supervision of, and examination by, the authority in such jurisdiction in charge of the administration of the banking laws;

(iii) In the case of a trust created or organized outside of the United States, that is, outside the States and the District of Columbia, a bank or trust company, wherever incorporated, exercising fiduciary powers and subject to both supervision and examination by governmental authority;

(iv) Beginning on January 1, 1974, an insured credit union (within the meaning of section 101(6) of the Federal Credit Union Act, 12 U.S.C. 1752(6)).

*(3)* Although a bank is required to be the trustee of a qualified trust, another person, including the employer, may be granted the power in the trust instrument to control the investment of the trust funds either by directing investments, including reinvestments, disposals, and exchanges, or by disapproving proposed investments, including reinvestments, disposals, or exchanges.

*(4)* (i) This paragraph does not apply to a trust created or organized outside the States and the District of Columbia before October 10, 1962, if, on October 9, 1962, such trust is described in section 402(c) as an organization treated as if it was a trust exempt from tax under section 501(a).

(ii) In addition, the requirement that the trustee must be a bank does not apply to a qualified trust forming a part of a pension or profit-sharing plan if—

(a) The investments of all the funds in such trust are in annuity, endowment, or life insurance contracts, issued by a company which is a life insurance company as defined in section 801(a) during the taxable year immediately preceding the year that such contracts are originally purchased;

(b) All the proceeds which are, or may become, payable under the contract are payable directly to the employee or his beneficiary;

(c) The plan contains a provision to the effect that the employer is to substitute a bank as a trustee or custodian of the contracts if the employer is notified by the district director that such substitution is required because the trustee is not keeping such records, or making such returns, or rendering such statements, as are required by forms or regulations.

However, a qualified trust may only purchase insurance protection to the extent permitted under a qualified plan (see paragraph (b)(1)(i) and (ii) of § 1.401-1).

*(5)* An employer may designate several trusts (or custodial accounts) or a trust or trusts and an annuity plan or plans as constituting parts of a single plan which is intended to satisfy the requirements for qualification. However, each trust (or custodial account) so designated which is part of a plan covering an owner-employee must satisfy the requirements of this paragraph. Thus, for example, if all other requirements for qualification are satisfied by the plan, a qualified profit-sharing plan may provide that a portion of the contributions under the plan will be paid to a custodial account, the custodian of which is a bank, for investment in stock of a regulated investment company, and the remainder of such contributions will be paid to a trust, the trustee of which is not a bank, for investment in annuity contracts.

**(d) Profit-sharing plan.** *(1)* A profit-sharing plan, as defined in paragraph (b)(1)(ii) of § 1.401-1, which covers any owner-employee must contain a definite formula for determining the contributions to be made by the employer on behalf of employees, other than owner-employees. A formula to be definite must specify the portion of profits to be contributed to the trust and must also define profits for plan purposes. A definite formula may contain a variable factor, if the value of such factor may not vary at the discretion of the employer. For example, the percentage of profits to be contributed each year may differ depending on the amount of profits. On the other hand, a formula which, for example, specifies that profits for plan purposes are not to exceed the cash on hand at the time the employer contribution is made is not a definite formula. The requirement that the plan formula be definite is satisfied if such formula limits the amount to be contributed on behalf of all employees covered under the plan to the amount which permits self-employed individuals to obtain the maximum deduction under section 404(a). However, even though the plan formula is definite, the plan must satisfy all the other requirements for qualification, including the requirement that the contributions under the plan not discriminate in favor of any self-employed individual, and the requirement that the plan be for the exclusive benefit of the employees in general.

*(2)* A definite contribution formula constitutes an integral part of a qualified profit-sharing plan and may not be amended except for a valid business reason.

*(3)* The requirement that a profit-sharing plan contain a definite formula for determining the amount of contributions to be made on behalf of employees does not apply to contributions which are made on behalf of owner-employees. However, such contributions are subject to the requirement that they be nondiscriminatory with respect to other employees and must not exceed the limitations on allowable and deductible contributions which may be made by owner-employees.

**(e) Requirements as to coverage.** *(1) Coverage of all employees.* The coverage requirements contained in section 401(a)(3) do not apply to a plan which covers any owner-employee. However, such a plan must satisfy the coverage requirements of section 401(d), including section 401(d)(3). Accordingly, a plan which covers an owner-employee must benefit each employee of the trade or business (other than any owner-employee who does not consent to be covered under the plan) whose customary period of employment has been for more than 20 hours a week for more than five months during each of three consecutive periods of twelve calendar months. Therefore, a plan may not provide, for example, that an employee, other than an owner-employee, is ineligible to participate because he does not consent to be a participant or because he does not consent to make reasonable contributions under the plan.

*(2) Period of service.* (i) In determining whether an employee renders service to the same employer, and, therefore, must be covered under the plan of such employer, a partnership is considered to be one employer during the entire period prior to the time it is terminated within the meaning of section 708 (see paragraph (e)(2) of § 1.401-10).

(ii) In the case of a common-law employee who becomes an employee within the meaning of section 401(c)(1) with respect to the same trade or business, his period of employment is the aggregate of his service as a common-law employee and an employee within the meaning of section 401(c)(1).

(iii) In determining whether any employee, including any owner-employee, has three years of service, past service of any such employee may be taken into account as provided in paragraph (b) of § 1.401-10. Thus, if an employer takes into account past service for any owner-employee, he must take into account the past service of all his other employees to the same extent. However, a plan may provide for coverage after a period of service which is shorter than three years, but in no case may the plan require a waiting period for employees which is longer than that required for the owner-employees.

**(f) Discrimination in contributions or benefits.** *(1)* Variations in contributions or benefits may be provided under the plan so long as the plan does not discriminate, either as to contributions or benefits, in favor of officers, employees whose principal duties consist in supervising the work of other employees, or highly compensated employees, as against other employees (see § 1.401-4). For the purpose of determining whether the provisions of a plan which provide contributions or benefits for an owner-employee result in the prohibited discrimination, an owner-employee, like other self-employed individuals, is considered a highly compensated employee (see paragraph (d) of § 1.401-11). Whether or not a plan is discriminatory is determined by the actual operation of the plan as well as by its formal provisions.

*(2)* The provisions of section 401(a)(5), relating to certain plan provisions which will not in and of themselves be considered discriminatory, are not applicable to any plan which covers any owner-employee. Such a plan must, instead, satisfy the requirements of section 401(a)(10) and section 401(d)(6). Accordingly, a plan is not discriminatory within the meaning of section 401(a)(4) merely because the contributions or benefits provided for the employees covered under the plan bear a uniform relationship to the total compensation, or to the basic or regular rate of compensation, of

such employees. The total compensation or the basic or regular rate of compensation of an owner-employee is computed in accordance with the provisions of paragraph (d)(2) of § 1.401-11.

*(3)* Even though the contributions under the plan do not bear a uniform relationship to the total compensation, or the basic or regular rate of compensation, of the employees covered thereunder and the plan would otherwise be considered discriminatory within the meaning of section 401(a)(4), the plan shall not be considered discriminatory if such variation is due to employer contributions on behalf of any owner-employee which are required, under the plan, to be applied to pay premiums or other consideration on one or more level premium contracts described in section 401(e)(3)(A). In a taxable year to which the foregoing exception applies and, therefore, one in which the contributions under the plan would otherwise be discriminatory, the employer contributions to pay such premiums or other consideration must be the only employer contributions made for the owner-employee, and the contributions for such taxable year under such plan must not be in excess of the amount permitted to be paid toward the purchase of such a contract under the provisions of section 401(e)(3). Furthermore, the exception described in this subparagraph only applies to contributions made under a plan which otherwise satisfies the requirements of section 401(a)(4) and the regulations thereunder. Thus, if a plan provides for the purchase, in accordance with section 401(e)(3), of a level premium contract for an owner-employee, then such plan must provide either that the benefits for all employees are nondiscriminatory or, in the case of a money-purchase type of plan, that the contributions for all employees are based on compensation determined in a nondiscriminatory manner. For example, since the contributions on behalf of the owner-employee are based on his earned income during the period preceding the purchase of the contract, the contributions for other employees must be based on their compensation during the same period if this will result in larger contributions on their behalf.

*(4)* In the case of a plan which covers any owner-employee, the contributions or benefits provided under the plan cannot vary with respect to years of service except as provided in subparagraph (5) of this paragraph.

*(5)* The provisions of section 401(d)(3) do not preclude the coverage of employees with less than three years of service if such coverage is provided on a nondiscriminatory basis. However, a plan will not be disqualified merely because the contributions or benefits for employees who have less than three years of service are not as favorable as the contributions or benefits for employees having more than three years of service.

**(g) Nonforfeitable rights.** *(1)* (i) Except as provided in subparagraph (2) of this paragraph, if an owner-employee is covered under the plan of his employer, each employee's rights to the contributions, or to the benefits derived from the contributions, of such employer must be nonforfeitable at the time such contributions are paid to, or under, the plan. The employees who must obtain such nonforfeitable rights include the self-employed individuals who are covered under the plan. As to what constitutes nonforfeitable rights of an employee, see paragraph (a)(2) of § 1.402(b)-1.

(ii) Under section 401(d)(2), it is necessary that each employee obtain nonforfeitable rights to the employer contributions under the plan on his behalf from the time such contributions are paid. Thus, each employee must have a nonforfeitable interest to the portion of the funds under the plan which is allocable to the employer contributions made under the plan on his behalf.

*(2)* The provisions of subparagraph (1) of this paragraph do not apply to the extent that employer contributions on behalf of any employee must remain forfeitable in order to satisfy the requirements of paragraph (c) of § 1.401-4. However, employer contributions on behalf of employees whose rights are required to remain forfeitable to satisfy such requirements must be nonforfeitable except for such contingency.

**(h) Integration with social security.** *(1)* If a qualified plan covers any owner-employee, then the rules relating to the integration of such plan with the contributions or benefits under the Social Security Act are provided in this paragraph. Accordingly, the provisions of paragraph (e) of § 1.401-3 and paragraph (c) of § 1.401-11 do not apply to such a plan. In the case of a plan which provides contributions or benefits for any owner-employee, integration of the plan with the Social Security Act for any taxable year of the employer can take place only if not more than one-third of the employer contributions under the plan which are deductible under section 404 for that year are made on behalf of the owner-employees. If such requirement is satisfied, then the plan may be integrated with the contributions or benefits under the Social Security Act in accordance with the rules of subparagraph (3) of this paragraph.

*(2)* (i) For purposes of subparagraph (1) of this paragraph, in determining the total amount of employer contributions which are deductible under section 404, the provisions of section 404(a), including the provisions of section 404(a)(9) (relating to plans benefiting self-employed individuals), and section 404(e) (relating to the special limitations for self-employed individuals) are taken into account, but the provisions of section 404(a)(10), (relating to the special limitation on the amount allowed as a deduction for self-employed individuals) are not taken into account.

(ii) The amount of deductible employer contributions which are made on behalf of all owner-employees for the year is compared with the amount of deductible employer contributions for the year made on behalf of all employees covered under the plan (including self-employed individuals who are not owner-employees and owner-employees) for the purpose of determining whether the deductible contributions by the employer on behalf of owner-employees are not more than one-third of the total deductible contributions.

*(3)* If a plan covering an owner-employee satisfies the requirement of subparagraph (1) of this paragraph, and if the employer wishes to integrate such plan with the contributions or benefits under the Social Security Act, then—

(i) The employer contributions under the plan on behalf of any owner-employee shall be reduced by an amount determined by multiplying the earned income of such owner-employee which is derived from the trade or business with respect to which the plan is established and which does not exceed the maximum which may be treated as self-employment income under section 1402(b)(1), by the rate of tax imposed under section 1401(a); and

(ii) The employer contributions under the plan on behalf of any employee other than an owner-employee may be reduced by an amount not in excess of the amount determined by multiplying the employee's wages under section 3121(a)(1) by the rate of tax imposed under section 3111(a). For purposes of this subdivision, the earned income of a self-employed individual which is derived from the trade or business with respect to which the plan is established and which is treated as self-employment income under section 1402(b)(1), shall be treated as "wages" under section 3121(a)(1).

*(4)* A money purchase pension plan or a profit-sharing plan may provide that such plan will be integrated with the Social Security Act only for such taxable years of the employer in which the requirements for integration are satisfied. However, a qualified plan cannot provide that employer contributions are only to be made for taxable years in which the integration requirements are satisfied.

**(i) Limit on contributions on behalf of an owner-employee.** *(1)* Section 401(d)(5) requires that a plan which covers any owner-employee must contain provisions which restrict the employer contributions that may be made on behalf of any owner-employee for each taxable year to an amount no greater than that which is deductible under section 404. In computing the amount deductible under section 404 for purposes of section 401(d)(5) and this paragraph, the limitations contained in section 404(a)(9) and (e), relating to special limitations for self-employed individuals, are taken into account, but such amount is determined without regard to section 404(a)(10), relating to the special limitation on the amount allowed as a deduction for self-employed individuals. Accordingly, a qualified plan which covers any owner-employee cannot permit employer contributions to be made on behalf of such owner-employee in excess of 10 percent of the earned income which is derived by such owner-employee from the trade or business with respect to which the plan is established, or permit the employer to contribute more than $2,500 on behalf of any such owner-employee for any taxable year.

*(2)* (i) In determining whether the plan permits contributions to be made in excess of the limitations of subparagraph (1) of this paragraph, employer contributions under the plan which are allocable to the purchase of life, accident, health, or other insurance are not to be taken into account. To determine the amount of employer contributions under the plan which are allocable to the purchase of life, accident, health, or other insurance, see paragraph (f) of § 1.404(e)-1 and paragraph (b) of § 1.72-16. However, contributions for such insurance can be made only to the extent otherwise permitted under sections 401 through 404 and the regulations thereunder.

(ii) A further exception to the limit on the amount of contributions which an employer may make under the plan on behalf of an owner-employee is made in the case of contributions which are required, under the plan, to be applied to pay premiums or other consideration for one or more annuity, endowment, or life insurance contracts described in section 401(e)(3) (see section 401(e)(3) and the regulations thereunder).

**(j) Excess contributions.** The provisions of section 401(e) define the term "excess contribution" and indicate the consequences of making such a contribution (see § 1.401-13). However, section 401(d)(8) provides that a qualified plan which provides contributions or benefits for any owner-employee must contain certain provisions which complement the rules contained in section 401(e). Under section 401(d)(8), a qualified plan must provide that—

*(1)* The net amount of any excess contribution (determined in accordance with the provisions of § 1.401-13) must be returned to the owner-employee on whose behalf it is made, together with the net income earned on such excess contribution;

*(2)* For each taxable year for which the trust is considered to be a nonqualified trust with respect to an owner-employee under section 401(e)(2) because the net amount of an excess contribution and the earnings thereon have not been returned to such owner-employee, the income of the trust for that taxable year attributable to the interest of such owner-employee is to be paid to him.

*(3)* If an excess contribution is determined to be willfully made (within the meaning of section 401(e)(2)(E)), the entire interest of the owner-employee on whose behalf such contribution was made is required to be distributed to such owner-employee. Furthermore, the plan must require the distribution of an owner-employee's entire interest under the plan if a willful excess contribution is determined to have been made under any other plan in which the owner-employee is covered as an owner-employee.

**(k) Contributions of property under a qualified plan.** *(1)* The contribution of property, other than money, prior to January 1, 1975, by the person who is the employer (within the meaning of section 401(c)(4)) to a qualified trust forming a part of a plan which covers employees some or all of whom are owner-employees who control (within the meaning of section 401(d)(9)(B) and the regulations thereunder) the trade or business with respect to which the plan is established is a prohibited transaction between such trust and the employer-grantor of such trust (see section 503(g) prior to its repeal by Sec. 2003(b)(5) of the Employee Retirement Income Security Act of 1974 (88 Stat. 978)).

*(2)* A contribution of property, other than money, prior to January 1, 1975, to a qualified trust by an owner-employee who controls, or a member of a group of owner-employees who together control, the trade or business with respect to which the plan is established, or a contribution of property, other than money, to a qualified trust by a member of such an owner-employee's family (as defined in section 267(c)(4)), is a prohibited transaction. (See section 503(g) prior to its repeal by section 2003(b)(5) of the Employee Retirement Income Security Act of 1974 (88 Stat. 978)).

*(3)* See section 4975 and the regulations thereunder with respect to rules relating to the contribution of property, other than money, made after December 31, 1974.

**(l) Controlled trades or businesses.** *(1) Plans covering an owner-employee who controls another trade or business.* (i) A plan must not cover any owner-employee, or group of two or more owner-employees, if such owner-employee, or group of owner-employees, control (within the meaning of subparagraph (3) of this paragraph) any other trade or business, unless the employees of such other trade or business controlled by such owner-employee, or such group of owner-employees, are included in a plan which satisfies the requirements of section 401(a), including the qualification requirements of section 401(d). The employees who must be covered under the plan of the trade or business which is controlled include the self-employed individuals who are not owner-employees and the owner-employees who consent to be covered by such plan. Accordingly, the employer must determine whether any owner-employee, or group of owner-employees, who may participate in the plan which is established by such employer controls any other trade or business, and whether the requirements of this subparagraph are satisfied with respect to the plan established in such other trade or business. The plan of an employer may exclude an owner-employee who controls another trade or business from coverage under the plan even though such owner-employee consents to be covered, if a plan which satisfies the requirements of subdivision (ii) of this subparagraph has not been established in the trade or business which such owner-employee controls.

(ii) The qualified plan which the owner-employee, or owner-employees, are required to provide for the employees of the trade or business which they control must provide contributions and benefits which are not less favorable than the contributions and benefits provided for the owner-employee, or owner-employees, under the plan of any trade or business which they do not control. Thus, for example, if the contributions or benefits for the owner-employee under the plan of the trade or business which he does not control are computed on the basis of his total (as compared to basic or regular rate) of compensation, then the contributions or benefits for employees covered under the plan of the trade or business which the owner controls must be computed on the basis of their total compensation. However, the requirements of this subdivision cannot be satisfied if the benefits and contributions provided under the plan for the employees of the trade or business which is controlled are not comparable to those provided under the plan covering the owner-employee, or group of owner-employees, in the trade or business which they do not control. Thus, for example, if the owner-employee is covered by a pension plan in the trade or business which he does not control, he may not satisfy the requirements of this subdivision by establishing a profit-sharing plan in the trade or business which he does control.

(iii) If an individual is covered as an owner-employee under the plans of two or more trades or businesses which he does not control and such individual controls a trade or business, then the contributions or benefits of the employees under the plan of the trade or business which he does control must be as favorable as those provided for him under the most favorable plan of the trade or business which he does not control.

*(2) Owner-employees who control more than one trade or business.* If the plan provides contributions or benefits for an owner-employee who controls, or group of owner-employees who together control, the trade or business with respect to which the plan is established, and such owner-employee, or group of owner-employees, also control as owner-employees one or more other trades or businesses, plans must be established with respect to such controlled trades or businesses so that when taken together they form a single plan which satisfies the requirements of section 401(a) and (d) with respect to the employees of all the controlled trades or businesses.

*(3) Control defined.* (i) For purposes of this paragraph, an owner-employee, or a group of two or more owner-employees, shall be considered to control a trade or business if such owner-employee, or such group of two or more owner-employees together—

(a) Own the entire interest in an unincorporated trade or business, or

(b) In the case of a partnership, own more than 50 percent of either the capital interest or the profits interest in such partnership.

In determining whether an owner-employee, or group of owner-employees, control a trade or business within the meaning of the preceding sentence, it is immaterial whether or not such individuals could be covered under a plan established with respect to the trade or business. For example, if an individual who is an owner-employee has a 60-percent capital interest in another trade or business, such individual controls such trade or business and the provisions of this paragraph apply even though the individual derives no earned income, as defined in section 401(c)(2), from the controlled trade or business. For purposes of determining the ownership interest of an owner-employee, or group of owner-employees, an owner-employee, or group of owner-employees, is treated as owning any interest in a partnership which is owned, directly or indirectly, by a partnership controlled by such owner-employee, or group of owner-employees.

(ii) The provisions of subparagraphs (1) and (2) of this paragraph apply only if the owner-employee who controls, or the group of owner-employees who control, a trade or business, or trades or businesses, within the meaning of subdivision (i) of this subparagraph is the same owner-employee, or group of owner-employees, covered under the plan intended to satisfy the requirements for qualification. Thus, for example, if A is a 50-percent partner in both the AB and AC partnership, and if the AB partnership wishes to establish a plan covering A and B, the provisions of subparagraphs (1) and (2) of this paragraph do not apply, since A does not control either partnership, and since B has no interest in the AC partnership.

**(m) Distribution of benefits.** *(1)* (i) Section 401(d)(4)(B) requires that a qualified plan which provides contributions or benefits for any owner-employee must not provide for the payment of benefits to such owner-employee at any time before he has attained age 59½. An exception to the foregoing rule permits a qualified plan to provide for the distribution of benefits to an owner-employee prior to the time he attains age 59½ if he is disabled. For taxable years beginning after December 31, 1966, see section 72(m)(7) and paragraph (f) of § 1.72-17 for the meaning of disabled. For taxable years beginning before January 1, 1967, see section 213(g)(3) for the meaning of disabled. In general, both sections 72(m)(7) and 213(g)(3) provide that an individual is considered disabled if he is unable to engage in any substantial gainful activity because of a medically determinable physical or mental impairment which can be expected to result in death or to be of long-continued and indefinite duration. In addition, section 401(d)(4)(B) does not preclude the distribution of benefits to the estate or other beneficiary of a deceased owner-employee prior to the time the owner-employee would have attained age 59½ if he had lived.

(ii) A qualified plan must provide that if, despite the restrictions in the plan to the contrary, an amount is prematurely distributed, or made available, to a participant in such plan who is, or has been, an owner-employee, then no contribution shall be made under the plan by, or for, such individual during any of the 5 taxable years of the plan beginning after the distribution is made.

*(2)* (i) The provisions of subparagraph (1) of this paragraph preclude an owner-employee who is a participant in a qualified pension or profit-sharing plan of his employer from withdrawing any part of the funds accumulated on his behalf except as provided in such subparagraph (1). However, the distribution of an owner-employee's interest, or any portion of such interest, after he attains age 59½ is determined by the provisions of the plan. Thus, for example, if a qualified pension plan provides that the normal retirement age under the plan is age 65, an owner-employee would not be entitled to a distribution of an amount under the plan merely because he attained age 59½.

(ii) The provisions of subparagraph (1) of this paragraph do not preclude the establishment of a profit-sharing plan which provides for the distribution of all, or part, of participants' accounts after a fixed number of years. However, such a plan must not permit a distribution of any amount to any owner-employee prior to the time the owner-employee has attained 59½ or becomes disabled within the meaning of section 72(m)(7) or section 213(g)(3), whichever is applicable. On the other hand, if a distribution would have been made under the plan to an owner-employee but for the fact that he had not attained age 59½, then the amount of such distribution (including any increment earned on such amount) must be distributed to such owner-employee at such time as he attains age 59½.

*(3)* A qualified pension, annuity, or profit-sharing plan which covers an owner-employee must provide that the distribution of an owner-employee's entire interest under the plan must begin prior to the end of the taxable year in which he attains the age of 70½, and such distribution must satisfy the requirements of section 401(a)(9) and paragraph (e) of § 1.401-11. Furthermore, section 401(d)(7) provides that, if an owner-employee dies prior to the time his entire interest has been distributed to him, such owner-employee's entire remaining interest under the plan must, in general, either be distributed to his beneficiary, or beneficiaries, within 5 years, or be used within that period to purchase an immediate annuity for his beneficiary, or beneficiaries. However, a distribution within 5 years of the death of the owner-employee is not required if the distribution of his interest has commenced and such distribution is for a term certain over a period not extending beyond the joint life and survivor expectancy of the owner-employee and his spouse. Thus, for example, an annuity for the joint life and survivor expectancy of an owner-employee and his spouse which guarantees payments for 10 years is a distribution which is payable over a period which does not exceed the joint life and survivor expectancy of the owner-employee and his spouse if such expectancy is at least 10 years at the time the distribution first commences.

---

T.D. 6675, 9/16/63, amend T.D. 6982, 11/12/68, T.D. 6985, 12/26/68, T.D. 7428, 8/13/76, T.D. 7611, 4/19/79, T.D. 8635, 12/19/95.

---

### § 1.401-13 Excess contributions on behalf of owner-employees.

**(a) Introduction.** *(1)* The provisions of this section prescribe the rules relating to the treatment of excess contributions made under a qualified pension, annuity, or profit-sharing plan on behalf of a self-employed individual who is an owner-employee (as defined in paragraph (d) of § 1.401-10). Paragraph (b) of this section defines the term "excess contribution". Paragraph (c) of this section describes an exception to the definition of an excess contribution in the case of contributions which are applied to any pay premiums on certain annuity, endowment, or life insurance contracts. Paragraph (d) of this section describes the effect of making an excess contribution which is not determined to have been willfully made, and paragraph (e) of this section describes the effect of making an excess contribution which is determined to have been willfully made.

*(2)* Under section 401(c)(1), certain self-employed individuals are treated as employees for purposes of section 401. In addition, under section 401(c)(4), a proprietor is treated as his own employer, and the partnership is treated as the employer of the partners. Under section 404, certain contributions on behalf of a self-employed individual are treated as deductible and taken into consideration in determining the amount allowed as a deduction under section 404(a). Such contributions are treated under section 401 and the regulations thereunder as employer contributions on behalf of the self-employed individual. However, in some cases, additional contributions may be made on behalf of a self-employed individual. Such contributions are not taken into consideration in determining the amount deductible under section 404 and are not taken into consideration in computing the amount allowed as a deduction under section 404(a). For purposes of section 401 and the regulations thereunder, such contributions are treated as employee contributions by the self-employed individual. If a self-employed individual is an owner-employee within the meaning of section 401(c)(3) and paragraph (d) of § 1.401-10, then this section prescribes the rules applicable if contributions are made in excess of those permitted to be made under section 401.

**(b) Excess contributions defined.** *(1)* (i) Except as provided in paragraph (c) relating to contributions which are applied to pay premiums on certain annuity, endowment, or life insurance contracts, an excess contribution is any amount described in subparagraphs (2) through (4) of this paragraph.

(ii) For purposes of determining if the amount of any contribution made under the plan on behalf of an owner-employee is an excess contribution, the amount of any contribution made under the plan which is allocable to the purchase of life, accident, health, or other insurance is not taken into account. The amount of any contribution which is allocable to the cost of insurance protection is determined in accordance with the provisions of paragraph (f) of § 1.404(e)-1 and paragraph (b) of § 1.72-16.

*(2)* (i) In the case of a taxable year of the plan for which employer contributions are made on behalf of only owner-employees, an excess contribution is the amount of any contribution for such taxable year on behalf of such owner-employee which is not deductible under section 404 (determined without regard to section 404(a)(10)). This rule applies irrespective of whether the plan provides for contributions on behalf of common-law employees, or self-employed individuals who are not owner-employees, when such employees or individuals become eligible for coverage under the plan, and irrespective of whether contributions are in fact made for such employees or such individuals for other taxable years of the plan.

(ii) In the case of a taxable year of the plan for which employer contributions are made on behalf of both owner-employees and either common-law employees or self-employed individuals who are not owner-employees, an excess contribution is the amount of any employer contribution on behalf of any owner-employee for such taxable year which exceeds the amount deductible under section 404 (determined without regard to section 404(a)(10)) unless such amount may be treated as an employee contribution under the plan in accordance with the rules of paragraph (d)(3) of § 1.401-11 and is a permissible employee contribution under subparagraph (3) of this paragraph.

*(3)* (i) In the case of a taxable year of the plan for which employer contributions are made on behalf of both an owner-employee and either common-law employees or self-employed individuals who are not owner-employees, employee contributions on behalf of an owner-employee may be made for such taxable year of the plan. However, the amount of such contributions, if any, which is described in subdivisions (ii), (iii), or (iv) of this subparagraph is an excess contribution.

(ii) An excess contribution is the amount of any employee contribution made on behalf of any owner-employee during a taxable year of the plan at a rate in excess of the rate of contributions which may be made as employee contributions by common-law employees, or by self-employed individuals who are not owner-employees, during such taxable year of the plan.

(iii) An excess contribution is the amount of any employee contribution made on behalf of an owner-employee which exceeds the lesser of $2,500 or 10 percent of the earned income (as defined in paragraph (c) of § 1.401-10) of such owner-employee for his taxable year in which such contributions are made.

(iv) In the case of a taxable year of an owner-employee in which contributions are made on behalf of such owner-employee under more than one plan, an excess contribution is the amount of any employee contribution made on behalf of such owner-employee under all such plans during such taxable year which exceeds $2,500. If such an excess contribution is made, the amount of the excess contribution made on behalf of the owner-employee with respect to any one of such plans is the amount by which the employee contribution on his behalf under such plan for the year exceeds an amount which bears the same ratio to $2,500 as the earned income of the owner-employee derived from the trade or business with respect to which the plan is established bears to his earned income derived from the trades or businesses with respect to which all such plans are established.

*(4)* An excess contribution is the amount of any contribution on behalf of an owner-employee for any taxable year of the plan with respect to which the plan is treated, under section 401(e)(2), as not meeting the requirements of section 401(d) with respect to such owner-employee.

**(c) Contributions for premiums on certain annuity, endowment, or life insurance contracts.** *(1)* The term "excess contribution" does not include the amount of any employer contributions on behalf of an owner-employee which, under the provisions of the plan, is expressly required to be applied (either directly or through a trustee) to pay the premiums or other consideration for one or more annuity, endowment, or life insurance contracts, if—

(i) The employer contributions so applied meet the requirements of subparagraphs (2) through (4) of this paragraph, and

(ii) The total employer contributions required to be applied annually to pay premiums on behalf of any owner-employee for contracts described in this paragraph do not exceed $2,500. For purposes of computing such $2,500 limit, the total employer contributions includes amounts which are allocable to the purchase of life, accident, health, or other insurance.

*(2)* (i) The employer contributions must be paid under a plan which satisfies all the requirements for qualification. Accordingly, for example, contributions can be paid under the plan for life insurance protection only to the extent otherwise permitted under sections 401 through 404 and the regulations thereunder. However, certain of the requirements for qualification are modified with respect to a plan described in this paragraph (see section 401(a)(10)(A)(ii) and (d)(5)).

(ii) A plan described in this paragraph is not disqualified merely because a contribution is made on behalf of an owner-employee by his employer during a taxable year of the employer for which the owner-employee has no earned income. On the other hand, a plan will fail to qualify if a contribution is made on behalf of an owner-employee which results in the discrimination prohibited by section 401(a)(4) as modified by section 401(a)(10)(A)(ii) (see paragraph (f)(3) of § 1.401-12).

*(3)* The employer contributions must be applied to pay premiums or other consideration for a contract issued on the life of the owner-employee. For purposes of this subparagraph, a contract is not issued on the life of an owner-employee unless all the proceeds which are, or may become, payable under the contract are payable directly, or through a trustee of a trust described in section 401(a) and exempt from tax under section 501(a), to the owner-employee or to the beneficiary named in the contract or under the plan. Accordingly, for example, a nontransferable face-amount certificate (as defined in section 401(g) and the regulations thereunder) is considered an annuity on the life of the owner-employee if the proceeds of such contract are payable only to the owner-employee or his beneficiary.

*(4)* (i) For any taxable year of the employer, the amount of contributions by the employer on behalf of the owner-employee which is applied to pay premiums under the contracts described in this paragraph must not exceed the average of the amounts deductible under section 404 (determined without regard to section 404(a)(10)) by such employer on behalf of such owner-employee for the most recent three taxable years of the employer (ending prior to the date the latest contract was entered into or modified to provide additional benefits), in which the owner-employee derived earned income from the trade or business with respect to which the plan is established. However, if such owner-employee has not derived earned income for at least three taxable years preceding such date, then, in determining the "average of the amounts deductible", only so many of such taxable years as such owner-employee was engaged in such trade or business and derived earned income therefrom are taken into account.

(ii) For the purpose of making the computation described in subdivision (i) of this subparagraph, the taxable years taken into account include those years in which the individual derived earned income from the trade or business but was not an owner-employee with respect to such trade or business. Furthermore, taxable years of the employer preceding the taxable year in which a qualified plan is established are taken into account. If such taxable years began prior to January 1, 1963, the amount deductible is determined as if section 404 included section 404(a)(8), (9), (10), and (e).

*(5)* The amount of any employer contribution which is not deductible but which is not treated as an excess contribution because of the provisions of this paragraph shall be taken into account as an employee contribution made on behalf of the owner-employee during the owner-employee's taxable year with, or within which, the taxable year of the person treated as his employer under section 401(c)(4) ends. However, such contribution is only treated as an employee contribution made on behalf of the owner-employee for the purpose of determining whether any other employee contribution made on behalf of the owner-employee during such period is an excess contribution described in paragraph (b)(3) of this section.

**(d) Effect of an excess contribution which is not willfully made.** *(1)* If an excess contribution (as defined in paragraph (b) of this section) is made on behalf of an owner-employee, and if such contribution is not willfully made, then the provisions of this paragraph describe the effect of such an excess contribution. However, if the excess contribution made on behalf of an owner-employee is determined to have been willfully made, then the provisions of paragraph (e) of this section are applicable to such contribution.

*(2)* (i) This paragraph does not apply to an excess contribution if the net amount of such excess contribution (as de-

fined in subparagraph (4) of this paragraph) and the net income attributable to such amount are repaid to the owner-employee on whose behalf the excess contribution was made at any time before the end of six months beginning on the day on which the district director sends notice (by certified or registered mail) of the amount of the excess contribution to the trust, insurance company, or other person to whom such excess contribution was paid. The net income attributable to the net amount of the excess contribution is the aggregate of the amounts of net income attributable to the net amount of the excess contribution for each year of the plan beginning with the taxable year of the plan within which the excess contribution is made and ending with the close of the taxable year of the plan immediately preceding the taxable year of the plan in which the net amount of the excess contribution is repaid. The amount of net income attributable to the net amount of the excess contribution for each year is the amount of net income earned under the plan during the year which is allocated in a reasonable manner to the net amount of the excess contribution. For example, the amount of net income earned under the plan for the year which is attributable to the net amount of an excess contribution can be computed as the amount which bears the same ratio to the amount of the "net income attributable to the interest of the owner-employee under the plan" for such taxable year (determined in accordance with the provisions of subparagraph (5)(ii) of this paragraph) as the net amount of the excess contribution bears to the aggregate amount standing to the account of the owner-employee at the end of that year (including the net amount of any excess contribution).

(ii) The notice described in subdivision (i) of this subparagraph shall not be mailed prior to the time that the amount of the tax under chapter 1 of the Code of the owner-employee to whom the excess contribution is to be repaid has been finally determined for his taxable year in which such excess contribution was made. For purposes of this subdivision, a final determination of the amount of tax liability of the owner-employee includes—

(a) A decision by the Tax Court of the United States, or a judgment, decree, or other order by any court of competent jurisdiction, which has become final;

(b) A closing agreement authorized by section 7121; or

(c) The expiration of the period of limitation on suits by the taxpayer for refund, unless suit is instituted prior to the expiration of such period.

(iii) For purposes of this subparagraph, an amount is treated as repaid to an owner-employee if an adequate adjustment is made to the account of the owner-employee. An adequate adjustment is made to the account of an owner-employee, for example, if the amount of the excess contribution (without any reduction for any loading or other administrative charge) and the net income attributable to such amount is taken into account as a contribution under the plan for the current year. In such a case, the gross income of the owner-employee for his taxable year in which such adjustment is made includes the amount of the net income attributable to the excess contribution.

(iv) If the net amount of the excess contribution and the net income attributable thereto is repaid, within the period described in subdivision (i) of this subparagraph, to the owner-employee on whose behalf such contribution was made, then the net income attributable to the excess contribution is, pursuant to section 61(a), includible in the gross income of the owner-employee for his taxable year in which such amount is distributed, or made available, to him. However, such amount is not a distribution to which section 402 or 403 and section 72 apply (see subparagraph (6) of this paragraph).

*(3)* (i) If the net amount of any excess contribution (as defined in subparagraph (4) of this paragraph) and the net income attributable to that excess contribution are not repaid to the owner-employee on whose behalf the excess contribution was made before the end of the six-month period described in subparagraph (2)(i) of this paragraph, the plan under which the excess contribution has been made is considered, for purposes of section 404, as not satisfying the requirements for qualification with respect to such owner-employee for all taxable years of the plan described in subdivision (ii) of this subparagraph. However, such disqualification only applies to the interest of the owner-employee on whose behalf an excess contribution has been made and does not disqualify the plan with respect to the other participants thereunder.

(ii) The taxable years referred to in subdivision (i) of this subparagraph include the taxable year of the plan within which the excess contribution is made and each succeeding taxable year of the plan until the beginning of the taxable year of the plan in which the trust, insurance company, or other person to whom such excess contribution was paid repays to such owner-employee—

(a) The net amount of the excess contribution, and

(b) The amount of income attributable to his interest under the plan which is includible in his gross income for any taxable year by reason of the provisions of subparagraph (5) of this paragraph.

*(4)* For purposes of this paragraph, the net amount of an excess contribution is the amount of such excess contribution, as defined in paragraph (b) of this section, reduced by the amount of any loading charge or other administrative charge ratably allocable to such excess contribution.

*(5)* (i) If a plan is considered as not meeting the requirements for qualification with respect to an owner-employee by reason of the provisions of subparagraph (3) of this paragraph for any taxable year of the plan, such owner-employee's gross income for any of his taxable years with or within which such taxable year of the plan ends shall, for purposes of chapter 1 of the Code, include the portion of the net income earned under the plan for such taxable year of the plan which is attributable to the interest of the owner-employee under the plan.

(ii) For purposes of this subparagraph, the term "net income" means the net income earned under the plan determined in accordance with generally accepted accounting principles consistently applied, and the "net income attributable to the interest of the owner-employee under the plan" is the amount which bears the same ratio to the aggregate amount of net income earned under the plan for the taxable year of the plan as the amount standing to the account of the owner-employee at the end of that year (including the amount of any excess contribution which is credited to his account) bears to the aggregate amount of all funds under the plan for all employees at the end of that year (including the aggregate amount of excess contributions credited to the accounts of all owner-employees for that year).

(iii) The provisions of this subparagraph may be illustrated by the following example:

*Example.* A is an owner-employee covered under the X Employees' Pension Trust who files his return on the basis of a calendar year. An excess contribution was made on behalf of A during the plan year beginning on January 1, 1966. The net amount of the excess contribution and the net income attributable thereto was not repaid to A before the end of the six-month period described in subparagraph (2)(i) of this paragraph. Accordingly, the net income earned under the plan during 1966 which is attributable to A's interest is to be included in his gross income for 1966. Assume that the trust which forms a part of the pension plan of the X Company also files its returns on a calendar year basis, and that during 1966 the trust had a gross income of $4,000 (including a long-term capital gain of $2,500) and expenses of $500. Assume, further, that the amount standing to A's account on December 31, 1966 (including the amount of the excess contribution), was $20,000, and that on that date the amount funded under the plan for all employees (including A) is $140,000. Then the net income of the trust for 1966 is $3,500 ($4,000 – $500). The net income attributable to the interest of A under the plan is $500 (the amount which bears the same ratio to $3,500 as $20,000 bears to $140,000). Accordingly, $500 is included in A's gross income in accordance with the provisions of section 401(e)(2)(B) as the "net income attributable to the interest of the owner-employee under the plan".

*(6)* The provisions of section 402 or 403 and section 72 do not apply to any amount distributed, or made available, to an owner-employee which is described in this paragraph. Accordingly, for example, the provisions of section 72(m)(5)(A)(i), relating to amounts subject to the penalty tax imposed by section 72(m), do not apply to the amount of the net income attributable to the interest of an owner-employee (as defined in subparagraph (5)(ii) of this paragraph) which is includible in his gross income. Furthermore, in such a case, the provisions of section 401(d)(5)(C) do not apply to such amount.

*(7)* Certain adjustments will be required with respect to the interest of an owner-employee after any amount previously allocated to his account has been returned to him pursuant to the provisions of this paragraph. For example, if the determination of whether life insurance benefits provided under the plan are incidental is made, in part, with regard to the contributions allocated to the accounts of the participants covered under the plan, an adjustment may have to be made with respect to the life insurance purchased under the plan for any owner-employee after any amount previously allocated to his account has been repaid to him. Furthermore, if, for example, an owner-employee has received annuity payments which were taxable under the exclusion ratio rule of section 72, and if such exclusion ratio took into account any amount credited to the account of the owner-employee which is subsequently repaid to him, then such exclusion ratio must be recomputed after the adjustment in such owner-employee's account has taken place.

*(8)* Notwithstanding any other provision of law, in any case in which the plan is treated as not satisfying the requirements for qualification with respect to any owner-employee by reason of the provisions of section 401(e), the period for assessing, with respect to such owner-employee, any deficiency arising by reason of—

(i) The disallowance of any deduction under section 404 by reason of the provisions of subparagraph (3) of this paragraph, or

(ii) The inclusion of amounts in the gross income of the owner-employee by reason of the provisions of subparagraph (5) of this paragraph,

shall not expire prior to 18 months after the day the district director mails the notice with respect to the excess contribution (described in subparagraph (2)(i) of this paragraph) which gives rise to such disallowance or inclusion. Thus, for example, notwithstanding the provisions of section 6212(c) (relating to the restriction on the determination of additional deficiencies), if, after a final determination by the Tax Court of the income tax liability of an owner-employee for a taxable year in which an excess contribution was made, the amount of such excess contribution and the net income attributable thereto is not paid to the owner-employee before the end of the six-month period described in subparagraph (2)(i) of this paragraph, an additional deficiency assessment may be made for such taxable year with respect to such excess contribution.

**(e) Effect of an excess contribution which is determined to have been willfully made.** If an excess contribution (as defined in paragraph (b) of this section) on behalf of an owner-employee is determined to have been willfully made, then—

*(1)* Only the provisions of this paragraph apply to such contribution;

*(2)* There shall be distributed to the owner-employee on whose behalf such contribution was willfully made his entire interest in all plans in which he is a participant as an owner-employee;

*(3)* The amount distributed under each such plan is an amount to which section 72 does apply (see section 72(m)(5)(A)(iii)); and

*(4)* For purposes of section 404, no plan in which such individual is covered as an owner-employee shall be considered as meeting the requirements for qualification with respect to such owner-employee for any taxable year of the plan beginning with or within the calendar year in which it is determined that the excess contribution has been willfully made and with or within the five calendar years following such year.

**(f) Years to which this section applies.** This section applies to contributions made in taxable years of employers beginning before January 1, 1976. Thus, for example, in the case of willful contributions made in taxable years of employers beginning before January 1, 1976, paragraphs (e)(1), (2), and (3) of this section apply to such taxable years beginning on or after such date. However, in such a case, because the application of paragraph (e)(4) of this section affects contributions made in taxable years of employers beginning on or after January 1, 1976, paragraph (e)(4) of this section does not apply to such taxable years; see paragraph (c) of § 1.401(e)-4 (relating to transitional rules for excess contributions).

T.D. 6676, 9/16/63, amend T.D. 7636, 8/9/79.

## § 1.401-14 Inclusion of medical benefits for retired employees in qualified pension or annuity plans.

***Caution:*** The Treasury has not yet amended Reg § 1.401-14 to reflect changes made by P.L. 101-508, P.L. 101-239, P.L. 99-514, P.L. 93-406.

**(a) Introduction.** Under section 401(h) a qualified pension or annuity plan may make provision for the payment of sickness, accident, hospitalization, and medical expenses for retired employees, their spouses, and their dependents. The term "medical benefits described in section 401(h)" is used in this section to describe such payments.

**(b) In general.** *(1) Coverage.* Under section 401(h), a qualified pension or annuity plan may provide for the payment of medical benefits described in section 401(h) only for retired employees, their spouses, or their dependents. To be "retired" for purposes of eligibility to receive medical benefits described in section 401(h), an employee must be eligible to receive retirement benefits provided under the pension plan, or else be retired by an employer providing such medical benefits by reason of permanent disability. For purposes of the preceding sentence, an employee is not considered to be eligible to receive retirement benefits provided under the plan if he is still employed by the employer and a separation from employment is a condition to receiving the retirement benefits.

*(2) Discrimination.* A plan which provides medical benefits described in section 401(h) must not discriminate in favor of officers, shareholders, supervisory employees, or highly compensated employees with respect to coverage and with respect to the contributions or benefits under the plan. The determination of whether such a plan so discriminates is made with reference to the retirement portion of the plan as well as the portion providing the medical benefits described in section 401(h). Thus, for example, a plan will not be qualified under section 401 if it discriminates in favor of employees who are officers or shareholders with respect to either portion of the plan.

*(3) Funding medical benefits.* Contributions to provide the medical benefits described in section 401(h) may be made either on a contributory or non-contributory basis, without regard to whether the contributions to fund the retirement benefits are made on a similar basis. Thus, for example, the contributions to fund the medical benefits described in section 401(h) may be provided for entirely out of employer contributions even though the retirement benefits under the plan are determined on the basis of both employer and employee contributions.

*(4) Definitions.* For purposes of section 401(h) and this section:

(i) The term "dependent" shall have the same meaning as that assigned to it by section 152, and

(ii) The term "medical expense" means expenses for medical care as defined in section 213(e)(1).

**(c) Requirements.** The requirements which must be met for a qualified pension or annuity plan to provide medical benefits described in section 401(h) are set forth in subparagraphs (1) through (5) of this paragraph.

*(1) Benefits.* (i) The plan must specify the medical benefits described in section 401(h) which will be available and must contain provisions for determining the amount which will be paid.

Such benefits, when added to any life insurance protection provided for under the plan, must be subordinate to the retirement benefits provided by such plan. For purposes of this section, life insurance protection includes any benefit paid under the plan on behalf of an employee-participant as a result of the employee-participant's death to the extent such payment exceeds the amount of the reserve to provide the retirement benefits for the employee-participant existing at his death. The medical benefits described in section 401(h) are considered subordinate to the retirement benefits if at all times the aggregate of contributions (made after the date on which the plan first includes such medical benefits) to provide such medical benefits and any life insurance protection does not exceed 25 percent of the aggregate contributions (made after such date) other than contributions to fund past service credits.

(ii) The meaning of the term "subordinate" may be illustrated by the following example:

*Example.* The X Corporation amends its qualified pension plan to provide medical benefits described in section 401(h) effective for the taxable year 1964. The total contributions under the plan (excluding those for past service credits) for the taxable year 1964 are $125,000, allocated as follows: $100,000 for retirement benefits, $10,000 for life insurance protection, and $15,000 for medical benefits described in section 401(h). The medical benefits described in section 401(h) are considered subordinate to the retirement benefits since the portion of the contributions allocated to the medical benefits described in section 401(h) ($15,000) and to life insurance protection after such medical benefits were included in the plan ($10,000), or $25,000, does not exceed 25 percent of $125,000. For the taxable year 1965, the X Corporation contributes $140,000 (exclusive of contributions for past service credits) allocated as follows: $100,000 for retirement benefits, $10,000 for life insurance protection, and $30,000 for medical benefits described in section 401(h). The medical benefits described in section 401(h) are considered subordinate to the retirement benefits since the aggregate contributions allocated to the medical benefits described in section 401(h) ($45,000) and to life insurance protection after such medical benefits were included in the plan ($20,000) or $65,000 does not exceed 25 percent of $265,000, the aggregate of the contributions made in 1964 and 1965.

*(2) Separate accounts.* Where medical benefits described in section 401(h) are provided for under a qualified pension or annuity plan, a separate account must be maintained with respect to contributions to fund such benefits. The separation required by this section is for recordkeeping purposes only. Consequently, the funds in the medical benefits account need not be separately invested. They may be invested with funds set aside for retirement purposes without identification of which investment properties are allocable to each account. However, where the investment properties are not allocated to each account, the earnings on such properties must be allocated to each account in a reasonable manner.

*(3) Reasonable and ascertainable.* Section 401(h) further requires that amounts contributed to fund medical benefits therein described must be reasonable and ascertainable. For the rules relating to the deduction of such contributions, see paragraph (f) of § 1.404(a)-3. The employer must, at the time he makes a contribution, designate that portion of such contribution allocable to the funding of medical benefits.

*(4) Impossibility of diversion prior to satisfaction of all liabilities.* Section 401(h) further requires that it must be impossible, at any time prior to the satisfaction of all liabilities under the plan to provide for the payment of medical benefits described in section 401(h), for any part of the corpus or income of the medical benefits account to be (within the taxable year or thereafter) used for, or diverted to, any purpose other than the providing of such benefits. Consequently, a plan which, for example, under its terms, permits funds in the medical benefits account to be used for any retirement benefit provided under the plan does not satisfy the requirements of section 401(h) and will not qualify under section 401(a). However, the payment of any necessary or appropriate expenses attributable to the administration of the medical benefits account does not affect the qualification of the plan.

*(5) Reversion upon satisfaction of all liabilities.* The plan must provide that any amounts which are contributed to fund medical benefits described in section 401(h) and which remain in the medical benefits account upon the satisfaction of all liabilities arising out of the operation of the medical benefits portion of the plan are to be returned to the employer.

*(6) Forfeitures.* The plan must expressly provide that in the event an individual's interest in the medical benefits ac-

count is forfeited prior to termination of the plan an amount equal to the amount of the forfeiture must be applied as soon as possible to reduce employer contributions to fund the medical benefits described in section 401(h).

**(d) Effective date.** This section applies to taxable years of a qualified pension or annuity plan beginning after October 23, 1962.

T.D. 6722, 4/13/64.

**§ 1.401(a)-1 Post-ERISA qualified plans and qualified trusts; in general.**

*Caution:* The Treasury has not yet amended Reg § 1.401(a)-1 to reflect changes made by P.L. 98-397.

**(a) Introduction.** *(1) In general.* This section and the following regulation sections under section 401 reflect the provisions of section 401 after amendment by the Employee Retirement Income Security Act of 1974 (Pub. L. 93-406) ("ERISA").

*(2) [Reserved]*

**(b) Requirements for pension plans.** *(1) Definitely determinable benefits.* (i) In order for a pension plan to be a qualified plan under section 401(a), the plan must be established and maintained by an employer primarily to provide systematically for the payment of definitely determinable benefits to its employees over a period of years, usually for life, after retirement or attainment of normal retirement age (subject to paragraph (b)(2) of this section). A plan does not fail to satisfy this paragraph (b)(1)(i) merely because the plan provides, in accordance with section 401(a)(36), that a distribution may be made from the plan to an employee who has attained age 62 and who is not separated from employment at the time of such distribution.

(ii) Section 1.401-1(b)(1)(i), a pre-ERISA regulation, provides rules applicable to this requirement, and that regulation is applicable except as otherwise provided.

(iii) The use of the type of plan provision described in § 1.415(a)-1(d)(1) which automatically freezes or reduces the rate of benefit accrual or the annual addition to insure that the limitations of section 415 will not be exceeded, will not be considered to violate the requirements of this subparagraph provided that the operation of such provision precludes discretion by the employer.

*(2) Normal retirement age.* (i) General rule. The normal retirement age under a plan must be an age that is not earlier than the earliest age that is reasonably representative of the typical retirement age for the industry in which the covered workforce is employed.

(ii) Age 62 safe harbor. A normal retirement age under a plan that is age 62 or later is deemed to be not earlier than the earliest age that is reasonably representative of the typical retirement age for the industry in which the covered workforce is employed.

(iii) Age 55 to age 62. In the case of a normal retirement age that is not earlier than age 55 and is earlier than age 62, whether the age is not earlier than the earliest age that is reasonably representative of the typical retirement age for the industry in which the covered workforce is employed is based on all of the relevant facts and circumstances.

(iv) Under age 55. A normal retirement age that is lower than age 55 is presumed to be earlier than the earliest age that is reasonably representative of the typical retirement age for the industry in which the covered workforce is employed, unless the Commissioner determines that under the facts and circumstances the normal retirement age is not earlier than the earliest age that is reasonably representative of the typical retirement age for the industry in which the covered workforce is employed.

(v) Age 50 safe harbor for qualified public safety employees. A normal retirement age under a plan that is age 50 or later is deemed to be not earlier than the earliest age that is reasonably representative of the typical retirement agė for the industry in which the covered workforce is employed if substantially all of the participants in the plan are qualified public safety employees (within the meaning of section 72(t)(10)(B)).

*(3) Benefit distribution prior to retirement.* For purposes of paragraph (b)(1)(i) of this section, retirement does not include a mere reduction in the number of hours that an employee works. Accordingly, benefits may not be distributed prior to normal retirement age solely due to a reduction in the number of hours that an employee works.

*(4) Effective date.* Except as otherwise provided in this paragraph (b)(4), paragraphs (b)(2) and (3) of this section are effective May 22, 2007. In the case of a governmental plan (as defined in section 414(d)), paragraphs (b)(2) and (3) of this section are effective for plan years beginning on or after January 1, 2009. In the case of a plan maintained pursuant to one or more collective bargaining agreements that have been ratified and are in effect on May 22, 2007, paragraphs (b)(2) and (3) of this section do not apply before the first plan year that begins after the last of such agreements terminate determined without regard to any extension thereof (or, if earlier, May 24, 2010. See § 1.411(d)-4, A-12, for a special transition rule in the case of a plan amendment that increases a plan's normal retirement age pursuant to paragraph (b)(2) of this section.

T.D. 7748, 12/30/80, amend T.D. 9319, 4/4/2007, T.D. 9325, 5/21/2007.

PAR. 2. In § 1.401(a)-1, paragraph (b)(1)(i) is amended by adding text before the period at the end of the current sentence and a new second sentence, and paragraph (b)(1)(iv) is added to read as follows:

**Proposed § 1.401(a)-1 Post-ERISA qualified plans and qualified trusts; in general.** [*For Preamble, see ¶ 152,601*]

* * * * *

• *Caution:* This Notice of Proposed Rulemaking was partially finalized by TD 9325, 05/21/2007. Subpara. (b)(1)(iv) of prop. reg. 1.401(a)-1 and prop reg. 1.401(a)-3 remain proposed.

**(b)** * * *

*(1)*

* * * * *

(iv) Benefits may not be distributed prior to normal retirement age solely due to a reduction in hours. However, notwithstanding anything provided elsewhere in paragraph (b) of this section (including the pre-ERISA rules under § 1.401-1), an employee may be treated as partially retired for purposes of paragraph (b)(1)(i) of this section to the extent provided under § 1.401(a)-3 relating to a bona fide phased retirement program.

* * * * *

### § 1.401(a)-2 Impossibility of diversion under qualified plan or trust.

*Caution:* The Treasury has not yet amended Reg § 1.401(a)-2 to reflect changes made by P.L. 101-508, P.L. 101-239.

**(a) General rule.** Section 401(a)(2) requires that in order for a trust to be qualified, it must be impossible under the trust instrument (in the taxable year and at any time thereafter before the satisfaction of all liabilities to employees or their beneficiaries covered by the trust) for any part of the trust corpus or income to be used for, or diverted to, purposes other than for the exclusive benefit of those employees or their beneficiaries. Section 1.401-2, a pre-ERISA regulation, provides rules under section 401(a)(2) and that regulation is applicable except as otherwise provided.

**(b) Section 415 suspense account.** Notwithstanding paragraph (a) of this section, a plan, or trust forming part of a plan, may provide for the reversion to the employer, upon termination of the plan, of amounts contributed to the plan that exceed the limitations imposed under section 415(c), to the extent set forth in rules prescribed by the Commissioner in revenue rulings, notices, or other guidance published in the Internal Revenue Bulletin (see § 601.601(d)(2) of this chapter).

T.D. 7748, 12/30/80, amend T.D. 9319, 4/4/2007.

### Proposed § 1.401(a)-3 Benefits during phased retirement. [*For Preamble, see ¶ 152,601*]

• *Caution:* This Notice of Proposed Rulemaking was partially finalized by TD 9325, 05/21/2007. Subpara. (b)(1)(iv) of prop. reg. 1.401(a)-1 and prop reg. 1.401(a)-3 remain proposed.

**(a) Introduction.** *(1) General rule.* Under section 401(a), a qualified pension plan may provide for the distribution of phased retirement benefits in accordance with the limitations of this paragraph (a) to the extent that an employee is partially retired under a bona fide phased retirement program, as defined in paragraph (c) of this section, provided the requirements set forth in paragraphs (d) and (e) of this section are satisfied.

*(2) Limitation on benefits paid during phased retirement period.* (i) Benefits limited to pro rata retirement benefit. The phased retirement benefits paid during the phased retirement period cannot exceed the phased retirement accrued benefit payable in the optional form of benefit applicable at the annuity starting date for the employee's phased retirement benefit.

(ii) Availability of early retirement subsidies, etc. Except as provided in paragraph (a)(2)(iii) of this section, all early retirement benefits, retirement-type subsidies, and optional forms of benefit available upon full retirement must be available with respect to the portion of an employee's phased retirement accrued benefit that is payable as a phased retirement benefit.

(iii) Limitation on optional forms of payment. Phased retirement benefits may not be paid in the form of a single sum or other form that constitutes an eligible rollover distribution under section 402(c)(4).

*(3) Limited to full-time employees who are otherwise eligible to commence benefits.* Phased retirement benefits are only permitted to be made available to an employee who, prior to the phased retirement period, normally maintains a full-time work schedule and who would otherwise be eligible to commence retirement benefits immediately if he or she were to fully retire.

*(4) Authority of Commissioner to adopt other rules.* The Commissioner, in revenue rulings, notices, or other guidance published in the Internal Revenue Bulletin (see § 601.601(d)(2)(ii)(b) of this chapter), may adopt additional rules regarding the coordination of partial retirement under a phased retirement program and the qualification rules of section 401(a).

**(b) Definitions.** *(1) In general.* The definitions set forth in this paragraph (b) apply for purposes of this section.

*(2) Phased retirement program.* The term *phased retirement program* means a written, employer-adopted program pursuant to which employees may reduce the number of hours they customarily work beginning on or after a date specified under the program and commence phased retirement benefits during the phased retirement period, as provided under the plan.

*(3) Phased retirement period.* The term *phased retirement period* means the period of time that the employee and employer reasonably expect the employee to work reduced hours under the phased retirement program.

*(4) Phased retirement accrued benefit.* The term *phased retirement accrued benefit* means the portion of the employee's accrued benefit equal to the product of the employee's total accrued benefit on the annuity starting date for the employee's phased retirement benefit, and one minus the employee's work schedule fraction.

*(5) Phased retirement benefit.* The term *phased retirement benefit* means the benefit paid to an employee upon the employee's partial retirement under a phased retirement program, based on some or all of the employee's phased retirement accrued benefit, and payable in the optional form of benefit applicable at the annuity starting date.

*(6) Work schedule.* With respect to an employee, the term *work schedule* means the number of hours the employee is reasonably expected to work annually during the phased retirement period (determined in accordance with paragraph (c)(4) of this section).

*(7) Full-time work schedule.* With respect to an employee, the term *full-time work schedule* means the number of hours the employee would normally work during a year if the employee were to work on a full-time basis, determined in a reasonable and consistent manner.

*(8) Work schedule fraction.* With respect to an employee, the term *work schedule fraction* means a fraction, the numerator of which is the employee's work schedule and the denominator of which is the employee's full-time work schedule.

**(c) Bona fide phased retirement program.** *(1) Definition generally.* The term *bona fide phased retirement program* means a phased retirement program that satisfies paragraphs (c)(2) through (5) of this section.

*(2) Limitation to individuals who have attained age 59½.* A bona fide phased retirement program must be limited to

employees who have attained age 59½. A plan is permitted to impose additional requirements for eligibility to participate in a bona fide phased retirement program, such as limiting eligibility to either employees who have satisfied additional age or service conditions (or combination thereof) specified in the program or employees whose benefit may not be distributed without consent under section 411(a)(11).

*(3) Participation must be voluntary.* An employee's participation in a bona fide phased retirement program must be voluntary.

*(4) Reduction in hours requirement.* An employee who participates in a bona fide phased retirement program must reasonably be expected (by both the employer and employee) to reduce, by 20 percent or more, the number of hours the employee customarily works. This requirement is satisfied if the employer and employee enter into an agreement, in good faith, under which they agree that the employee will reduce, by 20 percent or more, the number of hours the employee works during the phased retirement period.

*(5) Limited to employees who are not key-employee owners.* Phased retirement benefits are not permitted to be made available to a key employee who is described in section 416(i)(1)(A)(ii) or (iii).

**(d) Conditions for commencement of phased retirement benefit.** *(1) Imputed accruals based on full-time schedule.* (i) General rule. During the phased retirement period, in addition to being entitled to payment of the phased retirement benefit, the employee must be entitled to participate in the plan in the same manner as if the employee still maintained a full-time work schedule (including calculation of average earnings, imputation of compensation in accordance with § 1.414(s)-1(f), and imputation of service in accordance with the service-crediting rules under § 1.401(a)(4)-11(d)), and must be entitled to the same benefits (including early retirement benefits, retirement-type subsidies, and optional forms of benefits) upon full retirement as a similarly situated employee who has not elected phased retirement, except that the years of service credited under the plan for any plan year during the phased retirement period is determined under paragraph (d)(1)(ii) or (iii) of this section, whichever is applicable.

(ii) Method for crediting years of service for full plan years. The years of service credited under the plan for any full plan year during the phased retirement period is multiplied by an adjustment ratio that is equal to the ratio of the employee's actual hours worked during that year to the number of hours that would be worked by the employee during that year under a full-time work schedule. Alternatively, on a reasonable and consistent basis, the adjustment ratio may be based on the ratio of an employee's actual compensation during the year to the compensation that would be paid to the employee during the year if he or she had maintained a full-time work schedule.

(iii) Method for crediting years of service for partial plan years. In the case of a plan year only a portion of which is during a phased retirement period for an employee, the method described in paragraphs (d)(1)(i) and (ii) of this section is applied with respect to that portion of the plan year. Thus, for example, if an employee works full time until October 1 of a calendar plan year and works one-third time from October 1 through December 31 of the year, then the employee is credited with 10 months for that year (9 months plus ⅓ of 3 months).

*(2) Ancillary benefits during phased retirement period.* (i) Death benefits. If an employee dies while receiving phased retirement benefits, death benefits are allocated between the phased retirement benefit and the benefit that would be payable upon subsequent full retirement. See also § 1.401(a)-20, A-9. Thus, if an employee dies after the annuity starting date for the phased retirement benefit, death benefits are paid with respect to the phased retirement benefit in accordance with the optional form elected for that benefit, and death benefits are paid with respect to the remainder of the employee's benefit in accordance with the plan's provisions regarding death during employment.

(ii) Other ancillary benefits. To the extent provided under the terms of the plan, ancillary benefits, other than death benefits described in paragraph (d)(2)(i) of this section, are permitted to be provided during the phased retirement period.

*(3) Calculation of benefit at full retirement.* (i) In general. Upon full retirement following partial retirement under a phased retirement program, the employee's total accrued benefit under the plan (including the employee's accruals during the phased retirement period, determined in accordance with paragraph (d)(1) of this section) is offset by the portion of the employee's phased retirement accrued benefit that is being distributed as a phased retirement benefit at the time of full retirement.

(ii) Adjustment for prior payments. If, before full retirement, the employee's phased retirement benefit has been reduced under paragraph (d)(4) of this section, then the employee's accrued benefit under the plan is also offset upon full retirement by an amount that is actuarially equivalent to the phased retirement benefit payments that have been made during the phased retirement period that were not made with respect to the portion of the phased retirement accrued benefit that is applied as an offset under paragraph (d)(3)(i) of this section at the time of full retirement.

(iii) Election of optional form with respect to net benefit. Upon full retirement, an employee is entitled to elect, in accordance with section 417, an optional form of benefit with respect to the net accrued benefit determined under paragraph (d)(3)(i) and (ii) of this section.

(iv) New election permitted for phased retirement benefit. A plan is permitted to provide that, upon full retirement, an employee may elect, in accordance with section 417 and without regard to paragraph (a)(2)(iii) of this section, a new optional form of benefit with respect to the portion of the phased retirement accrued benefit that is being distributed as a phased retirement benefit. Any such new optional form of benefit is calculated at the time of full retirement as the actuarial equivalent of the future phased retirement benefits (without offset for the phased retirement benefits previously paid).

*(4) Prospective reduction in phased retirement benefit if hours are materially greater than expected.* (i) General rule. Except as otherwise provided in this paragraph (d)(4), a plan must compare annually the number of hours actually worked by an employee during the phased retirement testing period and the number of hours the employee was reasonably expected to work during the testing period for purposes of calculating the work schedule fraction. For this purpose, the phased retirement testing period is the 12 months preceding the comparison date (or such longer period permitted under paragraph(d)(4)(iv) of this section, or any shorter period that applies if there is a comparison date as a result of an agreed increase under paragraph (d)(4)(vi) of this section). In the event that the actual hours worked (determined on an annual

basis) during the phased retirement testing period exceeds the work schedule, then, except as provided in paragraph (d)(4)(ii) or (v) of this section, the employee's phased retirement benefit must be reduced in accordance with the method provided in paragraph (d)(4)(iii) of this section, effective as of an adjustment date specified in the plan that is not more than 3 months later than the comparison date.

(ii) Permitted variance in hours. A plan is not required to reduce the phased retirement benefit unless the hours worked during the phased retirement testing period are materially greater than the hours that would be expected to be worked under the work schedule. For this purpose, the employee's hours worked (determined on annual basis) are materially greater than the employee's work schedule if either—

(A) The employee's hours worked (determined on an annual basis) are more than 133⅓ percent of the employee's work schedule; or

(B) The employee's hours worked (determined on an annual basis) exceed 90 percent of the full-time work schedule.

(iii) Adjustment method. If a phased retirement benefit must be reduced under paragraph (d)(4) of this section, a new (i.e., reduced) phased retirement benefit must be calculated as provided in this paragraph (d)(4)(iii). First, an adjusted work schedule is determined. The adjusted work schedule is an annual schedule based on the number of hours the employee actually worked during the phased retirement testing period. The adjusted work schedule is applied to the employee's accrued benefit that was used to calculate the prior phased retirement benefit. This results in a new phased retirement accrued benefit for purposes of paragraph (b)(4) of this section. Second, a new phased retirement benefit is determined, based on the new phased retirement accrued benefit and payable in the same optional form of benefit (i.e., using the same annuity starting date and the same early retirement factor and other actuarial adjustments) as the prior phased retirement benefit. If an employee is receiving more than one phased retirement benefit (as permitted under paragraph (e)(2) of this section) and a reduction is required under paragraph (d)(4) of this section, then the reduction is applied first to the most recently commencing phased retirement benefit (and then, if necessary, to the next most recent phased retirement benefit, etc.).

(iv) Comparison date for phased retirement testing period. The comparison date is any date chosen by the employer on a reasonable and consistent basis and specified in the plan, such as the last day of the plan year, December 31, or the anniversary of the annuity starting date for the employee's phased retirement benefit. As an alternative to testing the hours worked during the 12 months preceding the comparison date, the plan may, on a reasonable and consistent basis, provide that the comparison of actual hours worked to the work schedule be based on a cumulative period that exceeds 12 months beginning with either the annuity starting date for the employee's phased retirement benefit or any later date specified in the plan.

(v) Exceptions to comparison requirement. (A) In general. The comparison of hours described in paragraph (d)(4) of this section is not required in the situations set forth in this paragraph (d)(4)(v).

(B) Employees recently commencing phased retirement. No comparison is required for an employee who commenced phased retirement benefits within the 12-month period preceding the comparison date.

(C) Employees with short phased retirement periods. No comparison is required during the first 2 years of an employee's phased retirement period if—

(1) The employee has entered into an agreement with the employer under which the employee's phased retirement period will not exceed 2 years and the employee will fully retire at the end of such period; and

(2) The employee fully retires after a phased retirement period not in excess of 2 years.

(D) Employees with proportional pay reduction. No comparison is required for any phased retirement testing period if the amount of compensation paid to the employee during that period does not exceed the compensation that would be paid to the employee if he or she had maintained a full-time work schedule multiplied by the work schedule fraction.

(E) Employees at or after normal retirement age. No comparison is required for any phased retirement testing period ending within 3 months before the employee's normal retirement age or any time thereafter.

(vi) Agreement to increase hours. (A) General rule. In the event that the employer and the employee agree to increase prospectively the hours under the employee's work schedule prior to normal retirement age, then, notwithstanding the exceptions provided in paragraphs (d)(4)(v)(B) through (D) of this section, the plan must treat the effective date of the agreement to increase the employee's hours as a comparison date for purposes of paragraph (d)(4)(iv) of this section. For purposes of this paragraph (d)(4)(vi), with respect to an employee, the term new work schedule means the greater of the actual number of hours the employee worked (determined on an annual basis) during the prior phased retirement testing period or the annual number of hours the employee reasonably expects to work under the new agreement.

(B) Required adjustments. If the employee's hours under the new work schedule are materially greater (within the meaning of paragraph (d)(4)(ii) of this section) than the hours the employee would be expected to work (based on the employee's prior work schedule), the employer is required to reduce the employee's phased retirement benefit, effective as of the date of the increase, based on the new work schedule. In this case, the employee's new work schedule is used for future comparisons under paragraph (d)(4) of this section.

(C) Permitted adjustments. If the employee's hours under the new work schedule are not materially greater (within the meaning of paragraph (d)(4)(ii) of this section) than the hours the employee would be expected to work (based on the employee's prior work schedule), the employer is permitted, but not required, to reduce the employee's phased retirement benefit, effective as of the date of the increase, based on the new work schedule. If the benefit is so reduced, the employee's new work schedule is used for future comparisons under paragraph (d)(4) of this section. If the employee's phased retirement benefit is not so reduced, future comparisons are determined using the employee's prior work schedule.

**(e) Other rules.** *(1) Highly compensated employees.* An employee who partially retires under a phased retirement program and who was a highly compensated employee, as defined in section 414(q), immediately before the partial retirement is considered to be a highly compensated employee during the phased retirement period, without regard to the compensation actually paid to the employee during the phased retirement period.

*(2) Multiple phased retirement benefits permitted.* (i) In general. A plan is permitted to provide one or more additional phased retirement benefits prospectively to an employee who is receiving a phased retirement benefit if the conditions set forth in paragraph (e)(2)(ii) of this section are satisfied. At the later annuity starting date for the additional phased retirement benefit, the additional phased retirement benefits may not exceed the amount permitted to be paid based on the excess of—

(A) The employee's phased retirement accrued benefit at the later annuity starting date, over

(B) The portion of the employee's phased retirement accrued benefit at the earlier annuity starting date that is being distributed as a phased retirement benefit.

(ii) Conditions. The additional phased retirement benefit described in paragraph (e)(2)(i) of this section may be provided only if—

(A) The prior phased retirement benefit was not based on the employee's entire phased retirement accrued benefit at the annuity starting date for the prior phased retirement benefit, or

(B) The employee's work schedule at the later annuity starting date is less than the employee's work schedule that was used to calculate the prior phased retirement benefit.

*(3) Application of section 411(d)(6).* In accordance with § 1.411(d)-4, A-1(b)(1), the right to receive a partial distribution of an employee's accrued benefit as a phased retirement benefit is treated as an optional form of payment that is separate from the right to receive a full distribution of the accrued benefit upon full retirement.

*(4) Application of nondiscrimination rules.* The right to receive a phased retirement benefit is a benefit, right, or feature that is subject to § 1.401(a)(4)-4.

**(f) Examples.** The following examples illustrate the application of this section:

*Example (1).* (i) Employer's Plans. Plan X (as in effect prior to amendment to reflect the phased retirement program described below) is a defined benefit plan maintained by Employer M. Plan X provides an accrued benefit of 1.5% of the average of an employee's highest three years of pay (based on the highest 36 consecutive months of pay), times years of service (with 1,000 hours of service required for a year of service), payable as a life annuity beginning at age 65. Plan X permits employees to elect to commence actuarially reduced distributions at any time after the later of termination of employment or attainment of age 50, except that if an employee retires after age 55 and completion of 20 years of service, the applicable reduction is only 3% per year for the years between ages 65 and 62 and 6% per year for the years between ages 62 to 55. Plan X permits employees to select, with spousal consent, a single life annuity, a joint and contingent annuity with the employee having the right to select any beneficiary and a continuation percentage of 50%, 75%, or 100%, or a 10-year certain and life annuity.

(ii) Phased Retirement Program. Employer M adopts a voluntary phased retirement program that will only be available for employees who retire during the two-year period from February 1, 2006 to January 31, 2008. The program will not be available to employees who are not entitled to an immediate pension or who are 1 percent owners. Employer M has determined that employees typically begin to retire after attainment of age 55 with at least 15 years of service. Accordingly, to increase retention of certain employees, the program will provide that employees in certain specified work positions who have reached age 59½ and completed 15 years of service may elect phased retirement. The program permits phased retirement to be implemented through a reduction of 25%, 50%, or 75% in the number of hours expected to be worked for up to 5 years following phased retirement (other reduced schedules may be elected with the approval of M), with the employee's compensation during the phased retirement period to be based on what a similar full-time employee would be paid, reduced by the applicable percentage reduction in hours expected to be worked. In order to participate in the program, the employee and the employer must enter into an agreement under which the employee will reduce his or her hours accordingly. The agreement also provides that the employee's compensation during phased retirement will be reduced by that same percentage. The program is announced to employees in the fall of 2005.

(iii) Plan Provisions Regarding Phased Retirement Benefit. (A) Plan X is amended, prior to February 1, 2006, to provide that an employee who elects phased retirement under M's phased retirement program is permitted to commence benefits with respect to a portion of his or her accrued retirement benefit (the employee's phased retirement accrued benefit), based on the applicable percentage reduction in hours expected to be worked. For example, for a 25% reduction in hours, the employee is entitled to commence benefits with respect to 25% of his or her accrued benefit. Plan X permits an employee who commences phased retirement to elect, with spousal consent, from any of the optional forms provided under the plan.

(B) During the phased retirement period, the employee will continue to accrue benefits (without regard to the plan's 1,000 hour requirement), with his or her pay for purposes of calculating benefits under Plan X increased by the ratio of 100 percent to the percentage of full-time pay that will be paid during phased retirement and with the employee's service credit to be equal to the product of the same percentage times the service credit that would apply if the employee were working full time. Upon the employee's subsequent full retirement, his or her total accrued benefit will be based on the resulting highest three years of pay and total years of service, offset by the phased retirement accrued benefit. The retirement benefit payable upon subsequent full retirement is in addition to the phased retirement benefit. Plan X does not provide for a new election with respect to the phased retirement benefit.

(C) In the case of death during the phased retirement period, the employee will be treated as a former employee to the extent of his or her phased retirement benefit and as an active employee to the extent of the retirement benefit that would be due upon full retirement.

(D) Because the terms of the phased retirement program provide that the employee's compensation during phased retirement will be reduced by that same percentage as applies to calculate phased retirement benefits, Plan X does not have provisions requiring annual testing of hours actually worked.

(iv) Application to a Specific Employee. (A) Phased retirement benefit. Employee E is age 59½ with 20 years of credited service. Employee E's compensation is $90,000, and E's highest three years of pay is $85,000. Employee E elects phased retirement on April 1, 2006 and elects to reduce hours by 50% beginning on July 1, 2006. Thus, E's annuity starting date for the phased retirement benefit is July 1, 2006. Employee E's total accrued benefit as of July 1, 2006 as a single life annuity payable at normal retirement age is equal to $25,500 per year (1.5% times $85,000 times 20 years of service). Thus, Employee E's phased retirement accrued benefit as of July 1, 2006 as a single life annuity payable at normal retirement age is equal to $12,750 per year ($25,500 times 1 minus E's work schedule fraction of 50%). Accordingly, Employee E's phased retirement benefit payable as a straight life annuity commencing on July 1, 2006 is equal to $9,690 per year ($12,750 per year times 76% (100% minus the applicable reduction for early retirement equal to 3% for 3 years and 6% for an additional 2½ years)). Employee E elects a joint and 50% survivor annuity, with E's spouse as the contingent annuitant. Under Plan X, the actuarial factor for this form of benefit is 90%, so E's benefit is $8,721 per year.

(B) Death during phased retirement. If Employee E were to die on or after July 1, 2006 and before subsequent full retirement, E's spouse would be entitled to a 50% survivor annuity based on the joint and 50% survivor annuity being paid to E, plus a qualified preretirement survivor annuity that complies with section 417 with respect to the additional amount that would be paid to E if he or she had fully retired on the date of E's death.

(C) Subsequent full retirement benefit. Three years later, Employee E fully retires from Employer M. Throughout this period, E's compensation has been 50% of the compensation that would have been paid to E if he or she were working full time. Consequently, no adjustment in E's phased retirement benefit is required. E's highest consecutive 36 months of compensation would be $95,000 if E had not elected phased retirement and E has been credited with 1½ years of service credit for the 3 years of phased retirement (.50 times 3 years). Accordingly, prior to offset for E's phased retirement accrued benefit, E's total accrued benefit as of July 1, 2009 as a single life annuity commencing at normal retirement age is equal to $30,637.50 per year ($95,000 times 1.5% times 21.5 years of service) and, after the offset for E's phased retirement accrued benefit, E's retirement benefit as a single life annuity commencing at normal retirement age is equal to $17,887.50 ($30,637.50 minus $12,750). Thus, the amount of E's additional early retirement benefit payable as a straight life annuity at age 62½ is equal to $16,545.94 per year ($17,887.50 per year times 92.5% (100% minus 3% for 2½ years)). Employee E elects, with spousal consent, a 10-year certain and life annuity that applies to the remainder of E's accrued benefit. This annuity is in addition to the previously elected joint and 50% survivor annuity payable as E's phased retirement benefit.

*Example (2).* (i) Same Plan and Phased Retirement Program, Except Annual Testing Required. The facts with respect to the Plan X and M's phased retirement program are the same as in Example 1, except that the program does not provide that the employee's compensation during phased retirement will be reduced by that same percentage as is applied to calculate phased retirement benefits, but instead the compensation depends on the number of hours worked by the employee. Plan X provides for annual testing on a calendar year basis and for an employee's phased retirement benefit to be reduced proportionately if the hours worked exceed a threshold, under provisions which reflect the variance permitted paragraph (d)(4)(ii) of this section.

(ii) Employee Has Small Increase in Hours. The facts with respect to Employee E are the same as in Example 1, except that E's full time work schedule would result in 2,000 hours worked annually, E's work schedule fraction is 50%, and E works 500 hours from July 1, 2006 through December 31, 2006, 1,000 hours in 2007, 1,200 hours in 2008, and 600 hours from January 1, 2009 through E's full retirement on June 30, 2009.

(iii) Application of Testing Rules. No comparison of hours is required for the partial testing period that occurs in 2006. For 2007, no reduction is required in E's phased retirement benefit as a result of the hours worked by E during 2007 because the hours did not exceed E's work schedule (50% of 2,000). For 2008, although the hours worked by E exceeded E's work schedule, no reduction is required because the hours worked in 2008 were not materially greater than E's work schedule (1,200 is not more than the variance permitted under paragraph (d)(4)(ii) of this section, which is 133⅓% of 1,000). E's total accrued benefit upon E's retirement on July 1, 2009 would be based on 21.65 years of service to reflect the actual hours worked from July 1, 2006 through June 30, 2009.

*Example (3).* (i) Same Plan and Phased Retirement Program, Except Material Increase in Hours. The facts with respect to the Plan X and M's phased retirement program are the same as in Example 2, except E works 1,400 hours in 2008 and 700 hours in the first half of 2009.

(ii) Application of Testing Rules. No comparison of hours is required for the partial testing period that occurs in 2006. For 2007, no reduction is required in E's phased retirement benefit as a result of the hours worked by E during 2007 because the hours did not exceed 50% of 2,000. However, the hours worked by E during 2008 exceed 133⅓% of E's work schedule (50% of 2,000), so that the phased retirement benefit paid to E during 2009 must be reduced. The reduction is effective March 1, 2009. The new phased retirement benefit of $5,232.60 is based on 30% of the participant's accrued benefit as of July 1, 2006, payable as a joint and 50% survivor annuity commencing on that date (30% times $25,500 times the early retirement factor of 76% times the joint and 50% factor of 90%). This is equivalent to reducing the previously elected joint and 50% survivor annuity payable with respect to E by 40% (400 "excess" hours divided by the 1,000 hour expected reduction). When E retires fully on July 1, 2009, E's total accrued benefit as of July 1, 2009 as a single life annuity commencing at normal retirement age is $31,065 per year ($95,000 times 1.5% times 21.8 years of service). This accrued benefit is offset by (A) E's phased retirement accrued benefit (which is $7,650 (600 divided by 2,000 times $25,500)) plus (B) the actuarial equivalent of 40% of the payments that were made to E from January 1, 2008 through February 28, 2009.

*Example (4).* (i) Same Plan and Phased Retirement Program, Except Employer and Employee Agree to Decrease Hours. The facts with respect to the Plan X and M's phased retirement program are the same as in Example 2, except before 2008, E enters into an agreement with M to decrease E's number of hours worked from 50% of full time to 25% of full time. E works 500 hours in 2008 and 250 hours in 2009.

(ii) Application of Multiple Benefit Rule. Under paragraph (e)(2) of this section, Plan M may provide for an additional phased retirement benefit to be offered to E for 2008. The maximum increase would be for the phased retirement benefit paid to E during 2009 to be increased based on a phased retirement accrued benefit equal to 75% of E's accrued benefit (1,500 divided by 2,000). Thus, the amount being paid to E would be increased, effective January 1, 2008, based on the excess of 75% of E's total accrued benefit on December 31, 2007, over E's original phased retirement accrued benefit of $12,750. Employee E would have the right to elect, with spousal consent, any annuity form offered under Plan X (with the actuarial adjustment for time of commencement and form of payment to be based on the age of E and any contingent beneficiary (and E's service, if applicable) on June 1, 2008), which would be in addition to the previously elected joint and 50% survivor annuity payable as E's original phased retirement benefit. When E retires fully on July 1, 2009, Employee E's total accrued benefit as of July 1, 2009 would be offset by (A) E's original phased retirement accrued benefit plus (B) the phased retirement accrued benefit for which additional phased retirement benefits were payable beginning in 2008.

**(g) Effective date.** The rules of this section apply to plan years beginning on or after the date of publication of the Treasury decision adopting these rules as final regulations in the Federal Register.

**§ 1.401(a)-4 Optional forms of benefit (before 1994).**

***Caution:*** The Treasury has not yet amended Reg § 1.401(a)-4 to reflect changes made by P.L. 105-34.

Q-1. How does section 401(a)(4) apply to optional forms of benefits?

A-1. **(a) In general.** *(1) Scope.* The nondiscrimination requirements of section 401(a)(4) apply to the amount of contributions or benefits, optional forms of benefit, and other benefits, rights and features (e.g., actuarial assumptions, methods of benefit calculation, loans, social security supplements, and disability benefits) under a plan. This section addresses the application of section 401(a)(4) only to optional forms of benefit under a plan. Generally, the determination of whether an optional form is nondiscriminatory under section 401(a)(4) is made by reference to the availability of such optional form, and not by reference to the utilization or actual receipt of such optional form. See Q&A-2 of this section. Even though an optional form of benefit under a plan may be nondiscriminatory under section 401(a)(4) and this § 1.401(a)-4 because the availability of such optional form does not impermissibly favor employees in the highly compensated group, such plan may fail to satisfy section 401(a)(4) with respect to the amount of contributions or benefits or with respect to other benefits, rights and features if, for example, the method of calculation or the amount or value of benefits payable under such optional form impermissibly favors the highly compensated group. See § 1.411(d)-4, Q&A-1 for the definition of "optional form of benefit."

*(2) Nondiscrimination requirements.* Each optional form of benefit provided under a plan is subject to the nondiscrimination requirement of section 401(a)(4) and thus the availability of each optional form of benefit must not discriminate in favor of the employees described in section 401(a)(4) in whose favor discrimination is prohibited (the "highly compensated group"). See paragraph (b) of this Q&A-1 for a description of the employees included in such group. This is true without regard to whether a particular optional form of benefit is the actuarial equivalent of any other optional form of benefit under the plan. Thus, for example, a plan may not condition, or otherwise limit, the availability of a single sum distribution of an employee's benefit in a manner that impermissibly favors the highly compensated group.

**(b) Highly compensated group.** For plan years commencing prior to the applicable effective date for the amendment made to section 401(a)(4) by section 1114 of the Tax Reform Act of 1986 (TRA '86), the highly compensated group consists of those employees who are officers, shareholders, or highly compensated. For plan years beginning on or after the applicable effective date of the amendments to section 401(a)(4) made by TRA '86, the highly compensated group consists of those employees who are highly compensated within the meaning of section 414(q). The amendment to section 401(a)(4) made by section 1114 of TRA '86 is generally effective for plan years commencing after December 31, 1988. See section 1114(a) of TRA '86.

Q-2. How is it determined whether an optional form of benefit satisfies the nondiscrimination requirements of section 401(a)(4)?

A-2. **(a) Nondiscrimination requirement.** *(1) In general.* An optional form of benefit under a plan is nondiscriminatory under section 401(a)(4) only if the requirements of paragraphs (a)(2) and (a)(3) of this Q&A-2 are satisfied with respect to such optional form. The determination of whether an optional form of benefit satisfies these requirements is made by reference to the availability of the optional form, and not by reference to the utilization or actual receipt of such optional form. Thus, an optional form of benefit that satisfies the requirements of paragraphs (a)(2) and (a)(3) of this Q&A-2 is nondiscriminatory under section 401(a)(2) even though the highly compensated group disproportionately utilizes such optional form. However, the composition of the group of employees who actually receive benefits in an optional form may be relevant in determining whether such optional form satisfies the requirement of paragraph (a)(3) of this Q&A-2 with respect to effective availability.

*(2) Current availability.* (i) Plan years prior to TRA '86 effective date. Except as provided in paragraph (a)(2)(iii) of this Q&A-2, for plan years prior to the effective date of the amendments made to section 401(b) by section 1112(a) of TRA '86, the requirement of this paragraph (a)(2) is satisfied only if the group of employees to whom the optional form is currently available satisfies either the seventy percent test of section 410(b)(1)(A) or the nondiscriminatory classification test of section 410(b)(1)(B).

(ii) Plan years commencing on or after TRA '86 effective date. Except as provided in paragraph (a)(2)(iii) of this Q&A-2, for plan years commencing on or after the effective date on which the amendments made to section 410(b) by section 1112(a) of TRA '86 first apply to a plan, the requirement of this paragraph (a)(2) is satisfied only if the group of employees to whom the optional form is currently available satisfies either the percentage test set forth in section 410(b)(1)(A), the ratio test set forth in section 410(b)(1)(B), or the nondiscriminatory classification test set forth in section 410(b)(2)(A)(i). The employer need not satisfy the average benefit percentage test in section 410(b)(2)(A)(ii) in order for the optional form to be currently available to a nondiscriminatory group of employees.

(iii) Special rule for certain governmental or church plans. Plans described in section 410(c) will be treated as satisfying the current availability test of this paragraph (a)(2) if the group of employees with respect to whom the optional form is currently available satisfies the requirements of section 401(a)(3) as in effect on September 1, 1974.

(iv) Effective date for TRA '86 amendments to section 410(b). The amendments to section 410(b) made by section 1112(a) of TRA '86 are generally effective for plan years commencing after December 31, 1988. See section 1112(e)(1) of TRA '86.

(v) Elimination of optional forms. (A) In general. Notwithstanding paragraphs (a)(2)(i) and (a)(2)(ii) of this Q&A-2, in the case of an optional form of benefit that has been eliminated under a plan with respect to specified employees for benefits accrued after the later of the eliminating amendment's adoption date or effective date, the determination of whether such optional form satisfies this paragraph (a)(2) with respect to such employees is to be made immediately prior to the elimination. Accordingly, if, as of the later of the adoption date or effective date of an amendment eliminating an optional form with respect to future benefit accruals, the current availability of such optional form immediately prior to such amendment satisfies this paragraph (a)(2), then the optional form will be treated as satisfying this paragraph (a)(2) for all subsequent years.

(B) Example. A profit-sharing plan that provides for a single sum distribution available to all employees on termination of employment is amended January 1, 1990, to eliminate such single sum optional form of benefit with respect to benefits accrued after January 1, 1991. As of January 1, 1991, the single sum optional form of benefit is available to a group of employees that satisfies the percentage test of section 410(b)(1)(A). As of January 1, 1995, all nonhighly compensated employees who were entitled to the single sum optional form of benefit have terminated from employment with the employer and taken a distribution of their benefits. The only remaining employees who have a right to take a portion of their benefits in the form of a single sum distribution on termination of employment are highly compensated employees. Because the availability of the single sum optional form of benefit satisfied the current availability test as of January 1, 1991, the availability of such optional form of benefit is deemed to continue to satisfy the current availability test of this paragraph (a)(2).

*(3) Effective availability.* (i) In general. The requirement of this paragraph (a)(3) is satisfied only if, based on the facts and circumstances, the group of employees to whom the optional form is effectively available does not substantially favor the highly compensated group. This is the case even if the optional form is, or has been, currently available to a group of employees that satisfies the applicable requirements in paragraph (a)(2)(i) or (ii) of this Q&A-2.

(ii) *Examples.* The provisions of paragraph (a)(3)(i) of this Q&A-2 can be illustrated by the following examples:

*Example (1).* Employer X maintains a defined benefit plan that covers both of the 2 highly compensated employees of the employer and 8 of the twelve nonhighly compensated employees of the employer. Plan X provides for a normal retirement benefit payable as an annuity and based on a normal retirement age of 65, and an early retirement benefit payable upon termination in the form of an annuity to employees who terminate from service with the employer on or after age 55 with 30 or more years of service. Each of the 2 employees of employer X who are in the highly compensated group currently meet the age and service requirement, or will have 30 years of service by the time they reach age 55. All but 2 of the 8 nonhighly compensated employees of employer X who are covered by the plan were hired on or after age 35 and thus, cannot qualify for the early retirement benefit provision. Even though the group of employees to whom the early retirement benefit is currently available does not impermissibly favor the highly compensated group by reason of disregarding age and service, these facts and circumstances indicate that the effective availability of the early retirement benefit in plan X substantially favors the highly compensated group.

*Example (2).* Assume the same facts as in *Example 1* except that the early retirement benefit is added by a plan amendment first adopted, announced and effective December 1, 1991, and is available only to employees who terminate from employment with the employer prior to December 15, 1991. Further assume that all employees were hired prior to attaining age 25, and that the group of employees who have, or will have attained age 55 with 30 years of service, by December 15, 1991, satisfies the ratio test of section 410(b)(1)(B). Finally, assume that the only employees who terminate from employment with the employer during the two week period in which the early retirement benefit is available are employees in the highly compensated group. These facts and circumstances indicate that the effective availability of the early retirement benefit substantially favors the highly compensated group. This is the case even though the limitation of the early retirement benefit to a specified period satisfies section 411(d)(6).

*Example (3).* Employer Y amends plan Y on June 30, 1990, to provide for a single sum distribution for employees who terminate from employment with the employer after June 30, 1990, and prior to January 1, 1991. The availability of this single sum distribution is conditioned on the employee having a particular disability at the time of termination of employment. The only employee of the employer who meets this disability requirement at the time of the amendment and thereafter through December 31, 1990, is a highly compensated employee. Generally, a disability condition with respect to the availability of a single sum distribution may be disregarded in determining whether the current availability of such optional form of benefit is discriminatory. However, these facts and circumstances indicate that the effective availability of the optional form of benefit substantially favors the highly compensated group.

*Example (4).* Employer Z maintains a money purchase pension plan that covers all employees of the employer. The plan provides for distribution in the form of a joint and survivor annuity, a life annuity, or equal installments over 10 years. During the 1992 calendar year the employer winds up his business. In December of 1992, only two employees remain in the employment of the employer, both of whom are highly compensated. Employer Z then amends the plan to provide for a single sum distribution to employees who terminate from employment on or after the date of the amendment. Both highly compensated employees terminate from employment on December 31, 1992, taking a single sum distribution of their benefits. These facts and circumstances indicate that the effective availability of the single sum optional form of benefit substantially favors the highly compensated group.

**(b) Application of tests.** *(1) Current availability.* (i) In general. Except as otherwise provided in this paragraph (b), in determining whether an optional form of benefit that is subject to specified eligibility conditions is currently available to an employee for purposes of paragraph (a) of this Q&A-2, the determination of current availability generally is to be based on the current facts and circumstances with respect to the employee (e.g., the employee's current compensation or the employee's current net worth). Thus, for example, the fact that an employee may, in the future, satisfy an eligibility condition generally does not cause an optional form of benefit to be treated as currently available to such employee.

(ii) Exceptions for age, service, employment termination and certain other conditions. (A) Age and service conditions. For purposes of applying paragraph (a)(2) of this Q&A-2, except as provided in paragraph (b)(1)(ii)(B) of this Q&A-2, an age condition, a service condition, or both are to be disregarded. For example, an employer that maintains a plan that provides for an early retirement benefit payable as an annuity for employees in division A, subject to a requirement that the employee has attained his or her 55th birthday and has at least twenty years of service with the employer, is to disregard the age and service conditions in determining the group of employees to whom the early retirement annuity benefit is currently available. Thus, the early retirement annuity benefit is treated as currently available to all employees of division A, without regard to their ages or years of service and without regard to whether they could potentially meet the age and service conditions prior to attaining the plan's normal retirement age.

(B) Exception for certain age and service conditions. Age and service conditions that must be satisfied within a specified period of time may not be disregarded pursuant to paragraph (b)(1)(ii)(A) of this Q&A-2. However, in determining the current availability of an optional form of benefit subject to such an age condition, service condition, or both, an employer may project the age and service of employees to the last date on which the optional form of benefit subject to the age condition or service condition (or both) is available under the plan. An employer's ability to project age and service to the last date on which the optional form of benefit is available under the plan is not cut off by a plan termination occurring prior to that date. Thus, for example, assume that an employer maintaining a plan that permits employees terminating from employment on or after age 55 between June 1, 1991 to May 31, 1992, to elect a single sum distribution, decides to terminate the plan on December 31, 1991. In determining the group of employees to whom the single sum optional form of benefit is currently available, this employer may project employees' ages through May 31, 1992.

(C) Certain other conditions disregarded. Conditions on the availability of optional forms of benefit requiring termination of employment, death, satisfaction of a specified health condition (or failure to meet such condition), disability, hardship, marital status, default on a plan loan secured by a participant's account balance, or execution of a covenant not to compete may be disregarded in determining the group of employees to whom an optional form of benefit is currently available.

*(2) Employees taken into account.*For purposes of applying paragraph (a) of this Q&A-2, the tests are to be applied on the basis of the employer's nonexcludable employees (whether or not they are participants in the plan) in the same manner as such tests would be applied in determining whether the plan providing the optional form of benefit satisfies the tests under section 410(b).

*(3) Definition of "plan".*For purposes of applying paragraph (a) of this Q&A-2, the term "plan" has the meaning that such term has for purposes of determining whether the amount of contributions or benefits and whether other benefits, rights, and features are nondiscriminatory under section 401(a)(4).

*(4) Restructuring optional forms of benefit.* (i) In general. For purposes of applying paragraph (a) of this Q&A-2, the availability of two or more optional forms of benefit under a plan may be tested by restructuring such benefits into two or more restructured optional forms of benefit and testing the availability of such restructured optional forms of benefit. If two or more optional forms of benefit under a plan contain both common and distinct components, such optional forms of benefit may be restructured as a single optional form of benefit comprising the common component, and one or more optional forms of benefit comprising each distinct component. Components of optional forms of benefit may be treated as common only if they are identical with respect to all characteristics taken into account under Q&A-1(b) of § 1.411(d)-4. The availability of each restructured optional form of benefit must satisfy the applicable nondiscrimination requirements of paragraph (a) of this Q&A-2.

(ii) Example. A profit-sharing plan covering all the employees of an employer provides a single sum distribution option upon termination from employment for all employees earning less than $50,000 and a single sum distribution option upon termination from employment after the attainment of age 55 for all employees earning $50,000 or more. These distribution options are identical in all other respects. For purposes of applying section 401(a)(4), such optional forms of benefit may be restructured into two different optional forms of benefit: (A) a single sum distribution option upon termination from employment after the attainment of age 55 for all employees (i.e., the common component), and (B) a single sum distribution option upon termination from employment before the attainment of age 55 for all employees earning less than $50,000. The availability of each of these restructured optional forms of benefit must satisfy section 401(a)(4).

**(c) Commissioner may provide additional tests.**The Commissioner may provide such additional factors, tests, and safe harbors as are necessary or appropriate for purposes of determining whether the availability of an optional form of benefit is discriminatory under section 401(a)(4). In addition, the Commissioner may provide that additional eligibility conditions not related directly or indirectly to compensation or wealth may be disregarded under paragraph (b)(1)(ii)(C) of this Q&A-2 in determining the current availability of an optional form of benefit. The Commissioner may provide such additional guidance only through the publication of revenue rulings, notices or other documents of general applicability.

Q-3. May a plan condition the availability of an optional form of benefit on employer discretion?

A-3. No. Even if the availability of an optional form of benefit that is conditioned on employer discretion satisfies the nondiscrimination requirements of section 401(a)(4), the plan providing the optional form of benefit will fail to satisfy certain other requirements of section 401(a), including, in applicable circumstances, the definitely determinable requirement of section 401(a) and the requirements of section 401(a)(25) and section 411(d)(6). See § 1.411(d)-4.

Q-4. Will a plan provision violate section 401(a)(4) merely because it requires that an employee who terminates from service with the employer receive a single sum distribution in the event that the present value of the employee's benefit is not more than $3,500, as permitted by sections 411(a)(11) and 417(e)?

A-4. No. A plan will not be treated as discriminatory under section 401(a)(4) merely because the plan mandates a single sum distribution when the present value of an employee's benefit is not more than $3,500, as permitted by sections 411(a)(11) and 417(e). This is an exception to the general principles of this section. (No similar provision exists excepting such single sum distributions from the limits on employer discretion under section 411(d)(6). See § 1.411(d)-4 Q&A-4.)

Q-5. If the availability of an optional form of benefit discriminates, or may reasonably be expected to discriminate, in favor of the highly compensated group, what acceptable alternatives exist for amending the plan without violating section 411(d)(6)?

A-5. **(a) Transitional rules.** *(1) In general.* The following rules apply for purposes of making necessary amendments to existing plans (as defined in Q&A-6 of this section) under which the availability of an optional form of benefit violates the nondiscrimination requirements of section 401(a)(4) or may reasonably be expected to violate such requirements. These transitional rules are provided under the authority of section 411(d)(6), which allows the elimination of certain optional forms of benefit if permitted by regulations, and section 7805(b).

*(2) Nondiscrimination.* (i) In general. The determination of whether the availability of an optional form of benefit violates section 401(a)(4) is to be made in accordance with Q&A-2 of this section. In addition, the availability of a particular optional form of benefit may reasonably be expected to violate the nondiscrimination requirements of section 401(a)(4) if, under the applicable facts and circumstances, there is a significant possibility that the current availability of such optional form of benefit will impermissibly favor the highly compensated group. This determination must be made on the basis of the seventy percent test of section 410(b)(1)(A) or the nondiscriminatory classification test of section 410(b)(1)(B) as such tests existed prior to the effective date of the amendments made to section 410(b) by section 1112(a) of TRA '86. Thus, a condition may not reasonably be expected to discriminate for purposes of these rules merely because it results in a significant possibility that discrimination will result because of the amendments made to section 410(b) by section 1112(a) of TRA '86. In addition, the availability of an optional form of benefit may not reasonably be expected to discriminate merely because of an age or service condition that may be disregarded in determining the current availability of such optional form of benefit under paragraph (b)(1)(ii)(A) of Q&A-2 of this section. Similarly, the availability of an optional form of benefit may not reasonably be expected to discriminate merely because of an age or service condition that, after permitted projection, does not cause such optional form to fail to satisfy the requirement of this paragraph (a)(2).

(ii) Examples. The provisions of paragraph (a)(2)(i) of this Q&A-5 can be illustrated by the following examples:

*Example (1).* A plan provides that a single sum distribution option is available only to (A) employees earning $50,000 or more in the final year of employment, (B) employees who furnish evidence that they have a net worth above a certain specified amount, and (C) employees who present a letter from an accountant or attorney declaring that it is in the employee's best interest to receive a single sum distribution. Whether the availability of such optional form of benefit discriminates depends on whether it meets the requirements of Q&A-2 of this § 1.401(a)-4. However, each of the specified conditions limiting the availability of the optional form of benefit may reasonably be expected to discriminate in favor of the highly compensated group in operation because of the likelihood of a significant positive correlation between the ability to meet any of the specified conditions and membership in the highly compensated group.

*Example (2).* A plan limits the availability of a single sum distribution option to employees employed in one particular division of the employer's company. All the employees of the company are participants in the plan. During the 1988 plan year, the division employs individuals who represent a nondiscriminatory classification of that company's employees (under section 410(b)(1)(B) prior to the effective date of the amendments made to section 410(b) by section 1112(a) of TRA '86) and is unlikely to cease employing such a nondiscriminatory classification in the future. The availability of a single sum distribution under this plan does not result in discrimination during the 1988 plan year and may not reasonably be expected to do so.

**(b) Transitional alternatives.** If the availability of an optional form of benefit under an existing plan is discriminatory under section 401(a)(4), the plan must be amended either to eliminate the optional form of benefit or to make the availability of the optional form of benefit nondiscriminatory. For example, the availability of an optional form of benefit may be made nondiscriminatory by making such benefit available to sufficient additional employees who are not in the highly compensated group or by imposing nondiscriminatory objective criteria on its availability such that the group of employees to whom the benefit is available is nondiscriminatory. See Q&A-6 of § 1.411(d)-4 for requirements with respect to such objective criteria. If, under an existing plan, the availability of an optional form of benefit may reasonably be expected to discriminate, the plan may be amended in the same manner permitted where the availability of an optional form of benefit is discriminatory. See paragraph (d) of this Q&A-5 for rules limiting the period during which the availability of optional forms of benefit may be eliminated or reduced under this paragraph.

**(c) Compliance and amendment date provisions.** *(1) Operational compliance requirement.* On or before the applicable effective date for the plan (see Q&A-6 of this section), the plan sponsor must select one of the alternatives permitted under paragraph (b) of this Q&A-5 with respect to each affected optional form of benefit and the plan must be operated in accordance with this selection. This is an operational requirement and does not require a plan amendment prior to the period set forth in paragraph (c)(2) of this Q&A-5. There is no special reporting requirement under the Code or this section with respect to this selection.

*(2) Deferred amendment date.* If paragraph (c)(1) of this Q&A-5 is satisfied, a plan amendment conforming the plan to the particular alternative selected under paragraph (b) of this Q&A-5 must be adopted within the time period permitted for amending plans in order to meet the requirements of section 410(b) as amended by TRA '86. Such conforming amendment must be consistent with the sponsor's selection as reflected by plan practice during the period from the effective date to the date the amendment is adopted. Thus, for example, if an existing calendar year noncollectively bargained defined benefit plan has a single sum distribution form subject to a discriminatory condition, that was available as of January 30, 1986 (subject to such condition), and such employer makes one or more single sum distributions available on or after the first day of the first plan year commencing on or after January 1, 1989, and before the plan amendment, then such employer may not adopt a plan amendment eliminating the single sum distribution form. Instead, such employer must adopt an amendment making the distribution form available to a nondiscriminatory group of employees while retaining the availability of such distribution form with respect to the group of employees to whom the benefit is already available. Similarly, any objective criteria that are adopted as part of such amendment must be consistent with the plan practice for the applicable period prior to the amendment. A conforming amendment under this paragraph (c)(2) must be made with respect to each optional form of benefit for which such amendment is required and must be retroactive to the applicable effective date.

**(d) Limitation on transitional alternatives.**The transitional alternatives permitting the elimination or reduction of optional forms of benefit will not violate section 411(d)(6) during the period prior to the applicable effective date for the plan (see Q&A-6 of this section). After the applicable effective date, any amendment (other than one described in paragraph (c)(2) of this Q&A-5) that eliminates or reduces an optional form of benefit or imposes new objective criteria restricting the availability of such optional form of benefit will fail to qualify for the exception to section 411(d)(6) provided in this Q&A-5. This is the case without regard to whether the availability of the optional form of benefit is discriminatory or may reasonably be expected to be discriminatory.

Q-6. For what period are the rules of this section effective?

A-6. **(a) General effective date.** *(1) In general.* Except as otherwise provided in this section, the provisions of this section are effective January 30, 1986, and do not apply to plan years beginning on or after January 1, 1994. For rules applicable to plan years beginning on or after January 1, 1994, see §§ 1.401(a)(4)-1 through 1.401(a)(4)-13.

*(2) Plans of tax-exempt organizations.* In the case of plans maintained by organizations exempt from income taxation under section 501(a), including plans subject to section 403(b)(12)(A)(i) (nonelective plans), except as otherwise provided in this section, the provisions of this section are effective January 30, 1986, and do not apply to plan years beginning on or after January 1, 1996. For rules applicable to plan years beginning on or after January 1, 1996, see §§ 1.401(a)(4)-1 through 1.401(a)(4)-13.

**(b) New plans.** *(1) In general.* Unless otherwise provided in paragraph (b)(2) of this Q&A-6, plans that are either adopted or made effective on or after January 30, 1986, are "new plans". With respect to such new plans, this section is effective January 30, 1986. This effective date is applicable to such plans whether or not they are collectively bargained.

*(2) Exception with respect to certain new plans.* Plans that are new plans as defined in paragraph (b)(1) of this Q&A-6, under which the availability of an optional form of benefit is discriminatory or may reasonably be expected to be discriminatory, and that receive a favorable determination letter that covered such plan provisions with respect to an application submitted prior to July 11, 1988, will be treated as existing plans with respect to such optional form of benefit for purposes of the transitional rules of this section. Thus, such plans are eligible for the compliance and amendment alternatives set forth in the transitional rule in Q&A-5 of this section.

**(c) Existing plans.** *(1) In general.* Plans that are both adopted and in effect prior to January 30, 1986, are "existing plans". In addition, new plans described in paragraph (b)(2) of this Q&A-6 are treated as existing plans with respect to certain forms of benefit. Subject to the limitations in paragraph (d) of this Q&A-6, the effective dates set forth in paragraphs (c)(2) and (c)(3) of this Q&A-6 apply to these existing plans for purposes of this section.

*(2) Existing noncollectively bargained plans.* With respect to existing noncollectively bargained plans, this section is effective for the first day of the first plan year commencing on or after January 1, 1989.

*(3) Existing collectively bargained plans.* With respect to existing collectively bargained plans, this section is effective for the later of the first day of the first plan year commencing on or after January 1, 1989, or the first day of the first plan year that the requirements of section 410(b) as amended by TRA '86 apply to such plan.

**(d) Delayed effective dates not applicable to new optional forms of benefit or conditions.** *(1) In general.* The delayed effective dates in paragraph (c)(2) and (3) of this Q&A-6 for existing plans are applicable with respect to an optional form of benefit only if both the optional form of benefit and any applicable condition either causing the availability of such optional form of benefit to be discriminatory or making it reasonable to expect that the availability of such optional form will be discriminatory were both adopted and in effect prior to January 30, 1986. If the preceding sentence is not satisfied with respect to an optional form of benefit, this section is effective with respect to such optional form of benefit as if the plan were a new plan.

*(2) Exception for certain amendments covered by a favorable determination letter.* If a condition causing the availability of an optional form of benefit to be discriminatory, or to be reasonably expected to discriminate, was adopted or made effective on or after January 30, 1986, and a favorable determination letter that covered such plan provision is or was received with respect to an application submitted before July 11, 1988, the effective date of this section with respect to such provision is the applicable effective date determined under the rules with respect to existing plans, as though such provision had been adopted and in effect prior to January 30, 1986.

**(e) Transitional rule effective date.**The transitional rule provided in Q&A-5 of this section is effective January 30, 1986.

T.D. 8212, 7/8/88, amend T.D. 8360, 9/12/91, T.D. 8485, 8/30/93.

### § 1.401(a)-11 Qualified joint and survivor annuities.

**(a) General rule.** *(1) Required provisions.* A trust, to which section 411 (relating to minimum vesting standards) applies without regard to section 411(e)(2), which is a part of a plan providing for the payment of benefits in any form of a life annuity (as defined in paragraph (b)(1) of this section), shall not constitute a qualified trust under section 401(a)(11) and this section unless such plan provides that:

(i) Unless the election provided in paragraph (c)(1) of this section has been made, life annuity benefits will be paid in a form having the effect of a qualified joint and survivor annuity (as defined in paragraph (b)(2) of this section) with respect to any participant who—

(A) Begins to receive payments under such plan on or after the date the normal retirement age is attained, or

(B) Dies (on or after the date the normal retirement age is attained) while in active service of the employer maintaining the plan, or

(C) In the case of a plan which provides for the payment of benefits before the normal retirement age, begins to receive payments under such plan on or after the date the qualified early retirement age (as defined in paragraph (b)(4) of this section) is attained, or

(D) Separates from service on or after the date the normal retirement age (or the qualified early retirement age) is attained and after satisfaction of eligibility requirements for the payment of benefits under the plan (except for any plan requirement that there be filed a claim for benefits) and thereafter dies before beginning to receive such benefits;

(ii) Any participant may elect, as provided in paragraph (c)(1) of this section, not to receive life annuity benefits in the form of a qualified joint and survivor annuity; and

(iii) If the plan provides for the payment of benefits before the normal retirement age, any participant may elect, as provided in paragraph (c)(2) of this section, that life annuity benefits be payable as an early survivor annuity (as defined in paragraph (b)(3) of this section) upon his death in the event that he—

(A) Attains the qualified early retirement age (as defined in paragraph (b)(4) of this section), and

(B) Dies on or before the day normal retirement age is attained while employed by an employer maintaining the plan.

*(2) Certain cash-outs.* A plan will not fail to satisfy the requirements of section 401(a)(11) and this section merely because it provides that if the present value of the entire nonforfeitable benefit derived from employer contributions of a participant at the time of his separation from service does not exceed $1,750 (or such smaller amount as the plan may specify), such benefit will be paid to him in a lump sum.

*(3) Illustrations.* The provisions of subparagraph (1) of this paragraph may be illustrated by the following examples:

*Example (1).* The X Corporation Defined Contribution Plan was established in 1960. As in effect on January 1, 1974, the plan provided that, upon the participant's retirement, the participant may elect to receive the balance of his account in the form of (1) a single-sum cash payment, (2) a single-sum distribution consisting of X Corporation stock, (3) five equal annual cash payments, (4) a life annuity, or (5) a combination of options (1) through (4). The plan also provided that, if a participant did not elect another form of distribution, the balance of his account would be distributed to him in the form of a single-sum cash payment upon his retirement. Assume that section 401(a)(11) and this section became applicable to the plan as of its plan year beginning January 1, 1976, with respect to persons who were active participants in the plan as of such date (see paragraph (f) of this section). If X Corporation Defined Contribution Plan continues to allow the life annuity payment option after December 31, 1975, it must be amended to provide that if a participant elects a life annuity option the life annuity benefit will be paid in a form having the effect of a qualified joint and survivor annuity, except to the extent that the participant elects another form of benefit payment. However, the plan can continue to provide that, if no election is made, the balance will be paid as a single-sum cash payment. If the trust is not so amended, it will fail to qualify under section 401(a).

*Example (2).* The Y Corporation Retirement Plan provides that plan benefits are payable only in the form of a life annuity and also provides that a participant may retire before the normal retirement age of 65 and receive a benefit if he has completed 30 years of service. Under this plan, an employee who begins employment at the age of 18 will be eligible to receive retirement benefits at the age of 48 if he then has 30 years of service. This plan must allow a participant to elect in the time and manner prescribed in paragraph (c)(2) of this section an early survivor annuity (defined in paragraph (b)(3) of this section) to be payable on the death of the participant if death occurs while the participant is in active service for the employer maintaining the plan and on or after the date the participant reaches the qualified early retirement age of 55 (the later of the date the participant reaches the earliest retirement age (age 48) or 10 years before normal retirement age (age 55)) but before the day after the day the participant reaches normal retirement age (age 65).

*Example (3).* Assume the same facts as in Example (2). A, B, and C began employment with Y Corporation when they each attained age 18. A retires and begins to receive benefit payments at age 48 after completing 30 years of service. The plan is not required to pay a qualified joint and survivor annuity to A and his spouse at any time. B does not elect an early survivor annuity at age 55, but retires at age 57 after completing 39 years of service. Unless B makes an election under subparagraph (1)(ii) of this paragraph, the plan is required to pay a qualified joint and survivor annuity to B and his spouse. C makes no elections described in subparagraph (1) of this paragraph, and dies while in active service at age 66 after completing 48 years of service. The plan is required to pay a qualified survivor annuity to C's spouse.

**(b) Definitions.** As used in this section. *(1) Life annuity.* (i) The term "life annuity" means an annuity that provides retirement payments and requires the survival of the participant or his spouse as one of the conditions for any payment or possible payment under the annuity. For example, annuities that make payments for 10 years or until death, whichever occurs first or whichever occurs last, are life annuities.

(ii) However, the term "life annuity" does not include an annuity, or that portion of an annuity, that provides those benefits which, under section 411(a)(9), would not be taken into account in the determination of the normal retirement benefit or early retirement benefit. For example, "social security supplements" described in the fourth sentence of section 411(a)(9) are not considered to be life annuities for the purposes of this section, whether or not an early retirement benefit is provided under the plan.

*(2) Qualified joint and survivor annuity.* The term "qualified joint and survivor annuity" means an annuity for the life of the participant with a survivor annuity for the life of his spouse which is neither (i) less than one-half of, nor (ii) greater than, the amount of the annuity payable during the joint lives of the participant and his spouse. For purposes of the preceding sentence, amounts described in § 1.401(a)-11(b)(1)(ii) may be disregarded. A qualified joint and survivor annuity must be at least the actuarial equivalent of the normal form of life annuity or, if greater, of any optional form of life annuity offered under the plan. Equivalence may be determined, on the basis of consistently applied reasonable actuarial factors, for each participant or for all participants or reasonable groupings of participants, if such determination does not result in discrimination in favor of employees who are officers, shareholders, or highly compensated. An annuity is not a qualified joint and survivor annuity if payments to the spouse of a deceased participant are terminated, or reduced, because of such spouse's remarriage.

*(3) Early survivor annuity.* The term "early survivor annuity" means an annuity for the life of the participant's spouse the payments under which must not be less than the payments which would have been made to the spouse under the joint and survivor annuity if the participant had made the election described in paragraph (c)(2) of this section immediately prior to his retirement and if his retirement had occurred on the day before his death and within the period during which an election can be made under such paragraph (c)(2). For example, if a participant would be entitled to a single life annuity of $100 per month or a reduced amount under a qualified joint and survivor annuity of $80 per month, his spouse is entitled to a payment of at least $40 per month. However, the payments may be reduced to reflect the number of months of coverage under the survivor annuity pursuant to paragraph (e) of this section.

*(4) Qualified early retirement age.* The term "qualified early retirement age" means the latest of—

(i) The earliest date, under the plan, on which the participant could elect (without regard to any requirement that approval of early retirement be obtained) to receive retirement benefits (other than disability benefits),

(ii) The first day of the 120th month beginning before the participant reaches normal retirement age, or

(iii) The date on which the participant begins participation.

*(5) Normal retirement age.* The term "normal retirement age" has the meaning set forth in section 411(a)(8).

*(6) Annuity starting date.* The term "annuity starting date" means the first day of the first period with respect to which an amount is received as a life annuity, whether by reason of retirement or by reason of disability.

*(7) Day.* The term "day" means a calendar day.

**(c) Elections.** *(1) Election not to take joint and survivor annuity form.* (i) In general. (A) A plan shall not be treated as satisfying the requirements of this section unless it provides that each participant may elect, during the election period described in subdivision (ii) of this subparagraph, not to receive a qualified joint and survivor annuity. However, if a plan provides that a qualified joint and survivor annuity is the only form of benefit payable under the plan with respect to a married participant, no election need be provided.

(B) The election shall be in writing and clearly indicate that the participant is electing to receive all or, if permitted by the plan, part of his benefits under the plan in a form other than that of a qualified joint and survivor annuity. A plan will not fail to meet the requirements of this section merely because the plan requires the participant to obtain the written approval of his spouse in order for the participant to make this election or if the plan provides that such approval is not required.

(ii) Election period. (A) For purposes of the election described in paragraph (c)(1)(i) of this section, the plan shall provide an election period which shall include a period of at least 90 days following the furnishing of all of the applicable information required by subparagraph (3)(i) of this paragraph and ending prior to commencement of benefits. In no event may the election period end earlier than the 90th day before the commencement of benefits. Thus, for example, the commencement of benefits may be delayed until the end of such election period because the amount of payments to be made to a participant cannot be ascertained before the end of such period; see § 1.401(a)-14(d).

If a participant makes a request for additional information as provided in subparagraph (3)(iii) of this paragraph on or before the last day of the election period, the election period shall be extended to the extent necessary to include at least the 90 calendar days immediately following the day the requested additional information is personally delivered or mailed to the participant. Notwithstanding the immediately preceding sentence, a plan may provide in cases in which the participant has been furnished by mail or personal delivery all of the applicable information required by subparagraph (3)(i) of this paragraph, that a request for such additional information must be made on or before a date which is not less than 60 days from the date of such mailing or delivery; and if the plan does so provide, the election period shall be extended to the extent necessary to include at least the 60 calendar days following the day the requested additional information is personally delivered or mailed to the participant.

(B) In the case of a participant in a plan to which this subparagraph applies who separated from service after section 401(a)(11) and this section became applicable to such plan with respect to such participant, and to whom an election required by this subparagraph has not been previously made available (and will not become available in normal course), the plan must provide an election to receive the balance of his benefits (properly adjusted, if applicable, for payments received, prior to the exercise of such election, in the form of a qualified joint and survivor annuity) in a form other than that of a qualified joint and survivor annuity. The provisions of paragraph (c)(1)(ii)(A) shall apply except that in no event shall the election period end before the 90th day after the date on which notice of the availability of such election and the applicable information required by subparagraph (3)(i) of this paragraph is given directly to the participant. If such notice and information is given by mail, it shall be treated as given on the date of mailing. If such participant has died, such election shall be made available to such participant's personal representative.

*(2) Election of early survivor annuity.* (i) In general. (A) A plan described in paragraph (a)(1)(iii) of this section shall not be treated as satisfying the requirements of this section unless it provides that each participant may elect, during the period described in subdivision (ii) of this subparagraph, an early survivor annuity as described in paragraph (a)(1)(iii) of this section. Breaks in service after the participant has attained the qualified early retirement age neither invalidate a previous election or revocation nor prevent an election from being made or revoked during the election period.

(B) The election shall be in writing and clearly indicate that the participant is electing the early survivor annuity form.

(C) A plan is not required to provide an election under this subparagraph if—

(1) The plan provides that an early survivor annuity is the only form of benefit payable under the plan with respect to a married participant who dies while employed by an employer maintaining the plan,

(2) In the case of a defined contribution plan, the plan provides a survivor benefit at last equal in value to the vested portion of the participant's account balance, if the participant dies while in active service with an employer maintaining the plan, or

(3) In the case of a defined benefit plan, the plan provides a survivor benefit at least equal in value to the present value of the vested portion of the participant's normal form of the accrued benefit payable at normal retirement age (determined immediately prior to death), if the participant dies while in active service with an employer maintaining the plan. Any present values must be determined in accordance with either the actuarial assumptions or factors specified in the plan, or a variable standard independent of employer discretion for converting optional benefits specified in the plan.

(ii) Election period. (A) For purposes of the election described in paragraph (c)(2)(i) of this section the plan shall provide an election period which, except as provided in the following sentence, shall begin not later than the later of either the 90th day before a participant attains the qualified early retirement age or the date on which his participation begins, and shall end on the date the participant terminates his employment. If such a plan contains a provision that any election made under this subparagraph does not become effective or ceases to be effective if the participant dies within a certain period beginning on the date of such election, the election period prescribed in this subdivision (ii) shall begin not later than the later of (1) a date which is 90 days plus such certain period before the participant attains the qualified early retirement age or (2) the date on which his participation begins. For example, if a plan provides that an election made under this subparagraph does not become effective if the participant dies less than 2 years after the date of such election, the period for making an election under this subparagraph must begin not later than the later of (1) 2 years and 90 days before the participant attains the qualified early retirement age, or (2) the date on which his participation begins. However, the election period for an individual who was an active participant on the date this section became effective with regard to the plan need not begin earlier than such effective date.

(B) In the case of a participant in a plan to which this subparagraph applies who dies after section 401(a)(11) and this section became applicable to such plan with respect to such participant and to whom an election required by this subparagraph has not been previously made available, the plan must give the participant's surviving spouse or, if dead, such spouse's personal representative the option of electing an early survivor annuity. The plan may reduce the surviving spouse's annuity to take into account any benefits already received. The period for making such election shall not end before the 90th day after the date on which written notice of the availability of such election and applicable information required by subparagraph (3)(i) of this paragraph is given directly to such surviving spouse or personal representative. If such notice and information is given by mail, it shall be treated as given on the date of mailing.

*(3) Information to be provided by plan.* For rules regarding the information required to be provided with respect to the election to waive a QJSA or a QPSA, see § 1.417(a)(3)-1.

*(4) Election is revocable.* A plan to which this section applies must provide that any election made under this paragraph may be revoked in writing during the specified election period, and that after such election has been revoked, another election under this paragraph may be made during the specified election period.

*(5) Election by surviving spouse.* A plan will not fail to meet the requirements of section 401(a)(11) and this section merely because it provides that the spouse of a deceased participant may elect to have benefits paid in a form other than a survivor annuity. If the plan provides that such a spouse may make such an election, the plan administrator must furnish to this spouse, within a reasonable amount of time after a written request has been made by this spouse, a written explanation in nontechnical language of the survivor annuity and any other form of payment which may be selected. This explanation must state the financial effect (in terms of dollars) of each form of payment. A plan need not respond to more than one such request.

**(d) Permissible additional plan provisions.** *(1) In general.* A plan will not fail to meet the requirements of section 401(a)(11) and this section merely because it contains one or more of the provisions described in paragraphs (d)(2) through (5) of this section.

*(2) Claim for benefits.* A plan may provide that as a condition precedent to the payment of benefits, a participant must express in writing to the plan administrator the form in which he prefers benefits to be paid and provide all the information reasonably necessary for the payment of such benefits. However, if a participant files a claim for benefits with the plan administrator and provides the plan administrator with all the information necessary for the payment of benefits but does not indicate a preference as to the form for the payment of benefits, benefits must be paid in the form of a qualified joint and survivor annuity if the participant has attained the qualified early retirement age unless such participant has made an effective election not to receive benefits in such form. For rules relating to provisions in a plan to the effect that a claim for benefits must be filed before the payment of benefits will commence, see § 1.401(a)-14.

*(3) Marriage requirements.* A plan may provide that a joint and survivor annuity will be paid only if—

(i) The participant and his spouse have been married to each other throughout a period (not exceeding one year) ending on the annuity starting date.

(ii) The spouse of the participant is not entitled to receive a survivor annuity (whether or not the election described in paragraph (c)(2) of this section has been made) unless the participant and his spouse have been married to each other throughout a period (not exceeding one year) ending on the date of such participant's death.

(iii) The same spouse must satisfy the requirements of subdivisions (i) and (ii) of this subparagraph.

(iv) The participant must notify the plan administrator (as defined by section 414(g)) of his marital status within any reasonable time period specified in the plan.

*(4) Effect of participant's death on an election or revocation of an election under paragraph (c).* A plan may provide that any election described in paragraph (c) of this section or any revocation of any such election does not become effective or ceases to be effective if the participant dies within a period, not in excess of 2 years, beginning on the date of such election or revocation. However, a plan containing a provision described in the preceding sentence shall not satisfy the requirements of this section unless it also provides that any such election or any revocation of any such election will be given effect in any case in which—

(i) The participant dies from accidental causes,

(ii) A failure to give effect to the election or revocation would deprive the participant's survivor of a survivor annuity, and

(iii) Such election or revocation is made before such accident occurred.

*(5) Benefit option approval by third party.* (i) A plan may provide that an optional form of benefit elected by a participant is subject to the approval of an administrative committee or similar third party. However, the administrative committee cannot deny a participant any of the benefits required by section 401(a)(11). For example, if a plan offers a life annuity option, the committee may deny the participant a qualified joint and survivor annuity only by denying the participant access to all life annuity options without knowledge of whether the participant wishes to receive a qualified joint and survivor annuity. Alternatively, if the committee knows which form of life annuity the participant has chosen before the committee makes its decision, the committee cannot withhold its consent for payment of a qualified joint and survivor annuity event though it denies all other life annuity options. This subparagraph (5) only applies before the effective date of the amendment made to section 411(d)(6) by section 301 of the Retirement Equity Act of 1984. See section 411(d)(6) and the regulations thereunder for rules limiting employer discretion.

(ii) The provisions of this subparagraph may be illustrated by the following example:

*Example.* In 1980 plan M provides that the automatic form of benefit is a single sum distribution. The plan also permits, subject to approval by the administrative committee, the election of several optional forms of life annuity. On the election form that is reviewed by the administrative committee the participant indicates whether any life annuity option is preferred, without indicating the particular life annuity chosen. Thus, the committee approves or disapproves the election without knowledge of whether a qualified joint and survivor annuity will be elected. The administrative committee approval provision in Plan M does not cause the plan to fail to satisfy this section. On the other hand, if the form indicates which form of life annuity is preferred, committee disapproval of any election of the qualified joint and survivor annuity would cause the plan to fail to satisfy this section.

**(e) Costs of providing qualified joint and survivor annuity form or early survivor annuity form.** A plan may take into account in any equitable manner consistent with generally accepted actuarial principles applied on a consistent basis any increased costs resulting from providing qualified joint and survivor annuity and early survivor annuity benefits. A plan may give a participant the option of paying premiums only if it provides another option under which an out-of-pocket expense by the participant is not required.

**(f) Application and effective date.** Section 401(a)(11) and this section shall apply to a plan only with respect to plan years beginning after December 31, 1975, and shall apply only if—

*(1)* The participant's annuity starting date did not fall within a plan year beginning before January 1, 1976, and

*(2)* The participant was an active participant in the plan on or after the first day of the first plan year beginning after December 31, 1975.

For purposes of this paragraph, the term "active participant" means a participant for whom benefits are being accrued under the plan on his behalf (in the case of a defined benefit plan), the employer is obligated to contribute to or under the plan on his behalf (in the case of a defined contribution plan other than a profit-sharing plan), or the employer either is obligated to contribute to or under the plan on his behalf or would have been obligated to contribute to or under the plan on his behalf if any contribution were made to or under the plan (in the case of a profit-sharing plan).

If benefits under a plan are provided by the distribution to the participants of individual annuity contracts, the annuity starting date will be considered for purposes of this paragraph to fall within a plan year beginning before January 1, 1976, with respect to any such individual contract that was distributed to the participant during a plan year beginning before January 1, 1976, if no premiums are paid with respect to such contract during a plan year beginning after December 31, 1975. In the case of individual annuity contracts that are distributed to participants before January 1, 1978, and which contain an option to provide a qualified joint and survivor annuity, the requirements of this section will be considered to have been satisfied if, not later than January 1, 1978, holders of individual annuity contracts who are participants described in the first sentence of this paragraph are given an opportunity to have such contracts amended, so as to provide for a qualified joint and survivor annuity in the absence of a contrary election, within a period of not less than one year from the date such opportunity was offered. In no event, however, shall the preceding sentence apply with respect to benefits attributable to premiums paid after December 31, 1977.

**(g) Effect of REA 1984.** *(1) In general.* The Retirement Equity Act of 1984 (REA 1984) significantly changed the qualified joint and survivor annuity rules generally effective for plan years beginning after December 31, 1984. The new survivor annuity rules are primarily in sections 401(a)(11) and 417 as revised by REA 1984 and §§ 1.401(a)-20 and 417(e)-1.

*(2) Regulations after REA 1984.* (i) REA and the regulations thereunder to the extent inconsistent with pre-REA 1984 section 401(a)(11) and this section are controlling for years to which REA 1984 applies. See e.g., paragraphs (a)(1) and (2) of this section, relating to required provisions and certain cash-outs, respectively and (e), relating to costs of providing annuities, for rules that are inconsistent with REA 1984 and, therefore, are not applicable to REA 1984 years.

(ii) To the extent that the pre-REA 1984 law either is the same as or consistent with REA 1984 and the new regulations hereunder, the rules in this section shall continue to apply for years to which REA 1984 applies. (See, e.g., paragraph (c) (relating to how information is furnished participants and spouses) and paragraph (b) (defining a life annuity) for some of the rules that apply to REA 1984 years.) The rules in this section shall not apply for such years to the extent that they are inconsistent with REA 1984 and the regulations thereunder.

(iii) The Commissioner may provide additional guidance as to the continuing effect of the various rules in this section for years to which REA 1984 applies.

---

T.D. 7458, 1/4/77, amend T.D. 7510, 10/3/77, T.D. 8219, 8/19/88, T.D. 9099, 12/16/2003.

---

### § 1.401(a)-12 Mergers and consolidations of plans and transfers of plan assets.

***Caution:*** The Treasury has not yet amended Reg § 1.401(a)-12 to reflect changes made by P.L. 96-364.

A trust will not be qualified under section 401 unless the plan of which the trust is a part provides that in the case of any merger or consolidation with, or transfer of assets or liabilities to, another plan after September 2, 1974, each participant in the plan would receive a minimum benefit if the plan terminated immediately after the merger, consolidation, or transfer. This benefit must be equal to or greater than the benefit the participant would have been entitled to receive immediately before the merger, consolidation, or transfer if the plan in which he was a participant had then terminated. This section applies to a multiemployer plan only to the extent determined by the Pension Benefit Guaranty Corporation. For additional rules concerning mergers or consolidations of plans and transfers of plan assets, see section 414(l) and § 1.414(l)-1.

---

T.D. 7638, 8/16/79.

---

### § 1.401(a)-13 Assignment or alienation of benefits.

**(a) Scope of the regulations.** This section applies only to plans to which section 411 applies without regard to section 411(e)(2). Thus, for example, it does not apply to a governmental plan, within the meaning of section 414(d); a church plan, within the meaning of section 414(e), for which there has not been made the election under section 410(a) to have the participation, vesting, funding, etc. requirements apply; or a plan which at no time after September 2, 1974, provided for employer contributions.

**(b) No assignment or alienation.** *(1) General rule.* Under section 401(a)(13), a trust will not be qualified unless the plan of which the trust is a part provides that benefits provided under the plan may not be anticipated, assigned (either at law or in equity), alienated or subject to attachment, garnishment, levy, execution or other legal or equitable process.

*(2) Federal tax levies and judgments.* A plan provision satisfying the requirements of subparagraph (1) of this paragraph shall not preclude the following:

(i) The enforcement of a Federal tax levy made pursuant to section 6331.

(ii) The collection by the United States on a judgment resulting from an unpaid tax assessment.

**(c) Definition of assignment and alienation.** *(1) In general.* For purposes of this section, the terms "assignment" and "alienation" include—

(i) Any arrangement providing for the payment to the employer of plan benefits which otherwise would be due the participant under the plan, and

(ii) Any direct or indirect arrangement (whether revocable or irrevocable) whereby a party acquires from a participant or beneficiary a right or interest enforceable against the plan in, or to, all or any part of a plan benefit payment which is, or may become, payable to the participant or beneficiary.

*(2) Specific arrangements not considered an assignment or alienation.* The terms "assignment" and "alienation" do not include, and paragraph (e) of this section does not apply to, the following arrangements:

(i) Any arrangement for the recovery of amounts described in section 4045(b) of the Employee Retirement Income Security Act of 1974, 88 Stat. 1027 (relating to the recapture of certain payments),

(ii) Any arrangement for the withholding of Federal, State or local tax from plan benefit payments,

(iii) Any arrangement for the recovery by the plan of overpayments of benefits previously made to a participant,

(iv) Any arrangement for the transfer of benefit rights from the plan to another plan, or

(v) Any arrangement for the direct deposit of benefit payments to an account in a bank, savings and loan association or credit union, provided such arrangement is not part of an arrangement constituting an assignment or alienation. Thus, for example, such an arrangement could provide for the direct deposit of a participant's benefit payments to a bank account held by the participant and the participant's spouse as joint tenants.

**(d) Exceptions to general rule prohibiting assignments or alienations.** *(1) Certain voluntary and revocable assignments or alienations.* Notwithstanding paragraph (b)(1) of this section, a plan may provide that once a participant or beneficiary begins receiving benefits under the plan, the participant or beneficiary may assign or alienate the right to future benefit payments provided that the provision is limited to assignments or alienations which—

(i) Are voluntary and revocable;

(ii) Do not in the aggregate exceed 10 percent of any benefit payment; and

(iii) Are neither for the purpose, nor have the effect, of defraying plan administration costs.

For purposes of this subparagraph, an attachment, garnishment, levy, execution, or other legal or equitable process is not considered a voluntary assignment or alienation.

*(2) Benefits assigned or alienated as security for loans.* (i) Notwithstanding paragraph (b)(1) of this section, a plan may provide for loans from the plan to a participant or a beneficiary to be secured (by whatever means) by the participant's accrued nonforfeitable benefit provided that the following conditions are met.

(ii) The plan provision providing for the loans must be limited to loans from the plan. A plan may not provide for the use of benefits accrued or to be accrued under the plan as security for a loan from a party other than the plan, regardless of whether these benefits are nonforfeitable within the meaning of section 411 and the regulations thereunder.

(iii) The loan, if made to a participant or beneficiary who is a disqualified person (within the meaning of section 4975(e)(2)), must be exempt from the tax imposed by section 4975 (relating to the tax imposed on prohibited transactions) by reason of section 4975(d)(1). If the loan is made to a participant or beneficiary who is not a disqualified person, the loan must be one which would be exempt from the tax imposed by section 4975 by reason of section 4975(d)(1) if the loan were made to a disqualified person.

**(e) Special rule for certain arrangements.** *(1) In general.* For purposes of this section and notwithstanding paragraph (c)(1) of this section, an arrangement whereby a participant or beneficiary directs the plan to pay all, or any portion, of a plan benefit payment to a third party (which includes the participant's employer) will not constitute an "assignment or alienation" if—

(i) It is revocable at any time by the participant or beneficiary; and

(ii) The third party files a written acknowledgement with the plan administrator pursuant to subparagraph (2) of this paragraph.

*(2) Acknowledgement requirement for third party arrangements.* In accordance with paragraph (e)(1)(ii) of this section, the third party is required to file a written acknowledgement with the plan administrator. This acknowledgement must state that the third party has no enforceable right in, or to, any plan benefit payment or portion thereof (except to the extent of payments actually received pursuant to the terms of the arrangement). A blanket written acknowledgement for all participants and beneficiaries who are covered under the arrangement with the third party is sufficient. The written acknowledgement must be filed with the plan administrator no later than the later of—

(i) August 18, 1978; or

(ii) 90 days after the arrangement is entered into.

**(f) Effective date.** Section 401(a)(13) is applicable as of January 1, 1976, and the plan provision required by this section must be effective as of that date. However, regardless of when the provision is adopted, it will not affect—

*(1)* Attachments, garnishments, levies, or other legal or equitable process permitted under the plan that are made before January 1, 1976;

*(2)* Assignments permitted under the plan that are irrevocable on December 31, 1975, including assignments made before January 1, 1976, as security for loans to a participant or beneficiary from a party other than the plan; and

*(3)* Renewals or extensions of loans described in subparagraph (2) of this paragraph, if—

(i) The principal amount of the obligation outstanding on December 31, 1975 (or, if less, the principal amount outstanding on the date of renewal or extension), is not increased;

(ii) The loan, as renewed or extended, does not bear a rate of interest in excess of the rate prevailing for similar loans at the time of the renewal or extension; and

(iii) With respect to loans that are renewed or extended to bear a variable interest rate, the formula for determining the applicable rate is consistent with the formula or formulae prevailing for similar loans at the time of the renewal or extension.

For purposes of subparagraphs (2) and (3) of this paragraph, a loan from a party other than the plan made after December 31, 1975, will be treated as a new loan. This is so even if the lender's security interest for the loan arises from an assignment of the participant's accrued nonforfeitable benefit made before that date.

**(g) Special rules for qualified domestic relations orders.** *(1) Definition.* The term "qualified domestic relations order" (QDRO) has the meaning set forth in section 414(p). For purposes of the Internal Revenue Code, a QDRO also includes any domestic relations order described in section 303(d) of the Retirement Equity Act of 1984.

*(2) Plan amendments.* A plan will not fail to satisfy the qualification requirements of section 401(a) or 403(a) merely because it does not include provisions with regard to a QDRO.

*(3) Waiver of distribution requirements.* A plan shall not be treated as failing to satisfy the requirements of sections 401(a) and (k) and 409(d) solely because of a payment to an alternate payee pursuant to a QDRO. This is the case even if the plan provides for payments pursuant to a QDRO to an alternate payee prior to the time it may make payments to a participant. Thus, for example, a pension plan may pay an alternate payee even though the participant may not receive a distribution because he continues to be employed by the employer.

*(4) Coordination with section 417.* (i) Former spouse. (A) In general. Under section 414(p)(5), a QDRO may provide that a former spouse shall be treated as the current spouse of a participant for all or some purposes under sections 401(a)(11) and 417.

(B) Consent. (1) To the extent a former spouse is treated as the current spouse of the participant by reason of a QDRO, any current spouse shall not be treated as the current spouse. For example, assume H is divorced from W, but a QDRO provides that H shall be treated as W's current spouse with respect to all of W's benefits under a plan. H will be treated as the surviving spouse under the QPSA and QJSA unless W obtains H's consent to waive the QPSA or QJSA or both. The fact that W married S after W's divorce from H is disregarded. If, however, the QDRO had provided that H shall be treated as W's current spouse only with respect to benefits that accrued prior to the divorce, then H's consent would be needed by W to waive the QPSA or QJSA with respect to benefits accrued before the divorce. S's consent would be required with respect to the remainder of the benefits.

(2) In the preceding examples, if the QDRO ordered that a portion of W's benefit (either through separate accounts or a percentage of the benefit) must be distributed to H rather than ordering that H be treated as W's spouse, the survivor annuity requirements of sections 401(a)(11) and 417 would not apply to the part of W's benefit awarded H. Instead, the terms of the QDRO would determine how H's portion of W's accrued benefit is paid. W is required to obtain S's consent if W elects to waive either the QJSA or QPSA with respect to the remaining portion of W's benefit.

(C) Amount of the QPSA or QJSA. (1) Where, because of a QDRO, more than one individual is to be treated as the surviving spouse, a plan may provide that the total amount to be paid in the form of a QPSA or survivor portion of a QJSA may not exceed the amount that would be paid if there were only one surviving spouse. The QPSA or survivor portion of the QJSA, as the case may be, payable to each surviving spouse must be paid as an annuity based on the life of each such spouse.

(2) Where the QDRO splits the participant's accrued benefit between the participant and a former spouse (either through separate accounts or percentage of the benefit), the surviving spouse of the participant is entitled to a QPSA or QJSA based on the participant's accrued benefit as of the date of death or the annuity starting date, less the separate account or percentage that is payable to the former spouse. The calculation is made as if the separate account or percentage had been distributed to the participant prior to the relevant date.

(ii) Current spouse. Under section 414(p)(5), even if the applicable election periods (i.e., the first day of the year in which the participant attains age 35 and 90 days before the annuity starting date) have not begun, a QDRO may provide that a current spouse shall not be treated as the current spouse of the participant for all or some purposes under sections 401(a)(11) and 417. A QDRO may provide that the current spouse waives all future rights to a QPSA or QJSA.

(iii) Effects on benefits. (A) A plan is not required to provide additional vesting or benefits because of a QDRO.

(B) If an alternate payee is treated pursuant to a QDRO as having an interest in the plan benefit, including a separate account or percentage of the participant's account, then the QDRO cannot provide the alternate payee with a greater right to designate a beneficiary for the alternate payee's benefit amount than the participant's right. The QJSA or QPSA provisions of section 417 do not apply to the spouse of an alternate payee.

(C) If the former spouse who is treated as a current spouse dies prior to the participant's annuity starting date, then any actual current spouse of the participant is treated as the current spouse, except as otherwise provided in a QDRO.

(iv) Section 415 requirements. Even though a participant's benefits are awarded to an alternate payee pursuant to a QDRO, the benefits are benefits of the participant for purposes of applying the limitations of section 415 to the participant's benefits.

---

T.D. 7534, 2/15/78, amend T.D. 8219, 8/19/88.

---

PAR. 2. For each entry listed in the "Location" column, remove the language in the "Remove" column and add the language in the "Add" column in its place.

PAR. 2. For each entry listed in the "Location" column, remove the language in the "Remove" column and add the language in the "Add" column in its place.

PAR. 2. For each entry listed in the "Location" column, remove the language in the "Remove" column and add the language in the "Add" column in its place.

PAR. 2. For each entry listed in the "Location" column, remove the language in the "Remove" column and add the language in the "Add" column in its place.

PAR. 2. For each entry listed in the "Location" column, remove the language in the "Remove" column and add the language in the "Add" column in its place.

**Proposed § 1.401(a)-13** [*For Preamble, see ¶ 153,065*]

| Location | Remove | Add |
|---|---|---|
| 1.401(a)-13(g)(4)(ii), first sentence | 90 days | 180 days. |
| 1.401(a)-20, A-4, third sentence | 90 days | 180 days. |
| 1.401(a)-20, A-10(a), fifth and sixth sentences. | 90 days | 180 days. |
| 1.401(a)-20, A-16, sixth sentence. | 90 days | 180 days. |
| 1.401(a)-20, A-24(a)(1), fifth sentence. | 90 days | 180 days. |
| 1.402(f)-1, A-2(a), first sentence. | 90 days | 180 days. |
| 1.411(a)-11(c)(2)(ii) | 90 days | 180 days. |
| 1.411(a)-11(c)(2)(iii)(A), first sentence. | 90 days | 180 days. |
| 1.417(e)-1(b)(3)(i) | 90 days | 180 days. |
| 1.417(e)-1(b)(3)(ii), first sentence. | 90 days | 180 days. |
| 1.417(e)-1(b)(3)(iii) | 90 days | 180 days. |
| 1.417(e)-1(b)(3)(vi), second sentence. | 90 days | 180 days. |
| 1.417(e)-1(b)(3)(vii) | 90 days | 180 days. |
| 1.417(e)-1(b)(3)(vii) | 90-day | 180-day. |

### § 1.401(a)-14 Commencement of benefits under qualified trusts.

*Caution:* The Treasury has not yet amended Reg § 1.401(a)-14 to reflect changes made by P.L. 98-369.

**(a) In general.** Under section 401(a)(14), a trust to which section 411 applies (without regard to section 411(e)(2)) is not qualified under section 401 unless the plan of which such trust is a part provides that the payment of benefits under the plan to the participant will begin not later than the 60th day after the close of the plan year in which the latest of the following events occurs:

*(1)* The attainment by the participant of age 65, or, if earlier, the normal retirement age specified under the plan,

*(2)* The 10th anniversary of the date on which the participant commenced participation in the plan,

*(3)* The termination of the participant's service with the employer, or

*(4)* The date specified in an election made pursuant to paragraph (b) of this section.

Notwithstanding the preceding sentence, a plan may require that a participant file a claim for benefits before payment of benefits will commence.

**(b) Election of later date.** *(1) General rule.* A plan may permit a participant to elect that the payment to him of any benefit under a plan will commence at a date later than the dates specified under paragraphs (a)(1), (2), and (3) of this section.

*(2) Manner of election.* A plan permitting an election under this paragraph shall require that such election must be made by submitting to the plan administrator a written statement, signed by the participant, which describes the benefit and the date on which the payment of such benefit shall commence.

*(3) Restriction.* An election may not be made pursuant to a plan provision permitted by this paragraph if the exercise of such election will cause benefits payable under the plan with respect to the participant in the event of his death to be more than "incidental" within the meaning of paragraph (b)(1)(i) of § 1.401-1.

**(c) Special early retirement rule.** *(1) Separation prior to early retirement age.* A trust forming part of a plan which provides for the payment of an early retirement benefit is not qualified under section 401 unless, upon satisfaction of the age requirement for such early retirement benefit, a participant who:

(i) Satisfied the service requirements for such early retirement benefit, but

(ii) Separated from service (with any nonforfeitable right to an accrued benefit) before satisfying such age requirement,

is entitled to receive not less than the reduced normal retirement benefit described in paragraph (c)(2) of this section. A plan may establish reasonable conditions for payments of early retirement benefits (including for example, a requirement that a claim for benefits be made) if the conditions are equally applicable to participants who separate from service when eligible for an early retirement benefit and participants who separate from service earlier.

*(2) Reduced normal retirement benefit.* For purposes of this section, the reduced normal retirement benefit is the benefit to which the participant would have been entitled under the plan at normal retirement age, reduced in accordance with reasonable actuarial assumptions.

*(3) Separation prior to effective date of this section.* The provisions of this paragraph shall not apply in the case of a plan participant who separates from service before attainment of early retirement age and prior to the effective date of this section set forth in paragraph (e) of this section.

*(4) Illustration.* The provisions of this paragraph may be illustrated by the following example:

*Example.* The X Corporation Defined Benefit Plan provides that a normal retirement benefit will be payable to a participant upon attainment of age 65. The plan also provides that an actuarially reduced retirement benefit will be payable, upon application, to any participant who has completed 10 years of service with the X Corporation and attained age 60. When he is 55 years of age and has completed 10 years of service with X Corporation, A, a participant in the plan, leaves the service of X Corporation and does not return. The plan will not be qualified under section 401 unless, upon attainment of age 60 and application for benefits, A is entitled to receive a reduced normal retirement benefit described in subparagraph (2) of this paragraph.

**(d) Retroactive payment rule.** If the amount of the payment required to commence on the date determined under this section cannot be ascertained by such date, or if it is not possible to make such payment on such date because the plan administrator has been unable to locate the participant after making reasonable efforts to do so, a payment retroactive to such date may be made no later than 60 days after the earliest date on which the amount of such payment can be ascertained under the plan or the date on which the participant is located (whichever is applicable).

**(e) Effective date.** This section shall apply to a plan for those plan years to which section 411 of the Code applies without regard to section 411(e)(2).

---

T.D. 7436, 9/23/76.

---

### § 1.401(a)-15 Requirement that plan benefits are not decreased on account of certain Social Security increases.

**(a) In general.** Under section 401(a)(15), a trust which is part of a plan to which section 411 applies (without regard to section 411(e)(2)) is not qualified under section 401 unless, under the plan of which such trust is a part:

*(1) Benefit being received by participant or beneficiary.* A benefit (including a death or disability benefit) being received under the plan by a participant or beneficiary (other than a participant to whom subparagraph (2)(ii) of this paragraph applies, or a beneficiary of such a participant) is not decreased by reason of any post-separation social security benefit increase effective after the later of—

(i) September 2, 1974, or

(ii) The date of first receipt of any retirement benefit, death benefit, or disability benefit under the plan by the participant or by a beneficiary of the participant (whichever receipt occurs first).

*(2) Benefit to which participant separated from service has nonforfeitable right.* In the case of a benefit to which a participant has a nonforfeitable right under such plan—

(i) If such participant is separated from service and does not subsequently return to service and resume participation in the plan, such benefit is not decreased by reason of any post-separation social security benefit increase effective after the later of September 2, 1974, or separation from service, or

(ii) If such participant is separated from service and subsequently returns to service and resumes participation in the plan, such benefit is not decreased by reason of any post-separation social security benefit increase effective after September 2, 1974, which occurs during separation from service and which would decrease such benefit to a level below the level of benefits to which he would have been entitled had he not returned to service after his separation.

**(b) Post-separation social security benefit increase.** For purposes of this section, the term "post-separation social security benefit increase" means, with respect to a participant or a beneficiary of the participant, an increase in a benefit level or wage base under title II of the Social Security Act (whether such increase is a result of an amendment of such title II or is a result of the application of the provisions of such title II) occurring after the earlier of such participant's separation from service or commencement of benefits under the plan.

**(c) Illustrations.** The provisions of paragraphs (a) and (b) of this section may be illustrated by the following examples:

*Example (1).* A plan to which section 401(a)(15) applies provides an annual benefit at the normal retirement age, 65, in the form of a stated benefit formula amount less a specified percentage of the primary insurance amount payable under title II of the Social Security Act. The plan provides no early retirement benefits. In the case of a participant who separates from service before age 65 with a nonforfeitable right to a benefit under the plan, the plan defines the primary insurance amount as the amount which the participant is entitled to receive under title II of the Social Security Act at age 65, multiplied by the ratio of the number of years of service with the employer to the number of years of service the participant would have had if he had worked for the employer until age 65. The plan does not satisfy the requirements of section 401(a)(15), because social security increases that occur after a participant's separation from service will reduce the benefit the participant will receive under the plan.

*Example (2).* A plan to which section 401(a)(15) applies provides an annual benefit at the normal retirement age, 65, in the form of a stated benefit formula amount less a specified percentage of the primary insurance amount payable under title II of the Social Security Act. The plan provides no early retirement benefits. In the case of a participant who separates from service before age 65 with a nonforfeitable right to a benefit under the plan, the plan defines the primary insurance amount as the amount which the participant is entitled to receive under title II of the Social Security Act at age 65 based upon the assumption that he will continue to receive until reaching age 65 compensation which would be treated as wages for purposes of the Social Security Act at the same rate as he received such compensation at the time he separated from service, but determined without regard to any post-separation social security benefit increase, multiplied by the ratio of the number of years of service with the employer to the number of years of service the participant would have had if he had worked for the employer until age 65. The plan satisfies the requirements of section 401(a)(15), because social security increases that occur after a participant's separation from service will not reduce the benefit the participant will receive under the plan.

**(d) Other Federal or State laws.** To the extent applicable, the rules discussed in this section will govern classifications under a plan supplementing the benefits provided by other Federal or State laws, such as the Railroad Retirement Act of 1937. See section 206(b) of the Employee Retirement Income Security Act of 1974 (Public Law 93-406, 88 Stat. 864).

**(e) Effect on prior law.** Nothing in this section shall be construed as amending or modifying the rules applicable to post-separation social security increases prior to September 2, 1974. See paragraph (e) of § 1.401-3.

**(f) Effective date.** Section 401(a)(15) and this section shall apply to a plan only with respect to plan years to which section 411 (relating to minimum vesting standards) is applicable to the plan without regard to section 411(e)(2).

---

T.D. 7434, 9/27/76.

---

### § 1.401(a)-16 Limitations on benefits and contributions under qualified plans.

A trust will not be a qualified trust and a plan will not be a qualified plan if the plan provides for benefits or contributions which exceed the limitations of section 415. Section 415 and the regulations thereunder provide rules concerning these limitations on benefits and contributions.

---

T.D. 7748, 12/30/80.

---

## § 1.401(a)-19 Nonforfeitability in case of certain withdrawals.

**(a) Application of section.** Section 401(a)(19) and this section apply to a plan to which section 411(a) applies. (See section 411(e) and § 1.411(a)-2 for applicability of section 411).

**(b) Prohibited forfeitures.** *(1) General rule.* A plan to which this section applies is not a qualified plan (and a trust forming a part of such plan is not a qualified trust) if, under such plan, any part of a participant's accrued benefit derived from employer contributions is forfeitable solely because a benefit derived from the participant's contributions under the plan is voluntarily withdrawn by him after he has become a 50 percent vested participant.

*(2) 50 percent vested participant.* For purposes of subparagraph (1) of this paragraph, a participant is a 50 percent vested participant when he has a nonforfeitable right (within the meaning of section 411 and the regulations thereunder) to at least 50 percent of his accrued benefit derived from employer contributions. Whether or not a participant is 50 percent vested shall be determined by the ratio of the participant's total nonforfeitable employer-derived accrued benefit under the plan to his total employer-derived accrued benefit under the plan.

*(3) Certain forfeitures.* Paragraph (b)(1) of this section does not apply in the case of a forfeiture permitted by section 411(a)(3)(D)(iii) and § 1.411(a)-7(d)(3) (relating to forfeitures of certain benefits accrued before September 2, 1974).

**(c) Supersession.** Section 11.401(a)(19) of the Temporary Income Tax Regulations under the Employee Retirement Income Security Act of 1974 is superseded by this section.

T.D. 7501, 8/22/77.

## § 1.401(a)-20 Requirements of qualified joint and survivor annuity and qualified preretirement survivor annuity.

***Caution:*** The Treasury has not yet amended Reg § 1.401(a)-20 to reflect changes made by P.L. 105-34, P.L. 104-188.

Q-1. What are the survivor annuity requirements added to the Code by the Retirement Equity Act of 1984 (REA 1984)?

A-1. REA 1984 replaced section 401(a)(11) with a new section 401(a)(11) and added section 417. Plans to which new section 401(a)(11) applies must comply with the requirements of sections 401(a)(11) and 417 in order to remain qualified under sections 401(a) or 403(a). In general, these plans must provide both a qualified joint and survivor annuity (QJSA) and a qualified preretirement survivor annuity (QPSA) to remain qualified. These survivor annuity requirements are applicable to any benefit payable under a plan, including a benefit payable to a participant under a contract purchased by the plan and paid by a third party.

Q-2. Must annuity contracts purchased and distributed to a participant or spouse by a plan subject to the survivor annuity requirements of sections 401(a)(11) and 417 satisfy the requirements of those sections?

A-2. Yes. Rights and benefits under section 401(a)(11) or 417 may not be eliminated or reduced because the plan uses annuity contracts to provide benefits merely because (a) such a contract is held by a participant or spouse instead of a plan trustee, or (b) such contracts are distributed upon plan termination. Thus, the requirements of sections 401(a)(11) and 417 apply to payments under the annuity contracts, not to the distributions of the contracts.

Q-3. What plans are subject to the survivor annuity requirements of section 401(a)(11)?

A-3. **(a)** Section 401(a)(11) applies to any defined benefit plan and to any defined contribution plan that is subject to the minimum funding standards of section 412. This section also applies to any participant under any other defined contribution plan unless all of the following conditions are satisfied—

*(1)* The plan provides that the participant's nonforfeitable accrued benefit is payable in full, upon the participant's death, to the participant's surviving spouse (unless the participant elects, with spousal consent that satisfies the requirements of section 417(a)(2), that such benefit be provided instead to a designated beneficiary);

*(2)* The participant does not elect the payment of benefits in the form of a life annuity; and

*(3)* With respect to the participant, the plan is not a transferee or an offset plan. (See Q&A 5 of this section.)

**(b)** A defined contribution plan not subject to the minimum funding standards of section 412 will not be treated as satisfying the requirement of paragraph (a)(1) unless both of the following conditions are satisfied—

*(1)* The benefit is available to the surviving spouse within a reasonable time after the participant's death. For this purpose, availability within the 90-day period following the date of death is deemed to be reasonable and the reasonableness of longer periods shall be determined based on the particular facts and circumstances. A time period longer than 90 days, however, is deemed unreasonable if it is less favorable to the surviving spouse than any time period under the plan that is applicable to other distributions. Thus, for example, the availability of a benefit to the surviving spouse would be unreasonable if the distribution was required to be made by the close of the plan year including the participant's death while distributions to employees who separate from service were required to be made within 90 days of separation.

*(2)* The benefit payable to the surviving spouse is adjusted for gains or losses occurring after the participant's death in accordance with plan rules governing the adjustment of account balances for other plan distributions. Thus, for example, the plan may not provide for distributions of an account balance to a surviving spouse determined as of the last day of the quarter in which the participant's death occurred with no adjustments of an account balance for gains or losses after death if the plan provides for such adjustments for a participant who separates from service within a quarter.

**(c)** For purposes of determining the extent to which section 401(a)(11) applies to benefits under an employee stock ownership plan (as defined in section 4975(e)(7)), the portion of a participant's accrued benefit that is subject to section 409(h) is to be treated as though such benefit were provided under a defined contribution plan not subject to section 412.

**(d)** The requirements set forth in section 401(a)(11) apply to other employee benefit plans that are covered by applicable provisions under Title I of the Employee Retirement Income Security Act of 1974. For purposes of applying the regulations under sections 401(a)(11) and 417, plans subject to ERISA section 205 are treated as if they were described in section 401(a). For example, to the extent that section 205 covers section 403(b) contracts and custodial accounts they are treated as section 401(a) plans. Individual retirement plans (IRAs), including IRAs to which contributions are made under simplified employee pensions described in section 408(k) and IRAs that are treated as plans subject to Title I, are not subject to these requirements.

Q-4. What rules apply to a participant who elects a life annuity option under a defined contribution plan not subject to section 412?

A-4. If a participant elects at any time (irrespective of the applicable election period defined in section 417(a)(6)) a life annuity option under a defined contribution plan not subject to section 412, the survivor annuity requirements of sections 401(a)(11) and 417 will always thereafter apply to all of the participant's benefits under such plan unless there is a separate accounting of the account balance subject to the election. A plan may allow a participant to elect an annuity option prior to the applicable election period described in section 417(a)(6). If a participant elects an annuity option, the plan must satisfy the applicable written explanation, consent, election, and withdrawal rules of section 417, including waiver of the QJSA within 90 days of the annuity starting date. If a participant selecting such an option dies, the surviving spouse must be able to receive the QPSA benefit described in section 417(c)(2) which is a life annuity, the actuarial equivalent of which is not less than 50 percent of the nonforfeitable account balance (adjusted for loans as described in Q&A 24(d) of this section). The remaining account balance may be paid to a designated nonspouse beneficiary.

Q-5. How do sections 401(a)(11) and 417 apply to transferee plans which are defined contribution plans not subject to section 412?

A-5. **(a) Transferee plans.** Although the survivor annuity requirements of sections 401(a)(11) and 417 generally do not apply to defined contribution plans not subject to section 412, such plans are subject to the survivor annuity requirements to the extent that they are transferee plans with respect to any participant. A defined contribution plan is a transferee plan with respect to any participant if the plan is a direct or indirect transferee of such participant's benefits held on or after January 1, 1985, by:

*(1)* A defined benefit plan,

*(2)* A defined contribution plan subject to section 412, or

*(3)* A defined contribution plan that is subject to the survivor annuity requirements of sections 401(a)(11) and 417 with respect to that participant. If through a merger, spinoff, or other transaction having the effect of a transfer, benefits subject to the survivor annuity requirements of sections 401(a)(11) and 417 are held under a plan that is not otherwise subject to such requirements, such benefits will be subject to the survivor annuity requirements even though they are held under such plan. Even if a plan satisfies the survivor annuity requirements, other rules apply to these transactions. See, e.g., section 411(d)(6) and the regulations thereunder. A transfer made before January 1, 1985, and any rollover contribution made at any time, are not transactions that subject the transferee plan to the survivor annuity requirements with respect to a participant. If a plan is a transferee plan with respect to a participant, the survivor annuity requirements do not apply with respect to other plan participants solely because of the transfer. Any plan that would not otherwise be subject to the survivor annuity requirements of sections 401(a)(11) and 417 whose benefits are used to offset benefits in a plan subject to such requirements is subject to the survivor annuity requirements with respect to those participants whose benefits are offset. Thus, if a stock bonus or profit-sharing plan offsets benefits under a defined benefit plan, such a plan is subject to the survivor annuity requirements.

**(b) Benefits covered.** The survivor annuity requirements apply to all accrued benefits held for a participant with respect to whom the plan is a transferee plan unless there is an acceptable separate accounting between the transferred benefits and all other benefits under the plan. A separate accounting is not acceptable unless gains, losses, withdrawals, contributions, forfeitures, and other credits or charges are allocated on a reasonable and consistent basis between the accrued benefits subject to the survivor annuity requirements and other benefits. If there is an acceptable separate accounting between transferred benefits and any other benefits under the plan, only the transferred benefits are subject to the survivor annuity requirements.

Q-6. Is a frozen or terminated plan required to satisfy the survivor annuity requirements of sections 401(a)(11) and 417?

A-6. In general, benefits provided under a plan that is subject to the survivor annuity requirements of sections 401(a)(11) and 417 must be provided in accordance with those requirements even if the plan is frozen or terminated. However, any plan that has a termination date prior to September 17, 1985, and that distributed all remaining assets as soon as administratively feasible after the termination date, is not subject to the survivor annuity requirements. The date of termination is determined under section 411(d)(3) and § 1.411(d)-2(c).

Q-7. If the Pension Benefit Guaranty Corporation (PBGC) is administering a plan, are benefits payable in the form of a OPSA or QJSA?

A-7. Yes, the PBGC will pay benefits in such forms.

Q-8. How do the survivor annuity requirements of sections 401(a)(11) and 417 apply to participants?

A-8. **(a)** If a participant dies before the annuity starting date with vested benefits attributable to employer or employee contributions (or both), benefits must be paid to the surviving spouse in the form of a QPSA. If a participant survives until the annuity starting date with vested benefits attributable to employer or employee contributions (or both), benefits must be provided to the participant in the form of a QJSA.

**(b)** A participant may waive the QPSA or the QJSA (or both) if the applicable notice, election, and spousal consent requirements of section 417 are satisfied.

**(c)** Benefits are not required to be paid in the form of a QPSA or QJSA if at the time of death or distribution the participant was vested only in employee contributions and such death occurred, or distribution commenced, before October 22, 1986.

**(d)** Certain mandatory distributions. A distribution may occur without satisfying the spousal consent requirements of section 417(a) and (e) if the present value of the nonforfeitable benefit does not exceed the cash-out limit in effect under § 1.411(a)-11(c)(3)(ii). See § 1.417(e)-1.

Q-9. May separate portions of a participant's accrued benefit be subject to QPSA and QJSA requirements at any particular point in time?

A-9. **(a) Dual QPSA and QJSA rights.** One portion of a participant's benefit may be subject to the QPSA and another portion to the QJSA requirements at the same time. For example, in order for a money purchase pension plan to distribute any portion of a married participant's benefit to the participant, the plan must distribute such portion in the form of a QJSA (unless the plan satisfies the applicable consent requirements of section 417(a) and (e) with respect to such portion of the participant's benefit). This rule applies even if the distribution is merely an in service distribution attributable to voluntary employee contributions and regardless of whether the participant has attained the normal retirement age under the plan. The QJSA requirements apply to such a distribution because the annuity starting date has occurred with respect to this portion of the participant's benefit. In the event of a participant's death following the commencement of a distribution in the form of a QJSA, the remaining payments must be made to the surviving spouse under the QJSA. In addition, the plan must satisfy the QPSA requirements with respect to any portion of the participant's benefits for which the annuity starting date had not yet occurred.

**Example.** Assume that participant A has a $100,000 account balance in a money purchase pension plan. A makes an in-service withdrawal of $20,000 attributable to voluntary employee contributions. The QJSA requirements apply to A's withdrawal of the $20,000. Accordingly, unless the QJSA form is properly waived such amount must be distributed in the form of a QJSA. A's remaining account balance ($80,000) remains subject to the QPSA requirements because the annuity starting date has not occurred with respect to the $80,000. (If A survives until the annuity starting date, the $80,000 would be subject to the QJSA requirements.) If A died on the day following the annuity starting date for the withdrawal, A's spouse would be entitled to a QPSA with a value equal to at least $40,000 with respect to the $80,000 account balance, in addition to any survivor benefit without respect to the $20,000. If the $20,000 payment to A had been the first payment of an annuity purchased with the entire $100,000 account balance rather than an in-service distribution, then the QJSA requirements would apply to the entire account balance at the time of the annuity starting date. In such event, the plan would have no obligation to provide A's spouse with a QPSA benefit upon A's death. Of course, A's spouse would receive the QJSA benefit (if the QJSA had not been waived) based on the full $100,000.

Q-10. What is the relevance of the annuity starting date with respect to the survivor benefit requirements?

A-10. **(a) Relevance.** The annuity starting date is relevant to whether benefits are payable as either a QJSA or QPSA, or other selected optional form of benefit. If a participant is alive on the annuity starting date, the benefits must be payable as a QJSA. If the participant is not alive on the annuity starting date, the surviving spouse must receive a QPSA. The annuity starting date is also used to determine when a spouse may consent to and a participant may waive a QJSA. A waiver is only effective if it is made 90 days before the annuity starting date. Thus, a deferred annuity cannot be selected and a QJSA waived until 90 days before payments commence under the deferred annuity. In some cases, the annuity starting date will have occurred with respect to a portion of the participant's accrued benefit and will not have occurred with respect to the remaining portion. (See Q&A-9.)

**(b) Annuity starting date.** *(1) General rule.*For purposes of sections 401(a)(11), 411(a)(11) and 417, the annuity starting date is the first day of the first period for which an amount is paid as an annuity or any other form.

*(2) Annuity payments.* The annuity starting date is the first date for which an amount is paid, not the actual date of payment. Thus, if participant A is to receive annuity payments as of the first day of the first month after retirement but does not receive any payments until three months later, the annuity starting date is the first day of the first month. For example, if an annuity is to commence on January 1, January 1 is the annuity starting date even though the payment for January is not actually made until a later date. In the case of a deferred annuity, the annuity starting date is the date for which the annuity payments are to commence, not the date that the deferred annuity is elected or the date the deferred annuity contract is distributed.

*(3) Administrative delay.* A payment shall not be considered to occur after the annuity starting date merely because actual payment is reasonably delayed for calculation of the benefit amount if all payments are actually made.

*(4) Forfeitures on death.* Prior to the annuity starting date, section 411(a)(3)(A) allows a plan to provide for a forfeiture of a participant's benefit, except in the case of a QPSA or a spousal benefit described in section 401(a)(11)(B)(iii)(I). Once the annuity starting date has occurred, even if actual payment has not yet been made, a plan must pay the benefit in the distribution form elected.

*(5) Surviving spouses, alternate payees, etc.*The definition of "annuity starting date" for surviving spouses, other beneficiaries and alternate payees under section 414(p) is the same as it is for participants.

**(c) Disability auxiliary benefit.** *(1) General rule.* The annuity starting date for a disability benefit is the first day of the first period for which the benefit becomes payable unless the disability benefit is an auxiliary benefit. The payment of any auxiliary disability benefits is disregarded in determining the annuity starting date. A disability benefit is an auxiliary benefit if upon attainment of early or normal retirement age, a participant receives a benefit that satisfies the accrual and vesting rules of section 411 without taking into account the disability benefit payments up to that date.

*(2) Example.* (i) Assume that participant A at age 45 is entitled to a vested accrued benefit of $100 per month commencing at age 65 in the form a joint and survivor annuity under Plan X. If prior to age 65 A receives a disability benefit under Plan X and the payment of such benefit does not reduce the amount of A's retirement benefit of $100 per month commencing at age 65, any disability benefit payments made to A between ages 45 and 65 are auxiliary benefits. Thus, A's annuity starting date does not occur until A attains age 65. A's surviving spouse B would be entitled to receive a QPSA if A died before age 65. B would be entitled to receive the survivor portion of a QJSA (unless waived) if A died after age 65. The QPSA payable to B upon A's death prior to age 65 would be computed by reference to the QJSA that would have been payable to A and B had A survived to age 65.

(ii) If in the above example A's benefit payable at age 65 is reduced to $99 per month because a disability benefit is provided to A prior to age 65, the disability benefit would not be an auxiliary benefit. The benefit of $99 per month payable to A at age 65 would not, without taking into account the disability benefit payments to A prior to age 65, satisfy the minimum vesting and accrual rules of section 411. Accordingly, the first day of the first period for which the disability payments are to be made to A would constitute A's annuity starting date, and any benefit paid to A would be required to be paid in the form of a QJSA (unless waived by A with the consent of B).

**(d) Other rules.** *(1) Suspension of benefits.* If benefit payments are suspended after the annuity starting date pursuant to a suspension of benefits described in section 411(a)(3)(B) after an employee separates from service, the recommencement of benefit payments after the suspension is not treated as a new annuity starting date unless the plan provides otherwise. In such case, the plan administrator is not required to provide new notices nor to obtain new waivers for the recommenced distributions if the form of distribution is the same as the form that was appropriately selected prior to the suspension. If benefits are suspended for an employee who continues in service without a separation and who never receives payments, the commencement of payments after the period of suspension is treated as the annuity starting date unless the plan provides otherwise.

*(2) Additional accruals.* In the case of an annuity starting date that occurs on or after normal retirement age, such date applies to any additional accruals after the annuity starting date, unless the plan provides otherwise. For example, if a participant who continues to accrue benefits elects to have benefits paid in an optional form at normal retirement age, the additional accruals must be paid in the optional form selected unless the plan provides otherwise. In the case of an annuity starting date that occurs prior to normal retirement age, such date does not apply to any additional accruals after such date.

Q-11. Do the survivor annuity requirements apply to benefits derived from both employer and employee contributions?

A-11. Yes. The survivor annuity benefit requirements apply to benefits derived from both employer and employee contributions. Benefits are not required to be paid in the form of a QPSA or QJSA if the participant was vested only in employee contributions at the time of death or a distribution and such death or distribution occurred before October 22, 1986. All benefits provided under a plan, including benefits attributable to rollover contributions, are subject to the survivor annuity requirements.

Q-12. To what benefits do the survivor annuity requirements of sections 401(a)(11) and 417 apply?

A-12. **(a) Defined benefit plans.** Under a defined benefit plan, sections 401(a)(11) and 417 apply only to benefits in which a participant was vested immediately prior to death. They do not apply to benefits to which a participant's beneficiary becomes entitled by reason of death or to the proceeds of a life insurance contract to the extent such proceeds exceed the present value of the participant's nonforfeitable benefits that existed immediately prior to death.

**(b) Defined contribution plans.** Sections 401(a)(11) and 417 apply to all nonforfeitable benefits which are payable under a defined contribution plan, whether nonforfeitable before or upon death, including the proceeds of insurance contracts.

Q-13. Does the rule of section 411(a)(3)(A) which permits forfeitures on account of death apply to a QPSA or the spousal benefit described in section 401(a)(11)(B)(iii)?

A-13. No. Section 411(a)(3)(A) permits forfeiture on account of death prior to the time all the events fixing payment occur. However, this provision does not operate to deprive a surviving spouse of a QPSA or the spousal benefit described in section 401(a)(11)(B)(iii). Therefore, sections 401(a)(11) and 417 apply to benefits that were nonforfeitable immediately prior to death (determined without regard to section 411(a)(3)(A)). Thus, in the case of the death of a married participant in a defined contribution plan not subject to section 412 which provides that, upon a participant's death, the entire nonforfeitable accrued benefit is payable to the participant's spouse, the nonforfeitable benefit is determined without regard to the provisions of section 411(a)(3)(A).

Q-14. Do sections 411(a)(11), 401(a)(11) and 417 apply to accumulated deductible employee contributions, as defined in section 72(o)(5)(B) (Accumulated DECs)?

A-14. **(a) Employee consent, section 411.** The requirements of section 411(a)(11) apply to Accumulated DECs. Thus, Accumulated DECs may not be distributed without participant consent unless the applicable exemptions apply.

**(b) Survivor requirements.** Accumulated DECs are treated as though held under a separate defined contribution plan that is not subject to section 412. Thus, section 401(a)(11) applies to Accumulated DECs only as provided in section 401(a)(11)(B)(iii). All Accumulated DECs are treated in this manner, including Accumulated DECs that are the only benefit held under a plan and Accumulated DECs that are part of a defined benefit or a defined contribution plan.

**(c) Effective date.** Sections 401(a)(11) and 411(a)(11) shall not apply to distributions of accumulated DECs until the first plan year beginning after December 31, 1988.

Q-15. How do the survivor annuity requirements of sections 401(a)(11) and 417 apply to a defined benefit plan that includes an accrued benefit based upon a contribution to a separate account or mandatory employee contributions?

A-15. **(a) 414(k) plans.** In the case of a section 414(k) plan that includes both a defined benefit plan and a separate account, the rules of sections 401(a)(11) and 417 apply separately to the defined benefit portion and the separate account portion of the plan. The separate account portion is subject to the survivor annuity requirements of sections 401(a)(11) and 417 and the special QPSA rules in section 417(c)(2).

**(b) Employee contributions.** *(1) Voluntary.* In the case of voluntary employee contributions to a defined benefit plan, the plan must maintain a separate account with respect to the voluntary employee contributions. This separate account is subject to the survivor annuity requirements of sections 401(a)(11) and 417 and the special QPSA rules in section 417(c)(2).

*(2) Mandatory.* In the case of a defined benefit plan providing for mandatory employee contributions, the entire accrued benefit is subject to the survivor annuity requirements of sections 401(a)(11) and 417 as a defined benefit plan.

**(c) Accumulated DECs.** See Q&A 14 of this section for the rule applicable to accumulated deductible employee contributions.

Q-16. Can a plan provide a benefit form more valuable than the QJSA and if a plan offers more than one annuity option satisfying the requirements of a QJSA, is spousal consent required when the participant chooses among the various forms?

A-16. In the case of an unmarried participant, the QJSA may be less valuable than other optional forms of a benefit payable under the plan. In the case of married participant, the QJSA must be at least as valuable as any other optional form of benefit payable under the plan at the same time. Thus, if a plan has two joint and survivor annuities that would satisfy the requirements for a QJSA, but one has a greater actuarial value than the other, the more valuable joint and survivor annuity is the QJSA. If there are two or more actuarially equivalent joint and survivor annuities that satisfy the requirements for a QJSA, the plan must designate which one is the QJSA and, therefore, the automatic form of benefit payment. A plan, however, may allow a participant to elect out of such a QJSA, without spousal consent, in favor of another actuarially equivalent joint and survivor annuity that satisfies the QJSA conditions. Such an election is not subject to the requirement that it be made within the 90-day period before the annuity starting date. For example, if a plan designates a joint and 100% survivor annuity as the QJSA and also offers an actuarially equivalent joint and 50% survivor annuity that would satisfy the requirements of a QJSA, the participant may elect the joint and 50% survivor annuity without spousal consent. The participant, however, does need spousal consent to elect a joint and survivor annuity that was not actuarially equivalent to the automatic QJSA. A plan does not fail to satisfy the requirements of this Q&A-16 merely because the amount payable under an optional form of benefit that is subject to the minimum present value requirement of section 417(e)(3) is calculated using the applicable interest rate (and, for periods when required, the applicable mortality table) under section 417(e)(3).

Q-17. When must distributions to a participant under a QJSA commence?

A-17. **(a) QJSA benefits upon earliest retirement.** A plan must permit a participant to receive a distribution in the form of a QJSA when the participant attains the earliest retirement age under the plan. Written consent of the participant is required. However, the consent of the participant's spouse is not required. Any payment not in the form of a QJSA is subject to spousal consent. For example, if the participant separates from service under a plan that allows for distributions on separation from service or if a plan allows for in-service distributions, the participant may receive a QJSA without spousal consent in such events. Payments in any other form, including a single sum, would require waiver of the QJSA by the participant's spouse.

**(b) Earliest retirement age.** *(1)* This paragraph (b) defines the term "earliest retirement age" for purposes of sections 401(a)(11), 411(a)(11) and 417.

*(2)* In the case of a plan that provides for voluntary distributions that commence upon the participant's separation from service, earliest retirement age is the earliest age at which a participant could separate from service and receive a distribution. Death of a participant is treated as a separation from service.

*(3)* In the case of a plan that provides for in-service distributions, earliest retirement age is the earliest age at which such distributions may be made.

*(4)* In the case of a plan not described in subparagraph (2) or (3) of this paragraph, the rule below applies. Earliest retirement age is the early retirement age determined under the plan, or if no early retirement age, the normal retirement age determined under the plan. If the participant dies or separates from service before such age, then only the participant's actual years of service at the time of the participant's separation from service or death are taken into account. Thus, in the case of a plan under which benefits are not payable until the attainment of age 65, or upon attainment of age 55 and completion of 10 years of service, the earliest retirement age of a participant who died or separated from service with 8 years of service is when the participant would have attained age 65 (if the participant had survived). On the other hand, if a participant died or separated from service after 10 years of service, the earliest retirement age is when the participant would have attained age 55 (if the participant had survived).

Q-18. What is a qualified preretirement survivor annuity (QPSA) in a defined benefit plan?

A-18. A QPSA is an immediate annuity for the life of the surviving spouse of a participant. Each payment under a QPSA under a defined benefit plan is not to be less than the payment that would have been made to the survivor under the QJSA payable under the plan if (a) in the case of a participant who dies after attaining the earliest retirement age under the plan, the participant had retired with a QJSA on the day before the participant's death, and (b) in the case of a participant who dies on or before the participant's earliest retirement age under the plan, the participant had separated from service at the earlier of the actual time of separation or death, survived until the earliest retirement age, retired at that time with a QJSA, and died on the day thereafter. If the participant elects before the annuity starting date a form of joint and survivor annuity that satisfies the requirements for a QJSA and dies before the annuity starting date, the elected form is treated as the QJSA and the QPSA must be based on such form.

Q-19. What rules apply in determining the amount and forfeitability of a QPSA?

A-19. The QPSA is calculated as of the earliest retirement age if the participant dies before such time, or at death if the participant dies after the earliest retirement age. The plan must make reasonable actuarial adjustments to reflect a payment earlier or later than the earliest retirement age. A defined benefit plan may provide that the QPSA is forfeited if the spouse does not survive until the date prescribed under the plan for commencement of the QPSA *(i.e.,* the earliest retirement age). Similarly, if the spouse survives past the participant's earliest retirement age (or other earlier QPSA distribution date under the plan) and elects after the death of the participant to defer the commencement of the QPSA to a later date, a defined benefit plan may provide for a forfeiture of the QPSA benefit if the spouse does not survive until the deferred commencement date. The account balance in a defined contribution plan may not be forfeited even though the spouse does not survive until the time the account balance is used to purchase the QPSA. See Q&A-17 of this section for the meaning of earliest retirement age.

Q-20. What preretirement survivor annuity benefits must a defined contribution plan subject to the survivor annuity requirements of sections 401(a)(11) and 417 provide?

A-20. A defined contribution plan that is subject to the survivor annuity requirements of sections 401(a)(11) and 417 must provide a preretirement survivor annuity with a value which is not less than 50 percent of the nonforfeitable account balance of the participant as of the date of the participant's death. If a contributory defined contribution plan has a forfeiture provision permitted by section 411(a)(3)(A), not more than a proportional percent of the account balance attributable to contributions that may not be forfeited at death (for example, employee and section 401(k) contributions) may be used to satisfy the QPSA benefit. Thus, for example, if the QPSA benefit is to be provided from 50 percent of the account balance, not more than 50 percent of the nonforfeitable contributions may be used for the QPSA.

Q-21. May a defined benefit plan charge the participant for the cost of the QPSA benefit?

A-21. Prior to the later of the time the plan allows the participant to waive the QPSA or provides notice of the ability to waive the QPSA, a defined benefit plan may not charge the participant for the cost of the QPSA by reducing the participant's plan benefits or by any other method. The preceding sentence does not apply to any charges prior to the first plan year beginning after December 31, 1988. Once the participant is given the opportunity to waive the QPSA or the notice of the QPSA if later, the plan may charge the participant for the cost of the QPSA. A charge for the QPSA that reasonably reflects the cost of providing the QPSA will not fail to satisfy section 411 even if it reduces the accrued benefit.

Q-22. When must distributions to a surviving spouse under a QPSA commence?

A-22. **(a)** In the case of a defined benefit plan, the plan must permit the surviving spouse to direct the commencement of payments under QPSA no later than the month in which the participant would have attained the earliest retirement age. However, a plan may permit the commencement of payments at an earlier date.

**(b)** In the case of a defined contribution plan, the plan must permit the surviving spouse to direct the commencement of payments under the QPSA within a reasonable time after the participant's death.

Q-23. Must a defined benefit plan obtain the consent of a participant and the participant's spouse to commence payments in the form of a QJSA in order to avoid violating section 415 or 411(b)?

A-23. No. A defined benefit plan may commence distributions in the form of a QJSA without the consent of the participant and spouse, even if consent would otherwise be required (see § 1.417(e)-1(b)), to the extent necessary to avoid a violation of section 415 or 411(b). For example, assume a plan has a normal retirement age of 55. A is a married participant, age 55, and has accrued a $75,000 joint and 100 percent survivor annuity that satisfies section 415. If an actuarial increase would be required under section 411 because of deferred commencement and the increase would cause the benefit to exceed the applicable limit under section 415, the plan may commence payment of a QJSA at age 55 without the participant's election or consent and without the spouse's consent.

Q-24. What are the rules under sections 401(a)(11) and 417 applicable to plan loans?

A-24. **(a) Consent rules.** *(1)* A plan does not satisfy the survivor annuity requirements of sections 401(a)(11) and 417 unless the plan provides that, at the time the participant's accrued benefit is used as security for a loan, spousal consent to such use is obtained. Consent is required even if the accrued benefit is not the primary security for the loan. No spousal consent is necessary if, at the time the loan is secured, no consent would be required for a distribution under section 417(a)(2)(B). Spousal consent is not required if the plan or the participant is not subject to section 401(a)(11) at the time the accrued benefit is used as security, or if the total accrued benefit subject to the security is not in excess of the cash-out limit in effect under § 1.411(a)-11(c)(3)(ii). The spousal consent must be obtained no earlier than the beginning of the 90-day period that ends on the date on which the loan is to be so secured. The consent is subject to the requirements of section 417(a)(2). Therefore, the consent must be in writing, must acknowledge the effect of the loan and must be witnessed by a plan representative or a notary public.

*(2)* Participant consent is deemed obtained at the time the participant agrees to use his accrued benefit as security for a loan for purposes of satisfying the requirements for participant consent under sections 401(a)(11), 411(a)(11) and 417.

**(b) Change in status.** If spousal consent is obtained or is not required under paragraph (a) of this Q&A 24 at the time the benefits are used as security, spousal consent is not required at the time of any setoff of the loan against the accrued benefit resulting from a default, even if the participant is married to a different spouse at the time of the setoff. Similarly, in the case of a participant who secured a loan while unmarried, no consent is required at the time of a setoff of the loan against the accrued benefit even if the participant is married at the time of the setoff.

**(c) Renegotiation.** For purposes of obtaining any required spousal consent, any renegotiation, extension, renewal, or other revision of a loan shall be treated as a new loan made on the date of the renegotiation, extension, renewal, or other revision.

**(d) Effect on benefits.** For purposes of determining the amount of a QPSA or QJSA, the accrued benefit of a participant shall be reduced by any security interest held by the plan by reason of a loan outstanding to the participant at the time of death or payment, if the security interest is treated as payment in satisfaction of the loan under the plan. A plan may offset any loan outstanding at the participant's death which is secured by the participant's account balance against the spousal benefit required to be paid under section 401(a)(11)(B)(iii).

**(e) Effective date.** Loans made prior to August 19, 1985, are deemed to satisfy the consent requirements of paragraph (a) of this Q&A 24.

Q-25. How do the survivor annuity requirements of sections 401(a)(11) and 417 apply with respect to participants who are not married or to surviving spouses and participants who have a change in marital status?

A-25. **(a) Unmarried participant rule.** Plans subject to the survivor annuity requirements of sections 401(a)(11) and 417 must satisfy those requirements applicable to QJSAs with respect to participants who are not married. A QJSA for a participant who is not married is an annuity for the life of the participant. Thus, an unmarried participant must be provided the written explanation described in section 417(a)(3)(A) and a single life annuity unless another form of benefit is elected by the participant. An unmarried participant is deemed to have waived the QPSA requirements. This deemed waiver is null and void if the participant later marries.

**(b) Marital status change.** *(1) Remarriage.* If a participant is married on the date of death, payments to a surviving spouse under a QPSA or QJSA must continue even if the surviving spouse remarries.

*(2) One-year rule.* (i) A plan is not required to treat a participant as married unless the participant and the participant's spouse have been married throughout the one-year period ending on the earlier of (A) the participant's annuity starting date or (B) the date of the participant's death. Nevertheless, for purposes of the preceding sentence, a participant and the participant's spouse must be treated as married throughout the one-year period ending on the participant's annuity starting date even though they are married to each other for less than one year before the annuity starting date if they remain married to each other for at least one year. See section 417(d)(2). If a plan adopts the one-year rule provided in section 417(d), the plan must treat the participant and spouse who are married on the annuity starting date as married and must provide benefits which are to commence on the annuity starting date in the form of a QJSA unless the participant (with spousal consent) elects another form of

benefit. The plan is not required to provide the participant with a new or retroactive election or the spouse with a new consent when the one-year period is satisfied. If the participant and the spouse do not remain married for at least one year, the plan may treat the participant as having not been married on the annuity starting date. In such event, the plan may provide that the spouse loses any survivor benefit right; further, no retroactive correction of the amount paid the participant is required.

(ii) *Example.* Plan X provides that participants who are married on the annuity starting date for less than one year are treated as unmarried participants. Plan X provides benefits in the form of a QJSA or an optional single sum distribution. Participant A was married 6 months prior to the annuity starting date. Plan X must treat A as married and must commence payments to A in the form of a QJSA unless another form of benefit is elected by A with spousal consent. If a QJSA is paid and A is divorced from his spouse S, within the first year of the marriage, S will no longer have any survivor rights under the annuity (unless a QDRO provides otherwise). If A continues to be married to S, and A dies within the one-year period, Plan X may treat A as unmarried and forfeit the OJSA benefit payable to S.

*(3) Divorce.* If a participant divorces his spouse prior to the annuity starting date, any elections made while the participant was married to his former spouse remain valid, unless otherwise provided in a QDRO, or unless the participant changes them or is remarried. If a participant dies after the annuity starting date, the spouse to whom the participant was married on the annuity starting date is entitled to the QJSA protection under the plan. The spouse is entitled to this protection (unless waived and consented to by such spouse) even if the participant and spouse are not married on the date of the participant's death, except as provided in a QDRO.

Q-26. In the case of a defined contribution plan not subject to section 412, does the requirement that a participant's nonforfeitable accrued benefit be payable in full to a surviving spouse apply to a spouse who has been married to the participant for less than one year?

A-26. A plan may provide that a spouse who has not been married to a participant throughout the one-year period ending on the earlier of (a) the participant's annuity starting date or (b) the date of the participant's death is not treated as a surviving spouse and is not required to receive the participant's account balance. The special exception described in section 417(d)(2) and Q&A 25 of this section does not apply.

Q-27. Are there circumstances when spousal consent to a participant's election to waive the QJSA or the QPSA is not required?

A-27. Yes. If it is established to the satisfaction of a plan representative that there is no spouse or that the spouse cannot be located, spousal consent to waive the QJSA or the QPSA is not required. If the spouse is legally incompetent to give consent, the spouse's legal guardian, even if the guardian is the participant, may give consent. Also, if the participant is legally separated or the participant has been abandoned (within the meaning of local law) and the participant has a court order to such effect, spousal consent is not required unless a QDRO provides otherwise. Similar rules apply to a plan subject to the requirements of section 401(a)(11)(B)(iii)(I).

Q-28. Does consent contained in an antenuptial agreement or similar contract entered into prior to marriage satisfy the consent requirements of sections 401(a)(11) and 417?

A-28. No. An agreement entered into prior to marriage does not satisfy the applicable consent requirements, even if the agreement is executed within the applicable election period.

Q-29. If a participant's spouse consents under section 417(a)(2)(A) to the participant's waiver of a survivor annuity form of benefit, is a subsequent spouse of the same participant bound by the consent?

A-29. No. A consent under section 417(a)(2)(A) by one spouse is binding only with respect to the consenting spouse. See Q&A-24 of this section for an exception in the case of plan benefits securing plan loans.

Q-30. Does the spousal consent requirement of section 417(a)(2)(A) require that a spouse's consent be revocable?

A-30. No. A plan may preclude a spouse from revoking consent once it has been given. Alternatively, a plan may also permit a spouse to revoke a consent after it has been given, and thereby to render ineffective the participant's prior election not to receive a QPSA or QJSA. A participant must always be allowed to change his election during the applicable election period. Spousal consent is required in such cases to the extent provided in Q&A 31, except that spousal consent is never required for a QJSA or QPSA.

Q-31. What rules govern a participant's waiver of a QPSA or QJSA under section 417(a)(2)?

A-31. **(a) Specific beneficiary.** Both the participant's waivers of a QPSA and QJSA and the spouse's consents thereto must state the specific nonspouse beneficiary (including any class of beneficiaries or any contingent beneficiaries) who will receive the benefit. Thus, for example, if spouse B consents to participant A's election to waive a QPSA, and to have any benefits payable upon A's death before the annuity starting date paid to A's children, A may not subsequently change beneficiaries without the consent of B (except if the change is back to a QPSA). If the designated beneficiary is a trust, A's spouse need only consent to the designation of the trust and need not consent to the designation of trust beneficiaries or any changes of trust beneficiaries.

**(b) Optional form of benefit.** *(1) QJSA.* Both the participant's waiver of a QJSA (and any required spouse's consent thereto) must specify the particular optional form of benefit. The participant who has waived a QJSA with the spouse's consent in favor of another form of benefit may not subsequently change the optional form of benefit without obtaining the spouse's consent (except back to a QJSA). Of course, the participant may change the form of benefit if the plan so provides after the spouse's death or a divorce (other than as provided in a QDRO). A participant's waiver of a QJSA (and any required spouse's consent thereto) made prior to the first plan year beginning after December 31, 1986, is not required to specify the optional form of benefit.

*(2) QPSA.* A participant's waiver of a QPSA and the spouse's consent thereto are not required to specify the optional form of any preretirement benefit. Thus, a participant who waives the QPSA with spousal consent may subsequently change the form of the preretirement benefit, but not the nonspouse beneficiary, without obtaining the spouse's consent.

*(3) Change in form.* After the participant's death, a beneficiary may change the optional form of survivor benefit as permitted by the plan.

**(c) General consent.** In lieu of satisfying paragraphs (a) and (b) of this Q&A 31, a plan may permit a spouse to execute a general consent that satisfies the requirements of this paragraph (c). A general consent permits the participant to waive a QPSA or QJSA, and change the designated beneficiary or the optional form of benefit payment without any requirement of further consent by such spouse. No general consent is valid unless the general consent acknowledges that the spouse has the right to limit consent to a specific beneficiary and a specific optional form of benefit, where applicable, and that the spouse voluntarily elects to relinquish both of such rights. Notwithstanding the previous sentence, a spouse may execute a general consent that is limited to certain beneficiaries or forms of benefit payment. In such case, paragraphs (a) and (b) of this Q& A 31 shall apply to the extent that the limited general consent is not applicable and this paragraph (c) shall apply to the extent that the limited general consent is applicable. A general consent, including a limited general consent, is not effective unless it is made during the applicable election period. A general consent executed prior to October 22, 1986 does not have to satisfy the specificity requirements of this Q&A 31.

Q-32. What rules govern a participant's waiver of the spousal benefit under section 401(a)(11)(B)?

A-32. **(a) Application.** In the case of a defined contribution plan that is not subject to the survivor annuity requirements of sections 401(a)(11) and 417, a participant may waive the spousal benefit of section 401(a)(11)(B)(iii) if the conditions of paragraph (b) are satisfied. In general, a spousal benefit is the nonforfeitable account balance on the participant's date of death.

**(b) Conditions.** In general, the same conditions, other than the age 35 requirement, that apply to the participant's waiver of a QPSA and the spouse's consent thereto apply to the participant's waiver of the spousal benefit and the spouse's consent thereto. See Q&A-31. Thus, the participant's waiver of the spousal benefit must state the specific nonspouse beneficiary who will receive such benefit. The waiver is not required to specify the optional form of benefit. The participant may change the optional form of benefit, but not the nonspouse beneficiary, without obtaining the spouse's consent.

Q-33. When and in what manner, may a participant waive a spousal benefit or a QPSA?

A-33. **(a) Plans not subject to section 401(a)(11).** A participant's in a plan that is not subject to the survivor annuity requirements of section 401(a)(11) (because of subparagraph (B)(iii) thereof) may waive the spousal benefit at any time, provided that no such waiver shall be effective unless the spouse has consented to the waiver. The spouse may consent to a waiver of the spousal benefit at any time, even prior to the participant attaining age 35. No spousal consent is required for a payment to the participant or the use of the accrued benefit as security for a plan loan to the participant.

**(b) Plans subject to section 401(a)(11).** A participant in a plan subject to the survivor annuity requirements of section 401(a)(11) generally may waive the QPSA benefit (with spousal consent) only on or after the first day of the plan year in which the participant attains age 35. However, a plan may provide for an earlier waiver (with spousal consent), provided that a written explanation of the QPSA is given to the participant and such waiver becomes invalid upon the beginning of the plan year in which the participant's 35th birthday occurs. If there is no new waiver after such date, the participant's spouse must receive the QPSA benefit upon the participant's death.

Q-34. Must the written explanations required by section 417(a)(3) be provided to nonvested participants?

A-34. Such written explanations must be provided to nonvested participants who are employed by an employer maintaining the plan. Thus, they are not required to be provided to those nonvested participants who are no longer employed by such an employer.

Q-35. When must a plan provide the written explanation, required by section 417(a)(3)(B), of the QPSA to a participant?

A-35. **(a) General rule.** A plan must provide the written explanation of the QPSA to a participant within the applicable period. Except as provided in paragraph (b), the applicable period means, with respect to a participant, whichever of the following periods ends last:

*(1)* The period beginning with the first day of the plan year in which the participant attains age 32 and ending with the close of the plan year preceding the plan year in which the participant attains age 35.

*(2)* A reasonable period ending after the individual becomes a participant.

*(3)* A reasonable period ending after the QPSA is no longer fully subsidized.

*(4)* A reasonable period ending after section 401(a)(11) first applies to the participant. Section 401(a)(11) would first apply when a benefit is transferred from a plan not subject to the survivor annuity requirements of section 401(a)(11) to a plan subject to such section or at the time of an election of an annuity under a defined contribution plan described in section 401(a)(11)(B)(iii).

**(b) Pre-35 separations.** In the case of a participant who separates from service before attaining age 35, the applicable period means the period beginning one year before the separation from service and ending one year after such separation. If such a participant returns to service, the plan must also comply with paragraph (a).

**(c) Reasonable period.** For purposes of applying paragraph (a), a reasonable period ending after the enumerated events described in paragraphs (a)(2), (3) and (4) is the end of the one-year period beginning with the date the applicable event occurs. The applicable period for such events begins one year prior to the occurrence of the enumerated events.

**(d) Transition rule.** In the case of an individual who was a participant in the plan on August 23, 1984, and, as of that date had attained age 34, the plan will satisfy the requirement of section 417(a)(3)(B) if it provided the explanation not later than December 31, 1985.

Q-36. How do plans satisfy the requirements of providing participants explanations of QPSAs and QJSAs?

A-36. For rules regarding the explanation of QPSAs and QJSAs required under section 417(a)(3), see § 1.417(a)(3)-1. However, the rules of § 1.401(a)-20, Q&A-36, as it appeared in 26 CFR part 1 revised April 1, 2003, apply to the explanation of a QJSA under section 417(a)(3) for an annuity starting date prior to February 1, 2006.

Q-37. What are the consequences of fully subsidizing the cost of either a QJSA or a QPSA in accordance with section 417(a)(5)?

A-37. If a plan fully subsidizes a QJSA or QPSA in accordance with section 417(a)(5) and does not allow a participant to waive such QJSA or QPSA or to select a nonspouse beneficiary, the plan is not required to provide the written explanation required by section 417(a)(3). However, if the plan offers an election to waive the benefit or designate a beneficiary, it must satisfy the election, consent, and notice requirements of section 417(a)(1), (2), and (3), with respect to such subsidized QJSA or QPSA, in accordance with section 417(a)(5).

Q-38. What is a fully subsidized benefit?

A-38. **(a) QJSA.** *(1) General rule.* A fully subsidized QJSA is one under which no increase in cost to, or decrease in actual amounts received by, the participant may result from the participant's failure to elect another form of benefit.

*(2) Examples.*

*Example (1).* If a plan provides a joint and survivor annuity and a single sum option, the plan does not fully subsidize the joint and survivor annuity, regardless of the actuarial value of the joint and survivor annuity because, in the event of the participant's early death, the participant would have received less under the annuity than he would have received under the single sum option.

*Example (2).* If a plan provides for a life annuity of $100 per month and a joint and 100% survivor benefit of $99 per month, the plan does not fully subsidize the joint and survivor benefit.

**(b) QPSA.** A QPSA is fully subsidized if the amount of the participant's benefit is not reduced because of the QPSA coverage and if no charge to the participant under the plan is made for the coverage. Thus, a QPSA is fully subsidized in a defined contribution plan.

Q-39. When do the survivor annuity requirements of sections 401(a)(11) and 417 apply to plans?

A-39. Sections 401(a)(11) and 417 generally apply to plan years beginning after December 31, 1984. Sections 302 and 303 of REA 1984 provide specific effective dates and transitional rules under which the QJSA or QPSA (or pre-REA 1984 section 401(a)(11)) requirements may be applicable to particular plans or with respect to benefits provided to (as amended by REA 1984) particular participants. In general, the section 401(a)(11) (as amended by REA 1984) survivor annuity requirements do not apply with respect to a participant who does not have at least one hour of service or one hour of paid leave under the plan after August 22, 1984.

Q-40. Are there special effective dates for plans maintained pursuant to collective bargaining agreements?

A-40. Yes. Section 302(b) of REA 1984 as amended by section 1898(g) of the Tax Reform Act of 1986 provides a special deferred effective date for such plans. Whether a plan is described in section 302(b) of REA 1984 is determined under the principles applied under section 1017(c) of the Employee Retirement Income Security Act of 1974. See H.R. Rep. No. 1280, 93d Cong., 2d Sess. 266 (1974). In addition, a plan will not be treated as maintained under a collective bargaining agreement unless the employee representatives satisfy section 7701(a)(46) of the Internal Revenue Code after March 31, 1984. See § 301.7701-17T for other requirements for a plan to be considered to be collectively bargained. Nothing in section 302(b) of REA 1984 denies a participant or spouse the rights set forth in sections 303(c)(2), 303(c)(3), 303(e)(1), and 303(e)(2) of REA 1984.

Q-41. What is one hour of service or paid leave under the plan for purposes of the transition rules in section 303 of REA 1984?

A-41. One hour of service or paid leave under the plan is one hour of service or paid leave recognized or required to be recognized under the plan for any purpose, *e.g.*, participation, vesting percentage, or benefit accrual purposes. For plans that do not compute hours of service, one hour of service or paid leave means any service or paid leave recognized or required to be recognized under the plan for any purpose.

Q-42. Must a plan be amended to provide for the QPSA required by section 303(c)(2) of REA 1984, or for the survivor annuities required by section 303(e) of REA 1984?

A-42. A plan will not fail to satisfy the qualification requirements of section 401(a) or 403(a) merely because it is not amended to provide the QPSA required by section 303(c)(2) or the survivor annuities required by section 303(e). The plan must, however, satisfy those requirements in operation.

Q-43. Is a participant's election, or a spouse's consent to an election, with respect to a QPSA, made before August 23, 1984, valid?

A-43. No.

Q-44. Is spousal consent required for certain survivor annuity elections made by the participant after December 31, 1984, and before the first plan year to which new sections 401(a)(11) and 417 apply?

A-44. Yes. Section 303(c)(3) of REA 1984 provides that any election not to take a QJSA made after December 31, 1984, and before the date sections 401(a)(11) and 417 apply to the plan by a participant who has 1 hour of service or leave under the plan after August 23, 1984, is not effective unless the spousal consent requirements of section 417 are met with respect to such election. Unless the participant's annuity starting date occurred before January 1, 1985, the spousal consent required by section 417(a)(2) and (e) must be obtained even though the participant elected the benefit prior to January 1, 1985. The plan is not required to be amended to comply with section 303(c)(3) of REA 1984, but the plan must satisfy this requirement in operation.

Q-45. Are there special rules for certain participants who separated from service prior to August 23, 1984?

A-45. Yes. Section 303(e) of REA 1984 provides special rules for certain participants who separated from service before August 23, 1984. Section 303(e)(1), which applies only to plans subject to section 401(a)(11) of the Code (as in effect on August 22, 1984), provides that participants whose annuity starting date did not occur before August 24, 1984, and who had one hour of service on or after September 2, 1974, but not in a plan year beginning after December 31, 1975, may elect to receive the benefits required to be provided under section 401(a)(11) of the Code (as in effect on August 22, 1984). Section 303(e)(2) provides that certain participants who had one hour of service in a plan year beginning on or after January 1, 1976, but not after August 22, 1984, may elect QPSA coverage under new sections 401(a)(11) and 417 in plans subject to these provisions. Section 303(e)(4)(A) requires plans or plan administrators to notify those participants of the provisions of section 303(e).

Q-46. When must a plan provide the notice required by section 303(e)(4)(A) of REA 1984?

A-46. The notice required by section 303(e)(4)(A) must be provided no later than the earlier of:

**(a)** The date the first summary annual report provided after September 17, 1985, is distributed to participants; or

**(b)** September 30, 1985. A plan will not fail to satisfy the preceding sentence if the plan provides a fully subsidized QPSA with respect to any participant described in section 303(e) who dies on or after July 19, 1985, and before the notice is received. If the plan ceases to fully subsidize the QPSA, the cessation must not be effective until the notice is given. For this purpose, an annuity payable to a nonspouse beneficiary elected by the participant, in lieu of a spouse, shall satisfy the QPSA requirement, so long as the survivor benefit is fully subsidized. The notice required by this paragraph must be in writing and sent to the participant's last known address.

Q-47. Is there another time when plans must provide notice of the right, described in section 303(e)(1) of REA '84, to elect a pre-REA 1984 qualified joint and survivor annuity?

A-47. Yes. Notice of this right must also be provided to a participant at the time the participant applies for benefit payments.

---

T.D. 8219, 8/19/88, amend T.D. 8794, 12/18/98, T.D. 8891, 7/18/2000, T.D. 9099, 12/16/2003, T.D. 9256, 3/23/2006.

PAR. 2. For each entry listed in the "Location" column, remove the language in the "Remove" column and add the language in the "Add" column in its place.

PAR. 2. For each entry listed in the "Location" column, remove the language in the "Remove" column and add the language in the "Add" column in its place.

PAR. 2. For each entry listed in the "Location" column, remove the language in the "Remove" column and add the language in the "Add" column in its place.

PAR. 2. For each entry listed in the "Location" column, remove the language in the "Remove" column and add the language in the "Add" column in its place.

PAR. 2. For each entry listed in the "Location" column, remove the language in the "Remove" column and add the language in the "Add" column in its place.

**Proposed § 1.401(a)-20** [*For Preamble, see ¶ 153,065*]

| Location | Remove | Add |
|---|---|---|
| 1.401(a)-13(g)(4)(ii), first sentence | 90 days | 180 days. |
| 1.401(a)-20, A-4, third sentence | 90 days | 180 days. |
| 1.401(a)-20, A-10(a), fifth and sixth sentences. | 90 days | 180 days. |
| 1.401(a)-20, A-16, sixth sentence. | 90 days | 180 days. |
| 1.401(a)-20, A-24(a)(1), fifth sentence. | 90 days | 180 days. |
| 1.402(f)-1, A-2(a), first sentence. | 90 days | 180 days. |
| 1.411(a)-11(c)(2)(ii) | 90 days | 180 days. |
| 1.411(a)-11(c)(2)(iii)(A), first sentence. | 90 days | 180 days. |
| 1.417(e)-1(b)(3)(i) | 90 days | 180 days. |
| 1.417(e)-1(b)(3)(ii), first sentence. | 90 days | 180 days. |
| 1.417(e)-1(b)(3)(iii) | 90 days | 180 days. |
| 1.417(e)-1(b)(3)(vi), second sentence. | 90 days | 180 days. |
| 1.417(e)-1(b)(3)(vii) | 90 days | 180 days. |
| 1.417(e)-1(b)(3)(vii) | 90-day | 180-day. |

### § 1.401(a)-21 Rules relating to the use of an electronic medium to provide applicable notices and to make participant elections.

**(a) Introduction.** *(1) In general.* (i) Permission to use an electronic medium. This section provides rules relating to the use of an electronic medium to provide applicable notices and to make participant elections as defined in paragraph (e)(1) and (6) of this section with respect to retirement plans, employee benefit arrangements, and individual retirement plans described in paragraph (a)(2) of this section. The rules in this section reflect the provisions of the Electronic Signatures in Global and National Commerce Act, Public Law 106-229 (114 Stat. 464 (2000) (E-SIGN)).

(ii) Notices and elections required to be in writing or in written form. (A) In general. The rules of this section must be satisfied in order to use an electronic medium to provide an applicable notice or to make a participant election if the notice or election is required to be in writing or in written form under the Internal Revenue Code, Department of Treasury regulations, or other guidance issued by the Commissioner.

(B) Rules relating to applicable notices. An applicable notice that is provided using an electronic medium is treated as being provided in writing or in written form if and only if the requirements of paragraph (a)(5) of this section are satisfied and either the consumer consent requirements of paragraph (b) of this section or the requirements for exemption from the consumer consent requirements under paragraph (c) of this section are satisfied. For example, in order to provide a section 402(f) notice electronically, a qualified plan must satisfy either the consumer consent requirements of paragraph (b) of this section or the requirements for exemption under paragraph (c) of this section. If a plan fails to satisfy either of these requirements, the plan must provide the section 402(f) notice using a written paper document in order to satisfy the requirements of section 402(f).

(C) Rules relating to participant elections. A participant election that is made using an electronic medium is treated as being provided in writing or in written form if and only if the requirements of paragraphs (a)(5) and (d) of this section are satisfied.

(iii) Safe harbor method for applicable notices and participant elections that are not required to be in writing or written form. For an applicable notice or a participant election that is not required to be in writing or in written form, the rules of this section provide a safe harbor method for using an electronic medium to provide the applicable notice or to make the participant election.

*(2) Application of rules.* (i) Notices, elections, or consents under retirement plans. The rules of this section apply to any

applicable notice or any participant election relating to the following retirement plans: A qualified retirement plan under section 401(a) or 403(a); a section 403(b) plan; a simplified employee pension (SEP) under section 408(k); a simple retirement plan under section 408(p); or an eligible governmental plan under section 457(b).

(ii) Notices, elections, or consents under other employee benefit arrangements. The rules of this section also apply to any applicable notice or any participant election relating to the following employee benefit arrangements: An accident and health plan or arrangement under sections 104(a)(3) and 105; a cafeteria plan under section 125; an educational assistance program under section 127; a qualified transportation fringe program under section 132; an Archer MSA under section 220; or a health savings account under section 223.

(iii) Notices, elections, or consents under individual retirement plans. The rules of this section also apply to any applicable notice or any participant election relating to individual retirement plans, including a Roth IRA under section 408A; or a deemed IRA under a qualified employer plan described in section 408(q).

*(3) Limitation on application of rules.* (i) In general. The rules of this section do not apply to any notice, election, consent, disclosure, or obligation required under the provisions of title I or IV of the Employee Retirement Income Security Act of 1974, as amended (ERISA), over which the Department of Labor or the Pension Benefit Guaranty Corporation has interpretative and enforcement authority. For example, the rules in 29 CFR 2520.104b-1 of the Department of Labor Regulations apply with respect to an employee benefit plan providing disclosure documents, such as a summary plan description or a summary annual report. The rules in this section also do not apply to Internal Revenue Code section 411(a)(3)(B) (relating to suspension of benefits), Internal Revenue Code section 4980B(f)(6) (relating to an individual's COBRA rights), or any other Internal Revenue Code provision over which Department of Labor or the Pension Benefit Guaranty Corporation has similar interpretative authority.

(ii) Recordkeeping and other requirements. The rules in this section only apply with respect to applicable notices and participant elections relating to an individual's rights under a retirement plan, an employee benefit arrangement, or an individual retirement plan. Thus, the rules in this section do not alter the otherwise applicable requirements under the Internal Revenue Code, such as the requirements relating to tax reporting, tax records, or substantiation of expenses. See section 6001 for rules relating to the maintenance of records, statements, and special returns. See also section 101(e) of E-SIGN, which provides that if an electronic record of an applicable notice or a participant election is not maintained in a form that is capable of being retained and accurately reproduced for later reference, then the legal effect, validity, or enforceability of such electronic record may be denied.

*(4) General requirements related to applicable notices and participant elections.* The rules of this section supplement the general requirements related to each applicable notice and participant election. Thus, in addition to satisfying the rules for timing and content, the rules in this section must be satisfied.

*(5) Requirements related to the design of an electronic system used to deliver applicable notices and to make participant elections.* (i) The electronic system must take into account the content of a notice. With respect to the content of an applicable notice, the electronic system must be reasonably designed to provide the information in the notice to a recipient in a manner that is no less understandable to the recipient than a written paper document.

(ii) Identification of the significance of information in the notice. The electronic system must be designed to alert the recipient, at the time an applicable notice is provided, to the significance of the information in the notice (including identification of the subject matter of the notice), and provide any instructions needed to access the notice, in a manner that is readily understandable.

**(b) Consumer consent requirements.** *(1) Requirements.* With respect to an applicable notice, the consumer consent requirements of this paragraph (b) are satisfied if—

(i) The requirements in paragraphs (b)(2) through (4) of this section are satisfied; and

(ii) In accordance with section 101(c)(6) of E-SIGN, the applicable notice is not provided through the use of oral communication or a recording of an oral communication.

*(2) Consent.* (ii) In general. The recipient must affirmatively consent to the delivery of the applicable notice using an electronic medium. This consent must be either—

(A) Made electronically in a manner that reasonably demonstrates that the recipient can access the applicable notice in the electronic medium in the form that will be used to provide the notice; or

(B) Made using a written paper document (or using another form not described in paragraph (b)(2)(i)(A) of this section), but only if the recipient confirms the consent electronically in a manner that reasonably demonstrates that the recipient can access the applicable notice in the electronic medium in the form that will be used to provide the notice.

(ii) Withdrawal of consumer consent. The consent to receive electronic delivery requirement of this paragraph (b)(2) is not satisfied if the recipient withdraws his or her consent before the applicable notice is delivered.

*(3) Required disclosure statement.* The recipient, prior to consenting under paragraph (b)(2)(i) of this section, must be provided with a clear and conspicuous statement containing the disclosures described in paragraphs (b)(3)(i) through (v) of this section:

(i) Right to receive paper document. (A) In general. The statement informs the recipient of any right to have the applicable notice be provided using a written paper document or other nonelectronic form.

(B) Post-consent request for paper copy. The statement informs the recipient how, after having provided consent to receive the applicable notice electronically, the recipient may, upon request, obtain a paper copy of the applicable notice and whether any fee will be charged for such copy.

(ii) Right to withdraw consumer consent. The statement informs the recipient of the right to withdraw consent to receive electronic delivery of an applicable notice on a prospective basis at any time and explains the procedures for withdrawing that consent and any conditions, consequences, or fees in the event of the withdrawal.

(iii) Scope of the consumer consent. The statement informs the recipient whether the consent to receive electronic delivery of an applicable notice applies only to the particular transaction that gave rise to the applicable notice or to other identified transactions that may be provided or made available during the course of the parties' relationship. For example, the statement may provide that a recipient's consent to receive electronic delivery will apply to all future applicable notices of the recipient relating to the employee benefit arrangement until the recipient is no longer a participant in the employee benefit arrangement (or withdraws the consent).

(iv) Description of the contact procedures. The statement describes the procedures to update information needed to contact the recipient electronically.

(v) Hardware or software requirements. The statement describes the hardware and software requirements needed to access and retain the applicable notice.

*(4) Post-consent change in hardware or software requirements.* If, after a recipient provides consent to receive electronic delivery, there is a change in the hardware or software requirements needed to access or retain the applicable notice and such change creates a material risk that the recipient will not be able to access or retain the applicable notice in electronic format—

(i) The recipient must receive a statement of—

(A) The revised hardware or software requirements for access to and retention of the applicable notice; and

(B) The right to withdraw consent to receive electronic delivery without the imposition of any fees for the withdrawal and without the imposition of any condition or consequence that was not previously disclosed in paragraph (b)(3) of this section; and

(ii) The recipient must reaffirm consent to receive electronic delivery in accordance with the requirements of paragraph (b)(2) of this section.

**(c) Exemption from consumer consent requirements.** *(1) In general.* This paragraph (c) is satisfied if the conditions in paragraphs (c)(2) and (3) of this section are satisfied. This paragraph (c) constitutes an exemption from the consumer consent requirements of section 101(c) of E-SIGN pursuant to the authority granted in section 104(d)(1) of E-SIGN.

*(2) Effective ability to access.* For purposes of this paragraph (c), the electronic medium used to provide an applicable notice must be a medium that the recipient has the effective ability to access.

*(3) Free paper copy of applicable notice.* At the time the applicable notice is provided, the recipient must be advised that he or she may request and receive the applicable notice in writing on paper at no charge, and, upon request, that applicable notice must be provided to the recipient at no charge.

**(d) Special rules for participant elections.** *(1) In general.* This paragraph (d) is satisfied if the conditions described in the following paragraphs (d)(2) through (6) are satisfied:

*(2) Effective ability to access.* The electronic medium under an electronic system used to make a participant election must be a medium that the person who is eligible to make the election is effectively able to access. If the appropriate individual is not effectively able to access the electronic medium for making the participant election, the participant election will not be treated as made available to that individual. Thus, for example, the participant election will not be treated as made available to that individual for purposes of the rules under section 401(a)(4).

*(3) Authentication.* The electronic system used in making participant elections is reasonably designed to preclude any person other than the appropriate individual from making the election. Whether this condition is satisfied is based on facts and circumstances, including whether the participant election has the potential for a conflict of interest between the individuals involved in the election. See Examples 3, 4, and 5 of paragraph (f) of this section for illustrations of electronic systems that satisfy the authentication requirement of this paragraph (d)(3).

*(4) Opportunity to review.* The electronic system used in making participant elections provides the person making the participant election with a reasonable opportunity to review, confirm, modify, or rescind the terms of the election before the election becomes effective.

*(5) Confirmation of action.* The person making the participant election receives, within a reasonable time, a confirmation of the effect of the election under the terms of the plan or arrangement through either a written paper document or an electronic medium under a system that satisfies the requirements of either paragraph (b) or (c) of this section (as if the confirmation were an applicable notice).

*(6) Participant elections, including spousal consents, that are required to be witnessed by a plan representative or a notary public.* (i) In general. In the case of a participant election which is required to be witnessed by a plan representative or a notary public (such as a spousal consent under section 417), the signature of the individual making the participant election is witnessed in the physical presence of a plan representative or a notary public.

(ii) Electronic notarization permitted. If the requirements of paragraph (d)(6)(i) of this section are satisfied, an electronic notarization acknowledging a signature (in accordance with section 101(g) of E-SIGN and State law applicable to notary publics) will not be denied legal effect if the signature of the individual is witnessed in the physical presence of a notary public.

(iii) Delegation to Commissioner. In guidance published in the Internal Revenue Bulletin, the Commissioner may provide that the use of procedures under an electronic system is deemed to satisfy the physical presence requirement under paragraph (d)(6)(i) of this section, but only if those procedures with respect to the electronic system provide the same safeguards for participant elections as are provided through the physical presence requirement. See § 601.601(d)(2)(ii)(b) of this chapter.

**(e) Definitions.** The definitions in this paragraph (e) apply for purposes of this section.

*(1) Applicable notice.* The term applicable notice includes any notice, report, statement, or other document required to be provided to a recipient under a retirement plan, employee benefit arrangement, or individual retirement plan as described in paragraph (a)(2) of this section.

*(2) Electronic.* The term electronic means technology having electrical, digital, magnetic, wireless, optical, electromagnetic, voice-recording systems, or similar capabilities.

*(3) Electronic medium.* The term electronic medium means an electronic method of communication (e.g., Web site, electronic mail, telephonic system, magnetic disk, and CD-ROM).

*(4) Electronic record.* The term electronic record means an applicable notice or a participant election that is created, generated, sent, communicated, received, or stored by electronic media.

*(5) Electronic system.* The term electronic system means a system designed for creating, generating, sending, receiving, storing, retrieving, displaying, or processing information that makes use of any electronic medium.

*(6) Participant election.* The term participant election includes any consent, election, request, agreement, or similar communication made by or from a participant, beneficiary,

alternate payee, or an individual entitled to benefits under a retirement plan, employee benefit arrangement, or individual retirement plan as described in paragraph (a)(2) of this section.

*(7) Recipient.* The term recipient means a plan participant, beneficiary, employee, alternate payee, or any other person to whom an applicable notice is to be provided.

**(f) Examples.** The following examples illustrate the rules of this section. Examples 1, 2, 3, and 6 assume that the requirements of paragraph (a)(4) and (5) of this section are satisfied.

*Example (1).* (i) Facts involving using the consumer consent requirements to deliver a section 402(f) notice via e-mail. Plan A, a qualified plan, permits participants to request benefit distributions from the plan on Plan A's Internet Web site. Under Plan A's system for such transactions, a participant must enter his or her account number, personal identification number (PIN), and his or her e-mail address to which the notice is to be sent. The participant's PIN and account number must match the information in Plan A's records in order for the transaction to proceed. Participant H requests a distribution from Plan A on Plan A's Web site, and, at the time of the request for distribution, a disclosure statement appears on the computer screen that explains that Participant H can consent to receive the section 402(f) notice electronically. The disclosure statement provides information relating to the consent, including how to receive a paper copy of the notice, how to withdraw consent, the hardware and software requirements, and the procedures for accessing the section 402(f) notice, which is in a file format from a specific spreadsheet program. After reviewing the disclosure statement, which satisfies the requirements of paragraph (b)(3) of this section, Participant H consents to receive the section 402(f) notice via e-mail by selecting the consent button at the end of the disclosure statement. As a part of the consent procedure, an e-mail is sent to Participant H's e-mail address in order to demonstrate that Participant H can access the spreadsheet program. In the e-mail, Participant H is prompted to answer a question from the spreadsheet program, which is in an attachment to the e-mail. Once Participant H correctly answers the question, the section 402(f) notice is then delivered to Participant H via e-mail.

(ii) Conclusion. In this Example 1, Plan A's delivery of the section 402(f) notice to Participant H satisfies the requirements of paragraph (b) of this section.

*Example (2).* (i) Facts. (A) Facts involving using the alternative method to deliver a section 411(a)(11) notice via e-mail. Plan B, a qualified plan, permits participants to request benefit distributions from the plan on Plan B's Internet Web site. Under Plan B's system for such transactions, a participant must enter his or her account number and personal identification number (PIN), and his or her e-mail address to which the notice is to be sent. The participant's PIN and account number must match the information in Plan B's records in order for the transaction to proceed. After Participant K, a single employee, requests a distribution from Plan B on Plan B's Internet Web site, the plan administrator provides Participant K with a section 411(a)(11) notice in an attachment to an e-mail. Plan B sends the e-mail with a request for a computer generated notification that the message was received and opened. The e-mail instructs Participant K to read the attachment for important information regarding the request for a distribution. In addition, the e-mail also states that Participant K may request the section 411(a)(11) notice on a written paper document and that, if Participant K requests the notice on a written paper document, it will be provided at no charge. Plan B receives notification indicating that the e-mail was received and opened by Participant K.

(B) Facts involving making a participant's consent to a distribution. In order to consent to a distribution, Plan B requires a participant to enter the participant's account number and PIN in order to preclude any person other than the participant from making the election. After the authentication process, Participant K completes a distribution request form on the Web site. After completing the request form, the Web site provides a summary of the information entered on the form and gives Participant K an opportunity to review or modify the distribution request form before the transaction is completed. Within a reasonable period of time after Participant K consents to the distribution, the plan administrator, by e-mail, sends confirmation of the terms (including the form) of the distribution to Participant K and advises Participant K that, upon request, the confirmation may be provided to Participant K on a written paper document at no charge. Plan B retains an electronic copy of the consent to the distribution in a form that is capable of being retained and accurately reproduced for later reference by Participant K.

(ii) Conclusion. In this Example 2, Plan B's delivery of the section 411(a)(11) notice and the electronic system used to make Participant K's consent to a distribution satisfy the requirements of paragraphs (a), (c), and (d) of this section.

*Example (3).* (i) Facts involving the transmission of a spousal consent via electronic notarization. Plan C, a qualified money purchase pension plan, permits a married participant to request a plan loan through the Plan C's Internet Web site with the notarized consent of the spouse. Under Plan C's system for requesting a plan loan, a participant must enter his or her account number, personal identification number (PIN), and his or her e-mail address. The information entered by the participant must match the information in Plan C's records in order for the transaction to proceed. Participant M, a married participant, is effectively able to access the Web site available to apply for a plan loan. In order to apply for a loan, Plan C requires a participant to enter the participant's account number and PIN in order to preclude any person other than the participant from making the election. Participant M completes the loan application on Plan C's Web site. Within a reasonable period of time after submitting the plan loan application, the plan administrator, by e-mail, sends Participant M the loan application, including all attachments setting forth the terms of the loan agreement and all other required information. In the e-mail, Plan C also notifies Participant M that, upon request, the loan application may be provided to Participant M on a written paper document at no charge. Plan C then instructs Participant M that, in order for the loan application to proceed, Participant M must submit to the plan administrator a notarized spousal consent form. Participant M and M's spouse go to a notary public and the notary witnesses Participant M's spouse signing the spousal consent for the loan agreement on an electronic signature capture pad with adequate security. After witnessing M's spouse signing the spousal consent, the notary public sends an e-mail with an electronic acknowledgement that is attached to or logically associated with the signature of M's spouse to the plan administrator. The electronic acknowledgement is in accordance with section 101(g) of E-SIGN and the relevant State law applicable to notary publics. After the plan receives the e-mail, Plan C sends an e-mail to Participant M, giving M a reasonable period to review and confirm the completed loan application and to determine whether the loan application should be modified or rescinded. In addition, the e-mail to Participant

M also provides that M may request the completed loan application on a written paper document and that, if M requests the written paper document, it will be provided at no charge. Plan C retains an electronic copy of the loan agreement, including the spousal consent, in a form that is capable of being retained and accurately reproduced for later reference by all parties.

(ii) Conclusion. In this Example 3, the transmission of the plan loan agreement satisfies the requirements of paragraphs (a), (c), and (d) of this section. By requiring that the spouse sign the spousal consent on an electronic signature capture pad in the physical presence of a notary public, the electronic system satisfies the requirement that the system be reasonably designed to preclude any person other than the appropriate individual from making the election. Thus, the electronic notarization of spousal consent satisfies the requirements of paragraphs (a) and (d) of this section.

*Example (4).* (i) Facts. (A) Facts involving using the alternative method of compliance to deliver a section 411(a)(11) notice via an automated telephone system. A qualified profit-sharing plan (Plan D) permits participants to request distributions through an automated telephone system. Under Plan D's system for such transactions, a participant must enter his or her account number and personal identification number (PIN); this information must match the information in Plan D's records in order for the transaction to proceed. Plan D provides only the following distribution options: single-sum payment; and annual installments over 5, 10, or 20 years. Participant N, a single participant, requests a distribution from Plan D by following the applicable instructions on the automated telephone system. After Participant N has requested the distribution, the automated telephone system recites the section 411(a)(11) notice over the phone. The automated telephone system also advises Participant N that, upon request, the notice may be provided on a written paper document and that, if Participant N so requests, the notice will be provided on a written paper document at no charge.

(B) Facts involving making a participant's consent to a distribution via an automated telephone system. In order to consent to a distribution, Plan D requires a participant to enter the participant's account number and PIN in order to preclude any person other than the participant from making the election. Participant N requests a distribution by entering information on the automated telephone system. After completing the request, the automated telephone system provides a oral summary of the information entered and gives Participant N an opportunity to review or modify the distribution request before the transaction is completed. Plan D's automated telephone system confirms the distribution request to Participant N and advises Participant N that, upon request, a confirmation may be provided on a written paper document at no charge. Plan D retains an electronic copy of the consent to the distribution in a form that is capable of being retained and accurately reproduced for later reference by Participant N.

(ii) Conclusion. In this Example 4, because Plan D has relatively few and simple distribution options, the provision of the section 411(a)(11) notice through the automated telephone system is no less understandable to the participant than a written paper notice for purposes of paragraph (a)(5)(i) of this section. In addition, the automated telephone procedures of Plan D satisfy the applicable requirements of paragraphs (a), (c), and (d) of this section.

*Example (5).* (i) Facts. Same facts as Example 4 of this paragraph (f), except that, pursuant to Plan D's system for processing such transactions, a participant who so requests is transferred to a customer service representative whose conversation with the participant is recorded. The customer service representative provides the section 411(a)(11) notice from a prepared text and processes the participant's distribution in accordance with the predetermined instructions from the plan administrator.

(ii) Conclusion. As in Example 4 of this paragraph (f), because Plan D has relatively few and simple distribution options, the provision of the section 411(a)(11) notice through the automated telephone system is no less understandable to the participant than a written paper notice for purposes of paragraph (a)(4) of this section. Further, in this Example 5, the customer service telephone procedures of Plan D satisfy the requirements of paragraphs (a), (c), and (d) of this section.

*Example (6).* (i) Facts. Plan E, a qualified plan, permits participants to request distributions by e-mail on the employer's e-mail system. Under this system, a participant must enter his or her account number, personal identification number (PIN), and e-mail address. This information must match that in Plan E's records in order for the transaction to proceed. If a participant requests a distribution by e-mail, the plan administrator provides the participant with a section 411(a)(11) notice by e-mail. The plan administrator also advises the participant by e-mail that he or she may request the section 411(a)(11) notice on a written paper document and that, if the participant requests the notice on a written paper document, it will be provided at no charge. Participant Q requests a distribution and receives the section 411(a)(11) notice from the plan administrator by reply e-mail. However, before Participant Q elects a distribution, Q terminates employment. Following termination of employment, Participant Q no longer has access to the employer's e-mail system.

(ii) Conclusion. In this Example 6, Plan E does not satisfy the participant election requirements under paragraph (d) of this section because Participant Q is not effectively able to access the electronic medium used to make the participant election. Plan E must provide Participant Q with the opportunity to make the participant election through a written paper document or another system that Participant Q is effectively able to access, such as the automated telephone systems described in Example 4 and Example 5 of this paragraph (f).

**(g) Effective date.** The rules provided in this section apply to applicable notices provided, and to participant elections made, on or after January 1, 2007. However, a retirement plan, an employee benefit arrangement, or an individual retirement plan that provides an applicable notice or makes a participant election that complies with the requirements set forth in these regulations on or after October 1, 2000, and before January 1, 2007, will not be treated as failing to provide an applicable notice or to make a participant election merely because the notice or election was not in writing or written form.

---

T.D. 9294, 10/19/2006

---

### § 1.401(a)-30 Limit on elective deferrals.

**(a) General rule.** A trust that is part of a plan under which elective deferrals may be made during a calendar year is not qualified under section 401(a) unless the plan provides that the elective deferrals on behalf of an individual under the plan and all other plans, contracts, or arrangements of the employer maintaining the plan may not exceed the applicable limit for the individual's taxable year beginning in the calendar year. A plan may incorporate the applicable limit by reference. In the case of a plan maintained by more than one employer to which section 413(b) or (c) applies, section 401(a)(30) and this section are applied as if each employer maintained a separate plan. See § 1.402(g)-1(e) for rules permitting the distribution of excess deferrals to prevent disqualification of a plan or trust for failure to comply in operation with section 401(a)(30).

**(b) Definitions.** For purposes of this section:

*(1) Applicable limit.* The term "applicable limit" has the meaning provided in § 1.402(g)-1(d).

*(2) Elective deferrals.* The term "elective deferrals" has the meaning provided in § 1.402(g)-1(b).

**(c) Effective date.** *(1) In general.* Except as otherwise provided in this paragraph (c), this section is effective for plan years beginning after December 31, 1987.

*(2) Transition rule.* For plan years beginning in 1988, a plan may rely on a reasonable interpretation of the law as in effect on December 31, 1987.

*(3) Deferrals under collective bargaining agreements.* In the case of a plan maintained pursuant to one or more collective bargaining agreements between employee representatives and one or more employers ratified before March 1, 1986, this section does not apply to contributions made pursuant to a collective bargaining agreement for plan years beginning before the earlier of:

(i) The later of January 1, 1988, or the date on which the last collective bargaining agreement terminates (determined without regard to any extension thereof after February 28, 1986), or

(ii) January 1, 1989.

T.D. 8357, 8/8/91.

## § 1.401(a)-50 Puerto Rican trusts; election to be treated as a domestic trust.

**(a) In general.** Section 401(a) requires, among other things, that a trust forming part of a pension, profit-sharing, or stock bonus plan must be created or organized in the United States to be a qualified trust. Section 1022(i)(2) of the Employee Retirement Income Security Act of 1974 (ERISA) (88 Stat. 942) provides that trusts under certain pension, etc., plans created or organized in Puerto Rico whose administrators have made the election referred to in section 1022(i)(2) are to be treated as trusts created or organized in the United States for purposes of section 401(a). Thus, if a plan otherwise satisfies the qualification requirements of section 401(a), any trust forming part of the plan for which an election is made will be treated as a qualified trust under that section.

**(b) Manner and effect of election.** A plan administrator may make an election under ERISA section 1022(i)(2) by filing a statement making the election, along with a copy of the plan, with the Director's Representative of the Internal Revenue Service in Puerto Rico. The statement making the election must indicate that it is being made under ERISA section 1022(i)(2). The statement may also be filed in conjunction with a written request for a determination letter. If the election is made with a written request for a determination letter, the election may be conditioned upon issuance of a favorable determination letter and will be irrevocable upon issuance of such letter. Otherwise, once made, an election is irrevocable. It is generally effective for plan years beginning after the date it has been made. However, an election made before March 3, 1983 may, at the option of the plan administrator at the time he or she makes the election, be considered to have been made on any date between September 2, 1974, and the actual date of the election. The election will then be effective for plan years beginning on or after the date chosen by the plan administrator.

**(c) Annuities, custodial accounts, etc.** See section 401(f) for rules relating to the treatment of certain annuities, custodial accounts or other contracts, as trusts for purposes of section 401(a).

**(d) Source of plan distributions to participants and beneficiaries residing outside the United States.** Except as provided under section 871(f) (relating to amounts received as an annuity by nonresident aliens), the amount of a distribution from an electing plan that is to be treated as income from sources within the United States is determined as described below. The portion of the distribution considered to be a return of employer contributions is to be treated as income from sources within the United States in an amount equal to the portion of the distribution considered to be a return of employer contributions multiplied by the following fraction:

$$\frac{\text{Days of performance of labor or services within the United States for the employer.}}{\text{Total days of performance of labor or services for the employer.}}$$

The days of performance of labor or services within the United States shall not include the time period for which the employee's compensation is deemed not to be income from sources within the United States under subtitle A of the Code. Thus, for example, if an employee's compensation was not deemed to be income from sources within the United States under section 861(a)(3), then the time the employee was present in the United States while such compensation was earned would not be included in determining the days of performance of labor or services within the United States in the numerator of the above fraction. In addition, days of performance of labor or services for the employer in both the numerator and denominator of the above fraction are limited to days of plan participation by the employee and any service used for determining an employee's accrued benefit under the plan. The remaining portion of the distribution, that is, any amount other than the portion of the distribution considered to be a return of employer contributions, is not to be treated as income from sources within the United States. For example, if a distribution consists of amounts representing employer contributions, employee contributions, and earnings on employer and employee contributions, no part of the portion of the distribution attributable to employee contributions, or earnings on employer and employee contributions, will be treated as income from sources within the United States.

T.D. 7859, 12/1/82.

## § 1.401(a)(2)-1 Refund of mistaken employer contributions and withdrawal liability payments to multiemployer plans.

**(a) Introduction.** *(1) In general.* Section 401(a)(2) provides that a contribution or payment of withdrawal liability made to a multiemployer plan due to a mistake of fact or mistake of law can be returned to the employer under certain conditions. This section specifies the conditions under which an employer's contribution or payment may be returned.

*(2) Effective dates.* This section applies to refunds made after July 22, 2002.

**(b) Conditions for return of contribution.** *(1) In general.* In the case of a contribution or a withdrawal liability payment to a multiemployer plan which was made because of a mistake of fact or a mistake of law, the plan will not violate section 401(a)(2) merely because the contribution or payment is returned within six months after the date on which the plan administrator determines that the contribution or payment was the result of a mistake of fact or law. The contribution or payment is considered as returned within the required period if the employer establishes a right to a refund of the amount mistakenly contributed or paid by filing a claim with the plan administrator within six months after the date on which the plan administrator determines that a mistake did occur. For purposes of this section, plan administrator is defined in section 414(g) and the regulations thereunder.

*(2) Applicable conditions.* (i) In general. The employer making the contribution or withdrawal liability payment to a multiemployer plan must demonstrate that an excessive contribution or overpayment has been made due to a mistake of fact or law. A mistake of fact or law relating to plan qualification under section 401 or to trust exemption under section 501 is not considered to be a mistake of fact or law which entitles an employer to a refund under this section. For purposes of this section, a multiemployer plan is defined in section 414(f) and the regulations thereunder.

(ii) Amount to be returned. (A) General rule. The amount to be returned to the employer is the excess of the amount contributed or paid over the amount that would have been contributed or paid had no mistake been made. This amount is the excess contribution or overpayment. Except as provided in paragraph (b)(2)(ii)(B) of this section, interest or earnings attributable to an excess contribution shall not be returned to the employer, and any losses attributable to an excess contribution must reduce the amount returned to the employer. For purposes of the previous sentence, the application of plan-wide investment experience to the excess contribution would be an acceptable method of calculating losses. A refund of a mistaken contribution must in no event reduce a participant's account balance in a defined contribution plan to an amount less than that amount which would properly have been in that participant's account had no mistake occurred. Thus, to the extent that the refund of an excess contribution would reduce a participant's account balance in a defined contribution plan to an amount less than the amount which would properly be in the participant's account had no mistake occurred, the return of the excess contribution would be prohibited by this section.

(B) Overpayment of withdrawal liability. In the case of an overpayment of withdrawal liability established by the plan sponsor under section 4219(c)(2) of ERISA, the plan will not fail to satisfy section 401(a)(2) if, in accordance with Pension Benefit Guaranty Corporation regulations regarding the overpayments of withdrawal liability (29 CFR 4219.31(d)), the overpayment, with interest, is returned to the employer.

**(c) Amount refunded includible in employer's income.** In general, the amount of the excess contribution or overpayment must be included in gross income by the employer if the excess contribution or overpayment resulted in a tax benefit in a prior year. Any interest credited or paid on the refund of mistaken withdrawal liability payments must also be included in gross income by the employer.

**(d) Application of section 412.** An amount returned under paragraph (b)(2)(ii) of this section is charged to the funding standard account under section 412 in the year in which the amount is returned.

---

T.D. 9005, 7/19/2002.

---

## § 1.401(a)(4)-0 Table of contents.

This section contains a listing of the major headings of §§ 1.401(a)(4)-1 through 1.401(a)(4)-13.

*§ 1.401(a)(4)-3 Nondiscrimination in amount of employer-provided benefits under a defined benefit plan.*

(a) Introduction.

(1) Overview.

(2) Alternative methods of satisfying nondiscriminatory amount requirement.

(b) Safe harbors.

(1) In general.

(2) Uniformity requirements.

(3) Safe harbor for unit credit plans.

(4) Safe harbor for plans using fractional accrual rule.

(5) Safe harbor for insurance contract plans.

(6) Use of safe harbors not precluded by certain plan provisions.

(c) General test for nondiscrimination in amount of benefits.

(1) General rule.

(2) Satisfaction of section 410(b) by a rate group.

(3) Certain violations disregarded.

(4) Examples.

(d) Determination of accrual rates.

(1) Definitions.

(2) Rules of application.

(3) Optional rules.

(4) Examples.

(e) Compensation rules.

(1) In general.

(2) Average annual compensation.

(3) Examples.

(f) Special rules.

(1) In general.

(2) Certain qualified disability benefits.

(3) Accruals after normal retirement age.

(4) Early retirement window benefits.

(5) Unpredictable contingent event benefits.

(6) Determination of benefits on other than plan-year basis.

(7) Adjustments for certain plan distributions.

(8) Adjustment for certain QPSA charges.

(9) Disregard of certain offsets.

(10) Special rule for multiemployer plans.

*§ 1.401(a)(4)-4 Nondiscriminatory availability of benefits, rights, and features.*

(a) Introduction.

(b) Current availability.

(1) General rule.

(2) Determination of current availability.

(3) Benefits, rights, and features that are eliminated prospectively.

(c) Effective availability.

(1) General rule.

(2) Examples.

(d) Special rules.

(1) Mergers and acquisitions.

(2) Frozen participants.

(3) Early retirement window benefits.

(4) Permissive aggregation of certain benefits, rights, or features.

(5) Certain spousal benefits.

(6) Special ESOP rules.

(7) Special testing rule for unpredictable contingent event benefits.

(e) Definitions.

(1) Optional form of benefit.

(2) Ancillary benefit.

(3) Other right or feature.

*§ 1.401(a)(4)-5 Plan amendments and plan terminations.*

(a) Introduction.

(1) Overview.

(2) Facts-and-circumstances determination.

(3) Safe harbor for certain grants of benefits for past periods.

(4) Examples.

(b) Pre-termination restrictions.

(1) Required provisions in defined benefit plans.

(2) Restriction of benefits upon plan termination.

(3) Restrictions on distributions.

(4) Operational restrictions on certain money purchase pension plans.

*§ 1.401(a)(4)-6 Contributory defined benefit plans.*

(a) Introduction.

(b) Determination of employer-provided benefit.

(1) General rule.

(2) Composition-of-work-force method.

(3) Minimum-benefit method.

(4) Grandfather rules for plans in existence on May 14, 1990.

(5) Government-plan method.

(6) Cessation of employee contributions.

(c) Rules applicable in determining whether employee-provided benefits are nondiscriminatory in amount.

(1) In general.

(2) Same rate of contributions.

(3) Total-benefits method.

(4) Grandfather rule for plans in existence on May 14, 1990.

*§ 1.401(a)(4)-7 Imputation of permitted disparity.*

(a) Introduction.

(b) Adjusting allocation notes.

(1) In general.

(2) Employees whose plan year compensation does not exceed taxable wage base.

(3) Employees whose plan year compensation exceeds taxable wage base.

(4) Definitions.

(5) Example.

(c) Adjusting accrual rates.

(1) In general.

(2) Employees whose average annual compensation does not exceed covered compensation.

T.D. 8360, 9/12/91, amend T.D. 8485, 8/30/93, T.D. 8954, 6/28/2001.

### § 1.401(a)(4)-1 Nondiscrimination requirements of section 401(a)(4).

**(a) In general.** Section 401(a)(4) provides that a plan is a qualified plan only if the contributions or the benefits provided under the plan do not discriminate in favor of HCEs. Whether a plan satisfies this requirement depends on the form of the plan and on its effect in operation. In making this determination, intent is irrelevant. This section sets forth the exclusive rules for determining whether a plan satisfies section 401(a)(4). A plan that complies in form and operation with the rules in this section therefore satisfies section 401(a)(4).

**(b) Requirements a plan must satisfy.** *(1) In general.* In order to satisfy section 401(a)(4), a plan must satisfy each of the requirements of this paragraph (b).

*(2) Nondiscriminatory amount of contributions or benefits.* (i) General rule. Either the contributions or the benefits provided under the plan must be nondiscriminatory in amount. It need not be shown that both the contributions and the benefits provided are nondiscriminatory in amount, but only that either the contributions alone or the benefits alone are nondiscriminatory in amount.

(ii) Defined contribution plans. (A) General rule. A defined contribution plan satisfies this paragraph (b)(2) if the contributions allocated under the plan (including forfeitures) are nondiscriminatory in amount under § 1.401(a)(4)-2. Alternatively, a defined contribution plan (other than an ESOP) satisfies this paragraph (b)(2) if the equivalent benefits provided under the plan are nondiscriminatory in amount under § 1.401(a)(4)-8(b). Section 1.401(a)(4)-8(b) includes a safe-harbor testing method for contributions provided under a target benefit plan.

(B) Section 401(k) plans and section 401(m) plans. A section 401(k) plan is deemed to satisfy this paragraph (b)(2) because § 1.410(b)-9 defines a section 401(k) plan as a plan consisting of elective contributions under a qualified cash or deferred arrangement (i.e., one that satisfies section 401(k)(3), the nondiscriminatory amount requirement applicable to qualified cash or deferred arrangements). A section 401(m) plan satisfies this paragraph (b)(2) only if the plan satisfies §§ 1.401(m)-1(b) and 1.401(m)-2. Contributions under a nonqualified cash or deferred arrangement, elective contributions described in § 1.401(k)-1(a)(5)(i) that fail to satisfy the allocation and compensation requirements of § 1.401(k)-2(a)(4)(i), matching contributions that fail to satisfy § 1.401(m)-2(a)(4)(iii), and qualified nonelective contributions treated as elective or matching contributions for certain purposes under §§ 1.401(k)-2(a)(6) and 1.401(m)-2(a)(6), respectively, are not subject to the special rule in this paragraph (b)(2)(ii)(B), because they are not treated as part of a section 401(k) plan or section 401(m) plan as those terms are defined in § 1.410(b)-9. The contributions described in the preceding sentence must satisfy paragraph (b)(2)(ii)(A) of this section.

(iii) Defined benefit plans. A defined benefit plan satisfies this paragraph (b)(2) if the benefits provided under the plan are nondiscriminatory in amount under § 1.401(a)(4)-3. Alternatively, a defined benefit plan satisfies this paragraph (b)(2) if the equivalent allocations provided under the plan are nondiscriminatory in amount under § 1.401(a)(4)-8(c). Section 1.401(a)(4)-8(b) includes a safe-harbor testing method for benefits provided under a cash balance plan. In addition, § 1.401(a)(4)-8(d) provides a safe-harbor testing method for benefits provided under a defined benefit plan that is part of a floor-offset arrangement.

*(3) Nondiscriminatory availability of benefits, rights, and features.* All benefits, rights, and features provided under the plan must be made available in the plan in a nondiscriminatory manner. Rules for determining whether this requirement is satisfied are set forth in § 1.401(a)(4)-4.

*(4) Nondiscriminatory effect of plan amendments and terminations.* The timing of plan amendments must not have the effect of discriminating significantly in favor of HCEs. Rules for determining whether this requirement is satisfied are set forth in § 1.401(a)(4)-5(a). Section 1.401(a)(4)-5(b) provides additional requirements regarding plan terminations.

**(c) Application of requirements.** *(1) In general.* The requirements of paragraph (b) of this section must be applied in accordance with the rules set forth in this paragraph (c).

*(2) Interpretation.* The provisions of §§ 1.401(a)(4)-1 through 1.401(a)(4)-13 must be interpreted in a reasonable manner consistent with the purpose of preventing discrimination in favor of HCEs.

*(3) Plan-year basis of testing.* The requirements of paragraph (b) of this section are generally applied on the basis of the plan year and on the basis of the terms of the plan in effect during the plan year. Thus, unless otherwise provided, the compensation, contributions, benefit accruals, and other items used to apply these requirements must be determined with respect to the plan year being tested. However, § 1.401(a)(4)-11(g) provides rules allowing for corrective amendments made after the close of the plan year to be taken into account in satisfying certain requirements under paragraph (b) of this section.

*(4) Application of section 410(b) rules.* (i) Relationship between sections 401(a)(4) and 410(b). To be a qualified plan, a plan must satisfy both sections 410(b) and 401(a)(4). Section 410(b) requires that a plan benefit a nondiscriminatory group of employees, and section 401(a)(4) requires that the contributions or benefits provided to employees benefiting under the plan not discriminate in favor of HCEs. Consistent with this requirement, the definition of a plan subject to testing under section 401(a)(4) is the same as the definition of a plan subject to testing under section 410(b), i.e., the plan determined after applying the mandatory disaggregation rules of § 1.410(b)-7(c) and the permissive aggregation rules of § 1.410(b)-7(d). In addition, whichever testing option is used for the plan year under § 1.410(b)-8(a) (e.g., quarterly testing) must also be used for purposes of determining whether the plan satisfies section 401(a)(4) for the plan year.

(ii) Special rules for certain aggregated plans. Special rules are set forth in § 1.401(a)(4)-9(b) for applying the nondiscriminatory amount and availability requirements of paragraphs (b)(2) and (b)(3) of this section to a plan that includes one or more defined benefit plans and one or more defined contribution plans that have been permissively aggregated under § 1.410(b)-7(d).

(iii) Restructuring. In certain circumstances, a plan may be restructured on the basis of employee groups and treated as comprising two or more plans, each of which is treated as a separate plan that must independently satisfy sections 401(a)(4) and 410(b). Rules relating to restructuring plans for purposes of applying the requirements of paragraph (b) of this section are set forth in § 1.401(a)(4)-9(c).

(iv) References to section 410(b). Except as otherwise specifically provided, references to satisfying section 410(b) in §§ 1.401(a)(4)-1 through 1.401(a)(4)-13 mean satisfying

§ 1.410(b)-2 (taking into account any special rules available in satisfying that section, other than the permissive aggregation rules of § 1.410(b)-7(d)). In the case of a plan described in section 410(c)(1) that has not made the election described in section 410(d) and is not subject to section 403(b)(12)(A)(i), references in §§ 1.401(a)(4)-1 through 1.401(a)(4)-13 to satisfying section 410(b) mean satisfying section 410(c)(2).

*(5) Collectively-bargained plans.* The requirements of paragraph (b) of this section are treated as satisfied by a collectively-bargained plan that automatically satisfies section 410(b) under § 1.410(b)-2(b)(7).

*(6) Former employees.* In applying the nondiscriminatory amount and availability requirements of paragraphs (b)(2) and (b)(3) of this section, former employees are tested separately from active employees, unless otherwise provided. Rules for applying paragraphs (b)(2) and (b)(3) of this section to former employees are set forth in § 1.401(a)(4)-10.

*(7) Employee-provided contributions and benefits.* In applying the nondiscriminatory amount requirement of paragraph (b)(2) of this section, employee-provided contributions and benefits are tested separately from employer-provided contributions and benefits, unless otherwise provided. Rules for determining the amount of employer-provided benefits under a defined benefit plan that include employee contributions not allocated to separate accounts are set forth in § 1.401(a)(4)-6(b), and rules for applying paragraph (b)(2) of this section to employee contributions under such a plan are set forth in § 1.401(a)(4)-6(c). See paragraph (b)(2)(ii)(B) of this section for rules applicable to employee contributions allocated to separate accounts.

*(8) Allocation of earnings.* Notwithstanding any other provision in §§ 1.401(a)(4)-1 through 1.401(a)(4)-13, a defined contribution plan does not satisfy paragraph (b)(2) of this section if the manner in which income, expenses, gains, or losses are allocated to accounts under the plan discriminates in favor of HCEs or former HCEs.

*(9) Rollovers, transfers, and buybacks.* In applying the requirements of paragraph (b) of this section, rollover (including direct rollover) contributions described in section 402(c), 402(e)(6), 403(a)(4), 403(a)(5), or 408(d)(3), elective transfers described in § 1.411(d)-4, Q&A-3(b), transfers of assets and liabilities described in section 414(l), and employee buybacks are treated in accordance with the rules set forth in § 1.401(a)(4)-11(b).

*(10) Vesting.* A plan does not satisfy the nondiscriminatory amount requirement of paragraph (b)(2) of this section unless it satisfies § 1.401(a)(4)-11(c) with respect to the manner in which employees vest in their accrued benefits.

*(11) Crediting service.* A plan does not satisfy paragraphs (b)(2) and (b)(3) of this section unless it satisfies § 1.401(a)(4)-11(d) with respect to the manner in which employees' service is credited under the plan. Service other than actual service with the employer may not be taken into account in determining whether the plan satisfies paragraphs (b)(2) and (b)(3) of this section except as provided in § 1.401(a)(4)-11(d).

*(12) Governmental plans.* The rules of this section apply to a governmental plan within the meaning of section 414(d), except as provided in §§ 1.401(a)(4)-11(f) and 1.401(a)(4)-13(b).

*(13) Employee stock ownership plans.* [Reserved]

*(14) Section 401(h) benefits.* In applying the requirements of paragraph (b) of this section, the portion of a plan providing benefits described in section 401(h) is tested separately from the portion of the same plan providing retirement benefits, and thus is not required to satisfy this section. Rules applicable to section 401(h) benefits are set forth in § 1.401-14(b)(2).

*(15) Definitions.* In applying the requirements of this section, the definitions in § 1.401(a)(4)-12 govern.

*(16) Effective dates and fresh-start rules.* In applying the requirements of this section, the effective dates set forth in § 1.401(a)(4)-13 govern. Section 1.401(a)(4)-13 also provides certain transition and fresh-start rules that apply for purposes of this section.

**(d) Additional guidance.** The Commissioner may, in revenue rulings, notices, and other guidance, published in the Internal Revenue Bulletin, provide any additional guidance that may be necessary or appropriate in applying the nondiscrimination requirements of section 401(a)(4), including additional safe harbors and alternative methods and procedures for satisfying those requirements. See § 601.601(d)(2)(ii)(b) of this chapter.

---

T.D. 8360, 9/12/91, amend T.D. 8485, 8/30/93, T.D. 9169, 12/28/2004.

---

### § 1.401(a)(4)-2 Nondiscrimination in amount of employer contributions under a defined contribution plan.

**(a) Introduction.** *(1) Overview.* This section provides rules for determining whether the employer contributions allocated under a defined contribution plan are nondiscriminatory in amount as required by § 1.401(a)(4)-1(b)(2)(ii)(A). Certain defined contribution plans that provide uniform allocations are permitted to satisfy this requirement by meeting one of the safe harbors in paragraph (b) of this section. Plans that do not provide uniform allocations may satisfy this requirement by satisfying the general test in paragraph (c) of this section. See § 1.401(a)(4)-1(b)(2)(ii)(B) for the exclusive tests applicable to section 401(k) plans and section 401(m) plans.

*(2) Alternative methods of satisfying nondiscriminatory amount requirement.* A defined contribution plan is permitted to satisfy paragraph (b)(2) or (c) of this section on a restructured basis pursuant to § 1.401(a)(4)-9(c). Alternatively, a defined contribution plan (other than an ESOP) is permitted to satisfy the nondiscriminatory amount requirement of § 1.401(a)(4)-1(b)(2)(ii)(A) on the basis of equivalent benefits pursuant to § 1.401(a)(4)-8(b).

**(b) Safe harbors.** *(1) In general.* The employer contributions allocated under a defined contribution plan are nondiscriminatory in amount for a plan year if the plan satisfies either of the safe harbors in paragraph (b)(2) or (b)(3) of this section. Paragraph (b)(4) of this section provides exceptions for certain plan provisions that do not cause a plan to fail to satisfy this paragraph (b).

*(2) Safe harbor for plans with uniform allocation formula.* (i) General rule. A defined contribution plan satisfies the safe harbor in this paragraph (b)(2) for a plan year if the plan allocates all amounts taken into account under paragraph (c)(2)(ii) of this section for the plan year under an allocation formula that allocates to each employee the same percentage of plan year compensation, the same dollar amount, or the same dollar amount for each uniform unit of service (not to exceed one week) performed by the employee during the plan year.

(ii) Permitted disparity. If a plan satisfies section 401(l) in form, differences in employees' allocations under the plan attributable to uniform disparities permitted under § 1.401(l)-

2 (including differences in disparities that are deemed uniform under § 1.401(l)-2(c)(2)) do not cause the plan to fail to satisfy this paragraph (b)(2).

*(3) Safe harbor for plans with uniform points allocation formula.* (i) General rule. A defined contribution plan (other than an ESOP) satisfies the safe harbor in this paragraph (b)(3) for a plan year if it satisfies both of the following requirements:

(A) The plan must allocate amounts under a uniform points allocation formula. A uniform points allocation formula defines each employee's allocation for the plan year as the product of the total of all amounts taken into account under paragraph (c)(2)(ii) of this section and a fraction, the numerator of which is the employee's points for the plan year and the denominator of which is the sum of the points of all employees in the plan for the plan year. For this purpose, an employee's points for a plan year equal the sum of the employee's points for age, service, and units of plan year compensation for the plan year. Under a uniform points allocation formula, each employee must receive the same number of points for each year of age, the same number of points for each year of service, and the same number of points for each unit of plan year compensation. (See § 1.401(a)(4)-11(d)(3) regarding service that may be taken into account as years of service.) A uniform points allocation formula need not grant points for both age and service, but it must grant points for at least one of them. If the allocation formula grants points for years of service, the plan is permitted to limit the number of years of service taken into account to a single maximum number of years of service. A uniform points allocation formula need not grant points for units of plan year compensation, but if it does, the unit used must be a single dollar amount for all employees that does not exceed $200.

(B) For the plan year, the average of the allocation rates for the HCEs in the plan must not exceed the average of the allocation rates for the NHCEs in the plan. For this purpose, allocation rates are determined in accordance with paragraph (c)(2) of this section, without imputing permitted disparity and without grouping allocation rates under paragraphs (c)(2)(iv) and (v) of this section, respectively.

(ii) Example. The following example illustrates the safe harbor in this paragraph (b)(3):

*Example.* (a) Plan A has a single allocation formula that applies to all employees, under which each employee's allocation for the plan year equals the product of the total of all amounts taken into account for all employees for the plan year under paragraph (c)(2)(ii) of this section and a fraction, the numerator of which is the employee's points for the plan year and the denominator of which is the sum of the points of all employees for the plan year. Plan A grants each employee 10 points for each year of service (including pre-participation service and imputed service credited under Plan A that satisfies § 1.401(a)(4)-11(d)(3)) and one point for each $100 of plan year compensation. For the 1994 plan year, the total allocations are $71,200, and the total points for all employees are 7,120. Each employee's allocation for the 1994 plan year is set forth in the table below.

| Employee | Years of Service | Plan Year Compensation | Points | Amount of Allocation | Allocation Rate |
|---|---|---|---|---|---|
| H1 | 20 | $150,000 | 1,700 | $17,000 | 11.3% |
| H2 | 10 | $150,000 | 1,600 | $16,000 | 10.7% |
| H3 | 30 | $100,000 | 1,300 | $13,000 | 13.0% |
| H4 | 3 | $100,000 | 1,030 | $10,300 | 10.3% |
| N1 | 10 | $ 40,000 | 500 | $ 5,000 | 12.5% |
| N2 | 5 | $ 35,000 | 400 | $ 4,000 | 11.4% |
| N3 | 3 | $ 30,000 | 330 | $ 3,300 | 11.0% |
| N4 | 1 | $ 25,000 | 260 | $ 2,600 | 10.4% |
| Total | — | — | 7,120 | $71,200 | — |

(b) Under these facts, for the 1994 plan year, Plan A allocates amounts under a uniform points allocation formula within the meaning of paragraph (b)(3)(i)(A) of this section.

(c) For the 1994 plan year, the average allocation rate for the HCEs (H1 through H4) is 11.3 percent, and the average allocation rate for NHCEs (N1 through N4) is 11.3 percent. Because the average of the allocation rates for the HCEs does not exceed the average of the allocation rates for the NHCEs, Plan A satisfies paragraph (b)(3)(i)(B) of this section and, thus, the safe harbor in this paragraph (b)(3) for the 1994 plan year.

*(4) Use of safe harbors not precluded by certain plan provisions.* (i) In general. A plan does not fail to satisfy this paragraph (b) merely because the plan contains one or more of the provisions described in this paragraph (b)(4). Unless otherwise provided, any such provision must apply uniformly to all employees.

(ii) Entry dates. The plan provides one or more entry dates during the plan year as permitted by section 410(a)(4).

(iii) Certain conditions on allocations. The plan provides that an employee's allocation for the plan year is conditioned on either the employee's employment on the last day of the plan year or the employee's completion of a minimum number of hours of service during the plan year (not to exceed 1,000), or both. Such a provision may include an exception from this condition for all employees whose employment terminates during the plan year or only for those employees whose employment terminates during the plan year on account of one or more of the following circumstances: retirement, disability, death, or military service.

(iv) Certain limits on allocations. The plan limits allocations otherwise provided under the allocation formula to a maximum dollar amount or a maximum percentage of plan year compensation, limits the dollar amount of plan year compensation taken into account in determining the amount of allocations, or applies the restrictions of section 409(n) or the limits of section 415.

(v) Lower allocations for HCEs. The allocations provided to one or more HCEs under the plan are less than the allocations that would otherwise be provided to those employees if the plan satisfied this paragraph (b) (without regard to this paragraph (b)(4)(v)).

(vi) Multiple formulas. (A) General rule. The plan provides that an employee's allocation under the plan is the greater of the allocations determined under two or more formulas, or is the sum of the allocations determined under two or more formulas. This paragraph (b)(4)(vi) does not apply to a plan unless each of the formulas under the plan satisfies the requirements of paragraph (b)(4)(vi)(B) through (D) of this section.

(B) Sole formulas. The formulas must be the only formulas under the plan.

(C) Separate testing. Each of the formulas must separately satisfy this paragraph (b). A formula that is available solely to some or all NHCEs is deemed to satisfy this paragraph (b)(4)(vi)(C).

(D) Availability. (1) General rule. All of the formulas must be available on the same terms to all employees.

(2) Formulas for NHCEs. A formula does not fail to be available on the same terms to all employees merely because the formula is not available to any HCEs, but is available to some or all NHCEs on the same terms as all of the other formulas in the plan.

(3) Top-heavy formulas. In the case of a plan that provides the greater of the allocations under two or more formulas, one of which is a top-heavy formula, the top-heavy formula does not fail to be available on the same terms to all employees merely because it is available solely to all non-key employees on the same terms as all the other formulas under the plan. Furthermore, the top-heavy formula does not fail to be available on the same terms as the other formulas under the plan merely because it is conditioned on the plan's being top-heavy within the meaning of section 416(g). Finally, the top-heavy formula does not fail to be available on the same terms as the other formulas under the plan merely because it is available to all employees described in § 1.416-1, Q&A M-10 (i.e., all non-key employees who have not separated from service as of the last day of the plan year). The preceding sentence does not apply, however, unless the plan would satisfy section 410(b) if all employees who are benefiting under the plan solely as a result of receiving allocations under the top-heavy formula were treated as not currently benefiting under the plan. For purposes of this paragraph (b)(4)(vi)(D)(3), a top-heavy formula is a formula that provides the minimum benefit described in section 416(c)(2) (taking into account, if applicable, the modification in section 416(h)(2)(A)(ii)(II)).

(E) Provisions may be applied more than once. The provisions of this paragraph (b)(4)(vi) may be applied more than once. For example, a plan satisfies this paragraph (b) if an employee's allocation under the plan is the greater of the allocations under two or more formulas, and one or more of those formulas is the sum of the allocations under two or more other formulas, provided that each of the formulas under the plan satisfies the requirements of paragraph (b)(4)(vi)(B) through (D) of this section.

(F) Examples. The following examples illustrate the rules in this paragraph (b)(4)(vi):

*Example (1).* Under Plan A, each employee's allocation equals the sum of the allocations determined under two formulas. The first formula provides an allocation of five percent of plan year compensation. The second formula provides an allocation of $100. Plan A satisfies this paragraph (b)(4)(vi).

*Example (2).* Under Plan B, each employee's allocation equals the greater of the allocations determined under two formulas. The first formula provides an allocation of seven percent of plan year compensation and is available to all employees who complete at least 1,000 hours of service during the plan year and who have not separated from service as of the last day of the plan year. The second formula is a top-heavy formula that provides an allocation of three percent of plan year compensation and that is available to all employees described in § 1.416-1, Q&A M-10. Plan B does not satisfy the general rule in paragraph (b)(4)(vi)(D)(1) of this section because the two formulas are not available on the same terms to all employees (i.e., an employee is required to complete 1,000 hours of service during the plan year to receive an allocation under the first formula, but not under the second formula). Nonetheless, because the second formula is a top-heavy formula, the special availability rules for top-heavy formulas in paragraph (b)(4)(vi)(D)(3) of this section apply. Thus, the second formula does not fail to be available on the same terms as the first formula merely because the second formula is available to all employees described in § 1.416-1, Q&A M-10, as long as the plan would satisfy section 410(b) if all employees who are benefiting under the plan solely as a result of receiving allocations under the top-heavy formula were treated as not currently benefiting under the plan. This is true even if the plan conditions the availability of the second formula on the plan's being top-heavy for the plan year.

*Example (3).* The facts are the same as in Example 2, except that the first formula is available to all employees who have not separated from service as of the last day of the plan year, regardless of whether they complete at least 1,000 hours of service during the plan year. Plan B still does not satisfy the general rule in paragraph (b)(4)(vi)(D)(1) of this section because the two formulas are not available on the same terms to all employees (i.e., the second formula is only available to all non-key employees). Nonetheless, because the second formula is a top-heavy formula, the special availability rules for top-heavy formulas in paragraph (b)(4)(vi)(D)(3) of this section apply. Thus, the second formula does not fail to be available on the same terms as the first formula merely because the second formula is available solely to all non-key employees.

**(c) General test for nondiscrimination in amount of contributions.** *(1) General rule.* The employer contributions allocated under a defined contribution plan are nondiscriminatory in amount for a plan year if each rate group under the plan satisfies section 410(b). For purposes of this paragraph (c), a rate group exists under a plan for each HCE and consists of the HCE and all other employees in the plan (both HCEs and NHCEs) who have an allocation rate greater than or equal to the HCE's allocation rate. Thus, an employee is in the rate group for each HCE who has an allocation rate less than or equal to the employee's allocation rate.

*(2) Determination of allocation rates.* (i) General rule. The allocation rate for an employee for a plan year equals the sum of the allocations to the employee's account for the plan year, expressed either as a percentage of plan year compensation or as a dollar amount.

(ii) Allocations taken into account. The amounts taken into account in determining allocation rates for a plan year include all employer contributions and forfeitures that are allocated or treated as allocated to the account of an employee under the plan for the plan year, other than amounts described in paragraph (c)(2)(iii) of this section. For this purpose, employer contributions include annual additions described in § 1.415(c)-1(b)(4) (regarding amounts arising from certain transactions between the plan and the employer). In the case of a defined contribution plan subject to section 412, an employer contribution is taken into account in the plan year for which it is required to be contributed and allocated to employees' accounts under the plan, even if all or part of the required contribution is not actually made.

(iii) Allocations not taken into account. Allocations of income, expenses, gains, and losses attributable to the balance in an employee's account are not taken into account in determining allocation rates.

(iv) Imputation of permitted disparity. The disparity permitted under section 401(l) may be imputed in accordance with the rules of § 1.401(a)(4)-7.

(v) Grouping of allocation rates. (A) General rule. An employer may treat all employees who have allocation rates within a specified range above and below a midpoint rate chosen by the employer as having an allocation rate equal to the midpoint rate within that range. Allocation rates within a given range may not be grouped under this paragraph (c)(2)(v) if the allocation rates of HCEs within the range generally are significantly higher than the allocation rates of NHCEs in the range. The specified ranges within which all employees are treated as having the same allocation rate may not overlap and may be no larger than provided in paragraph (c)(2)(v)(B) of this section. Allocation rates of employees that are not within any of these specified ranges are determined without regard to this paragraph (c)(2)(v).

(B) Size of specified ranges. The lowest and highest allocation rates in the range must be within five percent (not five percentage points) of the midpoint rate. If allocation rates are determined as a percentage of plan year compensation, the lowest and highest allocation rates need not be within five percent of the midpoint rate, if they are no more than one quarter of a percentage point above or below the midpoint rate.

(vi) Consistency requirement. Allocation rates must be determined in a consistent manner for all employees for the plan year.

*(3) Satisfaction of section 410(b) by a rate group.* (i) General rule. For purposes of determining whether a rate group satisfies section 410(b), the rate group is treated as if it were a separate plan that benefits only the employees included in the rate group for the plan year. Thus, for example, under § 1.401(a)(4)-1(c)(4)(iv), the ratio percentage of the rate group is determined taking into account all nonexcludable employees regardless of whether they benefit under the plan. Paragraphs (c)(3)(ii) and (iii) of this section provide additional special rules for determining whether a rate group satisfies section 410(b).

(ii) Application of nondiscriminatory classification test. A rate group satisfies the nondiscriminatory classification test of § 1.410(b)-4 (including the reasonable classification requirement of § 1.410(b)-4(b)) if and only if the ratio percentage of the rate group is greater than or equal to the lesser of—

(A) The midpoint between the safe and the unsafe harbor percentages applicable to the plan; and

(B) The ratio percentage of the plan.

(iii) Application of average benefit percentage test. A rate group satisfies the average benefit percentage test of § 1.410(b)-5 if the plan of which it is a part satisfies § 1.410(b)-5 (without regard to § 1.410(b)-5(f)). In the case of a plan that relies on § 1.410(b)-5(f) to satisfy the average benefit percentage test, each rate group under the plan satisfies the average benefit percentage test (if applicable) only if the rate group separately satisfies § 1.410(b)-5(f).

*(4) Examples.* The following examples illustrate the general test in this paragraph (c):

*Example (1).* Employer X maintains two defined contribution plans, Plan A and Plan B, that are aggregated and treated as a single plan for purposes of sections 410(b) and 401(a)(4) pursuant to § 1.410(b)-7(d). For the 1994 plan year, Employee M has plan year compensation of $10,000 and receives an allocation of $200 under Plan A and an allocation of $800 under Plan B. Employee M's allocation rate under the aggregated plan for the 1994 plan year is 10 percent (i.e., $1,000 divided by $10,000).

*Example (2).* The employees in Plan C have the following allocation rates (expressed as a percentage of plan year compensation): 2.75 percent, 2.80 percent, 2.85 percent, 3.25 percent, 6.65 percent, 7.33 percent, 7.34 percent, and 7.35 percent. Because the first four rates are within a range of no more than one quarter of a percentage point above and below 3.0 percent (a midpoint rate chosen by the employer), under paragraph (c)(2)(v) of this section the employer may treat the employees who have those rates as having an allocation rate of 3.0 percent (provided that the allocation rates of HCEs within the range generally are not significantly higher than the allocation rates of NHCEs within the range). Because the last four rates are within a range of no more than five percent above and below 7.0 percent (a midpoint rate chosen by the employer), the employer may treat the employees who have those rates as having an allocation rate of 7.0 percent (provided that the allocation rates of HCEs within the range generally are not significantly higher than the allocation rates of NHCEs within the range).

*Example (3).* (a) Employer Y has only six nonexcludable employees, all of whom benefit under Plan D. The HCEs are H1 and H2, and the NHCEs are N1 through N4. For the 1994 plan year, H1 and N1 through N4 have an allocation rate of 5.0 percent of plan year compensation. For the same plan year, H2 has an allocation rate of 7.5 percent of plan year compensation.

(b) There are two rate groups under Plan D. Rate group 1 consists of H1 and all those employees who have an allocation rate greater than or equal to H1's allocation rate (5.0 percent). Thus, rate group 1 consists of H1, H2, and N1 through N4. Rate group 2 consists only of H2 because no other employee has an allocation rate greater than or equal to H2's allocation rate (7.5 percent).

(c) The ratio percentage for rate group 2 is zero percent—i.e., zero percent (the percentage of all nonhighly compensated nonexcludable employees who are in the rate group) divided by 50 percent (the percentage of all highly compensated nonexcludable employees who are in the rate group). Therefore rate group 2 does not satisfy the ratio percentage test under § 1.410(b)-2(b)(2). Rate group 2 also does not satisfy the nondiscriminatory classification test of § 1.410(b)-4 (as modified by paragraph (c)(3) of this section). Rate group 2 therefore does not satisfy section 410(b) and, as a result, Plan D does not satisfy the general test in paragraph (c)(1) of this section. This is true regardless of whether rate group 1 satisfies § 1.410(b)-2(b)(2).

*Example (4).* (a) The facts are the same as in Example 3, except that N4 has an allocation rate of 8.0 percent.

(b) There are two rate groups in Plan D. Rate group 1 consists of H1 and all those employees who have an allocation rate greater than or equal to H1's allocation rate (5.0

percent). Thus, rate group 1 consists of H1, H2 and N1 through N4. Rate group 2 consists of H2, and all those employees who have an allocation rate greater than or equal to H2's allocation rate (7.5 percent). Thus, rate group 2 consists of H2 and N4.

(c) Rate group 1 satisfies the ratio percentage test under § 1.410(b)-2(b)(2) because the ratio percentage of the rate group is 100 percent—i.e., 100 percent (the percentage of all nonhighly compensated nonexcludable employees who are in the rate group) divided by 100 percent (the percentage of all highly compensated nonexcludable employees who are in the rate group).

(d) Rate group 2 does not satisfy the ratio percentage test of § 1.410(b)-2(b)(2) because the ratio percentage of the rate group is 50 percent—i.e., 25 percent (the percentage of all nonhighly compensated nonexcludable employees who are in the rate group) divided by 50 percent (the percentage of all highly compensated nonexcludable employees who are in the rate group).

(e) However, rate group 2 does satisfy the nondiscriminatory classification test of § 1.410(b)-4 because the ratio percentage of the rate group (50 percent) is greater than the safe harbor percentage applicable to the plan under § 1.410(b)-4(c)(4) (45.5 percent).

(f) Under paragraph (c)(3)(iii) of this section, rate group 2 satisfies the average benefit percentage test, if Plan D satisfies the average benefit percentage test. (The requirement that Plan D satisfy the average benefit percentage test applies even though Plan D satisfies the ratio percentage test and would ordinarily not need to run the average benefit percentage test.) If Plan D satisfies the average benefit percentage test, then rate group 2 satisfies section 410(b) and thus, Plan D satisfies the general test in paragraph (c)(1) of this section, because each rate group under the plan satisfies section 410(b).

*Example (5).* (a) Plan E satisfies section 410(b) by satisfying the nondiscriminatory classification test of § 1.410(b)-4 and the average benefit percentage test of § 1.410(b)-5 (without regard to § 1.410(b)-5(f)). See § 1.410(b)-2(b)(3). Plan E uses the facts-and-circumstances requirements of § 1.410(b)-4(c)(3) to satisfy the nondiscriminatory classification test of § 1.410(b)-4. The safe and unsafe harbor percentages applicable to the plan under § 1.410(b)-4(c)(4) are 29 and 20 percent, respectively. Plan E has a ratio percentage of 22 percent.

(b) Rate group 1 under Plan E has a ratio percentage of 23 percent. Under paragraph (c)(3)(ii) of this section, the rate group satisfies the nondiscriminatory classification requirement of § 1.410(b)-4, because the ratio percentage of the rate group (23 percent) is greater than the lesser of—

(1) The ratio percentage for the plan as a whole (22 percent); and

(2) The midpoint between the safe and unsafe harbor percentages (24.5 percent).

(c) Under paragraph (c)(3)(iii) of this section, the rate group satisfies section 410(b) because the plan satisfies the average benefit percentage test of § 1.410(b)-5.

---

T.D. 8360, 9/12/91, amend T.D. 8485, 8/30/93, T.D. 9319, 4/4/2007.

---

### § 1.401(a)(4)-3 Nondiscrimination in amount of employer-provided benefits under a defined benefit plan.

***Caution:*** The Treasury has not yet amended Reg § 1.401(a)(4)-3 to reflect changes made by P.L. 104-188.

**(a) Introduction.** *(1) Overview.* This section provides rules for determining whether the employer-provided benefits under a defined benefit plan are nondiscriminatory in amount as required by § 1.401(a)(4)-1(b)(2)(iii). Certain defined benefit plans that provide uniform benefits are permitted to satisfy this requirement by meeting one of the safe harbors in paragraph (b) of this section. Plans that do not provide uniform benefits may satisfy this requirement by satisfying the general test in paragraph (c) of this section. Paragraph (d) of this section provides rules for determining the individual benefit accrual rates needed for the general test. Paragraph (e) of this section provides rules for determining compensation for purposes of applying the requirements of this section. Paragraph (f) of this section provides additional rules that apply generally for purposes of both the safe harbors in paragraph (b) of this section and the general test in paragraph (c) of this section. See § 1.401(a)(4)-6 for rules for determining the amount of employer-provided benefits under a contributory DB plan, and for determining whether the employee-provided benefits under such a plan are nondiscriminatory in amount.

*(2) Alternative methods of satisfying nondiscriminatory amount requirement.* A defined benefit plan is permitted to satisfy paragraph (b) or (c) of this section on a restructured basis pursuant to § 1.401(a)(4)-9(c). Alternatively, a defined benefit plan is permitted to satisfy the nondiscriminatory amount requirement of § 1.401(a)(4)-1(b)(2)(iii) on the basis of equivalent allocations pursuant to § 1.401(a)(4)-8(c). In addition, a defined benefit plan that is part of a floor-offset arrangement is permitted to satisfy this section pursuant to § 1.401(a)(4)-8(d).

**(b) Safe harbors.** *(1) In general.* The employer-provided benefits under a defined benefit plan are nondiscriminatory in amount for a plan year if the plan satisfies each of the uniformity requirements of paragraph (b)(2) of this section and any one of the safe harbors in paragraphs (b)(3) (unit credit plans), (b)(4) (fractional accrual plans), and (b)(5) (insurance contract plans) of this section. Paragraph (b)(6) of this section provides exceptions for certain plan provisions that do not cause a plan to fail to satisfy this paragraph (b). Paragraph (f) of this section provides additional rules that apply in determining whether a plan satisfies this paragraph (b).

*(2) Uniformity requirements.* (i) Uniform normal retirement benefit. The same benefit formula must apply to all employees. The benefit formula must provide all employees with an annual benefit payable in the same form commencing at the same uniform normal retirement age. The annual benefit must be the same percentage of average annual compensation or the same dollar amount for all employees who will have the same number of years of service at normal retirement age. (See § 1.401(a)(4)-11(d)(3) regarding service that may be taken into account as years of service.) The annual benefit must equal the employee's accrued benefit at normal retirement age (within the meaning of section 411(a)(7)(A)(i)) and must be the normal retirement benefit under the plan (within the meaning of section 411(a)(9)).

(ii) Uniform post-normal retirement benefit. With respect to an employee with a given number of years of service at any age after normal retirement age, the annual benefit commencing at that employee's age must be the same percentage of average annual compensation or the same dollar amount that would be payable commencing at normal retirement age to an employee who had that same number of years of service at normal retirement age.

(iii) Uniform subsidies. Each subsidized optional form of benefit available under the plan must be currently available (within the meaning of § 1.401(a)(4)-4(b)(2)) to substantially all employees. Whether an optional form of benefit is considered subsidized for this purpose may be determined using any reasonable actuarial assumptions.

(iv) No employee contributions. The plan must not be a contributory DB plan.

(v) Period of accrual. Each employee's benefit must be accrued over the same years of service that are taken into account in applying the benefit formula under the plan to that employee. For this purpose, any year in which the employee benefits under the plan (within the meaning of § 1.410(b)-3(a)) is included as a year of service in which a benefit accrues. Thus, for example, a plan does not satisfy the safe harbor in paragraph (b)(4) of this section unless the plan uses the same years of service to determine both the normal retirement benefit under the plan's benefit formula and the fraction by which an employee's fractional rule benefit is multiplied to derive the employee's accrued benefit as of any plan year.

(vi) Examples. The following examples illustrate the rules in this paragraph (b)(2):

*Example (1).* Plan A provides a normal retirement benefit equal to two percent of average annual compensation times each year of service commencing at age 65 for all employees. Plan A provides that employees of Division S receive their benefit in the form of a straight life annuity and that employees of Division T receive their benefit in the form of a life annuity with an automatic cost-of-living increase. Plan A does not provide a uniform normal retirement benefit within the meaning of paragraph (b)(2)(i) of this section because the annual benefit is not payable in the same form to all employees.

*Example (2).* Plan B provides a normal retirement benefit equal to 1.5 percent of average annual compensation times each year of service at normal retirement age for all employees. The normal retirement age under the plan is the earlier of age 65 or the age at which the employee completes 10 years of service, but in no event earlier than age 62. Plan B does not provide a uniform normal retirement benefit within the meaning of paragraph (b)(2)(i) of this section because the same uniform normal retirement age does not apply to all employees.

*Example (3).* Plan C is an accumulation plan under which the benefit for each year of service equals one percent of plan year compensation payable in the same form to all employees commencing at the same uniform normal retirement age. Under paragraph (e)(2) of this section, an accumulation plan may substitute plan year compensation for average annual compensation. Plan C provides a uniform normal retirement benefit within the meaning of paragraph (b)(2)(i) of this section, because all employees with the same number of years of service at normal retirement age will receive an annual benefit that is treated as the same percentage of average annual compensation.

*Example (4).* The facts are the same as in Example 3, except that the benefit for each year of service equals one percent of plan year compensation increased by reference to the increase in the cost of living from the year of service to normal retirement age. Plan C does not provide a uniform normal retirement benefit, because the annual benefit defined by the benefit formula can vary for employees with the same number of years of service at normal retirement age, depending on the age at which those years of service were credited to the employee under the plan.

*Example (5).* Plan D provides a normal retirement benefit of 50 percent of average annual compensation at normal retirement age (age 65) for employees with 30 years of service at normal retirement age. Plan D provides that, in the case of an employee with less than 30 years of service at normal retirement age, the normal retirement benefit is reduced on a pro rata basis for each year of service less than 30. However, if an employee with less than 30 years of service at normal retirement age continues to work past normal retirement age, Plan D provides that the additional years of service worked past normal retirement age are taken into account for purposes of the 30 years of service requirement. Thus, an employee who has 26 years of service at age 65 but who does not retire until age 69 with 30 years of service will receive a benefit of 50 percent of average annual compensation. Plan D provides uniform post-normal retirement benefits within the meaning of paragraph (b)(2)(ii) of this section.

*Example (6).* (a) Plan E is amended on February 14, 1994, to provide an early retirement window benefit that consists of an unreduced early retirement benefit to employees who terminate employment after attainment of age 55 with 10 years of service and between June 1, 1994, and November 30, 1994. The early retirement window benefit is a single subsidized optional form of benefit. Paragraph (b)(2)(iii) of this section requires that the subsidized optional form of benefit be currently available (within the meaning of § 1.401(a)(4)-4(b)(2)) to substantially all employees. Section 1.401(a)(4)-4(b)(2)(ii)(A)(2) provides that age and service requirements are not disregarded in determining the current availability of an optional form of benefit if those requirements must be satisfied within a specified period of time. Thus, the early retirement window benefit is not currently available to an employee unless the employee will satisfy the eligibility requirements for the early retirement window benefit by the close of the early retirement window benefit period. Plan E will fail to satisfy paragraph (b)(2)(iii) of this section unless substantially all of the employees satisfy the eligibility requirements for the early retirement window benefit by November 30, 1994. However, see § 1.401(a)(4)-9(c)(6), Example 2, for an example of how a plan with an early retirement window benefit may be restructured into two component plans, each of which satisfies the safe harbors of this paragraph (b).

(b) A similar analysis would apply if, instead of an unreduced early retirement benefit, the early retirement window benefit consisted of a special schedule of early retirement factors, defined by starting with the plan's usual schedule and then treating each employee eligible for the early retirement window benefit as being five years older than the employee actually is, but not older than the employee's normal retirement age.

*Example (7).* Plan F generally provides a normal retirement benefit of 1.5 percent of an employee's average annual compensation multiplied by the employee's years of service with the employer. For employees transferred outside of the group of employees covered by the plan, the plan's benefit formula takes into account only years of service prior to the transfer, but determines average annual compensation taking into account section 414(s) compensation both before and after the transfer. Plan F does not satisfy the requirements of paragraph (b)(2)(v) of this section with respect to transferred employees, because their benefits are accrued over years of service (i.e., after transfer) that are not taken into account in applying the plan's benefit formula to them. However, see Example 2 of paragraph (b)(6)(x)(B) of this section for an example of how a plan that continues to take transferred employees' section 414(s) compensation into account after their transfer may still satisfy this paragraph (b).

*(3) Safe harbor for unit credit plans.* (i) General rule. A plan satisfies the safe harbor in this paragraph (b)(3) for a plan year if it satisfies both of the following requirements:

(A) The plan must satisfy the 133 1/3 percent accrual rule of section 411(b)(1)(B).

(B) Each employee's accrued benefit under the plan as of any plan year must be determined by applying the plan's benefit formula to the employee's years of service and (if applicable) average annual compensation, both determined as of that plan year.

(ii) Example. The following example illustrates the rules in this paragraph (b)(3):

*Example.* Plan A provides that the accrued benefit of each employee as of any plan year equals the employee's average annual compensation times a percentage that depends on the employee's years of service determined as of that plan year. The percentage is two percent for each of the first 10 years of service, plus 1.5 percent for each of the next 10 years of service, plus two percent for all additional years of service. Plan A satisfies this paragraph (b)(3).

*(4) Safe harbor for plans using fractional accrual rule.* (i) General rule. A plan satisfies the safe harbor in this paragraph (b)(4) for a plan year if it satisfies each of the following requirements:

(A) The plan must satisfy the fractional accrual rule of section 411(b)(1)(C).

(B) Each employee's accrued benefit under the plan as of any plan year before the employee reaches normal retirement age must be determined by multiplying the employee's fractional rule benefit (within the meaning of § 1.411(b)-1(b)(3)(ii)(A)) by a fraction, the numerator of which is the employee's years of service determined as of the plan year, and the denominator of which is the employee's projected years of service as of normal retirement age.

(C) The plan must satisfy one of the following requirements:

(1) Under the plan, it must be impossible for any employee to accrue in a plan year a portion of the normal retirement benefit described in paragraph (b)(2)(i) of this section that is more than one third larger than the portion of the same benefit accrued in that or any other plan year by any other employee, when each portion of the benefit is expressed as a percentage of each employee's average annual compensation or as a dollar amount. In making this determination, actual and potential employees in the plan with any amount of service at normal retirement must be taken into account (other than employees with more than 33 years of service at normal retirement age). In addition, in the case of a plan that satisfies section 401(l) in form, an employee is treated as accruing benefits at a rate equal to the excess benefit percentage in the case of a defined benefit excess plan or at a rate equal to the gross benefit percentage in the case of an offset plan.

(2) The normal retirement benefit under the plan must be a flat benefit that requires a minimum of 25 years of service at normal retirement age for an employee to receive the unreduced flat benefit, determined without regard to section 415. For this purpose, a flat benefit is a benefit that is the same percentage of average annual compensation or the same dollar amount for all employees who have a minimum number of years of service at normal retirement age (e.g., 50 percent of average annual compensation), with a pro rata reduction in the flat benefit for employees who have less than the minimum number of years of service at normal retirement age. An employee is permitted to accrue the maximum benefit permitted under section 415 over a period of less than 25 years, provided that the flat benefit under the plan, determined without regard to section 415, can accrue over no less than 25 years.

(3) The plan must satisfy the requirements of paragraph (b)(4)(i)(C)(2) of this section (other than the requirement that the minimum number of years of service for receiving the unreduced flat benefit is at least 25 years), and, for the plan year, the average of the normal accrual rates for all nonhighly compensated nonexcludable employees must be at least 70 percent of the average of the normal accrual rates for all highly compensated nonexcludable employees. The averages in the preceding sentence are determined taking into account all nonexcludable employees (regardless of whether they benefit under the plan). In addition, contributions and benefits under other plans of the employer are disregarded. For purposes of this paragraph (b)(4)(i)(C)(3), normal accrual rates are determined under paragraph (d) of this section.

(ii) Examples. The following examples illustrate the rules in this paragraph (b)(4). In each example, it is assumed that the plan has never permitted employee contributions.

*Example (1).* Plan A provides a normal retirement benefit equal to 1.6 percent of average annual compensation times each year of service up to 25. Plan A further provides that an employee's accrued benefit as of any plan year equals the employee's fractional rule benefit multiplied by a fraction, the numerator of which is the employee's years of service as of the plan year, and the denominator of which is the employee's projected years of service as of normal retirement age. The greatest benefit that an employee could accrue in any plan year is 1.6 percent of average annual compensation (this is the case for an employee with 25 or fewer years of projected service at normal retirement age). Among potential employees with 33 or fewer years of projected service at normal retirement age, the lowest benefit that an employee could accrue in any plan year is 1.212 percent of average annual compensation (this is the case for an employee with 33 years of projected service at normal retirement age). Plan A satisfies paragraph (b)(4)(i)(C)(1) of this section because 1.6 percent is not more than one third larger than 1.212 percent.

*Example (2).* Plan B provides a normal retirement benefit equal to 1.0 percent of average annual compensation up to the integration level, and 1.6 percent of average annual compensation above the integration level, times each year of service up to 35. Plan B further provides that an employee's accrued benefit as of any plan year equals the employee's fractional rule benefit multiplied by a fraction, the numerator of which is the employee's years of service as of the plan year and the denominator of which is the employee's projected years of service as of normal retirement age. For purposes of satisfying the one third larger rule in paragraph (b)(4)(i)(C)(1) of this section, because Plan B satisfies section 401(l) in form, all employees with less than 35 projected years of service are assumed to accrue benefits at the rate of 1.6 percent of average annual compensation (the excess benefit percentage under the plan). Plan B satisfies paragraph (b)(4)(i)(C) of this section because all employees with 33 or fewer years of projected service at normal retirement age accrue in each plan year a benefit of 1.6 percent of average annual compensation.

*Example (3).* Plan C provides a normal retirement benefit equal to four percent of average annual compensation times each year of service up to 10 and one percent of average annual compensation times each year of service in excess of 10 and not in excess of 30. Plan C further provides that an employee's accrued benefit as of any plan year equals the employee's fractional rule benefit multiplied by a fraction, the numerator of which is the employee's years of service as of the plan year, and the denominator of which is the employee's projected years of service as of normal retirement age. The greatest benefit that an employee could accrue in any plan year is four percent of average annual compensation (this is the case for an employee with 10 or fewer years of projected service at normal retirement age). Among employees with 33 or fewer years of projected service at normal retirement age, the lowest benefit that an employee could accrue in a plan year is 1.82 percent of average annual compensation (this is the case of an employee with 33 years of projected service at normal retirement age). Plan C fails to satisfy this paragraph (b)(4) because four percent is more than one third larger than 1.82 percent. See also § 1.401(a)(4)-9(c)(6), Example 3.

*Example (4).* Plan D provides a normal retirement benefit of 100 percent of average annual compensation, reduced by four percentage points for each year of service below 25 the employee has at normal retirement age. Plan D further provides that an employee's accrued benefit as of any plan year is equal to the employee's fractional rule benefit multiplied by a fraction, the numerator of which is the employee's years of service as of the plan year, and the denominator of which is the employee's projected years of service at normal retirement age. In the case of an employee who has five years of service as of the current plan year, and who is projected to have 10 years of service at normal retirement age, the employee's fractional rule benefit would be 40 percent of average annual compensation, and the employee's accrued benefit as of the current plan year would be 20 percent of average annual compensation (the fractional rule benefit multiplied by a fraction of five years over 10 years). Plan D satisfies this paragraph (b)(4).

*Example (5).* The facts are the same as in Example 4, except that the normal retirement benefit is 125 percent of average annual compensation, reduced by five percentage points for each year of service below 25 that the employee has at normal retirement age. Plan D satisfies this paragraph (b)(4), even though an employee may accrue the maximum benefit allowed under section 415 (i.e., 100 percent of the participant's average compensation for the high three years of service) in less than 25 years.

*Example (6).* The facts are the same as in Example 1, except that the plan determines each employee's accrued benefit by multiplying the employee's projected normal retirement benefit (rather than the fractional rule benefit) by the fraction described in Example 1. In determining an employee's projected normal retirement benefit, the plan defines each employee's average annual compensation as the average annual compensation the employee would have at normal retirement age if the employee's annual section 414(s) compensation in future plan years equaled the employee's plan year compensation for the prior plan year. Under these facts, Plan A does not satisfy paragraph (b)(4)(i)(B) of this section because the employee's accrued benefit is determined on the basis of a projected normal retirement benefit that is not the same as the employee's fractional rule benefit determined in accordance with § 1.411(b)-1(b)(3)(ii)(A).

*Example (7).* Plan E provides a normal retirement benefit of 50 percent of average annual compensation, with a pro rata reduction for employees with less than 30 years of service at normal retirement age. Plan E further provides that an employee's accrued benefit as of any plan year is equal to the employee's fractional rule benefit multiplied by a fraction, the numerator of which is the employee's years of service as of the plan year, and the denominator of which is the employee's projected years of service at normal retirement age. For purposes of determining this fraction, the plan limits the years of service taken into account for an employee to the number of years the employee has participated in the plan. However, all years of service (including years of service before the employee commenced participation in the plan) are taken into account in determining an employee's normal retirement benefit under the plan's benefit formula. Plan E fails to satisfy this paragraph (b)(4) because the years of service over which benefits accrue differ from the years of service used in applying the benefit formula under the plan. See paragraph (b)(2)(v) of this section.

*Example (8).* (a) Plan F provides a normal retirement benefit equal to 2.0 percent of average annual compensation, plus 0.65 percent of average annual compensation above covered compensation, for each year of service up to 25. Plan F further provides that an employee's accrued benefit as of any plan year equals the sum of—

(1) The employee's fractional rule benefit (determined as if the normal retirement benefit under the plan equaled 2.0 percent of average annual compensation for each year of service up to 25) multiplied by a fraction, the numerator of which is the employee's years of service as of the plan year and the denominator of which is the employee's projected years of service as of normal retirement age; plus

(2) 0.65 percent of the employee's average annual compensation above covered compensation multiplied by the employee's years of service (up to 25) as of the current plan year.

(b) Although Plan F satisfies the fractional accrual rule of section 411(b)(1)(C), the plan fails to satisfy this paragraph (b)(4) because the plan does not determine employees' accrued benefits in accordance with paragraph (b)(4)(i)(B) of this section.

*(5) Safe harbor for insurance contract plans.* A plan satisfies the safe harbor in this paragraph (b)(5) if it satisfies each of the following requirements:

(i) The plan must satisfy the accrual rule of section 411(b)(1)(F).

(ii) The plan must be an insurance contract plan within the meaning of section 412(i).

(iii) The benefit formula under the plan must be one that would satisfy the requirements of paragraph (b)(4) of this section if the stated normal retirement benefit under the formula accrued ratably over each employee's period of plan participation through normal retirement age in accordance with paragraph (b)(4)(i)(B) of this section. Thus, the benefit formula may not recognize years of service before an employee commenced participation in the plan because, otherwise, the definition of years of service for determining the normal retirement benefit would differ from the definition of years of service for determining the accrued benefit under paragraph (b)(4)(i)(B) of this section. See paragraph (b)(4)(ii), Example 7, of this section. Notwithstanding the foregoing, an insurance contract plan adopted and in effect on September 19, 1991, may continue to recognize years of service prior to an employee's participation in the plan for an employee who is a participant in the plan on that date to the extent provided by the benefit formula in the plan on such date.

(iv) The scheduled premium payments under an individual or group insurance contract used to fund an employee's normal retirement benefit must be level annual payments to normal retirement age. Thus, payments may not be scheduled to cease before normal retirement age.

(v) The premium payments for an employee who continues benefiting after normal retirement age must be equal to the amount necessary to fund additional benefits that accrue under the plan's benefit formula for the plan year.

(vi) Experience gains, dividends, forfeitures, and similar items must be used solely to reduce future premiums.

(vii) All benefits must be funded through contracts of the same series. Among other requirements, contracts of the same series must have cash values based on the same terms (including interest and mortality assumptions) and the same conversion rights. A plan does not fail to satisfy this requirement, however, if any change in the contract series or insurer applies on the same terms to all employees. But see § 1.401(a)(4)-5(a)(4), Example 12 (change in insurer considered a plan amendment subject to § 1.401(a)(4)-5(a)).

(viii) If permitted disparity is taken into account, the normal retirement benefit stated under the plan's benefit formula must satisfy § 1.401(l)-3. For this purpose, the 0.75-percent factor in the maximum excess or offset allowance in § 1.401(l)-3(b)(2)(i) or (b)(3)(i), respectively, adjusted in accordance with § 1.401(l)-3(d)(9) and (e), is reduced by multiplying the factor by 0.80.

*(6) Use of safe harbors not precluded by certain plan provisions.* (i) In general. A plan does not fail to satisfy this paragraph (b) merely because the plan contains one or more of the provisions described in this paragraph (b)(6). Unless otherwise provided, any such provision must apply uniformly to all employees.

(ii) Section 401(l) permitted disparity. The plan takes permitted disparity into account in a manner that satisfies section 401(l) in form. Thus, differences in employees' benefits under the plan attributable to uniform disparities permitted under § 1.401(l)-3 (including differences in disparities that are deemed uniform under § 1.401(l)-3(c)(2)) do not cause a plan to fail to satisfy this paragraph (b).

(iii) Different entry dates. The plan provides one or more entry dates during the plan year as permitted by section 410(a)(4).

(iv) Certain conditions on accruals. The plan provides that an employee's accrual for the plan year is less than a full accrual (including a zero accrual) because of a plan provision permitted by the year-of-participation rules of section 411(b)(4).

(v) Certain limits on accruals. The plan limits benefits otherwise provided under the benefit formula or accrual method to a maximum dollar amount or to a maximum percentage of average annual compensation (e.g., by limiting service taken into account in the benefit formula) or in accordance with section 401(a)(5)(D), applies the limits of section 415, or limits the dollar amount of compensation taken into account in determining benefits.

(vi) Dollar accrual per uniform unit of service. The plan determines accruals based on the same dollar amount for each uniform unit of service (not to exceed one week) performed by each employee with the same number of years of service under the plan during the plan year. The preceding sentence applies solely for purposes of the unit credit safe harbor in paragraph (b)(3) of this section.

(vii) Prior benefits accrued under a different formula. The plan determines benefits for years of service after a fresh-start date for all employees under a benefit formula and accrual method that differ from the benefit formula and accrual method previously used to determine benefit accruals for employees in a fresh-start group for years of service before the fresh-start date. This paragraph (b)(6)(vii) applies solely to plans that satisfy § 1.401(a)(4)-13(c) with respect to the fresh start.

(viii) Employee contributions. The plan is a contributory DB plan that would satisfy the requirements of paragraph (b) of this section if the plan's benefit formula provided benefits at employees' employer-provided benefit rates determined under § 1.401(a)(4)-6(b). This paragraph (b)(6)(viii) does not apply to a plan tested under paragraph (b)(4) or (b)(5) of this section unless the plan satisfies one of the methods in § 1.401(a)(4)-6(b)(4) through (b)(6). A minimum benefit added to the plan solely to satisfy § 1.401(a)(4)-6(b)(3) is not taken into account in determining whether this paragraph (b)(6)(viii) is satisfied.

(ix) Certain subsidized optional forms. The plan provides a subsidized optional form of benefit that is available to fewer than substantially all employees because the optional form of benefit has been eliminated prospectively as provided in § 1.401(a)(4)-4(b)(3).

(x) Lower benefits for HCEs. (A) General rule. The benefits (including any subsidized optional form of benefit) provided to one or more HCEs under the plan are inherently less valuable to those HCEs (determined by applying the principles of § 1.401(a)(4)-4(d)(4)) than the benefits that would otherwise be provided to those HCEs if the plan satisfied this paragraph (b) (determined without regard to this paragraph (b)(6)(x)). These inherently less valuable benefits are deemed to satisfy this paragraph (b).

(B) Examples. The following examples illustrate the rules in this paragraph (b)(6)(x):

*Example (1).* Plan A would satisfy this paragraph (b) (determined without regard to this paragraph (b)(6)(x)), except for the fact that it fails to satisfy the requirement of paragraph (b)(2)(iii) of this section (i.e., a subsidized optional form must be available to substantially all employees on similar terms). Each subsidized optional form in the plan is available to all the NHCEs on similar terms, but one of the subsidized optional forms of benefit is not available to any of the HCEs. Plan A satisfies this paragraph (b), because Plan A is a safe harbor plan with respect to the NHCEs and provides inherently less valuable benefits to the HCEs.

*Example (2).* (a) Plan B would satisfy this paragraph (b) (determined without regard to this paragraph (b)(6)(x)), except for the fact that some employees are not being credited with years of service under the plan, but are continuing to accrue benefits as a result of compensation increases. These are employees who have been transferred from the employer that sponsors Plan B to another member of the controlled group whose employees are not covered by Plan B. For these employees, Plan B fails to satisfy the requirement of paragraph (b)(2)(v) of this section (i.e., each employee's benefit must accrue over the same years of service used in applying the benefit formula).

(b) Plan B is restructured into two component plans under the provisions of § 1.401(a)(4)-9(c). One component plan (Component Plan B1) consists of all NHCEs who are not being credited with years of service under the plan's benefit formula but are continuing to accrue benefits as a result of compensation increases, and the other component plan (Component Plan B2) consists of the balance of the employees.

(c) Component Plan B1 satisfies this section and section 410(b), because it benefits only NHCEs.

(d) Component Plan B2 is treated as satisfying this paragraph (b), because Plan B would satisfy this paragraph (b) (determined without regard to this paragraph (b)(6)(x)) with respect to the employees in Component Plan B2 but for the fact that it provides inherently less valuable benefits to some HCEs in that component plan (i.e., the employees who are credited only with compensation increases rather than both years of service and compensation increases).

(e) Under § 1.401(a)(4)-9(c), if Component Plan B2 satisfies section 410(b), then Plan B satisfies this section.

(xi) Multiple formulas. (A) General rule. The plan provides that an employee's benefit under the plan is the greater of the benefits determined under two or more formulas, or is the sum of the benefits determined under two or more formulas. This paragraph (b)(6)(xi) does not apply to a plan unless each of the formulas under the plan satisfies the requirements of paragraph (b)(6)(xi)(B) through (D) of this section.

(B) Sole formulas. The formulas must be the only formulas under the plan.

(C) Separate testing. Each of the formulas must separately satisfy the uniformity requirements of paragraph (b)(2) of this section and also separately satisfy one of the safe harbors in paragraphs (b)(3) through (b)(5) of this section. A formula that is available solely to some or all NHCEs is deemed to satisfy this paragraph (b)(6)(xi)(C).

(D) Availability. (1) General rule. All of the formulas must be available on the same terms to all employees.

(2) Formulas for NHCEs. A formula does not fail to be available on the same terms to all employees merely because the formula is not available to any HCEs, but is available to some or all NHCEs on the same terms as all of the other formulas in the plan.

(3) Top-heavy formulas. Rules parallel to those in § 1.401(a)(4)-2(b)(4)(vi)(D)(3) apply in the case of a plan that provides the greater of the benefits under two or more formulas, one of which is a top-heavy formula. For purposes of this paragraph (b)(6)(xi)(D)(3), a top-heavy formula is a formula that provides a benefit equal to the minimum benefit described in section 416(c)(1) (taking into account, if applicable, the modification in section 416(h)(2)(A)(ii)(I)).

(E) Provisions may be applied more than once. The provisions of this paragraph (b)(6)(xi) may be applied more than once. See § 1.401(a)(4)-2(b)(4)(vi)(E) for an example of the application of these provisions more than once.

(F) Examples. The following examples illustrate the rules in this paragraph (b)(6)(xi):

*Example (1).* Under Plan A, each employee's benefit equals the sum of the benefits determined under two formulas. The first formula provides one percent of average annual compensation per year of service. The second formula provides $10 per year of service. Plan A is eligible to apply the rules in this paragraph (b)(6)(xi).

*Example (2).* Under Plan B, each employee's benefit equals the greater of the benefits determined under two formulas. The first formula provides $15 per year of service and is available to all employees who complete at least 500 hours of service during the plan year. The second formula provides 1.5 percent of average annual compensation per year of service and is available to all employees who complete at least 1,000 hours of service during the plan year. Plan B does not satisfy this paragraph (b)(6)(xi) because the two formulas are not available on the same terms to all employees.

*Example (3).* Under Plan C, each employee's benefit equals the greater of the benefits determined under two formulas. The first formula provides $15 per year of service and is available to all employees who complete at least 1,000 hours of service during the plan year. The second formula provides the minimum benefit described in section 416(c)(1) and is available to all non-key employees who complete at least 1,000 hours of service during the plan year. Plan C does not satisfy the general rule in paragraph (b)(6)(xi)(D)(1) of this section because the two formulas are not available on the same terms to all employees (i.e., the second formula is only available to all non-key employees). Nonetheless, because the second formula is a top-heavy formula, the special availability rules for top-heavy formulas in paragraph (b)(6)(xi)(D)(3) of this section apply. Thus, the second formula does not fail to be available on the same terms as the first formula merely because the second formula is available solely to all non-key employees on the same terms. This is true even if the plan conditions the availability of the second formula on the plan's being top-heavy for the plan year.

*Example (4).* Under Plan D, each employee's benefit equals the greater of the benefits determined under two formulas. The first formula is available to all employees and provides a benefit equal to 1.5 percent of average annual compensation per year of service. The second formula is only available to NHCEs and provides a benefit equal to two percent of average annual compensation per year of service, minus two percent of the primary insurance amount per year of service. The amount of the offset is not limited to the maximum permitted offset under § 1.401(l)-3(b). Under paragraph (b)(6)(xi)(D)(2) of this section, both formulas are treated as available to all employees on the same terms. Furthermore, even though the second formula does not satisfy any of the safe harbors in this paragraph (b), the formula is deemed to satisfy the separate testing requirement under paragraph (b)(6)(xi)(C) of this section, because the formula is available solely to some or all NHCEs.

*Example (5).* Plan E is a unit credit plan that provides a benefit of one percent of average annual compensation per year of service to all employees. In 1994, the plan is amended to provide a benefit of two percent of average annual compensation per year of service after 1993, while continuing to provide a benefit of one percent of average annual compensation per year of service for all years of service before 1994. Thus, the plan's amended benefit formula provides a benefit equal to the sum of the benefits determined under two benefit formulas: one percent of average annual compensation per year of service, plus one percent of average annual compensation per year of service after 1993. Plan E satisfies this paragraph (b)(6)(xi).

*Example (6).* The facts are the same as in Example 5, except that the plan amendment in 1994 decreases the benefit to 0.75 percent of average annual compensation per year of service after 1993, while retaining the one-percent formula for all years of service before 1994. Thus, the plan's amended benefit formula provides a benefit equal to the sum of the benefits determined under two benefit formulas: 0.75 percent of average annual compensation per year of service, plus 0.25 percent of average annual compensation per year of service before 1994. Under these facts, the second formula does not separately satisfy any of the safe harbors in this paragraph (b) because the years of service over which each employee's benefit accrues under the second formula (i.e., all years of service) are not the same years of service that are taken into account in applying the benefit formula under the plan to that employee (i.e., years of service before 1994). See paragraph (b)(2)(v) of this section. But see paragraph (b)(6)(vii) of this section and § 1.401(a)(4)-13, which provide rules under which Plan E, as amended, may be able to satisfy this paragraph (b).

*Example (7).* Plan F provides a benefit to all employees of one percent of average annual compensation per year of service. Employee M was hired as the president of the employer in December 1994 and was not a HCE under section 414(q) during the 1994 calendar plan year. In 1994, Plan F is amended to provide a benefit that is the greater of the benefit determined under the pre-existing formula in the plan and a new formula that is available solely to some NHCEs (including Employee M). The new formula does not satisfy the uniformity requirements of paragraph (b)(2) of this section, because it provides a different benefit for some NHCEs than for other NHCEs. As a result of this change, Employee M receives a higher accrual in 1994 than the NHCEs who are not eligible for the new formula. In 1995, when Employee M first becomes a HCE, the second formula no longer applies to Employee M. It would be inconsistent with the purpose of preventing discrimination in favor of HCEs for Plan F to use the special rule for a formula that is available solely to some or all NHCEs to satisfy the separate testing requirement of paragraph (b)(6)(xi)(C) of this section for the 1994 calendar plan year. See § 1.401(a)(4)-1(c)(2).

**(c) General test for nondiscrimination in amount of benefits.** *(1) General rule.* The employer-provided benefits under a defined benefit plan are nondiscriminatory in amount for a plan year if each rate group under the plan satisfies section 410(b). For purposes of this paragraph (c)(1), a rate group exists under a plan for each HCE and consists of the HCE and all other employees (both HCEs and NHCEs) who have a normal accrual rate greater than or equal to the HCE's normal accrual rate, and who also have a most valuable accrual rate greater than or equal to the HCE's most valuable accrual rate. Thus, an employee is in the rate group for each HCE who has a normal accrual rate less than or equal to the employee's normal accrual rate, and who also has a most valuable accrual rate less than or equal to the employee's most valuable accrual rate.

*(2) Satisfaction of section 410(b) by a rate group.* For purposes of determining whether a rate group satisfies section 410(b), the same rules apply as in § 1.401(a)(4)-2(c)(3). See paragraph (c)(4) of this section and § 1.401(a)(4)-2(c)(4), Example 3 through Example 5, for examples of this rule.

*(3) Certain violations disregarded.* A plan is deemed to satisfy paragraph (c)(1) of this section if the plan would satisfy that paragraph by treating as not benefiting no more than five percent of the HCEs in the plan, and the Commissioner determines that, on the basis of all of the relevant facts and circumstances, the plan does not discriminate with respect to the amount of employer-provided benefits. For this purpose, five percent of the number of HCEs may be determined by rounding to the nearest whole number (e.g., 1.4 rounds to 1 and 1.5 rounds to 2). Among the relevant factors that the Commissioner may consider in making this determination are—

(i) The extent to which the plan has failed the test in paragraph (c)(1) of this section;

(ii) The extent to which the failure is for reasons other than the design of the plan;

(iii) Whether the HCEs causing the failure are five-percent owners or are among the highest paid nonexcludable employees;

(iv) Whether the failure is attributable to an event that is not expected to recur (e.g., a plant closing); and

(v) The extent to which the failure is attributable to benefits accrued under a prior benefit structure or to benefits accrued when a participant was not a HCE.

*(4) Examples.* The following examples illustrate the rules in this paragraph (c):

*Example (1).* (a) Employer X has 1100 nonexcludable employees, N1 through N1000, who are NHCEs, and HI through H100, who are HCEs. Employer X maintains Plan A, a defined benefit plan that benefits all of these nonexcludable employees. The normal and most valuable accrual rates (determined as a percentage of average annual compensation) for the employees in Plan A for the 1994 plan year are listed in the following table.

| Employee | Normal Accrual Rate | Most Valuable Accrual Rate |
|---|---|---|
| N1 through N100 | 1.0 | 1.4 |
| N101 through N500 | 1.5 | 3.0 |
| N501 through N750 | 2.0 | 2.65 |
| N751 through N1000 | 2.3 | 2.8 |
| H1 through H50 | 1.5 | 2.0 |
| H51 through H100 | 2.0 | 2.65 |

(b) There are 100 rate groups in Plan A because there are 100 HCEs in Plan A.

(c) Rate group 1 consists of H1 and all those employees who have a normal accrual rate greater than or equal to H1's normal accrual rate (1.5 percent) and who also have a most valuable accrual rate greater than or equal to H1's most valuable accrual rate (2.0 percent). Thus, rate group 1 consists of HI through H100 and N101 through N1000.

(d) Rate group 1 satisfies the ratio percentage test of § 1.410(b)-2(b)(2) because the ratio percentage of the rate group is 90 percent, i.e., 90 percent (the percentage of all nonhighly compensated nonexcludable employees who are in the rate group) divided by 100 percent (the percentage of all highly compensated nonexcludable employees who are in the rate group).

(e) Because H1 through H50 have the same normal accrual rates and the same most valuable accrual rates, the rate group with respect to each of them is identical. Thus, because rate group 1 satisfies section 410(b), rate groups 2 through 50 also satisfy section 410(b).

(f) Rate group 51 consists of H51 and all those employees who have a normal accrual rate greater than or equal to H51's normal accrual rate (2.0 percent) and who also have a most valuable accrual rate greater than or equal to H51's most valuable accrual rate (2.65 percent). Thus, rate group 51 consists of H51 through H100 and N501 through N1000. (Even though N101 through N500 have a most valuable accrual rate (3.0 percent) greater than H51's most valuable accrual rate (2.65 percent), they are not included in this rate group because their normal accrual rate (1.5 percent) is less than H51's normal accrual rate (2.0 percent).)

(g) Rate group 51 satisfies the ratio percentage test of § 1.410(b)-2(b)(2) because the ratio percentage of the rate group is 100 percent, i.e., 50 percent (the percentage of all nonhighly compensated nonexcludable employees who are in the rate group) divided by 50 percent (the percentage of all highly compensated nonexcludable employees who are in the rate group).

(h) Because H51 through H100 have the same normal accrual rates and the same most valuable accrual rates, the rate group with respect to each of them is identical. Thus, because rate group 51 satisfies section 410(b), rate groups 52 through 100 also satisfy section 410(b).

(i) The employer-provided benefits under Plan A are nondiscriminatory in amount because each rate group under the plan satisfies section 410(b).

*Example (2).* The facts are the same as in Example 1, except that H96 has a most valuable accrual rate of 3.5. Each of the rate groups is the same as in Example 1, except that rate group 96 consists solely of H96 because no other employee has a most valuable accrual rate greater than 3.5. Because the plan would satisfy the test in paragraph (c)(1) of this section by treating H96 (who constitutes less than five percent of the HCEs in the plan) as not benefiting, the Commissioner may determine under paragraph (c)(3) of this section that, on the basis of all of the relevant facts and circumstances, the plan does not discriminate with respect to the amount of benefits.

**(d) Determination of accrual rates.** *(1) Definitions.* (i) Normal accrual rate. The normal accrual rate for an employee for a plan year is the increase in the employee's accrued benefit (within the meaning of section 411(a)(7)(A)(i)) during the measurement period, divided by the employee's testing service during the measurement period, and expressed either as a dollar amount or as a percentage of the employee's average annual compensation.

(ii) Most valuable accrual rate. The most valuable accrual rate for an employee for a plan year is the increase in the employee's most valuable optional form of payment of the accrued benefit during the measurement period, divided by the employee's testing service during the measurement period, and expressed either as a dollar amount or as a percentage of the employee's average annual compensation. The employee's most valuable optional form of payment of the accrued benefit is determined by calculating for the employee the normalized QJSA associated with the accrued benefit that is potentially payable in the current or any future plan year at any age under the plan and selecting the largest (per year of testing service). If the plan provides a QSUPP, the most valuable accrual rate also takes into account the QSUPP payable in conjunction with the QJSA at each age under the plan. Thus, the most valuable accrual rate reflects the value of all benefits accrued or treated as accrued under section 411(d)(6) that are payable in any form and at any time under the plan, including early retirement benefits, retirement-type subsidies, early retirement window benefits, and QSUPPs. In addition, the most valuable accrual rate must take into account any such benefits that are available during a plan year, even if the benefits cease to be available before the end of the current or any future plan year.

(iii) Measurement period. The measurement period can be—

(A) The current plan year;

(B) The current plan year and all prior years; or

(C) The current plan year and all prior and future years.

(iv) Testing service. (A) General rule. Testing service means an employee's years of service as defined in the plan for purposes of applying the benefit formula under the plan, subject to the requirements of paragraph (d)(1)(iv)(B) of this section. Alternatively, testing service means service determined for all employees in a reasonable manner that satisfies the requirements of paragraph (d)(1)(iv)(B) of this section. For example, the number of plan years that an employee has benefited under the plan within the meaning of § 1.410(b)-3(a) is an acceptable definition of testing service because it determines service in a reasonable manner and satisfies paragraph (d)(1)(iv)(B) of this section. See also § 1.401(a)(4)-11(d)(3) (additional limits on service that may be taken into account as testing service).

(B) Requirements for testing service. (1) Employees not credited with years of service under the benefit formula. An employee must be credited with testing service for any year in which the employee benefits under the plan (within the meaning of § 1.410(b)-3(a)), unless that year is part of a period of service that may not be taken into account under § 1.401(a)(4)-11(d)(3). This rule applies even if the employee does not receive service credit under the benefit formula for that year (e.g., because of a service cap in the benefit formula or because of a transfer out of the group of employees covered by the plan).

(2) Current year testing service. In the case of a measurement period that is the current plan year, testing service for the plan year equals one (1).

*(2) Rules of application.* (i) Consistency requirement. Both normal and most valuable accrual rates must be determined in a consistent manner for all employees for the plan year. Thus, for example, the same measurement periods must be used, and the rules of this paragraph (d)(2) and any available options described in paragraph (d)(3) of this section must be applied consistently. If plan benefits are not expressed as straight life annuities beginning at employees' testing ages, they must be normalized.

(ii) Determining plan benefits, service and compensation. (A) In general. Potential plan benefits, testing service, and average annual compensation must be determined in a reasonable manner, reflecting actual or projected service and compensation only through the end of the measurement period. The determination of potential plan benefits is not reasonable if it incorporates an assumption that, in future years, an employee's compensation will increase or the employee will terminate employment before the employee's testing age (other than the assumptions under paragraph (d)(1)(ii) of this section that the employee's service will end in connection with the payment of each potential QJSA in future years).

(B) Section 415 limits. For purposes of determining accrual rates under this paragraph (d), plan benefits are generally determined without regard to whether those benefits are permitted to be paid under section 415. However, plan provisions implementing any of the limits of section 415 may be taken into account in applying this paragraph (d) if the plan does not provide for benefit increases resulting from section 415(d)(1) adjustments for former employees who were employees in a plan year in which such plan provisions were taken into account in applying this paragraph (d). If the limits of section 415 are taken into account under this paragraph (d)(2)(ii)(B) as of the end of the measurement period, they must also be taken into account as of the beginning of the measurement period. If the limits of section 415 are not taken into account in testing the plan for the current plan year, but were taken into account in testing the plan for the preceding plan year, any resulting increase in the accrued benefits taken into account in testing the plan is treated as an increase in accrued benefits during the current plan year.

(iii) Requirements for measurement period that includes future years. (A) Discriminatory pattern of accruals. A measurement period that includes future years (as described in paragraph (d)(1)(iii)(C) of this section) may not be used if the pattern of accruals under the plan discriminates in favor of HCEs (i.e., if projected benefits for HCEs are relatively frontloaded when compared to the degree of frontloading or backloading for NHCEs). This determination is made based on all of the relevant facts and circumstances.

(B) Future-period limitation. Future years beginning after an employee's attainment of the employee's testing age (or after the employee's assumed termination in the case of most valuable accrual rates) may not be included in the measurement period.

*(3) Optional rules.* (i) Imputation of permitted disparity. The disparity permitted under section 401(l) may be imputed in accordance with the rules of § 1.401(a)(4)-7.

(ii) Grouping of accrual rates. (A) General rule. An employer may treat all employees who have accrual rates within a specified range above and below a midpoint rate chosen by the employer as having an accrual rate equal to the midpoint rate within that range. Accrual rates within a given range may not be grouped under this paragraph (d)(3)(ii) if the accrual rates of HCEs within the range generally are significantly higher than the accrual rates of NHCEs in the range. The specified ranges within which all employees are treated as having the same accrual rate may not overlap and may be no larger than provided in paragraph (d)(3)(ii)(B) of this section. Accrual rates of employees that are not within any of these specified ranges are determined without regard to this paragraph (d)(3)(ii).

(B) Size of specified ranges. In the case of normal accrual rates, the lowest and highest accrual rates in the range must be within five percent (not five percentage points) of the midpoint rate. In the case of most valuable accrual rates, the lowest and highest accrual rates in the range must be within 15 percent (not 15 percentage points) of the midpoint rate. If accrual rates are determined as a percentage of average annual compensation, the lowest and highest accrual rates need not be within five percent (or 15 percent) of the midpoint rate, if they are no more than one twentieth of a percentage point above or below the midpoint rate.

(iii) Fresh-start alternative. (A) General rule. Notwithstanding the definition of measurement period provided in paragraph (d)(1)(iii) of this section, a measurement period for a fresh-start group is permitted to be limited to the period beginning after the fresh-start date with respect to that group if the plan makes a fresh start that satisfies § 1.401(a)(4)-13(c) (without regard to § 1.401(a)(4)-13(c)(2)(i) and (ii)). If the measurement period is so limited or the measurement period is the plan year (whether or not so limited), any compensation adjustments during the measurement period to the frozen accrued benefit as of the fresh-start date that are permitted under the rules of § 1.401(a)(4)-13(d) may be disregarded in determining the increase in accrued benefits during the measurement period, but only if—

(1) The plan makes a fresh start as of the fresh-start date that satisfies § 1.401(a)(4)-13(c) (without regard to § 1.401(a)(4)-13(c)(2)(ii)) in conjunction with a bona fide amendment to the benefit formula or accrual method under the plan; and

(2) The amendment provides for adjustments to employees' frozen accrued benefits as of the fresh-start date in accordance with the rules of § 1.401(a)(4)-13(d).

(B) Application of consistency requirements. Limiting the application of the fresh-start alternative in this paragraph (d)(3)(iii) to a fresh-start group that consists of fewer than all employees does not violate the consistency requirement of paragraph (d)(2)(i) of this section.

(iv) Floor on most valuable accrual rate. In lieu of determining an employee's most valuable accrual rate in accordance with the definition in paragraph (d)(1)(ii) of this section, an employer may determine an employee's most valuable accrual rate for the current plan year as the employee's highest most valuable accrual rate determined for any prior plan year. This option may be used only if the employee's normal accrual rate has not changed significantly from the normal accrual rate for the relevant prior plan year and, there have been no plan amendments in the interim period since that prior plan year that affect the determination of most valuable accrual rate.

*(4) Examples.* The following examples illustrate the rules in this paragraph (d):

*Example (1).* The employees in Plan A have the following normal accrual rates (expressed as percentage of average annual compensation): 0.8 percent, 0.83 percent, 0.9 percent, 1.9 percent, 2.0 percent, and 2.1 percent. Because the first three rates are within a range of no more than one twentieth of a percentage point above or below 0.85 percent (a midpoint rate chosen by the employer), the employer may treat the employees who have those rates as having an accrual rate of 0.85 percent (provided that the accrual rates of HCEs within the range are not significantly higher than the accrual rates for NHCEs within the range). Because the last three rates are within a range of no more than five percent above or below 2.0 percent (a midpoint rate chosen by the employer), the employer may treat the employees who have those rates as having an accrual rate of 2.0 percent (provided that the accrual rates of HCEs within the range are not significantly higher than the accrual rates for NHCEs within the range).

*Example (2).* Employer X maintains a plan under which headquarters employees accrue a benefit of 1.25 percent of average compensation for the first 10 years of service and 0.75 percent of average compensation for subsequent years of service, while all other employees accrue a benefit of one percent of compensation for all years of service. Assume that the group of headquarters employees does not satisfy section 410(b). Under these facts, the pattern of accruals under the plan discriminates in favor of HCEs, and, therefore, under paragraph (d)(2)(iii)(A) of this section, the measurement period for determining accrual rates under the plan may not include future service.

**(e) Compensation rules.** *(1) In general.* This paragraph (e) provides rules for determining average annual compensation. Safe harbor plans that satisfy paragraph (b) of this section must determine benefits either as a dollar amount unrelated to employees' compensation or as a percentage of each employee's average annual compensation. In contrast, plans that must satisfy the general test of paragraph (c) of this section are not required under this section to determine benefits under any particular definition of compensation or in any particular manner, but the accrual rates used in testing these plans must be expressed either as a dollar amount or determined as a percentage of each employee's average annual compensation.

*(2) Average annual compensation.* (i) General rule. An employee's average annual compensation is the average of the employee's annual section 414(s) compensation determined over the averaging period in the employee's compensation history during which the average of the employee's annual section 414(s) compensation is the highest. For this purpose, an averaging period must consist of three or more consecutive 12-month periods, but need not be longer than the employee's period of employment. An employee's compensation history may begin at any time, but must be continuous, be no shorter than the averaging period, and end in the current plan year.

(ii) Certain permitted modifications to average annual compensation. (A) Use of plan year compensation. If the measurement period for determination of accrual rates is the current plan year, or the plan is an accumulation plan that satisfies paragraph (b) of this section, then plan year compensation may be substituted for average annual compensation.

(B) Drop-out years. Any of the following types of 12-month periods in an employee's compensation history may be disregarded in determining the employee's average annual compensation (including for purposes of the requirement to average section 414(s) compensation over consecutive 12-month periods), but only if the plan disregards the employee's compensation for those periods in determining benefits—

(1) The 12-month period in which the employee terminates employment;

(2) All 12-month periods in which the employee performs no services; or

(3) All 12-month periods in which the employee performs services for less than a specified number of hours or specified period of time in the 12-month period. The specified number of hours or specified period of time may be selected by the employer, but may not exceed three quarters of the time that an employee in the same job category working on a full-time basis would perform services during that 12-month period.

(C) Drop-out months within 12-month periods. If a plan determines an employee's average annual compensation using 12-month periods that do not end on a fixed date (e.g., average annual compensation as of a date is defined as the average of the employee's section 414(s) compensation for the 60 consecutive months within the compensation history in which the average is highest), then, for purposes of determining a 12-month period, any of the following type of months may be disregarded (including for purposes of the requirement to average section 414(s) compensation over consecutive 12-month periods), but only if the plan disregards the employee's compensation for those months in determining benefits—

(1) The month in which the employee terminates employment;

(2) All months in which the employee performs no services; or

(3) All months in which the employee performs services for less than a specified number of hours or specified period of time in the month. The specified number of hours or specified period of time may be selected by the employer, but may not exceed three quarters of the time that an employee in the same job category working on a full-time basis would perform services during that month.

(D) Employees working less than full-time. In the case of an employee who normally works less than full-time, the rules in paragraphs (e)(2)(ii)(B)(3) and (e)(2)(ii)(C)(3) of this section may be applied in relation to that employee's normal work schedule (instead of a full-time employee's work schedule) by prorating the specified number of hours or specified period of time, based on the employee's normal work schedule as a fraction of a full-time schedule.

(E) Exception from consecutive-periods requirement for certain plans. The requirement that the periods taken into account under paragraph (e)(2)(i) of this section be consecutive does not apply in the case of a plan that is not a section 401(l) plan, provided that it does not take permitted disparity into account under § 1.401(a)(4)-7. This paragraph (e)(2)(ii)(E) applies only if the plan does not take into account whether 12-month periods of compensation are consecutive in determining average compensation for purposes of calculating benefits.

(iii) Consistency requirements. Average annual compensation must be determined in a consistent manner for all employees.

*(3) Examples.* The following examples illustrate the rules in this paragraph (e):

*Example (1).* Plan A is a defined benefit plan. Plan A determines benefits on the basis of the average of each employee's annual compensation for the five consecutive plan years (or the employee's period of employment, if shorter) during the employee's compensation history in which the average of the employee's annual compensation is the highest. The compensation history used for this purpose is the last 10 plan years, plus the current plan year. In determining compensation for each plan year in the compensation history, Plan A defines compensation using a single definition that satisfies section 414(s) as a safe harbor definition under § 1.414(s)-1(c). Plan A determines benefits on the basis of average annual compensation.

*Example (2).* Plan B is a defined benefit plan. Plan B determines benefits on the basis of the average of each employee's compensation for the five consecutive 12-month periods (or the employee's period of employment, if shorter) during the employee's compensation history in which the average of the employee's annual compensation is the highest. The compensation history used for this purpose is the 10 consecutive 12-month periods ending on the employee's termination date. In determining the average, Plan B disregards all months in which the employee performs services for less than 100 hours (60 percent of a full-time work schedule of 173 hours). In the case of an employee whose normal work schedule is less than a full-time schedule, Plan B disregards all months in which that employee performs services for less than 60 percent of the employee's normal work schedule. Plan B defines compensation for each 12-month period using a single definition that satisfies § 1.414(s)-1. Plan B determines benefits on the basis of average annual compensation.

*Example (3).* (a) The facts are the same as in Example 1, except that, for plan years prior to 1996, the compensation for a plan year was determined under a rate of pay definition of compensation that satisfies section 414(s), while, for plan years after 1995, the compensation for a plan year is determined using a definition that satisfies section 414(s) as a safe harbor definition under § 1.414(s)-1(c).

(b) The underlying definition of compensation for each plan year in the employee's compensation history is section

414(s) compensation, because for each plan year the definition satisfies the requirements for section 414(s) compensation under § 1.401(a)(4)-12. Therefore, Plan A determines benefits on the basis of average annual compensation, even though the underlying definition used to measure the amount of compensation for each plan year in an employee's compensation history is not the same for all plan years.

*Example (4).* The facts are the same as in Example 1, except that Plan A determines benefits on the basis of the average of the employee's annual section 414(s) compensation for the five consecutive 12-month periods ending on June 30 during the employee's compensation history in which the average is highest. An employee's compensation history begins when the employee commences participation in the plan and ends in the current plan year. In the case of an employee with less than five consecutive years of plan participation as of June 30, the compensation history is extended prior to the employee's commencement of participation to include the five consecutive 12-month periods ending on June 30 of the current plan year (or the employee's total period of employment, if shorter). Plan A determines benefits on the basis of average annual compensation.

*Example (5).* The facts are the same as in Example 4, except that Plan A determines benefits on the basis of the average of each employee's compensation for the employee's entire compensation history. Plan A determines benefits on the basis of average annual compensation.

**(f) Special rules.** *(1) In general.* The special rules in this paragraph (f) apply for purposes of applying the provisions of this section to a defined benefit plan. Any special rule provided in this paragraph (f) that is optional must, if used, apply uniformly to all employees.

*(2) Certain qualified disability benefits.* In general, qualified disability benefits (within the meaning of section 411(a)(9)) are not taken into account under this section. However, a qualified disability benefit that results from the crediting of compensation or service for a period of disability in the same manner as actual compensation or service is credited under a plan's benefit formula is permitted to be taken into account under this section as an accrued benefit upon the employee's return to service with the employer following the period of disability, provided that the qualified disability benefit is then treated in the same manner as an accrued benefit for all purposes under the plan.

*(3) Accruals after normal retirement age.* (i) General rule. An employee's accruals for any plan year after the plan year in which the employee attains normal retirement age are taken into account for purposes of this section. However, any plan provision that provides for increases in an employee's accrued benefit solely because the employee has delayed commencing benefits beyond the normal retirement age applicable to the employee under the plan may be disregarded, but only if—

(A) The same uniform normal retirement age applies to all employees; and

(B) The percentage factor used to increase the employee's accrued benefit is no greater than the largest percentage factor that could be applied to increase actuarially the employee's accrued benefit using any standard mortality table and any standard interest rate.

(ii) Examples. The following examples illustrate the rules of this paragraph (f)(3). In each example, it is assumed that the plan satisfies the requirements of paragraph (f)(3)(i)(A) and (B) of this section.

*Example (1).* Plan A provides a benefit of two percent of average annual compensation per year of service for all employees. In addition, Plan A provides an actuarial increase in an employee's accrued benefit of six percent for each year that an employee defers commencement of benefits beyond normal retirement age. For employees who continue in service beyond normal retirement age, the employee's two-percent accrual for the current plan year is offset by the six-percent actuarial increase, as permitted under section 411(b)(1)(H)(iii)(II). For purposes of this section, the actuarial increase (and hence the offset) may be disregarded, and thus all employees may be treated as if they were accruing at the rate of two percent of average annual compensation per year.

*Example (2).* The facts are the same as in Example 1, except that the employee's two-percent accrual for the current plan year is not offset by the six-percent actuarial increase. The employer may disregard the actuarial increase and thus may treat all employees as if they were accruing at the rate of two percent of average annual compensation per year.

*(4) Early retirement window benefits.* (i) General rule. In applying the requirements of this section, all early retirement benefits, retirement-type subsidies, QSUPPs, and other optional forms of benefit under a plan, and changes in the plan's benefit formula, are taken into account regardless of whether they are permanent features of the plan or are offered only to employees whose employment terminates within a limited period of time. Additional rules and examples relevant to the testing of early retirement window benefits are found in Example 6 of paragraph (b)(2)(vi) of this section; paragraph (b)(2)(ii)(A)(2), Example 2 of paragraph (c)(2), paragraph (d)(3), and Example 3 of paragraph (e)(1)(iii) of § 1.401(a)(4)-4; paragraph (c)(4)(i) and Example 2 of paragraph (c)(6) of § 1.401(a)(4)-9; and the definition of benefit formula in § 1.401(a)(4)-12.

(ii) Special rules. (A) Year in which early retirement window benefit taken into account. Notwithstanding paragraph (f)(4)(i) of this section, an early retirement window benefit is disregarded for purposes of determining whether a plan satisfies this section with respect to an employee for all plan years other than the first plan year in which the benefit is currently available (within the meaning of § 1.401(a)(4)-4(b)(2)) to the employee. For purposes of this paragraph (f)(4)(ii)(A), in determining which plan years the benefit is currently available, an early retirement window benefit that consists of a temporary change in the plan's benefit formula is treated as an optional form of benefit.

(B) Treatment of early retirement window benefit that consists of temporary change in benefit formula. An early retirement window benefit is disregarded for purposes of determining an employee's normal accrual rate, even if the early retirement window benefit consists of a temporary change in a plan's benefit formula. However, if an early retirement window benefit consists of a temporary change in a plan's benefit formula, the plan does not satisfy paragraph (b) of this section during the period for which the change is effective unless the plan satisfies paragraph (b) of this section both reflecting the temporary change in the benefit formula and disregarding that change.

(C) Effect of early retirement window benefit on most valuable accrual rate. In determining an employee's most valuable optional form of payment of the accrued benefit (which is used in determining the employee's most valuable accrual rate under paragraphs (d)(1)(ii) and (f)(4)(i) of this section), an early retirement window benefit that is currently available to the employee (within the meaning of paragraph (f)(4)(ii)(A) of this section) and that is not disregarded for a plan year under paragraph (f)(4)(ii)(A) of this section is taken into account in that plan year with respect to the employee's accrued benefit as of the earliest of the employee's date of termination, the close of the early retirement window, or the last day of that plan year.

(D) Effect of early retirement window benefit on average benefit percentage test. Notwithstanding paragraph (c)(2) of this section, a rate group under a plan that provides an early retirement window benefit is deemed to satisfy the average benefit percentage test of § 1.410(b)-5 if—

(1) All rate groups under the plan would satisfy the ratio percentage test of § 1.410(b)-2(b)(2) if the early retirement window benefit were disregarded; and

(2) The group of employees to whom the early retirement window benefit is currently available (within the meaning of paragraph (f)(4)(ii)(A) of this section) satisfies section 410(b) without regard to the average benefit percentage test of § 1.410(b)-5.

(iii) Early retirement window benefit defined. For purposes of this paragraph (f)(4), an early retirement window benefit is an early retirement benefit, retirement-type subsidy, QSUPP, or other optional form of benefit under a plan that is available, or a change in the plan's benefit formula that is applicable, only to employees who terminate employment within a limited period specified by the plan (not to exceed one year) under circumstances specified by the plan. A benefit does not fail to be described in the preceding sentence merely because the plan contains provisions under which certain employees may receive the benefit even though, for bona fide business reasons, they terminate employment within a reasonable period after the end of the limited period. An amendment to an early retirement window benefit that merely extends the periods in the preceding sentences is not treated as a separate early retirement window benefit, provided that the periods, as extended, satisfy the preceding sentences. However, any other amendment to an early retirement window benefit creates a separate early retirement window benefit.

(iv) Examples. The following examples illustrate the rules of this paragraph (f)(4):

*Example (1).* (a) Plan A provides a benefit of one percent of average annual compensation per year of service and satisfies the requirements of paragraph (b)(2) of this section. Thus, the plan provides the same benefit to all employees with the same years of service under the Plan. Plan A is amended to treat all employees with ten or more years of service who terminate employment after attainment of age 55 and between March 1, 1999, and January 31, 2000, as if they had an additional five years of service under the benefit formula. However, in order to ensure the orderly implementation of the early retirement window, the plan amendment provides that designated employees in the human resources department who would otherwise be eligible for the early retirement window benefit are eligible to be treated as having the additional five years of service only if they terminate between January 1, 2000, and April 30, 2000.

(b) The additional benefits provided under this amendment are tested as benefits provided to employees rather than former employees. The effect of this amendment is temporarily to change the benefit formula for employees who are eligible for the early retirement window benefit because the amendment changes (albeit temporarily) the amount of the benefit payable to those employees at normal retirement age. See the definition of benefit formula in § 1.401(a)(4)-12. Assume that the additional years of service credited to employees eligible for the window benefit do not represent past service (within the meaning of § 1.401(a)(4)-11(d)(3)(i)(B)) or preparticipation or imputed service (within the meaning of § 1.401(a)(4)-11(d)(3)(ii)(A) or (B), respectively) and thus may not be taken into account as years of service. See § 1.401(a)(4)-11(d)(3)(i)(A) (regarding years of service that may not be taken into account under § 1.401(a)(4)-1(b)(2)). Thus, the window-eligible employees are entitled to a larger benefit (as a percentage of average annual compensation) than other employees with the same number of years of service, and the plan does not satisfy the uniform normal retirement benefit requirement of paragraph (b)(2)(i) of this section.

(c) Plan A is restructured under the provisions of § 1.401(a)(4)-9(c) into two component plans: Component Plan A1, consisting of all employees who are not eligible for the early retirement window benefit and all of their accruals and benefits, rights, and features under the plan, and Component Plan A2, consisting of all employees who are eligible for the early retirement window benefit (including the designated employees in the human resource department) and all of their accruals and benefits, rights, and features under the plan.

(d) Component Plan A1 still satisfies paragraph (b) of this section, because there has been no change for the employees in that component plan. Similarly, Component Plan A2 satisfies paragraph (b) of this section disregarding the change in the benefit formula.

(e) Because the early retirement window benefit consists of a temporary change in the benefit formula, paragraph (f)(4)(ii)(B) of this section requires that the plan satisfy the requirements of paragraph (b) of this section reflecting the change in order to remain a safe harbor plan. After reflecting the change, Component Plan A2 still provides the same benefit (albeit higher than under the regular benefit formula) to all employees with the same years of service that may be taken into account in testing the plan, and thus the benefit formula (as temporarily amended) satisfies the requirements of paragraphs (b)(2)(i) and (ii) of this section.

(f) Since Component Plan A2 also satisfies all of the other requirements of paragraph (b)(2) of this section and the safe harbor of paragraph (b)(3) of this section reflecting the change in the benefit formula, Component Plan A2 satisfies this paragraph (b) both reflecting and disregarding the change in the benefit formula. Thus, Component Plan A2 satisfies paragraph (b) of this section.

*Example (2).* The facts are the same as in Example 1, except that Plan A's benefit formula used the maximum amount of permitted disparity under section 401(l) prior to the amendment. The analysis is the same as in paragraphs (a) through the first sentence of paragraph (e) of Example 1. In order to satisfy the requirements of paragraph (b)(2) of this section, a plan that uses permitted disparity must satisfy the requirements of section 401(l) after reflecting the change in the benefit formula. Because, as stated in Example 1, the additional five years of service may not be taken into account for purposes of satisfying paragraph (b) of this section, the disparity that results from crediting that service exceeds the maximum permitted disparity under section 401(l). Thus, Component Plan A2 does not satisfy the requirements of paragraph (b) of this section.

*Example (3).* The facts are the same as in Example 1, except that Plan A is tested under the general test in paragraph (c) of this section. The early retirement window benefit is disregarded for purposes of determining the normal accrual rates, but is taken into account in 1999 for purposes of determining the most valuable accrual rates, of employees who were eligible for the early retirement window benefit (regardless of whether they elected to receive it). As stated in Example 1, the additional five years of service do not represent past service, pre-participation service, or imputed service, and thus under § 1.401(a)(4)-11(d)(3)(i)(A) may not be taken into account as testing service.

*(5) Unpredictable contingent event benefits.* (i) General rule. In general, an unpredictable contingent event benefit (within the meaning of section 412(l)(7)(B)(ii)) is not taken into account under this section until the occurrence of the contingent event. Thus, the special rule in § 1.401(a)(4)-4(d)(7) (treating the contingent event as having occurred) does not apply for purposes of this section. In the case of an unpredictable contingent event that is expected to result in the termination from employment of certain employees within a period of time consistent with the rules for defining an early retirement window benefit in paragraph (f)(4)(iii) of this section, the unpredictable contingent event benefit available to those employees is permitted to be treated as an early retirement window benefit, thus permitting the rules of paragraph (f)(4) of this section to be applied to it.

(ii) Example. The following example illustrates the rules of this paragraph (f)(5):

*Example.* (a) Employer X operates various manufacturing plants and maintains Plan A, a defined benefit plan that covers all of its nonexcludable employees. Plan A provides an early retirement benefit under which employees who retire after age 55 but before normal retirement age and who have at least 10 years of service receive a benefit equal to their normal retirement benefit reduced by four percent per year for each year prior to normal retirement age. Plan A also provides a plant-closing benefit under which employees who satisfy the conditions for receiving the early retirement benefit and who work at a plant where operations have ceased and whose employment has been terminated will receive an unreduced normal retirement benefit. The plant-closing benefit is an unpredictable contingent event benefit.

(b) During the 1997 plan year, Employer X had no plant closings. Therefore, the plant-closing benefit is not taken into account for the 1997 plan year in determining accrual rates or in applying the safe harbors in paragraph (b) of this section.

(c) During the 1998 plan year, Employer X begins to close one plant. Employees M through Z, who are employees at the plant that is closing, are expected to terminate employment with Employer X during the plan year and will satisfy the conditions for the plant-closing benefit. Therefore, in testing Plan A under this section for the 1998 plan year, the availability of the plant-closing benefit to Employees M through Z must be taken into account in determining their accrual rates or in determining whether the plan satisfies one of the safe harbors under paragraph (b) of this section.

(d) Because the employees eligible for the unpredictable contingent event benefit are expected to terminate employment with Employer X during a period consistent with the rules for defining an early retirement window benefit, in testing Plan A under this section for the 1998 plan year, the special rules in paragraph (f)(4)(ii) of this section may be applied. Thus, for example, normal accrual rates may be determined without reference to the unpredictable contingent event benefit.

(e) Despite the closing of the plant, Employee Q remains an employee into the 1999 plan year. Under paragraph (f)(4)(ii)(A) of this section, the availability of the plant-closing benefit to Employee Q may be disregarded in the 1999 plan year.

*(6) Determination of benefits on other than plan-year basis.* For purposes of this section, accruals are generally determined based on the plan year. Nevertheless, an employer may determine accruals on the basis of any period ending within the plan year as long as the period is at least 12 months in duration. For example, accruals for all employees may be determined based on accrual computation periods ending within the plan year.

*(7) Adjustments for certain plan distributions.* For purposes of this section, an employee's accrued benefit includes the actuarial equivalent of prior distributions of accrued benefits from the plan to the employee if the years of service taken into account in determining the accrued benefits that were distributed continue to be taken into account under the plan for purposes of determining the employee's current accrued benefit. For purposes of this paragraph (f)(7), actuarial equivalence must be determined in a uniform manner for all employees using reasonable actuarial assumptions. A standard interest rate and a standard mortality table are among the assumptions considered reasonable for this purpose. Thus, for example, if an employee has commenced receipt of benefits in accordance with the minimum distribution requirements of section 401(a)(9), and the plan reduces the employee's accrued benefit to take into account the amount of the distributions, the employee's accrued benefit for purposes of this section is restored to the value it would have had if the distributions had not occurred.

*(8) Adjustment for certain QPSA charges.* For purposes of this section, an employee's accrued benefit includes the cost of a qualified preretirement survivor annuity (QPSA) that reduces the employee's accrued benefit otherwise determined under the plan, as permitted under § 1.401(a)-20, Q&A-21. Thus, an employee's accrued benefit for purposes of this section is determined as if the cost of the QPSA had not been charged against the accrued benefit. This paragraph (f)(8) applies only if the QPSA charges apply uniformly to all employees.

*(9) Disregard of certain offsets.* (i) General rule. For purposes of this section, an employee's accrued benefit under a plan includes that portion of the benefit that is offset under an offset provision described in § 1.401(a)(4)-11(d)(3)(i)(D). The rule in the preceding sentence applies only to the extent that the benefit by which the benefit under the plan being tested is offset is attributable to periods for which the plan being tested credits pre-participation service (within the meaning of § 1.401(a)(4)-11(d)(3)(ii)(A)) that satisfies § 1.401(a)(4)-11(d)(3)(iii) or past service (within the meaning of § 1.401(a)(4)-11(d)(3)(i)(B)), and only if—

(A) The benefit under the plan being tested is offset by either—

(1) Benefits under a qualified defined benefit plan or defined contribution plan (whether or not terminated); or

(2) Benefits under a foreign plan that are reasonably expected to be paid; and,

(B) If any portion of the benefit that is offset is nonforfeitable (within the meaning of section 411), that portion is offset by a benefit (or portion of a benefit) that is also nonforfeitable (or vested, in the case of a foreign plan).

(ii) Examples. The following examples illustrate the rules in this paragraph (f)(9):

*Example (1).* (a) Employer X maintains two qualified defined benefit plans, Plan A and Plan B. Plan B provides that, whenever an employee transfers to Plan B from Plan A, the service that was credited under Plan A is credited in determining benefits under Plan B. The Plan A service credited under Plan B is pre-participation service that satisfies § 1.401(a)(4)-11(d)(3)(iii). Plan B offsets the benefits determined under Plan B by the employee's vested benefits under Plan A. Plan A does not credit additional benefit service or accrual service after employees transfer to Plan B.

(b) The Plan B provision providing for an offset of benefits under Plan A satisfies § 1.401(a)(4)-11(d)(3)(i)(D). This is because the provision applies to similarly-situated employees and the benefits under Plan A that are offset against the Plan B benefits are attributable to pre-participation service taken into account under Plan B.

(c) This paragraph (f)(9) applies in determining the benefits that are taken into account under this section for employees in Plan B who are transferred from Plan A. This is because the offset provision is described in § 1.401(a)(4)-11(d)(3)(i)(D), the benefits under the other plan by which the benefits under the plan being tested are offset are attributable solely to pre-participation service that satisfies § 1.401(a)(4)-11(d)(3)(iii), and the benefits are offset solely by vested benefits under another qualified plan. Thus, for example, the accrual rates of employees in Plan B are determined as if there were no offset, i.e., by adding back the benefits that are offset to the net benefits under Plan B.

(d) The result would be the same even if Plan A continued to recognize compensation paid after the transfer in the determination of benefits under Plan A. However, if Plan A continued to credit benefit or accrual service after the transfer, then, to the extent that Plan B's offset of benefits under Plan A increased as a result, the additional benefits offset under Plan B would not be added back in determining the benefits under Plan B that are taken into account under this section.

*Example (2).* The facts are the same as in Example 1, except that Plan A is not a plan described in paragraph (f)(9)(i)(A) of this section. None of the benefits under Plan B that are offset by benefits under Plan A may be added back in determining the benefits under Plan B that are taken into account under this section. Thus, benefits under Plan B are tested on a net basis.

*(10) Special rule for multiemployer plans.* For purposes of this section, if a multiemployer plan increases benefits for service prior to a specific date subject to a plan provision requiring employees to complete a specified amount of service (not to exceed five years) after that date, then benefits are permitted to be determined disregarding the service condition, provided that the condition is applicable to all employees in the multiemployer plan (including collectively bargained employees).

---

T.D. 8360, 9/12/91, amend T.D. 8485, 8/30/93.

---

## § 1.401(a)(4)-4 Nondiscriminatory availability of benefits, rights, and features.

***Caution:*** The Treasury has not yet amended Reg § 1.401(a)(4)-4 to reflect changes made by P.L. 105-34, P.L. 104-188.

**(a) Introduction.** This section provides rules for determining whether the benefits, rights, and features provided under a plan (i.e., all optional forms of benefit, ancillary benefits, and other rights and features available to any employee under the plan) are made available in a nondiscriminatory manner. Benefits, rights, and features provided under a plan are made available to employees in a nondiscriminatory manner only if each benefit, right, or feature satisfies the current availability requirement of paragraph (b) of this section and the effective availability requirement of paragraph (c) of this section. Paragraph (d) of this section provides special rules for applying these requirements. Paragraph (e) of this section defines optional form of benefit, ancillary benefit, and other right or feature.

**(b) Current availability.** *(1) General rule.* The current availability requirement of this paragraph (b) is satisfied if the group of employees to whom a benefit, right, or feature is currently available during the plan year satisfies section 410(b) (without regard to the average benefit percentage test of § 1.410(b)-5). In determining whether the group of employees satisfies section 410(b), an employee is treated as benefiting only if the benefit, right, or feature is currently available to the employee.

*(2) Determination of current availability.* (i) General rule. Whether a benefit, right, or feature that is subject to specified eligibility conditions is currently available to an employee generally is determined based on the current facts and circumstances with respect to the employee (e.g., current compensation, accrued benefit, position, or net worth).

(ii) Certain conditions disregarded. (A) Certain age and service conditions. (1) General rule. Notwithstanding paragraph (b)(2)(i) of this section, any specified age or service condition with respect to an optional form of benefit or a social security supplement is disregarded in determining whether the optional form of benefit or the social security supplement is currently available to an employee. Thus, for example, an optional form of benefit that is available to all employees who terminate employment on or after age 55 with at least 10 years of service is treated as currently available to an employee, without regard to the employee's current age or years of service, and without regard to whether the employee could potentially meet the age and service conditions prior to attaining the plan's normal retirement age.

(2) Time-limited age or service conditions not disregarded. Notwithstanding paragraph (b)(2)(ii)(A)(1) of this section, an age or service condition is not disregarded in determining the current availability of an optional form of benefit or social security supplement if the condition must be satisfied within a limited period of time. However, in determining the current availability of an optional form of benefit or a social security supplement subject to such an age or service condition, the age and service of employees may be projected to the last date by which the age condition or service condition must be satisfied in order to he eligible for the optional form of benefit or social security supplement under the plan. Thus, for example, an optional form of benefit that is available only to employees who terminate employment between July 1, 1995, and December 31, 1995, after attainment of age 55 with at least 10 years of service is treated as currently available to an employee only if the employee could satisfy those age and service conditions by December 31, 1995.

(B) Certain other conditions. Specified conditions on the availability of a benefit, right, or feature requiring a specified percentage of the employee's accrued benefit to be nonforfeitable, termination of employment, death, satisfaction of a specified health condition (or failure to meet such condition), disability, hardship, family status, default on a plan loan secured by a participant's account balance, execution of a covenant not to compete, application for benefits or similar ministerial or mechanical acts, election of a benefit form, execution of a waiver of rights under the Age Discrimination in Employment Act or other federal or state law, or absence from service, are disregarded in determining the employees to whom the benefit, right, or feature is currently available. In addition, if a multiemployer plan includes a reasonable condition that limits eligibility for an ancillary benefit, or other right or feature, to those employees who have recent service under the plan (e.g., a condition on a death benefit that requires an employee to have a minimum number of hours credited during the last two years) and the condition applies to all employees in the multiemployer plan (including the collectively bargained employees) to whom the ancillary benefit, or other right or feature, is otherwise currently available, then the condition is disregarded in determining the employees to whom the ancillary benefit, or other right or feature, is currently available.

(C) Certain conditions relating to mandatory cash-outs. In the case of a plan that provides for mandatory cash-outs of all terminated employees who have a vested accrued benefit with an actuarial present value less than or equal to a specified dollar amount (not to exceed the cash-out limit in effect under § 1.411(a)-11(c)(3)(ii)) as permitted by sections 411(a)(11) and 417(e), the implicit condition on any benefit, right, or feature (other than the mandatory cash-out) that requires the employee to have a vested accrued benefit with an actuarial present value in excess of the specified dollar amount is disregarded in determining the employees to whom the benefit, right, or feature is currently available.

(D) Other dollar limits. A condition that the amount of an employee's vested accrued benefit or the actuarial present value of that benefit be less than or equal to a specified dollar amount is disregarded in determining the employees to whom the benefit, right, or feature is currently available.

(E) Certain conditions on plan loans. In the case of an employee's right to a loan from the plan, the condition that an employee must have an account balance sufficient to be eligible to receive a minimum loan amount specified in the plan (not to exceed $1,000) is disregarded in determining the employees to whom the right is currently available.

*(3) Benefits, rights, and features that are eliminated prospectively.* (i) Special testing rule. Notwithstanding paragraph (b)(1) of this section, a benefit, right, or feature that is eliminated with respect to benefits accrued after the later of the eliminating amendment's adoption or effective date (the elimination date), but is retained with respect to benefits accrued as of the elimination date, and that satisfies this paragraph (b) as of the elimination date, is treated as satisfying this paragraph (b) for all subsequent periods. This rule does not apply if the terms of the benefit, right, or feature (including the employees to whom it is available) are changed after the elimination date.

(ii) Elimination of a benefit, right, or feature. (A) General rule. For purposes of this paragraph (b)(3), a benefit, right, or feature provided to an employee is eliminated with respect to benefits accrued after the elimination date if the amount or value of the benefit, right, or feature depends solely on the amount of the employee's accrued benefit (within the meaning of section 411(a)(7)) as of the elimination date, including subsequent income, expenses, gains, and losses with respect to that benefit in the case of a defined contribution plan.

(B) Special rule for benefits, rights, and features that are not section 411(d)(6)-protected benefits. Notwithstanding paragraph (b)(3)(ii)(A) of this section, in the case of a benefit, right, or feature under a defined contribution plan that is not a section 411(d)(6)-protected benefit (within the meaning of § 1.411(d)-4, Q&A-1), e.g., the availability of plan loans, for purposes of this paragraph (b)(3)(ii) each employee's accrued benefit as of the elimination date may be treated, on a uniform basis, as consisting exclusively of the dollar amount of the employee's account balance as of the elimination date.

(C) Special rule for benefits, rights, and features that depend on adjusted accrued benefits. For purposes of this paragraph (b)(3), a benefit, right, or feature provided to an employee under a plan that has made a fresh start does not fail to be eliminated as of an elimination date that is the fresh-start date merely because it depends solely on the amount of the employee's adjusted accrued benefit (within the meaning of § 1.401(a)(4)-13(d)(8)).

**(c) Effective availability.** *(1) General rule.* Based on all of the relevant facts and circumstances, the group of employees to whom a benefit, right, or feature is effectively available must not substantially favor HCEs.

*(2) Examples.* The following examples illustrate the rules of this paragraph (c):

*Example (1).* Employer X maintains Plan A, a defined benefit plan that covers both of its highly compensated nonexcludable employees and nine of its 12 nonhighly compensated nonexcludable employees. Plan A provides for a normal retirement benefit payable as an annuity and based on a normal retirement age of 65, and an early retirement benefit payable upon termination in the form of an annuity to employees who terminate from service with the employer on or after age 55 with 30 or more years of service. Both HCEs of Employer X currently meet the age and service requirement, or will have 30 years of service by the time they reach age 55. All but two of the nine NHCEs of Employer X who are covered by Plan A were hired on or after age 35 and, thus, cannot qualify for the early retirement benefit. Even though the group of employees to whom the early retirement benefit is currently available satisfies the ratio percentage test of § 1.410(b)-2(b)(2) when age and service are disregarded pursuant to paragraph (b)(2)(ii)(A) of this section, absent other facts, the group of employees to whom the early retirement benefit is effectively available substantially favors HCEs.

*Example (2).* Employer Y maintains Plan B, a defined benefit plan that provides for a normal retirement benefit payable as an annuity and based on a normal retirement age of 65. By a plan amendment first adopted and effective December 1, 1998, Employer Y amends Plan B to provide an early retirement benefit that is available only to employees who terminate employment by December 15, 1998, and who are at least age 55 with 30 or more years of service. Assume that all employees were hired prior to attaining age 25 and that the group of employees who have, or will have, attained age 55 with 30 years of service by December 15, 1998, satisfies the ratio percentage test of § 1.410(b)-2(b)(2). Assume, further, that the employer takes no steps to inform all eligible employees of the early retirement option on a timely basis and that the only employees who terminate from employment with the employer during the two-week period in which the early retirement benefit is available are HCEs. Under these facts, the group of employees to whom this early retirement window benefit is effectively available substantially favors HCEs.

*Example (3).* Employer Z amends Plan C on June 30, 1999, to provide for a single sum optional form of benefit for employees who terminate from employment with Employer Z after June 30, 1999, and before January 1, 2000. The availability of this single sum optional form of benefit is conditioned on the employee's having a particular disability at the time of termination of employment. The only employee of the employer who meets this disability requirement at the time of the amendment and thereafter through December 31, 1999, is a HCE. Under paragraph (b)(2)(ii)(B) of this section, the disability condition is disregarded in determining the current availability of the single sum optional form of benefit. Nevertheless, under these facts, the group of employees to whom the single sum optional form of benefit is effectively available substantially favors HCEs.

**(d) Special rules.** *(1) Mergers and acquisitions.* (i) Special testing rule. A benefit, right, or feature available under a plan solely to an acquired group of employees is treated as satisfying paragraphs (b) and (c) of this section during the period that each of the following requirements is satisfied:

(A) The benefit, right, or feature must satisfy paragraphs (b) and (c) of this section (determined without regard to the special rule in section 410(b)(6)(C)) on the date that is selected by the employer as the latest date by which an employee must be hired or transferred into the acquired trade or business for an employee to be included in the acquired group of employees. This determination is made with reference to the plan of the current employer and its nonexcludable employees.

(B) The benefit, right, or feature must be available under the plan of the current employer after the transaction on the same terms as it was available under the plan of the prior employer before the transaction. This requirement is not violated merely because of a change made to the benefit, right, or feature that is permitted by section 411(d)(6), provided that—

(1) The change is a replacement of the benefit, right, or feature with another benefit, right, or feature that is available to the same employees as the original benefit, right, or feature, and the original benefit, right, or feature is of inherently equal or greater value (within the meaning of paragraph (d)(4)(i)(A) of this section) than the benefit, right, or feature that replaces it; or

(2) The change is made before January 12, 1993.

(ii) Scope of special testing rule. This paragraph (d)(1) applies only to benefits, rights, and features with respect to benefits accruing under the plan of the current employer, and not to benefits, rights, and features with respect to benefits accrued under the plan of the prior employer (unless, pursuant to the transaction, the plan of the prior employer becomes the plan of the current employer, or the assets and liabilities with respect to the acquired group of employees under the plan of the prior employer are transferred to the plan of the current employer in a plan merger, consolidation, or other transfer described in section 414(l)).

(iii) Example. The following example illustrates the rules of this paragraph (d)(1):

*Example.* Employer X maintains Plan A, a defined benefit plan with a single sum optional form of benefit for all employees. Employer Y acquires Employer X and merges Plan A into Plan B, a defined benefit plan maintained by Employer Y that does not otherwise provide a single sum optional form of benefit. Employer Y continues to provide the single sum optional form of benefit under Plan B on the same terms as it was offered under Plan A to all employees who were acquired in the transaction with Employer X (and to no other employees). The optional form of benefit satisfies paragraphs (b) and (c) of this section immediately following the transaction (determined without taking into account section 410(b)(6)(C)) when tested with reference to Plan B and Employer Y's nonexcludable employees. Under these facts, Plan B is treated as satisfying this section with respect to the single sum optional form of benefit for the plan year of the transaction and all subsequent plan years.

*(2) Frozen participants.* A plan must satisfy the nondiscriminatory availability requirement of this section not only with respect to benefits, rights, and features provided to employees who are currently benefiting under the plan, but also separately with respect to benefits, rights, and features provided to nonexcludable employees with accrued benefits who are not currently benefiting under the plan (frozen participants). Thus, each benefit, right, and feature available to any frozen participant under the plan is separately subject to the requirements of this section. A plan satisfies paragraphs (b) and (c) of this section with respect to a benefit, right, or feature available to any frozen participant under the plan only if one or more of the following requirements is satisfied:

(i) The benefit, right, or feature must be one that would satisfy paragraphs (b) and (c) of this section if it were not available to any employee currently benefiting under the plan.

(ii) The benefit, right, or feature must be one that would satisfy paragraphs (b) and (c) of this section if all frozen participants were treated as employees currently benefiting under the plan.

(iii) No change in the availability of the benefit, right, or feature may have been made that is first effective in the current plan year with respect to a frozen participant.

(iv) Any change in the availability of the benefit, right, or feature that is first effective in the current plan year with respect to a frozen participant must be made in a nondiscriminatory manner. Thus, any expansion in the availability of the benefit, right, or feature to any highly compensated frozen participant must be applied on a consistent basis to all nonhighly compensated frozen participants. Similarly, any contraction in the availability of the benefit, right, or feature that affects any nonhighly compensated frozen participant must be applied on a consistent basis to all highly compensated frozen participants.

*(3) Early retirement window benefits.* If a benefit, right, or feature meets the definition of an early retirement window benefit in § 1.401(a)(4)-3(f)(4)(iii) (or would meet that definition if the definition applied to all benefits, rights, and features), the benefit, right, or feature is disregarded for purposes of applying this section with respect to an employee for all plan years other than the first plan year in which the benefit is currently available to the employee.

*(4) Permissive aggregation of certain benefits, rights, or features.* (i) General rule. An optional form of benefit, ancillary benefit, or other right or feature may be aggregated with another optional form of benefit, ancillary benefit, or other right or feature, respectively, and the two may be treated as a single optional form of benefit, ancillary benefit, or other right or feature, if both of the following requirements are satisfied:

(A) One of the two optional forms of benefit, ancillary benefit, or other rights or features must in all cases be of inherently equal or greater value than the other. For this purpose, one benefit, right, or feature is of inherently equal or greater value than another benefit, right, or feature only if, at any time and under any conditions, it is impossible for any employee to receive a smaller amount or a less valuable right under the first benefit, right, or feature than under the second benefit, right, or feature.

(B) The optional form of benefit, ancillary benefit, or other right or feature of inherently equal or greater value must separately satisfy paragraphs (b) and (c) of this section (without regard to this paragraph (d)(4)).

(ii) Aggregation may be applied more than once. The aggregation rule in this paragraph (d)(4) may be applied more than once. Thus, for example, an optional form of benefit may be aggregated with another optional form of benefit that itself constitutes two separate optional forms of benefit that are aggregated and treated as a single optional form of benefit under this paragraph (d)(4).

(iii) Examples. The following examples illustrate the rules in this paragraph (d)(4):

*Example (1).* Plan A is a defined benefit plan that provides a single sum optional form of benefit to all employees. The single sum optional form of benefit is available on the same terms to all employees, except that, for employees in Division S, a five-percent discount factor is applied and, for employees of Division T, a seven-percent discount factor is applied. Under paragraph (e)(1) of this section, the single sum optional form of benefit constitutes two separate optional forms of benefit. Assume that the single sum optional form of benefit available to employees of Division S separately satisfies paragraphs (b) and (c) of this section without taking into account this paragraph (d)(4). Because a lower discount factor is applied in determining the single sum optional form of benefit available to employees of Division S than is applied in determining the single sum optional form of benefit available to employees of Division T, the first single sum optional form of benefit is of inherently greater value than the second single sum optional form of benefit. Under these facts, these two single sum optional forms of benefit may be aggregated and treated as a single optional form of benefit for purposes of this section.

*Example (2).* The facts are the same as in Example 1, except that, in order to receive the single sum optional form of benefit, employees of Division S (but not employees of Division T) must have completed at least 20 years of service. The single sum optional form of benefit available to employees of Division S is not of inherently equal or greater value than the single sum optional form of benefit available to employees of Division T, because an employee of Division S who terminates employment with less than 20 years of service would receive a smaller single sum amount (i.e., zero) than a similarly-situated employee of Division T who terminates employment with less than 20 years of service. Under these facts, the two single sum optional forms of benefit may not be aggregated and treated as a single optional form of benefit for purposes of this section.

*(5) Certain spousal benefits.* In the case of a plan that includes two or more plans that have been permissively aggregated under § 1.410(b)-7(d), the aggregated plan satisfies this section with respect to the availability of any nonsubsidized qualified joint and survivor annuities, qualified preretirement survivor annuities, or spousal death benefits described in section 401(a)(11), if each plan that is part of the aggregated plan satisfies section 401(a)(11). Whether a benefit is considered subsidized for this purpose may be determined using any reasonable actuarial assumptions. For purposes of this paragraph (d)(5), a qualified joint and survivor annuity, qualified preretirement survivor annuity, or spousal death benefit is deemed to be nonsubsidized if it is provided under a defined contribution plan.

*(6) Special ESOP rules.* An ESOP does not fail to satisfy paragraphs (b) and (c) of this section merely because it makes an investment diversification right or feature or a distribution option available solely to all qualified participants (within the meaning of section 401(a)(28)(B)(iii)), or merely because the restrictions of section 409(n) apply to certain individuals.

*(7) Special testing rule for unpredictable contingent event benefits.* A benefit, right, or feature that is contingent on the occurrence of an unpredictable contingent event (within the meaning of section 412(l)(7)(B)(ii)) is tested under this section as if the event had occurred. Thus, the current availability of a benefit that becomes an optional form of benefit upon the occurrence of an unpredictable contingent event is tested by deeming the event to have occurred and by disregarding age and service conditions on the eligibility for that benefit to the extent permitted for optional forms of benefit under paragraph (b)(2) of this section.

**(e) Definitions.** *(1) Optional form of benefit.* (i) General rule. The term optional form of benefit means a distribution alternative (including the normal form of benefit) that is available under a plan with respect to benefits described in section 411(d)(6)(A) or a distribution alternative that is an early retirement benefit or retirement-type subsidy described in section 411(d)(6)(B)(i), including a QSUPP. Except as provided in paragraph (e)(1)(ii) of this section, different optional forms of benefit exist if a distribution alternative is not payable on substantially the same terms as another distribution alternative. The relevant terms include all terms affecting the value of the optional form, such as the method of benefit calculation and the actuarial assumptions used to determine the amount distributed. Thus, for example, different optional forms of benefit may result from differences in terms relating to the payment schedule, timing, commencement, medium of distribution (e.g., in cash or in kind), election rights, differences in eligibility requirements, or the portion of the benefit to which the distribution alternative applies.

(ii) Exceptions. (A) Differences in benefit formula or accrual method. A distribution alternative available under a defined benefit plan does not fail to be a single optional form of benefit merely because the benefit formulas, accrual methods, or other factors (including service-computation methods and definitions of compensation) underlying, or the manner in which employees vest in, the accrued benefit that is paid in the form of the distribution alternative are different for different employees to whom the distribution alternative is available. Notwithstanding the foregoing, differences in the normal retirement ages of employees or in the form in which the accrued benefit of employees is payable at normal retirement age under a plan are taken into account in determining whether a distribution alternative constitutes one or more optional forms of benefit.

(B) Differences in allocation formula. A distribution alternative available under a defined contribution plan does not fail to be a single optional form of benefit merely because the allocation formula or other factors (including service-computation methods, definitions of compensation, and the manner in which amounts described in § 1.401(a)(4)-2(c)(2)(iii) are allocated) underlying, or the manner in which employees vest in, the accrued benefit that is paid in the form of the distribution alternative are different for different employees to whom the distribution alternative is available.

(C) Distributions subject to section 417(e). A distribution alternative available under a defined benefit plan does not fail to be a single optional form of benefit merely because, in determining the amount of a distribution, the plan applies a lower interest rate to determine the distribution for employees with a vested accrued benefit having an actuarial present value not in excess of $25,000, as required by section 417(e)(3) and § 1.417(e)-1.

(D) Differences attributable to uniform normal retirement age. A distribution alternative available under a defined benefit plan does not fail to be a single optional form of benefit, to the extent that the differences are attributable to differences in normal retirement dates among employees, provided that the differences do not prevent the employees from having the same uniform normal retirement age under the definition of uniform normal retirement age in § 1.401(a)(4)-12.

(iii) Examples. The following examples illustrate the rules in this paragraph (e)(1):

*Example (1).* Plan A is a defined benefit plan that benefits all employees of Divisions S and T. The plan offers a qualified joint and 50-percent survivor annuity at normal retirement age, calculated by multiplying an employee's single life annuity payment by a factor. For an employee of Division S whose benefit commences at age 65, the plan provides a factor of 0.90, but for a similarly-situated employee of Division T the plan provides a factor of 0.85. The qualified joint and survivor annuity is not available to employees of Divisions S and T on substantially the same terms, and thus it constitutes two separate optional forms of benefit.

*Example (2).* Plan B is a defined benefit plan that benefits all employees of Divisions U and V. The plan offers a single sum distribution alternative available on the same terms and determined using the same actuarial assumptions, to all employees. However, different benefit formulas apply to employees of each division. Under the exception provided in paragraph (e)(1)(ii)(A) of this section, the single sum optional form of benefit available to employees of Division U is not a separate optional form of benefit from the single sum optional form of benefit available to employees of Division V.

*Example (3).* Defined benefit Plan C provides an early retirement benefit based on a schedule of early retirement factors that is a single optional form of benefit. Plan C is amended to provide an early retirement window benefit that consists of a temporary change in the plan's benefit formula (e.g., the addition of five years of service to an employee's actual service under the benefit formula) applicable in determining the benefits for certain employees who terminate employment within a limited period of time. Under the exception provided in paragraph (e)(1)(ii)(A) of this section, the early retirement optional form of benefit available to window-eligible employees is not a separate optional form of benefit from the early retirement optional form of benefit available to the other employees.

*(2) Ancillary benefit.* The term ancillary benefit means social security supplements (other than QSUPPs), disability benefits not in excess of a qualified disability benefit described in section 411(a)(9), ancillary life insurance and health insurance benefits, death benefits under a defined contribution plan, preretirement death benefits under a defined benefit plan, shut-down benefits not protected under section 411(d)(6), and other similar benefits. Different ancillary benefits exist if an ancillary benefit is not available on substantially the same terms as another ancillary benefit. Principles similar to those in paragraph (e)(1)(ii) of this section apply in making this determination.

*(3) Other right or feature.* (i) General rule. The term other right or feature generally means any right or feature applicable to employees under the plan. Different rights or features exist if a right or feature is not available on substantially the same terms as another right or feature.

(ii) Exceptions to definition of other right or feature. Notwithstanding paragraph (e)(3)(i) of this section, a right or feature is not considered an other right or feature if it—

(A) Is an optional form of benefit or an ancillary benefit under the plan;

(B) Is one of the terms that are taken into account in determining whether separate optional forms of benefit or ancillary benefits exist, or that would be taken into account but for paragraph (e)(1)(ii) of this section (e.g., benefit formulas or the manner in which benefits vest); or

(C) Cannot reasonably be expected to be of meaningful value to an employee (e.g., administrative details).

(iii) Examples. Other rights and features include, but are not limited to—

(A) Plan loan provisions (other than those relating to a distribution of an employee's accrued benefit upon default under a loan);

(B) The right to direct investments;

(C) The right to a particular form of investment, including, for example, a particular class or type of employer securities (taking into account, in determining whether different forms of investment exist, any differences in conversion, dividend, voting, liquidation preference, or other rights conferred under the security);

(D) The right to make each rate of elective contributions described in § 1.401(k)-6 (determining the rate based on the plan's definition of the compensation out of which the elective contributions are made (regardless of whether that definition satisfies section 414(s)), but also treating different rates as existing if they are based on definitions of compensation or other requirements or formulas that are not substantially the same);

(E) The right to make after-tax employee contributions to a defined benefit plan that are not allocated to separate accounts;

(F) The right to make each rate of after-tax employee contributions described in § 1.401(m)-1(a)(3) (determining the rate based on the plan's definition of the compensation out of which the after-tax employee contributions are made (regardless of whether that definition satisfies section 414(s)), but also treating different rates as existing if they are based on definitions of compensation or other requirements or formulas that are not substantially the same);

(G) The right to each rate of allocation of matching contributions described in § 1.401(m)-1(a)(2) (determining the rate using the amount of matching, elective, and after-tax employee contributions determined after any corrections under §§ 1.401(k)-2(b)(1)(i), 1.401(m)-2(b)(1)(i), but also treating different rates as existing if they are based on definitions of compensation or other requirements or formulas that are not substantially the same);

(H) The right to purchase additional retirement or ancillary benefits under the plan; and

(I) The right to make rollover contributions and transfers to and from the plan.

---

T.D. 8360, 9/12/91, amend T.D. 8485, 8/30/93, T.D. 8794, 12/18/98, T.D. 8891, 7/18/2000, T.D. 9169, 12/28/2004.

---

**§ 1.401(a)(4)-5 Plan amendments and plan terminations.**

**(a) Introduction.** *(1) Overview.* This paragraph (a) provides rules for determining whether the timing of a plan amendment or series of amendments has the effect of discriminating significantly in favor of HCEs or former HCEs. For purposes of this section, a plan amendment includes, for example, the establishment or termination of the plan, and any change in the benefits, rights, or features, benefit formulas, or allocation formulas under the plan. Paragraph (b) of this section sets forth additional requirements that must be satisfied in the case of a plan termination.

*(2) Facts-and-circumstances determination.* Whether the timing of a plan amendment or series of plan amendments has the effect of discriminating significantly in favor of HCEs or former HCEs is determined at the time the plan amendment first becomes effective for purposes of section 401(a), based on all of the relevant facts and circumstances. These include, for example, the relative numbers of current and former HCEs and NHCEs affected by the plan amendment, the relative length of service of current and former HCEs and NHCEs, the length of time the plan or plan provision being amended has been in effect, and the turnover of employees prior to the plan amendment. In addition, the relevant facts and circumstances include the relative accrued benefits of current and former HCEs and NHCEs before and after the plan amendment and any additional benefits provided to current and former HCEs and NHCEs under other plans (including plans of other employers, if relevant). In the case of a plan amendment that provides additional benefits based on an employee's service prior to the amendment, the relevant facts and circumstances also include the benefits that employees and former employees who do not benefit under the amendment would have received had the plan, as amended, been in effect throughout the period on which the additional benefits are based.

*(3) Safe harbor for certain grants of benefits for past periods.* The timing of a plan amendment that credits (or increases benefits attributable to) years of service for a period in the past is deemed not to have the effect of discriminating significantly in favor of HCEs or former HCEs if the period for which the service credit (or benefit increase) is granted does not exceed the five years immediately preceding the year in which the amendment first becomes effective, the service credit (or benefit increase) is granted on a reasonably uniform basis to all employees, benefits attributable to the period are determined by applying the current plan formula, and the service credited is service (including pre-participation or imputed service) with the employer or a previous employer that may be taken into account under § 1.401(a)(4)-11(d)(3) (without regard to § 1.401(a)(4)-11(d)(3)(i)(B)). However, this safe harbor is not available if the plan amendment granting the service credit (or increasing benefits) is part of a pattern of amendments that has the effect of discriminating significantly in favor of HCEs or former HCEs.

*(4) Examples.* The following examples illustrate the rules in this paragraph (a):

*Example (1).* Plan A is a defined benefit plan that covered both HCEs and NHCEs for most of its existence. The employer decides to wind up its business. In the process of ceasing operations, but at a time when the plan covers only HCEs, Plan A is amended to increase benefits and thereafter is terminated. The timing of this plan amendment has the effect of discriminating significantly in favor of HCEs.

*Example (2).* Plan B is a defined benefit plan that provides a social security supplement that is not a QSUPP. After substantially all of the HCEs of the employer have benefited from the supplement, but before a substantial number of NHCEs have become eligible for the supplement, Plan B is amended to reduce significantly the amount of the supplement. The timing of this plan amendment has the effect of discriminating significantly in favor of HCEs.

*Example (3).* Plan C is a defined benefit plan that contains an ancillary life insurance benefit available to all employees. The plan is amended to eliminate this benefit at a time when life insurance payments have been made only to beneficiaries of HCEs. Because all employees received the benefit of life insurance coverage before Plan C was amended, the timing of this plan amendment does not have the effect of discriminating significantly in favor of HCEs or former HCEs.

*Example (4).* Plan D provides for a benefit of one percent of average annual compensation per year of service. Ten years after Plan D is adopted, it is amended to provide a benefit of two percent of average annual compensation per year of service, including years of service prior to the amendment. The amendment is effective only for employees currently employed at the time of the amendment. The ratio of HCEs to former HCEs is significantly higher than the ratio of NHCEs to former NHCEs. In the absence of any additional factors, the timing of this plan amendment has the effect of discriminating significantly in favor of HCEs.

*Example (5).* The facts are the same as in Example 4, except that, in addition, the years of prior service are equivalent between HCEs and NHCEs who are current employees, and the group of current employees with prior service would satisfy the nondiscriminatory classification test of § 1.410(b)-4 in the current and all prior plan years for which past service credit is granted. The timing of this plan amendment does not have the effect of discriminating significantly in favor of HCEs or former HCEs.

*Example (6).* Employer V maintains Plan E, an accumulation plan. In 1994, Employer V amends Plan E to provide that the compensation used to determine an employee's benefit for all preceding plan years shall not be less than the employee's average annual compensation as of the close of the 1994 plan year. The years of service and percentage increases in compensation for HCEs are reasonably comparable to those of NHCEs. In addition, the ratio of HCEs to former HCEs is reasonably comparable to the ratio of NHCEs to former NHCEs. The timing of this plan amendment does not have the effect of discriminating significantly in favor of HCEs or former HCEs.

*Example (7).* Employer W currently has six nonexcludable employees, two of whom, H1 and H2, are HCEs, and the remaining four of whom, N1 through N4, are NHCEs. The ratio of HCEs to former HCEs is significantly higher than the ratio of NHCEs to former NHCEs. Employer W establishes Plan F, a defined benefit plan providing a benefit of one percent of average annual compensation per year of service, including years of service prior to the establishment of the plan. H1 and H2 each have 15 years of prior service, N1 has nine years of past service, N2 has five years, N3 has three years, and N4 has one year. The timing of this plan establishment has the effect of discriminating significantly in favor of HCEs.

*Example (8).* Assume the same facts as in Example 7, except that N1 through N4 were hired in the current year, and Employer W never employed any NHCEs prior to the current year. Thus, no NHCEs would have received additional benefits had Plan F been in existence during the preceding

15 years. The timing of this plan establishment does not have the effect of discriminating significantly in favor of HCEs or former HCEs.

*Example (9).* The facts are the same as in Example 7, except that Plan F limits the grant of past service credit to five years, and the grant of past service otherwise satisfies the safe harbor in paragraph (a)(3) of this section. The timing of this plan establishment is deemed not to have the effect of discriminating significantly in favor of HCEs or former HCEs.

*Example (10).* The facts are the same as in Example 9, except that, five years after the establishment of Plan F, Employer W amends the plan to provide a benefit equal to two percent of average annual compensation per year of service, taking into account all years of service since the establishment of the plan. The ratio of HCEs to former HCEs who terminated employment during the five-year period since the establishment of the plan is significantly higher than the ratio of NHCEs to former NHCEs who terminated employment during the five-year period since the establishment of the plan. Although the amendment described in this example might separately satisfy the safe harbor in paragraph (a)(3) of this section, the safe harbor is not available with respect to the amendment because, under these facts, the amendment is part of a pattern of amendments that has the effect of discriminating significantly in favor of HCEs.

*Example (11).* Employer Y maintains Plan G, a defined benefit plan, covering all its employees. In 1995, Employer Y acquires Division S from Employer Z. Some of the employees of Division S had been covered under a defined benefit plan maintained by Employer Z. Soon after the acquisition, Employer Y amends Plan G to cover all employees of Division S and to credit those who were in Division S's defined benefit plan with years of service for years of employment with Employer Z. Because the timing of the plan amendment was determined by the timing of the transaction, the timing of this plan amendment does not have the effect of discriminating significantly in favor of HCEs or former HCEs. See also § 1.401(a)(4)-11(d)(3) for other rules regarding the crediting of pre-participation service.

*Example (12).* Plan H is an insurance contract plan within the meaning of section 412(i). For all plan years before 1999, Plan H purchases insurance contracts from Insurance Company J. In 1999, Plan H shifts future purchases of insurance contracts to Insurance Company K. The shift in insurance companies is a plan amendment subject to this paragraph (a).

**(b) Pre-termination restrictions.** *(1) Required provisions in defined benefit plans.* A defined benefit plan has the effect of discriminating significantly in favor of HCEs or former HCEs unless it incorporates provisions restricting benefits and distributions as described in paragraph (b)(2) and (3) of this section at the time the plan is established or, if later, as of the first plan year to which §§ 1.401(a)(4)-1 through 1.401(a)(4)-13 apply to the plan under § 1.401(a)(4)-13(a) or (b). This paragraph (b) does not apply if the Commissioner determines that such provisions are not necessary to prevent the prohibited discrimination that may occur in the event of an early termination of the plan. The restrictions in this paragraph (b) apply to a plan within the meaning of § 1.410(b)-7(b) (i.e., a section 414(l) plan). Any plan containing a provision described in this paragraph (b) satisfies section 411(d)(2) and does not fail to satisfy section 411(a) or (d)(3) merely because of the provision.

*(2) Restriction of benefits upon plan termination.* A plan must provide that, in the event of plan termination, the benefit of any HCE (and any former HCE) is limited to a benefit that is nondiscriminatory under section 401(a)(4).

*(3) Restrictions on distributions.* (i) General rule. A plan must provide that, in any year, the payment of benefits to or on behalf of a restricted employee shall not exceed an amount equal to the payments that would be made to or on behalf of the restricted employee in that year under—

(A) A straight life annuity that is the actuarial equivalent of the accrued benefit and other benefits to which the restricted employee is entitled under the plan (other than a social security supplement); and

(B) A social security supplement, if any, that the restricted employee is entitled to receive.

(ii) Restricted employee defined. For purposes of this paragraph (b), the term restricted employee generally means any HCE or former HCE. However, an HCE or former HCE need not be treated as a restricted employee in the current year if the HCE or former HCE is not one of the 25 (or a larger number chosen by the employer) nonexcludable employees and former employees of the employer with the largest amount of compensation in the current or any prior year. Plan provisions defining or altering this group can be amended at any time without violating section 411(d)(6).

(iii) Benefit defined. For purposes of this paragraph (b), the term benefit includes, among other benefits, loans in excess of the amounts set forth in section 72(p)(2)(A), any periodic income, any withdrawal values payable to a living employee or former employee, and any death benefits not provided for by insurance on the employee's or former employee's life.

(iv) Nonapplicability in certain cases. The restrictions in this paragraph (b)(3) do not apply, however, if any one of the following requirements is satisfied:

(A) After taking into account payment to or on behalf of the restricted employee of all benefits payable to or on behalf of that restricted employee under the plan, the value of plan assets must equal or exceed 110 percent of the value of current liabilities, as defined in section 412(l)(7).

(B) The value of the benefits payable to or on behalf of the restricted employee must be less than one percent of the value of current liabilities before distribution.

(C) The value of the benefits payable to or on behalf of the restricted employee must not exceed the amount described in section 411(a)(11)(A) (restrictions on certain mandatory distributions).

(v) Determination of current liabilities. For purposes of this paragraph (b), any reasonable and consistent method may be used for determining the value of current liabilities and the value of plan assets.

*(4) Operational restrictions on certain money purchase pension plans.* A money purchase pension plan that has an accumulated funding deficiency, within the meaning of section 412(a), or an unamortized funding waiver, within the meaning of section 412(d), must comply in operation with the restrictions on benefits and distributions as described in paragraphs (b)(2) and (b)(3) of this section. Such a plan does not fail to satisfy section 411(d)(6) merely because of restrictions imposed by the requirements of this paragraph (b)(4).

---

T.D. 8360, 9/12/91, amend T.D. 8485, 8/30/93.

---

## § 1.401(a)(4)-6 Contributory defined benefit plans.

**(a) Introduction.** This section provides rules necessary for determining whether a contributory DB plan satisfies the nondiscriminatory amount requirement of § 1.401(a)(4)-1(b)(2). Paragraph (b) of this section provides rules for determining the amount of benefits derived from employer contributions (employer-provided benefits) under a contributory DB plan for purposes of determining whether the plan satisfies § 1.401(a)(4)-1(b)(2) with respect to such amounts. Paragraph (c) of this section provides the exclusive rules for determining whether a contributory DB plan satisfies § 1.401(a)(4)-1(b)(2) with respect to the amount of benefits derived from employee contributions not allocated to separate accounts (employee-provided benefits). See § 1.401(a)(4)-1(b)(2)(ii)(B) for the exclusive tests applicable to employee contributions allocated to separate accounts under a section 401(m) plan.

**(b) Determination of employer-provided benefit.** *(1) General rule.* An employee's employer-provided benefit under a contributory DB plan for purposes of section 401(a)(4) equals the difference between the employee's total benefit and the employee's employee-provided benefit under the plan. The rules of section 411(c) generally must be used to determine the employee's employer-provided benefit for this purpose. However, paragraphs (b)(2) through (b)(6) of this section provide alternative methods for determining the employee's employer-provided benefit.

*(2) Composition-of-workforce method.* (i) General rule. A contributory DB plan that satisfies paragraph (b)(2)(ii)(A) and (B) of this section may determine employees' employer-provided benefit rates under the rules of paragraph (b)(2)(iii) of this section.

(ii) Eligibility requirements. (A) Uniform rate of employee contributions. A contributory DB plan satisfies this paragraph (b)(2)(ii)(A) if all employees make employee contributions at the same rate, expressed as a percentage of plan year compensation (the employee contribution rate). A plan does not fail to satisfy this paragraph (b)(2)(ii)(A) merely because it eliminates employee contributions for all employees with plan year compensation below a specified contribution breakpoint that is either a stated dollar amount or a stated percentage of covered compensation (within the meaning of § 1.401(l)-1(c)(7)); or merely because all employees make employee contributions at the same rate (expressed as a percentage of plan year compensation) with respect to plan year compensation up to the contribution breakpoint (base employee contribution rate) and at a higher rate (expressed as a percentage of plan year compensation) that is the same for all employees with respect to plan year compensation above the contribution breakpoint (excess employee contribution rate). A plan described in paragraph (c)(4)(i) of this section that satisfies paragraph (c)(4)(iii) of this section is deemed to satisfy this paragraph.

(B) Demographic requirements. (1) In general. A contributory DB plan satisfies this paragraph (b)(2)(ii)(B) if it satisfies either of the demographic tests in paragraph (b)(2)(ii)(B)(2) or (3) of this section.

(2) Minimum percentage test. This test is satisfied only if more than 40 percent of the NHCEs in the plan have attained ages at least equal to the plan's target age, and more than 20 percent of the NHCEs in the plan have attained ages at least equal to the average attained age of the HCEs in the plan. For this purpose, a plan's target age is the lower of age 50 or the average attained age of the HCEs in the plan minus X years, where X equals 20 minus the product of five times the employee contribution rate under the plan. In no case, however, may X years be fewer than zero (0) years. Thus, for example, if the average attained age of the HCEs in the plan is 53 and the employee contribution rate is two percent of plan year compensation, the plan's target age is 43 years (i.e., 53 − (20 − (5 × 2))).

(3) Ratio test. This test is satisfied only if the percentage of all nonhighly compensated nonexcludable employees, who are in the plan and who have attained ages at least equal to the average attained age of the HCEs in the plan, is at least 70 percent of the percentage of all highly compensated nonexcludable employees, who are in the plan and who have attained ages at least equal to the average attained age of the HCEs in the plan. Attained ages must be determined as of the beginning of the plan year. In lieu of determining the actual distribution of the attained ages of the HCEs, an employer may assume that 50 percent of all HCEs have attained ages at least equal to the average attained age of the HCEs.

(iii) Determination of employer-provided benefit. (A) Safe harbor plans other than section 401(l) plans. For purposes of applying the exception to the safe harbor in § 1.401(a)(4)-3(b)(6)(viii) with respect to employer-provided benefits under a plan other than a section 401(l) plan, the employee's entire accrued benefit is treated as employer-provided.

(B) Section 401(l) plans. (1) General rule. For purposes of applying the exception to the safe harbor in § 1.401(a)(4)-3(b)(6)(viii) with respect to employer-provided benefits under a section 401(l) plan, an employee's base benefit percentage and excess benefit percentage are reduced, or an employee's gross benefit percentage is reduced, by subtracting the product of the employee contribution rate and the factor determined under paragraph (b)(2)(iv) of this section from the respective percentages for the plan year. For this purpose, the employee contribution rate is the highest rate of employee contributions applicable to any potential level of plan year compensation for that plan year under the plan.

(2) Excess plans with varying contribution rates. In the case of a defined benefit excess plan described in the second sentence of paragraph (b)(2)(ii)(A) of this section, solely for purposes of reducing an employee's base benefit percentage as required under paragraph (b)(2)(iii)(B)(1) of this section, it may be assumed that the employee's employee contribution rate equals the weighted average of the base employee contribution rate and the excess employee contribution rate. In determining this weighted average, the weight of the base employee contribution rate is equal to a fraction, the numerator of which is the lesser of the integration level and the contribution breakpoint and the denominator of which is the integration level. The weight of the excess employee contribution rate is equal to the difference between one and the weight of the base employee contribution rate.

(3) Offset plans with varying contribution rates. In the case of an offset plan described in the second sentence of paragraph (b)(2)(ii)(A) of this section, an equivalent adjustment to the alternative method in paragraph (b)(2)(iii)(B)(2) of this section may be made to the offset percentage.

(C) Employer-provided benefits under the general test. For purposes of applying the general test of § 1.401(a)(4)-3(c) with respect to employer-provided benefits, an employee's normal and most valuable accrual rates otherwise determined under § 1.401(a)(4)-3(d) (without applying any of the options under § 1.401(a)(4)-3(d)(3) other than the fresh-start alternative of § 1.401(a)(4)-3(d)(3)(iii)) are each reduced by subtracting the product of the employee's contributions (expressed as a percentage of plan year compensation) and the factor determined under paragraph (b)(2)(iv) of this section from the respective accrual rates. A plan may then apply the optional rules in § 1.401(a)(4)-3(d)(3)(i) and (ii) to this resulting accrual rate.

(D) Additional limitation. A plan may not use the composition-of-workforce method provided in this paragraph (b)(2) to determine an employee's base benefit percentage, excess benefit percentage, gross benefit percentage, offset percentage, or accrual rates unless employee contributions have been made at the same rate (or rates) throughout the period after the fresh-start date or throughout the measurement period used to determine accrual rates.

(iv) Determination of plan factor. The factor for a plan is determined under the following table based on the average entry age of the employees in the plan and on whether the plan determines benefits based on average compensation. For this purpose, average entry age equals the average attained age of all employees in the plan, minus the average years of participation of all employees in the plan. A plan is treated as determining benefits based on average compensation if it determines benefits based on compensation averaged over a specified period not exceeding five consecutive years (or the employee's entire period of employment with the employer, if shorter).

**TABLE OF FACTORS**

| | Factors | |
|---|---|---|
| Average Entry Age | Average Compensation Benefit Formula | Other Formulas |
| Less than 30 | 0.5 | 0.75 |
| 30 to 40 | 0.4 | 0.6 |
| Over 40 | 0.2 | 0.3 |

(v) Examples. The following examples illustrate the rules of this paragraph (b)(2):

*Example (1).* Plan A is a contributory DB plan that is a defined benefit excess plan providing a benefit equal to 2.0 percent of employees' average annual compensation at or below covered compensation, plus 2.5 percent of average annual compensation above covered compensation, times years of service up to 35. Under the plan, average annual compensation is determined using a five-consecutive-year period for purposes of § 1.401(a)(4)-3(e)(2). The plan requires employee contributions at a rate of four percent of plan year compensation for all employees. Assume that the plan satisfies the demographic requirements of paragraph (b)(2)(ii)(B) of this section. Under these facts, the plan satisfies the eligibility requirements of paragraph (b)(2)(ii) of this section. Assume, further, that the average attained age for all employees in the plan is 55, and that the average years of participation of all employees in the plan is 10. The average entry age for the plan is therefore 45, and, accordingly, the appropriate factor under the table is 0.2. Thus, in applying the safe harbor requirements of § 1.401(a)(4)-3(b) to this plan for the plan year (including the requirements of § 1.401(l)-3), the employee's base benefit percentage and excess benefit percentage are each reduced by 0.8 percent (4 percent × 0.2) and equal 1.2 percent and 1.7 percent, respectively.

*Example (2).* The facts are the same as in Example 1, except that the employee contribution rate is two percent of plan year compensation up to the covered compensation level, and four percent for plan year compensation at or above that contribution breakpoint. The employer elects to apply the alternative method in paragraph (b)(2)(iii)(B)(2) of this section to determine the reduction in the base benefit percentage. Because the contribution breakpoint is equal to the integration level, the weight of the employee contribution rate below the contribution breakpoint is 100 percent, and the weight of the employee contribution rate above the contribution breakpoint is zero. Thus, the weighted average of employee contribution rates is two percent. Under the alternative method in paragraph (b)(2)(iii)(B)(2) of this section, the reduction in the employee's base benefit percentage is 0.4. In applying the safe harbor requirements of § 1.401(a)(4)-3(b) to this plan (including the requirements of § 1.401(l)-3), the employee's base benefit percentage is 1.6 percent, and the employee's excess benefit percentage is 1.7.

*Example (3).* The facts are the same as in Example 1, except that the employee contribution rate is two percent of plan year compensation up to 50 percent of the covered compensation level, and four percent for plan year compensation at or above that contribution breakpoint. Because the contribution breakpoint is equal to 50 percent of the integration level, the weight of the employee contribution rate below the contribution breakpoint is 50 percent, and the weight of the employee contribution rate above the contribution breakpoint is 50 percent. Thus, the weighted average of employee contribution rates is three percent. Under the alternative method in paragraph (b)(2)(iii)(B)(2) of this section, the reduction in the employee's base benefit percentage is 0.6. In applying the safe harbor requirements of § 1.401(a)(4)-3(b) to this plan (including the requirements of § 1.401(l)-3), the employee's base benefit percentage is 1.4 percent, and the employee's excess benefit percentage is 1.7.

*Example (4).* The facts are the same as in Example 1, except that the plan is tested using the general test in § 1.401(a)(4)-3(c). Assume Employee M benefits under Plan A and has a normal accrual rate for the plan year (calculated with respect to Employee M's total accrued benefit) of 2.2 percent of average annual compensation. In applying the general test in § 1.401(a)(4)-3(c) with respect to employer-provided benefits, this rate is reduced by 0.8 to yield a normal accrual rate of 1.4 percent. This rate may then be adjusted using either of the optional rules in § 1.401(a)(4)-3(d)(3)(i) or (ii).

*(3) Minimum-benefit method.* (i) Application of uniform factors. A contributory DB plan that satisfies the uniform rate requirement of paragraph (b)(2)(ii)(A) of this section and the minimum benefit requirement of paragraph (b)(3)(ii) of this section may apply the adjustments provided in paragraph (b)(2)(iii) of this section as if the average entry age of employees in the plan were within the range of 30 to 40, without regard to the actual demographics of the employees in the plan.

(ii) Minimum benefit requirement. This requirement is satisfied if the plan provides that, in plan years beginning on or after the effective date of these regulations, as set forth in § 1.401(a)(4)-13(a) and (b), each employee will accrue a benefit that equals or exceeds the sum of—

(A) The accrued benefit derived from employee contributions made for plan years beginning on or after the effective date of these regulations, determined in accordance with section 411(c); and

(B) Fifty percent of the total benefit accrued in plan years beginning on or after the effective date of these regulations, as determined under the plan benefit formula without regard to that portion of the formula designed to satisfy the minimum benefit requirement of this paragraph (b)(3)(ii).

(iii) Example. The following example illustrates the minimum-benefit method of this paragraph (b)(3):

*Example.* Plan A is contributory DB plan. For the plan year beginning in 1994, Employee M participates in Plan A and accrues a benefit under the terms of the plan (without regard to the minimum benefit requirement of paragraph (b)(3)(ii) of this section) of $3,000. The portion of Employee M's benefit accrual for the plan year beginning in 1994 derived from employee contributions is $2,000, determined by applying the rules of section 411(c) to such contributions. The requirement of paragraph (b)(3)(ii) of this section is not satisfied for the plan year beginning in 1994 unless the plan provides that Employee M's benefit accrual for the plan year beginning in 1994 is equal to $3,500 ($2,000 + (50 percent x $3,000)).

*(4) Grandfather rule for plans in existence on May 14, 1990.* A contributory DB plan that satisfies paragraph (c)(4) of this section may determine an employee's employer-provided benefit by subtracting from the employee's total benefit the employee-provided benefits determined using any reasonable method set forth in the plan, provided that it is the same method used in determining whether the plan satisfies paragraph (c)(4)(ii)(D) of this section.

*(5) Government-plan method.* A contributory DB plan that is established and maintained for its employees by the government of any state or political subdivision or by any agency or instrumentality thereof may treat an employee's total benefit as entirely employer-provided.

*(6) Cessation of employee contributions.* If a contributory DB plan provides that no employee contributions may be made to the plan after the last day of the first plan year beginning on or after the effective date of these regulations, as set forth in § 1.401(a)(4)-13(a) and (b), the plan may treat an employee's total benefit as entirely employer-provided.

**(c) Rules applicable in determining whether employee-provided benefits are nondiscriminatory in amount.** *(1) In general.* A contributory DB plan satisfies § 1.401(a)(4)-1(b)(2) with respect to the amount of employee-provided benefits for a plan year only if the plan satisfies the requirements of paragraph (c)(2), (c)(3), or (c)(4) of this section for the plan year. This requirement applies regardless of the method used to determine the amount of employer-provided benefits under paragraph (b) of this section.

*(2) Same rate of contributions.* This requirement is satisfied for a plan year if the employee contribution rate (within the meaning of paragraph (b)(2)(ii)(A) of this section) is the same for all employees for the plan year.

*(3) Total-benefits method.* This requirement is satisfied for a plan year if—

(i) The total benefits (i.e., the sum of employer-provided and employee-provided benefits) under the plan would satisfy § 1.401(a)(4)-3 if all benefits were treated as employer-provided benefits; and

(ii) The plan's contribution requirements satisfy paragraph (b)(2)(ii)(A) of this section.

*(4) Grandfather rules for plans in existence on May 14, 1990.* (i) In general. This requirement is satisfied for a plan year if the plan contained provisions as of May 14, 1990, that meet the requirements of paragraph (c)(4)(ii) or (c)(4)(iii) of this section.

(ii) Graded contribution rates. The plan's provisions meet the requirements of this paragraph (c)(4)(ii) if all the following requirements are met:

(A) The provisions require employee contributions at a greater rate (expressed as a percentage of compensation) at higher levels of compensation than at lower levels of compensation.

(B) The required rate of employee contributions is not increased after May 14, 1990, although the level of compensation at which employee contributions are required may be increased or decreased.

(C) All employees are permitted to make employee contributions under the plan at a uniform rate with respect to all compensation, beginning no later than the last day of the first plan year to which these regulations apply, as set forth in § 1.401(a)(4)-13(a) and (b).

(D) The benefits provided on account of employee contributions at lower levels of compensation are comparable to those provided on account of employee contributions at higher levels of compensation.

(iii) Prior year compensation. The plan's provisions meet the requirements of this paragraph (c)(4)(iii) if they are part of a plan maintained by more than one employer that requires employee contributions and the rate of required employee contributions, expressed as a percentage of compensation for the last calendar year ending before the beginning of the plan year, is the same for all employees.

T.D. 8360, 9/12/91, amend T.D. 8485, 8/30/93.

## § 1.401(a)(4)-7 Imputation of permitted disparity.

**(a) Introduction.** In determining whether a plan satisfies section 401(a)(4) with respect to the amount of contributions or benefits, section 401(a)(5)(C) allows the disparities permitted under section 401(l) to be taken into account. For purposes of satisfying the safe harbors of §§ 1.401(a)(4)-2(b)(2) and 1.401(a)(4)-3(b), permitted disparity may be taken into account only by satisfying section 401(l) in form in accordance with § 1.401(l)-2 or § 1.401(l)-3, respectively. For purposes of the general tests of §§ 1.401(a)(4)-2(c) and 1.401(a)(4)-3(c), permitted disparity may be taken into account only in accordance with the rules of this section. In general, this section allows permitted disparity to be arithmetically imputed with respect to employer-provided contributions or benefits by determining an adjusted allocation or accrual rate that appropriately accounts for the permitted disparity with respect to each employee. Paragraph (b) of this section provides rules for imputing permitted disparity with respect to employer-provided contributions by adjusting each employee's unadjusted allocation rate. Paragraph (c) of this section provides rules for imputing permitted disparity with respect to employer-provided benefits by adjusting each employee's unadjusted accrual rate. Paragraph (d) of this section provides rules of general application.

**(b) Adjusting allocation rates.** *(1) In general.* The rules in this paragraph (b) produce an adjusted allocation rate for each employee by determining the excess contribution percentage under the hypothetical formula that would yield the allocation actually received by the employee, if the plan took into account the full disparity permitted under section 401(l)(2) and used the taxable wage base as the integration level. This adjusted allocation rate is used to determine whether the amount of contributions under the plan satisfies the general test of § 1.401(a)(4)-2(c) and to apply the average benefit percentage test on the basis of contributions under § 1.410(b)-5(d). Paragraphs (b)(2) and (b)(3) of this section apply to employees whose plan year compensation does not exceed and does exceed, respectively, the taxable wage base, and paragraph (b)(4) of this section provides definitions.

*(2) Employees whose plan year compensation does not exceed taxable wage base.* If an employee's plan year compensation does not exceed the taxable wage base, the employee's adjusted allocation rate is the lesser of the A rate and the B rate determined under the formulas below, where the permitted disparity rate and the unadjusted allocation rate are determined under paragraph (b)(4)(ii) and (iv) of this section, respectively.

A Rate = 2 × unadjusted allocation rate

B Rate = unadjusted allocation rate + permitted disparity rate

*(3) Employees whose plan year compensation exceeds taxable wage base.* If an employee's plan year compensation exceeds the taxable wage base, the employee's adjusted allocation rate is the lesser of the C rate and the D rate determined under the formulas below, where allocations and the permitted disparity rate are determined under paragraph (b)(4)(i) and (ii) of this section, respectively.

$$\text{C Rate} = \frac{\text{allocations}}{\text{plan year compensation} - \frac{1}{2}\text{ taxable wage base}}$$

$$\text{D Rate} = \frac{\text{allocations} + (\text{permitted disparity rate} \times \text{taxable wage base})}{\text{plan year compensation}}$$

*(4) Definitions.* In applying this paragraph (b), the following definitions govern—

(i) Allocations. Allocations means the amount determined by multiplying the employee's plan year compensation by the employee's unadjusted allocation rate.

(ii) Permitted disparity rate. (A) General rule. Permitted disparity rate means the rate in effect as of the beginning of the plan year under section 401(l)(2)(A)(ii) (e.g., 5.7 percent for plan years beginning in 1990).

(B) Cumulative permitted disparity limit. Notwithstanding paragraph (b)(4)(ii)(A) of this section, the permitted disparity rate is zero for an employee who has benefited under a defined benefit plan taken into account under § 1.401(l)-5(a)(3) for a plan year that begins on or after one year from the first day of the first plan year to which these regulations apply, as set forth in § 1.401(a)(4)-13(a) and (b), if imputing permitted disparity would result in a cumulative disparity fraction for the employee, as defined in § 1.401(l)-5(c)(2), that exceeds 35. See § 1.401(l)-5(c)(1) for special rules for determining whether an employee has benefited under a defined benefit plan for this purpose.

(iii) Taxable wage base. Taxable wage base means the taxable wage base, as defined in § 1.401(l)-1(c)(32), in effect as of the beginning of the plan year.

(iv) Unadjusted allocation rate. Unadjusted allocation rate means the employee's allocation rate determined under § 1.401(a)(4)-2(c)(2)(i) for the plan year (expressed as a percentage of plan year compensation), without imputing permitted disparity under this section.

*(5) Example.* The following example illustrates the rules in this paragraph (b):

*Example.* (a) Employees M and N participate in a defined contribution plan maintained by Employer X. Employee M has plan year compensation of $30,000 in the 1990 plan year and has an unadjusted allocation rate of five percent. Employee N has plan year compensation of $100,000 in the 1990 plan year and has an unadjusted allocation rate of eight percent. The taxable wage base in 1990 is $51,300.

(b) Because Employee M's plan year compensation does not exceed the taxable wage base, Employee M's A rate is 10 percent (2 × 5 percent), and Employee M's B rate is 10.7 percent (5 percent + 5.7 percent). Thus, Employee M's adjusted allocation rate is 10 percent, the lesser of the A rate and the B rate.

(c) Employee N's allocations are $8,000 (8 percent × $100,000). Because Employee N's plan year compensation exceeds the taxable wage base, Employee N's C rate is 10.76 percent ($8,000 divided by ($100,000 – (1/2 × $51,300))), and Employee N's D rate is 10.92 percent (($8,000 + (5.7 percent × $51,300)) divided by $100,000). Thus, Employee N's adjusted allocation rate is 10.76 percent, the lesser of the C rate and the D rate.

**(c) Adjusting accrual rates.** *(1) In general.* The rules in this paragraph (c) produce an adjusted accrual rate for each employee by determining the excess benefit percentage under the hypothetical plan formula that would yield the employer-provided accrual actually received by the employee, if the plan took into account the full permitted disparity under section 401(l)(3)(A) in each of the first 35 years of an employee's testing service under the plan and used the employee's covered compensation as the integration level. This adjusted accrual rate is used to determine whether the amount of employer-provided benefits under the plan satisfies the alternative safe harbor for flat benefit plans under § 1.401(a)(4)-3(b)(4)(i)(C)(3) or the general test of § 1.401(a)(4)-3(c), and to apply the average benefit percentage test on the basis of benefits under § 1.410(b)-5. Paragraphs (c)(2) and (c)(3) of this section apply to employees whose average annual compensation does not exceed and does exceed, respectively, covered compensation, and paragraph (c)(4) of this section provides definitions. Paragraph (c)(5) of this section provides a special rule for employees with negative unadjusted accrual rates.

*(2) Employees whose average annual compensation does not exceed covered compensation.* If an employee's average annual compensation does not exceed the employee's covered compensation, the employee's adjusted accrual rate is the lesser of the A rate and the B rate determined under the formulas below, where the permitted disparity factor and the unadjusted accrual rate are determined under paragraph (c)(4)(iii) and (v) of this section, respectively.

A Rate = 2 × unadjusted accrual rate

B Rate = unadjusted accrual rate + permitted disparity factor

*(3) Employees whose average annual compensation exceeds covered compensation.* If an employee's average annual compensation exceeds the employee's covered compensation, the employee's adjusted accrual rate is the lesser of the C rate and D rate determined under the formulas below,

where the employer-provided accrual and the permitted disparity factor are determined under paragraph (c)(4)(ii) and (iii) of this section, respectively.

$$\text{C Rate} = \frac{\text{employer-provided accrual}}{\text{average annual compensation} - \tfrac{1}{2}\ \text{covered compensation}}$$

$$\text{D Rate} = \frac{\text{employer-provided accrual} + (\text{permitted disparity factor} \times \text{covered compensation})}{\text{average annual compensation}}$$

*(4) Definitions.* For purposes of this paragraph (c), the following definitions apply.

(i) Covered compensation. Covered compensation means covered compensation as defined in § 1.401(l)-1(c)(7). Notwithstanding § 1.401(l)-1(c)(7)(iii), an employee's covered compensation must be automatically adjusted each plan year for purposes of applying this paragraph (c).

(ii) Employer-provided accrual. Employer-provided accrual means the amount determined by multiplying the employee's average annual compensation by the employee's unadjusted accrual rate.

(iii) Permitted disparity factor. (A) General rule. Permitted disparity factor for an employee means the sum of the employee's annual permitted disparity factors determined under paragraph (c)(4)(iii)(B) of this section for each of the years in the measurement period used for determining the employee's accrual rate in § 1.401(a)(4)-3(d)(1), divided by the employee's testing service during that measurement period.

(B) Annual permitted disparity factor. (1) Definition. An employee's annual permitted disparity factor is generally 0.75 percent adjusted, pursuant to § 1.401(l)-3(e), using as the age at which benefits commence the lesser of age 65 or the employee's testing age. No adjustments are made in the annual permitted disparity factor unless an employee's testing age is different from the employee's social security retirement age. An annual permitted disparity factor that is less than the annual permitted disparity factor described in the first sentence of this paragraph (c)(4)(iii)(B)(1) may be used if it is a uniform percentage of that factor (e.g., 50 percent of the annual permitted disparity factor) or a fixed percentage (e.g., 0.65 percent) for all employees.

(2) Annual permitted disparity factor after 35 years.

For purposes of determining the sum described in paragraph (c)(4)(iii)(A) of this section, the annual permitted disparity factor for each of the employee's first 35 years of testing service is the amount described in paragraph (c)(4)(iii)(B)(1) of this section, and the annual permitted disparity factor in any subsequent year equals zero. This rule applies regardless of whether the end of the measurement period extends beyond an employee's first 35 years of testing service. Thus, for example, if the measurement period is the current plan year and the employee completed 35 years of testing service prior to the beginning of the current plan year, under this paragraph (c)(4)(iii)(B)(2) the annual permitted disparity factor in the current plan year (and hence the sum of the annual permitted disparity factors for each year in the measurement period) is zero.

(3) Cumulative permitted disparity limit. The 35 years used in paragraph (c)(4)(iii)(B)(2) of this section must be reduced by the employee's cumulative disparity fraction, as defined in § 1.401(l)-5(c)(2), but determined solely with respect to the employee's total years of service under all plans taken into account under § 1.401(l)-5(a)(3) during the measurement period, other than the plan being tested.

(iv) Social security retirement age. Social security retirement age means social security retirement age as defined in section 415(b)(8).

(v) Unadjusted accrual rate. Unadjusted accrual rate means the normal or most valuable accrual rate, whichever is being determined for the employee under § 1.401(a)(4)-3(d), expressed as a percentage of average annual compensation, without imputing permitted disparity under this section.

*(5) Employees with negative unadjusted accrual rates.* Notwithstanding the formulas in paragraph (c)(2) and (c)(3) of this section, if an employee's unadjusted accrual rate is less than zero, the employee's adjusted accrual rate is deemed to be the employee's unadjusted accrual rate.

*(6) Example.* The following example illustrates the rules in this paragraph (c):

*Example.* (a) Employees M and N participate in a defined benefit plan that uses a normal retirement age of 65. The plan is being tested for the plan year under § 1.401(a)(4)-3(c), using unadjusted accrual rates determined using a plan year measurement period under § 1.401(a)(4)-3(d)(1)(iii)(A). Employee M has an unadjusted normal accrual rate of 1.48 percent, average annual compensation of $21,000, and an employer-provided accrual of $311 (1.48 percent × $21,000). Employee N has an unadjusted normal accrual rate of 1.7 percent, average annual compensation of $106,000, and an employer-provided accrual of $1,802 (1.7 percent × $106,000). The covered compensation of both Employees M and N is $25,000, and social security retirement age for both employees is 65. Neither employee has testing service of more than 35 years and neither has ever participated in another plan.

(b) Because Employee M's average annual compensation does not exceed covered compensation, Employee M's A rate is 2.96 percent (2.0 × 1.48 percent), and Employee M's B rate is 2.23 percent (1.48 percent + 0.75 percent). Thus, Employee M's adjusted accrual rate is 2.23 percent, the lesser of the A rate and the B rate.

(c) Because Employee N's average annual compensation exceeds covered compensation, Employee N's C rate is 1.93 percent ($1,802/($106,000 − (0.5 × $25,000))), and Employee N's D rate is 1.88 percent (($1,802 + (0.75 percent × $25,000))/$106,000). Thus, Employee N's adjusted accrual rate is 1.88 percent, the lesser of the C rate and the D rate.

**(d) Rules of general application.** *(1) Eligible plans.* The rules in this section may be used only for those plans to which the permitted disparity rules of section 401(l) are available. See § 1.401(l)-1(a)(3).

*(2) Exceptions from consistency requirements.* A plan does not fail to satisfy the consistency requirements of § 1.401(a)(4)-2(c)(2)(vi) or § 1.401(a)(4)-3(d)(2)(i) merely

because the plan does not impute disparity for some employees to the extent required to comply with paragraph (d)(3) of this section, or because the plan does not impute disparity for any employees (including self-employed individuals within the meaning of section 401(c)(1)) who are not covered by any of the taxes under section 3111(a), section 3221, or section 1401.

*(3) Overall permitted disparity.* The annual overall permitted disparity limits of § 1.401(l)-5(b) apply to the employer-provided contributions and benefits for an employee under all plans taken into account under § 1.401(l)-5(a)(3). Thus, if an employee who benefits under the plan for the current plan year also benefits under a section 401(l) plan for the plan year ending with or within the current plan year, permitted disparity may not be imputed for that employee for the plan year. See § 1.401(l)-5(b)(9), Example 4. Similarly, if an employee who benefits under the plan for the current plan year also benefits under another plan of the employer for the plan year ending with or within the current plan year, disparity may be imputed for that employee under only one of the plans.

T.D. 8360, 9/12/91, amend T.D. 8485, 8/30/93.

## § 1.401(a)(4)-8 Cross-testing.

***Caution:*** The Treasury has not yet amended Reg § 1.401(a)(4)-8 to reflect changes made by P.L. 104-188.

**(a) Introduction.** This section provides rules for testing defined benefit plans on the basis of equivalent employer-provided contributions and defined contribution plans on the basis of equivalent employer-provided benefits under § 1.401(a)(4)-1(b)(2). Paragraphs (b)(1) and (c)(1) of this section provide general tests for nondiscrimination based on individual equivalent accrual or allocation rates determined under paragraphs (b)(2) and (c)(2) of this section, respectively. Paragraphs (b)(3), (c)(3), and (d) of this section provide additional safe-harbor testing methods for target benefit plans, cash balance plans, and defined benefit plans that are part of floor-offset arrangements, respectively, that generally may be satisfied on a design basis.

**(b) Nondiscrimination in amount of benefits provided under a defined contribution plan.** *(1) General rule and gateway.* (i) General rule. Equivalent benefits under a defined contribution plan (other than an ESOP) are nondiscriminatory in amount for a plan year if—

(A) The plan would satisfy § 1.401(a)(4)-2(c)(1) for the plan year if an equivalent accrual rate, as determined under paragraph (b)(2) of this section, were substituted for each employee's allocation rate in the determination of rate groups; and

(B) For plan years beginning on or after January 1, 2002, the plan satisfies one of the following conditions—

(1) The plan has broadly available allocation rates (within the meaning of paragraph (b)(1)(iii) of this section) for the plan year;

(2) The plan has age-based allocation rates that are based on either a gradual age or service schedule (within the meaning of paragraph (b)(1)(iv) of this section) or a uniform target benefit allocation (within the meaning of paragraph (b)(1)(v) of this section) for the plan year; or

(3) The plan satisfies the minimum allocation gateway of paragraph (b)(1)(vi) of this section for the plan year.

(ii) Allocations after testing age. A plan does not fail to satisfy paragraph (b)(1)(i)(A) of this section merely because allocations are made at the same rate for employees who are older than their testing age (determined without regard to the current-age rule in paragraph (4) of the definition of testing age in § 1.401(a)(4)-12) as they are made for employees who are at that age.

(iii) Broadly available allocation rates. (A) In general. A plan has broadly available allocation rates for the plan year if each allocation rate under the plan is currently available during the plan year (within the meaning of § 1.401(a)(4)-4(b)(2)), to a group of employees that satisfies section 410(b) (without regard to the average benefit percentage test of § 1.410(b)-5). For this purpose, if two allocation rates could be permissively aggregated under § 1.401(a)(4)-4(d)(4), assuming the allocation rates were treated as benefits, rights or features, they may be aggregated and treated as a single allocation rate. In addition, the disregard of age and service conditions described in § 1.401(a)(4)-4(b)(2)(ii)(A) does not apply for purposes of this paragraph (b)(1)(iii)(A).

(B) Certain transition allocations. In determining whether a plan has broadly available allocation rates for the plan year within the meaning of paragraph (b)(1)(iii)(A) of this section, an employee's allocation may be disregarded to the extent that the allocation is a transition allocation for the plan year. In order for an allocation to be a transition allocation, the allocation must comply with the requirements of paragraph (b)(1)(iii)(C) of this section and must be either—

(1) A defined benefit replacement allocation within the meaning of paragraph (b)(1)(iii)(D) of this section; or

(2) A pre-existing replacement allocation or pre-existing merger and acquisition allocation, within the meaning of paragraph (b)(1)(iii)(E) of this section.

(C) Plan provisions relating to transition allocations. (1) In general. Plan provisions providing for transition allocations for the plan year must specify both the group of employees who are eligible for the transition allocations and the amount of the transition allocations.

(2) Limited plan amendments. Allocations are not transition allocations within the meaning of paragraph (b)(1)(iii)(B) of this section for the plan year if the plan provisions relating to the allocations are amended after the date those plan provisions are both adopted and effective. The preceding sentence in this paragraph (b)(1)(iii)(C)(2) does not apply to a plan amendment that reduces transition allocations to HCEs, makes de minimis changes in the calculation of the transition allocations (such as a change in the definition of compensation to include section 132(f) elective reductions), or adds or removes a provision permitted under paragraph (b)(1)(iii)(C)(3) of this section.

(3) Certain permitted plan provisions. An allocation does not fail to be a transition allocation within the meaning of paragraph (b)(1)(iii)(B) of this section merely because the plan provides that each employee who is eligible for a transition allocation receives the greater of such allocation and the allocation for which the employee would otherwise be eligible under the plan. In a plan that contains such a provision, for purposes of determining whether the plan has broadly available allocation rates within the meaning of paragraph (b)(1)(iii)(A) of this section, the allocation for which an employee would otherwise be eligible is considered currently available to the employee, even if the employee's transition allocation is greater.

(D) Defined benefit replacement allocation. An allocation is a defined benefit replacement allocation for the plan year if it is provided in accordance with guidance prescribed by the Commissioner published in the Internal Revenue Bulletin (see § 601.601(d)(2)(ii)(b) of this chapter) and satisfies the following conditions—

(1) The allocations are provided to a group of employees who formerly benefitted under an established nondiscriminatory defined benefit plan of the employer or of a prior employer that provided age-based equivalent allocation rates;

(2) The allocations for each employee in the group were reasonably calculated, in a consistent manner, to replace the retirement benefits that the employee would have been provided under the defined benefit plan if the employee had continued to benefit under the defined benefit plan;

(3) Except as provided in paragraph (b)(1)(iii)(C) of this section, no employee who receives the allocation receives any other allocations under the plan for the plan year; and

(4) The composition of the group of employees who receive the allocations is nondiscriminatory.

(E) Pre-existing transition allocations. (1) Pre-existing replacement allocations. An allocation is a pre-existing replacement allocation for the plan year if the allocation satisfies the following conditions—

(i) The allocations are provided pursuant to a plan provision adopted before June 29, 2001;

(ii) The allocations are provided to employees who formerly benefitted under a defined benefit plan of the employer; and

(iii) The allocations for each employee in the group are reasonably calculated, in a consistent manner, to replace some or all of the retirement benefits that the employee would have received under the defined benefit plan and any other plan or arrangement of the employer if the employee had continued to benefit under such defined benefit plan and such other plan or arrangement.

(2) Pre-existing merger and acquisition allocations. An allocation is a pre-existing merger and acquisition allocation for the plan year if the allocation satisfies the following conditions—

(i) The allocations are provided solely to employees of a trade or business that has been acquired by the employer in a stock or asset acquisition, merger, or other similar transaction occurring prior to August 28, 2001, involving a change in the employer of the employees of the trade or business;

(ii) The allocations are provided only to employees who were employed by the acquired trade or business before a specified date that is no later than two years after the transaction (or January 1, 2002, if earlier);

(iii) The allocations are provided pursuant a plan provision adopted no later than the specified date; and

(iv) The allocations for each employee in the group are reasonably calculated, in a consistent manner, to replace some or all of the retirement benefits that the employee would have received under any plan of the employer if the new employer had continued to provide the retirement benefits that the prior employer was providing for employees of the trade or business.

(F) Successor employers. An employer that accepts a transfer of assets (within the meaning of section 414(l)) from the plan of a prior employer may continue to treat any transition allocations provided under that plan as transition allocations under paragraph (b)(1)(iii)(B) of this section, provided that the successor employer continues to satisfy the applicable requirements set forth in paragraphs (b)(1)(iii)(C) through (E) of this section for the plan year.

(iv) Gradual age or service schedule. (A) In general. A plan has a gradual age or service schedule for the plan year if the allocation formula for all employees under the plan provides for a single schedule of allocation rates under which—

(1) The schedule defines a series of bands based solely on age, years of service, or the number of points representing the sum of age and years of service (age and service points), under which the same allocation rate applies to all employees whose age, years of service, or age and service points are within each band; and

(2) The allocation rates under the schedule increase smoothly at regular intervals, within the meaning of paragraphs (b)(1)(iv)(B) and (C) of this section.

(B) Smoothly increasing schedule of allocation rates. A schedule of allocation rates increases smoothly if the allocation rate for each band within the schedule is greater than the allocation rate for the immediately preceding band (i.e., the band with the next lower number of years of age, years of service, or age and service points) but by no more than 5 percentage points. However, a schedule of allocation rates will not be treated as increasing smoothly if the ratio of the allocation rate for any band to the rate for the immediately preceding band is more than 2.0 or if it exceeds the ratio of allocation rates between the two immediately preceding bands.

(C) Regular intervals. A schedule of allocation rates has regular intervals of age, years of service or age and service points, if each band, other than the band associated with the highest age, years of service, or age and service points, is the same length. For this purpose, if the schedule is based on age, the first band is deemed to be of the same length as the other bands if it ends at or before age 25. If the first age band ends after age 25, then, in determining whether the length of the first band is the same as the length of other bands, the starting age for the first age band is permitted to be treated as age 25 or any age earlier than 25. For a schedule of allocation rates based on age and service points, the rules of the preceding two sentences are applied by substituting 25 age and service points for age 25. For a schedule of allocation rates based on service, the starting service for the first service band is permitted to be treated as one year of service or any lesser amount of service.

(D) Minimum allocation rates permitted. A schedule of allocation rates under a plan does not fail to increase smoothly at regular intervals, within the meaning of paragraphs (b)(1)(iv)(B) and (C) of this section, merely because a minimum uniform allocation rate is provided for all employees or the minimum benefit described in section 416(c)(2) is provided for all non-key employees (either because the plan is top heavy or without regard to whether the plan is top heavy) if the schedule satisfies one of the following conditions— (1) The allocation rates under the plan that are greater than the minimum allocation rate can be included in a hypothetical schedule of allocation rates that increases smoothly at regular intervals, within the meaning of paragraphs (b)(1)(iv)(B) and (C) of this section, where the hypothetical schedule has a lowest allocation rate no lower than 1% of plan year compensation; or

(2) For a plan using a schedule of allocation rates based on age, for each age band in the schedule that provides an allocation rate greater than the minimum allocation rate, there could be an employee in that age band with an equivalent accrual rate that is less than or equal to the equivalent accrual rate that would apply to an employee

whose age is the highest age for which the allocation rate equals the minimum allocation rate.

(v) Uniform target benefit allocations. A plan has allocation rates that are based on a uniform target benefit allocation for the plan year if the plan fails to satisfy the requirements for the safe harbor testing method in paragraph (b)(3) of this section merely because the determination of the allocations under the plan differs from the allocations determined under that safe harbor testing method for any of the following reasons—

(A) The interest rate used for determining the actuarial present value of the stated plan benefit and the theoretical reserve is lower than a standard interest rate;

(B) The stated benefit is calculated assuming compensation increases at a specified rate; or

(C) The plan computes the current year contribution using the actual account balance instead of the theoretical reserve.

(vi) Minimum allocation gateway. (A) General rule. A plan satisfies the minimum allocation gateway of this paragraph (b)(1)(vi) if each NHCE has an allocation rate that is at least one third of the allocation rate of the HCE with the highest allocation rate.

(B) Deemed satisfaction. A plan is deemed to satisfy the minimum allocation gateway of this paragraph (b)(1)(vi) if each NHCE receives an allocation of at least 5% of the NHCE's compensation within the meaning of section 415(c)(3), measured over a period of time permitted under the definition of plan year compensation.

(vii) Determination of allocation rate. For purposes of paragraph (b)(1)(i)(B) of this section, allocations and allocation rates are determined under § 1.401(a)(4)-2(c)(2), but without taking into account the imputation of permitted disparity under § 1.401(a)(4)-7. However, in determining whether the plan has broadly available allocation rates as provided in paragraph (b)(1)(iii) of this section, differences in allocation rates attributable solely to the use of permitted disparity described in § 1.401(l)-2 are disregarded.

(viii) Examples. The following examples illustrate the rules in this paragraph (b)(1):

*Example (1).* (i) Plan M, a defined contribution plan without a minimum service requirement, provides an allocation formula under which allocations are provided to all employees according to the following schedule:

| Completed years of service | Allocation rate (in percent) | Ratio of allocation rate for band to allocation rate for immediately preceding band |
|---|---|---|
| 0–5 | 3.0 | [1] |
| 6–10 | 4.5 | 1.50 |
| 11–15 | 6.5 | 1.44 |
| 16–20 | 8.5 | 1.31 |
| 21–25 | 10.0 | 1.18 |
| 26 or more | 11.5 | 1.15 |

[1] Not applicable

(ii) Plan M provides that allocation rates for all employees are determined using a single schedule based solely on service, as described in paragraph (b)(1)(iv)(A)(1) of this section. Therefore, if the allocation rates under the schedule increase smoothly at regular intervals as described in paragraph (b)(1)(iv)(A)(2) of this section, then the plan has a gradual age or service schedule described in paragraph (b)(1)(iv) of this section.

(iii) The schedule of allocation rates under Plan M does not increase by more than 5 percentage points between adjacent bands and the ratio of the allocation rate for any band to the allocation rate for the immediately preceding band is never more than 2.0 and does not increase. Therefore, the allocation rates increase smoothly as described in paragraph (b)(1)(iv)(B) of this section. In addition, the bands (other than the highest band) are all 5 years long, so the increases occur at regular intervals as described in paragraph (b)(1)(iv)(C) of this section. Thus, the allocation rates under the plan's schedule increase smoothly at regular intervals as described in paragraph (b)(1)(iv)(A)(2) of this section. Accordingly, the plan has a gradual age or service schedule described in paragraph (b)(1)(iv) of this section.

(iv) Under paragraph (b)(1)(i) of this section, Plan M satisfies the nondiscrimination in amount requirement of § 1.401(a)(4)-1(b)(2) on the basis of benefits if it satisfies paragraph (b)(1)(i)(A) of this section, regardless of whether it satisfies the minimum allocation gateway of paragraph (b)(1)(vi) of this section.

*Example (2).* (i) The facts are the same as in Example 1, except that the 4.5% allocation rate applies for all employees with 10 years of service or less.

(ii) Plan M provides that allocation rates for all employees are determined using a single schedule based solely on service, as described in paragraph (b)(1)(iv)(A)(1) of this section. Therefore, if the allocation rates under the schedule increase smoothly at regular intervals as described in paragraph (b)(1)(iv)(A)(2) of this section, then the plan has a gradual age or service schedule described in paragraph (b)(1)(iv) of this section.

(iii) The bands (other than the highest band) in the schedule are not all the same length, since the first band is 10 years long while other bands are 5 years long. Thus, the schedule does not have regular intervals as described in paragraph (b)(1)(iv)(C) of this section. However, under paragraph (b)(1)(iv)(D) of this section, the schedule of allocation rates does not fail to increase smoothly at regular intervals merely because the minimum allocation rate of 4.5% results in a first band that is longer than the other bands, if either of the conditions of paragraph (b)(1)(iv)(D)(1) or (2) of this section is satisfied.

(iv) In this case, the schedule of allocation rates satisfies the condition in paragraph (b)(1)(iv)(D)(1) of this section because the allocation rates under the plan that are greater than the 4.5% minimum allocation rate can be included in the following hypothetical schedule of allocation rates that increases smoothly at regular intervals and has a lowest allocation rate of at least 1% of plan year compensation:

| Completed years of service | Allocation rate (in percent) | Ratio of allocation rate for band to allocation rate for immediately preceding band |
|---|---|---|
| 0–5 | 2.5 | [1] |
| 6–10 | 4.5 | 1.80 |
| 11–15 | 6.5 | 1.44 |
| 16–20 | 8.5 | 1.31 |
| 21–25 | 10.0 | 1.18 |
| 26 or more | 11.5 | 1.15 |

[1] Not applicable

(v) Accordingly, the plan has a gradual age or service schedule described in paragraph (b)(1)(iv) of this section. Under paragraph (b)(1)(i) of this section, Plan M satisfies the nondiscrimination in amount requirement of § 1.401(a)(4)-1(b)(2) on the basis of benefits if it satisfies paragraph (b)(1)(i)(A) of this section, regardless of whether it satisfies the minimum allocation gateway of paragraph (b)(1)(vi) of this section.

*Example (3).* (i) Plan N, a defined contribution plan, provides an allocation formula under which allocations are provided to all employees according to the following schedule:

| Age | Allocation rate (in percent) | Ratio of allocation rate for band to allocation rate for immediately preceding band |
|---|---|---|
| Under 25 ...... | 3.0 | [1] |
| 25–34......... | 6.0 | 2.00 |
| 35–44......... | 9.0 | 1.50 |
| 45–54......... | 12.0 | 1.33 |
| 55–64......... | 16.0 | 1.33 |
| 65 or older ..... | 21.0 | 1.31 |

[1] Not applicable

(ii) Plan N provides that allocation rates for all employees are determined using a single schedule based solely on age, as described in paragraph (b)(1)(iv)(A)(1) of this section. Therefore, if the allocation rates under the schedule increase smoothly at regular intervals as described in paragraph (b)(1)(iv)(A)(2) of this section, then the plan has a gradual age or service schedule described in paragraph (b)(1)(iv) of this section.

(iii) The schedule of allocation rates under Plan N does not increase by more than 5 percentage points between adjacent bands and the ratio of the allocation rate for any band to the allocation rate for the immediately preceding band is never more than 2.0 and does not increase. Therefore, the allocation rates increase smoothly as described in paragraph (b)(1)(iv)(B) of this section. In addition, the bands (other than the highest band and the first band, which is deemed to be the same length as the other bands because it ends prior to age 25) are all 5 years long, so the increases occur at regular intervals as described in paragraph (b)(1)(iv)(C) of this section. Thus, the allocation rates under the plan's schedule increase smoothly at regular intervals as described in paragraph (b)(1)(iv)(A)(2) of this section. Accordingly, the plan has a gradual age or service schedule described in paragraph (b)(1)(iv) of this section.

(iv) Under paragraph (b)(1)(i) of this section, Plan N satisfies the nondiscrimination in amount requirement of § 1.401(a)(4)-1(b)(2) on the basis of benefits if it satisfies paragraph (b)(1)(i)(A) of this section, regardless of whether it satisfies the minimum allocation gateway of paragraph (b)(1)(vi) of this section.

*Example (4).* (i) Plan O, a defined contribution plan, provides an allocation formula under which allocations are provided to all employees according to the following schedule:

| Age | Allocation rate (in percent) | Ratio of allocation rate for band to allocation rate for immediately preceding band |
|---|---|---|
| Under 40 ...... | 3 | [1] |
| 40–44......... | 6 | 2.00 |
| 45–49......... | 9 | 1.50 |
| 50–54......... | 12 | 1.33 |
| 55–59......... | 16 | 1.33 |
| 60–64......... | 20 | 1.25 |
| 65 or older ..... | 25 | 1.25 |

[1] Not applicable

(ii) Plan O provides that allocation rates for all employees are determined using a single schedule based solely on age, as described in paragraph (b)(1)(iv)(A)(1) of this section. Therefore, if the allocation rates under the schedule increase smoothly at regular intervals as described in paragraph (b)(1)(iv)(A)(2) of this section, then the plan has a gradual age or service schedule described in paragraph (b)(1)(iv) of this section.

(iii) The bands (other than the highest band) in the schedule are not all the same length, since the first band is treated as 15 years long while other bands are 5 years long. Thus, the schedule does not have regular intervals as described in paragraph (b)(1)(iv)(C) of this section. However, under paragraph (b)(1)(iv)(D) of this section, the schedule of allocation rates does not fail to increase smoothly at regular intervals merely because the minimum allocation rate of 3% results in a first band that is longer than the other bands, if either of the conditions of paragraph (b)(1)(iv)(D)(1) or (2) of this section is satisfied.

(iv) In this case, in order to define a hypothetical schedule that could include the allocation rates in the actual schedule of allocation rates, each of the bands below age 40 would have to be 5 years long (or be treated as 5 years long). Accordingly, the hypothetical schedule would have to provide for a band for employees under age 30, a band for employees in the range 30-34 and a band for employees age 35-39.

(v) The ratio of the allocation rate for the age 40-44 band to the next lower band is 2.0. Accordingly, in order for the applicable allocations rates under this hypothetical schedule to increase smoothly, the ratio of the allocation rate for each band in the hypothetical schedule below age 40 to the allocation rate for the immediately preceding band would have to be 2.0. Thus, the allocation rate for the hypothetical band applicable for employees under age 30 would be .75%, the allocation rate for the hypothetical band for employees in the range 30-34 would be 1.5% and the allocation rate for employees in the range 35-39 would be 3%.

(vi) Because the lowest allocation rate under any possible hypothetical schedule is less than 1% of plan year compensation, Plan O will be treated as satisfying the requirements of paragraphs (b)(1)(iv)(B) and (C) of this section only if the schedule of allocation rates satisfies the steepness condition described in paragraph (b)(1)(iv)(D)(2) of this section. In this case, the steepness condition is not satisfied because the equivalent accrual rate for an employee age 39 is 2.81%, but there is no hypothetical employee in the band for ages 40-44 with an equal or lower equivalent accrual rate (since the lowest equivalent accrual rate for hypothetical employees within this band is 3.74% at age 44).

(vii) Since the schedule of allocation rates under the plan does not increase smoothly at regular intervals, Plan O's schedule of allocation rates is not a gradual age or service schedule. Further, Plan O does not provide uniform target benefit allocations. Therefore, under paragraph (b)(1)(i) of this section, Plan O cannot satisfy the nondiscrimination in amount requirement of § 1.401(a)(4)-1(b)(2) for the plan year on the basis of benefits unless either Plan O provides for broadly available allocation rates for the plan year as described in paragraph (b)(1)(iii) of this section (i.e., the allocation rate at each age is provided to a group of employees that satisfies section 410(b) without regard to the average benefit percentage test), or Plan O satisfies the minimum allocation gateway of paragraph (b)(1)(vi) of this section for the plan year.

*Example (5).* (i) Plan P is a profit-sharing plan maintained by Employer A that covers all of Employer A's employees, consisting of two HCEs, X and Y, and 7 NHCEs. Employee X's compensation is $170,000 and Employee Y's compensation is $150,000. The allocation for Employees X and Y is $30,000 each, resulting in an allocation rate of 17.65% for Employee X and 20% for Employee Y. Under Plan P, each NHCE receives an allocation of 5% of compensation within the meaning of section 415(c)(3), measured over a period of time permitted under the definition of plan year compensation.

(ii) Because the allocation rate for X is not currently available to any NHCE, Plan P does not have broadly available allocation rates within the meaning of paragraph (b)(1)(iii) of this section. Furthermore, Plan P does not provide for age based-allocation rates within the meaning of paragraph (b)(1)(iv) or (v) of this section. Thus, under paragraph (b)(1)(i) of this section, Plan P can satisfy the nondiscrimination in amount requirement of § 1.401(a)(4)-1(b)(2) for the plan year on the basis of benefits only if Plan P satisfies the minimum allocation gateway of paragraph (b)(1)(vi) of this section for the plan year.

(iii) The highest allocation rate for any HCE under Plan P is 20%. Accordingly, Plan P would satisfy the minimum allocation gateway of paragraph (b)(1)(vi) of this section if all NHCEs have an allocation rate of at least 6.67%, or if all NHCEs receive an allocation of at least 5% of compensation within the meaning of section 415(c)(3) (measured over a period of time permitted under the definition of plan year compensation).

(iv) Under Plan P, each NHCE receives an allocation of 5% of compensation within the meaning of section 415(c)(3) (measured over a period of time permitted under the definition of plan year compensation). Accordingly, Plan P satisfies the minimum allocation gateway of paragraph (b)(1)(vi) of this section.

(v) Under paragraph (b)(1)(i) of this section, Plan P satisfies the nondiscrimination in amount requirement of § 1.401(a)(4)-1(b)(2) on the basis of benefits if it satisfies paragraph (b)(1)(i)(A) of this section.

*(2) Determination of equivalent accrual rates.* (i) Basic definition. An employee's equivalent accrual rate for a plan year is the annual benefit that is the result of normalizing the increase in the employee's account balance during the measurement period, divided by the number of years in which the employee benefited under the plan during the measurement period, and expressed either as a dollar amount or as a percentage of the employee's average annual compensation. A measurement period that includes future years may not be used for this purpose.

(ii) Rules of application. (A) Determination of account balance. The increase in the account balance during the measurement period taken into account under paragraph (b)(2)(i) of this section does not include income, expenses, gains, or losses allocated during the measurement period that are attributable to the account balance as of the beginning of the measurement period, but does include any additional amounts that would have been included in the increase in the account balance but for the fact that they were previously distributed (including a reasonable adjustment for interest). In the case of a measurement period that is the current plan year, an employer may also elect to disregard the income, expenses, gains, and losses allocated during the current plan year that are attributable to the increase in account balance since the beginning of the year, and thus, determine the increase in account balance during the plan year taking into account only the allocations described in § 1.401(a)(4)-2(c)(2)(ii). In addition, an employer may disregard distributions made to a NHCE as well as distributions made to any employee in plan years beginning before a selected date no later than January 1, 1986.

(B) Normalization. The account balances determined under paragraph (b)(2)(ii)(A) of this section are normalized by treating them as single-sum benefits that are immediately and unconditionally payable to the employee. A standard interest rate, and a straight life annuity factor that is based on the same or a different standard interest rate and on a standard mortality table, must be used in normalizing these benefits. In addition, no mortality may be assumed prior to the employee's testing age.

(iii) Options. Any of the optional rules in § 1.401(a)(4)-3(d)(3) (e.g., imputation of permitted disparity) may be applied in determining an employee's equivalent accrual rate by substituting the employee's equivalent accrual rate (determined without regard to the option) for the employee's normal accrual rate (i.e., not most valuable accrual rate) in that section where appropriate. For this purpose, however, the last sentence of the fresh-start alternative in § 1.401(a)(4)-3(d)(3)(iii)(A) (dealing with compensation adjustments to the frozen accrued benefit) is not applicable. No other options are available in determining an employee's equivalent accrual rate except those (e.g., selection of alternative measurement periods) specifically provided in this paragraph (b)(2). Thus, for example, none of the optional special rules in § 1.401(a)(4)-3(f) (e.g., determination of benefits on other than a plan year basis under § 1.401(a)(4)-3(f)(6)) is available.

(iv) Consistency rule. Equivalent accrual rates must be determined in a consistent manner for all employees for the plan year. Thus, for example, the same measurement periods and standard interest rates must be used, and any available options must be applied consistently if at all.

*(3) Safe-harbor testing method for target benefit plans.* (i) General rule. A target benefit plan is a money purchase pension plan under which contributions to an employee's account are determined by reference to the amounts necessary to fund the employee's stated benefit under the plan. Whether a target benefit plan satisfies section 401(a)(4) with respect to an equivalent amount of benefits is generally determined under paragraphs (b)(1) and (b)(2) of this section. A target benefit plan is deemed to satisfy section 401(a)(4) with respect to an equivalent amount of benefits, however, if each of the following requirements is satisfied:

(A) Stated benefit formula. Each employee's stated benefit must be determined as the straight life annuity commencing at the employee's normal retirement age under a formula that would satisfy the requirements of § 1.401(a)(4)-3(b)(4)(i)(C)(1) or (2), and that would satisfy each of the uniformity requirements in § 1.401(a)(4)-3(b)(2) (taking into account the relevant exceptions provided in § 1.401(a)(4)-3(b)(6)), if the plan were a defined benefit plan with the same benefit formula. In determining whether these requirements are satisfied, the rules of § 1.401(a)(4)-3(f) do not apply, and, in addition, except as provided in paragraph (b)(3)(vii) of this section, an employee's stated benefit at normal retirement age under the stated benefit formula is deemed to accrue ratably over the period ending with the plan year in which the employee is projected to reach normal retirement age and beginning with the latest of: the first plan year in which the employee benefited under the plan, the first plan year taken into account in the stated benefit formula, and any plan year immediately following a plan year in which the plan did not satisfy this paragraph (b)(3). Thus, except as provided in paragraph (b)(3)(vii) of this section, under § 1.401(a)(4)-3(b)(2)(v) an employee's stated benefit may not take into account service in years prior to the first plan year that the employee benefited under the plan, and an employee's stated benefit may not take into account service in plan years prior to the current plan year unless the plan satisfied this paragraph (b)(3) in all of those prior plan years.

(B) Employer and employee contributions. Employer contributions with respect to each employee must be based exclusively on the employee's stated benefit using the method provided in paragraph (b)(3)(iv) of this section, and forfeitures and any other amounts under the plan taken into account under § 1.401(a)(4)-2(c)(2)(ii) (other than employer contributions) are used exclusively to reduce employer contributions. Employee contributions (if any) may not be used to fund the stated benefit.

(C) Permitted disparity. If permitted disparity is taken into account, the stated benefit formula must satisfy § 1.401(l)-3. For this purpose, the 0.75-percent factor in the maximum excess or offset allowance in § 1.401(l)-3(b)(2)(i) or (b)(3)(i), respectively, as adjusted in accordance with § 1.401(l)-3(d)(9) (and, if the employee's normal retirement age is not the employee's social security retirement age, § 1.401(l)-3(e)), is further reduced by multiplying the factor by 0.80.

(ii) Changes in stated benefit formula. A plan does not fail to satisfy paragraph (b)(3)(i) of this section merely because the plan determines each employee's stated benefit in the current plan year under a stated benefit formula that differs from the stated benefit formula used to determine the employee's stated benefit in prior plan years.

(iii) Stated benefits after normal retirement age. A target benefit plan may limit increases in the stated benefit after normal retirement age consistent with the requirements applicable to defined benefit plans under section 411(b)(1)(H) (without regard to section 411(b)(1)(H)(iii)), provided that the limitation applies on the same terms to all employees. Thus, post-normal retirement benefits required under § 1.401(a)(4)-3(b)(2)(ii) must be provided under the stated benefit formula, subject to any uniformly applicable service cap under the formula.

(iv) Method for determining required employer contributions. (A) General rule. An employer's required contribution to the account of an employee for a plan year is determined based on the employee's stated benefit and the amount of the employee's theoretical reserve as of the date the employer's required contribution is determined for the plan year (the determination date). Paragraph (b)(3)(iv)(B) of this section provides rules for determining an employee's theoretical reserve. Paragraph (b)(3)(iv)(C) and (D) of this section provides rules for determining an employer's required contributions.

(B) Theoretical reserve. (1) Initial theoretical reserve. An employee's theoretical reserve as of the determination date for the first plan year in which the employee benefits under the plan, the first plan year taken into account under the stated benefit formula (if that is the current plan year), or the first plan year immediately following any plan year in which the plan did not satisfy this paragraph (b)(3), is zero.

(2) Theoretical reserve in subsequent plan years. An employee's theoretical reserve as of the determination date for a plan year (other than a plan year described in paragraph (b)(3)(iv)(B)(1) of this section) is the employee's theoretical reserve as of the determination date for the prior plan year, plus the employer's required contribution for the prior plan year (as limited by section 415, but without regard to the additional contributions described in paragraph (b)(3)(v) of this section) both increased by interest from the determination date for the prior plan year through the determination date for the current plan year, but not beyond the determination date for the plan year that includes the employee's normal retirement date. (Thus, an employee's theoretical reserve as of the determination date for a plan year does not include the amount of the employer's required contribution for the plan year.) The interest rate for determining employer contributions that was in effect on the determination date in the prior plan year must be applied to determine the required interest adjustment for this period. For plan years beginning after the effective date applicable to the plan under § 1.401(a)(4)-13(a) or (b), a standard interest rate must be used, and may not be changed except on the determination date for a plan year.

(C) Required contributions for employees under normal retirement age. The required employer contributions with respect to an employee whose attained age is less than the employee's normal retirement age must be determined for each plan year as follows:

(1) Determine the employee's fractional rule benefit (within the meaning of § 1.411(b)-1(b)(3)(ii)(A)) under the plan's stated benefit formula as if the plan were a defined benefit plan with the same benefit formula.

(2) Determine the actuarial present value of the fractional rule benefit determined in paragraph (b)(3)(iv)(C)(1) of this section as of the determination date for the current plan year, using a standard interest rate and a standard mortality table that are set forth in the plan and that are the same for all employees, and assuming no mortality before the employee's normal retirement age.

(3) Determine the excess, if any, of the amount determined in paragraph (b)(3)(iv)(C)(2) of this section over the employee's theoretical reserve for the current plan year determined under paragraph (b)(3)(iv)(B) of this section.

(4) Determine the required employer contribution for the current plan year by amortizing on a level annual basis, using the same interest rate used for paragraph (b)(3)(iv)(C)(2) of this section, the result in paragraph (b)(3)(iv)(C)(3) of this section over the period beginning with the determination date for the current plan year and ending with the determination date for the plan year in which the employee is projected to reach normal retirement age.

(D) Required contributions for employees over normal retirement age. The required employer contributions with respect to an employee whose attained age equals or exceeds the employee's normal retirement age is the excess, if any, of the actuarial present value, as of the determination date for the current plan year, of the employee's stated benefit for the current plan year (determined using an immediate straight life annuity factor based on a standard interest rate and a standard mortality table, for an employee whose attained age equals the employee's normal retirement age) over the employee's theoretical reserve as of the determination date.

(v) Effect of section 415 and 416 requirements. A target benefit plan does not fail to satisfy this paragraph (b)(3) merely because required contributions under the plan are limited by section 415 in a plan year. Similarly, a target benefit plan does not fail to satisfy this paragraph (b)(3) merely because additional contributions are made consistent with the requirements of section 416(c)(2) (regardless of whether the plan is top-heavy).

(vi) Certain conditions on allocations. A target benefit plan does not fail to satisfy this paragraph (b)(3) merely because required contributions under the plan are subject to the conditions on allocations permitted under § 1.401(a)(4)-2(b)(4)(iii).

(vii) Special rules for target benefit plans qualified under prior law. (A) Service taken into account prior to satisfaction of this paragraph. For purposes of determining whether the stated benefit formula satisfies paragraph (b)(3)(i)(A) of this section (e.g., whether the period over which an employee's stated benefit is deemed to accrue is the same as the period taken into account under the stated benefit formula as required by paragraph (b)(3)(i)(A) of this section), a target benefit plan that was adopted and in effect on September 19, 1991, is deemed to have satisfied this paragraph (b)(3), and an employee is treated as benefiting under the plan, in any year prior to the effective date applicable to the plan under § 1.401(a)(4)-13(a) or (b) that was taken into account in the stated benefit formula under the plan on September 19, 1991, if the plan satisfied the applicable nondiscrimination requirements for target benefit plans for that prior year.

(B) Initial theoretical reserve. Notwithstanding paragraph (b)(3)(iv)(B)(1) of this section, a target benefit plan under which the stated benefit formula takes into account service for an employee for plan years prior to the first plan year in which the plan satisfied this paragraph (b)(3), as permitted under paragraph (b)(3)(vii)(A) of this section, must determine an initial theoretical reserve for the employee as of the determination date for the last plan year beginning before such plan year under the rules of § 1.401(a)(4)-13(e).

(C) Satisfaction of prior law. In determining whether a plan satisfied the applicable nondiscrimination requirements for target benefit plans for any period prior to the effective date applicable to the plan under § 1.401(a)(4)-13(a) or (b), no amendments after September 19, 1991, other than amendments necessary to satisfy section 401(l), are taken into account.

(viii) Examples. The following examples illustrate the rules in this paragraph (b)(3):

*Example (1).* (a) Employer X maintains a target benefit plan with a calendar plan year that bases contributions on a stated benefit equal to 40 percent of each employee's average annual compensation, reduced pro rata for years of participation less than 25, payable annually as a straight life annuity commencing at normal retirement age. The UP-84 mortality table and an interest rate of 7.5 percent are used to calculate the contributions necessary to fund the stated benefit. Required contributions are determined on the last day of each plan year. The normal retirement age under the plan is 65. Employee M is 39 years old in 1994, has participated in the plan for six years, and has average annual compensation equal to $60,000 for the 1994 plan year. Assume that Employee M's theoretical reserve as of the last day of the 1993 plan year is $13,909, determined under § 1.401(a)(4)-13(e), and that required employer contributions for 1993 were determined using an interest rate of six percent.

(b) Under these facts, Employer X's 1994 required contribution to fund Employee M's stated benefit is $1,318, calculated as follows:

(1) Employee M's fractional rule benefit is $24,000 (40 percent of Employee M's average annual compensation of $60,000).

(2) The actuarial present value of Employee M's fractional rule benefit as of the last day of the 1994 plan year is $30,960 (Employee M's fractional rule benefit of $24,000 multiplied by 1.290, the actuarial present value factor for an annual straight life annuity commencing at age 65 applicable to a 39-year-old employee, determined using the stated interest rate of 7.5 percent and the UP-84 mortality table, and assuming no mortality before normal retirement age).

(3) The actuarial present value of Employee M's fractional rule benefit ($30,960) is reduced by Employee M's theoretical reserve as of the last day of the 1994 plan year. The theoretical reserve on that day is $14,744—the $13,909 theoretical reserve as of the last day of the 1993 plan year, increased by interest for one year at the rate of six percent. Because the required contribution for the 1993 plan year is taken into account under § 1.401(a)(4)-13(e)(2) in determining the theoretical reserve as of the last day of the 1993 plan year, it is not added to the theoretical reserve again in this paragraph (b)(3) of this Example 1. The resulting difference is $16,216 ($30,960 − $14,744).

(4) The $16,216 excess of the actuarial present value of Employee M's fractional rule benefit over Employee M's theoretical reserve is multiplied by 0.0813, the amortization factor applicable to a 39-year-old employee determined using the stated interest rate of 7.5 percent. The product of $1,318 is the amount of the required employer contribution for Employee M for the 1994 plan year.

*Example (2).* (a) The facts are the same as in Example 1, except that as of January 1, 1995, the plan's stated benefit formula is amended to provide for a stated benefit equal to 45 percent of average annual compensation, reduced pro rata for years of participation less than 25, payable annually as a straight life annuity commencing at normal retirement age. For the 1995 plan year, Employee M's average annual compensation continues to be $60,000. The mortality table used for the calculation of the employer's required contributions remains the same as in the prior plan year, but the plan's stated interest rate is changed to 8.0 percent effective as of December 31, 1995.

(b) Under these facts, Employer X's required contribution for Employee M is $1,290, calculated as follows:

(1) Employee M's fractional rule benefit is $27,000 (45 percent of $60,000).

(2) The actuarial present value of Employee M's fractional rule benefit as of the last day of the 1995 plan year is $32,319 ($27,000 multiplied by 1.197, the actuarial present value factor for an annuity commencing at age 65 applicable to a 40-year-old employee, determined using the stated interest rate of 8.0 percent and the UP-84 mortality table, and assuming no mortality before normal retirement age).

(3) The actuarial present value of Employee M's fractional rule benefit ($32,319) is reduced by Employee M's theoretical reserve as of the last day of the 1995 plan year. The theoretical reserve as of that day is $17,267—the $14,744 theoretical reserve as of the last day of the 1994 plan year plus the $1,318 required contribution for the 1994

plan year, both increased by interest for one year at the rate of 7.5 percent. The resulting difference is $15,052 ($32,319 – $17,267).

(4) The result in paragraph (b)(3) of this Example 2 is multiplied by 0.0857, the amortization factor applicable to a 40-year-old employee determined using the stated interest rate of 8.0 percent. The product, $1,290, is the amount of the required employer contribution for Employee M for the 1995 plan year.

**(c) Nondiscrimination in amount of contributions under a defined benefit plan.** *(1) General rule.* Equivalent allocations under a defined benefit plan are nondiscriminatory in amount for a plan year if the plan would satisfy § 1.401(a)(4)-3(c)(1) (taking into account § 1.401(a)(4)-3(c)(3)) for the plan year if an equivalent normal and most valuable allocation rate, as determined under paragraph (c)(2) of this section, were substituted for each employee's normal and most valuable accrual rate, respectively, in the determination of rate groups.

*(2) Determination of equivalent allocation rates.* (i) Basic definitions. An employee's equivalent normal and most valuable allocation rates for a plan year are, respectively, the actuarial present value of the increase over the plan year in the benefit that would be taken into account in determining the employee's normal and most valuable accrual rates for the plan year, expressed either as a dollar amount or as a percentage of the employee's plan year compensation. In the case of a contributory DB plan, the rules in § 1.401(a)(4)-6(b)(1), (b)(5), or (b)(6) must be used to determine the amount of each employee's employer-provided benefit that would be taken into account for this purpose.

(ii) Rules for determining actuarial present value. The actuarial present value of the increase in an employee's benefit must be determined using a standard interest rate and a standard mortality table, and no mortality may be assumed prior to the employee's testing age.

(iii) Options. The optional rules in § 1.401(a)(4)-2(c)(2)(iv) (imputation of permitted disparity) and (v) (grouping of rates) may be applied to determine an employee's equivalent normal and most valuable allocation rates by substituting those rates (determined without regard to the option) for the employee's allocation rate in that section where appropriate. In addition, the limitations under section 415 may be taken into account under § 1.401(a)(4)-3(d)(2)(ii)(B), and qualified disability benefits may be taken into account as accrued benefits under § 1.401(a)(4)-3(f)(2), in determining the increase in an employee's accrued benefit during a plan year for purposes of paragraph (c)(2)(i) of this section, if those rules would otherwise be available. No other options are available in determining an employee's equivalent normal and most valuable allocations rate except those (e.g., selection of alternative standard interest rates) specifically provided in this paragraph (c)(2). Thus, while all of the mandatory rules in § 1.401(a)(4)-3(d) and (f) for determining the amount of benefits used to determine an employee's normal and most valuable accrual rates (e.g., the treatment of early retirement window benefits in § 1.401(a)(4)-3(f)(4)) are applicable in determining an employee's equivalent normal and most valuable allocation rates, none of the optional rules under § 1.401(a)(4)-3 is available (except the options relating to the section 415 limits and qualified disability benefits noted above).

(iv) Consistency rule. Equivalent allocation rates must be determined in a consistent manner for all employees for the plan year. Thus, for example, the same standard interest rates must be used, and any available options must be applied consistently if at all.

*(3) Safe harbor testing method for cash balance plans.* (i) General rule. A cash balance plan is a defined benefit plan that defines benefits for each employee by reference to the employee's hypothetical account. An employee's hypothetical account is determined by reference to hypothetical allocations and interest adjustments that are analogous to actual allocations of contributions and earnings to an employee's account under a defined contribution plan. Because a cash balance plan is a defined benefit plan, whether it satisfies section 401(a)(4) with respect to the equivalent amount of contributions is generally determined under paragraphs (c)(1) and (c)(2) of this section. However, a cash balance plan that satisfies each of the requirements in paragraphs (c)(3)(ii) through (xi) of this section is deemed to satisfy section 401(a)(4) with respect to an equivalent amount of contributions.

(ii) Plan requirements in general. The plan must be an accumulation plan. The benefit formula under the plan must provide for hypothetical allocations for each employee in the plan that satisfy paragraph (c)(3)(iii) of this section, and interest adjustments to these hypothetical allocations that satisfy paragraph (c)(3)(iv) of this section. The benefit formula under the plan must provide that these hypothetical allocations and interest adjustments are accumulated as a hypothetical account for each employee, determined in accordance with paragraph (c)(3)(v) of this section. The plan must provide that an employee's accrued benefit under the plan as of any date is an annuity that is the actuarial equivalent of the employee's projected hypothetical account as of normal retirement age, determined in accordance with paragraph (c)(3)(vi) of this section. In addition, the plan must satisfy paragraphs (c)(3)(vii) through (xi) of this section (to the extent applicable) regarding optional forms of benefit, past service credits, post-normal retirement age benefits, certain uniformity requirements, and changes in the plan's benefit formula, respectively.

(iii) Hypothetical allocations. (A) In general. The hypothetical allocations provided under the plan's benefit formula must satisfy either paragraph (c)(3)(iii)(B) or (C) of this section. Paragraph (c)(3)(iii)(B) of this section provides a design-based safe harbor that does not require the annual comparison of hypothetical allocations under the plan. Paragraph (c)(3)(iii)(C) of this section requires the annual comparison of hypothetical allocations.

(B) Uniform hypothetical allocation formula. To satisfy this paragraph (c)(3)(iii)(B), the plan's benefit formula must provide for hypothetical allocations for all employees in the plan for all plan years of amounts that would satisfy § 1.401(a)(4)-2(b)(3) for each such plan year if the hypothetical allocations were the only allocations under a defined contribution plan for the employees for those plan years. Thus, the plan's benefit formula must provide for hypothetical allocations for all employees in the plan for all plan years that are the same percentage of plan year compensation or the same dollar amount. In determining whether the hypothetical allocations satisfy § 1.401(a)(4)-2(b)(3), the only provisions of § 1.401(a)(4)-2(b)(5) that apply are § 1.401(a)(4)-2(b)(5)(ii) (section 401(l) permitted disparity), (iii) (entry dates), (vi) (certain limits on allocations), and (vii) (dollar allocation per uniform unit of service). Thus, for example, the plan's benefit formula may take permitted disparity into account in a manner allowed under § 1.401(l)-2 for defined contribution plans.

(C) Modified general test. To satisfy this paragraph (c)(3)(iii)(C), the plan's benefit formula must provide for hypothetical allocations for all employees in the plan for the plan year that would satisfy the general test in § 1.401(a)(4)-2(c) for the plan year, if the hypothetical allocations were the only allocations for the employees taken into account under § 1.401(a)(4)-2(c)(2)(ii) under a defined contribution plan for the plan year. In determining whether the hypothetical allocations satisfy § 1.401(a)(4)-2(c), the provisions of § 1.401(a)(4)-2(c)(2)(iii) through (v) apply. Thus, for example, permitted disparity may be imputed under § 1.401(a)(4)-2(c)(2)(iv) in accordance with the rules of § 1.401(a)(4)-7(b) applicable to defined contribution plans.

(iv) Interest adjustments to hypothetical allocations. (A) General rule. The plan benefit formula must provide that the dollar amount of the hypothetical allocation for each employee for a plan year is automatically adjusted using an interest rate that satisfies paragraph (c)(3)(iv)(B) of this section, compounded no less frequently than annually, for the period that begins with a date in the plan year and that ends at normal retirement age. This requirement is not satisfied if any portion of the interest adjustments to a hypothetical allocation are contingent on the employee's satisfaction of any requirement. Thus, for example, the interest adjustments to a hypothetical allocation must be provided through normal retirement age, even though the employee terminates employment or commences benefits before that age.

(B) Requirements with respect to interest rates. The interest rate must be a single interest rate specified in the plan that is the same for all employees in the plan for all plan years. The interest rate must be either a standard interest rate or a variable interest rate. If the interest rate is a variable interest rate, it must satisfy paragraph (c)(3)(iv)(C) of this section.

(C) Variable interest rates. (1) General rule. The plan must specify the variable interest rate, the method for determining the current value of the variable interest rate, and the period (not to exceed 1 year) for which the current value of the variable interest rate applies. Permissible variable interest rates are listed in paragraph (c)(3)(iv)(C)(2) of this section. Permissible methods for determining the current value of the variable interest rate are provided in paragraph (c)(3)(iv)(C)(3) of this section.

(2) Permissible variable interest rates. The variable interest rate specified in the plan must be one of the following—

(i) The rate on 3-month Treasury Bills,

(ii) The rate on 6-month Treasury Bills,

(iii) The rate on 1-year Treasury Bills,

(iv) The yield on 1-year Treasury Constant Maturities,

(v) The yield on 2-year Treasury Constant Maturities,

(vi) The yield on 5-year Treasury Constant Maturities,

(vii) The yield on 10-year Treasury Constant Maturities,

(viii) The yield on 30-year Treasury Constant Maturities, or

(ix) The single interest rate such that, as of a single age specified in the plan, the actuarial present value of a deferred straight life annuity of an amount commencing at the normal retirement age under the plan, calculated using that interest rate and a standard mortality table but assuming no mortality before normal retirement age, is equal to the actuarial present value, as of the single age specified in the plan, of the same annuity calculated using the section 417(e) rates applicable to distributions in excess of $25,000 (determined under § 1.417(e)-1(d)), and the same mortality assumptions.

(3) Current value of variable interest rate. The current value of the variable interest rate that applies for a period must be either the value of the variable interest rate determined as of a specified date in the period or the immediately preceding period, or the average of the values of the variable interest rate as of two or more specified dates during the current period or the immediately preceding period. The value as of a date of the rate on a Treasury Bill is the average auction rate for the week or month in which the date falls, as reported in the Federal Reserve Bulletin. The value as of a date of the yield on a Treasury Constant Maturity is the average yield for the week, month, or year in which the date falls, as reported in the Federal Reserve Bulletin. (The Federal Reserve Bulletin is published by the Board of Governors of the Federal Reserve System and is available from Publication Services, Mail Stop 138, Board of Governors of the Federal Reserve System, Washington D.C. 20551.) The plan may limit the current value of the variable interest rate to a maximum (not less than the highest standard interest rate), or a minimum (not more than the lowest standard interest rate), or both.

(v) Hypothetical account. (A) Current value of hypothetical account. As of any date, the current value of an employee's hypothetical account must equal the sum of all hypothetical allocations and the respective interest adjustments to each such hypothetical allocation provided through that date for the employee under the plan's benefit formula (without regard to any interest adjustments provided under the plan's benefit formula for periods after that date).

(B) Value of hypothetical account as of normal retirement age. Under paragraph (c)(3)(vi) of this section, the value of an employee's hypothetical account must be determined as of normal retirement age in order to determine the employee's accrued benefit as of any date at or before normal retirement age. As of any date at or before normal retirement age, the value of an employee's hypothetical account as of normal retirement age must equal the sum of each hypothetical allocation provided through that date for the employee under the plan's benefit formula, plus the interest adjustments provided through normal retirement age on each of those hypothetical allocations for the employee under the plan's benefit formula (without regard to any hypothetical allocations that might be provided after that date under the plan's benefit formula). If the interest rate specified in the plan is a variable interest rate, the plan must specify that the determination in the preceding sentence is made by assuming that the current value of the variable interest rate for all future periods is either the current value of the variable interest rate for the current period or the average of the current values of the variable interest rate for the current period and one or more periods immediately preceding the current period (not to exceed 5 years in the aggregate).

(vi) Determination of accrued benefit. (A) Definition of accrued benefit. The plan must provide that at any date at or before normal retirement age the accrued benefit (within the meaning of section 411(a)(7)(A)(i)) of each employee in the plan is an annuity commencing at normal retirement age that is the actuarial equivalent of the employee's hypothetical account as of normal retirement age (as determined under paragraph (c)(3)(v)(B) of this section). The separate benefit that each employee accrues for a plan year is an annuity that is the actuarial equivalent of the employee's hypothetical allocation for that plan year, including the automatic adjustments for interest through normal retirement age required under paragraph (c)(3)(iv) of this section.

(B) Normal form of benefit. The annuity specified in paragraph (c)(3)(vi)(A) of this section must provide an annual benefit payable in the same form at the same uniform normal retirement age for all employees in the plan. The annual benefit must be the normal retirement benefit under the plan (within the meaning of section 411(a)(9)) under the plan.

(C) Determination of actuarial equivalence. For purposes of this paragraph (c)(3)(vi) and paragraph (c)(3)(ix) of this section, actuarial equivalence must be determined using a standard mortality table and either a standard interest rate or the interest rate specified in the plan for making interest adjustments to hypothetical allocations. If the interest rate used is the interest rate specified in the plan, and that rate is a variable interest rate, the assumed value of the variable interest rate for all future periods must be the same value that would be assumed for purposes of paragraph (c)(3)(v)(B) of this section. The same actuarial assumptions must be used for all employees in the plan.

(D) Effect of section 415 and 416 requirements. A plan does not fail to satisfy this paragraph (c)(3)(vi) merely because the accrued benefits under the plan are limited by section 415, or merely because the accrued benefits under the plan are the greater of the accrued benefits otherwise determined under the plan and the minimum benefit described in section 416(c)(1) (regardless of whether the plan is top-heavy).

(vii) Optional forms of benefit. (A) In general. The plan must satisfy the uniform subsidies requirement of § 1.401(a)(4)-3(b)(2)(iv) with respect to all subsidized optional forms of benefit.

(B) Limitation on subsidies. Unless hypothetical allocations are determined under a uniform hypothetical allocation formula that satisfies paragraph (c)(3)(iii)(B) of this section, the actuarial present value of any QJSA provided under the plan must not be greater than the single sum distribution to the employee that would satisfy paragraph (c)(3)(vii)(C) of this section assuming that it was distributed to the employee on the date of commencement of the QJSA.

(C) Distributions subject to section 417(e). Except as otherwise required under section 415(b), if the plan provides for a distribution alternative that is subject to the interest rate restrictions under section 417(e), the actuarial present value of the benefit paid to an employee under the distribution alternative must equal the nonforfeitable percentage (determined under the plan's vesting schedule) of the greater of the following two amounts—

(1) The current value of the employee's hypothetical account as of the date the distribution commences, calculated in accordance with paragraph (c)(3)(v)(A) of this section.

(2) The actuarial present value (calculated in accordance with § 1.417(e)-1(d)) of the employee's accrued benefit.

(D) Determination of actuarial present value. For purposes of this paragraph (c)(3)(vii), actuarial present value must be determined using a reasonable interest rate and mortality table. A standard interest rate and a standard mortality table are considered reasonable for this purpose.

(viii) Past service credit. The benefit formula under the plan may not provide for hypothetical allocations in the current plan year that are attributable to years of service before the current plan year, unless each of the following requirements is satisfied—

(A) The years of past service credit are granted on a uniform basis to all current employees in the plan.

(B) Hypothetical allocations for the current plan year are determined under a uniform hypothetical allocation formula that satisfies paragraph (c)(3)(iii)(B) of this section.

(C) The hypothetical allocations attributable to the years of past service would have satisfied the uniform hypothetical allocation formula requirement of paragraph (c)(3)(iii)(B) of this section, and the interest adjustments to those hypothetical allocations would have satisfied paragraph (c)(3)(iv)(A) of this section, if the plan provision granting past service had been in effect for the entire period for which years of past service are granted to any employee. In order to satisfy this requirement, the hypothetical allocation attributable to a year of past service must be adjusted for interest in accordance with paragraph (c)(3)(iv) of this section for the period (including the retroactive period) beginning with the year of past service to which the hypothetical allocation is attributable and ending at normal retirement age. If the interest rate specified in the plan is a variable interest rate, the interest adjustments for the period prior to the current plan year either must be based on the current value of the variable interest rate for the period in which the grant of past service first becomes effective or must be reconstructed based on the then current value of the variable interest rate that would have applied during each prior period.

(ix) Employees beyond normal retirement age. In the case of an employee who commences receipt of benefits after normal retirement age, the plan must provide that interest adjustments continue to be made to an employee's hypothetical account until the employee's benefit commencement date. In the case of an employee described in the previous sentence, the employee's accrued benefit is defined as an annuity that is the actuarial equivalent of the employee's hypothetical account determined in accordance with paragraph (c)(3)(v)(A) of this section as of the date of benefit commencement.

(x) Additional uniformity requirements. In addition to any uniformity requirements provided elsewhere in this paragraph (c)(3), the plan must satisfy the uniformity requirements in § 1.401(a)(4)-3(b)(2)(v) (uniform vesting and service requirements) and (vi) (no employee contributions). A plan does not fail to satisfy the uniformity requirements of this paragraph (c)(3)(x) or any other uniformity requirement provided in this paragraph (c)(3) merely because the plan contains one or more of the provisions described in § 1.401(a)(4)-3(b)(8)(iv) (prior vesting schedules), (v) (certain conditions on accruals), or (xi) (multiple definitions of service).

(xi) Changes in benefit formula, allocation formula, or interest rates. A plan does not fail to satisfy this paragraph (c)(3) merely because the plan is amended to change the benefit formula, hypothetical allocation formula, or the interest rate used to adjust hypothetical allocations for plan years after a fresh-start date, provided that the accrued benefits for plan years beginning after the fresh-start date are determined in accordance with § 1.401(a)(4)-13(c), as modified by § 1.401(a)(4)-13(f).

**(d) Safe-harbor testing method for defined benefit plans that are part of a floor-offset arrangement.** *(1) General rule.* A defined benefit plan that is part of a floor-offset arrangement is deemed to satisfy the nondiscriminatory amount requirement of § 1.401(a)(4)-1(b)(2) if all of the following requirements are satisfied:

(i) Under the floor-offset arrangement, the accrued benefit (as defined in section 411(a)(7)(A)(i)) that would otherwise be provided to an employee under the defined benefit plan must be reduced solely by the actuarial equivalent of all or part of the employee's account balance attributable to employer contributions under a defined contribution plan maintained by the same employer (plus the actuarial equivalent of all or part of any prior distributions from that portion of the account balance). If any portion of the benefit that is being offset is nonforfeitable, that portion may be offset only by a benefit (or portion of a benefit) that is also nonforfeitable. In determining the actuarial equivalent of amounts provided under the defined contribution plan, an interest rate no higher than the highest standard interest rate must be used, and no mortality may be assumed in determining the actuarial equivalent of any prior distributions from the defined contribution plan or for periods prior to the benefit commencement date under the defined benefit plan.

(ii) The defined benefit plan may not be a contributory DB plan (unless it satisfies § 1.401(a)(4)-6(b)(6)), and benefits under the defined benefit plan may not be reduced by any portion of the employee's account balance under the defined contribution plan (or prior distributions from that account) that are attributable to employee contributions.

(iii) The defined benefit plan and the defined contribution plan must benefit the same employees.

(iv) The offset under the defined benefit plan must be applied to all employees on the same terms.

(v) All employees must have available to them under the defined contribution plan the same investment options and the same options with respect to the timing of preretirement distributions.

(vi) The defined benefit plan must satisfy the uniformity requirements of § 1.401(a)(4)-3(b)(2) and the unit credit safe harbor in § 1.401(a)(4)- 3(b)(3) without taking into account the offset described in paragraph (d)(1)(i) of this section (i.e., on a gross-benefit basis), and the defined contribution plan must satisfy any of the tests in § 1.401(a)(4)-2(b) or (c). Alternatively, the defined benefit plan must satisfy any of the tests in § 1.401(a)(4)-3(b) or (c) without taking into account the offset described in paragraph (d)(1)(i) of this section, and the defined contribution plan must satisfy the uniform allocation safe harbor in § 1.401(a)(4)-2(b)(2).

(vii) The defined contribution plan may not be a section 401(k) plan or a section 401(m) plan.

*(2) Application of safe-harbor testing method to qualified offset arrangements.* A defined benefit plan that is part of a qualified offset arrangement as defined in section 1116(f)(5) of the Tax Reform Act of 1986, Public Law No. 99-514, is deemed to satisfy the requirements of paragraph (d)(1)(vi) and (vii) of this section, if the only defined contribution plans included in the qualified offset arrangement are section 401(k) plans, section 401(m) plans, or both, and the defined benefit plan would satisfy the requirements of paragraph (d)(1)(vi) of this section assuming the elective contributions for each employee under the defined contribution plan were the same (either as a dollar amount or as a percentage of compensation) for all plan years since the establishment of the plan.

T.D. 8360, 9/12/91, amend T.D. 8485, 8/30/93, T.D. 8954, 6/28/2001.

### § 1.401(a)(4)-9 Plan aggregation and restructuring.

**(a) Introduction.** Two or more plans that are permissively aggregated and treated as a single plan under § 1.410(b)-7(d) must also be treated as a single plan for purposes of section 401(a)(4). See § 1.401(a)(4)-12 (definition of plan). An aggregated plan is generally tested under the same rules applicable to single plans. Paragraph (b) of this section, however, provides special rules for determining whether a plan that consists of one or more defined contribution plans and one or more defined benefit plans (a DB/DC plan) satisfies section 401(a)(4) with respect to the amount of employer-provided benefits and the availability of benefits, rights, and features. Paragraph (c) of this section provides rules allowing a plan to be treated as consisting of separate component plans and allowing the component plans to be tested separately under section 401(a)(4).

**(b) Application of nondiscrimination requirements to DB/DC plans.** *(1) General rule.* Except as provided in paragraph (b)(2) of this section, whether a DB/DC plan satisfies section 401(a)(4) is determined using the same rules applicable to a single plan. In addition, paragraph (b)(3) of this section provides an optional rule for demonstrating nondiscrimination in availability of benefits, rights, and features provided under a DB/DC plan.

*(2) Special rules for demonstrating nondiscrimination in amount of contributions or benefits.* (i) Application of general tests. A DB/DC plan satisfies section 401(a)(4) with respect to the amount of contributions or benefits for a plan year if it would satisfy § 1.401(a)(4)-3(c)(1) (without regard to the special rule in § 1.401(a)(4)-3(c)(3)) for the plan year if an employee's aggregate normal and most valuable allocation rates, as determined under paragraph (b)(2)(ii)(A) of this section, or an employee's aggregate normal and most valuable accrual rates, as determined under paragraph (b)(2)(ii)(B) of this section, were substituted for each employee's normal and most valuable accrual rates, respectively, in the determination of rate groups.

(ii) Determination of aggregate rates. (A) Aggregate allocation rates. An employee's aggregate normal and most valuable allocation rates are determined by treating all defined contribution plans that are part of the DB/DC plan as a single plan, and all defined benefit plans that are part of the DB/DC plan as a separate single plan; and determining an allocation rate and equivalent normal and most valuable allocation rates for the employee under each plan under §§ 1.401(a)(4)-2(c)(2) and 1.401(a)(4)-8(c)(2), respectively. The employee's aggregate normal allocation rate is the sum of the employee's allocation rate and equivalent normal allocation rate determined in this manner, and the employee's aggregate most valuable allocation rate is the sum of the employee's allocation rate and equivalent most valuable allocation rate determined in this manner.

(B) Aggregate accrual rates. An employee's aggregate normal and most valuable accrual rates are determined by treating all defined contribution plans that are part of the DB/DC plan as a single plan, and all defined benefit plans that are part of the DB/DC plan as a separate single plan; and determining an equivalent accrual rate and normal and most valuable accrual rates for the employee under each plan under §§ 1.401(a)(4)-8(b)(2) and 1.401(a)(4)-3(d), respectively. The employee's aggregate normal accrual rate is the sum of the employee's equivalent accrual rate and the normal accrual rate determined in this manner, and the employee's aggregate most valuable accrual rate is the sum of the employee's equivalent accrual rate and most valuable accrual rate determined in this manner.

(iii) Options applied on an aggregate basis. The optional rules in § 1.401(a)(4)-2(c)(2)(iv) (imputation of permitted disparity) and (v) (grouping of rates) may not be used to determine an employee's allocation or equivalent allocation rate, but may be applied to determine an employee's aggregate normal and most valuable allocation rates by substituting those rates (determined without regard to the option) for the employee's allocation rate in that section where appropriate. The optional rules in § 1.401(a)(4)-3(d)(3) (e.g., imputation of permitted disparity) may not be used to determine an employee's accrual or equivalent accrual rate, but may be applied to determine an employee's aggregate normal and most valuable accrual rate by substituting those rates (determined without regard to the option) for the employee's normal and most valuable accrual rates, respectively, in that section where appropriate.

(iv) Consistency rule. (A) General rule. Aggregate normal and most valuable allocation rates and aggregate normal and most valuable accrual rates must be determined in a consistent manner for all employees for the plan year. Thus, for example, the same measurement periods and interest rates must be used, and any available options must be applied consistently, if at all, for the entire DB/DC plan. Consequently, options that are not permitted to be used under § 1.401(a)(4)-8 in cross-testing a defined contribution plan or a defined benefit plan (such as measurement periods that include future periods, non-standard interest rates, the option to disregard compensation adjustments described in § 1.401(a)(4)-13(d), or the option to disregard plan provisions providing for actuarial increases after normal retirement age under § 1.401(a)(4)-3(f)(3)) may not be used in testing a DB/DC plan on either a benefits or contributions basis, because their use would inevitably result in inconsistent determinations under the defined contribution and defined benefit portions of the plan.

(B) Exception for section 415 alternative. A DB/DC plan does not fail to satisfy the consistency rule in paragraph (b)(2)(iv)(A) of this section merely because the limitations under section 415 are not taken into account, or may not be taken into account, under § 1.401(a)(4)-3(d)(2)(ii)(B) in determining employees' accrual or equivalent allocation rates under the defined benefit portion of the plan, even though those limitations are applied in determining employees' allocation and equivalent accrual rates under the defined contribution portion of the plan.

(v) Eligibility for testing on a benefits basis. (A) General rule. For plan years beginning on or after January 1, 2002, unless, for the plan year, a DB/DC plan is primarily defined benefit in character (within the meaning of paragraph (b)(2)(v)(B) of this section) or consists of broadly available separate plans (within the meaning of paragraph (b)(2)(v)(C) of this section), the DB/DC plan must satisfy the minimum aggregate allocation gateway of paragraph (b)(2)(v)(D) of this section for the plan year in order to be permitted to demonstrate satisfaction of the nondiscrimination in amount requirement of § 1.401(a)(4)-1(b)(2) on the basis of benefits.

(B) Primarily defined benefit in character. A DB/DC plan is primarily defined benefit in character if, for more than 50% of the NHCEs benefitting under the plan, the normal accrual rate for the NHCE attributable to benefits provided under defined benefit plans that are part of the DB/DC plan exceeds the equivalent accrual rate for the NHCE attributable to contributions under defined contribution plans that are part of the DB/DC plan.

(C) Broadly available separate plans. A DB/DC plan consists of broadly available separate plans if the defined contribution plan and the defined benefit plan that are part of the DB/DC plan each would satisfy the requirements of section 410(b) and the nondiscrimination in amount requirement of § 1.401(a)(4)-1(b)(2) if each plan were tested separately and assuming that the average benefit percentage test of § 1.410(b)-5 were satisfied. For this purpose, all defined contribution plans that are part of the DB/DC plan are treated as a single defined contribution plan and all defined benefit plans that are part of the DB/DC plan are treated as a single defined benefit plan. In addition, if permitted disparity is used for an employee for purposes of satisfying the separate testing requirement of this paragraph (b)(2)(v)(C) for plans of one type, it may not be used in satisfying the separate testing requirement for plans of the other type for the employee.

(D) Minimum aggregate allocation gateway. (1) General rule. A DB/DC plan satisfies the minimum aggregate allocation gateway if each NHCE has an aggregate normal allocation rate that is at least one third of the aggregate normal allocation rate of the HCE with the highest such rate (HCE rate), or, if less, 5% of the NHCE's compensation, provided that the HCE rate does not exceed 25% of compensation. If the HCE rate exceeds 25% of compensation, then the aggregate normal allocation rate for each NHCE must be at least 5% increased by one percentage point for each 5-percentage-point increment (or portion thereof) by which the HCE rate exceeds 25% (e.g., the NHCE minimum is 6% for an HCE rate that exceeds 25% but not 30%, and 7% for an HCE rate that exceeds 30% but not 35%).

(2) Deemed satisfaction. A plan is deemed to satisfy the minimum aggregate allocation gateway of this paragraph (b)(2)(v)(D) if the aggregate normal allocation rate for each NHCE is at least 7½% of the NHCE's compensation within the meaning of section 415(c)(3), measured over a period of time permitted under the definition of plan year compensation.

(3) Averaging of equivalent allocation rates for NHCEs. For purposes of this paragraph (b)(2)(v)(D), a plan is permitted to treat each NHCE who benefits under the defined benefit plan as having an equivalent normal allocation rate equal to the average of the equivalent normal allocation rates under the defined benefit plan for all NHCEs benefitting under that plan.

(E) Determination of rates. For purposes of this paragraph (b)(2)(v), the normal accrual rate and the equivalent normal allocation rate attributable to defined benefit plans, the equivalent accrual rate attributable to defined contribution plans, and the aggregate normal allocation rate are determined under paragraph (b)(2)(ii) of this section, but without taking into account the imputation of permitted disparity under § 1.401(a)(4)-7, except as otherwise permitted under paragraph (b)(2)(v)(C) of this section.

(F) Examples. The following examples illustrate the application of this paragraph (b)(2)(v):

*Example (1).* (i) Employer A maintains Plan M, a defined benefit plan, and Plan N, a defined contribution plan. All HCEs of Employer A are covered by Plan M (at a 1% accrual rate), but are not covered by Plan N. All NHCEs of Employer A are covered by Plan N (at a 3% allocation rate), but are not covered by Plan M. Because Plan M does not satisfy section 410(b) standing alone, Plans M and N are aggregated for purposes of satisfying sections 410(b) and 401(a)(4).

(ii) Because none of the NHCEs participate in the defined benefit plan, the aggregated DB/DC plan is not primarily defined benefit in character within the meaning of paragraph (b)(2)(v)(B) of this section nor does it consist of broadly available separate plans within the meaning of paragraph (b)(2)(v)(C) of this section. Accordingly, the aggregated Plan M and Plan N must satisfy the minimum aggregate allocation gateway of paragraph (b)(2)(v)(D) of this section in order be permitted to demonstrate satisfaction of the nondiscrimination in amount requirement of § 1.401(a)(4)-1(b)(2) on the basis of benefits.

*Example (2).* (i) Employer B maintains Plan O, a defined benefit plan, and Plan P, a defined contribution plan. All of the six employees of Employer B are covered under both Plan O and Plan P. Under Plan O, all employees have a uniform normal accrual rate of 1% of compensation. Under Plan P, Employees A and B, who are HCEs, receive an allocation rate of 15%, and participants C, D, E and F, who are NHCEs, receive an allocation rate of 3%. Employer B aggregates Plans O and P for purposes of satisfying sections 410(b) and 401(a)(4). The equivalent normal allocation and normal accrual rates under Plans O and P are as follows:

| Employee | Equivalent normal allocation rates for the 1% accural under plan O (defined benefit plan) (in percent) | Equivalent normal accural rates for the 15%/3% allocation under plan P (defined contribution plan) (in percent) |
|---|---|---|
| HCE A (age 55) | 3.93 | 3.82 |
| HCE B (age 50) | 2.61 | 5.74 |
| C (age 60) | 5.91 | .51 |
| D (age 45) | 1.74 | 1.73 |
| E (age 35) | .77 | 3.90 |
| F (age 25) | .34 | 8.82 |

(ii) Although all of the NHCEs benefit under Plan O (the defined benefit plan), the aggregated DB/DC plan is not primarily defined benefit in character because the normal accrual rate attributable to defined benefit plans (which is 1% for each of the NHCEs) is greater than the equivalent accrual rate under defined contribution plans only for Employee C. In addition, because the 15% allocation rate is available only to HCEs, the defined contribution plan cannot satisfy the requirements of § 1.401(a)(4)-2 and does not have broadly available allocation rates within the meaning of § 1.401(a)(4)-8(b)(1)(iii). Further, the defined contribution plan does not satisfy the minimum allocation gateway of § 1.401(a)(4)-8(b)(1)(vi) (3% is less than ⅓ of the 15% HCE rate). Therefore, the defined contribution plan within the DB/DC plan cannot separately satisfy § 1.401(a)(4)-1(b)(2) and does not constitute a broadly available separate plan within the meaning of paragraph (b)(2)(v)(C) of this section. Accordingly, the aggregated plans are permitted to demonstrate satisfaction of the nondiscrimination in amounts requirement of § 1.401(a)(4)-1(b)(2) on the basis of benefits only if the aggregated plans satisfy the minimum aggregate allocation gateway of paragraph (b)(2)(v)(D) of this section.

(iii) Employee A has an aggregate normal allocation rate of 18.93% under the aggregated plans (3.93% from Plan O plus 15% from Plan P), which is the highest aggregate normal allocation rate for any HCE under the plans. Employee F has an aggregate normal allocation rate of 3.34% under the aggregated plans (.34% from Plan O plus 3% from Plan P) which is less than the 5% aggregate normal allocation rate that Employee F would be required to have to satisfy the minimum aggregate allocation gateway of paragraph (b)(2)(v)(D) of this section.

(iv) However, for purposes of satisfying the minimum aggregate allocation gateway of paragraph (b)(2)(v)(D) of this section, Employer B is permitted to treat each NHCE who benefits under Plan O (the defined benefit plan) as having an equivalent allocation rate equal to the average of the equivalent allocation rates under Plan O for all NHCEs benefitting under that plan. The average of the equivalent allocation rates for all of the NHCEs under Plan O is 2.19% (the sum of 5.91%, 1.74%, .77%, and .34%, divided by 4). Accordingly, Employer B is permitted to treat all of the NHCEs as having an equivalent allocation rate attributable to Plan O equal to 2.19%. Thus, all of the NHCEs can be treated as having an aggregate normal allocation rate of 5.19% for this purpose (3% from the defined contribution plan and 2.19% from the defined benefit plan) and the aggregated DB/DC plan satisfies the minimum aggregate allocation gateway of paragraph (b)(2)(v)(D) of this section.

*(3) Optional rules for demonstrating nondiscrimination in availability of certain benefits, rights, and features.* (i) Current availability. A DB/DC plan is deemed to satisfy § 1.401(a)(4)-4(b)(1) with respect to the current availability of a benefit, right, or feature other than a single sum benefit, loan, ancillary benefit, or benefit commencement date (including the availability of in-service withdrawals), that is provided under only one type of plan (defined benefit or defined contribution) included in the DB/DC plan, if the benefit, right, or feature is currently available to all NHCEs in all plans of the same type as the plan under which it is provided.

(ii) Effective availability. The fact that it may be difficult or impossible to provide a benefit, right, or feature described in paragraph (b)(3)(i) of this section under a plan of a different type than the plan or plans under which it is provided is one of the factors taken into account in determining whether the plan satisfies the effective availability requirement of § 1.401(a)(4)-4(c)(1).

**(c) Plan restructuring.** *(1) General rule.* A plan may be treated, in accordance with this paragraph (c), as consisting of two or more component plans for purposes of determining whether the plan satisfies section 401(a)(4). If each of the component plans of a plan satisfies all of the requirements of sections 401(a)(4) and 410(b) as if it were a separate plan, then the plan is treated as satisfying section 401(a)(4).

*(2) Identification of component plans.* A plan may be restructured into component plans, each consisting of all the allocations, accruals, and other benefits, rights, and features provided to a selected group of employees. The employer may select the group of employees used for this purpose in any manner, and the composition of the groups may be changed from plan year to plan year. Every employee must be included in one and only one component plan under the same plan for a plan year.

*(3) Satisfaction of section 401(a)(4) by a component plan.* (i) General rule. The rules applicable in determining whether a component plan satisfies section 401(a)(4) are the same as those applicable to a plan. Thus, for this purpose, any reference to a plan in section 401(a)(4) and the regulations thereunder (other than this paragraph (c)) is interpreted as a reference to a component plan. As is true for a plan, whether a component plan satisfies the uniformity and other requirements applicable to safe harbor plans under §§ 1.401(a)(4)-2(b) and 1.401(a)(4)-3(b) is determined on a design basis. Thus, for example, plan provisions are not disregarded merely because they do not currently apply to employees in the component plan if they will apply to those employees as a result of the mere passage of time.

(ii) Restructuring not available for certain testing purposes. The safe harbor in § 1.401(a)(4)-2(b)(3) for plans with uniform points allocation formulas is not available in testing (and thus cannot be satisfied by) contributions under a component plan. Similarly, component plans cannot be used for purposes of determining whether a plan provides broadly available allocation rates (as defined in § 1.401(a)(4)-8(b)(1)(iii)), determining whether a plan has a gradual age or service schedule (as defined in § 1.401(a)(4)-8(b)(1)(iv)), determining whether a plan has allocation rates that are based on a uniform target benefit allocation (as defined in § 1.401(a)(4)-8(b)(1)(v)), or determining whether a plan is primarily defined benefit in character or consists of broadly available separate plans (as defined in paragraphs (b)(2)(v)(B) and (C) of this section). In addition, the minimum allocation gateway of § 1.401(a)(4)-8(b)(1)(vi) and the minimum aggregate allocation gateway of paragraph (b)(2)(v)(D) of this section cannot be satisfied on the basis of component plans. See §§ 1.401(k)-1(b)(4)(iv)(B) and 1.401(m)-1(b)(4)(iv)(B) for rules regarding the inapplicability of restructuring to section 401(k) plans and section 401(m) plans.

*(4) Satisfaction of section 410(b) by a component plan.* (i) General rule. The rules applicable in determining whether a component plan satisfies section 410(b) are generally the same as those applicable to a plan. However, a component plan is deemed to satisfy the average benefit percentage test of § 1.410(b)-5 if the plan of which it is a part satisfies § 1.410(b)-5 (without regard to § 1.410(b)-5(f)). In the case of a component plan that is part of a plan that relies on § 1.410(b)-5(f) to satisfy the average benefit percentage test, the component plan is deemed to satisfy the average benefit percentage test only if the component plan separately satisfies § 1.410(b)-5(f). In addition, all component plans of a plan are deemed to satisfy the average benefit percentage test if the plan makes an early retirement window benefit (within the meaning of § 1.401(a)(4)-3(f)(4)(iii)) currently available (within the meaning of § 1.401(a)(4)-3(f)(4)(ii)(A)) to a group of employees that satisfies section 410(b) (without regard to the average benefit percentage test), and if it would not be necessary for the plan or any rate group or component plan of the plan to satisfy that test in order for the plan to satisfy sections 401(a)(4) and 410(b) in the absence of the early retirement window benefit.

(ii) Relationship to satisfaction of section 410(b) by the plan. Satisfaction of section 410(b) by a component plan is relevant solely for purposes of determining whether the plan of which it is a part satisfies section 401(a)(4), and not for purposes of determining whether the plan satisfies section 410(b) itself. The plan must still independently satisfy section 410(b) in order to be a qualified plan. Similarly, satisfaction of section 410(b) by a plan is relevant solely for purposes of determining whether the plan, and not the component plan, satisfies section 410(b). Thus, for example, a component plan that does not satisfy the ratio percentage test of § 1.410(b)-2(b)(2) must still satisfy the average benefit test of § 1.410(b)-2(b)(3), even though the plan of which it is a part satisfies the ratio percentage test.

*(5) Effect of restructuring under other sections.* The restructuring rules provided in this paragraph (c) apply solely for purposes of sections 401(a)(4) and 401(l), and those portions of sections 410(b), 414(s), and any other provisions that are specifically applicable in determining whether the requirements of section 401(a)(4) are satisfied. Thus, for example, a component plan is not treated as a separate plan under section 401(a)(26).

*(6) Examples.* The following examples illustrate the rules in this paragraph (c):

*Example (1).* Employer X maintains a defined benefit plan. The plan provides a normal retirement benefit equal to 1.0 percent of average annual compensation times years of service to employees at Plant S, and 1.5 percent of average annual compensation times years of service to employees at Plant T. Under paragraph (c)(2) of this section, the plan may be treated as consisting of two component defined benefit plans, one providing retirement benefits equal to 1.0 percent of average annual compensation times years of service to the employees at Plant S, and another providing benefits equal to 1.5 percent of average annual compensation times years of service to employees at Plant T. If each component plan satisfies sections 401(a)(4) and 410(b) as if it were a separate plan under the rules of this paragraph (c), then the entire plan satisfies section 401(a)(4).

*Example (2).* (a) Employer Y maintains Plan A, a defined benefit plan, for its Employees M, N, O, P, Q, and R. Plan A provides benefits under a uniform formula that satisfies the requirements of § 1.401(a)(4)-3(b)(2) and (b)(3) before it is amended on February 14, 1994. The amendment provides an early retirement window benefit that is a subsidized optional form of benefit under § 1.401(a)(4)-3(b)(2)(iii) and that is available on the same terms to all employees who satisfy the eligibility requirements for the window. The early retirement window benefit is available only to employees who retire between June 1, 1994, and November 30, 1994.

(b) Assume that Employees M, N, and O will be eligible to receive the window benefit by the end of the window period and Employees P, Q, and R will not. Because substantially all employees will not satisfy the eligibility requirements for the early retirement window benefit by the close of the early retirement window benefit period, Plan A fails to satisfy the uniform subsidies requirement of § 1.401(a)(4)-3(b)(2)(iii). See § 1.401(a)(4)-3(b)(2)(vi), Example 6.

(c) Under paragraph (c)(2) of this section, Employees M, N, O, P, Q, and R may be grouped into two component plans, one consisting of Employees M, N, and O and all their accruals and other benefits, rights, and features under the plan (including the early retirement window benefit), and another consisting of Employees P, Q, and R, and all their accruals and other benefits, rights, and features under the plan. Each of the component plans identified in this manner satisfies the uniform subsidies requirement of § 1.401(a)(4)-3(b)(2)(iii), and thus satisfies § 1.401(a)(4)-3(b). The entire plan satisfies section 401(a)(4) under the rules of this paragraph (c), if each of these component plans also satisfies section 410(b) as if it were a separate plan (including, if applicable, the reasonable classification requirement of § 1.410(b)-4(b), and taking into account the special rule of paragraph (c)(4)(i) of this section that forgives the average benefit percentage test in certain situations in which the average benefit percentage test would be required solely as a result of the early retirement window benefit).

*Example (3).* (a) Employer Z maintains Plan B, a defined benefit plan with a benefit formula that provides two percent of average annual compensation for each year of service up to 20 to each employee. Assume that Plan B would satisfy the fractional accrual rule safe harbor in § 1.401(a)(4)-3(b)(4), except that some employees accrue a portion of their normal retirement benefit in the current plan year that is more than one third larger than the portion of the same benefit accrued by other employees for the current plan year, and the plan therefore fails to satisfy the one-third-larger-requirement of § 1.401(a)(4)-3(b)(4)(i)(C)(1).

(b) Employer Z restructures Plan B into two plans, one covering employees with 30 years or less of service at normal retirement age, and the other covering all other employees. Each component plan would separately satisfy the one-third-larger requirement of § 1.401(a)(4)-3(b)(4)(i)(C)(1) if the only employees taken into account were those employees included in the component plan in the current plan year. Under paragraph (c)(3)(i) of this section and § 1.401(a)(4)-3(b)(4)(i)(C)(1), however, the component plans do not satisfy the one-third-larger requirement because the safe harbor determination is made taking into account the effect of the plan benefit formula on any potential employee in the component plan (other than employees with more than 33 years of service at normal retirement age), and not just those employees included in the component plan in the current plan year.

T.D. 8360, 9/12/91, amend T.D. 8485, 8/30/93, T.D. 8954, 6/28/2001, T.D. 9169, 12/28/2004.

### § 1.401(a)(4)-10 Testing of former employees.

**(a) Introduction.** This section provides rules for determining whether a plan satisfies the nondiscriminatory amount and nondiscriminatory availability requirements of § 1.401(a)(4)-1(b)(2) and (3), respectively, with respect to former employees. Generally, this section is relevant only in the case of benefits provided through an amendment to the plan effective in the current plan year. See the definitions of employee and former employee in § 1.401(a)(4)-12.

**(b) Nondiscrimination in amount of contributions or benefits.** *(1) General rule.* A plan satisfies § 1.401(a)(4)-1(b)(2) with respect to the amount of contributions or benefits provided to former employees if, under all of the relevant facts and circumstances, the amount of contributions or benefits provided to former employees does not discriminate significantly in favor of former HCEs. For this purpose, contributions or benefits provided to former employees includes all contributions or benefits provided to former employees or, at the employer's option, only those contributions or benefits arising out of the amendment providing the contributions or benefits. A plan under which no former employee currently benefits (within the meaning of § 1.410(b)-3(b)) is deemed to satisfy this paragraph (b).

*(2) Permitted disparity.* Section 401(l) and § 1.401(a)(4)-7 generally apply to benefits provided to former employees in the same manner as those provisions apply to employees. Thus, for example, for purposes of determining a former employee's cumulative permitted disparity limit, the sum of the former employee's total annual disparity fractions (within the meaning of § 1.401(l)-5) as an employee continues to be taken into account. However, the permitted disparity rate applicable to a former employee is determined under § 1.401(l)-3(e) as of the age the former employee commenced receipt of benefits, not as of the date the employee receives the accrual for the current plan year.

*(3) Examples.* The following examples illustrate the rules in this paragraph (b):

*Example (1).* Employer X maintains a section 401(l) plan, Plan A, that uses maximum permitted disparity. Plan A is amended to increase the benefits of all former employees in pay status. The percentage increase for each former employee is reasonably comparable to the adjustment in social security benefits under section 215(i)(2)(A) of the Social Security Act since the former employee commenced receipt of benefits. Plan A does not fail to satisfy this paragraph (b) merely because of the amendment.

*Example (2).* The facts are the same as in Example 1, except that the amendment provides an across-the-board 20 percent increase in benefits for all former employees in pay status. The cost of living has increased at an average rate of three percent in the two years preceding the amendment, and some HCEs have retired and become former HCEs during that period. Because this amendment increases the disparity in the plan formula beyond the maximum permitted disparity adjusted for any reasonable approximation of the increase in the cost of living since the HCEs retired, Plan A discriminates significantly in favor of former HCEs, and thus does not satisfy this paragraph (b).

*Example (3).* The facts are the same as an Example 1, except that Plan A is only amended to increase the benefits of former employees in pay status who terminated employment with Employer X after attaining early retirement age. The determination of whether the amendment causes Plan A to fail to satisfy this paragraph (b) must take into account the relative numbers of former HCEs and former NHCEs who have terminated employment with Employer X after attaining early retirement age.

**(c) Nondiscrimination in availability of benefits, rights, or features.** A plan satisfies section 401(a)(4) with respect to the availability of benefits, rights, and features provided to former employees if any change in the availability of any benefit, right, or feature to any former employee is applied in a manner that, under all of the relevant facts and circumstances, does not discriminate significantly in favor of former HCEs. For purposes of demonstrating that a plan satisfies section 401(a)(4) with respect to the availability of loans provided to former employees, an employer may treat former employees who are parties in interest within the meaning of section 3(14) of the Employee Retirement Income Security Act of 1974 as employees.

T.D. 8360, 9/12/91, amend T.D. 8485, 8/30/93.

### § 1.401(a)(4)-11 Additional rules.

**(a) Introduction.** This section provides additional rules for determining whether a plan satisfies section 401(a)(4). Paragraph (b) of this section provides rules for the treatment of the portion of an employee's accrued benefit or account balance that is attributable to rollovers, transfers between plans, and employee buybacks. Paragraph (c) of this section provides rules regarding vesting. Paragraph (d) of this section provides rules regarding service crediting. Paragraph (e) of this section, regarding family aggregation, and paragraph (f) of this section, regarding governmental plans, are reserved. Paragraph (g) of this section provides rules regarding the extent to which corrective amendments may be made for purposes of section 401(a).

**(b) Rollovers, transfers, and buybacks.** *(1) Rollovers and elective transfers.* The portion of an employee's accrued benefit or account balance under a plan that is attributable to rollover (including direct rollover) contributions to the plan that are described in section 402(c), 402(e)(6), 403(a)(4), 403(a)(5), or 408(d)(3), or elective transfers to the plan that are described in § 1.411(d)-4, Q&A-3(b), is not taken into account in determining whether the plan satisfies the nondiscriminatory amount requirement of § 1.401(a)(4)-1(b)(2).

*(2) Other transfers.* [Reserved]

*(3) Employee buybacks.* (i) Rehired employee buyback of previous service. An employee's repayment to a plan of a prior distribution from the plan (including reasonable interest from the time of the distribution) that results in the restoration of the employee's accrued benefit under the plan (or the service associated with that accrued benefit) that would oth-

erwise be disregarded in determining the employee's accrued benefit in accordance with section 411 on account of the distribution is not treated as an employee contribution for purposes of §§ 1.401(a)(4)-1 through 1.401(a)(4)-13.

(ii) Make-up of missed employee contributions. If a contributory DB plan gives all employees who did not make employee contributions for a prior period the right to make the missed contributions at a later date (including reasonable interest from the time of the missed contributions) and, once the contributions have been made, determines benefits under the plan by treating the employee contributions (excluding the interest) as if they were actually made during that prior period, then those contributions must satisfy § 1.401(a)(4)-6(c) as if they were employee contributions actually made during that prior period. Thus, for example, § 1.401(a)(4)-6(c)(2) is not satisfied for the current plan year if the employee contribution rate (within the meaning of § 1.401(a)(4)-6(b)(2)(ii)(A) but determined without regard to the interest) for the employees making up missed contributions is different than the employee contribution rate applicable to other employees during the prior period. The rule in this paragraph (b)(3)(ii) may be extended to employees who did not make employee contributions for a period of service that is or would otherwise have been credited under the plan and that preceded their participation in the plan.

**(c) Vesting.** *(1) General rule.* A plan satisfies this paragraph (c) if the manner in which employees vest in their accrued benefits under the plan does not discriminate in favor of HCEs. Whether the manner in which employees vest in their accrued benefits under a plan discriminates in favor of HCEs is determined under this paragraph (c) based on all of the relevant facts and circumstances, taking into account any relevant provisions of sections 401(a)(5)(E), 411(a)(10), 411(d)(1), 411(d)(2), 411(d)(3), 411(e), and 420(c)(2), and taking into account any plan provisions that affect the nonforfeitability of employees' accrued benefits (e.g., plan provisions regarding suspension of benefits permitted under section 411(a)(3)(B)), other than the method of crediting years of service for purposes of applying the vesting schedule provided in the plan.

*(2) Deemed equivalence of statutory vesting schedules.* For purposes of this paragraph (c), the manner in which employees vest in their accrued benefits under the vesting schedules in section 411(a)(2)(A) and (B) are treated as equivalent to one another, and the manner in which employees vest in their accrued benefits under the vesting schedules in section 416(b)(1)(A) and (B) are treated as equivalent to one another.

*(3) Safe harbor for vesting schedules.* The manner in which employees vest in their accrued benefits under a plan is deemed not to discriminate in favor of HCEs if each combination of plan provisions that affect the nonforfeitability of any employee's accrued benefit would satisfy the nondiscriminatory availability requirements of § 1.401(a)(4)-4 if that combination were an other right or feature.

*(4) Examples.* The following examples illustrate the rules in this paragraph (c):

*Example (1).* Plan A provides the six-year graded vesting schedule described in section 416(b)(1)(B). In 1996, Plan A is amended to provide the five-year vesting schedule described in section 411(a)(2)(A). To comply with section 411(a)(10)(B), the plan amendment also provides that all employees with at least three years of service may elect to retain the prior vesting schedule. The manner in which employees vest in their accrued benefits under Plan A does not discriminate in favor of HCEs merely because the prior vesting schedule continues to apply to the accrued benefits of electing employees, even if, at the time of the election or in future years, the prior vesting schedule applies only to a group of employees that does not satisfy section 410(b).

*Example (2).* The facts are the same as in Example 1, except that, for administrative convenience in complying with section 411(a)(10)(B), the plan amendment automatically provides all employees employed on the date of the amendment with the higher of the nonforteitable percentages determined under either schedule. The manner in which employees vest in their accrued benefits under Plan A does not discriminate in favor of HCEs merely because, for administrative convenience in complying with section 411(a)(10), the amendment exceeds the requirements of section 411(a)(10). The result would be the same if the plan amendment automatically provided the higher of the nonforteitable percentages only to those employees with at least three years of service.

*Example (3).* (a) Employer Y maintains Plan B covering all of its employees. On January 1, 1996, Employer Y sells Division M to Employer Z, and all of the employees in Division M become employees of Employer Z. Employer Y obtains a determination letter that the resulting cessation of participation by these employees in Plan B constitutes a partial termination. Therefore, in order to satisfy section 411(d)(3), Plan B fully vests the accrued benefit of each of the employees of Division M whose participation in Plan B ceased as a result of the sale on January 1, 1996.

(b) The manner in which employees vest in their accrued benefits under Plan B does not discriminate in favor of HCEs merely because, in order to satisfy section 411(d)(3), the accrued benefits of all employees affected by the partial termination become fully vested. This is true even if the affected group of employees does not satisfy section 410(b).

*Example (4).* (a) The facts are the same as in Example 3, except that Employer Y does not obtain a determination letter that the sale of Division M to Employer Z will cause a partial termination. Instead, based on its reasonable belief that the sale will cause a partial termination, and in order to ensure that Plan B will satisfy section 411(d)(3), Employer Y amends Plan B to vest fully the accrued benefit on January 1, 1996 of each of the employees it reasonably believes to be an affected employee.

(b) The manner in which employees vest in their accrued benefits under Plan B does not discriminate in favor of HCEs merely because, based on Employer Y's reasonable belief that the sale will cause a partial termination, Plan B is amended to vest fully the accrued benefits of each of the employees it reasonably believes to be an affected employee.

**(d) Service-crediting rules.** *(1) Overview.* (i) In general. A defined benefit plan or a defined contribution plan does not satisfy this paragraph (d) with respect to the manner in which service is credited under the plan unless the plan satisfies paragraph (d)(2) of this section. Paragraph (d)(3) of this section provides rules for determining whether service other than actual service with the employer may be taken into account in determining whether a defined benefit plan or a defined contribution plan satisfies § 1.401(a)(4)-1(b)(2) or (b)(3). (However, for purposes of cross-testing a defined contribution plan, only years in which the employee benefited under the plan may be taken into account in determining equivalent accrual rates. See § 1.401(a)(4)-8(b)(2)(i).) The rules of this paragraph (d) apply separately to service credited under a plan for each different purpose under the plan, including, but not limited to: application of the benefit formula (benefit service), application of the accrual method (accrual service), application of the vesting schedule (vesting service), entitlement to benefits, rights, and features (entitlement service), application of the requirements for eligibility to participate in the plan (eligibility service).

(ii) Special rule for pre-effective date service. A plan is deemed to satisfy this paragraph (d) with respect to service credited for periods prior to the effective date applicable to the plan under § 1.401(a)(4)-13(a) or (b) under a plan provision adopted and in effect as of February 11, 1993 (and any such service may be taken into account for purposes of satisfying § 1.401(a)(4)-1(b)(2) or (b)(3)), if the plan satisfied the applicable nondiscrimination requirements with respect to the service that were in effect for all relevant periods prior to the applicable effective date.

*(2) Manner of crediting service.* (i) General rule. A plan satisfies this paragraph (d)(2) if, on the basis of all of the relevant facts and circumstances, the manner in which employees' service is credited for all purposes under the plan does not discriminate in favor of HCEs.

(ii) Equivalent service-crediting methods. For purposes of this paragraph (d)(2), a service-crediting method used for a specified purpose that is based on hours of service, as provided in 29 CFR 2530.200b-2, and a service-crediting method used for the same purpose that is based on one of the equivalencies set forth in 29 CFR 2530.200b-3, are treated as equivalent if the service-crediting methods are otherwise the same.

(iii) Safe harbor for service-crediting. The manner in which service is credited under a plan for a specified purpose is deemed to satisfy this paragraph (d)(2) if each combination of service-crediting provisions applied for that purpose would satisfy the nondiscriminatory availability requirements of § 1.401(a)(4)-4 if that combination were an other right or feature.

(iv) Examples. The following examples illustrate the rules in this paragraph (d)(2):

*Example (1).* (a) Plan A covers both salaried employees and hourly employees. All of the HCEs in Plan A are salaried employees. For administrative convenience, salaried employees in Plan A (none of whom are part-time) have their years of service calculated in accordance with the elapsed time provisions in § 1.410(a)-7. Hourly employees in Plan A (most of whom are scheduled to work 2,000 hours in a year) have their hours of service calculated in accordance with 29 CFR 2530.200b-2 and are credited with a year of service for each plan year in which they complete 1,000 hours of service.

(b) Plan A does not fail to satisfy this paragraph (d)(2) merely because different service-crediting provisions are applied to salaried and hourly employees for administrative convenience. The service-crediting provisions for hourly employees in Plan A are reasonably comparable to the service-crediting provisions for salaried employees. This is because the amount of service credited to hourly employees who complete fewer than 1,000 hours of service before termination of employment (i.e., quit, retirement, discharge, or death) during the plan year (and are treated less favorably than the salaried employees with the same period of employment during the plan year) is balanced by the amount of service credited to hourly employees who complete more than 1,000 hours of service before termination of employment during the plan year (who are treated more favorably than the salaried employees with the same period of employment during the plan year).

*Example (2).* (a) The facts are the same as in Example 1, except Plan A requires hourly employees to complete 2,000 hours of service in order to be credited with a full year of service, with a pro rata reduction for hourly employees who complete fewer than 2,000 hours of service.

(b) Plan A does not fail to satisfy this paragraph (d)(2) merely because different service-crediting provisions are applied to salaried and hourly employees for administrative convenience. The service-crediting provisions for hourly employees in Plan A are reasonably comparable to the service-crediting provisions for salaried employees. This is because the amount of service credited to hourly employees whose employment terminates (i.e., quit, retire, are discharged, or die) during the plan year is reasonably comparable to the amount of service credited to salaried employees whose employment is terminated during the plan year with the same period of employment during the plan year.

*(3) Service-crediting period.* (i) Limitation on service taken into account. (A) General rule. Except as otherwise provided in this paragraph (d)(3), service for periods in which an employee does not perform services as an employee of the employer or in which the employee did not participate in the plan may not be taken into account in determining whether the plan satisfies § 1.401(a)(4)-1(b)(2) and (b)(3). In addition, in determining whether a plan satisfies § 1.401(a)(4)-1(b)(2) and (b)(3), no more than one year of service may be taken into account with respect to any 12-consecutive-month period (with adjustments for shorter periods, if appropriate) unless the additional service is required to be credited under section 410 or 411, whichever is applicable.

(B) Past service. Notwithstanding paragraph (d)(3)(i)(A) of this section, service for periods in which an employee performed services as an employee of the employer and did not participate in a plan, but in which the employee would have participated in the plan but for the fact that the plan (or the plan amendment extending coverage to the employee) was not in existence during that period, may be taken into account in determining whether the plan satisfies § 1.401(a)(4)-1(b)(2) and (b)(3). This is because service for such periods generally would have been credited for the employee but for the timing of the plan establishment or amendment, and the timing of the plan establishment or amendment must satisfy § 1.401(a)(4)-5(a).

(C) Pre-participation and imputed service. Notwithstanding paragraph (d)(3)(i)(A) of this section, to the extent that a plan treats pre-participation service and imputed service as actual service with the employer, such service may be taken into account in determining whether the plan satisfies § 1.401(a)(4)-1(b)(2) and (b)(3) if the service satisfies each of the requirements in paragraph (d)(3)(iii) of this section taking into account, in the case of imputed service, the additional rules in paragraph (d)(3)(iv) of this section.

(D) Additional limitations on service-crediting in the case of certain offsets. Notwithstanding paragraphs (d)(3)(i)(B) and (C) of this section, if a plan credits benefit service or accrual service under paragraph (d)(3)(i)(B) or (C) of this section for a period before an employee becomes a participant in the plan, but offsets the benefits determined under the plan by benefits under another plan (whether or not qualified or terminated) that are attributable to the same period for which that service is credited, then that service may not be taken into account for purposes of determining whether the first plan satisfies § 1.401(a)(4)-1(b)(2) or (b)(3) unless the offset provision applies on the same basis to all similarly-situated employees (within the meaning of paragraph (d)(3)(iii)(A) of this section).

(ii) Definitions. (A) Pre-participation service. For purposes of this section, pre-participation service includes all years of service credited under a plan for years of service with the employer or a prior employer for periods before the employee commenced or recommenced participation in the plan (other than past service described in paragraph (d)(3)(i)(B) of this section).

(B) Imputed service. For purposes of this section, imputed service includes any service credited for periods after an employee has commenced participation in a plan while the employee is not performing services as an employee for the employer (including a period in which the employee performs services for another employer, e.g., a joint venture), or while the employee has a reduced work schedule and would not otherwise be credited with service at the level being credited under the general terms of the plan.

(iii) Requirements for pre-participation and imputed service. (A) Provision applied to all similarly-situated employees. (1) General rule. A plan provision crediting pre-participation service or imputed service to any HCE must apply on the same terms to all similarly-situated NHCEs. Whether two employees are similarly situated for this purpose must be determined based on reasonable business criteria, generally taking into account only the circumstances resulting in the employees being covered under the plan or being granted imputed service and on the situation of the employees (e.g., the plan in which the employees benefit or the employer by which they are employed) during the period for which the pre-participation service or imputed service is credited. For example, employees who enter a plan as a result of a particular merger and who participated in the same plan of a prior employer are generally similarly situated. As another example, employees who are transferred to different joint ventures or different spun-off divisions are generally not similarly situated.

(2) Examples. The following examples illustrate the rules in this paragraph (d)(3)(iii)(A):

*Example (1).* Employer X maintains defined benefit Plans A and B and defined contribution Plan C. Plan A covers all employees who work at the headquarters of Employer X. Plan B covers some employees in Division M of Employer X, and Plan C covers the other employees of Division M. Plans B and C have not been aggregated for purposes of satisfying section 401(a)(4) or 410(b) for the period for which service is being credited. Plan A provides that, whenever an employee covered by Plan B transfers from Division M to the headquarters, the employee's service credited under Plan B is credited under Plan A, and the employee's benefit under Plan A is offset by the employee's benefit under Plan B. However, Plan A provides for no similar recognition of service or offset for employees covered by Plan C who transfer from Division M to the headquarters. Plan A does not fail to satisfy this paragraph (d)(3)(iii)(A) merely because it credits service for employees transferring from Plan B but not from Plan C, because it is reasonable to treat employees participating in different plans that have not been aggregated as not being similarly situated.

*Example (2).* The facts are the same as in Example 1, except that Employer X acquires two trades or businesses from different employers. Employees of the acquired trades or businesses become employees of Division M and become covered by Plan B. In addition, Plan B is amended to credit service with one of the trades or businesses but not the other. Plan B does not fail to satisfy this paragraph (d)(3)(iii)(A) merely because it credits service for one acquired trade or business but not another, because it is reasonable to treat employees of one acquired trade or business as not similarly situated to employees of another acquired trade or business.

(B) Legitimate business reason. (1) General rule. There must be a legitimate business reason, based on all of the relevant facts and circumstances, for a plan to credit imputed service or for a plan to credit pre-participation service for a period of service with another employer.

(2) Relevant facts and circumstances when crediting service with another employer. The following are examples of relevant facts and circumstances for determining whether a legitimate business reason exists for a plan to credit pre-participation or imputed service for a period of service with another employer as service with the employer: whether one employer has a significant ownership, control, or similar interest in, or relationship with, the other employer (though not enough to cause the two employers to be treated as a single employer under section 414); whether the two employers share interrelated business operations; whether the employers maintain the same multiple employer plan; whether the employers share similar attributes, such as operation in the same industry or the same geographic area; and whether the employees are an acquired group of employees or the employees became employed by the other employer in a transaction between the two employers that was a stock or asset acquisition, merger, or other similar transaction involving a change in the employer of the employees of a trade or business. Other factors may also be relevant for this purpose, such as the plan's treatment of service with other employers with which the employer has a similar relationship and the type of service being credited (e.g., vesting service as compared to benefit service or accrual service). A legitimate business reason is deemed to exist for a plan to credit military service as service with the employer.

(3) Examples. The following examples illustrate the rules in this paragraph (d)(3)(iii)(B):

*Example (1).* Twenty unrelated employers jointly sponsor a multiple-employer plan that covers all employees of the employers. From time to time, employees transfer employment among the employers. There is a legitimate business reason for a disaggregated portion of the plan that benefits the employees of one of the employers to treat service with any of the other employers as service with the employer.

*Example (2).* Employer X owns 20 percent of the outstanding stock of Employer Y. From time to time, employees transfer from Employer X to Employer Y at the request of Employer X. Employer X maintains defined benefit Plan A. Plan A provides that years of service include an employee's years of service with Employer Y. There is a legitimate business reason for Plan A to credit service with Employer Y because Employer X, through its 20-percent ownership interest, benefits from the service that the transferred employees provide to Employer Y.

*Example (3).* Employer Z manufactures widgets and belongs to the National Widget Manufacturers' Association. From time to time, Employer Z hires employees from other widget manufacturers. Employer Z maintains a defined benefit plan, Plan B, which credits pre-participation service for periods of service with all other members of the Association located in the western half of the United States as service with Employer Z. There is a legitimate business reason for Plan B to treat service with other members of the Association as service with Employer Z.

(C) No significant discrimination. (1) General rule. Based on all of the relevant facts and circumstances, a plan provision crediting pre-participation or imputed service must not by design or in operation discriminate significantly in favor of HCEs.

(2) Relevant facts and circumstances. The following are examples of relevant facts and circumstances for determining whether a plan provision crediting pre-participation service or imputed service discriminates significantly in favor of HCEs: whether the service credit does not duplicate benefits but merely makes an employee whole (i.e., prevents the employee from being disadvantaged with respect to benefits by a change in job or employer or provides the employee with benefits comparable to those of other employees); the degree of business ties between the current employer and the prior employer, such as the degree of ownership interest or other affiliation; the degree of excess coverage under section 410(b) of NHCEs for the plan crediting the service, taking into account employees who are credited with pre-participation service; whether the other employer maintains a qualified plan for its employees; the existence of reciprocal service credit under other plans of the employer or the prior employer; the circumstances underlying the employee's transfer into the group of employees covered by the plan; the type of service being credited; and the relative number of employees other than five-percent owners or the most highly-paid HCEs of the employer (determined without regard to the one officer rule of section 414(q)(5)(B)) who are being credited with pre-participation service or imputed service. The relative number referred to in the last factor is determined taking into account all employees who have been over time, or are reasonably expected to be in the future, credited with such service.

(3) Examples. The following examples illustrate the rules in this paragraph (d)(3)(iii)(C). It is assumed that facts not described in an example do not, in the aggregate, suggest that the relevant plan provision either does or does not discriminate significantly in favor of HCEs.

*Example (1).* (a) Employer U maintains defined benefit Plans A and B. Plan A covers all employees who work at the headquarters of Employer U. Plan B covers all employees of Division M of Employer U. Plan A provides that, whenever an employee transfers from Division M to the headquarters, the employee's service credited under Plan B is credited under Plan A, and the employee's benefit under Plan A is offset by the employee's benefit under Plan B. Employees, including a meaningful number of NHCEs, are periodically transferred from Division M to the headquarters of Employer U for bona fide business reasons.

(b) The Plan A provision crediting service under Plan B does not discriminate significantly in favor of HCEs. The provision is designed only to prevent employees from being disadvantaged by being transferred from Division M to the headquarters, and a meaningful number of NHCEs can be expected to benefit from it.

*Example (2).* (a) The facts are the same as in Example 1, except that the only employees transferred from Division M to the headquarters of Employer U are HCEs (but not the most highly-paid HCEs of Employer U).

(b) Employer U determines that Plan A would have satisfied sections 401(a)(4) and 410(b) for the period for which the transferred employees are being credited with pre-participation service had the employees participated in Plan A during that period. This determination is based on test results under sections 401(a)(4) and 410(b) for the current year, taking into account significant demographic changes over this period.

(c) The Plan A provision crediting service under Plan B does not significantly discriminate in favor of HCEs in the current year. This conclusion is based on the fact that the circumstances underlying the transfers indicate that they were made for bona fide business reasons, that Plan A would have satisfied sections 401(a)(4) and 410(b) had the transferred employees participated in Plan A during the period for which the pre-participation service is credited, and that the transferred employees are not the most highly-paid HCEs of Employer U.

*Example (3).* (a) The facts are the same as in Example 1, except that the only employee who is transferred from Division M to the headquarters of Employer U is Employee P, who is among the most highly-paid HCEs of Employer U. Plan A provides an unreduced early retirement benefit at age 55 for employees with 20 years of service, but Plan B's early retirement benefits are not subsidized. Employee P is transferred to the headquarters with 20 years of service credited under Plan B and shortly before attainment of age 55. Employee P is expected to retire upon reaching age 55.

(b) The Plan A provision crediting service under Plan B discriminates significantly in favor of HCEs in the year of the transfer. This is because the circumstances underlying this transfer (i.e., its occurrence shortly before Employee P's expected retirement and the fact that the transfer significantly increased Employee P's early retirement benefits) indicate that Employee P was transferred to the headquarters primarily to obtain the higher pension benefits provided under Plan A.

(c) Because of this conclusion, the pre-participation service credited to Employee P cannot be taken into account in determining whether Plan A satisfies § 1.401(a)(4)-1(b)(2) and (b)(3). Thus, if Plan A credits the service, it cannot be a safe harbor plan because the benefit formula will take into account service that may not be taken into account under this paragraph (d)(3). In addition, Employee P's accrual rates under the general test in § 1.401(a)(4)-3(c) are likely to be higher than those of other employees because, while the pre-participation service may be used to determine Employee P's benefits under Plan A, the service must be disregarded in determining Employee P's testing service. Also, if Employee P's pre-participation service is used in determining Employee P's entitlement to a benefit, right, or feature under Plan A, the fact that the service must be disregarded in determining Employee P's entitlement service for purposes of § 1.401(a)(4)-4 may cause the benefit, right, or feature to be treated as a separate benefit, right, or feature that is currently available only to Employee P.

*Example (4).* (a) Employer V manufactures widgets and belongs to the National Widget Manufacturers' Association. Each member of the Association maintains a defined benefit plan that credits pre-participation service for periods of service with other members and offsets benefits under the plan by benefits under the plans of the other members. Employer V maintains defined benefit Plan C. Employer V periodically hires employees from other widget manufacturers who are not among its most highly-paid HCEs. In 1997, however, the only employee hired by Employer V from another member of the Association is Employee Q, who is among Employer V's most highly-paid HCEs. Employee Q receives pre-participation service credit in accordance with the terms of Plan

C. Some of the plans maintained by other members of the Association credited pre-participation service to NHCEs for the same period for which the pre-participation service is credited to Employee Q.

(b) The provision of Plan C crediting pre-participation service with other members of the Association does not discriminate significantly in 1997, despite the fact that the only employee who received pre-participation service credit under the provision in that year was among the most highly-paid HCEs of Employer V. This conclusion is based on the relative number of employees other than Employer V's most highly-paid HCEs who have been credited in the past, or are reasonably expected to be credited in the future, with pre-participation service for periods of service with other members of the Association, and the fact that other employees who are NHCEs are being credited with pre-participation service under a reciprocal agreement.

*Example (5).* Employer W owns 79 percent of the outstanding stock of Employer X. From time to time, employees transfer from Employer W to Employer X at the request of Employer W. The only employees who have ever been transferred are HCEs. Employer W maintains a defined benefit plan, Plan D, which credits employees transferred to Employer X with imputed benefit and accrual service while employed by Employer X. Employer X maintains no qualified plan. Plan D would fail either section 401(a)(4) or section 410(b) in the current plan year if the individuals employed by Employer X were treated as employed by Employer W. In addition, Plan D would fail either section 401(a)(4) or section 410(b) in the current plan year if the portion of Plan D covering the transferred employees were treated as maintained by Employer X. The Plan D provision crediting imputed benefit and accrual service to employees transferred to Employer X significantly discriminates in favor of HCEs in the current plan year.

*Example (6).* The facts are the same as in Example 5, except that Plan D credits the individuals who transfer to Employer X only with imputed vesting and entitlement service. The Plan D provision crediting imputed vesting and entitlement service to individuals transferred to Employer X does not significantly discriminate in favor of HCEs in the current plan year, because there is less potential for discrimination when the only types of service being imputed are vesting and entitlement service.

(iv) Additional rules for imputed service. (A) Legitimate business reasons for crediting imputed service. (1) General rule. A legitimate business reason does not exist for a plan to impute service after an individual has permanently ceased to perform services as an employee (within the meaning of § 1.410(b)-9) for the employer maintaining the plan, i.e., is not expected to resume performing services as an employee for the employer. The preceding sentence does not apply in the case of an individual who is not performing services for the employer because of disability or is performing services for another employer under an arrangement (such as a transfer of the employee to another employer) that provides some ongoing business benefit to the original employer. The first sentence in this paragraph (d)(3)(iv)(A)(1) also does not apply in the case of vesting and entitlement service if the employee is performing services for another employer that is being treated under the plan as actual service with the original employer.

(2) Certain presumptions applicable. Whether an individual has permanently ceased to perform services as an employee for an employer is determined taking into account all of the relevant facts and circumstances. There is a rebuttable presumption for a period of up to two years that an individual who has ceased to perform services as an employee for an employer is nonetheless expected to resume performing services as an employee for the employer, if the employer continues to treat the individual as an employee for significant purposes unrelated to the plan. After two years, there is a rebuttable presumption that an individual who has ceased to perform services as an employee for the employer is not expected to resume performing services as an employee for the employer. The fact that an individual is absent to perform jury duty or military service automatically rebuts the latter presumption. Other evidence, such as the employer's layoff policy, the terms of an employment contract, or specific leave to pursue a degree requiring more than two years of study, may also rebut this presumption.

(3) Imputed service for part-time employees. Rules similar to the rules in paragraph (d)(3)(iv)(A)(1) and (2) of this section apply in the case of an employee whose work hours are temporarily reduced and who therefore would normally be credited with service at a reduced rate, but who continues to be credited with service at the same rate as before the reduction (e.g., an employee who continues to be credited with service as if the employee were a full-time employee during a temporary change from a full-time to a part-time work schedule).

(B) Additional factors for determining whether a provision crediting imputed service discriminates significantly. In addition to the factors described in paragraph (d)(3)(iii)(C)(2) of this section, relevant facts and circumstances for determining whether a plan provision crediting imputed service during a leave of absence or a period of reduced services discriminates significantly include any employer policies or practices that restrict the ability of employees to take leaves of absence or work temporarily on a part-time basis, respectively.

(v) Satisfaction of other service-crediting rules. A plan does not fail to satisfy this paragraph (d)(3) merely because it credits service to the extent necessary to satisfy the service-crediting rules in section 410(a), 411(a), 413, or 414(a), § 1.410(a)-7 (elapsed-time method of service-crediting) or 29 CFR 2530.200b-2 (regarding hours of service to be credited), whichever is applicable, or 29 CFR 2530.204-2(d) (regarding double proration of service and compensation).

**(e) Family aggregation rules.[Reserved]**

**(f) Governmental plans.[Reserved]**

**(g) Corrective amendments.** *(1) In general.* A corrective amendment that satisfies the rules of this paragraph (g) is taken into account for purposes of satisfying certain section 401(a) requirements for a plan year, by treating the corrective amendment as if it were adopted and effective as of the first day of the plan year. These rules apply in addition to the rules of section 401(b). Paragraph (g)(2) of this section describes the scope of the corrective amendments that are permitted to be made. Paragraph (g)(3) of this section specifies the conditions under which a corrective amendment may be made. Paragraph (g)(4) of this section provides a rule prohibiting a corrective amendment from being taken into account to the extent that it does not have substance. Paragraph (g)(5) of this section discusses the effect of the corrective amendments permitted under this paragraph (g) under provisions other than section 401(a).

*(2) Scope of corrective amendments.* For purposes of satisfying the minimum coverage requirements of section 410(b), the nondiscriminatory amount requirement of § 1.401(a)(4)-1(b)(2), or the nondiscriminatory plan amendment requirement of § 1.401(a)(4)-1(b)(4), a corrective

amendment may retroactively increase accruals or allocations for employees who benefited under the plan during the plan year being corrected, or may grant accruals or allocations to individuals who did not benefit under the plan during the plan year being corrected. In addition, for purposes of satisfying the nondiscriminatory current availability requirement of § 1.401(a)(4)-4(b) for benefits, rights, or features, a corrective amendment may make a benefit, right, or feature available to employees to whom it was previously not available. A corrective amendment may not, however, correct for a failure to incorporate the pre-termination restrictions of § 1.401(a)(4)-5(b).

*(3) Conditions for corrective amendments.* (i) In general. A corrective amendment is not taken into account prior to its adoption under this paragraph (g) unless it satisfies each of the requirements of paragraph (g)(3)(ii) through (vii) of this section, whichever are applicable. Thus, for example, if any of the applicable requirements are not satisfied, any additional accruals arising from an amendment adopted after the end of a plan year are not given retroactive effect and, thus, are tested in the plan year in which the amendment is adopted.

(ii) Benefits not reduced. Except as permitted under paragraph (g)(3)(vi)(C)(2) of this section, the corrective amendment may not result in a reduction of an employee's benefits (including any benefit, right, or feature), determined based on the terms of the plan in effect immediately before the amendment.

(iii) Amendment effective for all purposes. For purposes of determining an employee's rights and benefits under the plan, the corrective amendment must generally be effective as if the amendment had been made on the first day of the plan year being corrected. Thus, if the corrective amendment is made after the close of the plan year being corrected, an employee's allocations or accruals, along with the associated benefits, rights, and features, must be increased to the level at which they would have been had the amendment been in effect for the entire preceding plan year. Accordingly, such increases are taken into account for testing purposes as if the increases had actually occurred in the prior plan year. However, to the extent that an amendment makes a benefit, right, or feature available to a group of employees, the amendment does not fail to satisfy this paragraph (g)(3)(iii) merely because it is not effective prior to the date of adoption and, therefore, the benefit, right, or feature is not made currently available to those employees before that date.

(iv) Time when amendment must be adopted and put into effect. (A) General rule. Any corrective amendment intended to apply to the preceding plan year must be adopted and implemented on or before the 15th day of the 10th month after the close of the plan year in order to be taken into account for the preceding plan year.

(B) Determination letter requested by employer or plan administrator. If, on or before the end of the period set forth in paragraph (g)(3)(iv)(A) of this section, the employer or plan administrator files a request pursuant to § 601.201(o) of this chapter (Statement of Procedural Rules) for a determination letter on the amendment, the initial or continuing qualification of the plan, or the trust that is part of the plan, the period set forth in paragraph (g)(3)(iv)(A) of this section is extended in the same manner as provided for an extension of the remedial amendment period under § 1.401(b)-1(d)(3).

(v) Corrective amendment for coverage or amounts testing. (A) Retroactive benefits must be provided to nondiscriminatory group. Except as provided in paragraph (g)(3)(v)(B) of this section, if the corrective amendment is adopted after the close of the plan year, the additional allocations or accruals for the preceding year resulting from the corrective amendment must separately satisfy section 401(a)(4) for the preceding plan year and must benefit a group of employees that separately satisfies section 410(b) (determined by applying the same rules as are applied in determining whether a component plan separately satisfies section 410(b) under § 1.401(a)(4)-9(c)(4)). Thus, for example, in applying the rules of this paragraph (g)(3)(v), an employer may not aggregate the additional accruals or allocations for the preceding plan year resulting from the corrective amendment with the other accruals or allocations already provided under the terms of the plan as in effect during the preceding plan year without regard to the corrective amendment.

(B) Corrective amendment to conform to safe harbor. The requirements of paragraph (g)(3)(v)(A) of this section need not be met if the corrective amendment is for purposes of conforming the plan to one of the safe harbors in § 1.401(a)(4)-2(b) or § 1.401(a)(4)-3(b) (including for purposes of applying the requirements of those safe harbors under the optional testing methods in § 1.401(a)(4)-8(b)(3) or (c)(3)), or ensuring that the plan continues to meet one of those safe harbors.

(vi) Conditions for corrective amendment of the availability of benefits, rights, and features. A corrective amendment may not be taken into account under this paragraph (g) for purposes of satisfying § 1.401(a)(4)-4(b) for a given plan year unless—

(A) The corrective amendment is not part of a pattern of amendments being used to correct repeated failures with respect to a particular benefit, right, or feature;

(B) The relevant provisions of the plan immediately after the corrective amendment with respect to the benefit, right, or feature (including a corrective amendment eliminating the benefit, right, or feature) remain in effect until the end of the first plan year beginning after the date of the amendment; and

(C) The corrective amendment either—

(1) Expands the group of employees to whom the benefit, right, or feature is currently available so that for each plan year in which the corrective amendment is taken into account in determining whether the plan satisfies § 1.401(a)(4)-4(b), the group of employees to whom the benefit, right, or feature is currently available, after taking into account the amendment, satisfies the nondiscriminatory classification requirement of § 1.410(b)-4 (and thus the current availability requirement of § 1.401(a)(4)-4(b)) with a ratio percentage greater than or equal to the lesser of—

(i) The safe harbor percentage applicable to the plan; and

(ii) The ratio percentage of the plan; or

(2) Eliminates the benefit, right, or feature (to the extent permitted under section 411(d)(6)) on or before the last day of the plan year for which the corrective amendment is taken into account.

(vii) Special rules for section 401(k) plans and section 401(m) plans. (A) Minimum coverage requirements. In the case of a section 401(k) plan, a corrective amendment may only be taken into account for purposes of satisfying § 1.410(b)-3(a)(2)(i) under this paragraph (g) for a given plan year to the extent that the corrective amendment grants qualified nonelective contributions within the meaning of § 1.401(k)-6 (QNECs) to nonhighly compensated nonexcludable employees who were not eligible employees within the meaning of § 1.401(k)-6 for the given plan year, and the amount of the QNECs granted to each nonhighly compensated nonexcludable employee equals the product of the nonhighly compensated nonexcludable employee's plan year compensation and the actual deferral percentage (within the meaning of section 401(k)(3)(B)) for the given plan year for the group of NHCEs who are eligible employees. Similarly, in the case of a section 401(m) plan, a corrective amendment may only be taken into account for purposes of satisfying § 1.410(b)-3(a)(2)(i) under this paragraph (g) for a given plan year to the extent that the corrective amendment grants qualified nonelective contributions (QNECs) to nonhighly compensated nonexcludable employees who were not eligible employees within the meaning of § 1.401(m)-5 for the given plan year, and the amount of the QNECs granted to each nonhighly compensated nonexcludable employee equals the product of the nonhighly compensated nonexcludable employee's plan year compensation and the actual contribution percentage (within the meaning of section 401(m)(3)) for the given plan year for the group of NHCEs who are eligible employees.

(B) Correction of rate of match. In the case of a section 401(m) plan, allocations for a given plan year granted under a corrective amendment to NHCEs who made contributions for the plan year eligible for a matching contribution may be treated as matching contributions. These allocations treated as matching contributions may be taken into account for purposes of satisfying the current availability requirement of § 1.401(a)(4)-4(b) with respect to the right to a rate of match, but may not be taken into account for satisfying other amounts testing.

*(4) Corrective amendments must have substance.* A corrective amendment is not taken into account in determining whether a plan satisfies section 401(a)(4) or 410(b) to the extent the amendment affects nonvested employees whose employment with the employer terminated on or before the close of the preceding year, and who therefore would not have received any economic benefit from the amendment if it had been made in the prior year. Similarly, in determining whether the requirements of paragraph (g)(3)(vi)(C)(1) of this section are satisfied, a corrective amendment making a benefit, right, or feature available to employees is not taken into account to the extent the benefit, right, or feature is not currently available to any of those employees immediately after the amendment. However, a plan will not fail to satisfy the requirements of paragraph (g)(3)(vi)(C)(1) of this section by operation of the provisions in this paragraph (g)(4) if the benefit, right, or feature is made available to all employees in the plan as of the date of the amendment.

*(5) Effect under other statutory requirements.* A corrective amendment under this paragraph (g) is treated as if it were adopted and effective as of the first day of the plan year only for the specific purposes described in this paragraph (g). Thus, for example, the corrective amendment is taken into account not only for purposes of sections 401(a)(4) and 410(b), but also for purposes of determining whether the plan satisfies sections 401(l). By contrast, the amendment is not given retroactive effect for purposes of section 404 (deductions for employer contributions) or section 412 (minimum funding standards), unless otherwise provided for in rules applicable to those sections.

*(6) Examples.* The following examples illustrate the rules in this paragraph (g):

*Example (1).* Employer U maintains a calendar year defined benefit plan that in 1994 is tested using the safe harbor for flat benefit plans in § 1.401(a)(4)-3(b)(4). In 1996, Employer U is concerned that the plan will not satisfy the demographic requirement in § 1.401(a)(4)-3(b)(4)(i)(C)(3) for the 1995 plan year because the average of the normal accrual rates for all NHCEs is less than 70 percent of the average of the normal accrual rates for all HCEs. Provided the corrective amendment would otherwise satisfy this paragraph (g), Employer U may make a corrective amendment to the plan to increase the number of NHCEs so that the amended plan satisfies the safe harbor for the 1995 plan year. The corrective amendment need not satisfy paragraph (g)(3)(v)(A) of this section because Employer U is retroactively amending the plan to conform to a safe harbor in § 1.401(a)(4)-3(b). See paragraph (g)(3)(v)(B) of this section.

*Example (2).* (a) Employer V maintains a calendar year defined contribution plan covering all the employees in Division M and Division N. Under the plan, only employees in Division M have the right to direct the investments in their account. For plan years prior to 1996, the plan met the current availability requirement of § 1.401(a)(4)-4(b) because the employees in Division M were a group of employees that satisfied the nondiscriminatory classification test of § 1.410(b)-4. Because of attrition in the employee population in Division M in 1996, the group of employees to whom the right to direct investments is available during that plan year no longer meets the nondiscriminatory classification test of § 1.410(b)-4. Thus, the right to direct investments under the plan does not meet the current availability requirement of § 1.401(a)(4)-4(b) during the 1996 plan year.

(b) Employer V may amend the plan in 1997 (but on or before October 15) to make the right to direct investments available from the date of the corrective amendment to a larger group of employees and the corrective amendment may be taken into account for purposes of satisfying the current availability requirement of § 1.401(a)(4)-4(b) for 1996 if the amendment satisfies this paragraph (g). Thus, for example, the group of employees to whom the right to direct investments is currently available, after taking into account the corrective amendment, must satisfy the nondiscriminatory classification test of § 1.410(b)-4 for 1996 using a safe harbor percentage (or if lower, the ratio percentage of the plan for 1996). In addition, the corrective amendment making the right to direct investments available to a larger group of employees must remain in effect through the end of the 1998 plan year.

(c) In order for Employer V to take the corrective amendment into account for purposes of satisfying the current availability requirement of § 1.401(a)(4)-4(b) for the portion of the 1997 plan year before the amendment, the group of employees to whom the right to direct investments is currently available, taking into account the amendment, must satisfy the nondiscriminatory classification test of § 1.410(b)-4 for 1997 using a safe harbor percentage (or if lower, the ratio percentage of the plan for 1997).

(d) Alternatively, if Employer V adopts the corrective amendment before the end of the 1996 plan year, the corrective amendment need only remain in force through the end of the 1997 plan year, or the corrective amendment may eliminate the right to direct investments (provided that the elimination remains in effect through the end of the 1997 plan year).

*Example (3).* The facts are the same as in Example 2. In 1997, Employer V makes a corrective amendment to extend the plan to employees of Division O as well as Divisions M and N. Assume that the corrective amendment satisfies paragraph (g)(3)(v)(A) of this section, and thus, may be taken into account for purposes of satisfying the nondiscriminatory amounts requirement of § 1.401(a)(4)-1(b)(2) or the minimum coverage requirements of section 410(b). However, the employees in Division O will not be taken into account in determining whether the right to direct investments meets the current availability requirements of § 1.401(a)(4)-4(b) unless the corrective amendment meets the requirements of paragraph (g)(3)(vi) of this section. Thus, for example, the group of employees to whom the right to direct investments is made available as a result of the expansion of coverage, after taking into account the corrective amendment, must satisfy the nondiscriminatory clarification test of § 1.410(b)-4 for 1996 using a safe harbor percentage (or if lower, the ratio percentage of the plan for 1996). In addition, the amendment making the right to direct investments available to a larger group of employees must remain in effect through the end of the 1998 plan year.

*Example (4).* Employer W maintains a defined benefit plan that covers all employees and that offsets an employee's benefit by the employee's projected primary insurance amount. The plan is not eligible to use the safe harbors under § 1.401(a)(4)-3(b) because the plan does not satisfy section 401(l). Under the plan, the accrual rates for all HCEs (determined under the general test of § 1.401(a)(4)-3(c)) for 1998 are less than 1.5 percent of average annual compensation, and the accrual rates for all NHCEs (determined under the general test of § 1.401(a)(4)-3(c)) for 1998 are two percent of average annual compensation. If Employer W adopts a corrective amendment adopted in 1999 that retroactively increases HCEs' benefits under the plan so that their accrual rates equal those of the NHCEs, the corrective amendment may not be taken into account in testing the 1998 plan year (i.e., the accruals that result from the corrective amendment are treated as 1999 accruals), because the accruals for the 1998 plan year resulting from the corrective amendment would not separately satisfy sections 410(b) and 401(a)(4). This is the case even if, after taking the amendment into account, the plan would satisfy sections 410(b) and 401(a)(4) for the 1998 plan year.

*Example (5).* Employer X maintains two plans—Plan A and Plan B. Plan A satisfies the ratio percentage test of § 1.410(b)-2(b)(2), but Plan B does not. Thus, in order to satisfy section 410(b), Plan B must satisfy the average benefits test of § 1.410(b)-2(b)(3). The average benefit percentage of Plan B is 60 percent. Employer X may take into account a corrective amendment that increases the accruals under either Plan A or Plan B so that the average benefit percentage meets the 70 percent requirement of the average benefits test, if the amendment satisfies paragraph (g)(3)(v) of this section.

*Example (6).* Employer Y maintains Plan C, which does not satisfy section 401(a)(4) in a plan year. Under the terms of paragraph (g)(2) of this section, Employer Y amends Plan C to increase the benefits of certain employees retroactively. In designing the amendment, Employer Y identifies those employees who have terminated without vested benefits during the period after the end of the prior plan year and before the adoption date of the amendment, and the amendment provides increases in benefits primarily to those employees. It would be inconsistent with the purpose of preventing discrimination in favor of HCEs for Plan C to treat the amendment as retroactively effective under this paragraph (g). See § 1.401(a)(4)-1(c)(2).

*Example (7).* Employer Z maintains both a section 401(k) plan and a section 401(m) plan that provides matching contributions at a rate of 50 percent with respect to elective contributions under the section 401(k) plan. In plan year 1995, the section 401(k) plan fails to satisfy the actual deferral percentage test of section 401(k)(3). In order to satisfy section 401(k)(3), Employer Z makes corrective distributions to HCEs H1 through H10 of their excess contributions as provided under § 1.401(k)-2(b). The matching contributions that H1 through H10 had received on account of their excess contributions are not forfeited, however. Thus, the effective rate of matching contributions provided to H1 through H10 is increased as a result of the corrective distributions. See § 1.401(a)(4)-4(e)(3)(iii)(G). Since no NHCE in the section 401(m) plan is provided with an equivalent rate of matching contributions, the rate of matching contributions provided to H1 through H10 does not satisfy the nondiscriminatory availability requirement of § 1.401(a)(4)-4 in plan year 1995. Employer Z makes a corrective amendment by October 15, 1996, that grants allocations to NHCEs who made contributions for the 1995 plan year eligible for a matching contribution. Employer Z may treat the allocations granted under the corrective amendment to those NHCEs as matching contributions for the 1995 plan year and, as a result, take them into account in determining whether the availability of the rate of matching contributions provided to H1 through H10 satisfies the current availability requirement of § 1.401(a)(4)-4(b) for the 1995 plan year.

---

T.D. 8360, 9/12/91, amend T.D. 8485, 8/30/93, T.D. 9169, 12/28/2004.

---

### § 1.401(a)(4)-12 Definitions.

***Caution:*** The Treasury has not yet amended Reg § 1.401(a)(4)-12 to reflect changes made by P.L. 104-188.

Unless otherwise provided, the definitions in this section govern in applying the provisions of §§ 1.401(a)(4)-1 through 1.401(a)(4)-13.

*Accumulation plan.* Accumulation plan means a defined benefit plan under which the benefit of every employee for each plan year is separately determined, using plan year compensation (if benefits are determined as a percentage of compensation rather as than a dollar amount) separately calculated for the plan year, and each employee's total accrued benefit as of the end of a plan year is the sum of the separately determined benefit for that plan year and the total accrued benefit as of the end of the preceding plan year.

*Acquired group of employees.* Acquired group of employees means employees of a prior employer who become employed by the employer in a transaction between the employer and the prior employer that is a stock or asset acquisition, merger, or other similar transaction involving a change in the employer of the employees of a trade or business, plus employees hired by or transferred into the acquired trade or business on or before a date selected by the employer that is within the transition period defined in section 410(b)(6)(C)(ii). In addition, in the case of a transaction prior to the effective date of these regulations, the date by which employees must be hired by or transferred into the acquired trade or business in order to be included in the acquired group of employees may be any date prior to February 11, 1993, without regard to whether it is later than the end of the transition period defined in section 410(b)(6)(C)(ii).

*Actuarial equivalent.* An amount or benefit is the actuarial equivalent of, or is actuarially equivalent to, another amount or benefit at a given time if the actuarial present value of the two amounts or benefits (calculated using the same actuarial assumptions) at that time is the same.

*Actuarial present value.* Actuarial present value means the value as of a specified date of an amount or series of amounts due thereafter, where each amount is—

(1) Multiplied by the probability that the condition or conditions on which payment of the amount is contingent will be satisfied; and

(2) Discounted according to an assumed rate of interest to reflect the time value of money.

*Ancillary benefit.* Ancillary benefit is defined in § 1.401(a)(4)-4(e)(2).

*Average annual compensation.* Average annual compensation is defined in § 1.401(a)(4)-3(e)(2).

*Base benefit percentage.* Base benefit percentage is defined in § 1.401(l)-1(c)(3).

*Benefit formula.* Benefit formula means the formula a defined benefit plan applies to determine the accrued benefit (within the meaning of section 411(a)(7)(A)(i)) in the form of an annual benefit commencing at normal retirement age of an employee who continues in service until normal retirement age. Thus, for example, the benefit formula does not include the accrual method the plan applies (in conjunction with the benefit formula) to determine the accrued benefit of an employee who terminates employment before normal retirement age. For purposes of this definition, a change in plan provisions that applies only to certain employees who terminate within a limited period of time (e.g., an early retirement window benefit) is treated as a change in the plan's benefit formula for the employees to whom the change is potentially applicable during the period that the change is potentially applicable to them. The preceding sentence applies only to the extent that the change in plan provisions would result in a change in the benefit formula if it were permanent and applied without regard to when the employees' employment was terminated.

*Benefit right, or feature.* Benefit, right, or feature means an optional form of benefit, an ancillary benefit, or an other right or feature within the meaning of § 1.401(a)(4)-4(e).

*Contributory DB plan.* Contributory DB plan means a defined benefit plan that includes employee contributions not allocated to separate accounts.

*Defined benefit excess plan.* Defined benefit excess plan is defined in § 1.401(l)-1(c)(16)(i).

*Defined benefit plan.* Defined benefit plan is defined in § 1.410(b)-9.

*Defined contribution plan.* Defined contribution plan is defined in § 1.410(b)-9.

*Determination date.* Determination date is defined in § 1.401(a)(4)-8(b)(3)(iv)(A).

*Employee.* With respect to a plan for a given plan year, employee means an employee (within the meaning of § 1.410(b)-9) who benefits as an employee under the plan for the plan year (within the meaning of § 1.410(b)-3).

*Employer.* Employer is defined in § 1.410(b)-9.

*ESOP.* ESOP is defined in § 1.410(b)-9.

*Excess benefit percentage.* Excess benefit percentage is defined in § 1.401(l)-1(c)(14).

*Former employee.* With respect to a plan for a given plan year, former employee means a former employee (within the meaning of § 1.410(b)-9).

*Former HCE.* Former HCE means a highly compensated former employee as defined in § 1.410(b)-9.

*Former NHCE.* Former NHCE means a former employee who is not a former HCE.

*Fresh-start date.* Fresh-start date is defined in § 1.401(a)(4)-13(c)(5)(iii).

*Fresh-start group.* Fresh-start group is defined in § 1.401(a)(4)-13(c)(5)(ii).

*Gross benefit percentage.* Gross benefit percentage is defined in § 1.401(l)-1(c)(18).

*HCE.* HCE means a highly compensated employee as defined in § 1.410(b)-9 who benefits under the plan for the plan year (within the meaning of § 1.410(b)-3).

*Integration level.* Integration level is defined in § 1.401(l)-1(c)(20).

*Measurement period.* Measurement period is defined in § 1.401(a)(4)-3(d)(1)(iii).

*Multiemployer plan.* Multiemployer plan is defined in § 1.410(b)-9.

*NHCE.* NHCE means an employee who is not a HCE.

*Nonexcludable employee.* Nonexcludable employee means an employee within the meaning of § 1.410(b)-9, other than an excludable employee with respect to the plan as determined under § 1.410(b)-6. A nonexcludable employee may be either a highly or nonhighly compensated nonexcludable employee, depending on the nonexcludable employee's status under section 414(q).

*Normalize.* With respect to a benefit payable to an employee in a particular form, normalize means to convert the benefit to an actuarially equivalent straight life annuity commencing at the employee's testing age. The actuarial assumptions used in normalizing a benefit must be reasonable and must be applied on a gender-neutral basis. A standard interest rate and a standard mortality table are among the assumptions considered reasonable for this purpose.

*Offset plan.* Offset plan is defined in § 1.401(l)-1(c)(24).

*Optional form of benefit.* Optional form of benefit is defined in § 1.401(a)(4)-4(e)(1).

*Other right or feature.* Other right or feature is defined in § 1.401(a)(4)-4(e)(3).

*Plan.* Plan means a plan within the meaning of § 1.410(b)-7(a) and (b), after application of the mandatory disaggregation rules of § 1.410(b)-7(c) and the permissive aggregation rules of § 1.410(b)-7(d).

*Plan year.* Plan year is defined in § 1.410(b)-9.

*Plan year compensation. (1) In general.* Plan year compensation means section 414(s) compensation for the plan year determined by measuring section 414(s) compensation during one of the periods described in paragraphs (2) through (4) of this definition. Whichever period is selected must be applied uniformly to determine the plan year compensation of every employee.

*(2) Plan year.* This period consists of the plan year.

*(3) Twelve-month period ending in the plan year.* This period consists of a specified 12-month period ending with or within the plan year, such as the calendar year or the period for determining benefit accruals described in § 1.401(a)(4)-3(f)(6).

*(4) Period of plan participation during the plan year.* This period consists of the portion of the plan year during which the employee is a participant in the plan. This period may be used to determine plan year compensation for the plan year in which participation begins, the plan year in which participation ends, or both. This period may be used to determine

plan year compensation when substituted for average annual compensation in § 1.401(a)(4)-3(e)(2)(ii)(A) only if the plan year is also the period for determining benefit accruals under the plan rather than another period as permitted under § 1.401(a)(4)-3(f)(6). Further, selection of this period must be made on a reasonably consistent basis from plan year to plan year in a manner that does not discriminate in favor of HCEs.

*(5) Special rule for new employees.* Notwithstanding the uniformity requirement of paragraph (1) of this definition, if employees' plan year compensation for a plan year is determined based on a 12-month period ending within the plan year under paragraph (3) of this definition, then the plan year compensation of any employees whose date of hire was less than 12 months before the end of that 12-month period must be determined uniformly based either on the plan year or on the employees' periods of participation during the plan year, as provided in paragraphs (2) and (4), respectively, of this definition.

*QJSA.* QJSA means a qualified joint and survivor annuity as defined in section 417(b).

*QSUPP. (1) In general.* QSUPP or qualified social security supplement means a social security supplement that meets each of the requirements in paragraphs (2) through (6) of this definition.

*(2) Accrual.* (i) General rule. The amount of the social security supplement payable at any age for which the employee is eligible for the social security supplement must be equal to the lesser of—

(A) The employee's old-age insurance benefit, unreduced on account of age, under title II of the Social Security Act; and

(B) The accrued social security supplement, determined under one of the methods in paragraph (2)(ii) through (iv) of this definition.

(ii) Section 401(l) plans. In the case of a section 401(l) plan that is a defined benefit excess plan, each employee's accrued social security supplement equals the employee's average annual compensation up to the integration level, multiplied by the disparity provided by the plan for the employee's years of service used in determining the employee's accrued benefit under the plan. In the case of a section 401(l) plan that is an offset plan, each employee's accrued social security supplement equals the dollar amount of the offset accrued for the employee under the plan.

(iii) PIA offset plan. In the case of a PIA offset plan, each employee's accrued social security supplement equals the dollar amount of the offset accrued for the employee under the plan. For this purpose, a PIA offset plan is a plan that reduces an employee's benefit by an offset based on a stated percentage of the employee's primary insurance amount under the Social Security Act.

(iv) Other plans. In the case of any other plan, each employee's social security supplement accrues ratably over the period beginning with the later of the employee's commencement of participation in the plan or the effective date of the social security supplement and ending with the earliest age at which the social security supplement is payable to the employee. The effective date of the social security supplement is the later of the effective date of the amendment adding the social security supplement or the effective date of the amendment modifying an existing social security supplement to comply with the requirements of this definition. If, by the end of the first plan year to which these regulations apply, as set forth in § 1.401(a)(4)-13(a) and (b), an amendment is made to a social security supplement in existence on September 19, 1991, the employer may treat the accrued portion of the social security supplement, as determined under the plan without regard to amendments made after September 19, 1991, as included in the employee's accrued social security supplement, provided that the remainder of the social security supplement is accrued under the otherwise-applicable method.

*(3) Vesting.* The plan must provide that an employee's right to the accrued social security supplement becomes nonforfeitable within the meaning of section 411 as if it were an early retirement benefit.

*(4) Eligibility.* The plan must impose the same eligibility conditions on receipt of the social security supplement as on receipt of the early retirement benefit in conjunction with which the social security supplement is payable. Furthermore, if the service required for an employee to become eligible for the social security supplement exceeds 15 years, then the ratio percentage of the group of employees who actually satisfy the eligibility conditions on receipt of the QSUPP in the current plan year must equal or exceed the unsafe harbor percentage applicable to the plan under § 1.410(b)-4(c)(4)(ii).

*(5) QJSA.* At each age, the most valuable QSUPP commencing at that age must be payable in conjunction with the QJSA commencing at that age. In addition, the plan must provide that, in the case of a social security supplement payable in conjunction with a QJSA, the social security supplement will be paid after the employee's death on the same terms as the QJSA, but in no event for a period longer than the period for which the social security supplement would have been paid to the employee had the employee not died. For example, if the QJSA is in the form of a joint annuity with a 50-percent survivor's benefit, the social security supplement must provide a 50-percent survivor's benefit. When section 417(c) requires the determination of a QJSA for purposes of determining a qualified pre-retirement survivor's annuity as defined in section 417(c) (QPSA), the social security supplement payable in conjunction with that QJSA must be paid in conjunction with the QPSA.

*(6) Protection.* The plan must specifically provide that the social security supplement is treated as an early retirement benefit that is protected under section 411(d)(6) (other than for purposes of sections 401(a)(11) and 417). Thus, the accrued social security supplement must continue to be payable notwithstanding subsequent amendment of the plan (including the plan's termination), and an employee may meet the eligibility requirements for the social security supplement after plan termination.

*Qualified plan.* Qualified plan means a plan that satisfies section 401(a). For this purpose, a qualified plan includes an annuity plan described in section 403(a).

*Rate group.* Rate group is defined in § 1.401(a)(4)-2(c)(1) or is defined in § 1.401(a)(4)-3(c)(1).

*Ratio percentage.* Ratio percentage is defined in § 1.410(b)-9.

*Section 401(a)(17) employee.* Section 401(a)(17) employee is defined in § 1.401(a)(17)-1(e)(2)(ii).

*Section 401(k) plan.* Section 401(k) plan is defined in § 1.410(b)-9.

*Section 401(l) plan.* Section 401(l) plan is defined in § 1.410(b)-9.

*Section 401(m) plan.* Section 401(m) plan is defined in § 1.410(b)-9.

*Section 414(s) compensation. (1) General rule.* When used with reference to compensation for a plan year, 12-month period, or other specified period, section 414(s) compensation means compensation measured using an underlying definition that satisfies section 414(s) for the applicable plan year. Whether an underlying definition of compensation satisfies section 414(s) is determined on a year-by-year basis, based on the provisions of section 414(s) in effect for the applicable plan year and, if relevant, the employer's HCEs and NHCEs for that plan year. See § 1.414(s)-1(i) for transition rules for plan years beginning before the effective date applicable to the plan under § 1.401(a)(4)-13(a) or (b). For a plan year or 12-month period beginning before January 1, 1988, any underlying definition of compensation may be used to measure the amount of employees' compensation for purposes of this definition, provided that the definition was nondiscriminatory based on the facts and circumstances in existence for that plan year or for the plan year in which that 12-month period ends.

*(2) Determination period for section 414(S) nondiscrimination requirement.* (i) General rule. If an underlying definition of compensation must satisfy the nondiscrimination requirement in § 1.414(s)-1(d)(3) in order to satisfy section 414(s) for a plan year, any one of the following determination periods may be used to satisfy the nondiscrimination requirement—

(A) The plan year;

(B) The calendar year ending in the plan year; or

(C) The 12-month period ending in the plan year that is used to determine the underlying definition of compensation.

(ii) Exception for partial plan year compensation. Notwithstanding the general rule in paragraph (2)(i) of this definition, if the period for measuring the underlying compensation is the portion of the plan year during which each employee is a participant in the plan (as provided in paragraph (4) of the definition of plan year compensation in this section), that period must be used as the determination period.

*(3) Plans using permitted disparity.* In the case of a section 401(l) plan or a plan that imputes permitted disparity in accordance with § 1.401(a)(4)-7, an underlying definition of compensation is not section 414(s) compensation if the definition results in significant under inclusion of compensation for employees.

*(4) Double proration of service and compensation.* If a defined benefit plan prorates benefit accruals as permitted under section 411(b)(4)(B) by crediting less than full years of participation, then compensation for a plan year, 12-month period, or other specified period that is used to determine the amount of an employee's benefits under the plan will not fail to be section 414(s) compensation, merely because the amount of compensation for that period is adjusted to reflect the equivalent of full-time compensation to the extent necessary to satisfy the requirements of 29 CFR 2530.204-2(d) (regarding double proration of service and compensation). This adjustment is disregarded in determining whether the underlying definition of compensation used satisfies the requirements of section 414(s). Thus, for example, if the underlying definition of compensation is an alternative definition that must satisfy the nondiscrimination requirement of § 1.414(s)-1(d)(3), in determining whether that requirement is satisfied with regard to the underlying definition, the compensation included for any employee is determined without any adjustment to reflect the equivalent of full-time compensation required by 29 CFR 2530.204-2(d).

*Social security supplement.* Social security supplement is defined in § 1.411(a)-7(c)(4)(ii).

*Standard interest rate.* Standard interest rate means an interest rate that is neither less than 7.5 percent nor greater than 8.5 percent, compounded annually. The Commissioner may, in revenue rulings, notices, and other guidance of general applicability, change the definition of standard interest rate.

*Standard mortality table.* Standard mortality table means one of the following tables: the UP-1984 Mortality Table (Unisex); the 1983 Group Annuity Mortality Table (1983 GAM) (Female); the 1983 Group Annuity Mortality Table (1983 GAM) (Male); the 1983 Individual Annuity Mortality Table (1983 IAM) (Female); the 1983 Individual Annuity Mortality Table (1983 IAM) (Male); the 1971 Group Annuity Mortality Table (1971 GAM) (Female); the 1971 Group Annuity Mortality Table (1971 GAM) (Male); the 1971 Individual Annuity Mortality Table (1971 IAM) (Female); or the 1971 Individual Annuity Mortality Table (1971 IAM) (Male). These standard mortality tables are available from the Society of Actuaries, 475 N. Martingale Road, Suite 800, Schaumberg, Illinois 60173. The Commissioner may, in revenue rulings, notices, and other guidance of general applicability, change the definition of standard mortality table. See § 601.601(d)(2)(ii)(b) of this Chapter. The applicable mortality table under section 417(e)(3)(A)(ii)(I) is also a standard mortality table.

*Straight life annuity.* Straight life annuity means an annuity payable in equal installments for the life of the employee that terminates upon the employee's death.

*Testing age.* With respect to an employee, testing age means the age determined for the employee under the following rules:

*(1)* If the plan provides the same uniform normal retirement age for all employees, the employee's testing age is the employee's normal retirement age under the plan.

*(2)* If a plan provides different uniform normal retirement ages for different employees or different groups of employees, the employee's testing age is the employee's latest normal retirement age under any uniform normal retirement age under the plan, regardless of whether that particular uniform normal retirement age actually applies to the employee under the plan.

*(3)* If the plan does not provide a uniform normal retirement age, the employee's testing age is 65.

*(4)* If an employee is beyond the testing age otherwise determined for the employee under paragraphs (1) through (3) of this definition, the employee's testing age is the employee's current age. The rule in the preceding sentence does not apply in the case of a defined benefit plan that fails to satisfy the requirements of § 1.401(a)(4)-3(f)(3)(i) (permitting certain increases in benefits that commence after normal retirement age to be disregarded).

*Testing service.* Testing service is defined in § 1.401(a)(4)-3(d)(1)(iv).

*Uniform normal retirement age. (1) General rule.* Uniform normal retirement age means a single normal retirement age under the plan that does not exceed the maximum age in paragraph (2) of this definition and that is the same for all of the employees in a given group. A group of employees does not fail to have a uniform normal retirement age merely because the plan contains provisions described in paragraphs (3) and (4) of this definition.

*(2) Maximum age.* The maximum age is generally 65. However, if all employees have the same social security retirement age (within the meaning of section 415(b)(8)), the maximum age is the employees' social security retirement age. Thus, for example, a component plan has a uniform normal retirement age of 67 if it defines normal retirement age as social security retirement age and all employees in the component plan have a social security retirement age of 67.

*(3) Stated anniversary date. (i) General rule.* A group of employees does not fail to have a uniform normal retirement age merely because the plan provides that the normal retirement age of all employees in the group is the later of a stated age (not exceeding the maximum age in paragraph (2) of this definition) or a stated anniversary no later than the fifth anniversary of the time each employee commenced participation in the plan. For employees who commenced participation in the plan before the first plan year beginning on or after January 1, 1988, the stated anniversary date may be later than the anniversary described in the preceding sentence if it is no later than the earlier of the tenth anniversary of the date the employee commenced participation in the plan (or such earlier anniversary selected by the employer, if less than 10) or the fifth anniversary of the first day of the first plan year beginning on or after January 1, 1988.

*(ii) Use of service other than anniversary of commencement of participation.* In lieu of using a stated anniversary date as permitted under paragraph (3)(i) of this definition, a plan may use a stated number of years of service measured on another basis, provided that the determination is made on a basis that satisfies section 411(a)(8) and that the stated number of years of service does not exceed the number of anniversaries permitted under paragraph (3)(i) of this definition. For example, a uniform normal retirement age could be based on the earlier of the fifth anniversary of the commencement of participation and the completion of five years of vesting service.

*(4) Conversion of normal retirement age to normal retirement date.* A group of employees does not fail to have a uniform normal retirement age merely because a defined benefit plan provides for the commencement of normal retirement benefits on different retirement dates for different employees if each employee's normal retirement date is determined on a reasonable basis with reference to an otherwise uniform normal retirement age and the difference between the normal retirement date and the uniform normal retirement age cannot exceed six months for any employee. Thus, for example, benefits under a plan do not fail to commence at a uniform normal retirement age of age 62 for purposes of § 1.401(a)(4)-3(b)(2)(i), merely because the plan's normal retirement date is defined as the last day of the plan year nearest attainment of age 62.

*Year of service.* Year of service means a year of service as defined in the plan for a specific purpose, including the method of crediting service for that purpose under the plan.

T.D. 8360, 9/12/91, amend T.D. 8485, 8/30/93, T.D. 8954, 6/28/2001.

### § 1.401(a)(4)-13 Effective dates and fresh-start rules.

**(a) General effective dates.** *(1) In general.* Except as otherwise provided in this section, §§ 1.401(a)(4)-1 through 1.401(a)(4)-13 apply to plan years beginning on or after January 1, 1994.

*(2) Plans of tax-exempt organizations.* In the case of plans maintained by organizations exempt from income taxation under section 501(a), including plans subject to section 403(b)(12)(A)(i) (nonelective plans), §§ 1.401(a)(4)-1 through 1.401(a)(4)-13 apply to plan years beginning on or after January 1, 1996.

*(3) Compliance during transition period.* For plan years beginning before the effective date of these regulations, as set forth in paragraph (a)(1) and (2) of this section, and on or after the first day of the first plan year to which the amendments made to section 410(b) by section 1112(a) of the Tax Reform Act of 1986 (TRA '86) apply, a plan must be operated in accordance with a reasonable, good faith interpretation of section 401(a)(4), taking into account pre-existing guidance and the amendments made by TRA '86 to related provisions of the Code (including, for example, sections 401(l), 401(a)(17), and 410(b)). Whether a plan is operated in accordance with a reasonable, good faith interpretation of section 401(a)(4) will generally be determined on the basis of all the relevant facts and circumstances, including the extent to which an employer has resolved unclear issues in its favor. A plan will be deemed to be operated in accordance with a reasonable, good faith interpretation of section 401(a)(4) if it is operated in accordance with the terms of §§ 1.401(a)(4)-1 through 1.401(a)(4)-13.

**(b) Effective date for governmental plans.** In the case of governmental plans described in section 414(d), including plans subject to section 403(b)(12)(A)(i) (nonelective plans), §§ 1.401(a)(4)-1 through 1.401(a)(4)-13 apply to plan years beginning on or after the later of January 1, 1996, or 90 days after the opening of the first legislative session beginning on or after January 1, 1996, of the governing body with authority to amend the plan, if that body does not meet continuously. Such plans are deemed to satisfy section 401(a)(4) for plan years before that effective date. For purposes of this paragraph (b), the governing body with authority to amend the plan is the legislature, board, commission, council, or other governing body with authority to amend the plan.

**(c) Fresh-start rules for defined benefit plans.** *(1) Introduction.* This paragraph (c) provides rules that must be satisfied in order to use the fresh-start testing options for defined benefit plans in § 1.401(a)(4)-3(b)(6)(vii) and (d)(3)(iii), relating to the safe harbors and the general test, respectively. Those fresh-start options are designed to allow a plan to be tested without regard to benefits accrued before a selected fresh-start date. To the extent provided in paragraph (d) of this section, those options also may be used to disregard certain increases in benefits attributable to compensation increases after a fresh-start date. Although this paragraph (c) generally requires a plan to be amended to freeze employees' accrued benefits as of a fresh-start date and to provide any additional accrued benefits after the fresh-start date solely in accordance with certain specified formulas, certain of these requirements do not apply to a plan that is tested under the general test of § 1.401(a)(4)-3(c). See § 1.401(a)(4)-3(b)(6)(vii) and (d)(3)(iii).

*(2) General rule.* A defined benefit plan satisfies this paragraph (c) if—

(i) Accrued benefits of employees in the fresh-start group are frozen as of the fresh-start date in accordance with paragraph (c)(3) of this section;

(ii) Accrued benefits after the fresh-start date for employees in the fresh-start group are determined under one of the fresh-start formulas in paragraph (c)(4) of this section; and

(iii) paragraph (c)(5) of this section is satisfied.

*(3) Definition of frozen.* (i) General rule. An employee's accrued benefit under a plan is frozen as of the fresh-start

date if it is determined as if the employee terminated employment with the employer as of the fresh-start date (or the date the employee actually terminated employment with the employer, if earlier), and without regard to any amendment to the plan adopted after that date, other than amendments recognized as effective as of or before that date under section 401(b) or § 1.401(a)(4)-11(g). The assumption that an employee has terminated employment applies solely for purposes of this paragraph (c)(3). Thus, for example, the fresh start has no effect on the service taken into account for purposes of determining vesting and eligibility for benefits, rights, and features under the plan.

(ii) Permitted compensation adjustments. An employee's accrued benefit under a plan that satisfies paragraph (d) of this section does not fail to be frozen as of the fresh-start date merely because the plan makes the adjustments described in paragraph (d)(7) and (8) of this section with regard to the fresh-start date. In addition, if the frozen accrued benefit of an employee under the plan includes top-heavy minimum benefits, an employee's accrued benefit under a plan does not fail to be frozen as of the fresh-start date merely because the plan increases the frozen accrued benefit of each employee in the fresh-start group solely to the extent necessary to comply with the average compensation requirement of section 416(c)(1)(D)(i).

(iii) Permitted changes in optional forms. An employee's accrued benefit under a plan does not fail to be frozen as of the fresh-start date merely because the plan provides a new optional form of benefit with respect to the frozen accrued benefit, if—

(A) The optional form is provided with respect to each employee's entire accrued benefit (i.e., accrued both before and after the fresh-start date);

(B) The plan provided meaningful coverage as of the fresh-start date, as described in paragraph (d)(4) of this section; and

(C) The plan provides meaningful current benefit accruals as described in paragraph (d)(6) of this section.

(iv) Floor-offset plans. In the case of a plan that was a floor-offset plan described in § 1.401(a)(4)-8(d) prior to the fresh-start date, an employee's accrued benefit as of the fresh-start date does not fail to be frozen merely because the actuarial equivalent of the account balance in the defined contribution plan that is offset against the defined benefit plan varies as a result of investment return that is different from the assumed interest rate used to determine the actuarial equivalent of the account balance.

*(4) Fresh-start formulas.* (i) Formula without wear-away. An employee's accrued benefit under the plan is equal to the sum of—

(A) The employee's frozen accrued benefit; and

(B) The employee's accrued benefit determined under the formula applicable to benefit accruals in the current plan year (current formula) as applied to the employee's years of service after the fresh-start date.

(ii) Formula with wear-away. An employee's accrued benefit under the plan is equal to the greater of—

(A) The employee's frozen accrued benefit; or

(B) The employee's accrued benefit determined under the current formula as applied to the employee's total years of service (before and after the fresh-start date) taken into account under the current formula.

(iii) Formula with extended wear-away. An employee's accrued benefit under the plan is equal to the greater of—

(A) The amount determined under paragraph (c)(4)(i) of this section; or

(B) The amount determined under paragraph (c)(4)(ii)(B) of this section.

*(5) Rules of application.* (i) Consistency requirement. This paragraph (c)(5) is not satisfied unless the fresh-start rules in this paragraph (c) (and paragraph (d) of this section, if applicable) are applied consistently to all employees in the fresh-start group. Thus, for example, the same fresh-start date and fresh-start formula (within the meaning of paragraph (c)(4) of this section) must apply to all employees in the fresh-start group. Similarly, if a plan makes a fresh start for all employees with accrued benefits on the fresh-start date and, for a later plan year, is aggregated for purposes of section 401(a)(4) with another plan that did not make the same fresh start, the aggregated plan must make a new fresh start in order to use the fresh-start rules for that later plan year or any subsequent plan year.

(ii) Definition of fresh-start group. Generally, the fresh-start group with respect to a fresh start consists of all employees who have accrued benefits as of the fresh-start date and have at least one hour of service with the employer after that date. However, a fresh-start group with respect to a fresh start may consist exclusively of all employees who have accrued benefits as of the fresh-start date, have at least one hour of service with the employer after that date, and are—

(A) Section 401(a)(17) employees;

(B) Members of an acquired group of employees (provided the fresh-start date is the date determined under paragraph (c)(5)(iii)(B) of this section); or

(C) Employees with a frozen accrued benefit that is attributable to assets and liabilities transferred to the plan as of a fresh-start date in connection with the transfer (provided the fresh-start date is the date determined under paragraph (c)(5)(iii)(C) of this section) and for whom the current formula is different from the formula used to determine the frozen accrued benefit.

(iii) Definition of fresh-start date. Generally, the fresh-start date is the last day of a plan year. However, a plan may use a fresh-start date other than the last day of the plan year if—

(A) The plan satisfied the safe harbor rules of § 1.401(a)(4)-3(b) for the period from the beginning of the plan year through the fresh-start date;

(B) The fresh-start group is an acquired group of employees, and the fresh-start date is the latest date of hire or transfer into an acquired trade or business selected by the employer for any employees to be included in the acquired group of employees; or

(C) The fresh-start group is the group of employees with a frozen accrued benefit that is attributable to assets and liabilities transferred to the plan and the fresh-start date is the date as of which the employees begin accruing benefits under the plan.

*(6) Examples.* The following examples illustrate the rules in this paragraph (c):

*Example (1).* (a) Employer X maintains a defined benefit plan with a calendar plan year. The plan formula provides an employee with a normal retirement benefit at age 65 of one percent of average annual compensation up to covered compensation multiplied by the employee's years of service for Employer X, plus 1.5 percent of average annual compensation in excess of covered compensation, multiplied by the employee's years of service for Employer X up to 40.

(b) For plan years beginning after 1994, Employer X amends the plan formula to provide a normal retirement benefit of 0.75 percent of average annual compensation up to covered compensation multiplied by the employee's total years of service for Employer X up to 35, plus 1.4 percent of average annual compensation in excess of covered compensation multiplied by the employee's years of service for Employer X up to 35. For plan years after 1994, each employee's accrued benefit is determined under the fresh-start formula in paragraph (c)(4)(iii) of this section (formula with extended wear-away), using December 31, 1994, as the fresh-start date.

(c) As of December 31, 1994, Employee M has 10 years of service for Employer X, has average annual compensation of $38,000, and has covered compensation of $30,000. Employee M's accrued benefit as of December 31, 1994, is therefore $4,200 ((1 percent × $30,000 × 10 years) + (1.5 percent × $8,000 × 10 years)). As of December 31, 1995, Employee M has 11 years of service for Employer X, has average annual compensation of $40,000 (determined by taking into account compensation before and after the fresh-start date), and has covered compensation of $32,000. Employee M's accrued benefit as of December 31, 1995, is $4,552, the greater of—

(1) $4,552, the sum of Employee M's accrued benefit frozen as of December 31, 1994, ($4,200) and the amended formula applied to Employee M's years of service after 1994 ((0.75 percent × $32,000 × 1 year) + (1.4 percent × $8,000 × 1 year), or $352); or

(2) $3,872, the amended formula applied to Employee M's total years of service ((0.75 percent × $32,000 × 11 years) + (1.4 percent × $8,000 × 11 years)).

*Example (2).* (a) Employer Y maintains a defined benefit plan, Plan A, that has a calendar plan year. For the 1995 plan year, Plan A satisfies the requirements for a safe harbor plan in § 1.401(a)(4)-3(b). Employer Y selects a date in 1995 for all the employees, freezes the employees' accrued benefits as of that date under the rules of paragraph (c)(3) of this section, and, in accordance with the rules of this paragraph (c), amends Plan A to determine benefits for all employees after that date using the formula with wear-away described in paragraph (c)(4)(ii) of this section. The new benefit formula would satisfy the requirements for a safe harbor plan in § 1.401(a)(4)-3(b) if all accrued benefits were determined under it.

(b) Because Plan A satisfied the requirements for a safe harbor plan for the period from the beginning of the plan year through the selected date, paragraph (c)(5)(iii)(A) of this section permits the selected date to be a fresh-start date, even if it is not the last day of the plan year. Thus, Plan A satisfies the requirements in this paragraph (c) for a fresh start as of the fresh-start date.

(c) Under § 1.401(a)(4)-3(b)(6)(vii), a plan does not fail to satisfy the requirements of § 1.401(a)(4)-3(b), merely because of benefits accrued under a different formula prior to a fresh-start date. Thus, Plan A still satisfies the safe harbor requirements of § 1.401(a)(4)-3(b) after the amendment to the benefit formula. Because Plan A satisfied the requirements for a safe harbor plan for the period from the beginning of the plan year, taking the amendment into account, Employer Y may select any date within the plan year (which may be the same date as the first fresh-start date) and apply the fresh-start rules in this paragraph (c) a second time as of that date.

**(d) Compensation adjustments to frozen accrued benefits.** *(1) Introduction.* In addition to the fresh-start rules in paragraph (c) of this section, this paragraph (d) sets forth requirements that must be satisfied in order for a plan to disregard increases in benefits accrued as of a fresh-start date that are attributable to increases in employees' compensation after the fresh-start date.

*(2) In general.* In the case of a defined benefit plan that is tested under the safe harbors in § 1.401(a)(4)-3(b) or § 1.401(a)(4)-8(c)(3), an employee's adjusted accrued benefit (determined under the rules in paragraph (d)(8) of this section) may be substituted for the employee's frozen accrued benefit in applying the formulas in paragraph (c)(4) of this section (or paragraph (f)(2) of this section, if applicable) if paragraphs (d)(3) through (d)(7) of this section are satisfied. Thus, for example, in determining whether such a plan satisfies § 1.401(a)(4)-3(b), any compensation adjustments to the employee's frozen accrued benefit described in paragraph (d)(8) of this section are disregarded. Similarly, in the case of a defined benefit plan tested under the general test in § 1.401(a)(4)-3(c), the compensation adjustments described in paragraph (d)(8) of this section may be disregarded under the rules of § 1.401(a)(4)-3(d)(3)(iii) if paragraphs (d)(3) through (d)(7) of this section are satisfied. Of course, any increases in accrued benefits exceeding these adjustments must be taken into account under the general test, and a plan providing such excess increases generally will fail to satisfy the safe harbor requirements of § 1.401(a)(4)-3(b). Where paragraphs (d)(3) through (d)(7) of this section are satisfied with respect to a plan as of the fresh-start date, but one or more of those paragraphs fail to be satisfied for a later plan year, further compensation adjustments described in paragraph (d)(8) of this section may not be disregarded in testing the plan under § 1.401(a)(4)-3.

*(3) Plan requirements.* (i) Pre-fresh-start date. As of the fresh-start date, the plan must have contained a benefit formula under which benefits of each employee in the fresh-start group that are accrued as of the fresh-start date and are attributable to service before the fresh-start date would be affected by the employee's compensation after the fresh-start date. A plan satisfies this requirement, for example, if it based benefits on an employee's highest average pay over a fixed period of years or on an employee's average pay over the employee's entire career with the employer. A plan does not satisfy this paragraph (d)(3)(i) if the Commissioner determines, based on all of the relevant facts and circumstances, that the plan provision described in the first sentence of this paragraph (d)(3) was added primarily in order to provide additional benefits to HCEs that are disregarded under the special testing rules described in this paragraph (d).

(ii) Post-fresh-start date. The plan by its terms must provide that the accrued benefits of each employee in the fresh-start group after the fresh-start date be at least equal to the employee's adjusted accrued benefit (i.e., the frozen accrued benefit as of the fresh-start date, adjusted as provided under paragraph (d)(7) of this section, plus the compensation adjustments described in paragraph (d)(8) of this section).

*(4) Meaningful coverage as of fresh-start date.* The plan must have provided meaningful coverage as of the fresh-start date. A plan provided meaningful coverage as of the fresh-start date if the group of employees with accrued benefits under the plan as of the fresh-start date satisfied the minimum coverage requirements of section 410(b) as in effect on

that date (determined without regard to section 410(b)(6)(C)). In order to satisfy the requirement in the preceding sentence, an employer may amend the plan to grant past service credit under the formula in effect as of the fresh-start date to NHCEs, if the amount of past service granted them is reasonably comparable, on average, to the amount of past service HCEs have under the plan. Any benefit increase that results from the grant of past service credit to a NHCE under this paragraph (d)(4) is included in the employee's frozen accrued benefit.

*(5) Meaningful ongoing coverage.* (i) General rule. The fresh-start group must have satisfied the minimum coverage requirements of section 410(b) for all plan years from the first plan year beginning after the fresh-start date through the current plan year. Thus, if a fresh-start group fails to satisfy the minimum coverage requirements of section 410(b) for any plan year, this paragraph (d)(5) is not satisfied for that plan year or any subsequent plan year; however, such a failure is not taken into account in determining whether this paragraph (d)(5) is satisfied for any previous plan year.

(ii) Alternative rules. Notwithstanding paragraph (d)(5)(i) of this section, a fresh-start group is deemed to satisfy this paragraph (d)(5) for all plan years following the fresh-start date if any one of the following requirements is satisfied:

(A) Section 410(b) coverage for first five years. The fresh-start group must have satisfied the minimum coverage requirements of section 410(b) for the first five plan years beginning after the fresh-start date.

(B) Ratio percentage coverage as of fresh-start date. The fresh-start group must have satisfied the ratio percentage test of § 1.410(b)-2(b)(2) as of the fresh-start date.

(C) Fresh start for acquired group of employees. The fresh-start group must consist of an acquired group of employees that satisfied the minimum coverage requirements of section 410(b) (determined without regard to section 410(b)(6)(C)) as of the fresh-start date.

(D) Fresh start before applicable effective date. The fresh-start date with respect to the fresh-start group must have been on or before the effective date applicable to the plan under paragraph (a) or (b) of this section.

*(6) Meaningful current benefit accruals.* The benefit formula and accrual method under the plan that apply to the fresh-start group in the aggregate must provide benefit accruals in the current plan year (other than increases in benefits accrued as of the fresh-start date) at a rate that is meaningful in comparison to the rate at which benefits accrued for the fresh-start group in plan years beginning before the fresh-start date. Whether this requirement is satisfied with respect to a fresh-start group that does not include all employees in the plan with an hour of service after the fresh-start date may be determined taking into account the rate at which benefits are provided to other employees in the plan.

*(7) Minimum benefit adjustment.* (i) In general. In the case of a section 401(l) plan or a plan that imputes disparity under § 1.401(a)(4)-7, the plan must make the minimum benefit adjustment described in paragraph (d)(7)(ii) or (iii) of this section.

(ii) Excess or offset plans. In the case of a plan that is a defined benefit excess plan as of the fresh-start date, each employee's frozen accrued benefit is adjusted so that the base benefit percentage is not less than 50 percent of the excess benefit percentage. In the case of a plan that is a PIA offset plan (as defined in paragraph (2)(iii) of the definition of QSUPP in § 1.401(a)(4)-12) as of the fresh-start date, each employee's offset as applied to determine the frozen accrued benefit is adjusted so that it does not exceed 50 percent of the benefit determined without applying the offset.

(iii) Other plans. In the case of a plan that is not described in paragraph (d)(7)(ii) of this section, each employee's frozen accrued benefit is adjusted in a manner that is economically equivalent to the adjustment required under that paragraph, taking into account the plan's benefit formula, accrual rate, and relevant employee factors, such as period of service.

*(8) Adjusted accrued benefit.* (i) General rule. The term adjusted accrued benefit means an employee's frozen accrued benefit that is adjusted as provided in paragraph (d)(7) of this section and then multiplied by a fraction (not less than one), the numerator of which is the employee's compensation for the current plan year and the denominator of which is the employee's compensation as of the fresh-start date determined under the same definition. For purposes of this adjustment, the compensation definition must be either the same compensation definition and formula used to determine the frozen accrued benefit or average annual compensation (determined without regard to § 1.401(a)(4)-3(e)(2)(ii)(A) (use of plan year compensation)).

(ii) Alternative formula for pre-effective-date fresh starts. In the case of a fresh-start date before the effective date that applies to the plan under paragraph (a) or (b) of this section, the adjusted accrued benefit may be determined by multiplying the frozen accrued benefit by a fraction (not less than one) determined under this paragraph (d)(8)(ii). The numerator of the fraction is the employee's average annual compensation for the current plan year. The denominator of the fraction is the employee's reconstructed average annual compensation as of the fresh-start date. An employee's reconstructed average annual compensation is determined by—

(A) Selecting a single plan year beginning after the fresh-start date but beginning not later than the last day of the first plan year to which these regulations apply under paragraph (a) or (b) of this section;

(B) Determining the employee's average annual compensation for the selected plan year under the same method used to determine the employee's average annual compensation for the current plan year under this paragraph (d)(8)(ii); and

(C) Multiplying the employee's average annual compensation for the selected plan year by a fraction, the numerator of which is the employee's compensation as of the fresh-start date determined under the same compensation definition and formula used to determine the employee's frozen accrued benefit and the denominator of which is the employee's compensation for the selected plan year determined under the compensation definition and formula used to determine the employee's frozen accrued benefit.

(iii) Effect of section 401(a)(17). In determining the numerators and the denominators of the fractions described in this paragraph (d)(8), the annual compensation limit under section 401(a)(17) generally applies. See, however, § 1.401(a)(17)-1(e)(4) for special rules applicable to section 401(a)(17) employees.

(iv) Option to make less than the full permitted adjustment. A plan may limit the increase in an employee's frozen accrued benefit for the current and all future years to a percentage (not more than 100 percent) of the increase otherwise provided under this paragraph (d)(8). Furthermore, the plan may, at any time, terminate all future adjustments permitted under this paragraph (d).

(v) Alternative determination of adjusted accrued benefit. In lieu of applying the fractions in paragraph (d)(8)(i) or (ii) of this section, a plan may determine an employee's adjusted accrued benefit by substituting the employee's compensation for the current plan year (determined under the same compensation formula and underlying definition of compensation used to determine the employee's frozen accrued benefit) in the benefit formula used to determine the frozen accrued benefit. For this purpose, insignificant changes in the underlying definition of compensation to reflect current compensation practices will not be treated as a change in the definition of compensation. A plan may apply the alternative in this paragraph (d)(8)(v), only if it is reasonable to expect as of the fresh-start date that, over time, the use of this method instead of the general rule of paragraph (d)(8)(i) will not discriminate significantly in favor of HCEs.

*(9) Examples.* The following examples illustrate the rules of this paragraph (d).

*Example (1).* (a) Employer X maintains a defined benefit plan that is an excess plan with a calendar plan year. For plan years before 1989, the plan is integrated with benefits provided under the Social Security Act, providing each employee with a normal retirement benefit equal to one percent of the employee's average annual compensation in excess of the employee's covered compensation, multiplied by the employee's years of service for Employer X. The benefit formula thus provides no benefit with respect to average annual compensation up to covered compensation.

(b) As of December 31, 1988, Employee M has 10 years of service for Employer X and has covered compensation of $25,000 and average annual compensation of $20,000. Employee M's average annual compensation has never exceeded $20,000. Therefore, as of December 31, 1988, Employee M's accrued benefit under the plan is zero.

(c) Effective with the 1989 plan year, the plan is amended to provide each employee with a normal retirement benefit of 0.6 percent of average annual compensation up to covered compensation plus 1.2 percent of average annual compensation in excess of covered compensation, multiplied by the employee's years of service up to 35. The plan also provides that, for plan years after 1988, each employee's accrued benefit is determined under the formula in paragraph (c)(4)(i) of this section (formula without wear-away) and, in applying the fresh-start formula, each employee's frozen accrued benefit under paragraph (c)(4)(i) of this section will be adjusted under this paragraph (d), using the same compensation definition and formula used to determine the frozen accrued benefit under paragraph (d)(8)(i) of this section.

(d) The plan uses the permitted disparity of section 401(l) and thus must also make the minimum benefit adjustment under paragraph (d)(7) of this section. Because the excess benefit percentage under the plan for years before 1989 was one percent, the plan must provide a base benefit percentage for those years of at least 0.5 percent. After the minimum benefit adjustment, Employee M's accrued benefit as of December 31, 1988, is $1,000 (0.5 percent × $20,000 × 10 years).

(e) As of December 31, 1992, Employee M has 14 years of service and has covered compensation of $30,000 and average annual compensation of $35,000. Employee M's adjusted accrued benefit as of December 31, 1992, is $1,750 ($1,000 × $35,000/$20,000), and Employee M's accrued benefit as of December 31, 1992, is $2,710 (the sum of $1,750 plus $960 ((0.6 percent × $30,000 × 4 years) plus (1.2 percent × $5,000 × 4 years))).

*Example (2).* (a) The facts are the same as in Example 1, except that in determining adjusted accrued benefits, the plan specifies the alternative method of paragraph (d)(8)(v) of this section. This method may be used because it is reasonable to expect as of the fresh-start date that, over time, the use of this method instead of the general rule of paragraph (d)(8)(i) will not discriminate significantly in favor of HCEs.

(b) As of December 31, 1992, Employee M's adjusted accrued benefit is $2,000 (10 years of service prior to the fresh-start date × (0.5 percent of $30,000 + 1.0 percent of the excess of $35,000 over $30,000)).

(c) Alternatively, Employer X may choose to use the method of paragraph (d)(8)(v) of this section but freezes the covered compensation level at the dollar level in place as of the fresh-start date. In such case, Employee M's adjusted accrued benefit as of December 31, 1992, would have been $2,250 (10 years of service prior to the fresh-start date × (0.5 percent of $25,000 + 1.0 percent of the excess of $35,000 over $25,000)). This method may be used because it is reasonable to expect as of the fresh-start date that, over time, the use of this method instead of the general rule of paragraph (d)(8)(i) will not discriminate significantly in favor of HCEs.

*Example (3).* (a) The facts are the same as in Example 1, except that for plan years before 1989, the plan provided a minimum benefit to certain employees equal to $120 per year of service. Employee M is entitled to the minimum benefit, and thus, Employee M's frozen accrued benefit as of December 31, 1988 was $1,200 (the greater of 10 years of service × $120 and $1,000, Employee M's benefit under the underlying formula, after the minimum benefit adjustment of paragraph (d)(7) of this section).

(b) Employer X's plan specifies instead the alternative method of adjusting accrued benefits described in paragraph (d)(8)(v) of this section. (The fact that a minimum benefit applying to certain employees is not adjusted under the alternative method of paragraph (d)(8)(v) of this section, but would be adjusted under the general rule of paragraph (d)(8)(i) of this section does not change the conclusion in Example 2, that the plan may apply the alternative method).

**(e) Determination of initial theoretical reserve for target benefit plans.** *(1) General rule.* In the case of a target benefit plan the stated benefit formula under which takes into account service for years in which the plan did not satisfy § 1.401(a)(4)-8(b)(3), as permitted under § 1.401(a)(4)-8(b)(3)(vii), the theoretical reserve as of the determination date for the last plan year beginning before the first day of the first plan year in which the plan satisfies § 1.401(a)(4)-8(b)(3) of an employee who was a participant in the plan on that determination date, is determined as follows:

(i) Determine the actuarial present value, as of that determination date, of the stated benefit that the employee is projected to have at the employee's normal retirement age, using the actuarial assumptions, the provisions of the plan, and the employee's compensation as of that determination date. For an employee whose attained age equals or exceeds the employee's normal retirement age, determine the actuarial present value of the employee's stated benefit at the employee's current age, but using an immediate straight life annuity factor for an employee whose attained age equals the employee's normal retirement age.

(ii) Calculate the actuarial present value of future required employer contributions (without regard to limitations under section 415 or additional contributions described in § 1.401(a)(4)-8(b)(3)(v)) as of that determination date (i.e., the actuarial present value of the level contributions due for each plan year through the end of the plan year in which the employee attains normal retirement age). This calculation is made assuming that the required contribution in each future year will be equal to the required contribution for the plan year that includes that determination date, and applying the interest rate that was used in determining that required contribution.

(iii) Determine the excess, if any, of the amount determined in paragraph (e)(1)(i) of this section over the amount determined in paragraph (e)(1)(ii) of this section. This excess is the employee's theoretical reserve on that determination date.

*(2) Example.* The following example illustrates the determination of an employee's theoretical reserve.

*Example.* (a) A target benefit plan was adopted and in effect before September 19, 1991, and satisfied the requirements of Rev. Rul. 76-464, 1976-2 C.B. 115, with respect to all years credited under the stated benefit formula through 1993. The plan provides a stated benefit equal to 40 percent of compensation, payable annually as a straight life annuity beginning at normal retirement age. Normal retirement age under the plan is 65. The stated interest rate under the plan is six percent. The determination date for required contributions under the plan is the last day of the plan year. Employee M is 38 years old on the determination date for the 1993 plan year, has participated in the plan for five years, and has compensation equal to $60,000 in 1993. The amount of employer contribution to Employee M's account for 1993 was $2,468.

(b) Under these facts, Employee M's theoretical reserve is equal to $13,909, calculated as follows:

(1) The actuarial present value of Employee M's stated benefit is calculated using the actuarial assumptions, provisions of the plan and Employee M's compensation as of the determination date for the 1993 plan year. This amount is equal to $46,512, Employee M's stated benefit of $24,000 ($60,000 multiplied by 40 percent), multiplied by 1.938, the actuarial present value factor applicable to a participant who is 38 years old using a stated interest rate of six percent.

(2) The actuarial present value of future employer contributions is calculated assuming that the required contribution in each future year will be equal to the required contribution for the 1993 plan year and assuming the same interest rate as was used in determining that contribution. This amount is equal to $32,603, which is equal to the amount of the level annual employer contribution ($2,468) multiplied by a factor of 13.2105 (the temporary annuity factor for a period of 27 years, assuming the six percent interest rate that was used to determine the required employer contribution).

(3) Employee M's theoretical reserve is $13,909, the excess of the amount determined in paragraph (b)(1) of this Examples over the amount determined in paragraph (b)(2) of this Example.

**(f) Special fresh-start rules for cash balance plans.** *(1) In general.* In order to satisfy the optional testing method of § 1.401(a)(4)-8(c)(3) after a fresh-start date, a cash balance plan must apply the rules of paragraph (c) of this section as modified under this paragraph (f). Paragraph (f)(2) of this section provides an alternative formula that may be used in addition to the formulas in paragraphs (c)(2) through (c)(4) of this section. Paragraph (f)(3) of this section sets forth certain limitations on use of the formulas in paragraph (c) or (f)(2) of this section.

*(2) Alternative formula.* (i) In general. An employee's accrued benefit under the plan is equal to the greater of—

(A) The employee's frozen accrued benefit, or

(B) The employee's accrued benefit determined under the plan's benefit formula applicable to benefit accruals in the current plan year as applied to years of service after the fresh-start date, modified in accordance with paragraph (f)(2)(ii) of this section.

(ii) Addition of opening hypothetical account. As of the first day after the fresh-start date, the plan must credit each employee's hypothetical account with an amount equal to the employee's opening hypothetical account (determined under paragraph (f)(2)(iii) of this section), adjusted for interest for the period that begins on the first day after the fresh-start date and that ends at normal retirement age. The interest adjustment in the preceding sentence must be made using the same interest rate applied to the hypothetical allocation for the first plan year beginning after the fresh-start date.

(iii) Determination of opening hypothetical account. (A) General rule. An employee's opening hypothetical account equals the actuarial present value of the employee's frozen accrued benefit as of the fresh-start date. For this purpose, if the plan provides for a single sum distribution as of the fresh-start date, the actuarial present value of the employee's frozen accrued benefit as of the fresh-start date equals the amount of a single sum distribution payable under the plan on that date, assuming that the employee terminated employment on the fresh-start date, the employee's accrued benefit was 100-percent vested, and the employee satisfied all eligibility requirements under the plan for the single sum distribution. If the plan does not offer a single sum distribution as of the fresh-start date, the actuarial present value of the employee's frozen accrued benefit as of the fresh-start date must be determined using a standard mortality table and the applicable section 417(e) rates, as defined in § 1.417(e)-1(d).

(B) Alternative opening hypothetical account. Alternatively, the employee's opening hypothetical account is the greater of the opening hypothetical account determined under paragraph (f)(2)(ii)(A) of this section and the employee's hypothetical account as of the fresh-start date determined in accordance with § 1.401(a)(4)-8(c)(3)(v)(A) calculated under the plan's benefit formula applicable to benefit accruals in the current plan year as applied to the employee's total years of service through the fresh-start date in a manner that satisfies the past service credit rules of § 1.401(a)(4)-8(c)(3)(viii).

*(3) Limitations on formulas.* (i) Past service restriction. If the plan does not satisfy the uniform hypothetical allocation formula requirement of § 1.401(a)(4)-8(c)(3)(iii)(B) as of the fresh-start date, under § 1.401(a)(4)-8(c)(3)(viii) the plan may not provide for past service credits, and thus may not use the formula in paragraph (c)(3) of this section (formula with wear-away), the formula in paragraph (c)(4) of this section (formula with extended wear-away), or the alternative determination of the opening hypothetical account in paragraph (f)(2)(iii)(B) of this section.

(ii) Change in interest rate. If the interest rate used to adjust employees' hypothetical allocations under § 1.401(a)(4)-8(c)(3)(iv) for the plan year is different from the interest rate used for this purpose in the immediately preceding plan year, the plan must use the formula in paragraph (c)(2) of this section (formula without wear-away).

(iii) Meaningful benefit requirement. A plan is permitted to use the formula provided in paragraph (f)(2) of this section only if the plan satisfies paragraphs (d)(3) through (d)(5) of this section (regarding coverage as of fresh-start date, current benefit accruals, and minimum benefit adjustment, respectively).

T.D. 8360, 9/12/91, amend T.D. 8485, 8/30/93.

### § 1.401(a)(5)-1 Special rules relating to nondiscrimination requirements.

**(a) In general.** Section 401(a)(5) sets out certain provisions that will not of themselves be discriminatory within the meaning of section 410(b)(2)(A)(i) or section 401(a)(4). The exceptions specified in section 401(a)(5) are not an exclusive enumeration, but are merely a recital of provisions frequently encountered that will not of themselves constitute prohibited discrimination in contributions or benefits. See section 401(a)(4) and the regulations thereunder for the basic nondiscrimination rules. See § 1.410(b)-4 for the rule of section 410(b)(2)(A)(i) (relating to the nondiscriminatory classification test that is part of the minimum coverage requirements) referred to in section 401(a)(5)(A). See paragraphs (b) through (f) of this section for special rules used in applying the section 401(a)(4) nondiscrimination requirements under the remaining provisions of section 401(a)(5).

**(b) Salaried or clerical employees.** A plan does not fail to satisfy the nondiscrimination requirements of section 401(a)(4) merely because contributions or benefits provided under the plan are limited to salaried or clerical employees.

**(c) Uniform relationship to compensation.** A plan does not fail to satisfy the nondiscrimination requirements of section 401(a)(4) merely because the contributions or benefits of, or on behalf of, the employees under the plan bear a uniform relationship to the compensation (within the meaning of section 414(s)) of those employees.

**(d) Certain disparity permitted.** Under section 401(a)(5)(C), a plan does not discriminate in favor of highly compensated employees (as defined in section 414(q)), within the meaning of section 401(a)(4), in the amount of employer-provided contributions or benefits solely because—

*(1)* In the case of a defined contribution plan, employer contributions allocated to the accounts of employees favor highly compensated employees in a manner permitted by section 401(l) (relating to permitted disparity in plan contributions and benefits), and

*(2)* In the case of a defined benefit plan, employer-provided benefits favor highly compensated employees in a manner permitted by section 401(l) (relating to permitted disparity in plan contributions and benefits).

See §§ 1.401(l)-1 through 1.401(l)-6 for rules under which a plan may satisfy section 401(l) for purposes of the safe harbors of §§ 1.401(a)(4)-2(b)(3) and 1.401(a)(4)-3(b).

**(e) Defined benefit plans integrated with social security.** *(1) In general.* Under section 401(a)(5)(D), a defined benefit plan does not discriminate in favor of highly compensated employees (as defined in section 414(q)) with respect to the amount of employer-provided contributions or benefits solely because the plan provides that, with respect to each employee, the employer-provided accrued retirement benefit under the plan is limited to the excess (if any) of—

(i) The employee's final pay from the employer, over

(ii) The employer-provided retirement benefit created under the Social Security Act and attributable to service by the employee for the employer.

*(2) Final pay.* For purposes of paragraph (e)(1)(i) of this section, an employee's final pay from the employer as of a plan year is the employee's compensation (as defined in section 414(q)(7)) for the year (ending with or within the 5-plan-year period ending with the plan year in which the employee terminates from employment with the employer) in which the employee receives the highest compensation from the employer. Notwithstanding the preceding sentence, final pay for each employee under the plan may be determined with reference to the 5-plan-year period ending with the plan year before the plan year in which the employee terminates from employment with the employer. In determining an employee's final pay, the plan may specify any 12-month period (ending with or within the applicable 5-plan-year period) as a year provided the specified 12-month period is uniformly and consistently applied with respect to all employees. In determining an employee's final pay, compensation for any year in excess of the applicable limit under section 401(a)(17) for the year may not be taken into account.

*(3) Rules for determining amount of employer-provided social security retirement benefit.* For purposes of paragraph (e)(1)(ii) of this section, the following rules apply.

(i) The employer-provided retirement benefit on which any reduction or offset in the employee's accrued retirement benefit is based is limited solely to the employer-provided primary insurance amount payable under section 215 of the Social Security Act attributable to service by the employee for the employer.

(ii) The employer-provided primary insurance amount attributable to service by the employee for the employer is determined by multiplying the employer-provided portion of the employee's projected primary insurance amount by a fraction (not exceeding 1), the numerator of which is the employee's number of complete years of covered service for the employer under the Social Security Act, and the denominator of which is 35.

*(4) Projected primary insurance amount.* (i) As of a plan year, an employee's projected primary insurance amount is the primary insurance amount, determined as of the close of the plan year (the "determination date"), payable to the employee upon attainment of the employee's social security retirement age (as determined under section 415(b)(8)), assuming the employee's annual compensation from the employer that is treated as wages for purposes of the Social Security Act remains the same from the plan year until the employee's attainment of social security retirement age. With respect to service by the employee for the employer before the determination date, the actual compensation paid to the employee by the employer during all periods of service of the employee for the employer covered by the Social Security Act must be used in determining an employee's projected primary insurance amount. With respect to years before the employee's commencement of service for the employer, in determining the employee's projected primary insurance amount, it may be assumed that the employee received compensation in an amount computed by using a six-percent salary scale projected backwards from the determination date to the employee's 21st birthday. However, if the employee provides the employer with satisfactory evidence of the employee's actual past compensation for the prior years treated as wages under the Social Security Act at the time the compensation was earned and the actual past compensation results in a smaller projected primary insurance amount, the plan must use the actual past compensation. The plan administrator must give clear written notice to each employee of the employee's right to supply actual compensation history

and of the financial consequences of failing to supply the history. The notice must be given each time the summary plan description is provided to the employee and must also be given upon the employee's separation from service. The notice must also state that the employee can obtain the actual compensation history from the Social Security Administration. In determining the employee's projected primary insurance amount, the employer may not take into account any compensation from any other employer while the employee is employed by the employer.

(ii) As of a plan year, the employer-provided portion of the employee's projected primary insurance amount under the Social Security Act is 50 percent of the employee's projected primary insurance amount (as determined under paragraph (e)(4)(i) of this section).

*(5) Employer-provided accrued retirement benefit.* For purposes of this section, the employee's employer-provided accrued retirement benefit as of a plan year is the employee's accrued retirement benefit under the plan (determined on an actual basis and not on a projected basis) attributable to employer contributions under the plan. With respect to plans that provide for employee contributions, see section 411(c) for rules relating to allocation of accrued benefits between employer contributions and employee contributions.

*(6) Additional rules.* (i) As of a plan year, paragraph (e)(1) of this section does not apply to the extent that its application would result in a decrease in an employee's accrued benefit. See sections 411(b)(1)(G) and 411(d)(6).

(ii) Section 401(a)(5)(D) and this paragraph (e) do not apply to a plan maintained by an employer, determined for purposes of the Federal Insurance Contributions Act or the Railroad Retirement Tax Act, as applicable, that does not pay any wages within the meaning of section 3121(a) or compensation within the meaning of section 3231(e). For this purpose, a plan maintained for a self-employed individual within the meaning of section 401(c)(1), who is also subject to the tax under section 1401, is deemed to be a plan maintained by an employer that pays wages within the meaning of section 3121(a).

(iii) If a plan provides for the payment of an employee's accrued retirement benefit (whether or not subsidized) commencing before an employee's social security retirement age, the projected employer-provided primary insurance amount attributable to service by the employee for the employer (as determined under paragraphs (e)(3) and (e)(4) of this section) that may be applied as an offset to limit the employee's accrued retirement benefit must be reduced in accordance with § 1.401(l)-3(e)(1). The reduction is made by multiplying the employee's projected employer-provided primary insurance amount by a fraction, the numerator of which is the appropriate factor under § 1.401(l)-3(e)(1), and the denominator of which is 0.75 percent.

(iv) The Commissioner may, in revenue rulings, notices or other documents of general applicability, prescribe additional rules that may be necessary or appropriate to carry out the purposes of this section, including rules relating to the determination of an employee's projected primary insurance amount attributable to the employee's service for former employers and rules applying section 401(a)(5)(D) with respect to an employer that pays wages within the meaning of section 3121(a) or compensation within the meaning of section 3231(e) for some years and not for other years.

*(7) Examples.* The following examples illustrate this paragraph (e).

*Example (1).* Employer Z maintains a noncontributory defined benefit plan that uses the calendar year as its plan year. The plan provides a normal retirement benefit, commencing at age 65, equal to $500 a year, multiplied by the employee's years of service for Z, limited to the excess of the amount of the employee's final pay from Z (as determined in accordance with paragraph (e)(2) of this section) over the employee's employer-provided primary insurance amount attributable to the employee's service for Z. If an employee's social security retirement age is greater than 65, the plan provides for reduction of the employee's employer-provided primary insurance amount in accordance with paragraph (e)(6)(iii) of this section. The plan provides no limitation on the number of years of service taken into account in determining benefits under the plan. Employee A retires on July 6, 1995, at A's social security retirement age of 65 with 35 years of service for Z. The plan uses the plan year as the 12 month period for determining an employee's year of final highest pay from the employer. A's compensation for A's final 5 plan years is as follows:

| | |
|---|---|
| 1995 plan year | $10,500 |
| 1994 plan year | $20,000 |
| 1993 plan year | $18,000 |
| 1992 plan year | $17,000 |
| 1991 plan year | $16,500 |

A's annual primary insurance amount under social security, determined as of A's social security retirement age, is $9,000, of which $4,500 is the employer-provided portion attributable to A's service for Z ($9,000 × 50 percent × 35/35). Under the plan's benefit formula (disregarding the final pay limitation), A would be entitled to receive a normal retirement benefit of $17,500 ($500 × 35 years). However, under the plan, A's otherwise determined normal retirement benefit of $17,500 is limited to the excess of the amount of A's final pay from Z over A's employer-provided primary insurance amount under social security attributable to A's service for Z. Accordingly, A's normal retirement benefit is determined to be $15,500 ($20,000 (A's final pay from Z) less $4,500 (A's employer-provided primary insurance amount attributable to A's service for Z)) rather than $17,500. The final pay limitation in Z's plan satisfies section 401(a)(5)(D) and this paragraph (e). Accordingly, the plan maintained by Z does not discriminate in favor of highly compensated employees within the meaning of section 401(a)(4) merely because of the final pay limitation contained in the plan.

*Example (2).* Assume the same facts as in Example 1, except that A has 32 years of service for Z when A retires at A's social security retirement age. Under the plan's benefit formula (disregarding the final pay limitation), A would be entitled to receive an annual normal retirement benefit of $16,000 ($500 × 32 years). However, the plan provides that A's normal retirement benefit of $16,000 will be limited to $15,500 ($20,000 (the amount of A's final pay from Z) less $4,500 (½ of A's primary insurance amount under the Social Security Act)). The final pay limitation does not satisfy this paragraph (e). The portion of A's employer-provided primary insurance amount under the Social Security Act attributable to A's service for Z is 32/35 × $4,500, or $4,114. Therefore, to satisfy this paragraph (e), the final pay provision in Z's plan may not limit A's otherwise determined normal retirement benefit of $16,000 to less than $15,886 ($20,000 (the amount of X's final pay) − $4,114 (the portion of A's employer-provided primary insurance amount attributable to A's service for Z)).

*Example (3).* (a) Employer X maintains a noncontributory defined benefit plan that uses the calendar year as its plan year. The formula for determining benefits under the plan provides a normal retirement benefit at age 65 equal to 90 percent of an employee's final average compensation, with the benefit reduced by 1/30th for each year of the employee's service less than 30 and limited to the employee's final pay (as determined in accordance with paragraph (e)(2) of this section) less the employee's employer-provided primary insurance amount under social security attributable to the employee's service for X. The plan determines an employee's employer-provided projected primary insurance amount under social security attributable to the employee's service for X in accordance with paragraph (e)(3) of this section and applies the reductions applicable under paragraph (e)(6)(iii) of this section if benefits commence before social security retirement age. The plan determines an employee's accrued benefit under the fractional accrual method of section 411(b)(1)(C).

(b) Employee A commences participation in the plan on January 1, 1990, when A is 35 years of age. A's social security retirement age is age 67. As of the close of the 2014 plan year, A's final average compensation from X is $15,000; A's final pay from X is $15,400 and A's projected employer-provided annual primary insurance amount under social security attributable to A's service for X is $4,000 (after the reduction applicable under paragraph (e)(6)(iii) of this section). Under the plan formula, A's accrued benefit as of the close of the 2014 plan year is $11,250 (90 percent × $15,000 × 25/30). As of the close of the 2014 plan year, the plan's final pay limitation does not affect A's benefit because A's benefit under the plan as of the close of the plan year and before application of the final pay limitation ($11,250) does not exceed A's final pay of $15,400 from X, determined as of the close of the plan year, less A's employer-provided projected primary insurance amount under social security attributable to A's service for X ($4,000).

(c) Assume that, as of the close of the 2015 plan year, A's final average compensation from X is $14,500 and A's final pay from X is $15,400. Assume also that as of the close of the 2015 plan year, A's employer-provided primary insurance amount attributable to A's service for X is $4,200 (after the reduction applicable under paragraph (e)(6)(iii) of this section). Accordingly, A's benefit as of the close of the 2015 plan year and before application of the final pay limitation is $11,310 (90 percent × $14,500 × 26/30). Under the plan's final pay limitation, A's accrued benefit of $11,310 would be limited to $11,200, the amount of A's final pay from X ($15,400), less A's employer-provided projected primary insurance amount under social security attributable to A's service for X ($4,200). However, the plan's final pay limitation may not be applied to limit A's accrued benefit for the 2015 plan year to an amount below $11,250, which was A's accrued benefit under the plan at the close of the prior plan year. The foregoing is further illustrated in the following table for the plan years presented above and for additional years of service performed by A for X.

**TABLE**

| 1 | 2 | 3 | 4 | 5 | 6 | 7 |
|---|---|---|---|---|---|---|
| Years of service | Final average compensation | Benefit under plan formula (Column 2 × 0.9 × years of service ÷ 30 | Final pay | Employer–provided projected primary insurance amount under social security attributable to service for employer | Benefit if final pay reduction is applied in full (Column 4 – Column 5) | Benefit to which A is entitled (smaller of Column 6 or Column 3, but not less than Column 7 for prior year |
| 25 | $15,000 | $11,250 | $15,400 | $4,000 | $11,400 | $11,250 |
| 26 | $14,500 | $11,310 | $15,400 | $4,200 | $11,200 | $11,250 |
| 27 | $15,500 | $12,555 | $15,800 | $4,400 | $11,400 | $11,400 |
| 28 | $15,500 | $13,020 | $16,000 | $4,500 | $11,500 | $11,500 |
| 29 | $15,000 | $13,050 | $16,000 | $4,800 | $11,200 | $11,500 |
| 30 | $14,500 | $13,050 | $16,000 | $5,000 | $11,000 | $11,500 |

**(f) Certain benefits not taken into account.** In determining whether a plan satisfies section 401(a)(4) and this section, other benefits created under state or federal law (e.g., worker's compensation benefits or black lung benefits) may not be taken into account.

**(g) More than one plan treated as single plan. [Reserved]**

**(h) Effective date.** *(1) In general.* Except as provided in paragraph (h)(2) of this section, this section is effective for plan years beginning on or after January 1, 1994.

*(2) Plans of tax-exempt organizations.* In the case of plans maintained by organizations exempt from income taxation under section 501(a), including plans subject to section 403(b)(12)(A)(i) (nonelective plans), this section is effective for plan years beginning on or after January 1, 1996.

*(3) Compliance during transition period.* For plan years beginning before the effective date of these regulations, as set forth in paragraphs (h)(1) and (h)(2) of this section, and on or after the first day of the first plan year to which the amendments made to section 401(a)(5) by section 1111(b) of the Tax Reform Act of 1986 (TRA '86) apply, a plan must be operated in accordance with a reasonable, good faith interpretation of section 401(a)(5), taking into account pre-existing guidance and the amendments made by TRA '86 to related provisions of the Code. Whether a plan is operated in accordance with a reasonable, good faith interpretation of section 401(a)(5) will generally be determined based on all of the relevant facts and circumstances, including the extent to which an employer has resolved unclear issues in its favor. A plan will be deemed to be operated in accordance with a reasonable, good faith interpretation of section

401(a)(5) if it is operated in accordance with the terms of this section.

---

T.D. 8359, 9/12/91, amend T.D. 8486, 8/31/93.

---

**Proposed § 1.401(a)(5)-1 Special rules relating to nondiscrimination requirements.** [*For Preamble, see ¶ 151,125*]

• ***Caution:*** This Notice of Proposed Rulemaking was partially finalized by TD 8359, 9/19/91. Proposed Reg. 1.401-3 and 1.401(a)(5)-1 remain proposed.

**(a) Salaried or clerical employees.** [Reserved]

**(b) Contributions and benefits may bear uniform relationship to compensation.** [Reserved]

**(c) Certain disparity permitted.** *(1)* Under section 401(a)(5)(C), a plan does not discriminate in favor of highly compensated employees (as defined in section 414(q) and the regulations thereunder) with respect to the amount of employer-derived benefits or employer contributions within the meaning of section 401(a)(4) solely because—

(i) In the case of a defined contribution plan, employer contributions (and forfeitures) allocated to the accounts of participants favor highly compensated employees in a manner permitted by section 401(l) (relating to permitted disparity in plan contributions and benefits) and the regulations thereunder, and

(ii) In the case of a defined benefit plan, employer-derived benefits favor highly compensated employees in a manner permitted by section 401(l) (relating to permitted disparity in plan contributions and benefits) and the regulations thereunder.

**(d) Defined benefit plans integrated with social security.** *(1) In general.* Under section 401(a)(5)(D), a defined benefit plan does not discriminate in favor of highly compensated employees (as defined in section 414(q) and the regulations thereunder) with respect to the amount of employer-derived benefits or employer contributions within the meaning of section 401(a)(4) solely because the plan provides that, with respect to each participant, the employer- derived accrued retirement benefit under the plan is limited to the excess (if any) of—

(i) The participant's final pay from the employer, over

(ii) The employer-derived retirement benefit created under the Social Security Act and attributable to service by the participant for the employer.

*(2) Final pay.* For purposes of paragraph (d)(1)(i) of this section, a participant's final pay from the employer as of a plan year is the participant's compensation (as defined in section 414(q)(7)) and the regulations thereunder) during the year (ending with or within the 5-plan year period ending with the plan year in which the participant terminates from employment with the employer) in which the participant receives the highest compensation from the employer. In determining a participant's year of highest final pay, the plan may specify any 12-month period (ending with or within the period described in the preceding sentence) as a year provided the specified 12-month period is uniformly and consistently applied with respect to all participants. In addition, a plan may not take into account for any year any compensation in excess of the applicable limit under section 401(a)(17) for such year.

*(3) Rules for determining amount of employer-derived social security retirement benefit.* For purposes of paragraph (d)(1)(ii) of this section, the following rules shall apply—

(i) The employer-derived retirement benefit on which any reduction or offset in the participant's accrued retirement benefit is based is limited solely to the employer-derived primary insurance amount payable under section 215 of the Social Security Act attributable to service by the participant for the employer.

(ii) The employer-derived primary insurance amount attributable to service by the participant for the employer is determined by multiplying the employer- derived portion of the participant's projected primary insurance amount by a fraction (not exceeding 1), the numerator of which is the participant's number of complete years of covered service for the employer under the Social Security Act and the denominator of which is 35.

*(4) Projected primary insurance amount.* (i) As of a plan year, a participant's projected primary insurance amount is the primary insurance amount (determined as of the close of the plan year) payable to the participant upon attainment of the participant's social security retirement age (as determined under section 216(1) of the Social Security Act), assuming the participant's annual compensation from the employer that is treated as wages for purposes of the Social Security Act remains the same from the plan year until the participant's attainment of social security retirement age. With respect to service by the participant for the employer before the determination date, the actual compensation paid to the participant by the employer during all periods of service of the participant for the employer covered by the Social Security Act shall be used in determining a participant's projected primary insurance amount. With respect to years before the participant's commencement of service for the employer, in determining the participant's projected primary insurance amount, it may be assumed that the participant received compensation for such service in an amount computed by using a six percent salary scale projected backwards from the determination date to the participant's 21st birthday. However, if the participant provides the employer with satisfactory evidence of the participant's actual past compensation for such prior years treated as wages under the Social Security Act at the time the compensation was earned, the plan must use such actual past compensation. The plan must give clear written notice to each participant of the participant's right to supply actual compensation history and of the financial consequences of failing to supply such history. The notice must be given each time the summary plan description is provided to the participant and must also be given upon the participant's separation from service. The notice must also state that the participant can obtain the actual compensation history from the Social Security Administration. The employer may not take into account any compensation from any other employer while the participant is employed by the employer for purposes of determining the participant's projected primary insurance amount.

(ii) As of a plan year, the employer-derived portion of the participant's projected primary insurance amount under the Social Security Act is 50 percent of the participant's projected primary insurance amount (as determined under paragraph (d)(4)(i) of this section) under such Act.

*(5) Employer-derived accrued retirement benefit.* For purposes of this section, the participant's employer-derived accrued retirement benefit as of a plan year is the participant's accrued retirement benefit under the plan (determined on an actual basis and not on a projected basis) attributable to employer contributions under the plan. With respect to plans that provide for employee contributions, see section 411(c) (and the regulations thereunder) for rules relating to the allocation of accrued benefits between employer contributions and employee contributions.

*(6) Additional rules.* (i) As of a plan year, paragraph (d)(1) of this section shall not apply to the extent that its application would provide a participant with an accrued retirement benefit that is lower than the minimum benefit the plan is required to provide under section 416 and the regulations thereunder.

(ii) As of a plan year, paragraph (d)(1) of this section shall not apply to the extent that its application would result in a decrease in a participant's accrued benefit. See sections 411(b)(1)(G) and 411(d)(6).

(iii) Section 401(a)(5)(D) and paragraph (d) of this section do not apply to a plan maintained by an employer that is not subject to the tax imposed by section 3111 or section 3221.

(iv) If a plan provides for the payment of a participant's accrued retirement benefit (whether or not subsidized) commencing before a participant's social security retirement age, the projected employer-derived primary insurance amount attributable to service by the participant for the employer (as determined under paragraphs (d)(3) and (4) of this section) that may be applied as an offset to limit the participant's accrued retirement benefit must be reduced in accordance with the provisions of § 1.401(l)-3(e)(1).

(v) The Commissioner may, in revenue rulings, notices or other documents of general applicability, prescribe such additional rules as may be necessary or appropriate to carry out the purposes of this section, including rules relating to the determination of a participant's projected primary insurance amount attributable to the participant's service for former employers and rules applying section 401(a)(5)(D) with respect to an employer that is subject to the tax imposed by section 3111 or section 3221 for certain years and is not subject to either of such taxes for other years.

*(7) Examples.* The provisions of this paragraph (d) may be illustrated by the following examples:

*Example (1).* Employer Z maintains a noncontributory defined benefit plan that uses the calendar year as its plan year. The plan provides a normal retirement benefit, commencing at a participant's social security retirement age, equal to $500 a year, multiplied by the participant's years of credited service for Z. However, the plan provides that a participant's otherwise determined normal retirement benefit is limited to a normal retirement benefit equal to the excess of the amount of the participant's year of highest final pay from Z (as determined in accordance with paragraph (d)(2) of this section) over the participant's employer-derived primary insurance amount attributable to the participant's employment by Z. The plan provides no limitation on the number of years of credited service taken into account in determining benefits under the plan. Participant A retires on July 6, 1995, at A's social security retirement age with 35 years of credited service for Z. The plan uses the plan year as the 12 month period for determining a participant's year of final highest pay from the employer. A's compensation for A's final 5 plan years is as follows: 1995 plan year–$10,500, 1994 plan year–$20,000, 1993 plan year–$18,000, 1992 plan year–$17,000, 1991 plan year–$16,500.

Assume that A's annual primary insurance amount under social security, attributable to A's employment by Z and determined as of A's social security retirement age, is $9,000, of which $4,500 is attributable to contributions made by Z on behalf of A under the Federal Insurance Contribution Act. Under the plan's benefit formula (disregarding the final pay limitation provision), A would be entitled to receive an annual normal retirement benefit of $17,500 ($500 x 35 years). However, under the plan, A's otherwise determined normal retirement benefit of $17,500 is limited to a normal retirement benefit equal to the excess of the amount of A's year of highest final pay from Z over A's employer-derived primary insurance amount under social security attributable to A's employment by Z. Accordingly, A's normal retirement benefit is determined to be $15,500 ($20,000 (X's year of highest final pay from Z) less $4,500 (employer-derived primary insurance amount attributable to A's employment by Z)) rather than $17,500. The final pay limitation provision in Z's plan satisfies the requirements of section 401(a)(5)(D) and paragraph (d) of this section. Accordingly, the plan maintained by Z does not discriminate in favor of highly compensated employees within the meaning of section 401(a)(4) merely because of the final pay limitation provision contained in the plan.

*Example (2).* Assume the same facts as in Example (1), except that A has 32 years of credited service and employment by Z when A retires at A's social security retirement age. Under the plan's benefit formula (disregarding the final pay limitation provision), A would be entitled to receive an annual normal retirement benefit of $16,000 ($500 x 32 years). However, the plan provides that A's annual normal retirement benefit of $16,000 will be limited to $15,500 ($20,000 (the amount of A's year of highest final pay from Z) less $4,500 ( 1/2 of A's primary insurance amount under the Social Security Act)). The final pay limitation provision does not satisfy the requirements of paragraph (d)(1) of this section. The portion of A's employer-derived primary insurance amount under the Social Security Act attributable to A's service for Z is 32/35 x $4,500, or $4,114. Therefore, to satisfy the requirements of paragraph (d)(1) of this section, the final pay provision in Z's plan may not limit A's otherwise determined normal retirement benefit of $16,000 to less than $15,886 ($20,000 (the amount of X's year of highest final pay)-$4,114 (the portion of A's employer-derived primary insurance amount attributable to A's service for Z)).

*Example (3).* (a) Employer X maintains a noncontributory defined benefit plan that uses the calendar year as its plan year. The formula for determining benefits under the plan provides a normal retirement benefit equal to 90% of a participant's final average compensation with such benefit reduced by 1/30th for each year of credited service less than 30 years a participant has when the participant attains normal retirement age. The plan provides, however, that a participant's accrued benefit or normal retirement benefit under the plan is limited to an amount equal to the participant's year of highest final pay (as determined in accordance with paragraph (d)(2) of this section) less the participant's employer-derived primary insurance amount under social security attributable to the participant's service for X. The plan determines a participant's employer-derived projected primary insurance amount under social security attributable to the participant's service for X in accordance with paragraph (d)(3) of this section.

(b) Participant A commences participation in the plan on January 1, 1990, when A is 36 years of age. A's social security retirement age is age 67 and the plan uses the fractional rule for purposes of determining a participant's accrued benefit. As of the close of the 2014 plan year, A's final average compensation from X is $15,000; A's year of highest final pay from X is $15,400, and A's projected employer-derived annual primary insurance amount under social security attributable to A's service for X is $4,000. Under the plan formula, A's benefit as of the close of the 2014 plan year is $11,250 (90% x $15,000 x 25/30). As of the close of the 2014 plan year, the plan's final pay limitation provision is not applied to A because A's benefit under the plan as of the close of the plan year ($11,250) does not exceed A's year of highest final pay of $15,400 from X, determined as of the close of the plan year, less A's employer-dervied projected primary insurance amount under social security attributable to A's service for X ($4,000).

(c) Assume that as of the close of the 2015 plan year, A's final average compensation from X is $14,500 and A's year of highest final pay from X is $15,400. Assume also that as of the close of the 2015 plan year, A's employer-derived primary insurance amount attributable to A's service for X is $4,200. Accordingly, under the plan's benefit formula, A's benefit as of the close of the 2015 plan year is $11,310 (90% x $14,500 x 26/30). Under the plan's final pay limitation provision, A's benefit of $11,310 as of the close of the 2015 plan year would be limited to $11,200, the amount of A's year of highest final pay from X (15,400), less A's employer-derived projected primary insurance amount under social security attributable to A's service for X ($4,200). However, the plan's final pay, limitation provision may not be applied to limit A's accrued benefit for the 2015 plan year to an amount below $11,250, which was A's accrued benefit under the plan at the close of the prior play year. The foregoing is further illustrated in the following table for the plan years presented above and for additional plan years of credited service performed by A for X.

**TABLE**

| 1<br>Years of credited service | 2<br>Final average compensation | 3<br>Benefit under plan formula (Column 2 × 0.90 × years of service/30) | 4<br>Final pay | 5<br>Employer–derived projected primary insurance amount under social security attributable to service for employer | 6<br>Benefit if final pay reduction is applied in full (Column 4 – Column 5) | 7<br>Benefit to which A is entitled (smaller of Column 6 or Column 3, but not less than Column 7 for prior year) |
|---|---|---|---|---|---|---|
| 25 | $15,000 | $11,250 | $15,400 | $4,000 | $11,400 | $11,250 |
| 26 | $14,500 | $11,310 | $15,400 | $4,200 | $11,200 | $11,250 |
| 27 | $15,500 | $12,555 | $15,800 | $4,400 | $11,400 | $11,400 |
| 28 | $15,500 | $13,020 | $16,000 | $4,500 | $11,500 | $11,500 |
| 29 | $15,000 | $13,050 | $16,000 | $4,800 | $11,200 | $11,500 |
| 30 | $14,500 | $13,050 | $16,000 | $5,000 | $11,000 | $11,500 |

**(e) Certain benefits not taken into account.** In determining whether a plan satisfies section 401(a)(4) and this section, other benefits created under state or federal law (e.g., worker's compensation benefits or black lung benefits) may not be taken into account.

**(f) More than one plan treated as a single plan.** [Reserved]

### § 1.401(a)(9)-0 Required minimum distributions; table of contents.

This table of contents lists the regulations relating to required minimum distributions under section 401(a)(9) of the Internal Revenue Code as follows:



T.D. 8987, 4/16/2002, amend T.D. 9130, 6/14/2004.

### § 1.401(a)(9)-1 Minimum distribution requirement in general.

Q-1. What plans are subject to the minimum distribution requirement under section 401(a)(9), this section, and §§ 1.401(a)(9)-2 through 1.401(a)(9)-9?

A-1. Under section 401(a)(9), all stock bonus, pension, and profit-sharing plans qualified under section 401(a) and annuity contracts described in section 403(a) are subject to required minimum distribution rules. See this section and §§ 1.401(a)(9)-2 through 1.401(a)(9)-9 for the distribution rules applicable to these plans. Under section 403(b)(10), annuity contracts or custodial accounts described in section 403(b) are subject to required minimum distribution rules.

See § 1.403(b)-6(e) for the distribution rules applicable to these annuity contracts or custodial accounts. Under section 408(a)(6) and 408(b)(3), individual retirement plans (including, for some purposes, Roth IRAs under section 408A) are subject to required minimum distribution rules. See § 1.408-8 for the distribution rules applicable to individual retirement plans and see § 1.408A-6 for the distribution rules applicable to Roth IRAs under section 408A. Under section 457(d)(2), certain deferred compensation plans for employees of tax exempt organizations or state and local government employees are subject to required minimum distribution rules.

Q-2. Which employee account balances and benefits held under qualified trusts and plans are subject to the distribution rules of section 401(a)(9), this section, and §§ 1.401(a)(9)-2 through 1.401(a)(9)-9?

A-2. **(a) In general.** The distribution rules of section 401(a)(9) apply to all account balances and benefits in existence on or after January 1, 1985. This section and §§ 1.401(a)(9)-2 through 1.401(a)(9)-9 apply for purposes of determining required minimum distributions for calendar years beginning on or after January 1, 2003.

**(b) Beneficiaries.** (1) The distribution rules of this section and §§ 1.401(a)(9)-2 through 1.401(a)(9)-9 apply to account balances and benefits held for the benefit of a beneficiary for calendar years beginning on or after January 1, 2003, even if the employee died prior to January 1, 2003. Thus, in the case of an employee who died prior to January 1, 2003, the designated beneficiary must be redetermined in accordance with the provisions of § 1.401(a)(9)-4 and the applicable distribution period (determined under § 1.401(a)(9)-5 or 1.401(a)(9)-6, whichever is applicable) must be reconstructed for purposes of determining the amount required to be distributed for calendar years beginning on or after January 1, 2003.

(2) A designated beneficiary that is receiving payments under the 5-year rule of section 401(a)(9)(B)(ii), either by affirmative election or default provisions, may, if the plan so provides, switch to using the life expectancy rule of section 401(a)(9)(B)(iii) provided any amounts that would have been required to be distributed under the life expectancy rule of section 401(a)(9)(B)(iii) for all distribution calendar years before 2004 are distributed by the earlier of December 31, 2003 or the end of the 5-year period determined under A-2 of § 1.401(a)(9)-3.

**(c) Trust documentation.** If a trust fails to meet the rule of A-5 of § 1.401(a)(9)-4 (permitting the beneficiaries of the trust, and not the trust itself, to be treated as the employee's designated beneficiaries) solely because the trust documentation was not provided to the plan administrator by October 31 of the calendar year following the calendar year in which the employee died, and such documentation is provided to the plan administrator by October 31, 2003, the beneficiaries of the trust will be treated as designated beneficiaries of the employee under the plan for purposes of determining the distribution period under section 401(a)(9).

**(d) Special rule for governmental plans.** Notwithstanding anything to the contrary in this A-2, a governmental plan (within the meaning of section 414(d)), or an eligible governmental plan described in § 1.457-2(f), is treated as having complied with section 401(a)(9) for all years to which section 401(a)(9) applies to the plan if the plan complies with a reasonable and good faith interpretation of section 401(a)(9).

Q-3. What specific provisions must a plan contain in order to satisfy section 401(a)(9)?

A-3. **(a) Required provisions.** In order to satisfy section 401(a)(9), the plan must include the provisions described in this paragraph reflecting section 401(a)(9). First, the plan must generally set forth the statutory rules of section 401(a)(9), including the incidental death benefit requirement in section 401(a)(9)(G). Second, the plan must provide that distributions will be made in accordance with this section and §§ 1.401(a)(9)-2 through 1.401(a)(9)-9. The plan document must also provide that the provisions reflecting section 401(a)(9) override any distribution options in the plan inconsistent with section 401(a)(9). The plan also must include any other provisions reflecting section 401(a)(9) that are prescribed by the Commissioner in revenue rulings, notices, and other guidance published in the Internal Revenue Bulletin. See § 601.601(d)(2)(ii)(b) of this chapter.

**(b) Optional provisions.** The plan may also include written provisions regarding any optional provisions governing plan distributions that do not conflict with section 401(a)(9) and the regulations thereunder.

**(c) Absence of optional provisions.** Plan distributions commencing after an employee's death will be required to be made under the default provision set forth in § 1.401(a)(9)-3 for distributions unless the plan document contains optional provisions that override such default provisions. Thus, if distributions have not commenced to the employee at the time of the employee's death, distributions after the death of an employee are to be made automatically in accordance with the default provisions in A-4(a) of § 1.401(a)(9)-3 unless the plan either specifies in accordance with A-4(b) of § 1.401(a)(9)-3 the method under which distributions will be made or provides for elections by the employee (or beneficiary) in accordance with A-4(c) of § 1.401(a)(9)-3 and such elections are made by the employee or beneficiary.

---

T.D. 8987, 4/16/2002, amend T.D. 9130, 6/14/2004, T.D. 9340, 7/23/2007, T.D. 9459, 9/4/2009.

---

PAR. 2. Section 1.401(a)(9)-1 as proposed to be added at 52 FR 28075, July 27, 1987, is amended by:

1. Revising Q&A D-5.
2. Revising Q&A D-6.
3. Adding Q&A D-7.

The additions and revisions read as follows:

**Proposed § 1.401(a)(9)-1 Required distributions from trust and plans.** [*For Preamble, see ¶ 151,831*]

* * * * *

D. *Determination of the Designated Beneficiary.*

* * * * * D-5. Q. If a trust is named as a beneficiary of an employee, will the beneficiaries of the trust with respect to the trust's interest in the employee's benefit be treated as having been designated as beneficiaries of the employee under the plan for purposes of determining the distribution period under section 401(a)(9)(A)(ii)?

A. (a) Pursuant to D-2A of this section, only an individual may be a designated beneficiary for purposes of determining the distribution period under section 401(a)(9)(A)(ii). Consequently, a trust itself may not be the designated beneficiary even though the trust is named as a beneficiary. However, if the requirements of paragraph (b) of this D-5 are met, distributions made to the trust will be treated as paid to the beneficiaries of the trust with respect to the trust's interest in the employee's benefit, and the beneficiaries of the trust will be treated as having been designated as beneficiaries of the employee under the plan for purposes of determining the distribution period under section 401(a)(9)(A)(ii). If, as of any date on or after the employee's required beginning date, a trust is named as a beneficiary of the employee and the requirements in paragraph (b) of this D-5 are not met, the employee will be treated as not having a designated beneficiary under the plan for purposes of section 401(a)(9)(A)(ii). Consequently, for calendar years beginning after that date, distribution must be made over the employee's life (or over the period which would have been the employee's remaining life expectancy determined as if no beneficiary had been designated as of the employee's required beginning date).

(b) The requirements of this paragraph (b) are met if, as of the later of the date on which the trust is named as a beneficiary of the employee, or the employee's required beginning date, and as of all subsequent periods during which the trust is named as a beneficiary, the following requirements are met:

(1) The trust is a valid trust under state law, or would be but for the fact that there is no corpus.

(2) The trust is irrevocable or will, by its terms, become irrevocable upon the death of the employee.

(3) The beneficiaries of the trust who are beneficiaries with respect to the trust's interest in the employee's benefit are identifiable from the trust instrument within the meaning of D-2 of this section.

(4) The documentation described in D-7 of this section has been provided to the plan administrator.

(c) In the case of payments to a trust having more than one beneficiary, see E-5 of this section for the rules for determining the designated beneficiary whose life expectancy will be used to determine the distribution period. If the beneficiary of the trust named as beneficiary is another trust, the beneficiaries of the other trust will be treated as having been designated as beneficiaries of the employee under the plan for purposes of determining the distribution period under section 401(a)(9)(A)(ii), provided that the requirements of paragraph (b) of this D-5 are satisfied with respect to such other trust in addition to the trust named as beneficiary.

D-6. Q. If a trust is named as a beneficiary of an employee, will the beneficiaries of the trust with respect to the trust's interest in the employee's benefit be treated as designated beneficiaries under the plan with respect to the employee for purposes of determining the distribution period under section 401(a)(9)(B)(iii) and (iv)?

A. (a) If a trust is named as a beneficiary of an employee and the requirements of paragraph (b) of D-5 of this section are satisfied as of the date of the employee's death or, in the case of the documentation described in D-7 of this section, by the end of the ninth month beginning after the employee's date of death, then distributions to the trust for purposes of section 401(a)(9) will be treated as being paid to the appropriate beneficiary of the trust with respect to the trust's interest in the employee's benefit, and all beneficiaries of the trust with respect to the trust's interest in the employee's benefit will be treated as designated beneficiaries of the employee under the plan for purposes of determining the distribution period under section 401(a)(9)(B)(iii) and (iv). If the beneficiary of the trust named as beneficiary is another trust, the beneficiaries of the other trust will be treated as having been designated as beneficiaries of the employee under the plan for purposes of determining the distribution period under section 401(a)(9)(B)(iii) and (iv), provided that the requirements of paragraph (b) of D-5 of this section are satisfied with respect to such other trust in addition to the trust named as beneficiary. If a trust is named as a beneficiary of an employee and if the requirements of paragraph (b) of D-5 of this section are not satisfied as of the dates specified in the first sentence of this paragraph, the employee will be treated as not having a designated beneficiary under the plan. Consequently, distribution must be made in accordance with the five-year rule in section 401(a)(9)(B)(ii).

(b) The rules of D-5 of this section and this D-6 also apply for purposes of applying the provisions of section 401(a)(9)(B)(iv)(II) if a trust is named as a beneficiary of the employee's surviving spouse. In the case of payments to a trust having more than one beneficiary, see E-5 of this section for the rules for determining the designated beneficiary whose life expectancy will be used to determine the distribution period.

D-7. Q. If a trust is named as a beneficiary of an employee, what documentation must be provided to the plan administrator so that the beneficiaries of the trust who are beneficiaries with respect to the trust's interest in the employee's benefit are identifiable to the plan administrator?

A. (a) Required distributions commencing before death. In order to satisfy the requirement of paragraph (b)(4) of D-5 of this section for distributions required under section 401(a)(9) to commence before the death of an employee, the employee must comply with either paragraph (a)(1) or (2) of this D-7:

(1) The employee provides to the plan administrator a copy of the trust instrument and agrees that if the trust instrument is amended at any time in the future, the employee will, within a reasonable time, provide to the plan administrator a copy of each such amendment.

(2) The employee—

(i) Provides to the plan administrator a list of all of the beneficiaries of the trust (including contingent and remainderman beneficiaries with a description of the conditions on their entitlement);

(ii) Certifies that, to the best of the employee's knowledge, this list is correct and complete and that the requirements of paragraphs (b)(1), (2), and (3) of D-5 of this section are satisfied;

(iii) Agrees to provide corrected certifications to the extent that an amendment changes any information previously certified; and

(iv) Agrees to provide a copy of the trust instrument to the plan administrator upon demand.

(b) Required distributions after death. In order to satisfy the documentation requirement of this D-7 for required distributions after death, by the end of the ninth month beginning after the death of the employee, the trustee of the trust must either—

(1) Provide the plan administrator with a final list of all of the beneficiaries of the trust (including contingent and remainderman beneficiaries with a description of the conditions on their entitlement) as of the date of death; certify that, to the best of the trustee's knowledge, this list is correct and complete and that the requirements of paragraph (b)(1), (2), and (3) of D-5 of this section are satisfied as of the date of death; and agree to provide a copy of the trust instrument to the plan administrator upon demand; or

(2) Provide the plan administrator with a copy of the actual trust document for the trust that is named as a benefici-

ary of the employee under the plan as of the employee's date of death.

(c) Relief for discrepancy between trust instrument and employee certifications or earlier trust instruments. (1) If required distributions are determined based on the information provided to the plan administrator in certifications or trust instruments described in paragraph (a)(1), (a)(2) or (b) of this D-7, a plan will not fail to satisfy section 401(a)(9) merely because the actual terms of the trust instrument are inconsistent with the information in those certifications or trust instruments previously provided to the plan administrator, but only if the plan administrator reasonably relied on the information provided and the minimum required distributions for calendar years after the calendar year in which the discrepancy is discovered are determined based on the actual terms of the trust instrument. For purposes of determining whether the plan satisfies section 401(a)(9) for calendar years after the calendar year in which the discrepancy is discovered, if the actual beneficiaries under the trust instrument are different from the beneficiaries previously certified or listed in the trust instrument previously provided to the plan administrator, or the trust instrument specifying the actual beneficiaries does not satisfy the other requirements of paragraph (b) of D-5 of this section, the minimum required distribution will be determined by treating the beneficiaries of the employee as having been changed in the calendar year in which the discrepancy was discovered to conform to the corrected information and by applying the change in beneficiary provisions of E-5 of this section.

(2) For purposes of determining the amount of the excise tax under section 4974, the minimum required distribution is determined for any year based on the actual terms of the trust in effect during the year.

* * * * *

**§ 1.401(a)(9)-2 Distributions commencing during an employee's lifetime.**

Q-1. In the case of distributions commencing during an employee's lifetime, how must the employee's entire interest be distributed in order to satisfy section 401(a)(9)(A)?

A-1. (a) In order to satisfy section 401(a)(9)(A), the entire interest of each employee must be distributed to such employee not later than the required beginning date, or must be distributed, beginning not later than the required beginning date, over the life of the employee or joint lives of the employee and a designated beneficiary or over a period not extending beyond the life expectancy of the employee or the joint life and last survivor expectancy of the employee and the designated beneficiary.

(b) Section 401(a)(9)(G) provides that lifetime distributions must satisfy the incidental death benefit requirements.

(c) The amount required to be distributed for each calendar year in order to satisfy section 401(a)(9)(A) and (G) generally depends on whether a distribution is in the form of distributions under a defined contribution plan or annuity payments under a defined benefit plan or under an annuity contract. For the method of determining the required minimum distribution in accordance with section 401(a)(9)(A) and (G) from an individual account under a defined contribution plan, see § 1.401(a)(9)-5. For the method of determining the required minimum distribution in accordance with section 401(a)(9)(A) and (G) in the case of annuity payments from a defined benefit plan or an annuity contract, see § 1.401(a)(9)-6.

Q-2. For purposes of section 401(a)(9)(C), what does the term required beginning date mean?

A-2. (a) Except as provided in paragraph (b) of this A-2 with respect to a 5-percent owner, as defined in paragraph (c) of this A-2, the term required beginning date means April 1 of the calendar year following the later of the calendar year in which the employee attains age 70½ or the calendar year in which the employee retires from employment with the employer maintaining the plan.

(b) In the case of an employee who is a 5-percent owner, the term required beginning date means April 1 of the calendar year following the calendar year in which the employee attains age 70½.

(c) For purposes of section 401(a)(9), a 5-percent owner is an employee who is a 5-percent owner (as defined in section 416) with respect to the plan year ending in the calendar year in which the employee attains age 70½.

(d) Paragraph (b) of this A-2 does not apply in the case of a governmental plan (within the meaning of section 414(d)) or a church plan. For purposes of this paragraph, the term church plan means a plan maintained by a church for church employees, and the term church means any church (as defined in section 3121(w)(3)(A)) or qualified church-controlled organization (as defined in section 3121(w)(3)(B)).

(e) A plan is permitted to provide that the required beginning date for purposes of section 401(a)(9) for all employees is April 1 of the calendar year following the calendar year in which an employee attains age 70½ regardless of whether the employee is a 5-percent owner.

Q-3. When does an employee attain age 70½?

A-3. An employee attains age 70½ as of the date six calendar months after the 70th anniversary of the employee's birth. For example, if an employee's date of birth was June 30, 1933, the 70th anniversary of such employee's birth is June 30, 2003. Such employee attains age 70½ on December 30, 2003. Consequently, if the employee is a 5-percent owner or retired, such employee's required beginning date is April 1, 2004. However, if the employee's date of birth was July 1, 1933, the 70th anniversary of such employee's birth would be July 1, 2003. Such employee would then attain age 70½ on January 1, 2004 and such employee's required beginning date would be April 1, 2005.

Q-4. Must distributions made before the employee's required beginning date satisfy section 401(a)(9)?

A-4. Lifetime distributions made before the employee's required beginning date for calendar years before the employee's first distribution calendar year, as defined in A-1(b) of § 1.401(a)(9)-5, need not be made in accordance with section 401(a)(9). However, if distributions commence before the employee's required beginning date under a particular distribution option, such as in the form of an annuity, the distribution option fails to satisfy section 401(a)(9) at the time distributions commence if, under terms of the particular distribution option, distributions to be made for the employee's first distribution calendar year or any subsequent distribution calendar year will fail to satisfy section 401(a)(9).

Q-5. If distributions have begun to an employee during the employee's lifetime (in accordance with section 401(a)(9)(A)(ii)), how must distributions be made after an employee's death?

A-5. Section 401(a)(9)(B)(i) provides that if the distribution of the employee's interest has begun in accordance with section 401(a)(9)(A)(ii) and the employee dies before his entire interest has been distributed to him, the remaining portion of such interest must be distributed at least as rapidly as under the distribution method being used under section 401(a)(9)(A)(ii) as of the date of his death. The amount required to be distributed for each distribution calendar year following the calendar year of death generally depends on whether a distribution is in the form of distributions from an individual account under a defined contribution plan or annuity payments under a defined benefit plan. For the method of determining the required minimum distribution in accordance with section 401(a)(9)(B)(i) from an individual account, see § 1.401(a)(9)-5. In the case of annuity payments from a defined benefit plan or an annuity contract, see § 1.401(a)(9)-6.

Q-6. For purposes of section 401(a)(9)(B), when are distributions considered to have begun to the employee in accordance with section 401(a)(9)(A)(ii)?

A-6. **(a) General rule.** Except as otherwise provided in A-10 of § 1.401(a)(9)-6, distributions are not treated as having begun to the employee in accordance with section 401(a)(9)(A)(ii) until the employee's required beginning date, without regard to whether payments have been made before that date. Thus, section 401(a)(9)(B)(i) only applies if an employee dies on or after the employee's required beginning date. For example, if employee A retires in 2003, the calendar year A attains age 65½, and begins receiving installment distributions from a profit-sharing plan over a period not exceeding the joint life and last survivor expectancy of A and A's spouse, benefits are not treated as having begun in accordance with section 401(a)(9)(A)(ii) until April 1, 2009 (the April 1 following the calendar year in which A attains age 70½). Consequently, if A dies before April 1, 2009 (A's required beginning date), distributions after A's death must be made in accordance with section 401(a)(9)(B)(ii) or (iii) and (iv) and § 1.401(a)(9)-3, and not section 401(a)(9)(B)(i). This is the case without regard to whether the plan has distributed the minimum distribution for the first distribution calendar year (as defined in A-1(b) of § 1.401(a)(9)-5) before A's death.

(b) If a plan provides, in accordance with A-2(e) of this section, that the required beginning date for purposes of section 401(a)(9) for all employees is April 1 of the calendar year following the calendar year in which an employee attains age 70½, an employee who dies on or after the required beginning date determined under the plan terms is treated as dying after the employee's distributions have begun for purposes of this A-6 even though the employee dies before the April 1 following the calendar year in which the employee retires.

T.D. 8987, 4/16/2002, amend T.D. 9130, 6/14/2004.

## § 1.401(a)(9)-3 Death before required beginning date.

Q-1. If an employee dies before the employee's required beginning date, how must the employee's entire interest be distributed in order to satisfy section 401(a)(9)?

A-1. (a) Except as otherwise provided in A-10 of § 1.401(a)(9)-6, if an employee dies before the employee's required beginning date (and, thus, before distributions are treated as having begun in accordance with section 401(a)(9)(A)(ii)), distribution of the employee's entire interest must be made in accordance with one of the methods described in section 401(a)(9)(B)(ii) or (iii) and (iv). One method (the 5-year rule in section 401(a)(9)(B)(ii)) requires that the entire interest of the employee be distributed within 5 years of the employee's death regardless of who or what entity receives the distribution. Another method (the life expectancy rule in section 401(a)(9)(B)(iii) and (iv)) requires that any portion of an employee's interest payable to (or for the benefit of) a designated beneficiary be distributed, commencing within one year of the employee's death, over the life of such beneficiary (or over a period not extending beyond the life expectancy of such beneficiary). Section 401(a)(9)(B)(iv) provides special rules where the designated beneficiary is the surviving spouse of the employee, including a special commencement date for distributions under section 401(a)(9)(B)(iii) to the surviving spouse.

(b) See A-4 of this section for the rules for determining which of the methods described in paragraph (a) of this A-1 applies. See A-3 of this section to determine when distributions under the exception to the 5-year rule in section 401(a)(9)(B)(iii) and (iv) must commence. See A-2 of this section to determine when the 5-year period in section 401(a)(9)(B)(ii) ends. For distributions using the life expectancy rule in section 401(a)(9)(B)(iii) and (iv), see § 1.401(a)(9)-4 in order to determine the designated beneficiary under section 401(a)(9)(B)(iii) and (iv), see § 1.401(a)(9)-5 for the rules for determining the required minimum distribution under a defined contribution plan, and see § 1.401(a)(9)-6 for required minimum distributions under defined benefit plans.

Q-2. By when must the employee's entire interest be distributed in order to satisfy the 5-year rule in section 401(a)(9)(B)(ii)?

A-2. In order to satisfy the 5-year rule in section 401(a)(9)(B)(ii), the employee's entire interest must be distributed by the end of the calendar year which contains the fifth anniversary of the date of the employee's death. For example, if an employee dies on January 1, 2003, the entire interest must be distributed by the end of 2008, in order to satisfy the 5-year rule in section 401(a)(9)(B)(ii).

Q-3. When are distributions required to commence in order to satisfy the life expectancy rule in section 401(a)(9)(B)(iii) and (iv)?

A-3. **(a) Nonspouse beneficiary.** In order to satisfy the life expectancy rule in section 401(a)(9)(B)(iii), if the designated beneficiary is not the employee's surviving spouse, distributions must commence on or before the end of the calendar year immediately following the calendar year in which the employee died. This rule also applies to the distribution of the entire remaining benefit if another individual is a designated beneficiary in addition to the employee's surviving spouse. See A-2 and A-3 of § 1.401(a)(9)-8, however, if the employee's benefit is divided into separate accounts.

**(b) Spousal beneficiary.** In order to satisfy the rule in section 401(a)(9)(B)(iii) and (iv), if the sole designated beneficiary is the employee's surviving spouse, distributions must commence on or before the later of—

(1) The end of the calendar year immediately following the calendar year in which the employee died; and

(2) The end of the calendar year in which the employee would have attained age 70½.

Q-4. How is it determined whether the 5-year rule in section 401(a)(9)(B)(ii) or the life expectancy rule in section 401(a)(9)(B)(iii) and (iv) applies to a distribution?

A-4. **(a) No plan provision.** If a plan does not adopt an optional provision described in paragraph (b) or (c) of this A-4 specifying the method of distribution after the death of an employee, distribution must be made as follows:

(1) If the employee has a designated beneficiary, as determined under § 1.401(a)(9)-4, distributions are to be made in accordance with the life expectancy rule in section 401(a)(9)(B)(iii) and (iv).

(2) If the employee has no designated beneficiary, distributions are to be made in accordance with the 5-year rule in section 401(a)(9)(B)(ii).

**(b) Optional plan provisions.** A plan may adopt a provision specifying either that the 5-year rule in section 401(a)(9)(B)(ii) will apply to certain distributions after the death of an employee even if the employee has a designated beneficiary or that distribution in every case will be made in accordance with the 5-year rule in section 401(a)(9)(B)(ii). Further, a plan need not have the same method of distribution for the benefits of all employees in order to satisfy section 401(a)(9).

**(c) Elections.** A plan may adopt a provision that permits employees (or beneficiaries) to elect on an individual basis whether the 5-year rule in section 401(a)(9)(B)(ii) or the life expectancy rule in section 401(a)(9)(B)(iii) and (iv) applies to distributions after the death of an employee who has a designated beneficiary. Such an election must be made no later than the earlier of the end of the calendar year in which distribution would be required to commence in order to satisfy the requirements for the life expectancy rule in section 401(a)(9)(B)(iii) and (iv) (see A-3 of this section for the determination of such calendar year) or the end of the calendar year which contains the fifth anniversary of the date of death of the employee. As of the last date the election may be made, the election must be irrevocable with respect to the beneficiary (and all subsequent beneficiaries) and must apply to all subsequent calendar years. If a plan provides for the election, the plan may also specify the method of distribution that applies if neither the employee nor the beneficiary makes the election. If neither the employee nor the beneficiary elects a method and the plan does not specify which method applies, distribution must be made in accordance with paragraph (a) of this A-4.

Q-5. If the employee's surviving spouse is the employee's sole designated beneficiary and such spouse dies after the employee, but before distributions have begun to the surviving spouse under section 401(a)(9)(B)(iii) and (iv), how is the employee's interest to be distributed?

A-5. Pursuant to section 401(a)(9)(B)(iv)(II), if the surviving spouse is the employee's sole designated beneficiary and dies after the employee, but before distributions to such spouse have begun under section 401(a)(9)(B)(iii) and (iv), the 5-year rule in section 401(a)(9)(B)(ii) and the life expectancy rule in section 401(a)(9)(B)(iii) are to be applied as if the surviving spouse were the employee. In applying this rule, the date of death of the surviving spouse shall be substituted for the date of death of the employee. However, in such case, the rules in section 401(a)(9)(B)(iv) are not available to the surviving spouse of the deceased employee's surviving spouse.

Q-6. For purposes of section 401(a)(9)(B)(iv)(II), when are distributions considered to have begun to the surviving spouse?

A-6. Distributions are considered to have begun to the surviving spouse of an employee, for purposes of section 401(a)(9)(B)(iv)(II), on the date, determined in accordance with A-3 of this section, on which distributions are required to commence to the surviving spouse, even though payments have actually been made before that date. See A-11 of § 1.401(a)(9)-6 for a special rule for annuities.

T.D. 8987, 4/16/2002, amend T.D. 9130, 6/14/2004.

### § 1.401(a)(9)-4 Determination of the designated beneficiary.

Q-1. Who is a designated beneficiary under section 401(a)(9)(E)?

A-1. A designated beneficiary is an individual who is designated as a beneficiary under the plan. An individual may be designated as a beneficiary under the plan either by the terms of the plan or, if the plan so provides, by an affirmative election by the employee (or the employee's surviving spouse) specifying the beneficiary. A beneficiary designated as such under the plan is an individual who is entitled to a portion of an employee's benefit, contingent on the employee's death or another specified event. For example, if a distribution is in the form of a joint and survivor annuity over the life of the employee and another individual, the plan does not satisfy section 401(a)(9) unless such other individual is a designated beneficiary under the plan. A designated beneficiary need not be specified by name in the plan or by the employee to the plan in order to be a designated beneficiary so long as the individual who is to be the beneficiary is identifiable under the plan. The members of a class of beneficiaries capable of expansion or contraction will be treated as being identifiable if it is possible, to identify the class member with the shortest life expectancy. The fact that an employee's interest under the plan passes to a certain individual under a will or otherwise under applicable state law does not make that individual a designated beneficiary unless the individual is designated as a beneficiary under the plan. See A-6 of § 1.401(a)(9)-8 for rules which apply to qualified domestic relation orders.

Q-2. Must an employee (or the employee's spouse) make an affirmative election specifying a beneficiary for a person to be a designated beneficiary under section 40l(a)(9)(E)?

A-2. No, a designated beneficiary is an individual who is designated as a beneficiary under the plan whether or not the designation under the plan was made by the employee. The choice of beneficiary is subject to the requirements of sections 401(a)(11), 414(p), and 417.

Q-3. May a person other than an individual be considered to be a designated beneficiary for purposes of section 401(a)(9)?

A-3. No, only individuals may be designated beneficiaries for purposes of section 401(a)(9). A person that is not an individual, such as the employee's estate, may not be a designated beneficiary. If a person other than an individual is designated as a beneficiary of an employee's benefit, the employee will be treated as having no designated beneficiary for purposes of section 401(a)(9), even if there are also individuals designated as beneficiaries. However, see A-5 of this section for special rules that apply to trusts and A-2 and A-3 of § 1.401(a)(9)-8 for rules that apply to separate accounts.

Q-4. When is the designated beneficiary determined?

A-4. **(a) General rule.** In order to be a designated beneficiary, an individual must be a beneficiary as of the date of death. Except as provided in paragraph (b) and § 1.401(a)(9)-6, the employee's designated beneficiary will be determined based on the beneficiaries designated as of the date of death who remain beneficiaries as of September 30 of the calendar year following the calendar year of the employee's death. Consequently, except as provided in § 1.401(a)(9)-6, any person who was a beneficiary as of the date of the employee's death, but is not a beneficiary as of that September 30 (e.g., because the person receives the entire benefit to which the person is entitled before that September 30), is not taken into account in determining the employee's designated beneficiary for purposes of determining the distribution period for required minimum distributions after the employee's death. Accordingly, if a person disclaims entitlement to the employee's benefit, pursuant to a disclaimer that satisfies section 2518 by that September 30 thereby allowing other beneficiaries to receive the benefit in lieu of that person, the disclaiming person is not taken into account in determining the employee's designated beneficiary.

**(b) Surviving spouse.** As provided in A-5 of § 1.401(a)(9)-3, if the employee's spouse is the sole designated beneficiary as of September 30 of the calendar year following the calendar year of the employee's death, and the surviving spouse dies after the employee and before the date on which distributions have begun to the surviving spouse under section 401(a)(9)(B)(iii) and (iv), the rule in section 401(a)(9)(B)(iv)(II) will apply. Thus, for example, the relevant designated beneficiary for determining the distribution period after the death of the surviving spouse is the designated beneficiary of the surviving spouse. Similarly, such designated beneficiary will be determined based on the beneficiaries designated as of the date of the surviving spouse's death and who remain beneficiaries as of September 30 of the calendar year following the calendar year of the surviving spouse's death. Further, if, as of that September 30, there is no designated beneficiary under the plan with respect to that surviving spouse, distribution must be made in accordance with the 5-year rule in section 401(a)(9)(B)(ii) and A-2 of § 1.401(a)(9)-3.

**(c) Deceased beneficiary.** For purposes of this A-4, an individual who is a beneficiary as of the date of the employee's death and dies prior to September 30 of the calendar year following the calendar year of the employee's death without disclaiming continues to be treated as a beneficiary as of the September 30 of the calendar year following the calendar year of the employee's death in determining the employee's designated beneficiary for purposes of determining the distribution period for required minimum distributions after the employee's death, without regard to the identity of the successor beneficiary who is entitled to distributions as the beneficiary of the deceased beneficiary. The same rule applies in the case of distributions to which A-5 of § 1.401(a)(9)-3 applies so that, if an individual is designated as a beneficiary of an employee's surviving spouse as of the spouse's date of death and dies prior to September 30 of the year following the year of the surviving spouse's death, that individual will continue to be treated as a designated beneficiary.

Q-5. If a trust is named as a beneficiary of an employee, will the beneficiaries of the trust with respect to the trust's interest in the employee's benefit be treated as having been designated as beneficiaries of the employee under the plan for purposes of determining the distribution period under section 401(a)(9)?

A-5. (a) If the requirements of paragraph (b) of this A-5 are met with respect to a trust that is named as the beneficiary of an employee under the plan, the beneficiaries of the trust (and not the trust itself) will be treated as having been designated as beneficiaries of the employee under the plan for purposes of determining the distribution period under section 401(a)(9).

(b) The requirements of this paragraph (b) are met if, during any period during which required minimum distributions are being determined by treating the beneficiaries of the trust as designated beneficiaries of the employee, the following requirements are met—

(1) The trust is a valid trust under state law, or would be but for the fact that there is no corpus.

(2) The trust is irrevocable or will, by its terms, become irrevocable upon the death of the employee.

(3) The beneficiaries of the trust who are beneficiaries with respect to the trust's interest in the employee's benefit are identifiable within the meaning of A-1 of this section from the trust instrument.

(4) The documentation described in A-6 of this section has been provided to the plan administrator.

(c) In the case of payments to a trust having more than one beneficiary, see A-7 of § 1.401(a)(9)-5 for the rules for determining the designated beneficiary whose life expectancy will be used to determine the distribution period and A-3 of this section for the rules that apply if a person other than an individual is designated as a beneficiary of an employee's benefit. However, the separate account rules under A-2 of § 1.401(a)(9)-8 are not available to beneficiaries of a trust with respect to the trust's interest in the employee's benefit.

(d) If the beneficiary of the trust named as beneficiary of the employee's interest is another trust, the beneficiaries of the other trust will be treated as being designated as beneficiaries of the first trust, and thus, having been designated by the employee under the plan for purposes of determining the distribution period under section 401(a)(9)(A)(ii), provided that the requirements of paragraph (b) of this A-5 are satisfied with respect to such other trust in addition to the trust named as beneficiary.

Q-6. If a trust is named as a beneficiary of an employee, what documentation must be provided to the plan administrator?

A-6. **(a) Required minimum distributions before death.** If an employee designates a trust as the beneficiary of his or her entire benefit and the employee's spouse is the sole beneficiary of the trust, in order to satisfy the documentation requirements of this A-6 so that the spouse can be treated as the sole designated beneficiary of the employee's benefits (if the other requirements of paragraph (b) of A-5 of this section are satisfied), the employee must either—

(1) Provide to the plan administrator a copy of the trust instrument and agree that if the trust instrument is amended at any time in the future, the employee will, within a reasonable time, provide to the plan administrator a copy of each such amendment; or

(2) Provide to the plan administrator a list of all of the beneficiaries of the trust (including contingent and remaindermen beneficiaries with a description of the conditions on their entitlement sufficient to establish that the spouse is the sole beneficiary) for purposes of section 401(a)(9); certify that, to the best of the employee's knowledge, this list is correct and complete and that the requirements of paragraph (b)(1), (2), and (3) of A-5 of this section are satisfied; agree that, if the trust instrument is amended at any time in the future, the employee will, within a reasonable time, provide to the plan administrator corrected certifications to the extent that the amendment changes any information previously certified; and agree to provide a copy of the trust instrument to the plan administrator upon demand.

**(b) Required minimum distributions after death.** In order to satisfy the documentation requirement of this A-6 for required minimum distributions after the death of the employee (or spouse in a case to which A-5 of § 1.401(a)(9)-3 applies), by October 31 of the calendar year immediately following the calendar year in which the employee died, the trustee of the trust must either—

(1) Provide the plan administrator with a final list of all beneficiaries of the trust (including contingent and remaindermen beneficiaries with a description of the conditions on their entitlement) as of September 30 of the calendar year following the calendar year of the employee's death; certify that, to the best of the trustee's knowledge, this list is correct and complete and that the requirements of paragraph (b)(1), (2), and (3) of A-5 of this section are satisfied; and agree to provide a copy of the trust instrument to the plan administrator upon demand; or

(2) Provide the plan administrator with a copy of the actual trust document for the trust that is named as a beneficiary of the employee under the plan as of the employee's date of death.

**(c) Relief for discrepancy between trust instrument and employee certifications or earlier trust instruments.** (1) If required minimum distributions are determined based on the information provided to the plan administrator in certifications or trust instruments described in paragraph (a) or (b) of this A-6, a plan will not fail to satisfy section 401(a)(9) merely because the actual terms of the trust instrument are inconsistent with the information in those certifications or trust instruments previously provided to the plan administrator, but only if the plan administrator reasonably relied on the information provided and the required minimum distributions for calendar years after the calendar year in which the discrepancy is discovered are determined based on the actual terms of the trust instrument.

(2) For purposes of determining the amount of the excise tax under section 4974, the required minimum distribution is determined for any year based on the actual terms of the trust in effect during the year.

---

T.D. 8987, 4/16/2002, amend T.D. 9130, 6/14/2004.

---

### § 1.401(a)(9)-5 Required minimum distributions from defined contribution plans.

Q-1. If an employee's benefit is in the form of an individual account under a defined contribution plan, what is the amount required to be distributed for each calendar year?

A-1. **(a) General rule.** If an employee's accrued benefit is in the form of an individual account under a defined contribution plan, the minimum amount required to be distributed for each distribution calendar year, as defined in paragraph (b) of this A-1, is equal to the quotient obtained by dividing the account (determined under A-3 of this section) by the applicable distribution period (determined under A-4 or A-5 of this section, whichever is applicable). However, the required minimum distribution amount will never exceed the entire account balance on the date of the distribution. See A-8 of this section for rules that apply if a portion of the employee's account is not vested. Further, the minimum distribution required to be distributed on or before an employee's required beginning date is always determined under section 401(a)(9)(A)(ii) and this A-1 and not section 401(a)(9)(A)(i).

**(b) Distribution calendar year.** A calendar year for which a minimum distribution is required is a distribution calendar year. If an employee's required beginning date is April 1 of the calendar year following the calendar year in which the employee attains age 70½, the employee's first distribution calendar year is the year the employee attains age 70½. If an employee's required beginning date is April 1 of the calendar year following the calendar year in which the employee retires, the employee's first distribution calendar year is the calendar year in which the employee retires. In the case of distributions to be made in accordance with the life expectancy rule in § 1.401(a)(9)-3 and in section 401(a)(9)(B)(iii) and (iv), the first distribution calendar year is the calendar year containing the date described in A-3(a) or A-3(b) of § 1.401(a)(9)-3, whichever is applicable.

**(c) Time for distributions.** The distribution required to be made on or before the employee's required beginning date shall be treated as the distribution required for the employee's first distribution calendar year (as defined in paragraph (b) of this A-1). The required minimum distribution for other distribution calendar years, including the required minimum distribution for the distribution calendar year in which the employee's required beginning date occurs, must be made on or before the end of that distribution calendar year.

**(d) Minimum distribution incidental benefit requirement.** If distributions of an employee's account balance under a defined contribution plan are made in accordance with this section, the minimum distribution incidental benefit requirement of section 401(a)(9)(G) is satisfied. Further, with respect to the retirement benefits provided by that account balance, to the extent the incidental benefit requirement of § 1.401-1(b)(1)(i) requires a distribution, that requirement is deemed to be satisfied if distributions satisfy the minimum distribution incidental benefit requirement of section 401(a)(9)(G) and this section.

**(e) Annuity contracts.** Instead of satisfying this A-1, the minimum distribution requirement may be satisfied by the purchase of an annuity contract from an insurance company in accordance with A-4 of § 1.401(a)(9)-6 with the employee's entire individual account. If such an annuity is purchased after distributions are required to commence (the required beginning date, in the case of distributions commencing before death, or the date determined under A-3 of § 1.401(a)(9)-3, in the case of distributions commencing after death), payments under the annuity contract purchased will satisfy section 401(a)(9) for distribution calendar years after the calendar year of the purchase if payments under the annuity contract are made in accordance with § 1.401(a)(9)-6. In such a case, payments under the annuity contract will be treated as distributions from the individual account for purposes of determining if the individual account satisfies section 401(a)(9) for the calendar year of the purchase. An employee may also purchase an annuity contract with a portion of the employee's account under the rules of A-2(a)(3) of § 1.401(a)(9)-8.

Q-2. If an employee's benefit is in the form of an individual account and, in any calendar year, the amount distributed exceeds the minimum required, will credit be given in subsequent calendar years for such excess distribution?

A-2. If, for any distribution calendar year, the amount distributed exceeds the minimum required, no credit will be given in subsequent calendar years for such excess distribution.

Q-3. What is the amount of the account of an employee used for determining the employee's required minimum distribution in the case of an individual account?

A-3. (a) In the case of an individual account, the benefit used in determining the required minimum distribution for a distribution calendar year is the account balance as of the last valuation date in the calendar year immediately preceding that distribution calendar year (valuation calendar year) adjusted in accordance with paragraphs (b) and (c) of this A-3.

(b) The account balance is increased by the amount of any contributions or forfeitures allocated to the account balance as of dates in the valuation calendar year after the valuation date. For this purpose, contributions that are allocated to the account balance as of dates in the valuation calendar year after the valuation date, but that are not actually made during the valuation calendar year, are permitted to be excluded.

(c) The account balance is decreased by distributions made in the valuation calendar year after the valuation date.

(d) If an amount is distributed by one plan and rolled over to another plan (receiving plan), A-2 of § 1.401(a)(9)-7 provides additional rules for determining the benefit and required minimum distribution under the receiving plan. If an amount is transferred from one plan (transferor plan) to another plan (transferee plan), A-3 and A-4 of § 1.401(a)(9)-7 provide additional rules for determining the amount of the required minimum distribution and the benefit under both the transferor and transferee plans.

Q-4. For required minimum distributions during an employee's lifetime, what is the applicable distribution period?

A-4. **(a) General rule.** Except as provided in paragraph (b) of this A-4, the applicable distribution period for required minimum distributions for distribution calendar years up to and including the distribution calendar year that includes the employee's date of death is determined using the Uniform Lifetime Table in A-2 of § 1.401(a)(9)-9 for the employee's age as of the employee's birthday in the relevant distribution calendar year. If an employee dies on or after the required beginning date, the distribution period applicable for calculating the amount that must be distributed during the distribution calendar year that includes the employee's death is determined as if the employee had lived throughout that year. Thus, a minimum required distribution, determined as if the employee had lived throughout that year, is required for the year of the employee's death and that amount must be distributed to a beneficiary to the extent it has not already been distributed to the employee.

**(b) Spouse is sole beneficiary.** *(1) General rule.* Except as otherwise provided in paragraph (b)(2) of this A-4, if the sole designated beneficiary of an employee is the employee's surviving spouse, for required minimum distributions during the employee's lifetime, the applicable distribution period is the longer of the distribution period determined in accordance with paragraph (a) of this A-4 or the joint life expectancy of the employee and spouse using the employee's and spouse's attained ages as of the employee's and the spouse's birthdays in the distribution calendar year. The spouse is sole designated beneficiary for purposes of determining the applicable distribution period for a distribution calendar year during the employee's lifetime only if the spouse is the sole beneficiary of the employee's entire interest at all times during the distribution calendar year.

*(2) Change in marital status.* If the employee and the employee's spouse are married on January 1 of a distribution calendar year, but do not remain married throughout that year (i.e., the employee or the employee's spouse die or they become divorced during that year), the employee will not fail to have a spouse as the employee's sole beneficiary for that year merely because they are not married throughout that year. If an employee's spouse predeceases the employee, the spouse will not fail to be the employee's sole beneficiary for the distribution calendar year that includes the date of the spouse's death solely because, for the period remaining in that year after the spouse's death, someone other than the spouse is named as beneficiary. However, the change in beneficiary due to the death or divorce of the spouse will be effective for purposes of determining the applicable distribution period under section 401(a)(9) in the distribution calendar year following the distribution calendar year that includes the date of the spouse's death or divorce.

Q-5. For required minimum distributions after an employee's death, what is the applicable distribution period?

A-5. **(a) Death on or after the employee's required beginning date.** If an employee dies after distribution has begun as determined under A-6 of § 1.401(a)(9)-2 (generally on or after the employee's required beginning date), in order to satisfy section 401(a)(9)(B)(i), the applicable distribution period for distribution calendar years after the distribution calendar year containing the employee's date of death is either—

(1) If the employee has a designated beneficiary as of the date determined under A-4 of § 1.401(a)(9)-4, the longer of—

(i) The remaining life expectancy of the employee's designated beneficiary determined in accordance with paragraph (c)(1) or (2) of this A-5; and

(ii) The remaining life expectancy of the employee determined in accordance with paragraph (c)(3) of this A-5; or

(2) If the employee does not have a designated beneficiary as of the date determined under A-4 of § 1.401(a)(9)-4, the remaining life expectancy of the employee determined in accordance with paragraph (c)(3) of this A-5.

**(b) Death before an employee's required beginning date.** If an employee dies before distribution has begun, as determined under A-5 of § 1.401(a)(9)-2 (generally before the employee's required beginning date), in order to satisfy section 401(a)(9)(B)(iii) or (iv) and the life expectancy rule described in A-1 of § 1.401(a)(9)-3, the applicable distribution period for distribution calendar years after the distribution calendar year containing the employee's date of death is determined in accordance with paragraph (c) of this A-5. See A-4 of § 1.401(a)(9)-3 to determine when the 5-year rule of in section 401(a)(9)(B)(ii) applies (e.g., there is no designated beneficiary or the 5-year rule is elected or specified by plan provision).

**(c) Life expectancy.** *(1) Nonspouse designated beneficiary.* Except as otherwise provided in paragraph (c)(2), the applicable distribution period measured by the beneficiary's remaining life expectancy is determined using the beneficiary's age as of the beneficiary's birthday in the calendar year immediately following the calendar year of the employee's death. In subsequent calendar years, the applicable distribution period is reduced by one for each calendar year that has elapsed after the calendar year immediately following the calendar year of the employee's death.

*(2) Spouse designated beneficiary.* If the surviving spouse of the employee is the employee's sole beneficiary, the applicable distribution period is measured by the surviving spouse's life expectancy using the surviving spouse's birthday for each distribution calendar year after the calendar year of the employee's death up through the calendar year of the spouse's death. For calendar years after the calendar

year of the spouse's death, the applicable distribution period is the life expectancy of the spouse using the age of the spouse as of the spouse's birthday in the calendar year of the spouse's death, reduced by one for each calendar year that has elapsed after the calendar year of the spouse's death.

*(3) No designated beneficiary.* If the employee does not have a designated beneficiary, the applicable distribution period measured by the employee's remaining life expectancy is the life expectancy of the employee using the age of the employee as of the employee's birthday in the calendar year of the employee's death. In subsequent calendar years the applicable distribution period is reduced by one for each calendar year that has elapsed after the calendar year of the employee's death.

Q-6. What life expectancies must be used for purposes of determining required minimum distributions under section 401(a)(9)?

A-6. Life expectancies for purposes of determining required minimum distributions under section 401(a)(9) must be computed using the Single Life Table in A-1 of § 1.401(a)(9)-9 and the Joint and Last Survivor Table in A-3 of § 1.401(a)(9)-9.

Q-7. If an employee has more than one designated beneficiary, which designated beneficiary's life expectancy will be used to determine the applicable distribution period?

A-7. **(a) General rule.** (1) Except as otherwise provided in paragraph (c) of this A-7, if more than one individual is designated as a beneficiary with respect to an employee as of the applicable date for determining the designated beneficiary under A-4 of § 1.401(a)(9)-4, the designated beneficiary with the shortest life expectancy will be the designated beneficiary for purposes of determining the applicable distribution period.

(2) See A-3 of § 1.401(a)(9)-4 for rules that apply if a person other than an individual is designated as a beneficiary and see A-2 and A-3 of § 1.401(a)(9)-8 for special rules that apply if an employee's benefit under a plan is divided into separate accounts and the beneficiaries with respect to a separate account differ from the beneficiaries of another separate account.

**(b) Contingent beneficiary.** Except as provided in paragraph (c)(1) of this A-7, if a beneficiary's entitlement to an employee's benefit after the employee's death is a contingent right, such contingent beneficiary is nevertheless considered to be a beneficiary for purposes of determining whether a person other than an individual is designated as a beneficiary (resulting in the employee being treated as having no designated beneficiary under the rules of A-3 of § 1.401(a)(9)-4) and which designated beneficiary has the shortest life expectancy under paragraph (a) of this A-7.

**(c) Successor beneficiary.** (1) A person will not be considered a beneficiary for purposes of determining who is the beneficiary with the shortest life expectancy under paragraph (a) of this A-7, or whether a person who is not an individual is a beneficiary, merely because the person could become the successor to the interest of one of the employee's beneficiaries after that beneficiary's death. However, the preceding sentence does not apply to a person who has any right (including a contingent right) to an employee's benefit beyond being a mere potential successor to the interest of one of the employee's beneficiaries upon that beneficiary's death. Thus, for example, if the first beneficiary has a right to all income with respect to an employee's individual account during that beneficiary's life and a second beneficiary has a right to the principal but only after the death of the first income beneficiary (any portion of the principal distributed during the life of the first income beneficiary to be held in trust until that first beneficiary's death), both beneficiaries must be taken into account in determining the beneficiary with the shortest life expectancy and whether only individuals are beneficiaries.

(2) If the individual beneficiary whose life expectancy is being used to calculate the distribution period dies after September 30 of the calendar year following the calendar year of the employee's death, such beneficiary's remaining life expectancy will be used to determine the distribution period without regard to the life expectancy of the subsequent beneficiary.

(3) This paragraph (c) is illustrated by the following examples:

Example 1. (i) Employer M maintains a defined contribution plan, Plan X. Employee A, an employee of M, died in 2005 at the age of 55, survived by spouse, B, who was 50 years old. Prior to A's death, M had established an account balance for A in Plan X. A's account balance is invested only in productive assets. A named a testamentary trust (Trust P) established under A's will as the beneficiary of all amounts payable from A's account in Plan X after A's death. A copy of the Trust P and a list of the trust beneficiaries were provided to the plan administrator of Plan X by October 31 of the calendar year following the calendar year of A's death. As of the date of A's death, the Trust P was irrevocable and was a valid trust under the laws of the state of A's domicile. A's account balance in Plan X was includible in A's gross estate under § 2039.

(ii) Under the terms of Trust P, all trust income is payable annually to B, and no one has the power to appoint Trust P principal to any person other than B. A's children, who are all younger than B, are the sole remainder beneficiaries of the Trust P. No other person has a beneficial interest in Trust P. Under the terms of the Trust P, B has the power, exercisable annually, to compel the trustee to withdraw from A's account balance in Plan X an amount equal to the income earned on the assets held in A's account in Plan X during the calendar year and to distribute that amount through Trust P to B. Plan X contains no prohibition on withdrawal from A's account of amounts in excess of the annual required minimum distributions under section 401(a)(9). In accordance with the terms of Plan X, the trustee of Trust P elects, in order to satisfy section 401(a)(9), to receive annual required minimum distributions using the life expectancy rule in section 401(a)(9)(B)(iii) for distributions over a distribution period equal to B's life expectancy. If B exercises the withdrawal power, the trustee must withdraw from A's account under Plan X the greater of the amount of income earned in the account during the calendar year or the required minimum distribution. However, under the terms of Trust P, and applicable state law, only the portion of the Plan X distribution received by the trustee equal to the income earned by A's account in Plan X is required to be distributed to B (along with any other trust income.)

(iii) Because some amounts distributed from A's account in Plan X to Trust P may be accumulated in Trust P during B's lifetime for the benefit of A's children, as remaindermen beneficiaries of Trust P, even though access to those amounts are delayed until after B's death, A's children are beneficiaries of A's account in Plan X in addition to B and B is not the sole designated beneficiary of A's account. Thus the designated beneficiary used to determine the distribution period from A's account in Plan X is the beneficiary with the shortest life expectancy. B's life expectancy is the shortest of all the potential beneficiaries of the testamentary trust's interest in A's account in Plan X (including remainder beneficiaries). Thus, the distribution period for purposes of section 401(a)(9)(B)(iii) is B's life expectancy. Because B is not the sole designated beneficiary of the testamentary trust's interest in A's account in Plan X, the special rule in 401(a)(9)(B)(iv) is not available and the annual required minimum distributions from the account to Trust M must begin no later than the end of the calendar year immediately following the calendar year of A's death.

Example 2. (i) The facts are the same as Example 1 except that the testamentary trust instrument provides that all amounts distributed from A's account in Plan X to the trustee while B is alive will be paid directly to B upon receipt by the trustee of Trust P.

(ii) In this case, B is the sole designated beneficiary of A's account in Plan X for purposes of determining the designated beneficiary under section 401(a)(9)(B)(iii) and (iv). No amounts distributed from A's account in Plan X to Trust P are accumulated in Trust P during B's lifetime for the benefit of any other beneficiary. Therefore, the residuary beneficiaries of Trust P are mere potential successors to B's interest in Plan X. Because B is the sole beneficiary of the testamentary trust's interest in A's account in Plan X, the annual required minimum distributions from A's account to Trust P must begin no later than the end of the calendar year in which A would have attained age 70½, rather than the calendar year immediately following the calendar year of A's death.

Q-8. If a portion of an employee's individual account is not vested as of the employee's required beginning date, how is the determination of the required minimum distribution affected?

A-8. If the employee's benefit is in the form of an individual account, the benefit used to determine the required minimum distribution for any distribution calendar year will be determined in accordance with A-1 of this section without regard to whether or not all of the employee's benefit is vested. If any portion of the employee's benefit is not vested, distributions will be treated as being paid from the vested portion of the benefit first. If, as of the end of a distribution calendar year (or as of the employee's required beginning date, in the case of the employee's first distribution calendar year), the total amount of the employee's vested benefit is less than the required minimum distribution for the calendar year, only the vested portion, if any, of the employee's benefit is required to be distributed by the end of the calendar year (or, if applicable, by the employee's required beginning date). However, the required minimum distribution for the subsequent distribution calendar year must be increased by the sum of amounts not distributed in prior calendar years because the employee's vested benefit was less than the required minimum distribution.

Q-9. Which amounts distributed from an individual account are taken into account in determining whether section 401(a)(9) is satisfied and which amounts are not taken into account in determining whether section 401(a)(9) is satisfied?

A-9. **(a) General rule.** Except as provided in paragraph (b), all amounts distributed from an individual account are distributions that are taken into account in determining whether section 401(a)(9) is satisfied, regardless of whether the amount is includible in income. Thus, for example, amounts that are excluded from income as recovery of investment in the contract under section 72 are taken into account for purposes of determining whether section 401(a)(9) is satisfied for a distribution calendar year. Similarly, amounts excluded from income as net unrealized appreciation on employer securities also are amounts distributed for purposes of determining if section 401(a)(9) is satisfied.

**(b) Exceptions.** The following amounts are not taken into account in determining whether the required minimum amount has been distributed for a calendar year:

(1) Elective deferrals (as defined in section 402(g)(3)) and employee contributions that, pursuant to rules prescribed by the Commissioner in revenue rulings, notices, or other guidance published in the Internal Revenue Bulletin (see § 601.601(d)(2) of this chapter), are returned to the employee (together with the income allocable thereto) in order to comply with the section 415 limitations.

(2) Corrective distributions of excess deferrals as described in § 1.402(g)-1(e)(3), together with the income allocable to these distributions.

(3) Corrective distributions of excess contributions under a qualified cash or deferred arrangement under section 401(k)(8) and excess aggregate contributions under section 401(m)(6), together with the income allocable to these distributions.

(4) Loans that are treated as deemed distributions pursuant to section 72(p).

(5) Dividends described in section 404(k) that are paid on employer securities. (Amounts paid to the plan that, pursuant to section 404(k)(2)(A)(iii)(II), are included in the account balance and subsequently distributed from the account lose their character as dividends.)

(6) The costs of life insurance coverage (P.S. 58 costs).

(7) Similar items designated by the Commissioner in revenue rulings, notices, and other guidance published in the Internal Revenue Bulletin. See § 601.601(d)(2)(ii)(b) of this chapter.

---

T.D. 8987, 4/16/2002, amend T.D. 9130, 6/14/2004, T.D. 9319, 4/4/2007.

---

## § 1.401(a)(9)-6 Required minimum distributions for defined benefit plans and annuity contracts.

*Caution:* The Treasury has not yet amended Reg § 1.401(a)(9)-6 to reflect changes made by P.L. 109-280.

Q-1. How must distributions under a defined benefit plan be paid in order to satisfy section 401(a)(9)?

A-1. **(a) General rules.** In order to satisfy section 401(a)(9), except as otherwise provided in this section, distributions of the employee's entire interest under a defined benefit plan must be paid in the form of periodic annuity payments for the employee's life (or the joint lives of the employee and beneficiary) or over a period certain that does not exceed the maximum length of the period certain determined in accordance with A-3 of this section. The interval between payments for the annuity must be uniform over the entire distribution period and must not exceed one year. Once payments have commenced over a period, the period may only be changed in accordance with A-13 of this section. Life (or joint and survivor) annuity payments must satisfy the minimum distribution incidental benefit requirements of A-2 of this section. Except as otherwise provided in this section (such as permitted increases described in A-14 of this section), all payments (whether paid over an employee's life, joint lives, or a period certain) also must be nonincreasing.

**(b) Life annuity with period certain.** The annuity may be a life annuity (or joint and survivor annuity) with a period certain if the life (or lives, if applicable) and period certain each meet the requirements of paragraph (a) of this A-1. For purposes of this section, if distributions are permitted to be made over the lives of the employee and the designated beneficiary, references to a life annuity include a joint and survivor annuity.

**(c) Annuity commencement.** (1) Annuity payments must commence on or before the employee's required beginning date (within the meaning of A-2 of § 1.401(a)(9)-2). The first payment, which must be made on or before the employee's required beginning date, must be the payment which is required for one payment interval. The second payment need not be made until the end of the next payment interval even if that payment interval ends in the next calendar year. Similarly, in the case of distributions commencing after death in accordance with section 401(a)(9)(B)(iii) and (iv), the first payment, which must be made on or before the date determined under A-3(a) or (b) (whichever is applicable) of § 1.401(a)(9)-3, must be the payment which is required for one payment interval. Payment intervals are the periods for which payments are received, e.g., bimonthly, monthly, semi-annually, or annually. All benefit accruals as of the last day of the first distribution calendar year must be included in the calculation of the amount of annuity payments for payment intervals ending on or after the employee's required beginning date.

(2) This paragraph (c) is illustrated by the following example:

**Example.** A defined benefit plan (Plan X) provides monthly annuity payments of $500 for the life of unmarried participants with a 10-year period certain. An unmarried, retired participant (A) in Plan X attains age 70½ in 2005. In order to meet the requirements of this paragraph, the first monthly payment of $500 must be made on behalf of A on or before April 1, 2006, and the payments must continue to be made in monthly payments of $500 thereafter for the life and 10-year period certain.

**(d) Single sum distributions.** In the case of a single sum distribution of an employee's entire accrued benefit during a distribution calendar year, the amount that is the required minimum distribution for the distribution calendar year (and thus not eligible for rollover under section 402(c)) is determined using either the rule in paragraph (d)(1) or the rule in paragraph (d)(2) of this A-1.

(1) The portion of the single sum distribution that is a required minimum distribution is determined by treating the single sum distribution as a distribution from an individual account plan and treating the amount of the single sum distribution as the employee's account balance as of the end of the relevant valuation calendar year. If the single sum distribution is being made in the calendar year containing the required beginning date and the required minimum distribution for the employee's first distribution calendar year has not been distributed, the portion of the single sum distribution that represents the required minimum distribution for the employee's first and second distribution calendar years is not eligible for rollover.

(2) The portion of the single sum distribution that is a required minimum distribution is permitted to be determined by expressing the employee's benefit as an annuity that would satisfy this section with an annuity starting date as of the first day of the distribution calendar year for which the required minimum distribution is being determined, and treating one year of annuity payments as the required minimum distribution for that year, and not eligible for rollover. If the single sum distribution is being made in the calendar year containing the required beginning date and the required minimum distribution for the employee's first distribution calendar year has not been made, the benefit must be expressed as an annuity with an annuity starting date as of the first day of the first distribution calendar year and the payments for the first two distribution calendar years would be treated as required minimum distributions, and not eligible for rollover.

**(e) Death benefits.** The rule in paragraph (a) of this A-1, prohibiting increasing payments under an annuity applies to payments made upon the death of an employee. However, for purposes of this section, an ancillary death benefit described in this paragraph (e) may be disregarded in applying that rule. Such an ancillary death benefit is excluded in determining an employee's entire interest and the rules prohibiting increasing payments do not apply to such an ancillary death benefit. A death benefit with respect to an employee's benefit is an ancillary death benefit for purposes of this A-1 if—

(1) It is not paid as part of the employee's accrued benefit or under any optional form of the employee's benefit; and

(2) The death benefit, together with any other potential payments with respect to the employee's benefit that may be provided to a survivor, satisfy the incidental benefit requirement of § 1.401-1(b)(1)(i).

**(f) Additional guidance.** Additional guidance regarding how distributions under a defined benefit plan must be paid in order to satisfy section 401(a)(9) may be issued by the Commissioner in revenue rulings, notices, or other guidance published in the Internal Revenue Bulletin. See § 601.601(d)(2)(ii)(b) of this chapter.

Q-2. How must distributions in the form of a life (or joint and survivor) annuity be made in order to satisfy the minimum distribution incidental benefit (MDIB) requirement of section 401(a)(9)(G) and the distribution component of the incidental benefit requirement of § 1.401-1(b)(1)(i)?

A-2. **(a) Life annuity for employee.** If the employee's benefit is paid in the form of a life annuity for the life of the employee satisfying section 401(a)(9) without regard to the MDIB requirement, the MDIB requirement of section 401(a)(9)(G) will be satisfied.

**(b) Joint and survivor annuity, spouse beneficiary.** If the employee's sole beneficiary, as of the annuity starting date for annuity payments, is the employee's spouse and the distributions satisfy section 401(a)(9) without regard to the MDIB requirement, the distributions to the employee will be deemed to satisfy the MDIB requirement of section 401(a)(9)(G). For example, if an employee's benefit is being distributed in the form of a joint and survivor annuity for the lives of the employee and the employee's spouse and the spouse is the sole beneficiary of the employee, the amount of the periodic payment payable to the spouse would not violate the MDIB requirement if it was 100 percent of the annuity payment payable to the employee, regardless of the difference in the ages between the employee and the employee's spouse.

**(c) Joint and survivor annuity, nonspouse beneficiary. (1) Explanation of rule.** If distributions commence under a distribution option that is in the form of a joint and survivor annuity for the joint lives of the employee and a beneficiary other than the employee's spouse, the minimum distribution incidental benefit requirement will not be satisfied as of the date distributions commence unless under the distribution option, the annuity payments to be made on and after the employee's required beginning date will satisfy the conditions of this paragraph (c). The periodic annuity payment payable to the survivor must not at any time on and after the employee's required beginning date exceed the applicable percentage of the annuity payment payable to the employee using the table in paragraph (c)(2) of this A-2. The applicable percentage is based on the adjusted employee/beneficiary age difference. The adjusted employee/beneficiary age difference is determined by first calculating the excess of the age of the employee over the age of the beneficiary based on their ages on their birthdays in a calendar year. Then, if the employee is younger than age 70, the age difference determined in the previous sentence is reduced by the number of years that the employee is younger than age 70 on the employee's birthday in the calendar year that contains the annuity starting date. In the case of an annuity that provides for increasing payments, the requirement of this paragraph (c) will not be violated merely because benefit payments to the beneficiary increase, provided the increase is determined in the same manner for the employee and the beneficiary.

**(2) Table.**

| Adjusted employee/beneficiary age difference | Applicable percentage |
|---|---|
| 10 years or less | 100 |
| 11 | 96 |
| 12 | 93 |
| 13 | 90 |
| 14 | 87 |
| 15 | 84 |
| 16 | 82 |
| 17 | 79 |
| 18 | 77 |
| 19 | 75 |
| 20 | 73 |
| 21 | 72 |
| 22 | 70 |
| 23 | 68 |
| 24 | 67 |
| 25 | 66 |
| 26 | 64 |
| 27 | 63 |
| 28 | 62 |
| 29 | 61 |
| 30 | 60 |
| 31 | 59 |
| 32 | 59 |
| 33 | 58 |
| 34 | 57 |
| 35 | 56 |
| 36 | 56 |
| 37 | 55 |
| 38 | 55 |
| 39 | 54 |
| 40 | 54 |
| 41 | 53 |
| 42 | 53 |
| 43 | 53 |
| 44 and greater | 52 |

**(3) Example.** This paragraph (c) is illustrated by the following example:

**Example.** Distributions commence on January 1, 2003 to an employee (Z), born March 1, 1937, after retirement at age 65. Z's daughter (Y), born February 5, 1967, is Z's beneficiary. The distributions are in the form of a joint and survivor annuity for the lives of Z and Y with payments of $500 a month to Z and upon Z's death of $500 a month to Y, i.e., the projected monthly payment to Y is 100 percent of the monthly amount payable to Z. Accordingly, under A-10 of this section, compliance with the rules of this section is determined as of the annuity starting date. The adjusted employee/beneficiary age difference is calculated by taking the excess of the employee's age over the beneficiary's age and subtracting the number of years the employee is younger than age 70. In this case, Z is 30 years older than Y and is commencing benefit 4 years before attaining age 70 so the adjusted employee-beneficiary age difference is 26 years. Under the table in the paragraph (c)(2) of this A-2, the applicable percentage for a 26-year adjusted employee/beneficiary age difference is 64 percent. As of January 1, 2003 (the annuity starting date) the plan does not satisfy the MDIB requirement because, as of such date, the distribution option provides that, as of Z's required beginning date, the monthly payment to Y upon Z's death will exceed 66 percent of Z's monthly payment.

**(d) Period certain and annuity features.** If a distribution form includes a period certain, the amount of the annuity payments payable to the beneficiary need not be reduced during the period certain, but in the case of a joint and survivor annuity with a period certain, the amount of the annuity payments payable to the beneficiary must satisfy paragraph (c) of this A-2 after the expiration of the period certain.

**(e) Deemed satisfaction of incidental benefit rule.** Except in the case of distributions with respect to an employee's benefit that include an ancillary death benefit described in paragraph A-1(e) of this section, to the extent the incidental benefit requirement of § 1.401-1(b)(1)(i) requires a distribution, that requirement is deemed to be satisfied if distributions satisfy the minimum distribution incidental benefit requirement of this A-2. If the employee's benefits include an ancillary death benefit described in paragraph A-1(e) of this section, the benefits (including the ancillary death benefit) must be distributed in accordance with the incidental benefit requirement described in § 1.401-1(b)(1)(i) and the benefits (excluding the ancillary death benefit) must also satisfy the minimum distribution incidental benefit requirement of this A-2.

Q-3. How long is a period certain under a defined benefit plan permitted to extend?

A-3. **(a) Distributions commencing during the employee's life.** The period certain for any annuity distributions commencing during the life of the employee with an annuity starting date on or after the employee's required beginning date generally is not permitted to exceed the applicable distribution period for the employee (determined in accordance with the Uniform Lifetime Table in A-2 of § 1.401(a)(9)-9) for the calendar year that contains the annuity starting date. See A-10 of this section for the rule for annuity payments with an annuity starting date before the required beginning date. However, if the employee's sole beneficiary is the employee's spouse, the period certain is permitted to be as long as the joint life and last survivor expectancy of the employee and the employee's spouse, if longer than the applicable distribution period for the employee, provided the period certain is not provided in conjunction with a life annuity under A-1(b) of this section.

**(b) Distributions commencing after the employee's death.** (1) If annuity distributions commence after the death of the employee under the life expectancy rule (under section 401(a)(9)(B)(iii) or (iv)), the period certain for any distributions commencing after death cannot exceed the applicable distribution period determined under A-5(b) of § 1.401(a)(9)-5 for the distribution calendar year that contains the annuity starting date.

(2) If the annuity starting date is in a calendar year before the first distribution calendar year, the period certain may not exceed the life expectancy of the designated beneficiary using the beneficiary's age in the year that contains the annuity starting date.

Q-4. Will a plan fail to satisfy section 401(a)(9) merely because distributions are made from an annuity contract which is purchased from an insurance company?

A-4. A plan will not fail to satisfy section 401(a)(9) merely because distributions are made from an annuity contract which is purchased with the employee's benefit by the plan from an insurance company, as long as the payments satisfy the requirements of this section. If the annuity contract is purchased after the required beginning date, the first payment interval must begin on or before the purchase date and the payment required for one payment interval must be made no later than the end of such payment interval. If the payments actually made under the annuity contract do not meet the requirements of section 401(a)(9), the plan fails to satisfy section 401(a)(9). See also A-14 of this section permitting certain increases under annuity contracts.

Q-5. In the case of annuity distributions under a defined benefit plan, how must additional benefits that accrue after the employee's first distribution calendar year be distributed in order to satisfy section 401(a)(9)?

A-5. **(a)** In the case of annuity distributions under a defined benefit plan, if any additional benefits accrue in a calendar year after the employee's first distribution calendar year, distribution of the amount that accrues in the calendar year must commence in accordance with A-1 of this section beginning with the first payment interval ending in the calendar year immediately following the calendar year in which such amount accrues.

**(b)** A plan will not fail to satisfy section 401(a)(9) merely because there is an administrative delay in the commencement of the distribution of the additional benefits accrued in a calendar year, provided that the actual payment of such amount commences as soon as practicable. However, payment must commence no later than the end of the first calendar year following the calendar year in which the additional benefit accrues, and the total amount paid during such first calendar year must be no less than the total amount that was required to be paid during that year under A-5(a) of this section.

Q-6. If a portion of an employee's benefit is not vested as of December 31 of a distribution calendar year, how is the determination of the required minimum distribution affected?

A-6. In the case of annuity distributions from a defined benefit plan, if any portion of the employee's benefit is not vested as of December 31 of a distribution calendar year, the portion that is not vested as of such date will be treated as not having accrued for purposes of determining the required minimum distribution for that distribution calendar year. When an additional portion of the employee's benefit becomes vested, such portion will be treated as an additional accrual. See A-5 of this section for the rules for distributing benefits which accrue under a defined benefit plan after the employee's first distribution calendar year.

Q-7. If an employee (other than a 5-percent owner) retires after the calendar year in which the employee attains age 70½, for what period must the employee's accrued benefit under a defined benefit plan be actuarially increased?

A-7. **(a) Actuarial increase starting date.** If an employee (other than a 5-percent owner) retires after the calendar year in which the employee attains age 70½, in order to satisfy section 401(a)(9)(C)(iii), the employee's accrued benefit under a defined benefit plan must be actuarially increased to take into account any period after age 70½ in which the employee was not receiving any benefits under the plan. The actuarial increase required to satisfy section 401(a)(9)(C)(iii) must be provided for the period starting on the April 1 following the calendar year in which the employee attains age 70½, or January 1, 1997, if later.

**(b) Actuarial increase ending date.** The period for which the actuarial increase must be provided ends on the date on which benefits commence after retirement in an amount sufficient to satisfy section 401(a)(9).

**(c) Nonapplication to plan providing same required beginning date for all employees.** If, as permitted under A-2(e) of § 1.401(a)(9)-2, a plan provides that the required beginning date for purposes of section 401(a)(9) for all employees is April 1 of the calendar year following the calendar year in which the employee attains age 70½ (regardless of whether the employee is a 5-percent owner) and the plan makes distributions in an amount sufficient to satisfy section 401(a)(9) using that required beginning date, no actuarial increase is required under section 401(a)(9)(C)(iii).

**(d) Nonapplication to governmental and church plans.** The actuarial increase required under this A-7 does not apply to a governmental plan (within the meaning of section 414(d)) or a church plan. For purposes of this paragraph, the term church plan means a plan maintained by a church for church employees, and the term church means any church (as defined in section 3121(w)(3)(A)) or qualified church-controlled organization (as defined in section 3121(w)(3)(B)).

Q-8. What amount of actuarial increase is required under section 401(a)(9)(C)(iii)?

A-8. In order to satisfy section 401(a)(9)(C)(iii), the retirement benefits payable with respect to an employee as of the end of the period for actuarial increases (described in A-7 of this section) must be no less than: the actuarial equivalent of the employee's retirement benefits that would have been payable as of the date the actuarial increase must commence under paragraph (a) of A-7 of this section if benefits had commenced on that date; plus the actuarial equivalent of any additional benefits accrued after that date; reduced by the actuarial equivalent of any distributions made with respect to the employee's retirement benefits after that date. Actuarial equivalence is determined using the plan's assumptions for determining actuarial equivalence for purposes of satisfying section 411.

Q-9. How does the actuarial increase required under section 401(a)(9)(C)(iii) relate to the actuarial increase required under section 411?

A-9. In order for any of an employee's accrued benefit to be nonforfeitable as required under section 411, a defined benefit plan must make an actuarial adjustment to an accrued benefit, the payment of which is deferred past normal retirement age. The only exception to this rule is that generally no actuarial adjustment is required to reflect the period during which a benefit is suspended as permitted under section 203(a)(3)(B) of the Employee Retirement Income Security Act of 1974 (ERISA) (88 Stat. 829). The actuarial increase required under section 401(a)(9)(C)(iii) for the period described in A-7 of this section is generally the same as, and not in addition to, the actuarial increase required for the same period under section 411 to reflect any delay in the payment of retirement benefits after normal retirement age. However, unlike the actuarial increase required under section 411, the actuarial increase required under section 401(a)(9)(C)(iii) must be provided even during any period during which an employee's benefit has been suspended in accordance with ERISA section 203(a)(3)(B).

Q-10. What rule applies if distributions commence to an employee on a date before the employee's required beginning date over a period permitted under section 401(a)(9)(A)(ii) and the distribution form is an annuity under which distributions are made in accordance with the provisions of A-1 of this section?

A-10. **(a) General rule.** If distributions commence to an employee on a date before the employee's required beginning date over a period permitted under section 401(a)(9)(A)(ii) and the distribution form is an annuity under which distributions are made in accordance with the provisions of A-1 of this section, the annuity starting date will be treated as the required beginning date for purposes of applying the rules of this section and § 1.401(a)(9)-2. Thus, for example, the designated beneficiary distributions will be determined as of the annuity starting date. Similarly, if the employee dies after the annuity starting date but before the required beginning date determined under A-2 of § 1.401(a)(9)-2, after the employee's death, the remaining portion of the employee's interest must continue to be distributed in accordance with this section over the remaining period over which distributions commenced. The rules in § 1.401(a)(9)-3 and section 401(a)(9)(B)(ii) or (iii) and (iv) do not apply.

**(b) Period certain.** If, as of the employee's birthday in the year that contains the annuity starting date, the age of the employee is under 70, the following rule applies in applying the rule in paragraph (a) of A-3 of this section. The applicable distribution period for the employee is the distribution period for age 70, determined in accordance with the Uniform Lifetime Table in A-2 of § 1.401(a)(9)-9, plus the excess of 70 over the age of the employee as of the employee's birthday in the year that contains the annuity starting date.

**(c) Adjustment to employee/beneficiary age difference.** See A-2(c)(1) of this section for the determination of the adjusted employee/ beneficiary age difference in the case of an employee whose age on the annuity starting date is less than 70.

Q-11. What rule applies if distributions commence to the surviving spouse of an employee over a period permitted under section 401(a)(9)(B)(iii)(II) before the date on which distributions are required to commence and the distribution form is an annuity under which distributions are made as of the date distributions commence in accordance with the provisions of A-1 of this section.

A-11. If distributions commence to the surviving spouse of an employee over a period permitted under section 401(a)(9)(B)(iii)(II) before the date on which distributions are required to commence and the distribution form is an annuity under which distributions are made as of the date distributions commence in accordance with the provisions of A-1 of this section, distributions will be considered to have begun on the actual commencement date for purposes of section 401(a)(9)(B)(iv)(II). Consequently, in such case, A-5 of § 1.401(a)(9)-3 and section 401(a)(9)(B)(ii) and (iii) will not apply upon the death of the surviving spouse as though the surviving spouse were the employee. Instead, the annuity distributions must continue to be made, in accordance with the provisions of A-1 of this section, over the remaining period over which distributions commenced.

Q-12. In the case of an annuity contract under an individual account plan that has not yet been annuitized, how is section 401(a)(9) satisfied with respect to the employee's or beneficiary's entire interest under the annuity contract for the period prior to the date annuity payments so commence?

A-12. **(a) General rule.** Prior to the date that an annuity contract under an individual account plan is annuitized, the interest of an employee or beneficiary under that contract is treated as an individual account for purposes of section 401(a)(9). Thus, the required minimum distribution for any year with respect to that interest is determined under § 1.401(a)(9)-5 rather than this section. See A-1 of § 1.401(a)(9)-5 for rules relating to the satisfaction of section 401(a)(9) in the year that annuity payments commence and A-2(a)(3) of § 1.401(a)(9)-8.

**(b) Entire interest.** For purposes of applying the rules in § 1.401(a)(9)-5, the entire interest under the annuity contract as of December 31 of the relevant valuation calendar year is treated as the account balance for the valuation calendar year described in A-3 of § 1.401(a)(9)-5. The entire interest under an annuity contract is the dollar amount credited to the employee or beneficiary under the contract plus the actuarial present value of any additional benefits (such as survivor benefits in excess of the dollar amount credited to the employee or beneficiary) that will be provided under the contract. However, paragraph (c) of this A-12 describes certain additional benefits that may be disregarded in determining the employee's entire interest under the annuity contract. The actuarial present value of any additional benefits described under this A-12 is to be determined using reasonable actuarial assumptions, including reasonable assumptions as to future distributions, and without regard to an individual's health.

**(c) Exclusions.** **(1)** The actuarial present value of any additional benefits provided under an annuity contract described in paragraph (b) of this A-12 may be disregarded if the sum of the dollar amount credited to the employee or beneficiary under the contract and the actuarial present value of the additional benefits is no more than 120 percent of the dollar amount credited to the employee or beneficiary under the contract and the contract provides only for the following additional benefits:

(i) Additional benefits that, in the case of a distribution, are reduced by an amount sufficient to ensure that the ratio of such sum to the dollar amount credited does not increase as a result of the distribution, and

(ii) An additional benefit that is the right to receive a final payment upon death that does not exceed the excess of the premiums paid less the amount of prior distributions.

**(2)** If the only additional benefit provided under the contract is the additional benefit described in paragraph (c)(1)(ii) of this A-12, the additional benefit may be disregarded regardless of its value in relation to the dollar amount credited to the employee or beneficiary under the contract.

**(3)** The Commissioner in revenue rulings, notices, or other guidance published in the Internal Revenue Bulletin (see § 601.601(d)(2) of this chapter) may provide additional guidance on additional benefits that may be disregarded.

**(d) Examples.** The following examples, which use a 5 percent interest rate and the Mortality Table provided in Rev. Rul. 2001-62 (2001-2 C.B. 632), illustrate the application of the rules in this A-12:

**Example 1.** (i) G is the owner of a variable annuity contract (Contract S) under an individual account plan which has not been annuitized. Contract S provides a death benefit until the end of the calendar year in which the owner attains the age of 84 equal to the greater of the current Contract S notional account value (dollar amount credited to G under the contract) and the largest notional account value at any previous policy anniversary reduced proportionally for subsequent partial distributions (High Water Mark). Contract S provides a death benefit in calendar years after the calendar year in which the owner attains age 84 equal to the current notional account value. Contract S provides that assets within the contract may be invested in a Fixed Account at a guaranteed rate of 2 percent. Contract S provides no other additional benefits.

(ii) At the end of 2008, when G has an attained age of 78 and 9 months the notional account value of Contract S (after the distribution for 2008 of 4.93% of the notional account value as of December 31, 2007) is $550,000, and the High Water Mark, before adjustment for any withdrawals from Contract S in 2008 is $1,000,000. Thus, Contract S will provide additional benefits (i.e. the death benefits in excess of the notional account value) through 2014, the year S turns 84. The actuarial present value of these additional benefits at the end of 2008 is determined to be $84,300 (15 percent of the notional account value). In making this determination, the following assumptions are made: on the average, deaths occur mid-year; the investment return on his notional account value is 2 percent per annum; and minimum required distributions (determined without regard to additional benefits under the Contract S) are made at the end of each year. The following table summarizes the actuarial methodology used in determining the actuarial present value of the additional benefit.

| Year | Death benefit during year | End-of-year notional account before withdrawal | Average notional account | Withdrawal at end of year | End-of-year notional account after withdrawal |
|---|---|---|---|---|---|
| 2008 | $1,000,000 | .............. | .............. | ............ | $550,000 |
| 2009 | 950,739[1] | $561,000[2] | $555,500[3] | $28,205[4] | 532,795 |
| 2010 | 901,983 | 543,451 | 538,123 | 28,492 | 514,959 |
| 2011 | 853,749 | 525,258 | 520,109 | 28,769 | 496,490 |
| 2012 | 806,053 | 506,419 | 501,454 | 29,034 | 477,385 |
| 2013 | 758,916 | 486,933 | 482,159 | 29,287 | 457,645 |
| 2014 | 712,356 | 466,798 | 462,222 | 29,525 | 437,273 |

[1] $1,000,000 death benefit reduced 4.93 percent for withdrawal during 2008.
[2] Notional account value at end of prior year (after distribution) increased by 2 percent return for year.
[3] Average of $550,000 notional account value at end of prior year (after distribution) and $561,000 notional account value at end of current year (before distribution).
[4] December 31, 2008 notional account (before distribution) divided by uniform lifetime table age 79 factor of 19.5.

| Year | Survivorship to start of year | Interest discount to end of 2008 | Mortality rate during year | Discounted additional benefits within year |
|---|---|---|---|---|
| 2008 | ............ | .......... | .......... | .......... |
| 2009 | 1.00000 | .97590 | .04426[5] | 17,070 |
| 2010 | .95574 | .92943[6] | .04946 | 15,987[7] |
| 2011 | .90847[8] | .88517 | .05519 | 14,807 |
| 2012 | .85833 | .84302 | .06146 | 13,546 |
| 2013 | .80558 | .80288 | .06788 | 12,150 |
| 2014 | .75090 | .76464 | .07477 | 10,739 |
| | ............ | .......... | .......... | $84,300 |

[5] One-quarter age 78 rate plus three-quarters age 79 rate.
[6] Five percent discounted 18 months (1.05[caret](-1.5)).
[7] Blended age 79/age 80 mortality rate (.04946) multiplied by the $363,860 excess of death benefit over the average notional account value (901,983 less 538,123) multiplied by .95574 probability of survivorship to the start of 2010 multiplied by 18 month interest discount of .92943.
[8] Survivorship to start of preceding year (.95574) multiplied by probability of survivorship during prior year (1-.04946).

(iii) Because Contract S provides that, in the case of a distribution, the value of the additional death benefit (which is the only additional benefit available under the contract) is reduced by an amount that is at least proportional to the reduction in the notional account value and, at age 78 and 9 months, the sum of the notional account value (dollar amount credited to the employee under the contract) and the actuarial present value of the additional death benefit is no more than 120 percent of the notional account value, the exclusion under paragraph (c)(2) of this A-12 is applicable for 2009. Therefore, for purposes of applying the rules in § 1.401(a)(9)-5, the entire interest under Contract S may be determined as the notional account value (i.e. without regard to the additional death benefit).

**Example 2.** (i) The facts are the same as in (Example 1 except that the notional account value is $450,000 at the end of 2008. In this instance, the actuarial present value of the death benefit in excess of the notional account value in 2008 is determined to be $108,669 (24 percent of the notional account value). The following table summarizes the actuarial methodology used in determining the actuarial present value of the additional benefit.

| Year | Death benefit during year | End-of-year notional account before withdrawal | Average notional account | Withdrawal at end of year | End-of-year notional account after withdrawal |
|---|---|---|---|---|---|
| 2008 | $1,000,000 | .............. | .............. | ............ | $450,000 |
| 2009 | 950,739 | $459,000 | $454,500 | $23,077 | 435,923 |
| 2010 | 901,983 | 444,642 | 440,282 | 23,311 | 421,330 |
| 2011 | 853,749 | 429,757 | 425,543 | 23,538 | 406,219 |
| 2012 | 806,053 | 414,343 | 410,281 | 23,755 | 390,588 |
| 2013 | 758,916 | 398,399 | 394,494 | 23,962 | 374,437 |
| 2014 | 712,356 | 381,926 | 378,181 | 24,157 | 357,768 |

| Year | Survivorship to start of year | Interest discount to end of 2008 | Mortality rate during year | Discounted additional benefits within year |
|---|---|---|---|---|
| 2008 | ............ | .......... | .......... | ............ |
| 2009 | 1.00000 | .97590 | .04426 | $21,432 |
| 2010 | .95574 | .92943 | .04946 | 20,286 |
| 2011 | .90847 | .88517 | .05519 | 19,004 |
| 2012 | .85833 | .84302 | .06146 | 17,601 |
| 2013 | .80558 | .80288 | .06788 | 15,999 |
| 2014 | .75090 | .76464 | .07477 | 14,347 |
| | ............ | .......... | .......... | $108,669 |

(ii) Because the sum of the notional account balance and the actuarial present value of the additional death benefit is more than 120 percent of the notional account value, the exclusion under paragraph (b)(1) of this A-12 does not apply for 2009. Therefore, for purposes of applying the rules in § 1.401(a)(9)-5, the entire interest under Contract S must include the actuarial present value of the additional death benefit.

Q-13. When can an annuity payment period be changed?

A-13. **(a) In general.** An annuity payment period may be changed in accordance with the provisions set forth in paragraph (b) of this A-13 or in association with an annuity payment increase described in A-14 of this section.

**(b) Reannuitization.** If, in a stream of annuity payments that otherwise satisfies section 401(a)(9), the annuity payment period is changed and the annuity payments are modified in association with that change, this modification will not cause the distributions to fail to satisfy section 401(a)(9) provided the conditions set forth in paragraph (c) of this A-13 are satisfied, and either—

**(1)** The modification occurs at the time that the employee retires or in connection with a plan termination;

**(2)** The annuity payments prior to modification are annuity payments paid over a period certain without life contingencies; or

**(3)** The annuity payments after modification are paid under a qualified joint and survivor annuity over the joint lives of the employee and a designated beneficiary, the employee's spouse is the sole designated beneficiary, and the modification occurs in connection with the employee becoming married to such spouse.

**(c) Conditions.** In order to modify a stream of annuity payments in accordance with paragraph (b) of this A-13, the following conditions must be satisfied—

**(1)** The future payments under the modified stream satisfy section 401(a)(9) and this section (determined by treating the date of the change as a new annuity starting date and the actuarial present value of the remaining payments prior to modification as the entire interest of the participant);

**(2)** For purposes of sections 415 and 417, the modification is treated as a new annuity starting date;

**(3)** After taking into account the modification, the annuity stream satisfies section 415 (determined at the original annuity starting date, using the interest rates and mortality tables applicable to such date); and

**(4)** The end point of the period certain, if any, for any modified payment period is not later than the end point available under section 401(a)(9) to the employee at the original annuity starting date.

**(d) Examples.** For the following examples in this A-13, assume that the Applicable Interest Rate throughout the period from 2005 through 2008 is 5 percent and throughout 2009 is 4 percent, the Applicable Mortality Table throughout the period from 2005 to 2009 is the table provided in Rev. Rul. 2001-62 (2001-C.B. 632) and the section 415 limit in 2005 at age 70 for a straight life annuity is $255,344:

**Example 1.** (i) A participant (D), who has 10 years of participation in a frozen defined benefit plan (Plan W), attains age 70½ in 2005. D is not retired and elects to receive distributions from Plan W in the form of a straight life (i.e. level payment) annuity with annual payments of $240,000 per year beginning in 2005 at a date when D has an attained age of 70. Plan W offers non-retired employees in pay status the opportunity to modify their annuity payments due to an associated change in the payment period at retirement. Plan W treats the date of the change in payment period as a new annuity starting date for the purposes of sections 415 and 417. Thus, for example, the plan provides a new qualified and joint survivor annuity election and obtains spousal consent.

(ii) Plan W determines modifications of annuity payment amounts at retirement such that the present value of future new annuity payment amounts (taking into account the new associated payment period) is actuarially equivalent to the present value of future pre-modification annuity payments (taking into account the pre-modification annuity payment period). Actuarial equivalency for this purpose is determined using the Applicable Interest Rate and the Applicable Mortality Table as of the date of modification.

(iii) D retires in 2009 at the age of 74 and, after receiving four annual payments of $240,000, elects to receive his remaining distributions from Plan W in the form of an immediate final lump sum payment (calculated at 4 percent interest) of $2,399,809.

(iv) Because payment of retirement benefits in the form of an immediate final lump sum payment satisfies (in terms of form) section 401(a)(9), the condition under paragraph (c)(1) of this A-13 is met.

(v) Because Plan W treats a modification of an annuity payment stream at retirement as a new annuity starting date for purposes of sections 415 and 417, the condition under paragraph (c)(2) of this A-13 is met.

(vi) After taking into account the modification, the annuity stream determined as of the original annuity starting date consists of annual payments beginning at age 70 of $240,000, $240,000, $240,000, $240,000, and $2,399,809. This benefit stream is actuarially equivalent to a straight life annuity at age 70 of $250,182, an amount less than the section 415 limit determined at the original annuity starting date, using the interest and mortality rates applicable to such date. Thus, the condition under paragraph (c)(3) of this A-13 is met.

(vii) Thus, because a stream of annuity payments in the form of a straight life annuity satisfies section 401(a)(9), and because each of the conditions under paragraph (c) of this A-13 are satisfied, the modification of annuity payments to D described in this example meets the requirements of this A-13.

**Example 2.** The facts are the same as in Example 1 except that the straight life annuity payments are paid at a rate of $250,000 per year and after D retires the lump sum payment at age 75 is $2,499,801. Thus, after taking into account the modification, the annuity stream determined as of the original annuity starting date consists of annual payments beginning at age 70 of $250,000, $250,000, $250,000, $250,000, and $2,499,801. This benefit stream is actuarially equivalent to a straight life annuity at age 70 of $260,606, an amount greater than the section 415 limit determined at the original annuity starting date, using the interest and mortality rates applicable to such date. Thus, the lump sum payment to D fails to satisfy the condition under paragraph (c)(3) of this A-13. Therefore, the lump sum payment to D fails to meet the requirements of this A-13 and thus fails to satisfy the requirements of section 401(a)(9).

**Example 3.** (i) A participant (E), who has 10 years of participation in a frozen defined benefit plan (Plan X), attains age 70½ and retires in 2005 at a date when his attained age is 70. E was born in 1935. E elects to receive annual distributions from Plan X in the form of a 27 year period certain annuity (i.e., a 27 year annuity payment period without a life contingency) paid at a rate of $37,000 per year beginning in 2005 with future payments increasing at a rate of 4 percent per year (i.e., the 2006 payment will be $38,480, the 2007 payment will be $40,019 and so on). Plan X offers participants in pay status whose annuity payments are in the form of a term-certain annuity the opportunity to modify their payment period at any time and treats such modifications as a new annuity starting date for the purposes of sections 415 and 417. Thus, for example, the plan provides a new qualified and joint survivor annuity election and obtains spousal consent.

(ii) Plan X determines modifications of annuity payment amounts such that the present value of future new annuity payment amounts (taking into account the new associated payment period) is actuarially equivalent to the present value of future pre-modification annuity payments (taking into account the pre-modification annuity payment period). Actuarial equivalency for this purpose is determined using 5 percent and the Applicable Mortality Table as of the date of modification.

(iii) In 2008, E, after receiving annual payments of $37,000, $38,480, and $40,019, elects to receive his remaining distributions from Plan W in the form of a straight life annuity paid with annual payments of $92,133 per year.

(iv) Because payment of retirement benefits in the form of a straight life annuity satisfies (in terms of form) section 401(a)(9), the condition under paragraph (c)(1) of this A-13 is met.

(v) Because Plan X treats a modification of an annuity payment stream at retirement as a new annuity starting date for purposes of sections 415 and 417, the condition under paragraph (c)(2) of this A-13 is met.

(vi) After taking into account the modification, the annuity stream determined as of the original annuity starting date consists of annual payments beginning at age 70 of $37,000, $38,480, $40,019, and a straight life annuity beginning at age 73 of $92,133. This benefit stream is equivalent to a straight life annuity at age 70 of $82,539, an amount less than the section 415 limit determined at the original annuity starting date, using the interest and mortality rates applicable to such date. Thus, the condition under paragraph (c)(3) of this A-13 is met.

(vii) Thus, because a stream of annuity payments in the form of a straight life annuity satisfies section 401(a)(9), and because each of the conditions under paragraph (c) of this A-13 are satisfied, the modification of annuity payments to E described in this example meets the requirements of this A-13.

Q-14. Are annuity payments permitted to increase?

A-14. **(a) General rules.** Except as otherwise provided in this section, all annuity payments (whether paid over an employee's life, joint lives, or a period certain) must be nonincreasing or increase only in accordance with one or more of the following —

**(1)** With an annual percentage increase that does not exceed the percentage increase in an eligible cost-of-living index as defined in paragraph (b) of this A-14 for a 12-month period ending in the year during which the increase occurs or the prior year;

**(2)** With a percentage increase that occurs at specified times (e.g., at specified ages) and does not exceed the cumulative total of annual percentage increases in an eligible cost-of-living index as defined in paragraph (b) of this A-14 since the annuity starting date, or if later, the date of the most recent percentage increase. However, in cases providing such a cumulative increase, an actuarial increase may not be provided to reflect the fact that increases were not provided in the interim years;

**(3)** To the extent of the reduction in the amount of the employee's payments to provide for a survivor benefit, but only if there is no longer a survivor benefit because the beneficiary whose life was being used to determine the period described in section 401(a)(9)(A)(ii) over which payments were being made dies or is no longer the employee's beneficiary pursuant to a qualified domestic relations order within the meaning of section 414(p);

**(4)** To pay increased benefits that result from a plan amendment;

**(5)** To allow a beneficiary to convert the survivor portion of a joint and survivor annuity into a single sum distribution upon the employee's death; or

**(6)** To the extent increases are permitted in accordance with paragraph (c) or (d) of this A-14.

**(b)(1)** For purposes of this A-14, an eligible cost-of-living index means an index described in paragraphs (b)(2), (b)(3), or (b)(4) of this A-14.

**(2)** A consumer price index that is based on prices of all items (or all items excluding food and energy) and issued by the Bureau of Labor Statistics, including an index for a specific population (such as urban consumers or urban wage earners and clerical workers) and an index for a geographic area or areas (such as a given metropolitan area or state).

**(3)** A percentage adjustment based on a cost-of-living index described in paragraph (b)(2) of this A-14, or a fixed percentage if less. In any year when the cost-of-living index is lower than the fixed percentage, the fixed percentage may be treated as an increase in an eligible cost-of-living index, provided it does not exceed the sum of:

(i) The cost-of-living index for that year, and

(ii) The accumulated excess of the annual cost-of-living index from each prior year over the fixed annual percentage used in that year (reduced by any amount previously utilized under this paragraph (b)(3)(ii)).

**(4)** A percentage adjustment based on the increase in compensation for the position held by the employee at the time of retirement, and provided under either the terms of a governmental plan within the meaning of section 414(d) or under the terms of a nongovernmental plan as in effect on April 17, 2002.

**(c) Additional permitted increases for annuity payments under annuity contracts purchased from insurance companies.** In the case of annuity payments paid from an annuity contract purchased from an insurance company, if the total future expected payments (determined in accordance with paragraph (e)(3) of this A-14) exceed the total value being annuitized (within the meaning of paragraph (e)(1) of this A-14), the payments under the annuity will not fail to satisfy the nonincreasing payment requirement in A-1(a) of this section merely because the payments are increased in accordance with one or more of the following —

**(1)** By a constant percentage, applied not less frequently than annually;

**(2)** To provide a final payment upon the death of the employee that does not exceed the excess of the total value being annuitized (within the meaning of paragraph (e)(1) of this A-14) over the total of payments before the death of the employee;

**(3)** As a result of dividend payments or other payments that result from actuarial gains (within the meaning of paragraph (e)(2) of this A-14), but only if actuarial gain is measured no less frequently than annually and the resulting dividend payments or other payments are either paid no later than the year following the year for which the actuarial experience is measured or paid in the same form as the payment of the annuity over the remaining period of the annuity (beginning no later than the year following the year for which the actuarial experience is measured); and

**(4)** An acceleration of payments under the annuity (within the meaning of paragraph (e)(4) of this A-14).

**(d) Additional permitted increases for annuity payments from a qualified trust.** In the case of annuity payments paid under a defined benefit plan qualified under section 401(a) (other than annuity payments under an annuity contract purchased from an insurance company that satisfy paragraph (c) of this section), the payments under the annuity will not fail to satisfy the nonincreasing payment requirement in A-1(a) of this section merely because the payments are increased in accordance with one of the following—

**(1)** By a constant percentage, applied not less frequently than annually, at a rate that is less than 5 percent per year;

**(2)** To provide a final payment upon the death of the employee that does not exceed the excess of the actuarial present value of the employee's accrued benefit (within the meaning of section 411(a)(7)) calculated as the annuity starting date using the applicable interest rate and the applicable mortality table under section 417(e) (or, if greater, the total amount of employee contributions) over the total of payments before the death of the employee; or

**(3)** As a result of dividend payments or other payments that result from actuarial gains (within the meaning of paragraph (e)(2) of this A-14), but only if—

(i) Actuarial gain is measured no less frequently than annually;

(ii) The resulting dividend payments or other payments are either paid no later than the year following the year for which the actuarial experience is measured or paid in the same form as the payment of the annuity over the remaining period of the annuity (beginning no later than the year following the year for which the actuarial experience is measured);

(iii) The actuarial gain taken into account is limited to actuarial gain from investment experience;

(iv) The assumed interest used to calculate such actuarial gains is not less than 3 percent; and

(v) The payments are not increasing by a constant percentage as described in paragraph (d)(1) of this A-14.

**(e) Definitions.** For purposes of this A-14, the following definitions apply—

**(1)** Total value being annuitized means—

(i) In the case of annuity payments under a section 403(a) annuity plan or under a deferred annuity purchased by a section 401(a) trust, the value of the employee's entire interest (within the meaning of A-12 of this section) being annuitized (valued as of the date annuity payments commence);

(ii) In the case of annuity payments under an immediate annuity contract purchased by a trust for a defined benefit plan qualified under section 401(a), the amount of the premium used to purchase the contract; and

(iii) In the case of a defined contribution plan, the value of the employee's account balance used to purchase an immediate annuity under the contract.

**(2)** Actuarial gain means the difference between an amount determined using the actuarial assumptions (i.e., investment return, mortality, expense, and other similar assumptions) used to calculate the initial payments before adjustment for any increases and the amount determined under the actual experience with respect to those factors. Actuarial gain also includes differences between the amount determined using actuarial assumptions when an annuity was purchased or commenced and such amount determined using actuarial assumptions used in calculating payments at the time the actuarial gain is determined.

**(3)** Total future expected payments means the total future payments expected to be made under the annuity contract as of the date of the determination, calculated using the Single Life Table in A-1 of § 1.401(a)(9)-9 (or, if applicable, the Joint and Last Survivor Table in A-3 of in § 1.401(a)(9)-9) for annuitants who are still alive, without regard to any increases in annuity payments after the date of determination, and taking into account any remaining period certain.

**(4)** Acceleration of payments means a shortening of the payment period with respect to an annuity or a full or partial commutation of the future annuity payments. An increase in the payment amount will be treated as an acceleration of payments in the annuity only if the total future expected payments under the annuity (including the amount of any payment made as a result of the acceleration) is decreased as a result of the change in payment period.

**(f) Examples.** Paragraph (c) of this A-14 is illustrated by the following examples:

**Example 1.** Variable annuity. A retired participant (Z1) in defined contribution plan X attains age 70 on March 5, 2005, and thus, attains age 70½ in 2005. Z1 elects to purchase annuity Contract Y1 from Insurance Company W in 2005. Contract Y1 is a single life annuity contract with a 10-year period certain. Contract Y1 provides for an initial annual payment calculated with an assumed interest rate (AIR) of 3 percent. Subsequent payments are determined by multiplying the prior year's payment by a fraction the numerator of which is 1 plus the actual return on the separate account assets underlying Contract Y1 since the preceding payment and the denominator of which is 1 plus the AIR during that period. The value of Z1's account balance in Plan X at the time of purchase is $105,000, and the purchase price of Contract Y1 is $105,000. Contract Y1 provides Z1 with an initial payment of $7,200 at the time of purchase in 2005. The total future expected payments to Z1 under Contract Y1 are $122,400, calculated as the initial payment of $7,200 multiplied by the age 70 life expectancy of 17 provided in the Single Life Table in A-1 of § 1.401(a)(9)-9. Because the total future expected payments on the purchase date exceed the total value used to purchase Contract Y1 and payments may only increase as a result of actuarial gain, with such increases, beginning no later than the next year, paid in the same form as the payment of the annuity over the remaining period of the annuity, distributions received by Z1 from Contract Y1 meet the requirements under paragraph (c)(3) of this A-14.

**Example 2.** Participating annuity. A retired participant (Z2) in defined contribution plan X attains age 70 on May 1, 2005, and thus, attains age 70½ in 2005. Z2 elects to purchase annuity Contract Y2 from Insurance Company W in 2005. Contract Y2 is a participating single life annuity contract with a 10-year period certain. Contract Y2 provides for level annual payments with dividends paid in a lump sum in the year after the year for which the actuarial experience is measured or paid out levelly beginning in the year after the year for which the actuarial gain is measured over the remaining lifetime and period certain, i.e., the period certain ends at the same time as the original period certain. Dividends are determined annually by the Board of Directors of Company W based upon a comparison of actual actuarial experience to expected actuarial experience in the past year. The value of Z2's account balance in Plan X at the time of purchase is $265,000, and the purchase price of Contract Y2 is $265,000. Contract Y2 provides Z2 with an initial payment of $16,000 in 2005. The total future expected payments to Z2 under Contract Y2 are calculated as the annual initial payment of $16,000 multiplied by the age 70 life expectancy of 17 provided in the Single Life Table in A-1 of § 1.401(a)(9)-9 for a total of $272,000. Because the total future expected payments on the purchase date exceeds the total value used to purchase Contract Y2 and payments may only increase as a result of actuarial gain, with such increases, beginning no later than the next year, paid in the same form as the payment of the annuity over the remaining period of the annuity, distributions received by Z2 from Contract Y2 meet the requirements under paragraph (c)(3) of this A-14.

**Example 3.** Participating annuity with dividend accumulation. The facts are the same as in Example 2 except that the annuity provides a dividend accumulation option under which Z2 may defer receipt of the dividends to a time selected by Z2. Because the dividend accumulation option permits dividends to be paid later than the end of the year following the year for which the actuarial experience is measured or as a stream of payments that only increase as a result of actuarial gain, with such increases beginning no later than the next year, paid in the same form as the payment of the annuity over the remaining period of the annuity in Example 2, the dividend accumulation option does not meet the requirements of paragraph (c)(3) of this A-14. Neither does the dividend accumulation option fit within any of the other increases described in paragraph (c) of this A-14. Accordingly, the dividend accumulation option causes the contract, and consequently any distributions from the contract, to fail to meet the requirements of this A-14 and thus fail to satisfy the requirements of section 401(a)(9).

**Example 4.** Participating annuity with dividends used to purchase additional death benefits. The facts are the same as in Example 2 except that the annuity provides an option under which actuarial gain under the contract is used to provide additional death benefit protection for Z2. Because this option permits payments as a result of actuarial gain to be paid later than the end of the year following the year for which the actuarial experience is measured or as a stream of payments that only increase as a result of actuarial gain, with such increases beginning no later than the next year, paid in the same form as the payment of the annuity over the remaining period of the annuity in Example 2, the option does not meet the requirements of paragraph (c)(3) of this A-14. Neither does the option fit within any of the other increases described in paragraph (c) of this A-14. Accordingly, the addition of the option causes the contract, and consequently any distributions from the contract, to fail to meet the requirements of this A-14 and thus fail to satisfy the requirements of section 401(a)(9).

**Example 5.** Annuity with a fixed percentage increase. A retired participant (Z3) in defined contribution plan X attains age 70½ in 2005. Z3 elects to purchase annuity contract Y3 from Insurance Company W. Contract Y3 is a single life annuity contract with a 20-year period certain (which does not exceed the maximum period certain permitted under A-3(a) of this section) with fixed annual payments increasing 3 percent each year. The value of Z3's account balance in Plan X at the time of purchase is $110,000, and the purchase price of Contract Y3 is $110,000. Contract Y3 provides Z3 with an initial payment of $6,000 at the time of purchase in 2005. The total future expected payments to Z3 under Contract Y3 are $120,000, calculated as the initial annual payment of $6,000 multiplied by the period certain of 20 years. Because the total future expected payments on the purchase date exceed the total value used to purchase Contract Y3 and payments only increase as a constant percentage applied not less frequently than annually, distributions received by Z3 from Contract Y3 meet the requirements under paragraph (c)(1) of this A-14.

**Example 6.** Annuity with excessive increases. The facts are the same as in Example 5 except that the initial payment is $5,400 and the annual rate of increase is 4 percent. In this example, the total future expected payments are $108,000, calculated as the initial payment of $5,400 multiplied by the period certain of 20 years. Because the total future expected payments are less than the total value of $110,000 used to purchase Contract Y3, distributions received by Z3 do not meet the requirements under paragraph (c) of this A-14 and thus fail to meet the requirements of section 401(a)(9).

**Example 7.** Annuity with full commutation feature. (i) A retired participant (Z4) in defined contribution Plan X attains age 78 in 2005. Z4 elects to purchase Contract Y4 from Insurance Company W. Contract Y4 provides for a single life annuity with a 10 year period certain (which does not exceed the maximum period certain permitted under A-3(a) of this section) with annual payments. Contract Y4 provides that Z4 may cancel Contract Y4 at any time before Z4 attains age 84, and receive, on his next payment due date, a final payment in an amount determined by multiplying the initial payment amount by a factor obtained from Table M of Contract Y4 using the Y4's age as of Y4's birthday in the calendar year of the final payment. The value of Z4's account balance in Plan X at the time of purchase is $450,000, and the purchase price of Contract Y4 is $450,000. Contract Y4 provides Z4 with an initial payment in 2005 of $40,000. The factors in Table M are as follows:

| Age at final payment | Factor |
|---|---|
| 79 | 10.5 |
| 80 | 10.0 |
| 81 | 9.5 |
| 82 | 9.0 |
| 83 | 8.5 |
| 84 | 8.0 |

(ii) The total future expected payments to Z4 under ContractY4 are $456,000, calculated as the initial payment of 40,000 multiplied by the age 78 life expectancy of 11.4 provided in the Single Life Table in A-1 of § 1.401(a)(9)-9. Because the total future expected payments on the purchase date exceed the total value being annuitized (i.e., the $450,000 used to purchase Contract Y4), the permitted increases set forth in paragraph (c) of this A-14 are available. Furthermore, because the factors in Table M are less than the life expectancy of each of the ages in the Single Life Table provided in A-1 of § 1.401(a)(9)-9, the final payment is always less than the total future expected payments. Thus, the final payment is an acceleration of payments within the meaning of paragraph (c)(4) of this A-14.

(iii) As an illustration of the above, if Participant Z4 were to elect to cancel Contract Y4 on the day before he was to attain age 84, his contractual final payment would be $320,000. This amount is determined as $40,000 (the annual payment amount due under Contract Y4) multiplied by 8.0 (the factor in Table M for the next payment due date, age

84). The total future expected payments under Contract Y4 at age 84 before the final payment is $324,000, calculated as the initial payment amount multiplied by 8.1, the age 84 life expectancy provided in the Single Life Table in A-1 of § 1.401(a)(9)-9. Because $320,000 (the total future expected payments under the annuity contract, including the amount of the final payment) is less than $324,000 (the total future expected payments under the annuity contract, determined before the election), the final payment is an acceleration of payments within the meaning of paragraph (c)(4) of this A-14.

**Example 8.** Annuity with partial commutation feature. (i) The facts are the same as in Example 7 except that the annuity provides Z4 may request, at any time before Z4 attains age 84, an ad hoc payment on his next payment due date with future payments reduced by an amount equal to the ad hoc payment divided by the factor obtained from Table M (from Example 7) corresponding to Z4's age at the time of the ad hoc payment. Because, at each age, the factors in Table M are less than the corresponding life expectancies in the Single Life Table in A-1 of § 1.401(a)(9)-9, total future expected payments under Contract Y4 will decrease after an ad hoc payment. Thus, ad hoc distributions received by Z4 from Contract Y4 will satisfy the requirements under paragraph (c)(4) of this A-4.

(ii) As an illustration of paragraph (i) of this Example 8, if Z4 were to request, on the day before he was to attain age 84, an ad hoc payment of $100,000 on his next payment due date, his recalculated annual payment amount would be reduced to $27,500. This amount is determined as $40,000 ( the amount of Z4's next annual payment) reduced by $12,500 (his $100,000 ad hoc payment divided by the Table M factor at age 84 of 8.0). Thus, Z4's total future expected payments after the ad hoc payment (and including the ad hoc payment) are equal to $322,750 ($100,000 plus $27,500 multiplied by the Single Life Table value of 8.1). Note that this $322,750 amount is less than the amount of Z4's total future expected payments before the ad hoc payment ($324,000, determined as $40,000 multiplied by 8.1), and the requirements under paragraph (c)(4) of this A-4 are satisfied.

**Example 9.** Annuity with excessive increases. (i) A retired participant (Z5) in defined contribution plan X attains age 70½ in 2005. Z5 elects to purchase annuity Contract Y5 from Insurance Company W in 2005 with a premium of $1,000,000. Contract Y5 is a single life annuity contract with a 20-year period certain. Contract Y5 provides for an initial payment of $200,000, a second payment one year from the time of purchase of $40,000, and 18 succeeding annual payments each increasing at a constant percentage rate of 4.5 percent from the preceding payment.

(ii) Contract Y5 fails to meet the requirements of section 401(a)(9) because the total future expected payments without regard to any increases in the annuity payment, calculated as $200,000 in year one and $40,000 in each of years two through twenty, is only $960,000 (i.e., an amount that does not exceed the total value used to purchase the annuity).

Q-15. Are there special rules applicable to payments made under a defined benefit plan or annuity contract to a surviving child?

A-15. Yes, pursuant to section 401(a)(9)(F), payments under a defined benefit plan or annuity contract that are made to an employee's child until such child reaches the age of majority (or dies, if earlier) may be treated, for purposes of section 401(a)(9), as if such payments were made to the surviving spouse to the extent they become payable to the surviving spouse upon cessation of the payments to the child. For purposes of the preceding sentence, a child may be treated as having not reached the age of majority if the child has not completed a specified course of education and is under the age of 26. In addition, a child who is disabled within the meaning of section 72(m)(7) when the child reaches the age of majority may be treated as having not reached the age of majority so long as the child continues to be disabled. Thus, when payments described in this paragraph A-15 become payable to the surviving spouse because the child attains the age of majority, recovers from a disabling illness, dies, or completes a specified course of education, there is not an increase in benefits under A-1 of this section. Likewise, the age of child receiving such payments is not taken into consideration for purposes of the minimum incidental benefit requirement of A-2 of this section.

Q-16. What are the rules for determining required minimum distributions for defined benefit plans and annuity contracts for calendar years 2003, 2004, and 2005?

A-16. A distribution from a defined benefit plan or annuity contract for calendar years 2003, 2004, and 2005 will not fail to satisfy section 401(a)(9) merely because the payments do not satisfy A-1 through A-15 of this section, provided the payments satisfy section 401(a)(9) based on a reasonable and good faith interpretation of the provisions of section 401(a)(9).

T.D. 9130, 6/14/2004, amend T.D. 9459, 9/4/2009.

### § 1.401(a)(9)-7 Rollovers and transfers.

Q-1. If an amount is distributed by one plan (distributing plan) and is rolled over to another plan, is the required minimum distribution under the distributing plan affected by the rollover?

A-1. No, if an amount is distributed by one plan and is rolled over to another plan, the amount distributed is still treated as a distribution by the distributing plan for purposes of section 401(a)(9), notwithstanding the rollover. See A-1 of § 1.402(c)-2 for the definition of a rollover and A-7 of § 1.402(c)-2 for rules for determining the portion of any distribution that is not eligible for rollover because it is a required minimum distribution.

Q-2. If an amount is distributed by one plan (distributing plan) and is rolled over to another plan (receiving plan), how are the benefit and the required minimum distribution under the receiving plan affected?

A-2. If an amount is distributed by one plan (distributing plan) and is rolled over to another plan (receiving plan), the benefit of the employee under the receiving plan is increased by the amount rolled over for purposes of determining the required minimum distribution for the calendar year immediately following the calendar year in which the amount rolled over is distributed. If the amount rolled over is received after the last valuation date in the calendar year under the receiving plan, the benefit of the employee as of such valuation date, adjusted in accordance with A-3 of § 1.401(a)(9)-5, will be increased by the rollover amount valued as of the date of receipt. In addition, if the amount rolled over is received in a different calendar year from the calendar year in which it is distributed, the amount rolled over is deemed to have been received by the receiving plan in the calendar year in which it was distributed.

Q-3. In the case of a transfer of an amount of an employee's benefit from one plan (transferor plan) to another plan (transferee plan), are there any special rules for satisfying section 401(a)(9) or determining the employee's benefit under the transferor plan?

A-3. (a) In the case of a transfer of an amount of an employee's benefit from one plan (transferor plan) to another (transferee plan), the transfer is not treated as a distribution by the transferor plan for purposes of section 401(a)(9). Instead, the benefit of the employee under the transferor plan is decreased by the amount transferred. However, if any portion of an employee's benefit is transferred in a distribution calendar year with respect to that employee, in order to satisfy section 401(a)(9), the transferor plan must determine the amount of the required minimum distribution with respect to that employee for the calendar year of the transfer using the employee's benefit under the transferor plan before the transfer. Additionally, if any portion of an employee's benefit is transferred in the employee's second distribution calendar year but on or before the employee's required beginning date, in order to satisfy section 401(a)(9), the transferor plan must determine the amount of the minimum distribution requirement for the employee's first distribution calendar year based on the employee's benefit under the transferor plan before the transfer. The transferor plan may satisfy the minimum distribution requirement for the calendar year of the transfer (and the prior year if applicable) by segregating the amount which must be distributed from the employee's benefit and not transferring that amount. Such amount may be retained by the transferor plan and must be distributed on or before the date required under section 401(a)(9).

(b) For purposes of determining any required minimum distribution for the calendar year immediately following the calendar year in which the transfer occurs, in the case of a transfer after the last valuation date for the calendar year of the transfer under the transferor plan, the benefit of the employee as of such valuation date, adjusted in accordance with A-3 of § 1.401(a)(9)-5, will be decreased by the amount transferred, valued as of the date of the transfer.

Q-4. If an amount of an employee's benefit is transferred from one plan (transferor plan) to another plan (transferee plan), how are the benefit and the required minimum distribution under the transferee plan affected?

A-4. In the case of a transfer from one plan (transferor plan) to another (transferee plan), the benefit of the employee under the transferee plan is increased by the amount transferred in the same manner as if it were a plan receiving a rollover contribution under A-2 of this section.

Q-5. How is a spinoff, merger or consolidation (as defined in § 1.414(l)-1) treated for purposes of determining an employee's benefit and required minimum distribution under section 401(a)(9)?

A-5. For purposes of determining an employee's benefit and required minimum distribution under section 401(a)(9), a spinoff, a merger, or a consolidation (as defined in § 1.414(l)-1) will be treated as a transfer of the benefits of the employees involved. Consequently, the benefit and required minimum distribution of each employee involved under the transferor and transferee plans will be determined in accordance with A-3 and A-4 of this section.

T.D. 8987, 4/16/2002.

## § 1.401(a)(9)-8 Special rules.

Q-1. What distribution rules apply if an employee is a participant in more than one plan?

A-1. If an employee is a participant in more than one plan, the plans in which the employee participates are not permitted to be aggregated for purposes of testing whether the distribution requirements of section 401(a)(9) are met. The distribution of the benefit of the employee under each plan must separately meet the requirements of section 401(a)(9). For this purpose, a plan described in section 414(k) is treated as two separate plans, a defined contribution plan to the extent benefits are based on an individual account and a defined benefit plan with respect to the remaining benefits.

Q-2. If an employee's benefit under a defined contribution plan is divided into separate accounts (or under a defined benefit plan is divided into segregated shares), do the distribution rules in section 401(a)(9) and these regulations apply separately to each separate account?

A-2. **(a) Defined contribution plan.** (1) Except as otherwise provided in this A-2, if an employee's benefit under a defined contribution plan is divided into separate accounts under the plan, the separate accounts will be aggregated for purposes of satisfying the rules in section 401(a)(9). Thus, except as otherwise provided in this A-2, all separate accounts, including a separate account for employee contributions under section 72(d)(2), will be aggregated for purposes of section 401(a)(9).

(2) If the employee's benefit in a defined contribution plan is divided into separate accounts and the beneficiaries with respect to one separate account differ from the beneficiaries with respect to the other separate accounts of the employee under the plan, for years subsequent to the calendar year containing the date as of which the separate accounts were established, or date of death if later, such separate account under the plan is not aggregated with the other separate accounts under the plan in order to determine whether the distributions from such separate account under the plan satisfy section 401(a)(9). Instead, the rules in section 401(a)(9) separately apply to such separate account under the plan. However, the applicable distribution period for each such separate account is determined disregarding the other beneficiaries of the employee's benefit only if the separate account is established on a date no later than the last day of the year following the calendar year of the employee's death. For example, if, in the case of a distribution described in section 401(a)(9)(B)(iii) and (iv), the only beneficiary of a separate account under the plan established on a date no later than the end of the year following the calendar year of the employee's death is the employee's surviving spouse, and beneficiaries other than the surviving spouse are designated with respect to the other separate accounts with respect to the employee, distribution of the spouse's separate account under the plan need not commence until the date determined under the first sentence in A-3(b) of § 1.401(a)(9)-3, even if distribution of the other separate accounts under the plan must commence at an earlier date. Similarly, in the case of a distribution after the death of an employee to which section 401(a)(9)(B)(i) does not apply, distribution from a separate account of an employee established on a date no later than the end of the year following the year of the employee's death may be made over a beneficiary's life expectancy in accordance with section 401(a)(9)(B)(iii) and (iv) even though distributions from other separate accounts under the plan with different beneficiaries are being made in accordance with the 5-year rule in section 401(a)(9)(B)(ii).

(3) A portion of an employee's account balance under a defined contribution plan is permitted to be used to purchase an annuity contract while another portion stays in the account. In that case, the remaining account under the plan must be distributed in accordance with § 1.401(a)(9)-5 in order to satisfy section 401(a)(9) and the annuity payments under the annuity contract must satisfy § 1.401(a)(9)-6 in order to satisfy section 401(a)(9).

**(b) Defined benefit plan.** The rules of paragraph (a)(2) and (3) of this A-2 also apply to benefits under a defined benefit plan where the benefits under the plan are separated into separate identifiable components which are separately distributed.

Q-3. What are separate accounts for purposes of section 401(a)(9)?

A-3. For purposes of section 401(a)(9), separate accounts in an employee's account are separate portions of an employee's benefit reflecting the separate interests of the employee's beneficiaries under the plan as of the date of the employee's death for which separate accounting is maintained. The separate accounting must allocate all post-death investment gains and losses, contributions, and forfeitures, for the period prior to the establishment of the separate accounts on a pro rata basis in a reasonable and consistent manner among the separate accounts. However, once the separate accounts are actually established, the separate accounting can provide for separate investments for each separate account under which gains and losses from the investment of the account are only allocated to that account, or investment gain or losses can continue to be allocated among the separate accounts on a pro rata basis. A separate accounting must allocate any post-death distribution to the separate account of the beneficiary receiving that distribution.

Q-4. If a distribution is required to be made to an employee by section 401(a)(9)(A) or is required to be made to a surviving spouse under section 401(a)(9)(B), must the distribution be made even if the employee, or spouse where applicable, fails to consent to a distribution while a benefit is immediately distributable?

A-4. Yes, section 411(a)(11) and section 417(e) (see §§ 1.411(a)(11)-1(c)(2) and 1.417(e)-1(c)) require employee and spousal consent to certain distributions of plan benefits while such benefits are immediately distributable. If an employee's normal retirement age is later than the employee's required beginning date and, therefore, benefits are still immediately distributable, the plan must, nevertheless, distribute plan benefits to the employee (or where applicable, to the spouse) in a manner that satisfies the requirements of section 401(a)(9). Section 401(a)(9) must be satisfied even though the employee (or spouse, where applicable) fails to consent to the distribution. In such a case, the plan may distribute in the form of a qualified joint and survivor annuity (QJSA) or in the form of a qualified preretirement survivor annuity (QPSA), as applicable, and the consent requirements of sections 411(a)(11) and 417(e) are deemed to be satisfied if the plan has made reasonable efforts to obtain consent from the employee (or spouse if applicable) and if the distribution otherwise meets the requirements of section 417. If, because of section 401(a)(11)(B), the plan is not required to distribute in the form of a QJSA to a employee or a QPSA to a surviving spouse, the plan may distribute the required minimum distribution amount to satisfy section 401(a)(9) and the consent requirements of sections 411(a)(11) and 417(e) are deemed to be satisfied if the plan has made reasonable efforts to obtain consent from the employee (or spouse if applicable) and if the distribution otherwise meets the requirements of section 417.

Q-5. Who is an employee's spouse or surviving spouse for purposes of section 401(a)(9)?

A-5. Except as otherwise provided in A-6(a) of this section (in the case of distributions of a portion of an employee's benefit payable to a former spouse of an employee pursuant to a qualified domestic relations order), for purposes of section 401(a)(9), an individual is a spouse or surviving spouse of an employee if such individual is treated as the employee's spouse under applicable state law. In the case of distributions after the death of an employee, for purposes of determining whether, under the life expectancy rule in section 401(a)(9)(B)(iii) and (iv), the provisions of section 401(a)(9)(B)(iv) apply, the spouse of the employee is determined as of the date of death of the employee.

Q-6. In order to satisfy section 401(a)(9), are there any special rules which apply to the distribution of all or a portion of an employee's benefit payable to an alternate payee pursuant to a qualified domestic relations order as defined in section 414(p) (QDRO)?

A-6. (a) A former spouse to whom all or a portion of the employee's benefit is payable pursuant to a QDRO will be treated as a spouse (including a surviving spouse) of the employee for purposes of section 401(a)(9), including the minimum distribution incidental benefit requirement, regardless of whether the QDRO specifically provides that the former spouse is treated as the spouse for purposes of sections 401(a)(11) and 417.

(b)(1) If a QDRO provides that an employee's benefit is to be divided and a portion is to be allocated to an alternate payee, such portion will be treated as a separate account (or segregated share) which separately must satisfy the requirements of section 401(a)(9) and may not be aggregated with other separate accounts (or segregated shares) of the employee for purposes of satisfying section 401(a)(9). Except as otherwise provided in paragraph (b)(2) of this A-6, distribution of such separate account allocated to an alternate payee pursuant to a QDRO must be made in accordance with section 401(a)(9). For example, in general, distribution of such account will satisfy section 401(a)(9)(A) if required minimum distributions from such account during the employee's lifetime begin not later than the employee's required beginning date and the required minimum distribution is determined in accordance with § 1.401(a)(9)-5 for each distribution calendar year (using an applicable distribution period determined under A-4 of § 1.401(a)(9)-5 for the employee in the distribution calendar year either using the Uniform Lifetime Table in A-2 of § 1.401(a)(9)-9 or using the joint life expectancy of the employee and a spousal alternate payee in the distribution calendar year if the spousal alternate payee is more than 10 years younger than the employee). The determination of whether distribution from such account after the death of the employee to the alternate payee will be made in accordance with section 401(a)(9)(B)(i) or section 401(a)(9)(B)(ii) or (iii) and (iv) will depend on whether distributions have begun as determined under A-6 of § 1.401(a)(9)-2 (which provides, in general, that distributions are not treated as having begun until the employee's required beginning date even though payments may actually have begun before that date). For example, if the alternate payee dies before the employee and distribution of the separate account allocated to the alternate payee pursuant to the QDRO is to be made to the alternate payee's beneficiary, such beneficiary may be treated as a designated beneficiary for purposes of determining the minimum distribution required from such account after the death of the employee if the beneficiary of the alternate payee is an individual and if such beneficiary is a beneficiary under the plan or specified to or in the plan. Specification in or pursuant to the QDRO is treated as specification to the plan.

(2) Distribution of the separate account allocated to an alternate payee pursuant to a QDRO will satisfy the requirements of section 401(a)(9)(A)(ii) if such account is to be distributed, beginning not later than the employee's required beginning date, over the life of the alternate payee (or over a period not extending beyond the life expectancy of the alternate payee). Also, if the plan permits the employee to elect whether distribution upon the death of the employee will be made in accordance with the 5-year rule in section 401(a)(9)(B)(ii) or the life expectancy rule in section 401(a)(9)(B)(iii) and (iv) pursuant to A-4(c) of § 1.401(a)(9)-3, such election is to be made only by the alternate payee for purposes of distributing the separate account allocated to the alternate payee pursuant to the QDRO. If the alternate payee dies after distribution of the separate account allocated to the alternate payee pursuant to a QDRO has begun (determined under A-6 of § 1.401(a)(9)-2) but before the employee dies, distribution of the remaining portion of that portion of the benefit allocated to the alternate payee must be made in accordance with the rules in § 1.401(a)(9)-5 or 1.401(a)(9)-6 for distributions during the life of the employee. Only after the death of the employee is the amount of the required minimum distribution determined in accordance with the rules of section 401(a)(9)(B).

(c) If a QDRO does not provide that an employee's benefit is to be divided but provides that a portion of an employee's benefit (otherwise payable to the employee) is to be paid to an alternate payee, such portion will not be treated as a separate account (or segregated share) of the employee. Instead, such portion will be aggregated with any amount distributed to the employee and will be treated as having been distributed to the employee for purposes of determining whether section 401(a)(9) has been satisfied with respect to that employee.

Q-7. Will a plan fail to satisfy section 401(a)(9) merely because it fails to distribute an amount otherwise required to be distributed by section 401(a)(9) during the period in which the issue of whether a domestic relations order is a QDRO is being determined?

A-7. A plan will not fail to satisfy section 401(a)(9) merely because it fails to distribute an amount otherwise required to be distributed by section 401(a)(9) during the period in which the issue of whether a domestic relations order is a QDRO is being determined pursuant to section 414(p)(7), provided that the period does not extend beyond the 18-month period described in section 414(p)(7)(E). To the extent that a distribution otherwise required under section 401(a)(9) is not made during this period, any segregated amounts, as defined in section 414(p)(7)(A), will be treated as though the amounts are not vested during the period and any distributions with respect to such amounts must be made under the relevant rules for nonvested benefits described in either A-8 of § 1.401(a)(9)-5 or A-6 of § 1.401(a)(9)-6, as applicable.

Q-8. Will a plan fail to satisfy section 401(a)(9) where an individual's distribution from the plan is less than the amount otherwise required to satisfy section 401(a)(9) because distributions were being paid under an annuity contract issued by a life insurance company in state insurer delinquency proceedings and have been reduced or suspended by reasons of such state proceedings?

A-8. A plan will not fail to satisfy section 401(a)(9) merely because an individual's distribution from the plan is less than the amount otherwise required to satisfy section 401(a)(9) because distributions were being paid under an annuity contract issued by a life insurance company in state insurer delinquency proceedings and have been reduced or suspended by reasons of such state proceedings. To the extent that a distribution otherwise required under section 401(a)(9) is not made during the state insurer delinquency proceedings, this amount and any additional amount accrued during this period will be treated as though such amounts are not vested during the period and any distributions with respect to such amounts must be made under the relevant rules for nonvested benefits described in either A-8 of § 1.401(a)(9)-5 or A-6 of § 1.401(a)(9)-6, as applicable.

Q-9. Will a plan fail to qualify as a pension plan within the meaning of section 401(a) solely because the plan permits distributions to commence to an employee on or after April 1 of the calendar year following the calendar year in which the employee attains age 70½ even though the employee has not retired or attained the normal retirement age under the plan as of the date on which such distributions commence?

A-9. No, a plan will not fail to qualify as a pension plan within the meaning of section 401(a) solely because the plan permits distributions to commence to an employee on or after April 1 of the calendar year following the calendar year in which the employee attains age 70½ even though the employee has not retired or attained the normal retirement age under the plan as of the date on which such distributions commence. This rule applies without regard to whether the employee is a 5-percent owner with respect to the plan year ending in the calendar year in which distributions commence.

Q-10. Is the distribution of an annuity contract a distribution for purposes of section 401(a)(9)?

A-10. No, the distribution of an annuity contract is not a distribution for purposes of section 401(a)(9).

Q-11. Will a payment by a plan after the death of an employee fail to be treated as a distribution for purposes of section 401(a)(9) solely because it is made to an estate or a trust?

A-11. A payment by a plan after the death of an employee will not fail to be treated as a distribution for purposes of section 401(a)(9) solely because it is made to an estate or a trust. As a result, the estate or trust which receives a payment from a plan after the death of an employee need not distribute the amount of such payment to the beneficiaries of the estate or trust in accordance with section 401(a)(9)(B). Pursuant to A-3 of § 1.401(a)(9)-4, an estate may not be a designated beneficiary. Thus, pursuant to A-4 of § 1.401(a)(9)-3, distribution to the estate must satisfy the 5-year rule in section 401(a)(9)(B)(iii) if the distribution to the employee had not begun (as defined in A-6 of § 1.401(a)(9)-2) as of the employee's date of death. However, see A-5 and A-6 of § 1.401(a)(9)-4 for provisions under which beneficiaries of a trust with respect to the trust's interest in an employee's benefit are treated as having been designated as beneficiaries of the employee under the plan.

Q-12. Will a plan fail to satisfy section 411(d)(6) if the plan is amended to eliminate the availability of an optional form of benefit to the extent that the optional form does not satisfy section 401(a)(9)?

A-12. No, pursuant to section 411(d)(6)(B), a plan will not fail to satisfy section 411(d)(6) merely because the plan is amended to eliminate the availability of an optional form of benefit to the extent that the optional form does not satisfy section 401(a)(9). (See also A-3 of § 1.401(a)(9)-1, which requires a plan to provide that, notwithstanding any other plan provision, it will not distribute benefits under any option that does not satisfy section 401(a)(9).)

Q-13. Is a plan disqualified merely because it pays benefits under a designation made before January 1, 1984, in accordance with section 242(b)(2) of the Tax Equity and Fiscal Responsibility Act (TEFRA)?

A-13. No, even though the distribution requirements added by TEFRA were retroactively repealed by the Tax Reform Act of 1984 (TRA of 1984), the transitional election rule in section 242(b) of TEFRA was preserved. Satisfaction of the spousal consent requirements of section 417(a) and (e) (added by the Retirement Equity Act of 1984) will not be considered a revocation of the pre-1984 designation. However, sections 401(a)(11) and 417 must be satisfied with respect to any distribution subject to those sections. The election provided in section 242(b) of TEFRA is hereafter referred to as a section 242(b)(2) election.

Q-14. If an amount is transferred from one plan (transferor plan) to another plan (transferee plan), may the transferee plan distribute the amount transferred in accordance with a section 242(b)(2) election made under either the transferor plan or under the transferee plan?

A-14. (a) If an amount is transferred from one plan (transferor plan) to another plan (transferee plan), the amount transferred may be distributed in accordance with a section 242(b)(2) election made under the transferor plan if the employee did not elect to have the amount transferred and if the amount transferred is separately accounted for by the transferee plan. However, only the benefit attributable to the amount transferred, plus earnings thereon, may be distributed in accordance with the section 242(b)(2) election made under the transferor plan. If the employee elected to have the amount transferred, the transfer will be treated as a distribution and rollover of the amount transferred for purposes of this section.

(b) In the case in which an amount is transferred from one plan to another plan, the amount transferred may not be distributed in accordance with a section 242(b)(2) election made under the transferee plan. If a section 242(b)(2) election was made under the transferee plan, the amount transferred must be separately accounted for. If the amount transferred is not separately accounted for under the transferee plan, the section 242(b)(2) election under the transferee plan is revoked and section 401(a)(9) will apply to subsequent distributions by the transferee plan.

(c) A merger, spinoff, or consolidation, as defined in § 1.414(l)-1(b), will be treated as a transfer for purposes of the section 242(b)(2) election.

Q-15. If an amount is distributed by one plan (distributing plan) and rolled over into another plan (receiving plan), may the receiving plan distribute the amount rolled over in accordance with a section 242(b)(2) election made under either the distributing plan or the receiving plan?

A-15. No, if an amount is distributed by one plan (distributing plan) and rolled over into another plan (receiving plan), the receiving plan must distribute the amount rolled over in accordance with section 401(a)(9) whether or not the employee made a section 242(b)(2) election under the distributing plan. Further, if the amount rolled over was not distributed in accordance with the election, the election under the distributing plan is revoked and section 401(a)(9) will apply to all subsequent distributions by the distributing plan. Finally, if the employee made a section 242(b)(2) election under the receiving plan and such election is still in effect, the amount rolled over must be separately accounted for under the receiving plan and distributed in accordance with section 401(a)(9). If amounts rolled over are not separately accounted for, any section 242(b)(2) election under the receiving plan is revoked and section 401(a)(9) will apply to subsequent distributions by the receiving plan.

Q-16. May a section 242(b)(2) election be revoked after the date by which distributions are required to commence in order to satisfy section 401(a)(9) and this section of the regulations?

A-16. Yes, a section 242(b)(2) election may be revoked after the date by which distributions are required to commence in order to satisfy section 401(a)(9) and this section of the regulations. However, if the section 242(b)(2) election is revoked after the date by which distributions are required to commence in order to satisfy section 401(a)(9) and this section of the regulations and the total amount of the distributions which would have been required to be made prior to the date of the revocation in order to satisfy section 401(a)(9), but for the section 242(b)(2) election, have not been made, the plan must distribute by the end of the calendar year following the calendar year in which the revocation occurs the total amount not yet distributed which was required to have been distributed to satisfy the requirements of section 401(a)(9) and continue distributions in accordance with such requirements.

T.D. 8987, 4/16/2002, amend T.D. 9130, 6/14/2004.

### § 1.401(a)(9)-9 Life expectancy and distribution period tables.

Q-1. What is the life expectancy for an individual for purposes of determining required minimum distributions under section 401(a)(9)?

A-1. The following table, referred to as the Single Life Table, is used for determining the life expectancy of an individual:

**Single Life Table**

| Age | Life Expectancy | Age | Life Expectancy | Age | Life Expectancy | Age | Life Expectancy |
|---|---|---|---|---|---|---|---|
| 0 | 82.4 | 29 | 54.3 | 58 | 27.0 | 87 | 6.7 |
| 1 | 81.6 | 30 | 53.3 | 59 | 26.1 | 88 | 6.3 |
| 2 | 80.6 | 31 | 52.4 | 60 | 25.2 | 89 | 5.9 |
| 3 | 79.7 | 32 | 51.4 | 61 | 24.4 | 90 | 5.5 |
| 4 | 78.7 | 33 | 50.4 | 62 | 23.5 | 91 | 5.2 |
| 5 | 77.7 | 34 | 49.4 | 63 | 22.7 | 92 | 4.9 |
| 6 | 76.7 | 35 | 48.5 | 64 | 21.8 | 93 | 4.6 |

| | | | | | | | |
|---|---|---|---|---|---|---|---|
| 7 | 75.8 | 36 | 47.5 | 65 | 21.0 | 94 | 4.3 |
| 8 | 74.8 | 37 | 46.5 | 66 | 20.2 | 95 | 4.1 |
| 9 | 73.8 | 38 | 45.6 | 67 | 19.4 | 96 | 3.8 |
| 10 | 72.8 | 39 | 44.6 | 68 | 18.6 | 97 | 3.6 |
| 11 | 71.8 | 40 | 43.6 | 69 | 17.8 | 98 | 3.4 |
| 12 | 70.8 | 41 | 42.7 | 70 | 17.0 | 99 | 3.1 |
| 13 | 69.9 | 42 | 41.7 | 71 | 16.3 | 100 | 2.9 |
| 14 | 68.9 | 43 | 40.7 | 72 | 15.5 | 101 | 2.7 |
| 15 | 67.9 | 44 | 39.8 | 73 | 14.8 | 102 | 2.5 |
| 16 | 66.9 | 45 | 38.8 | 74 | 14.1 | 103 | 2.3 |
| 17 | 66.0 | 46 | 37.9 | 75 | 13.4 | 104 | 2.1 |
| 18 | 65.0 | 47 | 37.0 | 76 | 12.7 | 105 | 1.9 |
| 19 | 64.0 | 48 | 36.0 | 77 | 12.1 | 106 | 1.7 |
| 20 | 63.0 | 49 | 35.1 | 78 | 11.4 | 107 | 1.5 |
| 21 | 62.1 | 50 | 34.2 | 79 | 10.8 | 108 | 1.4 |
| 22 | 61.1 | 51 | 33.3 | 80 | 10.2 | 109 | 1.2 |
| 23 | 60.1 | 52 | 32.3 | 81 | 9.7 | 110 | 1.1 |
| 24 | 59.1 | 53 | 31.4 | 82 | 9.1 | 111+ | 1.0 |
| 25 | 58.2 | 54 | 30.5 | 83 | 8.6 | | |
| 26 | 57.2 | 55 | 29.6 | 84 | 8.1 | | |
| 27 | 56.2 | 56 | 28.7 | 85 | 7.6 | | |
| 28 | 55.3 | 57 | 27.9 | 86 | 7.1 | | |

Q-2. What is the applicable distribution period for an individual account for purposes of determining required minimum distributions during an employee's lifetime under section 401(a)(9)?

A-2. Table for determining distribution period. The following table, referred to as the Uniform Lifetime Table, is used for determining the distribution period for lifetime distributions to an employee in situations in which the employee's spouse is either not the sole designated beneficiary or is the sole designated beneficiary but is not more than 10 years younger than the employee.

**Uniform Lifetime Table**

| Age of employee | Distribution period | Age of employee | Distribution period |
|---|---|---|---|
| 70 | 27.4 | 92 | 10.2 |
| 71 | 26.5 | 93 | 9.6 |
| 72 | 25.6 | 94 | 9.1 |
| 73 | 24.7 | 95 | 8.6 |
| 74 | 23.8 | 96 | 8.1 |
| 75 | 22.9 | 97 | 7.6 |
| 76 | 22.0 | 98 | 7.1 |
| 77 | 21.2 | 99 | 6.7 |
| 78 | 20.3 | 100 | 6.3 |
| 79 | 19.5 | 101 | 5.9 |
| 80 | 18.7 | 102 | 5.5 |
| 81 | 17.9 | 103 | 5.2 |
| 82 | 17.1 | 104 | 4.9 |
| 83 | 16.3 | 105 | 4.5 |
| 84 | 15.5 | 106 | 4.2 |
| 85 | 14.8 | 107 | 3.9 |
| 86 | 14.1 | 108 | 3.7 |
| 87 | 13.4 | 109 | 3.4 |
| 88 | 12.7 | 110 | 3.1 |
| 89 | 12.0 | 111 | 2.9 |
| 90 | 11.4 | 112 | 2.6 |
| 91 | 10.8 | 113 | 2.4 |
| 92 | 10.2 | 114 | 2.1 |
| 93 | 9.6 | 115+ | 1.9 |

Q-3. What is the joint life and last survivor expectancy of an individual and beneficiary for purposes of determining required minimum distributions under section 401(a)(9)?

A-3. The following table, referred to as the Joint and Last Survivor Table, is used for determining the joint and last survivor life expectancy of two individuals:

**Joint and Last Survivor Table**

| AGES | 0 | 1 | 2 | 3 | 4 | 5 | 6 | 7 | 8 | 9 |
|---|---|---|---|---|---|---|---|---|---|---|
| 0 | 90.0 | 89.5 | 89.0 | 88.6 | 88.2 | 87.8 | 87.4 | 87.1 | 86.8 | 86.5 |
| 1 | 89.5 | 89.0 | 88.5 | 88.1 | 87.6 | 87.2 | 86.8 | 86.5 | 86.1 | 85.8 |
| 2 | 89.0 | 88.5 | 88.0 | 87.5 | 87.1 | 86.6 | 86.2 | 85.8 | 85.5 | 85.1 |
| 3 | 88.6 | 88.1 | 87.5 | 87.0 | 86.5 | 86.1 | 85.6 | 85.2 | 84.8 | 84.5 |
| 4 | 88.2 | 87.6 | 87.1 | 86.5 | 86.0 | 85.5 | 85.1 | 84.6 | 84.2 | 83.8 |
| 5 | 87.8 | 87.2 | 86.6 | 86.1 | 85.5 | 85.0 | 84.5 | 84.1 | 83.6 | 83.2 |
| 6 | 87.4 | 86.8 | 86.2 | 85.6 | 85.1 | 84.5 | 84.0 | 83.5 | 83.1 | 82.6 |
| 7 | 87.1 | 86.5 | 85.8 | 85.2 | 84.6 | 84.1 | 83.5 | 83.0 | 82.5 | 82.1 |
| 8 | 86.8 | 86.1 | 85.5 | 84.8 | 84.2 | 83.6 | 83.1 | 82.5 | 82.0 | 81.6 |
| 9 | 86.5 | 85.8 | 85.1 | 84.5 | 83.8 | 83.2 | 82.6 | 82.1 | 81.6 | 81.0 |
| 10 | 86.2 | 85.5 | 84.8 | 84.1 | 83.5 | 82.8 | 82.2 | 81.6 | 81.1 | 80.6 |
| 11 | 85.9 | 85.2 | 84.5 | 83.8 | 83.1 | 82.5 | 81.8 | 81.2 | 80.7 | 80.1 |
| 12 | 85.7 | 84.9 | 84.2 | 83.5 | 82.8 | 82.1 | 81.5 | 80.8 | 80.2 | 79.7 |
| 13 | 85.4 | 84.7 | 84.0 | 83.2 | 82.5 | 81.8 | 81.1 | 80.5 | 79.9 | 79.2 |
| 14 | 85.2 | 84.5 | 83.7 | 83.0 | 82.2 | 81.5 | 80.8 | 80.1 | 79.5 | 78.9 |
| 15 | 85.0 | 84.3 | 83.5 | 82.7 | 82.0 | 81.2 | 80.5 | 79.8 | 79.1 | 78.5 |
| 16 | 84.9 | 84.1 | 83.3 | 82.5 | 81.7 | 81.0 | 80.2 | 79.5 | 78.8 | 78.1 |
| 17 | 84.7 | 83.9 | 83.1 | 82.3 | 81.5 | 80.7 | 80.0 | 79.2 | 78.5 | 77.8 |
| 18 | 84.5 | 83.7 | 82.9 | 82.1 | 81.3 | 80.5 | 79.7 | 79.0 | 78.2 | 77.5 |
| 19 | 84.4 | 83.6 | 82.7 | 81.9 | 81.1 | 80.3 | 79.5 | 78.7 | 78.0 | 77.3 |
| 20 | 84.3 | 83.4 | 82.6 | 81.8 | 80.9 | 80.1 | 79.3 | 78.5 | 77.7 | 77.0 |
| 21 | 84.1 | 83.3 | 82.4 | 81.6 | 80.8 | 79.9 | 79.1 | 78.3 | 77.5 | 76.8 |
| 22 | 84.0 | 83.2 | 82.3 | 81.5 | 80.6 | 79.8 | 78.9 | 78.1 | 77.3 | 76.5 |
| 23 | 83.9 | 83.1 | 82.2 | 81.3 | 80.5 | 79.6 | 78.8 | 77.9 | 77.1 | 76.3 |
| 24 | 83.8 | 83.0 | 82.1 | 81.2 | 80.3 | 79.5 | 78.6 | 77.8 | 76.9 | 76.1 |
| 25 | 83.7 | 82.9 | 82.0 | 81.1 | 80.2 | 79.3 | 78.5 | 77.6 | 76.8 | 75.9 |
| 26 | 83.6 | 82.8 | 81.9 | 81.0 | 80.1 | 79.2 | 78.3 | 77.5 | 76.6 | 75.8 |
| 27 | 83.6 | 82.7 | 81.8 | 80.9 | 80.0 | 79.1 | 78.2 | 77.4 | 76.5 | 75.6 |
| 28 | 83.5 | 82.6 | 81.7 | 80.8 | 79.9 | 79.0 | 78.1 | 77.2 | 76.4 | 75.5 |
| 29 | 83.4 | 82.6 | 81.6 | 80.7 | 79.8 | 78.9 | 78.0 | 77.1 | 76.2 | 75.4 |
| 30 | 83.4 | 82.5 | 81.6 | 80.7 | 79.7 | 78.8 | 77.9 | 77.0 | 76.1 | 75.2 |
| 31 | 83.3 | 82.4 | 81.5 | 80.6 | 79.7 | 78.8 | 77.8 | 76.9 | 76.0 | 75.1 |
| 32 | 83.3 | 82.4 | 81.5 | 80.5 | 79.6 | 78.7 | 77.8 | 76.8 | 75.9 | 75.0 |
| 33 | 83.2 | 82.3 | 81.4 | 80.5 | 79.5 | 78.6 | 77.7 | 76.8 | 75.9 | 74.9 |
| 34 | 83.2 | 82.3 | 81.3 | 80.4 | 79.5 | 78.5 | 77.6 | 76.7 | 75.8 | 74.9 |
| 35 | 83.1 | 82.2 | 81.3 | 80.4 | 79.4 | 78.5 | 77.6 | 76.6 | 75.7 | 74.8 |
| 36 | 83.1 | 82.2 | 81.3 | 80.3 | 79.4 | 78.4 | 77.5 | 76.6 | 75.6 | 74.7 |
| 37 | 83.0 | 82.2 | 81.2 | 80.3 | 79.3 | 78.4 | 77.4 | 76.5 | 75.6 | 74.6 |
| 38 | 83.0 | 82.1 | 81.2 | 80.2 | 79.3 | 78.3 | 77.4 | 76.4 | 75.5 | 74.6 |
| 39 | 83.0 | 82.1 | 81.1 | 80.2 | 79.2 | 78.3 | 77.3 | 76.4 | 75.5 | 74.5 |

| AGES | 0 | 1 | 2 | 3 | 4 | 5 | 6 | 7 | 8 | 9 |
|---|---|---|---|---|---|---|---|---|---|---|
| 40 | 82.9 | 82.1 | 81.1 | 80.2 | 79.2 | 78.3 | 77.3 | 76.4 | 75.4 | 74.5 |
| 41 | 82.9 | 82.0 | 81.1 | 80.1 | 79.2 | 78.2 | 77.3 | 76.3 | 75.4 | 74.4 |
| 42 | 82.9 | 82.0 | 81.1 | 80.1 | 79.1 | 78.2 | 77.2 | 76.3 | 75.3 | 74.4 |
| 43 | 82.9 | 82.0 | 81.0 | 80.1 | 79.1 | 78.2 | 77.2 | 76.2 | 75.3 | 74.3 |
| 44 | 82.8 | 81.9 | 81.0 | 80.0 | 79.1 | 78.1 | 77.2 | 76.2 | 75.3 | 74.3 |
| 45 | 82.8 | 81.9 | 81.0 | 80.0 | 79.1 | 78.1 | 77.1 | 76.2 | 75.2 | 74.3 |
| 46 | 82.8 | 81.9 | 81.0 | 80.0 | 79.0 | 78.1 | 77.1 | 76.1 | 75.2 | 74.3 |
| 47 | 82.8 | 81.9 | 80.9 | 80.0 | 79.0 | 78.0 | 77.1 | 76.1 | 75.2 | 74.2 |
| 48 | 82.8 | 81.9 | 80.9 | 80.0 | 79.0 | 78.0 | 77.1 | 76.1 | 75.2 | 74.2 |
| 49 | 82.7 | 81.8 | 80.9 | 79.9 | 79.0 | 78.0 | 77.0 | 76.1 | 75.1 | 74.2 |
| 50 | 82.7 | 81.8 | 80.9 | 79.9 | 79.0 | 78.0 | 77.0 | 76.0 | 75.1 | 74.1 |
| 51 | 82.7 | 81.8 | 80.9 | 79.9 | 78.9 | 78.0 | 77.0 | 76.0 | 75.1 | 74.1 |
| 52 | 82.7 | 81.8 | 80.9 | 79.9 | 78.9 | 78.0 | 77.0 | 76.0 | 75.1 | 74.1 |
| 53 | 82.7 | 81.8 | 80.8 | 79.9 | 78.9 | 77.9 | 77.0 | 76.0 | 75.0 | 74.1 |
| 54 | 82.7 | 81.8 | 80.8 | 79.9 | 78.9 | 77.9 | 76.9 | 76.0 | 75.0 | 74.0 |
| 55 | 82.6 | 81.8 | 80.8 | 79.8 | 78.9 | 77.9 | 76.9 | 76.0 | 75.0 | 74.0 |
| 56 | 82.6 | 81.7 | 80.8 | 79.8 | 78.9 | 77.9 | 76.9 | 76.0 | 75.0 | 74.0 |
| 57 | 82.6 | 81.7 | 80.8 | 79.8 | 78.9 | 77.9 | 76.9 | 75.9 | 75.0 | 74.0 |
| 58 | 82.6 | 81.7 | 80.8 | 79.8 | 78.8 | 77.9 | 76.9 | 75.9 | 75.0 | 74.0 |
| 59 | 82.6 | 81.7 | 80.8 | 79.8 | 78.8 | 77.9 | 76.9 | 75.9 | 74.9 | 74.0 |
| 60 | 82.6 | 81.7 | 80.8 | 79.8 | 78.8 | 77.8 | 76.9 | 75.9 | 74.9 | 73.9 |

| | | | | | | | | | | |
|---|---|---|---|---|---|---|---|---|---|---|
| 61 | 82.6 | 81.7 | 80.8 | 79.8 | 78.8 | 77.8 | 76.9 | 75.9 | 74.9 | 73.9 |
| 62 | 82.6 | 81.7 | 80.7 | 79.8 | 78.8 | 77.8 | 76.9 | 75.9 | 74.9 | 73.9 |
| 63 | 82.6 | 81.7 | 80.7 | 79.8 | 78.8 | 77.8 | 76.8 | 75.9 | 74.9 | 73.9 |
| 64 | 82.5 | 81.7 | 80.7 | 79.8 | 78.8 | 77.8 | 76.8 | 75.9 | 74.9 | 73.9 |
| 65 | 82.5 | 81.7 | 80.7 | 79.8 | 78.8 | 77.8 | 76.8 | 75.8 | 74.9 | 73.9 |
| 66 | 82.5 | 81.7 | 80.7 | 79.7 | 78.8 | 77.8 | 76.8 | 75.8 | 74.9 | 73.9 |
| 67 | 82.5 | 81.7 | 80.7 | 79.7 | 78.8 | 77.8 | 76.8 | 75.8 | 74.9 | 73.9 |
| 68 | 82.5 | 81.6 | 80.7 | 79.7 | 78.8 | 77.8 | 76.8 | 75.8 | 74.8 | 73.9 |
| 69 | 82.5 | 81.6 | 80.7 | 79.7 | 78.8 | 77.8 | 76.8 | 75.8 | 74.8 | 73.9 |
| 70 | 82.5 | 81.6 | 80.7 | 79.7 | 78.8 | 77.8 | 76.8 | 75.8 | 74.8 | 73.9 |
| 71 | 82.5 | 81.6 | 80.7 | 79.7 | 78.7 | 77.8 | 76.8 | 75.8 | 74.8 | 73.8 |
| 72 | 82.5 | 81.6 | 80.7 | 79.7 | 78.7 | 77.8 | 76.8 | 75.8 | 74.8 | 73.8 |
| 73 | 82.5 | 81.6 | 80.7 | 79.7 | 78.7 | 77.8 | 76.8 | 75.8 | 74.8 | 73.8 |
| 74 | 82.5 | 81.6 | 80.7 | 79.7 | 78.7 | 77.8 | 76.8 | 75.8 | 74.8 | 73.8 |
| 75 | 82.5 | 81.6 | 80.7 | 79.7 | 78.7 | 77.8 | 76.8 | 75.8 | 74.8 | 73.8 |
| 76 | 82.5 | 81.6 | 80.7 | 79.7 | 78.7 | 77.8 | 76.8 | 75.8 | 74.8 | 73.8 |
| 77 | 82.5 | 81.6 | 80.7 | 79.7 | 78.7 | 77.7 | 76.8 | 75.8 | 74.8 | 73.8 |
| 78 | 82.5 | 81.6 | 80.7 | 79.7 | 78.7 | 77.7 | 76.8 | 75.8 | 74.8 | 73.8 |
| 79 | 82.5 | 81.6 | 80.7 | 79.7 | 78.7 | 77.7 | 76.8 | 75.8 | 74.8 | 73.8 |

| AGES | 0 | 1 | 2 | 3 | 4 | 5 | 6 | 7 | 8 | 9 |
|---|---|---|---|---|---|---|---|---|---|---|
| 80 | 82.5 | 81.6 | 80.7 | 79.7 | 78.7 | 77.7 | 76.8 | 75.8 | 74.8 | 73.8 |
| 81 | 82.4 | 81.6 | 80.7 | 79.7 | 78.7 | 77.7 | 76.8 | 75.8 | 74.8 | 73.8 |
| 82 | 82.4 | 81.6 | 80.7 | 79.7 | 78.7 | 77.7 | 76.8 | 75.8 | 74.8 | 73.8 |
| 83 | 82.4 | 81.6 | 80.7 | 79.7 | 78.7 | 77.7 | 76.8 | 75.8 | 74.8 | 73.8 |
| 84 | 82.4 | 81.6 | 80.7 | 79.7 | 78.7 | 77.7 | 76.8 | 75.8 | 74.8 | 73.8 |
| 85 | 82.4 | 81.6 | 80.6 | 79.7 | 78.7 | 77.7 | 76.8 | 75.8 | 74.8 | 73.8 |
| 86 | 82.4 | 81.6 | 80.6 | 79.7 | 78.7 | 77.7 | 76.7 | 75.8 | 74.8 | 73.8 |
| 87 | 82.4 | 81.6 | 80.6 | 79.7 | 78.7 | 77.7 | 76.7 | 75.8 | 74.8 | 73.8 |
| 88 | 82.4 | 81.6 | 80.6 | 79.7 | 78.7 | 77.7 | 76.7 | 75.8 | 74.8 | 73.8 |
| 89 | 82.4 | 81.6 | 80.6 | 79.7 | 78.7 | 77.7 | 76.7 | 75.8 | 74.8 | 73.8 |
| 90 | 82.4 | 81.6 | 80.6 | 79.7 | 78.7 | 77.7 | 76.7 | 75.8 | 74.8 | 73.8 |
| 91 | 82.4 | 81.6 | 80.6 | 79.7 | 78.7 | 77.7 | 76.7 | 75.8 | 74.8 | 73.8 |
| 92 | 82.4 | 81.6 | 80.6 | 79.7 | 78.7 | 77.7 | 76.7 | 75.8 | 74.8 | 73.8 |
| 93 | 82.4 | 81.6 | 80.6 | 79.7 | 78.7 | 77.7 | 76.7 | 75.8 | 74.8 | 73.8 |
| 94 | 82.4 | 81.6 | 80.6 | 79.7 | 78.7 | 77.7 | 76.7 | 75.8 | 74.8 | 73.8 |
| 95 | 82.4 | 81.6 | 80.6 | 79.7 | 78.7 | 77.7 | 76.7 | 75.8 | 74.8 | 73.8 |
| 96 | 82.4 | 81.6 | 80.6 | 79.7 | 78.7 | 77.7 | 76.7 | 75.8 | 74.8 | 73.8 |
| 97 | 82.4 | 81.6 | 80.6 | 79.7 | 78.7 | 77.7 | 76.7 | 75.8 | 74.8 | 73.8 |
| 98 | 82.4 | 81.6 | 80.6 | 79.7 | 78.7 | 77.7 | 76.7 | 75.8 | 74.8 | 73.8 |
| 99 | 82.4 | 81.6 | 80.6 | 79.7 | 78.7 | 77.7 | 76.7 | 75.8 | 74.8 | 73.8 |
| 100 | 82.4 | 81.6 | 80.6 | 79.7 | 78.7 | 77.7 | 76.7 | 75.8 | 74.8 | 73.8 |
| 101 | 82.4 | 81.6 | 80.6 | 79.7 | 78.7 | 77.7 | 76.7 | 75.8 | 74.8 | 73.8 |
| 102 | 82.4 | 81.6 | 80.6 | 79.7 | 78.7 | 77.7 | 76.7 | 75.8 | 74.8 | 73.8 |
| 103 | 82.4 | 81.6 | 80.6 | 79.7 | 78.7 | 77.7 | 76.7 | 75.8 | 74.8 | 73.8 |
| 104 | 82.4 | 81.6 | 80.6 | 79.7 | 78.7 | 77.7 | 76.7 | 75.8 | 74.8 | 73.8 |
| 105 | 82.4 | 81.6 | 80.6 | 79.7 | 78.7 | 77.7 | 76.7 | 75.8 | 74.8 | 73.8 |
| 106 | 82.4 | 81.6 | 80.6 | 79.7 | 78.7 | 77.7 | 76.7 | 75.8 | 74.8 | 73.8 |
| 107 | 82.4 | 81.6 | 80.6 | 79.7 | 78.7 | 77.7 | 76.7 | 75.8 | 74.8 | 73.8 |
| 108 | 82.4 | 81.6 | 80.6 | 79.7 | 78.7 | 77.7 | 76.7 | 75.8 | 74.8 | 73.8 |
| 109 | 82.4 | 81.6 | 80.6 | 79.7 | 78.7 | 77.7 | 76.7 | 75.8 | 74.8 | 73.8 |
| 110 | 82.4 | 81.6 | 80.6 | 79.7 | 78.7 | 77.7 | 76.7 | 75.8 | 74.8 | 73.8 |
| 111 | 82.4 | 81.6 | 80.6 | 79.7 | 78.7 | 77.7 | 76.7 | 75.8 | 74.8 | 73.8 |
| 112 | 82.4 | 81.6 | 80.6 | 79.7 | 78.7 | 77.7 | 76.7 | 75.8 | 74.8 | 73.8 |
| 113 | 82.4 | 81.6 | 80.6 | 79.7 | 78.7 | 77.7 | 76.7 | 75.8 | 74.8 | 73.8 |
| 114 | 82.4 | 81.6 | 80.6 | 79.7 | 78.7 | 77.7 | 76.7 | 75.8 | 74.8 | 73.8 |
| 115+ | 82.4 | 81.6 | 80.6 | 79.7 | 78.7 | 77.7 | 76.7 | 75.8 | 74.8 | 73.8 |

| AGES | 10 | 11 | 12 | 13 | 14 | 15 | 16 | 17 | 18 | 19 |
|---|---|---|---|---|---|---|---|---|---|---|
| 10 | 80.0 | 79.6 | 79.1 | 78.7 | 78.2 | 77.9 | 77.5 | 77.2 | 76.8 | 76.5 |
| 11 | 79.6 | 79.0 | 78.6 | 78.1 | 77.7 | 77.3 | 76.9 | 76.5 | 76.2 | 75.8 |
| 12 | 79.1 | 78.6 | 78.1 | 77.6 | 77.1 | 76.7 | 76.3 | 75.9 | 75.5 | 75.2 |
| 13 | 78.7 | 78.1 | 77.6 | 77.1 | 76.6 | 76.1 | 75.7 | 75.3 | 74.9 | 74.5 |
| 14 | 78.2 | 77.7 | 77.1 | 76.6 | 76.1 | 75.6 | 75.1 | 74.7 | 74.3 | 73.9 |
| 15 | 77.9 | 77.3 | 76.7 | 76.1 | 75.6 | 75.1 | 74.6 | 74.1 | 73.7 | 73.3 |
| 16 | 77.5 | 76.9 | 76.3 | 75.7 | 75.1 | 74.6 | 74.1 | 73.6 | 73.1 | 72.7 |

| | | | | | | | | | | |
|---|---|---|---|---|---|---|---|---|---|---|
| 17 | 77.2 | 76.5 | 75.9 | 75.3 | 74.7 | 74.1 | 73.6 | 73.1 | 72.6 | 72.1 |
| 18 | 76.8 | 76.2 | 75.5 | 74.9 | 74.3 | 73.7 | 73.1 | 72.6 | 72.1 | 71.6 |
| 19 | 76.5 | 75.8 | 75.2 | 74.5 | 73.9 | 73.3 | 72.7 | 72.1 | 71.6 | 71.1 |
| 20 | 76.3 | 75.5 | 74.8 | 74.2 | 73.5 | 72.9 | 72.3 | 71.7 | 71.1 | 70.6 |
| 21 | 76.0 | 75.3 | 74.5 | 73.8 | 73.2 | 72.5 | 71.9 | 71.3 | 70.7 | 70.1 |
| 22 | 75.8 | 75.0 | 74.3 | 73.5 | 72.9 | 72.2 | 71.5 | 70.9 | 70.3 | 69.7 |
| 23 | 75.5 | 74.8 | 74.0 | 73.3 | 72.6 | 71.9 | 71.2 | 70.5 | 69.9 | 69.3 |
| 24 | 75.3 | 74.5 | 73.8 | 73.0 | 72.3 | 71.6 | 70.9 | 70.2 | 69.5 | 68.9 |
| 25 | 75.1 | 74.3 | 73.5 | 72.8 | 72.0 | 71.3 | 70.6 | 69.9 | 69.2 | 68.5 |
| 26 | 75.0 | 74.1 | 73.3 | 72.5 | 71.8 | 71.0 | 70.3 | 69.6 | 68.9 | 68.2 |
| 27 | 74.8 | 74.0 | 73.1 | 72.3 | 71.6 | 70.8 | 70.0 | 69.3 | 68.6 | 67.9 |
| 28 | 74.6 | 73.8 | 73.0 | 72.2 | 71.3 | 70.6 | 69.8 | 69.0 | 68.3 | 67.6 |
| 29 | 74.5 | 73.6 | 72.8 | 72.0 | 71.2 | 70.4 | 69.6 | 68.8 | 68.0 | 67.3 |
| 30 | 74.4 | 73.5 | 72.7 | 71.8 | 71.0 | 70.2 | 69.4 | 68.6 | 67.8 | 67.1 |
| 31 | 74.3 | 73.4 | 72.5 | 71.7 | 70.8 | 70.0 | 69.2 | 68.4 | 67.6 | 66.8 |
| 32 | 74.1 | 73.3 | 72.4 | 71.5 | 70.7 | 69.8 | 69.0 | 68.2 | 67.4 | 66.6 |
| 33 | 74.0 | 73.2 | 72.3 | 71.4 | 70.5 | 69.7 | 68.8 | 68.0 | 67.2 | 66.4 |
| 34 | 73.9 | 73.0 | 72.2 | 71.3 | 70.4 | 69.5 | 68.7 | 67.8 | 67.0 | 66.2 |
| 35 | 73.9 | 73.0 | 72.1 | 71.2 | 70.3 | 69.4 | 68.5 | 67.7 | 66.8 | 66.0 |
| 36 | 73.8 | 72.9 | 72.0 | 71.1 | 70.2 | 69.3 | 68.4 | 67.6 | 66.7 | 65.9 |
| 37 | 73.7 | 72.8 | 71.9 | 71.0 | 70.1 | 69.2 | 68.3 | 67.4 | 66.6 | 65.7 |
| 38 | 73.6 | 72.7 | 71.8 | 70.9 | 70.0 | 69.1 | 68.2 | 67.3 | 66.4 | 65.6 |
| 39 | 73.6 | 72.7 | 71.7 | 70.8 | 69.9 | 69.0 | 68.1 | 67.2 | 66.3 | 65.4 |
| 40 | 73.5 | 72.6 | 71.7 | 70.7 | 69.8 | 68.9 | 68.0 | 67.1 | 66.2 | 65.3 |
| 41 | 73.5 | 72.5 | 71.6 | 70.7 | 69.7 | 68.8 | 67.9 | 67.0 | 66.1 | 65.2 |
| 42 | 73.4 | 72.5 | 71.5 | 70.6 | 69.7 | 68.8 | 67.8 | 66.9 | 66.0 | 65.1 |
| 43 | 73.4 | 72.4 | 71.5 | 70.6 | 69.6 | 68.7 | 67.8 | 66.8 | 65.9 | 65.0 |
| 44 | 73.3 | 72.4 | 71.4 | 70.5 | 69.6 | 68.6 | 67.7 | 66.8 | 65.9 | 64.9 |
| 45 | 73.3 | 72.3 | 71.4 | 70.5 | 69.5 | 68.6 | 67.6 | 66.7 | 65.8 | 64.9 |
| 46 | 73.3 | 72.3 | 71.4 | 70.4 | 69.5 | 68.5 | 67.6 | 66.6 | 65.7 | 64.8 |
| 47 | 73.2 | 72.3 | 71.3 | 70.4 | 69.4 | 68.5 | 67.5 | 66.6 | 65.7 | 64.7 |
| 48 | 73.2 | 72.2 | 71.3 | 70.3 | 69.4 | 68.4 | 67.5 | 66.5 | 65.6 | 64.7 |
| 49 | 73.2 | 72.2 | 71.2 | 70.3 | 69.3 | 68.4 | 67.4 | 66.5 | 65.6 | 64.6 |

| AGES | 10 | 11 | 12 | 13 | 14 | 15 | 16 | 17 | 18 | 19 |
|---|---|---|---|---|---|---|---|---|---|---|
| 50 | 73.1 | 72.2 | 71.2 | 70.3 | 69.3 | 68.4 | 67.4 | 66.5 | 65.5 | 64.6 |
| 51 | 73.1 | 72.2 | 71.2 | 70.2 | 69.3 | 68.3 | 67.4 | 66.4 | 65.5 | 64.5 |
| 52 | 73.1 | 72.1 | 71.2 | 70.2 | 69.2 | 68.3 | 67.3 | 66.4 | 65.4 | 64.5 |
| 53 | 73.1 | 72.1 | 71.1 | 70.2 | 69.2 | 68.3 | 67.3 | 66.3 | 65.4 | 64.4 |
| 54 | 73.1 | 72.1 | 71.1 | 70.2 | 69.2 | 68.2 | 67.3 | 66.3 | 65.4 | 64.4 |
| 55 | 73.0 | 72.1 | 71.1 | 70.1 | 69.2 | 68.2 | 67.2 | 66.3 | 65.3 | 64.4 |
| 56 | 73.0 | 72.1 | 71.1 | 70.1 | 69.1 | 68.2 | 67.2 | 66.3 | 65.3 | 64.3 |
| 57 | 73.0 | 72.0 | 71.1 | 70.1 | 69.1 | 68.2 | 67.2 | 66.2 | 65.3 | 64.3 |
| 58 | 73.0 | 72.0 | 71.0 | 70.1 | 69.1 | 68.1 | 67.2 | 66.2 | 65.2 | 64.3 |
| 59 | 73.0 | 72.0 | 71.0 | 70.1 | 69.1 | 68.1 | 67.2 | 66.2 | 65.2 | 64.3 |
| 60 | 73.0 | 72.0 | 71.0 | 70.0 | 69.1 | 68.1 | 67.1 | 66.2 | 65.2 | 64.2 |
| 61 | 73.0 | 72.0 | 71.0 | 70.0 | 69.1 | 68.1 | 67.1 | 66.2 | 65.2 | 64.2 |
| 62 | 72.9 | 72.0 | 71.0 | 70.0 | 69.0 | 68.1 | 67.1 | 66.1 | 65.2 | 64.2 |
| 63 | 72.9 | 72.0 | 71.0 | 70.0 | 69.0 | 68.1 | 67.1 | 66.1 | 65.2 | 64.2 |
| 64 | 72.9 | 71.9 | 71.0 | 70.0 | 69.0 | 68.0 | 67.1 | 66.1 | 65.1 | 64.2 |
| 65 | 72.9 | 71.9 | 71.0 | 70.0 | 69.0 | 68.0 | 67.1 | 66.1 | 65.1 | 64.2 |
| 66 | 72.9 | 71.9 | 70.9 | 70.0 | 69.0 | 68.0 | 67.1 | 66.1 | 65.1 | 64.1 |
| 67 | 72.9 | 71.9 | 70.9 | 70.0 | 69.0 | 68.0 | 67.0 | 66.1 | 65.1 | 64.1 |
| 68 | 72.9 | 71.9 | 70.9 | 70.0 | 69.0 | 68.0 | 67.0 | 66.1 | 65.1 | 64.1 |
| 69 | 72.9 | 71.9 | 70.9 | 69.9 | 69.0 | 68.0 | 67.0 | 66.1 | 65.1 | 64.1 |
| 70 | 72.9 | 71.9 | 70.9 | 69.9 | 69.0 | 68.0 | 67.0 | 66.0 | 65.1 | 64.1 |
| 71 | 72.9 | 71.9 | 70.9 | 69.9 | 69.0 | 68.0 | 67.0 | 66.0 | 65.1 | 64.1 |
| 72 | 72.9 | 71.9 | 70.9 | 69.9 | 69.0 | 68.0 | 67.0 | 66.0 | 65.1 | 64.1 |
| 73 | 72.9 | 71.9 | 70.9 | 69.9 | 68.9 | 68.0 | 67.0 | 66.0 | 65.0 | 64.1 |
| 74 | 72.9 | 71.9 | 70.9 | 69.9 | 68.9 | 68.0 | 67.0 | 66.0 | 65.0 | 64.1 |
| 75 | 72.8 | 71.9 | 70.9 | 69.9 | 68.9 | 68.0 | 67.0 | 66.0 | 65.0 | 64.1 |
| 76 | 72.8 | 71.9 | 70.9 | 69.9 | 68.9 | 68.0 | 67.0 | 66.0 | 65.0 | 64.1 |
| 77 | 72.8 | 71.9 | 70.9 | 69.9 | 68.9 | 68.0 | 67.0 | 66.0 | 65.0 | 64.1 |
| 78 | 72.8 | 71.9 | 70.9 | 69.9 | 68.9 | 67.9 | 67.0 | 66.0 | 65.0 | 64.0 |
| 79 | 72.8 | 71.9 | 70.9 | 69.9 | 68.9 | 67.9 | 67.0 | 66.0 | 65.0 | 64.0 |
| 80 | 72.8 | 71.9 | 70.9 | 69.9 | 68.9 | 67.9 | 67.0 | 66.0 | 65.0 | 64.0 |

| | | | | | | | | | | |
|---|---|---|---|---|---|---|---|---|---|---|
| 81 | 72.8 | 71.8 | 70.9 | 69.9 | 68.9 | 67.9 | 67.0 | 66.0 | 65.0 | 64.0 |
| 82 | 72.8 | 71.8 | 70.9 | 69.9 | 68.9 | 67.9 | 67.0 | 66.0 | 65.0 | 64.0 |
| 83 | 72.8 | 71.8 | 70.9 | 69.9 | 68.9 | 67.9 | 67.0 | 66.0 | 65.0 | 64.0 |
| 84 | 72.8 | 71.8 | 70.9 | 69.9 | 68.9 | 67.9 | 67.0 | 66.0 | 65.0 | 64.0 |
| 85 | 72.8 | 71.8 | 70.9 | 69.9 | 68.9 | 67.9 | 66.9 | 66.0 | 65.0 | 64.0 |
| 86 | 72.8 | 71.8 | 70.9 | 69.9 | 68.9 | 67.9 | 66.9 | 66.0 | 65.0 | 64.0 |
| 87 | 72.8 | 71.8 | 70.9 | 69.9 | 68.9 | 67.9 | 66.9 | 66.0 | 65.0 | 64.0 |
| 88 | 72.8 | 71.8 | 70.9 | 69.9 | 68.9 | 67.9 | 66.9 | 66.0 | 65.0 | 64.0 |
| 89 | 72.8 | 71.8 | 70.9 | 69.9 | 68.9 | 67.9 | 66.9 | 66.0 | 65.0 | 64.0 |

| AGES | 10 | 11 | 12 | 13 | 14 | 15 | 16 | 17 | 18 | 19 |
|---|---|---|---|---|---|---|---|---|---|---|
| 90 | 72.8 | 71.8 | 70.9 | 69.9 | 68.9 | 67.9 | 66.9 | 66.0 | 65.0 | 64.0 |
| 91 | 72.8 | 71.8 | 70.9 | 69.9 | 68.9 | 67.9 | 66.9 | 66.0 | 65.0 | 64.0 |
| 92 | 72.8 | 71.8 | 70.9 | 69.9 | 68.9 | 67.9 | 66.9 | 66.0 | 65.0 | 64.0 |
| 93 | 72.8 | 71.8 | 70.9 | 69.9 | 68.9 | 67.9 | 66.9 | 66.0 | 65.0 | 64.0 |
| 94 | 72.8 | 71.8 | 70.8 | 69.9 | 68.9 | 67.9 | 66.9 | 66.0 | 65.0 | 64.0 |
| 95 | 72.8 | 71.8 | 70.8 | 69.9 | 68.9 | 67.9 | 66.9 | 66.0 | 65.0 | 64.0 |
| 96 | 72.8 | 71.8 | 70.8 | 69.9 | 68.9 | 67.9 | 66.9 | 66.0 | 65.0 | 64.0 |
| 97 | 72.8 | 71.8 | 70.8 | 69.9 | 68.9 | 67.9 | 66.9 | 66.0 | 65.0 | 64.0 |
| 98 | 72.8 | 71.8 | 70.8 | 69.9 | 68.9 | 67.9 | 66.9 | 66.0 | 65.0 | 64.0 |
| 99 | 72.8 | 71.8 | 70.8 | 69.9 | 68.9 | 67.9 | 66.9 | 66.0 | 65.0 | 64.0 |
| 100 | 72.8 | 71.8 | 70.8 | 69.9 | 68.9 | 67.9 | 66.9 | 66.0 | 65.0 | 64.0 |
| 101 | 72.8 | 71.8 | 70.8 | 69.9 | 68.9 | 67.9 | 66.9 | 66.0 | 65.0 | 64.0 |
| 102 | 72.8 | 71.8 | 70.8 | 69.9 | 68.9 | 67.9 | 66.9 | 66.0 | 65.0 | 64.0 |
| 103 | 72.8 | 71.8 | 70.8 | 69.9 | 68.9 | 67.9 | 66.9 | 66.0 | 65.0 | 64.0 |
| 104 | 72.8 | 71.8 | 70.8 | 69.9 | 68.9 | 67.9 | 66.9 | 66.0 | 65.0 | 64.0 |
| 105 | 72.8 | 71.8 | 70.8 | 69.9 | 68.9 | 67.9 | 66.9 | 66.0 | 65.0 | 64.0 |
| 106 | 72.8 | 71.8 | 70.8 | 69.9 | 68.9 | 67.9 | 66.9 | 66.0 | 65.0 | 64.0 |
| 107 | 72.8 | 71.8 | 70.8 | 69.9 | 68.9 | 67.9 | 66.9 | 66.0 | 65.0 | 64.0 |
| 108 | 72.8 | 71.8 | 70.8 | 69.9 | 68.9 | 67.9 | 66.9 | 66.0 | 65.0 | 64.0 |
| 109 | 72.8 | 71.8 | 70.8 | 69.9 | 68.9 | 67.9 | 66.9 | 66.0 | 65.0 | 64.0 |
| 110 | 72.8 | 71.8 | 70.8 | 69.9 | 68.9 | 67.9 | 66.9 | 66.0 | 65.0 | 64.0 |
| 111 | 72.8 | 71.8 | 70.8 | 69.9 | 68.9 | 67.9 | 66.9 | 66.0 | 65.0 | 64.0 |
| 112 | 72.8 | 71.8 | 70.8 | 69.9 | 68.9 | 67.9 | 66.9 | 66.0 | 65.0 | 64.0 |
| 113 | 72.8 | 71.8 | 70.8 | 69.9 | 68.9 | 67.9 | 66.9 | 66.0 | 65.0 | 64.0 |
| 114 | 72.8 | 71.8 | 70.8 | 69.9 | 68.9 | 67.9 | 66.9 | 66.0 | 65.0 | 64.0 |
| 115+ | 72.8 | 71.8 | 70.8 | 69.9 | 68.9 | 67.9 | 66.9 | 66.0 | 65.0 | 64.0 |

| AGES | 20 | 21 | 22 | 23 | 24 | 25 | 26 | 27 | 28 | 29 |
|---|---|---|---|---|---|---|---|---|---|---|
| 20 | 70.1 | 69.6 | 69.1 | 68.7 | 68.3 | 67.9 | 67.5 | 67.2 | 66.9 | 66.6 |
| 21 | 69.6 | 69.1 | 68.6 | 68.2 | 67.7 | 67.3 | 66.9 | 66.6 | 66.2 | 65.9 |
| 22 | 69.1 | 68.6 | 68.1 | 67.6 | 67.2 | 66.7 | 66.3 | 65.9 | 65.6 | 65.2 |
| 23 | 68.7 | 68.2 | 67.6 | 67.1 | 66.6 | 66.2 | 65.7 | 65.3 | 64.9 | 64.6 |
| 24 | 68.3 | 67.7 | 67.2 | 66.6 | 66.1 | 65.6 | 65.2 | 64.7 | 64.3 | 63.9 |
| 25 | 67.9 | 67.3 | 66.7 | 66.2 | 65.6 | 65.1 | 64.6 | 64.2 | 63.7 | 63.3 |
| 26 | 67.5 | 66.9 | 66.3 | 65.7 | 65.2 | 64.6 | 64.1 | 63.6 | 63.2 | 62.8 |
| 27 | 67.2 | 66.6 | 65.9 | 65.3 | 64.7 | 64.2 | 63.6 | 63.1 | 62.7 | 62.2 |
| 28 | 66.9 | 66.2 | 65.6 | 64.9 | 64.3 | 63.7 | 63.2 | 62.7 | 62.1 | 61.7 |
| 29 | 66.6 | 65.9 | 65.2 | 64.6 | 63.9 | 63.3 | 62.8 | 62.2 | 61.7 | 61.2 |
| 30 | 66.3 | 65.6 | 64.9 | 64.2 | 63.6 | 62.9 | 62.3 | 61.8 | 61.2 | 60.7 |
| 31 | 66.1 | 65.3 | 64.6 | 63.9 | 63.2 | 62.6 | 62.0 | 61.4 | 60.8 | 60.2 |
| 32 | 65.8 | 65.1 | 64.3 | 63.6 | 62.9 | 62.2 | 61.6 | 61.0 | 60.4 | 59.8 |
| 33 | 65.6 | 64.8 | 64.1 | 63.3 | 62.6 | 61.9 | 61.3 | 60.6 | 60.0 | 59.4 |
| 34 | 65.4 | 64.6 | 63.8 | 63.1 | 62.3 | 61.6 | 60.9 | 60.3 | 59.6 | 59.0 |
| 35 | 65.2 | 64.4 | 63.6 | 62.8 | 62.1 | 61.4 | 60.6 | 59.9 | 59.3 | 58.6 |
| 36 | 65.0 | 64.2 | 63.4 | 62.6 | 61.9 | 61.1 | 60.4 | 59.6 | 59.0 | 58.3 |
| 37 | 64.9 | 64.0 | 63.2 | 62.4 | 61.6 | 60.9 | 60.1 | 59.4 | 58.7 | 58.0 |
| 38 | 64.7 | 63.9 | 63.0 | 62.2 | 61.4 | 60.6 | 59.9 | 59.1 | 58.4 | 57.7 |
| 39 | 64.6 | 63.7 | 62.9 | 62.1 | 61.2 | 60.4 | 59.6 | 58.9 | 58.1 | 57.4 |
| 40 | 64.4 | 63.6 | 62.7 | 61.9 | 61.1 | 60.2 | 59.4 | 58.7 | 57.9 | 57.1 |
| 41 | 64.3 | 63.5 | 62.6 | 61.7 | 60.9 | 60.1 | 59.3 | 58.5 | 57.7 | 56.9 |
| 42 | 64.2 | 63.3 | 62.5 | 61.6 | 60.8 | 59.9 | 59.1 | 58.3 | 57.5 | 56.7 |
| 43 | 64.1 | 63.2 | 62.4 | 61.5 | 60.6 | 59.8 | 58.9 | 58.1 | 57.3 | 56.5 |
| 44 | 64.0 | 63.1 | 62.2 | 61.4 | 60.5 | 59.6 | 58.8 | 57.9 | 57.1 | 56.3 |
| 45 | 64.0 | 63.0 | 62.2 | 61.3 | 60.4 | 59.5 | 58.6 | 57.8 | 56.9 | 56.1 |
| 46 | 63.9 | 63.0 | 62.1 | 61.2 | 60.3 | 59.4 | 58.5 | 57.7 | 56.8 | 56.0 |

| | | | | | | | | | | |
|---|---|---|---|---|---|---|---|---|---|---|
| 47 | 63.8 | 62.9 | 62.0 | 61.1 | 60.2 | 59.3 | 58.4 | 57.5 | 56.7 | 55.8 |
| 48 | 63.7 | 62.8 | 61.9 | 61.0 | 60.1 | 59.2 | 58.3 | 57.4 | 56.5 | 55.7 |
| 49 | 63.7 | 62.8 | 61.8 | 60.9 | 60.0 | 59.1 | 58.2 | 57.3 | 56.4 | 55.6 |
| 50 | 63.6 | 62.7 | 61.8 | 60.8 | 59.9 | 59.0 | 58.1 | 57.2 | 56.3 | 55.4 |
| 51 | 63.6 | 62.6 | 61.7 | 60.8 | 59.9 | 58.9 | 58.0 | 57.1 | 56.2 | 55.3 |
| 52 | 63.5 | 62.6 | 61.7 | 60.7 | 59.8 | 58.9 | 58.0 | 57.1 | 56.1 | 55.2 |
| 53 | 63.5 | 62.5 | 61.6 | 60.7 | 59.7 | 58.8 | 57.9 | 57.0 | 56.1 | 55.2 |
| 54 | 63.5 | 62.5 | 61.6 | 60.6 | 59.7 | 58.8 | 57.8 | 56.9 | 56.0 | 55.1 |
| 55 | 63.4 | 62.5 | 61.5 | 60.6 | 59.6 | 58.7 | 57.8 | 56.8 | 55.9 | 55.0 |
| 56 | 63.4 | 62.4 | 61.5 | 60.5 | 59.6 | 58.7 | 57.7 | 56.8 | 55.9 | 54.9 |
| 57 | 63.4 | 62.4 | 61.5 | 60.5 | 59.6 | 58.6 | 57.7 | 56.7 | 55.8 | 54.9 |
| 58 | 63.3 | 62.4 | 61.4 | 60.5 | 59.5 | 58.6 | 57.6 | 56.7 | 55.8 | 54.8 |
| 59 | 63.3 | 62.3 | 61.4 | 60.4 | 59.5 | 58.5 | 57.6 | 56.7 | 55.7 | 54.8 |
| AGES | 20 | 21 | 22 | 23 | 24 | 25 | 26 | 27 | 28 | 29 |
| 60 | 63.3 | 62.3 | 61.4 | 60.4 | 59.5 | 58.5 | 57.6 | 56.6 | 55.7 | 54.7 |
| 61 | 63.3 | 62.3 | 61.3 | 60.4 | 59.4 | 58.5 | 57.5 | 56.6 | 55.6 | 54.7 |
| 62 | 63.2 | 62.3 | 61.3 | 60.4 | 59.4 | 58.4 | 57.5 | 56.5 | 55.6 | 54.7 |
| 63 | 63.2 | 62.3 | 61.3 | 60.3 | 59.4 | 58.4 | 57.5 | 56.5 | 55.6 | 54.6 |
| 64 | 63.2 | 62.2 | 61.3 | 60.3 | 59.4 | 58.4 | 57.4 | 56.5 | 55.5 | 54.6 |
| 65 | 63.2 | 62.2 | 61.3 | 60.3 | 59.3 | 58.4 | 57.4 | 56.5 | 55.5 | 54.6 |
| 66 | 63.2 | 62.2 | 61.2 | 60.3 | 59.3 | 58.4 | 57.4 | 56.4 | 55.5 | 54.5 |
| 67 | 63.2 | 62.2 | 61.2 | 60.3 | 59.3 | 58.3 | 57.4 | 56.4 | 55.5 | 54.5 |
| 68 | 63.1 | 62.2 | 61.2 | 60.2 | 59.3 | 58.3 | 57.4 | 56.4 | 55.4 | 54.5 |
| 69 | 63.1 | 62.2 | 61.2 | 60.2 | 59.3 | 58.3 | 57.3 | 56.4 | 55.4 | 54.5 |
| 70 | 63.1 | 62.2 | 61.2 | 60.2 | 59.3 | 58.3 | 57.3 | 56.4 | 55.4 | 54.4 |
| 71 | 63.1 | 62.1 | 61.2 | 60.2 | 59.2 | 58.3 | 57.3 | 56.4 | 55.4 | 54.4 |
| 72 | 63.1 | 62.1 | 61.2 | 60.2 | 59.2 | 58.3 | 57.3 | 56.3 | 55.4 | 54.4 |
| 73 | 63.1 | 62.1 | 61.2 | 60.2 | 59.2 | 58.3 | 57.3 | 56.3 | 55.4 | 54.4 |
| 74 | 63.1 | 62.1 | 61.2 | 60.2 | 59.2 | 58.2 | 57.3 | 56.3 | 55.4 | 54.4 |
| 75 | 63.1 | 62.1 | 61.1 | 60.2 | 59.2 | 58.2 | 57.3 | 56.3 | 55.3 | 54.4 |
| 76 | 63.1 | 62.1 | 61.1 | 60.2 | 59.2 | 58.2 | 57.3 | 56.3 | 55.3 | 54.4 |
| 77 | 63.1 | 62.1 | 61.1 | 60.2 | 59.2 | 58.2 | 57.3 | 56.3 | 55.3 | 54.4 |
| 78 | 63.1 | 62.1 | 61.1 | 60.2 | 59.2 | 58.2 | 57.3 | 56.3 | 55.3 | 54.4 |
| 79 | 63.1 | 62.1 | 61.1 | 60.2 | 59.2 | 58.2 | 57.2 | 56.3 | 55.3 | 54.3 |
| 80 | 63.1 | 62.1 | 61.1 | 60.1 | 59.2 | 58.2 | 57.2 | 56.3 | 55.3 | 54.3 |
| 81 | 63.1 | 62.1 | 61.1 | 60.1 | 59.2 | 58.2 | 57.2 | 56.3 | 55.3 | 54.3 |
| 82 | 63.1 | 62.1 | 61.1 | 60.1 | 59.2 | 58.2 | 57.2 | 56.3 | 55.3 | 54.3 |
| 83 | 63.1 | 62.1 | 61.1 | 60.1 | 59.2 | 58.2 | 57.2 | 56.3 | 55.3 | 54.3 |
| 84 | 63.0 | 62.1 | 61.1 | 60.1 | 59.2 | 58.2 | 57.2 | 56.3 | 55.3 | 54.3 |
| 85 | 63.0 | 62.1 | 61.1 | 60.1 | 59.2 | 58.2 | 57.2 | 56.3 | 55.3 | 54.3 |
| 86 | 63.0 | 62.1 | 61.1 | 60.1 | 59.2 | 58.2 | 57.2 | 56.2 | 55.3 | 54.3 |
| 87 | 63.0 | 62.1 | 61.1 | 60.1 | 59.2 | 58.2 | 57.2 | 56.2 | 55.3 | 54.3 |
| 88 | 63.0 | 62.1 | 61.1 | 60.1 | 59.2 | 58.2 | 57.2 | 56.2 | 55.3 | 54.3 |
| 89 | 63.0 | 62.1 | 61.1 | 60.1 | 59.1 | 58.2 | 57.2 | 56.2 | 55.3 | 54.3 |
| 90 | 63.0 | 62.1 | 61.1 | 60.1 | 59.1 | 58.2 | 57.2 | 56.2 | 55.3 | 54.3 |
| 91 | 63.0 | 62.1 | 61.1 | 60.1 | 59.1 | 58.2 | 57.2 | 56.2 | 55.3 | 54.3 |
| 92 | 63.0 | 62.1 | 61.1 | 60.1 | 59.1 | 58.2 | 57.2 | 56.2 | 55.3 | 54.3 |
| 93 | 63.0 | 62.1 | 61.1 | 60.1 | 59.1 | 58.2 | 57.2 | 56.2 | 55.3 | 54.3 |
| 94 | 63.0 | 62.1 | 61.1 | 60.1 | 59.1 | 58.2 | 57.2 | 56.2 | 55.3 | 54.3 |
| 95 | 63.0 | 62.1 | 61.1 | 60.1 | 59.1 | 58.2 | 57.2 | 56.2 | 55.3 | 54.3 |
| 96 | 63.0 | 62.1 | 61.1 | 60.1 | 59.1 | 58.2 | 57.2 | 56.2 | 55.3 | 54.3 |
| 97 | 63.0 | 62.1 | 61.1 | 60.1 | 59.1 | 58.2 | 57.2 | 56.2 | 55.3 | 54.3 |
| 98 | 63.0 | 62.1 | 61.1 | 60.1 | 59.1 | 58.2 | 57.2 | 56.2 | 55.3 | 54.3 |
| 99 | 63.0 | 62.1 | 61.1 | 60.1 | 59.1 | 58.2 | 57.2 | 56.2 | 55.3 | 54.3 |
| AGES | 20 | 21 | 22 | 23 | 24 | 25 | 26 | 27 | 28 | 29 |
| 100 | 63.0 | 62.1 | 61.1 | 60.1 | 59.1 | 58.2 | 57.2 | 56.2 | 55.3 | 54.3 |
| 101 | 63.0 | 62.1 | 61.1 | 60.1 | 59.1 | 58.2 | 57.2 | 56.2 | 55.3 | 54.3 |
| 102 | 63.0 | 62.1 | 61.1 | 60.1 | 59.1 | 58.2 | 57.2 | 56.2 | 55.3 | 54.3 |
| 103 | 63.0 | 62.1 | 61.1 | 60.1 | 59.1 | 58.2 | 57.2 | 56.2 | 55.3 | 54.3 |
| 104 | 63.0 | 62.1 | 61.1 | 60.1 | 59.1 | 58.2 | 57.2 | 56.2 | 55.3 | 54.3 |
| 105 | 63.0 | 62.1 | 61.1 | 60.1 | 59.1 | 58.2 | 57.2 | 56.2 | 55.3 | 54.3 |
| 106 | 63.0 | 62.1 | 61.1 | 60.1 | 59.1 | 58.2 | 57.2 | 56.2 | 55.3 | 54.3 |
| 107 | 63.0 | 62.1 | 61.1 | 60.1 | 59.1 | 58.2 | 57.2 | 56.2 | 55.3 | 54.3 |
| 108 | 63.0 | 62.1 | 61.1 | 60.1 | 59.1 | 58.2 | 57.2 | 56.2 | 55.3 | 54.3 |

| | | | | | | | | | | |
|---|---|---|---|---|---|---|---|---|---|---|
| 109 | 63.0 | 62.1 | 61.1 | 60.1 | 59.1 | 58.2 | 57.2 | 56.2 | 55.3 | 54.3 |
| 110 | 63.0 | 62.1 | 61.1 | 60.1 | 59.1 | 58.2 | 57.2 | 56.2 | 55.3 | 54.3 |
| 111 | 63.0 | 62.1 | 61.1 | 60.1 | 59.1 | 58.2 | 57.2 | 56.2 | 55.3 | 54.3 |
| 112 | 63.0 | 62.1 | 61.1 | 60.1 | 59.1 | 58.2 | 57.2 | 56.2 | 55.3 | 54.3 |
| 113 | 63.0 | 62.1 | 61.1 | 60.1 | 59.1 | 58.2 | 57.2 | 56.2 | 55.3 | 54.3 |
| 114 | 63.0 | 62.1 | 61.1 | 60.1 | 59.1 | 58.2 | 57.2 | 56.2 | 55.3 | 54.3 |
| 115+ | 63.0 | 62.1 | 61.1 | 60.1 | 59.1 | 58.2 | 57.2 | 56.2 | 55.3 | 54.3 |

| AGES | 30 | 31 | 32 | 33 | 34 | 35 | 36 | 37 | 38 | 39 |
|---|---|---|---|---|---|---|---|---|---|---|
| 30 | 60.2 | 59.7 | 59.2 | 58.8 | 58.4 | 58.0 | 57.6 | 57.3 | 57.0 | 56.7 |
| 31 | 59.7 | 59.2 | 58.7 | 58.2 | 57.8 | 57.4 | 57.0 | 56.6 | 56.3 | 56.0 |
| 32 | 59.2 | 58.7 | 58.2 | 57.7 | 57.2 | 56.8 | 56.4 | 56.0 | 55.6 | 55.3 |
| 33 | 58.8 | 58.2 | 57.7 | 57.2 | 56.7 | 56.2 | 55.8 | 55.4 | 55.0 | 54.7 |
| 34 | 58.4 | 57.8 | 57.2 | 56.7 | 56.2 | 55.7 | 55.3 | 54.8 | 54.4 | 54.0 |
| 35 | 58.0 | 57.4 | 56.8 | 56.2 | 55.7 | 55.2 | 54.7 | 54.3 | 53.8 | 53.4 |
| 36 | 57.6 | 57.0 | 56.4 | 55.8 | 55.3 | 54.7 | 54.2 | 53.7 | 53.3 | 52.8 |
| 37 | 57.3 | 56.6 | 56.0 | 55.4 | 54.8 | 54.3 | 53.7 | 53.2 | 52.7 | 52.3 |
| 38 | 57.0 | 56.3 | 55.6 | 55.0 | 54.4 | 53.8 | 53.3 | 52.7 | 52.2 | 51.7 |
| 39 | 56.7 | 56.0 | 55.3 | 54.7 | 54.0 | 53.4 | 52.8 | 52.3 | 51.7 | 51.2 |
| 40 | 56.4 | 55.7 | 55.0 | 54.3 | 53.7 | 53.0 | 52.4 | 51.8 | 51.3 | 50.8 |
| 41 | 56.1 | 55.4 | 54.7 | 54.0 | 53.3 | 52.7 | 52.0 | 51.4 | 50.9 | 50.3 |
| 42 | 55.9 | 55.2 | 54.4 | 53.7 | 53.0 | 52.3 | 51.7 | 51.1 | 50.4 | 49.9 |
| 43 | 55.7 | 54.9 | 54.2 | 53.4 | 52.7 | 52.0 | 51.3 | 50.7 | 50.1 | 49.5 |
| 44 | 55.5 | 54.7 | 53.9 | 53.2 | 52.4 | 51.7 | 51.0 | 50.4 | 49.7 | 49.1 |
| 45 | 55.3 | 54.5 | 53.7 | 52.9 | 52.2 | 51.5 | 50.7 | 50.0 | 49.4 | 48.7 |
| 46 | 55.1 | 54.3 | 53.5 | 52.7 | 52.0 | 51.2 | 50.5 | 49.8 | 49.1 | 48.4 |
| 47 | 55.0 | 54.1 | 53.3 | 52.5 | 51.7 | 51.0 | 50.2 | 49.5 | 48.8 | 48.1 |
| 48 | 54.8 | 54.0 | 53.2 | 52.3 | 51.5 | 50.8 | 50.0 | 49.2 | 48.5 | 47.8 |
| 49 | 54.7 | 53.8 | 53.0 | 52.2 | 51.4 | 50.6 | 49.8 | 49.0 | 48.2 | 47.5 |
| 50 | 54.6 | 53.7 | 52.9 | 52.0 | 51.2 | 50.4 | 49.6 | 48.8 | 48.0 | 47.3 |
| 51 | 54.5 | 53.6 | 52.7 | 51.9 | 51.0 | 50.2 | 49.4 | 48.6 | 47.8 | 47.0 |
| 52 | 54.4 | 53.5 | 52.6 | 51.7 | 50.9 | 50.0 | 49.2 | 48.4 | 47.6 | 46.8 |
| 53 | 54.3 | 53.4 | 52.5 | 51.6 | 50.8 | 49.9 | 49.1 | 48.2 | 47.4 | 46.6 |
| 54 | 54.2 | 53.3 | 52.4 | 51.5 | 50.6 | 49.8 | 48.9 | 48.1 | 47.2 | 46.4 |
| 55 | 54.1 | 53.2 | 52.3 | 51.4 | 50.5 | 49.7 | 48.8 | 47.9 | 47.1 | 46.3 |
| 56 | 54.0 | 53.1 | 52.2 | 51.3 | 50.4 | 49.5 | 48.7 | 47.8 | 47.0 | 46.1 |
| 57 | 54.0 | 53.0 | 52.1 | 51.2 | 50.3 | 49.4 | 48.6 | 47.7 | 46.8 | 46.0 |
| 58 | 53.9 | 53.0 | 52.1 | 51.2 | 50.3 | 49.4 | 48.5 | 47.6 | 46.7 | 45.8 |
| 59 | 53.8 | 52.9 | 52.0 | 51.1 | 50.2 | 49.3 | 48.4 | 47.5 | 46.6 | 45.7 |
| 60 | 53.8 | 52.9 | 51.9 | 51.0 | 50.1 | 49.2 | 48.3 | 47.4 | 46.5 | 45.6 |
| 61 | 53.8 | 52.8 | 51.9 | 51.0 | 50.0 | 49.1 | 48.2 | 47.3 | 46.4 | 45.5 |
| 62 | 53.7 | 52.8 | 51.8 | 50.9 | 50.0 | 49.1 | 48.1 | 47.2 | 46.3 | 45.4 |
| 63 | 53.7 | 52.7 | 51.8 | 50.9 | 49.9 | 49.0 | 48.1 | 47.2 | 46.3 | 45.3 |
| 64 | 53.6 | 52.7 | 51.8 | 50.8 | 49.9 | 48.9 | 48.0 | 47.1 | 46.2 | 45.3 |
| 65 | 53.6 | 52.7 | 51.7 | 50.8 | 49.8 | 48.9 | 48.0 | 47.0 | 46.1 | 45.2 |
| 66 | 53.6 | 52.6 | 51.7 | 50.7 | 49.8 | 48.9 | 47.9 | 47.0 | 46.1 | 45.1 |
| 67 | 53.6 | 52.6 | 51.7 | 50.7 | 49.8 | 48.8 | 47.9 | 46.9 | 46.0 | 45.1 |
| 68 | 53.5 | 52.6 | 51.6 | 50.7 | 49.7 | 48.8 | 47.8 | 46.9 | 46.0 | 45.0 |
| 69 | 53.5 | 52.6 | 51.6 | 50.6 | 49.7 | 48.7 | 47.8 | 46.9 | 45.9 | 45.0 |

| AGES | 30 | 31 | 32 | 33 | 34 | 35 | 36 | 37 | 38 | 39 |
|---|---|---|---|---|---|---|---|---|---|---|
| 70 | 53.5 | 52.5 | 51.6 | 50.6 | 49.7 | 48.7 | 47.8 | 46.8 | 45.9 | 44.9 |
| 71 | 53.5 | 52.5 | 51.6 | 50.6 | 49.6 | 48.7 | 47.7 | 46.8 | 45.9 | 44.9 |
| 72 | 53.5 | 52.5 | 51.5 | 50.6 | 49.6 | 48.7 | 47.7 | 46.8 | 45.8 | 44.9 |
| 73 | 53.4 | 52.5 | 51.5 | 50.6 | 49.6 | 48.6 | 47.7 | 46.7 | 45.8 | 44.8 |
| 74 | 53.4 | 52.5 | 51.5 | 50.5 | 49.6 | 48.6 | 47.7 | 46.7 | 45.8 | 44.8 |
| 75 | 53.4 | 52.5 | 51.5 | 50.5 | 49.6 | 48.6 | 47.7 | 46.7 | 45.7 | 44.8 |
| 76 | 53.4 | 52.4 | 51.5 | 50.5 | 49.6 | 48.6 | 47.6 | 46.7 | 45.7 | 44.8 |
| 77 | 53.4 | 52.4 | 51.5 | 50.5 | 49.5 | 48.6 | 47.6 | 46.7 | 45.7 | 44.8 |
| 78 | 53.4 | 52.4 | 51.5 | 50.5 | 49.5 | 48.6 | 47.6 | 46.6 | 45.7 | 44.7 |
| 79 | 53.4 | 52.4 | 51.5 | 50.5 | 49.5 | 48.6 | 47.6 | 46.6 | 45.7 | 44.7 |
| 80 | 53.4 | 52.4 | 51.4 | 50.5 | 49.5 | 48.5 | 47.6 | 46.6 | 45.7 | 44.7 |
| 81 | 53.4 | 52.4 | 51.4 | 50.5 | 49.5 | 48.5 | 47.6 | 46.6 | 45.7 | 44.7 |
| 82 | 53.4 | 52.4 | 51.4 | 50.5 | 49.5 | 48.5 | 47.6 | 46.6 | 45.6 | 44.7 |
| 83 | 53.4 | 52.4 | 51.4 | 50.5 | 49.5 | 48.5 | 47.6 | 46.6 | 45.6 | 44.7 |
| 84 | 53.4 | 52.4 | 51.4 | 50.5 | 49.5 | 48.5 | 47.6 | 46.6 | 45.6 | 44.7 |

| | | | | | | | | | | |
|---|---|---|---|---|---|---|---|---|---|---|
| 85 | 53.3 | 52.4 | 51.4 | 50.4 | 49.5 | 48.5 | 47.5 | 46.6 | 45.6 | 44.7 |
| 86 | 53.3 | 52.4 | 51.4 | 50.4 | 49.5 | 48.5 | 47.5 | 46.6 | 45.6 | 44.6 |
| 87 | 53.3 | 52.4 | 51.4 | 50.4 | 49.5 | 48.5 | 47.5 | 46.6 | 45.6 | 44.6 |
| 88 | 53.3 | 52.4 | 51.4 | 50.4 | 49.5 | 48.5 | 47.5 | 46.6 | 45.6 | 44.6 |
| 89 | 53.3 | 52.4 | 51.4 | 50.4 | 49.5 | 48.5 | 47.5 | 46.6 | 45.6 | 44.6 |
| 90 | 53.3 | 52.4 | 51.4 | 50.4 | 49.5 | 48.5 | 47.5 | 46.6 | 45.6 | 44.6 |
| 91 | 53.3 | 52.4 | 51.4 | 50.4 | 49.5 | 48.5 | 47.5 | 46.6 | 45.6 | 44.6 |
| 92 | 53.3 | 52.4 | 51.4 | 50.4 | 49.5 | 48.5 | 47.5 | 46.6 | 45.6 | 44.6 |
| 93 | 53.3 | 52.4 | 51.4 | 50.4 | 49.5 | 48.5 | 47.5 | 46.6 | 45.6 | 44.6 |
| 94 | 53.3 | 52.4 | 51.4 | 50.4 | 49.5 | 48.5 | 47.5 | 46.6 | 45.6 | 44.6 |
| 95 | 53.3 | 52.4 | 51.4 | 50.4 | 49.5 | 48.5 | 47.5 | 46.5 | 45.6 | 44.6 |
| 96 | 53.3 | 52.4 | 51.4 | 50.4 | 49.5 | 48.5 | 47.5 | 46.5 | 45.6 | 44.6 |
| 97 | 53.3 | 52.4 | 51.4 | 50.4 | 49.5 | 48.5 | 47.5 | 46.5 | 45.6 | 44.6 |
| 98 | 53.3 | 52.4 | 51.4 | 50.4 | 49.5 | 48.5 | 47.5 | 46.5 | 45.6 | 44.6 |
| 99 | 53.3 | 52.4 | 51.4 | 50.4 | 49.5 | 48.5 | 47.5 | 46.5 | 45.6 | 44.6 |
| 100 | 53.3 | 52.4 | 51.4 | 50.4 | 49.5 | 48.5 | 47.5 | 46.5 | 45.6 | 44.6 |
| 101 | 53.3 | 52.4 | 51.4 | 50.4 | 49.5 | 48.5 | 47.5 | 46.5 | 45.6 | 44.6 |
| 102 | 53.3 | 52.4 | 51.4 | 50.4 | 49.5 | 48.5 | 47.5 | 46.5 | 45.6 | 44.6 |
| 103 | 53.3 | 52.4 | 51.4 | 50.4 | 49.5 | 48.5 | 47.5 | 46.5 | 45.6 | 44.6 |
| 104 | 53.3 | 52.4 | 51.4 | 50.4 | 49.5 | 48.5 | 47.5 | 46.5 | 45.6 | 44.6 |
| 105 | 53.3 | 52.4 | 51.4 | 50.4 | 49.4 | 48.5 | 47.5 | 46.5 | 45.6 | 44.6 |
| 106 | 53.3 | 52.4 | 51.4 | 50.4 | 49.4 | 48.5 | 47.5 | 46.5 | 45.6 | 44.6 |
| 107 | 53.3 | 52.4 | 51.4 | 50.4 | 49.4 | 48.5 | 47.5 | 46.5 | 45.6 | 44.6 |
| 108 | 53.3 | 52.4 | 51.4 | 50.4 | 49.4 | 48.5 | 47.5 | 46.5 | 45.6 | 44.6 |
| 109 | 53.3 | 52.4 | 51.4 | 50.4 | 49.4 | 48.5 | 47.5 | 46.5 | 45.6 | 44.6 |

| AGES | 30 | 31 | 32 | 33 | 34 | 35 | 36 | 37 | 38 | 39 |
|---|---|---|---|---|---|---|---|---|---|---|
| 110 | 53.3 | 52.4 | 51.4 | 50.4 | 49.4 | 48.5 | 47.5 | 46.5 | 45.6 | 44.6 |
| 111 | 53.3 | 52.4 | 51.4 | 50.4 | 49.4 | 48.5 | 47.5 | 46.5 | 45.6 | 44.6 |
| 112 | 53.3 | 52.4 | 51.4 | 50.4 | 49.4 | 48.5 | 47.5 | 46.5 | 45.6 | 44.6 |
| 113 | 53.3 | 52.4 | 51.4 | 50.4 | 49.4 | 48.5 | 47.5 | 46.5 | 45.6 | 44.6 |
| 114 | 53.3 | 52.4 | 51.4 | 50.4 | 49.4 | 48.5 | 47.5 | 46.5 | 45.6 | 44.6 |
| 115+ | 53.3 | 52.4 | 51.4 | 50.4 | 49.4 | 48.5 | 47.5 | 46.5 | 45.6 | 44.6 |

| AGES | 40 | 41 | 42 | 43 | 44 | 45 | 46 | 47 | 48 | 49 |
|---|---|---|---|---|---|---|---|---|---|---|
| 40 | 50.2 | 49.8 | 49.3 | 48.9 | 48.5 | 48.1 | 47.7 | 47.4 | 47.1 | 46.8 |
| 41 | 49.8 | 49.3 | 48.8 | 48.3 | 47.9 | 47.5 | 47.1 | 46.7 | 46.4 | 46.1 |
| 42 | 49.3 | 48.8 | 48.3 | 47.8 | 47.3 | 46.9 | 46.5 | 46.1 | 45.8 | 45.4 |
| 43 | 48.9 | 48.3 | 47.8 | 47.3 | 46.8 | 46.3 | 45.9 | 45.5 | 45.1 | 44.8 |
| 44 | 48.5 | 47.9 | 47.3 | 46.8 | 46.3 | 45.8 | 45.4 | 44.9 | 44.5 | 44.2 |
| 45 | 48.1 | 47.5 | 46.9 | 46.3 | 45.8 | 45.3 | 44.8 | 44.4 | 44.0 | 43.6 |
| 46 | 47.7 | 47.1 | 46.5 | 45.9 | 45.4 | 44.8 | 44.3 | 43.9 | 43.4 | 43.0 |
| 47 | 47.4 | 46.7 | 46.1 | 45.5 | 44.9 | 44.4 | 43.9 | 43.4 | 42.9 | 42.4 |
| 48 | 47.1 | 46.4 | 45.8 | 45.1 | 44.5 | 44.0 | 43.4 | 42.9 | 42.4 | 41.9 |
| 49 | 46.8 | 46.1 | 45.4 | 44.8 | 44.2 | 43.6 | 43.0 | 42.4 | 41.9 | 41.4 |
| 50 | 46.5 | 45.8 | 45.1 | 44.4 | 43.8 | 43.2 | 42.6 | 42.0 | 41.5 | 40.9 |
| 51 | 46.3 | 45.5 | 44.8 | 44.1 | 43.5 | 42.8 | 42.2 | 41.6 | 41.0 | 40.5 |
| 52 | 46.0 | 45.3 | 44.6 | 43.8 | 43.2 | 42.5 | 41.8 | 41.2 | 40.6 | 40.1 |
| 53 | 45.8 | 45.1 | 44.3 | 43.6 | 42.9 | 42.2 | 41.5 | 40.9 | 40.3 | 39.7 |
| 54 | 45.6 | 44.8 | 44.1 | 43.3 | 42.6 | 41.9 | 41.2 | 40.5 | 39.9 | 39.3 |
| 55 | 45.5 | 44.7 | 43.9 | 43.1 | 42.4 | 41.6 | 40.9 | 40.2 | 39.6 | 38.9 |
| 56 | 45.3 | 44.5 | 43.7 | 42.9 | 42.1 | 41.4 | 40.7 | 40.0 | 39.3 | 38.6 |
| 57 | 45.1 | 44.3 | 43.5 | 42.7 | 41.9 | 41.2 | 40.4 | 39.7 | 39.0 | 38.3 |
| 58 | 45.0 | 44.2 | 43.3 | 42.5 | 41.7 | 40.9 | 40.2 | 39.4 | 38.7 | 38.0 |
| 59 | 44.9 | 44.0 | 43.2 | 42.4 | 41.5 | 40.7 | 40.0 | 39.2 | 38.5 | 37.8 |
| 60 | 44.7 | 43.9 | 43.0 | 42.2 | 41.4 | 40.6 | 39.8 | 39.0 | 38.2 | 37.5 |
| 61 | 44.6 | 43.8 | 42.9 | 42.1 | 41.2 | 40.4 | 39.6 | 38.8 | 38.0 | 37.3 |
| 62 | 44.5 | 43.7 | 42.8 | 41.9 | 41.1 | 40.3 | 39.4 | 38.6 | 37.8 | 37.1 |
| 63 | 44.5 | 43.6 | 42.7 | 41.8 | 41.0 | 40.1 | 39.3 | 38.5 | 37.7 | 36.9 |
| 64 | 44.4 | 43.5 | 42.6 | 41.7 | 40.8 | 40.0 | 39.2 | 38.3 | 37.5 | 36.7 |
| 65 | 44.3 | 43.4 | 42.5 | 41.6 | 40.7 | 39.9 | 39.0 | 38.2 | 37.4 | 36.6 |
| 66 | 44.2 | 43.3 | 42.4 | 41.5 | 40.6 | 39.8 | 38.9 | 38.1 | 37.2 | 36.4 |
| 67 | 44.2 | 43.3 | 42.3 | 41.4 | 40.6 | 39.7 | 38.8 | 38.0 | 37.1 | 36.3 |
| 68 | 44.1 | 43.2 | 42.3 | 41.4 | 40.5 | 39.6 | 38.7 | 37.9 | 37.0 | 36.2 |
| 69 | 44.1 | 43.1 | 42.2 | 41.3 | 40.4 | 39.5 | 38.6 | 37.8 | 36.9 | 36.0 |
| 70 | 44.0 | 43.1 | 42.2 | 41.3 | 40.3 | 39.4 | 38.6 | 37.7 | 36.8 | 35.9 |

| | | | | | | | | | | |
|---|---|---|---|---|---|---|---|---|---|---|
| 71 | 44.0 | 43.0 | 42.1 | 41.2 | 40.3 | 39.4 | 38.5 | 37.6 | 36.7 | 35.9 |
| 72 | 43.9 | 43.0 | 42.1 | 41.1 | 40.2 | 39.3 | 38.4 | 37.5 | 36.6 | 35.8 |
| 73 | 43.9 | 43.0 | 42.0 | 41.1 | 40.2 | 39.3 | 38.4 | 37.5 | 36.6 | 35.7 |
| 74 | 43.9 | 42.9 | 42.0 | 41.1 | 40.1 | 39.2 | 38.3 | 37.4 | 36.5 | 35.6 |
| 75 | 43.8 | 42.9 | 42.0 | 41.0 | 40.1 | 39.2 | 38.3 | 37.4 | 36.5 | 35.6 |
| 76 | 43.8 | 42.9 | 41.9 | 41.0 | 40.1 | 39.1 | 38.2 | 37.3 | 36.4 | 35.5 |
| 77 | 43.8 | 42.9 | 41.9 | 41.0 | 40.0 | 39.1 | 38.2 | 37.3 | 36.4 | 35.5 |
| 78 | 43.8 | 42.8 | 41.9 | 40.9 | 40.0 | 39.1 | 38.2 | 37.2 | 36.3 | 35.4 |
| 79 | 43.8 | 42.8 | 41.9 | 40.9 | 40.0 | 39.1 | 38.1 | 37.2 | 36.3 | 35.4 |

| AGES | 40 | 41 | 42 | 43 | 44 | 45 | 46 | 47 | 48 | 49 |
|---|---|---|---|---|---|---|---|---|---|---|
| 80 | 43.7 | 42.8 | 41.8 | 40.9 | 40.0 | 39.0 | 38.1 | 37.2 | 36.3 | 35.4 |
| 81 | 43.7 | 42.8 | 41.8 | 40.9 | 39.9 | 39.0 | 38.1 | 37.2 | 36.2 | 35.3 |
| 82 | 43.7 | 42.8 | 41.8 | 40.9 | 39.9 | 39.0 | 38.1 | 37.1 | 36.2 | 35.3 |
| 83 | 43.7 | 42.8 | 41.8 | 40.9 | 39.9 | 39.0 | 38.0 | 37.1 | 36.2 | 35.3 |
| 84 | 43.7 | 42.7 | 41.8 | 40.8 | 39.9 | 39.0 | 38.0 | 37.1 | 36.2 | 35.3 |
| 85 | 43.7 | 42.7 | 41.8 | 40.8 | 39.9 | 38.9 | 38.0 | 37.1 | 36.2 | 35.2 |
| 86 | 43.7 | 42.7 | 41.8 | 40.8 | 39.9 | 38.9 | 38.0 | 37.1 | 36.1 | 35.2 |
| 87 | 43.7 | 42.7 | 41.8 | 40.8 | 39.9 | 38.9 | 38.0 | 37.0 | 36.1 | 35.2 |
| 88 | 43.7 | 42.7 | 41.8 | 40.8 | 39.9 | 38.9 | 38.0 | 37.0 | 36.1 | 35.2 |
| 89 | 43.7 | 42.7 | 41.7 | 40.8 | 39.8 | 38.9 | 38.0 | 37.0 | 36.1 | 35.2 |
| 90 | 43.7 | 42.7 | 41.7 | 40.8 | 39.8 | 38.9 | 38.0 | 37.0 | 36.1 | 35.2 |
| 91 | 43.7 | 42.7 | 41.7 | 40.8 | 39.8 | 38.9 | 37.9 | 37.0 | 36.1 | 35.2 |
| 92 | 43.7 | 42.7 | 41.7 | 40.8 | 39.8 | 38.9 | 37.9 | 37.0 | 36.1 | 35.1 |
| 93 | 43.7 | 42.7 | 41.7 | 40.8 | 39.8 | 38.9 | 37.9 | 37.0 | 36.1 | 35.1 |
| 94 | 43.7 | 42.7 | 41.7 | 40.8 | 39.8 | 38.9 | 37.9 | 37.0 | 36.1 | 35.1 |
| 95 | 43.6 | 42.7 | 41.7 | 40.8 | 39.8 | 38.9 | 37.9 | 37.0 | 36.1 | 35.1 |
| 96 | 43.6 | 42.7 | 41.7 | 40.8 | 39.8 | 38.9 | 37.9 | 37.0 | 36.1 | 35.1 |
| 97 | 43.6 | 42.7 | 41.7 | 40.8 | 39.8 | 38.9 | 37.9 | 37.0 | 36.1 | 35.1 |
| 98 | 43.6 | 42.7 | 41.7 | 40.8 | 39.8 | 38.9 | 37.9 | 37.0 | 36.0 | 35.1 |
| 99 | 43.6 | 42.7 | 41.7 | 40.8 | 39.8 | 38.9 | 37.9 | 37.0 | 36.0 | 35.1 |
| 100 | 43.6 | 42.7 | 41.7 | 40.8 | 39.8 | 38.9 | 37.9 | 37.0 | 36.0 | 35.1 |
| 101 | 43.6 | 42.7 | 41.7 | 40.8 | 39.8 | 38.9 | 37.9 | 37.0 | 36.0 | 35.1 |
| 102 | 43.6 | 42.7 | 41.7 | 40.8 | 39.8 | 38.9 | 37.9 | 37.0 | 36.0 | 35.1 |
| 103 | 43.6 | 42.7 | 41.7 | 40.8 | 39.8 | 38.9 | 37.9 | 37.0 | 36.0 | 35.1 |
| 104 | 43.6 | 42.7 | 41.7 | 40.8 | 39.8 | 38.8 | 37.9 | 37.0 | 36.0 | 35.1 |
| 105 | 43.6 | 42.7 | 41.7 | 40.8 | 39.8 | 38.8 | 37.9 | 37.0 | 36.0 | 35.1 |
| 106 | 43.6 | 42.7 | 41.7 | 40.8 | 39.8 | 38.8 | 37.9 | 37.0 | 36.0 | 35.1 |
| 107 | 43.6 | 42.7 | 41.7 | 40.8 | 39.8 | 38.8 | 37.9 | 37.0 | 36.0 | 35.1 |
| 108 | 43.6 | 42.7 | 41.7 | 40.8 | 39.8 | 38.8 | 37.9 | 37.0 | 36.0 | 35.1 |
| 109 | 43.6 | 42.7 | 41.7 | 40.7 | 39.8 | 38.8 | 37.9 | 37.0 | 36.0 | 35.1 |
| 110 | 43.6 | 42.7 | 41.7 | 40.7 | 39.8 | 38.8 | 37.9 | 37.0 | 36.0 | 35.1 |
| 111 | 43.6 | 42.7 | 41.7 | 40.7 | 39.8 | 38.8 | 37.9 | 37.0 | 36.0 | 35.1 |
| 112 | 43.6 | 42.7 | 41.7 | 40.7 | 39.8 | 38.8 | 37.9 | 37.0 | 36.0 | 35.1 |
| 113 | 43.6 | 42.7 | 41.7 | 40.7 | 39.8 | 38.8 | 37.9 | 37.0 | 36.0 | 35.1 |
| 114 | 43.6 | 42.7 | 41.7 | 40.7 | 39.8 | 38.8 | 37.9 | 37.0 | 36.0 | 35.1 |
| 115+ | 43.6 | 42.7 | 41.7 | 40.7 | 39.8 | 38.8 | 37.9 | 37.0 | 36.0 | 35.1 |

| AGES | 50 | 51 | 52 | 53 | 54 | 55 | 56 | 57 | 58 | 59 |
|---|---|---|---|---|---|---|---|---|---|---|
| 50 | 40.4 | 40.0 | 39.5 | 39.1 | 38.7 | 38.3 | 38.0 | 37.6 | 37.3 | 37.1 |
| 51 | 40.0 | 39.5 | 39.0 | 38.5 | 38.1 | 37.7 | 37.4 | 37.0 | 36.7 | 36.4 |
| 52 | 39.5 | 39.0 | 38.5 | 38.0 | 37.6 | 37.2 | 36.8 | 36.4 | 36.0 | 35.7 |
| 53 | 39.1 | 38.5 | 38.0 | 37.5 | 37.1 | 36.6 | 36.2 | 35.8 | 35.4 | 35.1 |
| 54 | 38.7 | 38.1 | 37.6 | 37.1 | 36.6 | 36.1 | 35.7 | 35.2 | 34.8 | 34.5 |
| 55 | 38.3 | 37.7 | 37.2 | 36.6 | 36.1 | 35.6 | 35.1 | 34.7 | 34.3 | 33.9 |
| 56 | 38.0 | 37.4 | 36.8 | 36.2 | 35.7 | 35.1 | 34.7 | 34.2 | 33.7 | 33.3 |
| 57 | 37.6 | 37.0 | 36.4 | 35.8 | 35.2 | 34.7 | 34.2 | 33.7 | 33.2 | 32.8 |
| 58 | 37.3 | 36.7 | 36.0 | 35.4 | 34.8 | 34.3 | 33.7 | 33.2 | 32.8 | 32.3 |
| 59 | 37.1 | 36.4 | 35.7 | 35.1 | 34.5 | 33.9 | 33.3 | 32.8 | 32.3 | 31.8 |
| 60 | 36.8 | 36.1 | 35.4 | 34.8 | 34.1 | 33.5 | 32.9 | 32.4 | 31.9 | 31.3 |
| 61 | 36.6 | 35.8 | 35.1 | 34.5 | 33.8 | 33.2 | 32.6 | 32.0 | 31.4 | 30.9 |
| 62 | 36.3 | 35.6 | 34.9 | 34.2 | 33.5 | 32.9 | 32.2 | 31.6 | 31.1 | 30.5 |
| 63 | 36.1 | 35.4 | 34.6 | 33.9 | 33.2 | 32.6 | 31.9 | 31.3 | 30.7 | 30.1 |
| 64 | 35.9 | 35.2 | 34.4 | 33.7 | 33.0 | 32.3 | 31.6 | 31.0 | 30.4 | 29.8 |
| 65 | 35.8 | 35.0 | 34.2 | 33.5 | 32.7 | 32.0 | 31.4 | 30.7 | 30.0 | 29.4 |
| 66 | 35.6 | 34.8 | 34.0 | 33.3 | 32.5 | 31.8 | 31.1 | 30.4 | 29.8 | 29.1 |

| | | | | | | | | | | |
|---|---|---|---|---|---|---|---|---|---|---|
| 67 | 35.5 | 34.7 | 33.9 | 33.1 | 32.3 | 31.6 | 30.9 | 30.2 | 29.5 | 28.8 |
| 68 | 35.3 | 34.5 | 33.7 | 32.9 | 32.1 | 31.4 | 30.7 | 29.9 | 29.2 | 28.6 |
| 69 | 35.2 | 34.4 | 33.6 | 32.8 | 32.0 | 31.2 | 30.5 | 29.7 | 29.0 | 28.3 |
| 70 | 35.1 | 34.3 | 33.4 | 32.6 | 31.8 | 31.1 | 30.3 | 29.5 | 28.8 | 28.1 |
| 71 | 35.0 | 34.2 | 33.3 | 32.5 | 31.7 | 30.9 | 30.1 | 29.4 | 28.6 | 27.9 |
| 72 | 34.9 | 34.1 | 33.2 | 32.4 | 31.6 | 30.8 | 30.0 | 29.2 | 28.4 | 27.7 |
| 73 | 34.8 | 34.0 | 33.1 | 32.3 | 31.5 | 30.6 | 29.8 | 29.1 | 28.3 | 27.5 |
| 74 | 34.8 | 33.9 | 33.0 | 32.2 | 31.4 | 30.5 | 29.7 | 28.9 | 28.1 | 27.4 |
| 75 | 34.7 | 33.8 | 33.0 | 32.1 | 31.3 | 30.4 | 29.6 | 28.8 | 28.0 | 27.2 |
| 76 | 34.6 | 33.8 | 32.9 | 32.0 | 31.2 | 30.3 | 29.5 | 28.7 | 27.9 | 27.1 |
| 77 | 34.6 | 33.7 | 32.8 | 32.0 | 31.1 | 30.3 | 29.4 | 28.6 | 27.8 | 27.0 |
| 78 | 34.5 | 33.6 | 32.8 | 31.9 | 31.0 | 30.2 | 29.3 | 28.5 | 27.7 | 26.9 |
| 79 | 34.5 | 33.6 | 32.7 | 31.8 | 31.0 | 30.1 | 29.3 | 28.4 | 27.6 | 26.8 |
| 80 | 34.5 | 33.6 | 32.7 | 31.8 | 30.9 | 30.1 | 29.2 | 28.4 | 27.5 | 26.7 |
| 81 | 34.4 | 33.5 | 32.6 | 31.8 | 30.9 | 30.0 | 29.2 | 28.3 | 27.5 | 26.6 |
| 82 | 34.4 | 33.5 | 32.6 | 31.7 | 30.8 | 30.0 | 29.1 | 28.3 | 27.4 | 26.6 |
| 83 | 34.4 | 33.5 | 32.6 | 31.7 | 30.8 | 29.9 | 29.1 | 28.2 | 27.4 | 26.5 |
| 84 | 34.3 | 33.4 | 32.5 | 31.7 | 30.8 | 29.9 | 29.0 | 28.2 | 27.3 | 26.5 |
| 85 | 34.3 | 33.4 | 32.5 | 31.6 | 30.7 | 29.9 | 29.0 | 28.1 | 27.3 | 26.4 |
| 86 | 34.3 | 33.4 | 32.5 | 31.6 | 30.7 | 29.8 | 29.0 | 28.1 | 27.2 | 26.4 |
| 87 | 34.3 | 33.4 | 32.5 | 31.6 | 30.7 | 29.8 | 28.9 | 28.1 | 27.2 | 26.4 |
| 88 | 34.3 | 33.4 | 32.5 | 31.6 | 30.7 | 29.8 | 28.9 | 28.0 | 27.2 | 26.3 |
| 89 | 34.3 | 33.3 | 32.4 | 31.5 | 30.7 | 29.8 | 28.9 | 28.0 | 27.2 | 26.3 |

| AGES | 50 | 51 | 52 | 53 | 54 | 55 | 56 | 57 | 58 | 59 |
|---|---|---|---|---|---|---|---|---|---|---|
| 90 | 34.2 | 33.3 | 32.4 | 31.5 | 30.6 | 29.8 | 28.9 | 28.0 | 27.1 | 26.3 |
| 91 | 34.2 | 33.3 | 32.4 | 31.5 | 30.6 | 29.7 | 28.9 | 28.0 | 27.1 | 26.3 |
| 92 | 34.2 | 33.3 | 32.4 | 31.5 | 30.6 | 29.7 | 28.8 | 28.0 | 27.1 | 26.2 |
| 93 | 34.2 | 33.3 | 32.4 | 31.5 | 30.6 | 29.7 | 28.8 | 28.0 | 27.1 | 26.2 |
| 94 | 34.2 | 33.3 | 32.4 | 31.5 | 30.6 | 29.7 | 28.8 | 27.9 | 27.1 | 26.2 |
| 95 | 34.2 | 33.3 | 32.4 | 31.5 | 30.6 | 29.7 | 28.8 | 27.9 | 27.1 | 26.2 |
| 96 | 34.2 | 33.3 | 32.4 | 31.5 | 30.6 | 29.7 | 28.8 | 27.9 | 27.0 | 26.2 |
| 97 | 34.2 | 33.3 | 32.4 | 31.5 | 30.6 | 29.7 | 28.8 | 27.9 | 27.0 | 26.2 |
| 98 | 34.2 | 33.3 | 32.4 | 31.5 | 30.6 | 29.7 | 28.8 | 27.9 | 27.0 | 26.2 |
| 99 | 34.2 | 33.3 | 32.4 | 31.5 | 30.6 | 29.7 | 28.8 | 27.9 | 27.0 | 26.2 |
| 100 | 34.2 | 33.3 | 32.4 | 31.5 | 30.6 | 29.7 | 28.8 | 27.9 | 27.0 | 26.1 |
| 101 | 34.2 | 33.3 | 32.4 | 31.5 | 30.6 | 29.7 | 28.8 | 27.9 | 27.0 | 26.1 |
| 102 | 34.2 | 33.3 | 32.4 | 31.4 | 30.5 | 29.7 | 28.8 | 27.9 | 27.0 | 26.1 |
| 103 | 34.2 | 33.3 | 32.4 | 31.4 | 30.5 | 29.7 | 28.8 | 27.9 | 27.0 | 26.1 |
| 104 | 34.2 | 33.3 | 32.4 | 31.4 | 30.5 | 29.6 | 28.8 | 27.9 | 27.0 | 26.1 |
| 105 | 34.2 | 33.3 | 32.3 | 31.4 | 30.5 | 29.6 | 28.8 | 27.9 | 27.0 | 26.1 |
| 106 | 34.2 | 33.3 | 32.3 | 31.4 | 30.5 | 29.6 | 28.8 | 27.9 | 27.0 | 26.1 |
| 107 | 34.2 | 33.3 | 32.3 | 31.4 | 30.5 | 29.6 | 28.8 | 27.9 | 27.0 | 26.1 |
| 108 | 34.2 | 33.3 | 32.3 | 31.4 | 30.5 | 29.6 | 28.8 | 27.9 | 27.0 | 26.1 |
| 109 | 34.2 | 33.3 | 32.3 | 31.4 | 30.5 | 29.6 | 28.7 | 27.9 | 27.0 | 26.1 |
| 110 | 34.2 | 33.3 | 32.3 | 31.4 | 30.5 | 29.6 | 28.7 | 27.9 | 27.0 | 26.1 |
| 111 | 34.2 | 33.3 | 32.3 | 31.4 | 30.5 | 29.6 | 28.7 | 27.9 | 27.0 | 26.1 |
| 112 | 34.2 | 33.3 | 32.3 | 31.4 | 30.5 | 29.6 | 28.7 | 27.9 | 27.0 | 26.1 |
| 113 | 34.2 | 33.3 | 32.3 | 31.4 | 30.5 | 29.6 | 28.7 | 27.9 | 27.0 | 26.1 |
| 114 | 34.2 | 33.3 | 32.3 | 31.4 | 30.5 | 29.6 | 28.7 | 27.9 | 27.0 | 26.1 |
| 115+ | 34.2 | 33.3 | 32.3 | 31.4 | 30.5 | 29.6 | 28.7 | 27.9 | 27.0 | 26.1 |

| AGES | 60 | 61 | 62 | 63 | 64 | 65 | 66 | 67 | 68 | 69 |
|---|---|---|---|---|---|---|---|---|---|---|
| 60 | 30.9 | 30.4 | 30.0 | 29.6 | 29.2 | 28.8 | 28.5 | 28.2 | 27.9 | 27.6 |
| 61 | 30.4 | 29.9 | 29.5 | 29.0 | 28.6 | 28.3 | 27.9 | 27.6 | 27.3 | 27.0 |
| 62 | 30.0 | 29.5 | 29.0 | 28.5 | 28.1 | 27.7 | 27.3 | 27.0 | 26.7 | 26.4 |
| 63 | 29.6 | 29.0 | 28.5 | 28.1 | 27.6 | 27.2 | 26.8 | 26.4 | 26.1 | 25.7 |
| 64 | 29.2 | 28.6 | 28.1 | 27.6 | 27.1 | 26.7 | 26.3 | 25.9 | 25.5 | 25.2 |
| 65 | 28.8 | 28.3 | 27.7 | 27.2 | 26.7 | 26.2 | 25.8 | 25.4 | 25.0 | 24.6 |
| 66 | 28.5 | 27.9 | 27.3 | 26.8 | 26.3 | 25.8 | 25.3 | 24.9 | 24.5 | 24.1 |
| 67 | 28.2 | 27.6 | 27.0 | 26.4 | 25.9 | 25.4 | 24.9 | 24.4 | 24.0 | 23.6 |
| 68 | 27.9 | 27.3 | 26.7 | 26.1 | 25.5 | 25.0 | 24.5 | 24.0 | 23.5 | 23.1 |
| 69 | 27.6 | 27.0 | 26.4 | 25.7 | 25.2 | 24.6 | 24.1 | 23.6 | 23.1 | 22.6 |
| 70 | 27.4 | 26.7 | 26.1 | 25.4 | 24.8 | 24.3 | 23.7 | 23.2 | 22.7 | 22.2 |
| 71 | 27.2 | 26.5 | 25.8 | 25.2 | 24.5 | 23.9 | 23.4 | 22.8 | 22.3 | 21.8 |
| 72 | 27.0 | 26.3 | 25.6 | 24.9 | 24.3 | 23.7 | 23.1 | 22.5 | 22.0 | 21.4 |

| | | | | | | | | | | |
|---|---|---|---|---|---|---|---|---|---|---|
| 73 | 26.8 | 26.1 | 25.4 | 24.7 | 24.0 | 23.4 | 22.8 | 22.2 | 21.6 | 21.1 |
| 74 | 26.6 | 25.9 | 25.2 | 24.5 | 23.8 | 23.1 | 22.5 | 21.9 | 21.3 | 20.8 |
| 75 | 26.5 | 25.7 | 25.0 | 24.3 | 23.6 | 22.9 | 22.3 | 21.6 | 21.0 | 20.5 |
| 76 | 26.3 | 25.6 | 24.8 | 24.1 | 23.4 | 22.7 | 22.0 | 21.4 | 20.8 | 20.2 |
| 77 | 26.2 | 25.4 | 24.7 | 23.9 | 23.2 | 22.5 | 21.8 | 21.2 | 20.6 | 19.9 |
| 78 | 26.1 | 25.3 | 24.6 | 23.8 | 23.1 | 22.4 | 21.7 | 21.0 | 20.3 | 19.7 |
| 79 | 26.0 | 25.2 | 24.4 | 23.7 | 22.9 | 22.2 | 21.5 | 20.8 | 20.1 | 19.5 |
| 80 | 25.9 | 25.1 | 24.3 | 23.6 | 22.8 | 22.1 | 21.3 | 20.6 | 20.0 | 19.3 |
| 81 | 25.8 | 25.0 | 24.2 | 23.4 | 22.7 | 21.9 | 21.2 | 20.5 | 19.8 | 19.1 |
| 82 | 25.8 | 24.9 | 24.1 | 23.4 | 22.6 | 21.8 | 21.1 | 20.4 | 19.7 | 19.0 |
| 83 | 25.7 | 24.9 | 24.1 | 23.3 | 22.5 | 21.7 | 21.0 | 20.2 | 19.5 | 18.8 |
| 84 | 25.6 | 24.8 | 24.0 | 23.2 | 22.4 | 21.6 | 20.9 | 20.1 | 19.4 | 18.7 |
| 85 | 25.6 | 24.8 | 23.9 | 23.1 | 22.3 | 21.6 | 20.8 | 20.1 | 19.3 | 18.6 |
| 86 | 25.5 | 24.7 | 23.9 | 23.1 | 22.3 | 21.5 | 20.7 | 20.0 | 19.2 | 18.5 |
| 87 | 25.5 | 24.7 | 23.8 | 23.0 | 22.2 | 21.4 | 20.7 | 19.9 | 19.2 | 18.4 |
| 88 | 25.5 | 24.6 | 23.8 | 23.0 | 22.2 | 21.4 | 20.6 | 19.8 | 19.1 | 18.3 |
| 89 | 25.4 | 24.6 | 23.8 | 22.9 | 22.1 | 21.3 | 20.5 | 19.8 | 19.0 | 18.3 |
| 90 | 25.4 | 24.6 | 23.7 | 22.9 | 22.1 | 21.3 | 20.5 | 19.7 | 19.0 | 18.2 |
| 91 | 25.4 | 24.5 | 23.7 | 22.9 | 22.1 | 21.3 | 20.5 | 19.7 | 18.9 | 18.2 |
| 92 | 25.4 | 24.5 | 23.7 | 22.9 | 22.0 | 21.2 | 20.4 | 19.6 | 18.9 | 18.1 |
| 93 | 25.4 | 24.5 | 23.7 | 22.8 | 22.0 | 21.2 | 20.4 | 19.6 | 18.8 | 18.1 |
| 94 | 25.3 | 24.5 | 23.6 | 22.8 | 22.0 | 21.2 | 20.4 | 19.6 | 18.8 | 18.0 |
| 95 | 25.3 | 24.5 | 23.6 | 22.8 | 22.0 | 21.1 | 20.3 | 19.6 | 18.8 | 18.0 |
| 96 | 25.3 | 24.5 | 23.6 | 22.8 | 21.9 | 21.1 | 20.3 | 19.5 | 18.8 | 18.0 |
| 97 | 25.3 | 24.5 | 23.6 | 22.8 | 21.9 | 21.1 | 20.3 | 19.5 | 18.7 | 18.0 |
| 98 | 25.3 | 24.4 | 23.6 | 22.8 | 21.9 | 21.1 | 20.3 | 19.5 | 18.7 | 17.9 |
| 99 | 25.3 | 24.4 | 23.6 | 22.7 | 21.9 | 21.1 | 20.3 | 19.5 | 18.7 | 17.9 |

| AGES | 60 | 61 | 62 | 63 | 64 | 65 | 66 | 67 | 68 | 69 |
|---|---|---|---|---|---|---|---|---|---|---|
| 100 | 25.3 | 24.4 | 23.6 | 22.7 | 21.9 | 21.1 | 20.3 | 19.5 | 18.7 | 17.9 |
| 101 | 25.3 | 24.4 | 23.6 | 22.7 | 21.9 | 21.1 | 20.2 | 19.4 | 18.7 | 17.9 |
| 102 | 25.3 | 24.4 | 23.6 | 22.7 | 21.9 | 21.1 | 20.2 | 19.4 | 18.6 | 17.9 |
| 103 | 25.3 | 24.4 | 23.6 | 22.7 | 21.9 | 21.0 | 20.2 | 19.4 | 18.6 | 17.9 |
| 104 | 25.3 | 24.4 | 23.5 | 22.7 | 21.9 | 21.0 | 20.2 | 19.4 | 18.6 | 17.8 |
| 105 | 25.3 | 24.4 | 23.5 | 22.7 | 21.9 | 21.0 | 20.2 | 19.4 | 18.6 | 17.8 |
| 106 | 25.3 | 24.4 | 23.5 | 22.7 | 21.9 | 21.0 | 20.2 | 19.4 | 18.6 | 17.8 |
| 107 | 25.2 | 24.4 | 23.5 | 22.7 | 21.8 | 21.0 | 20.2 | 19.4 | 18.6 | 17.8 |
| 108 | 25.2 | 24.4 | 23.5 | 22.7 | 21.8 | 21.0 | 20.2 | 19.4 | 18.6 | 17.8 |
| 109 | 25.2 | 24.4 | 23.5 | 22.7 | 21.8 | 21.0 | 20.2 | 19.4 | 18.6 | 17.8 |
| 110 | 25.2 | 24.4 | 23.5 | 22.7 | 21.8 | 21.0 | 20.2 | 19.4 | 18.6 | 17.8 |
| 111 | 25.2 | 24.4 | 23.5 | 22.7 | 21.8 | 21.0 | 20.2 | 19.4 | 18.6 | 17.8 |
| 112 | 25.2 | 24.4 | 23.5 | 22.7 | 21.8 | 21.0 | 20.2 | 19.4 | 18.6 | 17.8 |
| 113 | 25.2 | 24.4 | 23.5 | 22.7 | 21.8 | 21.0 | 20.2 | 19.4 | 18.6 | 17.8 |
| 114 | 25.2 | 24.4 | 23.5 | 22.7 | 21.8 | 21.0 | 20.2 | 19.4 | 18.6 | 17.8 |
| 115+ | 25.2 | 24.4 | 23.5 | 22.7 | 21.8 | 21.0 | 20.2 | 19.4 | 18.6 | 17.8 |

| AGES | 70 | 71 | 72 | 73 | 74 | 75 | 76 | 77 | 78 | 79 |
|---|---|---|---|---|---|---|---|---|---|---|
| 70 | 21.8 | 21.3 | 20.9 | 20.6 | 20.2 | 19.9 | 19.6 | 19.4 | 19.1 | 18.9 |
| 71 | 21.3 | 20.9 | 20.5 | 20.1 | 19.7 | 19.4 | 19.1 | 18.8 | 18.5 | 18.3 |
| 72 | 20.9 | 20.5 | 20.0 | 19.6 | 19.3 | 18.9 | 18.6 | 18.3 | 18.0 | 17.7 |
| 73 | 20.6 | 20.1 | 19.6 | 19.2 | 18.8 | 18.4 | 18.1 | 17.8 | 17.5 | 17.2 |
| 74 | 20.2 | 19.7 | 19.3 | 18.8 | 18.4 | 18.0 | 17.6 | 17.3 | 17.0 | 16.7 |
| 75 | 19.9 | 19.4 | 18.9 | 18.4 | 18.0 | 17.6 | 17.2 | 16.8 | 16.5 | 16.2 |
| 76 | 19.6 | 19.1 | 18.6 | 18.1 | 17.6 | 17.2 | 16.8 | 16.4 | 16.0 | 15.7 |
| 77 | 19.4 | 18.8 | 18.3 | 17.8 | 17.3 | 16.8 | 16.4 | 16.0 | 15.6 | 15.3 |
| 78 | 19.1 | 18.5 | 18.0 | 17.5 | 17.0 | 16.5 | 16.0 | 15.6 | 15.2 | 14.9 |
| 79 | 18.9 | 18.3 | 17.7 | 17.2 | 16.7 | 16.2 | 15.7 | 15.3 | 14.9 | 14.5 |
| 80 | 18.7 | 18.1 | 17.5 | 16.9 | 16.4 | 15.9 | 15.4 | 15.0 | 14.5 | 14.1 |
| 81 | 18.5 | 17.9 | 17.3 | 16.7 | 16.2 | 15.6 | 15.1 | 14.7 | 14.2 | 13.8 |
| 82 | 18.3 | 17.7 | 17.1 | 16.5 | 15.9 | 15.4 | 14.9 | 14.4 | 13.9 | 13.5 |
| 83 | 18.2 | 17.5 | 16.9 | 16.3 | 15.7 | 15.2 | 14.7 | 14.2 | 13.7 | 13.2 |
| 84 | 18.0 | 17.4 | 16.7 | 16.1 | 15.5 | 15.0 | 14.4 | 13.9 | 13.4 | 13.0 |
| 85 | 17.9 | 17.3 | 16.6 | 16.0 | 15.4 | 14.8 | 14.3 | 13.7 | 13.2 | 12.8 |
| 86 | 17.8 | 17.1 | 16.5 | 15.8 | 15.2 | 14.6 | 14.1 | 13.5 | 13.0 | 12.5 |
| 87 | 17.7 | 17.0 | 16.4 | 15.7 | 15.1 | 14.5 | 13.9 | 13.4 | 12.9 | 12.4 |
| 88 | 17.6 | 16.9 | 16.3 | 15.6 | 15.0 | 14.4 | 13.8 | 13.2 | 12.7 | 12.2 |

| | | | | | | | | | | |
|---|---|---|---|---|---|---|---|---|---|---|
| 89 | 17.6 | 16.9 | 16.2 | 15.5 | 14.9 | 14.3 | 13.7 | 13.1 | 12.6 | 12.0 |
| 90 | 17.5 | 16.8 | 16.1 | 15.4 | 14.8 | 14.2 | 13.6 | 13.0 | 12.4 | 11.9 |
| 91 | 17.4 | 16.7 | 16.0 | 15.4 | 14.7 | 14.1 | 13.5 | 12.9 | 12.3 | 11.8 |
| 92 | 17.4 | 16.7 | 16.0 | 15.3 | 14.6 | 14.0 | 13.4 | 12.8 | 12.2 | 11.7 |
| 93 | 17.3 | 16.6 | 15.9 | 15.2 | 14.6 | 13.9 | 13.3 | 12.7 | 12.1 | 11.6 |
| 94 | 17.3 | 16.6 | 15.9 | 15.2 | 14.5 | 13.9 | 13.2 | 12.6 | 12.0 | 11.5 |
| 95 | 17.3 | 16.5 | 15.8 | 15.1 | 14.5 | 13.8 | 13.2 | 12.6 | 12.0 | 11.4 |
| 96 | 17.2 | 16.5 | 15.8 | 15.1 | 14.4 | 13.8 | 13.1 | 12.5 | 11.9 | 11.3 |
| 97 | 17.2 | 16.5 | 15.8 | 15.1 | 14.4 | 13.7 | 13.1 | 12.5 | 11.9 | 11.3 |
| 98 | 17.2 | 16.4 | 15.7 | 15.0 | 14.3 | 13.7 | 13.0 | 12.4 | 11.8 | 11.2 |
| 99 | 17.2 | 16.4 | 15.7 | 15.0 | 14.3 | 13.6 | 13.0 | 12.4 | 11.8 | 11.2 |
| 100 | 17.1 | 16.4 | 15.7 | 15.0 | 14.3 | 13.6 | 12.9 | 12.3 | 11.7 | 11.1 |
| 101 | 17.1 | 16.4 | 15.6 | 14.9 | 14.2 | 13.6 | 12.9 | 12.3 | 11.7 | 11.1 |
| 102 | 17.1 | 16.4 | 15.6 | 14.9 | 14.2 | 13.5 | 12.9 | 12.2 | 11.6 | 11.0 |
| 103 | 17.1 | 16.3 | 15.6 | 14.9 | 14.2 | 13.5 | 12.9 | 12.2 | 11.6 | 11.0 |
| 104 | 17.1 | 16.3 | 15.6 | 14.9 | 14.2 | 13.5 | 12.8 | 12.2 | 11.6 | 11.0 |
| 105 | 17.1 | 16.3 | 15.6 | 14.9 | 14.2 | 13.5 | 12.8 | 12.2 | 11.5 | 10.9 |
| 106 | 17.1 | 16.3 | 15.6 | 14.8 | 14.1 | 13.5 | 12.8 | 12.2 | 11.5 | 10.9 |
| 107 | 17.0 | 16.3 | 15.6 | 14.8 | 14.1 | 13.4 | 12.8 | 12.1 | 11.5 | 10.9 |
| 108 | 17.0 | 16.3 | 15.5 | 14.8 | 14.1 | 13.4 | 12.8 | 12.1 | 11.5 | 10.9 |
| 109 | 17.0 | 16.3 | 15.5 | 14.8 | 14.1 | 13.4 | 12.8 | 12.1 | 11.5 | 10.9 |
| AGES | 70 | 71 | 72 | 73 | 74 | 75 | 76 | 77 | 78 | 79 |
| 110 | 17.0 | 16.3 | 15.5 | 14.8 | 14.1 | 13.4 | 12.7 | 12.1 | 11.5 | 10.9 |
| 111 | 17.0 | 16.3 | 15.5 | 14.8 | 14.1 | 13.4 | 12.7 | 12.1 | 11.5 | 10.8 |
| 112 | 17.0 | 16.3 | 15.5 | 14.8 | 14.1 | 13.4 | 12.7 | 12.1 | 11.5 | 10.8 |
| 113 | 17.0 | 16.3 | 15.5 | 14.8 | 14.1 | 13.4 | 12.7 | 12.1 | 11.4 | 10.8 |
| 114 | 17.0 | 16.3 | 15.5 | 14.8 | 14.1 | 13.4 | 12.7 | 12.1 | 11.4 | 10.8 |
| 115+ | 17.0 | 16.3 | 15.5 | 14.8 | 14.1 | 13.4 | 12.7 | 12.1 | 11.4 | 10.8 |

| AGES | 80 | 81 | 82 | 83 | 84 | 85 | 86 | 87 | 88 | 89 |
|---|---|---|---|---|---|---|---|---|---|---|
| 80 | 13.8 | 13.4 | 13.1 | 12.8 | 12.6 | 12.3 | 12.1 | 11.9 | 11.7 | 11.5 |
| 81 | 13.4 | 13.1 | 12.7 | 12.4 | 12.2 | 11.9 | 11.7 | 11.4 | 11.3 | 11.1 |
| 82 | 13.1 | 12.7 | 12.4 | 12.1 | 11.8 | 11.5 | 11.3 | 11.0 | 10.8 | 10.6 |
| 83 | 12.8 | 12.4 | 12.1 | 11.7 | 11.4 | 11.1 | 10.9 | 10.6 | 10.4 | 10.2 |
| 84 | 12.6 | 12.2 | 11.8 | 11.4 | 11.1 | 10.8 | 10.5 | 10.3 | 10.1 | 9.9 |
| 85 | 12.3 | 11.9 | 11.5 | 11.1 | 10.8 | 10.5 | 10.2 | 9.9 | 9.7 | 9.5 |
| 86 | 12.1 | 11.7 | 11.3 | 10.9 | 10.5 | 10.2 | 9.9 | 9.6 | 9.4 | 9.2 |
| 87 | 11.9 | 11.4 | 11.0 | 10.6 | 10.3 | 9.9 | 9.6 | 9.4 | 9.1 | 8.9 |
| 88 | 11.7 | 11.3 | 10.8 | 10.4 | 10.1 | 9.7 | 9.4 | 9.1 | 8.8 | 8.6 |
| 89 | 11.5 | 11.1 | 10.6 | 10.2 | 9.9 | 9.5 | 9.2 | 8.9 | 8.6 | 8.3 |
| 90 | 11.4 | 10.9 | 10.5 | 10.1 | 9.7 | 9.3 | 9.0 | 8.6 | 8.3 | 8.1 |
| 91 | 11.3 | 10.8 | 10.3 | 9.9 | 9.5 | 9.1 | 8.8 | 8.4 | 8.1 | 7.9 |
| 92 | 11.2 | 10.7 | 10.2 | 9.8 | 9.3 | 9.0 | 8.6 | 8.3 | 8.0 | 7.7 |
| 93 | 11.1 | 10.6 | 10.1 | 9.6 | 9.2 | 8.8 | 8.5 | 8.1 | 7.8 | 7.5 |
| 94 | 11.0 | 10.5 | 10.0 | 9.5 | 9.1 | 8.7 | 8.3 | 8.0 | 7.6 | 7.3 |
| 95 | 10.9 | 10.4 | 9.9 | 9.4 | 9.0 | 8.6 | 8.2 | 7.8 | 7.5 | 7.2 |
| 96 | 10.8 | 10.3 | 9.8 | 9.3 | 8.9 | 8.5 | 8.1 | 7.7 | 7.4 | 7.1 |
| 97 | 10.7 | 10.2 | 9.7 | 9.2 | 8.8 | 8.4 | 8.0 | 7.6 | 7.3 | 6.9 |
| 98 | 10.7 | 10.1 | 9.6 | 9.2 | 8.7 | 8.3 | 7.9 | 7.5 | 7.1 | 6.8 |
| 99 | 10.6 | 10.1 | 9.6 | 9.1 | 8.6 | 8.2 | 7.8 | 7.4 | 7.0 | 6.7 |
| 100 | 10.6 | 10.0 | 9.5 | 9.0 | 8.5 | 8.1 | 7.7 | 7.3 | 6.9 | 6.6 |
| 101 | 10.5 | 10.0 | 9.4 | 9.0 | 8.5 | 8.0 | 7.6 | 7.2 | 6.9 | 6.5 |
| 102 | 10.5 | 9.9 | 9.4 | 8.9 | 8.4 | 8.0 | 7.5 | 7.1 | 6.8 | 6.4 |
| 103 | 10.4 | 9.9 | 9.4 | 8.8 | 8.4 | 7.9 | 7.5 | 7.1 | 6.7 | 6.3 |
| 104 | 10.4 | 9.8 | 9.3 | 8.8 | 8.3 | 7.9 | 7.4 | 7.0 | 6.6 | 6.3 |
| 105 | 10.4 | 9.8 | 9.3 | 8.8 | 8.3 | 7.8 | 7.4 | 7.0 | 6.6 | 6.2 |
| 106 | 10.3 | 9.8 | 9.2 | 8.7 | 8.2 | 7.8 | 7.3 | 6.9 | 6.5 | 6.2 |
| 107 | 10.3 | 9.8 | 9.2 | 8.7 | 8.2 | 7.7 | 7.3 | 6.9 | 6.5 | 6.2 |
| 108 | 10.3 | 9.7 | 9.2 | 8.7 | 8.2 | 7.7 | 7.3 | 6.8 | 6.4 | 6.1 |
| 109 | 10.3 | 9.7 | 9.2 | 8.7 | 8.2 | 7.7 | 7.2 | 6.8 | 6.4 | 6.1 |
| 110 | 10.3 | 9.7 | 9.2 | 8.6 | 8.1 | 7.7 | 7.2 | 6.8 | 6.4 | 6.0 |
| 111 | 10.3 | 9.7 | 9.1 | 8.6 | 8.1 | 7.6 | 7.2 | 6.8 | 6.3 | 6.0 |
| 112 | 10.2 | 9.7 | 9.1 | 8.6 | 8.1 | 7.6 | 7.2 | 6.7 | 6.3 | 5.9 |
| 113 | 10.2 | 9.7 | 9.1 | 8.6 | 8.1 | 7.6 | 7.2 | 6.7 | 6.3 | 5.9 |
| 114 | 10.2 | 9.7 | 9.1 | 8.6 | 8.1 | 7.6 | 7.1 | 6.7 | 6.3 | 5.9 |

| 115+ | 10.2 | 9.7 | 9.1 | 8.6 | 8.1 | 7.6 | 7.1 | 6.7 | 6.3 | 5.9 |
|---|---|---|---|---|---|---|---|---|---|---|

| AGES | 90 | 91 | 92 | 93 | 94 | 95 | 96 | 97 | 98 | 99 |
|---|---|---|---|---|---|---|---|---|---|---|
| 90 | 7.8 | 7.6 | 7.4 | 7.2 | 7.1 | 6.9 | 6.8 | 6.6 | 6.5 | 6.4 |
| 91 | 7.6 | 7.4 | 7.2 | 7.0 | 6.8 | 6.7 | 6.5 | 6.4 | 6.3 | 6.1 |
| 92 | 7.4 | 7.2 | 7.0 | 6.8 | 6.6 | 6.4 | 6.3 | 6.1 | 6.0 | 5.9 |
| 93 | 7.2 | 7.0 | 6.8 | 6.6 | 6.4 | 6.2 | 6.1 | 5.9 | 5.8 | 5.6 |
| 94 | 7.1 | 6.8 | 6.6 | 6.4 | 6.2 | 6.0 | 5.9 | 5.7 | 5.6 | 5.4 |
| 95 | 6.9 | 6.7 | 6.4 | 6.2 | 6.0 | 5.8 | 5.7 | 5.5 | 5.4 | 5.2 |
| 96 | 6.8 | 6.5 | 6.3 | 6.1 | 5.9 | 5.7 | 5.5 | 5.3 | 5.2 | 5.0 |
| 97 | 6.6 | 6.4 | 6.1 | 5.9 | 5.7 | 5.5 | 5.3 | 5.2 | 5.0 | 4.9 |
| 98 | 6.5 | 6.3 | 6.0 | 5.8 | 5.6 | 5.4 | 5.2 | 5.0 | 4.8 | 4.7 |
| 99 | 6.4 | 6.1 | 5.9 | 5.6 | 5.4 | 5.2 | 5.0 | 4.9 | 4.7 | 4.5 |
| 100 | 6.3 | 6.0 | 5.8 | 5.5 | 5.3 | 5.1 | 4.9 | 4.7 | 4.5 | 4.4 |
| 101 | 6.2 | 5.9 | 5.6 | 5.4 | 5.2 | 5.0 | 4.8 | 4.6 | 4.4 | 4.2 |
| 102 | 6.1 | 5.8 | 5.5 | 5.3 | 5.1 | 4.8 | 4.6 | 4.4 | 4.3 | 4.1 |
| 103 | 6.0 | 5.7 | 5.4 | 5.2 | 5.0 | 4.7 | 4.5 | 4.3 | 4.1 | 4.0 |
| 104 | 5.9 | 5.6 | 5.4 | 5.1 | 4.9 | 4.6 | 4.4 | 4.2 | 4.0 | 3.8 |
| 105 | 5.9 | 5.6 | 5.3 | 5.0 | 4.8 | 4.5 | 4.3 | 4.1 | 3.9 | 3.7 |
| 106 | 5.8 | 5.5 | 5.2 | 4.9 | 4.7 | 4.5 | 4.2 | 4.0 | 3.8 | 3.6 |
| 107 | 5.8 | 5.4 | 5.1 | 4.9 | 4.6 | 4.4 | 4.2 | 3.9 | 3.7 | 3.5 |
| 108 | 5.7 | 5.4 | 5.1 | 4.8 | 4.6 | 4.3 | 4.1 | 3.9 | 3.7 | 3.5 |
| 109 | 5.7 | 5.3 | 5.0 | 4.8 | 4.5 | 4.3 | 4.0 | 3.8 | 3.6 | 3.4 |
| 110 | 5.6 | 5.3 | 5.0 | 4.7 | 4.5 | 4.2 | 4.0 | 3.8 | 3.5 | 3.3 |
| 111 | 5.6 | 5.3 | 5.0 | 4.7 | 4.4 | 4.2 | 3.9 | 3.7 | 3.5 | 3.3 |
| 112 | 5.6 | 5.3 | 4.9 | 4.7 | 4.4 | 4.1 | 3.9 | 3.7 | 3.5 | 3.2 |
| 113 | 5.6 | 5.2 | 4.9 | 4.6 | 4.4 | 4.1 | 3.9 | 3.6 | 3.4 | 3.2 |
| 114 | 5.6 | 5.2 | 4.9 | 4.6 | 4.3 | 4.1 | 3.9 | 3.6 | 3.4 | 3.2 |
| 115+ | 5.5 | 5.2 | 4.9 | 4.6 | 4.3 | 4.1 | 3.8 | 3.6 | 3.4 | 3.1 |

| AGES | 100 | 101 | 102 | 103 | 104 | 105 | 106 | 107 | 108 | 109 |
|---|---|---|---|---|---|---|---|---|---|---|
| 100 | 4.2 | 4.1 | 3.9 | 3.8 | 3.7 | 3.5 | 3.4 | 3.3 | 3.3 | 3.2 |
| 101 | 4.1 | 3.9 | 3.7 | 3.6 | 3.5 | 3.4 | 3.2 | 3.1 | 3.1 | 3.0 |
| 102 | 3.9 | 3.7 | 3.6 | 3.4 | 3.3 | 3.2 | 3.1 | 3.0 | 2.9 | 2.8 |
| 103 | 3.8 | 3.6 | 3.4 | 3.3 | 3.2 | 3.0 | 2.9 | 2.8 | 2.7 | 2.6 |
| 104 | 3.7 | 3.5 | 3.3 | 3.2 | 3.0 | 2.9 | 2.7 | 2.6 | 2.5 | 2.4 |
| 105 | 3.5 | 3.4 | 3.2 | 3.0 | 2.9 | 2.7 | 2.6 | 2.5 | 2.4 | 2.3 |
| 106 | 3.4 | 3.2 | 3.1 | 2.9 | 2.7 | 2.6 | 2.4 | 2.3 | 2.2 | 2.1 |
| 107 | 3.3 | 3.1 | 3.0 | 2.8 | 2.6 | 2.5 | 2.3 | 2.2 | 2.1 | 2.0 |
| 108 | 3.3 | 3.1 | 2.9 | 2.7 | 2.5 | 2.4 | 2.2 | 2.1 | 1.9 | 1.8 |
| 109 | 3.2 | 3.0 | 2.8 | 2.6 | 2.4 | 2.3 | 2.1 | 2.0 | 1.8 | 1.7 |
| 110 | 3.1 | 2.9 | 2.7 | 2.5 | 2.3 | 2.2 | 2.0 | 1.9 | 1.7 | 1.6 |
| 111 | 3.1 | 2.9 | 2.7 | 2.5 | 2.3 | 2.1 | 1.9 | 1.8 | 1.6 | 1.5 |
| 112 | 3.0 | 2.8 | 2.6 | 2.4 | 2.2 | 2.0 | 1.9 | 1.7 | 1.5 | 1.4 |
| 113 | 3.0 | 2.8 | 2.6 | 2.4 | 2.2 | 2.0 | 1.8 | 1.6 | 1.5 | 1.3 |
| 114 | 3.0 | 2.7 | 2.5 | 2.3 | 2.1 | 1.9 | 1.8 | 1.6 | 1.4 | 1.3 |
| 115+ | 2.9 | 2.7 | 2.5 | 2.3 | 2.1 | 1.9 | 1.7 | 1.5 | 1.4 | 1.2 |

| AGES | 110 | 111 | 112 | 113 | 114 | 115+ |
|---|---|---|---|---|---|---|
| 110 | 1.5 | 1.4 | 1.3 | 1.2 | 1.1 | 1.1 |
| 111 | 1.4 | 1.2 | 1.1 | 1.1 | 1.0 | 1.0 |
| 112 | 1.3 | 1.1 | 1.0 | 1.0 | 1.0 | 1.0 |
| 113 | 1.2 | 1.1 | 1.0 | 1.0 | 1.0 | 1.0 |
| 114 | 1.1 | 1.0 | 1.0 | 1.0 | 1.0 | 1.0 |
| 115+ | 1.1 | 1.0 | 1.0 | 1.0 | 1.0 | 1.0 |

Q-4. May the tables under this section be changed?

A-4. The Single Life Table, Uniform Lifetime Table and Joint and Last Survivor Table provided in A-1 through A-3 of this section may be changed by the Commissioner in revenue rulings, notices, and other guidance published in the Internal Revenue Bulletin. See § 601.601(d)(2)(ii)(b) of this chapter.

T.D. 8987, 4/16/2002.

### § 1.401(a)(17)-1 Limitation on annual compensation.

***Caution:*** The Treasury has not yet amended Reg § 1.401(a)(17)-1 to reflect changes made by P.L. 107-16, P.L. 103-465.

**(a) Compensation limit requirement.** *(1) In general.* In order to be a qualified plan, a plan must satisfy section

401(a)(17). Section 401(a)(17) provides an annual compensation limit for each employee under a qualified plan. This limit applies to a qualified plan in two ways. First, a plan may not base allocations, in the case of a defined contribution plan, or benefit accruals, in the case of a defined benefit plan, on compensation in excess of the annual compensation limit. Second, the amount of an employee's annual compensation that may be taken into account in applying certain specified nondiscrimination rules under the Internal Revenue Code is subject to the annual compensation limit. These two limitations are set forth in paragraphs (b) and (c) of this section, respectively. Paragraph (d) of this section provides the effective dates of section 401(a)(17), the amendments made by section 13212 of the Omnibus Budget Reconciliation Act of 1993 (OBRA '93), and this section. Paragraph (e) of this section provides rules for determining post-effective-date accrued benefits under the fresh-start rules.

*(2) Annual compensation limit for plan years beginning before January 1, 1994.* For purposes of this section, for plan years beginning prior to the OBRA '93 effective date, annual compensation limit means $200,000, adjusted as provided by the Commissioner. The amount of the annual compensation limit is adjusted at the same time and in the same manner as under section 415(d). The base period for the annual adjustment is the calendar quarter ending December 31, 1988, and the first adjustment is effective on January 1, 1990. Any increase in the annual compensation limit is effective as of January 1 of a calendar year and applies to any plan year beginning in that calendar year. In any plan year beginning prior to the OBRA '93 effective date, if compensation for any plan year beginning prior to the statutory effective date is used for determining allocations or benefit accruals, or when applying any nondiscrimination rule, then the annual compensation limit for the first plan year beginning on or after the statutory effective date (generally $200,000) must be applied to compensation for that prior plan year.

*(3) Annual compensation limit for plan years beginning on or after January 1, 1994.* (i) In general. For purposes of this section, for plan years beginning on or after the OBRA '93 effective date, annual compensation limit means $150,000, adjusted as provided by the Commissioner. The adjusted dollar amount of the annual compensation limit is determined by adjusting the $150,000 amount for changes in the cost of living as provided in paragraph (a)(3)(ii) of this section and rounding this adjusted dollar amount as provided in paragraph (a)(3)(iii) of this section. Any increase in the annual compensation limit is effective as of January 1 of a calendar year and applies to any plan year beginning in that calendar year. For example, if a plan has a plan year beginning July 1, 1994, and ending June 30, 1995, the annual compensation limit in effect on January 1, 1994 ($150,000), applies to the plan for the entire plan year.

(ii) Cost of living adjustment. The $150,000 amount is adjusted for changes in the cost of living by the Commissioner at the same time and in the same manner as under section 415(d). The base period for the annual adjustment is the calendar quarter ending December 31, 1993.

(iii) Rounding of adjusted compensation limit. After the $150,000, adjusted in accordance with paragraph (a)(3)(ii) of this section, exceeds the annual compensation limit for the prior calendar year by $10,000 or more, the annual compensation limit will be increased by the amount of such excess, rounded down to the next lowest multiple of $10,000.

*(4) Additional guidance.* The Commissioner may, in revenue rulings and procedures, notices, and other guidance, published in the Internal Revenue Bulletin (see § 601.601(d)(2)(ii)(b) of this chapter), provide any additional guidance that may be necessary or appropriate concerning the annual limits on compensation under section 401(a)(17).

**(b) Plan limit on compensation.** *(1) General rule.* A plan does not satisfy section 401(a)(17) unless it provides that the compensation taken into account for any employee in determining plan allocations or benefit accruals for any plan year is limited to the annual compensation limit. For purposes of this rule, allocations and benefit accruals under a plan include all benefits provided under the plan, including ancillary benefits.

*(2) Plan-year-by-plan-year requirement.* For purposes of this paragraph (b), the limit in effect for the current plan year applies only to the compensation for that year that is taken into account in determining plan allocations or benefit accruals for the year. The compensation for any prior plan year taken into account in determining an employee's allocations or benefit accruals for the current plan year is subject to the applicable annual compensation limit in effect for that prior year. Thus, increases in the annual compensation limit apply only to compensation taken into account for the plan year in which the increase is effective. In addition, if compensation for any plan year beginning prior to the OBRA '93 effective date is used for determining allocations or benefit accruals in a plan year beginning on or after the OBRA '93 effective date, then the annual compensation limit for that prior year is the annual compensation limit in effect for the first plan year beginning on or after the OBRA '93 effective date (generally $150,000).

*(3) Application of limit to a plan year.* (i) In general. For purposes of applying this paragraph (b), the annual compensation limit is applied to the compensation for the plan year on which allocations or benefit accruals are based.

(ii) Compensation for the plan year. If a plan determines compensation used in determining allocations or benefit accruals for a plan year based on compensation for the plan year, then the annual compensation limit that applies to the compensation for the plan year is the limit in effect for the calendar year in which the plan year begins. Alternatively, if a plan determines compensation used in determining allocations or benefit accruals for the plan year on the basis of compensation for a 12-consecutive-month period, or periods, ending no later than the last day of the plan year, then the annual compensation limit applies to compensation for each of those periods based on the annual compensation limit in effect for the respective calendar year in which each 12-month period begins.

(iii) Compensation for a period of less than 12-months. (A) Proration required. If compensation for a period of less than 12 months is used for a plan year, then the otherwise applicable annual compensation limit is reduced in the same proportion as the reduction in the 12-month period. For example, if a defined benefit plan provides that the accrual for each month in a plan year is separately determined based on the compensation for that month and the plan year accrual is the sum of the accruals for all months, then the annual compensation limit for each month is 1/12th of the annual compensation limit for the plan year. In addition, if the period for determining compensation used in calculating an employee's allocation or accrual for a plan year is a short plan year (i.e., shorter than 12 months), the annual compensation limit is an amount equal to the otherwise applicable annual compensation limit multiplied by a fraction, the numerator of which is the number of months in the short plan year, and the denominator of which is 12.

(B) No proration required for participation for less than a full plan year. Notwithstanding paragraph (b)(3)(iii)(A) of this section, a plan is not treated as using compensation for less than 12 months for a plan year merely because the plan formula provides that the allocation or accrual for each employee is based on compensation for the portion of the plan year during which the employee is a participant in the plan. In addition, no proration is required merely because an employee is covered under a plan for less than a full plan year, provided that allocations or benefit accruals are otherwise determined using compensation for a period of at least 12 months. Finally, notwithstanding paragraph (b)(3)(iii)(A) of this section, no proration is required merely because the amount of elective contributions (within the meaning of § 1.401(k)-6), matching contributions (within the meaning of § 1.401(m)-5), or employee contributions (within the meaning of § 1.401(m)-5) that is contributed for each pay period during a plan year is determined separately using compensation for that pay period.

*(4) Limits on multiple employer and multiemployer plans.* For purposes of this paragraph (b), in the case of a plan described in section 413(c) or 414(f) (a plan maintained by more than one employer), the annual compensation limit applies separately with respect to the compensation of an employee from each employer maintaining the plan instead of applying to the employee's total compensation from all employers maintaining the plan.

*(5) Family aggregation.* [Reserved]

*(6) Examples.* The following examples illustrate the rules in this paragraph (b).

*Example (1).* Plan X is a defined benefit plan with a calendar year plan year and bases benefits on the average of an employee's high 3 consecutive years' compensation. The OBRA '93 effective date for Plan X is January 1, 1994. Employee A's high 3 consecutive years' compensation prior to the application of the annual compensation limits is $160,000 (1994), $155,000 (1993), and $135,000 (1992). To satisfy this paragraph (b), Plan X cannot base plan benefits for Employee A in 1994 on compensation in excess of $145,000 (the average of $150,000 (A's 1994 compensation capped by the annual compensation limit), $150,000 (A's 1993 compensation capped by the $150,000 annual compensation limit applicable to all years before 1994), and $135,000 (A's 1992 compensation capped by the $150,000 annual compensation limit applicable to all years before 1994)). For purposes of determining the 1994 accrual, each year (1994, 1993, and 1992), not the average of the 3 years, is subject to the 1994 annual compensation limit of $150,000.

*Example (2).* Assume the same facts as Example 1, except that Employee A's high 3 consecutive years' compensation prior to the application of the limits is $185,000 (1997), $175,000 (1996), and $165,000 (1995). Assume that the annual compensation limit is first adjusted to $160,000 for plan years beginning on or after January 1, 1997. Plan X cannot base plan benefits for Employee A in 1997 on compensation in excess of $153,333 (the average of $160,000 (A's 1997 compensation capped by the 1997 limit), $150,000 (A's 1996 compensation capped by the 1996 limit), and $150,000 (A's 1995 compensation capped by the 1995 limit)).

*Example (3).* Plan Y is a defined benefit plan that bases benefits on an employee's high consecutive 36 months of compensation ending within the plan year. Employee B's high 36 months are the period September 1995 to August 1998, in which Employee B earned $50,000 in each month. Assume that the annual compensation limit is first adjusted to $160,000 for plan years beginning on or after January 1, 1997. The annual compensation limit is $150,000, $150,000, and $160,000 in 1995, 1996, and 1997, respectively. To satisfy this paragraph (b), Plan Y cannot base Employe B's plan benefits for the 1998 plan year on compensation in excess of $153,333. This amount is determined by applying the applicable annual compensation limit to compensation for each of the three 12-consecutive-month periods. The September 1995 to August 1996 period is capped by the annual compensation limit of $150,000 for 1995; the September 1996 to August 1997 period is capped by the annual compensation limit of $150,000 for 1996; and the September 1997 to August 1998 period is capped by the annual compensation limit of $160,000 for 1997. The average of these capped amounts is the annual compensation limit applicable in determining benefits for the 1998 year.

*Example (4).* (a) Employer P is a partnership. Employer P maintains Plan Z, a profit-sharing plan that provides for an annual allocation of employer contributions of 15 percent of plan year compensation for employees other than self-employed individuals, and 13.0435 percent of plan year compensation for self-employed individuals. The plan year of Plan Z is the calendar year. The OBRA '93 effective date for Plan Z is January 1, 1994. In order to satisfy section 401(a)(17), as amended by OBRA '93, the plan provides that, beginning with the 1994 plan year, the plan year compensation used in determining the allocation of employer contributions for each employee may not exceed the annual limit in effect for the plan year under OBRA '93. Plan Z defines compensation for self-employed individuals (employees within the meaning of section 401(c)(1)) as the self-employed individual's net profit from self-employment attributable to Employer P minus the amount of the self-employed individual's deduction under section 164(f) for one-half of self-employment taxes. Plan Z defines compensation for all other employees as wages within the meaning of section 3401(a). Employee C and Employee D are partners of Employer P and thus are self-employed individuals. Neither Employee C nor Employee D owns an interest in any other business or is a common-law employee in any business. For the 1994 calendar year, Employee C has net profit from self-employment of $80,000, and Employee D has net profit from self-employment of $175,000. The deduction for Employee C under section 164(f) for one-half of self-employment taxes is $4,828. The deduction for Employee D under section 164(f) for one-half of self-employment taxes is $6,101.

(b) The plan year compensation under the plan formula for Employee C is $75,172 ($80,000 minus $4,828). The allocation of employer contributions under the plan allocation formula for 1994 for Employee C is $9,805 ($75,172 (Employee C's plan year compensation for 1994) multiplied by 13.0435%). The plan year compensation under the plan formula before application of the annual limit under section 401(a)(17) for Employee D is $168,899 ($175,000 minus $6101). After application of the annual limit, the plan year compensation for the 1994 plan year for Employee D is $150,000 (the annual limit for 1994). Therefore, the allocation of employer contributions under the plan allocation formula for 1994 for Employee D is $19,565 ($150,000 (Employee D's plan year compensation after application of the annual limit for 1994) multiplied by 13.0435%).

*Example (5).* The facts are the same as in Example 4, except that Plan Z provides that plan year compensation for self-employed individuals is defined as earned income within the meaning of section 401(c)(2) attributable to Employer P. In addition, Plan Z provides for an annual allocation of employer contributions of 15 percent of plan year compensation for all employees in the plan, including self-employed individuals, such as Employees C and D. The net profit from self-employment for Employee C and the net profit from self-employment for Employee D are the same as provided in Example 4. However, the earned income of Employee C determined in accordance with section 401(c)(2) is $65,367 ($80,000 minus $4,828 minus $9,805). The earned income of Employee D determined in accordance with section 401(c)(2) is $146,869 ($175,000 minus $6,101 minus $22,030). Therefore, the allocation of employer contributions under the plan allocation formula for 1994 for Employee C is $9,805 ($65,367 (Employee C's plan year compensation for 1994) multiplied by 15%). Employee D's earned income for 1994 does not exceed the 1994 annual limit of $150,000. Therefore, the allocation of employer contributions under the plan allocation formula for 1994 for Employee D is $22,030 ($146,869 (Employee D's plan year compensation for 1994) multiplied by 15%).

**(c) Limit on compensation for nondiscrimination rules.** *(1) General rule.* The annual compensation limit applies for purposes of applying the nondiscrimination rules under sections 401(a)(4), 401(a)(5), 401(l), 401(k)(3), 401(m)(2), 403(b)(12), 404(a)(2) and 410(b)(2). The annual compensation limit also applies in determining whether an alternative method of determining compensation impermissibly discriminates under section 414(s)(3). Thus, for example, the annual compensation limit applies when determining a self-employed individual's total earned income that is used to determine the equivalent alternative compensation amount under § 1.414(s)-1(g)(1). This paragraph (c) provides rules for applying the annual compensation limit for these purposes. For purposes of this paragraph (c), compensation means the compensation used in applying the applicable nondiscrimination rule.

*(2) Plan-year-by-plan-year requirement.* For purposes of this paragraph (c), when applying an applicable nondiscrimination rule for a plan year, the compensation for each plan year taken into account is limited to the applicable annual compensation limit in effect for that year, and an employee's compensation for that plan year in excess of the limit is disregarded. Thus, if the nondiscrimination provision is applied on the basis of compensation determined over a period of more than one year (for example, average annual compensation), the annual compensation limit in effect for each of the plan years that is taken into account in determining the average applies to the respective plan year's compensation. In addition, if compensation for any plan year beginning prior to the OBRA '93 effective date is used when applying any nondiscrimination rule in a plan year beginning on or after the OBRA '93 effective date, then the annual compensation limit for that prior year is the annual compensation limit for the first plan year beginning on or after the OBRA '93 effective date (generally $150,000).

*(3) Plan-by-plan limit.* For purposes of this paragraph (c), the annual compensation limit applies separately to each plan (or group of plans treated as a single plan) of an employer for purposes of the applicable nondiscrimination requirement. For this purpose, the plans included in the testing group taken into account in determining whether the average benefit percentage test of § 1.410(b)-5 is satisfied are generally treated as a single plan.

*(4) Application of limit to a plan year.* The rules provided in paragraph (b)(3) of this section regarding the application of the limit to a plan year apply for purposes of this paragraph (c).

*(5) Limits on multiple employer and multiemployer plans.* The rule provided in paragraph (b)(4) of this section regarding the application of the limit to multiple employer and multiemployer plans applies for purposes of this paragraph (c).

**(d) Effective date.** *(1) Statutory effective date.* (i) General rule. Except as otherwise provided in this paragraph (d), section 401(a)(17) applies to a plan as of the first plan year beginning on or after January 1, 1989. For purposes of this section, statutory effective date generally means the first day of the first plan year that section 401(a)(17) is applicable to a plan. In the case of governmental plans, statutory effective date means the first day of the first plan year for which the plan is not deemed to satisfy section 401(a)(17) by reason of paragraph (d)(4) of this section.

(ii) Exception for collectively bargained plans. In the case of a plan maintained pursuant to one or more collective bargaining agreements between employee representatives and one or more employers ratified before March 1, 1986, section 401(a)(17) applies to allocations and benefit accruals for plan years beginning on or after the earlier of—

(A) January 1, 1991; or

(B) The later of January 1, 1989, or the date on which the last of the collective bargaining agreements terminates (determined without regard to any extension or renegotiation of any agreement occurring after February 28, 1986). For purposes of this paragraph (d)(1)(ii), the rules of § 1.410(b)-10(a)(2) apply for purposes of determining whether a plan is maintained pursuant to one or more collective bargaining agreements, and any extension or renegotiation of a collective bargaining agreement, which extension or renegotiation is ratified after February 28, 1986, is to be disregarded in determining the date on which the agreement terminates.

*(2) OBRA '93 effective date.* (i) In general. For purposes of this section, OBRA '93 effective date means the first day of the first plan year beginning on or after January 1, 1994, except as provided in this paragraph (d)(2).

(ii) Exception for collectively bargained plans. (A) In general. In the case of a plan maintained pursuant to one or more collective bargaining agreements between employee representatives and 1 or more employers ratified before August 10, 1993, OBRA '93 effective date means the first day of the first plan year beginning on or after the earlier of—

(1) The latest of—

(i) January 1, 1994;

(ii) The date on which the last of such collective bargaining agreements terminates (without regard to any extension, amendment, or, modification of such agreements on or after August 10, 1993); or

(iii) In the case of a plan maintained pursuant to collective bargaining under the Railway Labor Act, the date of execution of an extension or replacement of the last of such collective bargaining agreements in effect on August 10, 1993; or

(2) January 1, 1997.

(B) Determination of whether plan is collectively bargained. For purposes of this paragraph (d)(2)(ii), the rules of § 1.410(b)-10(a)(2) apply for purposes of determining whether a plan is maintained pursuant to one or more collective bargaining agreements, except that August 10, 1993, is substituted for March 1, 1986, as the date before which the collective bargaining agreements must be ratified.

*(3) Regulatory effective date.* This § 1.401(a)(17)-1 applies to plan years beginning on or after the OBRA '93 effective date. However, in the case of a plan maintained by an organization that is exempt from income taxation under section 501(a), including plans subject to section 403(b)(12)(A)(i) (nonelective plans), this § 1.401(a)(17)-1 applies to plan years beginning on or after January 1, 1996. For plan years beginning before the effective date of these regulations and on or after the statutory effective date, a plan must be operated in accordance with a reasonable, good faith interpretation of section 401(a)(17), taking into account, if applicable, the OBRA '93 reduction to the annual compensation limit under section 401(a)(17).

*(4) Special rules for governmental plans.* (i) Deemed satisfaction by governmental plans. In the case of governmental plans described in section 414(d), including plans subject to section 403(b)(12)(A)(i) (nonelective plans), section 401(a)(17) is considered satisfied for plan years beginning before the later of January 1, 1996, or 90 days after the opening of the first legislative session beginning on or after January 1, 1996, of the governing body with authority to amend the plan, if that body does not meet continuously. For purposes of this paragraph (d)(4), the term governing body with authority to amend the plan means the legislature, board, commission, council, or other governing body with authority to amend the plan.

(ii) Transition rule for governmental plans. (A) In general. In the case of an eligible participant in a governmental plan (within the meaning of section 414(d)), the annual compensation limit under this section shall not apply to the extent that the application of the limitation would reduce the amount of compensation that is allowed to be taken into account under the plan below the amount that was allowed to be taken into account under the plan as in effect on July 1, 1993. Thus, for example, if a plan as in effect on July 1, 1993, determined benefits without any reference to a limit on compensation, then the annual compensation limit in effect under this section will not apply to any eligible participant in any future year.

(B) Eligible participant. For purposes of this paragraph (d)(4)(ii), an eligible participant is an individual who first became a participant in the plan prior to the first day of the first plan year beginning after the earlier of—

(1) The last day of the plan year by which a plan amendment to reflect the amendments made by section 13212 of OBRA '93 is both adopted and effective; or

(2) December 31, 1995.

(C) Plan must be amended to incorporate limits. This paragraph (d)(4)(ii) shall not apply to any eligible participant in a plan unless the plan is amended so that the plan incorporates by reference the annual compensation limit under section 401(a)(17), effective with respect to noneligible participants for plan years beginning after December 31, 1995 (or earlier, if the plan amendment so provides).

*(5) Benefits earned prior to effective date.* (i) In general. Allocations under a defined contribution plan or benefits accrued under a defined benefit plan for plan years beginning before the statutory effective date are not subject to the annual compensation limit. Allocations under a defined contribution plan or benefits accrued under a defined benefit plan for plan years beginning on or after the statutory effective date, but before the OBRA '93 effective date, are subject to the annual compensation limit under paragraph (a)(2) of this section. However these allocations or accruals are not subject to the OBRA '93 reduction to the annual compensation limit described in paragraph (a)(3) of this section.

(ii) Allocation for a plan. The allocations for a plan year include amounts described in § 1.401(a)(4)-2(c)(ii) or § 1.401(m)-1(a)(3) plus the earnings, expenses, gains, and losses attributable to those amounts.

(iii) Benefits accrued for years before the effective date. The benefits accrued for plan years prior to a specified date by any employee are the employee's benefits accrued under the plan, determined as if those benefits had been frozen (as defined in § 1.401(a)(4)-13(c)(3)(i)) as of the day immediately preceding such specified date. Thus, for example, benefits accrued for those plan years generally do not include any benefits accrued under an amendment increasing prior benefits that is adopted after the date on which the employee's benefits under the plan must be treated as frozen.

**(e) Determination of post-effective-date accrued benefits.** *(1) In general.* The plan formula that is used to determine the amount of allocations or benefit accruals for plan years beginning on or after the dates described in paragraph (d)(1) or (2) must comply with section 401(a)(17) as in effect on such date. This paragraph (e) provides rules for applying section 401(a)(17) in the case of section 401(a)(17) employees who accrue additional benefits under a defined benefit plan in a plan year beginning on or after the relevant effective date. Paragraph (e)(2) of this section contains definitions used in applying these rules. Paragraphs (e)(3) and (e)(4) of this section explain the application of the fresh-start rules in § 1.401(a)(4)-13 to the determination of the accrued benefits of section 401(a)(17) employees.

*(2) Definitions.* For purposes of this paragraph (e), the following definitions apply:

(i) Section 401(a)(17) employee. An employee is a section 401(a)(17) employee as of a date, on or after the statutory effective date, if the employee's current accrued benefit as of that date is based on compensation for a year prior to the statutory effective date that exceeded the annual compensation limit for the first plan year beginning on or after the statutory effective date. In addition, an employee is a section 401(a)(17) employee as of a date, on or after the OBRA '93 effective date, if the employee's current accrued benefit as of that date is based on compensation for a year prior to the OBRA '93 effective date that exceeded the annual compensation limit for the first plan year beginning on or after the OBRA '93 effective date. For this purpose, a current accrued benefit is not treated as based on compensation that exceeded the relevant annual compensation limit, if a plan makes a fresh start using the formula with wear-away described in § 1.401(a)(4)-13(c)(4)(ii), and the employee's accrued benefit determined under § 1.401(a)(4)-13(c)(4)(ii)(B), taking into account the annual compensation limit, exceeds the employee's frozen accrued benefit (or, if applicable, the employee's adjusted accrued benefit) as of the fresh-start date.

(ii) Section 401(a)(17) fresh-start date. Section 401(a)(17) fresh-start date means a fresh-start date as defined in § 1.401(a)(4)-12 not earlier than the last day of the last plan year beginning before the statutory effective date, and not later than the last day of the last plan year beginning before the effective date of these regulations.

(iii) OBRA '93 fresh-start date. OBRA '93 fresh-start date means a fresh-start date as defined in § 1.401(a)(4)-12 not earlier than the last day of the last plan year beginning before the OBRA '93 effective date, and not later than the last day of the last plan year beginning before the effective date of these regulations.

(iv) Section 401(a)(17) frozen accrued benefit. Section 401(a)(17) frozen accrued benefit means the accrued benefit for any section 401(a)(17) employee frozen (as defined in § 1.401(a)(4)-13(c)(3)(i)) as of the last day of the last plan year beginning before the statutory effective date.

(v) OBRA '93 frozen accrued benefit. OBRA '93 frozen accrued benefit means the accrued benefit for any section 401(a)(17) employee frozen (as defined in § 1.401(a)(4)-13(c)(3)(i)) as of the OBRA '93 fresh-start date.

*(3) Application of fresh-start rules.* (i) General rule. In order to satisfy section 401(a)(17), a defined benefit plan must determine the accrued benefit of each section 401(a)(17) employee by applying the fresh-start rules in § 1.401(a)(4)-13(c). The fresh-start rules must be applied using a section 401(a)(17) fresh-start date and using the plan benefit formula, after amendment to comply with section 401(a)(17) and this section, as the formula applicable to benefit accruals in the current plan year. In addition, the fresh-start rules must be applied to determine the accrued benefit of each section 401(a)(17) employee using an OBRA '93 fresh-start date and using the plan benefit formula, after amendment to comply with the reduction in the section 401(a)(17) annual compensation limit described in paragraph (a)(3) of this section, as the formula applicable to benefit accruals in the current plan year.

(ii) Consistency rules in § 1.401(a)(4)-13(c) and (d). (A) General rule. In applying the fresh-start rules of § 1.401(a)(4)-13(c) and (d), the group of section 401(a)(17) employees is a fresh-start group. See § 1.401(a)(4)-13(c)(5)(ii)(A). Thus, the consistency rules of those sections govern, unless otherwise provided. For example, if the plan is using a fresh-start date applicable to all employees and is not adjusting frozen accrued benefits under § 1.401(a)(4)-13(d) for employees who are not section 401(a)(17) employees, then the frozen accrued benefits for section 401(a)(17) employees may not be adjusted under § 1.401(a)(4)-13(d) or this paragraph (e).

(B) Determination of adjusted accrued benefit. If the fresh-start rules of § 1.401(a)(4)-13(c) and (d) are applied to determine the benefits of all employees after a fresh-start date, the plan will not fail to satisfy the consistency requirement of § 1.401(a)(4)-13(c)(5)(i) merely because the plan makes the adjustment described in § 1.401(a)(4)-13(d) to the frozen accrued benefits of employees who are not section 401(a)(17) employees, but does not make the adjustment to the frozen accrued benefits of section 401(a)(17) employees. In addition, the plan does not fail to satisfy the consistency requirement of § 1.401(a)(4)-13(c)(5)(i) merely because the plan makes the adjustment described in § 1.401(a)(4)-13(d) for section 401(a)(17) employees on the basis of the compensation formula that was used to determine the frozen accrued benefit (as required under paragraph (e)(4)(iii) of this section) but makes the adjustment for employees who are not section 401(a)(17) employees on the basis of any other method provided in § 1.401(a)(4)-13(d)(8).

*(4) Permitted adjustments to frozen accrued benefit of section 401(a)(17) employees.* (i) General rule. Except as otherwise provided in paragraphs (e)(4)(ii) and (iii) of this section, the rules in § 1.401(a)(4)-13(c)(3) (permitting certain adjustments to frozen accrued benefits) apply to section 401(a)(17) frozen accrued benefits or OBRA '93 frozen accrued benefits.

(ii) Option forms of benefit. After either the section 401(a)(17) fresh-start date or the OBRA '93 fresh-start date, a plan may be amended either to provide a new optional form of benefit or to make an optional form of benefit available with respect to the section 401(a)(17) frozen accrued benefit or the OBRA '93 frozen accrued benefit, provided that the optional form of benefit is not subsidized. Whether an optional form is subsidized may be determined using any reasonable actuarial assumptions.

(iii) Adjusting section 401(a)(17) accrued benefits. (A) In general. If the plan adjusts accrued benefits for employees under the rules of § 1.401(a)(4)-13(d) as of a fresh-start date, the adjusted accrued benefit (within the meaning of § 1.401(a)(4)-13(d)) for each section 401(a)(17) employee must be determined after the fresh-start date by reference to the plan's compensation formula that was actually used to determine the frozen accrued benefit as of the fresh-start date. For this purpose, the plan's compensation formula incorporates the plan's underlying compensation definition and compensation averaging period. In making the adjustment, the denominator of the adjustment fraction described in § 1.401(a)(4)-13(d)(8)(i) is the employee's compensation as of the fresh-start date using the plan's compensation formula as of that date and, in the case of an OBRA '93 fresh-start date, reflecting the annual compensation limits that applied as of the fresh-start date. The numerator of the adjustment fraction is the employee's updated compensation (i.e., compensation for the current plan year within the meaning of § 1.401(a)(4)-13(d)(8)), determined after applying the annual compensation limits to each year's compensation that is used in the plan's compensation formula as of the fresh-start date. Similarly, in applying the alternative rule in § 1.401(a)(4)-13(d)(8)(v), the updated compensation that is substituted must be determined after applying the annual compensation limits to each year's compensation that is used in the plan's compensation formula. Thus, no adjustment will be permitted unless the updated compensation (determined after applying the annual compensation limit) exceeds the compensation that was used to determine the employee's frozen accrued benefit.

(B) Multiple fresh starts. If a plan makes more than one fresh start with respect to a section 401(a)(17) employee, the employee's frozen accrued benefit as of the latest fresh-start date will either be determined by applying the current benefit formula to the employee's total years of service as of that fresh-start date or will consist of the sum of the employee's frozen accrued benefit (or adjusted accrued benefit (as defined in § 1.401(a)(4)-13(d)(8)(i))) as of the previous fresh-start date plus additional frozen accruals since the previous fresh start. If the frozen accrued benefit consists of such a sum, in making the adjustments described in paragraph (e)(4)(iii)(A) of this section, separate adjustments must be made to that previously frozen accrued benefit (or adjusted accrued benefit) and the additional frozen accruals to the extent that the frozen accrued benefit and the additional accruals have been determined using different compensation formulas or different compensation limits (i.e., the section 401(a)(17) limit before and after the reduction in limit described in paragraph (a)(3) of this section). In this case, if the plan is applying the adjustment fraction of § 1.401(a)(4)-13(d)(8)(i), the denominator of the separate adjustment fraction for adjusting each portion of the frozen accrued benefit must reflect the actual compensation formula, and, if applicable, compensation limit, originally used for determining that portion. For example, the frozen accrued benefit of a section 401(a)(17) employee as of the OBRA '93 fresh-start date may be based on the sum of the section 401(a)(17) frozen accrued benefit (determined without any annual compensation limit) plus benefit accruals in the years between the statutory effective date and the OBRA '93 effective date (based on compensation that was subject to the annual compensation limits for those years). In this example, in adjusting the section 401(a)(17) frozen accrued benefit, the denominator of the adjustment fraction does not reflect any annual compensation limit. Similarly, in adjusting the frozen accruals for years between the statutory effective date and the OBRA '93 effective date, the denominator of the adjustment fraction reflects the level of the annual compensation limit in effect for those years.

*(5) Examples.* The following examples illustrate the rules in this paragraph (e).

*Example (1).* (a) Employer X maintains Plan Y, a calendar year defined benefit plan providing an annual benefit for each year of service equal to 2 percent of compensation averaged over an employee's high 3 consecutive calendar years' compensation. Section 401(a)(17) applies to Plan Y in 1989. As of the close of the last plan year beginning before January 1, 1989 (i.e., the 1988 plan year), Employee A, with 5 years of service, had accrued a benefit of $25,000 which equals 10 percent (2 percent multiplied by 5 years of service) of average compensation of $250,000. Employer X decides to comply with the provisions of this section for plan years before the effective date of this section. Employer X decides to make the amendment effective for plan years beginning on or after January 1, 1989, and uses December 31, 1988 as the section 401(a)(17) fresh-start date. Plan Y, as amended, provides that, in determining an employee's benefit, compensation taken into account is limited in accordance with the provisions of this section to the annual compensation limit under section 401(a)(17), and that, for section 401(a)(17) employees, the employee's accrued benefit is the greater of—

(i) The employee's benefit under the plan's benefit formula (after the plan formula is amended to comply with section 401(a)(17)) as applied to the employee's total years of service; and

(ii) The employee's accrued benefit as of December 31, 1988, determined as though the employee terminated employment on that date without regard to any plan amendments after that date. Employer X decides not to amend Plan Y to provide for the adjustments permitted under § 1.401(a)(4)-13(d) to the accrued benefit of section 401(a)(17) employees as of December 31, 1988.

(b) Under Plan Y, Employee A's accrued benefit at the end of 1989 is $25,000, which is the greater of Employee A's accrued benefit as of the last day of the 1988 plan year ($25,000), and $24,000, which is Employee A's benefit based on the plan's benefit formula applied to Employee A's total years of service ($200,000 multiplied by (2 percent multiplied by 6 years of service)). The formula of Plan Y applicable to section 401(a)(17) employees for calculating their accrued benefits for years after the section 401(a)(17) fresh-start date is the formula in § 1.401(a)-13(c)(4)(ii) (formula with wear-away). The fresh-start formula is applied using a benefit formula for the 1989 plan year that satisfies section 401(a)(17) and this section, and the December 31, 1988 fresh-start date used for the plan is a section 401(a)(17) fresh-start date within the meaning of paragraph (e)(2)(ii) of this section. Thus, Plan Y, as amended, satisfies paragraph (e)(3)(i) of this section for plan years commencing prior to the OBRA '93 effective date.

*Example (2).* Assume the same facts as in Example 1, except that the plan formula provides that effective January 1, 1989, for section 401(a)(17) employees, an employee's benefit will equal the sum of the employee's accrued benefit as of December 31, 1988 (determined as though the employee terminated employment on that date and without regard to any amendments after that date), and 2 percent of compensation averaged over an employee's high 3 consecutive years' compensation times years of service taking into account only years of service after December 31, 1988. Thus, under Plan Y's formula, Employee A's accrued benefit as of December 31, 1989 is $29,000, which is equal to the sum of $25,000 (Employee A's accrued benefit as of December 31, 1988) plus $4,000 ($200,000 multiplied by (2 percent multiplied by 1 year of service)). The formula of Plan Y applicable to section 401(a)(17) employees for calculating their accrued benefits for years after the section 401(a)(17) fresh-start date is the formula in § 1.401(a)-13(c)(4)(i) (formula without wear-away). The fresh-start formula is applied using a benefit formula for the 1989 plan year that satisfies section 401(a)(17) and this section, and the December 31, 1988 fresh-start date used for the plan is a section 401(a)(17) fresh-start date within the meaning of paragraph (e)(2)(ii) of this section. Thus, Plan Y, as amended, satisfies paragraph (e)(3)(i) of this section for plan years commencing prior to the OBRA '93 effective date.

*Example (3).* (a) Assume the same facts as in Example 1, except that the plan formula provides that effective January 1, 1989, an employee's benefit equals the greater of the plan formulas in Example 1 and Example 2. The formula of Plan Y applicable to section 401(a)(17) employees for calculating their accrued benefits for years after the section 401(a)(17) fresh-start date is the formula in § 1.401(a)-13(c)(4)(iii) (formula with extended wear-away). The fresh-start formula is applied using a benefit formula for the 1989 plan year that satisfies section 401(a)(17) and this section, and the December 31, 1988 fresh-start date used for the plan is a section 401(a)(17) fresh-start date within the meaning of paragraph (e)(2)(ii) of this section. Thus, Plan Y, as amended, satisfies paragraph (e)(3)(i) of this section for plan years commencing prior to the OBRA '93 effective date.

(b) Assume that for each of the years 1991-93 Employee A's annual compensation under the plan compensation formula, disregarding the amendment to comply with section 401(a)(17) is $300,000. The annual compensation limit is adjusted to $222,220, $228,860, and $235,840 for plan years beginning January 1, 1991, 1992, and 1993, respectively. Because Employer X has decided to amend Plan Y to comply with the provisions of this section effective for plan years beginning on or after January 1, 1989, and has used December 31, 1988 as the section 401(a)(17) fresh-start date, the compensation that may be taken into account for plan benefits in 1993 cannot exceed $228,973 (the average of $222,220, $228,860, and $235,840). Therefore, as of December 31, 1993, the benefit determined under the fresh-start formula with wear-away would be $45,795 ($228,973 multiplied by (2 percent multiplied by 10 years of service)). The benefit determined under the fresh-start formula without wear-away would be $47,897, which is equal to $25,000 (Employee A's section 401(a)(17) frozen accrued benefit) plus $22,897 ($228,973 multiplied by (2 percent multiplied by 5 years of service)). Because Employee A's accrued benefit is being determined using the fresh-start formula with extended wear-away, Employee A's accrued benefit as of December 31, 1993, is equal to $47,897, the greater of the two amounts.

*Example (4).* (a) Assume the same facts as in Example 3, except that Plan Y satisfies § 1.401(a)(4)-13(d)(3) through (d)(7) and that the amendment to Plan Y effective for plan years beginning after December 31, 1988, also provided for adjustments to the section 401(a)(17) frozen accrued benefit in accordance with § 1.401(a)(4)-13(d) using the fraction described in § 1.401(a)(4)-13(d)(8)(i).

(b) As of December 31, 1993, the numerator of Employee A's compensation fraction is $228,973 (the average of Employee A's annual compensation for 1991, 1992, and 1993, as limited by the respective annual limit for each of those years). The denominator of Employee A's compensation fraction determined in accordance with paragraph (e)(4)(iii) of this section is $250,000 (the average of Employee A's high 3 consecutive calendar year compensation as of December 31, 1988, determined without regard to section 401(a)(17)). Therefore, Employee A's compensation fraction is $228,973/$250,000. Because the compensation adjustment fraction is less than 1, Employee A's section 401(a)(17) frozen accrued benefit is not adjusted. Therefore, Employee A's accrued benefit as of December 31, 1993, would still be $47,897, which is equal to $25,000 (Employee A's section 401(a)(17) frozen accrued benefit) plus $22,897 ($228,973 multiplied by (2 percent multiplied by 5 years of service).

*Example (5).* (a) Assume the same facts as in Example 3, except that as of January 1, 1994, Plan Y is amended to provide that benefits will be determined based on compensation of $150,000 (the limit in effect under section 401(a)(17) for plan years beginning on or after the OBRA '93 effective date) and that for section 401(a)(17) employees, each employee's accrued benefit will be determined under § 1.401(a)(4)-13(c)(4)(i) (formula without wear-away) using December 31, 1993 as the OBRA '93 fresh-start date.

(b) Assume that for each of the years 1996-98 Employee A's annual compensation under the plan compensation definition, disregarding the amendment to comply with section 401(a)(17), is $400,000. Assume that the annual compensation limit is first adjusted to $160,000 for plan years beginning on or after January 1, 1997, and is not adjusted for the plan year beginning on or after January 1, 1998. The compensation that may be taken into account for the 1998 plan year cannot exceed $156,667 (the average of $150,000 for 1996, $160,000 for 1997, and $160,000 for 1998).

(c) Therefore, at the end of December 31, 1998, Employee A's accrued benefit is $63,564, which is equal to $47,897 (Employee A's OBRA '93 frozen accrued benefit) plus $15,667 ($156,667 multiplied by (2 percent multiplied by 5 years of service)).

*Example (6).* (a) Assume the same facts as in Example 5, except that, for the fresh-start group (in this case the section 401(a)(17) employees), the amendments to Plan Y provide for adjustments to the section 401(a)(17) frozen accrued benefit and the OBRA '93 frozen accrued benefit in accordance with § 1.401(a)(4)-13(d) using the fraction described in § 1.401(a)(4)-13(d)(8)(i).

(b) Employee A's frozen accrued benefit as of December 31, 1993, is adjusted as of December 31, 1998, as follows:

(1) Employee A's frozen accrued benefit as of December 31, 1993, is the sum of Employee A's section 401(a)(17) frozen accrued benefit ($25,000) and Employee A's frozen accruals for the years 1989-93 ($22,897).

(2) The numerator of Employee A's adjustment fraction is $156,667 (the average of $150,000, $160,000, and $160,000). The denominator of Employee A's adjustment fraction with respect to Employee A's section 401(a)(17) frozen accrued benefit is $250,000, and the denominator of Employee A's adjustment fraction with respect to the rest of Employee A's frozen accrued benefit is $228,973 (the average of Employee A's annual compensation for 1991, 1992, and 1993, as limited by the respective annual limit for each of those years).

(3) Employee A's section 401(a)(17) frozen accrued benefit as adjusted through December 31, 1998, remains $25,000. The compensation adjustment fraction determined in accordance with paragraph (e)(4)(iii) of this section is less than one ($156,667 divided by $250,000).

(4) Employee A's frozen accruals for the years 1989-93, as adjusted through December 31, 1998, remain $22,897 because the adjustment fraction is less than one ($156,667 divided by $228,973).

(5) Employee A's adjusted accrued benefit as of December 31, 1998, equals $47,897 (the sum of the $25,000 and $22,897 amounts from paragraphs (b)(3) and (b)(4), respectively, of this Example).

(c) Employee A's section 401(a)(17) frozen accrued benefit will not be adjusted for compensation increases until the numerator of the fraction used to adjust that frozen accrued benefit exceeds the denominator of $250,000 used in determining those accruals. Similarly, the portion of Employee A's OBRA '93 frozen accrued benefit attributable to the frozen accruals for the years 1989-1993 will not be adjusted for compensation increases until the numerator of the fraction used to adjust those frozen accruals exceeds the denominator of $228,973 used in determining those accruals.

---

T.D. 8362, 9/12/91, amend T.D. 8547, 6/23/94, T.D. 9169, 12/28/2004.

---

### § 1.401(a)(26)-0 Table of contents.

This section contains a listing of the headings of §§ 1.401(a)(26)-1 through 1.401(a)(26)-9.

T.D. 8375, 12/2/91.

**§ 1.401(a)(26)-1 Minimum participation requirements.**

***Caution:*** The Treasury has not yet amended Reg § 1.401(a)(26)-1 to reflect changes made by P.L. 104-188.

**(a) General rule.** A plan is a qualified plan for a plan year only if the plan satisfies section 401(a)(26) for the plan year. A plan that satisfies any of the exceptions described in paragraph (b) of this section passes section 401(a)(26) automatically for the plan year. A plan that does not satisfy one of the exceptions in paragraph (b) of this section must satisfy § 1.401(a)(26)-2(a). In addition, a defined benefit plan must satisfy § 1.401(a)(26)-3 with respect to its prior benefit structure. Finally, a defined benefit plan that benefits former employees (for example, a defined benefit plan that is amended to provide an ad hoc cost-of-living adjustment to former employees) must separately satisfy § 1.401(a)(26)-4 with respect to its former employees.

**(b) Exceptions to section 401(a)(26).** *(1) Plans that do not benefit any highly compensated employees.* A plan, other than a frozen defined benefit plan as defined in § 1.401(a)(26)-2(b), satisfies section 401(a)(26) for a plan year if the plan is not a top-heavy plan under section 416 and the plan meets the following requirements:

(i) The plan benefits no highly compensated employee or highly compensated former employee of the employer; and

(ii) The plan is not aggregated with any other plan of the employer to enable the other plan to satisfy section 401(a)(4) or 410(b). The plan may, however, be aggregated with the employer's other plans for purposes of the average benefit percentage test in section 410(b)(2)(A)(ii).

*(2) Multiemployer plans.* (i) In general. The portion of a multiemployer plan that benefits only employees included in a unit of employees covered by a collective bargaining agreement may be treated as a separate plan that satisfies section 401(a)(26) for a plan year.

(ii) Multiemployer plans covering noncollectively bargained employees. (A) In general. The rule provided in paragraph (b)(2)(i) does not apply to the portion of a multiemployer plan that benefits employees who are not included in any collective bargaining unit covered by a collective bargaining agreement. Thus, the portion of the plan benefiting these employees must separately satisfy section 401(a)(26).

(B) Special testing rule. A multiemployer plan that benefits employees who are not included in any collective bargaining unit covered by a collective bargaining agreement satisfies section 401(a)(26) if the plan benefits 50 employees. For purposes of this special testing rule, employees who are included in a unit of employees covered by a collective bargaining agreement may be included in determining whether the plan benefits 50 employees.

*(3) Certain underfunded defined benefit plans.* (i) In general. A defined benefit plan is deemed to satisfy section 401(a)(26) for a plan year if all of the conditions of paragraphs (b)(3)(ii) through (b)(3)(iv) of this section are satisfied with respect to the plan for the plan year.

(ii) Eligible plans. This condition is satisfied for a plan year only if the plan is subject to Title IV of the Employee Retirement Income Security Act of 1974 (ERISA) for the plan year or, if the plan is not a Title IV plan under ERISA, it is not a top-heavy plan within the meaning of section 416. This condition does not apply for plan years beginning before January 1, 1992.

(iii) Actuarial certification. This condition is satisfied for a plan year only if the employer's timely filed actuarial report, as required by section 6059, evidences that the plan does not have sufficient assets to satisfy all liabilities under the plan (determined in accordance with section 401(a)(2)).

(iv) Cessation of all benefit accruals. This condition is satisfied for a plan year only if, for the plan year, no employee or former employee is benefiting within the meaning of § 1.401(a)(26)-5(a) or (b). For this purpose, an employee is not treated as benefiting solely by reason of being a non-key employee receiving minimum benefit accruals required by section 416.

*(4) Section 401(k) plan maintained by employers that include certain governmental or tax-exempt entities.* Section 401(k)(4)(B) prevents certain State and local governments and tax-exempt organizations from maintaining a qualified cash or deferred arrangement. A plan (or portion of a plan) that is either a section 401(k) plan or a section 401(m) plan that is provided under the same general arrangement as a section 401(k) plan may be treated as a separate plan that satisfies section 401(a)(26) for a plan year if the following requirements are satisfied:

(i) The section 401(k) plan is maintained by an employer who has employees precluded from being eligible employees under the arrangement by reason of section 401(k)(4)(B), and

(ii) More than 95 percent of the employees of the employer who are not precluded from being eligible employees under a section 401(k) plan by reason of section 401(k)(4)(B) benefit under the section 401(k) plan.

*(5) Certain acquisitions or dispositions.* (i) General rule. Rules similar to the rules prescribed under section 410(b)(6)(C) apply under section 401(a)(26). Pursuant to these rules, the requirements of section 401(a)(26) are treated as satisfied for certain plans of an employer involved in an acquisition or disposition (transaction) for the transition period. The transition period begins on the date of the transaction and ends on the last day of the first plan year beginning after the date of the transaction.

(ii) Special rule for transactions that occur in the plan year prior to the first plan year to which section 401(a)(26) applies. Where there has been a transaction described in section 410(b)(6)(C) in the plan year prior to the first plan year in which section 401(a)(26) applies to a plan, the plan satisfies section 401(a)(26) for the transition period if the plan benefited 50 employees or 40 percent of the employees of the employer immediately prior to the transaction.

(iii) Definition of "acquisition" and "disposition." For purposes of this paragraph (b)(5), the terms "acquisition" and "disposition" refer to an asset or stock acquisition, merger, or other similar transaction involving a change in employer of the employees of a trade or business.

**(c) Additional rules.** The Commissioner may, in revenue rulings, notices, and other guidance of general applicability, provide any additional rules that may be necessary or appropriate in applying the minimum participation requirements of section 401(a)(26).

T.D. 8375, 12/2/91, amend T.D. 8487, 8/31/93.

### § 1.401(a)(26)-2 Minimum participation rule.

***Caution:*** The Treasury has not yet amended Reg § 1.401(a)(26)-2 to reflect changes made by P.L. 104-188.

**(a) General rule.** A plan satisfies this paragraph (a) for a plan year only if the plan benefits at least the lesser of—

*(1)* 50 employees of the employer, or

*(2)* 40 percent of the employees of the employer.

**(b) Frozen plans.** A plan under which no employee or former employee benefits (within the meaning of § 1.401(a)(26)-5(a) or (b)), is a frozen plan for purposes of this section and satisfies paragraph (a) of this section automatically. Thus, a frozen defined contribution plan satisfies section 401(a)(26) automatically and a frozen defined benefit plan satisfies section 401(a)(26) for a plan year by satisfying the prior benefit structure requirements in § 1.401(a)(26)-3. For purposes of the rule in this paragraph (b), a defined benefit plan that provides only the minimum benefits for non-key employees required by section 416 is a frozen defined benefit plan.

**(c) Plan.** "Plan" means a plan within the meaning of § 1.410(b)-7(a) and (b), after the application of the mandatory disaggregation rules of paragraph (d)(1) of this section and, if applicable, the permissive disaggregation rules of paragraph (d)(2) of this section.

**(d) Disaggregation of certain plans.** *(1) Mandatory disaggregation.* (i) ESOPs and non-ESOPs. The portion of a plan that is an ESOP and the portion of the plan that is not an ESOP are treated as separate plans for purposes of section 401(a)(26), except as otherwise permitted under § 54.4975-11(e) of this Chapter.

(ii) Plans maintained by more than one employer. (A) Multiple employer plans. If a plan benefits employees of more than one employer and those employees are not included in a unit of employees covered by one or more collective bargaining agreements, the plan is a multiple employer plan. A multiple employer plan is treated as separate plans, each of which is maintained by a separate employer and must separately satisfy section 401(a)(26) by reference only to that employer's employees.

(B) Multiemployer plans. The portion of a multiemployer plan that benefits employees who are included in one or more units of employees covered by one or more collective bargaining agreements and the portion of that plan that benefits employees who are not included in a unit of employees covered pursuant to any collective bargaining agreement are treated as separate plans. The portion of a multiemployer plan that benefits employees who are not included in a unit of employees covered by a collective bargaining agreement is a multiple employer plan as described in paragraph (d)(1)(ii)(A) of this section. This paragraph (d)(1)(ii)(B) does not apply to the extent that the special testing rule in § 1.401(a)(26)-1(b)(2)(ii) applies. Also, this paragraph (d)(1)(B)(2) does not apply for purposes of prior benefit structure testing under § 1.401(a)(26)-3.

(iii) Defined benefit plans with other arrangements. (A) In general. A defined benefit plan is treated as comprising separate plans if, under the facts and circumstances, there is an arrangement (either under or outside the plan) that has the effect of providing any employee with a greater interest in a portion of the assets of a plan in a way that has the effect of creating separate accounts. Separate plans are not created, however, merely because a partnership agreement provides for allocation among partners, in proportion to their partnership interests, of either the cost of funding the plan or surplus assets upon plan termination.

(B) Examples. The following examples illustrate certain situations in which other arrangements relating to a defined benefit plan are or are not treated as creating separate plans:

*Example (1).* Employer A maintains a defined benefit plan under which each highly compensated employee can direct the investment of the portion of the plan's assets that represents the accumulated contributions with respect to that employee's plan benefits. In addition, by agreement outside the plan, if the product of the employee's investment direction exceeds the value needed to fund that employee's benefits, Employer A agrees to make a special payment to the participant. In this case, each separate portion of the pool of assets over which an employee has investment authority is a separate plan for the employee.

*Example (2).* Employer B is a partnership that maintains a defined benefit plan. The partnership agreement provides that, upon termination of the plan, a special allocation of any excess plan assets after reversion is made to the partnership on the basis of partnership share. This arrangement does not create separate plans with respect to the partners.

(iv) Plans benefiting employees of qualified separate lines of business. If an employer is treated as operating qualified separate lines of business for purposes of section 401(a)(26) in accordance with § 1.414(r)-1(b), the portion of a plan that benefits employees of one qualified separate line of business is treated as a separate plan from the portions of the same plan that benefit employees of the other qualified separate lines of business of the employer. See §§ 1.414(r)-1(c)(3) and 1.414(r)-9 (separate application of section 401(a)(26) to the employees of a qualified separate line of business). The rule in this paragraph (d)(6) does not apply to a plan that is tested under the special rule for employer-wide plans in § 1.414(r)-1(c)(3)(ii) for a plan year.

*(2) Permissive disaggregation.* (i) Plans benefiting collectively bargained employees. For purposes of section 401(a)(26), an employer may treat the portion of a plan that benefits employees who are included in a unit of employees covered by a collective bargaining agreement as a plan separate from the portion of a plan that benefits employees who are not included in such a collective bargaining unit. This paragraph (d)(2)(i) applies separately to each collective bargaining agreement. Thus, for example, the portion of a plan that benefits employees included in a unit of employees covered by one collective bargaining agreement may be treated as a plan that is separate from the portion of the plan that benefits employees included in a unit of employees covered by another collective bargaining agreement.

(ii) Plans benefiting otherwise excludable employees. If an employer applies section 401(a)(26) separately to the portion of a plan that benefits only employees who satisfy age and service conditions under the plan that are lower than the greatest minimum age and service conditions permissible under section 410(a), the plan is treated as comprising separate plans, one benefiting the employees who have not satisfied the lower minimum age and service but not the greatest minimum age and service conditions permitted under section 410(a) and one benefiting employees who have satisfied the greatest minimum age and service conditions permitted under section 410(a). See § 1.401(a)(26)-6(b)(1)(ii) for rules concerning testing of otherwise excludable employees.

T.D. 8375, 12/2/91.

### § 1.401(a)(26)-3 Rules applicable to a defined benefit plan's prior benefit structure.

***Caution:*** The Treasury has not yet amended Reg § 1.401(a)(26)-3 to reflect changes made by P.L. 104-88.

**(a) General rule.** A defined benefit plan that does not meet one of the exceptions in § 1.401(a)(26)-1(b) must satisfy paragraph (c) of this section with respect to its prior benefit structure. Defined contribution plans are not subject to this section.

**(b) Prior benefit structure.** Each defined benefit plan has only one prior benefit structure, and all accrued benefits under the plan as of the beginning of a plan year (including benefits rolled over or transferred to the plan) are included in the prior benefit structure for the year.

**(c) Testing a prior benefit structure.** *(1) General rule.* A plan's prior benefit structure satisfies this paragraph if the plan provides meaningful benefits to a group of employees that includes the lesser of 50 employees or 40 percent of the employer's employees. Thus, a plan satisfies the requirements of this paragraph (c) if at least 50 employees or 40 percent of the employer's employees currently accrue meaningful benefits under the plan. Alternatively, a plan satisfies this paragraph if at least 50 employees and former employees or 40 percent of the employer's employees and former employees have meaningful accrued benefits under the plan.

*(2) Meaningful benefits.* Whether a plan is providing meaningful benefits, or whether individuals have meaningful accrued benefits under a plan, is determined on the basis of all the facts and circumstances. The relevant factors in making this determination include, but are not limited to, the following: the level of current benefit accruals; the comparative rate of accruals under the current benefit formula compared to prior rates of accrual under the plan; the projected accrued benefits under the current benefit formula compared to accrued benefits as of the close of the immediately preceding plan year; the length of time the current benefit formula has been in effect; the number of employees with accrued benefits under the plan; and the length of time the plan has been in effect. A rule for determining whether an offset plan provides meaningful benefits is provided in § 1.401(a)(26)-5(a)(2). A plan does not satisfy this paragraph (c) if it exists primarily to preserve accrued benefits for a small group of employees and thereby functions more as an individual plan for the small group of employees or for the employer.

**(d) Multiemployer plan rule.** A multiemployer plan is deemed to satisfy the prior benefit structure rule in paragraph (c)(1) of this section for a plan year if the multiemployer plan provides meaningful benefits to at least 50 employees for a plan year, or 50 employees have meaningful accrued benefits under the plan. For purposes of this paragraph, all employees benefiting under the multiemployer plan may be considered, whether or not these employees are included in a unit of employees covered pursuant to any collective bargaining agreement.

T.D. 8375, 12/2/91.

### § 1.401(a)(26)-4 Testing former employees.

***Caution:*** The Treasury has not yet amended Reg § 1.401(a)(26)-4 to reflect changes made by P.L. 105-34, P.L. 104-188.

**(a) Scope.** This section applies to any defined benefit plan that benefits former employees in a plan year within the meaning of § 1.401(a)(26)-5(b) and does not meet one of the exceptions in § 1.401(a)(26)-1(b).

**(b) Minimum participation rule for former employees.** Except as set forth in paragraph (c) of this section, a plan that is subject to this section must benefit at least the lesser of:

*(1)* 50 former employees of the employer, or

*(2)* 40 percent of the former employees of the employer.

**(c) Special rule.** A plan satisfies the minimum participation rule in paragraph (b) of this section if the plan benefits at least five former employees, and if either:

*(1)* More than 95 percent of all former employees with vested accrued benefits under the plan benefit under the plan for the plan year, or

*(2)* At least 60 percent of the former employees who benefit under the plan for the plan year are nonhighly compensated former employees.

**(d) Excludable former employees.** *(1) General rule.* Whether a former employee is an excludable former employee for purposes of this section is determined under § 1.401(a)(26)-6(c).

*(2) Exception.* Solely for purposes of paragraph (c) of this section, the rule in § 1.401(a)(26)(c)(4) (regarding vested accrued benefits eligible for mandatory distribution) does not apply to any former employee having a vested accrued benefit. Thus, a former employee who has a vested accrued benefit is not an excludable former employee merely because that vested accrued benefit does not exceed the cash-out limit in effect under § 1.411(a)-11(c)(3)(ii).

T.D. 8375, 12/2/91, amend T.D. 8794, 12/18/98, T.D. 8891, 7/18/2000.

### § 1.401(a)(26)-5 Employees who benefit under a plan.

**(a) Employees benefiting under a plan.** *(1) In general.* Except as provided in paragraph (a)(2) of this section, an employee is treated as benefiting under a plan for a plan year if and only if, for that plan year, the employee would be treated as benefiting under the provisions of § 1.410(b)-3(a), without regard to § 1.410(b)-3(a)(iv).

*(2) Sequential or concurrent benefit offset arrangements.* (i) In general. An employee is treated as accruing a benefit under a plan that includes an offset or reduction of benefits that satisfies either paragraph (a)(2)(ii) or (a)(2)(iii) of this section if either the employee accrues a benefit under the plan for the year, or the employee would have accrued a benefit if the offset or reduction portion of the benefit formula were disregarded. In addition, an employee is treated as accruing a meaningful benefit for purposes of prior benefit structure testing under § 1.401(a)(26)-3 if the employee would have accrued a meaningful benefit if the offset or reduction portion of the benefit formula were disregarded.

(ii) Offset by sequential or grandfathered benefits. An offset or reduction of benefits under a defined benefit plan satisfies this paragraph (a)(2) if the benefit formula provides that an employee will not accrue additional benefits under the current portion of the benefit formula until the employee has accrued, under such portion, a benefit in excess of such employee's benefit under one or more formulas in effect for prior years that are based wholly on prior years of service. The prior benefit may have accrued under the same or a separate plan, may be provided under the same or a separate plan and may relate to service with the same or previous employers. Benefits will not fail to be treated as based wholly on prior years if they are based, directly or indirectly, on compensation earned after such prior years (including compensation earned in the current year), if they are adjusted to reflect increases in the section 415 limitations, or if they are increased to provide an ad hoc cost of living adjustment designed to adjust, in whole or in part, for inflation. Furthermore, benefits do not fail to be treated as based wholly on prior years merely because the benefits (e.g., early retirement benefits) are subject to an age or years of service condition and, in applying the condition or conditions, the current and prior years are taken into account.

(iii) Concurrent benefit offset arrangements. (A) General rule. An offset or reduction of benefits under a defined benefit plan satisfies the requirements of this paragraph (a)(2)(iii) if the benefit formula provides a benefit that is offset or reduced by contributions or benefits under another plan that is maintained by the same employer and the following additional requirements are met:

(1) The contributions or benefits under a plan that are used to offset or reduce the benefits under the positive portion of the formula being tested accrued under such other plan;

(2) The employees who benefit under the formula being tested also benefit under the other plan on a reasonable and uniform basis; and

(3) The contributions or benefits under the plan that are used to offset or reduce the benefits under the formula being tested are not used to offset or reduce that employee's benefits under any other plan or any other formula.

(B) Special rules for certain section 414(n) employer-recipients. The same employer requirement in the concurrent benefit offset rule in paragraph (a)(2)(iii)(A) of this section is waived for certain section 414(n) employer-recipients. Under this exception, an employer-recipient (within the meaning of sections 414(n) and (o)) may treat contributions or benefits the recipient organization plan provided the following requirements are met: the employer-recipient maintains a plan covering leased employees (which employees are treated as employees of the employer-recipient within the meaning of sections 414(n)(2) and 414(o)(2)); the leased employees are also covered under a plan maintained by the leasing organization; and contributions or benefits under the plan maintained by the employer-recipient are offset or reduced by the contributions or benefits under the leasing organization plan that are attributable to service with the recipient organization. Also, for purposes of the benefiting condition requirement in paragraph (a)(2)(iii)(A)(2) of this section, the employees of the employer-recipient who are not leased from the leasing organization are not required to benefit under the plan of the leasing organization.

**(b) Former employees benefiting under a plan.** A former employee is treated as benefiting for a plan year if and only if the former employee would be treated as benefiting under the rules in § 1.410(b)-3(b).

---

T.D. 8375, 12/2/91.

---

## § 1.401(a)(26)-6 Excludable employees.

***Caution:*** The Treasury has not yet amended Reg § 1.401(a)(26)-6 to reflect changes made by P.L. 105-34, P.L. 104-188.

**(a) In general.** For purposes of applying section 401(a)(26) with respect to either employees, former employees, or both employees and former employees, as applicable, all employees other than excludable employees described in paragraph (b) of this section, all former employees other than excludable former employees described in paragraph (c) of this section, or both, as the case may be, must be taken into account. Except as specifically provided otherwise in this section, the rules of this section are applied by reference only to the particular plan and must be applied on a uniform and consistent basis.

**(b) Excludable employees.** An employee is an excludable employee if the employee is covered by one or more of the following exclusions:

*(1) Minimum age and service exclusions.* (i) In general. If a plan applies minimum age and service eligibility conditions permissible under section 410(a)(1) and excludes all employees who do not meet those conditions from benefiting under the plan, then all employees who fail to satisfy those conditions may be treated as excludable employees with respect to that plan. An employee is treated as meeting the age and service requirements on the date any employee with the same age and service would be eligible to commence participation in the plan, as provided in section 410(b)(4)(C).

(ii) Plans benefiting otherwise excludable employees. An employer may treat a plan benefiting otherwise excludable employees as two separate plans, one for the otherwise excludable employees and one for the other employees benefiting under the plan. The effect of this rule is that employees who would be excludable under paragraph (b)(1) of this section (applied without regard to section 410(a)(1)(B)), but for the fact that the plan does not apply the greatest permissible minimum age and service conditions, may be treated as excludable employees with respect to the plan. This treatment is only available if each of the following conditions is satisfied:

(A) The plan under which the otherwise excludable employees benefit also benefits employees who are not otherwise excludable.

(B) The plan under which the otherwise excludable employees benefit satisfies section 401(a)(26), both by reference only to otherwise excludable employees and by reference only to employees who are not otherwise excludable.

(C) The contributions or benefits provided to the otherwise excludable employees (expressed as percentages of compensation) are not greater than the contributions or benefits provided to the employees who are not otherwise excludable under the plan.

(D) No highly compensated employee is included in the group of otherwise excludable employees for more than one plan year.

(iii) Examples. The following examples illustrate some of the minimum-age-and-service exclusion requirements:

*Example (1).* Employer X maintains a defined contribution plan, Plan X, under which employees who have not completed 1 year of service are not eligible to participate. Employer X has six employees. Two of the employees participate in Plan X. The other four employees have not completed 1 year of service and are therefore not eligible to participate in Plan X. The four employees who have not completed 1 year of service are excludable employees and may be disregarded for purposes of applying the minimum participation test. Therefore, Plan X satisfies section 401(a)(26) because both of the two employees who must be considered are participants in Plan X.

*Example (2).* Employer Y has 100 employees and maintains two plans, Plan 1 and Plan 2. Plan 1 provides that employees who have not completed 1 year of service are not eligible to participate. Plan 2 has no minimum age or service requirement. Twenty of Y's employees do not meet the minimum service requirement under Plan 1. Each plan satisfies the ratio test under section 410(b)(1)(B). In testing Plan 1 to determine whether it satisfies section 401(a)(26), the 20 employees not meeting the minimum age and service requirement under Plan 1 are treated as excludable employees. In testing Plan 2 to determine whether it satisfies section 401(a)(26), no employees are treated as excludable employees because Plan 2 does not have a minimum age or service requirement.

*(2) Certain air pilots.* An employee who is excluded from consideration under section 410(b)(3)(B) (relating to certain air pilots) may be treated as an excludable employee.

*(3) Certain nonresident aliens.* (i) In general. An employee who is excluded from consideration under section 410(b)(3)(C) (relating to certain nonresident aliens) may be treated as an excludable employee.

(ii) Special treaty rule. In addition, an employee who is a nonresident alien (within the meaning of section 7701(b)(1)(B)) and who does receive earned income (within the meaning of section 911(d)(2)) from the employer that constitutes income from sources within the United States (within the meaning of section 861(a)(3)) is permitted to be excluded, if all of the employee's earned income from the employer from sources within the United States is exempt from United States income tax under an applicable income tax convention. This paragraph (b)(3)(ii) applies only if all employees described in the preceding sentence are so excluded.

*(4) Employees covered pursuant to a collective bargaining agreement.* When testing a plan benefiting only noncollectively bargained employees, an employee who is excluded from consideration under section 410(b)(3)(A) (exclusion for employees included in a unit of employees covered by a collective bargaining agreement) may be treated as an excludable employee. This rule may be applied separately to each collective bargaining agreement. See § 1.401(a)(26)-8 for the definitions of the terms "collective bargaining agreement," "collectively bargained employee," and "covered pursuant to a collective bargaining agreement."

*(5) Employees not covered pursuant to a collective bargaining agreement.* When testing a plan that benefits only employees who are included in a group of employees who are covered pursuant to a collective bargaining agreement, an employee who is not included in the group of employees who are covered by the collective bargaining agreement may be treated as an excludable employee.

*(6) Examples.* The following examples illustrate the excludable employee rules that relate to employees covered pursuant to collective bargaining agreements. For purposes of these examples assume that no other exclusion rules are applicable.

*Example (1).* Employer W has 70 collectively bargained employees and 30 noncollectively bargained employees. Employer W maintains Plan W, which benefits only the 30 noncollectively bargained employees. The 70 collectively bargained employees may be treated as excludable employees and thus may be disregarded in applying section 401(a)(26) to Plan W.

*Example (2).* Assume the same facts as Example 1, except that the Commissioner has determined that the employee representative is not a bona fide employee representative under section 7701(a)(46) and thus there are no "collectively bargained employees." In this case, all employees of W must be considered in determining whether section 401(a)(26) is met.

*Example (3).* Employer X has 30 collectively bargained employees and 70 noncollectively bargained employees. Employer X maintains Plan X, which benefits only the 30 collectively bargained employees. Employer X may treat the non-collectively bargained employees as excludable employees and disregard them in applying section 401(a)(26) to the collectively bargained plan.

*Example (4).* Assume the same facts as Example 3, except that the Commissioner has determined that the employee representative is not a bona fide employee representative under section 7701(a)(46) and thus there is no recognized collective bargaining agreement. In this case, Employer X may not treat the non-collectively bargained employees of X as excludable employees.

*Example (5).* Assume the same facts as Example 3, except that 3 percent of the 30 collectively bargained employees are professionals. In this case, Employer X may not treat the non-collectively bargained employees of X as excludable employees.

*Example (6).* Employer Y has 100 collectively bargained employees. Thirty of Y's employees are represented by Collective Bargaining Unit 1 and covered under Plan 1. Seventy of Y's employees are represented by Collective Bargaining Unit 2 and covered under Plan 2. For purposes of testing Plan 1, the employees of Collective Bargaining Unit 2 may be treated as excludable employees. Similarly, for purposes of testing Plan 2, the employees of Collective Bargaining Unit 1 may be treated as excludable employees.

*(7) Certain terminating employees.* (i) In general. An employee may be treated as an excludable employee for a plan year with respect to a particular plan if—

(A) The employee does not benefit under the plan for the plan year,

(B) The employee is eligible to participate in the plan,

(C) The plan has a minimum period of service requirement or a requirement that an employee be employed on the last day of the plan year (last-day requirement) in order for an employee to accrue a benefit or receive an allocation for the plan year,

(D) The employee fails to accrue a benefit or receive an allocation under the plan solely because of the failure to satisfy the minimum period of service or lastly requirement,

(E) The employee terminates employment during the plan year with no more than 500 hours of service, and the employee is not an employee as of the last day of the plan year (for purposes of this paragraph (b)(7)(i)(E), a plan that uses the elapsed time method of determining years of service may use either 91 consecutive calendar days or 3 consecutive calendar months instead of 500 hours of service, provided it uses the same convention for all employees during a plan year), and

(F) If this paragraph (b)(7) is applied with respect to any employee with respect to a plan for a plan year, it is applied with respect to all employees with respect to the plan for the plan year.

(ii) Hours of service. For purposes of this paragraph (b)(7),the term "hour of service" has the same meaning as set forth in 29 CFR § 2530.200b-2 under the general method of crediting service for the employee. If one of the equivalencies set forth in 29 CFR § 2530.200b-3 is used for crediting service under the plan, the 500-hour requirement must be adjusted accordingly.

*(8) Employees of qualified separate lines of business.* If an employer is treated as operating qualified separate lines of business for purposes of section 401(a)(26) in accordance with § 1.414(r)-1(b), in testing a plan that benefits employees of one qualified separate line of business, the employees of the other qualified separate lines of business of the employer are treated as excludable employees. See §§ 1.414(r)-1(c)(3) and 1.414(r)-9 (separate application of section 401(a)(26) to the employees of a qualified separate line of business). The rule in this paragraph (b)(8) does not apply to a plan that is tested under the special rule for employer-wide plans in § 1.414(r)-1(c)(3)(ii) for a plan year.

**(c) Former employees.** *(1) In general.* For purposes of applying section 401(a)(26) with respect to former employees, all former employees of the employer are taken into account, except that the employer may treat a former employee described in paragraphs (c)(2) through (c)(4) of this section as an excludable former employee. If any of the former employee exclusion rules under paragraphs (c)(2) through (c)(4) of this section is applied, it must be applied to all former employees for the plan year on a consistent basis.

*(2) Employees terminated before a specified date.* The employer may treat a former employee as excludable if—

(i) The former employee became a former employee either prior to January 1, 1984, or prior to the tenth calendar year preceding the calendar year in which the current plan year begins, and

(ii) The former employee became a former employee in a calendar year that precedes the earliest calendar year in which any former employee who benefits under the plan in the current plan year became a former employee.

*(3) Previously excludable employees.* The employer may treat a former employee as excludable if the former employee was an excludable employee (or would have been an excludable employee if these regulations had been in effect) under the rules of paragraphs (a) and (b) of this section during the plan year in which the former employee became a former employee. If the employer treats a former employee as excludable pursuant to this paragraph (c)(3), the former employee is not taken into account with respect to a plan even if the former employee is benefiting under the plan.

*(4) Vested accrued benefits eligible for mandatory distribution.* A former employee may be treated as an excludable former employee if the present value of the former employee's vested accrued benefit does not exceed the cash-out limit in effect under § 1.411(a)-11(c)(3)(ii). This determination is made in accordance with the rules of sections 411(a)(11) and 417(e).

**(d) Certain police or firefighters.** An employer may apply section 401(a)(26) separately with respect to any classification of qualified public safety employees for whom a separate plan is maintained. Thus, for purposes of testing a separate plan covering a class of qualified public safety employees, all employees who are not in that classification are treated as excludable employees. Also, such employees need not be taken into account in determining whether or not any other plan satisfies section 401(a)(26). For purposes of this paragraph (d), "qualified public safety employee" means any employee of any police department or fire department organized and operated by a State or political subdivision if the employee provides police protection, firefighting services, or emergency medical services for any area within the jurisdiction of a State or political subdivision.

T.D. 8375, 12/2/91, amend T.D. 8794, 12/18/98, T.D. 8891, 7/18/2000.

## § 1.401(a)(26)-7 Testing methods.

**(a) Testing on each day of the plan year.** A plan satisfies section 401(a)(26) for a plan year only if the plan satisfies section 401(a)(26) on each day of the plan year. An employee benefits on a day if the employee is a participant for such day and the employee benefits under the plan for the year under the rules in § 1.401(a)(26)-5.

**(b) Simplified testing method.** A plan is treated as satisfying the requirements of paragraph (a) of this section if it satisfies section 401(a)(26) on any single plan day during the plan year, but only if that day is reasonably representative of the employer's workforce and the plan's coverage. A plan does not have to be tested on the same day each plan year.

**(c) Retroactive correction.** If a plan fails to satisfy section 401(a)(26) for a plan year, the plan may be retroactively amended during the same period and under the same conditions as provided for in § 1.401(a)(4)-11(g)(3) through (g)(5) to satisfy section 401(a)(26). A plan merger that occurs by the end of the period provided in § 1.401(a)(4)-11(g)(3)(iv) is treated solely for purposes of section 401(a)(26) as if it were effective as of the first day of the plan year. The rule of this paragraph (c) may be illustrated by the following example.

*Example.* Assume that an employer with 500 employees maintains two defined contribution plans. Plan A benefits 45 employees. Plan B benefits 50 employees. Immediately before the end of the period provided for in § 1.401(a)(4)-11(g)(3)(iv), the employer expands coverage under Plan A to benefit 20 more employees retroactively for the plan year. Thus, Plan A satisfies paragraph (a) of this section for the plan year. Alternatively, before the end of the period provided for in § 1.401(a)(4)-11(g)(3)(iv), or later if a later period is applicable under section 401(b), the employer could merge Plan A with Plan B to satisfy section 401(a)(26).

T.D. 8375, 12/2/91.

## § 1.401(a)(26)-8 Definitions.

In applying this section and §§ 1.401(a)(26)-1 through 1.401(a)(26)-9 the definitions in this section govern unless otherwise provided.

Collective bargaining agreement. "Collective bargaining agreement" means an agreement that the Secretary of Labor finds to be a collective bargaining agreement between employee representatives and the employer that satisfies § 301.7701-17T. Employees described in section 413(b)(8) who are employees of the union or the plan and are treated as employees of an employer are not employees covered pursuant to a collective bargaining agreement for purposes of section 401(a)(26) unless the employees are actually covered pursuant to such an agreement.

Collectively bargained employee. "Collectively bargained employee" means a collectively bargained employee within the meaning of § 1.410(b)-6(d)(2).

Covered by a collective bargaining agreement. "Covered by a collective bargaining agreement" means covered by a collective bargaining agreement within the meaning of § 1.410(b)-6(d)(2)(iii).

Defined benefit plan. "Defined benefit plan" means a defined benefit plan within the meaning of § 1.410(b)-9.

Defined contribution plan. "Defined contribution plan" means a defined contribution plan within the meaning of § 1.410(b)-9.

Employee. "Employee" means an employee, within the meaning of § 1.410(b)-9.

Employer. "Employer" means the employer within the meaning of § 1.410(b)-9.

ESOP. "ESOP" means an employee stock ownership plan within the meaning of section 4975(e)(7) or a tax credit employee stock ownership plan within the meaning of section 409(a).

Former employee. "Former employee" means a former employee within the meaning of § 1.410(b)-9.

Highly compensated employee. "Highly compensated employee" means an employee who is highly compensated within the meaning of section 414(q).

Highly compensated former employee. "Highly compensated former employee" means a former employee who is highly compensated within the meaning of section 414(q)(9).

Multiemployer plan. "Multiemployer plan" means a multiemployer plan within the meaning of section 414(f).

Noncollectively bargained employee. "Noncollectively bargained employee" means an employee who is not a collectively bargained employee.

Nonhighly compensated employee. "Nonhighly compensated employee" means an employee who is not a highly compensated employee.

Nonhighly compensated former employee. "Nonhighly compensated former employee" means a former employee who is not a highly compensated former employee.

Plan. "Plan" means plan as defined in § 1.401(a)(26)-2(c).

Plan year. "Plan year" means the plan year of the plan as defined in the written plan document. In the absence of a specifically designated plan year, the plan year is deemed to be the calendar year.

Professional employee. "Professional employee" means a professional employee as defined in § 1.410(b)-9.

Section 401(k) plan. "Section 401(k) plan" means a plan consisting of elective contributions described in § 1.401(k)-1(g)(3) under a qualified cash or deferred arrangement described in § 1.401(k)-1(a)(4)(i).

Section 401(m) plan. "Section 401(m) plan" means a plan consisting of employee contributions described in § 1.401(m)-1(f)(6) or matching contributions described in § 1.401(m)-1(f)(12), or both.

T.D. 8375, 12/2/91.

**§ 1.401(a)(26)-9 Effective dates and transition rules.**

***Caution:*** The Treasury has not yet amended Reg § 1.401(a)(26)-9 to reflect changes made by P.L. 104-188.

**(a) In general.** Except as provided in paragraphs (b), (c), and (d) of this section, section 401(a)(26) and the regulations thereunder apply to plan years beginning on or after January 1, 1989.

**(b) Transition rules.** *(1) Governmental plans and certain section 403(b) annuities.* Section 401(a)(26) is treated as satisfied for plan years beginning before the later of January 1, 1996, or 90 days after the opening of the first legislative session beginning on or after January 1, 1996, of the governing body with authority to amend the plan, if that body does not meet continuously, in the case of governmental plans described in section 414(d), including plans subject to section 403(b)(12)(A)(i) (nonelective plans). For purposes of this paragraph (b)(1), the term "governing body with authority to amend the plan" means the legislature, board, commission, council, or other governing body with authority to amend the plan.

*(2) Early retirement "window-period" benefits.* Early retirement benefits available under a plan only to employees who retire within a limited period of time, not to exceed one year, are treated as satisfying section 401(a)(26) if such benefits are provided under plan terms that were adopted and in effect on or before March 14, 1989.

*(3) Employees who do not benefit because of a minimum-period-of-service requirement or a last-day requirement.* For the first plan year beginning after December 31, 1988, and before January 1, 1990, employees who are eligible to participate under the plan and who fail to accrue a benefit solely because of the failure to satisfy either a minimum-period-of-service requirement of 1000 hours of service or less or a last-day requirement may be treated as benefiting under the plan.

*(4) Certain plan terminations.* (i) In general. Except as provided in paragraph (b)(4)(ii) of this section, if a plan terminates after section 401(a)(26) becomes effective with respect to the plan (as determined under paragraph (a) of this section), the plan is not treated as a qualified plan upon termination unless it complies with section 401(a)(26) and the regulations thereunder (to the extent they are applicable) for all periods for which section 401(a)(26) is effective with respect to the plan.

(ii) Exception. Notwithstanding paragraphs (a) and (b)(4)(i) of this section, a plan does not fail to be treated as a qualified plan upon termination merely because the plan fails to satisfy the requirements of section 401(a)(26) and the regulations thereunder if the plan is terminated with a termination date on or before December 31, 1989, and either of the following conditions is satisfied:

(A) In the case of a defined benefit plan, no highly compensated employee has an accrued benefit under the plan exceeding the lesser of either the benefit the employee had accrued as of the close of the last plan year beginning before January 1, 1989, or the benefit the employee would have accrued as of the close of the last plan year under the terms of the plan in effect and applicable with respect to the employee on December 13, 1988.

(B) In the case of a defined contribution plan, no highly compensated employee receives a contribution allocation for any plan year beginning after December 31, 1988. For this purpose, a contribution allocation with respect to an employee for a plan year beginning before January 1, 1989, may be treated as a contribution allocation for a plan year beginning after December 31, 1988, if the allocation for the prior year exceeds the allocation that the employee would have received for such year under the terms of the plan in effect and applicable with respect to the employee on December 13, 1988. An allocation of forfeitures to highly compensated employees with respect to contributions made for plan years beginning before January 1, 1988, does not cause a defined contribution plan to fail to satisfy the conditions of this paragraph (b)(4)(ii)(B).

*(5) ESOPs and non-ESOPs.* Notwithstanding paragraph (a) of this section and § 54.4975-11(a)(5) of this Chapter, an employer may treat the rule in § 1.401(a)(26)-2(d)(1)(i), regarding mandatory disaggregation of ESOPs and non-ESOPs as not effective for plan years beginning before January 1, 1990.

**(c) Waiver of excise tax on reversions.** *(1) In general.* Pursuant to section 1112(e)(3) of the Tax Reform Act of 1986 (TRA '86), if certain conditions are satisfied, a waiver of the excise tax under section 4980 applies with respect to any employer reversion that occurs by rein of the termination or merger of a plan before the first year to which section 401(a)(26) applies to the plan. In general, the applicable conditions are that the plan must have been in existence on August 16, 1986; that if section 401(a)(26) was in effect for the plan year including August 16, 1986, the plan would have failed to satisfy the requirements of section 401(a)(26) and would have continued to fail the requirements at all times thereafter; that the plan satisfies the applicable conditions in paragraph (b)(4)(ii)(A) or (B) of this section; and that certain requirements regarding asset or liability transfers and mergers and spinoffs involving the plan after August 16, 1986, are satisfied.

*(2) Termination date.* An employer reversion with respect to a plan is eligible for the section 4980 excise tax waiver only if the employer reversion occurs by reason of the termination of the plan with a termination date prior to the first plan year for which section 401(a)(26) applies to the plan. Solely for purposes of this waiver, the employer reversion is treated as satisfying this paragraph (c)(2) even though the plan's termination date is during the first plan year for which section 401(a)(26) applies to the plan if the plan's termination date is on or before May 31, 1989. If the termination date occurs in the first plan year for which section 401(a)(26) applied to the plan and the employer receives a reversion that is eligible for the waiver of the section 4980 tax, the plan is subject to the interest rate restriction set forth in section 1112(e)(3)(B) of TRA '86 as amended.

*(3) Failure to satisfy section 401(a)(26).* An employer reversion with respect to a plan is eligible for the excise tax waiver only if the plan was in existence on August 16, 1986, and, if section 401(a)(26) had applied to the plan for the plan year including such date, the plan would have failed to satisfy section 401(a)(26) for the plan year and continuously thereafter until the plan's termination or merger. For purposes of this paragraph (c)(3), a plan is treated as though it would have failed to satisfy section 401(a)(26) before such section actually applied to the plan only if the plan (as defined under section 414(l)) failed to benefit at least the lesser of 50 employees or 40 percent of the employer's employees. In general, this determination is to be made on the basis of only the applicable statutory provisions, without regard to the regulations under section 401(a)(26). Thus, for example, the prior benefit structure rules in § 1.401(a)(26)-3 do not apply in determining whether a plan would have failed to satisfy section 401(a)(26) for plan years beginning prior to the effective date of section 401(a)(26) with respect to the plan.

**(d) Special rule for collective bargaining agreements.** In the case of a plan maintained pursuant to one or more collective bargaining agreements (as defined in § 1.401(a)(26)-8(a)) that were ratified before March 1, 1986, section 401(a)(26) and the regulations thereunder shall not apply to plan years beginning before the earlier of—

*(1)* January 1, 1991, or

*(2)* The later of—

(i) January 1, 1989, or

(ii) The date on which the last of such collective bargaining agreements terminates. For purposes of this paragraph (d), any extension or renegotiation of any collective bargaining agreement that is ratified after February 28, 1986, is disregarded in determining the date on which such collective bargaining agreement terminates.

---

T.D. 8375, 12/2/91, amend T.D. 8487, 8/31/93.

---

### § 1.401(a)(31)-1 Requirement to offer direct rollover of eligible rollover distributions; questions and answers.

***Caution:*** The Treasury has not yet amended Reg § 1.401(a)(31)-1 to reflect changes made by P.L. 104-188.

The following questions and answers relate to the qualification requirement imposed by section 401(a)(31) of the Internal Revenue Code of 1986, pertaining to the direct rollover option for eligible rollover distributions from pension, profit-sharing, and stock bonus plans. Section 401(a)(31) was added by section 522(a) of the Unemployment Compensation Amendments of 1992, Public Law 102-318, 106 Stat. 290 (UCA). For additional UCA guidance under sections 402(c), 402(f), 403(b)(8) and (10), and 3405(c), see §§ 1.402(c)-2, 1.402(f)-1, and 1.403(b)-7(b), and § 31.3405(c)-1 of this chapter, respectively.

*List of Questions*

Q-1. What are the direct rollover requirements under section 401(a)(31)?

Q-2. Does section 401(a)(31) require that a qualified plan permit a direct rollover to be made to a qualified trust that is not part of a defined contribution plan?

Q-3. What is a *direct rollover* that satisfies section 401(a)(31), and how is it accomplished?

Q-4. Is providing a distributee with a check for delivery to an eligible retirement plan a reasonable means of accomplishing a direct rollover?

Q-5. Is an eligible rollover distribution that is paid to an eligible retirement plan in a direct rollover currently includible in gross income or subject to 20-percent withholding?

Q-6. What procedures may a plan administrator prescribe for electing a direct rollover, and what information may the plan administrator require a distributee to provide when electing a direct rollover?

Q-7. May the plan administrator treat a distributee as having made an election under a default procedure where the distributee does not affirmatively elect to make or not make a direct rollover within a certain time period?

Q-8. May the plan administrator establish a deadline after which the distributee may not revoke an election to make or not make a direct rollover?

Q-9. Must the plan administrator permit a distributee to elect to have a portion of an eligible rollover distribution paid to an eligible retirement plan in a direct rollover and to have the remainder of that distribution paid to the distributee?

Q-10. Must the plan administrator allow a distributee to divide an eligible rollover distribution into two or more separate distributions to be paid in direct rollovers to two or more eligible retirement plans?

Q-11. Will a plan satisfy section 401(a)(31) if the plan administrator does not permit a distributee to elect a direct rollover if his or her eligible rollover distributions during a year are reasonably expected to total less than $200?

Q-12. Is a plan administrator permitted to treat a distributee's election to make or not make a direct rollover with respect to one payment in a series of periodic payments as applying to all subsequent payments in the series?

Q-13. Is the eligible retirement plan designated by a distributee to receive a direct rollover distribution required to accept the distribution?

Q-14. If a plan accepts an invalid rollover contribution, whether or not as a direct rollover, how will the contribution be treated for purposes of applying the qualification requirements of section 401(a) or 403(a) to the plan?

Q-15. For purposes of applying the plan qualification requirements of section 401(a), is an eligible rollover distribution that is paid to an eligible retirement plan in a direct rollover a distribution and rollover or is it a transfer of assets and liabilities?

Q-16. Must a direct rollover option be provided for an eligible rollover distribution that is in the form of a plan loan offset amount?

Q-17. Must a direct rollover option be provided for an eligible rollover distribution from a qualified plan distributed annuity contract?

Q-18. What assumptions may a plan administrator make regarding whether a benefit is an eligible rollover distribution?

Q-19. When must a qualified plan be amended to comply with section 401(a)(31)?

Questions and Answers

Q-1. What are the direct rollover requirements under section 401(a)(31)?

A-1. **(a) General rule.** To satisfy section 401(a)(31), added by UCA, a plan must provide that if the distributee of any eligible rollover distribution elects to have the distribution paid directly to an eligible retirement plan, and specifies the eligible retirement plan to which the distribution is to be paid, then the distribution will be paid to that eligible retirement plan in a direct rollover described in Q&A-3 of this section. Thus, the plan must give the distributee the option of having his or her distribution paid in a direct rollover to an eligible retirement plan specified by the distributee. For purposes of section 401(a)(31) and this section, eligible rollover distribution has the meaning set forth in section 402(c)(4) and § 1.402(c)-2, Q&A-3 through Q&A-10 and Q&A-14, except as otherwise provided in Q&A-2 of this section, eligible retirement plan has the meaning set forth in section 402(c)(8)(B) and § 1.402(c)-2, Q&A-2.

**(b) Related Internal Revenue Code provisions.** *(1) Mandatory withholding.* If a distributee of an eligible rollover distribution does not elect to have the eligible rollover distribution paid directly from the plan to an eligible retirement plan in a direct rollover under section 401(a)(31), the eligible rollover distribution is subject to 20-percent income tax withholding under section 3405(c). See § 31.3405(c)-1 of this chapter for guidance concerning the withholding requirements applicable to eligible rollover distributions.

*(2) Notice requirement.* Section 402(f) requires the plan administrator of a qualified plan to provide, within a reasonable period of time before making an eligible rollover distribution, a written explanation to the distributee of the distributee's right to elect a direct rollover and the withholding consequences of not making that election. The explanation also is required to provide certain other relevant information relating to the taxation of distributions. See § 1.402(f)-1 for guidance concerning the written explanation required under section 402(f).

*(3) Section 403(b) annuities.* Section 403(b)(10) provides that requirements similar to those imposed by section 401(a)(31) apply to annuities described in section 403(b). See § 1.403(b)-7(b) for guidance concerning the direct rollover requirements for distributions from annuities described in section 403(b).

**(c) Effective date.** *(1) Statutory effective date.* Section 401(a)(31) applies to eligible rollover distributions made on or after January 1, 1993.

*(2) Regulatory effective date.* This section applies to eligible rollover distributions made on or after October 19, 1995. For eligible rollover distributions made on or after January 1, 1993 and before October 19, 1995, § 1.401(a)(31)-1T (as it appeared in the April 1, 1995 edition of 26 CFR part 1), applies. However, for any distribution made on or after January 1, 1993 but before October 19, 1995, a plan may satisfy section 401(a)(31) by substituting any or all provisions of this section for the corresponding provisions of § 1.401(a)(31)-1T, if any.

Q-2. Does section 401(a)(31) require that a qualified plan permit a direct rollover to be made to a qualified trust that is not part of a defined contribution plan?

A-2. No. Section 401(a)(31)(D) limits the types of qualified trusts that are treated as eligible retirement plans to defined contribution plans that accept eligible rollover distributions. Therefore, although a plan is permitted, at a participant's election, to make a direct rollover to any type of eligible retirement plan, as defined in section 402(c)(8)(B) (including a defined benefit plan), a plan will not fail to satisfy section 401(a)(31) solely because the plan will not permit a direct rollover to a qualified trust that is part of a defined benefit plan. In contrast, if a distributee elects a direct rollover of an eligible rollover distribution to an annuity plan described in section 403(a), that distribution must be paid to the annuity plan, even if the recipient annuity plan is a defined benefit plan.

Q-3. What is a *direct rollover* that satisfies section 401(a)(31), and how is it accomplished?

A-3. A direct rollover that satisfies section 401(a)(31) is an eligible rollover distribution that is paid directly to an eligible retirement plan for the benefit of the distributee. A direct rollover may be accomplished by any reasonable means of direct payment to an eligible retirement plan. Reasonable means of direct payment include, for example, a wire transfer or the mailing of a check to the eligible retirement plan. If payment is made by check, the check must be negotiable only by the trustee of the eligible retirement plan. If the payment is made by wire transfer, the wire transfer must be directed only to the trustee of the eligible retirement plan. In the case of an eligible retirement plan that does not have a trustee (such as a custodial individual retirement account or an individual retirement annuity), the custodian of the plan or issuer of the contract under the plan, as appropriate, should be substituted for the trustee for purposes of this Q&A-3, and Q&A-4 of this section.

Q-4. Is providing a distributee with a check for delivery to an eligible retirement plan a reasonable means of accomplishing a direct rollover?

A-4. Providing the distributee with a check and instructing the distributee to deliver the check to the eligible retirement plan is a reasonable means of direct payment, provided that the check is made payable as follows: [Name of the trustee] as trustee of [name of the eligible retirement plan]. For example, if the name of the eligible retirement plan is "Individual Retirement Account of John Q. Smith," and the name of the trustee is "ABC Bank," the payee line of a check would read "ABC Bank as trustee of Individual Retirement Account of John Q. Smith." Unless the name of the distributee is included in the name of the eligible retirement plan, the check also must indicate that it is for the benefit of the distributee. If the eligible retirement plan is not an individual retirement account or an individual retirement annuity, the payee line of the check need not identify the trustee by name. For example, the payee line of a check for the benefit of distributee Jane Doe might read, "Trustee of XYZ Corporation Savings Plan FBO Jane Doe."

Q-5. Is an eligible rollover distribution that is paid to an eligible retirement plan in a direct rollover currently includible in gross income or subject to 20-percent withholding?

A-5. No. An eligible rollover distribution that is paid to an eligible retirement plan in a direct rollover is not currently includible in the distributee's gross income under section 402(c) and is exempt from the 20-percent withholding imposed under section 3405(c)(2). However, when any portion of the eligible rollover distribution is subsequently distributed from the eligible retirement plan, that portion will be includible in gross income to the extent required under section 402, 403, or 408.

Q-6. What procedures may a plan administrator prescribe for electing a direct rollover, and what information may the plan administrator require a distributee to provide when electing a direct rollover?

A-6. **(a) Permissible procedures.** Except as otherwise provided in paragraph (b) of this Q&A-6, the plan administrator may prescribe any procedure for a distributee to elect a direct rollover under section 401(a)(31), provided that the procedure is reasonable. The procedure may include any reasonable requirement for information or documentation from the distributee in addition to the items of adequate information specified in § 31.3405(c)-1(b), Q&A-7 of this chapter. For example, it would be reasonable for the plan administrator to require that the distributee provide a statement from the designated recipient plan that the plan will accept the direct rollover for the benefit of the distributee and that the recipient plan is, or is intended to be, an individual retirement account, an individual retirement annuity, a qualified annuity plan described in section 403(a), or a qualified trust described in section 401(a), as applicable. In the case of a designated recipient plan that is a qualified trust, it also would be reasonable for the plan administrator to require a statement that the qualified trust is not excepted from the definition of an eligible retirement plan by section 401(a)(31)(D) (i.e., is not a defined benefit plan).

**(b) Impermissible procedures.** A plan will fail to satisfy section 401(a)(31) if the plan administrator prescribes any unreasonable procedure, or requires information or documentation, that effectively eliminates or substantially impairs the distributee's ability to elect a direct rollover. For example, it would effectively eliminate or substantially impair the distributee's ability to elect a direct rollover if the recipient plan required the distributee to obtain an opinion of counsel stating that the eligible retirement plan receiving the rollover is a qualified plan or individual retirement account. Similarly, it would effectively eliminate or substantially impair the distributee's ability to elect a direct rollover if the distributing plan required a letter from the recipient eligible retirement plan stating that, upon request by the distributing plan, the recipient plan will automatically return any direct rollover amount that the distributing plan advises the recipient plan was paid incorrectly. It would also effectively eliminate or substantially impair the distributee's ability to elect a direct rollover if the distributing plan required, as a condition for making a direct rollover, a letter from the recipient eligible retirement plan indemnifying the distributing plan for any liability arising from the distribution.

Q-7. May the plan administrator treat a distributee as having made an election under a default procedure where the distributee does not affirmatively elect to make or not make a direct rollover within a certain time period?

A-7. Yes, the plan administrator may establish a default procedure whereby any distributee who fails to make an affirmative election is treated as having either made or not made a direct rollover election. However, the plan administrator may not make a distribution under any default procedure unless the distributee has received an explanation of the default procedure and an explanation of the direct rollover option as required under section 402(f) and § 1.402(f)-1, Q&A-1 and unless the timing requirements described in § 1.402(f)-1, Q&A-2 and Q&A-3 have been satisfied with respect to the explanations of both the default procedure and the direct rollover option.

Q-8. May the plan administrator establish a deadline after which the distributee may not revoke an election to make or not make a direct rollover?

A-8. Yes, but the plan administrator is not permitted to prescribe any deadline or time period with respect to revocation of a direct rollover election that is more restrictive for the distributee than that which otherwise applies under the plan to revocation of the form of distribution elected by the distributee.

Q-9. Must the plan administrator permit a distributee to elect to have a portion of an eligible rollover distribution paid to an eligible retirement plan in a direct rollover and to have the remainder of that distribution paid to the distributee?

A-9. Yes, the plan administrator must permit a distributee to elect to have a portion of an eligible rollover distribution paid to an eligible retirement plan in a direct rollover and to have the remainder paid to the distributee. However, the plan administrator is permitted to require that, if the distributee elects to have only a portion of an eligible rollover distribution paid to an eligible retirement plan in a direct rollover, that portion be equal to at least a specified minimum amount, provided the specified minimum amount is less than or equal to $500 or any greater amount as prescribed by the Commissioner in revenue rulings, notices, and other guidance published in the Internal Revenue Bulletin. See § 601.601(d)(2)(ii)(b) of this chapter. If the entire amount of the eligible rollover distribution is less than or equal to the specified minimum amount, the plan administrator need not allow the distributee to divide the distribution.

Q-10. Must the plan administrator allow a distributee to divide an eligible rollover distribution into two or more separate distributions to be paid in direct rollovers to two or more eligible retirement plans?

A-10. No. The plan administrator is not required (but is permitted) to allow the distributee to divide an eligible rollover distribution into separate distributions to be paid to two or more eligible retirement plans in direct rollovers. Thus, the plan administrator may require that the distributee select a single eligible retirement plan to which the eligible rollover distribution (or portion thereof) will be distributed in a direct rollover.

Q-11. Will a plan satisfy section 401(a)(31) if the plan administrator does not permit a distributee to elect a direct rollover if his or her eligible rollover distributions during a year are reasonably expected to total less than $200?

A-11. Yes. A plan will satisfy section 401(a)(31) even though the plan administrator does not permit any distributee to elect a direct rollover with respect to eligible rollover distributions during a year that are reasonably expected to total less than $200 or any lower minimum amount specified by the plan administrator. The rules described in § 31.3405(c)-1, Q&A-14 of this chapter (relating to whether withholding under section 3405(c) is required for an eligible rollover distribution that is less than $200) also apply for purposes of determining whether a direct rollover election under section 401(a)(31) must be provided for an eligible rollover distribution that is less than $200 or the lower specified amount.

Q-12. Is a plan administrator permitted to treat a distributee's election to make or not make a direct rollover with respect to one payment in a series of periodic payments as applying to all subsequent payments in the series?

A-12. (a) Yes. A plan administrator is permitted to treat a distributee's election to make or not make a direct rollover with respect to one payment in a series of periodic payments as applying to all subsequent payments in the series, provided that:

(1) The employee is permitted at any time to change, with respect to subsequent payments, a previous election to make or not make a direct rollover; and

(2) The written explanation provided under section 402(f) explains that the election to make or not make a direct rollover will apply to all future payments unless the employee subsequently changes the election.

(b) See § 1.402(f)-1, Q&A-3 for further guidance concerning the rules for providing section 402(f) notices when eligible rollover distributions are made in a series of periodic payments.

Q-13. Is the eligible retirement plan designated by a distributee to receive a direct rollover distribution required to accept the distribution?

A-13. No. Although section 401(a)(31) requires qualified plans to provide distributees the option to make a direct rollover of their eligible rollover distributions to an eligible retirement plan, it imposes no requirement that any eligible retirement plan accept rollovers. Thus, a plan can refuse to accept rollovers. Alternatively, a plan can limit the circumstances under which it will accept rollovers. For example, a plan can limit the types of plans from which it will accept a rollover or limit the types of assets it will accept in a rollover (such as accepting only cash or its equivalent).

Q-14. If a plan accepts an invalid rollover contribution, whether or not as a direct rollover, how will the contribution be treated for purposes of applying the qualification requirements of section 401(a) or 403(a) to the plan?

A-14. **(a) Acceptance of invalid rollover contribution.** If a plan accepts an invalid rollover contribution, the contribution will be treated, for purposes of applying the qualification requirements of section 401(a) or 403(a) to the receiving plan, as if it were a valid rollover contribution, if the following two conditions are satisfied. First, when accepting the amount from the employee as a rollover contribution, the plan administrator of the receiving plan reasonably concludes that the contribution is a valid rollover contribution. While evidence that the distributing plan is the subject of a determination letter from the Commissioner indicating that the distributing plan is qualified would be useful to the receiving plan administrator in reasonably concluding that the contribution is a valid rollover contribution, it is not necessary for the distributing plan to have such a determination letter in order for the receiving plan administrator to reach that conclusion. Second, if the plan administrator of the receiving plan later determines that the contribution was an invalid rollover contribution, the amount of the invalid rollover contribution, plus any earnings attributable thereto, is distributed to the employee within a reasonable time after such determination.

**(b) Definitions.** For purposes of this Q&A-14:

(1) An invalid rollover contribution is an amount that is accepted by a plan as a rollover within the meaning of § 1.402(c)-2, Q&A-1 (or as a rollover contribution within the meaning of section 408(d)(3)(A)(ii)) but that is not an eligible rollover distribution from a qualified plan (or an amount described in section 408(d)(3)(A)(ii)) or that does not satisfy the other requirements of section 401(a)(31), 402(c), or 408(d)(3) for treatment as a rollover or a rollover contribution.

(2) A valid rollover contribution is a contribution that is accepted by a plan as a rollover within the meaning of § 1.402(c)-2, Q&A-1 or as a rollover contribution within the meaning of section 408(d)(3) and that satisfies the requirements of section 401(a)(31), 402(c), or 408(d)(3) for treatment as a rollover or a rollover contribution.

**(c) Examples.** The provisions of paragraph (a) of this Q&A-14 are illustrated by the following examples:

Example 1. (i) Employer X maintains for its employees Plan M, a profit sharing plan qualified under section 401(a). Plan M provides that any employee of Employer X may make a rollover contribution to Plan M. Employee A is an employee of Employer X, will not have attained age 70½ by the end of the year, and has a vested account balance in Plan O (a plan maintained by Employee A's prior employer). Employee A elects a single sum distribution from Plan O and elects that it be paid to Plan M in a direct rollover.

(ii) Employee A provides the plan administrator of Plan M with a letter from the plan administrator of Plan O stating that Plan O has received a determination letter from the Commissioner indicating that Plan O is qualified.

(iii) Based upon such a letter, absent facts to the contrary, a plan administrator may reasonably conclude that Plan O is qualified and that the amount paid as a direct rollover is an eligible rollover distribution.

Example 2. (i) The facts are the same as Example 1, except that, instead of the letter provided in paragraph (ii) of Example 1, Employee A provides the plan administrator of Plan M with a letter from the plan administrator of Plan O representing that Plan O satisfies the requirements of section 401(a) (or representing that Plan O is intended to satisfy the requirements of section 401(a) and that the administrator of Plan O is not aware of any Plan O provision or operation that would result in the disqualification of Plan O).

(ii) Based upon such a letter, absent facts to the contrary, a plan administrator may reasonably conclude that Plan O is qualified and that the amount paid as a direct rollover is an eligible rollover distribution.

Example 3. (i) Same facts as Example 1, except that Employee A elects to receive the distribution from Plan O and wishes to make a rollover contribution described in section 402 rather than a direct rollover.

(ii) When making the rollover contribution, Employee A certifies that, to the best of Employee A's knowledge, Employee A is entitled to the distribution as an employee and not as a beneficiary, the distribution from Plan O to be contributed to Plan M is not one of a series of periodic payments, the distribution from Plan O was received by Employee A not more than 60 days before the date of the rollover contribution, and the entire amount of the rollover contribution would be includible in gross income if it were not being rolled over.

(iii) As support for these certifications, Employee A provides the plan administrator of Plan M with two statements from Plan O. The first is a letter from the plan administrator of Plan O, as described in Example 1, stating that Plan O has received a determination letter from the Commissioner indicating that Plan O is qualified. The second is the distribution statement that accompanied the distribution check. The distribution statement indicates that the distribution is being made by Plan O to Employee A, indicates the gross amount of the distribution, and indicates the amount withheld as Federal income tax. The amount withheld as Federal income tax is 20 percent of the gross amount of the distribution. Employee A contributes to Plan M an amount not greater than the gross amount of the distribution stated in the letter from Plan O and the contribution is made within 60 days of the date of the distribution statement from Plan O.

(iv) Based on the certifications and documentation provided by Employee A, absent facts to the contrary, a plan administrator may reasonably conclude that Plan O is qualified and that the distribution otherwise satisfies the requirements of section 402(c) for treatment as a rollover contribution.

Example 4. (i) The facts are the same as in Example 3, except that, rather than contributing the distribution from Plan O to Plan M, Employee A contributes the distribution from Plan O to IRA P, an individual retirement account described in section 408(a). After the contribution of the distribution from Plan O to IRA P, but before the year in which Employee A attains age 70½, Employee A requests a distribution from IRA P and decides to contribute it to Plan M as a rollover contribution. To make the rollover contribution, Employee A endorses the check received from IRA P as payable to Plan M.

(ii) In addition to providing the certifications described in Example 3 with respect to the distribution from Plan O, Employee A certifies that, to the best of Employee A's knowledge, the contribution to IRA P was not made more than 60 days after the date Employee A received the distribution from Plan O, no amount other than the distribution from Plan O has been contributed to IRA P, and the distribution from IRA P was received not more than 60 days earlier than the rollover contribution to Plan M.

(iii) As support for these certifications, in addition to the two statements from Plan O described in Example 3, Employee A provides copies of statements from IRA P. The statements indicate that the account is identified as an IRA, the account was established within 60 days of the date of the letter from Plan O informing Employee A that an amount had been distributed, and the opening balance in the IRA does not exceed the amount of the distribution described in the letter from Plan O. There is no indication in the statements that any additional contributions have been made to IRA P since the account was opened. The date on the check from IRA P is less than 60 days before the date that Employee A makes the contribution to Plan M.

(iv) Based on the certifications and documentation provided by Employee A, absent facts to the contrary, a plan administrator may reasonably conclude that Plan O is qualified and that the contribution by Employee A is a rollover contribution described in section 408(d)(3)(A)(ii) that satisfies the other requirements of section 408(d)(3) for treatment as a rollover contribution.

Q-15. For purposes of applying the plan qualification requirements of section 401(a), is an eligible rollover distribution that is paid to an eligible retirement plan in a direct rollover a distribution and rollover or is it a transfer of assets and liabilities?

A-15. For purposes of applying the plan qualification requirements of section 401(a), a direct rollover is a distribution and rollover of the eligible rollover distribution and not a transfer of assets and liabilities. For example, if the consent requirements under section 411(a)(11) or sections 401(a)(11) and 417(a)(2) apply to the distribution, they must be satisfied before the eligible rollover distribution may be distributed in a direct rollover. Similarly, the direct rollover is not a transfer of assets and liabilities that must satisfy the requirements of section 414(l). Finally, a direct rollover is not a transfer of benefits for purposes of applying the requirements under section 411(d)(6), as described in § 1.411(d)-4, Q&A-3. Therefore, for example, the eligible retirement plan is not required to provide, with respect to amounts paid to it in a direct rollover, the same optional forms of benefits that were provided under the plan that made the direct rollover. The direct rollover requirements of section 401(a)(31) do not affect the ability of a qualified plan to make an elective or nonelective transfer of assets and liabilities to another qualified plan in accordance with applicable law (such as section 414(l)).

Q-16. Must a direct rollover option be provided for an eligible rollover distribution that is in the form of a plan loan offset amount?

A-16. A plan will not fail to satisfy section 401(a)(31) merely because the plan does not permit a distributee to elect a direct rollover of an eligible rollover distribution in the form of a plan loan offset amount. Section 1.402(c)-2(b), Q&A-9 defines a plan loan offset amount, in general, as a distribution that occurs when, under the terms governing a plan loan, the participant's accrued benefit is reduced (offset) in order to repay the loan. A plan administrator is permitted to allow a direct rollover of a participant note for a plan loan to a qualified trust described in section 401(a) or a qualified annuity plan described in section 403(a). See § 1.402(c)-2, Q&A-9 for examples illustrating the rules for plan loan offset amounts that are set forth in this Q&A-16. See § 31.3405(c)-1, Q&A-11 of this chapter for guidance concerning special withholding rules that apply to a distribution in the form of a plan loan offset amount.

Q-17. Must a direct rollover option be provided for an eligible rollover distribution from a qualified plan distributed annuity contract?

A-17. Yes. If any amount to be distributed under a qualified plan distributed annuity contract is an eligible rollover distribution (in accordance with § 1.402(c)-2), Q&A-10 the annuity contract must satisfy section 401(a)(31) in the same manner as a qualified plan under section 401(a). Section 1.402(c)-2, Q&A-10 defines a qualified plan distributed annuity contract as an annuity contract purchased for a participant, and distributed to the participant, by a qualified plan.

In the case of a qualified plan distributed annuity contract, the payor under the contract is treated as the plan administrator. See § 31.3405(c)-1, Q&A-13 of this chapter concerning the application of mandatory 20-percent withholding requirements to distributions from a qualified plan distributed annuity contract.

Q-18. What assumptions may a plan administrator make regarding whether a benefit is an eligible rollover distribution?

A-18. **(a) General rule.** For purposes of section 401(a)(31), a plan administrator may make the assumptions described in paragraphs (b) and (c) of this Q&A-18 in determining the amount of a distribution that is an eligible rollover distribution for which a direct rollover option must be provided. Section 31.3405(c)-1, Q&A-10 of this chapter provides assumptions for purposes of complying with section 3405(c). See § 1.402(c)-2, Q&A-15 concerning the effect of these assumptions for purposes of section 402(c).

**(b) $5,000 death benefit.** A plan administrator is permitted to assume that a distribution from the plan that qualifies for the $5,000 death benefit exclusion under section 101(b) is the only death benefit being paid with respect to a deceased employee that qualifies for that exclusion. Thus, to the extent that such a distribution would be excludible from gross income based on this assumption, the plan administrator is permitted to assume that it is not an eligible rollover distribution.

**(c) Determination of designated beneficiary.** For the purpose of determining the amount of the minimum distribution required to satisfy section 401(a)(9)(A) for any calendar year, the plan administrator is permitted to assume that there is no designated beneficiary.

Q-19. When must a qualified plan be amended to comply with section 401(a)(31)?

A-19. Even though section 401(a)(31) applies to distributions from qualified plans made after on or after January 1, 1993, a qualified plan is not required to be amended before the last day by which amendments must be made to comply with the Tax Reform Act of 1986 and related provisions, as permitted in other administrative guidance of general applicability, provided that:

(a) In the interim period between January 1, 1993, and the date on which the plan is amended, the plan is operated in accordance with the requirements of section 401(a)(31); and

(b) The amendment applies retroactively to January 1, 1993.

---

T.D. 8619, 9/15/95, amend T.D. 8880, 4/20/2000, T.D. 9340, 7/23/2007.

---

PAR. 2. Section 1.401(a)(31)-1 is amended as follows:

1. Under the heading "List of Questions," redesignating Q-14 through Q-18 as Q-15 through Q-19, respectively, and adding new Q-14.

2. Under the heading "Question and Answers," removing designation (a) and the paragraph heading, and removing paragraph (b) from A-13.

3. Under the heading "Question and Answers," redesignating Q&A-14 through Q&A-18 as Q&A-15 through Q&A-19, respectively, and adding Q&A-14.

The additions read as follows:

**Proposed § 1.401(a)(31)-1 (09/19/1996) Requirement to offer direct rollover of eligible rollover distributions; questions and answers.** [*For Preamble, see ¶ 151,753*]

* * * * *

**List of questions**

* * * * *

Q-14. If a plan accepts an invalid rollover contribution, whether or not as a direct rollover, how will the contribution be treated for purposes of applying the qualification requirements of section 401(a) or 403(a) to the plan?

* * * * *

**Questions and answers**

* * * * *

Q-14. If a plan accepts an invalid rollover contribution, whether or not as a direct rollover, how will the contribution be treated for purposes of applying the qualification requirements of section 401(a) or 403(a) to the plan?

A-14. **(a) Acceptance of invalid rollover contribution.** If a plan accepts an invalid rollover contribution, the contribution will be treated, for purposes of applying the qualification requirements of section 401(a) or 403(a) to the receiving plan, as if it were a valid rollover contribution, if the following two conditions are satisfied. First, when accepting the amount from the employee as a rollover contribution, the plan administrator of the receiving plan reasonably concludes that the contribution is a valid rollover contribution. Second, if the plan administrator of the receiving plan later determines that the contribution was an invalid rollover contribution, the amount of the invalid rollover contribution, plus any earnings attributable thereto, is distributed to the employee within a reasonable time after such determination.

**(b) Definitions.** For purposes of this Q&A-14:

(1) An *invalid rollover contribution* is an amount that is accepted by a plan as a rollover within the meaning of Q&A-1 of § 1.402(c)-2 (or as a rollover contribution within the meaning of section 408(d)(3)(A)(ii)) but that is not an eligible rollover distribution from a qualified plan (or an amount described in section 408(d)(3)(A)(ii)) or that does not satisfy the other requirements of section 401(a)(31), 402(c), or 408(d)(3) for treatment as a rollover or a rollover contribution.

(2) A *valid rollover contribution* is a contribution that is accepted by a plan as a rollover within the meaning of Q&A-1 of § 1.402(c)-2 or as a rollover contribution within the meaning of section 408(d)(3) and that satisfies the requirements of section 401(a)(31), 402(c), or 408(d)(3) for treatment as a rollover or a rollover contribution.

(c) The provisions of paragraph (a) of this Q&A-14 are illustrated by the following examples:

*Example (1).* (a) Employer X maintains for its employees Plan M, a profit sharing plan qualified under section 401(a). Plan M provides that any employee of Employer X may make a rollover contribution to Plan M. Employee A is an employee of Employer X, will not have attained age 70½ by the end of the year, and has a vested account balance in Plan O (a plan maintained by Employee A's prior employer). Employee A elects a single sum distribution from Plan O and elects that it be paid to Plan M in a direct rollover.

(b) Employee A provides the plan administrator of Plan M with a letter from the plan administrator of Plan O stating that Plan O has received a determination letter from the Commissioner indicating that Plan O is qualified.

(c) Based upon such a letter, absent facts to the contrary, a plan administrator may reasonably conclude that Plan O is qualified and that the amount paid as a direct rollover is an eligible rollover distribution.

*Example (2).* (a) Same facts as Example 1, except that Employee A elects to receive the distribution from Plan O and wishes to make a rollover contribution described in section 402 rather than a direct rollover.

(b) When making the rollover contribution, Employee A certifies that, to the best of Employee A's knowledge, Employee A is entitled to the distribution as an employee and not as a beneficiary, the distribution from Plan O to be contributed to Plan M is not one of a series of periodic payments, the distribution from Plan O was received by Employee A not more than 60 days before the date of the rollover contribution, and the entire amount of the rollover contribution would be includible in gross income if it were not being rolled over.

(c) As support for these certifications, Employee A provides the plan administrator of Plan M with two statements from Plan O. The first is a letter from the plan administrator of Plan O, as described in Example 1, stating that Plan O has received a determination letter from the Commissioner indicating that Plan O is qualified. The second is the distribution statement that accompanied the distribution check. The distribution statement indicates that the distribution is being made by Plan O to Employee A, indicates the gross amount of the distribution, and indicates the amount withheld as Federal income tax. The amount withheld as Federal income tax is 20 percent of the gross amount of the distribution. Employee A contributes to Plan M an amount not greater than the gross amount of the distribution stated in the letter from Plan O and the contribution is made within 60 days of the date of the distribution statement from Plan O.

(d) Based on the certifications and documentation provided by Employee A, absent facts to the contrary, a plan administrator may reasonably conclude that Plan O is qualified and that the distribution otherwise satisfies the requirements of section 402(c) for treatment as a rollover contribution.

*Example (3).* (a) The facts are the same as in Example 2, except that, rather than contributing the distribution from Plan O to Plan M, Employee A contributes the distribution from Plan O to IRA P, an individual retirement account described in section 408(a). After the contribution of the distribution from Plan O to IRA P, but before the year in which Employee A attains age 70½, Employee A requests a distribution from IRA P and decides to contribute it to Plan M as a rollover contribution. To make the rollover contribution, Employee A endorses the check received from IRA P as payable to Plan M.

(b) In addition to providing the certifications described in Example 2 with respect to the distribution from Plan O, Employee A certifies that, to the best of Employee A's knowledge, the contribution to IRA P was made not more than 60 days after the date Employee A received the distribution from Plan O, no amount other than the distribution from Plan O has been contributed to IRA P, and the distribution from IRA P was received not more than 60 days earlier than the rollover contribution to Plan M.

(c) As support for these certifications, in addition to the two statements from Plan O described in Example 2, Employee A provides copies of statements from IRA P. The statements indicate that the account is identified as an IRA, the account was established within 60 days of the date of the letter from Plan O informing Employee A that an amount had been distributed, and the opening balance in the IRA does not exceed the amount of the distribution described in the letter from Plan O. There is no indication in the statements that any additional contributions have been made to IRA P since the account was opened. The date on the check from IRA P is less than 60 days before the date that Employee A makes the contribution to Plan M.

(d) Based on the certifications and documentation provided by Employee A, absent facts to the contrary, a plan administrator may reasonably conclude that Plan O is qualified and that the contribution by Employee A is a rollover contribution described in section 408(d)(3)(A)(ii) that satisfies the other requirements of section 408(d)(3) for treatment as a rollover contribution.

### § 1.401(a)(35)-1 Diversification requirements for certain defined contribution plans.

**(a) General rule.** *(1) Diversification requirements.* Section 401(a)(35) imposes diversification requirements on applicable defined contribution plans. A trust that is part of an applicable defined contribution plan is not a qualified trust under section 401(a) unless the plan—

(i) Satisfies the diversification election requirements for elective deferrals and employee contributions set forth in paragraph (b) of this section;

(ii) Satisfies the diversification election requirements for employer nonelective contributions set forth in paragraph (c) of this section;

(iii) Satisfies the investment option requirement set forth in paragraph (d) of this section; and

(iv) Does not apply any restrictions or conditions on investments in employer securities that violate the requirements of paragraph (e) of this section.

*(2) Definitions, effective dates, and transition rules.* The definitions of applicable defined contribution plan, employer security, parent corporation, and publicly traded are set forth in paragraph (f) of this section. Applicability dates and transition rules are set forth in paragraph (g) of this section.

**(b) Diversification requirements for elective deferrals and employee contributions invested in employer securities.** *(1) General rule.* With respect to any individual described in paragraph (b)(2) of this section, if any portion of the individual's account under an applicable defined contribution plan attributable to elective deferrals (as described in section 402(g)(3)(A)), employee contributions, or rollover contributions is invested in employer securities, then the plan satisfies the requirements of this paragraph (b) if the individual may elect to divest those employer securities and reinvest an equivalent amount in other investment options. The plan may limit the time for divestment and reinvestment to periodic, reasonable opportunities occurring no less frequently than quarterly.

*(2) Applicable individual with respect to elective deferrals and employee contributions.* An individual is described in this paragraph (b)(2) if the individual is—

(i) A participant;

(ii) An alternate payee who has an account under the plan; or

(iii) A beneficiary of a deceased participant.

**(c) Diversification requirements for employer nonelective contributions invested in employer securities.** *(1) General rule.* With respect to any individual described in paragraph (c)(2) of this section, if a portion of the individual's account under an applicable defined contribution plan attributable to employer nonelective contributions is invested in employer securities, then the plan satisfies the requirements of this paragraph (c) if the individual may elect to divest those employer securities and reinvest an equivalent amount in other investment options. The plan may limit the time for divestment and reinvestment to periodic, reasonable opportunities occurring no less frequently than quarterly.

*(2) Applicable individual with respect to employer nonelective contributions.* An individual is described in this paragraph (c)(2) if the individual is—

(i) A participant who has completed at least three years of service;

(ii) An alternate payee who has an account under the plan with respect to a participant who has completed at least three years of service; or

(iii) A beneficiary of a deceased participant.

*(3) Completion of three years of service.* For purposes of paragraph (c)(2) of this section, a participant completes three years of service on the last day of the vesting computation period provided for under the plan that constitutes the completion of the third year of service under section 411(a)(5). However, for a plan that uses the elapsed time method of crediting service for vesting purposes (or a plan that provides for immediate vesting without using a vesting computation period or the elapsed time method of determining vesting), a participant completes three years of service on the day immediately preceding the third anniversary of the participant's date of hire.

**(d) Investment options.** An applicable defined contribution plan must offer not less than three investment options, other than employer securities, to which an individual who has the right to divest under paragraph (b)(1) or (c)(1) of this section may direct the proceeds from the divestment of employer securities. Each of the three investment options must be diversified and have materially different risk and return characteristics. For this purpose, investment options that constitute a broad range of investment alternatives within the meaning of Department of Labor Regulation section 2550.404c-1(b)(3) are treated as being diversified and having materially different risk and return characteristics.

**(e) Restrictions or conditions on investments in employer securities.** *(1) Impermissible restrictions or conditions.* (i) General rule. Except as provided in paragraph (e)(2) of this section, an applicable defined contribution plan violates the requirements of this paragraph (e) if the plan imposes restrictions or conditions with respect to the investment of employer securities that are not imposed on the investment of other assets of the plan. A restriction or condition with respect to employer securities means—

(A) A restriction on an individual's right to divest an investment in employer securities that is not imposed on an investment that is not employer securities; or

(B) A benefit that is conditioned on investment in employer securities.

(ii) Indirect restrictions or conditions. (A) Except as provided in paragraph (e)(3) of this section, a plan violates the requirements of this paragraph (e) if the plan imposes a restriction or condition described in paragraph (e)(1)(i)(A) or (B) of this section either directly or indirectly.

(B) A plan imposes an indirect restriction on an individual's right to divest an investment in employer securities if, for example, the plan provides that a participant who divests his or her account balance with respect to the investment in employer securities is not permitted for a period of time thereafter to reinvest in employer securities.

(C) A plan does not impose an indirect restriction or condition merely because there are tax consequences that result from an individual's divestment of an investment in employer securities. Thus, the loss of the special treatment for net unrealized appreciation provided under section 402(e)(4) with respect to employer securities is disregarded. Similarly, a plan does not impose an impermissible restriction or condition merely because it provides that an individual may not reinvest divested amounts in the same employer securities account but is permitted to invest such divested amounts in another employer securities account where the only relevant difference between the separate accounts is the section 402(e)(4) cost (or other basis) of the trust in the shares held in each account. (See § 1.402(a)-1(b) for rules regarding section 402(e)(4).)

*(2) Permitted restrictions or conditions.* (i) In general. An applicable defined contribution plan does not violate the requirements of this paragraph (e) merely because it imposes a restriction or a condition set forth in paragraph (e)(2)(ii) or (e)(2)(iii) of this section.

(ii) Securities laws. A plan is permitted to impose a restriction or condition on the divestiture of employer securities that is either required in order to ensure compliance with applicable securities laws or is reasonably designed to ensure compliance with applicable securities laws. For example, it is permissible for a plan to limit divestiture rights for participants who are subject to section 16(b) of the Securities Exchange Act of 1934 (15 U.S.C. 78f) to a reasonable period (such as 3 to 12 days) following publication of the employer's quarterly earnings statements because it is reasonably designed to ensure compliance with Rule 10b-5 of the Securities and Exchange Commission.

(iii) Deferred application of the diversification requirements. (A) Becoming an applicable defined contribution plan. An applicable defined contribution plan is permitted to restrict the application of the diversification requirements of section 401(a)(35) and this section for up to 90 days after the plan becomes an applicable defined contribution plan (for example, a plan becoming an applicable defined contribution plan because the employer securities held under the plan become publicly traded).

(B) Loss of exception for indirect investments. In the case where an investment fund described in paragraph (f)(3)(ii)(A) of this section no longer meets the requirement in paragraph (f)(3)(ii)(B) of this section that the investment must be independent of the employer (including the situation where the fund no longer meets the percentage limitation rule in paragraph (f)(3)(ii)(C) of this section), the plan does not fail to satisfy the diversification requirements of section 401(a)(35) and this section merely because it does not offer those rights with respect to that investment fund for up to 90 days after the investment fund ceases to meet those requirements.

*(3) Permitted indirect restrictions or conditions.* (i) In general. An applicable defined contribution plan does not violate the requirements of this paragraph (e) merely because it imposes an indirect restriction or condition set forth in this paragraph (e)(3).

(ii) Limitation on investment in employer securities. A plan is permitted to limit the extent to which an individual's account balance can be invested in employer securities, provided the limitation applies without regard to a prior exercise of rights to divest employer securities. For example, a plan does not impose a restriction that violates this paragraph (e) merely because the plan prohibits a participant from investing additional amounts in employer securities if more than 10 percent of that participant's account balance is invested in employer securities.

(iii) Trading frequency. A plan is permitted to impose reasonable restrictions on the timing and number of investment elections that an individual can make to invest in employer securities, provided that the restrictions are designed to limit short-term trading in the employer securities. For example, a plan could provide that a participant may not elect to invest in employer securities if the employee has elected to divest employer securities within a short period of time, such as seven days, prior to the election to invest in employer securities.

(iv) Fees. The plan has not provided an indirect benefit that is conditioned on investment in employer securities merely because the plan imposes fees on other investment options that are not imposed on the investment in employer securities. In addition, the plan has not provided a restriction on the right to divest an investment in employer securities merely because the plan imposes a reasonable fee for the divestment of employer securities.

(v) Stable value or similar fund. A plan is permitted to allow transfers to be made into or out of a stable value or similar fund more frequently than a fund invested in employer securities for purposes of paragraph (e)(1)(ii) of this section. Thus, a plan that includes a broad range of investment alternatives as described in paragraph (d) of this section, including a stable value or similar fund, does not impose an impermissible restriction under paragraph (e)(1)(ii) of this section merely because it permits transfers into or out of that fund more frequently than other funds under the plan, provided that the plan would otherwise satisfy this paragraph (e) (taking into account any restrictions or conditions imposed with respect to the other investment options under the plan). For purposes of this section, a stable value fund or similar fund means an investment product or fund designed to preserve or guarantee principal and provide a reasonable rate of return, while providing liquidity for benefit distributions or transfers to other investment alternatives (such as a product or fund described in Department of Labor Regulation § 2550.404c-5(e)(4)(iv)(A) or (v)(A)).

(vi) Transfers out of a qualified default investment alternative (QDIA). A plan is permitted to provide for transfers out of a QDIA within the meaning of Department of Labor Regulation section 2550.404c-5(e) more frequently than a fund invested in employer securities.

(vii) Frozen funds. (A) General rule. A plan is permitted to prohibit any further investment in employer securities. Thus, a plan is not treated as imposing an indirect restriction merely because it provides that an employee that divests an investment in employer securities is not permitted to reinvest in employer securities, but only if the plan does not permit additional contributions or other investments to be invested in employer securities. For this purpose, a plan does not provide for further investment in employer securities merely because dividends paid on employer securities under the plan are reinvested in employer securities.

(B) Transitional relief for certain leveraged employee stock ownership plans (ESOPs). An employer stock fund does not fail to be a frozen fund under this paragraph (e)(3)(vii) merely because of the allocation of employer securities that are released as matching contributions from the plan's suspense account that holds employer securities acquired with an exempt loan under section 4975(d)(3). This paragraph (e)(3)(vii)(B) only applies to employer securities that were acquired in a plan year beginning before January 1, 2007, with the proceeds of an exempt loan within the meaning of section 4975(d)(3) which is not refinanced after the end of the last plan year beginning before January 1, 2007.

*(4) Delegation of authority to Commissioner.* The Commissioner may provide for additional permitted restrictions or conditions or permitted indirect restrictions or conditions in revenue rulings, notices, or other guidance published in the Internal Revenue Bulletin.

**(f) Definitions.** *(1) Application of definitions.* This paragraph (f) contains definitions that are applicable for purposes of this section.

*(2) Applicable defined contribution plan.* (i) General rule. Except as provided in this paragraph (f)(2), an applicable defined contribution plan means any defined contribution plan which holds employer securities that are publicly traded. See paragraph (f)(2)(iv) of this section for a special rule that treats certain plans that hold employer securities that are not publicly traded as applicable defined contribution plans and paragraph (f)(3)(ii) of this section for a special rule that treats certain plans as not holding publicly traded employer securities for purposes of this section.

(ii) Exception for certain ESOPs. An employee stock ownership plan (ESOP), as defined in section 4975(e)(7), is not an applicable defined contribution plan if the plan is a separate plan for purposes of section 414(l) with respect to any other defined benefit plan or defined contribution plan maintained by the same employer or employers and holds no contributions (or earnings thereunder) that are (or were ever) subject to section 401(k) or 401(m). Thus, an ESOP is an applicable defined contribution plan if the ESOP is a portion of a larger plan (whether or not that larger plan includes contributions that are subject to section 401(k) or 401(m)). For purposes of this paragraph (f)(2)(ii), a plan is not considered to hold amounts ever subject to section 401(k) or 401(m) merely because the plan holds amounts attributable to rollover amounts in a separate account that were previously subject to section 401(k) or 401(m).

(iii) Exception for one-participant plans. A one-participant plan, as defined in section 401(a)(35)(E)(iv), is not an applicable defined contribution plan.

(iv) Certain defined contribution plans treated as holding publicly traded employer securities. (A) General rule. A defined contribution plan holding employer securities that are not publicly traded is treated as an applicable defined contribution plan if any employer maintaining the plan or any member of a controlled group of corporations that includes such employer has issued a class of stock which is publicly traded. For purposes of this paragraph (f)(2)(iv), a controlled group of corporations has the meaning given such term by section 1563(a), except that "50 percent" is substituted for "80 percent" each place it appears.

(B) Exception for certain plans. Paragraph (f)(2)(iv)(A) of this section does not apply to a plan if—

(1) No employer maintaining the plan (or a parent corporation with respect to such employer) has issued stock that is publicly traded; and

(2) No employer maintaining the plan (or parent corporation with respect to such employer) has issued any special class of stock which grants to the holder or issuer particular rights, or bears particular risks for the holder or issuer, with respect to any employer maintaining the plan (or any mem-

ber of a controlled group of corporations that includes such employer) which has issued any stock that is publicly traded.

*(3) Employer security.* (i) General rule. Employer security has the meaning given such term by section 407(d)(1) of the Employee Retirement Income Security Act of 1974, as amended (ERISA).

(ii) Certain defined contribution plans or investment funds not treated as holding employer securities. (A) Exception for certain indirect investments. Subject to paragraphs (f)(3)(ii)(B) and (C) of this section, a plan (and an investment option described in paragraph (d) of this section) is not treated as holding employer securities for purposes of this section to the extent the employer securities are held indirectly as part of a broader fund that is—

(1) A regulated investment company described in section 851(a);

(2) A common or collective trust fund or pooled investment fund maintained by a bank or trust company supervised by a State or a Federal agency;

(3) A pooled investment fund of an insurance company that is qualified to do business in a State;

(4) An investment fund managed by an investment manager within the meaning of section 3(38) of ERISA for a multiemployer plan; or

(5) Any other investment fund designated by the Commissioner in revenue rulings, notices, or other guidance published in the Internal Revenue Bulletin.

(B) Investment must be independent. The exception set forth in paragraph (f)(3)(ii)(A) of this section applies only if the investment in the employer securities is held in a fund under which—

(1) There are stated investment objectives of the fund; and

(2) The investment is independent of the employer (or employers) and any affiliate thereof.

(C) Percentage limitation rule. For purposes of paragraph (f)(3)(ii)(B)(2) of this section, an investment in employer securities in a fund is not considered to be independent of the employer (or employers) and any affiliate thereof if the aggregate value of the employer securities held in the fund is in excess of 10 percent of the total value of all of the fund's investments for the plan year. The determination of whether the value of employer securities exceeds 10 percent of the total value of the fund's investments for the plan year is made as of the end of the preceding plan year. The determination can be based on the information in the latest disclosure of the fund's portfolio holdings that was filed with the Securities and Exchange Commission (SEC) in that preceding plan year.

*(4) Parent corporation.* Parent corporation has the meaning given such term by section 424(e).

*(5) Publicly traded.* (i) In general. A security is publicly traded if it is readily tradable on an established securities market.

(ii) Readily tradable on an established securities market. For purposes of this paragraph (f)(5), except as provided by the Commissioner in revenue rulings, notices, or other guidance published in the Internal Revenue Bulletin, a security is readily tradable on an established securities market if—

(A) The security is traded on a national securities exchange that is registered under section 6 of the Securities Exchange Act of 1934 (15 U.S.C. 78f); or

(B) The security is traded on a foreign national securities exchange that is officially recognized, sanctioned, or supervised by a governmental authority and the security is deemed by the SEC as having a "ready market" under SEC Rule 15c3-1 (17 CFR 240.15c3-1).

**(g) Applicability date and transition rules.** *(1) Statutory effective date.* (i) General rule. Except as otherwise provided in this paragraph (g) and section 901(c)(3)(A) and (B) of the Pension Protection Act of 2006, Public Law 109-280 (120 Stat. 780 (2006)) (PPA '06), section 401(a)(35) is effective for plan years beginning after December 31, 2006.

(ii) Collectively bargained plans. (A) Delayed statutory effective date. In the case of a plan maintained pursuant to one or more collective bargaining agreements between employee representatives and one or more employers ratified on or before August 17, 2006, section 401(a)(35) is effective for plan years beginning after the earlier of—

(1) The later of—

(i) December 31, 2007; or

(ii) The date on which the last such collective bargaining agreement terminates (determined without regard to any extension thereof); or

(2) December 31, 2008.

(B) Treatment of plans with both collectively bargained and non-collectively bargained employees. If a collective bargaining agreement applies to some, but not all, of the plan participants, the definition of whether the plan is considered a collectively bargained plan for purposes of this paragraph (g)(1)(ii) is made in the same manner as the definition of whether a plan is collectively bargained under section 436(f)(3).

*(2) Regulatory effective/applicability date.* This section is effective and applicable for plan years beginning on or after January 1, 2011.

*(3) Statutory transition rules.* (i) General rule. Pursuant to section 401(a)(35)(H), in the case of the portion of an account to which paragraph (c) of this section applies and that consists of employer securities acquired in a plan year beginning before January 1, 2007, the requirements of paragraph (c) of this section only apply to the applicable percentage of such securities.

(ii) Applicable percentage. (A) Phase-in percentage. For purposes of this paragraph (g)(3), the applicable percentage is determined as follows—

| Plan year to which paragraph (c) of this section applies: | The applicable percentage is: |
|---|---|
| 1st | 33 |
| 2nd | 66 |
| 3rd and following | 100 |

(B) Special rule. For a plan for which the special effective date under section 901(c)(3) of PPA '06 applies, the applicable percentage under this paragraph (g)(3)(ii) is determined without regard to the delayed effective date in section 901(c)(3)(A) and (B) of PPA '06.

(iii) Nonapplication for participants age 55 with three years of service. Paragraph (g)(3)(i) of this section does not apply to an individual who is a participant who attained age 55 and had completed at least three years of service (as defined in paragraph (c)(3) of this section) before the first day of the first plan year beginning after December 31, 2005.

(iv) Separate application by class of securities. This paragraph (g)(3) applies separately with respect to each class of securities.

T.D. 9484, 5/19/2010.

### § 1.401(b)-1 Certain retroactive changes in plan.

**(a) General rule.** Under section 401(b) a stock bonus, pension, profit-sharing, annuity, or bond purchase plan which does not satisfy the requirements of section 401(a) on any day solely as a result of a disqualifying provision (as defined in paragraph (b) of this section) shall be considered to have satisfied such requirements on such date if, on or before the last day of the remedial amendment period (as determined under paragraphs (d), (e) and (f) of this section) with respect to such disqualifying provision, all provisions of the plan which are necessary to satisfy all requirements of sections 401(a), 403(a), or 405(a) are in effect and have been made effective for all purposes for the whole of such period. Under some facts and circumstances, it may not be possible to amend a plan retroactively so that all provisions of the plan which are necessary to satisfy the requirements of section 401(a) are in fact made effective for the whole remedial amendment period. If it is not possible, the requirements of this section will not be satisfied even if the employer adopts a retroactive plan amendment which, in form, appears to satisfy such requirements. Section 401(b) does not permit a plan to be made retroactively effective, for qualification purposes, for a taxable year prior to the taxable year of the employer in which the plan was adopted by such employer.

**(b) Disqualifying provisions.** For purposes of this section, with respect to a plan described in paragraph (a) of this section, the term "disqualifying provision" means:

*(1)* A provision of a new plan, the absence of a provision from a new plan, or an amendment to an existing plan, which causes such plan to fail to satisfy the requirements of the Code applicable to qualification of such plan as of the date such plan or amendment is first made effective.

*(2)* A plan provision which results in the failure of the plan to satisfy the qualification requirements of the Code by reason of a change in such requirements—

(i) Effected by the Employee Retirement Income Security Act of 1974 (Pub. L. 93-406, 88 Stat. 829), hereafter referred to as "ERISA," or the Tax Equity and Fiscal Responsibility Act of 1982 (Pub. L. 97-248, 96 Stat. 324), hereafter referred to as "TEFRA," or

(ii) Effective before the first day of the first plan year beginning after December 31, 1989 and that is effected by the Tax Reform Act of 1986 (Pub. L. 99-514, 100 Stat. 2085, 2489), hereafter referred to as "TRA '86," the Omnibus Budget Reconciliation Act of 1986, (Pub. L. 99-509, 100 Stat. 1879), hereinafter referred to as "OBRA '86," or the Omnibus Budget Reconciliation Act of 1987 (Pub. L. 100-203, 101 Stat. 1330, hereafter referred to as "OBRA '87." For purposes of this paragraph (b)(2)(ii), a disqualifying provision includes any plan provision that is integral to a qualification requirement changed by TRA '86, OBRA '86, or OBRA '87 or any requirement treated by the Commissioner, directly or indirectly, as if section 1140 of TRA '86 applied to it, but only to the extent such provision is effective before the first day of the first plan year beginning after December 31, 1989. With respect to disqualifying provisions described in this paragraph (b)(2)(ii) effective before the first day of the first plan year which begins after December 31, 1988, there must be compliance with the conditions of section 1140 of TRA '86 (other than the requirement that the plan amendment be made on or before the last day of the first plan year beginning after December 31, 1988), including operation in accordance with the plan provision as of its effective date with respect to the plan.

*(3)* A plan provision designated by the Commissioner, at the Commissioner's discretion, as a disqualifying provision that either—

(i) Results in the failure of the plan to satisfy the qualification requirements of the Internal Revenue Code by reason of a change in those requirements; or

(ii) Is integral to a qualification requirement of the Internal Revenue Code that has been changed.

**(c) Special rules applicable to disqualifying provisions.** *(1) Absence of plan provision.* For purposes of paragraphs (b)(2) and (3) of this section, a disqualifying provision includes the absence from a plan of a provision required by, or, if applicable, integral to the applicable change to the qualification requirements of the Internal Revenue Code, if the plan was in effect on the date the change became effective with respect to the plan.

*(2) Method of designating disqualifying provisions.* The Commissioner may designate a plan provision as a disqualifying provision pursuant to paragraph (b)(3) of this section only in revenue rulings, notices, and other guidance published in the Internal Revenue Bulletin. See § 601.601(d)(2) of this chapter.

*(3) Authority to impose limitations.* In the case of a provision that has been designated as a disqualifying provision by the Commissioner pursuant to paragraph (b)(3) of this section, the Commissioner may impose limits and provide additional rules regarding the amendments that may be made with respect to that disqualifying provision during the remedial amendment period. The Commissioner may provide guidance in revenue rulings, notices, and other guidance published in the Internal Revenue Bulletin. See § 601.601(d)(2) of this chapter.

**(d) Remedial amendment period.** *(1)* The remedial amendment period with respect to a disqualifying provision begins:

(i) In the case of a provision of, or absence of a provision from, a new plan, described in paragraph (b)(1) of this section, the date the plan is put into effect,

(ii) In the case of an amendment to an existing plan, described in paragraph (b)(1) of this section, the date the plan amendment is adopted or put into effect (whichever is earlier),

(iii) In the case of a disqualifying provision described in paragraph (b)(2) of this section, the date on which the change effected by ERISA, TEFRA TRA, '86, OBRA '86, OBRA '87, or a qualification requirement that is treated, directly or indirectly, as subject to the conditions of section 1140 of TRA '86 described in paragraph (b)(2) of this section, became effective with respect to such plan or, in the case of a provision, described in paragraph (b)(2)(ii) of this section, that is integral to such qualification requirement, the first day on which the plan was operated in accordance with such provision, or

(iv) In the case of a disqualifying provision described in paragraph (b)(3)(i) of this section, the date on which the change effected by an amendment to the Internal Revenue Code became effective with respect to the plan; or

(v) In the case of a disqualifying provision described in paragraph (b)(3)(ii) of this section, the first day on which the plan was operated in accordance with such provision, as amended, unless another time is specified by the Commissioner in revenue rulings, notices, and other guidance published in the Internal Revenue Bulletin. See § 601.601(d)(2) of this chapter.

*(2)* Unless further extended as provided by paragraph (e) of this section, the remedial amendment period ends with the latest of:

(i) In the case of a plan maintained by one employer, the time prescribed by law, including extensions, for filing the income tax return (or partnership return of income) of the employer for the employer's taxable year in which falls the latest of:

(A) The date on which the remedial amendment period begins,

(B) The date on which a plan amendment described in paragraph (b)(1) of this section is adopted, or

(C) The date on which a plan amendment described in paragraph (b)(1) of this section is made effective,

(ii) In the case of a plan maintained by one employer, the last day of the plan year within which falls the latest of:

(A) The date on which the remedial amendment period begins,

(B) The date on which a plan amendment described in paragraph (b)(1) of this section is adopted, or

(C) The date on which a plan amendment described in paragraph (b)(1) of this section is made effective,

(iii) In the case of a plan maintained by more than one employer, the last day of the tenth month following the last day of the plan year in which falls the latest of:

(A) The date on which the remedial amendment period begins,

(B) The date on which a plan amendment described in paragraph (b)(1) of this section is adopted, or

(C) The date of which a plan amendment described in paragraph (b)(1) of this section is made effective, or

(iv) December 31, 1976, but only in the case of a plan to which section 411 (relating to minimum vesting standards) applies without regard to section 411(e)(2), and only in the case of a remedial amendment period which began on or after September 2, 1974.

*(3)* For purposes of paragraphs (d)(2)(i), (d)(2)(ii) and (d)(2)(iii) of this section, for any disqualifying provision described in paragraph (b)(2)(ii) of this section, the remedial amendment period shall be deemed to have begun with the first day of the first plan year which begins after December 31, 1988.

*(4)* For purposes of this paragraph (d)(2) of this section, a master or prototype plan shall not be considered to be a plan maintained by more than one employer, and whether or not a plan is maintained solely by an affiliated group of corporations (within the meaning of section 1504) which files a consolidated income tax return pursuant to section 1501 for a taxable year within which falls the latest of the dates described in paragraph (d)(2)(i) of this section, such plan shall be deemed to be maintained by one employer.

**(e) Extensions of remedial amendment period.** *(1) Opinion letter request by sponsoring organization of master or prototype plan.* In the case of an employer who has adopted a master or prototype plan, a remedial amendment period that began on or after September 2, 1974, shall not end prior to the later of:

(i) June 30, 1977, or

(ii) The last day of the month that is six months after the month in which:

(A) The opinion letter with respect to the request of the sponsoring organization is issued by the Internal Revenue Service,

(B) Such request is withdrawn, or

(C) Such request is otherwise disposed of by the Internal Revenue Service. The rules contained in this subparagraph apply only if the sponsoring organization of such master or prototype plan has, after September 2, 1974, and on or before December 31, 1976, filed a request for an opinion letter with respect to the initial or continuing qualification of the plan (or a trust which is part of the plan). The provisions of this paragraph (e)(1) apply to a master or prototype plan adopted to replace another plan even though the remedial amendment period applicable to the replaced plan has expired at the time of adoption of the replacement plan.

*(2) Notification letter request by law firm sponsor of district-approved plan.* In the case of an employer who has adopted a pattern plan, a remedial amendment period that began on or after September 2, 1974, shall not end prior to the later of:

(i) June 30, 1977, or

(ii) The last day of the month that is six months after the month in which:

(A) The notification letter with respect to the request of the sponsoring law firm is issued by the Internal Revenue Service,

(B) Such request is withdrawn, or

(C) Such request is otherwise disposed of by the Internal Revenue Service. The rules contained in this subparagraph shall apply only if the sponsoring law firm of such pattern plan has, on or before December 31, 1976, filed a request for a notification letter with the Internal Revenue Service with respect to the initial or continuing qualification of the plan (or a trust which is part of the plan). The provisions of this paragraph (e)(2) apply to a pattern plan adopted to replace another plan even though the remedial amendment period applicable to the replaced plan has expired at the time of the adoption of the replacement plan.

*(3) Determination letter request by employer or plan administrator.* If on or before the end of a remedial amendment period determined without regard to this paragraph (e), or in a case to which paragraph (e)(1) or (2) of this section applies, on or before the 90th day following the later of the dates described in paragraph (e)(1) or (2) of this section, the employer or plan administrator files a request pursuant to § 601.201(s) of this chapter (Statement of Procedural Rules). for a determination letter with respect to the initial or continuing qualification of the plan, or a trust which is part of such plan, such remedial amendment period shall be extended until the expiration of 91 days after:

(i) The date on which notice of the final determination with respect to such request for a determination letter is issued by the Internal Revenue Service, such request is withdrawn, or such request is otherwise finally disposed of by the Internal Revenue Service, or

(ii) If a petition is timely filed with the United States Tax Court for a declaratory judgment under section 7476 with respect to the final determination (or the failure of the Internal Revenue Service to make a final determination) in response to such request, the date on which the decision of the United States Tax Court in such proceeding becomes final.

*(4) Transitional rule.* In the case of a request for a determination letter described in and filed within the time prescribed in paragraph (e)(3) of this section with respect to which a final determination is issued by the Internal Revenue Service on or before September 28, 1976 the remedial amendment period described in paragraph (d) of this section shall not end prior to the expiration of 150 days beginning on the date of such final determination by the Internal Revenue Service.

*(5) Disqualifying provision prior to September 2, 1974.* If the remedial amendment period with respect to a disqualifying provision described in paragraph (b)(1) of this section began prior to September 2, 1974, and the provisions of paragraphs (e)(5)(i), (ii) and (iii) of this section are satisfied, the remedial amendment period described in paragraph (d) shall not end prior to December 31, 1976. This subparagraph shall apply only if—

(i) A request pursuant to § 601.201 of this chapter for a determination letter with respect to the initial or continuing qualification of the plan (or a trust which is part of the plan) was filed not later than the later of:

(A) The time prescribed by law, including extensions, for filing the income tax return (or partnership return of income) of the employer for the employer's taxable year in which falls the date on which the remedial amendment period began, or

(B) The date 6 months after the close of such taxable year,

(ii) The employer, either:

(A) While such request for a determination letter is or was under consideration by the Internal Revenue Service or,

(B) Promptly after the date on which notice of the final determination with respect to such request for a determination letter is issued by the Internal Revenue Service, such request is withdrawn, or such request is otherwise finally disposed of by the Internal Revenue Service, adopts or adopted either a plan amendment retroactive to the date on which the remedial amendment period began, or a prospective plan amendment, and

(iii) The amendment described in paragraph (e)(5)(ii) of this section would have resulted in the plan's satisfying the requirements of section 401(a) of the Code from the beginning of the remedial amendment period to the date such amendment was made if this section had been in effect during such period, and in the case of a prospective amendment, if such amendment had been made retroactive to such beginning date.

**(f) Discretionary extensions.** At his discretion, the Commissioner may extend the remedial amendment period or may allow a particular plan to be amended after the expiration of its remedial amendment period and any applicable extension of such period. In determining whether such an extension will be granted, the Commissioner shall consider, among other factors, whether substantial hardship to the employer would result if such an extension were not granted, whether such an extension is in the best interest of plan participants, and whether the granting of the extension is adverse to the interests of the Government. The mere absence of final regulations with respect to issues covered under the Special Reliance Procedure announced by the Internal Revenue Service in Technical Information Release 1416 on November 5, 1975, and as extended by Internal Revenue Service News Release IR-1616 on May 14, 1976, shall not be deemed to satisfy the criteria of this paragraph. With regard to a particular plan, a request for extension of time pursuant to this paragraph shall be submitted prior to the expiration of the remedial amendment period determined without regard to this paragraph, or within such time thereafter as the Internal Revenue Service may consider reasonable under the circumstances. The request should be submitted to the appropriate District Director, determined under § 601.201(s)(3)(xii) of this chapter (Statement of Procedural Rules). This subparagraph applies to disqualifying provisions that were adopted or became effective prior to September 2, 1974, as well as disqualifying provisions adopted or made effective on or after September 2, 1974.

T.D. 7437, 9/23/76, amend T.D. 7896, 5/26/83, T.D. 7997, 12/27/84, T.D. 8217, 8/8/88, T.D. 8727, 7/31/97, T.D. 8871, 2/3/2000.

### § 11.401(d)(1)-1 Nonbank trustees of trusts benefiting owner-employees.

**(a) Effective dates.** *(1) General rule.* For a plan not in existence on January 1, 1974, this section shall apply to the first plan year commencing after September 2, 1974, and all subsequent plan years.

*(2) Existing plans.* For a plan in existence on January 1, 1974, this section shall apply to the first plan year commencing after December 31, 1975, and all subsequent plan years.

**(b) In general.** For plan years to which this section applies, the trustee of a trust described in § 1.401-12(c)(1)(i) may (notwithstanding § 1.401-12(c)) be a person other than a bank (within the meaning of section 401(d)(1)) if he demonstrates to the satisfaction of the Commissioner that the manner in which he will administer trusts will be consistent with the requirements of section 401. Such demonstration must be made by a written application to the Commissioner of Internal Revenue, Attention: E:EP, Internal Revenue Service, Washington, D.C. 20224. Such application must meet the requirements set forth in paragraphs (c) to (g) of this section.

**(c) Fiduciary ability.** The applicant must demonstrate in detail his ability to act within the accepted rules of fiduciary conduct. Such demonstration must include the following elements of proof:

*(1) Continuity.* (i) The applicant must assure the uninterrupted performance of its fiduciary duties notwithstanding the death or change of its owners. Thus, for example, there must be sufficient diversity in the ownership of the applicant to ensure that the death or change of owners will not interrupt the conduct of its business. Therefore, the applicant cannot be an individual.

(ii) Sufficient diversity in the ownership of an incorporated applicant means that individuals each of whom owns more than 20 percent of the voting stock in the applicant own, in the aggregate, no more than 50 percent of such stock.

(iii) Sufficient diversity in the ownership of an applicant which is a partnership means that—

(A) Individuals each of whom owns more than 20 percent of the profits interest in the partnership own, in the aggregate, no more than 50 percent of such profits interest, and

(B) Individuals each of whom owns more than 20 percent of the capital interest in the partnership own, in the aggregate, no more than 50 percent of such capital interest.

(iv) For purposes of this subparagraph, the ownership of stock and of capital and profits interests shall be determined in accordance with the rules for constructive ownership of stock provided in section 1563(e) and (f)(2). For this purpose, the rules for constructive ownership of stock provided in section 1563(e) and (f)(2) shall apply to a capital or profits interest in a partnership as if it were a stock interest.

*(2) Established location.* The applicant must have an established place of business in the United States where he is accessible during every business day.

*(3) Fiduciary experience.* The applicant must have fiduciary experience or expertise sufficient to ensure that he will be able to perform his fiduciary duties. Evidence of fiduciary experience must include proof that a significant part of the business of the applicant consists of exercising fiduciary powers similar to those he will exercise if his application is approved. Evidence of fiduciary expertise must include proof that the applicant employs personnel experienced in the administration of fiduciary powers similar to those he will exercise if his application is approved.

*(4) Fiduciary responsibility.* The applicant must assure compliance with the rules of fiduciary conduct set out in paragraph (f) of this section.

*(5) Financial responsibility.* The applicant must exhibit a high degree of solvency commensurate with the obligations imposed by this section. Among the factors to be taken into account are the applicant's net worth, his liquidity, and his ability to pay his debts as they come due.

**(d) Capacity to account.** The applicant must demonstrate in detail his experience and competence with respect to accounting for the interests of a large number of individuals (including calculating and allocating income earned and paying out distributions to payees). Examples of accounting for the interests of a large number of individuals include accounting for the interests of large number of shareholders in a regulated investment company and accounting for the interests of a large number of variable annuity contract holders.

**(e) Fitness to handle funds.** *(1) In general.* The applicant must demonstrate in detail his experience and competence with respect to other activities normally associated with the handling of retirement funds.

*(2) Examples.* Examples of activities normally associated with the handling of retirement funds include:

(i) To receive, issue receipts for, and safely keep securities;

(ii) To collect income;

(iii) To execute such ownership certificates, to keep such records, make such returns, and render such statements as are required for Federal tax purposes;

(iv) To give proper notification regarding all collections;

(v) To collect matured or called principal and properly report all such collections;

(vi) To exchange temporary for definitive securities;

(vii) To give proper notification of calls, subscription rights, defaults in principal or interest, and the formation of protective committees;

(viii) To buy, sell, receive, or deliver securities on specific directions.

**(f) Rules of fiduciary conduct.** *(1) Administration of fiduciary powers.* The applicant must demonstrate that under applicable regulatory requirements, corporate or other governing instruments, or its established operating procedures:

(i) (A) The owners or directors of the applicant will be responsible for the proper exercise of fiduciary powers by the applicant. Thus, all matters pertinent thereto, including the determination of policies, the investment and disposition of property held in a fiduciary capacity, and the direction and review of the actions of all employees utilized by the applicant in the exercise of his fiduciary powers, will be the responsibility of the owners or directors. In discharging this responsibility, the owners or directors may assign to designated employees, by action duly recorded, the administration of such of the applicant's fiduciary powers as may be proper to assign.

(B) A written record will be made of the acceptance and of the relinquishment or closing out of all fiduciary accounts, and of the assets held for each account.

(C) At least once during each period of 12 months all the assets held in or for each fiduciary account where the applicant has investment responsibilities will be reviewed to determine the advisability of retaining or disposing of such assets.

(ii) All employees taking part in the performance of the applicant's fiduciary duties will be adequately bonded. Nothing in this subdivision shall require any person to be bonded in contravention of section 412(d) of the Employee Retirement Income Security Act of 1974 (29 U.S.C. 1112(d)).

(iii) The applicant will designate, employ, or retain legal counsel who will be readily available to pass upon fiduciary matters and to advise the applicant.

(iv) In order to segregate the performance of his fiduciary duties from other business activities, the applicant will maintain a separate trust division under the immediate supervision of an individual designated for that purpose. The trust division may utilize the personnel and facilities of other divisions of the applicant, and other divisions of the applicant may utilize the personnel and facilities of the trust division, as long as the separate identity of the trust division is preserved.

*(2) Adequacy of net worth.* (i) Not less frequently than once during each calendar year the applicant will determine the value of the assets held by him in trust. Such assets will be valued at their current value, except that the assets of an employee benefit plan to which section 103(b)(3)(A) of the Employee Retirement Income Security Act of 1974 (29 U.S.C. 1023(b)(3)(A)) applies will be considered to have the value stated in the most recent annual report of the plan.

(ii) No fiduciary account will be accepted by the applicant unless his net worth (determined as of the end of the most recent taxable year) exceeds the greater of—

(A) $100,000, or

(B) Four percent of the value of all of the assets held by the applicant in trust (determined as of the most recent valuation date).

(iii) The applicant will take whatever lawful steps are necessary (including the relinquishment of fiduciary accounts) to ensure that his net worth (determined as of the close of each taxable year) exceeds the greater of—

(A) $50,000, or

(B) Two percent of the value of all of the assets held by the applicant in trust (determined as of the most recent valuation date).

*(3) Audits.* (i) The applicant will at least once during each period of 12 months cause detailed audits of the fiduciary books and records to be made by an independent qualified public accountant, and at such time will ascertain whether the fiduciary accounts have been administered in accordance with law, this section, and sound fiduciary principles. Such audits shall be conducted in accordance with generally accepted auditing standards, and shall involve such tests of the fiduciary books and records of the applicant as are considered necessary by the independent qualified public accountant.

(ii) In the case of an applicant who is regulated, supervised, and subject to periodic examination by a State or Federal agency, such applicant may adopt an adequate continuous audit system in lieu of the periodic audits required by paragraph (f)(3)(i) of this section.

(iii) A report of the audits and examinations required under this subparagraph, together with the action taken thereon, will be noted in the fiduciary records of the applicant.

*(4) Funds awaiting investment or distribution.* Funds held in a fiduciary capacity by the applicant awaiting investment or distribution will not be held uninvested or undistributed any longer than is reasonable for the proper management of the account.

*(5) Custody of investments.* (i) Except for investments pooled in a common investment fund in accordance with the provisions of paragraph (f)(6) of this section, the investments of each account will not be commingled with any other property.

(ii) Fiduciary assets requiring safekeeping will be deposited in an adequate vault. A permanent record will be kept of fiduciary assets deposited in or withdrawn from the vault.

*(6) Common investment funds.* Where not in contravention of local law the assets of an account may be pooled in a common investment fund (as defined in paragraph (f)(8)(iii) of this section) which must be administered as follows:

(i) Each common investment fund must be established and maintained in accordance with a written agreement, containing appropriate provisions as to the manner in which the fund is to be operated, including provisions relating to the investment powers and a general statement of the investment policy of the applicant with respect to the fund; the allocation of income, profits and losses; the terms and conditions governing the admission or withdrawal of participations in the fund; the auditing of accounts of the applicant with respect to the fund; the basis and method of valuing assets in the fund, setting forth specific criteria for each type of asset; the minimum frequency for valuation of assets of the fund; the period following each such valuation date during which the valuation may be made (which period in usual circumstances may not exceed 10 business days); the basis upon which the fund may be terminated; and such other matters as may be necessary to define clearly the rights of participants in the fund. A copy of the agreement must be available at the principal office of the applicant for inspection during all business hours, and upon request a copy of the agreement must be furnished to any interested person.

(ii) All participations in the common investment fund must be on the basis of a proportionate interest in all of the assets.

(iii) Not less frequently than once during each period of 3 months applicant must determine the value of the assets in the fund as of the date set for the valuation of assets. No participation may be admitted to or withdrawn from the fund except (A) on the basis of such valuation and (B) as of such valuation date. No participation may be admitted to or withdrawn from the fund unless a written request for or notice of intention of taking such action has been entered on or before the valuation date in the fiduciary records of the applicant. No request or notice may be canceled or countermanded after the valuation date.

(iv) (A) The applicant must at least once during each period of 12 months cause an adequate audit to be made of the common investment fund by a qualified public accountant.

(B) The applicant must at least once during each period of 12 months prepare a financial report of the fund which, based upon the above audit, must contain a list of investments in the fund showing the cost and current market value of each investment; a statement for the period since the previous report showing purchases, with cost; sales, with profit or loss and any other investment changes; income and disbursements; and an appropriate notation as to any investments in default.

(C) The applicant must transmit and certify the accuracy of the financial report to the administrator of each plan participating in the common investment fund within 120 days after the end of the plan year.

(v) When participations are withdrawn from a common investment fund, distributions may be made in cash or ratably in kind, or partly in cash and partly in kind, provided that all distributions as of any one valuation date must be made on the same basis.

(vi) If for any reason an investment is withdrawn in kind from a common investment fund for the benefit of all participants in the fund at the time of such withdrawal and such investment is not distributed ratably in kind, it must be segregated and administered or realized upon for the benefit ratably of all participants in the common investment fund at the time of withdrawal.

*(7) Books and records.* (i) The applicant must keep his fiduciary records separate and distinct from other records. All fiduciary records must be so kept and retained for as long as the contents thereof may become material in the administra-

tion of any internal revenue law. The fiduciary records must contain full information relative to each account.

(ii) The applicant must keep an adequate record of all pending litigation to which he is a party in connection with the exercise of fiduciary powers.

*(8) Definitions.* For purposes of this paragraph and paragraph (c)(5) of this section—

(i) The term "account" or "fiduciary account" means a trust described in section 401(a) (including a custodial account described in section 401(f), a custodial account described in section 403(b)(7), or an individual retirement account described in section 408(a) (including a custodial account described in section 408(h)).

(ii) The term "administrator" means an administrator as defined in section 3(16)(A) of the Employee Retirement Income Security Act of 1974, 29 U.S.C. 1002(16)(A).

(iii) The term "common investment fund" means a trust which satisfied the following requirements:

(A) The trust consists of all or part of the assets of several accounts which have been established with the applicant, and

(B) The trust is described in section 401(a) and exempt from tax under section 501(a), or is a common investment fund described in § 1.408-2(b)(5) (as published with notice of proposed rule making in the FEDERAL REGISTER on February 21, 1975, at 40 FR 7661), or both.

(iv) The term "employee benefit plan" means an employee benefit plan as defined in section 3(2) of the Employee Retirement Income Security Act of 1974, 29 U.S.C. 1002(2).

(v) The term "fiduciary records" means all matters which are written, transcribed, recorded, received or otherwise come into the possession of the applicant and are necessary to preserve information concerning the acts and events relevant to the fiduciary activities of the applicant.

(vi) The term "qualified public accountant" means a qualified public accountant as defined in section 103(a)(3)(D) of the Employee Retirement Income Security Act of 1974, 29 U.S.C. 1023(a)(3)(D).

(vii) The term "net worth" means the amount of the applicant's assets less the amount of his liabilities, as determined in accordance with generally accepted accounting principles.

**(g) Special rules.** *(1) Passive trustee.* (i) An applicant who undertakes to act only as a passive trustee may be relieved of one or more of the requirements of this section upon clear and convincing proof that such requirements are not germane, under all the facts and circumstances, to the manner in which he will administer any trust. A trustee is a passive trustee only if under the written trust instrument he has no discretion to direct the investment of the trust funds or any other aspect of the business administration of the trust, but is merely authorized to acquire and hold particular investments specified by the trust instrument. Thus, for example, in the case of an applicant who undertakes merely to acquire and hold the stock of a single regulated investment company, the requirements of paragraph (f)(1)(i)(C), (1)(iv), and (6) of this section shall not apply and no negative inference shall be drawn from the applicant's failure to demonstrate his experience or competence with respect to the activities described in paragraph (e)(2)(v) to (viii) of this section.

(ii) The determination letter issued to an applicant who is approved by reason of this subparagraph shall state that the applicant is authorized to act only as a passive trustee.

*(2) Federal or State regulation.* Evidence that an appellant is subject to Federal or State regulation with respect to one or more relevant factors shall be given weight in proportion to the extent that such regulatory standards are consonant with the requirements of section 401.

*(3) Savings account.* (i) An applicant will be approved to act as trustee under this subparagraph if the following requirements are satisfied:

(A) The applicant is a credit union, industrial loan company, savings and loan association, or other financial institution designated by the Commissioner;

(B) The investment of the trust assets will be solely in deposits in the applicant;

(C) Deposits in the applicant are insured (up to the dollar limit prescribed by applicable law) by an agency or instrumentality of the United States or a State.

(ii) Any applicant who satisfies the requirements of this subparagraph is hereby approved, and (notwithstanding paragraph (b) of this section) is not required to submit a written application. This approval takes effect on the first day after December 22, 1976, on which the applicant satisfies the requirements of this subparagraph, and continues in effect for so long as the applicant continues to satisfy those requirements.

*(4) Notification of Commissioner.* The applicant must notify the Commissioner in writing of any change which affects the continuing accuracy of any representation made in the application required by this section, whether the change occurs before or after the applicant receives a determination letter. Such notification must be addressed to Commissioner of Internal Revenue, Attention: E:EP, Internal Revenue Service, Washington, D.C. 20224.

*(5) Substitution of trustee.* No applicant shall be approved unless he undertakes to act as trustee only under trust instruments which contain a provision to the effect that the employer is to substitute another trustee upon notification by the Commissioner that such substitution is required because the applicant has failed to comply with the requirements of this section or is not keeping such records, or making such returns, or rendering such statements as are required by forms or regulations.

*(6) Revocation.* Approval of the application required by this section may be revoked for any good and sufficient reason.

---

T.D. 7383, 10/15/75, amend T.D. 7448, 12/17/76.

---

### § 1.401(e)-1 Definitions relating to plans covering self-employed individuals.

***Caution:*** The Treasury has not yet amended Reg § 1.401(e)-1 to reflect changes made by P.L. 103-66.

**(a) "Keogh" or "H.R. 10" plans, in general.** *(1) Introduction and organization of regulations.* Certain self-employed individuals may be covered by a qualified pension, annuity, or profit-sharing plan. This section contains definitions contained in section 401(c) relating to plans covering self-employed individuals and is applicable to employer taxable years beginning after December 31, 1975, unless otherwise specified.

The provisions of section 401(a) relating to qualification requirements which are generally applicable to all qualified plans, and other provisions relating to the special rules under section 401(b), (f), (g), (h), and (i), are also generally applicable to any plan covering a self-employed individual. However, in addition to such requirements and special rules, any plan covering a self-employed individual is subject to the rules contained in §§ 1.401(e)-2, (e)-5, and (j)-1 through (j)-5. Section 1.401(e)-2 contains general rules, § 1.401(e)-5 contains a special rule limiting the contribution and benefit base to the first $100,000 of annual compensation, and § 1.401(j)-1 through (j)-5 contains special rules for defined benefit plans. Section 1.401(e)-3 contains special rules which are applicable to plans covering self-employed individuals when one or more of such individuals is an owner-employee within the meaning of section 401(c)(3). Section 1.401(e)-4 contains rules relating to contributions on behalf of owner-employees for premiums on annuity, etc., contracts and a transitional rule for certain excess contributions made on behalf of owner-employees for employer taxable years beginning before January 1, 1976. The provisions of this section and of §§ 1.401(e)-2 through 1.401(e)-5 are applicable to employer taxable years beginning after December 31, 1975, unless otherwise specified.

*(2) [Reserved]*

---

T.D. 7636, 8/9/79.

---

**§ 1.401(e)-2 General rules relating to plans covering self-employed individuals.**

**(a) "Keogh" or "H.R. 10" plans; introduction and organization of regulations.** This section provides certain rules which supplement, and modify, the qualification requirements of section 401(a) and the special rules provided by § 1.401(b)-1 and other special rules under subsections (f), (g), (h), and (i) of section 401 in the case of a qualified pension, annuity, or profit-sharing plan which covers a self-employed individual who is an employee within the meaning of section 401(c)(1). Section 1.401(e)-1(a)(1) sets forth other provisions which also supplement, and modify, these requirements and special rules in the case of a plan described in this section. The provisions of this section apply to employer taxable years beginning after December 31, 1975, unless otherwise specified.

**(b) [Reserved]**

---

T.D. 7636, 8/9/79.

---

**§ 1.401(e)-3 Requirements for qualification of trusts and plans benefiting owner-employees.**

**(a) "Keogh" or "H.R. 10" plans covering owner-employees; introduction and organization of regulations.** This section prescribes the additional requirements which must be met for qualification of a trust forming part of a pension or profit-sharing plan, or of an annuity plan, which covers any self-employed individual who is an owner-employee as defined in section 401(c)(3). These additional requirements are prescribed in section 401(d) and are made applicable to such a trust by section 401(a)(10)(B) and to an annuity plan by section 404(a)(2). However, to the extent that the provisions of §§ 1.401(e)-1 and 1.401(e)-2 are not modified by the provisions of this section such provisions are also applicable to a plan which covers an owner-employee. The provisions of this section apply to taxable years beginning after December 31, 1975, unless otherwise specified.

**(b) [Reserved]**

---

T.D. 7636, 8/9/79.

---

**§ 1.401(e)-4 Contributions for premiums on annuity, etc., contracts and transitional rule for certain excess contributions.**

**(a) In general.** The provisions of this section prescribe the rules specified in section 401(e) relating to certain contributions made under a qualified pension, annuity, or profit-sharing plan on behalf of a self-employed individual who is an owner-employee (as defined in section 401(c)(3) and the regulations thereunder) in taxable years of the employer beginning after December 31, 1975. In addition, such plans are also subject to the limitations on contributions and benefits under section 415 for years beginning after December 31, 1975. However, the defined contribution compensation limitation described in section 415(c)(1)(B) will not apply to any contribution described in this section provided that the requirements specified in section 415(c)(7) and § 1.415-6(h) are satisfied. Solely for the purpose of applying section 4972(b) (relating to excise tax on excess contributions for self-employed individuals) to other contributions made by an owner-employee as an employee, the amount of any employer contribution which is not deductible under section 404 for the employer's taxable year but which is described in section 401(e) and this section shall be taken into account as a contribution made by such owner-employee as an employee during the taxable year of his employer in which such contribution is made.

**(b) Contributions described in section 401(e).** *(1)* An employer contribution on behalf of an owner-employee is described in section 401(e), if—

(i) Under the provisions of the plan, the contribution is expressly required to be applied (either directly or through a trustee) to pay the premiums or other consideration for one or more annuity, endowment, or life insurance contracts on the life of the owner-employee.

(ii) The employer contributions so applied meet the requirements of subparagraphs (2) through (5) of this paragraph.

(iii) The amount of the contribution exceeds the amount deductible under section 404 with respect to contributions made by the employer on behalf of the owner-employee under the plan, and

(iv) The total employer contributions required to be applied annually to pay premiums on behalf of any owner-employee for contracts described in this paragraph do not exceed $7,500. For purposes of computing such $7,500 limit, the total employer contributions include amounts which are allocable to the purchase of life, accident, health, or other insurance.

**Note.**—This is an example.

*(2)* (i) The employer contributions must be paid under a plan which satisfies all the requirements for qualification. Accordingly, for example, contributions can be paid under the plan for life insurance protection only to the extent otherwise permitted under sections 401 through 404 and the regulations thereunder. However, certain of the requirements for qualification are modified with respect to a plan described in this paragraph (see section 401(a)(10)(A)(ii) and (d)(5)).

(ii) A plan described in this paragraph is not disqualified merely because a contribution is made on behalf of an owner-employee by his employer during a taxable year of the employer for which the owner-employee has no earned income. On the other hand, a plan will fail to qualify if a contribution is made on behalf of an owner-employee which results in the discrimination prohibited by section 401(a)(4) as modified by section 401(a)(10)(A)(ii).

*(3)* The employer contributions must be applied to pay premiums or other consideration for a contract issued on the life of the owner-employee. For purposes of this subparagraph, a contract is not issued on the life of an owner-employee unless all the proceeds which are, or may become, payable under the contract are payable directly, or through a trustee of a trust described in section 401(a) and exempt from tax under section 501(a), to the owner-employee or to the beneficiary named in the contract or under the plan. For example, a nontransferable face-amount certificate described in section 401(g) and the regulations thereunder is considered an annuity on the life of the owner-employee if the proceeds of such contract are payable only to the owner-employee or his beneficiary.

*(4)* (i) For any taxable year of the employer, the amount of contributions by the employer on behalf of the owner-employee which is applied to pay premiums under the contracts described in this paragraph must not exceed the average of the amounts deductible under section 404 by such employer on behalf of such owner-employee for the most recent three taxable years of the employer which are described in the succeeding sentence. The three employer taxable years described in the preceding sentence must be years, ending prior to the date the latest contract was entered into or modified to provide additional, benefits, in which the owner-employee derived earned income from the trade or business with respect to which the plan is established. However, if such owner-employee has not derived earned income for at least three taxable years preceding such date, then, in determining the "average of the amounts deductible", only so many of such taxable years as such owner-employee was engaged in such trade or business and derived earned income therefrom are taken into account.

(ii) For the purpose of making the computation described in subdivision (i) of this subparagraph, the taxable years taken into account include those years in which the individual derived earned income from the trade or business but was not an owner-employee with respect to such trade or business. Furthermore, taxable years of the employer preceding the taxable year in which a qualified plan is established are taken into account.

(iii) For purposes of making the computations described in subdivisions (i) and (ii) of this subparagraph for any taxable year of the employer the average of the amounts deductible under section 404 by the employer on behalf of an owner-employee for the most recent three relevant taxable years of the employer shall be determined as if section 404, as in effect for the taxable year for which the computation is to be made, had been in effect for all three such years.

*(5)* For any taxable year of an employer in which contributions are made on behalf of an individual as an owner-employee under more than one plan, the amount of contributions described in this section by the employer on behalf of such an owner-employee under all such plans must not exceed $7,500.

**(c) Transitional rule for excess contributions.** *(1)* (i) The rules of this paragraph are inapplicable to a plan which was not in existence for any taxable year of an employer which begins before January 1, 1976. For taxable years of an employer which begin before January 1, 1976, the rules with respect to excess contributions on behalf of owner-employees set forth in section 401(d)(5) and (8) and in section 401(e), as these sections were in effect on September 1, 1974, prior to their amendment by section 2001(e) of the Employee Retirement Income Security Act of 1974 (hereinafter in this paragraph referred to as the "Act") (88 Stat. 954), shall apply except as provided by subparagraph (2) of this paragraph. Section 1.401-13 generally provides the rules for excess contributions on behalf of owner-employees set forth in these sections.

(ii) Notwithstanding the provisions of subdivision (i) of this subparagraph, the rules set forth in such subsections (d)(5) and (8) and (e) of section 401 with respect to excess contributions for such taxable years beginning before January 1, 1976, apply even though the application of those rules affects a subsequent taxable year. Thus, for example, if, in 1975, a nonwillful excess contribution described in section 401(e)(1) (prior to such amendment) is made on behalf of an owner-employee, the plan will not be qualified unless the provisions required by subparagraphs (A) and (B) of such 401(d)(8) are contained in the plan and made applicable to excess contributions made for such taxable years beginning before January 1, 1976. In such case, the effect of such contribution on the plan, the employer, and the owner-employee would be determined under paragraph (2) of section 401(e), as in effect on September 1, 1974. By reason of section 401(e)(2)(F), as in effect on September 1, 1974, the period for assessing any deficiency by reason of the excess contribution will not expire until the expiration of the 6-month period described in section 401(e)(2)(C), as in effect on September 1, 1974, even if the first day of such 6-month period falls in a taxable year beginning after December 31, 1975. For the rules applicable to a willful excess contribution, which generally divide an owner-employee's interest in a plan into two parts on the basis of employer taxable years beginning before and after December 31, 1975, see § 1.72-17A(e)(2)(v). In the case of a willful excess contribution, the rule specified in section 401(e)(2)(E)(iii), as in effect on September 1, 1974, shall not apply to any taxable year of an employer beginning on or after January 1, 1976. Thus, for example, if a willful excess contribution was made to a plan on behalf of an owner-employee with respect to his employer's taxable year beginning January 1, 1975, the plan would not meet, for purposes of section 404, the requirements of section 401(d) with respect to that owner-employee for such year, but the 5 taxable years following such year would be unaffected because those years begin on or after January 1, 1976.

*(2)* (i) For purposes of applying the excess contribution rules with respect to the employer taxable years specified in subparagraph (1) of this paragraph for such an employer taxable year which begins after December 31, 1973, see section 404(e) and § 1.404(e)-1A for rules increasing the limitation on the amount of allowable employer deductions on behalf of owner-employees under section 404. For purposes of applying subparagraphs (A) and (B)(i) of section 401(e)(1) prior to the amendment made by section 2001(e)(3) of the Act (88 Stat. 954), the employer deduction allowable by section 404(e)(4) with respect to an owner-employee in a defined contribution plan shall be deemed not to be an excess contribution (see § 1.404(e)-1A(c)(4)).

(ii) For purposes of applying the excess contribution rules with respect to the employer taxable years specified in subparagraph (1) of this paragraph to an employer's plan which was not in existence on January 1, 1974, or to a plan in existence on January 1, 1974, which elects under section 1017(d) of the Act (88 Stat. 934), in accordance with regulations, to have the funding provisions of section 412 apply to such an existing plan, see section 404(a)(1), (a)(6), and (a)(7), as amended by section 1013(c)(1), (2), and (3) of the Act (88 Stat. 922 and 923) for rules modifying the amount of employer deductions on behalf of owner-employees.

T.D. 7636, 8/9/79.

### § 1.401(e)-5 Limitation of contribution and benefit bases to first $100,000 of annual compensation in case of plans covering self-employed individuals.

***Caution:*** The Treasury has not yet amended Reg § 1.401(e)-5 to reflect changes made by P.L. 103-66.

**(a) General rules.** *(1) General rule.* Under section 401(a)(17), a plan maintained by an employer which provided contributions or benefits for employees some or all of whom are employees within the meaning of section 401(c)(1) is a qualified plan only if the annual compensation of each employee taken into account under the plan does not exceed the first $100,000 of such compensation. For purposes of applying section 401(a)(17) and the preceding sentence, all plans maintained by such an employer with respect to the same trade or business shall be treated as a single plan. See also sections 401(d)(9) and (10) (relating to controlled trades or businesses where a plan covers an owner-employee who controls more than one trade or business); section 404(e) (relating to special limitations for self-employed individuals); section 413(b)(7) (relating to determination of limitations provided by section 404(a) in the case of certain plans maintained pursuant to a collective bargaining agreement); and section 413(c)(6) (relating to determination of limitations provided by section 404(a) in the case of certain plans maintained by more than one employer).

*(2) Special section 414(b), (c) rule.* This subparagraph (2) applies to plans maintained by employers that are trades or businesses (whether or not incorporated) that are under common control within the meaning of section 414(c). All such plans that are described in paragraph (a)(1) and § 1.401(e)-6(a) (so called "Subchapter S plans") shall be treated as a single plan in applying the limitation of paragraph (a)(1).

**(b) Integrated plans.** *(1)* In the case of a qualified plan, other than a plan described in section 414(j), which is integrated with the Social Security Act (chapter 21 of the Code), or with contributions or benefits under chapter 2 of the Code (relating to tax on self-employment income) or under any other Federal or State law, the $100,000 limitation described in subparagraph (a) shall be determined without regard to any adjustments to contributions or benefits under the plan on account of such integration. See also subsections (a)(5), (a)(15), and (d)(6) of section 401 and the regulations thereunder for other rules with respect to plans which are integrated.

*(2)* In the case of a qualified defined benefit plan described in section 414(j), see section 401(j)(4) for a special prohibition against integration.

**(c) Application of nondiscrimination requirement.** *(1)* This paragraph shall apply—

(i) In the case of a plan which provides contributions or benefits for employees some or all of whom are employees within the meaning of section 401(c)(1) and

(ii) For a year in which the compensation of any employee covered by the plan exceeds $100,000. In the case of an employee who is an employee within the meaning of section 401(c)(1), compensation includes earned income within the meaning of section 401(c)(2).

*(2)* In applying section 401(a)(4) under the circumstances described in subparagraph (1) of this paragraph, the determination whether the rate of contributions or benefits under the plan discriminates in favor of highly compensated employees shall be made as if the compensation for the year of each employee described in the first sentence of subparagraph (1)(ii) of this paragraph were $100,000, rather than the compensation actually received by him for such year.

**(d) Examples.** The provisions of this section may be illustrated by the following examples:

*Example (1).* A, a self-employed individual, has established the P Profit-Sharing Plan, which covers A and his two common law employees, B and C. A's taxable year and the plan's plan year are both the calendar year. For 1976, A has earned income of $150,000, and B and C each receive compensation of less than $100,000 from A. If he wishes to contribute $7,500 to the plan on his behalf for 1976, A must also contribute to the accounts of B and C under the plan amounts at least equal to 7½ percent of their respective compensation for 1976.

*Example (2).* D, an owner-employee within the meaning of section 401(c)(3), is a participant in the Q Qualified Defined Contribution Plan, which, in 1975, satisfies the requirements of section 401(d)(6) and all other integration requirements applicable to qualified defined contribution plans. The taxable years of D, the employer of D within the meaning of section 401(c)(4), and the plan are all calendar years. The plan provides for an integration level of $13,200 and a contribution rate of 5 percent of compensation in excess of $13,200. For 1975, D has earned income of $115,000. The maximum amount of earned income upon which D's contribution can be determined is $86,800, and the contribution based upon this maximum amount of earned income is $4,340, computed as follows:

| | |
|---|---|
| Maximum annual compensation which may be taken into account | $100,000 |
| Less: Social Security Act integration level | 13,200 |
| Plan contribution base | $ 86,800 |
| Multiplied by: Contribution rate (percent) | 5 |
| Total | $ 4,340 |

**(e) Years to which section applies.** This section applies to taxable years of an employer beginning after December 31, 1975. However, if employer contributions made under a plan for any employee for taxable years of an employer beginning after December 31, 1973, exceed the amounts permitted to be deducted for that employee under section 404(e), as in effect on September 1, 1974, this section applies to such taxable years of an employer.

Thus, for example, a plan of a calendar year employer which was adopted on January 1, 1974, would be subject to this section in 1974, if the employer made a contribution on behalf of any employee within the meaning of section 401(c)(1) for such year in excess of the $2,500 or 10 percent earned income limit, whichever is applicable to that employee, specified in section 404(e)(1) as in effect prior to the amendment to such Code section made by section 2001(a)(1)(A) of the Employee Retirement Income Security Act of 1974 (88 Stat. 952). The plan described in the proceeding sentence would also be subject to this section in 1974, if the employer made a contribution on behalf of any employee within the meaning of section 401(c)(1) which is allowable as a deduction only because of the addition of paragraph (4) to Code section 404(e) made by section 2001(a)(3) of such Act (88 Stat. 952).

T.D. 7636, 8/9/79.

## § 1.401(e)-6 Special rules for shareholder-employees.

**(a) Limitation of contributions and benefit bases to first $100,000 of annual compensation in case of plans covering shareholder-employees.** *(1)* Under section 401(a)(17), a plan which provides contributions or benefits for employees, some or all of whom are shareholder-employees within the meaning of section 1379(d), is subject to the same limitation on annual compensation as a plan which provides such contributions or benefits for employees some or all of whom are self-employed individuals within the meaning of section 401(c)(1). Thus, a plan which provides contributions or benefits for such shareholder-employees is subject to the rules provided by § 1.401(e)-5, unless otherwise specified. See also section 1379. In the case of plans maintained by employers that are corporations described in section 414(b) and that are described in this subparagraph (1), the same rule described in § 1.401(e)-5(a)(2) shall apply.

*(2)* Subparagraph (1) applies to taxable years of an electing small business corporation beginning after December 31, 1975. However, if corporate contributions made under a plan on behalf of any shareholder-employee for corporate taxable years beginning after December 31, 1973, exceed the lesser of the amount of contributions specified in section 1379(b)(1)(A) or (B), as in effect on September 1, 1974, for that shareholder-employee, subparagraph (1) applies to such corporate taxable years. Thus, for example if an electing small business corporation whose taxable year is the calendar year adopted a plan on January 1, 1974, the plan would be subject to the provisions of subparagraph (1) of this section in 1974, if the corporation made a contribution in excess of $2,500 on behalf of any shareholder-employee for such year.

**(b) [Reserved]**

T.D. 7636, 8/9/79.

## § 1.401(f)-1 Certain custodial accounts and annuity contracts.

**(a) Treatment of a custodial account or an annuity contract as a qualified trust.** Beginning on January 1, 1974, a custodial account or an annuity contract may be used, in lieu of a trust, under any qualified pension, profit-sharing, or stock bonus plan if the requirements of paragraph (b) of this section are met. A custodial account or an annuity contract may be used under such a plan, whether the plan covers common-law employees, self-employed individuals who are treated as employees by reason of section 401(c), or both. The use of a custodial account or annuity contract as part of a plan does not preclude the use of a trust or another custodial account or another annuity contract as part of the same plan. A plan under which a custodial account or an annuity contract is used may be considered in connection with other plans of the employer in determining whether the requirements of section 401 are satisfied. For regulations relating to the period before January 1, 1974, see § 1.401-8.

**(b) Rules applicable to custodial accounts and annuity contracts.** *(1)* Beginning on January 1, 1974, a custodial account or an annuity contract is treated as a qualified trust under section 401 if the following requirements are met:

(i) The custodial account or annuity contract would, except for that fact that it is not a trust, constitute a qualified trust under section 401; and

(ii) In the case of a custodial account, the custodian either is a bank or is another person who demonstrates, to the satisfaction of the Commissioner, that the manner in which he will hold the assets will be consistent with the requirements of section 401. This demonstration must be made in the same manner as the demonstration required by § 1.408-2(e).

*(2)* If a custodial account would, except for the fact that it is not a trust, constitute a qualified trust under section 401, it must, for example, be created pursuant to a written agreement which constitutes a valid contract under local law. In addition, the terms of the contract must make it impossible, prior to the satisfaction of all liabilities with respect to the employees and their beneficiaries covered by the plan. For any part of the funds of the custodial account to be used for, or diverted to, purposes other than for the exclusive benefit of the employees or their beneficiaries as provided for in the plan (see paragraph (a) of § 1.401-2).

*(3)* An annuity contract would, except for the fact that it is not a trust, constitute a qualified trust under section 401 if it is purchased by an employer for an employee under a plan which meets the requirements of section 404(a)(2) and the regulations thereunder, except that the plan may be either a pension or a profit-sharing plan.

**(c) Effect of this section.** *(1)* (i) Any custodial account or annuity contract which satisfies the requirements of paragraph (b) of this section is treated as a qualified trust for all purposes of the Internal Revenue Code of 1954. Such a custodial account or annuity contract is treated as a separate legal person which is exempt from the income tax under section 501(a). In addition, the person holding the assets of such account or holding such contract is treated as the trustee thereof. Accordingly, such person is required to file the returns described in sections 6033 and 6047 and to supply any other information which the trustee of a qualified trust is required to furnish.

(ii) Any procedure which has the effect of merely substituting one custodian for another shall not be considered as terminating or interrupting the legal existence of a custodial account which otherwise satisfies the requirements of paragraph (b) of this section.

*(2)* (i) The beneficiary of a custodial account which satisfies the requirements of paragraph (b) of this section is taxed in accordance with section 402. In determining whether the funds of a custodial account are distributed or made available to an employee or his beneficiary, the rules which under section 402(a) are applicable to trusts will also apply to the custodial account as though it were a separate legal person and not an agent of the employee.

(ii) If a custodial account which has qualified under section 401 fails to qualify under such section for any taxable year, such custodial account will not thereafter be treated as a separate legal person, and the funds in such account shall be treated as made available within the meaning of section 402(a)(1) to the employees for whom they are held.

*(3)* The beneficiary of an annuity contract which satisfies the requirements of paragraph (b) of this section is taxed as if he were the beneficiary of an annuity contract described in section 403(a).

**(d) Definitions.** For purposes of this section—

*(1)* The term "bank" means a bank as defined in section 408(n).

*(2)* The term "annuity" means an annuity as defined in section 401(g). Thus, any contract or certificate issued after December 31, 1962, which is transferable is not treated as a qualified trust under this section.

**(e) Other contracts.** For purposes of this section, other than the nontransferability restriction of paragraph (d)(2), a contract issued by an insurance company qualified to do business in a state shall be treated as an annuity contract. For purposes of the preceding sentence, the contract does not include a life, health or accident, property, casualty or liability insurance contract. For purposes of this paragraph, a contract which is issued by an insurance company will not be considered a life insurance contract merely because the contract provides incidental life insurance protection. The provisions of this paragraph are effective for taxable years beginning after December 31, 1975.

**(f) Cross reference.** For the requirement that the assets of an employee benefit plan be placed in trust, and exceptions thereto, see section 403 of the Employee Retirement Income Security Act of 1974, 29 U.S.C. 1103, and the regulations prescribed thereunder by the Secretary of Labor.

---

T.D. 7565, 9/14/78, amend T.D. 7748, 12/30/80, T.D. 8635, 12/19/95.

---

**§ 1.401(k)-0 Table of contents.**

This section contains first a list of section headings and then a list of the paragraphs in each section in §§ 1.401(k)-1 through 1.401(k)-6.

List of Sections



List of Paragraphs

*§ 1.401(k)-1 Certain cash or deferred arrangements.*

*§ 1.401(k)-2 ADP Test*

T.D. 8217, 8/8/88, amend T.D. 8357, 8/8/88, T.D. 8376, 12/2/91, T.D. 8581, 12/22/94, T.D. 9169, 12/28/2004, T.D. 9237, 12/30/2005, T.D. 9324, 4/27/2007, T.D. 9447, 2/23/2009.

PAR. 2. Section 1.401(k)-0 is amended by revising the entries for § 1.401(k)-3(g), (g)(1) and (g)(2) to read as follows:

**Proposed § 1.401(k)-0** [*For Preamble, see ¶ 153,107*]

*§ 1.401(k)-1 Table of Contents.*

* * * * *

*§ 1.401(k)-3 Safe harbor requirements.*

*      *      *      *      *

(g) Permissible reduction or suspension of safe harbor contributions.

(1) General rule.

(i) Matching contributions.

(ii) Nonelective contributions.

(2) Supplemental notice.

*      *      *      *      *

**§ 1.401(k)-1 Certain cash or deferred arrangements.**

***Caution:*** The Treasury has not yet amended Reg § 1.401(k)-1 to reflect changes made by P.L. 109-432.

**(a) General rules.** *(1) Certain plans permitted to include cash or deferred arrangements.* A plan, other than a profit-sharing, stock bonus, pre-ERISA money purchase pension, or rural cooperative plan, does not satisfy the requirements of section 401(a) if the plan includes a cash or deferred arrangement. A profit-sharing, stock bonus, pre-ERISA money purchase pension, or rural cooperative plan does not fail to satisfy the requirements of section 401(a) merely because the plan includes a cash or deferred arrangement. A cash or deferred arrangement is part of a plan for purposes of this section if any contributions to the plan, or accruals or other benefits under the plan, are made or provided pursuant to the cash or deferred arrangement.

*(2) Rules applicable to cash or deferred arrangements generally.* (i) Definition of cash or deferred arrangement. Except as provided in paragraphs (a)(2)(ii) and (iii) of this section, a cash or deferred arrangement is an arrangement under which an eligible employee may make a cash or deferred election with respect to contributions to, or accruals or other benefits under, a plan that is intended to satisfy the requirements of section 401(a) (including a contract that is intended to satisfy the requirements of section 403(a)).

(ii) Treatment of after-tax employee contributions. A cash or deferred arrangement does not include an arrangement under which amounts contributed under a plan at an employee's election are designated or treated at the time of contribution as after-tax employee contributions (e.g., by treating the contributions as taxable income subject to applicable withholding requirements). See also section 414(h)(1). A designated Roth contribution, however, is not treated as an after-tax contribution for purposes of this section, § 1.401(k)-2 through § 1.401(k)-6 and § 1.401(m)-1 through § 1.401(m)-5. A contribution can be an after-tax employee contribution under the rule of this paragraph (a)(2)(ii) even if the employee's election to make after-tax employee contributions is made before the amounts subject to the election are currently available to the employee.

(iii) Treatment of ESOP dividend election. A cash or deferred arrangement does not include an arrangement under an ESOP under which dividends are either distributed or invested pursuant to an election made by participants or their beneficiaries in accordance with section 404(k)(2)(A)(iii).

(iv) Treatment of elective contributions as plan assets. The extent to which elective contributions constitute plan assets for purposes of the prohibited transaction provisions of section 4975 and Title I of the Employee Retirement Income Security Act of 1974 (88 Stat. 829), Public Law 93-406, is determined in accordance with regulations and rulings issued by the Department of Labor. See 29 CFR 2510.3-102.

*(3) Rules applicable to cash or deferred elections generally.* (i) Definition of cash or deferred election. A cash or deferred election is any direct or indirect election (or modification of an earlier election) by an employee to have the employer either—

(A) Provide an amount to the employee in the form of cash (or some other taxable benefit) that is not currently available; or

(B) Contribute an amount to a trust, or provide an accrual or other benefit, under a plan deferring the receipt of compensation.

(ii) Automatic enrollment. For purposes of determining whether an election is a cash or deferred election, it is irrelevant whether the default that applies in the absence of an affirmative election is described in paragraph (a)(3)(i)(A) of this section (i.e., the employee receives an amount in cash or some other taxable benefit) or in paragraph (a)(3)(i)(B) of this section (i.e., the employer contributes an amount to a trust or provides an accrual or other benefit under a plan deferring the receipt of compensation).

(iii) Rules related to timing. (A) Requirement that amounts not be currently available. A cash or deferred election can only be made with respect to an amount that is not currently available to the employee on the date of the election. Further, a cash or deferred election can only be made with respect to amounts that would (but for the cash or deferred election) become currently available after the later of the date on which the employer adopts the cash or deferred arrangement or the date on which the arrangement first becomes effective.

(B) Contribution may not precede election. A contribution is made pursuant to a cash or deferred election only if the contribution is made after the election is made.

(C) Contribution may not precede services. (1) General rule. Contributions are made pursuant to a cash or deferred election only if the contributions are made after the employee's performance of service with respect to which the contributions are made (or when the cash or other taxable benefit would be currently available, if earlier).

(2) Exception for bona fide administrative considerations. The timing of contributions will not be treated as failing to satisfy the requirements of this paragraph (a)(3)(iii)(C) merely because contributions for a pay period are occasionally made before the services with respect to that pay period are performed, provided the contributions are made early in order to accommodate bona fide administrative considerations (for example, the temporary absence of the bookkeeper with responsibility to transmit contributions to the plan) and are not paid early with a principal purpose of accelerating deductions.

(iv) Current availability defined. Cash or another taxable benefit is currently available to the employee if it has been paid to the employee or if the employee is able currently to receive the cash or other taxable benefit at the employee's discretion. An amount is not currently available to an employee if there is a significant limitation or restriction on the employee's right to receive the amount currently. Similarly, an amount is not currently available as of a date if the employee may under no circumstances receive the amount before a particular time in the future. The determination of whether an amount is currently available to an employee does not depend on whether it has been constructively received by the employee for purposes of section 451.

(v) Certain one-time elections not treated as cash or deferred elections. A cash or deferred election does not include a one-time irrevocable election made no later than the employee's first becoming eligible under the plan or any other plan or arrangement of the employer that is described in section 219(g)(5)(A) (whether or not such other plan or arrangement has terminated), to have contributions equal to a specified amount or percentage of the employee's compensation (including no amount of compensation) made by the employer on the employee's behalf to the plan and a specified amount or percentage of the employee's compensation (including no amount of compensation) divided among all other plans or arrangements of the employer (including plans or arrangements not yet established) for the duration of the employee's employment with the employer, or in the case of a defined benefit plan to receive accruals or other benefits (including no benefits) under such plans. Thus, for example, employer contributions made pursuant to a one-time irrevocable election described in this paragraph are not treated as having been made pursuant to a cash or deferred election and are not includible in an employee's gross income by reason of § 1.402(a)-1(d). In the case of an irrevocable election made on or before December 23, 1994—

(A) The election does not fail to be treated as a one-time irrevocable election under this paragraph (a)(3)(v) merely because an employee was previously eligible under another plan of the employer (whether or not such other plan has terminated); and

(B) In the case of a plan in which partners may participate, the election does not fail to be treated as a one-time irrevocable election under this paragraph (a)(3)(v) merely because the election was made after commencement of employment or after the employee's first becoming eligible under any plan of the employer, provided that the election was made before the first day of the first plan year beginning after December 31, 1988, or, if later, March 31,1989.

(vi) Tax treatment of employees. An amount generally is includible in an employee's gross income for the taxable year in which the employee actually or constructively receives the amount. But for section 402(e)(3), an employee is treated as having received an amount that is contributed to an exempt trust or plan described in section 401(a) or 403(a) pursuant to the employee's cash or deferred election. This is the case even if the election to defer is made before the year in which the amount is earned, or before the amount is currently available. See § 1.402(a)-1(d).

(vii) Examples. The following examples illustrate the application of this paragraph (a)(3):

*Example (1).* (i) An employer maintains a profit-sharing plan under which each eligible employee has an election to defer an annual bonus payable on January 30 each year. The bonus equals 10% of compensation during the previous calendar year. Deferred amounts are not treated as after-tax employee contributions. The bonus is currently available on January 30.

(ii) An election made prior to January 30 to defer all or part of the bonus is a cash or deferred election, and the bonus deferral arrangement is a cash or deferred arrangement.

*Example (2).* (i) An employer maintains a profit-sharing plan which provides for discretionary profit sharing contributions and under which each eligible employee may elect to reduce his compensation by up to 10% and to have the employer contribute such amount to the plan. The employer pays each employee every two weeks for services during the immediately preceding two weeks. The employee's election to defer compensation for a payroll period must be made prior to the date the amount would otherwise be paid. The employer contributes to the plan the amount of compensation that each employee elected to defer, at the time it would otherwise be paid to the employee, and does not treat the contribution as an after-tax employee contribution.

(ii) The election is a cash or deferred election and the contributions are elective contributions.

*Example (3).* (i) The facts are the same as in Example 2, except that the employer makes a $10,000 contribution on January 31 of the plan year that is in addition to the contributions that satisfy the employer's obligation to make contributions with respect to cash or deferred elections for prior payroll periods. Employee A makes an election on February 15 to defer $2,000 from compensation that is not currently available and the employer reduces the employee's compensation to reflect the election.

(ii) None of the additional $10,000 contributed January 31 is a contribution made pursuant to Employee A's cash or deferred election, because the contribution was made before the election was made. Accordingly, the employer must make an additional contribution of $2,000 in order to satisfy its obligation to contribute an amount to the plan pursuant to Employee A's election. The $10,000 contribution may be allocated under the plan terms providing for discretionary profit sharing contributions.

*Example (4).* (i) The facts are the same as in Example 3, except that Employee A had an outstanding election to defer $500 from each payroll period's compensation. The $10,000 additional payment that is contributed early is not made early in order to accommodate bona fide administrative considerations.

(ii) None of the additional $10,000 contributed January 31 is a contribution made pursuant to Employee A's cash or deferred election for future payroll periods, because the contribution was made before the earlier of Employee A's performance of services to which the contribution is attributable or when the compensation would be currently available. Furthermore, the exception for early contributions in paragraph (a)(3)(iii)(C)(2) of this section does not apply. Accordingly, the employer must make an additional contribution of $500 per payroll period in order to satisfy its obligation to contribute an amount to the plan pursuant to Employee A's election. The $10,000 contribution may be allocated under the plan terms providing for discretionary profit sharing contributions.

*Example (5).* (i) Employer B establishes a money purchase pension plan in 1986. This is the first qualified plan established by Employer B. All salaried employees are eligible to participate under the plan. Hourly-paid employees are not eligible to participate under the plan. In 2000, Employer B establishes a profit-sharing plan under which all employees (both salaried and hourly) are eligible. Employer B permits all employees on the effective date of the profit-sharing plan to make a one-time irrevocable election to have Employer B contribute 5% of compensation on their behalf to the plan and make no other contribution to any other plan of Employer B (including plans not yet established) for the duration of the employee's employment with Employer B, and have their salaries reduced by 5%.

(ii) The election provided under the profit-sharing plan is not a one-time irrevocable election within the meaning of paragraph (a)(3)(v) of this section with respect to the salaried employees of Employer B who, before becoming eligible to participate under the profit-sharing plan, became eligible to participate under the money purchase pension plan. The election under the profit-sharing plan is a one-time irrevocable election within the meaning of paragraph (a)(3)(v) of this section with respect to the hourly employees, because they were not previously eligible to participate under another plan of the employer.

*(4) Rules applicable to qualified cash or deferred arrangements.* (i) Definition of qualified cash or deferred arrangement. A qualified cash or deferred arrangement is a cash or deferred arrangement that satisfies the requirements of paragraphs (b), (c), (d), and (e) of this section.

(ii) Treatment of elective contributions as employer contributions. Except as otherwise provided in § 1.401(k)-2(b)(3), elective contributions under a qualified cash or deferred arrangement (including designated Roth contributions) are treated as employer contributions. Thus, for example, elective contributions under such an arrangement are treated as employer contributions for purposes of sections 401(a), 401(k), 402, 404, 409, 411, 412, 415, 416, and 417.

(iii) Tax treatment of employees. Except as provided in section 402(g), 402A (effective for taxable years beginning after December 31, 2005), or § 1.401(k)-2(b)(3), elective contributions under a qualified cash or deferred arrangement are neither includible in an employee's gross income at the time the cash would have been includible in the employee's gross income (but for the cash or deferred election), nor at the time the elective contributions are contributed to the plan. See § 1.402(a)-1(d)(2)(i).

(iv) Application of nondiscrimination requirements to plan that includes a qualified cash or deferred arrangement. (A) Exclusive means of amounts testing. Elective contributions (including elective contributions that are designated Roth contributions) under a qualified cash or deferred arrangement satisfy the requirements of section 401(a)(4) with respect to amounts if and only if the amount of elective contributions satisfies the nondiscrimination test of section 401(k) under paragraph (b)(1) of this section. See § 1.401(a)(4)-1(b)(2)(ii)(B).

(B) Testing benefits, rights and features. A plan that includes a qualified cash or deferred arrangement must satisfy the requirements of section 401(a)(4) with respect to benefits, rights and features in addition to the requirements regarding amounts described in paragraph (a)(4)(iv)(A) of this section. For example, the right to make each level of elective contributions under a cash or deferred arrangement and the right to make designated Roth contributions are rights or features subject to the requirements of section 401(a)(4). See § 1.401(a)(4)-4(e)(3)(i) and (iii)(D). Thus, for example, if all employees are eligible to make a stated level of elective contributions under a cash or deferred arrangement, but that level of contributions can only be made from compensation in excess of a stated amount, such as the Social Security taxable wage base, the arrangement will generally favor HCEs with respect to the availability of elective contributions and thus will generally not satisfy the requirements of section 401(a)(4).

(C) Minimum coverage requirement. A qualified cash or deferred arrangement is treated as a separate plan that must satisfy the requirements of section 410(b). See § 1.410(b)-7(c)(1) for special rules. The determination of whether a cash or deferred arrangement satisfies the requirements of section 410(b) must be made without regard to the modifications to the disaggregation rules set forth in paragraph (b)(4)(v) of this section. See also § 1.401(a)(4)-11(g)(3)(vii)(A), relating to corrective amendments that may be made to satisfy the minimum coverage requirements of section 410(b).

*(5) Rules applicable to nonqualified cash or deferred arrangements.* (i) Definition of nonqualified cash or deferred arrangement. A nonqualified cash or deferred arrangement is a cash or deferred arrangement that fails to satisfy one or more of the requirements in paragraph (b), (c), (d) or (e) of this section.

(ii) Treatment of elective contributions as nonelective contributions. Except as specifically provided otherwise, elective contributions under a nonqualified cash or deferred arrangement are treated as nonelective employer contributions. Thus, for example, the elective contributions under such an arrangement are treated as nonelective employer contributions for purposes of sections 401(a) (including section 401(a)(4)) and 401(k), 404, 409, 411, 412, 415, 416, and 417 and are not subject to the requirements of section 401(m).

(iii) Tax treatment of employees. Elective contributions under a nonqualified cash or deferred arrangement are includible in an employee's gross income at the time the cash or other taxable amount that the employee would have received (but for the cash or deferred election) would have been includible in the employee's gross income. See § 1.402(a)-1(d)(1).

(iv) Qualification of plan that includes a nonqualified cash or deferred arrangement. (A) In general. A profit-sharing, stock bonus, pre-ERISA money purchase pension, or rural cooperative plan does not fail to satisfy the requirements of section 401(a) merely because the plan includes a nonqualified cash or deferred arrangement. In determining whether the plan satisfies the requirements of section 401(a)(4), the nondiscrimination tests of sections 401(k), paragraph (b)(1) of this section, section 401(m)(2) and § 1.401(m)-1(b) may not be used. See §§ 1.401(a)(4)-1(b)(2)(ii)(B) and 1.410(b)-9 (definition of section 401(k) plan).

(B) Application of section 401(a)(4) to certain plans. The amount of employer contributions under a nonqualified cash or deferred arrangement is treated as satisfying section 401(a)(4) if the arrangement is part of a collectively bargained plan that automatically satisfies the requirements of section 410(b). See §§ 1.401(a)(4)-(c)(5) and 1.410(b)-2(b)(7). Additionally, the requirements of sections 401(a)(4) and 410(b) do not apply to a governmental plan (within the meaning of section 414(d)) maintained by a State or local government or political subdivision thereof (or agency or instrumentality thereof). See sections 401(a)(5) and 410(c)(1)(A).

(v) Example. The following example illustrates the application of this paragraph (a)(5):

*Example.* (i) For the 2006 plan year, Employer A maintains a collectively bargained plan that includes a cash or deferred arrangement. Employer contributions under the cash or deferred arrangement do not satisfy the nondiscrimination test of section 401(k) and paragraph (b) of this section.

(ii) The arrangement is a nonqualified cash or deferred arrangement. The employer contributions under the cash or deferred arrangement are considered to be nondiscriminatory under section 401(a)(4), and the elective contributions are generally treated as employer contributions under paragraph (a)(5)(ii) of this section. Under paragraph (a)(5)(iii) of this section and under § 1.402(a)-1(d)(1), however, the elective contributions are includible in each employee's gross income.

*(6) Rules applicable to cash or deferred arrangements of self-employed individuals.* (i) Application of general rules. Generally, a partnership or sole proprietorship is permitted to maintain a cash or deferred arrangement, and individual partners or owners are permitted to make cash or deferred elec-

tions with respect to compensation attributable to services rendered to the entity, under the same rules that apply to other cash or deferred arrangements. For example, any contributions made on behalf of an individual partner or owner pursuant to a cash or deferred arrangement of a partnership or sole proprietorship are elective contributions unless they are designated or treated as after-tax employee contributions. In the case of a partnership, a cash or deferred arrangement includes any arrangement that directly or indirectly permits individual partners to vary the amount of contributions made on their behalf. Consistent with § 1.402(a)-1(d), the elective contributions under such an arrangement are includible in income and are not deductible under section 404(a) unless the arrangement is a qualified cash or deferred arrangement (i.e., the requirements of section 401(k) and this section are satisfied). Also, even if the arrangement is a qualified cash or deferred arrangement, the elective contributions are includible in gross income and are not deductible under section 404(a) to the extent they exceed the applicable limit under section 402(g). See also § 1.401(a)-30.

(ii) Treatment of matching contributions made on behalf of self-employed individuals. Under section 402(g)(8), matching contributions made on behalf of a self-employed individual are not treated as elective contributions made pursuant to a cash or deferred election, without regard to whether such matching contributions indirectly permit individual partners to vary the amount of contributions made on their behalf.

(iii) Timing of self-employed individual's cash or deferred election. For purposes of paragraph (a)(3)(iv) of this section, a partner's compensation is deemed currently available on the last day of the partnership taxable year and a sole proprietor's compensation is deemed currently available on the last day of the individual's taxable year. Accordingly, a self-employed individual may not make a cash or deferred election with respect to compensation for a partnership or sole proprietorship taxable year after the last day of that year. See § 1.401(k)-2(a)(4)(ii) for the rules regarding when these contributions are treated as allocated.

(iv) Special rule for certain payments to self-employed individuals. For purposes of sections 401(k) and 401(m), the earned income of a self-employed individual for a taxable year constitutes payment for services during that year. Thus, for example, if a partnership provides for cash advance payments during the taxable year to be made to a partner based on the value of the partner's services prior to the date of payment (and which do not exceed a reasonable estimate of the partner's earned income for the taxable year), a contribution of a portion of these payments to a profit sharing plan in accordance with an election to defer the portion of the advance payments does not fail to be made pursuant to a cash or deferred election within the meaning of paragraph (a)(3)(iii) of this section merely because the contribution is made before the amount of the partner's earned income is finally determined and reported. However, see § 1.401(k)-2(a)(4)(ii) for rules on when earned income is treated as received.

**(b) Coverage and nondiscrimination requirements.** *(1) In general.* A cash or deferred arrangement satisfies this paragraph (b) for a plan year only if—

(i) The group of eligible employees under the cash or deferred arrangement (including any employees taken into account for purposes of section 410(b) pursuant to § 1.401(a)(4)-11(g)(3)(vii)(A)) satisfies the requirements of section 410(b) (including the average benefit percentage test, if applicable); and

(ii) The cash or deferred arrangement satisfies—

(A) The ADP test of section 401(k)(3) described in § 1.401(k)-2;

(B) The ADP safe harbor provisions of section 401(k)(12) described in § 1.401(k)-3; or

(C) The ADP safe harbor provisions of section 401(k)(13) described in § 1.401(k)-3; or

(D) The SIMPLE 401(k) provisions of section 401(k)(11) described in § 1.401(k)-4.

*(2) Automatic satisfaction by certain plans.* Notwithstanding paragraph (b)(1) of this section, a governmental plan (within the meaning of section 414(d)) maintained by a State or local government or political subdivision thereof (or agency or instrumentality thereof) shall be treated as meeting the requirements of this paragraph (b).

*(3) Anti-abuse provisions.* This section and §§ 1.401(k)-2 through 1.401(k)-6 are designed to provide simple, practical rules that accommodate legitimate plan changes. At the same time, the rules are intended to be applied by employers in a manner that does not make use of changes in plan testing procedures or other plan provisions to inflate inappropriately the ADP for NHCEs (which is used as a benchmark for testing the ADP for HCEs) or to otherwise manipulate the nondiscrimination testing requirements of this paragraph (b). Further, this paragraph (b) is part of the overall requirement that benefits or contributions not discriminate in favor of HCEs. Therefore, a plan will not be treated as satisfying the requirements of this paragraph (b) if there are repeated changes to plan testing procedures or plan provisions that have the effect of distorting the ADP so as to increase significantly the permitted ADP for HCEs, or otherwise manipulate the nondiscrimination rules of this paragraph, if a principal purpose of the changes was to achieve such a result.

*(4) Aggregation and restructuring.* (i) In general. This paragraph (b)(4) contains the exclusive rules for aggregating and disaggregating plans and cash or deferred arrangements for purposes of this section, and §§ 1.401(k)-2 through 1.401(k)-6.

(ii) Aggregation of cash or deferred arrangements within a plan. Except as otherwise specifically provided in this paragraph (b)(4), all cash or deferred arrangements included in a plan are treated as a single cash or deferred arrangement and a plan must apply a single test under paragraph (b)(1)(ii) of this section with respect to all such arrangements within the plan. Thus, for example, if two groups of employees are eligible for separate cash or deferred arrangements under the same plan, all contributions under both cash or deferred arrangements must be treated as made under a single cash or deferred arrangement subject to a single test, even if they have significantly different features, such as different limits on elective contributions.

(iii) Aggregation of plans. (A) In general. For purposes of this section and §§ 1.401(k)-2 through 1.401(k)-6, the term plan means a plan within the meaning of § 1.410(b)-7(a) and (b), after application of the mandatory disaggregation rules of § 1.410(b)-7(c), and the permissive aggregation rules of § 1.410(b)-7(d), as modified by paragraph (b)(4)(v) of this section. Thus, for example, two plans (within the meaning of § 1.410(b)-7(b)) that are treated as a single plan pursuant to the permissive aggregation rules of § 1.410(b)-7(d) are treated as a single plan for purposes of sections 401(k) and (m).

(B) Plans with inconsistent ADP testing methods. Pursuant to paragraph (b)(4)(ii) of this section, a single testing method must apply with respect to all cash or deferred arrangements under a plan. Thus, in applying the permissive aggregation rules of § 1.410(b)-7(d), an employer may not aggregate plans (within the meaning of § 1.410(b)-7(b)) that apply inconsistent testing methods. For example, a plan (within the meaning of § 1.410(b)-7(b)) that applies the current year testing method may not be aggregated with another plan that applies the prior year testing method. Similarly, an employer may not aggregate a plan (within the meaning of § 1.410(b)-7(b)) using the ADP safe harbor provisions of section 401(k)(12) and another plan that is using the ADP test of section 401(k)(3).

(iv) Disaggregation of plans and separate testing. (A) In general. If a cash or deferred arrangement is included in a plan (within the meaning of § 1.410(b)-7(b)) that is mandatorily disaggregated under the rules of section 410(b) (as modified by this paragraph (b)(4)), the cash or deferred arrangement must be disaggregated in a consistent manner. For example, in the case of an employer that is treated as operating qualified separate lines of business under section 414(r), if the eligible employees under a cash or deferred arrangement are in more than one qualified separate line of business, only those employees within each qualified separate line of business may be taken into account in determining whether each disaggregated portion of the plan complies with the requirements of section 401(k), unless the employer is applying the special rule for employer-wide plans in § 1.414(r)-1(c)(2)(ii) with respect to the plan. Similarly, if a cash or deferred arrangement under which employees are permitted to participate before they have completed the minimum age and service requirements of section 410(a)(1) applies section 410(b)(4)(B) for determining whether the plan complies with section 410(b)(1), then the arrangement must be treated as two separate arrangements, one comprising all eligible employees who have met the age and service requirements of section 410(a)(1) and one comprising all eligible employees who have not met the age and service requirements under section 410(a)(1), unless the plan is using the rule in § 1.401(k)-2(a)(1)(iii)(A).

(B) Restructuring prohibited. Restructuring under § 1.401(a)(4)-9(c) may not be used to demonstrate compliance with the requirements of section 401(k). See § 1.401(a)(4)-9(c)(3)(ii).

(v) Modifications to section 410(b) rules. (A) Certain disaggregation rules not applicable. The mandatory disaggregation rules relating to section 401(k) plans and section 401(m) plans set forth in § 1.410(b)-7(c)(1) and ESOP and non-ESOP portions of a plan set forth in § 1.410(b)-7(c)(2) shall not apply for purposes of this section and §§ 1.401(k)-2 through 1.401(k)-6. Accordingly, notwithstanding § 1.410(b)-7(d)(2), an ESOP and a non-ESOP which are different plans (within the meaning of section 414(l), as described in § 1.410(b)-7(b)) are permitted to be aggregated for these purposes.

(B) Permissive aggregation of collective bargaining units. Notwithstanding the general rule under section 410(b) and § 1.410(b)-7(c) that a plan that benefits employees who are included in a unit of employees covered by a collective bargaining agreement and employees who are not included in the collective bargaining unit is treated as comprising separate plans, an employer can treat two or more separate collective bargaining units as a single collective bargaining unit for purposes of this section and §§ 1.401(k)-2 through 1.401(k)-6, provided that the combinations of units are determined on a basis that is reasonable and reasonably consistent from year to year. Thus, for example, if a plan benefits employees in three categories (e.g., employees included in collective bargaining unit A, employees included in collective bargaining unit B, and employees who are not included in any collective bargaining unit), the plan can be treated as comprising three separate plans, each of which benefits only one category of employees. However, if collective bargaining units A and B are treated as a single collective bargaining unit, the plan will be treated as comprising only two separate plans, one benefiting all employees who are included in a collective bargaining unit and another benefiting all other employees. Similarly, if a plan benefits only employees who are included in collective bargaining unit A and employees who are included in collective bargaining unit B, the plan can be treated as comprising two separate plans. However, if collective bargaining units A and B are treated as a single collective bargaining unit, the plan will be treated as a single plan. An employee is treated as included in a unit of employees covered by a collective bargaining agreement if and only if the employee is a collectively bargained employee within the meaning of § 1.410(b)-6(d)(2).

(C) Multiemployer plans. Notwithstanding § 1.410(b)-7(c)(4)(ii)(C), the portion of the plan that is maintained pursuant to a collective bargaining agreement (within the meaning of § 1.413-1(a)(2)) is treated as a single plan maintained by a single employer that employs all the employees benefiting under the same benefit computation formula and covered pursuant to that collective bargaining agreement. The rules of paragraph (b)(4)(v)(B) of this section (including the permissive aggregation of collective bargaining units) apply to the resulting deemed single plan in the same manner as they would to a single employer plan, except that the plan administrator is substituted for the employer where appropriate and that appropriate fiduciary obligations are taken into account. The noncollectively bargained portion of the plan is treated as maintained by one or more employers, depending on whether the noncollectively bargaining unit employees who benefit under the plan are employed by one or more employers.

(vi) Examples. The following examples illustrate the application of this paragraph (b)(4):

*Example (1).* (i) Employer A maintains Plan V, a profit-sharing plan that includes a cash or deferred arrangement in which all of the employees of Employer A are eligible to participate. For purposes of applying section 410(b), Employer A is treated as operating qualified separate lines of business under section 414(r) in accordance with § 1.414(r)-1(b). However, Employer A applies the special rule for employer-wide plans in § 1.414(r)-1(c)(2)(ii) to the portion of its profit-sharing plan that consists of elective contributions under the cash or deferred arrangement (and to no other plans or portions of plans).

(ii) Under these facts, the requirements of this section and §§ 1.401(k)-2 through 1.401(k)-6 must be applied on an employer-wide rather than a qualified separate line of business basis.

*Example (2).* (i) Employer B maintains Plan W, a profit-sharing plan that includes a cash or deferred arrangement in which all of the employees of Employer B are eligible to participate. For purposes of applying section 410(b), the plan treats the cash or deferred arrangement as two separate plans, one for the employees who have completed the minimum age and service eligibility conditions under section 410(a)(1) and the other for employees who have not completed the conditions. The plan provides that it will satisfy the section 401(k) safe harbor requirement of § 1.401(k)-3 with respect to the employees who have met the minimum age and service conditions and that it will meet the ADP test requirements of § 1.401(k)-2 with respect to the employees who have not met the minimum age and service conditions.

(ii) Under these facts, the cash or deferred arrangement must be disaggregated on a consistent basis with the disaggregation of Plan W. Thus, the requirements of § 1.401(k)-2 must be applied by comparing the ADP for eligible HCEs who have not completed the minimum age and service conditions with the ADP for eligible NHCEs for the applicable year who have not completed the minimum age and service conditions.

*Example (3).* (i) Employer C maintains Plan X, a stock-bonus plan including an ESOP. The plan also includes a cash or deferred arrangement for participants in the ESOP and non-ESOP portions of the plan.

(ii) Pursuant to paragraph (b)(4)(v)(A) of this section the ESOP and non-ESOP portions of the stock-bonus plan are a single cash or deferred arrangement for purposes of this section and §§ 1.401(k)-2 through 1.401(k)-6. However, as provided in paragraph (a)(4)(iv)(C) of this section, the ESOP and non-ESOP portions of the plan are still treated as separate plans for purposes of satisfying the requirements of section 410(b).

**(c) Nonforfeitability requirements.** *(1) General rule.* A cash or deferred arrangement satisfies this paragraph (c) only if the amount attributable to an employee's elective contributions are immediately nonforfeitable, within the meaning of paragraph (c)(2) of this section, are disregarded for purposes of applying section 411(a)(2) to other contributions or benefits, and the contributions remain nonforfeitable even if the employee makes no additional elective contributions under a cash or deferred arrangement.

*(2) Definition of immediately nonforfeitable.* An amount is immediately nonforfeitable if it is immediately nonforfeitable within the meaning of section 411, and would be nonforfeitable under the plan regardless of the age and service of the employee or whether the employee is employed on a specific date. An amount that is subject to forfeitures or suspensions permitted by section 411(a)(3) does not satisfy the requirements of this paragraph (c).

*(3) Example.* The following example illustrates the application of this paragraph (c):

*Example.* (i) Employees B and C are covered by Employer Y's stock bonus plan, which includes a cash or deferred arrangement. All employees participating in the plan have a nonforfeitable right to a percentage of their account balance derived from all contributions (including elective contributions) as shown in the following table:

| Years of service | Nonforfeitable percentage |
|---|---|
| Less than 1 | 0 |
| 1 | 20 |
| 2 | 40 |
| 3 | 60 |
| 4 | 80 |
| 5 or more | 100 |

(ii) The cash or deferred arrangement does not satisfy paragraph (c) of this section because elective contributions are not immediately nonforfeitable. Thus, the cash or deferred arrangement is a nonqualified cash or deferred arrangement.

**(d) Distribution limitation.** *(1) General rule.* A cash or deferred arrangement satisfies this paragraph (d) only if amounts attributable to elective contributions may not be distributed before one of the following events, and any distributions so permitted also satisfy the additional requirements of paragraphs (d)(2) through (5) of this section (to the extent applicable)—

(i) The employee's death, disability, or severance from employment;

(ii) In the case of a profit-sharing, stock bonus or rural cooperative plan, the employee's attainment of age 59½, or the employee's hardship; or

(iii) The termination of the plan.

*(2) Rules applicable to distributions upon severance from employment.* An employee has a severance from employment when the employee ceases to be an employee of the employer maintaining the plan. An employee does not have a severance from employment if, in connection with a change of employment, the employee's new employer maintains such plan with respect to the employee. For example, a new employer maintains a plan with respect to an employee by continuing or assuming sponsorship of the plan or by accepting a transfer of plan assets and liabilities (within the meaning of section 414(l)) with respect to the employee.

*(3) Rules applicable to hardship distributions.* (i) Distribution must be on account of hardship. A distribution is treated as made after an employee's hardship for purposes of paragraph (d)(1)(ii) of this section if and only if it is made on account of the hardship. For purposes of this rule, a distribution is made on account of hardship only if the distribution both is made on account of an immediate and heavy financial need of the employee and is necessary to satisfy the financial need. The determination of the existence of an immediate and heavy financial need and of the amount necessary to meet the need must be made in accordance with nondiscriminatory and objective standards set forth in the plan.

(ii) Limit on maximum distributable amount. (A) General rule. A distribution on account of hardship must be limited to the maximum distributable amount. The maximum distributable amount is equal to the employee's total elective contributions as of the date of distribution, reduced by the amount of previous distributions of elective contributions. Thus, the maximum distributable amount does not include earnings, QNECs or QMACs, unless grandfathered under paragraph (d)(3)(ii)(B) of this section.

(B) Grandfathered amounts. If the plan so provides, the maximum distributable amount may be increased for amounts credited to the employee's account as of a date specified in the plan that is no later than December 31, 1988, or if later, the end of the last plan year ending before July 1, 1989 (or in the case of a collectively bargained plan, the earlier of—

(1) The later of January 1, 1989, or the date on which the last of the collective bargaining agreements in effect on March 1, 1986 terminates (determined without regard to any extension thereof after February 28, 1986); or

(2) January 1, 1991 and consisting of—

(i) Income allocable to elective contributions;

(ii) Qualified nonelective contributions and allocable income; and

(iii) Qualified matching contributions and allocable income.

(iii) Immediate and heavy financial need. (A) In general. Whether an employee has an immediate and heavy financial need is to be determined based on all the relevant facts and circumstances. Generally, for example, the need to pay the funeral expenses of a family member would constitute an immediate and heavy financial need. A distribution made to an employee for the purchase of a boat or television would generally not constitute a distribution made on account of an immediate and heavy financial need. A financial need may be immediate and heavy even if it was reasonably foreseeable or voluntarily incurred by the employee.

(B) Deemed immediate and heavy financial need. A distribution is deemed to be on account of an immediate and heavy financial need of the employee if the distribution is for—

(1) Expenses for (or necessary to obtain) medical care that would be deductible under section 213(d) (determined without regard to whether the expenses exceed 7.5% of adjusted gross income);

(2) Costs directly related to the purchase of a principal residence for the employee (excluding mortgage payments);

(3) Payment of tuition, related educational fees, and room and board expenses, for up to the next 12 months of post-secondary education for the employee, or the employee's spouse, children, or dependents (as defined in section 152, and, for taxable years beginning on or after January 1, 2005, without regard to section 152(b)(1), (b)(2) and (d)(1)(B));

(4) Payments necessary to prevent the eviction of the employee from the employee's principal residence or foreclosure on the mortgage on that residence;

(5) Payments for burial or funeral expenses for the employee's deceased parent, spouse, children or dependents (as defined in section 152, and, for taxable years beginning on or after January 1, 2005, without regard to section 152(d)(1)(B)); or

(6) Expenses for the repair of damage to the employee's principal residence that would qualify for the casualty deduction under section 165 (determined without regard to whether the loss exceeds 10% of adjusted gross income).

(iv) Distribution necessary to satisfy financial need. (A) Distribution may not exceed amount of need. A distribution is treated as necessary to satisfy an immediate and heavy financial need of an employee only to the extent the amount of the distribution is not in excess of the amount required to satisfy the financial need. For this purpose, the amount required to satisfy the financial need may include any amounts necessary to pay any federal, state, or local income taxes or penalties reasonably anticipated to result from the distribution.

(B) No alternative means available. A distribution is not treated as necessary to satisfy an immediate and heavy financial need of an employee to the extent the need may be relieved from other resources that are reasonably available to the employee. This determination generally is to be made on the basis of all the relevant facts and circumstances. For purposes of this paragraph (d)(3)(iv), the employee's resources are deemed to include those assets of the employee's spouse and minor children that are reasonably available to the employee. Thus, for example, a vacation home owned by the employee and the employee's spouse, whether as community property, joint tenants, tenants by the entirety, or tenants in common, generally will be deemed a resource of the employee. However, property held for the employee's child under an irrevocable trust or under the Uniform Gifts to Minors Act (or comparable State law) is not treated as a resource of the employee.

(C) Employer reliance on employee representation. For purposes of paragraph (d)(3)(iv)(B) of this section, an immediate and heavy financial need generally may be treated as not capable of being relieved from other resources that are reasonably available to the employee, if the employer relies upon the employee's representation (made in writing or such other form as may be prescribed by the Commissioner), unless the employer has actual knowledge to the contrary, that the need cannot reasonably be relieved—

(1) Through reimbursement or compensation by insurance or otherwise;

(2) By liquidation of the employee's assets;

(3) By cessation of elective contributions or employee contributions under the plan;

(4) By other currently available distributions (including distribution of ESOP dividends under section 404(k)) and nontaxable (at the time of the loan) loans, under plans maintained by the employer or by any other employer; or

(5) By borrowing from commercial sources on reasonable commercial terms in an amount sufficient to satisfy the need.

(D) Employee need not take counterproductive actions. For purposes of this paragraph (d)(3)(iv), a need cannot reasonably be relieved by one of the actions described in paragraph (d)(3)(iv)(C) of this section if the effect would be to increase the amount of the need. For example, the need for funds to purchase a principal residence cannot reasonably be relieved by a plan loan if the loan would disqualify the employee from obtaining other necessary financing.

(E) Distribution deemed necessary to satisfy immediate and heavy financial need. A distribution is deemed necessary to satisfy an immediate and heavy financial need of an employee if each of the following requirements are satisfied—

(1) The employee has obtained all other currently available distributions (including distribution of ESOP dividends under section 404(k), but not hardship distributions) and nontaxable (at the time of the loan) loans, under the plan and all other plans maintained by the employer; and

(2) The employee is prohibited, under the terms of the plan or an otherwise legally enforceable agreement, from making elective contributions and employee contributions to the plan and all other plans maintained by the employer for at least 6 months after receipt of the hardship distribution.

(F) Definition of other plans. For purposes of paragraph (d)(3)(iv)(C)(4) and (E)(1) of this section, the phrase plans maintained by the employer means all qualified and nonqualified plans of deferred compensation maintained by the employer, including a cash or deferred arrangement that is part of a cafeteria plan within the meaning of section 125. However, it does not include the mandatory employee contribution portion of a defined benefit plan or a health or welfare benefit plan (including one that is part of a cafeteria plan). In addition, for purposes of paragraph (d)(3)(iv)(E)(2) of this section, the phrase plans maintained by the employer also includes a stock option, stock purchase, or similar plan maintained by the employer. See § 1.401(k)-6 for the continued treatment of suspended employees as eligible employees.

(v) Commissioner may expand standards. The Commissioner may prescribe additional guidance of general applicability, published in the Internal Revenue Bulletin (see § 601.601(d)(2) of this chapter), expanding the list of deemed immediate and heavy financial needs and prescribing additional methods for distributions to be deemed necessary to satisfy an immediate and heavy financial need.

*(4) Rules applicable to distributions upon plan termination.* (i) No alternative defined contribution plan. A distribution may not be made under paragraph (d)(1)(iii) of this section if the employer establishes or maintains an alternative

defined contribution plan. For purposes of the preceding sentence, the definition of the term "employer" contained in § 1.401(k)-6 is applied as of the date of plan termination, and a plan is an alternative defined contribution plan only if it is a defined contribution plan that exists at any time during the period beginning on the date of plan termination and ending 12 months after distribution of all assets from the terminated plan. However, if at all times during the 24-month period beginning 12 months before the date of plan termination, fewer than 2% of the employees who were eligible under the defined contribution plan that includes the cash or deferred arrangement as of the date of plan termination are eligible under the other defined contribution plan, the other plan is not an alternative defined contribution plan. In addition, a defined contribution plan is not treated as an alternative defined contribution plan if it is an employee stock ownership plan as defined in section 4975(e)(7) or 409(a), a simplified employee pension as defined in section 408(k), a SIMPLE IRA plan as defined in section 408(p), a plan or contract that satisfies the requirements of section 403(b), or a plan that is described in section 457(b) or (f).

(ii) Lump sum requirement for certain distributions. A distribution may be made under paragraph (d)(1)(iii) of this section only if it is a lump sum distribution. The term lump sum distribution has the meaning provided in section 402(e)(4)(D) (without regard to section 402(e)(4)(D)(i)(I), (II), (III) and (IV)). In addition, a lump sum distribution includes a distribution of an annuity contract from a trust that is part of a plan described in section 401(a) and which is exempt from tax under section 501(a) or an annuity plan described in 403(a).

*(5) Rules applicable to all distributions.* (i) Exclusive distribution rules. Amounts attributable to elective contributions may not be distributed on account of any event not described in this paragraph (d), such as completion of a stated period of plan participation or the lapse of a fixed number of years. For example, if excess deferrals (and income) for an employee's taxable year are not distributed within the time prescribed in § 1.402(g)-1(e)(2) or (3), the amounts may be distributed only on account of an event described in this paragraph (d). Pursuant to section 401(k)(8), the prohibition on distributions set forth in this section does not apply to a distribution of excess contributions under § 1.401(k)-2(b).

(ii) Deemed distributions. The cost of life insurance (determined under section 72) is not treated as a distribution for purposes of section 401(k)(2) and this paragraph (d). The making of a loan is not treated as a distribution, even if the loan is secured by the employee's accrued benefit attributable to elective contributions or is includible in the employee's income under section 72(p). However, the reduction, by reason of default on a loan, of an employee's accrued benefit derived from elective contributions is treated as a distribution.

(iii) ESOP dividend distributions. A plan does not fail to satisfy the requirements of this paragraph (d) merely by reason of a dividend distribution described in section 404(k)(2).

(iv) Limitations apply after transfer. The limitations of this paragraph (d) generally continue to apply to amounts attributable to elective contributions (including QNECs and qualified matching contributions taken into account for the ADP test under § 1.401(k)-2(a)(6)) that are transferred to another qualified plan of the same or another employer. Thus, the transferee plan will generally fail to satisfy the requirements of section 401(a) and this section if transferred amounts may be distributed before the times specified in this paragraph (d). In addition, a cash or deferred arrangement fails to satisfy the limitations of this paragraph (d) if it transfers amounts to a plan that does not provide that the transferred amounts may not be distributed before the times specified in this paragraph (d). The transferor plan does not fail to comply with the preceding sentence if it reasonably concludes that the transferee plan provides that the transferred amounts may not be distributed before the times specified in this paragraph (d). What constitutes a basis for a reasonable conclusion is determined under standards comparable to those under the rules related to acceptance of rollover distributions. See § 1.401(a)(31)-1, A-14. The limitations of this paragraph (d) cease to apply after the transfer, however, if the amounts could have been distributed at the time of the transfer (other than on account of hardship), and the transfer is an elective transfer described in § 1.411(d)-4, Q&A-3(b)(1). The limitations of this paragraph (d) also do not apply to amounts that have been paid in a direct rollover to the plan after being distributed by another plan.

*(6) Examples.* The following examples illustrate the application of this paragraph (d):

*Example (1).* Employer M maintains Plan V, a profit-sharing plan that includes a cash or deferred arrangement. Elective contributions under the arrangement may be withdrawn for any reason after two years following the end of the plan year in which the contributions were made. Because the plan permits distributions of elective contributions before the occurrence of one of the events specified in section 401(k)(2)(B) and this paragraph (d), the cash or deferred arrangement is a nonqualified cash or deferred arrangement and the elective contributions are currently includible in income under section 402.

*Example (2).* (i) Employer N maintains Plan W, a profit-sharing plan that includes a cash or deferred arrangement. Plan W provides for distributions upon a participant's severance from employment, death or disability. All employees of Employer N and its wholly owned subsidiary, Employer O, are eligible to participate in Plan W. Employer N agrees to sell all issued and outstanding shares of Employer O to an unrelated entity, Employer T, effective on December 31, 2006. Following the transaction, Employer O will be a wholly owned subsidiary of Employer T. Additionally, individuals who are employed by Employer O on the effective date of the sale continue to be employed by Employer O following the sale. Following the transaction, all employees of Employer O will cease to participate in Plan W and will become eligible to participate in the cash or deferred arrangement maintained by Employer T, Plan X. No assets will be transferred from Plan W to Plan X, except in the case of a direct rollover within the meaning of section 401(a)(31).

(ii) Employer O ceases to be a member of Employer N's controlled group as a result of the sale. Therefore, employees of Employer O who participated in Plan W will have a severance from employment and are eligible to receive a distribution from Plan W.

*Example (3).* (i) Employer Q maintains Plan Y, a profit-sharing plan that includes a cash or deferred arrangement. Plan Y, the only plan maintained by Employer Q, does not provide for loans. However, Plan Y provides that elective contributions under the arrangement may be distributed to an eligible employee on account of hardship using the deemed immediate and heavy financial need provisions of paragraph (d)(3)(iii)(B) of this section and provisions regarding distributions necessary to satisfy financial need of paragraphs (d)(3)(iv)(A) through (D) of this section. Employee A is an eligible employee in Plan Y with an account balance of $50,000 attributable to elective contributions made by Employee A. The total amount of elective contributions made by Employee A, who has not previously received a distribution from Plan Y, is $20,000. Employee A requests a $15,000 hardship distribution of his elective contributions to pay 6 months of college tuition and room and board expenses for his dependent. At the time of the distribution request, the sole asset of Employee A (that is reasonably available to Employee A within the meaning of paragraph (d)(3)(iv)(B) of this section) is a savings account with an available balance of $10,000.

(ii) A distribution is made on account of hardship only if the distribution both is made on account of an immediate and heavy financial need of the employee and is necessary to satisfy the financial need. Under paragraph (d)(3)(iii)(B) of this section, a distribution for payment of up to the next 12 months of post-secondary education and room and board expenses for Employee A's dependent is deemed to be on account of an immediate and heavy financial need of Employee A.

(iii) A distribution is treated as necessary to satisfy Employee A's immediate and heavy financial need to the extent the need may not be relieved from other resources reasonably available to Employee A. Under paragraph (d)(3)(iv)(B) of this section, Employee A's $10,000 savings account is a resource that is reasonably available to the employee and must be taken into account in determining the amount necessary to satisfy Employee A's immediate and heavy financial need. Thus, Employee A may receive a distribution of only $5,000 of his elective contributions on account of this hardship, plus an amount necessary to pay any federal, state, or local income taxes or penalties reasonably anticipated to result from the distribution.

*Example (4).* (i) The facts are the same as in Example 3. Employee B, another employee of Employer Q has an account balance of $25,000, attributable to Employee B's elective contributions. The total amount of elective contributions made by Employee B, who has not previously received a distribution from Plan Y, is $15,000. Employee B requests a $10,000 distribution of his elective contributions to pay 6 months of college tuition and room and board expenses for his child. Employee B makes a written representation (with respect to which Employer Q has no actual knowledge to the contrary) that the need cannot reasonably be relieved:

(A) Through reimbursement or compensation by insurance or otherwise;

(B) By liquidation of the employee's assets;

(C) By cessation of elective contributions or employee contributions under the plan;

(D) By other distributions or nontaxable (at the time of the loan) loans from plans maintained by the employer or by any other employer; or

(E) By borrowing from commercial sources on reasonable commercial terms in an amount sufficient to satisfy the need.

(ii) Under paragraph (d)(3)(iii)(B) of this section, a distribution for payment of up to the next 12 months of post-secondary education and room and board expenses for Employee B's child is deemed to be on account of an Employee B's immediate and heavy financial need. In addition, because Employer Q can rely on Employee B's written representation, the distribution is considered necessary to satisfy Employee B's immediate and heavy financial need. Therefore, Employee B may receive a $10,000 distribution of his elective contributions on account of hardship plus an amount necessary to pay any federal, state, or local income taxes or penalties reasonably anticipated to result from the distribution.

*Example (5).* (i) The facts are the same as in Example 3, except Plan Y provides for hardship distributions using the safe harbor rule of paragraph (d)(3)(iv)(E) of this section. Accordingly, Plan Y provides for a 6 month suspension of an eligible employee's elective contributions and employee contributions to the plan after the receipt of a hardship distribution by such eligible employee.

(ii) Under paragraph (d)(3)(iii)(B) of this section, a distribution for payment of up to the next 12 months of post-secondary education and room and board expenses for Employee A's dependent is deemed to be on account of an Employee A's immediate and heavy financial need. In addition, because Employee A is not eligible for any other distribution or loan from Plan Y and Plan Y suspends Employee A's elective contributions and employee contributions following receipt of the hardship distribution, the distribution will be deemed necessary to satisfy Employee A's immediate and heavy financial need (and Employee A is not required to first liquidate his savings account). Therefore, Employee A may receive a $15,000 distribution of his elective contributions on account of hardship plus an amount necessary to pay any federal, state, or local income taxes or penalties reasonably anticipated to result from the distribution.

*Example (6).* Employer R maintains a pre-ERISA money purchase pension plan that includes a cash or deferred arrangement that is not a rural cooperative plan. Elective contributions under the arrangement may be distributed to an employee on account of hardship. Under paragraph (d)(1) of this section, hardship is a permissible distribution event only in a profit-sharing, stock bonus or rural cooperative plan. Since elective contributions under the arrangement may be distributed before a permissible distribution event occurs, the cash or deferred arrangement does not satisfy this paragraph (d), and is not a qualified cash or deferred arrangement. Moreover, the plan is not a qualified plan because a money purchase pension plan may not provide for payment of benefits upon hardship. See § 1.401-1(b)(1)(i).

**(e) Additional requirements for qualified cash or deferred arrangements.** *(1) Qualified plan requirement.* A cash or deferred arrangement satisfies this paragraph (e) only if the plan of which it is a part is a profit-sharing, stock bonus, pre-ERISA money purchase or rural cooperative plan that otherwise satisfies the requirements of section 401(a) (taking into account the cash or deferred arrangement). A plan that includes a cash or deferred arrangement may provide for other contributions, including employer contributions (other than elective contributions), employee contributions, or both. However, except as expressly permitted under section 401(m), 410(b)(2)(A)(ii) or 416(c)(2)(A), elective contributions and matching contributions taken into account under § 1.401(k)-2(a) may not be taken into account for purposes of determining whether any other contributions under any plan (including the plan to which the contributions are made) satisfy the requirements of section 401(a).

*(2) Election requirements.* (i) Cash must be available. A cash or deferred arrangement satisfies this paragraph (e) only if the arrangement provides that the amount that each eligible employee may defer as an elective contribution is available to the employee in cash. Thus, for example, if an eligible employee is provided the option to receive a taxable benefit (other than cash) or to have the employer contribute on the employee's behalf to a profit-sharing plan an amount equal to the value of the taxable benefit, the arrangement is not a qualified cash or deferred arrangement. Similarly, if an em-

ployee has the option to receive a specified amount in cash or to have the employer contribute an amount in excess of the specified cash amount to a profit-sharing plan on the employee's behalf, any contribution made by the employer on the employee's behalf in excess of the specified cash amount is not treated as made pursuant to a qualified cash or deferred arrangement, but would be treated as a matching contribution. This cash availability requirement applies even if the cash or deferred arrangement is part of a cafeteria plan within the meaning of section 125.

(ii) Frequency of elections. A cash or deferred arrangement satisfies this paragraph (e) only if the arrangement provides an employee with an effective opportunity to make (or change) a cash or deferred election at least once during each plan year. Whether an employee has an effective opportunity is determined based on all the relevant facts and circumstances, including the adequacy of notice of the availability of the election, the period of time during which an election may be made, and any other conditions on elections.

*(3) Separate accounting requirement.* (i) General rule. A cash or deferred arrangement satisfies this paragraph (e) only if the portion of an employee's benefit subject to the requirements of paragraphs (c) and (d) of this section is determined by an acceptable separate accounting between that portion and any other benefits. Separate accounting is not acceptable unless contributions and withdrawals are attributed to the separate accounts and gains, losses, and other credits or charges are separately allocated on a reasonable and consistent basis to the accounts subject to the requirements of paragraphs (c) and (d) of this section and to other accounts. Subject to section 401(a)(4), forfeitures are not required to be allocated to the accounts in which benefits are subject to paragraphs (c) and (d) of this section. The separate accounting requirement of this paragraph (e)(3)(i) applies at the time the elective contribution is contributed to the plan and continues to apply until the contribution is distributed under the plan.

(ii) Satisfaction of separate accounting requirement. The requirements of paragraph (e)(3)(i) of this section are treated as satisfied if all amounts held under a plan that includes a qualified cash or deferred arrangement (and, if applicable, under another plan to which QNECs and QMACs are made) are subject to the requirements of paragraphs (c) and (d) of this section.

*(4) Limitations on cash or deferred arrangements of state and local governments.* (i) General rule. A cash or deferred arrangement does not satisfy the requirements of this paragraph (e) if the arrangement is adopted after May 6, 1986, by a State or local government or political subdivision thereof, or any agency or instrumentality thereof (a governmental unit). For purposes of this paragraph (e)(4), an employer that has made a legally binding commitment to adopt a cash or deferred arrangement is treated as having adopted the arrangement on that date.

(ii) Rural cooperative plans and Indian tribal governments. This paragraph (e)(4) does not apply to a rural cooperative plan or to a plan of an employer which is an Indian tribal government (as defined in section 7701(a)(40)), a subdivision of an Indian tribal government (determined in accordance with section 7871(d)), an agency or instrumentality of an Indian tribal government or subdivision thereof, or a corporation chartered under Federal, State or tribal law which is owned in whole or in part by any of the entities in this paragraph (e)(4)(ii).

(iii) Adoption after May 6, 1986. A cash or deferred arrangement is treated as adopted after May 6, 1986, with respect to all employees of any employer that adopts the arrangement after such date.

(iv) Adoption before May 7, 1986. If a governmental unit adopted a cash or deferred arrangement before May 7, 1986, then any cash or deferred arrangement adopted by the unit at any time is treated as adopted before that date. If an employer adopted an arrangement prior to such date, all employees of the employer may participate in the arrangement.

*(5) One-year eligibility requirement.* A cash or deferred arrangement satisfies this paragraph (e) only if no employee is required to complete a period of service with the employer maintaining the plan extending beyond the period permitted under section 410(a)(1) (determined without regard to section 410(a)(1)(B)(i)) to be eligible to make a cash or deferred election under the arrangement.

*(6) Other benefits not contingent upon elective contributions.* (i) General rule. A cash or deferred arrangement satisfies this paragraph (e) only if no other benefit is conditioned (directly or indirectly) upon the employee's electing to make or not to make elective contributions under the arrangement. The preceding sentence does not apply to—

(A) Any matching contribution (as defined in § 1.401(m)-1(a)(2)) made by reason of such an election;

(B) Any benefit, right or feature (such as a plan loan) that requires, or results in, an amount to be withheld from an employee's pay (e.g. to pay for the benefit or to repay the loan), to the extent the cash or deferred arrangement restricts elective contributions to amounts available after such withholding from the employee's pay (after deduction of all applicable income and employment taxes);

(C) Any reduction in the employer's top-heavy contributions under section 416(c)(2) because of matching contributions that resulted from the elective contributions; or

(D) Any benefit that is provided at the employee's election under a plan described in section 125(d) in lieu of an elective contribution under a qualified cash or deferred arrangement.

(ii) Definition of other benefits. For purposes of this paragraph (e)(6), other benefits include, but are not limited to, benefits under a defined benefit plan; nonelective contributions under a defined contribution plan; the availability, cost, or amount of health benefits; vacations or vacation pay; life insurance; dental plans; legal services plans; loans (including plan loans); financial planning services; subsidized retirement benefits; stock options; property subject to section 83; and dependent care assistance. Also, increases in salary, bonuses or other cash remuneration (other than the amount that would be contributed under the cash or deferred election) are benefits for purposes of this paragraph (e)(6). The ability to make after-tax employee contributions is a benefit, but that benefit is not contingent upon an employee's electing to make or not make elective contributions under the arrangement merely because the amount of elective contributions reduces dollar-for-dollar the amount of after-tax employee contributions that may be made. Additionally, benefits under any other plan or arrangement (whether or not qualified) are not contingent upon an employee's electing to make or not to make elective contributions under a cash or deferred arrangement merely because the elective contributions are or are not taken into account as compensation under the other plan or arrangement for purposes of determining benefits.

(iii) Effect of certain statutory limits. Any benefit under an excess benefit plan described in section 3(36) of the Employee Retirement Income Security Act of 1974 (88 Stat. 829), Public Law 93-406, that is dependent on the employee's electing to make or not to make elective contributions is not treated as contingent. Deferred compensation under a nonqualified plan of deferred compensation that is dependent on an employee's having made the maximum elective deferrals under section 402(g) or the maximum elective contributions permitted under the terms of the plan also is not treated as contingent.

(iv) Nonqualified deferred compensation. Except as otherwise provided in paragraph (e)(6)(iii) of this section, participation in a nonqualified deferred compensation plan is treated as contingent for purposes of this paragraph (e)(6) to the extent that an employee may receive additional deferred compensation under the nonqualified plan to the extent the employee makes or does not make elective contributions.

(v) Plan loans and distributions. A loan or distribution of elective contributions is not a benefit conditioned on an employee's electing to make or not make elective contributions under the arrangement merely because the amount of the loan or distribution is based on the amount of the employee's account balance.

(vi) Examples. The following examples illustrate the application of this paragraph (e)(6):

*Example (1).* Employer T maintains a cash or deferred arrangement for all of its employees. Employer T also maintains a nonqualified deferred compensation plan for two highly paid executives, Employees R and C. Under the terms of the nonqualified deferred compensation plan, R and C are eligible to participate only if they do not make elective contributions under the cash or deferred arrangement. Participation in the nonqualified plan is a contingent benefit for purposes of this paragraph (e)(6), because R's and C's participation is conditioned on their electing not to make elective contributions under the cash or deferred arrangement.

*Example (2).* Employer T maintains a cash or deferred arrangement for all its employees. Employer T also maintains a nonqualified deferred compensation plan for two highly paid executives, Employees R and C. Under the terms of the arrangements, Employees R and C may defer a maximum of 10% of their compensation, and may allocate their deferral between the cash or deferred arrangement and the nonqualified deferred compensation plan in any way they choose (subject to the overall 10% maximum). Because the maximum deferral available under the nonqualified deferred compensation plan depends on the elective deferrals made under the cash or deferred arrangement, the right to participate in the nonqualified plan is a contingent benefit for purposes of this paragraph (e)(6).

*(7) Plan provision requirement.* A plan that includes a cash or deferred arrangement satisfies this paragraph (e) only if it provides that the nondiscrimination requirements of section 401(k) will be met. Thus, the plan must provide for satisfaction of one of the specific alternatives described in paragraph (b)(1)(ii) of this section and, if with respect to that alternative there are optional choices, which of the optional choices will apply. For example, a plan that uses the ADP test of section 401(k)(3), as described in paragraph (b)(1)(ii)(A) of this section, must specify whether it is using the current year testing method or prior year testing method. Additionally, a plan that uses the prior year testing method must specify whether the ADP for eligible NHCEs for the first plan year is 3% or the ADP for the eligible NHCEs for the first plan year. Similarly, a plan that uses the safe harbor method of section 401(k)(12), as described in paragraph (b)(1)(ii)(B) of this section, must specify whether the safe harbor contribution will be the nonelective safe harbor contribution or the matching safe harbor contribution and is not permitted to provide that ADP testing will be used if the requirements for the safe harbor are not satisfied. In addition, a plan that uses the safe harbor method of section 401(k)(13), as described in paragraph (b)(1)(ii)(C) of this section, must specify the default percentages that apply for the plan year and whether the safe harbor contribution will be the nonelective safe harbor contribution or the matching safe harbor contribution, and is not permitted to provide that ADP testing will be used if the requirements for the safe harbor are not satisfied. For purposes of this paragraph (e)(7), a plan may incorporate by reference the provisions of section 401(k)(3) and § 1.401(k)-2 if that is the nondiscrimination test being applied. The Commissioner may, in guidance of general applicability, published in the Internal Revenue Bulletin (see § 601.601(d)(2) of this chapter), specify the options that will apply under the plan if the nondiscrimination test is incorporated by reference in accordance with the preceding sentence.

*(8) Section 415 compensation required.* With respect to compensation that is paid (or would have been paid but for a cash or deferred election) in plan years beginning on or after July 1, 2007, a cash or deferred arrangement satisfies this paragraph (e) only if cash or deferred elections can only be made with respect to amounts that are compensation within the meaning of section 415(c)(3) and § 1.415(c)-2. Thus, for example, the arrangement is not a qualified cash or deferred arrangement if an eligible employee who is not in qualified military service (as that term is defined in section 414(u)) and who is not permanently and totally disabled (as defined in section 22(e)(3)) can make a cash or deferred election with respect to an amount paid after severance from employment, unless the amount is paid by the later of 2½ months after severance from employment or the end of the year that includes the date of severance from employment and is described in § 1.415(c)-2(e)(3)(ii) or (iii).

**(f) Special rules for designated Roth contributions.** *(1) In general.* The term designated Roth contribution means an elective contribution under a qualified cash or deferred arrangement that, to the extent permitted under the plan, is--

(i) Designated irrevocably by the employee at the time of the cash or deferred election as a designated Roth contribution that is being made in lieu of all or a portion of the pretax elective contributions the employee is otherwise eligible to make under the plan;

(ii) Treated by the employer as not excludible from the employee's gross income (in accordance with paragraph (f)(2) of this section);

(iii) Maintained by the plan in a separate account (in accordance with paragraph (f)(3) of this section).

*(2) Inclusion treatment.* An elective contribution is generally treated as not excludible from gross income if it is treated as includible in gross income by the employer (e.g., by treating the contribution as wages subject to applicable income tax withholding). However, in the case of a self-employed individual, an elective contribution is treated as not excludible from gross income only if the individual does not claim a deduction for such amount. If an elective contribution would not have been includible in gross income if the amount had been paid directly to the employee (rather than being subject to a cash or deferral election), the elective contribution is nevertheless permitted to be a designated Roth

contribution, provided the employee is entitled to treat the amount as an investment in the contract pursuant to section 72(f)(2).

*(3) Separate accounting required.* Under the separate accounting requirement of this paragraph (f)(3), contributions and withdrawals of designated Roth contributions must be credited and debited to a designated Roth account maintained for the employee and the plan must maintain a record of the employee's investment in the contract (that is, designated Roth contributions that have not been distributed) with respect to the employee's designated Roth account. In addition, gains, losses, and other credits or charges must be separately allocated on a reasonable and consistent basis to the designated Roth account and other accounts under the plan. However, forfeitures may not be allocated to the designated Roth account and no contributions other than designated Roth contributions and rollover contributions described in section 402A(c)(3)(B) may be allocated to such account. The separate accounting requirement applies at the time the designated Roth contribution is contributed to the plan and must continue to apply until the designated Roth account is completely distributed. See A-13 of § 1.402A-1 for additional requirements for separate accounting.

*(4) Designated Roth contributions must satisfy rules applicable to elective contributions.* (i) In general. A designated Roth contribution must satisfy the requirements applicable to elective contributions made under a qualified cash or deferred arrangement. Thus, for example, a designated Roth contribution must satisfy the requirements of paragraphs (c) and (d) of this section and is treated as an employer contribution for purposes of sections 401(a), 401(k), 402, 404, 409, 411, 412, 415, 416 and 417. In addition, the designated Roth contributions are treated as elective contributions for purposes of the ADP test. Similarly, the designated Roth account under the plan is subject to the rules of section 401(a)(9)(A) and (B) in the same manner as an account that contains pre-tax elective contributions.

(ii) Special rules for direct rollovers. A direct rollover from a designated Roth account under a qualified cash or deferred arrangement may only be made to another designated Roth account under an applicable retirement plan described in section 402A(e)(1) or to a Roth IRA described in section 408A, and only to the extent the rollover is permitted under the rules of section 402(c). Moreover, a participant's designated Roth account and the participant's other accounts under a plan are treated as accounts held under two separate plans (within the meaning of section 414(l)) for purposes of applying the automatic rollover rules for mandatory distributions under section 401(a)(31)(B)(i)(I) and the special rules in A-9 through A-11 of § 1.401(a)(31)-1.

*(5) Rules regarding designated Roth contribution elections.* (i) Frequency of elections. The rules under paragraph (e)(2)(ii) of this section regarding frequency of elections apply in the same manner to both pre-tax elective contributions and designated Roth contributions. Thus, an employee must have an effective opportunity to make (or change) an election to make designated Roth contributions at least once during each plan year.

(ii) Default elections. (A) In the case of a plan that provides for both pre-tax elective contributions and designated Roth contributions and in which, under paragraph (a)(3)(ii) of this section, the default in the absence of an affirmative election is to make a contribution under the cash or deferred arrangement, the plan terms must provide the extent to which the default contributions are pre-tax elective contributions and the extent to which the default contributions are designated Roth contributions.

(B) If the default contributions under the plan are designated Roth contributions, then an employee who has not made an affirmative election is deemed to have irrevocably designated the contributions (in accordance with section 402A(c)(1)(B)) as designated Roth contributions.

*(6) Effective date.* Section 402A and the provisions of this section 1.401(k)-1(f) apply to taxable years beginning after December 31, 2005.

**(g) Effective dates.** *(1) General rule.* Except as otherwise provided in this paragraph (g), this section and §§ 1.401(k)-2 through 1.401(k)-6 apply to plan years that begin on or after January 1, 2006.

*(2) Early implementation permitted.* A plan is permitted to apply the rules of this section and §§ 1.401(k)-2 through 1.401(k)-6 to any plan year that ends after December 29, 2004, provided the plan applies all the rules of this section and §§ 1.401(k)-2 through 1.401(k)-6 and all the rules of §§ 1.401(m)-1 through 1.401(m)-5, to the extent applicable, for that plan year and all subsequent plan years.

*(3) Collectively bargained plans.* In the case of a plan maintained pursuant to one or more collective bargaining agreements between employee representatives and one or more employers in effect on the date described in paragraph (g)(1) of this section, the provisions of this section and §§ 1.401(k)-2 through 1.401(k)-6 apply to the later of the first plan year beginning after the termination of the last such agreement or the first plan year described in paragraph (g)(1) of this section.

*(4) Applicability of prior regulations.* For any plan year before a plan applies this section and §§ 1.401(k)-2 through 1.401(k)-6 (either the first plan year beginning on or after January 1, 2006, or such earlier year, as provided in paragraph (g)(2) of this section), § 1.401(k)-1 (as it appeared in the April 1, 2004 edition of 26 CFR part 1) applies to the plan to the extent that section, as it so appears, reflects the statutory provisions of section 401(k) as in effect for the relevant year.

T.D. 8217, 8/8/88, amend T.D. 8357, 8/9/91, T.D. 8376, 12/2/91, T.D. 8581, 12/22/94, T.D. 9169, 12/28/2004, T.D. 9237, 12/30/2005, T.D. 9319, 4/4/2007, T.D. 9324, 4/27/2007, T.D. 9447, 2/23/2009.

## § 1.401(k)-2 ADP test.

**(a) Actual deferral percentage (ADP) test.** *(1) In general.* (i) ADP test formula. A cash or deferred arrangement satisfies the ADP test for a plan year only if—

(A) The ADP for the eligible HCEs for the plan year is not more than the ADP for the eligible NHCEs for the applicable year multiplied by 1.25; or

(B) The excess of the ADP for the eligible HCEs for the plan year over the ADP for the eligible NHCEs for the applicable year is not more than 2 percentage points, and the ADP for the eligible HCEs for the plan year is not more than the ADP for the eligible NHCEs for the applicable year multiplied by 2.

(ii) HCEs as sole eligible employees. If, for the applicable year for determining the ADP of the NHCEs for a plan year, there are no eligible NHCEs (i.e., all of the eligible employees under the cash or deferred arrangement for the applicable year are HCEs), the arrangement is deemed to satisfy the ADP test for the plan year.

(iii) Special rule for early participation. If a cash or deferred arrangement provides that employees are eligible to participate before they have completed the minimum age and service requirements of section 410(a)(1)(A), and if the plan applies section 410(b)(4)(B) in determining whether the cash or deferred arrangement meets the requirements of section 410(b)(1), then in determining whether the arrangement meets the requirements under paragraph (a)(1) of this section, either—

(A) Pursuant to section 401(k)(3)(F), the ADP test is performed under the plan (determined without regard to disaggregation under § 1.410(b)-7(c)(3)), using the ADP for all eligible HCEs for the plan year and the ADP of eligible NHCEs for the applicable year, disregarding all NHCEs who have not met the minimum age and service requirements of section 410(a)(1)(A); or

(B) Pursuant to § 1.401(k)-1(b)(4), the plan is disaggregated into separate plans and the ADP test is performed separately for all eligible employees who have completed the minimum age and service requirements of section 410(a)(1)(A) and for all eligible employees who have not completed the minimum age and service requirements of section 410(a)(1)(A).

*(2) Determination of ADP.* (i) General rule. The ADP for a group of eligible employees (either eligible HCEs or eligible NHCEs) for a plan year or applicable year is the average of the ADRs of the eligible employees in that group for that year. The ADP for a group of eligible employees is calculated to the nearest hundredth of a percentage point.

(ii) Determination of applicable year under current year and prior year testing method. The ADP test is applied using the prior year testing method or the current year testing method. Under the prior year testing method, the applicable year for determining the ADP for the eligible NHCEs is the plan year immediately preceding the plan year for which the ADP test is being performed. Under the prior year testing method, the ADP for the eligible NHCEs is determined using the ADRs for the eligible employees who were NHCEs in that preceding plan year, regardless of whether those NHCEs are eligible employees or NHCEs in the plan year for which the ADP test is being calculated. Under the current year testing method, the applicable year for determining the ADP for the eligible NHCEs is the same plan year as the plan year for which the ADP test is being performed. Under either method, the ADP for eligible HCEs is the average of the ADRs of the eligible HCEs for the plan year for which the ADP test is being performed. See paragraph (c) of this section for additional rules for the prior year testing method.

*(3) Determination of ADR.* (i) General rule. The ADR of an eligible employee for a plan year or applicable year is the sum of the employee's elective contributions taken into account with respect to such employee for the year, determined under the rules of paragraphs (a)(4) and (5) of this section, and the qualified nonelective contributions and qualified matching contributions taken into account with respect to such employee under paragraph (a)(6) of this section for the year, divided by the employee's compensation taken into account for the year. The ADR is calculated to the nearest hundredth of a percentage point. If no elective contributions, qualified nonelective contributions, or qualified matching contributions are taken into account under this section with respect to an eligible employee for the year, the ADR of the employee is zero.

(ii) ADR of HCEs eligible under more than one arrangement. (A) General rule. Pursuant to section 401(k)(3)(A), the ADR of an HCE who is an eligible employee in more than one cash or deferred arrangement of the same employer is calculated by treating all contributions with respect to such HCE under any such arrangement as being made under the cash or deferred arrangement being tested. Thus, the ADR for such an HCE is calculated by accumulating all contributions under any cash or deferred arrangement (other than a cash or deferred arrangement described in paragraph (a)(3)(ii)(B) of this section) that would be taken into account under this section for the plan year, if the cash or deferred arrangement under which the contribution was made applied this section and had the same plan year. For example, in the case of a plan with a 12-month plan year, the ADR for the plan year of that plan for an HCE who participates in multiple cash or deferred arrangements of the same employer is the sum of all contributions during such 12-month period that would be taken into account with respect to the HCE under all such arrangements in which the HCE is an eligible employee, divided by the HCE's compensation for that 12-month period (determined using the compensation definition for the plan being tested), without regard to the plan year of the other plans and whether those plans are satisfying this section or § 1.401(k)-3.

(B) Plans not permitted to be aggregated. Cash or deferred arrangements under plans that are not permitted to be aggregated under § 1.401(k)-1(b)(4) (determined without regard to the prohibition on aggregating plans with inconsistent testing methods set forth in § 1.401(k)-1(b)(4)(iii)(B) and the prohibition on aggregating plans with different plan years set forth in § 1.410(b)-7(d)(5)) are not aggregated under this paragraph (a)(3)(ii).

(iii) Examples. The following examples illustrate the application of this paragraph (a)(3):

*Example (1).* (i) Employee A, an HCE with compensation of $120,000, is eligible to make elective contributions under Plan S and Plan T, two profit-sharing plans maintained by Employer H with calendar year plan years, each of which includes a cash or deferred arrangement. During the current plan year, Employee A makes elective contributions of $6,000 to Plan S and $4,000 to Plan T.

(ii) Under each plan, the ADR for Employee A is determined by dividing Employee A's total elective contributions under both arrangements by Employee A's compensation taken into account under the plan for the year. Therefore, Employee A's ADR under each plan is 8.33% ($10,000/$120,000).

*Example (2).* (i) The facts are the same as in Example 1, except that Plan T defines compensation (for deferral and testing purposes) to exclude all bonuses paid to an employee. Plan S defines compensation (for deferral and testing purposes) to include bonuses paid to an employee. During the current year, Employee A's compensation included a $10,000 bonus. Therefore, Employee A's compensation under Plan T is $110,000 and Employee A's compensation under Plan S is $120,000.

(ii) Employee A's ADR under Plan T is 9.09% ($10,000/$110,000) and under Plan S, Employee A's ADR is 8.33% ($10,000/$120,000).

*Example (3).* (i) Employer J sponsors two profit-sharing plans, Plan U and Plan V, each of which includes a cash or deferred arrangement. Plan U's plan year begins on July 1 and ends on June 30. Plan V has a calendar year plan year. Compensation under both plans is limited to the participant's compensation during the period of participation. Employee B is an HCE who participates in both plans. Employee B's monthly compensation and elective contributions to each plan for the 2005 and 2006 calendar years are as follows:

| Calendar year | Monthly compensation | Monthly elective contribution to Plan U | Monthly elective contribution to Plan V |
|---|---|---|---|
| 2005 . . . . . . . . . . . . . . . . . . . . . . . . . . . . | $10,000 | $500 | $400 |
| 2006 . . . . . . . . . . . . . . . . . . . . . . . . . . . . | 11,500 | 700 | 550 |

(ii) Under Plan U, Employee B's ADR for the plan year ended June 30, 2006, is equal to Employee B's total elective contributions under Plan U and Plan V for the plan year ending June 30, 2006, divided by Employee B's compensation for that period. Therefore, Employee B's ADR under Plan U for the plan year ending June 30, 2006, is (($900 x 6) + ($1,250 x 6)) / (($10,000 x 6) + ($11,500 x 6)), or 10%.

(iii) Under Plan V, Employee B's ADR for the plan year ended December 31, 2005, is equal to total elective contributions under Plan U and V for the plan year ending December 31, 2005, divided by Employee B's compensation for that period. Therefore, Employee B's ADR under Plan V for the plan year ending December 31, 2005, is ($10,800/$120,000), or 9%.

*Example (4).* (i) The facts are the same as Example 3, except that Employee B first becomes eligible to participate in Plan U on January 1, 2006.

(ii) Under Plan U, Employee B's ADR for the plan year ended June 30, 2006, is equal to Employee B's total elective contributions under Plan U and V for the plan year ending June 30, 2006, divided by Employee B's compensation for that period. Therefore, Employee B's ADR under Plan U for the plan year ending June 30, 2006, is (($400 x 6) + ($1,250 x 6)) / (($10,000 x 6) + ($11,500 x 6)), or 7.67%.

*(4) Elective contributions taken into account under the ADP test.* (i) General rule. An elective contribution is taken into account in determining the ADR for an eligible employee for a plan year or applicable year only if each of the following requirements is satisfied—

(A) The elective contribution is allocated to the eligible employee's account under the plan as of a date within that year. For purposes of this rule, an elective contribution is considered allocated as of a date within a year only if—

(1) The allocation is not contingent on the employee's participation in the plan or performance of services on any date subsequent to that date; and

(2) The elective contribution is actually paid to the trust no later than the end of the 12-month period immediately following the year to which the contribution relates.

(B) The elective contribution relates to compensation that either—

(1) Would have been received by the employee in the year but for the employee's election to defer under the arrangement; or

(2) Is attributable to services performed by the employee in the year and, but for the employee's election to defer, would have been received by the employee within 2½ months after the close of the year, but only if the plan provides for elective contributions that relate to compensation that would have been received after the close of a year to be allocated to such prior year rather than the year in which the compensation would have been received.

(ii) Elective contributions for partners and self-employed individuals. For purposes of this paragraph (a)(4), a partner's distributive share of partnership income is treated as received on the last day of the partnership taxable year and a sole proprietor's compensation is treated as received on the last day of the individual's taxable year. Thus, an elective contribution made on behalf of a partner or sole proprietor is treated as allocated to the partner's account for the plan year that includes the last day of the partnership taxable year, provided the requirements of paragraph (a)(4)(i) of this section are met.

(iii) Elective contributions for HCEs. Elective contributions of an HCE must include any excess deferrals, as described in § 1.402(g)-1(a), even if those excess deferrals are distributed, pursuant to § 1.402(g)-1(e).

*(5) Elective contributions not taken into account under the ADP test.* (i) General rule. Elective contributions that do not satisfy the requirements of paragraph (a)(4)(i) of this section may not be taken into account in determining the ADR of an eligible employee for the plan year or applicable year with respect to which the contributions were made, or for any other plan year. Instead, the amount of the elective contributions must satisfy the requirements of section 401(a)(4) (without regard to the ADP test) for the plan year for which they are allocated under the plan as if they were nonelective contributions and were the only nonelective contributions for that year. See §§ 1.401(a)(4)-1(b)(2)(ii)(B) and 1.410(b)-7(c)(1).

(ii) Elective contributions for NHCEs. Elective contributions of an NHCE shall not include any excess deferrals, as described in § 1.402(g)-1(a), to the extent the excess deferrals are prohibited under section 401(a)(30). However, to the extent that the excess deferrals are not prohibited under section 401(a)(30), they are included in elective contributions even if distributed pursuant to § 1.402(g)-1(e).

(iii) Elective contributions treated as catch-up contributions. Elective contributions that are treated as catch-up contributions under section 414(v) because they exceed a statutory limit or employer-provided limit (within the meaning of § 1.414(v)-1(b)(1)) are not taken into account under paragraph (a)(4) of this section for the plan year for which the contributions were made, or for any other plan year.

(iv) Elective contributions used to satisfy the ACP test. Except to the extent necessary to demonstrate satisfaction of the requirement of § 1.401(m)-2(a)(6)(ii), elective contributions taken into account for the ACP test under § 1.401(m)-2(a)(6) are not taken into account under paragraph (a)(4) of this section.

(v) Additional elective contributions pursuant to section 414(u). Additional elective contributions made pursuant to section 414(u) by reason of an eligible employee's qualified military service are not taken into account under paragraph (a)(4) of this section for the plan year for which the contributions are made, or for any other plan year.

(vi) Default elective contributions pursuant to section 414(w). Default elective contributions made under an eligible automatic contribution arrangement (within the meaning of § 1.414(w)-1(b)) that are distributed pursuant to § 1.414(w)-1(c) for plan years beginning on or after January 1, 2008, are not taken into account under paragraph (a)(4) of this section for the plan year for which the contributions are made, or for any other plan year.

*(6) Qualified nonelective contributions and qualified matching contributions that may be taken into account under the ADP test.* Qualified nonelective contributions and qualified matching contributions may be taken into account in determining the ADR for an eligible employee for a plan year or applicable year but only to the extent the contributions satisfy the following requirements—

(i) Timing of allocation. The qualified nonelective contribution or qualified matching contribution is allocated to the employee's account as of a date within that year within the meaning of paragraph (a)(4)(i)(A) of this section. Consequently, under the prior year testing method, in order to be taken into account in calculating the ADP for the eligible NHCEs for the applicable year, a qualified nonelective contribution or qualified matching contribution must be contributed no later than the end of the 12-month period immediately following the applicable year even though the applicable year is different than the plan year being tested.

(ii) Requirement that amount satisfy section 401(a)(4). The amount of nonelective contributions, including those qualified nonelective contributions taken into account under this paragraph (a)(6) and those qualified nonelective contributions taken into account for the ACP test of section 401(m)(2) under § 1.401(m)-2(a)(6), satisfies the requirements of section 401(a)(4). See § 1.401(a)(4)-1(b)(2). The amount of nonelective contributions, excluding those qualified nonelective contributions taken into account under this paragraph (a)(6) and those qualified nonelective contributions taken into account for the ACP test of section 401(m)(2) under § 1.401(m)-2(a)(6), satisfies the requirements of section 401(a)(4). See § 1.401(a)(4)-1(b)(2). In the case of an employer that is applying the special rule for employer-wide plans in § 1.414(r)-1(c)(2)(ii) with respect to the cash or deferred arrangement, the determination of whether the qualified nonelective contributions satisfy the requirements of this paragraph (a)(6)(ii) must be made on an employer-wide basis regardless of whether the plans to which the qualified nonelective contributions are made are satisfying the requirements of section 410(b) on an employer-wide basis. Conversely, in the case of an employer that is treated as operating qualified separate lines of business, and does not apply the special rule for employer-wide plans in § 1.414(r)-1(c)(2)(ii) with respect to the cash or deferred arrangement, then the determination of whether the qualified nonelective contributions satisfy the requirements of this paragraph (a)(6)(ii) is not permitted to be made on an employer-wide basis regardless of whether the plans to which the qualified nonelective contributions are made are satisfying the requirements of section 410(b) on that basis.

(iii) Aggregation must be permitted. The plan that contains the cash or deferred arrangement and the plan or plans to which the qualified nonelective contributions or qualified matching contributions are made, are plans that would be permitted to be aggregated under § 1.401(k)-1(b)(4). If the plan year of the plan that contains the cash or deferred arrangement is changed to satisfy the requirement under § 1.410(b)-7(d)(5) that aggregated plans have the same plan year, qualified nonelective contributions and qualified matching contributions may be taken into account in the resulting short plan year only if such qualified nonelective contributions and qualified matching contributions could have been taken into account under an ADP test for a plan with the same short plan year.

(iv) Disproportionate contributions not taken into account. (A) General rule. Qualified nonelective contributions cannot be taken into account for a plan year for an NHCE to the extent such contributions exceed the product of that NHCE's compensation and the greater of 5% or two times the plan's representative contribution rate. Any qualified nonelective contribution taken into account under an ACP test under § 1.401(m)-2(a)(6) (including the determination of the representative contribution rate for purposes of § 1.401(m)-2(a)(6)(v)(B)), is not permitted to be taken into account for purposes of this paragraph (a)(6) (including the determination of the representative contribution rate under paragraph (a)(6)(iv)(B) of this section).

(B) Definition of representative contribution rate. For purposes of this paragraph (a)(6)(iv), the plan's representative contribution rate is the lowest applicable contribution rate of any eligible NHCE among a group of eligible NHCEs that consists of half of all eligible NHCEs for the plan year (or, if greater, the lowest applicable contribution rate of any eligible NHCE in the group of all eligible NHCEs for the plan year and who is employed by the employer on the last day of the plan year).

(C) Definition of applicable contribution rate. For purposes of this paragraph (a)(6)(iv), the applicable contribution rate for an eligible NHCE is the sum of the qualified matching contributions taken into account under this paragraph (a)(6) for the eligible NHCE for the plan year and the qualified nonelective contributions made for the eligible NHCE for the plan year, divided by the eligible NHCE's compensation for the same period.

(D) Special rule for prevailing wage contributions. Notwithstanding paragraph (a)(6)(iv)(A) of this section, qualified nonelective contributions that are made in connection with an employer's obligation to pay prevailing wages under the Davis-Bacon Act (46 Stat. 1494), Public Law 71-798, Service Contract Act of 1965 (79 Stat. 1965), Public Law 89-286, or similar legislation can be taken into account for a plan year for an NHCE to the extent such contributions do not exceed 10 percent of that NHCE's compensation.

(v) Qualified matching contributions. Qualified matching contributions satisfy this paragraph (a)(6) only to the extent that such qualified matching contributions are matching contributions that are not precluded from being taken into account under the ACP test for the plan year under the rules of § 1.401(m)-2(a)(5)(ii).

(vi) Contributions only used once. Qualified nonelective contributions and qualified matching contributions cannot be taken into account under this paragraph (a)(6) to the extent such contributions are taken into account for purposes of satisfying any other ADP test, any ACP test, or the requirements of § 1.401(k)-3, 1.401(m)-3 or 1.401(k)-4. Thus, for example, matching contributions that are made pursuant to § 1.401(k)-3(c) cannot be taken into account under the ADP test. Similarly, if a plan switches from the current year testing method to the prior year testing method pursuant to § 1.401(k)-2(c), qualified nonelective contributions that are taken into account under the current year testing method for a year may not be taken into account under the prior year testing method for the next year.

*(7) Examples.* The following examples illustrate the application of this paragraph (a):

*Example (1).* (i) Employer X has three employees, A, B, and C. Employer X sponsors a profit-sharing plan (Plan Z) that includes a cash or deferred arrangement. Each year, Employer X determines a bonus attributable to the prior year. Under the cash or deferred arrangement, each eligible employee may elect to receive none, all or any part of the bonus in cash. X contributes the remainder to Plan Z. The portion of the bonus paid in cash, if any, is paid 2 months after the end of the plan year and thus is included in compensation for the following plan year. Employee A is an HCE, while Employees B and C are NHCEs. The plan uses the current year testing method and defines compensation to include elective contributions and bonuses paid during each plan year. In February of 2005, Employer X determined that no bonuses will be paid for 2004. In February of 2006, Employer X provided a bonus for each employee equal to 10% of regular compensation for 2005. For the 2005 plan year, A, B, and C have the following compensation and make the following elections:

| Employee | Compensation | Elective contribution |
|---|---|---|
| A | $100,000 | $4,340 |
| B | 60,000 | 2,860 |
| C | 45,000 | 1,250 |

(ii) For each employee, the ratio of elective contributions to the employee's compensation for the plan year is:

| Employee | Ratio of elective contribution to compensation | ADR (percent) |
|---|---|---|
| A | $4,340/$100,000 | 4.34 |
| B | 2,860/60,000 | 4.77 |
| C | 1,250/45,000 | 2.78 |

(iii) The ADP for the HCEs (Employee A) is 4.34%. The ADP for the NHCEs is 3.78% ((4.77% + 2.78%)/2). Because 4.34% is less than 4.73% (3.78% multiplied by 1.25), the plan satisfies the ADP test under paragraph (a)(1)(i) of this section.

*Example (2).* (i) The facts are the same as in Example 1, except that elective contributions are made pursuant to a salary reduction agreement throughout the plan year, and no bonuses are paid. As provided by section 414(s)(2), Employer X includes elective contributions in compensation. During the year, B and C defer the same amount as in Example 1, but A defers $5,770. Thus, the compensation and elective contributions for A, B, and C are:

| Employee | Compensation | Elective contributions | ADR (percent) |
|---|---|---|---|
| A | $100,000 | $5,770 | 5.77 |
| B | 60,000 | 2,860 | 4.77 |
| C | 45,000 | 1,250 | 2.78 |

(ii) The ADP for the HCEs (Employee A) is 5.77%. The ADP for the NHCEs is 3.78% ((4.77% + 2.78%)/2). Because 5.77% exceeds 4.73% (3.78% x 1.25), the plan does not satisfy the ADP test under paragraph (a)(1)(i) of this section. However, because the ADP for the HCEs does not exceed the ADP for the NHCEs by more than 2 percentage points and the ADP for the HCEs does not exceed the ADP for the NHCEs multiplied by 2 (3.78% x 2 = 7.56%), the plan satisfies the ADP test under paragraph (a)(1)(ii) of this section.

*Example (3).* (i) Employees D through L are eligible employees in Plan T, a profit-sharing plan that contains a cash or deferred arrangement. The plan is a calendar year plan that uses the prior year testing method. Plan T provides that elective contributions are included in compensation (as provided under section 414(s)(2)). Each eligible employee may elect to defer up to 6% of compensation under the cash or deferred arrangement. Employees D and E are HCEs. The compensation, elective contributions, and ADRs of Employees D and E for the 2006 plan year are shown below:

| Employee | Compensation for 2006 plan year | Elective contributions for 2006 plan year | ADR for 2006 plan year (percent) |
|---|---|---|---|
| D | $100,000 | $10,000 | 10 |
| E | 95,000 | 4,750 | 5 |

(ii) During the 2005 plan year, Employees F through L were eligible NHCEs. The compensation, elective contributions and ADRs of Employees F through L for the 2005 plan year are shown in the following table:

| Employee | Compensation for 2005 plan year | Elective contributions for 2005 plan year | ADR for 2005 plan year (percent) |
|---|---|---|---|
| F | $60,000 | $3,600 | 6 |
| G | 40,000 | 1,600 | 4 |
| H | 30,000 | 1,200 | 4 |
| I | 20,000 | 600 | 3 |
| J | 20,000 | 600 | 3 |
| K | 10,000 | 300 | 3 |
| L | 5,000 | 150 | 3 |

(iii) The ADP for 2006 for the HCEs is 7.5%. Because Plan T is using the prior year testing method, the applicable year for determining the NHCE ADP is the prior plan year (i.e., 2005). The NHCE ADP is determined using the ADRs for NHCEs eligible during the prior plan year (without regard to whether they are eligible under the plan during the plan year). The ADP for the NHCEs is 3.71% (the sum of the individual ADRs, 26%, divided by 7 employees). Because 7.5% exceeds 4.64% (3.71% x 1.25), Plan T does not satisfy the ADP test under paragraph (a)(1)(i) of this section. In addition, because the ADP for the HCEs exceeds the ADP for the NHCEs by more than 2 percentage points, Plan T does not satisfy the ADP test under paragraph (a)(1)(ii) of this section. Therefore, the cash or deferred arrangement fails to be a qualified cash or deferred arrangement unless the ADP failure is corrected under paragraph (b) of this section.

*Example (4)*. (i) Plan U is a calendar year profit-sharing plan that contains a cash or deferred arrangement and uses the current year testing method. Plan U provides that elective contributions are included in compensation (as provided under section 414(s)(2)). The following amounts are contributed under Plan U for the 2006 plan year: QNECs equal to 2% of each employee's compensation; Contributions equal to 6% of each employee's compensation that are not immediately vested under the terms of the plan; 3% of each employee's compensation that the employee may elect to receive as cash or to defer under the plan. Both types of nonelective contributions are made for the HCEs (employees M and N) and the NHCEs (employees O through S) for the plan year and are contributed after the end of the plan year and before the end of the following plan year. In addition, neither type of nonelective contributions is used for any other ADP or ACP test.

(ii) For the 2006 plan year, the compensation, elective contributions, and actual deferral ratios of employees M through S are shown in the following table:

| Employee | Compensation | Elective contributions | Actual deferral ratio (percent) |
|---|---|---|---|
| M | $100,000 | $3,000 | 3 |
| N | 100,000 | 2,000 | 2 |
| O | 60,000 | 1,800 | 3 |
| P | 40,000 | 0 | 0 |
| Q | 30,000 | 0 | 0 |
| R | 5,000 | 0 | 0 |
| S | 20,000 | 0 | 0 |

(iii) The elective contributions alone do not satisfy the ADP test of section 401(k)(3) and paragraph (a)(1) of this section because the ADP for the HCEs, consisting of employees M and N, is 2.5% and the ADP for the NHCEs is 0.6%.

(iv) The 2% QNECs satisfies the timing requirement of paragraph (a)(6)(i) of this section because it is paid within 12-month after the plan year for which allocated. All nonelective contributions also satisfy the requirements relating to section 401(a)(4) set forth in paragraph (a)(6)(ii) of this section (because all employees receive an 8% nonelective contribution and the nonelective contributions excluding the QNECs is 6% for all employees). In addition, the QNECs are not disproportionate under paragraph (a)(6)(iv) of this section because no QNEC for an NHCE exceeds the product of the plan's applicable contribution rate (2%) and that NHCE's compensation.

(v) Because the rules of paragraph (a)(6) of this section are satisfied, the 2% QNECs may be taken into account in applying the ADP test of section 401(k)(3) and paragraph (a)(1) of this section. The 6% nonelective contributions, however, may not be taken into account because they are not QNECs.

(vi) If the 2% QNECs are taken into account, the ADP for the HCEs is 4.5%, and the actual deferral percentage for the NHCEs is 2.6%. Because 4.5% is not more than two percentage points greater than 2.6 percent, and not more than two times 2.6, the cash or deferred arrangement satisfies the ADP test of section 401(k)(3) under paragraph (a)(1)(ii) of this section.

*Example (5).* (i) The facts are the same as Example 4, except the plan uses the prior year testing method. In addition, the NHCE ADP for the 2005 plan year (the prior plan year) is 0.8% and no QNECs are contributed for the 2005 plan year during 2005 or 2006.

(ii) In 2007, it is determined that the elective contributions alone do not satisfy the ADP test of section 401(k)(3) and paragraph (a)(1) of this section for 2006 because the 2006 ADP for the eligible HCEs, consisting of employees M and N, is 2.5% and the 2005 ADP for the eligible NHCEs is 0.8%. An additional QNEC of 2% of compensation is made for each eligible NHCE in 2007 and allocated for 2005.

(iii) The 2% QNECs that are made in 2007 and allocated for the 2005 plan year do not satisfy the timing requirement of paragraph (a)(6)(i) of this section for the applicable year for the 2005 plan year because they were not contributed before the last day of the 2006 plan year. Accordingly, the 2% QNECs do not satisfy the rules of paragraph (a)(6) of this section and may not be taken into account in applying the ADP test of section 401(k)(3) and paragraph (a)(1) of this section for the 2006 plan year. The cash or deferred arrangement fails to be a qualified cash or deferred arrangement unless the ADP failure is corrected under paragraph (b) of this section.

*Example (6).* (i) The facts are the same as Example 4, except that the ADP for the HCEs is 4.6% and there is no 6% nonelective contribution under the plan. The employer would like to take into account the 2% QNEC in determining the ADP for the NHCEs but not in determining the ADP for the HCEs.

(ii) The elective contributions alone fail the requirements of section 401(k) and paragraph (a)(1) of this section because the HCE ADP for the plan year (4.6%) exceeds 0.75% (0.6% x 1.25) and 1.2% (0.6% x 2).

(iii) The 2% QNECs may not be taken into account in determining the ADP of the NHCEs because they fail to satisfy the requirements relating to section 401(a)(4) set forth in paragraph (a)(6)(ii) of this section. This is because the amount of nonelective contributions, excluding those QNECs that would be taken into account under the ADP test, would be 2% of compensation for the HCEs and 0% for the NHCEs. Therefore, the cash or deferred arrangement fails to be a qualified cash or deferred arrangement unless the ADP failure is corrected under paragraph (b) of this section.

*Example (7).* (i) The facts are the same as Example 6, except that Employee R receives a QNEC in an amount of $500 and no QNECs are made on behalf of the other employees.

(ii) If the QNEC could be taken into account under paragraph (a)(6) of this section, the ADP for the NHCEs would be 2.6% and the plan would satisfy the ADP test. The QNEC is disproportionate under paragraph (a)(6)(iv) of this section, and cannot be taken into account under paragraph (a)(6) of this section, to the extent it exceeds the greater of 5% and two times the plan's representative contribution rate (0%), multiplied by Employee R's compensation. The plan's representative contribution rate is 0% because it is the lowest applicable contribution rate among a group of NHCEs that is at least half of all NHCEs, or all the NHCEs who are employed on the last day of the plan year. Therefore, the QNEC may be taken into account under the ADP test only to the extent it does not exceed 5% times Employee R's compensation (or $250) and the cash or deferred arrangement fails to satisfy the ADP test and must correct under paragraph (b) of this section.

*Example (8).* (i) The facts are the same as in Example 4 except that the plan changes from the current year testing method to the prior year testing method for the following plan year (2007 plan year). The ADP for the HCEs for the 2007 plan year is 3.5%.

(ii) The 2% QNECs may not be taken into account in determining the ADP for the NHCEs for the applicable year (2006 plan year) in satisfying the ADP test for the 2007 plan year because they were taken into account in satisfying the ADP test for the 2006 plan year. Accordingly, the NHCE ADP for the applicable year is 0.6%. The elective contributions for the plan year fail the requirements of section 401(k) and paragraph (a)(1) of this section because the HCE ADP for the plan year (3.5%) exceeds the ADP limit of 1.2% (the greater of 0.75% (0.6% x 1.25) and 1.2% (0.6% x 2)), determined using the applicable year ADP for the NHCEs. Therefore, the cash or deferred arrangement fails to be a qualified cash or deferred arrangement unless the ADP failure is corrected under paragraph (b) of this section.

*Example (9).* (i) (A) Employer N maintains Plan X, a profit sharing plan that contains a cash or deferred arrangement and that uses the current year testing method. Plan X provides for employee contributions, elective contributions, and matching contributions. Matching contributions on behalf of NHCEs are qualified matching contributions (QMACs) and are contributed during the 2005 plan year. Matching contributions on behalf of HCEs are not QMACs, because they fail to satisfy the nonforfeitability requirement of § 1.401(k)-1(c). The elective contributions and matching contributions with respect to HCEs for the 2005 plan year are shown in the following table:

| | Elective contributions | Total matching contributions | Matching contributions that are not QMACs | QMACs |
|---|---|---|---|---|
| Highly compensated employees .............. | 15% | 5% | 5% | 0% |

(B) The elective contributions and matching contributions with respect to the NHCEs for the 2005 plan year are shown in the following table:

| | Elective contributions | Total matching contributions | Matching contributions that are not QMACs | QMACs |
|---|---|---|---|---|
| Nonhighly compensated employees ........... | 11% | 4% | 0% | 4% |

(ii) The plan fails to satisfy the ADP test of section 401(k)(3)(A) and paragraph (a)(1) of this section because the ADP for HCEs (15%) is more than 125% of the ADP for NHCEs (11%), and more than 2 percentage points greater than 11%. However, the plan provides that QMACs may be used to meet the requirements of section 401(k)(3)(A)(ii) provided that they are not used for any other ADP or ACP test. QMACs equal to 1% of compensation are taken into account for each NHCE in applying the ADP test. After this adjustment, the applicable ADP and ACP (taking into account the provisions of § 1.401(m)-2(a)(5)(ii)) for the plan year are as follows:

| | Actual deferral percentage | Actual contribution percentage |
|---|---|---|
| HCEs.................................... | 15 | 5 |
| Nonhighly compensated employees ........... | 12 | 3 |

(iii) The elective contributions and QMACs taken into account for purposes of the ADP test of section 401(k)(3) satisfy the requirements of section 401(k)(3)(A)(ii) under paragraph (a)(1)(ii) of this section because the ADP for HCEs (15%) is not more than the ADP for NHCEs multiplied by 1.25 (12% x 1.25 = 15%).

**(b) Correction of excess contributions.** *(1) Permissible correction methods.* (i) In general. A cash or deferred arrangement does not fail to satisfy the requirements of section 401(k)(3) and paragraph (a)(1) of this section if the employer, in accordance with the terms of the plan that includes the cash or deferred arrangement, uses any of the following correction methods—

(A) Qualified nonelective contributions or qualified matching contributions. The employer makes qualified nonelective contributions or qualified matching contributions that are taken into account under this section and, in combination with other amounts taken into account under paragraph (a) of this section, allow the cash or deferred arrangement to satisfy the requirements of paragraph (a)(1) of this section.

(B) Excess contributions distributed. Excess contributions are distributed in accordance with paragraph (b)(2) of this section.

(C) Excess contributions recharacterized. Excess contributions are recharacterized in accordance with paragraph (b)(3) of this section.

(ii) Combination of correction methods. A plan may provide for the use of any of the correction methods described in paragraph (b)(1)(i) of this section, may limit elective contributions in a manner designed to prevent excess contributions from being made, or may use a combination of these methods, to avoid or correct excess contributions. Similarly, a plan may permit an HCE with elective contributions for a year that includes both pre-tax elective contributions and designated Roth contributions to elect whether the excess contributions are to be attributed to pre-tax elective contributions or designated Roth contributions. A plan may permit an HCE to elect whether any excess contributions are to be recharacterized or distributed. If the plan uses a combination of correction methods, any contribution made under paragraph (b)(1)(i)(A) of this section must be taken into account before application of the correction methods in paragraph (b)(1)(i)(B) or (C) of this section.

(iii) Exclusive means of correction. A failure to satisfy the requirements of paragraph (a)(1) of this section may not be corrected using any method other than the ones described in paragraphs (b)(1)(i) and (ii) of this section. Thus, excess contributions for a plan year may not remain unallocated or be allocated to a suspense account for allocation to one or more employees in any future year. In addition, excess contributions may not be corrected using the retroactive correction rules of § 1.401(a)(4)-11(g). See § 1.401(a)(4)-11(g)(3)(vii) and (5).

*(2) Corrections through distribution.* (i) General rule. This paragraph (b)(2) contains the rules for correction of excess contributions through a distribution from the plan. Correction through a distribution generally involves a 4-step process. First, the plan must determine, in accordance with paragraph (b)(2)(ii) of this section, the total amount of excess contributions that must be distributed under the plan. Second, the plan must apportion the total amount of excess contributions among HCEs in accordance with paragraph (b)(2)(iii) of this section. Third, the plan must determine the income allocable to excess contributions in accordance with paragraph (b)(2)(iv) of this section. Finally, the plan must distribute the apportioned excess contributions and allocable income in ac-

cordance with paragraph (b)(2)(v) of this section. Paragraph (b)(2)(vi) of this section provides rules relating to the tax treatment of these distributions. Paragraph (b)(2)(vii) provides other rules relating to these distributions.

(ii) Calculation of total amount to be distributed. The following procedures must be used to determine the total amount of the excess contributions to be distributed—

(A) Calculate the dollar amount of excess contributions for each HCE. The amount of excess contributions attributable to a given HCE for a plan year is the amount (if any) by which the HCE's contributions taken into account under this section must be reduced for the HCE's ADR to equal the highest permitted ADR under the plan. To calculate the highest permitted ADR under a plan, the ADR of the HCE with the highest ADR is reduced by the amount required to cause that HCE's ADR to equal the ADR of the HCE with the next highest ADR. If a lesser reduction would enable the arrangement to satisfy the requirements of paragraph (b)(2)(ii)(C) of this section, only this lesser reduction is used in determining the highest permitted ADR.

(B) Determination of the total amount of excess contributions. The process described in paragraph (b)(2)(ii)(A) of this section must be repeated until the arrangement would satisfy the requirements of paragraph (b)(2)(ii)(C) of this section. The sum of all reductions for all HCEs determined under paragraph (b)(2)(ii)(A) of this section is the total amount of excess contributions for the plan year.

(C) Satisfaction of ADP. A cash or deferred arrangement satisfies this paragraph (b)(2)(ii)(C) if the arrangement would satisfy the requirements of paragraph (a)(1)(ii) of this section if the ADR for each HCE were determined after the reductions described in paragraph (b)(2)(ii)(A) of this section.

(iii) Apportionment of total amount of excess contributions among the HCEs. The following procedures must be used in apportioning the total amount of excess contributions determined under paragraph (b)(2)(ii) of this section among the HCEs:

(A) Calculate the dollar amount of excess contributions for each HCE. The contributions of the HCE with the highest dollar amount of contributions taken into account under this section are reduced by the amount required to cause that HCE's contributions to equal the dollar amount of the contributions taken into account under this section for the HCE with the next highest dollar amount of contributions taken into account under this section. If a lesser apportionment to the HCE would enable the plan to apportion the total amount of excess contributions, only the lesser apportionment would apply.

(B) Limit on amount apportioned to any individual. For purposes of this paragraph (b)(2)(iii), the amount of contributions taken into account under this section with respect to an HCE who is an eligible employee in more than one plan of an employer is determined by taking into account all contributions otherwise taken into account with respect to such HCE under any plan of the employer during the plan year of the plan being tested as being made under the plan being tested. However, the amount of excess contributions apportioned for a plan year with respect to any HCE must not exceed the amount of contributions actually contributed to the plan for the HCE for the plan year. Thus, in the case of an HCE who is an eligible employee in more than one plan of the same employer to which elective contributions are made and whose ADR is calculated in accordance with paragraph (a)(3)(ii) of this section, the amount required to be distributed under this paragraph (b)(2)(iii) shall not exceed the contributions actually contributed to the plan and taken into account under this section for the plan year.

(C) Apportionment to additional HCEs. The procedure in paragraph (b)(2)(iii)(A) of this section must be repeated until the total amount of excess contributions determined under paragraph (b)(2)(ii) of this section has been apportioned.

(iv) Income allocable to excess contributions. (A) General rule. For plan years beginning on or after January 1, 2008, the income allocable to excess contributions is equal to the allocable gain or loss through the end of the plan year. See paragraph (b)(2)(iv)(D) of this section for rules that apply to plan years beginning before January 1, 2008.

(B) Method of allocating income. A plan may use any reasonable method for computing the income allocable to excess contributions, provided that the method does not violate section 401(a)(4), is used consistently for all participants and for all corrective distributions under the plan for the plan year, and is used by the plan for allocating income to participant's accounts. See § 1.401(a)(4)-1(c)(8). A plan will not fail to use a reasonable method for computing the income allocable to excess contributions merely because the income allocable to excess contributions is determined on a date that is no more than 7 days before the distribution.

(C) Alternative method of allocating plan year income. A plan may allocate income to excess contributions for the plan year by multiplying the income for the plan year allocable to the elective contributions and other amounts taken into account under this section (including contributions made for the plan year), by a fraction, the numerator of which is the excess contributions for the employee for the plan year, and the denominator of which is the sum of the—

(1) Account balance attributable to elective contributions and other contributions taken into account under this section as of the beginning of the plan year, and

(2) Any additional amount of such contributions made for the plan year.

(D) Plan years before 2008. For plan years beginning before January 1, 2008, the income allocable to excess contributions is determined under § 1.401(k)-2(b)(2)(iv) (as it appeared in the April 1, 2007, edition of 26 CFR part 1).

(v) Distribution. Within 12 months after the close of the plan year in which the excess contribution arose, the plan must distribute to each HCE the excess contributions apportioned to such HCE under paragraph (b)(2)(iii) of this section and the allocable income. Except as otherwise provided in this paragraph (b)(2)(v) and paragraph (b)(4)(i) of this section, a distribution of excess contributions must be in addition to any other distributions made during the year and must be designated as a corrective distribution by the employer. In the event of a complete termination of the plan during the plan year in which an excess contribution arose, the corrective distribution must be made as soon as administratively feasible after the date of termination of the plan, but in no event later than 12 months after the date of termination. If the entire account balance of an HCE is distributed prior to when the plan makes a distribution of excess contributions in accordance with this paragraph (b)(2), the distribution is deemed to have been a corrective distribution of excess contributions (and income) to the extent that a corrective distribution would otherwise have been required.

(vi) Tax treatment of corrective distributions. (A) Corrective distributions for plan years beginning on or after January 1, 2008. Except as provided in this paragraph (b)(2)(vi), for plan years beginning on or after January 1, 2008, a corrective distribution of excess contributions (and allocable income) is includible in the employee's gross income for the employee's taxable year in which distributed. In addition, the corrective distribution is not subject to the early distribution tax of section 72(t). See paragraph (b)(5) of this section for additional rules relating to the employer excise tax on amounts distributed more than 2½ months (6 months in the case of certain plans that include an eligible automatic contribution arrangement within the meaning of section 414(w)) after the end of the plan year. See also § 1.402(c)-2, A-4 for restrictions on rolling over distributions that are excess contributions.

(B) Corrective distributions for plan years beginning before January 1, 2008. The tax treatment of corrective distributions for plan years beginning before January 1, 2008, is determined under § 1.401(k)-2(b)(2)(vi) (as it appeared in the April 1, 2007, edition of 26 CFR Part 1). If the total amount of excess contributions, determined under this paragraph (b)(2), and excess aggregate contributions determined under § 1.401(m)-2(b)(2) distributed to a recipient under a plan for any plan year is less than $100 (excluding income), a corrective distribution of excess contributions (and income) is includible in the gross income of the recipient in the taxable year of the recipient in which the corrective distribution is made, except to the extent provided in paragraph (b)(2)(vi)(C) of this section.

(C) Corrective distributions attributable to designated Roth contributions. Notwithstanding paragraphs (b)(2)(vi)(A) and (B) of this section, a distribution of excess contributions is not includible in gross income to the extent it represents a distribution of designated Roth contributions. However, the income allocable to a corrective distribution of excess contributions that are designated Roth contributions is included in gross income in accordance with paragraph (b)(2)(vi)(A) or (B) of this section (i.e., in the same manner as income allocable to a corrective distribution of excess contributions that are pre-tax elective contributions).

(vii) Other rules. (A) No employee or spousal consent required. A corrective distribution of excess contributions (and income) may be made under the terms of the plan without regard to any notice or consent otherwise required under sections 411(a)(11) and 417.

(B) Treatment of corrective distributions as elective contributions. Excess contributions are treated as employer contributions for purposes of sections 404 and 415 even if distributed from the plan.

(C) No reduction of required minimum distribution. A distribution of excess contributions (and income) is not treated as a distribution for purposes of determining whether the plan satisfies the minimum distribution requirements of section 401(a)(9). See § 1.401(a)(9)-5, A-9(b).

(D) Partial distributions. Any distribution of less than the entire amount of excess contributions (and allocable income) with respect to any HCE is treated as a pro rata distribution of excess contributions and allocable income.

(viii) Examples. The following examples illustrate the application of this paragraph (b)(2). For purposes of these examples, none of the plans provide for catch-up contributions under section 414(v). The examples are as follows:

*Example (1).* (i) Plan P, a calendar year profit-sharing plan that includes a cash or deferred arrangement, provides for distribution of excess contributions to HCEs to the extent necessary to satisfy the ADP test. For the 2006 plan year, Employee A, an HCE, has elective contributions of $12,000 and $200,000 in compensation, for an ADR of 6%, and Employee B, a second HCE, has elective contributions of $8,960 and compensation of $128,000, for an ADR of 7%. The ADP for the NHCEs is 3% for the 2006 plan year. Under the ADP test, the ADP of the two HCEs under the plan may not exceed 5% (i.e., 2 percentage points more than the ADP of the NHCEs under the plan). The ADP for the 2 HCEs under the plan is 6.5%. Therefore, there must be a correction of excess contributions for the 2006 plan year.

(ii) The total amount of excess contributions for the HCEs is determined under paragraph (b)(2)(ii) of this section as follows: the elective contributions of Employee B (the HCE with the highest ADR) are reduced by $1,280 in order to reduce his ADR to 6% ($7,680/ $128,000), which is the ADR of Employee A.

(iii) Because the ADP of the HCEs determined after the $1,280 reduction to Employee B still exceeds 5%, further reductions in elective contributions are necessary in order to reduce the ADP of the HCEs to 5%. The elective contributions of Employee A and Employee B are each reduced by 1% of compensation ($2,000 and $1,280 respectively). Because the ADP of the HCEs determined after the reductions equals 5%, the plan would satisfy the requirements of (a)(1)(ii) of this section.

(iv) The total amount of excess contributions ($4,560 = $1,280+$2,000+$1,280) is apportioned among the HCEs under paragraph (b)(2)(iii) of this section first to the HCE with the highest amount of elective contributions. Therefore, Employee A is apportioned $3,040 (the amount required to cause Employee A's elective contributions to equal the next highest dollar amount of elective contributions).

(v) Because the total amount of excess contributions has not been apportioned, further apportionment is necessary. The balance ($1,520) of the total amount of excess contributions is apportioned equally among Employee A and Employee B ($760 to each).

(vi) Therefore, the cash or deferred arrangement will satisfy the requirements of paragraph (a)(1) of this section if, by the end of the 12 month period following the end of the 2006 plan year, Employee A receives a corrective distribution of excess contributions equal to $3,800 ($3,040 + $760) and allocable income and Employee B receives a corrective distribution of $760 and allocable income.

*Example (2).* (i) The facts are the same as in Example 1, except Employee A's ADR is based on $3,000 of elective contributions to this plan and $9,000 of elective contributions to another plan of the employer.

(ii) The total amount of excess contributions ($4,560 = $1,280+$2,000+$1,280) is apportioned among the HCEs under paragraph (b)(2)(iii) of this section first to the HCE with the highest amount of elective contributions. The amount of elective contributions for Employee A is $12,000. Therefore, Employee A is apportioned $3,040 (the amount required to cause Employee A's elective contributions to equal the next highest dollar amount of elective contributions). However, pursuant to paragraph (b)(2)(iii)(B) of this section, no more than the amount actually contributed to the plan may be apportioned to an HCE. Accordingly, no more than $3,000 may be apportioned to Employee A. Therefore, the remaining $1,560 must be apportioned to Employee B.

(iii) The cash or deferred arrangement will satisfy the requirements of paragraph (a)(1) of this section if, by the end of the 12 month period following the end of the 2006 plan year, Employee A receives a corrective distribution of excess contributions equal to $3,000 (total amount of elective contributions actually contributed to the plan for Employee A) and allocable income and Employee B receives a corrective distribution of $1,560 and allocable income.

*(3) Recharacterization of excess contributions.* (i) General rule. Excess contributions are recharacterized in accordance with this paragraph (b)(3) only if the excess contributions that would have to be distributed under (b)(2) of this section if the plan was correcting through distribution of excess contributions are recharacterized as described in paragraph (b)(3)(ii) of this section, and all of the conditions set forth in paragraph (b)(3)(iii) of this section are satisfied.

(ii) Treatment of recharacterized excess contributions. Recharacterized excess contributions are includible in the employee's gross income as if such amounts were distributed under paragraph (b)(2) of this section. The recharacterized excess contributions are treated as employee contributions for purposes of section 72, sections 401(a)(4), 401(m), § 1.401(k)-1(d) and § 1.401(k)-2. This requirement is not treated as satisfied unless the payor or plan administrator reports the recharacterized excess contributions as employee contributions to the Internal Revenue Service and the employee by timely providing such Federal tax forms and accompanying instructions and timely taking such other action as is prescribed by the Commissioner in revenue rulings, notices and other guidance published in the Internal Revenue Bulletin (see § 601.601(d)(2) of this chapter) as well as the applicable Federal tax forms and accompanying instructions.

(iii) Additional rules. (A) Time of recharacterization. Excess contributions may not be recharacterized under this paragraph (b)(3) after 2½ months after the close of the plan year to which the recharacterization relates. Recharacterization is deemed to have occurred on the date on which the last of those HCEs with excess contributions to be recharacterized is notified in accordance with paragraph (b)(3)(ii) of this section.

(B) Employee contributions must be permitted under plan. The amount of recharacterized excess contributions, in combination with the employee contributions actually made by the HCE, may not exceed the maximum amount of employee contributions (determined without regard to the ACP test of section 401(m)(2)) permitted under the provisions of the plan as in effect on the first day of the plan year.

(C) Treatment of recharacterized excess contributions. Recharacterized excess contributions continue to be treated as employer contributions for all purposes under the Internal Revenue Code (other than those specified in paragraph (b)(3)(ii) of this section), including section 401(a) and sections 404, 409, 411, 412, 415, 416, and 417. Thus, for example, recharacterized excess contributions remain subject to the requirements of § 1.401(k)-1(c); must be deducted under section 404; and are treated as employer contributions described in section 415(c)(2)(A).

*(4) Rules applicable to all corrections.* (i) Coordination with distribution of excess deferrals. (A) Treatment of excess deferrals that reduce excess contributions. The amount of excess contributions (and allocable income) to be distributed under paragraph (b)(2) of this section or the amount of excess contributions recharacterized under paragraph (b)(3) of this section with respect to an employee for a plan year, is reduced by any amounts previously distributed to the employee from the plan to correct excess deferrals for the employee's taxable year ending with or within the plan year in accordance with section 402(g)(2).

(B) Treatment of excess contributions that reduce excess deferrals. Under § 1.402(g)-1(e), the amount required to be distributed to correct an excess deferral to an employee for a taxable year is reduced by any excess contributions (and allocable income) previously distributed or excess contributions recharacterized with respect to the employee for the plan year beginning with or within the taxable year. The amount of excess contributions includible in the gross income of the employee, and the amount of excess contributions reported by the payer or plan administrator as includible in the gross income of the employee, does not include the amount of any reduction under § 1.402(g)-1(e)(6).

(ii) Forfeiture of match on distributed excess contributions. A matching contribution is taken into account under section 401(a)(4) even if the match is with respect to an elective contribution that is distributed or recharacterized under this paragraph (b). This requires that, after correction of excess contributions, each level of matching contributions be currently and effectively available to a group of employees that satisfies section 410(b). See § 1.401(a)(4)-4(e)(3)(iii)(G). Thus, a plan that provides the same rate of matching contributions to all employees will not meet the requirements of section 401(a)(4) if elective contributions are distributed under this paragraph (b) to HCEs to the extent needed to meet the requirements of section 401(k)(3), while matching contributions attributable to those elective contributions remain allocated to the HCEs' accounts. Under section 411(a)(3)(G) and § 1.411(a)-4(b)(7), a plan may forfeit matching contributions attributable to excess contributions, excess aggregate contributions or excess deferrals to avoid a violation of section 401(a)(4). See also § 1.401(a)(4)-11(g)(3)(vii)(B) regarding the use of additional allocations to the accounts of NHCEs for the purpose of correcting a discriminatory rate of matching contributions.

(iii) Permitted forfeiture of QMAC. Pursuant to section 401(k)(8)(E), a qualified matching contribution is not treated as forfeitable under § 1.401(k)-1(c) merely because under the plan it is forfeited in accordance with paragraph (b)(4)(ii) of this section or § 1.414(w)-1(d)(2).

(iv) No requirement for recalculation. If excess contributions are distributed or recharacterized in accordance with paragraphs (b)(2) and (3) of this section, the cash or deferred arrangement is treated as meeting the nondiscrimination test of section 401(k)(3) regardless of whether the ADP for the HCEs, if recalculated after the distributions or recharacterizations, would satisfy section 401(k)(3).

(v) Treatment of excess contributions that are catch-up contributions. A cash or deferred arrangement does not fail to meet the requirements of section 401(k)(3) and paragraph (a)(1) of this section merely because excess contributions that are catch-up contributions because they exceed the ADP limit, as described in § 1.414(v)-1(b)(1)(iii), are not corrected in accordance with this paragraph (b).

*(5) Failure to timely correct.* (i) Failure to correct within 2½ months after end of plan year. If a plan does not correct excess contributions within 2½ months after the close of the plan year for which the excess contributions are made, the employer will be liable for a 10% excise tax on the amount of the excess contributions. See section 4979 and § 54.4979-1 of this chapter. Qualified nonelective contributions and qualified matching contributions properly taken into account under paragraph (a)(6) of this section for a plan year may enable a plan to avoid having excess contributions, even if the contributions are made after the close of the 2½ month period.

(ii) Failure to correct within 12 months after end of plan year. If excess contributions are not corrected within 12 months after the close of the plan year for which they were made, the cash or deferred arrangement will fail to satisfy the requirements of section 401(k)(3) for the plan year for which the excess contributions are made and all subsequent plan years during which the excess contributions remain in the trust.

(iii) Special rule for eligible automatic contribution arrangements. In the case of excess contributions under a plan that includes an eligible automatic contribution arrangement within the meaning of section 414(w), 6 months is substituted for 2½ months in paragraph (b)(5)(i) of this section. The additional time described in this paragraph (b)(5)(iii) applies to a distribution of excess contributions for a plan year beginning on or after January 1, 2010 only where all the eligible NHCEs and eligible HCEs are covered employees under the eligible automatic contribution arrangement (within the meaning of § 1.414(w)-1(e)(3)) for the entire plan year (or for the portion of the plan year that the eligible NHCEs and eligible HCEs are eligible employees).

**(c) Additional rules for prior year testing method.** *(1) Rules for change in testing method.* (i) General rule. A plan is permitted to change from the prior year testing method to the current year testing method for any plan year. A plan is permitted to change from the current year testing method to the prior year testing method only in situations described in paragraph (c)(1)(ii) of this section. For purposes of this paragraph (c)(1), a plan that uses the safe harbor method described in § 1.401(k)-3 or a SIMPLE 401(k) plan is treated as using the current year testing method for that plan year.

(ii) Situations permitting a change to the prior year testing method. The situations described in this paragraph (c)(1)(ii) are:

(A) The plan is not the result of the aggregation of two or more plans, and the current year testing method was used under the plan for each of the 5 plan years preceding the plan year of the change (or if lesser, the number of plan years the plan has been in existence, including years in which the plan was a portion of another plan).

(B) The plan is the result of the aggregation of two or more plans, and for each of the plans that are being aggregated (the aggregating plans), the current year testing method was used for each of the 5 plan years preceding the plan year of the change (or if lesser, the number of plan years since that aggregating plan has been in existence, including years in which the aggregating plan was a portion of another plan).

(C) A transaction described in section 410(b)(6)(C)(i) and § 1.410(b)-2(f) occurs and—

(1) As a result of the transaction, the employer maintains both a plan using the prior year testing method and a plan using the current year testing method; and

(2) The change from the current year testing method to the prior year testing method occurs within the transition period described in section 410(b)(6)(C)(ii).

*(2) Calculation of ADP under the prior year testing method for the first plan year.* (i) Plans that are not successor plans. If, for the first plan year of any plan (other than a successor plan), the plan uses the prior year testing method, the plan is permitted to use either that first plan year as the applicable year for determining the ADP for eligible NHCEs, or use 3% as the ADP for eligible NHCEs, for applying the ADP test for that first plan year. A plan (other than a successor plan) that uses the prior year testing method but has elected for its first plan year to use that year as the applicable year is not treated as changing its testing method in the second plan year and is not subject to the limitations on double counting on QNECs under paragraph (a)(6)(vi) of this section for the second plan year.

(ii) First plan year defined. For purposes of this paragraph (c)(2), the first plan year of any plan is the first year in which the plan provides for elective contributions. Thus, the rules of this paragraph (c)(2) do not apply to a plan (within the meaning of § 1.410(b)-7(b)) for a plan year if for such plan year the plan is aggregated under § 1.401(k)-1(b)(4) with any other plan that provided for elective contributions in the prior year.

(iii) Successor plans. A plan is a successor plan if 50% or more of the eligible employees for the first plan year were eligible employees under a qualified cash or deferred arrangement maintained by the employer in the prior year. If a plan that is a successor plan uses the prior year testing method for its first plan year, the ADP for the group of NHCEs for the applicable year must be determined under paragraph (c)(4) of this section.

*(3) Plans using different testing methods for the ADP and ACP test.* Except as otherwise provided in this paragraph (c)(3), a plan may use the current year testing method or prior year testing method for the ADP test for a plan year without regard to whether the current year testing method or prior year testing method is used for the ACP test for that year. For example, a plan may use the prior year testing method for the ADP test and the current year testing method for its ACP test for the plan year. However, plans that use different testing methods under this paragraph (c)(3) cannot use—

(i) The recharacterization method of paragraph (b)(3) of this section to correct excess contributions for a plan year;

(ii) The rules of § 1.401(m)-2(a)(6)(ii) to take elective contributions into account under the ACP test (rather than the ADP test); or

(iii) The rules of paragraph (a)(6)(v) of this section to take qualified matching contributions into account under the ADP test (rather than the ACP test).

*(4) Rules for plan coverage changes.* (i) In general. A plan that uses the prior year testing method and experiences a plan coverage change during a plan year satisfies the requirements of this section for that year only if the plan provides that the ADP for the NHCEs for the plan year is the weighted average of the ADPs for the prior year subgroups.

(ii) Optional rule for minor plan coverage changes. If a plan coverage change occurs and 90% or more of the total number of the NHCEs from all prior year subgroups are from a single prior year subgroup, then, in lieu of using the weighted averages described in paragraph (c)(4)(i) of this section, the plan may provide that the ADP for the group of eligible NHCEs for the prior year under the plan is the ADP of the NHCEs for the prior year of the plan under which that single prior year subgroup was eligible.

(iii) Definitions. The following definitions apply for purposes of this paragraph (c)(4):

(A) Plan coverage change. The term plan coverage change means a change in the group or groups of eligible employees under a plan on account of—

(1) The establishment or amendment of a plan;

(2) A plan merger or spinoff under section 414(l);

(3) A change in the way plans (within the meaning of § 1.410(b)-7(b)) are combined or separated for purposes of § 1.401(k)-1(b)(4) (e.g., permissively aggregating plans not previously aggregated under § 1.410(b)-7(d), or ceasing to permissively aggregate plans under § 1.410(b)-7(d));

(4) A reclassification of a substantial group of employees that has the same effect as amending the plan (e.g., a transfer of a substantial group of employees from one division to another division); or

(5) A combination of any of paragraphs (c)(4)(iii)(A)(1) through (4) of this section.

(B) Prior year subgroup. The term prior year subgroup means all NHCEs for the prior plan year who, in the prior year, were eligible employees under a specific plan maintained by the employer that included a qualified cash or deferred arrangement and who would have been eligible employees in the prior year under the plan being tested if the plan coverage change had first been effective as of the first day of the prior plan year instead of first being effective during the plan year. The determination of whether an NHCE is a member of a prior year subgroup is made without regard to whether the NHCE terminated employment during the prior year.

(C) Weighted average of the ADPs for the prior year subgroups. The term weighted average of the ADPs for the prior year subgroups means the sum, for all prior year subgroups, of the adjusted ADPs for the plan year. The term adjusted ADP with respect to a prior year subgroup means the ADP for the prior plan year of the specific plan under which the members of the prior year subgroup were eligible employees on the first day of the prior plan year, multiplied by a fraction, the numerator of which is the number of NHCEs in the prior year subgroup and denominator of which is the total number of NHCEs in all prior year subgroups.

(iv) Examples. The following examples illustrate the application of this paragraph (c)(4):

*Example (1).* (i) Employer B maintains two calendar year plans, Plan O and Plan P, each of which includes a cash or deferred arrangement. The plans were not permissively aggregated under § 1.410(b)-7(d) for the 2005 plan year. Both plans use the prior year testing method. Plan O had 300 eligible employees who were NHCEs for the 2005 plan year, and their ADP for that year was 6%. Sixty of the eligible employees who were NHCEs for the 2005 plan year under Plan O, terminated their employment during that year. Plan P had 100 eligible employees who were NHCEs for 2005, and the ADP for those NHCEs for that plan was 4%. Plan O and Plan P are permissively aggregated under § 1.410(b)-7(d) for the 2006 plan year.

(ii) The permissive aggregation of Plan O and Plan P for the 2006 plan year under § 1.410(b)-7(d) is a plan coverage change that results in treating the plans as one plan (Plan OP) for purposes of § 1.401(k)-1(b)(4). Therefore, the prior year ADP for the NHCEs under Plan OP for the 2006 plan year is the weighted average of the ADPs for the prior year subgroups: the Plan O prior year subgroup and the Plan P prior year subgroup.

(iii) The Plan O prior year subgroup consists of the 300 employees who, in the 2005 plan year, were eligible NHCEs under Plan O and who would have been eligible under Plan OP for the 2005 plan year if Plan O and Plan P had been permissively aggregated for that plan year. The Plan P prior year subgroup consists of the 100 employees who, in the 2005 plan year, were eligible NHCEs under Plan P and would have been eligible under Plan OP for the 2005 plan year if Plan O and Plan P had been permissively aggregated for that plan year.

(iv) The weighted average of the ADPs for the prior year subgroups is the sum of the adjusted ADP for the Plan O prior year subgroup and the adjusted ADP for the Plan P prior year subgroup. The adjusted ADP for the Plan O prior year subgroup is 4.5%, calculated as follows: 6% (the ADP for the NHCEs under Plan O for the 2005 plan year) x 300/400 (the number of NHCEs in the Plan O prior year subgroup divided by the total number of NHCEs in all prior year subgroups). The adjusted ADP for the Plan P prior year subgroup is 1%, calculated as follows: 4% (the ADP for the NHCEs under Plan P for the 2005 plan year) x 100/400 (the number of NHCEs in the Plan P prior year subgroup divided by the total number of NHCEs in all prior year subgroups). Thus, the prior year ADP for NHCEs under Plan OP for the 2006 plan year is 5.5% (the sum of adjusted ADPs for the prior year subgroups, 4.5% plus 1%).

(v) As provided in paragraph (c)(4)(iii)(B) of this section, the determination of whether an NHCE is a member of a prior year subgroup is made without regard to whether that NHCE terminated employment during the prior year. Thus, the prior ADP for the NHCEs under Plan OP for the 2006 plan year is unaffected by the termination of the 60 NHCEs covered by Plan O during the 2005 plan year.

*Example (2).* (i) The facts are the same as Example 1, except that the 60 employees who terminated employment during the 2005 plan are instead spun-off to another plan.

(ii) The permissive aggregation of Plan O and Plan P for the 2006 plan year under § 1.410(b)-7(d) is a plan coverage change that results in treating the plans as one plan (Plan OP) for purposes of § 1.401(k)-1(b)(4) and the spin-off of the 60 employees is a plan coverage change. Therefore, the prior year ADP for the NHCEs under Plan OP for the 2006 plan year is the weighted average of the ADPs for the prior year subgroups: the Plan O prior year subgroup and the Plan P prior year subgroup.

(iii) For purposes of determining the prior year subgroups, the employees who would have been eligible employees in the prior year under the plan being tested are determined as if both plan coverage changes had first been effective as of the first day of the prior plan year. The Plan O prior year subgroup consists of the 240 employees who, in the 2005 plan year, were eligible NHCEs under Plan O and would have been eligible under Plan OP for the 2005 plan year if the spin-off had occurred at the beginning of the 2005 plan year and Plan O and Plan P had been permissively aggregated under § 1.410(b)-7(d) for that plan year. The Plan P prior year subgroup consists of the 100 employees who, in the 2005 plan year, were eligible NHCEs under Plan P and would have been eligible under Plan OP for the 2005 plan year if Plan O and Plan P had been permissively aggregated under § 1.410(b)-7(d) for that plan year.

(iv) The weighted average of the ADPs for the prior year subgroups is the sum of the adjusted ADP with respect to the prior year subgroup consisting of eligible NHCEs from Plan O and the adjusted ADP with respect to the prior year subgroup consisting of eligible NHCEs from Plan P. The adjusted ADP for the prior year subgroup consisting of eligible NHCEs under Plan O is 4.23%, calculated as follows: 6% (the ADP for the NHCEs under Plan O for the 2005 plan year) x 240/340 (the number of NHCEs in that prior year subgroup divided by the total number of NHCEs in all prior year subgroups). The adjusted ADP for the prior year subgroup consisting of the eligible NHCEs from Plan P is 1.18%, calculated as follows: 4% (the ADP for the NHCEs under Plan P for the 2005 plan year) x 100/340 (the number of NHCEs in that prior year subgroup divided by the total number of NHCEs in all prior year subgroups). Thus, the prior year ADP for NHCEs under Plan OP for the 2006 plan year is 5.41% (the sum of adjusted ADPs for the prior year subgroups, 4.23% plus 1.18%).

*Example (3).* (i) The facts are the same as in Example 1, except that instead of Plan O and Plan P being permissively aggregated for the 2006 plan year, 200 of the employees eligible under Plan O were spun-off from Plan O and merged into Plan P.

(ii) The spin-off from Plan O and merger to Plan P for the 2006 plan year are plan coverage changes for Plan P. Therefore, the prior year ADP for the NHCEs under Plan P for the 2006 plan year is the weighted average of the ADPs for the prior year subgroups under Plan P. There are 2 subgroups under Plan P for the 2006 plan year. The Plan O prior year subgroup consists of the 200 employees who, in the 2005 plan year, were eligible NHCEs under Plan O and who would have been eligible under Plan P for the 2005 plan year if the spin-off and merger had occurred on the first day of the 2005 plan year. The Plan P prior year subgroup consists of the 100 employees who, in the 2005 plan year, were eligible NHCEs under Plan P for the 2005 plan year.

(iii) The weighted average of the ADPs for the prior year subgroups is the sum of the adjusted ADP for the Plan O prior year subgroup and the adjusted ADP for the Plan P prior year subgroup. The adjusted ADP for the Plan O prior year subgroup is 4.0%, calculated as follows: 6% (the ADP for the NHCEs under Plan O for the 2005 plan year) x 200/300 (the number of NHCEs in the Plan O prior year subgroup divided by the total number of NHCEs in all prior year subgroups). The adjusted ADP for the Plan P prior year subgroup is 1.33%, calculated as follows: 4% (the ADP for the NHCEs under Plan P for the 2005 plan year) x 100/300 (the number of NHCEs in the Plan P prior year subgroup divided by the total number of NHCEs in all prior year subgroups). Thus, the prior year ADP for NHCEs under Plan P for the 2006 plan year is 5.33% (the sum of adjusted ADPs for the 2 prior year subgroups, 4.0% plus 1.33%).

(iv) The spin-off from Plan O for the 2006 plan year is a plan coverage change for Plan O. Therefore, the prior year ADP for the NHCEs under Plan O for the 2006 plan year is the weighted average of the ADPs for the prior year subgroups under Plan O. In this case, there is only one prior year subgroup under Plan O, the employees who were NHCEs of Employer B for the 2005 plan year and who were eligible for the 2005 plan year under Plan O. Because there is only one prior year subgroup under Plan O, the weighted average of the ADPs for the prior year subgroup under Plan O is equal to the NHCE ADP for the prior year (2005 plan year) under Plan O, or 6%.

*Example (4).* (i) Employer C maintains a calendar year plan, Plan Q, which includes a cash or deferred arrangement that uses the prior year testing method. Plan Q covers employees of Division A and Division B. In 2005, Plan Q had 500 eligible employees who were NHCEs, and the ADP for those NHCEs for 2005 was 2%. Effective January 1, 2006, Employer C amends the eligibility provisions under Plan Q to exclude employees of Division B effective January 1, 2006. In addition, effective on that same date, Employer C establishes a new calendar year plan, Plan R, which includes a cash or deferred arrangement that uses the prior year testing method. The only eligible employees under Plan R are the 100 employees of Division B who were eligible employees under Plan Q.

(ii) Plan R is a successor plan, within the meaning of paragraph (c)(2)(iii) of this section (because all of the employees were eligible employees under Plan Q in the prior year). Therefore, Plan R cannot use the first plan year rule set forth in paragraph (c)(2)(i) of this section.

(iii) The amendment to the eligibility provisions of Plan Q and the establishment of Plan R are plan coverage changes within the meaning of paragraph (c)(4)(iii)(A) of this section for Plan Q and Plan R. Accordingly, each plan must determine the NHCE ADP for the 2006 plan year under the rules set forth in paragraph (c)(4) of this section.

(iv) The prior year ADP for NHCEs under Plan Q is the weighted average of the ADPs for the prior year subgroups. Plan Q has only one prior year subgroup (because the only NHCEs who would have been eligible employees under Plan Q for the 2005 plan year if the amendment to the Plan Q eligibility provisions had occurred as of the first day of that plan year were eligible employees under Plan Q). Therefore, for purposes of the 2006 plan year under Plan Q, the ADP for NHCEs for the prior year is the weighted average of the ADPs for the prior year subgroups, or 2%, the same as if the plan amendment had not occurred.

(v) Similarly, Plan R has only one prior year subgroup (because the only NHCEs who would have been eligible employees under Plan R for the 2005 plan year if the plan were established as of the first day of that plan year were eligible employees under Plan Q). Therefore, for purposes of the 2006 testing year under Plan R, the ADP for NHCEs for the prior year is the weighted average of the ADPs for the prior year subgroups, or 2%, the same as that of Plan Q.

*Example (5).* (i) The facts are the same as in Example 4, except that the provisions of Plan R extend eligibility to 50 hourly employees who previously were not eligible employees under any qualified cash or deferred arrangement maintained by Employer C.

(ii) Plan R is a successor plan (because 100 of Plan R's 150 eligible employees were eligible employees under another qualified cash or deferred arrangement maintained by Employer C in the prior year). Therefore, Plan R cannot use the first plan year rule set forth in paragraph (c)(2)(i) of this section.

(iii) The establishment of Plan R is a plan coverage change that affects Plan R. Because the 50 hourly employees were not eligible employees under any qualified cash or deferred arrangement of Employer C for the prior plan year, they do not comprise a prior year subgroup. Accordingly, Plan R still has only one prior year subgroup. Therefore, for purposes of the 2006 testing year under Plan R, the ADP for NHCEs for the prior year is the weighted average of the ADPs for the prior year subgroups, or 2%, the same as that of Plan Q.

T.D. 9169, 12/28/2004, amend T.D. 9237, 12/30/2005, T.D. 9447, 2/23/2009.

**§ 1.401(k)-3 Safe harbor requirements.**

**(a) ADP test safe harbor.** *(1) Section 401(k)(12) safe harbor.* A cash or deferred arrangement satisfies the ADP safe harbor provision of section 401(k)(12) for a plan year if the arrangement satisfies the safe harbor contribution requirement of paragraph (b) or (c) of this section for the plan year, the notice requirement of paragraph (d) of this section, the plan year requirements of paragraph (e) of this section, and the additional rules of paragraphs (f), (g), and (h) of this section, as applicable.

*(2) Section 401(k)(13) safe harbor.* For plan years beginning on or after January 1, 2008, a cash or deferred arrangement satisfies the ADP safe harbor provision of section

401(k)(13) for a plan year if the arrangement is described in paragraph (j) of this section and satisfies the safe harbor contribution requirement of paragraph (k) of this section for the plan year, the notice requirement of paragraph (d) of this section (modified to include the information set forth in paragraph (k)(4) of this section), the plan year requirements of paragraph (e) of this section, and the additional rules of paragraphs (f), (g), and (h) of this section, as applicable. A cash or deferred arrangement that satisfies the requirements of this paragraph (a)(2) is referred to as a qualified automatic contribution arrangement.

*(3) Requirements applicable to safe harbor contributions.* Pursuant to section 401(k)(12)(E)(ii) and section 401(k)(13)(D)(iv), the safe harbor contribution requirement of paragraph (b), (c), or (k) of this section must be satisfied without regard to section 401(l). The contributions made under paragraph (b) or (c) of this section (and the corresponding contributions under paragraph (k) of this section) are referred to as safe harbor nonelective contributions and safe harbor matching contributions.

**(b) Safe harbor nonelective contribution requirement.** *(1) General rule.* The safe harbor nonelective contribution requirement of this paragraph is satisfied if, under the terms of the plan, the employer is required to make a qualified nonelective contribution on behalf of each eligible NHCE equal to at least 3% of the employee's safe harbor compensation.

*(2) Safe harbor compensation defined.* For purposes of this section, safe harbor compensation means compensation as defined in § 1.401(k)-6 (which incorporates the definition of compensation in § 1.414(s)-1); provided, however, that the rule in the last sentence of § 1.414(s)-1(d)(2)(iii) (which generally permits a definition of compensation to exclude all compensation in excess of a specified dollar amount) does not apply in determining the safe harbor compensation of NHCEs. Thus, for example, the plan may limit the period used to determine safe harbor compensation to the eligible employee's period of participation.

**(c) Safe harbor matching contribution requirement.** *(1) In general.* The safe harbor matching contribution requirement of this paragraph (c) is satisfied if, under the plan, qualified matching contributions are made on behalf of each eligible NHCE in an amount determined under the basic matching formula of section 401(k)(12)(B)(i)(I), as described in paragraph (c)(2) of this section, or under an enhanced matching formula of section 401(k)(12)(B)(i)(II), as described in paragraph (c)(3) of this section.

*(2) Basic matching formula.* Under the basic matching formula, each eligible NHCE receives qualified matching contributions in an amount equal to the sum of—

(i) 100% of the amount of the employee's elective contributions that do not exceed 3% of the employee's safe harbor compensation; and

(ii) 50% of the amount of the employee's elective contributions that exceed 3% of the employee's safe harbor compensation but that do not exceed 5% of the employee's safe harbor compensation.

*(3) Enhanced matching formula.* Under an enhanced matching formula, each eligible NHCE receives a matching contribution under a formula that, at any rate of elective contributions by the employee, provides an aggregate amount of qualified matching contributions at least equal to the aggregate amount of qualified matching contributions that would have been provided under the basic matching formula of paragraph (c)(2) of this section. In addition, under an enhanced matching formula, the ratio of matching contributions on behalf of an employee under the plan for a plan year to the employee's elective contributions may not increase as the amount of an employee's elective contributions increases.

*(4) Limitation on HCE matching contributions.* The safe harbor matching contribution requirement of this paragraph (c) is not satisfied if the ratio of matching contributions made on account of an HCE's elective contributions under the cash or deferred arrangement for a plan year to those elective contributions is greater than the ratio of matching contributions to elective contributions that would apply with respect to any eligible NHCE with elective contributions at the same percentage of safe harbor compensation.

*(5) Use of safe harbor match not precluded by certain plan provisions.* (i) Safe harbor matching contributions on employee contributions. The safe harbor matching contribution requirement of this paragraph (c) will not fail to be satisfied merely because safe harbor matching contributions are made on both elective contributions and employee contributions if safe harbor matching contributions are made with respect to the sum of elective contributions and employee contributions on the same terms as safe harbor matching contributions are made with respect to elective contributions. Alternatively, the safe harbor matching contribution requirement of this paragraph (c) will not fail to be satisfied merely because safe harbor matching contributions are made on both elective contributions and employee contributions if safe harbor matching contributions on elective contributions are not affected by the amount of employee contributions.

(ii) Periodic matching contributions. The safe harbor matching contribution requirement of this paragraph (c) will not fail to be satisfied merely because the plan provides that safe harbor matching contributions will be made separately with respect to each payroll period (or with respect to all payroll periods ending with or within each month or quarter of a plan year) taken into account under the plan for the plan year, provided that safe harbor matching contributions with respect to any elective contributions made during a plan year quarter are contributed to the plan by the last day of the immediately following plan year quarter.

*(6) Permissible restrictions on elective contributions by NHCEs.* (i) General rule. The safe harbor matching contribution requirement of this paragraph (c) is not satisfied if elective contributions by NHCEs are restricted, unless the restrictions are permitted by this paragraph (c)(6).

(ii) Restrictions on election periods. A plan may limit the frequency and duration of periods in which eligible employees may make or change cash or deferred elections under a plan. However, an employee must have a reasonable opportunity (including a reasonable period after receipt of the notice described in paragraph (d) of this section) to make or change a cash or deferred election for the plan year. For purposes of this paragraph (c)(6)(ii), a 30-day period is deemed to be a reasonable period to make or change a cash or deferred election.

(iii) Restrictions on amount of elective contributions. A plan is permitted to limit the amount of elective contributions that may be made by an eligible employee under a plan, provided that each NHCE who is an eligible employee is permitted (unless the employee is restricted under paragraph (c)(6)(v) of this section) to make elective contributions in an amount that is at least sufficient to receive the maximum amount of matching contributions available under the plan for the plan year, and the employee is permitted to elect any lesser amount of elective contributions. However, a plan may require eligible employees to make cash or deferred elections in whole percentages of compensation or whole dollar amounts.

(iv) Restrictions on types of compensation that may be deferred. A plan may limit the types of compensation that may be deferred by an eligible employee under a plan, provided that each eligible NHCE is permitted to make elective contributions under a definition of compensation that would be a reasonable definition of compensation within the meaning of § 1.414(s)-1(d)(2). Thus, the definition of compensation from which elective contributions may be made is not required to satisfy the nondiscrimination requirement of § 1.414(s)-1(d)(3).

(v) Restrictions due to limitations under the Internal Revenue Code. A plan may limit the amount of elective contributions made by an eligible employee under a plan—

(A) Because of the limitations of section 402(g) or 415; or

(B) Because, on account of a hardship distribution, an employee's ability to make elective contributions has been suspended for 6 months in accordance with § 1.401(k)-1(d)(3)(iv)(E).

*(7) Examples.* The following examples illustrate the safe harbor contribution requirement of this paragraph (c):

*Example (1).* (i) Beginning January 1, 2006, Employer A maintains Plan L covering employees in Divisions D and E, each of which includes HCEs and NHCEs. Plan L contains a cash or deferred arrangement and provides qualified matching contributions equal to 100% of each eligible employee's elective contributions up to 3% of compensation and 50% of the next 2% of compensation. For purposes of the matching contribution formula, safe harbor compensation is defined as all compensation within the meaning of section 415(c)(3) (a definition that satisfies section 414(s)). Also, each employee is permitted to make elective contributions from all safe harbor compensation within the meaning of section 415(c)(3) and may change a cash or deferred election at any time. Plan L limits the amount of an employee's elective contributions for purposes of section 402(g) and section 415, and, in the case of a hardship distribution, suspends an employee's ability to make elective contributions for 6 months in accordance with § 1.401(k)-1(d)(3)(iv)(E). All contributions under Plan L are nonforfeitable and are subject to the withdrawal restrictions of section 401(k)(2)(B). Plan L provides for no other contributions and Employer A maintains no other plans. Plan L is maintained on a calendar-year basis, and all contributions for a plan year are made within 12 months after the end of the plan year.

(ii) Based on these facts, matching contributions under Plan L are safe harbor matching contributions because they are qualified matching contributions equal to the basic matching formula. Accordingly, Plan L satisfies the safe harbor contribution requirement of this paragraph (c).

*Example (2).* (i) The facts are the same as in Example 1, except that instead of providing a basic matching contribution, Plan L provides a qualified matching contribution equal to 100% of each eligible employee's elective contributions up to 4% of safe harbor compensation.

(ii) Plan L's formula is an enhanced matching formula because each eligible NHCE receives safe harbor matching contributions at a rate that, at any rate of elective contributions, provides an aggregate amount of qualified matching contributions at least equal to the aggregate amount of qualified matching contributions that would have been received under the basic safe harbor matching formula, and the rate of matching contributions does not increase as the rate of an employee's elective contributions increases. Accordingly, Plan L satisfies the safe harbor contribution requirement of this paragraph (c).

*Example (3).* (i) The facts are the same as in Example 2, except that instead of permitting each employee to make elective contributions from all compensation within the meaning of section 415(c)(3), each employee's elective contributions under Plan L are limited to 15% of the employee's basic compensation. Basic compensation is defined under Plan L as compensation within the meaning of section 415(c)(3), but excluding overtime pay.

(ii) The definition of basic compensation under Plan L is a reasonable definition of compensation within the meaning of § 1.414(s)-1(d)(2).

(iii) Plan L will not fail to satisfy the safe harbor contribution requirement of this paragraph (c) merely because Plan L limits the amount of elective contributions and the types of compensation that may be deferred by eligible employees, provided that each eligible NHCE may make elective contributions equal to at least 4% of the employee's safe harbor compensation.

*Example (4).* (i) The facts are the same as in Example 1, except that Plan L provides that only employees employed on the last day of the plan year will receive a safe harbor matching contribution.

(ii) Even if the plan that provides for employee contributions and matching contributions satisfies the minimum coverage requirements of section 410(b)(1) taking into account this last-day requirement, Plan L would not satisfy the safe harbor contribution requirement of this paragraph (c) because safe harbor matching contributions are not made on behalf of all eligible NHCEs who make elective contributions.

(iii) The result would be the same if, instead of providing safe harbor matching contributions, Plan L provides for a 3% safe harbor nonelective contribution that is restricted to eligible employees under the cash or deferred arrangement who are employed on the last day of the plan year.

*Example (5).* (i) The facts are the same as in Example 1, except that instead of providing qualified matching contributions under the basic matching formula to employees in both Divisions D and E, employees in Division E are provided qualified matching contributions under the basic matching formula, while safe harbor matching contributions continue to be provided to employees in Division D under the enhanced matching formula described in Example 2.

(ii) Even if Plan L satisfies § 1.401(a)(4)-4 with respect to each rate of matching contributions available to employees under the plan, the plan would fail to satisfy the safe harbor contribution requirement of this paragraph (c) because the rate of matching contributions with respect to HCEs in Division D at a rate of elective contributions between 3% and 5% would be greater than that with respect to NHCEs in Division E at the same rate of elective contributions. For example, an HCE in Division D who would have a 4% rate of elective contributions would have a rate of matching contributions of 100% while an NHCE in Division E who would have the same rate of elective contributions would have a lower rate of matching contributions.

**(d) Notice requirement.** *(1) General rule.* The notice requirement of this paragraph (d) is satisfied for a plan year if each eligible employee is given notice of the employee's rights and obligations under the plan and the notice satisfies the content requirement of paragraph (d)(2) of this section and the timing requirement of paragraph (d)(3) of this section. The notice must be in writing or in such other form as may be approved by the Commissioner. See § 1.401(a)-21 of this chapter for rules permitting the use of electronic media to provide applicable notices to recipients with respect to retirement plans.

*(2) Content requirement.* (i) General rule. The content requirement of this paragraph (d)(2) is satisfied if the notice is—

(A) Sufficiently accurate and comprehensive to inform the employee of the employee's rights and obligations under the plan; and

(B) Written in a manner calculated to be understood by the average employee eligible to participate in the plan.

(ii) Minimum content requirement. Subject to the requirements of paragraph (d)(2)(iii) of this section, a notice is not considered sufficiently accurate and comprehensive unless the notice accurately describes—

(A) The safe harbor matching contribution or safe harbor nonelective contribution formula used under the plan (including a description of the levels of safe harbor matching contributions, if any, available under the plan);

(B) Any other contributions under the plan or matching contributions to another plan on account of elective contributions or employee contributions under the plan (including the potential for discretionary matching contributions) and the conditions under which such contributions are made;

(C) The plan to which safe harbor contributions will be made (if different than the plan containing the cash or deferred arrangement);

(D) The type and amount of compensation that may be deferred under the plan;

(E) How to make cash or deferred elections, including any administrative requirements that apply to such elections;

(F) The periods available under the plan for making cash or deferred elections;

(G) Withdrawal and vesting provisions applicable to contributions under the plan; and

(H) Information that makes it easy to obtain additional information about the plan (including an additional copy of the summary plan description) such as telephone numbers, addresses and, if applicable, electronic addresses, of individuals or offices from whom employees can obtain such plan information.

(iii) References to SPD. A plan will not fail to satisfy the content requirements of this paragraph (d)(2) merely because, in the case of information described in paragraph (d)(2)(ii)(B) of this section (relating to any other contributions under the plan), paragraph (d)(2)(ii)(C) of this section (relating to the plan to which safe harbor contributions will be made) or paragraph (d)(2)(ii)(D) of this section (relating to the type and amount of compensation that may be deferred under the plan), the notice cross-references the relevant portions of a summary plan description that provides the same information that would be provided in accordance with such paragraphs and that has been provided (or is concurrently provided) to employees.

*(3) Timing requirement.* (i) General rule. The timing requirement of this paragraph (d)(3) is satisfied if the notice is provided within a reasonable period before the beginning of the plan year (or, in the year an employee becomes eligible, within a reasonable period before the employee becomes eligible). The determination of whether a notice satisfies the timing requirement of this paragraph (d)(3) is based on all of the relevant facts and circumstances.

(ii) Deemed satisfaction of timing requirement. The timing requirement of this paragraph (d)(3) is deemed to be satisfied if at least 30 days (and no more than 90 days) before the beginning of each plan year, the notice is given to each eligible employee for the plan year. In the case of an employee who does not receive the notice within the period described in the previous sentence because the employee becomes eligible after the 90th day before the beginning of the plan year, the timing requirement is deemed to be satisfied if the notice is provided no more than 90 days before the employee becomes eligible (and no later than the date the employee becomes eligible). Thus, for example, the preceding sentence would apply in the case of any employee eligible for the first plan year under a newly established plan that provides for elective contributions, or would apply in the case of the first plan year in which an employee becomes eligible under an existing plan that provides for elective contributions. If it is not practicable for the notice to be provided on or before the date specified in the plan that an employee becomes eligible, the notice will nonetheless be treated as provided timely if it is provided as soon as practicable after that date and the employee is permitted to elect to defer from all types of compensation that may be deferred under the plan earned beginning on the date the employee becomes eligible.

**(e) Plan year requirement.** *(1) General rule.* Except as provided in this paragraph (e) or in paragraph (f) of this section, a plan will fail to satisfy the requirements of sections 401(k)(12), 401(k)(13), and this section unless plan provisions that satisfy the rules of this section are adopted before the first day of the plan year and remain in effect for an entire 12-month plan year. In addition, except as provided in paragraph (g) of this section, a plan which includes provisions that satisfy the rules of this section will not satisfy the requirements of § 1.401(k)-1(b) if it is amended to change such provisions for that plan year. Moreover, if, as described under paragraph (h)(4) of this section, safe harbor matching or nonelective contributions will be made to another plan for a plan year, provisions under that other plan specifying that the safe harbor contributions will be made and providing that the contributions will be QNECs or QMACs must also be adopted before the first day of that plan year.

*(2) Initial plan year.* A newly established plan (other than a successor plan within the meaning of § 1.401(k)-2(c)(2)(iii)) will not be treated as violating the requirements of this paragraph (e) merely because the plan year is less than 12 months, provided that the plan year is at least 3 months long (or, in the case of a newly established employer that establishes the plan as soon as administratively feasible after the employer comes into existence, a shorter period). Similarly, a cash or deferred arrangement will not fail to satisfy the requirement of this paragraph (e) if it is added to an existing profit sharing, stock bonus, or pre-ERISA money purchase pension plan for the first time during that year provided that—

(i) The plan is not a successor plan; and

(ii) The cash or deferred arrangement is made effective no later than 3 months prior to the end of the plan year.

*(3) Change of plan year.* A plan that has a short plan year as a result of changing its plan year will not fail to satisfy the requirements of paragraph (e)(1) of this section merely because the plan year has less than 12 months, provided that—

(i) The plan satisfied the requirements of this section for the immediately preceding plan year; and

(ii) The plan satisfies the requirements of this section (determined without regard to paragraph (g) of this section) for the immediately following plan year (or for the immediately following 12 months if the immediately following plan year is less than 12 months).

*(4) Final plan year.* A plan that terminates during a plan year will not fail to satisfy the requirements of paragraph (e)(1) of this section merely because the final plan year is less than 12 months, provided that the plan satisfies the requirement of this section through the date of termination and either—

(i) The plan would satisfy the requirements of paragraph (g) of this section, treating the termination of the plan as a reduction or suspension of safe harbor matching contributions, other than the requirement that employees have a reasonable opportunity to change their cash or deferred elections and, if applicable, employee contribution elections; or

(ii) The plan termination is in connection with a transaction described in section 410(b)(6)(C) or the employer incurs a substantial business hardship comparable to a substantial business hardship described in section 412(d).

**(f) Plan amendments adopting safe harbor nonelective contributions.** *(1) General rule.* Notwithstanding paragraph (e)(1) of this section, a plan that provides for the use of the current year testing method may be amended after the first day of the plan year and no later than 30 days before the last day of the plan year to adopt the safe harbor method of this section, effective as of the first day of the plan year, using nonelective contributions under paragraph (b) of this section, but only if the plan provides the contingent and follow-up notices described in this section. A plan amendment made pursuant to this paragraph (f)(1) for a plan year may provide for the use of the safe harbor method described in this section solely for that plan year and a plan sponsor is not limited in the number of years for which it is permitted to adopt an amendment providing for the safe harbor method of this section using nonelective contributions under paragraph (b) of this section and this paragraph (f).

*(2) Contingent notice provided.* A plan satisfies the requirement to provide the contingent notice under this paragraph (f)(2) if it provides a notice that would satisfy the requirements of paragraph (d) of this section, except that, in lieu of setting forth the safe harbor contributions used under the plan as set forth in paragraph (d)(2)(ii)(A) of this section, the notice specifies that the plan may be amended during the plan year to include the safe harbor nonelective contribution and that, if the plan is amended, a follow-up notice will be provided.

*(3) Follow-up notice requirement.* A plan satisfies the requirement to provide a follow-up notice under this paragraph (f)(3) if, no later than 30 days before the last day of the plan year, each eligible employee is given a notice that states that the safe harbor nonelective contributions will be made for the plan year. The notice must be in writing or in such other form as may be prescribed by the Commissioner and is permitted to be combined with a contingent notice provided under paragraph (f)(2) of this section for the next plan year.

**(g) Permissible reduction or suspension of safe harbor matching contributions.** *(1) General rule.* A plan that provides for safe harbor matching contributions will not fail to satisfy the requirements of section 401(k)(3) for a plan year merely because the plan is amended during a plan year to reduce or suspend safe harbor matching contributions on future elective contributions (and, if applicable, employee contributions) provided that—

(i) All eligible employees are provided the supplemental notice in accordance with paragraph (g)(2) of this section;

(ii) The reduction or suspension of safe harbor matching contributions is effective no earlier than the later of 30 days after eligible employees are provided the notice described in paragraph (g)(2) of this section and the date the amendment is adopted;

(iii) Eligible employees are given a reasonable opportunity (including a reasonable period after receipt of the supplemental notice) prior to the reduction or suspension of safe harbor matching contributions to change their cash or deferred elections and, if applicable, their employee contribution elections;

(iv) The plan is amended to provide that the ADP test will be satisfied for the entire plan year in which the reduction or suspension occurs using the current year testing method described in § 1.401(k)-2(a)(2)(ii); and

(v) The plan satisfies the requirements of this section (other than this paragraph (g)) with respect to amounts deferred through the effective date of the amendment.

*(2) Notice of suspension requirement.* The notice of suspension requirement of this paragraph (g)(2) is satisfied if each eligible employee is given a notice (in writing or such other form as prescribed by the Commissioner) that explains—

(i) The consequences of the amendment which reduces or suspends matching contributions on future elective contributions and, if applicable, employee contributions;

(ii) The procedures for changing their cash or deferred election and, if applicable, their employee contribution elections; and

(iii) The effective date of the amendment.

**(h) Additional rules.** *(1) Contributions taken into account.* A contribution is taken into account for purposes of this section for a plan year if and only if the contribution would be taken into account for such plan year under the rules of § 1.401(k)-2(a) or 1.401(m)-2(a). Thus, for example, a safe harbor matching contribution must be made within 12 months of the end of the plan year. Similarly, an elective contribution that would be taken into account for a plan year under § 1.401(k)-2(a)(4)(i)(B)(2) must be taken into account for such plan year for purposes of this section, even if the compensation would have been received after the close of the plan year.

*(2) Use of safe harbor nonelective contributions to satisfy other nondiscrimination tests.* A safe harbor nonelective contribution used to satisfy the nonelective contribution requirement under paragraph (b) of this section may also be taken into account for purposes of determining whether a plan satisfies section 401(a)(4). Thus, these contributions are not subject to the limitations on qualified nonelective contributions under § 1.401(k)-2(a)(6)(ii), but are subject to the rules generally applicable to nonelective contributions under section 401(a)(4). See § 1.401(a)(4)-1(b)(2)(ii). However, pursuant to section 401(k)(12)(E)(ii) and section 401(k)(13)(D)(iv), to the extent they are needed to satisfy the safe harbor contribution requirement of paragraph (b) of this section, safe harbor nonelective contributions may not be taken into account under any plan for purposes of section 401(l) (including the imputation of permitted disparity under § 1.401(a)(4)-7).

*(3) Early participation rules.* Section 401(k)(3)(F) and § 1.401(k)-2(a)(1)(iii)(A), which provide an alternative nondiscrimination rule for certain plans that provide for early participation, do not apply for purposes of section 401(k)(12), section 401(k)(13), and this section. Thus, a plan is not treated as satisfying this section with respect to the eligible employees who have not completed the minimum age and service requirements of section 410(a)(1)(A) unless the plan satisfies the requirements of this section with respect to such eligible employees. However, a plan is permitted to apply the rules of section 410(b)(4)(B) to treat the plan as two separate plans for purposes of section 410(b) and apply the safe harbor requirements of this section to one plan and apply the requirements of § 1.401(k)-2 to the other plan. See § 1.401(k)-1(b)(4)(vi), Example 2.

*(4) Satisfying safe harbor contribution requirement under another defined contribution plan.* Safe harbor matching or nonelective contributions may be made to the plan that contains the cash or deferred arrangement or to another defined contribution plan that satisfies section 401(a) or 403(a). If safe harbor contributions are made to another defined contribution plan, the safe harbor plan must specify the plan to which the safe harbor contributions are made and the contribution requirement of paragraph (b) or (c) of this section must be satisfied in the other defined contribution plan in the same manner as if the contributions were made to the plan that contains the cash or deferred arrangement. Consequently, the plan to which the contributions are made must have the same plan year as the plan containing the cash and deferred arrangement and each employee eligible under the plan containing the cash or deferred arrangement must be eligible under the same conditions under the other defined contribution plan. The plan to which the safe harbor contributions are made need not be a plan that can be aggregated with the plan that contains the cash or deferred arrangement.

*(5) Contributions used only once.* Safe harbor matching or nonelective contributions cannot be used to satisfy the requirements of this section with respect to more than one plan.

**(i)** [Reserved].

**(j) Qualified automatic contribution arrangement.** *(1) Automatic contribution requirement.* (i) In general. A cash or deferred arrangement is described in this paragraph (j) if it is an automatic contribution arrangement described in paragraph (j)(1)(ii) of this section where the default election under that arrangement is a contribution equal to the qualified percentage described in paragraph (j)(2) of this section multiplied by the eligible employee's compensation from which elective contributions are permitted to be made under the cash or deferred arrangement. For plan years beginning on or after January 1, 2010, the compensation used for this purpose must be safe harbor compensation as defined under paragraph (b)(2) of this section.

(ii) Automatic contribution arrangement. An automatic contribution arrangement is a cash or deferred arrangement within the meaning of § 1.401(k)-1(a)(2) that provides that, in the absence of an eligible employee's affirmative election, a default election applies under which the employee is treated as having made an election to have a specified contribution made on his or her behalf under the plan. The default election begins to apply with respect to an eligible employee no earlier than a reasonable period of time after receipt of the notice describing the automatic contribution arrangement. The default election ceases to apply with respect to an eligible employee for periods of time with respect to which the employee has an affirmative election that is currently in effect to—

(A) Have elective contributions made in a different amount on his or her behalf (in a specified amount or percentage of compensation); or

(B) Not have any elective contributions made on his or her behalf.

(iii) Exception to automatic enrollment for certain current employees. An automatic contribution arrangement will not fail to be a qualified automatic contribution arrangement merely because the default election provided under paragraph (j)(1)(i) of this section is not applied to an employee who was an eligible employee under the cash or deferred arrangement (or a predecessor arrangement) immediately prior to the effective date of the qualified automatic contribution arrangement and on that effective date had an affirmative election in effect (that remains in effect) to—

(A) Have elective contributions made on his or her behalf (in a specified amount or percentage of compensation); or

(B) Not have elective contributions made on his or her behalf.

*(2) Qualified percentage.* (i) In general. A percentage is a qualified percentage only if it—

(A) Is uniform for all employees (except to the extent provided in paragraph (j)(2)(iii) of this section);

(B) Does not exceed 10 percent; and

(C) Satisfies the minimum percentage requirements of paragraph (j)(2)(ii) of this section.

(ii) Minimum percentage requirements. (A) Initial-period requirement. The minimum percentage requirement of this paragraph (j)(2)(ii)(A) is satisfied only if the percentage that applies for the initial period is at least 3 percent. For this purpose, the initial period begins when the employee first has contributions made pursuant to a default election under an arrangement that is intended to be a qualified automatic contribution arrangement for a plan year and ends on the last day of the following plan year.

(B) Second-year requirement. The minimum percentage requirement of this paragraph (j)(2)(ii)(B) is satisfied only if the percentage that applies for the plan year immediately following the last day described in paragraph (j)(2)(ii)(A) of this section is at least 4 percent.

(C) Third-year requirement. The minimum percentage requirement of this paragraph (j)(2)(ii)(C) is satisfied only if the percentage that applies for the plan year immediately following the plan year described in paragraph (j)(2)(ii)(B) of this section is at least 5 percent.

(D) Later years requirement. A percentage satisfies the minimum percentage requirement of this paragraph (j)(2)(ii)(D) only if the percentage that applies for all plan years following the plan year described in paragraph (j)(2)(ii)(C) of this section is at least 6 percent.

(iii) Exception to uniform percentage requirement. A plan does not fail to satisfy the uniform percentage requirement of paragraph (j)(2)(i)(A) of this section merely because—

(A) The percentage varies based on the number of years (or portions of years) since the beginning of the initial period for an eligible employee;

(B) The rate of elective contributions under a cash or deferred election that is in effect for an employee immediately prior to the effective date of the default percentage under the qualified automatic contribution arrangement is not reduced;

(C) The rate of elective contributions is limited so as not to exceed the limits of sections 401(a)(17), 402(g) (determined with or without catch-up contributions described in section 402(g)(1)(C) or 402(g)(7)), and 415; or

(D) The default election provided under paragraph (j)(1)(i) of this section is not applied during the period an employee is not permitted to make elective contributions in order for the plan to satisfy the requirements of § 1.401(k)-3(c)(6)(v)(B).

(iv) Treatment of periods without default contributions. The minimum percentages described in paragraph (j)(2)(ii) of this section are based on the date the initial period begins, regardless of whether the employee is eligible to make elective contributions under the plan after that date. Thus, for example, if an employee is ineligible to make contributions under the plan for 6 months because the employee had a hardship withdrawal and the 6-month period includes a date as of which the default minimum percentage is increased, then the default percentage must reflect that increase when the employee is permitted to resume contributions. However, for purposes of determining the date the initial period described in paragraph (j)(2)(ii)(A) of this section begins, a plan is permitted to treat an employee who for an entire plan year did not have contributions made pursuant to a default election under the qualified automatic contribution arrangement as if the employee had not had such contributions made for any prior plan year as well.

**(k) Modifications to contribution requirements and notice requirements for automatic contribution safe harbor.** *(1) In general.* A cash or deferred arrangement satisfies the contribution requirements of this paragraph (k) only if it satisfies the contribution requirements of either paragraph (b) or (c) of this section, as modified by the rules of paragraphs (k)(2) and (k)(3) of this section. In addition, a cash or deferred arrangement satisfies the notice requirement of section 401(k)(13)(E) only if the notice satisfies the additional requirements of paragraph (k)(4) of this section.

*(2) Lower matching requirement.* In applying the requirement of paragraph (c) of this section in the case of a cash or deferred arrangement, the basic matching formula is modified so that each eligible NHCE must receive the sum of—

(i) 100 percent of the employee's elective contributions that do not exceed 1 percent of the employee's safe harbor compensation; and

(ii) 50 percent of the employee's elective contributions that exceed 1 percent of the employee's safe harbor compensation but that do not exceed 6 percent of the employee's safe harbor compensation.

*(3) Modified nonforfeiture requirement.* A cash or deferred arrangement described in paragraph (j) of this section will not fail to satisfy the requirements of paragraph (b) or (c) of this section, as applicable, merely because the safe harbor contributions are not qualified nonelective contributions or qualified matching contributions provided that—

(i) The contributions are subject to the withdrawal restrictions that apply to QNECs and QMACs, as set forth in § 1.401(k)-1(d); and

(ii) Any employee who has completed 2 years of service (within the meaning of section 411(a)) has a nonforfeitable right to the account balance attributable to the safe harbor contributions.

*(4) Additional notice requirements.* (i) In general. A notice satisfies the requirements of this paragraph (k)(4) only if it includes the additional information described in paragraph (k)(4)(ii) of this section and satisfies the timing requirements of paragraph (k)(4)(iii) of this section.

(ii) Additional information. A notice satisfies the additional information requirement of this paragraph (k)(4)(ii) only if it explains—

(A) The level of elective contributions which will be made on the employee's behalf if the employee does not make an affirmative election;

(B) The employee's right under the arrangement to elect not to have elective contributions made on the employee's behalf (or to elect to have such contributions made in a different amount or percentage of compensation); and

(C) How contributions under the arrangement will be invested (including, in the case of an arrangement under which the employee may elect among 2 or more investment options, how contributions will be invested in the absence of an investment election by the employee).

(iii) Timing requirements. A notice satisfies the timing requirements of this paragraph (k)(4)(iii) only if it is provided sufficiently early so that the employee has a reasonable period of time after receipt of the notice to make the elections described under paragraph (k)(4)(ii)(B) and (C) of this section. However, the requirement in the preceding sentence that an employee have a reasonable period of time after receipt of the notice to make an alternative election does not permit a plan to make the default election effective any later than the earlier of—

(A) The pay date for the second payroll period that begins after the date the notice is provided; and

(B) The first pay date that occurs at least 30 days after the notice is provided.

---

T.D. 9169, 12/28/2004, amend T.D. 9294, 10/19/2006, T.D. 9447, 02/23/2009.

---

PAR. 3. Section 1.401(k)-3 is amended by:

1. Revising paragraph (e)(4)(ii).

2. Revising paragraph (g).

The revisions read as follows:

**Proposed § 1.401(k)-3 Safe harbor requirements.** [*For Preamble, see ¶ 153,107*]

* * * * *

**(e)** * * *

*(4)* * * *

(ii) The plan termination is in connection with a transaction described in section 410(b)(6)(C) or the employer incurs a substantial business hardship comparable to a substantial business hardship described in section 412(c).

* * * * *

**(g) Permissible reduction or suspension of safe harbor contributions.** *(1) General rule.* (i) Matching contributions. A plan that provides for safe harbor matching contributions intended to satisfy the requirements of paragraph (c) of this section for a plan year will not fail to satisfy the requirements of section 401(k)(3) merely because the plan is amended during the plan year to reduce or suspend safe harbor matching contributions on future elective contributions (and, if applicable, employee contributions) provided that—

(A) All eligible employees are provided the supplemental notice in accordance with paragraph (g)(2) of this section;

(B) The reduction or suspension of safe harbor matching contributions is effective no earlier than the later of 30 days after eligible employees are provided the supplemental notice described in paragraph (g)(2) of this section and the date the amendment is adopted;

(C) Eligible employees are given a reasonable opportunity (including a reasonable period after receipt of the supplemental notice) prior to the reduction or suspension of safe harbor matching contributions to change their cash or deferred elections and, if applicable, their employee contribution elections;

(D) The plan is amended to provide that the ADP test will be satisfied for the entire plan year in which the reduction or suspension occurs using the current year testing method described in § 1.401(k)-2(a)(2)(ii); and

(E) The plan satisfies the requirements of this section (other than this paragraph (g)) with respect to amounts deferred through the effective date of the amendment.

(ii) Nonelective contributions. A plan that provides for safe harbor nonelective contributions intended to satisfy the requirements of paragraph (b) of this section for the plan year will not fail to satisfy the requirements of section 401(k)(3) merely because the plan is amended during the plan year to reduce or suspend safe harbor nonelective contributions provided that—

(A) The employer incurs a substantial business hardship (comparable to a substantial business hardship described in section 412(c));

(B) The amendment is adopted after May 18, 2009;

(C) All eligible employees are provided the supplemental notice in accordance with paragraph (g)(2) of this section;

(D) The reduction or suspension of safe harbor nonelective contributions is effective no earlier than the later of 30 days after eligible employees are provided the supplemental notice described in paragraph (g)(2) of this section and the date the amendment is adopted;

(E) Eligible employees are given a reasonable opportunity (including a reasonable period after receipt of the supplemental notice) prior to the reduction or suspension of nonelective contributions to change their cash or deferred elections and, if applicable, their employee contribution elections;

(F) The plan is amended to provide that the ADP test will be satisfied for the entire plan year in which the reduction or suspension occurs using the current year testing method described in § 1.401(k)-2(a)(2)(ii); and

(G) The plan satisfies the requirements of this section (other than this paragraph (g)) with respect to safe harbor compensation paid through the effective date of the amendment.

*(2) Supplemental notice.* The supplemental notice requirement of this paragraph (g)(2) is satisfied if each eligible employee is given a notice (in writing or such other form as prescribed by the Commissioner) that explains—

(i) The consequences of the amendment which reduces or suspends future safe harbor contributions;

(ii) The procedures for changing their cash or deferred elections and, if applicable, their employee contribution elections; and

(ii) The effective date of the amendment.

**§ 1.401(k)-4 SIMPLE 401(k) plan requirements.**

**(a) General rule.** A cash or deferred arrangement satisfies the SIMPLE 401(k) plan provision of section 401(k)(11) for a plan year if the arrangement satisfies the requirements of paragraphs (b) through (i) of this section for that year. A plan that contains a cash or deferred arrangement that satisfies this section is referred to as a SIMPLE 401(k) plan. Pursuant to section 401(k)(11), a SIMPLE 401(k) plan is treated as satisfying the ADP test of section 401(k)(3)(A)(ii) for that year.

**(b) Eligible employer.** *(1) General rule.* A SIMPLE 401(k) plan must be established by an eligible employer. Eligible employer for purposes of this section means, with respect to any plan year, an employer that had no more than 100 employees who each received at least $5,000 of SIMPLE compensation, as defined in paragraph (e)(5) of this section, from the employer for the prior calendar year.

*(2) Special rule.* An eligible employer that establishes a SIMPLE 401(k) plan for a plan year and that fails to be an eligible employer for any subsequent plan year, is treated as an eligible employer for the 2 plan years following the last plan year the employer was an eligible employer. If the failure is due to any acquisition, disposition, or similar transaction involving an eligible employer, the preceding sentence applies only if the provisions of section 410(b)(6)(C)(i) are satisfied.

**(c) Exclusive plan.** *(1) General rule.* The SIMPLE 401(k) plan must be the exclusive plan for each SIMPLE 401(k) plan participant for the plan year. This requirement is satisfied if there are no contributions made, or benefits accrued, for services during the plan year on behalf of any SIMPLE 401(k) plan participant under any other qualified plan maintained by the employer. Other qualified plan for purposes of this section means any plan, contract, pension, or trust described in section 219(g)(5)(A) or (B).

*(2) Special rule.* A SIMPLE 401(k) plan will not be treated as failing the requirements of this paragraph (c) merely because any SIMPLE 401(k) plan participant receives an allocation of forfeitures under another plan of the employer.

**(d) Election and notice.** *(1) General rule.* An eligible employer establishing or maintaining a SIMPLE 401(k) plan must satisfy the election and notice requirements in paragraphs (d)(2) and (3) of this section.

*(2) Employee elections.* (i) Initial plan year of participation. For the plan year in which an employee first becomes eligible under the SIMPLE 401(k) plan, the employee must be permitted to make a cash or deferred election under the plan during a 60-day period that includes either the day the employee becomes eligible or the day before.

(ii) Subsequent plan years. For each subsequent plan year, each eligible employee must be permitted to make or modify his cash or deferred election during the 60-day period immediately preceding such plan year.

(iii) Election to terminate. An eligible employee must be permitted to terminate his cash or deferred election at any time. If an employee does terminate his cash or deferred election, the plan is permitted to provide that such employee cannot have elective contributions made under the plan for the remainder of the plan year.

*(3) Employee notices.* The employer must notify each eligible employee within a reasonable time prior to each 60-day election period, or on the day the election period starts, that he or she can make a cash or deferred election, or mod-

ify a prior election, if applicable, during that period. The notice must state whether the eligible employer will make the matching contributions described in paragraph (e)(3) of this section or the nonelective contributions described in paragraph (e)(4) of this section.

**(e) Contributions.** *(1) General rule.* A SIMPLE 401(k) plan satisfies the contribution requirements of this paragraph (e) for a plan year only if no contributions may be made to the SIMPLE 401(k) plan during such year, other than contributions described in this paragraph (e) and rollover contributions described in § 1.402(c)-2, Q&A-1(a).

*(2) Elective contributions.* Subject to the limitations on annual additions under section 415, each eligible employee must be permitted to make an election to have up to $10,000 of elective contributions made on the employee's behalf under the SIMPLE 401(k) plan for a plan year. The $10,000 limit is increased beginning in 2006 in the same manner as the $160,000 amount is adjusted under section 415(d), except that pursuant to section 408(p)(2)(E)(ii) the base period shall be the calendar quarter beginning July 1, 2004 and any increase which is not a multiple of $500 is rounded to the next lower multiple of $500.

*(3) Matching contributions.* Each plan year, the eligible employer must contribute a matching contribution to the account of each eligible employee on whose behalf elective contributions were made for the plan year. The amount of the matching contribution must equal the lesser of the eligible employee's elective contributions for the plan year or 3% of the eligible employee's SIMPLE compensation for the entire plan year.

*(4) Nonelective contributions.* For any plan year, in lieu of contributing matching contributions described in paragraph (e)(3) of this section, an eligible employer may, in accordance with plan terms, contribute a nonelective contribution to the account of each eligible employee in an amount equal to 2% of the eligible employee's SIMPLE compensation for the entire plan year. The eligible employer may limit the nonelective contributions to those eligible employees who received at least $5,000 of SIMPLE compensation from the employer for the entire plan year.

*(5) SIMPLE compensation.* Except as otherwise provided, the term SIMPLE compensation for purposes of this section means the sum of wages, tips, and other compensation from the eligible employer subject to federal income tax withholding (as described in section 6051(a)(3)) and the employee's elective contributions made under any other plan, and if applicable, elective deferrals under a section 408(p) SIMPLE IRA plan, a section 408(k)(6) SARSEP, or a plan or contract that satisfies the requirements of section 403(b), and compensation deferred under a section 457 plan, required to be reported by the employer on Form W-2 (as described in section 6051(a)(8)). For self-employed individuals, SIMPLE compensation means net earnings from self-employment determined under section 1402(a) prior to subtracting any contributions made under the SIMPLE 401(k) plan on behalf of the individual.

**(f) Vesting.** All benefits attributable to contributions described in paragraph (e) of this section must be nonforfeitable at all times.

**(g) Plan year.** The plan year of a SIMPLE 401(k) plan must be the whole calendar year. Thus, in general, a SIMPLE 401(k) plan can be established only on January 1 and can be terminated only on December 31. However, in the case of an employer that did not previously maintain a SIMPLE 401(k) plan, the establishment date can be as late as October 1 (or later in the case of an employer that comes into existence after October 1 and establishes the SIMPLE 401(k) plan as soon as administratively feasible after the employer comes into existence).

**(h) Other rules.** A SIMPLE 401(k) plan is not treated as a top-heavy plan under section 416. See section 416(g)(4)(G).

T.D. 9169, 12/28/2004.

## § 1.401(k)-5 Special rules for mergers, acquisitions and similar events. [Reserved]

T.D. 9169, 12/28/2004.

## § 1.401(k)-6 Definitions.

Unless otherwise provided, the definitions of this section govern for purposes of section 401(k) and the regulations thereunder.

Actual contribution percentage (ACP) test. Actual contribution percentage test or ACP test means the test described in § 1.401(m)-2(a)(1).

Actual deferral percentage (ADP). Actual deferral percentage or ADP means the ADP of the group of eligible employees as defined in § 1.401(k)-2(a)(2).

Actual deferral percentage (ADP) test. Actual deferral percentage test or ADP test means the test described in § 1.401(k)-2(a)(1).

Actual deferral ratio (ADR). Actual deferral ratio or ADR means the ADR of an eligible employee as defined in § 1.401(k)-2(a)(3).

Cash or deferred arrangement. Cash or deferred arrangement is defined in § 1.401(k)-1(a)(2).

Cash or deferred election. Cash or deferred election is defined in § 1.401(k)-1(a)(3).

Compensation. Compensation means compensation as defined in section 414(s) and § 1.414(s)-1. The period used to determine an employee's compensation for a plan year must be either the plan year or the calendar year ending within the plan year. Whichever period is selected must be applied uniformly to determine the compensation of every eligible employee under the plan for that plan year. A plan may, however, limit the period taken into account under either method to that portion of the plan year or calendar year in which the employee was an eligible employee, provided that this limit is applied uniformly to all eligible employees under the plan for the plan year. In the case of an HCE whose ADR is determined under § 1.401(k)-2(a)(3)(ii), period of participation includes periods under another plan for which elective contributions are aggregated under § 1.401(k)-2(a)(3)(ii). See also section 401(a)(17) and § 1.401(a)(17)-1(c)(1).

Current year testing method. Current year testing method means the testing method described in § 1.401(k)-2(a)(2)(ii) or 1.401(m)-2(a)(2)(ii) under which the applicable year is the current plan year.

Elective contributions. Elective contributions means employer contributions made to a plan pursuant to a cash or deferred election under a cash or deferred arrangement (whether or not the arrangement is a qualified cash or deferred arrangement under § 1.401(k)-1(a)(4)).

Designated Roth account. Designated Roth account means a separate account maintained by a plan to which only designated Roth contributions (including income, expenses, gains and losses attributable thereto) are made.

Designated Roth contributions. Designated Roth contributions means designated Roth contributions as defined in § 1.401(k)-1(f)(1).

Eligible employee—(1) General rule. Eligible employee means an employee who is directly or indirectly eligible to make a cash or deferred election under the plan for all or a portion of the plan year. For example, if an employee must perform purely ministerial or mechanical acts (e.g., formal application for participation or consent to payroll withholding) in order to be eligible to make a cash or deferred election for a plan year, the employee is an eligible employee for the plan year without regard to whether the employee performs the acts.

(2) Conditions on eligibility. An employee who is unable to make a cash or deferred election because the employee has not contributed to another plan is also an eligible employee. By contrast, if an employee must perform additional service (e.g., satisfy a minimum period of service requirement) in order to be eligible to make a cash or deferred election for a plan year, the employee is not an eligible employee for the plan year unless the service is actually performed. See § 1.401(k)-1(e)(5), however, for certain limits on the use of minimum service requirements. An employee who would be eligible to make elective contributions but for a suspension due to a distribution, a loan, or an election not to participate in the plan, is treated as an eligible employee for purposes of section 401(k)(3) for a plan year even though the employee may not make a cash or deferred election by reason of the suspension. Finally, an employee does not fail to be treated as an eligible employee merely because the employee may receive no additional annual additions because of section 415(c)(1).

(3) Certain one-time elections. An employee is not an eligible employee merely because the employee, no later than the employee's first becoming eligible to make a cash or deferred election under any plan or arrangement of the employer (described in section 219(g)(5)(A)), is given the one-time opportunity to elect, and the employee does in fact elect, not to be eligible to make a cash or deferred election under the plan or any other plan or arrangement maintained by the employer (including plans not yet established) for the duration of the employee's employment with the employer. This rule applies in addition to the rules in § 1.401(k)-1(a)(3)(v) relating to the definition of a cash or deferred election. In no event is an election made after December 23, 1994, treated as a one-time irrevocable election under this paragraph if the election is made by an employee who previously became eligible under another plan or arrangement (whether or not terminated) of the employer.

Eligible HCE. Eligible HCE means an eligible employee who is an HCE.

Eligible NHCE. Eligible NHCE means an eligible employee who is not an HCE.

Employee. Employee means an employee within the meaning of § 1.410(b)-9.

Employee stock ownership plan (ESOP). Employee stock ownership plan or ESOP means the portion of a plan that is an ESOP within the meaning of § 1.410(b)-7(c)(2).

Employer. Employer means an employer within the meaning of § 1.410(b)-9.

Excess contributions. Excess contributions means, with respect to a plan year, the amount of total excess contributions apportioned to an HCE under § 1.401(k)-2(b)(2)(iii).

Excess deferrals. Excess deferrals means excess deferrals as defined in § 1.402(g)-1(e)(3).

Highly compensated employee (HCE). Highly compensated employee or HCE has the meaning provided in section 414(q).

Matching contributions. Matching contributions means matching contributions as defined in § 1.401(m)-1(a)(2).

Nonelective contributions. Nonelective contributions means employer contributions (other than matching contributions) with respect to which the employee may not elect to have the contributions paid to the employee in cash or other benefits instead of being contributed to the plan.

Non-employee stock ownership plan (non-ESOP). Non-employee stock ownership plan or non-ESOP means the portion of a plan that is not an ESOP within the meaning of § 1.410(b)-7(c)(2).

Non-highly compensated employee (NHCE). Non-highly compensated employee or NHCE means an employee who is not an HCE. Plan. Plan is defined in § 1.401(k)-1(b)(4).

Pre-ERISA money purchase pension plan. (1) Pre-ERISA money purchase pension plan is a pension plan—

(i) That is a defined contribution plan (as defined in section 414(i));

(ii) That was in existence on June 27, 1974, and as in effect on that date, included a salary reduction agreement; and

(iii) Under which neither the employee contributions nor the employer contributions, including elective contributions, may exceed the levels (as a percentage of compensation) provided for by the contribution formula in effect on June 27, 1974.

(2) A plan was in existence on June 27, 1974, if it was a written plan adopted on or before that date, even if no funds had yet been paid to the trust associated with the plan.

Pre-tax elective contributions. Pre-tax elective contributions means elective contributions under a qualified cash or deferred arrangement that are not designated Roth contributions.

Prior year testing method. Prior year testing method means the testing method under which the applicable year is the prior plan year, as described in § 1.401(k)-2(a)(2)(ii) or 1.401(m)-2(a)(2)(ii).

Qualified matching contributions (QMACs). Qualified matching contributions or QMACs means matching contributions that, except as provided otherwise in § 1.401(k)-1(c) and (d), satisfy the requirements of § 1.401(k)-1(c) and (d) as though the contributions were elective contributions, without regard to whether the contributions are actually taken into account under the ADP test under § 1.401(k)-2(a)(6) or the ACP test under § 1.401(m)-2(a)(6). Thus, the matching contributions must satisfy the vesting requirements of § 1.401(k)-1(c) and be subject to the distribution requirements of § 1.401(k)-1(d) when they are contributed to the plan. See also § 1.401(k)-2(b)(4)(iii) for a rule providing that a matching contribution does not fail to qualify as a QMAC solely because it is forfeitable under section 411(a)(3)(G) as a result of being a matching contribution with respect to an excess deferral, excess contribution, or excess aggregate contribution, or it is forfeitable under § 1.414(w)-1(d)(2).

Qualified nonelective contributions (QNECs). Qualified nonelective contributions or QNECs means employer contributions, other than elective contributions or matching contributions, that, except as provided otherwise in § 1.401(k)-1(c) and (d), satisfy the requirements of § 1.401(k)-1(c) and (d) as though the contributions were elective contributions, without regard to whether the contributions are actually taken into account under the ADP test under § 1.401(k)-2(a)(6) or the ACP test under § 1.401(m)-2(a)(6). Thus, the nonelective contributions must satisfy the vesting requirements of § 1.401(k)-1(c) and be subject to the distribution requirements of § 1.401(k)-1(d) when they are contributed to the plan.

Rural cooperative plans. Rural cooperative plan means a plan described in section 401(k)(7).

T.D. 9169, 12/28/2004, amend T.D. 9237, 12/30/2005, T.D. 9447, 02/23/2009.

## § 1.401(l)-0 Table of contents.

This section contains a listing of the headings of §§ 1.401(l)-1 through 1.401(l)-6.

(1) In general.
(2) Maximum excess allowance.
(3) Maximum offset allowance.
(4) Rules of application.
(i) Disparity provided for the plan year.
(ii) Reductions in disparity rate.
(iii) Normal and optional forms of benefit.
(A) In general.
(B) Level annuity forms.
(C) Other forms.
(D) Post-retirement cost-of-living adjustments.
(1) In general.
(2) Requirements.
(E) Section 417(e) exception.
(5) Examples.
(c) Uniform disparity.
(1) In general.
(2) Deemed uniformity.
(i) In general.
(ii) Use of fractional accrual and disparity for 35 years.
(iii) Use of fractional accrual and disparity for fewer than 35 years.
(iv) Different social security retirement ages.
(v) Reduction for integration level.
(vi) Overall permitted disparity.
(A) In general.
(B) Unit credit plans.
(C) Fractional accrual plans.
(vii) Non-FICA employees.
(viii) Average annual compensation adjustment for offset plan.
(ix) PIA offsets.
(3) Examples.
(d) Requirements for integration level or offset compensation.
(1) In general.
(2) Covered compensation.
(3) Uniform percentage of covered compensation.
(4) Single dollar amount.
(5) Intermediate amount.
(6) Intermediate amount safe harbor.
(7) Prorated integration level for short plan year.
(8) Demographic requirements.
(i) In general.
(ii) Attained age requirement.
(iii) Nondiscrimination requirement.
(A) Minimum percentage test.
(B) Ratio test.
(C) High dollar amount test.
(D) Individual disparity reductions.
(9) Reduction in the 0.75 percent factor if integration or offset level exceeds covered compensation.
(i) In general.
(ii) Uniform percentage of covered compensation.
(iii) Single dollar amount.
(A) Plan-wide reduction.
(B) Individual reductions.
(iv) Reductions.
(A) Table.
(B) Interpolation.
(10) Examples.
(e) Adjustments to the 0.75-percent factor for benefits commencing at ages other than social security retirement age.
(1) In general.
(2) Adjustments.
(i) Benefits commencing on or after age 55 and before social security retirement age.
(ii) Benefits commencing after social security retirement age and on or before age 70.
(iii) Benefits commencing before age 55.
(iv) Benefits commencing after age 70.
(3) Tables.
(4) Benefit commencement date.
(i) In general.
(ii) Qualified social security supplement.
(5) Examples.
(f) Benefits, rights, and features.
(1) Defined benefit excess plan.
(2) Offset plan.
(3) Examples.
(g) No reductions in 0.75-percent factor for ancillary benefits.
(h) Benefits attributable to employee contributions not taken into account.
(i) Multiple integration levels. [Reserved]
(j) Additional rules.

*§ 1.401(l)-4 Special rules for railroad plans.*

(a) In general.
(b) Defined contribution plans.
(1) In general.
(2) Single integration level method.
(i) In general.
(ii) Definitions.
(3) Two integration level method.
(i) In general.
(ii) Total disparity requirement.
(iii) Intermediate disparity requirement.
(iv) Definitions.
(c) Defined benefit excess plans.
(1) In general.
(2) Single integration level method.
(i) In general.
(ii) Definitions.
(3) Two integration level method.
(i) In general.
(ii) Employee with lower covered compensation.
(iii) Employee with lower railroad retirement covered compensation.
(iv) Definitions.

T.D. 8359, 9/12/91, amend T.D. 8486, 8/31/93.

### § 1.401(l)-1 Permitted disparity in employer-provided contributions or benefits.

**(a) Permitted disparity.** *(1) In general.* Section 401(a)(4) provides that a plan is a qualified plan only if the amount of contributions or benefits provided under the plan does not discriminate in favor of highly compensated employees. See § 1.401(a)(4)-1(b)(2). Section 401(a)(5)(C) provides that a plan does not discriminate in favor of highly compensated employees merely because of disparities in employer-provided contributions or benefits provided to, or on behalf of, employees under the plan that are permitted under section 401(l). Thus, if a plan satisfies section 401(l), permitted disparities in employer-provided contributions or benefits under a plan are disregarded, by reason of section 401(a)(5)(C), in determining whether the plan satisfies any of the safe harbors under §§ 1.401(a)(4)-2(b)(2) and 1.401(a)(4)-3(b). However, even if disparities in employer-provided contributions or benefits under a plan are permitted under section 401(l) and thus do not cause the plan to fail to satisfy the § 1.401(a)(4)-1(b)(2), the plan may still fail to satisfy section 401(a)(4) for other reasons. Similarly, even if disparities in employer-provided contributions or benefits under a plan are not permitted under section 401(l) and thus may not be disregarded under section 401(a)(4) by reason of section 401(l), the plan may still be found to be nondiscriminatory under the tests of section 401(a)(4), including the rules for imputing permitted disparity under § 1.401(a)(4)-7.

*(2) Overview.* Rules relating to disparities in employer-provided contributions under a defined contribution plan are provided in § 1.401(l)-2. For rules relating to disparities in employer-provided benefits under a defined benefit plan, see § 1.401(l)-3. For rules relating to the application of section 401(l) to a plan maintained by a railroad employer, see § 1.401(l)-4. For rules relating to the overall permitted disparity limits, see § 1.401(l)-5. For rules relating to the effective date of section 401(l), see § 1.401(l)-6.

*(3) Exclusive rules.* The rules provided in §§ 1.401(l)-1 through 1.401(l)-6 are the exclusive means for a plan to satisfy sections 401(l) and 401(a)(5)(C). Accordingly, a plan that provides disparities in employer-provided contributions or benefits that are not permitted under §§ 1.401(l)-1 through 1.401(l)-6 does not satisfy section 401(l) or 401(a)(5)(C).

*(4) Exceptions.* Sections 401(a)(5)(C) and 401(l) are not available in the following arrangements—

(i) A plan maintained by an employer, determined for purposes of the Federal Insurance Contributions Act or the Railroad Retirement Tax Act, as applicable, that does not pay any wages within the meaning of section 3121(a) or compensation within the meaning of section 3231(e). For this purpose, a plan maintained for a self-employed individual within the meaning of section 401(c)(1), who is also subject to the tax under section 1401, is deemed to be a plan maintained by an employer that pays wages within the meaning of section 3121(a).

(ii) A plan, or the portion of a plan, that is an employee stock ownership plan described in section 4975(e)(7) (an ESOP) or a tax credit employee stock ownership plan described in section 409(a) (a TRASOP), except as provided in § 54.4975-11(a)(7)(ii) of this chapter, which contains a limited exception to this rule for certain ESOPs in existence on November 1, 1977.

(iii) With respect to elective contributions as defined in § 1.401(k)-6 under a qualified cash or deferred arrangement as defined in § 1.401(k)-1(a)(4)(i) or with respect to employee or matching contributions defined in § 1.401(m)-1(a)(3) or (a)(2), respectively.

(iv) With respect to contributions to a simplified employee pension made under a salary reduction arrangement described in section 408(k)(6) (a SARSEP).

*(5) Additional rules.* The Commissioner may, in revenue rulings, notices, or other documents of general applicability, prescribe additional rules that may be necessary or appropriate to carry out the purposes of section 401(l), including rules applying section 401(l) with respect to an employer that pays wages within the meaning of section 3121(a) or compensation within the meaning of section 3231(e) for some years and not other years.

**(b) Relationship to other requirements.** Unless explicitly provided otherwise, section 401(l) does not provide an exception to any other requirement under section 401(a). Thus, for example, even if the plan complies with section 401(l), the plan may not provide a benefit lower than the minimum benefit required under section 416. Moreover, a plan may not adjust benefits in any manner that results in a decrease in any employee's accrued benefit in violation of section 411(d)(6) and section 411(b)(1)(G). However, a plan does not fail to satisfy section 401(l) merely because, in order to ensure compliance with section 411, an employee's accrued benefit under the plan is defined as the greater of the employee's previously accrued benefit and the benefit determined under a strict application of the plan's benefit formula and accrual method. See section 401(a)(15) for additional rules relating to circumstances under which plan benefits may not be decreased because of increases in social security benefits.

**(c) Definitions.** In applying §§ 1.401(l)-1 through 1.401(l)-6, the definitions in this paragraph (c) govern unless otherwise provided.

*(1) Accumulation plan.* "Accumulation plan" means an accumulation plan within the meaning of § 1.401(a)(4)-12.

*(2) Average annual compensation.* "Average annual compensation" means average annual compensation within the meaning of § 1.401(a)(4)-3(e)(2).

*(3) Base benefit percentage.* "Base benefit percentage" means the rate at which employer-provided benefits are determined under a defined benefit excess plan with respect to an employee's average annual compensation at or below the integration level (expressed as a percentage of such average annual compensation).

*(4) Base contribution percentage.* "Base contribution percentage" means the rate at which employer contributions are allocated to the account of an employee under a defined contribution excess plan with respect to the employee's plan year compensation at or below the integration level (expressed as a percentage of such plan year compensation).

*(5) Benefit formula.* "Benefit formula" means benefit formula within the meaning of § 1.401(a)(4)-12.

*(6) Benefit, right, or feature.* "Benefit, right, or feature" means a benefit, right, or feature within the meaning of § 1.401(a)(4)-12.

*(7) Covered compensation.* (i) In general. "Covered compensation" for an employee means the average (without indexing) of the taxable wage bases in effect for each calendar year during the 35-year period ending with the last day of the calendar year in which the employee attains (or will attain) social security retirement age. A 35-year period is used for all individuals regardless of the year of birth of the individual. In determining an employee's covered compensation for a plan year, the taxable wage base for all calendar years beginning after the first day of the plan year is assumed to be the same as the taxable wage base in effect as of the beginning of the plan year. An employee's covered compensation for a plan year beginning after the 35-year period applicable under this paragraph (c)(7)(i) is the employee's covered compensation for the plan year during which the 35-year period ends. An employee's covered compensation for a plan year beginning before the 35-year period applicable under this paragraph (c)(7)(i) is the taxable wage base in effect as of the beginning of the plan year.

(ii) Special rules. (A) Rounded table. For purposes of determining the amount of an employee's covered compensation under paragraph (c)(7)(i) of this section, a plan may use tables, provided by the Commissioner, that are developed by rounding the actual amounts of covered compensation for different years of birth.

(B) Proposed regulation definition. For plan years beginning before January 1, 1995, in lieu of the definition of covered compensation contained in paragraph (c)(7)(i) of this section, a plan may define covered compensation as the average (without indexing) of the taxable wage bases in effect for each calendar year during the 35-year period ending with the last day of the calendar year preceding the calendar year in which the employee attains (or will attain) social security retirement age.

(iii) Period for using covered compensation amount. A plan must generally provide that an employee's covered compensation is automatically adjusted for each plan year. However, a plan may use an amount of covered compensation for employees equal to each employee's covered compensation (as defined in paragraph (c)(7)(i) or (c)(7)(ii) of this section) for a plan year earlier than the current plan year, provided the earlier plan year is the same for all employees and is not earlier than the later of—

(A) the plan year that begins 5 years before the current plan year, and

(B) the plan year beginning in 1989.

In the case of an accumulation plan, the benefit accrued for an employee in prior years is not affected by changes in the employee's covered compensation that occur in later years.

*(8) Defined benefit plan.* "Defined benefit plan" means a defined benefit plan within the meaning of § 1.410(b)-9.

*(9) Defined contribution plan.* "Defined contribution plan" means a defined contribution plan within the meaning

of § 1.410(b)-9. In addition, for purposes of §§ 1.401(l)-1 through 1.401(l)-6, a defined contribution plan includes a simplified employee pension as defined in section 408(k) (SEP), other than a SEP (or portion or a SEP) that is a salary reduction arrangement described in section 408(k)(6) (SARSEP).

*(10) Disparity.* "Disparity" means—

(i) In the case of a defined contribution excess plan, the amount by which the excess contribution percentage exceeds the base contribution percentage,

(ii) In the case of a defined benefit excess plan, the amount by which the excess benefit percentage exceeds the base benefit percentage, and

(iii) In the case of an offset plan, the offset percentage.

*(11) Employee.* "Employee" means employee within the meaning of § 1.401(a)(4)-12.

*(12) Employer.* "Employer" means the employer within the meaning of § 1.410(b)-9.

*(13) Employer contributions.* "Employer contributions" means all amounts taken into account with respect to an employee under a plan under § 1.401(a)(4)-2(c)(2)(ii).

*(14) Excess benefit percentage.* "Excess benefit percentage" means the rate at which employer-provided benefits are determined under a defined benefit excess plan with respect to an employee's average annual compensation above the integration level (expressed as a percentage of such average annual compensation).

*(15) Excess contribution percentage.* "Excess contribution percentage" means the rate at which employer contributions are allocated to the account of an employee under a defined contribution excess plan with respect to the employee's plan year compensation above the integration level (expressed as a percentage of such plan year compensation).

*(16) Excess plan.* (i) Defined benefit excess plan. "Defined benefit excess plan" means a defined benefit plan under which the rate at which employer-provided benefits are determined with respect to average annual compensation above the integration level under the plan (expressed as a percentage of such average annual compensation) is greater than the rate at which employer-provided benefits are determined with respect to average annual compensation at or below the integration level (expressed as a percentage of such average annual compensation).

(ii) Defined contribution excess plan. "Defined contribution excess plan" means a defined contribution plan under which the rate at which employer contributions are allocated to the account of an employee with respect to plan year compensation above the integration level (expressed as a percentage of such plan year compensation) is greater than the rate at which employer contributions are allocated to the account of an employee with respect to plan year compensation at or below the integration level (expressed as a percentage of such plan year compensation).

*(17) Final average compensation.* (i) In general. "Final average compensation" for an employee means the average of the employee's annual section 414(s) compensation for the 3-consecutive-year period ending with or within the plan year or for the employee's period of employment if shorter. The year in which an employee terminates employment may be disregarded in determining final average compensation. The definition of final average compensation used in the plan must be applied consistently with respect to all employees. For example, if the plan provides that the year in which the employee terminates employment is disregarded in determining final average compensation, the year must be disregarded for all employees who terminate employment in that year. The plan may specify any 3-consecutive-year period ending in the plan year, provided the period is determined consistently for all employees. See § 1.401(a)(4)-11(d)(3)(iii) and § 1.414(s)-1(f) for rules permitting service and compensation with another employer to be taken into account for purposes of nondiscrimination testing, including satisfying section 401(l).

(ii) Limitations. In determining an employee's final average compensation under this paragraph (c)(17), annual section 414(s) compensation for any year in excess of the taxable wage base in effect at the beginning of that year must not be taken into account. A plan may provide that each employee's final average compensation for a plan year is limited to the employee's average annual compensation for the plan year.

(iii) Determination of section 414(s) compensation. A plan must use the same definition of section 414(s) compensation to determine final average compensation as the plan uses to determine average annual compensation (or plan year compensation in the case of an accumulation plan).

*(18) Gross benefit percentage.* "Gross benefit percentage" means the rate at which employer-provided benefits are determined under an offset plan (before application of the offset) with respect to an employee's average annual compensation (expressed as a percentage of average annual compensation).

*(19) Highly compensated employee.* "Highly compensated employee" means HCE within the meaning of § 1.401(a)(4)-12.

*(20) Integration level.* "Integration level" means the dollar amount specified in an excess plan at or below which the rate of employer-provided contributions or benefits (expressed in each case as a percentage of an employee's plan year compensation or average annual compensation up to the specified dollar amount) under the plan is less than the rate of employer-provided contributions or benefits (expressed in each case as a percentage of the employee's plan year compensation or average annual compensation above the specified dollar amount) under the plan above such dollar amount.

*(21) Nonexcludable employee.* "Nonexcludable employee" means nonexcludable employee within the meaning of § 1.401(a)(4)-12.

*(22) Nonhighly compensated employee.* "Nonhighly compensated employee" means NHCE within the meaning of § 1.401(a)(4)-12.

*(23) Offset level.* "Offset level" means the dollar limit specified in the plan on the amount of each employee's final average compensation taken into account in determining the offset under an offset plan.

*(24) Offset percentage.* "Offset percentage" means the rate at which an employee's employer-provided benefit is reduced or offset under an offset plan (expressed as a percentage of the employee's final average compensation up to the offset level).

*(25) Offset plan.* "Offset plan" means a defined benefit plan that is not a defined benefit excess plan and that provides that each employee's employer-provided benefit is reduced or offset by a specified percentage of the employee's final average compensation up to the offset level under the plan.

*(26) PIA.* "PIA" or "primary insurance amount" means the old-age insurance benefit under section 202 of the Social Security Act (42 U.S.C. 402) payable to each employee at a single age that is not earlier than age 62 and not later than age 65. PIA must be determined under the Social Security Act as in effect at the time the employee's offset is determined. Thus, it is determined without assuming any future increases in compensation, any future increases in the taxable wage base, any changes in the formulas used under the Social Security Act to determine PIA (for example, changes in the breakpoints), or any future increases in the consumer price index. However, it may be assumed that the employee will continue to receive compensation at the same rate as that received at the time the offset is being determined, until reaching the single age described in the first sentence of this paragraph (c)(26). PIA must be determined in a consistent manner for all employees and in accordance with revenue rulings or other guidance provided by the Commissioner.

*(27) Plan.* "Plan" means a plan within the meaning of § 1.401(a)(4)-12 or a component plan treated as a plan under § 1.401(a)(4)-9(c).

*(28) Plan year compensation.* "Plan year compensation" means plan year compensation within the meaning of § 1.401(a)(4)-12.

*(29) Qualified plan.* "Qualified plan" means a qualified plan within the meaning of § 1.401(a)(4)-12.

*(30) Section 401(l) plan.* "Section 401(l) plan" means a section 401(l) plan within the meaning of § 1.401(a)(4)-12.

*(31) Section 414(s) compensation.* "Section 414(s) compensation means section 414(s) compensation within the meaning of § 1.401(a)(4)-12.

*(32) Social security retirement age.* "Social security retirement age" for an employee means the social security retirement age of the employee as determined under section 415(b)(8).

*(33) Straight life annuity.* "Straight life annuity" means a straight life annuity within the meaning of § 1.401(a)(4)-12.

*(34) Taxable wage base.* "Taxable wage base" means the contribution and benefit base under section 230 of the Social Security Act (42 U.S.C. § 430).

*(35) Year of service.* "Year of service" means a year of service as defined in the plan for purposes of the benefit formula and the accrual method under the plan, unless the context clearly indicates otherwise. See § 1.401(a)(4)-11(d)(3) for rules on years of service that may be taken into account for purposes of nondiscrimination testing, including satisfying section 401(l).

---

T.D. 8359, 9/12/91, amend T.D. 8486, 8/31/93, T.D. 9169, 12/28/2004.

---

### § 1.401(l)-2 Permitted disparity for defined contribution plans.

**(a) Requirements.** *(1) In general.* Disparity in the rates of employer contributions allocated to employees' accounts under a defined contribution plan is permitted under section 401(l) and this section for a plan year only if the plan satisfies paragraphs (a)(2) through (a)(5) of this section. A plan that otherwise satisfies this paragraph (a) will not be considered to fail section 401(l) merely because it contains one or more provisions described in § 1.401(a)(4)-2(b)(4). See § 1.401(a)(4)-8(b)(3)(i)(C) for special rules applicable to target benefit plans.

*(2) Excess plan requirement.* The plan must be a defined contribution excess plan.

*(3) Maximum disparity.* The disparity for all employees under the plan must not exceed the maximum permitted disparity prescribed in paragraph (b) of this section.

*(4) Uniform disparity.* The disparity for all employees under the plan must be uniform within the meaning of paragraph (c) of this section.

*(5) Integration level.* The integration level specified in the plan must satisfy paragraph (d) of this section.

**(b) Maximum permitted disparity.** *(1) In general.* The disparity provided for the plan year must not exceed the maximum excess allowance as defined in paragraph (b)(2) of this section. In addition, the plan must satisfy the overall permitted disparity limits of § 1.401(l)-5.

*(2) Maximum excess allowance.* The maximum excess allowance for a plan year is the lesser of—

(i) The base contribution percentage, or

(ii) The greater of—

(A) 5.7 percent, reduced as required under paragraph (d) of this section, or

(B) The percentage rate of tax under section 3111(a), in effect as of the beginning of the plan year, that is attributable to the old age insurance portion of the Old Age, Survivors and Disability Insurance provisions of the Social Security Act, reduced as required under paragraph (d) of this section. For a year in which the percentage rate of tax described in this paragraph (b)(2)(ii)(B) exceeds 5.7 percent, the Commissioner will publish the rate of such tax and a revised table under paragraph (d)(4) of this section.

**(c) Uniform disparity.** *(1) In general.* The disparity provided under a plan is uniform only if the plan uses the same base contribution percentage and the same excess contribution percentage for all employees in the plan.

*(2) Deemed uniformity.* (i) In general. The disparity under a plan does not fail to be uniform for purposes of this paragraph (c) merely because the plan contains one or more of the provisions described in paragraphs (c)(2)(ii) and (iii) of this section.

(ii) Overall permitted disparity. The plan provides that, in the case of each employee who has reached the cumulative permitted disparity limit applicable to the employee under § 1.401(l)-5(c), employer contributions are allocated to the account of the employee with respect to the employee's total plan year compensation at the excess contribution percentage.

(iii) Non-FICA employees. The plan provides that, in the case of each employee under the plan with respect to whom none of the taxes under section 3111(a), section 3221, or section 1401 is required to be paid, employer contributions are allocated to the account of the employee with respect to the employee's total plan year compensation at the excess contribution percentage.

**(d) Integration level.** *(1) In general.* The integration level under the plan must satisfy paragraph (d)(2), (d)(3), or (d)(4) of this section, as modified by paragraph (d)(5) of this section in the case of a short plan year. If a reduction applies to the disparity factor under this paragraph (d), the reduced factor is used for all purposes in determining whether the permitted disparity rules for defined contribution plans are satisfied.

*(2) Taxable wage base.* The requirement of this paragraph (d)(2) is satisfied only if the integration level under the plan

for each employee is the taxable wage base in effect as of the beginning of the plan year.

*(3) Single dollar amount.* The requirement of this paragraph (d)(3) is satisfied only if the integration level under the plan for all employees is a single dollar amount (either specified in the plan or determined under a formula specified in the plan) that does not exceed the greater of $10,000 or 20 percent of the taxable wage base in effect as of the beginning of the plan year.

*(4) Intermediate amount.* The requirement of this paragraph (d)(4) is satisfied only if—

(i) the integration level under the plan for all employees is a single dollar amount (either specified in the plan or determined under a formula specified in the plan) that is greater than the highest amount determined under paragraph (d)(3) of this section and less than the taxable wage base, and

(ii) the plan adjusts the factor determined under paragraph (b)(2)(ii) of this section in accordance with the table below.

**TABLE**

| If the integration level | | The 5.7 percent factor in the maximum excess allowance is reduced to — |
|---|---|---|
| Is more than | But not more than | |
| Greater of $10,000 or 20% of taxable wage base. | 80% of taxable wage base. | 4.3% |
| 80% of taxable wage base. | Amount less than taxable wage base. | 5.4% |

*(5) Prorated integration level for short plan year.* If a plan uses paragraph (2) or (4) of the definition of plan year compensation under § 1.401(a)(4)-12 (i.e., section 414(s) compensation for the plan year or the period of plan participation) and has a plan year that comprises fewer than 12 months, the integration level under the plan for each employee must be an amount equal to the otherwise applicable integration level described in paragraph (d)(2), (d)(3), or (d)(4) of this section, multiplied by a fraction, the numerator of which is the number of months in the plan year, and the denominator of which is 12. No adjustment to the maximum excess allowance is required as a result of the application of this paragraph (d)(5), other than any adjustment already required under paragraph (d)(4) of this section.

**(e) Examples.** The following examples illustrate this section. In each example, 5.7 percent exceeds the percentage rate of tax described in paragraph (b)(2)(ii)(B) of this section.

*Example (1).* Employer X maintains a profit-sharing plan with the calendar year as its plan year. For the 1989 plan year, the plan provides that the account of each employee who has plan year compensation in excess of the taxable wage base in effect at the beginning of the plan year will receive an allocation for the plan year of 5.7 percent of plan year compensation in excess of the taxable wage base. The plan provides that no allocation will be made to the account of any employee for the plan year with respect to plan year compensation not in excess of the taxable wage base. The maximum excess allowance is exceeded for the 1989 plan year because the excess contribution percentage (5.7 percent) for the plan year exceeds the base contribution percentage (0 percent) for the plan year by more than the lesser of the base contribution percentage (0 percent) or the percentage determined under paragraph (b)(2)(ii) of this section (5.7 percent) for the plan year.

*Example (2).* Employer Y maintains a money purchase pension plan with the calendar year as its plan year. For the 1990 plan year, the plan provides that the account of each employee will receive an allocation of 5 percent of the employee's plan year compensation up to the taxable wage base in effect at the beginning of the plan year plus an allocation of 10 percent of the employee's plan year compensation in excess of the taxable wage base. The maximum excess allowance is not exceeded for the plan year because the excess contribution percentage (10 percent) for the plan year does not exceed the base contribution percentage (5 percent) for the plan year by more than the lesser of the base contribution percentage (5 percent) or the percentage determined under paragraph (b)(2)(ii) of this section (5.7 percent) for the plan year.

*Example (3).* Assume the same facts as in Example 2, except that the plan provides that, with respect to plan year compensation in excess of the taxable wage base, the account of each employee will receive an allocation for the plan year of 12 percent of such compensation. The maximum excess allowance is exceeded for the plan year because the excess contribution percentage (12 percent) for the plan year exceeds the base contribution percentage (5 percent) for the plan year by more than the lesser of the base contribution percentage (5 percent) or the percentage determined under paragraph (b)(2)(ii) of this section (5.7 percent) for the plan year.

*Example (4).* Employer Z maintains a money purchase pension plan with a plan year beginning July 1 and ending June 30. The taxable wage base for the 1990 calendar year is $51,300 and the taxable wage base for the 1991 calendar year is $53,400. For the plan year beginning July 1, 1990, and ending June 30, 1991, the plan provides that the account of each employee will receive an allocation of 4 percent of the employee's plan year compensation up to $53,400 plus an allocation of 6 percent of the employee's plan year compensation in excess of $53,400. Although the excess contribution percentage (6 percent) for the plan year does not exceed the base contribution percentage (4 percent) for the plan year by more than the lesser of the base contribution percentage (4 percent) or the percentage determined under paragraph (b)(2)(ii) of this section (5.7 percent), the plan does not satisfy paragraph (a)(5) of this section because the integration level of $53,400 exceeds the maximum permitted integration level of $51,300 (the taxable wage base in effect as of the beginning of the plan year).

*Example (5).* Assume the same facts as in Example 4, except that for the plan year beginning July 1, 1990, and ending June 30, 1991, the plan provides that the account of each employee will receive an allocation of 5 percent of the employee's plan year compensation up to $30,000 plus an allocation of 9 percent of the employee's plan year compensation in excess of $30,000. The integration level of $30,000 is 58 percent of the taxable wage base of $51,300 for the 1990 calendar year. The maximum excess allowance is not exceeded for the plan year because the excess contribution percentage (9 percent) for the plan year does not exceed the base contribution percentage (5 percent) for the plan year by more than the lesser of the base contribution percentage (5 percent) or the percentage determined under paragraphs (b)(2)(ii) and (d) of this section (4.3 percent) for the plan year.

T.D. 8359, 9/12/91, amend T.D. 8486, 8/31/93.

### § 1.401(l)-3 Permitted disparity for defined benefit plans.

**(a) Requirements.** *(1) In general.* Disparity in the rates of employer-provided benefits under a defined benefit plan is permitted under section 401(l) and this section for a plan year only if the plan satisfies paragraphs (a)(2) through (a)(6) of this section. A plan that otherwise satisfies this paragraph (a) will not be considered to fail section 401(l) merely because it contains one or more provisions described in § 1.401(a)(4)-3(b)(6) (such as multiple formulas). Section 401(a)(5)(D) and § 1.401(a)(5)-1(d) provide other rules under which benefits provided under a defined benefit plan (including defined benefit excess and offset plans) may be limited. See § 1.401(a)(4)-3(b)(5)(viii) for special rules under which an insurance contract plan may satisfy § 1.401(a)(4)-1(b)(2) and section 401(l). See § 1.401(a)(4)-8(c)(3)(iii)(B) for special rules applicable to cash balance plans.

*(2) Excess or offset plan requirement.* The plan must be a defined benefit excess plan or an offset plan.

*(3) Maximum disparity.* The disparity for all employees under the plan must not exceed the maximum permitted disparity prescribed in paragraph (b) of this section.

*(4) Uniform disparity.* The disparity for all employees under the plan must be uniform within the meaning of paragraph (c) of this section.

*(5) Integration or offset level.* The integration or offset level specified in the plan must satisfy paragraph (d) of this section.

*(6) Benefits, rights, and features.* The benefits, rights, and features provided under the plan must satisfy paragraph (f)(1) of this section.

**(b) Maximum permitted disparity.** *(1) In general.* In the case of a defined benefit excess plan, the disparity provided for the plan year may not exceed the maximum excess allowance as defined in paragraph (b)(2) of this section. In the case of an offset plan, the disparity provided for the plan year may not exceed the maximum offset allowance as defined in paragraph (b)(3) of this section. In addition, either type of plan must satisfy the overall permitted disparity limits of § 1.401(l)-5.

*(2) Maximum excess allowance.* The maximum excess allowance for a plan year is the lesser of—

(i) 0.75 percent, reduced as required under paragraphs (d) and (e) of this section, or

(ii) The base benefit percentage for the plan year.

*(3) Maximum offset allowance.* The maximum offset allowance for a plan year is the lesser of—

(i) 0.75 percent, reduced as required under paragraphs (d) and (e) of this section, or

(ii) One-half of the gross benefit percentage, multiplied by a fraction (not to exceed one), the numerator of which is the employee's average annual compensation, and the denominator of which is the employee's final average compensation up to the offset level.

*(4) Rules of application.* (i) Disparity provided for the plan year. Disparity provided for the plan year generally means the disparity provided under the plan's benefit formula for the employee's year of service with respect to the plan year. However, if a plan determines each employee's accrued benefit under the fractional accrual method of section 411(b)(1)(C), disparity provided under the plan also means the disparity in the benefit accrued for the employee for the plan year. Thus, a plan using the fractional accrual method must satisfy this paragraph (b) with respect to the plan's benefit formula and with respect to the benefits accrued for the plan year.

(ii) Reduction in disparity rate. Any reductions in the 0.75-percent factor required under paragraphs (d) and (e) of this section are cumulative.

(iii) Normal and optional forms of benefit. (A) In general. A plan satisfies the maximum permitted disparity requirement of this paragraph (b) only if the plan satisfies this paragraph (b) with respect to each optional form of benefit (including the normal form of benefit) provided under the plan.

(B) Level annuity forms. In the case of an optional form of benefit payable as a level annuity over a period of not less than the life of the employee, the optional form must satisfy the maximum permitted disparity requirement of this paragraph (b). Thus, for example, if the form of a defined benefit plan's normal retirement benefit is an annuity for life with a 10-year certain feature and the plan permits employees to elect an optional form of benefit in the form of a straight life annuity, the plan must satisfy the maximum disparity requirement of this paragraph (b) with respect to each of the optional forms of benefit. An annuity that decreases only after the death of the employee, or that decreases only after the death of either the employee or the joint annuitant, is considered a level annuity for purposes of this paragraph (b).

(C) Other forms. In the case of an optional form of benefit that is not described in paragraph (b)(4)(iii)(B) of this section, the optional form must satisfy the maximum permitted disparity requirement of this paragraph (b), when the respective portions of the optional form are normalized under the rules of § 1.401(a)(4)-12 to a straight life annuity commencing at the same time as the optional form of benefit, regardless of whether the straight life annuity form is actually provided under the plan. In the case of a defined benefit excess plan, the respective portions are the portion of the optional form attributable to average annual compensation up to the integration level (the "base portion") and the portion of the optional form attributable to average annual compensation in excess of the integration level (the "excess portion"). In the case of an offset plan, the respective portions are the optional form determined without regard to the offset (the "gross amount") and the offset applied to the gross amount to determine the optional form (the "offset amount").

(D) Post-retirement cost-of-living adjustments. (1) In general. A benefit does not fail to be a level annuity described in paragraph (b)(4)(iii)(B) of this section merely because it provides an automatic post-retirement cost-of-living adjustment that satisfies paragraph (b)(4)(iii)(D)(2) of this section. Thus, increases in the employee's annuity pursuant to such a cost-of-living adjustment do not cause the disparity provided under the optional form of benefit to exceed the maximum disparity permitted under this paragraph (b). For rules on ad hoc post-retirement cost-of-living adjustments, see § 1.401(a)(4)-10(b).

(2) Requirements. A cost-of-living adjustment satisfies this paragraph (b)(4)(iii)(D)(2) if—

(i) It is included in the accrued benefit of all employees, and

(ii) It increases, on a uniform and consistent basis, the benefits of all former employees who are no younger than age 62, at a rate no greater than adjustments to social security benefits under section 215(i)(2)(A) of the Social Security Act that have occurred since the later of the employee's attainment of age 62 or commencement of benefits.

(E) Section 417(e) exception. A plan will not fail to satisfy this paragraph (b) merely because the disparity in a benefit that is subject to the interest rate restrictions of sections 401(a)(11) and 417(e) exceeds the maximum disparity that would otherwise be allowed under this paragraph (b) if the increase in disparity is required to satisfy § 1.417(e)-1(d). In applying the exception in this paragraph (b)(4)(iii)(E), for purposes of determining what is required under § 1.417(e)-1(d), a plan may use the rate described in § 1.417(e)-1(d)(2)(i) for all employees, without regard to whether the present value of an employee's vested benefit exceeds $25,000.

*(5) Examples.* The following examples illustrate this paragraph (b). Unless otherwise provided, the following facts apply. The plan is noncontributory and is the only plan ever maintained by the employer. The plan uses a normal retirement age of 65 and contains no provision that would require a reduction in the 0.75-percent factor under paragraph (b)(2) or (b)(3) of this section. In the case of a defined benefit excess plan, the plan uses each employee's covered compensation as the integration level; in the case of an offset plan, the plan uses each employee's covered compensation as the offset level and provides that an employee's final average compensation is limited to the employee's average annual compensation. Each example discusses the benefit formula applicable to an employee who has a social security retirement age of 65.

*Example (1).* Plan N is a defined benefit excess plan that provides a normal retirement benefit of 0.5 percent of average annual compensation in excess of the integration level, for each year of service. The plan provides no benefits with respect to average annual compensation up to the integration level. The disparity provided under the plan exceeds the maximum excess allowance because the excess benefit percentage (0.5 percent) exceeds the base benefit percentage (0 percent) by more than the base benefit percentage (0 percent).

*Example (2).* Plan O is an offset plan that provides a normal retirement benefit equal to 2 percent of average annual compensation, minus 0.75 percent of final average compensation up to the offset level, for each year of service up to 35. The disparity provided under the plan satisfies this paragraph (b) because the offset percentage (0.75 percent) does not exceed the maximum offset allowance equal to the lesser of 0.75 percent or one-half of the gross benefit percentage (1 percent).

*Example (3).* Plan P is a defined benefit excess plan that provides a normal retirement benefit of 0.5 percent of average annual compensation up to the integration level, plus 1.25 percent of average annual compensation in excess of the integration level, for each year of service up to 35. The disparity provided under the plan exceeds the maximum excess allowance because the excess benefit percentage (1.25 percent) exceeds the base benefit percentage (0.5 percent) by more than the base benefit percentage (0.5 percent).

*Example (4).* Plan Q is an offset plan that provides a normal retirement benefit of 1 percent of average annual compensation, minus 0.75 percent of final average compensation up to the offset level, for each year of service up to 35. The disparity under the plan exceeds the maximum offset allowance because the offset percentage exceeds one-half of the gross benefit percentage (0.5 percent).

*Example (5).* (a) Plan R is an offset plan that provides a normal retirement benefit of 1 percent of average annual compensation, minus 0.5 percent of final average compensation up to the offset level, for each year of service up to 35. The plan determines an employee's average annual compensation using an averaging period comprising five consecutive 12-month periods and taking into account the employee's compensation for the ten consecutive 12-month periods ending with the plan year. The plan does not provide that an employee's final average compensation is limited to the employee's average annual compensation.

(b) Employee A has average annual compensation of $20,000, final average compensation of $25,000, and covered compensation of $32,000. The maximum offset allowance applicable to Employee A for the plan year under paragraph (b)(3) of this section is one-half of the gross benefit percentage multiplied by the ratio, not to exceed one, of Employee A's average annual compensation to Employee A's final average compensation up to the offset level. Thus, the maximum offset allowance is 0.4 percent (½ × 1 percent × $20,000/$25,000). With respect to Employee A, the benefit formula provides an offset that exceeds the maximum offset allowance. The plan must therefore reduce Employee A's offset percentage to 0.4 percent. (Under paragraph (c)(2)(viii) of this section, Employee A's adjusted disparity rate is deemed uniform.)

(c) Alternatively, under § 1.401(l)-1(c)(17)(ii) (the definition of final average compensation), the plan could specify that an employee's final average compensation is limited to the amount of the employee's average annual compensation. Thus, the ratio of average annual compensation to final average compensation would always be equal to at least one, and the maximum offset allowance under the plan would be one-half of the gross benefit percentage.

*Example (6).* Plan S is a defined benefit excess plan that provides a base benefit percentage of 1 percent of average annual compensation up to the integration level for each year of service. The plan also provides, for each of the first 10 years of service, an excess benefit percentage of 1.85 percent of average annual compensation in excess of the integration level. For each year of service after 10, the plan provides an excess benefit percentage of 1.65 percent of the employee's average annual compensation in excess of the integration level. The disparity provided under the plan exceeds the maximum excess allowance because the excess benefit percentage for each of the first ten years of service (1.85 percent) exceeds the base benefit percentage (1 percent) by more than 0.75 percent.

*Example (7).* The facts are the same as in *Example 6*, except that the plan provides an excess benefit percentage of 1.65 percent of average annual compensation in excess of the integration level for each of the first 10 years of service and an excess benefit percentage of 1.85 percent of average annual compensation in excess of the integration level for each year of service after 10. The disparity provided under the plan exceeds the maximum excess allowance because the excess benefit percentage for each year of service after 10 (1.85 percent) exceeds the base benefit percentage (1 percent) by more than 0.75 percent.

*Example (8).* Plan T is a defined benefit excess plan that provides a normal retirement benefit of 1.0 percent of average annual compensation up to the integration level, plus 1.7 percent of average annual compensation in excess of the integration level, for each year of service up to 35, payable in the form of a joint and survivor annuity. The plan also allows an employee to receive the retirement benefit in the form of an actuarially equivalent straight life annuity. The actuarially equivalent straight life annuity equals 1.09 percent of average annual compensation up to the integration level, plus 1.85 percent of average annual compensation in excess of the integration level, for each year of service up 35. The disparity provided under the plan with respect to the straight life annuity form of benefit (0.76 percent) exceeds the maximum excess allowance because the excess benefit percentage (1.85 percent) exceeds the base benefit percentage (1.09 percent) by more than 0.75 percent.

*Example (9).* Plan U is a defined benefit excess plan that provides a normal retirement benefit of 1.0 percent of average annual compensation up to the integration level, plus 1.7 percent of average annual compensation in excess of the integration level, for each year of service up to 35, payable in the form of a straight life annuity. Plan U provides a single sum optional form of benefit at normal retirement age equal to 100 times the monthly annuity payable at that age. Thus, if an employee elects the single sum optional form of benefit, the base portion of the single sum benefit is 8.33 percent (100 times 1.0 percent/12) of average annual compensation up to the integration level per year of service, and the excess portion of the single sum benefit is 14.17 percent (100 times 1.7 percent/12) of average annual compensation in excess of the integration level per year of service. Each respective portion of the single sum option is normalized to a straight life annuity commencing at normal retirement age, using 8-percent interest and the UP-84 mortality table. After normalization, the base portion of the benefit is 1.02 percent of average annual compensation up to the integration level, and the excess portion of the benefit is 1.73 percent of average annual compensation in excess of the integration level. The single sum optional form of benefit satisfies this paragraph (b) because the disparity provided in the optional form of benefit does not exceed the maximum excess allowance.

**(c) Uniform disparity.** *(1) In general.* The disparity provided under a defined benefit excess plan is uniform only if the plan uses the same base benefit percentage and the same excess benefit percentage for all employees with the same number of years of service. The disparity provided under an offset plan is uniform only if the plan uses the same gross benefit percentage and the same offset percentage for all employees with the same number of years of service. The disparity provided under a plan that determines each employee's accrued benefit under the fractional accrual method of section 411(b)(1)(C) is uniform only if the plan satisfies one of the deemed uniformity rules of paragraph (c)(2)(ii) or (iii) of this section.

*(2) Deemed uniformity.* (i) In general. The disparity provided under a plan does not fail to be uniform for purposes of this paragraph (c) merely because the plan contains one or more of the provisions described in paragraphs (c)(2)(ii) through (ix) of this section.

(ii) Use of fractional accrual and disparity for 35 years. The plan contains a benefit formula as described in paragraphs (c)(2)(ii)(A) and (B) of this section, and the plan determines each employee's accrued benefit under the method described in § 1.401(a)(4)-3(b)(4)(i)(B), i.e., by multiplying the employee's fractional rule benefit (within the meaning of § 1.411(b)-1(b)(3)(ii)(A)) by a fraction, the numerator of which is the employee's years of service determined as of the plan year, and the denominator of which is the employee's projected years of service as of normal retirement age.

(A) For each year of service at least up to 35, the plan formula provides the same base benefit percentage and the same excess benefit percentage for all employees in the case of a defined benefit excess plan or the same gross benefit percentage and the same offset percentage for all employees in the case of an offset plan.

(B) For each additional year of service, the benefit formula provides a uniform percentage of all average annual compensation that is no greater than the excess benefit percentage or the gross benefit percentage under paragraph (c)(2)(ii)(A) of this section, whichever is applicable.

(iii) Use of fractional accrual and disparity for fewer than 35 years. The plan contains a benefit formula as described in paragraphs (c)(2)(iii)(A) through (C) of this section, and the plan determines each employee's accrued benefit under the method described in § 1.401(a)(4)-3(b)(4)(i)(B).

(A) For each year in the employee's initial period of service comprising fewer than 35 years, the benefit formula provides the same base benefit percentage and the same excess benefit percentage for all employees in the case of a defined benefit excess plan or the same gross benefit percentage and the same offset percentage for all employees in the case of an offset plan.

(B) For each year of service after the initial period and at least up to 35, the benefit formula provides a uniform percentage of all average annual compensation, that is equal to the excess benefit percentage or the gross benefit percentage under paragraph (c)(2)(iii)(A) of this section.

(C) For each year of service after the period described in paragraph (c)(2)(iii)(B) of this section, the benefit formula provides a uniform percentage of all average annual compensation that is no greater than the excess benefit percentage or the gross benefit percentage under paragraph (c)(2)(iii)(A) of this section.

(iv) Different social security retirement ages. The benefit formula uses the same excess benefit percentage or the same gross benefit percentage for all employees with the same number of years of service and, for employees with social security retirement ages later than age 65, adjusts the 0.75-percent factor in the maximum excess or offset allowance as required under paragraph (e)(1) of this section, by increasing the base benefit percentage in the case of a defined benefit excess plan, or reducing the offset percentage in the case of an offset plan.

(v) Reduction for integration level. The plan uses an integration level or offset level greater than each employee's covered compensation and makes individual reductions in the 0.75-percent factor, as permitted under paragraph (d)(9)(iii)(B) of this section, by increasing the base benefit percentage in the case of a defined benefit excess plan or reducing the offset percentage in the case of an offset plan.

(vi) Overall permitted disparity. (A) In general. The benefit formula provides that, with respect to each employee's years of service after reaching the cumulative permitted disparity limit applicable to the employee under § 1.401(l)-5(c), employer-provided benefits are determined with respect to the employee's total average annual compensation at a rate equal to the nondisparate percentage. For purposes of this paragraph (c)(2)(vi), the nondisparate percentage is generally the excess benefit percentage or gross benefit percentage otherwise applicable under the benefit formula to an employee with the same number of years of service.

(B) Unit credit plans. In the case of a unit credit plan described in section 1.401(a)(4)-3(b)(3), if the 411(b)(1)(B) limit percentage is less than the nondisparate percentage, the 411(b)(1)(B) limit percentage must be substituted for the nondisparate percentage. For this purpose, the 411(b)(1)(B) limit percentage is 133⅓ percent of the smallest base benefit percentage, or 133⅓ percent of the smallest difference between the gross benefit percentage and the offset percentage, whichever is applicable, where the smallest base benefit percentage or difference is determined by reference to the benefit formula as applied to employees with no more years of service than the employee.

(C) Fractional accrual plans. In the case of a fractional accrual plan described in section 1.401(a)(4)-3(b)(4), the benefit formula must provide for the nondisparate percentage with respect to years of service after the employee would reach the cumulative permitted disparity limit applicable to the employee under section 1.401(l)-5(c) as modified by this paragraph (c)(2)(vi)(C). Solely for purposes of this paragraph (c)(2)(vi)(C), the employee's annual disparity fractions (and thus the year in which the employee would reach the cumulative permitted disparity limit) are determined using the disparity provided under the benefit formula (rather than the special rule for fractional accrual plans in section 1.401(l)-5(b)(8)(v)).

(vii) Non-FICA employees. The plan provides that, in the case of each employee under the plan with respect to whom none of the taxes under section 3111(a), section 3221, or section 1401 is required to be paid, employer-provided benefits are determined with respect to the employee's total average annual compensation at the excess benefit percentage or gross benefit percentage applicable to an employee with the same number of years of service.

(viii) Average annual compensation adjustment for offset plan. In the case of each employee whose final average compensation exceeds the employee's average annual compensation, the plan adjusts the offset percentage as required under paragraph (b)(3)(ii) of this section in order to satisfy the maximum offset allowance.

(ix) PIA offsets. In the case of an offset plan, the plan provides that the offset applied to each employee's benefit is the lesser of a specified percentage of the employee's PIA and an offset that otherwise satisfies the requirements of this section (the "section 401(l) overlay"). The specified percentage of PIA must be the same for all employees with the same number of years of service. In the case of a plan that determines each employee's accrued benefit under the fractional accrual method of section 411(b)(1)(C), the specified percentage of PIA is deemed to be the same for all employees with the same number of years of service if the plan satisfies either of the deemed uniformity rules in paragraph (c)(2)(ii) or (iii) of this section, substituting "offset, expressed as a percentage of PIA, per year of service" for the term "offset percentage" (in addition to satisfying either of those rules with respect to the section 401(l) overlay).

*(3) Examples.* The following examples illustrate this paragraph (c). Unless otherwise provided, the following facts apply. The plan is noncontributory and is the only plan ever maintained by the employer. The plan uses a normal retirement age of 65 and contains no provision that would require a reduction in the 0.75-percent factor under paragraph (b)(2) or (b)(3) of this section. In the case of a defined benefit excess plan, the plan uses each employee's covered compensation as the integration level; in the case of an offset plan, the plan uses each employee's covered compensation as the offset level and provides that an employee's final average compensation is limited to the employee's average annual compensation. Each example discusses the benefit formula applicable to an employee who has a social security retirement age of 65.

*Example (1).* Plan M is a defined benefit excess plan that satisfies the 133⅓ percent accrual rule of section 411(b)(1)(B). The plan provides a normal retirement benefit of 1.0 percent of average annual compensation up to the integration level, plus 1.65 percent of average annual compensation in excess of the integration level, for each year of service up to 25. The plan also provides a benefit of 1.0 percent of all average annual compensation for each year of service in excess of 25. The disparity provided under the plan is uniform because the plan uses the same base and excess benefit percentages for all employees with the same number of years of service. If the plan formula were the same except that it used a different excess benefit percentage for some of the years of service between one and 25, the disparity under the plan would continue to be uniform.

*Example (2).* Plan O is a defined benefit excess plan that provides a normal retirement benefit of 50 percent of average annual compensation up to the integration level and 68.75 percent of average annual compensation in excess of the integration level, multiplied by a fraction, the numerator of which is the employee's service, up to 25 years, and the denominator of which is 25. The plan determines an employee's accrued benefit as described in § 1.401(a)(4)-3(b)(4)(i)(B). The benefit formula thus provides a base benefit percentage of 2 percent (50 percent × 1/25) and an excess benefit percentage of 2.75 percent (68.75 percent × 1/25) for each of an employee's first 25 years of service and no benefit for years of service after 25. The disparity provided under the plan is not uniform within the meaning of this paragraph (c) because the benefit formula does not satisfy either of the uniform disparity rules for fractional accrual plans under paragraphs (c)(2)(ii) and (iii) of this section.

*Example (3).* Plan P is an offset plan that provides a normal retirement benefit of 2 percent of average annual compensation for each year of service up to 35, minus 0.75 percent of the final average compensation up to the offset level for each year of service up to 25. The plan determines an employee's accrued benefit under the method described in § 1.401(a)(4)-3(b)(4)(i)(B). Because the formula under the plan provides the same gross benefit percentage and offset percentage for 25 years of service (fewer than 35) and, for years of service after 25 and up to 35, provides a benefit at a uniform rate (equal to the gross benefit percentage) of all average annual compensation, and the plan accrues the benefit ratably, the disparity under the plan is deemed to be uniform under paragraph (c)(2)(iii) of this section.

*Example (4).* Plan Q is an offset plan that benefits employees with social security retirement ages of 65, 66, and 67. For each year of service up to 35, the plan provides a normal retirement benefit equal to 2 percent of average annual compensation, minus an offset based on the employee's final average compensation up to the offset level. For employees with a social security retirement age of 65, the offset percentage is 0.75 percent; for employees with a social security retirement age of 66, the offset percentage is 0.70 percent; and for employees with a social security retirement age of 67, the offset percentage is 0.65 percent. The disparity under the plan is deemed to be uniform under paragraph (c)(2)(iv) of this section because the plan uses the same gross benefit percentage for all employees and reduces the offset percentage for employees with social security retirement ages of 66 and 67 to comply with the adjustments in the 0.75-percent factor in the maximum excess or offset allowance required under paragraph (e)(1) of this section. (Because Plan Q effectively provides unreduced benefits prior to the social security retirement age for employees with social security retirement ages of 66 and 67, the 0.75-percent factor in the maximum offset allowance must be reduced to 0.70 percent and 0.65 percent, respectively.) Alternatively, Plan Q could satisfy this paragraph (c) if it provided a uniform offset percentage of 0.65 percent for all employees because 0.65 percent is the maximum offset allowance under the plan for an employee with a social security retirement age of 67.

*Example (5).* Plan R is an offset plan that provides a normal retirement benefit of 2 percent of average annual compensation, minus an offset determined as a percentage of total final average compensation, for each year of service up to 35. For an employee whose final average compensation does not exceed the employee's covered compensation, the offset percentage is 0.75 percent. For an employee whose final average compensation exceeds the employee's covered compensation, the plan reduces the offset percentage, as required by paragraph (d) of this section. The reduced offset percentage is determined by comparing the employee's final average compensation to the employee's covered compensation as permitted under paragraph (d)(9)(iii)(B) of this section. The disparity provided under the plan is deemed uniform under paragraph (c)(2)(v) of this section because the plan uses the same gross benefit percentage for all employees and makes individual reductions in the 0.75-percent factor, as permitted under paragraph (d)(9)(iii)(B) of this section, by reducing the offset percentage in the case of an employee whose final average compensation exceeds covered compensation.

**(d) Requirements for integration or offset level.** *(1) In general.* The integration level under a defined benefit excess plan or the offset level under an offset plan must satisfy paragraphs (d)(2), (d)(3), (d)(4), (d)(5) or (d)(6) of this section, as modified by paragraph (d)(7) of this section in the case of a short plan year. Paragraph (d)(8) of this section contains demographic tests that apply to certain defined benefit plans. Paragraph (d)(9) of this section explains certain reductions required in the 0.75-percent factor under paragraph (b)(2) or (b)(3) of this section. Paragraph (d)(10) of this section contains examples. If a reduction applies to the 0.75-percent factor under this paragraph (d), the reduced factor is used for all purposes in determining whether the permitted disparity rules for defined benefit plans are satisfied.

*(2) Covered compensation.* The requirement of this paragraph (d)(2) is satisfied only if the integration or offset level under the plan for each employee is the employee's covered compensation.

*(3) Uniform percentage of covered compensation.* The requirement of this paragraph (d)(3) is satisfied only if—

(i) The integration or offset level under the plan for each employee is a uniform percentage (greater than 100 percent) of each employee's covered compensation,

(ii) In the case of a defined benefit excess plan, the integration level does not exceed the taxable wage base in effect for the plan year, and, in the case of an offset plan, the offset level does not exceed the employee's final average compensation, and

(iii) The plan adjusts the 0.75-percent factor in the maximum excess or offset allowance in accordance with paragraph (d)(9) of this section.

*(4) Single dollar amount.* The requirement of this paragraph (d)(4) is satisfied only if the integration or offset level under the plan for all employees is a single dollar amount (either specified in the plan or determined under a formula specified in the plan) that does not exceed the greater of $10,000 or one-half of the covered compensation of an individual who attains social security retirement age in the calendar year in which the plan year begins. In the case of a calendar year in which no individual could attain social security retirement age, for example, the year 2003, this rule is applied using covered compensation of an individual attaining social security retirement age in the preceding calendar year.

*(5) Intermediate amount.* The requirement of this paragraph (d)(5) is satisfied only if—

(i) The integration or offset level under the plan for all employees is a single dollar amount (either specified in the plan or determined under a formula specified in the plan) that is greater than the highest amount determined under paragraph (d)(4) of this section,

(ii) In the case of a defined benefit excess plan, the single dollar amount does not exceed the taxable wage base in effect for the plan year, and, in the case of an offset plan, the single dollar amount does not exceed the employee's final average compensation,

(iii) The plan satisfies the demographic requirements of paragraph (d)(8) of this section, and

(iv) The plan adjusts the 0.75-percent factor in the maximum excess or offset allowance in accordance with paragraph (d)(9) of this section.

For purposes of this paragraph (d)(5), an offset level of each employee's final average compensation is considered a single dollar amount determined under a formula specified in the plan.

*(6) Intermediate amount safe harbor.* The requirement of this paragraph (d)(6)is satisfied only if—

(i) The integration or offset level under the plan for all employees is a single dollar amount described in paragraph (d)(5) of this section, and

(ii) The 0.75-percent factor in the maximum excess or offset allowance under paragraph (b)(2) or (b)(3) of this section is reduced to the lesser of the adjusted factor determined under paragraph (d)(9) of this section or 80 percent of the otherwise applicable factor under paragraph (b)(2) or (b)(3) of this section, determined without regard to paragraph (d)(9) of this section.

*(7) Prorated integration level for short plan year.* If an accumulation plan uses paragraph (2) or (4) of the definition of plan year compensation under § 1.401(a)(4)-12 (i.e., section 414(s) compensation for the plan year or the period of plan participation) and has a plan year that comprises fewer than 12 months, the integration or offset level under the plan for each employee must be an amount equal to the otherwise applicable integration or offset level described in paragraph (d)(2), (d)(3), (d)(4), (d)(5), or (d)(6) of this section, multiplied by a fraction, the numerator of which is the number of months in the plan year and the denominator of which is 12. No adjustment to the maximum excess or offset allowance is required as a result of the application of this paragraph (d)(7), other than any adjustment already required under paragraph (d)(6) or (d)(9) of this section.

*(8) Demographic requirements.* (i) In general. A plan that satisfies the demographic requirements of paragraphs (d)(8)(ii) and (iii) of this section may use an integration level described in paragraph (d)(5) of this section.

(ii) Attained age requirement. The requirement of this paragraph (d)(8)(ii) is satisfied only if the average attained age of the nonhighly compensated employees in the plan is not greater than the greater of—

(A) Age 50, or

(B) 5 plus the average attained age of the highly compensated employees in the plan. For purposes of this paragraph (d)(8)(ii), attained ages are determined as of the beginning of the plan year.

(iii) Nondiscrimination requirement. The requirement of this paragraph (d)(8)(iii) is satisfied only if at least one of the following tests in paragraphs (d)(8)(iii)(A) through (D) of this section is satisfied.

(A) Minimum percentage test. This test is satisfied only if more than 50 percent of the nonhighly compensated employees in the plan have average annual compensation at least equal to 120 percent of the integration or offset level.

(B) Ratio test. This test is satisfied only if the percentage of nonhighly compensated nonexcludable employees, who are in the plan and who have average annual compensation at least equal to 120 percent of the integration or offset level, is at least 70 percent of the percentage of highly compensated nonexcludable employees who are employees in the plan.

(C) High dollar amount test. This test is satisfied only if the integration or offset level exceeds 150 percent of the covered compensation of an individual who attains social security retirement age in the calendar year in which the plan year begins. In the case of a calendar year in which no individual could attain social security requirement age, for example, the year 2003, this rule is applied using covered compensation of an individual attaining social security retirement age in the preceding calendar year.

(D) Individual disparity reductions. This test is satisfied only if the plan is an offset plan that uses an offset level of each employee's final average compensation and makes individual disparity reductions as permitted under paragraph (d)(9)(iii)(B) of this section.

*(9) Reduction in the 0.75-percent factor if integration or offset level exceeds covered compensation.* (i) In general. If the integration or offset level specified under the plan is each employee's covered compensation as of the plan year, no reduction in the 0.75-percent factor in the maximum excess or offset allowance is required for the plan year under this paragraph (d)(9). If a plan specifies an integration or offset level that exceeds an employee's covered compensation, the 0.75-percent factor in the maximum excess or offset allowance must be reduced as required in paragraph (d)(9)(ii) or (iii) of this section. Paragraph (d)(9)(iv) of this section contains a table of the applicable reductions.

(ii) Uniform percentage of covered compensation. If a plan specifies an integration or offset level that is a uniform percentage (in excess of 100 percent) of each employee's covered compensation, the 0.75-percent factor in the maximum excess or offset allowance must be reduced in accordance with the table in paragraph (d)(9)(iv) of this section. Thus, for example, if a plan specifies an integration or offset level of 120 percent of each employee's covered compensation, the 0.75-percent factor in the maximum excess or offset allowance must be reduced to 0.69 percent in accordance with the table because the specified integration or offset level is more than covered compensation but not more than 125 percent of covered compensation.

(iii) Single dollar amount. If a plan specifies an integration or offset level of a single dollar amount as permitted under paragraph (d)(5) of this section (for example, $30,000), the applicable reduction in the maximum excess or offset allowance must be determined under paragraph (d)(9)(iii)(A) or (B) of this section, as specified under the plan.

(A) Plan-wide reduction. The applicable reduction in the maximum excess or offset allowance under the table in paragraph (d)(9)(iv) of this section may be determined by comparing the single dollar amount specified in the plan to the covered compensation of an individual attaining social security retirement age in the calendar year in which the plan year begins. Thus, for example, if a plan specifies a single integration or offset level of $30,000 that is uniformly applicable to all employees for a plan year and the covered compensation of an individual attaining social security retirement age in the calendar year in which the plan year begins is $20,000, the 0.75-percent factor in the maximum excess or offset allowance must be reduced to 0.60 percent for all employees in accordance with the table in paragraph (d)(9)(iv) of this section because the specified integration or offset level of $30,000 is more than 125 percent of $20,000 but not more than 150 percent of $20,000. In the case of a calendar year in which no individual could attain social security retirement age (for example, 2003), the comparison is made with covered compensation of an individual who attained social security retirement age in the preceding calendar year. If an offset plan uses an offset level of each employee's final average compensation, the reduction under this paragraph (d)(9)(iii)(A) is determined by comparing the highest possible amount of final average compensation to the covered compensation of an individual attaining social security retirement age in the calendar year in which the plan year begins.

(B) Individual reductions. The applicable reduction in the maximum excess or offset allowance under the table in paragraph (d)(9)(iv) of this section may be determined by comparing the single dollar amount specified in the plan to the covered compensation of each employee under the plan. Thus, for example, if a plan specified a single integration or offset level of $30,000 that is uniformly applicable to all employees for a plan year, the 0.75-percent factor in the maximum excess or offset allowance must be reduced to 0.60 percent for an employee with covered compensation of $20,000, but need not be reduced for an employee whose covered compensation is $30,000 or greater.

(iv) Reductions. (A) Table.

TABLE

| If the integration or offset level is | the permitted disparity factor is |
|---|---|
| 100 percent of covered compensation | 0.75 percent |
| 125 percent of covered compensation | 0.69 percent |
| 150 percent of covered compensation | 0.60 percent |
| 175 percent of covered compensation | 0.53 percent |
| 200 percent of covered compensation | 0.47 percent |
| The taxable wage base or final average compensation | 0.42 percent |

(B) Interpolation. If the integration or offset level used under a plan is between the percentages of covered compensation in the table, the permitted disparity factor applicable to the plan can be determined either by straight-line interpolation between the permitted disparity factors in the table or by rounding the integration or offset level up to the next highest percentage of covered compensation in the table.

*(10) Examples.* The following examples illustrate this paragraph (d). Unless otherwise provide, the following facts apply. The plan is noncontributory and is the only plan ever maintained by the employer. The plan uses a normal retirement age of 65 and contains no provision that would require a reduction in the 0.75-percent factor under paragraph (b)(2) or (b)(3) of this section. In the case of an offset plan, the plan provides that an employee's final average compensation is limited to the employee's average annual compensation. Each example discusses the benefit formula applicable to an employee who has a social security retirement age of 65.

*Example (1).* (a) Plan M is a defined benefit excess plan that uses the calendar year as its plan year. For the 1989 plan year, the plan uses an integration level of $20,000, which is 118 percent of the 1989 covered compensation of $16,968 for an individual reaching social security retirement age in 1989. The plan may use that integration level without satisfying paragraph (d)(8) of this section, provided the adjustment to the 0.75-percent factor required under paragraph (d)(6) of this section is made. That adjustment is the lesser of the factor determined under paragraph (d)(9) of this section or 80 percent of the factor otherwise applicable under paragraph (b)(2) or (b)(3) of this section.

(b) The plan determines the factor under paragraph (d)(9) of this section by comparing the integration level to the covered compensation of an individual attaining social security retirement age in the calendar year in which the plan year begins and by rounding the integration level up to 125 percent of that covered compensation amount. The 0.75-percent factor is therefore replaced by 0.69 percent pursuant to the table in paragraph (d)(9) of this section. The 0.69-percent factor is 92 percent of the 0.75-percent factor. Because the lesser of 80 percent and 92 percent is 80 percent, the 0.75-percent factor is reduced to 0.6 percent (80 percent of 0.75 percent) under paragraph (d)(6) of this section. The 0.6-percent factor applies to benefits commencing at age 65 for an employee with a social security retirement age of 65. In determining normal retirement benefits for employees with social security retirement ages of 66 or 67, the applicable factors for benefits commencing at age 65 are, respectively, 0.56 percent (80 percent of 0.7 percent) and 0.52 percent (80 percent of 0.65 percent).

(c) The plan could also determine the factor under paragraph (d)(9) of this section by comparing the integration level to the covered compensation of each employee under the plan, or by straight line interpolation between the disparity factors contained in the table in paragraph (d)(9) of this section, or both. (Of course, if the plan satisfied paragraph (d)(8) of this section, the plan could use the factor determined under paragraph (d)(9) of this section.)

*Example (2).* (a) Plan N, an accumulation plan, is a defined benefit excess plan that, for each year of service up to 35, accrues a normal retirement benefit of 1 percent of plan year compensation up to the taxable wage base, plus 1.75 percent of plan year compensation above the taxable wage base, for each year of service up to 35. An employee's total retirement benefit is the sum of the accruals for all years. The plan satisfies paragraph (d)(8) of this section.

(b) Because the plan uses the taxable wage base (an amount above covered compensation) as the integration level, it must reduce the 0.75-percent factor in the maximum excess allowance as required under paragraphs (d)(5) and (d)(9) of this section. The reduced factor, if determined on a plan-wide basis under paragraph (d)(9)(iii)(A) of this section, is 0.42 percent. The plan must therefore reduce the disparity in the plan so that it does not exceed 0.42 percent.

*Example (3).* (a) For the 1990 plan year, Plan O provides a normal retirement benefit of 2 percent of average annual compensation, minus a percentage of final average compensation up to $48,000, for each year of service up to 35. The plan satisfies paragraph (d)(8) of this section. As permitted under paragraph (d)(9) of this section, the plan provides that each employee's offset percentage is determined by comparing $48,000 to the employee's covered compensation and by rounding the result up to the next highest percentage of covered compensation.

(b) Employee A has a social security retirement age of 66 and covered compensation of $40,000. Because the plan provides for commencement of Employee A's benefit at age 65, the 0.75-percent factor in the maximum offset allowance is reduced to 0.7 percent under paragraph (e)(1) of this section (the "paragraph (e) factor"). In addition, because $48,000 is rounded up to 125 percent of Employee A's covered compensation, the 0.75-percent factor in the maximum offset allowance is reduced to 0.69 percent under paragraph (d)(9) of this section (the "paragraph (d) factor"). The reductions are cumulative under paragraph (b)(3)(ii) of this section.

(c) The cumulative reductions can be made by multiplying the paragraph (e) factor by the ratio of the paragraph (d) factor to 0.75 percent or by multiplying the paragraph (d) factor by the ratio of the paragraph (e) factor to 0.75 percent. The disparity factor for Employee A is therefore 0.64 percent ((0.7 percent × 0.69 percent/0.75 percent) or (0.69 percent × 0.7 percent/0.75 percent)).

*Example (4).* Plan P is an offset plan that uses the calendar year as the plan year and uses an offset level of each employee's final average compensation. Assume that the taxable wage bases for 1990-1992 are the following:

| | |
|---|---|
| 1990 | $51,300 |
| 1991 | $53,400 |
| 1992 | $58,000 |

Employee B's final average compensation, determined as of the close of the 1992 plan year, is the average of Employee B's annual compensation for the period 1990-1992. Employee B's annual compensation for each year is the following:

| | |
|---|---|
| 1990 | $47,000 |
| 1991 | $59,000 |
| 1992 | $65,000 |

For purposes of determining the offset applied to Employee B's employer-provided benefit under the plan. Employee B's final average compensation as of the close of the 1992 plan year is $52,800 ($47,000 + $53,400 + $58,000)/3). This is because annual compensation in excess of the taxable wage base in effect at the beginning of the year may not be taken into account in determining an employee's final average compensation or in determining the employee's offset. If the plan determines the offset applied to Employee B's benefit by reference to compensation in excess of $52,800, the plan fails to satisfy this paragraph (d).

**(e) Adjustments to the 0.75-percent factor for benefits commencing at ages other than social security retirement age.** *(1) In general.* The 0.75-percent factor in the maximum excess allowance and in the maximum offset allowance applies to a benefit commencing at an employee's social security retirement age. Except as provided in paragraph (g) of this section, if a benefit payable to an employee under a defined benefit excess plan or a defined offset plan commences at an age before the employee's social security retirement age (including a benefit payable at the normal retirement age under the plan), the 0.75-percent factor in the maximum excess allowance or in the maximum offset allowance, respectively, is reduced in accordance with paragraph (e)(2)(i) of this section. If a benefit payable to an employee under a defined benefit excess plan or a defined benefit offset plan commences at an age after the employee's social security retirement age, the 0.75-percent factor in the maximum excess allowance or in the maximum offset allowance, respectively, may be increased in accordance with paragraph (e)(2)(ii) of this section. Paragraph (e)(4) of this section provides rules on the age at which a benefit commences. See paragraph (f) of this section for the requirements applicable to optional forms of benefit.

*(2) Adjustments.* (i) Benefits commencing on or after age 55 and before social security retirement age. If benefits commence before an employee's social security retirement age, the 0.75-percent factor in the maximum excess allowance and in the maximum offset allowance must be reduced for such early commencement of benefits in accordance with the tables set forth in paragraph (e)(3) of this section.

(ii) Benefits commencing after social security retirement age and on or before age 70. If benefits commence after an employee's social security retirement age, the 0.75-percent factor in the maximum excess allowance and in the maximum offset allowance may be increased for such delayed commencement of benefits in accordance with the tables set forth in paragraph (e)(3) of this section.

(iii) Benefits commencing before age 55. If benefits commence before the employee attains age 55, the 0.75-percent factor in the maximum excess allowance and in the maximum offset allowance is further reduced (on a monthly basis to reflect the month in which benefits commence) to a factor that is the actuarial equivalent of the 0.75-percent factor, as adjusted under the tables in paragraph (e)(3) of this section, applicable to a benefit commencing in the month in which the employee attains age 55. In determining actuarial equivalence for this purpose, a reasonable interest rate must be used. In addition, a reasonable mortality table must be used to determine the actuarial present value, as defined in § 1.401(a)(4)-12, of the benefits commencing at age 55 and at the earlier commencement age, and a reasonable mortality table may be used to determine the actuarial present value at the earlier commencement age of the benefits commencing at age 55. A standard interest rate and a standard mortality table, as defined in § 1.401(a)(4)-12, are considered reasonable.

(iv) Benefits commencing after age 70. If benefits commence after the employee attains age 70, the 0.75-percent factor in the maximum excess allowance and in the maximum offset allowance may be further increased (on a monthly basis to reflect the month in which benefits commence) to a factor that is the actuarial equivalent of the 0.75-percent factor (as adjusted in accordance with this paragraph (e)) applicable to a benefit commencing in the month in which the employee attains age 70. In determining actuarial equivalence for this purpose, a reasonable interest rate must be used. In addition, a reasonable mortality table must be used to determine the actuarial present value, as defined in § 1.401(a)(4)-12, of the benefits commencing at age 70 and at the later commencement age, and a reasonable mortality table may be used to determine the value at the later commencement age of the benefits commencing at age 70. A standard interest rate and a standard mortality table, as defined in § 1.401(a)(4)-12, are considered reasonable.

*(3) Tables.* Tables I, II, and III provide the adjustments in the 0.75-percent factor in the maximum excess allowance and in the maximum offset allowance applicable to benefits commencing on or after age 55 and on or before age 70 to an employee who has a social security retirement age of 65, 66 or 67. Table IV is a simplified table for a plan that uses a single disparity factor of 0.65 percent for all employees at age 65. The factors in the following tables are applicable to benefits that commence in the month the employee attains the specified age. Accordingly, if benefits commence in a month other than the month in which the employee attains the specified age, appropriate adjustments in the 0.75-percent factor in the maximum excess allowance and the maximum offset allowance must be made. For this purpose, adjustments may be based on straight-line interpolation from the factors in the tables or in accordance with the methods of adjustment specified in paragraphs (e)(2)(iii) and (iv) of this section.

**TABLE I**

*Social security retirement age 67*

| Age at which benefits commence | Annual factor in maximum excess allowance and maximum offset allowance (percent) |
|---|---|
| 70 | 1.002 |
| 69 | 0.908 |
| 68 | 0.825 |
| 67 | 0.750 |
| 66 | 0.700 |
| 65 | 0.650 |
| 64 | 0.600 |
| 63 | 0.550 |
| 62 | 0.500 |
| 61 | 0.475 |
| 60 | 0.450 |

| | |
|---|---|
| 59 | 0.425 |
| 58 | 0.400 |
| 57 | 0.375 |
| 56 | 0.344 |
| 55 | 0.316 |

**TABLE II**

*Social security retirement age 66*

| Age at which benefits commence | Annual factor in maximum excess allowance and maximum offset allowance (percent) |
|---|---|
| 70 | 1.101 |
| 69 | 0.998 |
| 68 | 0.907 |
| 67 | 0.824 |
| 66 | 0.750 |
| 65 | 0.700 |
| 64 | 0.650 |
| 63 | 0.600 |
| 62 | 0.550 |
| 61 | 0.500 |
| 60 | 0.475 |
| 59 | 0.450 |
| 58 | 0.425 |
| 57 | 0.400 |
| 56 | 0.375 |
| 55 | 0.344 |

**TABLE III**

*Social security retirement age 65*

| Age at which benefits commence | Annual factor in maximum excess allowance and maximum offset allowance (percent) |
|---|---|
| 70 | 1.209 |
| 69 | 1.096 |
| 68 | 0.996 |
| 67 | 0.905 |
| 66 | 0.824 |
| 65 | 0.750 |
| 64 | 0.700 |
| 63 | 0.650 |
| 62 | 0.600 |
| 61 | 0.550 |
| 60 | 0.500 |
| 59 | 0.475 |
| 58 | 0.450 |
| 57 | 0.425 |
| 56 | 0.400 |
| 55 | 0.375 |

**TABLE IV**

*Simplified table*

| Age at which benefits commence | Annual factor in maximum excess allowance and maximum offset allowance (percent) |
|---|---|
| 70 | 1.048 |
| 69 | 0.950 |
| 68 | 0.863 |
| 67 | 0.784 |
| 66 | 0.714 |
| 65 | 0.650 |
| 64 | 0.607 |
| 63 | 0.563 |
| 62 | 0.520 |
| 61 | 0.477 |
| 60 | 0.433 |
| 59 | 0.412 |
| 58 | 0.390 |
| 57 | 0.368 |
| 56 | 0.347 |
| 55 | 0.325 |

*(4) Benefit commencement date.* (i) In general. Except as provided in paragraph (e)(4)(ii) of this section, a benefit commences for purposes of this paragraph (e) on the first day of the period for which the benefit is paid under the plan.

(ii) Qualified social security supplement. If a plan uses a qualified social security supplement, as defined in § 1.401(a)(4)-12, to provide an aggregate benefit at retirement before social security retirement age that is a uniform percentage of average annual compensation, benefits will be considered to commence on the first day of the period for which the qualified social security supplement is no longer payable. In order for this paragraph (e)(4)(ii) to apply, the uniform percentage must be equal to the excess benefit percentage in the case of an excess plan or the gross benefit percentage in the case of an offset plan.

*(5) Examples.* The following examples illustrate this paragraph (e). Unless otherwise provided, the following facts apply. The plan is noncontributory and is the only plan ever maintained by the employer. The plan uses a normal retirement age of 65 and contains no provision that would require a reduction in the 0.75-percent factor under paragraph (b)(2) or (b)(3) of this section. In the case of a defined benefit excess plan, the plan uses each employee's covered compensation as the integration level; in the case of an offset plan, the plan uses each employee's covered compensation as the offset level and provides that an employee's final average compensation is limited to the employee's average annual compensation. Each example discusses the benefit formula applicable to an employee who has a social security retirement age of 65.

*Example (1).* Plan M is a defined benefit excess plan that, for an employee with a social security retirement age of 65, provides a normal retirement benefit of 1.25 percent of average annual compensation up to the integration level, plus 2.0 percent of average annual compensation in excess of the integration level, for each year of service up to 35. For an employee with at least 20 years of service, the plan provides a benefit commencing at age 55 that is equal to the benefit payable at age 65. For that employee, the disparity provided under the plan at age 55 is 0.75 percent (2 percent − 1.25 percent). Because this disparity exceeds the 0.375 percent factor provided in the table for a benefit payable at age 55 to an employee with a social security retirement age of 65, the plan fails to satisfy paragraphs (b) and (e) of this section with respect to the early retirement benefit.

*Example (2).* Assume the same facts as in Example 1, except that the base benefit percentage under the plan is 1.75 percent. Thus, the disparity provided under the plan at age 55 is 0.25 percent (2 percent − 1.75 percent). Because the disparity does not exceed the 0.375 percent factor provided in the table for a benefit payable at age 55 to an employee with a social security retirement age of 65, the plan does not fail to satisfy paragraphs (b) and (e) of this section with respect to the early retirement benefit.

*Example (3).* Plan N is an offset plan that, for an employee with a social security retirement age of 65, provides a normal retirement benefit of 1.75 percent of average annual compensation, minus 0.75 percent of final average compensation up to the offset level, for each year of service up to 35. For an employee with at least 20 years of service, the plan provides a benefit commencing at age 55 that is equal to the benefit payable at age 65. For that employee, the disparity provided under the plan at age 55 is 0.75 percent. Because this disparity exceeds the 0.375-percent factor provided in the table for an offset applied to a benefit payable at age 55 to an employee with a social security retirement age of 65, the plan fails to satisfy paragraphs (b) and (e) of this section with respect to the early retirement benefit. The plan would not fail to satisfy paragraphs (b) and (e) of this section with respect to the early retirement benefit if the applicable factor for determining the offset applied to the benefit were reduced to 0.375 percent.

*Example (4).* Plan O is defined benefit excess plan that, for an employee with a social security retirement age of 65, provides a normal retirement benefit of 1.25 percent of average annual compensation up to the integration level, plus 2.0 percent of average annual compensation in excess of the integration level, for each year of service up to 35. The plan provides benefits commencing before normal retirement age with the following reductions:

| Age | Percentage of normal retirement benefit |
|---|---|
| 64 | 90% |
| 63 | 85% |
| 62 | 80% |

Under the plan, a benefit payable at age 64 is equal to 90 percent of the normal retirement benefit payable at age 65. Thus, the excess benefit percentage under the plan is 1.8 percent, the base benefit percentage under the plan is 1.125 percent, and the disparity provided under the plan at age 64 is 0.675 percent. Similarly, a benefit payable at age 63 is equal to 85 percent of the normal retirement benefit payable at age 65. Thus, the excess benefit percentage under the plan is 1.7 percent, the base benefit percentage under the plan is 1.0625 percent, and the disparity provided under the plan at age 63 is 0.6375 percent. Finally, a benefit payable at age 62 is equal to 80 percent of the normal retirement benefit payable at age 65. Thus, the excess benefit percentage under the plan is 1.6 percent, the base benefit percentage under the plan is 1.0 percent, and the disparity provided under the plan at age 62 is 0.6 percent. Because the disparities provided under the plan at each early commencement age do not exceed the factors provided in the applicable table in paragraph (e)(3) of this section, the plan does not fail to satisfy paragraphs (b) and (e) of this section with respect to the early retirement benefits.

*Example (5).* Plan P is defined benefit excess plan that provides a normal retirement benefit of 0.75 percent of average annual compensation up to the integration level, plus 1.5 percent of average annual compensation in excess of the integration level, for each year of service up to 35. The plan does not provide any benefits, other than normal retirement benefits, commencing before an employee's social security retirement age. Employee A, born in 1947, has a social security retirement age of 66. Because the plan provides for the distribution of normal retirement benefits before Employee A's social security retirement age, the 0.75-percent factor in the maximum excess allowance applicable to Employee A must be reduced to 0.70 percent in accordance with this paragraph (e). Accordingly, the disparity provided to A under the plan exceeds the maximum excess allowance because the excess benefit percentage (1.5 percent) exceeds the base benefit percentage (0.75 percent) by more than the maximum excess allowance of 0.70 percent, as reduced in accordance with this paragraph (e).

*Example (6).* Assume the same facts as in Example 5, except that the plan also provides an early retirement benefit, commencing at age 62, to an employee who satisfies the conditions for early retirement specified in the plan. The early retirement benefit is based upon the employee's accrued benefit at early retirement age and equals the amount that would have been paid commencing at the employee's normal retirement age based upon the employee's average annual compensation, covered compensation and years of service at the date of the employee's early retirement. Employee B, who has a social security retirement age of 65, meets the conditions for early retirement under the plan and retires at age 62 with 30 years of service. At the time of early retirement, Employee B has average annual compensation of $20,000 and covered compensation of $16,000. Under the plan's benefit formula, Employee B has accrued a normal retirement benefit, commencing at age 65, of $5,400 ((22.5 percent × $16,000) + (45 percent × $4,000)) based on Employee B's average annual compensation, covered compensation and years of service at early retirement. Accordingly, under the plan's early retirement provisions, Employee B is entitled to receive, commencing at early retirement, a benefit of $5,400. Because the early retirement benefit is a benefit commencing at age 62 (before Employee B's social security retirement age), the 0.75-percent factor in the maximum excess allowance must be reduced to 0.60 percent in accordance with this paragraph (e). Accordingly, the disparity provided to Employee B under the plan at early retirement exceeds the maximum excess allowance.

*Example (7).* (a) Plan Q is a defined benefit excess plan that provides a normal retirement benefit of 1.35 percent of average annual compensation up to the integration level, plus 2 percent of average annual compensation in excess of the integration level, for each year of service up to 35. The plan provides that an employee with 10 years of service at age 55 may receive an unreduced retirement benefit. The plan also provides that employee with a supplemental benefit of 0.65 percent of average annual compensation up to the integration level for each year of service up to 35, payable from early retirement until age 65. The supplemental benefit is a qualified social security supplement under § 1.401(a)(4)-12. The effect of the supplement is to provide an employee with a uniform benefit of 2 percent of average annual compensation from early retirement until age 65, when the supplement is no longer payable. Therefore, for purposes of this paragraph (e), the employee's benefit will be considered to commence at age 65.

(b) Assume that Plan Q is instead an offset plan that provides a normal retirement benefit of 2 percent of average annual compensation, minus 0.65 percent of final average compensation up to the offset level, for each year of service up to 35. The plan provides the same early retirement benefit on the same conditions, except that the supplement is 0.65 percent of an employee's final average compensation up to the offset level. An employee at age 55 thus receives a uniform benefit of 2 percent of average annual compensation until age 65, when the supplement is no longer payable. Therefore, for purposes of this paragraph (e), the employee's benefit will be considered to commence at age 65.

**(f) Benefits, rights, and features.** *(1) Defined benefit excess plan.* In the case of a defined benefit excess plan, each benefit, right, or feature provided under the plan with respect to employer-provided benefits attributable to average annual compensation above the integration level (an "excess benefit, right, or feature") must also be provided on the same terms with respect to employer-provided benefits attributable to average annual compensation up to the integration level (a "base benefit, right, or feature"). Alternatively, an excess benefit, right, or feature may be provided on different terms than the base benefit, right, or feature, if the terms used to determine the base benefit, right, or feature produce a benefit, right, or feature of inherently equal or greater value than the benefit, right, or feature that would be produced under the terms used to determine the excess benefit, right or feature.

*(2) Offset plan.* In the case of an offset plan, each benefit, right, or feature provided under the plan with respect to employer-provided benefits before application of the offset (a "gross benefit, right, or feature") must be provided on the same terms as those used to determine the offset applied to the gross benefit, right, or feature. Alternatively, a gross benefit, right, or feature may be provided on different terms from those used to determine the offset applied to the gross benefit, right, or feature, if the terms used to determine the gross benefit, right, or feature produce a benefit, right, or feature of inherently equal or greater value than the benefit, right, or feature that would be produced under the terms used to determine the offset applied to the gross benefit, right, or feature. In addition, if benefits commence before an employee's normal retirement age, the gross benefit percentage under the plan must be reduced by a number of percentage points that is not less than the number of percentage points by which the offset percentage must be reduced, from normal retirement age to the age at which benefits commence, under the rules of paragraph (e) of this section.

*(3) Examples.* The following examples illustrate this paragraph (f). Unless otherwise provided, the following facts apply. The plan is noncontributory and is the only plan ever maintained by the employer. The plan uses a normal retirement age of 65 and contains no provision that would require a reduction in the 0.75-percent factor under paragraph (b)(2) or (b)(3) of this section. In the case of a defined benefit excess plan, the plan uses each employee's covered compensation as the integration level; in the case of an offset plan, the plan uses each employee's covered compensation as the offset level and provides that an employee's final average compensation is limited to the employee's average annual compensation. Each example discusses the benefit formula applicable to an employee who has a social security retirement age of 65. All optional forms of benefit under each plan are provided on the same terms.

*Example (1).* Plan M is a defined benefit excess plan that provides a normal retirement benefit of 1 percent of average annual compensation up to the integration level, plus 1.65 percent of average annual compensation above the integration level, for each year of service up to 35. The plan provides an early retirement benefit for any employee who terminates employment at or after age 55 with 10 or more years of service. In determining an employee's early retirement, the 1.65 percent excess benefit percentage is reduced in accordance with the table in paragraph (e)(3) of this section for a plan that uses a single disparity factor of 0.65 percent for all employees at age 65. However, a larger reduction factor is applied to determine the base benefit percentage at early retirement. The plan violates this paragraph (f) because the excess early retirement benefit is not provided on the same terms as the base early retirement benefit, nor do the terms used to determine the base early retirement benefit produce an early retirement benefit of inherently equal or greater value than the early retirement benefit that would be produced under the terms used to determine the excess benefit, right, or feature.

*Example (2).* The facts are the same as in Example 1 except that the plan determines the early retirement benefit by applying the same reduction factors under paragraph (e)(3) of this section to the base and excess benefit percentages. Furthermore, if an employee terminates employment at or after age 55 with 30 or more years of service, the plan provides that the base benefit percentage of 1 percent is not reduced. Although the excess early retirement benefit is provided on different terms than the base early retirement benefit, the plan satisfies this paragraph (f) because the terms used to determine the base early retirement benefit produce an early retirement of inherently equal or greater value than the early retirement benefit that would be produced under the terms used to determine the excess benefit, right, or feature.

*Example (3).* Plan N is an offset plan that provides a normal retirement benefit of 2 percent of average annual compensation, minus 0.65 percent of final average compensation up to the offset level, for each year of service up to 35. In determining the qualified joint and survivor ("QJSA") form of the normal retirement benefit, the plan applies a factor of 80 percent to the gross benefit percentage and a factor of 100 percent to the offset percentage. Thus, the QJSA form is 1.6 percent of average annual compensation, minus 0.65 percent of final average compensation up to the offset level, for each year of service up to 35. The plan violates this paragraph (f) because the gross QJSA form is not provided on the same terms as the terms used to determine the offset applied to the QJSA, nor does it produce a QJSA benefit that is of inherently equal or greater value than the QJSA benefit that would be produced under the terms used to determine the offset under the plan.

*Example (4).* Plan O is a defined benefit excess plan that provides a normal retirement benefit of 1 percent of average annual compensation up to the integration level, plus 1.65 percent of average annual compensation above the integration level, for each year of service up to 35. The plan also provides a single sum optional form of benefit determined by applying a single interest rate and mortality assumption to the entire normal retirement benefit. The plan satisfies this paragraph (f) because the excess optional form is provided on the same terms as the base optional form. The plan would also satisfy this paragraph (f) if it used a lower interest rate to determine the base optional form than used to determine the excess optional form because the lower interest rate would produce an optional form of inherently equal or greater value than the optional form produced by using the same interest rate.

*Example (5).* Plan R is a defined benefit excess plan that provides a normal retirement benefit of 1 percent of average annual compensation up to the integration level, plus 1.65 percent of average annual compensation above the integration level, for each year of service up to 35. If an employee continues to work after normal retirement age, the plan provides that the employee receives credit for additional years of service up to the service limit of 35. The plan also provides that the disparity provided under the plan will increase as permitted under paragraph (e) of this section for benefits commencing after social security retirement age. However, the plan does not provide an increase in the base benefit percentage to reflect the fact that the employee has delayed commencement of benefits past normal retirement age. Thus, for example, for an employee at age 68, the plan provides a benefit of 1 percent of average annual compensation up to the integration level, plus 1.86 percent of average annual compensation above the integration level, for each year of service up to 35. The plan violates this paragraph (f) because the excess benefit provided for an employee after normal retirement age is not provided on the same terms as the base benefit, nor do the terms used to determine the base benefit produce a benefit of inherently equal or greater value than the benefit that would be produced under the terms used to determine the excess benefit.

*Example (6).* Plan Q is an offset plan that provides a normal retirement benefit of 2 percent of average annual compensation, minus 0.65 percent of final average compensation up to the offset level, for each year of service up to 35. In accordance with paragraph (e) of this section, the plan reduces the offset percentage under the plan for early retirement and provides a benefit at age 55 of 2 percent of average annual compensation, minus 0.325 percent of final average compensation up to the offset level, for each year of service up to 35. However, the early retirement benefit does not meet this paragraph (f) because an employee's gross benefit percentage is not reduced for early retirement.

*Example (7).* The facts are the same as in Example 6 except that the plan reduces the gross benefit percentage for early retirement at age 55 to 1.675 percent. Because the gross benefit percentage is reduced by 0.325 percent (from 2.0 percent to 1.675 percent), the same percentage point reduction made in the offset percentage (from 0.65 percent to 0.325 percent), the early retirement benefit meets this paragraph (f).

**(g) No reductions in 0.75-percent factor for ancillary benefits.** For purposes of applying the maximum excess allowance or the maximum offset allowance under paragraph (b)(2) or (3) of this section, no reduction is made to the 0.75-percent factor merely because the plan provides disparity in qualified disability benefits (within the meaning of section 411(a)(9)) or preretirement death benefits and the relevant benefits are payable before an employee's social security retirement age.

**(h) Benefits attributable to employee contributions not taken into account.** Benefits attributable to employee contributions to a defined benefit plan are not taken into account in determining whether the disparity provided under a defined benefit excess plan or an offset plan exceeds the maximum permitted disparity described in paragraph (b) of this section. See § 1.401(a)(4)-6(b) for methods of determining the employer-provided benefit under a plan that includes employee contributions not allocated to separate accounts (i.e., a contributory DB plan), including § 1.401(a)(4)-6(b)(2)(iii)(B) for adjustments to the base and excess benefit percentages or the gross benefit percentage under a section 401(l) plan. If, after adjustment, the employee's base benefit percentage or gross benefit percentage (whichever is applicable) is less than zero, such percentage is deemed to be zero for purposes of the maximum excess allowance or maximum offset allowance under paragraph (b)(2) or (3) of this section.

**(i) Multiple integration levels. [Reserved].**

**(j) Additional rules.** The Commissioner may, in revenue rulings, notices or other documents of general applicability, prescribe additional rules as may be necessary or appropriate to carry out the purposes of this section, including updated tables under paragraphs (d) and (e) of this section providing for reductions in the 0.75-percent factor in the maximum excess allowance and in the maximum offset allowance and rules in paragraph (h) of this section for determining the portion of an employee's benefit attributable to employee contributions.

T.D. 8359, 9/12/91, amend T.D. 8486, 8/31/93.

**§ 1.401(l)-4 Special rules for railroad plans.**

**(a) In general.** Section 401(l)(6) provides that, in the case of a plan maintained by a railroad employer that covers employees who are entitled to benefits under the Railroad Retirement Act of 1974, in determining whether such a plan satisfies section 401(l), rules similar to the rules under section 401(l) apply and such rules take into account the employer-derived portion of tier 2 and supplemental annuity benefits provided under the railroad retirement system. In general, for purposes of determining whether a defined contribution plan or a defined benefit plan maintained by a railroad employer and covering employees described in the preceding sentence, satisfies section 401(l), the employer-derived portion of an employee's tier 2 benefits and supplementary annuity benefits under the Railroad Retirement Act of 1974 are treated as though such benefits were provided by the railroad employer under a qualified plan. Paragraph (b) of this section contains rules for defined contribution plans. Paragraph (c) of this section contains rules for defined benefit excess plans. Paragraph (d) of this section contains rules for offset plans. Paragraph (e) of this section contains definitions and additional rules of application.

**(b) Defined contribution plans.** *(1) In general.* A defined contribution plan maintained by a railroad employer satisfies section 401(l) and § 1.401(l)-2 for a plan year only if the plan satisfies paragraph (b)(2) or (b)(3) of this section for the plan year.

*(2) Single integration level method.* (i) In general. A plan satisfies this paragraph (b)(2) if—

(A) The plan specifies a single integration level for all employees that does not exceed the railroad retirement taxable wage base in effect as of the beginning of the plan year,

(B) The plan uses the same base contribution percentage and the same excess contribution percentage for all employees, and

(C) The excess contribution percentage does not exceed the sum of 11.4 percentage points and the base contribution percentage.

(ii) Definitions. The following definitions govern for purposes of this paragraph (b)(2).

(A) "Base contribution percentage" means the rate at which employer contributions are allocated to the account of an employee under the plan with respect to the employee's plan year compensation at or below the railroad retirement taxable wage base (expressed as a percentage of such plan year compensation).

(B) "Excess contribution percentage" means the rate at which employer contributions are allocated to the account of an employee under the plan with respect to the employee's plan year compensation above the railroad retirement taxable wage base (expressed as a percentage of such plan year compensation).

*(3) Two integration level method.* (i) In general. A plan satisfies this paragraph (b)(3) if—

(A) The plan specifies two integration levels for all employees, equal to the railroad retirement taxable wage base in effect as of the beginning of the plan year and the taxable wage base in effect as of the beginning of the plan year, and

(B) The plan satisfies paragraphs (b)(3)(ii) and (iii) of this section.

(ii) Total disparity requirement. A plan satisfies this paragraph (b)(3)(ii) if—

(A) The plan uses the same base contribution percentage and the same excess contribution percentage for all employees, and

(B) The excess contribution percentage does not exceed the sum of 11.4 percentage points and the base contribution percentage.

(iii) Intermediate disparity requirement. A plan satisfies this paragraph (b)(3)(iii) if—

(A) The plan uses the same base contribution percentage and the same intermediate contribution percentage for all employees, and

(B) The intermediate contribution percentage does not exceed the sum of 5.7 percentage points and the base contribution percentage.

(iv) Definitions. The following definitions govern for purposes of this paragraph (b)(3).

(A) "Base contribution percentage" means the rate at which employer contributions are allocated to the account of an employee under the plan with respect to the employee's plan year compensation at or below the railroad retirement taxable wage base (expressed as a percentage of such plan year compensation).

(B) "Intermediate contribution percentage" means the rate at which employer contributions are allocated to the account of an employee under the plan with respect to the employee's plan year compensation between the railroad retirement taxable wage base and the taxable wage base (expressed as a percentage of such plan year compensation).

(C) "Excess contribution percentage" means the rate at which employer contributions are allocated to the account of an employee under the plan with respect to the employee's plan year compensation above the taxable wage base (expressed as a percentage of such plan year compensation).

**(c) Defined benefit excess plans.** *(1) In general.* A defined benefit excess plan maintained by a railroad employer satisfies section 401(l) and § 1.401(l)-3 for a plan year only if the plan satisfies paragraph (c)(2) or (c)(3) of this section for the plan year.

*(2) Single integration level method.* (i) In general. A plan satisfies this paragraph (c)(2) if—

(A) The plan specifies a single integration level for all employees that does not exceed railroad retirement covered compensation,

(B) The plan uses the same base benefit percentage and the same excess benefit percentage for all employees, and

(C) The excess benefit percentage does not exceed the lesser of—

(1) Two times the sum of 0.56 percent and the base benefit percentage, or

(2) 0.56 percent plus the base benefit percentage plus 0.75 percent.

(ii) Definitions. The following definitions govern for purposes of this paragraph (c)(2).

(A) "Base benefit percentage" means the rate at which employer-provided benefits are determined under the plan with respect to an employee's average annual compensation at or below the employee's railroad retirement covered compensation (expressed as a percentage of such average annual compensation).

(B) "Excess benefit percentage" means the rate at which employer-provided benefits are determined under the plan with respect to an employee's average annual compensation above the employee's railroad retirement covered compensation (expressed as a percentage of such average annual compensation).

*(3) Two integration level method.* (i) In general. A plan satisfies this paragraph (c)(3) for a plan year if—

(A) The plan specifies two integration levels for all employees, equal to each employee's railroad retirement covered compensation and each employee's covered compensation, and

(B) The plan satisfies paragraphs (c)(3)(ii) and (iii) of this section.

(ii) Employee with lower covered compensation. A plan satisfies this paragraph (c)(3)(ii) if, with respect to each employee whose lower integration level is the employee's covered compensation—

(A) The plan uses the same base benefit percentage and the same intermediate benefit percentage for all employees,

(B) The intermediate benefit percentage does not exceed the base benefit percentage by more than the lesser of 0.75 percent or the base benefit percentage,

(C) The plan uses the same intermediate benefit percentage and the same excess benefit percentage for all employees, and

(D) The excess benefit percentage does not exceed the intermediate benefit percentage by more than 0.56 percent.

(iii) Employee with lower railroad retirement covered compensation. A plan satisfies this paragraph (c)(3)(iii) if, with respect to each employee whose lower integration level is the employee's railroad retirement covered compensation—

(A) The plan uses the same base benefit percentage and the same excess benefit percentage for all employees,

(B) The excess benefit percentage does not exceed the lesser of—

(1) Two times the sum of 0.56 percent and the base benefit percentage, or

(2) The sum of 0.56 percent plus the base benefit percentage plus 0.75 percent,

(C) The plan uses the same base benefit percentage and the same intermediate benefit percentage for all employees, and

(D) The intermediate benefit percentage does not exceed the sum of 0.56 percent plus the base benefit percentage.

(iv) Definitions. The following definitions govern for purposes of this paragraph (c)(3).

(A) "Base benefit percentage" means the rate at which employer-provided benefits are determined under the plan with respect to an employee's average annual compensation at or below the lower integration level specified in the plan (expressed as a percentage of such average annual compensation).

(B) "Intermediate benefit percentage" means the rate at which employer-provided benefits are determined under the plan with respect to an employee's average annual compensation between the lower and higher integration levels specified in the plan (expressed as a percentage of such average annual compensation).

(C) "Excess benefit percentage" means the rate at which employer-provided benefits are determined under the plan with respect to an employee's average annual compensation above the higher integration level specified in the plan (expressed as a percentage of such average annual compensation).

**(d) Offset plans.** *(1) In general.* An offset plan maintained by a railroad employer satisfies section 401(l) and § 1.401(l)-3 for a plan year only if—

(i) The plan satisfies § 1.401(l)-3 for the plan year without regard to the offset for the employer-derived portion of tier 2 and supplementary annuity benefits provided under the railroad retirement system, and

(ii) The offset for the employer-derived portion of tier 2 and supplementary annuity benefits provided under the railroad retirement system does not exceed the maximum tier 2 and supplementary annuity offset allowance.

*(2) Maximum tier 2 and supplementary annuity offset allowance.* For purposes of paragraph (d)(1) of this section, the maximum tier 2 and supplementary annuity offset allowance for a plan year is equal to 0.56 percent of the employee's railroad retirement covered compensation for the plan year.

**(e) Additional rules.** *(1) Definitions.* The following definitions govern for purposes of this section.

(i) "Railroad retirement taxable wage base" means the applicable base, as determined under section 3231(e)(2)(B)(ii), for purposes of the tax under section 3221(b) (the tier 2 tax).

(ii) Railroad retirement covered compensation for an employee means 12 multiplied by the average of the 60 highest monthly railroad retirement taxable wage bases in effect for the employee's period of employment. The monthly railroad retirement taxable wage base is determined by dividing the railroad retirement taxable wage base for the calendar year in which the month occurs by 12. An employee's railroad retirement covered compensation for the plan year is determined as of the beginning of the plan year. A plan must provide that an employee's railroad retirement covered compensation is automatically adjusted for each plan year. See § 1.401(l)-1(b) for rules relating to prohibited decreases in an employee's accrued benefit within the meaning of section 411(d)(6) or section 411(b)(1)(G).

*(2) Adjustments to 0.75-percent factor.* The 0.75-percent factor in the maximum excess allowance and in the maximum offset allowance is subject to the reductions prescribed in § 1.401(l)-3(d) and (e), except that in the case of an employee with at least 30 years of service with a railroad employer, the following tables are substituted for Tables I through III contained in § 1.401(l)-3(e)(3).

**TABLE I**

Social security retirement age 67

| Age at which benefits commence | Annual factor in maximum excess allowance and maximum offset allowance (percent) |
|---|---|
| 66 | 0.750 |
| 65 | 0.750 |
| 64 | 0.750 |
| 63 | 0.750 |
| 62 | 0.750 |
| 61 | 0.525 |
| 60 | 0.525 |
| 59 | 0.508 |
| 58 | 0.490 |
| 57 | 0.472 |
| 56 | 0.433 |
| 55 | 0.398 |

**TABLE II**

Social security retirement age 66

| Age at which benefits commence | Annual factor in maximum excess allowance and maximum offset allowance (percent) |
|---|---|
| 65 | 0.750 |
| 64 | 0.750 |
| 63 | 0.750 |
| 62 | 0.750 |
| 61 | 0.563 |
| 60 | 0.563 |
| 59 | 0.544 |
| 58 | 0.525 |
| 57 | 0.506 |
| 56 | 0.488 |
| 55 | 0.447 |

**TABLE III**

Social security retirement age 65

| Age at which benefits commence | Annual factor in maximum excess allowance and maximum offset allowance (percent) |
|---|---|
| 64 | 0.750 |
| 63 | 0.750 |
| 62 | 0.750 |
| 61 | 0.600 |
| 60 | 0.600 |
| 59 | 0.580 |
| 58 | 0.560 |
| 57 | 0.540 |
| 56 | 0.520 |
| 55 | 0.500 |

*(3) Adjustments to 0.56-percent factor.* The 0.56-percent factor for defined benefit excess plans and offset plans under paragraphs (c) and (d) of this section respectively is subject to the reductions prescribed in § 1.401(l)-3(d) and (e), except that, for purposes of applying this paragraph (e)(3)—

(i) "Railroad retirement covered compensation" is substituted for "covered compensation" in § 1.401(l)-3(d),

(ii) The reductions under § 1.401(l)-3(d) are made by multiplying the 0.56-percent factor by the ratio of the applicable factor from the table in § 1.401(l)-3(d)(9)(iv)(A) to 0.75, and

(iii) The following tables are substituted for Tables I through III set forth in § 1.401(l)-3(e)(3).

(A) Tables applicable to 0.56% factor for employees covered by tier 2 of railroad retirement with 30 or more years of railroad service

**TABLE I**

Social security retirement age 67

| Age at which benefits commence | Annual factor in maximum excess allowance and maximum offset allowance (percent) |
|---|---|
| 66 | 0.560 |
| 65 | 0.560 |
| 64 | 0.560 |

| | |
|---|---|
| 63 | 0.560 |
| 62 | 0.560 |
| 61 | 0.560 |
| 60 | 0.560 |
| 59 | 0.541 |
| 58 | 0.523 |
| 57 | 0.504 |
| 56 | 0.462 |
| 55 | 0.425 |

**TABLE II**

Social security retirement age 66

| Age at which benefits commence | Annual factor in maximum excess allowance and maximum offset allowance (percent) |
|---|---|
| 65 | 0.560 |
| 64 | 0.560 |
| 63 | 0.560 |
| 62 | 0.560 |
| 61 | 0.560 |
| 60 | 0.560 |
| 59 | 0.541 |
| 58 | 0.523 |
| 57 | 0.504 |
| 56 | 0.485 |
| 55 | 0.445 |

**TABLE III**

Social security retirement age 65

| Age at which benefits commence | Annual factor in maximum excess allowance and maximum offset allowance (percent) |
|---|---|
| 64 | 0.560 |
| 63 | 0.560 |
| 62 | 0.560 |
| 61 | 0.560 |
| 60 | 0.560 |
| 59 | 0.541 |
| 58 | 0.523 |
| 57 | 0.504 |
| 56 | 0.485 |
| 55 | 0.467 |

(B) Tables applicable to 0.56% factor for employees covered by tier 2 of railroad retirement with less than 30 years of railroad service

**TABLE I**

Social security retirement age 67

| Age at which benefits commence | Annual factor in maximum excess allowance and maximum offset allowance (percent) |
|---|---|
| 66 | 0.523 |
| 65 | 0.485 |
| 64 | 0.448 |
| 63 | 0.420 |
| 62 | 0.392 |
| 61 | 0.379 |
| 60 | 0.366 |
| 59 | 0.353 |
| 58 | 0.340 |
| 57 | 0.327 |
| 56 | 0.300 |
| 55 | 0.275 |

**TABLE II**

Social security retirement age 66

| Age at which benefits commence | Annual factor in maximum excess allowance and maximum offset allowance (percent) |
|---|---|
| 65 | 0.523 |
| 64 | 0.485 |
| 63 | 0.448 |
| 62 | 0.420 |
| 61 | 0.392 |
| 60 | 0.378 |
| 59 | 0.364 |
| 58 | 0.350 |
| 57 | 0.336 |
| 56 | 0.322 |
| 55 | 0.295 |

**TABLE III**

Social security retirement age 65

| Age at which benefits commence | Annual factor in maximum excess allowance and maximum offset allowance (percent) |
|---|---|
| 64 | 0.523 |
| 63 | 0.485 |
| 62 | 0.448 |
| 61 | 0.418 |
| 60 | 0.388 |
| 59 | 0.373 |
| 58 | 0.358 |
| 57 | 0.343 |
| 56 | 0.329 |
| 55 | 0.314 |

*(4) Overall permitted disparity.* The overall permitted disparity rules of § 1.401(l)-5 apply to employees who benefit under a plan maintained by a railroad employer.

T.D. 8359, 9/12/91.

## § 1.401(l)-5 Overall permitted disparity limits.

**(a) Introduction.** *(1) In general.* The maximum excess allowance and maximum offset allowance limit the disparity that can be provided under a plan for a plan year. The overall permitted disparity rules apply to limit the disparity provided for a plan year if an employee benefits under more than one plan maintained by the employer (the "annual overall permitted disparity limit") and to limit the disparity provided for an employee's total years of service, either in a single plan or in more than one plan of the employer (the "cumulative overall permitted disparity limit"). The overall permitted disparity rules take into account the disparity provided under a section 401(l) plan and the permitted disparity imputed under a plan that satisfies section 401(a)(4) by relying on § 1.401(a)(4)-7. A plan that is not a section 401(l) plan is generally deemed to impute permitted disparity under § 1.401(a)(4)-7 unless established otherwise. Paragraph (b) of this section provides rules on the annual overall permitted disparity limit. Paragraph (c) of this section provides rules on the cumulative overall permitted disparity limit.

*(2) Plan requirements.* In order to satisfy section 401(l), a plan must provide that the overall permitted disparity limits may not be exceeded and must specify how employer-provided contributions or benefits under the plan are adjusted, if necessary, to satisfy the overall permitted disparity limits.

Any adjustments made to satisfy the overall permitted disparity limits must be made in a uniform manner for all employees.

*(3) Plans taken into account.* For purposes of this section, all plans of the employer are taken into account. In addition, all plans of any other employer are taken into account for all periods of service with the other employer for which the employee receives credit for purposes of benefit accrual under any plan of the current employer.

**(b) Annual overall permitted disparity limit.** *(1) In general.* If, in the plan year, an employee benefits under more than one plan, the annual overall permitted disparity limit is satisfied only if the employee's total annual disparity fraction, as defined in paragraph (b)(2) of this section, does not exceed one. Paragraphs (b)(3) through (b)(8) of this section explain the determination of an employee's annual disparity fractions. Paragraph (b)(9) of this section provides examples.

*(2) Total annual disparity fraction.* An employee's total annual disparity fraction is the sum of the employee's annual disparity fractions, as defined in paragraphs (b)(3) through (b)(7) of this section. An employee's total annual disparity fraction is determined as of the end of the current plan year, based on the employee's annual disparity fractions under all plans with plan years ending in the current plan year.

*(3) Annual defined contribution plan disparity fraction.* For a plan year, the annual defined contribution plan disparity fraction for an employee benefiting under a defined contribution plan that is a section 401(l) plan is a fraction—

(i) The numerator of which is the disparity provided under the plan for the plan year, and

(ii) The denominator of which is the maximum excess allowance under § 1.401(l)-2(b)(2) for the plan year.

*(4) Annual defined benefit excess plan disparity fraction.* For a plan year, the annual defined benefit excess plan disparity fraction for an employee benefiting under a defined benefit excess plan that is a section 401(l) plan is a fraction—

(i) The numerator of which is the disparity provided under the plan for the plan year, and

(ii) The denominator of which is the maximum excess allowance under § 1.401(l)-3(b)(2) for the plan year.

*(5) Annual offset plan disparity fraction.* (i) In general. For a plan year, the annual offset plan disparity fraction for an employee benefiting under an offset plan that is a section 401(l) plan is a fraction—

(A) The numerator of which is the disparity provided under the plan for the plan year; and

(B) The denominator of which is the maximum offset allowance under § 1.401(l)-3(b)(3) for the plan year.

(ii) PIA offset plans. In the case of an offset plan that applies an offset of a specified percentage of the employee's PIA, as permitted under § 1.401(l)-3(c)(2)(ix), the numerator of the annual offset plan disparity fraction is the offset percentage used in the section 401(l) overlay under the plan.

*(6) Annual imputed disparity fraction.* For a plan year, the annual imputed disparity fraction for an employee benefiting under a plan that imputes permitted disparity with respect to the employee under § 1.401(a)(4)-7 is one.

*(7) Annual nondisparate fraction.* For a plan year, the annual nondisparate fraction for an employee benefiting under a plan that neither is a section 401(l) plan nor imputes permitted disparity under § 1.401(a)(4)-7 is zero.

*(8) Determination of fraction.* (i) General rule. A separate annual disparity fraction is generally determined for each plan under which the employee benefits. Thus, for example, if two plans are aggregated and treated as a single plan for purposes of section 401(a)(4), a single annual disparity fraction applies to the aggregated plan.

(ii) Multiple formulas. If a plan provides an allocation or benefit equal to the sum of two or more formulas, each formula is considered a separate plan for purposes of this section. If a plan provides an allocation or benefit equal to the greater of two or more formulas, an annual disparity fraction is calculated for the employee under each formula and the largest of the fractions is the employee's annual disparity fraction under the plan.

(iii) Offset arrangements. (A) In general. If an employee benefits under two plans taken into account under paragraph (a)(3) of this section as described in paragraph (b)(8)(iii)(B) or (C) of this section, the employee's annual disparity fraction under both plans is the larger of the annual disparity fractions calculated separately under each plan.

(B) Defined benefit plans. The employee's employer-provided accrued benefit under a defined benefit plan is offset by the employee's total employer-provided accrued benefit under another defined benefit plan or by the actuarial equivalent (as defined in § 1.401(a)(4)-12) of the employee's total account balance under a defined contribution plan that is attributable to employer contributions.

(C) Defined contribution plans. The amount allocated to the employee's account under a defined contribution plan is offset by the total amount allocated to the employee's account under another defined contribution plan.

(iv) Applicable percentages. The disparity provided under a plan is determined on the base and excess percentages under an excess plan and the offset percentage under an offset plan, regardless of whether the employee's plan year or average annual compensation exceeds the integration or offset level under the plan.

(v) Fractional accrual plans. If a section 401(l) plan determines each employee's accrued benefit under the fractional accrual method of section 411(b)(1)(C), the numerator of an employee's annual disparity fraction is based on the disparity provided in the benefit accrued for the employee for the plan year.

*(9) Examples.* The following examples illustrate this paragraph (b). Except as otherwise provided, each plan is a section 401(l) plan.

*Example (1).* (a) Employee A benefits for the plan year under a defined contribution excess plan, Plan X, and a defined benefit excess plan, Plan Y, of the employer. Plans X and Y have the same plan year. Employee A benefits under no other plan of the employer for the plan year of any other plan ending in the plan year of Plans X and Y. Plan X provides a base contribution percentage of 5 percent and an excess contribution percentage of 7 percent, thus providing Employee A with disparity of 2 percent for the plan year. The maximum excess allowance for the plan year under Plan X is 5 percent. Plan Y provides a base benefit percentage of 1 percent and an excess benefit percentage of 1.35 percent, thus providing Employee A with disparity of 0.35 percent for the plan year. The maximum excess allowance for the plan year under Plan Y is 0.75 percent.

(b) Employee A's annual defined contribution plan disparity fraction under Plan X for the plan year is 0.4 (2 percent divided by 5 percent). Employee A's annual defined benefit excess plan disparity fraction under Plan Y for the plan year is 0.47 (0.35 percent divided by 0.75 percent). Employee A's total annual disparity fraction is the sum of 0.4 and 0.47 or 0.87. Because Employee A's total annual disparity fraction does not exceed one, the plans satisfy the annual overall permitted disparity limit with respect to Employee A for the plan year.

*Example (2).* (a) The facts are the same as in Example 1, except that Plan Y is a defined contribution plan, rather than a defined benefit plan. Plan X and Plan Y cover the same employees and are identical in their terms except for the base and excess contribution percentages provided under the plans. Plan Y provides a base contribution percentage of 3 percent and an excess contribution percentage of 6 percent, thus providing Employee A with disparity of 3 percent for the plan year. The maximum excess allowance for the plan year under Plan Y is 3 percent.

(b) Employee A's annual defined contribution plan disparity fraction under Plan X for the plan year is 0.4 (2 percent divided by 5 percent). Employee A's annual defined contribution plan disparity fraction under Plan Y for the plan year is 1 (3 percent divided by 3 percent). Because Employee A's total annual disparity fraction (the sum of 0.4 and 1 or 1.4) exceeds one, the plans do not satisfy the annual overall permitted disparity requirements with respect to Employee A for the plan year.

(c) Plan X and Plan Y are aggregated for purposes of section 401(a)(4) and form a single section 401(l) plan. Under the plan, the base contribution percentage is 8 percent (5 percent plus 3 percent), and the excess contribution percentage is 13 percent (7 percent plus 6 percent). A single annual defined contribution plan disparity fraction is determined for Employee A for the plan year, the numerator of which is the disparity of 5 percent provided under the plan (13 percent minus 8 percent), and the denominator of which is 5.7 percent, the maximum excess allowance that applies to the plan. Because Employee A's only annual disparity fraction of 0.88 (5 percent divided by 5.7 percent) does not exceed one, Employee A's total annual disparity fraction also does not exceed one. The plan thus satisfies the annual overall permitted disparity limit with respect to Employee A for the plan year.

*Example (3).* Assume the same facts as in Example 2, except that Plan X and Plan Y use different integration levels. Therefore, when Plan X and Plan Y are aggregated to form a single plan for purposes of section 401(a)(4), the single plan does not satisfy section 401(l). In applying the general test of § 1.401(a)(4)-2(c), the plan imputes disparity under § 1.401(a)(4)-7. Employee A's only annual disparity fraction is the annual imputed disparity fraction of one. Employee A's total annual disparity fraction is also one, and the plan satisfies the annual overall permitted disparity limit with respect to Employee A for the plan year.

*Example (4).* (a) Employee B participates in two plans: Plan M, which is a section 401(l) plan, and Plan N, which is subject to the general test under § 1.401(a)(4)-3(c). Plan M provides that the disparity provided an employee for the plan year will be reduced to the extent necessary to satisfy the annual overall permitted disparity limits. The employer wishes to impute permitted disparity under § 1.401(a)(4)-7 in order for Plan N to satisfy section 401(a)(4). Employee B's imputed disparity fraction under Plan N is therefore one, and Plan M provides no disparity for Employee B for the plan year. As a result, Plan M provides disparity that is neither uniform nor deemed uniform under § 1.401(l)-3(c); Plan M therefore does not satisfy section 401(l).

(b) Assume instead that Plan M provides that the annual overall permitted disparity limits must be satisfied without reducing the disparity provided for an employee under Plan M, thus requiring a reduction in the employee's annual disparity fraction under another plan. In that case, the disparity provided under Plan M would be uniform for the plan year and Plan M would continue to satisfy section 401(l). However, imputation of permitted disparity with respect to Employee B would not be allowed under Plan N.

**(c) Cumulative permitted disparity limit.** *(1) In general.* (i) Employees who benefit under defined benefit plans. In the case of an employee who has benefited under one or more defined benefit plans for a plan year described in paragraph (c)(1)(v) of this section, the cumulative permitted disparity limit is satisfied if the employee's cumulative disparity fraction, as defined in paragraph (c)(2) of this section, does not exceed 35.

(ii) Employees who do not benefit under defined benefit plans. In the case of an employee who has not benefited under a defined benefit plan for any plan year described in paragraph (c)(1)(v) of this section, the cumulative permitted disparity limit is satisfied.

(iii) Certain plan years disregarded. For purposes of this paragraph (c), an employee is not treated as benefiting under a defined benefit plan for a plan year described in paragraph (c)(1)(v) of this section if the employer can establish that for that plan year the defined benefit plan was not a section 401(l) plan and did not impute permitted disparity under § 1.401(a)(4)-7.

(iv) Determination of type of plan. For purposes of this paragraph (c), a target benefit plan that relies on the special rule of § 1.401(a)(4)-8(b)(3) to satisfy section 401(a)(4) and a DB/DC plan within the meaning of § 1.401(a)(4)-9(a) are treated as defined benefit plans. Similarly, a cash balance plan that relies on the special rule of § 1.401(a)(4)-8(c)(3) to satisfy section 401(a)(4) is treated as a defined contribution plan.

(v) Applicable plan years. In applying paragraphs (c)(1)(i), (ii), and (iii) of this section, for purposes of determining whether an employee benefits under a defined benefit plan, the applicable plan years are all plan years that begin on or after the regulatory effective date, as set forth in § 1.401(l)-6(b), or, in the case of governmental plans, as set forth in § 1.401(a)(4)-13(b).

(vi) Transition rule for defined contribution plans. A defined contribution plan is deemed to satisfy the cumulative permitted disparity limit for the first plan year to which these regulations apply, as set forth in § 1.401(l)-6(b), or, in the case of governmental plans, as set forth in § 1.401(a)(4)-13(b).

*(2) Cumulative disparity fraction.* An employee's cumulative disparity fraction is the sum of the employee's total annual disparity fractions, as defined in paragraph (b)(2) of this section, attributable to the employee's total years of service under all plans.

*(3) Determination of total annual disparity fractions for prior years.* For each of the employee's years of service credited as of the end of the last plan year beginning before January 1, 1989, not to exceed 35, under all plans as of that time that are taken into account under paragraph (a)(3) of this section (whether or not terminated), the employee's total annual disparity fraction is one. Therefore, if, before the first plan year beginning on or after January 1, 1989, an employee never participated in or benefited under any plan taken into account under paragraph (a)(3) of this section, the

employee's total annual disparity fractions are determined without regard to this paragraph (c)(3). An employer may apply the rule in this paragraph (c)(3) with respect to all employees, using a year (including the current year) that is chosen by the employer and is later than 1989. Thus, for example, in lieu of calculating annual disparity fractions for all plan years, the employer may assume that the full disparity limit has been used in each prior plan year for which an employee has been credited with a year of service.

*(4) Special rules for greater of formulas and offset arrangements.* (i) Greater of formulas. (A) In general. A defined benefit plan that is a section 401(l) plan and that provides a benefit equal to the greater of the benefits determined under two or more formulas is deemed to satisfy the cumulative permitted disparity limit with respect to an employee if each of the requirements in paragraphs (c)(4)(i)(B) and (C) of this section is satisfied. For this purpose, a plan that uses a fresh-start formula that determines the accrued benefit as the greater of two amounts under § 1.401(a)(4)-13(c)(4)(ii) or (iii) provides a benefit equal to the greater of the benefits determined under two or more formulas.

(B) Separate satisfaction by formulas. Each formula under the plan would satisfy the cumulative permitted disparity limit if it were the only formula under the plan. In the case of a current formula that applies to the employee's total years of service (as, for example, under § 1.401(a)(4)-13(c)(4)(ii)(B) or (iii)(B)), for purposes of determining whether that formula would satisfy the cumulative permitted disparity limit if it were the only formula under the plan, the special rule for prior years under paragraph (c)(3) of this section may be disregarded.

(C) Single plan. The employee has never benefited under another plan taken into account under paragraph (a)(3) of this section that is a section 401(l) plan or that satisfies section 401(a)(4) by relying on § 1.401(a)(4)-7. For this purpose, if the benefit under the plan is offset in an offset arrangement described in paragraph (b)(8)(iii)(B) of this section, the other plan is disregarded. In addition, a plan does not fail the requirements of this paragraph (c)(4)(i)(C) merely because the employee benefits under another defined benefit plan, provided that—

(1) With respect to each benefit formula under the plan, no years of service taken into account under that benefit formula are taken into account under a benefit formula of the other plan; and

(2) Paragraph (c)(4)(i)(B) of this section would be satisfied if the plans were treated as a single plan that provided a benefit equal to the greater of the benefits provided under two or more formulas. For this purpose, a formula consists of the sum of a formula for the years of service taken into account under one plan and a formula for the years of service taken into account under the other plan. Thus, each possible combination of the formulas under the plans must satisfy paragraph (c)(4)(i)(B) of this section.

(ii) Offset arrangements. (A) In general. If a defined benefit plan is a section 401(l) plan and the benefit under the plan (the gross benefit plan) is offset by the benefit under another plan (the offsetting plan) in an offset arrangement described in paragraph (b)(8)(iii)(B) of this section, the gross benefit plan is deemed to satisfy the cumulative permitted disparity limit with respect to an employee if each of the requirements in paragraphs (c)(4)(ii)(B) and (C) of this section is satisfied.

(B) Separate satisfaction by plans. This requirement is satisfied if the gross benefit plan would satisfy the cumulative disparity limit if no offset applied, and the offsetting plan satisfies the cumulative permitted disparity limit, not taking into account the gross benefit plan.

(C) No other plan. Except for the plans in the offset arrangement, the employee has never benefited under another plan taken into account under paragraph (a)(3) of this section that is a section 401(l) plan or that satisfies section 401(a)(4) by relying on § 1.401(a)(4)-7. An offset arrangement does not fail the requirements of this paragraph (c)(4)(ii)(C) merely because the employee benefits under another defined benefit plan, provided no years of service taken into account under a benefit formula of any plan in the offset arrangement are also taken into account under a benefit formula of the other plan.

*(5) Examples.* The following examples illustrate this paragraph (c). In each example the plan is noncontributory and, unless provided otherwise, is the only plan ever maintained by the employer. Each plan uses a normal retirement age of 65 and contains no provision that would require a reduction in the 0.75-percent factor under § 1.401(l)-3(b)(2) or (3). Each example discusses the benefit formula applicable to an employee who has a social security retirement age of 65.

*Example (1).* Plan M is a defined benefit excess plan that provides a normal retirement benefit of 1 percent of average annual compensation up to covered compensation, plus 1.75 percent of average annual compensation above covered compensation, for each year of service without limit. The disparity provided under the plan for the plan year is 0.75 percent, the excess benefit percentage of 1.75 percent minus the base benefit percentage of 1 percent. The maximum excess allowance for the plan year is 0.75 percent. Thus, each employee's annual defined benefit excess plan disparity fraction under the plan for each plan year is one. Because the plan contains no limit on the years of service taken into account under the plan, the sum of the total annual disparity fractions for a potential employee with more than 35 years of service will exceed 35. In addition, the plan does not provide that the overall permitted disparity limits may not be exceeded as required by paragraph (a)(2) of this section. The plan therefore does not satisfy the cumulative permitted disparity limit of this paragraph (c).

*Example (2).* Plan N is an offset plan that provides a normal retirement benefit of 2 percent of average annual compensation, minus 0.75 percent of final average compensation up to the lesser of covered compensation and average annual compensation, for each year of service up to 35. The disparity provided under the plan for the plan year is 0.75 percent, the offset percentage. The maximum offset allowance for the plan year is 0.75 percent. Thus, each employee's annual offset plan disparity fraction under the plan for each plan year is one. Because the plan limits the years of service taken into account under the plan to 35, the sum of the total annual disparity fractions for an employee cannot exceed 35. The plan therefore satisfies the cumulative permitted disparity limit of this paragraph (c).

*Example (3).* Plan O is a defined benefit excess plan that provides a normal retirement benefit of 0.75 percent of average annual compensation up to covered compensation, plus 1.25 percent of average annual compensation above covered compensation for each year of service up to 45. The disparity provided under the plan for the plan year is 0.5 percent, the excess benefit percentage of 1.25 percent minus the base benefit percentage of 0.75 percent. The maximum excess allowance for the plan year is 0.75 percent. Thus, each employee's annual defined benefit excess plan disparity fraction under the plan for each plan year is 0.67 (0.5 percent divided by 0.75 percent). Because the plan limits the years of service taken into account under the plan to 45, the sum of the total annual disparity fractions for an employee cannot exceed 30 (0.67 × 45). The plan therefore satisfies the cumulative permitted disparity limit of this paragraph (c).

*Example (4).* (a) Plan P is a defined contribution excess plan. Plan P provides a base contribution percentage of 6 percent and an excess contribution percentage of 11.7 percent, thus providing disparity of 5.7 percent for the plan year. Because the maximum excess allowance for each plan year under Plan P is 5.7 percent, each employee's annual defined contribution plan disparity fraction under Plan P for each plan year is one. Plan Q is a defined benefit excess plan maintained by the same employer. Plan Q provides a base benefit percentage of 1 percent and an excess benefit percentage of 1.75 percent for each year of service up to 35, thus providing disparity of 0.75 percent for the plan year. Because the maximum excess allowance for each plan year under Plan Q is 0.75 percent, each employee's annual defined benefit excess plan disparity fraction under Plan Q for each plan year is one.

(b) Employee A benefits under Plan P for the 1980 through the 1994 plan years. The sum of Employee A's total annual disparity fractions under Plan P is 15. (Under paragraph (c)(3)(i) of this section, Employee A's annual disparity fraction for each year of service as of the end of the 1988 plan year is one). As of the 1995 plan year, Employee A no longer benefits under Plan P and begins to benefit under Plan Q for the first time. In order to satisfy the cumulative permitted disparity limit of this paragraph (c), Plan Q must provide that no disparity will be provided if the sum of an employee's total annual disparity fractions reaches 35, taking into account the employee's annual defined contribution plan disparity fractions under Plan P as well as the employee's annual defined benefit excess plan disparity fractions under Plan Q. Thus, after Employee A has benefited under Plan Q for 20 years, Plan Q may not provide any disparity in additional benefits accrued for Employee A.

*Example (5).* (a) Plan O is a noncontributory defined benefit excess plan. Plan O provides an employee whose social security retirement age is 65 with the greater of the benefits determined under two formulas. The first formula provides a benefit of 1 percent of average annual compensation up to covered compensation, plus 1.75 percent of average annual compensation above covered compensation, for each year of service up to 35. The second formula provides a benefit of 1 percent of average annual compensation up to covered compensation, plus 1.6 percent of average annual compensation above covered compensation, for each year of service up to 40.

(b) Under paragraph (b)(4) of this section, an employee's annual defined benefit excess plan fraction for each of the 35 years under the first formula is 0.75/0.75 or one, and an employee's annual defined benefit excess plan fraction for each of the 40 years under the second formula is 0.6/0.75 or 0.8. Under paragraph (b)(8)(ii) of this section, an employee's annual defined benefit excess plan fraction (and total annual disparity fraction because the employee benefits only under Plan O) for the plan year is the larger fraction under the two formulas or one. Therefore, after 35 years, the employee has a cumulative disparity fraction of 35. The disparity provided under the second formula for years of service after 35 thus exceeds the cumulative permitted disparity limit unless the plan qualifies for the special rule in paragraph (c) (4) (i) of this section.

(c) Assume the condition in paragraph (c)(4)(i)(C) of this section is satisfied because no employee has benefited under another plan taken into account under paragraph (a)(3) of this section. In addition, the largest cumulative disparity fraction possible under the first formula is 35 times one or 35, and the largest cumulative disparity fraction possible under the second formula is 40 times 0.8 or 32. Thus, the requirement of paragraph (c)(4)(i)(B) of this section is also satisfied because each formula would satisfy the cumulative permitted disparity limit if it were the only formula under the plan. Under paragraph (c)(4)(i) of this section, the plan is deemed to satisfy the cumulative permitted disparity limit with respect to an employee whose social security retirement age is 65.

**(d) Additional rules.** The Commissioner may prescribe additional rules under this section as the Commissioner considers appropriate. Additional rules may include (without being limited to) rules for computing the fractions described in this section with respect to terminated plans, rules for applying the overall permitted disparity limits to employees who benefit under plans maintained by railroad employers, and rules for determining which plans do not satisfy section 401(l) if the overall permitted disparity limits are exceeded.

---

T.D. 8359, 9/12/91, amend T.D. 8486, 8/31/93.

---

### § 1.401(l)-6 Effective dates and transition rules.

**(a) Statutory effective date.** *(1) In general.* Except as otherwise provided in paragraph (a)(2) of this section, section 401(a)(5)(C) is effective for plan years beginning on or after January 1, 1989, and section 401(l) is effective with respect to plan years, and benefits attributable to plan years, beginning on or after January 1, 1989. The preceding sentence is applicable to a plan without regard to whether the plan was in existence as of a particular date.

*(2) Collectively bargained plans.* (i) In the case of a plan maintained pursuant to 1 or more collective bargaining agreements between employee representatives and 1 or more employers ratified before March 1, 1986, sections 401(a)(5) and 401(l) are applicable for plan years beginning on or after the later of—

(A) January 1, 1989; or

(B) The date on which the last of such collective bargaining agreements terminates (determined without regard to any extension of any such agreement occurring on or after March 1, 1986). However, notwithstanding the preceding sentence, sections 401(a)(5) and 401(l) apply to plans described in this paragraph (a)(2) no later than the first plan year beginning after January 1, 1991.

(ii) For purposes of paragraph (a)(2)(i)(B) of this section, a change made after October 22, 1986, in the terms or conditions of a collectively bargained plan, pursuant to a collective bargaining agreement ratified before March 1, 1986, is not treated as a change in the terms and conditions of the plan.

(iii) In the case of a collectively bargained plan described in paragraph (a)(2)(i) of this section, if the date in paragraph (a)(2)(i)(B) of this section precedes November 15, 1988, then the date in this paragraph (a)(2) is replaced with the date on which the last of any collective bargaining agreements in effect on November 15, 1988, terminates, provided that the plan complies during this period with a reasonable good faith interpretation of section 401(l).

(iv) Whether a plan is maintained pursuant to a collective bargaining agreement is determined under the principles applied under section 1017(c) of the Employee Retirement Income Security Act of 1974. See H.R. Rep. No. 1280, 93d Cong., 2d Sess. 266 (1974). In addition, a plan is not treated as maintained under a collective bargaining agreement unless the employee representatives satisfy section 7701(a)(46) of the Internal Revenue Code after March 31, 1984. See § 301.7701-17T of this chapter for other requirements for a plan to be considered to be collectively bargained.

**(b) Regulatory effective date.** *(1) In general.* Except as otherwise provided in paragraph (b)(2) of this section, §§ 1.401(l)-1 through 1.401(l)-6 apply to plan years beginning on or after January 1, 1994.

*(2) Plans of tax-exempt organizations.* In the case of plans maintained by an organization exempt from income taxation under section 501(a), including plans subject to section 403(b)(12)(A)(i) (nonelective plans), §§ 1.401(l)-1 through 1.401(l)-6 apply to plan years beginning on or after January 1, 1996.

*(3) Defined contribution plans.* A defined contribution plan satisfies section 401(l) with respect to a plan year beginning on or after the effective date of these regulations, as set forth in paragraphs (b)(1) and (b)(2) of this section, if it satisfies the applicable requirements of §§ 1.401(l)-1 through 1.401(l)-5 for the plan year.

*(4) Defined benefit plans.* A defined benefit excess plan or offset plan satisfies section 401(l) with respect to all plan years, and benefits attributable to all plan years, beginning on or after the effective date of these regulations, as set forth in paragraphs (b)(1) and (b)(2) of this section, by satisfying the applicable requirements of §§ 1.401(l)-1 through 1.401(l)-5 and the requirements of § 1.401(a)(4)-13(c) (and § 1.401(a)(4)-13(d), if applicable), using a fresh-start date that is on or after December 31, 1988, and before the effective date of these regulations. A defined benefit excess plan or offset plan that does not satisfy section 401(l) with respect to all plan years beginning on or after the effective date of these regulations may, under the rules of § 1.401(a)(4)-13(c) (and § 1.401(a)(4)-13(d), if applicable), satisfy section 401(l) for plan years beginning after a fresh-start date by satisfying the applicable requirements of §§ 1.401(l)-1 through 1.401(l)-5 after the fresh-start date.

**(c) Compliance during transition period.** For plan years beginning on or after January 1, 1989, and before the effective date of these regulations, as set forth in paragraph (b) of this section, a plan must be operated in accordance with a reasonable, good faith interpretation of section 401(l). Whether a plan is operated in accordance with a reasonable, good faith interpretation of section 401(l) will generally be determined based on all of the relevant facts and circumstances, including the extent to which an employer has resolved unclear issues in its favor. A plan will be deemed to be operated in accordance with a reasonable, good faith interpretation of section 401(l) if it is operated in accordance with the terms of §§ 1.401(l)-1 through 1.401(l)-5.

T.D. 8359, 9/12/91, amend T.D. 8486, 8/31/93.

## § 1.401(m)-0 Table of contents.

This section contains first a list of section headings and then a list of the paragraphs in each section in §§ 1.401(m)-1 through 1.401(m)-5.

List of Sections



List of Paragraphs

T.D. 8357, 8/8/91, amend T.D. 8376, 12/2/91, T.D. 8581, 12/22/94, T.D. 9169, 12/28/2004, T.D. 9237, 12/30/2005, T.D. 9447, 2/23/2009.

PAR. 4. Section 1.401(m)-0 is amended by revising the entries for § 1.401(m)-3(h), (h)(1) and (h)(2) in their entirety to read as follows:

**Proposed § 1.401(m)-0 Table of Contents.** [*For Preamble, see ¶ 153,107*]

*   *   *   *   *



*   *   *   *   *

### § 1.401(m)-1 Employee contributions and matching contributions.

***Caution:*** The Treasury has not yet amended Reg § 1.401(m)-1 to reflect changes made by P.L. 104-188.

**(a) General nondiscrimination rules.** *(1) Nondiscriminatory amount of contributions.* (i) Exclusive means of amounts testing. A defined contribution plan does not satisfy section 401(a) for a plan year unless the amount of employee contributions and matching contributions to the plan for the plan year satisfies section 401(a)(4). The amount of employee contributions and matching contributions under a plan satisfies the requirements of section 401(a)(4) with respect to amounts if and only if the amount of employee contributions and matching contributions satisfies the nondiscrimination test of section 401(m) under paragraph (b) of this section and the plan satisfies the additional requirements of paragraph (c) of this section. See § 1.401(a)(4)-1(b)(2)(ii)(B).

(ii) Testing benefits, rights and features. A plan that provides for employee contributions or matching contributions must satisfy the requirements of section 401(a)(4) relating to benefits, rights and features in addition to the requirement regarding amounts described in paragraph (a)(1)(i) of this section. For example, the right to make each level of employee contributions and the right to each level of matching contributions under the plan are benefits, rights or features subject to the requirements of section 401(a)(4). See § 1.401(a)(4)-4(e)(3)(i) and (iii)(F) through (G).

*(2) Matching contributions.* (i) In general. For purposes of section 401(m), this section and §§ 1.401(m)-2 through 1.401(m)-5, matching contributions are—

(A) Any employer contribution (including a contribution made at the employer's discretion) to a defined contribution plan on account of an employee contribution to a plan maintained by the employer;

(B) Any employer contribution (including a contribution made at the employer's discretion) to a defined contribution plan on account of an elective deferral; and

(C) Any forfeiture allocated on the basis of employee contributions, matching contributions, or elective deferrals.

(ii) Employer contributions made on account of an employee contribution or elective deferral. Whether an employer contribution is made on account of an employee contribution or an elective deferral is determined on the basis of all the relevant facts and circumstances, including the relationship between the employer contribution and employee actions outside the plan. An employer contribution made to a defined contribution plan on account of contributions made by an employee under an employer-sponsored savings arrangement that are not held in a plan that is intended to be a qualified plan or other arrangement described in § 1.402(g)-1(b) is not a matching contribution.

(iii) Employer contributions not on account of an employee contribution or elective deferral. (A) General rule. Employer contributions are not matching contributions made on account of elective deferrals if they are contributed before the cash or deferred election is made or before the employees' performance of services with respect to which the elective deferrals are made (or when the cash that is subject to the cash or deferred elections would be currently available, if earlier). In addition, an employer contribution is not a matching contribution made on account of an employee contribution if it is contributed before the employee contribution.

(B) Exceptions for forfeitures and released ESOP shares. The rule of paragraph (a)(3)(iii)(A) of this section does not apply to a forfeiture that is allocated as a matching contribution. In addition, an allocation of shares from an ESOP loan suspense account described in § 54.4975-11(c) and (d) of this chapter will not fail to be treated as a matching contribution solely because the employer contribution that resulted in the release and allocation of those shares from the suspense account is made before the employees' performance of services with respect to which the elective deferrals are made (or when the cash that is subject to the cash or deferred elections would be currently available, if earlier) provided that—

(1) The contribution is for a required payment that is due under the loan terms; and

(2) The contribution is not made early with a principal purpose of accelerating deductions.

(C) Exception for bona fide administrative considerations. The timing of contributions will not be treated as failing to satisfy the requirements of this paragraph (a)(3)(iii) merely because contributions are occasionally made before the employees' performance of services with respect to which the elective deferrals are made (or when the cash that is subject to the cash or deferred elections would be currently available, if earlier) in order to accommodate bona fide administrative considerations and are not paid early with a principal purpose of accelerating deductions.

*(3) Employee contributions.* (i) In general. For purposes of section 401(m), this section and §§ 1.401(m)-2 through 1.401(m)-5, employee contributions are contributions to a plan that are designated or treated at the time of contribution as after-tax employee contributions (e.g., by treating the contributions as taxable income subject to applicable withholding requirements) and are allocated to an individual account for each eligible employee to which attributable earnings and losses are allocated. See § 1.401(k)-1(a)(2)(ii). The term employee contributions includes—

(A) Employee contributions to the defined contribution portion of a plan described in section 414(k);

(B) Employee contributions applied to the purchase of whole life insurance protection or survivor benefit protection under a defined contribution plan;

(C) Amounts attributable to excess contributions within the meaning of section 401(k)(8)(B) that are recharacterized as employee contributions under § 1.401(k)-2(b)(3); and

(D) Employee contributions to a plan or contract that satisfies the requirements of section 403(b).

(ii) Certain contributions not treated as employee contributions. The term employee contributions does not include designated Roth contributions, repayment of loans, rollover contributions, repayment of distributions described in section 411(a)(7)(C), or employee contributions that are transferred to the plan from another plan.

(iii) Qualified cost-of-living arrangements. Employee contributions to a qualified cost-of-living arrangement described in section 415(k)(2)(B) are treated as employee contributions to a defined contribution plan, without regard to the requirement that the employee contributions be allocated to an individual account to which attributable earnings and losses are allocated.

**(b) Nondiscrimination requirements for amount of contributions.** *(1) Matching contributions and employee contributions.* The matching contributions and employee contributions under a plan satisfy this paragraph (b) for a plan year only if the plan satisfies—

(i) The ACP test of section 401(m)(2) described in § 1.401(m)-2;

(ii) The ACP safe harbor provisions of section 401(m)(11) described in § 1.401(m)-3; or

(iii) The ACP safe harbor provisions of section 401(m)(12) described in § 1.401(m)-3; or

(iv) The SIMPLE 401(k) provisions of sections 401(k)(11) and 401(m)(10) described in § 1.401(k)-4.

*(2) Automatic satisfaction by certain plans.* Notwithstanding paragraph (b)(1) of this section, the requirements of this section are treated as satisfied with respect to employee contributions and matching contributions under a collectively bargained plan (or the portion of a plan) that automatically satisfies section 410(b). See §§ 1.401(a)(4)-1(c)(5) and 1.410(b)-2(b)(7). Additionally, the requirements of sections 401(a)(4) and 410(b) do not apply to a governmental plan (within the meaning of section 414(d)) maintained by a State or local government or political subdivision thereof (or agency or instrumentality thereof) and, accordingly such plans are not required to comply with this section. See sections 401(a)(5)(G), 403(b)(12)(C) and 410(c)(1)(A).

*(3) Anti-abuse provisions.* Sections 1.401(m)-1 through 1.401(m)-5 are designed to provide simple, practical rules that accommodate legitimate plan changes. At the same time, the rules are intended to be applied by employers in a manner that does not make use of changes in plan testing procedures or other plan provisions to inflate inappropriately the ACP for NHCEs (which is used as a benchmark for testing the ACP for HCEs) or to otherwise manipulate the nondiscrimination testing requirements of this paragraph (b). Further, this paragraph (b) is part of the overall requirement that benefits or contributions not discriminate in favor of HCEs. Therefore, a plan will not be treated as satisfying the requirements of this paragraph (b) if there are repeated

changes to plan testing procedures or plan provisions that have the effect of distorting the ACP so as to increase significantly the permitted ACP for HCEs, or otherwise manipulate the nondiscrimination rules of this paragraph, if a principal purpose of the changes was to achieve such a result.

*(4) Aggregation and restructuring.* (i) In general. This paragraph (b)(4) contains the exclusive rules for aggregating and disaggregating plans that provide for employee contributions and matching contributions for purposes of this section and §§ 1.401(m)-2 through 1.401(m)-5.

(ii) Aggregation of employee contributions and matching contributions within a plan. Except as otherwise specifically provided in this paragraph (b)(4) and § 1.401(m)-3(j)(6), a plan must be subject to a single test under paragraph (b)(1) of this section with respect to all employee contributions and matching contributions and all eligible employees under the plan. Thus, for example, if two groups of employees are eligible for matching contributions under a plan, all employee contributions and matching contributions under the plan must be subject to a single test, even if they have significantly different features, such as different rates of match.

(iii) Aggregation of plans. (A) In general. The term plan means a plan within the meaning of § 1.410(b)-7(a) and (b), after application of the mandatory disaggregation rules of § 1.410(b)-7(c), and the permissive aggregation rules of § 1.410(b)-7(d), as modified by paragraph (b)(4)(v) of this section. Thus, for example, two plans (within the meaning of § 1.410(b)-7(b)) that are treated as a single plan pursuant to the permissive aggregation rules of § 1.410(b)-7(d) are treated as a single plan for purposes of sections 401(k) and 401(m).

(B) Arrangements with inconsistent ACP testing methods. Pursuant to paragraph (b)(4)(ii) of this section, a single testing method must apply with respect to all employee contributions and matching contributions and all eligible employees under a plan. Thus, in applying the permissive aggregation rules of § 1.410(b)-7(d), an employer may not aggregate plans (within the meaning of § 1.410(b)-7(b)) that apply inconsistent testing methods. For example, a plan (within the meaning of § 1.410(b)-7) that applies the current year testing method may not be aggregated with another plan that applies the prior year testing method. Similarly, an employer may not aggregate a plan (within the meaning of § 1.410(b)-7) that is using the ACP safe harbor provisions of section 401(m)(11) or 401(m)(12) and another plan that is using the ACP test of section 401(m)(2).

(iv) Disaggregation of plans and separate testing. (A) In general. If employee contributions or matching contributions are included in a plan (within the meaning of § 1.410(b)-7(b)) that is mandatorily disaggregated under the rules of section 410(b) (as modified by this paragraph (b)(4)), the matching contributions and employee contributions under that plan must be disaggregated in a consistent manner. For example, in the case of an employer that is treated as operating qualified separate lines of business under section 414(r), if the eligible employees under a plan which provides for employee contributions or matching contributions are in more than one qualified separate line of business, only those employees within each qualified separate line of business may be taken into account in determining whether each disaggregated portion of the plan complies with the requirements of section 401(m), unless the employer is applying the special rule for employer-wide plans in § 1.414(r)-1(c)(2)(ii) with respect to the plan. Similarly, if a plan that provides for employee contributions or matching contributions under which employees are permitted to participate before they have completed the minimum age and service requirements of section 410(a)(1) applies section 410(b)(4)(B) for determining whether the plan complies with section 410(b)(1), then the plan must be treated as two separate plans, one comprising all eligible employees who have met the minimum age and service requirements of section 410(a)(1) and one comprising all eligible employees who have not met the minimum age and service requirements of section 410(a)(1), unless the plan is using the rule in § 1.401(m)-2(a)(1)(iii)(A).

(B) Restructuring prohibited. Restructuring under § 1.401(a)(4)-9(c) may not be used to demonstrate compliance with the requirements of section 401(m). See § 1.401(a)(4)-9(c)(3)(ii).

(v) Certain disaggregation rules not applicable. The mandatory disaggregation rules relating to section 401(k) plans and section 401(m) plans set forth in § 1.410(b)-7(c)(1) and to ESOP and non-ESOP portions of a plan set forth in § 1.410(b)-7(c)(2) shall not apply for purposes of this section and §§ 1.401(m)-2 through 1.401(m)-5. Accordingly, notwithstanding § 1.410(b)-7(d)(2), an ESOP and a non-ESOP which are different plans (within the meaning of section 414(l), as described in § 1.410(b)-7(b)) are permitted to be aggregated for these purposes.

**(c) Additional requirements.** *(1) Separate testing for employee contributions and matching contributions.* Under § 1.410(b)-7(c)(1), the group of employees who are eligible to make employee contributions or eligible to receive matching contributions must satisfy the requirements of section 410(b) as if those employees were covered under a separate plan. The determination of whether the separate plan satisfies the requirements of section 410(b) must be made without regard to the modifications to the disaggregation rules set forth in paragraph (b)(4)(v) of this section. In addition, except as expressly permitted under section 401(k), 410(b)(2)(A)(ii), or 416(c)(2)(A), employee contributions, matching contributions and elective contributions taken into account under § 1.401(m)-2(a)(6) may not be taken into account for purposes of determining whether any other contributions under any plan (including the plan to which the employee contributions or matching contributions are made) satisfy the requirements of section 401(a). See also § 1.401(a)(4)-11(g)(3)(vii) for special rules relating to corrections of violations of the minimum coverage requirements or discriminatory rates of matching contributions.

*(2) Plan provision requirement.* A plan that provides for employee contributions or matching contributions satisfies this section only if it provides that the nondiscrimination requirements of section 401(m) will be met. Thus, the plan must provide for satisfaction of one of the specific alternatives described in paragraph (b)(1) of this section and, if with respect to that alternative there are optional choices, which of the optional choices will apply. For example, a plan that uses the ACP test of section 401(m)(2), as described in paragraph (b)(1)(i) of this section, must specify whether it is using the current year testing method or prior year testing method. Additionally, a plan that uses the prior year testing method must specify whether the ACP for eligible NHCEs for the first plan year is 3% or the ACP for the eligible NHCEs for the first plan year. Similarly, a plan that uses the safe harbor method of section 401(m)(11), as described in paragraph (b)(1)(ii) of this section, must specify whether the safe harbor contribution will be the nonelective safe harbor contribution or the matching safe harbor contribution and is not permitted to provide that ACP testing will be used if the requirements for the safe harbor are not satisfied. Similarly, a plan that uses the safe harbor method of

section 401(m)(11) or 401(m)(12), as described in paragraphs (b)(1)(ii) and (b)(1)(iii) of this section, must specify the default percentages that apply for the plan year and whether the safe harbor contribution will be the nonelective safe harbor contribution or the matching safe harbor contribution, and is not permitted to provide that ACP testing will be used if the requirements for the safe harbor are not satisfied. The Commissioner may, in guidance of general applicability, published in the Internal Revenue Bulletin (see § 601.601(d)(2) of this chapter), specify the options that will apply under the plan if the nondiscrimination test is incorporated by reference in accordance with the preceding sentence.

**(d) Effective date.** *(1) General rule.* Except as otherwise provided in this paragraph (d), this section and §§ 1.401(m)-2 through 1.401(m)-5 apply to plan years that begin on or after January 1, 2006.

*(2) Early implementation permitted.* A plan is permitted to apply the rules of this section and §§ 1.401(m)-2 through 1.401(m)-5 to any plan year that ends after December 29, 2004, provided the plan applies all the rules of this section and §§ 1.401(m)-2 through 1.401(m)-5 and all the rules of §§ 1.401(k)-1 through 1.401(k)-6, to the extent applicable, for that plan year and all subsequent plan years.

*(3) Applicability of prior regulations.* For any plan year, before a plan applies this section and §§ 1.401(m)-2 through 1.401(m)-5 (either the first plan year beginning on or after January 1, 2006 or such earlier year, as provided in paragraph (d)(2) of this section), § 1.401(m)-1 and § 1.401(m)-2 (as they appeared in the April 1, 2004 edition of 26 CFR part 1) apply to the plan to the extent those sections, as they so appear, reflect the statutory provisions of section 401(m) as in effect for the relevant year.

---

T.D. 8357, 8/8/91, amend T.D. 8376, 12/2/91, T.D. 8581, 12/22/94, T.D. 9169, 12/28/2004, T.D. 9447, 2/23/2009.

---

### § 1.401(m)-2 ACP test.

**(a) Actual contribution percentage (ACP) test.** *(1) In general.* (i) ACP test formula. A plan satisfies the ACP test for a plan year only if—

(A) The ACP for the eligible HCEs for the plan year is not more than the ACP for the eligible NHCEs for the applicable year multiplied by 1.25; or

(B) The excess of the ACP for the eligible HCEs for the plan year over the ACP for the eligible NHCEs for the applicable year is not more than 2 percentage points, and the ACP for the eligible HCEs for the plan year is not more than the ACP for the eligible NHCEs for the applicable year multiplied by 2.

(ii) HCEs as sole eligible employees. If, for the applicable year there are no eligible NHCEs (i.e., all of the eligible employees under the plan for the applicable year are HCEs), the plan is deemed to satisfy the ACP test.

(iii) Special rule for early participation. If a plan providing for employee contributions or matching contributions provides that employees are eligible to participate before they have completed the minimum age and service requirements of section 410(a)(1)(A), and if the plan applies section 410(b)(4)(B) in determining whether the plan meets the requirements of section 410(b)(1), then in determining whether the plan meets the requirements under paragraph (a)(1) of this section either—

(A) Pursuant to section 401(m)(5)(C), the ACP test is performed under the plan (determined without regard to disaggregation under § 1.410(b)-7(c)(3)), using the ACP for all eligible HCEs for the plan year and the ACP of eligible NHCEs for the applicable year, disregarding all NHCEs who have not met the minimum age and service requirements of section 410(a)(1)(A); or

(B) Pursuant to § 1.401(m)-1(b)(4), the plan is disaggregated into separate plans and the ACP test is performed separately for all eligible employees who have completed the minimum age and service requirements of section 410(a)(1)(A) and for all eligible employees who have not completed the minimum age and service requirements of section 410(a)(1)(A).

*(2) Determination of ACP.* (i) General rule. The ACP for a group of eligible employees (either eligible HCEs or eligible NHCEs) for a plan year or applicable year is the average of the ACRs of eligible employees in the group for that year. The ACP for a group of eligible employees is calculated to the nearest hundredth of a percentage point.

(ii) Determination of applicable year under current year and prior year testing method. The ACP test is applied using the prior year testing method or the current year testing method. Under the prior year testing method, the applicable year for determining the ACP for the eligible NHCEs is the plan year immediately preceding the plan year for which the ACP test is being calculated. Under the prior year testing method, the ACP for the eligible NHCEs is determined using the ACRs for the eligible employees who were NHCEs in that preceding plan year, regardless of whether those NHCEs are eligible employees or NHCEs in the plan year for which the ACP test is being performed. Under the current year testing method, the applicable year for determining the ACP for eligible NHCEs is the same plan year as the plan year for which the ACP test is being calculated. Under either method, the ACP for the eligible HCEs is determined using the ACRs of eligible employees who are HCEs for the plan year for which the ACP test is being performed. See paragraph (c) of this section for additional rules for the prior year testing method.

*(3) Determination of ACR.* (i) General rule. The ACR of an eligible employee for the plan year or applicable year is the sum of the employee contributions and matching contributions taken into account with respect to such employee (determined under the rules of paragraphs (a)(4) and (5) of this section), and the qualified nonelective and elective contributions taken into account under paragraph (a)(6) of this section for the year, divided by the employee's compensation taken into account for the year. The ACR is calculated to the nearest hundredth of a percentage point. If no employee contributions, matching contributions, elective contributions, or qualified nonelective contributions are taken into account under this section with respect to an eligible employee for the year, the ACR of the employee is zero.

(ii) ACR of HCEs eligible under more than one plan. (A) General rule. Pursuant to section 401(m)(2)(B), the ACR of an HCE who is an eligible employee in more than one plan of an employer to which matching contributions or employee contributions are made is calculated by treating all contributions with respect to such HCE under any such plan as being made under the plan being tested. Thus, the ACR for such an HCE is calculated by accumulating all matching contributions and employee contributions under any plan (other than a plan described in paragraph (a)(3)(ii)(B) of this section) that would be taken into account under this section for the plan year, if the plan under which the contribution was made applied this section and had the same plan year. For example, in the case of a plan with a 12-month plan year, the

ACR for the plan year of that plan for an HCE who participates in multiple plans of the same employer that provide for matching contributions or employee contributions is the sum of all such contributions during such 12-month period that would be taken into account with respect to the HCE under all plans in which the HCE is an eligible employee, divided by the HCE's compensation for that 12-month period (determined using the compensation definition for the plan being tested), without regard to the plan year of the other plans and whether those plans are satisfying this section or § 1.401(m)-3.

(B) Plans not permitted to be aggregated. Contributions under plans that are not permitted to be aggregated under § 1.401(m)-1(b)(4) (determined without regard to the prohibition on aggregating plans with inconsistent testing methods set forth in § 1.401(m)-1(b)(4)(iii)(B) and the prohibition on aggregating plans with different plan years set forth in § 1.410(b)-7(d)(5)) are not aggregated under this paragraph (a)(3)(ii).

(iii) Example. The following example illustrates the application of paragraph (a)(3)(ii) of this section. See also § 1.401(k)-2(a)(3)(iii) for additional examples of the application of the parallel rule under section 401(k)(3)(A). The example is as follows:

*Example.* Employee A, an HCE with compensation of $120,000, is eligible to make employee contributions under Plan S and Plan T, two calendar-year profit-sharing plans of Employer H. Plan S and Plan T use the same definition of compensation. Plan S provides a match equal to 50% of each employee's contributions and Plan T has no match. During the current plan year, Employee A elects to contribute $4,000 in employee contributions to Plan T and $4,000 in employee contributions to Plan S. There are no other contributions made on behalf of Employee A. Each plan must calculate Employee A's ACR by dividing the total employee contributions by Employee A and matching contributions under both plans by $120,000. Therefore, Employee A's ACR under each plan is 8.33% ($4,000 + $4,000 + $2,000/$120,000).

*(4) Employee contributions and matching contributions taken into account under the ACP test.* (i) Employee contributions. An employee contribution is taken into account in determining the ACR for an eligible employee for the plan year or applicable year in which the contribution is made. For purposes of the preceding sentence, an amount withheld from an employee's pay (or a payment by the employee to an agent of the plan) is treated as contributed at the time of such withholding (or payment) if the funds paid are transmitted to the trust within a reasonable period after the withholding (or payment).

(ii) Recharacterized elective contributions. Excess contributions recharacterized in accordance with § 1.401(k)-2(b)(3) are taken into account as employee contributions for the plan year that includes the time at which the excess contribution is includible in the gross income of the employee under § 1.401(k)-2(b)(3)(ii).

(iii) Matching contributions. A matching contribution is taken into account in determining the ACR for an eligible employee for a plan year or applicable year only if each of the following requirements is satisfied—

(A) The matching contribution is allocated to the employee's account under the terms of the plan as of a date within that year;

(B) The matching contribution is made on account of (or the matching contribution is allocated on the basis of) the employee's elective deferrals or employee contributions for that year; and

(C) The matching contribution is actually paid to the trust no later than the end of the 12-month period immediately following the year that contains that date.

*(5) Employee contributions and matching contributions not taken into account under the ACP test.* (i) General rule. Matching contributions that do not satisfy the requirements of paragraph (a)(4)(iii) of this section may not be taken into account in the ACP test for the plan year with respect to which the contributions were made, or for any other plan year. Instead, the amount of the matching contributions must satisfy the requirements of section 401(a)(4) (without regard to the ACP test) for the plan year for which they are allocated under the plan as if they were nonelective contributions and were the only nonelective contributions for that year. See §§ 1.401(a)(4)-1(b)(2)(ii)(B) and 1.410(b)-7(c)(1).

(ii) Disproportionate matching contributions.

(A) Matching contributions in excess of 100%. A matching contribution with respect to an elective deferral for an NHCE is not taken into account under the ACP test to the extent it exceeds the greatest of:

(1) 5% of compensation;

(2) the employee's elective deferrals for a year; and

(3) the product of 2 times the plan's representative matching rate and the employee's elective deferrals for a year.

(B) Representative matching rate. For purposes of this paragraph (a)(5)(ii), the plan's representative matching rate is the lowest matching rate for any eligible NHCE among a group of NHCEs that consists of half of all eligible NHCEs in the plan for the plan year who make elective deferrals for the plan year (or, if greater, the lowest matching rate for all eligible NHCEs in the plan who are employed by the employer on the last day of the plan year and who make elective deferrals for the plan year).

(C) Definition of matching rate. For purposes of this paragraph (a)(5)(ii), the matching rate for an employee generally is the matching contributions made for such employee divided by the employee's elective deferrals for the year. If the matching rate is not the same for all levels of elective deferrals for an employee, the employee's matching rate is determined assuming that an employee's elective deferrals are equal to 6 percent of compensation.

(D) Application to matching contributions that match employee contributions. If a plan provides a match with respect to the sum of the employee's employee contributions and elective deferrals, that sum is substituted for the amount of the employee's elective deferrals in paragraphs (a)(5)(ii) (A) and (C) of this section and employees who make either employee contributions or elective deferrals are taken into account under paragraph (a)(5)(ii)(B) of this section. Similarly, if a plan provides a match with respect to the employee's employee contributions, but not elective deferrals, the employee's employee contributions are substituted for the amount of the employee's elective deferrals in paragraphs (a)(5)(ii) (A) and (C) of this section and employees who make employee contributions are taken into account under paragraph (a)(5)(ii)(B) of this section.

(iii) Qualified matching contributions used to satisfy the ADP test. Qualified matching contributions that are taken into account for the ADP test of section 401(k)(3) under § 1.401(k)-2(a)(6) are not taken into account in determining an eligible employee's ACR.

(iv) Matching contributions taken into account under safe harbor provisions. A plan that satisfies the ACP safe harbor requirements of section 401(m)(11) or 401(m)(12) for a plan year but nonetheless must satisfy the requirements of this section because it provides for employee contributions for such plan year is permitted to apply this section disregarding all matching contributions with respect to all eligible employees. In addition, a plan that satisfies the ADP safe harbor requirements of § 1.401(k)-3 for a plan year using qualified matching contributions but does not satisfy the ACP safe harbor requirements of section 401(m)(11) or 401(m)(12) for such plan year is permitted to apply this section by excluding matching contributions with respect to all eligible employees that do not exceed 4 percent (3½ percent in the case of a plan that satisfies the ADP safe harbor under section 401(k)(13)) of each employee's compensation. If a plan disregards matching contributions pursuant to this paragraph (a)(5)(iv), the disregard must apply with respect to all eligible employees.

(v) Treatment of forfeited matching contributions. A matching contribution that is forfeited because the contribution to which it relates is treated as an excess contribution, excess deferral, excess aggregate contribution, or default elective contribution that is distributed under section 414(w), is not taken into account for purposes of this section.

(vi) Additional employee contributions or matching contributions pursuant to section 414(u). Additional employee contributions and matching contributions made by reason of an eligible employee's qualified military service under section 414(u) are not taken into account under paragraph (a)(4) of this section for the plan year for which the contributions are made, or for any other plan year.

*(6) Qualified nonelective contributions and elective contributions that may be taken into account under the ACP test.* Qualified nonelective contributions and elective contributions may be taken into account in determining the ACR for an eligible employee for a plan year or applicable year, but only to the extent the contributions satisfy the following requirements—

(i) Timing of allocation. The qualified nonelective contribution is allocated to the employee's account as of a date within that year (within the meaning of § 1.401(k)-2(a)(4)(i)(A)) and the elective contribution satisfies § 1.401(k)-2(a)(4)(i). Consequently, under the prior year testing method, in order to be taken into account in calculating the ACP for the group of eligible NHCEs for the applicable year, a qualified nonelective contribution must be contributed no later than the end of the 12-month period following the applicable year even though the applicable year is different than the plan year being tested.

(ii) Elective contributions taken into account under the ACP test. Elective contributions may be taken into account for the ACP test only if the cash or deferred arrangement under which the elective contributions are made is required to satisfy the ADP test in § 1.401(k)-2(a)(1) and, then only to the extent that the cash or deferred arrangement would satisfy that test, including such elective contributions in the ADP for the plan year or applicable year. Thus, for example, elective deferrals made pursuant to a salary reduction agreement under an annuity described in section 403(b) are not permitted to be taken into account in an ACP test. Similarly, elective contributions under a cash or deferred arrangement that is using the section 401(k) safe harbor described in § 1.401(k)-3 cannot be taken into account in an ACP test. In addition, for plan years ending on or after November 8, 2007, elective contributions which are not permitted to be taken into account for the ADP test for the plan year under § 1.401(k)-2(a)(5)(ii), (iii), (v), or (vi) are not permitted to be taken into account for the ACP test.

(iii) Requirement that amount satisfy section 401(a)(4). The amount of nonelective contributions, including those qualified nonelective contributions taken into account under this paragraph (a)(6) and those qualified nonelective contributions taken into account for the ADP test under paragraph § 1.401(k)-2(a)(6), and the amount of nonelective contributions, excluding those qualified nonelective contributions taken into account under this paragraph (a)(6) for the ACP test and those qualified nonelective contributions taken into account for the ADP test under paragraph § 1.401(k)-2(a)(6), satisfies the requirements of section 401(a)(4). See § 1.401(a)(4)-1(b)(2). In the case of an employer that is applying the special rule for employer-wide plans in § 1.414(r)-1(c)(2)(ii) with respect to the plan, the determination of whether the qualified nonelective contributions satisfy the requirements of this paragraph (a)(6)(iii) must be made on an employer-wide basis regardless of whether the plans to which the qualified nonelective contributions are made are satisfying the requirements of section 410(b) on an employer-wide basis. Conversely, in the case of an employer that is treated as operating qualified separate lines of business, and does not apply the special rule for employer-wide plans in § 1.414(r)-1(c)(2)(ii) with respect to the plan, then the determination of whether the qualifiednonelective contributions satisfy the requirements of this paragraph (a)(6)(iii) is not permitted to be made on an employer-wide basis regardless of whether the plans to which the qualified nonelective contributions are made are satisfying the requirements of section 410(b) on that basis.

(iv) Aggregation must be permitted. The plan that provides for employee or matching contributions and the plan or plans to which the qualified nonelective contributions or elective contributions are made are plans that would be permitted to be aggregated under § 1.401(m)-1(b)(4). If the plan year of the plan that provides for employee or matching contributions is changed to satisfy the requirement under § 1.410(b)-7(d)(5) that aggregated plans have the same plan year, qualified nonelective contributions and elective contributions may be taken into account in the resulting short plan year only if such qualified nonelective and elective contributions could have been taken into account under an ADP test for a plan with that same short plan year.

(v) Disproportionate contributions not taken into account. (A) General rule. Qualified nonelective contributions cannot be taken into account for an applicable year for an NHCE to the extent such contributions exceed the product of that NHCE's compensation and the greater of 5% and 2 times the plan's representative contribution rate. Any qualified nonelective contribution taken into account in an ADP test under § 1.401(k)-2(a)(6) (including the determination of the representative contribution rate for purposes of § 1.401(k)-2(a)(6)(iv)(B)) is not permitted to be taken into account for purposes of this paragraph (a)(6) (including the determination of the representative contribution rate for purposes of paragraph (a)(6)(v)(B) of this section).

(B) Definition of representative contribution rate. For purposes of this paragraph (a)(6)(v), the plan's representative contribution rate is the lowest applicable contribution rate of any eligible NHCE among a group of eligible NHCEs that consists of half of all eligible NHCEs for the plan year (or, if greater, the lowest applicable contribution rate of any eligible NHCE in the group of all eligible NHCEs for the applicable year and who is employed by the employer on the last day of the applicable year).

(C) Definition of applicable contribution rate. For purposes of this paragraph (a)(6)(v), the applicable contribution rate for an eligible NHCE is the sum of the matching contributions taken into account under this section for the employee for the plan year and the qualified nonelective contributions made for that employee for the plan year, divided by that employee's compensation for the same period.

(D) Special rule for prevailing wage contributions. Notwithstanding paragraph (a)(6)(v)(A) of this section, qualified nonelective contributions that are made in connection with an employer's obligation to pay prevailing wages under the Davis-Bacon Act (46 Stat. 1494), Pub. L. 71-798, Service Contract Act of 1965 (79 Stat. 1965), Pub. L. 89-286, or similar legislation can be taken into account for a plan year for an NHCE to the extent such contributions do not exceed 10 percent of that NHCE's compensation.

(vi) Contribution only used once. Qualified nonelective contributions cannot be taken into account under this paragraph (a)(6) to the extent such contributions are taken into account for purposes of satisfying any other ACP test, any ADP test, or the requirements of § 1.401(k)-3, 1.401(m)-3 or 1.401(k)-4. Thus, for example, qualified nonelective contributions that are made pursuant to § 1.401(k)-3(b) cannot be taken into account under the ACP test. Similarly, if a plan switches from the current year testing method to the prior year testing method pursuant to § 1.401(m)-2(c)(1), qualified nonelective contributions that are taken into account under the current year testing method for a plan year may not be taken into account under the prior year testing method for the next plan year.

*(7) Examples.* The following examples illustrate the application of this paragraph (a). See § 1.401(k)-2(a)(6) for additional examples of the parallel rules under section 401(k)(3)(A). The examples are as follows:

*Example (1).* (i) Employer L maintains Plan U, a profit-sharing plan under which $.50 matching contributions are made for each dollar of employee contributions. Plan U uses the current year testing method. The chart below shows the average employee contributions (as a percentage of compensation) and matching contributions (as a percentage of compensation) for Plan U's HCEs and NHCEs for the 2006 plan year:

| | Employee contributions (percentage) | Matching contributions (percentage) | Actual contribution (percentage) |
|---|---|---|---|
| Highly compensated employees ................. | 4 | 2 | 6 |
| Nonhighly compensated employees .............. | 3 | 1.5 | 4.5 |

(ii) The matching rate for all NHCEs is 50% and thus the matching contributions are not disproportionate under paragraph (a)(5)(ii) of this section. Accordingly, they are taken into account in determining the ACR of eligible employees.

(iii) Because the ACP for the HCEs (6.0%) exceeds 5.63% (4.5% x 1.25), Plan U does not satisfy the ACP test under paragraph (a)(1)(i)(A) of this section. However, because the ACP for the HCEs does not exceed the ACP for the NHCEs by more than 2 percentage points and the ACP for the HCEs does not exceed the ACP for the NHCEs multiplied by 2 (4.5% x 2 = 9%), the plan satisfies the ACP test under paragraph (a)(1)(i)(B) of this section.

*Example (2).* (i) Employees A through F are eligible employees in Plan V, a profit-sharing plan of Employer M that includes a cash or deferred arrangement and permits employee contributions. Under Plan V, a $.50 matching contribution is made for each dollar of elective contributions and employee contributions. Plan V uses the current year testing method and does not provide for elective contributions to be taken into account in determining an eligible employee's ACR. For the 2006 plan year, Employees A and B are HCEs and the remaining employees are NHCEs. The compensation, elective contributions, employee contributions, and matching contributions for the 2006 plan year are shown in the following table:

| Employee | Compensation | Elective contributions | Employee contributions | Matching contributions |
|---|---|---|---|---|
| A ............................ | $190,000 | $15,000 | $3,500 | $9,250 |
| B ............................ | 100,000 | 5,000 | 10,000 | 7,500 |
| C ............................ | 85,000 | 12,000 | 0 | 6,000 |
| D ............................ | 70,000 | 9,500 | 0 | 4,750 |
| E ............................ | 40,000 | 10,000 | 0 | 5,000 |
| F ............................ | 10,000 | 0 | 0 | 0 |

(ii) The matching rate for all NHCEs is 50% and thus the matching contributions are not disproportionate under paragraph (a)(5)(ii) of this section. Accordingly, they are taken into account in determining the ACR of eligible employees, as shown in the following table:

| Employee | Compensation | Employee contributions | Matching contributions | ACR (percent) |
|---|---|---|---|---|
| A | $190,000 | $3,500 | $9,250 | 6.71 |
| B | 100,000 | 10,000 | 7,500 | 17.50 |
| C | 85,000 | 0 | 6,000 | 7.06 |
| D | 70,000 | 0 | 4,750 | 6.79 |
| E | 40,000 | 0 | 5,000 | 12.50 |
| F | 10,000 | 0 | 0 | 0 |

(iii) The ACP for the HCEs is 12.11% ((6.71% + 17.50%)/2). The ACP for the NHCEs is 6.59% ((7.06% + 6.79% + 12.50% + 0.%)/4). Plan V fails to satisfy the ACP test under paragraph (a)(1)(i)(A) of this section because the ACP of HCEs is more than 125% of the ACP of the NHCEs (6.59% x 1.25 = 8.24%). In addition, Plan V fails to satisfy the ACP test under paragraph (a)(1)(i)(B) of this section because the ACP for the HCEs exceeds the ACP of the other employees by more than 2 percentage points (6.59% + 2% = 8.59%). Therefore, the plan fails to satisfy the requirements of section 401(m)(2) and paragraph (a)(1) of this section unless the ACP failure is corrected under paragraph (b) of this section.

*Example (3).* (i) The facts are the same as Example 2, except that the plan provides that the NHCEs' elective contributions may be used to meet the requirements of section 401(m) to the extent needed under that section.

(ii) Pursuant to paragraph (a)(6)(ii) of this section, the $10,000 of elective contributions for Employee E may be taken into account in determining the ACP rather than the ADP to the extent that the plan satisfies the requirements of § 1.401(k)-2(a)(1) excluding from the ADP this $10,000. In this case, if the $10,000 were excluded from the ADP for the NHCEs, the ADP for the HCEs is 6.45% (7.89% + 5.00%) /2 and the ADP for the NHCEs would be 6.92% (14.12% + 13.57% + 0% +0%)/4) and the plan would satisfy the requirements of § 1.401(k)-2(a)(1) excluding from the ADP the elective contributions for NHCEs that are taken into account under section 401(m).

(iii) After taking into account the $10,000 of elective contributions for Employee E in the ACP test, the ACP for the NHCEs is 12.84% (7.06% + 6.79% + 37.50 % + 0%) /4. Therefore the plan satisfies the ACP test because the ACP for the HCEs (12.11%) is less than 1.25 times the ACP for the NHCEs.

*Example (4).* (i) The facts are the same as Example 2, except that Plan V provides for a higher than 50% match rate on the elective contributions and employee contributions for all NHCEs. The match rate is defined as the rate, rounded up to the next whole percent, necessary to allow the plan to satisfy the ACP test, but not in excess of 100%. In this case, an increase in the match rate from 50% to 74% will be sufficient to allow the plan to satisfy the ACP test. Thus, for the 2006 plan year, the compensation, elective contributions, employee contributions, matching contributions at a 74% match rate of the eligible NHCEs (employees C through F) are shown in the following table:

| Employee | Compensation | Elective contributions | Employee contributions | Matching contributions |
|---|---|---|---|---|
| C | $85,000 | $12,000 | $0 | $8,880 |
| D | 70,000 | 9,500 | 0 | 7,030 |
| E | 40,000 | 10,000 | 0 | 7,400 |
| F | 10,000 | 0 | 0 | 0 |

(ii) The matching rate for all NHCEs is 74% and thus the matching contributions are not disproportionate under paragraph (a)(5)(ii) of this section. Therefore, the matching contributions may be taken into account in determining the ACP for the NHCEs.

(iii) The ACP for the NHCEs is 9.75% (10.45% + 10.04% + 18.50% + 0%)/4. Because the ACP for the HCEs (12.11%) is less than 1.25 times the ACP for the NHCEs, the plan satisfies the requirements of section 401(m).

*Example (5).* (i) The facts are the same as Example 4, except that: Employee E's elective contributions are $2,000 (rather than $10,000) and pursuant to paragraph (a)(6)(ii) of this section, the $2,000 of elective contributions for Employee E are taken into account in determining the ACP rather than the ADP. In addition, Plan V provides that the higher match rate is not limited to 100% and applies only for a specified group of NHCEs. The only member of that group is Employee E. Under the plan provision, the higher match rate is a 400% match. Thus, for the 2006 plan year, the compensation, elective contributions, employee contributions, matching contributions of the eligible NHCEs (employees C through F) are shown in the following table:

| Employee | Compensation | Elective contributions | Employee contributions | Matching contributions |
|---|---|---|---|---|
| C | $85,000 | $12,000 | $0 | $6,000 |
| D | 70,000 | 9,500 | 0 | 4,750 |
| E | 40,000 | 2,000 | 0 | 8,000 |
| F | 10,000 | 0 | 0 | 0 |

(ii) If the entire matching contribution made on behalf of Employee E were taken into account under the ACP test, Plan V would satisfy the test, because the ACP for the NHCEs would be 9.71% (7.06% + 6.79% + 25.00% + 0%)/4. Because the ACP for the HCEs (12.11%) is less than 1.25 times what the ACP for the NHCEs would be, the plan would satisfy the requirements of section 401(m).

(iii) Pursuant to paragraph (a)(5)(ii) of this section, however, matching contributions for an eligible NHCE that exceed the greatest of 5% of compensation, the employee's elective deferrals and 2 times the product of the plan's representative matching rate and the employee's elective deferrals cannot be taken into account in applying the ACP test. The plan's representative matching rate is the lowest matching rate for any eligible employee in a group of NHCEs that is at least half of all eligible employees who are NHCEs in the plan for the plan year who make elective contributions for the plan year. For Plan V, the group of NHCEs who make such contributions consists of Employees C, D and E. The matching rates for these three employees are 50%, 50% and 400% respectively. The lowest matching rate for a group of NHCEs that is at least half of all the NHCEs who make elective contributions (or 2 NHCEs) is 50%. Because 400% is more than twice the plan's representative matching rate and the matching contributions exceed 5% of compensation, the full amount of matching contributions is not taken into account. Only $2,000 of the matching contributions made on behalf of Employee E (matching contributions that do not exceed the greatest of 5% of compensation, the employee's elective deferrals, or the product of 100% (2 times the representative matching rate) and the employee's elective deferrals) satisfy the requirements of paragraph (a)(5)(ii) of this section and may be taken into account under the ACP test. Accordingly, the ACP for the NHCEs is 5.96% (7.06% + 6.79% + 10% + 0%)/4 and the plan fails to satisfy the requirements of section 401(m)(2) and paragraph (a)(1) of this section unless the ACP failure is corrected under paragraph (b) of this section.

*Example (6).* (i) The facts are the same as Example 2, except that Plan V provides a QNEC equal to 13% of pay for Employee F that will be taken into account under the ACP test to the extent the contributions satisfy the requirements of paragraph (a)(6) of this section.

(ii) Pursuant to paragraph (a)(6)(v) of this section, a QNEC cannot be taken into account in determining an NHCE's ACR to the extent it exceeds the greater of 5% and the product of the employee's compensation and the plan's representative contribution rate. The plan's representative contribution rate is two times the lowest applicable contribution rate for any eligible employee in a group of NHCEs that is at least half of all eligible employees who are NHCEs in the plan for the plan year. For Plan V, the applicable contribution rates for Employees C, D, E and F are 7.06%, 6.79%, 12.5% and 13% respectively. The lowest applicable contribution rate for a group of NHCEs that is at least half of all the NHCEs is 12.50% (the lowest applicable contribution rate for the group of NHCEs that consists of Employees E and F).

(iii) Under paragraph (a)(6)(v)(B) of this section, the plan's representative contribution rate is 2 times 12.50% or 25.00%. Accordingly, the QNECs for Employee F can be taken into account under the ACP test only to the extent they do not exceed 25.00% of compensation. In this case, all of the QNECs for Employee F may be taken into account under the ACP test.

(iv) After taking into account the QNECs for Employee F, the ACP for the NHCEs is 9.84% (7.06% + 6.79% + 12.50% + 13%)/4. Because the ACP for the HCEs (12.11%) is less than 1.25 times the ACP for the NHCEs, the plan satisfies the requirements of section 401(m)(2) and paragraph (a)(1) of this section.

**(b) Correction of excess aggregate contributions.** *(1) Permissible correction methods.* (i) In general. A plan that provides for employee contributions or matching contributions does not fail to satisfy the requirements of section 401(m)(2) and paragraph (a)(1) of this section if the employer, in accordance with the terms of the plan, uses either of the following correction methods—

(A) Additional contributions. The employer makes additional contributions that are taken into account for the ACP test under this section that, in combination with the other contributions taken into account under this section, allow the plan to satisfy the requirements of paragraph (a)(1) of this section.

(B) Excess aggregate contributions distributed or forfeited. Excess aggregate contributions are distributed or forfeited in accordance with paragraph (b)(2) of this section.

(ii) Combination of correction methods. A plan may provide for the use of either of the correction methods described in paragraph (b)(1)(i) of this section, may limit employee contributions or matching contributions in a manner that prevents excess aggregate contributions from being made, or may use a combination of these methods, to avoid or correct excess aggregate contributions. If a plan uses a combination of correction methods, any contributions made under paragraph (b)(1)(i)(A) of this section must be taken into account before application of the correction method in paragraph (b)(1)(i)(B) of this section.

(iii) Exclusive means of correction. A failure to satisfy the requirements of paragraph (a)(1) of this section may not be corrected using any method other than one described in paragraph (b)(1)(i) or (ii) of this section. Thus, excess aggregate contributions for a plan year may not be corrected by forfeiting vested matching contributions, distributing nonvested matching contributions, recharacterizing matching contributions, or not making matching contributions required under the terms of the plan. Similarly, excess aggregate contributions for a plan year may not remain unallocated or be allocated to a suspense account for allocation to one or more employees in any future year. In addition, excess aggregate contributions may not be corrected using the retroactive correction rules of § 1.401(a)(4)-11(g). See § 1.401(a)(4)-11(g)(3)(vii) and (5).

*(2) Correction through distribution.* (i) General rule. This paragraph (b)(2) contains the rules for correction of excess aggregate contributions through a distribution from the plan. Correction through a distribution generally involves a 4-step process. First, the plan must determine, in accordance with paragraph (b)(2)(ii) of this section, the total amount of excess aggregate contributions that must be distributed under the plan. Second, the plan must apportion the total amount of excess aggregate contributions among the HCEs in accordance with paragraph (b)(2)(iii) of this section. Third, the plan must determine the income allocable to excess aggregate contributions in accordance with paragraph (b)(2)(iv) of this section. Finally, the plan must distribute the apportioned contributions, together with allocable income (or forfeit the apportioned matching contributions, if forfeitable) in accordance with paragraph (b)(2)(v) of this section. Paragraph (b)(2)(vi) of this section provides rules relating to the tax treatment of these distributions.

(ii) Calculation of total amount to be distributed. The following procedures must be used to determine the total amount of the excess aggregate contributions to be distributed—

(A) Calculate the dollar amount of excess aggregate contributions for each HCE. The amount of excess aggregate contributions attributable to an HCE for a plan year is the amount (if any) by which the HCE's contributions taken into account under this section must be reduced for the HCE's ACR to equal the highest permitted ACR under the plan. To calculate the highest permitted ACR under a plan, the ACR of the HCE with the highest ACR is reduced by the amount required to cause that HCE's ACR to equal the ACR of the HCE with the next highest ACR. If a lesser reduction would enable the plan to satisfy the requirements of paragraph (b)(2)(ii)(C) of this section, only this lesser reduction applies.

(B) Determination of the total amount of excess aggregate contributions. The process described in paragraph (b)(2)(ii)(A) of this section must be repeated until the plan would satisfy the requirements of paragraph (b)(2)(ii)(C) of this section. The sum of all reductions for all HCEs determined under paragraph (b)(2)(ii)(A) of this section is the total amount of excess aggregate contributions for the plan year.

(C) Satisfaction of ACP. A plan satisfies this paragraph (b)(2)(ii)(C) if the plan would satisfy the requirements of paragraph (a)(1)(i) of this section if the ACR for each HCE were determined after the reductions described in paragraph (b)(2)(ii)(A) of this section.

(iii) Apportionment of total amount of excess aggregate contributions among the HCEs. The following procedures must be used in apportioning the total amount of excess aggregate contributions determined under paragraph (b)(2)(ii) of this section among the HCEs—

(A) Calculate the dollar amount of excess aggregate contributions for each HCE. The contributions with respect to the HCE with the highest dollar amount of contributions taken account under this section are reduced by the amount required to cause that HCE's contributions to equal the dollar amount of contributions taken into account under this section for the HCE with the next highest dollar amount of such contributions. If a lesser apportionment to the HCE would enable the plan to apportion the total amount of excess aggregate contributions, only the lesser apportionment would apply.

(B) Limit on amount apportioned to any HCE. For purposes of this paragraph (b)(2)(iii), the contributions for an HCE who is an eligible employee in more than one plan of an employer to which matching contributions and employee contributions are made is determined by adding together all contributions otherwise taken into account in determining the ACR of the HCE under the rules of paragraph (a)(3)(ii) of this section. However, the amount of contributions apportioned with respect to an HCE must not exceed the amount of contributions taken into account under this section that were actually made on behalf of the HCE to the plan for the plan year. Thus, in the case of an HCE who is an eligible employee in more than one plan of the same employer to which employee contributions or matching contributions are made and whose ACR is calculated in accordance with paragraph (a)(3)(ii) of this section, the amount distributed under this paragraph (b)(2)(iii) will not exceed such contributions actually contributed to the plan for the plan year that are taken into account under this section for the plan year.

(C) Apportionment to additional HCEs. The procedure in paragraph (b)(2)(iii)(A) of this section must be repeated until the total amount of excess aggregate contributions have been apportioned.

(iv) Income allocable to excess aggregate contributions—-(A) General rule. For plan years beginning on or after January 1, 2008, the income allocable to excess aggregate contributions is equal to the allocable gain or loss through the end of the plan year. See paragraph (b)(2)(iv)(D) of this section for rules that apply to plan years beginning before January 1, 2008.

(B) Method of allocating income. A plan may use any reasonable method for computing the income allocable to excess aggregate contributions, provided that the method does not violate section 401(a)(4), is used consistently for all participants and for all corrective distributions under the plan for the plan year, and is used by the plan for allocating income to participants' accounts. See § 1.401(a)(4)-1(c)(8). A plan will not fail to use a reasonable method for computing the income allocable to excess contributions merely because the income allocable to excess aggregate contributions is determined on a date that is no more than 7 days before the distribution.

(C) Alternative method of allocating income for the plan year. A plan may allocate income to excess aggregate contributions for the plan year by multiplying the income for the plan year allocable to employee contributions, matching contributions and other amounts taken into account under this section (including the contributions for the year), by a fraction, the numerator of which is the excess aggregate contributions for the employee for the plan year, and the denominator of which is the sum of the

(1) Account balance attributable to employee contributions and matching contributions and other amounts taken into account under this section as of the beginning of the plan year; and

(2) Any additional such contributions for the plan year.

(D) Plan years before 2008. For plan years beginning before January 1, 2008, the income allocable to excess aggregate contributions is determined under § 1.401(m)-2(b)(2)(iv) (as it appeared in the April 1, 2007, edition of 26 CFR part 1).

(E) Allocable income for recharacterized elective contributions. If recharacterized elective contributions are distributed as excess aggregate contributions, the income allocable to the excess aggregate contributions is determined as if recharacterized elective contributions had been distributed as excess contributions. Thus, income must be allocated to the recharacterized amounts distributed using the methods in § 1.401(k)-2(b)(2)(iv).

(v) Distribution and forfeiture. Within 12 months after the close of the plan year in which the excess aggregate contribution arose, the plan must distribute to each HCE the contributions apportioned to such HCE under paragraph (b)(2)(iii) of this section (and the allocable income) to the extent they are vested or forfeit such amounts, if forfeitable. Except as otherwise provided in this paragraph (b)(2)(v), a distribution of excess aggregate contributions must be in addition to any other distributions made during the year and must be designated as a corrective distribution by the employer. In the event of a complete termination of the plan during the plan year in which an excess aggregate contribution arose, the corrective distribution must be made as soon as administratively feasible after the date of termination of the plan, but in no event later than 12 months after the date of termination. If the entire account balance of an HCE is distributed prior to when the plan makes a distribution of excess aggregate contributions in accordance with this paragraph (b)(2), the distribution is deemed to have been a corrective distribution of excess aggregate contributions (and income) to the extent that a corrective distribution would otherwise have been required.

(vi) Tax treatment of corrective distributions. (A) Corrective distributions for plan years beginning on or after January 1, 2008. Except as otherwise provided in this paragraph (b)(2)(vi), for plan years beginning on or after January 1, 2008, a corrective distribution of excess aggregate contributions (and allocable income) is includible in the employee's gross income in the taxable year of the employee in which distributed. The portion of the distribution that is treated as an investment in the contract and is therefore not subject to tax under section 72 is determined without regard to any plan contributions other than those distributed as excess aggregate contributions. Regardless of when the corrective distribution is made, it is not subject to the early distribution tax of section 72(t). See paragraph (b)(4) of this section for additional rules relating to the employer excise tax on amounts distributed more than 2½ months (6 months in the case of certain plans that include an eligible automatic contribution arrangement within the meaning of section 414(w)) after the end of the plan year. See also § 1.402(c)-2, A-4, prohibiting rollover of distributions that are excess aggregate contributions.

(B) Corrective distributions for plan years beginning before January 1, 2008. The tax treatment of corrective distributions for plan years beginning before January 1, 2008, is determined under § 1.401(m)-2(b)(2)(vi) (as it appeared in the April 1, 2007, edition of 26 CFR Part 1). If the total amount of excess aggregate contributions determined under this paragraph (b)(2), and excess contributions determined under § 1.401(k)-2(b)(2) distributed to a recipient under a plan for any plan year is less than $100 (excluding income), a corrective distribution of excess aggregate contributions (and income) is includible in gross income in the recipient's taxable year in which the corrective distribution is made, except to the extent the corrective distribution is a return of employee contributions, or as provided in paragraph (b)(2)(vi)(C) of this section.

(C) Corrective distributions attributable to designated Roth contributions. Notwithstanding paragraphs (b)(2)(vi)(A) and (B) of this section, a distribution of excess aggregate contributions is not includible in gross income to the extent it represents a distribution of designated Roth contributions. However, the income allocable to a corrective distribution of excess aggregate contributions that are designated Roth contributions is taxed in accordance with paragraph (b)(2)(vi)(A) or (B) of this section (i.e., in the same manner as income allocable to a corrective distribution of excess aggregate contributions that are not designated Roth contributions).

*(3) Other rules.* (i) No employee or spousal consent required. A distribution of excess aggregate contributions (and income) may be made under the terms of the plan without regard to any notice or consent otherwise required under sections 411(a)(11) and 417.

(ii) Treatment of corrective distributions and forfeited contributions as employer contributions. Excess aggregate contributions (other than amounts attributable to employee contributions), including forfeited matching contributions, are treated as employer contributions for purposes of sections 404 and 415 even if distributed from the plan. Forfeited matching contributions that are reallocated to the accounts of other participants for the plan year in which the forfeiture occurs are treated under section 415 as annual additions for the participants to whose accounts they are reallocated and for the participants from whose accounts they are forfeited.

(iii) No reduction of required minimum distribution. A distribution of excess aggregate contributions (and income) is not treated as a distribution for purposes of determining whether the plan satisfies the minimum distribution requirements of section 401(a)(9). See § 1.401(a)(9)-5, A-9(b).

(iv) Partial correction. Any distribution of less than the entire amount of excess aggregate contributions (and allocable income) is treated as a pro rata distribution of excess aggregate contributions and allocable income.

(v) Matching contributions on excess contributions, excess referrals and excess aggregate contributions. (A) Corrective distributions not permitted. A matching contribution may not be distributed merely because the contribution to which it relates is treated as an excess contribution, excess deferral, or excess aggregate contribution.

(B) Coordination with section 401(a)(4). A matching contribution is taken into account under section 401(a)(4) even if the match is distributed, unless the distributed contribution is an excess aggregate contribution. This requires that, after correction of excess aggregate contributions, each level of matching contributions be currently and effectively available to a group of employees that satisfies section 410(b). See § 1.401(a)(4)-4(e)(3)(iii)(G). Thus, a plan that provides the same rate of matching contributions to all employees will not meet the requirements of section 401(a)(4) if employee contributions are distributed under this paragraph (b) to HCEs to the extent needed to meet the requirements of section 401(m)(2), while matching contributions attributable to employee contributions remain allocated to the HCEs' accounts. This is because the level of matching contributions will be higher for a group of employees that consists entirely of HCEs. Under section 411(a)(3)(G) and § 1.411(a)-4(b)(7), a plan may forfeit matching contributions attributable to excess contributions, excess aggregate contributions and excess deferrals to avoid a violation of section 401(a)(4). See also § 1.401(a)(4)-11(g)(3)(vii)(B) regarding the use of additional allocations to the accounts of NHCEs for the purpose of correcting a discriminatory rate of matching contributions. A plan is permitted to provide for which contributions are to be distributed to satisfy the ACP test so as to avoid discriminatory matching rates that would otherwise violate section 401(a)(4). For example, the plan may provide that unmatched employee contributions will be distributed before matched employee contributions.

(vi) No requirement for recalculation. If the distributions and forfeitures described in paragraph (b)(2) of this section are made, the employee contributions and matching contributions are treated as meeting the nondiscrimination test of section 401(m)(2) regardless of whether the ACP for the HCEs, if recalculated after the distributions and forfeitures, would satisfy section 401(m)(2).

*(4) Failure to timely correct.* (i) Failure to correct within 2½ months after end of plan year. If a plan does not correct excess aggregate contributions within 2½ months after the close of the plan year for which the excess aggregate contributions are made, the employer will be liable for a 10% excise tax on the amount of the excess aggregate contributions. See section 4979 and § 54.4979-1 of this chapter. Qualified nonelective contributions properly taken into account under paragraph (a)(6) of this section for a plan year may enable a plan to avoid having excess aggregate contributions, even if the contributions are made after the close of the 2½ month period.

(ii) Failure to correct within 12 months after end of plan year. If excess aggregate contributions are not corrected within 12 months after the close of the plan year for which they were made, the plan will fail to meet the requirements of section 401(a)(4) for the plan year for which the excess aggregate contributions were made and all subsequent plan years in which the excess aggregate contributions remain in the trust.

(iii) Special rule for eligible automatic contribution arrangements. In the case of excess aggregate contributions under a plan that includes an eligible automatic contribution arrangement (within the meaning of section 414(w)), 6 months is substituted for 2½ months in paragraph (b)(4)(i) of this section. The additional time described in this paragraph (b)(4)(iii) applies to a distribution of excess aggregate contributions for a plan year beginning on or after January 1, 2010 only where all the eligible NHCEs and eligible HCEs are covered employees under the eligible automatic contribution arrangement (within the meaning of § 1.414(w)-1(e)(3)) for the entire plan year (or for the portion of the plan year that the eligible NHCEs and eligible HCEs are eligible employees).

*(5) Examples.* The following examples illustrate the application of this paragraph. See also § 1.401(k)-2(b) for additional examples of the parallel correction rules applicable to cash or deferred arrangements. For purposes of these examples, none of the plans provide for catch-up contributions under section 414(v). The examples are as follows:

*Example (1).* (i) Employer L maintains a plan that provides for employee contributions and fully vested matching contributions. The plan provides that failures of the ACP test are corrected by distribution. In 2006, the ACP for the eligible NHCEs is 6%. Thus, the ACP for the eligible HCEs may not exceed 8%. The three HCEs who participate have the following compensation, contributions, and ACRs:

| Employee | Compensation | Employee contributions and matching contributions | Actual contribution ratio (percent) |
|---|---|---|---|
| A | 200,000 | 14,000 | 7 |
| B | 150,000 | 13,500 | 9 |
| C | 100,000 | 12,000 | 12 |
| | | | Average 9.33 |

(ii) The total amount of excess aggregate contributions for the HCEs is determined under paragraph (b)(2)(ii) of this section as follows: the matching and employee contributions of Employee C (the HCE with the highest ACR) is reduced by 3% of compensation (or $3,000) in order to reduce the ACR of that HCE to 9%, which is the ACR of Employee B.

(iii) Because the ACP of the HCEs determined after the $3,000 reduction still exceeds 8%, further reductions in matching contributions and employee contributions are necessary in order to reduce the ACP of the HCEs to 8%. The employee contributions and matching contributions for Employees B and C are reduced by an additional .5% of compensation or $1,250 ($750 and $500 respectively). Because the ACP of the HCEs determined after the reductions now equals 8%, the plan would satisfy the requirements of (a)(1)(ii) of this section.

(iv) The total amount of excess aggregate contributions ($4,250) is apportioned among the HCEs under paragraph (b)(2)(iii) of this section first to the HCE with the highest amount of matching contributions and employee contributions. Therefore, Employee A is apportioned $500 (the amount required to cause A's matching contributions and employee contributions to equal the next highest dollar amount of matching contributions and employee contributions).

(v) Because the total amount of excess aggregate contributions has not been apportioned, further apportionment is necessary. The balance ($3,750) of the total amount of excess aggregate contributions is apportioned equally among Employees A and B ($1,500 to each, the amount required to cause their contributions to equal the next highest dollar amount of matching contributions and employee contributions).

(vi) Because the total amount of excess aggregate contributions has not been apportioned, further apportionment is necessary. The balance ($750) of the total amount of excess aggregate contributions is apportioned equally among Employees A, B and C ($250 to each, the amount required to allocate the total amount of excess aggregate contributions for the plan).

(vii) Therefore, the plan will satisfy the requirements of paragraph (a)(1) of this section if, by the end of the 12 month period following the end of the 2006 plan year, Employee A receives a corrective distribution of excess aggregate contributions equal to $2,250 ($500 + $1,500 + $250) and allocable income, Employee B receives a corrective distribution of $250 and allocable income and Employee C receives a corrective distribution of $1,750 ($1,500 + $250) and allocable income.

*Example (2).* (i) Employee D is the sole HCE who is eligible to participate in a cash or deferred arrangement maintained by Employer M. The plan that includes the arrangement, Plan X, permits employee contributions and provides a fully vested matching contribution equal to 50% of elective contributions. Plan X is a calendar year plan. Plan X corrects excess contributions by recharacterization and provides that failures of the ACP test are corrected by distribution. For the 2006 plan year, D's compensation is $200,000, and D's elective contributions are $15,000. The actual deferral percentages and actual contribution percentages for Employee D and the other eligible employees under Plan X are shown in the following table:

| | Actual deferral percentage | Actual contribution percentage |
|---|---|---|
| Employee D | 7.5 | 3.75 |
| NHCEs | 4 | 2 |

(ii) In February 2007, Employer M determines that D's actual deferral ratio must be reduced to 6%, or $12,000, which requires a recharacterization of $3,000 as an employee contribution. This increases D's actual contribution ratio to 5.25% ($7,500 in matching contributions plus $3,000 recharacterized as employee contributions, divided by $200,000 in compensation). Since D's actual contribution ratio must be limited to 4% for Plan X to satisfy the actual contribution percentage test, Plan X must distribute 1.25% or $2,500 of D's employee contributions and matching contributions together with allocable income. If $2,500 in matching contributions and allocable income is distributed, this will correct the excess aggregate contributions and will not result in a discriminatory rate of matching contributions. See Example 8.

*Example (3).* (i) The facts are the same as in Example 2, except that Employee D also had elective contributions under Plan Y, maintained by an employer unrelated to M. In January 2007, D requests and receives a distribution of $1,200 in excess deferrals from Plan X. Pursuant to the terms of Plan X, D forfeits the $600 match on the excess deferrals to correct a discriminatory rate of match.

(ii) The $3,000 that would otherwise have been recharacterized for Plan X to satisfy the actual deferral percentage test is reduced by the $1,200 already distributed as an excess deferral, leaving $1,800 to be recharacterized. See § 1.401(k)-2(b)(4)(i)(A). D's actual contribution ratio is now 4.35% ($7,500 in matching contributions plus $1,800 in recharacterized contributions less $600 forfeited matching contributions attributable to the excess deferrals, divided by $200,000 in compensation).

(iii) The matching and employee contributions for Employee D must be reduced by .35% of compensation in order to reduce the ACP of the HCEs to 4%. The plan must provide for forfeiture of additional matching contributions to prevent a discriminatory rate of matching contributions. See Example 8.

*Example (4).* (i) The facts are the same as in Example 3, except that D does not request a distribution of excess deferrals until March 2007. Employer X has already recharacterized $3,000 as employee contributions.

(ii) Under § 1.402(g)-1(e)(6), the amount of excess deferrals is reduced by the amount of excess contributions that are recharacterized. Because the amount recharacterized is greater than the excess deferrals, Plan X is neither required nor permitted to make a distribution of excess deferrals, and the recharacterization has corrected the excess deferrals.

*Example (5).* (i) For the 2006 plan year, Employee F defers $10,000 under Plan M and $6,000 under Plan N. Plans M and N, which have calendar plan years are maintained by unrelated employers. Plan M provides a fully vested, 100% matching contribution, does not take elective contributions into account under section 401(m) or take matching contributions into account under section 401(k) and provides that excess contributions and excess aggregate contributions are corrected by distribution. Under Plan M, Employee F is allocated excess contributions of $600 and excess aggregate contributions of $1,600. Employee F timely requests and receives a distribution of the $1,000 excess deferral from Plan M and, pursuant to the terms of Plan M, forfeits the corresponding $1,000 matching contribution.

(ii) No distribution is required or permitted to correct the excess contributions because $1,000 has been distributed by Plan M as excess deferrals. The distribution required to correct the excess aggregate contributions (after forfeiting the matching contribution) is $600 ($1,600 in excess aggregate contributions minus $1,000 in forfeited matching contributions). If Employee F had corrected the excess deferrals of $1,000 by withdrawing $1,000 from Plan N, Plan M would have had to correct the $600 excess contributions in Plan M by distributing $600. Since Employee F then would have forfeited $600 (instead of $1,000) in matching contributions, Employee F would have had $1,000 ($1,600 in excess aggregate contributions minus $600 in forfeited matching contributions) remaining of excess aggregate contributions in Plan M. These would have been corrected by distributing an additional $1,000 from Plan M.

*Example (6).* (i) Employee G is the sole HCE in a profit sharing plan under which the employer matches 100% of employee contributions up to 2% of compensation, and 50% of employee contributions up to the next 4% of compensation. For the 2008 plan year, Employee G has compensation of $100,000 and makes a 7% employee contribution of $7,000. Employee G receives a 4% matching contribution or $4,000. Thus, Employee G's actual contribution ratio (ACR) is 11%. The actual contribution percentage for the NHCEs is 5%, and the employer determines that Employee G's ACR must be reduced to 7% to comply with the rules of section 401(m).

(ii) In this case, the plan satisfies the requirements of section if it distributes the unmatched employee contributions of $1,000, and $2,000 of matched employee contributions with their related matches of $1,000. This would leave Employee G with 4% employee contributions, and 3% matching contributions, for an ACR of 7%. Alternatively, the plan could distribute all matching contributions and satisfy this section. However, the plan could not distribute $4,000 of Employee G's employee contributions without forfeiting the related matching contributions because this would result in a discriminatory rate of matching contributions. See also Example 7.

*Example (7).* (i) Employee H is an HCE in Employer X's profit sharing plan, which matches 100% of employee contributions up to 5% of compensation. The matching contribution is vested at the rate of 20% per year. In 2006, Employee H makes $5,000 in employee contributions and receives $5,000 of matching contributions. Employee H is 60% vested in the matching contributions at the end of the 2006 plan year. In February 2007, Employer X determines that Employee H has excess aggregate contributions of $1,000. The plan provides that only matching contributions will be distributed as excess aggregate contributions.

(ii) Employer X has two options available in distributing Employee H's excess aggregate contributions. The first option is to distribute $600 of vested matching contributions and forfeit $400 of nonvested matching contributions. These amounts are in proportion to Employee H's vested and nonvested interests in all matching contributions. The second option is to distribute $1,000 of vested matching contributions, leaving the nonvested matching contributions in the plan.

(iii) If the second option is chosen, the plan must also provide a separate vesting schedule for vesting these nonvested matching contributions. This is necessary because the nonvested matching contributions must vest as rapidly as they would have had no distribution been made. Thus, 50% must vest in each of the next 2 years.

(iv) The plan will not satisfy the nondiscriminatory availability requirement of section 401(a)(4) if only nonvested matching contributions are forfeited because the effect is that matching contributions for HCEs vest more rapidly than those for NHCEs. See § 1.401(m)-2(b)(3)(v)(B).

*Example (8).* (i) Employer Y maintains a calendar year profit sharing plan that includes a cash or deferred arrangement. Elective contributions are matched at the rate of 100%. After-tax employee contributions are permitted under the plan only for NHCEs and are matched at the same rate. No employees make excess deferrals. Employee J, an HCE, makes an $8,000 elective contribution and receives an $8,000 matching contribution.

(ii) Employer Y performs the actual deferral percentage (ADP) and the actual contribution percentage (ACP). To correct failures of the ADP and ACP tests, the plan distributes to A $1,000 of excess contributions and $500 of excess aggregate contributions. After the distributions, Employee J's contributions for the year are $7,000 of elective contributions and $7,500 of matching contributions. As a result, Employee J has received a higher effective rate of matching contributions than NHCEs ($7,000 of elective contributions matched by $7,500 is an effective matching rate of 107 percent). If this amount remains in Employee J's account without correction, it will cause the plan to fail to satisfy section 401(a)(4), because only an HCE receives the higher matching contribution rate. The remaining $500 matching contribution may be forfeited (but not distributed) under section 411(a)(3)(G), if the plan so provides. The plan could instead correct the discriminatory rate of matching contributions by making additional allocations to the accounts of NHCEs. See § 1.401(a)(4)-11(g)(3)(vii)(B) and (6), Example 7.

**(c) Additional rules for prior year testing method.** *(1) Rules for change in testing method.* A plan is permitted to change from the prior year testing method to the current year testing method for any plan year. A plan is permitted to change from the current year testing method to the prior year testing method only in situations described in § 1.401(k)-2(c)(1)(ii). For purposes of this paragraph (c)(1), a plan that uses the safe harbor method described in § 1.401(m)-3 or a SIMPLE 401(k) plan is treated as using the current year testing method for that plan year

*(2) Calculation of ACP under the prior year testing method for the first plan year.* (i) Plans that are not successor plans. If, for the first plan year of any plan (other than a successor plan), a plan uses the prior year testing method, the plan is permitted to use either that first plan year as the applicable year for determining the ACP for the eligible NHCEs, or 3% as the ACP for eligible NHCEs, for applying the ACP test for that first plan year. A plan (other than a successor plan) that uses the prior year testing method but has elected for its first plan year to use that year as the applicable year for determining the ACP for the eligible NHCEs is not treated as changing its testing method in the second plan year and is not subject to the limitations on double counting under paragraph (a)(6)(vi) of this section for the second plan year.

(ii) First plan year defined. For purposes of this paragraph (c)(2), the first plan year of any plan is the first year in which the plan provides for employee contributions or matching contributions. Thus, the rules of this paragraph (c)(2) do not apply to a plan (within the meaning of § 1.410(b)-7) for a plan year if for such plan year the plan is aggregated under § 1.401(m)-1(b)(4) with any other plan that provides for employee or matching contributions in the prior year.

(iii) Plans that are successor plans. A plan is a successor plan if 50% or more of the eligible employees for the first plan year were eligible employees under another plan maintained by the employer in the prior year that provides for employee contributions or matching contributions. If a plan that is a successor plan uses the prior year testing method for its first plan year, the ACP for the group of NHCEs for the applicable year must be determined under paragraph (c)(4) of this section.

*(3) Plans using different testing methods for the ACP and ADP test.* Except as otherwise provided in this paragraph (c)(3), a plan may use the current year testing method or prior year testing method for the ACP test for a plan year without regard to whether the current year testing method or prior year testing method is used for the ADP test for that year. For example, a plan may use the prior year testing method for the ACP test and the current year testing method for its ADP test for the plan year. However, plans that use different testing methods under this paragraph (c)(3) cannot use—

(i) The recharacterization method of § 1.401(k)-2(b)(3) to correct excess contributions for a plan year;

(ii) The rules of paragraph (a)(6)(ii) of this section to take elective contributions into account under the ACP test (rather than the ADP test); or

(iii) The rules of paragraph § 1.401(k)-2(a)(6) to take qualified matching contributions into account under the ADP test (rather than the ACP test).

*(4) Rules for plan coverage change.* (i) In general. A plan that uses the prior year testing method that experiences a plan coverage change during a plan year satisfies the requirements of this section for that year only if the plan provides that the ACP for the NHCEs for the plan year is the weighted average of the ACPs for the prior year subgroups.

(ii) Optional rule for minor plan coverage changes. If a plan coverage change occurs and 90% or more of the total number of the NHCEs from all prior year subgroups are from a single prior year subgroup, then, in lieu of using the weighted averages described in paragraph (c)(4)(i) of this section, the plan may provide that the ACP for the group of eligible NHCEs for the prior year under the plan is the ACP of the NHCEs for the prior year of the plan under which that single prior year subgroup was eligible.

(iii) Definitions. The following definitions apply for purposes of this paragraph (c)(4)—

(A) Plan coverage change. The term plan coverage change means a change in the group or groups of eligible employees under a plan on account of—

(1) The establishment or amendment of a plan;

(2) A plan merger or spinoff under section 414(l);

(3) A change in the way plans (within the meaning of § 1.410(b)-7) are combined or separated for purposes of § 1.401(m)-1(b)(4) (e.g., permissively aggregating plans not previously aggregated under § 1.410(b)-7(d), or ceasing to permissively aggregate plans under § 1.410(b)-7(d));

(4) A reclassification of a substantial group of employees that has the same effect as amending the plan (e.g., a transfer of a substantial group of employees from one division to another division); or

(5) A combination of any of paragraphs (c)(4)(iii)(A)(1) through (4) of this section.

(B) Prior year subgroup. The term prior year subgroup means all NHCEs for the prior plan year who, in the prior year, were eligible employees under a specific plan that provides for employee contributions or matching contributions maintained by the employer and who would have been eligible employees in the prior year under the plan being tested if the plan coverage change had first been effective as of the first day of the prior plan year instead of first being effective during the plan year. The determination of whether an NHCE is a member of a prior year subgroup is made without regard to whether the NHCE terminated employment during the prior year.

(C) Weighted average of the ACPs for the prior year subgroups. The term weighted average of the ACPs for the prior year subgroups means the sum, for all prior year subgroups, of the adjusted ACPs for the plan year. The term adjusted ACP with respect to a prior year subgroup means the ACP for the prior plan year of the specific plan under which the members of the prior year subgroup were eligible employees on the first day of the prior plan year, multiplied by a fraction, the numerator of which is the number of NHCEs in the prior year subgroup and denominator of which is the total number of NHCEs in all prior year subgroups.

(iv) Example. The following example illustrate the application of this paragraph (c)(4). See also § 1.401(k)-2(c)(4) for examples of the parallel rules applicable to the ADP test. The example is as follows:

*Example.* (i) Employer B maintains two plans, Plan N and Plan P, each of which provides for employee contributions or matching contributions. The plans were not permissively aggregated under § 1.410(b)-7(d) for the 2005 testing year. Both plans use the prior year testing method. Plan N had 300 eligible employees who were NHCEs for 2005, and their ACP for that year was 6%. Plan P had 100 eligible employees who were NHCEs for 2005, and the ACP for those NHCEs for that plan was 4%. Plan N and Plan P are permissively aggregated under § 1.410(b)-7(d) for the 2006 plan year.

(ii) The permissive aggregation of Plan N and Plan P for the 2006 testing year under § 1.410(b)-7(d) is a plan coverage change that results in treating the plans as one plan (Plan NP). Therefore, the prior year ACP for the NHCEs under Plan NP for the 2006 testing year is the weighted average of the ACPs for the prior year subgroups.

(iii) The first step in determining the weighted average of the ACPs for the prior year subgroups is to identify the prior year subgroups. With respect to the 2006 testing year, an employee is a member of a prior year subgroup if the employee was an NHCE of Employer B for the 2005 plan year, was an eligible employee for the 2005 plan year under any section 401(k) plan maintained by Employer B, and would have been an eligible employee in the 2005 plan year under Plan NP if Plan N and Plan P had been permissively aggregated under § 1.410(b)-7(d) for that plan year. The NHCEs who were eligible employees under separate plans for the 2005 plan year comprise separate prior year subgroups. Thus, there are two prior year subgroups under Plan NP for the 2006 testing year: the 300 NHCEs who were eligible employees under Plan N for the 2005 plan year and the 100 NHCEs who were eligible employees under Plan P for the 2005 plan year.

(iv) The weighted average of the ACPs for the prior year subgroups is the sum of the adjusted ACP with respect to the prior year subgroup that consists of the NHCEs who were eligible employees under Plan N, and the adjusted ACP with respect to the prior year subgroup that consists of the NHCEs who were eligible employees under Plan P. The adjusted ACP for the prior year subgroup that consists of the NHCEs who were eligible employees under Plan N is 4.5%, calculated as follows: 6% (the ACP for the NHCEs under Plan N for the prior year) x 300/400 (the number of NHCEs in that prior year subgroup divided by the total number of NHCEs in all prior year subgroups), which equals 4.5%. The adjusted ACP for the prior year subgroup that consists of the NHCEs who were eligible employees under Plan P is 1%, calculated as follows: 4% (the ACP for the NHCEs under Plan P for the prior year) x 100/400 (the number of NHCEs in that prior year subgroup divided by the total number of NHCEs in all prior year subgroups), which equals 1%. Thus, the prior year ACP for NHCEs under Plan NP for the 2006 testing year is 5.5% (the sum of adjusted ACPs for the prior year subgroups, 4.5% plus 1%).

---

T.D. 8357, 8/8/91, amend T.D. 8581, 12/22/94, T.D. 9169, 12/28/2004, T.D. 9237, 12/30/2005, T.D. 9447, 2/23/2009.

---

### § 1.401(m)-3 Safe harbor requirements.

**(a) ACP test safe harbor.** *(1) Section 401(m)(11) safe harbor.* Matching contributions under a plan satisfy the ACP safe harbor provisions of section 401(m)(11) for a plan year if the plan satisfies the safe harbor contribution requirement of paragraph (b) or (c) of this section for the plan year, the limitations on matching contributions of paragraph (d) of this section, the notice requirement of paragraph (e) of this section, the plan year requirements of paragraph (f) of this section, and the additional rules of paragraphs (g), (h) and (j) of this section, as applicable.

*(2) Section 401(m)(12) safe harbor.* For a plan year beginning on or after January 1, 2008, matching contributions under a plan satisfy the ACP safe harbor provisions of section 401(m)(12) for a plan year if the matching contributions are made with respect to an automatic contribution arrangement described in paragraph § 1.401(k)-3(j) that satisfies the safe harbor requirements of § 1.401(k)-3, the limitations on matching contributions of paragraph (d) of this section, the notice requirement of paragraph (e) of this section, the plan year requirements of paragraph (f) of this section, and the

additional rules of paragraphs (g), (h) and (j) of this section, as applicable.

*(3) Requirements applicable to safe harbor contributions.* Pursuant to sections 401(k)(12)(E)(ii) and 401(k)(13)(D)(iv), the safe harbor contribution requirement of paragraph (b) or (c) of this section and § 1.401(k)-3(k) must be satisfied without regard to section 401(l). The contributions made under paragraphs (b) and (c) of this section and § 1.401(k)-3(k) are referred to as safe harbor nonelective contributions and safe harbor matching contributions.

**(b) Safe harbor nonelective contribution requirement.** A plan satisfies the safe harbor nonelective contribution requirement of this paragraph (b) if it satisfies the safe harbor nonelective contribution requirement of § 1.401(k)-3(b).

**(c) Safe harbor matching contribution requirement.** A plan satisfies the safe harbor matching contribution requirement of this paragraph (c) if it satisfies the safe harbor matching contribution requirement of § 1.401(k)-3(c).

**(d) Limitation on contributions.** *(1) General rule.* A plan that provides for matching contributions meets the requirements of this section only if it satisfies the limitations on contributions set forth in this paragraph (d).

*(2) Matching rate must not increase.* A plan that provides for matching contributions meets the requirements of this paragraph (d) only if the ratio of matching contributions on behalf of an employee under the plan for a plan year to the employee's elective deferrals and employee contributions, does not increase as the amount of an employee's elective deferrals and employee contributions increases.

*(3) Limit on matching contributions.* A plan that provides for matching contributions satisfies the requirements of this section only if—

(i) Matching contributions are not made with respect to elective deferrals or employee contributions that exceed 6% of the employee's safe harbor compensation (within the meaning of § 1.401(k)-3(b)(2)); and

(ii) Matching contributions that are discretionary do not exceed 4% of the employee's safe harbor compensation.

*(4) Limitation on rate of match.* A plan meets the requirements of this section only if the ratio of matching contributions on behalf of an HCE to that HCE's elective deferrals or employee contributions (or the sum of elective deferrals and employee contributions) for that plan year is no greater than the ratio of matching contributions to elective deferrals or employee contributions (or the sum of elective deferrals and employee contributions) that would apply with respect to any NHCE for whom the elective deferrals or employee contributions (or the sum of elective deferrals and employee contributions) are the same percentage of safe harbor compensation. An employee is taken into account for purposes of this paragraph (d)(4) if the employee is an eligible employee under the cash or deferred arrangement with respect to which the contributions required by paragraph (b) or (c) of this section are being made for a plan year. A plan will not fail to satisfy this paragraph (d)(4) merely because the plan provides that matching contributions will be made separately with respect to each payroll period (or with respect to all payroll periods ending with or within each month or quarter of a plan year) taken into account under the plan for the plan year, provided that matching contributions with respect to any elective deferrals or employee contributions made during a plan year quarter are contributed to the plan by the last day of the immediately following plan year quarter.

*(5) HCEs participating in multiple plans.* The rules of section 401(m)(2)(B) and § 1.401(m)-2(a)(3)(ii) apply for purposes of determining the rate of matching contributions under paragraph (d)(4) of this section. However, a plan will not fail to satisfy the safe harbor matching contribution requirements of this section merely because an HCE participates during the plan year in more than one plan that provides for matching contributions, provided that—

(i) The HCE is not simultaneously an eligible employee under two plans that provide for matching contributions maintained by an employer for a plan year; and

(ii) The period used to determine compensation for purposes of determining matching contributions under each such plan is limited to periods when the HCE participated in the plan.

*(6) Permissible restrictions on elective deferrals by NHCEs.* (i) General rule. A plan does not satisfy the safe harbor requirements of this section, if elective deferrals or employee contributions by NHCEs are restricted, unless the restrictions are permitted by this paragraph (d)(6).

(ii) Restrictions on election periods. A plan may limit the frequency and duration of periods in which eligible employees may make or change contribution elections under a plan. However, an employee must have a reasonable opportunity (including a reasonable period after receipt of the notice described in paragraph (e) of this section) to make or change a contribution election for the plan year. For purposes of this section, a 30-day period is deemed to be a reasonable period to make or change a contribution election.

(iii) Restrictions on amount of contributions. A plan is permitted to limit the amount of contributions that may be made by an eligible employee under a plan, provided that each NHCE who is an eligible employee is permitted (unless the employee is restricted under paragraph (d)(6)(v) of this section) to make contributions in an amount that is at least sufficient to receive the maximum amount of matching contributions available under the plan for the plan year, and the employee is permitted to elect any lesser amount of contributions. However, a plan may require eligible employees to make contribution elections in whole percentages of compensation or whole dollar amounts.

(iv) Restrictions on types of compensation that may be deferred. A plan may limit the types of compensation that may be deferred or contributed by an eligible employee under a plan, provided that each eligible NHCE is permitted to make contributions under a definition of compensation that would be a reasonable definition of compensation within the meaning of § 1.414(s)-1(d)(2). Thus, the definition of compensation from which contributions may be made is not required to satisfy the nondiscrimination requirement of § 1.414(s)-1(d)(3).

(v) Restrictions due to limitations under the Internal Revenue Code. A plan may limit the amount of contributions made by an eligible employee under a plan—

(A) Because of the limitations of section 402(g) or section 415; or

(B) Because, on account of a hardship distribution, an employee's ability to make contributions has been suspended for 6 months in accordance with § 1.401(k)-1(d)(3)(iv)(E).

**(e) Notice requirement.** A plan satisfies the notice requirement of this paragraph (e) if it satisfies the notice requirement of § 1.401(k)-3(d).

**(f) Plan year requirement.** *(1) General rule.* Except as provided in this paragraph (f) or in paragraph (g) of this section, a plan will fail to satisfy the requirements of section 401(m)(11), section 401(m)(12), and this section unless plan provisions that satisfy the rules of this section are adopted before the first day of that plan year and remain in effect for an entire 12-month plan year. In addition, except as provided in paragraph (h) of this section, a plan which includes provisions that satisfy the rules of this section will not satisfy the requirements of § 1.401(m)-1(b) if it is amended to change such provisions for that plan year. Moreover, if, as described in paragraph (j)(4) of this section, safe harbor matching or nonelective contributions will be made to another plan for a plan year, provisions under that other plan specifying that the safe harbor contributions will be made and providing that the contributions will be QNECs or QMACs must also be adopted before the first day of that plan year.

*(2) Initial plan year.* A newly established plan (other than a successor plan within the meaning of § 1.401(m)-2(c)(2)(iii)) will not be treated as violating the requirements of this paragraph (f) merely because the plan year is less than 12 months, provided that the plan year is at least 3 months long (or, in the case of a newly established employer that establishes the plan as soon as administratively feasible after the employer comes into existence, a shorter period). Similarly, a plan will not fail to satisfy the requirements of this paragraph (f) for the first plan year in which matching contributions are provided under the plan provided that—

(i) The plan is not a successor plan; and

(ii) The amendment providing for matching contributions is made effective at the same time as the adoption of a cash or deferred arrangement that satisfies the requirements of § 1.401(k)-3, taking into account the rules of § 1.401(k)-3(e)(2).

*(3) Change of plan year.* A plan that has a short plan year as a result of changing its plan year will not fail to satisfy the requirements of paragraph (f)(1) of this section merely because the plan year has less than 12 months, provided that—

(i) The plan satisfied the requirements of this section for the immediately preceding plan year; and

(ii) The plan satisfies the requirements of this section (determined without regard to paragraph (h) of this section) for the immediately following plan year or for the immediately following 12 months if the immediately following plan year is less than 12 months.

*(4) Final plan year.* A plan that terminates during a plan year will not fail to satisfy the requirements of paragraph (f)(1) of this section merely because the final plan year is less than 12 months, provided that the plan satisfies the requirement of this section through the date of termination and either—

(i) he plan would satisfy the requirements of paragraph (h) of this section, treating the termination of the plan as a reduction or suspension of safe harbor matching contributions, other than the requirement that employees have a reasonable opportunity to change their cash or deferred elections and, if applicable, employee contribution elections; or

(ii) The plan termination is in connection with a transaction described in section 410(b)(6)(C) or the employer incurs a substantial business hardship, comparable to a substantial business hardship described in section 412(d).

**(g) Plan amendments adopting nonelective safe harbor contributions.** Notwithstanding paragraph (f)(1) of this section, a plan that provides for the use of the current year testing method may be amended after the first day of the plan year and no later than 30 days before the last day of the plan year to adopt the safe harbor method of this section, effective as of the first day of the plan year, using nonelective contributions under paragraph (b) of this section if the plan satisfies the requirements of § 1.401(k)-3(f).

**(h) Permissible reduction or suspension of safe harbor matching contributions.** *(1) General rule.* A plan that provides for safe harbor matching contributions will not fail to satisfy the requirements of section 401(m)(2) for a plan year merely because the plan is amended during a plan year to reduce or suspend safe harbor matching contributions on future elective deferrals and, if applicable, employee contributions provided—

(i) All eligible employees are provided the supplemental notice in accordance with paragraph (h)(2) of this section;

(ii) The reduction or suspension of safe harbor matching contributions is effective no earlier than the later of 30 days after eligible employees are provided the notice described in paragraph (h)(2) of this section and the date the amendment is adopted;

(iii) Eligible employees are given a reasonable opportunity (including a reasonable period after receipt of the supplemental notice) prior to the reduction or suspension of safe harbor matching contributions to change their cash or deferred elections and, if applicable, their employee contribution elections;

(iv) The plan is amended to provide that the ACP test will be satisfied for the entire plan year in which the reduction or suspension occurs using the current year testing method described in § 1.401(m)-2(a)(1)(ii); and

(v) The plan satisfies the requirements of this section (other than this paragraph (h)) with respect to amounts deferred through the effective date of the amendment.

*(2) Notice of suspension requirement.* The notice of suspension requirement of this paragraph (h)(2) is satisfied if each eligible employee is given notice that satisfies the requirements of § 1.401(k)-3(g)(2).

**(i)** [Reserved]

**(j) Other rules.** *(1) Contributions taken into account.* A contribution is taken into account for purposes of this section for a plan year under the same rules as § 1.401(k)-3(h)(1).

*(2) Use of safe harbor nonelective contributions to satisfy other nondiscrimination tests.* A safe harbor nonelective contribution used to satisfy the nonelective contribution requirement under paragraph (b) of this section may also be taken into account for purposes of determining whether a plan satisfies section 401(a)(4) under the same rules as § 1.401(k)-3(h)(2).

*(3) Early participation rules.* Section 401(m)(5)(C) and § 1.401(m)-2(a)(1)(iii)(A), which provide an alternative nondiscrimination rule for certain plans that provide for early participation, do not apply for purposes of section 401(m)(11), section 401(m)(12), and this section. Thus, a plan is not treated as satisfying this section with respect to the eligible employees who have not completed the minimum age and service requirements of section 410(a)(1)(A) unless the plan satisfies the requirements of this section with respect to such eligible employees.

*(4) Satisfying safe harbor contribution requirement under another defined contribution plan.* Safe harbor matching or nonelective contributions may be made to another defined contribution plan under the same rules as § 1.401(k)-3(h)(4). Consequently, each NHCE under the plan providing for

matching contributions must be eligible under the same conditions under the other defined contribution plan and the plan to which the contributions are made must have the same plan year as the plan providing for matching contributions.

*(5) Contributions used only once.* Safe harbor matching or nonelective contributions cannot be used to satisfy the requirements of this section with respect to more than one plan.

*(6) Plan must satisfy ACP with respect to employee contributions.* If the plan provides for employee contributions, in addition to satisfying the requirements of this section, it must also satisfy the ACP test of § 1.401(m)-2. See § 1.401(m)-2(a)(5)(iv) for special rules under which the ACP test is permitted to be performed disregarding some or all matching when this section is satisfied with respect to the matching contributions.

T.D. 9169, 12/28/2004, amend T.D. 9447, 2/23/2009.

PAR. 5. Section 1.401(m)-3 is amended by:

1. Revising paragraph (f)(4)(ii).

2. Revising paragraph (h).

The revisions read as follows:

**Proposed § 1.401(m)-3 Safe harbor requirements.** [*For Preamble, see ¶ 153,107*]

* * * * *

**(f)** * * *

*(4)* * * *

(ii) The plan termination is in connection with a transaction described in section 410(b)(6)(C) or the employer incurs a substantial business hardship, comparable to a substantial business hardship described in section 412(c).

* * * * *

**(h) Permissible reduction or suspension of safe harbor contributions.** *(1) General rule.* (i) Matching contributions. A plan that provides for safe harbor matching contributions intended to satisfy the requirements of paragraph (c) of this section for a plan year will not fail to satisfy the requirements of section 401(m)(2) merely because the plan is amended during the plan year to reduce or suspend safe harbor matching contributions on future elective deferrals and, if applicable, employee contributions provided that—

(A) All eligible employees are provided the supplemental notice in accordance with paragraph (h)(2) of this section;

(B) The reduction or suspension of safe harbor matching contributions is effective no earlier than the later of 30 days after eligible employees are provided the supplemental notice described in paragraph (h)(2) of this section and the date the amendment is adopted;

(C) Eligible employees are given a reasonable opportunity (including a reasonable period after receipt of the supplemental notice) prior to the reduction or suspension of safe harbor matching contributions to change their cash or deferred elections and, if applicable, their employee contribution elections;

(D) The plan is amended to provide that the ACP test will be satisfied for the entire plan year in which the reduction or suspension occurs using the current year testing method described in § 1.401(m)-2(a)(2)(ii); and

(E) The plan satisfies the requirements of this section (other than this paragraph (h)) with respect to amounts deferred through the effective date of the amendment.

(ii) Nonelective contributions. A plan that provides for safe harbor nonelective contributions intended to satisfy the requirements of paragraph (b) of this section will not fail to satisfy the requirements of section 401(m)(2) for the plan year merely because the plan is amended during the plan year to reduce or suspend safe harbor nonelective contributions provided that—

(A) The employer incurs a substantial business hardship (comparable to a substantial business hardship described in section 412(c));

(B) The amendment is adopted after May 18, 2009;

(C) All eligible employees are provided the supplemental notice in accordance with paragraph (h)(2) of this section;

(D) The reduction or suspension of safe harbor nonelective contributions is effective no earlier than the later of 30 days after eligible employees are provided the supplemental notice described in paragraph (h)(2) of this section and the date the amendment is adopted;

(E) Eligible employees are given a reasonable opportunity (including a reasonable period after receipt of the supplemental notice) prior to the reduction or suspension of nonelective contributions to change their cash or deferred elections and, if applicable, their employee contribution elections;

(F) The plan is amended to provide that the ACP test will be satisfied for the entire plan year in which the reduction or suspension occurs using the current year testing method described in § 1.401(m)-2(a)(2)(ii); and

(G) The plan satisfies the requirements of this section (other than this paragraph (h)) with respect to safe harbor compensation paid through the effective date of the amendment.

*(2) Supplemental notice.* The supplemental notice requirement of this paragraph (h)(2) is satisfied if each eligible employee is given a notice that satisfies the requirements of § 1.401(k)-3(g)(2).

**§ 1.401(m)-4 Special rules for mergers, acquisitions and similar events. [Reserved]**

T.D. 9169, 12/28/2004.

**§ 1.401(m)-5 Definitions.**

Unless otherwise provided, the definitions of this section govern for purposes of section 401(m) and the regulations thereunder.

Actual contribution percentage (ACP). Actual contribution percentage or ACP means the ACP of the group of eligible employees as defined in § 1.401(m)-2(a)(2)(i).

Actual contribution percentage (ACP) test. Actual contribution percentage test or ACP test means the test described in § 1.401(m)-2(a)(1).

Actual contribution ratio (ACR). Actual contribution ratio or ACR means the ACR of an eligible employee as defined in § 1.401(m)-2(a)(3).

Actual deferral percentage (ADP) test. Actual deferral percentage test or ADP test means the test described in § 1.401(k)-2(a)(1).

Compensation. Compensation means compensation as defined in section 414(s) and § 1.414(s)-1. The period used to determine an employee's compensation for a plan year must be either the plan year or the calendar year ending within the plan year. Whichever period is selected must be applied uniformly to determine the compensation of every eligible employee under the plan for that plan year. A plan may, however, limit the period taken into account under either method to that portion of the plan year or calendar year in which the employee was an eligible employee, provided that this limit is applied uniformly to all eligible employees under the plan for the plan year. See also section 401(a)(17) and § 1.401(a)(17)-1(c)(1). For this purpose, in case of an HCE whose ACR is determined under § 1.401(m)-2(a)(3)(ii), period of participation includes periods under another plan for which matching contributions or employee contributions are aggregated under § 1.401(m)-2(a)(3)(ii).

Current year testing method. Current year testing method means the testing method under which the applicable year is the current plan year, as described in § 1.401(k)-2(a)(2)(ii) or 1.401(m)-2(a)(2)(ii)

Designated Roth contributions. Designated Roth contributions means designated Roth contributions as defined in § 1.401(k)-1(f)(1).

Elective contributions. Elective contributions means elective contributions as defined in § 1.401(k)-6.

Elective deferrals. Elective deferrals means elective deferrals described in section 402(g)(3).

Eligible employee—(1) General rule. Eligible employee means an employee who is directly or indirectly eligible to make an employee contribution or to receive an allocation of matching contributions (including matching contributions derived from forfeitures) under the plan for all or a portion of the plan year. For example, if an employee must perform purely ministerial or mechanical acts (e.g., formal application for participation or consent to payroll withholding) in order to be eligible to make an employee contribution for a plan year, the employee is an eligible employee for the plan year without regard to whether the employee performs these acts.

(2) Conditions on eligibility. An employee who is unable to make employee contributions or to receive an allocation of matching contributions because the employee has not contributed to another plan is also an eligible employee. By contrast, if an employee must perform additional service (e.g., satisfy a minimum period of service requirement) in order to be eligible to make an employee contribution or to receive an allocation of matching contributions for a plan year, the employee is not an eligible employee for the plan year unless the service is actually performed. An employee who would be eligible to make employee contributions but for a suspension due to a distribution, a loan, or an election not to participate in the plan, is treated as an eligible employee for purposes of section 401(m) for a plan year even though the employee may not make employee contributions or receive an allocation of matching contributions by reason of the suspension. Finally, an employee does not fail to be treated as an eligible employee merely because the employee may receive no additional annual additions because of section 415(c)(1).

(3) Certain one-time elections. An employee is not an eligible employee merely because the employee, no later than the employee's first becoming eligible under any plan or arrangement described in section 219(g)(5)(A) and providing for employee or matching contributions, is given a one-time opportunity to elect, and the employee in fact does elect, not to be eligible to make employee contributions or to receive allocations of matching contributions under the plan or any other plan or arrangement maintained by the employer (including plans not yet established) for the duration of the employee's employment with the employer. In no event is an election made after December 23, 1994, treated as a one-time irrevocable election under this paragraph if the election is made by an employee who previously became eligible under another plan or arrangement (whether or not terminated) of the employer.

Eligible HCE. Eligible HCE means an eligible employee who is an HCE.

Eligible NHCE. Eligible NHCE means an eligible employee who is not an HCE.

Employee. Employee means an employee within the meaning of § 1.410(b)-9.

Employee contributions. Employee contributions means employee contributions as defined in § 1.401(m)-1(a)(3).

Employee stock ownership plan (ESOP). Employee stock ownership plan or ESOP the portion of a plan that is an ESOP within the meaning of § 1.410(b)-7(c)(2).

Employer. Employer means an employer within the meaning of § 1.410(b)-9.

Excess aggregate contributions. Excess aggregate contributions means, with respect to a plan year, the amount of excess aggregate contributions apportioned to an HCE under § 1.401(m)-2(b)(2)(iii).

Excess contributions. Excess contributions means with respect to a plan year, the amount of excess contributions apportioned to an HCE under § 1.401(k)-2(b)(2)(iii).

Excess deferrals. Excess deferrals means excess deferrals as defined in § 1.402(g)-1(e)(3).

Highly compensated employee (HCE). Highly compensated employee or HCE has the meaning provided in section 414(q).

Matching contributions. Matching contribution is defined in § 1.401(m)-1(a)(2).

Nonelective contributions. Nonelective contributions means employer contributions (other than matching contributions) with respect to which the employee may not elect to have the contributions paid to the employee in cash or other benefits instead of being contributed to the plan.

Non-employee stock ownership plan (non-ESOP). Non-employee stock ownership plan or non-ESOP means the portion of a plan that is not an ESOP within the meaning of § 1.410(b)-7(c)(2).

Non-highly compensated employee (NHCE). Non-highly compensated employee or NHCE means an employee who is not an HCE.

Plan. Plan means plan as defined in § 1.401(m)-1(b)(4).

Prior year testing method. Prior year testing method means the testing method under which the applicable year is the prior plan year, as described in § 1.401(k)-2(a)(2)(ii) or 1.401(m)-2(a)(2)(ii)

Qualified matching contributions (QMAC). Qualified matching contributions or QMAC means matching contributions that satisfy the requirements of § 1.401(k)-1(c) and (d) at the time the contribution is made, without regard to whether the contributions are actually taken into account as elective contributions under § 1.401(k)-2(a)(6). See also § 1.401(k)-2(b)(4)(iii) for a rule providing that a matching contribution does not fail to qualify as a QMAC solely because it is forfeitable under section 411(a)(3)(G) because it is a matching contribution with respect to an excess deferral, excess contribution, or excess aggregate contribution.

Qualified nonelective contributions (QNEC). Qualified nonelective contributions or QNEC means employer contributions, other than elective contributions or matching contributions, that satisfy the requirements of § 1.401(k)-1(c) and (d) at the time the contribution is made, without regard to whether the contributions are actually taken into account under the ADP test under § 1.401(k)-2(a)(6) or the ADP test under § 1.401(m)-2(a)(6).

T.D. 9169, 12/28/2004, amend T.D. 9237, 12/30/2005.

PAR. 9.

Section 1.402(a) is amended.

**Proposed § 1.402(a) Statutory provisions; taxability of beneficiary of employees' trust; exempt trust.** [*For Preamble, see ¶ 150,135*]

• ***Caution:*** Proposed section 1.62-1 was finalized by TD 7399, 2/3/76. Proposed sections 1.72-4, 1.72-13, 1.101-2, 1.122-1, 1.402(a)-1, 1.402(e)-2, 1.402(e)-3, 1.403(a)-1, 1.403(a)-2, 1.405-3, 1.652(b)-1, 1.1304-2 and 11.402(e)(4)(B)-1 remain proposed.

* * * * *

**§ 1.402(a)-1 Taxability of beneficiary under a trust which meets the requirements of section 401(a).**

***Caution:*** The Treasury has not yet amended Reg § 1.402(a)-1 to reflect changes made by P.L. 100-647, P.L. 99-514, P.L. 98-397, P.L. 98-369, P.L. 96-608, P.L. 96-222, P.L. 95-30, P.L. 94-455, P.L. 94-267.

**(a) In general.** *(1)* (i) Section 402 relates to the taxation of the beneficiary of an employees' trust. If an employer makes a contribution for the benefit of an employee to a trust described in section 401(a) for the taxable year of the employer which ends within or with a taxable year of the trust for which the trust is exempt under section 501(a), the employee is not required to include such contribution in his income except for the year or years in which such contribution is distributed or made available to him. It is immaterial in the case of contributions to an exempt trust whether the employee's rights in the contributions to the trust are forfeitable or nonforfeitable either at the time the contribution is made to the trust or thereafter.

(ii) The provisions of section 402(a) relate only to a distribution by a trust described in section 401(a) which is exempt under section 501(a) for the taxable year of the trust in which the distribution is made. With two exceptions, the distribution from such an exempt trust when received or made available is taxable to the distributee to the extent provided in section 72 (relating to annuities). First, for taxable years beginning before January 1, 1964, section 72(e)(3) (relating to the treatment of certain lump sums), as in effect before such date, shall not apply to such distributions. For taxable years beginning after December 31, 1963, such distributions may be taken into account in computations under sections 1301 through 1305 (relating to income averaging). Secondly, certain total distributions described in section 402(a)(2) are taxable as long-term capital gains. For the treatment of such total distributions, see subparagraph (6) of this paragraph. Under certain circumstances, an amount representing the unrealized appreciation in the value of the securities of the employer is excludable from gross income for the year of distribution. For the rules relating to such exclusion, see paragraph (b) of this section. Furthermore, the exclusion provided by section 105(d) is applicable to a distribution from a trust described in section 401(a) and exempt under section 501(a) if such distribution constitutes wages or payments in lieu of wages for a period during which an employee is absent from work on account of a personal injury or sickness. See § 1.72-15 for the rules relating to the tax treatment of accident or health benefits received under a plan to which section 72 applies.

(iii) Except as provided in paragraph (b) of this section, a distribution of property by a trust described in section 401(a) and exempt under section 501(a) shall be taken into account by the distributee at its fair market value. In the case of a distribution of a life insurance contract, retirement income contract, endowment contract, or other contract providing life insurance protection, or any interest therein, the policy cash value and all other rights under such contract (including any supplemental agreements thereto and whether or not guaranteed) are included in determining the fair market value of the contract. In addition, in the case of a transfer of property that occurs on or after August 29, 2005 where a trust described in section 401(a) and exempt under section 501(a) transfers property to a plan participant or beneficiary in exchange for consideration and where the fair market value of the property transferred exceeds the value of the consideration, then the excess of the fair market value of the property transferred by the trust over the value of the consideration received by the trust is treated as a distribution to the distributee under the plan for all purposes under the Internal Revenue Code. Where such a transfer occurs before that date, the excess of the fair market value of the property transferred by the trust over the value of the consideration received by the trust is includible in the gross income of the participant or beneficiary under section 61. However, such a transfer of a life insurance contract, retirement income contract, endowment contract, or other contract providing life insurance protection occurring before that date is not treated as a distribution for purposes of applying the requirements of subchapter D of chapter 1 of subtitle A of the Internal Revenue Code.

(iv) If a trust is exempt for the taxable year in which the distribution occurs, but was not so exempt for one or more prior taxable years under section 501(a) (or under section 165(a) of the Internal Revenue Code of 1939 for years to which such section was applicable), the contributions of the employer which were includible in the gross income of the employee for the taxable year when made shall, in accordance with section 72(f), also be treated as part of the consideration paid by the employee.

(v) If the trust is not exempt at the time the distribution is received by or made available to the employee, see section 402(b) and paragraph (b) of § 1.402(b)-1.

(vi) For the treatment of amounts paid to provide medical benefits described in section 401(h) as defined in paragraph (a) of § 1.401-14, see paragraph (h) of § 1.72-15.

*(2)* If a trust described in section 401(a) and exempt under section 501(a) purchases an annuity contract for an employee and distributes it to the employee in a year in which the trust is exempt, and the contract contains a cash surrender value which may be available to an employee by surrendering the contract, such cash surrender value will not be considered income to the employee unless and until the contract is surrendered. For the rule as to nontransferability of annuity contracts issued after 1962, see § 1.401-9(b)(1). For additional requirements regarding distributions of annuity contracts, see, e.g., §§ 1.401(a)-20, Q&A-2, 1.401(a)(31)-1, Q&A-17, and 1.401(a)(9)-6, Q&A-4. However, the distribution of an annuity contract must be treated as a lump sum distribution for purposes of determining the amount of tax under the 10-year averaging rule of section 402(e) (as in effect prior to amendment by the Tax Reform Act of 1986, Public Law 99-514, 100 Stat. 2085). If, however, the contract distributed by such exempt trust is a life insurance contract, retirement income contract, endowment contract, or other contract providing life insurance protection, the fair market value of the contract at the time of distribution must be included in the distributee's income in accordance with the provisions of section 402(a), except to the extent that, within 60 days after the distribution of the contract, all or any portion of such value is irrevocably converted into a contract under which no part of any proceeds payable on death at any time would be excludable under section 101(a) (relating to life insurance proceeds), or the contract is treated as a rollover contribution under section 402(c). If the contract distributed by such trust is a transferable annuity contract, or a retirement income, endowment, or other life insurance contract and such contract is not treated as a rollover contribution under section 402(c), then, notwithstanding the preceding sentence, the fair market value of the contract is includible in the distributee's gross income unless, within such 60 days, such contract is made nontransferable.

*(3)* For the rules applicable to premiums paid by a trust described in section 401(a) and exempt under section 501(a) for the purchase of retirement income, endowment, or other contracts providing life insurance protection payable upon the death of the employee-participant, see paragraph (b) of § 1.72-16.

*(4)* For the rules applicable to the amounts payable by reason of the death of an employee under a contract providing life insurance protection, or an annuity contract, purchased by a trust described in section 401(a) and exempt under section 501(a), see paragraph (c) of § 1.72-16.

*(5)* If pension or annuity payments or other benefits are paid or made available to the beneficiary of a deceased employee or a deceased retired employee by a trust described in section 401(a) which is exempt under section 501(a), such amounts are taxable in accordance with the rules of section 402(a) and this section. In case such amounts are taxable under section 72, the "investment in the contract" shall be determined by reference to the amount contributed by the employee and by applying the applicable rules of sections 72 and 101(b)(2)(D). In case the amounts paid to, or includible in the gross income of, the beneficiaries of the deceased employee or deceased retired employee constitute a distribution to which subparagraph (6) of this paragraph is applicable, the extent to which the distribution is taxable is determined by reference to the contributions of the employee, by reference to any prior distributions which were excludable from gross income as a return of employee contributions, and by applying the applicable rules of sections 72 and 101(b).

*(6)* (i) If the total distributions payable with respect to any employee under a trust described in section 401(a) which in the year of distribution is exempt under section 501(a) are paid to, or includible in the gross income of, the distributee within one taxable year of the distributee on account of the employee's death or other separation from the service, or death after such separation from service, the amount of such distribution, to the extent it exceeds the net amount contributed by the employee, shall be considered a gain from the sale or exchange of a capital asset held for more than six months. The total distributions payable are includible in the gross income of the distributee within one taxable year if they are made available to such distributee and the distributee fails to make a timely election under section 72(h) to receive an annuity in lieu of such total distributions. The "net amount contributed by the employee" is the amount actually contributed by the employee plus any amounts considered to be contributed by the employee under the rules of section 72(f), 101(b), and subparagraph (3) of this paragraph, reduced by any amounts theretofore distributed to him which were excludable from gross income as a return of employee contributions. See, however, paragraph (b) of this section for rules relating to the exclusion of amounts representing net unrealized appreciation in the value of securities of the employer corporation. In addition, all or part of the amount otherwise includible in gross income under this paragraph by a nonresident alien individual in respect of a distribution by the United States under a qualified pension plan may be excludable from gross income under section 402(a)(4). For rules relating to such exclusion, see paragraph (c) of this section. For additional rules relating to the treatment of total distributions described in this subdivision in the case of a nonresident alien individual, see sections 871 and 1441 and the regulations thereunder.

(ii) The term "total distributions payable" means the balance to the credit of an employee which becomes payable to a distributee on account of the employee's death or other separation from the service or on account of his death after separation from the service. Thus, distributions made before a total distribution (for example, annuity payments received by the employee after retirement), will not defeat application of the capital gains treatment with respect to the total distributions received by a beneficiary upon the death of the employee after retirement. However, a distribution on separation from service will not receive capital gains treatment unless it constitutes the total amount in the employee's account at the time of his separation from service. If the total amount in the employee's account at the time of his death or other separation from the service or death after separation from the service is paid or includible in the gross income of the distributee within one taxable year of the distributee, such amount is entitled to the capital gains treatment notwithstanding that in a later taxable year an additional amount, attributable to the last year of service, is credited to the account of the employee and distributed.

(iii) If an employee retires and commences to receive an annuity but subsequently, in some succeeding taxable year, is paid a lump sum in settlement of all future annuity payments, the capital gains treatment does not apply to such lump sum settlement paid during the lifetime of the employee since it is not a payment on account of separation from the service, or death after separation, but is on account of the settlement of future annuity payments.

(iv) If the "total distributions payable" are paid or includible in the gross income of several distributees within one taxable year on account of the employee's death or other separation from the service or on account of his death after separation from the service, the capital gains treatment is applicable. The total distributions payable are paid within one taxable year of the distributees when, for example, a portion of such total is distributed in cash to one distributee and the balance is used to purchase an annuity contract which is distributed to the other distributee. However, if the share of any distributee is not paid or includible in his gross income within the same taxable year in which the shares of the other distributees are paid or includible in their gross income, none of the distributees is entitled to the capital gains treatment, since the total distributions payable are not paid or includible in the distributees' gross income within one taxable year. For example, if the total distributions payable are made available to each of two distributees and one elects to receive his share in cash while the other makes a timely election under section 72(h) to receive his share in installment payments from the trust, the capital gains treatment does not apply to either distributee.

(v) For regulations as to certain plan terminations, see § 1.402(e)-1.

(vi) The term "total distributions payable" does not include United States Retirement Plan Bonds held by a trust to the credit of an employee. Thus, a distribution by a qualified trust may constitute a total distributions payable with respect to an employee even though the trust retains retirement plan bonds registered in the name of such employee. Similarly, the proceeds of a retirement plan bond received as a part of the total amount to the credit of an employee will not be entitled to capital gains treatment. See section 405(e) and paragraph (a)(4) of § 1.405-3.

(vii) For purposes of determining whether the total distributions payable to an employee have been distributed within one taxable year, the term "total distributions payable" includes amounts held by a trust to the credit of an employee which are attributable to contributions on behalf of the employee while he was a self-employed individual in the business with respect to which the plan was established. Thus, a distribution by a qualified trust is not a total distributions payable with respect to an employee if the trust retains amounts which are so attributable.

(viii) The term "total distributions payable" does not include any amount which has been placed in a separate account for the funding of medical benefits described in section 401(h) as defined in paragraph (a) of § 1.401-14. Thus, a distribution by a qualified trust may constitute a total distributions payable with respect to an employee even though the trust retains amounts attributable to the funding of medical benefits described in section 401(h).

*(7)* The capital gains treatment provided by section 402(a)(2) and subparagraph (6) of this paragraph is not applicable to distributions paid to a distributee to the extent such distributions are attributable to contributions made on behalf of an employee while he was a self-employed individual in the business with respect to which the plan was established. For the taxation of such amounts, see § 1.72-18. For the rules for determining the amount attributable to contributions on behalf of an employee while he was self-employed, see paragraphs (b)(4) and (c)(2) of such section.

*(8)* For purposes of this section, the term "employee" includes a self-employed individual who is treated as an employee under section 401(c)(1), and paragraph (b) of § 1.401-10, and the term "employer" means the person treated as the employer of such individual under section 401(c)(4).

**(b) Distributions including securities of the employer corporation.** *(1) In general.* (i) If a trust described in section 401(a) which is exempt under section 501(a) makes a distribution to a distributee, and such distribution includes securities of the employer corporation, the amount of any net unrealized appreciation in such securities shall be excluded from the distributee's income in the year of such distribution to the following extent:

(A) If the distribution constitutes a total distribution to which the regulations of paragraph (a)(6) of this section are applicable, the amount to be excluded is the entire net unrealized appreciation attributable to that part of the total distribution which consists of securities of the employer corporation; and

(B) If the distribution is other than a total distribution to which paragraph (a)(6) of this section is applicable, the amount to be excluded is that portion of the net unrealized appreciation in the securities of the employer corporation which is attributable to the amount considered to be contributed by the employee to the purchase of such securities.

The amount of net unrealized appreciation which is excludable under the regulations of (a) and (b) of this subdivision shall not be included in the basis of the securities in the hands of the distributee at the time of distribution for purposes of determining gain or loss on their subsequent disposition. In the case of a total distribution the amount of net unrealized appreciation which is not included in the basis of the securities in the hands of the distributee at the time of distribution shall be considered as a gain from the sale or exchange of a capital asset held for more than six months to the extent that such appreciation is realized in a subsequent taxable transaction. However, if the net gain realized by the distributee in a subsequent taxable transaction exceeds the amount of the net unrealized appreciation at the time of distribution, such excess shall constitute a long-term or short-term capital gain depending upon the holding period of the securities in the hands of the distributee.

(ii) For purposes of section 402(a) and of this section, the term "securities" means only shares of stock and bonds or debentures issued by a corporation with interest coupons or in registered form, and the term "securities of the employer corporation" includes securities of a parent or subsidiary corporation (as defined in subsections (e) and (f) of section 425) of the employer corporation.

*(2) Determination of net unrealized appreciation.* (i) The amount of net unrealized appreciation in securities of the employer corporation which are distributed by the trust is the excess of the market value of such securities at the time of distribution over the cost or other basis of such securities to the trust. Thus, if a distribution consists in part of securities which have appreciated in value and in part of securities which have depreciated in value, the net unrealized appreciation shall be considered to consist of the net increase in value of all of the securities included in the distribution. For this purpose, two or more distributions made by a trust to a distributee in a single taxable year of the distributee shall be treated as a single distribution.

(ii) For the purpose of determining the net unrealized appreciation on a distributed security of the employer corporation, the cost or other basis of such security to the trust shall be computed in accordance with whichever of the following rules is applicable:

(A) If a security was earmarked for the account of a particular employee at the time it was purchased by or contributed to the trust so that the cost or other basis of such security to the trust is reflected in the account of such employee, such cost or other basis shall be used.

(B) If as of the close of each taxable year of the trust (or other specified period of time not in excess of 12 consecutive calendar months) the trust allocates among the accounts of participating employees all securities acquired by the trust during the period (exclusive of securities unallocated under a plan providing for allocation in whole shares only), the cost or other basis to the trust of any securities allocated as of the close of a particular allocation period shall be the average cost or other basis to the trust of all securities of the same type which were purchased or otherwise acquired by the trust during such allocation period. For purposes of determining the average cost to the trust of securities included in a subsequent allocation, the actual cost to the trust of the securities unallocated as of the close of a prior allocation period shall be deemed to be the average cost or other basis to the trust of securities of the same type allocated as of the close of such prior allocation period.

(C) In a case where neither (a) nor (b) of this subdivision is applicable, if the trust fund, or a specified portion thereof, is invested exclusively in one particular type of security of the employer corporation, and if during the period the distributee participated in the plan none of such securities has been sold except for the purpose of paying benefits under the trust or for the purpose of enabling the trustee to obtain funds with which to exercise rights which have accrued to the trust, the cost or other basis to the trust of all securities distributed to such distributee shall be the total amount credited to the account of such distributee (or such portion thereof as was available for investment in such securities) reduced by the amount available for investment but uninvested on the date of distribution. If at the time of distribution to a particular distributee a portion of the amount credited to his account is forfeited, appropriate adjustment shall be made with respect thereto in determining the cost or other basis to the trust of the securities distributed.

(D) (1) In all other cases, there shall be used the average cost (or other basis) to the trust of all securities of the employer corporation of the type distributed to the distributee which the trust has on hand at the time of the distribution, or which the trust had on hand on a specified inventory date which date does not precede the date of distribution by more than twelve calendar months. If a distribution includes securities of the employer corporation of more than one type, the average cost (or other basis) to the trust of each type of security distributed shall be determined. The average cost to the trust of securities of the employer corporation on hand on a specified inventory date (or on hand at the time of distribution) shall be computed on the basis of their actual cost, considering the securities most recently purchased to be those on hand, or by means of a moving average calculated by subtracting from the total cost of securities on hand immediately preceding a particular sale or distribution an amount computed by multiplying the number of securities sold or distributed by the average cost of all securities on hand preceding such sale or distribution.

(2) These methods of computing average cost may be illustrated by the following examples:

*Example (1).* A, a distributee who makes his income tax returns on the basis of a calendar year, receives on August 1, 1954, in a total distribution, to which paragraph (a)(6) of this section is applicable, ten shares of class D stock of the employer corporation. On July 1, 1954 (the specified inventory date of the trust), the trust had on hand 80 shares of class D stock. The average cost of the 10 shares distributed, on the basis of the actual cost method, is $100 computed as follows:

| Shares | Purchase date | Cost per share | Total cost |
|---|---|---|---|
| 20 | June 24, 1954 | $101 | $2,020 |
| 40 | Jan. 10, 1953 | 102 | 4,080 |
| 20 | Oct. 20, 1952 | 95 | 1,900 |
| 80 | | | 8,000 |

*Example (2).* B, a distributee who makes his income tax returns on the basis of a calendar year, receives on October 31, 1954, in a total distribution, to which paragraph (a)(6) of this section is applicable, 20 shares of class E stock of the employer corporation. The specified inventory date of the trust is the last day of each calendar year. The trust had on hand on December 31, 1952, 1,000 shares of class E stock of the employer corporation. During the calendar year 1953 the trust distributed to four distributees a total of 100 shares of such stock and acquired, through a number of purchases, a total of 120 shares. The average cost of the 20 shares distributed to B, on the basis of the moving average method, is $52 computed as follows:

| | Shares | Total cost | Average cost |
|---|---|---|---|
| On hand Dec. 31, 1952 ........ | 1,000 | $50,000 | $50 |
| Distributed during 1953 at average cost of $50.......... | 100 | 5,000 | ..... |
| | 900 | 45,000 | ..... |
| Purchased during 1953 ......... | 120 | 8,040 | ..... |
| On hand Dec. 31, 1953 ........ | 1,020 | 53,040 | 52 |

(3) *Unrealized appreciation attributable to employee contributions.* In any case in which it is necessary to determine the amount of net unrealized appreciation in securities of the employer corporation which is attributable to contributions made by an employee:

(i) The cost or other basis of the securities to the trust and the amount of net unrealized appreciation shall first be determined in accordance with the regulations in subparagraph (2) of this paragraph;

(ii) The amount contributed by the employee to the purchase of the securities shall be solely the portion of his actual contributions to the trust properly allocable to such securities, and shall not include any part of the increment in the trust fund expended in the purchase of the securities;

(iii) The amount of net unrealized appreciation in the securities distributed which is attributable to the contributions of the employee shall be that proportion of the net unrealized appreciation determined under the regulations of subparagraph (2) of this paragraph which the contributions of the employee properly allocable to such securities bear to the cost or other basis to the trust of the securities;

(iv) If a distribution consists solely of securities of the employer corporation, the contributions of the employee expended in the purchase of such securities shall be allocated to the securities distributed in a manner consistent with the principles set forth in subparagraph (2)(ii)(a), (b), (c), or (d) of this paragraph, whichever is applicable. Thus, the amount of the employee's contribution which can be identified as having been expended in the purchase of a particular security shall be allocated to such security, and the amount of such contribution which cannot be so identified shall be allocated ratably among the securities distributed. If a distribution consists in part of securities of the employer corporation and in part of cash or other property, appropriate allocation of a portion of the employee's contribution to such cash or other property shall be made unless such allocation is inconsistent with the terms of the plan or trust.

(v) The application of this subparagraph may be illustrated by the following example:

*Example.* A trust distributes ten shares of stock issued by the employer corporation each of which has an average cost to the trust of $100, consisting of employee contributions in the amount of $60 and employer contributions in the amount of $40, and on the date of distribution has a fair market value of $180. The portion of the net unrealized appreciation attributable to the contributions of the employee with respect to each of the shares of stock is $48 computed as follows:

| | |
|---|---|
| (1) Value of one share of stock on distribution ...... | $180 |
| (2) Employee contributions ...................... | 60 |
| (3) Employer contributions ...................... | 40 |
| (4) Total contributions ........................ | 100 |
| (5) Net unrealized appreciation ................... | 80 |
| (6) Portion of net unrealized appreciation attributable to employee contributions 60/100 (amount of employee contributions (item 2) over total contributions (item 4) of $80 (item 5)).......... | 48 |

(vi) For the purpose of determining gain or loss to the distributee in the year or years in which any share of stock referred to in the example in subdivision (v) of this subparagraph is sold or otherwise disposed of in a taxable transaction, the basis of each such share in the hands of the distributee at the time of the distribution by the trust will be $132 computed as follows:

| | |
|---|---|
| (a) Employee contributions ...................... | $ 60 |
| (b) Employer contributions (taxable as ordinary income in the year the securities were distributed) ................................ | 40 |
| (c) Portion of net unrealized appreciation attributable to employer contributions (item (5) minus item (6)) (taxable as ordinary income in the year the securities were distributed) .................. | 32 |
| (d) Basis of stock ............................ | 132 |

*(4) Change in exempt status of trust.* For principles applicable in making appropriate adjustments if the trust was not exempt for one or more years before the year of distribution, see paragraph (a) of this section.

**(c) Certain distributions by United States to nonresident alien individuals.** *(1)* This paragraph applies to a distribution—

(i) Which is made by the United States under a pension plan described in section 401(a);

(ii) Which is made in respect of services performed by an employee of the United States; and

(iii) Which is received by, or made available to, a nonresident alien individual (including a nonresident alien individual who is a beneficiary of a deceased employee) during a taxable year beginning after December 31, 1959.

The amount of such a distribution that is includible in the gross income of the nonresident alien individual under section 402(a)(1) or (2) shall not exceed an amount which bears the same ratio to the amount which would be includible in gross income if it were not for this paragraph, as—

(a) The aggregate basic salary paid by the United States to the employee for his services in respect of which the distribution is being made, reduced by the amount of such basic salary which was not includible in the employee's gross income by reason of being from sources without the United States, bears to

(b) The aggregate basic salary paid by the United States to the employee for his services in respect of which the distribution is being made.

See section 402(a)(4). See, also, paragraph (a) of this section for rules relating to the amount that is includible in gross income under section 402(a) (1) or (2) in the case of a distribution under a pension plan described in section 401(a).

*(2)* For purposes of applying section 402(a)(4) and this paragraph to distributions under the Civil Service Retirement Act (5 U.S.C. 2251), the term "basic salary" shall have the meaning provided in section 1(d) of such Act. In applying section 402(a)(4) and this paragraph to distributions under any other qualified pension plan of the United States, such term shall have a similar meaning. Thus, for example, "basic salary" does not, in any case, include bonuses, allowances, or overtime pay.

*(3)* The rules in this paragraph may be illustrated by the following examples:

*Example (1).* A, a retired employee of the United States who performed all of his services for the United States in a foreign country, receives, in respect of such services, a monthly pension of $200 under the Civil Service Retirement Act (a pension plan described in section 401(a)). A received an aggregate basic salary for his services for the United States of $100,000. A was a nonresident alien individual during the whole of his employment with the United States and, therefore, his basic salary from the United States was not includible in his gross income by reason of being from sources without the United States. A would be required, under section 72 but without regard to section 402(a)(4) and this paragraph, to include $60 of each monthly pension payment in his gross income. The amount that is includible in A's gross income under section 402(a)(1) with respect to the monthly payments received during taxable years beginning after December 31, 1959, and while A is a nonresident alien individual, is computed as follows:

| | |
|---|---|
| (i) Amount of distribution includible in gross income under section 72 without regard to section 402(a)(4) ........................ | $60 |
| (ii) Aggregate basic salary for services for United States .................................. | 100,000 |
| (iii) Aggregate basic salary for services for United States reduced by amount of such salary not includible in A's gross income by reason of being from sources without the United States | 0 |
| (iv) Amount includible in A's gross income under section 402(a)(1)(iii) ÷ (ii) × (i), or $0 \ $100,000 × $60) ........................ | 0 |

*Example (2).* B, a retired employee of the United States who performed services for the United States both in a foreign country and in the United States, receives, in respect of such services, a monthly pension of $240 under the Civil Service Retirement Act. B received an aggregate basic salary for his services for the United States of $120,000; $80,000 of which was for his services performed in the United States, and $40,000 of which was for his services performed in the foreign country. B was a nonresident alien individual during the whole of his employment with the United States and, consequently, the $40,000 basic salary for his services performed in the foreign country was not includible in his gross income by reason of being from sources without the United States. B would be required, under section 72 but without regard to section 402(a)(4) and this paragraph, to include $165 of each monthly pension in his gross income. The amount that is includible in B's gross income under section 402(a)(1) with respect to the monthly payments received during taxable years beginning after December 31, 1959, and while B is a nonresident alien individual, is computed as follows:

| | |
|---|---|
| (i) Amount of distribution includible in gross income under section 72 without regard to section 402(a)(4) | $165 |
| (ii) Aggregate basic salary for services for United States | 120,000 |
| (iii) Aggregate basic salary for services for United States reduced by amount of such salary not includible in B's gross income by reason of being from sources without the United States ($120,000 – $40,000) | 80,000 |
| (iv) Amount includible in B's gross income under section 402(a)(1)((iii) ÷ (ii) × (i), or $80,000\$120,000 × $165) | 110 |

**(d) Salary reduction, cash or deferred arrangements.** *(1) Inclusion in income.* Whether a contribution to an exempt trust or plan described in section 401(a) or 403(a) is made by the employer or the employee is determined on the basis of the particular facts and circumstances of each case. Nevertheless, an amount contributed to a plan or trust will, except as otherwise provided under paragraph (d)(2) of this section, be treated as contributed by the employee if it was contributed at the employee's election, even though the election was made before the year in which the amount was earned by the employee or before the year in which the amount became currently available to the employee. Any amount treated as contributed by the employee is includible in the gross income of the employee for the year in which the amount would have been received by the employee but for the election. Thus, for example, amounts contributed to an exempt trust or plan by reason of a salary reduction agreement under a cash or deferred arrangement are treated as received by the employee when they would have been received by the employee but for the election to defer. Accordingly, they are includible in the gross income of the employee for that year (except as provided under paragraph (d)(2) of this section). See § 1.401(k)-1(a)(3)(iv) and (2)(iv) for the meaning of currently available and cash or deferred arrangement, respectively.

*(2) Amounts not included in income.* (i) Qualified cash or deferred arrangement. Elective contributions as defined in § 1.401(k)-6 for a plan year made by an employer on behalf of an employee pursuant to a cash or deferred election under a qualified cash or deferred arrangement, as defined in § 1.401(k)-1(a)(4)(i), are not treated as received by or distributed to the employee or as employee contributions. For plan years beginning after December 31, 1992, whether a cash or deferred election is made under a qualified cash or deferred arrangement is determined without regard to the special rules for certain collectively bargained plans contained in § 1.401(k)-1(a)(5)(iv)(B). As a result, elective contributions under these plans are treated as employee contributions for purposes of this section if the cash or deferred arrangement does not satisfy the actual deferral percentage test of section 401(k)(3) or otherwise fails to be a qualified cash or deferred arrangement.

(ii) Matching contributions. Matching contributions described in § 1.401(m)-1(a)(2) and section 401(m)(4) are not treated as contributed by an employee merely because they are made by the employer as a result of an employee's election.

(iii) Effect of certain one-time elections. Amounts contributed to an exempt plan or trust described in section 401(a) or 403(a) pursuant to the one-time irrevocable employee election to participate in a plan described in § 1.401(k)-1(a)(3)(v) are not treated as contributed by an employee. Similarly, amounts contributed to an exempt plan or trust described in section 401(a) or 403(a) in which self-employed individuals may participate pursuant to the one-time irrevocable election described in § 1.401(k)-1(a)(3)(v)(B) are not treated as contributed by an employee.

*(3) Effective date and transition rules.* (i) Effective date. In the case of a plan or trust that does not include a salary reduction or cash or deferred arrangement in existence on June 27, 1974, this paragraph applies to taxable years ending after that date.

(ii) Transition rule for cash or deferred arrangements in existence on June 27, 1974. (A) General rule. In the case of a plan or trust that includes a salary reduction or a cash or deferred arrangement in existence on June 27, 1974, this paragraph applies to plan years beginning after December 31, 1979 (or, in the case of a pre-ERISA money purchase plan, as defined in § 1.401(k)-6, plan years beginning after July 18, 1984). For plan years beginning prior to January 1, 1980 (or, in the case of a pre-ERISA money purchase plan, plan years beginning before July 19, 1984), the taxable year of inclusion in gross income of the employee of any amount so contributed by the employer to the trust is determined in a manner consistent with Rev. Rul. 56-497, 1956-2 CB 284, Rev. Rul. 63-180, 1963-2 CB 189, and Rev. Rul. 68-89, 1968-1 CB 402.

(B) Meaning of cash or deferred arrangement in existence on June 27, 1974. A cash or deferred arrangement is considered as in existence on June 27, 1974, if, on or before that date, it was reduced to writing and adopted by the employer (including, in the case of a corporate employer, formal approval by the employer's board of directors and, if required, shareholders), even though no amounts had been contributed pursuant to the terms of the arrangement as of that date.

(iii) Reasonable interpretation for plan years beginning after 1979 and before 1992. For plan years beginning after December 31, 1979 (or in the case of a pre-ERISA money purchase plan, plan years beginning after July 18, 1984) and before January 1, 1992, a reasonable interpretation of the rules set forth in section 401(k) (as in effect during those years) may be relied upon to determine whether contributions were made under a qualified cash or deferred arrangement.

(iv) Special rule for collectively bargained plans. For plan years beginning before January 1, 1993, a nonqualified cash or deferred arrangement will be treated as satisfying section 401(k)(3) solely for purposes of paragraph (d)(2)(i) of this section if it is part of a plan (or portion of a plan) that automatically satisfies section 401(a)(4) under § 1.401-1(a)(5)(iv)(B), relating to certain collectively bargained plans.

(v) Special rule for governmental plans. For plan years beginning before the later of January 1, 1996, or 90 days after the opening of the first legislative session beginning on or after January 1, 1996, of the governing body with authority to amend the plan, if that body does not meet continuously, in the case of governmental plans described in section 414(d), a nonqualified cash or deferred arrangement will be treated as satisfying section 401(k)(3) solely for purposes of paragraph (d)(2)(i) of this section if it is part of a plan adopted by a state or local government before May 6, 1986. For purposes of this paragraph (d)(3)(v), the term *governing body with authority to amend the plan* means the legislature, board, commission, council, or other governing body with authority to amend the plan.

T.D. 6203, 9/24/56, amend T.D. 6485, 7/29/60, T.D. 6497, 10/19/60, T.D. 6676, 9/16/63, T.D. 6717, 3/27/64, T.D. 6722, 4/13/64, T.D. 6823, 5/5/65, T.D. 6885, 6/1/66, T.D. 6887, 6/23/66, T.D. 8217, 8/8/88, T.D. 8357, 8/8/91, T.D. 8581, 12/22/94, T.D. 9169, 12/28/2004, T.D. 9223, 8/26/2005.

PARAGRAPH 1. Section 1.402(a)-1(a)(9), as set forth in paragraph 10 of the appendix to the notice of proposed rulemaking of April 30, 1975, is revised by adding a new sentence at the end thereof to read as follows:

**Proposed § 1.402(a)-1 Taxability of beneficiary under a trust which meets the requirements of section 401(a).** [*For Preamble, see ¶ 150,475*]

**(a) In general.** * * *

*(9)* * * * In the case of a lump sum distribution received by or made available to a recipient in a taxable year of the recipient beginning after December 31, 1975, the recipient may elect, in accordance with section 402(e)(4)(L) and § 1.402(e)-14, to treat all calendar years of an employee's active participation in all plans in which the employee has been an active participant as years of active participation after December 31, 1973. If a recipient makes the election, no portion of any distribution received by or made available to the recipient with respect to the employee (whether in the recipient's taxable year for which the election is made, or thereafter) is taxable to the recipient as long-term capital gain under section 402(a)(2) and this subparagraph.

* * * * *

PAR. 10. Section 1.402(a)-1 is amended by revising paragraphs (a)(1)(ii), (a)(1)(iii), (a)(2), (a)(5), (a)(6), (a)(7), (a)(9), and (b)(1) to read as follows:

**Proposed § 1.402(a)-1 Taxability of beneficiary under a trust which meets the requirements of section 401(a).** [*For Preamble, see ¶ 150,135*]

• ***Caution:*** Proposed section 1.62-1 was finalized by TD 7399, 2/3/76. Proposed sections 1.72-4, 1.72-13, 1.101-2, 1.122-1, 1.402(a)-1, 1.402(e)-2, 1.402(e)-3, 1.403(a)-1, 1.403(a)-2, 1.405-3, 1.652(b)-1, 1.1304-2 and 11.402(e)(4)(B)-1 remain proposed.

**(a) In general.** *(1)* * * *

(ii) The provisions of section 402(a) relate only to a distribution by a trust which is described in section 401(a) and which is exempt under section 501(a) for the taxable year of the trust in which the distribution is made. With three exceptions, the distribution from such an exempt trust when received or made available is taxable to the distributee or recipient to the extent provided in section 72 (relating to annuities). First, for taxable years beginning before January 1, 1964, section 72(e)(3) (relating to the treatment of certain lump sums), as in effect before such date, shall not apply to such distributions. For taxable years beginning after December 31, 1963, such distributions may be taken into account in computations under sections 1301 through 1305 (relating to income averaging). For treatment of such total distributions, see (a)(6) of this section. Secondly, if the taxable year ends after December 31, 1969 and begins before January 1, 1974, the portion of the distribution treated as long-term capital gain is subject to the limitation under section 402(a)(5), as in effect on December 31, 1973. Thirdly, for taxable years beginning after December 31, 1973, a certain portion, described in section 402(a)(2), of a lump sum distribution, as defined in section 402(e)(4)(A) is taxable as long-term capital gain and a certain portion, described in section 402(e)(4)(E), may be taxable under section 402(e). For the treatment of such lump sum distributions, see paragraph (a)(9) of this section. Under certain circumstances, an amount representing the unrealized appreciation in the value of the securities of the employer is excludable from gross income for the year of distribution. For the rules relating to such exclusion, see paragraph (b) of this section. Furthermore, the exclusion provided by section 105(d) is applicable to a distribution from a trust described in section 401(a) and exempt under section 501(a) if such distribution constitutes wages or payments in lieu of wages for a period during which an employee is absent from work on account of a personal injury or sickness. See § 1.72-15 for the rules relating to the tax treatment of accident or health benefits received under a plan to which section 72 applies.

(iii) Except as provided in paragraph (b) of this section, a distribution of property (other than an annuity contract) by a trust described in section 401(a) and exempt under section 501(a) shall be taken into account by the recipient at its fair market value. For valuation of an annuity contract, see § 1.402(e)-2(c)(1)(ii)(F).

* * * * *

*(2)* If a trust described in section 401(a) and exempt under section 501(a) purchases an annuity contract for an employee and distributes it to the employee in a year for which the trust is exempt, and the contract contains a cash surrender value which may be available to an employee by surrendering the contract, such cash surrender value will not be considered income to the employee unless and until the contract is surrendered. For the rule as to nontransferability of annuity contracts issued after 1962, see paragraph (b)(1) of § 1.401-9. However, the distribution of an annuity contract must be treated as a lump sum distribution under section 402(e) for purposes of determining the separate tax imposed under section 402(e)(1)(A). If, however, the contract distributed by such exempt trust is a retirement income, endowment, or other life insurance contract and is distributed after October 26, 1956, the entire cash value of such contract at the time of distribution must be included in the distributee's income in accordance with the provisions of section 402(a), except to the extent that, within 60 days after the distribution of such contract, (i) all or any portion of such value is irrevocably converted into a contract under which no part of any proceeds payable on death at any time would be excludable under section 101(a) (relating to life insurance proceeds), or (ii) such contract is treated as a rollover contribution under section 402(a)(5), as in effect after December 31, 1973. If the contract distributed by such trust is a transferable annuity contract issued after 1962, or a retirement income, endow-

ment, or other life insurance contract which is distributed after 1962 (whether or not transferable), then notwithstanding the preceding sentence the entire cash value of the contract is includible in the distributee's gross income, unless within such 60 days such contract is also made nontransferable.

* * * * *

*(5)* If pension or annuity payments or other benefits are paid or made available to the beneficiary of a deceased employee or a deceased retired employee by a trust described in section 401(a) which is exempt under section 501(a), such amounts are taxable in accordance with the rules of section 402(a) and this section. In case such amounts are taxable under section 72, the "investment in the contract" shall be determined by reference to the amount contributed by the employee and by applying the applicable rules of sections 72 and 101(b)(2)(D). In case the amounts paid to, or includible in the gross income of, the beneficiaries of the deceased employee or deceased retired employee constitute a distribution to which paragraph (a)(6) or (9) (whichever applies) of this section is applicable, the extent to which the distribution is taxable is determined by reference to the contributions of the employee, by reference to any prior distributions which were excludable from gross income as a return of employee contributions, and by applying the applicable rules of sections 72 and 101(b).

*(6)* This subparagraph applies in the case of a total distribution made in a taxable year of the distributee or payee ending before January 1, 1970.

(i) If the total distributions payable with respect to any employee under a trust described in section 401(a) which in the year of distribution is exempt under section 501(a) are paid to, or includible in the gross income of, the distributee within one taxable year of the distributee on account of the employee's death or other separation from the service, or death after such separation from service, the amount of such distribution, to the extent it exceeds the net amount contributed by the employee, shall be considered a gain from the sale or exchange of a capital asset held for more than six months. The total distributions payable are includible in the gross income of the distributee within one taxable year if they are made available to such distributee and the distributee fails to make a timely election under section 72(h) to receive an annuity in lieu of such total distributions. The "net amount contributed by the employee" is the amount actually contributed by the employee plus any amounts considered to be contributed by the employee under the rules of section 72(f), 101(b), and paragraph (a)(3) of this section, reduced by any amounts theretofore distributed to him which were excludable from gross income as a return of employee contributions. See, however, paragraph (b) of this section for rules relating to the exclusion of amounts representing net unrealized appreciation in the value of securities of the employer corporation. In addition, all or part of the amount otherwise includible in gross income under this paragraph by a nonresident alien individual in respect of a distribution by the United States under a qualified pension plan may be excludable from gross income under section 402(a)(4). For rules relating to such exclusion, see paragraph (c) of this section. For additional rules relating to the treatment of total distributions described in this subdivision in the case of a nonresident alien individual, see sections 871 and 1441 and the regulations thereunder.

* * * * *

*(7)* The capital gains treatment provided by section 402(a)(2), as in effect for taxable years beginning before January 1, 1974, and paragraph (a)(6) of this section is not applicable to distributions paid during such years to a distributee to the extent such distributions are attributable to contributions made on behalf of an employee while he was a self-employed individual in the business with respect to which the plan was maintained. For the taxation of such amounts, see § 1.72-18. For the rules for determining the amount attributable to contributions on behalf of an employee while he was self-employed, see paragraphs (b)(4) and (c)(2) of such section.

* * * * *

*(9)* For taxable years beginning after December 31, 1973, in the case of a lump sum distribution (as defined in section 402(e)(4)(A)) made to a recipient which is an individual, estate, or trust, so much of the total taxable amount (as defined in section 402(e)(4)(D) and § 1.402(e)-2(d)(2)) of such lump sum distribution as is equal to the product of such total taxable amount multiplied by a fraction—

(i) The numerator of which is the number of calendar years of active participation (as determined under § 1.402(e)-2(d)(3)(ii)) by the employee in such plan before January 1, 1974, and

(ii) The denominator of which is the number of calendar years of active participation (as determined under § 1.402(e)-2(d)(3)(ii)) by the employee in such plan,

shall be treated as gain from the sale or exchange of a capital asset held for more than six months. For purposes of this subparagraph, in the case of an individual who at no time during his participation under the plan is an employee within the meaning of section 401(c)(1), determination of whether any distribution is a lump sum distribution shall be made without regard to the requirement that an election be made under section 402(e)(4)(B) and § 1.402(e)-3.

**(b) Distributions including securities of the employer corporation.** *(1) In general.* (i) If a trust described in section 401(a) which is exempt under section 501(a) makes a distribution to a distributee, and such distribution includes securities of the employer corporation, the amount of any net unrealized appreciation in such securities shall be excluded from the distributee's income in the year of such distribution to the following extent:

(A) If the distribution constitutes a total distribution to which the regulations of paragraph (a)(6) of this section are applicable, or if the distribution would constitute a lump sum distribution as defined in section 402(e)(4)(A) (without regard to section 402(e)(4)(H)), the amount to be excluded is the entire net unrealized appreciation attributable to that part of the distribution which consists of securities of the employer corporation; and

(B) If the distribution is other than a total distribution to which paragraph (a)(6) of this section is applicable, or if the distribution is other than a lump sum distribution as defined in section 402(e)(4)(A) (without regard to section 402(e)(4)(H)), the amount to be excluded is that portion of the net unrealized appreciation in the securities of the employer corporation which is attributable to the amount considered to be contributed by the employee to the purchase of such securities.

The amount of net unrealized appreciation which is excludable under the regulations of (b)(1)(i)(A) and (B) of this shall not be included in the basis of the securities in the hands of the distributee at the time of distribution for purposes of determining gain or loss on their subsequent disposition. Further, the amount of net unrealized appreciation which is not included in the basis of the securities in the hands of the distributee at the time of distribution shall be considered as a gain from the sale or exchange of a capital asset held for more than six months to the extent that such appreciation is realized in a subsequent taxable transaction. However, if the net gain realized by the distributee in a subsequent taxable transaction exceeds the amount of the net unrealized appreciation at the time of distribution, such excess shall constitute a long-term or short-term capital gain depending upon the holding period of the securities in the hands of the distributee.

(ii) (A) For purposes of section 402(a) and of this section, the term "securities" means only shares of stock and bonds or debentures issued by a corporation with interest coupons or in registered form, and the term "securities of the employer corporation" includes securities of a parent or subsidiary corporation (as defined in subsections (e) and (f) of section 425) of the employer corporation.

(B) For purposes of this paragraph, for taxable years beginning after December 31, 1973, the term "distributee" means "recipient".

* * * * *

PAR. 7. Section 1.402(a)-1 is amended by removing the last two sentences of paragraph (a)(1)(ii) and adding a new sentence in their place and by adding a new paragraph (e) to read as follows:

**Proposed § 1.402(a)-1 Taxability of beneficiary under a trust which meets the requirements of section 401(a).** [*For Preamble, see ¶ 152,901*]

**(a)** * * *

*(1)*

(i) * * *

(ii) * * * Paragraph (e) of this section provides rules relating to use of a qualified pension, annuity, profit-sharing, or stock bonus plan to provide accident or health benefits or coverage otherwise described in section 104, 105, or 106.

* * * * *

**(e) Medical, accident, etc. benefits paid from a qualified pension, annuity, profit-sharing, or stock bonus plan.** *(1) Payment of premiums.*

(i) General rule. The payment of premiums from a qualified trust for accident or health insurance, including a qualified long-term care insurance contract under section 7702B, constitutes a distribution under section 402(a) to the participant against whose benefit the premium is charged. The amount of the distribution equals the amount of the premium charged against the participant's benefits under the plan. If a defined contribution plan pays these premiums from a current year contribution or forfeiture that has not been allocated to a participant's account, then the amount of the premium for each participant will be treated as first being allocated to the participant and then charged against the participant's benefits under the plan, so that the amount of the distribution is treated in the same manner as determined under the preceding sentence. Except as described in paragraphs (e)(2) and (3) of this section, a distribution described in this paragraph (e)(1) is not excludable from gross income.

(ii) Treatment of amounts received through accident or health insurance. To the extent that the premium for accident or health insurance constitutes a distribution under this paragraph (e)(1), amounts received through accident or health insurance are neither attributable to contributions by the employer which are not includible in the gross income of the employee nor are such amounts paid by the employer. Accordingly, amounts received through the accident or health insurance for personal injuries or sickness are excludable from gross income under section 104(a)(3) and are not treated as distributions from the plan. If amounts received through accident or health insurance are paid to the plan instead of the employee, these amounts are treated as having been paid to the employee and then contributed by the employee to the plan (and these amounts must satisfy the qualification requirements applicable to employee contributions).

*(2) Medical benefits for retired employees provided under an account described in section 401(h).* The payment of medical benefits described in section 401(h) under a pension or annuity plan is treated in the same manner as a payment of accident or health benefits attributable to employer contributions, or employer-provided coverage under an accident or health plan. See § 1.401-14(a) for the definition of medical benefits described in section 401(h). Accordingly, amounts applied for the payment of accident or health benefits, or for the payment of accident or health coverage, from a section 401(h) account are not includible in the gross income of the participant on whose behalf such contributions are made to the extent they are excludible from gross income under section 104, 105, or 106.

*(3) Distributions to eligible retired public safety officers.* See section 402(l) for a limited exclusion from gross income for distributions used to pay for certain accident or health premiums (including premiums for qualified long-term care insurance contracts). This limited exclusion applies to eligible retired public safety officers, as defined in section 402(l)(4)(B).

*(4) Effect of making a distribution of insurance premiums on qualification.* See § 1.401-1(b)(1) for rules concerning the types and amount of medical coverage and benefits that are permitted to be provided under a plan that is part of a trust described in section 401(a). For example, § 1.401-1(b)(1)(ii) provides that a profit-sharing plan is primarily a plan of deferred compensation, but the amounts allocated to the account of a participant may be used to provide incidental accident or health insurance for the participant and the participant's family. See also, section 401(k)(2)(B) for certain restrictions on the distribution of elective contributions.

*(5) Application of this paragraph (e).* This paragraph (e) applies to the payment of premiums charged against the benefits of a beneficiary or an alternate payee in the same manner as the payment of premiums charged against the account of a participant.

*(6) Example.* The provisions of this paragraph (e) are illustrated by the following example:

*Example.* (i) Facts. Employer sponsors a profit-sharing plan qualified under section 401(a). The plan provides solely for non-elective employer profit-sharing contributions. The plan's trustee enters into a contract with a third-party insurance carrier to provide health insurance for certain plan participants. The insurance policy provides for the payment of medical expenses incurred by those participants. The plan limits the amounts used to provide medical benefits with respect to a participant to 25 percent of the funds held in the participant's account. The trustee makes monthly payments of $1,000 to pay the premiums due for Participant A's health insurance. The trustee also reduces Participant A's account balance by $1,000 at the time of each premium payment. In June of a year, Participant A is admitted to the hospital for covered medical care, and in July of the same year, the health insurer pays the hospital $5,000 for the medical care provided to Participant A in June.

(ii) Conclusion. Under paragraph (e)(1) of this section, each of the trustee's payments of $1,000 constitutes a distribution under section 402(a) to Participant A on the date of each payment. To the extent provided under section 213, the amount of these distributions constitutes payments for medical care. The $5,000 payment to the hospital is excludable from Participant A's gross income under section 104(a)(3) and is not treated as a distribution from the plan.

### § 1.402(a)(5)-1T Rollovers of partial distributions from qualified trusts and annuities (temporary).

***Caution:*** The Treasury has not yet amended Reg § 1.402(a)(5)-1T to reflect changes made by P.L. 100-647, P.L. 99-514, P.L. 99-272.

Q-1. Can an employee or the surviving spouse of a deceased employee roll over to an individual retirement account or annuity, described in section 408(a) or (b), the taxable portion of a partial distribution from a qualified trust described in section 401(a), a qualified plan described in section 403(a), or a tax-sheltered annuity contract under section 403(b)?

A-1. Yes. For distributions made after July 18, 1984, the taxable portion of a partial distribution may be rolled over within 60 days of the distribution to an individual retirement account or annuity.

Q-2. Are there special requirements applicable to rollovers of partial distributions?

A-2. Yes. Section 402(a)(5)(D)(i) specifies that no part of a partial distribution may be rolled over unless the distribution is equal to at least 50 percent of the balance to the credit of the employee in the contract or plan immediately before the distribution, and the distribution is not one of a series of periodic payments. For purposes of this section, the balance to the credit of an employee does not include any accumulated deductible employee contributions (within the meaning of section 72(o)). In addition, in calculating the balance to the credit for purposes of the 50 percent test, qualified plans are not to be aggregated with other qualified plans and tax-sheltered annuity contracts are not to be aggregated with other tax-sheltered annuity contracts. Also, in applying the 50 percent test to a surviving spouse, the balance to the credit is the maximum amount the spouse is entitled to receive under the plan or contract, rather than the total balance to the credit of the employee. The rollover of a partial distribution may result in adverse tax consequences; see section 402(a)(5)(D)(iii) and (iv).

Q-3. Are there any other requirements applicable to rollovers of partial distribution?

A-3. Yes. Section 402(a)(5)(D)(i)(III) requires the employee to elect, in conformance with Treasury regulations, to treat a contribution of a partial distribution to an IRA as a rollover contribution. An election is made by designating, in writing, to the trustee or issuer of the IRA at the time of the contribution that the contribution is to be treated as a rollover contribution. This requirement of a written designation to the trustee or issuer of the IRA is effective for contributions paid to the trustee or issuer of the IRA after March 20, 1986. For contributions paid to the trustee or issuer before March 21, 1986, an election is made by computing the individual's income tax liability on the income tax return for the taxable year in which the distribution occurs in a manner consistent with not including the distribution (or portion thereof) in gross income. Both such elections are irrevocable, except that an election made on an income tax return filed before March 21, 1986 is revocable.

Q-4. Does the election requirement apply to rollovers of qualified total distributions or rollover contributions described in section 402(a) (5) or (7), 403(a)(4), 403(b)(8), 405(d)(3), or 408(d)(3) to individual retirement accounts and annuities (IRAs)?

A-4. Yes. No amounts may be treated as a rollover contribution to an IRA under section 402(a)(5), 402(a)(7), 403(a)(4), 403(b)(8), 405(d)(3) (as amended by section 491(c) of the TRA of 1984), or 408(d)(3) unless the requirements described in Q&A-3 of this section are satisfied. Thus, once any portion of a total distribution is irrevocably designated as a rollover contribution, such distribution is not taxable under section 402 or 403 and therefore, is not eligible for the special capital gains and separate tax treatment under section 402(a) and (e). Election requirements for rollover contributions to IRAs described in this Q&A-4 are subject to the same effective date rules set forth in Q&A-3.

---

T.D. 8073, 1/29/86.

---

### § 1.402(b)-1 Treatment of beneficiary of a trust not exempt under section 501(a).

***Caution:*** The Treasury has not yet amended Reg § 1.402(b)-1 to reflect changes made by P.L. 100-647, P.L. 99-514.

**(a) Taxation by reason of employer contributions made after August 1, 1969.** *(1) Taxation of contributions.* Section 402(b) provides rules for taxing an employee on contributions made on his behalf by an employer to an employees' trust that is not exempt under section 501(a). In general, any such contributions made after August 1, 1969, during a taxable year of the employer which ends within or with a taxable year of the trust for which it is not so exempt shall be included as compensation in the gross income of the employee for his taxable year during which the contribution is made, but only to the extent that the employee's interest in such contribution is substantially vested at the time the contribution is made. The preceding sentence does not apply to contracts referred to in the transitional rule of paragraph (d)(1)(ii) or (iii) of this section. For the definition of the terms "substantially vested" and "substantially nonvested" see § 1.83-3(b).

*(2) Determination of amount of employer contributions.* If, for an employee, the actual amount of employer contributions referred to in paragraph (a)(1) of this section for any taxable year of the employee is not determinable or for any other reason is not known, then, except as set forth in rules prescribed by the Commissioner in revenue rulings, notices, or other guidance published in the Internal Revenue Bulletin (see § 601.601(d)(2)(ii)(b) of this chapter), such amount shall be either—

(i) The excess of—

(A) The amount determined as of the end of such taxable year in accordance with the formula described in § 1.403(b)-1(d)(4), as it appeared in the April 1, 2006, edition of 26 CFR Part 1; over

(B) The amount determined as of the end of the prior taxable year in accordance with the formula described in paragraph (a)(2)(i)(A) of this section; or

(ii) The amount determined under any other method utilizing recognized actuarial principles that are consistent with the provisions of the plan under which such contributions are made and the method adopted by the employer for funding the benefits under the plan.

**(b) Taxability of employee when rights under nonexempt trust change from nonvested to vested.** *(1) In general.* If rights of an employee under a trust become substantially vested during a taxable year of the employee (ending after August 1, 1969), and a taxable year of the trust for which it is not exempt under section 501(a) ends with or within such year, the value of the employee's interest in the trust on the date of such change shall be included in his gross income for such taxable year, to the extent provided in paragraph (b)(3) of this section. When an employees' trust that was exempt under section 501(a) ceases to be so exempt, an employee shall include in his gross income only amounts contributed to the trust during a taxable year of the employer that ends within or with a taxable year of the trust in which it is not so exempt (to the same extent as if the trust had not been so exempt in all prior taxable years).

*(2) Value of an employee's interest in a trust.* (i) For purposes of this section, the term "the value of an employee's interest in a trust" means the amount of the employee's beneficial interest in the net fair market value of all the assets in the trust as of any date on which some or all of the employee's interest in the trust becomes substantially vested. The net fair market value of all the assets in the trust is the total amount of the fair market values (determined without regard to any lapse restriction, as defined in § 1.83-3(h)) of all the assets in the trust, less the amount of all the liabilities (including taxes) to which such assets are subject or which the trust has assumed (other than the rights of any employee in such assets), as of the date on which some or all of the employee's interest in the trust becomes substantially vested.

(ii) If a separate account in a trust for the benefit of two or more employees is not maintained for each employee, the value of the employee's interest in such trust is determined in accordance with rules prescribed by the Commissioner under the authority in paragraph (a)(2) of this section.

(iii) If there is no valuation of a nonexempt trust's assets on the date of the change referred to in paragraph (b)(1) of this section, the value of an employee's interest in such trust is determined by taking the weighted average of the values on the nearest valuation dates occurring before and after the date of such change. The average is to be determined in the manner described in § 20.2031-2(b)(1).

*(3) Extent to which value of an employee's interest is includible in gross income.* For purposes of paragraph (b)(1) of this section, there shall be included in the gross income of the employee for his taxable year in which his rights under the trust become substantially vested only that portion of the value of his interest in the trust that is attributable to contributions made by the employer after August 1, 1969. However, the preceding sentence shall not apply—

(i) To the extent such value is attributable to a contribution made on the date of such change, and

(ii) To the extent such value is attributable to contributions described in paragraph (d)(1)(ii) or (iii) of this section (relating to contributions made pursuant to a binding contract entered into before April 22, 1969).

For purposes of this paragraph (3), if the value of an employee's interest in a trust which is attributable to contributions made by the employer after August 1, 1969, is not known, it shall be deemed to be an amount which bears the same ratio to the value of the employee's interest as the contributions made by the employer after such date bear to the total contributions made by the employer.

*(4) Partial vesting.* For purposes of paragraph (b)(1) of this section, if only part of an employee's interest in the trust becomes substantially vested during any taxable year, then only the corresponding part of the value of the employee's interest in such trust is includible in his gross income for such year. In such a case, it is first necessary to compute, under the rules in paragraphs (b)(1) and (2) of this section, the amount that would be includible if his entire interest had changed to a substantially vested interest during such year. The amount that is includible under this paragraph (4) is the amount determined under the preceding sentence multiplied by the percent of the employee's interest which became substantially vested during the taxable year.

*(5) Basis.* The basis of any employee's interest in a trust to which this section applies shall be increased by the amount included in his gross income under this section.

*(6) Treatment as owner of trust.* In general, a beneficiary of a trust to which this section applies may not be considered to be the owner under subpart E, part I, subchapter J, chapter I of the Code of any portion of such trust which is attributable to contributions to such trust made by the employer after August 1, 1969, or to incidental contributions made by the employee after such date. However, where contributions made by the employee are not incidental when compared to contributions made by the employer, such beneficiary shall be considered to be the owner of the portion of the trust attributable to contributions made by the employee, if the applicable requirements of such subpart E are satisfied. For purposes of this paragraph (6), contributions made by an employee are not incidental when compared to contributions made by the employer if the employee's total contributions as of any date exceed the employer's total contributions on behalf of the employee as of such date.

*(7) Example.* The provisions in this paragraph may be illustrated by the following example:

*Example.* On January 1, 1968 M corporation establishes an employees' trust, which is not exempt under section 501(a), for some of its employees, including A, reserving the right to discontinue contributions at any time. M corporation contributes $5,000 on A's behalf to the trust on February 1, 1968. At the time of contribution 50 percent of A's interest was substantially vested. On January 1, 1971, and January 1, 1974, M corporation makes additional $5,000 contributions to the trust on A's behalf. A's interest in the trust changed from a 50 percent substantially vested interest to a 100 percent substantially vested interest in the trust on December 31, 1974. Assume that the value of A's interest in the trust on December 31, 1974, which is attributable to employer contributions made after August 1, 1969, is calculated to be $11,000 under paragraph (b)(3) of this section. The amount includible in A's gross income for 1971 and 1974 is computed as follows:

1971

(i) Amount of M corporation's contribution made on January 1, 1971, to the trust which is includible in A's gross income under paragraph (b)(1) of this section (50 percent substantially vested interest in the trust times $5,000 contribution)—$2,500.

1974

(i) Amount of M corporation's contribution made on January 1, 1974, to the trust which is includible in A's gross income under paragraph (b)(1) of this section (50 percent substantially vested interest in the trust times $5,000 contribution)—$2,500.

(ii) Amount which would have been includible if A's entire interest had changed to a substantially vested interest (value of employee's interest in the trust attributable to employer contributions made after August 1, 1969)— $11,000.

(iii) Percent of A's interest that became substantially vested on December 31, 1974—50 percent.

(iv) Amount includible in A's gross income for 1974 in respect of his percentage change from a substantially nonvested to a substantially vested interest in the trust (50 percent of $11,000)—$5,500.

(v) Total amount includible in A's gross income for 1974 ((i) plus (iv))—$8,000.

**(c) Taxation of distributions from trust not exempt under section 501(a).** *(1) In general.* Any amount actually distributed or made available to any distributee by an employees' trust in a taxable year in which it is not exempt under section 501(a) shall be taxable under section 72 (relating to annuities) to the distributee in the taxable year in which it is so distributed or made available. For taxable years beginning after December 31, 1963, such amounts may be taken into account in computations under sections 1301 through 1305 (relating to income averaging). If, for example, the distribution from such a trust consists of an annuity contract, the amount of the distribution shall be considered to be the entire value of the contract at the time of distribution. Such value is includible in the gross income of the distributee to the extent that such value exceeds the investment in the contract, determined by applying sections 72 and 101(b). The distributions by such a trust shall be taxed as provided in section 72 whether or not the employee's rights to the contributions become substantially vested beforehand. For rules relating to the treatment of employer contributions to a nonexempt trust as part of the consideration paid by the employee, see section 72(f). For rules relating to the treatment of the limited exclusion allowable under section 101(b)(2)(D) as additional consideration paid by the employee, see the regulations under that section.

*(2) Distributions before annuity starting date.* Any amount distributed or made available to any distributee before the annuity starting date (as defined in section 72(c)(4)) by an employees' trust in a taxable year in which it is not exempt under section 501(a) shall be treated as distributed in the following order—

(i) First, from that portion of the employee's interest in the trust attributable to contributions made by the employer after August 1, 1969 (other than those referred to in paragraph (d)(1)(ii) or (iii) of this section) that has not been previously includible in the employee's gross income, to the extent that such a distribution is permitted under the trust (or the plan of which the trust is a part);

(ii) Second, from that portion of the employee's interest in the trust attributable to contributions made by the employer on or before August 1, 1969 (or contributions referred to in paragraph (d)(1)(ii) or (iii) of this section);

(iii) Third, from the remaining portion of the employee's interest in the trust attributable to contributions made by the employer.

If the employee has made contributions to the trust, amounts attributable thereto shall be treated as distributed prior to any amounts attributable to the employer's contributions, to the extent provided by the trust (or the plan of which the trust is a part). However, the portion of such amounts attributable to income earned on the employee's contributions made after August 1, 1969, shall be treated as distributed prior to any return of such contributions.

**(d) Taxation by reason of employer contributions made on or before August 1, 1969.** *(1)* Except as provided in section 402(d) (relating to taxable years beginning before January 1, 1977), any contribution to a trust made by an employer on behalf of an employee—

(i) On or before August 1, 1969, or

(ii) After such date, pursuant to a binding contract (as defined in § 1.83-3(b)(2)) entered into before April 22, 1969, or

(iii) After August 1, 1969, pursuant to a written plan in which the employee participated on April 22, 1969, and under which the obligation of the employer on such date was essentially the same as under a binding written contract, during a taxable year of the employer which ends within or with a taxable year of the trust for which the trust is not exempt under section 501(a) shall be included in income of the employee for his taxable year during which the contribution is made, if the employee's beneficial interest in the contribution is nonforfeitable at the time the contribution is made. If the employee's beneficial interest in the contribution is forfeitable at the time the contribution is made, even though his interest becomes nonforfeitable later the amount of such contribution is not required to be included in the income of the employee at the time his interest becomes nonforfeitable.

*(2)* (i) An employee's beneficial interest in the contribution is nonforfeitable, within the meaning of sections 402(b), 403(c), and 404(a)(5) prior to the amendments made thereto by the Tax Reform Act of 1969 and section 403(b), at the time the contribution is made if there is no contingency under the plan that may cause the employee to lose his rights in the contribution. Similarly, an employee's rights under an annuity contract purchased for him by his employer change from forfeitable to nonforfeitable rights within the meaning of section 403(d) prior to the repeal thereof by the Tax Reform Act of 1969 at that time when, for the first time, there is no contingency which may cause the employee to lose his rights under the contract. For example, if under the terms of a pension plan, an employee upon termination of his services before the retirement date, whether voluntarily or involuntarily, is entitled to a deferred annuity contract to be purchased with the employer's contributions made on his behalf, or is entitled to annuity payments which the trustee is obligated to make under the terms of the trust instrument based on the contributions made by the employer on his behalf, the employee's beneficial interest in such contributions is nonforfeitable.

(ii) On the other hand, if, under the terms of a pension plan, an employee will lose the right to any annuity purchased from, or to be provided by, contributions made by the employer if his services should be terminated before retirement, his beneficial interest in such contributions is forfeitable.

(iii) The mere fact that an employee may not live to the retirement date, or may live only a short period after the retirement date, and may not be able to enjoy the receipt of annuity or pension payments, does not make his beneficial interest in the contributions made by the employer on his behalf forfeitable. If the employer's contributions have been irrevocably applied to purchase an annuity contract for the employee, or if the trustee is obligated to use the employer's contributions to provide an annuity for the employee provided only that the employee is alive on the dates the annuity payments are due, the employee's rights in the employer's contributions are nonforfeitable.

T.D. 6203, 9/24/56, amend T.D. 6783, 12/23/64, T.D. 6885, 6/1/66, T.D. 7554, 7/21/78, T.D. 9340, 7/23/2007.

### § 1.402(c)-1 Taxability of beneficiary of certain foreign situs trusts.

Section 402(c) has the effect of treating, for purposes of section 402, the distributions from a trust which at the time of the distribution is located outside the United States in the same manner as distributions from a trust which is located in the United States. If the trust would qualify for exemption from tax under section 501(a) except for the fact that it fails to comply with the provisions of paragraph (a)(3)(i) of § 1.401-1, which restricts qualification to trusts created or organized in the United States and maintained here, section 402(a) and § 1.402(a)-1 are applicable to the distributions from such a trust. Thus, for example, a total distribution from such a trust is entitled to the long-term capital gains treatment of section 402(a)(2), except in the case of a nonresident alien individual (see sections 871 and 1441 and the regulations thereunder). However, if the plan fails to meet any requirement of section 401 and the regulations thereunder in addition to paragraph (a)(3)(i) of § 1.401-1, section 402(b) and § 1.402(b)-1 are applicable to the distributions from such a trust.

T.D. 6203, 9/24/56.

### § 1.402(c)-2 Eligible rollover distributions; questions and answers.

***Caution:*** The Treasury has not yet amended Reg § 1.402(c)-2 to reflect changes made by P.L. 107-16, P.L. 105-206, P.L. 104-188.

The following questions and answers relate to the rollover rules under section 402(c) of the Internal Revenue Code of 1986, as added by sections 521 and 522 of the Unemployment Compensation Amendments of 1992, Public Law 102-318, 106 Stat. 290 (UCA). For additional UCA guidance under sections 401(a)(31), 402(f), 403(b)(8) and (10), and 3405(c), see §§ 1.401(a)(31)-1, 1.402(f)-1, and 1.403(b)-7(b), and § 31.3405(c)-1 of this chapter, respectively.

*List of Questions*

Q-1. What is the rule regarding distributions that may be rolled over to an eligible retirement plan?

Q-2. What is an *eligible retirement plan* and a *qualified plan*?

Q-3. What is an *eligible rollover distribution*?

Q-4. Are there other amounts that are not eligible rollover distributions?

Q-5. For purposes of determining whether a distribution is an eligible rollover distribution, how is it determined whether a series of payments is a series of substantially equal periodic payments over a period specified in section 402(c)(4)(A)?

Q-6. What types of variations in the amount of a payment cause the payment to be independent of a series of substantially equal periodic payments and thus not part of the series?

Q-7. When is a distribution from a plan a required minimum distribution under section 401(a)(9)?

Q-8. How are amounts that are not includible in gross income allocated for purposes of determining the required minimum distribution?

Q-9. What is a distribution of a plan loan offset amount and is it an eligible rollover distribution?

Q-10. What is a qualified plan distributed annuity contract, and is an amount paid under such a contract a distribution of the balance to the credit of the employee in a qualified plan for purposes of section 402(c)?

Q-11. If an eligible rollover distribution is paid to an employee, and the employee contributes all or part of the eligible rollover distribution to an eligible retirement plan within 60 days, is the amount contributed not currently includible in gross income?

Q-12. How does section 402(c) apply to a distributee who is not the employee?

Q-13. Must an employee's (or spousal distributee's) election to treat a contribution of an eligible rollover distribution to an individual retirement plan as a rollover contribution be irrevocable?

Q-14. How is the $5,000 death benefit exclusion under section 101(b) treated for purposes of determining the amount that is an eligible rollover distribution?

Q-15. May an employee (or spousal distributee) roll over more than the plan administrator determines to be an eligible rollover distribution using an assumption described in § 1.401(a)(31)-1, Q&A-18?

Q-16. Is a rollover from a qualified plan to an individual retirement account or individual retirement annuity treated as a rollover contribution for purposes of the one-year look-back rollover limitation of section 408(d)(3)(B)?

Questions and Answers

Q-1. What is the rule regarding distributions that may be rolled over to an eligible retirement plan?

A-1. **(a) General rule.** Under section 402(c), as added by UCA, any portion of a distribution from a qualified plan that is an eligible rollover distribution described in section 402(c)(4) may be rolled over to an eligible retirement plan described in section 402(c)(8)(B). For purposes of section 402(c) and this section, a rollover is either a direct rollover as described in § 1.401(a)(31)-1, Q&A-3 or a contribution of an eligible rollover distribution to an eligible retirement plan that satisfies the time period requirement in section 402(c)(3) and Q&A-11 of this section and the designation requirement described in Q&A-13 of this section. See Q&A-2 of this section for the definition of an eligible retirement plan and a qualified plan.

**(b) Related Internal Revenue Code provisions.** *(1) Direct rollover option.* Section 401(a)(31), added by UCA, requires qualified plans to provide a distributee of an eligible rollover distribution the option to elect to have the distribution paid directly to an eligible retirement plan in a direct rollover. See § 1.401(a)(31)-1 for further guidance concerning this direct rollover option.

*(2) Notice requirement.* Section 402(f) requires the plan administrator of a qualified plan to provide, within a reasonable time before making an eligible rollover distribution, a written explanation to the distributee of the distributee's right to elect a direct rollover and the withholding consequences of not making that election. The explanation also is required to provide certain other relevant information relating to the taxation of distributions. See § 1.402(f)-1 for guidance concerning the written explanation required under section 402(f).

*(3) Mandatory income tax withholding.* If a distributee of an eligible rollover distribution does not elect to have the eligible rollover distribution paid directly from the plan to an eligible retirement plan in a direct rollover under section 401(a)(31), the eligible rollover distribution is subject to 20-

percent income tax withholding under section 3405(c). See § 31.3405(c)-1 of this chapter for provisions relating to the withholding requirements applicable to eligible rollover distributions.

*(4) Section 403(b) annuities.* See § 1.403(b)-7(b) for guidance concerning the direct rollover requirements for distributions from annuities described in section 403(b).

**(c) Effective date.** *(1) Statutory effective date.* Section 402(c), added by UCA, applies to eligible rollover distributions made on or after January 1, 1993, even if the event giving rise to the distribution occurred on or before January 1, 1993 (e.g. termination of the employee's employment with the employer maintaining the plan before January 1, 1993), and even if the eligible rollover distribution is part of a series of payments that began before January 1, 1993.

*(2) Regulatory effective date.* This section applies to any distribution made on or after October 19, 1995. For eligible rollover distributions made on or after January 1, 1993 and before October 19, 1995, § 1.402(c)-2T (as it appeared in the April 1, 1995 edition of 26 CFR part 1), applies. However, for any distribution made on or after January 1, 1993 but before October 19, 1995, any or all of the provisions of this section may be substituted for the corresponding provisions of § 1.402(c)-2T, if any.

Q-2. What is an *eligible retirement plan* and a *qualified plan*?

A-2. An eligible retirement plan, under section 402(c)(8)(B), means a qualified plan or an individual retirement plan. For purposes of section 402(c) and this section, a qualified plan is an employees' trust described in section 401(a) which is exempt from tax under section 501(a) or an annuity plan described in section 403(a). An individual retirement plan is an individual retirement account described in section 408(a) or an individual retirement annuity (other than an endowment contract) described in section 408(b).

Q-3. What is an *eligible rollover distribution*?

A-3. **(a) General rule.** Unless specifically excluded, an eligible rollover distribution means any distribution to an employee (or to a spousal distributee described in Q&A-12(a) of this section) of all or any portion of the balance to the credit of the employee in a qualified plan. Thus, except as specifically provided in Q&A-4(b) of this section, any amount distributed to an employee (or such a spousal distributee) from a qualified plan is an eligible rollover distribution, regardless of whether it is a distribution of a benefit that is protected under section 411(d)(6).

**(b) Exceptions.** An eligible rollover distribution does not include the following:

(1) Any distribution that is one of a series of substantially equal periodic payments made (not less frequently than annually) over any one of the following periods—

(i) The life of the employee (or the joint lives of the employee and the employee's designated beneficiary);

(ii) The life expectancy of the employee (or the joint life and last survivor expectancy of the employee and the employee's designated beneficiary); or

(iii) A specified period of ten years or more;

(2) Any distribution to the extent the distribution is a required minimum distribution under section 401(a)(9); or

(3) The portion of any distribution that is not includible in gross income (determined without regard to the exclusion for net unrealized appreciation described in section 402(e)(4)). Thus, for example, an eligible rollover distribution does not include the portion of any distribution that is excludible from gross income under section 72 as a return of the employee's investment in the contract (e.g., a return of the employee's after-tax contributions), but does include net unrealized appreciation.

Q-4. Are there other amounts that are not eligible rollover distributions?

A-4. Yes. The following amounts are not eligible rollover distributions:

(a) Elective deferrals (as defined in section 402(g)(3)) and employee contributions that, pursuant to rules prescribed by the Commissioner in revenue rulings, notices, or other guidance published in the Internal Revenue Bulletin (see § 601.601(d)(2) of this chapter), are returned to the employee (together with the income allocable thereto) in order to comply with the section 415 limitations.

(b) Corrective distributions of excess deferrals as described in § 1.402(g)-1(e)(3), together with the income allocable to these corrective distributions.

(c) Corrective distributions of excess contributions under a qualified cash or deferred arrangement described in § 1.401(k)-2(b)(2) and excess aggregate contributions described in § 1.401(m)-2(b)(2), together with the income allocable to these distributions.

(d) Loans that are treated as deemed distributions pursuant to section 72(p).

(e) Dividends paid on employer securities as described in section 404(k).

(f) The costs of life insurance coverage (P.S. 58 costs).

(g)Prohibited allocations that are treated as deemed distributions pursuant to section 409(p).

(h) A distribution that is a permissible withdrawal from an eligible automatic contribution arrangement within the meaning of section 414(w).

(i) [Reserved]

(j) Similar items designated by the Commissioner in revenue rulings, notices, and other guidance published in the Internal Revenue Bulletin. See § 601.601(d)(2)(ii)(b) of this chapter.

Q-5. For purposes of determining whether a distribution is an eligible rollover distribution, how is it determined whether a series of payments is a series of substantially equal periodic payments over a period specified in section 402(c)(4)(A)?

A-5. **(a) General rule.** Generally, whether a series of payments is a series of substantially equal periodic payments over a specified period is determined at the time payments begin, and by following the principles of section 72(t)(2)(A)(iv), without regard to contingencies or modifications that have not yet occurred. Thus, for example, a joint and 50-percent survivor annuity will be treated as a series of substantially equal payments at the time payments commence, as will a joint and survivor annuity that provides for increased payments to the employee if the employee's beneficiary dies before the employee. Similarly, for purposes of determining if a disability benefit payment is part of a series of substantially equal payments for a period described in section 402(c)(4)(A), any contingency under which payments cease upon recovery from the disability may be disregarded.

**(b) Certain supplements disregarded.** For purposes of determining whether a distribution is one of a series of payments that are substantially equal, social security supplements described in section 411(a)(9) are disregarded. For example, if a distributee receives a life annuity of $500 per month, plus a social security supplement consisting of payments of $200 per month until the distributee reaches the age at which social security benefits of not less than $200 a month begin, the $200 supplemental payments are disregarded and, therefore, each monthly payment of $700 made before the social security age and each monthly payment of $500 made after the social security age is treated as one of a series of substantially equal periodic payments for life. A series of payments that are not substantially equal solely because the amount of each payment is reduced upon attainment of social security retirement age (or, alternatively, upon commencement of social security early retirement, survivor, or disability benefits) will also be treated as substantially equal as long as the reduction in the actual payments is level and does not exceed the applicable social security benefit.

**(c) Changes in the amount of payments or the distributee.** If the amount (or, if applicable, the method of calculating the amount) of the payments changes so that subsequent payments are not substantially equal to prior payments, a new determination must be made as to whether the remaining payments are a series of substantially equal periodic payments over a period specified in Q&A-3(b)(1) of this section. This determination is made without taking into account payments made or the years of payment that elapsed prior to the change. However, a new determination is not made merely because, upon the death of the employee, the spouse or former spouse of the employee becomes the distributee. Thus, once distributions commence over a period that is at least as long as either the first annuitant's life or 10 years (e.g., as provided by a life annuity with a five-year or ten-year-certain guarantee), then substantially equal payments to the survivor are not eligible rollover distributions even though the payment period remaining after the death of the employee is or may be less than the period described in section 402(c)(4)(A). For example, substantially equal periodic payments made under a life annuity with a five-year term certain would not be an eligible rollover distribution even when paid after the death of the employee with three years remaining under the term certain.

**(d) Defined contribution plans.** The following rules apply in determining whether a series of payments from a defined contribution plan constitute substantially equal periodic payments for a period described in section 402(c)(4)(A):

*(1) Declining balance of years.* A series of payments from an account balance under a defined contribution plan will be considered substantially equal payments over a period if, for each year, the amount of the distribution is calculated by dividing the account balance by the number of years remaining in the period. For example, a series of payments will be considered substantially equal payments over 10 years if the series is determined as follows. In year 1, the annual payment is the account balance divided by 10; in year 2, the annual payment is the remaining account balance divided by 9; and so on until year 10 when the entire remaining balance is distributed.

*(2) Reasonable actuarial assumptions.* If an employee's account balance under a defined contribution plan is to be distributed in annual installments of a specified amount until the account balance is exhausted, then, for purposes of determining if the period of distribution is a period described in section 402(c)(4)(A), the period of years over which the installments will be distributed must be determined using reasonable actuarial assumptions. For example, if an employee has an account balance of $100,000, elects distributions of $12,000 per year until the account balance is exhausted, and the future rate of return is assumed to be 8% per year, the account balance will be exhausted in approximately 14 years. Similarly, if the same employee elects a fixed annual distribution amount and the fixed annual amount is less than or equal to $10,000, it is reasonable to assume that a future rate of return will be greater than 0% and, thus, the account will not be exhausted in less than 10 years.

**(e) Series of payments beginning before January 1, 1993.** Except as provided in paragraph (c) of this Q&A, if a series of periodic payments began before January 1, 1993, the determination of whether the post-December 31, 1992 payments are a series of substantially equal periodic payments over a specified period is made by taking into account all payments made, including payments made before January 1, 1993. For example, if a series of substantially equal periodic payments beginning on January 1, 1983, is scheduled to be paid over a period of 15 years, payments in the series that are made after December 31, 1992, will not be eligible rollover distributions even though they will continue for only five years after December 31, 1992, because the pre-January 1, 1993 payments are taken into account in determining the specified period.

Q-6. What types of variations in the amount of a payment cause the payment to be independent of a series of substantially equal periodic payments and thus not part of the series?

A-6. **(a) Independent payments.** Except as provided in paragraph (b) of this Q&A, a payment is treated as independent of the payments in a series of substantially equal payments, and thus not part of the series, if the payment is substantially larger or smaller than the other payments in the series. An independent payment is an eligible rollover distribution if it is not otherwise excepted from the definition of eligible rollover distribution. This is the case regardless of whether the payment is made before, with, or after payments in the series. For example, if an employee elects a single payment of half of the account balance with the remainder of the account balance paid over the life expectancy of the distributee, the single payment is treated as independent of the payments in the series and is an eligible rollover distribution unless otherwise excepted. Similarly, if an employee's surviving spouse receives a survivor life annuity of $1,000 per month plus a single payment on account of death of $7,500, the single payment is treated as independent of the payments in the annuity and is an eligible rollover distribution unless otherwise excepted (e.g., $5,000 of the $7,500 might qualify to be excluded from gross income as a death benefit under section 101(b)).

**(b) Special rules.** *(1) Administrative error or delay.* If, due solely to reasonable administrative error or delay in payment, there is an adjustment after the annuity starting date to the amount of any payment in a series of payments that otherwise would constitute a series of substantially equal payments described in section 402(c)(4)(A) and this section, the adjusted payment or payments will be treated as part of the series of substantially equal periodic payments and will not be treated as independent of the payments in the series. For example, if, due solely to reasonable administrative delay, the first payment of a life annuity is delayed by two months and reflects an additional two months worth of benefits, that payment will be treated as a substantially equal payment in the series rather than as an independent payment. The result will not change merely because the amount of the adjustment is paid in a separate supplemental payment.

*(2) Supplemental payments for annuitants.* A supplemental payment from a defined benefit plan to annuitants (e.g., retirees or beneficiaries) will be treated as part of a series of

substantially equal payments, rather than as an independent payment, provided that the following conditions are met—

(i) The supplement is a benefit increase for annuitants;

(ii) The amount of the supplement is determined in a consistent manner for all similarly situated annuitants;

(iii) The supplement is paid to annuitants who are otherwise receiving payments that would constitute substantially equal periodic payments; and

(iv) The aggregate supplement is less than or equal to the greater of 10% of the annual rate of payment for the annuity, or $750 or any higher amount prescribed by the Commissioner in revenue rulings, notices, and other guidance published in the Federal Register. See § 601.601(d)(2)(ii)(b) of this chapter.

*(3) Final payment in a series.* If a payment in a series of payments from an account balance under a defined contribution plan represents the remaining balance to the credit and is substantially less than the other payments in the series, the final payment must nevertheless be treated as a payment in the series of substantially equal payments and may not be treated as an independent payment if the other payments in the series are substantially equal and the payments are for a period described in section 402(c)(4)(A) based on the rules provided in paragraph (d)(2) of Q&A-5 of this section. Thus, such final payment will not be an eligible rollover distribution.

Q-7. When is a distribution from a plan a required minimum distribution under section 401(a)(9)?

A-7. **(a) General rule.** Except as provided in paragraphs (b) and (c) of this Q&A, if a minimum distribution is required for a calendar year, the amounts distributed during that calendar year are treated as required minimum distributions under section 401(a)(9), to the extent that the total required minimum distribution under section 401(a)(9) for the calendar year has not been satisfied. Accordingly, these amounts are not eligible rollover distributions. For example, if an employee is required under section 401(a)(9) to receive a required minimum distribution for a calendar year of $5,000 and the employee receives a total of $7,200 in that year, the first $5,000 distributed will be treated as the required minimum distribution and will not be an eligible rollover distribution and the remaining $2,200 will be an eligible rollover distribution if it otherwise qualifies. If the total section 401(a)(9) required minimum distribution for a calendar year is not distributed in that calendar year (e.g., when the distribution for the calendar year in which the employee reaches age 70½ is made on the following April 1), the amount that was required but not distributed is added to the amount required to be distributed for the next calendar year in determining the portion of any distribution in the next calendar year that is a required minimum distribution.

**(b) Distribution before age 70½.** Any amount that is paid before January 1 of the year in which the employee attains (or would have attained) age 70½ will not be treated as required under section 401(a)(9) and, thus, is an eligible rollover distribution if it otherwise qualifies.

**(c) Special rule for annuities.** In the case of annuity payments from a defined benefit plan, or under an annuity contract purchased from an insurance company (including a qualified plan distributed annuity contract (as defined in Q&A-10 of this section)), the entire amount of any such annuity payment made on or after January 1 of the year in which an employee attains (or would have attained) age 70½ will be treated as an amount required under section 401(a)(9) and, thus, will not be an eligible rollover distribution.

Q-8. How are amounts that are not includible in gross income allocated for purposes of determining the required minimum distribution?

A-8. If section 401(a)(9) has not yet been satisfied by the plan for the year with respect to an employee, a distribution is made to the employee that exceeds the amount required to satisfy section 401(a)(9) for the year for the employee, and a portion of that distribution is excludible from gross income, the following rule applies for purposes of determining the amount of the distribution that is an eligible rollover distribution. The portion of the distribution that is excludible from gross income is first allocated toward satisfaction of section 401(a)(9) and then the remaining portion of the required minimum distribution, if any, is satisfied from the portion of the distribution that is includible in gross income. For example, assume an employee is required under section 401(a)(9) to receive a minimum distribution for a calendar year of $4,000 and the employee receives a $4,800 distribution, of which $1,000 is excludible from income as a return of basis. First, the $1,000 return of basis is allocated toward satisfying the required minimum distribution. Then, the remaining $3,000 of the required minimum distribution is satisfied from the $3,800 of the distribution that is includible in gross income, so that the remaining balance of the distribution, $800, is an eligible rollover distribution if it otherwise qualifies.

Q-9. What is a distribution of a plan loan offset amount, and is it an eligible rollover distribution?

A-9. **(a) General rule.** A distribution of a plan loan offset amount, as defined in paragraph (b) of this Q&A, is an eligible rollover distribution if it satisfies Q&A-3 of this section. Thus, an amount equal to the plan loan offset amount can be rolled over by the employee (or spousal distributee) to an eligible retirement plan within the 60-day period under section 402(c)(3), unless the plan loan offset amount fails to be an eligible rollover distribution for another reason. See § 1.401(a)(31)-1, Q&A-16 for guidance concerning the offering of a direct rollover of a plan loan offset amount. See § 31.3405(c)-1, Q&A-11 of this chapter for guidance concerning special withholding rules with respect to plan loan offset amounts.

**(b) Definition of plan loan offset amount.** For purposes of section 402(c), a distribution of a plan loan offset amount is a distribution that occurs when, under the plan terms governing a plan loan, the participant's accrued benefit is reduced (offset) in order to repay the loan (including the enforcement of the plan's security interest in a participant's accrued benefit). A distribution of a plan loan offset amount can occur in a variety of circumstances, e.g., where the terms governing a plan loan require that, in the event of the employee's termination of employment or request for a distribution, the loan be repaid immediately or treated as in default. A distribution of a plan loan offset amount also occurs when, under the terms governing the plan loan, the loan is cancelled, accelerated, or treated as if it were in default (e.g., where the plan treats a loan as in default upon an employee's termination of employment or within a specified period thereafter). A distribution of a plan loan offset amount is an actual distribution, not a deemed distribution under section 72(p).

**(c) Examples.** The rules with respect to a plan loan offset amount in this Q&A-9, § 1.401(a)(31)-1, Q&A-16 and § 31.3405(c)-1, Q&A-11 of this chapter are illustrated by the following examples:

*Example (1).* (a) In 1996, Employee A has an account balance of $10,000 in Plan Y, of which $3,000 is invested in a plan loan to Employee A that is secured by Employee A's account balance in Plan Y. Employee A has made no after-tax employee contributions to Plan Y. Plan Y does not provide any direct rollover option with respect to plan loans. Upon termination of employment in 1996, Employee A, who is under age 70½, elects a distribution of Employee A's entire account balance in Plan Y, and Employee A's outstanding loan is offset against the account balance on distribution. Employee A elects a direct rollover of the distribution.

(b) In order to satisfy section 401(a)(31), Plan Y must pay $7,000 directly to the eligible retirement plan chosen by Employee A in a direct rollover. When Employee A's account balance was offset by the amount of the $3,000 unpaid loan balance, Employee A received a plan loan offset amount (equivalent to $3,000) that is an eligible rollover distribution. However, under § 1.401(a)(31)-1, Q&A-16 Plan Y satisfies section 401(a)(31), even though a direct rollover option was not provided with respect to the $3,000 plan loan offset amount.

(c) No withholding is required under section 3405(c) on account of the distribution of the $3,000 plan loan offset amount because no cash or other property (other than the plan loan offset amount) is received by Employee A from which to satisfy the withholding. Employee A may roll over $3,000 to an eligible retirement plan within the 60 day period provided in section 402(c)(3).

*Example (2).* (a) The facts are the same as in Example 1, except that the terms governing the plan loan to Employee A provide that, upon termination of employment, Employee A's account balance is automatically offset by the amount of any unpaid loan balance to repay the loan. Employee A terminates employment but does not request a distribution from Plan Y. Nevertheless, pursuant to the terms governing the plan loan, Employee A's account balance is automatically offset by the amount of the $3,000 unpaid loan balance.

(b) The $3,000 plan loan offset amount attributable to the plan loan in this example is treated in the same manner as the $3,000 plan loan offset amount in Example 1.

*Example (3).* (a) The facts are the same as in Example 2, except that, instead of providing for an automatic offset upon termination of employment to repay the plan loan, the terms governing the plan loan require full repayment of the loan by Employee A within 30 days of termination of employment. Employee A terminates employment, does not elect a distribution from Plan Y, and also fails to repay the plan loan within 30 days. The plan administrator of Plan Y declares the plan loan to Employee A in default and executes on the loan by offsetting Employee A's account balance by the amount of the $3,000 unpaid loan balance.

(b) The $3,000 plan loan offset amount attributable to the plan loan in this example is treated in the same manner as the $3,000 plan loan offset amount in Example 1 and in Example 2. The result in this Example 3 is the same even though the plan administrator treats the loan as in default before offsetting Employee A's accrued benefit by the amount of the unpaid loan.

*Example (4).* (a) The facts are the same as in Example 1, except that Employee A elects to receive the distribution of the account balance that remains after the $3,000 offset to repay the plan loan, instead of electing a direct rollover of the remaining account balance.

(b) In this case, the amount of the distribution received by Employee A is $10,000, not $3,000. Because the amount of the $3,000 offset attributable to the loan is included in determining the amount that equals 20 percent of the eligible rollover distribution received by Employee A, withholding in the amount of $2,000 (20 percent of $10,000) is required under section 3405(c). The $2,000 is required to be withheld from the $7,000 to be distributed to Employee A in cash, so that Employee A actually receives a check for $5,000.

*Example (5).* The facts are the same as in Example 4, except that the $7,000 distribution to Employee A after the offset to repay the loan consists solely of employer securities within the meaning of section 402(e)(4)(E). In this case, no withholding is required under section 3405(c) because the distribution consists solely of the $3,000 plan loan offset amount and the $7,000 distribution of employer securities. This is the result because the total amount required to be withheld does not exceed the sum of the cash and the fair market value of other property distributed, excluding plan loan offset amounts and employer securities. Employee A may roll over the employer securities and $3,000 to an eligible retirement plan within the 60-day period provided in section 402(c)(3).

*Example (6).* Employee B, who is age 40, has an account balance in Plan Z, a profit sharing plan qualified under section 401(a) that includes a qualified cash or deferred arrangement described in section 401(k). Plan Z provides for no after-tax employee contributions. In 1990, Employee B receives a loan from Plan Z, the terms of which satisfy section 72(p)(2), and which is secured by elective contributions subject to the distribution restrictions in section 401(k)(2)(B). In 1996, the loan fails to satisfy section 72(p)(2) because Employee B stops repayment. In that year, pursuant to section 72(p), Employee B is taxed on a deemed distribution equal to the amount of the unpaid loan balance. Under Q&A-4 of this section, the deemed distribution is not an eligible rollover distribution. Because Employee B has not separated from service or experienced any other event that permits the distribution under section 401(k)(2)(B) of the elective contributions that secure the loan, Plan Z is prohibited from executing on the loan. Accordingly, Employee B's account balance is not offset by the amount of the unpaid loan balance at the time Employee B stops repayment on the loan. Thus, there is no distribution of an offset amount that is an eligible rollover distribution in 1996.

Q-10. What is a qualified plan distributed annuity contract, and is an amount paid under such a contract a distribution of the balance to the credit of the employee in a qualified plan for purposes of section 402(c)?

A-10. **(a) Definition of a qualified plan distributed annuity contract.** A qualified plan distributed annuity contract is an annuity contract purchased for a participant, and distributed to the participant, by a qualified plan.

**(b) Treatment of amounts paid as eligible rollover distributions.** Amounts paid under a qualified plan distributed annuity contract are payments of the balance to the credit of the employee for purposes of section 402(c) and are eligible rollover distributions, if they otherwise qualify. Thus, for example, if the employee surrenders the contract for a single sum payment of its cash surrender value, the payment would be an eligible rollover distribution to the extent it is includible in gross income and not a required minimum distribution under section 401(a)(9). This rule applies even if the annuity contract is distributed in connection with a plan termination. See § 1.401(a)(31)-1, Q&A-17 and § 31.3405(c)-1, Q&A-13 of this chapter concerning the direct rollover requirements and 20-percent withholding requirements, respectively, that apply to eligible rollover distributions from such an annuity contract.

Q-11. If an eligible rollover distribution is paid to an employee, and the employee contributes all or part of the eligible rollover distribution to an eligible retirement plan within 60 days, is the amount contributed not currently includible in gross income?

A-11. Yes, the amount contributed is not currently includible in gross income, provided that it is contributed to the eligible retirement plan no later than the 60th day following the day on which the employee received the distribution. If more than one distribution is received by an employee from a qualified plan during a taxable year, the 60-day rule applies separately to each distribution. Because the amount withheld as income tax under section 3405(c) is considered an amount distributed under section 402(c), an amount equal to all or any portion of the amount withheld can be contributed as a rollover to an eligible retirement plan within the 60-day period, in addition to the net amount of the eligible rollover distribution actually received by the employee. However, if all or any portion of an amount equal to the amount withheld is not contributed as a rollover, it is included in the employee's gross income to the extent required under section 402(a), and also may be subject to the 10-percent additional income tax under section 72(t). See § 1.401(a)(31)-1, Q&A-14, for guidance concerning the qualification of a plan that accepts a rollover contribution.

Q-12. How does section 402(c) apply to a distributee who is not the employee?

A-12. **(a) Spousal distributee.** If any distribution attributable to an employee is paid to the employee's surviving spouse, section 402(c) applies to the distribution in the same manner as if the spouse were the employee. The same rule applies if any distribution attributable to an employee is paid in accordance with a qualified domestic relations order (as defined in section 414(p)) to the employee's spouse or former spouse who is an alternate payee. Therefore, a distribution to the surviving spouse of an employee (or to a spouse or former spouse who is an alternate payee under a qualified domestic relations order), including a distribution of ancillary death benefits attributable to the employee, is an eligible rollover distribution if it meets the requirements of section 402(c)(2) and (4) and Q&A-3 through Q&A-10 and Q&A-14 of this section. However, a qualified plan (as defined in Q&A-2 of this section) is not treated as an eligible retirement plan with respect to a surviving spouse. Only an individual retirement plan is treated as an eligible retirement plan with respect to an eligible rollover distribution to a surviving spouse.

**(b) Non-spousal distributee.** A distributee other than the employee or the employee's surviving spouse (or a spouse or former spouse who is an alternate payee under a qualified domestic relations order) is not permitted to roll over distributions from a qualified plan. Therefore, those distributions do not constitute eligible rollover distributions under section 402(c)(4) and are not subject to the 20-percent income tax withholding under section 3405(c).

Q-13. Must an employee's (or spousal distributee's) election to treat a contribution of an eligible rollover distribution to an individual retirement plan as a rollover contribution be irrevocable?

A-13. **(a) In general.** Yes. In order for a contribution of an eligible rollover distribution to an individual retirement plan to constitute a rollover and, thus, to qualify for current exclusion from gross income, a distributee must elect, at the time the contribution is made, to treat the contribution as a rollover contribution. An election is made by designating to the trustee, issuer, or custodian of the eligible retirement plan that the contribution is a rollover contribution. This election is irrevocable. Once any portion of an eligible rollover distribution has been contributed to an individual retirement plan and designated as a rollover distribution, taxation of the withdrawal of the contribution from the individual retirement plan is determined under section 408(d) rather than under section 402 or 403. Therefore, the eligible rollover distribution is not eligible for capital gains treatment, five-year or ten-year averaging, or the exclusion from gross income for net unrealized appreciation on employer stock.

**(b) Direct rollover.** If an eligible rollover distribution is paid to an individual retirement plan in a direct rollover at the election of the distributee, the distributee is deemed to have irrevocably designated that the direct rollover is a rollover contribution.

Q-14. How is the $5,000 death benefit exclusion under section 101(b) treated for purposes of determining the amount that is an eligible rollover distribution?

A-14. To the extent that a death benefit is a distribution from a qualified plan, the portion of the distribution that is excluded from gross income under section 101(b) is not an eligible rollover distribution. See § 1.401(a)(31)-1, Q&A-18 for guidance concerning assumptions that a plan administrator may make with respect to whether and to what extent a distribution of a survivor benefit is excludible from gross income under section 101(b).

Q-15. May an employee (or spousal distributee) roll over more than the plan administrator determines to be an eligible rollover distribution using an assumption described in § 1.401(a)(31)-1, Q&A-18?

A-15. Yes. The portion of any distribution that an employee (or spousal distributee) may roll over as an eligible rollover distribution under section 402(c) is determined based on the actual application of section 402 and other relevant provisions of the Internal Revenue Code. The actual application of these provisions may produce different results than any assumption described in § 1.401(a)(31)-1, Q&A-18 that is used by the plan administrator. Thus, for example, even though the plan administrator calculates the portion of a distribution that is a required minimum distribution (and thus is not made eligible for direct rollover under section 401(a)(31)), by assuming that there is no designated beneficiary, the portion of the distribution that is actually a required minimum distribution and thus not an eligible rollover distribution is determined by taking into account the designated beneficiary, if any. If, by taking into account the designated beneficiary, a greater portion of the distribution is an eligible rollover distribution, the distributee may rollover the additional amount. Similarly, even though a plan administrator assumes that a distribution from a qualified plan is the only death benefit with respect to an employee that qualifies for the $5,000 death benefit exclusion under section 101(b), to the extent that the death benefit exclusion is allocated to a different death benefit, a greater portion of the distribution may actually be includible in gross income and, thus, be an eligible rollover distribution, and the surviving spouse may roll over the additional amount if it otherwise qualifies.

Q-16. Is a rollover from a qualified plan to an individual retirement account or individual retirement annuity treated as a rollover contribution for purposes of the one-year look-back rollover limitation of section 408(d)(3)(B)?

A-16. No. A distribution from a qualified plan that is rolled over to an individual retirement account or individual retirement annuity is not treated for purposes of section

408(d)(3)(B) as an amount received by an individual from an individual retirement account or individual retirement annuity which is not includible in gross income because of the application of section 408(d)(3).

T.D. 8619, 9/15/95, amend T.D. 8880, 4/20/2000, T.D. 9169, 12/28/2004, T.D. 9302, 12/19/2006, T.D. 9319, 4/4/2007, T.D. 9340, 7/23/2007, T.D. 9447, 2/23/2009.

PAR. 3. Section 1.402(c)-2 is amended by adding a sentence to the end of A-11 to read as follows:

**Proposed § 1.402(c)-2 Eligible rollover distributions; questions and answers.** [*For Preamble, see ¶ 151,753*]

* * * * *

Q-11. [Not amended.]

A-11. * * * See § 1.401(a)(31)-1, Q&A-14, for guidance concerning the qualification of a plan that accepts a rollover contribution.

* * * * *

PAR. 8. Section 1.402(c)-2 is amended by redesignating paragraph A-4(h) as paragraph A-4(i) and adding a new paragraph A-4(h) to read as follows:

**Proposed § 1.402(c)-2 Eligible rollover contributions; questions and answers.** [*For Preamble, see ¶ 152,901*]

* * * * *

Q-4.

A-4. * * * (h) Distributions of premiums for accident or health insurance under § 1.402(a)-1(e).

* * * * *

**§ 1.402(d)-1 Effect of section 402(d).**

**(a)** If the requirements of section 402(d) are met, a contribution made by an employer on behalf of an employee to a trust which is not exempt under section 501(a) shall not be included in the income of the employee in the year in which the contribution is made. Such contribution will be taxable to the employee, when received in later years, as provided in section 72 (relating to annuities). For taxable years beginning before January 1, 1964, section 72(e)(3) (relating to the treatment of certain lump sums), as in effect before such date, shall not apply to such contributions. For taxable years beginning after December 31, 1963, such contributions, when received, may be taken into account in computations under sections 1301 through 1305 (relating to income averaging). See paragraph (b) of § 1.403(c)-1. The intent and purpose of section 402(d) is to give those employees, covered under certain non-exempt trusts to which such section applies, essentially the same tax treatment as those covered by trusts described in section 401(a) and exempt under section 501(a), except that the capital gains treatment referred to in section 402(a)(2) does not apply.

**(b)** Every person claiming the benefit of section 402(d) must be able to demonstrate to the satisfaction of the Commissioner that all of the provisions of such section are met. The taxpayer must produce sufficient evidence to prove:

*(1)* That, before October 21, 1942, he was employed by the particular employer making the contribution in question and was at such time definitely covered by a written agreement, entered into before October 21, 1942, between himself and the employer, or between the employer and the trustee of a trust established by the employer before October 21, 1942, and that the contribution by the employer was made pursuant to such agreement. The fact that an employee may have been potentially covered is not sufficient. Evidence that the employment was entered into, or the agreement executed, "as of" a date before October 21, 1942, or that the agreement or trust instrument which did not theretofore meet the requirements of section 402(d) was modified or amended after October 20, 1942, so as to come within the provisions of such section, will not satisfy the requirements of section 402(d).

*(2)* That such contribution, pursuant to the terms of such agreement, was to be applied for the purchase of an annuity contract for the taxpayer. In the case of a contribution by the employer of an annuity contract purchased by such employer and transferred by him to the trustee of the trust, evidence should be presented to prove that such contract was purchased for the taxpayer by the employer pursuant to the terms of a written agreement between the employer and the employee or between the employer and the trustee, entered into before October 21, 1942.

*(3)* That under the written terms of the trust agreement the taxpayer is not entitled during his lifetime, except with the consent of the trustee, to any payments other than annuity payments under the annuity contract or contracts purchased by the trustee or by the employer and transferred to the trustee, and that the trustee may grant or withhold such consent free from control by the taxpayer, the employer, or any other person. However, such control will not be presumed from the fact that the trustee is himself an officer or employee of the employer. As used in section 402(d) the phrase "if . . . under the terms of the trust agreement the employee is not entitled" means that the trust instrument must make it impossible for the prohibited distribution to occur, whether by operation or natural termination of the trust, whether by power of revocation or amendment, other than with the consent of the trustee, whether by the happening of a contingency, by collateral arrangement, or any other means. It is not essential that the employer relinquish all power to modify or terminate the trust but it must be impossible, except with the consent of the trustee, for any payments under annuity contracts purchased by the trustee, or by the employer and transferred to the trustee, to be received by the taxpayer, directly or indirectly, other than as annuity payments.

*(4)* The nature and amount of such contribution and the extent to which income taxes have been paid thereon before January 1, 1949, and not credited or refunded.

*(5)* If it is claimed that section 402(d) applies to amounts contributed to a trust after June 1, 1949, the taxpayer must prove to the satisfaction of the Commissioner that the trust did not, on June 1, 1949, qualify for exemption under section 165(a) of the Internal Revenue Code of 1939. Where an employer buys an annuity contract which is transferred to the trustee, the date of the purchase of the annuity contract and not the date of the transfer to the trustee is the controlling date in determining whether or not the contribution was made to the trust after June 1, 1949.

T.D. 6203, 9/24/56, amend T.D. 6783, 12/23/64, T.D. 6885, 6/1/66.

PAR. 11. Section 1.402(e) is amended.

**Proposed § 1.402(e) Statutory provisions; tax on lump sum distributions.** [*For Preamble, see ¶ 150,135*]

• ***Caution:*** Proposed section 1.62-1 was finalized by TD 7399, 2/3/76. Proposed sections 1.72-4, 1.72-13, 1.101-2, 1.122-1, 1.402(a)-1, 1.402(e)-2,

1.402(e)-3, 1.403(a)-1, 1.403(a)-2, 1.405-3, 1.652(b)-1, 1.1304-2 and 11.402(e)(4)(B)-1 remain proposed.

**§ 1.402(e)-1 Certain plan terminations.**

Distributions made after December 31, 1953, and before January 1, 1955, as a result of the complete termination of an employees' trust described in section 401(a) which is exempt under section 501(a) shall be considered distributions on account of separation from service for purposes of section 402(a)(2) if the employer who established the trust is a corporation, and the termination of the plan is incident to the complete liquidation of the corporation before August 16, 1954, regardless of whether such liquidation is incident to a reorganization as defined in section 368.

T.D. 6203, 9/24/56.

PAR. 2.

Section 1.402(e)-2(d)(3) as set forth in paragraph 12 of the appendix to the notice of proposed rulemaking of April 30, 1975, is revised by adding a new subdivision (iii) to read as follows:

**Proposed § 1.402(e)-2 Treatment of certain lump sum distributions made after 1973.** [*For Preamble, see ¶ 150,475*]

* * * * *

**(d) Definitions.** * * *

*(3) Ordinary income portion.* * * *

(iii) In the case of a lump sum distribution received in a taxable year of the recipient beginning after December 31, 1975, the recipient may elect, in accordance with section 402(e)(4)(L) and § 1.402(e)-14, to treat all calendar years of an employee's active participation in all plans in which the employee has been an active participant as years of active participation after December 31, 1973. If a recipient makes the election, the ordinary income portion of any lump sum distribution received by the recipient with respect to the employee (whether in the recipient's taxable year for which the election is made, or thereafter) is equal to the total taxable amount of the distribution.

* * * * *

**Proposed § 1.402(e)-2 Treatment of certain lump sum distributions made after 1973.** [*For Preamble, see ¶ 150,135*]

• ***Caution:*** Proposed section 1.62-1 was finalized by TD 7399, 2/3/76. Proposed sections 1.72-4, 1.72-13, 1.101-2, 1.122-1, 1.402(a)-1, 1.402(e)-2, 1.402(e)-3, 1.403(a)-1, 1.403(a)-2, 1.405-3, 1.652(b)-1, 1.1304-2 and 11.402(e)(4)(B)-1 remain proposed.

***Caution:*** The Treasury has not yet amended Reg § 1.402(e)-2 to reflect changes made by P.L. 99-514, P.L. 94-267.

**(a) In general.** *(1) Tax imposed; deduction allowed.* For a taxable year, at the election of the recipient of a lump sum distribution, the ordinary income portion of such distribution is subject to the tax imposed by section 402(e)(1)(A) (hereinafter referred to as the "separate tax") and, under section 402(e)(3), an amount equal to such portion is allowable as a deduction from gross income (see section 62 (11), as added by sec. 2005(c)(9) of Pub. L. No. 93-406, and the regulations thereunder) to the extent such portion is included in the gross income of the taxpayer for such year. The separate tax imposed by section 402(e)(1)(A) is an addition to the tax otherwise imposed under chapter 1 of the Code and may be elected whether or not the tax otherwise imposed by such chapter is computed under part I of subchapter Q of such chapter (relating to income averaging). This section applies with respect to distributions or payments made, or made available, to a recipient after December 31, 1973, in taxable years of the recipient beginning after that date.

*(2) Cross references.* (i) Computation; ordinary method. Paragraph (b) of this section provides rules with respect to a distribution which is not a multiple distribution, and does not include an annuity contract.

(ii) Computation; special method (distribution including an annuity contract). Paragraph (c)(2) of this section provides rules with respect to a distribution which is a multiple distribution.

(iii) Lump sum distribution. For the definition of the term "lump sum distribution", see paragraph (d)(1) of this section.

(iv) Total taxable amount. For the definition of the term "total taxable amount", see paragraph (d)(2) of this section.

(v) Ordinary income portion. For the definition of the term "ordinary income portion", see paragraph (d)(3) of this section.

(vi) Multiple distribution. For the definition of the term "multiple distribution", see paragraph (c)(2)(ii)(E) of this section.

(vii) Election. For rules relating to the election of lump sum distribution treatment under this section, see § 1.402(e)-3.

**(b) Ordinary method.** *(1) In general.* In the case of a distribution which is not included in a multiple distribution, and which does not include an annuity contract, if the recipient elects (under § 1.402(e)-3) to treat such distribution as a lump sum distribution under this section, the tax imposed by section 402(e)(1)(A) for the recipient's taxable year is an amount equal to the initial separate tax (determined under paragraph (b)(2) of this section) for such taxable year, multiplied by a fraction—

(i) The numerator of which is the ordinary income portion (determined under paragraph (d)(3) of this section) of such lump sum distribution for such taxable year, and

(ii) The denominator of which is the total taxable amount (determined under paragraph (d)(2) of this section) of such lump sum distribution for such taxable year.

*(2) Computation of initial separate tax.* For purposes of subparagraph (1) of this paragraph, the initial separate tax is an amount equal to 10 times the tax which would be imposed by section 1(c) (relating to unmarried individuals (other than surviving spouses and heads of households)) if the recipient were an individual referred to in such section and the taxable income referred to in such section were an amount equal to one-tenth of the excess of—

(i) The total taxable amount (determined under paragraph (d)(2) of this section) of the lump sum distribution, over

(ii) The minimum distribution allowance (determined under paragraph (b)(3) of this section).

*(3) Computation of minimum distribution allowance.* For purposes of paragraph (b)(2)(ii) of this section, the minimum distribution allowance is the lesser of—

(i) $10,000, or

(ii) One-half of the total taxable amount of the lump sum distribution for the taxable year,

reduced (but not below zero) by 20 percent of the excess (if any) of such total taxable amount over $20,000.

*(4) Example.* The application of this paragraph is illustrated by the following example:

*Example.* (i) On December 22, 1975, A separates from the service of the M Corporation and receives a lump sum distribution of $65,000 from the M Corporation's contributory qualified plan. A's contributions to the plan as an employee were $15,000. A has been an active participant in the plan since February 20, 1966. A and his wife, B, are each age 50. Neither received an annuity contract from a qualified plan in 1974 or 1975. Neither received a lump sum distribution in 1974. A and B file a joint return for the calendar year 1975. Their income for 1975 consists of A's salary of $15,000 from the M Corporation and of $5,000 from the N Corporation. Their deductions for 1975 (other than deductions attributable to the distribution) consist of itemized deductions of $3,000. Their average base period income (determined under section 1302(b)(1)) for the four preceding taxable years (1971 through 1974) is $14,000. Assuming there are no changes in the applicable tax after 1974, A and B's income tax liability for 1975 is computed as follows.

(ii) A and B's gross income for 1975 is $70,000, computed by adding the total taxable amount of the lump sum distribution (determined under paragraph (d)(2) of this section) to their otherwise computed gross income [$15,000 + $5,000 + $65,000 − $15,000)]. Their adjusted gross income for 1975 is $40,000 [$70,000 − ($10,000 + $20,000)] computed by reducing their gross income by the sum of the lump sum distributing deduction allowed by section 402(e)(3) with respect to the ordinary income portion of the distribution [$50,000 × 24/120] and the deduction allowed by section 1202 with respect to the capital gains portion of the distribution [($50,000 × 96/120) × 0.5]. A and B's joint taxable income is $35,500 (their itemized deductions are $3,000 and their personal exemptions total $1,500). A and B choose to apply the income averaging rules of section 1301 for 1975. Thus, A and B's income tax liability not including the separate tax on the ordinary income portion of the distribution is $8,828.

(iii) The minimum distribution allowance with respect to A's distribution is $4,000 [$10,000 − (($50,000 − $20,000) × 0.2)]. The initial separate tax on A's distribution is 10 times the tax imposed by section 1(c), computed as if the taxable income therein described were $4,600 [$50,000 − $4,000]. Thus, A's initial separate tax is $8,160. The separate tax on A's distribution is computed by multiplying the initial separate tax and the quotient of the ordinary income portion divided by the total taxable amount. Thus, the separate tax on A's distribution is $1,632 [$8,160 × $10,000/$50,000].

(iv) A and B's total income tax liability for 1975 is the sum of the income tax as otherwise determined and the separate tax. Thus, A and B's total income tax liability for 1975 is $10,460 [$8,828 + $1,632].

**(c) Special method.** *(1) Computation of separate tax on distribution including annuity contract and lump sum distribution.* (i) Computation. In the case of a distribution which is not included in a multiple distribution and which includes an annuity contract, if the recipient elects (under § 1.402(e)-3) to treat the portion of such distribution not consisting of an annuity contract as a lump sum distribution under this section, the separate tax imposed by section 402(e)(1)(A) of the recipient's taxable year is the excess (if any) of the adjusted separate tax over the tax attributable to the annuity contract (determined under paragraph (c)(1)(iii) of this section).

(ii) Definitions. For purposes of this section—

(A) Adjusted separate tax. The *adjusted separate tax* is an amount equal to the adjusted initial separate tax multiplied by a fraction—

(1) The numerator of which is the ordinary income portion of the distribution, and

(2) The denominator of which is the total taxable amount (determined under paragraph (d)(2) of this section) of the lump sum distribution.

(B) Adjusted initial separate tax. The *adjusted initial separate tax* is an amount equal to 10 times the tax which would be imposed by section 1(c) (relating to unmarried individuals (other than surviving spouses and heads of households)) if the recipient were an individual referred to in such section and the taxable income referred to in such section were an amount equal to one-tenth of the excess of—

(1) the adjusted total taxable amount of the lump sum distribution, over

(2) The adjusted minimum distribution allowance.

(C) Adjusted total taxable amount. (1) For taxable years beginning before January 1, 1975, the adjusted total taxable amount is the sum of—

(i) The excess (if any) of the current actuarial value of annuity contracts distributed to the recipient, over the portion of the net amount contributed by the employee which is allocable to the contract, and

(ii) The total taxable amount (determined under paragraph (d)(2) of this section) of the lump sum distribution for the taxable year.

For purposes of (c)(1)(ii)(A)(1)(i) of this section, the net amount contributed by the employee which is allocable to the contract is an amount equal to the amounts considered contributed by the employee under the plan (determined by applying sections 72(f) and 101(b), and paragraph (b) of § 1.72-16) reduced by any amount theretofore distributed to the employee which were not includible in his gross income multiplied by a fraction, the numerator of which is the current actuarial value of the contract, and the denominator of which is the sum of such current actuarial value and the value of other property (including cash) distributed.

(2) For taxable years beginning after December 31, 1974, the adjusted total taxable amount is the sum of—

(i) The current actuarial value of annuity contracts distributed to the recipient, reduced by the excess, if any, of the net amount contributed by the employee (as defined in paragraph (d)(2)(ii)(A) of this section) over the cash and other property distributed, and

(ii) The total taxable amount (determined under paragraph (d)(2) of this section) of the lump sum distribution for the taxable year.

(D) Adjusted ordinary income portion. The adjusted ordinary income portion of a lump sum distribution is the amount which would be computed under paragraph (d)(3) of this section if "adjusted total taxable amount" is substituted for "total taxable amount" in such subparagraph.

(E) Adjusted minimum distribution allowance. The adjusted minimum distribution allowance is the lesser of—

(1) $10,000, or

(2) one-half of the adjusted total taxable amount of the lump sum distribution for the taxable year,

reduced (but not below zero) by 20 percent of the excess (if any) of the adjusted total taxable amount over $20,000.

(F) Current actuarial value. The current actuarial value of an annuity contract is the greater of—

(1) The cash value of the annuity contract (determined without regard to any loans under the contract) on the date of distribution, or

(2) The amount determined under the appropriate tables contained in publication No. 861, entitled "Annuity Factors for Lump Sum Distributions".

(iii) Tax attributable to an annuity contract. For purposes of subdivision (i) of this subparagraph, the tax attributable to an annuity contract is the product of—

(A) The quotient of the adjusted ordinary income portion (determined under paragraph (c)(1)(ii)(D) of this section) of the lump sum distribution divided by the adjusted total taxable amount (determined under paragraph (c)(1)(ii)(C) of this section), and

(B) 10 times the tax which would be imposed by section 1(c) (relating to unmarried individuals (other than surviving spouses and heads of households)) if the recipient were an individual referred to in such section and the taxable income were an amount equal to one-tenth of the excess of—

(1) The current actuarial value of the annuity contract, over

(2) The adjusted minimum distribution allowance multiplied by a fraction—

(i) The numerator of which is the current actuarial value of the annuity contract, and

(ii) The denominator of which is the adjusted total taxable amount (determined under paragraph (c)(1)(ii) of this section).

(iv) Examples. The application of this subparagraph is illustrated by the following examples:

*Example (1).* (i) On December 29, 1975, A separates from the service of the M Corporation and receives a distribution of the balance to the credit of his account under the M Corporation's noncontributory qualified plan. The distribution consists of cash of $44,000, and an annuity contract with a current actuarial value of $6,000. A has been a participant in the plan since March 26, 1966. A and his wife, B, are each age 50. Neither received a previous distribution from a qualified plan. A and B file a joint return for 1975. Their income for 1975, other than the distribution, consists of A's salary from the M Corporation of $15,000 and of $5,000 from the N Corporation. Their deductions (other than deductions attributable to the distribution) consist of itemized deductions of $3,000. They are not otherwise permitted to use income averaging for 1975 under section 1301. Assuming there are no changes in the applicable tax law after 1974, A and B's income tax liability for 1975 is computed as follows.

(ii) A and B's gross income for 1975 is $64,000, computed by adding the total taxable amount (determined under paragraph (d)(2) of this section) of the lump sum distribution to their otherwise computed gross income [$15,000 + $5,000 + $44,000]. Their adjusted gross income for 1975 is $37,600 [$64,000 − ($8,800 + $17,600)], computed by reducing their gross income by the sum of the lump sum distribution deduction allowed by section 402(e)(3) with respect to the ordinary income portion of the distribution [$44,000 × 24/120] and the deduction allowed by section 1202 with respect to the capital gains portion of the distribution [($44,000 × 96/120) × 0.5]. A and B's taxable income for 1975 is $33,100 (their itemized deductions are $3,000 and their personal exemptions total $1,500). Thus, A and B's income tax liability not including the separate tax on the ordinary income portion of the distribution is $9,122.

(iii) The adjusted total taxable amount of A's distribution is the sum of the current actuarial value of the annuity contract distributed and the total taxable amount of the lump sum distribution. Thus, the adjusted total taxable amount of A's distribution is $50,000 [$6,000 + $44,000]. The adjusted minimum distribution allowance with respect to A's distribution is the lesser of $10,000 or ½ of the adjusted total taxable amount, reduced by 20 percent of the excess (if any) of the adjusted total taxable amount over $20,000. Thus, the adjusted minimum distribution allowance with respect to A's distribution is $4,000 [$10,000 − (($50,000 − $20,000) × 0.2)]. The adjusted initial separate tax on A's distribution is computed by multiplying 10 times the tax imposed by section 1(c) computed as if the taxable income therein described were $4,600 [($50,000 − $4,000)/10]. Thus, A's adjusted initial separate tax is $8,160. The adjusted separate tax on A's distribution is computed by multiplying the adjusted initial separate tax by the quotient of the ordinary income portion divided by the total taxable amount. Thus, the adjusted separate tax on A's distribution is $1,632 ($8,160 × $8,800/$44,000). The tax attributable to the annuity contract is 10 times the tax that would be imposed by section 1(c) computed as if the taxable income of a person described therein were $552

$$\frac{[\$6{,}000 - (\$4{,}000 \times \$6{,}000/\$50{,}000)]}{10}$$

multiplied by the quotient described in the second preceding sentence. Thus, the tax attributable to the annuity contract is $156 [$778 × $8,800/$44,000)]. The separate tax on A's distribution is computed by reducing the adjusted separate tax by the tax attributable to the annuity contract. Thus, the separate tax on A's distribution is $1,476 [$1,632 − $156].

(iv) A and B's total income tax liability for 1975 is the sum of their income tax liability as otherwise determined, and the separate tax. Thus A and B's total income tax liability for 1975 is $10,598 [$9,122 + $1,476].

*Example (2).* (i) Assume the same facts as in example (1) except that the M Corporation's qualified plan is contributory and that A's contributions under the plan as an employee were $1,760, and the current actuarial value of the annuity contract which is distributed is $5,760.

(ii) A and B's gross income for 1975 is $62,240, computed by adding the total taxable amount (determined under paragraph (d)(2) of this section) of the lump sum distribution to their otherwise computed gross income [$15,000 + $5,000 + ($44,000 − $1,760)]. Their adjusted gross income for 1975 is $36,896 [$62,240 − ($8,448 + $16,896)], computed by reducing their gross income by the sum of the lump sum distribution deduction allowed by section 402(e)(3) with respect to the ordinary income portion of the distribution [$42,240 × 24/120] and the deduction allowed by section 1202 with respect to the capital gains portion of the distribution. [($42,240 × 96/120) × 0.5]. A and B's taxable income for 1976 is $82,396 (their itemized deductions are $3,000 and their personal exemptions total $1,500). Thus A and B's income tax liability not including the separate tax on the ordinary income portion of the distribution is $8,826.

(iii) The adjusted total taxable amount of A's distribution is the sum of the current actuarial value of the annuity contract distributed and the total taxable amount of the lump sum distribution. Thus, the adjusted total taxable amount of A's distribution is $48,000 [$5,760 + ($44,000 – $1,760)]. The adjusted minimum distribution allowance with respect to A's distribution is the lesser of $10,000 or ½ of the adjusted total taxable amount, reduced by 20 percent of the excess of the adjusted total taxable amount over $20,000. Thus, the adjusted minimum distribution allowance with respect to A's distribution is $4,400 [$10,000 – (($48,000 – $20,000) × 0.2)]. The adjusted initial separate tax on A's distribution is 10 times the tax imposed by section 1(c) computed as if the taxable income therein described were $4,360.

$$\frac{[(\$48{,}000 - \$4{,}400)]}{10}.$$

Thus, A's adjusted initial separate tax is $7,656. The adjusted separate tax on A's distribution is computed by multiplying the adjusted initial separate tax by the quotient of the ordinary income portion divided by the total taxable amount. Thus, the adjusted separate tax on A's distribution is $1,531 [$7,656 × $3,448/$42,240]. The tax attributable to the annuity contract is 10 times the tax that would be imposed by section 1(c) computed as if the taxable income of a person therein described were $523

$$\frac{[\$5{,}760 - (\$4{,}400 \times (\$5{,}760/\$48{,}000)]}{10}$$

multiplied by the quotient described in the second preceding sentence. Thus, the tax attributable to the annuity contract is $147 [$735 × $8,448/$42,240]. The separate tax on A's distribution is computed by reducing the adjusted separate tax by the tax attributable to the annuity contract. Thus, the separate tax on A's distribution is $1,384 [$1,531 – $147].

(iv) A and B's total income tax liability for 1975 is the sum of their income tax liability, as otherwise determined, and the separate tax. Thus A and B's total income tax liability for 1975 is $10,210 [$1,384 + $8,826].

*Example (3).* (i) On December 7, 1974, C separates from the service of P Corporation and receives a distribution of the balance to the credit of his account under the P Corporation's contributory qualified plan. The distribution consists of cash of $44,000, and an annuity contract with a current actuarial value of $6,000. C has been a participant in the plan since February 20, 1965. C's contributions under the plan as an employee were $2,000. C and his wife, D, are each age 50. Neither received a previous distribution from a qualified plan. C and D file a joint return for 1974. Their income for 1974, other than the distribution, consists of C's salary from the P Corporation of $20,000. Their deductions (other than deductions attributable to the distribution) consist of itemized deductions of $3,000. They are not otherwise permitted to use income averaging for 1974 under section 1301. C and D's income tax liability for 1974 is computed as follows.

(ii) C and D's gross income for 1974 is $62,240, computed by adding the total taxable amount (determined under paragraph (d)(2) of this section) of the lump sum distribution to their otherwise computed gross income [$20,000 + ($44,000 – $1,760)]. Their adjusted gross income for 1974 is $39,008 [$62,240 – ($4,224 + $19,008)], computed by reducing their gross income by the sum of the lump sum distribution deduction allowed by section 402(e)(3) with respect to the ordinary income portion of the distribution [$42,240 × 12/120] and the deduction allowed by section 1202 with respect to the capital gains portion of the distribution ($42,240 × 108/120) × 0.5]. C and D's taxable income for 1974 is $34,508 (their itemized deductions are $3,000 and their personal exemptions total $1,500). C and D's income tax liability for 1974 not including the separate tax on the ordinary income portion of the distribution is $9,713.

(iii) The adjusted total taxable amount of C's distribution is the sum of the current actuarial value of the annuity contract distributed and the total taxable amount of the lump sum distribution. Thus, the adjusted total taxable amount of C's distribution is $48,000 [($6,000 – $240) + ($44,000 – $1,760)]. The adjusted minimum distribution allowance with respect to C's distribution is the lesser of $10,000 or ½ of the adjusted total taxable amount, reduced by 20 percent of the excess of the adjusted total taxable amount over $20,000. Thus, the adjusted minimum distribution allowance with respect to C's distribution is $4,400 [$10,000 – (($48,000 – $20,000) × 0.2)]. The adjusted initial separate tax on C's distribution is 10 times the tax imposed by section 1(c) computed as if the taxable income therein described were $4,360

$$\frac{[(\$48{,}000 - \$4{,}400)]}{10}$$

Thus, C's adjusted initial separate tax is $7,656. The adjusted separate tax on C's distribution is computed by multiplying the adjusted initial separate tax by the quotient of the ordinary income portion divided by the total taxable amount. Thus, the adjusted separate tax on C's distribution is $766 ($7,656 × $4,224/$42,240). The tax attributable to the annuity contract is 10 times the tax imposed by section 1(c) computed as if the taxable income therein described were $523

$$\frac{[\$5{,}760 - (\$4{,}400 \times \$5{,}760/\$48{,}000)]}{10}$$

multiplied by the quotient described in the second preceding sentence. Thus, the amount attributable to the annuity contract is $74 [$735 × ($4,224/$42,240)]. The separate tax on C's distribution is computed by reducing the adjusted separate tax by the tax attributable to the annuity contract. Thus, the separate tax on C's distribution is $692 ($766 – $74)

(iv) C and D's total income tax liability for 1974 is the sum of their income tax liability otherwise determined, and the separate tax. Thus, C and D's total income tax liability for 1974 is $10,405 [$9,713 + $692].

*(2) Computation of separate tax in case of multiple distribution.* (i) Computation. In the case of a payment or distribution which is included in a multiple distribution, the separate tax imposed on such multiple distribution by section 402(e)(1)(A) for the recipient's taxable year is the excess (if any) of the modified separate tax, over the sum of—

(A) The aggregate amount of the separate tax imposed by section 402(e)(1)(A) paid during the lookback period, and

(B) The modified tax attributable to the annuity contract.

(ii) Definitions. For purposes of this section. (A) Modified separate tax. The term "modified separate tax" means an amount equal to the modified initial separate tax multiplied by a fraction—

(1) The numerator of which is the sum of the ordinary income portions of the lump sum distributions made within the lookback period, and

(2) The denominator of which is the sum of the total taxable amounts of the lump sum distributions made within the lookback period.

(B) Modified initial separate tax. The modified initial separate tax is an amount equal to 10 times the tax which would be imposed by section 1(c) (relating to unmarried individuals (other than surviving spouses and heads of households)) if the recipient were an individual referred to in such section and the taxable income referred to in such section were an amount equal to one-tenth of the excess of

(1) The modified total taxable amount of the lump sum distribution, over

(2) The modified minimum distribution allowance.

(C) Modified total taxable amount. The modified total taxable amount is the sum of the total taxable amounts (determined under paragraph (d)(2) of this section) of the distributions made during the lookback period and, in the case of a distribution made during such period to which paragraph (c)(1) of this section applied, the amount specified in paragraph (c)(1)(ii)(C)(1)(i) or (2)(i) of this section, whichever is applicable

(D) Modified minimum distribution allowance. The modified minimum distribution allowance is the lesser of—

(1) $10,000, or

(2) one-half of the modified total taxable amount,

reduced (but not below zero) by 20 percent of the excess of the modified total taxable amount over $20,000.

(E) Multiple distributions. A distribution or payment received during a taxable year of the recipient which begins with or within a lookback period and after December 31, 1973, is included in a multiple distribution for such lookback period if—

(1) Any part of such distribution or payment (i) is treated as a lump sum distribution under this section or (ii) consists of a contract which would constitute all or a part of a lump sum distribution (determined without regard to section 402(e)(4)(B) and § 1.402(e)-3), except for the fact that it is an annuity contract, and

(2) a distribution or payment received in another such taxable year is treated as a lump sum distribution under this section.

For purposes of this subdivision (E), if the recipient of a lump sum distribution is a trust and if a beneficiary of such trust is an employee with respect to the plan under which the distribution is made, or treated as the owner of such trust for purposes of subpart E of part I of subchapter J of chapter 1 of the Code (relating to grantors and others treated as substantial owners), then such employee or owner shall be treated as the sole recipient of the lump sum distribution. For purposes of this subdivision (E), the term "an employee with respect to the plan under which the distribution is made" means an individual who, immediately before the distribution is made, is a participant in the plan under which the distribution is made.

(F) Lookback period. The lookback period with respect to any recipient is a period of 6 consecutive taxable years ending on the last day of the taxable year of the recipient in which a payment or distribution which is a multiple distribution is made.

(iii) Modified tax attributable to an annuity contract. For purposes of subdivision (i) of this subparagraph, the modified tax attributable to an annuity contract is equal to the product of—

(A) The quotient of the sum of the ordinary income portions (determined under paragraph (d)(3) of the lump sum distributions received during the lookback period divided by the sum of the total taxable amounts (determined under paragraph (d)(2) of the distributions made during the lookback period, and

(B) 10 times the tax which would be imposed by section 1(c) (relating to unmarried individual (other than surviving spouses and heads of households)) if the recipient were an individual referred to in such section and the taxable income were an amount equal to one-tenth of the excess

(1) The sum of the amounts described in paragraph (c)(1)(ii)(C)(1)(i) or (2)(i) of this section in respect of the annuity contracts distributed during the lookback period, over

(2) The modified minimum distribution allowance multiplied by a fraction—

(i) The numerator of which is the sum of the amounts described in paragraph (C)(2)(iii)(B) in (1) of this section, and

(ii) The denominator of which is the modified total taxable amount (determined under paragraph (C)(2)(ii)(C) of this section).

(iv) The application of this subparagraph is illustrated by the following examples:

*Example (1).* (i) On December 7, 1976, A separates from the service of N Corporation and receives a distribution of the balance to the credit of his account under the N Corporation's noncontributory qualified plan. The distribution consists of cash of $4,000 and an annuity contract with a current actuarial value of $6,000. A has been a participant in the plan since October 13, 1967. A and his wife, B, are each age 50. A and B file a joint return for 1976. Their income for 1976, other than the distribution, consists of A's salary from N Corporation of $25,000 and interest income of $3,000. Their deductions (other than deductions attributable to the distribution) consist of itemized deductions of $2,100. They are not otherwise permitted to use income averaging for 1976 under section 1301. A received a distribution in 1975 from the M Corporation and elected lump sum treatment for such distribution. The ordinary income portion of such distribution was $10,000; the total taxable amount of such distribution was $50,000; the adjusted ordinary income portion and the adjusted total taxable amount of such distribution are the same as the ordinary income portion and the total taxable amount; and they paid a separate tax on such distribution of $1,632. Assuming there are no changes in the applicable tax law after 1974, A and B's gross income tax liability for 1976 is computed as follows:

(ii) A and B's gross income for 1976 is $32,000, computed by adding the total taxable amount (determined under paragraph (d)(2) of this section) of the lump sum distribution to their otherwise computed gross income [$25,000 + $3,000 + $4,000]. Their adjusted gross income for 1976 is $29,400 [$32,000 − ($1,200 + $1,400)], computed by reducing their gross income by the sum of the lump sum distribution deduction allowed by section 402(e)(3) with respect to the ordinary income portion of the distribution [$4,000 × 36/120] and the deduction allowed by section 1202 with respect to the capital gains portion of the distribution [($4,000 × (84/120)) × 0.5]. A and B's taxable income for 1976 is $25,800 (their itemized deductions are $2,100 and their personal exemptions total $1,500). Thus, A and B's income tax liability for 1976, not including the separate tax on the ordinary income portion of the distribution is $6,308.

(iii) The adjusted total taxable amount of A's distribution for 1976 is the sum of the current actuarial value of the annuity contract distributed and the total taxable amount of the lump sum distribution. Thus, the adjusted total taxable amount of A's 1976 distribution is $10,000 [$6,000 + $4,000]. The modified total taxable amount is $60,000 [$50,000 + $10,000]. The modified minimum distribution allowance with respect to A's 1976 distribution is the lesser of $10,000 or ½ of the modified total taxable amount, reduced by 20 percent of the excess (if any) of the modified total taxable amount over $20,000. Thus, the modified minimum distribution allowance with respect to A's 1976 distribution is $2,000 [$10,000 − (($60,000 − $20,000) × 0.2)]. The modified initial separate tax on A's 1976 distribution is computed by multiplying 10 times the tax imposed by section 1(c) computed as if the taxable income therein described were $5,800

$$\frac{[(\$60{,}000 - \$2{,}000)]}{10}$$

Thus, A's modified initial separate tax is $10,680. The modified separate tax on A's 1976 distribution is computed by multiplying the modified initial separate tax by the quotient of the sum of the ordinary income portions of the lump sum distributions received during the lookback period divided by the sum of the total taxable amounts of each lump sum distribution made during such period. Thus, the modified separate tax on A's 1976 distribution is $2,215 [$10,680 × ($10,000 + $1,200)/($50,000 + $4,000)]. The modified tax attributable to the annuity contract is 10 times the tax imposed by section 1(c) computed as if the taxable income of a person described therein were $580

$$\frac{[\$6{,}000 - ((\$6{,}000/\$60{,}000) \times \$2{,}000)]}{10}$$

multiplied by the quotient described in the second preceding sentence. Thus, the modified tax attributable to the annuity contract is $70 [$820 × ($10,000 + $1,200 + $4,000)]. The separate tax on A's 1976 distribution is computed by reducing the modified separate tax by the sum of the separate tax paid during the lookback period, and the modified tax attributable to the annuity contract. Thus, the separate tax on A's 1976 distribution is $413 [$2,215 − ($1,632 + $170)].

(iv) A and B's total income tax liability for 1976 is the sum of their income tax liability as otherwise determined, and the separate tax. Thus, A and B's total income tax liability for 1976 is $6,721 [$6,308 + $413].

*Example (2).* (i) Assume the same facts as in example (1) except that the N Corporation's qualified plan was contributory and that A's contributions under the plan as an employee were $800, and the current actuarial value of the annuity contract which is distributed is $4,800.

(ii) A and B's gross income for 1976 is $31,200, computed by adding the total taxable amount (determined under paragraph (d)(2) of this section) of the lump sum distribution to their otherwise computed gross income [$25,000 + $3,000 + ($4,000 − $800)]. Their adjusted gross income for 1976 is $29,120 [$31,200 − ($960 + $1,200)] computed by reducing their gross income by the sum of the lump sum distribution deduction allowed by section 402(e)(3) with respect to the ordinary income portion of the distribution [$3,200 × 36/120] and the deduction allowed by section 1202 with respect to the capital gains portion of the distribution [($3,200 × 84/120) × 0.5]. A and B's taxable deductions are $2,100 and their personal exemptions total $1,500). Thus, A and B's income tax liability for 1976, not including the separate tax on the ordinary income portion of the distribution, is $6,207.

(iii) The adjusted total taxable amount of A's distribution for 1976 is the sum of the current actuarial value of the annuity contract distributed and the total taxable amount of the lump sum distribution. Thus, the adjusted total taxable amount of A's 1976 distribution is $8,000 [($4,800 + ($4,000 − $800)]. The modified total taxable amount is $58,000 [$50,000 + $8,000]. The modified minimum distribution allowance with respect to A's 1976 distribution is the lesser of $10,000 or ½ of the modified total taxable amount reduced by the excess, if any, of such modified total taxable amount over $20,000. Thus, the modified minimum distribution allowance with respect to A's 1976 distribution is $2,400 [$10,000 − [(($8,000 + $50,000) − $20,000) × 0.2)]]. The modified initial separate tax on A's 1976 distribution is 10 times the tax imposed by section 1(c) computed as if the taxable income therein described were

$$\$5{,}560\ \frac{[(\$58{,}000 - \$2{,}400)]}{10}$$

Thus, A's modified initial separate tax is $10,176. The modified separate tax on A's 1976 distribution is computed by multiplying the modified initial separate tax by the quotient of the sum of the ordinary income portions of each lump sum distribution received during the lookback period divided by the sum of the total taxable amounts of each lump sum distribution made during such period. Thus, the modified separate tax on A's 1976 distribution is $2,096 [$10,176 × ($10,000 + $960)/($50,000 + $3,200)]. The modified tax attributable to the annuity contract is 10 times the tax imposed by section 1(c) computed as if the taxable income therein described were

$$\$460\ \frac{[(\$4{,}800 - (\$2{,}400 \times (\$4{,}800/\$58{,}000))]}{10}$$

multiplied by the quotient described in the second preceding sentence. Thus, the modified tax attributable to the annuity contract is $133 [$644 × ($10,000 + $960)/($50,000 + $3,200)]. The separate tax on A's 1976 distribution is computed by reducing the modified separate tax by the sum of the separate tax paid during the lookback period, and the modified tax attributable to the annuity contract. Thus, the separate tax on A's 1976 distribution is $331 [$2,096 − ($1,632 + $133)].

(iv) A and B's total income tax liability for 1976 is the sum of their income tax liability as otherwise determined, and the separate tax. Thus, A and B's total income tax liability for 1976 is $6,538 [$6,207 + $331].

*Example (3).* (i) Assume the same facts as in example (1) except that the distribution on December 7, 1976, from the N Corporation's noncontributory qualified plan consists only of an annuity contract with a current actuarial value of $6,000.

(ii) A and B's gross income for 1976 is $28,000, computed by adding the total taxable amount (determined under paragraph (d)(2) of this section) of the lump sum distribution to their otherwise computed gross income [$ 25,000 + $3,000 + 0]. Their adjusted gross income for 1976 is $28,000 [$28,000 − ($0 + $0)], computed by reducing their gross income by the sum of the lump sum distribution deduction allowed by section 402(e)(3) with respect to the ordinary income portion of the distribution [$0 × 36/120] and the deduction allowed by section 1202 with respect to the capital gains portion of the distribution [$0 + 84/120) + 0.5]. Their taxable income for 1976 is $24,000 (their itemized deductions are $2,100 and their personal exemptions total $1,500). Thus, A and B's income tax liability for 1976, not including the separate tax on the distribution is $5,804.

(iii) The adjusted total taxable amount of A's distribution for 1976 is the sum of the current actuarial value of the annuity contract distributed and the total taxable amount of the lump sum distribution. Thus, the adjusted total taxable amount of A's 1976 distribution is $6,000 [$6,000 + $0]. The modified total taxable amount is $56,000 [$6,000 + $50,000]. The modified minimum distribution allowance with respect to A's 1976 distribution is the lesser of $10,000 or ½ of the modified total taxable amount, reduced by 20 percent of the excess (if any) of the modified total taxable amount over $20,000. Thus, the modified minimum distribution allowance with respect to A's 1976 distribution is $2,800 [$10,000 – (($56,000 – $20,000) × 0.2)]. The modified initial separate tax on A's 1976 distribution is computed by multiplying 10 times the tax imposed by section 1(c) computed as if the taxable income therein described were $5,320

$$\frac{[\$56{,}000 - \$2{,}800]}{10}$$

Thus, A's modified initial separate tax is $9,672. The modified separate tax on A's 1976 distribution is computed by multiplying the modified initial separate tax by the quotient of the sum of the ordinary income portions of the lump sum distributions received during the lookback period divided by the sum of the total taxable amounts of each lump sum distribution made during such period. Thus, the modified separate tax on A's 1976 distribution is $1,934 [$9,672 × ($10,000 × $0/($50,000 × $0))]. The modified tax attributable to the annuity contract is 10 times the tax imposed by section 1(c) computed as if the taxable income of a person described therein were $570

$$\frac{[(\$6{,}000 - ((\$6{,}000/\$56{,}000) \times \$2{,}800))]}{10}$$

multiplied by the quotient described in the second preceding sentence. Thus, the modified tax attributable to the annuity contract is $161 [$805 × ($10,000 + $0)/($50,000 + $0)]. The separate tax on A's 1976 distribution is computed by reducing the modified separate tax by the sum of the separate tax paid during the lookback period, and the modified tax attributable to the annuity contract. Thus, the separate tax on A's 1976 distribution is $141 [$1,934 – ($1,632 + $161)].

(iv) A and B's total income tax liability for 1976 is the sum of their income tax liability as otherwise determined, and the separate tax. Thus, A and B's total income tax liability for 1976 is $5,945 [$5,804 + $141].

*Example (4).* (i) Assume the same facts as in example (3) except that the N Corporation's qualified plan was contributory and that A's contributions under the plan as an employee were $2,000.

(ii) A and B's gross income for 1976 is $28,000, computed by adding the total amount (determined under paragraph (d)(2) of this section) of the lump sum distribution to their otherwise computed gross income [$25,000 + $3,000 + 0]. Their adjusted gross income for 1976 is $28,000 [$28,000 – ($0 + $0)], computed by reducing their gross income by the sum of the lump sum distribution deduction allowed by section 402(e)(3) with respect to the ordinary income portion of the distribution [$0 × 36/120] and the deduction allowed by section 1202 with respect to the capital gains portion of the distribution [($0 × 84/120) × 0.5]. Their taxable income for 1976 is $24,400 (their itemized deductions are $2,100 and their personal exemptions total $1,500). Thus, A and B's income tax liability for 1976, not including the separate tax on the distribution is $5,804.

(iii) The adjusted total taxable amount of A's distribution for 1976 is the sum of the current actuarial value of the annuity contract distributed, reduced by the excess of the net amount contributed by the employee over the cash and other property distributed, and the total taxable amount of the lump sum distribution. Thus, the adjusted total taxable amount of A's 1976 distribution is $4,000 [($6,000 – $2,000) + $0]. The modified minimum distribution total taxable amount is $54,000. [$50,000 + allowance with respect to A's 1976 distributions is the lesser of $10,000 or ½ of the modified total taxable amount, reduced by 20 percent of the excess (if any) of the modified total taxable amount over $20,000. Thus, the modified minimum distribution allowance with respect to A's 1976 distribution is $3,200 [$10,000 – (($54,000 – $20,000) × 0.2)]. The modified initial separate tax on A's 1976 distribution is computed by multiplying 10 times the tax imposed by section 1(c) computed as if the taxable income therein described were $5,080

$$\frac{[\$54{,}000 - \$3{,}200]}{10}$$

Thus, A's modified initial separate tax is $9,168. The modified separate tax on A's 1976 distribution is computed by multiplying the modified initial separate tax by the quotient of the sum of the ordinary income portions of the lump sum distribution received during the lookback period divided by the sum of the total taxable amounts of each lump sum distribution made during such period. Thus, the modified separate tax on A's 1976 distribution is $1,833 [$9,168 × ($10,000 + $0)/($50,000 + $0)]. The modified tax attributable to the annuity contract is 10 times the tax imposed by section 1(c) computed as if the taxable income therein described were $376

$$\frac{[\$4{,}000 - ((\$4{,}000/\$54{,}000) \times \$3{,}200)]}{10}$$

multiplied by the quotient described in the second preceding sentence. Thus, the modified tax attributable to the annuity contract is $105 [$526 × ($10,000 + $0)/($50,000 + $0)]. The separate tax on A's 1976 distribution is computed by reducing the modified separate tax by the sum of the separate tax paid during the lookback period, and the modified tax attributable to the annuity contract. Thus, the separate tax on A's 1976 distribution is $96 [$1,833 – ($1,632 + $105)].

(iv) A and B's total income tax liability for 1976 is the sum of their income tax liability as otherwise determined, and the separate tax. Thus, A and B's total income tax liability for 1976 is $5,900 [$5,804 + $96].

**(d) Definitions.** *For purposes of this section and § 1.402(e)-3. (1) Lump sum distribution.* (i) For taxable years of a recipient beginning after December 31, 1973, the term "lump sum distribution" means the distribution or payment within one taxable year of the recipient of the balance under the plan to the credit of an employee which becomes payable, or is made available, to the recipient—

(A) On account of the employee's death,

(B) After the employee attains age 59½,

(C) In the case of an employee who at no time during his participation in the plan was an employee within the meaning of section 401(c)(1), on account of the employee's separation from the service, or

(D) In the case of an employee within the meaning of section 401(c)(1), after the employee has become disabled within the meaning of section 72(m)(7) and paragraph (f) of § 1.72-17,

from a trust forming part of a plan described in section 401(a) and which is exempt from tax under section 501(a) or from a plan described in section 403(a). Although periodic payments made under an annuity contract distributed under a plan described in the preceding sentence are taxed under section 72, solely for purposes of determining the adjusted total taxable amount or the modified total taxable amount, an annuity contract distributed from a plan described in the preceding sentence shall be treated as a lump sum distribution.

(ii) (A) A distribution or payment is not a lump sum distribution unless it constitutes the balance to the credit of the employee at the time the distribution or payment commences. For purposes of the preceding sentence, the time at which a distribution or payment commences shall be the date on which the requirements of subdivisions (A), (B), (C), or (D) (whichever is applicable) of paragraph (d)(1)(i) of this section are satisfied, disregarding any previous distribution which constituted the balance to the credit of the employee.

(B) A distribution made before the death of an employee (for example, annuity payments received by the employee after retirement) will not preclude an amount paid on account of the death of the employee from being treated as a lump sum distribution by the recipient. Further, if a distribution or payment constitutes the balance to the credit of the employee, such distribution or payment shall not be treated as other than a lump sum distribution merely because an additional amount, attributable to the last or a subsequent year of service, is credited to the account of the employee and distributed.

(C) The application of this subdivision may be illustrated by the following example:

*Example.* A, an individual who is a calendar year taxpayer, retires from services with the M Corporation on October 31, 1975 after attaining age 59½. A begins to receive monthly annuity payments under the M Corporation's qualified plan on November 1, 1975. On February 3, 1976. A takes the balance to his credit under the M Corporation's plan in lieu of any future annuity payments. The balance to the credit of A under the M Corporation's plan is distributed to him on February 3, 1976, and as of such date he had not previously received any amount constituting a lump sum distribution. Such payments and distributions are not to be treated as a lump sum distribution because they are not paid within 1 taxable year of the recipient.

(iii) A payment or distribution described in paragraph (d)(1)(i) of this section which is made to more than one person (except a payment or distribution made solely to two or more trusts), shall not be treated as a lump sum distribution, unless the entire amount paid or distributed is included in the income of the employee in respect of whom the payment or distribution is made. Thus, for example, a distribution of the balance to the credit of the employee after the death of the employee made to the surviving spouse and his children cannot be treated as a lump sum distribution by the surviving spouse and children. However, a distribution to the employee's estate can be treated as a lump sum distribution even though the estate subsequently distributes the amount received to the surviving spouse and children.

(iv) The term "balance to the credit of the employee" does not include United States Retirement Plan Bonds held by a trust to the credit of an employee. Thus, a distribution or payment by a plan described in subdivision (i) of this subparagraph may constitute a lump sum distribution with respect to an employee even though the trust retains retirement plan bonds registered in the name of such employee. Similarly, the proceeds of a retirement plan bond received as a part of the balance to the credit of an employee will not be entitled to be treated as a lump sum distribution. See section 405(e) and paragraph (a)(4) of § 1.405-3.

(v) The term "balance to the credit of the employee" includes any amount to the credit of the employee under any plan which is required to be aggregated under the provisions of section 402(e)(4)(C) and paragraph (e)(1) of this section.

(vi) The term "balance to the credit of the employee" does not include any amount which has been placed in a separate account for the funding of medical benefits described in section 401(h) as defined in paragraph (a) of § 1.401-14. Thus, a distribution or payment by a plan described in subdivision (i) of this subparagraph may constitute the "balance to the credit of the employee" with respect to an employee even though the trust retains amounts attributable to the funding of medical benefits described in section 401(h).

(vii) The term "balance to the credit of the employee" includes any amount which is not forfeited under the plan as of the close of the taxable year of the recipient within which the distribution is made except that in the case of an employee who has separated from the service and incurs a break in service (within the meaning of section 411), such term does not include an amount which is forfeited at the close of the plan year, beginning with or within such taxable year, by reason of such break in service.

(viii) The balance to the credit of the employee is includible in the gross income of the recipient if the recipient fails to make a timely election under section 72(h) to receive an annuity in lieu of such balance.

*(2) Total taxable amount.* (i) The term "total taxable amount" means, with respect to a lump sum distribution described in the first sentence of paragraph (d)(1)(i) of this section, the amount of such lump sum distribution which exceeds the sum of—

(A) The net amount contributed by the employee, and

(B) The net unrealized appreciation attributable to that part of the distribution which consists of the securities of the employer corporation so distributed.

(ii) For purposes of paragraph (d)(2)(i)(A) of this section, the term "net amount contributed by the employee" means—

(A) For taxable years beginning after December 31, 1974, the amount actually contributed by the employee plus any amounts considered to be contributed by the employee under the rules of sections 72(f) and 101(b), and paragraph (b) of § 1.72-16, reduced by any amounts theretofore distributed to him which were excludable from gross income as a return of employee contributions.

(B) For taxable years beginning before January 1, 1975, an amount equal to the product of the amounts considered contributed by the employee under the plan (determined by applying sections 72(f) and 101(b), and paragraph (b) of § 1.72-16) reduced by any amount theretofore distributed to the employee which were not includible in his gross income, multiplied by a fraction—

(i) The numerator of which is the excess, if any, of the sum of the current actuarial value of the annuity contract distributed and the value of the other property (including cash) distributed, over such current actuarial value, and

(ii) The denominator of which is the sum of the current actuarial value of the annuity contract distributed and the value of other property (including cash) distributed.

(iii) The provisions of this subparagraph may be illustrated by the following examples:

*Example (1).* A, age 60, receives a lump sum distribution from the M Corporation's noncontributory qualified plan on November 24, 1975. The distribution of $25,000 consists of cash and M Corporation securities with net unrealized appreciation of $15,000. The total taxable amount of the distribution to A is $10,000.

*Example (2).* B, age 60, receives a lump sum distribution from the N Corporation's contributory qualified plan on December 29, 1975. The distribution consists of $25,000 in cash. B's contributions under the plan as an employee are $5,000. The total taxable amount of the distribution to B is $20,000.

*Example (3).* W receives a lump sum distribution on April 1, 1975, from the M Corporation's noncontributory qualified plan as beneficiary of H on account of H's death. The distribution consists of $25,000 in cash. The total taxable amount of distribution to W is $20,000 if W is otherwise allowed a $5,000 exclusion under section 101(b).

*(3) Ordinary income portion.* (i) The ordinary income portion of a lump sum distribution is the product of the total taxable amount of the lump sum distribution, multiplied by a fraction—

(A) the numerator of which is the number of calendar years of active participation by the employee in the plan after December 31, 1973, under which the lump sum distribution is made, and

(B) the denominator of which is the total number of calendar years of active participation by the employee in such plan.

(ii) For purposes of computing the fraction described in subdivision (i) of this subparagraph, the number of calendar years of active participation shall be the number of calendar months during the period beginning with the first month in which the employee became a participant under the plan and ending with the earliest of—

(A) The month in which the employee receives a lump sum distribution under the plan,

(B) In the case of an employee who is not an employee within the meaning of section 401(c)(1), the month in which the employee separates from the service,

(C) The month in which the employee dies, or

(D) In the case of an employee within the meaning of section 401(c)(1) who receives a lump sum distribution on account of disability, the first month in which he becomes disabled within the meaning of section 72(m)(7) and paragraph (f) of § 1.72-17.

In computing the months of active participation, in the case of active participation before January 1, 1974, a part of a calendar year in which the employee was an active participant under the plan shall be counted as 12 months, and in the case of active participation after December 31, 1973, a part of a calendar month in which an individual is an active participant under the plan shall be counted as 1 month. Thus, for example, if A, an individual, became an active participant under a plan on December 31, 1965, and continued to be an active participant under the plan until May 7, 1976, A has 108 (12 × 9) months of active participation under the plan before January 1, 1974, and A has 29 (12 + 12 + 5) months of active participation after December 31, 1973. For special rule in case of aggregation of plans, see paragraph (e) (1)(ii) of this section.

*(4) Employee; employer.* The term "employee" includes an employee within the meaning of section 401(c)(1) and the employer of such individual is the person treated as his employer under section 401(c)(4).

*(5) Securities.* The terms "securities" and "securities of the employer corporation" shall have the meanings provided in sections 402(a)(3)(A) and 402(a)(3)(B), respectively.

**(e) Special rules.** *(1) Aggregation.* (i) Aggregation of trusts and plans. (A) For purposes of determining the balance to the credit of an employee, all trusts described in section 401(a) and which are exempt from tax under section 501(a) and which are part of a plan shall be treated as a single trust; all pension plans described in section 401(a) maintained by an employer shall be treated as a single plan; all profit-sharing plans described in section 401(a) maintained by an employer shall be treated as a single plan; and all stock bonus plans described in section 401(a) maintained by an employer shall be treated as a single plan. For purposes of this subdivision (i), an annuity contract shall be considered to be a trust.

(B) Trusts which are not described in section 401(a) or which are not exempt from tax under section 501(a), and annuity contracts which do not satisfy the requirements of section 404(a)(2) shall not be taken into account for purposes of subdivision (i) of this subparagraph.

(ii) Computation of ordinary income portion. The ordinary income portion of a distribution from two or more plans (which are treated as a single plan under subdivision (i) of this subparagraph) shall be computed by aggregating all of the amounts which would constitute the ordinary income portion of a lump sum distribution if each plan maintained by the employer were not subject to the application of subdivision (i) of this subparagraph.

(iii) Examples. The application of this subparagraph is illustrated by the following examples:

*Example (1).* M Corporation maintains a qualified profit-sharing plan and a qualified defined benefit pension plan. A, who has participated in each plan for 5 years and is age 55, separates from the service on December 5, 1975. On December 5, 1975, A receives a distribution of the balance to the credit of his account under the profit-sharing plan. Payment of his pension benefits, however, will not commence until he attains age 65. A is entitled to treat his profit-sharing distribution as a lump sum distribution.

*Example (2).* Assume the same facts as in example (1) except that instead of a profit-sharing plan, M Corporation maintains a qualified money purchase pension plan. A is not entitled to have the amount received from the money purchase pension plan treated as a lump sum distribution.

*Example (3).* Assume the same facts as in example (2) except that the trust forming part of the defined benefit pension maintained by M Corporation is not a qualified trust. A is entitled to have the amount received from the money purchase plan treated as a lump sum distribution.

*Example (4).* N Corporation maintains profit-sharing plan X and profit-sharing plan Y which plans are qualified and are noncontributory. A is a participant in each plan. A has been a participant in the profit-sharing plan X since October 13, 1966 and a participant in profit-sharing plan Y since its inception on May 9, 1968. A, at age 55, separates from the service on December 5, 1975. He receives the balance to his credit from each plan upon separation. He receives $50,000 from profit-sharing plan X and $60,000 from profit-sharing plan Y. The ordinary income portion of his distribution from the N Corporation plans is $25,000 [($50,000 × (24/120)) + ($60,000 × (24/90))].

*(2) Community property laws.* (i) Except as provided in paragraph (e)(2)(ii) of this section, the provisions of this section shall be applied without regard to community property laws.

(ii) In applying the provisions of section 402(e)(3), relating to the allowance of a deduction from gross income of the ordinary income portion of a lump sum distribution, community property laws shall not be disregarded. Thus, for example, if A, a married individual subject to the community property laws of a jurisdiction, receives a lump sum distribution of which the ordinary income portion is $10,000, and he and his wife, B, file separate returns for the taxable year, generally, one half of the total taxable amount of the lump sum distribution is includible in A's gross income, and he will be entitled to a deduction under section 402(e)(3) of $5,000. In this case, the other half of the total taxable amount is includible in B's gross income, and she will be entitled to a deduction of $5,000. The entire amount of the lump sum distribution, however, must be taken into account by A in computing the separate tax imposed by section 402(e)(1)(A).

*(3) Minimum period of service.* For purposes of computing the separate tax imposed by section 402(e)(1)(A), no amount distributed or paid to an employee may be treated as a lump sum distribution under section 402(e)(4)(A) and this section unless he has been a participant in the plan for at least 5 full taxable years of such employee (preceding his taxable year in which such amount is distributed or paid). Thus, for example, if an amount, which would otherwise be a lump sum distribution, is distributed to A, an employee who has completed only 4 of his taxable years of participation in the plan before the first day of the taxable year in which the amount is distributed, A is not entitled to use the provisions of section 402(e) to compute the tax on the ordinary income portion of the amount distributed. If the amount were distributed to A's beneficiary on account of A's death, however, A's beneficiary could treat the distribution as a lump sum distribution under section 402(e) and this section.

*(4) Amounts subject to penalty.* Section 402(e) and this section do not apply to an amount described in section 72(m)(5)(A)(ii) and § 1.72-17(e)(1)(i)(b) to the extent the provisions of section 72(m)(5) apply to such amount.

*(5) Distributions including securities of the employer corporation.* For rules relating to distributions including securities of the employer corporation, see § 1.402(a)-1(b).

*(6) Liability for tax.* (i) Except as provided in subdivision (ii) of this subparagraph the recipient shall be liable for the tax imposed by section 402 (e)(1)(A).

(ii) (A) In any case in which the recipient of a lump sum distribution is a trust, if a beneficiary of such trust, is—

(1) An employee with respect to the plan under which the distribution is made, or

(2) Treated as the owner of such trust for purposes of subpart E of part I of subchapter J of chapter 1 of the Code (relating to grantors and others treated as substantial owners),

then such employee or the owner shall be treated as the sole recipient of the lump sum distribution. For purposes of (1) of this subdivision, the term "an employee with respect to the plan under which the distribution is made" means and individual who, immediately before the distribution is made, is a participant in the plan under which the distribution is made.

(B) (1) In any case in which a lump sum distribution is made within a taxable year with respect to an individual only to two or more trusts, if a beneficiary of any one of such trusts is not treated as the sole recipient of the distribution by reason of the application of (A) of this subdivision (ii), the separate tax imposed by section 402(e)(1)(A) shall be computed as if the distribution were made to a single recipient consisting of all of such trusts, but the liability for such separate tax shall be allocated among the trusts according to the relative portions of the total taxable amount of the distribution received by each trust.

(2) In any case in which a lump sum distribution is made in a succeeding taxable year in a lookback period with respect to a trust described in (1) of this subdivision (B), the separate tax imposed by section 402(1)(A) shall be computed as if the amount described in section 402(e)(2)(A) (relating to the amount of tax imposed by section 402(e)(1)(A) paid with respect to other distributions in a lookback period) includes the separate tax determined in (1) of this subdivision (B) (without regard to the allocation described therein).

*(7) Change in exempt status of trust.* For principles applicable in making appropriate adjustments if the trust was not exempt for one or more years before the year of distribution, see § 1.402(a)-1(a)(1)(iv).

**(f) Reporting.** *(1) Information required.* An employer who maintains a plan described in section 401(a) or 403(a), under which a distribution or payment which may be treated as a lump sum distribution is made in a taxable year of the recipient beginning after December 31, 1973, shall communicate (or cause to be communicated) in writing, to the recipient on Form 1099 R the following information (where applicable):

(i) The gross amount of such distribution (including the value of any United States retirement plan bonds distributed to or held for the recipient);

(ii) The total taxable amount of such distribution;

(iii) The ordinary income portion and capital gain element of such distribution;

(iv) The net amount contributed by the employee (within the meaning of paragraph (d)(2)(ii) of this section);

(v) The portions of such distribution excludable from the gross income of the recipient under paragraph (c) of § 1.72-16 and paragraph (b) of § 1.402(a)-1;

(vi) The value of any United States retirement plan bonds distributed to or held for the recipient in excess of the net amount contributed by the employee (within the meaning of paragraph (d)(2)(ii) of this section) included in the basis of such bonds;

(vii) The current actuarial value of any annuity contract distributed as part of the balance to the credit of the employee in excess of the net amount contributed by the employee (within the meaning of paragraph (d)(2)(ii) of this section) considered to be an investment in the contract;

(viii) The net unrealized appreciation on any securities of the employer corporation.

*(2) Alternate method of communication.* The obligation of the employer to communicate the information described in subparagraph (1) of this paragraph to the recipient shall be satisfied if the fiduciary of the trust or the payer of such distribution communicates the information to the recipient.

*(3) Taxable year of recipient.* The report required by this paragraph may be prepared, at the option of the employer as if the taxable year of each employee were the calendar year.

*(4) Failure to satisfy requirements.* In the event that the requirements of this paragraph are not satisfied, the information required to be furnished under this paragraph shall be furnished as part of the return required to be filed under section 6058 and the regulations thereunder.

**Proposed § 1.402(e)-3 Election to treat an amount as a lump sum distribution.** [*For Preamble, see ¶ 150,135*]

• ***Caution:*** Proposed section 1.62-1 was finalized by TD 7399, 2/3/76. Proposed sections 1.72-4, 1.72-13, 1.101-2, 1.122-1, 1.402(a)-1, 1.402(e)-2,

1.402(e)-3, 1.403(a)-1, 1.403(a)-2, 1.405-3, 1.652(b)-1, 1.1304-2 and 11.402(e)(4)(B)-1 remain proposed.

***Caution:*** The Treasury has not yet amended Reg § 1.402(e)-3 to reflect changes made by P.L. 99-514, P.L. 97-34.

**(a) In general.** For purposes of sections 402, 403, and this section, an amount which is described in section 402(e)(4)(A) and which is not an annuity contract may be treated as a lump sum distribution under section 402(e)(4)(A) only if the taxpayer elects for the taxable year to have all such amounts received during such year so treated. Not more than one election may be made under this section with respect to an employee after such employee has attained age 59½.

**(b) Taxpayers eligible to make the election.** Individuals, estates, and trusts are the only taxpayers eligible to make the election provided by this section. In the case of a lump sum distribution made with respect to an employee to 2 or more trusts, the election provided by this section shall be made by the employee or by the personal representative of a deceased employee.

**(c) Procedure for making election.** *(1) Time and scope of election.* An election under this section shall be made for each taxable year to which such election is to apply. The election shall be made before the expiration of the period (including extensions thereof) prescribed in section 6511 for making a claim for credit or refund of the assessed tax imposed by chapter 1 of subtitle A of the Code for such taxable year.

*(2) Manner of making election.* An election by the taxpayer with respect to a taxable year shall be made by filing Form 4972 as a part of the taxpayer's income tax return or amended return for the taxable year.

*(3) Revocation of election.* An election made pursuant to this section may be revoked within the time prescribed in subparagraph (1) of this paragraph for making an election, only if there is filed, within such time, an amended income tax return for such taxable year, which includes a statement revoking the election and is accompanied by payment of any tax attributable to the revocation. If an election for a taxable year is revoked, another election may be made for that taxable year under paragraphs (c)(1) and (2) of this section.

*(4) Effect of election on subsequent distribution.* An election made pursuant to this section shall be an election to treat an annuity contract distributed after December 31, 1973, in a lookback period (as defined in § 1.402(e)-2(c)(2)(iii)(F)) beginning after such date as a lump sum distribution in the taxable year of the recipient in which such contract is distributed.

**Proposed § 1.402(e)-14 Election to treat pre-1974 participation as post-1973 participation (the "402(e)(4)(L) election").** [*For Preamble, see ¶ 150,475*]

**(a) In general.** Under section 402(e)(4)(L) and this section, the recipient of a lump sum distribution may elect to treat all calendar years of an employee's active participation in all plans in which the employee has been an active participant as years of active participation after December 31, 1973. This election is the "402(e)(4)(L) election." For rules relating to the treatment of distributions made on behalf of an employee with respect to whom the election is made, see § 1.402(a)-1(a)(9) (relating to the capital gains portion of a lump sum distribution) and § 1.402(e)-2(d)(3)(iii) (relating to the ordinary income portion of a lump sum distribution). For purposes of this section the term "lump sum distribution" means a lump sum distribution as defined in section 402(e)(4)(A), without regard to section 402(e)(4)(B).

**(b) Taxpayers not eligible to make the election.** A taxpayer may not make the 402(e)(4)(L) election with respect to a lump sum distribution made on behalf of an employee, if—

*(1)* The taxpayer received a prior lump sum distribution made on behalf of the employee in a taxable year of the employee (or in a year that would have been a taxable year of the employee, but for the death of the employee) beginning after December 31, 1975, and

*(2)* A portion of that prior lump sum distribution was treated as long-term capital gain under section 402(a)(2) or 403(a)(2).

**(c) Time and scope of election.** *(1) In general.* The 402(e)(4)(L) election shall be made for the first lump sum distribution made with respect to an employee to which the election is to apply. The election does not apply to a lump sum distribution received by the recipient with respect to another employee. The 402(e)(4)(L) election is irrevocable. A revocation under § 1.402(e)-3 of the election to apply the separate tax to a lump sum distribution will not revoke a 402(e)(4)(L) election.

*(2) Application of separate tax.* Nothing in section 402(e)(4)(L) and this section changes the requirements which must be satisfied in order for a lump sum distribution to be eligible for application of the separate tax under section 402(e). Accordingly, a lump sum distribution is not taxable under section 402(e) merely because the 402(e)(4)(L) election is made with respect to, or otherwise applies to, the distribution.

*(3) Example.* The provisions of subparagraph (2) of this paragraph may be illustrated by the following example:

*Example.* (i) A, a calendar year taxpayer aged 59½, separates from the service of A's employer, the M Corporation, on October 31, 1976. On December 15, 1976, A receives a distribution of the balance to A's credit under the M Corporation qualified profit sharing plan. A has been an active participant in the plan since January 1, 1971. The distribution is a lump sum distribution within the meaning of section 402(e)(4)(A) which satisfies the requirements of section 402(e)(4)(C), relating to the aggregation of certain trusts and plans, and section 402(e)(4)(H), relating to a minimum period of participation in the plan.

(ii) A makes the 402(e)(4)(L) election with respect to the distribution. Under section 402(e)(4)(L), all years of A's active participation in all plans in which A has been an active participant are treated as years of active participation after December 31, 1973. Accordingly, no portion of the distribution is taxable as long-term capital gain under section 402(a)(2), and the total taxable amount of the distribution is "ordinary income" for purposes of section 402(e). A also makes the section 402(e)(4)(B) election for A's taxable year in which A receives the distribution. Accordingly, the total taxable amount of the distribution is taxable under the 10-year averaging provisions of section 402(e) (the separate tax).

(iii) On January 15, 1977, A receives a distribution of the balance of A's credit under the M Corporation qualified pension plan. A has been an active participant in the plan since January 1, 1958. The distribution is a lump sum distribution within the meaning of section 402(e)(4)(A) which satisfies the requirements of section 402(e)(4)(C), relating to the aggregation of certain trusts and plans, and section 402(e)(4)(H), relating to a minimum period of participation in the plan. No portion of the distribution is taxable as long-term capital gain under section 402(a)(2) because A made the 402(e)(4)(L) election with respect to A's 1976 distribution. In addition, no portion of the distribution is taxable under the 10-year averaging provisions of section 402(e) because A made a prior election under section 402(e)(4)(B) with respect to a distribution made on A's behalf and after A was age 59½ (the 1976 distribution).

**(d) Manner of making election.** The 402(e)(4)(L) election shall be made in the manner indicated on the form filed pursuant to section 402(e)(4)(B) and § 1.402(e)-3(c)(2) before the expiration of the period prescribed in § 1.402(e)-3 for making the election to apply the separate tax to the ordinary income portion of a lump sum distribution.

**(e) Effective date.** Taxpayers eligible under this section to make the 402(e)(4)(L) election may make the election with respect to a lump sum distribution received after December 31, 1975, and in a taxable year of the recipient beginning after that date.

### § 11.402(e)(4)(A)-1 Lump sum distributions in the case of an employee who has separated from service.

**(a) Balance to the credit of an employee.** Section 402(e)(4)(A) provides that in order for a distribution or payment from a qualified plan to be a lump sum distribution, the distribution or payment must represent the employee's balance under the plan. The employee's balance does not include any amount which is forfeited under the plan (even though the amount may be reinstated) as of the close of the taxable year of the recipient within which the distribution is made. In addition, in the case of an employee who has separated from service, the employee's balance does not include an amount which is subject to forfeiture not later than the close of the plan year within which the employee incurs a one-year break in service (within the meaning of section 411) if—

*(1)* By reason of the break in service, the amount is actually forfeited at or prior to the close of that plan year, and

*(2)* The break in service occurs within 25 months after the employee's separation from service. In the case of a plan which uses the elapsed time method of crediting service, the break in service may occur within 25 months of the employee's severance from service. See Department of Labor regulations relating to the elapsed time method for the date an employee severs from service.

An employee may assume that an amount subject to forfeiture will be treated as forfeited by the date prescribed in subparagraphs (1) and (2) of this paragraph if, under the plan, forfeiture will occur not later than that date. Therefore, he may assume that a distribution is a lump sum distribution at the time it is made, if the other requirements for lump sum distributions are satisfied. However, if the amount is not forfeited by that date, the amount will be taken into account in determining the balance to the credit of the employee. Accordingly, the distribution will not be a lump sum distribution because it did not include the employee's entire balance under the plan.

**(b) Rollover contribution.** As described in paragraph (a) of this section, an employee may assume that a distribution is a lump sum distribution even though part of the balance of his account has not been forfeited at the time the distribution is made. He may then roll the distribution over as a contribution to an individual retirement arrangement pursuant to section 402(a)(5) or 403(a)(4). It may be subsequently determined that the distribution is not a lump sum distribution because an amount subject to forfeiture was not in fact forfeited within the time required in paragraph (a) of this section. In that case, the contribution will be an excess contribution to the individual retirement arrangement, deemed made in the first taxable year of the employee in which it can be determined that an amount subject to forfeiture will not be forfeited.

**(c) Effective date.** This section is effective for distributions made in taxable years of recipients beginning after December 31, 1973.

---

T.D. 7488, 5/26/77.

---

### § 11.402(e)(4)(B)-1 Election to treat an amount as a lump sum distribution.

**(a) In general.** For purposes of sections 402, 403, and this section, an amount which is described in section 402(e)(4)(A) and which is not an annuity contract may be treated as a lump sum distribution under section 402(e)(4)(A) only if the taxpayer elects for the taxable year to have all such amounts received during such year so treated. Not more than one election may be made under this section with respect to an employee after such employee has attained age 59½.

**(b) Taxpayers eligible to make the election.** Individuals, estates, and trusts are the only taxpayers eligible to make the election provided by this section. In the case of a lump sum distribution made with respect to an employee to 2 or more trusts, the election provided by this section shall be made by the employee or by the personal representative of a deceased employee.

**(c) Procedure for making election.** *(1) Time and scope of election.* An election under this section shall be made for each taxable year to which such election is to apply. The election shall be made before the expiration of the period (including extension thereof) prescribed in section 6511 for making a claim for credit or refund of the assessed tax imposed by chapter 1 of subtitle A of the Code for such taxable year.

*(2) Manner of making election.* An election by the taxpayer with respect to a taxable year shall be made by filing Form 4972 as a part of the taxpayer's income tax return or amended return for the taxable year.

*(3) Revocation of election.* An election made pursuant to this section may be revoked within the time prescribed in subparagraph (1) of this paragraph for making an election, only if there is filed, within such time, an amended income tax return for such taxable year, which includes a statement revoking the election and is accompanied by payment of any tax attributable to the revocation. If an election for a taxable year is revoked, another election may be made for that taxable year under subparagraphs (1) and (2) of this paragraph.

---

T.D. 7339, 1/3/75.

---

PAR. 21. Section 11.402(e)(4)(B)-1 is revoked.

**Proposed § 11.402(e)(4)(B)-1 [Revoked]** [*For Preamble, see ¶ 150,135*]

• ***Caution:*** Proposed section 1.62-1 was finalized by TD 7399, 2/3/76. Proposed sections 1.72-4, 1.72-13, 1.101-2, 1.122-1, 1.402(a)-1, 1.402(e)-2,

1.402(e)-3, 1.403(a)-1, 1.403(a)-2, 1.405-3, 1.652(b)-1, 1.1304-2 and 11.402(e)(4)(B)-1 remain proposed.

### § 1.402(f)-1 Required explanation of eligible rollover distributions; questions and answers.

***Caution:*** The Treasury has not yet amended Reg § 1.402(f)-1 to reflect changes made by P.L. 109-280.

The following questions and answers concern the written explanation requirement imposed by section 402(f) of the Internal Revenue Code of 1986 relating to distributions eligible for rollover treatment. Section 402(f) was amended by section 521(a) of the Unemployment Compensation Amendments of 1992, Public Law 102-318, 106 Stat. 290 (UCA). For additional UCA guidance under sections 401(a)(31), 402(c), 403(b)(8) and (10), and 3405(c), see §§ 1.401(a)(31)-1, 1.402(c)-2, 1.403(b)-7(b), and 31.3405(c)-1 of this chapter, respectively.

*List of Questions*

Q-1. What are the requirements for a written explanation under section 402(f)?

Q-2. When must the plan administrator provide the section 402(f) notice to a distributee?

Q-3. Must the plan administrator provide a separate section 402(f) notice for each distribution in a series of periodic payments that are eligible rollover distributions?

Q-4. May a plan administrator post the section 402(f) notice as a means of providing it to distributees?

Questions and Answers

Q-1. What are the requirements for a written explanation under section 402(f)?

A-1. **(a) General rule.** Under section 402(f), as amended by UCA, the plan administrator of a qualified plan is required, within a reasonable period of time before making an eligible rollover distribution, to provide the distributee with the written explanation described in section 402(f) (section 402(f) notice). The section 402(f) notice must be designed to be easily understood and must explain the following: the rules under which the distributee may elect that the distribution be paid in the form of a direct rollover to an eligible retirement plan; the rules that require the withholding of tax on the distribution if it is not paid in a direct rollover; the rules under which the distributee may defer tax on the distribution if it is contributed in a rollover to an eligible retirement plan within 60 days of the distribution; and if applicable, certain special rules regarding the taxation of the distribution as described in section 402(d) (averaging with respect to lump sum distributions) and (e) (other rules including treatment of net unrealized appreciation). See § 1.401(a)(31)-1, Q&A-7 for additional information that must be provided if a plan provides a default procedure regarding the election of a direct rollover.

**(b) Model section 402(f) notice.** The plan administrator will be deemed to have complied with the requirements of paragraph (a) of this Q&A-1 relating to the contents of the section 402(f) notice if the plan administrator provides the applicable model section 402(f) notice published by the Internal Revenue Service for this purpose in a revenue ruling, notice, or other guidance published in the Internal Revenue Bulletin. See § 601.601(d)(2)(ii)(b) of this chapter.

**(c) Delegation to Commissioner.** The Commissioner, in revenue rulings, notices, and other guidance, published in the Internal Revenue Bulletin, may modify, or provide any additional guidance with respect to, the notice requirement of this section. See § 601.601(d)(2)(ii)(b) of this chapter.

**(d) Effective date.** *(1) Statutory effective date.* Section 402(f) applies to eligible rollover distributions made after December 31, 1992.

*(2) Regulatory effective date.* This section applies to eligible rollover distributions made on or after October 19, 1995. For eligible rollover distributions made on or after January 1, 1993 and before October 19, 1995, section 1.402(c)-2T, Q&A-11 through 15 (as it appeared in the April 1, 1995 edition of 26 CFR part 1), apply. However, for any distribution made on or after January 1, 1993 but before October 19, 1995, a plan administrator or payor may satisfy the requirements of section 402(f) by substituting any or all provisions of this section for the corresponding provisions of § 1.402(c)-1T, Q&A-11 through 15, if any.

Q-2. When must the plan administrator provide the section 402(f) notice to a distributee?

A-2. The plan administrator must provide the section 402(f) notice to a distributee at a time that satisfies either paragraph (a) or (b) of this Q&A-2.

**(a)** This paragraph (a) is satisfied if the plan administrator provides a distributee with the section 402(f) notice no less than 30 days and no more than 90 days before the date of a distribution. However, if the distributee, after having received the section 402(f) notice, affirmatively elects a distribution, a plan will not fail to satisfy section 402(f) merely because the distribution is made less than 30 days after the section 402(f) notice was provided to the distributee, provided the plan administrator clearly indicates to the distributee that the distributee has a right to consider the decision of whether or not to elect a direct rollover for at least 30 days after the notice is provided. The plan administrator may use any method to inform the distributee of the relevant time period, provided that the method is reasonably designed to attract the attention of the distributee. For example, this information could be either provided in the section 402(f) notice or stated in a separate document (e.g., attached to the election form) that is provided at the same time as the notice. For purposes of satisfying the requirement in the first sentence of paragraph (a) of this Q&A-2, the plan administrator may substitute the annuity starting date, within the meaning of § 1.401(a)-20, Q&A-10, for the date of the distribution.

**(b)** This paragraph (b) is satisfied if the plan administrator—

*(1)* Provides a distributee with the section 402(f) notice;

*(2)* Provides the distributee with a summary of the section 402(f) notice within the time period described in paragraph (a) of this Q&A-2; and

*(3)* If the distributee so requests after receiving the summary described in paragraph (b)(2) of this Q&A-2, provides the section 402(f) notice to the distributee without charge and no less than 30 days before the date of a distribution (or the annuity starting date), subject to the rules for the distributee's waiver of that 30-day period. The summary described in paragraph (b)(2) of this Q&A-2 must set forth a summary of the principal provisions of the section 402(f) notice, must refer the distributee to the most recent version of the section 402(f) notice (and, in the case of a notice provided in any document containing information in addition to the notice, must identify that document and must provide a reasonable indication of where the notice may be found in that document, such as by index reference or by section heading), and must advise the distributee that, upon request, a copy of the section 402(f) notice will be provided without charge.

Q-3. Must the plan administrator provide a separate section 402(f) notice for each distribution in a series of periodic payments that are eligible rollover distributions?

A-3. No. In the case of a series of periodic payments that are eligible rollover distributions, the plan administrator is permitted to satisfy section 402(f) with respect to each payment in the series by providing the section 402(f) notice prior to the first payment in the series, in accordance with the rules in Q&A-1 and Q&A-2 of this section, and providing the notice at least once annually for as long as the payments continue. However, see § 1.401(a)(31)-1 for additional guidance if the plan administrator intends to treat a distributee's election to make or not make a direct rollover with respect to one payment in a series of periodic payments as applicable to all subsequent payments in the series (absent a subsequent change of election).

Q-4. May a plan administrator post the section 402(f) notice as a means of providing it to distributees?

A-4. No. The posting of the section 402(f) notice will not be considered provision of the notice. The written notice must be provided individually to any distributee of an eligible rollover distribution within the time period described in Q&A-2 and Q&A-3 of this section.

Q-5. Will the requirements of section 402(f) be satisfied if a plan administrator provides a distributee with the section 402(f) notice or the summary of the notice described in paragraph (b)(2) of Q&A-2 of this section other than through a written paper document?

A-5. Yes. See § 1.401(a)-21 of this chapter for rules permitting the use of electronic media to provide applicable notices to recipients with respect to retirement plans.

T.D. 8219, 8/19/88, amend T.D. 8619, 9/15/95, T.D. 8873, 2/7/2000, T.D. 9294, 10/19/2006, T.D. 9340, 7/23/2007.

PAR. 2. For each entry listed in the "Location" column, remove the language in the "Remove" column and add the language in the "Add" column in its place.

PAR. 2. For each entry listed in the "Location" column, remove the language in the "Remove" column and add the language in the "Add" column in its place.

PAR. 2. For each entry listed in the "Location" column, remove the language in the "Remove" column and add the language in the "Add" column in its place.

PAR. 2. For each entry listed in the "Location" column, remove the language in the "Remove" column and add the language in the "Add" column in its place.

PAR. 2. For each entry listed in the "Location" column, remove the language in the "Remove" column and add the language in the "Add" column in its place.

**Proposed § 1.402(f)-1** [*For Preamble, see ¶ 153,065*]

| Location | Remove | Add |
|---|---|---|
| 1.401(a)-13(g)(4)(ii), first sentence | 90 days | 180 days. |
| 1.401(a)-20, A-4, third sentence | 90 days | 180 days. |
| 1.401(a)-20, A-10(a), fifth and sixth sentences. | 90 days | 180 days. |
| 1.401(a)-20, A-16, sixth sentence. | 90 days | 180 days. |
| 1.401(a)-20, A-24(a)(1), fifth sentence. | 90 days | 180 days. |
| 1.402(f)-1, A-2(a), first sentence. | 90 days | 180 days. |
| 1.411(a)-11(c)(2)(ii) | 90 days | 180 days. |
| 1.411(a)-11(c)(2)(iii)(A), first sentence. | 90 days | 180 days. |
| 1.417(e)-1(b)(3)(i) | 90 days | 180 days. |
| 1.417(e)-1(b)(3)(ii), first sentence. | 90 days | 180 days. |
| 1.417(e)-1(b)(3)(iii) | 90 days | 180 days. |
| 1.417(e)-1(b)(3)(vi), second sentence. | 90 days | 180 days. |
| 1.417(e)-1(b)(3)(vii) | 90 days | 180 days. |
| 1.417(e)-1(b)(3)(vii) | 90-day | 180-day. |

**§ 1.402(g)-0 Limitation on exclusion for elective deferrals, table of contents.**

This section contains the captions that appear in § 1.402(g)-1.

---

T.D. 8357, 8/8/91.

---

### § 1.402(g)-1 Limitation on exclusion for elective deferrals.

***Caution:*** The Treasury has not yet amended Reg § 1.402(g)-1 to reflect changes made by P.L. 110-458, P.L. 107-147, P.L. 107-16, P.L. 103-465.

**(a) In general.** The excess of an individual's elective deferrals for any taxable year over the applicable limit for the year may not be excluded from gross income under sections 402(a)(8), 402(h)(1)(B), 403(b), 408(k)(6), or 501(c)(18). Thus, an individual's elective deferrals in excess of the applicable limit for a taxable year (that is, the individual's excess deferrals for the year) must be included in gross income for the year, except to the extent the excess deferrals are comprised of designated Roth contributions, and thus, are already includible in gross income. A designated Roth contribution is treated as an excess deferral only to the extent that the total amount of designated Roth contributions for an individual exceeds the applicable limit for the taxable year or the designated Roth contributions are identified as excess deferrals and the individual receives a distribution of the excess deferrals and allocable income under paragraph (e)(2) or (e)(3) of this section.

**(b) Elective deferrals.** An individual's elective deferrals for a taxable year are the sum of the following:

*(1)* Any elective contribution under a qualified cash or deferred arrangement (as defined in section 401(k)) to the extent not includible in the individual's gross income for the taxable year on account of section 402(a)(8) (before applying the limits of section 402(g) or this section).

*(2)* Any employer contribution to a simplified employee pension (as defined in section 408(k)) to the extent not includible in the individual's gross income for the taxable year on account of section 402(h)(1)(B) (before applying the limits of section 402(g) or this section).

*(3)* Any employer contribution to an annuity contract under section 403(b) under a salary reduction agreement (within the meaning of section 3121(a)(5)(D)) to the extent not includible in the individual's gross income for the taxable year on account of section 403(b) (before applying the limits of section 402(g) or this section).

*(4)* Any employee contribution designated as deductible under a trust described in section 501(c)(18) to the extent deductible from the individual's income for the taxable year on account of section 501(c)(18) (before applying the limits of section 402(g) or this section). For purposes of this section, the employee contribution is treated as though it were excluded from the individual's gross income.

*(5)* Any designated Roth contributions described in section 402A (before applying the limits of section 402(g) or this section).

*(6)* Any elective employer contributions to a SIMPLE retirement account, on behalf of an employee pursuant to a qualified salary reduction arrangement as described in section 408(p)(2) (before applying the limits of section 402(g) or this section).

**(c) Certain one-time irrevocable elections.** An employer contribution is not treated as an elective deferral under paragraph (b) of this section if the contribution is made pursuant to a one-time irrevocable election made by the employee:

*(1)* In the case of an annuity contract under section 403(b), at the time of initial eligibility to participate in the salary reduction agreement;

*(2)* In the case of a qualified cash or deferred arrangement, at a time when, under § 1.401(k)-1(a)(3)(v), the election is not treated as a cash or deferred election;

*(3)* In the case of a trust described in section 501(c)(18), at the time of initial eligibility to have the employer contribute on the employee's behalf to the trust.

**(d) Applicable limit.** *(1) In general.* Except as provided under paragraph (d)(2) of this section, the applicable limit for an individual's taxable year is the applicable dollar amount set forth in section 402(g)(1)(B). This applicable dollar amount is increased for the taxable year beginning in 2007 and later years in the same manner as the dollar amount under section 415(b)(1)(A) is adjusted pursuant to section 415(d). See § 1.402(g)-2 for the treatment of catch-up contributions described in section 414(v).

*(2) Special adjustment for elective deferrals with respect to section 403(b) annuity contracts for certain long-term employees.* The applicable limit for an individual who is a qualified employee (as defined in section 402(g)(7)(C)) and has elective deferrals described in paragraph (b)(3) or (5) of this section for a taxable year is adjusted by increasing the applicable limit otherwise determined under paragraph (d)(1) of this section in accordance with section 402(g)(7).

**(e) Treatment of excess deferrals.** *(1) Plan qualification.* (i) Effect of excess deferrals. For plan years beginning before January 1, 1988, a plan, annuity contract, simplified employee pension, or trust does not fail to meet the requirements of section 401(a), section 403(b), section 408(k), or section 501(c)(18), respectively, merely because excess deferrals are made with respect to the plan, contract, pension, or trust. For plan years beginning after December 31, 1987, see section 401(a)(30) and § 1.401(a)-30 for the effect of excess deferrals on the qualification of a plan or trust under section 401(a). For purposes of determining whether a plan or trust complies in operation with section 401(a)(30), excess deferrals that are distributed under paragraph (e)(2) or (3) of this section are disregarded. Similar rules apply to annuity contracts under section 403(b), simplified employee pensions under section 408(k), and plans or trusts under section 501(c)(18).

(ii) Treatment of excess deferrals as employer contributions. For other purposes of the Code, including sections 401(a)(4), 401(k)(3), 404, 409, 411, 412, and 416, excess deferrals must be treated as employer contributions even if they are distributed in accordance with paragraph (e)(2) or (3) of this section. However, excess deferrals of a nonhighly compensated employee are not taken into account under section 401(k)(3) (the actual deferral percentage test) to the extent the excess deferrals are prohibited under section 401(a)(30). Excess deferrals are also treated as employer contributions for purposes of section 415 unless distributed under paragraph (e)(2) or (3) of this section.

(iii) Definition of excess deferrals. The term "excess deferrals" means the excess of an individual's elective deferrals for any taxable year, as defined in § 1.402(g)-1(b), over the applicable limit under section 402(g)(1) for the taxable year.

*(2) Correction of excess deferrals after the taxable year.* Correction of excess deferrals after the taxable year. A plan may provide that if any amount is an excess deferral under paragraph (a) of this section:

(i) Not later than the first April 15 (or such earlier date specified in the plan) following the close of the individual's taxable year, the individual may notify each plan under which elective deferrals were made of the amount of the excess deferrals received by the plan. If any designated Roth contributions were made to a plan, the notification must also identify the extent, if any, to which the excess deferrals are comprised of designated Roth contributions. A plan may provide that an individual is deemed to have notified the plan of excess deferrals (including the portion of excess deferrals that are comprised of designated Roth contributions) to the extent the individual has excess deferrals for the taxable year calculated by taking into account only elective deferrals under the plan and other plans of the same employer and the plan may provide the extent to which such excess deferrals are comprised of designated Roth contributions. A plan may instead provide that the employer may notify the plan on behalf of the individual under these circumstances.

(ii) Not later than the first April 15 following the close of the taxable year, the plan may distribute to the individual the amount designated under paragraph (e)(2)(i) of this section (and any income allocable to that amount).

*(3) Correction of excess deferrals during taxable year.* (i) A plan may provide that an individual who has excess deferrals for a taxable year may receive a corrective distribution of excess deferrals during the same year. This corrective distribution may be made only if all of the following conditions are satisfied:

(A) The individual designates the distribution as an excess deferral. A plan may provide that an individual is deemed to have designated the distribution to the extent the individual has excess deferrals for the taxable year calculated by taking into account only elective deferrals under the plan and other plans of the same employer. If any designated Roth contributions were made to a plan, the notification must identify the extent to which, if any, the excess deferrals are comprised of designated Roth contributions. A plan may provide that an individual is deemed to have notified the plan of excess deferrals (including the portion of excess deferrals that are comprised of designated Roth contributions) for the taxable year calculated by taking into account only elective deferrals under the plan and other plans of the same employer and the plan may provide the extent to which such excess deferrals are comprised of designated Roth contributions.

(B) The correcting distribution is made after the date on which the plan received the excess deferral.

(C) The plan designates the distribution as a distribution of excess deferrals.

(ii) The provisions of this paragraph (e)(3) are illustrated by the following example:

*Example.* S is a 62 year old individual who participates in Employer Y's qualified cash or deferred arrangement. In January 1991, S withdraws $5,000 from Y's cash or deferred arrangement. From February through September, S defers $900 per month. On October 1, S leaves Employer Y and becomes employed by Employer Z (unrelated to Y). During the remainder of 1991, S defers $1,800 under Z's qualified cash or deferred arrangement. In January 1992, S realizes that S has deferred a total of $9,000 in 1991, and therefore has a $525 excess deferral ($9,000 minus $8,475, the applicable limit for 1991). An additional $525 must be distributed to S before April 15, 1992, to correct the excess deferral. The $5,000 withdrawal did not correct the excess deferral because it occurred before the excess deferral was made.

*(4) Plan provisions.* In order to distribute excess deferrals pursuant to paragraphs (e)(2) or (e)(3) of this section, a plan must contain language permitting distribution of excess deferrals. A plan may require the notification in paragraphs (e)(2) and (e)(3) of this section to be in writing and may require that the employee certify or otherwise establish that the designated amount is an excess deferral. A plan need not permit distribution of excess deferrals.

*(5) Income allocable to excess deferrals.* (i) General rule. The income allocable to excess deferrals for a taxable year that begins on or after January 1, 2007 is equal to the sum of the allocable gain or loss for the taxable year of the individual and, to the extent the excess deferrals are or will be credited with gain or loss for the period after the close of the taxable year and prior to the distribution (the gap period) if the total account were to be distributed, the allocable gain or loss during that period. The income allocable to excess deferrals for a taxable year that begins before 2007 is determined using the 1.402(g)-1(e)(5) (as it appeared in the April 1, 2006 edition of 26 CFR Part 1).

(ii) Method of allocating income. A plan may use any reasonable method for computing the income allocable to excess deferrals, provided that the method does not violate section 401(a)(4), is used consistently for all participants and for all corrective distributions under a plan for the plan year, and is used by the plan for allocating income to participants' accounts. See § 1.401(a)(4)-1(c)(8). A plan will not fail to use a reasonable method for computing the income allocable to excess deferrals merely because the income allocable to excess deferrals is determined on a date that is no more than 7 days before the distribution.

(iii) Alternative method of allocating taxable year income. A plan may determine the income allocable to excess deferrals for the taxable year by multiplying the income for the taxable year allocable to elective deferrals by a fraction. The numerator of the fraction is the excess deferrals by the employee for the taxable year. The denominator of the fraction is equal to the sum of:

(A) The total account balance of the employee attributable to elective deferrals as of the beginning of the taxable year, plus

(B) The employee's elective deferrals for the taxable year.

(iv) Safe harbor method of allocating gap period income. Under the safe harbor method, income on excess deferrals for the gap period is equal to 10 percent of the income allocable to excess deferrals for the taxable year (calculated under the method described in paragraph (e)(5)(iii) of this section), multiplied by the number of calendar months that have elapsed since the end of the taxable year. For purposes of calculating the number of calendar months that have elapsed under the safe harbor method, a corrective distribution that is made on or before the fifteenth day of the month is treated as made on the last day of the preceding month. A distribution made after the fifteenth day of the month is treated as made on the first day of the next month.

(v) Alternative method for allocating taxable year and gap period income. A plan may determine the allocable gain or loss for the aggregate of the taxable year and the gap period by applying the alternative method provided by paragraph (e)(5)(iii) of this section to this aggregate period. This is accomplished by substituting the income for the taxable year and the gap period for the income for the taxable year and by substituting the elective deferrals for the taxable year and the gap period for the elective deferrals for the taxable year in determining the fraction that is multiplied by that income.

*(6) Coordination with distribution or recharacterization of excess contributions.* The amount of excess deferrals that may be distributed under this paragraph (e) with respect to an employee for a taxable year is reduced by any excess contributions previously distributed or recharacterized with respect to the employee for the plan year beginning with or within the taxable year. In the event of a reduction under this paragraph (e)(6), the amount of excess contributions includible in the gross income of the employee and reported by the employer as a distribution of excess contributions is reduced by the amount of the reduction under this paragraph (e)(6). See § 1.401(k)-2(b)(4)(i). In no case may an individual receive from a plan as a corrective distribution for a taxable year under paragraph (e)(2) or (e)(3) of this section an amount in excess of the individual's total elective deferrals under the plan for the taxable year.

*(7) No employee or spousal consent required.* A corrective distribution of excess deferrals (and income) may be made under the terms of the plan without regard to any notice or consent otherwise required under sections 411(a)(11) or 417.

*(8) Tax treatment.* (i) Corrective distributions on or before April 15 after close of taxable year. A corrective distribution of excess deferrals within the period described in paragraph (e)(2) or (e)(3) of this section is excludable from the employee's gross income. However, the income allocable to excess deferrals is includible in the employee's gross income for the taxable year in which the allocable income is distributed. The corrective distribution of excess deferrals (and income) is not subject to the early distribution tax of section 72(t) and is not treated as a distribution for purposes of applying the excise tax under section 4980A.

(ii) Special rule for 1987 and 1988 excess deferrals. Income on excess deferrals for 1987 or 1988 that were timely distributed on or before April 17, 1989, may be reported by the recipient either in the year described in paragraph (e)(8)(i) of this section, or in the year in which the employee would have received the elective deferrals had the employee originally elected to receive the amounts in cash.

(iii) Distributions of excess deferrals after correction period. If excess deferrals (and income) for a taxable year are not distributed within the period described in paragraphs (e)(2) and (e)(3) of this section, they may only be distributed when permitted under section 401(k)(2)(B). These amounts are includible in gross income when distributed, and are treated for purposes of the distribution rules otherwise applicable to the plan as elective deferrals (and income) that were excludable from the individual's gross income under section 402(g). Thus, any amount includible in gross income for any taxable year under this section that is not distributed by April 15 of the following taxable year is not treated as an investment in the contract for purposes of section 72 and is includible in the employee's gross income when distributed from the plan. Excess deferrals that are distributed under this paragraph (e)(8)(iii) are treated as employer contributions for purposes of section 415 when they are contributed to the plan.

(iv) Distributions of excess deferrals from a designated Roth account. The rules of paragraph (e)(8)(iii) of this section generally apply to distributions of excess deferrals that are designated Roth contributions and the attributable income. Thus, if a designated Roth account described in section 402A includes any excess deferrals, any distribution of amounts attributable to those excess deferrals are includible in gross income (without adjustment for any return of investment in the contract under section 72(e)(8)). In addition, such distributions cannot be qualified distributions described in section 402A(d)(2) and are not eligible rollover distributions within the meaning of section 402(c)(4). For this purpose, if a designated Roth account includes any excess deferrals, any distributions from the account are treated as attributable to those excess deferrals until the total amount distributed from the designated Roth account equals the total of such deferrals and attributable income.

*(9) No reduction of required minimum distribution.* A distribution of excess deferrals (and income) under paragraphs (e)(2) and (e)(3) of this section is not treated as a distribution for purposes of determining whether the plan meets the minimum distribution requirements of section 401(a)(9).

*(10) Partial correction.* Any distribution under paragraphs (e)(2) or (e)(3) of this section of less than the entire amount of excess deferrals (and income) is treated as a pro rata distribution of excess deferrals and income.

*(11) Examples.* The provisions of this paragraph are illustrated by the following examples. Assume in Examples 1 and 2 that there is no income or loss allocable to the elective deferrals.

*Example (1).* Employee A is a 60-year old highly compensated employee who participates in Employer M's cash or deferred arrangement. During the period of January through September of 1988, A contributed $7,000 to the arrangement in elective deferrals. During the same period A also contributed $813 in elective deferrals under a plan of an unrelated employer. In December of 1988, A made a withdrawal of $1,000 from Employer M's plan but did not designate this as a withdrawal of an excess deferral. In January of 1989, A notifies Employer M of an excess deferral, specifying a distribution of $500 for 1988. To correct the excess deferrals, A must receive this additional $500 even though A has already withdrawn $1,000 for 1988. A may exclude from income in 1988 only $7,313. However, if the $500 is distributed by April 15, 1989, the distribution is excludable from A's gross income in 1989. Even if A withdraws the $500, M must take into account the entire $7,000 in computing A's actual deferral percentage for 1988.

*Example (2).* (i) Corporation X maintains a cash or deferred arrangement. The plan year is the calendar year. For plan year 1989, all 10 of X's employees are eligible to participate in the plan. The employees' compensation, contributions, and actual deferral ratios are shown in the following table:

| Employee | Compensation | Contribution | Actual Deferral Ratio |
|---|---|---|---|
| A | $140,000 | $7,000 | 5.0% |
| B | 70,000 | 7,000 | 10.0 |
| C | 70,000 | 7,000 | 10.0 |
| D | 45,000 | 2,250 | 5.0 |
| E | 40,000 | 4,000 | 10.0 |
| F | 35,000 | 1,750 | 5.0 |
| G | 35,000 | 350 | 1.0 |
| H | 30,000 | 3,000 | 10.0 |
| I | 17,500 | 0 | 0.0 |
| J | 17,500 | 0 | 0.0 |

(ii) Employees A, B, and C are highly compensated employees within the meaning of section 414(q). Employees D, E, F, G, H, I, and J are nonhighly compensated employees. The actual deferral percentages for the highly compensated employees and nonhighly compensated employees are 8.33 percent and 4.43 percent, respectively. These percentages do not satisfy the requirements of section 401(k)(3)(A)(ii). The actual deferral percentage for the highly compensated employees may not exceed 6.43 percent.

(iii) The plan reduces the actual deferral ratios of B and C to 7.14 percent by distributing $2,002 ($7,000 – .0714 × $70,000) to each in January 1990. Section 401(k)(3)(A)(ii) is therefore satisfied.

(iv) In February 1990, B notifies X that B made elective deferrals of $2,000 under a qualified cash or deferred arrangement maintained by an unrelated employer in 1989, and requests distribution of $2,000 from X's plan. However, since B has already received a distribution of $2,002 to meet the ADP test, no additional amounts are required or are permitted to be distributed as excess deferrals by this plan, and the prior distribution of excess contributions has corrected the excess deferrals. But X must report $2,000 as a distribution of an excess deferral and $2 as a distribution of an excess contribution.

*Example (3).* Employee T has excess deferrals of $1,000. The income attributable to excess deferrals is $100. T properly notifies the employer, and requests a distribution of the excess deferral (and income) on February 1. The plan distributes $1,000 to T by April 15. Because the plan did not distribute any additional amount as income, $909 is treated as a distribution of excess deferrals, and $91 is treated as a distribution of earnings. With respect to amounts remaining in the account, $91 is treated as an elective deferral and is not included in T's investment in the contract. Because it was not distributed by the required date, the $91 is includible in gross income upon distribution as well as in the year of deferral.

**(f) Community property laws.** This section is applied without regard to community property laws.

**(g) Effective date.** *(1) In general.* Except as otherwise provided, the provisions of this section are effective for taxable years beginning after December 31, 1986.

*(2) Deferrals under collective bargaining agreements.* In the case of a plan maintained pursuant to one or more collective bargaining agreements between employee representatives and one or more employers ratified before March 1, 1986, the provisions of this section do not apply to contributions made pursuant to the collective bargaining agreement for taxable years beginning before the earlier of January 1, 1989, or the date on which the agreement terminates (determined without regard to any extension thereof after February 28, 1986). These contributions under a collective bargaining agreement are taken into account for purposes of applying this section to elective deferrals under plans not described in this paragraph (g)(2).

*(3) Transition rule.* For taxable years beginning before January 1, 1992, a plan or an individual may rely on a reasonable interpretation of the rules set forth in section 402(g), as in effect during those years.

*(4) Partnership cash or deferred arrangements.* For purposes of section 402(g), employer contributions for any plan year beginning after December 31, 1986, and before January 1, 1989, under an arrangement that directly or indirectly permits individual partners to vary the amount of contributions made on their behalf will be treated as elective contributions only if the arrangement was intended to satisfy and did satisfy the nondiscrimination test of section 401(k)(3) and § 1.401(k)-1(b) for the plan year.

T.D. 8357, 8/8/91, amend T.D. 8581, 12/22/94, T.D. 9169, 12/28/2004, T.D. 9324, 4/27/2007.

## § 1.402(g)-2 Increased limit for catch-up contributions.

**(a) General rule.** Under section 402(g)(1)(C), in determining the amount of elective deferrals that are includible in gross income under section 402(g) for a catch-up eligible participant (within the meaning of § 1.414(v)-1(g)), the otherwise applicable dollar limit under section 402(g)(1)(B) (as increased under section 402(g)(7), to the extent applicable) shall be further increased by the applicable dollar catch-up limit as set forth under § 1.414(v)-1(c)(2).

**(b) Participants in multiple plans.** Paragraph (a) of this section applies without regard to whether the applicable employer plans (within the meaning of section 414(v)(6)) treat the elective deferrals as catch-up contributions. Thus, a catch-up eligible participant who makes elective deferrals under applicable employer plans of two or more employers that in total exceed the applicable dollar amount under section 402(g)(1) by an amount that does not exceed the applicable dollar catch-up limit under either plan may exclude the elective deferrals from gross income, even if neither applicable employer plan treats those elective deferrals as catch-up contributions.

**(c) Effective date.** *(1) Statutory effective date.* Section 402(g)(1)(C) applies to contributions in taxable years beginning on or after January 1, 2002.

*(2) Regulatory effective date.* Paragraphs (a) and (b) of this section apply to contributions in taxable years beginning on or after January 1, 2004.

T.D. 9072, 7/7/2003.

## § 1.402(g)(3)-1 Employer contributions to purchase a section 403(b) contract under a salary reduction agreement.

**(a) General rule.** With respect to an annuity contract under section 403(b), except as provided in paragraph (b) of this section, an elective deferral means an employer contribution to purchase an annuity contract under section 403(b) under a salary reduction agreement within the meaning of section 3121(a)(5)(D).

**(b) Special rule.** Notwithstanding paragraph (a) of this section, for purposes of section 403(b), an elective deferral only includes a contribution that is made pursuant to a cash or deferred election (as defined at § 1.401(k)-1(a)(3)). Thus, for purposes of section 402(g)(3)(C), an elective deferral does not include a contribution that is made pursuant to an employee's one-time irrevocable election made on or before the employee's first becoming eligible to participate under the employer's plans or a contribution made as a condition of employment that reduces the employee's compensation.

**(c) Applicable date.** This section is applicable for taxable years beginning after December 31, 2008.

T.D. 9340, 7/23/2007.

**§ 1.402A-1 Designated Roth Accounts.**

Q-1. What is a designated Roth account?

A-1. A designated Roth account is a separate account under a qualified cash or deferred arrangement under a section 401(a) plan, or under a section 403(b) plan, to which designated Roth contributions are permitted to be made in lieu of elective contributions and that satisfies the requirements of § 1.401(k)-1(f) (in the case of a section 401(a) plan) or § 1.403(b)-3(c) (in the case of a section 403(b) plan).

Q-2. How is a distribution from a designated Roth account taxed?

A-1. (a) The taxation of a distribution from a designated Roth account depends on whether or not the distribution is a qualified distribution. A qualified distribution from a designated Roth account is not includible in the distributee's gross income.

(b) Except as otherwise provided in paragraph (c) of this A-2, a qualified distribution is a distribution that is both—

(1) Made after the 5-taxable-year period of participation defined in A-4 of this section has been completed; and

(2) Made on or after the date the employee attains age 59½, made to a beneficiary or the estate of the employee on or after the employee's death, or attributable to the employee's being disabled within the meaning of section 72(m)(7).

(c) A distribution from a designated Roth account is not a qualified distribution to the extent it consists of a distribution of excess deferrals and attributable income described in § 1.402(g)-1(e). See A-11 of this section for other amounts that are not treated as qualified distributions, including excess contributions described in section 401(k)(8), and excess aggregate contributions described in section 401(m)(8), and income, on any of these excess amounts.

Q-3. How is a distribution from a designated Roth account taxed if it is not a qualified distribution?

A-3. Except as provided in A-11 of this section, a distribution from a designated Roth account that is not a qualified distribution is taxable to the distributee under section 402 in the case of a plan qualified under section 401(a) and under section 403(b)(1) in the case of a section 403(b) plan. For this purpose, a designated Roth account is treated as a separate contract under section 72. Thus, except as otherwise provided in A-5 of this section for a rollover, if a distribution is before the annuity starting date, the portion of any distribution that is includible in gross income as an amount allocable to income on the contract and the portion not includible in gross income as an amount allocable to investment in the contract is determined under section 72(e)(8), treating the designated Roth account as a separate contract. Similarly, in the case of any amount received as an annuity, if a distribution is on or after the annuity starting date, the portion of any annuity payment that is includible in gross income as an amount allocable to income on the contract and the portion not includible in gross income as an amount allocable to investment in the contract is determined under section 72(b) or (d), as applicable, treating the designated Roth account as a separate contract. For purposes of section 72, designated Roth contributions are described in section 72(f)(1) or 72(f)(2), to the extent applicable.

Q-4. What is the 5-taxable-year period of participation described in A-2 of this section?

A-4. (a) The 5-taxable-year period of participation described in A-2 of this section for a plan is the period of 5 consecutive taxable years that begins with the first day of the first taxable year in which the employee makes a designated Roth contribution to any designated Roth account established for the employee under the same plan and ends when 5 consecutive taxable years have been completed. For this purpose, the first taxable year in which an employee makes a designated Roth contribution is the year in which the amount is includible in the employee's gross income. Notwithstanding the preceding, however, a contribution that is returned as an excess deferral or excess contribution does not begin the 5 taxable-year period of participation. Similarly, a contribution returned as a permissible withdrawal under section 414(w) does not begin the 5 taxable-year period of participation.

(b) Generally, an employee's 5-taxable-year period of participation is determined separately for each plan (within the meaning of section 414(l)) in which the employee participates. Thus, if an employee has elective deferrals made to designated Roth accounts under two or more plans, the employee may have two or more different 5-taxable-year periods of participation, depending on when the employee first had contributions made to a designated Roth account under each plan. However, if a direct rollover contribution of a distribution from a designated Roth account under another plan is made by the employee to the plan, the 5-taxable-year period of participation begins on the first day of the employee's taxable year in which the employee first had designated Roth contributions made to such other designated Roth account, if earlier than the first taxable year in which a designated Roth contribution is made to the plan. See A-5(c) of this section for additional rules on determining the start of the 5-taxable-year of participation in the case of an indirect rollover.

(c) The beginning of the 5-taxable-year period of participation is not redetermined for any portion of an employee's designated Roth account. This is true even if the entire designated Roth account is distributed during the 5-taxable-year period of participation and the employee subsequently makes additional designated Roth contributions under the plan.

(d) The rule in paragraph (c) of this section applies if the employee dies or the account is divided pursuant to a qualified domestic relations order (QDRO), and thus, a portion of the account is not payable to the employee and is payable to the employee's beneficiary or an alternate payee. In the case of distribution to an alternate payee or beneficiary, generally, the age, death, or disability of the employee is used to determine whether the distribution to an alternate payee or beneficiary is qualified. However, if an alternate payee or a spousal beneficiary rolls the distribution into a designated Roth account in a plan maintained by his or her own employer, such individual's age, disability, or death is used to determine whether a distribution from the recipient plan is qualified. In addition, if the rollover is a direct rollover contribution to the alternate payee's or spousal beneficiary's own designated Roth account, the 5-taxable-year period of participation under the recipient plan begins on the earlier of the date the employee's 5-taxable-year period of participation began under the distributing plan or the date the 5-taxable-year period of participation applicable to the alternate payee's or spousal beneficiary's designated Roth account began under the recipient plan.

(e) If a designated Roth contribution is made by a reemployed veteran for a year of qualified military service pursuant to section 414(u) that is before the year in which the contribution is actually made, the contribution is treated as having been made in the year of qualified military service to which the contribution relates, as designated by the reemployed veteran. Reemployed veterans may identify the year of qualified military service for which a contribution is made for other purposes, such as for entitlement to a match, and the treatment for the 5-taxable-year period of participation rule follows that identification. In the absence of such designation, for purposes of determining the first year of the five years of participation under section 402A(d)(2)(B), the contribution is treated as relating to the first year of qualified military service for which the reemployed veteran could have made designated Roth contributions under the plan, or if later the first taxable year in which designated Roth contributions could be made under the plan.

Q-5. How do the taxation rules apply to a distribution from a designated Roth account that is rolled over?

A-5. (a) An eligible rollover distribution from a designated Roth account is permitted to be rolled over into another designated Roth account or a Roth IRA, and the amount rolled over is not currently includible in gross income. In accordance with section 402(c)(2), to the extent that a portion of a distribution from a designated Roth account is not includible in income (determined without regard to the rollover), if that portion of the distribution is to be rolled over into a designated Roth account, the rollover must be accomplished through a direct rollover (i.e., a 60-day rollover to another designated Roth account is not available for this portion of the distribution). For this purpose, any amount paid in a direct rollover is treated as a separate distribution from any amount paid directly to the employee. If a distribution from a designated Roth account is instead made to the employee, the employee would still be able to roll over the entire amount (or any portion thereof) into a Roth IRA within the 60-day period described in section 402(c)(3).

(b) In the case of an eligible rollover distribution from a designated Roth account that is not a qualified distribution and not paid as a direct rollover contribution, if less than the entire amount of the distribution is rolled over, the part that is rolled over is deemed to consist first of the portion of the distribution that is attributable to income under section 72(e)(8).

(c) If an employee receives a distribution from a designated Roth account, the portion of the distribution that would be includible in gross income is permitted to be rolled over into a designated Roth account under another plan. In such a case, § 1.402A-2, A-3, provides for additional reporting by the recipient plan. In addition, the employee's period of participation under the distributing plan is not carried over to the recipient plan for purposes of satisfying the 5-taxable-year period of participation requirement under the recipient plan. Generally, the taxable year in which the recipient plan accepts such rollover contribution is the taxable year that begins the participant's new 5-taxable-year period of participation. However, if the participant is rolling over to a plan in which the participant already has a pre-existing designated Roth account with a longer period of participation, the starting date of the recipient account is used to measure the participant's 5-taxable-year period of participation.

(d) The following example illustrates the application of this A-5:

Example. Employee B receives a $14,000 eligible rollover distribution that is not a qualified distribution from B's designated Roth account, consisting of $11,000 of investment in the contract and $3,000 of income. Within 60 days of receipt, Employee B rolls over $7,000 of the distribution into a Roth IRA. The $7,000 is deemed to consist of $3,000 of income and $4,000 of investment in the contract. Because the only portion of the distribution that could be includible in gross income (the income) is rolled over, none of the distribution is includible in Employee B's gross income.

(e) This A-5 applies for taxable years beginning on or after January 1, 2006.

Q-6. In the case of a rollover contribution to a designated Roth account, how is the amount that is treated as investment in the contract under section 72 determined?

A-6. (a) If a distribution from a designated Roth account is rolled over to another designated Roth account in a direct rollover, the amount of the rollover contribution allocated to investment in the contract in the recipient designated Roth account is the amount that would not have been includible in gross income (determined without regard to section 402(e)(4)) if the distribution had not been rolled over. Thus, if an amount that is a qualified distribution is rolled over, the entire amount of the rollover contribution is allocated to investment in the contract.

(b) If the entire account balance of a designated Roth account is rolled over to another designated Roth account in a direct rollover, and, at the time of the distribution, the investment in the contract exceeds the balance in the designated Roth account, the investment in the contract in the distributing plan is included in the investment in the contract of the recipient plan.

Q-7. After a qualified distribution from a designated Roth account has been made, how is the remaining investment in the contract of the designated Roth account determined under section 72?

A-7. (a) The portion of any qualified distribution that is treated as a recovery of investment in the contract is determined in the same manner as if the distribution were not a qualified distribution. (See A-3 of this section) Thus, the remaining investment in the contract in a designated Roth account after a qualified distribution is determined in the same manner after a qualified distribution as it would be determined if the distribution were not a qualified distribution.

(b) The following example illustrates the application of this A-7:

Example. Employee C receives a $12,000 distribution, which is a qualified distribution that is attributable to the employee being disabled within the meaning of section 72(m)(7), from C's designated Roth account. Immediately prior to the distribution, the account consisted of $21,850 of investment in the contract (i.e., designated Roth contributions) and $1,150 of income. For purposes of determining recovery of investment in the contract under section 72, the distribution is deemed to consist of $11,400 of investment in the contract [$12,000 x 21,850/(1,150 + 21,850)], and $600 of income [$12,000 2006 × 1,150/(1,150 + 21,850)]. Immediately after the distribution, C's designated Roth account consists of $10,450 of investment in the contract and $550 of income. This determination of the remaining investment in the contract will be needed if C subsequently is no longer disabled and takes a nonqualified distribution from the designated Roth account.

Q-8. What is the relationship between the accounting for designated Roth contributions as investment in the contract for purposes of section 72 and their treatment as elective deferrals available for a hardship distribution under section 401(k)(2)(B)?

A-8. (a) There is no relationship between the accounting for designated Roth contributions as investment in the contract for purposes of section 72 and their treatment as elective deferrals available for a hardship distribution under section 401(k)(2)(B). A plan that makes a hardship distribution under section 401(k)(2)(B) from elective deferrals that includes designated Roth contributions must separately determine the amount of elective deferrals available for hardship and the amount of investment in the contract attributable to designated Roth contributions for purposes of section 72. Thus, the entire amount of a hardship distribution is treated as reducing the otherwise maximum distributable amount for purposes of applying the rule in section 401(k)(2)(B) and § 1.401(k)-1(d)(3)(ii) that generally limits hardship distributions to the principal amount of elective deferrals made less the amount of elective deferrals previously distributed from the plan, even if a portion of the distribution is treated as income under section 72(e)(8).

(b) The following example illustrates the application of this A-8:

Example. The facts are the same as in the Example in A-7 of this section, except that instead of being disabled, Employee C is receiving a hardship distribution. In addition, Employee C has made elective deferrals that are not designated Roth contributions totaling $20,000 and has received no previous distributions of elective deferrals from the plan. The adjustment to the investment in the contract is the same as in A-7 of this section, but for purposes of determining the amount of elective deferrals available for future hardship distribution, the entire amount of the distribution is subtracted from the maximum distributable amount. Thus, Employee C has only $29,850 ($41,850-$12,000) available for hardship distribution from C's designated Roth account.

Q-9. Can an employee have more than one separate contract for designated Roth contributions under a plan qualified under section 401(a) or a section 403(b) plan?

A-9. (a) Except as otherwise provided in paragraph (b) of this A-9, for purposes of section 72, there is only one separate contract for an employee with respect to the designated Roth contributions under a plan. Thus, if a plan maintains one separate account for designated Roth contributions made under the plan and another separate account for rollover contributions received from a designated Roth account under another plan (so that the rollover account is not required to be subject to the distribution restrictions otherwise applicable to the account consisting of designated Roth contributions made under the plan), both separate accounts are considered to be one contract for purposes of applying section 72 to the distributions from either account.

(b) If a separate account with respect to an employee's accrued benefit consisting of designated Roth contributions is established and maintained for an alternate payee pursuant to a qualified domestic relations order and another designated Roth account is maintained for the employee, each account is treated as a separate contract for purposes of section 72. The alternate payee's designated Roth account is also a separate contract for purposes of section 72 with respect to any other account maintained for that alternate payee. Similarly, if separate accounts are established and maintained for different beneficiaries after the death of an employee, the separate account for each beneficiary is treated as a separate contract under section 72 and is also a separate contract with respect to any other account maintained for that beneficiary under the plan that is not a designated Roth account. When the separate account is established for an alternate payee or for a beneficiary (after an employee's death), each separate account must receive a proportionate amount attributable to investment in the contract.

Q-10. What is the tax treatment of employer securities distributed from a designated Roth account?

A-10. (a) If a distribution of employer securities from a designated Roth account is not a qualified distribution, section 402(e)(4)(B) applies. Thus, in the case of a lump-sum distribution that includes employer securities, unless the taxpayer elects otherwise, net unrealized appreciation attributable to the employer securities is not includible in gross income; and such net unrealized appreciation is not included in the basis of the distributed securities and is capital gain to the extent such appreciation is realized in a subsequent taxable transaction.

(b) In the case of a qualified distribution of employer securities from a designated Roth account, the distributee's basis in the distributed securities for purposes of subsequent disposition is their fair market value at the time of distribution.

Q-11. Can an amount described in A-4 of § 1.402(c)-2 with respect to a designated Roth account be a qualified distribution?

A-11. No. An amount described in A-4 of § 1.402(c)-2 with respect to a designated Roth account cannot be a qualified distribution. Such an amount is taxable under the rules of §§ 1.72-16(b), 1.72(p)-1, A-11 through A-13, 1.402(g)-1(e)(8), 1.401(k)-2(b)(2)(vi), 1.401(m)-2(b)(2)(vi), or 1.404(k)-1T. Thus, for example, loans that are treated as deemed distributions pursuant to section 72(p), or dividends paid on employer securities as described in section 404(k) are not qualified distributions even if the deemed distributions occur or the dividends are paid after the employee attains age 59½ and the 5-taxable-year period of participation defined in A-4 of this section has been satisfied. However, if a dividend is reinvested in accordance with section 404(k)(2)(A)(iii)(II), the amount of such a dividend is not precluded from being a qualified distribution if later distributed. Further, an amount is not precluded from being a qualified distribution merely because it is described in section 402(c)(4) as an amount not eligible for rollover. Thus, a hardship distribution is not precluded from being a qualified distribution.

Q-12. If any amount from a designated Roth account is included in a loan to an employee, do the plan aggregation rules of section 72(p)(2)(D) apply for purposes of determining the total amount an employee is permitted to borrow from the plan, even though the designated Roth account generally is treated as a separate contract under section 72?

A-12. Yes. If any amount from a designated Roth account is included in a loan to an employee, notwithstanding the general rule that the designated Roth account is treated as a separate contract under section 72, the plan aggregation rules of section 72(p)(2)(D) apply for purposes of determining the maximum amount the employee is permitted to borrow from the plan and such amount is based on the total of the designated Roth contribution amounts and the other amounts under the plan. To the extent a loan is from a designated Roth account, the repayment requirement of section 72(p)(2)(C) must be satisfied separately with respect to that portion of the loan and with respect to the portion of the loan from other accounts under the plan.

Q-13. Does a transaction or accounting methodology involving an employee's designated Roth account and any other accounts under the plan or plans of an employer that has the effect of transferring value from the other accounts into the designated Roth account violate the separate accounting requirement of section 402A?

A-13. (a) Yes. Any transaction or accounting methodology involving an employee's designated Roth account and any other accounts under the plan or plans of an employer that has the effect of directly or indirectly transferring value from another account into the designated Roth account violates the separate accounting requirement under section 402A. However, any transaction that merely exchanges investments between accounts at fair market value will not violate the separate accounting requirement.

(b) In the case of an annuity contract which contains both a designated Roth account and any other accounts, the Commissioner may prescribe additional guidance of general applicability, published in the Internal Revenue Bulletin (see 601.601(d)(2) of this chapter), to provide additional rules for allocation of income, expenses, gains and losses among the accounts under the contract.

(c) This A-13 applies to designated Roth accounts for taxable years beginning on or after January 1, 2006.

Q-14. How is an annuity contract that is distributed from a designated Roth account treated for purposes of section 402A?

A-14. A qualified plan distributed annuity contract within the meaning of § 1.402(c)-2, A-10(a) that is distributed from a designated Roth account is not treated as a distribution for purposes of section 402 or 402A. Instead, the amounts paid under the annuity contract are treated as distributions for purposes of sections 402 and 402A. Thus, the period after the annuity contract is distributed and before a payment from the annuity contract is made is included in determining whether the five-year period of participation is satisfied. Further, for purposes of determining if a distribution is a qualified distribution, the determination of whether a distribution is made on or after the date the employee attains age 59½, made to a beneficiary or the estate of the employee on or after the employee's death, or attributable to the employee's being disabled within the meaning of section 72(m)(7) is made based on the facts at the time the distribution is made from the annuity contract. Thus for example, if an employee first makes a designated Roth contribution to a designated Roth account in 2006 at age 56, receives a distributed annuity contract within the meaning of § 1.402(c)-2, A-10(a) in 2007 purchased only with assets from the designated Roth account, and then receives a distribution from the contract in 2011 at age 60, the distribution is a qualified distribution.

Q-15. When are section 402A and this § 1.402A-1 applicable?

A-15. Section 402A is applicable for taxable years beginning on or after January 1, 2006. Except as otherwise provided in A-5 and A-13 of this section, the rules of this § 1.402A-1 apply for taxable years beginning on or after January 1, 2007.

T.D. 9324, 4/27/2007, amend T.D. 9340, 7/23/2007

## § 1.402A-2 Reporting and recordkeeping requirements with respect to designated Roth accounts.

Q-1. Who is responsible for keeping track of the 5-taxable-year period of participation and the investment in the contract, i.e., the amount of unrecovered designated Roth contributions for the employee?

A-1. The plan administrator or other responsible party with respect to a plan with a designated Roth account is responsible for keeping track of the 5-taxable-year period of participation for each employee and the amount of investment in the contract (unrecovered designated Roth contributions) on behalf of such employee. For purposes of the preceding sentence, in the absence of actual knowledge to the contrary, the plan administrator or other responsible party is permitted to assume that an employee's taxable year is the calendar year. In the case of a direct rollover from another designated Roth account, the plan administrator or other responsible party of the recipient plan can rely on reasonable representations made by the plan administrator or responsible party with respect to the plan with the other designated Roth account. See A-2 of this section for statements required in the case of rollovers.

Q-2. In the case of an eligible rollover distribution from a designated Roth account, what additional information must be provided with respect to such distribution?

A-2. (a) Pursuant to section 6047(f), if an amount is distributed from a designated Roth account, the plan administrator or other responsible party with respect to the plan must provide a statement as described below in the following situations—

(1) In the case of a direct rollover of a distribution from a designated Roth account under a plan to a designated Roth account under another plan, the plan administrator or other responsible party must provide to the plan administrator or responsible party of the recipient plan either a statement indicating the first year of the 5-taxable-year period described in A-1 of this section and the portion of the distribution that is attributable to investment in the contract under section 72, or a statement that the distribution is a qualified distribution.

(2) If the distribution is not a direct rollover to a designated Roth account under another plan, the plan administrator or responsible party must provide to the employee, upon request, the same information described in paragraph (a)(1) of this A-2, except the statement need not indicate the first year of the 5-taxable-year period described in A-1 of this section.

(b) The statement described in paragraph (a) of this A-2 must be provided within a reasonable period following the direct rollover or distributee request but in no event later than 30 days following the direct rollover or distributee request.

Q-3. If a plan qualified under section 401(a) or a section 403(b) plan accepts a 60-day rollover of earnings from a designated Roth account, what report to the IRS must be provided with respect to such rollover contribution?

A-3. To the extent required in Forms and Instructions, if a plan qualified under section 401(a), or a section 403(b) plan, accepts a rollover contribution (other than a direct rollover contribution) under section 402(c)(2), or section 403(b)(8)(B), of the portion of a distribution from a designated Roth account that would have been includable in gross income, the plan administrator or other responsible party for the recipient plan must notify the Commissioner of its acceptance of the rollover contribution no later than the due date for filing Form 1099-R, "Distributions From Pensions,

Annuities, Retirement or Profit-Sharing Plans, IRAs, Insurance Contracts, etc.,." The Forms and Instructions will specify the address to which the notification is required to be sent and will require inclusion of the employee's name and social security number, the amount rolled over, the year in which the rollover contribution was made, and such other information as the Commissioner may prescribe in order to determine that the amount rolled over is a valid rollover contribution.

Q-4. When is this § 1.402A-2 applicable?

A-4. The rules of this § 1.402A-2 are applicable for taxable years beginning on or after January 1, 2007.

T.D. 9324, 4/27/2007.

PAR. 13. Section 1.403(a) is amended.

**Proposed § 1.403(a) Statutory provisions; taxation of employee annuities; qualified annuity plan.** [*For Preamble, see ¶ 150,135*]

• ***Caution:*** Proposed section 1.62-1 was finalized by TD 7399, 2/3/76. Proposed sections 1.72-4, 1.72-13, 1.101-2, 1.122-1, 1.402(a)-1, 1.402(e)-2, 1.402(e)-3, 1.403(a)-1, 1.403(a)-2, 1.405-3, 1.652(b)-1, 1.1304-2 and 11.402(e)(4)(B)-1 remain proposed.

**§ 1.403(a)-1 Taxability of beneficiary under a qualified annuity plan.**

***Caution:*** The Treasury has not yet amended Reg § 1.403(a)-1 to reflect changes made by P.L. 99-514, P.L. 93-406.

**(a)** An employee or retired or former employee for whom an annuity contract is purchased by his employer is not required to include in his gross income the amount paid for the contract at the time such amount is paid, whether or not his rights to the contract are forfeitable, if the annuity contract is purchased under a plan which meets the requirements of section 404(a)(2). For purposes of the preceding sentence, it is immaterial whether the employer deducts the amounts paid for the contract under such section 404(a)(2). See §§ 1.403(b)-1 through 1.403(b)-10 for rules relating to annuity contracts which are not purchased under qualified plans but which are purchased by organizations described in section 501(c)(3) and exempt under section 501(a) or which are purchased for employees who perform services for certain public schools.

**(b)** The amounts received by or made available to any employee referred to in paragraph (a) of this section under such annuity contract shall be included in gross income of the employee for the taxable year in which received or made available, as provided in section 72 (relating to annuities), except that certain total distributions described in section 403(a)(2) are taxable as long-term capital gains. For the treatment of such total distributions, see § 1.403(a)-2. However, for taxable years beginning before January 1, 1964, section 72(e)(3) (relating to the treatment of certain lump sums), as in effect before such date, shall not apply to such amounts. For taxable years beginning after December 31, 1963, such amounts may be taken into account in computations under sections 1301 through 1305 (relating to income averaging).

**(c)** If upon the death of an employee or of a retired employee, the widow or other beneficiary of such employee is paid, in accordance with the terms of the annuity contract relating to the deceased employee, an annuity or other death benefit, the extent to which the amounts received by or made available to the beneficiary must be included in the beneficiary's income under section 403(a) shall be determined in accordance with the rules presented in paragraph (a)(5) of § 1.402(a)-1.

**(d)** An individual contract issued after December 31, 1962, or a group contract, which provides incidental life insurance protection may be purchased under a qualified annuity plan. For the rules as to nontransferability of such contracts issued after December 31, 1962, see § 1.401-9. For the rules relating to the taxation of the cost of the life insurance protection and the proceeds thereunder, see § 1.72-16. Section 403(a) is not applicable to premiums paid after October 26, 1956, for individual contracts which were issued prior to January 1, 1963, and which provide life insurance protection.

**(e)** As to inclusion of full-time life insurance salesmen within the class of persons considered to be employees, see section 7701(a)(20).

**(f)** For purposes of this section and § 1.403(a)-2, the term "employee" includes a self-employed individual who is treated as an employee under section 401(c)(1) and paragraph (b) of § 1.401-10, and the term "employer" means the person treated as the employer of such individual under section 401(c)(4). For the rules relating to annuity plans covering self-employed individuals, see section 404(a)(2) and §§ 1.404(a)-8 and 1.401-10 through 1.401-13.

**(g)** For the treatment of amounts paid to provide medical benefits described in section 401(h) as defined in § 1.401-14, see paragraph (h) of § 1.72-15.

T.D. 6203, 9/24/56, amend T.D. 6676, 9/16/63, T.D. 6722, 4/13/64, T.D. 6783, 12/23/64, T.D. 6885, 6/1/66, T.D. 9340, 7/23/2007.

PAR. 14. Section 1.403(a)-1(b)(1) and (2) are amended to read as follows:

**Proposed § 1.403(a)-1 Taxability of beneficiary under a qualified annuity plan.** [*For Preamble, see ¶ 150,135*]

• ***Caution:*** Proposed section 1.62-1 was finalized by TD 7399, 2/3/76. Proposed sections 1.72-4, 1.72-13, 1.101-2, 1.122-1, 1.402(a)-1, 1.402(e)-2, 1.402(e)-3, 1.403(a)-1, 1.403(a)-2, 1.405-3, 1.652(b)-1, 1.1304-2 and 11.402(e)(4)(B)-1 remain proposed.

* * * * *

**(b)** The amounts received by or made available to any employee referred to in paragraph (a) of this section under an annuity contract shall be included in the gross income of the employee for the taxable year in which received or made available, as provided in section 72 (relating to annuities), except that—

*(1)* For taxable years beginning before January 1, 1970, certain total distributions described in section 403(a)(2) (as in effect for such years) are taxable as long-term capital gains (see § 1.403(a)-2 for rules applicable to such amounts), and

*(2)* For taxable years beginning after December 31, 1973, a portion of a lump sum distribution (as defined by section 402(e)(4)(A)) is treated as long-term capital gains (see paragraph (d) of § 1.403(a)-2 for rules applicable to such portion and see § 1.402(e)-2 for the computation of the separate tax on the portion of a lump sum distribution not treated as long-term capital gains). For taxable years beginning before January 1, 1964, section 72(e)(3) (relating to treatment of certain lump sums), as in effect before such date, shall not apply to an amount described in this paragraph. For taxable years beginning after December 31, 1963, such amounts may be taken into account in computations under section 1301 through 1305 (relating to income averaging).

* * * * *

PAR. 9. Section 1.403(a)-1 is amended by revising paragraph (g) to read as follows:

**Proposed § 1.403(a)-1 Taxability of beneficiary under a qualified annuity plan.** [*For Preamble, see ¶ 152,901*]

* * * * *

**(g)** The rules of § 1.402(a)-1(e) apply for purposes of determining the treatment of amounts paid to provide accident and health insurance benefits.

**§ 1.403(a)-2 Capital gains treatment for certain distributions.**

***Caution:*** The Treasury has not yet amended Reg § 1.403(a)-2 to reflect changes made by P.L. 100-647, P.L. 99-514, P.L. 98-397, P.L. 96-222, P.L. 95-30, P.L. 94-455, P.L. 94-267, P.L. 93-406.

**(a)** If the total amounts payable with respect to any employee for whom an annuity contract has been purchased by an employer under a plan which—

*(1)* Is a plan described in section 403(a)(1) and § 1.403(a)-1, and

*(2)* Requires that refunds of contributions with respect to annuity contracts purchased under such plan be used to reduce subsequent premiums on the contracts under the plan,

are paid to, or includible in gross income of, the payee within one taxable year of the payee by reason of the employee's death or other separation from the service, or death after such separation from the service, such total payments, to the extent they exceed the net amount contributed by the employee, shall be considered a gain from the sale or exchange of a capital asset held for more than six months. The "net amount contributed by the employee" is the amount actually contributed by the employee plus any amounts considered to be contributed by the employee under the rules of sections 72(f), 101(b), and paragraph (d) of § 1.403(a)-1, reduced by any amounts theretofore distributed to him which were excludable from his gross income as a return of employee contributions. For example, if under an annuity contract purchased under a plan described in this section, the total distributions payable to the employee's widow are paid to her in the year in which the employee dies, in the amount of $8,000, and if $5,000 thereof is excludable under section 101(b), and if the employee made contributions of $600 and had received no payments, the remaining amount of $2,400 will be considered a gain from the sale or exchange of a capital asset held for more than six months.

**(b)** *(1)* The term "total amounts" means the balance to the credit of an employee with respect to all annuities under the annuity plan which becomes payable to the payee by reason of the employee's death or other separation from the service, or by reason of his death after separation from the service. If an employee commences to receive annuity payments on retirement and then a lump sum payment is made to his widow upon his death, the capital gains treatment applies to the lump sum payment, but it does not apply to amounts received before the time the "total amounts" become payable. However, if the total amount to the credit of the employee at the time of his death or other separation from the service or death after separation from the service is paid or includible in the gross income of the payee within one taxable year of the payee, such amount is entitled to the capital gains treatment notwithstanding that in a later taxable year an additional amount is credited to the employee and paid to the payee.

*(2)* If more than one annuity contract is received under the plan, the capital gains treatment does not apply to any amount received on the surrender thereof unless all contracts under the plan with respect to a particular employee are surrendered either at the time of the employee's death or other separation from the service or death after separation from the service. Thus, if an employee receives two contracts on separation from the service and surrenders one of them in the year of separation and receives payments under the other until his death, the capital gains treatment is applicable to the balance paid to his beneficiary on his death if paid within one taxable year of the beneficiary. The amount received by the employee on surrender of the contract in the year of his separation from the service, however, would not receive capital gains treatment since the balance to the credit of the employee with respect to all amounts under the plan did not become payable at that time.

*(3)* If an employee retires and commences to receive an annuity but subsequently in some succeeding taxable year, he is paid a lump sum in settlement of all future annuity payments, the capital gains treatment does not apply to such lump sum settlement paid during the lifetime of the employee since it is not a payment on account of separation from the service, or death after separation, but is on account of the settlement of future annuity payments.

*(4)* If the "total amounts" payable under all annuity contracts under the plan with respect to a particular employee are paid or includible in the gross income of several payees within one taxable year on account of the employee's death or other separation from the service or on account of his death after separation from the service, the capital gains treatment is applicable. Thus, if the balance to the credit of a deceased employee under all annuity contracts provided under an annuity plan becomes payable to two payees, the capital gains treatment is applicable provided the "total amounts" payable are received by or includible in the gross income of both payees within the same taxable year. However, if the "total amounts" payable are made available to each payee and one elects to receive his share in cash while the other makes a timely election under section 72(h) to receive his share as an annuity, the capital gains treatment does not apply to either payee.

*(5)* For purposes of determining whether the total amounts payable to an employee have been paid within one taxable year, the term "total amounts" includes amounts under a plan which are attributable to contributions on behalf of an individual while he was self-employed in the business with respect to which the plan was established. Thus, the "total amounts" payable are not paid within one taxable year if amounts remain payable which are so attributable.

*(6)* The term "total amounts" does not include any amount which has been placed in a separate account for the funding of benefits described in section 401(h). Thus, a dis-

tribution under a qualified annuity plan may constitute a distribution of the total amounts payable with respect to an employee even though amounts attributable to the funding of section 401(h) medical benefits as defined in paragraph (a) of § 1.401-14 are not so distributed.

**(c)** The provisions of this section are not applicable to any amounts paid to a payee to the extent such amounts are attributable to contributions made on behalf of an employee while he was a self-employed individual in the business with respect to which the plan was established. For the taxation of such amounts, see § 1.72-18. For the rules for determining the amount attributable to contributions on behalf of an employee while he was self-employed, see paragraphs (b)(4) and (c)(2) of such section.

T.D. 6203, 9/24/56, amend T.D. 6676, 9/16/63, T.D. 6722, 4/13/64.

PAR. 4. Section 1.403(a)-2(e)(3), as set forth in paragraph 15 of the appendix to the notice of proposed rulemaking of April 30, 1975, is revised by adding, immediately after subdivision (ii) thereof, a new sentence to read as follows:

**Proposed § 1.403(a)-2 Capital gains treatment for certain distributions.** [*For Preamble, see ¶ 150,475*]

* * * * *

**(e)** * * *

*(3)* * * *

(i) * * *

(ii) * * * In the case of a lump sum distribution received by or made available to a recipient in a taxable year of the recipient beginning after December 31, 1975, the recipient may elect, in accordance with section 402(e)(4)(L), and § 1.402(e)-14, to treat all calendar years of an employee's active participation in all plans in which the employee has been an active participant as years of active participation after December 31, 1973. If a recipient makes the election, no portion of any distribution received by or made available to the recipient with respect to the employee (whether in the recipient's taxable year for which the election is made, or thereafter) is taxable to the recipient as long-term capital gain under section 403(a)(2) and this subparagraph.

* * * * *

PAR. 15. Section 1.403(a)-2(a)(1) and (b) are amended; (c) is revised, (d) and (e) are added to read as follows:

**Proposed § 1.403(a)-2 Capital gains treatment for certain distributions.** [*For Preamble, see ¶ 150,135*]

• ***Caution:*** Proposed section 1.62-1 was finalized by TD 7399, 2/3/76. Proposed sections 1.72-4, 1.72-13, 1.101-2, 1.122-1, 1.402(a)-1, 1.402(e)-2, 1.402(e)-3, 1.403(a)-1, 1.403(a)-2, 1.405-3, 1.652(b)-1, 1.1304-2 and 11.402(e)(4)(B)-1 remain proposed.

**(a)** For taxable years beginning before January 1, 1970, if the total amounts payable with respect to any employee for whom an annuity contract has been purchased by an employer under a plan which—

*(1)* Is a plan described in section 403(a)(1) and § 1.403(a)-1, and

* * * * *

**(b)** For taxable years beginning before January 1, 1970—

*(1)* The term "total amounts" means the balance to the credit of an employee with respect to all annuities under the annuity plan which becomes payable to the payee by reason of the employee's death or other separation from the service, or by reason of his death after separation from the service. If an employee commences to receive annuity payments on retirement and then a lump sum payment is made to his widow upon his death, the capital gains treatment applies to the lump sum payment, but it does not apply to amounts received before the time the "total amounts" become payable. However, if the total amount to the credit of the employee at the time of his death or other separation from the service or death after separation from the service, is paid or includible in the gross income of the payee within one taxable year of the payee, such amount is entitled to the capital gains treatment notwithstanding that in a later taxable year an additional amount is credited to the employee and paid to the payee.

* * * * *

**(c)** For taxable years beginning before January 1, 1970, the provisions of this section are not applicable to any amounts paid to a payee to the extent such amounts are attributable to contributions made on behalf of an employee while he was a self-employed individual in the business with respect to which the plan was established. For the taxation of such amounts, see § 1.72-18. For such years for the rules for determining the amount attributable to contributions on behalf of an employee while he was self-employed, see paragraphs (b)(4) and (c)(2) of such section.

**(d)** For taxable years ending after December 31, 1969, and beginning before January 1, 1974, the portion of the total amounts described in paragraph (b)(1) of this section treated as gain from the sale or exchange of a capital asset held for more than six months is subject to the limitation of section 403(a)(2)(C), as in effect on December 31, 1973.

**(e)** For taxable years beginning after December 31, 1973—

*(1)* If a lump sum distribution (as defined in section 402(e)(4)(A) and the regulations thereunder) is received by, or made available to, the recipient under an annuity contract described in subparagraph (2)(i) of this paragraph, the ordinary income portion (as defined in section 402(e)(4)(E) and the regulations thereunder) of such distribution shall be taxable in accordance with the provisions of section 402(e) and the regulations thereunder and the portion of such distribution determined under paragraph (3) of this section shall be treated in accordance with the provisions of paragraph (2) of this section.

*(2)* If—

(i) An annuity contract is purchased by an employer for an employee under a plan described in section 403(a)(1) and § 1.403(a)-1,

(ii) Such plan requires that refunds of contributions with respect to annuity contracts purchased under the plan be used to reduce subsequent premiums on the contracts under the plan, and

(iii) A lump sum distribution (as defined in section 402(e)(4)(A) and the regulations thereunder) is paid to the recipient, the amount described in paragraph (e)(3) of this section shall be treated as gain from the sale or exchange of a capital asset held for more than 6 months.

*(3)* For purposes of paragraph (e)(2) of this section, the portion of a lump sum distribution treated as gain from the sale or exchange of a capital asset held for more than 6 months is an amount equal to the total taxable amount of the lump sum distribution (as defined in section 402(e)(4)(D) and the regulations thereunder) multiplied by a fraction—

(i) The numerator of which is the number of calendar years of active participation (as determined under § 1.402(e)-2(d)(3)(ii)) by the employee in such plan before January 1, 1974, and

(ii) The denominator of which is the number of calendar years of active participation (as determined under § 1.402(e)-2(d)(3)(ii)) by the employee in such plan.

*(4)* For purposes of this paragraph—

(i) In the case of an employee who is an employee without regard to section 401(c)(1), the determination of whether or not an amount is a lump sum distribution shall be made without regard to the requirements of section 402(e)(4)(B) and § 1.402(e)-3.

(ii) No distribution to any taxpayer other than an individual, estate, or trust may be treated as a lump sum distribution under this section.

**§ 1.403(b)-0 Taxability of beneficiary under annuity purchased by a section 501(c)(3) organization or public school.**

This section lists the headings that appear in §§ 1.403(b)-1 through 1.403(b)-11.

*§ 1.403(b)-1 General overview of taxability under an annuity contract purchased by a section 501(c)(3) organization or a public school.*

*§ 1.403(b)-2 Definitions.*

(a) Application of definitions.

(b) Definitions.

*§ 1.403(b)-3 Exclusion for contributions to purchase section 403(b) contracts.*

(a) Exclusion for section 403(b) contracts.

(b) Application of requirements.

(c) Special rules for designated Roth section 403(b) contributions.

(d) Effect of failure.

*§ 1.403(b)-4 Contribution limitations.*

(a) Treatment of contributions in excess of limitations.

(b) Maximum annual contribution.

(c) Section 403(b) elective deferrals.

(d) Employer contributions for former employees.

(e) Special rules for determining years of service.

(f) Excess contributions of deferrals.

*§ 1.403(b)-5 Nondiscrimination rules.*

(a) Nondiscrimination rules for contributions other than section 403(b) elective deferrals.

(b) Universal availability required for section 403(b) elective deferrals.

(c) Plan required.

(d) Church plans exception.

(e) Other rules.

*§ 1.403(b)-6 Timing of distributions and benefits.*

(a) Distributions generally.

(b) Distributions from contracts other than custodial accounts or amounts attributable to section 403(b) elective deferrals.

(c) Distributions from custodial accounts that are not attributable to section 403(b) elective deferrals.

(d) Distribution of section 403(b) elective deferrals.

(e) Minimum required distributions for eligible plans.

(f) Loans.

(g) Death benefits and other incidental benefits.

(h) Special rule regarding severance from employment.

*§ 1.403(b)-7 Taxation of distributions and benefits.*

(a) General rules for when amounts are included in gross income.

(b) Rollovers to individual retirement arrangements and other eligible retirement plans.

(c) Special rules for certain corrective distributions.

(d) Amounts taxable under section 72(p)(1).

(e) Special rules relating to distributions from a designated Roth account.

(f) Certain rules relating to employment taxes.

*§ 1.403(b)-8 Funding.*

(a) Investments.

(b) Contributions to the plan.

(c) Annuity contracts.

(d) Custodial accounts.

(e) Retirement income accounts.

(f) Combining assets.

*§ 1.403(b)-9 Special rules for church plans.*

(a) Retirement income accounts.

(b) Retirement income account defined.

(c) Special deduction rule for self-employed ministers.

*§ 1.403(b)-10 Miscellaneous provisions.*

(a) Plan terminations and frozen plans.

(b) Contract exchanges and plan-to-plan transfers.

(c) Qualified domestic relations orders.

(d) Rollovers to a section 403(b) contract.

(e) Deemed IRAs.

(f) Defined benefit plans.

(g) Other rules relating to section 501(c)(3) organizations.

*§ 1.403(b)-11 Applicable date.*

(a) General rule.

(b) Collective bargaining agreements.

(c) Church conventions.

(d) Special rules for plans that exclude certain types of employees from elective deferrals.

(e) Special rules for plans that permit in-service distributions.

(f) Special rule for life insurance contracts.

(g) Special rule for contracts received in an exchange.

---

T.D. 9340, 7/23/2007.

---

**§ 1.403(b)-1 General overview of taxability under an annuity contract purchased by a section 501(c)(3) organization or a public school.**

***Caution:*** The Treasury has not yet amended Reg § 1.403(b)-1 to reflect changes made by P.L. 107-16, P.L. 105-34, P.L. 104-188, P.L. 100-647, P.L. 99-514.

Section 403(b) and §§ 1.403(b)-2 through 1.403(b)-10 provide rules for the Federal income tax treatment of an annuity purchased for an employee by an employer that is either a tax-exempt entity under section 501(c)(3) (relating to certain religious, charitable, scientific, or other types of organizations) or a public school, or for a minister described in section 414(e)(5)(A). See section 403(a) (relating to qualified annuities) for rules regarding the taxation of an annuity purchased under a qualified annuity plan that meets the requirements of section 404(a)(2), and see section 403(c) (relating to nonqualified annuities) for rules regarding the taxation of other types of annuities.

T.D. 6203, 9/24/56, amend T.D. 6783, 12/23/64, T.D. 6885, 6/1/66, T.D. 7748, 12/30/80, T.D. 7836, 9/23/82, T.D. 8115, 12/16/86, T.D. 9340, 7/23/2007.

**§ 1.403(b)-2 Definitions.**

**(a) Application of definitions.** The definitions set forth in this section are applicable for purposes of § 1.403(b)-1, this section and §§ 1.403(b)-3 through 1.403(b)-11.

**(b) Definitions.** *(1)* Accumulated benefit means the total benefit to which a participant or beneficiary is entitled under a section 403(b) contract, including all contributions made to the contract and all earnings thereon.

*(2)* Annuity contract means a contract that is issued by an insurance company qualified to issue annuities in a State and that includes payment in the form of an annuity. See § 1.401(f)-1(d)(2) and (e) for the definition of an annuity, and see § 1.403(b)-8(c)(3) for a special rule for certain State plans. See also §§ 1.403(b)-8(d) and 1.403(b)-9(a) for additional rules regarding the treatment of custodial accounts and retirement income accounts as annuity contracts.

*(3)* Beneficiary means a person who is entitled to benefits in respect of a participant following the participant's death or an alternate payee pursuant to a qualified domestic relations order, as described in § 1.403(b)-10(c).

*(4)* Catch-up amount or catch-up limitation for a participant for a taxable year means a section 403(b) elective deferral permitted under section 414(v) (as described in § 1.403(b)-4(c)(2)) or section 402(g)(7) (as described in § 1.403(b)-4(c)(3)).

*(5)* Church means a church as defined in section 3121(w)(3)(A) and a qualified church-controlled organization as defined in section 3121(w)(3)(B).

*(6)* Church-related organization means a church or a convention or association of churches, including an organization described in section 414(e)(3)(A).

*(7)* Elective deferral means an elective deferral under § 1.402(g)-1 (with respect to an employer contribution to a section 403(b) contract) and any other amount that constitutes an elective deferral under section 402(g)(3).

*(8)* (i) Eligible employer means—

(A) A State, but only with respect to an employee of the State performing services for a public school;

(B) A section 501(c)(3) organization with respect to any employee of the section 501(c)(3) organization;

(C) Any employer of a minister described in section 414(e)(5)(A), but only with respect to the minister; or

(D) A minister described in section 414(e)(5)(A), but only with respect to a retirement income account established for the minister.

(ii) An entity is not an eligible employer under paragraph (a)(8)(i)(A) of this section if it treats itself as not being a State for any other purpose of the Internal Revenue Code, and a subsidiary or other affiliate of an eligible employer is not an eligible employer under paragraph (a)(8)(i) of this section if the subsidiary or other affiliate is not an entity described in paragraph (a)(8)(i) of this section.

*(9)* Employee means a common-law employee performing services for the employer, and does not include a former employee or an independent contractor. Subject to any rules in § 1.403(b)-1, this section, and §§ 1.403(b)-3 through 1.403(b)-11 that are specifically applicable to ministers, an employee also includes a minister described in section 414(e)(5)(A) when performing services in the exercise of his or her ministry.

*(10)* Employee performing services for a public school means an employee performing services as an employee for a public school of a State. This definition is not applicable unless the employee's compensation for performing services for a public school is paid by the State. Further, a person occupying an elective or appointive public office is not an employee performing services for a public school unless such office is one to which an individual is elected or appointed only if the individual has received training, or is experienced, in the field of education. The term public office includes any elective or appointive office of a State.

*(11)* Includible compensation means the employee's compensation received from an eligible employer that is includible in the participant's gross income for Federal income tax purposes (computed without regard to section 911) for the most recent period that is a year of service. Includible compensation for a minister who is self-employed means the minister's earned income as defined in section 401(c)(2) (computed without regard to section 911) for the most recent period that is a year of service. Includible compensation does not include any compensation received during a period when the employer is not an eligible employer. Includible compensation also includes any elective deferral or other amount contributed or deferred by the eligible employer at the election of the employee that would be includible in the gross income of the employee but for the rules of sections 125, 132(f)(4), 402(e)(2), 402(h)(1)(B), 402(k), or 457(b). The amount of includible compensation is determined without regard to any community property laws. See section 415(c)(3)(A) through (D) for additional rules, and see § 1.403(b)-4(d) for a special rule regarding former employees.

*(12)* Participant means an employee for whom a section 403(b) contract is currently being purchased, or an employee or former employee for whom a section 403(b) contract has previously been purchased and who has not received a distribution of his or her entire accumulated benefit under the contract.

*(13)* Plan means a plan as described in § 1.403(b)-3(b)(3).

*(14)* Public school means a State-sponsored educational organization described in section 170(b)(1)(A)(ii) (relating to educational organizations that normally maintain a regular faculty and curriculum and normally have a regularly enrolled body of pupils or students in attendance at the place where educational activities are regularly carried on).

*(15)* Retirement income account means a defined contribution program established or maintained by a church-related organization to provide benefits under section 403(b) for its employees or their beneficiaries as described in § 1.403(b)-9.

*(16)* Section 403(b) contract; section 403(b) plan. (i) Section 403(b) contract means a contract that satisfies the requirements of § 1.403(b)-3. If for any taxable year an employer contributes to more than one section 403(b) contract for a participant or beneficiary, then, under section 403(b)(5), all such contracts are treated as one contract for purposes of section 403(b) and § 1.403(b)-1, this section, and §§ 1.403(b)-3 through 1.403(b)-11. See also § 1.403(b)-3(b)(1).

(ii) Section 403(b) plan means the plan of the employer under which the section 403(b) contracts for its employees are maintained.

*(17)* Section 403(b) elective deferral; designated Roth contribution. (i) Section 403(b) elective deferral means an elective deferral that is an employer contribution to a section 403(b) plan for an employee. See § 1.403(b)-5(b) for additional rules with respect to a section 403(b) elective deferral.

(ii) Designated Roth contribution under a section 403(b) plan means a section 403(b) elective deferral that satisfies § 1.403(b)-3(c).

*(18)* Section 501(c)(3) organization means an organization that is described in section 501(c)(3) (relating to certain religious, charitable, scientific, or other types of organizations) and exempt from tax under section 501(a).

*(19)* Severance from employment means that the employee ceases to be employed by the employer maintaining the plan. See § 1.401(k)-1(d) for additional guidance concerning severance from employment. See also § 1.403(b)-6(h) for a special rule under which severance from employment is determined by reference to employment with the eligible employer.

*(20)* State means a State, a political subdivision of a State, or any agency or instrumentality of a State. For this purpose, the District of Columbia is treated as a State. In addition, for purposes of determining whether an individual is an employee performing services for a public school, an Indian tribal government is treated as a State, as provided under section 7871(a)(6)(B). See also section 1450(b) of the Small Business Job Protection Act of 1996 (110 Stat. 1755, 1814) for special rules treating certain contracts purchased in a plan year beginning before January 1, 1995, that include contributions by an Indian tribal government as section 403(b) contracts, whether or not those contributions are for employees performing services for a public school.

*(21)* Year of service means each full year during which an individual is a full-time employee of an eligible employer, plus fractional credit for each part of a year during which the individual is either a full-time employee of an eligible employer for a part of the year or a part-time employee of an eligible employer. See § 1.403(b)-4(e) for rules for determining years of service.

---

T.D. 8619, 9/15/95, amend T.D. 8880, 4/20/2000, T.D. 9340, 7/23/2007.

---

### § 1.403(b)-3 Exclusion for contributions to purchase section 403(b) contracts.

**(a) Exclusion for section 403(b) contracts.** Amounts contributed by an eligible employer for the purchase of an annuity contract for an employee are excluded from the gross income of the employee under section 403(b) only if each of the requirements in paragraphs (a)(1) through (9) of this section is satisfied. In addition, amounts contributed by an eligible employer for the purchase of an annuity contract for an employee pursuant to a cash or deferred election (as defined at § 1.401(k)-1(a)(3)) are not includible in an employee's gross income at the time the cash would have been includible in the employee's gross income (but for the cash or deferred election) if each of the requirements in paragraphs (a)(1) through (9) of this section is satisfied. However, the preceding two sentences generally do not apply to designated Roth contributions; see paragraph (c) of this section and § 1.403(b)-7(e) for special taxation rules that apply with respect to designated Roth contributions under a section 403(b) plan.

*(1) Not a contract issued under qualified plan or eligible governmental plan.* The annuity contract is not purchased under a qualified plan (under section 401(a) or 403(a)) or an eligible governmental plan under section 457(b).

*(2) Nonforfeitability.* The rights of the employee under the annuity contract (disregarding rights to future premiums) are nonforfeitable. An employee's rights under a contract fail to be nonforfeitable unless the employee for whom the contract is purchased has at all times a fully vested and nonforfeitable right (as defined in regulations under section 411) to all benefits provided under the contract. See paragraph (d)(2) of this section for additional rules regarding the nonforfeitability requirement of this paragraph (a)(2).

*(3) Nondiscrimination.* In the case of an annuity contract purchased by an eligible employer other than a church, the contract is purchased under a plan that satisfies section 403(b)(12) (relating to nondiscrimination requirements, including universal availability). See § 1.403(b)-5.

*(4) Limitations on elective deferrals.* In the case of an elective deferral, the contract satisfies section 401(a)(30) (relating to limitations on elective deferrals). A contract does not satisfy section 401(a)(30) as required under this paragraph (a)(4) unless the contract requires that all elective deferrals for an employee not exceed the limits of section 402(g)(1), including elective deferrals for the employee under the contract and any other elective deferrals under the plan under which the contract is purchased and under all other plans, contracts, or arrangements of the employer. See § 1.401(a)-30.

*(5) Nontransferability.* The contract is not transferable. This paragraph (a)(5) does not apply to a contract issued before January 1, 1963. See section 401(g).

*(6) Minimum required distributions.* The contract satisfies the requirements of section 401(a)(9) (relating to minimum required distributions). See § 1.403(b)-6(e).

*(7) Rollover distributions.* The contract provides that, if the distributee of an eligible rollover distribution elects to have the distribution paid directly to an eligible retirement plan, as defined in section 402(c)(8)(B), and specifies the eligible retirement plan to which the distribution is to be paid, then the distribution will be paid to that eligible retirement plan in a direct rollover. See § 1.403(b)-7(b)(2).

*(8) Limitation on incidental benefits.* The contract satisfies the incidental benefit requirements of section 401(a). See § 1.403(b)-6(g).

*(9) Maximum annual additions.* The annual additions to the contract do not exceed the applicable limitations of section 415(c) (treating contributions and other additions as annual additions). See paragraph (b) of this section and § 1.403(b)-4(b) and (f).

**(b) Application of requirements.** *(1) Aggregation of contracts.* In accordance with section 403(b)(5), for purposes of determining whether this section is satisfied, all section 403(b) contracts purchased for an individual by an employer are treated as purchased under a single contract. Additional aggregation rules apply under section 402(g) for purposes of satisfying paragraph (a)(4) of this section and under section 415 for purposes of satisfying paragraph (a)(9) of this section.

*(2) Disaggregation for excess annual additions.* In accordance with the last sentence of section 415(a)(2), if an excess annual addition is made to a contract that otherwise satisfies the requirements of this section, then the portion of the contract that includes such excess annual addition fails to be a section 403(b) contract (as further described in paragraph (d)(1) of this section) and the remaining portion of the contract is a section 403(b) contract. This paragraph (b)(2) is not satisfied unless, for the year of the excess and each year thereafter, the issuer of the contract maintains separate accounts for each such portion. Thus, the entire contract fails to be a section 403(b) contract if an excess annual addition is made and a separate account is not maintained with respect to the excess.

*(3) Plan in form and operation.* (i) A contract does not satisfy paragraph (a) of this section unless it is maintained pursuant to a plan. For this purpose, a plan is a written defined contribution plan, which, in both form and operation, satisfies the requirements of § 1.403(b)-1, § 1.403(b)-2, this section, and §§ 1.403(b)-4 through 1.403(b)-11. For purposes of § 1.403(b)-1, § 1.403(b)-2, this section, and §§ 1.403(b)-4 through 1.403(b)-11, the plan must contain all the material terms and conditions for eligibility, benefits, applicable limitations, the contracts available under the plan, and the time and form under which benefit distributions would be made. For purposes of § 1.403(b)-1, § 1.403(b)-2, this section, and §§ 1.403(b)-4 through 1.403(b)-11, a plan may contain certain optional features that are consistent with but not required under section 403(b), such as hardship withdrawal distributions, loans, plan-to-plan or annuity contract-to-annuity contract transfers, and acceptance of rollovers to the plan. However, if a plan contains any optional provisions, the optional provisions must meet, in both form and operation, the relevant requirements under section 403(b), this section, and §§ 1.403(b)-4 through 1.403(b)-11.

(ii) The plan may allocate responsibility for performing administrative functions, including functions to comply with the requirements of section 403(b) and other tax requirements. Any such allocation must identify responsibility for compliance with the requirements of the Internal Revenue Code that apply on the basis of the aggregated contracts issued to a participant under a plan, including loans under section 72(p) and the conditions for obtaining a hardship withdrawal under § 1.403(b)-6. A plan is permitted to assign such responsibilities to parties other than the eligible employer, but not to participants (other than employees of the employer a substantial portion of whose duties are administration of the plan), and may incorporate by reference other documents, including the insurance policy or custodial account, which thereupon become part of the plan.

(iii) This paragraph (b)(3) applies to contributions to an annuity contract by a church only if the annuity is part of a retirement income account, as defined in § 1.403(b)-9.

*(4) Exclusion limited for former employees.* (i) General rule. Except as provided in paragraph (b)(4)(ii) of this section and in § 1.403(b)-4(d), the exclusion from gross income provided by section 403(b) does not apply to contributions made for former employees. For this purpose, a contribution is not made for a former employee if the contribution is with respect to compensation that would otherwise be paid for a payroll period that begins before severance from employment.

(ii) Exceptions. The exclusion from gross income provided by section 403(b) applies to contributions made for former employees with respect to compensation described in § 1.415(c)-2(e)(3)(i) (relating to certain compensation paid by the later of ½ months after severance from employment or the end of the limitation year that includes the date of severance from employment), and compensation described in § 1.415(c)-2(e)(4), § 1.415(c)-2(g)(4), or § 1.415(c)-2(g)(7) (relating to compensation paid to participants who are permanently and totally disabled or relating to qualified military service under section 414(u)).

**(c) Special rules for designated Roth section 403(b) contributions.** *(1)* The rules of § 1.401(k)-1(f)(1) and (2) for designated Roth contributions under a qualified cash or deferred arrangement apply to designated Roth contributions under a section 403(b) plan. Thus, a designated Roth contribution under a section 403(b) plan is a section 403(b) elective deferral that is designated irrevocably by the employee at the time of the cash or deferred election as a designated Roth contribution that is being made in lieu of all or a portion of the section 403(b) elective deferrals the employee is otherwise eligible to make under the plan; that is treated by the employer as includible in the employee's gross income at the time the employee would have received the amount in cash if the employee had not made the cash or deferred election (such as by treating the contributions as wages subject to applicable withholding requirements); and that is maintained in a separate account (within the meaning of § 1.401(k)-1(f)(2)).

*(2)* A designated Roth contribution under a section 403(b) plan must satisfy the requirements applicable to section 403(b) elective deferrals. Thus, for example, designated Roth contributions under a section 403(b) plan must satisfy the requirements of § 1.403(b)-6(d). Similarly, a designated Roth account under a section 403(b) plan is subject to the rules of sections 401(a)(9)(A) and (B) and § 1.403(b)-6(e).

**(d) Effect of failure.** *(1) General rules.* (i) If a contract includes any amount that fails to satisfy the requirements of section 403(b), § 1.403(b)-1, § 1.403(b)-2, this section, or §§ 1.403(b)-4 through 1.403(b)-11, then, except as otherwise provided in paragraph (d)(2) of this section (relating to failure to satisfy nonforfeitability requirements) or § 1.403(b)-4(f) (relating to excess contributions under section 415 and excess deferrals under section 402(g)), the contract is not a section 403(b) contract. In addition, section 403(b)(5) and paragraph (b)(1) of this section provide that, for purposes of determining whether a contract satisfies section 403(b), all section 403(b) contracts purchased for an individual by an employer are treated as purchased under a single contract. Thus, except as provided in paragraph (b)(2) of this section or as otherwise provided in this paragraph (d), a failure to satisfy section 403(b) with respect to any contract issued to an individual by an employer adversely affects all contracts issued to that individual by that employer.

(ii) In accordance with paragraph (b)(3) of this section, a failure to operate in accordance with the terms of a plan adversely affects all of the contracts issued by the employer to the employee or employees with respect to whom the operational failure occurred. Such a failure does not adversely affect any other contract if the failure is neither a failure to satisfy the nondiscrimination requirements of § 1.403(b)-5 (a nondiscrimination failure) nor a failure of the employer to be an eligible employer as defined in § 1.403(b)-2 (an employer eligibility failure). However, any failure that is not an operational failure adversely affects all contracts issued under the plan, including: a failure to have contracts issued pursuant to a written defined contribution plan which, in form, satisfies the requirements of § 1.403(b)-1, § 1.403(b)-2, this section, and §§ 1.403(b)-4 through 1.403(b)-11 (a written plan failure); a nondiscrimination failure; or an employer eligibility failure.

(iii) See other applicable Internal Revenue Code provisions for the treatment of a contract that is not a section 403(b) contract, such as sections 61, 83, 402(b), and 403(c). Thus, for example, section 403(c) (relating to nonqualified annuities) applies if any annuity contract issued by an insurance company fails to satisfy section 403(b), based on the value of the contract at the time of the failure. However, see paragraph (d)(2) of this section for special rules with respect to the nonforfeitability requirement of paragraph (a)(2) of this section.

*(2) Failure to satisfy nonforfeitability requirement.* (i) Treatment before contract becomes nonforfeitable. If an annuity contract issued by an insurance company would qualify as a section 403(b) contract but for the failure to satisfy the nonforfeitability requirement of paragraph (a)(2) of this section, then the contract is treated as a contract to which section 403(c) applies. See § 1.403(b)-8(d)(4) for a rule under which a custodial account that fails to satisfy the nonforfeitability requirement of paragraph (a)(2) of this section is treated as a section 401(a) qualified plan for certain purposes.

(ii) Treatment when contract becomes nonforfeitable. (A) In general. Notwithstanding paragraph (d)(2)(i) of this section, on or after the date on which the participant's interest in a contract described in paragraph (d)(2)(i) of this section becomes nonforfeitable, the contract may be treated as a section 403(b) contract if no election has been made under section 83(b) with respect to the contract, the participant's interest in the contract has been subject to a substantial risk of forfeiture (as defined in section 83) before becoming nonforfeitable, each contribution under the contract that is subject to a different vesting schedule is maintained in a separate account, and the contract has at all times satisfied the requirements of paragraph (a) of this section other than the nonforfeitability requirement of paragraph (a)(2) of this section. Thus, for example, for the current year and each prior year, no contribution can have been made to the contract that would cause the contract to fail to be a section 403(b) contract as a result of contributions exceeding the limitations of section 415 (except to the extent permitted under paragraph (b)(2) of this section) or to fail to satisfy the nondiscrimination rules described in § 1.403(b)-5. See also § 1.403(b)-10(a)(1) for a special rule in connection with termination of a section 403(b) plan.

(B) Partial vesting. For purposes of applying this paragraph (d), if only a portion of a participant's interest in a contract becomes nonforfeitable in a year, then the portion that is nonforfeitable and the portion that fails to be nonforfeitable are each treated as separate contracts. In addition, for purposes of applying this paragraph (d), if a contribution is made to an annuity contract in excess of the limitations of section 415(c) and the excess is maintained in a separate account, then the portion of the contract that includes the excess contributions account and the remainder are each treated as separate contracts. Thus, if an annuity contract that includes an excess contributions account changes from forfeitable to nonforfeitable during a year, then the portion that is not attributable to the excess contributions account constitutes a section 403(b) contract (assuming it otherwise satisfies the requirements to be a section 403(b) contract) and is not included in gross income, and the portion that is attributable to the excess contributions account is included in gross income in accordance with section 403(c). See § 1.403(b)-4(f) for additional rules.

---

T.D. 8987, 4/16/2002, amend T.D. 9130, 6/14/2004, T.D. 9340, 7/23/2007.

---

### § 1.403(b)-4 Contribution limitations.

**(a) Treatment of contributions in excess of limitations.** The exclusion provided under § 1.403(b)-3(a) applies to a participant only if the amounts contributed by the employer for the purchase of an annuity contract for the participant do not exceed the applicable limit under sections 415 and 402(g), as described in this section. Under § 1.403(b)-3(a)(4), a section 403(b) contract is required to include the limits on elective deferrals imposed by section 402(g), as described in paragraph (c) of this section. See paragraph (f) of this section for special rules concerning excess contributions and deferrals. Rollover contributions made to a section 403(b) contract, as described in § 1.403(b)-10(d), are not taken into account for purposes of the limits imposed by section 415, § 1.403(b)-3(a)(9), section 402(g), § 1.403(b)-3(a)(4), and this section, but after-tax employee contributions are taken into account under section 415, § 1.403(b)-3(a)(9), and paragraph (b) of this section.

**(b) Maximum annual contribution.** *(1) General rule.* In accordance with section 415(a)(2) and § 1.403(b)-3(a)(9), the contributions for any participant under a section 403(b) contract (namely, employer nonelective contributions (including matching contributions), section 403(b) elective deferrals, and after-tax employee contributions) are not permitted to exceed the limitations imposed by section 415. Under section 415(c), contributions are permitted to be made for participants in a defined contribution plan, subject to the limitations set forth therein (which are generally the lesser of a dollar limit for a year or the participant's compensation for the year). For purposes of section 415, contributions made for a participant are aggregated to the extent applicable under sections 414(b), (c), (m), (n), and (o). For purposes of section 415(a)(2), §§ 1.403(b)-1 through 1.403(b)-3, this section, and §§ 1.403(b)-5 through 1.403(b)-11, a contribution means any annual addition, as defined in section 415(c).

*(2) Special rules.* See section 415(k)(4) for a special rule under which contributions to section 403(b) contracts are generally aggregated with contributions under other arrangements in applying section 415. For purposes of applying section 415(c)(1)(B) (relating to compensation) with respect to a section 403(b) contract, except as provided in section 415(c)(3)(C), a participant's includible compensation (as defined in § 1.403(b)-2) is substituted for the participant's compensation, as described in section 415(c)(3)(E). Any age 50 catch-up contributions under paragraph (c)(2) of this section are disregarded in applying section 415.

**(c) Section 403(b) elective deferrals.** *(1) Basic limit under section 402(g)(1).* In accordance with section 402(g)(1)(A), the section 403(b) elective deferrals for any individual are included in the individual's gross income to the extent the amount of such deferrals, plus all other elective deferrals for the individual, for the taxable year exceeds the applicable dollar amount under section 402(g)(1)(B). The applicable annual dollar amount under section 402(g)(1)(B) is

$15,000, adjusted for cost-of-living after 2006 in the manner described in section 402(g)(4). See § 1.403(b)-5(b) for a universal availability rule that applies if any employee is permitted to have any section 403(b) elective deferrals made on his or her behalf.

*(2) Age 50 catch-up.* (i) In general. In accordance with section 414(v) and the regulations thereunder, a section 403(b) contract may provide for catch-up contributions for a participant who is age 50 by the end of the year, provided that such age 50 catch-up contributions do not exceed the catch-up limit under section 414(v)(2) for the taxable year. The maximum amount of additional age 50 catch-up contributions for a taxable year under section 414(v) is $5,000, adjusted for cost-of-living after 2006 in the manner described in section 414(v)(2)(C). For additional requirements, see regulations under section 414(v).

(ii) Coordination with special section 403(b) catch-up. In accordance with sections 414(v)(6)(A)(ii) and 402(g)(7)(A), the age 50 catch-up described in this paragraph (c)(2) may apply for any taxable year in which a participant also qualifies for the special section 403(b) catch-up under paragraph (c)(3) of this section.

*(3) Special section 403(b) catch-up for certain organizations.* (i) Amount of the special section 403(b) catch-up. In the case of a qualified employee of a qualified organization for whom the basic section 403(b) elective deferrals for any year are not less than the applicable dollar amount under section 402(g)(1)(B), the section 403(b) elective deferral limitation of section 402(g)(1) for the taxable year of the qualified employee is increased by the least of—

(A) $3,000;

(B) The excess of—

(1) $15,000, over

(2) The total elective deferrals described in section 402(g)(7)(A)(ii) made for the qualified employee by the qualified organization for prior years; or

(C) The excess of—

(1) $5,000 multiplied by the number of years of service of the employee with the qualified organization, over

(2) The total elective deferrals (as defined at § 1.403(b)-2) made for the employee by the qualified organization for prior years.

(ii) Qualified organization. (A) For purposes of this paragraph (c)(3), qualified organization means an eligible employer that is—

(1) An educational organization described in section 170(b)(1)(A)(ii);

(2) A hospital;

(3) A health and welfare service agency (including a home health service agency);

(4) A church-related organization; or

(5) Any organization described in section 414(e)(3)(B)(ii).

(B) All entities that are in a church-related organization or an organization controlled by a church-related organization under section 414(e)(3)(B)(ii) are treated as a single qualified organization (so that years of service and any special section 403(b) catch-up elective deferrals previously made for a qualified employee for a church or other entity within a church-related organization or an organization controlled by the church-related organization are taken into account for purposes of applying this paragraph (c)(3) to the employee with respect to any other entity within the same church-related organization or organization controlled by a church-related organization).

(C) For purposes of this paragraph (c)(3)(ii), a health and welfare service agency means—

(1) An organization whose primary activity is to provide services that constitute medical care as defined in section 213(d)(1) (such as a hospice);

(2) A section 501(c)(3) organization whose primary activity is the prevention of cruelty to individuals or animals;

(3) An adoption agency; or

(4) An agency that provides substantial personal services to the needy as part of its primary activity (such as a section 501(c)(3) organization that either provides meals to needy individuals, is a home health service agency, provides services to help individuals who have substance abuse, or provides help to the disabled).

(iii) Qualified employee. For purposes of this paragraph (c)(3), qualified employee means an employee who has completed at least 15 years of service (as defined under paragraph (e) of this section) taking into account only employment with the qualified organization. Thus, an employee who has not completed at least 15 years of service (as defined under paragraph (e) of this section) taking into account only employment with the qualified organization is not a qualified employee.

(iv) Coordination with age 50 catch-up. In accordance with sections 402(g)(1)(C) and 402(g)(7), any catch-up amount contributed by an employee who is eligible for both an age 50 catch-up and a special section 403(b) catch-up is treated first as an amount contributed as a special section 403(b) catch-up to the extent a special section 403(b) catch-up is permitted, and then as an amount contributed as an age 50 catch-up (to the extent the catch-up amount exceeds the maximum special section 403(b) catch-up after taking into account sections 402(g) and 415(c), this paragraph (c)(3), and any limitations on the special section 403(b) catch-up that are imposed by the terms of the plan).

*(4) Coordination with designated Roth contributions.* See regulations under section 402A for rules for determining whether an elective deferral is a pre-tax elective deferral or a designated Roth contribution.

*(5) Examples.* The provisions of this paragraph (c) are illustrated by the following examples:

*Example (1).* (i) Facts illustrating application of the basic dollar limit. Participant B, who is 45, is eligible to participate in a State university section 403(b) plan in 2006. B is not a qualified employee, as defined in paragraph (c)(3)(iii) of this section. The plan permits section 403(b) elective deferrals, but no other employer contributions are made under the plan. The plan provides limitations on section 403(b) elective deferrals up to the maximum permitted under paragraphs (c)(1) and (3) of this section and the additional age 50 catch-up amount described in paragraph (c)(2) of this section. For 2006, B will receive includible compensation of $42,000 from the eligible employer. B desires to elect to have the maximum section 403(b) elective deferral possible contributed in 2006. For 2006, the basic dollar limit for section 403(b) elective deferrals under paragraph (c)(1) of this section is $15,000 and the additional dollar amount permitted under the age 50 catch-up is $5,000.

(ii) Conclusion. B is not eligible for the age 50 catch-up in 2006 because B is 45 in 2006. B is also not eligible for the special section 403(b) catch-up under paragraph (c)(3) of this section because B is not a qualified employee. Accordingly, the maximum section 403(b) elective deferral that B may elect for 2006 is $15,000.

*Example (2).* (i) Facts illustrating application of the includible compensation limitation. The facts are the same as in Example 1, except B's includible compensation is $14,000.

(ii) Conclusion. Under section 415(c), contributions may not exceed 100 percent of includible compensation. Accordingly, the maximum section 403(b) elective deferral that B may elect for 2006 is $14,000.

*Example (3).* (i) Facts illustrating application of the age 50 catch-up. Participant C, who is 55, is eligible to participate in a State university section 403(b) plan in 2006. The plan permits section 403(b) elective deferrals, but no other employer contributions are made under the plan. The plan provides limitations on section 403(b) elective deferrals up to the maximum permitted under paragraphs (c)(1) and (c)(3) of this section and the additional age 50 catch-up amount described in paragraph (c)(2) of this section. For 2006, C will receive includible compensation of $48,000 from the eligible employer. C desires to elect to have the maximum section 403(b) elective deferral possible contributed in 2006. For 2006, the basic dollar limit for section 403(b) elective deferrals under paragraph (c)(1) of this section is $15,000 and the additional dollar amount permitted under the age 50 catch-up is $5,000. C does not have 15 years of service and thus is not a qualified employee, as defined in paragraph (c)(3)(iii) of this section.

(ii) Conclusion. C is eligible for the age 50 catch-up in 2006 because C is 55 in 2006. C is not eligible for the special section 403(b) catch-up under paragraph (c)(3) of this section because C is not a qualified employee (as defined in paragraph (c)(3)(iii) of this section). Accordingly, the maximum section 403(b) elective deferral that C may elect for 2006 is $20,000 ($15,000 plus $5,000).

*Example (4).* (i) Facts illustrating application of both the age 50 and the special section 403(b) catch-up. The facts are the same as in Example 3, except that C is a qualified employee for purposes of the special section 403(b) catch-up provisions in paragraph (c)(3) of this section. For 2006, the maximum additional section 403(b) elective deferral for which C qualifies under the special section 403(b) catch-up under paragraph (c)(3) of this section is $3,000.

(ii) Conclusion. The maximum section 403(b) elective deferrals that C may elect for 2006 is $23,000. This is the sum of the basic limit on section 403(b) elective deferrals under paragraph (c)(1) of this section equal to $15,000, plus the $3,000 additional special section 403(b) catch-up amount for which C qualifies under paragraph (c)(3) of this section, plus the additional age 50 catch-up amount of $5,000.

*Example (5).* (i) Facts illustrating calculation of years of service with a predecessor organization for purposes of the special section 403(b) catch-up. Participant A is an employee of hospital H and is eligible to participate in a section 403(b) plan of H in 2006. A does not have 15 years of service with H, but A has previously made special section 403(b) catch-up deferrals to a section 403(b) plan maintained by hospital P which has since been acquired by H.

(ii) Conclusion. The special section 403(b) catch-up amount for which A qualifies under paragraph (c)(3) of this section must be calculated taking into account A's prior years of service and section 403(b) elective deferrals with the predecessor hospital if and only if A did not have any severance from service in connection with the acquisition.

*Example (6).* (i) Facts illustrating application of the age 50 catch-up and the section 415(c) dollar limitation. The facts are the same as in Example 4, except that the employer makes a nonelective contribution for each employee equal to 20 percent of C's compensation (which is $48,000). Thus, the employer makes a nonelective contribution for C for 2006 equal to $9,600. The plan provides that a participant is not permitted to make section 403(b) elective deferrals to the extent the section 403(b) elective deferrals would result in contributions in excess of the maximum permitted under section 415 and provides that contributions are reduced in the following order: the special section 403(b) catch-up elective deferrals under paragraph (c)(3) of this section are reduced first; the age 50 catch-up elective deferrals under paragraph (c)(2) of this section are reduced second; and then the basic section 403(b) elective deferrals under paragraph (c)(1) of this section are reduced. For 2006, the applicable dollar limit under section 415(c)(1)(A) is $44,000.

(ii) Conclusion. The maximum section 403(b) elective deferral that C may elect for 2006 is $23,000. This is the sum of the basic limit on section 403(b) elective deferrals under paragraph (c)(1) of this section equal to $15,000, plus the $3,000 additional special section 403(b) catch-up amount for which C qualifies under paragraph (c)(3) of this section, plus the additional age 50 catch-up amount of $5,000. The limit in paragraph (b) of this section would not be exceeded because the sum of the $9,600 nonelective contribution and the $23,000 section 403(b) elective deferrals does not exceed the lesser of $49,000 (which is the sum of $44,000 plus the $5,000 additional age 50 catch-up amount) or $53,000 (which is the sum of C's includible compensation for 2006 ($48,000) plus the $5,000 additional age 50 catch-up amount).

*Example (7).* (i) Facts further illustrating application of the age 50 catch-up and the section 415(c) dollar limitation. The facts are the same as in Example 6, except that C's includible compensation for 2006 is $58,000 and the plan provides for a nonelective contribution equal to 50 percent of includible compensation, so that the employer nonelective contribution for C for 2006 is $29,000 (50 percent of $58,000).

(ii) Conclusion. The maximum section 403(b) elective deferral that C may elect for 2006 is $20,000. A section 403(b) elective deferral in excess of this amount would exceed the sum of the limit in section 415(c)(1)(A) plus the additional age 50 catch-up amount, because the sum of the employer's nonelective contribution of $29,000 plus a section 403(b) elective deferral in excess of $20,000 would exceed $49,000 (the sum of the $44,000 limit in section 415(c)(1)(A) plus the $5,000 additional age 50 catch-up amount). (Note that a section 403(b) elective deferral in excess of $20,000 would also exceed the limitations of section 402(g) unless a special section 403(b) catch-up were permitted.)

*Example (8).* (i) Facts further illustrating application of the age 50 catch-up and the section 415(c) dollar limitation. The facts are the same as in Example 7, except that the plan provides for a nonelective contribution for C equal to $44,000 (which is the limit in section 415(c)(1)(A)).

(ii) Conclusion. The maximum section 403(b) elective deferral that C may elect for 2006 is $5,000. A section 403(b) elective deferral in excess of this amount would exceed the sum of the limit in section 415(c)(1)(A) plus the additional age 50 catch-up amount ($5,000), because the sum of the employer's nonelective contribution of $44,000 plus a section 403(b) elective deferral in excess of $5,000 would exceed $49,000 (the sum of the $44,000 limit in section 415(c)(1)(A) plus the $5,000 additional age 50 catch-up amount).

*Example (9).* (i) Facts illustrating application of the age 50 catch-up and the section 415(c) includible compensation limitation. The facts are the same as in Example 7, except that C's includible compensation for 2006 is $28,000, so that the employer nonelective contribution for C for 2006 is $14,000 (50 percent of $28,000).

(ii) Conclusion. The maximum section 403(b) elective deferral that C may elect for 2006 is $19,000. A section 403(b) elective deferral in excess of this amount would exceed the sum of the limit in section 415(c)(1)(B) plus the additional age 50 catch-up amount, because C's includible compensation is $28,000 and the sum of the employer's nonelective contribution of $14,000 plus a section 403(b) elective deferral in excess of $19,000 would exceed $33,000 (which is the sum of 100 percent of C's includible compensation plus the $5,000 additional age 50 catch-up amount).

*Example (10).* (i) Facts illustrating that section 403(b) elective deferrals cannot exceed compensation otherwise payable. Employee D is age 60, has includible compensation of $14,000, and wishes to contribute section 403(b) elective deferrals of $20,000 for the year. No nonelective contributions are made for Employee D.

(ii) Conclusion. Because a contribution is a section 403(b) elective deferral only if it relates to an amount that would otherwise be included in the participant's compensation, the effective limitation on section 403(b) elective deferrals for a participant whose compensation is less than the basic dollar limit for section 403(b) elective deferrals is the participant's compensation. Thus, D cannot make section 403(b) elective deferrals in excess of D's actual compensation, which is $14,000, even though the basic dollar limit exceeds that amount.

*Example (11).* (i) Facts illustrating calculation of the special section 403(b) catch-up. For 2006, employee E, who is age 53, is eligible to participate in a section 403(b) plan of hospital H, which is a section 501(c)(3) organization. H's plan permits section 403(b) elective deferrals and provides for an employer contribution of 10 percent of a participant's compensation. The plan provides limitations on section 403(b) elective deferrals up to the maximum permitted under paragraphs (c)(1), (2), and (3) of this section. For 2006, E's includible compensation is $50,000. E wishes to elect to have the maximum section 403(b) elective deferral possible contributed in 2006. E has previously made $62,000 of section 403(b) elective deferrals under the plan, but has never made an election for a special section 403(b) catch-up elective deferral. For 2006, the basic dollar limit for section 403(b) elective deferrals under paragraph (c)(1) of this section is $15,000, the additional dollar amount permitted under the age 50 catch-up is $5,000, E's employer will make a nonelective contribution of $5,000 (10% of $50,000 compensation), and E is a qualified employee of a qualified employer as defined in paragraph (c)(3) of this section.

(ii) Conclusion. The maximum section 403(b) elective deferrals that E may elect under H's section 403(b) plan for 2006 is $23,000. This is the sum of the basic limit on section 403(b) elective deferrals for 2006 under paragraph (c)(1) of this section equal to $15,000, plus the $3,000 maximum additional special section 403(b) catch-up amount for which D qualifies in 2006 under paragraph (c)(3) of this section, plus the additional age 50 catch-up amount of $5,000. The limitation on the additional special section 403(b) catch-up amount is not less than $3,000 because the limitation at paragraph (c)(3)(i)(B) of this section is $15,000 ($15,000 minus zero) and the limitation at paragraph (c)(3)(i)(C) of this section is $13,000 ($5,000 times 15, minus $62,000 of total deferrals in prior years). These conclusions would be unaffected if H were an eligible governmental employer under section 457(b) that has a section 457(b) eligible governmental plan and E were in the past to have made annual deferrals to that plan, because contributions to a section 457(b) eligible governmental plan do not constitute elective deferrals; and these conclusions would also be the same if H had a section 401(k) plan and E were in the past to have made elective deferrals to that plan, assuming that those elective deferrals did not exceed $10,000 ($5,000 times 15, minus the sum of $62,000 plus $10,000, equals $3,000), so as to result in the limitation at paragraph (c)(3)(i)(C) of this section being less than $3,000.

*Example (12).* (i) Facts illustrating calculation of the special section 403(b) catch-up in the next calendar year. The facts are the same as in Example 11, except that, for 2007, E has includible compensation of $60,000. For 2007, E now has previously made $85,000 of section 403(b) elective deferrals ($62,000 deferred before 2006, plus the $15,000 in basic section 403(b) elective deferrals in 2006, the $3,000 maximum additional special section 403(b) catch-up amount in 2006, plus the $5,000 age 50 catch-up amount in 2006). However, the $5,000 age 50 catch-up amount deferred in 2006 is disregarded for purposes of applying the limitation at paragraph (c)(3)(i)(C) of this section to determine the special section 403(b) catch-up amount. Thus, for 2007, only $80,000 of section 403(b) elective deferrals are taken into account in applying the limitation at paragraph (c)(3)(i)(C) of this section. For 2007, the basic dollar limit for section 403(b) elective deferrals under paragraph (c)(1) of this section is assumed to be $16,000, the additional dollar amount permitted under the age 50 catch-up is assumed to be $5,000, and E's employer contributes $6,000 (10% of $60,000) as a non-elective contribution.

(ii) Conclusion. The maximum section 403(b) elective deferral that D may elect under H's section 403(b) plan for 2007 is $21,000. This is the sum of the basic limit on section 403(b) elective deferrals under paragraph (c)(1) of this section equal to $16,000, plus the additional age 50 catch-up amount of $5,000. E is not entitled to any additional special section 403(b) catch-up amount for 2007 under paragraph (c)(3) of this section due to the limitation at paragraph (c)(3)(i)(C) of this section (16 times $5,000 equals $80,000, minus D's total prior section 403(b) elective deferrals of $80,000 equals zero).

**(d) Employer contributions for former employees.** *(1) Includible compensation deemed to continue for nonelective contributions.* For purposes of applying paragraph (b) of this section, a former employee is deemed to have monthly includible compensation for the period through the end of the taxable year of the employee in which he or she ceases to be an employee and through the end of each of the next five taxable years. The amount of the monthly includible compensation is equal to one twelfth of the former employee's includible compensation during the former employee's most recent year of service. Accordingly, nonelective employer contributions for a former employee must not exceed the limitation of section 415(c)(1) up to the lesser of the dollar amount in section 415(c)(1)(A) or the former employee's annual includible compensation based on the former employee's average monthly compensation during his or her most recent year of service.

*(2) Examples.* The provisions of paragraph (d)(1) of this section are illustrated by the following examples:

*Example (1).* (i) Facts. Private college M is a section 501(c)(3) organization operated on the basis of a June 30 fiscal year that maintains a section 403(b) plan for its employees. In 2004, M amends the plan to provide for a temporary early retirement incentive under which the college will make a nonelective contribution for any participant who satisfies certain minimum age and service conditions and who retires before June 30, 2006. The contribution will equal 110 percent of the participant's rate of pay for one year and will be payable over a period ending no later than the end of the fifth fiscal year that begins after retirement. It is assumed for purposes of this Example 1 that, in accordance with § 1.401(a)(4)-10(b) and under the facts and circumstances, the post-retirement contributions made for participants who satisfy the minimum age and service conditions and retire before June 30, 2006, do not discriminate in favor of former employees who are highly compensated employees. Employee A retires under the early retirement incentive on March 12, 2006, and A's annual includible compensation for the period from March 1, 2005, through February 28, 2006 (which is A's most recent one year of service) is $30,000. The applicable dollar limit under section 415(c)(1)(A) is assumed to be $44,000 for 2006 and $45,000 for 2007. The college contributes $30,000 for A for 2006 and $3,000 for A for 2007 (totaling $33,000 or 110 percent of $30,000). No other contributions are made to a section 403(b) contract for A for those years.

(ii) Conclusion. The contributions made for A do not exceed A's includible compensation for 2006 or 2007.

*Example (2).* (i) Facts. Private college N is a section 501(c)(3) organization that maintains a section 403(b) plan for its employees. The plan provides for N to make monthly nonelective contributions equal to 20 percent of the monthly includible compensation for each eligible employee. In addition, the plan provides for contributions to continue for 5 years following the retirement of any employee after age 64 and completion of at least 20 years of service (based on the employee's average annual rate of base salary in the preceding 3 calendar years ended before the date of retirement). It is assumed for purposes of this Example 2 that, in accordance with § 1.401(a)(4)-10(b) and under the facts and circumstances, the post-retirement contributions made for participants who satisfy the minimum age and service conditions do not discriminate in favor of former employees who are highly compensated employees. Employee B retires on July 1, 2006, at age 64 after completion of 20 or more years of service. At that date, B's annual includible compensation for the most recently ended fiscal year of N is $72,000 and B's average monthly rate of base salary for 2003 through 2005 is $5,000. N contributes $1,200 per month (20 percent of 1/12th of $72,000) from January of 2006 through June of 2006 and contributes $1,000 (20 percent of $5,000) per month for B from July of 2006 through June of 2011. The applicable dollar limit under section 415(c)(1)(A) is $44,000 for 2006 through 2011. No other contributions are made to a section 403(b) contract for B for those years.

(ii) Conclusion. The contributions made for B do not exceed B's includible compensation for any of the years from 2006 through 2010.

*Example (3).* (i) Facts. A public university maintains a section 403(b) under which it contributes annually 10% of compensation for participants, including for the first 5 calendar years following the date on which the participant ceases to be an employee. The plan provides that if a participant who is a former employee dies during the first 5 calendar years following the date on which the participant ceases to be an employee, a contribution is made that is equal to the lesser of—

(A) The excess of the individual's includible compensation for that year over the contributions previously made for the individual for that year; or

(B) The total contributions that would have been made on the individual's behalf thereafter if he or she had survived to the end of the 5-year period.

(ii) Individual C's annual includible compensation is $72,000 (so that C's monthly includible compensation is $6,000). A $600 contribution is made for C for January of the first taxable year following retirement (10% of individual C's monthly includible compensation of $6,000). Individual C dies during February of that year. The university makes a contribution for individual C for February equal to $11,400 (C's monthly includible compensation for January and February, reduced by $600).

(iii) Conclusion. The contribution does not exceed the amount of individual C's includible compensation for the taxable year for purposes of section 415(c), but any additional contributions would exceed C's includible compensation for purposes of section 415(c).

*(3) Disabled employees.* See also section 415(c)(3)(C) which sets forth a special rule under which compensation may be treated as continuing for purposes of section 415 for certain former employees who are disabled.

**(e) Special rules for determining years of service.** *(1) In general.* For purposes of determining a participant's includible compensation under paragraph (b)(2) of this section and a participant's years of service under paragraphs (c)(3) (special section 403(b) catch-up for qualified employees of certain organizations) and (d) (employer contributions for former employees) of this section, an employee must be credited with a full year of service for each year during which the individual is a full-time employee of the eligible employer for the entire work period, and a fraction of a year for each part of a work period during which the individual is a full-time or part-time employee of the eligible employer. An individual's number of years of service equals the aggregate of the annual work periods during which the individual is employed by the eligible employer.

*(2) Work period.* A year of service is based on the employer's annual work period, not the employee's taxable year. For example, in determining whether a university professor is employed full time, the annual work period is the school's academic year. However, in no case may an employee accumulate more than one year of service in a twelve-month period.

*(3) Service with more than one eligible employer.* (i) General rule. With respect to any section 403(b) contract of an eligible employer, except as provided in paragraph (e)(3)(ii) of this section, any period during which an individual is not an employee of that eligible employer is disregarded for purposes of this paragraph (e).

(ii) Special rule for church employees. With respect to any section 403(b) contract of an eligible employer that is a church-related organization, any period during which an individual is an employee of that eligible employer and any other eligible employer that is a church-related organization that has an association (as defined in section 414(e)(3)(D)) with that eligible employer is taken into account on an aggregated basis, but any period during which an individual is not an employee of a church-related organization or is an employee of a church-related organization that does not have an association with that eligible employer is disregarded for purposes of this paragraph (e).

*(4) Full-time employee for full year.* Each annual work period during which an individual is employed full time by the eligible employer constitutes one year of service. In determining whether an individual is employed full-time, the amount of work which he or she actually performs is compared with the amount of work that is normally required of individuals performing similar services from which substantially all of their annual compensation is derived.

*(5) Other employees.* (i) An individual is treated as performing a fraction of a year of service for each annual work period during which he or she is a full-time employee for part of the annual work period and for each annual work period during which he or she is a part-time employee either for the entire annual work period or for a part of the annual work period.

(ii) In determining the fraction that represents the fractional year of service for an individual employed full time for part of an annual work period, the numerator is the period of time (such as weeks or months) during which the individual is a full-time employee during that annual work period, and the denominator is the period of time that is the annual work period.

(iii) In determining the fraction that represents the fractional year of service of an individual who is employed part time for the entire annual work period, the numerator is the amount of work performed by the individual, and the denominator is the amount of work normally required of individuals who perform similar services and who are employed full time for the entire annual work period.

(iv) In determining the fraction representing the fractional year of service of an individual who is employed part time for part of an annual work period, the fractional year of service that would apply if the individual were a part-time employee for a full annual work period is multiplied by the fractional year of service that would apply if the individual were a full-time employee for the part of an annual work period.

*(6) Work performed.* For purposes of this paragraph (e), in measuring the amount of work of an individual performing particular services, the work performed is determined based on the individual's hours of service (as defined under section 410(a)(3)(C)), except that a plan may use a different measure of work if appropriate under the facts and circumstances. For example, a plan may provide for a university professor's work to be measured by the number of courses taught during an annual work period in any case in which that individual's work assignment is generally based on a specified number of courses to be taught.

*(7) Most recent one-year period of service.* For purposes of paragraph (d) of this section, in the case of a part-time employee or a full-time employee who is employed for only part of the year determined on the basis of the employer's annual work period, the employee's most recent periods of service are aggregated to determine his or her most recent one-year period of service. In such a case, there is first taken into account his or her service during the annual work period for which the last year of service's includible compensation is being determined; then there is taken into account his or her service during his or her next preceding annual work period based on whole months; and so forth until the employee's service equals, in the aggregate, one year of service.

*(8) Less than one year of service considered as one year.* If, at the close of a taxable year, an employee has, after application of all of the other rules in this paragraph (e), some portion of one year of service (but has accumulated less than one year of service), the employee is deemed to have one year of service. Except as provided in the previous sentence, fractional years of service are not rounded up.

*(9) Examples.* The provisions of this paragraph (e) are illustrated by the following examples:

*Example (1).* (i) Facts. Individual G is employed half-time in 2004 and 2005 as a clerk by H, a hospital which is a section 501(c)(3) organization. G earns $20,000 from H in each of those years, and retires on December 31, 2005.

(ii) Conclusion. For purposes of determining G's includible compensation during G's last year of service under paragraph (d) of this section, G's most recent periods of service are aggregated to determine G's most recent one-year period of service. In this case, since D worked half-time in 2004 and 2005, the compensation D earned in those two years are aggregated to produce D's includible compensation for D's last full year in service. Thus, in this case, the $20,000 that D earned in 2004 and 2005 for D's half-time work are aggregated, so that D has $40,000 of includible compensation for D's most recent one-year of service for purposes of applying paragraphs (b)(2), (c)(3), and (d) of this section.

*Example (2).* (i) Facts. Individual H is employed as a part-time professor by public University U during the first semester of its two-semester 2004-2005 academic year. While H teaches one course generally for 3 hours a week during the first semester of the academic year, U's full-time faculty members generally teach for 9 hours a week during the full academic year.

(ii) Conclusion. For purposes of calculating how much of a year of service H performs in the 2004-2005 academic year (before application of the special rules of paragraphs (e)(7) and (8) of this section concerning less than one year of service), paragraph (e)(5)(iv) of this section is applied as follows: since H teaches one course at U for 3 hours per week for 1 semester and other faculty members at U teach 9 hours per week for 2 semesters, H is considered to have completed $3/18$ or $1/6$ of a year of service during the 2004-2005 academic year, determined as follows:

(A) The fractional year of service if H were a part-time employee for a full year is $3/9$ (number of hours employed divided by the usual number of hours of work required for that position).

(B) The fractional year of service if H were a full-time employee for half of a year is $1/2$ (one semester, divided by the usual 2-semester annual work period).

(C) These fractions are multiplied to obtain the fractional year of service: $3/9$ times $1/2$, or $3/18$, equals $1/6$ of a year of service.

**(f) Excess contributions or deferrals.** *(1) Inclusion in gross income.* Any contribution made for a participant to a section 403(b) contract for the taxable year that exceeds either the maximum annual contribution limit set forth in paragraph (b) of this section or the maximum annual section 403(b) elective deferral limit set forth in paragraph (c) of this section constitutes an excess contribution that is included in gross income for that taxable year. See § 1.403(b)-3(d)(1)(iii) and (2)(i) for additional rules, including special rules relating to contracts that fail to be nonforfeitable. See also section 4973 for an excise tax applicable with respect to excess contributions to a custodial account and section 4979(f)(2)(B) for a special rule applicable if excess matching contributions, excess after-tax employee contributions, and excess section 403(b) elective deferrals do not exceed $100.

*(2) Separate account required for certain excess contributions; distribution of excess elective deferrals.* A contract to which a contribution is made that exceeds the maximum annual contribution limit set forth in paragraph (b) of this section is not a section 403(b) contract unless the excess contribution is held in a separate account which constitutes a separate account for purposes of section 72. See also § 1.403(b)-3(a)(4) and paragraph (f)(4) of this section for additional rules with respect to the requirements of section 401(a)(30) and any excess deferral.

*(3) Ability to distribute excess contributions.* A contract does not fail to satisfy the requirements of § 1.403(b)-3, the distribution rules of § 1.403(b)-6 or 1.403(b)-9, or the funding rules of § 1.403(b)-8 solely by reason of a distribution made from a separate account under paragraph (f)(2) of this section or made under paragraph (f)(4) of this section.

*(4) Excess section 403(b) elective deferrals.* A section 403(b) contract may provide that any excess deferral as a result of a failure to comply with the limitation under paragraph (c) of this section for a taxable year with respect to any section 403(b) elective deferral made for a participant by the employer will be distributed to the participant, with allocable net income, no later than April 15 of the following taxable year or otherwise in accordance with section 402(g). See section 402(g)(2)(A) for rules permitting the participant to allocate excess deferrals among the plans in which the participant has made elective deferrals, and see section 402(g)(2)(C) for special rules to determine the tax treatment of such a distribution.

*(5) Examples.* The provisions of this paragraph (f) are illustrated by the following examples:

*Example (1).* (i) Facts. Individual D's employer makes a $46,000 contribution for 2006 to an individual annuity insurance policy for Individual D that would otherwise be a section 403(b) contract. The contribution does not include any elective deferrals and the applicable limit under section 415(c) is $44,000 for 2006. The $2,000 section 415(c) excess is put into a separate account under the policy. Employer includes $2,000 in D's gross income as wages for 2006 and, to the extent of the amount held in the separate account for the section 415(c) excess contribution, does not treat the account as a contract to which section 403(b) applies.

(ii) Conclusion. The separate account for the section 415(c) excess contribution is a contract to which section 403(c) applies, but the excess contribution does not cause the rest of the contract to fail section 403(b).

*Example (2).* (i) Facts. Same facts as Example 1, except that the contribution is made to purchase mutual funds that are held in a custodial account, instead of an individual annuity insurance policy.

(ii) Conclusion. The conclusion is the same as in Example 1, except that the purchase constitutes a transfer described in section 83.

*Example (3).* (i) Facts. Same facts as Example 1, except that the amount held in the separate account for the section 415(c) excess contribution is subsequently distributed to D.

(ii) Conclusion. The distribution is included in gross income to the extent provided under section 72 relating to distributions from a section 403(c) contract.

*Example (4).* (i) Facts. Individual E makes section 403(b) elective deferrals totaling $15,500 for 2006, when E is age 45 and the applicable limit on section 403(b) elective deferrals is $15,000. On April 14, 2007, the plan refunds the $500 excess along with applicable earnings of $65.

(ii) Conclusion. The $565 payment constitutes a distribution of an excess deferral under paragraph (f)(4) of this section. Under section 402(g), the $500 excess deferral is included in E's gross income for 2006. The additional $65 is included in E's gross income for 2007 and, because the distribution is made by April 15, 2007 (as provided in section 402(g)(2)), the $65 is not subject to the additional 10 percent income tax on early distributions under section 72(t).

T.D. 9340, 7/23/2007.

### § 1.403(b)-5 Nondiscrimination rules.

**(a) Nondiscrimination rules for contributions other than section 403(b) elective deferrals.** *(1) General rule.* Under section 403(b)(12)(A)(i), employer contributions and after-tax employee contributions to a section 403(b) plan must satisfy all of the following requirements (the nondiscrimination requirements) in the same manner as a qualified plan under section 401(a):

(i) Section 401(a)(4) (relating to nondiscrimination in contributions and benefits), taking section 401(a)(5) into account.

(ii) Section 401(a)(17) (limiting the amount of compensation that can be taken into account).

(iii) Section 401(m) (relating to matching and after-tax employee contributions).

(iv) Section 410(b) (relating to minimum coverage).

*(2) Nonapplication to section 403(b) elective deferrals.* The requirements of this paragraph (a) do not apply to section 403(b) elective deferrals.

*(3) Compensation for testing.* Except as may otherwise be specifically permitted under the provisions referenced in paragraph (a)(1) of this section, compliance with those provisions is tested using compensation as defined in section 414(s) (and without regard to section 415(c)(3)(E)). In addition, for purposes of paragraph (a)(1) of this section, there may be excluded employees who are permitted to be excluded under paragraph (b)(4)(ii)(D) and (E) of this section. However, as provided in paragraph (b)(4)(i) of this section, the exclusion of any employee listed in paragraph (b)(4)(ii)(D) or (E) of this section is subject to the conditions applicable under section 410(b)(4).

*(4) Employer aggregation rules.* See regulations under section 414(b), (c), (m), and (o) for rules treating entities as a single employer for purposes of the nondiscrimination requirements.

*(5) Special rules for governmental plans.* Paragraphs (a)(1)(i), (iii), and (iv) of this section do not apply to a governmental plan as defined in section 414(d) (but contributions to a governmental plan must comply with paragraphs (a)(1)(ii) and (b) of this section).

**(b) Universal availability required for section 403(b) elective deferrals.** *(1) General rule.* Under section 403(b)(12)(A)(ii), all employees of the eligible employer must be permitted to have section 403(b) elective deferrals contributed on their behalf if any employee of the eligible employer may elect to have the organization make section 403(b) elective deferrals. Further, the employee's right to make elective deferrals also includes the right to designate section 403(b) elective deferrals as designated Roth contributions.

*(2) Effective opportunity required.* For purposes of paragraph (b)(1) of this section, an employee is not treated as being permitted to have section 403(b) elective deferrals contributed on the employee's behalf unless the employee is provided an effective opportunity that satisfies the requirements of this paragraph (b)(2). Whether an employee has an effective opportunity is determined based on all the relevant facts and circumstances, including notice of the availability of the election, the period of time during which an election may be made, and any other conditions on elections. A section 403(b) plan satisfies the effective opportunity requirement of this paragraph (b)(2) only if, at least once during each plan year, the plan provides an employee with an effective opportunity to make (or change) a cash or deferred election (as defined at § 1.401(k)-1(a)(3)) between cash or a contribution to the plan. Further, an effective opportunity includes the right to have section 403(b) elective deferrals made on his or her behalf up to the lesser of the applicable limits in § 1.403(b)-4(c) (including any permissible catch-up elective deferrals under § 1.403(b)-4(c)(2) and (3)) or the applicable limits under the contract with the largest limitation, and applies to part-time employees as well as full-time employees. An effective opportunity is not considered to exist if there are any other rights or benefits (other than rights or benefits listed in § 1.401(k)-1(e)(6)(i)(A), (B), or (D)) that are conditioned (directly or indirectly) upon a participant making or failing to make a cash or deferred election with respect to a contribution to a section 403(b) contract.

*(3) Special rules.* (i) In the case of a section 403(b) plan that covers the employees of more than one section 501(c)(3) organization, the universal availability requirement of this paragraph (b) applies separately to each common law entity (that is, applies separately to each section 501(c)(3) organization). In the case of a section 403(b) plan that covers the employees of more than one State entity, this requirement applies separately to each entity that is not part of a common payroll. An eligible employer may condition the employee's right to have section 403(b) elective deferrals made on his or her behalf on the employee electing a section 403(b) elective deferral of more than $200 for a year.

(ii) For purposes of this paragraph (b)(3), an employer that historically has treated one or more of its various geographically distinct units as separate for employee benefit purposes may treat each unit as a separate organization if the unit is operated independently on a day-to-day basis. Units are not geographically distinct if such units are located within the same Standard Metropolitan Statistical Area (SMSA).

*(4) Exclusions.* (i) Exclusions for special types of employees. A plan does not fail to satisfy the universal availability requirement of this paragraph (b) merely because it excludes one or more of the types of employees listed in paragraph (b)(4)(ii) of this section. However, the exclusion of any employee listed in paragraph (b)(4)(ii)(D) or (E) of this section is subject to the conditions applicable under section 410(b)(4). Thus, if any employee listed in paragraph (b)(4)(ii)(D) of this section has the right to have section 403(b) elective deferrals made on his or her behalf, then no employee listed in that paragraph (b)(4)(ii)(D) of this section may be excluded under this paragraph (b)(4) and, if any employee listed in paragraph (b)(4)(ii)(E) of this section has the right to have section 403(b) elective deferrals made on his or her behalf, then no employee listed in that paragraph (b)(4)(ii)(E) of this section may be excluded under this paragraph (b)(4).

(ii) List of special types of excludible employees. The following types of employees are listed in this paragraph (b)(4)(ii):

(A) Employees who are eligible under another section 403(b) plan, or a section 457(b) eligible governmental plan, of the employer which permits an amount to be contributed or deferred at the election of the employee.

(B) Employees who are eligible to make a cash or deferred election (as defined at § 1.401(k)-1(a)(3)) under a section 401(k) plan of the employer.

(C) Employees who are non-resident aliens described in section 410(b)(3)(C).

(D) Subject to the conditions applicable under section 410(b)(4) (including section 410(b)(4)(B) permitting separate testing for employees not meeting minimum age and service requirements), employees who are students performing services described in section 3121(b)(10).

(E) Subject to the conditions applicable under section 410(b)(4), employees who normally work fewer than 20 hours per week (or such lower number of hours per week as may be set forth in the plan).

(iii) Special rules. (A) A section 403(b) plan is permitted to take into account coverage under another plan, as permitted in paragraphs (b)(4)(ii)(A) and (B) of this section, only if the rights to make elective deferrals with respect to that coverage would satisfy paragraphs (b)(2) and (4)(i) of this section if that coverage were provided under the section 403(b) plan.

(B) For purposes of paragraph (b)(4)(ii)(E) of this section, an employee normally works fewer than 20 hours per week if and only if—

(1) For the 12-month period beginning on the date the employee's employment commenced, the employer reasonably expects the employee to work fewer than 1,000 hours of service (as defined in section 410(a)(3)(C)) in such period; and

(2) For each plan year ending after the close of the 12-month period beginning on the date the employee's employment commenced (or, if the plan so provides, each subsequent 12-month period), the employee worked fewer than 1,000 hours of service in the preceding 12-month period. (See, however, section 202(a)(1) of the Employee Retirement Income Security Act of 1974 (ERISA) (88 Stat. 829) Public Law 93-406, and regulations under section 410(a) of the Internal Revenue Code applicable with respect to plans that are subject to Title I of ERISA.)

**(c) Plan required.** Contributions to an annuity contract do not satisfy the requirements of this section unless the contributions are made pursuant to a plan, as defined in § 1.403(b)-3(b)(3), and the terms of the plan satisfy this section.

**(d) Church plans exception.** This section does not apply to a section 403(b) contract purchased by a church (as defined in § 1.403(b)-2).

**(e) Other rules.** This section only reflects requirements of the Internal Revenue Code applicable for purposes of section 403(b) and does not include other requirements. Specifically, this section does not reflect the requirements of ERISA that may apply with respect to section 403(b) arrangements, such as the vesting requirements at 29 U.S.C. 1053.

T.D. 9340, 7/23/2007.

### § 1.403(b)-6 Timing of distributions and benefits.

**(a) Distributions generally.** This section provides special rules regarding the timing of distributions from, and the benefits that may be provided under, a section 403(b) contract, including limitations on when early distributions can be made (in paragraphs (b) through (d) of this section), required minimum distributions (in paragraph (e) of this section), and special rules relating to loans (in paragraph (f) of this section) and incidental benefits (in paragraph (g) of this section).

**(b) Distributions from contracts other than custodial accounts or amounts attributable to section 403(b) elective deferrals.** Except as provided in paragraph (c) of this section relating to distributions from custodial accounts, paragraph (d) of this section relating to distributions attributable to section 403(b) elective deferrals, § 1.403(b)-4(f) (relating to correction of excess deferrals), or § 1.403(b)-10(a) (relating to plan termination), a section 403(b) contract is permitted to distribute retirement benefits to the participant no earlier than upon the earlier of the participant's severance from employment or upon the prior occurrence of some event, such as after a fixed number of years, the attainment of a stated age, or disability. See § 1.401-1(b)(1)(ii) for additional guidance. This paragraph (b) does not apply to after-tax employee contributions or earnings thereon.

**(c) Distributions from custodial accounts that are not attributable to section 403(b) elective deferrals.** Except as provided in § 1.403(b)-4(f) (relating to correction of excess deferrals) or § 1.403(b)-10(a) (relating to plan termination), distributions from a custodial account, as defined in § 1.403(b)-8(d)(2), may not be paid to a participant before the participant has a severance from employment, dies, becomes disabled (within the meaning of section 72(m)(7)), or attains age 59½. Any amounts transferred out of a custodial account to an annuity contract or retirement income account, including earnings thereon, continue to be subject to this paragraph (c). This paragraph (c) does not apply to distributions that are attributable to section 403(b) elective deferrals.

**(d) Distribution of section 403(b) elective deferrals.** *(1) Limitation on distributions.* (i) General rule. Except as provided in § 1.403(b)-4(f) (relating to correction of excess deferrals) or § 1.403(b)-10(a) (relating to plan termination), distributions of amounts attributable to section 403(b) elective deferrals may not be paid to a participant earlier than the earliest of the date on which the participant has a severance from employment, dies, has a hardship, becomes disabled (within the meaning of section 72(m)(7)), or attains age 59½.

(ii) Special rule for pre-1989 section 403(b) elective deferrals. For special rules relating to amounts held as of the close of the taxable year beginning before January 1, 1989 (which does not apply to earnings thereon), see section 1123(e)(3) of the Tax Reform Act of 1986 (100 Stat. 2085, 2475) Public Law 99-514, and section 1011A(c)(11) of the Technical and Miscellaneous Revenue Act of 1988 (102 Stat. 3342, 3476) Public Law 100-647.

*(2) Hardship rules.* A hardship distribution under this paragraph (d) has the same meaning as a distribution on account of hardship under § 1.401(k)-1(d)(3) and is subject to the rules and restrictions set forth in § 1.401(k)-1(d)(3) (including limiting the amount of a distribution in the case of hardship to the amount necessary to satisfy the hardship). In addition, a hardship distribution is limited to the aggregate dollar amount of the participant's section 403(b) elective deferrals under the contract (and may not include any income thereon), reduced by the aggregate dollar amount of the distributions previously made to the participant from the contract.

*(3) Failure to keep separate accounts.* If a section 403(b) contract includes both section 403(b) elective deferrals and other contributions and the section 403(b) elective deferrals are not maintained in a separate account, then distributions may not be made earlier than the later of—

(i) Any date permitted under paragraph (d)(1) of this section; and

(ii) Any date permitted under paragraph (b) or (c) of this section with respect to contributions that are not section 403(b) elective deferrals (whichever applies to the contributions that are not section 403(b) elective deferrals).

**(e) Minimum required distributions for eligible plans.** *(1) In general.* Under section 403(b)(10), a section 403(b) contract must meet the minimum distribution requirements of section 401(a)(9) (in both form and operation). See section 401(a)(9) for these requirements.

*(2) Treatment as IRAs.* For purposes of applying the distribution rules of section 401(a)(9) to section 403(b) contracts, the minimum distribution rules applicable to individual retirement annuities described in section 408(b) and individual retirement accounts described in section 408(a) apply to section 403(b) contracts. Consequently, except as otherwise provided in this paragraph (e), the distribution rules in section 401(a)(9) are applied to section 403(b) contracts in accordance with the provisions in § 1.408-8 for purposes of determining required minimum distributions.

*(3) Required beginning date.* The required beginning date for purposes of section 403(b)(10) is April 1 of the calendar year following the later of the calendar year in which the employee attains 70½ or the calendar year in which the employee retires from employment with the employer maintaining the plan. The required beginning date for purposes of section 403(b)(10) is April 1 of the calendar year following the later of the calendar year in which the employee attains age 70½ or the calendar year in which the employee retires from employment with the employer maintaining the plan. However, for any section 403(b) contract that is not part of a governmental plan or church plan, the required beginning date for a 5-percent owner is April 1 of the calendar year following the calendar year in which the employee attains age 70½.

*(4) Surviving spouse rule does not apply.* The special rule in § 1.408-8, A-5 (relating to spousal beneficiaries), does not apply to a section 403(b) contract. Thus, the surviving spouse of a participant is not permitted to treat a section 403(b) contract as the spouse's own section 403(b) contract, even if the spouse is the sole beneficiary.

*(5) Retirement income accounts.* For purposes of § 1.401(a)(9)-6, A-4 (relating to annuity contracts), annuity payments provided with respect to retirement income accounts do not fail to satisfy the requirements of section 401(a)(9) merely because the payments are not made under an annuity contract purchased from an insurance company, provided that the relationship between the annuity payments and the retirement income accounts is not inconsistent with any rules prescribed by the Commissioner in revenue rulings, notices, or other guidance published in the Internal Revenue Bulletin (see § 601.601(d)(2)(ii)(b) of this chapter). See also § 1.403(b)-9(a)(5) for additional rules relating to annuities payable from a retirement income account.

(6) *Special rules for benefits accruing before December 31, 1986.* (i) The distribution rules provided in section 401(a)(9) do not apply to the undistributed portion of the account balance under the section 403(b) contract valued as of December 31, 1986, exclusive of subsequent earnings (pre-'87 account balance). The distribution rules provided in section 401(a)(9) apply to all benefits under section 403(b) contracts accruing after December 31, 1986 (post-'86 account balance), including earnings after December 31, 1986. Consequently, the post-'86 account balance includes earnings after December 31, 1986, on contributions made before January 1, 1987, in addition to the contributions made after December 31, 1986, and earnings thereon.

(ii) The issuer or custodian of the section 403(b) contract must keep records that enable it to identify the pre-'87 account balance and subsequent changes as set forth in paragraph (d)(6)(iii) of this section and provide such information upon request to the relevant employee or beneficiaries with respect to the contract. If the issuer or custodian does not keep such records, the entire account balance is treated as subject to section 401(a)(9).

(iii) In applying the distribution rules in section 401(a)(9), only the post-'86 account balance is used to calculate the required minimum distribution for a calendar year. The amount of any distribution from a contract is treated as being paid from the post-'86 account balance to the extent the distribution is required to satisfy the minimum distribution requirement with respect to that contract for a calendar year. Any amount distributed in a calendar year from a contract in excess of the required minimum distribution for a calendar year with respect to that contract is treated as paid from the pre-'87 account balance, if any, of that contract.

(iv) If an amount is distributed from the pre-'87 account balance and rolled over to another section 403(b) contract, the amount is treated as part of the post-'86 account balance in that second contract. However, if the pre-'87 account balance under a section 403(b) contract is directly transferred to another section 403(b) contract (as permitted under § 1.403(b)-10(b)), the amount transferred retains its character as a pre-'87 account balance, provided the issuer of the transferee contract satisfies the recordkeeping requirements of paragraph (e)(6)(ii) of this section.

(v) The distinction between the pre-'87 account balance and the post-'86 account balance provided for under this paragraph (e)(6) of this section has no relevance for purposes of determining the portion of a distribution that is includible in income under section 72.

(vi) The pre-'87 account balance must be distributed in accordance with the incidental benefit requirement of § 1.401-1(b)(1)(i). Distributions attributable to the pre-'87 account balance are treated as satisfying this requirement if all distributions from the section 403(b) contract (including distributions attributable to the post-'86 account balance) satisfy the requirements of § 1.401-1(b)(1)(i) without regard to this section, and distributions attributable to the post-'86 account balance satisfy the rules of this paragraph (e) (without regard to this paragraph (e)(6)). Distributions attributable to the pre-'87 account balance are treated as satisfying the incidental benefit requirement if all distributions from the section 403(b) contract (including distributions attributable to both the pre-'87 account balance and the post-'86 account balance) satisfy the rules of this paragraph (e) (without regard to this paragraph (e)(6)).

(7) *Application to multiple contracts for an employee.* The required minimum distribution must be separately determined for each section 403(b) contract of an employee. However, because, as provided in paragraph (e)(2) of this section, the distribution rules in section 401(a)(9) apply to section 403(b) contracts in accordance with the provisions in § 1.408?8, the required minimum distribution from one section 403(b) contract of an employee is permitted to be distributed from another section 403(b) contract in order to satisfy section 401(a)(9). Thus, as provided in § 1.408?8, A-9, with respect to IRAs, the required minimum distribution amount from each contract is then totaled and the total minimum distribution taken from any one or more of the individual section 403(b) contracts. However, consistent with the rules in § 1.408?8, A-9, only amounts in section 403(b) contracts that an individual holds as an employee may be aggregated. Amounts in section 403(b) contracts that an individual holds as a beneficiary of the same decedent may be aggregated, but such amounts may not be aggregated with amounts held in section 403(b) contracts that the individual holds as the employee or as the beneficiary of another decedent. Distributions from section 403(b) contracts do not satisfy the minimum distribution requirements for IRAs, nor do distributions from IRAs satisfy the minimum distribution requirements for section 403(b) contracts.

(8) *Special rule for governmental plans.* A section 403(b) contract that is part of a governmental plan (within the meaning of section 414(d)) is treated as having complied with section 401(a)(9) for all years to which section 401(a)(9) applies to the contract, if the contract complies with a reasonable and good faith interpretation of section 401(a)(9).

**(f) Loans.** The determination of whether the availability of a loan, the making of a loan, or a failure to repay a loan made from an issuer of a section 403(b) contract to a participant or beneficiary is treated as a distribution (directly or indirectly) for purposes of this section, and the determination of whether the availability of the loan, the making of the loan, or a failure to repay the loan is in any other respect a violation of the requirements of section 403(b) and §§ 1.403(b)-1 through 1.403(b)-5, this section and §§ 1.403(b)-7 through 1.403(b)-11 depends on the facts and circumstances. Among the facts and circumstances are whether the loan has a fixed repayment schedule and bears a reasonable rate of interest, and whether there are repayment safeguards to which a prudent lender would adhere. Thus, for example, a loan must bear a reasonable rate of interest in order to be treated as not being a distribution. However, a plan loan offset is a distribution for purposes of this section. See § 1.72(p)-1, Q&A-13. See also § 1.403(b)-7(d) relating to the application of section 72(p) with respect to the taxation of a loan made under a section 403(b) contract. (Further, see section 408(b)(1) of Title I of ERISA and 29 CFR 2550.408b-1 of the Department of Labor regulations concerning additional requirements applicable with respect to plans that are subject to Title I of ERISA.)

**(g) Death benefits and other incidental benefits.** An annuity is not a section 403(b) contract if it fails to satisfy the incidental benefit requirement of § 1.401-1(b)(1)(ii) (in form or in operation). For purposes of this paragraph (g), to the extent the incidental benefit requirement of § 1.401-1(b)(1)(ii) requires a distribution of the participant's or beneficiary's accumulated benefit, that requirement is deemed to be satisfied if distributions satisfy the minimum distribution requirements of section 401(a)(9). In addition, if a contract issued by an insurance company qualified to issue annuities in a State includes provisions under which, in the event a participant becomes disabled, benefits will be provided by the insurance carrier as if employer contributions were continued until benefit distribution commences, then that benefit is treated as an incidental benefit (as insurance for a deferred annuity benefit in the event of disability) that must satisfy the incidental benefit requirement of § 1.401-1(b)(1)(ii) (taking into account any other incidental benefits provided under the plan).

**(h) Special rule regarding severance from employment.** For purposes of this section, severance from employment occurs on any date on which an employee ceases to be an employee of an eligible employer, even though the employee may continue to be employed either by another entity that is treated as the same employer where either that other entity is not an entity that can be an eligible employer (such as transferring from a section 501(c)(3) organization to a for-profit subsidiary of the section 501(c)(3) organization) or in a capacity that is not employment with an eligible employer (for example, ceasing to be an employee performing services for a public school but continuing to work for the same State employer). Thus, this paragraph (h) does not apply if an employee transfers from one section 501(c)(3) organization to another section 501(c)(3) organization that is treated as the same employer or if an employee transfers from one public school to another public school of the same State employer.

**(i) Certain limitations do not apply to rollover contributions.** The limitations on distributions in paragraphs (b) through (d) of this section do not apply to amounts held in a separate account for eligible rollover distributions as described in § 1.403(b)-10(d).

---

T.D. 9340, 7/23/2007, amend T.D. 9459, 9/4/2009.

---

PAR. 10. Section 1.403(b)-6 is amended by adding a sentence following the first sentence of paragraph (g) to read as follows:

**Proposed § 1.403(b)-6 Timing of distributions and benefits.** [*For Preamble, see ¶ 152,901*]

* * * * *

**(g) Death benefits and other incidental benefits.** * * * The rules of § 1.402(a)-1(e) apply for purposes of determining when incidental benefits are treated as distributed and included in gross income. See §§ 1.72-15 and 1.72-16. * * *

* * * * *

**§ 1.403(b)-7 Taxation of distributions and benefits.**

**(a) General rules for when amounts are included in gross income.** Except as provided in this section (or in § 1.403(b)-10(c) relating to payments pursuant to a qualified domestic relations order), amounts actually distributed from a section 403(b) contract are includible in the gross income of the recipient participant or beneficiary (in the year in which so distributed) under section 72 (relating to annuities). For an additional income tax that may apply to certain early distributions that are includible in gross income, see section 72(t).

**(b) Rollovers to individual retirement arrangements and other eligible retirement plans.** *(1) Timing of taxation of rollovers.* In accordance with sections 402(c), 403(b)(8), and 403(b)(10), a direct rollover in accordance with section 401(a)(31) is not includible in the gross income of a participant or beneficiary in the year rolled over. In addition, any payment made in the form of an eligible rollover distribution (as defined in section 402(c)(4)) is not includible in gross income in the year paid to the extent the payment is contributed to an eligible retirement plan (as defined in section 402(c)(8)(B)) within 60 days, including the contribution to the eligible retirement plan of any property distributed. For this purpose, the rules of section 402(c)(2) through (7) and (c)(9) apply. Thus, to the extent that a portion of a distribution (including a distribution from a designated Roth account) would be excluded from gross income if it were not rolled over, if that portion of the distribution is to be rolled over into an eligible retirement plan that is not an IRA, the rollover must be accomplished through a direct rollover of the entire distribution to a plan qualified under section 401(a) or a section 403(b) plan and that plan must agree to separately account for the amount not includible in income (so that a 60-day rollover to a plan qualified under section 401(a) or another section 403(b) plan is not available for this portion of the distribution). Any direct rollover under this paragraph (b)(1) is a distribution that is subject to the distribution requirements of § 1.403(b)-6.

*(2) Requirement that contract provide rollover options for eligible rollover distributions.* As required in § 1.403(b)-3(a)(7), an annuity contract is not a section 403(b) contract unless the contract provides that if the distributee of an eligible rollover distribution elects to have the distribution paid directly to an eligible retirement plan (as defined in section 402(c)(8)(B)) and specifies the eligible retirement plan to which the distribution is to be paid, then the distribution will be paid to that eligible retirement plan in a direct rollover. For purposes of determining whether a contract satisfies this requirement, the provisions of section 401(a)(31) apply to the annuity as though it were a plan qualified under section 401(a) unless otherwise provided in section 401(a)(31). Thus, the special rule in § 1.401(k)-1(f)(3)(ii) with respect to distributions from a designated Roth account that are expected to total less than $200 during a year applies to designated Roth accounts under a section 403(b) plan. In applying the provisions of this paragraph (b)(2), the payor of the eligible rollover distribution from the contract is treated as the plan administrator.

*(3) Requirement that contract payor provide notice of rollover option to distributees.* To ensure that the distributee of an eligible rollover distribution from a section 403(b) contract has a meaningful right to elect a direct rollover, section 402(f) requires that the distributee be informed of the option. Thus, within a reasonable time period before making the initial eligible rollover distribution, the payor must provide an explanation to the distributee of his or her right to elect a direct rollover and the income tax withholding consequences of not electing a direct rollover. For purposes of satisfying the reasonable time period requirement, the plan timing rule provided in section 402(f)(1) and § 1.402(f)-1 applies to section 403(b) contracts.

*(4) Mandatory withholding upon certain eligible rollover distributions from contracts.* If a distributee of an eligible rollover distribution from a section 403(b) contract does not elect to have the eligible rollover distribution paid directly to an eligible retirement plan in a direct rollover, the eligible rollover distribution is subject to 20-percent income tax withholding imposed under section 3405(c). See section 3405(c) and § 31.3405(c)-1 of this chapter for provisions regarding the withholding requirements relating to eligible rollover distributions.

*(5) Automatic rollover for certain mandatory distributions under section 401(a)(31).* In accordance with section 403(b)(10), a section 403(b) plan is required to comply with section 401(a)(31) (including automatic rollover for certain

mandatory distributions) in the same manner as a qualified plan.

**(c) Special rules.** See section 402(g)(2)(C) for special rules to determine the tax treatment of a distribution of excess deferrals, and see § 1.401(m)-1(e)(3)(v) for the tax treatment of corrective distributions of after-tax employee contributions and matching contributions to comply with section 401(m). See sections 402(l) and 403(b)(2) for a special rule regarding distributions for certain retired public safety officers made from a governmental plan for the direct payment of certain premiums.

**(d) Amounts taxable under section 72(p)(1).** In accordance with section 72(p), the amount of any loan from a section 403(b) contract to a participant or beneficiary (including any pledge or assignment treated as a loan under section 72(p)(1)(B)) is treated as having been received as a distribution from the contract under section 72(p)(1), except to the extent set forth in section 72(p)(2) (relating to loans that do not exceed a maximum amount and that are repayable in accordance with certain terms) and § 1.72(p)-1. See generally § 1.72(p)-1. Thus, except to the extent a loan satisfies section 72(p)(2), any amount loaned from a section 403(b) contract to a participant or beneficiary (including any pledge or assignment treated as a loan under section 72(p)(1)(B)) is includible in the gross income of the participant or beneficiary for the taxable year in which the loan is made. A deemed distribution is not an actual distribution for purposes of § 1.403(b)-6, as provided at § 1.72(p)-1, Q&A-12 and Q&A-13. (Further, see section 408(b)(1) of Title I of ERISA concerning the effect of noncompliance with Title I loan requirements for plans that are subject to Title I of ERISA.)

**(e) Special rules relating to distributions from a designated Roth account.** If an amount is distributed from a designated Roth account under a section 403(b) plan, the amount, if any, that is includible in gross income and the amount, if any, that may be rolled over to another section 403(b) plan is determined under § 1.402A-1. Thus, the designated Roth account is treated as a separate contract for purposes of section 72. For example, the rules of section 72(b) must be applied separately to annuity payments with respect to a designated Roth account under a section 403(b) plan and separately to annuity payments with respect to amounts attributable to any other contributions to the section 403(b) plan.

**(f) Aggregation of contracts.** In accordance with section 403(b)(5), the rules of this section are applied as if all annuity contracts for the employee by the employer are treated as a single contract.

**(g) Certain rules relating to employment taxes.** With respect to contributions under the Federal Insurance Contributions Act (FICA) under Chapter 21, see section 3121(a)(5)(D) for a special rule relating to section 403(b) contracts. With respect to income tax withholding on distributions from section 403(b) contracts, see section 3405 generally. However, see section 3401 for income tax withholding applicable to annuity contracts or custodial accounts that are not section 403(b) contracts or for cases in which an annuity contract or custodial account ceases to be a section 403(b) contract. See also § 1.72(p)-1, Q&A-15, and § 35.3405(c)-1, Q&A-11 of this chapter, for special rules relating to income tax withholding for loans made from certain employer plans, including section 403(b) contracts.

---

T.D. 9340, 7/23/2007.

---

**§ 1.403(b)-8 Funding.**

**(a) Investments.** Section 403(b) and § 1.403(b)-3(a) only apply to amounts held in an annuity contract (as defined in § 1.403(b)-2), including a custodial account that is treated as an annuity contract under paragraph (d) of this section, or a retirement income account that is treated as an annuity contract under § 1.403(b)-9.

**(b) Contributions to the plan.** Contributions to a section 403(b) plan must be transferred to the insurance company issuing the annuity contract (or the entity holding assets of any custodial or retirement income account that is treated as an annuity contract) within a period that is not longer than is reasonable for the proper administration of the plan. For purposes of this requirement, the plan may provide for section 403(b) elective deferrals for a participant under the plan to be transferred to the annuity contract within a specified period after the date the amounts would otherwise have been paid to the participant. For example, the plan could provide for section 403(b) elective deferrals under the plan to be contributed within 15 business days following the month in which these amounts would otherwise have been paid to the participant.

**(c) Annuity contracts.** *(1) Generally.* As defined in § 1.403(b)-2, and except as otherwise permitted under this section, an annuity contract means a contract that is issued by an insurance company qualified to issue annuities in a State and that includes payment in the form of an annuity. This paragraph (c) sets forth additional rules regarding annuity contracts.

*(2) Certain insurance contracts.* Neither a life insurance contract, as defined in section 7702, an endowment contract, a health or accident insurance contract, nor a property, casualty, or liability insurance contract meets the definition of an annuity contract. See § 1.401(f)-4(e). If a contract issued by an insurance company qualified to issue annuities in a State provides death benefits as part of the contract, then that coverage is permitted, assuming that those death benefits do not cause the contract to fail to satisfy any requirement applicable to section 403(b) contracts, for example, assuming that those benefits satisfy the incidental benefit requirement of § 1.401-1(b)(1)(i), as required by § 1.403(b)-6(g).

*(3) Special rule for certain contracts.* This paragraph (c)(3) applies in the case of a contract issued under a State section 403(b) plan established on or before May 17, 1982, or for an employee who becomes covered for the first time under the plan after May 17, 1982, unless the Commissioner had before that date issued any written communication (either to the employer or financial institution) to the effect that the arrangement under which the contract was issued did not meet the requirements of section 403(b). The requirement that the contract be issued by an insurance company qualified to issue annuities in a State does not apply to a contract described in the preceding sentence if one of the following two conditions is satisfied and that condition has been satisfied continuously since May 17, 1982—

(i) Benefits under the contract are provided from a separately funded retirement reserve that is subject to supervision of the State insurance department; or

(ii) Benefits under the contract are provided from a fund that is separate from the fund used to provide statutory benefits payable under a state retirement system and that is part of a State teachers retirement system (including a state university retirement system) to purchase benefits that are unrelated to the basic benefits provided under the retirement system, and the death benefit provided under the contract does not at any time exceed the larger of the reserve or the contribution made for the employee.

**(d) Custodial accounts.** *(1) Treatment as a section 403(b) contract.* Under section 403(b)(7), a custodial account is treated as an annuity contract for purposes of §§ 1.403(b)-1 through 1.403(b)-7, this section and §§ 1.403(b)-9 through 1.403(b)-11. See section 403(b)(7)(B) for special rules regarding the tax treatment of custodial accounts and section 4973(c) for an excise tax that applies to excess contributions to a custodial account.

*(2) Custodial account defined.* A custodial account means a plan, or a separate account under a plan, in which an amount attributable to section 403(b) contributions (or amounts rolled over to a section 403(b) contract, as described in § 1.403(b)-10(d)) is held by a bank or a person who satisfies the conditions in section 401(f)(2), if—

(i) All of the amounts held in the account are invested in stock of a regulated investment company (as defined in section 851(a) relating to mutual funds);

(ii) The requirements of § 1.403(b)-6(c) (imposing restrictions on distributions with respect to a custodial account) are satisfied with respect to the amounts held in the account;

(iii) The assets held in the account cannot be used for, or diverted to, purposes other than for the exclusive benefit of plan participants or their beneficiaries (for which purpose, assets are treated as diverted to the employer if the employer borrows assets from the account); and

(iv) The account is not part of a retirement income account.

*(3) Effect of definition.* The requirement in paragraph (d)(2)(i) of this section is not satisfied if the account includes any assets other than stock of a regulated investment company.

*(4) Treatment of custodial account.* A custodial account is treated as a section 401 qualified plan solely for purposes of subchapter F of subtitle A and subtitle F of the Internal Revenue Code with respect to amounts received by it (and income from investment thereof). This treatment only applies to a custodial account that constitutes a section 403(b) contract under §§ 1.403(b)-1 through 1.403(b)-7, this section and §§ 1.403(b)-9 through 1.403(b)-11 or that would constitute a section 403(b) contract under §§ 1.403(b)-1 through 1.403(b)-7, this section and §§ 1.403(b)-9 through 1.403(b)-11 if the amounts held in the account were to satisfy the nonforfeitability requirement of § 1.403(b)-3(a)(2).

**(e) Retirement income accounts.** See § 1.403(b)-9 for special rules under which a retirement income account for employees of a church-related organization is treated as a section 403(b) contract for purposes of §§ 1.403(b)-1 through 1.403(b)-7, this section and §§ 1.403(b)-9 through 1.403(b)-11.

**(f) Combining assets.** To the extent permitted by the Commissioner in revenue rulings, notices, or other guidance published in the Internal Revenue Bulletin (see § 601.601(d)(2)(ii)(b) of this chapter), trust assets held under a custodial account and trust assets held under a retirement income account, as described in § 1.403(b)-9(a)(6), may be invested in a group trust with trust assets held under a qualified plan or individual retirement plan. For this purpose, a trust includes a custodial account that is treated as a trust under section 401(f).

---

T.D. 9340, 7/23/2007.

---

### § 1.403(b)-9 Special rules for church plans.

**(a) Retirement income accounts.** *(1) Treatment as a section 403(b) contract.* Under section 403(b)(9), a retirement income account for employees of a church-related organization (as defined in § 1.403(b)-2) is treated as an annuity contract for purposes of §§ 1.403(b)-1 through 1.403(b)-8, this section, § 1.403(b)-10 and § 1.403(b)-11.

*(2) Retirement income account defined.* (i) In general. A retirement income account means a defined contribution program established or maintained by a church-related organization under which—

(A) There is separate accounting for the retirement income account's interest in the underlying assets (namely, there must be sufficient separate accounting in order for it to be possible at all times to determine the retirement income account's interest in the underlying assets and to distinguish that interest from any interest that is not part of the retirement income account);

(B) Investment performance is based on gains and losses on those assets; and

(C) The assets held in the account cannot be used for, or diverted to, purposes other than for the exclusive benefit of plan participants or their beneficiaries (and for this purpose, assets are treated as diverted to the employer if there is a loan or other extension of credit from assets in the account to the employer).

(ii) Plan required. A retirement income account must be maintained pursuant to a program which is a plan (as defined in § 1.403(b)-3(b)(3)) and the plan document must state (or otherwise evidence in a similarly clear manner) the intent to constitute a retirement income account.

*(3) Ownership or use constitutes distribution.* Any asset of a retirement income account that is owned or used by a participant or beneficiary is treated as having been distributed to that participant or beneficiary. See §§ 1.403(b)-6 and 1.403(b)-7 for rules relating to distributions.

*(4) Coordination of retirement income account with custodial account rules.* A retirement income account that is treated as an annuity contract is not a custodial account (as defined in § 1.403(b)-8(d)(2)), even if it is invested solely in stock of a regulated investment company.

*(5) Life annuities.* A retirement income account may distribute benefits in a form that includes a life annuity only if—

(i) The amount of the distribution form has an actuarial present value, at the annuity starting date, equal to the participant's or beneficiary's accumulated benefit, based on reasonable actuarial assumptions, including regarding interest and mortality; and

(ii) The plan sponsor guarantees benefits in the event that a payment is due that exceeds the participant's or beneficiary's accumulated benefit.

*(6) Combining retirement income account assets with other assets.* For purposes of § 1.403(b)-8(f) relating to combining assets, retirement income account assets held in trust (including a custodial account that is treated as a trust under section 401(f)) are subject to the same rules regarding combining of assets as custodial account assets. In addition, retirement income account assets are permitted to be commingled in a common fund with amounts devoted exclusively to church purposes (such as a fund from which unfunded pension payments are made to former employees of the church). However, unless otherwise permitted by the Commissioner, no assets of the plan sponsor, other than retirement income

account assets, may be combined with custodial account assets or any other assets permitted to be combined under § 1.403(b)-8(f). This paragraph (a)(6) is subject to any additional rules issued by the Commissioner in revenue rulings, notices, or other guidance published in the Internal Revenue Bulletin (see § 601.601(d)(2)(ii)(b) of this chapter).

*(7) Trust treated as tax exempt.* A trust (including a custodial account that is treated as a trust under section 401(f)) that includes no assets other than assets of a retirement income account is treated as an organization that is exempt from taxation under section 501(a).

**(b) No compensation limitation up to $10,000.** See section 415(c)(7) for special rules regarding certain annual additions not exceeding $10,000.

**(c) Special deduction rule for self-employed ministers.** See section 404(a)(10) for a special rule regarding the deductibility of a contribution made by a self-employed minister.

T.D. 9340, 7/23/2007.

## § 1.403(b)-10 Miscellaneous provisions.

**(a) Plan terminations and frozen plans.** *(1) In general.* An employer is permitted to amend its section 403(b) plan to eliminate future contributions for existing participants or to limit participation to existing participants and employees (to the extent consistent with § 1.403(b)-5). A section 403(b) plan is permitted to contain provisions that provide for plan termination and that allow accumulated benefits to be distributed on termination. However, in the case of a section 403(b) contract that is subject to the distribution restrictions in § 1.403(b)-6(c) or (d) (relating to custodial accounts and section 403(b) elective deferrals), termination of the plan and the distribution of accumulated benefits is permitted only if the employer (taking into account all entities that are treated as the same employer under section 414(b), (c), (m), or (o) on the date of the termination) does not make contributions to any section 403(b) contract that is not part of the plan during the period beginning on the date of plan termination and ending 12 months after distribution of all assets from the terminated plan. However, if at all times during the period beginning 12 months before the termination and ending 12 months after distribution of all assets from the terminated plan, fewer than 2 percent of the employees who were eligible under the section 403(b) plan as of the date of plan termination are eligible under the alternative section 403(b) contract, the alternative section 403(b) contract is disregarded. To the extent a contract fails to satisfy the nonforfeitability requirement of § 1.403(b)-3(a)(2) at the date of plan termination, the contact is not, and cannot later become, a section 403(b) contract. In order for a section 403(b) plan to be considered terminated, all accumulated benefits under the plan must be distributed to all participants and beneficiaries as soon as administratively practicable after termination of the plan. For this purpose, delivery of a fully paid individual insurance annuity contract is treated as a distribution. The mere provision for, and making of, distributions to participants or beneficiaries upon plan termination does not cause a contract to cease to be a section 403(b) contract. See § 1.403(b)-7 for rules regarding the tax treatment of distributions, including § 1.403(b)-7(b)(1) under which an eligible rollover distribution is not included in gross income if paid in a direct rollover to an eligible retirement plan or if transferred to an eligible retirement plan within 60 days.

*(2) Employers that cease to be eligible employers.* An employer that ceases to be an eligible employer may no longer contribute to a section 403(b) contract for any subsequent period, and the contract will fail to satisfy § 1.403(b)-3(a) if any further contributions are made with respect to a period after the employer ceases to be an eligible employer.

**(b) Contract exchanges and plan-to-plan transfers.** *(1) Contract exchanges and transfers.* (i) General rule. If the conditions in paragraph (b)(2) of this section are met, a section 403(b) contract held under a section 403(b) plan is permitted to be exchanged for another section 403(b) contract held under that section 403(b) plan. Further, if the conditions in paragraph (b)(3) of this section are met, a section 403(b) plan is permitted to provide for the transfer of its assets (including any assets held in a custodial account or retirement income account that are treated as section 403(b) contracts) to another section 403(b) plan. In addition, if the conditions in paragraph (b)(4) of this section (relating to permissive service credit and repayments under section 415) are met, a section 403(b) plan is permitted to provide for the transfer of its assets to a qualified plan under section 401(a). However, neither a qualified plan nor an eligible governmental plan under section 457(b) may transfer assets to a section 403(b) plan, and a section 403(b) plan may not accept such a transfer. In addition, a section 403(b) contract may not be exchanged for an annuity contract that is not a section 403(b) contract. Neither a plan-to-plan transfer nor a contract exchange permitted under this paragraph (b) is treated as a distribution for purposes of the distribution restrictions at § 1.403(b)-6. Therefore, such a transfer or exchange may be made before severance from employment or another distribution event. Further, no amount is includible in gross income by reason of such a transfer or exchange.

(ii) ERISA rules. See § 1.414(l)-1 for other rules that are applicable to section 403(b) plans that are subject to section 208 of the Employee Retirement Income Security Act of 1974 (88 Stat. 829, 865).

*(2) Requirements for contract exchange within the same plan.* (i) General rule. A section 403(b) contract of a participant or beneficiary may be exchanged under paragraph (b)(1) of this section for another section 403(b) contract of that participant or beneficiary under the same section 403(b) plan if each of the following conditions are met:

(A) The plan under which the contract is issued provides for the exchange.

(B) The participant or beneficiary has an accumulated benefit immediately after the exchange that is at least equal to the accumulated benefit of that participant or beneficiary immediately before the exchange (taking into account the accumulated benefit of that participant or beneficiary under both section 403(b) contracts immediately before the exchange).

(C) The other contract is subject to distribution restrictions with respect to the participant that are not less stringent than those imposed on the contract being exchanged, and the employer enters into an agreement with the issuer of the other contract under which the employer and the issuer will from time to time in the future provide each other with the following information:

(1) Information necessary for the resulting contract, or any other contract to which contributions have been made by the employer, to satisfy section 403(b), including information concerning the participant's employment and information that takes into account other section 403(b) contracts or qualified employer plans (such as whether a severance from

employment has occurred for purposes of the distribution restrictions in § 1.403(b)-6 and whether the hardship withdrawal rules of § 1.403(b)-6(d)(2) are satisfied).

(2) Information necessary for the resulting contract, or any other contract to which contributions have been made by the employer, to satisfy other tax requirements (such as whether a plan loan satisfies the conditions in section 72(p)(2) so that the loan is not a deemed distribution under section 72(p)(1)).

(ii) Accumulated benefit. The condition in paragraph (b)(2)(i)(B) of this section is satisfied if the exchange would satisfy section 414(l)(1) if the exchange were a transfer of assets.

(iii) Authority for future guidance. Subject to such conditions as the Commissioner determines to be appropriate, the Commissioner may issue rules of general applicability, in revenue rulings, notices, or other guidance published in the Internal Revenue Bulletin (see § 601.601(d)(2)(ii)(b) of this chapter), permitting an exchange of one section 403(b) contract for another section 403(b) contract for an exchange that does not satisfy paragraph (b)(2)(i)(C) of this section. Any such rules must require the resulting contract to set forth procedures that the Commissioner determines are reasonably designed to ensure compliance with those requirements of section 403(b) or other tax provisions that depend on either information concerning the participant's employment or information that takes into account other section 403(b) contracts or other employer plans (such as whether a severance from employment has occurred for purposes of the distribution restrictions in § 1.403(b)-6, whether the hardship withdrawal rules of § 1.403(b)-6(d)(2) are satisfied, and whether a plan loan constitutes a deemed distribution under section 72(p)).

*(3) Requirements for plan-to-plan transfers.* (i) In general. A plan-to-plan transfer under paragraph (b)(1) of this section from a section 403(b) plan to another section 403(b) plan is permitted if each of the following conditions are met—

(A) In the case of a transfer for a participant, the participant is an employee or former employee of the employer (or the business of the employer) for the receiving plan.

(B) In the case of a transfer for a beneficiary of a deceased participant, the participant was an employee or former employee of the employer (or business of the employer) for the receiving plan.

(C) The transferor plan provides for transfers.

(D) The receiving plan provides for the receipt of transfers.

(E) The participant or beneficiary whose assets are being transferred has an accumulated benefit immediately after the transfer that is at least equal to the accumulated benefit of that participant or beneficiary immediately before the transfer.

(F) The receiving plan provides that, to the extent any amount transferred is subject to any distribution restrictions under § 1.403(b)-6, the receiving plan imposes restrictions on distributions to the participant or beneficiary whose assets are being transferred that are not less stringent than those imposed on the transferor plan.

(G) If a plan-to-plan transfer does not constitute a complete transfer of the participant's or beneficiary's interest in the section 403(b) plan, the transferee plan treats the amount transferred as a continuation of a pro rata portion of the participant's or beneficiary's interest in the section 403(b) plan (for example, a pro rata portion of the participant's or beneficiary's interest in any after-tax employee contributions).

(ii) Accumulated benefit. The condition in paragraph (b)(3)(i)(D) of this section is satisfied if the transfer would satisfy section 414(l)(1).

*(4) Purchases of permissive service credit by contract-to-plan transfers from a section 403(b) contract to a qualified plan.* (i) General rule. If the conditions in paragraph (b)(4)(ii) of this section are met, a section 403(b) plan may provide for the transfer of assets held in the plan to a qualified defined benefit plan that is a governmental plan (as defined in section 414(d)).

(ii) Conditions for plan-to-plan transfers. A transfer may be made under this paragraph (b)(4) only if the transfer is either—

(A) For the purchase of permissive service credit (as defined in section 415(n)(3)(A)) under the receiving defined benefit plan; or

(B) A repayment to which section 415 does not apply by reason of section 415(k)(3).

**(c) Qualified domestic relations orders.** In accordance with the second sentence of section 414(p)(9), any distribution from an annuity contract under section 403(b) (including a distribution from a custodial account or retirement income account that is treated as a section 403(b) contract) pursuant to a qualified domestic relations order is treated in the same manner as a distribution from a plan to which section 401(a)(13) applies. Thus, for example, a section 403(b) plan does not fail to satisfy the distribution restrictions set forth in § 1.403(b)-6(b), (c), or (d) merely as a result of distribution made pursuant to a qualified domestic relations order under section 414(p), so that such a distribution is permitted without regard to whether the employee from whose contract the distribution is made has had a severance from employment or another event permitting a distribution to be made under section 403(b). In the case of a plan that is subject to Title I of ERISA, see also section 206(d)(3) of ERISA under which the prohibition against assignment or alienation of plan benefits under section 206(d)(1) of ERISA does not apply to an order that is determined to be a qualified domestic relations order.

**(d) Rollovers to a section 403(b) contract.** *(1) General rule.* A section 403(b) contract may accept a contribution that is an eligible rollover distribution (as defined in section 402(c)(4)) made from another eligible retirement plan (as defined in section 402(c)(8)(B)). Any amount contributed to a section 403(b) contract as an eligible rollover distribution is not taken into account for purposes of the limits in § 1.403(b)-4, but, except as otherwise specifically provided (for example, at § 1.403(b)-6(i)), is otherwise treated in the same manner as an amount held under a section 403(b) contract for purposes of §§ 1.403(b)-3 through 1.403(b)-9 and this section.

*(2) Special rules relating to after-tax employee contributions and designated Roth contributions.* A section 403(b) plan that receives an eligible rollover distribution that includes after-tax employee contributions or designated Roth contributions is required to obtain information regarding the employee's section 72 basis in the amount rolled over. A section 403(b) plan is permitted to receive an eligible rollover distribution that includes designated Roth contributions only if the plan permits employees to make elective deferrals that are designated Roth contributions.

**(e) Deemed IRAs.** See regulations under section 408(q) for special rules relating to deemed IRAs.

**(f) Defined benefit plans.** *(1) Defined benefit plans generally.* Except for a TEFRA church defined benefit plan as defined in paragraph (f)(2) of this section, section 403(b) does not apply to any contributions or accrual under a defined benefit plan.

*(2) TEFRA church defined benefit plans.* See section 251(e)(5) of the Tax Equity and Fiscal Responsibility Act of 1982, Public Law 97-248, for a provision permitting certain arrangements established by a church-related organization and in effect on September 3, 1982 (a TEFRA church defined benefit plan) to be treated as section 403(b) contract even though it is a defined benefit arrangement. In accordance with section 403(b)(1), for purposes of applying section 415 to a TEFRA church defined benefit plan, the accruals under the plan are limited to the maximum amount permitted under section 415(c) when expressed as an annual addition, and, for this purpose, the rules at § 1.402(b)-1(a)(2) for determining the present value of an accrual under a nonqualified defined benefit plan also apply for purposes of converting the accrual under a TEFRA church defined benefit plan to an annual addition. See section 415(b) for additional limits applicable to TEFRA church defined benefit plans.

**(g) Other rules relating to section 501(c)(3) organizations.** See section 501(c)(3) and regulations thereunder for the substantive standards for tax-exemption under that section, including the requirement that no part of the organization's net earnings inure to the benefit of any private shareholder or individual. See also sections 4941 (self dealing), 4945 (taxable expenditures), and 4958 (excess benefit transactions), and the regulations thereunder, for rules relating to excise taxes imposed on certain transactions involving organizations described in section 501(c)(3).

---

T.D. 9340, 7/23/2007.

---

### § 1.403(b)-11 Applicable dates.

**(a) General rule.** Except as otherwise provided in this section, §§ 1.403(b)-1 through 1.403(b)-10 apply for taxable years beginning after December 31, 2008.

**(b) Collective bargaining agreements.** In the case of a section 403(b) plan maintained pursuant to one or more collective bargaining agreements that have been ratified and in effect on July 26, 2007, §§ 1.403(b)-1 through 1.403(b)-10 do not apply before the earlier of—

*(1)* The date on which the last of the collective bargaining agreements terminates (determined without regard to any extension thereof after July 26, 2007); or

*(2)* July 26, 2010.

**(c) Church conventions; retirement income account.** *(1)* In the case of a section 403(b) plan maintained by a church-related organization for which the authority to amend the plan is held by a church convention (within the meaning of section 414(e)), §§ 1.403(b)-1 through 1.403(b)-10 do not apply before the first day of the first plan year that begins after December 31, 2009.

*(2)* In the case of a loan or other extension of credit to the employer that was entered into under a retirement income account before July 26, 2007, the plan does not fail to satisfy § 1.403(b)-9(a)(2)(i)(C) on account of the loan or other extension of credit if the plan takes reasonable steps to eliminate the loan or other extension of credit to the employer before the applicable date for § 1.403(b)-9(a)(2) or as promptly as practical thereafter (including taking steps after July 26, 2007 and before the applicable date).

**(d) Special rules for plans that exclude certain types of employees from elective deferrals.** *(1)* If, on July 26, 2007, a plan excludes any of the following categories of employees, then the plan does not fail to satisfy § 1.403(b)-5(b) as a result of that exclusion before the first day of the first taxable year that begins after December 31, 2009:

(i) Employees who make a one-time election to participate in a governmental plan described in section 414(d) that is not a section 403(b) plan.

(ii) Professors who are providing services on a temporary basis to another educational organization (as defined under section 170(b)(1)(A)(ii)) for up to one year and for whom section 403(b) contributions are being made at a rate no greater than the rate each such professor would receive under the section 403(b) plan of the original educational organization.

(iii) Employees who are affiliated with a religious order and who have taken a vow of poverty where the religious order provides for the support of such employees in their retirement from eligibility to make elective deferrals.

*(2)* If, on July 26, 2007, a plan excludes employees who are covered by a collective bargaining agreement from eligibility to make elective deferrals, the plan does not fail to satisfy § 1.403(b)-5(b) (relating to universal availability) as a result of that exclusion before the later of—

(i) The first day of the first taxable year that begins after December 31, 2008; or

(ii) The earlier of—

(A) The date on which the related collective bargaining agreement terminates (determined without regard to any extension thereof after July 26, 2007); or

(B) July 26, 2010.

*(3)* In the case of a governmental plan (as defined in section 414(d)) for which the authority to amend the plan is held by a legislative body that meets in legislative session, the plan does not fail to satisfy § 1.403(b)-5(b) as a result of any exclusion in paragraph (d)(1)(i), (d)(1)(ii),(d)(1)(iii), or (d)(2) of this section before the earlier of—

(i) The close of the first regular legislative session of the legislative body with the authority to amend the plan that begins on or after January 1, 2009; or

(ii) January 1, 2011.

**(e) Special rules for plans that permit in-service distributions.** *(1)* Section 1.403(b)-6(b) does not apply to a contract issued by an insurance company before January 1, 2009.

*(2)* Any amendment to comply with the requirements of § 1.403(b)-6 (disregarding paragraph (e)(1) of this section) that is adopted before January 1, 2009, or such later date as may be permitted under guidance issued by the Commissioner in revenue rulings, notices, or other guidance published in the Internal Revenue Bulletin (see § 601.601(d)(2)(ii)(b) of this chapter), does not violate section 204(g) of the Employee Retirement Income Security Act of 1974 to the extent the amendment eliminates or reduces a right to receive benefit distributions during employment.

**(f) Special rule for life insurance contracts.** Section 1.403(b)-8(c)(2) does not apply to a contract issued before September 24, 2007.

**(g) Special rule for contracts received in an exchange.** Section 1.403(b)-10(b)(2) does not apply to a contract received in an exchange that occurred on or before September 24, 2007 if the exchange (including the contract received in the exchange) satisfies such rules as the Commissioner has prescribed in guidance of general applicability at the time of the exchange.

**(h) Special rule for coordination with regulations under section 415.** Section 1.403(b)-3(b)(4)(ii) is applicable for taxable years beginning on or after July 1, 2007.

**(i) Special rule for coordination with regulations under section 402A.** Sections 1.403(b)-3(c), 1.403(b)-7(e), and 1.403(b)-10(d)(2) are applicable with respect to taxable years beginning on or after January 1, 2007.

T.D. 9340, 7/23/2007.

**§ 1.403(c)-1 Taxability of beneficiary under a nonqualified annuity.**

**(a) Taxability of vested interest in premiums.** If after August 1, 1969, an employer (whether or not exempt under section 501(a) or 521(a)) pays premiums for an annuity contract for the benefit of an employee, the amount of such premiums shall be included as compensation in the gross income of the employee for the taxable year during which such premiums are paid, but only to the extent that the employee's rights in such premiums are substantially vested (as defined in § 1.83-3(b)) at the time such premiums are paid. The preceding sentence shall not apply to contracts referred to in the transitional rule of paragraph (d)(1), (ii), or (iii) of this section, or to premiums subject to § 1.403(a)-1(a) or excludible under § 1.403(b)-3. If an employer has purchased annuity contracts and transferred them to a trust (other than one described in section 401(a)) that is to provide annuity contracts or benefits for his employees, the amounts so paid shall be treated as contributions to a trust described in section 402(b). For the rules relating to the taxation of the cost of life insurance protection when rights in a life insurance contract are substantially nonvested, see § 1.83-1(a)(2).

**(b) Taxability of employee when rights under annuity contract change from nonvested to vested.** *(1) In general.* If, during a taxable year of an employee ending after August 1, 1969, the rights of such employee under an annuity contract purchased for him by an employer (whether or not exempt under section 501(a) or 521(a)) become substantially vested, the value of the annuity contract on the date of such change shall be included in the employee's gross income for such year, to the extent provided in paragraph (b)(2) of this section. The preceding sentence shall not apply, however, to an annuity contract purchased and held as part of a plan which met at the time of such purchase, and continues to meet, the requirements of section 404(a)(2) or an annuity contract referred to in paragraph (d)(1)(ii) or (iii) of this section. For purposes of this section, the value of an annuity contract on the date the employee's rights become substantially vested means the cash surrender value of such contract on such date.

*(2) Extent to which value of annuity contract is includible in employee's gross income.* For purposes of paragraph (b)(1) of this section, the only amount includible in the gross income of the employee is that portion of the value of the contract on the date of the change that is attributable to premiums which were paid by the employer after August 1, 1969, and which were not excludible from the employee's gross income under § 1.403(b)-3. However, the includible portion does not include—

(i) The value attributable to a premium paid on the date of such change, and

(ii) The value attributable to premiums described in the transitional rule of paragraph (d)(1)(ii) or (iii) of this section. See § 1.403(b)-3(2) for the treatment of an amount otherwise includible in gross income under section 403(c) as an employer contribution for purposes of the exclusion under section 403(b).

*(3) Partial vesting.* If, during any taxable year of an employee, only part of his beneficial interest in an annuity contract becomes substantially vested, then only the corresponding part of the value of the annuity contract on the date of such change is includible in the employee's gross income for such taxable year. In such a case, it is first necessary to compute, under the rules in paragraphs (b)(1) and (2) of this section but without regard to any exclusion allowable under § 1.403(b)-3, the amount which would be includible in the employee's gross income for the taxable year if his entire beneficial interest in the annuity contract had changed to a substantially vested interest during such year. The amount that is includible under this (3) (without regard to the section 403(b) exclusion) is equal to the amount determined under the preceding sentence multiplied by the percent of the employee's beneficial interest which became substantially vested during the taxable year.

**(c) Amounts paid or made available under an annuity contract.** The amounts paid or made available to the employee under an annuity contract subject to this section shall be included in the gross income of the employee for the taxable year in which paid or made available, as provided in section 72 (relating to annuities). Such amounts may be taken into account in computations under sections 1301 through 1305 (relating to income averaging). For rules relating to the treatment of employer contributions as part of the consideration paid by the employee, see section 72(f). See also section 101(b)(2)(D) for rules relating to the treatment of the limited exclusion provided thereunder as part of the consideration paid by the employee.

**(d) Taxability of beneficiary under a nonqualified annuity on or before August 1, 1969.** *(1)* Except as provided in section 402(d) (relating to taxable years beginning before January 1, 1977), if an employer purchases an annuity contract and if the amounts paid for the contract—

(i) On or before August 1, 1969, or

(ii) After such date, if pursuant to a binding written contract (as defined in § 1.83-8(b)(2)) entered into before April 22, 1969, or

(iii) After August 1, 1969, pursuant to a written plan in which the employee participated on April 22, 1969 and under which the obligation of the employer is essentially the same as under a binding written contract, are not subject to paragraph (a) of § 1.403(a)-1 or paragraph (a) of § 1.403(b)-1, the amount of such contribution shall, to the extent it is not excludible under paragraph (b) of § 1.403(b)-1, be included in the income of the employee for the taxable year during which such contribution is made if, at the time the contribution is made, the employee's rights under the annuity contract are nonforfeitable, except for failure to pay future premiums. If the annuity contract was purchased by an employer which is not exempt from tax under section 501(a) or section 521(a), and if the employee's rights under the annuity contract in such a case were forfeitable at the time the employer's contribution was made for the annuity contract, even though they become nonforfeitable later the amount of such contribution is not required to be included in the income of the employee at the time his rights under the contract become nonforfeitable. On the other hand, if the annuity contract is purchased by an employer which is exempt from tax under section 501(a) or section 521(a), all or part of the value of the contract may be includible in the employee's gross income at the time his rights under the contract become nonforfeitable (see section 403(d) prior to the repeal thereof by the Tax Reform Act of 1969 and the regulations thereunder). As to what constitutes nonforfeitable rights of an employee, see § 1.402(b)-1(d)(2). The amounts received by or made available to the employee under the annuity contract shall be included in the gross income of the employee for the taxable year in which received or made available, as provided in section 72 (relating to annuities). For taxable years beginning before January 1, 1964, section 72(e)(3) (relating to the treatment of certain lump sums), as in effect before such date, shall not apply to such amounts. For taxable years beginning after December 31, 1963, such amounts may be taken into account in computations under sections 1301 through 1305 (relating to income averaging). For rules relating to the treatment of employer contributions as part of the consideration paid by the employee, see section 72(f). See also section 101(b)(2)(D) for rules relating to the treatment of the limited exclusion provided thereunder as part of the consideration paid by the employee.

*(2)* If an employer has purchased annuity contracts and transferred them to a trust, or if an employer has made contributions to a trust for the purpose of providing annuity contracts for his employees as provided in section 402(d) (see paragraph (a) of § 1.402(d)-1), the amount so paid or contributed is not required to be included in the income of the employee, but any amount received by or made available to the employee under the annuity contract shall be includible in the gross income of the employee for the taxable year in which received or made available, as provided in section 72 (relating to annuities). For taxable years beginning before January 1, 1964, section 72(e)(3) (relating to the treatment of certain lump sums), as in effect before such date, shall not apply to any amount received by or made available to the employee under the annuity contract. For taxable years beginning after December 31, 1963, amounts received by or made available to the employee under the annuity contract may be taken into account in computations under sections 1301 through 1305 (relating to income averaging). In such case the amount paid or contributed by the employer shall not constitute consideration paid by the employee for such annuity contract in determining the amount of annuity payments required to be included in his gross income under section 72 unless the employee has paid income tax for any taxable year beginning before January 1, 1949, with respect to such payment or contribution by the employer for such year and such tax is not credited or refunded to the employee. In the event such tax has been paid and not credited or refunded the amount paid or contributed by the employer for such year shall constitute consideration paid by the employee for the annuity contract in determining the amount of the annuity required to be included in the income of the employee under section 72.

*(3)* For taxable years beginning before January 1, 1958, the provisions contained in section 403(c) prior to the amendment made thereto by the Tax Reform Act of 1969 were included in section 403(b) of the Internal Revenue Code of 1954. Therefore, the regulations contained in this paragraph shall, for such taxable years, be considered as the regulations under section 403(b) as in effect for such taxable years. For the rules with respect to contributions paid after August 1, 1969, see paragraphs (a), (b), and (c) of this section.

---

T.D. 6783, 12/23/64, amend T.D. 6885, 6/1/66, T.D. 7554, 7/21/78, T.D. 9340, 7/23/2007.

---

### § 1.404(a)-1 Contributions of an employer to an employees' trust or annuity plan and compensation under a deferred payment plan; general rule.

***Caution:*** The Treasury has not yet amended Reg § 1.404(a)-1 to reflect changes made by P.L. 100-647, P.L. 100-203, P.L. 99-514, P.L. 98-369, P.L. 97-248, P.L. 97-34, P.L. 93-406.

**(a)** *(1)* Section 404(a) prescribes limitations upon deductions for amounts contributed by an employer under a pension, annuity, stock bonus, or profit-sharing plan, or under any plan of deferred compensation. It is immaterial whether the plan covers present employees only, or present and former employees, or only former employees. Section 404(a) also governs the deductibility of unfunded pensions and death benefits paid directly to former employees or their beneficiaries (see § 1.404(a)-12). For taxable years beginning after 1962, certain self-employed individuals may be covered by pension, annuity, or profit-sharing plans. For the rules relating to the deduction of contributions on behalf of such individuals, see paragraph (a)(2) of § 1.404(a)-8 and § 1.404(e)-1.

*(2)* Section 404(a) does not apply to a plan which does not defer the receipt of compensation. Furthermore, section 404(a) does not apply to deductions for contributions under a plan which is solely a dismissal wage or unemployment benefit plan, or a sickness, accident, hospitalization, medical expense, recreation, welfare, or similar benefit plan, or a combination thereof. For example, if under a plan an employer contributes 5 percent of each employee's compensation per month to a fund out of which employees who are laid off will be paid benefits for temporary periods, but employees who are not laid off have no rights to the funds, such a plan is an unemployment benefit plan, and the deductibility of the contributions to it is determined under section 162. As to the deductibility of such contributions, see § 1.162-9.

*(3)* If, however, the contributions to a pension, profit-sharing, stock bonus, or other plan of deferred compensation can be used to provide any of the benefits referred to in subparagraph (2) of this paragraph, then, except as provided in section 404(c), section 404(a) applies to the entire contribution to the plan. Thus, if in the example described in subparagraph (2) of this paragraph, the employer's contribution on behalf of each employee is set up as a separate account, and if any amount which remains in an employee's account at the time of retirement is paid to him at such time, the deductibility of the contributions to the plan is determined under section 404(a). For the regulations for determining whether the benefits referred to in subparagraph (2) of this paragraph can be included in a qualified pension or profit-sharing plan, see § 1.401-1(b).

*(4)* As to inclusion of full-time life insurance salesmen within the class of persons considered to be employees, see section 7701(a)(20).

**(b)** In order to be deductible under section 404(a), contributions must be expenses which would be deductible under section 162 (relating to trade or business expenses) or 212 (relating to expenses for production of income) if it were not for the provision in section 404(a) that they are deductible, if at all, only under section 404(a). Contributions may therefore be deducted under section 404(a) only to the extent that they are ordinary and necessary expenses during the taxable year in carrying on the trade or business or for the production of income and are compensation for personal services actually rendered. In no case is a deduction allowable under section 404(a) for the amount of any contribution for the benefit of an employee in excess of the amount which, together with other deductions allowed for compensation for such employee's services, constitutes a reasonable allowance for compensation for the services actually rendered. What constitutes a reasonable allowance depends upon the facts in the particular case. Among the elements to be considered in determining this are the personal services actually rendered in prior years as well as the current year and all compensation and contributions paid to or for such employee in prior years as well as in the current year. Thus, a contribution which is in the nature of additional compensation for services performed in prior years may be deductible, even if the total of such contributions and other compensation for the current year would be in excess of reasonable compensation for services performed in the current year, provided that such total plus all compensation and contributions paid to or for such employee in prior years represents a reasonable allowance for all services rendered by the employee by the end of the current year. A contribution under a plan which is primarily for the benefit of shareholders of the employer is not deductible. Such a contribution may constitute a dividend within the meaning of section 316. See also §§ 1.162-6 and 1.162-8. In addition to the limitations referred to above, deductions under section 404(a) are also subject to further conditions and limitations particularly provided therein.

**(c)** Deductions under section 404(a) are generally allowable only for the year in which the contribution or compensation is paid, regardless of the fact that the taxpayer may make his returns on the accrual method of accounting. Exceptions are made in the case of overpayments as provided in paragraphs (1), (3), and (7) of section 404(a), and, as provided by section 404(a)(6), in the case of payments made by a taxpayer on the accrual method of accounting not later than the time prescribed by law for filing the return for the taxable year of accrual (including extensions thereof). This latter provision is intended to permit a taxpayer on the accrual method to deduct such accrued contribution or compensation in the year of accrual, provided payment is actually made not later than the time prescribed by law for filing the return for the taxable year of accrual (including extensions thereof), but this provision is not applicable unless, during the taxable year on account of which the contribution is made, the taxpayer incurs a liability to make the contribution, the amount of which is accruable under section 461 for such taxable year. See section 461 and the regulations thereunder. There is another exception in the case of certain taxpayers who are required to make additional contributions as a result of the Act of June 15, 1955 (Public Law 74, 84th Cong., 69 Stat 134), and the regulations thereunder.

---

T.D. 6203, 9/24/56, amend T.D. 6676, 9/16/63.

---

### § 1.404(a)-1T Questions and answers relating to deductibility of deferred compensation and deferred benefits for employees (temporary).

Q-1. How does the amendment of section 404(b) by the Tax Reform Act of 1984 affect the deduction of contributions or compensation under section 404(a)?

A-1. As amended by the Tax Reform Act of 1984, section 404(b) clarifies that section 404(a) shall govern the deduction of contributions paid and compensation paid or incurred by the employer under a plan, or method or arrangement, deferring the receipt of compensation or providing for deferred benefits to employees, their spouses, or their dependents. See section 404(b) and § 1.404(b)-1T. Section 404(a) and (d) requires that such a contribution or compensation be paid or incurred for purposes of section 162 or 212 and satisfy the requirements for deductibility under either of those sections. However, notwithstanding the above, section 404 does not apply to contributions paid or accrued with respect to a "welfare benefit fund" (as defined in section 419(e)) after July 18, 1984, in taxable years of employers (and payors) ending after that date. Also, section 463 shall govern the deduction of vacation pay by a taxpayer that has elected the application of such section. For rules relating to the deduction of contributions paid or accrued with respect to a welfare benefit fund, see section 419, § 1.419-1T and § 1.419A-2T. For rules relating to the deduction of vacation pay for which an election is made under section 463, see § 301.9100-16T of this chapter and § 1.463-1T.

---

T.D. 8073, 1/29/86, amend T.D. 8435, 9/18/92.

---

### § 1.404(a)-2 Information to be furnished by employer claiming deductions; taxable years ending before December 31, 1971.

**(a)** For the first taxable year for which a deduction from gross income is claimed under section 404(a)(1), (2), (3), or (7), the employer must file the following information (unless such information has been previously filed in accordance with the regulations under section 23(p) of the Internal Revenue Code of 1939) for each plan involved to establish that it meets the requirements of section 401(a) or 404(a)(2), and that deductions claimed do not exceed the amount allowable under paragraphs (1), (2), (3), and (7) of section 404(a), as the case may be:

*(1)* Verified copies of all the instruments constituting or evidencing the plan, including trust indentures, group annuity contracts, specimen copy of each type of individual contract, and specimen copy of formal announcement and comprehensive detailed description to employees, with all amendments to any such instruments.

*(2)* A statement describing the plan which identifies it and which sets forth the name or names of the employers, the effective date of the plan and of any amendments thereto, the method of distribution or of disbursing benefits (whether by trustee, insurance company, or otherwise), the dates when the instruments or amendments were executed, the date of formal announcement and the dates when comprehensive detailed description of the plan and of each amendment thereto were made available to employees generally, the dates when the plan and when the trust or the contract evidencing the plan and of any amendments thereto were put into effect so that contributions thereunder were irrevocable and a summary of the provisions and rules relating to—

(i) Employee eligibility requirements for participation in the plan,

(ii) Employee contributions,

(iii) Employer contributions,

(iv) The basis or formula for determining the amount of each type of benefit and the requirements for obtaining such benefits and the vesting conditions,

(v) The medium of funding (e. g., self-insured, unit purchase group annuity contract, individual level annual premium retirement endowment insurance contracts, etc) and, if not wholly insured, the medium of contributions and the kind of investments, and

(vi) The discontinuance or modification of the plan and distributions or benefit payments upon liquidation or termination.

*(3)* A tabulation in columnar form showing the information specified below with respect to each of the 25 highest paid employees covered by the plan in the taxable year, listed in order of their nondeferred compensation (where there are several plans of deferred compensation, the information for each of the plans may be shown on a single tabulation without repetition of the information common to the several plans):

(i) Name.

(ii) Whether an officer.

(iii) Percentage of each class of stock owned directly or indirectly by the employee or members of his family.

(iv) Whether the principal duties consist in supervising the work of other employees.

(v) Year of birth.

(vi) Length of service for employer to the close of the year.

(vii) Total nondeferred compensation paid or accrued during the taxable year with a breakdown of such compensation into the following components:

(a) Basic compensation and overtime pay,

(b) Other direct payments, such as bonuses and commissions,

(c) Compensation paid other than in cash, such as goods, services, insurance not directly related to the benefits or provided from funds under the plan, etc.

(viii) Amount allocated during the year for the benefit of the employee or his beneficiary (including any insurance provided thereby or directly related thereto), less the employee's contributions during the year, under each other plan of deferred compensation.

(ix) Amount allocated during the year for the benefit of the employee or his beneficiary (including any insurance provided thereby or directly related thereto), less the employee's contributions during the year, under the plan. If a profit-sharing or stock bonus plan, also a breakdown of such amounts into the following components:

(a) Amounts originally allocated in the year, and

(b) Amounts reallocated in the year.

(x) Amounts of employee contributions during the year under the plan,

(xi) If a pension or annuity plan,

(a) The retirement age and date and the form of the retirement benefit,

(b) The annual rate or amount of the retirement benefit, and

(c) The aggregate of all of the employee's contributions under the plan,

all based, in the case of an employee who is not on retirement benefit under the plan, upon the assumption of his continued employment at his current rate of compensation until his normal retirement age (or the end of the current year if later) and retirement on such date with the normal form of retirement benefit under the plan.

*(4)* The following totals:

(i) Total nondeferred compensation paid or accrued during the taxable year for all employees covered under the plan and also for all employees of the employer.

(ii) Total amount allocated during the year for the benefit of employees, former or retired employees, or their beneficiaries (including any insurance provided thereby or directly related thereto), less employee contributions during the year under the plan and, if a profit-sharing or stock bonus plan, also a breakdown of such total into the following components:

(a) Amount originally allocated in the year, and

(b) Amount reallocated in the year.

*(5)* A schedule showing the total number of employees as of the close of the year for each of the following groups, based on reasonable estimates:

(i) All employees ineligible for coverage under the plan because of requirements as to employment classification, specifying the reasons applicable to the group (as, for example, temporary, seasonal, part time, hourly pay basis, etc.).

(ii) All employees ineligible for coverage under the plan because of requirements as to length of service and not included in subdivision (i) of this subparagraph.

(iii) All employees ineligible for coverage under the plan because of requirements as to minimum age and not included in subdivision (i) or (ii) of this subparagraph.

(iv) All employees ineligible for coverage under the plan solely because of requirements as to minimum rate of compensation.

(v) All employees ineligible for coverage under the plan other than those employees included in subdivision (i), (ii), (iii), or (iv) of this subparagraph, specifying the reason applicable to the group.

(vi) All employees ineligible for coverage under the plan for any reasons, which should be the sum of subdivisions (i) to (v), inclusive, of this subparagraph.

(vii) All employees, eligible for coverage but not covered under the plan.

(viii) All employees covered under the plan.

(ix) All employees of the employer, which should be the sum of subdivisions (vi),(vii), and (viii) of this subparagraph.

If it is claimed that the requirements of section 401(a)(3)(A) are satisfied, also the data and computations necessary to show that such requirements are satisfied.

*(6)* In the case of a trust, a detailed balance sheet and a detailed statement of receipts and disbursements during the year; in the case of a nontrusteed annuity plan, a detailed statement of the names of the insurers, the contributions paid by the employer and by the employees, and a statement as to the amounts and kinds of premium refunds or similar credits made available and the disposition of such credits in the year.

*(7)* If a pension or annuity plan, a detailed description of all the methods, factors, and assumptions used in determining costs and in adjusting the costs for actual experience under the plan (including any loadings, contingency reserves, or special factors and the basis of any insured costs or liabilities involved therein) explaining their source and application in sufficient detail to permit ready analysis and verification thereof, and, in the case of a trust, a detailed description of the basis used in valuing the investments held.

*(8)* A statement of the applicable limitations under section 404(a)(1), (2), (3), or (7) and an explanation of the method of determining such limitations, a summary of the data, and a statement of computations necessary to determine the allowable deductions for the taxable year. Also, in the case of a pension or annuity plan, a summary of the costs or liabilities and adjustments for the year under the plan based on the application of the methods, factors, and assumptions used

under the plan, in sufficient detail to permit ready verification of the reasonableness thereof.

*(9)* A statement of the contributions paid under the plan for the taxable year showing the date and amount of each payment. Also, a summary of the deductions claimed for the taxable year for the plan with a breakdown of the deductions claimed into the following components:

(i) For contributions paid in the taxable year before giving effect to the provisions of paragraph (7) of section 404(a).

(ii) For contributions paid in prior taxable years beginning after December 31, 1941, in accordance with the carryover provisions of paragraphs (1) and (3) of section 404(a), before giving effect to the provisions of paragraph (7) thereof, and in accordance with the carryover provisions of section 404(d).

(iii) Any reductions or increases in the deductions in accordance with the provisions of paragraph (7) of section 404(a). However, if the information in this subdivision is filed prior to the filing of the information required by subparagraph (8) of this paragraph, then, in determining the limit of deduction under paragraph (7) of section 404(a), the applicable percentage of the compensation otherwise paid or accrued during the year may be used.

**(b)** For taxable years subsequent to the year for which all of the applicable information under paragraph (a) of this section (or corresponding provisions of prior regulations) has been filed, information is to be filed only to the following extent:

*(1)* If there is any change in the plan, instruments, methods, factors, or assumptions upon which the data and information specified in paragraph (a)(1), (2), or (7) of this section are based, a detailed statement explaining the change and its effect is to be filed only for the taxable year in which the change is put into effect. However, if there is no such change, unless otherwise requested by the district director, merely a statement that there is no such change is to be filed.

*(2)* The information specified in paragraph (a)(3) of this section which has been filed for a taxable year, unless otherwise requested by the district director and so long as the plan and the method and basis of allocations are not changed, is to be filed for subsequent years only to the extent of showing in the tabulation such information with respect to employees who, at any time in the taxable year, own, directly or indirectly, more than 5 percent of the voting stock, considering stock so owned by an individual's spouse or minor lineal descendant as owned by the individual for this purpose.

*(3)* The information specified in paragraph (a)(4), (5), (6), (8), and (9) of this section.

In the case of corporate employers, the information required to be submitted by this paragraph shall, except as otherwise provided by the Commissioner, be filed on Form 2950 for taxable years ending on or after December 31, 1961. In the case of other employers, the information required to be submitted by this paragraph shall, except as otherwise provided by the Commissioner, be filed on Form 2950 for taxable years ending on or after December 31, 1962.

**(c)** If a deduction is claimed under section 404(a)(5) for the taxable year, the taxpayer shall furnish such information as is necessary to show that the deduction is not allowable under the other paragraphs of section 404(a), that the amount paid is an ordinary and necessary expense or an expense for the production of income, and that the employees' rights to, or derived from, such employer's contribution or such compensation were nonforfeitable at the time the contribution or compensation was paid. In the case of corporate employers, the information required to be submitted by this paragraph shall, except as otherwise provided by the Commissioner, be filed on Form 2950 for taxable years ending on or after December 31, 1961. In the case of other employers, the information required to be submitted by this paragraph shall, except as otherwise provided by the Commissioner, be filed on Form 2950 for taxable years ending on or after December 31, 1962.

**(d)** For the purpose of the information required by this section, contributions paid in a taxable year shall include those deemed to be so paid in accordance with the provisions of section 404(a)(6) and shall exclude those deemed to be paid in the prior taxable year in accordance with such provisions. As used in this section, "taxable year" refers to the taxable year of the employer and, unless otherwise requested by the district director, a "year" which is not specified as a "taxable year" may be taken as the taxable year of the employer or as the plan, trust, valuation, or group contract year with respect to which deductions are being claimed provided the same rule is followed consistently so that there is no gap or overlap in the information furnished for each item. In any case the date or period to which each item of information furnished relates should be clearly shown. All the information required by this section should be filed with the tax return for the taxable year in which the deduction is claimed, except that, unless sooner requested by the district director, such information, other than that specified in paragraph (a)(4)(i) and (9) of this section, may be filed within 12 months after the close of the taxable year provided there is filed with the tax return a statement that the information cannot reasonably be filed therewith, setting forth the reasons therefor.

**(e)** In any case all the information and data required by this section must be filed in the office of the district director in which the employer files his tax returns and must be filed independently of any information and data otherwise submitted in connection with a determination of the qualification of the trust or plan under section 401(a). The district director may, in addition, require any further information that he considers necessary to determine allowable deductions under section 404 or qualification under section 401. For taxable years ending on or before December 31, 1961, the district director may waive the filing of such information required by this section which he finds unnecessary in a particular case. For taxable years ending after December 31, 1961, the Commissioner may waive the filing of such information.

**(f)** Records substantiating all data and information required by this section to be filed must be kept at all times available for inspection by internal revenue officers at the main office or place of business of the employer.

**(g)** In the case of a plan which covers employees, some or all of whom are self-employed individuals and with respect to which a deduction is claimed under section 404(a)(1), (2), (3), or (7) paragraphs (a) and (b) of this section, and the provision of paragraph (d) of this section relating to the time for filing the information required by this section, shall not apply, but in lieu of the information required to be submitted by paragraphs (a) and (b) of this section, the employer shall, with the return for the taxable year in which the deduction is claimed, submit the information required by the form provided by the Internal Revenue Service for such purpose.

**(h)** When a custodial account forms a part of a plan for which a deduction is claimed under section 404(a)(1), (2),

(3), or (7), the information which under this section is to be submitted with respect to a qualified trust must be submitted with respect to such custodial account. Thus, for purposes of this section—

*(1)* The term "trust" includes custodial account,

*(2)* The term "trustee" includes custodian, and

*(3)* The term "trust indenture" includes custodial agreement.

(i) Except as provided under § 1.503(d)-1(a) and § 601.201 of this chapter (statement of Procedural Rules) in the case of a request for the determination of qualification of a trust under section 401 and exemption under section 501, paragraphs (a) through (h) of this section shall not apply for taxable years ending on or after December 31, 1971. For information to be furnished for taxable years ending on or after December 31, 1971, see § 1.404(a)-2A.

T.D. 6203, 9/24/56, amend T.D. 6599, 5/9/62, T.D. 6676, 9/16/63, T.D. 7168, 3/8/72.

### § 1.404(a)-2A Information to be furnished by employer; taxable years ending on or after December 31, 1971, and before December 31, 1975.

**(a) In general.** For any taxable year ending on or after December 31, 1971, and before December 31, 1975, any employer who maintains a pension, annuity, stock bonus, profit-sharing, or other funded plan of deferred compensation shall file the forms prescribed by this section. An employer (including a self-employed individual) maintaining such a plan shall furnish such information as is required by the forms and the instructions relating thereto. The forms shall be filed in the manner and at the time prescribed under paragraph (c) of this section. See § 1.404(a)-2 with respect to information to be furnished for taxable years ending before December 31, 1971. For purposes of this section, in the case of a plan of several employers described in § 1.401-1(d), each employer shall be deemed to be maintaining a separate plan corresponding to the plan of which the trust is a part. For information required to be furnished with respect to a funded deferred compensation plan maintained by an employer who is exempt from tax under section 501(a), see § 1.6033-2(a)(2)(ii)*(i)*.

**(b) Forms.** The forms prescribed by this section are:

*(1)* Form 4848, generally relating to information concerning the qualification of the plan, and deductions for contributions made on behalf of employees or self-employed individuals,

*(2)* Form 4849, generally relating to the financial position of the trust, fund, or custodial or fiduciary account which is a part of the plan, and

*(3)* For any taxable year ending on or after December 31, 1971, and before December 31, 1972, Forms 2950 and 2950SE, relating to the identification of plans to which an employer has made a contribution and information with respect to a deduction for a contribution made on behalf of a self-employed individual, respectively.

**(c) Filing requirements.** *(1)* Form 4848 shall be filed by the employer for each taxable year during which he maintains a pension, annuity, stock bonus, profit-sharing, or other funded plan of deferred compensation. Such form shall be filed on or before the 15th day of the 5th month following the close of the employer's taxable year. For rules relating to the extension of time for filing, see section 6081 and the regulations thereunder and the instructions for Form 4848.

*(2)* Form 4849 shall be filed by the employer as an attachment to Form 4848 for each taxable year during which he maintains a pension, annuity, stock bonus, profit-sharing, or other funded plan of deferred compensation unless the employer (i) has been notified in writing that Form 4849 will be filed by the fiduciary for such plan as an attachment to Form 990-P or (ii) is not required to file Form 4849 under the instructions relating thereto.

*(3)* For any taxable year ending on or after December 31, 1971, and before December 31, 1972, Form 2950 shall be filed with the employer's tax return for any such taxable year during which a pension, annuity, stock bonus, profit-sharing, or other funded plan of deferred compensation is maintained.

*(4)* For any taxable year ending on or after December 31, 1971, and before December 31, 1972, Form 2950SE shall be filed by each self-employed individual with his income tax return for any such taxable year in which he claims a deduction for contributions made on his behalf.

**(d) Additional information.** In addition to the information otherwise required to be furnished by this section, the district director may require any further information that he considers necessary to determine allowable deductions under section 404 or qualification under section 401.

**(e) Records.** Records substantiating all data and information required by this section to be filed must be kept at all times available for inspection by internal revenue officers at the main office or place of business of the employer.

T.D. 7168, 3/8/72, amend T.D. 7223, 11/20/72, T.D. 7551, 7/3/78.

### § 1.404(a)-3 Contributions of an employer to or under an employees' pension trust or annuity plan that meets the requirements of section 401(a); application of section 404(a)(1).

***Caution:*** The Treasury has not yet amended Reg § 1.404(a)-3 to reflect changes made by P.L. 101-508, P.L. 100-647, P.L. 100-203, P.L. 99-514, P.L. 98-369, P.L. 97-248, P.L. 97-34, P.L. 93-406.

**(a)** If contributions are paid by an employer to or under a pension trust or annuity plan for employees and the general conditions and limitations applicable to deductions for such contributions are satisfied (see § 1.404(a)-1), the contributions are deductible under section 404(a)(1) or (2) if the further conditions provided therein are also satisfied. As used in this section, a "pension trust" means a trust forming part of a pension plan and an "annuity plan" means a pension plan under which retirement benefits are provided under annuity or insurance contracts without a trust. This section is also applicable to contributions to a foreign situs pension trust which could qualify for exemption under section 501(a) except that it is not created or organized and maintained in the United States. For the meaning of "pension plan" as used in this section, see paragraph (b)(1)(i) of § 1.401-1. Where disability pensions, insurance, or survivorship benefits incidental and directly related to the retirement benefits under a pension or annuity plan are provided for the employees or their beneficiaries by contributions under the plan, deductions on account of such incidental benefits are also covered under section 404(a)(1) or (2). See paragraph (b)(2) of § 1.72-16 as to taxability to employees of cost of incidental life insurance protection. Similarly, where medical benefits described in section 401(h) as defined in paragraph (a) of § 1.401-14 are provided for retired employees, their spouses, or their dependents under the plan, deductions on account of such subordinate benefits are also covered under section 404(a)(1) or (2). In order to be deductible under section 404(a)(1), contributions to a pension trust must be paid in a taxable year of the employer which ends with or within a year of the trust for which it is exempt under section 501(a). Contributions paid in such a taxable year of the employer may be carried over and deducted in a succeeding taxable year of the employer in accordance with section 404(a)(1)(D), whether or not such succeeding taxable year ends with or within a taxable year of the trust for which it is exempt under section 501(a). See § 1.404(a)-7 for rules relating to the limitation on the amount deductible in such a succeeding taxable year of the employer. See § 1.404(a)-8 as to conditions for deductions under section 404(a)(2) in the case of an annuity plan. In either case, the deductions are also subject to further limitations provided in section 404(a)(1). The limitations provided in section 404(a)(1) are, with an exception provided for certain years under subparagraph (A) thereof (see § 1.404(a)-4), based on the actuarial costs of the plan.

**(b)** In determining costs for the purpose of limitations under section 404(a)(1), the effects of expected mortality and interest must be discounted and the effects of expected withdrawals, changes in compensation, retirements at various ages, and other pertinent factors may be discounted or otherwise reasonably recognized. A properly weighted retirement age based on adequate analyses of representative experience may be used as an assumed retirement age. Different basic assumptions or rates may be used for different classes of risks or different groups where justified by conditions or required by contract. In no event shall costs for the purpose of section 404(a)(1) exceed costs based on assumptions and methods which are reasonable in view of the provisions and coverage of the plan, the funding medium, reasonable expectations as to the effects of mortality and interest, reasonable and adequate regard for other factors such as withdrawal and deferred retirement (whether or not discounted) which can be expected to reduce costs materially, reasonable expenses of operation, and all other relevant conditions and circumstances. In any case, in determining the costs and limitations, an adjustment shall be made on account of any experience more favorable than that assumed in the basis of limitations for prior years. Unless such adjustments are consistently made every year by reducing the limitations otherwise determined by any decrease in liability or cost arising from experience in the next preceding taxable year which was more favorable than the assumptions on which the costs and limitations were based, the adjustment shall be made by some other method approved by the Commissioner.

**(c)** The amount of a contribution to a pension or annuity plan that is deductible under section 404(a)(1) or (2) depends upon the methods, factors, and assumptions which are used to compute the costs of the plan and the limitation of section 404(a)(1) which is applied. Since the amount that is deductible for one taxable year may affect the amount that is deductible for other taxable years, the methods, factors, and assumptions used in determining costs and the method of determining the limitation which have been used for determining the deduction for a taxable year for which the return has been filed shall not be changed for such taxable year, except when the Commissioner determines that the methods, factors, assumptions, or limitations were not proper, or except when a change is necessitated by reason of the use of different methods, factors, assumptions, or limitations for another taxable year. However, different methods, factors, and assumptions, or a different method of determining the limitation, if they are proper, may be used in determining the deduction for a subsequent taxable year.

**(d)** Any expenses incurred by the employer in connection with the plan, such as trustee's and actuary's fees, which are not provided for by contributions under the plan are deductible by the employer under section 162 (relating to trade or business expenses), or 212 (relating to expenses for production of income) to the extent that they are ordinary and necessary.

**(e)** In case deductions are allowable under section 404(a)(3), as well as under section 404(a)(1) or (2), the limitations under section 404(a)(1) and (3) are determined and applied without giving effect to the provisions of section 404(a)(7) but the amounts allowable as deductions are subject to the further limitations provided in section 404(a)(7). See § 1.404(a)-13.

**(f)** *(1)* Amounts contributed by an employer under the plan for the funding of medical benefits described in section 401(h) as defined in paragraph (a) of § 1.401-14 must satisfy the general requirements which are applicable to deductions allowable under section 404 and which are set forth in § 1.404(a)-1 including, for example, the requirements described in paragraph (b) of such section. Accordingly, such amounts must constitute an ordinary and necessary expense relating to either the trade or business or the production of income and must not, when added to all other compensation paid by the employer to the employee on whose behalf such a contribution is made, constitute more than reasonable compensation. However, in determining the amount which is deductible with respect to contributions to provide retirement benefits under the plan, amounts contributed for the funding of medical benefits described in section 401(h) shall not be taken into consideration.

*(2)* The amounts deductible with respect to employer contributions to fund medical benefits described in section 401(h) shall not exceed the total cost of providing such benefits. The total cost of providing such benefits shall be determined in accordance with any generally accepted actuarial method which is reasonable in view of the provisions and coverage of the plan, the funding medium, and other applicable considerations. The amount deductible for any taxable year with respect to such cost shall not exceed the greater of—

(i) An amount determined by distributing the remaining unfunded costs of past and current service credits as a level amount, or as a level percentage of compensation, over the remaining future service of each employee, or

(ii) 10 percent of the cost which would be required to completely fund or purchase such medical benefits.

In determining the amount deductible, an employer must apply either subdivision (i) of this subparagraph for all employees or subdivision (ii) of this subparagraph for all employees. If contributions paid by an employer in a taxable year to fund such medical benefits under a pension or annuity plan exceed the limitations of this subparagraph but otherwise satisfy the conditions for deduction under section 404, then the excess contributions are carried over and are deductible in succeeding taxable years of the employer which end with or within taxable years of the trust for which it is exempt under section 501(a) in order of time to the extent of the difference between the amount paid and deductible in each succeeding year and the limitation applicable to such year under this subparagraph. For purposes of subdivision (i) of this subparagraph, if the remaining future service of an employee is one year or less, it shall be treated as one year.

T.D. 6203, 9/24/56, amend T.D. 6534, 1/19/61, T.D. 6722, 4/31/64, T.D. 7168, 3/8/72.

### § 1.404(a)-4 Pension and annuity plans; limitations under section 404(a)(1)(A).

***Caution:*** The Treasury has not yet amended Reg § 1.404(a)-4 to reflect changes made by P.L. 100-647, P.L. 100-203, P.L. 99-514, P.L. 98-369, P.L. 97-248, P.L. 97-34, P.L. 93-406.

**(a)** Subject to the applicable general conditions and limitations (see § 1.404(a)-3), the initial limitation under section 404(a)(1)(A) is 5 percent of the compensation otherwise paid or accrued during the taxable year to all employees under the pension or annuity plan. This initial 5-percent limitation applies to the first taxable year for which a deduction is allowed for contributions to or under such a plan and also applies to any subsequent year (other than one described in paragraph (d) of this section) for which the 5-percent figure is not reduced as provided in this section. For years to which the initial 5-percent limitation applies, no adjustment on account of prior experience is required. If the contributions do not exceed the initial 5-percent limitation in the first taxable year to which this limitation applies, the taxpayer need not submit actuarial data for such year.

**(b)** For the first taxable year following the first year to which the initial 5-percent limitation applies, and for every fifth year thereafter, or more frequently where preferable to the taxpayer, the taxpayer shall submit with his return an actuarial certification of the amount reasonably necessary to provide the remaining unfunded cost of past and current service credits of all employees under the plan with a statement explaining all the methods, factors, and assumptions used in determining such amount. This amount may be determined as the sum of (1) the unfunded past service cost as of the beginning of the year, and (2) the normal cost for the year. Such costs shall be determined by methods, factors, and assumptions appropriate as a basis of limitations under section 404(a)(1)(C). Whenever requested by the district director, a similar certification and statement shall be submitted for the year or years specified in such request. The district director will make periodical examinations of such data at not less than 5-year intervals. Based upon such examinations the Commissioner will reduce the limitation under section 404(a)(1)(A) below the 5-percent limitation for the years with respect to which he finds that the 5-percent limitation exceeds the amount reasonably necessary to provide the remaining unfunded cost of past and current service credits of all employees under the plan. Where the limitation is so reduced, the reduced limitation shall apply until the Commissioner finds that a subsequent actuarial valuation shows a change to be necessary. Such subsequent valuation may be made by the taxpayer at any time and submitted to the district director with a request for a change in the limitation. See, however, paragraph (d) of this section with respect to taxable years to which the limitation under section 404(a)(1)(A) does not apply.

**(c)** For the purpose of limitations under section 404(a)(1)(A), "compensation otherwise paid or accrued" means all of the compensation paid or accrued except that for which a deduction is allowable under a plan that qualifies under section 401(a), including a plan that qualifies under section 404(a)(2). Where two or more pension or annuity plans cover the same employee, under section 404(a)(1)(A) the deductions with respect to each such plan are subject to the limitations applicable to the particular plan and the total deductions for all such plans are also subject to the limitations which would be applicable thereto if they constituted a single plan. Where, because of the particular provisions applicable to a large class of employees under a plan, the costs with respect to such employees are nominal in comparison with their compensation, after the first year to which the initial 5-percent limitation applies, deductions under section 404(a)(1)(A) are subject to limitations determined by considering the plan applicable to such class as if it were a separate plan. Deductions are allowable to the extent of the applicable limitations under section 404(a)(1)(A) even where these are greater than the applicable limitations under section 404(a)(1)(B) or section 404(a)(1)(C).

**(d)** The limitation under section 404(a)(1)(A) shall not be used for purposes of determining the amount deductible for a taxable year of the employer which ends with or within a taxable year of the pension trust during which it is not exempt under section 501(a), or, in the case of an annuity plan, during which it does not meet the requirements of section 404(a)(2), or which ends after the trust or plan has terminated. See § 1.404(a)-7 for rules relating to the limitation which is applicable for purposes of determining the amount deductible for such a taxable year of the employer.

T.D. 6203, 9/24/56, amend T.D. 6534, 1/19/61.

### § 1.404(a)-5 Pension and annuity plans; limitations under section 404(a)(1)(B).

***Caution:*** The Treasury has not yet amended Reg § 1.404(a)-5 to reflect changes made by P.L. 100-647, P.L. 100-203, P.L. 99-514, P.L. 98-369, P.L. 97-248, P.L. 97-34, P.L. 93-406.

**(a)** Subject to the applicable general conditions and limitations (see § 1.404(a)-3), under section 404(a)(1)(B), deductions may be allowed to the extent of limitations based on costs determined by distributing the remaining unfunded cost of the past and current service credits with respect to all employees covered under the trust or plan as a level amount or level percentage of compensation over the remaining service of each such employee except that, as to any three individuals with respect to whom more than 50 percent of such remaining unfunded cost attributable to such individuals shall be distributed evenly over a period of at least five taxable years. See, however, paragraph (e) of this section with respect to taxable years to which the limitation under section 404(a)(1)-(B) does not apply.

**(b)** The statutory limitation for any taxable year under section 404(a)(1)-(B) is any excess of the amount of the costs described in paragraph (a) of this section for the year over the amount allowable as a deduction under section 404(a)(1)(A).

**(c)** For this purpose, such excess, adjusted for prior experience, may be computed for each year as follows, all determinations being made as of the beginning of the year:

*(1)* Determine the value of all benefits expected to be paid after the beginning of the year for all employees, any former employees, and any other beneficiaries, then covered under the plan.

*(2)* If employees contribute under the plan, determine the value of all contributions expected to be made after the beginning of the year by employees then covered under the plan.

*(3)* Determine the value of all funds of the plan as of the beginning of the year.

*(4)* Determine the amount remaining to be distributed as a level amount or as a level percentage of compensation over the remaining future service of each employee by subtracting from subparagraph (1) of this paragraph the sum of subparagraphs (2) and (3) of this paragraph.

*(5)* Determine the value of all compensation expected to be paid after the beginning of the year to all employees then covered under the plan.

*(6)* Determine an accrual rate for each employee by dividing subparagraph (5) of this paragraph into subparagraph (4) of this paragraph.

*(7)* Compute the excess under section 404(a)(1)(B) for the year by multiplying the compensation paid to all employees covered under the plan during the year by any excess of subparagraph (6) of this paragraph over 5 percent. In general, where this method is used, the limitation under section 404(a)(1)(B) will be equal to the excess so computed without further adjustment on account of prior favorable experience, provided all the factors and assumptions used are reasonable in view of all applicable considerations (see § 1.404(a)-3) and provided subparagraph (5) of this paragraph is not less than five times the annual rate of compensation in effect at the beginning of the year.

**(d)** Instead of determining the excess deductible under section 404(a)(1)(B) by the method shown in paragraph (c), such excess may be based upon cost determined by some other method which is reasonable and appropriate under the circumstances. Thus, such excess may be based on the amounts necessary with respect to each individual covered employee to provide the remaining unfunded cost of all his benefits under the plan distributed as a level amount over the period remaining until the normal commencement of his retirement benefits, in accordance with other generally accepted actuarial methods which are reasonable and appropriate in view of the provisions of the plan, the funding medium, and other applicable considerations.

**(e)** The limitation under section 404(a)(1)(B) shall not be used for purposes of determining the amount deductible for a taxable year of the employer which ends with or within a taxable year of the pension trust during which it is not exempt under section 501(a), or, in the case of an annuity plan, during which it does not meet the requirements of section 404(a)(2), or which ends after the trust or plan has terminated. See § 1.404(a)-7 for rules relating to the limitation which is applicable for purposes of determining the amount deductible for such a taxable year of the employer.

T.D. 6203, 9/24/56, amend T.D. 6534, 1/19/61.

### § 1.404(a)-6 Pension and annuity plans; limitations under section 404(a)(1)(C).

***Caution:*** The Treasury has not yet amended Reg § 1.404(a)-6 to reflect changes made by P.L. 100-647, P.L. 100-203, P.L. 99-514, P.L. 98-369, P.L. 97-248, P.L. 97-34, P.L. 93-406.

**(a) Application to a taxable year of the employer which ends with or within a taxable year of the pension trust or annuity plan for which it is exempt under section 501(a) or meets the requirements of section 404(a)(2).** *(1)* The rules in this paragraph are applicable with respect to the limitation under section 404(a)(1)(C) for taxable years of the employer which end with or within a taxable year of the pension trust for which it is exempt under section 501(a), or, in the case of an annuity plan, during which it meets the requirements of section 404(a)(2). See paragraph (b) of this section for rules relating to the limitation under section 404(a)(1)(C) for other taxable years of the employer.

*(2)* Subject to the applicable general conditions and limitations (see § 1.404(a)-3), in lieu of amounts deductible under the limitations of section 404(a)(1)(A) and section 404(a)(1)(B), deductions may be allowed under section 404(a)(1)(C) to the extent of limitations based on normal and past service or supplementary costs of providing benefits under the plan. "Normal cost" for any year is the amount actuarially determined which would be required as a contribution by the employer in such year to maintain the plan if the plan had been in effect from the beginning of service of each then included employee and if such costs for prior years had been paid and all assumptions as to interest, mortality, time of payment, etc., had been fulfilled. Past service or supplementary cost at any time is the amount actuarially determined which would be required at such time to meet all the future benefits provided under the plan which would not be met by future normal costs and employee contributions with respect to the employees covered under the plan at such time.

*(3)* The limitation under section 404(a)(1)(C) for any taxable year to which this paragraph applies is the sum of normal cost for the year plus an amount not in excess of one-tenth of the past service or supplementary cost as of the date the past service or supplementary credits are provided under the plan. For this purpose, the normal cost may be determined by any generally accepted actuarial methods and may be expressed either as (i) the aggregate of level amounts with respect to each employee covered under the plan, (ii) a level percentage of payroll with respect to each employee covered under the plan, or (iii) the aggregate of the single premium or unit costs for the unit credits accruing during the year with respect to each employee covered under the plan, provided, in any case, that the method is reasonable in view of the provisions and coverage of the plan, the funding medium, and other applicable considerations. The limitation may include one-tenth of the past service or supplementary cost as of the date the provisions resulting in such cost were put into effect, but it is subject to adjustments for prior favorable experience. See § 1.404(a)-3. In any case, past service or supplementary costs shall not be included in the limitation for any year in which the amount required to fund fully or to purchase such past service or supplementary credits has been deducted, since no deduction is allowable for any amount (other than the normal cost) which is paid in after such credits are fully funded or purchased.

**(b) Application to a taxable year of the employer which does not end with or within a taxable year of the pension trust or annuity plan for which it is exempt under section 501(a) or meets the requirements of section 404(a)(2).** *(1)* The rules in this paragraph are applicable with respect to the limitation under section 404(a)(1)(C) for taxable years of the employer which end with or within a taxable year of the pension trust during which it is not exempt under section 501(a), or, in the case of an annuity plan, during which it does not meet the requirements of section 404(a)(2), or which end after the trust or plan has terminated. Since contributions paid in such taxable years of the employer are not deductible under section 404(a)(1) or (2) (except as provided in section 404(a)(6)), the limitation under section 404(a)(1)(C) for such taxable years relates only to the amount of any excess contributions that may be carried over to such taxable years under section 404(a)(1)(D).

(2) Subject to the applicable general conditions and limitations (see § 1.404(a)-3), deductions may be allowed under section 404(a)(1)(C) for taxable years of the employer to which this paragraph applies to the extent of limitations based on past service or supplementary costs of providing benefits under the plan. For definition of the "past service or supplementary cost at any time", see paragraph (a)(2) of this section.

(3) The limitation under section 404(a)(1)(C) for any taxable year to which this paragraph applies is an amount not in excess of one-tenth of the past service or supplementary cost as of the date the past service or supplementary credits are provided under the plan. The limitation under section 404(a)(1)(C) is subject, however, to adjustments for prior favorable experience. In any case, no amounts are deductible under section 404(a)(1)(C) for any year to which this paragraph applies if the amount required to fund fully or to purchase the past service or supplementary credits has been deducted in prior taxable years of the employer.

T.D. 6203, 9/24/56, amend T.D. 6534, 1/19/61.

### § 1.404(a)-7 Pension and annuity plans; contributions in excess of limitations under section 404(a)(1); application of section 404(a)(1)(D).

***Caution:*** The Treasury has not yet amended Reg § 1.404(a)-7 to reflect changes made by P.L. 107-16, P.L. 100-647, P.L. 100-203, P.L. 99-514, P.L. 98-369, P.L. 97-248, P.L. 97-34, P.L. 93-406.

When contributions paid by an employer in a taxable year to or under a pension or annuity plan exceed the limitations applicable under section 404(a)(1) but otherwise satisfy the conditions for deduction under section 404(a)(1) or (2), then in accordance with section 404(a)(1)(D), the excess contributions are carried over and are deductible in succeeding taxable years of the employer in order of time pursuant to the following rules:

**(a)** In the case of a succeeding taxable year of the employer which ends with or within a taxable year of the pension trust during which it is not exempt under section 501(a), or, in the case of an annuity plan, during which it meets the requirements of section 404(a)(2), such excess contributions are deductible to the extent of the difference between the amount paid and deductible in such succeeding taxable year and the limitation applicable to such year under section 404(a)(1)(A), (B), or (C).

**(b)** In the case of a succeeding taxable year of the employer which ends with or within a taxable year of the pension trust during which it is not exempt under section 501(a), or, in the case of an annuity plan, during which it does not meet the requirements of section 404(a)(2), or which ends after the trust or plan has terminated, such excess contributions are deductible to the extent of the limitation applicable to such year under section 404(a)(1)(C) (see paragraph (b) of § 1.404(a)-6).

The provisions of section 404(a)(1)(D) are to be applied before giving effect to the provisions of section 404(a)(7) for any year. The carryover provisions of section 404(a)(1)(D), before effect has been given to section 404(a)(7), may be illustrated by the following example for a plan put into effect in a taxable year ending December 31, 1954:

**Taxable Year Ending Dec. 31, 1954**

| | |
|---|---|
| Amount of contributions paid in year | $100,000 |
| Limitation applicable to year | 60,000 |
| Amount deductible for year | 60,000 |
| Excess carried over to succeeding years | 40,000 |

**Taxable Year Ending Dec. 31, 1955**

| | |
|---|---|
| Amount of contributions paid in year | $ 25,000 |
| Carried over from previous years | 40,000 |
| Total deductible subject to limitation | 65,000 |
| Limitation applicable to year | 50,000 |
| Amount deductible for year | 50,000 |
| Excess carried over to succeeding years | 15,000 |

**Taxable Year Ending Dec. 31, 1956**

| | |
|---|---|
| Amount of contributions paid in year | $ 10,000 |
| Carried over from previous years | 15,000 |
| Total deductible subject to limitation | 25,000 |
| Limitation applicable to year | 45,000 |
| Amount deductible for year | 25,000 |
| Excess carried over to succeeding years | None |

T.D. 6203, 9/24/56, amend T.D. 6534, 1/19/61.

### § 1.404(a)-8 Contributions of an employer under an employees' annuity plan which meets the requirements of section 401(a); application of section 404(a)(2).

***Caution:*** The Treasury has not yet amended Reg § 1.404(a)-8 to reflect changes made by P.L. 100-647, P.L. 100-203, P.L. 99-514, P.L. 98-369, P.L. 97-248, P.L. 97-34, P.L. 93-406.

**(a)** If contributions are paid by an employer under an annuity plan for employees and the general conditions and limitations applicable to deductions for such contributions are satisfied (see § 1.404(a)-1), the contributions are deductible under section 404(a)(2) if the further conditions provided therein are satisfied. For the meaning of "annuity plan" as used here, see § 1.404(a)-3. In order that contributions by the employer may be deducted under section 404(a)(2), all of the following conditions must be satisfied:

*(1)* The contributions must be paid toward the purchase of retirement annuities (or for disability, severance, insurance, survivorship benefits incidental and directly related to such annuities, or medical benefits described in section 401(h) as defined in paragraph (a) of § 1.404(h)-1) under an annuity plan for the exclusive benefit of the employer's employees or their beneficiaries.

*(2)* The contributions must be paid in a taxable year of the employer which ends with or within a year of the plan for which it meets the applicable requirements set forth in section 401(a)(3), (4), (5), (6), (7), (8), (11), (12), (13), (14), (15), (16), and (19). In the case of a plan which covers a self-employed individual, the contributions must be paid in a taxable year of the employer which ends with or within a year of the plan for which it also meets the requirements of section 401(a)(9), (10), (17), and (18) and of section 401(d) (other than paragraph (1)). In the case of a plan which covers a shareholder-employee within the meaning of section 1379(d), the contributions must be paid in a taxable year of the employer which ends with or within a year of the plan for which it also meets the requirements of section 401(a)(17) and (18). See section 401(a) and the regulations thereunder for the requirements and the applicable effective dates of the respective paragraphs set forth in section 401(a). Any contributions of an employer which are paid in a taxable year of the employer ending with or within a year of the

plan for which it meets the applicable requirements of section 401 may be carried over and deducted in a succeeding taxable year of the employer in accordance with section 404(a)(1)(D), whether or not such succeeding taxable year ends with or within a taxable year of the plan for which it meets the requirements set out in section 401(a) and (d). See section 401(b) and the regulations thereunder for special rules allowing certain plan amendments to be given retroactive effect. See section 404(a)(6) for a special rule for determining the time when a contribution is deemed to have been made.

*(3)* There must be a definite written arrangement between the employer and the insurer that refunds of premiums, if any, shall be applied within the taxable year of the employer in which received or within the next succeeding taxable year toward the purchase of retirement annuities (or for disability, severance, insurance, survivorship benefits incidental and directly related to such annuities, or medical benefits described in section 401(h) as defined in paragraph (a) of § 1.401(h)-1) under the plan. For the purpose of this condition, "refunds of premiums" means payments by the insurer on account of credits such as dividends, experience rating credits, or surrender or cancellation credits. The arrangement may be in the form of contract provisions or written directions of the employer or partly in one form and partly in another. This condition will be considered satisfied where—

(i) All credits are applied regularly, as they are determined, toward the premiums next due under the contracts before any further employer contributions are so applied, and

(ii) Under the arrangement,

(A) No refund of premiums may be made during continuance of the plan unless applied as aforesaid, and

(B) If refunds of premiums may be made after discontinuance or termination, whichever is applicable, of the plan on account of surrenders or cancellations before all retirement annuities provided under the plan with respect to service before its discontinuance or termination have been purchased, such refunds will be applied in the taxable year of the employer in which received, or in the next succeeding taxable year to purchase retirement annuities for employees by a procedure which does not contravene the conditions of section 401(a)(4). If the plan also includes medical benefits described in section 401(h) as defined in paragraph (a) of § 1.401(h)-1, any refund of premiums attributable to such benefits must, in accordance with these rules, be applied toward the purchase of medical benefits described in section 401(h).

*(4)* Any amounts described in subparagraph (3) of this paragraph which are attributable to contributions on behalf of a self-employed individual must be applied toward the purchase of retirement benefits. Amounts which are so applied are not contributions and thus are not taken into consideration in determining—

(i) The amount deductible with respect to contributions on his behalf, nor

(ii) In the case of an owner-employee, the maximum amount of contributions that may be made on his behalf.

**(b)** Where the above conditions are satisfied, the amounts deductible under section 404(a)(2) are governed by the limitations provided in section 404(a)(1). See §§ 1.404(a)-3 to 1.404(a)-7, inclusive.

---

T.D. 6203, 9/24/56, amend T.D. 6534, 1/19/61, T.D. 6676, 9/16/63, T.D. 6722, 4/13/64, T.D. 7501, 8/22/77.

---

**§ 1.404(a)-9 Contributions of an employer to an employees' profit-sharing or stock bonus trust that meets the requirements of section 401(a); application of section 404(a)(3)(A).**

***Caution:*** The Treasury has not yet amended Reg § 1.404(a)-9 to reflect changes made by P.L. 107-16, P.L. 104-188, P.L. 100-647, P.L. 100-203, P.L. 99-514, P.L. 98-369, P.L. 97-248, P.L. 97-34, P.L. 93-406.

**(a)** If contributions are paid by an employer to a profit-sharing or stock bonus trust for employees and the general conditions and limitations applicable to deductions for such contributions are satisfied (see § 1.404(a)-1), the contributions are deductible under section 404(a)(3)(A) if the further conditions provided therein are also satisfied. In order to be deductible under the first, second, or third sentence of section 404(a)(3)(A), the contributions must be paid (or deemed to have been paid under section 404(a)(6)) in a taxable year of the employer which ends with or within a taxable year of the trust for which it is exempt under section 501(a) and the trust must not be designed to provide retirement benefits for which the contributions can be determined actuarially. Excess contributions paid in such a taxable year of the employer may be carried over and deducted in a succeeding taxable year of the employer in accordance with the third sentence of section 404(a)(3)(A), whether or not such succeeding taxable year ends with or within a taxable year of the trust for which it is exempt under section 501(a). This section is also applicable to contributions to a foreign situs profit-sharing or stock bonus trust which could qualify for exemption under section 501(a) except that it is not created or organized and maintained in the United States.

**(b)** The amount of deductions under section 404(a)(3)(A) for any taxable year is subject to limitations based on the compensation otherwise paid or accrued by the employer during such taxable year to employees who are beneficiaries under the plan. For purposes of computing this limitation, the following rules are applicable:

*(1)* In the case of a taxable year of the employer which ends with or within a taxable year of the trust for which it is exempt under section 501(a), the limitation shall be based on the compensation otherwise paid or accrued by the employer during such taxable year of the employer to the employees who, in such taxable year of the employer, are beneficiaries of the trust funds accumulated under the plan.

*(2)* In the case of a taxable year of the employer which ends with or within a taxable year of the trust during which it is not exempt under section 501(a), or which ends after the trust has terminated, the limitation shall be based on the compensation otherwise paid or accrued by the employer during such taxable year of the employer to the employees who, at any time during the one-year period ending on the last day of the last calendar month during which the trust was exempt under section 501(a), were beneficiaries of the trust funds accumulated under the plan.

For purposes of this paragraph, "compensation otherwise paid or accrued" means all of the compensation paid or accrued except that for which a deduction is allowable under a plan that qualifies under section 401(a), including a plan that qualifies under section 404(a)(2). The limitations under section 404(a)(3)(A) apply to the total amount deductible for contributions to the trust regardless of the manner in which the funds of the trust are invested, applied, or distributed, and no other deduction is allowable on account of any benefits provided by contributions to the trust or by the funds thereof. Where contributions are paid to two or more profit-sharing or stock bonus trusts satisfying the conditions for deduction under section 404(a)(3)(A), such trusts are considered as a single trust in applying these limitations.

**(c)** The primary limitation on deductions for a taxable year is 15 percent of the compensation otherwise paid or accrued by the employer during such taxable year to the employees who are beneficiaries under the plan. See paragraph (b) of this section for rules for determining who are the beneficiaries under the plan.

**(d)** In order that the deductions may average 15 percent of compensation otherwise paid or accrued over a period of years, where contributions in some taxable year are less than the primary limitation but contributions in some succeeding taxable year exceed the primary limitation, deductions in each succeeding year are subject to a secondary limitation instead of to the primary limitation. The secondary limitation for any year is equal to the lesser of (1) twice the primary limitation for the year, or (2) any excess of (i) the aggregate of the primary limitations for the year and for all prior years over (ii) the aggregate of the deductions allowed or allowable under the limitations provided in section 404(a)(3)(A) for all prior years. Since contributions paid into a profit-sharing or stock bonus trust are deductible under section 404(a)(3)(A) only if they are paid (or deemed to have been paid under section 404(a)(6)) in a taxable year of the employer which ends with or within a taxable year of the trust for which it is exempt under section 501(a), the secondary limitation described in this paragraph is not applicable with respect to determining amounts deductible for a taxable year of the employer which ends with or within a taxable year of the trust during which it is not exempt under section 501(a), or which ends after the trust has terminated. See paragraph (e) of this section for rules relating to amounts which are deductible in such a taxable year.

**(e)** In any case when the contributions in a taxable year exceed the amount allowable as a deduction for the year under section 404(a)(3)(A), the excess is deductible in succeeding taxable years, in order of time, in accordance with the following limitations:

(1) If the succeeding taxable year ends with or within a taxable year of the trust for which it is exempt under section 501(a), such excess is deductible in any such succeeding taxable year in which the contributions are less than the primary limitation for that year; but the total deduction for such succeeding taxable year cannot exceed the lesser of (i) the primary limitation for such year, or (ii) the sum of the contributions in such year and the excess contributions not deducted under the limitations of section 404(a)(3)(A) for prior years.

(2) If the succeeding taxable year ends with or within a taxable year of the trust during which it is not exempt under section 501(a), or if such succeeding taxable year ends after the trust has terminated, the total deduction for such succeeding taxable year cannot exceed the lesser of (i) the primary limitation for such succeeding taxable year, or (ii) the excess contributions not deducted under the limitations of section 404(a)(3)(A) for prior years.

In no case, however, are excess contributions deductible in a succeeding taxable year if such contributions were not paid (or deemed to have been paid under section 404(a)(6)) in a taxable year of the employer which ends with or within a taxable year of the trust for which it is exempt under section 501(a).

**(f)** In case of deductions are allowable under section 404(a)(1) or (2), as well as under section 404(a)(3)(A), the limitations under section 404(a)(1) and (3)(A) are determined and applied without giving effect to the provisions of section 404(a)(7), but the amounts allowable as deductions are subject to the further limitations provided in section 404(a)(7). See § 1.404(a)-13.

**(g)** The provisions of section 404(a)(3)(A) before giving effect to section 404(a)(7), may be illustrated as follows:

| | Taxable (calendar) years | | | | | | |
|---|---|---|---|---|---|---|---|
| | 1954 | 1955 | 1956 | 1957 | 1958 | 1959 | 1960 |
| 1. Amount of contributions: | | | | | | | |
| (i) In taxable year | $65 | $10 | $15 | $100 | $ 70 | $ 40 | $30 |
| (ii) Carried over from prior taxable years | 0 | 8 | 0 | 0 | 4 | 5 | 3 |
| 2. Primary limitation applicable to year: | | | | | | | |
| 15 percent of covered compensation in year[1] | 57 | 54 | 51 | 48 | 45 | 42 | 39 |
| 3. Secondary limitation applicable to year: | | | | | | | |
| (i) Twice primary limitation | | | | 96 | 90 | 84 | |
| (ii) (a) Aggregate primary limitations (see item 2) | | | | 210 | 255 | 297 | |
| (b) Aggregate prior deductions (see item 4 (iii)) | | | | 90 | 186 | 255 | |
| (c) Excess of (a) over (b) | | | | 120 | 69 | 42 | |
| (iii) Lesser of (i) or (ii) | | | | 96 | 69 | 42 | |
| 4. Amount deductible for year on account of: | | | | | | | |
| (i) Contributions in year | 57 | 10 | 15 | 96 | 69 | 40 | 30 |
| (ii) Contributions carried over | 0 | 8 | 0 | 0 | 0 | 2 | 3 |
| (iii) Total | 57 | 18 | 15 | 96 | 69 | 42 | 33 |
| 5. Excess contribution carried over to succeeding years | 8 | 0 | 0 | 4 | 5 | 3 | 0 |

[1] Compensation otherwise paid or accrued during the year to the employees who are beneficiaries of trust funds accumulated under the plan in the year.

T.D. 6203, 9/24/56, amend T.D. 6534, 1/19/61.

**§ 1.404(a)-10 Profit-sharing plan of an affiliated group; application of section 404(a)(3)(B).**

***Caution:*** The Treasury has not yet amended Reg § 1.404(a)-10 to reflect changes made by P.L. 100-647, P.L. 100-203, P.L. 99-514, P.L. 98-369, P.L. 97-248, P.L. 97-34, P.L. 93-406.

**(a)** Section 404(a)(3)(B) allows a corporation a deduction to the extent provided in paragraphs (b) and (c) of this section for a contribution which it makes for another corporation to a profit-sharing plan or a stock bonus plan under which contributions are determined by reference to profits, provided the following tests are met:

*(1)* The corporation for which the contribution is made and the contributing corporation are members of an affiliated group of corporations as defined in section 1504, relating to the filing of consolidated returns, and both such corporations participate in the plan. However, it is immaterial whether all the members of such group participate in the plan.

*(2)* The corporation for which the contribution is made is required under the plan to make the contribution, but such corporation is prevented from making such contribution because it has neither current nor accumulated earnings or profits, or because its current and accumulated earnings or profits are insufficient to make the required contribution. To the extent that such a corporation has any current or accumulated earnings or profits, it is not considered to be prevented from making its required contribution to the plan.

*(3)* The contribution is made out of the current or accumulated earnings or profits of the contributing corporation.

**(b)** The amount that is deductible under section 404(a)(3)(B) is determined by applying the rules of section 404(a)(3)(A) and § 1.404(a)-9 as if the contribution were made by the corporation for which it is made. For example, the primary limitation described in paragraph (e) of § 1.404(a)-9 is determined by reference to the compensation otherwise paid or accrued to the employees of the corporation for which the contribution is made, and the secondary limitation described in paragraph (d) of § 1.404(a)-9 and the contribution carryover described in paragraph (c) of § 1.404(a)-9 are determined by reference to the prior contributions and deductions of such corporation. The contributing corporation may deduct the amount so determined subject to the limitations contained in paragraph (c) of this section. The contributing corporation shall not treat such amount as a contribution made by it in applying the rules of section 404(a)(3)(A) and § 1.404(a)-9 either for the taxable year for which the contribution is made or for succeeding taxable years. The corporation for which the contribution is made shall treat the contribution as having been made by it in applying the rules of section 404(a)(3)(A) and § 1.404(a)-9 for succeeding taxable years.

**(c)** The allowance of the deduction under section 404(a)(3)(B) does not depend upon whether the affiliated group does or does not file a consolidated return. If a consolidated return is filed, it is immaterial which of the participating corporations makes the contribution and takes the deduction or how the contribution or the deduction is allocated among them. However, if a consolidated return is not filed, the contribution which is deductible under section 404(a)(3)(B) by each contributing corporation shall be limited to that portion of its total current and accumulated earnings or profits (adjusted for its contribution deductible without regard to section 404(a)(3)(B)) which the prevented contribution bears to the total current and accumulated earnings or profits of all the participating members of the group having such earnings or profits (adjusted for all contributions deductible without regard to section 404(a)(3)(B)). For the purpose of this section, current earnings or profits shall be computed as of the close of the taxable year without diminution by reason of any dividends during the taxable year, and accumulated earnings or profits shall be computed as of the beginning of the taxable year.

**(d)** The application of section 404(a)(3)(B) may be illustrated by the following example in which the affiliated group does not file a consolidated return:

| (1) | (2) | (3) | (4) | (5) | (6) | (7) | (8) | (9) | (10) | (11) |
|---|---|---|---|---|---|---|---|---|---|---|
| A | ($10,000) | ($140,000) | ($150,000) | $200,000 | 1/5 | $6,000 | | | | |
| B | (5,000) | 105,000 | 100,000 | 300,000 | 3/10 | 9,000 | $9,000 | $91,000 | 6/326 × 91,000 | $1,674.85 |
| C | 75,000 | 175,000 | 250,000 | 500,000 | 1/2 | 15,000 | 15,000 | 235,000 | 6/326 × 235,000 | 4,325.15 |
| Total | 60,000 | 140,000 | 200,000 | 1,000,000 | | 30,000 | 24,000 | 326,000 | | 6,000.00 |

**Column**
(1) Member.
(2) Earnings and profits of the taxable year.
(3) Accumulated earnings and profits at beginning of taxable year.
(4) Total current and accumulated earnings and profits (column 2 plus column 3).
(5) Compensation of participating employees.
(6) Contribution formula; 50 percent of consolidated earnings and profits, allocated among participating members in proportion of covered payroll of each to covered payroll of consolidated group.
(7) Individual contribution had it not been prevented.
(8) Individual contribution made by each employer for its own employees.
(9) Balance of accumulated earnings and profits (column 4 minus column 8).
(10) Proportion of make-up contribution.
(11) Make-up contribution.

T.D. 6203, 9/24/56.

**§ 1.404(a)-11 Trusts created or organized outside the United States; application of section 404(a)(4).**

In order that a trust may constitute a qualified trust under section 401(a) and be exempt under section 501(a), it must be created or organized in the United States and maintained at all times as a domestic trust. See paragraph (a) of § 1.401-1. Paragraph (4) of section 404(a) provides, however, that an employer which is a resident, a corporation, or other entity of the United States, making contributions to a foreign stock bonus, pension, or profit-sharing trust, shall be allowed deductions for such contributions, under the applicable conditions and within the prescribed limits of section 404(a), if such foreign trust would qualify for exemption under section 501(a) except for the fact that it is a trust created, organized, or maintained outside the United States. Moreover, if a nonresident alien individual, foreign corporation, or other entity is engaged in trade or business within the United States and makes contributions to a foreign stock bonus, pension, or profit-sharing trust, which would qualify under section 401(a) and be exempt under section 501(a) except that it is created, organized, or maintained outside the United States, such contributions are deductible subject to the conditions and limitations of section 404(a) and to the extent allowed by section 873 or 882(c).

T.D. 6203, 9/24/56.

**§ 1.404(a)-12 Contributions of an employer under a plan that does not meet the requirements of section 401(a); application of section 404(a)(5).**

***Caution:*** The Treasury has not yet amended Reg § 1.404(a)-12 to reflect changes made by P.L. 104-188, P.L. 100-203.

**(a) In general.** Section 404(a)(5) covers all cases for which deductions are allowable under section 404(a) (for contributions paid by an employer under a stock bonus, pension, profit sharing, or annuity plan or for any compensation paid on account of any employee under a plan deferring the receipt of such compensation) but not allowable under paragraph (1), (2), (3), (4), or (7) of such section. For the rules with respect to the taxability of an employee when rights under a nonexempt trust become substantially vested, see section 402(b) and the regulations thereunder.

**(b) Contributions made after August 1, 1969.** *(1) In general.* A deduction is allowable for a contribution paid after August 1, 1969, under section 404(a)(5) only in the taxable year of the employer in which or with which ends the taxable year of an employee in which an amount attributable to such contribution is includible in his gross income as compensation, and then only to the extent allowable under section 404(a). See § 1.404(a)-1. For example, if an employer A contributes $1,000 to the account of its employee E for its taxable (calendar) year 1977, but the amount in the account attributable to that contribution is not includible in E's gross income until his taxable (calendar) year 1980 (at which time the includible amount is $1,150), A's deduction for that contribution is $1,000 in 1980 (if allowable under section 404(a)). For purposes of this (1), a contribution is considered to be so includible where the employee or his beneficiary excludes it from his gross income under section 101(b) or subchapter N. To the extent that property of the employer is transferred in connection with such a contribution, such transfer will constitute a disposition of such property by the employer upon which gain or loss is recognized, except as provided in section 1032 and the regulations thereunder. The amount of gain or loss recognized from such disposition shall be the difference between the value of such property used to measure the deduction allowable under this section and the employer's adjusted basis in such property.

*(2) Special rule for unfunded pensions and certain death benefits.* If unfunded pensions are paid directly to former employees, such payments are includible in their gross income when paid, and accordingly, such amounts are deductible under section 404(a)(5) when paid. Similarly, if amounts are paid as a death benefit to the beneficiaries of an employee (for example, by continuing his salary for a reasonable period), and if such amounts meet the requirements of section 162 or 212, such amounts are deductible under section 404(a)(5) in any case when they are not includible under the other paragraphs of section 404(a).

*(3) Separate accounts for funded plans with more than one employee.* In the case of a funded plan under which more than one employee participates, no deduction is allowable under section 404(a)(5) for any contribution unless separate accounts are maintained for each employee. The requirement of separate accounts does not require that a separate trust be maintained for each employee. However, a separate account must be maintained for each employee to which employer contributions under the plan are allocated, along with any income earned thereon. In addition, such accounts must be sufficiently separate and independent to qualify as separate shares under section 663(c). Nothing shall preclude a trust which loses its exemption under section 501(a) from setting up such accounts and meeting the separate account requirement of section 404(a)(5) with respect to the taxable years in which such accounts are set up and maintained.

**(c) Contributions paid on or before August 1, 1969.** No deduction is allowable under section 404(a)(5) for any contribution paid on or before August 1, 1969, by an employer under a stock bonus, pension, profit-sharing, or annuity plan, or for any compensation paid on account of any employee under a plan deferring the receipt of such compensation, except in the year when paid, and then only to the extent allowable under section 404(a). See § 1.404(a)-1. If payments are made under such a plan and the amounts are not deductible under the other paragraphs of section 404(a), they are deductible under section 404(a)(5) to the extent that the rights of individual employees to, or derived from, such employer's contribution or such compensation are nonforfeitable at the time the contribution or compensation is paid. If unfunded pensions are paid directly to former employees, their rights to such payments are nonforfeitable, and accordingly, such amounts are deductible under section 404(a)(5) when paid. Similarly, if amounts are paid as a death benefit to the beneficiaries of an employee (for example, by continuing his salary for a reasonable period), and if such amounts meet the requirements of section 162 or 212, such amounts are deductible under section 404(a)(5) in any case where they are not deductible under the other paragraphs of section 404(a). As to what constitutes nonforfeitable rights of an employee in other cases, see § 1.402(b)-1(d)(2). If an amount is accrued but not paid during the taxable year, no deduction is allowable for such amount for such year. If an amount is paid during the taxable year to a trust or under a plan and the employee's rights to such amount are forfeitable at the time the amount is paid, no deduction is allowable for such amount for any taxable year.

T.D. 6203, 9/24/56, amend T.D. 7554, 7/21/78.

**§ 1.404(a)-13 Contributions of an employer where deductions are allowable under section 404(a)(1) or (2) and also under section 404(a)(3); application of section 404(a)(7).**

***Caution:*** The Treasury has not yet amended Reg § 1.404(a)-13 to reflect changes made by P.L. 107-147, P.L. 107-16, P.L. 100-647, P.L. 100-203, P.L. 99-514, P.L. 98-369, P.L. 97-248, P.L. 97-34, P.L. 93-406.

**(a)** Where deductions are allowable under section 404(a)(1) or (2) on account of contributions under a pension or annuity plan and deductions are also allowable under section 404(a)(3) for the same taxable year on account of contributions to a profit-sharing or stock bonus trust, the total deductions under these sections are subject to the provisions of section 404(a)(7) unless no employee who is a beneficiary under the trusts or plans for which deductions are allowable under section 404(a)(1) or (2) is also a beneficiary under the trusts for which deductions are allowable under section 404(a)(3). The provisions of section 404(a)(7) apply only to deductions for overlapping trusts or plans, i.e., for all trusts or plans for which deductions are allowable under section 404(a)(1), (2), or (3) except (1) any trust or plan for which deductions are allowable under section 404(a)(1) or (2) and which does not cover any employee who is also covered under a trust for which deductions are allowable under section 404(a)(3), and (2) any trust for which deductions are allowable under section 404(a)(3) and which does not cover any employee who is also covered under a trust or plan for which deductions are allowable under section 404(a)(1) or (2). The limitations under section 404(a)(7) for any taxable year of the employer are based on the compensation otherwise paid or accrued during the year by the employer to all employees who, in such year, are beneficiaries of the funds accumulated under one or more of the overlapping trusts or plans. For purposes of the preceding sentence, if the taxable year of the employer with respect to which the limitation is being computed ends with or within a taxable year of any of the overlapping trusts or plans during which any such trust is not exempt under section 501(a) or, in the case of a plan, during which it does not meet the requirements of section 404(a)(2), or if such taxable year of the employer ends after any such trust or plan has terminated, then, with respect to such trust or plan, those employees, and only those employees, who, at any time during the one-year period ending on the last day of the last calendar month during which the trust was exempt under section 501(a), or the plan met the requirements of section 404(a)(2), were beneficiaries of the funds accumulated under such trust or plan shall be considered the beneficiaries of such trust or plan in the taxable year of the employer with respect to which the limitation is being computed. For purposes of this paragraph, "compensation otherwise paid or accrued" means all of the compensation paid or accrued except that for which a deduction is allowable under a plan that qualifies under section 401(a), including a plan that qualifies under section 404(a)(2).

**(b)** Under section 404(a)(7), any excess of the total amount otherwise deductible for the taxable year under section 404(a)(1), (2), or (3) as contributions to overlapping trusts or plans over 25 percent of the compensation otherwise paid or accrued during the year to all the employees who are beneficiaries under such trusts or plans, is not deductible for such year but is deductible for succeeding taxable years, in order of time, so that the total deduction for contributions to such trusts or plans for a succeeding taxable year is equal to the lesser of—

*(1)* 30 percent of the compensation otherwise paid or accrued during the taxable year to all the employees who are beneficiaries under such trusts or plans in the year, or

*(2)* The sum of (i) the smaller of (a) 25 percent of the compensation otherwise paid or accrued during the taxable year to all the employees who are beneficiaries under such trusts or plans in the year, or (b) the total of the amounts otherwise deductible under section 404(a)(1), (2), or (3), for the year for such trusts or plans and (ii) any carryover to the year from prior years under section 404(a)(7), i.e., any excess otherwise deductible under section 404(a)(1), (2), or (3) but not deducted for a prior taxable year because of the limitations under section 404(a)(7).

**(c)** The limitations under section 404(a)(7) are determined and applied after all the limitations, deductions otherwise allowable, and carryovers under section 404(a)(1), (2), and (3) have been determined and applied, and, in particular, after effect has been given to the carryover provision in section 404(a)(1)(D) and in the second and third sentences of section 404(a)(3)(A). Where the limitations under section 404(a)(7) reduce the total amount deductible, the excess deductible in succeeding years is treated as a carryover which is distinct from, and additional to, any excess contributions carried over and deductible in succeeding years under the provisions in section 404(a)(1)(D) or in the third sentence of section 404(a)(3)(A). The application of the provisions of section 404(a)(7) and the treatment of carryovers for a case where the taxable years are calendar years and the overlapping trusts or plans consist of a pension trust and a profit-sharing trust put into effect in 1954 and covering the same employees may be illustrated as follows:

**Illustration of Application of Provisions of Section 404(a)(7) and of Treatment of Carryovers for Overlapping Pension and Profit-Sharing Trusts Put into Effect in 1954 and Covering the Same Employees**

[All figure represent thousands of dollars and all taxable (calendar) years of the employer are years which end with or within a taxable year of the trust for which it is exempt under section 501(a)]

| | Taxable (calendar) years | | | |
|---|---|---|---|---|
| | 1954 | 1955 | 1956 | 1957 |
| **Before Giving Effect to Section 404(a)(7)** | | | | |
| Pensions trust contributions and limitations, deductions, and carryovers under section 404(a)(1): | | | | |
| 1. Contributions paid in year | $215 | $ 85 | $140 | $ 60 |
| 2. Contributions carried over from prior years | 0 | 5 | 0 | 20 |
| 3. Total deductible for year subject to limitation | 215 | 90 | 140 | 80 |
| 4. Limitation applicable to year | 210 | 175 | 120 | 85 |
| 5. Amount deductible for year | 210 | 90 | 120 | 80 |
| 6. Contributions carried over to succeeding years | 5 | 0 | 20 | 0 |
| Profit-sharing trust contributions and limitations, deductions, and carryovers under section 404(a)(3): | | | | |
| 7. Contributions paid in year | 200 | 125 | 105 | 65 |
| 8. Contributions carried over from prior years | 0 | 35 | 10 | 0 |
| 9. Total deduction for year subject to limitation | 200 | 160 | 115 | 65 |
| 10. Limitation applicable to year | 165 | 150 | 135 | 110[1] |
| 11. Amount deductible for year | 165 | 150 | 115 | 65 |
| 12. Contributions carried over to succeeding years | 35 | 10 | 0 | 0 |

[1] Includes carryover of 20 from 1956.

| **Application of Section 404(a)(7)** | | | | |
|---|---|---|---|---|
| 13. Amount deductible for year under section 404(a)(7): | | | | |
| (1) 30 percent of compensation covered in year[2] | ([3]) | 300 | 270 | 180 |
| (2)(i) (a) 25 percent of compensation covered in year[2] | 275 | 250 | 225 | 150 |
| (b) Total amount otherwise deductible for year: item 5 plus item 11 | 375 | 240 | 235 | 145 |
| (c) Smaller of (a) or (b) | 275 | 240 | 225 | 145 |
| (ii) Carryover from prior years under section 404(a)(7) | 0 | 100 | 40 | 10 |
| (iii) Sum of (i)(c) and (ii) | 275 | 340 | 265 | 155 |
| (3) Amount deductible: Lesser of (1) or (2)(iii) | 275 | 300 | 265 | 155 |
| 14. Carryover to succeeding years under section 404(a)(7): item 13(2)(ii) plus item 13(2)(i)(b) minus item 13(3) | 100 | 40 | 10 | 0 |

[2] Compensation otherwise paid or accrued during the year to the employees who are beneficiaries under the trusts in the year.
[3] 30 percent limitation not applicable to first year of plan.

T.D. 6203, 9/24/56, amend T.D. 6534, 1/19/61.

## § 1.404(a)-14 Special rules in connection with the Employee Retirement Income Security Act of 1974.

***Caution:*** The Treasury has not yet amended Reg § 1.404(a)-14 to reflect changes made by P.L. 100-647, P.L. 100-203, P.L. 99-514, P.L. 98-369, P.L. 97-248, P.L. 97-34.

**(a) Purpose of this section.** This section provides rules for determining the deductible limit under section 404(a)(1)(A) of the Internal Revenue Code of 1954 for defined benefit plans.

**(b) Definitions.** For purposes of this section—

*(1) Section 404(a).* The term "old section 404(a)" means section 404(a) as in effect on September 1, 1974. Any reference to section 404 without the designation "old" is a reference to section 404 as amended by the Employee Retirement Income Security Act of 1974.

*(2) Ten-year amortization base.* The term "10-year amortization base" means either the past service and other supplementary pension and annuity credits described in section 404(a)(1)(A)(iii) or any base established in accordance with paragraph (g) of this section. A plan may have several 10-year amortization bases to reflect different plan amendments, changes in actuarial assumptions, changes in funding method, and experience gains and losses of previous years.

*(3) Limit adjustment.* The term "limit adjustment" with respect to any 10-year amortization base is the lesser of—

(i) The level annual amount necessary to amortize the base over 10 years using the valuation rate, or

(ii) The unamortized balance of the base,

in each case using absolute values (solely for the purpose of determining which is the lesser). To compute the level amortization amount, the base may be divided by the present value of an annuity of one dollar, obtained from standard annuity tables on the basis of a given interest rate (the valuation rate) and a known period (the amortization period).

*(4) Absolute value.* The term "absolute value" for any number is the value of that number, treating negative numbers as if they were positive numbers. For example, the absolute value of 5 is 5 and the absolute value of minus 3 is 3. On the other hand, the true value of minus 3 is minus 3. This term is relevant to the computation of the limit adjustment described in paragraph (b)(3) and the remaining amor-

tization period of combined bases described in paragraph (i)(3) of this section.

*(5) Valuation rate.* The term "valuation rate" means the assumed interest rate used to value plan liabilities.

**(c) Use of plan in determining deductible limit for employer's taxable year.** Although the deductible limit applies for an employer's taxable year, the deductible limit is determined on the basis of a plan year. If the employer's taxable year coincides with the plan year, the deductible limit for the taxable year is the deductible limit for the plan year that coincides with that year. If the employer's taxable year does not coincide with the plan year, the deductible limit under section 404(a)(1)(A)(i), (ii), or (iii) for a given taxable year of the employer is one of the following alternatives:

*(1)* The deductible limit determined for the plan year commencing within the taxable year.

*(2)* The deductible limit determined for the plan year ending within the taxable year, or

*(3)* A weighted average of alternatives (1) and (2). Such an average may be based, for example, upon the number of months of each plan year falling within the taxable year.

The employer must use the same alternative for each taxable year unless consent to change is obtained from the Commissioner under section 446(e).

**(d) Computation of deductible limit for a plan year.** *(1) General rules.* The computation of the deductible limit for a plan year is based on the funding methods, actuarial assumptions, and benefit structure used for purposes of section 412, determined without regard to section 412(g) (relating to the alternative minimum funding standard), for the plan year. The method of valuing assets for purposes of section 404 must be the same method of valuing assets used for purposes of section 412.

*(2) Special adjustments of computations under section 412.* To apply the rules of this section *(i.e.,* rules regarding the computation of normal cost with aggregate type funding methods, unfunded liabilities, and the full funding limitation described in paragraph (k) of the section, where applicable) with respect to a given plan year in computing deductible limits under section 404(a)(1)(A), the following adjustments must be made:

(i) There must be excluded from the total assets of the plan the amount of any plan contribution for a plan year for which the plan was qualified under section 401(a), 403(a) or 405(a) that has not been previously deducted, even though that amount may have been credited to the funding standard account under section 412(b)(3). In the case of a plan using a spread gain funding method which maintains an unfunded liability *(e.g.,* the frozen initial liability method, but not the aggregate method), the amount described in the preceding sentence must be included in the unfunded liability of the plan.

(ii) There must be included in the total assets of the plan for a plan year the amount of any plan contribution that has been deducted with respect to a prior plan year, even though that amount is considered under section 412 to be contributed in a plan year subsequent to that prior plan year. In the case of a plan using a spread gain funding method which does not maintain an unfunded liability, the amount described in the preceding sentence must be excluded from the unfunded liability of the plan.

The special adjustments described in paragraph (d)(2)(i) and (ii) of this section apply on a year-by-year basis for purposes of section 404(a)(1)(A) only. Thus, the adjustments have no effect on the computation of the minimum funding requirement under section 412.

**(e) Special computation rules under section 404(a)(1)(A)(i).** *(1) In general.* For purposes of determining the deductible limit under section 404(a)(1)(A)(i), the deductible limit with respect to a plan year is the sum of—

(i) The amount required to satisfy the minimum funding standard of section 412(a) (determined without regard to section 412(g)) for the plan year and

(ii) An amount equal to the includible employer contributions. The term "includible employer contributions" means employer contributions which were required by section 412 for the plan year immediately preceding such plan year, and which were not deductible under section 404(a) for the prior taxable year of the employer solely because they were not contributed during the prior taxable year (determine with regard to section 404(a)(6)).

*(2) Rule for an employer using alternative minimum funding standard account and computing its deduction under section 404(a)(1)(A)(i).* This paragraph (e)(2) applies if the minimum funding requirements for the plan are determined under the alternative minimum funding standard described in section 412(g) for both the current plan year and the immediately preceding plan year. In that case, the deductible limit under section 404(a)(1)(A)(i) (regarding the minimum funding requirement of section 412) for the current year is the sum of the amount determined under the rules of paragraph (e)(1) of this section.

(i) Plus the charge under section 412(b)(2)(D), and

(ii) Less the credit under section 412(b)(3)(D), that would be required if in the current plan year the use of the alternative method were discontinued.

**(f) Special computation rules under section 404(a)(1)(A)(ii) and (iii).** *(1) In general.* Subject to the full funding limitation described in paragraph (k) of this section, the deductible limit under section 404(a)(1)(A)(ii) and (iii) is the normal cost of the plan (determined in accordance with paragraph (d) of this section).

*(2) Adjustments in calculating limit under section 404(a)(1)(A)(iii).* In calculating the deductible limit under section 404(a)(1)(A)(iii), the normal cost of the plan is—

(i) Decreased by the limit adjustments to any unamortized bases required by paragraph (g) of this section, for example, bases that are due to a net experience gain, a change in actuarial assumptions, a change in funding method, or a plan provision or amendment which decreases the accrued liability of the plan, and

(ii) Increased by the limit adjustments of any unamortized 10-year amortization bases required by paragraph (g) or (j) of this section, for example, bases that are due to a net experience loss, a change in actuarial assumptions, a change in funding method, or a plan provision or amendment which increases the accrued liability.

*(3) Timing for computations and interest adjustments under section 404(a)(1)(A)(ii) and (iii).* Regardless of the actual time when contributions are made to a plan, in computing the deductible limit under section 404(a)(1)(A)(ii) and (iii) the normal cost and limit adjustments shall be computed as of the date when contributions are assumed to be made ("the computation date") and adjusted for interest at the valuation rate from the computation date to the earlier of—

(i) The last day of the plan year used to compute the deductible limit for the taxable year, or

(ii) The last day of that taxable year.

For additional provisions relating to the timing of computations and interest adjustments, see paragraph (h)(6) of this section (relating to the timing of computations and interest adjustments in the maintenance of 10-year amortization bases). For taxable years beginning before April 22, 1981, computations under the preceding sentence may, as an alternative, be based on prior published positions of the Internal Revenue Service under section 404(a).

*(4) Special limit under section 404(a)(1)(A)(ii).* If the deduction for the plan year is determined solely on the basis of section 404(a)(1)(A)(ii) (that is, without regard to clauses (i) or (iii)), the special limitation contained in section 404(a)(1)(A)(ii), regarding the unfunded cost with respect to any three individuals, applies, notwithstanding the rules contained in paragraphs (d)(2) and (f)(1) of this section.

**(g) Establishment of a 10-year amortization base.** *(1) Experience gains and losses.* In the case of a plan valued by the use of a funding method which is an immediate gain type of funding method (and therefore separately amortizes rather than includes experience gains and losses as a part of the normal cost of the plan), a 10-year amortization base must be established in any plan year equal to the net experience gain or loss required under section 412 to be determined with respect to that plan year. The base to be maintained in accordance with paragraph (h) of this section. Such a base must not be established if the deductible limit is determined by use of a funding method which is a spread gain type of funding method (under which experience gains and losses are spread over future periods as a part of the plan's normal cost). Examples of the immediate gain type of funding method are the unit credit method, entry age normal cost method, and the individual level premium cost method. Examples of the spread gain type of funding method are the aggregate cost method, frozen initial liability cost method, and the attained age normal cost method.

*(2) Change in actuarial assumptions.* (i) If the creation of an amortization base is required under the rules of section 412(b)(2)(B)(v) or (3)(B)(iii) (as applied to the funding method used by the plan), a 10-year amortization base must be established at the time of a change in actuarial assumptions used to value plan liabilities. The amount of the base is the difference between the accrued liability calculated on the basis of the new assumptions and the accrued liability calculated on the basis of the old assumptions. Both computations of accrued liability are made as of the date of the change in assumptions.

(ii) A plan using a funding method of the spread gain type does not directly determine an accrued liability. If a plan using such a method is required under section 412(b)(2)(B)(v) or (3)(B)(iii) to create an amortization base, it must establish a base as described in paragraph (g)(2)(i) of this section for a change in actuarial assumptions by determining an accrued liability on the basis of another funding method (of the immediate gain type) that does determine an accrued liability. (The aggregate method is an example of a funding method that is not required under section 412(b)(2)(B)(v) or (3)(B)(iii) to create an amortization base.) The funding method chosen to determine the accrued liability of the plan in these cases must be the same method used to establish all other 10-year amortization bases maintained by the plan, if any. These bases must be maintained in accordance with paragraph (h) of this section.

*(3) Past service or supplemental credits.* A 10-year base must be established when a plan is established or amended, if the creation of an amortizable base is required under the rules of section 412(b)(2)(B)(ii) or (iii), or (b)(3)(B)(i) (as applied to the funding method used by the plan). The amount of the base is the accrued liability arising from, or the decrease in accrued liability resulting from, the establishment or amendment of the plan. The base must be maintained in accordance with paragraph (h) of this section.

*(4) Change in funding method.* If a change in funding method results in an increase or decrease in an unfunded liability required to be amortized under section 412, a 10-year base must be established equal to the increase or decrease in unfunded liability resulting from the change in funding method. The base must be maintained in accordance with paragraph (h) of this section.

**(h) Maintenance of 10-year amortization base.** *(1) In general.* Each time a 10-year amortization base is established, whether by a change in funding method, by plan amendment, by change in actuarial assumptions, or by experience gains and losses, the base must, except as provided in paragraph (i) of this section, be separately maintained in order to determine when the unamortized amount of the base is zero. The sum of the unamortized balances of all of the 10-year bases must equal the plan's unfunded liability with the adjustments described in paragraph (d) of this section, if applicable. When the unamortized amount of a base is zero, the deductible limit is no longer adjusted to reflect the amortization of the base.

*(2) First year's base.* See either paragraph (g) or paragraph (i) of this section for rules applicable with respect to the first year of a base.

*(3) Succeeding year's base.* For any plan year after the first year of a base, the unamortized amount of the base is equal to—

(i) The unamortized amount of the base as of the valuation date in the prior plan year, plus

(ii) Interest at the valuation rate from the valuation date in the prior plan year to the valuation date in the current plan year on the amount described in subdivision (i), minus

(iii) The contribution described in paragraph (h)(4) of this section with respect to the base for the prior plan year.

The valuation date is the date as of which plan liabilities are valued under section 412(c)(9). If such a valuation is performed less often than annually for purposes of section 412, bases must be adjusted for purposes of section 404 each year as of the date on which a section 412 valuation would be performed were it required on an annual basis. See paragraph (b)(3) of this section for the definition of valuation rate.

*(4) Contribution allocation with respect to each base.* A portion of the total contribution for the prior plan year is allocated to each base. Generally, this portion equals the product of—

(i) The total contribution described in paragraph (h)(6) of this section with respect to all bases, and

(ii) The ratio of the amount described in paragraph (b)(3)(i) of this section with respect to the base to the sum (using true rather than absolute values) of such amounts with respect to all remaining bases.

However, if the result of this computation with respect to a particular base exceeds the amount necessary to amortize such base fully, the smaller amount shall be deemed the contribution made with respect to such base. The unallocated excess with respect to a now fully amortized base shall be allocated among the other bases as indicated above.

*(5) Other allocation methods.* The Commissioner may authorize the use of methods other than the method described

in paragraph (h)(4) of this section for allocating contributions to bases.

*(6) Total contribution for all bases.* The contribution with respect to all bases for the prior plan year (see paragraph (h)(3)(iii) of this section) is the difference between—

(i) The sum of (A) the total deduction (including a carryover deduction) for the prior year, (B) interest on the actual contributions for the prior year (whether or not deductible) at the valuation rate for the period between the dates as of which the contributions are credited under section 412 and the valuation date in the current plan year, and (C) interest on the carryover described in section 404(a)(1)(D) that is available at the beginning of the prior taxable year at the valuation rate for the period between the current and prior valuation dates, and

(ii) The normal cost for the prior plan year and interest on it at the valuation rate from the date as of which the normal cost is calculated to the current valuation date.

*(7) Effect of failure to contribute normal cost plus interest on unamortized amounts.* The failure to make a contribution at least equal to the sum of the normal cost plus interest on the unamortized amounts has the following effects under the preceding rules of this section—

(i) It does not create a new base.

(ii) It results in an increase in the unamortized amount of each base and consequently extends the time before the base is fully amortized.

(iii) The limit adjustment for any base is not increased (in absolute terms) even if the unamortized amount computed under paragraph (h) of this section exceeds the initial 10-year amortization base. Thus, if the total unamortized amount of the plan's bases at the beginning of the plan year is $100,000 (which is also the unfunded liability of the plan), and a required $50,000 normal cost contribution is not made for the plan year, the following effects occur. The total unamortized balance of the plan's bases increases by the $50,000 normal cost for the year (adjusted for interest), plus interest on the $100,000 balance of the bases; and, because of that increase, it will take a longer period to amortize the remaining balance of the bases. (The annual amortization amount does not change.)

*(8) Required adjustment to a 10-year base limit adjustment if valuation rate changed.* If there is a change in the valuation rate, the limit adjustment for all unamortized 10-year amortization bases must be changed, in addition to establishing a new base as provided in paragraph (g)(2) of this section. The new limit adjustment for any base is the level amount necessary to amortize the unamortized amount of the base over the remaining amortization period using the new valuation rate. The remaining amortization period of the base is the number of years at the end of which the unamortized amount of the base would be zero if the contribution made with respect to that base equaled the limit adjustment each year. This calculation of the remaining period is made on the basis of the valuation rate used before the change. Both the remaining amortization period and the revised limit adjustment may be determined through the use of standard annuity tables. The remaining period may be computed in terms of fractional years, or it may be rounded off to a full year. The unamortized amount of the base as of the valuation date and the remaining amortization period of that base shall not be changed by any change in the valuation rate.

**(i) Combining bases.** *(1) General method.* For purposes of section 404 only, and not for purposes of section 412, different 10-year amortization bases may be combined into a single 10-year amortization base if such single base satisfies all of the requirements of paragraph (i)(2), (3), and (4) of this section at the time of the combining of the different bases.

*(2) Unamortized amount.* The unamortized amount of the single base equals the sum, as of the date the combination is made, of the unamortized amount of the bases being combined (treating negative bases as having negative unamortized amounts).

*(3) Remaining amortization period.* The remaining amortization period of the single base is equal to (i) the sum of the separate products of (A) the unamortized amount of each of these bases (using absolute values) and (B) its remaining amortization period, divided by (ii) the sum of the unamortized amounts of each of the bases (using absolute values). For purposes of this paragraph (i)(3), the remaining amortization period of each base being combined is that number of years at the end of which the unamortized amount of the base would be zero if the contribution made with respect to that base equaled the limit adjustment of that base in each year. This number may be determined through the use of standard annuity tables. The remaining amortization period described in this paragraph may be computed in terms of fractional years, or it may be rounded off to a whole year.

*(4) Limit Adjustment.* The limit adjustment for the single base is the level amount necessary to amortize the unamortized amount of the combined base over the remaining amortization period described in paragraph (i)(3) of this section, using the valuation rate. This amount may be determined through the use of standard annuity tables.

*(5) Fresh start alternative.* In lieu of combining different 10-year amortization bases, a plan may replace all existing bases with one new 10-year amortization base equal to the unfunded liability of the plan as of the time the new base is being established. This unfunded liability must be determined in accordance with the general rules of paragraphs (d) and (f) of this section. The unamortized amount of the base and the limit adjustment for the base will be determined as though the base were newly established.

**(j) Initial 10-year amortization base for existing plan.** *(1) In general.* In the case of a plan in existence before the effective date of section 404(a), the 10-year amortization base on the effective date of section 404(a) is the sum of all 10 percent bases existing immediately before section 404(a) became effective for the plan, determined under the rules of old section 404(a).

*(2) Limit adjustment.* The limit adjustment for the initial base is the lesser of the unamortized amount of such base or the sum of the amounts determined under paragraph (b)(3) of this section using the original balances of the remaining bases (under old section 404(a) rules) as the amount to be amortized.

*(3) Unamortized amount.* The employer may choose either to establish a single initial base reflecting both all prior 10-percent bases and the experience gain or loss for the immediately preceding actuarial period, or to establish a separate base for the prior 10-percent bases and another for the experience gain or loss for the immediately preceding period. If the initial 10-year amortization base reflects the net experience gain or loss from the immediately preceding actuarial period, the unamortized amount of the initial base shall equal the total unfunded liability on the effective date of section 404(a) determined in accordance with the general rules of paragraphs (d) and (f) of this section. If, however, a separate base will be used to reflect that gain or loss, the unam-

ortized amount of the initial base shall equal such unfunded liability on the effective date of section 404(a), reduced by the net experience loss or increased by the net experience gain for the immediately preceding actuarial period. In this case, a separate 10-year amortization base must be established on the effective date equal to the net experience gain or loss. Thus, if the effective date unfunded liability is $100,000 and an experience loss of $15,000 is recognized on that date, and if the loss is to be treated as a separate base, the unamortized balances of the two bases would be $85,000 and $15,000. If the unfunded liability were the same $100,000, but a gain of $15,000 instead of a loss were recognized on that date, the unamortized balances of the two bases would be $115,000 and a credit base of $15,000. In both cases, if only one 10-year base is to be established on the effective date, its unamortized balance would be $100,000 (the unfunded liability of the plan). See paragraphs (d) and (f) for rules for determining the unfunded liability of the plan.

**(k) Effect of full funding limit on 10-year-amortization bases.** The amount deductible under section 404(a)(1)(A)(i), (ii), or (iii) for a plan year may not exceed the full funding limitation for that year. See section 412 and paragraphs (d), (e), and (f) of this section for rules to be used in the computation of the full funding limitation. If the total deductible contribution (including carryover) for a plan year equals or exceeds the full funding limitation for the year, all 10-year amortization bases maintained by the plan will be considered fully amortized, and the deductible limit for subsequent plan years will not be adjusted to reflect the amortization of these bases.

**(l) Transitional rules.** *(1) Plan years beginning before April 22, 1981.* In determining the deductible limit for plan years beginning before April 22, 1981, a contribution will be deductible under section 404(a)(1)(A) if the computation of the deductible limit is based on an interpretation of section 404(a)(1)(A) that is reasonable when considered with prior published positions of the Internal Revenue Service. A computation of the deductible limit may satisfy the preceding sentence even if it does not satisfy the rules contained in paragraphs (c) through (i) of this section.

*(2) Transitional approaches.* The deductible limit determined for the first plan year with respect to which a plan applies the rules contained in paragraphs (c) through (i) of this section must be computed using one of the following approaches—

(i) The plan (whether or not in existence before the effective date of section 404(a)) may apply the rules of paragraph (j) for establishing the initial base for an existing plan, treating 10-year bases (if any) as 10 percent bases in adding bases.

(ii) The plan may apply the fresh start alternative for combining bases under paragraph (i)(5).

(iii) The plan may retroactively establish 10-year amortization bases for years with respect to which section 404(a)(1)(A) and the rules of this section would have applied but for the transition rule contained in paragraph (l)(1) of this section. Contributions actually deducted are used in retroactively establishing and maintaining these bases under paragraph (h). However, a deduction already taken shall not be recomputed because of the retroactive establishment of a base.

**(m) Effective date of section 404(a).** In the case of a plan which was in existence on January 1, 1974, section 404(a) generally applies for contributions on account of taxable years of an employer ending with or within plan years beginning after December 31, 1974. In the case of a plan not in existence on January 1, 1974, section 404(a) generally applies for contributions on account of taxable years of an employer ending with or within plan years beginning after September 4, 1974. See § 1.410(a)-2(c) for rules concerning the time of plan existence. See also § 1.410(a)-2(d), which provides that a plan in existence on January 1, 1974, may elect to have certain provisions, including the amendments to section 404(a) contained in section 1013 of the Employee Retirement Income Security Act of 1974, apply to a plan year beginning after September 2, 1974, and before the otherwise applicable effective date contained in that section.

---

T.D. 7760, 1/16/81.

---

### § 11.404(a)(6)-1 Time when contributions to "H.R. 10" plans considered made.

**(a) In general.** Section 404(a)(6), as amended by section 1013(c)(2) of the Employee Retirement Income Security Act of 1974, provides that for purposes of paragraphs (1), (2), and (3) of section 404(a), a taxpayer shall be deemed to have made a payment on the last day of the preceding taxable year if the payment is on account of such taxable year and is made not later than the time prescribed by law for filing the return for such taxable year (including extensions thereof). Under section 1017(b) of the Employee Retirement Income Security Act of 1974 (prior to its amendment by the Tax Reduction Act of 1975), in the case of a plan which was in existence on January 1, 1974, the foregoing provision generally applies for contributions on account of taxable years of an employer ending with or within plan years beginning after December 31, 1975. In the case of a plan not in existence on January 1, 1974, the foregoing provision generally applies for contributions on account of taxable years of an employer ending with or within plan years beginning after September 2, 1974. See § 11.410(a)-2(c) for time a plan is considered in existence. See also § 11.410(a)-2(d), which provides that a plan in existence on January 1, 1974 may elect to have certain provisions, including the amendment to section 404(a)(6) contained in section 1013 of the Employee Retirement Income Security Act of 1974, apply to a plan year beginning after September 2, 1974, and before the otherwise applicable effective date contained in that section.

**(b) "H.R. 10" plans may elect new provision.** Under section 402 of the Tax Reduction Act of 1975 (89 Stat. 47), in the case of a plan which was in existence on January 1, 1974, and which provides contributions or benefits for employees some or all of whom are employees within the meaning of section 401(c)(1) of the Code and § 1.401-10(b), the provision described in paragraph (a) of this section shall apply for taxable years of an employer ending with or within plan years beginning after December 31, 1974, but only if the employer (within the meaning of section 401(c)(4) of the Code and § 1.401-10(e)) elects to have such provisions apply as provided in paragraph (c) of this section.

**(c) Manner of election.** The election described in paragraph (b) of this section shall be considered to be made if the employer (as described in paragraph (b) of this section)—

*(1)* Makes a contribution which relates to his preceding taxable year within the time prescribed in paragraph (a) of this section to a plan described in paragraph (b) of this section, and

*(2)* Claims a deduction for such contribution on his tax return for such year (or, in the case of a contribution by a partnership on behalf of a partner, the contribution is shown on Schedule K of the partnership tax return for such year); no formal statement is necessary. In the case of an employer whose income tax return for the year on account of which the payment is made is required to be filed (determined without regard to extensions of time) on or before April 15, 1976, and who made a payment within the time prescribed in paragraph (a) of this section, the election also may be made by filing an amended return or claim for refund with respect to such year on or before September 30, 1976.

**(d) Election is irrevocable.** Any election made under paragraph (c) of this section, once made, shall be irrevocable.

**(e) Examples.** The rules of this section are illustrated by the following examples.

*Example (1).* On October 15, 1976, the ABC Partnership made a contribution to the ABC Profit Sharing Plan and Trust on behalf of partners and common-law employees with respect to the plan year ending December 31, 1975. The ABC Profit Sharing Trust was exempt under section 501(a) throughout 1975. The contribution for both partners and employees was reflected on the partnership return for the calendar year 1975 which was filed on October 10, 1976; proper extensions of the due date of the partnership return had been received, extending the due date to October 15, 1976. The election is valid since all requirements of this section have been met.

*Example (2).* The XYZ Partnership made a plan contribution on April 10, 1976, with respect to the plan year ending December 31, 1975, but the amount contributed for 1975 was not reflected in the partnership return filed for the calendar year 1975 on April 15, 1976. However, the XYZ Partnership filed an amended partnership return for the year 1975 on September 30, 1976, claiming a deduction for the employee-related contribution and setting forth on Schedule K the contribution relating to partners. The election is valid, since the contribution on account of 1975 was made within the time required, and was shown on the amended tax return of the employer for 1975 filed within the time prescribed in paragraph (c)(2) of this section.

*Example (3).* Mr. Smith, a sole proprietor whose taxable year is the calendar year, made a contribution to the Smith Profit Sharing Plan and Trust on April 15, 1976, for the plan year which began December 1, 1974, and ended November 30, 1975. The plan was in existence on January 1, 1974. Since the contribution was made within the time prescribed by this section and was on account of a taxable year of the employer ending within a plan year which began after December 31, 1974, the contribution may be deducted on Mr. Smith's return for 1975, even though the contribution was for a plan year beginning before December 31, 1974.

*Example (4).* The DEF Partnership, reporting its income on the basis of a fiscal year ending June 30, made a contribution to its "H.R. 10" plan which was in existence on January 1, 1974, and whose plan year was the calendar year. The contribution was made on September 30, 1975, and was on account of the taxable year of the partnership ending June 30, 1975. The contribution was properly reflected in the partnership return for the fiscal year ending June 30, 1975. The partnership's election to have section 404(a)(6), as amended, apply to its fiscal year ending June 30, 1975, is valid since that year ended with or within a plan year beginning after December 31, 1974.

T.D. 7402, 2/4/76.

### § 1.404(a)(8)-1T Deductions for plan contributions on behalf of self-employed individuals (temporary).

Q: How does the amendment to section 404(a)(8)(D), made by section 713(d)(6) of the Tax Reform Act of 1984 (TRA of 1984), affect section 404(a)(8)(C)?

A: In applying the rules of section 404(a)(8)(C), the Service will treat the amendment to section 404(a)(8)(D) as also having been made to section 404(a)(8)(C), pending enactment of technical corrections to TRA of 1984. The effect of treating the amendment as having also been made to section 404(a)(8)(C) is to increase the amount of contributions on behalf of a self-employed individual that will be treated as satisfying section 162 or 212. Generally, therefore, a contribution on behalf of a self-employed individual is treated as satisfying section 162 or 212 if it is not in excess of the individual's earned income for the year, determined without regard to the deduction allowed by section 404 for the self-employed individual's contribution.

T.D. 8073, 1/29/86.

### § 1.404(b)-1 Method of contribution, etc., having the effect of a plan; effect of section 404(b).

***Caution:*** The Treasury has not yet amended Reg § 1.404(b)-1 to reflect changes made by P.L. 93-406.

Section 404(a) is not confined to formal stock bonus, pension, profit-sharing, and annuity plans, or deferred compensation plans, but it includes any method of contributions or compensation having the effect of a stock bonus, pension, profit-sharing, or annuity plan, or similar plan deferring the receipt of compensation. Thus, where a corporation pays pensions to a retired employee or employees or to their beneficiaries in such amounts as may be determined from time to time by the board of directors or responsible officers of the company, or where a corporation is under an obligation, whether funded or unfunded, to pay a pension or other deferred compensation to an employee or his beneficiaries, there is a method having the effect of a plan deferring the receipt of compensation for which deductions are governed by section 404(a). If an employer on the accrual basis defers paying any compensation to an employee until a later year or years under an arrangement having the effect of a stock bonus, pension, profit-sharing, or annuity plan, or similar plan deferring the receipt of compensation, he shall not be allowed a deduction until the year in which the compensation is paid. This provision is not intended to cover the case where an employer on the accrual basis defers payment of compensation after the year of accrual merely because of inability to pay such compensation in the year of accrual, as, for example, where the funds of the company are not sufficient to enable payment of the compensation without jeopardizing the solvency of the company, or where the liability accrues in the earlier year, but the amount payable cannot be exactly determined until the later year.

T.D. 6203, 9/24/56.

### § 1.404(b)-1T Method or arrangement of contributions, etc., deferring the receipt of compensation or providing for deferred benefits (temporary).

Q-1. As amended by the Tax Reform Act of 1984, what does section 404(b) of the Internal Revenue Code provide?

A-1. As amended, section 404(b) clarifies that any plan, or method or arrangement, deferring the receipt of compensation or providing for deferred benefits (other than compensation) is to be treated as a plan deferring the receipt of compensation for purposes of section 404(a) and (d). Accordingly, section 404(a) and (d) (in the case of employees and nonemployees; respectively) shall govern the deduction of contributions paid or compensation paid or incurred with respect to such a plan, or method or arrangement. Section 404(a) and (d) requires that such a contribution or compensation be paid or incurred for purposes of section 162 or 212 and satisfy the requirements for deductibility under either of those sections. Thus, for example, under section 404(a)(5) and (b), if otherwise deductible under section 162 or 212, a contribution paid or incurred with respect to a nonqualified plan, or method or arrangement, providing for deferred benefits is deductible in the taxable year of the employer in which or with which ends the taxable year of the employee in which the amount attributable to the contribution is includible in the gross income of the employee (without regard to any applicable exclusion under Chapter 1, Subtitle A, of the Internal Revenue Code). Section 404(a) and (d) applies to all compensation and benefit plans, or methods or arrangements, however denominated, which defer the receipt of any amount of compensation or benefit, including fees or other payments. Thus, a limited partnership (using the accrual method of accounting) may not accrue deductions for a fee owed to an unrelated person (using the cash method of accounting) who performs services for the partnership until the partnership taxable year in which or with which ends the taxable year of the service provider in which the fee is included in income. However, notwithstanding the above, section 404 does not apply to contributions paid or accrued with respect to a "welfare benefit fund" (as defined in section 419(e)) after July 18, 1984, in taxable years of employers (and payors) ending after that date. Also, section 463 shall govern the deduction of vacation pay by a taxpayer that has elected the application of such section. For rules relating to the deduction of contributions paid or accrued with respect to a welfare benefit fund, see section 419, § 1.419-1T and § 1.419A-2T. For rules relating to the deduction of vacation pay for which an election is made under section 463, see § 301.9100-16T of this chapter and § 1.463-1T.

Q-2. When does a plan, or method or arrangement, defer the receipt of compensation or benefits for purposes of section 404(a), (b), and (d)?

A-2. (a) For purposes of section 404(a), (b), and (d), a plan, or method or arrangement, defers the receipt of compensation or benefits to the extent it is one under which an employee receives compensation or benefits more than a brief period of time after the end of the employer's taxable year in which the services creating the right to such compensation or benefits are performed.

The determination of whether a plan, or method or arrangement, defers the receipts of compensation or benefits is made separately with respect to each employee and each amount of compensation or benefit. Compensation or benefits received by an employee's spouse or dependent or any other person, but taxable to the employee, are treated as received by the employee for purposes of section 404. An employee is determined to receive compensation or benefits within or beyond a brief period of time after the end of the employer's taxable year under the rules provided in this Q&A. For the treatment of expenses with respect to transactions between related taxpayers, see section 267.

(b)(1) A plan, or method or arrangement, shall be presumed to be one deferring the receipt of compensation for more than a brief period of time after the end of an employer's taxable year to the extent that compensation is received after the 15th day of the 3rd calendar month after the end of the employer's taxable year in which the related services are rendered ("the 2½ month period"). Thus, for example, salary under an employment contract or a bonus under a year-end bonus declaration is presumed to be paid under a plan, or method or arrangement, deferring the receipt of compensation, to the extent that the salary or bonus is received beyond the applicable 2½ month period. Further, salary or a year-end bonus received beyond the applicable 2½ month period by one employee shall be presumed to constitute payment under a plan, or method or arrangement, deferring the receipt of compensation for such employee even though salary or bonus payments to all other employees are not similarly treated because they are received within the 2½ month period. Benefits are "deferred benefits" if, assuming the benefits were cash compensation, such benefits would be considered deferred compensation. Thus, a plan, or method or arrangement, shall be presumed to be one providing for deferred benefits to the extent benefits for services are received by an employee after the 2½ month period following the end of the employer's taxable year in which the related services are rendered.

(2) The taxpayer may rebut the presumption established under the previous subparagraph with respect to an amount of compensation or benefits only by setting forth facts and circumstances the preponderance of which demonstrates that it was impracticable, either administratively or economically, to avoid the deferral of the receipt by an employee of the amount of compensation or benefits beyond the applicable 2½ month period and that, as of the end of the employer's taxable year such impracticability was unforeseeable. For example, the presumption may be rebutted with respect to an amount of compensation to the extent that receipt of such amount is deferred beyond the applicable 2½ month period (i) either because the funds of the employer were not sufficient to make the payment within the 2½ month period without jeopardizing the solvency of the employer or because it was not reasonably possible to determine within the 2½ month period whether payment of such amount was to be made, and (ii) the circumstance causing the deferral described in (i) was unforeseeable as of the close of the employer's taxable year. Thus, the presumption with respect to the receipt of an amount of compensation or benefit is not rebutted to the extent it was foreseeable, as of the end of the employer's taxable year, that the amount would be received after the applicable 2½ month period. For example, if, as of the end of the employer's taxable year, it is foreseeable that calculation of a year-end bonus to be paid to an employee under a given formula will not be completed and thus the bonus will not be received (and is in fact not received) by the end of the applicable 2½ month period, the presumption that the bonus is deferred compensation is not rebutted.

(c) A plan, or method or arrangement, shall not be considered as deferring the receipt of compensation or benefits for more than a brief period of time after the end of the employer's taxable year to the extent that compensation or benefits are received by the employee on or before the end of the applicable 2½ month period. Thus, for example, salary under an employment contract or a bonus under a year-end bonus declaration is not considered paid under a plan, or method or arrangement, deferring the receipt of compensation to the extent that such salary or bonus is received by the employee on or before the end of the applicable 2½ month period.

(d) Solely for purposes of applying the rules of paragraphs (b) and (c) of this Q&A, in the case of an employer's taxable year ending on or after July 18, 1984, and on or before March 21, 1986, compensation or benefits that relate to services rendered in such taxable year shall be deemed to have been received within the applicable 2½ month period if such receipt actually occurs after such 2½ month period but on or before March 21, 1986.

Q-3. When does section 404(b), as amended by the Tax Reform Act of 1984, become effective?

A-3. With the exceptions discussed below, section 404(b), as amended, and the rules under Q&A-2 are effective with respect to amounts paid or incurred after July 18, 1984, in taxable years of employers (and payors) ending after that date. In the case of an extended vacation pay plan maintained pursuant to a collective bargaining agreement (a) between employee representatives and one or more employers, and (b) in effect on June 22, 1984, section 404(b) is not effective before the date on which such collective bargaining agreement terminates (determined without regard to any extension thereof agreed to after June 22, 1984). For purposes of the preceding sentence, any plan amendment made pursuant to a collective bargaining agreement relating to the plan which amends the plan solely to conform to any requirement added under section 512 of the Tax Reform Act of 1984 shall not be treated as a termination of such collective bargaining agreement. For purposes of this section, an "extended vacation pay plan" is one under which covered employees gradually over a specified period of years earn the right to additional vacation benefits, no part of which, under the terms of the plan, can be taken until the end of the specified period.

T.D. 8073, 1/29/86, amend T.D. 8435, 9/18/92.

### § 1.404(c)-1 Certain negotiated plans; effect of section 404(c).

*Caution:* The Treasury has not yet amended Reg § 1.404(c)-1 to reflect changes made by P.L. 93-406.

**(a)** Section 404(a) does not apply to deductions for contributions paid by an employer under a negotiated plan which meets the following conditions:

*(1)* The contributions under the plan are held in trust for the purpose of paying, either from principal or income or both, for the benefit of employees and their families, at least medical or hospital care, and pensions on retirement or death of employees; and

*(2)* Such plan was established before January 1, 1954, as a result of an agreement between employee representatives and the Government of the United States during a period of Government operation, under seizure powers, of a major part of the productive facilities of the industry in which such employer is engaged.

If these conditions are met, such contributions shall be deductible under section 162, to the extent that they constitute ordinary and necessary business expenses.

**(b)** The term "as a result of an agreement" is intended primarily to cover a trust established under the terms of an agreement referred to in paragraph (a)(2) of this section. It will also include a trust established under a plan of an employer, or group of employers, who are in competition with the employers whose facilities were seized by reason of producing the same commodity, and who would therefore be expected to establish such a trust as a reasonable measure to maintain a sound position in the labor market producing the commodity. Thus, for example, if a trust was established under such an agreement in the bituminous coal industry, a similar trust established about the same time in the anthracite coal industry would be covered by this provision.

**(c)** If any such trust becomes qualified for exemption under section 501(a), the deductibility of contributions by an employer to such trust on or after the date of such qualification would no longer be governed by section 404(c), even though the trust may later lose its exemption under section 501(a).

T.D. 6203, 9/24/56.

### § 1.404(d)-1T Questions and answers relating to deductibility of deferred compensation and deferred benefits for independent contractors (temporary).

Q-1. How does the amendment of section 404(b) by the Tax Reform Act of 1984 affect the deduction of contributions or compensation under section 404(d)?

A-1. As amended by the Tax Reform Act of 1984, section 404(b) clarifies that section 404(d) shall govern the deduction of contributions paid and compensation paid or incurred by a payor under a plan, or method or arrangement, deferring the receipt of compensation or providing for deferred benefits for service providers with respect to which there is no employer-employee relationship. In such a case, section 404(a) and (b) and the regulations thereunder apply as if the person providing the services were the employee and the person to whom the services are provided were the employer. Section 404(a) requires that such a contribution or compensation be paid or incurred for purposes of section 162 or 212 and satisfy the requirements for deductibility under either of those sections. However, notwithstanding the above, section 404 does not apply to contributions paid or accrued with respect to a "welfare benefit fund" (as defined in section 419(e)) after June 18, 1984, in taxable years of employers (and payors) ending after that date. Also, section 463 shall govern the deduction of vacation pay by a taxpayer that has elected under such section. For rules relating to the deduction of contributions paid or accrued with respect to a welfare benefit fund, see section 419, § 1.419-1T and § 1.419A-2T. For rules relating to the deduction of vacation pay for which an election is made under section 463, see § 301.9100-16T of this chapter and § 1.463-1T.

T.D. 8073, 1/29/86, amend T.D. 8435, 9/18/92.

### § 1.404(e)-1 Contributions on behalf of a self-employed individual to or under a pension, annuity, or profit-sharing plan meeting the requirements of section 401; application of section 404(a)(8), (9), and (10) and section 404(e) and (f).

**(a) In general.** *(1)* The Self-Employed Individuals Tax Retirement Act of 1962 (76 Stat. 809) permits certain self-employed individuals to be treated as employees for purposes of pension, annuity, and profit-sharing plans included in paragraph (1), (2), or (3) of section 404(a). Therefore, for taxable years of an employer beginning after December 31, 1962, employer contributions to qualified plans on behalf of self-employed individuals are deductible under section 404 subject to the limitations of paragraphs (b) and (c) of this section.

*(2)* In the case of contributions to qualified plans on behalf of self-employed individuals, the amount deductible differs from the amount allowed as a deduction. In general, the amount deductible is 10 percent of the earned income derived by the self-employed individual from the trade or business with respect to which the plan is established, or $2,500, whichever is the lesser. This is the amount referred to in section 401 when reference is made to the amounts which may be deducted under section 404 or the amount of contributions deductible under section 404. Thus, this is the amount taken into consideration in determining whether contributions under the plan are discriminatory. The amount allowed as a deduction with respect to contributions on behalf of a self-employed individual is one-half of the amount deductible. The amount allowed as a deduction is relevant only for purposes of determining the amount an employer may deduct from gross income.

**(b) Determination of the amount deductible.** *(1)* If a plan covers employees, some of whom are self-employed individuals, the determination of the amount deductible is made on the basis of independent consideration of the common-law employees and of the self-employed individuals. See subparagraphs (2) and (3) of this paragraph. For purposes of determining the amount deductible with respect to contributions on behalf of a self-employed individual, such contributions shall be considered to satisfy the conditions of section 162 (relating to trade or business expenses) or 212 (relating to expenses for the production of income), but only to the extent that such contributions do not exceed the earned income of such individual derived from the trade or business with respect to which the plan is established. However, the portion of such contribution, if any, attributable to the purchase of life, accident, health, or other insurance protection shall be considered payment of a personal expense which does not satisfy the requirements of section 162 or 212. See paragraph (f) of this section. For the additional rules applicable where contributions are made by more than one employer on behalf of a self-employed individual, see paragraph (d) of this section.

*(2)* If contributions are made to a plan included in section 404(a)(1), (2), or (3) on behalf of employees, some of whom are self-employed individuals, the amount deductible with respect to contributions on behalf of the common-law employees covered under the plan shall be determined as if such employees were the only employees for whom contributions and benefits are provided under the plan. Accordingly, for purposes of such determination, the percentage of compensation limitations of section 404(a)(1), (3), and (7) are applicable only with respect to the compensation otherwise paid or accrued during the taxable year by the employer to the common-law employees. Similarly, the costs referred to in section 404(a)(1)(B) and (C) shall be the costs of funding the benefits of the common-law employees. Also, the provisions of section 404(a)(1)(D), (3), and (7), relating to certain carryover deductions, shall be applicable only to amounts contributed, or to the amounts deductible, on behalf of such employees.

*(3)* If contributions are made to a plan included in section 404(a)(1), (2), or (3) on behalf of individuals some or all of whom are self-employed individuals, the amount deductible in any taxable year with respect to contributions on behalf of such individuals shall be determined as follows:

(i) The provisions of section 404(a)(1), (2), (3), and (7) shall be applied as if such individuals were the only participants for whom contributions and benefits are provided under the plan. Thus, the costs referred to in such provisions shall be the costs of funding the benefits of the self-employed individuals. If such costs are less than an amount equal to the amount determined under subdivision (iii) of this subparagraph, the maximum amount deductible with respect to such individuals shall be the costs of their benefits.

(ii) The provisions of section 404(a)(1)(D), the second and third sentences of section 404(a)(3)(A), and the second sentence of section 404(a)(7), relating to certain carryover deductions, are not applicable to contributions on behalf of self-employed individuals. Contributions on behalf of self-employed individuals are deductible, if at all, only in the taxable year in which the contribution is paid or deemed paid under section 404(a)(6).

(iii) The amount deductible for the taxable year of the employer with respect to contributions on behalf of a self-employed individual shall not exceed the lesser of $2,500 or 10 percent of the earned income derived by such individual for such taxable year from the trade or business with respect to which the plan is established.

(iv) If a self-employed individual receives in any taxable year earned income with respect to which deductions are allowable to two or more employers, the aggregate amounts deductible shall not exceed the lesser of $2,500 or 10 percent of such earned income. See paragraph (d) of this section.

**(c) Special limitation on the amount allowed as a deduction for self-employed individuals.** The amount allowed as a deduction under section 404(a)(1), (2), (3), and (7) in any taxable year with respect to contributions made on behalf of a self-employed individual shall be an amount equal to one-half of the amount deductible with respect to such contributions under paragraph (b)(3) of this section. However, for purposes of section 401, the amount which may be deducted, or the amount deductible, under section 404 with respect to contributions made on behalf of self-employed individuals shall be determined without regard to the special limitation of this paragraph.

**(d) Rules applicable where contributions are made by more than one employer on behalf of a self-employed individual.** *(1)* Under paragraph (b)(3)(iv) of this section, if a self-employed individual receives in any taxable year earned income with respect to which deductions are allowable to two or more employers, the aggregate amounts deductible shall not exceed the lesser of $2,500 or 10 percent of such earned income. This limitation does not apply to contributions made under a plan on behalf of an employee who is not self-employed in the trade or business with respect to which the plan is established, even though such employee may be covered as a self-employed individual under a plan or plans established by other trades or businesses.

*(2)* In any case in which the application of subparagraph (1) of this paragraph reduces the amount otherwise deductible, the amount deductible by each employer shall be that amount which bears the same ratio to the aggregate amount deductible with respect to all trades or businesses (as determined in subparagraph (1) of this paragraph) as the earned income derived from that employer bears to the aggregate of the earned income derived from all of the trades or businesses with respect to which plans are established. The amount allowed as a deduction to each employer is one-half of the amount determined (in accordance with the preceding sentence) to be deductible by such employer.

**(e) Partner's distributive share of contributions and deductions.** For purposes of sections 702(a)(8) and 704, a partner's distributive share of contributions on behalf of self-employed individuals under a qualified pension, annuity, or profit-sharing plan is the contribution made on his behalf, and his distributive share of deductions allowed the partnership under section 404 for contributions on behalf of self-employed individuals is that portion of the deduction which is attributable to contributions made on his behalf under the plan. The contribution on behalf of a partner and the deduction with respect thereto must be accounted for separately by such partner, for his taxable year with or within which the partnership's taxable year ends, as an item described in section 702(a)(8).

**(f) Contributions allocable to insurance protection.** For purposes of determining the amount deductible with respect to contributions on behalf of a self-employed individual, amounts allocable to the purchase of life, accident, health, or other insurance protection shall not be taken into account. Such amounts are neither deductible nor considered as contributions for purposes of determining the maximum amount of contributions that may be made on behalf of an owner-employee. The amount of a contribution allocable to insurance shall be an amount equal to a reasonable net premium cost, as determined by the Commissioner, for such amount of insurance for the appropriate period. See paragraph (b)(5) of § 1.72-16.

**(g) Rules applicable to loans.** For purposes of section 404, any amount paid, directly or indirectly, by an owner-employee in repayment of any loan which under section 72(m)(4)(B) was treated as an amount received from a qualified trust or plan shall be treated as a contribution to such trust or under such plan on behalf of such owner-employee.

**(h) Definitions.** For purposes of section 404 and the regulations thereunder—

*(1)* The term "employee" includes an employee as defined in section 401(c)(1) and paragraph (b) of § 1.401-10, and the term "employer" means the person treated as the employer of such individual under section 401(c)(4);

*(2)* The term "owner-employee" means an owner-employee as defined in section 401(c)(3) and paragraph (d) of § 1.401-10;

*(3)* The term "earned income" means earned income as defined in section 401(c)(2) and paragraph (c) of § 1.401-10; and

*(4)* The term "compensation" when used with respect to an individual who is an employee described in subparagraph (1) of this paragraph shall be considered to be a reference to the earned income of such individual derived from the trade or business with respect to which the plan is established.

**(i) Years to which this section applies.** This section applies to taxable years of employers beginning before January 1, 1974. For taxable years beginning after December 31, 1973, see § 1.404(e)-1A.

---

T.D. 6676, 9/16/63, amend T.D. 7636, 8/9/79.

---

### § 1.404(e)-1A Contributions on behalf of a self-employed individual to or under a qualified pension, annuity, or profit-sharing plan.

***Caution:*** The Treasury has not yet amended Reg § 1.404(e)-1A to reflect changes made by P.L. 100-647, P.L. 99-514, P.L. 98-369, P.L. 97-248.

**(a) In general.** This section provides rules relating to employer contributions to qualified plans on behalf of self-employed individuals described in subsections (a)(8) and (9), (e), and (f) of section 404. Unless otherwise specifically provided, this section applies to taxable years of an employer beginning after December 31, 1973. See section 1.404(e)-1 for rules relating to plans for self-employed individuals for taxable years beginning before January 1, 1974. Paragraph (b) of this section provides general rules of deductibility, paragraph (c) provides rules relating to defined contribution plans, paragraph (d) provides rules relating to defined benefit plans, paragraph (e) provides rules relating to combinations of plans, paragraph (f) provides rules for partnerships, paragraph (g) provides rules for insurance, paragraph (h) provides rules for loans, and paragraph (i) provides definitions.

**(b) Determination of the amount deductible.** *(1)* If a defined contribution plan covers employees, some of whom are self-employed individuals, the determination of the amount deductible is made on the basis of independent consideration of the common-law employees and of the self-employed individuals. See subparagraphs (2) and (3) of this paragraph. For purposes of determining the amount deductible with respect to contributions on behalf of a self-employed individual, such contributions shall be considered to satisfy the conditions of section 162 (relating to trade or business expenses) or 212 (relating to expenses for the production of income), but only to the extent that such contributions do not exceed the earned income of such individual derived from the trade or business with respect to which the plan is established. However, the portion of such contribution, if any, attributable to the purchase of life, accident, health, or other insurance protection shall be considered payment of a personal expense which does not satisfy the requirements of section 162 or 212. See paragraph (g) of this section.

*(2)* (i) If contributions are made on behalf of employees, some of whom are self-employed individuals, to a defined contribution plan described in section 414(i) and included in section 404(a)(1), (2), or (3), the amount deductible with respect to contributions on behalf of the common-law employees covered under the plan shall be determined as if such employees were the only employees for whom contributions and benefits are provided under the plan. Accordingly, for purposes of such determination, the percentage of compensation limitations of section 404(a)(3) and (7) are applicable only with respect to the compensation otherwise paid or accrued during the taxable year by the employer with respect to the common-law employees. Similarly, the costs referred to in section 404(a)(1)(A) and (B) shall be the costs of funding the benefits of the common-law employees. Also, the provisions of section 404(a)(1)(D), (3), and (7), relating to certain carryover deductions, shall be applicable only to amounts contributed or to the amounts deductible on behalf of such employees.

(ii) The amount deductible, by reason of contributions on behalf of employees to a defined benefit plan, shall be determined without regard to the self-employed or common law status of each employee.

*(3)* (i) If contributions are made on behalf of individuals, some or all of whom are self-employed individuals, to a defined contribution plan described in section 414(i) and included in section 404(a)(1), (2), or (3), the amount deductible in any taxable year with respect to contributions on behalf of such individuals shall be determined as follows:

(A) The provisions of section 404(a)(1), (2), (3), and (7) shall be applied as if such individuals were the only participants for whom contributions and benefits are provided under the plan. Thus, the costs referred to in such provisions shall be the costs of funding the benefits of the self-employed individuals. If such costs are less than an amount equal to the amount determined under paragraph (c) of this section, the maximum amount deductible with respect to such individuals shall be the cost of their benefits.

(B) The provisions of section 404(a)(1), (D), the third sentence of section 404(a)(3), (A), and the second sentence of section 404(a)(7), relating to certain carryover deductions are applicable to contributions on behalf of self-employed individuals made in taxable years of an employer beginning after December 31, 1975.

(C) For any employer taxable year in applying the 15 percent limit on deductible contributions set forth section in 404(a)(3) and the 25 percent limit in section 404(a)(7) for any taxable year of the employer, the amount deductible under section 404(e)(4) and paragraph (c)(4) of this section (relating to the minimum deduction of $750 or 100 percent of earned income) shall be substituted for such limits with respect to the self-employed individuals on whose behalf contributions are deductible under section 404(e)(4) for the taxable year of the employer. In addition, although the limitations of section 415 are applicable to the plan for plan years beginning after December 31, 1975, the defined contribution compensation limitation described in section 415(c)(1)(B) shall not be less than the amount deductible under section 404(e)(4) and paragraph (c)(4) of this section with respect to any self-employed individual for the taxable year of the employer ending with or within the limitation year. The special rule in the second sentence of paragraph (3)(A) of section 404(a) is not applicable in determining the amounts deductible on behalf of self-employed individuals.

(ii) The limitations of this subparagraph are not applicable to a defined benefit plan for self-employed individuals.

**(c) Defined contribution plans.** *(1)* Under section 404(e)(1) in the case of a defined contribution plan, as defined in section 414(i), the amount deductible for the taxable year of the employer with respect to contributions on behalf of a self-employed individual shall not exceed the lesser of $7,500 or 15 percent of the earned income derived by such individual for such taxable year from the trade or business with respect to which the plan is established.

*(2)* Under section 404(e)(2)(A) if a self-employed individual receives in any taxable year earned income with respect to which deductions are allowable to two or more employers under two or more defined contribution plans the aggregate amounts deductible shall not exceed the lesser of $7,500 or 15 percent of such earned income. This limitation does not apply to contributions made under a plan on behalf of an employee who is not self-employed in the trade or business with respect to which the plan is established.

*(3)* Under section 404(e)(2)(B) in any case in which the applicable limitation of subparagraph (2) of this paragraph reduces the amount otherwise deductible with respect to contributions on behalf of any employee within the meaning of section 401(c)(1), the amount deductible by each employer for such employee shall be that amount which bears the same ratio to the aggregate amount deductible for such employee with respect to all trades or businesses (as determined in subparagraph (1) of this paragraph) as his earned income derived from the employer bears to the aggregate of his earned income derived from all of the trades or businesses with respect to which plans are established.

Under section 404(e)(4), notwithstanding the provisions of subparagraphs (1) and (2) of this paragraph, the limitations on the amount deductible for the taxable year of the employer with respect to contributions on behalf of a self-employed individual shall not be less than the lesser of $750 or 100 percent of the earned income derived by such individual for such taxable year from the trade or business with respect to which the plan is established. If such individual receives in any taxable year earned income with respect to which deductions are allowable to two or more employers, 100 percent of such earned income shall be taken into account for purposes of the limitations determined under this subparagraph. This subparagraph does not apply to any taxable year beginning after December 31, 1975, to any employee whose adjusted gross income for that taxable year is greater than $15,000. In applying the preceding sentence, the adjusted gross income of an employee for a taxable year is determined separately for each individual, without regard to any community property laws, and without regard to the deduction allowable under section 404(a).

**(d) Defined benefit plans.** In the case of a defined benefit plan, as defined in section 401(j), the special limitations provided by section 404(e) and paragraph (c) of this section do not apply. See section 401(j) for requirements applicable to defined benefit plans.

**(e) Combination of plans.** For special rules applied if a self-employed individual in any taxable year is a participant in both a defined benefit plan and a defined contribution plan, see section 401(j) and the regulations thereunder.

**(f) Partner's distributive share of contributions and deductions.** *(1)* For purposes of sections 702(a)(8) and 704 in the case of a defined contribution plan, a partner's distributive share of contributions on behalf of self-employed individuals under such a plan is the contribution made on his behalf, and his distributive share of deductions allowed the partnership under section 404 for contributions on behalf of a self-employed individual is that portion of the deduction which is attributable to contributions made on his behalf under the plan. The contribution on behalf of a partner and the deduction with respect thereto must be accounted for separately by such partner, for his taxable year with or within which the partnership's taxable year ends, as an item described in section 702(a)(8).

*(2)* In the case of a defined benefit plan, a partner's distributive share of contributions on behalf of self-employed individuals and his distributive share of deductions allowed the partnership under section 404 for such contributions is determined in the same manner as his distributive share of partnership taxable income. See section 704, relating to the determination of the distributive share and the regulations thereunder.

**(g) Contributions allocable to insurance protection.** Under Section 404(e)(3), for purposes of determining the amount deductible with respect to contributions on behalf of a self-employed individual, amounts allocable to the purchase of life, accident, health, or other insurance protection shall not be taken into account. Such amounts are neither deductible nor considered as contributions for purposes of determining the maximum amount of contributions that may be made on behalf of an owner-employee. The amount of a contribution allocable to insurance shall be an amount equal to a reasonable net premium cost, as determined by the Commissioner, for such amount of insurance for the appropriate period. See paragraph (b)(5) of § 1.72-16.

**(h) Rules applicable to loans.** Under section 404(f), for purposes of section 404, any amount paid, directly or indirectly, by an owner-employee in repayment of any loan which under section 72(m)(4)(B) was treated as an amount received from a qualified trust or plan shall be treated as a contribution to such trust or under such plan on behalf of such owner-employee.

**(i) Definitions.** Under section 404(a)(8), for purposes of section 404 and the regulations thereunder—

*(1)* The term "employee" includes an employee as defined in section 401(c)(1) and the term "employer" means the person treated as the employer of such individual under section 401(c)(4);

*(2)* The term "owner-employee" means an owner-employee as defined in section 401(c)(3);

*(3)* The term "earned income" means earned income as defined in section 401(c)(2); and

*(4)* The term "compensation" when used with respect to an individual who is an employee described in subparagraph (1) of this paragraph shall be considered to be a reference to the earned income of such individual derived from the trade or business with respect to which the plan is established.

T.D. 7636, 8/9/79.

**§ 1.404(g)-1 Deduction of employer liability payments.**

***Caution:*** The Treasury has not yet amended Reg § 1.404(g)-1 to reflect changes made by P.L. 99-272.

**(a) General rule.** Employer liability payments shall be treated as contributions to a stock bonus, pension, profit-sharing, or annuity plan to which section 404 applies. Such payments that satisfy the limitations of this section shall be deductible under section 404 when paid without regard to any other limitations in section 404.

**(b) Employer liability payments.** For purposes of this section, employer liability payments mean:

*(1)* Any payment to the Pension Benefit Guaranty Corporation (PBGC) for termination or withdrawal liability imposed under section 4062 (without regard to section 4062(b)(2)), 4063, or 4064 of the Employee Retirement Insurance Security Act of 1974 (ERISA). Any bond or escrow payment furnished under section 4063 of ERISA shall not be considered as a payment of liability until applied against the liability of the employer.

*(2)* Any payment to a non-multiemployer plan pursuant to a commitment to the PBGC made in accordance with PBGC Determination of Plan Sufficiency and Termination of Sufficient Plans. See PBGC regulations, 29 CFR 2617.13(b) for rules concerning these commitments. Such payments shall not exceed an amount necessary to provide for, and used to fund, the benefits guaranteed under section 4022 or ERISA.

*(3)* Any payment to a multiemployer plan for withdrawal liability imposed under part 1 of subtitle E of title IV of ERISA. Any bond or escrow payment furnished under such part shall not be considered as a payment of liability until applied against the liability of the employer.

**(c) Limitations, etc.** *(1) Permissible expenses.* A payment shall be deductible under section 404(g) and this section only if the payment satisfies the conditions of section 162 or section 212. Payments made by an entity which is liable for such payments because it is a member of a commonly controlled group of corporations, or trades or businesses, within the meaning of section 414(b) or (c), shall not fail to satisfy such conditions merely because the entity did not directly employ participants in the plan with respect to which the liability payments were made.

*(2) Qualified plan.* A payment shall be deductible under section 404(g) and this section only if the payment is made in a taxable year of the employer ending within or with a taxable year of the trust for which the trust is exempt under section 501(a). For purposes of this paragraph, the payment timing rules of section 404(a)(6) shall apply.

*(3) Full funding limitation.* (i) If the employer liability payment is to a plan, the total amount deductible for such payment and for other plan contributions may not exceed an amount equal to the full funding limitation as defined in section 412(c)(7) for the taxable year with respect to which the contributions are deemed made under section 404.

(ii) If the total contributions to the plan for the taxable year including the employer liability payment exceed the amount equal to this full funding limitation, the employer liability payment shall be deductible first.

(iii) Any amount paid in a taxable year in excess of the amount deductible in such year under the full funding limitation shall be treated as a liability payment and be deductible in the succeeding taxable years in order of time to the extent of the difference between the employer liability payments made in each succeeding year and the maximum amount deductible for such year under the full funding limitation.

*(4) Maximum deduction allowable under section 404.* The amount deductible under section 404 is limited to the higher of the maximum amount deductible by the employer under section 404(a) or the amount otherwise deductible under section 404(g). If the contributions are to a plan to which more than one employer contributes, this limit shall apply to each employer separately rather than all employers in the aggregate. Thus, each employer may deduct the greater of its allocable share of the deduction determined under sections 404(a) and 413(b)(7) or 413(c)(6) or its allocable share of the amount deductible under section 404(g).

However, pursuant to the rule in subdivision (ii) of subparagraph (3), in determining each employer's allocable share under section 404(a), the total amount deductible under section 404(a) by all employers shall not exceed the difference between the full funding limitation and the total amount deductible by all employers under section 404(g).

*(5) Example.* The provisions of this paragraph may be illustrated by the following example:

*Example.* In the 1983 taxable year, Employer A makes a withdrawal liability payment of $700,000 to multiemployer Plan X to which Employer A and Employer B are required to contribute. Employer A's allocable share of the deduction allowable under sections 404(a) and 413(b)(7) in the 1983 taxable year is $600,000. Employer B's allocable share of the deduction allowable under section 404(a) and 413(b)(7) in the 1983 taxable year is $400,000.

The full funding limitation for the 1983 taxable year is $1,000,000. Based on paragraph (c)(4) of this section, Employer A may deduct $700,000, the amount of the withdrawal liability payment. However, the deduction of Employer B is limited to $300,000, the difference between the full funding limitation and the amount deductible under section 404(g).

**(d) Effective date etc.** *(1) General rule.* This section is effective for employer payments made after September 25, 1980.

*(2) Transitional rule.* For employer payments made before September 26, 1980, for purposes of section 404, any amount paid by an employer under section 4062, 4063, or 4064 of the Employee Retirement Income Security Act of 1974 shall be treated as a contribution to which section 404 applies by such employer to or under a stock bonus, pension, profit-sharing, or annuity plan.

T.D. 8085, 5/1/86.

**Proposed § 1.404(h)-1 Special rules for simplified employee pensions.** [*For Preamble, see ¶ 150,703*]

***Caution:*** The Treasury has not yet amended Reg § 1.404(h)-1 to reflect changes made by P.L. 107-147.

**(a) In general.** *(1)* Employer contributions to a simplified employee pension shall be treated as if they are made to a plan subject to the requirements of section 404. Employer contributions to a simplified employee pension are subject to the limitations of subparagraphs (2), (3), (4) and (5). For purposes of this paragraph participants means those employees who satisfy the age, service and other requirements to participate in a simplified employee pension. For purposes of this paragraph, "compensation" means all of the compensation paid by the employer except either that for which a deduction is allowable under section 404(h) for simplified employee pensions or that for which a deduction is allowable under a plan that qualifies under section 401(a), including a plan that qualifies under section 404(a)(2) or 405.

*(2)* Employer contributions made for a calendar year are deductible for the taxable year of the employer with which or within which the calendar year ends.

*(3)* Contributions made within 3½ months after the close of a calendar year are treated as if they were made on the last day of such calendar year if they are made on account of such calendar year.

*(4)* The amount deductible for a taxable year for a simplified employee pension shall not exceed 15 percent of the compensation paid to the employees who are participants during the calendar year ending with or within the taxable year.

*(5)* The excess of the amount contributed over the amount deductible for a taxable year shall be deductible in the succeeding taxable years in order of time subject to the 15 percent limit of subparagraph (4).

**(b) Effect on stock bonus and profit-sharing trust.** For any taxable year for which the employer has a deduction under section 404(h)(1), the otherwise applicable limitations in section 404(a)(3)(A) shall be reduced by the amount of the allowable deductions under section 404(h)(1) with respect to participants in the stock bonus or profit-sharing trust.

**(c) Effect on limit on deductions.** For any taxable year for which the employer has a allowable deduction under section 404(h)(1), the otherwise applicable 25 percent limitations in section 404(a)(7) shall be reduced by the amount of the allowable deductions under section 404(h)(1) with respect to participants in the stock bonus or profit-sharing trust.

**(d) Effect on self-employed individuals or shareholder-employee.** The limitations described in paragraphs (1), (2)(A), and (4) of section 404(e) or described in section 1379(b)(1) for any taxable year shall be reduced by the amount of the allowable deductions under section 404(h)(1) with respect to an employee within the meaning of section 401(c)(1) or a shareholder-employee (as defined in section 1379(d)).

**(e) Examples.** The provisions of this section may be illustrated by the following examples:

*Example (1).* Corporation X is a calendar-year taxpayer. On January 2, 1980, it adopts a simplified employee pension arrangement. At the end of 1980, it determines that it has paid $230,000 to all of its employees. Eight of its employees met its eligibility provisions for contributions to simplified employee pensions and their compensation totaled $140,000 before any contributions were made to their simplified employee pensions. Corporation X will be allowed to deduct its contributions to its employees' simplified employee pensions, not to exceed 15% of $140,000 or $21,000.

*Example (2).* Corporation Y is a calendar-year taxpayer which maintains a simplified employee pension agreement and a profit-sharing plan. The corporation has 100 employees. For the taxable year of 1980, it makes contributions to the simplified employee pensions of 75 of its employees. These contributions are 10 percent of compensation received in 1980. These same 75 employees are also participants in the corporation's profit-sharing plan. These 75 employees had total compensation paid during 1980 of $1,125,000. The corporation can deduct $112,500 under section 404(h) as its contributions to the simplified employee pension agreement. The corporation must reduce the otherwise applicable allowable deduction for contributions to the profit-sharing plan on behalf of these employees by the $112,500.

*Example (3).* Corporation Z is a calendar-year taxpayer which maintains a simplified employee pension arrangement and a profit-sharing plan. The corporation has 100 employees. For the taxable year 1980, it make contributions to the simplified employee pensions of 75 of its employees. These contributions are 10 percent of compensation received in 1980. Twenty-five of these employees are also participants in the corporation's profit-sharing plan. Each of these 75 employees had compensation for the year of $15,000, or total compensation of $1,125,000. The corporation deducts $112,500 under section 404(h) as its contribution to the simplified employee pension arrangement. The corporation must reduce the otherwise applicable allowable deduction for contributions to the profit-sharing plan on behalf of the 25 employees by $37,500, the amount contributed to the simplified employee pensions on behalf of employees covered by the profit-sharing plan.

*Example (4).* Corporation K is a taxpayer with a taxable year of December 1–November 30. On December 15, 1979, it adopts a simplified employee pension arrangement for its employees. It would like to make contributions to the plan on behalf of its employees for calendar year 1979. In order to make contributions to its employees' simplified employee pensions for calendar year 1979, the corporation must make the contributions by April 15, 1980. In order to receive a deduction for its taxable year ending November 30, 1980, for the contributions for calendar year 1979, the corporation must make the contributions by April 15, 1980.

**§ 1.404(k)-1T Questions and answers relating to the deductibility of certain dividend distributions (temporary).**

***Caution:*** The Treasury has not yet amended Reg § 1.404(k)-1T to reflect changes made by P.L. 107-147, P.L. 107-16, P.L. 104-188, P.L. 101-239, P.L. 99-514.

Q-1. What does section 404(k) provide?

A-1. Section 404(k) allows a corporation a deduction for dividends actually paid in accordance with section 404(k)(2) with respect to stock of such corporation held by an employee stock ownership plan (as defined in section 4975(e)(7)) maintained by the corporation (or by any other corporation that is a member of a "controlled group of corporations" within the meaning of section 409(l)(4) that includes the corporation), but only if such dividends may be immediately distributed under the terms of the plan and all of the applicable qualification and distribution rules. The deduction is allowed under section 404(k) for the taxable year of the corporation during which the dividends are received by the participants.

Q-2. Is the deductibility of dividends paid to plan participants under section 404(k) affected by a plan provision which permits participants to elect to receive or not receive payment of dividends?

A-2. No. Dividends actually paid in cash to plan participants in accordance with section 404(k) are deductible under section 404(k) despite such an election provision.

Q-3. Are dividends paid in cash directly to plan participants by the corporation and dividends paid to the plan and then distributed in cash to plan participants under section 404(k) treated as distributions under the plan holding stock to which the dividends relate for purposes of sections 72, 401 and 402?

A-3. Generally, yes. However, a deductible dividend under section 404(k) is treated for purposes of section 72 as paid under a contract separate from any other contract that is part of the plan. Thus, a deductible dividend is treated as a plan distribution and as paid under a separate contract providing only for payment of deductible dividends. Therefore, a deductible dividend under section 404(k) is a taxable plan distribution even though an employee has unrecovered employee contributions or basis in the plan.

T.D. 8073, 1/29/86.

**Proposed § 1.404(k)-2 Dividends paid by corporation not maintaining ESOP.** [*For Preamble, see ¶ 152,691*]

• ***Caution:*** This Notice of Proposed Rulemaking was partially finalized by TD 9282, 08/26/2006. Prop. reg. 1.404(k)-2 remains proposed.

Q-1. What corporation is entitled to the deduction provided under section 404(k) for applicable dividends paid on applicable employer securities of a C corporation held by an ESOP if the ESOP benefits employees of more than one corporation or if the corporation paying the dividend is not the corporation maintaining the plan?

A-1. **(a) In general.** Under section 404(k), only the corporation paying the dividend is entitled to the deduction with respect to applicable employer securities held by an ESOP. Thus, no deduction is permitted to a corporation maintaining the ESOP if that corporation does not pay the dividend.

**(b) Example.** (i) Facts. S is a U.S. corporation that is wholly owned by P, an entity organized under the laws of Country A that is classified as a corporation for Federal income tax purposes. P is not engaged in a U.S. trade or business. P has a single class of common stock that is listed on a stock exchange in a foreign country. In addition, these shares are listed on the New York Stock Exchange, in the form of American Depositary Shares, and are actively traded through American Depositary Receipts (ADRs) meeting the requirements of section 409(l). S maintains an ESOP for its employees. The ESOP holds ADRs of P on Date X and receives a dividend with respect to those employer securities. The dividends received by the ESOP constitute applicable dividends as described in section 404(k)(2).

(ii) Conclusion. P, as the payor of the dividend, is entitled to a deduction under section 404(k) with respect to the dividends, although as a foreign corporation P does not obtain a U.S. tax benefit from the deduction. No corporation other than the corporation paying the dividend is entitled to the deduction under section 404(k). Thus, because S did not pay the dividends, S is not entitled to a deduction under section 404(k). The answer would be the same if P is a U.S. C corporation.

Q-2. What is the effective date of this section?

A-2. This section applies with respect to dividends paid on or after the date these regulations are published as final regulations in the Federal Register.

**§ 1.404(k)-3 Disallowance of deduction for reacquisition payments.**

Q-1. Are payments to reacquire stock held by an ESOP applicable dividends that are deductible under section 404(k)(1)?

A-1. (a) Payments to reacquire stock held by an ESOP, including reacquisition payments that are used to make benefit distributions to participants or beneficiaries, are not deductible under section 404(k) because—

(1) Those payments do not constitute applicable dividends under section 404(k)(2); and

(2) The treatment of those payments as applicable dividends would constitute, in substance, an avoidance or evasion of taxation within the meaning of section 404(k)(5).

(b) See also § 1.162(k)-1 concerning the disallowance of deductions for amounts paid or incurred by a corporation in connection with the reacquisition of its stock from an ESOP.

Q-2. What is the effective date of this section?

A-2. This section applies with respect to payments to reacquire stock that are made on or after August 30, 2006.

T.D. 9282, 8/29/2006.

**Proposed § 1.404A-0 Table of contents.** [*For Preamble, see ¶ 151,519*]

This section 1.404A-0 lists the major headings that appear in §§ 1.404A-1 through 1.404A-7.

Closing year.
Contributions accumulated to pay deferred compensation.
Contributions to a trust.
Controlled foreign corporation.
Cumulative foreign amount.
Cumulative limitation.
Cumulative United States amount.
Deductions.
Earnings and profits.
Employer.
Equivalent of a trust.
Erroneous deduction.
Exclusive benefit.
Fixed or determinable benefits.
Full funding limitation.
Functional currency.
Funded method.
Initial aggregate amount.
Initial Cumulative foreign amount.
Initial Cumulative United States amount.
Initial section 404A(d) amounts.
Liability.
Majority domestic corporate shareholders.
Method of accounting.
Method (1) election.
Method (2) election.
New Method Opening Amount.
Noncontrolled foreign corporation.
Nonqualified individual.
Nonqualified plan.
Old Method Closing Amount.
Open period.
Open years.
Opening reserve.
Opening year.
Pay-as-you-go method.
Period of adjustment.
Permitted plan year.
Plan year.
Primary evidence.
Prior deduction.
Protective election.
Qualified business unit.
Qualified foreign plan.
Qualified funded plan.
Qualified reserve plan.
Reasonable actuarial assumptions.
Reductions in earnings and profits.
Reserve method.
Retirement annuity.
Retroactive effective date election.
Retroactive plan-by-plan election.
Revocation of election.
Secondary evidence.
Separate funding entity.
Short taxable year.
Single plan.
Substantial risk of forfeiture.
Substantiation quality data.
Taxable year of a controlled foreign corporation.
Taxable year of a noncontrolled foreign corporation.
Taxpayer.
Termination of election.
Transition period.
Trust.
Unit credit method.
United States tax significance.
Written plan.

(f) Application of other Code requirements.
(1) Deductibility requirement.
(2) Section 461 requirements.

*§ 1.404A-2 Rules for qualified funded plans.*

(a) In general.
(b) Payment to a trust.
(1) Contribution requirements.
(2) Trust requirements.
(3) Retirement annuity.
(4) Effect of reversion of overfunded contributions.
(5) Example.
(c) Contribution deemed made before payment.
(1) Time of payment to trust.
(2) Time of designation.
(3) Irrevocable designation.
(d) Limitation for qualified funded plans.
(1) Plans with fixed or determinable benefits.
(2) Plans without fixed or determinable benefits.
(3) Limitations where more than one type of plan is maintained.
(4) Carryover contributions.
(5) Additional rules.
(e) Examples.

*§ 1.404A-3 Rules for qualified reserve plans.*

(a) Amounts taken into account with respect to qualified reserve plans.
(1) General rule.
(2) Amounts less than zero.
(3) Exclusive rules for qualified reserve plans.
(b) Reasonable addition to a reserve for liabilities.
(1) General rule.
(2) Unit credit method required.
(3) Timing of valuation.
(4) Permissible actuarial assumptions.
(c) Ten-year amortization for certain changes in reserves.
(1) Actuarial valuation.
(2) Expected value of reserve.
(3) Special rule for certain cost of living adjustments.
(4) Anti-abuse rule.
(d) Examples.

*§ 1.404A-4 United States and foreign law limitations on amounts taken into account for qualified foreign plans.*

(a) In general.

(b) Cumulative limitation.

(c) Special rule for foreign corporations in pre-pooling years.

(d) Rules relating to foreign currency.

(1) Taxable years beginning after December 31, 1986.

(2) Taxable years beginning before January 1, 1987.

(3) Special rules for the net worth method of accounting.

(e) Maintenance of more than one type of qualified foreign plan by an employer.

(f) United States and foreign law limitations not applicable.

(g) Definitions.

(1) Cumulative United States amount.

(2) Cumulative foreign amount.

(3) Appropriate foreign tax law.

(4) Aggregate amount.

(h) Examples.

*§ 1.404A-5 Additional limitations on amounts taken into account for qualified foreign plans.*

(a) Restrictions for nonqualified individuals.

(1) General rule.

(2) Determination of service attribution.

(b) Records to be provided by taxpayer.

(1) In general.

(2) Primary evidence.

(3) Additional requirements.

(4) Secondary evidence.

(5) Foreign language.

(6) Additional information required by District Director.

(7) Authorized officer to complete documents.

(8) Transitional rules.

(c) Actuarial requirements.

(1) Reasonable actuarial assumptions.

(2) Full funding limitation.

*§ 1.404A-6 Elections under section 404A and changes in methods of accounting.*

(a) Elections, changes in accounting methods, and changes in plan years.

(1) In general.

(2) Single plan.

(b) Initial elections under section 404A.

(1) In general.

(2) Time for making election.

(3) Manner in which election is to be made.

(4) Other requirements for election.

(c) Termination of election when a plan ceases to be a qualified foreign plan.

(1) In general.

(2) Rules for changing method of accounting upon termination of election.

(d) Other changes in methods of accounting and changes in plan year.

(1) Application for consent.

(2) Procedures for other changes in method of accounting.

(3) Plan year.

(e) Application of section 481.

(1) In general.

(2) Period of adjustment.

(3) Allocation and source.

(4) Example.

(f) Computation of section 481(a) adjustment.

(1) In general.

(2) Old Method Closing Amount.

(3) New Method Opening Amount.

(4) Definitions and special rules.

(5) Examples.

(g) Initial section 404A(d) amounts.

(1) In general.

(2) Computation of amounts.

(3) Example.

*§ 1.404A-7 Effective date. retroactive elections, and transition rules.*

(a) In general.

(1) Effective date.

(2) Overview of retroactive elections for taxable years beginning before January 1, 1980.

(3) Overview of special transition rules for election, revocation, and re-election.

(b) Retroactive effective date elections for foreign subsidiaries.

(1) In general.

(2) Time and manner to make, perfect, or revoke election.

(3) Requirement to amend returns.

(c) Retroactive plan-by-plan elections for foreign subsidiaries.

(1) In general.

(2) Time and manner to make, perfect, or revoke election.

(3) Requirement to amend returns.

(4) Revocation after initial election and re-election permitted.

(5) Examples.

(d) Retroactive plan-by-plan qualified funded plan elections for plans of foreign branches.

(1) In general.

(2) Amounts allowed as a deduction.

(3) Definitions.

(4) Time and manner to make, perfect, or revoke election.

(5) Examples.

(e) Special transition rules for election, revocation and re-election.

(1) In general.

(2) Time and manner initially to elect, revoke and reelect.

(3) Revocation after initial election and re-election permitted.

(4) Example.

(f) Special data rules for retroactive elections.

(1) Retroactive calculation of section 481(a) adjustments.

(2) Determination of reasonable addition to a reserve in interim years.

(3) Protective elections.

(g) Definitions and special rules.

(1) Method (1) election.

(2) Protective or Method (2) election.

(3) Open years of the taxpayer.

(4) Retroactive period.

(5) Transition period.

(6) Open period.

**Proposed § 1.404A-1 General rules concerning deductions and adjustments to earnings and profits for foreign deferred compensation plans.** [*For Preamble, see ¶ 151,519*]

**(a) In general.** Section 404A provides the exclusive means by which an employer may take a deduction or reduce earnings and profits for deferred compensation in situations other than those in which a deduction or reduction of earnings and profits is permitted under section 404. A deduction or reduction of earnings and profits is permitted under section 404A for amounts paid or accrued by an employer under a foreign deferred compensation plan, in the taxable year in which the amounts are properly taken into account under §§ 1.404A-1 through 1.404A-7, if each of the following requirements is satisfied:

*(1)* The plan is a written plan maintained by the employer that provides deferred compensation.

*(2)* The plan is maintained for the exclusive benefit of the employer's employees or their beneficiaries.

*(3)* 90 percent or more of the amounts taken into account under the plan are attributable to services performed by nonresident aliens, the compensation for which is not subject to United States federal income tax.

*(4)* An election under § 1.404A-6 or 1.404A-7 is made to treat the plan as either a qualified funded plan or a qualified reserve plan and to select a plan year.

**(b) 90-percent test.** *(1) Reserve plans.* Paragraph (a)(3) of this section is not satisfied by a reserve plan unless 90 percent or more of the actuarial present value of the total vested benefits (i.e., benefits not subject to substantial risk of forfeiture) accrued under the plan is attributable to services performed by nonresident aliens, the compensation for which is not subject to United States federal income tax.

*(2) Funded plans.* (i) Individual account plans. Paragraph (a)(3) of this section is not satisfied by a funded plan with individual accounts unless 90 percent or more of the amounts allocated to individual accounts (as described in section 414(i)) under the plan are allocated to the accounts of nonresident aliens and are attributable to services the compensation for which is not subject to United States federal income tax.

(ii) Plans without individual accounts. Paragraph (a)(3) of this section is not satisfied by a funded plan not described in paragraphs (b)(2)(i) of this section unless 90 percent or more of the actuarial present value of the total benefits accrued under the plan is attributable to services performed by nonresident aliens the compensation for which is not subject to United States federal income tax.

**(c) Calculation of 90 percent amounts.** *(1) In general.* In determining whether the tests described in paragraphs (b)(1) and (b)(2)(ii) of this section are satisfied, accrued benefits and the actuarial present values of accrued benefits may be calculated under any reasonable method. See § 1.404A-5(a) for rules describing the calculation of accrued benefits attributable to services for which the compensation is subject to United States federal income tax.

*(2) Safe harbor.* The requirement of paragraph (a)(3) of this section will be deemed satisfied with respect to a plan if—

(i) The participants' benefits under the plan increase generally in proportion to their compensation taken into account under the plan; and

(ii) The sum of the following amounts does not exceed five percent of all compensation taken into account under the plan for the plan year—

(A) The compensation of United States citizens and residents taken into account under the plan; and

(B) Any other compensation subject to United States federal income tax taken into account under the plan.

*(3) Anti-abuse rule.* Notwithstanding paragraph (c)(2) of this section, the requirement of paragraph (a)(3) of this section will not be deemed satisfied under paragraph (c)(2) of this section if the Commissioner determines that a significant purpose of the plan is to secure benefits not otherwise eligible for tax benefits under the Internal Revenue Code to participants who are United States citizens or residents.

*(4) Example.* The principles of paragraphs (c)(2) and (c)(3) of this section are illustrated by the following example:

*Example.* A foreign branch of a domestic corporation maintains a deferred compensation plan under which benefits are based upon a participant's average compensation for the last five consecutive years of employment. The significant purposes of the plan do not include the provision of benefits otherwise unavailable under the Code to participants who are United States citizens or residents. The foreign branch maintains its books and records in its functional currency (FC). The taxpayer's taxable year and the plan year are coterminous with the calendar year. During the plan year in question, the compensation taken into account under the plan for all plan participants totals FC200 million. Of the FC200 million, FC6 million of the compensation taken into account under the plan is compensation for United States citizens and residents or otherwise subject to United States federal income tax. Because the FC6 million is less than five percent of all compensation taken into account under the plan for the plan year, the 90-percent requirement of paragraph (a)(3) of this section is deemed satisfied for this taxable year.

**(d) Deductions and reductions of earnings and profits.** Deductions and reductions of earnings and profits for amounts paid by an employer to a plan that provides deferred compensation that does not meet the requirements of paragraph (a) of this section are governed exclusively by section 404, without regard to whether the plan benefits foreign employees.

**(e) Definitions.** The following definitions apply for purposes of section 404A and §§ 1.404A-1 through 1.404A-7:

*Actuarial present value.* "Actuarial present value" is defined in § 1.401(a)(4)-12.

*Aggregate amount.* "Aggregate amount" is defined in § 1.404A-4(g)(4).

*Appropriate foreign tax law.* "Appropriate foreign tax law" is defined in § 1.404A-4(g)(3).

*Authorized officer.* "Authorized officer" is defined in § 1.404A-5(b)(7).

*Carryover contributions.* "Carryover contributions" are defined in § 1.404A-2(d)(4).

*Change in method of accounting.* "Change in method of accounting" is defined in § 1.404A-6(a).

*Closing year.* "Closing year" is defined in § 1.404A-6(f)(4)(ii).

*Contributions accumulated to pay deferred compensation.* "Contributions accumulated to pay deferred compensation" are defined in § 1.404A-2(b)(2).

*Contributions to a trust.* "Contributions to a trust" are defined in § 1.404A-2(b)(1).

*Controlled foreign corporation.* "Controlled foreign corporation" means a controlled foreign corporation as defined in sections 953(c)(1)(B) and 957.

*Cumulative foreign amount.* "Cumulative foreign amount" is defined in § 1.404A-4(g)(2).

*Cumulative limitation.* "Cumulative limitation" is defined in § 1,404A-4(b).

*Cumulative United States amount.* "Cumulative United States amount" is defined in § 1.404A-4(g)(1).

*Deductible limit.* "Deductible limit" is defined in § 1.404A-2(d)(1)(i).

*Deductions.* "Deductions" are defined in § 1.404A-1(f)(1).

*Deferred compensation. (i) In general.* "Deferred compensation" means any item the deductibility of which is determined by reference to section 404, without regard to whether section 404 permits a deduction and without regard to whether elections are made under § 1.404A-6 or 1.404A-7. Deferred compensation, as described in the preceding sentence, does not include deferred benefits described in section 404(b)(2)(B).

*(ii) Social security.* A plan under which a foreign government (including a political subdivision, agency or instrumentality thereof) makes a contribution or a direct payment to a participant (or the participant's beneficiary) does not provide deferred compensation to the extent of such contributions or payments. Thus, for example, a foreign country's social security system generally will not be considered as providing deferred compensation. However, the fact that employers are required to maintain the plan by reason of foreign law, or the fact that.ie plan supplements social security benefits provided by a foreign country, or provides benefits in lieu of such social security benefits, does not prevent a plan from providing deferred compensation.

*(iii) Termination indemnity plans.* The determination of whether a plan (including a termination indemnity plan) provides deferred compensation must generally be made under paragraph (i) of this definition in light of all of the facts and circumstances. Benefits paid under a plan, including a plan denominated a termination indemnity plan will generally be treated as deferred compensation if—

(A) A major purpose of the plan is to provide for the payment of retirement benefits;

(B) The plan has a benefit formula providing for payment based at least in part upon length of service;

(C) The plan provides for the payment of benefits to employees (or their beneficiaries) after the employee's retirement, death or other termination of employment; and

(D) It meets such other requirements as may be prescribed by the Commissioner in guidance of general applicability with respect to termination indemnity plans.

(iv) Example. The definition of deferred compensation is illustrated by the following example:

*Example.* A domestic corporation maintains a branch operation in foreign country F. F requires that all employers doing business in its country provide benefits to employees under a termination indemnity plan insured by F's government. The plan provides for payments to employees who terminate employment for any reason, including retirement, death, voluntary resignation and discharge for cause (other than for gross misconduct) and permits withdrawals for certain hardship conditions. Upon separation, the employee (or his or her beneficiary) receives an amount equal to the accumulation on the employer's books of one-thirteenth of his or her annual salary for each year of employment, with specified adjustments for interest and inflation. This termination indemnity plan provides deferred compensation as described in paragraph (e) of this section.

*Earnings and profits.* "Earnings and profits" means earnings and profits computed in accordance with sections 312 and 964(a) and, for taxable years beginning after December 31, 1986, section 986 and the regulations thereunder; and for purposes of section 902 in taxable years beginning before January 1, 1987, accumulated profits within the meaning of section 902(c) as in effect on the day before the enactment of the Tax Reform Act of 1986.

*Employer.* "Employer" means a person that maintains a plan for the payment of deferred compensation for services provided to it by its employees. "Employer" for purposes of the acceleration of the section 481(a) adjustment is defined in § 1.404A-6(e)(2)(iv).

*Equivalent of a trust.* "Equivalent of a trust" means a fund—

(i) The corpus and income of which is separately identifiable and segregated, through a separate legal entity, from the general assets of the employer;

(ii) The corpus and income of which is not subject, under the applicable foreign law, to the claims of the employer's creditors prior to the claims of employees and their beneficiaries under the plan;

(iii) The corpus and income of which, by law or by contract, cannot at any time prior to the satisfaction of all liabilities with respect to employees under the plan be used for, or diverted to, any purpose other than providing benefits under the plan; and

(iv) The corpus and income of which is held by a person who has a legally enforceable duty to operate the fund prudently.

*Erroneous deduction.* "Erroneous deduction" is defined in § 1.404A-7(d)(3)(ii).

*Exclusive benefit.* "Exclusive benefit" has the same meaning as in §§ 1.401-2 and 1.413-1(d).

*Fixed or determinable benefits.* "Fixed or determinable benefits" are defined in § 1.404A-2(d)(1)(i).

*Full funding limitation.* "Full funding limitation" is defined in § 1.404A-5(c)(2).

*Functional currency.* "Functional currency" (abbreviated as FC) means the functional currency of a taxpayer or a qualified business unit determined in accordance with section 985(b) and the regulations thereunder, or, for taxable years beginning before January 1, 1987, the currency in which the employer's books and records were maintained for United States tax purposes.

*Funded method.* "Funded method, is defined in § 1.404A-6(f)(2)(iv).

*Initial aggregate amount.* "Initial aggregate amount" is defined in § 1.404A-6(g)(2)(iii).

*Initial Cumulative foreign amount.* "Initial Cumulative foreign amount" is defined in § 1.404A-6(g)(2)(ii).

*Initial Cumulative United States amount.* "Initial Cumulative United States amount" is defined in § 1.404A-6(g)(2)(i).

*Initial section 404A(d) amounts.* "Initial section 404A(d) amounts" are defined in § 1.404A-6(g).

*Liability.* "Liability" is defined in § 1.404A-1(f)(2).

*Majority domestic corporate shareholders.* "Majority domestic corporate shareholders" are defined in § 1.404A-6(c)(2)(ii)(C).

*Method of accounting.* "Method of accounting" is defined in § 1.404A-6(a)(1).

*Method (1) election.* "Method (1) election" is defined in § 1.404A-7(g)(1).

*Method (2) election.* "Method (2) election" is defined in § 1.404A-7(g)(2).

*New Method Opening Amount.* "New Method Opening Amount" is defined in § 1.404A-6(f)(3).

*Noncontrolled foreign corporation.* "Noncontrolled foreign corporation" means a foreign corporation other than a controlled foreign corporation.

*Nonqualified individual.* "Nonqualified individual" is defined in § 1.404A-5(a)(1).

*Nonqualified plan.* "Nonqualified plan" is defined in § 1.404A-6(f)(3)(iii).

*Old Method Closing Amount.* "Old Method Closing Amount" is defined in § 1.404A-6(f)(2).

*Open period.* "Open period" is defined in § 1.404A-7(g)(6).

*Open years.* "Open years" are defined in § 1.404A-7(g)(3).

*Opening reserve.* "Opening reserve" is defined in § 1.404A-6(f)(3)(i).

*Opening year.* "Opening year" is defined in § 1.404A-6(f)(4)(i).

*Pay-as-you-go method.* "Pay-as-you-go method" is defined in § 1.404A-6(f)(2)(iii).

*Period of adjustment.* "Period of adjustment" is defined in § 1.404A-6(e)(2).

*Permitted plan year.* "Permitted plan year" means the plan year of a plan providing deferred compensation ending with or within the employer's taxable year.

*Plan year.* "Plan year" means the annual accounting period of a plan providing deferred compensation.

*Primary evidence.* "Primary evidence" is defined in § 1.404A-5(b)(2).

*Prior deduction.* "Prior deduction" is defined in § 1.404A-7(d)(3)(i).

*Protective election.* "Protective election" is defined in § 1.404A-7(g)(2).

*Qualified business unit.* "Qualified business unit" is defined in section 989(a).

*Qualified foreign plan.* "Qualified foreign plan" means a plan that meets the requirements of paragraph (a) of this section.

*Qualified funded plan.* "Qualified funded plan" means a qualified foreign plan for which an election has been made under § 1.404A-6 or 1.404A-7 by the taxpayer to treat the plan as a qualified funded plan.

*Qualified reserve plan.* "Qualified reserve plan" means a qualified foreign plan for which an election has been made by the taxpayer under § 1.404A-6 or 1.404A-7 to treat the plan as a qualified reserve plan.

*Reasonable actuarial assumptions.* "Reasonable actuarial assumptions" are defined in § 1.404A-5(c).

*Reductions in earnings and profits.* "Reductions in earnings and profits" are defined in § 1.404A-1(f)(1).

*Reserve method.* "Reserve method" is defined in § 1.404A-6(f)(2)(ii).

*Retirement annuity.* "Retirement annuity" is defined in § 1.404A-2(b)(3).

*Retroactive effective date election.* "Retroactive effective date election" is defined in § 1.404A-7(b)(1).

*Retroactive period.* "Retroactive period" is defined in § 1.404A-7(g)(4).

*Retroactive plan-by-plan election.* "Retroactive plan-by-plan election" is defined in § 1.404A-7(c)(1) and (d)(1).

*Revocation of election.* "Revocation of election" is defined in § 1.404A-6(d)(1).

*Secondary evidence.* "Secondary evidence" is defined in § 1.404A-5(b)(4).

*Separate funding entity.* "Separate funding entity" is defined in § 1.404A-6(f)(4)(iii).

*Short taxable year.* "Short taxable year" is defined in § 1.404A-7(d)(2).

*Single plan.* "Single plan" is defined in § 1.404A-6(a)(2).

*Substantial risk of forfeiture.* "Substantial risk of forfeiture" is defined in § 1.404A-3(b)(2).

*Substantiation quality data.* "Substantiation quality data" means less than precise data that is nevertheless the best data available for the plan year at reasonable expense.

*Taxable year of a controlled foreign corporation.* "Taxable year of a controlled foreign corporation" means the taxable year as defined in sections 441(b) and 7701(a)(23), subject to section 898.

*Taxable year of a noncontrolled foreign corporation.* "Taxable year of a noncontrolled foreign corporation" means the taxable year as defined in sections 441(b) and 7701(a)(23).

*Taxpayer.* "Taxpayer" is defined in section 7701(a)(14).

*Termination of election.* "Termination of election" is defined in § 1.404A-6(c)(1).

*Transition period.* "Transition period" is defined in § 1.404A-7(g)(5).

*Trust.* "Trust" means a trust (as defined in § 301.7701-4(a) of this chapter) or the equivalent of a trust.

*Unit credit method.* "Unit credit method" is defined in § 1.404A-3(b)(2).

*United States tax significance.* "United States tax significance" is defined in § 1.404A-6(b)(2)(ii).

*Written plan.* "Written plan" means a plan that is defined by plan instruments or required under the law of a foreign country, or both. An insurance contract can constitute a written plan.

**(f) Application of other Code requirements.** *(1) Deductibility requirement.* (i) In general. In order to deduct amounts under section 404A, amounts contributed to a qualified funded plan or properly added to a reserve with respect to a qualified reserve plan must otherwise be deductible. The standards under section 404 are to be used in determining whether an amount would otherwise be deductible for this purpose. Thus, amounts may be taken into account under section 404A only to the extent that they are ordinary and necessary expenses during the taxable year in carrying on a trade or business and are compensation for personal services actually rendered before the end of the year. Similarly, in order to reduce earnings and profits under section 404A by amounts contributed to a qualified funded plan or properly added to a reserve with respect to a qualified reserve plan, earnings and profits must otherwise be able to be reduced by such amounts under the general principles of sections 312, 901, 902, 960, and 964.

(ii) Capitalization requirements. In determining if an amount would otherwise be deductible (or able to be used to reduce earnings and profits) for purposes of paragraph (g)(1)(i) of this section, the fact that the amount is required to be capitalized (e.g., under section 263A) is ignored. Additionally, while section 404A and §§ 1.404A-1 through 1.404A-7 refer generally to permissible deductions or reductions of earnings and profits for deferred compensation, those references are intended to refer both to situations under which amounts may be taken into account as deductions or reductions of earnings and profits and to situations under which amounts may be taken into account through inclusion in the basis of inventory or through capitalization.

*(2) Section 461 requirements.* In determining whether any amount of deferred compensation may be taken into account under section 404A by an accrual method taxpayer, the conditions for accrual under section 461 must be met with respect to the amount by the last day of the taxable year. For this purpose, an amount determined under §§ 1.404A-1 through 1.404A-7 establishes the fact of the liability and determines the amount of the liability with reasonable accuracy. See § 1.461-4(d)(2)(iii), which generally provides that the economic performance requirement of section 461(h) is satisfied to the extent that any amount is otherwise properly taken into account under §§ 1.404A-1 through 1.404A-7.

**Proposed § 1.404A-2 Rules for qualified funded plans.**
*[For Preamble, see ¶ 151,519]*

**(a) In general.** Except as provided in this section and in §§ 1.404A-4 and 1.404A-5, the amount taken into account for a taxable year with respect to a qualified funded plan is the amount of the contributions paid by the employer to the trust in that year (regardless of whether the employer uses an accrual method of accounting). Accretions in a trust are not considered contributions to a plan.

**(b) Payment to a trust.** *(1) Contribution requirements.* Contributions paid under a qualified funded plan may not be taken into account unless they are—

(i) Paid to a trust which is operated in accordance with the requirements of section 401(a)(2);

(ii) Paid for a retirement annuity under which retirement benefits are provided and which is for the exclusive benefit of the employer's employees or their beneficiaries; or

(iii) Paid directly to a participant or beneficiary (rather than a trust).

*(2) Trust requirements.* (i) General rule. A contribution does not satisfy paragraph (b)(1)(i) of this section unless it is accumulated in the trust for the purpose of being distributed as deferred compensation. Whether a contribution is being accumulated in the trust for the purpose of being distributed as deferred compensation depends on the facts and circumstances. For purposes of paragraph (b)(1)(i) of this section, the fact that a trust has been (or has not been) involved in transactions that would be described in section 4975(c)(1)(and not exempted under section 4975(c)(2) or 4975(d)), e.g., contributions made in the form of a promissory note, if the plan were subject to section 4975(c)(1), is an important factor in determining whether the trust is not (or is) considered to be operated in accordance with the requirements of section 401(a)(2). In addition, a contribution to a trust does not satisfy paragraph (b)(1)(i) of this section unless it has substance.

(ii) Effective date. The section 4975(c)(1) factor in determining compliance with section 401(a)(2) provided in this paragraph (b)(2) is taken into account for all transactions entered into after May 7, 1993.

*(3) Retirement annuity.* A retirement annuity means a retirement annuity (as defined in section 404(a)(2)) except that the retirement annuity need not be part of a plan that meets the requirements of section 401(a) or 401(d). Notwithstanding the preceding sentence, the retirement annuity described therein need not be issued by an insurance company qualified to do business in a State in the United States if the taxpayer(s) and/or sponsoring employer(s) of the plan have shifted the risk of making payments under the plan to an entity that is qualified to do business in the country (or countries) where the plan is maintained.

*(4) Effect of reversion of overfunded contributions.* If any portion of a contribution to a trust may revert to the benefit of the employer before the satisfaction of all liabilities to employees or their beneficiaries covered by the trust, no amount of the contribution may be taken into account under this section.

*(5) Example.* The principles of paragraph (b) of this section are illustrated by the following example:

*Example.* A foreign subsidiary of a domestic corporation maintains a deferred compensation plan for its employees. The foreign subsidiary makes annual contributions under the plan to a trust. Each year after the contribution is made to the trust, the trustee lends the contribution back to the foreign subsidiary maintaining the plan. The foreign subsidiary executes promissory notes obligating it to repay the borrowed funds (at a reasonable rate of interest) to the trust and to pay any benefits due under the plan. Notwithstanding that the taxpayer may have designated the plan as a qualified funded plan, amounts may not be taken into account under section 404A with respect to contributions to the trust because the loans cause the trust to fail the requirements of section 401(a)(2). Even if the loans do not cause the trust to violate section 401(a)(2), the portion of any contribution that is loaned to the foreign subsidiary could not be taken into account because, to the extent of the loan (or loans), the contribution lacks substance and is not accumulated in the trust.

**(c) Contribution deemed made before payment.** *(1) Time of payment to trust.* Regardless of whether an employer uses the cash or an accrual method of accounting, for purposes of this section, a contribution to a trust that is paid after the close of an employer's taxable year is deemed to have been paid on the last day of that taxable year if—

(i) The payment is made on account of the taxable year and is made not later than the 15th day of the ninth month after the close of the taxable year;

(ii) The payment is treated by the plan in the same manner that the plan would treat a payment actually received on the last day of the taxable year; and

(iii) Either—

(A) The employer notifies the plan administrator or trustee in writing that the payment to the plan is designated on account of the taxable year;

(B) The taxpayer claims the payment as a deduction on its tax return for the taxable year; or

(C) The employer reduces earnings and profits with respect to the payment.

*(2) Time of designation.* Any designation of a payment pursuant to paragraph (c)(1)(iii)(A) of this section must occur not later than the time described in paragraph (c)(1)(i) of this section.

*(3) Irrevocable designation.* After a payment has been designated or claimed on a return in the manner provided in paragraph (c)(1)(iii)(A) of this section as being on account of a taxable year, the designation or claim may not be retracted or changed.

**(d) Limitation for qualified funded plans.** *(1) Plans with fixed or determinable benefits.* (i) Limit on amount taken into account. Contributions made to a qualified funded plan under which the benefits are fixed or determinable are not taken into account under this section to the extent they exceed the amount that would be taken into account under section 404(a)(1)(A)(ii) and (iii) (determined without regard to the last sentence of paragraph (A) of section 404(a)(1) and without regard to whether the trust is exempt under section 501(a)). Benefits are considered fixed or determinable for this purpose if either benefits under or contributions to the plan are definitely determinable within the meaning of § 1.401-1(b)(1)(i). The limit described in the first sentence of this paragraph (d)(1)(i) is determined on the basis of the permitted plan year of the qualified foreign plan. Thus, the limit for the employer's taxable year is the limit for the plan year ending with or within the employer's taxable year.

(ii) Actuarial valuation requirements. In determining the amount to be taken into account under this Section, an actuarial valuation must be made not less frequently than once every three years. However, an actuarial valuation must be made for the first plan year of the plan for which an election under § 1.404A-6 is in effect. For interim years, a reasonable actuarial determination of whether the full funding limit in § 1.404A-5(c)(2) applies to the qualified funded plan must be made. The Commissioner may require a full actuarial valuation in an interim year under appropriate circumstances. See § 1.404A-6 for rules on changes in methods of accounting.

*(2) Plans without fixed or determinable benefits.* Contributions made to a qualified funded plan under which the benefits are not fixed or determinable may not be taken into account under this section to the extent they exceed the limitations of section 404(a)(3) (determined without regard to whether the payment is made to a trust that is exempt under section 501(a)).

*(3) Limitations where more than one type of plan is maintained.* Where payments are made for a taxable year to more than one type of qualified funded plan, the amounts that may be taken into account for the taxable year with respect to the payments are subject to the limitations of section 404(a)(7). The amount that is taken into account under this paragraph (d)(3) is determined without regard to whether the payment satisfies the minimum funding standard described in section 412.

*(4) Carryover contributions.* In the event that the aggregate amount of contributions paid during an employer's taxable year in which an election under section 404A is in effect (reduced by an amount described in section 404A(g)(1)) exceeds the amount that may be taken into account under section 404A(a) and this section (Computed without regard to section 404A(d) and § 1.404A-4), the excess contributions are treated as an amount paid in the succeeding taxable year with respect to that qualified foreign plan. A carryover contribution is also taken into account in determining whether a carryover contribution exists for a succeeding taxable year.

*(5) Additional rules.* The Commissioner may prescribe additional rules for determining the amount that may be taken into account under this paragraph (d) in guidance of general applicability.

**(e) Examples.** The principles of this section are illustrated by the following examples:

*Example (1).* A qualified funded plan under which benefits are not fixed or determinable is maintained by a foreign branch of a domestic corporation. The foreign branch computes its income in units of local currency, the FC. The taxpayer's taxable year and the plan year are coterminous with the calendar year. The plan was established in 1985, and the taxpayer made an election to apply section 404A, a qualified funded plan election as described in § 1.404A-6. For the 1985 taxable year, the employer made a FC25,000 Contribution under the plan, and FC15,000 of that contribution could be taken into account under paragraph (d)(2) of this section. The cumulative foreign amount for the 1985 taxable year was FC20,000. The amount of the excess contribution carried forward was FC10,000 (FC25,000 – FC15,000), because the amount of the carryover contribution is determined without regard to section 404A(d) and § 1.404A-4.

*Example (2).* Assume the same facts as in Example 1, except that the entire FC25,000 contribution made under the plan may be taken into account under paragraph (d)(2) of this section. The amount of the excess contribution carried forward was zero, even though the cumulative United States amount may have exceeded the cumulative foreign amount for the taxable year, because the amount of the excess contribution is determined without regard to section 404A(d) and § 1.404A-4.

*Example (3).* P, a domestic corporation, owns all of the one class of stock of foreign corporation S. The taxable year for P is the calendar year. The taxable year for S is the fiscal year beginning on June 1. S made a contribution to its qualified funded plan on February 15, 1983, and notified the plan's trustee in writing that S designated the contribution as a payment on account of S's preceding taxable year (ending May 31, 1982). The contribution is taken into account in computing S's earnings and profits for S's taxable year ending May 31, 1982.

### Proposed § 1.404A-3 Rules for qualified reserve plans.

[*For Preamble, see ¶ 151,519*]

**(a) Amounts taken into account with respect to qualified reserve plans.** *(1) General rule.* Except as provided in §§ 1.404A-4 and 1.404A-5, the amount taken into account for a taxable year with respect to a qualified reserve plan equals the sum of—

(i) The reasonable addition during the permitted plan year to a reserve for liabilities under the plan as described in paragraph (b) of this section; and

(ii) The amortization of certain increases or decreases in the plan reserve over ten years, as described in paragraph (c) of this section.

*(2) Amounts less than zero.* If the amount to be taken into account under this section is less than zero, that amount

must be treated as an increase in income and earnings and profits for the taxable year.

*(3) Exclusive rules for qualified reserve plans.* No amounts may be taken into account with respect to a qualified reserve plan except as provided for in this section. Thus, for example, no deduction is allowed for benefit payments from the reserve. Similarly, no amount may be taken into account for any payments made by the employer that are used either to reinsure the liabilities or benefits under a qualified reserve plan or to fund separately all or a portion of the benefits under a qualified reserve plan. These amounts may, however, be taken into account as contributions to a qualified funded plan to the extent the requirements of § 1.404A-2 are satisfied.

**(b) Reasonable addition to a reserve for liabilities.** *(1) General rule.* Except as provided in § 1.404A-7(f)(2), the reasonable addition to a reserve for a plan year equals the increase in the reserve, determined under the unit credit method as described in paragraph (b)(2) of this section, that arises from the passage of time and from additional service and expected changes in compensation in the current plan year for employees who were included in the reserve as of the end of the prior plan year. Thus, the reasonable addition to the reserve includes an element of interest on the reserve as of the beginning of the plan year (less the interest on the benefit payments during the plan year) and the actuarial present value of the expected increase in vested benefits accrued during the current plan year for employees who were included in the reserve as of the end of the prior plan year, determined without reference to any plan amendment during the plan year.

*(2) Unit credit method required.* The reserve for the employer's liability must be determined under the unit credit method. Thus, the reserve must be the actuarial present value of the employer's liability, taking into account service and compensation only through the valuation date. In determining the reserve under this section, benefits that are subject to a substantial risk of forfeiture may not be taken into account. The term "substantial risk of forfeiture" has the meaning stated in section 83, except that the term "property" in all events includes benefits accrued under a qualified reserve plan.

*(3) Timing of valuation.* The determination of the reserve and the reasonable addition to the reserve must be made as of the last day of the plan year.

*(4) Permissible actuarial assumptions.* (i) Interest rates. (A) In general. Notwithstanding any other provision of §§ 1.404A-1 through 1.404A-7, no amount may be taken into account under section 404A with respect to a qualified reserve plan unless the rate (or rates) of interest for the plan that are selected by the employer are within the permissible range. The interest rate selected by the employer for the plan under this paragraph must remain in effect for that plan until the first plan year for which that rate is no longer within the permissible range. At that time, a new rate of interest must be selected by the employer from within the permissible range applicable at that time.

(B) Permissible range. For purposes of this paragraph (b)(4), the term "permissible range" means a rate of interest that is not more than 1.2 and not less than the product of 0.8 multiplied by the average rate of interest for the highest quality long-term corporate bonds denominated in the functional currency of the qualified business unit of the employer whose books reflect the plan's liabilities for the 15-year period ending on the last day before the beginning of the employer's taxable year. If there is no market in long-term corporate bonds denominated in the relevant functional currency, or if the qualified business unit computes its income or earnings and profits in dollars under § 1.985-3, the employer must use a rate that can be demonstrated clearly to reflect income, based on all relevant facts and circumstances, including appropriate rates of inflation and commercial practices.

(ii) Plan benefits. Except as otherwise provided by the Commissioner, changes in plan benefits or applicable foreign law that become effective (whether or not retroactively) in a future plan year may not be taken into account until the plan year the change is effective. Notwithstanding the above, the reserve calculation may take into account cost-of-living adjustments that are part of the employee's vested accrued benefit, using assumptions regarding cost-of-living adjustments that are consistent with the interest rate assumptions described in paragraph (b)(4)(i) of this section and the terms of the plan. Thus, for example, a cost-of-living adjustment that does not require any future service on the part of the employee and is not subject to employer discretion may be taken into account.

**(c) Ten-year amortization for certain changes in reserves.** *(1) Actuarial valuation.* Each plan year an actuarial valuation must be made as of the end of the plan year, comparing the actual reserve with the expected value of the reserve. Any difference between the actual reserve determined as of the end of the plan year and the expected value of the reserve as of that date must be amortized in level amounts of principal over ten years, beginning in the plan year of the actuarial valuation. This amortization applies regardless of whether the difference is attributable to changes in employee population, changes in plan provisions, or changes in actuarial assumptions.

*(2) Expected value of reserve.* The expected value of the reserve as of the end of the plan year is equal to the sum of the reserve as of the end of the prior plan year plus the reasonable addition to the reserve for the plan year described in paragraph (b) of this section less the benefit payments during the plan year. Thus, the expected value of the reserve is generally determined on the basis of the plan in effect and the actuarial assumptions used as of the end of the prior plan year, but, because it includes the reasonable addition to the reserve, includes the effect of expected changes in compensation, service and vesting during the current plan year.

*(3) Special rule for certain cost of living adjustments.* Notwithstanding the general rule that the increase in liability from a plan amendment is amortized over ten years, if under foreign law a shorter period for amortization is required, that shorter period shall be substituted for ten years in this paragraph (c) if the amendment is a cost of living adjustment that either—

(i) Relates primarily to retirees; or

(ii) Is for employees of a foreign corporation in a taxable year beginning before [insert date that is 90 days after the date of publication of final regulation in the FEDERAL REGISTER].

*(4) Anti-abuse rule.* The commissioner may reclassify any item included by a taxpayer as a reasonable addition to a reserve as instead subject to amortization over ten years if the Commissioner determines that the taxpayer's classification of that item circumvents the intent of section 404A(c)(4). Thus, for example, if the Commissioner determines that the vesting provisions of the plan cause the increase in vested benefits to be unreasonably large in a single plan year, the reasonable addition under paragraph (b) of this section must

be calculated without recognizing any changes in vesting for the plan year.

**(d) Examples.** The principles of this section are illustrated by the following examples:

*Example (1).* S, a foreign subsidiary of P, a domestic corporation, contributes funds to an irrevocable trust which is used to pay benefits provided under S's reserve plan. The trust does not satisfy the requirements of section 401(a), 404(a)(4), or 404(a)(5). The funds are not used to provide benefits in addition to those provided by the reserve plan. In 1984, the year the plan was adopted, S elected to treat the plan as a qualified reserve plan. In 1984 S also contributed an amount to the irrevocable trust. The fact that S contributed an amount to the trust has no effect on the computation of the amount that S is entitled to take into account under this section in 1984 (or in any other year). Furthermore, no additional amount may be taken into account for the amount of the contribution to the trust beyond the amount permitted to be taken into account under this section.

*Example (2).* (a) Employer Y hired 10,000 employees in 1980, each of whom was age 40 at the beginning of the year and earned FC10,000. The employees immediately commenced participation in the plan. The plan provided that the accrued benefit at the end of X years equaled: (X multiplied by one percent) multiplied by the highest one year's compensation. The plan vesting was 20 percent per year starting after two years of service with the employer. Under the plan, once an employee was vested in a benefit, the benefit could not be forfeited for any reason other than the death of the employee. Employees who terminate employment for reasons other than death or retirement receive an immediate single sum distribution in an amount equal to the actuarial present value (calculated at eight percent interest) of the vested accrued benefit (where the actuarial present value and the vested accrued benefit are determined as of the end of the prior plan year). Reserves and expected increases in the reserve were determined using eight percent interest, five percent assumed compensation increases, the UP-84 mortality table and assuming no pre-retirement terminations other than death. However as set forth in the relevant data below, the actual experience differed from these assumptions (e.g., the actual compensation did not increase five percent each year and the mortality and termination experience were different than assumed).

| Year | End of Year Age | Number of Deaths | Number of Terminations | Number of Employees Remaining |
|---|---|---|---|---|
| 1980 | 41 | 16 | 5 | 9,979 |
| 1981 | 42 | 18 | 5 | 9,956 |
| 1982 | 43 | 20 | 5 | 9,931 |
| 1983 | 44 | 25 | 5 | 9,901 |
| 1984 | 45 | 30 | 25 | 9,846 |

| Year | Compensation for Each Employee | End of Year Accrued Benefit for Each Employee | End of Year Vested Accrued Benefit for Each Employee |
|---|---|---|---|
| 1980 | 10,000 | 100 | 0 |
| 1981 | 10,000 | 200 | 0 |
| 1982 | 10,000 | 300 | 60 |
| 1983 | 12,000 | 480 | 192 |
| 1984 | 12,000 | 600 | 360 |

| Year | Benefit Payments | End of Year Actuarial Factor | End of Year Reserve for Vested Benefits |
|---|---|---|---|
| 1980 | 0 | 1.049706 | 0 |
| 1981 | 0 | 1.136328 | 0 |
| 1982 | 0 | 1.230380 | 733,134 |
| 1983 | 369 | 1.332564 | 2,533,194 |
| 1984 | 6,396 | 1.443638 | 5,117,062 |

(b) Computation of amounts taken into account for 1980. The amount taken into account for 1980 was zero because there was no reasonable addition to the reserve (i.e., no increase in the reserve on account of the passage of time, additional service or expected changes in compensation for employees who were included in the reserve at the end of the prior year) and there were no amounts that are subject to ten-year amortization under paragraph (c) of this section.

(c) Computation of amounts taken into account for 1981. There was no amount taken into account for 1981 for the same reason as in 1980.

(d) Computation of amount taken into account for 1982. The amount taken into account in 1982 was the sum of the reasonable addition to the reserve determined under paragraph (b) of this section and the amortization of certain increases in the plan reserve over ten years determined under paragraph (c) of this section. There was no reasonable addition to the reserve (i.e., no increase in the reserve on account of the passage of time, additional service or expected changes in compensation for employees who were included in the reserve at the end of the prior year) for the 1982 year because no employee was included in the reserve as of the end of 1981. There were no benefits paid during 1981. Thus, the expected value of the reserve at the end of 1982 was zero. However, the actual value of the reserve at the end of 1982 was FC733,134 (9,931 employees × 60 × 1.230380). The difference between the expected and actual values of the reserve was taken into account over ten years beginning in 1982. Thus, the total amount taken into account for 1982 was FC73,313.

(e) Computation of amount taken into account for 1983. Using the employee data as of the end of 1982 and the expected rate of compensation increase for 1983, each employee's accrued benefit was expected to be 420 (10,500 × 4 years × .01) as of the end of 1983. 40 percent of this accrued benefit, or 168, was expected to be vested. Thus, the expected increase in each employee's vested accrued benefit was 108 (the difference between 168 and the vested accrued benefit as of the end of the prior year (60) for those employees who were included in the reserve as of the end of the prior year). There were 9,931 employees included in the reserve as of the end of the prior year and 9,931 × $p_{43}$ were expected to be in the reserve as of the end of 1983. The actuarial present value factor for a deferred annuity of FC1 commencing at age 65 payable monthly is 1.332564. Thus, the actuarial present value of the expected increase in vested accrued benefits as of the end of the year was FC1,425,212 (9,931 employees × $p_{43}$ × 108 × 1.332564). The reasonable addition to the reserve also included an element of interest on the reserve as of the end of the prior year equal to FC58,651 (8 percent × 733,134) that is offset by the interest attributable to the actual benefits paid during the year (FC15, which is interest on the benefits paid during the year (FC369) from the date of payment through the end of the year). Thus, the reasonable addition to the reserve for 1983 was FC1,483,848 (1,425,212 + 58,651 − 15) and the expected reserve at the end of the year was FC2,216,613 (733,134 + 1,483,848 − 369). The actual reserve at the end of 1983 is FC2,533,194, so there was an actuarial loss of FC316,581 (2,533,194 − 2,216,613) which was amortized over 10 years beginning in 1983. Thus, the total amount taken into account in 1983 was FC1,588,819 (1,483,848 + 73,313 + 10 percent of 316,581).

(f) Computation of amount taken into account for 1984. Using the employee data as of the end of 1983 and the expected rate of compensation increase for 1984, each employee's accrued benefit was expected to be 630 (12,600 × 5 years × .01) as of the end of 1984 60 percent of this accrued benefit, or 378, was expected to be vested. Thus, the expected increase in each employee's vested accrued benefit was 186 (the difference between 378 and the vested accrued benefit as of the end of the prior year (192) for those employees who were included in the reserve as of the end of the prior year). There were 9,901 employees included in the reserve as of the end of the prior year and 9,901 × $p_{44}$ were expected to be in the reserve as of the end of 1984. The actuarial present value factor for a deferred annuity of FC1 commencing at age 65 payable monthly is 1.443638. Thus, the actuarial present value of the expected increase in vested accrued benefits as of the end of the year was FC2,650,355 (9,901 employees × $p_{44}$ × 186 × 1.443638). The reasonable addition to the reserve also included an element of interest on the reserve as of the end of the prior year equal to FC202,656 (8 percent × 2,533,194), offset by interest attributable to the actual benefits paid during the year (FC256, which is interest on the benefits paid during the year (FC6,396) from the date of payment through the end of the year). Thus, the reasonable addition to the reserve for 1984 was FC2,852,755 (2,650,355 + 202,656 − 256) and the expected reserve at the end of the year is FC5,379,553 (2,533,194 + 2,852,755 − 6,396). The actual reserve at the end of 1984 was FC5,117,062, so there was an actuarial gain of FC262,491 (5,379,553 − 5,117,062) which was amortized over 10 years beginning in 1984. Thus, the total amount taken into account in 1984 was FC2,931,477 (2,852,755 + 73,313 + 31,658 − 10 percent of 262,491).

(g) Alternative computation method. The amounts taken into account for 1982, 1983 and 1984 may also be illustrated as follows—

**1982**

*Worksheet For Calculating Amount Taken Into Account For Qualified Reserve Plans Under § 404A*

| | |
|---|---|
| (1) Reserve at end of Prior Year | 0 |
| (2) Interest on (1) to end of Current Year | 0 |
| (3) Present Value of the Expected Increase in Vested Accrued Benefits for employees who were included in the reserve as of the end of the prior year. | 0 |
| (4) Benefit Payments during current year | 0 |
| (5) Interest on (4) from date of payment through end of Current year | 0 |
| (6) Reasonable addition to the reserve (2) + (3) − (5) | 0 |
| (7) Expected value of reserve (1) + (6) − (4) | 0 |
| (8) Actual value of reserve | 733,134 |
| (9) Amount to be amortized (8) − (7) | 733,134 |
| (10) Remaining 10 Percent Bases from Prior Years (original amounts) (Item 12 from Prior Year) | 0 |
| (11) 10 percent Bases whose 10 years ended last year | 0 |
| (12) (9) + (10) − (11) | 733,134 |
| (13) 10 percent of (12) | 73,313 |
| (14) Amount Taken Into Account for Current Year [(6) + (13)] | 73,313 |

**1983**

*Worksheet For Calculating Amount Taken Into Account For Qualified Reserve Plans Under § 404A*

| | |
|---|---|
| (1) Reserve at end of Prior Year | 733,134 |
| (2) Interest on (1) to end of Current Year | 58,651 |
| (3) Present Value of the Expected Increase in Vested Accrued Benefits for employees who were included in the reserve as of the end of the prior year. | 1,425,212 |
| (4) Benefit Payments during current year | 369 |
| (5) Interest on (4) from date of payment through end of Current year | 15 |
| (6) Reasonable addition to the reserve (2) + (3) − (5) | 1,483,848 |
| (7) Expected value of reserve (1) + (6) −(4) | 2,216,613 |
| (8) Actual value of reserve | 2,533,194 |
| (9) Amount to be amortized (8) − (7) | 316,581 |
| (10) Remaining 10 Percent Bases from Prior Years (original amounts) (Item 12 from Prior Year) | 733,134 |
| (11) 10 percent Bases whose 10 years ended last year | 0 |
| (12) (9) + (10) − (11) | 1,049,715 |
| (13) 10 percent of (12) | 104,971 |
| (14) Amount Taken Into Account for Current Year [(6) + (13)] | 1,588,819 |

**1984**

*Worksheet For Calculating Amount Taken Into Account For Qualified Reserve Plans Under § 404A*

| | |
|---|---|
| (1) Reserve at end of Prior Year | 2,533,194 |
| (2) Interest on (1) to end of Current Year | 202,656 |
| (3) Present Value of the Expected Increase in Vested Accrued Benefits for employees who were included in the reserve as of the end of the prior year. | 2,650,355 |
| (4) Benefit Payments during current year | 6,396 |
| (5) Interest on (4) from date of payment through end of Current year | 256 |
| (6) Reasonable addition to the reserve (2) + (3) − (5) | 2,852,755 |
| (7) Expected value of reserve (1) + (6) − (4) | 5,379,553 |
| (8) Actual value of reserve | 5,117,062 |
| (9) Amount to be amortized (8) − (7) | (262,491) |
| (10) Remaining 10 Percent Bases from Prior Years (original amounts) (Item 12 from Prior Year) | 1,049,715 |
| (11) 10 percent Bases whose 10 years ended last year | 0 |

| | |
|---|---|
| (12) (9) + (10) − (11) | 787,224 |
| (13) 10 percent of (12) | 78,722 |
| (14) Amount Taken Into Account for Current Year [(6) + (13)] | 2,931,477 |

*Example (3).* (a) The facts are the same as in Example 2, except that the interest rate used to, determine the reserve as of the end of 1984 has been decreased to 7%.

(b) The amount taken into account for 1984 under the alternative calculation method is determined as follows:

**1984**

*Worksheet For Calculating Amount Taken Into Account For Qualified Reserve Plans Under § 404A*

| | |
|---|---|
| (1) Reserve at end of Prior Year | 2,533,194 |
| (2) Interest on (1) to end of Current Year | 202,656 |
| (3) Present Value of the Expected Increase in Vested Accrued Benefits for employees who were included in the reserve as of the end of the prior year. | 3,402,637 |
| (4) Benefit Payments during current year | 6,396 |
| (5) Interest on (4) from date of payment through end of Current year | 256 |
| (6) Reasonable addition to the reserve (2) + (3) − (5) | 3,605,037 |
| (7) Expected value of reserve (1) + (6) − (4) | 6,131,835 |
| (8) Actual value of reserve | 6,569,498 |
| (9) Amount to be amortized (8) − (7) | 437,663 |
| (10) Remaining 10 Percent Bases from Prior Years (original amounts) (Item 12 from Prior Year) | 1,049,715 |
| (11) 10 percent Bases whose 10 years ended last year | 0 |
| (12) (9) + (10) − (11) | 1,487,378 |
| (13) 10 percent of (12) | 148,738 |
| (14) Amount Taken Into Account for Current Year [(6) + (13)] | 3,753,775 |

**Proposed § 1.404A-4 United States and foreign law limitations on amounts taken into account for qualified foreign plans.** [*For Preamble, see ¶ 151,519*]

**(a) In general.** Section 404A(d) and this section place two limits on the amount taken into account for a taxable year with respect to a qualified foreign plan under section 404A(b) and (c) and §§ 1.404A-2 and 1.404A-3. First, as set forth in paragraph (b) of this section, the cumulative amounts that are or have been taken into account under section 404A through the end of the current year may not exceed the cumulative amounts deductible under foreign law in that period. Because the foreign law deduction is cumulative, however, amounts previously disallowed under this rule are taken into account in later years as the amount deductible under foreign law increases. Second, for taxable years beginning before January 1, 1987, or such later year determined under section 902(c)(3)(A), the rule in paragraph (c) of this section further limits the amount taken into account during those taxable years. Because section 404A(d) and this section apply solely to amounts that would otherwise be taken into account under § 1.404A-2 or 1.404A-3, these limitations are applied without regard to amounts taken into account under section 481 (i.e., without regard to the portion of a section 481(a) adjustment that is taken into account during any taxable year within the section 481(a) adjustment period, as defined in § 1.404A-6(e)(2)). See § 1.404A-6, however, for rules applying the section 404A(d) limitations to the calculation of the section 481(a) adjustment.

**(b) Cumulative limitation.** The amount taken into account with respect to a qualified foreign plan for any taxable year equals—

*(1)* The lesser of—

(i) The cumulative United States amount; or

(ii) The cumulative foreign amount;

*(2)* Reduced by the aggregate amount.

**(c) Special rule for foreign corporations in pre-pooling years.** For a taxable year of a foreign corporation beginning before January 1, 1987, or such later year determined under section 902(c)(3)(A), the reduction in earnings and profits determined under paragraph (b) of this section with respect to a qualified foreign plan may not exceed the amount allowed as a deduction under the appropriate foreign tax laws for such taxable year. See Example 3 of paragraph (h) of this section for an illustration of this rule.

**(d) Rules relating to foreign currency.** *(1) Taxable years beginning after December 31, 1986.* For taxable years beginning after December 31, 1986, the cumulative United States amount, the cumulative foreign amount, and the aggregate amount must be computed in the employer's functional currency. See generally section 964 and sections 985 through 989 for rules applicable to determining and translating into dollars the amount of income or loss of foreign branches and earnings and profits (or deficits in earnings and profits) of foreign corporations.

*(2) Taxable years beginning before January 1, 1987.* For taxable years beginning before January 1, 1987, the cumulative United States amount, the cumulative foreign amount, and the aggregate amount must be computed in the currency in which the foreign branch or foreign subsidiary kept its books and records. See Rev. Rul. 75-106, 1975-1 C.B. 31 (see § 601.601(d)(2)(ii)(b) of this chapter), for rules for determining the amount of income or loss of foreign branches using a net worth method of accounting. See Rev. Rul. 75-107, 1975-1 C.B. 32 (see § 601.601(d)(2)(ii)(b) of this chapter), for rules for determining the amount of income or loss of foreign branches using a profit and loss method of accounting. See sections 312, 902, and 1248 and the regulations thereunder for rules for determining the earnings and profits of noncontrolled foreign corporations. See section 964 and the regulations thereunder for rules for determining the earnings and profits of foreign corporations for purposes of subpart F.

*(3) Special rules for the net worth method of accounting.* For purposes of § 1.964-1(e)(4), an amount of deduction that is accrued but not paid at the end of the employer's taxable year with respect to a qualified funded plan must be treated as a short-term liability. In the case of a qualified reserve plan, for purposes of § 1.964-1(e), the amount of the reserve taken into account as a liability on the balance sheet as of the beginning of the taxable year must be limited to the aggregate amount and the amount of the reserve taken into account as a liability on the balance sheet as of the close of the taxable year must be limited to the sum of the aggregate amount and the amount taken into account for the taxable year. For purposes of § 1.964-1(e)(4), each annual increase in the aggregate amount must be treated as a long-term liability incurred on the last day of the employer's taxable year

to which the increase relates. As of the close of each taxable year, a portion of the aggregate amount equal to the amount of benefits expected to be paid during the succeeding taxable year must be reclassified as a short-term liability. The reclassified amount must be allocated to the annual increases in the aggregate amount on a first-in-first-out basis. Similar rules apply for purposes of determining the amount of reserve taken into account by a foreign branch using the net worth method of accounting for taxable years beginning before January 1, 1987, and by a qualified business unit that uses the United States dollar approximate separate transactions method of accounting under § 1.985-3 in a taxable year beginning after December 31, 1986.

**(e) Maintenance of more than one type of qualified foreign plan by an employer.** In determining the deduction or reduction in earnings and profits when an employer maintains one plan for purposes of foreign law that is treated as two separate plans for purposes of § 1.404A-6(a)(2), the cumulative United States amount for each plan must be combined for purposes of paragraphs (a) and (b) of this section. See Example 5 of paragraph (h) of this section for an illustration of this rule.

**(f) United States and foreign law limitations not applicable.** The limitations set forth in this section do not apply to the adjustments required by section 481, section 446(e) and section 2(e)(3)(A) of Public Law 96-603.

**(g) Definitions.** *(1) Cumulative United States amount.* The term "cumulative United States amount" means (with respect to a qualified foreign plan) the amount determined under section 404A (without regard to section 404A(d)) for the taxable year of the employer and for all consecutive prior taxable years for which an election under section 404A was in effect for the plan plus the "initial section 404A amount" within the meaning of § 1.404A-6(g)(2)(i).

*(2) Cumulative foreign amount.* The term "cumulative foreign amount" means (with respect to a qualified foreign plan) the cumulative amount allowed as a deduction under the appropriate foreign tax law for the taxable year of the employer and for all consecutive prior taxable years for which an election under section 404A was in effect for the plan plus the initial section 404A amount within the meaning of § 1.404A-6(g)(2)(ii).

*(3) Appropriate foreign tax law.* The appropriate foreign tax law is the income tax law of the country (other than the United States) that is the principal place of business of the qualified business unit of the employer whose books reflect the plan liabilities.

*(4) Aggregate amount.* The term "aggregate amount" means (with respect to a qualified foreign plan) amounts permitted to be taken into account under section 404A(d)(1) for all consecutive prior taxable years for which an election under section 404A was in effect for the Plan plus the initial section 404A amount required by § 1.404A-6(g)(2)(iii).

**(h) Examples.** The principles of this section are illustrated by the following examples:

*Example (1).* X, a foreign subsidiary of a domestic corporation, maintains its main office in foreign country A, and a branch, Y, in foreign country B. The functional currency of X is the FC. Y's functional currency is the local currency, LC. X maintains a qualified foreign plan for the benefit of X's employees in B. In the year the plan was adopted, a section 404A election was made for the plan. The appropriate foreign tax law is the tax law of B because all the employees covered by the plan are in B and plan liabilities are accounted for on Y's books. The tax law of B permits X to deduct contributions to the plan. The cumulative amount allowed as a deduction under the tax law of B is LC80. The cumulative United States amount with respect to the plan is LC100. Therefore, the cumulative limitation is LC80. The earnings and profits of X include the profit and loss for Y (reflecting a reduction for contributions to the plan, computed in LC and translated into FC under the principles of section 987).

*Example (2).* A qualified reserve plan is maintained by a foreign branch of a domestic corporation. The foreign branch computes its income under the profit and loss method of Rev. Rul. 75-107, 1975-1 C.B. 32 (see § 601.601(d)(2)(ii)(b) of this chapter), in units of the local currency, the FC. The foreign branch established the qualified reserve plan in 1985 and the taxpayer made the elections described in § 1.404A-6. The taxpayer's taxable year and the plan year is the calendar year. The assumed amounts taken into account under section 404A and appropriate foreign tax law for selected years and the computations under this section which follow from the amounts, in units of FC, are shown in the following table—

| | 1985 | 1986 | 1987 | 1988 |
|---|---|---|---|---|
| (1) Amount determined with respect to the plan under section 404A for the taxable year without regard to section 404A(d) | 800,000 | 900,000 | 300,000 | 1,000,000 |
| (2) Cumulative United States amount | 800,000 | 1,700,000 | 2,000,000 | 3,000,000 |
| (3) Cumulative foreign amount | 1,000,000 | 1,600,000 | 2,000,000 | 2,200,000 |
| (4) Lesser of cumulative United States or cumulative foreign amount | 800,000 | 1,600,000 | 2,000,000 | 2,200,000 |
| (5) Reduced by aggregate amount (cumulative sum of (6) for prior years) | (0) | (800,000) | (1,600,000) | (2,000,000) |
| | 800,000 | 800,000 | 400,000 | 200,000 |
| (6) Amount taken into account for the taxable year | 800,000 | 800,000 | 400,000 | 200,000 |

*Example (3).* Assume the same facts as in Example 2 for all taxable years, except that the qualified reserve plan is maintained by a foreign subsidiary of a domestic corporation. The foreign subsidiary computes its earnings and profits in units of the local currency, the FC. The foreign subsidiary's taxable year and the plan year are calendar years. The assumed amounts taken into account under section 404A and appropriate foreign law for selected years, and the computations under this section which follow from the amounts, in units of FC, are shown in the following table—

| | 1985 | 1986 | 1987 | 1988 |
|---|---|---|---|---|
| (1) Amount determined with respect to the plan under section 404A for the taxable year without regard to section 404A(d) | 800,000 | 900,000 | 300,000 | 1,000,000 |
| (2) Amount allowed as a deduction under the appropriate foreign tax laws for the taxable year | 1,000,000 | 600,000 | 400,000 | 200,000 |
| (3) cumulative United States amount | 800,000 | 1,700,000 | 2,000,000 | 3,000,000 |
| (4) cumulative foreign amount | 1,000,000 | 1,600,000 | 2,000,000 | 2,200,000 |
| (5) Lesser of cumulative United States or cumulative foreign amount | 800,000 | 1,600,000 | 2,000,000 | 2,200,000 |
| (6) Reduced by aggregate amount (cumulative sum of (7) or (8), whichever is applicable, for prior years) | (0) | (800,000) | (1,400,000) | (2,000,000) |
| | 800,000 | 800,000 | 600,000 | 200,000 |
| (7) Amount taken into account for taxable years before 1987 (lesser of (2) and (6)) | 800,000 | 600,000 | n/a | n/a |
| (8) Amount taken into account for taxable years after 1986 (same as (6)) | n/a | n/a | 600,000 | 200,000 |

*Example (4).* Z, a domestic corporation, maintains a retirement plan for employees employed in its foreign branch office. The foreign branch computes its income under the profit and loss method Rev. Rul. 75-107, 1975-1 C.B. 32 (see § 601.601(d)(2)(ii)(b) of this chapter), in units of local currency, the FC. The plan is a combination book reserve and funded plan, but is considered a single plan under foreign law. The total retirement benefits that a participant is eligible to receive is the sum of the benefits provided by the qualified reserve plan and the qualified funded plan. Pursuant to § 1.404A-6, in the year the plan was adopted, Z made a separate qualified reserve plan and funded plan election with respect to each portion of the foreign plan. The assumed deductions under section 404A and appropriate foreign law for selected years, and the computations under this section which follow from the deductions, are shown in the following table—

| | Qualified funded plan | | Qualified reserve plan | | Combined amount—qualified foreign plans | |
|---|---|---|---|---|---|---|
| | 1984 | 1985 | 1984 | 1985 | 1984 | 1985 |
| (1) Amount determined with respect to the qualified foreign plans under section 404A for the taxable year without regard to section 404A(d) | 40,000 | 90,000 | 30,000 | 80,000 | | |
| (2) Amount allowed as a deduction under the appropriate foreign tax laws for the taxable year | | | | | 60,000 | 185,000 |
| (3) Cumulative United States amount | 40,000 | 130,000 | 30,000 | 110,000 | | |
| (4) Combined cumulative United States amount (cumulative sum of (3)) | | | | | 70,000 | 240,000 |
| (5) Cumulative foreign amount (cumulative sum of (2)) | | | | | 60,000 | 245,000 |
| (6) Aggregate amount | | | | | 0 | 60,000 |
| (7) Lesser of combined cumulative United States amount or cumulative foreign amount ((4) or (5)) | | | | | 60,000 | 240,000 |
| (9) Reduced by the aggregate amount for the qualified funded and reserve plan (cumulative sum of (10) for prior years) | | | | | (0) | (60,000) |
| (10) Amount taken into account for taxable year | | | | | 60,000 | 180,000 |

*Example (5).* A qualified reserve plan is maintained by M, the foreign subsidiary of N, a domestic corporation. M computes its earnings and profits in units of the local currency, the FC. The taxable years of M and N and the plan year are the calendar year. M established the qualified reserve plan in 1984 and N made the elections described in § 1.404A-6. In, that year, the reasonable addition to the plan reserve under § 1.404A-3 was FC750,000. However, the amount allowed as a deduction under the appropriate foreign tax laws for the taxable year was FC650,000. The difference between the amount taken into account under § 1.404A-3 and the deduction under the appropriate foreign tax laws, FC100,000, could not be taken into account for any succeeding taxable year under § 1.404A-3, but it may later reduce M's earnings and profits pursuant to paragraph (a) of this section.

**Proposed § 1.404A-5 Additional limitations on amounts taken into account for qualified foreign plans.** [*For Preamble, see ¶ 151,519*]

**(a) Restrictions for nonqualified individuals.** *(1) General rule.* Notwithstanding any other provisions of §§ 1.404A-1 through 1.404A-7, no amount may be taken into account under section 404A for any contribution or amount accrued that is attributable to services performed either in the current or in a prior taxable year—

(i) By a citizen or resident of the United States who is a highly compensated employee (within the meaning of section 414(q)) (or, for taxable years beginning before January 1, 1989, by a citizen or resident of the United States who is an officer, shareholder, or highly compensated (within the meaning of § 1.410(b)-1(d)); or

(ii) In the United States, the compensation for which is subject to tax under chapter 1 of subtitle A of the Internal Revenue Code.

*(2) Determination of service attribution.* (i) Not limited to actual service. Service performed by individuals described in paragraph (a)(1)(i) of this section includes service credited to those individuals. Service performed in the United States includes service credited in relation (directly or indirectly) to any United States service.

(ii) Amounts attributable to service performed in the United States. The accrued benefit attributable to services described in this paragraph (a) is the excess, if any, of the total accrued benefit over the accrued benefit determined without credit for time spent performing services described in this paragraph (a) and without regard to the compensation levels for that time.

**(b) Records to be provided by taxpayer.** *(1) In general.* Notwithstanding any other provisions of §§ 1.404A-1 through 1.404A-7, no amount may be taken into account under section 404A for any contribution or amount accrued unless the taxpayer attaches a statement to its United States income tax return for any taxable year for which a qualified foreign plan maintained by an employer has United States tax significance. This statement must specify the name and type of qualified foreign plan; the cumulative United States amount, the cumulative foreign amount, and the aggregate amount with respect to the plan; the name and country of organization of the employer; and any other information the Commissioner may prescribe by forms and accompanying instructions or by revenue procedure.

*(2) Primary evidence.* The statement described in paragraph (b)(1) of this section and any required forms must be completed in good faith with all of the information called for and with the calculations referenced in paragraph (b)(1) of this section. Except as provided in paragraph (b)(4) of this section, one of the following documents must be attached to the United States income tax return—

(i) A statement from the foreign tax authorities specifying the amount of the deduction allowed in computing taxable income under the appropriate foreign tax law for the relevant year or years with respect to the qualified foreign plan; or

(ii) If the return under the appropriate foreign tax law shows the deduction for plan contributions or plan reserves as a separate identifiable item, a copy of the foreign tax return for the relevant year or years with respect to the qualified foreign plan.

*(3) Additional requirements.* The statement or return attached pursuant to paragraph (b)(2) of this section may be either the original, a duplicate original, a duly certified or authenticated copy, or a sworn copy. If only a sworn copy of a receipt or return is attached, there must be kept readily available for comparison on request the original, a duplicate original, or a duly certified or authenticated copy.

*(4) Secondary evidence.* Where the statement or return described in paragraph (b)(2)(i) or (b)(2)(ii) of this section is not available, all of the following information must be attached to the United States income tax return—

(i) A certified statement setting forth the cumulative foreign amount for each taxable year to which section 404A applies;

(ii) The excerpts from the employer's books and records showing either the change in the reserve or contributions made with respect to the plan for the taxable year to which section 404A applies; and

(iii) The computations of the foreign deduction relating to the plan to be established by data such as excerpts from the foreign law, assessment notices, or other documentary evidence.

*(5) Foreign language.* If the relevant returns, books, records or computations are not maintained in the English language, the taxpayer must furnish, upon request, a certified translation that is satisfactory to the District Director.

*(6) Additional information required by District Director.* If the taxpayer upon request of the District Director fails, without justification, to furnish any additional information that is significant, the provisions of section 982 will apply.

*(7) Authorized officer to complete documents.* The documents required by this section and by §§ 1.404A-6 and 1.404A-7 must be signed by an authorized officer of the taxpayer (as defined in section 6062 or 6063) who must verify under penalty of perjury that the statement and all other documents submitted are true and correct to his knowledge and belief.

*(8) Transitional rule—good faith effort.* For taxable years ending before [insert date that is 90 days after the date of publication of final regulations in the FEDERAL REGISTER] a taxpayer will be treated as satisfying this paragraph (b) if it makes a good faith effort to provide reasonable documentation.

**(c) Actuarial requirements.** *(1) Reasonable actuarial assumptions.* Except as otherwise specifically provided in §§ 1.404A-2 and 1.404A-3 and this paragraph (c), in the case of a qualified reserve plan or a qualified funded plan under which benefits are fixed or determinable, no amount may be taken into account under section 404A unless costs, liabilities, rates of interest, and other factors under the plan are determined on the basis of actuarial assumptions and methods each of which is reasonable (taking into account the experience of the plan and reasonable expectations), or which, in the aggregate, result in an amount being taken into account that is equivalent to that which would be determined if each such assumption and method were reasonable, and that, in combination, offer the actuary's best estimate of anticipated experience under the plan. For plan years beginning before January 1, 1988, the preceding sentence is satisfied if costs, liabilities, rates of interest, and other factors under the plan are determined on the basis of actuarial assumptions and methods that are reasonable in the aggregate (taking into account the experience of the plan and reasonable expectations) and that, in combination, offer the actuary's best estimate of anticipated experience under the plan. Except to the extent required under that paragraph, the interest rate determined under § 1.404A-3(b)(4) may not be considered in determining whether other actuarial assumptions are reasonable in the aggregate for this purpose.

*(2) Full funding limitation.* Notwithstanding any other provisions of §§ 1.404A-1 through 1.464A-7, no amount may be taken into account under section 404A if the amount causes the assets in the trust (in the case of a qualified funded plan) or if taking into account the amount causes the amount of the reserve (in the case of a qualified reserve

plan) to exceed the amount described in section 412(c)(7)(A)(i).

**Proposed § 1.404A-6 Elections under section 404A and changes in methods of accounting.** [*For Preamble, see ¶ 151,519*]

**(a) Elections, changes in accounting methods, and changes in plan years.** *(1) In general.* (i) Methods of accounting. An election under section 404A with respect to a qualified foreign plan constitutes the adoption of a method of accounting if the election is made in the taxable year in which the plan is adopted. Any election under section 404A with respect to a preexisting plan, however, constitutes a change in method of accounting requiring the Commissioner's consent under section 446(e) and an adjustment under section 481(a). Additionally, any other change in the method used to determine the amount taken into account under section 404A(a), as well as the revocation of any election under section 404A, constitutes a change in accounting method subject to the consent and adjustment requirements of sections 446(e) and 481(a). This section provides procedures for obtaining the Commissioner's consent to make certain changes in methods of accounting under section 404A. Additionally, § 1.404A-7 provides special procedural rules applicable (along with the rules under this section) for retroactive and transition period elections under section 404A.

(ii) Changes not involving accounting methods. Any change in treatment, adjustment, or correction described in § 1.446-1(e)(2)(ii)(b) (e.g., correction of computational errors) is not a change in accounting method. While a retroactive. qualified funded plan election under § 1.404A-7(c) constitutes a change in method of accounting, a mere election to apply the effective date of section 404A under § 1.404A-7(b) retroactively does not necessarily result in a change in accounting method. Additionally, a retroactive election for funded foreign branch plans under § 1.404A-7(d) will not be treated as a change in method of accounting, except to the extent that the taxpayer took erroneous deductions under its method of accounting prior to the beginning of its open period. Finally, a change of actuarial assumptions will not be treated as a change in method of accounting for purposes of this section.

*(2) Single plan.* (i) General rule. Except as otherwise provided, the rules of this section regarding elections, revocations, and re-elections, and the adoption or change of a plan year, apply separately (i.e., on a plan-by-plan basis) to each plan that qualifies as a single plan (as defined in § 1.414(l)-1(b)). For purposes of this definition, a separate reserve maintained by an employer exclusively for its liability under a plan is considered a plan asset that is available exclusively to pay benefits to employees who are covered by the plan and to their beneficiaries. Although a plan may be treated as a reserve plan under foreign law, this treatment is not binding for purposes of section 404A and this section.

(ii) Example. The principles of this paragraph (a)(2) are illustrated by the following example:

*Example.* S is a wholly-owned foreign subsidiary of P, a domestic corporation. S maintains a deferred compensation plan under local law to provide benefits to its employees upon retirement based upon years of service and the highest five-year average salary. S decided to account for 70 percent of its deferred compensation liabilities through an unfunded book reserve (Plan One), and to account for the remaining 30 percent through a trust equivalent (Plan Two). All of the assets of Plan One and Plan Two were available for payment of liabilities under their respective plans, and were only available for payment of liabilities under their respective plans. Thus, when deferred compensation was paid to S's employees, within the meaning of this paragraph (a)(2), 70 percent of the amount was paid by check drawn against the general assets of S and 30 percent of the amount paid was paid by check drawn on the assets of the trust equivalent. Pursuant to this section, P made a qualified reserve plan election for Plan One, which it defined as a plan of deferred compensation with liability for 70 percent of the amount of deferred compensation owing to each employee under S's deferred compensation plan. In addition, it made a qualified funded plan election for Plan Two, which it defined as a plan of deferred compensation with liability for the remaining 30 percent. Because S's reserve for its liability was treated as a plan asset with respect to 70 percent of the liability and the assets of the trust, Plan One met the requirements of a "single plan" under § 1.414(l)-1(b), and Plan Two was a separate "single plan". Thus, S could take into account only 70 percent of its liability to each employee under its deferred compensation plan when calculating the reasonable additions to the reserve under section 404A(c) for Plan One. Similarly, the full funding limitation and other calculations with respect to Plan Two may only be made with respect to 30 percent of S's liability to each employee under the foreign deferred compensation plan.

**(b) Initial elections under section 404A.** *(1) In general.* The Commissioner's consent to elect initially under section 404A to treat a single plan as a qualified funded plan or as a qualified reserve plan is granted automatically if the taxpayer complies with the requirements of this paragraph (b). Except as provided in § 1.404A-7, an initial election under this section with respect to any qualified foreign plan may be made only for a taxable year beginning after December 31, 1979.

*(2) Time for making election.* (i) Foreign branch plans. Except as provided in § 1.404A-7, the initial election for a qualified foreign plan maintained by a foreign branch must be made no later than the time prescribed by law for filing the United States return (including extensions) for the first taxable year for which the election is to be effective.

(ii) Foreign corporation plans. Except as provided in § 1.404A-7, the initial election for a qualified foreign plan maintained by a foreign corporation must be made no later than the time allowed for making elections under §§ 1.964-1 and 1.964-1T. Thus, the election under section 404A may be deferred until the earnings and profits of the foreign corporation have United States tax significance, as defined in §§ 1.964-1 and 1.964-1T. United States tax significance may occur in a number of ways, including, for example, a dividend distribution, an income inclusion under section 951(a), a section 1248 transaction, a step-up of basis by earnings and profits for purposes of valuing assets for interest allocation purposes under section 864(e), or an inclusion in income of the earnings of a qualified electing fund under section 1293(a)(1).

*(3) Manner in which election is to be made.* (i) Foreign branch plans. In the case of a qualified foreign plan maintained by a domestic corporation, the initial election must be made by the taxpayer by attaching a list of plans for which section 404A treatment is desired to a return filed within the time prescribed in paragraph (b)(2)(i) of this section.

(ii) Controlled foreign corporation plans. If a qualified foreign plan is maintained by a controlled foreign corporation, the initial election under this section must be made in the manner prescribed by §§ 1.964-1 and 1.964-1T and must include a list of all plans for which the election is made.

(iii) Noncontrolled foreign corporation plans. If a qualified foreign plan is maintained by a noncontrolled foreign corporation, the initial election under this section must be made in the manner prescribed by §§ 1.964-1 and 1.964-1T and must include a list of all plans for which the election is made, as if the noncontrolled foreign corporation were a controlled foreign corporation. In applying the rules of §§ 1.964-1 and 1.964-1T, the term "majority domestic corporate shareholders" is substituted for the term "controlling United States shareholders" wherever it appears in §§ 1.964-1 and 1.964-1T. The term "majority domestic corporate shareholders" has the meaning set forth in § 1.985-2(c)(3)(i).

*(4) Other requirements for election.* For each plan listed, pursuant to paragraph (b)(3) of this section, the taxpayer must designate whether it elects to treat the plan as a qualified funded plan or qualified reserve plan, and must designate a plan year. Additionally, for each plan listed, the taxpayer must disclose the amount of any section 481(a) adjustment, as well as the initial cumulative United States amount, the initial cumulative foreign amount, and the initial aggregate amount defined in paragraph (g) of this section. See § 1.404A-5(b) for rules on additional information required, signing and verifying required statements, and notices and forms necessary to elect under section 404A. Additionally, see § 1.404A-7(d)(1) for required agreement to assessment of tax for retroactive elections for funded foreign branch plans.

**(c) Termination of election when a plan ceases to be a qualified foreign plan.** *(1) In general.* An election under section 404A with respect to a foreign deferred compensation plan is terminated if at any time on or after the first day of the first taxable year for which the election is effective the plan ceases to be a qualified foreign plan by reason of a failure to satisfy the conditions of section 404A(e)(1) or (2). Thus, for example, the election is terminated (subject to the consent of the Commissioner) if more than 10 percent of the amounts taken into account under the plan are attributable to services performed by employees subject to United States federal income tax. As used in this section, the term "termination" refers only to situations under which a plan ceases to be a qualified foreign plan by reason of a failure to satisfy the conditions of section 404(e)(1) or (2). Thus, the term is distinguished from a voluntary revocation of an election (i.e., under paragraph (d)(1) of this section), which also causes a plan to cease to be a qualified foreign plan. Upon termination of an election under section 404A, a change in method of accounting is required. The conditional advance consent of the Commissioner is granted for this change in method of accounting. This conditional consent may be withdrawn, however, if the District Director determines that tax avoidance was a purpose of the termination or if the procedures in paragraph (c)(2) of this section are not satisfied.

*(2) Rules for changing method of accounting upon termination of election.* (i) Time for making change. (A) Foreign branch plans. Except as provided in § 1.404A-7, in the case of a plan of a foreign branch the change in method of accounting required upon termination of a section 404A election must be made no later than the time prescribed by law for filing the United States return (including extensions) for the taxable year in which the plan ceases to satisfy the requirements of section 404A(e)(1) or (2).

(B) Foreign corporation plans. Except as provided in § 1.404A-7, in the case of a plan of a foreign corporation the change in method of accounting required upon termination of a section 404A election shall be made no later than the first year after the termination in which the earnings and profits of the foreign corporation have United States tax significance, as defined in §§ 1.964-1 and 1.964-1T. See paragraph (b)(2)(ii) of this section for United States tax significance examples.

(ii) Procedures for changing method of accounting upon termination of election. (A) Foreign branch plans. The change in method of accounting required upon termination of a section 404A election with respect to a foreign branch plan must be made by attaching a statement to the return described in paragraph (c)(2)(i)(A) of this section disclosing the amount of any section 481 (a) adjustment (required under paragraph (e) of this section and computed in accordance with paragraph (f) of this section) arising upon the change.

(B) Controlled foreign corporation plans. The change in method of accounting required upon termination of a Section 404A election with respect to a controlled foreign corporation plan must be made in the manner prescribed by §§ 1.964-1 and 1.964-1T and must include disclosure of the amount of any section 481(a) adjustment (required under paragraph (e) of this section and computed in accordance with paragraph (f) of this section) arising upon the change.

(C) Noncontrolled foreign corporation plans. The change in method of accounting required upon termination of a section 404A election with respect to a noncontrolled foreign corporation plan must be made in the manner prescribed by §§ i.964-1 and 1.964-1T and must include disclosure of the amount of any section 481(a) adjustment (required under paragraph (e) of this section and computed in accordance with paragraph (f) of this section) arising upon the change. In applying the rules of §§ 1.964-1 and 1.964-1T, the term "majority domestic corporate shareholders" is substituted for the term "controlling United States shareholders" wherever it appears in §§ 1.964-1 and 1.964-1T. The term "majority domestic corporate shareholders" has the meaning set forth in § 1.985-2(c) (3)(i).

**(d) Other changes in methods of accounting and changes in plan year.** *(1) Application for consent.* Except as provided in paragraph (c) of this section or in § 1.404A-7, once an initial election under section 404A is effective with respect to a plan, the taxpayer must separately apply to obtain the express consent of the Commissioner prior to changing any method of accounting with respect to a foreign deferred compensation plan. Application for the consent of the Commissioner is required whether or not the method being changed is proper or permitted under the Internal Revenue Code and regulations thereunder. Any change in method of accounting not described in this paragraph (d)(1) must be made in accordance with the requirements of section 446(e) and the regulations thereunder. The procedures prescribed in this paragraph (d), however, are the exclusive procedures for making the following changes in method of accounting—

(i) Revocation of a section 404A election;

(ii) Re-election under section 404A following termination or revocation of a section 404A election;

(iii) Changing the treatment of a plan from a qualified funded plan to a qualified reserve plan (or the converse); or

(iv) Changing the actuarial funding method used to determine costs under a qualified funded plan.

*(2) Procedures for other changes in method of accounting.* (i) Foreign branch plans. To request consent to a change in method of accounting described in paragraph (d)(1) of this section, the taxpayer must file an application on Form 3115 with the Commissioner generally within 180 days after the beginning of the taxable year in which the change is re-

quested to be effective. In the case of a revocation of an election under section 404A, however, the 180-day period in the preceding sentence is extended to the time prescribed by law for filing the United States return for the taxable year of the change.

(ii) Foreign corporation plans. For a controlled foreign corporation or a noncontrolled foreign corporation, a request for consent to revocation or to another change in method of accounting must be made in accordance with the rules of §§ 1.964-1 and 1.964-1T.

*(3) Plan year.* A taxpayer must secure the consent of the Commissioner to change the plan year of a qualified foreign plan. Termination or revocation of a section 404A election will not effect a change in the plan year of the plan.

**(e) Application of section 481.** *(1) In general.* A change in method described in this section constitutes a change in method of accounting to which section 481 applies. Except as otherwise provided in this paragraph and in paragraph (f) of this section, this adjustment must be made in accordance with section 481 and the regulations thereunder in those circumstances. For purposes of section 481(a)(2), any change in method described in this section is considered a change in method of accounting initiated by the taxpayer.

*(2) Period of adjustment.* (i) In general. The section 481(a) adjustment period is determined under the rules of this paragraph (e)(2).

(ii) Election or re-election. In the case of an election or a re-election following termination or revocation, the section 481(a) adjustment required by paragraph (e)(1) of this section must be taken into account ratably over a 15-year period, beginning with the first taxable year for which the election or re-election is effective. This section 481(a) adjustment period also applies to a change from a qualified funded plan to a qualified reserve plan.

(iii) Termination or revocation of election and all other changes in method. The adjustment required by paragraph (e)(1) of this section for all changes in method (other than those described in paragraph (e)(2)(ii) of this section), including changes in election from a qualified reserve plan to a qualified funded plan, must be taken into account ratably over a six-year period, beginning with the first taxable year for which the change is effective. If unamortized section 481(a) adjustment amount (e.g., from a previous change) remains at the end of a change in method of accounting to which this paragraph (e)(2)(iii) applies, the net amount of all of the section 481(a) adjustments must be taken into account ratably over this six-year section 481(a) adjustment period.

(iv) Acceleration of section 481(a) adjustment. If the employer ceases to engage in the relevant trade or business at any time prior to the expiration of the applicable section 481(a) adjustment period provided in paragraph (e)(2)(ii) or (e)(2)(iii) of this section, the employer must take into account, in the taxable year of cessation, the balance of any section 481(a) adjustment not previously taken into account in computing taxable income (in the case of a branch) or earnings and profits (in the case of a foreign corporation). For purposes of this paragraph (e)(2)(iv), whether or not an employer ceases to engage in the trade or business is to be determined under administrative procedures issued under § 1.446-1(e). In applying those procedures, "employer" is to be defined in the same manner as "taxpayer" is defined under those procedures.

*(3) Allocation and source.* The amount of any net negative section 481(a) adjustment determined under this section and taken into account for a taxable year must be allocated and apportioned under § 1.861-8 in the same manner as a deduction or reduction in earnings and profits under section 404A. Any net positive section 481(a) adjustment that is taken into account for a taxable year first must be reduced by directly allocating to such adjustment the employer's section 404A expense that is subject to apportionment (including any amount that otherwise would be capitalized); to the extent a net positive section 481(a) adjustment exceeds the amount of the employer's section 404A expense for the taxable year, such excess must be sourced or otherwise classified in the same manner as section 404A deductions or reductions in earnings and profits are allocated and apportioned.

*(4) Example.* The principles of this paragraph (e) are illustrated by the following example:

*Example.* X, a domestic corporation, made an initial election under section 404A to treat an existing deferred compensation plan maintained by its foreign branch as a qualified reserve plan, effective beginning in X's 1985 taxable year. X's foreign branch maintains its books and records in FC, the functional currency. Previously, X had consistently used a permissible method of accounting with respect to the plan. The section 481(a) adjustment arising from X's change in accounting method upon its section 404A election was a negative FC150,000. Beginning with its 1985 taxable year, X took into account a negative FC10,000 each year (FC150,000/15). Effective beginning in X's 1988 taxable year X received the Commissioner's express consent to change from a qualified reserve plan to a qualified funded plan. The section 481(a) adjustment attributable solely to the 1988 change was a positive FC132,000. Beginning with its 1988 taxable year, and for each of the five succeeding taxable years, X took into account a positive FC2,000, as computed below.

| | |
|---|---|
| Negative 1985 section 481(a) adjustment | (FC150,000) |
| Less: 1985, 1986 & 1987 amounts taken into account | 30,000 |
| Subtotal | (120,000) |
| Positive 1988 section 481(a) adjustment | 132,000 |
| Net positive section 481(a) adjustment | 12,000 |
| Section 481(a) adjustment period | ÷ 6 |
| Net amount taken into account annually during section 481(a) adjustment period | FC2,000 |

**(f) Computation of section 481(a) adjustment.** *(1) In general.* For purposes of section 404A, except as provided in § 1.404A-7(f)(1)(ii)(C), the amount of the section 481(a) adjustment required under paragraph (e)(1) of this section equals—

(i) The Old Method Closing Amount; less

(ii) The New Method Opening Amount.

*(2) Old Method Closing Amount.* (i) In general. Except as otherwise provided in paragraph (f)(2)(ii), (iii),or (iv) of this section (or as otherwise prescribed by the Commissioner), the Old Method Closing Amount equals—

(A) The total of all past deductions taken with respect to liabilities under the plan; plus

(B) The net income earned directly or indirectly by any separate funding entity (e.g., account or trust) with respect to the plan, but only to the extent that such net income has not previously been taken into account in determining taxable income (in the case of a foreign branch) or earnings and profits (in the case of a foreign corporation); minus

(C) The total of all past payments under the plan made to plan participants and beneficiaries by the employer, the trust, or the separate funding entity.

(ii) Taxpayer formerly using a reserve method. (A) In general. If a taxpayer has consistently taken amounts with respect to the plan into account under a reserve method, the Old Method Closing Amount equals the closing reserve balance at the end of the closing year calculated under the taxpayer's reserve method. For purposes of the preceding sentence, a reserve method means a method of accrual based on the actuarial present value of expected future plan benefits.

(B) Former qualified reserve plan. To request the Commissioner's consent in the case of a former qualified reserve plan, the closing reserve balance must be adjusted for any unamortized increases or decreases to the reserve described in § 1.404A-3(c) that have not yet been taken into account. For example, if the closing reserve balance is FC100,000, but FC10,000 of the closing reserve balance consists of an unamortized increase in the reserve that has not previously been taken into account due to the ten-year amortization requirements of § 1.404A-3(c), the Old Method Closing Amount is FC90,000.

(iii) Taxpayer formerly using pay-as-you-go method. If the taxpayer has consistently taken amounts into account with respect to the plan based only on actual payments of plan benefits to participants and beneficiaries, the Old Method Closing Amount equals zero.

(iv) Taxpayer formerly using a funded method. (A) Payment to separate funding entity. If the taxpayer has consistently taken amounts into account with respect to the plan based only on actual payments to a separate funding entity and on payments by the employer (but not by the funding entity) to plan participants or beneficiaries, the Old Method Closing Amount equals the balance in the separate funding entity at the end of the closing year, including amounts attributable, directly or indirectly, to net investment income that has not previously been taken into account in determining taxable income (in the case of a foreign branch) or earnings and profits (in the case of a foreign corporation).

(B) Former qualified funded plan. In the case of a former qualified funded plan, the Old Method Closing Amount generally equals the amount described in paragraph (f)(2)(iv)(A) of this section, adjusted, however, by—

(1) Reducing the amount properly to reflect any net limitations under section 404A(b) and (g) (e.g., the full funding limitation for a qualified funded plan) that were applied in determining amounts taken into account under the former section 404A method of accounting; and

(2) Increasing the amount properly to reflect any amounts that are not paid during the closing year but that are permitted to be taken into account in the closing year under section 404A(b)(2)(relating to payments made after the close of the taxable year).

(v) Section 404A(d) limitation. In computing the Old Method Closing Amount upon the termination or revocation of an election under section 404A, the limitations of section 404A(d) and § 1.404A-4 must be taken into account. Thus, if the Old Method Closing Amount is determined under paragraph (f)(2)(ii)(B) or (f)(2)(iv)(B) of this section, the amount otherwise determined under those paragraphs shall be reduced by applying the section 404A(d) and § 1.404A-4 limitations to the extent the cumulative United States amount under § 1.404A-4 exceeds the cumulative foreign amount under § 1.404A-4.

*(3) New Method Opening Amount.* (i) Qualified reserve plan. In the case of an election to treat a plan as a qualified reserve plan, the New Method Opening Amount equals the balance of the reserve as of the end of the last day of the closing year, calculated under the rules of section 404A(c) and § 1.404A-3 based on plan information and data as of that date. The New Method Opening Amount must be reduced (or increased) for any unamortized increases (or decreases) to the reserve described in section 404A(c)(4) and § 1.404A-3(c).

(ii) Qualified funded plan. In the case of an election to be treated as a qualified funded plan, the New Method Opening Amount equals the amount of funds in the trust as of the beginning of the first day of the opening year, adjusted as necessary to take into account the rules of section 404A(b) and (g). If the separate funding entity does not qualify as a trust under § 1.404A-1(e), the New Method Opening Amount in the case of a qualified funded plan is zero because there is no balance in a trust as defined in § 1.404A-1(e).

(iii) Nonqualified plan. In the case of any plan that ceases to be a qualified foreign plan (either by reason of the termination or revocation of a section 404A election), the New Method Opening Amount is zero.

(iv) Section 404A(d) limitation. In computing the New Method Opening Amount upon an election under section 404A, the limitation on deductions of section 404A(d) and § 1.404A-4 must be taken into account. Thus, if the New Method Opening Amount is determined under paragraph (f)(2)(i) or (f)(2)(ii) of this section, the amount otherwise determined must be reduced to the extent the cumulative United States amount computed under § 1.404A-4 exceeds the cumulative foreign amount computed under § 1.404A-4. See paragraph (g) of this section for initialization of amounts taken into account under section 404A(d).

*(4) Definitions and special rules.* (i) Opening year. For purposes of this section, the *opening year* is the first taxable year for which the new method of accounting is effective with respect to a plan. For example, in the case of an election to treat a foreign corporation plan as a qualified reserve plan beginning in 1989, the opening year is 1989, even though the election may not be made until 1994 pursuant to paragraph (b)(2)(ii) of this section.

(ii) Closing year. For purposes of this section, the *closing year* is the taxable year immediately preceding the opening year.

(iii) Separate funding entity. A *separate funding entity* described in paragraphs (f)(2)(i)(B) and (f)(2)(iv) of this section is any entity that satisfies the first requirement in the definition of the equivalent of a trust in § 1.404A-1(e) (segregation in a separate legal entity) and, in practice, also satisfies the third requirement in that definition (dedication to payment of plan benefits) with respect to benefits under the relevant plan.

(iv) Special rules for Certain foreign corporation plans. In the case of a foreign corporation's plan for which no method has been used for some or all prior taxable years because no calculation of earnings and profits has been necessary for those years (see, e.g., paragraph (b)(2)(ii) of this section), the employer may assume that the old method has been consistent with any method actually used consistently in immediately prior years. If no calculation of earnings and profits has been made for prior years, in determining the Old Method closing Amount, the taxpayer may assume the method used was a method described in paragraph (f)(2)(iii) of this section. This assumed method used in the calculation of the Old Method Closing Amount must actually be used by the taxpayer for all the prior taxable years to the extent reductions of earnings and profits for those years are ever determined with respect to the plan.

(v) Reference to rules applicable in the case of failure to consider net investment income in computing section 481(a) adjustment. The treatment of net investment income earned by a funding vehicle that has not previously taken into account by the taxpayer in determining taxable income (in the case of a foreign branch) or earnings and profits (in the case of a foreign corporation), and that is not properly considered (as required under paragraphs (f)(2)(i)(B) and (f)(2)(iv)(A) of this section) in determining the amount of the section 481(a) adjustment for purposes of section 404A, is determined under other applicable provisions, which may include sections 61, 671 through 679, and 1001.

(vi) Certain section 481(a) adjustments treated as carryover contributions. In the case of an election for a plan to be treated as a qualified funded plan, any net positive section 481(a) adjustment is treated as a carryover contribution (within the meaning of § 1.404A-2(d)(4)) to the extent that the adjustment is attributable to limits (that would be taken into account under § 1.404A-2(d)(4)) on the amounts previously contributed to the trust under the plan that could be taken into account under section 404A.

*(5) Examples.* The principles of paragraph (f) of this section are illustrated by the following examples:

*Example (1).* Nonqualified reserve plan to qualified reserve plan. A foreign subsidiary of a domestic corporation established an irrevocable balance sheet reserve for pension expenses in 1981. The subsidiary maintains its books and records in FC, the functional currency. From 1981 through 1987, the taxpayer reduced earnings and profits of the foreign subsidiary by FC150,000, the amount of the pension liability which had accrued under the plan. This method of accounting was never challenged or changed by the District Director prior to the expiration of the statute of limitations for the 1981 through 1987 taxable years. Through December 31, 1987, the last day of the closing year, actual pension payments totalled FC15,000. For the 1988 taxable year, the taxpayer made an election for the plan to be treated as a qualified reserve plan. The reserve calculated under section 404A as of the first day of the 1988 taxable year, the opening year, and based upon employee census data as of that date, was FC175,000. The Old Method Closing Amount was FC135,000 (FC150,000 less FC15,000). The New Method Opening Amount was FC175,000. The section 481(a) adjustment was a negative FC40,000 (FC135,000 less FC175,000). This adjustment is to be taken into account over the 15-year section 481(a) adjustment period prescribed in paragraph (e)(2)(ii) of this section.

*Example (2).* Nonqualified reserve plan to qualified reserve plan. Assume the same facts as in Example 1, except that the reserve calculated under section 404A as of the first day of the 1988 taxable year and based upon employee census data as of that date was FC75,000. The Old Method Closing Amount was FC135,000 (FC150,000 less FC15,000). The New Method Opening Amount was FC75,000. The section 481(a) adjustment was a positive FC60,000 (FC135,000 less FC75,000). This adjustment is to be taken into account over the 15-year section 481(a) adjustment period prescribed in paragraph (e)(2)(ii) of this section.

*Example (3).* Nonqualified funded plan to qualified reserve plan. M, a domestic corporation, wholly owns N, a foreign corporation. N maintains its books and records in FC, the local currency. From 1981 through 1988, N maintained a nonqualified funded plan. During this period, N contributed FC55,000 to the separate funding entity administering the plan and reduced earnings and profits by FC55,000. The separate funding entity realized net income of FC17,000 from investment of plan assets and paid nothing to participants. None of the FC17,000 net investment income earned in the separate funding entity was taken into account in computing N's earnings and profits. As of the last day of N's 1988 taxable year, the closing year, the plan's fund balance was FC72,000, comprised of FC55,000 (excess contributions) and FC17,000 (investment income). The reserve calculated under section 404A as of the first day of the 1989 taxable year, the opening year, was FC100,000. Effective for M's 1989 taxable year, M elected under section 404A to treat N's funded plan as a qualified reserve plan. The Old Method Closing Amount was FC72000. The New Method Opening Amount was FC100,000; thus, if, in the future, N pays FC100,000 to plan participants or beneficiaries, that FC100,000 will not again reduce N's earnings and profits. The section 481(a) adjustment was a negative FC28,000 (FC72,000 less FC100,000). However, if the District Director later challenges and requires N to change its method of accounting for foreign deferred compensation used in determining its 1981 through 1988 earnings and profits in a taxable year prior to the 1989 taxable year, the section 481(a) adjustment could be changed from a negative FC28,000 to a negative FC100,000. Pursuant to the administrative procedures under section 446(e), the District Director, upon challenging the treatment of foreign deferred compensation in years prior to 1989, could require any necessary positive section 481(a) adjustment to be taken into account in one taxable year.

*Example (4).* Nonqualified funded clan to qualified funded plan. Y, a domestic corporation, wholly owns X, a foreign corporation. X maintains its books and records in FC, the local currency. From 1981 through 1988, X maintained a nonqualified funded plan. During this period, X reduced earnings and profits by contributions of FC55,000 to the plan. The plan paid participants FC30,000. As of the last day of Y's 1988 taxable year, the plan's fund balance was FC29,000, comprised of FC25,000 (net contributions) and FC4,000 (interest income that was never previously taken into account in determining earnings and profits). Effective for Y's 1989 taxable year, Y elected under section 404A to treat X's funded plan as a qualified funded plan. The Old Method Closing Amount was FC29,000. The New Method Opening Amount was FC29,000. The section 481(a) adjustment was zero (FC29,000 less FC29,000). See Example 3, however, for the effects on the section 481(a) adjustment of a successful challenge to X's method of accounting for foreign deferred compensation in years prior to 1989 by the District Director.

*Example (5).* Z, the wholly owned foreign subsidiary of Y, a domestic corporation, has maintained reserve plan for its employees, beginning in 1981. Z maintains its books and records in FC, the local currency. Effective for 1984, Y elected under section 404A to treat the plan as a qualified reserve plan. The only section 481(a) adjustment required was to take into account the limitation under section 404A(d). In 1981 through 1983, prior to the section 404A election, Z's earnings and profits were reduced by additions to the reserve. This method of accounting was never challenged or changed by the District Director prior to the expiration of the statute of limitations for the 1981 through 1983 taxable years. Thus, the Old Method Closing Amount equaled the balance in the reserve, which was FC300. To compute the New Method Opening Amount, the opening reserve took into account the lesser of the cumulative United States amount (FC300) or the cumulative foreign amount (FC90) as of the first day of 1984, the opening year. Thus, the New Method Opening Amount was FC90: The section 481(a) adjustment was therefore a positive FC210 (FC300 − FC90); 1/15 of this amount, FC14 (FC210/15), is being taken into account as an increase in earnings and profits each year over the 15-year section 481(a) adjustment period that began in 1984.

*Example (6).* Nonqualified reserve plan to qualified reserve plan. Assume the same facts as in Example 5 for all taxable years and the annual United States reduction, foreign reduction, cumulative United States amount, cumulative foreign amount and the section 481(a) adjustment shown below. The total annual reduction (or increase) in Z's earnings and profits was as follows—

| | 1984 | 1985 | 1986 | 1987 | 1988 | 1989 | 1990 |
|---|---|---|---|---|---|---|---|
| Amount determined under U.S. law with respect to the plan under section 404A for the taxable year without regard to section 404A(d) | FC(40) | FC(50) | FC(60) | FC(70) | FC(80) | FC(90) | FC(100) |
| Amount allowed as a deduction for the taxable year under the appropriate foreign tax laws | (70) | (260) | (50) | (40) | (30) | (20) | (10) |
| Cumulative U.S. amount | (340) | (390) | (450) | (520) | (600) | (690) | (790) |
| Cumulative foreign amount | (160) | (420) | (470) | (510) | (540) | (560) | (570) |
| Lesser of cumulative U.S. or foreign amount | (160) | (390) | (450) | (510) | (540) | (560) | (570) |
| Reduced by the aggregate amount | 90 | 160 | 390 | 440 | 510 | 540 | 560 |
| | (70) | (230) | (60) | (70) | (30) | (20) | (10) |
| Amount taken into account for the taxable year[1] | (70) | (230) | (50) | (70) | (30) | (20) | (10) |
| Positive section 481 adjustment | 14 | 14 | 14 | 14 | 14 | 14 | 14 |
| Total increase (reduction) in earnings and profits taken into account for the taxable year | FC(56) | FC(216) | FC(36) | FC(56) | FC(16) | FC(6) | FC(4) |

[1] The limitation in § 1.404A-4(c) applies to taxable years 1984, 1985 and 1986. In 1986, the amount deductible under the appropriate foreign tax law was less than the lower of (1) the cumulative U.S. amount, or, (2) the cumulative foreign amount (then reduced by the aggregate amount).

**(g) Initial section 404A(d) amounts.** *(1) In general.* By making an election under section 404A, a taxpayer adopts section 404A(d) a part of its method of accounting. Section 1.404A-4 provides rules to apply the limitations of section 404A(d) in taxable years when an election under section 404A is in effect. This paragraph (g) provides rules to compute initial amounts under section 404A(d) in the opening year. These rules are based on the rules to compute the New Method Opening Amount in paragraph (f)(3) of this section.

*(2) Computation of amounts.* As of the first day of the opening year, the initial section 404A(d) amounts are as follows:

(i) The initial cumulative United States amount equals the New Method Opening Amount without regard to any reduction under paragraph (f)(3)(iv) of this section.

(ii) The initial cumulative foreign amount equals the New Method Opening Amount computed as though the appropriate foreign tax law were the new method of accounting and without regard to paragraph (f)(3)(iv) of this section.

(iii) The initial aggregate amount equals the lesser of—

(A) The initial cumulative United States amount; and

(B) The initial cumulative foreign amount.

*(3) Example.* The principles of paragraph (g) of this section are illustrated by the following example:

*Example.* A foreign subsidiary of a domestic corporation maintains its books and record's in FC, the local currency. The subsidiary established a funded deferred compensation plan in 1983 but reduced earnings and profits on a Pay-as-you-go basis. The plan year and the taxable year of the domestic corporation and the subsidiary are the calendar year. For the 1990 taxable year, the domestic corporation elected to treat the plan as a qualified reserve plan. The balance in the separate funding entity as of January 1, 1990, the first day of the opening year, was FC90,000. The initial United States cumulative amount (the opening reserve) was FC150,000. The initial foreign cumulative amount (the balance in the separate funding entity) was FC90,000. The initial aggregate amount was FC90,000 (the lesser of FC90,000 or FC150,000). Since the subsidiary reduced earnings and profits on the pay-as-you-go method, the Old Method Closing Amount was zero. The section 481(a) adjustment was a negative FC90,000 (zero less FC90,000 (the lesser of FC150,000 or FC90,000)).

**Proposed § 1.404A-7 Effective date, retroactive elections, and transition rules.** [*For Preamble, see ¶ 151,519*]

**(a) In general.** *(1) Effective date.* Except as otherwise provided in this section, section 404A applies to taxable years beginning after December 31, 1979.

*(2) Overview of retroactive elections for taxable years beginning before January 1, 1980.* (i) Plans of foreign subsidiaries. Section 2(e)(2) of Public Law 96-603 permitted a taxpayer to make section 404A apply retroactively for all of its foreign subsidiaries. Paragraph (b) of this section describes and provides the time and manner to make, perfect, or revoke this retroactive effective date election. If a retroactive effective date election was made, the taxpayer was also eligible to make a qualified funded plan election or a qualified reserve plan election effective retroactively for any of its subsidiaries' plans that met the requirements of § 1.404A-1(a) (other than paragraph (4) thereof) for the relevant period. Paragraph (c) of this section describes and provides the time and manner to make, perfect, or revoke these retroactive plan-by-plan elections for foreign subsidiaries.

(ii) Plans of foreign branches. Section 2(e)(3) of Public Law 96-603 permitted a taxpayer to make a qualified funded plan election retroactively for any plans maintained by a foreign branch that met the requirements of § 1.404A-1(a) (other than paragraph (4) thereof) for the relevant period. Paragraph (d) of this section describes and provides the time and manner to make this retroactive plan-by-plan qualified funded plan election for plans maintained by foreign branches.

*(3) Overview of special transition rules for election, revocation, and re-election.* Paragraph (e) of this section provides the time and manner to make and revoke qualified funded plan and qualified reserve plan elections for a taxpayer's transition period.

**(b) Retroactive effective date elections for foreign subsidiaries.** *(1) In general.* Section 2(e)(2) of Public Law 96-603 permitted a taxpayer to make section 404A effective during the taxpayer's open period. If the election was made, the taxpayer accepted section 404A (including, for example, § 1.404A-1(d)) as the operative law for all foreign subsidiaries (whether or not controlled foreign corporations) during the taxpayer's entire open period. If the election was made, section 404A applies to all distributions from accumulated profits (or earnings and profits) earned after December 31, 1970 (unless the election is revoked pursuant to paragraph (b)(3) of this section, if applicable). If accumulated profits were earned prior to January 1, 1971, a change in method of accounting is required for the foreign subsidiary's taxable year that ends with or within the first taxable year in the taxpayer's open period. A section 481(a) adjustment is required for amounts taken into account prior to the beginning of the foreign subsidiary's year of change and must be computed applying the rules of § 1.404A-6(f).

*(2) Time and manner to make, perfect, or revoke election.* The retroactive effective date election described in paragraph (b)(1) of this section is not effective unless the election was actually made no later than the time prescribed by law for filing the United States return for the first taxable year ending on or after December 31, 1980, including extensions (whether or not the time was actually extended for filing the taxpayer's return), and unless the taxpayer perfects the election by filing a statement indicating the taxpayer's agreement to perfect the election with an amended return for the first taxable year ending on or after December 31, 1980, on or before [insert date that is 365 days after the date of publication of final regulations in the FEDERAL REGISTER]. In order to be effective, the perfection must be made in the manner provided in § 1.404A-6(b)(3)(ii) or (iii). An election that is not perfected is considered retroactively revoked.

*(3) Requirement to amend returns.* (i) In general. In addition to the amended return required by paragraph (b)(2) of this section, the taxpayer must file any other amended United States returns that are necessary to conform the treatment of all items affected by the election or revocation to the treatment consistent with the election or revocation within the time period described in paragraph (b)(2) of this section. If no adjustments are necessary, the amended return required by paragraph (b)(2) of this section must contain a statement to that effect.

(ii) Required statements. All amended returns required by this paragraph (b)(3) must be accompanied by a statement containing—

(A) The open years, open period and retroactive period of the taxpayer;

(B) The taxable year for which the election is perfected or revoked;

(C) A statement that the election (or elections) are perfected or revoked pursuant to the authority contained in § 1.404A-7; and

(D) A signature and verification as provided in § 1.404A-5(b)(7).

**(c) Retroactive plan-by-plan elections for foreign subsidiaries.** *(1) In general.* Any taxpayer that makes a retroactive effective date election described in paragraph (a)(2)(i) of this section under the rules of paragraph (b) of this section may, at its option, also elect to treat any foreign plan of a subsidiary that met the requirements of § 1.404A-1(a) (other than paragraph (4) thereof) for the relevant period as a qualified funded plan or as a qualified reserve plan under section 404A, beginning in any taxable year of the foreign subsidiary that ends with or within the taxpayer's open period (or for any earlier taxable year beginning after December 31, 1971, for which earnings and profits of the subsidiary had no United States tax significance). Alternatively, the taxpayer may decide to make no such plan-by-plan election with respect to any particular plan or plans of any of its foreign subsidiaries. Rules similar to those contained in § 1.404A-6 (including, where applicable, the requirement to obtain the consent of the Commissioner) are used to effect such plan-by-plan elections. If the plan existed in a taxable year beginning prior to the first year for which the election was effective, a change in method of accounting is required for the year of the election. The year of change for purposes of computing the section 481(a) adjustment is the first year that the election is effective.

*(2) Time and manner to make, perfect, or revoke election.* A taxpayer that is eligible to make a plan-by-plan election described in paragraph (c)(1) of this section may make or perfect such an election by attaching a statement to that effect on an amended return for the year that the election is to be effective on or before [insert date that is 365 days after the date of publication of final regulations in the FEDERAL REGISTER]. In order to be effective, the perfection of a plan-by-plan election must be made in the manner provided in § 1.404A-6(b)(3)(ii) or (iii). An election that is not perfected is considered retroactively revoked. Any election made or perfected under this paragraph (c) will continue in effect for taxable years beginning after the taxpayer's open period, unless revoked under paragraph (c)(4) or (e) of this section or § 1.404A-6.

*(3) Requirement to amend returns.* In addition to the amended return required by paragraph (c)(2) of this section, the taxpayer must file any other amended United States returns that are necessary to conform the treatment of all items affected by the election or revocation to the treatment consistent with the election or revocation. All amended returns must be accompanied by the statement described in paragraph (b)(3)(ii) of this section (substituting "made, perfected, or revoked" for "perfected or revoked" where applicable) and all of the information required by § 1.404A-6(b)(4) (and § 1.404A-6(c)(2)(ii), if applicable, in the case of a termination). If no adjustments are necessary, the amended return required by paragraph (c)(2) of this section must contain a statement to that effect.

*(4) Revocation after initial election and re-election permitted.* Any taxpayer that makes an initial election for any plan under paragraph (c)(2) of this section may, under the rules of that paragraph, revoke the election for any taxable year after the sixth consecutive taxable year for which the elec-

tion is effective, and may re-elect for any taxable year after the sixth consecutive taxable year for which the election is not in effect (regardless of whether the election is not in effect due to revocation or termination of the election as defined in § 1.404A-6(c)(1)). The consecutive changes in method of accounting described in the first sentence of this paragraph (c)(3) must be made under the rules in § 1.404A-6 regarding the section 481(a) adjustment period. The Commissioner may approve a letter ruling request (see § 601.201 of this chapter) to shorten the six-year waiting period upon a showing of extraordinary circumstances.

*(5) Examples.* The principles of paragraphs (b) and (c) of this section are illustrated by the following examples:

*Example (1).* P, a domestic corporation, wholly owns two foreign subsidiaries, S and T. S and T maintain their books and records in FC, the local currency. Since 1978, S and T have maintained unfunded pension plans for their respective employees. S maintained two plans, Plan 1 and Plan 2, and T maintained one plan. The plan years and the taxable years of all three corporations are the calendar year.

(i) For 1978 and 1979, P reduced the earnings and profits of S and T by the amount of the pension liability that had accrued under the plans as follows—

| Taxable year | S's Plan 1 | S's Plan 2 | T's plan |
|---|---|---|---|
| 1978 | FC30,000 | FC5,000 | FC70,000 |
| 1979 | 50,000 | 15,000 | 80,000 |
| Total reduction in earnings and profits | FC80,000 | FC20,000 | FC150,000 |
| Total reduction in earnings and profits | | | |
| S | FC100,000 | | |
| T | FC150,000 | | |

(ii) In 1981, P made a retroactive effective date election pursuant to section 2(e)(2) of Public Law 96-603 and paragraph (b) of this section for taxable years beginning after December 31, 1977, and ending before January 1, 1980, P's open period. Thus, with respect to its open periods P has made section 404A the operative law for all distributions of earnings and profits (or accumulated profits) earned after December 31, 1970 for S and T. The consequences of making or not making the retroactive plan-by-plan election under section 404A for each foreign plan will be determined as though section 404A had been in effect for those years. Accordingly, earnings and profits of S and T may not be reduced with respect to amounts accrued under their respective plans unless the plans met the requirements of § 1.404A-1(a) for those years in the open period.

(iii) P made a retroactive plan-by-plan election to treat S's Plan 1 as a qualified reserve plan for P's retroactive period. The amount taken into account under § 1.404A-3 for S's Plan 1 calculated under section 404A was FC25,000 for 1978 and FC35,000 for 1979. No election under section 404A was made for S's Plan 2 or for R's plan. Thus, no amount of the accrued but unpaid pension liability attributable to S's Plan 2 or to T's plan may reduce S's or T's respective 1978 and 1979 earnings and profits. P amended its tax returns for 1978 and 1979 to reflect the correct reduction of earnings and profits of FC25,000 and FC35,000 with respect to S's Plan 1 and no reduction for those years with respect to S's Plan 2 or T's plan. Since S's and T's plans were established during the open period, no section 481(a) adjustment is required.

*Example (2).* Q, a domestic corporation, has wholly owned R, a foreign subsidiary, since R's formation in 1968. R maintains its books and records in FC, the local currency. Since 1968, R maintained an unfunded pension plan for its employees. The plan year and the taxable year of both corporations is the calendar year. R since 1968, used a method of accounting under which it reduced earnings and profits by its accrued pension liability.

(i) R's earnings and profits were earned and distributed to Q as follows—

| Taxable year | Earnings and profits | Distribution of earnings and profits |
|---|---|---|
| 1968 | FC10,000 | |
| 1969 | 20,000 | |
| 1970 | 20,000 | |
| Subtotal | 50,000 | |
| 1971 | 30,000 | |
| 1972 | 30,000 | |
| 1973 | 30,000 | |
| 1974 | 30,000 | |
| 1975 | 30,000 | FC200,000 |
| Subtotal | 150,000 | |
| 1976 | 40,000 | |
| 1977 | 40,000 | |
| 1978 | 40,000 | |
| 1979 | 40,000 | |
| 1980 | 40,000 | |
| 1981 | 50,000 | |
| Subtotal | 250,000 | |
| Total | FC450,000 | |

(ii) In 1981, Q made a retroactive effective date election pursuant to section 2(e)(2) of Public Law 96-603 and paragraph (b)(1) of this section for its open period. As of December 31, 1980, Q's open period included the taxable years 1975 through 1979. Thus, with respect to those taxable years, Q has made section 404A the operative law for R. The consequences of making or not making the retroactive plan-by-plan election under section 404A for R's foreign plan will be determined as though section 404A had been in effect for those taxable years. Thus, the earnings and profits of R may not be reduced with respect to amounts accrued under R's plan, unless the plan met the requirements of § 1.404A-1(a) for those taxable years.

(iii) Q made a retroactive plan-by-plan election to treat R's plan as a qualified reserve plan effective beginning in 1971. Of the distribution of FC200,000 to Q in 1975, section 404A applies to FC150,000, because these accumulated profits (or earnings and profits) were earned in taxable years beginning after December 31, 1970 and were also distributed in 1975, within Q's open period. However, section 404A does not apply to the FC50,000 distribution made from accumulated profits earned before December 31, 1970. Since R's plan was established before Q's open period, a section 481(a) adjustment is required. This section 481(a) adjustment must be taken into account in determining earnings and profits beginning with the 1971 year of change.

**(d) Retroactive plan-by-plan qualified funded plan elections for certain plans of foreign branches.** *(1) In general.* Section 2(e)(3) of Public Law 96-603 permitted a taxpayer to make a qualified funded plan election retroactively for any plans maintained by a foreign branch that met the requirements of § 1.404A-1(a) (other than paragraph (4) thereof) for the relevant period. As a condition of making this election, a taxpayer is required to agree to the assessment of all deficiencies (including interest thereon) arising during those taxable Years within the open period (even those taxable years that are not opens years as defined in paragraph (g)(4) of this section) to the extent that the deficiencies arise from erroneous deductions claimed by the taxpayer with respect to all of the taxpayer's foreign branches that maintained a deferred compensation plan. For a taxpayer that agrees to the assessment of tax in an election under this paragraph (d), a change in method of accounting is necessary (and a section 481(a) adjustment is required in accordance with the provisions of § 1.404A-6) with respect to any erroneous deductions claimed by the taxpayer under its method of accounting in taxable years ending prior to the beginning of the open period. For such a change in method of accounting, the year of change is the first taxable year in the open period, and the method of accounting to which the taxpayer is required to change is the method permitted during the open period under this paragraph (d).

*(2) Amounts allowed a deduction.* If an election under section 2(e)(3) of Public Law 96-603 was made under the rules of this paragraph (d), the aggregate of the taxpayer's prior deductions is allowed as a deduction ratably over a 15-year period, beginning with the taxpayer's first taxable year beginning after December 31, 1979. A fractional part of a year which is a taxable year (as defined in sections 441(b) and 7701(a)(23)) is a taxable year for purposes of the 15-year period.

*(3) Definitions.* (i) Prior deduction. (A) In general. The term "prior deduction" means a deduction with respect to a qualified funded plan (i.e., a plan that met the requirements of § 1.404A-1(a) for the relevant period, and with respect to which a qualified funded plan election was made under the rules of this paragraph (d)) maintained by a foreign branch of a taxpayer for a taxable year beginning before January 1, 1980—

(1) That the taxpayer claimed;

(2) That was not allowable under the law in effect prior to the enactment of section 404A;

(3) With respect to which, on December 1, 1980, the assessment of a deficiency was not barred by any law or rule of law; and

(4) That would have been allowable if section 404A applied to taxable years beginning before January 1, 1980.

(B) Application of section 404A(d). Because the prior deductions are limited by the amounts that may be taken into account under section 404A, the computation of those prior deductions for the relevant taxable years is subject to the limitations described in section 404A(d) and § 1.404A-4. However, once the aggregate of prior deductions is calculated, the aggregate, or any portion thereof permitted to be taken into account over the 15-year period of paragraph (d)(2) of this section, is not subject to the limitations prescribed by section 404A(d) and § 1.404A-4.

(ii) Erroneous deduction. The term "erroneous deduction" means an amount that is not deductible under section 404(a) (including section 404(a)(5)), that was deducted on a taxpayer's income tax return with respect to a foreign deferred compensation plan.

*(4) Time and manner to make, perfect, or revoke election.* (i) In general. A plan-by-plan election described in paragraph (d)(1) of this section is not effective unless the election was actually made no later than the time Prescribed by law for filing the United States return for the first taxable year ending on or after December 31, 1980, including extensions (whether or not the time was actually extended for filing the taxpayer's return), and unless the taxpayer perfects the election by filing a statement indicating the taxpayer's agreement to perfect the election with an amended return for the first taxable year ending on or after December 31, 1980, on or before [insert date that is 365 days after the date of publication of final regulations in the FEDERAL REGISTER]. In order to be effective, the perfection must be made in the manner provided in § 1.404A-6(b)(3)(ii) or (iii). An election that is not perfected is considered retroactively revoked. Any election under this paragraph (d) will continue in effect for taxable years beginning after the taxpayer's open period, unless revoked under paragraph (e) of this section or § 1.404A-6.

(ii) Requirement to amend returns. In addition to the amended return required by paragraph (d)(4)(i) of this section, the taxpayer must file any other amended United States returns that are necessary to conform the treatment of all items affected by the election or revocation to the treatment consistent with the election or revocation under this paragraph (d) within the time period described in paragraph (d)(4)(i) of this section. All amended returns must be accompanied by the statement described in paragraph (b)(3)(ii) of this section and all of the information required by § 1.404A-6(b)(4) (and § 1.404A-6(c)(2)(ii), if applicable, in the case of a termination). If no adjustments are necessary, the amended return required by paragraph (d)(4)(i) of this section must contain a statement to that effect.

*(5) Examples.* The principles of this paragraph (d) are illustrated by the following examples:

*Example (1).* (i) During its open taxable years 1977 through 1979, X, a domestic corporation, maintained a nonqualified funded plan for the employees of its foreign branch. In 1981, X made a retroactive effective date election and a retroactive plan-by-plan election to treat this plan as a qualified funded plan. The amounts deducted on X's tax returns, the amount deductible under sections 404(a) and 404A (expressed in FC, the local currency) are as follows—

| | 1977 | 1978 | 1979 | Total |
|---|---|---|---|---|
| Amount deducted on tax return | FC100 | FC100 | FC100 | FC300 |
| Amount deductible under section 404(a) | 20 | 20 | 20 | FC60 |
| Amount deductible under section 404A | 90 | 90 | 90 | FC270 |

(ii) The assessment (including interest) for the open years 1977 through 1979 is based on adjustments to the erroneous deductions of FC240 (FC300 less FC60).

(iii) The amount of the prior deductions taken into account ratably over 15 years as provided in paragraph (d)(2). of this section, beginning in 1981, is a negative FC210 (FC60 less FC270).

(iv) No section 481(a) adjustment is required because X took no deductions with respect to the plan prior to the beginning of its open period.

*Example (2).* (i) Z, a domestic corporation, maintained a nonqualified funded foreign branch plan for its foreign employees, beginning in its 1965 (calendar) taxable year. In 1981, Z made a retroactive effective date election and a retroactive plan-by-plan election to treat this plan as a qualified funded plan. As of December 31, 1980, Z's 1965 taxable year was closed, but its 1978 taxable year was open. The amounts deducted on Z's tax returns, the amount deductible under sections 404(a) and 404A (expressed in FC, the local currency) are as follows—

| | 1965 | 1978 | Total |
|---|---|---|---|
| Amount deducted on tax return | FC20 | FC80 | FC100 |
| Amount deductible under section 404(a) | 5 | 6 | FC11 |
| Amount deductible under section 404A | 10 | 40 | FC60 |

(ii) Under paragraph (d)(1) of this section, Z agreed to an assessment of deficiencies for its 1978 taxable year based on its FC74 (FC80 – FC6) of erroneous deductions as defined in paragraph (d)(3)(ii) of this section.

(iii) The FC34 (FC40 – FC6) of prior deductions is permitted to be taken into account as a deduction over the 15-year period beginning with its 1980 taxable year as provided in paragraph (d)(2) of this section.

(iv) Additionally, because Z took erroneous deductions under its method of accounting prior to the beginning of its open period, it is required to change to the method of accounting permitted during the open period, and must take a section 481(a) adjustment (determined under the snapshot method of § 1.404A-6(f)) into account over the 15-year section 481(a) adjustment period of § 1.404A-6(e)(2)(ii) beginning in its 1978 year of change. See paragraph (d)(1) of this section.

*Example (3).* A foreign branch which computes its income under the profit and loss method of Rev. Rul. 75-107, 1975-1 C.B. 32 (see § 601.601(d)(2)(ii)(b) of this chapter), in units of local currency, the FC, maintains a qualified funded plan. In 1980, the taxpayer was eligible to make the elections described in this section, and did so during the 1980 taxable year. The amount determined under paragraph (d)(3)(i) of this section after taking into account the limitations prescribed § 1.404A-4(a) for the open period was FC1,500,000. For the 1980 taxable year, and as provided paragraph (d) of this section, FC100,000 of the prior deductions were deductible. The prior deductions allowed to be taken into account in the 1980 through 1994 taxable years are determined without regard to, and thus are not subject to, the limitations prescribed by § 1.404A-4(a).

**(e) Special transition rules for election, revocation and re-election.** *(1) In general.* This paragraph (e) provides the time and manner for making and revoking qualified funded plan and qualified reserve plan elections for a taxpayer's transition period. A taxpayer may make an election, revoke an election, and re-elect to treat any plan that met the requirements of § 1.404A-1(a) (other than paragraph (4) thereof) for the relevant period as a qualified funded plan or a qualified reserve plan under this paragraph (e) for the transition period without regard to whether a retroactive election is made under paragraph (b), (c), or (d) of this section. However, an election made under paragraph (c) or (d) of this section is deemed to continue in effect for taxable years beginning after December 31, 1979, unless revoked under paragraph (c)(4) of this section or this paragraph (e) or terminated or revoked under § 1.404A-6(f). See paragraphs (c)(2) and (d)(4)(i) of this section.

*(2) Time and manner initially to elect and revoke.* (i) In general. Taxpayers that wish to make an election under this paragraph (e) may have, but were not required to have, made a Method (1) or Method (2) election for the taxable year for which an election is made under this paragraph. Those taxpayers that wish to make (or perfect) an election under this paragraph (e) must attach a statement to that effect on an amended return for the year the election is to be effective on or before [insert date that is 365 days after the date of publication of final regulations in the FEDERAL REGISTER]. An election previously made that is not perfected is considered retroactively revoked.

(ii) Requirement to amend returns. In addition to the amended return required by paragraph (e)(2)(i) of this section, the taxpayer must file any other amended United States returns that are necessary to conform the treatment of all items affected by the election or revocation to the treatment consistent with the election or revocation under this paragraph (e) within the time period described in paragraph (e)(2)(i) of this section. All amended returns must be accompanied by the statement described in paragraph (b)(3)(ii) of this section (substituting "made, perfected, or revoked" for "perfected or revoked" where applicable) and all of the information required by § 1.404A-6(b)(4) (and § 1.404A-6(c)(2)(ii), if applicable, in the case of a termination). If no adjustments are necessary, the amended return required by paragraph (e)(2)(i) of this section must contain a statement to that effect.

*(3) Revocation after initial election and re-election permitted.* Any taxpayer that makes an initial election for any plan under paragraph (e)(2) of this section may, under the rules of that paragraph, revoke the election for any taxable year after the sixth consecutive taxable year for which the election is effective, and may re-elect for any taxable year after the sixth consecutive taxable year for which the election is not in effect (whether the election is not in effect due to either revocation or termination of the election as defined in § 1.404A-6(c)(1)). The consecutive changes in method of accounting described in the first sentence of this paragraph (e)(3) must be made under the rules in § 1.404A-6 regarding the section 481(a) adjustment period. The Commissioner may approve a letter ruling request to shorten the six-year waiting period upon a showing of extraordinary circumstances.

*(4) Example.* The principles of paragraph (e)(3) of this section are illustrated by the following example:

*Example.* (i) L, a domestic corporation, has wholly owned foreign subsidiary M, since M's formation in 1971. M maintained a funded plan for its employees from 1971 through 1991 The taxable year of L and M is the calendar year. In 1981, L made a Method (2) election. Within 365 days after the publication of the final regulations in the FEDERAL REGISTER, L perfected its retroactive effective date election for all its foreign subsidiaries. L's election terminated in 1975 due to its plan's violation of the requirements of section 404A(e)(2). Additionally, L perfected, revoked and re-elected on a plan-by-plan basis its election for M's plan, as follows—

| Plan-by-plan election effective | Plan-by-plan election terminated or revoked |
|---|---|
| 1971 - 1974 | 1975 - 1981 |
| 1982 - 1987 | 1988 - 1993 |

(ii) A section 481(a) adjustment is required for the years of change 1975, 1982 and 1988.

**(f) Special data rules for retroactive elections.** *(1) Retroactive calculation of section 481(a) adjustments.* (i) General rule. Retroactive elections may be made only if the taxpayer calculates the section 481(a) adjustment required by § 1.404A-6 based on substantiation quality data. Substantiation quality data generally must be current as of the date of the change in method of accounting. Nevertheless, if contemporaneous substantiation quality data is not readily available, the taxpayer may calculate the section 481(a) adjustment based on backward projections to earlier years from the first taxable year beginning before January 1, 1980, for which sufficient contemporaneous substantiation quality data is readily available. However, such projections must satisfy the substantiation requirements in paragraph (f)(1)(ii) of this section, however. Furthermore, the taxpayer may not use any of the approaches provided for under this paragraph (f) if circumstances indicate that the overall result is a material distortion of the amounts allowable.

(ii) Substantiation requirement for retroactive reserves. (A) In general. Although reasonable actuarial estimates and projections may be used, the calculation of the opening balance of the reserve for the first year for which a qualified reserve plan election under paragraph (c)(1) of this section is effective must nonetheless be based on some actual contemporaneous evidence. Thus, the opening balance may be based on actual aggregate covered payroll, the actual number of covered employees, or a contemporaneous actuarial valuation that used reasonable actuarial methods. For example, if the taxpayer has contemporaneous records of the number of covered employees and the aggregate covered payroll, it may estimate other actuarial information, such as average age and marital status, based on reasonable actuarial methods (e.g., using substantiation quality data as of another date and adjusting for actual or expected changes for the interim years). The resulting combination of actual contemporaneous evidence and reasonably estimated data may be used to calculate the opening reserve. If a contemporaneous actuarial valuation is used as the basis of an opening reserve, the results of the valuation must be adjusted to reflect any difference between the actuarial method used in that actuarial valuation and the unit credit method, as required by section 404A(c) and § 1.404A-3(b).

(B) Interpolation. In cases where an taxpayer can meet the substantiation requirement of paragraph (f)(1)(ii)(A) of this section for some years, but cannot meet that requirement in intervening years (including the year of the change in method of accounting), the taxpayer may interpolate a reserve balance for the intervening years based on reasonable actuarial methods. In the absence of evidence to the contrary, it is assumed that a pro rata allocation of amounts to those intervening years is a reasonable actuarial method. This paragraph (f)(1)(ii)(B) does not authorize any interpolation for years in which other evidence indicates that it would cause a material distortion (such as a year during which the work force was on strike and no deferred compensation benefits were accrued). In addition, this paragraph (f)(1)(ii)(B) does not authorize extrapolation of reserve balances to years that are not intervening years between years that meet the substantiation requirements of paragraph (f)(1)(ii)(A) of this section.

(C) Extrapolation. If the first year for which the taxpayer is able to meet the substantiation requirements of paragraph (f)(1)(ii)(A) of this section ("the substantiation year") is later than the year of the change in method of accounting, an taxpayer may use the approach described in this paragraph (f)(1)(ii)(C) to determine the section 481(a) adjustments described in § 1.404A-6(f) in years prior to the substantiation year. Under this approach, the taxpayer's closing balance under its prior method as of the date of the change in the method of accounting is compared with the opening balance in the substantiation year. If the closing balance exceeds the opening balance, the excess is the amount to be used in calculating the adjustment under section 481, as required by § 1.404A-6. However, if the closing balance of the taxpayer's reserve under its method used for years prior to the election under section 404A is less than the opening balance for the substantiation year, the opening balance as of the date of the change in method in accounting is assumed to be equal to the closing balance. Thus, if the closing balance is less than the opening balance for the substantiation year, there is no adjustment under section 481. In such a case, the difference between the opening balance as of the date of the change in method of accounting and the opening balance for the substantiation year is allocated to the years prior to the substantiation year based en reasonable actuarial methods using all available information.

*(2) Determination of reasonable addition to a reserve in interim years.* In the case of a qualified reserve plan that is using the interpolation option of paragraph (f)(1)(ii)(B) of this section or that is described in the last sentence in paragraph (f)(1)(ii)(C) of this section, none of the increase in the reserve in the intervening year is considered a reasonable addition to the reserve under § 1.404A-3(b). Thus, the entire amount of the increase must be considered an amount to be amortized over ten years under § 1.404A-3(c).

*(3) Protective elections.* For those taxpayers that relied on the prior position of the Internal Revenue Service by making a Method (1) election under which the section 481(a) adjustment was computed in a manner inconsistent with this section or by making a Method (2) election under which no section 481(a) adjustment was reflected in the original return, appropriate adjustments required by section 404A and its underlying regulations must be made on an amended return filed no later than [insert date that is 365 days after the date of publication of final regulations in the FEDERAL REGISTER] for the first year the election is effective and for all subsequent affected years for which a return has been filed. If no adjustments are necessary, an amended return should be filed for the first year stating that no adjustments are necessary.

**(g) Definitions and special rules.** *(1) Method (1) election.* The term "Method (1) election" means an election that was made under Method (1) (as defined in Ann. 81-114, 1981-28 I.R.B. 21) (see § 601.601(d)(2)(ii)(b) of this chapter) by claiming the deduction or credit allowable under section 404A on the taxpayer's income tax return for the first taxable year ending on or after December 31, 1980, including extensions (or an amended return filed no later than the end of the extended time period prescribed in section 6081, whether or not such time was actually extended for filing the taxpayer's return).

*(2) Protective or Method (2) election.* The term "protective election" or "Method (2) election" means an election that was made under Method (2) (as defined in Ann. 81-114, 1981-28 I.R.B. 21) (see § 601.601(d)(2)(ii)(b) of this chapter) without claiming deductions attributable to a qualified foreign plan on the taxpayer's income tax return (or, in the case of foreign subsidiaries, without taking into account reductions of earnings and profits).

*(3) Open years of the taxpayer.* The term "open years of the taxpayer" means open taxable years beginning after December 31, 1971, and for which, on December 31, 1980, the making of a refund, or the assessment of a deficiency, was not barred by any law or rule of law.

*(4) Retroactive period.* The term "retroactive period" means a taxpayer's taxable years (whether or not the making of a refund, or the assessment of a deficiency, was barred by any law or rule of law for any taxable year) in the following range—

(i) Any taxable year selected by the taxpayer between taxable years beginning after December 31, 1970 and before January 1, 1980 (the beginning taxable year); and

(ii) The last taxable year beginning before January 1, 1980 (the ending taxable year).

*(5) Transition period.* The term "transition period" means taxable years beginning after December 31, 1979, and before [ insert the date of publication of final regulations in the FEDERAL REGISTER].

*(6) Open period.* For purposes of this section, the term "open period" means, with respect to any taxpayer, all taxable years beginning after December 31, 1971, and beginning before January 1, 1980, and for which, on December 31, 1980, the making of a refund, or the assessment of a deficiency, was not barred by any law or rule of law.

PAR. 16. Section 1.405 is amended.

**Proposed § 1.405 Statutory provisions; qualified bond purchase plans.** [*For Preamble, see ¶ 150,135*]

• ***Caution:*** Proposed section 1.62-1 was finalized by TD 7399, 2/3/76. Proposed sections 1.72-4, 1.72-13, 1.101-2, 1.122-1, 1.402(a)-1, 1.402(e)-2, 1.402(e)-3, 1.403(a)-1, 1.403(a)-2, 1.405-3, 1.652(b)-1, 1.1304-2 and 11.402(e)(4)(B)-1 remain proposed.

**§ 1.405-1 Qualified bond purchase plans.**

***Caution:*** The Treasury has not yet amended Reg § 1.405-1 to reflect changes made by P.L. 98-369.

**(a) Introduction.** Section 405 relates to the requirements for qualification of, and the tax treatment of funds contributed to, retirement plans of an employer for the benefit of his employees which are funded through the purchase of United States retirement plan bonds. Such bonds may be purchased under a qualified bond purchase plan described in section 405(a) and paragraph (b) of this section. The qualified bond purchase plan is an alternative method of providing some of the deferred compensation benefits provided by plans described in section 401. In addition, retirement bonds may be purchased under a qualified pension or profit-sharing plan described in section 401. A qualified bond purchase plan or a qualified pension or profit-sharing plan under which retirement bonds are purchased may cover only common-law employees, self-employed individuals, or both. A qualified bond purchase plan may be established after December 31, 1962, and retirement bonds may be purchased by a qualified pension or profit-sharing plan after December 31, 1962. For the terms and conditions of the retirement bonds, see section 405(b) and Treasury Department Circular, Public Debt Series—No. 1-63.

**(b) Qualified bond purchase plans.** *(1)* A qualified bond purchase plan is a definite written program and arrangement which is communicated to the employees and established and maintained by an employer solely to purchase for and distribute to his employees or their beneficiaries retirement bonds. These bonds must be purchased in the name of the employee on whose behalf the contributions are made. The plan must be a permanent plan which meets the requirements of section 401(a)(3), (4), (5), (6), (7), (8), (16), and (19) and, if applicable, the requirements of section 401(a)(9) and (10) and of section 401(d) (other than paragraphs (1), (5)(B), (8), (16) and (19)). The rules set forth in the regulations relating to those provisions shall be applicable to qualified bond purchase plans.

*(2)* A qualified bond purchase plan must provide that an employee's right to the proceeds of a bond purchased in his name are nonforfeitable and will in no event inure to the benefit of the employer or be reallocated in any manner.

**(c) Benefits under a qualified bond purchase plan.** *(1)* Except as provided in subparagraph (2) of this paragraph, a qualified bond purchase plan must conform to the definition of a pension plan in paragraph (b)(1)(i) of § 1.401-1, or the definition of a profit-sharing plan in paragraph (b)(1)(ii) of § 1.401-1. For example, if the qualified bond purchase plan is a profit-sharing plan, the plan must include the definite allocation formula described in paragraph (b)(1)(ii) of § 1.401-1. In addition, if such a profit-sharing plan covers any owner-employee, the plan must also include the definite contribution formula described in section 401(d)(2)(B).

*(2)* (i) Under a qualified bond purchase plan, the bonds may be distributed to the employees at any time, and the plan need not prohibit the distribution or redemption of the bonds until the retirement of the employee. Accordingly, even though a qualified bond purchase plan is designed as a pension plan, it need not provide systematically for the payment of definitely determinable benefits. However, provisions for distribution must apply in a nondiscriminatory manner.

(ii) A qualified bond purchase plan which is designed as a pension plan may not contain a formula for contributions or benefits which might require the reallocation of amounts to an employee's credit or which might provide for the reversion of any amounts to the employer.

**(d) Contributions under a qualified bond purchase plan.** *(1)* The retirement bonds will be issued in the denominations of $50, $100, $500, and $1,000. Therefore, the contribution otherwise called for under the plan may not coincide with an amount that can be invested in retirement bonds. Accordingly, the plan must provide that the contributions on behalf of an individual employee for any year shall be rounded to the nearest multiple of $50.

*(2)* Since the employee's rights to any bonds purchased for him under a qualified bond purchase plan must be nonforfeitable, a qualified bond purchase plan must, in order to conform to the requirements of section 401(a)(4) with respect to the early termination of the plan, restrict the contributions on behalf of any employee to the amount which could be allocated to him under paragraph (c) of § 1.401-4.

**(e) Definitions.** For purposes of this section and §§ 1.405-2 and 1.405-3—

*(1)* The term "employee" includes an employee as defined in section 401(c)(1) and paragraph (b) of § 1.401-10, and the term "employer" means the person treated as the employer of such individual under section 401(c)(4);

*(2)* The term "owner-employee" means an owner-employee as defined in section 401(c)(3) and paragraph (d) of § 1.401-10;

*(3)* The term "earned income" means earned income as defined in section 401(c)(2) and paragraph (c) of § 1.401-10; and

*(4)* The term "retirement bond" means a United States Retirement Plan Bond, as described in section 405(b) and Treasury Department Circular, Public Debt Series—No. 1-63.

T.D. 6675, 9/16/63, amend T.D. 7748, 12/30/80.

## § 1.405-2 Deduction of contributions to qualified bond purchase plans.

***Caution:*** The Treasury has not yet amended Reg § 1.405-2 to reflect changes made by P.L. 98-369.

**(a) In general.** An employer shall be allowed a deduction for contributions paid to or under a qualified bond purchase plan in the same manner and to the same extent as if such contributions were made to a trust described in section 401(a) which is exempt from tax under section 501(a). A deduction will be allowed only for the taxable year in which the contributions are paid, or treated as paid, except as provided by section 404(a)(1), (3), and (7). For purposes of the deduction, a contribution is paid at the time the application for the bond is made and the full purchase price paid.

**(b) Rules for applying section 404.** If a qualified bond purchase plan is designed as a pension plan as defined in paragraph (b)(1)(i) of § 1.401-1, the limitations of section 404 applicable to qualified pension trusts shall apply. See §§ 1.404(a)-3 through 1.404(a)-7. Similarly, if a qualified bond purchase plan is designed as a profit-sharing plan as defined in paragraph (b)(1)(ii) of § 1.401-1, the limitations of section 404 applicable to qualified profit-sharing trusts shall apply. See §§ 1.404(a)-9 and 1.404(a)-10. In addition, if a qualified bond purchase plan designed as a pension plan covers some or all of the employees who are covered by a qualified profit-sharing plan established and maintained by the same employer, or if a qualified bond purchase plan which is designed as a profit-sharing plan covers some or all the employees who are also covered by a qualified pension or annuity plan established and maintained by the same employer, section 404(a)(7) is applicable. See § 1.404(a)-(13). Furthermore, if a qualified bond purchase plan covers employees some or all of whom are employees within the meaning of section 401(c)(1), the provisions of section 404(a)(8), (9), and (10) and 404(e) shall also apply.

**(c) Accrual method taxpayers.** In the case of a taxpayer using the accrual method of accounting, a contribution to a qualified bond purchase plan will be deemed paid on the last day of the year of accrual if—

*(1)* During the taxable year of accrual the taxpayer incurs a liability to make the contribution, the amount of which is accruable under section 461 for such taxable year, and

*(2)* Payment is in fact made no later than the time prescribed by the law for filing the return for the taxable year of accrual (including extensions thereof).

T.D. 6675, 9/16/63.

## § 1.405-3 Taxation of retirement bonds.

***Caution:*** The Treasury has not yet amended Reg § 1.405-3 to reflect changes made by P.L. 98-369.

**(a) In general.** *(1)* As in the case of employer contributions under a qualified pension, annuity, profit-sharing, or stock bonus plan, employer contributions on behalf of his common-law employees under a qualified bond purchase plan are not includible in the gross income of the employees when made, and employer contributions on behalf of self-employed individuals are deductible as provided in section 405(c) and § 1.405-2. Further, an employee or his beneficiary does not realize gross income upon the receipt of a retirement bond pursuant to a qualified bond purchase plan or from a trust described in section 401(a) which is exempt from tax under section 501(a). Upon redemption of such a bond, ordinary income will be realized to the extent the proceeds thereof exceed the basis (determined in accordance with paragraph (b) of this section) of the bond. The proceeds of a retirement bond are not entitled to the special tax treatment of section 72(n) and § 1.72-18.

*(2)* In the event a retirement bond is surrendered for partial redemption and reissuance of the remainder, the person surrendering the bond shall be taxable on the proceeds received to the extent such proceeds exceed the basis in the portion redeemed. In such case, the basis shall be determined (in accordance with paragraph (b) of this section) as if the portion redeemed and the portion reissued had been issued as separate bonds.

*(3)* In the event a retirement bond is redeemed after the death of the registered owner, the amount taxable (as determined in accordance with subparagraph (1) of this paragraph) is income in respect of a decedent under section 691.

*(4)* The provisions of section 402(a)(2) are not applicable to a retirement bond. In general, section 402(a)(2) provides for capital gains treatment of certain distributions from a qualified trust which constitute the total distributions payable with respect to any employee. The proceeds of a retirement bond received upon redemption will not be entitled to such capital gain treatment even though the bond is received as a part of, or as the whole of, such a total distribution. Nor will such a bond be taken into consideration in determining whether the distribution represents the total amount payable by the trust with respect to an employee. Thus, a distribution by a qualified trust may constitute a total distribution payable with respect to an employee for purposes of section 402(a)(2) even though the trust retains retirement bonds registered in the name of such employee.

**(b) Basis.** *(1)* This paragraph is applicable in determining the basis of any retirement bond distributed pursuant to a qualified bond purchase plan or distributed by a trust qualifying under section 401. In the case of such a bond purchased for an individual at the time he is a common-law employee, the basis is that portion of the purchase price attributable to employee contributions. In the case of such a bond purchased for an individual at the time he is a self-employed individual, the basis shall be determined under subparagraph (3) of this paragraph.

*(2)* At the time a retirement bond is purchased, there shall be indicated on the application for the retirement bond whether the individual for whom the retirement bond is purchased is a common-law employee or a self-employed individual, and in the case of common-law employees the amount of the purchase price, if any, attributable to the employee's contribution. The answers to these questions will appear on the retirement bond, and when the retirement bond is purchased for a common-law employee, the basis for the retirement bond is presumed to be the amount of the purchase price which the retirement bond indicates was contributed by the employee.

*(3)* (i) Except as provided in subdivision (ii) of this subparagraph, for purposes of determining the basis of retirement bonds purchased for an individual while he was a self-

employed individual, all such bonds redeemed during a taxable year shall be considered in the aggregate as a single retirement bond. The basis of such retirement bonds shall be the difference between the aggregate of their face amounts and the lesser of:

(a) One-half the aggregate of their face amounts, or

(b) The aggregate of the unused amounts allowed as a deduction at the end of the taxable year (as determined in subparagraph (4) of this paragraph).

(ii) The basis of a retirement bond purchased for a self-employed individual which is redeemed after his death is the amount determined by multiplying the face amount of such retirement bond by a fraction—

(a) The numerator of which is the aggregate of the face amounts of all the bonds registered in the individual's name at his death which were purchased while he was a self-employed individual reduced by the aggregate of the unused amounts allowed as a deduction at his death (as determined in subparagraph (4) of this paragraph), and

(b) The denominator of which is the aggregate of the face amounts of all such bonds.

*(4)* (i) In the case of retirement bonds purchased under a qualified bond purchase plan, the aggregate of the unused amounts allowed as a deduction at the end of any taxable year shall be an amount equal to the total of the amounts allowable for such taxable year, and the amounts allowed in all prior taxable years, as a deduction under section 405(c) for contributions used to purchase retirement bonds for the registered owner while he was a self-employed individual, reduced by an amount equal to the portion of the face amounts of such retirement bonds redeemed in prior taxable years which were included in the registered owner's gross income.

(ii) In the case of retirement bonds purchased by a trust described in section 401(a) and exempt under section 501(a), there shall be allocated to the retirement bond the deduction under section 404 attributable to the contributions used to purchase the retirement bond. The amount so allocated shall be treated in the same manner as the deduction allowed under section 405(c) for purposes of computing the unused amounts allowed as a deduction under subdivision (i) of this subparagraph. Further, the amount so allocated shall not be included in the investment in the contract for purposes of section 72 in determining the portion of the other assets distributed by the trust included in gross income.

*(5)* The application of the rule of subparagraphs (3) and (4) of this paragraph may be illustrated by the following examples:

*Example (1).* B, a self-employed individual, adopts a qualified bond purchase plan in 1963. During 1963 the plan purchased $2,000 worth of retirement bonds in his name. As a result of over-estimating his income for 1963, only $400 was allowed B as a deduction pursuant to section 405(c). In 1964, prior to B's retirement in June of that year, the plan purchased a $500 retirement bond in B's name for which a deduction was allowable pursuant to section 405(c) in the amount of $250. B redeemed a retirement bond with a face amount of $500 in September of 1964 and another with a face amount of $500 in October of 1964. Of the proceeds received in 1964 from the redemption of the bonds, $1,000 plus interest, B shall exclude from his gross income $500 (face amount of the retirement bonds, $1,000, less $500, one-half of the face amount, the latter being less than the aggregate of the unused amounts allowed as a deduction, $250 allowable for the taxable year in which the bonds were redeemed plus $400, the unused amounts allowed in prior taxable years, or $650). The aggregate of the unused amounts allowed as a deduction shall be reduced by the amount so excluded ($650 – $500 = $150). During the following year, B redeems another retirement bond with a face amount of $500. Of the proceeds received from the redemption of such retirement bond, $500 plus interest, B shall exclude from his gross income $350 (face amount of the retirement bonds, $500, less $150, the aggregate of the unused amounts allowed as a deduction, the latter being less than one-half of the face amount of the bond, $250). The aggregate of the unused amounts allowed as a deduction is reduced to zero ($150 – $150 = 0). Upon redemption of the remaining retirement bonds registered in B's name, B shall exclude from his gross income with respect to such proceeds an amount equal to the face amounts of the bonds redeemed.

*Example (2).* C, a self-employed individual, participated in a qualified bond purchase plan during the years 1963 through 1966. The plan purchased in his name retirement bonds in the aggregate of $10,000. C deducted $4,000 from his gross income for the four years ($1,000 for each year) with respect to the purchase of such retirement bonds. C retired in December of 1966 and during the following year redeemed one retirement bond with a face amount of $1,000. C excluded from his gross income $500 of the proceeds of the bond. C died without redeeming any of the remaining retirement bonds registered in his name. The basis of each remaining retirement bond shall be determined by multiplying the face amount of each retirement bond by

$$\frac{\$5{,}500}{\$9{,}000}$$

The numerator is the aggregate of the face amounts registered in C's name (as a self-employed individual) at his death, $9,000, reduced by the aggregate of the unused amounts allowed as a deduction at his death, $3,500 (amounts allowed as a deduction under section 405(c), $4,000, reduced by the portion of the face amount of the retirement bond redeemed by C which was included in C's gross income, $500), or $5,500. The denominator is the face amount of the retirement bonds registered in his name as a self-employed individual at his death, $9,000.

---

T.D. 6675, 9/16/63.

---

PAR. 17. Paragraph (4) of § 1.405-3(a) is revised to read as follows:

**Proposed § 1.405-3 Taxation of retirement bonds.** [*For Preamble, see ¶ 150,135*]

• ***Caution:*** Proposed section 1.62-1 was finalized by TD 7399, 2/3/76. Proposed sections 1.72-4, 1.72-13, 1.101-2, 1.122-1, 1.402(a)-1, 1.402(e)-2, 1.402(e)-3, 1.403(a)-1, 1.403(a)-2, 1.405-3, 1.652(b)-1, 1.1304-2 and 11.402(e)(4)(B)-1 remain proposed.

***Caution:*** The Treasury has not yet amended Reg § 1.405-3 to reflect changes made by P.L. 98-369.

**(a) In general.** * * *

*(4)* The provisions of section 402(a)(2) and (e) are not applicable to a retirement bond. In general, section 402(a)(2) provides for capital gains treatment of a portion of a lump

sum distribution as defined in section 402(e)(4)(A) and section 402(e) provides a special 10-year averaging of the ordinary income portion of such a lump sum distribution. The proceeds of a retirement bond received upon redemption will not be entitled to such capital gains treatment or 10-year averaging even though the bond is received as part of, or as the entire, balance to the credit of the employee. Nor will such a bond be taken into consideration in determining the balance to the credit of the employee. Thus, a distribution by a qualified trust may constitute a lump sum distribution for purposes of section 402(a)(2) and (e) even though the trust retains retirement bonds registered in the name of the employee.

### § 1.406-1 Treatment of certain employees of foreign subsidiaries as employees of the domestic corporation.

***Caution:*** The Treasury has not yet amended Reg § 1.406-1 to reflect changes made by P.L. 98-21.

**(a) Scope.** *(1) General rule.* For purposes of applying the rules in part 1 of subchapter D of chapter 1 of subtitle A of the Code and the regulations thereunder with respect to a pension, profit-sharing, or stock bonus plan described in section 401(a), an annuity plan described in section 403(a), or a bond purchase plan described in section 405(a), of a domestic corporation, an individual who is a citizen of the United States and who is an employee of a foreign subsidiary (as defined in section 3121(1)(8) and the regulations thereunder) of such domestic corporation shall be treated as an employee of such domestic corporation if the requirements of paragraph (b) of this section are satisfied.

*(2) Cross references.* For rules relating to nondiscrimination requirements and the determination of compensation, see paragraph (c) of this section. For rules under which termination of the status of an individual as an employee of the domestic corporation in certain instances will not be considered as separation from service for certain purposes, see paragraph (d) of this section. For rules regarding deductibility of contributions, see paragraph (e) of this section. For rules regarding treatment of such individual as an employee of the domestic corporation under related provisions, see paragraph (f) of this section.

**(b) Application of this section.** *(1) Requirements.* This section shall apply and the employee of the foreign subsidiary shall be treated as an employee of domestic corporation for the purposes set forth in paragraph (a)(1) of this section only if each of the following requirements is satisfied:

(i) The domestic corporation must have entered into an agreement under section 3121(1) to provide social security coverage which applies to the foreign subsidiary of which such individual is an employee and which has not been terminated under section 3121(1)(3) or (4).

(ii) The plan, referred to in paragraph (a)(1) of this section, must expressly provide for contributions or benefits for individuals who are citizens of the United States and who are employees of one or more of its foreign subsidiaries to which an agreement entered into by such domestic corporation under section 3121(1) applies. The plan must apply to all of the foreign subsidiaries to which such agreement applies.

(iii) Contributions under a funded plan of deferred compensation (whether or not a plan described in section 401(a), 403(a), or 405(a)) must not be provided by any other person with respect to the remuneration paid to such individual by the foreign subsidiary.

*(2) Supplementary rules.* Subparagraph (1)(ii) of this paragraph does not modify the requirements for qualification of a plan described in section 401(a), 403(a), or 405(a) and the regulations thereunder. It is not necessary that the plan provide benefits or contributions for all United States citizens who are employees of such foreign subsidiaries. If the plan is amended to cover individuals who are employees by reason of paragraph (a)(1) of this section, the plan will not qualify unless it meets the coverage requirements of section 410(b)(1) (section 401(a)(3), as in effect on September 1, 1974, for plan years to which section 410 does not apply; see § 1.410(a)-2 for the effective dates of section 410) and the nondiscrimination requirements of section 401(a)(4). In addition, the administrative rules contained in § 1.401(a)-3(e) (relating to the determination of the contributions or benefits provided by the employer under the Social Security Act) will also apply for purposes of determining whether the plan meets the requirements of section 401. For purposes of subparagraph (1)(iii) of this paragraph, contributions will not be considered as provided under a funded plan merely because the foreign subsidiary is required under the laws of the foreign jurisdiction to pay social insurance taxes or to make similar payments with respect to the wages paid to the employee.

**(c) Special rules.** *(1) Nondiscrimination requirements.* For purposes of applying sections 401(a)(4) and 410(b)(1)(B) (section 401(a)(3)(B), as in effect on September 1, 1974, for plan years to which section 410 does not apply) and the regulations thereunder (relating to nondiscrimination concerning benefits and contributions and coverage of employees) with respect to an employee of the foreign subsidiary who is treated as an employee of the domestic corporation under paragraph (a)(1) of this section—

(i) If the employee is an officer, shareholder, or (with respect to plan years to which section 410 does not apply) person whose principal duties consist in supervising the work of other employees of the foreign subsidiary of the domestic corporation, he shall be treated as having such capacity with respect to the domestic corporation; and

(ii) The determination as to whether the employee is a highly compensated employee shall be made by comparing his total compensation (determined under subparagraph (2) of this paragraph) with the compensation of all the employees of the domestic corporation (including individuals treated as employees of the domestic corporation pursuant to section 406 and this section).

*(2) Determination of compensation.* For purposes of applying section 401(a)(5) and the regulations thereunder, relating to classifications that will not be considered discriminatory, with respect to an employee of the foreign subsidiary who is treated as an employee of the domestic corporation under paragraph (a)(1) of this section—

(i) The total compensation of the employee shall be the remuneration of the employee from the foreign subsidiary (including any allowances that are paid to the employee because of his employment in a foreign country) which would constitute his total compensation if his services had been performed for the domestic corporation;

(ii) The basic or regular rate of compensation of the employee shall be determined for the employee in the same manner as it is determined under section 401 for other employees of the domestic corporation; and

(iii) The amount paid by the domestic corporation which is equivalent to the tax imposed with respect to the employee by section 3101 (relating to the tax on employees under the Federal Insurance Contributions Act) shall be treated as having been paid by the employee and shall be included in his compensation.

**(d) Termination of status as deemed employee not to be treated as separation from service for purposes of capital gain provisions and limitation of tax.** For purposes of applying the rules, relating to the treatment of certain distributions which are made after an employee's separation from service, set forth in section 72(n) as in effect on September 1, 1974 (with respect to taxable years ending after December 31, 1969, and to which section 402(e) does not apply), and in sections 402(a)(2) and (e) and 403(a)(2) (with respect to distributions or payments made after December 31, 1973, and in taxable years beginning after December 31, 1973) with respect to an employee of a foreign subsidiary who is treated as an employee of a domestic corporation under paragraph (a)(1) of this section, the employee shall not be considered as separated from the service of the domestic corporation solely by reason of the occurrence of any one or more of the following events:

*(1)* The termination, under the provisions of section 3121(1), of the agreement entered into by the domestic corporation under that section which covers the employment of the employee;

*(2)* The employee's becoming an employee of another foreign subsidiary of the domestic corporation with respect to which such agreement does not apply,

*(3)* The employee's ceasing to be an employee of the foreign subsidiary by reason of which employment he was treated as an employee of such domestic corporation, if he becomes an employee of another corporation controlled by such domestic corporation; or

*(4)* The termination of the provision of the plan described in paragraph (b)(1)(ii) of this section, for coverage of United States citizens who are employees of foreign subsidiaries covered by an agreement under section 3121(1).

For purposes of subparagraph (3) of this paragraph, a corporation is considered to be controlled by a domestic corporation if such domestic corporation owns directly or indirectly more than 50 percent of the voting stock of the corporation.

**(e) Deductibility of contributions.** *(1) In general.* For purposes of applying sections 404 and 405(c) with respect to the deduction for contributions made to or under a pension, profit-sharing, or stock bonus plan described in section 401(a), an annuity plan described in section 403(a), or a bond purchase plan described in section 405(a), by a domestic corporation, or by another corporation which is entitled to deduct its contributions under section 404(a)(3)(B), on behalf of an employee of a foreign subsidiary treated as an employee of the domestic corporation under paragraph (a)(1) of this section—

(i) Except as provided in subdivision (ii) of this subparagraph, no deduction shall be allowed to such domestic corporation or to any other corporation which would otherwise be entitled to deduct its contributions on behalf of such employee under one of such sections;

(ii) There shall be allowed as a deduction from the gross income of the foreign subsidiary which is effectively connected with the conduct of a trade or business within the United States (within the meaning of section 882 and the regulations thereunder) an amount which is allocable and apportionable to such gross income under the rules of § 1.861-8 and which in no event may exceed the amount which (but for subdivision (i) of this subparagraph) would be deductible under section 404 or section 405(c) by the domestic corporation if the individual were an employee of the domestic corporation and if his compensation were paid by the domestic corporation; and

(iii) Any reference to compensation shall be considered to be a reference to the total compensation of such individual (determined by applying paragraph (c)(2) of this section).

*(2) Year of deduction.* Any amount deductible by the foreign subsidiary under section 406(d) and this paragraph shall be deductible for its taxable year with or within which ends the taxable year of the domestic corporation for which the contribution was made.

*(3) Special rules.* Whether contributions to a plan on behalf of an employee of the foreign subsidiary who is treated as an employee of the domestic corporation under paragraph (a)(1) of this section, or whether forfeitures with regard to such employee, will require an inclusion in the income of the domestic corporation or an adjustment in the basis of its stock in the foreign subsidiary, shall be determined in accordance with the rules of general application of subtitle A of chapter 1 of the Code (relating to income taxes). For example, an unreimbursed contribution by the domestic corporation to a plan which meets the requirements of section 401(a) will be treated, to the extent each employee's rights to the contribution are nonforfeitable, as a contribution of capital to the foreign subsidiary to the extent that such contributions are made on behalf of the employees of such subsidiary.

**(f) Treatment as an employee of the domestic corporation under related provisions.** An individual who is treated as an employee of a domestic corporation under paragraph (a)(1) of this section shall also be treated as an employee of such domestic corporation, with respect to the plan having the provision described in paragraph (b)(1)(ii) of this section, for purposes of applying section 72(d) (relating to employees' annuities), section 72(f) (relating to special rules for computing employees' contributions), section 101(b) (relating to employees' death benefits), section 2039 (relating to annuities), and section 2517 (relating to certain annuities under qualified plans) and the regulations thereunder.

**(g) Nonexempt trust.** If the plan of the domestic corporation is a qualified plan described under section 401(a), the fact that a trust which forms a part of such plan is not exempt from tax under section 501(a) shall not affect the treatment of an employee of a foreign subsidiary as an employee of a domestic corporation under section 406(a) and paragraph (a)(1) of this section.

---

T.D. 7501, 8/22/77.

---

### § 1.407-1 Treatment of certain employees of domestic subsidiaries engaged in business outside the United States as employees of the domestic parent corporation.

*Caution:* The Treasury has not yet amended Reg § 1.407-1 to reflect changes made by P.L. 98-21.

**(a) Scope.** *(1) General rule.* For purposes of applying the rules in part 1 of subchapter D of chapter 1 of subtitle A of the Code and the regulations thereunder with respect to a pension, profit-sharing, or stock bonus plan described in section 401(a), an annuity plan described in section 403(a), or a bond purchase plan described in section 405(a), of a domestic parent corporation (as defined in paragraph (b)(3)(ii) of this section), an individual who is a citizen of the United States and who is an employee of a domestic subsidiary (as defined in paragraph (b)(3)(i) of this section) of such domestic parent corporation shall be treated as an employee of such domestic parent corporation if the requirements of paragraph (b) of this section are satisfied.

*(2) Cross-references.* For rules relating to nondiscrimination requirements and the determination of compensation, see paragraph (c) of this section. For rules under which termination of the status of an individual as an employee of the the domestic parent corporation in certain instances will not be considered as separation from service for certain purposes, see paragraph (d) of this section. For rules regarding deductibility of contributions, see paragraph (e) of this section. For rules regarding treatment of such individual as an employee of the domestic parent corporation under related provisions, see paragraph (f) of this section.

**(b) Application of this section.** *(1) Requirements.* This section shall apply and the employee of the domestic subsidiary shall be treated as an employee of the domestic parent corporation for the purposes set forth in paragraph (a)(1) of this section only if each of the following requirements is satisfied:

(i) The plan, referred to in paragraph (a)(1) of this section, must expressly provide for contributions or benefits for individuals who are citizens of the United States and who are employees of one or more of the domestic subsidiaries of the domestic parent corporation. The plan must apply to every domestic subsidiary.

(ii) Contributions under a funded plan of deferred compensation (whether or not a plan described in section 401(a), 403(a), or 405(a)) must not be provided by any other person with respect to the remuneration paid to such individual by the domestic subsidiary.

*(2) Supplementary rules.* Subparagraph (1)(i) of this paragraph does not modify the requirements for qualification of a plan described in section 401(a), 403(a), or 405(a) and the regulations thereunder. It is not necessary that the plan provide benefits or contributions for all United States citizens who are employees of such domestic subsidiaries. If the plan is amended to cover individuals who are employees by reason of paragraph (a)(1) of this section, the plan will not qualify unless it meets the coverage requirements of section 410(b)(1) (section 401(a)(3), as in effect on September 1, 1974, for plan years to which section 410 does not apply; see § 1.410(a)-2 for the effective dates of section 410) and the nondiscrimination requirements of section 410(a)(4). The administrative rules contained in § 1.401(a)-3(e) (relating to the determination of the contributions or benefits provided by the employer under the Social Security Act) will also apply for purposes of determining whether the plan meets the requirements of section 401. For purposes of subparagraph (1)(ii) of this paragraph, contributions will not be considered as provided under a funded plan merely because the domestic subsidiary employer pays the tax imposed by section 3111 (relating to tax on employers under the Federal Insurance Contributions Act) with respect to such employee or is required under the laws of a foreign jurisdiction to pay social insurance taxes or to make similar payments with respect to the wages paid to the employee.

*(3) Definitions.* (i) Domestic subsidiary. For purposes of this section, a corporation shall be treated as a domestic subsidiary for any taxable year only if each of the following requirements is satisfied:

(A) It is a domestic corporation 80 percent or more of the outstanding voting stock of which is owned by another domestic corporation;

(B) 95 percent or more of its gross income for the three-year period immediately preceding the close of its taxable year which ends on or before the close of the taxable year of such other domestic corporation (or for such part of such period during which it was in existence) was derived from sources without the United States, determined pursuant to sections 861 through 864 and the regulations thereunder; and

(C) 90 percent or more of its gross income for such period (or such part) was derived from the active conduct of a trade or business.

If for the period (or part thereof) referred to in (B) and (C) of this subdivision such corporation has no gross income, the provisions of (B) and (C) shall be treated as satisfied if it is reasonable to anticipate that, with respect to the first taxable year thereafter for which such corporation has gross income, such provisions will be satisfied.

(ii) Domestic parent corporation. The domestic parent corporation of any domestic subsidiary is the domestic corporation which owns 80 percent or more of the outstanding voting stock of such domestic subsidiary.

**(c) Special rules.** *(1) Nondiscrimination requirements.* For purposes of applying sections 401(a)(4) and 410(b)(1)(B) (section 401(a)(3)(B), as in effect on September 1, 1974, for plan years to which section 410 does not apply) and the regulations thereunder (relating to nondiscrimination concerning benefits and contributions and coverage of employees) with respect to an employee of the domestic subsidiary who is treated as an employee of the domestic parent corporation under paragraph (a)(1) of this section—

(i) If the employee is an officer, shareholder, or (with respect to plan years to which section 410 does not apply) a person whose principal duties consist in supervising the work of other employees of the domestic subsidiary of the domestic parent corporation, he shall be treated as having such capacity with respect to the domestic parent corporation; and

(ii) The determination as to whether the employee is a highly compensated employee shall be made by comparing his total compensation (determined under subparagraph (2) of this paragraph with the compensation of all the employees of the domestic parent corporation (including individuals treated as employees of the domestic parent corporation pursuant to section 407 and this section).

*(2) Determination of compensation.* For purposes of applying section 401(a)(5) and the regulations thereunder, relating to classifications that will not be considered discriminatory, with respect to an employee of the domestic subsidiary who is treated as an employee of the domestic parent corporation under paragraph (a)(1) of this section—

(i) The total compensation of the employee shall be the remuneration of the employee from the domestic subsidiary (including any allowances that are paid to the employee because of his employment in a foreign country) which would constitute his total compensation if his services had been performed for such domestic parent corporation; and

(ii) The basic or regular rate of compensation of the employee shall be determined for the employee in the same manner as it is determined under section 401 for other employees of the domestic parent corporation.

**(d) Termination of status as deemed employee not to be treated as separation from service for purposes of capital gain provisions and limitation of tax.** For purposes of applying the rules, relating to treatment of certain distributions which are made after an employee's separation from service, set forth in section 72(n) as in effect on September 1, 1974 (with respect to taxable years ending after December

31, 1969, and to which section 402(e) does not apply), and in sections 402(a)(2) and (e) and 403(a)(2) (with respect to distributions or payments made after December 31, 1973, and in taxable years beginning after December 31, 1973) with respect to an employee of a domestic subsidiary who is treated as an employee of a domestic parent corporation under paragraph (a)(1) of this section, the employee shall not be considered as separated from the service of the domestic parent corporation solely by reason of the occurrence of any one or more of the following events:

*(1)* The fact that the corporation of which such individual is an employee ceases, for any taxable year, to be a domestic subsidiary within the meaning of paragraph (b)(3)(i) of this section;

*(2)* The employee's ceasing to be an employee of the domestic subsidiary of such domestic parent corporation, if he becomes an employee of another corporation controlled by such domestic parent corporation; or

*(3)* the termination of the provision of the plan described in paragraph (b)(1)(i) of this section, requiring coverage of United States citizens who are employees of domestic subsidiaries of the domestic parent corporation.

For purposes of subparagraph (2) of this paragraph, a corporation is considered to be controlled by a domestic parent corporation if the domestic parent corporation owns directly or indirectly more than 50 percent of the voting stock of the corporation.

**(e) Deductibility of contributions.** *(1) In general.* For purposes of applying sections 404 and 405(c) with respect to the deduction for contributions made to or under a pension, profit-sharing, or stock bonus plan described in section 401(a), an annuity plan described in section 403(a), or a bond purchase plan described in section 405(a), by a domestic parent corporation, or by another corporation which is entitled to deduct its contributions under section 404(a)(3)(B), on behalf of an employee of a domestic subsidiary treated as an employee of the domestic parent corporation under paragraph (a)(1) of this section—

(i) Except as provided in subdivision (ii) of this subparagraph, no deduction shall be allowed to the domestic parent corporation which would otherwise be entitled to deduct its contributions on behalf of such employee under one of such sections;

(ii) There shall be allowed as a deduction to the domestic subsidiary of which such individual is an employee an amount equal to the amount which (but for subdivision (i) of this subparagraph) would be deductible under section 404 or section 405(c) by the domestic parent corporation if the individual were an employee of the domestic parent corporation and if his compensation were paid by the domestic corporation; and

(iii) Any reference to compensation shall be considered to be a reference to the total compensation of such individual (determined by applying paragraph (c)(2) of this section).

*(2) Year of deduction.* Any amount deductible by the domestic subsidiary under section 407(d) and this paragraph shall be deductible for its taxable year with or within which ends the taxable year of the domestic parent corporation for which the contribution was made.

*(3) Special rules.* Whether contributions to a plan on behalf of an employee of the domestic subsidiary who is treated as an employee of the domestic parent corporation under paragraph (a)(1) of this section, or whether forfeitures with regard to such employee, will require an inclusion in the income of the domestic parent corporation or an adjustment in the basis of its stock in the domestic subsidiary, shall be determined in accordance with the rules of general application of subtitle A of chapter 1 of the Code (relating to income taxes). For an example, an unreimbursed contribution by the domestic parent corporation to a plan which meets the requirements of section 401(a) will be treated, to the extent each employee's rights to the contribution are nonforfeitable, as a contribution of capital to the domestic subsidiary to the extent that such contributions are made on behalf of the employees of such subsidiary.

**(f) Treatment as an employee of the domestic parent corporation under related provisions.** An individual who is treated as an employee of a domestic parent corporation under paragraph (a)(1) of this section shall also be treated as an employee of such domestic corporation, with respect to the plan having the provision described in paragraph (b)(1)(i) of this section, for purposes of applying section 72(d) (relating to special rules for computing employees' contributions), section 72(f) (relating to special rules for computing employees' contributions), section 101(b) (relating to employees' death benefits), section 2039 (relating to annuities), and section 2517 (relating to certain annuities under qualified plans) and the regulations thereunder.

**(g) Nonexempt trust.** If the plan of the domestic parent corporation is a qualified plan described under section 401(a), the fact that a trust which forms a part of such plan is not exempt from tax under section 501(a) shall not affect the treatment of an employee of a domestic subsidiary as an employee of a domestic parent corporation under section 407(a) and paragraph (a)(1) of this section.

T.D. 7501, 8/22/77.

### § 1.408-1 General rules.

***Caution:*** The Treasury has not yet amended Reg § 1.408-1 to reflect changes made by P.L. 99-514, P.L. 98-369, P.L. 97-248, P.L. 97-34.

**(a) In general.** Section 408 prescribes rules relating to individual retirement accounts and individual retirement annuities. In addition to the rules set forth in §§ 1.408-2 and 1.408-3, relating respectively to individual retirement accounts and individual retirement annuities, the rules set forth in this section shall also apply.

**(b) Exemption from tax.** The individual retirement account or individual retirement annuity is exempt from all taxes under subtitle A of the Code other than the taxes imposed under section 511, relating to tax on unrelated business income of charitable, etc., organizations.

**(c) Sanctions.** *(1) Excess contributions.* If an individual retirement account or individual retirement annuity accepts and retains excess contributions, the individual on whose behalf the account is established or who is the owner of the annuity will be subject to the excise tax imposed by section 4973.

*(2) Prohibited transactions by owner or beneficiary of individual retirement account.* (i) Under section 408(e)(2), if, during any taxable year of the individual for whose benefit any individual retirement account is established, that individual or the individual's beneficiary engages in any transaction prohibited by section 4975 with respect to such account, such account ceases to be an individual retirement account as of the first day of such taxable year. In any case in which any individual retirement account ceases to be an individual retirement account by reason of the preceding sentence as of

the first day of any taxable year, section 408(d)(1) applies as if there were a distribution on such first day in an amount equal to the fair market value (on such first day) of all assets in the account (on such first day). The preceding sentence applies even though part of the fair market value of the individual retirement account as of the first day of the taxable year is attributable to excess contributions which may be returned tax-free under section 408(d)(4) or 408(d)(5).

(ii) If the trust with which the individual engages in any transaction described in subdivision (i) of this subparagraph is established by an employer or employee association under section 408(c), only the employee who engages in the prohibited transaction is subject to disqualification of his separate account.

*(3) Prohibited transaction by person other than owner or beneficiary of account.* If any person other than the individual on whose behalf an individual retirement account is established or the individual's beneficiary engages in any transaction prohibited by section 4975 with respect to such account, such person shall be subject to the taxes imposed by section 4975.

*(4) Pledging account as security.* Under section 408(e)(4), if, during any taxable year of the individual for whose benefit an individual retirement account is established, that individual uses the account or any portion thereof as security for a loan, the portion so used is treated as distributed to that individual.

*(5) Borrowing on annuity contract.* Under section 408(e)(3), if during any taxable year the owner of an individual retirement annuity borrows any money under or by use of such contract, the contract ceases to be an individual retirement annuity as of the first day of such taxable year. See § 1.408-3(c).

*(6) Premature distributions.* If a distribution (whether a deemed distribution or an actual distribution) is made from an individual retirement account, or individual retirement annuity, to the individual for whose benefit the account was established, or who is the owner of the annuity, before the individual attains age 59½ (unless the individual has become disabled within the meaning of section 72(m)(7)), the tax under Chapter 1 of the Code for the taxable year in which such distribution is received is increased under section 408(f)(1) or (f)(2). The increase equals 10 percent of the amount of the distribution which is includible in gross income for the taxable year. Except in the case of the credits allowable under section 31, 39, or 42, no credit can be used to offset the increased tax described in this subparagraph. See, however, § 1.408-4(c)(3).

**(d) Limitation on contributions and benefits.** An individual retirement account or individual retirement annuity is subject to the limitation on contributions and benefits imposed by section 415 for years beginning after December 31, 1975.

**(e) Community property laws.** Section 408 shall be applied without regard to any community property laws.

---

T.D. 7443, 12/3/76, amend T.D. 7642, 1/19/77, T.D. 7714, 8/7/80.

---

## § 1.408-2 Individual retirement accounts.

***Caution:*** The Treasury has not yet amended Reg § 1.408-2 to reflect changes made by P.L. 99-514, P.L. 98-369, P.L. 97-248, P.L. 97-34.

**(a) In general.** An individual retirement account must be a trust or a custodial account (see paragraph (d) of this section). It must satisfy the requirements of paragraph (b) of this section in order to qualify as an individual retirement account. It may be established and maintained by an individual, by an employer for the benefit of his employees (see paragraph (c) of this section), or by an employee association for the benefit of its members (see paragraph (c) of this section).

**(b) Requirements.** An individual retirement account must be a trust created or organized in the United States (as defined in section 7701(a)(9)) for the exclusive benefit of an individual or his beneficiaries. Such trust must be maintained at all times as a domestic trust in the United States. The instrument creating the trust must be in writing and the following requirements must be satisfied.

*(1) Amount of acceptable contributions.* Except in the case of a contribution to a simplified employee pension described in section 408(k) and a rollover contribution described in section 408(d)(3), 402(a)(5), 402(a)(7), 403(a)(4), 403(b)(8) or 409(b)(3)(C), the trust instrument must provide that contributions may not be accepted by the trustee for the taxable year in excess of $1,500 on behalf of any individual for whom the trust is maintained. An individual retirement account maintained as a simplified employee pension may provide for the receipt of up to $7,500 for a calendar year.

*(2) Trustee.* (i) The trustee must be a bank (as defined in section 408(n) and the regulations thereunder) or another person who demonstrates, in the manner described in paragraph (e) of this section, to the satisfaction of the Commissioner, that the manner in which the trust will be administered will be consistent with the requirements of section 408 and this section.

(ii) Section 11.408(a)(2)-1 of the Temporary Income Tax Regulations under the Employee Retirement Income Security Act of 1974 is superseded by this subparagraph (2).

*(3) Life insurance contracts.* No part of the trust funds may be invested in life insurance contracts. An individual retirement account may invest in annuity contracts which provide, in the case of death prior to the time distributions commence, for a payment equal to the sum of the premiums paid or, if greater, the cash value of the contract.

*(4) Nonforfeitability.* The interest of any individual on whose behalf the trust is maintained in the balance of his account must be nonforfeitable.

*(5) Prohibition against commingling.* (i) The assets of the trust must not be commingled with other property except in a common trust fund or common investment fund.

(ii) For purposes of this subparagraph, the term "common investment fund" means a group trust created for the purpose of providing a satisfactory diversification or investments or a reduction of administrative expenses for the individual participating trusts, and which group trust satisfies the requirements of section 408(c) (except that it need not be established by an employer or an association of employees) and the requirements of section 401(a) in the case of a group trust in which one of the individual participating trusts is an employees' trust described in section 401(a) which is exempt from tax under section 501(a).

(iii) For purposes of this subparagraph, the term "individual participating trust" means an employees' trust described in section 401(a) which is exempt from tax under section 501(a) or a trust which satisfies the requirements of section 408(a) provided that in the case of such an employees' trust, such trust would be permitted to participate in such a group trust if all the other individual participating trusts were employees' trusts described in section 401(a) which are exempt from tax under section 501(a).

*(6) Distribution of interest.* (i) The trust instrument must provide that the entire interest of the individual for whose benefit the trust is maintained must be distributed to him in accordance with paragraph (b)(6)(ii) or (iii) of this section.

(ii) Unless the provisions of paragraph (b)(6)(iii) of this section apply, the entire interest of the individual must be actually distributed to him not later than the close of his taxable year in which he attains age 70½.

(iii) In lieu of distributing the individual's entire interest as provided in paragraph (b)(6)(ii) of this section, the interest may be distributed commencing not later than the taxable year described in such paragraph (b)(6)(ii). In such case, the trust must expressly provide that the entire interest of the individual will be distributed to the individual and the individual's beneficiaries, in a manner which satisfies the requirements of paragraph (b)(6)(v) of this section, over any of the following periods (or any combination thereof)—

(A) The life of the individual,

(B) The lives of the individual and spouse,

(C) A period certain not extending beyond the life expectancy of the individual, or

(D) A period certain not extending beyond the joint life and last survivor expectancy of the individual and spouse.

(iv) The life expectancy of the individual or the joint life and last survivor expectancy of the individual and spouse cannot exceed the period computed by use of the expected return multiples in § 1.72-9, or, in the case of payments under a contract issued by an insurance company, the period computed by use of the mortality tables of such company.

(v) If an individual's entire interest is to be distributed over a period described in paragraph (b)(6)(iii) of this section, beginning in the year the individual attains 70½ the amount to be distributed each year must be not less than the lesser of the balance of the individual's entire interest or an amount equal to the quotient obtained by dividing the entire interest of the individual in the trust at the beginning of such year (including amounts not in the individual retirement account at the beginning of the year because they have been withdrawn for the purpose of making a rollover contribution to another individual retirement plan) by the life expectancy of the individual (or the joint life and last survivor expectancy of the individual and spouse (whichever is applicable)), determined in either case as of the date the individual attains age 70 in accordance with paragraph (b)(6)(iv) of this section, reduced by one for each taxable year commencing after the individual's attainment of age 70½. An annuity or endowment contract issued by an insurance company which provides for non-increasing payments over one of the periods described in paragraph (b)(6)(iii) of this section beginning not later than the close of the taxable year in which the individual attains age 70½ satisfies this provision. However, no distribution need be made in any year, or a lesser amount may be distributed, if beginning with the year the individual attains age 70½ the aggregate amounts distributed by the end of any year are at least equal to the aggregate of the minimum amounts required by this subdivision to have been distributed by the end of such year.

(vi) If an individual's entire interest is distributed in the form of an annuity contract, then the requirements of section 408(a)(6) are satisfied if the distribution of such contract takes place before the close of the taxable year described in subdivision (ii) of this subparagraph, and if the individual's interest will be paid over a period described in subdivision (iii) of this subparagraph and at a rate which satisfies the requirements of subdivision (v) of this subparagraph.

(vii) In determining whether paragraph (b)(6)(v) of this section is satisfied, all individual retirement plans maintained for an individual's benefit (except those under which he is a beneficiary described in section 408(a)(7)) at the close of the taxable year in which he reaches age 70½ must be aggregated. Thus, the total payments which such individual receives in any taxable year must be at least equal to the amount he would have been required to receive had all the plans been one plan at the close of the taxable year in which he attained age 70½.

*(7) Distribution upon death.* (i) The trust instrument must provide that if the individual for whose benefit the trust is maintained dies before the entire interest in the trust has been distributed to him, or if distribution has been commenced as provided in paragraph (b)(6) of this section to the surviving spouse and such spouse dies before the entire interest has been distributed to such spouse, the entire interest (or the remaining part of such interest if distribution thereof has commenced) must, within 5 years after the individual's death (or the death of the surviving spouse) be distributed or applied to the purchase of an immediate annuity for this beneficiary or beneficiaries (or the beneficiary or beneficiaries of the surviving spouse) which will be payable for the life of such beneficiary or beneficiaries (or for a term certain not extending beyond the life expectancy of such beneficiary or beneficiaries) and which annuity contract will be immediately distributed to such beneficiary or beneficiaries. A contract described in the preceding sentence is not includible in gross income upon distribution. Section 1.408-4(e) provides rules applicable to the taxation of such contracts. The first sentence of this paragraph (b)(7) shall have no application if distributions over a term certain commenced before the death of the individual for whose benefit the trust was maintained and the term certain is for a period permitted under paragraph (b)(6)(iii)(C) or (D) of this section.

(ii) Each such beneficiary (or beneficiary of a surviving spouse) may elect to treat the entire interest in the trust (or the remaining part of such interest if distribution thereof has commenced) as an account subject to the distribution requirements of section 408(a)(6) and paragraph (b)(6) of this section instead of those of section 408(a)(7) and paragraph (b)(7) of this section. Such an election will be deemed to have been made if such beneficiary treats the account in accordance with the requirements of section 408(a)(6) and paragraph (b)(6) of this section. An election will be considered to have been made by such beneficiary if either of the following occurs: (A) any amounts in the account (including any amounts that have been rolled over, in accordance with the requirements of section 408(d)(3)(A)(i), into an individual retirement account, individual retirement annuity, or retirement bond for the benefit of such individual) have not been distributed within the appropriate time period required by section 408(a)(7) and paragraph (b)(7) of this section; or (B) any additional amounts are contributed to the account (or to the account, annuity, or bond to which the beneficiary has rolled such amounts over, as described in (1) above) which are subject, or deemed to be subject, to the distribution requirements of section 408(a)(6) and paragraph (b)(6) of this section.

*(8) Definition of beneficiaries.* The term "beneficiaries" on whose behalf an individual retirement account is established includes (except where the context indicates otherwise) the estate of the individual, dependents of the individual, and any person designated by the individual to share in the benefits of the account after the death of the individual.

**(c) Accounts established by employers and certain association of employees.** *(1) In general.* A trust created or organized in the United States (as defined in section 7701(a)(9)) by an employer for the exclusive benefit of his employees or their beneficiaries, or by an association of employees for the exclusive benefit of its members or their beneficiaries, is treated as an individual retirement account if the requirements of paragraphs (c)(2) and (c)(3) of this section are satisfied under the written governing instrument creating the trust. A trust described in the preceding sentence is for the exclusive benefit of employees or members even though it may maintain an account for former employees or members and employees who are temporarily on leave.

*(2) General requirements.* The trust must satisfy the requirements of paragraphs (b)(1) through (7) of this section.

*(3) Special requirement.* There must be a separate accounting for the interest of each employee or member.

*(4) Definitions.* (i) Separate accounting. For purposes of paragraph (c)(3) of this section, the term "separate accounting" means that separate records must be maintained with respect to the interest of each individual for whose benefit the trust is maintained. The assets of the trust may be held in a common trust fund, common investment fund, or common fund for the account of all individuals who have an interest in the trust.

(ii) Employee association. For purposes of this paragraph and section 408(c), the term "employee association" means any organization composed of two or more employees, including but not limited to, an employee association described in section 501(c)(4). Such association may include employees within the meaning of section 401(c)(1). There must be, however, some nexus between the employees (e.g., employees of same employer, employees in the same industry, etc.) in order to qualify as an employee association described in this subdivision (ii).

**(d) Custodial accounts.** For purposes of this section and section 408(a), a custodial account is treated as a trust described in section 408(a) if such account satisfies the requirements of section 408(a) except that it is not a trust and if the assets of such account are held by a bank (as defined in section 401(d)(1) and the regulations thereunder) or such other person who satisfies the requirements of paragraph (b)(2)(ii) of this section. For purposes of this chapter, in the case of a custodial account treated as a trust by reason of the preceding sentence, the custodian of such account will be treated as the trustee thereof.

**(e) Nonbank trustee.** *(1) In general.* The trustee of a trust described in paragraph (b) of this section may be a person other than a bank if the person demonstrates to the satisfaction of the Commissioner that the manner in which the person will administer trusts will be consistent with the requirements of section 408. The person must demonstrate by written application that the requirements of paragraph (e)(2) to (e)(6) of this section will be met. The written application must be sent to the address prescribed by the Commissioner in revenue rulings, notices, and other guidance published in the Internal Revenue Bulletin (see § 601.601(d)(2)(ii)(b) of this chapter. For procedural and administrative rules, see paragraph (e)(7) of this section.

*(2) Fiduciary ability.* The applicant must demonstrate in detail its ability to act within the accepted rules of fiduciary conduct. Such demonstration must include the following elements of proof:

(i) Continuity. (A) The applicant must assure the uninterrupted performance of its fiduciary duties notwithstanding the death or change of its owners. Thus, for example, there must be sufficient diversity in the ownership of the applicant to ensure that the death or change of its owners will not interrupt the conduct of its business. Therefore, the applicant cannot be an individual.

(B) Sufficient diversity in the ownership of an incorporated applicant is demonstrated in the following circumstances:

(1) Individuals each of whom owns more than 20 percent of the voting stock in the applicant own, in the aggregate, no more than 50 percent of such stock;

(2) The applicant has issued securities registered under section 12(b) of the Securities Exchange Act of 1934 (15 U.S.C. 78l(b)) or required to be registered under section 12(g)(1) of that Act (15 U.S.C. 78l(g)(1)); or

(3) The applicant has a parent corporation within the meaning of section 1563(a)(1) that has issued securities registered under section 12(b) of the Securities Exchange Act of 1934 (15 U.S.C. 78l(b)) or required to be registered under Section 12(g)(1) of that Act (15 U.S.C. 78l(g)(1)).

(C) Sufficient diversity in the ownership of an applicant that is a partnership means that—

(1) Individuals each of whom owns more than 20 percent of the profits interest in the partnership own, in the aggregate, no more than 50 percent of such profits interest, and

(2) Individuals each of whom owns more than 20 percent of the capital interest in the partnership own, in the aggregate, no more than 50 percent of such capital interest.

(D) For purposes of this subdivision, the ownership of stock and of capital and profits interests shall be determined in accordance with the rules for constructive ownership of stock provided in section 1563(e) and (f)(2). For this purpose, the rules for constructive ownership of stock provided in section 1563(e) and (f)(2) shall apply to a capital or profits interest in a partnership as if it were a stock interest.

(ii) Established location. The applicant must have an established place of business in the United States where it is accessible during every business day.

(iii) Fiduciary experience. The applicant must have fiduciary experience or expertise sufficient to ensure that it will be able to perform its fiduciary duties. Evidence of fiduciary experience must include proof that a significant part of the business of the applicant consists of exercising fiduciary powers similar to those it will exercise if its application is approved. Evidence of fiduciary expertise must include proof that the applicant employs personnel experienced in the administration of fiduciary powers similar to those the applicant will exercise if its application is approved.

(iv) Fiduciary responsibility. The applicant must assure compliance with the rules of fiduciary conduct set out in paragraph (e)(5) of this section.

(v) Financial responsibility. The applicant must exhibit a high degree of solvency commensurate with the obligations imposed by this paragraph. Among the factors to be taken into account are the applicant's net worth, its liquidity, and its ability to pay its debts as they come due.

*(3) Capacity to account.* The applicant must demonstrate in detail its experience and competence with respect to accounting for the interests of a large number of individuals (including calculating and allocating income earned and paying out distributions to payees). Examples of accounting for the interests of a large number of individuals include accounting for the interests of a large number of shareholders in a regulated investment company and accounting for the

interests of a large number of variable annuity contract holders.

*(4) Fitness to handle funds.* (i) In general. The applicant must demonstrate in detail its experience and competence with respect to other activities normally associated with the handling of retirement funds.

(ii) Examples. Examples of activities normally associated with the handling of retirement funds include:

(A) To receive, issue receipts for, and safely keep securities;

(B) To collect income;

(C) To execute such ownership certificates, to keep such records, make such returns, and render such statements as are required for Federal tax purposes;

(D) To give proper notification regarding all collections;

(E) To collect matured or called principal and properly report all such collections;

(F) To exchange temporary for definitive securities;

(G) To give proper notification of calls, subscription rights, defaults in principal or interest, and the formation of protective committees;

(H) To buy, sell, receive, or deliver securities on specific directions.

*(5) Rules of fiduciary conduct.* The applicant must demonstrate that under applicable regulatory requirements, corporate or other governing instruments, or its established operating procedures:

(i) Administration of fiduciary powers. (A) (1) The owners or directors of the applicant will be responsible for the proper exercise of fiduciary powers by the applicant. Thus, all matters pertinent thereto, including the determination of policies, the investment and disposition of property held in a fiduciary capacity, and the direction and review of the actions of all employees utilized by the applicant in the exercise of its fiduciary powers, will be the responsibility of the owners or directors. In discharging this responsibility, the owners or directors may assign to designated employees, by action duly recorded, the administration of such of the applicant's fiduciary powers as may be proper to assign.

(2) A written record will be made of the acceptance and of the relinquishment or closing out of all fiduciary accounts, and of the assets held for each account.

(3) If the applicant has the authority or the responsibility to render any investment advice with regard to the assets held in or for each fiduciary account, the advisability of retaining or disposing of the assets will be determined at least once during each period of 12 months.

(B) All employees taking part in the performance of the applicant's fiduciary duties will be adequately bonded.

Nothing in this subdivision (i)(B) shall require any person to be bonded in contravention of section 412(d) of the Employee Retirement Income Security Act of 1974 (29 U.S.C. 1112(d)).

(C) The applicant will employ or retain legal counsel who will be readily available to pass upon fiduciary matters and to advise the applicant.

(D) In order to segregate the performance of its fiduciary duties from other business activities, the applicant will maintain a separate trust division under the immediate supervision of an individual designated for that purpose. The trust division may utilize the personnel and facilities of other divisions of the applicant, and other divisions of the applicant may utilize the personnel and facilities of the trust division, as long as the separate identity of the trust division is preserved.

(ii) Adequacy of net worth. (A) Initial net worth requirement. In the case of applications received after January 5, 1995, no initial application will be accepted by the Commissioner unless the applicant has a net worth of not less than $250,000 (determined as of the end of the most recent taxable year). Thereafter, the applicant must satisfy the adequacy of net worth requirements of paragraph (e)(5)(ii)(B) and (C) of this section.

(B) No fiduciary account will be accepted by the applicant unless the applicant's net worth (determined as of the end of the most recent taxable year) exceeds the greater of—

(1) $100,000, or

(2) Four percent (or, in the case of a passive trustee described in paragraph (e)(6)(i)(A) of this section, two percent) of the value of all of the assets held by the applicant in fiduciary accounts (determined as of the most recent valuation date).

(C) The applicant will take whatever lawful steps are necessary (including the relinquishment of fiduciary accounts) to ensure that its net worth (determined as of the close of each taxable year) exceeds the greater of—

(1) $50,000, or

(2) Two percent (or, in the case of a passive trustee described in paragraph (e)(6)(i)(A) of this section, one percent) of the value of all of the assets held by the applicant in fiduciary accounts (determined as of the most recent valuation date).

(D) Assets held by members of SIPC. (1) For purposes of satisfying the adequacy-of-net worth requirement of this paragraph, a special rule is provided for nonbank trustees that are members of the Securities Investor Protection Corporation (SIPC) created under the Securities Investor Protection Act of 1970 (SIPA)(15 U.S.C. § 78aaa et seq, as amended). The amount that the net worth of a nonbank trustee that is a member of SIPC must exceed is reduced by two percent for purposes of paragraph (e)(5)(ii)(B)(2), and one percent for purposes of paragraph (e)(5)(ii)(C)(2), of the value of assets (determined on an account-by-account basis) held for the benefit of customers (as defined in 15 U.S.C. § 78fff-2(e)(4)) in fiduciary accounts by the nonbank trustee to the extent of the portion of each account that does not exceed the dollar limit on advances described in 15 U.S.C. § 78fff-3(a), as amended, that would apply to the assets in that account in the event of a liquidation proceeding under the SIPA.

(2) The provisions of this special rule for assets held in fiduciary accounts by members of SIPC are illustrated in the following example.

*Example.* (a) Trustee X is a broker-dealer and is a member of the Securities Investment Protection Corporation. Trustee X also has been approved as a nonbank trustee for individual retirement accounts (IRAs) by the Commissioner but not as a passive nonbank trustee. Trustee X is the trustee for four IRAs. The total assets of each IRA (for which Trustee X is the trustee) as of the most recent valuation date before the last day of Trustee X's taxable year ending in 1995 are as follows: the total assets for IRA-1 is $3,000,000 (all of which is invested in securities); the value of the total assets for IRA-2 is $500,000 ($200,000 of which is cash and $300,000 of which is invested in securities), the value of the total assets for IRA-3 is $400,000 (all of which is invested in securities); and the value of the total assets of IRA-4 is $200,000 (all of which is cash). The value of all assets held in fiduciary accounts, as defined in § 1.408-2(e)(6)(viii)(A), is $4,100,000.

(b) The dollar limit on advances described in 15 U.S.C. § 78fff-3(a) that would apply to the assets in each account in the event of a liquidation proceeding under the Securities Investor Protection Act of 1970 in effect as of the last day of Trustee X's taxable year ending in 1995 is $500,000 per account (no more that $100,000 of which is permitted to be cash). Thus, the dollar limit that would apply to IRA-1 is $500,000; the dollar limit for IRA-2 is $400,000 ($100,000 of the cash and the $300,000 of the value of the securities); the dollar limit for IRA-3 is $400,000 (the full value of the account because the value of the account is less than $500,000 and no portion of the account is cash); and the dollar limit for IRA-4 is $100,000 (the entire account is cash and the dollar limit per account for cash is $100,000). The aggregate dollar limits of the four IRAs is $1,400,000.

(c) For 1996, the amount determined under § 1.408-2(e)(5)(ii)(B) is determined as follows for Trustee X: (1) four percent of $4,100,000 equals $164,000; (2) two percent of $1,400,000 equals $28,000; and (3) $164,000 minus $28,000 equals $136,000. Thus, because $136,000 exceeds $100,000 the minimum net worth necessary for Trustee X to accept new accounts for 1996 is $136,000.

(d) For 1996, the amount determined under § 1.408-2(e)(5)(ii)(C) for Trustee X is determined as follows: (1) two percent of $4,100,000 equals $82,000; (2) one percent of $1,400,000 equals $14,000; and (3) $82,000 minus $14,000 equals $68,000. Thus, because $68,000 exceeds $50,000, the minimum net worth necessary for Trustee X to avoid a mandatory relinquishment of accounts for 1996 is $68,000.

(E) The applicant will determine the value of the assets held by it in trust at least once in each calendar year and no more than 18 months after the preceding valuation. The assets will be valued at their fair market value, except that the assets of an employee pension benefit plan to which section 103(b)(3)(A) of the Employee Retirement Income Security Act of 1974 (29 U.S.C. 1023(b)(3)(A)) applies will be considered to have the value stated in the most recent annual report of the plan.

(iii) Audits. (A) At least once during each period of 12 months, the applicant will cause detailed audits of the fiduciary books and records to be made by a qualified public accountant. At that time, the applicant will ascertain whether the fiduciary accounts have been administered in accordance with law, this paragraph, and sound fiduciary principles. The audits shall be conducted in accordance with generally accepted auditing standards, and shall involve whatever tests of the fiduciary books and records of the applicant are considered necessary by the qualified public accountant.

(B) In the case of an applicant which is regulated, supervised, and subject to periodic examination by a State or Federal agency, such applicant may adopt an adequate continuous audit system in lieu of the periodic audits required by paragraph (e)(5)(iii)(A) of this section.

(C) A report of the audits and examinations required under this subdivision, together with the action taken thereon, will be noted in the fiduciary records of the applicant.

(iv) Funds awaiting investment or distribution. Funds held in a fiduciary capacity by the applicant awaiting investment or distribution will not be held uninvested or undistributed any longer than is reasonable for the proper management of the account.

(v) Custody of investments. (A) Except for investments pooled in a common investment fund in accordance with the provisions of paragraph (e)(5)(vi) of this section and for investments of accounts established under section 408(q) on or after August 1, 2003, the investments of each account will not be commingled with any other property.

(B) Assets of accounts requiring safekeeping will be deposited in an adequate vault. A permanent record will be kept of assets deposited in or withdrawn from the vault.

(vi) Common investment funds. The assets of an account may be pooled in a common investment fund (as defined in paragraph (e)(5)(viii)(C) of this section) if the applicant is authorized under applicable law to administer a common investment fund and if pooling the assets in a common investment fund is not in contravention of the plan documents or applicable law. The common investment fund must be administered as follows:

(A) Each common investment fund must be established and maintained in accordance with a written agreement, containing appropriate provisions as to the manner in which the fund is to be operated, including provisions relating to the investment powers and a general statement of the investment policy of the applicant with respect to the fund; the allocation of income, profits and losses; the terms and conditions governing the admission or withdrawal of participations in the funds; the auditing of accounts of the applicant with respect to the fund; the basis and method of valuing assets held by the fund, setting forth specific criteria for each type of asset; the minimum frequency for valuation of assets of the fund; the period following each such valuation date during which the valuation may be made (which period in usual circumstances may not exceed 10 business days); the basis upon which the fund may be terminated; and such other matters as may be necessary to define clearly the rights of participants in the fund. A copy of the agreement must be available at the principal office of the applicant for inspection during all business hours, and upon request a copy of the agreement must be furnished to the employer, the plan administrator, any participant or beneficiary of an account, or the individual for whose benefit the account is established or that individual's beneficiary.

(B) All participations in the common investment fund must be on the basis of a proportionate interest in all of the investments.

(C) Not less frequently than once during each period of 3 months the applicant must determine the value of the assets in the fund as of the date set for the valuation of assets. No participation may be admitted to or withdrawn from the fund except (1) on the basis of such valuation and (2) as of such valuation date. No participation may be admitted to or withdrawn from the fund unless a written request for or notice of intention of taking such action has been entered on or before the valuation date in the fiduciary records of the applicant. No request or notice may be canceled or countermanded after the valuation date.

(D) (1) The applicant must at least once during each period of 12 months cause an adequate audit to be made of the common investment fund by a qualified public accountant.

(2) The applicant must at least once during each period of 12 months prepare a financial report of the fund which, based upon the above audit, must contain a list of investments in the fund showing the cost and current value of each investment; a statement for the period since the previous re-

port showing purchases, with cost; sales, with profit or loss; any other investment changes; income and disbursements; and an appropriate notation as to any investments in default.

(3) The applicant must transmit and certify the accuracy of the financial report to the administrator of each plan participating in the common investment fund within 120 days after the end of the plan year.

(E) When participations are withdrawn from a common investment fund, distributions may be made in cash or ratably in kind, or partly in cash and partly in kind: *Provided,* That all distributions as of any one valuation date must be made on the same basis.

(F) If for any reason an investment is withdrawn in kind from a common investment fund for the benefit of all participants in the fund at the time of such withdrawal and such investment is not distributed ratably in kind, it must be segregated and administered or realized upon for the benefit ratably of all participants in the common investment fund at the time of withdrawal.

(vii) Books and records. (A) The applicant must keep its fiduciary records separate and distinct from other records. All fiduciary records must be so kept and retained for as long as the contents thereof may become material in the administration of any internal revenue law. The fiduciary records must contain full information relative to each account.

(B) The applicant must keep an adequate record of all pending litigation to which it is a party in connection with the exercise of fiduciary powers.

(viii) Definitions. For purposes of this paragraph (e)(5) and paragraph (e)(2)(v), and paragraph (e)(7) of this section—

(A) The term "account" or "fiduciary account" means a trust described in section 401(a) (including a custodial account described in section 401(f)), a custodial account described in section 403(b)(7), or an individual retirement account described in section 408(a) (including a custodial account described in section 408(h)).

(B) The term "plan administrator" means an administrator as defined in § 1.414(g)-1.

(C) The term "common investment fund" means a trust that satisfies the following requirements:

(1) The trust consists of all or part of the assets of several accounts that have been established with the applicant, and

(2) The trust is described in section 401(a) and is exempt from tax under section 501(a), or is a trust that is created for the purpose of providing a satisfactory diversification of investments or a reduction of administrative expenses for the participating accounts and that satisfies the requirements of section 408(c).

(D) The term "fiduciary records" means all matters which are written, transcribed, recorded, received or otherwise come into the possession of the applicant and are necessary to preserve information concerning the acts and events relevant to the fiduciary activities of the applicant.

(E) The term "qualified public accountant" means a qualified public accountant, as defined in section 103(a)(3)(D) of the Employee Retirement Income Security Act of 1974, 29 U.S.C. 1023(a)(3)(D), who is independent of the applicant.

(F) The term "net worth" means the amount of the applicant's assets less the amount of its liabilities, as determined in accordance with generally accepted accounting principles.

*(6) Special rules.* (i) Passive trustee. (A) An applicant that undertakes to act only as a passive trustee may be relieved of one or more of the requirements of this paragraph upon clear and convincing proof that such requirements are not germane, under all the facts and circumstances, to the manner in which the applicant will administer any trust. A trustee is a passive trustee only if under the written trust instrument the trustee has no discretion to direct the investment of the trust funds or any other aspect of the business administration of the trust, but is merely authorized to acquire and hold particular investments specified by the trust instrument. Thus, for example, in the case of an applicant that undertakes merely to acquire and hold the stock of regulated investment companies, the requirements of paragraph (e)(5)(i)(A)(3), (i)(D), and (vi) of this section shall not apply and no negative inference shall be drawn from the applicant's failure to demonstrate its experience of competence with respect to the activities described in paragraph (e)(4)(ii)(E) to (H) of this section.

(B) The notice of approval issued to an applicant that is approved by reason of this subdivision shall state that the applicant is authorized to act only as a passive trustee.

(ii) Federal or State regulation. Evidence that an applicant is subject to Federal or State regulation with respect to one or more relevant factors shall be given weight in proportion to the extent that such regulatory standards are consonant with the requirements of section 401. Such evidence may be submitted in addition to, or in lieu of, the specific proofs required by this paragraph.

(iii) Savings account. (A) An applicant will be approved to act as trustee under this subdivision if the following requirements are satisfied:

(1) The applicant is a credit union, industrial loan company, or other financial institution designated by the Commissioner;

(2) The investment of the trust assets will be solely in deposits in the applicant;

(3) Deposits in the applicant are insured (up to the dollar limit prescribed by applicable law) by an agency or instrumentality of the United States, or by an organization established under a special statute the business of which is limited to insuring deposits in financial institutions and providing related services.

(B) Any applicant that satisfies the requirements of this subdivision is hereby approved, and (notwithstanding subparagraph (2) of this paragraph) is not required to submit a written application. This approval takes effect on the first day after December 22, 1976, on which the applicant satisfies the requirements of this subdivision, and continues in effect for so long as the applicant continues to satisfy those requirements.

(C) If deposits are insured, but not in the manner provided in paragraph (e)(6)(iii)(A)(3) of this section, the applicant must submit an application. The application, notwithstanding subparagraph (2) of this paragraph, will be limited to a complete description of the insurance of applicant's deposits. The applicant will be approved if the Commissioner approves of the applicant's insurance.

(iv) Notification of Commissioner. The applicant must notify the Commissioner in writing of any change that affects the continuing accuracy of any representation made in the application required by this paragraph, whether the change occurs before or after the applicant receives a notice of approval. The notification must be addressed to the address prescribed by the Commissioner in revenue rulings, notices, and other guidance published in the Internal Revenue Bulletin (see § 601.601(d)(2)(ii)(b) of this chapter.

(v) Substitution of trustee. No applicant will be approved unless the applicant undertakes to act as trustee only under trust instruments which contain a provision to the effect that the grantor is to substitute another trustee upon notification by the Commissioner that such substitution is required because the applicant has failed to comply with the requirements of this paragraph or is not keeping such records, or making such returns, or rendering such statements as are required by forms or regulations.

*(7) Procedure and administration.* (i) Notice of approval. If the applicant is approved, a written notice of approval will be issued to the applicant. The notice of approval will state the day on which it becomes effective, and (except as otherwise provided therein) will remain effective until revoked. This paragraph does not authorize the applicant to accept any fiduciary account before such notice of approval becomes effective.

(ii) Notice of disapproval. If the applicant is not approved, a written notice will be furnished to the applicant containing a statement of the reasons why the applicant has not been approved.

(iii) Copy to be furnished. The applicant must not accept a fiduciary account until after the plan administrator or the person for whose benefit the account is to be established is furnished with a copy of the written notice of approval issued to the applicant. This provision is effective six months after April 20, 1979 for new accounts accepted thereafter. For accounts accepted before that date, the administrator must be notified before the later of the effective date of this provision or six months after acceptance of the account.

(iv) Grounds for revocation. The notice of approval issued to an applicant will be revoked if the Commissioner determines that the applicant is unwilling or unable to administer fiduciary accounts in a manner consistent with the requirements of this paragraph. Generally, the notice will not be revoked unless the Commissioner determines that the applicant has knowingly, willfully, or repeatedly failed to administer fiduciary accounts in a manner consistent with the requirements of this paragraph, or has administered a fiduciary account in a grossly negligent manner.

(v) Procedures for revocation. The notice of approval issued to an applicant may be revoked in accordance with the following procedures:

(A) If the Commissioner proposes to revoke the notice of approval issued to an applicant, the Commissioner will advise the applicant in writing of the proposed revocation and of the reasons therefor.

(B) Within 60 days after the receipt of such written advice, the applicant may protest the proposed revocation by submitting a written statement of facts, law, and arguments opposing such revocation to the address prescribed by the Commissioner in revenue rulings, notices, and other guidance published in the Internal Revenue Bulletin (see § 601.601(d)(2)(ii)(b) of this chapter. In addition, the applicant may request a conference in the National Office.

(C) If the applicant consents to the proposed revocation, either before or after a National Office conference, or if the applicant fails to file a timely protest, the Commissioner will revoke the notice of approval that was issued to the applicant.

(D) If, after considering the applicant's protest and any information developed in conference, the Commissioner determines that the applicant is unwilling or unable to administer fiduciary accounts in a manner consistent with the requirements of this paragraph, the Commissioner will revoke the notice of approval that was issued to the applicant and will furnish the applicant with a written statement of findings on which the revocation is based.

(E) If at any time the Commissioner determines that immediate action is necessary to protect the interest of the Internal Revenue Service or of any fiduciary account, the notice of approval issued to the applicant will be suspended at once, pending a final decision to be based on the applicant's protest and any information developed in conference.

*(8) Special rules for governmental units.* (i) In general. A governmental unit that seeks to qualify as a nonbank trustee of a deemed IRA that is part of its qualified employer plan must demonstrate to the satisfaction of the Commissioner that it is able to administer the trust in a manner that is consistent with the requirements of section 408. The demonstration must be made by written application to the Commissioner. Notwithstanding the requirement of paragraph (e)(1) of this section that a person must demonstrate by written application that the requirements of paragraphs (e)(2) through (e)(6) of this section will be met in order to qualify as a nonbank trustee, a governmental unit that maintains a plan qualified under section 401(a), 403(a), 403(b) or 457 need not demonstrate that all of these requirements will be met with respect to any individual retirement accounts maintained by that governmental unit pursuant to section 408(q). For example, a governmental unit need not demonstrate that it satisfies the net worth requirements of paragraph (e)(3)(ii) of this section if it demonstrates instead that it possesses taxing authority under applicable law. The Commissioner, in his discretion, may exempt a governmental unit from certain other requirements upon a showing that the governmental unit is able to administer the deemed IRAs in the best interest of the participants. Moreover, in determining whether a governmental unit satisfies the other requirements of paragraphs (e)(2) through (e)(6) of this section, the Commissioner may apply the requirements in a manner that is consistent with the applicant's status as a governmental unit.

(ii) Governmental unit. For purposes of this special rule, the term governmental unit means a state, political subdivision of a state, and any agency or instrumentality of a state or political subdivision of a state.

(iii) Additional rules. The Commissioner may in revenue rulings, notices, or other guidance of general applicability provide additional rules for governmental units seeking approval as nonbank trustees.

(iv) Effective/applicability date. This section is applicable for written applications made on or after June 18, 2007. The rules in this section also may be relied on for applications submitted on or after August 1, 2003 (or such earlier application as the Commissioner deems appropriate) and before June 18, 2007.

---

T.D. 7714, 8/7/80, amend T.D. 8635, 12/19/95, T.D. 9142, 7/21/2004, T.D. 9331, 6/15/2007.

---

**Proposed § 1.408-2 Special rules for governmental entities.** [*For Preamble, see ¶ 152,545*]

[The text of proposed § 1.408-2 paragraph (e)(8) is the same as the text of § 1.408-2(e)(8)T published elsewhere in this issue of the Federal Register].

PAR. 2. Section 1.408-2 is amended by revising paragraph (b)(1) to read as follows:

**Proposed § 1.408-2 Individual retirement accounts.** [*For Preamble, see ¶ 150,933*]

* * * * *

**(b)** * * * .

*(1) Amount of acceptable contributions.* Except in the case of a contribution to a simplified employee pension described in section 408(k) and a rollover contribution described in section 408(d)(3), 402(a)(5), 402(a)(7), 403(a)(4), 403(b)(8), 405(d)(3), or 409(b)(3)(C), the trust instrument must provide that contributions may not be accepted by the trustee for the taxable year in excess of $2,000 on behalf of any individual for whom the trust is maintained. An individual retirement account maintained as a simplified employee pension may provide for the receipt of up to the limits specified in section 408(j) for a calendar year.

* * * * *

PAR. 6. Section 1.408-2 is amended by revising paragraph (c)(3) to read as follows:

**Proposed § 1.408-2 Individual retirement accounts.** [*For Preamble, see ¶ 150,703*]

* * * * *

**(c)** * * *

*(3) Special requirement.* There must be a separate accounting for the interest of each employee or member (or spouse of an employee or member).

* * * * *

**§ 1.408-3 Individual retirement annuities.**

***Caution:*** The Treasury has not yet amended Reg § 1.408-3 to reflect changes made by P.L. 99-514, P.L. 98-369, P.L. 97-248, P.L. 97-34.

**(a) In general.** An individual retirement annuity is an annuity contract or endowment contract (described in paragraph (e)(1) of this section) issued by an insurance company which is qualified to do business under the law of the jurisdiction in which the contract is sold and which satisfies the requirements of paragraph (b) of this section. A participation certificate in a group contract issued by an insurance company described in this paragraph will be treated as an individual retirement annuity if the contract satisfies the requirements of paragraph (b) of this section; the certificate of participation sets forth the requirements of paragraphs (1) through (5) of section 408(b); the contract provides for a separate accounting of the benefit allocable to each participant-owner; and the group contract is for the exclusive benefit of the participant owners and their beneficiaries. For purposes of this title, a participant-owner of a group contract described in this paragraph shall be treated as the owner of an individual retirement annuity. A contract will not be treated as other than an individual retirement annuity merely because it provides for waiver of premium on disability. An individual retirement annuity contract which satisfies the requirements of section 408(b) need not be purchased under a trust if the requirements of paragraph (b) of this section are satisfied. An individual retirement endowment contract may not be held under a trust which satisfies the requirements of section 408(a). Distribution of the contract is not a taxable event. Distributions under the contract are includible in gross income in accordance with the provisions of § 1.408-4(e).

**(b) Requirements.** *(1) Transferability.* The annuity or the endowment contract must not be transferable by the owner. An annuity or endowment contract is transferable if the owner can transfer any portion of his interest in the contract to any person other than the issuer thereof. Accordingly, such a contract is transferable if the owner can sell, assign, discount, or pledge as collateral for a loan or as security for the performance of an obligation or for any other purpose his interest in the contract to any person other than the issuer thereof. On the other hand, a contract is not to be considered transferable merely because the contract contains: a provision permitting the individual to designate a beneficiary to receive the proceeds in the event of his death, a provision permitting the individual to elect a joint and survivor annuity, or other similar provisions.

*(2) Annual premium.* Except in the case of a contribution to a simplified employee pension described in section 408(k), the annual premium on behalf of any individual for the annuity or the endowment contract cannot exceed $1,500. Any refund of premiums must be applied before the close of the calendar year following the year of the refund toward the payment of future premiums or the purchase of additional benefits.

*(3) Distribution.* The entire interest of the owner must be distributed to him in the same manner and over the same period as described in § 1.408-2(b)(6).

*(4) Distribution upon death.* If the owner dies before the entire interest has been distributed to him, or if distribution has commenced to the surviving spouse, the remaining interest must be distributed in the same manner, over the same period, and to the same beneficiaries as described in § 1.408-2(b)(7).

*(5) Nonforfeitability.* The entire interest of the owner in the annuity or endowment contract must be nonforfeitable.

*(6) Flexible premium.[Reserved]*

**(c) Disqualification.** If during any taxable year the owner of an annuity borrows any money under the annuity or endowment contract or by use of such contract (including, but not limited to, pledging the contract as security for any loan), such contract will cease to be an individual retirement annuity as of the first day of such taxable year, and will not be an individual retirement annuity at any time thereafter. If an annuity or endowment contract which constitutes an individual retirement annuity is disqualified as a result of the preceding sentence, an amount equal to the fair market value of the contract as of the first day of the taxable year of the owner in which such contract is disqualified is deemed to be distributed to the owner. Such owner shall include in gross income for such year an amount equal to the fair market value of such contract as of such first day. The preceding sentence applies even though part of the fair market value of the individual retirement annuity as of the first day of the taxable year is attributable to excess contributions which may be returned tax-free under section 408(d)(4) or 408(d)(5).

**(d) Premature distribution tax on deemed distribution.** If the individual has not attained age 59½ before the beginning of the year in which the disqualification described in paragraph (c) of this section occurs, see section 408(f)(2) for additional tax on premature distributions.

**(e) Endowment contracts.** *(1) Additional requirement for endowment contracts.* No contract providing life insurance protection issued by a company described in paragraph (a) of this section shall be treated as an endowment contract for purposes of this section if—

(i) Such contract matures later than the taxable year in which the individual in whose name the contract is purchased attains the age of 70½;

(ii) Such contract is not for the exclusive benefit of such individual or his beneficiaries;

(iii) Premiums under the contract may increase over the term of the contract;

(iv) When all premiums are paid when due, the case value of such contract at maturity is less than the death benefit payable under the contract at any time before maturity;

(v) The death benefit does not, at some time before maturity, exceed the greater of the cash value or the sum of premiums paid under the contract;

(vi) Such contract does not provide for a cash value;

(vii) Such contract provides that the life insurance element of such contract may increase over the term of such contract, unless such increase is merely because such contract provides for the purchase of additional benefits;

(viii) Such contract provides insurance other than life insurance and waiver of premiums upon disability; or

(ix) Such contract is issued after November 6, 1978.

*(2) Treatment of proceeds under endowment contract upon death of individual.* In the case of the payment of a death benefit under an endowment contract upon the death of the individual in whose name the contract is purchased, the portion of such payment which is equal to the cash value immediately before the death of such individual is not excludable from gross income under section 101(a) and is treated as a distribution from an individual retirement annuity. The remaining portion, if any, of such payment constitutes current life insurance protection and is excludable under section 101(a). If a death benefit is paid under an endowment contract at a date or dates later than the death of the individual, section 101(d) is applicable only to the portion of the benefit which is attributable to the amount excludable under section 101(a).

---

T.D. 7714, 8/7/80.

---

PAR. 3. Section 1.408-3 is amended by revising paragraph (b)(2) to read as follows:

**Proposed § 1.408-3 Individual retirement annuities.** [*For Preamble, see ¶ 150,933*]

* * * * *

**(b)** * * *

*(2) Annual premium.* Except in the case of a contribution to a simplified employee pension described in section 408(k), the annual premium on behalf of any individual for the annuity cannot exceed $2,000. Any refund of premiums must be applied before the close of the calendar year following the year of the refund toward the payment of future premiums or the purchase of additional benefits. An individual retirement annuity maintained as a simplified employee pension may provide for an annual premium of up to the limits specified in section 408(j).

* * * * *

PAR. 7. Section 1.408-3 is revised by adding new paragraphs (b)(6) and (f). These added provisions read as follows:

**Proposed § 1.408-3 Individual retirement annuities.** [*For Preamble, see ¶ 150,703*]

* * * * *

**(b)** * * *

*(6) Flexible premium.* (i) In the case of annuity contracts issued after November 6, 1978, the premiums under such contracts are not fixed. See paragraph (f) for the definition of an annuity contract under which "the premiums are not fixed."

(ii) In the case of a fixed premium individual retirement annuity or individual retirement endowment contract issued before November 7, 1978, the issuer of such contract may offer the holder of the contract the option of exchanging such contract for a flexible premium contract. If such an exchange is made before January 1, 1981, the exchange shall not constitute a distribution and shall be nontaxable.

* * * * *

**(f) Flexible premium annuity contract.** *(1) In general.* A flexible premium retirement annuity contract shall be considered a contract under which "the premiums are not fixed" if it provides the following.

(i) At no time after the initial premium for the contract has been paid is there a specified renewal premium required.

(ii) The contract must allow for the continuance of the contract (as a paidup annuity) under its nonforfeiture provision if premium payments cease altogether.

(iii) The contract, if being continued on a paid-up basis (i.e., if it has not been terminated by a payment in cash), will be reinstated at any date prior to its maturity date upon payment of a premium to the insurer.

*(2) Exceptions.* (i) The insurer may require that if a premium is remitted, it will be accepted only if the amount remitted is some stated amount, not in excess of $50.

(ii) The contract may provide that if no premiums have been received under the contract for two (2) full years and the paid-up annuity benefit at maturity of the plan stipulated in the contract arising from the premium paid prior to such two-year period would be less than $20 a month, the insurer may, at its option, terminate the contract by payment in cash of the then present value of the paid-up benefit (computed on the same basis specified in the contract for determining the paid-up benefit).

*(3) Permissible provisions.* A flexible premium contract will not be considered to have fixed premiums merely because—

(i) A maximum limit (which may be expressed as a multiple of the premium paid in the first year of the contract) is placed on the amount of the premium that the insurer will accept in any year,

(ii) An annual charge is made against the policy value,

(iii) A fee (which may be composed of a flat dollar amount plus an amount equal to the required premium tax imposed by the state government) is charged upon the acceptance of each premium by the insurer, or

(iv) The contract requires a level annual premium for a supplementary benefit, such as a waiver of premium benefit.

**§ 1.408-4 Treatment of distributions from individual retirement arrangements.**

***Caution:*** The Treasury has not yet amended Reg § 1.408-4 to reflect changes made by P.L. 107-16, P.L. 101-239, P.L. 100-647, P.L. 99-514, P.L. 98-369, P.L. 97-248, P.L. 97-34.

**(a) General rule.** *(1) Inclusion in income.* Except as otherwise provided in this section, any amount actually paid or distributed or deemed paid or distributed from an individual retirement account or individual retirement annuity shall be included in the gross income of the payee or distributee for the taxable year in which the payment or distribution is received.

*(2) Zero basis.* Notwithstanding section 1015(d) or any other provision of the Code, the basis (or investment in the contract) of any person in such an account or annuity is zero. For purposes of this section, an assignment of an individual's rights under an individual retirement account or an individual retirement annuity shall, except as provided in § 1.408-4(g) (relating to transfer incident to divorce), be deemed a distribution to such individual from such account or annuity of the amount assigned.

**(b) Rollover contribution.** *(1) To individual retirement arrangement.* Paragraph (a)(1) of this section shall not apply to any amount paid or distributed from an individual retirement account or individual retirement annuity to the individual for whose benefit the account was established or who is the owner of the annuity if the entire amount received (including the same amount of money and any other property) is paid into an individual retirement account, annuity (other than an endowment contract), or bond created for the benefit of such individual not later than the 60th day after the day on which he receives the payment or distribution.

*(2) To qualified plan.* Paragraph (a)(1) of this section does not apply to any amount paid or distributed from an individual retirement account or individual retirement annuity to the individual for whose benefit the account was established or who is the owner of the annuity if—

(i) No amount in the account or no part of the value of the annuity is attributable to any source other than a rollover contribution from an employees' trust described in section 401(a) which is exempt from tax under section 501(a) or a rollover contribution from an annuity plan described in section 403(a) and the earnings on such sums, and

(ii) The entire amount received (including the same amount of money and any other property) represents the entire amount in the account and is paid into another such trust or plan (for the benefit of such individual) not later than the 60th day after the day on which the payment or distribution is received.

This subparagraph does not apply if any portion of the rollover contribution described in paragraph (b)(2)(i) of this section is attributable to an employees' trust forming part of a plan or an annuity under which the individual was an employee within the meaning of section 401(c)(1) at the time contributions were made on his behalf under the plan.

*(3) To section 403(b) contract. [Reserved]*

*(4) Frequency limitation.* (i) For taxable years beginning on or before December 31, 1977, paragraph (b)(1) of this section does not apply to any amount received by an individual from an individual retirement account, annuity or bond if at any time during the 3-year period ending on the day of receipt, the individual received any other amount from an individual retirement account, annuity or bond which was not includible in his gross income because of the application of paragraph (b)(1) of this section.

(ii) [Reserved]

**(c) Excess contributions returned before due date of return.** *(1) Excess contribution.* The rules in this paragraph (c) apply for purposes of determining net income attributable to IRA contributions made before January 1, 2004, and returned pursuant to section 408(d)(4). The rules in § 1.408-11 apply for purposes of determining net income attributable to IRA contributions made on or after January 1, 2004, and returned pursuant to section 408(d)(4). For purposes of this paragraph, excess contributions are the excess of the amounts contributed to an individual retirement account or paid for an individual retirement annuity during the taxable year over the amount allowable as a deduction under section 219 or 220 for the taxable year.

*(2) General rule.* (i) Paragraph (a)(1) of this section does not apply to the distribution of any excess contribution paid during a taxable year to an account or annuity if: the distribution is received on or before the date prescribed by law (including extensions) for filing the individual's return for such taxable year; no deduction is allowed under section 219 or section 220 with respect to the excess contribution; and the distribution is accompanied by the amount of net income attributable to the excess contribution as of the date of the distribution as determined under subdivision (ii).

(ii) The amount of net income attributable to the excess contributions is an amount which bears the same ratio to the net income earned by the account during the computation period as the excess contribution bears to the sum of the balance of the account as of the first day of the taxable year in which the excess contribution is made and the total contribution made for such taxable year. For purposes of this paragraph, the term "computation period" means the period beginning on the first day of the taxable year in which the excess contribution is made and ending on the date of the distribution from the account.

(iii) For purposes of paragraph (c)(2)(ii), the net income earned by the account during the computation period is the fair market value of the balance of the account immediately after the distribution increased by the amount of distributions from the account during the computation period, and reduced (but not below zero) by the sum of: (A) the fair market value of the balance of the account as of the first day of the taxable year in which the excess contribution is made and (B) the contributions to the account made during the computation period.

*(3) Time of inclusion.* (i) For taxable years beginning before January 1, 1977, the amount of net income determined under subparagraph (2) is includible in the gross income of the individual for the taxable year in which it is received. The amount of net income thus distributed is subject to the tax imposed by section 408(f)(1) for the year includible in gross income.

(ii) [Reserved]

*(4) Example.* The provisions of this paragraph may be illustrated by the following example:

*Example.* On January 1, 1975, A, age 55, who is a calendar-year taxpayer, contributes $1,500 to an individual retirement account established for his benefit. For 1975, A is entitled to a deduction of $1,400 under section 219. For 1975, A does not claim as deductions any other items listed in section 62. A's gross income for 1975 is $9,334. On April 1, 1976, $107 is distributed to A from his individual retirement account. As of such date, the balance of the account is $1,498 [$1,605 − $107]. There were no other distributions from the account as of such date. The net amount of income earned by the account is $105 [$1,498 + $107 − (0 + $1,500)]. The net income attributable to the excess contribution is $7. [$105 × ($100/$1,500)]. A's adjusted gross income for 1975 is his gross income for 1975 ($9,334) reduced by the amount allowable to A as a deduction under section 219 ($1,400), or $7,934. A will include the $7 of the $107 distributed on April 1, 1976, in his gross income for 1976. Further, A will pay an additional income tax of $.70 for 1976 under section 408(f)(1).

**(d) Deemed distribution.** *(1) General rule.* In any case in which an individual retirement account ceases to be an individual retirement account by reason of the application of section 408(e)(2), paragraph (a)(1) of this section shall apply as if there were a distribution on the first day of the taxable year in which such account ceases to be an individual retirement account of an amount equal to the fair market value on such day of all of the assets in the account on such day. In the case of a deemed distribution from an individual retirement annuity, see § 1.408-3(d).

*(2) Using account as security.* In any case in which an individual for whose benefit an individual retirement account is established uses, directly or indirectly, all or any portion of the account as security for a loan, paragraph (a)(1) of this section shall apply as if there were distributed on the first day of the taxable year in which the loan was made an amount equal to that portion of the account used as security for such loan.

**(e) Distribution of annuity contracts.** Paragraph (a)(1) of this section does not apply to any annuity contract which is distributed from an individual retirement account and which satisfies the requirements of paragraphs (b)(1), (3), (4) and (5) of section 408. Amounts distributed under such contracts will be taxable to the distributee under section 72. For purposes of applying section 72 to a distribution from such a contract, the investment in such contract is zero.

**(f) Treatment of assets distributed from an individual retirement account for the purchase of an endowment contract.** Under section 408(e)(5), if all, or any portion, of the assets of an individual retirement account are used to purchase an endowment contract described in § 1.408-3(e) for the benefit of the individual for whose benefit the account is established—

*(1)* The excess, if any, of the total amount of assets used to purchase such contract over the portion of the assets attributable to life insurance protection shall be treated as a rollover contribution described in section 408(d)(3), and

*(2)* The portion of the assets attributable to life insurance protection shall be treated as a distribution described in paragraph (a)(1) of this section, except that the provisions of section 408(f) shall not apply to such amount.

**(g) Transfer incident to divorce.** *(1) General rule.* The transfer of an individual's interest, in whole or in part, in an individual retirement account, individual retirement annuity, or a retirement bond, to his former spouse under a valid divorce decree or a written instrument incident to such divorce shall not be considered to be a distribution from such an account or annuity to such individual or his former spouse; nor shall it be considered a taxable transfer by such individual to his former spouse notwithstanding any other provision of Subtitle A of the Code.

*(2) Spousal account.* The interest described in this paragraph (g) which is transferred to the former spouse shall be treated as an individual retirement account of such spouse if the interest is an individual retirement account; an individual retirement annuity of such spouse if such interest is an individual retirement annuity; and a retirement bond of such spouse if such interest is a retirement bond.

---

T.D. 7714, 8/7/80, amend T.D. 9056, 5/2/2003.

---

PAR. 8. Section 1.408-4 is amended by: (1) Adding new paragraphs (b)(3), (b)(4)(ii), and (c)(3)(ii); and (2) adding a new paragraph (h). These added provisions read as follows:

**Proposed § 1.408-4 Treatment of distributions from individual retirement arrangements.** [*For Preamble, see ¶ 150,703*]

* * * * *

**(b) Rollover Contribution.** * * *

*(3) To section 403(b) contract.* Paragraph (a)(1) of this section does not apply to any amount paid or distributed from an individual retirement account or individual retirement annuity to the individual for whose benefit the account or annuity is maintained if—

(i) The entire amount received (including money and other property) represents the entire interest in the account or the entire value of the annuity,

(ii) No amount in the account and no part of the value of the annuity is attributable to any source other than a rollover contribution from an annuity contract described in section 403(b) and any earnings on such rollover,

(iii) The entire amount thereof is paid into an annuity contract described in section 403(b) (for the benefit of such individual) not later than the 60th day after the receipt of the payment or distribution, and

(iv) The distribution or transfer is made in a taxable year beginning after December 31, 1978.

*(4)* * * *

(ii) For taxable years beginning after December 31, 1977, paragraph (b)(1) of this section does not apply to any amount received by an individual from an individual retirement account, individual retirement annuity or retirement bond if at any time during the 1-year period ending on the day of receipt, the individual received any other amount from the individual retirement account, individual retirement annuity or retirement bond which was not includible in his gross income because of the application of paragraph (b)(1) of this section. This rule applies to each separate individual retirement account, individual retirement annuity, or retirement bond maintained by an individual. Thus, if an individual maintains two individual retirement accounts, IRA-1 and IRA-2, and rolls over the assets of IRA-1 into IRA-3, he is not precluded by this subdivision from making a tax-free rollover from IRA-2 to IRA-3 or any other IRA within one year after the rollover from IRA-1 to IRA-3.

**(c)** * * *

*(3) Time of inclusion.* * * *

(ii) For taxable years beginning after December 31, 1976, the amount of net income determined under subparagraph (2) is includible in the gross income of the individual in the taxable year in which such excess contribution is made. The amount of net income thus distributed is subject to the tax imposed by section 408(f)(1) for the year includible in gross income.

* * * * *

**(h) Certain distributions of excess contributions after due date of return for taxable year.** *(1) General rule.* In the case of any individual, if the aggregate contributions (other than valid rollover contributions) paid for any taxable year to an individual retirement account or for an individual retirement annuity do not exceed $1,750, section 408(d)(1) shall not apply to the distribution of any such contribution to the extent that such contribution exceeds the amount allowable as a deduction under section 219 or 220 for the taxable year for which the contribution was paid—

(i) If such distribution is received after the date described in section 408(d)(4),

(ii) But only to the extent that no deduction has been allowed under section 219 or 220 with respect to such excess contribution.

*(2) Excess rollover contribution attributable to erroneous information.* If the taxpayer reasonably relies on information supplied pursuant to subtitle F of the Internal Revenue Code of 1954 for determining the amount of a rollover contribution, but such information was erroneous, subparagraph (1) of this paragraph shall be applied by increasing the dollar limit set forth therein by that portion of the excess contribution which was attributable to such information.

*(3) Special rule for contributions to simplified employee pension.* If employer contributions on behalf of the individual are paid for the taxable year to a simplified employee pension, the dollar limitation of subparagraph (1) shall be the lesser of the amount of such contributions or $7,500. See § 1.219-3(a)(3)(iv) for a special rule where there is more than one employer.

*(4) Effective date.* (i) Subparagraphs (1) and (2) of this paragraph shall apply to distributions in taxable years beginning after December 31, 1975.

(ii) In the case of contributions for taxable years beginning before January 1, 1978, paragraph (5) of section 408(d) of the Internal Revenue Code of 1954 shall be applied as if such paragraph did not contain any dollar limitation.

*(5) Examples.* The provisions of this paragraph may be illustrated by the following examples:

*Example (1).* T a calendar-year taxpayer, had been a participant in a government pension plan for 6 years prior to separation from service on July 31, 1976. The plan required T to make mandatory contributions and as of July 31, 1976, these mandatory contributions totaled $6,000. Upon T separation from service, she was given the option of receiving back all of her mandatory contribution or leaving then with the plan. T elected to receive her mandatory contributions and attempted to roll over these amounts into an individual retirement account (IRA) in August of 1976. The trustee of the IRA accepted these funds and IRA was established. In March of 1977, T discovered that the funds she received from the government plan did not qualify for rollover treatment because they were employee contributions and withdrew all of the money from her IRA. T will not have to include any of the money withdrawn from the IRA in gross income for 1977 because the transitional rule of paragraph (h)(3)(ii) permits the withdrawal of all contributions which have not been allowed as deductions under section 219 or 220 made to IRA's for taxable years beginning before January 1, 1978, regardless of the amount of the contribution.

*Example (2).* (i) On April 1, 1980, A, a calendar-year taxpayer, receives a lump sum distribution satisfying the requirements of section 402(e)(4)(A) and (C) under the plan of A's employer. The distribution consists of $50,000 case. A made contributions under the plan totaling $8,000, and has received no prior distributions under the plan. However, on the form furnished to A by the employer on account of the distribution, A's contributions under the plan are listed as totaling only $4,500. A reasonably relied on this information.

(ii) A desires to establish an individual retirement account (as described in section 408(a)) with the cash received in the distribution. A desires to contribute the maximum amount permitted under the rollover rules. Under sections 402(a)(5)(B) and 402(a)(5)(D)(ii), A determines that the maximum rollover amount is $45,500, the total of the distribution ($50,000), less the amount listed as A's contributions under the plan ($4,500). The actual maximum rollover amount is $42,000, the total of the distribution ($50,000), less A's actual contribution under the plan ($8,000).

(iii) On May 23, 1980, A contributes $45,500 to an individual retirement account as a rollover contribution.

(iv) On May 1, 1981, A's employer furnishes A a corrected statement indicating that A's contributions under the plan were $8,000. On June 1, 1981, A withdraws $3,500 from the individual retirement account to correct the mistaken contribution. A will not have to include the $3,500 withdrawn from the individual retirement account in gross income for 1981 because the money was placed in the individual retirement account due to erroneous information furnished by the employer and reasonably relied upon by A and thus falls under the exception provided in section 408(d)(5)(B) to section 408(d)(1).

**§ 1.408-5 Annual reports by trustees or issuers.**

***Caution:*** The Treasury has not yet amended Reg § 1.408-5 to reflect changes made by P.L. 104-188, P.L. 99-514, P.L. 98-369.

**(a) In general.** The trustee of an individual retirement account or the issuer of an individual retirement annuity shall make annual calendar year reports concerning the status of the account or annuity. The report shall contain the information required in paragraph (b) and be furnished or filed in the manner and time specified in paragraph (c).

**(b) Information required to be included in the annual reports.** The annual calendar year report shall contain the following information for transactions occurring during the calendar year—

*(1)* The amount of contributions;

*(2)* The amount of distributions;

*(3)* In the case of an endowment contract, the amount of the premium paid allocable to the cost of life insurance;

*(4)* The name and address of the trustee or issuer; and

*(5)* Such other information as the Commissioner may require.

**(c) Manner and time for filing.** *(1)* The annual report shall be furnished to the individual on whose behalf the account is established or in whose name the annuity is purchased (or the beneficiary of the individual or owner). The report shall be furnished on or before the 30th day of June following the calendar year for which the report is required.

*(2)* The Commissioner may require the annual report to be filed with the Service at the time the Commissioner specifies.

**(d) Penalties.** Section 6693 prescribes penalties for failure to file the annual report.

**(e) Effective date.** This section shall apply to reports for calendar years after 1978.

**(f) Reports for years prior to 1979.** For years prior to 1979, a trustee or issuer shall make reports in the time and manner as the Commissioner requires.

---

T.D. 7714, 8/7/80.

---

Section 1.408-5 is revised to read as follows:

**Proposed § 1.408-5 Annual reports by trustees and issuers.** [*For Preamble, see ¶ 151,003*]

**(a) Requirement and form of report.** The trustee of an individual retirement account or the issuer of an individual retirement annuity (including an account or annuity that is a simplified employee pension) shall make annual calendar year reports on Form 5498 concerning the status of the account or annuity. The report shall contain the following information for transactions occurring during or after the calendar year that relate to such calendar year:

*(1)* The name, address, and identifying number of the trustee or issuer;

*(2)* The name, address, and identifying number of the participant (the individual on whose behalf the account is established or in whose name the annuity is purchased (or the beneficiary of the individual or owner));

*(3)* The amount of contributions (exclusive of rollover contributions) made during or after the calendar year that relate to such calendar year;

*(4)* The amount of rollover contributions made during the calendar year;

*(5)* In the case of an endowment contract, the amount of the premium allocable to the cost of life insurance paid either during or after the calendar year that relates to such calendar year; and

*(6)* Such other information as the Commissioner may require.

**(b) Manner and time for filing.** The report on Form 5498 shall be filed, accompanied by transmittal Form 1096, with the appropriate Internal Revenue Service Center. The report shall be filed on or before May 31 following the calendar year for which the report is required.

**(c) Statement to participants.** *(1)* Each trustee or issuer required to file Form 5498 under this section shall furnish the participant a statement containing the information required to be furnished on Form 5498 plus the value of the account or annuity at the end of the calendar year. A copy of Form 5498, containing the additional information specified in the previous sentence, may be used to satisfy the statement requirement of this paragraph. If a copy of Form 5498 is not used to satisfy the statement requirement of this paragraph, the statement shall contain the following language: "This information is being furnished to the Internal Revenue Service."

*(2)* Each statement required by this paragraph to be furnished to participants shall be furnished to such person on or before May 31 following the calendar year for which the report on Form 5498 is required.

**(d) Penalties.** Section 6693 prescribes penalties for failure to file an annual report required by this section.

**(e) Effective date.** In general, this section applies to reports for calendar years beginning with 1983. For additional requirements relating to the 1985 calendar year reports, see paragraph (f) of this section. For special requirements relating to the 1983 and 1984 calendar year reports, see paragraph (g) of this section. For requirements relating to pre-1983 calendar year reports, see 26 CFR 1.408-5 (1983).

**(f) Reports for calendar year 1985.** For calendar year 1985, both Form 5498 and the statement to the participant must report, as a separate entry, the amount of contributions made during the 1985 calendar year that relate to the 1984 calendar year. This also applies, in the case of the statement to the participant, to endowment contract premiums allocable to the cost of life insurance that are paid during the 1985 calendar year but that relate to the 1984 calendar year.

**(g) Reports for calendar years 1983 and 1984.** *(1)* For calendar years 1983 and 1984, neither Form 5498 nor the statement to the participant need identify the calendar year to which a contribution relates. The form and statement need only report the amount of contributions actually made during the calendar year. This also applies to endowment contract premiums allocable to the cost of life insurance and paid during the calendar year.

*(2)* For calendar years 1983 and 1984, Form 5498 need not report (but the statement to the participant must report), in the case of an endowment contract, the amount of the premium allocable to the cost of life insurance paid during the calendar year.

*(3)* For calendar year 1983, neither Form 5498 nor the statement to the participant need separately report rollover contributions made during the calendar year. Rollover contributions are to be aggregated with the amount of other contributions made during the calendar year.

*(4)* For calendar year 1983, the statement to the participant need not contain the language required by paragraph (c)(1) of this section.

*(5)* For calendar year 1983, Form 5498 shall be filed, and the statement to the participant shall be furnished, on or before June 30, 1984.

**(h) Related reports by trustees and issuers.** See § 1.408-7 for reports relating to distributions from individual retirement plans.

### § 1.408-6 Disclosure statements for individual retirement arrangements.

**(a) In general.** *(1) General rule.* Trustees and issuers of individual retirement accounts and annuities are, under the authority of section 408(i), required to provide disclosure statements. This section sets forth these requirements.

**(b) -(c) [Reserved]**

**(d) Requirements.** *(1) [Reserved]*

*(2) [Reserved]*

*(3) [Reserved]*

*(4) Disclosure statements.* (i) Under the authority contained in section 408(i), a disclosure statement shall be furnished in accordance with the provisions of this subparagraph by the trustee of an individual retirement account described in section 408(a) or the issuer of an individual retirement annuity described in section 408(b) or of an endowment contract described in section 408(b) to the individual (hereinafter referred to as the "benefited individual") for whom such an account, annuity, or contract is, or is to be, established.

(ii) (A) (1) The trustee or issuer shall furnish, or cause to be furnished, to the benefited individual, a disclosure statement satisfying the requirements of subdivisions (iii) through (viii) of this subparagraph, as applicable, and a copy of the governing instrument to be used in establishing the account, annuity, or endowment contract. The copy of such governing instrument need not be filled in with financial and other data pertaining to the benefited individual; however, such copy must be complete in all other respects. The disclosure statement and copy of the governing instrument must be received by the benefited individual at least seven days preceding the earlier of the date of establishment or purchase of the account, annuity, or endowment contract. A disclosure statement or copy of the governing instrument required by this subparagraph may be received by the benefited individual less than seven days preceding, but no later than, the earlier of the date of establishment or purchase, if the benefited individual is permitted to revoke the account, annuity, or endowment contract pursuant to a procedure which satisfies the requirements of subdivision (ii)(A)(2) of this subparagraph.

(2) A procedure for revocation satisfies the requirements of this subdivision (ii)(A)(2) of this subparagraph if the benefited individual is permitted to revoke the account, or endowment contract by mailing or delivering, at his option, a notice of revocation on or before a day not less than seven days after the earlier of the date of establishment or purchase and, upon revocation, is entitled to a return of the entire amount of the consideration paid by him for the account, annuity, or endowment contract without adjustment for such items as sales commissions, administrative expenses or fluctuation in market value. The procedure may require that the notice be in writing or that it be oral, or it may require both a written and an oral notice. If an oral notice is required or permitted, the procedure must permit it to be delivered by telephone call during normal business hours. If a written notice is required or permitted, the procedure must provide that, if mailed, it shall be deemed mailed on the date of the postmark (or if sent by certified or registered mail, the date of certification or registration) if it is deposited in the mail in the United States in an envelope, or other appropriate wrapper, first class postage prepaid, properly addressed.

(B) If after a disclosure statement has been furnished, or caused to be furnished, to the benefited individual pursuant to paragraph (d)(4)(ii)(A) of this section and—

(1) On or before the earlier of the date of establishment or purchase, or

(2) On or before the last day on which the benefited individual is permitted to revoke the account, annuity, or endowment contract (if the benefited individual has a right to revoke the account, annuity, or endowment contract pursuant to the rules of subdivision (ii)(A) of this subparagraph),

there becomes effective a material adverse change in the information set forth in such disclosure statement or a material change in the governing instrument to be used in establishing the account, annuity, or contract, the trustee or issuer shall furnish, or cause to be furnished, to the benefited individual such amendments to any previously furnished disclosure statement or governing instrument as may be necessary to adequately inform the benefited individual of such change. The trustee or issuer shall be treated as satisfying this subdivision (ii)(B) of this subparagraph only if material required to be furnished by this subdivision is received by the benefited individual at least seven days preceding the earlier of the date of establishment or purchase of the account, annuity, or endowment contract or if the benefited individual is permitted to revoke the account, annuity, or endowment contract on or before a date not less than seven days after the date on which such material is received, pursuant to a procedure for revocation otherwise satisfying the provisions of subdivision (ii)(A)(2) of this subparagraph.

(C) If the governing instrument is amended after the account, annuity, or endowment contract is no longer subject to revocation pursuant to subdivision (ii)(A) or (B) of this subparagraph, the trustee or issuer shall not later than the 30th day after the later of the date on which the amendment is adopted or becomes effective, deliver or mail to the last known address of the benefited individual a copy of such amendment and, if such amendment affects a matter described in subdivisions (iii) through (viii) of this subparagraph, a disclosure statement with respect to such matter meeting the requirements of subdivision (iv) of this subparagraph.

(D) For purposes of subdivision (ii)(A) and (B) of this subparagraph, if a disclosure statement, governing instrument, or an amendment to either, is mailed to the benefited individual, it shall be deemed (in the absence of evidence to the contrary) to be received by the benefited individual seven days after the date of mailing.

(E) In the case of a trust described in section 408(c) (relating to certain retirement savings arrangements for employees or members of associations of employees), the following special rules shall be applied:

(1) For purposes of this subparagraph, references to the benefited individual's account, annuity, or endowment contract shall refer to the benefited individual's interest in such trust, and

(2) The provisions of subdivision (ii) of this subparagraph shall be applied by substituting "the date on which the benefited individual's interest in such trust commences" for "the earlier of the date of establishment or purchase" wherever it appear therein.

Thus, for example, if an employer establishes a trust described in section 408(c) for the benefit of employees, and the trustee furnishes an employee with a disclosure statement and a copy of the governing instrument (as required by this subparagraph) on the date such employee's interest in the trust commences, such employee must be given a right to revoke such interest within a period of at least seven days. If any contribution has been made within such period (whether by the employee or by the employer), the full amount of such contribution must be paid to such employee pursuant to subdivision (ii)(A)(2) of this subparagraph.

(iii) The disclosure statement required by this subparagraph shall set forth in nontechnical language the following matters as such matters relate to the account, annuity, or endowment contract (as the case may be);

(A) Concise explanations of—

(1) The statutory requirements prescribed in section 408(a) (relating to an individual retirement account) or section 408(b) (relating to an individual retirement annuity and an endowment contract), and any additional requirements (whether or not required by law) that pertain to the particular retirement savings arrangement.

(2) The income tax consequences of establishing an account, annuity, or endowment contract (as the case may be) which meets the requirements of section 408(a) relating to an individual retirement account) or section 408(b) (relating to an individual retirement annuity and an endowment contract), including the deductibility of contributions to, the tax treatment of distributions (other than premature distributions) from, the availability of income tax free rollovers to and from, and the tax status of such account, annuity, or endowment contract.

(3) The limitations and restrictions on the deduction for retirement savings under section 219, including the ineligibility of certain individuals who are active participants in a plan described in section 219(b)(2)(A) or for whom amounts are contributed under a contract described in section 219(b)(2)(B) to make deductible contributions to an account or for an annuity or endowment contract.

(4) The circumstances under which the benefited individual may revoke the account, annuity, or endowment contract, and the procedure therefor (including the name, address, and telephone number of the person designated to receive notice of such revocation). Such explanation shall be prominently displayed at the beginning of the disclosure statement.

(B) Statements to the effect that—

(1) If the benefited individual or his beneficiary engages in a prohibited transaction, described in section 4975(c) with

respect to an individual retirement account, the account will lose its exemption from tax by reason of section 408(e)(2)(A), and the benefited individual must include in gross income, for the taxable year during which the benefited individual or his beneficiary engages in the prohibited transaction the fair market value of the account.

(2) If the owner of an individual retirement annuity or endowment contract described in section 408(b) borrows any money under, or by use of, such annuity or endowment contract, then, under section 408(e)(3), such annuity or endowment contract loses its section 408(b) classification, and the owner must include in gross income, for the taxable year during which the owner borrows any money under, or by use of, such annuity or endowment contract, the fair market value of the annuity or endowment contract.

(3) If a benefited individual uses all or any portion of an individual retirement account as security for a loan, then, under section 408(e)(4), the portion so used is treated as distributed to such individual and the benefited individual must include such distribution in gross income for the taxable year during which he so uses such account.

(4) An additional tax of 10 percent is imposed by section 408(f) on distributions (including amounts deemed distributed as the result of a prohibited loan or used as security for a loan) made before the benefited individual has attained age 59½, unless such distribution is made on account of death or disability, or unless a rollover contribution is made with such distribution.

(5) Sections 2039(e) (relating to exemption from estate tax of annuities under certain trusts and plans) and 2517 (relating to exemption from gift tax of specified transfers of certain annuities under qualified plans) apply (including the manner in which such sections apply) to the account, annuity, or endowment contract.

(6) Section 402(a)(2) and (e) (relating to tax on lump sum distributions) is not applicable to distributions from an account, annuity, or endowment contract.

(7) A minimum distribution is required under section 408(a)(6) or (7) and 408(b)(3) or (4) (including a brief explanation of the amount of minimum distribution) and that if the amount distributed from an account, annuity, or endowment contract during the taxable year of the payee is less than the minimum required during such year, an excise tax, which shall be paid by the payee, is imposed under section 4974, in an amount equal to 50 percent of the excess of the minimum required to be distributed over the amount actually distributed during the year.

(8) An excise tax is imposed under section 4973 on excess contributions (including a brief explanation of an excess contribution).

(9) The benefited individual must file Form 5329 (Return for Individual Retirement Savings Arrangement) with the Internal Revenue for each taxable year during which the account, annuity, or endowment contract is maintained.

(10) The account or contract has or has not (as the case may be) been approved as to form for use as an account, annuity, or endowment contract by the Internal Revenue Service. For purposes of this subdivision, if a favorable opinion or determination letter with respect to the form of a prototype trust, custodial account, annuity, or endowment contract has been issued by the Internal Revenue Service, or the instrument which establishes an individual retirement trust account or an individual retirement custodial account utilizes the precise language of a form currently provided by the Internal Revenue Service (including any additional language permitted by such form), such account or contract may be treated as approved as to form.

(11) The Internal Revenue Service approval is a determination only as to the form of the account, annuity, or endowment contract, and does not represent a determination of the merits of such account, annuity, or endowment contract.

(12) The proceeds from the account, annuity or endowment contract may be used by the benefited individual as a rollover contribution to another account or annuity or retirement bond in accordance with the provisions of section 408(d)(3).

(13) In the case of an endowment contract described in section 408(b), no deduction is allowed under section 219 for that portion of the amounts paid under the contract for the taxable year properly allocable to the cost of life insurance.

(14) If applicable, in the event that the benefited individual revokes the account, annuity, or endowment contract, pursuant to the procedure described in the disclosure statement (see subdivision (A)(4) of this subdivision (iii)), the benefited individual is entitled to a return of the entire amount of the consideration paid by him for the account, annuity, or endowment contract without adjustment for such items as sales commissions, administrative expenses or fluctuation in market value.

(15) Further information can be obtained from any district office of the Internal Revenue Service.

To the extent that information on the matters described in subdivisions (iii)(A) and (B) of this subparagraph is provided in a publication of the Internal Revenue Service relating to individual retirement savings arrangements, such publication may be furnished by the trustee or issuer in lieu of providing information relating to such matters in a disclosure statement.

(C) The financial disclosure required by paragraph (d)(4)(v), (vi), and (vii) of this section.

(iv) In the case of an amendment to the terms of an account, annuity, or endowment contract described in paragraph (d)(4)(i) of this section, the disclosure statement required by this subparagraph need not repeat material contained in the statement furnished pursuant to paragraph (d)(4)(iii) of this section, but it must set forth in nontechnical language those matters described in paragraph (d)(4)(iii) of this section which are affected by such amendment.

(v) With respect to an account, annuity, or endowment contract described in paragraph (d)(4)(i) of this section (other than an account or annuity which is to receive only a rollover contribution described in paragraph (d)(4)(vi) of this section and to which no deductible contributions will be made), the disclosure statement must set forth in cases where either an amount is guaranteed over period of time (such as in the case of a nonparticipating endowment or annuity contract), or a projection of growth of the value of the account, annuity, or endowment contract can reasonably be made (such as in the case of a participating endowment or annuity contract (other than a variable annuity) or passbook savings account), the following:

(A) To the extent that an amount is guaranteed,

(1) The amount, determined without regard to any portion of a contribution which is not deductible, that would be guaranteed to be available to the benefited individual if *(i)* level annual contributions in the amount of $1,000 were to be made on the first day of each year, and *(ii)* the benefited individual were to withdraw in a single sum the entire

amount of such account, annuity, or endowment contract at the end of each of the first five years during which contributions are to be made, at the end of the year in which the benefited individual attains the ages of 60, 65, and 70, and at the end of any other year during which the increase of the guaranteed available amount is less than the increase of the guaranteed available amount during any preceding year for any reason other than decrease of cessation of contributions, and

(2) A statement that the amount described in subdivision (v)(A)(1) of this subparagraph is guaranteed, and the period for which guaranteed;

(B) To the extent a projection of growth of the value of the account, annuity, or endowment contract can reasonably be made but the amounts are not guaranteed.

(1) The amount, determined without regard to any portion of a contribution which is not deductible, and upon the basis of an earnings rate no greater than, and terms no different from, those currently in effect, that would be available to the benefited individual if (i) level annual contributions in the amount of $1,000 were to be made on the first day of each year, and (ii) the benefited individual were to withdraw in a single sum the entire amount of such account, annuity, or endowment contract at the end of each of the first five years during which contributions are to be made, at the end of each of the years in which the benefited individual attains the ages of 60, 65, and 70, and at the end of any other year during which the increase of the available amount is less than the increase of the available amount during any preceding year for any reason other than decrease or cessation of contributions, and

(2) A statement that the amount described in paragraph (d)(4)(v)(B)(1) of this section is a projection and is not guaranteed and a statement of the earnings rate and terms on the basis of which the projection is made;

(C) The portion of each $1,000 contribution attributable to the cost of life insurance, which would not be deductible, for each year during which contributions are to be made; and

(D) The sales commission (including any commission attributable to the sale of life insurance), if any, to be charged in each year, expressed as a percentage of gross annual contributions (including any portion attributable to the cost of life insurance) to be made for each year.

(vi) With respect to an account or annuity described in paragraph (d)(4)(i) of this section to which a rollover contribution described in section 402(a)(5)(A), 403(a)(4)(A), 408(d)(3)(A) or 409(b)(3)(C) will be made, the disclosure statement must set forth, in cases where an amount is guaranteed over a period of time (such as in the case of a nonparticipating annuity contract, or a projection of growth of the value of the account or annuity can reasonably be made (such as in the case of a participating annuity contract (other than a variable annuity) or a passbook savings account), the following:

(A) To the extent guaranteed,

(1) The amount that would be guaranteed to be available to the benefited individual if (i) Such a rollover contribution in the amount of $1,000 were to be made on the first day of the year, (ii) No other contribution were to be made, and (iii) The benefited individual were to withdraw in a single sum the entire amount of such account or annuity at the end of each of the first five years after the contribution is made, at the end of the year in which the benefited individual attains the ages of 60, 65, and 70, and at the end of any other year during which the increase of the guaranteed available amount is less than the increase of the guaranteed available amount during any preceding year, and

(2) A statement that the amount described in paragraph (d)(vi)(A)(1) of this section is guaranteed;

(B) To the extent that a projection of growth of the value of the account or annuity can reasonably be made but the amounts are not guaranteed,

(1) The amount, determined upon the basis of an earnings rate no greater than, and terms no different from, those currently in effect, that would be available to the benefited individual if (i) such a rollover contribution in the amount of $1,000 were to be made on the first day of the year, (ii) no other contribution were to be made, and (iii) the benefited individual were to withdraw in a single sum the entire amount of such account or annuity at the end of each of the first five years after the contribution is made, at the end of each of the years in which the benefited individual attains the ages 60, 65, 70, and at the end of any other year during which the increase of the available amount is less than the increase of the available amount during any preceding year, and

(2) A statement that the amount described in paragraph (d)(4)(vi)(B)(1) of this section is a projection and is not guaranteed and a statement of the earnings rate and terms on the basis of which the projection is made; and

(C) The sales commission, if any, to be charged in each year, expressed as a percentage of the assumed $1,000 contribution.

(vii) With respect to an account, annuity, or endowment contract described in paragraph (d)(4)(i) of this section, in all cases not subject to paragraph (d)(4)(v) or (vi) of this section (such as in the case of a mutual fund or variable annuity), the disclosure statement must set forth information described in subdivision (A) through (C) of this subdivisions (vii) based (as applicable with respect to the type or types of contributions to be received by the account, annuity, or endowment contract) upon the assumption of (1) level annual contributions of $1,000 on the first day of each year, (2) a rollover contribution of $1,000 on the first day of the year and no other contributions, or (3) a rollover contribution of $1,000 on the first day of the year plus level annual contributions of $1,000 on the first day of each year.

(A) A description (in nontechnical language) with respect to the benefited individual's interest in the account, annuity, or endowment contract, of:

(1) Each type of charge, and the amount thereof, which may be made against a contribution,

(2) The method for computing and allocating annual earnings, and

(3) Each charge (other than those described in complying with paragraph (d)(4)(vii)(A)(1) of this section) which may be applied to such interest in determining the net amount of money available to the benefited individual and the method of computing each such charge;

(B) A statement that growth in value of the account, annuity, or endowment contract is neither guaranteed nor projected; and

(C) The portion of each $1,000 contribution attributable to the cost of life insurance, which would not be deductible, for every year during which contributions are to be made.

(viii) A disclosure statement, or an amendment thereto, furnished pursuant to the provisions of this subparagraph may contain information in addition to that required by paragraph (d)(4)(iii) through (vii) of this section. However, such disclosure statement will not be considered to comply with the provisions of this subparagraph if the substance of such additional material or the form in which it is presented causes such disclosure statement to be false or misleading with respect to the information required to be disclosed by this paragraph.

(ix) The provisions of section 6693, relating to failure to provide reports on individual retirement accounts or annuities, shall apply to any trustee or issuer who fails to furnish, or cause to be furnished, a disclosure statement, a copy of the governing instrument, or an amendment to either, as required by this paragraph.

(x) This section shall be effective for disclosure statements and copies of governing instruments mailed, or delivered without mailing, after February 14, 1977.

(xi) This section does not reflect the amendments made by section 1501 of the Tax Reform Act of 1976 (90 Stat. 1734) relating to retirement savings for certain married individuals.

T.D. 7714, 8/7/80.

PAR. 9. Section 1.408-6 is amended by removing paragraph (d)(4)(xi) and adding a new paragraph (b) to read as follows:

**Proposed § 1.408-6 Disclosure statements for individual retirement arrangements.** [*For Preamble, see ¶ 150,703*]

* * * * *

**(b) Disclosure statements for spousal individual retirement arrangements.** The trustee of an individual retirement account and the issuer of an individual retirement annuity shall furnish to the benefited individual of a spousal individual retirement arrangement a disclosure statement in accordance with paragraph (d). In the case of a spousal individual retirement arrangement that uses subaccounts, the benefited individual includes both the working and non-working spouse.

**§ 1.408-7 Reports on distributions from individual retirement plans.**

**(a) Requirement of report.** The trustee of an individual retirement account or the issuer of an individual retirement annuity who makes a distribution during any calendar year to an individual from such account or under such annuity shall make a report on Form W-2P (in the case of distributions that are not total distributions) or Form 1099R (in the case of total distributions), and their related transmittal forms, for such year. The return must show the name and address of the person to whom the distribution was made, the aggregate amount of such distribution, and such other information as is required by the forms.

**(b) Amount subject to this section.** The amounts subject to reporting under paragraph (a) include all amounts distributed or made available to which section 408(d) applies.

**(c) Time and place for filing.** The report required under this section for any calendar year shall be filed after the close of that year and on or before February 28 of the following year with the appropriate Internal Revenue Service Center.

**(d) Statement to recipients.** *(1)* Each trustee or issuer required to file Form 1099R or Form W-2P under this section shall furnish to the person whose identifying number is (or should be) shown on the forms a copy of the form.

*(2)* Each statement required by this paragraph to be furnished to recipients shall be furnished to such person after November 30 of the year of the distribution and on or before January 31 of the following year. However, for a distribution after December 31, 2008, the February 15 due date under section 6045 applies to the statement if the statement is furnished in a consolidated reporting statement under section 6045. See §§ 1.6045-1(k)(3), 1.6045-2(d)(2), 1.6045-3(e)(2), 1.6045-4(m)(3), and 1.6045-5(a)(3)(ii).

**(e) Effective date.** This section is effective for calendar years beginning after December 31, 1977.

T.D. 7714, 8/7/80, amend T.D. 9504, 10/12/2010.

**Proposed § 1.408-7 Simplified employee pension.** [*For Preamble, see ¶ 150,703*]

***Caution:*** The Treasury has not yet amended Reg § 1.408-7 to reflect changes made by P.L. 103-465, P.L. 103-66, P.L. 99-514, P.L. 98-369, P.L. 97-34.

**(a) In general.** The term "simplified employee pension" means an individual retirement account or individual retirement annuity described in section 408(a), (b) or (c) with respect to which the requirements of paragraphs (b), (d), (e), (g), and (h) of this section are met and the requirements of § 1.408-8 are met with respect to any calendar year.

**(b) Establishment of simplified employee pension.** In order to establish a simplified employee pension, the employer must execute a written instrument (hereafter referred to as the simplified employee pension arrangement) within the time prescribed for making deductible contributions. This instrument shall include: the name of the employer, the requirements for employee participation, the signature of a responsible official, and the definite allocation formula specified in section 408(k)(5) and paragraph (f) of this section.

**(c) Variation in contribution.** *(1) Permitted variations.* An employer's total contributions to its employees' simplified employee pensions may vary annually at the employer's discretion.

*(2) Salary reduction.* Contributions made to a simplified employee pension under an arrangement under which the contribution will be made only if the employee receives a reduction in compensation or forgoes a compensation increase shall be treated as employer contributions to a simplified employee pension only if the arrangement precludes an individual election by the employee. If there is an individual election, then the contribution shall be treated as an employee contribution.

**(d) Participation requirements.** *(1) Age and service requirements.* This paragraph is satisfied with respect to a simplified employee pension arrangement for a calendar year only if for such year the employer contributes to the simplified employee pension on behalf of each individual who is an employee at any time during the calendar year who has—

(i) Attained age 25,

(ii) Performed service for the employer during at least 3 of the immediately preceding 5 calendar years, and

(iii) Received at least $200 compensation from the employer for the calendar year.

*(2) Execution of documents.* The employer may execute any necessary documents on behalf of an employee who is entitled to a contribution to a simplified employee pension if the employee is unable or unwilling to execute such documents or the employer is unable to locate the employee.

*(3) Required employment.* An employer may not require that an employee be employed as of a particular date in order to receive a contribution for a calendar year.

*(4) Nonresident aliens and employees covered by collective-bargaining agreements.* An employer may exclude from participation in the simplified employee pension arrangement employees described in section 410(b)(2)(A) or 410(b)(2)(C).

*(5) Example.* The provisions of this paragraph may be illustrated by the following example:

*Example.* Corporation X maintains a simplified employee pension arrangement for its employees. Individual J worked for Corporation X while in graduate school in 1976, 1977, and 1978. J never worked more than 25 days in any particular year. In October of 1979, J began to work for Corporation X on a full-time basis. J earned $5,000 from Corporation X for 1979. J became 25 on December 31, 1979. Corporation X must make a contribution to a simplified employee pension maintained on behalf of J for 1979 because as of December 31, 1979, J had met the minimum age requirement of section 408(k)(2), had performed service for Corporation X in 3 of the 5 calendar years preceding 1979, and met the minimum compensation requirements of paragraph (d)(1)(iii).

**(e) Requirement of written allocation formula.** *(1) Requirement of definite written allocation formula.* Employer contributions to a simplified employee pension must be made under a definite written allocation formula which specifies—

(i) The requirements which an employee must satisfy to share in an allocation, and

(ii) The manner in which the amount allocated to each employee's account is computed.

*(2) Employer may vary formula.* An employer may vary the definite written allocation formula from year to year provided the simplified employee pension arrangement is amended by the permissible date for making contributions to indicate the new formula.

**(f) Treatment of contributions which exceed the written allocation formula.** *(1) General rule.* To the extent that employer contributions do not satisfy § 1.408-7(e)(1), the contributions shall be deemed to be contributions which are not made under a simplified employee pension arrangement except for purposes of section 408(a)(1), (b)(2)(B) and (d)(5). These contributions shall be deemed made to an individual retirement account or individual retirement annuity not maintained as part of a simplified employee pension arrangement.

*(2) Example.* This paragraph is illustrated by the following example:

*Example.* (i) Assume that in 1979 Corporation X adopts a simplified employee pension arrangement ("SEP Arrangement"). The arrangement calls for Corporation X to contribute the same percentage of each participant's compensation exclusive of SEP contributions to a simplified employee pension (Allocation Compensation). X has three employees, A, B and C, who satisfy the participation requirements of the SEP Arrangement. The compensation, the contributions to the individual simplified employee pension ("SEP") for A, B and C and the varying treatment of the contributions are set forth as follows:

| Employee | Gross income | Net compensation before contribution | SEP-IRA contribution | Ratio of SEP-IRA contributions to net compensation (percent) |
|---|---|---|---|---|
| A | $11,000 | $10,000 | $ 1,000 | 10 |
| B | 11,500 | 10,000 | 1,500 | 15 |
| C | 57,500 | 50,000 | 7,500 | 15 |
| Totals | 80,000 | $70,000 | $10,000 | |

(ii) Under the special rule of this paragraph, because only 10 percent of compensation was allocated to A, and the allocation formula provides that the same percentage will be allocated to each participant, a certain portion of the contribution to B and C under the SEP shall be deemed made to IRA's that are not part of the SEP Arrangement.

(iii) To determine A's and B's Allocation Compensation the respective total compensation included in A's and B's gross income must be divided by 1.10 (1 plus the percentage of Allocation Compensation contributed to A under the SEP Arrangement). The excess of compensation included in gross income over Allocation Compensation is considered as a contribution under the SEP. The following table shows the result of this calculation:

| Employee | Gross income | Allocation compensation[1] | SEP-IRA contribution | Deemed IRA contribution[2] |
|---|---|---|---|---|
| A | $11,000 | $10,000 | $1,000 | $ 0 |
| B | 11,500 | 10,455 | 1,045 | 455 |
| C | 57,500 | 52,273 | 5,227 | 2,273 |
| Totals | 80,000 | 72,728 | 7,272 | 2,728 |

[1] Gross income divided by 1.10.
[2] Also included in Allocation Compensation.

(iv) Under section 404(h) for purposes of computing Corporation X's deduction, only the $7,272 is considered as a contribution to a SEP Arrangement described in section 408(k) under the special rule. The allowable 404(h) deduction equals $10,909 (15% of the excess of total compensation of $80,000 over the SEP contribution of $7,272 or 15% of $72,728). The other $2,728 is payment of compensation and subject to the deduction rules of section 162 or 212. Similarly, the $2,728 would not be considered as an employer SEP contribution for purposes of exemption from FICA and FUTA taxes under sections 3121 and 3306.

(v) The effect of treating the $2,273 as a contribution to SEP's for purposes of section 408(a)(1), (b)(2)(B) and (d)(5) is to not disqualify the individual retirement arrangement of C for accepting non-SEP contributions in excess of $1,500 and to allow C to withdraw the excess contribution of $2,273 without including that amount in income under section 408(d)(1).

**(g) Permitted withdrawals.** A simplified employee pension meets the requirements of this paragraph only if—

*(1)* Employer contributions thereto are not conditioned on the retention in such pension of any portion of the amount contributed, and

*(2)* There is no prohibition imposed by the employer on withdrawals from the simplified employee pension.

See section 408(d) for rules concerning the taxation of withdrawals from individual retirement accounts and annuities. See section 408(f)(1) for penalties for premature withdrawals from individual retirement accounts and annuities.

**(h) Section 401(j) plan.** The requirements of this paragraph are met with respect to a simplified employee pension for a calendar year unless the employer maintains during any part of such year a plan—

*(1)* Some or all of the active participants in which are employees (within the meaning of section 401(c)(1)) or shareholder-employees (as defined in section 1379(d)), and

*(2)* To which section 401(j) applies.

### § 1.408-8 Distribution requirements for individual retirement plans.

The following questions and answers relate to the distribution rules for IRAs provided in sections 408(a)(6) and 408(b)(3).

Q-1. Is an IRA subject to the distribution rules provided in section 401(a)(9) for qualified plans?

A-1. (a) Yes, an IRA is subject to the required minimum distribution rules provided in section 401(a)(9). In order to satisfy section 401(a)(9) for purposes of determining required minimum distributions for calendar years beginning on or after January 1, 2003, the rules of §§ 1.401(a)(9)-1 through 1.401(a)(9)-9 and 1.401(a)(9)-6 for defined contribution plans must be applied, except as otherwise provided in this section. For example, whether the 5-year rule or the life expectancy rule applies to distributions after death occurring before the IRA owner's required beginning date is determined in accordance with § 1.401(a)(9)-3 and the rules of § 1.401(a)(9)-4 apply for purposes of determining an IRA owner's designated beneficiary. Similarly, the amount of the minimum distribution required for each calendar year from an individual account is determined in accordance with § 1.401(a)(9)-5. For purposes of this section, the term IRA means an individual retirement account or annuity described in section 408(a) or (b). The IRA owner is the individual for whom an IRA is originally established by contributions for the benefit of that individual and that individual's beneficiaries.

(b) For purposes of applying the required minimum distribution rules in §§ 1.401(a)(9)-1 through 1.401(a)(9)-9 and 1.401(a)(9)-6 for qualified plans, the IRA trustee, custodian, or issuer is treated as the plan administrator, and the IRA owner is substituted for the employee.

(c) See A-14 and A-15 of § 1.408A-6 for rules under section 401(a)(9) that apply to a Roth IRA.

Q-2. Are IRAs that receive employer contributions under a simplified employee pension (defined in section 408(k)) or a SIMPLE IRA (defined in section 408(p)) treated as IRAs for purposes of section 401(a)(9)?

A-2. Yes, IRAs that receive employer contributions under a simplified employee pension (defined in section 408(k)) or a SIMPLE plan (defined in section 408(p)) are treated as IRAs, rather than employer plans, for purposes of section 401(a)(9) and are, therefore, subject to the distribution rules in this section.

Q-3. In the case of distributions from an IRA, what does the term required beginning date mean?

A-3. In the case of distributions from an IRA, the term required beginning date means April 1 of the calendar year following the calendar year in which the individual attains age 70½.

Q-4. What portion of a distribution from an IRA is not eligible for rollover because the amount is a required minimum distribution?

A-4. The portion of a distribution that is a required minimum distribution from an IRA and thus not eligible for rollover is determined in the same manner as provided in A-7 of § 1.402(c)-2 for distributions from qualified plans. For example, if a minimum distribution is required under section 401(a)(9) for a calendar year, an amount distributed during a calendar year from an IRA is treated as a required minimum distribution under section 401(a)(9) to the extent that the total required minimum distribution for the year under section 401(a)(9) for that IRA has not been satisfied. This requirement may be satisfied by a distribution from the IRA or, as permitted under A-9 of this section, from another IRA.

Q-5. May an individual's surviving spouse elect to treat such spouse's entire interest as a beneficiary in an individual's IRA upon the death of the individual (or the remaining part of such interest if distribution to the spouse has commenced) as the spouse's own account?

A-5. (a) The surviving spouse of an individual may elect, in the manner described in paragraph (b) of this A-5, to treat the spouse's entire interest as a beneficiary in an individual's IRA (or the remaining part of such interest if distribution thereof has commenced to the spouse) as the spouse's own IRA. This election is permitted to be made at any time after the individual's date of death. In order to make this election, the spouse must be the sole beneficiary of the IRA and have an unlimited right to withdraw amounts from the IRA. If a trust is named as beneficiary of the IRA, this requirement is not satisfied even if the spouse is the sole beneficiary of the trust. If the surviving spouse makes the election, the required minimum distribution for the calendar year of the election and each subsequent calendar year is determined under section 401(a)(9)(A) with the spouse as IRA owner and not section 401(a)(9)(B) with the surviving spouse as the deceased IRA owner's beneficiary. However, if the election is made in the calendar year containing the IRA owner's death, the spouse is not required to take a required minimum distribution as the IRA owner for that calendar year. Instead, the spouse is required to take a required minimum distribution for that year, determined with respect to the deceased IRA owner under the rules of A-4(a) of § 1.401(a)(9)-5, to the extent such a distribution was not made to the IRA owner before death.

(b) The election described in paragraph (a) of this A-5 is made by the surviving spouse redesignating the account as an account in the name of the surviving spouse as IRA owner rather than as beneficiary. Alternatively, a surviving spouse eligible to make the election is deemed to have made the election if, at any time, either of the following occurs—

(1) Any amount in the IRA that would be required to be distributed to the surviving spouse as beneficiary under section 401(a)(9)(B) is not distributed within the time period required under section 401(a)(9)(B); or

(2) Any additional amount is contributed to the IRA which is subject, or deemed to be subject, to the lifetime distribution requirements of section 401(a)(9)(A).

(c) The result of an election described in paragraph (b) of this A-5 is that the surviving spouse shall then be considered the IRA owner for whose benefit the trust is maintained for all purposes under the Internal Revenue Code (e.g., section 72(t)).

Q-6. How is the benefit determined for purposes of calculating the required minimum distribution from an IRA?

A-6. For purposes of determining the minimum distribution required to be made from an IRA in any calendar year, the account balance of the IRA as of December 31 of the calendar year immediately preceding the calendar year for which distributions are required to be made is substituted in A-3 of § 1.401(a)(9)-5 for the account balance of the employee. Except as provided in A-7 and A-8 of this section, no adjustments are made for contributions or distributions after that date.

Q-7. What rules apply in the case of a rollover to an IRA of an amount distributed by a qualified plan or another IRA?

A-7. If the surviving spouse of an employee rolls over a distribution from a qualified plan, such surviving spouse may elect to treat the IRA as the spouse's own IRA in accordance with the provisions in A-5 of this section. In the event of any other rollover to an IRA of an amount distributed by a qualified plan or another IRA, the rules in § 1.401(a)(9)-7 will apply for purposes of determining the account balance for the receiving IRA and the required minimum distribution from the receiving IRA. However, because the value of the account balance is determined as of December 31 of the year preceding the year for which the required minimum distribution is being determined and not as of a valuation date in the preceding year, the account balance of the receiving IRA is only adjusted if the amount is not received in the calendar year in which the amount rolled over is distributed. In that case, for purposes of determining the required minimum distribution for the calendar year in which such amount is actually received, the account balance of the receiving IRA as of December 31 of the preceding year must be adjusted by the amount received in accordance with A-2 of § 1.401(a)(9)-7.

Q-8. What rules apply in the case of a transfer (including a recharacterization) from one IRA to another?

A-8. (a) General rule. In the case of a trustee-to-trustee transfer from one IRA to another IRA that is not a distribution and rollover, the transfer is not treated as a distribution by the transferor IRA for purposes of section 401(a)(9). Accordingly, the minimum distribution requirement with respect to the transferor IRA must still be satisfied. Except as provided in paragraph (b) of this A-8 for recharacterizations, after the transfer the employee's account balance and the required minimum distribution under the transferee IRA are determined in the same manner as an account balance and required minimum distribution are determined under an IRA receiving a rollover contribution under A-7 of this section.

(b) Recharacterizations. If an amount is contributed to a Roth IRA that is a conversion contribution or failed conversion contribution and that amount (plus net income allocable to that amount) is transferred to another IRA (transferee IRA) in a subsequent year as a recharacterized contribution, the recharacterized contribution (plus allocable net income) must be added to the December 31 account balance of the transferee IRA for the year in which the conversion or failed conversion occurred.

Q-9. Is the required minimum distribution from one IRA of an owner permitted to be distributed from another IRA in order to satisfy section 401(a)(9)?

A-9. Yes, the required minimum distribution must be calculated separately for each IRA. The separately calculated amounts may then be totaled and the total distribution taken from any one or more of the individual's IRAs under the rules set forth in this A-9. Generally, only amounts in IRAs that an individual holds as the IRA owner may be aggregated. However, amounts in IRAs that an individual holds as a beneficiary of the same decedent and which are being distributed under the life expectancy rule in section 401(a)(9)(B)(iii) or (iv) may be aggregated, but such amounts may not be aggregated with amounts held in IRAs that the individual holds as the IRA owner or as the beneficiary of another decedent. Distributions from section 403(b) contracts or accounts will not satisfy the distribution requirements from IRAs, nor will distributions from IRAs satisfy the distribution requirements from section 403(b) contracts or accounts. Distributions from Roth IRAs (defined in section 408A) will not satisfy the distribution requirements applicable to IRAs or section 403(b) accounts or contracts and distributions from IRAs or section 403(b) contracts or accounts will not satisfy the distribution requirements from Roth IRAs.

Q-10. Is any reporting required by the trustee, custodian, or issuer of an IRA with respect to the minimum amount that is required to be distributed from that IRA?

A-10. Yes, the trustee, custodian, or issuer of an IRA is required to report information with respect to the minimum amount required to be distributed from the IRA for each calendar year to individuals or entities, at the time, and in the manner, prescribed by the Commissioner in revenue rulings, notices, and other guidance published in the Internal Revenue Bulletin (see § 601.601(d)(2)(ii)(b) of this chapter) as well as the applicable Federal tax forms and accompanying instructions.

Q-11. Which amounts distributed from an IRA are taken into account in determining whether section 401(a)(9) is satisfied?

A-11. (a) General rule. Except as provided in paragraph (b) of this A-11, all amounts distributed from an IRA are taken into account in determining whether section 401(a)(9) is satisfied, regardless of whether the amount is includible in income.

(b) Amounts not taken into account. The following amounts are not taken into account in determining whether the required minimum amount with respect to an IRA for a calendar year has been distributed—

(1) Contributions returned pursuant to section 408(d)(4), together with the income allocable to these contributions;

(2) Contributions returned pursuant to section 408(d)(5);

(3) Corrective distributions of excess simplified employee pension contributions under section 408(k)(6)(C), together with the income allocable to these distributions; and

(4) Similar items designated by the Commissioner in revenue rulings, notices, and other guidance published in the Internal Revenue Bulletin. See § 601.601(d)(2)(ii)(b) of this chapter.

T.D. 8987, 4/16/2002, amend T.D. 9130, 6/14/2004.

**Proposed § 1.408-8 Nondiscrimination requirements for simplified employee pensions.** [*For Preamble, see ¶ 150,703*]

***Caution:*** The Treasury has not yet amended Reg § 1.408-8 to reflect changes made by P.L. 103-465, P.L. 103-66, P.L. 99-514, P.L. 98-369, P.L. 97-34.

**(a) In general.** The requirements of this section are met with respect to a simplified employee pension for a calendar year if for such year the contributions made by the employer to simplified employee pensions of its employees do not discriminate in favor of any employee who is—

*(1)* An officer,

*(2)* A shareholder, within the meaning of paragraph (b)(2),

*(3)* A self-employed individual, or

*(4)* Highly compensated.

**(b) Special rules.** *(1)* For purposes of this section, employees described in subparagraph (A) or (C) of section 410(b)(2) shall be excluded from consideration.

*(2)* An individual shall be considered a shareholder if he owns (with the application of section 318) more than 10 percent of the value of the stock of the employer.

**(c) Contributions must bear a uniform relationship to total compensation.** *(1) General rule.* Contributions shall be considered discriminatory unless employer contributions to its employees' simplified employee pensions bear a uniform relationship to the total compensation (not in excess of the first $100,000) of each employee maintaining a simplified employee pension. A rate of contribution which decreases as compensation increases shall be considered uniform.

*(2) Definition of compensation.* For purposes of this section, the term "compensation" has the meaning set forth in § 1.219-1, and is determined without regard to the employer contributions to the simplified employee pension arrangement.

*(3) Example.* The provisions of this paragraph may be illustrated by the following example:

*Example.* Corporation X maintains a simplified employee pension arrangement which allocates employer contributions in the manner described below. First, contributions made by June 30 of each year are allocated in proportion to compensation paid from January 1 to June 30. Second, contributions made between July 1 and December 31 are allocated in proportion to compensation paid during the same period.

In 1980, the salaries paid, and contributions allocated are shown below:

| Participant | Compensation[1] | Allocation[2] | Compensation[3] | Allocation[4] |
|---|---|---|---|---|
| A ....... | 10,000 | 500 | 10,000 | 1,000 |
| B ....... | 10,000 | 500 | 1,000 | 100 |
| C ....... | 10,000 | 500 | 15,000 | 1,500 |

[1] Jan 1, 1980 to June 30, 1980.
[2] June 30, 1980.
[3] July 1, 1980 to Dec. 31, 1980.
[4] Dec. 31, 1980.

For 1980, A, B, and C received allocations equal to 7.5 percent, 5.45 percent, and 8 percent of compensation, respectively. These contributions are discriminatory because they do not bear a uniform relationship to total compensation.

**(d) Treatment of certain contributions and taxes.** *(1) General rule.* (i) Except as provided in this paragraph, employer contributions do not meet the requirements of this section unless such contributions meet the requirements of this section without taking into account contributions or benefits under Chapter 2 of the Internal Revenue Code (relating to tax on self-employment income), Chapter 21 (relating to Federal Insurance Contribution Act), Title II of the Social Security Act, or any other Federal or State law ("Social Security Taxes"). If the employer does not maintain an integrated plan at any time during the taxable year, taxes paid under section 3111(a) (relating to tax on employers) with respect to an employee may, for purposes of this section, be taken into account as a contribution by the employer to an employee's simplified employee pension. If contributions are made to the simplified employee pension of an owner-employee, the preceding sentence shall not apply unless taxes paid by all such owner-employees under section 1401(a), and the taxes which would be payable under section 1401(a) by such owner-employees but for paragraphs (4) and (5) of section 1402(c), are taken into account as contributions by the employer on behalf of such owner-employees. The amount of such taxes shall be determined in a manner consistent with § 1.401-12(h)(3).

(ii) If contributions are made to the simplified employee pension of a self-employed individual who is not an owner-employee, the arrangement may be integrated. In such a case, the portion of the earned income of such individual which does not exceed the maximum amount which may be treated as self-employment income under section 1402(b)(1) shall be treated as "wages" under section 3121(a)(1) subject to the tax imposed by section 3111(a) and such tax shall be taken into account as employer contributions.

(iii) An employer may take into account as contributions amounts not in excess of such Social Security taxes. Thus, an employer may integrate using a rate less than the maximum rate of tax under section 3111(a) or compensation less than the maximum amount specified as wages under section 3121(a).

*(2) Integrated plan defined.* For purposes of subparagraph (1), the term "integrated plan" means a plan which meets the requirements of section 401(a), 403(a), or 405(a) but would not meet such requirements if contributions or benefits under Chapter 2 (relating to tax on self-employment income), Chapter 21 (relating to Federal Insurance Contributions Act), Title II of the Social Security Act, or any other Federal or State law were not taken into account.

**(e) Examples.** The provisions of this section may be illustrated by the following examples:

*Example (1).* Corporation M adopts a simplified employee pension arrangement. The corporation would like to contribute 7.5% of an employee's first $10,000 in compensation and 5% of all compensation above $10,000. The simplified employee pension arrangement which Corporation M adopts will not be considered discriminatory within the meaning of paragraph (c) of this section because the rate of contribution decreases as compensation increases.

*Example (2).* Corporation L adopts a simplified employee pension plan. It wishes to contribute to the simplified employee pension of each employee who is currently performing service. The corporation would like to contribute to the simplified employee pensions 5% of the total compensation of each employee who has completed up to 5 years of service and 7% of the total compensation of each employee who has completed more than 5 years of service. The simplified employee pension plan which Corporation L adopts will be considered discriminatory within the meaning of paragraph (c) of this section because the employer contributions do not bear a uniform relationship to each employee's total compensation.

**Proposed § 1.408-9 Reports for simplified employee pensions.** [*For Preamble, see ¶ 150,703*]

***Caution:*** The Treasury has not yet amended Reg § 1.408-9 to reflect changes made by P.L. 99-514, P.L. 98-369, P.L. 97-34.

**(a) Information to be furnished upon adoption of plan.** *(1)* An employer who adopts a definite written allocation formula for making contributions to an employee's simplified employee pension shall furnish the employee in writing the following information:

(i) A notice that the simplified employee pension arrangement has been adopted,

(ii) The requirements which an employee must meet in order to receive a contribution under the agreement,

(iii) The basis upon which the employer's contribution will be allocated to employees, and

(iv) Such other information that the Commissioner may require.

*(2)* The information in subparagraph (1) must be furnished to an employee no later than a reasonable time after the later of the time the employee becomes employed or the time of the adoption of the simplified employee pension arrangement.

*(3)* The Commissioner may relieve employers from furnishing any or all of the information specified in subparagraph (1).

**(b) Information to be furnished for a calendar year.** *(1)* For each calendar year, the employer shall furnish to the employee a written statement indicating the amount of employer contributions made to the employee's individual retirement account or individual retirement annuity under the simplified employee pension arrangement. This requirement is satisfied if the information is on the employee's W-2 for the calendar year for which the contribution is made. Amounts described in § 1.408-7(f)(1) which are not considered made under the simplified employee pension arrangement should not be included.

*(2)* The information required to be furnished by subparagraph (1) shall be furnished to the employee no later than the later of 30 days after the contribution or January 31 following the calendar year for which the contribution was made.

**(c)** The Internal Revenue Service may require reports to be filed with the Service with respect to employees who cannot be located by the employer (see § 1.408-7(d)(2)). Such reports shall include such information and shall be filed in the time and manner as the Commissioner specifies.

**(d) Effective date.** The provisions of this section are effective for calendar years beginning after December 31, 1978.

**Proposed § 1.408-10 Investment in collectibles.** [*For Preamble, see ¶ 150,933*]

**(a) In general.** The acquisition by an individual retirement account or by an individually-directed account under a plan described in section 401(a) of any collectible shall be treated (for purposes of section 402 and 408) as a distribution from such account in an amount equal to the cost to such account of such collectible.

**(b) Collectible defined.** For purposes of this section, the term " collectible" means—

*(1)* Any work of art,

*(2)* Any rug or antique,

*(3)* Any metal or gem,

*(4)* Any stamp or coin,

*(5)* Any alcoholic beverage,

*(6)* Any musical instrument,

*(7)* Any historical objects (documents, clothes, etc.), or

*(8)* Any other tangible personal property which the Commissioner determines is a "collectible" for purposes of this section.

**(c) Individually-directed account.** For purposes of this section, the term "individually-directed account" means an account under a plan that provides for individual accounts and that has the effect of permitting a plan participant to invest or control the manner in which the account will be invested.

**(d) Acquisition.** For purposes of this section, the term acquisition includes purchase, exchange, contribution, or any method by which an individual retirement account or individually-directed account may directly or indirectly acquire a collectible.

**(e) Cost.** For purposes of this section, cost means fair market value.

**(f) Premature withdrawal penalty.** The ten percent penalty described in sections 72(m)(5) and 408(f)(1) shall apply in the case of a deemed distribution from an individual retirement account described in paragraph (a) of this section.

**(g) Amounts subsequently distributed.** When a collectible is actually distributed from an individual retirement account or an individually-directed account, any amounts included in gross income because of this section shall not be included in gross income at the time when the collectible is actually distributed.

**(h) Effective date.** This section applies to property acquired after December 31, 1981, in taxable years ending after such date.

**§ 1.408-11 Net income calculation for returned or recharacterized IRA contributions.**

**(a) Net income calculation for returned IRA contributions.** *(1) General rule.* For purposes of returned contributions under section 408(d)(4), the net income attributable to a contribution made to an IRA is determined by allocating to the contribution a pro rata portion of the earnings on the assets in the IRA during the period the IRA held the contribution. This attributable net income is calculated by using the following formula:

Net Income = Contribution x (Adjusted Closing Balance - Adjusted Opening Balance) / Adjusted Opening Balance.

*(2) Special rule.* If an IRA is established with a contribution and no other contributions, distributions or transfers are made to or from that IRA, then the subsequent distribution of the entire account balance of the IRA pursuant to section 408(d)(4) will satisfy the requirement of that Internal Revenue Code section that the return of a contribution be accompanied by the amount of net income attributable to the contribution.

**(b) Definitions.** For purposes of this section the following definitions apply:

*(1) Adjusted opening balance.* The term adjusted opening balance means the fair market value of the IRA at the beginning of the computation period plus, the amount of any contributions or transfers (including the contribution that is distributed as a returned contribution pursuant to section 408(d)(4) and recharacterizations of contributions pursuant to section 408A(d)(6)) made to the IRA during the computation period.

*(2) Adjusted closing balance.* The term adjusted closing balance means the fair market value of the IRA at the end of the computation period plus the amount of any distributions or transfers (including recharacterizations of contributions pursuant to section 408A(d)(6)) made from the IRA during the computation period.

*(3) Computation period.* The term computation period means the period beginning immediately prior to the time that the contribution being returned was made to the IRA and ending immediately prior to the removal of the contribution. If more than one contribution was made as a regular contribution and is being returned from the IRA, the computation period begins immediately prior to the time the first contribution being returned was contributed.

*(4) Regular contribution.* The term regular contribution means an IRA contribution made by the IRA owner that is neither a trustee-to-trustee transfer from another IRA nor a rollover from another IRA or retirement plan.

**(c) Additional rules.** *(1)* When an IRA asset is not normally valued on a daily basis, the fair market value of the asset at the beginning of the computation period is deemed to be the most recent, regularly determined, fair market value of the asset, determined as of a date that coincides with or precedes the first day of the computation period. In addition, solely for purposes of this section, notwithstanding A-3 of § 1.408A-5, recharacterized contributions are taken into account for the period they are actually held in a particular IRA.

*(2)* In the case of an IRA that has received more than one regular contribution for a particular taxable year, the last regular contribution made to the IRA for the year is deemed to be the contribution that is distributed as a returned contribution under section 408(d)(4), up to the amount of the contribution identified by the IRA owner as the amount distributed as a returned contribution.

*(3)* In the case of an individual who owns multiple IRAs, the net income calculation is performed only on the IRA containing the contribution being returned, and that IRA is the IRA that must distribute the contribution.

**(d) Examples.** The following examples illustrate the net income calculation under section 408(d)(4) and this section:

*Example (1).* (i) On May 1, 2004, when her IRA is worth $4,800, Taxpayer A makes a $1,600 regular contribution to her IRA. Taxpayer A requests that $400 of the May 1, 2004, contribution be returned to her pursuant to section 408(d)(4). Pursuant to this request, on February 1, 2005, when the IRA is worth $7,600, the IRA trustee distributes to Taxpayer A the $400 plus attributable net income. During this time, no other contributions have been made to the IRA and no distributions have been made.

(ii) The adjusted opening balance is $6,400 [$4,800 + $1,600] and the adjusted closing balance is $7,600. Thus, the net income attributable to the $400 May 1, 2004, contribution is $75 [$400 x ($7,600-$6,400) ÷ $6,400]. Therefore, the total to be distributed on February 1, 2005, pursuant to § 408(d)(4) is $475.

*Example (2).* (i) Beginning in January 2004, Taxpayer B contributes $300 on the 15th of each month to an IRA for 2004, resulting in an excess regular contribution of $600 for that year. Taxpayer B requests that the $600 excess regular contribution be returned to her pursuant to section 408(d)(4). Pursuant to this request, on March 1, 2005, when the IRA is worth $16,000, the IRA trustee distributes to Taxpayer B the $600 plus attributable net income. The excess regular contributions to be returned are deemed to be the last two made in 2004: the $300 December 15 contribution and the $300 November 15 contribution. On November 15 the IRA was worth $11,000 immediately prior to the contribution. No distributions or transfers have been made from the IRA and no contributions or transfers, other than the monthly contributions (including $300 in January and February 2005), have been made.

(ii) As of the beginning of the computation period (November 15), the adjusted opening balance is $12,200 [$11,000 + $300 + $300 + $300 + $300] and the adjusted closing balance is $16,000. Thus, the net income attributable to the excess regular contributions is $187 [$600 x ($16,000 - $12,200) ÷ $12,200]. Therefore, the total to be distributed as returned contributions on March 1, 2005, to correct the excess regular contribution is $787 [$600 + $187].

T.D. 9056, 5/2/2003.

## § 1.408(q)-1 Deemed IRAs in qualified employer plans.

**(a) In general.** Under section 408(q), a qualified employer plan may permit employees to make voluntary employee contributions to a separate account or annuity established under the plan. If the requirements of section 408(q) and this section are met, such account or annuity is treated in the same manner as an individual retirement plan under section 408 or 408A (and contributions to such an account or annuity are treated as contributions to an individual retirement plan and not to the qualified employer plan). The account or annuity is referred to as a deemed IRA.

**(b) Types of IRAs.** If the account or annuity meets the requirements applicable to traditional IRAs under section 408, the account or annuity is deemed to be a traditional IRA, and if the account or annuity meets the requirements applicable to Roth IRAs under section 408A, the account or annuity is deemed to be a Roth IRA. Simplified employee pensions (SEPs) under section 408(k) and SIMPLE IRAs under section 408(p) may not be used as deemed IRAs.

**(c) Separate entities.** Except as provided in paragraphs (d) and (g) of this section, the qualified employer plan and the deemed IRA are treated as separate entities under the Internal Revenue Code and are subject to the separate rules applicable to qualified employer plans and IRAs, respectively. Issues regarding eligibility, participation, disclosure, nondiscrimination, contributions, distributions, investments, and plan administration are generally to be resolved under the separate rules (if any) applicable to each entity under the Internal Revenue Code.

**(d) Exceptions.** The following exceptions to treatment of a deemed IRA and the qualified employer plan as separate entities apply:

*(1)* The plan document of the qualified employer plan must contain the deemed IRA provisions and a deemed IRA must be in effect at the time the deemed IRA contributions are accepted. Notwithstanding the preceding sentence, employers that provided deemed IRAs for plan years beginning before January 1, 2004, (but after December 31, 2002) are not required to have such provisions in their plan documents before the end of such plan years.

*(2)* The requirements of section 408(a)(5) regarding commingling of assets do not apply to deemed IRAs. Accordingly, the assets of a deemed IRA may be commingled for investment purposes with those of the qualified employer plan. However, the restrictions on the commingling of plan and IRA assets with other assets apply to the assets of the qualified employer plan and the deemed IRA.

**(e) Application of distribution rules.** *(1)* Rules applicable to distributions from qualified employer plans under the Internal Revenue Code and regulations do not apply to distributions from deemed IRAs. Instead, the rules applicable to distributions from IRAs apply to distributions from deemed IRAs. Also, any restrictions that a trustee, custodian, or insurance company is permitted to impose on distributions from traditional and Roth IRAs may be imposed on distributions from deemed IRAs (for example, early withdrawal penalties on annuities).

*(2)* The required minimum distribution rules of section 401(a)(9) must be met separately with respect to the qualified employer plan and the deemed IRA. The determination

of whether a qualified employer plan satisfies the required minimum distribution rules of section 401(a)(9) is made without regard to whether a participant satisfies the required minimum distribution requirements with respect to the deemed IRA that is established under such plan.

**(f) Additional rules.** *(1) Trustee.* The trustee or custodian of an individual retirement account must be a bank, as required by section 408(a)(2), or, if the trustee is not a bank, as defined in section 408(n), the trustee must have received approval from the Commissioner to serve as a nonbank trustee or nonbank custodian pursuant to § 1.408-2(e). For further guidance regarding governmental units serving as nonbank trustees of deemed IRAs established under section 408(q), see § 1.408-2T(e)(8).

*(2) Trusts.* (i) General rule. Deemed IRAs that are individual retirement accounts may be held in separate individual trusts, a single trust separate from a trust maintained by the qualified employer plan, or in a single trust that includes the qualified employer plan. A deemed IRA trust must be created or organized in the United States for the exclusive benefit of the participants. If deemed IRAs are held in a single trust that includes the qualified employer plan, the trustee must maintain a separate account for each deemed IRA. In addition, the written governing instrument creating the trust must satisfy the requirements of section 408(a) (1), (2), (3), (4), and (6).

(ii) Application of section 408(a)(3). If deemed IRAs are held in a single trust that includes the qualified employer plan, section 408(a)(3) is treated as satisfied if no part of the separate accounts of any of the deemed IRAs is invested in life insurance contracts, regardless of whether the separate account for the qualified employer plan invests in life insurance contracts.

(iii) Separate accounts for traditional and Roth deemed IRAs. The rules of section 408A(b) and the regulations thereunder, requiring each Roth IRA to be clearly designated as a Roth IRA, will not fail to be satisfied solely because Roth deemed IRAs and traditional deemed IRAs are held in a single trust, provided that the trustee maintains separate accounts for the Roth deemed IRAs and traditional deemed IRAs of each participant, and each of those accounts is clearly designated as such.

*(3) Annuity contracts.* Deemed IRAs that are individual retirement annuities may be held under a single annuity contract or under separate annuity contracts. However, the contract must be separate from any annuity contract or annuity contracts of the qualified employer plan. In addition, the contract must satisfy the requirements of section 408(b) and there must be separate accounting for the interest of each participant in those cases where the individual retirement annuities are held under a single annuity contract.

*(4) Deductibility.* The deductibility of voluntary employee contributions to a traditional deemed IRA is determined in the same manner as if they were made to any other traditional IRA. Thus, for example, taxpayers with compensation that exceeds the limits imposed by section 219(g) may not be able to make contributions to deemed IRAs, or the deductibility of such contributions may be limited in accordance with sections 408 and 219(g). However, section 219(f)(5), regarding the taxable year in which amounts paid by an employer to an individual retirement plan are includible in the employee's income, is not applicable to deemed IRAs.

*(5) Rollovers and transfers.* The same rules apply to rollovers and transfers to and from deemed IRAs as apply to rollovers and transfers to and from other IRAs. Thus, for example, the plan may provide that an employee may request and receive a distribution of his or her deemed IRA account balance and may roll it over to an eligible retirement plan in accordance with section 408(d)(3), regardless of whether that employee may receive a distribution of any other plan benefits.

*(6) Nondiscrimination.* The availability of a deemed IRA is not a benefit, right or feature of the qualified employer plan under § 1.401(a)(4)-4.

*(7) IRA assets and benefits not taken into account in determining benefits under or funding of qualified employer plan.* Neither the assets held in the deemed IRA portion of the qualified employer plan, nor any benefits attributable thereto, shall be taken into account for purposes of:

(i) Determining the benefits of employees and their beneficiaries under the plan (within the meaning of section 401(a)(2)); or

(ii) Determining the plan's assets or liabilities for purposes of section 404 or 412.

**(g) Disqualifying defects.** *(1) Single trust.* If the qualified employer plan fails to satisfy the qualification requirements applicable to it, either in form or operation, any deemed IRA that is an individual retirement account and that is included as part of the trust of that qualified employer plan does not satisfy section 408(q). Accordingly, any account maintained under such a plan as a deemed IRA ceases to be a deemed IRA at the time of the disqualifying event. In addition, the deemed IRA also ceases to satisfy the requirements of sections 408(a) and 408A. Also, if any one of the deemed IRAs fails to satisfy the applicable requirements of sections 408 or 408A, and the assets of that deemed IRA are included as part of the trust of the qualified employer plan, section 408(q) does not apply and the plan will fail to satisfy the plan's qualification requirements.

*(2) Separate trusts and annuities.* If the qualified employer plan fails to satisfy its qualification requirements, either in form or operation, but the assets of a deemed IRA are held in a separate trust (or where a deemed IRA is an individual retirement annuity), then the deemed IRA does not automatically fail to satisfy the applicable requirements of section 408 or 408A. Instead, its status as an IRA will be determined by considering whether the account or the annuity satisfies the applicable requirements of sections 408 and 408A (including, in the case of individual retirement accounts, the prohibition against the commingling of assets under section 408(a)(5)). Also, if a deemed IRA fails to satisfy the requirements of a qualified IRA and the assets of the deemed IRA are held in a separate trust (or where the deemed IRA is an individual retirement annuity), the qualified employer plan will not fail the qualification requirements applicable to it under the Code solely because of the failure of the deemed IRA.

**(h) Definitions.** The following definitions apply for purposes of this section:

*(1) Qualified employer plan.* A qualified employer plan is a plan described in section 401(a), an annuity plan described in section 403(a), a section 403(b) plan, or a governmental plan under section 457(b).

*(2) Voluntary employee contribution.* A voluntary employee contribution is any contribution (other than a mandatory contribution within the meaning of section 411(c)(2)(C)) which is made by an individual as an employee under a qualified employer plan that allows employees to elect to make contributions to deemed IRAs and with

respect to which the individual has designated the contribution as a contribution to which section 408(q) applies.

*(3) Employee.* An employee includes any individual who is an employee under the rules applicable to the qualified employer plan under which the deemed IRA is established.

**(i) Effective date.** This section applies to accounts or annuities established under section 408(q) on or after August 1, 2003.

T.D. 9142, 7/21/2004.

### § 1.408A-0 Roth IRA; table of contents

This table of contents lists the regulations relating to Roth IRAs under section 408A of the Internal Revenue Code as follows:



T.D. 8816, 2/3/99.

### § 1.408A-1 Roth IRAs in general.

This section sets forth the following questions and answers that discuss the background and general features of Roth IRAs:

Q-1. What is a Roth IRA?

A-1. (a) A Roth IRA is a new type of individual retirement plan that individuals can use, beginning in 1998. Roth IRAs are described in section 408A, which was added by the Taxpayer Relief Act of 1997 (TRA 97), Public Law 105-34 (111 Stat. 788).

(b) Roth IRAs are treated like traditional IRAs except where the Internal Revenue Code specifies different treatment. For example, aggregate contributions (other than by a conversion or other rollover) to all an individual's Roth IRAs are not permitted to exceed $2,000 for a taxable year. Further, income earned on funds held in a Roth IRA is generally not taxable. Similarly, the rules of section 408(e), such as the loss of exemption of the account where the owner engages in a prohibited transaction, apply to Roth IRAs in the same manner as to traditional IRAs.

Q-2. What are the significant differences between traditional IRAs and Roth IRAs?

A-2. There are several significant differences between traditional IRAs and Roth IRAs under the Internal Revenue Code. For example, eligibility to contribute to a Roth IRA is subject to special modified AGI (adjusted gross income) limits; contributions to a Roth IRA are never deductible; qualified distributions from a Roth IRA are not includible in gross income; the required minimum distribution rules under section 408(a)(6) and (b)(3) (which generally incorporate the provisions of section 401(a)(9)) do not apply to a Roth IRA during the lifetime of the owner; and contributions to a Roth IRA can be made after the owner has attained age 70½.

T.D. 8816, 2/3/99.

### § 1.408A-2 Establishing Roth IRAs.

This section sets forth the following questions and answers that provide rules applicable to establishing Roth IRAs:

Q-1. Who can establish a Roth IRA?

A-1. Except as provided in A-3 of this section, only an individual can establish a Roth IRA. In addition, in order to be eligible to contribute to a Roth IRA for a particular year, an individual must satisfy certain compensation requirements and adjusted gross income limits (see § 1.408A-3 A-3).

Q-2. How is a Roth IRA established?

A-2. A Roth IRA can be established with any bank, insurance company, or other person authorized in accordance with § 1.408-2(e) to serve as a trustee with respect to IRAs. The document establishing the Roth IRA must clearly designate the IRA as a Roth IRA, and this designation cannot be changed at a later date. Thus, an IRA that is designated as a Roth IRA cannot later be treated as a traditional IRA. However, see § 1.408A-4 A-1(b)(3) for certain rules for converting a traditional IRA to a Roth IRA with the same trustee by redesignating the traditional IRA as a Roth IRA, and see § 1.408A-5 for rules for recharacterizing certain IRA contributions.

Q-3. Can an employer or an association of employees establish a Roth IRA to hold contributions of employees or members?

A-3. Yes. Pursuant to section 408(c), an employer or an association of employees can establish a trust to hold contributions of employees or members made under a Roth IRA. Each employee's or member's account in the trust is treated as a separate Roth IRA that is subject to the generally applicable Roth IRA rules. The employer or association of employees may do certain acts otherwise required by an individual, for example, establishing and designating a trust as a Roth IRA.

Q-4. What is the effect of a surviving spouse of a Roth IRA owner treating an IRA as his or her own?

A-4. If the surviving spouse of a Roth IRA owner treats a Roth IRA as his or her own as of a date, the Roth IRA is treated from that date forward as though it were established for the benefit of the surviving spouse and not the original Roth IRA owner. Thus, for example, the surviving spouse is treated as the Roth IRA owner for purposes of applying the minimum distribution requirements under section 408(a)(6) and (b)(3). Similarly, the surviving spouse is treated as the Roth IRA owner rather than a beneficiary for purposes of determining the amount of any distribution from the Roth IRA that is includible in gross income and whether the distribution is subject to the 10-percent additional tax under section 72(t).

T.D. 8816, 2/3/99.

### § 1.408A-3 Contributions to Roth IRAs.

This section sets forth the following questions and answers that provide rules regarding contributions to Roth IRAs:

Q-1. What types of contributions are permitted to be made to a Roth IRA?

A-1. There are two types of contributions that are permitted to be made to a Roth IRA: regular contributions and qualified rollover contributions (including conversion contributions). The term regular contributions means contributions other than qualified rollover contributions.

Q-2. When are contributions permitted to be made to a Roth IRA?

A-2. (a) The provisions of section 408A are effective for taxable years beginning on or after January 1, 1998. Thus, the first taxable year for which contributions are permitted to be made to a Roth IRA by an individual is the individual's taxable year beginning in 1998.

(b) Regular contributions for a particular taxable year must generally be contributed by the due date (not including extensions) for filing a Federal income tax return for that taxable year. (See § 1.408A-5 regarding recharacterization of certain contributions.)

Q-3. What is the maximum aggregate amount of regular contributions an individual is eligible to contribute to a Roth IRA for a taxable year?

A-3. (a) The maximum aggregate amount that an individual is eligible to contribute to all his or her Roth IRAs as a regular contribution for a taxable year is the same as the maximum for traditional IRAs: $2,000 or, if less, that individual's compensation for the year.

(b) For Roth IRAs, the maximum amount described in paragraph (a) of this A-3 is phased out between certain levels of modified AGI. For an individual who is not married, the dollar amount is phased out ratably between modified AGI of $95,000 and $110,000; for a married individual filing a joint return, between modified AGI of $150,000 and $160,000; and for a married individual filing separately, between modified AGI of $0 and $10,000. For this purpose, a married individual who has lived apart from his or her spouse for the entire taxable year and who files separately is treated as not married. Under section 408A(c)(3)(A), in applying the phase-out, the maximum amount is rounded up to the next higher multiple of $10 and is not reduced below $200 until completely phased out.

(c) If an individual makes regular contributions to both traditional IRAs and Roth IRAs for a taxable year, the maximum limit for the Roth IRA is the lesser of—

(1) The amount described in paragraph (a) of this A-3 reduced by the amount contributed to traditional IRAs for the taxable year; and

(2) The amount described in paragraph (b) of this A-3. Employer contributions, including elective deferrals, made under a SEP or SIMPLE IRA Plan on behalf of an individual (including a self-employed individual) do not reduce the amount of the individual's maximum regular contribution.

(d) The rules in this A-3 are illustrated by the following examples:

*Example (1).* In 1998, unmarried, calendar-year taxpayer B, age 60, has modified AGI of $40,000 and compensation of $5,000. For 1998, B can contribute a maximum of $2,000 to a traditional IRA, a Roth IRA or a combination of traditional and Roth IRAs.

*Example (2).* The facts are the same as in Example 1. However, assume that B violates the maximum regular contribution limit by contributing $2,000 to a traditional IRA and $2,000 to a Roth IRA for 1998. The $2,000 to B's Roth IRA would be an excess contribution to B's Roth IRA for 1998 because an individual's contributions are applied first to a traditional IRA, then to a Roth IRA.

*Example (3).* The facts are the same as in Example 1, except that B's compensation is $900. The maximum amount B can contribute to either a traditional IRA or a Roth (or a combination of the two) for 1998 is $900.

*Example (4).* In 1998, unmarried, calendar-year taxpayer C, age 60, has modified AGI of $100,000 and compensation of $5,000. For 1998, C contributes $800 to a traditional IRA and $1,200 to a Roth IRA. Because C's $1,200 Roth IRA contribution does not exceed the phased-out maximum Roth IRA contribution of $1,340 and because C's total IRA contributions do not exceed $2,000, C's Roth IRA contribution does not exceed the maximum permissible contribution.

Q-4. How is compensation defined for purposes of the Roth IRA contribution limit?

A-4. For purposes of the contribution limit described in A-3 of this section, an individual's compensation is the same as that used to determine the maximum contribution an individual can make to a traditional IRA. This amount is defined in section 219(f)(1) to include wages, commissions, professional fees, tips, and other amounts received for personal services, as well as taxable alimony and separate maintenance payments received under a decree of divorce or separate maintenance. Compensation also includes earned income as defined in section 401(c)(2), but does not include any amount received as a pension or annuity or as deferred compensation. In addition, under section 219(c), a married individual filing a joint return is permitted to make an IRA contribution by treating his or her spouse's higher compensation as his or her own, but only to the extent that the spouse's compensation is not being used for purposes of the spouse making a contribution to a Roth IRA or a deductible contribution to a traditional IRA.

Q-5. What is the significance of modified AGI and how is it determined?

A-5. Modified AGI is used for purposes of the phase-out rules described in A-3 of this section and for purposes of the $100,000 modified AGI limitation described in § 1.408A-4 A-2(a) (relating to eligibility for conversion). As defined in section 408A(c)(3)(C)(i), modified AGI is the same as adjusted gross income under section 219(g)(3)(A) (used to determine the amount of deductible contributions that can be made to a traditional IRA by an individual who is an active participant in an employer-sponsored retirement plan), except that any conversion is disregarded in determining modified AGI. For example, the deduction for contributions to an IRA is not taken into account for purposes of determining adjusted gross income under section 219 and thus does not apply in determining modified AGI for Roth IRA purposes.

Q-6. Is a required minimum distribution from an IRA for a year included in income for purposes of determining modified AGI?

A-6. (a) Yes. For taxable years beginning before January 1, 2005, any required minimum distribution from an IRA under section 408(a)(6) and (b)(3) (which generally incorporate the provisions of section 401(a)(9)) is included in income for purposes of determining modified AGI.

(b) For taxable years beginning after December 31, 2004, and solely for purposes of the $100,000 limitation applicable to conversions, modified AGI does not include any required minimum distributions from an IRA under section 408(a)(6) and (b)(3).

Q-7. Does an excise tax apply if an individual exceeds the aggregate regular contribution limits for Roth IRAs?

A-7. Yes. Section 4973 imposes an annual 6-percent excise tax on aggregate amounts contributed to Roth IRAs that exceed the maximum contribution limits described in A-3 of this section. Any contribution that is distributed, together with net income, from a Roth IRA on or before the tax return due date (plus extensions) for the taxable year of the contribution is treated as not contributed. Net income described in the previous sentence is includible in gross income for the taxable year in which the contribution is made. Aggregate excess contributions that are not distributed from a Roth IRA on or before the tax return due date (with extensions) for the taxable year of the contributions are reduced as a deemed Roth IRA contribution for each subsequent taxable year to the extent that the Roth IRA owner does not actually make regular IRA contributions for such years. Section 4973 applies separately to an individual's Roth IRAs and other types of IRAs.

T.D. 8816, 2/3/99.

## § 1.408A-4 Converting amounts to Roth IRAs.

This section sets forth the following questions and answers that provide rules applicable to Roth IRA conversions:

Q-1. Can an individual convert an amount in his or her traditional IRA to a Roth IRA?

A-1. (a) Yes. An amount in a traditional IRA may be converted to an amount in a Roth IRA if two requirements are satisfied. First, the IRA owner must satisfy the modified AGI limitation described in A-2(a) of this section and, if married, the joint filing requirement described in A-2(b) of this section. Second, the amount contributed to the Roth IRA must satisfy the definition of a qualified rollover contribution in section 408A(e) (i.e., it must satisfy the requirements for a rollover contribution as defined in section 408(d)(3), except that the one-rollover-per-year limitation in section 408(d)(3)(B) does not apply).

(b) An amount can be converted by any of three methods—

(1) An amount distributed from a traditional IRA is contributed (rolled over) to a Roth IRA within the 60-day period described in section 408(d)(3)(A)(i);

(2) An amount in a traditional IRA is transferred in a trustee-to-trustee transfer from the trustee of the traditional IRA to the trustee of the Roth IRA; or

(3) An amount in a traditional IRA is transferred to a Roth IRA maintained by the same trustee. For purposes of sections 408 and 408A, redesignating a traditional IRA as a Roth IRA is treated as a transfer of the entire account balance from a traditional IRA to a Roth IRA.

(c) Any converted amount is treated as a distribution from the traditional IRA and a qualified rollover contribution to the Roth IRA for purposes of section 408 and section 408A, even if the conversion is accomplished by means of a trustee-to-trustee transfer or a transfer between IRAs of the same trustee.

(d) A transaction that is treated as a failed conversion under § 1.408A-5 A-9(a)(1) is not a conversion.

Q-2. What are the modified AGI limitation and joint filing requirements for conversions?

A-2. (a) An individual with modified AGI in excess of $100,000 for a taxable year is not permitted to convert an amount to a Roth IRA during that taxable year. This $100,000 limitation applies to the taxable year that the funds are paid from the traditional IRA, rather than the year they are contributed to the Roth IRA.

(b) If the individual is married, he or she is permitted to convert an amount to a Roth IRA during a taxable year only if the individual and the individual's spouse file a joint return for the taxable year that the funds are paid from the traditional IRA. In this case, the modified AGI subject to the $100,000 limit is the modified AGI derived from the joint return using the couple's combined income. The only exception to this joint filing requirement is for an individual who has lived apart from his or her spouse for the entire taxable year. If the married individual has lived apart from his or her spouse for the entire taxable year, then such individual can treat himself or herself as not married for purposes of this paragraph, file a separate return and be subject to the $100,000 limit on his or her separate modified AGI. In all other cases, a married individual filing a separate return is not permitted to convert an amount to a Roth IRA, regardless of the individual's modified AGI.

Q-3. Is a remedy available to an individual who makes a failed conversion?

A-3. (a) Yes. See § 1.408A-5 for rules permitting a failed conversion amount to be recharacterized as a contribution to a traditional IRA. If the requirements in § 1.408A-5 are satisfied, the failed conversion amount will be treated as having been contributed to the traditional IRA and not to the Roth IRA.

(b) If the contribution is not recharacterized in accordance with § 1.408A-5, the contribution will be treated as a regular contribution to the Roth IRA and, thus, an excess contribution subject to the excise tax under section 4973 to the extent that it exceeds the individual's regular contribution limit. This is the result regardless of which of the three methods described in A-1(b) of this section applies to this transaction. Additionally, the distribution from the traditional IRA will not be eligible for the 4-year spread and will be subject to the additional tax under section 72(t) (unless an exception under that section applies).

Q-4. Do any special rules apply to a conversion of an amount in an individual's SEP IRA or SIMPLE IRA to a Roth IRA?

A-4. (a) An amount in an individual's SEP IRA can be converted to a Roth IRA on the same terms as an amount in any other traditional IRA.

(b) An amount in an individual's SIMPLE IRA can be converted to a Roth IRA on the same terms as a conversion from a traditional IRA, except that an amount distributed from a SIMPLE IRA during the 2-year period described in section 72(t)(6), which begins on the date that the individual first participated in any SIMPLE IRA Plan maintained by the individual's employer, cannot be converted to a Roth IRA. Pursuant to section 408(d)(3)(G), a distribution of an amount from an individual's SIMPLE IRA during this 2-year period is not eligible to be rolled over into an IRA that is not a SIMPLE IRA and thus cannot be a qualified rollover contribution. This 2-year period of section 408(d)(3)(G) applies separately to the contributions of each of an individual's employers maintaining a SIMPLE IRA Plan.

(c) Once an amount in a SEP IRA or SIMPLE IRA has been converted to a Roth IRA, it is treated as a contribution to a Roth IRA for all purposes. Future contributions under the SEP or under the SIMPLE IRA Plan may not be made to the Roth IRA.

Q-5. Can amounts in other kinds of retirement plans be converted to a Roth IRA?

A-5. No. Only amounts in another IRA can be converted to a Roth IRA. For example, amounts in a qualified plan or annuity plan described in section 401(a) or 403(a) cannot be converted directly to a Roth IRA. Also, amounts held in an annuity contract or account described in section 403(b) cannot be converted directly to a Roth IRA.

Q-6. Can an individual who has attained at least age 70½ by the end of a calendar year convert an amount distributed from a traditional IRA during that year to a Roth IRA before receiving his or her required minimum distribution with respect to the traditional IRA for the year of the conversion?

A-6. (a) No. In order to be eligible for a conversion, an amount first must be eligible to be rolled over. Section 408(d)(3) prohibits the rollover of a required minimum distribution. If a minimum distribution is required for a year with respect to an IRA, the first dollars distributed during that year are treated as consisting of the required minimum distribution until an amount equal to the required minimum distribution for that year has been distributed.

(b) As provided in A-1(c) of this section, any amount converted is treated as a distribution from a traditional IRA and a rollover contribution to a Roth IRA and not as a trustee-to-trustee transfer for purposes of section 408 and section 408A. Thus, in a year for which a minimum distribution is required (including the calendar year in which the individual attains age 70½), an individual may not convert the assets of an IRA (or any portion of those assets) to a Roth IRA to the extent that the required minimum distribution for the traditional IRA for the year has not been distributed.

(c) If a required minimum distribution is contributed to a Roth IRA, it is treated as having been distributed, subject to the normal rules under section 408(d)(1) and (2), and then contributed as a regular contribution to a Roth IRA. The amount of the required minimum distribution is not a conversion contribution.

Q-7. What are the tax consequences when an amount is converted to a Roth IRA?

A-7. (a) Any amount that is converted to a Roth IRA is includible in gross income as a distribution according to the rules of section 408(d)(1) and (2) for the taxable year in which the amount is distributed or transferred from the traditional IRA. Thus, any portion of the distribution or transfer that is treated as a return of basis under section 408(d)(1) and (2) is not includible in gross income as a result of the conversion.

(b) The 10-percent additional tax under section 72(t) generally does not apply to the taxable conversion amount. But see § 1.408A-6 A-5 for circumstances under which the taxable conversion amount would be subject to the additional tax under section 72(t).

(c) Pursuant to section 408A(e), a conversion is not treated as a rollover for purposes of the one-rollover-per-year rule of section 408(d)(3)(B).

Q-8. Is there an exception to the income-inclusion rule described in A-7 of this section for 1998 conversions?

A-8. Yes. In the case of a distribution (including a trustee-to-trustee transfer) from a traditional IRA on or before December 31, 1998, that is converted to a Roth IRA, instead of having the entire taxable conversion amount includible in income in 1998, an individual includes in gross income for 1998 only one quarter of that amount and one quarter of that amount for each of the next 3 years. This 4-year spread also applies if the conversion amount was distributed in 1998 and contributed to the Roth IRA within the 60-day period described in section 408(d)(3)(A)(i), but after December 31, 1998. However, see § 1.408A-6 A-6 for special rules requiring acceleration of inclusion if an amount subject to the 4-year spread is distributed from the Roth IRA before 2001.

Q-9. Is the taxable conversion amount included in income for all purposes?

A-9. Except as provided below, any taxable conversion amount includible in gross income for a year as a result of the conversion (regardless of whether the individual is using a 4-year spread) is included in income for all purposes. Thus, for example, it is counted for purposes of determining the taxable portion of social security payments under section 86 and for purposes of determining the phase-out of the $25,000 exemption under section 469(i) relating to the disallowance of passive activity losses from rental real estate activities. However, as provided in § 1.408A-3 A-5, the taxable conversion amount (and any resulting change in other elements of adjusted gross income) is disregarded for purposes of determining modified AGI for section 408A.

Q-10. Can an individual who makes a 1998 conversion elect not to have the 4-year spread apply and instead have the full taxable conversion amount includible in gross income for 1998?

A-10. Yes. Instead of having the taxable conversion amount for a 1998 conversion included over 4 years as provided under A-8 of this section, an individual can elect to include the full taxable conversion amount in income for 1998. The election is made on Form 8606 and cannot be made or changed after the due date (including extensions) for filing the 1998 Federal income tax return.

Q-11. What happens when an individual who is using the 4-year spread dies, files separately, or divorces before the full taxable conversion amount has been included in gross income?

A-11. (a) If an individual who is using the 4-year spread described in A-8 of this section dies before the full taxable conversion amount has been included in gross income, then the remainder must be included in the individual's gross income for the taxable year that includes the date of death.

(b) However, if the sole beneficiary of all the decedent's Roth IRAs is the decedent's spouse, then the spouse can elect to continue the 4-year spread. Thus, the spouse can elect to include in gross income the same amount that the decedent would have included in each of the remaining years of the 4-year period. Where the spouse makes such an election, the amount includible under the 4-year spread for the taxable year that includes the date of the decedent's death remains includible in the decedent's gross income and is reported on the decedent's final Federal income tax return. The election is made on either Form 8606 or Form 1040, in accordance with the instructions to the applicable form, for the taxable year that includes the decedent's date of death and cannot be changed after the due date (including extensions) for filing the Federal income tax return for the spouse's taxable year that includes the decedent's date of death.

(c) If a Roth IRA owner who is using the 4-year spread and who was married in 1998 subsequently files separately or divorces before the full taxable conversion amount has been included in gross income, the remainder of the taxable conversion amount must be included in the Roth IRA owner's gross income over the remaining years in the 4-year period (unless accelerated because of distribution or death).

Q-12. Can an individual convert a traditional IRA to a Roth IRA if he or she is receiving substantially equal periodic payments within the meaning of section 72(t)(2)(A)(iv) from that traditional IRA?

A-12. Yes. Not only is the conversion amount itself not subject to the early distribution tax under section 72(t), but the conversion amount is also not treated as a distribution for purposes of determining whether a modification within the meaning of section 72(t)(4)(A) has occurred. Distributions from the Roth IRA that are part of the original series of substantially equal periodic payments will be nonqualified distributions from the Roth IRA until they meet the requirements for being a qualified distribution, described in § 1.408A-6 A-1(b). The additional 10-percent tax under section 72(t) will not apply to the extent that these nonqualified distributions are part of a series of substantially equal periodic payments. Nevertheless, to the extent that such distributions are allocable to a 1998 conversion contribution with respect to which the 4-year spread for the resultant income inclusion applies (see A-8 of this section) and are received during 1998, 1999, or 2000, the special acceleration rules of § 1.408A-6 A-6 apply. However, if the original series of substantially equal periodic payments does not continue to be distributed in substantially equal periodic payments from the Roth IRA after the conversion, the series of payments will have been modified and, if this modification occurs within 5 years of the first payment or prior to the individual becoming disabled or attaining age 59½, the taxpayer will be subject to the recapture tax of section 72(t)(4)(A).

Q-13. Can a 1997 distribution from a traditional IRA be converted to a Roth IRA in 1998?

A-13. No. An amount distributed from a traditional IRA in 1997 that is contributed to a Roth IRA in 1998 would not be a conversion contribution. See A-3 of this section regarding the remedy for a failed conversion.

Q-14. What is the amount that is treated as a distribution, for purposes of determining income inclusion, when a conversion involves an annuity contract?

A-14. (a) In general—(1) Distribution of Fair Market Value Upon Conversion. Notwithstanding § 1.408-4(e), when part or all of a traditional IRA that is an individual retirement annuity described in section 408(b) is converted to a Roth IRA, for purposes of determining the amount includible in gross income as a distribution under § 1.408A-4, A-7, the amount that is treated as distributed is the fair market value of the annuity contract on the date the annuity contract is converted. Similarly, when a traditional IRA that is an individual retirement account described in section 408(a) holds an annuity contract as an account asset and the traditional IRA is converted to a Roth IRA, for purposes of determining the amount includible in gross income as a distribution under § 1.408A-4, A-7, the amount that is treated as distributed with respect to the annuity contract is the fair market value of the annuity contract on the date that the annuity contract is distributed or treated as distributed from the traditional IRA. The rules in this A-14 also apply to conversions from SIMPLE IRAs.

(2) Annuity contract surrendered. Paragraph (a)(1) of this paragraph A-14 does not apply to a conversion of a traditional IRA to the extent the conversion is accomplished by the complete surrender of an annuity contract for its cash value and the reinvestment of the cash proceeds in a Roth IRA, but only if the surrender extinguishes all benefits and other characteristics of the contract. In such a case, the cash from the surrendered contract is the amount reinvested in the Roth IRA.

(3) Definitions. The definitions set forth in § 1.408A-8 apply for purposes of this paragraph A-14.

(b) Determination of fair market value—(1) Overview—(i) Use of alternative methods. This paragraph (b) sets forth methods which may be used to determine the fair market value of an individual retirement annuity for purposes of paragraph (a)(1) of this paragraph A-14. However, if, because of the unusual nature of the contract, the value determined under one of these methods does not reflect the full value of the contract, that method may not be used.

(ii) Additional guidance. Additional guidance regarding the fair market value of an individual retirement annuity, including formulas to be used for determining fair market value, may be issued by the Commissioner in revenue rulings, notices, or other guidance published in the Internal Revenue Bulletin (see § 601.601(d)(2)(ii)(b)).

(2) Gift tax method—(i) Cost of contract or comparable contract. If with respect to an annuity, there is a comparable contract issued by the company which sold the annuity, the fair market value of the annuity may be established by the price of the comparable contract. If the conversion occurs soon after the annuity was sold, the comparable contract may be the annuity itself, and thus, the fair market value of the annuity may be established through the sale of the particular contract by the company (that is, the actual premiums paid for such contract).

(ii) Use of reserves where no comparable contract available. If with respect to an annuity, there is no comparable contract available in order to make the comparison described in paragraph (b)(2)(i) of this paragraph A-14, the fair market value may be established through an approximation that is based on the interpolated terminal reserve at the date of the conversion, plus the proportionate part of the gross premium last paid before the date of the conversion which covers the period extending beyond that date.

(3) Accumulation method. As an alternative to the gift tax method described in paragraph (b)(2) of this paragraph A-14, this paragraph (b)(3) provides a method that may be used for an annuity contract which has not been annuitized. The fair market value of such an annuity contract is permitted to be determined using the methodology provided in § 1.401(a)(9)-6, A-12, with the following modifications:

(i) All front-end loads and other non-recurring charges assessed in the twelve months immediately preceding the conversion must be added to the account value.

(ii) Future distributions are not to be assumed in the determination of the actuarial present value of additional benefits.

(iii) The exclusions provided under § 1.401(a)(9)-6, A-12(c)(1) and (c)(2), are not to be taken into account.

(c) Effective/applicability date. The provisions of this paragraph A-14 are applicable to any conversion in which an annuity contract is distributed or treated as distributed from a traditional IRA on or after August 19, 2005. However, for annuity contracts distributed or treated as distributed from a traditional IRA on or before December 31, 2008, taxpayers may instead apply the valuation methods in § 1.408A-4T (as it appeared in the April 1, 2008, edition of 26 CFR part 1) and Revenue Procedure 2006-13 (2006-1 CB 315) (See § 601.601(d)(2)(ii)(b)).

T.D. 8816, 2/3/99, amend T.D. 9220, 8/19/2005, T.D. 9418, 7/28/2008.

### § 1.408A-5 Recharacterized contributions.

This section sets forth the following questions and answers that provide rules regarding recharacterizing IRA contributions:

Q-1. Can an IRA owner recharacterize certain contributions (i.e., treat a contribution made to one type of IRA as made to a different type of IRA) for a taxable year?

A-1. (a) Yes. In accordance with section 408A(d)(6), except as otherwise provided in this section, if an individual makes a contribution to an IRA (the FIRST IRA) for a taxable year and then transfers the contribution (or a portion of the contribution) in a trustee-to-trustee transfer from the trustee of the FIRST IRA to the trustee of another IRA (the SECOND IRA), the individual can elect to treat the contribution as having been made to the SECOND IRA, instead of to the FIRST IRA, for Federal tax purposes. A transfer between the FIRST IRA and the SECOND IRA will not fail to be a trustee-to-trustee transfer merely because both IRAs are maintained by the same trustee. For purposes of section 408A(d)(6), redesignating the FIRST IRA as the SECOND IRA will be treated as a transfer of the entire account balance from the FIRST IRA to the SECOND IRA.

(b) This recharacterization election can be made only if the trustee-to-trustee transfer from the FIRST IRA to the SECOND IRA is made on or before the due date (including extensions) for filing the individual's Federal income tax return for the taxable year for which the contribution was made to the FIRST IRA. For purposes of this section, a conversion that is accomplished through a rollover of a distribution from a traditional IRA in a taxable year that, 60 days after the distribution (as described in section 408(d)(3)(A)(i)), is contributed to a Roth IRA in the next taxable year is treated as a contribution for the earlier taxable year.

Q-2. What is the proper treatment of the net income attributable to the amount of a contribution that is being recharacterized?

A-2. (a) The net income attributable to the amount of a contribution that is being recharacterized must be transferred to the SECOND IRA along with the contribution.

(b) If the amount of the contribution being recharacterized was contributed to a separate IRA and no distributions or additional contributions have been made from or to that IRA at any time, then the contribution is recharacterized by the trustee of the FIRST IRA transferring the entire account balance of the FIRST IRA to the trustee of the SECOND IRA. In this case, the net income (or loss) attributable to the contribution being recharacterized is the difference between the amount of the original contribution and the amount transferred.

(c)(1) If paragraph (b) of this A-2 does not apply, then, for purposes of determining net income attributable to IRA contributions, the net income attributable to the amount of a contribution is determined by allocating to the contribution a pro rata portion of the earnings on the assets in the IRA during the period the IRA held the contribution. This attributable net income is calculated by using the following formula:

Net Income = Contribution x (Adjusted Closing Balance - Adjusted Opening Balance) / Adjusted Opening Balance.

(2) For purposes of this paragraph (c), the following definitions apply:

(i) The term adjusted opening balance means the fair market value of the IRA at the beginning of the computation period plus the amount of any contributions or transfers (including the contribution that is being recharacterized pursuant to section 408A(d)(6) and any other recharacterizations) made to the IRA during the computation period.

(ii) The term adjusted closing balance means the fair market value of the IRA at the end of the computation period plus the amount of any distributions or transfers (including contributions returned pursuant to section 408(d)(4) and recharacterizations of contributions pursuant to section 408A(d)(6)) made from the IRA during the computation period.

(iii) The term computation period means the period beginning immediately prior to the time the particular contribution being recharacterized is made to the IRA and ending immediately prior to the recharacterizing transfer of the contribution. If a series of regular contributions was made to the IRA, and consecutive contributions in that series are being recharacterized, the computation period begins immediately prior to the time the first of the regular contributions being recharacterized was made.

(3) When an IRA asset is not normally valued on a daily basis, the fair market value of the asset at the beginning of the computation period is deemed to be the most recent, regularly determined, fair market value of the asset, determined as of a date that coincides with or precedes the first day of the computation period. In addition, solely for purposes of this paragraph (c), notwithstanding A-3 of this section, recharacterized contributions are taken into account for the period they are actually held in a particular IRA.

(4) In the case of an individual with multiple IRAs, the net income calculation is performed only on the IRA containing the particular contribution to be recharacterized, and that IRA is the IRA from which the recharacterizing transfer must be made.

(5) In the case of multiple contributions made to an IRA for a particular year that are eligible for recharacterization, the IRA owner can choose (by date and by dollar amount, not by specific assets acquired with those dollars) which contribution, or portion thereof, is to be recharacterized.

(6) The following examples illustrate the net income calculation under section 408A(d)(6) and this paragraph:

Example 1. (i) On March 1, 2004, when her Roth IRA is worth $80,000, Taxpayer A makes a $160,000 conversion contribution to the Roth IRA. Subsequently, Taxpayer A discovers that she was ineligible to make a Roth conversion contribution in 2004 and so she requests that the $160,000 be recharacterized to a traditional IRA pursuant to section 408A(d)(6). Pursuant to this request, on March 1, 2005, when the IRA is worth $225,000, the Roth IRA trustee transfers to a traditional IRA the $160,000 plus allocable net income. No other contributions have been made to the Roth IRA and no distributions have been made.

(ii) The adjusted opening balance is $240,000 [$80,000 + $160,000] and the adjusted closing balance is $225,000. Thus the net income allocable to the $160,000 is - $10,000 [$160,000 x ($225,000 - $240,000) ÷ $240,000]. Therefore, in order to recharacterize the March 1, 2004, $160,000 conversion contribution on March 1, 2005, the Roth IRA trustee must transfer from Taxpayer A's Roth IRA to her traditional IRA $150,000 [$160,000 - $10,000].

Example 2. (i) On April 1, 2004, when her traditional IRA is worth $100,000, Taxpayer B converts the entire amount, consisting of 100 shares of stock in ABC Corp. and 100 shares of stock in XYZ Corp., by transferring the shares to a Roth IRA. At the time of the conversion, the 100 shares of stock in ABC Corp. are worth $50,000 and the 100 shares of stock in XYZ Corp. are also worth $50,000. Taxpayer B decides that she would like to recharacterize the ABC Corp. shares back to a traditional IRA. However, B may choose only by dollar amount the contribution or portion thereof that is to be recharacterized. On the date of transfer, November 1, 2004, the 100 shares of stock in ABC Corp. are worth $40,000 and the 100 shares of stock in XYZ Corp. are worth

$70,000. No other contributions have been made to the Roth IRA and no distributions have been made.

(ii) If B requests that $50,000 (which was the value of the ABC Corp. shares at the time of conversion) be recharacterized, the net income allocable to the $50,000 is $5,000 [$50,000 x ($110,000 - $100,000) ÷ $100,000]. Therefore, in order to recharacterize $50,000 of the April 1, 2004, conversion contribution on November 1, 2004, the Roth IRA trustee must transfer from Taxpayer B's Roth IRA to a traditional IRA assets with a value of $55,000 [$50,000 + $5,000].

(iii) If, on the other hand, B requests that $40,000 (which was the value of the ABC Corp. shares on November 1) be recharacterized, the net income allocable to the $40,000 is $4,000 [$40,000 x ($110,000 - $100,000) / $100,000]. Therefore, in order to recharacterize $40,000 of the April 1, 2004, conversion contribution on November 1, 2004, the Roth IRA trustee must transfer from Taxpayer B's Roth IRA to a traditional IRA assets with a value of $44,000 [$40,000 + $4,000].

(iv) Regardless of the amount of the contribution recharacterized, the determination of that amount (or of the net income allocable thereto) is not affected by whether the recharacterization is accomplished by the transfer of shares of ABC Corp. or of shares of XYZ Corp.

(7) This paragraph (c) applies for purposes of determining net income attributable to IRA contributions, made on or after January 1, 2004. For purposes of determining net income attributable to IRA contributions made before January 1, 2004, see paragraph (c) of this A-2 of § 1.408A-5 (as it appeared in the April 1, 2003, edition of 26 CFR part 1).

Q-3. What is the effect of recharacterizing a contribution made to the FIRST IRA as a contribution made to the SECOND IRA?

A-3. The contribution that is being recharacterized as a contribution to the SECOND IRA is treated as having been originally contributed to the SECOND IRA on the same date and (in the case of a regular contribution) for the same taxable year that the contribution was made to the FIRST IRA. Thus, for example, no deduction would be allowed for a contribution to the FIRST IRA, and any net income transferred with the recharacterized contribution is treated as earned in the SECOND IRA, and not the FIRST IRA.

Q-4. Can an amount contributed to an IRA in a tax-free transfer be recharacterized under A-1 of this section?

A-4. No. If an amount is contributed to the FIRST IRA in a tax-free transfer, the amount cannot be recharacterized as a contribution to the SECOND IRA under A-1 of this section. However, if an amount is erroneously rolled over or transferred from a traditional IRA to a SIMPLE IRA, the contribution can subsequently be recharacterized as a contribution to another traditional IRA.

Q-5. Can an amount contributed by an employer under a SIMPLE IRA Plan or a SEP be recharacterized under A-1 of this section?

A-5. No. Employer contributions (including elective deferrals) under a SIMPLE IRA Plan or a SEP cannot be recharacterized as contributions to another IRA under A-1 of this section. However, an amount converted from a SEP IRA or SIMPLE IRA to a Roth IRA may be recharacterized under A-1 of this section as a contribution to a SEP IRA or SIMPLE IRA, including the original SEP IRA or SIMPLE IRA.

Q-6. How does a taxpayer make the election to recharacterize a contribution to an IRA for a taxable year?

A-6. (a) An individual makes the election described in this section by notifying, on or before the date of the transfer, both the trustee of the FIRST IRA and the trustee of the SECOND IRA, that the individual has elected to treat the contribution as having been made to the SECOND IRA, instead of the FIRST IRA, for Federal tax purposes. The notification of the election must include the following information: the type and amount of the contribution to the FIRST IRA that is to be recharacterized; the date on which the contribution was made to the FIRST IRA and the year for which it was made; a direction to the trustee of the FIRST IRA to transfer, in a trustee-to-trustee transfer, the amount of the contribution and net income allocable to the contribution to the trustee of the SECOND IRA; and the name of the trustee of the FIRST IRA and the trustee of the SECOND IRA and any additional information needed to make the transfer.

(b) The election and the trustee-to-trustee transfer must occur on or before the due date (including extensions) for filing the individual's Federal income tax return for the taxable year for which the recharacterized contribution was made to the FIRST IRA, and the election cannot be revoked after the transfer. An individual who makes this election must report the recharacterization, and must treat the contribution as having been made to the SECOND IRA, instead of the FIRST IRA, on the individual's Federal income tax return for the taxable year described in the preceding sentence in accordance with the applicable Federal tax forms and instructions.

(c) The election to recharacterize a contribution described in this A-6 may be made on behalf of a deceased IRA owner by his or her executor, administrator, or other person responsible for filing the final Federal income tax return of the decedent under section 6012(b)(1).

Q-7. If an amount is initially contributed to an IRA for a taxable year, then is moved (with net income attributable to the contribution) in a tax-free transfer to another IRA (the FIRST IRA for purposes of A-1 of this section), can the tax-free transfer be disregarded, so that the initial contribution that is transferred from the FIRST IRA to the SECOND IRA is treated as a recharacterization of that initial contribution?

A-7. Yes. In applying section 408A(d)(6), tax-free transfers between IRAs are disregarded. Thus, if a contribution to an IRA for a year is followed by one or more tax-free transfers between IRAs prior to the recharacterization, then for purposes of section 408A(d)(6), the contribution is treated as if it remained in the initial IRA. Consequently, an individual may elect to recharacterize an initial contribution made to the initial IRA that was involved in a series of tax-free transfers by making a trustee-to-trustee transfer from the last IRA in the series to the SECOND IRA. In this case the contribution to the SECOND IRA is treated as made on the same date (and for the same taxable year) as the date the contribution being recharacterized was made to the initial IRA.

Q-8. If a contribution is recharacterized, is the recharacterization treated as a rollover for purposes of the one-rollover-per-year limitation of section 408(d)(3)(B)?

A-8. No, recharacterizing a contribution under A-1 of this section is never treated as a rollover for purposes of the one-rollover-per-year limitation of section 408(d)(3)(B), even if the contribution would have been treated as a rollover contribution by the SECOND IRA if it had been made directly to the SECOND IRA, rather than as a result of a recharacterization of a contribution to the FIRST IRA.

Q-9. If an IRA owner converts an amount from a traditional IRA to a Roth IRA and then transfers that amount back to a traditional IRA in a recharacterization, may the IRA owner subsequently reconvert that amount from the traditional IRA to a Roth IRA?

A-9. (a)(1) Except as otherwise provided in paragraph (b) of this A-9, an IRA owner who converts an amount from a traditional IRA to a Roth IRA during any taxable year and then transfers that amount back to a traditional IRA by means of a recharacterization may not reconvert that amount from the traditional IRA to a Roth IRA before the beginning of the taxable year following the taxable year in which the amount was converted to a Roth IRA or, if later, the end of the 30-day period beginning on the day on which the IRA owner transfers the amount from the Roth IRA back to a traditional IRA by means of a recharacterization (regardless of whether the recharacterization occurs during the taxable year in which the amount was converted to a Roth IRA or the following taxable year). Thus, any attempted reconversion of an amount prior to the time permitted under this paragraph (a)(1) is a failed conversion of that amount. However, see sect;1.408A-4 A-3 for a remedy available to an individual who makes a failed conversion.

(2) For purposes of paragraph (a)(1) of this A-9, a failed conversion of an amount resulting from a failure to satisfy the requirements of sect;1.408A-4 A-1(a) is treated as a conversion in determining whether an IRA owner has previously converted that amount.

(b)(1) An IRA owner who converts an amount from a traditional IRA to a Roth IRA during taxable year 1998 and then transfers that amount back to a traditional IRA by means of a recharacterization may reconvert that amount once (but no more than once) on or after November 1, 1998 and on or before December 31, 1998; the IRA owner may also reconvert that amount once (but no more than once) during 1999. The rule set forth in the preceding sentence applies without regard to whether the IRA owner's initial conversion or recharacterization of the amount occurred before, on, or after November 1, 1998. An IRA owner who converts an amount from a traditional IRA to a Roth IRA during taxable year 1999 that has not been converted previously and then transfers that amount back to a traditional IRA by means of a recharacterization may reconvert that amount once (but no more than once) on or before December 31, 1999. For purposes of this paragraph (b)(1), a failed conversion of an amount resulting from a failure to satisfy the requirements of § 1.408A-4 A-1(a) is not treated as a conversion in determining whether an IRA owner has previously converted that amount.

(2) A reconversion by an IRA owner during 1998 or 1999 for which the IRA owner is not eligible under paragraph (b)(1) of this A-9 will be deemed an excess reconversion (rather than a failed conversion) and will not change the IRA owner's taxable conversion amount. Instead, the excess reconversion and the last preceding recharacterization will not be taken into account for purposes of determining the IRA owner's taxable conversion amount, and the IRA owner's taxable conversion amount will be based on the last reconversion that was not an excess reconversion (unless, after the excess reconversion, the amount is transferred back to a traditional IRA by means of a recharacterization). An excess reconversion will otherwise be treated as a valid reconversion.

(3) For purposes of this paragraph (b), any reconversion that an IRA owner made before November 1, 1998 will not be treated as an excess reconversion and will not be taken into account in determining whether any later reconversion is an excess reconversion.

(c) In determining the portion of any amount held in a Roth IRA or a traditional IRA that an IRA owner may not reconvert under this A-9, any amount previously converted (or reconverted) is adjusted for subsequent net income thereon.

Q-10. Are there examples to illustrate the rules in this section?

A-10. The rules in this section are illustrated by the following examples:

*Example (1).* In 1998, Individual C converts the entire amount in his traditional IRA to a Roth IRA. Individual C thereafter determines that his modified AGI for 1998 exceeded $100,000 so that he was ineligible to have made a conversion in that year. Accordingly, prior to the due date (plus extensions) for filing the individual's Federal income tax return for 1998, he decides to recharacterize the conversion contribution. He instructs the trustee of the Roth IRA (FIRST IRA) to transfer in a trustee-to-trustee transfer the amount of the contribution, plus net income, to the trustee of a new traditional IRA (SECOND IRA). The individual notifies the trustee of the FIRST IRA and the trustee of the SECOND IRA that he is recharacterizing his IRA contribution (and provides the other information described in A-6 of this section). On the individual's Federal income tax return for 1998, he treats the original amount of the conversion as having been contributed to the SECOND IRA and not the Roth IRA. As a result, for Federal tax purposes, the contribution is treated as having been made to the SECOND IRA and not to the Roth IRA. The result would be the same if the conversion amount had been transferred in a tax-free transfer to another Roth IRA prior to the recharacterization.

*Example (2).* In 1998, an individual makes a $2,000 regular contribution for 1998 to his traditional IRA (FIRST IRA). Prior to the due date (plus extensions) for filing the individual's Federal income tax return for 1998, he decides that he would prefer to contribute to a Roth IRA instead. The individual instructs the trustee of the FIRST IRA to transfer in a trustee-to-trustee transfer the amount of the contribution, plus attributable net income, to the trustee of a Roth IRA (SECOND IRA). The individual notifies the trustee of the FIRST IRA and the trustee of the SECOND IRA that he is recharacterizing his $2,000 contribution for 1998 (and provides the other information described in A-6 of this section). On the individual's Federal income tax return for 1998, he treats the $2,000 as having been contributed to the Roth IRA for 1998 and not to the traditional IRA. As a result, for Federal tax purposes, the contribution is treated as having been made to the Roth IRA for 1998 and not to the traditional IRA. The result would be the same if the conversion amount had been transferred in a tax-free transfer to another traditional IRA prior to the recharacterization.

*Example (3).* The facts are the same as in Example 2, except that the $2,000 regular contribution is initially made to a Roth IRA and the recharacterizing transfer is made to a traditional IRA. On the individual's Federal income tax return for 1998, he treats the $2,000 as having been contributed to the traditional IRA for 1998 and not the Roth IRA. As a result, for Federal tax purposes, the contribution is treated as having been made to the traditional IRA for 1998 and not the Roth IRA. The result would be the same if the contribution had been transferred in a tax-free transfer to another Roth IRA prior to the recharacterization, except that the only Roth IRA trustee the individual must notify is the one actually making the recharacterization transfer.

*Example (4).* In 1998, an individual receives a distribution from traditional IRA 1 and contributes the entire amount to traditional IRA 2 in a rollover contribution described in section 408(d)(3). In this case, the individual cannot elect to recharacterize the contribution by transferring the contribution amount, plus net income, to a Roth IRA, because an amount contributed to an IRA in a tax-free transfer cannot be recharacterized. However, the individual may convert (other than by recharacterization) the amount in traditional IRA 2 to a Roth IRA at any time, provided the requirements of § 1.408A-4 A-1 are satisfied.

---

T.D. 8816, 2/3/99, amend T.D. 9056, 5/2/2003.

---

**§ 1.408A-6 Distributions.**

This section sets forth the following questions and answers that provide rules regarding distributions from Roth IRAs:

Q-1. How are distributions from Roth IRAs taxed?

A-1. (a) The taxability of a distribution from a Roth IRA generally depends on whether or not the distribution is a qualified distribution. This A-1 provides rules for qualified distributions and certain other nontaxable distributions. A-4 of this section provides rules for the taxability of distributions that are not qualified distributions.

(b) A distribution from a Roth IRA is not includible in the owner's gross income if it is a qualified distribution or to the extent that it is a return of the owner's contributions to the Roth IRA (determined in accordance with A-8 of this section). A qualified distribution is one that is both—

(1) Made after a 5-taxable-year period (defined in A-2 of this section); and

(2) Made on or after the date on which the owner attains age 59½, made to a beneficiary or the estate of the owner on or after the date of the owner's death, attributable to the owner's being disabled within the meaning of section 72(m)(7), or to which section 72(t)(2)(F) applies (exception for first-time home purchase).

(c) An amount distributed from a Roth IRA will not be included in gross income to the extent it is rolled over to another Roth IRA on a tax-free basis under the rules of sections 408(d)(3) and 408A(e).

(d) Contributions that are returned to the Roth IRA owner in accordance with section 408(d)(4) (corrective distributions) are not includible in gross income, but any net income required to be distributed under section 408(d)(4) together with the contributions is includible in gross income for the taxable year in which the contributions were made.

Q-2. When does the 5-taxable-year period described in A-1 of this section (relating to qualified distributions) begin and end?

A-2. The 5-taxable-year period described in A-1 of this section begins on the first day of the individual's taxable year for which the first regular contribution is made to any Roth IRA of the individual or, if earlier, the first day of the individual's taxable year in which the first conversion contribution is made to any Roth IRA of the individual. The 5-taxable-year period ends on the last day of the individual's fifth consecutive taxable year beginning with the taxable year described in the preceding sentence. For example, if an individual whose taxable year is the calendar year makes a first-time regular Roth IRA contribution any time between January 1, 1998, and April 15, 1999, for 1998, the 5-taxable-year period begins on January 1, 1998. Thus, each Roth IRA owner has only one 5-taxable-year period described in A-1 of this section for all the Roth IRAs of which he or she is the owner. Further, because of the requirement of the 5-taxable-year period, no qualified distributions can occur before taxable years beginning in 2003. For purposes of this A-2, the amount of any contribution distributed as a corrective distribution under A-1(d) of this section is treated as if it was never contributed.

Q-3. If a distribution is made to an individual who is the sole beneficiary of his or her deceased spouse's Roth IRA and the individual is treating the Roth IRA as his or her own, can the distribution be a qualified distribution based on being made to a beneficiary on or after the owner's death?

A-3. No. If a distribution is made to an individual who is the sole beneficiary of his or her deceased spouse's Roth IRA and the individual is treating the Roth IRA as his or her own, then, in accordance with § 1.408A-2A-4, the distribution is treated as coming from the individual's own Roth IRA and not the deceased spouse's Roth IRA. Therefore, for purposes of determining whether the distribution is a qualified distribution, it is not treated as made to a beneficiary on or after the owner's death.

Q-4. How is a distribution from a Roth IRA taxed if it is not a qualified distribution?

A-4. A distribution that is not a qualified distribution, and is neither contributed to another Roth IRA in a qualified rollover contribution nor constitutes a corrective distribution, is includible in the owner's gross income to the extent that the amount of the distribution, when added to the amount of all prior distributions from the owner's Roth IRAs (whether or not they were qualified distributions) and reduced by the amount of those prior distributions previously includible in gross income, exceeds the owner's contributions to all his or her Roth IRAs. For purposes of this A-4, any amount distributed as a corrective distribution is treated as if it was never contributed.

Q-5. Will the additional tax under 72(t) apply to the amount of a distribution that is not a qualified distribution?

A-5. (a) The 10-percent additional tax under section 72(t) will apply (unless the distribution is excepted under section 72(t)) to any distribution from a Roth IRA includible in gross income.

(b) The 10-percent additional tax under section 72(t) also applies to a nonqualified distribution, even if it is not then includible in gross income, to the extent it is allocable to a conversion contribution, if the distribution is made within the 5-taxable-year period beginning with the first day of the individual's taxable year in which the conversion contribution was made. The 5-taxable-year period ends on the last day of the individual's fifth consecutive taxable year beginning with the taxable year described in the preceding sentence. For purposes of applying the tax, only the amount of the conversion contribution includible in gross income as a result of the conversion is taken into account. The exceptions under section 72(t) also apply to such a distribution.

(c) The 5-taxable-year period described in this A-5 for purposes of determining whether section 72(t) applies to a distribution allocable to a conversion contribution is separately determined for each conversion contribution, and need not be the same as the 5-taxable-year period used for purposes of determining whether a distribution is a qualified distribution under A-1(b) of this section. For example, if a calendar-year taxpayer who received a distribution from a traditional IRA on December 31, 1998, makes a conversion contribution by contributing the distributed amount to a Roth IRA on February 25, 1999 in a qualifying rollover contribution and makes a regular contribution for 1998 on the same date, the 5-taxable-year period for purposes of this A-5 begins on January 1, 1999, while the 5-taxable-year period for purposes of A-1(b) of this section begins on January 1, 1998.

Q-6. Is there a special rule for taxing distributions allocable to a 1998 conversion?

A-6. Yes. In the case of a distribution from a Roth IRA in 1998, 1999 or 2000 of amounts allocable to a 1998 conversion with respect to which the 4-year spread for the resultant income inclusion applies (see § 1.408A-4 A-8), any income deferred as a result of the election to years after the year of the distribution is accelerated so that it is includible in gross income in the year of the distribution up to the amount of the distribution allocable to the 1998 conversion (determined under A-8 of this section). This amount is in addition to the amount otherwise includible in the owner's gross income for that taxable year as a result of the conversion. However, this rule will not require the inclusion of any amount to the extent it exceeds the total amount of income required to be included over the 4-year period. The acceleration of income inclusion described in this A-6 applies in the case of a surviving spouse who elects to continue the 4-year spread in accordance with § 1.408A-4 A-11(b).

Q-7. Is the 5-taxable-year period described in A-1 of this section redetermined when a Roth IRA owner dies?

A-7. (a) No. The beginning of the 5-taxable-year period described in A-1 of this section is not redetermined when the Roth IRA owner dies. Thus, in determining the 5-taxable-year period, the period the Roth IRA is held in the name of a beneficiary, or in the name of a surviving spouse who treats the decedent's Roth IRA as his or her own, includes the period it was held by the decedent.

(b) The 5-taxable-year period for a Roth IRA held by an individual as a beneficiary of a deceased Roth IRA owner is determined independently of the 5-taxable-year period for the beneficiary's own Roth IRA. However, if a surviving spouse treats the Roth IRA as his or her own, the 5-taxable-year period with respect to any of the surviving spouse's Roth IRAs (including the one that the surviving spouse treats as his or her own) ends at the earlier of the end of either the 5-taxable-year period for the decedent or the 5-taxable-year period applicable to the spouse's own Roth IRAs.

Q-8. How is it determined whether an amount distributed from a Roth IRA is allocated to regular contributions, conversion contributions, or earnings?

A-8. (a) Any amount distributed from an individual's Roth IRA is treated as made in the following order (determined as of the end of a taxable year and exhausting each category before moving to the following category)—

(1) From regular contributions;

(2) From conversion contributions, on a first-in-first-out basis; and

(3) From earnings.

(b) To the extent a distribution is treated as made from a particular conversion contribution, it is treated as made first from the portion, if any, that was includible in gross income as a result of the conversion.

Q-9. Are there special rules for determining the source of distributions under A-8 of this section?

A-9. Yes. For purposes of determining the source of distributions, the following rules apply:

(a) All distributions from all an individual's Roth IRAs made during a taxable year are aggregated.

(b) All regular contributions made for the same taxable year to all the individual's Roth IRAs are aggregated and added to the undistributed total regular contributions for prior taxable years. Regular contributions for a taxable year include contributions made in the following taxable year that are identified as made for the taxable year in accordance with § 1.408A-3 A-2. For example, a regular contribution made in 1999 for 1998 is aggregated with the contributions made in 1998 for 1998.

(c) All conversion contributions received during the same taxable year by all the individual's Roth IRAs are aggregated. Notwithstanding the preceding sentence, all conversion contributions made by an individual during 1999 that were distributed from a traditional IRA in 1998 and with respect to which the 4-year spread applies are treated for purposes of A-8(b) of this section as contributed to the individual's Roth IRAs prior to any other conversion contributions made by the individual during 1999.

(d) A distribution from an individual's Roth IRA that is rolled over to another Roth IRA of the individual in accordance with section 408A(e) is disregarded for purposes of determining the amount of both contributions and distributions.

(e) Any amount distributed as a corrective distribution (including net income), as described in A-1(d) of this section, is disregarded in determining the amount of contributions, earnings, and distributions.

(f) If an individual recharacterizes a contribution made to a traditional IRA (FIRST IRA) by transferring the contribution to a Roth IRA (SECOND IRA) in accordance with § 1.408A-5, then, pursuant to § 1.408A-5 A-3, the contribution to the Roth IRA is taken into account for the same taxable year for which it would have been taken into account if the contribution had originally been made to the Roth IRA and had never been contributed to the traditional IRA. Thus, the contribution to the Roth IRA is treated as contributed to the Roth IRA on the same date and for the same taxable year that the contribution was made to the traditional IRA.

(g) If an individual recharacterizes a regular or conversion contribution made to a Roth IRA (FIRST IRA) by transferring the contribution to a traditional IRA (SECOND IRA) in accordance with § 1.408A-5, then pursuant to § 1.408A-5 A-3, the contribution to the Roth IRA and the recharacterizing transfer are disregarded in determining the amount of both contributions and distributions for the taxable year with respect to which the original contribution was made to the Roth IRA.

(h) Pursuant to § 1.408A-5 A-3, the effect of income or loss (determined in accordance with § 1.408A-5 A-2) occurring after the contribution to the FIRST IRA is disregarded in determining the amounts described in paragraphs (f) and (g) of this A-9. Thus, for purposes of paragraphs (f) and (g), the amount of the contribution is determined based on the original contribution.

Q-10. Are there examples to illustrate the ordering rules described in A-8 and A-9 of this section?

A-10. Yes. The following examples illustrate these ordering rules:

*Example (1).* In 1998, individual B converts $80,000 in his traditional IRA to a Roth IRA. B has a basis of $20,000 in the conversion amount and so must include the remaining $60,000 in gross income. He decides to spread the $60,000 income by including $15,000 in each of the 4 years 1998-2001, under the rules of § 1.408A-4 A-8. B also makes a regular contribution of $2,000 in 1998. If a distribution of $2,000 is made to B anytime in 1998, it will be treated as made entirely from the regular contributions, so there will be no Federal income tax consequences as a result of the distribution.

*Example (2).* The facts are the same as in Example 1, except that the distribution made in 1998 is $5,000. The distribution is treated as made from $2,000 of regular contributions and $3,000 of conversion contributions that were includible in gross income. As a result, B must include $18,000 in gross income for 1998: $3,000 as a result of the acceleration of amounts that otherwise would have been included in later years under the 4-year-spread rule and $15,000 includible under the regular 4-year-spread rule. In addition, because the $3,000 is allocable to a conversion made within the previous 5 taxable years, the 10-percent additional tax under section 72(t) would apply to this $3,000 distribution for 1998, unless an exception applies. Under the 4-year-spread rule, B would now include in gross income $15,000 for 1999 and 2000, but only $12,000 for 2001, because of the accelerated inclusion of the $3,000 distribution.

*Example (3).* The facts are the same as in Example 1, except that B makes an additional $2,000 regular contribution in 1999 and he does not take a distribution in 1998. In 1999, the entire balance in the account, $90,000 ($84,000 of contributions and $6,000 of earnings), is distributed to B. The distribution is treated as made from $4,000 of regular contributions, $60,000 of conversion contributions that were includible in gross income, $20,000 of conversion contributions that were not includible in gross income, and $6,000 of earnings. Because a distribution has been made within the 4-year-spread period, B must accelerate the income inclusion under the 4-year-spread rule and must include in gross income the $45,000 remaining under the 4-year-spread rule in addition to the $6,000 of earnings. Because $60,000 of the distribution is allocable to a conversion made within the previous 5 taxable years, it is subject to the 10-percent additional tax under section 72(t) as if it were includible in gross income for 1999, unless an exception applies. The $6,000 allocable to earnings would be subject to the tax under section 72(t), unless an exception applies. Under the 4-year-spread rule, no amount would be includible in gross income for 2000 or 2001 because the entire amount of the conversion that was includible in gross income has already been included.

*Example (4).* The facts are the same as in Example 1, except that B also makes a $2,000 regular contribution in each year 1999 through 2002 and he does not take a distribution in 1998. A distribution of $85,000 is made to B in 2002. The distribution is treated as made from the $10,000 of regular contributions (the total regular contributions made in the years 1998-2002), $60,000 of conversion contributions that were includible in gross income, and $15,000 of conversion contributions that were not includible in gross income. As a result, no amount of the distribution is includible in gross income; however, because the distribution is allocable to a conversion made within the previous 5 years, the $60,000 is subject to the 10-percent additional tax under section 72(t) as if it were includible in gross income for 2002, unless an exception applies.

*Example (5).* The facts are the same as in Example 4, except no distribution occurs in 2002. In 2003, the entire balance in the account, $170,000 ($90,000 of contributions and $80,000 of earnings), is distributed to B. The distribution is treated as made from $10,000 of regular contributions, $60,000 of conversion contributions that were includible in gross income, $20,000 of conversion contributions that were not includible in gross income, and $80,000 of earnings. As a result, for 2003, B must include in gross income the $80,000 allocable to earnings, unless the distribution is a qualified distribution; and if it is not a qualified distribution, the $80,000 would be subject to the 10-percent additional tax under section 72(t), unless an exception applies.

*Example (6).* Individual C converts $20,000 to a Roth IRA in 1998 and $15,000 (in which amount C had a basis of $2,000) to another Roth IRA in 1999. No other contributions are made. In 2003, a $30,000 distribution, that is not a qualified distribution, is made to C. The distribution is treated as made from $20,000 of the 1998 conversion contribution and $10,000 of the 1999 conversion contribution that was includible in gross income. As a result, for 2003, no amount is includible in gross income; however, because $10,000 is allocable to a conversion contribution made within the previous 5 taxable years, that amount is subject to the 10-percent additional tax under section 72(t) as if the amount were includible in gross income for 2003, unless an exception applies. The result would be the same whichever of C's Roth IRAs made the distribution.

*Example (7).* The facts are the same as in Example 6, except that the distribution is a qualified distribution. The result is the same as in Example 6, except that no amount would be subject to the 10-percent additional tax under section 72(t), because, to be a qualified distribution, the distribution must be made on or after the date on which the owner attains age 59½, made to a beneficiary or the estate of the owner on or after the date of the owner's death, attributable to the owner's being disabled within the meaning of section 72(m)(7), or to which section 72(t)(2)(F) applies (exception for a first-time home purchase). Under section 72(t)(2), each of these conditions is also an exception to the tax under section 72(t).

*Example (8).* Individual D makes a $2,000 regular contribution to a traditional IRA on January 1, 1999, for 1998. On April 15, 1999, when the $2,000 has increased to $2,500, D recharacterizes the contribution by transferring the $2,500 to a Roth IRA (pursuant to § 1.408A-5 A-1). In this case, D's regular contribution to the Roth IRA for 1998 is $2,000. The $500 of earnings is not treated as a contribution to the Roth IRA. The results would be the same if the $2,000 had decreased to $1,500 prior to the recharacterization.

*Example (9).* In December 1998, individual E receives a distribution from his traditional IRA of $300,000 and in January 1999 he contributes the $300,000 to a Roth IRA as a conversion contribution. In April 1999, when the $300,000 has increased to $350,000, E recharacterizes the conversion contribution by transferring the $350,000 to a traditional IRA. In this case, E's conversion contribution for 1998 is $0, because the $300,000 conversion contribution and the earnings of $50,000 are disregarded. The results would be the same if the $300,000 had decreased to $250,000 prior to the recharacterization. Further, since the conversion is disregarded, the $300,000 is not includible in gross income in 1998.

Q-11. If the owner of a Roth IRA dies prior to the end of the 5-taxable-year period described in A-1 of this section (relating to qualified distributions) or prior to the end of the

5-taxable-year period described in A-5 of this section (relating to conversions), how are different types of contributions in the Roth IRA allocated to multiple beneficiaries?

A-11. Each type of contribution is allocated to each beneficiary on a pro-rata basis. Thus, for example, if a Roth IRA owner dies in 1999, when the Roth IRA contains a regular contribution of $2,000, a conversion contribution of $6,000 and earnings of $1,000, and the owner leaves his Roth IRA equally to four children, each child will receive one quarter of each type of contribution. Pursuant to the ordering rules in A-8 of this section, an immediate distribution of $2,000 to one of the children will be deemed to consist of $500 of regular contributions and $1,500 of conversion contributions. A beneficiary's inherited Roth IRA may not be aggregated with any other Roth IRA maintained by such beneficiary (except for other Roth IRAs the beneficiary inherited from the same decedent), unless the beneficiary, as the spouse of the decedent and sole beneficiary of the Roth IRA, elects to treat the Roth IRA as his or her own (see A-7 and A-14 of this section).

Q-12. How do the withholding rules under section 3405 apply to Roth IRAs?

A-12. Distributions from a Roth IRA are distributions from an individual retirement plan for purposes of section 3405 and thus are designated distributions unless one of the exceptions in section 3405(e)(1) applies. Pursuant to section 3405(a) and (b), nonperiodic distributions from a Roth IRA are subject to 10-percent withholding by the payor and periodic payments are subject to withholding as if the payments were wages. However, an individual can elect to have no amount withheld in accordance with section 3405(a)(2) and (b)(2).

Q-13. Do the withholding rules under section 3405 apply to conversions?

A-13. Yes. A conversion by any method described in § 1.408A-4 A-1 is considered a designated distribution subject to section 3405. However, a conversion occurring in 1998 by means of a trustee-to-trustee transfer of an amount from a traditional IRA to a Roth IRA established with the same or a different trustee is not required to be treated as a designated distribution for purposes of section 3405. Consequently, no withholding is required with respect to such a conversion (without regard to whether or not the individual elected to have no withholding).

Q-14. What minimum distribution rules apply to a Roth IRA?

A-14. (a) No minimum distributions are required to be made from a Roth IRA under section 408(a)(6) and (b)(3) (which generally incorporate the provisions of section 401(a)(9)) while the owner is alive. The post-death minimum distribution rules under section 401(a)(9)(B) that apply to traditional IRAs, with the exception of the at-least-as-rapidly rule described in section 401(a)(9)(B)(i), also apply to Roth IRAs.

(b) The minimum distribution rules apply to the Roth IRA as though the Roth IRA owner died before his or her required beginning date. Thus, generally, the entire interest in the Roth IRA must be distributed by the end of the fifth calendar year after the year of the owner's death unless the interest is payable to a designated beneficiary over a period not greater than that beneficiary's life expectancy and distribution commences before the end of the calendar year following the year of death. If the sole beneficiary is the decedent's spouse, such spouse may delay distributions until the decedent would have attained age 70½ or may treat the Roth IRA as his or her own.

(c) Distributions to a beneficiary that are not qualified distributions will be includible in the beneficiary's gross income according to the rules in A-4 of this section.

Q-15. Does section 401(a)(9) apply separately to Roth IRAs and individual retirement plans that are not Roth IRAs?

A-15. Yes. An individual required to receive minimum distributions from his or her own traditional or SIMPLE IRA cannot choose to take the amount of the minimum distributions from any Roth IRA. Similarly, an individual required to receive minimum distributions from a Roth IRA cannot choose to take the amount of the minimum distributions from a traditional or SIMPLE IRA. In addition, an individual required to receive minimum distributions as a beneficiary under a Roth IRA can only satisfy the minimum distributions for one Roth IRA by distributing from another Roth IRA if the Roth IRAs were inherited from the same decedent.

Q-16. How is the basis of property distributed from a Roth IRA determined for purposes of a subsequent disposition?

A-16. The basis of property distributed from a Roth IRA is its fair market value (FMV) on the date of distribution, whether or not the distribution is a qualified distribution. Thus, for example, if a distribution consists of a share of stock in XYZ Corp. with an FMV of $40.00 on the date of distribution, for purposes of determining gain or loss on the subsequent sale of the share of XYZ Corp. stock, it has a basis of $40.00.

Q-17. What is the effect of distributing an amount from a Roth IRA and contributing it to another type of retirement plan other than a Roth IRA?

A-17. Any amount distributed from a Roth IRA and contributed to another type of retirement plan (other than a Roth IRA) is treated as a distribution from the Roth IRA that is neither a rollover contribution for purposes of section 408(d)(3) nor a qualified rollover contribution within the meaning of section 408A(e) to the other type of retirement plan. This treatment also applies to any amount transferred from a Roth IRA to any other type of retirement plan unless the transfer is a recharacterization described in § 1.408A-5.

Q-18. Can an amount be transferred directly from an education IRA to a Roth IRA (or distributed from an education IRA and rolled over to a Roth IRA)?

A-18. No amount may be transferred directly from an education IRA to a Roth IRA. A transfer of funds (or distribution and rollover) from an education IRA to a Roth IRA constitutes a distribution from the education IRA and a regular contribution to the Roth IRA (rather than a qualified rollover contribution to the Roth IRA).

Q-19. What are the Federal income tax consequences of a Roth IRA owner transferring his or her Roth IRA to another individual by gift?

A-19. A Roth IRA owner's transfer of his or her Roth IRA to another individual by gift constitutes an assignment of the owner's rights under the Roth IRA. At the time of the gift, the assets of the Roth IRA are deemed to be distributed to the owner and, accordingly, are treated as no longer held in a Roth IRA. In the case of any such gift of a Roth IRA made prior to October 1, 1998, if the entire interest in the Roth IRA is reconveyed to the Roth IRA owner prior to January 1, 1999, the Internal Revenue Service will treat the gift and reconveyance as never having occurred for estate tax, gift tax, and generation-skipping tax purposes and for purposes of this A-19.

T.D. 8816, 2/3/99.

### § 1.408A-7 Reporting.

This section sets forth the following questions and answers that relate to the reporting requirements applicable to Roth IRAs:

Q-1. What reporting requirements apply to Roth IRAs?

A-1. Generally, the reporting requirements applicable to IRAs other than Roth IRAs also apply to Roth IRAs, except that, pursuant to section 408A(d)(3)(D), the trustee of a Roth IRA must include on Forms 1099-R and 5498 additional information as described in the instructions thereto. Any conversion of amounts from an IRA other than a Roth IRA to a Roth IRA is treated as a distribution for which a Form 1099-R must be filed by the trustee maintaining the non-Roth IRA. In addition, the owner of such IRAs must report the conversion by completing Form 8606. In the case of a recharacterization described in § 1.408A-5 A-1, IRA owners must report such transactions in the manner prescribed in the instructions to the applicable Federal tax forms.

Q-2. Can a trustee rely on reasonable representations of a Roth IRA contributor or distributee for purposes of fulfilling reporting obligations?

A-2. A trustee maintaining a Roth IRA is permitted to rely on reasonable representations of a Roth IRA contributor or distributee for purposes of fulfilling reporting obligations.

T.D. 8816, 2/3/99.

### § 1.408A-8 Definitions.

This section sets forth the following question and answer that provides definitions of terms used in the provisions of §§ 1.408A-1 through 1.408A-7 and this section:

Q-1. Are there any special definitions that govern in applying the provisions of §§ 1.408A-1 through 1.408A-7 and this section?

A-1. Yes, the following definitions govern in applying the provisions of §§ 1.408A-1 through 1.408A-7 and this section. Unless the context indicates otherwise, the use of a particular term excludes the use of the other terms.

**(a) Different types of IRAs.** *(1) IRA.* Sections 408(a) and (b), respectively, describe an individual retirement account and an individual retirement annuity. The term *IRA* means an IRA described in either section 408(a) or (b), including each IRA described in paragraphs (a)(2) through (5) of this A-1. However, the term *IRA* does not include an education IRA described in section 530.

*(2) Traditional IRA.* The term *traditional IRA* means an individual retirement account or individual retirement annuity described in section 408(a) or (b), respectively. This term includes a SEP IRA but does not include a SIMPLE IRA or a Roth IRA.

*(3) SEP IRA.* Section 408(k) describes a simplified employee pension (SEP) as an employer-sponsored plan under which an employer can make contributions to IRAs established for its employees. The term *SEP IRA* means an IRA that receives contributions made under a SEP. The term SEP includes a salary reduction SEP (SARSEP) described in section 408(k)(6).

*(4) SIMPLE IRA.* Section 408(p) describes a SIMPLE IRA Plan as an employer-sponsored plan under which an employer can make contributions to SIMPLE IRAs established for its employees. The term *SIMPLE IRA* means an IRA to which the only contributions that can be made are contributions under a SIMPLE IRA Plan or rollovers or transfers from another SIMPLE IRA.

*(5) Roth IRA.* The term *Roth IRA* means an IRA that meets the requirements of section 408A.

**(b) Other defined terms or phrases.** *(1) 4-year spread.* The term *4-year spread* is described in § 1.408A-4 A-8.

*(2) Conversion.* The term *conversion* means a transaction satisfying the requirements of § 1.408A-4 A-1.

*(3) Conversion amount or conversion contribution.* The term *conversion amount or conversion contribution* is the amount of a distribution and contribution with respect to which a conversion described in § 1.408A-4 A-1 is made.

*(4) Failed conversion.* The term *failed conversion* means a transaction in which an individual contributes to a Roth IRA an amount transferred or distributed from a traditional IRA or Simple IRA (including a transfer by redesignation) in a transaction that does not constitute a conversion under § 1.408A-4 A-1.

*(5) Modified AGI.* The term *modified AGI* is defined in § 1.408A-3 A-5.

*(6) Recharacterization.* The term *recharacterization* means a transaction described in § 1.408A-5 A-1.

*(7) Recharacterized amount or recharacterized contribution.* The term *recharacterized amount or recharacterized contribution* means an amount or contribution treated as contributed to an IRA other than the one to which it was originally contributed pursuant to a recharacterization described in § 1.408A-5 A-1.

*(8) Taxable conversion amount.* The term *taxable conversion amount* means the portion of a conversion amount includible in income on account of a conversion, determined under the rules of section 408(d)(1) and (2).

*(9) Tax-free transfer.* The term *tax-free transfer* means a tax-free rollover described in section 402(c), 402(e)(6), 403(a)(4), 403(a)(5), 403(b)(8), 403(b)(10) or 408(d)(3), or a tax-free trustee-to-trustee transfer.

*(10) Treat an IRA as his or her own.* The phrase *treat an IRA as his or her own* means to treat an IRA for which a surviving spouse is the sole beneficiary as his or her own IRA after the death of the IRA owner in accordance with the terms of the IRA instrument or in the manner provided in the regulations under section 408(a)(6) or (b)(3).

*(11) Trustee.* The term *trustee* includes a custodian or issuer (in the case of an annuity) of an IRA (except where the context clearly indicates otherwise).

T.D. 8816, 2/3/99.

### § 1.408A-9 Effective date.

This section contains the following question and answer providing the effective date of § 1.408A-1 through 1.408A-8:

Q-1. To what taxable years do §§ 1.408A-1 through 1.408A-8 apply?

A-1. Sections 1.408A-1 through 1.408A-8 apply to taxable years beginning on or after January 1, 1998.

T.D. 8816, 2/3/99.

### § 1.408A-10 Coordination between designated Roth accounts and Roth IRAs.

Q-1. Can an eligible rollover distribution, within the meaning of section 402(c)(4), from a designated Roth account, as defined in A-1 of § 1.402A-1, be rolled over to a Roth IRA?

A-1. Yes. An eligible rollover distribution, within the meaning of section 402(c)(4), from a designated Roth account may be rolled over to a Roth IRA. For purposes of this section, a designated Roth account means a designated Roth account as defined in A-1 of § 1.402A-1.

Q-2. Can an eligible rollover distribution from a designated Roth account be rolled over to a Roth IRA even if the distributee is not otherwise eligible to make regular or conversion contributions to a Roth IRA?

A-2. Yes. An individual may establish a Roth IRA and roll over an eligible rollover distribution from a designated Roth account to that Roth IRA even if such individual is not eligible to make regular contributions or conversion contributions (as described in section 408A(c)(2) and (d)(3), respectively) because of the modified adjusted gross income limits in section 408A(b)(3).

Q-3. For purposes of the ordering rules on distributions from Roth IRAs, what portion of a distribution from a rollover contribution from a designated Roth account is treated as contributions?

A-3. (a) Under section 408A(d)(4), distributions from Roth IRAs are deemed to consist first of regular contributions, then of conversion contributions, and finally, of earnings. For purposes of section 408A(d)(4), the amount of a rollover contribution that is treated as a regular contribution is the portion of the distribution that is treated as investment in the contract under A-6 of § 1.402A-1, and the remainder of the rollover contribution is treated as earnings. Thus, the entire amount of any qualified distribution from a designated Roth account that is rolled over into a Roth IRA is treated as a regular contribution to the Roth IRA. Accordingly, a subsequent distribution from the Roth IRA in the amount of that rollover contribution is not includible in gross income under the rules of A-8 of § 1.408A-6.

(b) If the entire account balance of a designated Roth account is distributed to an employee and only a portion of the distribution is rolled over to a Roth IRA within the 60-day period described in section 402(c)(3), and at the time of the distribution, the investment in the contract exceeds the balance in the designated Roth account, the portion of investment in the contract that exceeds the amount used to determine the taxable amount of the distribution is treated as a regular contribution for purposes of section 408A(d)(4).

Q-4. In the case of a rollover from a designated Roth account to a Roth IRA, when does the 5-taxable-year period (described in section 408A(d)(2)(B) and A-1 of § 1.408A-6) for determining qualified distributions from a Roth IRA begin?

A-4. (a) The 5-taxable-year period for determining a qualified distribution from a Roth IRA (described in section 408A(d)(2)(B) and A-1 of § 1.408A-6) begins with the earlier of the taxable year described in A-2 of § 1.408A-6 or the taxable year in which a rollover contribution from a designated Roth account is made to a Roth IRA. The 5-taxable-year period described in this A-4 and the 5-taxable-year period of participation described in A-4 of § 1.402A-1 are determined independently.

(b) The following examples illustrate the application of this A-4:

Example 1. Employee D began making designated Roth contributions under his employer's 401(k) plan in 2006. Employee D, who is over age 59½, takes a distribution from D's designated Roth account in 2008, prior to the end of the 5-taxable-year period of participation used to determine qualified distributions from a designated Roth account. The distribution is an eligible rollover distribution and D rolls it over in accordance with sections 402(c) and 402A(c)(3) to D's Roth IRA, which was established in 2003. Any subsequent distribution from the Roth IRA of the amount rolled in, plus earnings thereon, would not be includible in gross income (because it would be a qualified distribution within the meaning of section 408A(d)(2)).

Example 2. The facts are the same as in Example 1, except that the Roth IRA is D's first Roth IRA and is established with the rollover in 2008, which is the only contribution made to the Roth IRA. If a distribution is made from the Roth IRA prior to the end of the 5-taxable-year period used to determine qualified distributions from a Roth IRA (which begins in 2008, the year of the rollover which established the Roth IRA) the distribution would not be a qualified distribution within the meaning of section 408A(d)(2), and any amount of the distribution that exceeded the portion of the rollover contribution that consisted of investment in the contract is includible in D's gross income.

Example 3. The facts are the same as in Example 2, except that the distribution from the designated Roth account and the rollover to the Roth IRA occur in 2011 (after the end of the 5-taxable-year period of participation used to determine qualified distributions from a designated Roth account). If a distribution is made from the Roth IRA prior to the expiration of the 5-taxable-year period used to determine qualified distributions from a Roth IRA, the distribution would not be a qualified distribution within the meaning of section 408A(d)(2), and any amount of the distribution that exceeded the amount rolled in is includible in D's gross income.

Q-5. Can amounts distributed from a Roth IRA be rolled over to a designated Roth account as defined in A-1 of § 1.402A-1?

A-5. No. Amounts distributed from a Roth IRA may be rolled over or transferred only to another Roth IRA and are not permitted to be rolled over to a designated Roth account under a section 401(a) or section 403(b) plan.

The same rule applies even if all the amounts in the Roth IRA are attributable to a rollover distribution from a designated Roth account in a plan.

Q-6. When is this § 1.408A-10 applicable?

A-6. The rules of this § 1.408A-10 apply for taxable years beginning on or after January 1, 2006.

T.D. 9324, 4/27/2007.

### § 1.409-1 Retirement bonds.

***Caution:*** The Treasury has not yet amended Reg § 1.409-1 to reflect changes made by P.L. 98-369.

**(a) In general** Section 409 authorizes the issuance of bonds under the Second Liberty Bond Act the purchase price of which would be deductible under section 219. Section 409 also prescribes the tax treatment of such bonds. See paragraph (b) of this section.

**(b) Income tax treatment of bonds.** *(1) General rule.* Except as provided in paragraph (b)(2) of this section, the entire proceeds upon redemption of a retirement bond described in section 409(a) shall be included in the gross income of the taxpayer entitled to such proceeds. If a bond has not been tendered for redemption by the registered owner before the close of the taxable year in which he attains age 70½, he must include in his gross income for such taxable year the amount of the proceeds he would have received if the bond had been redeemed at age 70½. The provisions of sections 72 and 1232 do not apply to a retirement bond.

*(2) Exceptions.* (i) If a retirement bond is redeemed within 12 months after the issue date, the proceeds are excluded from gross income if no deduction is allowed under section 219 on account of the purchase of such bond. For definition of issue date, see 31 CFR 346.1(c).

(ii) If a retirement bond is redeemed after the close of the taxable year in which the registered owner attains age 70½ the proceeds from the redemption of the bond are excludable from the gross income of the registered owner or his beneficiary to the extent that such proceeds were includible in the gross income of the registered owner for such taxable year.

(iii) If a retirement bond is surrendered for reissuance in the same or lesser face amount, the difference between current redemption value of the bond surrendered for reissuance and the current surrender value of the bond reissued is includible in the gross income of the registered owner.

*(3) Basis.* The basis of a retirement bond is zero.

**(c) Rollover.** The first sentence of paragraph (b)(1) of this section shall not apply in any case in which a retirement bond is redeemed by the registered owner before the close of the taxable year in which he attains the age of 70½ if he transfers the entire amount of the proceeds of such redemption to—

*(1)* An individual retirement account described in section 408(a) or an individual retirement annuity described in section 408(b) (other than an endowment contract described in § 1.408-3(e)), or

*(2)* An employees' trust which is described in section 401(a) which is exempt from tax under section 501(a), or an annuity plan described in section 403(a), for the benefit of the registered owner, on or before the 60th day after the day on which he received the proceeds of such redemption. This subparagraph shall not apply in the case of a transfer to a trust or plan described in (c)(2) of this section unless no part of the purchase price of the retirement bond redeemed is attributable to any source other than a rollover contribution from such an employees' trust or annuity plan (other than an annuity plan or employees' trust forming part of a plan under which the individual was an employee within the meaning of section 401(c)(1) at the time contributions were made on his behalf under the plan).

**(d) Additional tax.** *(1) Early redemption.* Except as provided in paragraph (d)(2) of this section, under section 409(c) if a retirement bond is redeemed by the registered owner before he attains age 59½, his tax under chapter 1 of the Code is increased by an amount equal to 10 percent of the proceeds of the redemption includible in his gross income for the taxable year. Except in the case of the credits allowable under sections 31, 39, or 42, no credit can be used to offset the tax described in the preceding sentence.

*(2) Limitations.* Paragraph (d)(1) of this section shall not apply if—

(i) During the taxable year of the registered owner in which a retirement bond is redeemed, the registered owner becomes disabled within the meaning of section 72(m)(7), or

(ii) A retirement bond is tendered for redemption in accordance with paragraph (b)(2)(i) of this section.

T.D. 7714, 8/7/80.

PAR. 7. Paragraph (b)(1) of § 1.409-1 is amended by removing the word "1232" from the last sentence thereof and adding in its place the phrase "1271 through 1275".

**Proposed § 1.409-1 [Amended.]** [*For Preamble, see ¶ 151,065*]

• ***Caution:*** Prop reg § 1.482-2 was finalized by T.D. 8204, 5/20/88. Prop regs §§ 1.163-7, 1.446-2, 1.483-1 through -5, 1.1001-1, 1.1012-1, 1.1271 through -3, 1.1272-1, 1.1273-1, 1.1273-2, 1.1274-1 throught -7, 1.1274A-1, 1.1275-1 through -3, and 1.1275-5 were withdrawn by the Treasury on 12/22/92, 57 Fed. Reg. 67050. Prop reg § 1.1275-4 was superseded by the Treasury on 12/16/94, Fed. Reg. 59, 64884, which was finalized by T.D. 8674, 6/11/96.

PAR. 11. Section 1.409-1 is amended by adding "or 220" after 219 each place it appears and by revising paragraph (c) to read as follows:

**Proposed § 1.409-1 Retirement bonds.** [*For Preamble, see ¶ 150,703*]

* * * * *

**(c) Rollover.** The first sentence of paragraph (b)(1) of this section shall not apply in any case in which a retirement bond is redeemed by the registered owner before the close of the taxable year in which he attains the age of 70½ if he transfers the entire amount of the proceeds of such redemption to—

*(1)* An individual retirement account described in section 408(a) or an individual retirement annuity described in section 408(b) (other than an endowment contract described in § 1.408-3(e)), or

*(2)* An employees' trust which is described in section 401(a) which is exempt from tax under section 501(a), an annuity plan described in section 403(a), or an annuity contract described in section 403(b), for the benefit of the registered owner,

on or before the 60th day after the day on which he received the proceeds of such redemption. This paragraph does not apply in the case of a transfer to such an employees' trust or such an annuity plan unless no part of the value of such proceeds is attributable to any source other than a rollover contribution from such an employees' trust or annuity plan (other than an annuity plan or a trust forming part of a plan under which the individual was an employee within the meaning of section 401(c)(1) at the time contributions were made on his behalf under the plan). This paragraph does not apply in the case of a transfer to an annuity contract described in section 403(b) unless no part of the value of such proceeds is attributable to any source other than a rollover contribution from such annuity contract.

**§ 1.409(p)-1 Prohibited allocation of securities in an S corporation.**

**(a) Organization of this section and definition.** *(1) Organization of this section.* Section 409(p) applies if a nonallocation year occurs in an ESOP that holds shares of stock of an S corporation that are employer securities. Paragraph (b) of this section sets forth the general rule under section 409(p)(1) and (2) prohibiting any accrual or allocation to a disqualified person in a nonallocation year. Paragraph (c) of this section sets forth rules under section 409(p)(3), (5), and (7) for determining whether a year is a nonallocation year, generally based on whether disqualified persons own at least 50 percent of the shares of the S corporation, either taking into account only the outstanding shares of the S corporation (including shares held by the ESOP) or taking into account both the outstanding shares and synthetic equity of the S corporation. Paragraphs (d), (e), and (f) of this section contain definitions of disqualified person under section 409(p)(4) and (5), deemed-owned ESOP shares under section 409(p)(4)(C), and synthetic equity under section 409(p)(6)(C). Paragraph (g) of this section contains a standard for determining when the principal purpose of the ownership structure of an S corporation constitutes an avoidance or evasion of section 409(p).

*(2) Definitions.* The following definitions apply for purposes of section 409(p) and this section, as well as for purposes of section 4979A, which imposes an excise tax on certain events.

(i) Deemed-owned ESOP shares has the meaning set forth in paragraph (e) of this section.

(ii) Disqualified person has the meaning set forth in paragraph (d) of this section.

(iii) Employer has the meaning set forth in § 1.410(b)-9.

(iv) Employer securities means employer securities within the meaning of section 409(l).

(v) ESOP means an employee stock ownership plan within the meaning of section 4975(e)(7).

(vi) Prohibited allocation has the meaning set forth in paragraph (b)(2) of this section.

(vii) S corporation means S corporation within the meaning of section 1361.

(viii) Synthetic equity has the meaning set forth in paragraph (f) of this section.

**(b) Prohibited allocation in a nonallocation year.** *(1) General rule.* Section 409(p)(1) provides that an ESOP holding employer securities consisting of stock in an S corporation must provide that no portion of the assets of the plan attributable to (or allocable in lieu of) such employer securities may, during a nonallocation year, accrue under the ESOP, or be allocated directly or indirectly under any plan of the employer (including the ESOP) meeting the requirements of section 401(a), for the benefit of any disqualified person.

*(2) Additional rules.* (i) Prohibited allocation definition. For purposes of section 409(p) and this section, a prohibited allocation means an impermissible accrual or an impermissible allocation. Whether there is impermissible accrual is determined under paragraph (b)(2)(ii) of this section and whether there is an impermissible allocation is determined under paragraph (b)(2)(iii) of this section. The amount of the prohibited allocation is equal to the sum of the amount of the impermissible accrual plus the amount of the impermissible allocation.

(ii) Impermissible accrual. There is an impermissible accrual to the extent that employer securities consisting of stock in an S corporation owned by the ESOP and any assets attributable thereto are held under the ESOP for the benefit of a disqualified person during a nonallocation year. For this purpose, assets attributable to stock in an S corporation owned by an ESOP include any distributions, within the meaning of section 1368, made on S corporation stock held in a disqualified person's account in the ESOP (including earnings thereon), plus any proceeds from the sale of S corporation securities held for a disqualified person's account in the ESOP (including any earnings thereon). Thus, in the event of a nonallocation year, all S corporation shares and all other ESOP assets attributable to S corporation stock, including distributions, sales proceeds, and earnings on either distributions or proceeds, held for the account of such disqualified person in the ESOP during that year are an impermissible accrual for the benefit of that person, whether attributable to contributions in the current year or in prior years.

(iii) Impermissible allocation. An impermissible allocation occurs during a nonallocation year to the extent that a contribution or other annual addition (within the meaning of section 415(c)(2)) is made with respect to the account of a disqualified person, or the disqualified person otherwise accrues additional benefits, directly or indirectly under the ESOP or any other plan of the employer qualified under section 401(a) (including a release and allocation of assets from a suspense account, as described at § 54.4975-11(c) and (d) of this chapter) that, for the nonallocation year, would have been added to the account of the disqualified person under the ESOP and invested in employer securities consisting of stock in an S corporation owned by the ESOP but for a provision in the ESOP that precludes such addition to the account of the disqualified person, and investment in employer securities during a nonallocation year.

(iv) Effects of prohibited allocation. (A) Deemed distribution. If a plan year is a nonallocation year, the amount of any prohibited allocation in the account of a disqualified person as of the first day of the plan year, as determined under this paragraph (b)(2), is treated as distributed from the ESOP (or other plan of the employer) to the disqualified person on the first day of the plan year. In the case of an impermissible accrual or impermissible allocation that is not in the account of the disqualified person as of the first day of the plan year, the amount of the prohibited allocation, as determined under this paragraph (b)(2), is treated as distributed on the date of the prohibited allocation. Thus, the fair market value of assets in the disqualified person's account that constitutes an impermissible accrual or allocation is included in gross income (to the extent in excess of any investment in the contract allocable to such amount) and is subject to any additional income tax that applies under section 72(t). A deemed distribution under this paragraph (b)(2)(iv)(A) is not an actual distribution from the ESOP. Thus, the amount of the prohibited allocation is not an eligible rollover distribution under section 402(c). However, for purposes of applying sections 72 and 402 with respect to any subsequent distribution from the ESOP, the amount that the disqualified person previously took into account as income as a result of the deemed distribution is treated as investment in the contract.

(B) Other effects. If there is a prohibited allocation, then the plan fails to satisfy the requirements of section 4975(e)(7) and ceases to be an ESOP. In such a case, the exemption from the excise tax on prohibited transactions for loans to leveraged ESOPs contained in section 4975(d)(3) would cease to apply to any loan (with the result that the employer would owe an excise tax with respect to the previously exempt loan). As a result of these failures, the plan would lose the prohibited transaction exemption for loans to an ESOP under section 4975(d)(3) of the Code and section 408(b)(3) of Title I of the Employee Retirement Income Security Act of 1974, as amended (ERISA). Finally, a plan that does not operate in accordance with its terms to reflect section 409(p) fails to satisfy the qualification requirements of section 401(a), which would cause the corporation's S election to terminate under section 1362. See also section 4979A(a) which imposes an excise tax in certain events, including a prohibited allocation under section 409(p).

(C) Example. The rules of this paragraph (b)(2)(iv) are illustrated by the following example:

*Example.* (i) Facts. Corporation M, an S corporation under section 1361, establishes Plan P as an ESOP in 2006, with a calendar plan year. Plan P is a qualified plan that includes terms providing that a prohibited allocation will not occur during a nonallocation year in accordance with section 409(p). On December 31, 2006, all of the 1,000 outstanding shares of stock of Corporation M, with a fair market value of $30 per share, are contributed to Plan P and allocated among accounts established within Plan P for the benefit of Corporation M's three employees, individuals A, B, and C, based on their compensation for 2006. As a result, on December 31, 2006, participant A's account includes 800 of the shares ($24,000); participant B's account includes 140 of the shares ($4,200); and participant C's account includes the remaining 60 shares ($1,800). The plan year 2006 is a nonallocation year, participants A and B are disqualified persons on December 31, 2006, and a prohibited allocation occurs for A and B on December 31, 2006.

(ii) Conclusion. On December 31, 2006, participants A and B each have a deemed distribution as a result of the prohibited allocation, resulting in income of $24,000 for participant A and $4,200 for participant B. Corporation M owes an excise tax under section 4979A, based on an amount involved of $28,200. Plan P ceases to be an ESOP on the date of the prohibited allocation (December 31, 2006) and also fails to satisfy the qualification requirements of section 401(a) on that date due to the failure to comply with the provisions requiring compliance with section 409(p). As a result of having an ineligible shareholder under section 1361(b)(1)(B), Corporation M ceases to be an S corporation under section 1361 on December 31, 2006.

(v) Prevention of prohibited allocation. (A) Transfer of account to non-ESOP. An ESOP may prevent a nonallocation year or a prohibited allocation during a nonallocation year by providing for assets (including S corporation securities) allocated to the account of a disqualified person (or a person reasonably expected to become a disqualified person absent a transfer described in this paragraph (b)(2)(v)(A)) to be transferred into a separate portion of the plan that is not an ESOP, as described in § 54.4975-11(a)(5) of this chapter, or to another plan of the employer that satisfies the requirements of section 401(a) and that is not an ESOP. Any such transfer must be effectuated by an affirmative action taken no later than the date of the transfer, and all subsequent actions (including benefit statements) generally must be consistent with the transfer having occurred on that date. In the event of such a transfer involving S corporation securities, the recipient plan is subject to tax on unrelated business taxable income under section 512.

(B) Relief from nondiscrimination requirement. Pursuant to this paragraph (b)(2)(v)(B), if a transfer described in paragraph (b)(2)(v)(A) of this section is made from an ESOP to a separate portion of the plan or to another qualified plan of the employer that is not an ESOP, then both the ESOP and the plan or portion of a plan that is not an ESOP do not fail to satisfy the requirements of § 1.401(a)(4)-4 merely because of the transfer. Further, subsequent to the transfer, that plan will not fail to satisfy the requirements of § 1.401(a)(4)-4 merely because of the benefits, rights, and features with respect to the transferred benefits if those benefits, rights, and features would satisfy the requirements of § 1.401(a)(4)-4 if the mandatory disaggregation rule for ESOPs at § 1.410(b)-7(c)(2) did not apply.

**(c) Nonallocation year.** A year is a nonallocation year if it is described in the general definition in paragraph (c)(1) of this section or if the special rule of paragraph (c)(3) of this section applies. *(1) General definition.* For purposes of section 409(p) and this section, a nonallocation year means a plan year of an ESOP during which, at any time, the ESOP holds any employer securities that are shares of an S corporation and either—

(i) Disqualified persons own at least 50 percent of the number of outstanding shares of stock in the S corporation (including deemed-owned ESOP shares); or

(ii) Disqualified persons own at least 50 percent of the sum of:

(A) The outstanding shares of stock in the S corporation (including deemed-owned ESOP shares); and

(B) The shares of synthetic equity in the S corporation owned by disqualified persons.

*(2) Attribution rules.* For purposes of this paragraph (c), the rules of section 318(a) apply to determine ownership of shares in the S corporation (including deemed-owned ESOP shares) and synthetic equity. However, for this purpose, section 318(a)(4) (relating to options to acquire stock) is disregarded and, in applying section 318(a)(1), the members of an individual's family include members of the individual's family under paragraph (d)(2) of this section. In addition, an individual is treated as owning deemed-owned ESOP shares of that individual notwithstanding the employee trust exception in section 318(a)(2)(B)(i). If the attribution rules in paragraph (f)(1) of this section apply, then the rules of paragraph (f)(1) of this section are applied before (and in addition to) the rules of this paragraph (c)(2).

*(3) Special rule for avoidance or evasion.* (i) Any ownership structure described in paragraph (g)(3) of this section results in a nonallocation year. In addition, each individual referred to in paragraph (g)(3) of this section is treated as a disqualified person and the individual's interest in the separate entity described in paragraph (g)(3) of this section is treated as synthetic equity.

(ii) Pursuant to section 409(p)(7)(B), the Commissioner, in revenue rulings, notices, and other guidance published in the Internal Revenue Bulletin (see § 601.601(d)(2)(ii)(b) of this chapter), may provide that a nonallocation year occurs in any case in which the principal purpose of the ownership structure of an S corporation constitutes an avoidance or evasion of section 409(p). For any year that is a nonallocation year under this paragraph (c)(3), the Commissioner may treat any person as a disqualified person. See paragraph (g) of this section for guidance regarding when the principal purpose of an ownership structure of an S corporation involving synthetic equity constitutes an avoidance or evasion of section 409(p).

*(4) Special rule for certain stock rights.* (i) For purposes of paragraph (c)(1) of this section, a person is treated as owning stock if the person has an exercisable right to acquire the stock, the stock is both issued and outstanding, and

the stock is held by persons other than the ESOP, the S corporation, or a related entity (as defined in paragraph (f)(3) of this section).

(ii) This paragraph (c)(4) applies only if treating persons as owning the shares described in paragraph (c)(4)(i) of this section results in a nonallocation year. This paragraph (c)(4) does not apply to a right to acquire stock of an S corporation held by a shareholder that is subject to Federal income tax that, under § 1.1361-1(l)(2)(iii)(A) or (l)(4)(iii)(C), would not be taken into account in determining if an S corporation has a second class of stock, provided that a principal purpose of the right is not the avoidance or evasion of section 409(p). Under the last sentence of paragraph (f)(2)(i) of this section, this paragraph (c)(4)(ii) does not apply for purposes of determining ownership of deemed-owned ESOP shares or whether an interest constitutes synthetic equity.

*(5) Application with respect to shares treated as owned by more than one person.* For purposes of applying paragraph (c)(1) of this section, if, by application of the rules of paragraph (c)(2), (c)(4), or (f)(1) of this section, any share is treated as owned by more than one person, then that share is counted as a single share and that share is treated as owned by disqualified persons if any of the owners is a disqualified person.

*(6) Effect of nonallocation year.* See paragraph (b) of this section for a prohibition applicable during a nonallocation year. See also section 4979A for an excise tax applicable in certain cases, including section 4979A(a)(3) and (4) which applies during a nonallocation year (whether or not there is a prohibited allocation during the year).

**(d) Disqualified persons.** A person is a disqualified person if the person is described in paragraph (d)(1), (d)(2), or (d)(3) of this section.

*(1) General definition.* For purposes of section 409(p) and this section, a disqualified person means any person for whom—

(i) The number of such person's deemed-owned ESOP shares of the S corporation is at least 10 percent of the number of the deemed-owned ESOP shares of the S corporation;

(ii) The aggregate number of such person's deemed-owned ESOP shares and synthetic equity shares of the S corporation is at least 10 percent of the sum of—

(A) The total number of deemed-owned ESOP shares of the S corporation; and

(B) The person's synthetic equity shares of the S corporation;

(iii) The aggregate number of the S corporation's deemed-owned ESOP shares of such person and of the members of such person's family is at least 20 percent of the number of deemed-owned ESOP shares of the S corporation; or

(iv) The aggregate number of the S corporation's deemed-owned ESOP shares and synthetic equity shares of such person and of the members of such person's family is at least 20 percent of the sum of—

(A) The total number of deemed-owned ESOP shares of the S corporation; and

(B) The synthetic equity shares of the S corporation owned by such person and the members of such person's family.

*(2) Treatment of family members; definition.* (i) Rule. Each member of the family of any person who is a disqualified person under paragraph (d)(1)(iii) or (iv) of this section and who owns any deemed-owned ESOP shares or synthetic equity shares is a disqualified person.

(ii) General definition. For purposes of section 409(p) and this section, member of the family means, with respect to an individual—

(A) The spouse of the individual;

(B) An ancestor or lineal descendant of the individual or the individual's spouse;

(C) A brother or sister of the individual or of the individual's spouse and any lineal descendant of the brother or sister; and

(D) The spouse of any individual described in paragraph (d)(2)(ii)(B) or (C) of this section.

(iii) Spouse. A spouse of an individual who is legally separated from such individual under a decree of divorce or separate maintenance is not treated as such individual's spouse under paragraph (d)(2)(ii) of this section.

*(3) Special rule for certain nonallocation years.* See paragraph (c)(3) of this section (relating to avoidance or evasion of section 409(p)) for special rules under which certain persons are treated as disqualified persons.

*(4) Example.* The rules of this paragraph (d) are illustrated by the following examples:

*Example (1).* (i) Facts. An S corporation has 800 outstanding shares, of which 100 are owned by individual O and 700 are held in an employee stock ownership plan (ESOP) during 2006, including 200 shares held in the ESOP account of O, 65 shares held in the ESOP account of participant P, 65 shares held in the ESOP account of participant Q who is P's spouse, and 14 shares held in the ESOP account of R, who is the daughter of P and Q. There are no unallocated suspense account shares in the ESOP. The S corporation has no synthetic equity.

(ii) Conclusion. Under paragraph (d)(1)(i) of this section, O is a disqualified person during 2006 because O's account in the ESOP holds at least 10% of the shares owned by the ESOP (200 is 28.6% of 700). During 2006, neither P, Q, nor R is a disqualified person under paragraph (d)(1)(i) of this section, because each of their accounts holds less than 10% of the shares owned by the ESOP. However, each of P, Q, and R is a disqualified person under paragraph (d)(1)(iii) of this section because P and members of P's family own at least 20% of the deemed-owned ESOP shares (144 (the sum of 65, 65 and 14) is 20.6% of 700). As a result, disqualified persons own at least 50% of the outstanding shares of the S corporation during 2006 (O's 100 directly owned shares, O's 200 deemed-owned shares, P's 65 deemed-owned shares, Q's 65 deemed-owned shares, and R's 14 deemed-owned shares are 55.5% of 800).

*Example (2).* (i) Facts. An S corporation has shares that are owned by an ESOP and various individuals. Individuals S and T are married and have a son, U. Individuals V and W are married and have a daughter, X. Individuals U and X are married. Individual V has a brother Y. Their percentages of the deemed-owned ESOP shares of the S corporation are as follows: T has 6%; U has 7%; and V has 8%. Neither S, W, X, nor Y has any deemed-owned ESOP shares and the S corporation has no synthetic equity. However, individual S and individual Y each own directly a number of shares of the outstanding shares of the S corporation.

(ii) Conclusion. In this example, individual U is a disqualified person under paragraph (d)(1) of this section (because U's family consists of S, T, U, V, W, and X, and, in the aggregate, those persons own more than 20% of the deemed-owned ESOP shares) and individual X is also a disqualified person under paragraph (d)(1) of this section (because T's family consists of S, T, U, V, W, and X, and, in the aggregate, those persons own more than 20% of the deemed-owned ESOP shares). Further, individuals T and V are each a disqualified person under paragraph (d)(2) of this section because each is a member of a family that includes one or more disqualified persons and each has deemed-owned ESOP shares. However, individuals S, W, and Y are not disqualified persons under this paragraph (d). For example, S does not own more than 10% of the deemed-owned ESOP shares, and S's family, which consists of S, T, U, and X, owns, in the aggregate, only 13% of the deemed-owned ESOP shares (X's parents are not members of S's family because the family members of a person do not include the parents-in-law of the person's descendants). Further, note that, for purposes of determining whether the ESOP has a nonallocation year under paragraph (c) of this section, the shares directly owned by S and Y would be taken into account as shares owned by disqualified persons under the attribution rules in paragraph (c)(2) of this section.

**(e) Deemed-owned ESOP shares.** For purposes of section 409(p) and this section, a person is treated as owning his or her deemed-owned ESOP shares. Deemed-owned ESOP shares owned by a person mean, with respect to any person—

*(1)* Any shares of stock in the S corporation constituting employer securities that are allocated to such person's account under the ESOP; and

*(2)* Such person's share of the stock in the S corporation that is held by the ESOP but is not allocated to the account of any participant or beneficiary (with such person's share to be determined in the same proportion as the shares released and allocated from a suspense account, as described at § 54.4975-11(c) and (d) of the Excise Tax Regulations, under the ESOP for the most recently ended plan year for which there were shares released and allocated from a suspense account, or if there has been no such prior release and allocation from a suspense account, then determined in proportion to a reasonable estimate of the shares that would be released and allocated in the first year of a loan repayment).

**(f) Synthetic equity and rights to acquire stock of the S corporation.** *(1) Ownership of synthetic equity.* For purposes of section 409(p) and this section, synthetic equity means the rights described in paragraph (f)(2) of this section. Synthetic equity is treated as owned by the person that has any of the rights specified in paragraph (f)(2) of the section. In addition, the attribution rules as set forth in paragraph (c)(2) of this section apply for purposes of attributing ownership of synthetic equity.

*(2) Synthetic equity.* (i) Rights to acquire stock of the S corporation. (A) General rule. Synthetic equity includes any stock option, warrant, restricted stock, deferred issuance stock right, stock appreciation right payable in stock, or similar interest or right that gives the holder the right to acquire or receive stock of the S corporation in the future. Rights to acquire stock in an S corporation with respect to stock that is, at all times during the period when such rights are effective, both issued and outstanding, and held by a person other than the ESOP, the S corporation, or a related entity are not synthetic equity but only if that person is subject to federal income taxes. (See also paragraph (c)(4) of this section.)

(B) Exception for certain rights of first refusal. A right of first refusal to acquire stock held by an ESOP is not treated as a right to acquire stock of an S corporation under this paragraph if the right to acquire stock would not be taken into account under § 1.1361-1(l)(2)(iii)(A) in determining if an S corporation has a second class of stock and the price at which the stock is acquired under the right of first refusal is not less than the price determined under section 409(h). See § 54.4975-11(d)(5) of the Excise Tax Regulations. The right of first refusal must also comply with the requirements of § 54.4975-7(b)(9) of the Excise Tax Regulations. This paragraph (f)(2)(i)(B) does not apply if, based on the facts and circumstances, the Commissioner finds that the right to acquire stock held by the ESOP constitutes an avoidance or an evasion of section 409(p). See also section 408(d) of ERISA, under which the exemption provided by section 408(e) of ERISA (and the related exemption at section 4975(d)(13) of the Code) does not apply to an owner-employee, including an employee or officer of an S corporation who is a 5 percent owner.

(ii) Special rule for certain stock rights. Synthetic equity also includes a right to a future payment (payable in cash or any other form other than stock of the S corporation) from an S corporation that is based on the value of the stock of the S corporation, such as appreciation in such value. Thus, for example, synthetic equity includes a stock appreciation right with respect to stock of an S corporation that is payable in cash or a phantom stock unit with respect to stock of an S corporation that is payable in cash.

(iii) Rights to acquire interests in or assets of an S corporation or a related entity. Synthetic equity includes a right to acquire stock or other similar interests in a related entity to the extent of the S corporation's ownership. Synthetic equity also includes a right to acquire assets of an S corporation or a related entity other than either rights to acquire goods, services, or property at fair market value in the ordinary course of business or fringe benefits excluded from gross income under section 132.

(iv) Special rule for nonqualified deferred compensation. (A) Synthetic equity also includes any of the following with respect to an S corporation or a related entity: any remuneration to which section 404(a)(5) applies; remuneration for which a deduction would be permitted under section 404(a)(5) if separate accounts were maintained; any right to receive property, as defined in § 1.83-3(e) of the Income Tax Regulations (including a payment to a trust described in section 402(b) or to an annuity described in section 403(c)) in a future year for the performance of services; any transfer of property in connection with the performance of services to which section 83 applies to the extent that the property is not substantially vested within the meaning of § 1.83-3(i) by the end of the plan year in which transferred; and a split-dollar life insurance arrangement under § 1.61-22(b) entered into in connection with the performance of services (other than one under which, at all times, the only economic benefit that will be provided under the arrangement is current life insurance protection as described in § 1.61-22(d)(3)). Synthetic equity also includes any other remuneration for services under a plan, method, or arrangement deferring the receipt of compensation to a date that is after the 15th day of the 3rd calendar month after the end of the entity's taxable year in which the related services are rendered. However, synthetic equity does not include benefits under a plan that is an eligible retirement plan within the meaning of section 402(c)(8)(B).

(B) For purposes of applying paragraph (f)(2)(iv)(A) of this section with respect to an ESOP, synthetic equity does not include any interest described in such paragraph (f)(2)(iv)(A) of this section to the extent that—

(1) The interest is nonqualified deferred compensation (within the meaning of section 3121(v)(2)) that was outstanding on December 17, 2004;

(2) The interest is an amount that was taken into account (within the meaning of § 31.3121(v)(2)-1(d) of this chapter) prior to January 1, 2005, for purposes of taxation under chapter 21 of the Internal Revenue Code (or income attributable thereto); and

(3) The interest was held before the first date on which the ESOP acquires any employer securities.

(v) No overlap among shares of deemed-owned ESOP shares or synthetic equity. Synthetic equity under this paragraph (f)(2) does not include shares that are deemed-owned ESOP shares (or any rights with respect to deemed-owned ESOP shares to the extent such rights are specifically provided under section 409(h)). In addition, synthetic equity under a specific subparagraph of this paragraph (f)(2) does not include anything that is synthetic equity under a preceding provision of paragraph (f)(2)(i), (ii), (iii), or (iv) of this section.

*(3) Related entity.* For purposes of this paragraph (f), related entity means any entity in which the S corporation holds an interest and which is a partnership, a trust, an eligible entity that is disregarded as an entity that is separate from its owner under § 301.7701-3 of this chapter, or a qualified subchapter S subsidiary under section 1361(b)(3).

*(4) Number of synthetic shares.* (i) Synthetic equity determined by reference to S corporation shares. In the case of synthetic equity that is determined by reference to shares of stock of the S corporation, the person who is entitled to the synthetic equity is treated as owning the number of shares of stock deliverable pursuant to such synthetic equity. In the case of synthetic equity that is determined by reference to shares of stock of the S corporation, but for which payment is made in cash or other property (besides stock of the S corporation), the number of shares of synthetic equity treated as owned is equal to the number of shares of stock having a fair market value equal to the cash or other property (disregarding lapse restrictions as described in § 1.83-3(i)). Where such synthetic equity is a right to purchase or receive S corporation shares, the corresponding number of shares of synthetic equity is determined without regard to lapse restrictions as described in § 1.83-3(i) or to any amount required to be paid in exchange for the shares. Thus, for example, if a corporation grants an employee of an S corporation an option to purchase 100 shares of the corporation's stock, exercisable in the future only after the satisfaction of certain performance conditions, the employee is the deemed owner of 100 synthetic equity shares of the corporation as of the date the option is granted. If the same employee were granted 100 shares of restricted S corporation stock (or restricted stock units), subject to forfeiture until the satisfaction of performance or service conditions, the employee would likewise be the deemed owner of 100 synthetic equity shares from the grant date. However, if the same employee were granted a stock appreciation right with regard to 100 shares of S corporation stock (whether payable in stock or in cash), the number of synthetic equity shares the employee is deemed to own equals the number of shares having a value equal to the appreciation at the time of measurement (determined without regard to lapse restrictions).

(ii) Synthetic equity determined by reference to shares in a related entity. In the case of synthetic equity that is determined by reference to shares of stock (or similar interests) in a related entity, the person who is entitled to the synthetic equity is treated as owning shares of stock of the S corporation with the same aggregate value as the number of shares of stock (or similar interests) of the related entity (with such value determined without regard to any lapse restriction as defined at § 1.83-3(i)).

(iii) Other synthetic equity. (A) General rule. In the case of any synthetic equity to which neither paragraph (f)(4)(i) of this section nor paragraph (f)(4)(ii) of this section apply, the person who is entitled to the synthetic equity is treated as owning on any date a number of shares of stock in the S corporation equal to the present value (on that date) of the synthetic equity (with such value determined without regard to any lapse restriction as defined at § 1.83-3(i)) divided by the fair market value of a share of the S corporation's stock as of that date.

(B) Use of annual or more frequent determination dates. A year is a nonallocation year if the thresholds in paragraph (c) of this section are met at any time during that year. However, for purposes of this paragraph (f)(4)(iii), an ESOP may provide that the number of shares of S corporation stock treated as owned by a person who is entitled to synthetic equity to which this paragraph (f)(4)(iii) applies is determined annually (or more frequently), as of the first day of the ESOP's plan year or as of any other reasonable determination date or dates during a plan year. If the ESOP so provides, the number of shares of synthetic equity to which this paragraph (f)(4)(iii) applies that are treated as owned by that person for any period from a given determination date through the date immediately preceding the next following determination date is the number of shares treated as owned on the given determination date.

(C) Use of triennial recalculations. (1) Although an ESOP must have a determination date that is no less frequent than annually, if the terms of the ESOP so provide, then the number of shares of synthetic equity with respect to grants of synthetic equity to which this paragraph (f)(4)(iii) applies may be fixed for a specified period from a determination date identified under the ESOP through the day before a determination date that is not later than the third anniversary of the identified determination date. Thus, the ESOP must provide for the number of shares of synthetic equity to which this paragraph (f)(4)(iii) applies to be re-determined not less frequently than every three years, based on the S corporation share value on a determination date that is not later than the third anniversary of the identified determination date and the aggregate present value of the synthetic equity to which this paragraph (f)(4)(iii) applies (including all grants made during the three-year period) on that determination date.

(2) However, additional accruals, allocations, or grants (to which this paragraph (f)(4)(iii) applies) that are made during such three-year period are taken into account on each determination date during that period, based on the number of synthetic equity shares resulting from the additional accrual, allocation, or grant (determined as of the determination date on or next following the date of the accrual, allocation, or grant). See Example 3 of paragraph (h) of this section for an example illustrating this paragraph (f)(4)(iii)(C).

(3) If, as permitted under this paragraph (f)(4)(iii)(C), an ESOP provides for the number of shares of synthetic equity to be fixed for a specified period from a determination date to a subsequent determination date, then that subsequent determination date can be changed to a new determination date, subject to the following conditions:

(i) The change in the subsequent determination date must be effectuated through a plan amendment adopted before the new determination date;

(ii) The new determination date must be earlier than the prior determination date (that is, the new determination date must be earlier than the determination date applicable in the absence of the plan amendment);

(iii) The conditions in paragraph (f)(4)(iii)(C)(2) of this section must be satisfied measured from the new determination date; and

(iv) Except to the extent permitted by the Commissioner in revenue rulings, notices, or other guidance published in the Internal Revenue Bulletin (see § 601.601(d)(2)(ii)(b) of this chapter), the change must be adopted in connection with either a change in the plan year of the ESOP or a merger, consolidation, or transfer of plan assets of the ESOP under section 414(l) (and the new determination date must consistent with that plan year change or section 414(l) event).

(4) Conditions for application of rules. This paragraph (f)(4)(iii)(C) only applies with respect to grants of synthetic equity to which this paragraph (f)(4)(iii) applies. In addition, paragraph (f)(4)(iii)(C) of this section applies only if the fair market value of a share of the S corporation securities on any determination date is not unrepresentative of the value of the S corporation securities throughout the rest of the plan year and only if the terms of the ESOP include provisions conforming to paragraph (f)(4)(iii)(C)(1) of this section which are consistently used by the ESOP for all persons. In addition, paragraph (f)(4)(iii)(C)(1) of this section applies only if the terms of the ESOP include provisions conforming to paragraphs (f)(4)(iii)(C)(1) of this section which are consistently used by the ESOP for all persons.

(iv) Adjustment of number of synthetic equity shares where ESOP owns less than 100 percent of S corporation. The number of synthetic shares otherwise determined under this paragraph (f)(4) is decreased ratably to the extent that shares of the S corporation are owned by a person who is not an ESOP and who is subject to Federal income taxes. For example, if an S corporation has 200 outstanding shares, of which individual A owns 50 shares and the ESOP owns the other 150 shares, and individual B would be treated under this paragraph (f)(4) as owning 100 synthetic equity shares of the S corporation but for this paragraph (f)(4)(iv), then, under the rule of this paragraph (f)(4)(iv), the number of synthetic shares treated as owned by B under this paragraph (f)(4) is decreased from 100 to 75 (because the ESOP only owns 75 percent of the outstanding stock of the S corporation, rather than 100 percent).

(v) Special rule for shares with greater voting power than ESOP shares. Notwithstanding any other provision of this paragraph (f)(4), if a synthetic equity right includes (directly or indirectly) a right to purchase or receive shares of S corporation stock that have per-share voting rights greater than the per-share voting rights of one or more shares of S corporation stock held by the ESOP, then the number of shares of deemed owned synthetic equity attributable to such right is not less than the number of shares that would have the same voting rights if the shares had the same per-share voting rights as shares held by the ESOP with the least voting rights. For example, if shares of S corporation stock held by the ESOP have one voting right per share, then an individual who holds an option to purchase one share with 100 voting rights is treated as owning 100 shares of synthetic equity.

**(g) Avoidance or evasion of section 409(p) involving synthetic equity.** *(1) General rule.* Paragraph (g)(2) of this section sets forth a standard for determining whether the principal purpose of the ownership structure of an S corporation involving synthetic equity constitutes an avoidance or evasion of section 409(p). Paragraph (g)(3) of this section identifies certain specific ownership structures that constitute an avoidance or evasion of section 409(p). See also paragraph (c)(3) of this section for a rule under which the ownership structures in paragraph (g)(3) of this section result in a nonallocation year for purposes of section 409(p).

*(2) Standard for determining when there is an avoidance or evasion of section 409(p) involving synthetic equity.* For purposes of section 409(p) and this section, whether the principal purpose of the ownership structure of an S corporation involving synthetic equity constitutes an avoidance or evasion of section 409(p) is determined by taking into account all the surrounding facts and circumstances, including all features of the ownership of the S corporation's outstanding stock and related obligations (including synthetic equity), any shareholders who are taxable entities, and the cash distributions made to shareholders, to determine whether, to the extent of the ESOP's stock ownership, the ESOP receives the economic benefits of ownership in the S corporation that occur during the period that stock of the S corporation is owned by the ESOP. Among the factors indicating that the ESOP receives those economic benefits include shareholder voting rights, the right to receive distributions made to shareholders, and the right to benefit from the profits earned by the S corporation, including the extent to which actual distributions of profits are made from the S corporation to the ESOP and the extent to which the ESOP's ownership interest in undistributed profits and future profits is subject to dilution as a result of synthetic equity. For example, the ESOP's ownership interest is not subject to dilution if the total amount of synthetic equity is a relatively small portion of the total number of shares and deemed-owned shares of the S corporation.

*(3) Specific transactions that constitute an avoidance or evasion of section 409(p) involving segregated profits.* Taking into account the standard in paragraph (g)(2) of this section, the principal purpose of the ownership structure of an S corporation constitutes an avoidance or evasion of section 409(p) in any case in which—

(i) The profits of the S corporation generated by the business activities of a specific individual or individuals are not provided to the ESOP, but are instead substantially accumulated and held for the benefit of the individual or individuals on a tax-deferred basis within an entity related to the S corporation, such as a partnership, trust, or corporation (such as in a subsidiary that is a disregarded entity), or any other method that has the same effect of segregating profits for the benefit of such individual or individuals (such as nonqualified deferred compensation described in paragraph (f)(2)(iv) of this section);

(ii) The individual or individuals for whom profits are segregated have rights to acquire 50 percent or more of those profits directly or indirectly (for example, by purchase of the subsidiary); and

(iii) A nonallocation year would occur if this section were separately applied with respect to either the separate entity or whatever method has the effect of segregating profits of the individual or individuals, treating such entity as a separate S corporation owned by an ESOP (or in the case of any other method of segregation of profits by treating those profits as the only assets of a separate S corporation owned by an ESOP).

**(h) Examples.** The rules of this section are illustrated by the following examples:

*Example (1).* Relating to determination of disqualified persons and nonallocation year if there is no synthetic equity. (i) Facts. Corporation X is a calendar year S corporation that maintains an ESOP. X has a single class of common stock, of which there are a total of 1,200 shares outstanding. X has no synthetic equity. In 2006, individual A, who is not an employee of X (and is not related to any employee of X), owns 100 shares directly, B, who is an employee of X, owns 100 shares directly, and the remaining 1,000 shares are owned by an ESOP maintained by X for its employees. The ESOP's 1,000 shares are allocated to the accounts of individuals who are employees of X (none of whom are related), as set forth in columns 1 and 2 in the following table:

| 1 Shareholders | 2 Deemed-owned ESOP shares (total of 1,000) | 3 Percentage deemed-owned ESOP shares | 4 Disqualified person |
|---|---|---|---|
| B | 330 | 33 | Yes. |
| C | 145 | 14.5 | Yes. |
| D | 75 | 7.5 | No. |
| E | 30 | 3 | No. |
| F | 20 | 2 | No. |
| Other participants | 400([1]) | ([2]) | No. |

(ii) Conclusion with respect to disqualified persons. As shown in column 4 in the table contained in paragraph (i) of Example 1, individuals B and C are disqualified persons for 2006 under paragraph (d)(1) of this section because each owns at least 10% of X's deemed-owned ESOP shares. However, the synthetic equity shares owned by any person do not affect the calculation for any other person's ownership of shares.

(iii) Conclusion with respect to nonallocation year. 2006 is not a nonallocation year under section 409(p) because disqualified persons do not own at least 50% of X's outstanding shares (the 100 shares owned directly by B, B's 330 deemed-owned ESOP shares, plus C's 145 deemed-owned ESOP shares equal only 47.9% of the 1,200 outstanding shares of X).

*Example (2).* Relating to determination of disqualified persons and nonallocation year if there is synthetic equity. (i) Facts. The facts are the same as in Example 1, except that, as shown in column 4 of the table in this Example 2, individuals E and F have options to acquire 110 and 130 shares, respectively, of the common stock of X from X:

| 1 Shareholder | 2 Deemed-owned ESOP shares (total of 1,000) | 3 Percentage deemed-owned ESOP share | 4 Options (240) | 5 Shareholder percentage of deemed-owned ESOP plus synthetic equity shares | 6 Disqualified person |
|---|---|---|---|---|---|
| B | 330 | 33 | | | Yes (col. 3). |
| C | 145 | 14.5 | | | Yes (col. 3). |
| D | 75 | 7.5 | | | No. |
| E | 30 | 3 | 110 | 11.1% ([30 + 91.7] divided by 1,091.7). | Yes (col. 5). |
| F | 20 | 2 | 130 | 11.6% ([20 + 108.3] divided by 1,108.3). | Yes (col. 5). |
| Other participants | 400[1] | ([2]) | | | No. |

[1] None exceeds 10 shares.
[2] 1% or less.

(ii) Conclusion with respect to disqualified persons. Individual E's synthetic equity shares are counted in determining whether E is a disqualified person for 2006, and individual F's synthetic equity shares are counted in determining whether F is a disqualified person for 2006. Applying the rule of paragraph (f)(4)(iv) of this section, E's option to acquire 110 shares of the S corporation converts under paragraph (f)(4)(iv) of this section, into 91.7 shares of synthetic equity (110 times the ratio of the 1,000 deemed-owned ESOP shares to the sum of the 1,000 deemed-owned ESOP shares plus the 200 shares held outside the ESOP by A and B). Similarly, F's option to acquire 130 shares of the S corporation converts into 108.3 shares of synthetic equity (130 times the ratio of the 1,000 deemed-owned ESOP shares to the sum of the 1,000 deemed-owned ESOP shares plus the 200 shares held outside the ESOP by A and B). However, the synthetic equity shares owned by any person do not affect the calculation for any other person's ownership of shares. Accordingly, as shown in column 6 in the table contained in paragraph (i) of Example 2, individuals B, C, E, and F are disqualified persons for 2006.

(iii) Conclusion with respect to nonallocation year. The 100 shares owned directly by B, B's 330 deemed-owned ESOP shares, C's 145 deemed-owned ESOP shares, E's 30 deemed-owned ESOP shares, E's 91.7 synthetic equity shares, F's 20 deemed-owned ESOP shares, plus F's 108.3 synthetic equity shares total 825, which equals 58.9% of 1,400, which is the sum of the 1,200 outstanding shares of X and the 200 shares of synthetic equity shares of X held by disqualified persons. Thus, 2006 is a nonallocation year for X's ESOP under section 409(p) because disqualified persons own at least 50% of the total shares of outstanding stock of

1. None exceed 10 shares.
2. 1% or less.

X and the total synthetic equity shares of X held by disqualified persons. In addition, independent of the preceding conclusion, 2006 would be a nonallocation year because disqualified persons own at least 50% of X's outstanding shares because the 100 shares owned directly by B, B's 330 deemed-owned ESOP shares, C's 145 deemed-owned ESOP shares, E's 30 deemed-owned ESOP shares, plus F's 20 deemed-owned ESOP shares equal 52.1% of the 1,200 outstanding shares of X.

*Example (3).* Relating to determination of number of shares of synthetic equity. (i) Facts. Corporation Y is a calendar year S corporation that maintains an ESOP. Y has a single class of common stock, of which there are a total of 1,000 shares outstanding, all of which are owned by the ESOP. Y has no synthetic equity, except for four grants of nonqualified deferred compensation that are made to an individual during the period from 2005 through 2011, as set forth in column 2 in the following table. The ESOP provides for the special rules in paragraph (f)(4)(iii) of this section to determine the number of shares of synthetic equity owned by that individual with a determination date of January 1 and the triennial rule redetermining value, as shown in columns 4 and 5:

| 1 Determination date | 2 Present value of nonqualified deferred compensation on determination date | 3 Share value on determination date | 4 New shares of synthetic equity on determination date | 5 Aggregate number of synthetic equity shares on determination date |
|---|---|---|---|---|
| January 1, 2005 | A grant is made on January 1, 2005 with a present value of $1,000. An additional grant of nonqualified deferred compensation with a present value of $775 is made on March 1, 2005 | $ 10 per share | 100 | 100 |
| January 1, 2006 | An additional grant is made on December 31, 2005 which has a present value of $800 on January 1, 2006. The March 1, 2005 grant has a present value on January 1, 2006 of $800. | $ 8 per share | 200 | 300 |
| January 1, 2007 | No new grants made | $ 12 per share | | 300 |
| January 1, 2008 | An additional grant is made on December 31, 2007 which has a present value of $3,000 on January 1, 2008. The grants made during 2005 through 2007 have an aggregate present value on January 1, 2008 of $3,750 | $ 15 per share | 200 | 450 |
| January 1, 2009 | No new grants are made | $ 11 per share | | 450 |
| January 1, 2010 | No new grants are made | $ 22 per share | | 450 |
| January 1, 2011. | No new grants are made. The grants made during 2005 through 2008 have an aggregate present value on January 1, 2011 of $7,600 | $ 20 per share | | 380 |

(ii) Conclusion. The grant made on January 1, 2005, is treated as 100 shares until the determination date in 2008. The grant made on March 1, 2005, is not taken into account until the 2006 determination date and its present value on that date, along with the then present value of the grant made on December 31, 2005, is treated as a number of shares that are based on the $8 per share value on the 2006 determination date, with the resulting number of shares continuing to apply until the determination date in 2008. On the January 1, 2008, determination date, the grant made on the preceding day is taken into account at its present value of $3,000 on January 1, 2008 and the $15 per share value on that date with the resulting number of shares (200) continuing to apply until the next determination date. In addition, on the January 1, 2008, determination date, the number of shares determined under other grants made between January 1, 2005 and December 31, 2007, must be revalued. Accordingly, the aggregate value of all nonqualified deferred compensation granted during that period is determined to be $3750 on January 1, 2008, and the corresponding number of shares of synthetic equity based on the $15 per share value is determined to be 250 shares on the 2008 determination date, with the resulting aggregate number of shares (450) continuing to apply until the determination date in 2011. On the January 1, 2011, determination date, the aggregate value of all nonqualified deferred compensation is determined to be $7,600 and the corresponding number of shares of synthetic equity based on the $20 per share value on the 2011 determination date is determined to be 380 shares (with the resulting number of shares continuing to apply until the day before the determination date in 2014, assuming no further grants are made).

**(i) Effective dates.** *(1) Statutory effective date.* (i) Except as otherwise provided in paragraph (i)(1)(ii) of this section, section 409(p) applies for plan years ending after March 14, 2001.

(ii) If an ESOP holding stock in an S corporation was established on or before March 14, 2001, and the election under section 1362(a) with respect to that S corporation was in effect on March 14, 2001, section 409(p) applies for plan years beginning on or after January 1, 2005.

*(2) Regulatory effective date.* This section applies for plan years beginning on or after January 1, 2006. For plan years beginning before January 1, 2006, § 1.409(p)-1T (as it appeared in the April 1, 2005, edition of 26 CFR part 1) applies.

T.D. 9302, 12/19/2006.

## § 1.409(p)-1T Prohibited allocation of securities in an S corporation (temporary).

• ***Caution:*** Under Code Sec. 7805, temporary regulations expire within three years of the date of issuance. This temporary regulation was issued on 7/18/2003.

**(a) Organization of this section.** Section 409(p) applies if a nonallocation year occurs in an employee stock ownership plan (ESOP), as defined in section 4975(e)(7), that holds shares of stock of an S corporation, as defined in section 1361, that are employer securities as defined in section 409(l). Paragraph (b) of this section sets forth the general rule under section 409(p)(1) and (2) prohibiting any accrual or allocation to a disqualified person in a nonallocation year. Paragraph (c) of this section sets forth rules under section 409(p)(3), (5), and (7) for determining whether a year is a nonallocation year, generally based on whether disqualified persons own at least 50 percent of the shares of the S corporation, either taking into account only the outstanding shares of the S corporation (including shares held by the ESOP) or taking into account both the outstanding shares and synthetic equity of the S corporation. Paragraphs (d), (e), and (f) of this section contain definitions of disqualified person under section 409(p)(4) and (5), deemed-owned ESOP shares under section 409(p)(4)(C), and synthetic equity under section 409(p)(6)(C). Paragraph (g) of this section contains a standard for determining when the principal purpose of the ownership structure of an S corporation constitutes an avoidance or evasion of section 409(p). The definitions used in section 409(p) and this section are also applicable for purposes of section 4979A, which imposes an excise tax on certain events, including a nonallocation year under section 409(p).

**(b) Prohibited allocation in a nonallocation year.** *(1) General rule.* An ESOP holding employer securities consisting of stock in an S corporation must provide that no portion of the assets of the plan attributable to (or allocable in lieu of) such employer securities may, during a nonallocation year, accrue under the ESOP, or be allocated directly or indirectly under any plan of the employer (including the ESOP) meeting the requirements of section 401(a), for the benefit of any disqualified person (a prohibited allocation).

*(2) Additional rules.* (i) Prohibited allocation definition. For purposes of section 409(p)(2)(A) and paragraph (b)(1) of this section, there is a prohibited allocation (i.e., assets accrue or are allocated as prohibited under paragraph (b)(1) of this section) if there is either an impermissible accrual as defined in paragraph (b)(2)(ii) of this section or an impermissible allocation as defined in paragraph (b)(2)(iii) of this section. The amount of the prohibited allocation is equal to the sum of the impermissible accrual plus the amount of the impermissible allocation (if any).

(ii) Impermissible accrual. There is an impermissible accrual to the extent (and only to the extent) that employer securities consisting of stock in an S corporation owned by the ESOP and any assets attributable thereto are held under the ESOP for the benefit of a disqualified person during a nonallocation year. For this purpose, assets attributable to S corporation securities include any distributions, within the meaning of section 1368, made on S corporation stock held in a disqualified person's account in the ESOP (including earnings thereon), plus any proceeds from the sale of S corporation securities held for a disqualified person's account in the ESOP (including any earnings thereon). Thus, for example, in the event of a nonallocation year, all S corporation shares and all other ESOP assets attributable to S corporation stock, including distributions, sales proceeds, and earnings on either the distribution or proceeds, held for the account of such disqualified person in the ESOP during that year are an impermissible accrual for the benefit of that person, whether attributable to contributions in the current year or in prior years.

(iii) Impermissible allocation. An impermissible allocation means any allocation for a disqualified person directly or indirectly under any plan of the employer qualified under section 401(a) that occurs during a nonallocation year to the extent that a contribution or other annual addition is made, or the disqualified person otherwise accrues additional benefits, under the ESOP or any other plan of the employer qualified under section 401(a) (including a release and allocation of assets from a suspense account, as described at § 54.4975-11(c) and (d) of this chapter) that, for the nonallocation year, would otherwise have been added to the account of the disqualified person under the ESOP and invested in employer securities consisting of stock in an S corporation owned by the ESOP but for a provision in the ESOP to comply with section 409(p).

(iv) Effects of prohibited allocation. (A) Deemed distribution. If there is a prohibited allocation, the amount of the prohibited allocation, as determined under this paragraph (b)(2), is treated as distributed from the ESOP (or other plan of the employer) to the disqualified person on the first day of the plan year on which there is an impermissible accrual or on the date of the allocation in the case of an additional impermissible accrual or impermissible allocation during the plan year but after the first day of the plan year. Thus, the fair market value of assets in the disqualified person's account that constitutes an impermissible accrual or allocation is included in gross income (to the extent in excess of any investment in the contract allocable to such amount) and is subject to any additional income tax that applies under section 72(t). A deemed distribution under this paragraph (b)(2)(iv)(A) is not an actual distribution from the ESOP. Thus, the amount of the prohibited allocation is not an eligible rollover distribution under section 402(c). However, for purposes of applying sections 72 and 402 with respect to any subsequent distribution from the ESOP, the amount that the disqualified person previously took into account as income as a result of the deemed distribution is treated as an investment in the contract.

(B) Other effects. If there is a prohibited allocation, then the plan fails to satisfy the requirements of section 4975(e)(7) and ceases to be an ESOP. In such a case, the exemption from the excise tax on prohibited transactions for loans to leveraged ESOPs contained in section 4975(d)(3) would cease to apply to any loan (with the result that the employer would owe an excise tax with respect to the previously exempt loan) and, further, the exception in section 512(e)(3) would not apply to the plan (with the result that the plan may owe income tax as a result of unrelated business taxable income under section 512 with respect to S corporation stock held by the plan). See also section 4979A(a) which imposes an excise tax in certain events, including a prohibited allocation under section 409(p).

(v) Prevention of prohibited allocation. (A) Transfer of account to non-ESOP. An ESOP may prevent a nonallocation year or a prohibited allocation during a nonallocation year by permitting assets (including S corporation securities) allocated to the account of a disqualified person (or a person reasonably expected to become a disqualified person absent a transfer described in this paragraph (b)(2)(v)(A)) to be transferred into a separate portion of the plan that is not an ESOP, as described in § 54.4975-11(a)(5) of this chapter, or to another plan of the employer that satisfies the requirements of section 401(a) (and that is not an ESOP). In the event of such a transfer involving S corporation securities, the recipient plan is subject to tax on unrelated business taxable income under section 512.

(B) Relief from nondiscrimination requirement. Pursuant to this paragraph (b)(2)(v)(B), if a transfer described in paragraph (b)(2)(v)(A) of this section is made from an ESOP to a separate portion of the plan or to another qualified plan of the employer that is not an ESOP, then both the ESOP and the plan or portion of a plan that is not an ESOP will not fail to satisfy the requirements of § 1.401(a)(4)-4 merely because of the transfer. Further, subsequent to the transfer, that plan will not fail to satisfy the requirements of § 1.401(a)(4)-4 merely because of the benefits, rights, or features with respect to the transferred benefits if those benefits, rights, or features would satisfy the requirements of § 1.401(a)(4)-4 if the mandatory disaggregation rule for ESOPs at § 1.410(b)-7(c)(2) did not apply.

**(c) Nonallocation year.** *(1) Definition generally.* For purposes of section 409(p) and this section, a nonallocation year means a plan year of an ESOP during which, at any time, the ESOP holds any employer securities that are shares of an S corporation and either—

(i) Disqualified persons own at least 50 percent of the number of outstanding shares of stock in the S corporation (including deemed-owned ESOP shares); or

(ii) Disqualified persons own at least 50 percent of the sum of:

(A) The outstanding shares of stock in the S corporation (including deemed-owned ESOP shares), plus

(B) The shares of synthetic equity in the S corporation owned by disqualified persons.

*(2) Attribution rules.* For purposes of this paragraph (c), the rules of section 318(a) apply to determine ownership of shares in the S corporation (including deemed-owned ESOP shares) and synthetic equity. However, for this purpose, section 318(a)(4) (relating to options to acquire stock) is disregarded and, in applying section 318(a)(1), the members of an individual's family include members of the individual's family under paragraph (d)(2) of this section. In addition, an individual is treated as owning deemed-owned ESOP shares of that individual notwithstanding the employee trust exception in section 318(a)(2)(B)(i). If the attribution rules in paragraph (f)(1) of this section apply, then the rules of paragraph (f)(1) of this section are applied before the rules of this paragraph (c)(2).

*(3) Special rule for avoidance or evasion.* (i) The ownership structures described in paragraph (g)(3) of this section result in a nonallocation year. In addition, under the ownership structures described in paragraph (g)(3) of this section, the individual referred to in paragraph (g)(3) of this section is treated as a disqualified person and that person's interest in the separate entity is treated as synthetic equity.

(ii) Under section 409(p)(7)(B), the Commissioner, in revenue rulings, notices, and other guidance published in the Internal Revenue Bulletin (see § 601.601(d)(2)(ii)(b) of this chapter), may provide that a nonallocation year occurs in any case in which the principal purpose of the ownership structure of an S corporation constitutes an avoidance or evasion of section 409(p). For any year that is a nonallocation year under this paragraph (c)(3), the Commissioner may treat any person as a disqualified person. See paragraph (g) of this section for guidance regarding when the principal purpose of an ownership structure of an S corporation involving synthetic equity constitutes an avoidance or evasion of section 409(p).

*(4) Special rule for certain stock rights.* (i) For purposes of paragraph (c)(1) of this section, a person is treated as owning stock that the person has a right to acquire if, at all times during the period when such right is effective, the stock that the person has the right to acquire is both issued and outstanding and is held by persons other than the ESOP, the S corporation, or a related entity (as defined in paragraph (f)(3) of this section).

(ii) This paragraph (c)(4) applies only if treating persons as owning the shares described in paragraph(c)(4)(i) of this section results in a nonallocation year. This paragraph (c)(4) does not apply to a right to acquire stock of an S corporation held by a shareholder subject to Federal income tax that, under § 1.1361-1(l)(2)(iii) or (l)(4)(iii)(C), would not be taken into account in determining if an S corporation has a second class of stock provided that a principal purpose of the right is not the avoidance or evasion of section 409(p). Under the last sentence of paragraph (f)(2)(i) of this section, this paragraph (c)(4)(ii) does not apply for purposes of determining ownership of deemed-owned ESOP shares or whether an interest constitutes synthetic equity.

*(5) Application with respect to shares treated as owned by more than one person.* For purposes of applying paragraph (c)(1) of this section, if, by application of the rules of paragraph (c)(2), (c)(4), or (f)(1) of this section, any share is treated as owned by more than one person, then that share is counted as a single share and that share is treated as owned by disqualified persons if any of the owners is a disqualified person.

*(6) Effect of nonallocation year.* See paragraph (b) of this section for a prohibition applicable during a nonallocation year. See also section 4979A for an excise tax applicable in certain cases, including section 4979A(a)(3) and (4) which applies during a nonallocation year (whether or not there is a prohibited allocation during the year).

**(d) Disqualified persons.** *(1) General definition.* For purposes of section 409(p) and this section, a disqualified person means any person for whom—

(i) The number of such person's deemed-owned ESOP shares of the S corporation is at least 10 percent of the number of the deemed-owned ESOP shares of the S corporation;

(ii) The aggregate number of such person's deemed-owned ESOP shares and synthetic equity shares of the S corporation is at least 10 percent of the sum of:

(A) The total number of deemed-owned ESOP shares, and

(B) The person's synthetic equity shares of the S corporation;

(iii) The aggregate number of the S corporation's deemed-owned ESOP shares of such person and of the members of such person's family is at least 20 percent of the number of deemed-owned ESOP shares of the S corporation; or

(iv) The aggregate number of the S corporation's deemed-owned ESOP shares and synthetic equity shares of such person and of the members of such person's family is at least 20 percent of the sum of:

(A) The total number of deemed-owned ESOP shares, and

(B) The synthetic equity shares of the S corporation owned by such person and the members of such person's family.

*(2) Treatment of family members; definition.* (i) Rule. Each member of the family of any person who is a disqualified person under paragraph (d)(1)(iii) or (iv) of this section is a disqualified person.

(ii) General definition. For purposes of section 409(p) and this section, member of the family means, with respect to an individual—

(A) The spouse of the individual;

(B) An ancestor or lineal descendant of the individual or the individual's spouse;

(C) A brother or sister of the individual or of the individual's spouse and any lineal descendant of the brother or sister; and

(D) The spouse of any individual described in paragraph (d)(2)(ii)(B) or (C) of this section.

(iii) Spouse. A spouse of an individual who is legally separated from such individual under a decree of divorce or separate maintenance is not treated as such individual's spouse under paragraph (d)(2)(ii)(A) of this section.

*(3) Special rule for certain nonallocation years.* See paragraph (c)(3) of this section (relating to avoidance or evasion of section 409(p)) for special rules permitting certain persons to be treated as disqualified persons in certain nonallocation years.

*(4) Example.* The rules of this paragraph (d) are illustrated by the following example:

*Example.* (i) Facts. An S corporation has 800 outstanding shares of which 100 are owned by individual O and 700 are held in an employee stock ownership plan (ESOP) during 2005, including 200 shares held in the ESOP account of O, 65 shares held in the ESOP account of participant P, and 40 shares held in the ESOP account of participant Q who is P's spouse. The S corporation has no synthetic equity.

(ii) Conclusion. O is a disqualified person during 2005 because O's account in the ESOP holds at least 10 percent of the shares owned by the ESOP (200 is 28.6 percent of 700). In addition, P is a disqualified person during 2005 because, under paragraph (d)(2) of this section, P is treated as owning the shares held by Q and P's total deemed-owned shares are thus at least 10 percent of the shares owned by the plan (65 plus 40 is more than 10 percent of 700). In addition, Q is a disqualified person as a result of the rules in paragraph (d)(2) of this section. As a result, disqualified persons own at least 50 percent of the outstanding shares of the S corporation during 2005 (O's 100 directly owned shares, O's 200 deemed-owned shares, P's 65 deemed-owned shares, plus Q's 40 deemed owned shares are 50.6 percent of 800).

**(e) Deemed-owned ESOP shares.** For purposes of section 409(p) and this section, a person is treated as owning his or her deemed-owned ESOP shares.

Deemed-owned ESOP shares mean, with respect to any person—

*(1)* Any shares of stock in the S corporation constituting employer securities that are allocated to such person's account under the ESOP; and

*(2)* Such person's share of the stock in the S corporation that is held by the ESOP but is not allocated to the account of any participant or beneficiary (with such person's share to be determined in the same proportion as the shares released and allocated from a suspense account, as described at § 54.4975-11(c) and (d) of this chapter, under the ESOP for the most recently ended plan year for which there were shares released and allocated from a suspense account, or if there has been no such prior release and allocation from a suspense account, then determined in proportion to a reasonable estimate of the shares that would be released and allocated in the first year of loan repayment).

**(f) Synthetic equity.** *(1) Ownership of synthetic equity.* For purposes of section 409(p) and this section, synthetic equity is treated as owned by a person in the same manner as stock is treated as owned by a person, directly or under the rules of section 318(a)(2) and (3). Synthetic equity means the rights described in paragraph (f)(2) of this section.

*(2) Synthetic equity.* (i) Rights to acquire stock of the S corporation. Synthetic equity includes any stock option, warrant, restricted stock, deferred issuance stock right, stock appreciation right payable in stock, or similar interest or right that gives the holder the right to acquire or receive stock of the S corporation in the future. Rights to acquire stock in an S corporation with respect to stock that is, at all times during the period when such rights are effective, both issued and outstanding and held by persons (who are subject to federal income taxes) other than the ESOP, the S corporation, or a related entity are not synthetic equity (but see paragraph (c)(4) of this section).

(ii) Special rule for certain stock rights. Synthetic equity also includes a right to a future payment (payable in cash or any other form other than stock of the S corporation) from an S corporation that is based on the value of the stock of the S corporation, such as appreciation in such value. Thus, synthetic equity includes a stock appreciation right with respect to stock of an S corporation that is payable in cash or a phantom stock unit with respect to stock of an S corporation that is payable in cash.

(iii) Rights to acquire interests in or assets of an S corporation or a related entity. Synthetic equity includes a right to acquire stock or other similar interests in a related entity to the extent of the S corporation's ownership. Synthetic equity also includes a right to acquire assets of an S corporation or a related entity other than either rights to acquire goods, services, or property at fair market value in the ordinary course of business or fringe benefits excluded from gross income under section 132.

(iv) Special rule for nonqualified deferred compensation. (A) Synthetic equity also includes any of the following with respect to an S corporation or a related entity: any remuneration to which section 404(a)(5) applies; remuneration for which a deduction would be permitted under section 404(a)(5) if separate accounts were maintained; any right to receive property to which section 83 applies (including a payment to a trust described in section 402(b) or to an annuity described in section 403(c)) in a future year for the performance of services; any transfer of property (to which section 83 applies) in connection with the performance of services to the extent that the property is not substantially vested within the meaning of § 1.83-3(i) by the end of the plan year in which transferred; and a split-dollar life insurance arrangement under § 1.61-22(b) entered into in connection with the performance of services (other than one under which, at all times, the only economic benefit that will be provided under the arrangement is current life insurance protection as described in § 1.61-22(d)(3)). Synthetic equity also includes any other remuneration for services under a plan, or method or arrangement, deferring the receipt of compensation to a date that is after the 15th day of the 3rd calendar month after the end of the entity's taxable year in which the related services are rendered. However, synthetic equity does not include benefits under a plan that is an eligible retirement plan within the meaning of section 402(c)(8)(B).

(B) For purposes of applying paragraph (f)(2)(iv)(A) of this section with respect to an ESOP, synthetic equity does not include any interest described in such paragraph (f)(2)(iv)(A) of this section to the extent that—

(1) The interest is nonqualified deferred compensation (within the meaning of section 3121(v)(2)) that was outstanding on December 17, 2004;

(2) The interest is an amount that was taken into account (within the meaning of § 31.3121(v)(2)-1(d) of this chapter) prior to January 1, 2005, for purposes of taxation under chapter 21 of the Internal Revenue Code (or income attributable thereto); and

(3) The interest was held before the first date on which the ESOP acquires any employer securities.

(v) No overlap among shares of deemed-owned ESOP shares or synthetic equity. Synthetic equity under this paragraph (f)(2) does not include shares that are deemed-owned ESOP shares (or any rights with respect to deemed-owned ESOP shares to the extent such rights are specifically permitted under section 409(h)). In addition, synthetic equity under a specific subparagraph of this paragraph (f)(2) does not include anything that is synthetic equity under paragraph (f)(2)(i), (ii), (iii) or (iv) of this section.

*(3) Related entity.* For purposes of this paragraph (f), related entity means any entity in which the S corporation holds an interest and which is a partnership, a trust, an eligible entity that is disregarded as an entity that is separate from its owner under § 301.7701-3 of this chapter, or a Qualified Subchapter S Subsidiary under section 1361(b)(3).

*(4) Number of synthetic shares.* (i) Synthetic equity determined by reference to S corporation shares. In the case of synthetic equity that is determined by reference to shares of stock of the S corporation, the person who is entitled to the synthetic equity is treated as owning the number of shares of stock deliverable pursuant to such synthetic equity. In the case of synthetic equity that is determined by reference to shares of stock of the S corporation, but for which payment is made in cash or other property (besides stock of the S corporation), the number of shares of synthetic equity treated as owned is equal to the number of shares of stock having a fair market value equal to the cash or other property (disregarding lapse restrictions as described in § 1.83-3(i)). Where such synthetic equity is a right to purchase or receive S corporation shares, the corresponding number of shares of synthetic equity is determined without regard to lapse restrictions as described in § 1.83-3(i) or to any amount required to be paid in exchange for the shares. Thus, for example, if a corporation grants an employee of an S corporation an option to purchase 100 shares of the corporation's stock, exercisable in the future only after the satisfaction of certain performance conditions, the employee is the deemed owner of 100 synthetic equity shares of the corporation as of the date the option is granted. If the same employee were granted 100 shares of restricted S corporation stock (or restricted stock units), subject to forfeiture until the satisfaction of performance or service conditions, the employee would likewise be the deemed owner of 100 synthetic equity shares from the grant date. However, if the same employee were granted a stock appreciation right with regard to 100 shares of S corporation stock (whether payable in stock or in cash), the number of synthetic equity shares the employee is deemed to own equals the number of shares having a value equal to the appreciation at the time of measurement (determined without regard to lapse restrictions).

(ii) Synthetic equity determined by reference to shares in a related entity. In the case of synthetic equity that is determined by reference to shares of stock (or similar interests) in a related entity, the person who is entitled to the synthetic equity is treated as owning shares of stock of the S corporation with the same aggregate value as the number of shares of stock (or similar interests) of the related entity (with such value determined without regard to any lapse restriction as defined at § 1.83-3(i)).

(iii) Other synthetic equity. (A) General rule. In the case of any synthetic equity to which neither paragraph (f)(4)(i) nor paragraph (f)(4)(ii) of this section apply, the person who is entitled to the synthetic equity is treated as owning on any date a number of shares of stock in the S corporation equal to the present value (on that date) of the synthetic equity (with such value determined without regard to any lapse restriction as defined at § 1.83-3(i)) divided by the fair market value of a share of the S corporation's stock as of that date.

(B) Special rules. (1) Use of annual or more frequent determination dates. For purposes of this paragraph (f)(4)(iii), while the determination of whether there is a nonallocation year depends on day-by-day determinations under paragraph (c) of this section, the number of shares of S corporation stock treated as owned by a person who is entitled to synthetic equity to which this paragraph (f)(4)(iii) applies is permitted to be determined only annually (or more frequently), as of the first day of the ESOP's plan year or as of any other reasonable determination date or dates during a plan year. If the ESOP so provides, the number of shares of synthetic equity to which this paragraph (f)(4)(iii) applies that are treated as owned by that person for any period from a given determination date through the date immediately preceding the next following determination date is the number of shares treated as owned on the given determination date.

(2) Use of triannual recalculations. In addition, if the terms of the ESOP so provide, then the number of shares of synthetic equity with respect to grants of synthetic equity to which this paragraph (f)(4)(iii) applies may be fixed for a specified period from a determination date identified under the ESOP through a date that is not later than the day before the determination date that is on or immediately preceding the third anniversary of the identified determination date. Additional accruals, allocations, or grants (to which this paragraph (f)(4)(iii) applies) that are made during such three-year period are taken into account on each determination date during that period, based on the number of synthetic equity shares resulting from the additional accrual, allocation, or grant (determined as of the determination date on or next following the date of the accrual, allocation, or grant). However, the ESOP must provide for the number of shares of synthetic equity to which this paragraph (f)(4)(iii) applies to be re-determined not less frequently than every three years, based on the S corporation share value on a determination date that is not later than the third anniversary of the identified determination date and the aggregate present value of the synthetic equity to which this paragraph (f)(4)(iii) applies (including all grants made during the three-year period) on that determination date. See Example 3 of paragraph (h) of this section for an example illustrating this paragraph (f)(4)(iii)(B)(2).

(3) Conditions for application of rules. Paragraph (f)(4)(iii)(B) of this section only applies with respect to grants of synthetic equity to which this paragraph (f)(4)(iii) applies. In addition, paragraph (f)(4)(iii)(B)(1) of this section

applies only if the fair market value of a share of the S corporation securities on any determination date is not unrepresentative of the value of the S corporation securities throughout the rest of the plan year. and only if the terms of the ESOP include provisions conforming to paragraph (f)(4)(iii)(B)(1) of this section which are consistently used by the ESOP for all persons. In addition, paragraph (f)(4)(iii)(B)(2) of this section applies only if the terms of the ESOP include provisions conforming to paragraphs (f)(4)(iii)(B)(1) and (2) of this section which are consistently used by the ESOP for all persons.

(iv) Adjustment of number of synthetic equity shares where ESOP owns less than 100% of S corporation. Under this paragraph (f)(4)(iv), the number of synthetic shares otherwise determined under this paragraph (f)(4) is decreased ratably to the extent that shares of the S corporation are owned by a person who is not an ESOP (and who is subject to Federal income taxes). For example, if an S corporation has 200 outstanding shares, of which individual A owns 50 shares and the ESOP owns the other 150 shares, and individual B would be treated under this paragraph (f)(4) as owning 200 synthetic equity shares of the S corporation but for this paragraph (f)(4)(iv), then, under the rule of this paragraph (f)(4)(iv), the number of synthetic shares treated as owned by B under this paragraph (f)(4) is decreased from 200 to 150 (because the ESOP only owns 75% of the outstanding stock of the S corporation, rather than 100%).

(v) Special rule for shares with greater voting power than ESOP shares. Notwithstanding any other provision of this paragraph (f)(4), if a synthetic equity right includes (directly or indirectly) a right to purchase or receive shares of S corporation stock that have per-share voting rights greater than the per-share voting rights of one or more shares of S corporation stock held by the ESOP, then the number of shares of deemed owned synthetic equity attributable to such right is not less than the number of shares that would have the same voting rights if the shares had the same per-share voting rights as shares held by the ESOP with the least voting rights. For example, if shares of S corporation stock held by the ESOP have one voting right per share, then an individual who holds an option to purchase one share with 100 voting rights is treated as owning 100 shares of synthetic equity.

**(g) Avoidance or evasion of section 409(p) involving synthetic equity.** *(1) General rule.* Paragraph (g)(2) of this section sets forth a standard for determining whether the principal purpose of the ownership structure of an S corporation involving synthetic equity constitutes an avoidance or evasion of section 409(p). Paragraph (g)(3) of this section identifies certain specific ownership structures that constitute an avoidance or evasion of section 409(p). See also paragraph (c)(3) of this section for a rule under which the ownership structures in paragraph (g)(3) result in a nonallocation year for purposes of section 409(p).

*(2) Standard for determining when there is an avoidance or evasion of section 409(p) involving synthetic equity.* For purposes of section 409(p) and this section, whether the principal purpose of the ownership structure of an S corporation involving synthetic equity constitutes an avoidance or evasion of section 409(p) is determined by taking into account all the surrounding facts and circumstances, including all features of the ownership of the S corporation's outstanding stock and related obligations (including synthetic equity), any shareholders who are taxable entities, and the cash distributions made to shareholders, to determine whether, to the extent of the ESOP's stock ownership, the ESOP receives the economic benefits of ownership in the S corporation that occur during the period that stock of the S corporation is owned by the ESOP. Among the factors indicating that the ESOP receives these economic benefits include shareholder voting rights, the right to receive distributions made to shareholders, and the right to benefit from the profits earned by the S corporation, including the extent to which actual distributions of profits are made from the S corporation to the ESOP and the extent to which the ESOP's ownership interest in undistributed profits and future profits is subject to dilution as a result of synthetic equity, for example, the ESOP's ownership interest is not subject to dilution if the total amount of synthetic equity is a relatively small portion of the total number of shares and deemed-owned shares of the S corporation.

*(3) Specific transactions that constitute an avoidance or evasion of section 409(p) involving segregated profits.* Taking into account the standard in paragraph (g)(2) of this section, the principal purpose of the ownership structure of an S corporation constitutes an avoidance or evasion of section 409(p) in any case in which—

(i) The profits of the S corporation generated by the business activities of a specific individual or individuals are not provided to the ESOP, but are instead substantially accumulated and held for the benefit of that individual or individuals on a tax-deferred basis within an entity related to the S corporation, such as a partnership, trust, or corporation (such as in a subsidiary that is a disregarded entity), or any other method that has the same effect of segregating profits for the benefit of such individual or individuals (such as nonqualified deferred compensation described in paragraph (f)(2)(iv) of this section);

(ii) The individual or individuals for whom profits are segregated have rights to acquire 50 percent or more of those profits directly or indirectly (for example, by purchase of the subsidiary); and

(iii) A nonallocation year would occur if this section were separately applied with respect to either the separate entity or whatever method has the effect of segregating profits of the individual or individuals, treating such entity as a separate S corporation owned by an ESOP (or in the case of any other method of segregation of profits by treating those profits as the only assets of a separate S corporation owned by an ESOP).

**(h) Examples.** The rules of this section are illustrated by the following examples:

*Example (1).* Relating to determination of disqualified persons and nonallocation year if there is no synthetic equity. (i) Facts. Corporation X is a calendar year S corporation that maintains an ESOP. X has a single class of common stock, of which there are a total of 1,200 shares outstanding. X has no synthetic equity. In 2006, individual A, who is not an employee of X (and is not related to any employee of X), owns 100 shares directly, individual B owns 100 shares directly, and the remaining 1,000 shares are owned by an ESOP maintained by X for its employees. The ESOP's 1,000 shares are allocated to the accounts of individuals who are employees of X (none of whom are related), as set forth in columns 1 and 2 in the following table:

| 1 Shareholders | 2 Deemed-owned ESOP shares (total of 1,000) | 3 Percentage deemed-owned ESOP shares | 4 Disqualified person |
|---|---|---|---|
| B | 330. | 33. | Yes |
| C | 145. | 14.5. | Yes |
| D | 75 | 7.5 | No |
| E | 30 | 3 | No |
| F | 20 | 2 | No |
| Other participants | 400 (none exceed 10 shares) | 1 or less | No |

(ii) Conclusion with respect to disqualified persons. As shown in column 4 in the table above, individuals B and C are disqualified persons for 2006 under paragraph (d)(1) of this section because each owns at least 10% of X's deemed-owned ESOP shares.

(iii) Conclusion with respect to nonallocation year. However, 2006 is not a nonallocation year under section 409(p) because disqualified persons do not own at least 50% of X's outstanding shares (the 100 shares owned directly by B, B's 330 deemed-owned ESOP shares, plus C's 145 deemed-owned ESOP shares equal only 47.9% of the 1,200 outstanding shares of X).

*Example (2).* Relating to determination of disqualified persons and nonallocation year if there is synthetic equity. (i) Facts. The facts are the same as in Example 1, except that, as shown in column 4 of the table in this example 2, individuals E and F have options to acquire 110 and 130 shares, respectively, of the common stock of X from X:

| 1 Shareholders | 2 Deemed-owned ESOP shares (total of 1,000) | 3 Percentage deemed-owned ESOP share | 4 Options (240) | 5 Shareholder percentage of deemed-owned ESOP plus synthetic equity shares | 6 Disqualified person |
|---|---|---|---|---|---|
| B | 330 | 33 | | | Yes (col. 3) |
| C | 145 | 14.5 | | | Yes (col. 3) |
| D | 75 | 7.5 | | | No |
| E | 30 | 3 | 110 | 11.1% ([30 + 91.7] divided by 1,091.7) | Yes (col. 5) |
| F | 20 | 2 | 130 | 11.6% ([20 + 108.3] divided by 1,108.3) | Yes (col. 5) |
| Other participants | 400 (none exceeds 10 shares) | 1 or less | | | No |

(ii) Conclusion with respect to disqualified persons. Applying the rule of paragraph (f)(4)(iv) of this section, E's option to acquire 110 shares of the S corporation converts into 91.7 shares of synthetic equity (110 times the ratio of the 1,000 deemed-owned ESOP shares to the sum of the 1,000 deemed-owned ESOP shares plus the 200 shares held outside the ESOP by A and B). Similarly, F's option to acquire 130 shares of the S corporation converts into 108.3 shares of synthetic equity (130 times the ratio of the 1,000 deemed-owned ESOP shares to the sum of the 1,000 deemed-owned ESOP shares plus the 200 shares held outside the ESOP by A and B). Accordingly, as shown in column 6 in the table above, individual E's synthetic equity shares are counted in determining whether E is a disqualified person for 2006, and individual F's synthetic equity shares are counted in determining whether F is a disqualified person for 2006, but the synthetic equity shares owned by any person do not affect the calculation for any other person's ownership of shares. Accordingly, individuals B, C, E, and F are disqualified persons for 2006.

(iii) Conclusion with respect to nonallocation year. The 100 shares owned directly by B, B's 330 deemed-owned ESOP shares, C's 145 deemed-owned ESOP shares, E's 30 deemed-owned ESOP shares, E's 91.7 synthetic equity shares, F's 20 deemed-owned ESOP shares, plus F's 108.3 synthetic equity shares total 825, which equals 58.9% of 1,400, which is the sum of the 1,200 outstanding shares of X and the 200 shares of synthetic equity shares of X held by disqualified persons. Thus, 2006 is a nonallocation year for X's ESOP under section 409(p) because disqualified persons own at least 50% of the total shares of outstanding stock of X and the total synthetic equity shares of X held by disqualified persons. In addition, independent of the preceding conclusion, 2006 would be a nonallocation year because disqualified persons own at least 50% of X's outstanding shares because the 100 shares owned directly by B, B's 330 deemed-owned ESOP shares, C's 145 deemed-owned ESOP shares, E's 30 deemed-owned ESOP shares, plus F's 20 deemed-owned ESOP shares equal 52.1% of the 1,200 outstanding shares of X.

*Example (3).* Relating to determination of number of shares of synthetic equity. (i) Facts. Corporation Y is a calendar year S corporation that maintains an ESOP. Y has a single class of common stock, of which there are a total of 1,000 shares outstanding, all of which are owned by the ESOP. Y has no synthetic equity, except for four grants of nonqualified deferred compensation that are made to an individual during the period from 2005 through 2011, as set forth in column 2 in the following table, and the ESOP uses the special rules in paragraph (f)(4)(iii) of this section to determine the number of shares of synthetic equity owned by that individual, as shown in columns 4 and 5:

| 1 Determination date | 2 Present value of nonqualified deferred compensation on determination date | 3 Share value on determination date | 4 New shares of synthetic equity on determination date | 5 Aggregate number of synthetic equity shares on determination date |
|---|---|---|---|---|
| January 1, 2005. | A grant is made on January 1, 2005 with a present value of $1,000. An additional grant of nonqualified deferred compensation with a present value of $775 is made on March 1, 2005 | $ 10 per share | 100 | 100 |
| January 1, 2006 | An additional grant is made on December 31, 2005 which has a present value of $800 on January 1, 2006. The March 1, 2005 grant has a present value on January 1, 2006 of $800. | $ 8 per share | 200 | 300 |
| January 1, 2007 | No new grants made | $ 12 per share | | 300 |
| January 1, 2008 | An additional grant is made on December 31, 2007 which has a present value of $3,000 on January 1, 2008. The grants made during 2005 through 2007 have an aggregate present value on January 1, 2008 of $3,750 | $ 15 per share | 200 | 450 |
| January 1, 2009 | No new grants are made | $ 11 per share | | 450 |
| January 1, 2010 | No new grants are made | $ 22 per share | | 450 |
| January 1, 2011. | No new grants are made. The grants made during 2005 through 2008 have an aggregate present value on January 1, 2011 of $7,600 | $ 20 per share | | 380 |

(ii) Conclusion. The grant made on January 1, 2005, is treated as 100 shares until the determination date in 2008. The grant made on March 1, 2005, is not taken into account until the 2006 determination date and its present value on that date, along with the then present value of the grant made on the preceding day, is treated as a number of shares that are based on the $8 per share value on the 2006 determination date, with the resulting number of shares continuing to apply until the determination date in 2008. On the January 1, 2008, determination date, the grant made on the preceding day is taken into account at its present value of $3,000 on January 1, 2008 and the $15 per share value on that date with the resulting number of shares (200) continuing to apply until the next determination date. In addition, on the January 1, 2008, determination date, the number of shares determined under other grants made between January 1, 2005 and December 31, 2007, must be revalued. Accordingly, the aggregate value of all nonqualified deferred compensation granted during that period is determined to be $3750 on January 1, 2008, and the corresponding number of shares of synthetic equity based on the $15 per share value is determined to be 250 shares on the 2008 determination date, with the resulting aggregate number of shares (450) continuing to apply until the determination date in 2011. On the January 1, 2011, determination date, the aggregate value of all nonqualified deferred compensation is determined to be $7,600 and the corresponding number of shares of synthetic equity based on the $20 per share value on the 2011 determination date is determined to be 380 shares (with the resulting number of shares continuing to apply until the determination date in 2014, assuming no further grants are made).

**(i) Effective dates.** *(1) Statutory effective date.* (i) Except as otherwise provided in paragraph (i)(1)(ii) of this section, section 409(p) applies for plan years ending after March 14, 2001.

(ii) If an ESOP holding stock in an S corporation was established on or before March 14, 2001, and the election under section 1362(a) with respect to that S corporation was in effect on March 14, 2001, section 409(p) applies for plan years beginning on or after January 1, 2005.

*(2) Regulation effective date.* (i) General effective date. Except as otherwise provided in paragraph (i)(2)(ii) of this section, this section applies for plan years beginning on or after January 1, 2005.

(ii) Rules for plan years beginning before January 1, 2005. (A) Except as provided in this paragraph (i)(2)(ii), § 1.409(p)-1T as in effect prior to December 17, 2004 (see § 1.409(p)-1T in 26 CFR part 1 revised as of April 1, 2004) applies for plan years ending after October 20, 2003, and beginning before January 1, 2005.

(B) Paragraphs (c)(3) and (g) of this section apply for plan years ending on or after December 31, 2004, but do not apply with respect to an interest held in a qualified subchapter S subsidiary (QSUB) of an S corporation or another entity to which paragraph (g)(3) of this section applies before March 15, 2004 if:

(1) All interests in the entity held by individuals who would be disqualified persons under paragraph (g)(3) of this section or under guidance issued by the Commissioner before March 15, 2004 are distributed to those individuals as compensation on or before March 15, 2004 and

(2) No such individual has been a participant in the ESOP of the S corporation at any time after October 20, 2003 and before March 15, 2004.

(C) Paragraph (f)(2)(iv)(B) of this section (providing that synthetic equity does not include certain preexisting nonqualified deferred compensation) applies for plan years ending before January 1, 2005.

(D) Paragraph (f)(4)(iv) of this section (permitting an adjustment of the number of synthetic equity shares where an ESOP owns less than 100% of an S corporation) applies for plan years ending before January 1, 2005.

(E) In no event does this paragraph (i)(2)(ii) apply for any plan year ending before January 1, 2005, for an ESOP holding stock in an S corporation that was established on or before March 14, 2001, if the election under section 1362(a) with respect to that S Corporation was in effect on March 14, 2001.

(iii) Transition rules. (A) Assets held in the account of a disqualified person as of the last day of the first plan year beginning before January 1, 2005, will not be treated as an impermissible accrual with respect to that disqualified person under paragraph (b)(2)((ii) of this section for the first plan year beginning on or after January 1, 2005, to the extent those assets are not held in that person's account on or after July 1, 2005. Thus, for example, to the extent the assets allocated to the account of a disqualified person as of the last day of the first plan year beginning before January 1, 2005, are transferred to a non-ESOP portion of the plan as described in paragraph (b)(2)(v)(A) of this section before July 1, 2005, those assets will not be treated as an impermissible accrual under paragraph (b)(2)((ii) of this section for the period from the first day of the first plan year beginning on or after January 1, 2005 through June 30, 2005. However, see section 4979A(a)(3), (a)(4), and (e)(2)(C) for excise tax provisions that apply to all deemed-owned shares during the first nonallocation year for the ESOP.

(B) An individual is not treated as a disqualified person during the period from the first day of the first plan year beginning on or after January 1, 2005 through June 30, 2005 if that person would not be a disqualified person during that period under the modified rules of this paragraph (i)(2)(iii)(B) as of any date during that same period. Further, solely for the purpose of determining whether the first plan year beginning on or after January 1, 2005 is a nonallocation year under section 409(p) and this section, if that plan year would not have been a nonallocation year under the modified rules of this paragraph (i)(2)(iii)(B), then synthetic equity that is not owned by a person on July 1, 2005 is disregarded during the period from the first day of the first plan year beginning on or after January 1, 2005 through June 30, 2005. For purposes of this paragraph (i)(2)(iii)(B), the modified rules of this paragraph (i)(2)(iii)(B) are the rules in § 1.409(p)-1T as in effect prior to December 17, 2004 (see § 1.409(p)-1T in 26 CFR Part 1 revised as of April 1, 2004), modified to exclude from the definition of synthetic equity any stock option, stock appreciation right (payable in cash or stock), or similar rights with respect to shares of the S corporation or a related entity where the facts and circumstances indicate that there is no reasonable likelihood that the holder of the right will receive the shares (or equivalent value). For this purpose, there is no reasonable likelihood that the holder of the right will receive the shares (or equivalent value) in any case in which the option is based on an exercise price that is more than 200% of the fair market value of the shares on the date of grant or the right (in the case of a stock appreciation right or similar right to acquire shares of the S corporation or a related entity) is payable only if the appreciation exceeds 100% of the fair market value of the shares on the date of grant.

(C) For the period from the first day of the first plan year beginning on or after January 1, 2005 through June 30, 2005, there is no nonallocation year under this section if there would be no nonallocation year under this section during that period if this section were applied without regard to paragraph (f)(4)(v) of this section (relating to voting rights).

(D) This paragraph (iii) does not apply to an ESOP for which the first plan year beginning on or after January 1, 2005 begins after June 30, 2005.

T.D. 9081, 7/18/2003, amend T.D. 9164, 12/16/2004.

## § 1.409A-0 Table of contents.

This section lists captions contained in §§ 1.409A-1, 1.409A-2, 1.409A-3, 1.409A-4, 1.409A-5 and 1.409A-6.

(B) Stock not readily tradable on an established securities market.

(1) In general.

(2) Presumption of reasonableness.

(3) Use of alternative methods.

(v) Modifications, extensions, substitutions, and assumptions of stock rights.

(A) Treatment of modified and extended stock rights.

(B) Modification in general.

(C) Extensions.

(1) In general.

(2) Certain extensions before April 10, 2007.

(3) Examples.

(D) Substitutions and assumptions of stock rights by reason of a corporate transaction.

(E) Acceleration of date when exercisable.

(F) Discretionary added benefits.

(G) Change in underlying stock increasing value.

(H) Change in the number of shares purchasable.

(I) Rescission of changes.

(J) Successive modifications and extensions.

(K) Modifications and extensions in effect on October 23, 2004.

(vi) Meaning and use of certain terms.

(A) Option.

(B) Date of grant of option.

(C) Stock.

(D) Exercise price.

(E) Exercise.

(F) Transfer.

(G) Readily tradable.

(H) Application to stock appreciation rights.

(6) Restricted property, section 402(b) trusts, and section 403(c) annuities.

(i) In general.

(ii) Promises to transfer property.

(7) Arrangements between partnerships and partners [Reserved].

(8) Certain foreign plans.

(i) Plans with respect to compensation covered by treaty or other international agreement.

(ii) Plans with respect to certain other compensation.

(iii) Tax equalization agreements.

(iv) Certain limited deferrals of a nonresident alien.

(v) Additional foreign plans.

(vi) Earnings.

(9) Separation pay plans.

(i) In general.

(ii) Collectively bargained separation pay plans.

(iii) Separation pay due to involuntary separation from service or participation in a window program.

(iv) Foreign separation pay plans.

(v) Reimbursements and certain other separation payments.

(A) In general.

(B) Medical benefits.

(C) In-kind benefits and direct service recipient payments.

(D) Limited payments.

(E) Limited period of time.

(vi) Window programs—definition.

(10) Certain indemnification and liability insurance plans.

(11) Legal settlements.

(12) Certain educational benefits.

(c) Plan.

(1) In general.

(2) Plan aggregation rules.

(i) In general.

(ii) Dual status.

(3) Establishment of plan.

(i) In general.

(ii) Initial deferral election provisions.

(iii) Subsequent deferral election provisions.

(iv) Payment accelerations.

(v) Six-month delay for specified employees.

(vi) Plan amendments.

(vii) Transition rule for written plan requirement.

(viii) Plan agregation rules.

(d) Substantial risk of forfeiture.

(1) In general.

(2) Stock rights.

(3) Enforcement of forfeiture condition.

(i) In general.

(ii) Examples.

(e) Performance-based compensation.

(1) In general.

(2) Payments based upon subjective performance criteria.

(3) Equity-based compensation.

(f) Service provider.

(1) In general.

(2) Independent contractors.

(i) In general.

(ii) Related person.

(iii) Significant services.

(iv) Management services.

(v) Services provided to related persons.

(g) Service recipient.

(h) Separation from service.

(1) Employees.

(i) In general.

(ii) Termination of employment.

(2) Independent contractors.

(i) In general.

(ii) Special rule.

(3) Definition of service recipient and employer.

(4) Asset purchase transactions.

(5) Dual status.

(6) Collectively bargained plans covering multiple employers.

(i) Specified employee.

(1) In general.

(2) Definition of compensation.
(3) Specified employee identification date.
(4) Specified employee effective date.
(5) Alternative methods of satisfying the six-month delay rule.
(6) Corporate transactions.
(i) Mergers and acquisitions of public service recipients.
(ii) Mergers and acquisitions of nonpublic service recipients.
(iii) Spinoffs.
(iv) Public offerings and other corporate transactions.
(v) Alternative methods of compliance.
(7) Nonresident alien employees.
(8) Elections affecting the identification of specified employees.
(j) Nonresident alien.
(k) Established securities market.
(l) Stock right.
(m) Separation pay plan.
(n) Involuntary separation from service.
(1) In general.
(2) Separations from service for good reason.
(i) In general.
(ii) Safe harbor.
(3) Special rule for certain collectively bargained plans.
(o) Earnings.
(p) In-kind benefits.
(q) Application of definitions and rules.

*§ 1.409A-2 Deferral elections.*

(a) Initial elections as to the time and form of payment.
(1) In general.
(2) Service recipient elections.
(3) General rule.
(4) Initial deferral election with respect to short-term deferrals.
(5) Initial deferral election with respect to certain forfeitable rights.
(6) Initial deferral election with respect to fiscal year compensation.
(7) First year of eligibility.
(i) In general.
(ii) Eligibility to participate.
(iii) Application to excess benefit plans.
(8) Initial deferral election with respect to performance-based compensation.
(9) Nonqualified deferred compensation plans linked to qualified employer plans or certain other arrangements.
(10) Changes in elections under a cafeteria plan.
(11) Initial deferral election with respect to certain separation pay.
(12) Initial deferral election with respect to certain commissions.
(i) Sales commission compensation.
(ii) Investment commission compensation.
(iii) Commission compensation and related persons.
(13) Initial deferral election with respect to compensation paid for final payroll period.
(i) In general.
(ii) Transition rule.
(14) Elections to annualize recurring part-year compensation.
(15) USERRA rights.
(b) Subsequent changes in time and form of payment.
(1) In general.
(2) Definition of payments for purposes of subsequent changes in the time and form of payment.
(i) In general.
(ii) Life annuities.
(A) In general.
(B) Certain features disregarded.
(C) Subsidized joint and survivor annuities.
(D) Actuarial assumptions and methods.
(iii) Installment payments.
(iv) Transition rule.
(3) Beneficiaries.
(4) Domestic relations orders.
(5) Coordination with prohibition against acceleration of payments.
(6) Application to multiple payment events.
(7) Delay of payments under certain circumstances.
(i) Payments subject to section 162(m).
(ii) Payments that would violate Federal securities laws or other applicable law.
(iii) Other events and conditions.
(8) USERRA rights.
(9) Examples.
(c) Special rules for certain resident aliens.

*§ 1.409A-3 Permissible payments.*

(a) In general.
(b) Designation of payment upon a permissible payment event.
(c) Designation of alternative specified dates or payment schedules based upon date of permissible event.
(d) When a payment is treated as made upon the designated payment date.
(e) Designation of time and form of payment with respect to earnings.
(f) Substitutions.
(g) Disputed payments and refusals to pay.
(h) Special rule for certain resident aliens.
(i) Definitions and special rules.
(1) Specified time or fixed schedule.
(i) In general.
(ii) Payment schedules with formula and fixed limitations.
(A) Individual limitations.
(B) Limitations on aggregate payments to all participants in substantially identical plans.
(iii) Payment schedules determined by timing of payments received by the service recipient.
(iv) Reimbursement or in-kind benefit plans.
(A) General rule.

(B) Medical reimbursement arrangements.

(v) Tax gross-up payments.

(vi) Examples.

(2) Separation from service—required delay in payment to a specified employee pursuant to a separation from service.

(i) In general.

(ii) Application of payment rules to delayed payments.

(3) Unforeseeable emergency.

(i) Definition.

(ii) Amount of payment permitted upon an unforeseeable emergency.

(iii) Payments due to an unforeseeable emergency.

(4) Disability.

(i) In general.

(ii) Limited plan definition of disability.

(iii) Determination of disability.

(5) Change in the ownership or effective control of a corporation, or a change in the ownership of a substantial portion of the assets of a corporation.

(i) In general.

(ii) Identification of relevant corporation.

(A) In general.

(B) Majority shareholder.

(C) Example.

(iii) Attribution of stock ownership.

(iv) Special rules for certain delayed payments pursuant to a change in control event.

(A) Certain transaction-based compensation.

(B) Certain nonvested compensation.

(v) Change in the ownership of a corporation.

(A) In general.

(B) Persons acting as a group.

(vi) Change in the effective control of a corporation.

(A) In general.

(B) Multiple change in control events.

(C) Acquisition of additional control.

(D) Persons acting as a group.

(vii) Change in the ownership of a substantial portion of a corporation's assets.

(A) In general.

(B) Transfers to a related person.

(C) Persons acting as a group.

(6) Certain back-to-back arrangements.

(i) In general.

(ii) Example.

(j) Prohibition on acceleration of payments.

(1) In general.

(2) Application to multiple payment events.

(3) Beneficiaries.

(4) Exceptions.

(i) In general.

(ii) Domestic relations order.

(iii) Conflicts of interest.

(A) Compliance with ethics agreements with the Federal government.

(B) Compliance with ethics laws or conflicts of interest laws.

(iv) Section 457 plans.

(v) Limited cashouts.

(vi) Payment of employment taxes.

(vii) Payment upon income inclusion under section 409A.

(viii) Cancellation of deferrals following an unforeseeable emergency or hardship distribution.

(ix) Plan terminations and liquidations.

(x) Certain distributions to avoid a nonallocation year under section 409(p).

(xi) Payment of state, local, or foreign taxes.

(xii) Cancellation of deferral elections due to disability.

(xiii) Certain offsets.

(xiv) Bona fide disputes as to a right to a payment.

(5) Nonqualified deferred compensation plans linked to qualified employer plans or certain other arrangements.

(6) Changes in elections under a cafeteria plan.

*§ 1.409A-4 Calculation of income inclusion [Reserved].*

*§ 1.409A-5 Funding [Reserved].*

*§ 1.409A-6 Application of section 409A and effective dates.*

(a) Statutory application and effective dates.

(1) Application to amounts deferred.

(i) In general.

(ii) Collectively bargained plans.

(2) Identification of date of deferral for statutory effective date purposes.

(3) Calculation of amount of compensation deferred for statutory effective date purposes.

(i) Nonaccount balance plans.

(ii) Account balance plans.

(iii) Equity-based compensation plans.

(iv) Earnings.

(v) Definition of plan.

(4) Material modifications.

(i) In general.

(ii) Adoptions of new plans.

(iii) Suspension or termination of a plan.

(iv) Changes to investment measures—account balance plans.

(v) Stock rights.

(vi) Rescission of modifications.

(vii) Definition of plan.

(b) Regulatory applicability date.

---

T.D. 9321, 4/10/2007.

---

PAR. 2. Section 1.409A-0 is amended by adding entries for § 1.409A-4 to read as follows:

**Proposed § 1.409A-0 Table of contents.** [*For Preamble, see ¶ 153,075*]

* * * * *

*§ 1.409A-4 Calculation of amount includible in income and additional income taxes.*

(a) Amount includible in income due to failure to meet the requirements of section 409A(a).

(1) In general.

(i) Calculation formula.

(ii) Each taxable year analyzed independently.

(A) In general.

(B) Treatment of certain deferred amounts otherwise subject to a substantial risk of forfeiture.

(iii) Examples.

(2) Identification of the portion of the total amount deferred for a taxable year that is subject to a substantial risk of forfeiture.

(i) In general.

(ii) Example.

(3) Identification of amount previously included in income.

(i) In general.

(ii) Examples.

(b) The total amount deferred under a plan for a taxable year.

(1) Application of general rules and specific rules for specific types of plans.

(2) General definition of total amount deferred.

(i) General calculation rules.

(ii) Actuarial assumptions and methods.

(A) Requirement of reasonable actuarial assumptions and methods.

(B) Use of an unreasonable actuarial assumption or method.

(iii) Crediting of earnings and losses.

(iv) Application of the general calculation rules to formula amounts.

(A) In general.

(B) Examples.

(v) Treatment of payment restrictions.

(vi) Treatment of alternative times and forms of a future payment.

(A) In general.

(B) Effect of status of service provider on available times and forms of payment.

(vii) Treatment of payment triggers based upon events.

(A) In general.

(B) Certain payment triggers disregarded.

(viii) Treatment of amounts that may qualify as short-term deferrals.

(ix) Examples.

(3) Account balance plans.

(i) In general.

(ii) Unreasonable rate of return.

(A) Application.

(B) Unreasonably high interest rate.

(C) Other rates of return.

(4) Reimbursement and in-kind benefit arrangements.

(5) Split-dollar life insurance arrangements.

(6) Stock rights.

(7) Anti-abuse provision.

(c) Additional 20 percent tax under section 409A(a)(1)(B)(i)(II).

(d) Premium interest tax under section 409A(a)(1)(B)(i)(I).

(1) In general.

(2) Identification of taxable year deferred amount was first deferred or vested.

(i) Method of identification.

(ii) Examples.

(3) Calculation of hypothetical underpayment for the taxable year during which a deferred amount was first deferred and vested.

(i) Calculation method.

(ii) Examples.

(4) Calculation of hypothetical premium underpayment interest.

(i) Calculation method.

(ii) Examples.

(e) Amounts includible in income under section 409A(b) [Reserved].

(f) Application of amounts included in income under section 409A to payments of amounts deferred.

(1) In general.

(2) Application of the plan aggregation rules.

(3) Examples.

(g) Forfeiture or other permanent loss of right to deferred compensation.

(1) Availability of deduction to the service provider.

(2) Application of the plan aggregation rules.

(3) Examples.

(h) Effective/applicability date.

* * * * *

**§ 1.409A-1 Definitions and covered plans.**

**(a) Nonqualified deferred compensation plan.** *(1) In general.* Except as otherwise provided in this paragraph (a), the term nonqualified deferred compensation plan means any plan (within the meaning of paragraph (c) of this section) that provides for the deferral of compensation (within the meaning of paragraph (b) of this section). Whether a plan provides for the deferral of compensation generally is determined at the time the service provider obtains a legally binding right to the compensation under the plan, and is not affected by any retroactive change to the plan to characterize the right as one that does not provide for the deferral of compensation. For example, amounts deferred under a nonqualified deferred compensation plan do not become an excluded death benefit if the plan is amended so that the amounts are payable only upon the death of the service provider. If a principal purpose of a plan is to achieve a result with respect to a deferral of compensation that is inconsistent with the purposes of section 409A, the Commissioner may treat the plan as a nonqualified deferred compensation plan for purposes of section 409A and the regulations thereunder.

*(2) Qualified employer plans.* The term nonqualified deferred compensation plan does not include a qualified employer plan. The term qualified employer plan means any of the following plans:

(i) Any plan described in section 401(a) and a trust exempt from tax under section 501(a) or that is described in section 402(d).

(ii) Any annuity plan described in section 403(a).

(iii) Any annuity contract described in section 403(b).

(iv) Any simplified employee pension (within the meaning of section 408(k)).

(v) Any simple retirement account (within the meaning of section 408(p)).

(vi) Any plan under which an active participant makes deductible contributions to a trust described in section 501(c)(18).

(vii) Any eligible deferred compensation plan (within the meaning of section 457(b)).

(viii) Any plan described in section 415(m).

(ix) Any plan described in § 1022(i)(2) of the Employee Retirement Income Security Act of 1974, Public Law 93-406 (88 Stat. 829, 942) (Sept. 2, 1974) (ERISA).

*(3) Certain foreign plans.* (i) With respect to an individual for a taxable year, the term nonqualified deferred compensation plan does not include any scheme, trust, arrangement, or plan maintained with respect to such individual, to the extent contributions made by or on behalf of such individual to such scheme, trust, arrangement, or plan, or credited allocations, accrued benefits, earnings, or other amounts constituting income, of such individual under such scheme, trust, arrangement, or plan, are excludable by such individual for Federal income tax purposes pursuant to any bilateral income tax convention, or other bilateral or multilateral agreement, to which the United States is a party.

(ii) Participation by nonresident aliens, certain resident aliens, and bona fide residents of possessions. With respect to an alien individual for a taxable year during which such individual is a nonresident alien, a resident alien classified as a resident alien solely under section 7701(b)(1)(A)(ii) (and not section 7701(b)(1)(A)(i)), or a bona fide resident of a possession (within the meaning of section 937(a)), the term nonqualified deferred compensation plan does not include any broad-based foreign retirement plan (within the meaning of paragraph (a)(3)(v) of this section).

(iii) Participation by U.S. citizens and lawful permanent residents. With respect to an individual for a given taxable year during which such individual is a U.S. citizen or a resident alien classified as a resident alien under section 7701(b)(1)(A)(i), other than an individual who is also a bona fide resident of a possession (within the meaning of section 937(a)), the term nonqualified deferred compensation plan does not include a broad-based foreign retirement plan (within the meaning of paragraph (a)(3)(v) of this section), but only with respect to a plan, or a portion of a plan where such portion may be distinguished, providing for nonelective deferrals of modified foreign earned income, and earnings with respect to such nonelective deferrals, and only to the extent that the amounts deferred under all such plans of the service recipient, or all portions of such plans, in which the service provider participates in such taxable year, do not exceed the applicable limits under section 415(b) (applied to nonaccount balance plans as defined in paragraph (c)(2)(i)(C) of this section) and section 415(c) (applied to account balance plans as defined in paragraph (c)(2)(i)(A) of this section) that would be applicable if such plans were plans subject to section 415 and the modified foreign earned income of such individual were treated as compensation for purposes of applying section 415(b) and (c). For purposes of this paragraph (a)(3)(iii), the term modified foreign earned income means foreign earned income as defined in section 911(b)(1) without regard to section 911(b)(1)(B)(iv) and without regard to the requirement that the income be attributable to services performed during the period described in section 911(d)(1)(A) or (B). The provisions of this paragraph (a)(3)(iii) do not apply to any individual with respect to any taxable year in which the individual is simultaneously eligible to participate in a broad-based foreign retirement plan and a qualified employer plan described in paragraph (a)(2) of this section. For purposes of this paragraph (a)(3)(iii), an individual is eligible to participate in a qualified employer plan if under the terms of the plan and without further amendment or action by the plan sponsor, the individual is eligible to make or receive contributions or accrue benefits under the plan (regardless of whether the individual has elected to participate in the plan).

(iv) Plans subject to a totalization agreement and similar plans. The term nonqualified deferred compensation plan does not include any social security system of a jurisdiction to the extent that benefits provided under or contributions made to the system are subject to an agreement entered into pursuant to section 233 of the Social Security Act (42 U.S.C. 433) with any foreign jurisdiction. In addition, the term nonqualified deferred compensation plan does not include a social security system of a foreign jurisdiction to the extent that benefits are provided under or contributions are made to a government-mandated plan as part of that foreign jurisdiction's social security system.

(v) Broad-based foreign retirement plan. The term broad-based foreign retirement plan means a scheme, trust, arrangement, or plan (regardless of whether sponsored by a U.S. person) that is written and that, in the case of an employer-maintained plan, satisfies the following conditions:

(A) The plan is nondiscriminatory insofar as the employees who, under the terms of the plan (alone or in combination with other comparable plans) and without further amendment or action by the employer, are eligible to make or receive contributions or accrue benefits under the plan other than earnings (regardless of whether the employee has elected to participate in the plan), are a wide range of employees, substantially all of whom are nonresident aliens, resident aliens classified as resident aliens solely under section 7701(b)(1)(A)(ii) (and not section 7701(b)(1)(A)(i)), or bona fide residents of a possession (within the meaning of section 937(a)), including rank and file employees.

(B) The plan (alone or in combination with other comparable plans) actually provides significant benefits for a substantial majority of such covered employees.

(C) The benefits actually provided under the plan to such covered employees are nondiscriminatory.

(D) The plan contains provisions or is the subject of tax law provisions or other legal restrictions that generally discourage employees from using plan benefits for purposes other than retirement or restrict access to plan benefits before separation from service, including (but not limited to), restricting in-service distributions except in events similar to an unforeseeable emergency (as defined in § 1.409A-3(i)(3)(i)) or hardship (as defined for purposes of section 401(k)(2)(B)(i)(IV)), or for educational purposes or the purchase of a primary residence.

*(4) Section 457 plans.* A nonqualified deferred compensation plan under section 457(f) may constitute a nonqualified deferred compensation plan for purposes of this paragraph (a). The rules of section 409A apply to nonqualified deferred

compensation plans separately and in addition to any requirements applicable to such plans under section 457(f). In addition, nonelective deferred compensation of non-employees described in section 457(e)(12) and a grandfathered plan or arrangement described in § 1.457-2(k)(4) may constitute a nonqualified deferred compensation plan for purposes of this paragraph (a). The term nonqualified deferred compensation plan does not include a length of service award to a bona fide volunteer under section 457(e)(11)(A)(ii). For purposes of the application of section 409A to a plan to which section 457 applies, a payment under the plan generally means the provision of cash or property to the service provider, provided that for purposes of the application of the short-term deferral rule set forth in paragraph (b)(4) of this section, the inclusion in income of an amount under section 457(f) is treated as a payment of the amount.

*(5) Certain welfare benefits.* The term nonqualified deferred compensation plan does not include a plan, or a portion of a plan, to the extent that the plan provides bona fide vacation leave, sick leave, compensatory time, disability pay, or death benefits. For these purposes, the terms "disability pay" and "death benefits" have the same meanings as provided in § 31.3121(v)(2)-1(b)(4)(iv)(C) of this chapter, provided that for purposes of this paragraph, such disability pay and death benefits may be provided through insurance and the lifetime benefits payable under the plan are not treated as including the value of any taxable term life insurance coverage or taxable disability insurance coverage provided under the plan. The term nonqualified deferred compensation plan also does not include any Archer Medical Savings Account as described in section 220, any Health Savings Account as described in section 223, or any other medical reimbursement arrangement, including a health reimbursement arrangement, that satisfies the requirements of section 105 and section 106 such that the benefits or reimbursements provided under such arrangement are not includible in income.

**(b) Deferral of compensation.** *(1) In general.* Except as otherwise provided in paragraphs (b)(3) through (b)(12) of this section, a plan provides for the deferral of compensation if, under the terms of the plan and the relevant facts and circumstances, the service provider has a legally binding right during a taxable year to compensation that, pursuant to the terms of the plan, is or may be payable to (or on behalf of) the service provider in a later taxable year. Such compensation is deferred compensation for purposes of section 409A, this section and §§ 1.409A-2 through 1.409A-6. A legally binding right to an amount that will be excluded from income when and if received does not constitute a deferral of compensation, unless the service provider has received the right in exchange for, or has the right to exchange the right for, an amount that will be includible in income (other than due to participation in a cafeteria plan described in section 125). A service provider does not have a legally binding right to compensation to the extent that compensation may be reduced unilaterally or eliminated by the service recipient or other person after the services creating the right to the compensation have been performed. However, if the facts and circumstances indicate that the discretion to reduce or eliminate the compensation is available or exercisable only upon a condition, or the discretion to reduce or eliminate the compensation lacks substantive significance, a service provider will be considered to have a legally binding right to the compensation. Whether the discretion to reduce or eliminate the compensation lacks substantive significance depends on all the relevant facts and circumstances. However, where the service provider to whom the compensation may be paid has effective control of the person retaining the discretion to reduce or eliminate the compensation, or has effective control over any portion of the compensation of the person retaining the discretion to reduce or eliminate the compensation, or is a member of the family (as defined in section 267(c)(4) applied as if the family of an individual includes the spouse of any member of the family) of the person retaining the discretion to reduce or eliminate the compensation, the discretion to reduce or eliminate the compensation will not be treated as having substantive significance. For this purpose, compensation is not considered subject to unilateral reduction or elimination merely because it may be reduced or eliminated by operation of the objective terms of the plan, such as the application of a nondiscretionary, objective provision creating a substantial risk of forfeiture. Similarly, a service provider does not fail to have a legally binding right to compensation merely because the amount of compensation is determined under a formula that provides for benefits to be offset by benefits provided under another plan (including a plan that is qualified under section 401(a)), or because benefits are reduced due to actual or notional investment losses, or, in a final average pay plan, subsequent decreases in compensation.

*(2) Earnings.* References to the deferral of compensation or deferred compensation include references to earnings. When the right to earnings is specified under the terms of the plan, the legally binding right to earnings arises at the time of the deferral of the compensation to which the earnings relate. A plan may provide that the time and form of payment of earnings is treated separately from the time and form of payment of the underlying compensation, so that, provided that the rules of section 409A are otherwise met, a plan may provide that earnings will be paid at a separate time or in a separate form from the payment of the underlying compensation. For the application of the deferral election rules to current payments of earnings and dividend equivalents, see § 1.409A-3(e).

*(3) Compensation payable pursuant to the service recipient's customary payment timing arrangement.* A deferral of compensation does not occur solely because compensation is paid after the last day of the service provider's taxable year pursuant to the timing arrangement under which the service recipient normally compensates service providers for services performed during a payroll period described in section 3401(b), or with respect to a non-employee service provider, a period not longer than the payroll period described in section 3401(b) or if no such payroll period exists, a period not longer than the earlier of the normal timing arrangement under which the service provider normally compensates non-employee service providers or 30 days after the end of the service provider's taxable year.

*(4) Short-term deferrals.* (i) In general. A deferral of compensation does not occur under a plan with respect to any payment (as defined in Sec. 1.409A-2(b)(2)) that is not a deferred payment, provided that the service provider actually or constructively receives such payment on or before the last day of the applicable 2 ½ month period. The following rules apply for purposes of this paragraph (b)(4)(i):

(A) The applicable 2 ½ month period is the period ending on the later of the 15th day of the third month following the end of the service provider's first taxable year in which the right to the payment is no longer subject to a substantial risk of forfeiture or the 15th day of the third month following the end of the service recipient's first taxable year in which the right to the payment is no longer subject to a substantial risk of forfeiture.

(B) A payment is treated as actually or constructively received if the payment is includible in income, including if the payment is includible in income under section 83, the economic benefit doctrine, section 402(b), or section 457(f).

(C) A right to a payment that is never subject to a substantial risk of forfeiture is considered to be no longer subject to a substantial risk of forfeiture on the first date the service provider has a legally binding right to the payment.

(D) A payment is a deferred payment if it is made pursuant to a provision of a plan that provides for the payment to be made or completed on or after any date, or upon or after the occurrence of any event, that will or may occur later than the end of the applicable 2 ½ month period, such as a separation from service, death, disability, change in control event, specified time or schedule of payment, or unforeseeable emergency, regardless of whether an amount is actually paid as a result of the occurrence of such a payment date or event during the applicable 2 ½ month period. If a plan provides that the service provider or service recipient may make an election under the plan (including an election under § 1.409A-2(a)(4)) of a different payment date, schedule, or event, such right is disregarded for this purpose. In such cases, whether a plan provides for a deferred payment is determined based on the payment date, schedule, or event that would apply if no such election were made, except that if the plan would not provide for a deferred payment absent such an election, and the service provider or service recipient makes such an election, whether the plan provides for a deferred payment is determined based upon the payment date, schedule, or event that the service provider or service recipient in fact elected.

(E) A stock right provides for a deferred payment if such right includes any provision pursuant to which the holder of the stock right will or may have the right to exercise the stock right after the applicable 2 ½ month period.

(F) This paragraph (b)(4)(i) is applied separately to each payment (as defined in § 1.409A-2(b)(2)) required to be made under a plan.

(G) If a plan provides for a deferred payment with respect to part of a payment (for example a life annuity or a series of installment amounts treated as a single payment), the plan provides for a deferred payment with respect to the entire payment.

(ii) Certain delayed payments. A payment that otherwise qualifies as a short-term deferral under paragraph (b)(4)(i) of this section but is made after the applicable 2 ½ month period may continue to qualify as a short-term deferral if the taxpayer establishes that it was administratively impracticable to make the payment by the end of the applicable 2 ½ month period and, as of the date upon which the legally binding right to the compensation arose, such impracticability was unforeseeable, or the taxpayer establishes that making the payment by the end of the applicable 2 ½ month period would have jeopardized the ability of the service recipient to continue as a going concern, and provided further that the payment is made as soon as administratively practicable or as soon as the payment would no longer have such effect. For purposes of this paragraph (b)(4)(ii), an action or failure to act of the service provider or a person under the service provider's control, such as a failure to provide necessary information or documentation, is not an unforeseeable event. In addition, a payment that otherwise qualifies as a short-term deferral under paragraph (b)(4)(i) of this section but is made after the applicable 2 ½ month period may continue to qualify as a short-term deferral if the taxpayer establishes that the service recipient reasonably anticipated that the service recipient's deduction with respect to such payment otherwise would not be permitted by application of section 162(m), and, as of the date the legally binding right to the payment arose, a reasonable person would not have anticipated the application of section 162(m) at the time of the payment, and provided further that the payment is made as soon as reasonably practicable following the first date on which the service recipient anticipates or reasonably should anticipate that, if the payment were made on such date, the service recipient's deduction with respect to such payment would no longer be restricted due to the application of section 162(m). For additional rules applicable to certain transaction-based compensation, see § 1.409A-3(i)(5)(iv)(A).

(iii) Examples. The following examples illustrate the provisions of this paragraph (b)(4). In these examples, except as otherwise noted, each employee and each employer has a calendar year taxable year and each employee is an individual who is employed by the specified employer.

*Example (1).* On November 1, 2008, Employer Z awards a bonus to Employee A such that Employee A has a legally binding right to the payment as of November 1, 2008, that is not subject to a substantial risk of forfeiture. The bonus plan does not provide for a payment date or a deferred payment. The bonus plan will not be considered to have provided for a deferral of compensation if the bonus is paid or made available to Employee A on or before March 15, 2009.

*Example (2).* Employer Y has a taxable year ending August 31. On November 1, 2008, Employer Y awards a bonus to Employee B so that Employee B has a legally binding right to the payment as of November 1, 2008, that is not subject to a substantial risk of forfeiture. The bonus plan does not provide for a payment date or a deferred payment. The bonus plan will not be considered to have provided for a deferral of compensation if the bonus is paid or made available to Employee B on or before November 15, 2009.

*Example (3).* On November 1, 2008, Employer X awards a bonus to Employee C such that Employee C has a legally binding right to the payment as of November 1, 2008. Under the bonus plan, Employee C will forfeit the bonus unless Employee C continues performing services through December 31, 2010. The right to the payment is subject to a substantial risk of forfeiture through December 31, 2010. Employee C has the right to make a written election not later than December 31, 2009, to receive the bonus on or after December 31, 2015, but Employee C does not make such election. The bonus plan does not provide for a default payment date or a deferred payment in the absence of an election by Employee C. The bonus plan will not be considered to have provided for a deferral of compensation if the bonus is paid or made available to Employee C on or before March 15, 2011.

*Example (4).* On November 1, 2008, Employer W awards a bonus to Employee D such that Employee D has a legally binding right to the payment as of November 1, 2008. Under the bonus plan, the bonus will be determined based on services performed during the period from January 1, 2009 through December 31, 2010. The bonus is scheduled to be paid as a lump sum payment on February 15, 2011. Under the bonus plan, Employee D will forfeit the bonus unless Employee D continues performing services through the scheduled payment date (February 15, 2011). Provided that at all times before the scheduled payment date Employee D is required to continue to perform services to retain the right to the bonus, and the bonus is paid on or before March 15,

2012, the bonus plan will not be considered to have provided for a deferral of compensation.

*Example (5).* On November 1, 2008, Employer V awards a bonus to Employee E such that Employee E has a legally binding right to the payment as of November 1, 2008. Under the bonus plan, Employee E will forfeit the bonus unless Employee E continues performing services through December 31, 2010. Under the bonus plan, the bonus is scheduled to be paid as a lump sum payment on July 1, 2011. By specifying a payment date after the applicable 2 ½ month period, the bonus plan provides for a deferred payment. The bonus plan provides for a deferral of compensation, and will not qualify as a short-term deferral regardless of whether the bonus is paid or made available on or before March 15, 2011 (and generally any payment before June 1, 2011 would constitute an impermissible acceleration of a payment).

*Example (6).* On November 1, 2008, Employer U awards a bonus to Employee F such that Employee F has a legally binding right to the payment as of November 1, 2008, that is not subject to a substantial risk of forfeiture. The bonus plan provides for a lump sum payment upon Employee F's separation from service. Because the separation from service is an event that may occur after the applicable 2 ½ month period, the bonus plan provides for a deferred payment and therefore provides for a deferral of compensation. Accordingly, the bonus plan will not qualify as a short-term deferral regardless of whether Employee F separates from service and the bonus is paid or made available on or before March 15, 2009.

*Example (7).* On November 1, 2008, Employer T grants Employee G a legally binding right to the payment of a life annuity with the first annuity payment on November 1, 2013, provided that Employee G continues performing services for Employer T continuously through November 1, 2013. Because the life annuity is treated as a single payment, and because all payments of the life annuity may not occur during the applicable 2 ½ month period, the plan provides for a deferred payment and none of the amounts payable under the annuity will qualify as a short-term deferral, so that section 409A applies to all amounts that are payable under the plan.

*Example (8).* On November 1, 2008, Employer S grants Employee H a stock right providing for an exercise price less than the fair market value of the underlying stock on November 1, 2008. The stock right is subject to a substantial risk of forfeiture requiring services through November 1, 2010. The stock right becomes exercisable when the substantial risk of forfeiture lapses and expires on November 1, 2013. Employee H continues providing services through November 1, 2010, at which time the substantial risk of forfeiture lapses. The stock right provides for a deferred payment and will not qualify as a short-term deferral regardless of whether Employee H exercises the stock right on or before March 15, 2011.

*(5) Stock options, stock appreciation rights, and other equity-based compensation.* (i) Stock rights. (A) Nonstatutory stock options not providing for the deferral of compensation. An option to purchase service recipient stock does not provide for a deferral of compensation if—

(1) The exercise price may never be less than the fair market value of the underlying stock (disregarding lapse restrictions as defined in § 1.83-3(i)) on the date the option is granted and the number of shares subject to the option is fixed on the original date of grant of the option;

(2) The transfer or exercise of the option is subject to taxation under section 83 and § 1.83-7; and

(3) The option does not include any feature for the deferral of compensation other than the deferral of recognition of income until the later of the following:

(i) The exercise or disposition of the option under § 1.83-7.

(ii) The time the stock acquired pursuant to the exercise of the option first becomes substantially vested (as defined in § 1.83-3(b)).

(B) Stock appreciation rights not providing for the deferral of compensation. A right to compensation based on the appreciation in value of a specified number of shares of service recipient stock occurring between the date of grant and the date of exercise of such right (a stock appreciation right) does not provide for a deferral of compensation if—

(1) Compensation payable under the stock appreciation right cannot be greater than the excess of the fair market value of the stock (disregarding lapse restrictions as defined in § 1.83-3(i)) on the date the stock appreciation right is exercised over an amount specified on the date of grant of the stock appreciation right (the stock appreciation right exercise price), with respect to a number of shares fixed on or before the date of grant of the right;

(2) The stock appreciation right exercise price may never be less than the fair market value of the underlying stock (disregarding lapse restrictions as defined in § 1.83-3(i)) on the date the right is granted; and

(3) The stock appreciation right does not include any feature for the deferral of compensation other than the deferral of recognition of income until the exercise of the stock appreciation right.

(C) Stock rights that may provide for the deferral of compensation. An option to purchase stock other than service recipient stock, or a stock appreciation right with respect to stock other than service recipient stock, generally will provide for the deferral of compensation within the meaning of this paragraph (b). If under the terms of an option to purchase service recipient stock (other than an incentive stock option described in section 422 or a stock option granted under an employee stock purchase plan described in section 423), the exercise price is or could become less than the fair market value of the stock (disregarding lapse restrictions as defined in § 1.83-3(i)) on the date of grant, the grant of the option generally will provide for the deferral of compensation within the meaning of this paragraph (b). If under the terms of a stock appreciation right with respect to service recipient stock, the compensation payable under the stock appreciation right is or could be any amount greater than, with respect to a predetermined number of shares, the excess of the fair market value of the stock (disregarding lapse restrictions as defined in § 1.83-3(i)) on the date the stock appreciation right is exercised over the fair market value of the stock (disregarding lapse restrictions as defined in § 1.83-3(i)) on the date of grant of the stock appreciation right, the grant of the stock appreciation right generally will provide for a deferral of compensation within the meaning of this paragraph (b).

(D) Feature for the deferral of compensation. To the extent a stock right provides a right other than the right to receive cash or stock on the date of exercise and such additional right would otherwise allow compensation to be deferred beyond the date of exercise, the entire arrangement (including the underlying stock right) provides for the deferral of compensation. For purposes of this paragraph (b)(5)(i), neither the right to receive substantially nonvested stock (as defined in § 1.83-3(b)) upon the exercise of a stock right, nor the right to pay the exercise price with previously acquired shares, constitutes a feature for the deferral of compensation.

(E) Rights to dividends. For purposes of this paragraph (b)(5)(i), the right, directly or indirectly contingent upon the exercise of a stock right, to receive an amount equal to all or part of the dividends or other distributions (other than stock dividends described in paragraph (b)(5)(v)(H) of this section) declared and paid on the number of shares underlying the stock right between the date of grant and the date of exercise of the stock right constitutes an offset to the exercise price of the stock option or an increase in the amount payable under the stock appreciation right (generally causing such stock right to be subject to section 409A). A plan providing a right to dividends or other distributions declared and paid on the number of shares underlying a stock right, the payment of which is not contingent upon, or otherwise payable on, the exercise of the stock right, may provide for a deferral of compensation, but the existence of the right to receive such an amount will not be treated as a reduction to the exercise price of (or an increase to the compensation payable under) the stock right. Thus, a right to such dividends or distributions that is not contingent, directly or indirectly, upon the exercise of a stock right will not cause the related stock right to fail to satisfy the requirements of the exclusion from the definition of a deferral of compensation provided in paragraphs (b)(5)(i)(A) and (B) of this section.

(ii) Statutory stock options. The grant of an incentive stock option as described in section 422, or the grant of an option under an employee stock purchase plan described in section 423 (including the grant of an option with an exercise price discounted in accordance with section 423(b)(6) and the accompanying regulations), does not constitute a deferral of compensation. However, the exclusion for statutory stock options under this paragraph (b)(5)(ii) does not apply to a modification, extension, or renewal of a statutory option that is treated as the grant of a new option that is not a statutory option. See § 1.424-1(e). In such event, the option is treated for purposes of this paragraph (b) as if it had been a nonstatutory stock option from the date of the original grant. Accordingly, if such modification, extension, or renewal of the stock option would have been treated as the grant of a new option or as causing the option to have had a deferral feature from the date of grant under paragraph (b)(5)(v) of this section, the modification, extension, or renewal of the stock option is treated as the grant of a new option or as causing the option to have had a deferral feature from the date of grant for purposes of this paragraph (b)(5).

(iii) Service recipient stock. (A) In general. Except as otherwise provided in paragraphs (b)(5)(iii)(B), (C), and (D) of this section, the term service recipient stock means a class of stock that, as of the date of grant, is common stock for purposes of section 305 and the regulations thereunder of a corporation that is an eligible issuer of service recipient stock (as defined in paragraph (b)(5)(iii)(E) of this section). Notwithstanding the foregoing, the term service recipient stock does not include a class of stock that has any preference as to distributions other than distributions of service recipient stock and distributions in liquidation of the issuer. The term service recipient stock also does not include any stock that is subject to a mandatory repurchase obligation (other than a right of first refusal), or a put or call right that is not a lapse restriction as defined in § 1.83-3(i), if the stock price under such right or obligation is based on a measure other than the fair market value (disregarding lapse restrictions as defined in § 1.83-3(i)) of the equity interest in the corporation represented by the stock.

(B) American depositary receipts. An American depositary receipt or American depositary share may constitute service recipient stock, to the extent that the stock traded on a foreign securities market to which the American depositary receipt or American depositary share relates qualifies as service recipient stock.

(C) Mutual company units. Mutual company units may constitute service recipient stock. For this purpose, the term mutual company unit means a fixed percentage of the overall value of a non-stock mutual company or association. For purposes of determining the value of the mutual company unit, the unit may be valued in accordance with the rules set forth in paragraph (b)(5)(iv)(B) of this section governing valuation of service recipient stock the shares of which are not traded on an established securities market, applied as if the mutual company were a stock corporation with one class of common stock and the number of shares of such stock determined according to such fixed percentage. For example, an appreciation right based on the appreciation of 10 mutual company units, where each unit is defined as one percent of the overall value of the mutual company, would be valued as if the appreciation right were based upon 10 shares of a corporation, with 100 shares of common stock (and no other class of stock), the shares of which are not readily tradable on an established securities market.

(D) Other entities. An interest in an entity other than a corporation or non-stock mutual company or association may constitute service recipient stock to the extent designated by the Commissioner in revenue procedures, notices, or other guidance published in the Internal Revenue Bulletin (see § 601.601(d)(2) of this chapter).

(E) Eligible issuer of service recipient stock. (1) In general. The term eligible issuer of service recipient stock means only the corporation for which the service provider provides direct services on the date of grant of the stock right (if the entity receiving such services is a corporation), and any corporation in a chain of corporations or other entities in which each corporation or other entity has a controlling interest in another corporation or other entity in the chain, ending with the corporation or other entity that has a controlling interest in the corporation or other entity for which the service provider provides direct services on the date of grant of the stock right. For this purpose, the term controlling interest has the same meaning as provided in § 1.414(c)-2(b)(2)(i), provided that the language "at least 50 percent" is used instead of "at least 80 percent" each place it appears in § 1.414(c)-2(b)(2)(i). In addition, where the use of such stock with respect to the grant of a stock right to such service provider is based upon legitimate business criteria, the term controlling interest has the same meaning as provided in § 1.414(c)-2(b)(2)(i), provided that the language "at least 20 percent" is used instead of "at least 80 percent" each place it appears in § 1.414(c)-2(b)(2)(i). For purposes of determining ownership of an interest in an organization, the rules of §§ 1.414(c)-3 and 1.414(c)-4 apply. The determination of whether a grant is based on legitimate business criteria is based on the facts and circumstances, focusing primarily on whether there is a sufficient nexus between the service provider and the issuer of the stock right so that the grant serves a legitimate non-tax business purpose other than simply providing compensation to the service provider that is excluded from the requirements of section 409A. For example, stock of a corporation that owns an interest in a joint venture involving an operating business, used with respect to stock rights granted to service providers of the joint venture who are former service providers of such corporation, generally will constitute use of service recipient stock based upon legitimate business criteria, and therefore could constitute service recipient stock with respect to such service providers if the corporation owns at least 20 percent of the joint venture and the other requirements of this paragraph (b)(5)(iii) are met. Similarly, the legitimate business criteria requirement generally would be met if the corporate venturer issued such a right to an employee of the joint venture who it reasonably expected would in the future become an employee of the corporate venturer. However, where a service provider has no real nexus with a corporate venturer, such as generally happens when the corporate venturer is a passive investor in the service recipient joint venture, a stock right issued to that employee on the investor corporation's stock generally would not be based upon legitimate business criteria. Similarly, where a corporation holds only a minority interest in an entity that in turn holds a minority interest in the entity for which the service provider performs services, such that the corporation holds only an insubstantial indirect interest in the entity receiving the services, legitimate business criteria generally would not exist for issuing a stock right on the corporation's stock to the service provider.

(2) Investment vehicles. Notwithstanding the provisions of paragraph (b)(5)(iii)(E)(1) of this section, except as to a service provider providing services directly to such corporation, for purposes of this paragraph (b)(5), an eligible issuer of service recipient stock does not include any corporation whose primary purpose is to serve as an investment vehicle with respect to the corporation's minority ownership interests in entities other than the service recipient.

(3) Corporate structures established or transactions undertaken for purposes of avoiding coverage under section 409A. Notwithstanding the provisions of paragraph (b)(5)(iii)(E)(1) of this section, an eligible issuer of service recipient stock does not include any corporation within a group of entities treated as a single service recipient if a purpose of the establishment of the structure of the ownership, or a purpose of a significant transaction between or among two or more entities comprising a single service recipient, is to provide deferred compensation not subject to the application of section 409A. If an entity becomes a member of a group of corporations or other entities treated as a single service recipient, and the primary source of income or value of such entity arises from the provision of management services to other members of the service recipient group, it is presumed that such structure was established for purposes of avoiding the application of section 409A if any stock rights are issued with respect to such entity.

(4) Substitutions and assumptions by reason of a corporate transaction. If the requirements of paragraph (b)(5)(v)(D) of this section are met such that the substitution of a new stock right pursuant to a corporate transaction for an outstanding stock right, or the assumption of an outstanding stock right pursuant to a corporate transaction, would not be treated as the grant of a new stock right or a change in the form of payment for purposes of this section and §§ 1.409A-2 through 1.409A-6, the stock underlying the stock right that replaced the stock right that is substituted or assumed will be treated as service recipient stock for purposes of applying this paragraph (b)(5) to the replacement stock rights if such underlying stock otherwise satisfies the requirements of paragraph (b)(5)(iii)(A) of this section. For example, if by reason of a spinoff transaction (under which the stock of a subsidiary corporation is distributed to the stockholders of a distributing corporation), a stock option to purchase distributing corporation stock is replaced with a stock option to purchase distributing corporation stock and a stock option to purchase the spun off subsidiary corporation's stock (each otherwise satisfying the requirements of paragraph (b)(5)(iii)(A) of this section), and where such substitution is not treated as a modification of the original stock option pursuant to paragraph (b)(5)(v)(D) of this section, both the distributing corporation stock and the subsidiary corporation stock are treated as service recipient stock for purposes of applying this paragraph (b)(5) to the replacement stock options.

(iv) Determination of the fair market value of service recipient stock. (A) Stock readily tradable on an established securities market. For purposes of paragraph (b)(5)(i) of this section, in the case of service recipient stock that is readily tradable on an established securities market, the fair market value of the stock may be determined based upon the last sale before or the first sale after the grant, the closing price on the trading day before or the trading day of the grant, the arithmetic mean of the high and low prices on the trading day before or the trading day of the grant, or any other reasonable method using actual transactions in such stock as reported by such market. The determination of fair market value also may be determined using an average selling price during a specified period that is within 30 days before or 30 days after the applicable valuation date, provided that the program under which the stock right is granted, including a program with a single participant, must irrevocably specify the commitment to grant the stock right with an exercise price set using such an average selling price before the beginning of the specified period. For this purpose, the term average selling price refers to the arithmetic mean of such selling prices on all trading days during the specified period, or the average of such prices over the specified period weighted based on the volume of trading of such stock on each trading day during such specified period. To satisfy this requirement, the service recipient must designate the recipient of the stock right, the number and class of shares of stock that are subject to the stock right, and the method for determining the exercise price including the period over which the averaging will occur, before the beginning of the specified averaging period. Notwithstanding the forgoing provisions of this paragraph (b)(5)(iv)(A), where applicable foreign law requires that a compensatory stock right be priced based upon a specific price averaging method and period, a stock right granted in accordance with such applicable foreign law will be treated as meeting the requirements of this paragraph (b)(5)(iv)(A), provided that the averaging period does not exceed 30 days.

(B) Stock not readily tradable on an established securities market. (1) In general. For purposes of paragraph (b)(5)(i) of this section, in the case of service recipient stock that is not readily tradable on an established securities market, the fair market value of the stock as of a valuation date means a value determined by the reasonable application of a reasonable valuation method. The determination whether a valuation method is reasonable, or whether an application of a valuation method is reasonable, is made based on the facts and circumstances as of the valuation date. Factors to be considered under a reasonable valuation method include, as applicable, the value of tangible and intangible assets of the corporation, the present value of anticipated future cash-flows of the corporation, the market value of stock or equity interests in similar corporations and other entities engaged in trades or businesses substantially similar to those engaged in by the corporation the stock of which is to be valued, the value of which can be readily determined through nondiscretionary, objective means (such as through trading prices on an established securities market or an amount paid in an arm's length private transaction), recent arm's length transactions involving the sale or transfer of such stock or equity interests, and other relevant factors such as control premiums or discounts for lack of marketability and whether the valuation method is used for other purposes that have a material economic effect on the service recipient, its stockholders, or its creditors. The use of a valuation method is not reasonable if such valuation method does not take into consideration in applying its methodology all available information material to the value of the corporation. Similarly, the use of a value previously calculated under a valuation method is not reasonable as of a later date if such calculation fails to reflect information available after the date of the calculation that may materially affect the value of the corporation (for example, the resolution of material litigation or the issuance of a patent) or the value was calculated with respect to a date that is more than 12 months earlier than the date for which the valuation is being used. The service recipient's consistent use of a valuation method to determine the value of its stock or assets for other purposes, including for purposes unrelated to compensation of service providers, is also a factor supporting the reasonableness of such valuation method.

(2) Presumption of reasonableness. For purposes of this paragraph (b)(5)(iv)(B), the use of any of the following methods of valuation is presumed to result in a reasonable valuation, provided that the Commissioner may rebut such a presumption upon a showing that either the valuation method or the application of such method was grossly unreasonable:

(i) A valuation of a class of stock determined by an independent appraisal that meets the requirements of section 401(a)(28)(C) and the regulations as of a date that is no more than 12 months before the relevant transaction to which the valuation is applied (for example, the date of grant of a stock option).

(ii) A valuation based upon a formula that, if used as part of a nonlapse restriction (as defined in Sec. 1.83-3(h)) with respect to the stock, would be considered to be the fair market value of the stock pursuant to Sec. 1.83-5, provided that such stock is valued in the same manner for purposes of any transfer of any shares of such class of stock (or any substantially similar class of stock) to the issuer or any person that owns stock possessing more than 10 percent of the total combined voting power of all classes of stock of the issuer (applying the stock attribution rules of Sec. 1.424-1(d)), other than an arm's length transaction involving the sale of all or substantially all of the outstanding stock of the issuer, and such valuation method is used consistently for all such purposes, and provided further that this paragraph (b)(5)(iv)(B)(2)(ii) does not apply with respect to stock subject to a stock right payable in stock, where the stock acquired pursuant to the exercise of the stock right is transferable other than through the operation of a nonlapse restriction.

(iii) A valuation, made reasonably and in good faith and evidenced by a written report that takes into account the relevant factors described in paragraph (b)(5)(iv)(B)(1) of this section, of illiquid stock of a start-up corporation. For this purpose, illiquid stock of a start-up corporation means service recipient stock of a corporation that has no material trade or business that it or any predecessor to it has conducted for a period of 10 years or more and has no class of equity securities that are traded on an established securities market (as defined in paragraph (k) of this section), where such stock is not subject to any put, call, or other right or obligation of the service recipient or other person to purchase such stock (other than a right of first refusal upon an offer to purchase by a third party that is unrelated to the service recipient or service provider and other than a right or obligation that constitutes a lapse restriction as defined in § 1.83-3(i)), and provided that this paragraph (b)(5)(iv)(B)(2)(iii) does not apply to the valuation of any stock if the service recipient or service provider may reasonably anticipate, as of the time the valuation is applied, that the service recipient will undergo a change in control event as described in § 1.409A-3(i)(5)(v) or § 1.409A-3(i)(5)(vii) within the 90 days following the action to which the valuation is applied, or make a public offering of securities within the 180 days following the action to which the valuation is applied. For purposes of this paragraph (b)(5)(iv)(B)(2)(iii), a valuation will not be treated as made reasonably and in good faith unless the valuation is performed by a person or persons that the corporation reasonably determines is qualified to perform such a valuation based on the person's or persons' significant knowledge, experience, education, or training. Generally, a person will be qualified to perform such a valuation if a reasonable individual, upon being apprised of such knowledge, experience, education, and training, would reasonably rely on the advice of such person with respect to valuation in deciding whether to accept an offer to purchase or sell the stock being valued. For this purpose, significant experience generally means at least five years of relevant experience in business valuation or appraisal, financial accounting, investment banking, private equity, secured lending, or other comparable experience in the line of business or industry in which the service recipient operates.

(3) Use of alternative methods. For purposes of this paragraph (b)(5), a different valuation method may be used for each separate action for which a valuation is relevant, provided that a single valuation method is used for each separate action and, once used, may not retroactively be altered. For example, one valuation method may be used to establish the exercise price of a stock option, and a different valuation method may be used to determine the value at the date of the repurchase of stock pursuant to a put or call right. However, once an exercise price or amount to be paid has been established, the exercise price or amount to be paid may not be changed through the retroactive use of another valuation method. In addition, notwithstanding the foregoing, where after the date of grant, but before the date of exercise or transfer, of the stock right, the service recipient stock to which the stock right relates becomes readily tradable on an established securities market, the service recipient must use the valuation method set forth in paragraph (b)(5)(iv)(A) of this section for purposes of determining the payment at the date of exercise or the purchase of the stock, as applicable.

(v) Modifications, extensions, substitutions, and assumptions of stock rights. (A) Treatment of modified and extended stock rights. A modification of the terms of a stock right within the meaning of paragraph (b)(5)(v)(B) of this section is considered to be the grant of a new stock right. The new stock right may or may not constitute a deferral of compensation under paragraph (b)(5)(i) of this section, determined at the date of grant of the new stock right. If there is an extension of a stock right (within the meaning of paragraph (b)(5)(v)(C) of this section), the stock right is treated as having had an additional deferral feature from the original date of grant of the stock right, and therefore will be treated as a plan providing for the deferral of compensation from the original grant date for purposes of this paragraph (b).

(B) Modification in general. Except as otherwise provided in paragraph (b)(5)(v) of this section, the term modification means any change in the terms of the stock right (or change in the terms of the plan pursuant to which the stock right was granted or in the terms of any other agreement governing the stock right) that may provide the holder of the stock right with a direct or indirect reduction in the exercise price of the stock right regardless of whether the holder in fact benefits from the change in terms. A change in the terms of the stock right shortening the period during which the stock right is exercisable is not a modification. It is not a modification to add a feature providing the ability to tender previously acquired stock for the stock purchasable under the stock right, or to withhold or have withheld shares of stock to facilitate the payment of the exercise price or the employment taxes or required withholding taxes resulting from the exercise of the stock right. In addition, it is not a modification for the grantor to exercise discretion specifically reserved under a stock right with respect to the transferability of the stock right.

(C) Extensions. (1) In general. An extension of a stock right refers to the provision to the holder of an additional period of time within which to exercise the stock right beyond the time originally prescribed under the terms of the stock right, the conversion or exchange of a stock right for a legally binding right to compensation in a future taxable year, or the addition of any feature for the deferral of compensation not permitted in paragraph (b)(5)(i)(A)(3) of this section (in the case of a stock option) or not permitted in paragraph (b)(5)(i)(B)(3) of this section (in the case of a stock appreciation right) to the terms of the stock right, other than at a time when the exercise price of the stock right equals or exceeds the fair market value of the service recipient stock that could be purchased (in the case of an option) or the fair market value of the service recipient stock used to determine the payment to the service provider (in the case of a stock appreciation right), and includes a renewal of such right that has such effect. It is not an extension if the exercise period of a stock right is extended to a date no later than the earlier of the latest date upon which the stock right could have expired by its original terms under any circumstances or the 10th anniversary of the original date of grant of the stock right. If the exercise period of a stock right is extended at a time when the exercise price of the stock right equals or exceeds the fair market value of the service recipient stock that could be purchased (in the case of an option) or the fair market value of the service recipient stock used to determine the payment to the service provider (in the case of a stock appreciation right), it is not an extension of the original stock right. Instead, in such a case, the original stock right is treated as modified rather than extended and a new stock right is treated as having been granted for purposes of this section. In addition, it is not an extension of a stock right if the expiration of the stock right is tolled while the holder cannot exercise the stock right because such an exercise would violate an applicable Federal, state, local, or foreign law, or would jeopardize the ability of the service recipient to continue as a going concern, provided that the period during which the stock right may be exercised is not extended more than 30 days after the exercise of the stock right first would no longer violate an applicable Federal, state, local, and foreign laws or would first no longer jeopardize the ability of the service recipient to continue as a going concern. For this purpose, a provision of foreign law shall be considered applicable only to foreign earned income (as defined under section 911(b)(1) without regard to section 911(b)(1)(B)(iv) and without regard to the requirement that the income be attributable to services performed during the period described in section 911(d)(1)(A) or (B)) from sources within the foreign country that promulgated such law.

(2) Certain extensions before April 10, 2007. An extension of a stock right before April 10, 2007 solely in order to provide the holder of such stock right an additional period of time beyond the time originally prescribed under the terms of such stock right within which to exercise the stock right is disregarded for purposes of applying the rules contained in paragraph (b)(5)(v)(C)(1) of this section. For purposes of applying the rules contained in paragraph (b)(5)(v)(C)(1) of this section on and after April 10, 2007, such a stock right is treated as having specified at the date of grant the time within which to exercise such stock right that was prescribed under the terms of such stock right in effect on April 10, 2007. Nothing in this paragraph (b)(5)(v)(C)(2) affects any other action treated as the extension of a stock right, including the addition of a deferral feature.

(3) Examples. The following examples illustrate the provisions of this paragraph (b)(5)(v)(C). In the examples, each employee is an individual employed by the specified employer, and each employee and each employer has a calendar year taxable year.

*Example (1).* On July 1, 2009, Employer Z grants Employee A a nonstatutory stock option that does not provide for the deferral of compensation in accordance with paragraph (b)(5)(i)(A) of this section. The terms of the nonstatutory stock option provide that the exercise period of the stock option expires on the earlier of July 1, 2019, or 3 months after Employee A's separation from service. On July 1, 2011, Employee A separates from service. On the same day, Employee A and Employer Z change the exercise period of the option so that it expires on July 1, 2013. Because the exercise period of the stock right is not extended beyond July 1, 2019, the change is not an extension for purposes of this paragraph (b)(5)(v)(C).

*Example (2).* The facts are the same as in Example 1 except that Employee A separates from service on July 1, 2018, and on the same day, Employee A and Employer Z change the exercise period of the option so that it expires on July 1, 2020. As of July 1, 2018, the fair market value of the underlying stock exceeds the exercise price. Because the exercise period of the stock right is extended beyond July 1, 2019, the change is an extension for purposes of this paragraph (b)(5)(v)(C).

*Example (3).* The facts are the same as in Example 2 except that as of July 1, 2018, the fair market value of the underlying stock is less than the exercise price of the option. Because the exercise period of the stock right is extended at a time when the fair market value of the underlying stock is less than the exercise price, the change is not an extension for purposes of this paragraph (b)(5)(v)(C) and the change is treated as a modification of the option, resulting in the extension of the exercise period being treated as the grant of a new option on July 1, 2018.

*Example (4).* On July 1, 2009, Employer Y grants to Employee B a stock appreciation right with respect to 200 shares of Employer Y common stock that does not provide for the deferral of compensation in accordance with paragraph (b)(5)(i)(B) of this section. Upon exercise of the stock appreciation right, Employee B is entitled to receive the excess of the fair market value of a share of Employer Y common stock on the date of exercise over $100 (the fair market value of a share of Employer Y common stock on July 1, 2009), multiplied by the number of shares with respect to which Employee B is exercising the right. The exercise period of the right expires on the earlier of July 1, 2019, or 3 months after Employee B separates from service. Employee B cannot exercise the stock appreciation right with respect to more than 100 shares unless Employee B continues to be employed by Employer Y through June 30, 2014. On July 1, 2011, when the fair market value of a share of Employer Y common stock is $200, Employee B and Employer Y amend the stock appreciation right to provide that the right will be exercisable only during calendar year 2018, except that before January 1, 2017, Employee B may elect to designate calendar year 2023 or any subsequent calendar year before 2033 as the year in which the right will be exercisable. The amendment constitutes an extension of the stock appreciation right under paragraph (b)(5)(v)(C)(1) of this section. Under paragraph (b)(5)(v)(A) of this section, the stock appreciation right is treated as having had an additional deferral feature from the original date of grant (July 1, 2009) of the right, and therefore is treated as a plan providing for the deferral of compensation from that date. During the period from July 1, 2009, through June 30, 2011, the provisions of the stock appreciation right relating to the time and form of payment did not satisfy the requirements of § 1.409A-3(a). Therefore, the stock appreciation right provides for a deferral of compensation that does not comply with section 409A.

(D) Substitutions and assumptions of stock rights by reason of a corporate transaction. If the requirements of § 1.424-1 (without regard to the requirement described in § 1.424-1(a)(2) that an eligible corporation be the employer of the optionee) would be met if the stock right were a statutory option, the substitution of a new stock right pursuant to a corporate transaction (as defined in § 1.424-1(a)(3)) for an outstanding stock right or the assumption of an outstanding stock right pursuant to a corporate transaction will not be treated as the grant of a new stock right or a change in the form of payment for purposes of this section and §§ 1.409A-2 through 1.409A-6. For purposes of the preceding sentence, the requirement of § 1.424-1(a)(5)(iii) will be deemed to be satisfied if the ratio of the exercise price to the fair market value of the shares subject to the stock right immediately after the substitution or assumption is not greater than the ratio of the exercise price to the fair market value of the shares subject to the stock right immediately before the substitution or assumption. In the case of a transaction described in section 355 in which the stock of the distributing corporation and the stock distributed in the transaction are both readily tradable on an established securities market immediately after the transaction, for purposes of this paragraph (b)(5)(v), the requirements of § 1.424-1(a)(5) related to the fair market value of the stock may be satisfied by—

(1) Using the last sale before or the first sale after the specified date as of which such valuation is being made, the closing price on the last trading day before or the trading day of a specified date, the arithmetic mean of the high and low prices on the last trading day before or the trading day of such specified date, or any other reasonable method using actual transactions in such stock as reported by such market on a specified date, for the stock of the distributing corporation and the stock distributed in the transaction, provided the specified date is designated before such specified date, and such specified date is not more than 60 days after the transaction;

(2) Using the arithmetic mean of such market prices on trading days during a specified period designated before the beginning of such specified period, where such specified period is not longer than 30 days and ends no later than 60 days after the transaction; or

(3) Using an average of such prices during such prespecified period weighted based on the volume of trading of such stock on each trading day during such prespecified period.

(E) Acceleration of date when exercisable. Although with respect to a stock right not immediately exercisable in full, a change in the terms of the right solely to accelerate or delay, within the original term of the stock right, the time at which the stock right (or any portion of such stock right) may be exercised is not a modification for purposes of this section, with respect to a stock right subject to section 409A, such an acceleration may constitute an impermissible acceleration of a payment date under § 1.409A-3(j) or a subsequent deferral under § 1.409A-2(b).

(F) Discretionary added benefits. If a change to a stock right provides, either by its terms or in substance, that the holder may receive an additional benefit under the stock right at the future discretion of the grantor, and the addition of such benefit would constitute a modification or extension, then the addition of such discretion is a modification or extension at the time that the stock right is changed to provide such discretion.

(G) Change in underlying stock increasing value. A change in the terms of the stock subject to a stock right that increases the value of the stock is a modification of such stock right, except to the extent that a new stock right is substituted for such stock right by reason of the change in the terms of the stock in accordance with paragraph (b)(5)(v)(D) of this section.

(H) Change in the number of shares purchasable. If a stock right is amended solely to increase the number of shares subject to the stock right, the increase is not considered a modification of the stock right but is treated as the grant of a new additional stock right to which the additional shares are subject. Notwithstanding the previous sentence, if the exercise price and number of shares subject to a stock right are proportionally adjusted to reflect a stock split (including a reverse stock split) or stock dividend, and the only effect of the stock split or stock dividend is to increase (or decrease) on a pro rata basis the number of shares owned by each shareholder of the class of stock subject to the stock right, then there is no modification of the stock right if it is proportionally adjusted to reflect the stock split or stock dividend and the aggregate exercise price of the stock right is not less than the aggregate exercise price before the stock split or stock dividend.

(I) Rescission of changes. A change to the terms of a stock right (or change in the terms of the plan pursuant to which the stock right was granted or in the terms of any other agreement governing the right) is not considered a modification or extension of the stock right to the extent the change in the terms of the stock right is rescinded by the earlier of the date the stock right is exercised or the last day of the service provider's taxable year during which such change occurred. Thus, for example, if the terms of a stock right granted to an individual employee with a calendar year taxable year are changed on March 1 in a manner that would result in an extension of the stock right, and the change is rescinded on November 1 of the same year, and the stock right is not exercised before the change is rescinded, the stock right is not considered extended under this paragraph (b)(5)(v).

(J) Successive modifications and extensions. The rules of this paragraph (b)(5)(v) apply as well to successive modifications and extensions.

(K) Modifications and extensions in effect on October 23, 2004. For purposes of the application of section 409A and these regulations to a stock right, if a legally binding right to a modification or extension of such stock right existed on October 23, 2004, such modification or extension is disregarded, and the stock right is treated as if granted with the terms and conditions in effect on October 23, 2004.

(vi) Meaning and use of certain terms. (A) Option. The term option means the right or privilege of an individual to purchase stock from a corporation by virtue of an offer of the corporation continuing for a stated period of time, whether or not irrevocable, to sell such stock at a price determined under paragraph (b)(5)(vi)(D) of this section, such individual being under no obligation to purchase. While no particular form of words is necessary, the option must express an offer to sell at the option price, the maximum number of shares purchasable under the option, and the period of time during which the offer remains open. The term option includes a warrant that meets the requirements of this paragraph (b)(5)(vi)(A). An option may be granted as part of or in conjunction with an employee stock purchase plan or subscription contract. An option must be in writing (in paper or electronic form) provided that such writing is adequate to establish an option right or privilege that is enforceable under applicable law.

(B) Date of grant of option. (1) The language the date of grant of the option, and similar phrases, refer to the date when the granting corporation completes the corporate action necessary to create the legally binding right constituting the option. A corporate action creating the legally binding right constituting the option is not considered complete until the date on which the maximum number of shares that can be purchased under the option and the minimum exercise price are fixed or determinable, and the class of underlying stock and the identity of the service provider is designated. Ordinarily, if the corporate action provides for an immediate offer of stock for sale to a service provider, or provides for a particular date on which such offer is to be made, the date of the granting of the option is the date of such corporate action if the offer is to be made immediately, or the date provided as the date of the offer, as the case may be. However, an unreasonable delay in the giving of notice of such offer to the service provider will be taken into account as indicating that the corporation provided that the offer was to be made at the subsequent date on which such notice is given.

(2) If the corporation imposes a condition on the granting of an option (as distinguished from a condition governing the exercise of the option), such condition generally will be given effect in accordance with the intent of the corporation. However, if the grant of an option is subject to approval by stockholders, the date of grant of the option will be determined as if the option had not been subject to such approval. A condition that does not require corporate action, such as the approval of, or registration with, some regulatory or government agency, for example, a stock exchange or the Securities and Exchange Commission, is ordinarily considered a condition upon the exercise of the option unless the corporate action clearly indicates that the option is not to be granted until such condition has been satisfied.

(3) In general, a condition imposed upon the exercise of an option will not operate to make ineffective the granting of the option. For example, on June 1, 2008, Corporation A grants to X, an employee, an option to purchase 5,000 shares of the corporation's common stock, exercisable by X on or after June 1, 2009, provided X is employed by the corporation on June 1, 2009, and provided that A's profits during the fiscal year preceding the year of exercise exceed $200,000. Such an option is granted to X on June 1, 2008, and will be treated as outstanding as of such date.

(C) Stock. The term stock means capital stock of any class, including voting or nonvoting common or preferred stock. Except as otherwise provided, the term stock includes both treasury stock and stock of original issue. Special classes of stock authorized to be issued to and held by employees are within the scope of the term stock for this purpose, provided such stock otherwise possesses the rights and characteristics of capital stock.

(D) Exercise price. The term exercise price means the consideration in cash or property that, pursuant to the terms of the option, is the price at which the stock subject to the option is purchased. The term exercise price does not include any amounts paid as interest under a deferred payment plan or treated as interest.

(E) Exercise. The term exercise, when used in reference to an option, means the act of acceptance by the holder of the option of the offer to sell contained in the option. In general, the time of exercise is the time when there is a sale or a contract to sell between the corporation and the individual. A promise to pay the exercise price does not constitute an exercise of the option unless the holder of the option is subject to personal liability on such promise. An agreement or undertaking by the service provider to make payments under a stock purchase plan does not constitute the exercise of an option to the extent the payments made remain subject to withdrawal by or refund to the service provider.

(F) Transfer. The term transfer, when used in reference to the transfer to an individual of a share of stock pursuant to the exercise of an option, means the transfer of ownership of such share, or the transfer of substantially all the rights of ownership. Such transfer must, within a reasonable time, be evidenced on the books of the corporation. A transfer may occur even if a share of stock is subject to a substantial risk of forfeiture or is not otherwise transferable immediately after the date of exercise. A transfer does not fail to occur merely because, under the terms of the arrangement, the individual may not dispose of the share for a specified period of time, or the share is subject to a right of first refusal or a right to acquire the share at the share's fair market value at the time of the sale.

(G) Readily tradable. For purposes of this section and §§ 1.409A-2 through 1.409A-6, stock is treated as readily tradable if it is regularly quoted by brokers or dealers making a market in such stock.

(H) Application to stock appreciation rights. For purposes of this section and §§ 1.409A-2 through 1.409A-6, the definitions provided in paragraphs (b)(5)(vi)(A) through (G) of this section may be applied by analogy to the issuance of, exercise of, or payment upon the exercise of, a stock appreciation right.

*(6) Restricted property, section 402(b) trusts, and section 403(c) annuities.* (i) In general. If a service provider receives property from, or pursuant to, a plan maintained by a service recipient, there is no deferral of compensation merely because the value of the property is not includible in income

by reason of the property being substantially nonvested (as defined in § 1.83-3(b)), or is includible in income solely due to a valid election under section 83(b). For purposes of this paragraph (b)(6)(i), a transfer of property includes the transfer of a beneficial interest in a trust or annuity plan, or a transfer to or from a trust or under an annuity plan, to the extent such a transfer is subject to section 83, section 402(b) or section 403(c). In addition, for purposes of this paragraph (b), a right to compensation income that will be required to be included in income under section 402(b)(4)(A) is not a deferral of compensation.

(ii) Promises to transfer property. A plan under which a service provider obtains a legally binding right to receive property in a future taxable year where the property will be substantially vested (as defined in § 1.83-3(b)) at the time of transfer of the property may provide for the deferral of compensation and, accordingly, may constitute a nonqualified deferred compensation plan. A legally binding right to receive property in a future taxable year where the property will be substantially nonvested (as defined in § 1.83-3(b)) at the time of transfer of the property will not provide for the deferral of compensation and, accordingly, will not constitute a nonqualified deferred compensation plan unless offered in conjunction with another legally binding right that constitutes a deferral of compensation.

*(7) Arrangements between partnerships and partners.* [Reserved.]

*(8) Certain foreign plans.* (i) Plans with respect to compensation covered by treaty or other international agreement. A plan in which a service provider participates does not provide for a deferral of compensation for purposes of this paragraph (b) to the extent that the compensation under the plan would have been excluded from gross income for Federal income tax purposes under the provisions of any bilateral income tax convention or other bilateral or multilateral agreement to which the United States is a party if the compensation had been paid to the service provider at the time that the legally binding right to the compensation first arose or, if later, the time that the legally binding right was no longer subject to a substantial risk of forfeiture.

(ii) Plans with respect to certain other compensation. A plan in which a service provider participates does not provide for a deferral of compensation for purposes of this paragraph (b) to the extent that compensation under the plan would not have been includible in gross income for Federal tax purposes if it had been paid to the service provider at the time that the legally binding right to the compensation first arose or, if later, the time that the legally binding right was no longer subject to a substantial risk of forfeiture, due to one of the following:

(A) The service provider was a nonresident alien at such time and the compensation would not have been includible in gross income under section 872.

(B) The service provider was a qualified individual (as defined in section 911(d)(1)) at such time, the compensation would have been foreign earned income within the meaning of section 911(b)(1) (without regard to section 911(b)(1)(B)(iv)) if paid at such time, and the amount of such compensation was equal to or less than the excess (if any) of the maximum exclusion amount under section 911(b)(2)(D) for such taxable year over the amount of foreign earned income actually excluded from gross income by such qualified individual for such taxable year under section 911(a)(1).

(C) The compensation would have been excludible from gross income under section 893.

(D) The compensation would have been excludible from gross income under section 931 or section 933.

(iii) Tax equalization agreements. A tax equalization agreement does not provide for a deferral of compensation if payments made under such tax equalization agreement are made no later than the end of the second taxable year of the service provider beginning after the taxable year of the service provider in which the service provider's U.S. Federal income tax return is required to be filed (including any extensions) for the year to which the compensation subject to the tax equalization payment relates, or, if later, the second taxable year of the service provider beginning after the latest such taxable year in which the service provider's foreign tax return or payment is required to be filed or made for the year to which the compensation subject to the tax equalization payment relates. Where such payments arise due to an audit, litigation or similar proceeding, the right to the payments will not be treated as resulting in a deferral of compensation if the payments are scheduled and made in accordance with the provisions of § 1.409A-3(i)(1)(v) (timing of tax gross-up payments). For purposes of this paragraph (b)(8)(iii), the term tax equalization agreement refers to an agreement, method, program, or other arrangement that provides payments intended to compensate the service provider for some or all of the excess of the taxes actually imposed by a foreign jurisdiction on the compensation paid by the service recipient to the service provider over the taxes that would be imposed if the compensation were subject solely to United States Federal, state, and local income tax, or some or all of the excess of the United States Federal, state, and local income tax actually imposed on the compensation paid by the service to the service provider over the taxes that would be imposed if the compensation were subject solely to taxes in the foreign jurisdiction, provided that the payment made under such agreement, method, program, or other arrangement may not exceed such excess and the amount necessary to compensate for the additional taxes on the amount paid under the agreement, method, program, or other arrangement.

(iv) Certain limited deferrals of a nonresident alien. With respect to a nonresident alien, a foreign plan does not provide for a deferral of compensation if the amounts deferred under the foreign plan based upon services performed by the nonresident alien in the United States (including amounts deferred based upon service credits or compensation received due to services performed in the United States) do not exceed the applicable dollar amount under section 402(g)(1)(B) for the taxable year. If the amounts deferred under the foreign plan based upon the services performed by the nonresident alien in the United States exceed the applicable dollar amount, an amount of such deferrals equal to such amount is treated as not deferred under a nonqualified deferred compensation plan. For purposes of this paragraph (b)(8)(iv), the term foreign plan means a plan that, together with all substantially similar plans, is maintained by a service recipient for a substantial number of participants, substantially all of whom are nonresident aliens or resident aliens classified as resident aliens solely under section 7701(b)(1)(A)(ii) (and not section 7701(b)(1)(A)(i)).

(v) Additional foreign plans. A plan in which a service provider participates does not provide for a deferral of compensation for purposes of this paragraph (b) to the extent designated by the Commissioner in revenue procedures, notices, or other guidance published in the Internal Revenue Bulletin (see § 601.601(d)(2) of this chapter).

(vi) Earnings. Earnings on compensation excluded from the definition of deferral of compensation pursuant to this paragraph (b)(8) are also not treated as a deferral of compensation.

*(9) Separation pay plans.* (i) In general. A plan that otherwise provides for a deferral of compensation under this paragraph (b) does not fail to provide a deferral of compensation merely because the right to payment of the compensation is conditioned upon a separation from service. However, paragraphs (b)(9)(ii), (iii), (iv), and (v) of this section provide rules concerning the extent to which certain separation pay plans do not provide for the deferral of compensation. The exceptions contained in paragraphs (b)(9)(ii), (iii), (iv), and (v) of this section may be used in combination, such that compensation under a plan that would be excepted under one of those paragraphs may be treated as excepted under another of those paragraphs, so that other compensation under a plan may be treated as excepted under the first of such paragraphs. Notwithstanding any other provision of this paragraph (b)(9), any payment or benefit, or entitlement to a payment or benefit, that acts as a substitute for, or replacement of, amounts deferred by the service recipient under a separate nonqualified deferred compensation plan constitutes a payment or a deferral of compensation under the separate nonqualified deferred compensation plan, and does not constitute a payment or deferral of compensation under a separation pay plan. If a service provider receives a payment at separation from service and also has a legally binding right to an amount of deferred compensation that would be forfeited upon the separation from service, whether the payment acts as an acceleration of vesting and substitute payment for the amount of deferred compensation forfeited, or whether the deferred compensation is treated as forfeited and the amount paid is treated as a separate payment of current compensation, is determined based on the facts and circumstances, provided that, where the separation from service is voluntary, it is presumed that the payment results from an acceleration of vesting followed by a payment of the deferred compensation that is subject to section 409A. Accordingly, any change in the payment schedule to accelerate or defer the payments would be subject to the rules of section 409A. The presumption that a right to a payment is not a new right, but is instead a right substituted for a pre-existing forfeited right, may be rebutted by demonstrating that the service provider would have obtained the right to the payment regardless of the forfeiture of the nonvested right. A factor indicating that the service provider would have obtained a right to a payment regardless of the forfeiture of the nonvested right is that the amount to which the service provider obtains a right is materially less than an amount equal to the present value of the forfeited amount multiplied by a fraction, the numerator of which is the period of service the service provider actually completed, and the denominator of which is the full period of service the service provider would have been required to complete to receive the full amount of the payment. For example, where a service provider is entitled to a future payment only if the service provider completes three years of service and at the time of termination the service provider has completed one year of service, the presumption could be rebutted if the payment to the service provider is materially less than the present value of one-third of the nonvested amount. Another such factor is that the payment to the service provider is of a type customarily made to service providers who separate from service with the service recipient and do not forfeit nonvested rights to deferred compensation (for example, a payment of accrued but unused leave or a payment for a release of actual or potential claims).

(ii) Collectively bargained separation pay plans. A separation pay plan does not provide for a deferral of compensation to the extent the plan is a collectively bargained separation pay plan that provides for separation pay only upon an involuntary separation from service or pursuant to a window program. Only the portion of the separation pay plan attributable to employees covered by a bona fide collective bargaining agreement is considered to be provided under a collectively bargained separation pay plan. A collectively bargained separation pay plan is a separation pay plan that meets the following conditions:

(A) The separation pay plan is contained within an agreement that the Secretary of Labor determines to be a collective bargaining agreement.

(B) The separation pay provided by the collective bargaining agreement was the subject of arm's length negotiations between employee representatives and one or more employers, and the agreement between employee representatives and one or more employers satisfies section 7701(a)(46).

(C) The circumstances surrounding the agreement evidence good faith bargaining between adverse parties over the separation pay to be provided under the agreement.

(iii) Separation pay due to involuntary separation from service or participation in a window program. A separation pay plan that is not described in paragraph (b)(9)(ii) of this section and that provides for separation pay only upon an involuntary separation from service (as defined in paragraph (n) of this section) or pursuant to a window program does not provide for a deferral of compensation to the extent that the separation pay, or portion of the separation pay, provided under the plan meets the following requirements:

(A) The separation pay (other than amounts described in paragraphs (b)(9)(iv) and (v) of this section) does not exceed two times the lesser of—

(1) The sum of the service provider's annualized compensation based upon the annual rate of pay for services provided to the service recipient for the taxable year of the service provider preceding the taxable year of the service provider in which the service provider has a separation from service with such service recipient (adjusted for any increase during that year that was expected to continue indefinitely if the service provider had not separated from service); or

(2) The maximum amount that may be taken into account under a qualified plan pursuant to section 401(a)(17) for the year in which the service provider has a separation from service.

(B) The plan provides that the separation pay described in paragraph (b)(9)(iii)(A) of this section must be paid no later than the last day of the second taxable year of the service provider following the taxable year of the service provider in which occurs the separation from service.

(iv) Foreign separation pay plans. A separation pay plan (including a plan providing payments upon a voluntary separation from service) does not provide for deferred compensation to the extent the plan provides for amounts of separation pay required to be provided under the applicable law of a foreign jurisdiction. For this purpose, a provision of foreign law shall be considered applicable only to foreign earned income (as defined under section 911(b)(1) without regard to section 911(b)(1)(B)(iv) and without regard to the requirement that the income be attributable to services performed during the period described in section 911(d)(1)(A) or (B)) from sources within the foreign country that promulgated such law.

(v) Reimbursements and certain other separation payments. (A) In general. To the extent a separation pay plan (including a plan providing payments upon a voluntary separation from service) entitles a service provider to payment by the service recipient of reimbursements that are not otherwise excludible from gross income for expenses that the service provider could otherwise deduct under section 162 or section 167 as business expenses incurred in connection with the performance of services (ignoring any applicable limitation based on adjusted gross income), or of reasonable outplacement expenses and reasonable moving expenses actually incurred by the service provider and directly related to the termination of services for the service recipient, such plan does not provide for a deferral of compensation to the extent such rights apply during a limited period of time (regardless of whether such rights extend beyond the limited period of time). For purposes of this paragraph (b)(9)(v)(A), the reimbursement of reasonable moving expenses includes the reimbursement of all or part of any loss the service provider actually incurs due to the sale of a primary residence in connection with a separation from service.

(B) Medical benefits. To the extent a separation pay plan (including a plan providing payments due to a voluntary separation from service) entitles a service provider to reimbursement by the service recipient of payments of medical expenses incurred and paid by the service provider but not reimbursed by a person other than the service recipient and allowable as a deduction under section 213 (disregarding the requirement of section 213(a) that the deduction is available only to the extent that such expenses exceed 7.5 percent of adjusted gross income), such plan does not provide for a deferral of compensation to the extent such rights apply during the period of time during which the service provider would be entitled (or would, but for such plan, be entitled) to continuation coverage under a group health plan of the service recipient under section 4980B (COBRA) if the service provider elected such coverage and paid the applicable premiums.

(C) In-kind benefits and direct service recipient payments. A service provider's entitlement to in-kind benefits from the service recipient, or a payment by the service recipient directly to the person providing the goods or services to the service provider, is treated as not providing for a deferral of compensation for purposes of this paragraph (b), if a right to reimbursement by the service recipient for a payment for such benefits, goods, or services by the service provider would not be treated as providing for a deferral of compensation under this paragraph (b)(9)(v).

(D) Limited payments. If not otherwise excluded, a taxpayer may treat a right or rights under a separation pay plan to a payment or payments as not providing for a deferral of compensation to the extent such payments in the aggregate do not exceed the applicable dollar amount under section 402(g)(1)(B) for the year of the separation from service.

(E) Limited period of time. For purposes of paragraphs (b)(9)(v)(A) and (C) of this section, a limited period of time in which expenses may be incurred, or in which in-kind benefits may be provided by the service recipient or a third party that the service recipient will pay, does not include periods beyond the last day of the second taxable year of the service provider following the taxable year of the service provider in which the separation from service occurred, provided that the period during which the reimbursements for such expenses must be paid may not extend beyond the third taxable year of the service provider following the taxable year of the service provider in which the separation from service occurred.

(vi) Window programs—definition. The term window program refers to a program established by a service recipient in connection with an impending separation from service to provide separation pay, where such program is made available by the service recipient for a limited period of time (no longer than 12 months) to service providers who separate from service during that period or to service providers who separate from service during that period under specified circumstances. A program will not be considered a window program if a service recipient establishes a pattern of repeatedly providing for similar separation pay in similar situations for substantially consecutive, limited periods of time. Whether the recurrence of these programs constitutes a pattern is determined based on the facts and circumstances. Although no one factor is determinative, relevant factors include whether the benefits are on account of a specific business event or condition, the degree to which the separation pay relates to the event or condition, and whether the event or condition is temporary or discrete or is a permanent aspect of the employer's business.

*(10) Certain indemnification and liability insurance plans.* A plan in which a service provider participates does not provide for a deferral of compensation for purposes of this paragraph (b) to the extent that the plan provides (to the extent permissible under applicable law), for the indemnification of, or the purchase of an insurance policy providing for payments of, all or part of the expenses incurred or damages paid or payable by a service provider with respect to a bona fide claim against the service provider or service recipient, including amounts paid or payable by the service provider upon the settlement of a bona fide claim against the service provider or service recipient, where such claim is based on actions or failures to act by the service provider in his or her capacity as a service provider of the service recipient.

*(11) Legal settlements.* An agreement to which a service provider is a party does not provide for a deferral of compensation for purposes of this paragraph (b) to the extent that the agreement provides for amounts paid as settlements or awards resolving bona fide legal claims based on wrongful termination, employment discrimination, the Fair Labor Standards Act, or worker's compensation statutes, including claims under applicable Federal, state, local, or foreign laws, or for reimbursements or payments of reasonable attorneys fees or other reasonable expenses incurred by the service provider related to such bona fide legal claims, regardless of whether such settlements, awards, or reimbursement or payment of expenses pursuant to such claims are treated as compensation or wages for Federal tax purposes. Whether the execution of a waiver of any or all of such types of claims indicates that the amounts are paid as an award or settlement of an actual bona fide claim for damages under applicable law is determined based on the facts and circumstances. This paragraph (b)(11) does not apply to any deferred amounts that did not arise as a result of an actual bona fide claim for damages under applicable law, such as amounts that would have been deferred or paid regardless of the existence of such claim, even if such amounts are paid or modified as part of a settlement or award resolving an actual bona fide claim. For this purpose, a provision of foreign law shall be considered applicable only to foreign earned income (as defined under section 911(b)(1) without regard to

section 911(b)(1)(B)(iv) and without regard to the requirement that the income be attributable to services performed during the period described in section 911(d)(1)(A) or (B)) from sources within the foreign country that promulgated such law.

*(12) Certain educational benefits.* A plan in which a service provider participates does not provide for a deferral of compensation to the extent the plan provides for taxable educational benefits. For purposes of this paragraph (b)(12), the term educational benefits refers solely to benefits provided to a service provider, consisting solely of educational assistance for the education of the service provider, as defined in section 127(c) and the accompanying regulations, and does not refer to any benefits provided for the education of any other person, including any spouse, child, or other family member of the service provider.

**(c) Plan.** *(1) In general.* The term plan includes any agreement, method, program, or other arrangement, including an agreement, method, program, or other arrangement that applies to one person or individual. A plan may be adopted unilaterally by the service recipient or may be negotiated or agreed to by the service recipient and one or more service providers or service provider representatives. An agreement, method, program, or other arrangement may constitute a plan regardless of whether it is an employee benefit plan under section 3(3) of ERISA, as amended (29 U.S.C. 1002(3)). The requirements of section 409A are applied as if a separate plan or plans is maintained for each service provider. For purposes of determining the terms of a plan, general provisions of the plan that purport to nullify noncompliant plan terms, or to supply any specific plan terms required by this section, § 1.409A-2 or § 1.409A-3, are disregarded.

*(2) Plan aggregation rules.* (i) In general. Except as otherwise provided, the following rules apply with respect to the application of this section and §§ 1.409A-2 through 1.409A-6 to deferrals of compensation with respect to a service provider:

(A) All deferrals of compensation at the election of that service provider under all plans of the service recipient that are account balance plans, except to the extent that the plan is described in paragraph (c)(2)(i)(D), (E), (F), (G), or (H) of this section, are treated as deferred under a single plan. For purposes of this paragraph, the term account balance plan means—

(1) An agreement, method, program, or other arrangement that is an account balance plan as defined in § 31.3121(v)(2)-1(c)(1)(ii)(A) of this chapter, including mandatorily bifurcating the agreement, method, program, or other arrangement in accordance with the rules provided in § 31.3121(v)-1(c)(1)(iii)(B) of this chapter; or

(2) An agreement, method, program, or other arrangement that would be described in paragraph (c)(2)(i)(A)(1) of this section if the service provider were an employee.

(B) All deferrals of compensation other than at the election of that service provider, including deferrals reflecting matching by the service recipient with respect to amounts a service provider elects to defer, under all plans of the service recipient that are account balance plans, except to the extent the plan is described in paragraph (c)(2)(i)(D), (E), (F), (G), or (H) of this section, are treated as deferred under a single plan. For purposes of this paragraph (c)(2)(i)(B), the term "account balance plan" has the same meaning as provided in paragraph (c)(2)(i)(A) of this section.

(C) All deferrals of compensation with respect to that service provider under all plans of the service recipient that are nonaccount balance plans, except to the extent such plan is described in paragraph (c)(2)(i)(D), (E), (F), (G), or (H) of this section, are treated as deferred under a single plan. For purposes of this paragraph (c)(2)(i)(C), the term nonaccount balance plan means—

(1) An agreement, method, program, or other arrangement that is a nonaccount balance plan as defined in § 31.3121(v)(2)-1(c)(2)(i) of this chapter, including mandatorily bifurcating the agreement, method, program, or other arrangement in accordance with the rules provided in § 31.3121(v)-1(c)(1)(iii)(B) of this chapter; or

(2) An agreement, method, program, or other arrangement that would be described in paragraph (c)(2)(i)(C)(1) of this section if the service provider were an employee.

(D) All deferrals of compensation with respect to that service provider under all separation pay plans (as defined in paragraph (m) of this section) of the service recipient to the extent an amount deferred under the plans is not described in paragraph (c)(2)(i)(E) of this section and is payable solely upon an involuntary separation from service within the meaning of paragraph (n) of this section or as a result of participation in a window program, are treated as deferred under a single plan.

(E) All deferrals of compensation with respect to that service provider under all plans of the service recipient to the extent such amounts deferred consist of rights to in-kind benefits or reimbursements of expenses, such as membership fees, or expenses related to aircraft or vehicle usage, to the extent that the right to the in-kind benefit or reimbursement, separately or in the aggregate, does not constitute a substantial portion of either the overall compensation earned by the service provider for performing services for the service recipient or the overall compensation received due to a separation from service, are treated as deferred under a single plan.

(F) All deferrals of compensation with respect to that service provider under all plans of the service recipient to the extent that the taxation of such compensation is governed by § 1.61-22 or § 1.7872-15 (split-dollar life insurance arrangements), or the taxation of such compensation would be governed by § 1.61-22 or § 1.7872-15 but for the operation of § 1.61-22(j) (effective date provisions), are treated as deferred under a single plan.

(G) All deferrals of compensation with respect to that service provider under all agreements, methods, programs, or other arrangements of the service recipient to the extent the deferrals under the agreements, methods, programs, or other arrangements are deferrals of amounts that would be treated as modified foreign earned income (meaning foreign earned income as defined under section 911(b)(1) without regard to section 911(b)(1)(B)(iv) and without regard to the requirement that the income be attributable to services performed during the period described in section 911(d)(1)(A) or (B)) if paid to the service provider at the time the amount is first deferred, and provided further that substantially all the participants in such agreements, methods, programs, or other arrangements and any substantially similar agreements, methods, programs, or other arrangements are nonresident aliens and that the service provider does not participate in a substantially identical agreement, method, program, or other arrangement that does not meet the requirements of this paragraph (c)(2)(i)(G) (a domestic arrangement), are treated as deferred under a single plan.

(H) All deferrals of compensation with respect to that service provider under all plans of the service recipient to the extent such plans are stock rights (as defined in paragraph (l) of this section) subject to section 409A, are treated as deferred under a single plan.

(I) All deferrals of compensation with respect to that service provider under all plans of the service recipient to the extent such plans are not described in paragraph (c)(2)(i)(A), (B), (C), (D), (E), (F), (G), or (H) of this section are treated as deferred under a single plan.

(ii) Dual status. Agreements, methods, programs, and other arrangements in which a service provider participates are not aggregated with other agreements, methods, programs, and other arrangements to the extent the service provider participates in one set of agreements, methods, programs, and other arrangements due to status as an employee of the service recipient (employee arrangements) and another set of agreements, methods, programs, and other arrangements due to status as an independent contractor of the service recipient (independent contractor arrangements). For example, where a service provider deferred amounts under an independent contractor arrangement while providing services as an independent contractor, and then becomes eligible for and defers amounts under a separate employee arrangement after being hired as an employee, the two arrangements will not be aggregated for purposes of this paragraph (c)(2). Where an employee also is a member of the board of directors of the service recipient (or a similar position with respect to a non-corporate service recipient), the arrangements under which the employee participates as a director (director arrangements) are not aggregated with employee arrangements, provided that the director arrangements are substantially similar to arrangements provided to service providers providing services only as directors (or similar positions with respect to non-corporate service recipients). For example, an employee director who participates in an employee arrangement and a director arrangement generally may treat the two arrangements as separate plans, provided that the director arrangement is substantially similar to arrangements providing benefits to non-employee directors. To the extent a plan in which an employee director participates is not substantially similar to arrangements in which non-employee directors participate, such plan is treated as an employee plan for purposes of this paragraph (c)(2). Director plans and independent contractor plans are aggregated for purposes of this paragraph (c)(2).

*(3) Establishment of plan.* (i) In general. A plan does not satisfy the requirements of section 409A and this section and §§ 1.409A-2 through 1.409A-3 and §§ 1.409A-5 through 1.409A-6, unless the plan is established and maintained by a service recipient in accordance with the requirements of this section, §§ 1.409A-2 through 1.409A-3 and §§ 1.409A-5 through 1.409A-6. For purposes of this paragraph (c)(3), a plan is established on the latest of the date on which it is adopted, the date on which it is effective, and the date on which the material terms of the plan are set forth in writing. The material terms of the plan may be set forth in writing in one or more documents. For purposes of this paragraph (c)(3)(i), a plan will be deemed to be set forth in writing if it is set forth in any other form that is approved by the Commissioner. The material terms of the plan include the amount (or the method or formula for determining the amount) of deferred compensation to be provided under the plan and the time and form of payment. Notwithstanding the foregoing, a plan will be deemed to be established as of the date the participant obtains a legally binding right to a deferral of compensation, provided that the plan is otherwise established under the rules of this paragraph (c)(3)(i) by the end of the taxable year of the service provider in which the legally binding right arises, or with respect to an amount not payable in the year immediately following the taxable year of the service provider in which the legally binding right arises (the subsequent year), the 15th day of the third month of the subsequent year.

(ii) Initial deferral election provisions. If a plan provides a service provider or a service recipient with an initial deferral election, the plan satisfies the requirements of this paragraph (c)(3) if the plan sets forth in writing, on or before the date the applicable election is required to be irrevocable to satisfy the requirements of § 1.409A-2(a), the conditions under which such election may be made.

(iii) Subsequent deferral election provisions. If a plan permits a subsequent deferral election described in § 1.409A-2(b), the plan satisfies the requirements of this paragraph (c)(3) if the plan sets forth in writing, on or before the date the election is required to be irrevocable to meet the requirements of § 1.409A-2(b), the conditions under which such election may be made.

(iv) Payment accelerations. Except as explicitly provided in § 1.409A-3, a plan is not required to set forth in writing the conditions under which a payment may be accelerated if such acceleration is permitted under § 1.409A-3(j)(4).

(v) Six-month delay for specified employees. A plan must provide that distributions to a specified employee may not be made before the date that is six months after the date of separation from service or, if earlier, the date of death (the six-month delay rule). The six-month delay rule, required for payments due to the separation from service of a specified employee, must be written in the plan. A plan does not fail to be established and maintained merely because it does not contain the six-month delay rule when the service provider who has a right to compensation deferred under such plan is not a specified employee. However, such provision must be set forth in writing on or before the date such service provider first becomes a specified employee. In general, this means the provision must be set forth in writing on or before the specified employee effective date (as defined in paragraph (i)(3) of this section) for the first list of specified employees that includes such service provider.

(vi) Plan amendments. In the case of an amendment that increases the amount deferred under a nonqualified deferred compensation plan, the plan is not considered established with respect to the additional amount deferred until the plan, as amended, is established in accordance with paragraph (c)(3)(i) of this section.

(vii) Transition rule for written plan requirement. For purposes of this paragraph (c)(3), a legally enforceable unwritten plan that was adopted and effective before December 31, 2007, is treated as established under this section as of the later of the date on which it was adopted or became effective, provided that the material terms of the plan are set forth in writing on or before December 31, 2007.

(viii) Plan aggregation rules. The plan aggregation rules of paragraph (c)(2)(i) of this section do not apply to the written plan requirements of this paragraph (c)(3). Accordingly, deferrals of compensation under an agreement, method, program, or other arrangement that fails to meet the requirements of section 409A solely due to a failure to meet the written plan requirements of this paragraph (c)(3) are not aggregated with deferrals of compensation under other agreements, methods, programs, or other arrangements that meet such requirements.

**(d) Substantial risk of forfeiture.** *(1) In general.* Compensation is subject to a substantial risk of forfeiture if entitlement to the amount is conditioned on the performance of substantial future services by any person or the occurrence of a condition related to a purpose of the compensation, and the possibility of forfeiture is substantial. For purposes of this paragraph (d), a condition related to a purpose of the compensation must relate to the service provider's performance for the service recipient or the service recipient's business activities or organizational goals (for example, the attainment of a prescribed level of earnings or equity value or completion of an initial public offering). For purposes of this paragraph (d), if a service provider's entitlement to the amount is conditioned on the occurrence of the service provider's involuntary separation from service without cause, the right is subject to a substantial risk of forfeiture if the possibility of forfeiture is substantial. An amount is not subject to a substantial risk of forfeiture merely because the right to the amount is conditioned, directly or indirectly, upon the refraining from the performance of services. Except as provided with respect to certain transaction-based compensation under § 1.409A-3(i)(5)(iv), the addition of any risk of forfeiture after the legally binding right to the compensation arises, or any extension of a period during which compensation is subject to a risk of forfeiture, is disregarded for purposes of determining whether such compensation is subject to a substantial risk of forfeiture. An amount will not be considered subject to a substantial risk of forfeiture beyond the date or time at which the recipient otherwise could have elected to receive the amount of compensation, unless the present value of the amount subject to a substantial risk of forfeiture (disregarding, in determining the present value, the risk of forfeiture) is materially greater than the present value of the amount the recipient otherwise could have elected to receive absent such risk of forfeiture. For this purpose, compensation that the service provider would receive for continuing to perform services regardless of whether the service provider elected to receive the amount that is subject to a substantial risk of forfeiture is not taken into account in determining whether the present value of the right to the amount subject to a substantial risk of forfeiture is materially greater than the amount the recipient otherwise could have elected to receive absent such risk of forfeiture. For example, a salary deferral generally may not be made subject to a substantial risk of forfeiture. But, for example, where a bonus plan provides an election between a cash payment or restricted stock units with a present value that is materially greater (disregarding the risk of forfeiture) than the present value of such cash payment and that will be forfeited absent continued services for a period of years, the right to the restricted stock units generally will be treated as subject to a substantial risk of forfeiture.

*(2) Stock rights.* A stock right is not subject to a substantial risk of forfeiture at the earlier of the first date the holder may exercise the stock right and receive cash or property that is substantially vested (as defined in § 1.83-3(b)) or the first date that the stock right is not subject to a forfeiture condition that would constitute a substantial risk of forfeiture. Accordingly, a stock option that the service provider may exercise immediately and receive substantially vested stock is not subject to a substantial risk of forfeiture, even if the stock option automatically terminates upon the service provider's separation from service.

*(3) Enforcement of forfeiture condition.* (i) In general. In determining whether the possibility of forfeiture is substantial in the case of rights to compensation granted by a service recipient to a service provider that owns a significant amount of the total combined voting power or value of all classes of equity of the service recipient (where the service provider's ownership is determined with application of the attribution rules under section 318 if the service recipient is a corporation, or if the service recipient is an entity that is not a corporation, with application by analogy of the attribution rules under section 318), all relevant facts and circumstances will be taken into account in determining whether the probability of the service recipient enforcing such condition is substantial, including—

(A) The service provider's relationship to other equity holders and the extent of their control, potential control and possible loss of control of the service recipient;

(B) The position of the service provider in the service recipient and the extent to which the service provider is subordinate to other service providers;

(C) The service provider's relationship to the officers and directors of the service recipient (or similar positions with respect to a noncorporate service recipient);

(D) The person or persons who must approve the service provider's discharge; and

(E) Past actions of the service recipient in enforcing the restrictions.

(ii) Examples. The following examples illustrate the rules of paragraph (d)(3)(i) of this section:

*Example (1).* A service provider would be considered as having deferred compensation subject to a substantial risk of forfeiture, but for the fact that the service provider owns 20 percent of the single class of stock in the transferor corporation. If the remaining 80 percent of the class of stock is owned by an unrelated individual (or members of such an individual's family) so that the possibility of the corporation enforcing a restriction on such rights is substantial, then such rights are subject to a substantial risk of forfeiture.

*Example (2).* A service provider would be considered as having deferred compensation subject to a substantial risk of forfeiture, but for the fact that the service provider, who is president of the corporation, also owns 4 percent of the voting power of all the stock of a corporation. If the remaining stock is so diversely held by the public that the president, in effect, controls the corporation, then the possibility of the corporation enforcing a restriction on the right to deferred compensation of the president is not substantial, and such rights are not subject to a substantial risk of forfeiture.

**(e) Performance-based compensation.** *(1) In general.* The term performance-based compensation means compensation the amount of which, or the entitlement to which, is contingent on the satisfaction of preestablished organizational or individual performance criteria relating to a performance period of at least 12 consecutive months. Organizational or individual performance criteria are considered preestablished if established in writing by not later than 90 days after the commencement of the period of service to which the criteria relates, provided that the outcome is substantially uncertain at the time the criteria are established. Performance-based compensation may include payments based on performance criteria that are not approved by a compensation committee of the board of directors (or similar entity in the case of a non-corporate service recipient) or by the stockholders or members of the service recipient. Performance-based compensation does not include any amount or portion of any amount that will be paid either regardless of performance, or based upon a level of performance that is substantially certain to be met at the time the criteria is established. In addition, except as provided in paragraph (e)(3) of this section, compensation is not performance-based compensation merely because the amount of such compensation is determined by reference to the value of the service recipient or the stock of the service recipient. Where a portion of an amount of compensation would qualify as performance-based compensation if the portion were the sole amount available under the plan, that portion of the award will not fail to qualify as performance-based compensation if that portion is designated separately or otherwise separately identifiable under the terms of the plan, and the amount of each portion is determined independently of the other. Compensation may be performance-based compensation where the amount will be paid regardless of satisfaction of the performance criteria due to the service provider's death, disability, or a change in control event (as defined in § 1.409A-3(i)(5)(i)), provided that a payment made under such circumstances without regard to the satisfaction of the performance criteria will not constitute performance-based compensation. For purposes of this paragraph (e)(1), a disability refers to any medically determinable physical or mental impairment resulting in the service provider's inability to perform the duties of his or her position or any substantially similar position, where such impairment can be expected to result in death or can be expected to last for a continuous period of not less than six months.

*(2) Payments based upon subjective performance criteria.* The term performance-based compensation includes payments based upon subjective performance criteria, provided that—

(i) The subjective performance criteria are bona fide and relate to the performance of the participant service provider, a group of service providers that includes the participant service provider, or a business unit for which the participant service provider provides services (which may include the entire organization); and

(ii) The determination that any subjective performance criteria have been met is not made by the participant service provider or a family member of the participant service provider (as defined in section 267(c)(4) applied as if the family of an individual includes the spouse of any member of the family), or a person under the effective control of the participant service provider or such a family member, and no amount of the compensation of the person making such determination is effectively controlled in whole or in part by the service provider or such a family member.

*(3) Equity-based compensation.* Compensation is performance-based compensation if it is based solely on an increase in the value of the service recipient, or a share of stock in the service recipient, after the date of a grant or award. However, compensation payable for a service period that is equal to the value of a predetermined number of shares of stock, and is variable only to the extent that the value of such shares appreciates or depreciates, generally will not be performance-based compensation. Notwithstanding the foregoing, the attainment of a prescribed value for the service recipient (or a portion thereof), or a share of stock in the service recipient, may be used as a preestablished organizational criterion for purposes of providing performance-based compensation, provided that the other requirements of paragraph (e)(1) of this section are satisfied. In addition, an award of equity-based compensation may constitute performance-based compensation if entitlement to the compensation is subject to a condition that would cause the award to otherwise qualify as performance-based compensation, such as a performance-based vesting condition. A provision that allows a service provider to defer compensation that would be realized upon the exercise of a stock right generally constitutes an additional deferral feature for purposes of the definition of a deferral of compensation under paragraph (b)(5) of this section.

**(f) Service provider.** *(1) In general.* The term service provider includes an individual, corporation, subchapter S corporation, partnership, personal service corporation (as defined in section 269A(b)(1)), noncorporate entity that would be a personal service corporation if it were a corporation, qualified personal service corporation (as defined in section 448(d)(2)), and noncorporate entity that would be a qualified personal service corporation if it were a corporation, for any taxable year in which such individual, corporation, subchapter S corporation, partnership, or other entity accounts for gross income from the performance of services under the cash receipts and disbursements method of accounting. The term service provider generally includes a person who has separated from service (a former service provider).

*(2) Independent contractors.* (i) In general. Except as otherwise provided in paragraph (f)(2)(iv) of this section, section 409A does not apply to an amount deferred under a plan between a service provider and service recipient with respect to a particular trade or business in which the service provider participates, including earnings credited to such deferred amount, if during the service provider's taxable year in which the service provider obtains a legally binding right to the payment of the amount deferred each of the following applies:

(A) The service provider is actively engaged in the trade or business of providing services, other than as an employee or as a member of the board of directors of a corporation (or similar position with respect to an entity that is not a corporation).

(B) The service provider provides significant services to two or more service recipients to which the service provider is not related and that are not related to one another (as defined in paragraph (f)(2)(ii) of this section).

(C) The service provider is not related to the service recipient, applying the definition of related person contained in paragraph (f)(2)(ii) of this section subject to the modification that the language "20 percent" is not used instead of "50 percent" each place "50 percent" appears in sections 267(b) and 707(b)(1).

(ii) Related person. For purposes of this paragraph (f)(2), a person is related to another person if the persons bear a relationship to each other that is specified in section 267(b) or 707(b)(1), subject to the modifications that the language "20 percent" is used instead of "50 percent" each place it appears in sections 267(b) and 707(b)(1), and section 267(c)(4) is applied as if the family of an individual includes the spouse of any member of the family; or the persons are engaged in trades or businesses under common control (within the meaning of section 52(a) and (b)). In addition, an individual is related to an entity if the individual is an officer of an entity that is a corporation, or holds a position substantially similar to an officer of a corporation with an entity that is not a corporation.

(iii) Significant services. Whether a service provider is providing significant services depends on the facts and circumstances of each case. However, for purposes of paragraph (f)(2)(i) of this section, a service provider who provides services to two or more service recipients to which the service provider is not related and that are not related to one another is deemed to be providing significant services to two or more of such service recipients for a given taxable year, if the revenues generated from the services provided to any service recipient or group of related service recipients during such taxable year do not exceed 70 percent of the total revenue generated by the service provider from the trade or business of providing such services. In addition, in the case of a service provider who has been providing services in a trade or business for a period of not less than three consecutive years, for purposes of paragraph (f)(2)(i) of this section, a service provider who provides services to two or more service recipients to which the service provider is not related and that are not related to one another is deemed to be providing significant services to two or more of such service recipients for a given taxable year if in each of the prior three taxable years the revenues generated from the services provided to any service recipient or group of related service recipients during such prior taxable years did not exceed 70 percent of the total revenue generated by the service provider from the trade or business of providing such services and, at the time an amount is deferred, the service provider does not know or have reason to anticipate that the revenues generated from the services provided to any service recipient or group of related service recipients during the current year will exceed 70 percent of the total revenue generated by the service provider from the trade or business of providing such services.

(iv) Management services. This paragraph (f)(2) does not apply to a service provider to the extent the service provider provides management services to a service recipient. For purposes of this paragraph (f)(2)(iv), the term management services means services that involve the actual or de facto direction or control of the financial or operational aspects of a trade or business of the service recipient, or investment management or advisory services provided to a service recipient whose primary trade or business includes the investment of financial assets (including investments in real estate), such as a hedge fund or a real estate investment trust.

(v) Services provided to related persons. Section 409A does not apply to an amount deferred under a plan that is a bona fide agreement, method, program, or other arrangement between a service provider and a related service recipient arising in the ordinary course of a particular trade or business in which the service provider is engaged to the extent that—

(A) The service provider provides services to the service recipient as an independent contractor;

(B) During the service provider's taxable year in which the amount is deferred, the service provider qualifies for the safe harbor provided in paragraph (f)(2)(iii) of this section with respect to such trade or business; and

(C) Such agreement, method, program, or other arrangement and the practices thereunder (including billing and collection practices), are substantially similar to the agreements, methods, programs, or other arrangements and practices applicable to one or more unrelated service recipients to whom the service provider provides substantial services and that produce a majority of the total revenue that the service provider earns from the trade or business of providing such services during the taxable year.

**(g) Service recipient.** Except as otherwise specifically provided in these regulations, the term service recipient means the person for whom the services are performed and with respect to whom the legally binding right to compensation arises, and all persons with whom such person would be considered a single employer under section 414(b) (employees of controlled group of corporations), and all persons with whom such person would be considered a single employer under section 414(c) (employees of partnerships, proprietorships, etc., under common control). For example, if the service provider is an employee, the service recipient generally is the employer (including all persons treated as a single employer under section 414(b) or (c)). Notwithstanding the foregoing, section 409A applies to a plan that provides for the deferral of compensation, even if the payment of the compensation is not made by the person for whom services are performed.

**(h) Separation from service.** *(1) Employees.* (i) In general. An employee separates from service with the employer if the employee dies, retires, or otherwise has a termination of employment with the employer. However, for purposes of this paragraph (h)(1), the employment relationship is treated as continuing intact while the individual is on military leave, sick leave, or other bona fide leave of absence if the period of such leave does not exceed six months, or if longer, so long as the individual retains a right to reemployment with the service recipient under an applicable statute or by contract. For purposes of this paragraph (h)(1), a leave of absence constitutes a bona fide leave of absence only if there is a reasonable expectation that the employee will return to perform services for the employer. If the period of leave exceeds six months and the individual does not retain a right to reemployment under an applicable statute or by contract, the employment relationship is deemed to terminate on the first date immediately following such six-month period. Notwithstanding the foregoing, where a leave of absence is due to any medically determinable physical or mental impairment that can be expected to result in death or can be expected to last for a continuous period of not less than six months, where such impairment causes the employee to be unable to perform the duties of his or her position of employment or any substantially similar position of employment, a 29-month period of absence may be substituted for such six-month period.

(ii) Termination of employment. Whether a termination of employment has occurred is determined based on whether the facts and circumstances indicate that the employer and employee reasonably anticipated that no further services would be performed after a certain date or that the level of bona fide services the employee would perform after such date (whether as an employee or as an independent contractor) would permanently decrease to no more than 20 percent of the average level of bona fide services performed (whether as an employee or an independent contractor) over the immediately preceding 36-month period (or the full period of services to the employer if the employee has been providing services to the employer less than 36 months). Facts and circumstances to be considered in making this determination include, but are not limited to, whether the employee continues to be treated as an employee for other purposes (such as continuation of salary and participation in employee benefit programs), whether similarly situated service providers have been treated consistently, and whether the employee is permitted, and realistically available, to perform services for other service recipients in the same line of business. An employee is presumed to have separated from service where the level of bona fide services performed decreases to a level equal to 20 percent or less of the average level of services performed by the employee during the immediately preceding 36-month period. An employee will be presumed not to have separated from service where the level of bona fide services performed continues at a level that is 50 percent or more of the average level of service performed by the employee during the immediately preceding 36-month period. No presumption applies to a decrease in the level of bona fide services performed to a level that is more than 20 percent and less than 50 percent of the average level of bona fide services performed during the immediately preceding 36-month period. The presumption is rebuttable by demonstrating that the employer and the employee reasonably anticipated that as of a certain date the level of bona fide services would be reduced permanently to a level less than or equal to 20 percent of the average level of bona fide services provided during the immediately preceding 36-month period or full period of services provided to the employer if the employee has been providing services to the service recipient for a period of less than 36 months (or that the level of bona fide services would not be so reduced). For example, an employee may demonstrate that the employer and employee reasonably anticipated that the employee would cease providing services, but that, after the original cessation of services, business circumstances such as termination of the employee's replacement caused the employee to return to employment. Although the employee's return to employment may cause the employee to be presumed to have continued in employment because the employee is providing services at a rate equal to the rate at which the employee was providing services before the termination of employment, the facts and circumstances in this case would demonstrate that at the time the employee originally ceased to provide services, the employee and the service recipient reasonably anticipated that the employee would not provide services in the future. Notwithstanding the foregoing provisions of this paragraph (h)(1)(ii), a plan may treat another level of reasonably anticipated permanent reduction in the level of bona fide services as a separation from service, provided that the level of reduction required must be designated in writing as a specific percentage, and the reasonably anticipated reduced level of bona fide services must be greater than 20 percent but less that 50 percent of the average level of bona fide services provided in the immediately preceding 36 months. The plan must specify the definition of separation from service on or before the date on which a separation from service is designated as a time of payment of the applicable amount deferred, and once designated, any change to the definition of separation from service with respect to such amount deferred will be subject to the rules regarding subsequent deferrals and the acceleration of payments. For purposes of this paragraph (h)(1)(ii), for periods during which an employee is on a paid bona fide leave of absence (as defined in paragraph (h)(1)(i) of this section) and has not otherwise terminated employment pursuant to paragraph (h)(1)(i) of this section, the employee is treated as providing bona fide services at a level equal to the level of services that the employee would have been required to perform to receive the compensation paid with respect to such leave of absence. Periods during which an employee is on an unpaid bona fide leave of absence (as defined in paragraph (h)(1)(i) of this section) and has not otherwise terminated employment pursuant to paragraph (h)(1)(i) of this section, are disregarded for purposes of this paragraph (h)(1)(ii) (including for purposes of determining the applicable 36-month (or shorter) period).

*(2) Independent contractors.* (i) In general. An independent contractor is considered to have a separation from service with the service recipient upon the expiration of the contract (or in the case of more than one contract, all contracts) under which services are performed for the service recipient if the expiration constitutes a good-faith and complete termination of the contractual relationship. An expiration does not constitute a good faith and complete termination of the contractual relationship if the service recipient anticipates a renewal of a contractual relationship or the independent contractor becoming an employee. For this purpose, a service recipient is considered to anticipate the renewal of the contractual relationship with an independent contractor if it intends to contract again for the services provided under the expired contract, and neither the service recipient nor the independent contractor has eliminated the independent contractor as a possible provider of services under any such new contract. Further, a service recipient is considered to intend to contract again for the services provided under an expired contract if the service recipient's doing so is conditioned only upon incurring a need for the services, the availability of funds, or both.

(ii) Special rule. Notwithstanding paragraph (h)(2)(i) of this section, a plan is considered to satisfy the requirement described in § 1.409A-3(a)(1) with respect to an amount payable upon a separation from service if, with respect to amounts payable to a service provider who is an independent contractor, the plan provides that—

(A) No amount will be paid to the service provider before a date at least 12 months after the day on which the contract expires under which the service provider performs services for the service recipient (or, in the case of more than one contract, all such contracts expire); and

(B) No amount payable to the service provider on that date will be paid to the service provider if, after the expiration of the contract (or contracts) and before that date, the service provider performs services for the service recipient as an independent contractor or an employee.

*(3) Definition of service recipient and employer.* For purposes of this paragraph (h), the term service recipient or employer means the service recipient as defined in paragraph (g) of this section, provided that in applying section 1563(a)(1), (2), and (3) for purposes of determining a controlled group of corporations under section 414(b), the language "at least 50 percent" is used instead of "at least 80 percent" each place it appears in section 1563(a)(1), (2), and (3), and in applying § 1.414(c)-2 for purposes of determining trades or businesses (whether or not incorporated) that are under common control for purposes of section 414(c), "at least 50 percent" is used instead of "at least 80 percent" each place it appears in § 1.414(c)-2. A plan may provide with respect to a deferral of compensation under the plan that in applying sections 1563(a)(1), (2), and (3) for purposes of determining a controlled group of corporations under section 414(b), another defined percentage greater than 50 percent, but not greater than 80 percent, is used instead of "at least 80 percent" at each place it appears in sections 1563(a)(1), (2), and (3), and in applying § 1.414(c)-2 for purposes of determining trades or businesses (whether or not incorporated) that are under common control for purposes of section 414(c), another defined percentage greater than 50 percent, but not greater than 80 percent, is used instead of "at least 80 percent" at each place it appears in § 1.414(c)-2. In addition, where the use of such definition of service recipient for purposes of determining a separation from service is based upon legitimate business criteria, the plan may provide that for purposes of a deferral of compensation under the plan that in applying sections 1563(a)(1), (2), and (3) for purposes of determining a controlled group of corporations

under section 414(b), the language "at least 20 percent" or another defined percentage not less than 20 percent but not greater than 50 percent is used instead of "at least 80 percent" at each place it appears in sections 1563(a)(1), (2), and (3), and in applying § 1.414(c)-2 for purposes of determining trades or businesses (whether or not incorporated) that are under common control for purposes of section 414(c), the language "at least 20 percent" or another defined percentage not less than 20 percent but not greater than 50 percent is used instead of "at least 80 percent" at each place it appears in § 1.414(c)-2. Where a definition of service recipient or employer other than the definition provided in the first sentence of this paragraph (h)(3) (the 50 percent standard) is used, the plan must designate in writing the alternate definition no later than the last date at which the time and form of payment of the applicable amount deferred must be elected in accordance with § 1.409A-2(a), and any change in the definition for such amounts deferred will constitute a change in the time and form of payment subject to the rules governing subsequent deferral elections under § 1.409A-2(b) and the acceleration of payments under § 1.409A-3(j).

*(4) Asset purchase transactions.* Where as part of a sale or other disposition of assets by one service recipient (seller) to an unrelated service recipient (buyer), a service provider of the seller would otherwise experience a separation from service with the seller, the seller and the buyer may retain the discretion to specify, and may specify, whether a service provider providing services to the seller immediately before the asset purchase transaction and providing services to the buyer after and in connection with the asset purchase transaction has experienced a separation from service for purposes of this paragraph (h), provided that the asset purchase transaction results from bona fide, arm's length negotiations, all service providers providing services to the seller immediately before the asset purchase transaction and providing services to the buyer after and in connection with the asset purchase transaction are treated consistently (regardless of position at the seller) for purposes of applying the provisions of any nonqualified deferred compensation plan, and such treatment is specified in writing no later than the closing date of the asset purchase transaction. For purposes of this paragraph (h)(4), references to a sale or other disposition of assets, or an asset purchase transaction, refer only to a transfer of substantial assets, such as a plant or division or substantially all the assets of a trade or business. For purposes of this paragraph (h)(4), whether a service recipient is related to another service recipient is determined under the rules provided in paragraph (f)(2)(ii) of this section.

*(5) Dual status.* If a service provider provides services both as an employee of a service recipient and as an independent contractor of a service recipient, the service provider must separate from service both as an employee and as an independent contractor to be treated as having separated from service. If a service provider ceases providing services as an independent contractor and begins providing services as an employee, or ceases providing services as an employee and begins providing services as an independent contractor, the service provider will not be considered to have a separation from service until the service provider has ceased providing services in both capacities. Notwithstanding the foregoing, if a service provider provides services both as an employee of a service recipient and a member of the board of directors of a corporate service recipient (or an analogous position with respect to a non-corporate service recipient), the services provided as a director are not taken into account in determining whether the service provider has a separation from service as an employee for purposes of a nonqualified deferred compensation plan in which the service provider participates as an employee that is not aggregated with any plan in which the service provider participates as a director under paragraph (c)(2)(ii) of this section. In addition, if a service provider provides services both as an employee of a service recipient and a member of the board of directors of a corporate service recipient (or an analogous position with respect to a non-corporate service recipient), the services provided as an employee are not taken into account in determining whether the service provider has a separation from service as a director for purposes of a nonqualified deferred compensation plan in which the service provider participates as a director that is not aggregated with any plan in which the service provider participates as an employee under paragraph (c)(2)(ii) of this section.

*(6) Collectively bargained plans covering multiple employers.* Notwithstanding the foregoing provisions of this paragraph (h), to the extent a plan is established pursuant to a bona fide collective bargaining agreement covering services performed by employees for multiple employers, such plan may define a separation from service in a reasonable manner that treats the employee as not having separated from service during periods in which the employee is not providing services but is available to perform services covered by the collective bargaining agreement for one or more employers, provided that the definition also provides that the employee must be deemed to have separated from service at a specified date not later than the end of any period of at least 12 consecutive months during which the employee has not provided any services covered by the collective bargaining agreement to any participating employer. This paragraph (h)(6) applies only if the definition of separation from service provided by the collective bargaining agreement was the subject of arm's length negotiations between employee representatives and two or more employers, the agreement between employee representatives and such employers satisfies section 7701(a)(46), and the circumstances surrounding the agreement evidence good faith bargaining between adverse parties over such definition.

**(i) Specified employee.** *(1) In general.* The term specified employee means a service provider who, as of the date of the service provider's separation from service, is a key employee of a service recipient any stock of which is publicly traded on an established securities market or otherwise. For purposes of this paragraph (i)(1), a service provider is a key employee if the service provider meets the requirements of section 416(i)(1)(A)(i), (ii), or (iii) (applied in accordance with the regulations thereunder and disregarding section 416(i)(5)) at any time during the 12-month period ending on a specified employee identification date. If a service provider is a key employee as of a specified employee identification date, the service provider is treated as a key employee for purposes of this paragraph (i) for the entire 12-month period beginning on the specified employee effective date.

*(2) Definition of compensation.* For purposes of identifying a specified employee by applying the requirements of section 416(i)(1)(A)(i), (ii), and (iii), the definition of compensation under § 1.415(c)-2(a) is used, applied as if the service recipient were not using any safe harbor provided in § 1.415(c)-2(d), were not using any of the elective special timing rules provided in § 1.415(c)-2(e), and were not using any of the elective special rules provided in § 1.415(c)-2(g). Notwithstanding the foregoing, a service recipient may elect to use any available definition of compensation under section 415 and the regulations thereunder in accordance with

the election requirements set forth in paragraph (i)(8) of this section, including any available safe harbor and any available election under the timing rules or special rules, provided that the definition is applied consistently to all employees of the service recipient for purposes of identifying specified employees. A service recipient may elect to use such an alternative definition regardless of whether another definition of compensation is being used for purposes of a qualified plan sponsored by the service recipient. However, once a list of specified employees has become effective, the service recipient cannot change the definition of compensation for purposes of identifying specified employees for the period with respect to which such list is effective.

*(3) Specified employee identification date.* Unless another date is designated in accordance with the requirements of this paragraph (i)(3) and paragraph (i)(8) of this section, the specified employee identification date is December 31. A service recipient may designate in accordance with the requirements of paragraph (i)(8) of this section any other date as the specified employee identification date, provided that a service recipient must use the same specified employee identification date with respect to all nonqualified deferred compensation plans, and any change to the specified employee identification date may not be effective for a period of at least 12 months. The service recipient may designate a specified employee identification date in each plan or in a separate document applicable to all plans, provided that the service recipient will not be treated as having designated a specified employee identification date before the designation is legally binding on the service recipient and all affected service providers. Any designation of a specified employee identification date made on or before December 31, 2007, may be applied to any separation from service occurring on or after January 1, 2005, unless and until subsequently changed pursuant to this paragraph (i)(3).

*(4) Specified employee effective date.* Unless another date is designated in accordance with the requirements of this paragraph (i)(4) and paragraph (i)(8) of this section, the specified employee effective date is the first day of the fourth month following the specified employee identification date. A service recipient may designate in accordance with the requirements of paragraph (i)(8) of this section any date following the specified employee identification date as the specified employee effective date, provided that such date may not be later than the first day of the fourth month following the specified employee identification date, and provided further that a service recipient must use the same specified employee effective date with respect to all nonqualified deferred compensation plans, and any change to the specified employee effective date may not be effective for a period of at least 12 months. The service recipient may designate a specified employee effective date through inclusion in each plan document or through a separate document applicable to all plans, provided that the service recipient will not be treated as having designated a specified employee effective date on any date before the designation is legally binding on the service recipient and all affected service providers. Any designation of a specified employee effective date made on or before December 31, 2007, may be applied to any separation from service occurring on or after January 1, 2005, unless and until subsequently changed pursuant to this paragraph (i)(4).

*(5) Alternative methods of satisfying the six-month delay rule.* A plan may provide, in accordance with the requirements of paragraph (i)(8) of this section, for an alternative method to identify service providers who will be subject to the six-month delay rule provided in section 409A(a)(2)(B)(i), provided that the alternative method is reasonably designed to include all specified employees (determined without respect to any available service recipient elections), the alternative method is an objectively determinable standard providing no direct or indirect election to any service provider regarding its application, and the alternative method results in either all service providers or no more than 200 service providers being identified in the class as of any date. Use of such an alternative method will not be treated as a change in the time and form of payment for purposes of § 1.409A-2(b) (the subsequent deferral rules), even if the service provider is not a specified employee when the payment is delayed.

*(6) Corporate transactions.* (i) Mergers and acquisitions of public service recipients. If as a result of a corporate transaction, two or more separate service recipients, more than one of which has stock outstanding that is publicly traded on an established securities market or otherwise immediately before the transaction, become one service recipient, any stock of which is publicly traded on an established securities market or otherwise immediately after the transaction (resulting public service recipient), the resulting public service recipient's next specified employee identification date and specified employee effective date following the corporate transaction are the specified employee identification date and specified employee effective date that the acquiring service recipient would have been required to use absent such transaction. For this purpose, in the case of a corporate merger, the acquiring service recipient is the service recipient that included the surviving corporation in such merger, in the case of an acquisition by a corporation of the stock of another corporation, the acquiring service recipient is the service recipient that included the corporation that acquired such stock, and in all other cases, the surviving service recipient is determined on the basis of all of the facts and circumstances. For the period between the transaction and the next specified employee effective date, the list of specified employees of the resulting public service recipient is determined by combining the lists of specified employees of all service recipients participating in the transaction that were in effect at the date of the corporate transaction, ranking such specified employees in order of the amount of compensation used to determine each specified employee's status as a specified employee, and treating the top 50 of such specified employees, plus any employees described in section 416(i)(1)(ii) or section 416(i)(1)(iii) and the regulations thereunder (relating to 1-percent and 5-percent owners) who are not included in such top 50 specified employees, as specified employees for the period between the corporate transaction and the next specified employee effective date. Alternatively, the resulting service recipient may elect in accordance with the requirements of paragraph (i)(8) of this section to use any reasonable method to determine the specified employees of the resulting service recipient, including the use of an alternative method of compliance described in paragraph (i)(5) of this section, provided that such method is adopted no later than 90 days after the corporate transaction and applied prospectively from the date the method is adopted.

(ii) Mergers and acquisitions of nonpublic service recipients. If as part of a corporate transaction a service recipient that does not have outstanding stock that is publicly traded on an established securities market or otherwise immediately before the transaction (initial private service recipient), and a service recipient with stock outstanding that is publicly traded on an established securities market or otherwise immediately before the transaction (initial public service recipient), become a single service recipient having stock that is publicly traded on an established securities market or otherwise immediately after the transaction (resulting public service recipient), the resulting public service recipient's next specified employee identification date and specified employee effective date following the corporate transaction are the specified employee identification date and specified employee effective date that the initial public service recipient would have been required to use absent such transaction. For the period after the date of the corporate transaction and before the next specified employee effective date, the specified employees of the initial public service recipient immediately before the transaction continue to be the specified employees of the resulting public service recipient, and no service providers of the initial private service recipient are required to be treated as specified employees.

(iii) Spinoffs. If as part of a corporate transaction, a service recipient with stock outstanding that is publicly traded on an established securities market or otherwise immediately before the transaction (initial public service recipient), becomes two or more separate service recipients, each with stock outstanding that is publicly traded on an established securities market or otherwise immediately after the transaction (post-transaction public service recipients), the next specified employee identification date of each of the post-transaction public service recipients is the specified employee identification date that the initial public service recipient would have been required to use absent such transaction. For the period after the date of the corporate transaction and before the next specified employee effective date, the specified employees of the initial public service recipient immediately before the transaction continue to be the specified employees of the post-transaction public service recipients.

(iv) Public offerings and other corporate transactions. If as part of an initial public offering or corporate transaction not described in paragraph (i)(6)(ii) or (iii) of this section, a service recipient with no outstanding stock that is publicly traded on an established securities market or otherwise immediately before such offering or other transaction (initial private service recipient), becomes one or more service recipients with stock outstanding that is publicly traded on an established securities market or otherwise immediately after such offering or other transaction (post-transaction public service recipient), each post-transaction public service recipient has a specified employee identification date of December 31 and a specified employee effective date of April 1, effective retroactively to the December 31 and April 1 next preceding the offering or other transaction for purposes of identifying the specified employees between the corporation transaction and the next December 31. Alternatively, a post-transaction public service recipient may elect in accordance with the requirements of paragraph (i)(8) of this section, a specified employee identification date and specified employee effective date on or before the date of the offering or other transaction. If a public service recipient makes such an election, for the period after the offering or other transaction and before the next specified employee effective date, the specified employees of the post-transaction public service recipient consist of the service providers that at the time of the offering or other transaction would have been classified as specified employees of the initial private service recipient, had the initial private service recipient elected the same specified employee identification date and specified employee effective date as selected by the post-transaction public service recipient, and had such initial private service recipient had stock publicly traded on an established securities market or otherwise as of the specified employee identification date preceding the transaction.

(v) Alternative methods of compliance. For purposes of this paragraph (i)(6), references to specified employees as of a corporate transaction or offering include any specified employees identified through the use of an alternative method described in paragraph (i)(5) of this section, where the use of such alternative method was established and effective at the time of the corporate transaction or offering.

*(7) Nonresident alien employees.* For purposes of determining whether an employee meets the requirements of section 416(i)(1)(A)(i), (ii), or (iii) (applied in accordance with the regulations thereunder and disregarding section 416(i)(5)), and therefore is a key employee, the incorporation of the rules of § 1.415(c)-2(g)(5) regarding the definition of compensation applies. Accordingly, the rule of § 1.415(c)-2(g)(5)(i), generally requiring the treatment as compensation of certain compensation excludible from an employee's gross income due to the location of the services or the identity of the employer, applies. In addition, a service recipient may elect in accordance with paragraph (i)(8) of this section to apply the rule of § 1.415(c)-2(g)(5)(ii) to not treat as compensation certain compensation excludible from an employee's gross income on account of the location of the services or the identity of the employer that is not effectively connected with the conduct of a trade or business within the United States. A service recipient may elect to apply the rule of § 1.415-2(g)(5)(ii) regardless of whether the service recipient has elected to apply the rule to a qualified plan sponsored by the service recipient; however, once a list of specified employees has become effective, any election of the rule for that period may not be changed. Notwithstanding the foregoing, any election of the rule made before January 1, 2008, may be effective with respect to any specified employee identification date on or before December 31, 2007.

*(8) Elections affecting the identification of specified employees.* The elections described in paragraphs (i)(2) through (7) of this section are effective only as of the date that all necessary corporate action has been taken to make such elections binding for purposes of all affected nonqualified deferred compensation plans in which the service providers of the service recipient that would become a specified employee due to the application of such election participate. Where a taxpayer attempts to make an election under paragraph (i)(2), (3), (4), (5), (6), or (7) of this section but such election is not binding on all the affected nonqualified deferred compensation plans and applied consistently to all such service providers, the election is not effective and the rule under paragraph (i)(2), (3), (4), (5), (6), or (7) of this section, as applicable, that would apply absent an election is applicable for identifying specified employees.

**(j) Nonresident alien.** *(1)* Except as provided in paragraph (j)(2) of this section, the term nonresident alien means an individual who is—

(i) A nonresident alien within the meaning of section 7701(b)(1)(B); or

(ii) A dual resident taxpayer within the meaning of § 301.7701(b)-7(a)(1) of this chapter with respect to any taxable year in which such individual is treated as a nonresident alien for purposes of computing the individual's U.S. income tax liability.

*(2)* The term nonresident alien does not include—

(i) A nonresident alien with respect to whom an election is in effect for the taxable year under section 6013(g) to be treated as a resident of the United States;

(ii) A former citizen or long-term resident (within the meaning of section 877(e)(2)) who expatriated after June 3, 2004, and has not complied with the requirements of section 7701(n); or

(iii) An individual who is treated as a citizen or resident of the United States for the taxable year under section 877(g).

**(k) Established securities market.** The term established securities market means an established securities market within the meaning of § 1.897-1(m).

**(l) Stock right.** The term stock right means a stock option (other than an incentive stock option described in section 422 or an option granted pursuant to an employee stock purchase plan described in section 423) or a stock appreciation right.

**(m) Separation pay plan.** The term separation pay plan means any plan that provides separation pay or, where a plan provides both amounts that are separation pay and that are not separation pay, that portion of the plan that provides separation pay. The term separation pay means any deferral of compensation (before the application of the exclusions from the definition of a deferral of compensation set forth in paragraph (b)(9) of this section) that will not be paid under any circumstances unless the service provider has had a separation from service, whether voluntary or involuntary, including payments in the form of reimbursements of expenses incurred, and the provision of in-kind benefits. A deferral of compensation that the service provider may receive without a separation from service does not become separation pay merely because the service provider elects to receive or receives the payment after or upon a separation from service. A deferral of compensation does not fail to be separation pay merely because the payment is conditioned upon the execution of a release of claims, noncompetition or nondisclosure provisions, or other similar requirements. Notwithstanding the foregoing, any amount, or entitlement to any amount, that acts as a substitute for, or replacement of, amounts deferred by the service recipient under a nonqualified deferred compensation plan constitutes a payment of compensation or deferral of compensation under such nonqualified deferred compensation plan.

**(n) Involuntary separation from service.** *(1) In general.* An involuntary separation from service means a separation from service due to the independent exercise of the unilateral authority of the service recipient to terminate the service provider's services, other than due to the service provider's implicit or explicit request, where the service provider was willing and able to continue performing services. An involuntary separation from service may include the service recipient's failure to renew a contract at the time such contract expires, provided that the service provider was willing and able to execute a new contract providing terms and conditions substantially similar to those in the expiring contract and to continue providing such services. The determination of whether a separation from service is involuntary is based on all the facts and circumstances. Any characterization of the separation from service as voluntary or involuntary by the service provider and the service recipient in the documentation of the separation from service is presumed to properly characterize the nature of the separation from service. However, the presumption may be rebutted where the facts and circumstances indicate otherwise. For example, if a separation from service is designated as a voluntary separation from service or resignation, but the facts and circumstances indicate that absent such voluntary separation from service the service recipient would have terminated the service provider's services, and that the service provider had knowledge that the service provider would be so terminated, the separation from service is involuntary.

*(2) Separations from service for good reason.* (i) In general. Notwithstanding paragraph (n)(1) of this section, a service provider's voluntary separation from service will be treated for purposes of this section and §§ 1.409A-2 through 1.409A-6 as an involuntary separation from service if the separation from service occurs under certain limited bona fide conditions, where the avoidance of the requirements of section 409A is not a purpose of the inclusion of these conditions in the plan or of the actions by the service recipient in connection with the satisfaction of these conditions, and a voluntary separation from service under such conditions effectively constitutes an involuntary separation from service. Generally such conditions will be prespecified under an agreement to provide compensation upon a separation from service for good reason. Such a good reason (or a similar condition) must be defined to require actions taken by the service recipient resulting in a material negative change to the service provider in the service relationship, such as the duties to be performed, the conditions under which such duties are to be performed, or the compensation to be received for performing such services. Other factors taken into account in determining whether a separation from service for good reason effectively constitutes an involuntary separation from service include the extent to which the payments upon a separation from service for good reason are in the same amount and are to be made at the same time and in the same form as payments available upon an actual involuntary separation from service, and whether the service provider is required to give the service recipient notice of the existence of the condition that would result in treatment as a separation from service for good reason and a reasonable opportunity to remedy the condition.

(ii) Safe harbor. For purposes of this section and §§ 1.409A-2 through 1.409A-6, if a plan provides that a voluntary separation from service will be treated as an involuntary separation from service if the separation from service occurs under certain express conditions, a separation from service satisfying the conditions set forth in the plan will be treated as an involuntary separation from the service if the necessary conditions (or set of conditions) require the following:

(A) The separation from service must occur during a predetermined limited period of time not to exceed two years following the initial existence of one or more of the following conditions arising without the consent of the service provider:

(1) A material diminution in the service provider's base compensation.

(2) A material diminution in the service provider's authority, duties, or responsibilities.

(3) A material diminution in the authority, duties, or responsibilities of the supervisor to whom the service provider is required to report, including a requirement that a service provider report to a corporate officer or employee instead of reporting directly to the board of directors of a corporation (or similar governing body with respect to an entity other than a corporation).

(4) A material diminution in the budget over which the service provider retains authority.

(5) A material change in the geographic location at which the service provider must perform the services.

(6) Any other action or inaction that constitutes a material breach by the service recipient of the agreement under which the service provider provides services.

(B) The amount, time, and form of payment upon the separation from service must be substantially identical to the amount, time and form of payment payable due to an actual involuntary separation from service, to the extent such a right exists.

(C) The service provider must be required to provide notice to the service recipient of the existence of the condition described in paragraph (n)(2)(ii)(A) of this section within a period not to exceed 90 days of the initial existence of the condition, upon the notice of which the service recipient must be provided a period of at least 30 days during which it may remedy the condition and not be required to pay the amount.

*(3) Special rule for certain collectively bargained plans.* Notwithstanding the foregoing, for purposes of this paragraph (n), to the extent a plan is subject to a bona fide collective bargaining agreement covering services performed for multiple employers under which an employee must separate from service with all such employers in order to receive a payment, such plan may use any reasonable definition of involuntary separation from service, provided that such definition is consistent with any definition of a separation from service adopted under paragraph (h)(6) of this section, and provided further that the definition of an involuntary separation from service provided by the collective bargaining agreement was the subject of arm's length negotiations between employee representatives and two or more employers, the agreement between employee representatives and such employers satisfies section 7701(a)(46), and the circumstances surrounding the agreement evidence good faith bargaining between adverse parties over such definition.

**(o) Earnings.** Whether a deferred amount constitutes earnings on an amount deferred, or actual or notional income attributable to an amount deferred, is determined under the principles defining income attributable to the amount taken into account under § 31.3121(v)(2)-1(d)(2) of this chapter. Accordingly, with respect to an account balance plan, earnings on an amount deferred generally include an amount credited on behalf of a service provider under the terms of the plan that reflects a rate of return that does not exceed either the rate of return on a predetermined actual investment or, if the income does not reflect the rate of return on a predetermined actual investment, a reasonable rate of interest. With respect to nonaccount balance plans, earnings on an amount deferred generally include an increase, due solely to the passage of time, in the present value of the future payments to which the service provider has obtained a legally binding right, the present value of which constituted the amount deferred (determined as of the date such amount was deferred), but only if the amount deferred was determined using reasonable actuarial assumptions and methods. A right to earnings on an amount deferred generally is treated as a right to a deferral of compensation for purposes of this section and §§ 1.409A-2 through 1.409A-6. However, for purposes of any provision of this section and §§ 1.409A-2 through 1.409A-6 referring to earnings on deferred compensation (or similar terms), the use of an unreasonable rate of return, or unreasonable actuarial assumptions and methods, generally will result in the treatment of some or all of such a right to deferred compensation as a right only to deferred compensation, and not a right to earnings on deferred compensation, so that the provision will not be applicable. With respect to plans that are neither account balance plans nor nonaccount balance plans, these rules apply by analogy.

**(p) In-kind benefits.** The term in-kind benefits refers to services provided to or on behalf of a service provider, such as financial planning services, or tangible personal or real property made available for use by or on behalf of the service provider, such as the use of an aircraft or vehicle, and does not refer to a transfer of property within the meaning of section 83 and the regulations thereunder, or a promise to transfer, or an option to purchase or receive, property in the future.

**(q) Application of definitions and rules.** The definitions and rules set forth in paragraphs (a) through (p) of this section apply for purposes of section 409A, this section, and §§ 1.409A-2 through 1.409A-6.

T.D. 9321, 4/10/2007.

## § 1.409A-2 Deferral elections.

**(a) Initial elections as to the time and form of payment.** *(1) In general.* A plan that is, or constitutes part of, a nonqualified deferred compensation plan meets the requirements of section 409A(a)(4)(B) only if under the terms of the plan, compensation for services performed during a service provider's taxable year (the service year) may be deferred at the service provider's election only if the election to defer such compensation is made and becomes irrevocable not later than the latest date permitted in this paragraph (a). An election will not be considered to be revocable merely because the service provider or service recipient may make an election to change the time and form of payment pursuant to paragraph (b) of this section, or the service recipient may accelerate the time of payment pursuant to § 1.409A-3(j)(4) (exceptions to prohibition on accelerated payments). Whether a plan provides a service provider an opportunity to elect the time or form of payment of compensation is determined based upon all the facts and circumstances surrounding the determination of the time and form of payment of the compensation. For purposes of this section, an election to defer includes an election as to the time of the payment, an election as to the form of the payment or an election as to both the time and the form of the payment, but does not include an election as to the medium of payment (for example, an election between a payment of cash or a payment of property). Except as otherwise expressly provided in this section, an election will not be considered made until such election becomes irrevocable under the terms of the applicable plan. Accordingly, a plan may provide that an election to defer may be changed at any time before the last permissible date for making such an election. Where a plan provides the service provider a right to make an initial deferral election, and further provides that the election remains in effect until terminated or modified by the service provider, the election will be treated as made as of the date such election becomes irrevocable as to compensation for services performed during the relevant service year. For example, where a plan provides that a service provider's election to defer a set percentage will remain in effect until changed or revoked, but that as of each December 31 the election becomes irrevocable with respect to salary payable in connection with services performed in the immediately following year, the initial deferral election with respect to salary payable with respect to services performed in the immediately following year will be deemed to have been made as of the December 31 upon which the election became irrevocable. For purposes of this paragraph (a), the reference to a service period or a performance period refers to the period of service for which the right to the compensation arises, and may include periods before the grant of a legally binding right to the compensation. For example, where a service recipient grants a bonus based upon services performed in the calendar year 2010, but retains the discretion to rescind the bonus until 2011 such that the promise of the bonus is not a legally binding right, the period of service or performance period to which the compensation relates is the calendar year 2010.

*(2) Service recipient elections.* A plan that provides for a deferral of compensation for services performed during a service provider's taxable year that does not provide the service provider with an opportunity to elect the time or form of payment of such compensation must designate the time and form of payment by no later than the later of the time the service provider first has a legally binding right to the compensation or, if later, the time the service provider would be required under this section to make such an election if the service provider were provided such an election. Such designation is treated as an initial deferral election for purposes of this section. Where a plan permits a service recipient to exercise discretion to disregard a service provider election as to the time or form of a payment, any service provider election that is subject to such discretion will be treated as revocable so long as such discretion may be exercised.

*(3) General rule.* A plan that is, or constitutes part of, a nonqualified deferred compensation plan meets the requirements of section 409A(a)(4)(B) if under the terms of the plan, compensation for services performed during a service provider's taxable year (the service year) may be deferred at the service provider's election only if the election to defer such compensation is made not later than the close of the service provider's taxable year next preceding the service year.

*(4) Initial deferral election with respect to short-term deferrals.* If a service provider has a legally binding right to a payment of compensation in a subsequent taxable year that, absent a deferral election, would be treated as a short-term deferral within the meaning of § 1.409A-1(b)(4), an election to defer such compensation may be made in accordance with the requirements of paragraph (b) of this section, applied as if the amount were a deferral of compensation and the scheduled payment date for the amount were the date the substantial risk of forfeiture lapses. Notwithstanding the requirements of paragraph (b) of this section, such a deferral election may provide that the deferred amounts will be payable upon a change in control event (as defined in § 1.409A-3(i)(5)) without regard to the five-year additional deferral requirement in paragraph (b) of this section.

*(5) Initial deferral election with respect to certain forfeitable rights.* If a service provider has a legally binding right to a payment in a subsequent year that is subject to a condition requiring the service provider to continue to provide services for a period of at least 12 months from the date the service provider obtains the legally binding right to avoid forfeiture of the payment, an election to defer such compensation may be made on or before the 30th day after the service provider obtains the legally binding right to the compensation, provided that the election is made at least 12 months in advance of the earliest date at which the forfeiture condition could lapse. For purposes of this paragraph (a)(5), a condition will not be treated as failing to require the service provider to continue to provide services for a period of at least 12 months from the date the service provider obtains the legally binding right merely because the condition immediately lapses upon the death or disability (as defined in § 1.409A-3(i)(4)) of the service provider, or upon a change in control event (as defined in § 1.409A-3(i)(5)), provided that if death, disability, or a change in control event occurs and the condition lapses before the end of such 12-month period, a deferral election may be given effect only if the deferral election is permitted under this section without regard to this paragraph (a)(5).

*(6) Initial deferral election with respect to fiscal year compensation.* In the case of a service recipient with a taxable year that is not the same as the taxable year of the service provider, a plan may provide that fiscal year compensation may be deferred at the service provider's election if the election to defer such compensation is made not later than the close of the service recipient's taxable year immediately preceding the first taxable year of the service recipient in which any services are performed for which such compensation is payable. For purposes of this paragraph (a)(6), the term fiscal year compensation means compensation relating to a period of service coextensive with one or more consecutive taxable years of the service recipient, of which no amount is paid or payable during the service recipient's taxable year or years constituting the period of service. For example, fiscal year compensation generally would include a bonus to an individual employee with a calendar year taxable year that is based on a service period consisting of the service recipient's two consecutive taxable years ending September 30, 2011, where the amount will be paid after the end of the second of such taxable years, but would not include either a bonus based on a service period consisting of one or more calendar years or salary that would otherwise be paid during such taxable years of the service recipient.

*(7) First year of eligibility.* (i) In general. In the case of the first year in which a service provider becomes eligible to participate in a plan, the service provider may make an initial deferral election within 30 days after the date the service provider becomes eligible to participate in such plan, with respect to compensation paid for services to be performed after the election. In the case of a plan that does not provide for service provider elections with respect to the time or form of a payment, the time and form of the payment must be specified on or before the date that is 30 days after the date the service provider first becomes eligible to participate in such plan. For compensation that is earned based upon a specified performance period (for example, an annual bonus), where a deferral election is made in the first year of eligibility but after the beginning of the performance period, the election must apply only to the compensation paid for services performed after the election. For this purpose, an election will be deemed to apply to compensation paid for services performed after the election if the election applies to no more than an amount equal to the total amount of the compensation for the performance period multiplied by the ratio of the number of days remaining in the performance period after the election over the total number of days in the performance period.

(ii) Eligibility to participate. For purposes of this paragraph (a)(7), a service provider is eligible to participate in a plan at any time during which, under the plan's terms and without further amendment or action by the service recipient, the service provider is eligible to accrue an amount of deferred compensation under the plan other than earnings on amounts previously deferred, even if the service provider has elected not to accrue (or has not elected to accrue) an amount of deferred compensation. Where a service provider has been paid all amounts deferred under a plan, and on and before the date of the last payment was not eligible to continue (or to elect to continue) to participate in the plan for periods after the last payment (other than through an election of a different time and form of payment with respect to the amounts paid), the service provider may be treated as initially eligible to participate in a plan as of the first date following such payment that the service provider becomes eligible to accrue an additional amount of deferred compensation. Where a service provider has ceased being eligible to participate in a plan (other than the accrual of earnings), regardless of whether all amounts deferred under the plan have been paid, and subsequently becomes eligible to participate in the plan again, the service provider may be treated as being initially eligible to participate in the plan if the service provider had not been eligible to participate in the plan (other than the accrual of earnings) at any time during the 24-month period ending on the date the service provider again becomes eligible to participate in the plan.

(iii) Application to excess benefit plans. For purposes of this paragraph (a)(7), a service provider is treated as initially eligible to participate in an excess benefit plan as of the first day of the service provider's taxable year immediately following the first year the service provider accrues a benefit under the excess benefit plan; and any election made within 30 days following such date is treated as applying to benefits accrued under such plan for services performed before the election. For purposes of this paragraph (a)(7), the term excess benefit plan means all nonqualified deferred compensation plans in which a service provider participates, to the extent such plans do not provide for an election between current compensation (including a short-term deferral) and deferred compensation and solely provide deferred compensation equal to the excess of the benefits the service provider would have accrued under a qualified employer plan (as defined in § 1.409A-1(a)(2)) in which the service provider also participates, in the absence of one or more of the limits incorporated into the plan to reflect one or more of the limits on contributions or benefits applicable to the qualified employer plan under the Internal Revenue Code, over the benefits the service provider actually accrues under the qualified employer plan. For purposes of this paragraph (a)(7), once a service provider has accrued a benefit or deferred compensation under a plan in any year, the service provider will not become eligible for an initial deferral election based upon an accrual or deferral under an excess benefit plan in a subsequent year, even if the benefit or deferred compensation accrued in a previous year is forfeited or eliminated.

*(8) Initial deferral election with respect to performance-based compensation.* In the case of any performance-based compensation (as defined in § 1.409A-1(e)), an initial deferral election may be made with respect to such performance-based compensation on or before the date that is six months before the end of the performance period, provided that the service provider performs services continuously from the later of the beginning of the performance period or the date the performance criteria are established through the date an election is made under this paragraph (a)(8), and provided further that in no event may an election to defer performance-based compensation be made after such compensation has become readily ascertainable. For purposes of this paragraph (a)(8), if the performance-based compensation is a specified or calculable amount, the compensation is readily ascertainable if and when the amount is first substantially certain to be paid. If the performance-based compensation is not a specified or calculable amount because, for example, the amount may vary based upon the level of performance, the compensation, or any portion of the compensation, is readily ascertainable when the amount is first both calculable and substantially certain to be paid. For this purpose, the performance-based compensation is bifurcated between the portion that is readily ascertainable and the amount that is not readily ascertainable. Accordingly, in general any minimum amount that is both calculable and substantially certain to be paid will be treated as readily ascertainable.

*(9) Nonqualified deferred compensation plans linked to qualified employer plans or certain other arrangements.* If a nonqualified deferred compensation plan provides that the amount deferred under the plan is determined under the formula for determining benefits under a qualified employer plan (as defined in § 1.409A-1(a)(2)) or a broad-based foreign retirement plan (as defined in § 1.409A-1(a)(3)(v)) maintained by the service recipient but applied without regard to one or more limitations applicable to the qualified employer plan under the Internal Revenue Code or to the broad-based foreign retirement plan under other applicable law, or that the amount deferred under the nonqualified deferred compensation plan is determined as an amount offset by some or all of the benefits provided under the qualified employer plan or the broad-based foreign retirement plan, an increase in amounts deferred under the nonqualified deferred compensation plan that results directly from the operation of the qualified employer plan or broad-based foreign retirement plan (other than service provider actions described in paragraphs (a)(9)(iii) and (iv) of this section) including changes in benefit limitations applicable to the qualified employer plan or the broad-based foreign retirement plan under the Internal Revenue Code or other applicable law does not constitute a deferral election under the nonqualified deferred compensation plan, provided that such operation does not otherwise result in a change in the time or form of a payment under the nonqualified deferred compensation plan, and provided further that such change in the amounts deferred under the nonqualified deferred compensation plan does not exceed that change in the amounts deferred under the qualified employer plan or the broad-based foreign retirement plan, as applicable. In addition, with respect to such a nonqualified deferred compensation plan, the following actions or failures to act will not constitute a deferral election under the nonqualified deferred compensation plan even if in accordance with the terms of the nonqualified deferred compensation plan, the actions or inactions result in an increase in the amounts deferred under the plan, provided that such actions or inactions do not otherwise affect the time or form of payment under the nonqualified deferred compensation plan and provided further that with respect to actions or inactions described in paragraphs (a)(9)(i) or (ii), the change in the amount deferred under the nonqualified deferred compensation plan does not exceed the change in the amounts deferred under the qualified employer plan or the broad-based foreign retirement plan, as applicable:

(i) A service provider's action or inaction under the qualified employer plan or broad-based foreign retirement plan with respect to whether to elect to receive a subsidized benefit or an ancillary benefit under the qualified employer plan or broad-based foreign retirement plan.

(ii) The amendment of a qualified employer plan or broad-based foreign retirement plan to add or remove a subsidized benefit or an ancillary benefit, or to freeze or limit future accruals of benefits under the qualified plan or freeze or limit future accruals of benefits or reduce existing benefits under the broad-based foreign retirement plan.

(iii) A service provider's action or inaction under a qualified employer plan with respect to elective deferrals and other employee pre-tax contributions subject to the contribution restrictions under section 401(a)(30) or section 402(g), including an adjustment to a deferral election under such qualified employer plan, provided that for any given taxable year, the service provider's action or inaction does not result in an increase in the amounts deferred under all nonqualified deferred compensation plans in which the service provider participates (other than amounts described in paragraph (a)(9)(iv) of this section) in excess of the limit with respect to elective deferrals under section 402(g)(1)(A), (B), and (C) in effect for the taxable year in which such action or inaction occurs.

(iv) A service provider's action or inaction under a qualified employer plan with respect to elective deferrals and other employee pre-tax contributions subject to the contribution restrictions under section 401(a)(30) or section 402(g), and after-tax contributions by the service provider to a qualified employer plan that provides for such contributions, that affects the amounts that are credited under one or more nonqualified deferred compensation plans as matching amounts or other similar amounts contingent on such elective deferrals, employee pre-tax contributions, or after-tax contributions, provided that the total of such matching or contingent amounts, as applicable, never exceeds 100 percent of the matching or contingent amounts that would be provided under the qualified employer plan absent any plan-based restrictions that reflect limits on qualified plan contributions under the Internal Revenue Code.

*(10) Changes in elections under a cafeteria plan.* A change in an election under a cafeteria plan does not constitute a deferral election with respect to an amount deferred under a nonqualified deferred compensation plan to the extent that the change in the amount deferred under the nonqualified deferred compensation plan results solely from the application of the change in amount eligible to be treated as compensation under the terms of the nonqualified deferred compensation plan resulting from the election change under the cafeteria plan, to a benefit formula under the nonqualified deferred compensation plan based upon the service provider's eligible compensation, and only to the extent that such change applies in the same manner as any other increase or decrease in compensation would apply to such benefit formula.

*(11) Initial deferral election with respect to certain separation pay.* In the case of separation pay (as defined in § 1.409A-1(m)), where such separation pay is the subject of bona fide, arm's length negotiations at the time of the separation from service, an initial deferral election may be made at any time up to the time the service provider obtains a legally binding right to the payment. This paragraph (a)(11) does not apply to any separation pay to which the service provider obtained a legally binding right before the negotiations at the time of the separation from service, including a right to a payment subject to a condition such as that the service provider separate from service other than for cause. In the case of separation pay due to participation in a window program (as defined in § 1.409A-1(b)(9)(vi)), an initial deferral election may be made at any time before the time the election to participate in the window program becomes irrevocable.

*(12) Initial deferral election with respect to certain commissions.* (i) Sales commission compensation. For purposes of this paragraph (a), a service provider earning sales commission compensation is treated as providing the services to which such compensation relates only in the service provider's taxable year in which the customer remits payment to the service recipient or, if applied consistently to all similarly situated service providers, the service provider's taxable year in which the sale occurs. For purposes of this paragraph (a)(12), the term sales commission compensation means compensation or portions of compensation earned by a service provider if a substantial portion of the services provided by such service provider to a service recipient consist of the direct sale of a product or service to an unrelated customer, the compensation paid by the service recipient to the service provider consists of either a portion of the purchase price for the product or service or an amount substantially all of which is calculated by reference to the volume of sales, and payment of the compensation is either contingent upon the service recipient receiving payment from an unrelated customer for the product or services or, if applied consistently to all similarly situated service providers, is contingent upon the closing of the sales transaction and such other requirements as may be specified by the service recipient before the closing of the sales transaction. For this purpose, a customer is treated as an unrelated customer only if the customer is not related to either the service provider or the service recipient. A person is treated as related to another person if the person would be treated as related to the other person under § 1.409A-1(f)(2)(ii) or the person would be treated as providing management services to the other person under § 1.409A-1(f)(2)(iv).

(ii) Investment commission compensation. For purposes of this paragraph (a), a service provider earning investment commission compensation is treated as providing the services to which such compensation relates over the 12 months preceding the date as of which the overall value of the assets or asset accounts is determined for purposes of the calculation of the investment commission compensation. For purposes of this paragraph (a)(12), the term investment commission compensation means the compensation or the portion of compensation earned by a service provider if a substantial portion of the services provided by such service provider to a service recipient to which such compensation relates consists of sales of financial products or other direct customer services to an unrelated customer with respect to customer assets or customer asset accounts, the customer retains the right to terminate the customer relationship and may move or liquidate the assets or asset accounts without undue delay (which may be subject to a reasonable notice period), such compensation consists of a portion of the value of the overall assets or asset account balance, an amount substantially all of which is calculated by reference to the increase in the value of the overall assets or account balance during a specified period, or both, and the value of the overall assets or account balance and investment commission compensation is determined at least annually. For this purpose, a customer is treated as an unrelated customer only if the customer is not related to either the service provider or the service recipient. A person is treated as related to another person if the person would be treated as related to the other person under § 1.409A-1(f)(2)(ii) or the person would be treated as providing management services to the other person under § 1.409A-1(f)(2)(iv).

(iii) Commission compensation and related persons. The rules of paragraphs (a)(12)(i) and (ii) of this section apply to sales commission compensation and investment commission compensation involving a related customer, provided that substantial sales from which commission compensation arises are made, or substantial services from which commission compensation arises are provided, to unrelated customers by the service recipient, the sales and service arrangement and the commission arrangement with respect to the related customer are bona fide, arise from the service recipient's ordinary course of business, and are substantially the same, both in terms and in practice, as the terms and practices applicable to unrelated customers (as defined in such paragraphs) to which individually or in the aggregate substantial sales are made or substantial services provided by the service recipient.

*(13) Initial deferral election with respect to compensation paid for final payroll period.* (i) In general. Unless a plan provides otherwise, compensation payable after the last day of the service provider's taxable year solely for services performed during the final payroll period described in section 3401(b) containing the last day of the service provider's taxable year or, with respect to a non-employee service provider, a period not longer than the payroll period described in section 3401(b), where such amount is payable pursuant to the timing arrangement under which the service recipient normally compensates service providers for services performed during a payroll period described in section 3401(b), or with respect to a non-employee service provider, a period not longer than the payroll period described in section 3401(b), is treated as compensation for services performed in the subsequent taxable year in which the payment is made. The preceding sentence does not apply to any compensation paid during such period for services performed during any period other than such final payroll period, such as a payment of an annual bonus. Any amendment of a plan after December 31, 2007, to add a provision providing for a differing treatment of such compensation may not be effective for 12 months from the date the amendment is executed and enacted.

(ii) Transition rule. For purposes of this paragraph (a)(13), a plan that was adopted and effective before December 31, 2007, whether written or unwritten, will be treated as designating such compensation for services performed in the taxable year in which the payroll period ends, unless otherwise set forth in writing before December 31, 2007.

*(14) Elections to annualize recurring part-year compensation.* In the case of a service provider receiving recurring part-year compensation, an election to defer all or a portion of the recurring part-year compensation to be earned during a particular service period is considered to meet the requirements of this paragraph (a) if the election is made before the services for which the recurring part-year compensation is paid begin, and the election does not defer payment of any of the recurring part-year compensation to a date beyond the last day of the 13th month following the first date of the service period. For purposes of this paragraph (a)(14), the term recurring part-year compensation means compensation paid for services rendered in a position that the service recipient and service provider reasonably anticipate will continue on similar terms and conditions in subsequent years, and will require services to be provided during successive service periods each of which comprises less than 12 months (for example, a teacher providing services during a school year comprised of 10 consecutive months), and each of which periods begins in one taxable year of the service provider and ends in the next such taxable year. The rules of this paragraph (a)(14) apply to a particular amount of compensation only once, so that an amount deferred under this rule may not again be treated as recurring part-year compensation for purposes of this paragraph and subject to a second deferral election under this paragraph (a)(14).

*(15) USERRA rights.* The requirements of this paragraph (a) are deemed satisfied to the extent an initial deferral election is provided to satisfy the requirements of the Uniformed Service Employment and Reemployment Rights Act of 1994, as amended, 38 U.S.C. 4301-4334.

**(b) Subsequent changes in time and form of payment.** *(1) In general.* A plan that permits under a subsequent election a delay in a payment or a change in the form of payment (a subsequent deferral election), including a subsequent deferral election made by a service provider or a service recipient, satisfies the requirements of section 409A(a)(4)(C) only if the conditions of this paragraph (b) are met. For purposes of this paragraph (b), except as otherwise expressly provided in this section, a subsequent deferral election is not considered made until such election becomes irrevocable under the terms of the plan. Accordingly, a plan may provide that a subsequent deferral election may be changed at any time before the last permissible date for making such a subsequent deferral election. Where a plan permits a subsequent deferral election, the requirements of this paragraph are satisfied only if the following conditions are met:

(i) The plan requires that such election not take effect until at least 12 months after the date on which the election is made.

(ii) In the case of an election related to a payment not described in § 1.409A-3(a)(2) (payment on account of disability), § 1.409A-3(a)(3) (payment on account of death), or § 1.409A-3(a)(6) (payment on account of the occurrence of an unforeseeable emergency), the plan requires that the payment with respect to which such election is made be deferred for a period of not less than five years from the date such payment would otherwise have been paid (or in the case of a life annuity or installment payments treated as a single payment, five years from the date the first amount was scheduled to be paid).

(iii) The plan requires that any election related to a payment described in § 1.409A-3(a)(4) (payment at a specified time or pursuant to a fixed schedule) be made not less than 12 months before the date the payment is scheduled to be paid (or in the case of a life annuity or installment payments treated as a single payment, 12 months before the date the first amount was scheduled to be paid).

*(2) Definition of payments for purposes of subsequent changes in the time or form of payment.* (i) In general. Except as provided in paragraphs (b)(2)(ii) and (iii) of this section, the term payment refers to each separately identified amount to which a service provider is entitled to payment under a plan on a determinable date, and includes amounts applied for the benefit of the service provider. An amount is separately identified only if the amount may be objectively determined under a nondiscretionary formula. For example, an amount identified as 10 percent of the account balance as of a specified payment date would be a separately identified amount. A payment includes the provision of any taxable benefit, including payment in cash or in kind. In addition, a payment includes, but is not limited to, the transfer, cancellation, or reduction of an amount of deferred compensation in exchange for benefits under a welfare benefit plan, a fringe benefit excludible under section 119 or section 132, or any other benefit that is excludible from gross income. For additional rules relating to the application of this paragraph (b) to amounts payable at a fixed time or pursuant to a fixed schedule, see § 1.409A-3(i)(1).

(ii) Life annuities. (A) In general. The entitlement to a life annuity is treated as the entitlement to a single payment.

Accordingly, an election to delay payment of a life annuity, or to change the form of payment of a life annuity, must be made at least 12 months before the scheduled commencement of the life annuity, and must defer the payment for a period of not less than five years from the originally scheduled commencement of the life annuity. For purposes of § 1.409A-1, this section, and §§ 1.409A-3 through 1.409A-6, the term life annuity means a series of substantially equal periodic payments, payable not less frequently than annually, for the life (or life expectancy) of the service provider, or a series of substantially equal periodic payments, payable not less frequently than annually, for the life (or life expectancy) of the service provider, followed upon the death or end of the life expectancy of the service provider by a series of substantially equal periodic payments, payable not less frequently than annually, for the life (or life expectancy) of the service provider's designated beneficiary (if any). Notwithstanding the foregoing, a schedule of payments does not fail to be an annuity solely because such plan provides for an immediate payment of the actuarial present value of all remaining annuity payments if the actuarial present value of the remaining annuity payments falls below a predetermined amount, and the immediate payment of such amount does not constitute an accelerated payment for purposes of § 1.409A-3(j), provided that such feature, including the predetermined amount, is established by no later than the time and form of payment is otherwise required to be established, and provided further that any change in such feature, including the predetermined amount, is a change in the time and form of payment. A change in designated beneficiary before any annuity payment has been made under the plan is not a change in the time or form of payment. A change in the form of a payment before any annuity payment has been made under the plan, from one type of life annuity to another type of life annuity with the same scheduled date for the first annuity payment, is not considered a change in the time and form of a payment, provided that the annuities are actuarially equivalent applying reasonable actuarial methods and assumptions. For purposes of this paragraph (b)(2)(ii), a requirement that a service provider obtain the consent of a spouse or other potential recipient of a survivor annuity to change a beneficiary or form of payment is disregarded, so that any annuity form that the service recipient could elect to receive with such consent is considered currently available.

(B) Certain features disregarded. Notwithstanding the foregoing provisions of this paragraph (b)(2)(ii), the following features are disregarded for purposes of determining whether a payment form is a life annuity within the meaning of this paragraph (b)(2)(ii), but are not disregarded for purposes of determining whether a life annuity is the actuarial equivalent of another life annuity except as otherwise provided in this paragraph (b)(2)(ii):

(1) Term certain features under which annuity payments continue for the longer of the life of the annuitant or a fixed period of time.

(2) Pop-up features under which payments increase upon the death of the beneficiary or another event that eliminates the right to a survivor annuity.

(3) Cash refund features under which payment is provided upon the death of the last annuitant in an amount that is not greater than the excess of the present value of the annuity at the annuity starting date over the total of payments before the death of the last annuitant.

(4) Features under which an annuity form of payment provides higher periodic payments before the expected commencement of benefits under the Social Security Act (42 U.S.C. ch. 7) or the Railroad Retirement Act (45 U.S.C. 231 et seq.) and lower periodic payments after such expected commencement date, so that the combined periodic payments under the arrangement and the Social Security Act or the Railroad Retirement Act, as applicable, are approximately level before and after such expected commencement date (Social Security or Railroad Retirement leveling features).

(5) Features providing for an increase in the annuity payment in a manner described in § 1.401(a)(9)-6, Q&A-14(a)(1) or (2) (eligible cost-of-living adjustments).

(C) Subsidized joint and survivor annuities. For purposes of this paragraph (b)(2)(ii), a joint and survivor annuity will not fail to be treated as actuarially equivalent to a single life annuity due solely to the value of a subsidized survivor annuity benefit, provided that the annual lifetime annuity benefit available to the service provider under the joint and survivor annuity is not greater than the annual lifetime annuity benefit available to the service provider under the single life annuity alternative, and provided that the annual survivor annuity benefit is not greater than the annual lifetime annuity benefit available to the service provider under the joint and survivor annuity.

(D) Actuarial assumptions and methods. For purposes of this paragraph (b)(2)(ii), at any given time the same actuarial assumptions and methods must be used in valuing each annuity payment option, in determining whether the payments are actuarially equivalent and such assumptions must be reasonable. This requirement applies over the entire term of the service provider's participation in the plan, such that the annuity payment must be actuarially equivalent at all times for the annuity payment options to be treated as one time and form of payment. There is no requirement that the same actuarial methods and assumptions be used over the term of a service provider's participation in a plan. Accordingly, a plan may change the actuarial assumptions and methods used to determine the life annuity payments provided that all of the actuarial assumptions and methods are reasonable.

(iii) Installment payments. The entitlement to a series of installment payments that is not a life annuity is treated as the entitlement to a single payment, unless the plan provides at all times with respect to the amount deferred that the right to the series of installment payments is to be treated as a right to a series of separate payments. For purposes of § 1.409A-1, this section, and §§ 1.409A-3 through 1.409A-6, a series of installment payments refers to an entitlement to the payment of a series of substantially equal periodic amounts to be paid over a predetermined period of years, except to the extent any increase (or decrease) in the amount reflects reasonable earnings (or losses) through the date the amount is paid. For this purpose, a series of installment payments over a predetermined period and a series of installment payments over a shorter or longer period, or a series of installment payments over the same predetermined period but with a different commencement date, are different times and forms of payment. Accordingly, a change in the predetermined period or the commencement date is a change in the time and form of payment. Notwithstanding the foregoing, a schedule of payments does not fail to be an installment payment solely because such plan provides for an immediate payment of all remaining installments if the present value of the deferred amount to be paid in the remaining installment payments falls below a predetermined amount, and the immediate payment of such amount does not constitute an accelerated payment for purposes of § 1.409A-3(j), provided that such feature including the predetermined amount is established by no later than the time and form of payment is otherwise required to be established, and provided further that any change in such feature including the predetermined amount is a change in the time and form of payment.

(iv) Transition rule. For purposes of this section, a plan that was adopted and effective before December 31, 2007, whether written or unwritten, that fails to make a designation as to whether the entitlement to a series of payments is to be treated as an entitlement to a series of separate payments under paragraph (b)(2)(iii) of this section, may make such designation on or before December 31, 2007, provided such designation is set forth in writing on or before December 31, 2007.

*(3) Beneficiaries.* The rules of this paragraph (b) governing changes in the time and form of payment apply to elections by beneficiaries with respect to the time and form of payment, as well as elections by service providers or service recipients with respect to the time and form of payment to beneficiaries. An election to change the identity of a beneficiary does not constitute a change in the time and form of payment merely because the election changes the identity of the recipient of the payment, if the time and form of the payment is not otherwise changed. In addition, an election to change the identity of a beneficiary before the initial payment of a life annuity does not constitute a change in the time and form of payment if the change in the time of payments stems solely from the different life expectancy of the new beneficiary, such as in the case of a joint and survivor annuity.

*(4) Domestic relations orders.* The rules of this paragraph (b) governing changes in the time and form of payment do not apply to elections by individuals other than a service provider, with respect to payments to a person other than the service provider, to the extent such elections are reflected in, or made in accordance with, the terms of a domestic relations order (as defined in section 414(p)(1)(B)).

*(5) Coordination with prohibition against acceleration of payments.* For purposes of applying the prohibition against the acceleration of payments in § 1.409A-3(j), the definition of payment is the same as the definition in paragraph (b)(2) of this section. Accordingly, a change in the form of a payment that results in a more rapid schedule for payments generally will not constitute an acceleration of a payment, if the change in the form of payment is made in compliance with the subsequent deferral rules. For example, a change in form from a 10-year installment payment treated as a single payment to a lump-sum payment would not constitute an acceleration if the change in the form of the payment is made in compliance with the requirements of paragraph (b)(1) of this section, generally meaning that the election to change to a lump-sum payment must be made at least 12 months before the installment payments were scheduled to commence and the lump-sum payment could not be made until at least five years after the date the installment payments were scheduled to commence. See § 1.409A-3(j)(4)(i) with respect to situations in which the failure to accelerate a payment or the modification of a plan term relating to certain accelerated payments will not be subject to the rules of this paragraph (b).

*(6) Application to multiple payment events.* In the case of a plan that permits a payment upon each of a number of potential permissible payment events, such as the earlier of a fixed date or separation from service, the requirements of paragraph (b)(1) of this section are applied separately to each payment (as defined in paragraph (b)(2) of this section) due upon each payment event. Notwithstanding the foregoing, the addition or deletion of a permissible payment event to a plan under which amounts were previously deferred is subject to the rules of this paragraph (b) where the addition or deletion of the permissible payment event may result in a change in the time or form of payment of the amount deferred. For application of the rules governing accelerations of payments to the addition of a permissible payment event to amounts deferred, see § 1.409A-3(j).

*(7) Delay of payments under certain circumstances.* A payment may be delayed to a date after the designated payment date under any of the circumstances described in this paragraph (b)(7), and the provision will not fail to meet the requirements of establishing a permissible payment event and the delay in the payment will not constitute a subsequent deferral election, so long as the service recipient treats all payments to similarly situated service providers on a reasonably consistent basis.

(i) Payments subject to section 162(m). A payment may be delayed to the extent that the service recipient reasonably anticipates that if the payment were made as scheduled, the service recipient's deduction with respect to such payment would not be permitted due to the application of section 162(m), provided that the payment is made either during the service provider's first taxable year in which the service recipient reasonably anticipates, or should reasonably anticipate, that if the payment is made during such year, the deduction of such payment will not be barred by application of section 162(m) or during the period beginning with the date of the service provider's separation from service and ending on the later of the last day of the taxable year of the service recipient in which the service provider separates from service or the 15th day of the third month following the service provider's separation from service, and provided further that where any scheduled payment to a specific service provider in a service recipient's taxable year is delayed in accordance with this paragraph, the delay in payment will be treated as a subsequent deferral election unless all scheduled payments to that service provider that could be delayed in accordance with this paragraph are also delayed. Where the payment is delayed to a date on or after the service provider's separation from service, the payment will be considered a payment upon a separation from service for purposes of the rules under § 1.409A-3(i)(2) (payments to specified employees upon a separation from service) and, in the case of a specified employee, the date that is six months after a service provider's separation from service is substituted for any reference to a service provider's separation from service in the first sentence of this paragraph. No election may be provided to the service provider with respect to the timing of the payment under this paragraph (b)(7)(i).

(ii) Payments that would violate Federal securities laws or other applicable law. A payment may be delayed where the service recipient reasonably anticipates that the making of the payment will violate Federal securities laws or other applicable law; provided that the payment is made at the earliest date at which the service recipient reasonably anticipates that the making of the payment will not cause such violation. The making of a payment that would cause inclusion in gross income or the application of any penalty provision or other provision of the Internal Revenue Code is not treated as a violation of applicable law.

(iii) Other events and conditions. A service recipient may delay a payment upon such other events and conditions as the Commissioner may prescribe in generally applicable guidance published in the Internal Revenue Bulletin (see § 601.601(d)(2) of this chapter). For additional rules applicable to certain delayed payments pursuant to a change in control event, see § 1.409A-3(i)(5)(iv). For additional rules applicable to amounts payable because of an unforeseeable emergency, see § 1.409A-3(i)(3).

*(8) USERRA rights.* The requirements of this paragraph (b) are deemed met to the extent an election to change the time or form of a payment of deferred compensation is provided to satisfy the requirements of the Uniformed Services Employment and Reemployment Rights Act of 1994, as amended, 38 U.S.C. 4301-4344.

*(9) Examples.* The following examples illustrate the application of the provisions of this section. For purposes of these examples, each employee is an individual with a calendar year taxable year, and is employed by the specified employer:

*Example (1).* Initial election to defer salary. Employer ZZ sponsors a plan under which Employee A may elect to defer a percentage of Employee A's salary. Employee A has participated in the plan in prior years. To satisfy the requirements of this section with respect to salary earned in calendar year 2008, if Employee A elects to defer any amount of such salary, the deferral election (including an election as to the time and form of payment) must be made no later than December 31, 2007.

*Example (2).* Designation of time and form of payment where an initial deferral election is not provided. Employer YY has a taxable year ending September 30. On July 1, 2008, Employer YY enters into a legally binding obligation to pay Employee B a $10,000 bonus. The amount is not subject to a substantial risk of forfeiture and does not qualify as performance-based compensation as described in § 1.409A-1(e). Employer YY does not provide Employee B an election as to the time and form of payment. Unless the amount is to be paid in accordance with the short-term deferral rule of § 1.409A-1(b)(4), Employer YY must specify the time and form of payment on or before July 1, 2008, to satisfy the requirements of this section.

*Example (3).* Initial election to defer bonus payable based on services during calendar year. Employer XX has a taxable year ending September 30. Employee C participates in a bonus plan under which Employee C is entitled to a bonus for services performed during the calendar year that, absent an election by Employee C, will be paid on March 15 of the following year. The amount is not subject to a substantial risk of forfeiture and does not qualify as performance-based compensation as described in § 1.409A-1(e). If Employee C elects to defer the payment of the bonus with respect to services rendered during calendar year 2008, Employee C must elect the time and form of payment not later than December 31, 2007, to satisfy the requirements of this section.

*Example (4).* Initial election to defer bonus payable based on services during fiscal year other than calendar year. Employer WW has a taxable year ending September 30. Employee D participates in a bonus plan under which Employee D is entitled to a bonus for services performed during Employer WW's fiscal year that, absent an election by Employee D, will be paid on December 15 of the calendar year in which the fiscal year ends. The amount is not subject to a substantial risk of forfeiture and does not qualify as performance-based compensation as described in § 1.409A-1(e). The amount qualifies as fiscal year compensation. If Employee D elects to defer the payment of the amount related to the fiscal year ending September 30, 2009, to satisfy the requirements of this section Employee D must elect the time and form of payment not later than September 30, 2008.

*Example (5).* Initial election to defer bonus payable only if service provider completes at least 12 months of services after the election. Employer VV has a calendar year taxable year. On March 1, 2008, Employer VV grants Employee E a $10,000 bonus, payable on March 1, 2010 (with reasonable interest), provided that Employee E continues performing services as an employee of Employer VV through March 1, 2010. The amount does not qualify as performance-based compensation as described in § 1.409A-1(e), and Employee E already participates in another account balance nonqualified deferred compensation plan. Employee E may make an initial deferral election on or before March 31, 2008 (within 30 days after obtaining a legally binding right), because at least 12 months of additional services are required after the date of election for the risk of forfeiture to lapse.

*Example (6).* Initial election to defer bonus that would otherwise constitute a short-term deferral. The same facts as Example 5, except that Employee E does not make an initial deferral election on or before March 31, 2008. Because the right to the compensation would not be treated as a deferral of compensation pursuant to § 1.409A-1(b)(4) absent a deferral election (because the arrangement would be treated as a short-term deferral), Employee E may make an initial deferral election provided that the election may not become effective for 12 months and must defer the payment at least 5 years from March 1, 2010 (the first date the payment could become substantially vested). Accordingly, Employee E may make an election before March 1, 2009, provided that the election defers the payment to a date on or after March 1, 2015 (other than a payment due to death, disability, unforeseeable emergency, or a change in control event).

*Example (7).* Initial election to defer sales commissions. Employer UU has a calendar year taxable year. As part of Employee F's services for Employer UU, Employee F sells refrigerators to customers unrelated to Employee F or Employer UU. Under the employment arrangement, Employee F is entitled to 10% of the sales price of any refrigerator Employee F sells, payable only upon the receipt of payment from the customer who purchased the refrigerator. For purposes of the initial deferral rule, Employee F is treated as performing the services related to each refrigerator sale in the calendar year in which each customer pays for the refrigerator.

*Example (8).* Initial election to defer renewal sales commissions. The same facts as Example 7, except that Employee F also sells warranties related to the refrigerators sold. Under the warranty arrangement, refrigerator warranty customers are entitled in a future year to extend the warranty for an additional cost to be paid at the time of the extension. Under Employee F's arrangement with Employer UU, Employee F is entitled to 10% of the amount paid for an extension of any warranty, payable upon the receipt of payment from the customer extending the warranty. For purposes of the initial deferral election rule, Employee F is treated as performing the services related to the amount paid for the extension of the warranty in the taxable year in which the customer pays for the warranty extension.

*Example (9).* Initial election to defer investment commissions. Employer TT is in the trade or business of managing financial assets for customer accounts. Customers who deposit funds in an account with Employer TT are entitled to remove the account balance of such account upon 60 days notice to Employer TT. Employee G sells financial products and provides continuing customer service to certain unrelated customers involving the deposit and maintenance of funds in customer accounts managed by Employer TT.

Under the employment arrangement, Employee G is entitled to a set percentage of the aggregate value of the assets held in the accounts of customers to whom Employee G sold financial products and provides customer service. Under the arrangement, the aggregate value of the assets held in the accounts is determined as of June 30 of each year, and unless Employee G elects to defer the payment, the amount is payable to Employee G in a lump sum on December 31 of the year in which the valuation is made. Employee G has no control over the valuation of the assets held in the accounts, or the calculation of the amount due Employee G. For purposes of the initial deferral rule, Employee G is treated as providing the services to which a payment relates during the July 1 through June 30 period ending on the June 30 date as of which the assets held in the account are valued.

*Example (10).* Initial election to defer part-year compensation. Employee H provides services as a teacher to Employer SS, a school system. The period of services routinely begins on the second Monday of August of one year and ends on the first Friday of June of the subsequent year. Employer SS provides an election to Employee H to receive the compensation for the period of services ratably over the period beginning on the second Monday of August of one year and ending on the last day of August of the subsequent year. Because the compensation constitutes recurring part-year compensation, as defined in paragraph (a)(14) of this section, and because the schedule will provide that all of the recurring part-year compensation is paid no later than September 30 of the subsequent year, Employee H will be deemed to have made a timely deferral election with respect to such recurring part-year compensation if Employee H elects before the first day of the service period to have the recurring part-year compensation paid under such schedule.

*Example (11).* Initial election to defer negotiated separation pay. Employer RR decides to terminate Employee J's employment involuntarily. As part of the process of terminating Employee J, Employer RR enters into bona fide, arm's length negotiations with respect to the terms of Employee J's termination of employment. As part of the process, Employer RR offers Employee J an amount that is in addition to any amounts to which Employee J is otherwise entitled, payable either as a lump sum payment at the end of 3 years or in 3 annual payments starting at the date of termination of employment. The election of the time and form of payment by Employee J may be made at any time before Employee J accepts the offer and obtains a legally binding right to the additional amount. The election may not apply to any amount to which Employee J already had a legally binding right.

*Example (12).* Election of time and form of payments under a window program. Employer QQ establishes a window program, as defined in § 1.409A-1(b)(9)(vi). Individuals who elect to terminate employment under the window program are entitled to receive an amount equal to 2 weeks pay multiplied by every year of service with Employer QQ. The individuals participating in the window program may elect to receive the payment as either a lump sum payment payable on the first day of the month after making the election to participate in the window program, or as a payment of 3 equal annual installments on each January 1 of the first 3 years following the election to participate in the window program. Employee K is eligible to participate in the window program. Employee K will be treated as making a timely deferral election if the election as to the time and form of payment is made on or before the date Employee K's election to participate in the window program becomes irrevocable.

*Example (13).* Initial election to defer salary earned during final payroll period beginning in one calendar year and ending in the subsequent calendar year. Employer PP pays the salary of its employees, including Employee L, on a bi-weekly basis. One bi-weekly payroll period runs from December 24, 2008, through January 6, 2009, with a scheduled payment date of January 13, 2009. Employer PP sponsors, and Employee L participates in, a nonqualified deferred compensation plan under which Employee L may defer a specified percentage of his annual salary. The plan does not specify that any salary compensation paid for the payroll period in which falls January 1 is to be treated as compensation for services performed during the year preceding the year in which falls that January 1. For purposes of applying the initial deferral election rules, Employee L is deemed to have performed the services for the payroll period December 24, 2008, through January 6, 2009, during the calendar year 2009.

*Example (14).* Application of deferral election rules and anti-acceleration rules to a nonqualified deferred compensation plan linked to a qualified plan. Employee M participates in a qualified retirement plan that is a defined benefit plan that offers a subsidized early retirement benefit to employees who have attained age 55 and completed 30 years of service. Employee M, who has attained age 55 and completed 30 years of service, also participates in a nonqualified deferred compensation plan, under which the benefit payable is calculated under a formula, with that benefit then reduced by any benefit that Employee M has accrued under the qualified retirement plan. In 2008, Employee M fails to elect the subsidized early retirement benefit under the qualified retirement plan, with the effect that the amounts payable under the nonqualified deferred compensation plan are increased by an amount equal to the reduction in the benefit payable under the qualified plan. In 2009, Employer NN amends the qualified retirement plan to increase benefits under the plan, resulting in a decrease in the amounts payable under the nonqualified deferred compensation plan equal to the increase in the benefit payable under the qualified plan. Neither of these actions constitutes a deferral election or an acceleration of a payment under the nonqualified deferred compensation plan.

*Example (15).* Subsequent deferral election. Employee N participates in a nonqualified deferred compensation plan. Employee N elects to be paid in a lump sum payment at the earlier of age 65 or separation from service. Employee N anticipates that he will work after age 65, and wishes to defer payment to a later date. Provided that Employee N continues in employment and makes the election by his 64th birthday, Employee N may elect to receive a lump sum payment at the earlier of age 70 or separation from service.

*Example (16).* Subsequent deferral election rule—change in form of payment from lump sum payment to life annuity. Employee P participates in a nonqualified deferred compensation plan. Employee P elects to be paid in a lump sum payment at age 65. Employee P wishes to change the payment form to a life annuity. Provided that Employee P makes the election on or before his 64th birthday, Employee P may elect to receive a life annuity commencing at age 70.

*Example (17).* Subsequent deferral election rule—change in form of payment from life annuity to lump sum payment. Employee Q participates in a nonqualified deferred compensation plan. Employee Q elects to be paid in a life annuity at age 65. Employee Q wishes to change the payment form to a lump sum payment. Provided that Employee Q makes the election on or before his 64th birthday, Employee Q may elect to receive a lump sum payment at age 70.

*Example (18).* Subsequent deferral election rule—installment payments designated as separate payments. Employee R, whose taxable year is the calendar year, participates in a nonqualified deferred compensation plan that provides for payment in a series of 5 equal annual amounts, each designated as a separate payment. The first payment is scheduled to be made on January 1, 2010. Provided that Employee R makes the election on or before January 1, 2009, Employee R may elect for the first payment scheduled to be made on January 1, 2010, to be made on January 1, 2015. If Employee R makes that election, but does not elect to defer the remaining payments, the remaining payments continue to be due upon January 1 of the 4 consecutive calendar years commencing on January 1, 2011.

*Example (19).* Subsequent deferral election rule—change in form of payment from installment payments not designated as separate payments to lump sum payment. Employee S participates in a nonqualified deferred compensation plan that provides for payment in a series of 5 equal annual amounts that are not designated as a series of 5 separate payments. The first amount is scheduled to be paid on January 1, 2010. Employee S wishes to receive the entire amount equal to the sum of all 5 of the amounts to be paid as a lump sum payment. Provided that Employee S makes the election on or before January 1, 2009, Employee S may elect to receive a lump sum payment on or after January 1, 2015.

*Example (20).* Subsequent deferral election rule—change in form of payment from installment payments designated as separate payments to lump sum payment. Employee T participates in a nonqualified deferred compensation plan that provides for payment in a series of 5 equal annual amounts each of which is designated as a separate payment. The first amount is scheduled to be paid on January 1, 2010. Employee T wishes to receive the entire amount equal to the sum of all 5 of the amounts in a single lump sum payment. Provided that Employee T makes the election on or before January 1, 2009, Employee T may elect to receive a lump sum payment on or after January 1, 2019.

*Example (21).* Subsequent deferral election rule—change in form of payment from one life annuity form to another life annuity form. Employee U participates in a nonqualified deferred compensation plan that permits Employee U to elect before Employee U's separation from service whether to be paid in the form of a single life annuity beginning on the first day of the month following Employee U's separation from service, or an annuity beginning on the first day of the month following Employee U's separation from service under which annuity payments continue for Employee U's lifetime but not less than 10 years. The two types of annuities are actuarially equivalent at all times applying reasonable actuarial methods and assumptions. For purposes of this section, the two types of annuities are treated as a single form of payment. Accordingly, the election provided under the plan is not treated as providing a subsequent deferral election or accelerated payment, and an election by Employee U under the plan between the two annuity options made before the first scheduled payment date for an annuity payment is not treated as a subsequent deferral election or an acceleration of a payment.

*Example (22).* Subsequent deferral election rule—change in time of payment from payment at specified age to payment at later of specified age or separation from service. Employee V participates in a nonqualified deferred compensation plan that provides for a lump sum payment at age 65. Employee V wishes to modify the plan so that the deferred amount will be payable upon the later of Employee V's attainment of a specified age or separation from service. Provided that Employee V makes such election on or before his 64th birthday, Employee V may modify the plan so Employee V will receive a lump sum payment upon the later of age 70 or separation from service.

*Example (23).* Subsequent deferral election rule—change in time of payment from payment at separation from service to payment at later of separation from service or specified age. Employee W participates in a nonqualified deferred compensation plan that provides for a lump sum payment at separation from service. Employee W wishes to make the payment payable upon the later of separation from service or a predetermined age. Provided that Employee W makes such election on or before the date 1 year before a separation from service, Employee W may elect to receive a lump sum payment upon the later of the date 5 years following a separation from service or at a specified age.

*Example (24).* Subsequent deferral election rule—change in time of payment from payment at separation from service to payment at a change in control event. Employee X participates in a nonqualified deferred compensation plan that provides for a lump sum payment at separation from service. Employee X wishes to change the payment provision such that the payment is payable upon a change in control event. A change in the distribution provision to provide for a payment only upon a change in control event will violate the rules governing payment provisions, because the change could result in an acceleration if the change in control event occurs before Employee X separates from service, or a subsequent deferral if the change in control does not occur until after Employee X separates from service. However, provided that Employee X makes such election on or before the date 1 year before a separation from service, Employee X may elect to receive a payment upon the later of a change in control event or 5 years following a separation from service.

**(c) Special rules for certain resident aliens.** For the first taxable year of an individual in which such individual is a resident alien, a nonqualified deferred compensation plan is deemed to meet the requirements of paragraph (a) of this section if, with respect to compensation payable for services performed during that first taxable year or with respect to compensation the right to which is subject to a substantial risk of forfeiture as of the first day of that first taxable year, an initial deferral election is made by the end of such first taxable year, provided that the initial deferral election may not apply to amounts that have already been paid or made available to the service provider before the election is made. For any year after the first taxable year in which an individual is classified as a resident alien, this paragraph (c) does not apply, provided that a taxable year may again be treated as the first taxable year in which an individual is classified as a resident alien if such individual is classified as a resident alien in that taxable year and has not been classified as a resident alien for the three consecutive taxable years immediately preceding that taxable year.

T.D. 9321, 4/10/2007.

## § 1.409A-3 Permissible payments.

**(a) In general.** The requirements of section 409A(a)(2)(A) are met only if the plan provides that an amount of deferred compensation under the plan may be paid only upon an event or at a time set forth in this paragraph (a):

*(1)* The service provider's separation from service (as defined in § 1.409A-1(h) and in accordance with paragraph (i)(2) of this section).

*(2)* The service provider becoming disabled (in accordance with paragraph (i)(4) of this section).

*(3)* The service provider's death.

*(4)* A time or a fixed schedule specified under the plan (in accordance with paragraph (i)(1) of this section).

*(5)* A change in the ownership or effective control of the corporation, or in the ownership of a substantial portion of the assets of the corporation (in accordance with paragraph (i)(5) of this section).

*(6)* The occurrence of an unforeseeable emergency (in accordance with paragraph (i)(3) of this section).

**(b) Designation of payment upon a permissible payment event.** Except as otherwise specified in this section, a plan provides for the payment upon an event described in paragraph (a)(1), (2), (3), (5), or (6) of this section if the plan provides the date of the event is the payment date, or specifies another payment date that is objectively determinable and nondiscretionary at the time the event occurs. A plan may also provide that a payment upon an event described in paragraph (a)(1), (2), (3), (5), or (6) of this section is to be made in accordance with a schedule that is objectively determinable and nondiscretionary based on the date the event occurs and that would qualify as a fixed schedule under paragraph (i)(1) of this section if the payment event were instead a fixed date, provided that the schedule must be fixed at the time the permissible payment event is designated. In addition, a plan may provide that a payment, including a payment that is part of a schedule, is to be made during a designated taxable year of the service provider that is objectively determinable and nondiscretionary at the time the payment event occurs such as, for example, a schedule of three substantially equal payments payable during the first three taxable years following the taxable year in which a separation from service occurs. A plan may also provide that a payment, including a payment that is part of a schedule, is to be made during a designated period objectively determinable and nondiscretionary at the time the payment event occurs, but only if the designated period both begins and ends within one taxable year of the service provider or the designated period is not more than 90 days and the service provider does not have a right to designate the taxable year of the payment (other than an election that complies with the subsequent deferral election rules of § 1.409A-2(b)). Where a plan provides for a period of more than one day following a payment event during which a payment may be made, such as within 90 days following the date of the event, the payment date for purposes of the subsequent deferral rules under § 1.409A-2(b) is treated as the first possible date upon which a payment could be made under the terms of the plan. A plan may provide for payment upon the earliest or latest of more than one event or time, provided that each event or time is described in paragraphs (a)(1) through (6) of this section. For examples illustrating the provisions of this paragraph, see paragraph (i)(1)(vi) of this section.

**(c) Designation of alternative specified dates or payment schedules based upon date of permissible event.** Except as otherwise provided in this paragraph (c), for an amount of deferred compensation under a plan, the plan may designate only one time and form of payment upon the occurrence of each event described in paragraph (a)(1), (2), (3), (5), or (6) of this section. For example, a plan does not satisfy the requirements of this paragraph (c) if it provides for one payment date or schedule of payments if a specified event occurs on a Monday, but another payment date or schedule of payments if the event occurs on any other day of the week. However, a plan that provides for a payment upon an event described in paragraph (a)(2), (3), (5), or (6) of this section may allow for an alternative payment schedule if the event occurs on or before one (but not more than one) specified date, provided that the addition or deletion of such a different time and form of payment applicable to an existing deferral is subject to § 1.409A-2(b) (subsequent deferral elections) and paragraph (j) of this section (accelerated payments). For example, a plan may provide that a service provider will receive a lump sum payment of the service provider's entire benefit under the plan on the first day of the month following a change in control event that occurs before the service provider attains age 55, but will receive 5 substantially equal annual payments commencing on the first day of the month following a change in control event that occurs on or after the service provider attains age 55. In the case of a plan that provides that a payment upon an event described in paragraph (a)(1) of this section (a payment upon a separation from service), a different time and form of payment may be designated with respect to a separation from service under each of the following conditions, provided that the addition or deletion of such a different time and form of payment applicable to an existing deferral is subject to § 1.409A-2(b) and paragraph (j) of this section:

*(1)* A separation from service during a limited period of time not to exceed two years following a change in control event (as defined in paragraph (i)(5) of this section).

*(2)* A separation from service before or after a specified date (for example, the attainment of a specified age), or a separation from service before or after a combination of a specified date, such as attaining a specified age, and a specified period of service determined under a predetermined, nondiscretionary, objective formula or pursuant to the method for crediting service under a qualified plan sponsored by the service recipient.

*(3)* A separation from service not described in paragraphs (c)(1) or (c)(2) of this section.

**(d) When a payment is treated as made upon the designated payment date.** Except as otherwise specified in this section, a payment is treated as made upon the date specified under the plan (including a date specified under paragraph (a)(4) of this section) if the payment is made at such date or a later date within the same taxable year of the service provider or, if later, by the 15th day of the third calendar month following the date specified under the plan and the service provider is not permitted, directly or indirectly, to designate the taxable year of the payment. In addition, a payment is treated as made upon the date specified under the plan (including a date specified under paragraph (a)(4) of this section) and is not treated as an accelerated payment if the payment is made no earlier than 30 days before the designated payment date and the service provider is not permitted, directly or indirectly to designate the taxable year of the payment. For purposes of this paragraph, if the date specified is only a designated taxable year of the service provider, or a period of time during such a taxable year, the date specified under the plan is treated as the first day of such taxable year or the first day of the period of time during such taxable year, as applicable. The payment with respect to a stock right generally occurs upon the exercise of the stock right, so that where a stock right designates a fixed exercise date, the stock right will be deemed to have been paid at such date if the exercise and payment occur on such date or a later date within the same taxable year of the service provider or, if later, by the 15th day of the third calendar month following the exercise date specified under the plan. If calculation of the amount of the payment is not administratively practicable due to events beyond the control of the service provider (or service provider's beneficiary), the payment will be treated as made upon the date specified under the plan if the payment is made during the first taxable year of the service provider in which the calculation of the amount of the payment is administratively practicable. For purposes of this paragraph, the inability of a service recipient to calculate the amount or timing of a payment due to a failure of a service provider (or service provider's beneficiary) to provide reasonably available information necessary to make such calculation does not constitute an event beyond the control of the service provider. Similarly, if the making of the payment at the date specified under the plan would jeopardize the ability of the service recipient to continue as a going concern, the payment will be treated as made upon the date specified under the plan if the payment is made during the first taxable year of the service provider in which the making of the payment would not have such effect.

**(e) Designation of time and form of payment with respect to earnings.** A nonqualified deferred compensation plan that provides for actual or notional earnings to be credited on amounts of deferred compensation may specify, in accordance with the requirements of § 1.409A-2(a) (initial deferral elections), that such earnings are treated separately from the right to the other amounts deferred under the plan for purposes of designating the time and form of payments under such plan, provided that to satisfy the requirements of this paragraph (e), actual or notional earnings must be credited at least annually. For these purposes, a right to dividend equivalents may be treated analogously to a right to actual or notional earnings on an amount of deferred compensation. For purposes of this paragraph (e), the term dividend equivalents means the right to an amount equal to all or a specified portion of dividends declared and paid, if any, on a specified number of shares of stock.

**(f) Substitutions.** Except as otherwise provided under these regulations, the payment of an amount as a substitute for a payment of deferred compensation will be treated as a payment of the deferred compensation. A forfeiture or voluntary relinquishment of an amount of deferred compensation will not be treated as a payment of the compensation, but there is no forfeiture or voluntary relinquishment for this purpose if an amount is paid, or a legally binding right to a payment is created, that acts as a substitute for the forfeited or voluntarily relinquished amount. Whether a payment or a right to a payment acts as a substitute for a payment of deferred compensation is determined based on all the facts and circumstances. However, where the payment of an amount results in an actual or potential reduction of, or current or future offset to, an amount of deferred compensation, or if the service provider receives a loan the repayment of which is secured by or may be accomplished through an offset of or a reduction in an amount deferred under a nonqualified deferred compensation plan, the payment or loan is a substitute for the deferred compensation. In addition, where a service provider's right to deferred compensation is made subject to anticipation, alienation, sale, transfer, assignment, pledge, encumbrance, attachment, or garnishment by creditors of the service provider or the service provider's beneficiary, the deferred compensation is treated as having been paid. For the treatment of certain offsets, see paragraph (j)(4)(xiii) of this section. Even where there is no explicit reduction or offset, the payment of an amount or creation of a new right to a payment proximate to the purported forfeiture or voluntary relinquishment of a right to deferred compensation is presumed to be a substitute for the deferred compensation. The presumption is rebuttable by a showing that the compensation paid would have been received regardless of the forfeiture or voluntary relinquishment of the right to deferred compensation. Factors indicating that a payment would have been received regardless of such forfeiture or voluntarily relinquishment include that the amount paid is materially less than the forfeited or relinquished amount, or consists of a type of payment customarily made in the ordinary course of business of the service recipient to service providers who do not forfeit or relinquish deferred compensation (for example, a payment of accrued but unused leave or a payment for a release of actual or potential claims). See § 1.409A-1(b)(9)(i) with respect to certain separation pay plans.

**(g) Disputed payments and refusals to pay.** If a service recipient fails to make a payment in whole or in part as of the date specified under a plan, either intentionally or unintentionally, other than with the express or implied consent of the service provider, the payment will be treated as made upon the date specified under the plan if the service provider accepts the portion (if any) of the payment that the service recipient is willing to make (unless such acceptance will result in a relinquishment of the claim to all or part of the remaining amount), makes prompt and reasonable, good faith efforts to collect the remaining portion of the payment, and any further payment (including payment of a lesser amount that satisfies the obligation to make the payment) is made no later than the end of the first taxable year of the service provider in which the service recipient and the service provider enter into a legally binding settlement of such dispute, the service recipient concedes that the amount is payable, or the service recipient is required to make such payment pursuant to a final and nonappealable judgment or other binding decision. For purposes of this paragraph (g), efforts to collect the payment will be presumed not to be prompt, reasonable, good faith efforts, unless the service provider provides notice to the service recipient within 90 days of the latest date upon which the payment could have been timely made in accordance with the terms of the plan and these regulations, and unless, if not paid, the service provider takes further enforcement measures within 180 days after such latest date. For purposes of this paragraph (g), a service recipient is not treated as having failed to make a payment where pursuant to the terms of the plan the service provider is required to request payment, or otherwise provide information or take any other action, and the service provider has failed to take such action. In addition, for purposes of this paragraph (g), the service provider is deemed to have requested that a payment not be made, rather than the service recipient having failed to make such payment, where the service recipient's decision to refuse to make the payment is made by the service provider or a member of the service provider's family (as defined in section 267(c)(4) applied as if the family of an individual includes the spouse of any member of the family), or any person or group of persons over whom the service provider or service provider's family member has effective control, or any person any portion of whose compensation is controlled the service provider or service provider's family member.

**(h) Special rule for certain resident aliens.** An agreement, method, program, or other arrangement that is, or constitutes part of, a nonqualified deferred compensation plan is deemed to meet the requirements of this section with respect to any amount payable in the first taxable year of the service provider in which a service provider is a resident alien, and with respect to any amount payable in a subsequent taxable year if no later than the last day of the first taxable year of the service provider in which the service provider is a resident alien, the plan is amended as necessary so that the times and forms of payment of amounts payable in a subsequent year comply with the provisions of this section. For any year after the first taxable year of an individual in which the individual is a resident alien, this paragraph (h) does not apply, provided that a taxable year may again be treated as the first taxable year in which an individual is a resident alien if such individual has not been a resident alien for at least three consecutive taxable years immediately preceding the taxable year in which the service provider is again a resident alien.

**(i) Definitions and special rules.** *(1) Specified time or fixed schedule.* (i) In general. Amounts are payable at a specified time or pursuant to a fixed schedule if objectively determinable amounts are payable at a date or dates that are nondiscretionary and objectively determinable at the time the amount is deferred. An amount is objectively determinable for this purpose if the amount is specifically identified or if the amount may be determined at the time payment is due pursuant to an objective, nondiscretionary formula specified at the time the amount is deferred (for example, 50 percent of a specified account balance). Except as otherwise provided in paragraph (i)(1) of this section, an amount is not objectively determinable if the amount of the payment is based all or in part upon the occurrence of an event, including the consummation of a transaction by, or a payment of an amount to, a service recipient. If an amount is payable in a service provider's taxable year (or pursuant to a fixed schedule of taxable years of the service provider) that is designated at the time the amount is deferred and that is objectively determinable, the amount is treated as payable at a specified time (or pursuant to a fixed schedule), provided that for purposes of the application of the subsequent deferral rules contained in § 1.409A-2(b), the specified time or fixed schedule of payments is deemed to refer to the first day of the relevant taxable year or years. A specified time or fixed schedule also includes the designation at the time the amount is deferred of a defined period or periods within the service provider's taxable year or taxable years that are objectively determinable, provided that no such defined period may begin within one taxable year and end within another taxable year, and provided further that for purposes of the application of the subsequent deferral rules contained in § 1.409A-2(b), the specified time or fixed schedule of payments is deemed to refer to the first day of the relevant period in which the payment will be made. A plan may provide that a payment upon the lapse of a substantial risk of forfeiture is to be made in accordance with a fixed schedule that is objectively determinable based on the date the substantial risk of forfeiture lapses (disregarding any discretionary acceleration of the lapse of the substantial risk of forfeiture), provided that the schedule must be fixed on the date the time and form of payment are designated, and any change in the fixed schedule will constitute a change in the time and form of payment. For example, a plan that provides for a bonus payment subject to the condition that the service provider complete three years of service, and subject to the further condition that such requirement of continued services will lapse upon the occurrence of an initial public offering, which condition if applied alone would constitute a substantial risk of forfeiture, may provide that a service provider is entitled to substantially equal payments on each of the first three anniversaries of the date the substantial risk of forfeiture lapses (the earlier of three years of service or the date of an initial public offering).

(ii) Payment schedules with formula and fixed limitations. (A) Individual limitations. A schedule of payments does not fail to be a fixed schedule of payments where the amount of a payment or payments that may be paid at a specified time or during a specified period is limited by an objective nondiscretionary formula or a specified amount that is not under the effective control of the service provider and is not subject to the exercise of discretion by the service recipient, where such limitation is established on or before the date the time and form of payment is otherwise required to be set under these regulations, and the plan specifies the time and form of any payment that will be made or completed after its original payment date due to the application of the limitation. A change in the limitation or a change in the time and form of any payment that exceeds the limitation is subject to the requirements of § 1.409A-2(b) (subsequent deferral elections) and paragraph (j) of this section (accelerated payments). For purposes of this paragraph, a plan provision that reduces a schedule of periodic payments on a dollar-for-dollar basis by the amount of Social Security payments received or receivable may be treated as a nondiscretionary, objective formula limitation, if such reduction does not otherwise affect the time of payment of the deferred compensation (other than a forfeiture due to the reduction), including changes based on the service provider's eligibility or elections related to Social Security benefits. Similarly, a plan provision that reduces a schedule of periodic payments on a dollar-for-dollar basis by the amount of bona fide disability pay (within the meaning of § 1.409A-1(a)(5)) received or receivable may be treated as a nondiscretionary, objective formula limitation, if the disability payments are made pursuant to a plan sponsored by the service recipient that covers a substantial number of service providers and was established before the service provider became disabled, and if such reduction does not otherwise affect the time of payment of the deferred compensation (other than a forfeiture due to the reduction). Whether an amendment to, or other change in the benefit payable under, such bona fide disability plan results in an acceleration of a payment for purposes of paragraph (j) of this section or a subsequent election to delay the time or change the form of payment for purposes of § 1.409A-2(b) is determined based on all of the relevant facts and circumstances.

(B) Limitations on aggregate payments to all participants in substantially identical plans. A schedule of payments does not fail to be a fixed schedule of payments where the amount of the aggregate payments that will be made during a specified period of time to all participants in substantially identical plans is limited by an objective nondiscretionary formula or specified amount that is not under the effective control of the service provider and is not subject to the exercise of discretion by the service recipient, where the limit is established on or before the date the time and form of payment of the amount deferred is otherwise required to be set under these regulations, the method of allocating payments among the participants where there is an overall limitation on the aggregate amount that may be paid to a group of service providers during a specified period is an objective nondiscretionary allocation method that is not under the effective control of the service provider and is not subject to the exercise of discretion by the service recipient, the method is established on or before the date the time and form of payment of the amount deferred is otherwise required to be set, and the plan specifies the time and form of any payment of any amount that will be paid after its original payment date due to the application of the limitation. A change in the limitation or a change in the time and form of payment of any payment that is not otherwise made at the scheduled payment date due to application of the formula limitation is subject to the requirements of § 1.409A-2(b) (subsequent deferral elections) and paragraph (j) of this section (accelerated payments).

(iii) Payment schedules determined by timing of payments received by the service recipient. A payment schedule determined by reference to the timing of payments received by the service recipient (not including payments from one entity to another entity where both entities are treated as part of a single service recipient), meets the requirements of a specified date or fixed schedule of payments if the following conditions are met:

(A) The payments due to the service recipient arise from bona fide and routine transactions in the ordinary course of business of the service recipient.

(B) The service provider does not have effective control of the service recipient, the person from whom such amounts are due, or the collection of any of the amounts due to the service recipient.

(C) The payment schedule provides an objective, nondiscretionary method of identification of the payments to the service recipient from which the amount of the payment from the service recipient to the service provider is determined.

(D) The payment schedule provides an objective, nondiscretionary schedule under which the payments will be made to the service provider.

(E) The payments to the service recipient from which the amount of the payments from service recipient to the service provider are determined result from sales of a type that the service recipient is in the trade or business of making and makes frequently, and either all such sales by the service recipient are taken into account for purposes of determining the payment to the service provider, or there is a legitimate, non-tax business reason for identifying the specific sales taken into account.

(iv) Reimbursement or in-kind benefit plans. (A) General rule. A plan that provides for reimbursements of expenses incurred by a service provider, or in-kind benefits, meets the requirements of a specified date or fixed schedule of payments with respect to such reimbursements or benefits if the following conditions are met:

(1) The plan provides an objectively determinable nondiscretionary definition of the expenses eligible for reimbursement or of the in-kind benefits to be provided.

(2) The plan provides for the reimbursement of expenses incurred or for the provision of the in-kind benefits during an objectively and specifically prescribed period (including the lifetime of the service provider).

(3) The plan provides that the amount of expenses eligible for reimbursement, or in-kind benefits provided, during a service provider's taxable year may not affect the expenses eligible for reimbursement, or in-kind benefits to be provided, in any other taxable year.

(4) The reimbursement of an eligible expense is made on or before the last day of the service provider's taxable year following the taxable year in which the expense was incurred.

(5) The right to reimbursement or in-kind benefits is not subject to liquidation or exchange for another benefit.

(B) Medical reimbursement arrangements. Notwithstanding the foregoing, an arrangement providing for the reimbursement of expenses referred to in section 105(b) will not be deemed to fail to meet the requirements of paragraph (i)(1)(iv)(A)(3) of this section solely because the arrangement provides for a limit on the amount of expenses that may be reimbursed under such arrangement over some or all of the period in which the reimbursement arrangement remains in effect.

(v) Tax gross-up payments. A plan providing a right to a tax gross-up payment will be treated as providing for payment at a specified time or on a fixed schedule of payments if the plan provides that payment will be made, and the payment is made, by the end of the service provider's taxable year next following the service provider's taxable year in which the service provider remits the related taxes. For purposes of this paragraph (i)(1)(v), the term tax gross-up payment refers to a payment to reimburse the service provider in an amount equal to all or a designated portion of the Federal, state, local, or foreign taxes imposed upon the service provider as a result of compensation paid or made available to the service provider by the service recipient, including the amount of additional taxes imposed upon the service provider due to the service recipient's payment of the initial taxes on such compensation. In addition, a right to the reimbursement of expenses incurred due to a tax audit or litigation addressing the existence or amount of a tax liability, whether Federal, state, local, or foreign, satisfies the requirement of a fixed time and form of payment if the right to the reimbursement provides that payment will be made, and the payment is made, by the end of the service provider's taxable year following the service provider's taxable year in which the taxes that are the subject of the audit or litigation are remitted to the taxing authority, or where as a result of such audit or litigation no taxes are remitted, the end of the service provider's taxable year following the service provider's taxable year in which the audit is completed or there is a final and nonappealable settlement or other resolution of the litigation. Nothing in this paragraph (i)(1)(v) otherwise alters the application of section 409A to the underlying compensation arrangement or other arrangement that results in the taxes subject to the right to the tax gross-up payment.

(vi) Examples. The following examples (in which each employee is an individual whose taxable year is the calendar year) illustrate the principles of paragraphs (a), (b), (c), (d), and (i)(1) of this section:

*Example (1).* Employee A provides services as an employee of Employer Z, but is not a specified employee. Employee A participates in a nonqualified deferred compensation plan providing for a lump sum payment payable on or before December 31 of the calendar year in which Employee A separates from service. The plan provides for a payment upon a separation from service in compliance with this section.

*Example (2).* Employee B provides services as an employee of Employer Y, but is not a specified employee. Employee B participates in a nonqualified deferred compensation plan providing for a lump sum payment payable on or before the 90th day immediately following the date upon which Employee B separates from service. Employer Y retains the sole discretion to determine when during the 90-day period the payment will be made. Although the plan does not specify a period during one calendar year in which the payment will be made, the plan provides for a payment upon a separation from service in compliance with this section because the period over which the payment may be made is not longer than 90 days.

*Example (3).* Employee C provides services as an employee of Employer X, but is not a specified employee. Employee C participates in a nonqualified deferred compensation plan providing for a lump sum payment payable on or before the 180th day following the date upon which Employee C separates from service. Employer X retains the sole discretion to determine when during the 180-day period the payment will be made. Because the plan does not specify a period during one calendar year in which the payment will be made, and because the period over which the payment may be made is longer than 90 days, the plan does not provide for a payment upon a separation from service that complies with this section.

*Example (4).* Employee D provides services as an employee of Employer W, but is not a specified employee. Employee D participates in a nonqualified deferred compensation plan providing for 10 installment payments payable on the first 10 anniversaries of the date Employee D separates from service, provided that no installment payment in any year may be more than 1% of Employer W's net income for the previous calendar year, and provided further that the excess over such limit that would otherwise be payable but is not paid due to application of the limit will become payable as of the first installment payment date at which time such amount, in combination with any installment payment otherwise due Employee D, does not exceed 1% of Employer W's net income for the previous calendar year. Provided that Employee D does not retain effective control of the calculation of Employer W's net income or the amount that Employee D will not be paid due to application of the limit, the plan provides for a schedule of payments upon a separation from service that complies with this section.

*Example (5).* Employee E and Employee F provide services as employees of Employer V, but neither is a specified employee. Employee E and Employee F both participate in substantially identical nonqualified deferred compensation plans providing for 10 installment payments payable on the first 10 anniversaries of the date the respective employee separates from service, provided that the total amount of installment payments in any year may not be more than 1% of Employer V's net income for the previous year, that where any payments are not made due to application of the limit the determination of the amount not paid to a particular employee will be made by applying the overall limit proportionately based upon the installment payment due the employee that year, and that the excess over such limit that would otherwise be payable but is not paid due to application of the limit will become payable as of the first installment payment date at which time such amount, in combination with any installment payments otherwise due the participants, does not exceed 1% of Employer V's net income for the previous calendar year. Provided that neither Employee E nor Employee F retains effective control of the calculation of Employer V's net income or the amount that the respective employee will not be paid due to application of the limit, the plan provides for a schedule of payments upon a separation from service that complies with this section.

*Example (6).* Employee G provides services as an employee of Employer U, but is not a specified employee. As a bona fide part of this employment relationship, Employee G provides professional services to clients of Employer U as part of the bona fide, ordinary course of Employer U's trade or business. Under an arrangement between Employee G and Employer U, Employer U agrees to pay Employee G upon Employee G's separation from service an amount equal to 5% of any amount collected from Company T, a client of Employer U for which Employee G performed services during his employment with Employer U, during the 36 months following Employee G's separation from service. Under the arrangement, the amounts due to Employee G based upon payments received by Employer U during any calendar year are payable to Employee G on April 1 of the subsequent calendar year. Provided that Employee G does not have effective control of Employer U, Company T, or the collection of any amounts due Employer Y from Company T, the arrangement provides for a schedule of payments upon a separation from service that complies with this section.

*Example (7).* Employee H provides services as an employee of Employer S, but is not a specified employee. Under a plan sponsored by Employer S, Employee H has a legally binding right upon a separation from service to the reimbursement of country club dues paid in the calendar year of the separation from service and each of the next 3 calendar years following the separation from service in an amount not to exceed $30,000 in any calendar year, provided that the amount of dues paid in any calendar year that are eligible for reimbursement equals only the amount actually expended during such calendar year, and the maximum amount available for reimbursement in any calendar year will not be increased or decreased to reflect the amount expended or reimbursed in a prior or subsequent calendar year. The plan further provides that any reimbursement must be paid to Employee H by December 31 of the calendar year following the year in which Employee H pays the country club dues. The reimbursement plan provides for a schedule of payments upon a separation from service that complies with this section.

*Example (8).* Employee J provides services as an employee of Employer Q, but is not a specified employee. Under a plan sponsored by Employer Q, Employee J has a legally binding right upon a separation from service to the reimbursement of country club dues paid during the calendar year in which the separation from service occurs and the next 3 calendar years in a total amount not to exceed $90,000. The plan further provides that any reimbursement must be paid to Employee J by December 31 of the calendar year following the year in which Employee J pays the country club dues. Because the reimbursement of a payment of country club dues in one calendar year may affect the amount of country club dues available for reimbursement in another calendar year, the plan does not provide for a schedule of payments upon a separation from service that complies with this section.

*(2) Separation from service—required delay in payment to a specified employee pursuant to a separation from service.* (i) In general. In the case of any service provider who is a specified employee (as defined in § 1.409A-1(i)) as of the date of a separation from service, the requirements of paragraph (a)(1) of this section permitting a payment upon a separation from service are satisfied only if payments may not be made before the date that is six months after the date of separation from service (or, if earlier than the end of the six-month period, the date of death of the specified employee). For this purpose, a service provider who is not a specified employee as of the date of a separation from ser-

vice will not be treated as subject to this requirement even if the service provider would have become a specified employee if the service provider had continued to provide services through the next specified employee effective date. Similarly, a service provider who is treated as a specified employee as of the date of a separation from service will be subject to this requirement even if the service provider would not have been treated as a specified employee after the next specified employee effective date had the specified employee continued providing services through the next specified employee effective date. Notwithstanding the foregoing, this paragraph (i)(2)(i) does not apply to a payment made under the circumstances described in paragraph (j)(4)(ii) (domestic relations order), (j)(4)(iii) (conflicts of interest), or (j)(4)(vi) (payment of employment taxes) of this section.

(ii) Application of payment rules to delayed payments. The required delay in payment is met if payments to which a specified employee would otherwise be entitled during the first six months following the date of separation from service are accumulated and paid on the first day of the seventh month following the date of separation from service, or if each payment to which a specified employee is otherwise entitled upon a separation from service is delayed by six months. A service recipient may retain discretion to choose which method will be implemented, provided that no direct or indirect election as to the method may be provided to the service provider. For an affected specified employee, a date upon which the plan or the service recipient designates that the payment will be made after the six-month delay is treated as a fixed payment date for purposes of paragraph (d) of this section once the separation from service has occurred.

*(3) Unforeseeable emergency.* (i) Definition. For purposes of §§ 1.409A-1 and 1.409A-2, this section, and §§ 1.409A-4 through 1.409A-6, an unforeseeable emergency is a severe financial hardship to the service provider resulting from an illness or accident of the service provider, the service provider's spouse, the service provider's beneficiary, or the service provider's dependent (as defined in section 152, without regard to section 152(b)(1), (b)(2), and (d)(1)(B)); loss of the service provider's property due to casualty (including the need to rebuild a home following damage to a home not otherwise covered by insurance, for example, not as a result of a natural disaster); or other similar extraordinary and unforeseeable circumstances arising as a result of events beyond the control of the service provider. For example, the imminent foreclosure of or eviction from the service provider's primary residence may constitute an unforeseeable emergency. In addition, the need to pay for medical expenses, including non-refundable deductibles, as well as for the costs of prescription drug medication, may constitute an unforeseeable emergency. Finally, the need to pay for the funeral expenses of a spouse, a beneficiary, or a dependent (as defined in section 152, without regard to section 152(b)(1), (b)(2), and (d)(1)(B)) may also constitute an unforeseeable emergency. Except as otherwise provided in this paragraph (i)(3)(i), the purchase of a home and the payment of college tuition are not unforeseeable emergencies. Whether a service provider is faced with an unforeseeable emergency permitting a distribution under this paragraph (i)(3)(i) is to be determined based on the relevant facts and circumstances of each case, but, in any case, a distribution on account of unforeseeable emergency may not be made to the extent that such emergency is or may be relieved through reimbursement or compensation from insurance or otherwise, by liquidation of the service provider's assets, to the extent the liquidation of such assets would not cause severe financial hardship, or by cessation of deferrals under the plan. A plan may provide for a payment upon a specific type or types of unforeseeable emergency, without providing for payment upon all unforeseeable emergencies, provided that any event upon which a payment may be made qualifies as an unforeseeable emergency.

(ii) Amount of payment permitted upon an unforeseeable emergency. Distributions because of an unforeseeable emergency must be limited to the amount reasonably necessary to satisfy the emergency need (which may include amounts necessary to pay any Federal, state, local, or foreign income taxes or penalties reasonably anticipated to result from the distribution). Determinations of amounts reasonably necessary to satisfy the emergency need must take into account any additional compensation that is available if the plan provides for cancellation of a deferral election upon a payment due to an unforeseeable emergency. See paragraph (j)(4)(viii) of this section. However, the determination of amounts reasonably necessary to satisfy the emergency need is not required to take into account any additional compensation that is available from a qualified employer plan as defined in § 1.409A-1(a)(2) (including any amount available by obtaining a loan under the plan), or that due to the unforeseeable emergency is available under another nonqualified deferred compensation plan (including a plan that would provide for deferred compensation except due to the application of the effective date provisions under § 1.409A-6). The payment may be made from any plan in which the service provider participates that provides for payment upon an unforeseeable emergency, provided that the plan under which the payment was made must be designated at the time of payment.

(iii) Payments due to an unforeseeable emergency. A service provider may retain discretion with respect to whether to apply for a payment upon an unforeseeable emergency, and a service recipient may retain discretion with respect to whether to make a payment available under the plan due to an unforeseeable emergency. A service provider who has experienced an unforeseeable emergency will not be treated as making a subsequent deferral election under § 1.409A-2(b) (subsequent deferral election rules) if the service provider does not apply for or elect to receive a payment available under the plan. A service recipient will not be treated as making a subsequent deferral election under § 1.409A-2(b) (subsequent deferral election rules) if the service recipient exercises its discretion not to make a payment otherwise available due to an unforeseeable emergency.

*(4) Disability.* (i) In general. For purposes of §§ 1.409A-1 and 1.409A-2, this section, and §§ 1.409A-4 through 1.409A-6, except as otherwise specifically provided, a service provider is considered disabled if the service provider meets one of the following requirements:

(A) The service provider is unable to engage in any substantial gainful activity by reason of any medically determinable physical or mental impairment that can be expected to result in death or can be expected to last for a continuous period of not less than 12 months.

(B) The service provider is, by reason of any medically determinable physical or mental impairment that can be expected to result in death or can be expected to last for a continuous period of not less than 12 months, receiving income replacement benefits for a period of not less than three months under an accident and health plan covering employees of the service provider's employer.

(ii) Limited plan definition of disability. A plan may provide for a payment upon any disability, and need not provide for a payment upon all disabilities, provided that any disability upon which a payment may be made under the plan complies with the provisions of this paragraph (i)(4).

(iii) Determination of disability. A plan may provide that a service provider will be deemed disabled if determined to be totally disabled by the Social Security Administration or Railroad Retirement Board. A plan may also provide that a service provider will be deemed disabled if determined to be disabled in accordance with a disability insurance program, provided that the definition of disability applied under such disability insurance program complies with the requirements of this paragraph (i)(4).

*(5) Change in the ownership or effective control of a corporation, or a change in the ownership of a substantial portion of the assets of a corporation.* (i) In general. Pursuant to section 409A(a)(2)(A)(v), a plan may permit a payment upon the occurrence of a change in the ownership of the corporation (as defined in paragraph (i)(5)(v) of this section), a change in effective control of the corporation (as defined in paragraph (i)(5)(vi) of this section), or a change in the ownership of a substantial portion of the assets of the corporation (as defined in paragraph (i)(5)(vii) of this section) (collectively referred to as a change in control event). To qualify as a change in control event, the occurrence of the event must be objectively determinable and any requirement that any other person or group, such as a plan administrator or compensation committee, certify the occurrence of a change in control event must be strictly ministerial and not involve any discretionary authority. The plan may provide for a payment on a particular type or types of change in control events, and need not provide for a payment on all such events, provided that each event upon which a payment is provided qualifies as a change in control event. For rules regarding the ability of the service recipient to terminate the plan and pay amounts of deferred compensation upon a change in control event, see paragraph (j)(4)(ix)(B) of this section.

(ii) Identification of relevant corporation. (A) In general. To constitute a change in control event with respect to the service provider, the change in control event must relate to—

(1) The corporation for whom the service provider is performing services at the time of the change in control event;

(2) The corporation that is liable for the payment of the deferred compensation (or all corporations liable for the payment if more than one corporation is liable) but only if either the deferred compensation is attributable to the performance of service by the service provider for such corporation (or corporations) or there is a bona fide business purpose for such corporation or corporations to be liable for such payment and, in either case, no significant purpose of making such corporation or corporations liable for such payment is the avoidance of Federal income tax; or

(3) A corporation that is a majority shareholder of a corporation identified in paragraph (i)(5)(ii)(A)(1) or (2) of this section, or any corporation in a chain of corporations in which each corporation is a majority shareholder of another corporation in the chain, ending in a corporation identified in paragraph (i)(5)(ii)(A)(1) or (2) of this section.

(B) Majority shareholder. For purposes of this paragraph (i)(5)(ii), a majority shareholder is a shareholder owning more than 50 percent of the total fair market value and total voting power of such corporation.

(C) Example. The following example illustrates the rules of this paragraph (i)(5)(ii):

*Example.* Corporation A is a majority shareholder of Corporation B, which is a majority shareholder of Corporation C. A change in ownership of Corporation B constitutes a change in control event to service providers performing services for Corporation B or Corporation C, and to service providers for which Corporation B or Corporation C is solely liable for payments under the plan (for example, former employees), but is not a change in control event as to Corporation A or any other corporation of which Corporation A is a majority shareholder unless the sale constitutes a change in the ownership of a substantial portion of Corporation A's assets (see paragraph (i)(5)(vii) of this section).

(iii) Attribution of stock ownership. For purposes of paragraph (i)(5) of this section, section 318(a) applies to determine stock ownership. Stock underlying a vested option is considered owned by the individual who holds the vested option (and the stock underlying an unvested option is not considered owned by the individual who holds the unvested option). For purposes of the preceding sentence, however, if a vested option is exercisable for stock that is not substantially vested (as defined by § 1.83-3(b) and (j)), the stock underlying the option is not treated as owned by the individual who holds the option.

(iv) Special rules for certain delayed payments pursuant to a change in control event. (A) Certain transaction-based compensation. Payments of compensation related to a change in control event described in paragraph (i)(5)(v) of this section (change in the ownership of a corporation) or paragraph (i)(5)(vii) of this section (change in the ownership of a substantial portion of a corporation's assets), that occur because a service recipient purchases its stock held by the service provider or because the service recipient or a third party purchases a stock right held by a service provider, or that are calculated by reference to the value of stock of the service recipient (collectively, transaction-based compensation), may be treated as paid at a designated date or pursuant to a payment schedule that complies with the requirements of section 409A if the transaction-based compensation is paid on the same schedule and under the same terms and conditions as apply to payments to shareholders generally with respect to stock of the service recipient pursuant to a change in control event described in paragraph (i)(5)(v) of this section (change in the ownership of a corporation) or as apply to payments to the service recipient pursuant to a change in control event described in paragraph (i)(5)(vii) of this section (change in the ownership of a substantial portion of a corporation's assets), and to the extent that the transaction-based compensation is paid not later than five years after the change in control event, the payment of such compensation will not violate the initial or subsequent deferral election rules set out in § 1.409A-2(a) and (b) solely as a result of such transaction-based compensation being paid pursuant to such schedule and terms and conditions. If before and in connection with a change in control event described in paragraph (i)(5)(v) or (i)(5)(vii) of this section, transaction-based compensation that would otherwise be payable as a result of such event is made subject to a condition on payment that constitutes a substantial risk of forfeiture (as defined in § 1.409A-1(d), without regard to the provisions of that section under which additions or extensions of forfeiture conditions are disregarded) and the transaction-based compensation is payable under the same terms and conditions as apply to payments made to shareholders generally with respect to stock of the service recipient pursuant to a change in control event described in paragraph (i)(5)(v) of this section or to payments to the service recipient pursuant to a change in control event described in paragraph (i)(5)(vii) of this section, for purposes of determining whether such transaction-based compensation is a short-term deferral the requirements of § 1.409A-1(b)(4) are applied as if the legally binding right to such transaction-based compensation arose on the date that it became subject to such substantial risk of forfeiture.

(B) Certain nonvested compensation. Notwithstanding the provisions of § 1.409A-1(d) (definition of a substantial risk of forfeiture) that disregard the extension or modification of a condition for purposes of determining whether a condition on payment constitutes a substantial risk of forfeiture, a condition that is a substantial risk of forfeiture that otherwise would lapse as a result of a change in control event described in paragraph (i)(5)(v) or (i)(5)(vii) of this section may be extended or modified before and in connection with such event to provide for a condition on payment that will not lapse as a result of such change in control event, and such extended or modified condition will be treated as continuing to subject the amount to a substantial risk of forfeiture, provided that the transaction constituting the change in control event is a bona fide arm's length transaction between the service recipient or its shareholders and one or more parties who are unrelated to the service recipient and service provider (applying the rules of § 1.409A-1(f)(2)(ii)) and the modified or extended condition to which the payment is subject would otherwise be treated as a substantial risk of forfeiture under § 1.409A-1(d) (without regard to the provisions disregarding additions or extensions of forfeiture conditions). In such a case, the continued application of a fixed schedule of payments based upon the lapse of the substantial risk of forfeiture, so that payments commence upon the lapse of the modified or extended condition on payment, will not be treated as a change in the fixed schedule of payments for purposes of § 1.409A-2(b) (subsequent deferral elections) or paragraph (j) of this section (prohibition on the acceleration of payments).

(v) Change in the ownership of a corporation. (A) In general. Except as provided in paragraph (i)(5)(vi)(C) of this section, a change in the ownership of a corporation occurs on the date that any one person, or more than one person acting as a group (as defined in paragraph (i)(5)(v)(B) of this section), acquires ownership of stock of the corporation that, together with stock held by such person or group, constitutes more than 50 percent of the total fair market value or total voting power of the stock of such corporation. A nonqualified deferred compensation plan may provide that amounts payable upon a change in the ownership of a corporation will be paid only if the conditions in the preceding sentence are satisfied but substituting a percentage specified in the plan that is higher than 50 percent for the words "50 percent" in the preceding sentence, but only if the provision is set forth in the plan no later than the date by which the time and form of payment must be established under § 1.409A-2. However, if any one person, or more than one person acting as a group, is considered to own more than 50 percent of the total fair market value or total voting power of the stock of a corporation (or such higher percentage specified in accordance with the preceding sentence), the acquisition of additional stock by the same person or persons is not considered to cause a change in the ownership of the corporation (or to cause a change in the effective control of the corporation (within the meaning of paragraph (i)(5)(vi) of this section)). An increase in the percentage of stock owned by any one person, or persons acting as a group, as a result of a transaction in which the corporation acquires its stock in exchange for property will be treated as an acquisition of stock for purposes of this section. This section applies only when there is a transfer of stock of a corporation (or issuance of stock of a corporation) and stock in such corporation remains outstanding after the transaction (see paragraph (i)(5)(vii) of this section for rules regarding the transfer of assets of a corporation). See § 1.280G-1, Q&A-27(d), Example 1, Example 2, Example 5, and Example 6.

(B) Persons acting as a group. For purposes of paragraph (i)(5)(v)(A) of this section, persons will not be considered to be acting as a group solely because they purchase or own stock of the same corporation at the same time, or as a result of the same public offering. However, persons will be considered to be acting as a group if they are owners of a corporation that enters into a merger, consolidation, purchase or acquisition of stock, or similar business transaction with the corporation. If a person, including an entity, owns stock in both corporations that enter into a merger, consolidation, purchase or acquisition of stock, or similar transaction, such shareholder is considered to be acting as a group with other shareholders only with respect to the ownership in that corporation before the transaction giving rise to the change and not with respect to the ownership interest in the other corporation. See § 1.280G-1, Q&A-27(d), Example 3 and Example 4.

(vi) Change in the effective control of a corporation. (A) In general. Notwithstanding that a corporation has not undergone a change in ownership under paragraph (i)(5)(v) of this section, a change in the effective control of the corporation occurs only on either of the following dates:

(1) The date any one person, or more than one person acting as a group (as determined under paragraph (i)(5)(v)(B) of this section), acquires (or has acquired during the 12-month period ending on the date of the most recent acquisition by such person or persons) ownership of stock of the corporation possessing 30 percent or more of the total voting power of the stock of such corporation. A nonqualified deferred compensation plan may provide that amounts payable upon an effective change in control of a corporation will be paid only if the conditions in the preceding sentence are satisfied but substituting a percentage specified in the plan that is higher than 30 percent for the word "30 percent" in the preceding sentence, but only if the percentage is set forth in the plan no later than the date by which the time and form of payment must be established under § 1.409A-2).

(2) The date a majority of members of the corporation's board of directors is replaced during any 12-month period by directors whose appointment or election is not endorsed by a majority of the members of the corporation's board of directors before the date of the appointment or election, provided that for purposes of this paragraph (i)(5)(vi)(A) the term corporation refers solely to the relevant corporation identified in paragraph (i)(5)(ii) of this section for which no other corporation is a majority shareholder for purposes of that paragraph. For example, if Corporation A is a publicly held corporation with no majority shareholder, and Corporation A is the majority shareholder of Corporation B, which is the majority shareholder of Corporation C, the term corporation for purposes of this paragraph (i)(5)(vi)(A)(2) would refer solely to Corporation A. A nonqualified deferred compensation plan may provide that amounts payable upon a change in the effective control of a corporation will be paid only if the conditions in the first sentence of this paragraph are satisfied substituting a portion of the members of the corporation's board of directors that is higher than the words "a majority

of the members of the corporation's board of directors" in the first sentence of this paragraph, but only if the higher portion is set forth in the plan no later than the date by which the time and form of payment must be established under § 1.409A-2(a)).

(B) Multiple change in control events. A change in effective control may occur in a transaction in which one of the two corporations involved in the transaction has a change in control event under paragraph (i)(5)(v) or (i)(5)(vii) of this section. Thus, for example, assume Corporation P transfers more than 40 percent of the total gross fair market value of its assets to Corporation O in exchange for 35 percent of O's stock. P has undergone a change in ownership of a substantial portion of its assets under paragraph (i)(5)(vii) of this section and O has a change in effective control under this paragraph (i)(5)(vi).

(C) Acquisition of additional control. If any one person, or more than one person acting as a group, is considered to effectively control a corporation (within the meaning of this paragraph (i)(5)(vi)), the acquisition of additional control of the corporation by the same person or persons is not considered to cause a change in the effective control of the corporation (or to cause a change in the ownership of the corporation within the meaning of paragraph (i)(5)(v) of this section).

(D) Persons acting as a group. Persons will not be considered to be acting as a group solely because they purchase or own stock of the same corporation at the same time, or as a result of the same public offering. However, persons will be considered to be acting as a group if they are owners of a corporation that enters into a merger, consolidation, purchase or acquisition of stock, or similar business transaction with the corporation. If a person, including an entity, owns stock in both corporations that enter into a merger, consolidation, purchase or acquisition of stock, or similar transaction, such shareholder is considered to be acting as a group with other shareholders in a corporation only with respect to the ownership in that corporation before the transaction giving rise to the change and not with respect to the ownership interest in the other corporation. See § 1.280G-1, Q&A-27(d), Example 4.

(vii) Change in the ownership of a substantial portion of a corporation's assets. (A) In general. A change in the ownership of a substantial portion of a corporation's assets occurs on the date that any one person, or more than one person acting as a group (as determined in paragraph (i)(5)(v)(B) of this section), acquires (or has acquired during the 12-month period ending on the date of the most recent acquisition by such person or persons) assets from the corporation that have a total gross fair market value equal to or more than 40 percent of the total gross fair market value of all of the assets of the corporation immediately before such acquisition or acquisitions (or such higher amount specified by the plan no later than the date by which the time and form of payment must be established under § 1.409A-2). For this purpose, gross fair market value means the value of the assets of the corporation, or the value of the assets being disposed of, determined without regard to any liabilities associated with such assets.

(B) Transfers to a related person. (1) There is no change in control event under this paragraph (i)(5)(vii) when there is a transfer to an entity that is controlled by the shareholders of the transferring corporation immediately after the transfer, as provided in this paragraph (i)(5)(vii)(B). A transfer of assets by a corporation is not treated as a change in the ownership of such assets if the assets are transferred to—

(i) A shareholder of the corporation (immediately before the asset transfer) in exchange for or with respect to its stock;

(ii) An entity, 50 percent or more of the total value or voting power of which is owned, directly or indirectly, by the corporation;

(iii) A person, or more than one person acting as a group, that owns, directly or indirectly, 50 percent or more of the total value or voting power of all the outstanding stock of the corporation; or

(iv) An entity, at least 50 percent of the total value or voting power of which is owned, directly or indirectly, by a person described in paragraph (i)(5)(vii)(B)(1)(iii) of this section.

(2) For purposes of this paragraph (i)(5)(vii)(B) and except as otherwise provided in this paragraph (i), a person's status is determined immediately after the transfer of the assets. For example, a transfer to a corporation in which the transferor corporation has no ownership interest before the transaction, but that is a majority-owned subsidiary of the transferor corporation after the transaction is not treated as a change in the ownership of the assets of the transferor corporation.

(C) Persons acting as a group. Persons will not be considered to be acting as a group solely because they purchase assets of the same corporation at the same time. However, persons will be considered to be acting as a group if they are owners of a corporation that enters into a merger, consolidation, purchase or acquisition of assets, or similar business transaction with the corporation. If a person, including an entity shareholder, owns stock in both corporations that enter into a merger, consolidation, purchase or acquisition of assets, or similar transaction, such shareholder is considered to be acting as a group with other shareholders in a corporation only to the extent of the ownership in that corporation before the transaction giving rise to the change and not with respect to the ownership interest in the other corporation. See § 1.280G-1, Q&A-27(d), Example 4.

*(6) Certain back-to-back arrangements.* (i) In general. This paragraph (i)(6) applies where a service provider is providing services to a service recipient (the intermediate service recipient), who in turn is providing services to another service recipient (the ultimate service recipient), the services provided by the service provider to the intermediate service recipient are closely related to the services provided by the intermediate service recipient to the ultimate service recipient, there is a nonqualified deferred compensation plan providing for payments by the ultimate service recipient to the intermediate service recipient (the ultimate service recipient plan), there is a nonqualified deferred compensation plan or other agreement, method, program, or other arrangement providing for payments of compensation by the intermediate service recipient to the service provider (the intermediate service recipient plan), and the intermediate service recipient plan provides for a payment upon the occurrence of an event described in paragraph (a)(1), (2), (3), (5), or (6) of this section. In such a case, notwithstanding the generally applicable limits on payments in paragraph (a) of this section, the ultimate service recipient plan may provide for a payment to the intermediate service recipient upon the occurrence of a payment event under the intermediate service recipient plan described in paragraph (a)(1), (2), (3), (5), or (6) of this section if the time and form of payment is defined as the same time and form of payment provided under the intermediate service recipient plan, the amount of the payment under the ul-

timate service recipient plan does not exceed the amount of the payment under the intermediate service recipient plan, and the ultimate service recipient plan and the intermediate service recipient plan otherwise satisfy the requirements of section 409A (regardless of whether such plan is subject to section 409A).

(ii) Example. The provisions of paragraph (i)(6)(i) of this section are illustrated by the following example:

*Example.* Company B (intermediate service recipient) provides services to Company C (ultimate service recipient). Employee A (service provider) provides services to Company B that are closely related to the services Company B provides to Company C. Pursuant to a nonqualified deferred compensation plan meeting the requirements of section 409A, Employee A is entitled to a payment of deferred compensation upon a separation from service with Company B (the intermediate service recipient plan). Under an arrangement between Company B and Company C (the ultimate service recipient plan), Company C agrees to pay an amount of deferred compensation to Company B upon Employee A's separation from service with Company B, in accordance with the time, form and amount of payment provided in the intermediate service recipient plan. Provided that the intermediate service recipient plan and the ultimate service recipient plan otherwise comply with the requirements of section 409A (regardless of whether such arrangements are subject to section 409A), Company C's payment to Company B of the amount due under the ultimate service recipient plan upon the separation from service of Employee A from Company B may constitute a permissible payment event for purposes of paragraph (a) of this section.

**(j) Prohibition on acceleration of payments.** *(1) In general.* Except as provided in paragraph (j)(4) of this section, a nonqualified deferred compensation plan may not permit the acceleration of the time or schedule of any payment or amount scheduled to be paid pursuant to the terms of the plan, and no such accelerated payment may be made whether or not provided for under the terms of such plan. For purposes of determining whether a payment of deferred compensation has been made, the rules of paragraph (f) of this section (substituted payments) apply. For purposes of this paragraph (j), an impermissible acceleration does not occur if payment is made in accordance with plan provisions or an election as to the time and form of payment in effect at the time of initial deferral (or added in accordance with the rules applicable to subsequent deferral elections under § 1.409A-2(b)) pursuant to which payment is required to be made on an accelerated schedule as a result of an intervening event that is an event described in paragraph (a)(1), (2), (3), (5), or (6) of this section. For example, a plan may provide that a participant will receive six installment payments commencing at separation from service, and also provide that if the participant dies after such payments commence but before all payments have been made, all remaining amounts will be paid in a lump sum payment. Additionally, it is not an acceleration of the time or schedule of payment of a deferral of compensation if a service recipient waives or accelerates the satisfaction of a condition constituting a substantial risk of forfeiture applicable to such deferral of compensation, provided that the requirements of section 409A (including the requirement that the payment be made upon a permissible payment event) are otherwise satisfied with respect to such deferral of compensation. For example, if a nonqualified deferred compensation plan provides for a lump sum payment of the vested benefit upon separation from service, and the benefit vests under the plan only after 10 years of service, it is not a violation of the requirements of section 409A if the service recipient reduces the vesting requirement to five years of service, even if a service provider becomes vested as a result and receives a payment in connection with a separation from service before the service provider would have completed 10 years of service. However, if the plan in this example had provided for a payment at a fixed date, rather than at separation from service, the date of payment could not be accelerated due to the accelerated vesting. For the definition of a payment for purposes of this paragraph (j), see § 1.409A-2(b)(5) (coordination of the subsequent deferral election rules with the prohibition on acceleration of payments). For other permissible payments, see § 1.409A-2(b)(2)(iii) (certain immediate payments of remaining installments) and paragraph (d) of this section (certain payments made no more than 30 days before the designated payment date).

*(2) Application to multiple payment events.* Generally, the addition of a permissible payment event, the deletion of a permissible payment event, or the substitution of one permissible payment event for another permissible payment event, results in an acceleration of a payment if the addition, deletion, or substitution could result in the payment being made at an earlier date than such payment would have been made absent such addition, deletion, or substitution. Notwithstanding the previous sentence, the addition of death, disability (as defined in paragraph (i)(4) of this section), or an unforeseeable emergency (as defined in paragraph (i)(3) of this section), as a potentially earlier alternative payment event to an amount previously deferred will not be treated as resulting in an acceleration of a payment, even if such addition results in the payment being paid at an earlier time than such payment would have been made absent the addition of the payment event. However, the addition of such a payment event as a potentially later alternative payment event generally is subject to the rules governing changes in the time and form of payment (see § 1.409A-2(b)).

*(3) Beneficiaries.* The rules of this paragraph (j) apply to elections by beneficiaries with respect to the time and form of payment, as well as elections by service providers or service recipients with respect to the time and form of payment to beneficiaries. An election to change the identity of a beneficiary does not constitute an acceleration of a payment merely because the election changes the identity of the recipient of the payment, if the time and form of the payment is not otherwise changed. In addition, an election before the commencement of a life annuity to change the identity of a beneficiary does not constitute an acceleration of a payment if the change in the time of payments stems solely from the different life expectancy of the new beneficiary, such as in the case of a joint and survivor annuity, and does not change the commencement date of the life annuity.

*(4) Exceptions.* (i) In general. Except as otherwise expressly provided, a plan may provide for the acceleration of a payment in accordance with paragraphs (j)(4)(ii) through (xiv) of this section, or may provide a service recipient discretion to accelerate payments in accordance with the provisions of paragraphs (j)(4)(ii) through (xiv) of this section. A plan may not provide a service provider discretion with respect to whether a payment will be accelerated, and a service recipient may not provide a service provider a direct or indirect election as to whether the service recipient's discretion to accelerate a payment will be exercised, even if such acceleration would be permitted under paragraphs (j)(4)(ii) through (xiv) of this section. Whether a service recipient has provided a service provider an election as to whether the ser-

vice recipient's discretion to accelerate a payment will be exercised is determined based on all the facts and circumstances, including whether similarly situated service providers have been treated differently. Except as otherwise provided in paragraphs (j)(4)(ii) through (xiv) of this section, the plan need not set forth the exception in writing, and provided all other requirements of this section are met, the making of such a payment or the addition of a plan term permitting the making of such a payment will not constitute the acceleration of a payment, and the failure to make such a payment or the deletion or modification of a plan term permitting the making of such a payment will not be subject to the rules regarding a change in the time and form of payment under § 1.409A-2(b).

(ii) Domestic relations order. A plan may provide for acceleration of the time or schedule of a payment under the plan to an individual other than the service provider, or a payment under such plan may be made to an individual other than the service provider, to the extent necessary to fulfill a domestic relations order (as defined in section 414(p)(1)(B)).

(iii) Conflicts of interest. (A) Compliance with ethics agreements with the Federal government. A plan may provide for acceleration of the time or schedule of a payment under the plan, or a payment may be made under a plan, to the extent necessary for any Federal officer or employee in the executive branch to comply with an ethics agreement with the Federal government.

(B) Compliance with ethics laws or conflicts of interest laws. A plan may provide for acceleration of the time or schedule of a payment under the plan, or a payment may be made under a plan, to the extent reasonably necessary to avoid the violation of an applicable Federal, state, local, or foreign ethics law or conflicts of interest law (including where such payment is reasonably necessary to permit the service provider to participate in activities in the normal course of his or her position in which the service provider would otherwise not be able to participate under an applicable rule). A payment is reasonably necessary to avoid the violation of a Federal, state, local, or foreign ethics law or conflicts of interest law if the payment is a necessary part of a course of action that results in compliance with a Federal, state, local, or foreign ethics law or conflicts of interest law that would be violated absent such course of action, regardless of whether other actions would also result in compliance with the Federal, state, local, or foreign ethics law or conflicts of interest law. For this purpose, a provision of foreign law is considered applicable only to foreign earned income (as defined under section 911(b)(1) without regard to section 911(b)(1)(B)(iv) and without regard to the requirement that the income be attributable to services performed during the period described in section 911(d)(1)(A) or (B)) from sources within the foreign country that promulgated such law.

(iv) Section 457 plans. A plan subject to section 457(f) may provide for an acceleration of the time or schedule of a payment to a service provider, or a payment may be made under such a plan, to pay Federal, state, local, and foreign income taxes due upon a vesting event, provided that the amount of such payment is not more than an amount equal to the Federal, state, local, and foreign income tax withholding that would have been remitted by the employer if there had been a payment of wages equal to the income includible by the service provider under section 457(f) at the time of the vesting.

(v) Limited cashouts. A plan may require or provide a service recipient discretion to require (or be amended to require or to provide a service recipient discretion to require), a mandatory lump sum payment of amounts deferred under the plan that do not exceed a specified amount, provided that such plan term or amendment is executed and effective, and any required exercise of service recipient discretion is evidenced in writing, no later than the date of such payment, and provided that—

(A) The payment results in the termination and liquidation of the entirety of the service provider's interest under the plan, including all agreements, methods, programs, or other arrangements with respect to which deferrals of compensation are treated as having been deferred under a single nonqualified deferred compensation plan under § 1.409A-1(c)(2); and

(B) The payment is not greater than the applicable dollar amount under section 402(g)(1)(B).

(vi) Payment of employment taxes. A plan may provide for the acceleration of the time or schedule of a payment, or a payment may be made under the plan, to pay the Federal Insurance Contributions Act (FICA) tax imposed under section 3101, section 3121(a), and section 3121(v)(2), or the Railroad Retirement Act tax imposed under section 3201, section 3211, section 3231(e)(1), and section 3231(e)(8), where applicable, on compensation deferred under the plan (the FICA or RRTA amount). Additionally, a plan may provide for the acceleration of the time or schedule of a payment, or a payment may be made under the plan, to pay the income tax at source on wages imposed under section 3401 or the corresponding withholding provisions of applicable state, local, or foreign tax laws as a result of the payment of the FICA or RRTA amount, and to pay the additional income tax at source on wages attributable to the pyramiding section 3401 wages and taxes. However, the total payment under this acceleration provision must not exceed the aggregate of the FICA or RRTA amount, and the income tax withholding related to such FICA or RRTA amount.

(vii) Payment upon income inclusion under section 409A. A plan may provide for the acceleration of the time or schedule of a payment, or a payment under such plan may be made, at any time the plan fails to meet the requirements of section 409A and these regulations. Such payment may not exceed the amount required to be included in income as a result of the failure to comply with the requirements of section 409A and these regulations.

(viii) Cancellation of deferrals following an unforeseeable emergency or hardship distribution. A plan may provide for a cancellation of a service provider's deferral election, or such a cancellation may be made, due to an unforeseeable emergency or a hardship distribution pursuant to § 1.401(k)-1(d)(3). The deferral election must be cancelled, not merely postponed or otherwise delayed. Accordingly, any later deferral election will be subject to the provisions governing initial deferral elections. See § 1.409A-2(a).

(ix) Plan terminations and liquidations. A plan may provide for the acceleration of the time and form of a payment, or a payment under such plan may be made, where the acceleration of the payment is made pursuant to a termination and liquidation of the plan in accordance with one of the following:

(A) The service recipient's termination and liquidation of the plan within 12 months of a corporate dissolution taxed under section 331, or with the approval of a bankruptcy court pursuant to 11 U.S.C. § 503(b)(1)(A), provided that the amounts deferred under the plan are included in the participants' gross incomes in the latest of the following years (or, if earlier, the taxable year in which the amount is actually or constructively received).

(1) The calendar year in which the plan termination and liquidation occurs.

(2) The first calendar year in which the amount is no longer subject to a substantial risk of forfeiture.

(3) The first calendar year in which the payment is administratively practicable.

(B) The service recipient's termination and liquidation of the plan pursuant to irrevocable action taken by the service recipient within the 30 days preceding or the 12 months following a change in control event (as defined in paragraph (i)(5) of this section), provided that this paragraph will only apply to a payment under a plan if all agreements, methods, programs, and other arrangements sponsored by the service recipient immediately after the time of the change in control event with respect to which deferrals of compensation are treated as having been deferred under a single plan under § 1.409A-1(c)(2) are terminated and liquidated with respect to each participant that experienced the change in control event, so that under the terms of the termination and liquidation all such participants are required to receive all amounts of compensation deferred under the terminated agreements, methods, programs, and other arrangements within 12 months of the date the service recipient irrevocably takes all necessary action to terminate and liquidate the agreements, methods, programs, and other arrangements. Solely for purposes of this paragraph (j)(4)(ix)(B), the applicable service recipient with the discretion to liquidate and terminate the agreements, methods, programs, and other arrangements is the service recipient that is primarily liable immediately after the transaction for the payment of the deferred compensation.

(C) The service recipient's termination and liquidation of the plan, provided that—

(1) The termination and liquidation does not occur proximate to a downturn in the financial health of the service recipient;

(2) The service recipient terminates and liquidates all agreements, methods, programs, and other arrangements sponsored by the service recipient that would be aggregated with any terminated and liquidated agreements, methods, programs, and other arrangements under § 1.409A-1(c) if the same service provider had deferrals of compensation under all of the agreements, methods, programs, and other arrangements that are terminated and liquidated;

(3) No payments in liquidation of the plan are made within 12 months of the date the service recipient takes all necessary action to irrevocably terminate and liquidate the plan other than payments that would be payable under the terms of the plan if the action to terminate and liquidate the plan had not occurred;

(4) All payments are made within 24 months of the date the service recipient takes all necessary action to irrevocably terminate and liquidate the plan; and

(5) The service recipient does not adopt a new plan that would be aggregated with any terminated and liquidated plan under § 1.409A-1(c) if the same service provider participated in both plans, at any time within three years following the date the service recipient takes all necessary action to irrevocably terminate and liquidate the plan.

(D) Such other events and conditions as the Commissioner may prescribe in generally applicable guidance published in the Internal Revenue Bulletin (see § 601.601(d)(2) of this chapter).

(x) Certain distributions to avoid a nonallocation year under section 409(p). A plan may provide for an acceleration of the time and form of a payment, or a payment may be made under such plan, to prevent the occurrence of a nonallocation year (within the meaning of section 409(p)(3)) in the plan year of an employee stock ownership plan next following the plan year in which such payment is made, provided that the amount distributed may not exceed 125 percent of the minimum amount of distribution necessary to avoid the occurrence of a nonallocation year. Solely for purposes of determining permissible distributions under this paragraph (j)(4)(x), synthetic equity (within the meaning of section 409(p)(6)(C) and § 1.409(p)-1(f)) granted during the plan year of the employee stock ownership plan in which such payment is made is disregarded for purposes of determining whether the subsequent plan year would result in a nonallocation year.

(xi) Payment of state, local, or foreign taxes. A plan may provide for an acceleration of the time and form of a payment, or a payment may be made under such plan, to reflect payment of state, local, or foreign tax obligations arising from participation in the plan that apply to an amount deferred under the plan before the amount is paid or made available to the participant (the state, local, or foreign tax amount). Such payment may not exceed the amount of such taxes due as a result of participation in the plan. Such payment may be made by distributions to the participant in the form of withholding pursuant to provisions of applicable state, local, or foreign law or by distribution directly to the participant. Additionally, an arrangement may provide for the acceleration of the time or schedule of payment, or a payment may be made under such arrangement, to pay the income tax at source on wages imposed under section 3401 as a result of such payment and to pay the additional income tax at source on wages imposed under section 3401 attributable to such additional section 3401 wages and taxes. However, the total payment under this acceleration provision must not exceed the aggregate of the state, local, and foreign tax amount, and the income tax withholding related to such state, local, and foreign tax amount.

(xii) Cancellation of deferral elections due to disability. A plan may provide for a cancellation of a service provider's deferral election, or a cancellation of such election may be made, where such cancellation occurs by the later of the end of the taxable year of the service provider or the 15th day of the third month following the date the service provider incurs a disability. For purposes of this paragraph, a disability refers to any medically determinable physical or mental impairment resulting in the service provider's inability to perform the duties of his or her position or any substantially similar position, where such impairment can be expected to result in death or can be expected to last for a continuous period of not less than six months.

(xiii) Certain offsets. A plan may provide for the acceleration of the time or schedule of a payment, or a payment may be made under such plan, as satisfaction of a debt of the service provider to the service recipient, where such debt is incurred in the ordinary course of the service relationship between the service recipient and the service provider, the entire amount of reduction in any of the service recipient's taxable years does not exceed $5,000, and the reduction is made at the same time and in the same amount as the debt otherwise would have been due and collected from the service provider.

(xiv) Bona fide disputes as to a right to a payment. A plan may provide for the acceleration of the time or schedule of one or more payments, or a payment may be made under such plan, where such payments occur as part of a settlement between the service provider and the service recipient of an arm's length, bona fide dispute as to the service provider's right to the deferred amount. Discretion to accelerate payments, other than due to an arm's length settlement of a bona fide dispute as to the service provider's right to the deferred amount, is not permitted under this paragraph (j)(4)(xiv). Whether a payment qualifies for the exception under this paragraph is based on all relevant facts and circumstances. A payment will be presumed not to meet this exception unless the payment is subject to a substantial reduction in the value of the payment made in relation to the amount that would have been payable had there been no dispute as to the service provider's right to the payment. For this purpose, a reduction that is less than 25 percent of the present value of the deferred amount in dispute generally is not a substantial reduction. In addition, a payment will be presumed not to meet this exception if the payment is made proximate to a downturn in the financial health of the service recipient.

*(5) Nonqualified deferred compensation plans linked to qualified employer plans or certain other arrangements.* If a nonqualified deferred compensation plan provides that the amount deferred under the plan is the amount determined under the formula determining benefits under a qualified employer plan (as defined in § 1.409A-1(a)(2)), or a broad-based foreign retirement plan (as defined in § 1.409A-1(a)(3)(v)) maintained by the service recipient but applied without regard to one or more limitations applicable to the qualified employer plan under the Internal Revenue Code or to the broad-based foreign retirement plan under other applicable law, or that the amount deferred under the nonqualified deferred compensation plan is determined as an amount offset by some or all of the benefits provided under the qualified employer plan or broad-based foreign retirement plan, a decrease in amounts deferred under the nonqualified deferred compensation plan that results directly from the operation of the qualified employer plan or broad-based foreign retirement plan (other than service provider actions described in paragraphs (j)(5)(iii) and (iv) of this section) including changes in benefit limitations applicable to the qualified employer plan or the broad-based foreign retirement plan under the Internal Revenue Code or other applicable law does not constitute an acceleration of a payment under the nonqualified deferred compensation plan, provided that such operation does not otherwise result in a change in the time or form of a payment under the nonqualified deferred compensation plan, and provided further that the change in the amounts deferred under the nonqualified deferred compensation plan does not exceed such change in the amounts deferred under the qualified employer plan or the broad-based foreign retirement plan, as applicable. In addition, with respect to such a nonqualified deferred compensation plan, the following actions or failures to act will not constitute an acceleration of a payment under the nonqualified deferred compensation plan even if in accordance with the terms of the nonqualified deferred compensation plan, the actions or inactions result in a decrease in the amounts deferred under the plan, provided that such actions or inactions do not otherwise affect the time or form of payment under the nonqualified deferred compensation plan, and provided further that with respect to actions or inactions described in paragraphs (j)(5)(i) and (ii) of this section, the change in the amount deferred under the nonqualified deferred compensation plan does not exceed the change in the amounts deferred under the qualified employer plan or the broad-based foreign retirement plan, as applicable:

(i) A service provider's action or inaction under the qualified employer plan or broad-based foreign retirement plan with respect to whether to elect to receive a subsidized benefit or an ancillary benefit under the qualified employer plan or broad-based foreign retirement plan.

(ii) The amendment of a qualified employer plan or broad-based foreign retirement plan to increase benefits provided under such plan, or to add or remove a subsidized benefit or an ancillary benefit.

(iii) A service provider's action or inaction under a qualified employer plan with respect to elective deferrals and other employee pre-tax contributions subject to the contribution restrictions under section 401(a)(30) or section 402(g), including an adjustment to a deferral election under such qualified employer plan, provided that for any given taxable year, the service provider's action or inaction does not result in a decrease in the amounts deferred under all nonqualified deferred compensation plans in which the service provider participates (other than amounts described in paragraph (j)(5)(iv) of this section) in excess of the limit with respect to elective deferrals under section 402(g)(1)(A), (B), and (C) in effect for the taxable year in which such action or inaction occurs.

(iv) A service provider's action or inaction under a qualified employer plan with respect to elective deferrals and other employee pre-tax contributions subject to the contributions restrictions under section 401(a)(30) or section 402(g), and after-tax contributions by the service provider to a qualified employer plan that provides for such contributions, that affects the amounts that are credited under one or more nonqualified deferred compensation plans as matching amounts or other similar amounts contingent on such elective deferrals, pre-tax contributions, or after-tax contributions, provided that the total of such matching or contingent amounts, as applicable, never exceeds 100 percent of the matching or contingent amounts that would be provided under the qualified employer plan absent any plan-based restrictions that reflect limits on qualified plan contributions under the Internal Revenue Code.

*(6) Changes in elections under a cafeteria plan.* A change in an election under a cafeteria plan (as defined in section 125(d)) does not result in an accelerated payment of an amount deferred under a nonqualified deferred compensation plan to the extent that the change in the amount deferred under the nonqualified deferred compensation plan results solely from the application of the change in amount eligible to be treated as compensation under the terms of the nonqualified deferred compensation plan resulting from the election change under the cafeteria plan, to a benefit formula under the nonqualified deferred compensation plan based upon the service provider's eligible compensation, and only to the extent that such change applies in the same manner as any other increase or decrease in compensation would apply to such benefit formula.

---

T.D. 9321, 4/10/2007.

---

**§ 1.409A-4 Calculation of income inclusion. [Reserved]**

T.D. 9321, 4/10/2007.

**Proposed § 1.409A-4 Calculation of amount includible in income and additional income taxes.** [*For Preamble, see ¶ 153,075*]

**(a) Amount includible in income due to failure to meet the requirements of section 409A(a).** *(1) In general.* (i) Calculation formula. The amount includible in income for a service provider's taxable year due to a failure to meet the requirements of section 409A(a) with respect to a plan is the excess (if any) of—

(A) The service provider's total amount deferred under the plan for the taxable year, including the amount of any payments of amounts deferred under the plan to (or on behalf of) the service provider during such taxable year; over

(B) The portion of such amount, if any, that is either subject to a substantial risk of forfeiture (as defined in § 1.409A-1(d) and applying paragraph (a)(1)(ii)(B) of this section) or has been previously included in income (as defined in § 1.409A-4(a)(3)).

(ii) Each taxable year analyzed independently. (A) In general. An amount is includible in income under section 409A(a) for a taxable year only if a plan fails to meet the requirements of section 409A(a) during such taxable year. Whether an amount is includible in income for a taxable year due to a failure to meet the requirements of section 409A(a) during such taxable year is determined independently of whether such amounts are also includible in income due to a failure to meet the requirements of section 409A(a) in a previous or subsequent taxable year. Accordingly, an amount may be includible in income for a taxable year during which a plan fails to meet the requirements of section 409A(a), even if the same amount was includible in income in a previous taxable year, except to the extent provided in § 1.409A-4(a)(3) (identification of amount previously included in income).

(B) Treatment of certain deferred amounts otherwise subject to a substantial risk of forfeiture. For purposes of determining the amount includible in income under section 409A(a) and paragraph (a)(1)(i) of this section, if the facts and circumstances indicate that a service recipient has a pattern or practice of permitting impermissible changes in the time and form of payment with respect to nonvested deferred amounts under one or more plans, an amount deferred under a plan that is otherwise subject to a substantial risk of forfeiture is not treated as subject to a substantial risk of forfeiture if an impermissible change in the time and form of payment (including an impermissible initial deferral election) applies to the amount deferred or if the facts and circumstances indicate that the amount deferred would be affected by such pattern or practice.

(iii) Examples. The following examples illustrate the provisions of this paragraph (a)(1). For each of the examples, Employee A is an individual taxpayer with a calendar year taxable year. Employee A has a total amount deferred under a nonqualified deferred compensation plan of $0 in 2010, $100,000 in 2011, and $250,000 in 2012. No payments are made under the plan. The plan under which the amounts are deferred fails to meet the requirements of section 409A(a) during 2011 and 2012. The examples read as follows:

*Example (1).* With respect to Employee A, at no time is any deferred amount subject to a substantial risk of forfeiture. Employee A has $100,000 includible in income under section 409A(a) for 2011, because no portion of the total deferred amount for 2011 is subject to a substantial risk of forfeiture or has previously been included in income. If that $100,000 is included in income for 2011, Employee A has $150,000 includible in income under section 409A(a) for 2012 because for the taxable year 2012 the $100,000 is previously included in income (see paragraphs (a)(1)(i)(B) and (a)(3) of this section). If that $100,000 is not included in income for 2011, Employee A has $250,000 includible in income under section 409A(a) for 2012. Employee A does not avoid the requirement to include $100,000 in income under section 409A(a) for 2011 by including $250,000 in income under section 409A(a) for 2012.

*Example (2).* The same facts as Example 1, except that, with respect to Employee A, the statute of limitations on assessments has expired for 2011, but has not expired for 2012. Employee A has $250,000 includible in income under section 409A(a) for 2012, because no portion of the total deferred amount for 2012 is subject to a substantial risk of forfeiture or has previously been included in income.

*(2) Identification of the portion of the total amount deferred for a taxable year that is subject to a substantial risk of forfeiture* (i) In general. The portion of the total amount deferred for a taxable year that is subject to a substantial risk of forfeiture (as defined in § 1.409A-1(d)) is determined as of the last day of the service provider's taxable year. Accordingly, an amount may be includible in income under section 409A(a) for a taxable year even if such amount is subject to a substantial risk of forfeiture during the taxable year if the substantial risk of forfeiture lapses during such taxable year, including if the substantial risk of forfeiture lapses after the date the nonqualified deferred compensation plan under which the amount is deferred first fails to meet the requirements of section 409A(a).

(ii) Example. The following example illustrates the provisions of this paragraph (a)(2): Employee B is an individual taxpayer with a calendar year taxable year. Employee B has a total amount deferred under a nonqualified deferred compensation plan of $0 for 2010, $100,000 for 2011, and $250,000 for 2012. No payments are made under the plan. Under the terms of the plan, if Employee B voluntarily separates from service before July 1, 2012, Employee B will forfeit 50 percent of the Employee B's total amount deferred under the plan. If Employee B voluntarily separates from service after June 30, 2012 but before July 1, 2013, Employee B will forfeit 20 percent of the total amount deferred under the plan. If Employee B voluntarily separates from service after June 30, 2013, Employee B will not forfeit any amount deferred under the plan. As of December 31, 2011, 50 percent of the total amount deferred under the plan ($50,000) is subject to a substantial risk of forfeiture, and the remaining amount deferred under the plan ($50,000) is not subject to a substantial risk of forfeiture. As of December 31, 2012, 20 percent of the total amount deferred under the plan ($50,000) is subject to a substantial risk of forfeiture, and the remaining amount deferred under the plan ($200,000) is not subject to a substantial risk of forfeiture. At all times the terms of the plan meet the requirements of section 409A(a) and the applicable regulations, and through May 31, 2012, the plan is operated in a manner that complies with the terms of the plan. On June 1, 2012, the plan is operated in a manner that fails to meet the requirements of section 409A(a). For purposes of determining the amount includible in income under section 409A(a), except as provided in paragraph (a)(1)(ii)(B) of this section, the portion of the total amount deferred for 2012 that is subject to a substantial risk of forfeiture is $50,000 (20 percent of $250,000).

*(3) Identification of amount previously included in income.* (i) In general. For purposes of this section, an amount is previously included in income only if the service provider has included the amount in income under an applicable provision of the Internal Revenue Code for a previous taxable year. An amount is treated as included in income for a taxable year only to the extent that the amount was properly includible in income and the service provider actually included the amount in income (including on an original or amended return or as a result of an IRS examination or a final decision of a court of competent jurisdiction). For future taxable years, the amount previously included in income is reduced to reflect any amount that was paid during the taxable year for which the amount was included in income, any amount allocated to a payment made under the plan under paragraph (f) of this section, and any amount deductible under paragraph (g) of this section.

(ii) Examples. The following examples illustrate the provisions of this paragraph (a)(3). For all of the examples, Employee C is an individual taxpayer with a calendar year taxable year. Employee C has a total amount deferred under a nonqualified deferred compensation plan of $0 in 2010, $100,000 in 2011, and $250,000 in 2012. With respect to Employee C, the statute of limitations on assessments has not expired for 2011 or 2012. Except as otherwise explicitly provided in the following examples, Employee C has not included in income for 2011 on any original or amended tax return any amount deferred under the plan, none of the $250,000 total amount deferred for 2012 has previously been included in income, no payments are made under the plan, and at no time is any deferred amount subject to a substantial risk of forfeiture. The plan under which the amounts are deferred fails to meet the requirements of section 409A(a) during 2011 and 2012. The examples read as follows:

*Example (1).* After filing an original Federal income tax return for 2011 that did not include any amount in income under section 409A(a), on April 1, 2013, Employee C files an amended Federal income tax return for 2011 and properly includes $100,000 in income under section 409A(a) for 2011. For purposes of determining the amount includible in income under section 409A(a) for 2012, $100,000 of the $250,000 total amount deferred for 2012 has previously been included in income with respect to the plan. For 2012, Employee C includes in income $150,000 under section 409A(a) on Employee C's original Federal income tax return. As of January 1, 2013, the amount that Employee C has previously included in income under section 409A(a) with respect to the plan is $250,000.

*Example (2).* The facts are the same as in Example 1, except that Employee C receives a $10,000 payment in 2011 so that the total amount deferred for 2012 is $240,000. For purposes of determining the amount includible in income under section 409A(a) for 2012, the $100,000 amount previously included in income is reduced by the $10,000 payment so that $90,000 of the $240,000 total amount deferred for 2012 has previously been included in income. For 2012, Employee C includes in income $150,000 under section 409A(a) on Employee C's original Federal income tax return. As of January 1, 2013, the amount that Employee C has previously included in income under section 409A(a) with respect to the plan is $240,000.

*Example (3).* The facts are the same as in Example 2. Due to deemed investment losses during 2013, Employee C has an $80,000 total amount deferred under the plan for 2013. On December 31, 2013, Employee C's total amount deferred ($80,000) is paid to Employee C as a single sum payment. Pursuant to paragraph (f) of this section, $80,000 of the $240,000 amount previously included in income is allocated to the $80,000 payment so that none of the $80,000 is includible in income. In addition, pursuant to paragraph (g) of this section, Employee C is entitled to deduct $160,000 for 2013 equal to the remaining amount previously included in income the right to which is permanently lost. Because the entire $240,000 amount previously included in income has been allocated to a payment under paragraph (f) of this section or was deductible under paragraph (g) of this section, no portion of such amount is treated as previously included in income for 2014 or any subsequent taxable year. As of January 1, 2014, the amount that Employee C has previously included in income under section 409A(a) with respect to the plan is $0.

**(b) The total amount deferred under a plan for a taxable year.** *(1) Application of general rules and specific rules for specific types of plans.* Paragraph (b)(2) of this section provides general rules governing the determination of the total amount deferred under a plan for a taxable year, including the treatment of plans providing for alternative times and forms of payment and plans providing for certain payments the amount of which is determined by a formula that includes one or more variables dependent upon future events (formula amounts). Paragraphs (b)(3) through (b)(6) of this section provide specific rules governing the determination of the total amount deferred under certain types of plans. Except as otherwise provided, any applicable rules of paragraphs (b)(3) through (b)(6) of this section are applied in conjunction with the general rules provided in paragraph (b)(2) of this section.

*(2) General definition of total amount deferred.* (i) General calculation rules. Except as otherwise provided, the total amount deferred for a taxable year equals the present value of the future payments to which the service provider has a legally binding right under the plan as of the last day of the taxable year, plus the amount of any payments of amounts deferred under the plan to (or on behalf of) the service provider during such taxable year. For purposes of this section, present value means the value, as of a specified date, of an amount or series of amounts due thereafter, determined in accordance with the rules and assumptions of this paragraph (b)(2), as applicable, where each amount is multiplied by the probability that the condition or conditions on which payment of the amount is contingent will be satisfied, also determined in accordance with the rules and assumptions set forth in this paragraph (b)(2), as applicable, discounted according to an assumed rate of interest to reflect the time value of money. For this purpose, a discount for the probability that an employee will die before commencement of benefit payments is permitted, but only to the extent that benefits will be forfeited upon death. In addition, the present value cannot be discounted for the probability that payments will not be made (or will be reduced) because of the unfunded status of the plan, the risk associated with any deemed or actual investment of amounts deferred under the plan, the risk that the service recipient, the trustee, or another party will be unwilling or unable to pay, the possibility of future plan amendments, the possibility of a future change in the law, or similar risks or contingencies. If the amount payable under a plan or the value of a benefit under a plan is expressed in a currency other than the U.S. dollar, the total amount deferred is translated from foreign currency into

U.S. dollars at the spot exchange rate on the last day of the service provider's taxable year. No adjustment is made to the total amount deferred to reflect the risk that the currency in which the amount payable or the value of the benefit is expressed may in the future increase or decrease in value with respect to the U.S. dollar or any other currency.

(ii) Actuarial assumptions and methods. (A) Requirement of reasonable actuarial assumptions and methods. For purposes of this section, the present value must be determined as of the last day of the service provider's taxable year using actuarial assumptions and methods that are reasonable as of that date, including an interest rate for purposes of discounting for present value that is reasonable as of that date.

(B) Use of an unreasonable actuarial assumption or method. If any actuarial assumption or method used to determine the total amount deferred for a taxable year under a plan is not reasonable, as determined by the Commissioner, then the total amount deferred is determined by the application of the AFR and, if applicable, the applicable mortality table under section 417(e)(3)(A)(ii)(I) (the 417(e) mortality table), both determined as of the last month of the taxable year for which the amount deferred is being determined. For purposes of this section, AFR means the appropriate applicable Federal rate (as defined pursuant to section 1274(d)) based on annual compounding, for the last month of the taxable year for which the amount includible in income is being determined. The period for which excess interest will be credited, beginning with the last day of the taxable year and ending with the date the excess interest will no longer be credited (determined in accordance with the payment timing assumptions set forth in paragraph (b)(2)(vi) and (vii) of this section) is used to determine the appropriate AFR (short-term, mid-term, or long-term).

(iii) Crediting of earnings and losses. The earnings and losses credited under a plan as of the last day of the service provider's taxable year pursuant to the plan are given effect only to the extent the plan's terms reasonably reflect the value of the service provider's rights under the plan. For example, a plan's method of determining the amount of such earnings or losses generally will be respected for purposes of determining the total amount deferred for the taxable year, provided that the earnings and losses are credited at least once per taxable year. If earnings and losses are not credited at least annually, the total amount deferred is calculated as if the earnings or losses were credited as of the last day of the taxable year. In addition, any change in the schedule for crediting earnings during the taxable year for which the total amount deferred is calculated that would reduce the earnings credited for a taxable year in which an amount is required to be included in income under section 409A(a) is disregarded for such taxable year. For example, if a plan is amended during a taxable year that is a calendar year to change the date for crediting earnings from December 31 to July 1 of that year and the plan fails to meet the requirements of section 409A(a) during that year, the amendment is disregarded for purposes of determining the total amount deferred for the year and December 31 is treated as the date for crediting earnings and losses. If no further changes are made to the plan with respect to the crediting of earnings and losses, for subsequent taxable years, July 1 is treated as the date for crediting earnings and losses.

(iv) Application of the general calculation rules to formula amounts. (A) In general. With respect to a right to a payment to which this paragraph applies, the amount payable for purposes of determining the total amount deferred for the taxable year must be determined based on all of the facts and circumstances existing as of the close of the last day of the taxable year. Such determination must reflect reasonable, good faith assumptions with respect to any contingencies as to the amount of the payment, both with respect to each contingency and with respect to all contingencies in the aggregate. An assumption based on the facts and circumstances as of the close of the last day of a taxable year may be reasonable even if the facts and circumstances change in a subsequent year so that if the amount payable were determined for such subsequent year, the amount payable would be a greater (or lesser) amount. In such a case, the increase (or decrease) due to the change in the facts and circumstances is treated as earnings (or losses). This paragraph (b)(2)(iv) applies to the extent that the amount payable in a future taxable year is a formula amount to the extent that the amount payable in a future taxable year is dependent upon factors that, after applying the assumptions and other rules set out in this section, are not determinable as of the end of the taxable year for which the total amount deferred is being calculated, so that the amount payable may not readily be determined as of the end of such taxable year under the other provisions of this section. If a portion of a deferred amount is determinable under the other rules of this paragraph (b)(2), the determination of the amount deferred with respect to such portion must be determined under the rules applicable to amounts that are not formula amounts, and only the balance of the deferred amount is determined under this paragraph.

(B) Examples. The following examples illustrate the provisions of this paragraph (b)(2)(iv):

*Example (1).* On January 1, 2020, a service provider receives a legally binding right to a payment of one percent of the service recipient's net profits for the calendar years 2020, 2021, and 2022, payable on the later of January 1, 2024 or the service provider's separation from service. The amount payable is a formula amount and this paragraph (b)(2)(iv) applies.

*Example (2).* On January 1, 2020, a service provider receives a legally binding right to a payment of the greater of one percent of the service recipient's net profits for the calendar years 2020, 2021, and 2022 or $10,000, payable on the later of January 1, 2024 or the service provider's separation from service. The portion of the amount payable that is a $10,000 payment, payable at the later of January 1, 2024 or the service provider's separation from service, is not a formula amount. The portion of the amount payable that is the excess, if any, of one percent of the service recipient's net profits for the calendar years 2020, 2021, and 2022 over $10,000 is a formula amount and this paragraph (b)(2)(iv) applies.

*Example (3).* On January 1, 2020, a service provider receives a legally binding right to payment equal to the value of 10,000 shares of service recipient stock, payable on the later of January 1, 2024 or the service provider's separation from service. Because the amount payable may increase or decrease only due to a change in value of a predetermined actual investment (10,000 shares of service recipient stock), the amount payable is not treated as a formula amount and this paragraph (b)(2)(iv) does not apply.

(v) Treatment of payment restrictions. Except as specifically provided, a restriction on the payment of all or part of a deferred amount that will or may lapse under the terms of the plan, including a risk of forfeiture that is not a substantial risk of forfeiture as defined in § 1.409A-1(d) or is disregarded under § 1.409A-4(a)(1)(ii)(B), is ignored for purposes of determining the total amount deferred under the plan. Accordingly, in calculating the total amount deferred, there is no reduction to account for a risk that the amount may be forfeited if the risk of forfeiture is not a substantial risk of forfeiture. For example, if an amount deferred is subject to forfeiture under a noncompetition provision applicable for a prescribed period, the forfeiture provision is disregarded for purposes of determining the total amount deferred for the taxable year.

(vi) Treatment of alternative times and forms of a future payment. (A) In general. For purposes of determining the total amount deferred for a taxable year, if payment of a deferred amount may be made at alternative times or in alternative forms, each amount deferred under the plan is treated as payable at the time and under the form of payment for which the present value is highest. A time and form of payment is available to the extent a deferred amount under the plan may be payable in such time and form of payment under the plan's terms. If the service recipient has commenced payment of a deferred amount in a time and form of payment under the plan, or the service provider or service recipient has elected a time and form of payment under the plan, and under the plan's terms neither party can change such time and form of payment without the consent of the other party (and such consent requirement has substantive significance), the time and form of payment elected or the time and form of payment in which payments have commenced is treated as the sole available time and form of payment for such amount. If an alternative time and form of payment is available only at the service recipient's discretion, the time and form of payment is not available unless the service provider has a legally binding right under the principles of § 1.409A-1(b)(1) to any additional value that would be generated by the service recipient's exercise of such discretion. For purposes of determining the value of each available time and form of payment, the assumptions and methods described in this paragraph (b)(2)(vi) are applied, and then the value of each available time and form of payment is determined in accordance with the other applicable rules provided in paragraph (b) of this section.

(B) Effect of status of service provider on available times and forms of payment. For purposes of determining whether a time and form of payment is available, if eligibility for a time and form of payment depends upon the service provider's status as of a future date, the service provider is assumed to continue in the service provider's status as of the last day of the taxable year. However, if the eligibility requirement is not bona fide and does not serve a bona fide business purpose, the eligibility requirement will be disregarded and the service provider will be treated as eligible for the alternative time and form of payment. For this purpose, an eligibility condition based upon the service provider's marital status (including status as a registered domestic partner or similar requirement), parental status, or status as a U.S. citizen or lawful permanent resident under section 7701(b)(6) is presumed to be bona fide and serve a bona fide business purpose. Notwithstanding the foregoing, if eligibility for a certain time or form of payment includes a bona fide requirement that the service provider provide additional services after the end of the taxable year, the time and form of payment is not treated as an available time and form of payment. The rules of this paragraph (b)(2)(vi)(B) apply regardless of whether the service provider's status changes during a subsequent taxable year.

(vii) Treatment of payment triggers based upon events. (A) In general. For purposes of determining the total amount deferred for a taxable year, if a payment trigger has occurred on or before the last day of the taxable year, a deferred amount payable upon such trigger is treated as payable at the time the payment is scheduled to be made under the terms of the plan. If the payment trigger has not occurred on or before the last day of the taxable year, the trigger is treated as occurring on the earliest possible date the trigger reasonably could occur based on the facts and circumstances as of the last day of the taxable year, and the deferred amount is treated as payable based upon the schedule of payments that would be triggered by such occurrence. Notwithstanding the foregoing, if the payment trigger requires a separation from service, a termination of employment, or other similar reduction or cessation of services, the service provider is treated as meeting such requirement as of the last day of the taxable year. For purposes of determining the earliest date the payment trigger reasonably could occur, whether the payment trigger actually occurs in a subsequent taxable year is disregarded. For purposes of this paragraph (b)(2)(vii), a payment trigger means an event (not including the mere passage of time) upon which an amount may become payable. Generally if an amount would be payable in a different time and form of payment depending upon some characteristic of an event, each type of event upon which an amount would become payable is treated as a separate payment trigger. For example, if an amount would be payable as a single sum payment if one subsidiary corporation of a service recipient that consists of multiple corporations is sold, but as an installment payment if another subsidiary corporation of the same service recipient is sold, then the sale of the one subsidiary corporation is treated as a separate payment trigger from the sale of the other subsidiary corporation.

(B) Certain payment triggers disregarded. The possibility that the following payment triggers will occur in the future is disregarded for purposes of determining the total amount deferred (but not for purposes of determining whether the plan otherwise complies with the requirements of section 409A(a)):

(1) A payment trigger that, if the trigger were the sole trigger determining when the amount would become payable, would cause the amount to be subject to a substantial risk of forfeiture, provided that if there is more than one payment trigger applicable to an amount that otherwise would be disregarded under this paragraph (b)(2)(vii)(B)(1), none of such payment triggers will be disregarded unless all such payment triggers, if applied in combination as the only payment triggers, would also cause the amount to be subject to a substantial risk of forfeiture.

(2) An unforeseeable emergency (as defined in § 1.409A-3(i)(3)).

(viii) Treatment of amounts that may qualify as short-term deferrals. For purposes of calculating the total amount deferred for a taxable year, the right to a payment that, under the terms of the arrangement and the facts and circumstances as of the last day of the taxable year, may be a short-term deferral as defined under § 1.409A-1(b)(4), is not included in the total amount deferred. In addition, even if such amount is not paid by the end of the applicable 2½ month period so that the amount is deferred compensation, the amount is not includible in the total amount deferred until the service provider's taxable year in which the applicable 2½ month period expires.

(ix) Examples. The following examples illustrate the provisions of paragraphs (b)(2)(vi) through (viii) of this section. For all of the examples, the service provider is an individual taxpayer who is an employee of the service recipient, the service provider has a calendar year taxable year, and the total amount deferred is being calculated for the taxable year ending December 31, 2010. In each case, the service provider is not entitled to earnings on the amount deferred. The examples read as follows:

*Example (1).* Employee D, who is employed by Employer Z, is entitled to commence receiving payments at age 65. The plan provides that Employee D will receive a single sum payment, except that, after Employee D attains age 62 but before Employee D attains age 64 (whether or not Employee D is then employed by Employer Z), Employee D can elect to receive payments as a single life annuity. Employee D is age 54 as of December 31, 2010. For purposes of determining the available times and forms of payment, Employee D is assumed to survive to age 62 and be eligible to elect a single life annuity. Accordingly, for purposes of determining the total amount deferred for 2010, the amount is treated as payable as either a single sum payment or a single life annuity, whichever is more valuable.

*Example (2).* Employee E is entitled to a single life annuity commencing on January 1, 2020 if Employee E is not married as of January 1, 2020. Employee E is entitled to either a single life annuity or a subsidized joint and survivor annuity commencing on January 1, 2020 if Employee E is married as of January 1, 2020. Employee E is not married as of December 31, 2010. For purposes of determining the total amount deferred for 2010, Employee E is assumed to remain unmarried indefinitely, so that the subsidized joint and survivor annuity is not an available form of payment. Accordingly, for purposes of determining the total amount deferred for 2010, the amount is treated as payable as a single life annuity commencing January 1, 2020.

*Example (3).* Employee F is entitled to a series of three payments of $1,000 due on January 1, 2020, January 1, 2021, and January 1, 2022. Under the plan's terms, Employer X has the discretion to accelerate one or more of the payments, provided that no payment may be made before January 1, 2020. Because there is no reduction in the amount payable if a payment is accelerated, an accelerated payment is more valuable than a payment made in accordance with the three-year schedule of payments. If Employee F does not have a legally binding right to a single sum payment on January 1, 2020 (or any other form of accelerated payment), then an accelerated payment is not an available time and form of payment and, for purposes of determining the total amount deferred for 2010, the amount is treated as payable as a series of three payments of $1,000 on January 1, 2020, January 1, 2021, and January 1, 2022.

*Example (4).* The facts are the same as in Example 3, except that Employer X has no discretion to accelerate one or more of the payments. Rather, Employee F has the right to accelerate one or more of the payments provided that a payment may not be paid at any date before the later of January 1, 2020 or the date 12 months after the date of such election. As of December 31, 2010, the earliest date upon which Employee F may elect to have a payment made is January 1, 2020. Because there is no reduction in the amount payable if a payment is accelerated, the earliest possible date of payment is the most valuable time and form of payment. Accordingly, for purposes of determining the total amount deferred for 2010, the amount is treated as payable as a single sum payment of $3,000 on January 1, 2020.

*Example (5).* Employee G is entitled to a single sum payment upon separation from service if Employee G separates from service before January 1, 2020 and a single life annuity if Employee G separates from service after December 31, 2019. As of December 31, 2010, Employee G has not separated from service. Under paragraph (b)(2)(vi)(A) of this section, the total amount deferred is determined based upon the amount that would be payable if Employee G separated from service on December 31, 2010. Accordingly, the single life annuity is not treated as an available time and form of payment, so that the amount is treated as payable as a single sum payment upon separation from service.

*Example (6).* Employee H is entitled to a single sum payment of deferred compensation upon the earlier of January 1, 2020 or an unforeseeable emergency. Because the payment upon an unforeseeable emergency is disregarded, for purposes of determining the total amount deferred, the deferred amount is treated as payable only on January 1, 2020.

*Example (7).* Employee I is entitled to a single sum payment of deferred compensation upon the earlier of January 1, 2020 or Employee I's involuntary separation from service. Under the facts and circumstances existing at the time the right to the payment was granted, if the deferred amount had been payable only upon Employee I's involuntary separation from service, the amount would have been subject to a substantial risk of forfeiture. Under paragraph (b)(2)(iv)(B) of this section, the right to a payment upon the Employee I's involuntary separation from service is disregarded, and the amount is treated as payable only on January 1, 2020.

*Example (8).* Employee J is entitled to a single sum payment of deferred compensation upon the earlier of January 1, 2020 or Employee J's separation from service. As of December 31, 2010, Employee J has not separated from service. Under paragraph (b)(2)(vi)(A) of this section, the total amount deferred is determined based upon the amount that would be payable if Employee J separated from service on December 31, 2010 and therefore had the right to receive the payment on December 31, 2010. The total amount deferred for 2010 is the greater of the amount that would be payable on December 31, 2010 or the present value of the amount that would be payable on January 1, 2020.

*Example (9).* Employee K is entitled to a single sum payment of deferred compensation upon the earlier of January 1, 2020 or the first day of the third month following Employee K's separation from service. As of December 31, 2010, Employee K has not separated from service. Under paragraph (b)(2)(vi)(A) of this section, the total amount deferred is determined based upon the amount that would be payable if Employee K separated from service on December 31, 2010, and therefore had a right to a payment on March 1, 2011. The total amount deferred for 2010 is the greater of the present value as of December 31, 2010 of the amount that would be payable on March 1, 2011 or the present value as of December 31, 2010 of the amount that would be payable on January 1, 2020.

*Example (10).* Employee L is entitled to a single sum payment of deferred compensation upon the earlier of January 1, 2020 or a separation from service that occurs on or before July 1, 2010. As of December 31, 2010, Employee L has not separated from service. For purposes of determining the total amount deferred, the right to be paid upon a separation from service on or before July 1, 2010 is ignored because it is no longer a possible payment trigger, and the amount is treated as payable only on January 1, 2020.

*Example (11).* Employee M is entitled to a single sum payment of deferred compensation upon the earliest of the date Employee M dies, Employee M attains age 65, or a child of Employee M becomes a full-time student at an accredited college or university (whether or not Employee M continues to be employed on such date). As of December 31, 2010, Employee M has a 10-year-old child who is in the fifth grade. For purposes of determining the total amount deferred, the earliest time that the payment reasonably could be due upon Employee M's child entering a college or university is August 1, 2018. Thus, the total amount deferred for 2010 is the more valuable of the amount that would be payable on the Employee M's 65th birthday and the amount that would be payable on August 1, 2018. Because any additional value that would be payable upon Employee M's death is a death benefit excluded from the definition of deferred compensation under section 409A(d)(1)(B) and § 1.409A-1(a)(5), that additional value, if any, is not required to be calculated.

*(3) Account balance plans.* (i) In general. For purposes of this section, if benefits are provided under a nonqualified deferred compensation plan that is described in § 1.409A-1(c)(2)(i)(A) or (B) (an account balance plan), the present value of the amount payable equals the amount credited to the service provider's account as of the last day of the taxable year, including both the principal amount credited to the account, and any earnings or losses attributable to the principal amounts credited to the account through the last day of the taxable year. For purposes of this section, earnings or losses means any increase or decrease in the amount credited to a service provider's account that is attributable to amounts previously credited to the service provider's account, regardless of whether the plan denominates that increase or decrease as earnings or losses. For rules related to the crediting of earnings, see paragraph (b)(2)(iii) of this section. For rules relating to earnings based on an unreasonable interest rate or a rate of return based on an investment other than a single predetermined actual investment or a single reasonable interest rate, see paragraph (b)(3)(ii) of this section.

(ii) Unreasonable rate of return. (A) Application. This paragraph (b)(3)(ii) applies to an account balance plan under which the amount of earnings or losses credited is not based on either a predetermined actual investment, within the meaning of § 31.3121(v)(2)-1(d)(2)(i)(B) of this chapter, or a rate of interest that is not higher than a reasonable rate of interest, within the meaning of § 31.3121(v)(2)-1(d)(2)(i)(C) of this chapter, as determined by the Commissioner.

(B) Unreasonably high interest rate. If the earnings or losses to be credited under a plan are based on an unreasonably high rate of interest, the amount deferred under the plan is equal to the present value as of the end of the taxable year (using a reasonable interest rate) of the amount that will be credited to the service recipient's account using the unreasonably high rate for the entire period for which the unreasonably high interest will be credited under the plan, beginning with the last day of such taxable year and ending with the date the unreasonably high interest will no longer be credited (determined in accordance with the payment timing assumptions set forth in paragraph (b)(2)(vi) and (vii) of this section). If the service recipient fails to use a reasonable interest rate to determine the amount includible in income, AFR will be used. For purposes of this section, AFR means the appropriate applicable Federal rate (as defined pursuant to section 1274(d)) based on annual compounding, for the last month of the taxable year for which the amount includible in income is being determined. The period described in the first sentence of this paragraph (b)(3)(ii)(B) is used to determine the appropriate AFR (short-term, mid-term, or long-term). For purposes of this paragraph (b)(3)(ii)(B), an unreasonably high interest rate includes a fixed interest rate that exceeds an interest rate that is reasonable, within the meaning of § 31.3121(v)(2)-1(d)(2)(i)(C) of this chapter.

(C) Other rates of return. If the amount of earnings or losses credited is based on a rate of return that is not an unreasonably high interest rate, within the meaning of paragraph (b)(3)(ii)(B) of this section, but is also not a predetermined actual investment, within the meaning of § 31.3121(v)(2)-1(d)(2)(i)(B) of this chapter or a rate of interest that is no more than a reasonable rate of interest, within the meaning of § 31.3121(v)(2)-1(d)(2)(i)(C) of this chapter , the amount payable is a formula amount.

*(4) Reimbursement and in-kind benefit arrangements.* For purposes of this section, if benefits for a service provider are provided under a nonqualified deferred compensation plan described in § 1.409A-1(c)(2)(i)(E) (a reimbursement arrangement), or under a nonqualified deferred compensation plan that would be described in § 1.409A-1(c)(2)(i)(E) except that the amounts, separately or in the aggregate, constitute a substantial portion of either the overall compensation earned by the service provider for performing services for the service recipient or the overall compensation received due to a separation from service, the arrangement is treated as providing for a formula amount to the extent that the expenses to be reimbursed are not explicitly identified to be a specific amount. Notwithstanding the foregoing, if the expenses eligible for reimbursement are limited, it is presumed that the limit reflects the reasonable amount of eligible expenses that the service provider will incur at the earliest possible date during the time period to which the limit applies, and for which the service provider will request reimbursement at the earliest possible date that the service provider may request reimbursement. This presumption may be rebutted only by demonstrating by clear and convincing evidence that it is unreasonable to assume that a service provider would incur such amount of expenses during the applicable time period. This presumption is not applicable to any reimbursement arrangement to which § 1.409A-3(i)(1)(iv)(B) applies (certain medical reimbursement arrangements). In addition, this paragraph (b)(4) also applies to an arrangement providing a service provider a right to in-kind benefits from the service recipient, or a payment by the service recipient directly to the person providing the goods or services to the service provider.

*(5) Split-dollar life insurance arrangements.* For purposes of this section, if benefits for a service provider are provided under a nonqualified deferred compensation plan described in § 1.409A-1(c)(2)(i)(F) (a split-dollar life insurance arrangement), the amount of the future payment to which the service provider is entitled is treated as the amount that would be includible in income under § 1.61-22 or § 1.7872-15 (as applicable) or, if those regulations are not applicable, the amount that would be includible in income under any other applicable guidance. For this purpose, the payment timing assumptions set forth in paragraph (b)(2)(vi) and (vii) of this section generally apply. However, in the case of an arrangement subject to § 1.7872-15, to the extent the assumptions set forth in paragraph (b)(2)(vi) and (vii) of this section conflict with the provisions of § 1.7872-15, the provisions of § 1.7872-15 apply, and the conflicting assumptions set forth in paragraph (b)(2)(vi) and (vii) of this section do not apply. In either case, for purposes of determining the total amount deferred under the plan for the taxable year, the benefits under the split-dollar life insurance arrangement are included only to the extent that the right to such benefits constitutes a right to deferred compensation under § 1.409A-1(b).

*(6) Stock rights.* If a stock right has not been exercised during the service recipient's taxable year, and remains outstanding as of the last day of the service provider's taxable year for which the total amount deferred is being calculated,

the total amount deferred under the stock right for such taxable year is the excess of the fair market value of the underlying stock on the last day of the service provider's taxable year (determined in accordance with § 1.409A-1(b)(5)(iv)) over the sum of the stock right's exercise price plus any amount paid for the stock right. If a stock right has been exercised during the service provider's taxable year, the payment amount for purposes of calculating the total amount deferred for the taxable year under the stock right is the excess of the fair market value of the underlying stock (as determined in accordance with § 1.409A-1(b)(5)(iv)) on the date of exercise over the sum of the exercise price of the stock right and any amount paid for the stock right.

*(7) Anti-abuse provision.* The Commissioner may disregard all or part of the rules of paragraphs (b)(2) through (b)(6) of this section or all or part of the plan's terms if the Commissioner determines based on all of the facts and circumstances that the plan terms have been established to eliminate or minimize the total amount deferred under the plan determined in accordance with the rules of paragraphs (b)(2) through (b)(6) of this section and if the rules of paragraphs (b)(2) through (b)(6) of this section were applied or such plan terms were given effect, the total amount deferred would not reasonably reflect the present value of the right. For example, if a plan provides that a deferred amount is payable upon a separation from service but also contains a provision that the amount will be forfeited upon a separation from service occurring on the last day of the service provider's taxable year (so that the application of paragraph (b)(2)(vii)(A) of this section treating the service provider as separating from service on the last day of the taxable year for purposes of determining the timing of the payment in calculating the total amount deferred would result in a zero amount deferred), the latter provision will be disregarded.

**(c) Additional 20 percent tax under section 409A(a)(1)(B)(i)(II).** With respect to an amount required to be included in income under section 409A(a) for a taxable year, the amount is subject to an additional income tax equal to 20 percent of the amount required to be included in income under section 409A(a).

**(d) Premium interest tax under section 409A(a)(1)(B)(i)(I).** *(1) In general.* With respect to an amount required to be included in income under section 409A(a) for a taxable year, the amount is subject to an additional income tax equal to the amount of interest at the underpayment rate plus one percentage point on the underpayments that would have occurred had the deferred compensation been includible in the service provider's gross income for the taxable year in which first deferred or, if later, the first taxable year in which such deferred compensation is not subject to a substantial risk of forfeiture. The amount required to be allocated to determine the additional tax described in this paragraph (d) is the amount required to be included in income under section 409A(a) for the taxable year, regardless of whether additional amounts were deferred under the plan in previous years.

*(2) Identification of taxable year deferred amount was first deferred or vested.* (i) Method of identification. The following method is applied for purposes of determining the taxable year or years in which an amount required to be included in income under section 409A(a) was first deferred and not subject to a substantial risk of forfeiture.

(A) For each taxable year preceding the taxable year for which the deferred amount is includible in income (the current taxable year) in which the service provider had an amount deferred under the plan that was not subject to a substantial risk of forfeiture (vested), ending with the later of the first taxable year in which the service provider had no vested amount deferred or the first taxable year beginning after December 31, 2004, calculate the vested total amount deferred for such year. For each year, include any deferred amount that was previously included in income under paragraph (a)(3) of this section but has not been paid, but exclude any amount paid to (or on behalf of) the service provider during such taxable year.

(B) Identify any payments made under the plan to (or on behalf of) the service provider for each taxable year identified in paragraph (d)(2)(i)(A) of this section.

(C) Identify any deemed net investment losses or other net decreases in the amount deferred (other than as a result of a payment) applicable to amounts that are vested for the current taxable year and each preceding taxable year identified in paragraph (d)(2)(i)(A) of this section.

(D) Starting with the first taxable year during which there was a payment identified under paragraph (d)(2)(i)(B) of this section or a loss identified under paragraph (d)(2)(i)(C) of this section (or both), subtract the total payments and loss for such taxable year from the amount determined under paragraph (d)(2)(i)(A) of this section for the earliest taxable year before such year in which there is such an amount, and from the amount determined under paragraph (d)(2)(i)(A) of this section for each subsequent taxable year ending before the taxable year in which the payment was made or the loss incurred. Do not reduce any taxable year-end balance below zero.

(E) Repeat this process for each subsequent taxable year during which there was a payment identified under paragraph (d)(2)(i)(B) of this section or a loss identified under paragraph (d)(2)(i)(C) of this section (or both).

(F) For each taxable year identified in paragraph (d)(2)(i)(A) of this section, determine the excess (if any) of the remaining amount deferred for the taxable year over the remaining amount deferred for the previous taxable year. Treat the amount deferred in taxable years beginning before January 1, 2005 as zero.

(G) Determine how much of the total amount deferred for the current taxable year was previously included in income in accordance with paragraph (a)(3) of this section.

(H) Subtract the amount determined in paragraph (d)(2)(i)(G) of this section from the excess amount determined in paragraph (d)(2)(i)(F) of this section for the earliest taxable year in which there is any such excess amount, but do not reduce the balance below zero. If the amount determined in paragraph (d)(2)(i)(G) of this section exceeds the amount determined in paragraph (d)(2)(i)(F) of this section for that earliest taxable year, subtract the excess from the amount determined in paragraph (d)(2)(i)(F) of this section for the next succeeding taxable year, but do not reduce the balance below zero. Repeat this process until the excess has been reduced to zero. The balance remaining with respect to each taxable year identified in paragraph (d)(2)(i)(A) of this section is the portion of the amount includible in income under section 409A(a) in the current taxable year that was first deferred and vested in that taxable year.

(ii) Examples. The following examples illustrate the provisions of paragraph (d)(2) of this section. In all of the following examples, the service provider is an individual taxpayer with a calendar year taxable year who elects to defer a portion of the bonus that would otherwise be payable to the service provider in each of Year 1 through Year 4. All amounts deferred are deferred under the same plan, and no amount deferred under the plan is ever subject to a substantial risk of forfeiture. The plan does not fail to meet the requirements of section 409A(a) in any year prior to Year 4, and no amounts deferred under the plan are otherwise includible in income until Year 4, except for payments actually made to the service provider. The service provider had no amount deferred under the plan prior to Year 1. The plan fails to meet the requirements of section 409A(a) in Year 4. The examples read as follows:

*Example (1).*

| | Year 1 | Year 2 | Year 3 | Year 4 |
|---|---|---|---|---|
| Opening Total Amount | 0 | 110 | 275 | 495 |
| Bonus Deferral | 100 | 150 | 200 | 250 |
| Net Gains (Losses) | 10 | 15 | 20 | 25 |
| Payments | 0 | 0 | 0 | 0 |
| Closing Total Amount | 110 | 275 | 495 | 770 |

(i) The amount required to be included in income under section 409A is 770. To calculate the premium interest tax, the 770 must be allocated to the year or years in which the amount was first deferred and vested.

(ii) Step A. Identification of vested total amount deferred excluding payments and including deferred amounts previously included in income.

| Year 1 | Year 2 | Year 3 |
|---|---|---|
| 110 | 275 | 495 |

(iii) Step B. Identification of any payments for each year other than Year 4.

| Year 1 | Year 2 | Year 3 |
|---|---|---|
| 0 | 0 | 0 |

(iv) Step C. Identification of any other decreases attributable to vested amounts.

| Year 1 | Year 2 | Year 3 | Year 4 |
|---|---|---|---|
| 0 | 0 | 0 | 0 |

(v) Steps D and E. Subtraction of payments and decreases from amounts deferred.

| Year 1 | Year 2 | Year 3 |
|---|---|---|
| 110 | 275 | 495 |
| -0 | -0 | -0 |
| 110 | 275 | 495 |

(vi) Step F. Subtraction of previous year total from each year's total.

| Year 1 | Year 2 | Year 3 |
|---|---|---|
| 110 | 275 | 495 |
| -0 | -110 | -275 |
| 110 | 165 | 220 |

(vii) Because no amount was previously included in income, Step G does not apply. Accordingly, the 770 is allocated such that 110 is treated as first deferred and vested in Year 1, 165 in Year 2, 220 in Year 3. The remainder (275) is treated as first deferred in Year 4, but is not required to be allocated for purposes of the premium interest tax because there is no hypothetical underpayment for such year.

*Example (2).*

| | Year 1 | Year 2 | Year 3 | Year 4 |
|---|---|---|---|---|
| Opening Total Amount | 0 | 110 | 235 | 365 |
| Bonus Deferral | 100 | 150 | 200 | 250 |
| Net Gains (Losses) | 10 | (25) | (30) | 25 |
| Payments | 0 | 0 | (40) | (50) |
| Closing Total Amount | 110 | 235 | 365 | 590 |

(i) The amount that is includible in income under section 409A(a) for Year 4 is the closing total amount (590), plus the amounts paid during Year 4 that were includible in income (50) or 640. To calculate the premium interest tax, the 640 must be allocated to the year or years in which the amount was first deferred and vested.

(ii) Step A. Identification of vested total amount deferred excluding payments and including deferred amounts previously included in income.

| Year 1 | Year 2 | Year 3 |
|---|---|---|
| 110 | 235 | 365 |

(iii) Step B. Identification of any payments for each year other than Year 4.

| Year 1 | Year 2 | Year 3 |
|---|---|---|
| 0 | 0 | (40) |

(iv) Step C. Identification of any other decreases attributable to vested amounts.

| Year 1 | Year 2 | Year 3 | Year 4 |
|---|---|---|---|
| 0 | (25) | (30) | 0 |

(v) Steps D and E. Subtraction of payments and decreases from amounts deferred.

| Year 1 | Year 2 | Year 3 |
|---|---|---|
| 110 | 235 | 365 |
| -25 (Year 2) | -40 (Year 3) | |
| -40 (Year 3) | -30 (Year 3) | |
| -30 (Year 3) | | |
| 15 | 165 | 365 |

(vi) Step F. Subtraction of previous year total from each year's total.

| Year 1 | Year 2 | Year 3 |
|---|---|---|
| 15 | 165 | 365 |
| -0 | -15 | -165 |
| 15 | 150 | 200 |

(vii) Because no amount was previously included in income, Step G does not apply. Accordingly, the 640 is allocated such that 15 is treated as first deferred and vested in Year 1, 150 in Year 2, and 200 in Year 3. The remaining amount includible in income under section 409A for Year 4 (275) is treated as first deferred in Year 4, but is not required to be allocated for purposes of the premium interest tax because there is no hypothetical underpayment for Year 4.

*Example (3).*

(i) The facts are the same as in Example 2 except 125 was previously included in income under paragraph (a)(3) of this section. Accordingly, of the 590 closing total amount for Year 4 plus the 50 payment during Year 4, or 640, only 515 (640 - 125) must be included in income under section 409A(a). To calculate the premium interest tax, the 125 must be allocated to the year or years in which such amount was first deferred.

(ii) Step G. Allocation of amounts previously included in income.

| Year 1 | Year 2 | Year 3 |
|---|---|---|
| 15 | 150 | 200 |
| -15 | -110 | -0 |
| 0 | 40 | 200 |

(iii) Accordingly, for purposes of calculating the premium interest tax, the 125 previously included in income is allocated so that of the 515 includible in income under section 409A(a), 0 is treated as first deferred and vested in Year 1, 40 in Year 2, and 200 in Year 3.

*(3) Calculation of hypothetical underpayment for the taxable year during which a deferred amount was first deferred and vested.* (i) Calculation method. The hypothetical underpayment for a taxable year is determined by treating as an additional cash payment of compensation to the service provider for such taxable year, the amount determined pursuant to paragraph (d)(2) of this section to be the portion of the amount includible in income under section 409A(a) that was first deferred and vested during such taxable year. The hypothetical underpayment is calculated based on the service provider's taxable income, credits, filing status, and other tax information for the year, based on the service provider's original return filed for such year, as adjusted by any examination for such year or any amended return the service provider filed for such year that was accepted by the Commissioner. The hypothetical underpayment must reflect the effect that such additional compensation would have had on the service provider's Federal income tax liability for such year, including the continued availability of any deductions taken, and the use of any carryovers such as carryover losses. For purposes of calculating a hypothetical underpayment in a subsequent year (whether or not a portion of the amount includible in income under section 409A(a) was first deferred and vested in the subsequent year), any changes to the service provider's Federal income tax liability for the subsequent year that would have occurred if the portion of the amount that was first deferred and vested during the previous taxable year had been included in the service provider's income for the previous year must be taken into account. Assumptions not based on the service provider's taxable income, credits, filing status, and other tax information for the year, based on the service provider's original return for such year, as adjusted by any examination for such year or any amended return the service provider filed for such year that was accepted by the Commissioner, may not be applied. For example, the service provider may not assume that some of the additional compensation would have been deferred under the terms of a qualified plan. If the service provider's Federal income tax liability for the taxable year in which an amount required to be included in income under section 409A(a) was first deferred and vested is adjusted (for example, by an amended return or IRS examination), and the adjustment affects the amount of the hypothetical underpayment, the service provider must recalculate the hypothetical underpayment and adjust the amount of premium interest tax due with respect to such inclusion in income under section 409A(a), as appropriate.

(ii) Examples. The following examples illustrate the provisions of paragraph (d)(3)(i) of this section. In all of the following examples, Employee N is an individual taxpayer with a calendar year taxable year. For the year 2020, Employee N has a total amount deferred of $100,000 which is includible in income under section 409A(a). For purposes of determining the premium interest tax, assume that $30,000 was first deferred and vested in 2018, $35,000 was first deferred and vested in 2019, and $35,000 was first deferred and vested in 2020. The first year that Employee N had a vested deferred amount under the plan was 2018. The examples read as follows:

*Example (1).* For the taxable years 2018 and 2019, Employee N has no carryover losses or other items a change in which could affect the adjusted gross income for a subsequent taxable year. Employee N determines the hypothetical underpayment for 2018 by assuming an additional cash compensation payment of $30,000 for 2018, and determining the hypothetical underpayment of Federal income tax that would result. Employee N determines the hypothetical underpayment for 2019 by assuming an additional cash compensation payment of $35,000 in 2019, and determining the hypothetical underpayment of Federal income tax for 2019 that would result. There is no hypothetical underpayment with respect to hypothetical income in 2020 because the tax payment would not have been due until 2021. Therefore, Employee N is not required to determine a hypothetical underpayment for 2020.

*Example (2).* The facts are the same as in Example 1, except that in 2018, Employee N had an excess charitable contribution the deduction of which was not permitted under section 170(b), and which was carried over to subsequent taxable years under section 170(d). For purposes of determining the hypothetical underpayment for 2018, Employee N uses the charitable contribution deduction that otherwise would have been available if the $30,000 compensation payment had actually been made. Employee N must then calculate the hypothetical underpayment for all subsequent years in a manner that eliminates the portion of any carryovers of excess contributions under section 170(d) related to the charitable contribution in 2018 that would not have been available in such subsequent years as a result of having been deducted in 2018.

*Example (3).* The facts are the same as in Example 2, except that in 2021 the IRS examines Employee N's 2018 return and determines that Employee N had $20,000 in unreported income for that year. In addition to paying the tax deficiency owed for 2018, Employee N must redetermine the hypothetical underpayment for 2018 and recalculate the premium interest tax owed for 2020.

*(4) Calculation of hypothetical premium underpayment interest.* (i) Calculation method. The amount of hypothetical premium underpayment interest is determined for any taxable year by applying the applicable rate of interest under section 6621 plus one percentage point to determine the underpayment interest under section 6601 that would be due for such underpayment as of the last day of the taxable year for which the amount deferred is includible in income under section 409A(a). The amount of additional income tax under paragraph (d)(2) of this section with respect to an amount required to be included in income under section 409A(a) is the sum of all of the hypothetical premium underpayment interest for all years in which there was determined a hypothetical underpayment.

(ii) Examples. The following examples illustrate the provisions of this paragraph (d)(4). In each of these examples, the service provider is an individual taxpayer with a calendar year taxable year. At all times the total amount deferred under the nonqualified deferred compensation plan is not subject to a substantial risk of forfeiture. The examples read as follows:

*Example (1).* Employee O has a total amount deferred under a nonqualified deferred compensation plan for 2010 of $100,000. The entire deferred amount was first deferred in 2006. For purposes of calculating the hypothetical premium underpayment interest tax, Employee O first must determine the hypothetical underpayment for taxable years 2006 through 2009 under the rules of paragraph (d)(3) of this section. Then Employee O must determine the underpayment interest under section 6601 that would have accrued, calculated using the applicable underpayment interest rate under section 6621 increased by one percentage point, applied through December 31, 2010. That amount is the premium interest tax that is due for 2010.

*Example (2).* Employee P has a total amount deferred under a nonqualified deferred compensation plan for 2010 of $100,000. $60,000 of that deferred amount was first deferred in 2006. $30,000 of that amount was first deferred in 2008. $10,000 of that amount was first deferred in 2010. For purposes of calculating the hypothetical premium underpayment interest tax, Employee P first must determine the hypothetical underpayment for taxable years 2006 through 2009 under the rules of paragraph (d)(3) of this section applying $60,000 of hypothetical additional compensation for 2006, and applying $30,000 of hypothetical additional compensation for 2008. The $10,000 of hypothetical additional compensation in 2010 would not result in a hypothetical underpayment because the Federal income tax applicable to that hypothetical additional compensation would not yet be due. Second, Employee P must determine the underpayment interest under section 6601 that would have accrued, calculated using the applicable underpayment interest rate under section 6621 increased by one percentage point, applied through December 31, 2010, for both the hypothetical underpayment occurring in 2006 and the hypothetical underpayment occurring in 2008. The sum of those two amounts is the premium interest tax that is due for 2010.

**(e) Amounts includible in income under section 409A(b) [Reserved].**

**(f) Application of amounts included in income under section 409A to payments of amounts deferred.** *(1) In general.* Section 409A(c) provides that any amount included in gross income under section 409A is not required to be included in gross income under any other provision of this chapter or any other rule of law later than the time provided in this section. An amount included in income under section 409A that has neither been paid in the taxable year the amount was included in income under section 409A nor served as the basis for a deduction under paragraph (g) of this section is allocated to the first payment of an amount deferred under the plan in any year subsequent to the year the amount was included in income under section 409A. To the extent the amount included in income under section 409A exceeds such payment, the excess is allocated to the next payment of an amount deferred under the plan. This process is repeated until the entire amount included in income under section 409A has been paid or the service provider has become entitled to a deduction under paragraph (g) of this section.

*(2) Application of the plan aggregation rules.* The plan aggregation rules of § 1.409A-1(c)(2) apply to the allocation of amounts previously included in income under section 409A to payments made under the plan. Accordingly, references to an amount deferred under a plan, or a payment of an amount deferred under a plan, refer to an amount deferred or a payment made under all arrangements in which a service provider participates that together are treated as a single plan under § 1.409A-1(c)(2).

*(3) Examples.* The following examples illustrate the provisions of this section. In each of these examples, the service provider is an individual taxpayer with a calendar year taxable year. Each service provider has a total amount deferred under a nonqualified deferred compensation plan of $0 for 2010, a total amount deferred under the plan of $100,000 for 2011, a total amount deferred under the plan of $250,000 for 2012, and a total amount deferred under the plan of $400,000 for 2013. At all times the total amount deferred under the plan is not subject to a substantial risk of forfeiture. During 2011, the plan fails to comply with section 409A(a) and each service provider includes $100,000 in income under section 409A. Except as otherwise provided in the following examples, the service provider does not receive any payments of amounts deferred under the plan. The examples read as follows:

*Example (1).* During 2012, Employee Q receives a $10,000 payment under the plan. During 2013, Employee Q receives a $150,000 payment under the plan. For 2012, $10,000 of the $100,000 included in income under section 409A(a) is allocated under paragraph (f)(1) of this section to the $10,000 payment, so that no amount is includible in gross income as a result of such payment and Employee Q retains $90,000 of amounts previously included in income under the plan to allocate to future plan payments. For 2013, the remaining $90,000 included in income under section 409A(a) is allocated to the $150,000 payment, so that only $60,000 is includible in income as a result of such payment.

*Example (2).* During 2012, Employee R receives a $10,000 payment under the plan. During 2014, Employee R receives a $50,000 payment, equaling the entire amount deferred under the plan. For 2012, $10,000 of the $100,000 previously included in income is allocated pursuant to paragraph (f)(1) of this section to the $10,000 payment, so that no amount is includible in gross income as a result of such payment. For 2014, $50,000 of the $90,000 remaining amount previously included in income is allocated pursuant to paragraph (f)(1) of this section to the $50,000 payment, so that no amount is includible in gross income as a result of such payment. Provided that the requirements of paragraph (g) of this section are otherwise met, Employee R is entitled to a deduction for 2014 equal to the remaining amount ($40,000) that was previously included in income under section 409A(a) that has not been allocated to a payment under the plan.

**(g) Forfeiture or other permanent loss of right to deferred compensation.** *(1) Availability of deduction to the service provider.* If a service provider has included a deferred amount in income under section 409A, but has not actually received payment of such deferred amount or otherwise allocated the amount included in income under paragraph (f) of this section, the service provider is entitled to a deduction for the taxable year in which the right to that amount of deferred compensation is permanently forfeited under the plan's terms or the right to the payment of the amount is otherwise permanently lost. The deduction to which the service provider is entitled equals the deferred amount included in income under section 409A in a previous year, less any portion of such deferred amount previously included in income under section 409A that was allocated under paragraph (f) of this section to amounts paid under the plan, including any deferred amount paid in the year the right to any remaining deferred compensation is permanently forfeited or otherwise lost. For this purpose, a mere diminution in the deferred amount under the plan due to deemed investment loss, actuarial reduction, or other decrease in the amount deferred is not treated as a permanent forfeiture or loss of the right if the service provider retains the right to an amount deferred under the plan (whether or not such right is subject to a substantial risk of forfeiture as defined in § 1.409A-1(d)). In addition, a deferred amount is not treated as permanently forfeited or otherwise lost if the obligation to make the payment of such deferred amount is substituted for another deferred amount or obligation to make a payment in a future year. However, a deferred amount is treated as permanently lost if the service provider's right to receive the payment of the deferred amount becomes wholly worthless during the taxable year. Whether the right to the payment of a deferred amount has become wholly worthless is determined based on all the facts and circumstances existing as of the last day of the relevant service provider taxable year.

*(2) Application of the plan aggregation rules.* For purposes of determining whether the right to a deferred amount is permanently forfeited or otherwise lost, the plan aggregation rules of § 1.409A-1(c) apply. Accordingly, if the right to an identified deferred amount under a plan is permanently forfeited or otherwise lost, but an additional amount remains deferred under the plan, the service provider is not entitled to a deduction.

*(3) Examples.* The following examples illustrate the provisions of this paragraph (g). In each example, the service provider is an individual taxpayer who has a calendar year taxable year and the service recipient does not experience bankruptcy at any time or otherwise discharge any obligation to make a payment of a deferred amount, except as expressly provided in the example. The examples read as follows:

*Example (1).* For 2010, Employee S has a total amount deferred under an elective account balance plan of $1,000,000. The plan fails to meet the requirements of section 409A(a) during 2010 and Employee S includes $1,000,000 in income under section 409A(a) for the year 2010. In 2011, Employee S experiences investment losses but no payments before July 1, 2011, such that Employee S's account balance under the plan is $500,000. On July 1, 2011, Employee S separates from service and receives a $500,000 payment equal to the entire amount deferred under the plan, and retains no other right to deferred compensation under the plan (including all arrangements aggregated with the arrangement under which the payment was made). For 2011, Employee S is entitled to deduct $500,000 (which is the amount Employee S previously included in income under section 409A(a) ($1,000,000) less the amount actually received by Employee S ($500,000)).

*Example (2).* For 2010, Employee T has a total amount deferred under an elective account balance plan of $1,000,000. The plan fails to meet the requirements of section 409A(a) for 2010 and Employee T includes $1,000,000 in income under section 409A(a) for 2010. For 2011, Employee T has a total amount deferred under the plan of $500,000, due solely to the deemed investment losses attributable to Employee T's account balance (with no payments being made during 2011). Because Employee T retains the right to an amount deferred under the plan, Employee T is not entitled to a deduction for 2011 as a result of the deemed investment losses.

*Example (3).* For 2010, Employee U has a total amount deferred under an elective account balance plan of $1,000,000. The elective account balance plan consists of one arrangement providing for salary deferrals with an amount deferred for 2010 of $600,000, and another arrangement providing for bonus deferrals with an amount deferred for 2010 of $400,000. The plan fails to meet the requirements of section 409A(a) during 2010 and Employee U includes $1,000,000 in income under section 409A(a) for 2010. On July 1, 2011, Employee U's account balance attributable to the salary deferral arrangement is $500,000, the reduction of which is due solely to deemed investment losses in 2011 and not any payments. On July 1, 2011, Employee U is paid the $500,000 equaling the entire account balance attributable to the salary deferral arrangement. On December 31, 2011, Employee U has an account balance attributable to the bonus deferral arrangement equal to $300,000. Because Employee U retains an amount deferred under the elective account balance plan, Employee U is not entitled to a deduction for 2011 as a result of the deemed investment losses.

**(h) Effective/applicability date.** The rules of this section apply to taxable years ending on or after the date of publication of the Treasury decision adopting these rules as final regulation in the Federal Register.

**§ 1.409A-5 Funding. [Reserved]**

---

T.D. 9321, 4/10/2007.

---

**§ 1.409A-6 Application of section 409A and effective dates.**

**(a) Statutory application and effective dates.** *(1) Application to amounts deferred.* (i) In general. Except as otherwise provided in this section, section 409A applies with respect to amounts deferred in taxable years beginning after December 31, 2004, and with respect to amounts deferred in taxable years beginning before January 1, 2005, if the plan under which the deferral is made is materially modified after October 3, 2004. For amounts deferred in taxable years beginning before January 1, 2005, under a plan that is materially modified after October 3, 2004, whether the plan complies with the requirements of section 409A and these regulations is determined by reference to the terms of the plan in effect as of, and any actions taken under the plan on or after, the date of the material modification. Section 409A is applicable with respect to earnings on amounts deferred only to the extent that section 409A is applicable with respect to the amounts deferred. Accordingly, section 409A does not apply with respect to earnings on amounts deferred before January 1, 2005, unless section 409A applies with respect to the amounts deferred. For this purpose, a right to earnings that is subject to a substantial risk of forfeiture (as defined in § 1.83-3(c)) or a requirement to perform further services, on an amount deferred that is not subject to a substantial risk of forfeiture (as defined in § 1.83-3(c)) or a requirement to perform further services, is not treated as earnings on the amount deferred, but a separate right to compensation. Except as otherwise provided in applicable guidance (see § 601.601(d)(2) of this chapter), the provisions of §§ 1.409A-1 through 1.409A-5 and this section provide the exclusive means of identifying agreements, methods, programs, or other arrangements subject to section 409A, and the exclusive means of satisfying the requirements of section 409A with respect to such agreements, methods, programs, or other arrangements.

(ii) Collectively bargained plans. Section 409A does not apply with respect to amounts deferred under a plan maintained pursuant to one or more bona fide collective bargaining agreements in effect on October 3, 2004, for the period ending on the earlier of the date on which the last of such collective bargaining agreements terminates (determined without regard to any extension thereof after October 3, 2004) or December 31, 2009.

*(2) Identification of date of deferral for statutory effective date purposes.* For purposes of determining whether section 409A is applicable with respect to an amount, the amount is considered deferred before January 1, 2005, if before January 1, 2005, the service provider had a legally binding right to be paid the amount, and the right to the amount was earned and vested. For purposes of this paragraph (a)(2), a right to an amount was earned and vested only if the amount was not subject to a substantial risk of forfeiture (as defined in § 1.83-3(c)) or a requirement to perform further services. Amounts to which the service provider did not have a legally binding right before January 1, 2005 (for example, because the service recipient retained discretion to reduce the amount), will not be considered deferred before January 1, 2005. In addition, amounts to which the service provider had a legally binding right before January 1, 2005, but the right to which was subject to a substantial risk of forfeiture or a requirement to perform further services after December 31, 2004, are not considered deferred before January 1, 2005, for purposes of the effective date. Notwithstanding the foregoing, an amount to which the service provider had a legally binding right before January 1, 2005, but for which the service provider was required to continue performing services to retain the right only through the completion of the payroll period (as defined in § 1.409A-1(b)(3)) that includes December 31, 2004, is not treated as subject to a requirement to perform further services (or a substantial risk of forfeiture) for purposes of the effective date. For purposes of this paragraph (a)(2), a stock option, stock appreciation right, or similar compensation that on or before December 31, 2004, was immediately exercisable for cash or substantially vested property (as defined in § 1.83-3(b)) is treated as earned and vested, regardless of whether the right would terminate if the service provider ceased providing services for the service recipient.

*(3) Calculation of amount of compensation deferred for statutory effective date purposes.* (i) Nonaccount balance plans. The amount of compensation deferred before January 1, 2005, under a nonqualified deferred compensation plan that is a nonaccount balance plan (as defined in § 1.409A-1(c)(2)(i)(C)), equals the present value of the amount to which the service provider would have been entitled under the plan if the service provider voluntarily terminated services without cause on December 31, 2004, and received a payment of the benefits available from the plan on the earliest possible date allowed under the plan to receive a payment of benefits following the termination of services, and received the benefits in the form with the maximum value.

Notwithstanding the foregoing, for any subsequent taxable year of the service provider, the grandfathered amount may increase to equal the present value of the benefit the service provider actually becomes entitled to, in the form and at the time actually paid, determined under the terms of the plan (including applicable limits under the Internal Revenue Code), as in effect on October 3, 2004, without regard to any further services rendered by the service provider after December 31, 2004, or any other events affecting the amount of or the entitlement to benefits (other than a participant election with respect to the time or form of an available benefit). For purposes of calculating the present value of a benefit under this paragraph (a)(3)(i), reasonable actuarial assumptions and methods must be used. Whether assumptions and methods are reasonable for this purpose is determined as of each date the benefit is valued for purposes of determining the grandfathered benefit, provided that any reasonable actuarial assumptions and methods that were used by the service recipient with respect to such benefit as of December 31, 2004, will continue to be treated as reasonable assumptions and methods for purposes of calculating the grandfathered benefit.

Actuarial assumptions and methods will be presumed reasonable if they are the same as those used to value benefits under a qualified plan sponsored by the service recipient the benefits under which are part of the benefit formula under, or otherwise impact the amount of benefits under, the nonaccount balance nonqualified deferred compensation plan.

(ii) Account balance plans. The amount of compensation deferred before January 1, 2005, under a nonqualified deferred compensation plan that is an account balance plan (as defined in § 1.409A-1(c)(2)(i)(A)), equals the portion of the service provider's account balance as of December 31, 2004, the right to which was earned and vested (as defined in paragraph (a)(2) of this section) as of December 31, 2004, plus any future contributions to the account, the right to which was earned and vested (as defined in paragraph (a)(2) of this section) as of December 31, 2004, to the extent such contributions are actually made.

(iii) Equity-based compensation plans. For purposes of determining the amounts deferred before January 1, 2005, under an equity-based compensation plan, the rules of paragraph (a)(3)(ii) of this section governing account balance plans are applied except that the account balance is deemed to be the amount of the payment available to the service provider on December 31, 2004 (or that would be available to the service provider if the right were immediately exercisable) the right to which is earned and vested (as defined in paragraph (a)(2) of this section) as of December 31, 2004. For this purpose, the payment available to the service provider excludes any exercise price or other amount that must be paid by the service provider.

(iv) Earnings. Earnings on amounts deferred under a plan before January 1, 2005, include only income (whether actual or notional) attributable to the amounts deferred under a plan as of December 31, 2004, or to such income. For example, notional interest earned under the plan on amounts deferred in an account balance plan as of December 31, 2004, generally will be treated as earnings on amounts deferred under the plan before January 1, 2005. Similarly, an increase in the amount of payment available pursuant to a stock option, stock appreciation right, or other equity-based compensation above the amount of payment available as of December 31, 2004, due to appreciation in the underlying stock after December 31, 2004, or accrual of other earnings such as dividends, is treated as earnings on the amount deferred. In the case of a nonaccount balance plan, earnings include the increase, due solely to the passage of time, in the present value of the future payments to which the service provider has obtained a legally binding right, the present value of which constituted the amounts deferred under the plan before January 1, 2005. Thus, for each year, there will be an increase (determined using the same interest rate used to determine the amounts deferred under the plan before January 1, 2005) resulting from the shortening of the discount period before the future payments are made, plus, if applicable, an increase in the present value resulting from the service provider's survivorship during the year. However, an increase in the potential benefits under a nonaccount balance plan due to, for example, an application of an increase in compensation after December 31, 2004, to a final average pay plan or subsequent eligibility for an early retirement subsidy, does not constitute earnings on the amounts deferred under the plan before January 1, 2005.

(v) Definition of plan. For purposes of paragraphs (a)(1), (2), and (3) of this section, the term "plan" has the meaning provided in § 1.409A-1(c), except that the plan aggregation rules do not apply for purposes of the actuarial assumptions and methods used in paragraph (a)(3)(i) of this section. Accordingly, different reasonable actuarial assumptions and methods may be used to calculate the amounts deferred by a service provider in two different agreements, methods, programs, or other arrangements each of which constitutes a nonaccount balance plan.

*(4) Material modifications.* (i) In general. Except as otherwise provided, a modification of a plan is a material modification if a benefit or right existing as of October 3, 2004, is materially enhanced or a new material benefit or right is added, and such material enhancement or addition affects amounts earned and vested before January 1, 2005. Such material benefit enhancement or addition is a material modification whether it occurs pursuant to an amendment or to the service recipient's exercise of discretion under the terms of the plan. For example, an amendment to a plan to add a provision that payments of deferred amounts earned and vested before January 1, 2005, may be allowed upon request if service providers are required to forfeit 20 percent of the amount of the payment (a haircut) would be a material modification to the plan. Similarly, a material modification would occur if a service recipient exercised discretion to accelerate vesting of a benefit under the plan to a date on or before December 31, 2004. However, it is not a material modification for a service recipient to exercise discretion over the time and manner of payment of a benefit to the extent such discretion is provided under the terms of the plan as of October 3, 2004. It is not a material modification for a service provider to exercise a right permitted under the plan as in effect on October 3, 2004. The amendment of a plan to bring the plan into compliance with the provisions of section 409A will not be treated as a material modification. However, a plan amendment or the exercise of discretion under the terms of the plan that materially enhances an existing benefit or right or adds a new material benefit or right will be considered a material modification even if the enhanced or added benefit would be permitted under section 409A. For example, the addition of a right to a payment upon an unforeseeable emergency of an amount earned and vested before January 1, 2005, would be considered a material modification. The reduction of an existing benefit is not a material modification. For example, the removal of a haircut provision generally would not constitute a material modification. The following modifications also are not material modifications for purposes of this paragraph (a)(4)(i):

(A) The establishment of or contributions to a trust or other arrangement from which benefits under the plan are to be paid is not a material modification of the plan, provided that the contribution to the trust or other arrangement would not otherwise cause an amount to be includible in the service provider's gross income.

(B) The modification of a provision requiring the immediate cancellation of a current deferral election, to require the cancellation of deferrals for the same length of time beginning with the first date at which the application of such cancellation would not violate section 409A (for example, the first date of the service provider's first taxable year following the cancellation).

(C) Compliance with a domestic relations order (as defined in § 1.409A-3(j)(4)(ii)) with respect to payments to an individual other than the service provider, or an amendment to a plan to require compliance with a domestic relations order with respect to payments to an individual other than the service provider.

(D) The modification of a plan providing a life annuity form of payment to permit an election between the existing life annuity form of payment and other forms of annuity payments that would be treated as a single form of payment with the existing life annuity form of payment under § 1.409A-2(b)(2)(ii).

(E) The modification of a grandfathered plan to add a limited cashout feature consistent with § 1.409A-3(j)(4)(v) (exception to prohibition on accelerated payments).

(ii) Adoptions of new plans. It is presumed that the adoption of a new plan or the grant of an additional benefit under an existing plan after October 3, 2004, and before January 1, 2005, constitutes a material modification of a plan. However, the presumption may be rebutted by demonstrating that the adoption of the plan or grant of the additional benefit was consistent with the service recipient's historical compensation practices. For example, the presumption that the grant of a discounted stock option on November 1, 2004, is a material modification of a plan may be rebutted by demonstrating that the grant was consistent with the historic practice of granting substantially similar discounted stock options (both as to terms and amounts) each November for a significant number of years. Notwithstanding paragraph (a)(4)(i) of this section and this paragraph (a)(4)(ii), the grant of an additional benefit under an existing plan that consists of a deferral of additional compensation not otherwise provided under the plan as of October 3, 2004, will be treated as a material modification of the plan only as to the additional deferral of compensation, if the plan explicitly identifies the additional deferral of compensation and provides that the additional deferral of compensation is subject to section 409A. Accordingly, amendments to conform a plan to the requirements of section 409A with respect to deferrals under a plan occurring after December 31, 2004, will not constitute a material modification of the plan with respect to amounts deferred that are earned and vested on or before December 31, 2004, provided that there is no concurrent material modification with respect to the amount of, or rights to, amounts deferred that were earned and vested on or before December 31, 2004. Similarly, a grant of an additional benefit under a new plan adopted after October 3, 2004, and before January 1, 2005, will not be treated as a material modification of an existing plan to the extent that the new plan explicitly identifies additional deferrals of compensation and provides that the additional deferrals of compensation are subject to section 409A.

(iii) Suspension or termination of a plan. A cessation of deferrals under, or termination of, a plan, pursuant to the provisions of such plan, is not a material modification. Amending a plan to provide participants an election whether to terminate participation in a plan generally constitutes a material modification of the plan.

(iv) Changes to investment measures—account balance plans. With respect to an account balance plan (as defined in § 1.409A-1(c)(2)(i)(A)), it is not a material modification to change a notional investment measure to, or to add to an existing investment measure, an investment measure that qualifies as a predetermined actual investment within the meaning of § 31.3121(v)(2)-1(d)(2) of this chapter or, for any given taxable year, reflects a reasonable rate of interest (determined in accordance with § 31.3121(v)(2)-1(d)(2)(i)(C) of this chapter).

(v) Stock rights. The modification, extension, or renewal of a stock right will not constitute a material modification of the stock right, if the modification, extension, or renewal would not be treated as the grant of a new stock right under § 1.409A-1(b)(5)(v)(A), and would not result in the stock right being treated as having had a deferral feature from the date of grant pursuant to § 1.409A-1(b)(5)(v)(C).

(vi) Rescission of modifications. Any modification to the terms of a plan that would inadvertently result in treatment as a material modification under this section is not considered a material modification of the plan to the extent the modification in the terms of the plan is rescinded by the earlier of a date before the right is exercised (if the change grants a discretionary right) or the last day of the taxable year of the service provider during which such change occurred. Thus, for example, if a service recipient modifies the terms of a plan on March 1 to allow an individual employee to elect a new change in the time or form of payment without realizing that such a change constituted a material modification that would subject the plan to the requirements of section 409A, and the modification is rescinded on November 1, then if no change in the time or form of payment has been made pursuant to the modification before November 1, the plan is not considered materially modified under this section.

(vii) Definition of plan. For purposes of this paragraph (a)(4), the term "plan" has the same meaning provided in § 1.409A-1(c), except that the plan aggregation rules of § 1.409A-1(c)(2) do not apply.

**(b) Regulatory applicability date.** § 1.409A-1, § 1.409A-2, § 1.409A-3 and this section are applicable for taxable years beginning on or after January 1, 2008.

T.D. 9321, 4/10/2007.

### § 1.410(a)-1 Minimum participation standards; general rules.

***Caution:*** The Treasury has not yet amended Reg § 1.410(a)-1 to reflect changes made by P.L. 104-188.

**(a) In general.** A plan is not a qualified plan (and a trust forming a part of such plan is not a qualified trust) unless the plan satisfies—

*(1)* The minimum age and service requirements of section 410(a)(1) and § 1.410(a)-3,

*(2)* The maximum age requirements of section 410(a)(2) and § 1.410(a)-4, and

*(3)* The minimum coverage requirements of section 410(b)(1) and § 1.410(b)-1.

**(b) Organization of regulations relating to minimum participation standards.** *(1) General rules.* This section prescribes general rules relating to the minimum participation standards provided by section 410.

*(2) Effective dates.* Section 1.410(a)-2 provides rules under section 1017 of the Employee Retirement Income Security Act of 1974 relating to effective dates under section 410.

*(3) Age and service conditions.* Section 1.410(a)-3 provides rules under section 410(a)(1) relating to minimum age and service conditions.

*(4) Maximum age and time of participation.* Section 1.410(a)-4 provides rules under section 410(a)(2) and (4) relating to maximum age and time of participation.

*(5) Year of service; breaks in service.* For rules relating to years of service and breaks in service, see 29 CFR Part 2530 (Department of Labor regulations relating to minimum standards for employee pension benefit plans). See § 1.410(a)-5 for rules under section 410(a)(3)(B) relating to seasonal industries and for certain rules under section 410(a)(5) relating to breaks in service.

*(6) Breaks in service.* Section 1.410(a)-6 provides special rules under section 1017(f) of the Employee Retirement Income Security Act of 1974 relating to amendment of break in service rules.

*(7) Elapsed time.* Section 1.410(a)-7 provides rules under sections 410 and 411 relating to the elapsed time method of crediting years of service.

*(8) Coverage.* Section 1.410(b)-1 provides rules relating to the minimum coverage requirements provided by section 410(b)(1).

*(9) Church election.* Section 1.410(d)-1 provides rules relating to the election by a church to have participation, vesting, funding, etc., provisions apply.

**(c) Application of participation standards to certain plans.** *(1) General rule.* Except as provided in subparagraph (2) of this paragraph, section 410 does not apply to—

(i) A governmental plan (within the meaning of section 414(d) and the regulations thereunder),

(ii) A church plan (within the meaning of section 414(e) and the regulations thereunder) which has not made the elections provided by section 410(d) and the regulations thereunder,

(iii) A plan which has not provided for employer contributions at any time after September 2, 1974, and

(iv) A plan established and maintained by a society, order, or association described in section 501(c)(8) or (9), if no part of the contributions to or under such plan are made by employers of participants in such plan.

*(2) Participation requirements.* A plan described in subparagraph (1) of this paragraph shall, for purposes of section 401(a), be treated as meeting the requirements of section 410 if such plan meets the coverage requirements resulting from the application of section 401(a)(3) as in effect on September 1, 1974. Such coverage requirements include the rules in § 1.410(b)-1(d) (special rules relating to minimum coverage requirements), that interpret statutory provisions substantially identical to section 401(a)(3) as in effect on September 1, 1974. In applying the rules of that paragraph (d) to plans described in this paragraph (c) employees whose principal duties consist in supervising the work of other employees shall be treated as officers, shareholders, and highly compensated employees.

**(d) Supersession.** Sections 11.410(a)-1 through 11.410(d)-1, inclusive, of the Temporary Income Tax Regulation under the Employee Retirement Income Security Act of 1974 are superseded by this section and §§ 1.410(a)-2 through 1.410(d)-1.

T.D. 7508, 9/14/77, amend T.D. 7703, 6/16/80, T.D. 7735, 11/10/80.

### § 1.410(a)-2 Effective dates.

**(a) Plans not in existence on January 1, 1974.** Under section 1017(a) of the Employee Retirement Income Security Act of 1974, in the case of a plan which was not in existence on January 1, 1974, section 410 and the regulations thereunder apply for plan years beginning after September 2, 1974. See paragraph (c) of this section for time plan is considered in existence.

**(b) Plans in existence on January 1, 1974.** Under section 1017(b) of the Employee Retirement Income Security Act of 1974, in the case of a plan which was in existence on January 1, 1974, section 410 and the regulations thereunder apply for plan years beginning after December 31, 1975. See paragraph (c) of this section for time plan is considered to be in existence.

**(c) Time of plan existence.** *(1) General rule.* For purposes of this section, a plan is considered to be in existence on a particular day if—

(i) The plan on or before that day was reduced to writing and adopted by the employer (including, in the case of a corporate employer, formal approval by the employer's board of directors and, if required, shareholders), even though no amounts had been contributed under the plan as of such day, and

(ii) The plan was not terminated on or before that day.

*(2) Collectively bargained plan.* Notwithstanding subparagraph (1) of this paragraph, a plan described in section 413(a), relating to a plan maintained pursuant to a collective bargaining agreement, is considered to be in existence on a particular day if—

(i) On or before that day there is a legally enforceable agreement to establish such a plan signed by the employer, and

(ii) The employer contributions to be made to the plan are set forth in the agreement.

*(3) Special rule.* If a plan is considered to be in existence on January 1, 1974, under subparagraph (1) of this paragraph, any other plan with which such existing plan is merged or consolidated shall also be considered to be in existence on such date.

**(d) Certain existing plans may elect new provisions.** *(1) In general.* The plan administrator (as defined in section 414(g)) of a plan that was in existence on January 1, 1974, may elect to have the provisions of the Code relating to participation, vesting, funding, and form of benefit (as in effect from time to time) apply to a plan year selected by the plan administrator which begins after September 2, 1974, but before the otherwise applicable effective dates determined under section 1017(b) or (c), 1021, or 1024 of the Employee Retirement Income Security Act of 1974, and to all subsequent plan years. The provisions referred to are the amendments to the Code made by sections 1011, 1012, 1013, 1015, 1016(a) (1) through (11) and (13) through (27), 1021, and 1022(b) of the Employee Retirement Income Security Act of 1974.

*(2) Election is irrevocable.* Any election made under this paragraph, once made, shall be irrevocable.

*(3) Procedure and time for making election.* An election under this paragraph shall be made by attaching a statement to either the annual return required under section 6058(a) (or an amended return) with respect to the plan which is filed for the first plan year for which the election is effective or to a written request for a determination letter relating to the qualification of the plan under section 401(a), 403(a), or 405(a) of the Code and, if trusteed, the exempt status under section 501(a) of the Code of a trust constituting a part of the plan. If the election is made with a written request for a determination letter, the election may be conditioned upon issuance of a favorable determination letter and will become irrevocable upon issuance of such letter. The statement shall indicate that the election is made under section 1017(d) of the Employee Retirement Income Security Act of 1974 and the first plan year for which the election is effective.

**(e) Examples.** The rules of this section are illustrated by the following examples:

*Example (1).* A plan is adopted on January 2, 1974, effective as of January 1, 1974. The plan is not considered to have been in existence on January 1, 1974.

*Example (2).* A plan was in existence on January 1, 1974, and was amended on November 1, 1974, to increase benefits. The fact that the plan was amended is not relevant and the amended plan is considered to be in existence on January 1, 1974.

*Example (3).* (i) A subsidiary business corporation is a member of a controlled group of corporations within the meaning of IRC section 1563(a). On November 1, 1974, the plan of the parent corporation is amended to provide coverage for employees of the subsidiary corporation. This amendment of the parent corporation's plan does not affect the effective date of section 410 with respect to the parent corporation's plan. No distinction is made for this purpose between employees of the parent corporation and employees of the subsidiary corporation.

(ii) If the subsidiary adopted a separate plan on November 1, 1974, under paragraph (a) of this section, section 410 would apply to that plan for its first plan year beginning after September 2, 1974. However, the adoption of a different plan by the subsidiary would not affect the time section 410 applies to the plan of the parent corporation. If, instead of adopting its own separate plan, the subsidiary merely executed an adoption agreement under the terms of the parent plan providing that a subsidiary, upon the execution of an adoption agreement, will become part of the parent plan, the effective date of section 410 with respect to such plan will not be affected by the adoption of the plan by the subsidiary.

T.D. 7508, 9/14/77.

### § 1.410(a)-3 Minimum age and service conditions.

***Caution:*** The Treasury has not yet amended Reg § 1.410(a)-3 to reflect changes made by P.L. 99-514, P.L. 98-397.

**(a) General rule.** Except as provided by paragraph (b) or (c) of this section, a plan is not a qualified plan (and a trust forming a part of such plan is not a qualified trust) if the plan requires, as a condition of participation in the plan, that an employee complete a period of service with the employer or employers maintaining the plan extending beyond the later of—

*(1) Age 25.* The date on which the employee attains the age of 25; or

*(2) One year of service.* The date on which the employee completes 1 year of service.

**(b) Special rule for plan with 3 year-100 percent vesting.** A plan which provides that after not more than 3 years of service each participant's right to his accrued benefit under the plan is completely nonforfeitable (within the meaning of section 411 and the regulations thereunder) at the time such benefit accrues satisfies the requirements of paragraph (a) of this section if the period of service required by the plan as a condition of participation does not extend beyond the later of—

*(1) Age 25.* The date on which the employee attains the age of 25; or

*(2) Three years of service.* The date on which the employee completes 3 years of service.

**(c) Special rule for employees of certain educational institutions.** A plan maintained exclusively for employees of an educational institution (as defined in section 170(b)(1)(A)(ii) by an employer exempt from tax under section 501(a) which provides that after 1 year of service each participant's right to his accrued benefit under the plan is completely nonforfeitable (within the meaning of section 411 and the regulations thereunder) at the time such benefit accrues satisfies the requirements of paragraph (a) of this section if the period of service required by the plan as a condition of participation does not extend beyond the later of—

*(1) Age 30.* The date on which the employee attains the age of 30; or

*(2) One year of service.* The date on which the employee completes 1 year of service.

**(d) Other conditions.** Section 410(a), § 1.410(a)-4, and this section relate solely to age and service conditions and do not preclude a plan from establishing conditions, other than conditions relating to age or service, which must be satisfied by plan participants. For example, such provisions would not preclude a qualified plan from requiring, as a condition of participation, that an employee be employed within a specified job classification. See section 410(b) and the regulations thereunder for rules with respect to coverage of employees under qualified plans.

**(e) Age and service requirements.** *(1) General rule.* For purposes of applying the rules of this section, plan provisions may be treated as imposing age or service requirements even though the provisions do not specifically refer to age or service. Plan provisions which have the effect of requiring an age or service requirement with the employer or employers maintaining the plan will be treated as if they imposed an age or service requirement. In general, a plan under which an employee cannot participate unless he retires will impose an age and service requirement. However, a plan may provide benefits which supplement benefits provided for employees covered under a pension plan, as defined in section 3(2) of the Employee Retirement Income Security Act of 1974, satisfying the requirements of section 410(a)(1) without violating the age and service rules.

*(2) Examples.* The rules of this paragraph are illustrated by the following examples:

*Example (1).* Corporation A is divided into two divisions. In order to work in division 2 an employee must first have been employed in division 1 for 5 years. A plan provision which required division 2 employment for participation will be treated as a service requirement because such a provision has the effect of requiring 5 years of service.

*Example (2).* Plan B requires as a condition of participation that each employee have had a driver's license for 15 years or more. This provision will be treated as an age requirement because such a provision has the effect of requiring an employee to attain a specified age.

*Example (3).* A plan which requires 1 year of service as a condition of participation also excludes a part-time or seasonal employee if his customary employment is for not more than 20 hours per week or 5 months in any plan year. The plan does not qualify because the provision could result in the exclusion by reason of a minimum service requirement of an employee who has completed a year of service. The plan would not qualify even though after excluding all such employees, the plan satisfied the coverage requirements of section 410(b).

*Example (4).* Employer A establishes a plan which covers employees after they retire and does not cover current employees unless they retire. Any employee who works past age 60 is treated as retired. The plan fails to satisfy the requirements of section 410(a) because the plan imposes a minimum age and service requirement in excess of that allowed by this section.

*Example (5).* Employer B establishes plan X, which provides that employees covered by qualified plan Y will receive benefits supplementing their benefits under plan Y to take into account cost of living increases after retirement. Plan X is not treated as imposing an age or service requirement.

*Example (6).* Employer C establishes a qualified plan satisfying the minimum age and service requirements. At a later time, entry into the plan is frozen so that employees not covered at that time cannot participate in the plan. The limitation on new participants is not treated as imposing a minimum age and service requirement.

T.D. 7508, 9/14/77.

### § 1.410(a)-3T Minimum age and service conditions (temporary).

**(a) [Reserved]**

**(b) Special rule for plan with 2-year 100 percent vesting.** A plan which provides that after not more than 2 years of service each participant's right to his or her accrued benefit under the plan is completely nonforfeitable (within the meaning of section 411 and the regulations thereunder) at the time such benefit accrues satisfies the requirements of paragraph (a) of this section if the period of service required by the plan as a condition of participation does not extend beyond the later of—

*(1) [Reserved]*

*(2) Two years of service.* The date on which the employee completes 2 years of service. For employees not described in § 1.411(a)-3T(e)(1), which describes employees with one hour of service in any plan year beginning after December 31, 1988, or later in the case of certain collectively bargained plans, the preceding sentence shall be applied by substituting "3 years of service" for "2 years of service".

T.D. 8170, 1/5/88.

### § 1.410(a)-4 Maximum age conditions and time of participation.

***Caution:*** The Treasury has not yet amended Reg § 1.410(a)-4 to reflect changes made by P.L. 99-509.

**(a) Maximum age conditions.** *(1) General rule.* A plan is not a qualified plan (and a trust forming a part of such plan is not a qualified trust) if the plan excludes from participation (on the basis of age) an employee who has attained an age specified by the plan unless—

(i) The plan is a defined benefit plan or a target benefit plan, and

(ii) The employee begins employment with the employer after the employee has attained an age specified by the plan, which age is not more than 5 years before normal retirement age (within the meaning of section 411(a)(8) and § 1.411(a)-7).

For purposes of this paragraph, a target benefit plan is a defined contribution plan under which the amount of employer contributions allocated to each participant is determined under a plan formula which does not allow employer discretion and on the basis of the amount necessary to provide a target benefit specified by the plan for such participant. Such target benefit must be the type of benefit which is provided by a defined benefit plan and the targeted benefit must not discriminate in favor of employees who are officers, shareholders, or highly compensated. For purposes of this paragraph, in the determination of the time an employee begins employment, any such time which is included in a period of service which may be disregarded under the break in service rules need not be taken into account.

*(2) Examples.* The rules provided by this paragraph are illustrated by the following examples:

*Example (1).* A defined benefit plan provides that an employee will become a participant upon completion of 3 years of service if at such time the employee is less than age 60. The normal retirement age under the plan is age 65. The plan also provides full and immediate vesting for each of the plan's participants. Under the plan, an employee hired at age 58 would be denied participation on account of service for the first 3 years and on account of maximum age for the remaining years even though the employee was hired more than 5 years prior to the normal retirement date. The plan therefore does not satisfy section 410(a)(2).

*Example (2).* A defined benefit plan provides a normal retirement age of the later of age 65 or completion of 10 years of service. Because no employee could ever be hired within 5 years of his normal retirement age, the plan could not exclude employees for being over a specified age.

*Example (3).* Prior to the effective date of section 410, a defined benefit plan with a normal retirement age of 65 contained a maximum age 55 requirement for participation. Because of the maximum age requirement, an employee hired at age 58 was excluded from the plan. This employee is age 61 at the time that section 410 first applies to the plan. The employee cannot be excluded from participation because of age. The exclusion under section 410(a)(2) is not applicable in this instance because the employee's age at the time of hire, 58, was not within 5 years of the normal retirement age specified in the plan.

*Example (4).* Employee A was hired at age 50 and participated in a defined benefit plan until separating from service at age 55 with 5 years of service and with no vested benefit. At age 61, employee A was rehired within 5 years of the normal retirement age of 65 after he incurred 6 consecutive breaks in service. Because A's consecutive number of 1-year breaks (6) exceeds his years of service prior to such breaks (5), his service before the breaks may be disregarded. Consequently A's initial employment date falling within such period may be disregarded and the plan could exclude A on account of his age because his employment commenced within 5 years of normal retirement age.

**(b) Time of participation.** *(1) General rule.* A plan is not a qualified plan (and a trust forming a part of such plan is not a qualified trust) unless under the plan any employee who has satisfied the applicable minimum age and service requirements specified in § 1.410(a)-3, and who is otherwise entitled to participate in the plan, commences participation in the plan no later than the earlier of—

(i) The first day of the first plan year beginning after the date on which such employee first satisfied such requirements, or

(ii) The date 6 months after the date on which he first satisfied such requirements,

unless such employee was separated from service and has not returned before the date referred to in subdivision (i) or (ii), whichever is applicable. If such separated employee returns to service after either of such dates without incurring a 1-year break in service, the employee must commence participation immediately upon his return. In the case of a plan using the elapsed time method described § 1-410(a)-7, such an employee who has a period of absence commencing before the date referred to in subdivision (i) or (ii) (whichever is applicable) must commence participation as of such applicable date no later than the date such absence ended. However, if an employee's prior service is disregarded on account of the plan's break-in-service rules then, for purposes of this subparagraph, such service is also disregarded for purposes of determining the date on which such employee first satisfied the minimum age and service requirements.

*(2) Examples.* The rules provided by this paragraph are illustrated by the following examples:

*Example (1).* A calendar year plan provides that an employee may enter the plan only on the first semi-annual entry date, January 1 or July 1, after he has satisfied the applicable minimum age and service requirements specified in section 410(a)(1). The plan satisfies the requirements of this paragraph because an employee is eligible to participate no later than the earlier of (1) the first day of the first plan year beginning after he satisfied the applicable minimum age and service requirements, or (2) the date 6 months after he satisfied such requirements.

*Example (2).* A plan provides that an employee is not eligible to participate until the first day of the first plan year beginning after he has satisfied the minimum age and service requirements of section 410(a)(1). In this case, an employee who satisfies the "6 month" rule described in subparagraph (1) of this paragraph will not be eligible to participate in the plan. Therefore, the plan does not satisfy the requirements of this paragraph.

*Example (3).* A calendar year plan provides that an employee may enter the plan only on the first semi-annual entry date, January 1 or July 1, after he has satisfied the applicable minimum age and service requirements specified in section 410(a)(1). Employee A after 10 years of service separated from service in 1976 with a vested benefit. On February 1, 1990, A returns to employment covered by the plan. Assuming A completes a year of service after his return, A must participate immediately on his return, February 1. A's prior service cannot be disregarded, because he had a vested benefit when he separated from service. Therefore, the plan may not postpone his participation until July 1.

*Example (4).* Assume the same facts as in example (3). The plan has the break-in-service rule described in section 410(a)(5)(D) and § 1.410(a)-5(c)(4). Employee B, after he had 5 years of service but no vested benefit incurs 5 consecutive 1-year breaks. Because B's prior service can be disregarded, the plan may postpone B's participation in the plan under the rule described in section 410(a)(4) and this paragraph.

T.D. 7508, 9/14/77, amend T.D. 7703, 6/16/80.

**Proposed § 1.410(a)-4A Maximum age conditions after 1987.** [*For Preamble, see ¶ 151,113*]

**(a) Maximum age conditions.** Under section 410(a)(2), a plan is not a qualified plan (and a trust forming a part of such plan is not a qualified trust) if the plan, either directly or indirectly, excludes any employee from participation on the basis of attaining a maximum age.

**(b) Effective date and transitional rule.** If a plan contains a provision that excludes an employee from participation on the basis of attaining a maximum age, the provision may not be applied in a plan year beginning on or after January 1, 1988, to any employee (regardless of when the employee first performed an hour of service for the employer) who is credited with at least 1 hour of service on or after January 1, 1988. For purposes of determining when such an employee (who is not otherwise ineligible to participate in the plan) must become eligible to participate in the plan under section 410(a)(1)(A)(ii), section 410(a)(1)(B) and the provisions of the plan, hours of service and years of service credited to the employee before the first plan year beginning on or after January 1, 1988, are taken into account in accordance with section 410 and the regulations thereunder and in accordance with 29 CFR Part 2530. Any employee who would be eligible to participate in the plan taking such service into account and whose entry date would be prior to the first day of the first plan year beginning on or after January 1, 1988, must participate in the plan as of the first day of such plan year.

**(c) Examples.** The provisions of this section may be illustrated by the following examples:

*Example (1).* Employer X maintains a defined benefit plan that uses a 12-month period beginning July 1 and ending June 30 as its plan year and that specifies a normal retirement age of 65. The plan provides that each employee of X is eligible to become a participant in the plan on the first entry date on or after the employee completes 1 year of service for X. The plan has 2 entry dates, July 1 and January 1. However, prior to the plan year beginning July 1, 1988, the plan contained a provision that excluded from participation any employee first hired within 5 years of attaining the plan's specified normal retirement age of 65. Employee A was hired by X on August 1, 1986 at age 62. A completes 1 year of service for X by August 1, 1987. If A performs at least one hour of service for X on or after January 1, 1988, the plan, in order to meet the requirements of section 410(a)(2), may not apply the maximum age provision to A on or after July 1, 1988, and A must be eligible to become a participant in the plan in accordance with the other eligibility rules contained in the plan, taking into account A's service with X performed prior to July 1, 1988 to the extent required under the terms of the plan or under section 410 and the regulations thereunder and under regulations in 29 CFR Part 2530. Accordingly, if A is still employed by X on July 1, 1988, A must become a participant in the plan on that date.

*Example (2).* Employer Y maintains a defined benefit plan that uses the calendar year as its plan year and that specifies a normal retirement age of 65. Employee B is first hired by Y in 1988 when B is age 66. In order for the plan to meet the requirements of section 410(a)(2), B may not be excluded from plan participation on the basis of B having attained a specified age.

**§ 1.410(a)-5 Year of service; break in service.**

***Caution:*** The Treasury has not yet amended Reg § 1.410(a)-5 to reflect changes made by P.L. 98-397.

**(a) Year of service.** For the rules relating to years of service under subparagraphs (A), (C), and (D) of section 410(a)(3), see regulations prescribed by the Secretary of Labor under 29 CFR Part 2530, relating to minimum standards for employee pension benefit plans.

Rules relating to a general rule for a year of service, hours of service, and maritime industries apply for purposes of section 410(a) and the regulations thereunder.

**(b) Seasonal industries.** For rules which relate to seasonal industries under section 410(a)(3)(B), see regulations prescribed by the Secretary of Labor under 29 CFR Part 2530, relating to minimum standards for employee pension benefit plans.

**(c) Breaks in service.** *(1) General rule.* This paragraph provides rules with respect to breaks in service under section 410(a)(5). Except as provided in subparagraphs (2), (3), (4), and (5) of this paragraph, all of an employee's years of service with the employer or employers maintaining a plan are taken into account in computing his period of service under the plan for purposes of section 410(a)(1) and § 1.410(a)-3.

*(2) Employees under 3-year 100 percent vesting schedule.* (i) General rule. In the case of an employee who incurs a 1-year break in service under a plan which provides that after not more than 3 years of service, each participant's right to his accrued benefit under the plan is completely nonforfeitable (within the meaning of section 411 and the regulations thereunder) at the time such benefit accrues, the employee's service before the break in service is not required to be taken into account after the break in service in determining the employee's years of service under section 410(a)(1) and § 1.410(a)-3 if such employee has not satisfied such service requirement.

(ii) Example. The rules of this subparagraph are illustrated by the following example:

*Example.* A qualified plan computing service by the actual counting of hours provides full and immediate vesting. The plan can not require as a condition of participation that an employee complete 3 consecutive years of service with the employer because the requirement as to consecutive years is not permitted under section 410(a)(5). However, such a plan can require 3 years without a break in service, i.e., 3 years with no intervening years in which the employee fails to complete more than 500 hours of service. Under a plan containing such a participation requirement, the following example illustrates when employees would become eligible to participate.

| Year | Hours of service completed | | |
|---|---|---|---|
| | Employee A | Employee B | Employee C |
| 1 | 1,000 | 1,000 | 1,000 |
| 2 | 1,000 | 1,000 | 500 |
| 3 | 1,000 | 700 | 1,000 |
| 4 | 1,000 | 1,000 | 700 |
| 5 | 1,000 | 1,000 | 1,000 |
| 6 | 1,000 | 1,000 | 1,000 |

**Note.**——Employee A will have satisfied the plan's service requirement at the end of year 3. Employee B at the end of year 4, and Employee C at the end of year 6.

*(3) One-year break in service.* (i) In general. In computing the period of service of an employee who has incurred a 1-year break in service, for purposes of section 410(a)(1) and § 1.410(a)-3, a plan may disregard the employee's service before the break until the employee completes a year of service after such break in service.

(ii) Examples. The rules provided by this subparagraph are illustrated by the following examples:

*Example (1).* Employee A completes a year of service under a plan computing service by the actual counting of hours for the 12-month period ending December 31, 1980, and incurs a 1-year break in service for the 12-month period ending December 31, 1981. The plan does not contain the provisions permitted by section 410(a)(5)(B) (relating to 3-year 100 percent vesting) and section 410(a)(5)(D) (relating to nonvested participants). Thereafter, he does not complete a year of service. As of January 1, 1982, in computing his period of service under the plan his service prior to December 31, 1981, is not required to be taken into account for purposes of section 410(a)(1) and § 1.410(a)-3.

*Example (2).* The employee in example (1) completes a year of service for the 12-month period ending December 31, 1982. Prior to December 31, 1982, in computing the employee's period of service as of any date occurring in 1982, the employee's service before December 31, 1981, is not required to be taken into account for purposes of section 410(a)(1) and § 11.410(a)-3. Because the employee completed a year of service for the 12-month period ending December 31, 1982, however, his period of service is redetermined as of January 1, 1982. Upon completion of a year of service for 1982, the employee's period of service, determined as of any date occurring in 1982, includes service prior to December 31, 1981.

*(4) Nonvested participants.* (i) General rule. In the case of a participant in a plan who does not have any nonforfeitable right under the plan to his employer-derived accrued benefit and who incurs a 1-year break in service, for purposes of section 410(a)(1) and § 1.410(a)-3 the plan may disregard his years of service prior to such break if the number of his consecutive 1-year breaks in service equals or exceeds his aggregate number of years of service prior to such break. In the case of a plan using the elapsed time method described in Department of Labor regulations, the plan may disregard such years of service prior to such break if the period of severance is at least 1 year and the period of severance equals or exceeds the prior period of service, whether or not consecutive, completed before such period of severance. The plan may in computing such aggregate numbers of years of service prior to such break disregard any years of service which could have been disregarded under this subparagraph by reasons of any prior break in service.

(ii) Examples. The rules of this subparagraph are illustrated by the following example:

*Example.* In 1980, A, who was hired at age 35, separates from the service of X Corporation after completing 4 years of service. At this time A had no vested benefits. In 1985, after incurring 5 consecutive one-year breaks in service, A was reemployed. Under section 410(a)(5)(D), A's 4 years of service may be disregarded because they are exceeded by the number of years of consecutive one-year breaks (5) after such service.

**(d) Special continuity rule for certain plans.** For special rules for computing years of service in the case of a plan maintained by more than one employer, see regulations prescribed by the Secretary of Labor under 29 CFR Part 2530, relating to minimum standards for employee pension benefit plans.

T.D. 7508, 9/14/77, amend T.D. 7703, 6/16/80.

### § 1.410(a)-6 Amendment of break in service rules; transition period.

**(a) In general.** Under section 1017(f)(1) of the Employee Retirement Income Security Act of 1974, a plan is not a qualified plan (and a trust forming a part of such plan is not a qualified trust) if the rules of the plan relating to breaks in service are amended, and—

*(1)* Such amendment is effective after January 1, 1974, and before the date on which section 410 becomes applicable to the plan, and

*(2)* Under such amendment, any employee's participation in the plan commences at any date later than the later of—

(i) The date on which his participation would commence under the break in service rules of section 410(a)(5), or

(ii) The earliest date on which his participation would commence under the plan as in effect on or after January 1, 1974.

**(b) Break in service rules.** For purposes of paragraph (a), the term "break in service rules" means the rules provided by a plan relating to circumstances under which a period of an employee's service or plan participation is disregarded for purposes of determining his rights to participate in the plan, if under such rules such service is disregarded by reason of the employee's failure to complete a required period of service within a specified period of time.

T.D. 7508, 9/14/77.

### § 1.410(a)-7 Elapsed time.

**(a) In general.** *(1) Introduction to elapsed time method of crediting service.* (i) 29 CFR § 2530.200b-2 sets forth the general method of crediting service for an employee. The general method is based upon the actual counting of hours of service during the applicable 12-consecutive-month computation period. The equivalencies set forth in 29 CFR § 2530.200b-3 are also methods for crediting hours of service during computation periods. Under the general method and the equivalencies an employee receives a year's credit (in units of years of service or years of participation) for a computation period during which the employee is credited with a specified number of hours of service. In general, an employee's statutory entitlement with respect to eligibility to participate, vesting and benefit accrual is determined by totalling the number of years' credit to which an employee is entitled.

(ii) Under the alternative method set forth in this section, by contrast, an employee's statutory entitlement with respect to eligibility to participate, vesting and benefit accrual is not based upon the actual completion of a specified number of hours of service during a 12-consecutive-month period. Instead, such entitlement is determined generally with reference to the total period of time which elapses while the employee is employed (i.e., while the employment relationship exists) with the employer or employers maintaining the plan. The alternative method set forth in this section is designed to enable a plan to lessen the administrative burdens associated with the maintenance of records of an employee's hours of service by permitting each employee to be credited with his or her total period of service with the employer or employers maintaining the plan, irrespective of the actual hours of service completed in any 12-consecutive-month period.

*(2) Overview of the operation of the elapsed time method.* (i) Under the elapsed time method of crediting service, a plan is generally required to take into account the period of time which elapses while the employee is employed (i.e., while the employment relationship exists) with the employer or employers maintaining the plan, regardless of the actual number of hours he or she completes during such period. Under this alternative method of crediting service, an employee's service is required to be taken into account for purposes of eligibility to participate and vesting as of the date he or she first performs an hour of service within the meaning of 29 CFR 2530.200b-2(a)(1) for the employer or employers maintaining the plan. Service is required to be taken into account for the period of time from the date the employee first performs such an hour of service until the date he or she severs from service with the employer or employers maintaining the plan.

(ii) The date the employee severs from service is the earlier of the date the employee quits, is discharged, retires or dies, or the first anniversary of the date the employee is absent from service for any other reason (e.g., disability, vacation, leave of absence, layoff, etc.). Thus, for example, if an employee quits, the severance from service date is the date the employee quits. On the other hand, if an employee is granted a leave of absence (and if no intervening event occurs), the severance from service date will occur one year after the date the employee was first absent on leave, and this one year of absence is required to be taken into account as service for the employer or employers maintaining the plan. Because the severance from service date occurs on the earlier of two possible dates (i.e., quit, discharge, retirement or death *or* the first anniversary of an absence from service for any other reason), a quit, discharge, retirement or death within the year after the beginning of an absence for any other reason results in an immediate severance from service. Thus, for example, if an employee dies at the end of a four-week absence resulting from illness, the severance from service date is the date of death, rather than the first anniversary date of the first day of absence for illness.

(iii) In addition, for purposes of eligibility to participate and vesting under the elapsed time method of crediting service, an employee who has severed from service by reason of a quit, discharge or retirement may be entitled to have a period of time of 12 months or less taken into account by the employer or employers maintaining the plan if the employee returns to service within a certain period of time and performs an hour of service within the meaning of 29 CFR 2530.200b-2(a)(1). In general, the period of time during which the employee must return to service begins on the date the employee severs from service as a result of a quit, discharge or retirement and ends on the first anniversary of such date. However, if the employee is absent for any other reason (e.g., layoff) and then quits, is discharged or retires, the period of time during which the employee may return and receive credit begins on the severance from service date and ends one year after the first day of absence (e.g., first day of layoff). As a result of the operation of these rules, a severance from service (e.g., a quit), or an absence (e.g., layoff) followed by a severance from service, never results in a period of time of more than one year being required to be taken into account after an employee severs from service or is absent from service.

(iv) For purposes of benefit accrual under the elapsed time method of crediting service, an employee is entitled to have his or her service taken into account from the date he or she begins to participate in the plan until the severance from service date. Periods of severance under any circumstances are not required to be taken into account. For example, a participant who is discharged on December 14, 1980 and rehired on October 14, 1981 is not required to be credited with the 10 month period of severance for benefit accrual purposes.

*(3) Overview of certain concepts relating to the elapsed time method.* (i) In general. The rules with respect to the elapsed time method of crediting service are based on certain concepts which are defined in paragraph (b) of this section. These concepts are applied in the substantive rules contained in paragraphs (c), (d), (e), (f) and (g) of this section. The purpose of this subparagraph is to summarize these concepts.

(ii) Employment commencement date. (A) A concept which is necessary in order to credit service accurately under any service crediting method is the establishment of a starting point for crediting service. The employment commencement date, which is the date on which an employee first performs an hour of service within the meaning of 29 CFR 2530.200b-2(a)(1) for the employer or employers maintaining the plan, is used to establish the date upon which an employee must begin to receive credit for certain purposes (e.g., eligibility to participate and vesting).

(B) In order to credit accurately an employee's total service with an employer or employers maintaining the plan, a plan also may provide for an "adjusted" employment commencement date (i.e., a recalculation of the employment commencement date to reflect noncreditable periods of severance) or a reemployment commencement date as defined in paragraph (b)(3) of this section. Fundamentally, all three concepts rely upon the performance of an hour of service to provide a starting point for crediting service. One purpose of these three concepts is to enable plans to satisfy the requirements of this section in a variety of ways.

(C) The fundamental rule with respect to these concepts is that any plan provision is permissible so long as it satisfies the minimum standards. Thus, for example, although the rules of this section provide that credit must begin on the employment commencement date, a plan is permitted to "adjust" the employment commencement date to reflect periods of time for which service is not required to be credited. Similarly, a plan may wish to credit service under the elapsed time method as discrete periods of service and provide for a reemployment commencement date. Certain plans may wish to provide for both concepts, although it is not a requirement of this section that plans so provide.

(iii) Severance from service date. Another fundamental concept of the elapsed time method of crediting service is the severance from service date, which is defined as the earlier of the date on which an employee quits, retires, is discharged or dies, or the first anniversary of the first date of absence for any other reason. One purpose of the severance from service date is to provide the endpoint for crediting service under the elapsed time method. As a general proposition, service is credited from the employment commencement date (i.e., the starting point) until the severance from service date (i.e., the endpoint). A complementary purpose of the severance from service date is to establish the starting point for measuring a period of severance from service in order to determine a "break in service" (see paragraph (a)(3)(v) of this section). A third purpose of such date is to establish the starting point for measuring the period of time which may be required to be taken into account under the service spanning rules (see paragraph (a)(3)(vi) of this section).

(iv) Period of service. A third elapsed time concept is the use of the "period of service" rather than the "year of service" in determining service to be taken into account for purposes of eligibility to participate, vesting and benefit accrual. For purposes of eligibility to participate and vesting, the period of service runs from the employment commencement date or reemployment commencement date until the severance from service date. For purposes of benefit accrual, a period of service runs from the date that a participant commences participation under the plan until the severance from service date. Because the endpoint of the period of service is marked by the severance from service date, an employee is credited with the period of time which runs during any absence from service (other than for reason of a quit, retirement, discharge or death) which is 12 months or less. Thus, for example, a three week absence for vacation is taken into account as part of a period of service and does not trigger a severance from service date.

(v) Period of severance. A period of severance begins on the severance from service date and ends when an employee returns to service with the employer or employers maintaining the plan. The purpose of the period of severance is to apply the statutory "break in service" rules to an elapsed time method of crediting service.

(vi) Service spanning. Under the elapsed time method of crediting service, a plan is required to credit periods of service and, under the service spanning rules, certain periods of severance of 12 months or less for purposes of eligibility to participate and vesting. Under the first service spanning rule, if an employee severs from service as a result of quit, discharge or retirement and then returns to service within 12 months, the period of severance is required to be taken into account. Also, a situation may arise in which an employee is absent from service for any reason other than quit, discharge, retirement or death and during the absence a quit, discharge or retirement occurs. The second service spanning rule provides in that set of circumstances that a plan is required to take into account the period of time between the severance from service date (i.e., the date of quit, discharge or retirement) and the first anniversary of the date on which the employee was first absent, if the employee returns to service on or before such first anniversary date.

*(4) Organization and applicability.* (i) The substantive rules for crediting service under the elapsed time method with respect to eligibility to participate are contained in paragraph (c), the rules with respect to vesting are contained in subparagraph (d), and the rules with respect to benefit accrual are contained in paragraph (e). The format of the rules is designed to enable a plan to use the elapsed time method of crediting service either for all purposes or for any one or combination of purposes under sections 410 and 411. Thus, for example, a plan may credit service for eligibility to participate purposes by the use of the general method of crediting service set forth in 29 CFR 2530.200b-2 or by the use of any of the equivalences set forth in 29 CFR 2530.200b-3, while the plan may credit service for vesting and benefit accrual purposes by the use of the elapsed time method of crediting service.

(ii) A plan using the elapsed time method of crediting service for one or more classifications of employees covered under the plan may use the general method of crediting service set forth in 29 CFR 2530.200b-2 or any of the equivalencies set forth in 29 CFR 2530.200b-3 for other classifications of employees, provided that such classifications are reasonable and are consistently applied. Thus, for example, a plan may provide that part-time employees are credited under the general method of crediting service set forth in 29 CFR 2530.200b-2 and full-time employees are credited under the elapsed time method. A classification, however, will not be deemed to be reasonable or consistently applied if such classification is designed with an intent to preclude an employee or employees from attaining his or her statutory entitlement with respect to eligibility to participate, vesting or benefit accrual. For example, a classification applied so that any full-time employee credited with less than 1,000 hours of service during a given 12-consecutive-month period would be considered part-time and subject to the general method of crediting service rather than the elapsed time method would not be reasonable.

(iii) Notwithstanding paragraph (a)(4)(i) and (ii) of this section, the use of the elapsed time method for some purposes or the use of the elapsed time method for some employees may, under certain circumstances, result in discrimination prohibited under section 401(a)(4), even though the use of the elapsed time method for such purposes, and for such employees, is permitted under this section.

*(5) More than one employer plans.* For special rules for computing years of service in the case of a plan maintained by more than one employer, see 29 CFR Part 2530 (Department of Labor regulations relating to minimum standards for employee pension benefit plans).

**(b) Definitions.** *(1) Employment commencement date.* For purposes of this section, the term "employment commencement date" shall mean the date on which the employee first performs an hour of service within the meaning of 29 CFR 2530.200b-2(a)(1) for the employer or employers maintaining the plan.

*(2) Severance from service date.* For purposes of this section, a "severance from service" shall occur on the earlier of—

(i) The date on which an employee quits, retires, is discharged or dies; or

(ii) The first anniversary of the first date of a period in which an employee remains absent from service (with or without pay) with the employer or employers maintaining the plan for any reason other than quit, retirement, discharge or death, such as vacation, holiday, sickness, disability, leave of absence or layoff.

*(3) Reemployment commencement date.* For purposes of this section, the term "reemployment commencement date" shall mean the first date, following a period of severance from service which is not required to be taken into account under the service spanning rules in paragraphs (c)(2)(iii) and (d)(1)(iii) of this section, on which the employee performs an hour of service within the meaning of 29 CFR 2530.200b-2(a)(1) for the employer or employers maintaining the plan.

*(4) Participation commencement date.* For purposes of this section, the term "participation commencement date" shall mean the date a participant first commences participation under the plan.

*(5) Period of severance.* For purposes of this section, the term "period of severance" shall mean the period of time commencing on the severance from service date and ending on the date on which the employee again performs an hour of service within the meaning of 29 CFR 2530.200b-2(a)(1) for an employer or employers maintaining the plan.

*(6) Period of service.* (i) General rule. For purposes of this section, the term "period of service" shall mean a period of service commencing on the employee's employment com-

mencement date or reemployment commencement date, whichever is applicable, and ending on the severance from service date.

(ii) Aggregation rule. Unless a plan provides in some manner for an "adjusted" employment commencement date or similar method of consolidating periods of service, periods of service shall be aggregated unless such periods may be disregarded under section 410(a)(5) or 411(a)(4).

(iii) Other federal law. Nothing in this section shall be construed to alter, amend, modify, invalidate, impair or supersede any law of the United States or any rule or regulation issued under such law. Thus, for example, nothing in this section shall be construed as denying an employee credit for a "period of service" if credit is required by a separate federal law. Furthermore, the nature and extent of such credit shall be determined under such law.

**(c) Eligibility to participate.** *(1) General rule.* For purposes of section 410(a)(1)(A), a plan generally may not require as a condition of participation in the plan that an employee complete a period of service with the employer or employers maintaining the plan extending beyond the later of—

(i) The date on which the employee attains the age of 25; or

(ii) The date on which the employee completes a one-year period of service.

See the regulations under section 410(a) (relating to eligibility to participate).

*(2) Determination of one-year period of service.* (i) For purposes of determining the date on which an employee satisfies the service requirement for initial eligibility to participate under the plan, a plan using the elapsed time method of crediting service shall provide that an employee who completes the 1-year period of service requirement on the first anniversary of his employment commencement date satisfies the minimum service requirement as of such date. In the case of an employee who fails to complete a one-year period of service on the first anniversary of his employment commencement date, a plan which does not contain a provision permitted by section 410(a)(5)(D) (rule of parity) shall provide for the aggregation of periods of service so that a one-year period of service shall be completed as of the date the employee completes 12 months of service (30 days are deemed to be a month in the case of the aggregation of fractional months) or 365 days of service.

(ii) For purposes of section 410(a)(1)(B)(i), a "3-year period of service" shall be deemed to be "3 years of service."

(iii) Service spanning rules. In determining a 1-year period of service for purposes of initial eligibility to participate and a period of service for purposes of retention of eligibility to participate, in addition to taking into account an employee's period of service, a plan shall take into account the following periods of severance—

(A) If an employee severs from service by reason of a quit, discharge or retirement and the employee then performs an hour of service within the meaning of 29 CFR 2530.200b-2(a)(1) within 12 months of the severance from service date, the plan is required to take into account the period of severance; and

(B) Notwithstanding paragraph (c)(2)(iii)(A) of this section, if an employee severs from service by reason of a quit, discharge or retirement during an absence from service of 12 months or less for any reason other than a quit, discharge, retirement or death, and then performs an hour of service within the meaning of 29 CFR 2530.200b-2(a)(1) within 12 months of the date on which the employee was first absent from service, the plan is required to take into account the period of severance.

(iv) For purposes of determining an employee's retention of eligibility to participate in the plan, a plan shall take into account an employee's entire period of service unless certain periods of service may be disregarded under section 410(a)(5) of the Code.

(v) Example. Employee W, age 31, completed 6 months of service and was laid off. After 2 months of layoff, W quit. Five months later, W returned to service. For purposes of eligibility to participate, W was required to be credited with 13 months of service (8 months of service and 5 months of severance). If, on the other hand, W had not returned to service within the first 10 months of severance (i.e., within 12 months after the first day of layoff), W would be required to be credited with only 8 months of service.

*(3) Entry date requirements.* (i) General rule. For purposes of section 410(a)(4), it is necessary for a plan to provide that any employee who has satisfied the minimum age and service requirements, and who is otherwise entitled to participate in the plan, commences participation in the plan no later than the earlier of—

(A) The first day of the first plan year beginning after the date on which such employee satisfied such requirements, or

(B) The date six months after the date on which he satisfied such requirements, unless such employee was separated from service before the date referred to in subdivision (i)(A) or (B), whichever is applicable. See the regulations under section 410(a) (relating to eligibility to participate).

(ii) Separation from service. (A) Definition. For purposes of this section, the term "separated from service" includes a severance from service or an absence from service for any reason other than a quit, discharge, retirement or death, regardless of the duration of such absence. Accordingly, if an employee is laid off for a period of six weeks, the employee shall be deemed to be "separated from service" during such period for purposes of the entry date requirements.

(B) Application. A period of severance which is taken into account under the service spanning rules in paragraph (c)(2)(iii) of this section or an absence of 12 months or less may result in an employee satisfying the plan's minimum service requirement during such period of time. In addition, once an employee satisfies the plan's minimum service requirement, either before or during such period of time, such period of time may contain an entry date applicable to such employee. In the case of an employee whose period of severance is taken into account and such period contains an entry date applicable to the employee, he or she shall be made a participant in the plan (if otherwise eligible) no later than the date on which he or she ended the period of severance. In the case of an employee whose period of absence contains an entry date applicable to such employee, he or she, no later than the date such absence ended, shall be made a participant in the plan (if otherwise eligible) as of the first applicable entry date which occurred during such absence from service.

(iii) Examples. For purposes of the following examples, assume that the plan provides for a minimum age requirement of 25 and a minimum service requirement of one year, and provides for semi-annual entry dates.

(A) Employee A, age 35, worked for 10 months in a job classification covered under the plan, became disabled for nine consecutive months and then returned to service. During the period of absence, A completed a 1-year period of service and passed a semi-annual entry date after satisfying the minimum service requirement. Accordingly, the plan is required to make A a participant no later than his return to service effective as of the applicable entry date.

(B) Employee B, after satisfying the minimum age and service requirements, quit work before the next semi-annual entry date, and then returned to service before incurring a 1-year period of severance, but after such semi-annual entry date. Employee B is entitled to become a participant immediately upon his return to service effective as of the date of his return.

*(4) Break in service.* For purposes of applying the break in service rules under section 410(a)(5)(B) and (C), the term "1-year period of severance" shall be substituted for the term "1-year break in service". A 1-year period of severance shall be determined on the basis of a 12-consecutive-month period beginning on the severance from service date and ending on the first anniversary of such date, provided that the employee during such 12-consecutive-month period does not perform an hour of service within the meaning of 29 CFR 2530.200b-2(a)(1) for the employer or employers maintaining the plan.

*(5) One-year hold-out.* (i) General rule. (A) For purposes of section 410(a)(5)(C), in determining the period of service of an employee who has incurred a 1-year period of severance, a plan may disregard the employee's period of service before such period of severance until the employee completes a 1-year period of service after such period of severance.

(B) Example. Assume that a plan provides for a minimum service requirement of 1-year and provides for semi-annual entry dates, but does not contain the provisions permitted by section 410(a)(5)(D) (relating to the rule of parity). Employee G, age 40, completed a seven-month period of service, quit and then returned to service 15 months later, thereby incurring a 1-year period of severance. After working four months, G was laid off for nine months and then returned to work again. Although the plan may hold employee G out from participation in the plan until the completion of a 1-year period of service after the 1-year (or greater) period of severance, once the 1-year hold-out is completed, the plan is required to provide the employee with such statutory entitlement as arose during the 1-year hold-out. Accordingly, employee G satisfied the 1-year hold-out requirement as of the eighth month of layoff, and G is entitled to become a participant in the plan immediately upon his return to service after the nine-month layoff effective as of the first applicable entry date occurring after the date on which he satisfied the 1-year of service requirement (i.e., the first applicable entry date after the first month of layoff). See the regulations under section 410(a) (relating to eligibility to participate).

*(6) Rule of parity.* (i) General rule. For purposes of section 410(a)(5)(D), in the case of a participant who does not have any nonforfeitable right under the plan to his accrued benefit derived from employer contributions and who incurs a 1-year period of severance, a plan, in determining an employee's period of service for purposes of section 410(a)(1), may disregard his period of service if his latest period of severance equals or exceeds his prior periods of service, whether or not consecutive, completed before such period of severance. See the regulations under section 410(a) (relating to eligibility to participate).

(ii) In determining whether a completely nonvested employee's service may be disregarded under the rule of parity, a plan is not permitted to apply the rule until the employee incurs a 1-year period of severance. Accordingly, a plan may not disregard a period of service of less than one year until an employee has incurred a period of severance of at least one year.

(iii) Example. Assume that a plan provides for a minimum service requirement of one year and provides for the rule of parity. An employee works for three months, quits and then is rehired 10 months later. Such employee is entitled to receive 13 months of credit for purposes of eligibility to participate and vesting (see the service spanning rules). Although the period of severance exceeded the period of service, the three months of service may not be disregarded because no 1-year period of severance occurred.

**(d) Vesting.** *(1) General rule.* (i) For purposes of section 411(a)(2), relating to vesting in accrued benefits derived from employer contributions, a plan which determines service to be taken in account on the basis of elapsed time shall provide that an employee is credited with a number of years of service equal to at least the number of whole years of the employee's period of service, whether or not such periods of service were completed consecutively.

(ii) In order to determine the number of whole years of an employee's period of service, a plan shall provide that nonsuccessive periods of service must be aggregated and that less than whole year periods of service (whether or not consecutive) must be aggregated on the basis that 12 months of service (30 days are deemed to be a month in the case of the aggregation of fractional months) or 365 days of service equal a whole year of service.

(iii) Service spanning rules. In determining a participant's period of service for vesting purposes, a plan shall take into account the following periods of severance—

(A) If an employee severs from service by reason of a quit, discharge or retirement and the employee then performs an hour of service within the meaning of 29 CFR 2530.200b-2(a)(1) within 12 months of the severance from service date, the plan is required to take into account the period of severance; and

(B) Notwithstanding paragraph (d)(1)(iii)(A) of this section, if an employee severs from service by reason of a quit, discharge or retirement during an absence from service of 12 months or less for any reason other than a quit, discharge, retirement or death, and then performs an hour of service within the meaning of 29 CFR 2530.200b-2(a)(1) within 12 months of the date on which the employee was first absent from service, the plan is required to take into account the period of severance.

(iv) For purposes of determining an employee's nonforfeitable percentage of accrued benefits derived from employer contributions, a plan, after calculating an employee's period of service in the manner prescribed in this paragraph, may disregard any remaining less than whole year, 12-month or 365-day period of service. Thus, for example, if a plan provides for the statutory five to fifteen year graded vesting, an employee with a period (or periods) of service which yield 5 whole year periods of service and an additional 321-day period of service is twenty-five percent vested in his or her employer-derived accrued benefits (based solely on the 5 whole year periods of service).

*(2) Service which may be disregarded.* (i) For purposes of section 411(a)(4), in determining the nonforfeitable percentage of an employee's right to his or her accrued benefits de-

rived from employer contributions, all of an employee's period or periods of service with an employer or employers maintaining the plan shall be taken into account unless such service may be disregarded under paragraph (d)(2)(ii) of this section.

(ii) For purposes of paragraph (d)(2)(i) of this section, the following periods of service may be disregarded—

(A) The period of service completed by an employee before the date on which he attains age 22;

(B) In the case of a plan which requires mandatory employee contributions, the period of service which falls within the period of time to which a particular employee contribution relates, if the employee had the opportunity to make a contribution for such period of time and failed to do so;

(C) The period of service during any period for which the employer did not maintain the plan or a predecessor plan;

(D) The period of service which is not required to be taken into account by reason of a period of severance which constitutes a break in service within the meaning of paragraph (d)(4) of this section;

(E) The period of service completed by an employee prior to January 1, 1971, unless the employee completes a period of service of at least 3 years at any time after December 31, 1970; and

(F) The period of service completed before the first plan year for which this section applies to the plan, if such service would have been disregarded under the plan rules relating to breaks in service in effect at that time. See the regulations under section 411(a) (relating to vesting).

*(3) Seasonal industry.* [Reserved]

*(4) Break in service.* For purposes of applying the break in service rules, the term "1-year period of severance" shall be substituted for the term "1-year break in service". A 1-year period of severance shall be a 12-consecutive-month period beginning on the severance from service date and ending on the first anniversary of such date, provided that the employee during such 12-consecutive-month period fails to perform an hour of service within the meaning of 29 CFR 2530.200b-2(a)(1) for an employer or employers maintaining the plan.

*(5) One-year hold-out.* For purposes of section 411(a)(6)(B), in determining the nonforfeitable percentage of the right to accrued benefits derived from employer contributions of an employee who has incurred a 1-year period of severance, the period of service completed before such period of severance is not required to be taken into account until the employee has completed a 1-year period of service after his return to service. See the regulations under section 411(a) (relating to vesting).

*(6) Vesting in pre-break accruals.* For purposes of section 411(a)(6)(C), a "1-year period of severance" shall be deemed to constitute a "1-year break in service." See the regulations under section 411(a) (relating to vesting).

*(7) Rule of parity.* (i) General rule. For purposes of section 411(a)(6)(D), in the case of an employee who is a nonvested participant in employer-derived benefits at the time he incurs a 1-year period of severance, the period of service completed by such participant before such period of severance is not required to be taken into account for purposes of determining the vested percentage of his or her right to employer-derived benefits if at such time the consecutive period of severance equals or exceeds his prior periods of service, whether or not consecutive, completed before such period of severance. See the regulations under section 411(a) (relating to vesting).

**(e) Benefit accrual.** *(1)* For purposes of section 411(b), a plan may provide that a participant's service with an employer or employers maintaining the plan shall be determined on the basis of the participant's total period of service beginning on the participation commencement date and ending on the severance from service date.

*(2)* Under section 411(b)(3)(A), a defined benefit pension plan may determine an employee's service for purposes of benefit accrual on any basis which is reasonable and consistent and which takes into account all service during the employee's participation in the plan which is included in a period of service required to be taken into account under section 410(a)(5) (relating to service which must be taken into account for purposes of determining an employee's eligibility to participate). A plan which provides for the determination of an employee's service with an employer or employers maintaining the plan on the basis permitted under paragraph (e)(1) of this section will be deemed to meet the requirements of section 411(b)(3)(A), provided that the plan meets the requirements of 29 CFR 2530.204-3, relating to plans which determine an employee's service for purposes of benefit accrual on a basis other than computation periods. Specifically, under 29 CFR § 2530.204-3, it must be possible to prove that, despite the fact that benefit accrual under such a plan is not based on computation periods, the plan's provisions meet at least one of the three benefit accrual rules of section 411(b)(1) under all circumstances. Further, 29 CFR § 2530.204-3 prohibits such a plan from disregarding service under section 411(b)(3)(C) (which would otherwise permit a plan to disregard service performed by an employee during a computation period in which the employee is credited with less than 1,000 hours). See the regulations under section 411(b) (relating to benefit accrual).

**(f) Transfers between methods of crediting service.** *(1) Single plan.* A plan may provide that an employee's service for purposes of eligibility to participate, vesting or benefit accrual shall be determined on the basis of computation periods under the general method set forth in 29 CFR 2530.200b-2 for certain classes of employees but under the alternative method permitted under this section for other classes of employees if the plan provides as follows—

(i) In the case of an employee who transfers from a class of employees whose service is determined on the basis of computation periods to a class of employees whose service is determined on the alternative basis permitted under this section, the employee shall receive credit for a period of service consisting of—

(A) A number of years equal to the number of years of service credited to the employee before the computation period during which the transfer occurs; and

(B) The greater of (1) the period of service that would be credited to the employee under the elapsed time method for his service during the entire computation period in which the transfer occurs or (2) the service taken into account under the computation periods method as of the date of the transfer.

In addition, the employee shall receive credit for service subsequent to the transfer commencing on the day after the last day of the computation period in which the transfer occurs.

(ii) In the case of an employee who transfers from a class of employees whose service is determined on the alternative basis permitted under this section to a class of employees whose service is determined on the basis of computation periods—

(A) The employee shall receive credit, as of the date of the transfer, for a number of years of service equal to the number of 1-year periods of service credited to the employee as of the date of the transfer, and

(B) The employee shall receive credit, in the computation period which includes the date of the transfer, for a number of hours of service determined by applying one of the equivalencies set forth in 29 CFR 2530.200b-3(e)(1) to any fractional part of a year credited to the employee under this section as of the date of the transfer. Such equivalency shall be set forth in the plan and shall apply to all similarly situated employees.

*(2) More than one plan.* In the case of an employee who transfers from a plan using either the general method of determining service on the basis of computation periods set forth in 29 CFR 2530.200b-2 or the method of determining service permitted under this section to a plan using the other method of determining service, all service required to be credited under the plan to which the employee transfers shall be determined by applying the rules of paragraph (f)(1) of this section.

**(g) Amendments to change method of crediting service.** A plan may be amended to change the method of crediting service for any purpose or for any class of employees between the general method set forth in 29 CFR 2530.200-2 and the method permitted under this section, if such amendment contains provisions under which each employee with respect to whom the method of crediting service is changed is treated in the same manner as an employee who transfers from one class of employees to another under paragraph (f)(1) of this section.

**(h) Transitional rule.** For plans in existence on June 17, 1980, the provisions of paragraph (f) of this section are effective for plan years beginning after December 31, 1983.

T.D. 7703, 6/16/80.

### § 1.410(a)-8 Five consecutive 1-year breaks in service, transitional rules under the Retirement Equity Act of 1984.

Sections 410(a)(5)(D) and 411(a)(6)(D), as amended by the Retirement Equity Act of 1984 (REA 1984), permit a plan to disregard years of service that were disregarded under the plan provisions satisfying those sections (as in effect on August 22, 1984) as of the day before the REA amendments apply to the plan. Under section 302(a) of REA 1984, the new break-in-service rules generally apply to plan years beginning after December 31, 1984. Thus, for example, assume a plan has a calendar plan year and disregarded years of service as permitted by sections 410(a)(5)(D) and 411(a)(6)(D) as in effect on August 22, 1984. An employee completed two years of service in 1981 and 1982, and then incurred two consecutive 1-year breaks in service in 1983 and 1984. The plans may disregard the prior years of service even though the employee did not incur five consecutive 1-year breaks in service. On the other hand, assume the employee completed three consecutive years of service beginning in 1980, and incurred two 1-year breaks in service in 1983 and 1984. Because, as of December 31, 1984, the years of service credited before 1983 could not be disregarded, whether the plan may subsequently disregard those years of service would be governed by the rules enacted by REA 1984.

T.D. 8219, 8/19/88.

### § 1.410(a)-8T Year of service; break in service (temporary).

**(a) [Reserved]**

**(b) [Reserved]**

**(c) Breaks in service.** *(1) [Reserved]*

*(2) Employees under 2-year 100 percent vesting schedule.* (i) General rule. In the case of an employee who incurs a 1-year break in service under a plan which provides that after not more than 2 years of service each participant's right to his accrued benefit under the plan is completely nonforfeitable (within the meaning of section 411 and the regulations thereunder) at the time such benefit accrues, the employee's service before the break in service is not required to be taken into account after the break in service in determining the employee's years of service under section 410(a)(1) and § 1.410(a)-3 if such employee has not satisfied such service requirement.

(ii) Example. The rules of this subparagraph are illustrated by the following example:

*Example.* A qualified plan computing service by the actual counting of hours provides full and immediate vesting. The plan can not require as a condition of participation that an employee complete 2 consecutive years of service with the employer because the requirement as to consecutive years is not permitted under section 410(a)(5). However, such a plan can require 2 years without a break in service, i.e., 2 years with no intervening years in which the employee fails to complete more than 500 hours of service. Under a plan containing such a participation requirement, the following example illustrates when employees would become eligible to participate.

| Year | Hours of service completed | | |
|---|---|---|---|
| | Employee A | Employee B | Employee C |
| 1 | 1,000 | 1,000 | 1,000 |
| 2 | 1,000 | 700 | 500 |
| 3 | 1,000 | 1,000 | 1,000 |
| 4 | 1,000 | 1,000 | 700 |
| 5 | 1,000 | 1,000 | 1,000 |

**Note.**——Employee A will have satisfied the plan's service requirement at the end of year 2, Employee B at the end of year 3, and Employee C at the end of year 5.

*(3) One-year break in service.* (i) [Reserved]

(ii) Examples. The rules provided by this subparagraph are illustrated by the following examples:

*Example (1).* Employee A completes a year of service under a plan computing service by the actual counting of hours for the 12-month period ending December 31, 1989, and incurs a 1-year break in service for the 12-month period ending December 31, 1990. The plan does not contain the provisions permitted by section 410(a)(5)(B) (relating to 2-year 100 percent vesting) and section 410(a)(5)(D) (relating to nonvested participants). Thereafter, he does not complete a year of service. As of January 1, 1991, in computing his period of service under the plan his service prior to December 31, 1990, is not required to be taken into account for purposes of section 410(a)(1) and § 1.410(a)-3.

*Example (2).* [Reserved]

T.D. 8170, 1/5/88.

### § 1.410(a)-9 Maternity and paternity absence.

**(a) Elapsed time.** *(1) Rule.* For purposes of applying the rules of § 1.410(a)-7 (relating to the elapsed time method of crediting service) to absences described in sections 410(a)(5)(E) and 411(a)(6)(E) (relating to maternity or paternity absence), the severance from service date of an employee who is absent from service beyond the first anniversary of the first day of absence by reason of a maternity or paternity absence described in section 410(a)(5)(E)(i) or 411(a)(6)(E)(i) is the second anniversary of the first day of such absence. The period between the first and second anniversaries of the first day of absence from work is neither a period of service nor a period of severance. This rule applies to maternity and paternity absences beginning on or after the first day of the first plan year in which the plan is required to credit service under sections 410(a)(5)(E) and 411(a)(6)(E).

*(2) Example.* The rules of this section are illustrated by the following example:

Assume an individual works until June 30, 1986; is first absent from employment on July 1, 1986, on account of maternity or paternity absence; and on July 1, 1989, performs an hour of service. The period of service must include the period from employment commencement date until June 30, 1987 (one year after the date of separation for any reason other than a quit, discharge, retirement, or death). The period from July 1, 1987, to June 30, 1988, is neither a period of service nor a period of severance. The period of severance would be from July 1, 1988, to June 30, 1989.

**(b) Other methods.** This paragraph provides a safe harbor for plans that compute years of service under the hours of service methods or permitted equivalencies. Such a plan will be treated as satisfying the requirements of sections 410(a)(5)(E) and 411(a)(6)(E) if the plan increases the minimum period of consecutive 1-year breaks required to disregard any service (or deprive any employee of any right) by one. Thus, a plan will satisfy sections 410(a)(5)(E) and 411(a)(6)(E) without having to compute service for maternity or paternity and sections 410(a)(5)(D) and 411(a)(4)(D) and (a)(6)(C), by increasing the period of consecutive breaks-in-service from 5 to 6.

T.D. 8219, 8/19/88.

### § 1.410(a)-9T Elapsed time (temporary).

**(a)** [Reserved]

**(b)** [Reserved]

**(c) Eligibility to participate.** *(1)* [Reserved]

*(2) Determination of one-year period of service.* (i) [Reserved]

(ii) For purposes of section 410(a)(1)(B)(i), a "2-year period of service" shall be deemed to be "2 years of service."

**(d) Vesting.** *(1) General rule.* (i) [Reserved]

(ii) [Reserved]

(iii) [Reserved]

(iv) For purposes of determining an employee's nonforfeitable percentage of accrued benefits derived from employer contributions, a plan, after calculating an employee's period of service in the manner prescribed in this paragraph, may disregard any remaining less than whole year, 12-month or 365-day period of service. Thus, for example, if a plan provides for the statutory three to seven year graded vesting, an employee with a period (or periods) of service which yields 3 whole year periods of service and an additional 321-day period of service is twenty percent vested in his or her employer-derived accrued benefits (based solely on the 3 whole year periods of service).

*(2) [Reserved]*

T.D. 8170, 1/5/88.

### § 1.410(b)-0 Table of contents.

This section contains a listing of the major headings of §§ 1.410(b)-1 through 1.410(b)-10.

---

T.D. 8363, 9/12/91, amend T.D. 8487, 8/31/93, T.D. 8548, 6/23/94, T.D. 9275, 7/20/2006.

---

### § 1.410(b)-1 Minimum coverage requirements (before 1994).

***Caution:*** The Treasury has not yet amended Reg § 1.410(b)-1 to reflect changes made by P.L. 99-514.

**(a) In general.** A plan is not a qualified plan (and a trust forming a part of the plan is not a qualified trust) unless the plan satisfies section 410(b)(1). For plan years prior to the applicable effective date set forth in § 1.410(b)-10, a plan satisfies section 410(b)(1) if it satisfies the requirements of paragraph (b)(1) or (b)(2) of this section. See also § 1.410(b)-2 for plan years beginning on or after the applicable effective date set forth in § 1.410(b)-10.

**(b) Coverage tests.** *(1) Percentage test.* A plan satisfies the requirements of this subparagraph if it benefits—

(i) Seventy percent or more of all employees, or

(ii) Eighty percent or more of all employees who are eligible to benefit under the plan if 70 percent or more of all the employees are eligible to benefit under the plan, excluding in each case employees who have not satisfied the minimum age and service requirements (if any) prescribed by the plan, as of the date coverage is tested, as a condition of participation and employees permitted to be excluded under paragraph (c) of this section. The percentage requirements of this subparagraph refer to a percentage of active employees, including employees temporarily on leave, such as those in the Armed Forces of the United States, if such employees are eligible under the plan.

*(2) Classification test.* A plan satisfies the requirements of section 410(b)(1) and this subparagraph if it benefits such employees as qualify under a classification of employees set up by the employer, which classification is found by the Internal Revenue Service not to be discriminatory in favor of employees who are officers, shareholders, or highly compensated. For purposes of this subparagraph, except as provided by paragraph (c) of this section, all active employees (including employees who do not satisfy the minimum age or service requirements of the plan) are taken into account.

**(c) Exclusion of certain employees.** Under section 410(b)(2), for purposes of section 410(b)(1) and paragraph (b) of this section, there shall be excluded from consideration employees described in subparagraphs (1), (2), and (3) of this paragraph.

*(1) Bargaining unit.* Under section 410(b)(2)(A) and this paragraph, there may be excluded from consideration employees not included in the plan who are included in a unit of employees covered by an agreement which the Secretary of Labor finds to be a collective bargaining agreement between employee representatives and one or more employers, if the Internal Revenue Service finds that retirement benefits were the subject of good faith bargaining between such employee representatives and such employer or employers. For purposes of determining whether such bargaining occurred, it is not material that such employees are not covered by another plan or that the plan was not considered in such bargaining.

*(2) Air pilots.* Under section 410(b)(2)(B) and this paragraph there may be excluded from consideration, in the case of a plan established or maintained pursuant to an agreement which the Secretary of Labor finds to be a collective bargaining agreement between air pilots represented in accordance with title II of the Railway Labor Act and one or more employers all employees not covered by such agreement. Section 410(b)(2)(B) and this subparagraph do not apply to a plan if the plan provides contributions or benefits for employees whose principal duties are not customarily performed aboard aircraft in flight.

*(3) Nonresident aliens.* Under section 410(b)(2)(C) and this paragraph, there may be excluded from consideration employees who are nonresident aliens and who receive no earned income (within the meaning of section 911(b) and the regulations thereunder) from the employer which constitutes income from sources within the United States (within the meaning of section 861(a)(3) and the regulations thereunder).

**(d) Special rules.** *(1) Highly compensated.* The classification of an employee as highly compensated for purposes of section 410(b)(1)(B) and § 1.410(b)-1(b)(2) is made on the basis of the facts and circumstances of each case, taking into account the level of the employee's compensation and the level of compensation paid by the employer to other employees, whether or not covered by the plan. Average compensation levels determined on a local, regional, or national basis, are not relevant for this purpose. Further, the classification of an employee as highly compensated is not made solely on the basis of the number or percentage of employees whose compensation exceeds, or is exceeded by, the employee's.

*(2) Discrimination.* The determination as to whether a plan discriminates in favor of employees who are officers, shareholders, or highly compensated is made on the basis of the facts and circumstances of each case, allowing a reasonable difference between the ratio of such employees benefited by the plan to all such employees of the employer and the ratio of the employees (other than officers, shareholders, or highly compensated) of the employer benefited by the plan to all employees (other than officers, shareholders, or highly compensated). A showing that a specified percentage of employees covered by a plan are not officers, shareholders, or highly compensated, is not in itself sufficient to establish that the plan does not discriminate in favor of employees who are officers, shareholders, or highly compensated.

*(3) Multiple plans.* (i) An employer may designate two or more plans as constituting a single plan which is intended to qualify for purposes of section 410(b)(1) and this section, in which case all plans so designated shall be considered as a single plan in determining whether the requirements of such section are satisfied by each of the separate plans. A determination that the combination of plans so designated does not satisfy such requirements does not preclude a determination that one or more of such plans, considered separately, satisfies such requirements.

(ii) Notwithstanding subdivision (i) of this subparagraph, a plan which is subject to the limitations of section 401(a)(17) of the Code or section 301(d)(3) of the Tax Reduction Act of 1975 cannot be considered with any other plan which covers any employee covered by such plan.

*(4) Profit-sharing plans.* Employees under a profit-sharing plan who receive the amounts allocated to their accounts before the expiration of a period of time or the occurrence of a contingency specified in the plan shall not be considered covered by the plan. Thus, in case a plan permits employees to receive immediately the amounts allocated to their accounts, or to have such amounts paid to a profit-sharing plan for them, the employees who receive the shares immediately shall not be considered covered by the plan.

*(5) Certain classifications.* See section 401(a)(5) and the regulations thereunder for rules relating to classifications of employees which are not considered to be discriminatory per se for purposes of section 410(b)(1)(B) and § 1.410(b)-1(b)(2).

*(6) Integration with Social Security Act.* See section 401(a)(5) and the regulations thereunder for rules relating to integration of plans with the Social Security Act.

*(7) Different age and service requirements.* (i) Application. The rules of this subparagraph (7) apply to a plan which must satisfy the minimum age and service requirements of section 410(a)(1)(A) in order to be a qualified plan. Accordingly, the rules are inapplicable to plans described in section 410(c)(1) (see § 1.410(a)-1(c)(1)); plans satisfying the alternative minimum age and service requirements of section 410(a)(1)(B) but not satisfying the requirements of section 410(a)(1)(A); and plans which provide contributions or benefits for employees, some or all of whom are owner-employees (see section 410(a)(10)).

(ii) General rules. A provision for different age and service requirements for present and future employees either upon establishment or subsequent amendment is not, of itself, discriminatory under section 401(b)(1)(B) even though present employees who are officers, shareholders, or highly compensated cannot meet the age and service requirements for future employees at the time the plan is established or amended and even though present participants who are officers, shareholders, or highly compensated would not have satisfied the age and service requirements for future employees at the time they became participants in the plan. Furthermore, prohibited discrimination will be deemed not to arise in operation, solely because of such different requirements, when future employees are added to the employer's work force.

*(8) Certain controlled groups.* In applying the percentage test and classification test described in paragraph (b)(1) and (2) of this section for a year, all the employees of corporations or trades and businesses whose employees are treated as employed by a single employer by reason of section 414(b) or (c) must be taken into account. The preceding sentence shall apply for a plan year if, on 1 day in each quarter of such plan year, such corporations are members of a controlled group of corporations (within the meaning of section 414(b)) of such trades or businesses are under common control (within the meaning of section 414(c)).

*(9) Transitional rule.* In the case of a cash and deferred profit-sharing plan, in existence on June 27, 1974, the re-

quirements of paragraph (b)(2) of this section are satisfied if over one-half of the participants in the plan are among the lowest paid two-thirds of all eligible employees. This subparagraph shall not apply after December 31, 1977.

**(e) Example.** The rules provided by this section are illustrated by the following example:

*Example.* An employer established a noncontributory defined benefit plan covering all employees of its ABC Division who are hired prior to age 60 and who are at least 25 years old. The normal retirement age under the plan is age 65. The employer has 100 employees including 20 employees who are under age 25 and 10 employees who were hired over age 60. The plan does not cover 15 employees who are over age 25 and were hired before age 60 because they are not in the ABC Division. Of these 15 excluded employees, 3 have less than 1 year of service. In addition, 12 of the 55 employees covered have less than one year of service. The plan can be shown not to satisfy the requirements of IRC section 410(b)(1)(A) as follows:

| | |
|---|---|
| (i) Number of Employees | 100 |
| (ii) Number of employees excluded on account of minimum age and service | 20 |
| (iii) (i) – (ii) | 80 |
| (iv) Number of employees who must be covered if plan is to satisfy IRC section 410(b)(1)(A), 70% of (iii) | 56 |
| (v) Number of employees actually covered | 55 |

Because the number of employees covered is less than the number of employees who must be covered, the plan does not satisfy the percentage coverage requirements of IRC section 410(b)(1)(A).

T.D. 7508, 9/14/77, amend T.D. 7735, 11/10/80, T.D. 8363, 9/12/91, T.D. 8487, 8/31/93.

## § 1.410(b)-2 Minimum coverage requirements (after 1993).

**(a) In general.** A plan is a qualified plan for a plan year only if the plan satisfies section 410(b) for the plan year. A plan satisfies section 410(b) for a plan year if and only if it satisfies paragraph (b) of this section with respect to employees for the plan year and paragraph (c) of this section with respect to former employees for the plan year. The rules in paragraphs (a), (b), and (c) of this section apply to all plans as a condition of qualification, including plans under which no employee is able to accrue any additional benefits (for example, frozen plans). Paragraphs (d), (e), and (f) of this section provide special rules for nonelective section 403(b) plans subject to section 403(b)(12)(A)(i), for governmental and church plans subject to section 410(c), and for certain acquisitions or dispositions, respectively. See § 1.410(b)-7 for rules for determining the "plan" subject to section 410(b).

**(b) Requirements with respect to employees.** *(1) In general.* A plan satisfies this paragraph (b) for a plan year if and only if it satisfies at least one of the tests in paragraphs (b)(2) through (b)(7) of this section for the plan year.

*(2) Ratio percentage test.* (i) In general. A plan satisfies this paragraph (b)(2) for a plan year if and only if the plan's ratio percentage for the plan year is at least 70 percent. This test incorporates both the percentage test of section 410(b)(1)(A) and the ratio test of section 410(b)(1)(B). See § 1.410(b)-9 for the definition of ratio percentage.

(ii) Examples. The following examples illustrate the ratio percentage test of this paragraph (b)(2).

*Example (1).* For a plan year, Plan A benefits 70 percent of an employer's nonhighly compensated employees and 100 percent of the employer's highly compensated employees. The plan's ratio percentage for the year is 70 percent (70 percent/100 percent), and thus the plan satisfies the ratio percentage test.

*Example (2).* For a plan year, Plan B benefits 40 percent of the employer's nonhighly compensated employees and 60 percent of the employer's highly compensated employees. Plan B fails to satisfy the ratio percentage test because the plan's ratio percentage is only 66.67 percent (40 percent/60 percent).

*(3) Average benefit test.* A plan satisfies this paragraph (b)(3) for a plan year if and only if the plan satisfies both the nondiscriminatory classification test of § 1.410(b)-4 and the average benefit percentage test of § 1.410(b)-5 for the plan year.

*(4) Certain tax credit employee stock ownership plans.* A plan satisfies this paragraph (b)(4) for a plan year if and only if the plan—

(i) Is a tax credit employee stock ownership plan (as defined in section 409(a)),

(ii) Is the only plan of the employer that is intended to qualify under section 401(a), and

(iii) Is a plan that satisfies the rule set forth in section 410(b)(6)(D).

This paragraph (b)(4) is available only for plan years for which the tax credit employee stock ownership plan receives contributions for which the employer is allowed a tax credit under section 41 (as in effect prior to its repeal by the Tax Reform Act of 1986) or section 48(n) (as in effect prior to its amendment by the Tax Reform Act of 1984). The requirement of this paragraph (b)(4) that the plan be the only plan of the employer that is intended to qualify under section 401(a) is not satisfied if the employer has only one plan, but that plan is treated as two or more separate plans under the mandatory disaggregation rules of § 1.410(b)-7(c).

*(5) Employers with no nonhighly compensated employees.* A plan satisfies this paragraph (b)(5) for a plan year if and only if the plan is maintained by an employer that has no nonhighly compensated employees at any time during the plan year.

*(6) Plans benefiting no highly compensated employees.* A plan satisfies this paragraph (b)(6) for a plan year if and only if the plan benefits no highly compensated employees for the plan year.

*(7) Plans benefiting collectively bargained employees.* A plan that benefits solely collectively bargained employees for a plan year satisfies this paragraph (b)(7) for the plan year. If a plan (within the meaning of § 1.410(b)-7(b)) benefits both collectively bargained employees and noncollectively bargained employees for a plan year, § 1.410(b)-7(c)(4) provides that the portion of the plan that benefits collectively bargained employees is treated as a separate plan from the portion of the plan that benefits noncollectively bargained employees. Thus, the mandatorily disaggregated portion of the plan that benefits the collectively bargained employees automatically satisfies this paragraph (b)(7) for the plan year and hence section 410(b). See § 1.410(b)-9 for the definitions of collectively bargained employee and noncollectively bargained employee.

**(c) Requirements with respect to former employees.** *(1) Former employees tested separately.* Former employees are tested separately from employees for purposes of section

410(b). Thus, former employees are disregarded in applying the ratio percentage test, the nondiscriminatory classification test, and the average benefit percentage test with respect to the coverage of employees under a plan, and employees are disregarded in applying this section with respect to the coverage of former employees under a plan.

*(2) Testing former employees.* A plan satisfies section 410(b) with respect to former employees if and only if, under all of the relevant facts and circumstances (including the group of nonexcludable former employees not benefiting under the plan), the group of former employees benefiting under the plan does not discriminate significantly in favor of highly compensated former employees.

**(d) Nonelective contributions under section 403(b) plans.** For plan years beginning on or after January 1, 1989, a plan subject to section 403(b)(12)(A)(i) with respect to nonelective contributions (i.e., contributions not made pursuant to a salary reduction agreement) is treated as a plan subject to the requirements of this section. For this purpose, a plan described in the preceding sentence must satisfy the requirements of this section without regard to section 410(c) and paragraph (e) of this section. For plan years beginning before the effective date set forth in § 1.410(b)-10(d), any plan described in section 410(c)(1)(A) (regarding governmental plans) satisfies the requirements of this section.

**(e) Certain governmental and church plans.** The requirements of section 410(b) do not apply to a plan described in section 410(c)(1) (other than a plan subject to section 403(b)(12)(A)(i) or a plan with respect to which an election has been made under section 410(d)). Such a plan must satisfy section 401(a)(3) as in effect on September 1, 1974. For this purpose, a plan that satisfies section 410(b) (without regard to this paragraph (e)) is treated as satisfying section 401(a)(3) as in effect on September 1, 1974. For plan years beginning before the effective date set forth in § 1.410(b)-10(d), any plan described in section 410(c)(1)(A) (regarding governmental plans) satisfies the requirements of this section and is thus treated as satisfying the requirements of section 401(a)(3) as in effect on September 1, 1974. See § 1.410(b)-10(b)(2) for a special rule for plans of tax-exempt organizations.

**(f) Certain acquisitions or dispositions.** Section 410(b)(6)(C) (relating to certain acquisitions or dispositions) provides a special rule whereby a plan may be treated as satisfying section 410(b) for a limited period of time after an acquisition or disposition if it satisfies section 410(b) (without regard to the special rule) immediately before the acquisition or disposition and there is no significant change in the plan or in the coverage of the plan other than the acquisition or disposition. For purposes of section 410(b)(6)(C) and this paragraph (f), the terms "acquisition" and "disposition" refer to an asset or stock acquisition, merger, or other similar transaction involving a change in employer of the employees of a trade or business.

**(g) Additional rules.** The Commissioner may, in revenue rulings, notices, and other guidance of general applicability, provide any additional rules that may be necessary or appropriate in applying the minimum coverage requirements of section 410(b), including (without limitation) additional rules limiting or expanding the methods in § 1.410(b)-5(d) and (e) for determining employee benefit percentages.

T.D. 8363, 9/12/91, amend T.D. 8487, 8/31/93, T.D. 8548, 6/23/94.

### § 1.410(b)-3 Employees and former employees who benefit under a plan.

**(a) Employees benefiting under a plan.** *(1) In general.* Except as provided in paragraph (a)(2) of this section, an employee is treated as benefiting under a plan for a plan year if and only if for that plan year, in the case of a defined contribution plan, the employer receives an allocation taken into account under section 1.401(a)(4)-2(c)(2)(ii), or in the case of a defined benefit plan, the employee has an increase in a benefit accrued or treated as an accrued benefit under section 411(d)(6).

*(2) Exceptions to allocation or accrual requirement.* (i) Section 401(k) and 401(m) plans. Notwithstanding paragraph (a)(1) of this section, an employee is treated as benefiting under a section 401(k) plan for a plan year if and only if the employee is an eligible employee as defined in § 1.401(k)-6 under the plan. Similarly, an employee is treated as benefiting under a section 401(m) plan for a plan year if and only if the employee is an eligible employee as defined in § 1.401(m)-5 under the plan for the plan year.

(ii) Section 415 Limits. (A) General rule for defined benefit plans. In determining whether an employee is treated as benefiting under a defined benefit plan for a plan year, plan provisions that implement the limits of section 415 are disregarded. Any plan provision that provides for increases in an employee's accrued benefit under the plan due solely to adjustments under section 415(d)(1), additional years of participation or service under section 415(b)(5), or changes in the defined contribution fraction under section 415(e) is also disregarded, but only if such provision applies uniformly to all employees in the plan.

(B) Defined benefit plans taking section 415 limits into account under section 401(a)(4) testing. Paragraph (a)(2)(ii)(A) of this section does not apply in the case of a defined benefit plan that uses the option in § 1.401(a)(4)-3(d)(2)(ii)(B) to take into account plan provisions implementing the provisions of section 415 in determining accrual rates under the section 401(a)(4) general test.

(C) Defined contribution plans. A defined contribution plan is permitted to apply the rule in the first sentence of paragraph (a)(2)(ii)(A) of this section in determining whether an employee is treated as benefiting under the plan, provided it applies the rule on a consistent basis for all employees in the plan.

(iii) Certain employees treated as benefiting. (A) In general. An employee is treated as benefiting under a plan for a plan year if the employee satisfies all of the applicable conditions for accruing a benefit or receiving an allocation for the plan year but fails to have an increase in accrued benefit or to receive an allocation solely because of one or more of the conditions set forth in paragraphs (a)(2)(iii)(B) through (F) of this section.

(B) Certain plan limits. The employee's benefit would otherwise exceed a limit that is applicable on a uniform basis to all employees in the plan. Thus, for example, if the formula under a defined benefit plan takes into account only the first 30 years of service for accrual purposes, an employee who has completed more than 30 years of service is still treated as benefiting under the plan.

(C) Benefits previously accrued. The benefit previously accrued by the employee is greater than the benefit that would be determined under the plan if the benefit previously accrued were disregarded. This could happen, for example, when the plan is applying the wear-away formula of § 1.401(a)(4)-13(c)(4)(ii) and the employee's frozen accrued benefit exceeds the benefit determined under the current formula.

(D) Benefit offset arrangements. The plan offsets the employee's current benefit accrual under an offset arrangement described in § 1.401(a)(4)-3(f)(9) (without regard to whether the offset is attributable to pre-participation service or past service).

(E) Target benefit plans. In the case of a target benefit plan that satisfies the nondiscriminatory amount requirement of § 1.401(a)(4)-1(b)(2) by satisfying the safe harbor in § 1.401(a)(4)-8(b)(3), the employee's theoretical reserve is greater than or equal to the actuarial present value of the fractional rule benefit.

(F) Post-normal retirement age adjustments. The employee has attained normal retirement age under a defined benefit plan and fails to accrue a benefit because of the provisions of section 411(b)(1)(H)(iii) regarding adjustments for delayed retirement.

(iv) Section 412(i) plans. (A) General rule. Notwithstanding paragraph (a)(1) of this section, an employee is treated as benefiting under an insurance contract plan within the meaning of section 412(i) for a plan year if and only if a premium is paid on behalf of the employee for the plan year.

(B) Exceptions. Notwithstanding paragraph (a)(2)(iv)(A) of this section, an employee is treated as benefiting under an insurance contract plan within the meaning of section 412(i) for a plan year if the sole reason that a premium is not paid on behalf of the employee is one of the reasons described in paragraph (a)(2)(iii) of this section. In addition, an employee is treated as benefiting under an insurance contract plan, within the meaning of section 412(i), that is a defined benefit plan if a premium is not paid on behalf of the employee solely because the insurance contracts that have previously been purchased on behalf of the employee guarantee to provide for the employee's projected normal retirement benefit without regard to future premium payments.

*(3) Examples.* The following examples illustrate the determination of whether an employee is benefiting under a plan for purposes of section 410(b).

*Example (1).* An employer has 35 employees who are eligible under a defined benefit plan. The plan requires 1,000 hours of service to accrue a benefit. Only 30 employees satisfy the 1,000-hour requirement and accrue a benefit. The five employees who do not satisfy the 1,000-hour requirement during the plan year are taken into account in testing the plan under section 410(b) but are treated as not benefiting under the plan.

*Example (2).* An employer maintains a section 401(k) plan. Only employees who are at least age 21 and who complete one year of service are eligible employees under the plan within the meaning of § 1.401(k)-6. Under the rule of paragraph (a)(2)(i) of this section, only employees who have satisfied these age and service conditions are treated as benefiting under the plan.

*Example (3).* The facts are the same as in Example 2, except that the employer also maintains a section 401(m) plan that provides matching contributions contingent on elective contributions under the section 401(k) plan. The matching contributions are contingent on employment on the last day of the plan year. Under § 1.401(m)-5, because matching contributions are contingent on employment on the last day of the plan year, not all employees who are eligible employees under the section 401(k) plan are eligible employees under the section 401(m) plan. Thus, employees who have satisfied the age and service conditions but who do not receive a matching contribution because they are not employed on the last day of the plan year are treated as not benefiting under the section 401(m) portion of the plan.

**(b) Former employees benefiting under a plan.** *(1) In general.* A former employee is treated as benefiting for a plan year if and only if the plan provides an allocation or benefit increase described in paragraph (a)(1) of this section to the former employee for the plan year. Thus, for example, a former employee benefits under a defined benefit plan for a plan year if the plan is amended to provide an ad hoc cost-of-living adjustment in the former employee's benefits. In contrast, because an increase in benefits payable under a plan pursuant to an automatic cost-of-living provision adopted and effective before the beginning of the plan year is previously accrued, a former employee is not treated as benefiting in a subsequent plan year merely because the former employee receives an increase pursuant to such an automatic cost-of-living provision. Any accrual or allocation for an individual during the plan year that arises from the individual's status as an employee is treated as an accrual or allocation of an employee. Similarly, any accrual or allocation for an individual during the plan year that arises from the individual's status as a former employee is treated as an accrual or allocation of a former employee. It is possible for an individual to accrue a benefit both as an employee and as a former employee in a given plan year. During the plan year in which an individual ceases performing services for the employer, the individual is treated as an employee in applying section 410(b) with respect to employees and is treated as a former employee in applying section 410(b) with respect to former employees.

*(2) Examples.* The following examples illustrate the determination of whether a former employee benefits under a plan for purposes of section 410(b).

*Example (1).* Employer A amends its defined benefit plan in the 1995 plan year to provide an ad hoc cost-of-living increase of 5 percent for all retirees. Former employees who receive this increase are treated as benefiting under the plan for the 1995 plan year.

*Example (2).* Employer B maintains a defined benefit plan with a calendar plan year. In the 1995 plan year, Employer B amends the plan to provide that an employee who has reached early retirement age under the plan and who retires before July 31 of the 1995 plan year will receive an unreduced benefit, even though the employee has not yet reached normal retirement age. This early retirement window benefit is provided to employees based on their status as employees. Thus, although individuals who take advantage of the benefit become former employees, the window benefit is treated as provided to employees and is not treated as a benefit for former employees.

*Example (3).* The facts are the same as Example 2, except that on September 1, 1995, Employer B also amends the defined benefit plan to provide an ad hoc cost-of-living increase effective for all former employees. An individual who ceases performing services for the employer before July 31, 1995, under the early retirement window, and then receives the ad hoc cost-of-living increase, is treated as benefiting for the 1995 plan year both as an employee with respect to the early retirement window, and as a former employee with respect to the ad hoc COLA.

T.D. 8363, 9/12/91, amend T.D. 8487, 8/31/93, T.D. 9169, 12/28/2004.

### § 1.410(b)-4 Nondiscriminatory classification test.

**(a) In general.** A plan satisfies the nondiscriminatory classification test of this section for a plan year if and only if, for the plan year, the plan benefits the employees who qualify under a classification established by the employer in accordance with paragraph (b) of this section, and the classification of employees is nondiscriminatory under paragraph (c) of this section.

**(b) Reasonable classification established by the employer.** A classification is established by the employer in accordance with this paragraph (b) if and only if, based on all the facts and circumstances, the classification is reasonable and is established under objective business criteria that identify the category of employees who benefit under the plan. Reasonable classifications generally include specified job categories, nature of compensation (i.e., salaried or hourly), geographic location, and similar bona fide business criteria. An enumeration of employees by name or other specific criteria having substantially the same effect as an enumeration by name is not considered a reasonable classification.

**(c) Nondiscriminatory classification.** *(1) General rule.* A classification is nondiscriminatory under this paragraph (c) for a plan year if and only if the group of employees included in the classification benefiting under the plan satisfies the requirements of either paragraph (c)(2) or (c)(3) of this section for the plan year.

*(2) Safe harbor.* A plan satisfies the requirement of this paragraph (c)(2) for a plan year if and only if the plan's ratio percentage is greater than or equal to the employer's safe harbor percentage, as defined in paragraph (c)(4)(i) of this section. See § 1.410(b)-9 for the definition of a plan's ratio percentage.

*(3) Facts and circumstances.* (i) General rule. A plan satisfies the requirements of this paragraph (c)(3) if and only if—

(A) The plan's ratio percentage is greater than or equal to the unsafe harbor percentage, as defined in paragraph (c)(4)(ii) of this section, and

(B) The classification satisfies the factual determination of paragraph (c)(3)(ii) of this section.

(ii) Factual determination. A classification satisfies this paragraph (c)(3)(ii) if and only if, based on all the relevant facts and circumstances, the Commissioner finds that the classification is nondiscriminatory. No one particular fact is determinative. Included among the facts and circumstances relevant in determining whether a classification is nondiscriminatory are the following—

(A) The underlying business reason for the classification. The greater the business reason for the classification, the more likely the classification is to be nondiscriminatory. Reducing the employer's cost of providing retirement benefits is not a relevant business reason.

(B) The percentage of the employer's employees benefiting under the plan. The higher the percentage, the more likely the classification is to be nondiscriminatory.

(C) Whether the number of employees benefiting under the plan in each salary range is representative of the number of employees in each salary range of the employer's workforce. In general, the more representative the percentages of employees benefiting under the plan in each salary range, the more likely the classification is to be nondiscriminatory.

(D) The difference between the plan's ratio percentage and the employer's safe harbor percentage. The smaller the difference, the more likely the classification is to be nondiscriminatory.

(E) The extent to which the plan's average benefit percentage (determined under § 1.410(b)-5) exceeds 70 percent.

*(4) Definitions.* (i) Safe harbor percentage. The safe harbor percentage of an employer is 50 percent, reduced by ¾ of a percentage point for each whole percentage point by which the nonhighly compensated employee concentration percentage exceeds 60 percent. See paragraph (c)(4)(iv) for a table that illustrates the safe harbor percentage and unsafe harbor percentage.

(ii) Unsafe harbor percentage. The unsafe harbor percentage of an employer is 40 percent, reduced by ¾ of a percentage point for each whole percentage point by which the nonhighly compensated employee concentration percentage exceeds 60 percent. However, in no case is the unsafe harbor percentage less than 20 percent.

(iii) Nonhighly compensated employee concentration percentage. The nonhighly compensated employee concentration percentage of an employer is the percentage of all the employees of the employer who are nonhighly compensated employees. Employees who are excludable employees for purposes of the average benefit test are not taken into account.

(iv) Table. The following table sets forth the safe harbor and unsafe harbor percentages at each nonhighly compensated employee concentration percentage:

| Nonhighly compensated employee concentration percentage | Safe harbor percentage | Unsafe harbor percentage |
|---|---|---|
| 0–60 | 50.00 | 40.00 |
| 61 | 49.25 | 39.25 |
| 62 | 48.50 | 38.50 |
| 63 | 47.75 | 37.75 |
| 64 | 47.00 | 37.00 |
| 65 | 46.25 | 36.25 |
| 66 | 45.50 | 35.50 |
| 67 | 44.75 | 34.75 |
| 68 | 44.00 | 34.00 |
| 69 | 43.25 | 33.25 |
| 70 | 42.50 | 32.50 |
| 71 | 41.75 | 31.75 |
| 72 | 41.00 | 31.00 |
| 73 | 40.25 | 30.25 |
| 74 | 39.50 | 29.50 |
| 75 | 38.75 | 28.75 |
| 76 | 38.00 | 28.00 |
| 77 | 37.25 | 27.25 |
| 78 | 36.50 | 26.50 |
| 79 | 35.75 | 25.75 |
| 80 | 35.00 | 25.00 |
| 81 | 34.25 | 24.25 |
| 82 | 33.50 | 23.50 |
| 83 | 32.75 | 22.75 |
| 84 | 32.00 | 22.00 |
| 85 | 31.25 | 21.25 |
| 86 | 30.50 | 20.50 |
| 87 | 29.75 | 20.00 |
| 88 | 29.00 | 20.00 |
| 89 | 28.25 | 20.00 |
| 90 | 27.50 | 20.00 |
| 91 | 26.75 | 20.00 |
| 92 | 26.00 | 20.00 |
| 93 | 25.25 | 20.00 |

| | | |
|---|---|---|
| 94 | 24.50 | 20.00 |
| 95 | 23.75 | 20.00 |
| 96 | 23.00 | 20.00 |
| 97 | 22.25 | 20.00 |
| 98 | 21.50 | 20.00 |
| 99 | 20.75 | 20.00 |

*(5) Examples.* The following examples illustrate the rules in this paragraph (c).

*Example (1).* Employer A has 200 nonexcludable employees, of whom 120 are nonhighly compensated employees and 80 are highly compensated employees. Employer A maintains a plan that benefits 60 nonhighly compensated employees and 72 highly compensated employees. Thus, the plan's ratio percentage is 55.56 percent ([60/120] / [72/80] = 50%/90% = 0.5556), which is below the percentage necessary to satisfy the ratio percentage test of § 1.410(b)-2(b)(2). The employer's nonhighly compensated employee concentration percentage is 60 percent (120/200); thus, Employer A's safe harbor percentage is 50 percent and its unsafe harbor percentage is 40 percent. Because the plan's ratio percentage is greater than the safe harbor percentage, the plan's classification satisfies the safe harbor of paragraph (c)(2) of this section.

*Example (2).* The facts are the same as in Example 1, except that the plan benefits only 40 nonhighly compensated employees. The plan's ratio percentage is thus 37.03 percent ([40/120] / [72/80] = 33.33%/90% = 0.3703). Under these facts, the plan's classification is below the unsafe harbor percentage and is thus considered discriminatory.

*Example (3).* The facts are the same as in Example 1, except that the plan benefits 45 nonhighly compensated employees. The plan's ratio percentage is thus 41.67 percent ([45/120] / [72/80] = 37.50%/90% = 0.4167), above the unsafe harbor percentage (40 percent) and below the safe harbor percentage (50 percent). The Commissioner may determine that the classification is nondiscriminatory after considering all the relevant facts and circumstances.

*Example (4).* Employer B has 10,000 nonexcludable employees, of whom 9,600 are nonhighly compensated employees and 400 are highly compensated employees. Employer B maintains a plan that benefits 600 nonhighly compensated employees and 100 highly compensated employees. Thus, the plan's ratio percentage is 25.00 percent ([ 600/9,600] / [100/400] = 6.25%/25% = 0.2500), which is below the percentage necessary to satisfy the ratio percentage test of § 1.410(b)-2(b)(2). Employer B's nonhighly compensated employee concentration percentage is 96 percent (9,600/10,000); thus, Employer B's safe harbor percentage is 23 percent, and its unsafe harbor percentage is 20 percent. Because the plan's ratio percentage (25.00 percent) is greater than the safe harbor percentage (23.00 percent), the plan's classification satisfies the safe harbor of paragraph (c)(2) of this section.

*Example (5).* The facts are the same as in Example 4, except that the plan benefits only 400 nonhighly compensated employees. The plan's ratio percentage is thus 16.67 percent ([400/9,600] / [100/400] = 4.17%/25% = 0.1667). The plan's ratio percentage is below the unsafe harbor percentage and thus the classification is considered discriminatory.

*Example (6).* The facts are the same as in Example 4, except that the plan benefits 500 nonhighly compensated employees. The plan's ratio percentage is thus 20.83 percent ([500/9,600] / [100/400] = 5.21%/25% = 0.2083), above the unsafe harbor percentage (20 percent) and below the safe harbor percentage (23 percent). The Commissioner may determine that the classification is nondiscriminatory after considering all the facts and circumstances.

T.D. 8363, 9/12/91.

### § 1.410(b)-5 Average benefit percentage test.

**(a) General rule.** A plan satisfies the average benefit percentage test of this section for a plan year if and only if the average benefit percentage of the plan for the plan year is at least 70 percent. A plan is deemed to satisfy this requirement if it satisfies paragraph (f) of this section for the plan year.

**(b) Determination of average benefit percentage.** The average benefit percentage of a plan for a plan year is the percentage determined by dividing the actual benefit percentage of the nonhighly compensated employees in plans in the testing group for the testing period that includes the plan year by the actual benefit percentage of the highly compensated employees in plans in the testing group for that testing period. See paragraph (d)(3)(ii) of this section for the definition of testing period.

**(c) Determination of actual benefit percentage.** The actual benefit percentage of a group of employees for a testing period is the average of the employee benefit percentages, calculated separately with respect to each of the employees in the group for the testing period. All nonexcludable employees of the employer are taken into account for this purpose, even if they are not benefiting under any plan that is taken into account.

**(d) Determination of employee benefit percentages.** *(1) Overview.* This paragraph (d) provides rules for determining employee benefit percentages. See paragraph (e) of this section for alternative methods for determining employee benefit percentages.

*(2) Employee contributions and employee-provided benefits disregarded.* Only employer-provided contributions and benefits are taken into account in determining employee benefit percentages. Therefore, employee contributions (including both employee contributions allocated to separate accounts and employee contributions not allocated to separate accounts), and benefits derived from such contributions, are not taken into account in determining employee benefit percentages.

*(3) Plans and plan years taken into account.* (i) Testing group. All plans included in the testing group under § 1.410(b)-7(e)(1), and only those plans, are taken into account in determining an employee's employee benefit percentage.

(ii) Testing period. An employee's employee benefit percentage is determined on the basis of plan years ending with or within the same calendar year. These plan years are referred to in this section as the relevant plan years or, in the aggregate, as the testing period.

*(4) Contributions or benefits basis.* Employee benefit percentages may be determined on either a contributions or a benefits basis. Employee benefit percentages for any testing period must be determined on the same basis (contributions or benefits) for all plans in the testing group.

*(5) Determination of employee benefit percentage.* (i) General rule. The employee benefit percentage for an employee for a testing period is the rate that would be determined for that employee for purposes of applying the general test for nondiscrimination in §§ 1.401(a)(4)-2, 1.401(a)(4)-3, 1.401(a)(4)-8 or 1.401(a)(4)-9, if all the plans in the testing group were aggregated for purposes of section

410(b). Thus, if employee benefit percentages are determined on a contributions basis, each employee's employee benefit percentage is the aggregate normal allocation rate that would be determined for the employee under § 1.401(a)(4)-9(b)(2)(ii)(A) (if the plans in the testing group include both defined benefit and defined contribution plans), the allocation rate that would be determined for the employee under § 1.401(a)(4)-2(c)(2) (if the plans in the testing group include only defined contribution plans), or the equivalent normal allocation rate that would be determined for the employee under § 1.401(a)(4)-8(c)(2) (if the plans in the testing group include only defined benefit plans). Similarly, if employee benefit percentages are determined on a benefits basis, each employee's employee benefit percentage is the aggregate normal accrual rate that would be determined for the employee under § 1.401(a)(4)-9(b)(2)(ii)(B), the normal accrual rate that would be determined for the employee under § 1.401(a)(4)-3(d), or the equivalent accrual rate that would be determined for the employee under § 1.401(a)(4)-8(b)(2), depending on whether the plans in the testing group include both defined benefit and defined contribution plans, only defined benefit plans, or only defined contribution plans.

(ii) Plans with differing plan years. If not all the plans in the testing group share the same plan year, § 1.410(b)-7(d)(5) would ordinarily prohibit them from being aggregated for purposes of section 410(b). In such a case, employee benefit percentages are determined by applying the rules of paragraph (d)(5)(i) of this section separately to each subset of plans in the testing group that share the same plan year (or the same accrual computation period) and aggregating the results for all plans in the testing group. Thus, an employee's employee benefit percentage is determined as the sum of these separate employee benefit percentages that are determined consistently for all the plans in the testing group (except for differences attributable solely to the differences in plan years).

(iii) Options and consistency requirements. In determining employee benefit percentages under this paragraph (d)(5), any optional or alternative methods or rules available for determining rates in §§ 1.401(a)(4)-2, 1.401(a)(4)-3, 1.401(a)(4)-8, or 1.401(a)(4)-9, whichever is applicable, may be applied. Thus, for example, employee benefit percentages may generally be calculated using any of the alternative methods of determining average annual compensation or plan year compensation under § 1.401(a)(4)-12, and using any underlying definition of compensation that satisfies section 414(s). Except as otherwise specifically permitted, the determination of employee benefit percentages must be made on a consistent basis for all employees and for all plans in the testing group as required by §§ 1.401(a)(4)-2(c)(2)(vi), 1.401(a)(4)-3(d)(2)(i), 1.401(a)(4)-8(b)(2)(iv), 1.401(a)(4)-8(c)(2)(iv) or 1.401(a)(4)-9(b)(2)(iv).

*(6) Permitted disparity.* (i) In general. Permitted disparity may be imputed in determining employee benefit percentages as provided in §§ 1.401(a)(4)-2, 1.401(a)(4)-3, 1.401(a)(4)-8, or 1.401(a)(4)-9, whichever is applicable. When separate employee benefit percentages are determined for individual plans under paragraph (e)(2) of this section (or for subsets of plans that have the same plan year as described in paragraph (d)(5)(ii) of this section), permitted disparity may be imputed for an employee only in one individual plan (or subset of plans) and may not be imputed for the same employee in another individual plan (or subset of plans). However, if the same average annual compensation or plan year compensation is used to determine employee benefit percentages in more than one plan, the employee's employee benefit percentages for those plans may be summed prior to imputing permitted disparity.

(ii) Plans which may not use permitted disparity. Permitted disparity may be reflected in the determination of rates only to the extent that the plans for which rates are being determined are plans for which the permitted disparity of section 401(l) is available. Thus, for example, if a section 401(k) plan is included in the testing group and permitted disparity is imputed under § 1.401(a)(4)-2(c)(iv), then employee benefit percentages are determined by first calculating an adjusted allocation rate (within the meaning of § 1.401(a)(4)-7(b)(1)) without regard to the amount of allocations under the section 401(k) plan and adding to it the allocation rate for the section 401(k) plan. See § 1.401(l)-1(a)(4) for a list of types of plans for which permitted disparity is not available.

*(7) Requirements for certain plans providing early retirement benefits.* (i) General rule. If any defined benefit plan in the testing group provides for early retirement benefits in addition to normal retirement benefits to any highly compensated employee, and the average actuarial reduction for any one of these benefits commencing in the five years prior to the plan's normal retirement age is less than four percent per year, then the aggregate most valuable allocation rate, equivalent most valuable allocation rate, aggregate most valuable accrual rate, or most valuable accrual rate must be substituted for the related normal rates in paragraph (d)(5) of this section.

(ii) Exception. Paragraph (d)(7)(i) of this section does not apply if early retirement benefits with average actuarial reductions described in that paragraph are currently available, within the meaning of § 1.401(a)(4)-4(b), under plans in the testing group to a percentage of nonhighly compensated employees that is at least 70 percent of the percentage of highly compensated employees to whom these benefits are currently available.

**(e) Additional optional rules.** *(1) Overview.* This paragraph (e) contains various alternative methods for determining employee benefit percentages for a testing period.

*(2) Determination of employee benefit percentages as the sum of separately determined rates.* (i) In general. Employee benefit percentages may be determined as the sum of separately determined employee benefit percentages for each of the plans in the testing group that are aggregated under paragraphs (d)(5)(i) or (ii) of this section, provided that these employee benefit percentages are determined on a consistent basis for all of these plans pursuant to paragraph (d)(5)(iii) of this section.

(ii) Exception from consistency requirement. The consistency requirement of paragraph (e)(2)(i) of this section is not violated merely because employee benefit percentages are not determined in a consistent manner for all of the plans in the testing group and the inconsistencies in determination of rates among plans are described in paragraph (e)(2)(iii) of this section. The exception in this paragraph (e)(2)(ii) applies only if it is reasonable to believe that the inconsistencies do not result in an average benefit percentage that is significantly higher than the average benefit percentage that would be determined had employee benefit percentages been determined on a consistent basis pursuant to paragraph (d)(5)(iii) of this section.

(iii) Permitted inconsistencies. The following inconsistencies between plans are permitted under this paragraph (e)(2)—

(A) Use of different underlying definitions of section 414(s) compensation in the determination of rates;

(B) Use of different definitions of average annual compensation;

(C) Use of different testing ages;

(D) Use of different fresh-start dates;

(E) Use of different actuarial assumptions for normalization; or

(F) Disregard of actuarial increases after normal retirement age and QPSA charges without regard to any requirement for uniformity in the actuarial increases or QPSA charges.

*(3) Determination of employee benefit percentages without regard to plans of another type.* (i) General rule. Employee benefit percentages may be determined under plans of one type (i.e., defined benefit plans or defined contribution plans) by treating all plans of the other type (i.e., defined contribution plans or defined benefit plans, respectively) as if they were not part of the testing group, using the method provided in this paragraph (e)(3). If this method is used to determine whether a defined contribution plan satisfies the average benefit percentage test, employee benefit percentages under all defined contribution plans in the testing group must be determined on a contributions basis, and benefits under any defined benefit plans may not be included in the employee benefit percentage. Similarly, if this method is used to determine whether a defined benefit plan satisfies the average benefit percentage test, employee benefit percentages under all defined benefit plans in the testing group must be determined on a benefits basis, and allocations under any defined contribution plans may not be included in the employee benefit percentage.

(ii) Restriction on use of separate testing group determination method. A plan does not satisfy the average benefit percentage test using the method provided in this paragraph (e)(3) unless each of the plans in the testing group of the other type (i.e., defined benefit plan or defined contribution plan) than the plan being tested satisfies the average benefit test of § 1.410(b)-2(b)(3) using the method in this paragraph (e)(3) or satisfies the ratio percentage test of § 1.410(b)-2(b)(2).

(iii) Treatment of permitted disparity. Although under the general rule of this paragraph (e)(3) plans of another type are disregarded in determining employee benefit percentages, the permitted disparity used by those plans (including any permitted disparity that is used by those plans to satisfy § 1.401(a)(4)-1(b)(2)) is nonetheless taken into account in determining the extent to which permitted disparity may be used in determining employee benefit percentages.

(iv) Example. The following example illustrates the rules of this paragraph (e)(3):

*Example.* Employer A maintains two defined benefit plans, neither of which covers a group of employees that satisfies the ratio percentage test of § 1.410(b)-2(b)(2), and a profit-sharing plan and a section 401(k) plan, each of which benefits a group of employees that satisfies the ratio percentage test of § 1.410(b)-2(b)(2). The defined benefit plans will satisfy the average benefit percentage test if the actual benefit percentage of all nonexcludable nonhighly compensated employees, computed on a benefits basis without regard to contributions under the profit-sharing plan or the section 401(k) plan, is at least 70 percent of the actual benefit percentage of all nonexcludable highly compensated employees, computed on a benefits basis without regard to contributions under the profit-sharing plan or the section 401(k) plan.

*(4) Simplified method for determining employee benefit percentages for certain defined benefit plans.* (i) In general. An employee's employee benefit percentage with respect to a plan may be determined under the simplified method of paragraph (e)(4)(ii) of this section, provided the following conditions are satisfied:

(A) The only plans included in the testing group are defined benefit plans, and employee benefit percentages under these plans are determined on a benefits basis.

(B) Employee benefit percentages under the plans in the testing group are not required to be determined by taking into account early retirement benefits under paragraph (d)(7) of this section.

(C) The plan is a safe harbor defined benefit plan described in § 1.401(a)(4)-3(b).

(ii) Simplified method. (A) Section 401(l) plans. Under the simplified method of this paragraph (e)(4)(ii), an employee's employee benefit percentage with respect to a section 401(l) plan described in § 1.401(a)(4)-3(b)(3) (i.e., a unit credit plan) may be deemed equal to the employee's excess benefit percentage or gross benefit percentage (as defined in § 1.401(l)-1(c)(14) or (18), respectively), whichever is applicable under the plan's benefit formula in the plan year. In the case of a section 401(l) plan described in § 1.401(a)(4)-3(b)(4) (i.e., a fractional accrual plan), an employee's employee benefit percentage with respect to that plan may be deemed equal to the rate at which the excess or gross benefit, whichever is applicable, accrues for the employee in the plan year, taking into account the plan's benefit formula and the employee's projected service at normal retirement age. The use of this simplified method will be treated as an imputation of permitted disparity. See paragraph (d)(6) of this section for a restriction on multiple use of permitted disparity.

(B) Other plans. Under the simplified method of this paragraph (e)(4)(ii), an employee's employee benefit percentage with respect to a plan described in § 1.401(a)(4)-3(b)(3) that is not a section 401(l) plan and that is not imputing permitted disparity may be deemed equal to the employee's benefit rate in the plan year under the plan's benefit formula. In the case of a plan described in § 1.401(a)(4)-3(b)(4) that is not a section 401(l) plan and that is not imputing permitted disparity, an employee's employee benefit percentage with respect to that plan may be deemed equal to the rate at which the benefit accrues for the employee in the plan year, taking into account the plan's benefit formula and an employee's projected service at normal retirement age.

*(5) Three-year averaging period.* An employee's employee benefit percentage may be determined for a testing period as the average of the employee's employee benefit percentages determined separately for the testing period and for the immediately preceding one or two testing periods (referred to in this section as an averaging period). Employee benefit percentages of a particular employee that are averaged together within an averaging period must be determined on a consistent basis for all testing periods within the averaging period.

*(6) Alternative methods of determining compensation.* Employee benefit percentages may be determined on the basis of any definition of compensation that satisfies § 1.414(s)-1(d) (without regard to whether the definition satisfies § 1.414(s)-1(d)(3)), provided that the same definition is used for all employees and it is reasonable to believe that

the definition does not result in an average benefit percentage that is significantly higher than the average benefit percentage that would be determined had employee benefit percentages been determined using a definition of compensation that also satisfies § 1.414(s)-1(d)(3).

**(f) Special rule for certain collectively bargained plans.** A plan (as determined without regard to the mandatory disaggregation rule of § 1.410(b)-7(c)(5)) that benefits both collectively bargained employees and noncollectively bargained employees is deemed to satisfy the average benefit percentage test of this section if—

*(1)* The provisions of the plan applicable to each employee in the plan are identical to the provisions of the plan applicable to every other employee in the plan, including the plan benefit or allocation formula, any optional forms of benefit, any ancillary benefit, and any other right or feature under the plan, and

*(2)* The plan would satisfy the ratio percentage test of § 1.410(b)-2(b)(2), if §§ 1.410(b)-6(d) and 1.410(b)-7(c)(5) (the excludable employee and mandatory disaggregation rules for collectively bargained and noncollectively bargained employees) did not apply.

T.D. 8363, 9/12/91, amend T.D. 8487, 8/31/93.

## § 1.410(b)-6 Excludable employees.

**(a) Employees.** *(1) In general.* For purposes of applying section 410(b) with respect to employees, all employees of the employer, other than the excludable employees described in paragraphs (b) through (i) of this section, are taken into account. Excludable employees are not taken into account with respect to a plan even if they are benefiting under the plan, except as otherwise provided in paragraph (b) of this section.

*(2) Rules of application.* Except as specifically provided otherwise, excludable employees are determined separately with respect to each plan for purposes of testing that plan under section 410(b). Thus, in determining whether a particular plan satisfies the ratio percentage test of § 1.410(b)-2(b)(2), paragraphs (b) through (i) of this section are applied solely with reference to that plan. Similarly, in determining whether two or more plans that are permissively aggregated and treated as a single plan under § 1.410(b)-7(d) satisfy the ratio percentage test of § 1.410(b)-2(b)(2), paragraphs (b) through (i) of this section are applied solely with reference to the deemed single plan. In determining whether a plan satisfies the average benefit percentage test of § 1.410(b)-5, the rules of this section are applied by treating all plans in the testing group as a single plan.

**(b) Minimum age and service exclusions.** *(1) In general.* If a plan applies minimum age and service eligibility conditions permissible under section 410(a)(1) and excludes all employees who do not meet those conditions from benefiting under the plan, then all employees who fail to satisfy those conditions are excludable employees with respect to that plan. An employee is treated as meeting the age and service requirements on the date that any employee with the same age and service (including service permitted to be taken into account for purposes of nondiscrimination testing under § 1.401(a)(4)-11(d)(3)) would be eligible to commence participation in the plan, as provided in section 410(b)(4)(C).

*(2) Multiple age and service conditions.* If a plan, including a plan for which an employer chooses the treatment under paragraph (b)(3) of this section, has two or more different sets of minimum age and service eligibility conditions, those employees who fail to satisfy all of the different sets of age and service conditions are excludable employees with respect to the plan. Except as provided in paragraph (b)(3) of this section, an employee who satisfies any one of the different sets of conditions is not an excludable employee with respect to the plan. Differences in the manner in which service is credited (e.g., hours of service calculated in accordance with 29 CFR 2530.200b-2 for hourly employees and elapsed time calculated in accordance with § 1.410(a)-7 for salaried employees) for purposes of applying a service condition are not taken into account in determining whether multiple age and service eligibility conditions exist.

*(3) Plans benefiting certain otherwise excludable employees.* (i) In general. An employer may treat a plan benefiting otherwise excludable employees as two separate plans, one for the otherwise excludable employees and one for the other employees benefiting under the plan. See § 1.410(b)-7(c)(3) regarding permissive disaggregation of plans benefiting otherwise excludable employees. The effect of this rule is that employees who would be excludable under paragraph (b)(1) of this section (applied without regard to section 410(a)(1)(B)) but for the fact that the plan does not apply the greatest permissible minimum age and service conditions may be treated as excludable employees with respect to the plan. This treatment is available only if the plan satisfies section 410(b) and § 1.410(b)-2 with respect to these otherwise excludable employees in the manner described in paragraph (b)(3)(ii) of this section.

(ii) Testing portion of plan benefiting otherwise excludable employees. In determining whether the plan that benefits employees who would otherwise be excludable under paragraph (b)(1) of this section (applied without regard to section 410(a)(1)(B)) satisfies section 410(b) and § 1.410(b)-2, employees who have satisfied the greatest permissible minimum age and service conditions with respect to the plan are excludable employees. In addition, if the plan being tested applies minimum age and service conditions and those conditions are less than the maximum permissible minimum age and service conditions, employees who have not satisfied the lower minimum age and service conditions actually provided for in the plan are excludable employees. Thus, for example, if the plan requires attainment of age 18 and 3 months of service, employees who have not attained age 18 or 3 months of service with the employer are excludable employees.

*(4) Examples.* The following examples illustrate the minimum age and service condition rules of this paragraph (b). In each example, the employer is not treated as operating qualified separate lines of business under section 414(r).

*Example (1).* An employer maintains Plan A for hourly employees and Plan B for salaried employees. Plan A has no minimum age or service condition. Plan B has no minimum age condition and requires 1 year of service. The employer treats Plans A and B as a single plan for purposes of section 410(b). Because Plan A imposes no minimum age or service condition, all employees of the employer automatically satisfy the minimum age and service conditions of Plan A. Therefore, no employees are excludable under this paragraph (b) in testing Plans A and B for purposes of section 410(b).

*Example (2).* An employer maintains three plans. Plan C benefits employees in Division C who satisfy the plan's minimum age and service condition of age 21 and 1 year of service. Plan D benefits employees in Division D who satisfy the plan's minimum age and service condition of age 18 and 1 year of service. Plan E benefits employees in Division E who satisfy the plan's minimum age and service condition of age 21 and 6 months of service. The employer treats Plans D and E as a single plan for purposes of section 410(b). In testing Plan C under the ratio percentage test or the nondiscriminatory classification test of section 410(b), employees who are not at least age 21 or who do not have at least 1 year of service are excludable employees under paragraph (b)(1) of this section. In testing Plans D and E, employees who do not satisfy the age and service requirements of either of the two plans are excludable employees under paragraph (b)(2) of this section. Thus, an employee is excludable with respect to Plans D and E only if the employee is not at least age 18 with at least 1 year of service or is not at least age 21 with at least 6 months of service. Thus, an employee who is 19 years old and has 11 months of service is excludable. Similarly, an employee who is 17 years old and has performed 2 years of service is also excludable.

*Example (3).* An employer maintains three plans. Plan F benefits all employees in Division F (the plan does not apply any minimum age or service condition). Plan G benefits employees in Division G who satisfy the plan's minimum age and service condition of age 18 and 1 year of service. Plan H benefits employees in Division H who satisfy the plan's minimum age and service condition of age 21 and 6 months of service. In testing the employer's plans under the average benefit percentage test provided in § 1.410(b)-5, Plans F, G, and H are treated as a single plan and, as such, use the lowest minimum age and service condition under the rule of paragraph (b)(2) of this section. Therefore, because Plan F does not apply any minimum age or service condition, no employee is excludable under this paragraph (b).

*Example (4).* An employer maintains Plan J, which does not apply any minimum age or service conditions. Plan J benefits all employees in Division 1 but does not benefit employees in Division 2. Although Plan J has no minimum age or service condition, the employer wants to exclude employees whose age and service is below the permissible minimums provided in section 410(b)(1)(A). The employer has 110 employees who either do not have 1 year of service or are not at least age 21. Of these 110 employees, 10 are highly compensated employees and 100 are nonhighly compensated employees. Five of these highly compensated employees, or 50 percent, work in Division 1 and thus benefit under Plan J. Thirty-five of these nonhighly compensated employees, or 35 percent, work in Division 1 and thus benefit under Plan J. Plan J satisfies the ratio percentage test of section 410(b) with respect to employees who do not satisfy the greatest permissible minimum age and service requirement because the ratio percentage of that group of employees is 70 percent. Thus, in determining whether or not Plan J satisfies section 410(b), the 110 employees may be treated as excludable employees in accordance with paragraph (b)(3)(i) of this section.

**(c) Certain nonresident aliens.** *(1) General rule.* An employee who is a nonresident alien (within the meaning of section 7701(b)(1)(B)) and who receives no earned income (within the meaning of section 911(d)(2)) from the employer that constitutes income from sources within the United States (within the meaning of section 861(a)(3)) is treated as an excludable employee.

*(2) Special treaty rule.* In addition, an employee who is a nonresident alien (within the meaning of section 7701(b)(1)(B)) and who does receive earned income (within the meaning of section 911(d)(2)) from the employer that constitutes income from sources within the United States (within the meaning of section 861(a)(3)) is permitted to be excluded, if all of the employee's earned income from the employer from sources within the United States is exempt from United States income tax under an applicable income tax convention. This paragraph (c)(2) applies only if all employees described in the preceding sentence are so excluded.

**(d) Collectively bargained employees.** *(1) General rule.* A collectively bargained employee is an excludable employee with respect to a plan that benefits solely noncollectively bargained employees. If a plan (within the meaning of § 1.410(b)-7(b)) benefits both collectively bargained employees and noncollectively bargained employees for a plan year, § 1.410(b)-7(c)(4) provides that the portion of the plan that benefits the collectively bargained employees is treated as a separate plan from the portion of the plan that benefits the noncollectively bargained employees. Thus, a collectively bargained employee is always an excludable employee with respect to the mandatorily disaggregated portion of any plan that benefits noncollectively bargained employees.

*(2) Definition of collectively bargained employee.* (i) In general. A collectively bargained employee is an employee who is included in a unit of employees covered by an agreement that the Secretary of Labor finds to be a collective bargaining agreement between employee representatives and one or more employers, provided that there is evidence that retirement benefits were the subject of good faith bargaining between employee representatives and the employer or employers. An employee is a collectively bargained employee regardless of whether the employee benefits under any plan of the employer. See section 7701(a)(46) and § 301.7701-17T of this chapter for additional requirements applicable to the collective bargaining agreement. An employee who performs hours of service during the plan year as both a collectively bargained employee and a noncollectively bargained employee is treated as a collectively bargained employee with respect to the hours of service performed as a collectively bargained employee and a noncollectively bargained employee with respect to the hours of service performed as a noncollectively bargained employee. See § 1.410(b)-7(c) for disaggregation rules for plans benefiting collectively bargained and noncollectively bargained employees.

(ii) Special rules for certain employees in multiemployer plans. (A) In general. For purposes of this paragraph (d), in testing the disaggregated portion of a multiemployer plan benefiting noncollectively bargained employees, a noncollectively bargained employee who benefits under the plan may be treated as a collectively bargained employee with respect to all of the employee's hours of service under the rules of paragraphs (d)(2)(ii)(B) through (E) of this section, if the employee is or was a member of a unit of employees covered by a collective bargaining agreement and that agreement or a successor agreement provides for the employee to benefit under the plan in the current plan year. For this purpose, provisions of a participation agreement or similar document are taken into account in determining whether a collective bargaining agreement provides for an employee to benefit under a multiemployer plan.

(B) Employees who were collectively bargained employees during a portion of the current plan year. An employee described in paragraph (d)(2)(ii)(A) of this section who performs services for one or more employers that are parties to the collective bargaining agreement, for the plan, or for the employee representative both as a collectively bargained employee and as a noncollectively bargained employee during a plan year may be treated as a collectively bargained employee for the plan year, provided that at least half of the employee's hours of service during the plan year are performed as a collectively bargained employee.

(C) Employees who were collectively bargained employees during the collective bargaining agreement. An employee described in paragraph (d)(2)(ii)(A) of this section who was a collectively bargained employee with respect to all of the employee's hours of service during a plan year (including employees who are treated as collectively bargained employees with respect to all of their hours of service during a plan year under paragraph (d)(2)(ii)(B) or (E) of this section) may be treated as a collectively bargained employee with respect to all of the employee's hours of service for the duration of the collective bargaining agreement applicable for such plan year or, if later, until the end of the following plan year. For this purpose, a collective bargaining agreement is applicable for a plan year if it provided for the employee to benefit in the plan and was effective for any portion of that plan year. This paragraph (d)(2)(ii)(C) does not apply unless the terms of the plan providing for benefit accruals treat the employee in a manner that is generally no more favorable than similarly-situated employees who are collectively bargained employees.

(D) Employees who previously were collectively bargained employees. An employee who was treated as a collectively bargained employee pursuant to paragraph (d)(2)(ii)(C) of this section may be treated as a collectively bargained employee with respect to all of the employee's hours of service after the end of the period described in paragraph (d)(2)(ii)(C) of this section, provided that the employee is performing services for one or more employers that are parties to the collective bargaining agreement, for the plan, or for the employee representative. This paragraph (d)(2)(ii)(D) does not apply unless the terms of the plan providing for benefit accruals treat the employee in a manner that is generally no more favorable than similarly-situated employees who are collectively bargained employees, and no more than five percent of the employees covered under the multiemployer plan are noncollectively bargained employees (determined without regard to this paragraph (d)(2)(ii)(D)). In determining whether more than five percent of the employees covered under the multiemployer plan are noncollectively bargained employees, those employees who are described in paragraphs (d)(2)(ii)(B) and (C) of this section are treated as collectively bargained employees.

(E) Transition rule. For a plan year beginning before the applicable effective date of these regulations as set forth in § 1.410(b)-10(b) or (d), any employee described in paragraph (d)(2)(ii)(A) of this section may be treated as a collectively bargained employee with respect all of the employee's hours of service for that plan year.

(F) Consistency requirement. The rules in paragraphs (d)(2)(i) and (ii) of this section must be applied to all employees on a reasonable and consistent basis for the plan year.

(iii) Covered by a collective bargaining agreement. (A) General rule. For purposes of paragraph (d)(2)(i) of this section, an employee is included in a unit of employees covered by a collective bargaining agreement if and only if the employee is represented by a bona fide employee representative that is a party to the collective bargaining agreement under which the plan is maintained. Thus, for example, an employee of either a plan or the employee representative that is a party to the collective bargaining agreement under which the plan is maintained is not included in a unit of employees covered by the collective bargaining agreement under which the plan is maintained merely because the employee is covered under the plan pursuant to an agreement entered into by the plan or employee representative on behalf of the employee (other than in the capacity of an employee representative with respect to the employee). This is the case even if all of such employees benefiting under the plan constitute only a de minimis percentage of the total employees benefiting under the plan.

(B) Plans covering professional employees. (1) In general. An employee is not considered included in a unit of employees covered by a collective bargaining agreement for a plan year for purposes of paragraph (d)(2)(iii)(A) of this section if, for the plan year, more than 2 percent of the employees who are covered pursuant to the agreement are professionals. This rule applies to all employees under the agreement, nonprofessionals as well as professionals. Thus, no employees covered by such an agreement are excludable employees with respect to employees who are not covered by a collective bargaining agreement.

(2) Multiple collective bargaining agreements. This paragraph (d)(2)(iii)(B) is applied separately with respect to each collective bargaining agreement. Thus, for example, if a plan benefits two groups of employees, one included in a unit of employees covered by collective bargaining agreement X, more than 2 percent of whom are professionals, and another included in a unit of employees covered by collective bargaining agreement Y, none of whom are professionals, the group covered by agreement X is not considered covered by a collective bargaining agreement and the group by agreement Y is considered covered by a collective bargaining agreement.

(3) Application of minimum coverage tests. If a plan covers more than 2 percent professional employees, no employees in the plan are treated as covered by a collective bargaining agreement. A plan that covers more than 2 percent professional employees must satisfy section 410(b) without regard to section 413(b) and the special rule in § 1.410(b)-2(b)(7) of this section (regarding collectively bargained plans). In such cases, all nonexcludable employees must be taken into account. For this purpose, employees included in other collective bargaining units are excludable employees. However, the employees who are not covered by a collective bargaining agreement and the employees who are covered by an agreement that has more than 2 percent professionals are not excludable employees.

(iv) Examples. The following examples illustrate the collective bargaining unit rules of this section.

*Example (1).* An employer has 700 collectively bargained employees (none of whom is a professional employee) and 300 noncollectively bargained employees (200 of whom are highly compensated employees). For purposes of applying the ratio percentage test of § 1.410(b)-2(b)(2) to Plan X, which benefits only the 300 noncollectively bargainee employees, the 700 collectively bargained employees are treated as excludable employees pursuant to paragraph (d) of this section.

*Example (2).* (i) An employer has 1,500 employees in the following categories:

| | Noncollectively Bargained Employees | Collectively Bargained Employees | Total |
|---|---|---|---|
| Highly Compensated Employees | 100 | 100 | 200 |
| Nonhighly Compensated Employees | 900 | 400 | 1,300 |

| Total | 1,000 | 500 | 1,500 |
|---|---|---|---|

The employer maintains Plan Y, which benefits 1,100 employees, including all of the noncollectively bargained employees (except for 100 nonhighly compensated employees who are noncollectively bargained employees), and 200 of the collectively bargained employees (including the 100 highly compensated employees who are collectively bargained employees). There are no professional employees covered by the collective bargaining agreement. In accordance with § 1.410(b)-7(c)(4), the employer must apply the ratio percentage test of § 1.410(b)-2(b)(2) to Plan Y as if the plan were two separate plans, one benefiting the noncollectively bargained employees and the other benefiting the collectively bargained employees.

(ii) In testing the portion of Plan Y that benefits the noncollectively bargained employees, the collectively bargained employees are excludable employees. That portion's ratio percentage is 88.89 percent ([800/900]/[100/100] = 88.89%/100% = 0.8889), and thus it satisfies the ratio percentage test. The portion of Plan Y that benefits collectively bargained employees automatically satisfies section 410(b) under the special rule in § 1.410(b)-2(b)(7).

**(e) Employees of qualified separate lines of business.** If an employer is treated as operating qualified separate lines of business for purposes of section 410(b) in accordance with § 1.414(r)-1(b), in testing a plan that benefits employees of one qualified separate line of business, the employees of the other qualified separate lines of business of the employer are treated as excludable employees. The rule in this paragraph (e) does not apply for purposes of satisfying the nondiscriminatory classification requirement of section 410(b)(5)(B). See §§ 1.414(r)-1(c)(2) and 1.414(r)-8 (separate application of section 410(b) to the employees of a qualified separate line of business). In addition, the rule in this paragraph (e) does not apply to a plan that is tested under the special rule for employer-wide plans in § 1.414(r)-1(c)(2)(ii) for a plan year.

**(f) Certain terminating employees.** *(1) In general.* An employee may be treated as an excludable employee for a plan year with respect to a particular plan if—

(i) The employee does not benefit under the plan for the plan year,

(ii) The employee is eligible to participate in the plan,

(iii) The plan has a minimum period of service requirement or a requirement that an employee be employed on the last day of the plan year (last-day requirement) in order for an employee to accrue a benefit or receive an allocation for the plan year,

(iv) The employee fails to accrue a benefit or receive an allocation under the plan solely because of the failure to satisfy the minimum period of service or last-day requirement,

(v) The employee terminates employment during the plan year with no more than 500 hours of service, and the employee is not an employee as of the last day of the plan year (for purposes of this paragraph (f)(1)(v), a plan that uses the elapsed time method of determining years of service may use either 91 consecutive calendar days or 3 consecutive calendar months instead of 500 hours of service, provided it uses the same convention for all employees during a plan year), and

(vi) If this paragraph (f) is applied with respect to any employee with respect to a plan for a plan year, it is applied with respect to all employees with respect to the plan for the plan year.

*(2) Hours of service.* For purposes of this paragraph (f), the term "hours of service" has the same meaning as provided for such term by 29 CFR 2530.200b-2 under the general method of crediting service for the employee. If one of the equivalencies set forth in 29 CFR 2530.200b-3 is used for crediting service under the plan, the 500-hour requirement must be adjusted accordingly.

*(3) Examples.* The following examples illustrate the provision of this paragraph (f).

*Example (1).* An employer has 35 employees who are eligible to participate under a defined contribution plan. The plan provides that an employee will not receive an allocation of contributions for a plan year unless the employee is employed by the employer on the last day of the plan year. Only 30 employees are employed by the employer on the last day of the plan year. Two of the five employees who terminated employment before the last day of the plan year had 500 or fewer hours of service during the plan year, and the remaining three had more than 500 hours of service during the year. Of the five employees who were no longer employed on the last day of the plan year, the two with 500 hours of service or less during the plan year are treated as excludable employees for purposes of section 410(b), and the remaining three who had over 500 hours of service during the plan year are taken into account in testing the plan under section 410(b) but are treated as not benefiting under the plan.

*Example (2).* An employer has 30 employees who are eligible to participate under a defined contribution plan. The plan requires 1,000 hours of service to receive an allocation of contributions or forfeitures. Ten employees do not receive an allocation because of their failure to complete 1,000 hours of service. Three of the 10 employees who failed to satisfy the minimum service requirement completed 500 or fewer hours of service and terminated their employment. Two of the employees completed more than 500, but fewer than 1,000 hours of service and terminated their employment. The remaining five employees did not terminate employment. Under the rule in paragraph (f) of this section, the three terminated employees who completed 500 or fewer hours of service are treated as excludable employees for the portion of the plan year they are employed. The other seven employees who do not receive an allocation are taken into account in testing the plan under section 410(b) but are treated as not benefiting under the plan.

*Example (3).* An employer maintains two plans, Plan A for salaried employees and Plan B for hourly employees. Of the 100 salaried employees, two do not receive an allocation under Plan A for the plan year because they terminate employment before completing 500 hours of service. Of the 300 hourly employees, 50 do not receive an allocation under Plan B for the plan year because they terminate employment before completing 500 hours. In applying section 410(b) to Plan A, the two employees who did not receive an allocation under Plan A are excludable employees, but the 50 who did not receive an allocation under Plan B are not excludable employees, because they were not eligible to participate under Plan A.

**(g) Employees of certain governmental or tax exempt entities.** *(1) Plans covered.* For purposes of testing either a section 401(k) plan, or a section 401(m) plan that is provided under the same general arrangement as a section 401(k) plan, an employer may treat as excludable those employees described in paragraphs (g)(2) and (3) of this section.

*(2) Employees of governmental entities.* Employees of governmental entities who are precluded from being eligible employees under a section 401(k) plan by reason of section 401(k)(4)(B)(ii) may be treated as excludable employees if more than 95 percent of the employees of the employer who are not precluded from being eligible employees by reason of section 401(k)(4)(B)(ii) benefit under the plan for the year.

*(3) Employees of tax exempt entities.* Employees of an organization described in section 403(b)(1)(A)(i) who are eligible to make salary reduction contributions under section 403(b) may be treated as excludable with respect to a section 401(k) plan, or a section 401(m) plan that is provided under the same general arrangement as a section 401 (k) plan, if—

(i) No employee of an organization described in section 403(b)(1)(A)(i) is eligible to participate in such section 401(k) plan or section 401(m) plan; and

(ii) At least 95 percent of the employees who are neither employees of an organization described in section 403(b)(1)(A)(i) nor employees of a governmental entity who are precluded from being eligible employees under a section 401(k) plan by reason of section 401(k)(4)(B)(ii) are eligible to participate in such section 401(k) plan or section 401 (m) plan.

**(h) Former employees.** *(1) In general.* For purposes of applying section 410(b) with respect to former employees, all former employees of the employer are taken into account, except that the employer may treat a former employee described in paragraph (h)(2) or (h)(3) of this section as an excludable former employee. If either (or both) of the former employee exclusion rules under paragraphs (h)(2) and (h)(3) of this section is applied, it must be applied to all former employees for the plan year on a consistent basis.

*(2) Employees terminated before a specified date.* The employer may treat a former employee as excludable if—

(i) The former employee became a former employee either prior to January 1, 1984, or prior to the tenth calendar year preceding the calendar year in which the current plan year begins, and

(ii) The former employee became a former employee in a calendar year that precedes the earliest calendar year in which any former employee who benefits under the plan in the current plan year became a former employee.

*(3) Previously excludable employees.* The employer may treat a former employee as excludable if the former employee was an excludable employee (or would have been an excludable employee if these regulations had been in effect) under the rules of paragraphs (b) through (g) of this section during the plan year in which the former employee became a former employee. If the employer treats a former employee as excludable pursuant to this paragraph (h)(3), the former employee is not taken into account with respect to a plan even if the former employee is benefiting under the plan.

**(i) Former employees treated as employees.** An employer may treat as excludable employees all formerly nonhighly compensated employees who are treated as employees of the employer under § 1.410(b)-9 solely because they have increases in accrued benefits under a defined benefit plan that are based on ongoing service or compensation credits (including imputed service or compensation) after they cease to perform services for the employer.

---

T.D. 8363, 9/12/91, amend T.D. 8376, 12/2/91, T.D. 8487, 8/31/93, T.D. 8548, 6/23/94, T.D. 9275, 7/20/2006.

---

## § 1.410(b)-7 Definition of plan and rules governing plan disaggregation and aggregation.

**(a) In general.** This section provides a definition of "plan." First, this section sets forth a definition of plan within the meaning of section 401(a) or 403(a). Then certain mandatory disaggregation and permissive aggregation rules are applied. The result is the definition of plan that applies for purposes of sections 410(b) and 401(a)(4). Thus, in general, the term "plan" as used in this section initially refers to a plan described in section 414(l) and to an annuity plan described in section 403(a), and the term "plan" as used in other sections under these regulations means the plan determined after application of this section. Paragraph (b) of this section provides that each single plan under section 414(l) is treated as a single plan for purposes of section 410(b). Paragraph (c) of this section describes the rules for certain plans that must be treated as comprising two or more separate plans, each of which is a single plan subject to section 410(b). Paragraph (d) of this section provides a rule permitting an employer to aggregate certain separate plans to form a single plan for purposes of section 410(b). Paragraph (e) of this section provides rules for determining the testing group of plans taken into account in determining whether a plan satisfies the average benefit percentage test of § 1.410(b)-5.

**(b) Separate asset pools are separate plans.** Each single plan within the meaning of section 414(l) is a separate plan for purposes of section 410(b). See § 1.414(l)-1(b). For example, if only a portion of the assets under a defined benefit plan is available, on an ongoing basis, to provide the benefits of certain employees, and the remaining assets are available only in certain limited cases to provide such benefits (but are available in all cases for the benefit of other employees), there are two separate plans. Similarly, the defined contribution portion of a plan described in section 414(k) is a separate plan from the defined benefit portion of that same plan. A single plan under section 414(l) is a single plan for purposes of section 410(b), even though the plan comprises separate written documents and separate trusts, each of which receives a separate determination letter from the Internal Revenue Service. A defined contribution plan does not comprise separate plans merely because it includes more than one trust, or merely because it provides for separate accounts and permits employees to direct the investment of the amounts allocated to their accounts. Further, a plan does not comprise separate plans merely because assets are separately invested in individual insurance or annuity contracts for employees.

**(c) Mandatory disaggregation of certain plans.** *(1) Section 401(k) and 401(m) plans.* The portion of a plan that is a section 401(k) plan and the portion that is not a section 401(k) plan are treated as separate plans for purposes of section 410(b). Similarly, the portion of a plan that is a section 401(m) plan and the portion that is not a section 401(m) plan are treated as separate plans for purposes of section 410(b). Thus, a plan that consists of elective contributions under a section 401(k) plan, employee and matching contributions under a section 401(m) plan, and contributions other than elective, employee, or matching contributions is treated as three separate plans for purposes of section 410(b). In addition, the portion of a plan that consists of contributions described in § 1.401(k)-2(a)(5) (i.e., contributions that fail to satisfy the allocation or compensation requirements applicable to elective contributions and are therefore required to be tested separately) and the portion of the plan that does not consist of such contributions are treated as separate plans for purposes of section 410(b). Similarly, the portion of a plan that consists of contributions described in § 1.410(m)-1(b)(4)(ii) (i.e., matching contributions that fail to satisfy the allocation and other requirements applicable to matching contributions and are therefore required to be tested separately) and the portion of the plan that does not consist of such contributions are treated as separate plans for purposes of section 410(b).

*(2) ESOPs and non-ESOPs.* The portion of a plan that is an ESOP and the portion of the plan that is not an ESOP are treated as separate plans for purposes of section 410(b), except as otherwise permitted under § 54.4975-11(e) of this Chapter.

*(3) Plans benefiting otherwise excludable employees.* If an employer applies section 410(b) separately to the portion of a plan that benefits only employees who satisfy age and service conditions under the plan that are lower than the greatest minimum age and service conditions permissible under section 410(a), the plan is treated as comprising separate plans, one benefiting the employees who have satisfied the lower minimum age and service conditions but not the greatest minimum age and service conditions permitted under section 410(a) and one benefiting employees who have satisfied the greatest minimum age and service conditions permitted under section 410(a). See § 1.410(b)-6(b)(3)(ii) for rules about testing otherwise excludable employees.

*(4) Plans benefiting certain disaggregation populations of employees.* (i) In general. (A) Single plan must be treated as separate plans. If a plan (i.e., a single plan within the meaning of section 414(l)) benefits employees of more than one disaggregation population, the plan must be disaggregated and treated as separate plans, each separate plan consisting of the portion of the plan benefiting the employees of each disaggregation population. See paragraph (c)(4)(ii) of this section for the definition of disaggregation population.

(B) Benefit accruals or allocations attributable to current status. Except as otherwise provided in paragraph (c)(4)(i)(C) of this section, in applying the rule of paragraph (c)(4)(i)(A) of this section, the portion of the plan benefiting employees of a disaggregation population consists of all benefits accrued by, or all allocations made to, employees while they were members of the disaggregation population.

(C) Exceptions for certain benefit accruals. (1) Attribution of benefits to first disaggregation population. If employees benefiting under a plan change from one disaggregation population to a second disaggregation population, benefits they accrue while members of the second disaggregation population that are attributable to years of service previously credited while the employees were members of the first disaggregation population may be treated as provided to them in their status as members of the first disaggregation population and thus included in the portion of the plan benefiting employees of the first disaggregation population. This special treatment is available only if it is applied on a consistent basis, if it does not result in significant discrimination in favor of highly compensated employees, and if the plan provision providing the additional benefits applies on the same terms to all similarly-situated employees. For example, if all formerly collectively bargained employees accrue additional benefits under a plan after becoming noncollectively bargained employees, then those benefit increases may be treated as included in the portion of the plan benefiting collectively bargained employees if they are attributable to years of service credited while the employees were collectively bargained (e.g., where the additional benefits result from compensation increases that occur while the employees are noncollectively bargained or from plan amendments affecting benefits earned while collectively bargained that are adopted while the employees are noncollectively bargained) and if such treatment does not result in significant discrimination in favor of highly compensated employees.

(2) Attribution of benefits to current disaggregation population. If employees benefiting under a plan change from one disaggregation population to another disaggregation population, benefits they accrue while members of the first disaggregation population may be treated as provided to them in their current status and thus included in the portion of the plan benefiting employees of the disaggregation population of which they are currently members. This special treatment is available only if it is applied on a consistent basis and if it does not result in significant discrimination in favor of highly compensated employees.

(D) Change in disaggregation populations. (1) Reasonable treatment. If, in previous years, the configuration of a plan's disaggregation populations differed from their configuration for the current year, for purposes of the benefits accrued by, or allocations made to, an employee for those years, the employee's status as a member of a current disaggregation population for those years must be determined on a reasonable basis. A different configuration occurs, for example, if disaggregation populations exist for the first time, such as when an employer is first treated as operating qualified separate lines of business, or if the existing disaggregation populations change, such as when an employer redesignates its qualified separate lines of business.

(2) Example. The following example illustrates the application of this paragraph (c)(4)(i)(D).

*Example.* (a) Employer X operates Divisions M and N, which are treated as qualified separate lines of business for the first time in 1998. Thus, the disaggregation populations of employees of Division M and employees of Division N exist for the first time. Since 1981 Employer X has maintained a defined benefit plan, Plan P, for employees of Division M. Plan P provides a normal retirement benefit of one percent of average annual compensation for each year of service up to 25. Employee A has worked for Division M since 1981 and has never worked for Division N. Employee B has worked for Division N since 1989 and worked for Division M from 1981 to 1988. Employee C has worked in the headquarters of Employer X since 1981. For the period 1981 to 1988 Employee C was credited with years of service under Plan P.

(b) For purposes of the benefits accrued by Employee A under Plan P during years 1981 through 1997, Employee A is reasonably treated as having been a member of the Division M disaggregation population for those years. For purposes of the benefits accrued by Employee B under Plan P during years 1981 through 1988, Employee B is reasonably treated as having been a member of the Division M disaggregation population for 1981 through 1988 and as having changed to the Division N disaggregation population for 1989 through 1997. For purposes of the benefits accrued by Employee C under Plan P during years 1981 through 1988, Employee C is reasonably treated as having been a member of the Division M disaggregation population for those years. Moreover, any benefit accruals for Employee B and Employee C in years after 1988, that result from increases in average annual compensation after 1988 and that are attributable to years of service credited for 1981 through 1988, may be treated as provided to Employee B and Employee C in their status as members of the Division M disaggregation population if the requirements of paragraph (c)(4)(i)(C)(1) of this section are otherwise met.

(ii) Definition of disaggregation population. (A) Plan benefiting employees of qualified separate lines of business. If an employer is treated as operating qualified separate lines of business for purposes of section 410(b) in accordance with § 1.414(r)-1(b), and a plan benefits employees of more than one qualified separate line of business, the employees of each qualified separate line of business are separate disaggregation populations. In this case, the portion of the plan benefiting the employees of each qualified separate line of business is treated as a separate plan maintained by that qualified separate line of business. However, employees of different qualified separate lines of business who are benefiting under a plan that is tested under the special rule for employer-wide plans in § 1.414(r)-1(c)(2)(ii) for a plan year are not separate disaggregation populations merely because they are employees of different qualified separate lines of business.

(B) Plan benefiting collectively bargained employees. If a plan benefits both collectively bargained employees and noncollectively bargained employees, the collectively bargained employees are one disaggregation population and the noncollectively bargained employees are another disaggregation population. If the population of collectively bargained employees includes employees covered under different collective bargaining agreements, the population of employees covered under each collective bargaining agreement is also a separate disaggregation population.

(C) Plan maintained by more than one employer. If a plan benefits employees of more than one employer, the employees of each employer are separate disaggregation populations. In this case, the portion of the plan benefiting the employees of each employer is treated as a separate plan maintained by that employer, which must satisfy section 410(b) by reference only to that employer's employees. However, for purposes of this paragraph (c)(4)(ii)(C), if the plan of one employer (or, in the case of a plan maintained by more than one employer, the plan provisions applicable to the employees of one employer) treats compensation or service with another employer as compensation or service with the first employer, then the current accruals attributable to that compensation or service are treated as provided to an employee of the first employer under the plan of the first employer (or the portion of a plan maintained by more than one employer benefiting employees of the first employer), and the provisions of paragraph (c)(4)(i)(C) of this section do not apply to those accruals. Thus, for example, if Plan A maintained by Employer X imputes service or compensation for an employee of Employer Y, then Plan A is not treated as benefiting the employees of more than one employer merely because of this imputation.

*(5) Additional rule for plans benefiting employees of more than one qualified separate line of business.* If a plan benefiting employees of more than one qualified separate line of business satisfies the reasonable classification requirement of § 1.410(b)-4(b) before the application of paragraph (c)(4) of this section, then any portion of the plan that is treated as a separate plan as a result of the application of paragraphs (c)(4)(i)(A) and (ii)(A) of this section is deemed to satisfy that requirement.

**(d) Permissive aggregation for ratio percentage and nondiscriminatory classification tests.** *(1) In general.* Except as provided in paragraphs (d)(2) and (d)(3) of this section, for purposes of applying the ratio percentage test of § 1.410(b)-2(b)(2) or the nondiscriminatory classification test of § 1.401(b)-4, an employer may designate two or more separate plans (determined after application of paragraph (b) of this section) as a single plan. If an employer treats two or more separate plans as a single plan under this paragraph, the plans must be treated as a single plan for all purposes under sections 401(a)(4) and 410(b).

*(2) Rules of disaggregation.* An employer may not aggregate portions of a plan that are disaggregated under the rules of paragraph (c) of this section. Similarly, an employer may not aggregate two or more separate plans that would be disaggregated under the rules of paragraph (c) of this section if they were portions of the same plan. In addition, an employer may not aggregate an ESOP with another ESOP, except as permitted under § 54.4975-11(e) of this Chapter.

*(3) Duplicative aggregation.* A plan may not be combined with two or more plans to form more than one single plan. Thus, for example, an employer that maintains plans A, B, and C may not aggregate plans A and B and plans A and C to form two single plans. However, the employer may apply the permissive aggregation rules of this paragraph (d) to form any one (and only one) of the following combinations: plan ABC, plans AB and C, plans AC and B, or plans A and BC.

*(4) Special rule for plans benefiting employees of a qualified separate line of business.* For purposes of paragraph (d)(1) of this section, an employer that is treated as operating qualified separate lines of business for purposes of section 410(b) in accordance with § 1.414(r)-1(b) is permitted to aggregate the portions of two or more plans that benefit employees of the same qualified separate line of business (regardless of whether the employer elects to aggregate the portions of the same plans that benefit employees of the other qualified separate lines of business of the employer), provided that none of the plans is tested under the special rule for employer-wide plans in § 1.414(r)-1(c)(2)(ii). Thus, the employer is permitted to apply paragraph (d)(1) of this section with respect to two or more separate plans determined after the application of paragraphs (b) and (c)(4) of this section, but may not aggregate a plan that is tested under the special rule for employer-wide plans in § 1.414(r)-1(c)(2)(ii) for a plan year with any portion of a plan that does not rely on that special rule for the plan year. In all other respects, the provisions of this paragraph (d) regarding permissive aggregation apply, including (but not limited to) the disaggregation rules under paragraph (d)(2) of this section (including the mandatory disaggregation rule of paragraph (c)(4) of this section), and the prohibition on duplicative aggregation under paragraph (d)(3) of this section. This paragraph (d)(4) applies only in the case of an employer that is treated as operating qualified separate lines of business for purposes of section 410(b) in accordance with § 1.414(r)-1(b). See §§ 1.414(r)-1(c)(2) and 1.414(r)-8 (separate application of section 410(b) to the employees of a qualified separate line of business).

*(5) Same plan year requirement.* Two or more plans may not be aggregated and treated as a single plan under this paragraph (d) unless they have the same plan year.

**(e) Determination of plans in testing group for average benefit percentage test.** *(1) In general.* For purposes of applying the average benefit percentage test of § 1.410(b)-5 with respect to a plan, all plans in the testing group must be taken into account. For this purpose, the plans in the testing group are the plan being tested and all other plans of the employer that could be permissively aggregated with that plan under paragraph (d) of this section. Whether two or more plans could be permissively aggregated under paragraph (d) of this section is determined (i) without regard to the rule in paragraph (d)(4) of this section that portions of two or more plans benefiting employees of the same line of business may not be aggregated if any of the plans is tested under the special rule for employer-wide plans in § 1.414(r)-1(c)(2)(ii), (ii) without regard to paragraph (d)(5) of this section, and (iii) by applying paragraph (d)(2) of this section without regard to paragraphs (c)(1) and (c)(2) of this section.

*(2) Examples.* the following example illustrates the rules of this paragraph (e).

*Example (1).* Employer X is treated as operating two qualified separate lines of business for purposes of section 410(b) in accordance with section 414(r), QSLOB1 and QSLOB2. Employer X must apply the rules in § 1.414(r)-8 to determine whether its plans satisfy section 410(b) on a qualified-separate-line-of-business basis. Employer X maintains the following plans:

(a) Plan A, the portion of Employer X's employer-wide section 401(k) plan that benefits all noncollectively bargained employees of QSLOB1,

(b) Plan B, the portion of Employer X's employer-wide section 401(k) plan that benefits all noncollectively bargained employees of QSLOB2,

(c) Plan C, a defined benefit plan that benefits all hourly noncollectively bargained employees of QSLOB1,

(d) Plan D, a defined benefit plan that benefits all collectively bargained employees of QSLOB1,

(e) Plan E, an ESOP that benefits all noncollectively bargained employees of QSLOB1,

(f) Plan F, a profit-sharing plan that benefits all salaried noncollectively bargained employees of QSLOB1.

Assume that Plan F does not satisfy the ratio percentage test of § 1.410(b)-2(b)(2) on a qualified-separate-line-of-business basis, but does satisfy the nondiscriminatory classification test of § 1.410(b)-4 on both an employer-wide and a qualified-separate-line-of-business basis. Therefore, to satisfy section 410(b), Plan F must satisfy the average benefit percentage test of § 1.410(b)-5 on a qualified-separate-line-of-business basis. The plans in the testing group used to determine whether Plan F satisfies the average benefit percentage test of § 1.410(b)-5 are Plans A, C, E, and F.

*Example (2).* The facts are the same as in Example 1, except that Employer X applies the special rule for employer-wide plans in § 1.414(r)-1(c)(2)(ii) to its employer-wide section 401(k) plan. To satisfy section 410(b), Plan F must satisfy the average benefit percentage test of § 1.410(b)-5. Since paragraph (c)(4) of this section no longer applies to Plans A and B, they are treated as a single plan (Plan AB). The plans in the testing group used to determine whether Plan F satisfies the average benefit percentage test of § 1.410(b)-5 are therefore Plans AB, C, E, and F. However, the employees of QSLOB2 continue to be excludable employees for purposes of determining whether Plan F satisfies the average benefit percentage test. See § 1.410(b)-6(e).

**(f) Section 403(b) plans.** In determining whether a plan satisfies section 410(b), a plan subject to section 403(b)(12)(A)(i) is disregarded. However, in determining whether a plan subject to section 403(b)(12)(A)(i) satisfies section 410(b), plans that are not subject to section 403(b)(12)(A)(i) may be taken into account.

T.D. 8363, 9/12/91, amend T.D. 8376, 12/2/91, T.D. 8487, 8/31/93, T.D. 8548, 6/23/94, T.D. 9169, 12/28/2004.

### § 1.410(b)-8 Additional rules.

**(a) Testing methods.** *(1) In general.* A plan must satisfy section 410(b) for a plan year using one of the testing options in paragraphs (a)(2) through (a)(4) of this section. Whichever testing option is used for the plan year must also be used for purposes of applying section 401(a)(4) to the plan for the plan year. The annual testing option in paragraph (a)(4) of this section must be used in applying section 410(b) to a section 401(k) plan or a section 401(m) plan, and in applying the average benefit percentage test of § 1.410(b)-5. For purposes of this paragraph (a), the plan provisions and other relevant facts as of the last day of the plan year regarding which employees benefit under the plan for the plan year are applied to the employees taken into account under the testing option used for the plan year. For this purpose, amendments retroactively correcting a plan in accordance with § 1.401(a)(4)-11(g) are taken into account as plan provisions in effect as of the last day of the plan year.

*(2) Daily testing option.* A plan satisfies section 410(b) for a plan year if it satisfies § 1.410(b)-2 on each day of the plan year, taking into account only those employees (or former employees) who are employees (or former employees) on that day.

*(3) Quarterly testing option.* A plan is deemed to satisfy section 410(b) for a plan year if the plan satisfies § 1.410(b)-2 on at least one day in each quarter of the plan year, taking into account for each of those days only those employees (or former employees) who are employees (or former employees) on that day. The preceding sentence does not apply if the plan's eligibility rules or benefit formula operate to cause the four quarterly testing days selected by the employer not to be reasonably representative of the coverage of the plan over the entire plan year.

*(4) Annual testing option.* A plan satisfies section 410(b) for a plan year if it satisfies § 1.410(b)-2 as of the last day of the plan year, taking into account all employees (or former employees) who were employees (or former employees) on any day during the plan year.

*(5) Example.* The following example illustrates this paragraph (a).

*Example.* Plan A is a defined contribution plan that is not a section 401(k) plan or a section 401(m) plan, and that conditions allocations on an employee's employment on the last day of the plan year. Plan A is being tested for the 1995 calendar plan year using the daily testing option in paragraph (a)(2) of this section. In testing the plan for compliance with section 410(b) on March 11, 1995, Employee X is taken into account because he was an employee on that day and was not an excludable employee with respect to Plan A on that day. Employee X was a participant in Plan A on March 11, 1995, was employed on December 31, 1995, and received an allocation under Plan A for the 1995 plan year. Under these facts, Employee X is treated as benefiting under Plan A on March 11, 1995, even though Employee X had not satisfied all of the conditions for receiving an allocation on that day, because Employee X satisfied all of those conditions as of the last day of the plan year.

**(b) Family member aggregation rule.** For purposes of section 410(b), and in accordance with section 414(q)(6), a highly compensated employee who is a 5-percent owner or one of the ten most highly compensated employees and any family member (or members) of such a highly compensated employee who is also an employee of the employer are to be treated as a single highly compensated employee. If any member of that group is benefiting under a plan, the deemed single employee is treated as benefiting under the plan. If no member of that group is benefiting under a plan, the deemed single employee is treated as not benefiting under the plan.

T.D. 8363, 9/12/91.

**§ 1.410(b)-9 Definitions.**

In applying this section and §§ 1.410(b)-2 through 1.410(b)-10, the definitions in this section govern unless otherwise provided.

Collectively bargained employee. "Collectively bargained employee" means a collectively bargained employee within the meaning of § 1.410(b)-6(d)(2).

Defined benefit plan. "Defined benefit plan" means a defined benefit plan within the meaning of section 414(j). The portion of a plan described in section 414(k) that does not consist of separate accounts is treated as a defined benefit plan.

Defined contribution plan. "Defined contribution plan" means a defined contribution plan within the meaning of section 414(i). The portion of a plan described in section 414(k) that consists of separate accounts is treated as a defined contribution plan.

Employee. "Employee" means an individual who performs services for the employer who is either a common law employee of the employer, a self-employed individual who is treated as an employee pursuant to section 401(c)(1), or a leased employee (not excluded under section 414(n)(5)) who is treated as an employee of the employer-recipient under section 414(n)(2) or 414(o)(2). Individuals that an employer treats as employees under section 414(n) pursuant to the requirements of section 414(o) are considered to be leased employees for purposes of this rule. In addition, an individual must be treated as an employee with respect to allocations under a defined contribution plan taken into account under § 1.401(a)(4)-2(c)(ii) and with respect to increases in accrued benefits (within the meaning of 411(a)(7)) under a defined benefit plan that are based on ongoing service or compensation (including imputed service or compensation) credits.

Employer. "Employer" means the employer maintaining the plan and those employers required to be aggregated with the employer under sections 414(b), (c), (m), or (o). An individual who owns the entire interest of an unincorporated trade or business is treated as an employer. Also, a partnership is treated as the employer of each partner and each employee of the partnership.

ESOP. "ESOP" or "employee stock ownership plan" means an employee stock ownership plan within the meaning of section 4975(e)(7) or a tax credit employee stock ownership plan within the meaning of section 409(a).

Former employee. "Former employee" means an individual who was, but has ceased to be, an employee of the employer (i.e., the individual has ceased performing services as an employee for the employer). An individual is treated as a former employee beginning on the day after the day on which the individual ceases performing services as an employee for the employer. Thus, an individual who ceases performing services as an employee for an employer during a plan year is both an employee and a former employee for the plan year. Notwithstanding the foregoing, an individual is an employee (and not a former employee) to the extent that the individual is treated as an employee with respect to the plan for the plan year under the definition of employee in this section.

Highly compensated employee. "Highly compensated employee" means an employee who is a highly compensated employee within the meaning of section 414(q) or a former employee treated as an employee under the definition of employee in this section who is a highly compensated former employee within the meaning of section 414(q).

Highly compensated former employee. "Highly compensated former employee" means a former employee who is a highly compensated former employee within the meaning of section 414(q).

Multiemployer plan. "Multiemployer plan" means a multiemployer plan within the meaning of section 414(f).

Noncollectively bargained employee. "Noncollectively bargained employee" means an employee who is not a collectively bargained employee.

Nonhighly compensated employee. "Nonhighly compensated employee" means an employee who is not a highly compensated employee.

Nonhighly compensated former employee. "Nonhighly compensated former employee" means a former employee who is not a highly compensated former employee.

Plan year. "Plan year" means the plan year of the plan as defined in the written plan document. In the absence of a specifically designated plan year, the plan year is deemed to be the calendar year.

Plan year compensation. "Plan year compensation" means plan year compensation within the meaning of § 1.401(a)(4)-12.

Professional employee. "Professional employee" means any highly compensated employee who, on any day of the plan year, performs professional services for the employer as an actuary, architect, attorney, chiropodist, chiropractor, dentist, executive, investment banker, medical doctor, optometrist, osteopath, podiatrist, psychologist, certified or other public accountant, stockbroker, or veterinarian, or in any other professional capacity determined by the Commissioner in a notice or other document of general applicability to constitute the performance of services as a professional.

Ratio percentage. With respect to a plan for a plan year, a plan's "ratio percentage" means the percentage (rounded to the nearest hundredth of a percentage point) determined by dividing the percentage of the nonhighly compensated employees who benefit under the plan by the percentage of the highly compensated employees who benefit under the plan. The percentage of the nonhighly compensated employees who benefit under the plan is determined by dividing the number of nonhighly compensated employees benefiting under the plan by the total number of nonhighly compensated employees of the employer. The percentage of the highly compensated employees who benefit under the plan is determined by dividing the number of highly compensated employees benefiting under the plan by the total number of highly compensated employees of the employer.

Section 401(k) plan. "Section 401(k) plan" means a plan consisting of elective contributions described in § 1.401(k)-6 under a qualified cash or deferred arrangement described in § 1.401(k)-2(a)(4)(i). Thus, a section 401(k) plan does not include a plan (or portion of a plan) that consists of contributions under a nonqualified cash or deferred arrangement, or qualified nonelective or qualified matching contributions treated as elective contributions under § 1.401(k)-1(a)(6).

Section 401(l) plan. "Section 401(l) plan" means a plan that—

(1) Provides for a disparity in employer-provided benefits or contributions that satisfies section 401(l) in form, and

(2) Relies on one of the safe harbors of § 1.401(a)(4)-2(b)(2), 1.401(a)(4)-3(b), 1.401(a)(4)-8(b)(3), or 1.401(a)(4)-8(c)(3)(iii)(B) to satisfy section 401(a)(4).

Section 401(m) plan. "Section 401(m) plan" means a plan consisting of employee contributions described in § 1.401(m)-1(f)(6) or matching contributions described in § 1.401(m)-1(a)(2), or both. Thus, a section 401(m) plan does not include a plan (or portion of a plan) that consists of elective contributions or qualified nonelective contributions treated as matching contributions under § 1.401(m)-1(b)(5).

T.D. 8363, 9/12/91, amend T.D. 8487, 8/31/93, T.D. 9169, 12/28/2004.

### § 1.410(b)-10 Effective dates and transition rules.

***Caution:*** The Treasury has not yet amended Reg § 1.410(b)-10 to reflect changes made by P.L. 105-34.

**(a) Statutory effective dates.** *(1) In general.* Except as set forth in paragraph (a)(2) of this section, the minimum coverage rules of section 410(b) as amended by section 1112 of the Tax Reform Act of 1986 apply to plan years beginning on or after January 1, 1989.

*(2) Special statutory effective date for collective bargaining agreements.* (i) In general. As provided for by section 1112(e)(2) of the Tax Reform Act of 1986, in the case of a plan maintained pursuant to one or more collective bargaining agreements between employee representatives and one or more employers ratified before March 1, 1986, the minimum coverage rules of section 410(b) as amended by section 1112 of the Tax Reform Act of 1986 do not apply to employees covered by any such agreement in plan years beginning before the earlier of—

(A) January 1, 1991; or

(B) The later of January 1, 1989, or the date on which the last of such collective bargaining agreements terminates (determined without regard to any extension thereof after February 28, 1986). For purposes of this paragraph (a)(2), any extension or renegotiation of a collective bargaining agreement, which extension or renegotiation is ratified after February 28, 1986, is to be disregarded in determining the date on which the agreement terminates.

(ii) Example. The following example illustrates this paragraph (a)(2).

*Example.* Employer A maintains Plan 1 pursuant to a collective bargaining agreement. Plan 1 covers 100 of Employer A's noncollectively bargained employees and 900 of Employer A's collectively bargained employees. Employer A also maintains Plan 2, which covers Employer A's other 400 noncollectively bargained employees. The collective bargaining agreement under which Plan 1 is maintained was entered into on January 1, 1986, and expires December 31, 1992. Because Plan 1 is a plan maintained pursuant to a collective bargaining agreement, section 410(b) applies to the first plan year beginning on or after January 1, 1991. In applying section 410(b) to Plan 2, the 100 noncollectively bargained employees in Plan 1 must be taken into account. The deferred effective date for plans maintained pursuant to a collective bargaining agreement is not applicable in determining how section 410(b) is applied to a plan that is not maintained pursuant to a collective bargaining agreement.

(iii) Plan maintained pursuant to a collective bargaining agreement. For purposes of this paragraph (a)(2), a plan is maintained pursuant to one or more collective bargaining agreements between employee representatives and one or more employers, if one or more of the agreements were ratified before March 1, 1986. Only plans maintained pursuant to agreements that the Secretary of Labor finds to be collective bargaining agreements and that satisfy section 7701(a)(46) are eligible for the deferred effective date under this paragraph (a)(2). A plan will not be treated as a plan maintained pursuant to one or more collective bargaining agreements eligible for the deferred effective date under this paragraph (a)(2) unless the plan would be a plan maintained pursuant to one or more collective bargaining agreements under the principles applied under section 1017(c) of the Employee Retirement Income Security Act of 1974. See H.R. Rep. No. 1280, 93rd Cong. 2d Sess. 266 (1974).

**(b) Regulatory effective dates.** *(1) In general.* Except as otherwise provided in this section, §§ 1.410(b)-2 through 1.410(b)-9 apply to plan years beginning on or after January 1, 1994.

*(2) Plans of tax-exempt organizations.* In the case of plans maintained by organizations exempt from income taxation under section 501(a), including plans subject to section 403(b)(12)(A)(i) (nonelective plans), §§ 1.410(b)-2 through 1.410(b)-9 apply to plan years beginning on or after January 1, 1996, to the extent such plans are subject to section 410(b).

**(c) Compliance during transition period.** For plan years beginning before the effective date of these regulations, as set forth in paragraph (b) of this section, and on or after the statutory effective date as set forth in paragraph (a) of this section, a plan must be operated in accordance with a reasonable, good faith interpretation of section 410(b). Whether a plan is operated in accordance with a reasonable, good faith interpretation of section 410(b) will generally be determined based on all of the relevant facts and circumstances, including the extent to which an employer has resolved unclear issues in its favor. If a plan's classification has been determined by the Commissioner to be nondiscriminatory and there have been no significant changes in or omissions of a material fact, the classification will be treated as nondiscriminatory for the relevant plan year. A plan will be deemed to be operated in accordance with a reasonable, good faith interpretation of section 410(b) if it is operated in accordance with the terms of §§ 1.410(b)-2 through 1.410(b)-9.

**(d) Effective date for governmental plans.** In the case of governmental plans described in section 414(d), including plans subject to section 403(b)(12)(A)(i) (nonelective plans) § 1.410(b)-2 through § 1.410(b)-10 apply to plan years beginning on or after January 1, 1996, or 90 days after the opening of the first legislative session beginning on or after January 1, 1996, of the governing body with authority to amend the plan, if that body does not meet continuously. Such plans are deemed to satisfy section 410(b) (and in the case of such plans that are not subject to section 403(b)(12)(A)(i), section 401(a)(3) as in effect on September 1, 1974) for plan years before that effective date. For purposes of this section, the governing body with authority to amend the plan is the legislature, board, commission, council, or other governing body with authority to amend the plan. See § 1.410(b)-2(d) and (e).

**(e) Effective date for provisions relating to exclusion of employees of certain tax exempt entities.** The provisions in § 1.410(b)-6(g) apply to plan years beginning after December 31, 1996. For plan years to which § 1.410(b)-6 applies that begin before January 1, 1997, § 1.410(b)-6(g) (as it appeared in the April 1, 2005 edition of 26 CFR part 1) applies.

T.D. 8363, 9/12/91, amend T.D. 8487, 8/31/93, T.D. 9275, 7/20/2006.

### § 1.410(d)-1 Election by church to have participation, vesting, funding, etc. provisions apply.

**(a) In general.** If a church or convention or association of churches which maintains any church plan, as defined in section 414(e), makes an election under this section, certain provisions of the Code and Title I of the Employee Retirement Income Security Act of 1974 (the "Act") shall apply to such church plan as if such plan were not a church plan. The provisions of the Code referred to are section 410 (relating to minimum participation standards), section 411 (relating to minimum vesting standards), section 412 (relating to minimum funding standards), section 4975 (relating to prohibited transactions), and paragraphs (11), (12), (13), (14), (15), and (19) of section 401(a) (relating to joint and survivor annuities, mergers and consolidations, assignment or alienation of benefits, time of benefit commencement, certain social security increases, and withdrawals of employee contributions, respectively).

**(b) Election is irrevocable.** An election under this section with respect to any church plan shall be binding with respect to such plan and, once made, shall be irrevocable.

**(c) Procedure for making election.** *(1) Time of election.* An election under this section may be made for plan years for which the provisions of section 410(d) of the Code apply to the church plan. By reason of section 1017(b) of the Act section 410(d) does not apply to a plan in existence on January 1, 1974, for plan years beginning before January 1, 1976. Section 1017(d) of the Act permits a plan administrator to elect to have certain provisions of the Code (including section 410(d)) apply to a plan before the otherwise applicable effective dates of such provisions. See § 1.410(a)-2(d). Therefore, for a plan in existence on January 1, 1974, an election under section 410(d) of the Code may be made for a plan year beginning before January 1, 1976, only if an election has been made under section 1017(d) of the Act with respect to that plan year.

*(2) By whom election is to be made.* The election provided by this section may be made only by the plan administrator of the church plan.

*(3) Manner of making election.* The plan administrator may elect to have the provisions of the Code described in paragraph (a) of this section apply to the church plan as if it were not a church plan by attaching the statement described in subparagraph (5) of this paragraph to either (i) the annual return required under section 6058(a) (or an amended return) with respect to the plan which is filed for the first plan year for which the election is effective or (ii) a written request for a determination letter relating to the qualification of the plan under section 401(a), 403(a), or 405(a) of the Code and, if trusteed, the exempt status under section 501(a) of the Code of a trust constituting a part of the plan.

*(4) Conditional election.* If an election is made with a written request for a determination letter, the election may be conditioned upon issuance of a favorable determination letter and will become irrevocable upon issuance of such letter.

*(5) Statement.* The statement described in subparagraph (3) of this paragraph shall indicate (i) that the election is made under section 410(d) of the Code and (ii) the first plan year for which it is effective.

T.D. 7508, 9/14/77.

### § 1.411(a)-1 Minimum vesting standards; general rules.

**(a) In general.** A plan is not a qualified plan (and a trust forming a part of such plan is not a qualified trust) unless—

*(1)* The plan provides that an employee's right to his normal retirement benefit (see § 1.411(a)-7(c)) is nonforfeitable (see § 1.411(a)-4) upon and after the attainment of normal retirement age (see § 1.411(a)-7(b)),

*(2)* The plan provides that an employee's right in his accrued benefit derived from his own contributions (see § 1.411(c)-1) are nonforfeitable at all times, and

*(3)* The plan satisfies the requirements of—

(A) Section 411(a)(2) and § 1.411(a)-3 (relating to vesting in accrued benefit derived from employer contributions), and

(B) In the case of a defined benefit plan, section 411(b)(1) and § 1.411(b)-1 (relating to accrued benefit).

**(b) Organization of regulations relating to minimum vesting standards.** *(1) General rules.* The section prescribes general rules relating to the minimum vesting standards provided by section 411.

*(2) Effective dates.* Section 1.411(a)-2 provides rules under section 1017 of the Employee Retirement Income Security Act of 1974 relating to effective dates under section 411.

*(3) Employer contributions.* Section 1.411(a)-3 provides rules under section 411(a)(2) relating to vesting in employer-derived accrued benefits.

*(4) Certain forfeitures.* Section 1.411(a)-4 provides rules under section 411(a)(3) relating to certain permitted forfeitures, suspensions, etc. under qualified plans.

*(5) Nonforfeitable percentage.* Section 1.411(a)-5 provides rules under section 411(a)(4) relating to service included in the determination of an employee's nonforfeitable percentage under section 411(a)(2) and § 1.411(a)-3.

*(6) Years of service; break in service.* Section 1.411(a)-6 provides rules under section 411(a)(5) and (6) of the Internal Revenue Code of 1954 relating to years of service and breaks in service. Rules prescribed by the Secretary of Labor, relating to years of service and breaks in service under part 2 of subtitle B of title I of the Employee Retirement Income Security Act of 1974 are provided under 29 CFR Part 2530 (Department of Labor regulations relating to minimum standard for employee pension benefit plans).

*(7) Definitions and special rules.* Section 1.411(a)-7 provides definitions and special rules under section 411(a)(7), (8), and (9), for purposes of section 411 and the regulations thereunder.

*(8) Changes in vesting schedule.* Section 1.411(a)-8 provides rules under section 411(a)(10) relating to changes in the vesting schedule of a plan.

*(9) Breaks in service.* Section 1.411(a)-9 provides special rules relating to breaks in service.

*(10) Accrued benefits.* See § 1.411(b)-1 for rules under section 411(b) relating to accrued benefit requirements under defined benefit plans.

*(11) Allocation of accrued benefits.* See § 1.411(c)-1 for rules under section 411(c) relating to allocation of accrued benefits between employer and employee contributions.

*(12) Discrimination, etc.* See § 1.411(d)-1 for rules relating to the coordination of section 411 with section 401(a)(4) (relating to discrimination) and other rules under section 411(d).

**(c) Application of standards to certain plans.** *(1) General rule.* Except as provided in subparagraph (2) of this paragraph, section 411 does not apply to—

(i) A governmental plan (within the meaning of section 414(d) and the regulations thereunder),

(ii) A church plan (within the meaning of section 414(e) and the regulations thereunder) which has not made the election provided by section 410(d) and the regulations thereunder,

(iii) A plan which has not provided for employer contributions at any time after September 2, 1974, and

(iv) A plan established and maintained by a society, order, or association described in section 501(c)(8) or (9), if no part of the contributions to or under such plan are made by employers of participants in such plan.

*(2) Vesting requirements.* A plan described in subparagraph (1) of this paragraph shall, for purposes of section 401(a), be treated as meeting the requirements of section 411 if such plan meets the vesting requirements resulting from the application of section 401(a)(4) and section 401(a)(7) as in effect on September 1, 1974.

**(d) Supersession.** Sections 11.411(a)-1 through 11.411(d)-3, inclusive, of the Temporary Income Tax Regulations under the Employee Retirement Income Security Act of 1974 are superseded by this section and §§ 1.411(a)-2 through 1.411(d)-3.

T.D. 7501, 8/22/77.

PAR. 3. Section 1.411(a)-1 is amended by revising paragraph (a)(3) to read as follows:

**Proposed § 1.411(a)-1 Minimum vesting standards; general rules.** [*For Preamble, see ¶ 151,113*]

**(a) In general.** * * *

*(3)* The plan satisfies the requirements of—

(i) Section 411(a)(2) and § 1.411(a)-3 (relating to vesting in accrued benefit derived from employer contributions),

(ii) In the case of a defined benefit plan, section 411(b)(1) and (3) (see §§ 1.411(b)-1 and 1.411(b)-2, relating to accrued benefit requirements, separate accounting and accruals and allocations after a specified age), and

(iii) In the case of a defined contribution plan, section 411(b)(2) and (3) (see §§ 1.411(b)-1(e)(2) and 1.411(b)-2, relating to accruals and allocations after a specified age and separate accounting).

* * * * *

### § 1.411(a)-2 Effective dates.

**(a) Plan not in existence on January 1, 1974.** Under section 1017(a) of the Employee Retirement Income Security Act of 1974, in the case of a plan which was not in existence on January 1, 1974, section 411 and the regulations thereunder apply for plan years beginning after September 2, 1974. See paragraph (c) of this section for time plan is considered in existence.

**(b) Plans in existence on January 1, 1974.** Under section 1017(b) of the Employee Retirement Income Security Act of 1974, in the case of a plan which was in existence on January 1, 1974, section 411 and the regulations thereunder apply for plan years beginning after December 31, 1975. See paragraph (c) of this section for time plan is considered to be in existence.

**(c) Time of plan existence.** *(1) General rule.* For purposes of this section, a plan is considered to be in existence on a particular day if—

(i) The plan on or before that day was reduced to writing and adopted by the employer (including, in the case of a corporate employer, formal approval by the employer's board of directors and, if required, shareholders), even though no amounts had been contributed under the plan as of such day, and

(ii) The plan was not terminated on or before that day.

For example, if a plan was adopted on January 2, 1974, effective as of January 1, 1974, the plan is not considered to have been in existence on January 1, 1974, because it was not both adopted and in writing on January 1, 1974.

*(2) Collectively-bargained plan.* Notwithstanding subparagraph (1) of this section, a plan described in section 413(c), relating to a plan maintained pursuant to a collective-bargaining agreement, is considered to be in existence on a particular day if—

(i) On or before that day there is a legally enforceable agreement to establish such a plan signed by the employer, and

(ii) The employer contributions to be made to the plan are set forth in the agreement.

*(3) Special rule.* If a plan is considered to be in existence under subparagraph (1) of this paragraph, any other plan with which such existing plan is merged or consolidated shall also be considered to be in existence on such date.

**(d) Existing plans under collective bargaining agreements.** For a special effective date rule for certain plans maintained pursuant to a collective bargaining agreement, see section 1017(c)(1) of the Employee Retirement Income Security Act of 1974 (88 Stat. 932).

**(e) Certain existing plans may elect new provisions.** The plan administrator may elect to have the provisions of the Code relating to participation, vesting, funding, and form of benefit apply to a selected plan year. See § 1.410(a)-2(d) for rules relating to such an election.

**(f) Application of rules.** The requirements of section 411 do not apply to employees who separate from service with the employer prior to the first plan year to which such requirements apply and who never return to service with the employer in a plan year to which section 411 applies.

T.D. 7501, 8/22/77.

### § 1.411(a)-3 Vesting in employer-derived benefits.

***Caution:*** The Treasury has not yet amended Reg § 1.411(a)-3 to reflect changes made by P.L. 104-188, P.L. 99-514.

**(a) In general.** *(1) Alternative requirements.* A plan is not a qualified plan (and a trust forming a part of such plan is not a qualified trust) unless the plan satisfies the requirements of section 411(a)(2) and this section. A plan satisfies the requirements of this section if it satisfies the requirements of paragraph (b), (c), or (d) of this section.

*(2) Composite arrangements.* A plan will not be considered to satisfy the requirements of paragraph (b), (c), or (d) of this section unless it satisfies all requirements of a particular one of such paragraphs with respect to all of an employee's years of service. A plan which, for example, satisfies the requirements of paragraph (b) (but not (c) or (d)) for an employee's first 9 years of service and satisfies the requirements of paragraph (c) (but not (b)) for all of his remaining years of service, does not satisfy the requirements of this section. A plan is not precluded from satisfying the requirement of one such paragraph with respect to one group of employees and another such paragraph with respect to another group provided that the groups are not so structured as to evade the requirements of this paragraph. For example, if plan A provides that employees who commence participation before age 30 are subject to the "rule of 45" vesting schedule and employees who commence participation after age 30 are subject to the full vesting after 10 years schedule, plan A would be so structured as to evade the requirements of this paragraph.

*(3) Plan amendments.* A plan which satisfies the requirements of a particular one of such paragraphs for each of an employee's years of service and which is amended so that, as amended, it satisfies the requirements of another such paragraph for all such years of service, satisfies the requirements of this section even though, as amended, it does not satisfy the requirements of the paragraph which were satisfied prior to the amendment. See § 1.411(a)-8 for rules relating to employee election where the vesting schedule is amended.

**(b) 10-year vesting.** A plan satisfies the requirements of section 411(a)(2)(A) and this paragraph if an employee who has completed 10 years of service has a nonforfeitable right to 100 percent of his accrued benefit derived from employer contributions.

**(c) 5- to 15-year vesting.** A plan satisfies the requirements of section 411(a)(2)(B) and this paragraph if an employee who has completed at least 5 years of service has a nonforfeitable right to a percentage of his accrued benefit derived from employer contribution which percentage is not less than the nonforfeitable percentage determined under the following table:

| Completed years of service | Nonforfeitable percentage |
|---|---|
| 5 | 25 |
| 6 | 30 |
| 7 | 35 |
| 8 | 40 |
| 9 | 45 |
| 10 | 50 |
| 11 | 60 |
| 12 | 70 |
| 13 | 80 |
| 14 | 90 |
| 15 or more | 100 |

**(d) Rule of 45.** A plan satisfies the requirements of section 411(a)(2)(C) and this paragraph if an employee is entitled to the greater of the two percentages determined under paragraph (d)(1) or (2) of this section.

*(1) Age and service test.* An employee who is not separated from the service, who has completed at least 5 years of service, and with respect to whom the sum of his age and years of service equals or exceeds 45, has a nonforfeitable right to a percentage of his accrued benefit derived from employer contributions which is not less than the nonforfeitable percentage corresponding to his number of completed years of service or to the sum of his age and completed years of service (whichever percentage is the lesser) determined under the following table:

| Completed years of service | Sum of age and service | Nonforfeitable percentage |
|---|---|---|
| 5 | 45 or 46 | 50 |
| 6 | 47 or 48 | 60 |
| 7 | 49 or 50 | 70 |
| 8 | 51 or 52 | 80 |
| 9 | 53 or 54 | 90 |
| 10 or more | 55 or more | 100 |

*(2) Service test.* An employee who has completed at least 10 years of service has a nonforfeitable right to a percentage of his accrued benefit derived from employer contributions determined under the following table:

| Completed years of service | Nonforfeitable percentage |
|---|---|
| 10 | 50 |
| 11 | 60 |
| 12 | 70 |
| 13 | 80 |
| 14 | 90 |
| 15 | 100 |

*(3) Computation of age.* For purposes of subparagraph (1) of this paragraph, the age of an employee is his age on his last birthday.

**(e) Examples.** The rules provided by this section are illustrated by the following examples:

*Example (1).* Plan B provides that each employee's rights to his employer-derived accrued benefit are nonforfeitable as follows:

| Completed years of service | Nonforfeitable percentage |
|---|---|
| 2 or less | 0 |
| 3 | 30 |
| 4 | 35 |
| 5 | 40 |
| 6 | 45 |
| 7 | 50 |
| 8 | 55 |
| 9 | 60 |
| 10 | 65 |
| 11 | 70 |
| 12 | 75 |
| 13 | 80 |
| 14 | 85 |
| 15 | 100 |

Plan B does not satisfy the requirements of paragraph (c) of this section (relating to 5-15-year vesting) because the nonforfeitable percentage provided by the plan after completion of 14 years of service (85 percent) is less than the percentage required by paragraph (c) of this section at that time (90 percent). The fact that the nonforfeitable percentage provided by the plan for years prior to the 13th year of service is greater than the percentage required under paragraph (c) of this section is immaterial. The plan fails to satisfy the requirements of paragraph (c) of this section even if it is demonstrated that the value of the vesting provided by the plan to the employee is at least equal to the value of the vesting rate required by that paragraph.

*Example (2).* Plan C provides for plan participation after the completion of 1 year of service. The plan provides that each employee's rights to his employer-derived accrued benefit are 100 percent nonforfeitable after 10 years of plan participation rather than service. The plan does not satisfy the requirements of paragraph (b) of this section because, under the plan, an employee obtains a 100 percent nonforfeitable right to his employer-derived accrued benefit only after completion of more than 10 years of service.

*Example (3).* Plan D provides that each employee's rights to his employer-derived accrued benefit are nonforfeitable in accordance with the following schedule:

| Completed years of service | Nonforfeitable percentage |
|---|---|
| 0–9 | 0 |
| 10 | 50 |
| 11 | 60 |
| 12 | 70 |
| 13 | 80 |
| 14 | 90 |
| 15 | 100 |

The plan does not satisfy the requirements of paragraph (b) of this section after the 9th year of service. It does not satisfy the requirements of paragraph (c) of this section for years prior to the 10th year of service. It does not satisfy the requirements of paragraph (d)(1) of this section for any year of service prior to the 10th year. The plan does not satisfy the requirements of this section because it does not satisfy the requirements of a particular one of the three paragraphs for each of an employee's years of service.

*Example (4).* Plan G provides that each employee's rights to his employer-derived accrued benefit are 100 percent nonforfeitable upon completion of 5 years of service. The plan satisfies the requirements of paragraphs (b), (c), and (d) of this section and, because it satisfies the requirements of at least one of such paragraphs for all of an employee's years of service, it satisfies the requirements of this section.

T.D. 7501, 8/22/77.

### § 1.411(a)-3T Vesting in employer-derived benefits (temporary).

***Caution:*** The Treasury has not yet amended Reg § 1.411(a)-3T to reflect changes made by P.L. 109-280, P.L. 104-188, P.L. 101-239, P.L. 99-514.

**(a) In general.** *(1) [Reserved]*

*(2) Composite arrangements.* A plan will not be considered to satisfy the requirements of paragraph (b), (c), or (d) of this section unless it satisfies all requirements of a particular one of such paragraphs with respect to all of an employee's years of service. A plan which, for example, satisfies the requirements of paragraph (b) (but not (c) or (d)) for an employee's first 4 years of service and satisfies the requirements of paragraph (c) (but not (b)) for all of his remaining years of service does not satisfy the requirements of this section. A plan is not precluded from satisfying the requirements of one such paragraph with respect to one group of employees and another such paragraph with respect to another group provided that the groups are not so structured as to evade the requirements of this paragraph.

*(3) [Reserved]*

**(b) 5-year vesting.** A plan satisfies the requirements of section 411(a)(2)(A) and this paragraph if an employee who has completed 5 years of service has a nonforfeitable right to 100 percent of his or her accrued benefits derived from employer contributions.

**(c) 3- to 7-year vesting.** A plan satisfies the requirements of section 411(a)(2)(B) and this paragraph if an employee who has completed at least 3 years of service has a nonforfeitable right to a percentage of his accrued benefit derived from employer contributions, which percentage is not less than the nonforfeitable percentage determined under the following table:

| Completed years of service | Nonforfeitable percentage |
|---|---|
| 3 | 20 |
| 4 | 40 |
| 5 | 60 |
| 6 | 80 |
| 7 or more | 100 |

**(d) Multiemployer plans.** A plan satisfies the requirements of section 411(a)(2)(C) and this paragraph if—

*(1)* The plan is a multiemployer plan (within the meaning of section 414(f)), and

*(2)* Under the plan—

(i) An employee who is covered pursuant to a collective bargaining agreement described in section 414(f)(1)(B) has a nonforfeitable right to 100 percent of the employee's accrued benefit derived from employer contributions not later than upon completion of 10 years of service, and

(ii) The requirements of paragraph (b) or (c) of this section are met with respect to employees who are not covered pursuant to a collective bargaining agreement described in section 414(f)(1)(B).

(iii) For purposes of this provision, an employee is not covered pursuant to a collective bargaining agreement unless the employee is represented by a bona fide employee representative that is a party to the collective bargaining agreement pursuant to which the multiemployer plan is maintained. Thus, for example, an employee of either the multiemployer plan or the employee representative is not covered pursuant to the collective bargaining agreement under which the plan is maintained even if the employee is covered pursuant to an agreement entered into by the multiemployer plan or employee representative on behalf of the employee and even if all such employees covered under the plan constitute only a de minimis percentage of the total employees covered under the plan.

**(e) Effective date.** *(1)* The provisions of this section apply to all employees who have one hour of service in any plan year beginning after—

(i) December 31, 1988, or

(ii) In the case of a plan maintained pursuant to one or more collective bargaining agreements between employee representatives and one or more employers ratified before March 1, 1986, for employees covered by any such agreement, the earlier of—

(A) The later of—

(1) January 1, 1989, or

(2) The date on which the last of such collective bargaining agreements terminates (determined without regard to any extension thereof after February 28, 1986), or

(B) January 1, 1991.

*(2)* For employees not described in paragraph (e)(1), above, the regulations in effect prior to January 1, 1989, shall be applied to determine the requirements of this section.

**(f) Examples.** The rules provided by this section are illustrated by the following examples:

*Example (1).* Plan B provides that each employee's rights to his employer-derived accrued benefit are nonforfeitable as follows:

| Completed years of service | Nonforfeitable percentage |
|---|---|
| 1 | 0 |
| 2 | 10 |
| 3 | 25 |
| 4 | 45 |
| 5 | 65 |
| 6 | 75 |
| 7 | 100 |

Plan B does not satisfy the requirements of paragraph (c) of this section (relating to 3- to 7-year vesting) because the nonforfeitable percentage provided by the plan after completion of 6 years of service (75 percent is less than the percentage required by paragraph (c) of this section at that time (80 percent). The fact that the nonforfeitable percentage provided by the plan for years prior to the 6th year of service as greater than the percentage required under paragraph (c) of this section is immaterial. The plan fails to satisfy the requirements of paragraph (c) of this section even if it is demonstrated that the value of the vesting provided by the plan to the employees is at least equal to the value of the vesting rate required by this paragraph.

*Example (2).* Plan C provides for plan participation after the completion of 1 year of service. The plan provides that each employee's rights to his employer-derived accrued benefits are 100 percent nonforfeitable after 5 years of plan participation rather than service. The plan does not satisfy the requirements of paragraph (b) of this section because, under the plan, an employee obtains a 100 percent nonforfeitable right to his or her employer-derived accrued benefit only after completion of more than 5 years of service.

*Example (3).* Plan D provides that each employee's rights to his employer-derived accrued benefits are nonforfeitable in accordance with the following schedule:

| Completed years of service | Nonforfeitable percentage |
|---|---|
| 0 to 4 | 0 |
| 5 | 60 |
| 6 | 80 |
| 7 | 100 |

The plan does not satisfy the requirements of paragraph (b) of this section after the 4th year of service. It does not satisfy the requirements of paragraph (c) of this section for years prior to the 5th year of service. The plan does not satisfy the requirements of this section because it does not satisfy the requirements of a particular one of the two paragraphs for each of an employee's years of service.

*Example (4).* Plan G provides that each employee's rights to his employer-derived accrued benefit are 100 percent nonforfeitable upon completion of 3 years of service. The plan satisfies the requirements of paragraphs (b) and (c) of this section and, because it satisfies the requirements of at least one of such paragraphs for all of an employee's years of service, it satisfies the requirements of this section.

T.D. 8170, 1/5/88.

## § 1.411(a)-4 Forfeitures, suspensions, etc.

**(a) Nonforfeitability.** Certain rights in an accrued benefit must be nonforfeitable to satisfy the requirements of section 411(a). This section defines the term "nonforfeitable" for purposes of these requirements. For purposes of section 411 and the regulations thereunder, a right to an accrued benefit is considered to be nonforfeitable at a particular time if, at that time and thereafter, it is an unconditional right. Except as provided by paragraph (b) of this section, a right which, at a particular time, is conditioned under the plan upon a subsequent event, subsequent performance, or subsequent forbearance which will cause the loss of such right is a forfeitable right at that time. Certain adjustments to plan benefits such as adjustments in excess of reasonable actuarial reductions, can result in rights being forfeitable. Rights which are conditioned upon a sufficiency of plan assets in the event of a termination or partial termination are considered to be forfeitable because of such condition. However, a plan does not violate the nonforfeitability requirements merely because in the event of a termination an employee does not have any recourse toward satisfaction of his nonforfeitable benefits from other than the plan assets or the Pension Benefit Guaranty Corporation. Furthermore, nonforfeitable rights are not considered to be forfeitable by reason of the fact that they may be reduced to take into account benefits which are provided under the Social Security Act or under any other Federal or State law and which are taken into account in determining plan benefits. To the extent that rights are not required to be nonforfeitable to satisfy the minimum vesting standards, or the nondiscrimination requirements of section 401(a)(4), they may be forfeited without regard to the limitations on forfeitability required by this section. The right of an employee to repurchase his accrued benefit for example under section 411(a)(3)(D), is an example of a right which is required to satisfy such standards. Accordingly, such a right is subject to the limitations on forfeitability. Rights which are required to be prospectively nonforfeitable under the vesting standards are nonforfeitable and may not be forfeited until it is determined that such rights are, in fact, in excess of the vesting standards. Thus, employees have a right to vest in the accrued benefits if they continue in employment of employers maintaining the plan unless a forfeitable event recognized by section 411 occurs. For example, if a plan covered employees in Division A of Corporation X under a plan utilizing a 10-year-100 percent vesting schedule, the plan could not forfeit employees' rights on account of their moving to service in Division B of Corporation X prior to completion of 10 years of service even though employees are not vested at that time.

**(b) Special rules.** For purposes of paragraph (a) of this section a right is not treated as forfeitable—

*(1) Death.* (i) General rule. In the case of a participant's right to his employer-derived accrued benefit, merely because such accrued benefit is forfeitable by the participant to the extent it has not been paid or distributed to him prior to his death. This subparagraph shall not apply to a benefit

which must be paid to a survivor in order to satisfy the requirements of section 401(a)(11).

(ii) Employee contributions. A participant's right in his accrued benefit derived from his own contributions must be nonforfeitable at all times. Such a right is not treated as forfeitable merely because, after commencement of annuity or pension payments in a benefit form provided under the plan, the participant dies without receiving payments equal in amount to his nonforfeitable accrued benefit derived from his contributions determined at the time of commencement.

*(2) Suspension of benefits upon reemployment of retiree.* In the case of certain suspensions of benefits under section 411(a)(3)(B), see regulations prescribed by the Secretary of Labor under 29 CFR Part 2530 (Department of Labor regulations relating to minimum standards for employee pension benefit plans).

*(3) Retroactive plan amendment.* In the case of a participant's right to his employer-derived accrued benefit, merely because such benefit is subject to reduction to the extent provided by a plan amendment described in section 412(c)(8) and the regulations thereunder, which amendment is given retroactive effective in accordance with such section.

*(4) Other forfeiture rules.* (i) Withdrawal of mandatory contributions. For rules allowing forfeitures on account of the withdrawal of mandatory contributions, see § 1.411(a)-7(d)(2) and (3).

(ii) Additional requirements. For additional requirements relating to nonforfeitability of benefits in the event of a withdrawal by the employee, see section 401(a)(19) and § 1.401(a)-19.

*(5) Multiemployer plan.* In the case of a multiemployer plan described in section 414(f), merely because an employee's accrued benefit which results from service with an employer before such employer was required to contribute to the plan is forfeitable on account of the cessation of contributions by the employer of the employee. This subparagraph shall not apply to an employee's accrued benefit with respect to an employer which accrued under a plan maintained by that employer prior to the adoption by that employer of the multiemployer plan.

*(6) Lost beneficiary; escheat.* In the case of a benefit which is payable, merely because the benefit is forfeitable on account of the inability to find the participant or beneficiary to whom payment is due, provided that the plan provides for reinstatement of the benefit if a claim is made by the participant or beneficiary for the forfeited benefit. In addition, a benefit which is lost by reason of escheat under applicable state law is not treated as a forfeiture.

*(7) Certain matching contributions.* A matching contribution (within the meaning of section 401(m)(4)(A) and § 1.401(m)-1(a)(2)) is not treated as forfeitable even if under the plan it may be forfeited under § 1.401(m)-2(b)(1) because the contribution to which it relates is treated as an excess contribution (within the meaning of Sec. § 1.401(k)-2(b)(2)(ii) and 1.401(k)-6), excess deferral (within the meaning of § 1.402(g)-1(e)(1)(iii)), excess aggregate contribution (within the meaning of § 1.401(m)-5), or a default elective contribution (within the meaning of § 1.414(w)-1(e)) that is withdrawn in accordance with the requirements of § 1.414(w)-1(c).

**(c) Examples.** The rules of this section are illustrated by the following examples:

*Example (1).* Corporation A's plan provides that an employee is fully vested in his employer-derived accrued benefit after completion of 5 years of service. The plan also provides that, if an employee works for a competitor he forfeits his rights in the plan. Such provision could result in the forfeiture of an employee's rights which are required to be nonforfeitable under section 411 and therefore the plan would not satisfy the requirements of section 411. If the plan limited the forfeiture to employees who completed less than 10 years of service, the plan would not fail to satisfy the requirements of section 411 because the forfeitures under this provision are limited to rights which are in excess of the minimum required to be nonforfeitable under section 411(a)(2)(A).

*Example (2).* Plan B provides that if an employee does not apply for benefits within 5 years after the attainment of normal retirement age, the employee loses his plan benefits. Such a plan provision could result in forfeiture of an employee's rights which are required to be nonforfeitable under section 411 and, therefore, the plan would not satisfy the requirements of section 411.

---

T.D. 7501, 8/22/77, amend T.D. 8357, 8/8/91, T.D. 9169, 12/28/2004, T.D. 9219, 8/11/2005, T.D. 9447, 2/23/2009.

---

### § 1.411(a)-4T Forfeitures, suspensions, etc. (temporary).

**(a) Nonforfeitability.** Certain rights in an accrued benefit must be nonforfeitable to satisfy the requirements of section 411(a). This section defines the term "nonforfeitable" for purposes of these requirements. For purposes of section 411 and the regulations thereunder, a right to an accrued benefit is considered to be nonforfeitable at a particular time if, at that time and thereafter, it is an unconditional right. Except as provided by paragraph (b) of this section, a right which, at a particular time, is conditioned under the plan upon a subsequent event, subsequent performance, or subsequent forbearance which will cause the loss of such right is a forfeitable right at that time. Certain adjustments to plan benefits, such as adjustments in excess of reasonable actuarial reductions, can result in rights being forfeitable. Rights which are conditioned upon a sufficiency of plan assets in the event of a termination or partial termination are considered to be forfeitable because of such condition. However, a plan does not violate the nonforfeitability requirements merely because in the event of a termination an employee does not have any recourse toward satisfaction of his nonforfeitable benefits from other than the plan assets, the Pension Benefit Guaranty Corporation, or a trust established and maintained pursuant to sections 4041(c)(3)(B)(ii) or (iii) and section 4049 of ERISA with respect to the plan. Furthermore, nonforfeitable rights are not considered to be forfeitable by reason of the fact that they may be reduced as allowed under sections 401(a)(5) and 401(l). To the extent that rights are not required to be nonforfeitable to satisfy the minimum vesting standards, or the nondiscrimination requirements of section 401(a)(4), they may be forfeited without regard to the limitations on forfeitability required by this section. The right of an employee to repurchase his accrued benefit for example under section 411(a)(3)(D), is an example of a right which is required to satisfy such standards. Accordingly, such a right is subject to the limitations on forfeitability. Rights which are required to be prospectively nonforfeitable under the vesting standards are nonforfeitable and may not be forfeited until it is determined that such rights are, in fact, in excess of the vesting standards. Thus, employees have a right to vest in the accrued benefits if they continue in employment of employers maintaining the plan unless a forfeitable event recognized by section 411 occurs. For example, if a plan covered employees in Division A of Corporation X under a plan utilizing a 5-year 100 percent vesting schedule, the plan could not forfeit employees' rights on account of their moving to service in Division B of Corporation X prior to completion of 5 years of service even though employees are not vested at that time.

**(b) [Reserved]**

**(c) Examples.** The rules of this section are illustrated by the following examples:

*Example (1).* Corporation A's plan provides that an employee is fully vested in his employer-derived accrued benefit after completion of 3 years of service. The plan also provides that if the employee works for a competitor he forfeits his rights in the plan. Such provision could result in the forfeiture of an employee's rights which are required to be nonforfeitable under section 411 and therefore the plan would not satisfy the requirements of section 411. If the plan limited the forfeiture to employees who completed less than 5 years of service, the plan would not fail to satisfy the requirements of section 411 because the forfeitures under this provision are limited to rights which are in excess of the minimum required to be nonforfeitable under section 411(a)(2)(A).

*Example (2).* [Reserved]

T.D. 8170, 1/5/88.

## § 1.411(a)-5 Service included in determination of nonforfeitable percentage.

***Caution:*** The Treasury has not yet amended Reg § 1.411(a)-5 to reflect changes made by P.L. 98-397, P.L. 96-364.

**(a) In general.** Under section 411(a)(4), for purposes of determining the nonforfeitable percentage of an employee's right to his employer-derived accrued benefit under section 411(a)(2) and § 1.411(a)-3, all of an employee's years of service with an employer or employers maintaining the plan shall be taken into account except that years of service described in paragraph (b) of this section may be disregarded.

**(b) Certain service.** For purposes of paragraph (a) of this section, the following years of service may be disregarded:

*(1) Service before age 22.* (i) In the case of a plan which satisfies the requirements of section 411(a)(2)(A) or (B) (relating to 10-year vesting and 5-15-year vesting, respectively), a year of service completed by an employee before he attains age 22.

(ii) In the case of a plan which does not satisfy the requirements of section 411(a)(2)(A) or (B), a year of service completed by an employee before he attains age 22 if the employee is not a participant (for purposes of section 410) in the plan at any time during such year.

(iii) For purposes of this subparagraph in the case of a plan utilizing computation periods, service during a computation period described in section 411(a)(5)(A) within which the employee attains age 22 may not be disregarded. In the case of a plan utilizing the elapsed time method described in § 1.410(a)-7, service on or after the date on which the employee attains age 22 may not be disregarded.

*(2) Contributory plans.* In the case of a plan utilizing computation periods, a year of service completed by an employee under a plan which requires mandatory contributions (within the meaning of section 411(c)(2)(C) and § 1.411(c)-1(c)(4)) to be made by the employee for such year, if the employee does not participate for such year solely because of his failure to make all mandatory contributions to the plan for such year. If the employee contributes any part of the mandatory contributions for the year, such year may not be excluded by reason of this subparagraph. In the case of a plan utilizing the elapsed time method described in § 1.410(a)-7, the service which may be disregarded is the period with respect to which the mandatory contribution is not made.

*(3) Plan not maintained.* (i) In general. An employee's years of service with an employer during any period for which the employer did not maintain the plan or a predecessor plan may be disregarded for purposes of section 411(a)(2). Paragraph (b)(3)(ii) of this section provides rules regarding the period prior to the adoption of a plan. Paragraph (b)(3)(iii) of this section provides rules regarding the period after the termination of a plan. Paragraph (b)(3)(iv) of this section provides rules regarding employers who have certain relationships with other employers maintaining the plan.

(ii) Period prior to adoption. The period for which a plan is not maintained by an employer includes the period before the plan was established. For purposes of this subdivision, a plan is established on the first day of the plan year in which the plan is adopted even though the plan is adopted after such first day. Except as provided in paragraph (b)(3)(iv) of this section if an employer adopts a plan which has previously been established by another employer or group of employers, the plan is not maintained by the adopting employer prior to the first day of the plan year in which the plan is adopted by the adopting employer. In the case of a transfer of assets or liabilities (including a merger or consolidation) involving two plans maintained by a single employer, the successor (or transferee) plan is treated as if it was established at the same time as the date of the establishment of the earliest component plan. In the case of a plan merger, consolidation, or transfer of plan assets or liabilities involving plans of two or more employers, the successor plan is treated as if it were established on each of the separate dates on which such component plan was established for the employees of each employer. Thus, for example, if employer A establishes a plan January 1, 1970, and employer B establishes a plan January 1, 1980, and the plans were subsequently merged, then the merged plan would be treated as if it were in existence on January 1, 1970, with respect to A's employees and as if it were in existence on January 1, 1980, with respect to B's employees.

(iii) Period after termination or withdrawal. The period for which a plan is not maintained by an employer includes the period after the plan is terminated. For purposes of this section, a plan is terminated at the date there is a termination of the plan within the meaning of section 411(d)(3)(A) and the regulations thereunder. Notwithstanding the preceding sentence, if contributions to or under a plan are made after termination, the plan is treated as being maintained until such contributions cease, whether or not accruals are made after such termination. If, after termination of a plan in circumstances under which the employer may be liable to the Pension Benefit Guaranty Corporation under section 4062 of the Act, employer contributions are made to or under the plan to fund benefits accrued at the time of termination, such contributions shall, for purposes of this paragraph, be deemed to be payments in satisfaction of employer liability to such Corporation rather than contributions to or under the plan. In the case of a plan maintained by more than one employer, the period for which the plan is not maintained by the withdrawing employer includes the period after the withdrawal from the plan.

(iv) Certain employers. For purposes of this subparagraph—

(A) Predecessor employers. Service with a predecessor employer who maintained the plan of the current employer is treated as service with such current employer (see section 414(a)(1) and the regulations thereunder), and certain service with a predecessor employer who did not maintain the plan of the current employer is treated as service with the current employer (see section 414(a)(2) and the regulations thereunder).

(B) Related employers. Service with an employer is treated as service for certain related employers for the period during which the employers are related. These related employers include members of a controlled group of corporations (within the meaning of section 1563(a), determined without regard to subsections (a)(4) and (e)(3)(C) thereof) and trades or businesses (whether or not incorporated) which are under common control (see section 414(b) and (c) and 29 CFR Part 2530, Department of Labor regulations relating to minimum standards for employee pension benefit plans).

(C) Plan maintained by more than one employer. Service with an employer who maintains a plan is treated as service for each other employer who maintains that plan for the period during which the employers are maintaining the plan (see section 413(B)(4) and (c)(3) and 29 CFR Part 2530, Department of Labor regulations relating to minimum standards for employee pension benefit plans).

(v) Predecessor Plan. (A) General rule. In the case of an employee who was covered by a predecessor plan, the time the successor of such plan is maintained for such employee includes the time the predecessor plan was maintained if, as of the later of the time the predecessor plan is terminated or the successor plan is established, the employee's years of service under the predecessor plan are not equalled or exceeded by the aggregate number of consecutive 1-year breaks in service occurring after such years of service. Years of service and breaks in service, without regard to whether the employee has nonforfeitable rights under the predecessor plan, are determined under section 411(a)(5) and (6) except that years between the termination date of the predecessor plan and the date of establishment of the successor plan do not count as years of service.

(B) Definition of predecessor plan. For purposes of this section, if—

(1) An employer establishes a retirement plan (within the meaning of section 7476(d)) qualified under subchapter D of chapter 1 of the Code within the 5-year period immediately preceding or following the date another such plan terminates, and

(2) The other plan is terminated during a plan year to which this section applies, the terminated plan is a predecessor plan with respect to such other plan.

(C) Example. The rules provided by this subparagraph are illustrated by the following example:

*Example.* (1) Employer X's qualified plan A terminated on January 1, 1977. Employer X established qualified plan B on January 1, 1981. Under paragraph (b)(3)(v)(B) of this section, plan A is a predecessor plan with respect to plan B because plan B is established within the 5-year period immediately following the date plan A terminated.

(2) Employee C was not covered by the A plan. Under the general rule in subdivision (v)(A) of this subparagraph, plan B is not maintained until January 1, 1981, with respect to Employee C.

(3) Employee D was covered by the A plan. On December 31, 1976, D had 4 years of service. D had 4 consecutive 1-year breaks in service because during the years between the termination of plan A and the establishment of plan B, he did not have more than 500 hours of service in any applicable computation period. Because D's consecutive 1-year breaks (4) equal his years of service prior to his breaks (4), plan B is not maintained until January 1, 1981, with respect to employee D.

(4) Employee E was covered by the A plan. On December 31, 1975, E had 6 years of service. E had a 1-year break in service in 1976. E also had 4 consecutive 1-year breaks in service for the period between plan A's termination and plan B's establishment. Because E's years of service (6) are not less than his consecutive 1-year breaks (5), plan B is maintained for E as of the establishment date of plan A.

*(4) Break in service.* A year of service which is not required to be taken into account by reason of a break in service (within the meaning of section 411(a)(6) and § 1.411(a)-6)).

*(5) Service before January 1, 1971.* A year of service completed by an employee prior to January 1, 1971, unless the employee completes at least 3 years of service at any time after December 31, 1970. For purposes of determining if an employee completes 3 years of service, whether or not consecutive, the exceptions of section 411(a)(4) are not applicable. For the meaning of the term "year of service", see regulations prescribed by the Secretary of Labor under 29 CFR Part 2530, relating to minimum standards for employee pension benefit plans.

*(6) Service before effective date.* A year of service completed before the first plan year for which this section applies to the plan, if such service would have been disregarded under the plan rules relating to breaks in service (whether or not such rules are so designated in the plan) as such rules were in effect from time to time under the plan. For this purpose, plan rules which result in the loss of prior vesting or benefit accruals of an employee, or which deny an employee eligibility to participate, by reason of separation or failure to complete a required period of service within a specified period of time (e.g., 300 hours in one year) will be considered break in service rules. See § 1.411(a)-9 for requirements relating to certain amendments to the break in service rules of a plan.

(ii) Examples. The rules of this subparagraph are illustrated by the following examples:

*Example (1).* The A plan in 1971 provides for immediate participation and vesting at normal retirement age. Employees accrue a unit benefit based on their compensation in each year. The plan provides that if an employee is not employed on the last day of the calendar year, he loses all accrued benefits. The requirement of employment on the last day of the year is a break in service rule because employees can lose benefits by reason of their separation. Accordingly, in the case of employees who separate and do not return by the close of the year, service which is completed prior to separation may be disregarded.

*Example (2).* The B plan in 1971 excludes from plan participation employees who work less than 1200 hours per year. Because years of less than 1200 hours are not taken into account under the B plan for eligibility to participate, such years are excluded under rules relating to breaks in service. Therefore, the years can be disregarded under this subparagraph.

*Example (3).* The C plan in 1971 provides for immediate participation and provides accruals and vesting credit for 1,200 hours or more in a given year. The plan provides that if a participant works less than 300 hours in a given year, he loses all prior vesting and benefit credits. The 300 hour rule is a break in service rule because the failure to complete 300 hours results in the loss of vesting and prior service credit. The 1,200 hour requirement is not a break in service rule because even though employees do not increase vesting or accrue benefits for service between 300 and 1,200 hours, they can not lose prior vesting or benefits for such service. Accordingly, the C plan can disregard completed years only on account of less than 300 hours of service by an employee.

**(c) Special continuity rule for certain plans.** For special rules for computing years of service in the case of a plan maintained by more than one employer, see 29 CFR Part 2530 (Department of Labor regulations relating to minimum standards for employee pension benefit plans).

T.D. 7501, 8/22/77, amend T.D. 7703, 6/16/80.

### § 1.411(a)-6 Year of service; hours of service; breaks in service.

***Caution:*** The Treasury has not yet amended Reg § 1.411(a)-6 to reflect changes made by P.L. 98-397.

**(a) Year of service.** Under section 411(a)(5)(A), for purposes of the regulations thereunder, the term "year of service" is defined in regulations prescribed by the Secretary of Labor under section 203(b)(2)(A) of the Employee Retirement Income Security Act of 1974. For special rules applicable to seasonal industries and maritime industries, see regulations prescribed by the Secretary of Labor under subparagraphs (C) and (D) of section 203(b)(2) of the Employee Retirement Income Security Act of 1974.

**(b) Hours of service.** Under section 411(a)(5)(B), for purposes of the regulations thereunder, the term "hours of service" has the meaning provided by section 410(a)(3)(C). See regulations prescribed by the Secretary of Labor under 29 CFR Part 2530, relating to minimum standards for employee pension benefit plans.

**(c) Breaks in service.** Under section 411(a)(6), for purposes of § 1.411(a)-5(b)(4) and of this paragraph—

*(1) In general.* (i) Year of service after 1-year break in service. In the case of any employee who has incurred a 1-year break in service, years of service completed before such break are not required to be taken into account until the employee has completed one year of service after his return to service.

(ii) Defined contribution plan. In the case of a participant in a defined contribution plan or in an insured defined benefit plan (which plan satisfies the requirements of section 411(b)(1)(F) and § 1.411(b)-1) who has incurred a 1-year break in service, years of service completed after such break are not required to be taken into account for purposes of determining the nonforfeitable percentage of the participant's right to employer-derived benefits which accrued before such break. This subdivision does not permit years of service completed before a 1-year break in service to be disregarded in determining the nonforfeitable percentage of a participant's right to employer-derived benefits which accrue after such break.

(iii) Nonvested participants. In the case of an employee who is a nonvested participant in employer-derived benefits at the time he incurs a 1-year break in service, years of service completed by such participant before such break are not required to be taken into account for purposes of determining the nonforfeitable percentage of his right to employer-derived benefits if at such time the number of consecutive 1-year breaks in service included in his most recent break in service equals or exceeds the aggregate number of his years of service, whether or not consecutive, completed before such break. In the case of a plan utilizing the elapsed time method described in § 1.410(a)-7, the condition in the preceding sentence shall be satisfied if the period of severance is at least one year and the consecutive period of severance equals or exceeds his prior period of service, whether or not consecutive, completed before such period of severance. In computing the aggregate number of years of service prior to such break, years of service which could have been disregarded under this subdivision by reason of any prior break in service may be disregarded.

*(2) One-year break in service defined.* The term "1-year break in service" means a calendar year, plan year, or other 12-consecutive month period designated by a plan (and not prohibited under regulations prescribed by the Secretary of Labor) during which the participant has not completed more than 500 hours of service. In the case of a plan utilizing the elapsed time method, the term "1-year break in service" means a 12-consecutive month period beginning on the severance from service date or any anniversary thereof and ending on the next succeeding anniversary of such date; provided, however, that the employee during such 12-consecutive-month period does not complete any hours of service within the meaning of 29 CFR Part 2530.200b-2(a) for the employer or employers maintaining the plan. See regulations prescribed by the Secretary of Labor under 29 CFR Part 2530, relating to minimum standards for employee pension benefit plans.

**(d) Examples.** The rules provided by this section are illustrated by the following examples:

*Example (1).* (i) X Corporation maintains a defined contribution plan to which section 411 applies. The plan uses the calendar year as the vesting computation period. In 1980, Employee A, who was hired at age 35, separates from the service of X Corporation after completing 4 years of service. At the time of his separation, Employee A had a nonforfeitable right to 25 percent of his employer-derived accrued benefit which was not distributed. In 1985, after incurring 5 consecutive one-year breaks in service, Employee A is reemployed by X Corporation and becomes an active participant in the plan. The plan provides that, for 1985 and all subsequent years, Employee A's previous years of service will not be taken into account for purposes of computing the nonforfeitable percentage of his employer-derived accrued benefit, solely because of his break in service.

(ii) The plan fails to satisfy section 411. Section 411(a)(6)(B) would permit the plan to disregard Employee A's prior service for purposes of computing his nonforfeitable percentage in 1985 only, but such service must be taken into account in subsequent years unless there is another break in service. Under section 411(a)(6)(C), the plan is not required to take Employee A's post-break service into account for purposes of computing his nonforfeitable right to his pre-break employer derived accrued benefits. This provision, however, would not permit the plan to disregard pre-break service in determining his nonforfeitable right to his benefit accrued after the break. The exception provided by section 411(a)(6)(D) does not apply in the case of a participant who has any nonforfeitable right to his accrued benefit derived from employer contributions.

*Example (2).* (i) X Corporation maintains a qualified plan to which sections 410 and 411 (relating to minimum participation standards and minimum vesting standards, respectively) apply. The plan permits participation upon completion of a year of service and provides that 100% of an employee's employer-derived accrued benefit vests after 10 years of service. The plan uses the calendar year as the vesting computation period. The plan provides that an employee who completes at least 1,000 hours of service in a 12-month period is credited with a year of service for participation and vesting purposes. The plan also provides that an employee who does not complete more than 500 hours of service in that 12-month period incurs a one-year break in service. The plan includes the rule described in section 411(a)(6)(D) for participation and vesting purposes. Under this rule, an employee's years of service prior to a break in service may be disregarded under certain circumstances if he has no vested right to any employer-derived benefit under the plan. The plan does not contain the rule described in section 411(a)(6)(B) (relating to the requirement of one year of service after a one-year break in service).

(ii) Employee A commences employment with the X Corporation on January 1, 1977. Employee A's employment history for 1977 through 1989 is as follows:

| Year ending December 31: | Hours of service completed |
|---|---|
| 1977 | 1,000 |
| 1978 | 800 |
| 1979 | 1,000 |
| 1980 | 400 |
| 1981 | 1,000 |
| 1982 | 0 |
| 1983 | 400 |
| 1984 | 1,000 |
| 1985 | 0 |
| 1986 | 0 |
| 1987 | 500 |
| 1988 | 200 |
| 1989 | 1,000 |

Employee A's status as a participant during this period is determined as follows:

*1978:* Employee A was a plan participant on January 1, 1978, because he completed a year of service (1,000 hours) in 1977. He did not complete a year of service in 1978 because he completed fewer than 1,000 hours in that year. Because he completed more than 500 hours of service in 1978, however, Employee A did not incur a one-year break in service that year.

*1979:* Employee A completes a year of service in 1979. Because he did not incur a one-year break in service in 1978, the plan may not disregard his 1977 service for purposes of determining his years of service as of January 1, 1979.

*1980:* Employee A incurs a one-year break in service in 1980.

*1981:* Because Employee A had completed 2 years of service prior to 1981 and had incurred one 1-year break in service prior to 1981, under section 411(a)(6)(D), the plan may not disregard his pre-1980 service in 1981. Employee A completes a year of service in 1981.

*1982:* Employee A incurs a one-year break in service in 1982.

*1983:* Employee A incurs a one-year break in service in 1983. As of the end of 1983, he has completed 3 years of service and has incurred 2 consecutive one-year breaks in service.

*1984:* Employee A completes a year of service in 1984. Under section 411(a)(6)(D), his pre-1982 service may not be disregarded in 1984 because, as of the beginning of 1984, his pre-1984 years of service (3) exceed his consecutive one-year breaks in service (2).

*1985-1988:* Employee A incurs 4 consecutive one-year breaks in service during the years 1985 through 1988.

*1989:* Employee A's pre-1989 service is disregarded in 1989 and all subsequent plan years because his years of service as of January 1, 1989, equal the number of consecutive one-year breaks he has incurred as of that date. Therefore, as of the beginning of 1989, Employee A is not a plan participant. Employee A completes a year of service in 1989. (Although section 411(a)(6)(D) does not prohibit the plan provision under which Employee A's pre-1989 service is disregarded, that section does not require such a provision in a qualified plan.)

T.D. 7501, 8/22/77, amend T.D. 7703, 6/16/80.

### § 1.411(a)-7 Definitions and special rules.

***Caution:*** The Treasury has not yet amended Reg § 1.411(a)-7 to reflect changes made by P.L. 101-239, P.L. 100-647, P.L. 99-514, P.L. 98-397.

**(a) Accrued benefit.** For purposes of section 411 and the regulations thereunder, the term "accrued benefit" means—

*(1) Defined benefit plan.* In the case of a defined benefit plan—

(i) If the plan provides an accrued benefit in the form of an annual benefit commencing at normal retirement age, such accrued benefit, or

(ii) If the plan does not provide an accrued benefit in the form described in subdivision (i) of this subparagraph, an annual benefit commencing at normal retirement age which is the actuarial equivalent (determined under section 411(c)(3) and § 1.411(c)-5) of the accrued benefit determined under the plan. In general, the term "accrued benefits" refers only to pension or retirement benefits. Consequently, accrued benefits do not include ancillary benefits not directly related to retirement benefits such as payment of medical expenses (or insurance premiums for such expenses), disability benefits not in excess of the qualified disability benefit (see section 411(a)(9) and paragraph (c)(3) of this section), life insurance benefits payable as a lump sum, incidental death benefits, current life insurance protection, or medical benefits described in section 401(h).

For purposes of this paragraph a subsidized early retirement benefit which is provided by a plan is not taken into account, except to the extent of determining the normal retirement benefit under the plan (see section 411(a)(9) and paragraph (c) of this section). The accrued benefit includes any optional settlement at normal retirement age under actuarial assumptions no less favorable than those which would be applied if the employee were terminating his employment at normal retirement age. The accrued benefit does not include any subsidized value in a joint and survivor annuity to the extent that the annual benefit of the joint and survivor annuity does not exceed the annual benefit of a single life annuity.

*(2) Defined contribution plan.* In the case of a defined contribution plan, the balance of the employee's account held under the plan.

**(b) Normal retirement age.** *(1) General rule.* For purposes of section 411 and the regulations thereunder, the term "normal retirement age" means the earlier of—

(i) The time specified by a plan at which a plan participant attains normal retirement age, or

(ii) The later of—

(A) The time the plan participant attains age 65, or

(B) The 10th anniversary of the date the plan participant commences participation in the plan.

If a plan, or the employer sponsoring the plan, imposes a requirement that an employee retire upon reaching a certain age, the normal retirement age may not exceed that mandatory retirement age. The preceding sentence will apply if the employer consistently enforces a mandatory retirement age rule, whether or not set forth in the plan or any related document.

For purposes of subdivision (i) of this subparagraph, if an age is not specified by a plan as the normal retirement age, then the normal retirement age under the plan is the earliest age beyond which the participant's benefits under the plan are not greater solely on account of his age or service. For purposes of subdivision (ii)(B) of this subparagraph participation commences on the first day of the first year in which the participant commenced his participation in the plan, except that years which may be disregarded under section 410(a)(5)(D) may be disregarded in determining when participation commenced.

*(2) Examples.* The provisions of this paragraph are illustrated by the following examples:

*Example (1).* Plan A defines normal retirement age as age 65. Under the plan, benefits payable to participants who retire at or after age 60 are not reduced on account of early retirement. For purposes of section 411 and the vesting regulations, normal retirement age under Plan A is age 65 (determined under subparagraph (1)(i) of this paragraph). This is true even if in operation all participants retire at age 60.

*Example (2).* Plan B does not specify any age as the normal retirement age. Under the plan, participants who have attained age 55 are entitled to benefits commencing upon retirement but the benefits of participants who retire before attaining age 70 are subject to reduction on account of early retirement. For purposes of section 411 and the vesting regulations the normal retirement age under Plan B is the later of (i) age 65, or (ii) the 10th anniversary of the date a plan participant commences participation in the plan (assuming such date is prior to age 70).

*Example (3).* The facts are the same as in example (2). Employee X first became a participant in Plan B on January 1, 1980 at age 53. His participation continued until December 31, 1980, when he separated from the service with no vested benefits. After incurring 5 consecutive 1-year breaks in service, Employee X again becomes an employee and a plan participant on January 1, 1986, at age 59. For purposes of section 411, Employee X's normal retirement age under Plan B is age 69, the 10th anniversary of the date on which his year of plan participation commenced. His participation in 1980 may be disregarded under the last sentence of paragraph (b)(1) of this section.

**(c) Normal retirement benefit.** *(1) In general.* For purposes of section 411 and the regulations thereunder, the term "normal retirement benefit" means the periodic benefit under the plan commencing upon early retirement (if any) or at normal retirement age, whichever benefit is greater.

*(2) Periodic benefit.* For purposes of subparagraph (1) of this paragraph—

(i) In the case of a plan under which a benefit is payable as an annuity in the same form upon early retirement and at normal retirement age, the greater benefit is determined by comparing the amount of such annuity payments.

(ii) In the case of a plan under which an annuity benefit payable upon early retirement is not in the same form as an annuity benefit payable at normal retirement age, the greater benefit is determined by converting the annuity benefit payable upon early retirement age into the same form of annuity benefit as is payable at normal retirement age and by comparing the amount of the converted early retirement benefit payment with the amount of the normal retirement benefit payment.

(iii) In the case of a plan which is integrated with the Social Security Act or any other Federal or State law, the periodic benefit payable upon and after early retirement age is adjusted for any increases in such benefits occurring on or after early retirement age which are taken into account under the plan. See however, section 401(a)(15) and the regulations thereunder.

*(3) Benefits included.* For purposes of this paragraph, the normal retirement benefit under a plan shall be determined without regard to ancillary benefits not directly related to retirement benefits such as medical benefits or disability benefits not in excess of the qualified disability benefit; see section 411(a)(7) and paragraph (a)(1) of this section. For this purpose, a qualified disability benefit is a disability benefit which is not in excess of the amount of the benefit which would be payable to the participant if he separated from service at normal retirement age.

*(4) Early retirement benefit; social security supplement.* (i) For purposes of this paragraph, the early retirement benefit under a plan shall be determined without regard to any social security supplement.

(ii) For purposes of this subparagraph, a social security supplement is a benefit for plan participants which—

(A) Commences before the age and terminates before the age when participants are entitled to old-age insurance benefits, unreduced on account of age, under title II of the Social Security Act, as amended (see section 202(a) and (g) of such Act), and

(B) Does not exceed such old-age insurance benefit.

*(5) Special limitation.* If a defined benefit plan bases its normal retirement benefits on employee compensation, the compensation must reflect the compensation which would have been paid for a full year of participation within the meaning of section 411(b)(3). If an employee works less than a full year of participation, the compensation used to determine benefits under the plan for such year of participation must be multiplied by the ratio of the number of hours for a complete year of participation to the number of hours worked in such year. A plan whose benefit formula is computed on a computation base which cannot decrease is not required to adjust employee compensation in the manner described in the previous sentence. Thus, for example, if a plan

provided a benefit based on an employee's compensation for his highest five consecutive years or a separate benefit for each year of participation based on the employee's compensation for such year the plan would not have to so adjust compensation. However, if a plan provided a benefit based on an employee's compensation for the employee's last five years or the five highest consecutive years out of the last 10 years, the compensation, would have to be so adjusted. For special rules for applying the limitations on proration of a year of participation for benefit accrual, see regulations prescribed by the Secretary of Labor under 29 CFR Part 2530, relating to minimum standards for employee pension benefit plans.

*(6) Examples.* The provisions of this paragraph are illustrated by the following examples:

*Example (1).* Plan A provides for a benefit equal to 1% of high 5 years compensation for each year of service and a normal retirement age of 65. The plan also provides for a full unreduced accrued benefit without any actuarial reduction for any employee at age 55 with 30 years of service. Even though the actuarial value of the early retirement benefit could exceed the value of the benefit at the normal age, the normal retirement benefit would not include the greater value of the early retirement benefit because actuarial subsidies are ignored.

*Example (2).* Plan B provides the following benefits: (1) at normal retirement age 65, $300/mo. for life and (2) at early retirement age 60, $400/mo. for life. The normal retirement benefit is $400/mo., the greater of the benefit payable at normal retirement age ($300) or early retirement ($400).

*Example (3).* Assume the same facts as example (2) except that the early retirement benefit of $400 is reduced to $300 upon attainment of age 65. If each employee's social security benefit at age 65 is not less than $100, the $100 would be considered to be a social security supplement and would therefore be ignored. Consequently, the normal retirement benefit would be $300.

*Example (4).* Plan C provides a benefit at normal retirement age equal to 1% per year of service, multiplied by the participant's compensation averaged over the 5 years immediately prior to retirement. An early retirement benefit is provided upon attainment of age 60 equal to the benefit accrued to date of early retirement reduced by 4 percent for each year by which the early retirement date precedes the normal retirement age of 65. Employee A was hired at age 30, participated immediately, and retired at age 65. Employee A's annual compensation was $50,000 between ages 55-60 and was reduced to $33,000 after age 60. The following table indicates the amount of annual benefit that would have been provided by the plan formula if the employee retired at or after 60:

| Age | Final average computed (1) | Percent accrued benefit (2) | Reduction (3) | Annual benefit (4) |
|---|---|---|---|---|
| 60 | $50,000 | 30 | 0.80 | $12,000 |
| 61 | 46,600 | 31 | .84 | 12,135 |
| 62 | 43,200 | 32 | .88 | 12,165 |
| 63 | 39,800 | 33 | .92 | 12,083 |
| 64 | 36,400 | 34 | .96 | 11,881 |
| 65 | 33,000 | 35 | 1.00 | 11,550 |

Note—Col. (1) times col. (2) times col. (3) equals col. (4).

The normal retirement benefit is the greater of the benefit payable at normal retirement age or the early retirement benefit. Employee A's normal retirement benefit is $12,165, the greatest annual benefit Employee A would be entitled to.

**(d) Rules relating to certain distributions and cash-outs of accrued benefits.** *(1) In general.* This paragraph sets forth vesting rules applicable to certain distributions from qualified plans and their related trusts (other than class year plans). Subparagraphs (2) and (3) set forth the exceptions to nonforfeitability on account of withdrawal of mandatory contributions provided by section 411(a)(3)(D). When a plan utilizes these exceptions with respect to a given participant's accrued benefit, such accrued benefit is not subject to the cash-out rules or vesting rules of subparagraphs (4) or (5), respectively. Section 411 prescribes certain requirements with respect to accrued benefits under a qualified plan. These requirements would generally not be satisfied if the plan disregarded service in computing accrued benefits even though amounts were distributed on account of such service. Subparagraph (4) of this paragraph sets forth rules under section 411(a)(7)(B) which allow a plan to make distributions and compute accrued benefits without regard to the accrued benefit attributable to the distribution. When a defined contribution plan utilizes this exception with respect to an accrued benefit, the plan is not required to satisfy the rules of subparagraph (5) of this paragraph. Subparagraph (5) of this paragraph sets forth a vesting requirement applicable to certain distributions from defined contribution plans. Subparagraph (6) sets forth other rules which pertain to the distribution rules of this paragraph.

*(2) Withdrawal of mandatory contribution.* (i) General rule. In the case of a participant's right to his employer-derived accrued benefit, a right is not treated as forfeitable merely because all or a portion of such benefit may be forfeited on account of the withdrawal by the participant of any amount attributable to his accrued benefit derived from his mandatory contributions (within the meaning of section 411(c)(2)(C) and § 1.411(c)-1) before he has become a 50 percent vested participant (within the meaning of § 1.401(a)-19(b)(2)). For purposes of determining the vested percentage, the plan may disregard service after the withdrawal. For example, assume that a plan utilizes 1000 hours for computing years of service and that for the computation period employee A had 1000 hours of service. If A was 40 percent vested at the beginning of the period but only had 800 hours at the time of the withdrawal, the plan could treat A as only 40 percent vested because service after the withdrawal can be disregarded. On the other hand, if A had 1000 hours at the time of the withdrawal, he must receive a year of service

for the computation period, even though service is not taken into account until the end of such period.

(ii) Plan repayment provision. (A) Subdivision (i) of this subparagraph shall not apply unless, at the time the amount described in such subdivision is withdrawn by the participant, the plan provides the employee with a right to restoration of his employer-derived accrued benefit to the extent forfeited in accordance with such subdivision upon repayment to the plan of the full amount of the withdrawal.

(B) In the case of a defined benefit plan (as defined in section 414(j)) the restoration of the employee's employer-derived accrued benefit may be conditioned upon repayment of interest on the full amount of the distribution. Such interest shall be computed on the amount of the distribution from the date of such distribution to the date of repayment, compounded annually from the date of distribution, at the rate determined under section 411(c)(2)(C) in effect on the date of repayment. A plan may provide for repayment of interest which is less than the amount determined under the preceding sentence.

(C) In the case of both defined benefit plans and defined contribution plans, the plan repayment provision described in this subparagraph may provide that the employee must repay the full amount of the distribution in order to have the forfeited benefit restored. The plan provision may not require that such repayment be made sooner than the time described in paragraph (d)(2)(ii)(D) of this section.

(D) (1) If a distribution is on account of separation from service, the time for repayment may not end before the earlier of—

(i) 5 years after the first day the employee is subsequently employed, or

(ii) The close of the first period of consecutive 1-year breaks in service commencing after the distribution.

If the distribution occurs for any other reason, the time for repayment may not end earlier than 5 years after the date of distribution. Nevertheless, a plan provision may provide for a longer period in which the employee may repay. For example, a plan could allow repayments to be made at any time before normal retirement age.

(2) In the case of a plan utilizing the elapsed time method, described in § 1.410(a)-7, the minimum time for repayment shall be determined as in paragraph (d)(2)(ii)(D)(1) of this section except as provided in this subdivision. The 5 consecutive 1-year break periods shall be determined by substituting the term "1-year period of severance" for the term "1-year break in service". Also, the repayment period both commences and closes in a manner determined by the Commissioner that is consistent with the rules in § 1.410(a)-7 and the substitution in section 411(a)(6)(C) and (D) of a 5-year break in service rule for the former 1-year break-in-service rule.

(E) A defined benefit plan using the break-in-service rule described in section 410(a)(5)(D) or a defined contribution plan using the break-in-service rule described in section 411(a)(6)(C) for determining employees' accrued benefits is not required to provide for repayment by an employee whose accrued benefit is disregarded by reason of a plan provision using these rules.

(iii) Computation of benefit. In the case of a defined contribution plan, the employer-derived accrued benefit required to be restored by this subparagraph shall not be less than the amount in the account balance of the employee which was forfeited, unadjusted by any subsequent gains or losses.

(iv) Delayed forfeiture. A defined contribution plan may, in lieu of the forfeiture and restoration described in this subparagraph, provide that the forfeiture does not occur until the expiration of the time for repayment described in subdivision (ii) of this subparagraph provided that the conditions of this subparagraph are satisfied.

*(3) Withdrawal of mandatory contributions; accruals before September 2, 1974.* (i) General rule. In the case of a participant's right to the portion of the employer-derived benefit which accrued prior to September 2, 1974, a right is not treated as forfeitable merely because all or part of such portion may be forfeited on account of the withdrawal by the participant of an amount attributable to his benefit derived from mandatory contributions (within the meaning of section 411(c)(2)(C) and § 1.411(c)-1(c)(4)) made by the participant before September 2, 1974, if the amount so subject to forfeiture is no more than proportional to such amounts withdrawn. This subparagraph shall not apply to any plan to which any mandatory contribution (within the meaning of section 411(c)(2)(C) and § 1.411(c)-1(c)(4)) is made after September 2, 1974.

(ii) Defined contribution plan. In the case of a defined contribution plan, the portion of a participant's employer-derived benefit which accrued prior to September 2, 1974, shall be determined on the basis of a separate accounting between benefits accruing before and after such date. Gains, losses, withdrawals, forfeitures, and other credits or charges must be separately allocated to such benefits. Any allocation made on a reasonable and consistent basis prior to September 1, 1977, shall satisfy the requirements of this subdivision.

(iii) Defined benefit plan. In the case of a defined benefit plan, the portion of a participant's employer-derived benefit which accrued prior to September 2, 1974, shall be determined in a manner consistent with the determination of an accrued benefit under section 411(b)(1)(D) (see § 1.411(b)-1(c)). Any method of determining such accrued benefit which the Commissioner finds to be reasonable shall satisfy the requirements of this subdivision.

*(4) Certain cash-outs of accrued benefits.* (i) Involuntary cash-outs. For purposes of determining an employee's right to an accrued benefit derived from employer contributions under a plan, the plan may disregard service performed by the employee with respect to which—

(A) The employee receives a distribution of the present value of his entire nonforfeitable benefit at the time of the distribution;

(B) The requirements of section 411(a)(11) are satisfied at the time of the distribution;

(C) The distribution is made due to the termination of the employee's participation in the plan; and

(D) The plan has a repayment provision which satisfies the requirements of paragraph (d)(4)(iv) of this section in effect at the time of the distribution.

(ii) Voluntary cash-outs. For purposes of determining an employee's accrued benefit derived from employer contributions under a plan, the plan may disregard service performed by the employee with respect to which—

(A) The employee receives a distribution of the present value of his nonforfeitable benefit attributable to such service at the time of such distribution,

(B) The employee voluntarily elects to receive such distribution,

(C) The distribution is made on a termination of the employee's participation in the plan, and

(D) The plan has a repayment provision in effect at the time of the distribution which satisfies the requirements of subdivision (iv) of this subparagraph.

A distribution shall be deemed to be made on termination of participation in the plan if it is made not later than the close of the second plan year following the plan year in which such termination occurs. For purposes of determining the nonforfeitable benefit, the plan may disregard service after the distribution as illustrated in subparagraph (2)(i) of this subparagraph.

(iii) Disregard of service. Service of an employee permitted to be disregarded under subdivision (i) or (ii) of this subparagraph is not required to be taken into account in computing the employee's accrued benefit under the plan. In the case of a voluntary distribution described in subdivision (ii) of this subparagraph which is less than the present value of the employee's total nonforfeitable benefit immediately prior to the distribution, the accrued benefit not required to be taken into account is such total accrued benefit multiplied by a fraction, the numerator of which is the amount of the distribution and the denominator of which is the present value of his total nonforfeitable benefit immediately prior to such distribution. For example, A who is 50 percent vested in an account balance of $1,000 receives a voluntary distribution of $250. The accrued benefit which can be disregarded equals $1,000 times $250/$500, or $500. However, such service may not by reason of this paragraph be disregarded for purposes of determining an employee's years of service under sections 410(a)(3) and 411(a)(4).

(iv) Plan repayment provision. (A) A plan repayment provision satisfies the requirements of this subdivision if, under the provision, the accrued benefit of an employee that is disregarded by a plan under this subparagraph is restored upon repayment to the plan by the employee of the full amount of the distribution. An accrued benefit is not restored unless all of the optional forms of benefit and subsidies relating to such benefit are also restored. A plan is not required to provide for repayment of an accrued benefit unless the employee—

(1) Received a distribution that is in a plan year to which section 411 applies (see § 1.411(a)-2), which distribution is less than the amount of his accrued benefit determined under the same optional form of benefit as the distribution was made, and

(2) Resumes employment covered under the plan.

(B) Example Plan A provides a single sum distribution equal to the present value of the normal form of the accrued benefit payable at normal retirement age which is a single life annuity. Plan A also provides a subsidized joint and survivor annuity and a subsidized early retirement annuity benefit. A participant who is fully vested and receives a single sum distribution equal to the present value of the single life annuity normal retirement benefit is not required to be provided the right under the plan to repay the distribution upon subsequent reemployment even though the participant received a distribution that did not reflect the value of the subsidy in the joint and survivor annuity or the value of the early retirement annuity subsidy. This is true whether or not the participant had satisfied at the time of the distribution all of the conditions necessary to receive the subsidies. However, if a participant does not receive his total accrued benefit in the optional form of benefit under which his benefit was distributed, the plan must provide for repayment. If the employee repays the distribution in accordance with section 411(a)(7), the plan must restore the employee's accrued benefit which would include the right to receive the subsidized joint and survivor annuity and the subsidized early retirement annuity benefit.

(C) A plan may impose the same conditions on repayments for the restoration of employer-derived accrued benefits that are allowed as conditions for restoration of employer-derived accrued benefits upon repayment of mandatory contributions under paragraphs (d)(2)(ii)(B), (C), (D) and (E) of this section.

(v) In the case of a defined contribution plan, the employer-derived accrued benefit required to be restored by this subparagraph shall not be less than the amount in the account balance of the employee, both the amount distributed and the amount forfeited, unadjusted by any subsequent gains or losses. Thus, for example, if an employee received a distribution of $250 when he was 25 percent vested in an account balance of $1,000, upon repayment of $250 the account balance may not be less than $1,000 even if, because of plan losses, the account balance, if not distributed, would have been reduced to $500.

(vi) For purposes of paragraph (d)(4)(i) of this section, a distribution shall be deemed to be made due to the termination of an employee's participation in the plan if it is made no later than the close of the second plan year following the plan year in which such termination occurs, or if such distribution would have been made under the plan by the close of such second plan year but for the fact that the present value of the nonforfeitable accrued benefit then exceeded the cash-out limit in effect under § 1.411(a)-11(c)(3)(ii). For purposes of determining the entire nonforfeitable benefit, the plan may disregard service after the distribution, as illustrated in paragraph (d)(2)(i) of this section.

(vii) Effective date. Paragraphs (d)(4)(i) and (vi) of this section apply to distributions made on or after March 22, 1999. However, an employer is permitted to apply paragraphs (d)(4)(i) and (vi) of this section to plan years beginning on or afterAugust 6, 1997. Otherwise, for distributions prior to March 22, 1999, §§ 1.411(a)-7 and 1.411(a)-7T, in effect prior to October 17, 2000 (as contained in 26 CFR part 1, revised as of April 1, 2000) apply.

*(5) Vesting requirement for defined contribution plans.* (i) Application. The requirements of this subparagraph apply to a defined contribution plan which makes distributions to employees from their accounts attributable to employer contributions at a time when—

(A) Employees are less than 100 percent vested in such accounts, and

(B) Under the plan, employees can increase their percentage of vesting in such accounts after the distributions.

(ii) Requirements. In order for a plan, to which this subparagraph applies, to satisfy the vesting requirements of section 411, account balances under the plan (with respect to which percentage vesting can increase) must be computed in a manner which satisfies either subdivision (iii)(A) or (B) of this subparagraph.

(iii) Permissible methods. A plan may provide for either of the following methods, but not both, for computing account balances with respect to which percentage vesting can increase and from which distributions are made:

(A) (1) A separate account is established for the employee's interest in the plan as of the time of the distribution, and

(2) At any relevant time the employee's vested portion of the separate account is not less than an amount ("X") determined by the formula: X = P(AB + (R × D)) − (R × D). For purposes of applying the formula: P is the vested percentage at the relevant time; AB is the account balance at the relevant time; D is the amount of the distribution; R is the ratio of the account balance at the relevant time to the account balance after distribution; and the relevant time is the time at which, under the plan, the vested percentage in the account cannot increase. A plan is not required to provide for separate accounts provided that account balances are maintained under a method that has the same effect as under this subdivision.

(B) At any relevant time the employee's vested portion is not less than an amount ("X") determined by the formula: X = P(AB + D) − D. For purposes of applying the formula, the terms have the same meaning as under subdivision (iii)(A) *(2)* of this subparagraph.

(C) An application of the methods described in subdivisions (iii)(a) and (B) of this subparagraph is illustrated by the following examples:

*Example (1).* The X defined contribution plan uses the method described in subdivision (iii)(A) of this subparagraph for computing account balances and the break in service rule described in section 411(a)(6)(C) (service after a 1-year break does not increase the vesting percentage in account balances accrued prior to the break). The plan distributes $250 to A when A's account balance prior to the distribution equals $1,000 and he is 25 percent vested. At the time of the distribution, A has not incurred a 1-year break so that his vesting percentage can increase. Six years later, when A is 60 percent vested, he incurs a 1-year break so that his vesting percentage cannot increase. At this time his separate account balance equals $1,500.

$$R = \frac{\$1,500}{\$750} \text{ or } 2$$

A's separate account must equal 60 percent ($1,500 + (2 × $250)) − (2 × $250) or 60 percent ($1,500 + $500) − $500, or $1,200 − $500 equals $700.

*Example (2).* The Y defined contribution plan uses the method described in subdivision (iii)(B) of this subparagraph for computing account balances and the break in service rule described in section 411(a)(6)(C). The plan distributes $250 to B when B's account balance prior to the distribution equals $1,000 and he is 25 percent vested. At the time of the distribution, B has not incurred a 1-year break so that his vesting percentage can increase. Six years later, when A is 60 percent vested, he incurs a 1-year break so that his vesting percentage cannot increase. At this time his account balance equals $1,500. B's separate account must equal 60 percent ($1,500 + $250) − $250, 60% of $1,750 − $250 equals $800.

*(6) Other rules.* (i) Distributions on separation or other event. None of the rules of this paragraph preclude distributions to employees upon separation from service or any other event recognized by the plan for commencing distributions. Such a distribution must, of course, satisfy the applicable qualification requirements pertaining to such distributions. For example, a profit-sharing plan could pay the vested portion of an account balance to an employee when he separated from service, but in order to satisfy section 411 of the plan might not be able to forfeit the nonvested account balance until the employee has a 1-year break in service. Similarly, the fact that a plan cannot disregard an accrued benefit attributable to service for which an employee has received a distribution because the plan does not satisfy the cash-out requirements of subparagraph (4) of this paragraph does not mean that the employee's accrued benefit (computed by taking into account such service) cannot be offset by the accrued benefit attributable to the distribution.

(ii) Joint and survivor requirements. See § 1.401 (a)-11(a)(2) (relating to joint and survivor annuities) for special rules applicable to certain distributions described in this paragraph.

(iii) Plan repayments. (A) Under subparagraphs (2) and (4) of this paragraph, a plan may be required to restore accrued benefits in the event of repayment by an employee.

(B) For purposes of applying the limitations of section 415(c) and (e), in the case of a defined contribution plan, the repayment by the employee and the restoration by the employer shall not be treated as annual additions.

(C) In the case of a defined contribution plan, the permissible sources for restoration of the accrued benefit are: income or gain to the plan, forfeitures, or employer contributions. Notwithstanding the provisions of § 1.401-1(b)(1)(ii), contributions may be made for such an accrued benefit by a profit-sharing plan even though there are no profits. In order for such a plan to be qualified, account balances (accrued benefits) generally must correspond to assets in the plan. Accordingly, there cannot be an unfunded account balance. However, an account balance will not be deemed to be unfunded in the case of a restoration if assets for the restored benefit are provided by the end of the plan year following the plan year in which the repayment occurs.

T.D. 7501, 8/22/77, amend T.D. 8038, 7/18/85, T.D. 8219, 8/19/88, T.D. 8794, 12/18/98, T.D. 8891, 7/18/2000.

PAR. 4. Section 1.411(a)-7 is amended by adding a new paragraph (b)(3) to read as follows:

**Proposed § 1.411(a)-7 Definitions and special rules.** [*For Preamble, see* ¶ *151,113*]

* * * * *

**(b) Normal retirement age.** * * *

*(3) Effect of Omnibus Budget Reconciliation Act of 1986 (OBRA). [Reserved]*

* * * * *

**§ 1.411(a)-8 Changes in vesting schedule.**

***Caution:*** The Treasury has not yet amended Reg § 1.411(a)-8 to reflect changes made by P.L. 104-188, P.L. 99-514.

**(a) Requirement of prior schedule.** Under section 411(a)(10)(A), for plan years for which section 411 applies, a plan will be treated as not meeting the minimum vesting standards of section 411(a)(2) if the plan does not satisfy the requirements of this paragraph. If the vesting schedule of a plan is amended, then as of the date such amendment is adopted, the plan satisfies the requirements of this paragraph if, under the plan as amended, in the case of an employee who is a participant on—

*(1)* The date the amendment is adopted, or

*(2)* The date the amendment is effective, if later

The nonforfeitable percentage (determined as of such date) of such employee's right to his employer-derived accrued benefit is not less than his percentage computed under the plan without regard to such amendment.

**(b) Election of former schedule.** *(1) In general.* Under section 411(a)(10)(B), for plan years for which section 411 applies, if the vesting schedule of a plan is amended, the plan will not be treated as meeting the minimum vesting standards of section 411(a)(2) unless the plan as amended, provides that each participant whose nonforfeitable percentage of his accrued benefit derived from employer contributions is determined under such schedule, and who has completed at least 5 years of service with the employer, may elect, during the election period, to have the nonforfeitable percentage of his accrued benefit derived from employer contributions determined without regard to such amendment. Notwithstanding the preceding sentence, no election need be provided for any participant whose nonforfeitable percentage under the plan, as amended, at any time cannot be less than such percentage determined without regard to such amendment.

*(2) Election period.* For purposes of subparagraph (1) of this paragraph, the election period under the plan must begin no later than the date the plan amendment is adopted and end no earlier than the latest of the following dates:

(i) The date which is 60 days after the day the plan amendment is adopted,

(ii) The date which is 60 days after the day the plan amendment becomes effective, or

(iii) The date which is 60 days after the day the participant is issued written notice of the plan amendment by the employer or plan administrator.

*(3) Service requirement.* For purposes of subparagraph (1) of this paragraph, a participant shall be considered to have completed 5 years of service if such participant has completed 5 years of service, whether or not consecutive, without regard to the exceptions of section 411(a)(4) prior to the expiration of the election period described in subparagraph (2) of this paragraph. For the meaning of the term "year of service", see regulations prescribed by the Secretary of Labor under 29 CFR Part 2530, relating to minimum standards for employee pension benefit plans.

*(4) Election only by participant.* The election described in subparagraph (1) of this paragraph is available only to an individual who is a participant in the plan at the time such election is made.

*(5) Election may be irrevocable.* A plan, as amended, shall not fail to meet the minimum vesting standards of section 411(a)(2) by reason of section 411(a)(10)(B) merely because such plan provides that the election described in subparagraph (1) of this paragraph is irrevocable.

*(6) Relationship with section 411(a)(2).* The election described in subparagraph (1) of this paragraph is available for a vesting schedule which does not satisfy the requirements of section 411(a)(2) only if under such schedule all participants have a 50 percent nonforfeitable right after 10 years of service, and a 100 percent nonforfeitable right after 15 years of service, in their employer-derived accrued benefit. If the vesting schedule provides less vesting than the percentages required by the preceding sentence, the plan can be amended to provide for such vesting.

**(c) Special rules.** *(1) Amendment of vesting schedule.* For purposes of this section, an amendment of a vesting schedule is each plan amendment which directly or indirectly affects the computation of the nonforfeitable percentage of employees' rights to employer-derived accrued benefits. Consequently, such an amendment, for example, includes each change in the plan which affects either the plan's computation of years of service or of vesting percentages for years of service.

*(2) Aggregation of amendments.* All plan amendments which are: (i) amendments of a vesting schedule within the meaning of subparagraph (1) of this paragraph and (ii) adopted and effective at the same time, shall be deemed to be a single amendment for purposes of applying the rules in paragraphs (a) and (b) of this section.

*(3) Relationship with section 411(d)(6).* For additional requirements relating to section 411(d)(6), see § 1.411(d)-3(a)(3).

---

T.D. 7501, 8/22/77, amend T.D. 9280, 8/8/2006.

---

### § 1.411(a)-8T Changes in vesting schedule (temporary).

**(a) [Reserved]**

**(b) Election of former schedule.** *(1) In general.* Under section 411(a)(10)(B), for plan years for which section 411 applies, if the vesting schedule of a plan is amended, the plan will not be treated as meeting the minimum vesting standards of section 411(a)(2) unless the plan as amended provides that each participant whose nonforfeitable percentage of his accrued benefit derived from employer contributions is determined under such schedule, and who has completed at least 3 years of service with the employer, may elect, during the election period, to have the nonforfeitable percentage of his accrued benefit derived from employer contributions determined without regard to such amendment. Notwithstanding the preceding sentence, no election need be provided for any participant whose nonforfeitable percentage under the plan, as amended, at any time cannot be less than such percentage determined without regard to such amendment. For employees not described in § 1.411(a)-3T(e)(1), this section shall be applied by substituting "5 years of service" for "3 years of service" where such language appears.

*(2) Election period.* For purposes of subparagraph (1) of this paragraph, the election period under the plan must begin no later than the date the plan amendment is adopted and end no earlier than the latest of the following dates:

(i) The date which is 60 days after the day the plan amendment is adopted,

(ii) The date which is 60 days after the day the plan amendment becomes effective, or

(iii) The date which is 60 days after the day the participant is issued written notice of the plan amendment by the employer or plan administrator.

*(3) Service requirement.* For purposes of subparagraph (1) of this paragraph, a participant shall be considered to have completed 3 years of service if such participant was completed 3 years of service, whether or not consecutive, without regard to the exceptions of section 411(a)(4) prior to the expiration of the election period described in subparagraph (2) of this paragraph. For the meaning of the term "year of service", see regulations prescribed by the Secretary of Labor under 29 CFR Part 2530, relating to minimum standards for employee pension benefit plans.

---

T.D. 8170, 1/5/88.

---

### § 1.411(a)-9 Amendment of break in service rules; transitional period.

**(a) In general.** Under section 1017(f)(2) of the Employee Retirement Income Security Act of 1974, a plan is not a qualified plan (and a trust forming a part of such plan is not a qualified trust) if the rules of the plan relating to breaks in service are amended, and—

*(1)* Such amendment is effective after January 1, 1974, and before the effective date of section 411, and

*(2)* Under such amendment, the nonforfeitable percentage of any employee's right to his employer-derived accrued benefit is less than the lesser of the nonforfeitable percentage of such employee's right to such benefit—

(i) Under the break in service rules provided by section 411(a)(6) and § 1.411(a)-6(c), or

(ii) The greatest such percentage under the plan as in effect on or after January 1, 1974 (provided the break in service rules of the plan were not in violation of any law or rule of law January 1, 1974).

**(b) Break in service rules.** For purposes of paragraph (a), the term "break in service rules" means the rules provided by a plan relating to circumstances under which a period of an employee's service or plan participation is disregarded, for purposes of determining the extent to which his rights to his accrued benefit under the plan are unconditional, if under such rules such service is disregarded by reason of the employee's failure to complete a required period of service within a specified period of time. For this purpose, plan rules which result in the loss of prior vesting or benefit accruals of an employee, or which deny an employee eligibility to participate, by reason of separation or failure to complete a required period of service within a specified period of time (e.g. 300 hours in one year) will be considered break in service rules. For purposes of section 411(b)(3), service described under the plan's break in service rules, as in effect before the effective date of section 411, need not be counted.

T.D. 7501, 8/22/77.

## § 1.411(a)-11 Restriction and valuation of distributions.

***Caution:*** The Treasury has not yet amended Reg § 1.411(a)-11 to reflect changes made by P.L. 109-280, P.L. 105-34, P.L. 103-465.

**(a) Scope.** *(1) In general.* Section 411(a)(11) restricts the ability of a plan to distribute any portion of a participant's accrued benefit without the participant's consent. Section 411(a)(11) also restricts the ability of defined benefit plans to distribute any portion of a participant's accrued benefit in optional forms of benefit without complying with specified valuation rules for determining the amount of the distribution. If the consent requirements or the valuation rules of this section are not satisfied, the plan fails to satisfy the requirements of section 411(a).

*(2) Accrued benefit.* For purposes of this section, an accrued benefit is valued taking into consideration the particular optional form in which the benefit is to be distributed. The value of an accrued benefit is the present value of the benefit in the distribution form determined under the plan. For example, a plan that provides a subsidized early retirement annuity benefit may specify that the optional single sum distribution form of benefit available at early retirement age is the present value of the subsidized early retirement annuity benefit. In this case, the subsidized early retirement annuity benefit must be used to apply the valuation requirements of this section and the resulting amount of the single sum distribution. However, if a plan that provides a subsidized early retirement annuity benefit specifies that the single sum distribution benefit available at early retirement age is the present value of the normal retirement annuity benefit, then the normal retirement annuity benefit is used to apply the valuation requirements of this section and the resulting amount of the single sum distribution available at early retirement age.

**(b) General consent rules.** A plan must satisfy the participant consent requirement with respect to the distribution of a participant's nonforfeitable accrued benefit with a present value in excess of the cash-out limit in effect under § 1.411(a)-11(c)(3)(ii). See paragraphs (c)(3) and (4) for situations where no consent is required.

**(c) Consent, etc. requirements.** *(1) General rule.* If an accrued benefit is immediately distributable, section 411(a)(11) permits plans to provide for the distribution of any portion of a participant's nonforfeitable accrued benefits only if the applicable consent requirements are satisfied.

*(2) Consent.* (i) No consent is valid unless the participant has received a general description of the material features of the optional forms of benefit available under the plan. In addition, so long as a benefit is immediately distributable, a participant must be informed of the right, if any, to defer receipt of the distribution. Furthermore, consent is not valid if a significant detriment is imposed under the plan on any participant who does not consent to a distribution. Whether or not a significant detriment is imposed shall be determined by the Commissioner by examining the particular facts and circumstances.

(ii) Consent of the participant to the distribution must not be made before the participant receives the notice of his or her rights specified in this paragraph (c)(2) and must not be made more than 90 days before the date the distribution commences.

(iii) A plan must provide a participant with notice of the rights specified in this paragraph (c)(2) at a time that satisfies either paragraph (c)(2)(iii)(A) or (B) of this section:

(A) This paragraph (c)(2)(iii)(A) is satisfied if the plan provides a participant with notice of the rights specified in this paragraph (c)(2) no less than 30 days and no more than 90 days before the date the distribution commences. However, if the participant, after having received this notice, affirmatively elects a distribution, a plan will not fail to satisfy the consent requirement of section 411(a)(11) merely because the distribution commences less than 30 days after the notice was provided to the participant, provided the plan administrator clearly indicates to the participant that the participant has a right to at least 30 days to consider whether to consent to the distribution. (B) This paragraph (c)(2)(iii)(B) is satisfied if the plan—

(1) Provides the participant with notice of the rights specified in this paragraph (c)(2);

(2) Provides the participant with a summary of the notice within the time period described in paragraph (c)(2)(iii)(A) of this section; and

(3) If the participant so requests after receiving the summary described in paragraph (c)(2)(iii)(B)(2) of this section, provides the notice to the participant without charge and no less than 30 days before the date the distribution commences, subject to the rules for the participant's waiver of that 30-day period. The summary described in paragraph (c)(2)(iii)(B)(2) of this section must advise the participant of the right, if any, to defer receipt of the distribution, must set forth a summary of the distribution options under the plan, must refer the participant to the most recent version of the notice (and, in the case of a notice provided in any document containing information in addition to the notice, must identify that document and must provide a reasonable indication of where the notice may be found in that document,

such as by index reference or by section heading), and must advise the participant that, upon request, a copy of the notice will be provided without charge.

(iv) For purposes of satisfying the requirements of this paragraph (c)(2), the plan administrator may substitute the annuity starting date, within the meaning of § 1.401(a)-20, Q&A-10, for the date the distribution commences.

(v) See § 1.401(a)-20, Q&A-24 for a special rule applicable to consents to plan loans.

*(3) Cash-out limit.* (i) Written consent of the participant is required before the commencement of the distribution of any portion of an accrued benefit if the present value of the nonforfeitable total accrued benefit is greater than the cash-out limit in effect under paragraph (c)(3)(ii) of this section on the date the distribution commences. The consent requirements are deemed satisfied if such value does not exceed the cash-out limit, and the plan may distribute such portion to the participant as a single sum. Present value for this purpose must be determined in the same manner as under section 417(e); see § 1.417(e)-1(d).

(ii) The cash-out limit in effect for a date is the amount described in section 411(a)(11)(A) for the plan year that includes that date. The cash-out limit in effect for dates in plan years beginning on or after August 6, 1997, is $5,000. The cash-out limit in effect for dates in plan years beginning before August 6, 1997, is $3,500.

(iii) Effective date. Paragraphs (c)(3)(i) and (ii) of this section apply to distributions made on or after October 17, 2000. However, an employer is permitted to apply the $5,000 cash-out limit described in paragraph (c)(3)(ii) of this section to plan years beginning on or after August 6, 1997. Otherwise, for distributions prior to October 17, 2000, §§ 1.411(a)-11 and 1.411(a)-11T in effect prior to October 17, 2000 (as contained in 26 CFR Part 1 revised as of April 1, 2000) apply.

*(4) Immediately distributable.* Participant consent is required for any distribution while it is immediately distributable, i.e., prior to the later of the time a participant has attained normal retirement age (as defined in section 411(a)(8)) or age 62. Once a distribution is no longer immediately distributable, a plan may distribute the benefit in the form of a QJSA in a case of a benefit subject to section 417 or in the normal form in other cases without consent.

*(5) Death of participant.* The consent requirements of section 411(a)(11) do not apply after the death of the participant.

*(6) QDROs.* The consent requirements of section 411(a)(11) do not apply to payments to an alternate payee, defined in section 414(p)(8), except as provided in a qualified domestic relations order pursuant to section 414(p).

*(7) Section 401(a)(9), etc.* The consent requirements of section 411(a)(11) do not apply to the extent that a distribution is required to satisfy the requirements of section 401(a)(9) or 415. See section 401(a)(9) and the regulations thereunder and § 1.401(a)-20 Q&A 23 for guidance on these requirements. Notwithstanding any provision to the contrary in section 401(a)(14) or § 1.401(a)-14, a plan may not distribute a participant's nonforfeitable accrued benefit with a present value in excess of the cash-out limit in effect under § 1.411(a)-11(c)(3)(ii) while the benefit is immediately distributable unless the participant consents to such distribution. The failure of a participant to consent is deemed to be an election to defer commencement of payment of the benefit for purposes of section 401(a)(14) and § 1.401(a)-14.

*(8) Delegation to Commissioner.* The Commissioner, in revenue rulings, notices, and other guidance published in the Internal Revenue Bulletin, may modify, or provide additional guidance with respect to, the notice and consent requirements of this section. See § 601.601(d)(2)(ii)(b) of this chapter.

**(d) Distribution valuation requirements.** In determining the present value of any distribution of any accrued benefit from a defined benefit plan, the plan must take into account specified valuation rules. For this purpose, the valuation rules are the same valuation rules for valuing distributions as set forth in section 417(e); see § 1.417(e)-1(d). This paragraph (d) applies both before and after the participant's death regardless of whether the accrued benefit is immediately distributable. This paragraph also applies whether or not the participant's consent is required under paragraphs (b) and (c) of this section.

**(e) Special rules.** *(1) Plan termination.* The requirements of this section apply before, on and after a plan termination. If a defined contribution plan terminates and the plan does not offer an annuity option (purchased from a commercial provider), then the plan may distribute a participant's accrued benefit without the participant's consent. The preceding sentence does not apply if the employer, or any entity within the same controlled group as the employer, maintains another defined contribution plan, other than an employee stock ownership plan (as defined in section 4975(e)(7)). In such a case, the participant's accrued benefit may be transferred without the participant's consent to the other plan if the participant does not consent to an immediate distribution from the terminating plan. See section 411(d)(6) and the regulations thereunder for other rules applicable to transferee plans and plan terminations.

*(2) ESOP dividends.* The requirements of this section do not apply to any distribution of dividends to which section 404(k) applies.

*(3) Other rules.* See § 1.401(a)-20 Q&As 14, 17 and 24 for other rules that apply to this section 411(a)(11) requirements.

**(f) Medium for notice and consent.** *(1) Notice.* The notice of a participant's rights described in paragraph (c)(2) of this section or the summary of that notice described in paragraph (c)(2)(iii)(B)(2) of this section must be provided on a written paper document. However, see § 1.401(a)-21 of this chapter for rules permitting the use of electronic media to provide applicable notices to recipients with respect to retirement plans.

*(2) Consent.* The consent described in paragraphs (c)(2) and (3) of this section must be given on a written paper document. However, see Sec. 1.401(a)-21 of this chapter for rules permitting the use of electronic media to make participant elections with respect to retirement plans.

---

T.D. 8219, 8/19/88, amend T.D. 8620, 9/15/95, T.D. 8794, 12/18/98, T.D. 8796, 12/17/98, T.D. 8873, 2/7/2000, T.D. 8891, 7/18/2000, amend T.D. 9294, 10/19/2006.

---

PAR. 2. For each entry listed in the "Location" column, remove the language in the "Remove" column and add the language in the "Add" column in its place.

PAR. 2. For each entry listed in the "Location" column, remove the language in the "Remove" column and add the language in the "Add" column in its place.

PAR. 2. For each entry listed in the "Location" column, remove the language in the "Remove" column and add the language in the "Add" column in its place.

PAR. 2. For each entry listed in the "Location" column, remove the language in the "Remove" column and add the language in the "Add" column in its place.

PAR. 2. For each entry listed in the "Location" column, remove the language in the "Remove" column and add the language in the "Add" column in its place.

**Proposed § 1.411(a)-11 Restriction and valuation of distributions.** [*For Preamble, see ¶ 153,065*]

* * * * *

**(c)** * * *

*(2) Consent.* (i) * * * In addition, so long as a benefit is immediately distributable, a participant must be informed of the right, if any, to defer receipt of the distribution and of the consequences of failing to defer such receipt. * * *

* * * * *

(iii) * * *

(B) * * *

*(3)* * * * The summary described in paragraph (c)(2)(iii)(B)(2) of this section must advise the participant of the right, if any, to defer receipt of the distribution and of the consequences of failing to defer such receipt, must set forth a summary of the distribution options under the plan, must refer the participant to the most recent version of the notice (and, in the case of a notice provided in any document containing information in addition to the notice, must identify that document and must provide a reasonable indication of where the notice may be found in that document, such as by index reference or by section heading), and must advise the participant that, upon request, a copy of the notice will be provided without charge.

* * * * *

(vi) Consequences of failing to defer. (A) A notice under this paragraph (c)(2) that is required to describe the consequences of failing to defer receipt of a distribution until it is no longer immediately distributable must, to the extent applicable under the plan and in a manner designed to be easily understood, provide the participant with the information set out in paragraphs (c)(2)(vi)(A)(1) through (5) of this section and explain why it is relevant to a decision whether to defer.

(1) A description of the following federal tax implications of failing to defer: differences in the timing of inclusion in taxable income of an immediately commencing distribution that is not rolled over (or not eligible to be rolled over) and a distribution that is deferred until it is no longer immediately distributable (including, as applicable, differences in the taxation of distributions of designated Roth contributions within the meaning of section 402A); application of the 10% additional tax on certain distributions before age 59½under section 72(t); and, in the case of a defined contribution plan, loss of the opportunity upon immediate commencement for future tax-favored treatment of earnings if the distribution is not rolled over (or not eligible to be rolled over) to an eligible retirement plan described in section 402(c)(8)(B).

(2) In the case of a defined benefit plan, a statement of the amount payable to the participant under the normal form of benefit both upon immediate commencement and upon commencement when the benefit is no longer immediately distributable (assuming no future benefit accruals). The statement need not vary based on the participant's marital status if the plan is permitted, pursuant to § 1.417(a)(3)-1(c)(2)(ii), to provide a QJSA explanation that does not vary based on the participant's marital status.

(3) In the case of a defined contribution plan, a statement that some currently available investment options in the plan may not be generally available on similar terms outside the plan and contact information for obtaining additional information on the general availability outside the plan of currently available investment options in the plan.

(4) In the case of a defined contribution plan, a statement that fees and expenses (including administrative or investment-related fees) outside the plan may be different from fees and expenses that apply to the participant's account and contact information for obtaining additional information on the fees and expenses that apply to the participant's account.

(5) An explanation of any provisions of the plan (and provisions of an accident or health plan maintained by the employer) that could reasonably be expected to materially affect a participant's decision whether to defer receipt of the distribution. Such provisions would include, for example: plan terms under which a participant who fails to defer may lose eligibility for retiree health coverage or eligibility for early retirement subsidies or social security supplements; plan terms under which the benefit of a rehired participant who failed to defer may be adversely affected by the decision not to defer; and, in the case of a defined contribution plan, plan terms under which undistributed benefits that otherwise are nonforfeitable become forfeitable upon the participant's death.

(B) Location of information; incorporation by reference. In general, the information required to be provided in a notice under this paragraph (c)(2)(vi) must appear together (for example, in a list of consequences of failing to defer). However, the notice will not be treated as failing to satisfy the requirements of this paragraph (c)(2)(vi) merely because the notice includes a cross-reference to where the required information may be found in notices or other information provided or made available to the participant, as long as the notice of consequences of failing to defer includes a statement of how the referenced information may be obtained without charge and explains why the referenced information is relevant to a decision whether to defer.

* * * * *

**(h) Consequences of Failing to Defer Effective/Applicability Date.** The provisions in paragraph (c) of this section that describe the requirement to notify participants of the consequences of failing to defer are effective for notices provided on or after the first day of the first plan year beginning on or after January 1, 2010.

PAR. 3. § 1.411(a)-11 [Amended]

Section 1.411(a)-11 is amended as follows:

1. The second sentence of paragraph (c)(2)(i) is revised.

2. The second sentence of paragraph (c)(2)(iii)(B)(3) is revised.

3. Paragraphs (c)(2)(vi) and (h) are added.

The additions and revisions read as follows:

**Proposed § 1.411(a)-11** [*For Preamble, see ¶ 153,065*]

| Location | Remove | Add |
|---|---|---|
| 1.401(a)-13(g)(4)(ii), first sentence | 90 days | 180 days. |
| 1.401(a)-20, A-4, third sentence | 90 days | 180 days. |
| 1.401(a)-20, A-10(a), fifth and sixth sentences. | 90 days | 180 days. |
| 1.401(a)-20, A-16, sixth sentence. | 90 days | 180 days. |
| 1.401(a)-20, A-24(a)(1), fifth sentence. | 90 days | 180 days. |
| 1.402(f)-1, A-2(a), first sentence. | 90 days | 180 days. |
| 1.411(a)-11(c)(2)(ii) | 90 days | 180 days. |
| 1.411(a)-11(c)(2)(iii)(A), first sentence. | 90 days | 180 days. |
| 1.417(e)-1(b)(3)(i) | 90 days | 180 days. |
| 1.417(e)-1(b)(3)(ii), first sentence. | 90 days | 180 days. |
| 1.417(e)-1(b)(3)(iii) | 90 days | 180 days. |
| 1.417(e)-1(b)(3)(vi), second sentence. | 90 days | 180 days. |
| 1.417(e)-1(b)(3)(vii) | 90 days | 180 days. |
| 1.417(e)-1(b)(3)(vii) | 90-day | 180-day. |

### § 1.411(a)(13)-1 Statutory hybrid plans.

**(a) In general.** This section sets forth certain rules that apply to statutory hybrid plans under section 411(a)(13). Paragraph (b) of this section describes special rules for certain statutory hybrid plans that determine benefits under a lump sum-based benefit formula. Paragraph (c) of this section describes the vesting requirement for statutory hybrid plans. Paragraphs (d) and (e) of this section contain definitions and effective/applicability dates, respectively.

**(b) Calculation of benefit by reference to hypothetical account balance or accumulated percentage.** *(1) Payment of a current balance or current value under a lump sum-based benefit formula.* Pursuant to section 411(a)(13)(A), a statutory hybrid plan that determines any portion of a participant's benefits under a lump sum-based benefit formula is not treated as failing to meet the following requirements solely because, with respect to benefits determined under that formula, the present value of those benefits is, under the terms of the plan, equal to the then-current balance of the hypothetical account maintained for the participant or to the then-current value of the accumulated percentage of the participant's final average compensation under that formula—

(i) Section 411(a)(2); or

(ii) With respect to the participant's accrued benefit derived from employer contributions, section 411(a)(11), 411(c), or 417(e).

*(2) Requirements that lump sum-based benefit formula must satisfy to obtain relief.* [Reserved].

*(3) Alternative forms of distribution under a lump sum-based benefit formula.* [Reserved].

*(4) Rules of application.* [Reserved].

**(c) Three-year vesting requirement.** *(1) In general.* Pursuant to section 411(a)(13)(B), if any portion of the participant's accrued benefit under a defined benefit plan is determined under a statutory hybrid benefit formula, the plan is treated as failing to satisfy the requirements of section 411(a)(2) unless the plan provides that the participant has a nonforfeitable right to 100 percent of the participant's accrued benefit if the participant has three or more years of service. Thus, this 3-year vesting requirement applies with respect to the entire accrued benefit of a participant under a defined benefit plan even if only a portion of the participant's accrued benefit under the plan is determined under a statutory hybrid benefit formula. Similarly, if the participant's accrued benefit under a defined benefit plan is, under the plan's terms, the larger of two (or more) benefit amounts, where each amount is determined under a different benefit formula (including a benefit determined pursuant to an offset among formulas within the plan or a benefit determined as the greater of a protected benefit under section 411(d)(6) and another benefit amount) and at least one of those formulas is a statutory hybrid benefit formula, the participant's entire accrued benefit under the defined benefit plan is subject to the 3-year vesting rule of section 411(a)(13)(B) and this paragraph (c). The rule described in the preceding sentence applies even if the larger benefit is ultimately the benefit determined under a formula that is not a statutory hybrid benefit formula.

*(2) Examples.* The provisions of this paragraph (c) are illustrated by the following examples:

*Example (1).* Employer M sponsors Plan X, a defined benefit plan under which each participant's accrued benefit is equal to the sum of the benefit provided under two benefit formulas. The first benefit formula is a statutory hybrid benefit formula, and the second formula is not. Because a portion of each participant's accrued benefit provided under Plan X is determined under a statutory hybrid benefit formula, the 3-year vesting requirement described in paragraph (c)(1) of this section applies to each participant's entire accrued benefit provided under Plan X.

*Example (2).* The facts are the same as in Example 1, except that the benefit formulas described in Example 1 only apply to participants for service performed in Division A of Employer M and a different benefit formula applies to participants for service performed in Division B of Employer M. Pursuant to the terms of Plan X, the accrued benefit of a participant attributable to service performed in Division B is based on a benefit formula that is not a statutory hybrid benefit formula. Therefore, the 3-year vesting requirement described in paragraph (c)(1) of this section does not apply to a participant with an accrued benefit under Plan X if the participant's benefit is solely attributable to service performed in Division B.

*Example (3).* Employer N sponsors defined benefit Plan Y, an independent plan that provides benefits based solely on a lump sum-based benefit formula, and defined benefit Plan Z, which provides benefits based on a formula which is not a statutory hybrid benefit formula, but which is a floor plan that provides for the benefits payable to a participant under Plan Z to be reduced by the amount of the vested accrued benefit payable under Plan Y. The formula under Plan Y is a statutory hybrid benefit formula. Accordingly, Plan Y is subject to the 3-year vesting requirement described in paragraph (c)(1) of this section. The formula provided under Plan Z, even taking into account the offset for vested accrued benefits under Plan Y, is not a statutory hybrid benefit formula. Therefore, Plan Z is not subject to the 3-year vesting requirement in paragraph (c)(1) of this section.

**(d) Definitions.** *(1) In general.* The definitions in this paragraph (d) apply for purposes of this section.

*(2) Accumulated benefit.* A participant's accumulated benefit at any date means the participant's benefit, as expressed under the terms of the plan, accrued to that date. For this purpose, if a participant's benefit is expressed under the terms of the plan as the current balance of a hypothetical account or the current value of an accumulated percentage of the participant's final average compensation, the participant's accumulated benefit is expressed in that manner regardless of how the plan defines the participant's accrued benefit. Thus, for example, the accumulated benefit of a participant may be expressed under the terms of the plan as either the current balance of a hypothetical account or the current value of an accumulated percentage of the participant's final average compensation, even if the plan defines the participant's accrued benefit as an annuity beginning at normal retirement age that is actuarially equivalent to that balance or value.

*(3) Lump sum-based benefit formula.* (i) In general. A lump sum-based benefit formula means a benefit formula used to determine all or any part of a participant's accumulated benefit under a defined benefit plan under which the accumulated benefit provided under the formula is expressed as the current balance of a hypothetical account maintained for the participant or as the current value of an accumulated percentage of the participant's final average compensation. A benefit formula is expressed as the current balance of a hypothetical account maintained for the participant if it is expressed as a current single-sum dollar amount. Whether a benefit formula is a lump sum-based benefit formula is determined based on how the accumulated benefit of a participant is expressed under the terms of the plan, and does not depend on whether the plan provides an optional form of benefit in the form of a single-sum payment.

(ii) Exception for employee contributions. For purposes of the definition of a lump sum-based benefit formula in paragraph (d)(3)(i) of this section, the benefit properly attributable to after-tax employee contributions, rollover contributions from eligible retirement plans under section 402(c)(8), and other similar employee contributions (such as repayments of distributions pursuant to section 411(a)(7)(C) and employee contributions that are pickup contributions pursuant to section 414(h)(2)) is disregarded. However, a benefit is not properly attributable to contributions described in this paragraph (d)(3)(ii) if the contributions are credited with interest at a rate that exceeds a reasonable rate of interest or if the conversion factors used to calculate such benefit are not actuarially reasonable. See section 411(c) for an example of a calculation of a benefit that is properly attributable to employee contributions.

*(4) Statutory hybrid benefit formula.* (i) In general. A statutory hybrid benefit formula means a benefit formula that is either a lump sum-based benefit formula or a formula that is not a lump sum-based benefit formula but that has an effect similar to a lump sum-based benefit formula.

(ii) Effect similar to a lump sum-based benefit formula. (A) In general. Except as provided in paragraphs (d)(4)(ii)(B) through (D) of this section, a benefit formula under a defined benefit plan that is not a lump sum-based benefit formula has an effect similar to a lump sum-based benefit formula if the formula provides that a participant's accumulated benefit is expressed as a benefit that includes the right to adjustments (including a formula that provides for indexed benefits under § 1.411(b)(5)-1(b)(2)) for a future period and the total dollar amount of those adjustments is reasonably expected to be smaller for the participant than for a similarly situated, younger individual (within the meaning of § 1.411(b)(5)-1(b)(5)) who is or could be a participant in the plan. A benefit formula that does not include adjustments for any future period is treated as a formula with an effect similar to a lump sum-based benefit formula if the formula would be described in the preceding sentence except for the fact that the adjustments are provided pursuant to a pattern of repeated plan amendments. See § 1.411(d)-4, A-1(c)(1).

(B) Exception for post-retirement benefit adjustments. Post-annuity starting date adjustments in the amount payable to a participant (such as cost-of-living increases) are disregarded in determining whether a benefit formula under a defined benefit plan has an effect similar to a lump sum-based benefit formula.

(C) Exception for certain variable annuity benefit formulas. If the assumed interest rate used for purposes of the adjustment of amounts payable to a participant under a variable annuity benefit formula is 5 percent or higher, then the variable annuity benefit formula is not treated as being reasonably expected to provide a smaller total dollar amount of future adjustments for the participant than for a similarly situated, younger individual who is or could be a participant in the plan, and thus such a variable annuity benefit formula does not have an effect similar to a lump sum-based benefit formula.

(D) Exception for employee contributions. Benefits that are disregarded under paragraph (d)(3)(ii) of this section (benefits properly attributable to certain employee contributions) are also disregarded for purposes of determining whether a benefit formula has an effect similar to a lump sum-based benefit formula,

*(5) Statutory hybrid plan.* A statutory hybrid plan means a defined benefit plan that contains a statutory hybrid benefit formula.

*(6) Variable annuity benefit formula.* A variable annuity benefit formula means any benefit formula under a defined benefit plan which provides that the amount payable is periodically adjusted by reference to the difference between the rate of return on plan assets (or specified market indices) and a specified assumed interest rate.

**(e) Effective/applicability date.** *(1) Statutory effective/applicability date.* (i) In general. Except as provided in paragraphs (e)(1)(ii) and (e)(1)(iii) of this section, section 411(a)(13) applies for periods beginning on or after June 29, 2005.

(ii) Calculation of benefits. Section 411(a)(13)(A) applies to distributions made after August 17, 2006.

(iii) Vesting. (A) Plans in existence on June 29, 2005. (1) General rule. In the case of a plan that is in existence on June 29, 2005 (regardless of whether the plan is a statutory hybrid plan on that date), section 411(a)(13)(B) applies to plan years that begin on or after January 1, 2008.

(2) Exception for plan sponsor election. See § 1.411(b)(5)-1(f)(1)(iii)(A)(2) for a special election for early application of section 411(a)(13)(B).

(B) Plans not in existence on June 29, 2005. In the case of a plan not in existence on June 29, 2005, section

411(a)(13)(B) applies to plan years that end on or after June 29, 2005.

(C) Collectively bargained plans. Notwithstanding paragraphs (e)(1)(iii)(A) and (B) of this section, in the case of a collectively bargained plan maintained pursuant to one or more collective bargaining agreements between employee representatives and one or more employers ratified on or before August 17, 2006, the requirements of section 411(a)(13)(B) do not apply to plan years that begin before the earlier of—

(1) The later of—

(i) The date on which the last of those collective bargaining agreements terminates (determined without regard to any extension thereof on or after August 17, 2006); or

(ii) January 1, 2008; or

(2) January 1, 2010.

(D) Treatment of plans with both collectively bargained and non-collectively bargained employees. In the case of a plan with respect to which a collective bargaining agreement applies to some, but not all, of the plan participants, the plan is considered a collectively bargained plan for purposes of paragraph (e)(1)(iii)(C) of this section if it is considered a collectively bargained plan under the rules of § 1.436-1(a)(5)(ii)(B).

(E) Hour of service required. Section 411(a)(13)(B) does not apply to a participant who does not have an hour of service after section 411(a)(13)(B) but would otherwise apply to the participant under the rules of paragraph (e)(1)(iii)(A), (B), or (C) of this section.

*(2) Effective/applicability date of regulations.* (i) In general. Except as provided in paragraph (e)(2)(ii) of this section, this section applies to plan years that begin on or after January 1, 2011. For the periods after the statutory effective date set forth in paragraph (e)(1) of this section and before the regulatory effective date set forth in the preceding sentence, the relief of section 411(a)(13)(A) applies and the 3-year vesting requirement of section 411(a)(13)(B) must be satisfied. During these periods, a plan is permitted to rely on the provisions of this section for purposes of applying the relief of section 411(a)(13)(A) and satisfying the requirements of section 411(a)(13)(B).

(ii) Special effective date. [Reserved].

(iii) Hour of service required. A benefit formula is not treated as having an effect similar to a lump sum-based benefit formula under paragraph (d)(4)(ii) of this section with respect to a participant who does not have an hour of service after the regulatory effective date set forth in paragraph (e)(2)(i) of this section.

---

T.D. 9505, 10/18/2010.

---

PAR. 2. Section 1.411(a)(13)-1 is amended by revising paragraphs (b)(2), (b)(3), (b)(4), and (e)(2)(ii) to read as follows:

**Proposed § 1.411(a)(13)-1 Statutory hybrid plans.** [*For Preamble, see ¶ 153,191*]

* * * * *

**(b)** * * *

*(2) Requirements that lump sum-based benefit formula must satisfy to obtain relief.* (i) In general. The relief of paragraph (b)(1) of this section does not apply with respect to benefits determined under a lump sum-based benefit formula unless the requirements of paragraphs (b)(2)(ii) through (iv) of this section are satisfied.

(ii) Benefit on or before normal retirement age. A plan satisfies this paragraph (b)(2)(ii) only if, at all times on or before normal retirement age, the then-current balance of the hypothetical account or the then-current value of the accumulated percentage of the participant's final average compensation is not less than the present value, determined using reasonable actuarial assumptions, of the portion of the participant's accrued benefit that is determined under the lump sum-based benefit formula. However, a plan is deemed to satisfy the requirement in the preceding sentence for periods before normal retirement age if, upon attainment of normal retirement age, the then-current balance of the hypothetical account or the then-current value of the accumulated percentage of the participant's final average compensation is actuarially equivalent (using reasonable actuarial assumptions) to the portion of the participant's accrued benefit that is determined under the lump sum-based benefit formula.

(iii) Benefit after normal retirement age. A plan satisfies this paragraph (b)(2)(iii) only if, as of each annuity starting date after normal retirement age, the then-current balance of the hypothetical account or the then-current value of the accumulated percentage of the participant's final average compensation—

(A) Satisfies the requirements of section 411(a)(2); or

(B) Would satisfy the requirements of section 411(a)(2) but for the fact that the plan suspends benefits in accordance with section 411(a)(3)(B).

(iv) Reductions limited. A plan satisfies this paragraph (b)(2)(iv) only if the balance of the hypothetical account or accumulated percentage of the participant's final average compensation may not be reduced except as a result of—

(A) Benefit payments under paragraph (b)(3) of this section;

(B) Qualified domestic relations orders under section 414(p);

(C) Forfeitures that are permitted under section 411(a) (such as charges for providing a qualified preretirement survivor annuity);

(D) Amendments that are permitted under section 411(d)(6); or

(E) Adjustments resulting from the application of interest credits (under the rules of § 1.411(b)(5)-1) that are negative for a period, for plans that express the accumulated benefit as the balance of a hypothetical account.

*(3) Alternative forms of distribution under a lump sum-based benefit formula.* (i) Payment of current account balance or current value. The relief of paragraph (b)(1) of this section applies with respect to a single-sum payment equal to the then-current balance of a hypothetical account maintained for the participant or the then-current value of an accumulated percentage of the participant's final average compensation.

(ii) Payment of benefits that are actuarially equivalent to current account balance or current value. With respect to the benefits under a lump sum-based benefit formula, the relief of paragraph (b)(1) of this section applies to an optional form of benefit that is determined as of the annuity starting date as the actuarial equivalent, using reasonable actuarial assumptions, of the then-current balance of a hypothetical account maintained for the participant or the then-current value of an accumulated percentage of the participant's final average compensation.

(iii) Payment of benefits based on immediate annuity. With respect to the benefits under a lump sum-based benefit formula, the relief of paragraph (b)(1) of this section applies to an optional form of benefit that is not subject to the minimum present value requirements of section 417(e) and that is determined under the plan as of the annuity starting date as the actuarial equivalent (using reasonable actuarial assumptions) of the optional form of benefit that—

(A) Commences as of the same annuity starting date;

(B) Is payable in the same generalized optional form (within the meaning of § 1.411(d)-3(g)(8)) as the accrued benefit; and

(C) Is the actuarial equivalent (using reasonable actuarial assumptions) of the then-current balance of a hypothetical account maintained for the participant or the then-current value of an accumulated percentage of the participant's final average compensation.

(iv) Payment of portion of current account balance or current value. The relief of paragraph (b)(1) of this section applies on a proportionate basis to a payment of a portion of the benefit under a lump sum-based benefit formula that is not paid in a form otherwise described in this paragraph (b)(3), such as a payment of a specified dollar amount or percentage of the then-current balance of a hypothetical account maintained for the participant or then-current value of an accumulated percentage of the participant's final average compensation. Thus, for example, if a plan that expresses the participant's entire accumulated benefit as the balance of a hypothetical account distributes 40 percent of the participant's then-current hypothetical account balance in a single payment, the plan is treated as satisfying the requirements of section 411(a) and the minimum present value rules of section 417(e) with respect to 40 percent of the participant's then-current accrued benefit. See paragraph (b)(3)(ii) or (iii) of this section for relief applicable with respect to a distribution with respect to the remainder (60 percent) of the participant's accumulated benefit.

(v) Conditions for applicability. This paragraph (b)(3) applies to a payment of benefits under a lump sum-based benefit formula only if the requirements of paragraph (b)(2) of this section are also satisfied.

*(4) Rules of application.* The relief of paragraph (b)(1) of this section applies only to the portion of the participant's benefit that is determined under a lump sum-based benefit formula and does not apply to any portion of the participant's benefit that is determined under a formula that is not a lump sum-based benefit formula. Thus, the following rules apply:

(iv) Greater-of formulas. Where the participant's accrued benefit equals the greater of the benefit under a lump sum-based benefit formula and the benefit under another formula, a single-sum payment of the participant's entire benefit must equal the greater of the then-current accumulated benefit under the lump sum-based benefit formula and the present value, determined in accordance with section 417(e), of the benefit under the other formula. Applying this rule where the non-lump sum-based benefit formula provides a benefit equal to a pro rata portion of the benefit determined by projecting a future hypothetical account balance (including future principal credits), a single-sum payment of the participant's entire benefit must equal the greater of the then-current balance of the hypothetical account and the present value, determined in accordance with section 417(e), of the pro-rata benefit determined by projecting the future hypothetical account balance.

(ii) "Sum-of" formulas. Where the accrued benefit equals the sum of the benefit under a lump sum-based benefit formula plus the excess of the benefit under another formula over the benefit under the lump sum-based benefit formula, a single-sum payment of the participant's entire benefit must equal the then-current accumulated benefit under the lump sum-based benefit formula plus the excess of the present value, determined in accordance with section 417(e), of the benefit under the other formula over the present value, determined in accordance with section 417(e), of the benefit under the lump sum-based benefit formula.

* * * * *

**(e)** * * *

*(2)* * * *

(ii) Special effective date. Paragraphs (b)(2), (b)(3), and (b)(4) of this section apply to plan years that begin on or after January 1, 2012.

* * * * *

### § 1.411(b)-1 Accrued benefit requirements.

***Caution:*** The Treasury has not yet amended Reg § 1.411(b)-1 to reflect changes made by P.L. 109-432, P.L. 99-509.

**(a) Accrued benefit requirements.** *(1) In general.* Under section 411(b), for plan years beginning after the applicable effective date of section 411, rules are provided for the determination of the accrued benefit to which a participant is entitled under a plan. Under a defined contribution plan, a participant's accrued benefit is the balance to the credit of the participant's account. Under a defined benefit plan, a participant's accrued benefit is his accrued benefit determined under the plan. A defined benefit plan is not a qualified plan unless the method provided by the plan for determining accrued benefits satisfies at least one of the alternative methods (described in paragraph (b) of this section) for determining accrued benefits with respect to all active participants under the plan. A defined benefit plan may provide that accrued benefits for participants are determined under more than one plan formula. In such a case, the accrued benefits under all such formulas must be aggregated in order to determine whether or not the accrued benefits under the plan for participants satisfy one of the alternative methods. A plan may satisfy different methods with respect to different classifications of employees, or separately satisfy one method with respect to the accrued benefits for each such classification, provided that such classifications are not so structured as to evade the accrued benefit requirements of section 411(b) and this section. (For example, if a plan provides that employees who commence participation at or before age 40 accrue benefits in a manner which satisfies the 133⅓ percent method of determining accrued benefits and employees who commence participation after age 40 accrue benefits in a manner which satisfies the 3 percent method of determining accrued benefits, the plan would be so structured as to evade the requirements of section 411(b).) A defined benefit plan does not satisfy the requirements of section 411(b) and this section merely because the accrued benefit is defined as the "reserve under the plan". Special rules are provided for the first two years of service by a participant, certain insured defined benefit plans, and certain reductions in accrued benefits due to increasing age or service. In addition, a special rule is provided with respect to accruals for service before the effective date of section 411.

*(2) Cross references.* (i) 3 percent method. For rules relating to the 3 percent method of determining accrued benefits, see paragraph (b)(1) of this section.

(ii) 133⅓ percent method. For rules relating to the 133⅓ percent method of determining accrued benefits, see paragraph (b)(2) of this section.

(iii) Fractional method. For rules relating to the fractional method of determining accrued benefits, see paragraph (b)(3) of this section.

(iv) Accruals before effective date. For rules relating to accruals for service before the effective date of section 411, see paragraph (c) of this section.

(v) First 2 years of service. For special rules relating to determination of accrued benefit for first 2 continuous years of service, see paragraph (d)(1) of this section.

(vi) Certain insured plans. For special rules relating to determination of accrued benefit under a defined benefit plan funded exclusively by insurance contracts, see paragraph (d)(2) of this section.

(vii) Accruals decreased by increasing age or service. For special rules relating to prohibition of decrease in accrued benefit on account of increasing age or service, see paragraph (d)(3) of this section.

(viii) Separate accounting. For rules relating to requirements for separate accounting, see paragraph (e) of this section.

(ix) Year of participation. For definition of "year of participation", see paragraph (f) of this section.

**(b) Defined benefit plans.** A defined benefit plan satisfies the requirements of section 411(b)(1) and this paragraph for a plan year to which section 411 and this section apply if it satisfies the requirements of subparagraph (1), (2), or (3) of this paragraph for such year.

*(1) 3 percent method.* (i) General rule. A defined benefit plan satisfies the requirements of this paragraph for a plan year if, as of the close of the plan year, the accrued benefit to which each participant is entitled, computed as if the participant separated from the service as of the close of such plan year, is not less than 3 percent of the 3 percent method benefit, multiplied by the number of years (not in excess of 33⅓) of his participation in the plan including years after his normal retirement age. For purposes of this subparagraph, the "3 percent method benefit" is the normal retirement benefit to which the participant would be entitled if he commenced participation at the earliest possible entry age for any individual who is or could be a participant under the plan and if he served continuously until the earlier of age 65 or the normal retirement age under the plan.

(ii) Special rules. (A) Compensation. In the case of a plan providing a retirement benefit based upon compensation during any period, the normal retirement benefit to which a participant would be entitled is determined as if he continued to earn annually the average rate of compensation which he earned during consecutive years of service, not in excess of 10, for which his compensation was the highest. For purposes of this subdivision (A), the number of consecutive years of service used in computing average compensation shall be the number of years of service specified under the plan (not in excess of 10) for computing normal retirement benefits.

(B) Social security, etc. For purposes of this subparagraph, for any plan year, social security benefits and all relevant factors used to compute benefits, e.g., consumer price index, are treated as remaining constant as of the beginning of the current plan year for all subsequent plan years.

(C) Computation in certain cases. In the case of any plan to which the provisions of section 411(b)(1)(D) and paragraph (c) of this section are applicable, for any plan year the accrued benefit of any participant shall not be less than the accrued benefit otherwise determined under this subparagraph, reduced by the excess of the accrued benefit determined under this subparagraph as of the first day of the first plan year to which section 411 applies over the accrued benefit determined under section 411(b)(1)(D) and paragraph (c) of this section and increased by the amount determined under paragraph (c)(2)(v) of this section.

(iii) Examples. The application of this subparagraph is illustrated by the following examples.

*Example (1).* The M Corporation's defined benefit plan provides an annual retirement benefit commencing at age 65 of $4 per month for each year of participation. As a condition of participation, the plan requires that an employee have attained age 25. The normal retirement age specified under the plan is age 65. The plan provides for no limit on the number of years of credited service. A, age 40, is a participant in the M Corporation's plan.

A has completed 12 years of participation in the plan of the M Corporation as of the close of the plan year. Under subdivision (i) of this subparagraph, the normal retirement benefit commencing at age 65 to which a participant would be entitled if he commenced participation at the earliest possible entry age (25) under the plan and served continuously until normal retirement age (65) is an annual benefit of $1,920 [40 × (12 × $4)]. Under paragraph (b)(1)(i) of this section, the plan does not satisfy the requirements of this subparagraph unless A has accrued an annual benefit of at least $691 [0.03 × ($1,920 × 12)] as of the close of the plan year. Under the M Corporation plan, A is entitled to an accrued benefit of $576 [(12 × 12) × $4] as of the close of the plan year. Thus, with respect to A, the accrued benefit provided under the M Corporation plan does not satisfy the requirements of this subparagraph.

*Example (2).* Assume the same facts as in example (1) except that the M Corporation's plan provides that only the first 30 years of participation are taken into account. Under subdivision (i) of this subparagraph, the normal retirement benefit commencing at age 65 to which a participant would be entitled if he commenced participation at the earliest possible entry age under the plan (25) and served continuously until normal retirement age (65) is an annual benefit of $1,440 [30 × $48]. Under paragraph (b)(1)(i) of this section, the plan does not satisfy the requirements of this subparagraph unless A has accrued an annual benefit of at least $518 [0.03 × ($1,440 × 12)] as of the close of the plan year. Under the M Corporation plan, A is entitled to an accrued benefit of $576 [12 × $48]. Thus, with respect to A, the accrued benefit provided under the M Corporation plan satisfies the requirements of this subparagraph.

*Example (3).* The N Corporation's defined benefit plan provides an annual retirement benefit commencing at age 65 of 50 percent of average compensation for the highest 3 consecutive years of compensation for an employee with 25 years of participation. A participant who separates from service before age 65 is entitled to 2 percent of average compensation for the highest 3 consecutive years of compensation for each year of participation not in excess of 25. The plan has no minimum age or service requirement for participation. The normal retirement age specified under the plan is age 65. On December 31, 1990, B, age 40, is a participant in the N Corporation's plan. B began employment with the N Corporation and became a participant in the N Corporation's plan on January 1, 1980. Under this subparagraph, the normal retirement benefit to which a participant would be entitled if he commenced participation at the earliest possible entry age (0) under the plan and served continuously until normal retirement age (65) is 50 percent of average compensation for the highest 3 consecutive years of compensation per year commencing at age 65. Under this subparagraph, B must have accrued an annual benefit of at least 16.5 percent of his highest 3 consecutive years of compensation per year commencing at age 65 [0.03 × 50 percent of average compensation for the highest 3 consecutive years of compensation × 11] as of the close of the plan year. Under the N Corporation plan, B has accrued an annual benefit of 22 percent of average compensation for his highest 3 consecutive years of compensation per year commencing at age 65. Thus, with respect to B, the accrued benefit under the N Corporation plan satisfies the requirements of this subparagraph.

*Example (4).* The P Corporation's defined benefit plan provides an annual retirement benefit commencing at age 65 of 50 percent of average compensation for the 3 consecutive years of compensation from the P Corporation next preceding normal retirement age. The plan has no minimum age or service requirement for participation. The normal retirement age under the plan is age 65. On December 31, 1990, C, age 55, separates from service with the P Corporation. C began employment with the P Corporation and became a participant in the P Corporation's plan on January 1, 1980. As of December 31, 1990, C's average compensation for the 3 consecutive years preceding his separation from service is $15,000. Under this subparagraph, the normal retirement benefit to which a participant would be entitled if he commenced participation at the earliest possible entry age (0) under the plan and served continuously until normal retirement age (65) is an annual benefit of 50 percent of average compensation for the 3 consecutive years of compensation from the P Corporation next preceding normal retirement age commencing at age 65. C must have accrued an annual benefit of at least $2,475 commencing at age 65 [0.03 × (0.50 × $15,000) × 11] as of his separation from the service with the P Corporation in order for the P Corporation's plan to satisfy the requirements of this subparagraph with respect to C.

*Example (5).* On December 31, 1985, the R Corporation's defined benefit plan provided an annual retirement benefit commencing at age 65 of $100 for each year of participation, not to exceed 30. As a condition of participation, the plan requires that an employee have attained age 25. The normal retirement age specified under the plan is age 65. The appropriate computation period is the calendar year. On January 1, 1986, the plan is amended to provide an annual retirement benefit commencing at age 65 of $200 for each year of participation (before and after the amendment), not to exceed 30. B, age 40, is a participant in the R Corporation's plan. B has completed 15 years of participation in the plan of the R Corporation as of December 31, 1990. Under paragraph (b)(1)(i) of this section, the normal retirement benefit commencing at age 65 to which a participant would be entitled if he commenced participation at the earliest possible entry age (25) under the plan and served continuously until normal retirement age (65) is an annual benefit of $6,000 [30 × 200]. Under subdivision (i) of this subparagraph, the plan does not satisfy the requirements of this subparagraph unless B has accrued an annual benefit of at least $2,700 [0.03 × $6,000 × 15] as of December 31, 1990. Under the R Corporation plan, B is entitled to an accrued benefit of $3,000 [$200 × 15] as of December 31, 1990. Thus, with respect to B, the accrued benefit provided under the R Corporation plan satisfies the requirements of this subparagraph.

*Example (6).* On December 31, 1995, the J Corporation's defined benefit plan provided an annual retirement benefit commencing at age 65 of $4,800 after 30 years of participation. The normal retirement age specified under the plan is age 65. The appropriate computation period is the calendar year. On January 1, 1996, the plan is amended to provide an annual retirement benefit commencing at age 65 of $6,000. A, age 40, is a participant in the J Corporation's plan since its adoption on January 1, 1986. Under paragraph (b)(1)(i) of this section, on December 31, 1995, the normal retirement benefit commencing at age 65 to which a participant would be entitled if he commenced participation at the earliest possible entry age (0) under the plan and served continuously until normal retirement age (65) is an annual benefit of $4,800. Under paragraph (b)(1)(i) of this section, on January 1, 1996, the normal retirement benefit commencing at age 65 to which a participant would be entitled if he commenced participation at the earliest possible entry age (0) under the plan and served continuously until normal retirement age (65) is an annual benefit of $6,000. Under subdivision (i) of this subparagraph, the plan does not satisfy the requirements of this subparagraph unless A has an accrued benefit on December 31, 1995 of at least $1,440 [$4,800 × 0.03 × 10] and an accrued benefit on January 1, 1996 of at least $2,000 [$6,000 × 0.03 × 10].

*Example (7).* The X Company's defined benefit plan provides an annual retirement benefit commencing at age 65 of $4 per month for each year of participation (not to exceed 30). As a condition of participation, the plan requires that an employee have attained age 25. The normal retirement age specified under the plan is age 65. D, age 68, is a participant in the X Company's plan. D has completed 20 years of participation in the X Company plan as of the close of the plan year. Under paragraph (b)(1)(i) of this section, the normal retirement benefit commencing at age 65 to which a participant would be entitled if he commenced participation at the earliest possible entry age (25) under the plan and served continuously until normal retirement age (65) is an annual benefit, commencing at age 65, of $1,440 [30 × $48]. Under paragraph (b)(1)(i) of this section, the plan does not satisfy the requirements of this subparagraph unless D has accrued an annual benefit, commencing at age 65, of $864 [0.03 × $1,440 × 20] as of the close of the plan year. Under the X Company plan, D has accrued an annual benefit, commencing at age 65, of $960 [20 × $48]. Thus, with respect to D the accrued benefit provided under the X Company plan satisfies the requirements of this subparagraph.

*Example (8).* Assume the same facts as in example (7) except that for purposes of determining accrued benefits under the plan the X Company's plan disregards all years of participation after normal retirement age. Under paragraph (b)(1)(i) of this section, the normal retirement benefit commencing at age 65 to which a participant would be entitled if he commenced participation at the earliest possible entry age (25) under the plan and served continuously until normal retirement age (65) is an annual benefit of $1,440 [30 × $48]. Under paragraph (b)(1)(i) of this section the plan does not satisfy the requirements of this subparagraph unless D has accrued an annual benefit, commencing at age 65, of $864 [0.03 × $1,440 × 20] as of the close of the plan year. Under the X Company's plan, D has accrued an annual benefit commencing at age 65, of $816 [17 × $48]. Thus, with respect to D, the accrued benefit provided under the X Company plan does not satisfy the requirements of this subparagraph.

*(2) 133⅓ percent rule.* (i) General rule. A defined benefit plan satisfies the requirements of this subparagraph for a particular plan year if—

(A) Under the plan the accrued benefit payable at the normal retirement age (determined under the plan) is equal to the normal retirement benefit (determined under the plan), and

(B) The annual rate at which any individual who is or could be a participant can accrue the retirement benefits payable at normal retirement age under the plan for any later plan year cannot be more than 133⅓ percent of the annual rate at which he can accrue benefits for any plan year beginning on or after such particular plan year and before such later plan year.

(ii) Special rules. For purposes of this subparagraph—

(A) Plan amendments. Any amendment to the plan which is in effect for the current plan year shall be treated as if it were in effect for all other plan years.

(B) Change in accrual rate. Any change in an accrual rate which change does not apply to any individual who is or could be a participant in the plan year is disregarded. Thus, for example, if for its plan year beginning January 1, 1980, a defined benefit plan provides an accrued benefit in plan year 1980 of 2 percent of a participant's average compensation for his highest 3 years of compensation for each year of service and provides that in plan year 1981 the accrued benefit will be 3 percent of such average compensation, the plan will be not be treated as failing to satisfy the requirements of this subparagraph for plan year 1980 because in plan year 1980 the change in the accrual rate does not apply to any individual who is or could be a participant in plan year 1980. However, if, for example, a defined benefit provided for an accrued benefit of 1 percent of a participant's average compensation for his highest 3 years of compensation for each of the first 10 years of service and 1.5 percent of such average compensation for each year of service thereafter, the plan will be treated as failing to satisfy the requirements of this subparagraph for the plan year even though no participant is actually accruing at the 1.5 percent rate because an individual who could be a participant and who had over 10 years of service would accrue at the 1.5 percent rate, which rate exceeds 133⅓ percent of the 1 percent rate.

(C) Early retirement benefits. The fact that certain benefits under the plan may be payable to certain participants before normal retirement age is disregarded. Thus, the requirements of subdivision (i) of this subparagraph must be satisfied without regard to any benefit payable prior to the normal retirement benefit (such as an early retirement benefit which is not the normal retirement benefit (see § 1.411(a)-7(c)).

(D) Social security, etc. For purposes of this paragraph, for any plan year, social security benefit and all relevant factors used to compute benefits, e.g., consumer price index, are treated as remaining constant as of the beginning of the current plan year for all subsequent plan years.

(E) Postponed retirement. A plan shall not be treated as failing to satisfy the requirements of this subparagraph for a plan year merely because no benefits under the plan accrue to a participant who continues service with the employer after such participant has attained normal retirement age.

(F) Computation of benefit. A plan shall not satisfy the requirements of this subparagraph if the base for the computation of retirement benefits changes solely by reason of an increase in the number of years of participation. Thus, for example, a plan will not satisfy the requirements of this subparagraph if it provides a benefit, commencing at normal retirement age, of the sum of (1) 1 percent of average compensation for a participant's first 3 years of participation multiplied by his first 10 years of participation (or, if less than 10 his total years of participation) and (2) 1 percent of average compensation for a participant's 3 highest years of participation multiplied by each year of participation subsequent to the 10th year.

(iii) Examples. The application of this subparagraph is illustrated by the following examples:

*Example (1).* On January 1, 1980, the R Corporation's defined benefit plan provides for an annual benefit (commencing at age 65) of a percentage of a participant's average compensation for the period of 5 consecutive years of participation for which his compensation is the highest. The percentage is 2 percent for each of the first 20 years of participation and 1 percent per year thereafter. The appropriate computation period is the calendar year. The R Corporation's plan satisfies the requirements of this subparagraph because the 133⅓ percent rule does not restrict subsequent accrual rate decreases.

*Example (2).* On January 1, 1980, the J Corporation's defined benefit plan provides for an annual benefit (commencing at age 65) of a percentage of a participant's average compensation for the period of his final 5 consecutive years of participation. The percentage is 1 percent for each of the first 5 years of participation; 1⅓ percent for each of the next 5 years of participation; and 1⁷⁄₉ percent for each year thereafter. The appropriate computation period is the calendar year. Even though no single accrual rate under the J Corporation's plan exceeds 133⅓ percent of the immediately preceding accrual rate, the J Corporation's plan does not satisfy the requirements of this subparagraph because the rate of accrual for all years of participation in excess of 10 (1⁷⁄₉ percent) exceeds 133⅓ percent of the rate of accrual for any of the first 5 years of participation (1 percent).

*Example (3).* On January 1, 1980, the C Corporation's defined benefit plan provides for an annual benefit (commencing at age 65) of a percentage of a participant's average compensation for the period of 3 consecutive years of participation for which his compensation is the highest. The percentage is 2 percent for each of the first 5 years of participation; 1 percent for each of the next 5 years of participation; and 1½ percent for each year thereafter. The appropriate computation period is the calendar year. Even though the average rate of accrual under the C Corporation's plan is not less rapidly than ratably, the C Corporation's plan does not satisfy the requirements of this subparagraph because the rate of accrual for all years of participation in excess of 10 (1½ percent) for any employee who is actually accruing benefits or who could accrue benefits exceeds 133⅓ percent of the rate of accrual for the sixth through tenth years of participation, respectively (1 percent).

*(3) Fractional rule.* (i) In general. A defined benefit plan satisfies the requirements of this paragraph if the accrued benefit to which any participant is entitled is not less than the fractional rule benefit multiplied by a fraction (not exceeding 1)—

(A) The numerator of which is his total number of years of participation in the plan, and

(B) The denominator of which is the total number of years he would have participated in the plan if he separated from the service at the normal retirement age under the plan.

(ii) Special rules. For purposes of this subparagraph—

(A) Fractional rule benefit. The "fractional rule benefit" is the annual benefit commencing at the normal retirement age under the plan to which a participant would be entitled if he continued to earn annually until such normal retirement age the same rate of compensation upon which his normal retirement benefit would be computed. Such rate of compensation shall be computed on the basis of compensation taken into account under the plan (but taking into account average compensation for no more than the 10 years of service immediately preceding the determination). For purposes of this subdivision (A), the normal retirement benefit shall be determined as if the participant had attained normal retirement age on the date any such determination is made.

(B) Social security, etc. For purposes of this subparagraph, for any plan year, social security benefits and all relevant factors used to compute benefits, e.g., consumer price index, are treated as remaining constant as of the beginning of the current plan year for all subsequent plan years.

(C) Postponed retirement. A plan shall not be treated as failing to satisfy the requirements of this subparagraph merely because no benefits under the plan accrue to a participant who continues service with the employer after such participant has attained normal retirement age under the plan.

(D) Computation in certain cases. In the case of any plan to which the provisions of section 411(b)(1)(D) and paragraph (c) of this section are applicable, for any plan year the accrued benefit of any participant shall not be less than the accrued benefit otherwise determined under this subparagraph, reduced by the excess of the accrued benefit determined under this subparagraph as of the first day of the first plan year to which section 411 applies over the accrued benefit determined under section 411(b)(1)(D) and paragraph (c) of this section and increased by the amount determined under paragraph (c)(2)(v) of this section.

(iii) Examples. The application of this subparagraph is illustrated by the following examples:

*Example (1).* The R Corporation's defined benefit plan provides an annual retirement benefit commencing at age 65 of 30 percent of a participant's average compensation for his highest 3 consecutive years of participation. If a participant separates from service prior to normal retirement age, the R Corporation's plan provides a benefit equal to an amount which bears the same ratio to 30 percent of such average compensation as the participant's actual number of years of participation in the plan bears to the number of years the participant would have participated in the plan had he separated from service at age 65. The plan further provides that normal retirement age is age 65. A, age 55, is a participant in the R Corporation's plan for the current year, and A has 15 years of participation in the R Corporation's plan. As of the current year, A's average compensation for his highest 3 years of compensation is $20,000. The R Corporation's plan satisfies the requirement of this subparagraph because if A separates from the service in the current year he will be entitled to an annual benefit of $3,600 commencing at age 65 [(0.3 × $20,000) × 15/25].

*Example (2).* The J Corporation's defined benefit plan provides a normal retirement benefit of 1 percent per year of a participant's average compensation from the employer. In the case of a participant who separates from service prior to normal retirement age (65), the plan provides that the annual benefit is an amount which is equal to 1 percent of such compensation multiplied by the number of years of plan participation actually completed by the participant. The plan year of the J Corporation's plan is the calendar year. B, age 55, is a participant in the J Corporation's plan for the current year. B became a participant in the J Corporation's plan on January 1, 1980. As of December 31, 1990, B's compensation history is as follows:

| Year | Compensation |
|---|---|
| 1980 | $17,000 |
| 1981 | 18,000 |
| 1982 | 20,000 |
| 1983 | 20,000 |
| 1984 | 21,000 |
| 1985 | 22,000 |
| 1986 | 23,000 |
| 1987 | 25,000 |
| 1988 | 26,000 |
| 1989 | 29,000 |
| 1990 | 32,000 |

If B separates from service on December 31, 1990, he would be entitled to an annual benefit of $2,530 commencing at age 65. Because the J Corporation's plan does not limit the number of years of compensation to be taken into account in determining the normal retirement benefit, B's rate of compensation or purposes of determining his normal retirement benefit is $23,600

$$\frac{[\$18{,}000 + \$20{,}000 + \$20{,}000 + \$21{,}000 + \$22{,}000 + \$23{,}000 + \$25{,}000 + \$26{,}000 + \$29{,}000 + \$32{,}000]}{10}$$

Under this subparagraph, B's accrued benefit under the J Corporation's plan as of December 31, 1990 must be not less than $2,561 per year commencing at age 65 [0.01 × ($17,000 + $18,000 + $20,000 + $20,000 + $21,000 + $22,000 + $23,000 + $25,000 + $26,000 + $29,000 + $32,000 + ($23,600 × 10)) × 11/21]. Thus, the J Corporation's plan would not satisfy the requirements of this subparagraph.

**(c) Accruals for service before effective date.** *(1) General rule.* For a plan year to which section 411 applies, a defined benefit plan does not satisfy the requirements of section 411(b)(1) and this section unless, under the plan, the accrued benefit of each participant for plan years beginning before section 411 applies is not less than the greater of—

(i) Such participant's accrued benefit (as of the day before section 411 applies) determined under the plan as in effect from time to time prior to September 2, 1974 (without regard to any amendment adopted after such date), or

(ii) One-half of the accrued benefit that would be determined with respect to the participant as of the day before section 411 applies if the participant's accrued benefit were computed for such prior plan years under a method which satisfies the requirements of section 411(b)(1)(A), (B), or (C) and paragraph (b)(1), (2), or (3) of this section. See 29 CFR Part 2530, Department of Labor regulations relating to minimum standards for employee pension benefit plans, for time participation deemed to begin.

*(2) Special rules.* (i) A plan shall not be deemed to fail to satisfy the requirements of section 411(b) and this section merely because the method for computing the accrued benefit of a participant for years of participation prior to the first plan year for which section 411 is effective with respect to

the plan is not the same method for computing the accrued benefit of a participant for years of participation subsequent to such plan year.

(ii) For purposes of paragraph (c)(1)(ii) of this section, section 411(b)(1)(A) and paragraph (b)(1) of this section shall be applied as if the participant separated from service with the employer on the day before the first day of the first plan year to which section 411 applies.

(iii) For purposes of paragraph (c)(1)(ii) of this section, section 411(b)(1)(B) and paragraph (b)(2) of this section shall be applied in the following manner:

(A) Except as provided in (c)(2)(iii)(B) of this section, section 411(b)(1)(B) and paragraph (b)(2) of this section shall be applied as if the participant separated from service with the employer on the day before the first day of the first plan year to which section 411 applies.

(B) In the case that the plan does not satisfy the requirements of section 411(b)(1)(B) and paragraph (b)(2) of this section at anytime prior to the day specified in (c)(2)(iii)(A) of this section, the plan shall be deemed revised to the extent necessary to satisfy the requirements of section 411(b)(1)(B) and paragraph (b)(2) of this section for all plan years beginning before the applicable effective date of section 411 and this section. For purposes of the preceding sentence, a plan shall not be deemed revised to the extent necessary to satisfy the requirements of section 411(b)(1)(B) and paragraph (b)(2) of this section for a plan year if the benefit a participant would receive if he were employed until normal retirement age is reduced by such revision or if the revised rate of accrual with respect to such accrued benefit does not otherwise satisfy the requirements of section 411(b)(1)(B) and paragraph (b)(2) of this section.

(iv) For purposes of paragraph (c)(1)(ii) of this section, section 411(b)(1)(C) and paragraph (b)(3) of this section shall be applied as if the participant separated from service on the day before the first day of the first plan year to which section 411 applies.

(v) The excess of the accrued benefit payable at normal retirement age of any participant determined under section 411(b)(1)(A), (B), or (C) (without regard to section 411(b)(1)(D)), and paragraph (b)(1), (2), or (3) of this section (without regard to this paragraph) as of the day before the first day of the first plan year to which section 411 and this section applies over the accrued benefit determined under paragraph (c)(1) of this section shall be accrued in accordance with the provisions of the plan as in effect after the applicable effective date of section 411, as if the plan had been initially adopted on such effective date.

**(d) Special rules.** *(1) First 2 years of service.* Notwithstanding paragraphs (1), (2), and (3) of paragraph (b) of this section, under section 411(b)(1)(E) and this subparagraph, a plan shall not be treated as failing to satisfy the requirements of paragraph (b) of this section solely because the accrual of benefits under the plan does not become effective until the employee has completed 2 continuous years of service. For purposes of this subparagraph, continuous years of service are years of service (within the meaning of section 410(a)(3)(A)) which are not separated by a break in service (within the meaning of section 410(a)(5)). For years of service beginning after such 2 years of service, the accrued benefit of an employee shall not be less than that to which the employee would be entitled if section 411(b)(1)(E) and this subparagraph did not apply. Thus, for example, a plan which otherwise satisfies the requirements of paragraph (b)(2) of this section provides for a rate of accrual of 1 percent of average compensation for the highest 3 years of compensation beginning with the third year of service of a participant shall not be treated as satisfying paragraph (b)(2) of this section because as of the time the employee completes 3 continuous years of service there is no accrual during the first 2 years of service. In addition, a plan which otherwise satisfies the requirements of paragraph (b)(1) of this section and which requires that an employee must attain age 25 and complete 1 year of service prior to becoming a participant will not satisfy the requirements of paragraph (b)(1) of this section if an employee who completes 2 years of service prior to attaining age 25 does not begin accruals immediately upon commencement of participation in the plan. For rules relating to years of service, see 29 CFR Part 2530, Department of Labor regulations relating to minimum standards for employee pension benefit plans.

*(2) Certain insured defined benefit plans.* Notwithstanding paragraphs (b)(1), (2), and (3) of this section, a defined benefit plan satisfies the requirements of paragraph (b) of this section if such plan is funded exclusively by the purchase of contracts from a life insurance company and such contracts satisfy the requirements of section 412(i)(2) and (3) and the regulations thereunder. The preceding sentence is applicable only if an employee's accrued benefit as of any applicable date is not less than the cash surrender value such employee's insurance contracts would have on such applicable date if the requirements of section 412(i)(4), (5), and (6) and the regulations thereunder were satisfied.

*(3) Accrued benefit may not decrease on account of increasing age or service.* Notwithstanding paragraphs (b)(1), (2), and (3) of this section and paragraphs (d)(1) and (2) of this section, a defined benefit plan shall be treated as not satisfying the requirements of paragraph (b) and (d) of this section if the participant's accrued benefit is reduced on account of any increase in his age or years of service. The preceding sentence shall not apply to social security supplements described in § 1.411(a)-7(c)(4).

**(e) Separate accounting.** A plan satisfies the requirements of this paragraph if the requirements of paragraph (e)(1) or (2) of this paragraph are met.

*(1) Defined benefit plan.* In the case of a defined benefit plan, the requirements of this paragraph are satisfied if the plan requires separate accounting for the portion of each employee's accrued benefit derived from any voluntary employee contributions permitted under the plan. For purposes of this subparagraph the term "voluntary employee contributions" means all employee contributions which are not mandatory contributions within the meaning of section 411(c)(2)(C) and the regulations thereunder. See § 1.411(c)-1(b)(1) for rules requiring the determination of such an accrued benefit by the use of a separate account.

*(2) Defined contribution plan.* In the case of a defined contribution plan, the requirements of this paragraph are not satisfied unless the plan requires separate accounting for each employee's accrued benefit. If a plan utilizes the break in service rule of section 411(a)(6)(C), an employee could have different percentages of vesting between pre-break and post-break accrued benefits. In such a case, the requirements of this paragraph are not satisfied unless the plan computes accrued benefits in a manner which takes into account different percentages. A plan which provides separate accounts for pre-break and post-break accrued benefits will be deemed to compute benefits in a reasonable manner.

**(f) Year of participation.** *(1) In general.* This paragraph is inapplicable to a defined contribution plan. For purposes of determining an employee's accrued benefit, a "year of participation" is a period of service determined under regulations prescribed by the Secretary of Labor in 29 CFR Part 2530, relating to minimum standards for employee pension benefit plans.

*(2) Additional rule relating to year of participation.* A trust shall not constitute a qualified trust if the plan of which such trust is a part provides for the crediting of a year of participation, or part thereof, and such credit results in the discrimination prohibited by section 401(a)(4).

**(g) Additional illustrations.** The application of this section may be illustrated by the following example:

*Example.* (i) The S Corporation established a defined benefit plan on January 1, 1980. The plan provides a minimum age for participation of age 25. The normal retirement age under the plan is age 65. The appropriate computation periods are the calendar year. The plan provides an annual benefit, commencing at age 65, equal to $96 per year of service for the first 25 years of service, and $48 per year of service for each additional year of service.

(ii) The plan of S Corporation does not satisfy the requirements of section 411(b)(1)(A) and paragraph (b)(1) of this section because the accrued benefit under the plan at some point will be less than the accrued benefit required under section 411(b)(1)(A) and paragraph (b)(1) of this section (i.e., 3 percent × normal retirement benefit × years of participation).

(iii) The plan of the S Corporation does satisfy the requirements of section 411(b)(1)(B) and paragraph (b)(2) of this section because the rate of benefit accrual is equal in each of the first 25 years of service and the rate decreases thereafter.

(iv) The plan of the S Corporation does satisfy the requirements of section 411(b)(1)(C) and paragraph (b)(3) of this section because the accrued benefit under the plan will equal or exceed the normal retirement benefit multiplied by the fraction described in paragraph (b)(3)(i) of this section.

---

T.D. 7501, 8/22/77.

---

PAR. 3. Section 1.411(b)-1 is amended by adding paragraph (b)(2)(ii)(G) and (b)(2)(ii)(H) to read as follows:

**Proposed § 1.411(b)-1 Accrued benefit requirements.** [*For Preamble, see ¶ 153,191*]

* * * * *

**(b)** * * *

*(2)* * * *

(ii) * * *

(G) Special rule for multiple formulas. [Reserved]

(H) Variable interest crediting rate under a statutory hybrid benefit formula. For plan years that begin on or after January 1, 2012, a plan that determines any portion of the participant's accrued benefit pursuant to a statutory hybrid benefit formula (as defined in § 1.411(a)(13)-1(d)(4)) that utilizes an interest crediting rate described in § 1.411(b)(5)-1(d) that is a variable rate that was less than zero for the prior plan year is not treated as failing to satisfy the requirements of paragraph (b)(2) of this section for the current plan year merely because the plan assumes for purposes of paragraph (b)(2) of this section that the variable rate is zero for the current plan year and all future plan years.

* * * * *

PAR. 2. Section 1.411(b)-1 is amended by adding new paragraph (b)(2)(ii)(G) to read as follows:

**Proposed § 1.411(b)-1 Accrued benefit requirements.** [*For Preamble, see ¶ 153,009*]

* * * * *

**(b)** * * *

*(2)* * * *

(ii) * * *

(G) Special rule for multiple formulas. (1) In general. Notwithstanding paragraph (a)(1) of this section, a plan that determines a participant's accrued benefit as the greatest of the benefits determined under two or more separate formulas is permitted, to the extent provided under this paragraph (b)(2)(ii)(G), to demonstrate satisfaction of section 411(b)(1)(B) and this paragraph (b) by demonstrating that each separate formula satisfies the requirements of section 411(b)(1)(B) and this paragraph (b).

(2) Separate bases requirement. A plan is eligible for separate testing under this paragraph (b)(2)(ii)(G) if each of the separate formulas uses a different basis for determining benefits. For example, a plan is eligible for this special rule if it provides an accrued benefit equal to the greater of the benefits under two formulas, one of which determines accrued benefits on the basis of highest average compensation and the other of which determines accrued benefits on the basis of career average compensation. As another example, a defined benefit plan that bases benefits on highest average compensation and that is amended to add a statutory hybrid benefit formula (as defined in § 1.411(a)(13)-1(d)(3)) that provides for pay credits to be made based on each year's compensation is eligible for this separate testing exception if the plan provides that one or more participants are entitled to the greater of the benefit determined under the statutory hybrid benefit formula and the benefit determined under the original formula.

(3) Plans with three or more formulas. If a plan determines a participant's benefits as the greatest of the benefits determined under three or more separate formulas, but two or more of the formulas use the same basis for determining benefits, then the plan may nonetheless apply paragraphs (b)(2)(ii)(G)(1) and (2) of this section by aggregating all benefit formulas that have the same basis and treating those aggregated formulas as a single formula for purposes of paragraphs (b)(2)(ii)(G)(1) and (2) of this section.

(4) Anti-abuse rule. A plan is not eligible for separate testing under this paragraph (b)(2)(ii)(G) if the Commissioner determines that the plan's use of separate formulas with different bases is structured to evade the requirement to aggregate formulas under paragraph (a)(1) of this section (for example, if the differences between the bases of the separate formulas are minor).

(5) Effective/applicability date. This paragraph (b)(2)(ii)(G) is applicable for plan years beginning on or after January 1, 2009.

**Proposed § 1.411(b)-2 Accruals and allocations after a specified age.** [*For Preamble, see ¶ 151,113*]

***Caution:*** The Treasury has not yet amended Reg § 1.411(b)-2 to reflect changes made by P.L. 109-432, P.L. 104-188.

**(a) In general.** Section 411(b)(1)(H) provides that a defined benefit plan does not satisfy the minimum vesting standards of section 411(a) if, under the plan, benefit accruals on behalf of a participant are discontinued or the rate of benefit accrual on behalf of a participant is reduced because of the participant's attainment of any age. Section 411(b)(2) provides that a defined contribution plan does not satisfy the minimum vesting standards of section 411(a) if, under the plan, allocations to a participant's account are reduced or discontinued or the rate of allocations to a participant's account is reduced because of the participant's attainment of any age. A defined benefit plan is not considered to discontinue benefit accruals or reduce the rate of benefit accrual on behalf of a participant because of the attainment of any age in violation of section 411(b)(1)(H) and a defined contribution plan is not considered to reduce or discontinue allocations to a participant's account or reduce the rate of allocations to a participant's account because of the attainment of any age in violation of section 411(b)(2) solely because of a positive correlation between increased age and a reduction or discontinuance in benefit accruals or account allocations under a plan. Thus, for example, if a defined benefit plan or a defined contribution plan provides for reduced or discontinued benefit accruals or account allocations on behalf of participants who have completed a specified number of years of credited service, the plan will not thereby fail to satisfy section 411(b)(1)(H) or (b)(2) solely because of a positive correlation between increased age and completion of the specified number of years of credited service. See paragraph (b)(2) of this section for rules relating to benefit and service limitations under defined benefit plans and paragraph (c)(2) of this section for rules relating to limitations on allocations under defined contribution plans. Also, if benefit accruals or the rate of benefit accrual on behalf of a participant in a defined benefit plan or allocations or the rate of allocations to the account of a participant in a defined contribution plan are reduced or discontinued under the plan and the reason for the reduction or discontinuance is neither directly nor indirectly related to the participant's attainment of a specified age, the plan does not thereby fail to satisfy the requirements of section 411(b)(1)(H) or (b)(2). Thus, for example, if a defined benefit plan is amended to cease or reduce the rate of benefit accrual for all plan participants, such cessation or reduction does not fail to satisfy the requirements of section 411(b)(1)(H).

**(b) Defined benefit plans.** *(1) In general.* (i) A defined benefit plan does not satisfy the minimum vesting standards of section 411(a) if, either directly or indirectly, because of the attainment of any age—

(A) A participant's accrual of benefits is discontinued or the rate of a participant's accrual of benefits is decreased, or

(B) A participant's compensation after the attainment of such age is not taken into account in determining the participant's accrual of benefits.

(ii) In determining whether a defined benefit plan satisfies paragraph (b)(1)(i) of this section, the subsidized portion of an early retirement benefit (whether provided on a temporary or permanent basis), a social security supplement (as defined in § 1.411(a)-7(c)(4)(ii)) and a qualified disability benefit (as defined in § 1.411(a)-7(c)(3)) are disregarded in determining the rate of a participant's accrual of benefits under the plan.

(iii) The provisions of paragraph (b)(1)(i) of this section may be illustrated by the following example. In the example, assume that the participant completes the hours of service in a plan year required under the plan to accrue a full benefit for the plan year.

*Example.* Employer X maintains a defined benefit plan that provides a normal retirement benefit of 1% of a participant's average annual compensation, multiplied by the participant's years of credited service under the plan. Normal retirement age under the plan is age 65. The plan contains no limitations (other than the limitations imposed by section 415) on the maximum amount of benefits the plan will pay to any participant or on the maximum number of years of credited service taken into account under the plan for purposes of determining the amount of any participant's normal retirement benefit. Participant A became a participant in the plan at age 25 and worked continuously for X until A retires at age 70. The plan will satisfy the requirements of section 411(b)(1)(H) and paragraph (b)(2) of this section if, under the plan's benefit formula, upon A's retirement, A has an accrued normal retirement benefit of at least 45% of A's average annual compensation (1% per year × 45 years).

*(2) Benefit and service limitations.* (i) In general. A defined benefit plan does not fail to satisfy section 411(b)(1)(H) and paragraph (b) of this section solely because the plan limits the amount of benefits a participant may accrue under the plan or limits the number of years of service or years of participation taken into account for purposes of determining the accrual of benefits under the plan (credited service). For this purpose, a limitation that is expressed as a percentage of compensation (whether averaged over a participant's total years of credited service for the employer or over a shorter period) and a limitation of the type described in section 401(a)(5)(D) are treated as permissible limitations on the amount of benefits a participant may accrue under the plan. However, in applying a limitation on the number of years of credited service that are taken into account under a plan, the plan may not take into account any year of service that is disregarded in determining the accrual of benefits under the plan (prior to the effective date of section 411(b)(1)(H) and this section) because of the attainment of any age.

(ii) Limitation not based on age. Any limitation on the amount of benefits a participant may accrue under the plan and any limitation on the number of years of credited service taken into account under the plan may not be based, directly or indirectly, on the attainment of any age. A limitation that is determined by reference to age or that is not determinable except by reference to age is considered a limitation directly based on age. Thus, a plan provision that, for purposes of benefit accrual, disregards years of service completed after a participant becomes eligible to receive social security benefits is considered a limitation directly based on age. Similarly, a plan provision that, for purposes of benefit accrual, disregards years of service completed after the sum of a participant's age and the participant's number of years of credited service equals a specified number, is considered a limitation directly based on age. Whether a limitation is indirectly based on age is determined with reference to all the facts and circumstances.

(iii) Examples. The provisions of paragraph (b)(2) of this section may be illustrated by the following examples. In each example, assume that the participant completes the hours of service in a plan year required under the plan to accrue a full benefit for the plan year.

*Example (1).* Assume the same facts as in the Example set forth in paragraph (b)(1)(ii) of this section, except that the plan provides that not more than 35 years of credited service will be taken into account in determining a participant's normal retirement benefit under the plan. Upon A's retirement at age 70, A will have a normal retirement benefit under the plan's benefit formula of 35% of A's average annual compensation (1% per year × 35 years). The plan will not fail to satisfy the requirements of section 411(b)(1)(H) and this paragraph (b) merely because the plan provides that the final 10 years of A's service under the plan is not taken into account in determining A's normal retirement benefit. The result would be the same if the plan provided that no participant could accrue a normal retirement benefit in excess of 35% of the participant's average annual compensation.

*Example (2).* Employer Y maintains a defined benefit plan that provides a normal retirement benefit of 50% of a participant's final average compensation. Normal retirement age under the plan is age 65. Other than the limitations imposed by section 415, the plan contains no provision that limits the accrual of the benefit payable to a participant who has less than a specified number of years of credited service for Y. Participant A is hired by Y at age 66 and commences participation in the plan at age 67. Under the plan's benefit formula, if A completes one year of credited service under the plan, A will be entitled to receive (subject to the limitations of section 415) a normal retirement benefit equal to 50% of A's final average compensation.

*(3) Different rates of benefit accrual.* (i) In general. A defined benefit plan does not fail to satisfy the requirements of section 411(b)(1)(H) and paragraph (b) of this section solely because the plan provides for the accrual of benefits at different rates with respect to participants under the plan. Accordingly, a plan under which a participant's accrued benefit is determined in accordance with the fractional rule described in section 411(b)(1)(C) and § 1.411(b)-1(b)(3) will not fail to satisfy the requirements of section 411(b)(1)(H) and paragraph (b) of this section solely because the rate at which a participant's normal retirement benefit accrues differs depending on the number of years of credited service a participant would have between the date of commencement of participation and the attainment of normal retirement age. In addition, a plan will not be treated as failing to satisfy section 411(b)(1)(H) and paragraph (b) of this section solely because the plan's benefit formula provides, on a uniform and consistent basis, a normal retirement benefit equal to, for example, 2% of average annual compensation multiplied by a participant's first 15 years of credited service and 1% of average annual compensation multiplied by a participant's years of credited service in excess of 15 years. The preceding sentence applies regardless of when the participant's normal retirement age occurs.

(ii) Differences not based on age. Any differences in the rate of benefit accrual described in paragraph (b)(3)(i) of this section may not be based, directly or indirectly, on the attainment of any age.

*(4) Certain adjustments for delayed retirement.* (i) In general. Under section 411(b)(1)(H)(iii), a plan may provide that benefit accruals that would otherwise be required under section 411(b)(1)(H)(i) and paragraph (b) of this section for a plan year are reduced (but not below zero) as set forth in paragraph (b)(4)(ii) and (iii) of this section. This paragraph (b)(4) applies for a plan year to a participant who, as of the end of the plan year, has attained normal retirement age under the plan.

(ii) Distribution of benefits. (A) A plan may provide that the benefit accrual otherwise required under section 411(b)(1)(H)(i) and paragraph (b) of this section for a plan year is reduced (but not below zero) by the actuarial equivalent of total plan benefit distributions (as determined under this paragraph (b)(4)(ii)) made to the participant by the close of the plan year.

(B) The plan benefit distributions described in this paragraph (b)(4)(ii) are limited to distributions made to the participant during plan years and periods with respect to which section 411(b)(1)(H)(i) and this section apply (including plan years and periods beginning before January 1, 1988) for which the plan could (without regard to section 401(a)(9) and the regulations thereunder) provide for the suspension of the participant's plan benefits in accordance with section 203(a)(3)(B) of the Employee Retirement Income Security Act of 1974 (ERISA) and regulations issued thereunder by the Department of Labor.

(C) For purposes of determining the total amount of plan benefit distributions that may be taken into account under this paragraph (b)(4)(ii) as of the close of a plan year, distributions shall be disregarded to the extent the total amount of distributions made to the participant by the close of the plan year exceeds the total amount of the distributions the participant would have received by the close of the plan year if the distributions had been made in accordance with the plan's normal form of benefit distribution. Accordingly, the plan is required to accrue a benefit for the plan year on behalf of a participant in accordance with the plan's benefit formula, taking into account all of the participant's years of credited service, reduced (but not below the participant's normal retirement benefit for the prior plan year) by the actuarial equivalent of total benefit distributions (taken into account under this paragraph (b)(4)(ii) made to the participant by the close of the plan year. If, by the close of the plan year, the actuarial equivalent of total plan benefit distributions made to the participant and taken into account under this paragraph (b)(4)(ii) is greater than the total benefit accruals required under section 411(b)(1)(H)(i) and paragraph (b) of this section for the plan years during which such distributions were made, the plan is not required under section 411(b)(1)(H)(i) and paragraph (b) of this section to accrue any benefit on behalf of the participant for the plan year.

(iii) Adjustment in benefits payable. (A) A plan may provide that the benefit accrual otherwise required under section 411(b)(1)(H)(i) and paragraph (b) of this section for the plan year is reduced (but not below zero) by the amount of any actuarial adjustment under the plan in the benefit payable for the plan year with respect to the participant because of a delay in the payment of plan benefits after the participant's attainment of normal retirement age.

(B) For purposes of paragraph (b)(4)(iii)(A) of this section, the actuarial adjustment may be taken into account for a plan year only to the extent it is made to the greater of the participant's retirement benefit as of the close of the prior plan year, including any actuarial adjustment made under the plan for the prior plan year, and the participant's normal retirement benefit as of the close of the prior play year determined by including benefit accruals required by section 411(b)(1)(H)(i) and paragraph (b) of this section. If the retirement benefit, as actuarially adjusted for the plan year in accordance with this paragraph (b)(4)(iii) for delayed payment, exceeds the normal retirement benefit, as determined by including benefit accruals required for the plan year by section 411(b)(1)(H)(i) and paragraph (b) of this section, the plan shall be required to provide the retirement benefit, as actuarially adjusted in accordance with this paragraph (b)(4)(iii) under the plan. Notwithstanding the provisions of this paragraph (b)(4)(iii)(B), in the case of a plan that suspends benefit payments in accordance with section 203(a)(3)(B) of the Employee Retirement Income Security Act of 1974 and the regulations issued thereunder by the Department of Labor, the plan does not fail to satisfy the requirements of section 411(b)(1)(H) and paragraph (b) of this section solely because the plan provides that the retirement benefit to which a participant is entitled as of the close of a plan year ending after the participant attains normal retirement age under the plan is the greater of the benefit payable at normal retirement age (not including benefit accruals otherwise required by section 411(b)(1)(H) and paragraph (b) of this section) actuarially adjusted under the plan to the close of the plan year for delayed payment, and the retirement benefit determined under the plan as of the close of the plan year determined by including benefit accruals required by section 411(b)(1)(H) and paragraph (b) of this section and determined without regard to any offset that would otherwise be applicable under this paragraph (b)(4)(iii).

(iv) Examples. The provisions of paragraph (b)(4) of this section may be illustrated by the following examples. In each example, assume that the participant completes the hours of service in a plan year required under the plan to accrue a full benefit for the plan year and assume that the participant is not married unless otherwise specified.

*Example (1).* Employer Y maintains a defined benefit plan that provides a normal retirement benefit of $20 per month multiplied by the participant's years of credited service. The plan contains no limit on the number of years of credited service taken into account for purposes of determining the normal retirement benefit provided by the plan. Participant A attains normal retirement age of 65 and continues in the full time service of Y. At age 65, A has 30 years of credited service under the plan and could receive a normal retirement benefit of $600 per month ($20 × 30 years) if A retires. The plan provides for the suspension of A's normal retirement benefit (in accordance with section 203(a)(3)(B) of the Employee Retirement Income Security Act of 1974 (ERISA) and regulations thereunder issued by the Department of Labor) during the period of A's continued employment with Y. Accordingly, the plan does not provide for an actuarial adjustment of A's normal retirement benefit because of delayed payment and the plan does not pay A's normal retirement benefit while A remains in the full time service of Y. If A retires at age 67, after completing two additional years of credited service for Y, A must receive additional accruals for the two years of credited service completed after attaining normal retirement age in order for the plan to satisfy section 411(b)(1)(H)(i). Accordingly, A is entitled to receive a normal retirement benefit of $640 per month ($20 × 32 years).

*Example (2).* Assume the same facts as in Example (1), except that the plan provides that at the time A's normal retirement benefit becomes payable, the amount of A's normal retirement benefit (determined as of A's normal retirement age and each year thereafter) will be actuarially increased for delayed retirement. The plan offsets this actuarial increase against benefit accruals in plan years ending after A's attainment of normal retirement age, as permitted by paragraph (b)(4)(iii) of this section. Accordingly, the plan does not provide for the suspension of normal retirement benefits (in accordance with section 203(a)(3)(B) of ERISA and regulations thereunder issued by the Department of Labor). Under section 411(b)(1)(H), the plan must provide A with a benefit of at least $620 per month after A completes 31 years of credited service for Y. However, under paragraph (b)(4)(iii) of this section, the plan is not required to provide A with a benefit accrual for A's additional year of credited service for Y because, under the plan, A will be entitled to receive, upon retirement at age 66 after completing 1 additional year of credited service for Y, an actuarially increased benefit of $672 per month. This monthly benefit of $672 is the greater of A's normal retirement benefit at normal retirement age ($20 × 30 years = $600) actuarially adjusted for delayed payment and A's normal retirement benefit ($20 × 31 years = $620) determined by taking into account A's year of credited service after attaining normal retirement age. Under the plan, A will be entitled to receive, upon retirement at age 67 after completing 2 additional years of credited service for Y after attaining normal retirement age, an actuarially increased benefit of $756 per month. This monthly benefit of $756 is the greater of A's actuarially adjusted normal retirement benefit at age 66 ($672) actuarially adjusted to $756 for delayed payment to age 67 and A's normal retirement benefit ($20 × 32 years = $640) determined by taking into account A's years of credited service after attaining normal retirement age.

*Example (3).* Assume the same facts as in Example (1), except that the plan neither provides for the suspension of normal retirement benefit payments (in accordance with section 203(a)(3)(B) of ERISA and regulations thereunder issued by the Department of Labor) nor provides for an actuarial increase in benefit payments because of delayed payment of benefits. Consequently, the plan provides that the normal retirement benefit will be paid to a participant, beginning at age 65 (normal retirement age) even though the participant remains in the service of Y and offsets the value of the benefit distributions against benefit accruals in plan years ending after the participant's attainment of normal retirement age, as permitted by paragraph (b)(4)(ii) of this section. Participant B (who remains in the full time service of Y) receives 12 monthly benefit payments prior to attainment of age 66. The total monthly benefit payments of $7,200 ($600 × 12 payments) have an actuarial value at age 66 of $7,559 (reflecting interest and mortality) which would produce a monthly benefit of $72 commencing at age 66. The benefit accrual for the year of credited service B completed after attaining normal retirement age is $20 per month ($20 × 1 year). Because the actuarial value (determined as a monthly benefit of $72) of the benefit payments made during the one year of credited service after B's attainment of normal retirement age exceeds the benefit accrual for the one year of credited service after B's attainment of normal retirement age exceeds the benefit accrual for the one year of credited service after B's attainment of normal retirement age, the plan is not required to accrue benefits on behalf of B for the one year of credited service after B's attainment of normal retirement age and the plan is not required to increase B's monthly benefit payment of $600 at age 66. Assume B receives 24 monthly benefit payments prior to B's retirement at age 67. The total monthly benefit payments of $14,400 ($600 × 24 payments have an actuarial value at age 67 of $15,839 (reflecting interest and mortality) which would produce a monthly benefit payment of $156 commencing at age 67. The benefit accrual for the two years of credited service B completed after attaining normal retirement age is $40 per month ($20 × 2 years). Because the actuarial value (determined as a monthly benefit of $156) of the benefit payments made during the two years of credited service after B's normal retirement age exceeds the benefit accrual for the two years of credited service after B's normal retirement age ($20 × 2 years = $40), the plan is not required to accrue benefits on behalf of B for the second year of credited service B completed after attaining normal retirement age and the plan is not required to increase B's monthly benefit payment of $600.

*Example (4).* Assume that Employer Z maintains a defined benefit plan that provides a normal retirement benefit of 2% of the average of a participant's high three consecutive years of compensation multiplied by the participant's years of credited service under the plan. The plan contains no limit on the number of years of credited service taken into account for purposes of determining the normal retirement benefit provided by the plan. Participant C, who has attained normal retirement age (age 65) under the plan, continues in the full time service of Z. At normal retirement age, C has average compensation of $20,000 for C's high three consecutive years and has 10 years of credited service under the plan. Thus, at normal retirement age, C is entitled to receive an annual normal retirement benefit of $4,000 ($20,000 × .02 × 10 years). Assume further that the plan provides for the suspension of N's normal retirement benefit (in accordance with section 203(a)(3)(B) of ERISA and regulations issued thereunder by the Department of Labor) during the period of C's continued employment with Z. Accordingly, the plan does not provide for the actuarial increase of C's normal retirement benefit because of delayed payment and the plan does not pay C's normal retirement benefit while C remains in the full time service of Z. At age 70, when C retires, C has average annual compensation for C's high three consecutive years of $35,000. Under section 411(b)(1)(H), C must be credited with 15 years of credited service for Z and C's increased compensation after attaining normal retirement age must be taken into account for purposes of determining C's normal retirement benefit. At age 70, C is entitled to receive an annual normal retirement benefit of $10,500 ($35,000 × .02 × 15 years).

*Example (5).* Assume the same facts as in Example (4), except that the payment of C's retirement benefit is not suspended (in accordance with section 203(a)(3)(B) of ERISA and regulations issued thereunder by the Department of Labor) and, accordingly, the plan provides that retirement benefits that commence after a participant's normal retirement age will be actuarially increased for late retirement. The plan offsets this actuarial increase against benefit accruals in plan years ending after C's attainment of normal retirement age, as permitted by paragraph (b)(4)(iii) of this section. Under this provision, at the close of each plan year after C's attainment of normal retirement age, C's retirement benefit is actuarially increased. Under this provision, the actuarial increase for the plan year is made to the greater of C's normal retirement benefit at the close of the prior plan year (including previous actuarial adjustments) and C's normal retirement benefit at the close of the prior plan year determined by including all benefit accruals. Accordingly, at the close of each plan year, C is entitled to receive an annual normal retirement benefit equal to the greater of C's normal retirement benefit (adjusted actuarially under the plan from the benefit to which C was entitled at the close of the prior plan year) determined at the close of the plan year and C's normal retirement benefit determined at the close of the plan year by taking into account C's years of credited service and benefit accruals after C's attainment of normal retirement age. The foregoing is illustrated in the following table with respect to certain years of credited service performed by C after attaining normal retirement age 65.

| Age | Years of credited service | Average compensation for high three consecutive years | Normal retirement benefit with additional accurate (.02 × column 2 × column 3) | Retirement benefit, as actuarially increased under the plan from the benefit at prior age (column 6) | Normal retirement benefit to which C is entitled (greater of column 4 and column 5) |
|---|---|---|---|---|---|
| 1 | 2 | 3 | 4 | 5 | 6 |
| 65 | 10 | $20,000 | $ 4,000 | N/A | $ 4,000 |
| 66 | 11 | 21,000 | 4,620 | 4,482 | 4,620 |
| 67 | 12 | 29,000 | 6,960 | 5,192 | 6,960 |
| 68 | 13 | 30,000 | 7,800 | 7,848 | 7,848 |
| 69 | 14 | 33,000 | 9,240 | 8,880 | 9,240 |
| 70 | 15 | 35,000 | 10,500 | 10,494 | 10,500 |

*Example (6).* Assume the same facts as in Example (4), except that C does not retire at age 70, but continues in the full time service of Z. Upon C's attainment of age 70, the plan commences benefit payments to C. The annual benefit paid to C in the first plan year is $10,500 ($35,000 × .02 × 15 years). In determining the annual benefit payable to C in each subsequent plan year, the plan offsets the value of benefit distributions made to the participant by the close of the prior plan year against benefit accruals in plan years during which such distributions were made, as permitted by paragraph (b)(4)(ii) of this section. Accordingly, for each subsequent plan year, C is entitled under the plan to receive benefit payments based on C's benefit (at the close of the prior plan year) determined under the plan formula by taking into account all of C's years of credited service, reduced (but not below C's normal retirement benefit for the prior plan year) by the value of total benefit distributions made to C by the close of the prior plan year. The foregoing is illustrated in the following table with respect to certain years of credited service performed by C while benefits were being distributed to C.

| Years of benefit distributions 1 | Years of credited service (as of close of the year) 2 | Average compensation for high three years 3 | Normal retirement benefit with additional accruals (02 × column 2 × column 3) 4 | Suspendible benefit distributions made during the year 5 | Cumulative suspendible distributions made as of close of the year 6 | Annual benefit that is actuarial equivalent of cumulative suspendible benefit distributions made as of close of the year 7 | Retirement benefit to which C is entitled at close of the year (column 4 − 7, but not less than column 8 for prior year) 8 |
|---|---|---|---|---|---|---|---|
| N/A ......... | 15 | $35,000 | $10,500 | N/A | N/A | N/A | $10,500 |
| 1............ | 16 | 35,000 | 11,200 | $10,500 | $10,500 | $1,472 | 10,500 |
| 2............ | 17 | 45,000 | 15,300 | 10,500 | 21,000 | 3,209 | 12,091 |
| 3............ | 18 | 50,000 | 18,000 | 12,091 | 33,091 | 5,510 | 12,490 |

**(c) Defined contribution plans.** *(1) In general.* A defined contribution plan (including a target benefit plan described in § 1.410(a)-4(a)(1)) does not satisfy the minimum vesting standards of section 411(a) if, either directly or indirectly, because of the attainment of any age—

(i) The allocation of employer contributions or forfeitures to the accounts of participants is discontinued, or

(ii) The rate at which the allocation of employer contributions or forfeitures is made to the accounts of participants is decreased.

*(2) Limitations on allocations.* (i) A defined contribution plan (including a target benefit plan described in § 1.410(A)-4(a)(1)) does not fail to satisfy the minimum vesting standards of section 411(a) solely because the plan limits the total amount of employer contributions and forfeitures that may be allocated to a participant's account (for a particular plan year or for the participant's total years of credited service under the plan) or solely because the plan limits the total number of years of credited service for which a participant's account may receive allocations of employer contributions and forfeitures. The limitations described in the preceding sentence may not be applied with respect to the allocation of gains, losses or income of the trust to the account of a participant. Furthermore, a defined contribution plan (including a target benefit plan) does not fail to satisfy section 411(a) solely because the plan limits the number of years of credited service that may be taken into account for purposes of determining the amount of, or the rate at which, employer contributions and forfeitures are allocated to a participant's account for a particular plan year. However, in applying a credited service limitation described in this paragraph (c)(2)(i), the plan may not take into account any year of service (prior to the effective date of section 411(b)(2) and paragraph (c) of this section) that is disregarded in determining allocations to a participant's account because of the participant's attainment of any age.

(ii) Any limitation described in paragraph (c)(2)(i) of this section may not be based, directly or indirectly, on the attainment of any age. The provisions of paragraph (b)(2)(ii) of this section shall also apply for purposes of this paragraph (c).

(iii) The Commissioner shall provide such additional rules as may be necessary or appropriate with respect to the application of section 411(b)(2) and this section to target benefit plans.

**(d) Benefits and forms of benefits subject to requirements.** *(1) General rule.* Except as provided in paragraph (d)(2) of this section, section 411(b)(1)(H) and (b)(2) and paragraphs (b) and (c) of this section apply to all benefits (and forms of benefits) provided under a defined benefit plan and a defined contribution plan, including accrued benefits, benefits described in section 411(d)(6), ancillary benefits and other rights and features provided under the plan. Accordingly, except as provided in paragraph (d)(2) of this section, benefit accruals under a defined benefit plan and allocations under a defined contribution plan will be considered to be reduced on account of the attainment of a specified age if optional forms of benefits, ancillary benefits, or other rights or features under the plan provided with respect to benefits or allocations attributable to credited service prior to the attainment of such age are not provided (on at least as favorable a basis to participants) with respect to benefits or allocations attributable to credited service after such age. Thus, for example, a plan may not provide a lump sum payment only with respect to benefits attributable to years of credited service before the attainment of a specified age. Similarly, except as provided in paragraph (d)(2) of this section, if an optional form of benefit is available under the plan at a specified age, the availability of such form of benefit, or the method for determining the manner in which such benefit is paid, may not, directly or indirectly, be denied or provided on terms less favorable to participants because of the attainment of any higher age. Similarly, if the method for determining the amount or the rate of the subsidized portion of a joint and survivor annuity or the subsidized portion of a joint and survivor annuity or the subsidized portion of a preretirement survivor annuity is less favorable with respect to participants who have attained a specified age than with respect to participants who have not attained such age, benefit accruals or account allocations under the plan will be considered to be reduced on account of the attainment of such age.

*(2) Special rule for certain benefits.* A plan will not fail to satisfy section 411(b)(1)(H) or paragraph (b) of this section merely because the following benefits, or the manner in which such benefits are provided under the plan, vary because of the attainment of any higher age.

(i) The subsidized portion of an early retirement benefit (whether provided on a temporary or permanent basis),

(ii) A qualified disability benefit (as defined in § 1.411(a)-7(c)(3)); and

(iii) A social security supplement (as defined in § 1.411(a)-7(c)(4)(ii)).

**(e) Coordination with certain provisions.** Notwithstanding section 411(b)(1)(H), (b)(2) and the preceding paragraphs of this section, the following rules shall apply.

*(1) Section 415 limitations.* No allocation to the account of a participant in a defined contribution plan (including a target benefit plan described in § 1.410(a)-4(a)(1)) shall be required for a limitation year by section 411(b)(2) and no benefit accrual with respect to a participant in a defined benefit plan shall be required for a limitation year by section 411(b)(1)(H)(i) to the extent that the allocation or accrual would cause the plan to exceed the limitations of section 415(b), (c), or (e) applicable to the participant for the limitation year.

*(2) Prohibited discrimination.* (i) No allocation to the account of a highly compensated employee in a defined contribution plan (including a target benefit plan) shall be required for a plan year by section 411(b)(2) to the extent the allocation would cause the plan to discriminate in favor of highly compensated employees within the meaning of section 401(a)(4).

(ii) No benefit accrual on behalf of a highly compensated employee in a defined benefit plan shall be required for a plan year by section 411(b)(1)(H)(i) to the extent such benefit accrual would cause the plan to discriminate in favor of highly compensated employees within the meaning of section 401(a)(4).

(iii) The Commissioner may provide additional rules relating to prohibited discrimination in favor of highly compensated employees.

*(3) Permitted disparity.* In the case of a plan that would fail to satisfy section 401(a)(4) except for the application of section 401(1), no allocation to the account of a participant in a defined contribution plan and no benefit accrual on behalf of a participant in a defined benefit plan shall be required under section 411(b)(1)(H) or (b)(2) for a plan year to the extent such allocation or accrual would cause the plan to fail to satisfy the requirements of section 401(1) and the regulations thereunder for the plan year.

**(f) Effective dates.** *(1) Noncollectively bargained plans.* (i) In general. Except as otherwise provided in paragraph (f)(2) of this section, section 411(b)(1)(H) and (b)(2) and paragraphs (b) and (c) of this section are effective for plan years beginning on or after January 1, 1988, with respect to a participant who is credited with at least 1 hour of service in a plan year beginning on or after January 1, 1988. Section 411(b)(1)(H) and (b)(2) and paragraphs (b) and (c) of this section are not effective with respect to a participant who is not credited with at least 1 hour of service in a plan year beginning on or after January 1, 1988.

(ii) Defined benefit plans. In the case of a participant who is credited with at least 1 hour of service in a plan year beginning on or after January 1, 1988, section 411(b)(1)(H) and paragraph (b) of this section are effective with respect to all years of service completed by the participant, including years of service completed before the first plan year beginning on or after January 1, 1988. Accordingly, in the case of a participant described in the preceding sentence, a defined benefit plan does not satisfy section 411(b)(1)(H) and paragraph (b) of this section for a plan year beginning on or after January 1, 1988, if the plan disregards, because of the participant's attainment of any age, any year of service completed by the participant or any compensation earned by the participant after attaining such age. However, a defined benefit plan is not required under section 411(b)(1)(H) and paragraph (b) of this section to take into account for benefit accrual purposes any year of service completed before an employee becomes a participant in the plan. See paragraph (b)(2) of this section for rules relating to benefit and service limitations that may be imposed by a defined benefit plan.

(iii) Defined contribution plans. Section 411(b)(2) and paragraph (c) of this section are not applicable with respect to allocations of employer contributions or forfeitures to the accounts of participants under a defined contribution plan for a plan year beginning before January 1, 1988. However, in the case of a defined contribution plan under which allocations to the accounts of participants for a plan year are determined on the basis of an allocation formula that takes into account service or compensation for the employer during prior plan years, section 411(b)(2) and paragraph (c) of this section are effective for plan years beginning on or after January 1, 1988, with respect to all years of service completed by the participant, including years of service completed before the first plan year beginning on or after January 1, 1988. Accordingly, in the case of a participant who has at least 1 hour of service in a plan year beginning on or after January 1, 1988, a defined contribution plan containing an allocation formula described in the preceding sentence does not satisfy section 411(b)(2) and paragraph (c) of this section with respect to allocations for a plan year beginning on or after January 1, 1988, if the plan disregards, because of the participant's attainment of any age, any year of service completed by the participant. See paragraph (c)(2) of this section for rules relating to limitations on allocations to the accounts of participants that may be imposed by a defined contribution plan.

(iv) Employee contributions. In applying paragraph (f)(1)(i), (ii) and (iii) of this section to plan years beginning on or after January 1, 1988, a year of service completed before the first plan year beginning on or after January 1, 1988, will not be treated as being disregarded under a plan on account of a participant's attainment of a specified age solely because such year of service is disregarded under the plan because the participant was not eligible to make voluntary or mandatory employee contributions (as well as contributions under a cash or deferred arrangement described in section 401(k)) under the plan for such year. A plan is not required to permit a participant to make voluntary or mandatory employee contributions (as well as contributions under a cash or deferred arrangement described in section 401(k)) for a plan year beginning before January 1, 1988, in order to satisfy section 411(b)(1)(H) or (b)(2) or paragraph (b) or (c) of this section for a plan year beginning on or after January 1, 1988.

(v) Hour of service. For purposes of this paragraph (f)(1), one hour of service means one hour of service recognized under the plan or required to be recognized under the plan by section 410 (relating to minimum participation standards) or section 411 (relating to minimum vesting standards). In the case of a plan that does not determine service on the basis of hours of service, one hour of service means any service recognized under the plan or required to be recognized under the plan by section 410 (relating to minimum participation standards) or section 411 (relating to minimum vesting standards).

(vi) Examples. The provisions of paragraph (f)(1) of this section may be illustrated by the following examples. In each example, assume that the participant completes the hours of service in a plan year required under the plan to accrue a full benefit or receive an allocation for the plan year.

*Example (1).* Employer X maintains a noncontributory defined benefit plan (that is not a collectively bargained plan) that provides a normal retirement benefit equal to 1% of a participant's average annual compensation for the participant's three consecutive years of highest compensation, multiplied by the participant's years of credited service under the plan. The plan contains no limit on the number of years of credited service taken into account for purposes of determining the normal retirement benefit provided by the plan. The plan uses the calendar year as its plan year. The plan specifies a normal retirement age of 65 and provides (prior to January 1, 1988) that no compensation earned and no service performed by a participant after attainment of normal retirement age will be taken into account in determining the participant's normal retirement benefit. Participant A attains normal retirement age on December 15, 1985. A continues in the full time service of X and has at least 1 hour of service for X during the plan year beginning on January 1, 1988. As of the plan year ending December 31, 1985, A had 35 years of credited service under the plan. In accordance with the plan provisions in effect prior to January 1, 1988, A's service and compensation during the 1986 and 1987 plan years is not taken into account in determining A's normal retirement benefit for those plan years. Beginning on January 1, 1988, the plan provisions that compensation earned and years of service completed after normal retirement age are not taken into account in determining a participant's normal retirement benefit may not be applied to A. Thus, as of the plan year beginning January 1, 1988, A's normal retirement benefit under the plan must be determined without regard to those provisions. Accordingly, beginning on January 1, 1988, the plan is required to take into account A's service for X and A's compensation from X during the 1986 and 1987 plan years for purposes of determining A's normal retirement benefit in order to satisfy section 411(b)(1)(H) and paragraph (b) of this section.

*Example (2).* Assume the same facts as in Example (1), except that the plan provides that, in determining a participant's normal retirement benefit under the plan (a) not more than 35 years of credited service will be taken into account and (b) no compensation earned after 35 years of credited service have been completed will be taken into account. Accordingly, the plan is not required to take into account A's service for X or A compensation from X during the 1986 and 1987 plan years for purposes of determining A's normal retirement benefit in order to satisfy section 411(b)(1)(H) and paragraph (b) of this section.

*Example (3).* Assume the same facts as in Example (1), except that A retires on December 5, 1987 and does not perform any hours of service for X after A's retirement. Accordingly, the plan is not required to take into account A's service for X and A's compensation from X during the 1986 and 1987 plan years for purposes of determining A's normal retirement benefit in order to satisfy section 411(b)(1)(H) and paragraph (b) of this section.

*Example (4).* Assume the same facts as in Example (1), except that the plan requires, as a condition to accruing benefits attributable to employer contributions under the plan, that a participant make employee contributions under the plan. The plan provides that a participant is not eligible to make employee contributions in a plan year beginning after the plan year in which the participant attains normal retirement age under the plan. Accordingly, A does not make employee contributions during the 1986 and 1987 plan years and, therefore, does not accrue in those plan years a benefit attributable to employer contributions. The plan is not required to take into account A's service for X and A's compensation from X during the 1986 and 1987 plan years in order to satisfy section 411(b)(1)(H) and paragraph (b) of this section. In addition, the plan is not required to permit A to make employee contributions to the plan for the 1986 and 1987 plan years in order to satisfy section 411(b)(1)(H) and paragraph (b) of this section.

*Example (5).* Employer Y maintains a profit-sharing plan (that is not a collectively bargained plan). The plan is the only qualified plan maintained by Y and uses the calendar year as its plan year. The formula under the plan for allocating employer contributions and forfeitures to the accounts of participants contains a years of service factor. Pursuant to the allocation formula containing the years of service factor, employer contributions and forfeitures for the plan year are allocated among the accounts of participants on the basis of one unit for each full $200 of compensation of the participant for the plan year and one unit for each year of credited service for Y completed by the participant. The plan contains no limit on the number of years of credited service taken into account for purposes of determining the allocation to the account of a participant for the plan year under the plan's allocation formula. The plan specifies a normal retirement age of 65 and provides (prior to January 1, 1988) that no service performed by a participant in a plan year beginning after the attainment of normal retirement age will be taken into account in determining the allocation to the participant's account for a plan year. Participant B attains normal retirement age on December 15, 1985. B continues in the full time service of Y and has at least 1 hour of service for Y during the plan year beginning January 1, 1988. As of the plan year ending December 31, 1985, B had 35 years of credited service under the plan. In accordance with the plan provisions in effect prior to January 1, 1988, B's service during the 1986 and 1987 plan year is not taken into account in determining the allocation of employer contributions and forfeitures to B's account for the 1986 and 1987 plan years. As of the plan year beginning January 1, 1988, the plan provision that years of service in plan years beginning after attainment of normal retirement age are not taken into account in determining the allocation of employer contributions and forfeitures to the accounts of participants may not be applied to B. Thus, the allocation of employer contributions and forfeitures to B's account for the 1988 plan year must be determined under the allocation formula contained in the plan without regard to that provision. Accordingly, the plan is required to take into account B's service for Y during the 1986 and 1987 plan years for purposes of determining the allocation of employer contributions and forfeitures to B's account for the 1988 plan year in order to satisfy section 411(b)(2) and paragraph (c) of this section. However, the plan is not required to provide any additional allocations to B's account under the plan for the 1986 or 1987 plan year in order to satisfy section 411(b)(2) and paragraph (c) of this section.

*Example (6).* Assume the same facts as in Example (5), except that the plan provides that, in determining the allocation of employer contributions and forfeitures to the account of a participant for a plan year, not more than 35 years of credited service for Y will be taken into account. Accordingly, the plan is not required to take into account B's service for Y during the 1986 or 1987 plan years for purposes of determining the allocation of employer contributions and forfeitures to B's account for the 1988 plan year under the allocation formula contained in the plan.

*(2) Collectively bargained plans.* (i) In the case of a plan maintained pursuant to 1 or more collective bargaining agreements between employee representatives and 1 or more employers, ratified before March 1, 1986, section 411(b)(1)(H) and (b)(2) is effective for benefits provided

under, and employees covered by, any such agreement with respect to plan years beginning on or after the later of—

(A) January 1, 1988, or

(B) The date on which the last of such collective bargaining agreements terminates (determinated without regard to any extension of any such agreement occurring on or after March 1, 1986).

However, notwithstanding the preceding sentence, section 411(b)(1)(H) and (b)(2) shall be effective for benefits provided under, and employees covered by, any agreement described in this paragraph (f)(2)(i) no later than with respect to the first plan year beginning on or after January 1, 1990.

(ii) The effective date provisions of paragraph (f)(1) of this section shall apply in the same manner to plans described in paragraph (f)(2)(i) of this section, except that the effective date determined under paragraph (f)(2)(i) of this section shall be substituted for the effective data determined under paragraph (f)(1) of this section.

(iii) In accordance with the provisions of paragraph (f)(2)(i) of this section, a plan described therein may be subject to different effective dates under section 411(b)(1)(H) and (b)(2) for employees who are covered by a collective bargaining agreement and employees who are not covered by a collective bargaining agreement.

(iv) For purposes of paragraph (f)(2)(i) of this section, the service crediting rules of paragraph (f)(1) of this section shall apply to a plan described in paragraph (f)(2)(i) of this section, except that in applying such rules the effective date determined under paragraph (f)(2)(i) of this section shall be substituted for the effective date determined under paragraph (f)(1) of this section. See paragraph (f)(1)(v) of this section for rules relating to the recognition of an hour of service.

*(3) Amendments to plans.* (i) Except as provided in paragraph (f)(3)(ii) of this section, plan amendments required by section 411(b)(1)(H) and (b)(2) (the applicable sections) shall not be required to be made before the first plan year beginning on or after January 1, 1989, if the following requirements are met—

(A) The plan is operated in accordance with the requirements of the applicable section for all periods before the first plan year beginning on or after January 1, 1989, for which such section is effective with respect to the plan; and

(B) Such plan amendments are adopted no later than the last day of the first plan year beginning on or after January 1, 1989, and are made effective retroactively for all periods for which the applicable section is effective with respect to the plan.

(ii) In the case of a collectively bargained plan described in paragraph (f)(2)(i) of this section that satisfies the requirements of paragraph (f)(3)(i) of this section (as modified by this paragraph (f)(3)(ii)), paragraph (f)(3)(i) shall be applied by substituting for "the first plan year beginning on or after January 1, 1989," the first plan year beginning on or after the later of—

(A) January 1, 1989, or

(B) The date on which the last of such collective bargaining agreements terminate (determined without regard to any extension of any such agreement occurring on or after March 1, 1986).

However, notwithstanding the preceding sentence, section 411(b)(1)(H) and (b)(2) shall be applicable to plans described in this paragraph (f)(3)(ii) no later than the first plan year beginning on or after January 1, 1990.

### § 1.411(b)(5)-1 Reduction in rate of benefit accrual under a defined benefit plan.

**(a) In general.** *(1) Organization of regulation.* This section sets forth certain rules for determining whether a reduction occurs in the rate of benefit accrual under a defined benefit plan because of the attainment of any age for purposes of section 411(b)(1)(H)(i). Paragraph (b) of this section describes safe harbors for certain plan designs (including statutory hybrid plans) that are deemed to satisfy the age discrimination rules under section 411(b)(1)(H). Paragraph (c) of this section describes rules relating to statutory hybrid plan conversion amendments. Paragraph (d) of this section describes rules restricting interest credits (or equivalent amounts) under a statutory hybrid plan to a market rate of return. Paragraph (e) of this section contains additional rules related to market rates of return. Paragraph (f) of this section contains effective/applicability dates.

*(2) Definitions.* The definitions of accumulated benefit, lump sum-based benefit formula, statutory hybrid benefit formula, statutory hybrid plan, and variable annuity benefit formula in § 1.411(a)(13)-1(d) apply for purposes of this section.

**(b) Safe harbors for certain plan designs.** *(1) Accumulated benefit testing.* (i) In general. Pursuant to section 411(b)(5)(A), and subject to paragraph (b)(1)(ii) of this section, a plan is not treated as failing to meet the requirements of section 411(b)(1)(H)(i) with respect to an individual who is or could be a participant if, as of any date, the accumulated benefit of the individual would not be less than the accumulated benefit of any similarly situated, younger individual who is or could be a participant. Thus, this test involves a comparison of the accumulated benefit of an individual who is or could be a participant in the plan with the accumulated benefit of each similarly situated, younger individual who is or could be a participant in the plan. See paragraph (b)(5) of this section for rules regarding whether a younger individual who is or could be a participant is similarly situated to a participant. The comparison described in this paragraph (b)(1)(i) is based on any one of the following benefit measures, each of which is referred to as a safe-harbor formula measure:

(A) The annuity payable at normal retirement age (or current age, if later) if the accumulated benefit of the participant under the terms of the plan is an annuity payable at normal retirement age (or current age, if later).

(B) The current balance of a hypothetical account maintained for the participant if the accumulated benefit of the participant under the terms of the plan is a balance of a hypothetical account.

(C) The current value of an accumulated percentage of the participant's final average compensation if the accumulated benefit of the participant under the terms of the plan is an accumulated percentage of final average compensation.

(ii) Benefit formulas for comparison. (A) In general. Except as provided in paragraphs (b)(1)(ii)(B), (C), and (D) of this section, the safe harbor provided by section 411(b)(5)(A) and paragraph (b)(1)(i) of this section is available with respect to an individual only if the individual's accumulated benefit under the plan is expressed in terms of only one safe-harbor formula measure and no similarly situated, younger individual who is or could be a participant has an accumulated benefit that is expressed in terms of any measure other than that same safe-harbor formula measure. Thus, for example, if a plan provides that the accumulated benefit of participants who are age 55 or over is expressed under the terms of the plan as a life annuity payable at normal retirement age (or current age, if later) as described in paragraph (b)(1)(i)(A) of this section and the plan provides that the accumulated benefit of participants who are younger than age 55 is expressed as the current balance of a hypothetical account as described in paragraph (b)(1)(i)(B) of this section, then the safe harbor described in section 411(b)(5)(A) and paragraph (b)(1)(i) of this section does not apply to individuals who are or could be participants who are age 55 or over.

(B) Sum-of benefit formulas. If a plan provides that a participant's accumulated benefit is expressed as the sum of benefits determined in terms of two or more benefit formulas, each of which is expressed in terms of a different safe-harbor formula measure, then the plan is deemed to satisfy paragraph (b)(1)(i) of this section with respect to an individual who is or could be a participant, provided that the plan satisfies the comparison described in paragraph (b)(1)(i) of this section separately for benefits determined in terms of each safe-harbor formula measure and no accumulated benefit of a similarly situated, younger individual who is or could be a participant is expressed other than as—

(1) The sum of benefits under two or more benefit formulas, each of which is expressed in terms of one of those same safe-harbor formula measures as is used for the participant's "sum-of" benefit;

(2) The greater of benefits under two or more benefit formulas, each of which is expressed in terms of any one of those same safe-harbor formula measures;

(3) The choice of benefits under two or more benefit formulas, each of which is expressed in terms of any one of those same safe-harbor formula measures; or

(4) A benefit that is determined in terms of only one of those same safe-harbor formula measures.

(C) Greater-of benefit formulas. If a plan provides that a participant's accumulated benefit is expressed as the greater of benefits under two or more benefit formulas, each of which is determined in terms of a different safe-harbor formula measure, then the plan is deemed to satisfy paragraph (b)(1)(i) of this section with respect to an individual who is or could be a participant, provided that the plan satisfies the comparison described in paragraph (b)(1)(i) of this section separately for benefits determined in terms of each safe-harbor formula measure and no accumulated benefit of a similarly situated, younger individual who is or could be a participant is expressed other than as—

(1) The greater of benefits determined under two or more benefit formulas, each of which is expressed in terms of one of those same safe-harbor formula measures as is used for the participant's "greater-of" benefit;

(2) The choice of benefits determined under two or more benefit formulas, each of which is expressed in terms of one of those same safe-harbor formula measures; or

(3) A benefit that is determined in terms of only one of those same safe-harbor formula measures.

(D) Choice-of benefit formulas. If a plan provides that a participant's accumulated benefit is determined pursuant to a choice by the participant between benefits determined in terms of two or more different safe-harbor formula measures, then the plan is deemed to satisfy paragraph (b)(1)(i) of this section with respect to an individual who is or could be a participant, provided that the plan satisfies the comparison described in paragraph (b)(1)(i) of this section separately for benefits determined in terms of each safe-harbor formula measure and no accumulated benefit of a similarly situated, younger individual who is or could be a participant is expressed other than as—

(1) The choice of benefits determined under two or more benefit formulas, each of which is expressed in terms of one of those same safe-harbor formula measures as is used for the participant's "choice-of" benefit; or

(2) A benefit that is determined in terms of only one of those same safe-harbor formula measures.

(iii) Disregard of certain subsidized benefits. For purposes of paragraph (b)(1)(i) of this section, any subsidized portion of any early retirement benefit that is included in a participant's accumulated benefit is disregarded. For this purpose, the subsidized portion of an early retirement benefit is the retirement-type subsidy within the meaning of § 1.411(d)-3(g)(6) that is contingent on a participant's severance from employment and commencement of benefits before normal retirement age.

(iv) Examples. The provisions of this paragraph (b)(1) are illustrated by the following examples:

*Example (1).* (i) Facts relating to formulas described in paragraph (b)(1)(i)(A) of this section. Employer X maintains a defined benefit plan that provides a straight life annuity payable commencing at normal retirement age (which is age 65) equal to 1 percent of the participant's highest 3 consecutive years' compensation times years of service and provides for suspension of benefits as permitted under section 411(a)(3)(B). In the case of a participant whose service continues after normal retirement age, the amount payable is the greater of (i) the benefit payable at normal retirement age, and for each year thereafter, actuarially increased to account for delayed commencement, and (ii) the retirement benefit determined under the formula at the date the employee's service ceases (calculated by including years of service and increases in compensation after normal retirement age).

(ii) Conclusion. Under these facts, the plan formula is a formula described in paragraph (b)(1)(i)(A) of this section. The formula is not a statutory hybrid benefit formula merely because the plan formula includes a benefit that is based on the participant's benefit at normal retirement age (and each year thereafter) that is actuarially increased for commencement after attainment of normal retirement age. In addition, the plan formula would satisfy the comparison under paragraph (b)(1)(i) of this section for each individual who is or could be a participant because, as of any date (including any date after normal retirement age), the accumulated benefit of the individual would not be less than the accumulated benefit of any similarly situated, younger individual who is or could be a participant.

*Example (2).* (i) Facts relating to formulas described in paragraph (b)(1)(i)(B) of this section. Employer Y maintains a defined benefit plan that expresses each participant's accumulated benefit as the balance of a hypothetical account. Under the formula, the hypothetical account balance of each participant is credited monthly with interest at a specified rate and the hypothetical account balance of each employee who is a participant is also credited with a pay credit under the plan equal to 7 percent of the participant's compensation for the month.

(ii) Conclusion. The plan formula is a lump sum-based benefit formula described in paragraph (b)(1)(i)(B) of this section and the formula would satisfy the comparison under paragraph (b)(1)(i) of this section for each individual who is or could be a participant because, as of any date, the hypothetical account balance of the individual would not be less than the hypothetical account balance of any similarly situated, younger individual who is or could be a participant.

*Example (3).* (i) Facts where plan suspends interest credits after normal retirement age. The facts are the same as in Example 2 except that the plan provides for suspension of benefits as permitted under section 411(a)(3)(B). Pursuant to the plan's suspension of benefits provision, the plan provides for interest credits to cease during service after normal retirement age or for the amount of the interest credits during this service to be reduced to reflect principal credits credited.

(ii) Conclusion. The plan does not satisfy the safe harbor in paragraph (b)(1)(i) of this section. Applying the rule of paragraph (b)(1)(i) of this section, the plan formula would fail to satisfy the safe harbor comparison under paragraph (b)(1)(i) of this section with respect to an individual whose benefits have been suspended because, as of any date after attainment of normal retirement age, the hypothetical account balance of this individual would be less than the hypothetical account balance of one or more similarly situated individuals who have not attained normal retirement age.

*Example (4).* (i) Facts providing greater-of benefits as described in paragraph (b)(1)(ii)(C) of this section. Employer Z sponsors a defined benefit plan that provides an accumulated benefit expressed as a straight life annuity commencing at the plan's normal retirement age (age 65), based on a percentage of average annual compensation times the participant's years of service. On November 2, 2011, the plan is amended effective as of January 1, 2012, to provide participants who have attained age 55 by January 1, 2012, with a benefit that is the greater of the benefit under the average annual compensation formula and a benefit that is based on the balance of a hypothetical account, which provides for annual pay credits of a specified percentage of the participant's compensation and annual interest credits based on the third segment rate.

(ii) Conclusion where plan provides greater-of benefits to older participants. The plan satisfies the safe harbor of paragraph (b)(1)(i) of this section with respect to all individuals who are or could be participants. Pursuant to the rules of paragraph (b)(1)(ii)(C) of this section, the plan satisfies the safe harbor with respect to individuals who have attained age 55 by January 1, 2012, because (A) with respect to the benefit described in paragraph (b)(1)(i)(A) of this section (the benefit based on average annual compensation, disregarding the benefit based on the balance of a hypothetical account), the accumulated benefit for any individual who is or could be a participant and who is at least age 55 on January 1, 2012, would in no event be less than the accumulated benefit for a similarly situated, younger individual who is or could be participant and who has not yet attained age 55 by January 1, 2012, (B) with respect to the benefit described in paragraph (b)(1)(i)(B) of this section (the benefit based on the balance of a hypothetical account, disregarding the benefit based on average annual compensation), the accumulated benefit for any individual who is or could be a participant and who is at least age 55 on January 1, 2012, would in no event be less than the accumulated benefit for a similarly situated, younger individual who is or could be a participant and who has not yet attained age 55 by January 1, 2012, and (C) the benefit of any individual who is or could be a participant who has not yet attained age 55 by January 1, 2012, is only expressed as an annuity payable at normal retirement age as described in paragraph (b)(1)(i)(A) of this section, and this safe-harbor formula measure applies also to participants who have attained age 55 by January 1, 2012. Furthermore, the plan satisfies the safe harbor with respect to individuals who have not yet attained age 55 by January 1, 2012, because the benefit of these individuals satisfies the general rule of paragraph (b)(1)(ii)(A) of this section.

(iii) Conclusion where plan provides greater-of benefits only to younger participants. If, instead of the facts in paragraph (i) of this Example 4, the plan had been amended to provide only participants who have not yet attained age 55 by January 1, 2012, with a benefit that is the greater of the benefit under the average annual compensation formula and a benefit that is based on the balance of a hypothetical account, then the safe harbor would not be satisfied with respect to individuals who have attained age 55 by January 1, 2012. Under paragraph (b)(1)(ii)(A) of this section, except as provided in paragraphs (b)(1)(ii)(B), (C), and (D) of this section, the safe harbor of paragraph (b)(1)(i) of this section is available only with respect to individuals over age 55, whose benefit is expressed in terms of only one safe-harbor formula measure, if no similarly situated, younger individual has an accumulated benefit that is expressed in terms of any measure other than that same safe-harbor formula measure. This is not the case under these facts. The greater-of rule of paragraph (b)(1)(ii)(C) of this section would not apply to individuals who have attained age 55 because the accumulated benefits of these individuals is not equal to the greater of benefits under two or more benefit formulas.

*Example (5).* (i) Facts where plan provides choice-of benefits to older participants. The facts are the same as in paragraph (i) of Example 4, except that for service after December 31, 2011, the amendment permits participants who have attained age 55 by January 1, 2012, to choose between benefits under the average annual compensation benefit formula or benefits under the hypothetical account balance formula (but, if a participant chooses the hypothetical account balance formula, his or her benefit under the plan is in no event to be less than the benefit determined under the average annual compensation benefit formula for service before January 1, 2012), while other participants receive benefits solely under the hypothetical account balance formula (but individuals who are participants on December 31, 2011, are in no event to receive less than the benefit determined under the average annual compensation benefit formula for service before January 1, 2012).

(ii) Conclusion where plan provides choice to older participants. The plan satisfies the safe harbor with respect to all individuals who are or could be participants. Pursuant to the rule of paragraph (b)(1)(ii)(D) of this section, the plan satisfies the safe harbor of paragraph (b)(1)(i) of this section with respect to individuals who have attained age 55 by January 1, 2012, and, pursuant to the rule of paragraph (b)(1)(ii)(A), the plan satisfies the safe harbor with respect to individuals who have not yet attained 55 by January 1, 2012.

(iii) Conclusion where plan provides choice-of benefits to older workers and greater-of benefits to younger participants. If, in addition to the facts in paragraph (i) of this Example 5, the plan were also to provide participants who had not yet attained age 55 by January 1, 2012, the greater of the benefits under the average annual compensation benefit formula or the benefits under the hypothetical account balance formula, then pursuant to the rules of paragraph (b)(1)(ii)(A) and (D) of this section, the safe harbor would not be satisfied with respect to participants who have attained age 55 by January 1, 2012.

*(2) Indexed benefits.* (i) In general. Except as provided in paragraph (b)(2)(iii) of this section, pursuant to section 411(b)(5)(E) and this paragraph (b)(2)(i), a defined benefit plan is not treated as failing to meet the requirements of sec-

tion 411(b)(1)(H) with respect to a participant solely because a benefit formula (other than a lump sum-based benefit formula) under the plan provides for the periodic adjustment of the participant's accrued benefit under the plan by means of the application of a recognized index or methodology. For purpose of the preceding sentence, a rate that does not exceed a market rate of return, as defined in paragraph (d) of this section, is deemed to be a recognized index or methodology. However, such a plan must satisfy the qualification requirements otherwise applicable to statutory hybrid plans, including the requirements of § 1.411(a)(13)-1(c) (relating to minimum vesting standards) and paragraph (c) of this section (relating to plan conversion amendments).

(ii) Similarly situated participant test. Paragraph (b)(2)(i) of this section does not apply unless the aggregate adjustments made to a participant's accrued benefit under the plan (determined as a percentage of the unadjusted accrued benefit) in a period would not be less than the aggregate adjustments for any similarly situated, younger participant. This test requires a comparison, for each period, of the aggregate adjustments for each individual who is or could be a participant in the plan for the period with the aggregate adjustments of each other similarly situated, younger individual who is or could be a participant in the plan for that period. See paragraph (b)(5) of this section for rules regarding whether each younger individual who is or could be a participant is similarly situated to a participant.

(iii) Protection against loss. (A) In general. Paragraph (b)(2)(i) of this section does not apply unless the plan satisfies section 411(b)(5)(E)(ii) and paragraph (d)(2) of this section (relating to preservation of capital).

(B) Exception for variable annuity benefit formulas. The requirement to satisfy section 411(b)(5)(B)(i)(II), as set forth in paragraph (d)(2) of this section, as well as section 411(b)(5)(E)(ii), as set forth in this paragraph (b)(2)(iii), does not apply in the case of a benefit provided under a variable annuity benefit formula as defined in § 1.411(a)(13)-1(d)(6).

*(3) Certain offsets permitted.* A plan is not treated as failing to meet the requirements of section 411(b)(1)(H) solely because the plan provides offsets against benefits under the plan to the extent the offsets are allowable in applying the requirements of section 401(a) and the applicable requirements of the Employee Retirement Income Security Act of 1974, Public Law 93-406 (88 Stat. 829 (1974)), and the Age Discrimination in Employment Act of 1967, Public Law 90-202 (81 Stat. 602 (1967)).

*(4) Permitted disparities in plan contributions or benefits.* A plan is not treated as failing to meet the requirements of section 411(b)(1)(H) solely because the plan provides a disparity in contributions or benefits with respect to which the requirements of section 401(l) are met.

*(5) Definition of similarly situated.* For purposes of paragraphs (b)(1) and (b)(2) of this section, an individual is similarly situated to another individual if the individual is identical to that other individual in every respect that is relevant in determining a participant's benefit under the plan (including period of service, compensation, position, date of hire, work history, and any other respect) except for age. In determining whether an individual is similarly situated to another individual, any characteristic that is relevant for determining benefits under the plan and that is based directly or indirectly on age is disregarded. For example, if a particular benefit formula applies to a participant on account of the participant's age, an individual to whom the benefit formula does not apply and who is identical to the participant in all other respects is similarly situated to the participant. By contrast, an individual is not similarly situated to a participant if a different benefit formula applies to the individual and the application of the different formula is not based directly or indirectly on age.

**(c) Special rules for plan conversion amendments.** *(1) In general.* Pursuant to section 411(b)(5)(B)(ii), (iii), and (iv), if there is a conversion amendment within the meaning of paragraph (c)(4) of this section with respect to a defined benefit plan, then the plan is treated as failing to meet the requirements of section 411(b)(1)(H) unless the plan, after the amendment, satisfies the requirements of paragraph (c)(2) of this section.

*(2) Separate calculation of post-conversion benefit.* (i) In general. A statutory hybrid plan satisfies the requirements of this paragraph (c)(2) if the plan provides that, in the case of an individual who was a participant in the plan immediately before the date of adoption of the conversion amendment, the participant's benefit at any subsequent annuity starting date is not less than the sum of—

(A) The participant's section 411(d)(6) protected benefit (as defined in § 1.411(d)-3(g)(14)) with respect to service before the effective date of the conversion amendment, determined under the terms of the plan as in effect immediately before the effective date of the conversion amendment; and

(B) The participant's section 411(d)(6) protected benefit with respect to service on and after the effective date of the conversion amendment, determined under the terms of the plan as in effect after the effective date of the conversion amendment.

(ii) Rules of application. For purposes of this paragraph (c)(2), except as provided in paragraph (c)(3) of this section, the benefits under paragraphs (c)(2)(i)(A) and (c)(2)(i)(B) of this section must each be determined in the same manner as if they were provided under separate plans that are independent of each other (for example, without any benefit offsets), and, except to the extent permitted under § 1.411(d)-3 or § 1.411(d)-4 (or other applicable law), each optional form of payment provided under the terms of the plan with respect to a participant's section 411(d)(6) protected benefit as in effect before the conversion amendment must be available thereafter to the extent of the plan's benefits for service prior to the effective date of the conversion amendment.

*(3) Establishment of opening hypothetical account balance or opening accumulated percentage.* (i) In general. Provided that the requirements of paragraph (c)(3)(ii) or (c)(3)(iii) of this section are satisfied, a statutory hybrid plan under which an opening hypothetical account balance or opening accumulated percentage of the participant's final average compensation is established as of the effective date of the conversion amendment does not fail to satisfy the requirements of paragraph (c)(2) of this section merely because benefits attributable to that opening hypothetical account balance or opening accumulated percentage (that is, benefits that are not described in paragraph (c)(2)(i)(B) of this section) are substituted for benefits described in paragraph (c)(2)(i)(A) of this section.

(ii) Comparison of benefits at annuity starting date. (A) Testing requirement. The requirements of this paragraph (c)(3)(ii) are satisfied with respect to an optional form of benefit payable at an annuity starting date only if the plan provides that the amount of the benefit payable in that optional form under the lump sum-based benefit formula that is attributable to the opening hypothetical account balance or opening accumulated percentage as described in paragraph (c)(3)(i) of this section is not less than the benefit under the comparable optional form of benefit under paragraph (c)(2)(i)(A) of this section. To satisfy this requirement, if the benefit under the optional form attributable to the opening hypothetical account balance or opening accumulated percentage is less than the benefit under the comparable optional form of benefit described in paragraph (c)(2)(i)(A) of this section, then the benefit attributable to the opening hypothetical account balance or opening accumulated percentage must be increased to the extent necessary to provide the minimum benefit described in this paragraph (c)(3)(ii). Thus, if a plan is using the option under this paragraph (c)(3)(ii) to satisfy paragraph (c)(2) of this section with respect to a participant, the participant must receive a benefit equal to not less than the sum of—

(1) The benefit described in paragraph (c)(2)(i)(B) of this section; and

(2) The greater of—

(i) The benefit attributable to the opening hypothetical account balance or attributable to the opening accumulated percentage of the participant's final average compensation as described in this paragraph (c)(3)(ii); or

(ii) The benefit described in paragraph (c)(2)(i)(A) of this section.

(B) Comparable optional form of benefit. If there was an optional form of benefit within the same generalized optional form of benefit (within the meaning of § 1.411(d)-3(g)(8)) that would have been available to the participant at that annuity starting date under the terms of the plan as in effect immediately before the effective date of the conversion amendment, then that optional form of benefit is the comparable optional form of benefit.

(C) Special rule for new post-conversion optional forms of benefit. If an optional form of benefit is available on the annuity starting date with respect to the benefit attributable to the opening hypothetical account balance or opening accumulated percentage, but no optional form within the same generalized optional form of benefit (within the meaning of § 1.411(d)-3(g)(8)) was available at that annuity starting date under the terms of the plan as in effect immediately prior to the effective date of the conversion amendment, then, for purposes of this paragraph (c)(3)(ii), the plan is treated as if such an optional form of benefit were available immediately prior to the effective date of the conversion amendment for purposes of this paragraph (c)(3)(ii). Thus, for example, if a single-sum optional form of payment is not available under the plan terms applicable to the accrued benefit described in paragraph (c)(2)(i)(A) of this section, but a single-sum optional form of payment is available with respect to the benefit attributable to the opening hypothetical account balance or opening accumulated percentage as of the annuity starting date, then, for purposes of this paragraph (c)(3)(ii), the plan is treated as if a single sum (which satisfies the requirements of section 417(e)(3)) were available under the terms of the plan as in effect immediately prior to the effective date of the conversion amendment.

(iii) Comparison of benefits at effective date of conversion amendment. [Reserved].

*(4) Conversion amendment.* (i) In general. An amendment is a conversion amendment that is subject to the requirements of this paragraph (c) with respect to a participant if—

(A) The amendment reduces or eliminates the benefits that, but for the amendment, the participant would have accrued after the effective date of the amendment under a benefit formula that is not a statutory hybrid benefit formula (and under which the participant was accruing benefits prior to the amendment); and

(B) After the effective date of the amendment, all or a portion of the participant's benefit accruals under the plan are determined under a statutory hybrid benefit formula.

(ii) Rules of application. (A) In general. Paragraphs (c)(4)(iii), (iv), and (v) of this section describe special rules that treat certain arrangements as conversion amendments. The rules described in those paragraphs apply both separately and in combination. Thus, for example, in an acquisition described in § 1.410(b)-2(f), if the buyer adopts an amendment under which a participant's benefits under the seller's plan that is not a statutory hybrid plan are coordinated with a separate plan of the buyer that is a statutory hybrid plan, such as through an offset of the participant's benefit under the buyer's plan by the participant's benefit under the seller's plan, the seller and buyer are treated as a single employer under paragraph (c)(4)(iv) of this section and they are treated as having adopted a conversion amendment under paragraph (c)(4)(iii) of this section. However, pursuant to paragraph (c)(4)(iii) of this section, if there is no coordination between the two plans, there is no conversion amendment.

(B) Covered amendments. Only amendments that eliminate or reduce accrued benefits described in section 411(a)(7), or a retirement-type subsidy described in section 411(d)(6)(B)(i), that would otherwise accrue as a result of future service are treated as amendments described in paragraph (c)(4)(i)(A) of this section.

(C) Operation of plan terms treated as covered amendment. If, under the terms of a plan, a change in the conditions of a participant's employment results in a reduction of the participant's benefits that would have accrued in the future under a benefit formula that is not a statutory hybrid benefit formula, the plan is treated for purposes of this paragraph (c)(4) as if such plan terms constitute an amendment that reduces the participant's benefits that would have accrued after the effective date of the change under a benefit formula that is not a statutory hybrid benefit formula. Thus, for example, if a participant transfers from an operating division that is covered by a non-statutory hybrid benefit formula to an operating division that is covered by a statutory hybrid benefit formula, there has been a conversion amendment and the effective date of the conversion amendment is the date of the transfer. For purposes of applying the effective date rule of paragraph (f)(1)(ii) of this section, the date that the relevant plan terms were adopted is treated as the adoption date of the amendment.

(iii) Multiple plans. An employer is treated as having adopted a conversion amendment if the employer adopts an amendment under which a participant's benefits under a plan that is not a statutory hybrid plan are coordinated with a separate plan that is a statutory hybrid plan, such as through a reduction (offset) of the benefit under the plan that is not a statutory hybrid plan.

(iv) Multiple employers. If the employer of an employee changes as a result of a transaction described in § 1.410(b)-2(f), then the two employers are treated as a single employer for purposes of this paragraph (c)(4).

(v) Multiple amendments. (A) In general. (1) General rule. For purposes of this paragraph (c)(4), a conversion amendment includes multiple amendments that result in a conversion amendment even if the amendments are not conversion amendments individually. For example, an employer is treated as having adopted a conversion amendment if the employer first adopts an amendment described in paragraph (c)(4)(i)(A) of this section and, at a later date, adopts an amendment that adds a benefit under a statutory hybrid benefit formula as described in paragraph (c)(4)(i)(B) of this section, if they are consolidated under paragraph (c)(4)(v)(A)(2) of this section.

(2) Delay between plan amendments. In determining whether a conversion amendment has been adopted, an amendment to provide a benefit under a statutory hybrid benefit formula is consolidated with a prior amendment to reduce non-statutory hybrid benefit formula benefits if the amendment providing benefits under a statutory hybrid benefit formula is adopted within three years after adoption of the amendment reducing non-statutory hybrid benefit formula benefits. Thus, the later adoption of the statutory hybrid benefit formula will cause the earlier amendment to be treated as part of a conversion amendment. In the case of an amendment to provide a benefit under a statutory hybrid benefit formula that is adopted more than three years after adoption of an amendment to reduce benefits under a non-statutory hybrid benefit formula, there is a presumption that the amendments are not consolidated unless the facts and circumstances indicate that adoption of the amendment to provide a benefit under a statutory hybrid benefit formula was intended at the time of reduction in the non-statutory hybrid benefit formula.

(B) Multiple conversion amendments. If an employer adopts multiple amendments reducing benefits described in paragraph (c)(4)(i)(A) of this section, each amendment is treated as a separate conversion amendment, provided that paragraph (c)(4)(i)(B) of this section is applicable at the time of the amendment (taking into account the rules of this paragraph (c)(4)).

(vi) Effective date of a conversion amendment. The effective date of a conversion amendment is, with respect to a participant, the date as of which the reduction of the participant's benefits described in paragraph (c)(4)(i)(A) of this section occurs. In accordance with section 411(d)(6), the date of a reduction of those benefits cannot be earlier than the date of adoption of the conversion amendment.

*(5) Examples.* The following examples illustrate the application of this paragraph (c):

*Example (1).* (i) Facts where plan does not establish opening hypothetical account balance for participants and participant elects life annuity at normal retirement age. Employer N sponsors Plan E, a defined benefit plan that provides an accumulated benefit, payable as a straight life annuity commencing at age 65 (which is Plan E's normal retirement age), based on a percentage of highest average compensation times the participant's years of service. Plan E permits any participant who has had a severance from employment to elect payment in the following optional forms of benefit (with spousal consent if applicable), with any payment not made in a straight life annuity converted to an equivalent form based on reasonable actuarial assumptions: A straight life annuity; and a 50 percent, 75 percent, or 100 percent joint and survivor annuity. The payment of benefits may commence at any time after attainment of age 55, with an actuarial reduction if the commencement is before normal retirement age. In addition, the plan offers a single-sum payment after attainment of age 55 equal to the present value of the normal retirement benefit using the applicable interest rate and mortality table under section 417(e)(3) in effect under the terms of the plan on the annuity starting date.

(ii) Facts relating to the conversion amendment. On January 1, 2012, Plan E is amended to eliminate future accruals under the highest average compensation benefit formula and to base future benefit accruals under a hypothetical account balance formula. For service on or after January 1, 2012, each participant's hypothetical account balance is credited monthly with a pay credit equal to a specified percentage of the participant's compensation during the month and also with interest based on the third segment rate described in section 430(h)(2)(C)(iii). With respect to benefits under the hypothetical account balance attributable to service on and after January 1, 2012, a participant is permitted to elect (with spousal consent if applicable) payment in the same generalized optional forms of benefit (even though different actuarial factors apply) as under the terms of the plan in effect before January 1, 2012, and also as a single-sum distribution. The plan provides for the benefit attributable to service before January 1, 2012, to be determined under the terms of the plan as in effect immediately before the effective date of the amendment, and the benefit attributable to service on and after January 1, 2012, to be determined separately, under the terms of the plan as in effect after the effective date of the amendment, with neither benefit offsetting the other in any manner. Thus, each participant's benefit is equal to the sum of the benefit attributable to service before January 1, 2012 (to be determined under the terms of the plan as in effect immediately before the effective date of the amendment), plus the benefit attributable to the participant's hypothetical account balance.

(iii) Facts relating to an affected participant. Participant A is age 62 on January 1, 2012. On December 31, 2011, A's benefit for years of service before January 1, 2012, payable as a straight life annuity commencing at A's normal retirement age (age 65), which is January 1, 2015, is $1,000 per month. On January 1, 2015, when Participant A has a severance from employment, the then-current hypothetical account balance, with pay credits and interest from January 1, 2012, to January 1, 2015, is $11,000. Using the conversion factors applicable under the plan on January 1, 2015, that balance is equivalent to a straight life annuity of $100 per month commencing on January 1, 2015. This benefit is in addition to the benefit attributable to service before January 1, 2012. Participant A elects (with spousal consent) a straight life annuity of $1,100 per month commencing January 1, 2015.

(iv) Conclusion. Participant A's benefit satisfies the requirements of paragraph (c) of this section because Participant A's benefit is not less than the sum of Participant A's section 411(d)(6) protected benefit (as defined in § 1.411(d)-3(g)(14)) with respect to service before the effective date of the conversion amendment, determined under the terms of the plan as in effect immediately before the effective date of the amendment, and Participant A's section 411(d)(6) protected benefit with respect to service on and after the effective date of the conversion amendment, determined under the terms of the plan as in effect after the effective date of the amendment.

*Example (2).* (i) Facts involving plan's establishment of opening hypothetical account balance and payment of preconversion accumulated benefit in life annuity at normal retirement age. Except as indicated in this Example 2, the facts are the same as the facts under paragraph (i) of Example 1.

(ii) Facts relating to the conversion amendment. On January 1, 2012, Plan E is amended to eliminate future accruals under the highest average compensation benefit formula and to provide future benefit accruals under a hypothetical account balance formula. An opening hypothetical account balance is established for each participant, and, under the plan's terms, that balance is equal to the present value of the participant's accumulated benefit on December 31, 2011 (payable as a straight life annuity at normal retirement age or immediately, if later), using the applicable interest rate and applicable mortality table under section 417(e)(3) on January 1, 2012. Under Plan E, the account based on this opening hypothetical account balance is maintained as a separate account from the account for accruals on or after January 1, 2012. The hypothetical account balance maintained for each participant for accruals on or after January 1, 2012, is credited monthly with a pay credit equal to a specified percentage of the participant's compensation during the month. A participant's hypothetical account balance (including both of the separate accounts) is credited monthly with interest based on the third segment rate described in section 430(h)(2)(C)(iii).

(iii) Facts relating to optional forms of benefit. Following severance from employment and attainment of age 55, a participant is permitted to elect (with spousal consent, if applicable) payment in the same generalized optional forms of benefit as under the plan in effect prior to January 1, 2012, with the amount payable calculated based on the hypothetical account balance on the annuity starting date and the applicable interest rate and applicable mortality table on the annuity starting date. The single-sum distribution is equal to the hypothetical account balance.

(iv) Facts relating to conversion protection. The plan provides that, as of a participant's annuity starting date, the plan will determine whether the benefit attributable to the opening hypothetical account balance payable in the particular optional form of benefit selected is equal to or greater than the benefit accrued under the plan through the date of conversion and payable in the same generalized optional form of benefit with the same annuity starting date. If the benefit attributable to the opening hypothetical account balance is equal to or greater than the pre-conversion benefit, the plan provides that such benefit is paid in lieu of the pre-conversion benefit, together with the benefit attributable to post-conversion pay-based principal credits. If the benefit attributable to the opening hypothetical account balance is less than the pre-conversion benefit, the plan provides that such benefit is increased sufficiently to provide the pre-conversion benefit, together with the benefit attributable to post-conversion pay-based principal credits.

(v) Facts relating to an affected participant. On January 1, 2012, the opening hypothetical account balance established for Participant A is $80,000, which is the present value of Participant A's straight life annuity of $1,000 per month commencing at January 1, 2015, using the applicable interest rate and applicable mortality table under section 417(e)(3) in effect on January 1, 2012. On January 1, 2012, the applicable interest rate for Participant A is equivalent to a level rate of 5.5 percent. Thereafter, Participant A's hypothetical account balance for subsequent accruals is credited monthly with a pay credit equal to a specified percentage of the participant's compensation during the month. In addition, Participant A's hypothetical account balance (including both of the separate accounts) is credited monthly with interest based on the third segment rate described in section 430(h)(2)(C)(iii).

(vi) Facts relating to calculation of the participant's benefit. Participant A has a severance from employment on January 1, 2015 at age 65, and elects (with spousal consent) a straight life annuity commencing January 1, 2015. On January 1, 2015, the opening hypothetical account balance, with interest credits from January 1, 2012, to January 1, 2015, has become $95,000, which, using the conversion factors under the plan on January 1, 2015, is equivalent to a straight life annuity of $1,005 per month commencing on January 1, 2015 (which is greater than the $1,000 a month payable at age 65 under the terms of the plan in effect before January 1, 2012). This benefit is in addition to the benefit determined using the hypothetical account balance for service after January 1, 2012.

(vii) Conclusion. The benefit satisfies the requirements of paragraph (c)(3)(ii)(A) of this section with respect to Participant A because A's benefit is not less than the sum of (A) the greater of Participant A's benefits attributable to the opening hypothetical account balance and A's section 411(d)(6) protected benefit (as defined in § 1.411(d)-3(g)(14)) with respect to service before the effective date of the conversion amendment, determined under the terms of the plan as in effect immediately before the effective date of the amendment, and (B) Participant A's section 411(d)(6) protected benefit with respect to service on and after the effective date of the conversion amendment, determined under the terms of the plan as in effect after the effective date of the amendment.

*Example (3).* (i) Facts involving a subsequent decrease in interest rates. The facts are the same as in Example 2, except that, because of a decrease in bond rates after January 1, 2012, and before January 1, 2015, the rate of interest credited in that period averages less than 5.5 percent, and, on January 1, 2015, the effective applicable interest rate under section 417(e)(3) under the plan's terms is 4.7 percent. As a result, Participant A's opening hypothetical account balance plus attributable interest credits has increased to only $87,000 on January 1, 2015, and, using the conversion factors under the plan on January 1, 2015, is equivalent to a straight life annuity commencing on January 1, 2015, of $775 per month. Under the terms of Plan E, the benefit attributable to A's opening hypothetical account balance is increased so that A's straight life annuity commencing on January 1, 2015, is $1,000 per month. This benefit is in addition to the benefit attributable to the hypothetical account balance for service after January 1, 2012.

(ii) Conclusion. The benefit satisfies the requirements of paragraph (c)(3)(ii)(A) of this section with respect to Participant A because A's benefit is not less than the sum of—

(A) The greater of A's benefits attributable to the opening hypothetical account balance and A's section 411(d)(6) protected benefit (as defined in § 1.411(d)-3(g)(14)) with respect to service before the effective date of the conversion amendment, determined under the terms of the plan as in effect immediately before the effective date of the amendment; and

(B) A's section 411(d)(6) protected benefit with respect to service on and after the effective date of the conversion amendment, determined under the terms of the plan as in effect after the effective date of the amendment.

*Example (4).* (i) Facts involving payment of a subsidized early retirement benefit. The facts are the same as in Example 2, except that under the terms of Plan E on December 31, 2011, a participant who retires before age 65 and after age 55 with 30 years of service has only a 3 percent per year actuarial reduction. Participant A has a severance from employment on January 1, 2013, when A is age 63 and has 30 years of service. On January 1, 2013, A's opening hypothetical account balance, with interest from January 1, 2012, to January 1, 2013, has become $86,000, which, using the conversion factors under the plan (as amended) on January 1, 2013, is equivalent to a straight life annuity commencing on January 1, 2013, of $850 per month.

(ii) Facts relating to calculation of the participant's benefit. Under the terms of Plan E on December 31, 2011, Participant A is entitled to a straight life annuity commencing on January 1, 2013, equal to at least $940 per month ($1,000 reduced by 3 percent for each of the 2 years that A's benefits commence before normal retirement age). Under the terms of Plan E, the benefit attributable to A's opening account balance is increased so that A is entitled to a straight life annuity of $940 per month commencing on January 1, 2015. This benefit is in addition to the benefit determined using the hypothetical account balance for service after January 1, 2012.

(iii) Conclusion. The benefit satisfies the requirements of paragraph (c)(3)(ii)(A) of this section with respect to Participant A because A's benefit is not less than the sum of—

(A) The greater of Participant A's benefits attributable to the opening hypothetical account balance (increased by attributable interest credits) and A's section 411(d)(6) protected benefit (as defined in § 1.411(d)-3(g)(14)) with respect to service before the effective date of the conversion amendment, determined under the terms of the plan as in effect immediately before the effective date of the amendment; and

(B) Participant A's section 411(d)(6) protected benefit with respect to service on and after the effective date of the conversion amendment, determined under the terms of the plan as in effect after the effective date of the amendment.

*Example (5).* (i) Facts involving addition of a single-sum payment option. The facts are the same as in Example 2, except that, before January 1, 2012, Plan E did not offer payment in a single-sum distribution for amounts in excess of $5,000. Plan E, as amended on January 1, 2012, offers payment in any of the available annuity distribution forms commencing at any time following severance from employment as were provided under Plan E before January 1, 2012. In addition, Plan E, as amended on January 1, 2012, offers payment in the form of a single sum attributable to service before January 1, 2012, which is the greater of the opening hypothetical account balance (increased by attributable interest credits) or a single-sum distribution of the straight life annuity payable at age 65 using the same actuarial factors as are used for mandatory cashouts for amounts equal to $5,000 or less under the terms of the plan on December 31, 2011. Participant B is age 40 on January 1, 2012, and B's opening hypothetical account balance (increased by attributable interest credits) is $33,000 (which is the present value, using the conversion factors under the plan (as amended) on January 1, 2012, of Participant B's straight life annuity of $1,000 per month commencing at January 1, 2037, which is when B will be age 65). Participant B has a severance from employment on January 1, 2015, and elects (with spousal consent) an immediate single-sum distribution. Participant B's opening hypothetical account balance (increased by attributable interest) on January 1, 2015, is $45,000. The present value, on January 1, 2015, of Participant B's benefit of $1,000 per month, commencing immediately using the actuarial factors for mandatory cashouts under the terms of the plan on December 31, 2011, would result in a single-sum payment of $44,750. Participant B is paid a single-sum distribution equal to the sum of $45,000 plus an amount equal to B's January 1, 2015, hypothetical account balance for benefit accruals for service after January 1, 2012.

(ii) Conclusion. Because, under Plan E, Participant B is entitled to the sum of—

(A) The greater of the $45,000 opening hypothetical account balance (increased by attributable interest credits) and $44,750 (present value of the benefit with respect to service prior to January 1, 2012, using the actuarial factors for mandatory cashout distributions under the terms of the plan on December 31, 2011); and

(B) An amount equal to B's hypothetical account balance for benefit accruals for service after January 1, 2012, the benefit satisfies the requirements of paragraph (c)(3)(ii)(A) of this section with respect to Participant B. If Participant B's hypothetical account balance under Plan E was instead less than $44,750 on January 1, 2015, Participant B would be entitled to a single-sum payment equal to the sum of $44,750 and an amount equal to B's hypothetical account balance for benefit accruals for service after January 1, 2012.

*Example (6).* (i) Facts involving addition of new annuity optional form of benefit. The facts are the same as in Example 2, except that, after December 31, 2011, and before January 1, 2015, Plan E is amended to offer payment in a 5-, 10-, or 15-year term certain and life annuity, using the same actuarial assumptions that apply for other optional forms of distribution. When Participant A has a severance from employment on January 1, 2015, A elects (with spousal consent) a 5-year term certain and life annuity commencing immediately equal to $935 per month. Application of the same actuarial assumptions to Participant A's benefit of $1,000 per month (under Plan E as in effect on December 31, 2011), commencing immediately on January 1, 2015, would result in a 5-year term certain and life annuity commencing immediately equal to $955 per month. Under the terms of Plan E, the benefit attributable to A's opening account balance is increased so that, using the conversion factors under the plan (as amended) on January 1, 2015, A's opening hypothetical account balance (increased by attributable interest credits) produces a 5-year term certain and life annuity commencing immediately equal to $955 per month commencing on January 1, 2015. This benefit is in addition to the benefit determined using the January 1, 2015, hypothetical account balance for service after January 1, 2012.

(ii) Conclusion. This benefit satisfies the requirements of paragraph (c)(3)(ii)(A) of this section with respect to Participant A.

*Example (7).* (i) Facts involving addition of distribution option before age 55. The facts are the same as in Example 5, except that Participant B (age 43) elects (with spousal consent) a straight life annuity commencing immediately on January 1, 2015. Under Plan E, the straight life annuity attributable to Participant B's opening hypothetical account balance at age 43 is $221 per month. Application of the same actuarial assumptions to Participant B's benefit of $1,000 per month commencing at age 65 (under Plan E as in effect on December 31, 2011) would result in a straight life annuity commencing immediately on January 1, 2015, equal to $219 per month.

(ii) Conclusion. Because, under its terms, Plan E provides that Participant B is entitled to an amount not less than the present value (using the same actuarial assumptions as apply on January 1, 2015, in converting the $45,000 hypothetical account balance attributable to the opening hypothetical account balance to the $221 straight life annuity) of Participant B's straight life annuity of $1,000 per month commencing at age 65, and the $221 straight life annuity is in addition to the benefit accruals for service after January 1, 2012, payment of the $221 monthly annuity would satisfy the requirements of paragraph (c)(3)(ii)(A) of this section with respect to Participant B.

**(d) Market rate of return.**

*(1) In general.* (i) Basic test. Subject to the rules of paragraph (e) of this section, a statutory hybrid plan satisfies the requirements of section 411(b)(1)(H) and this paragraph (d) only if, for any plan year, the interest crediting rate with respect to benefits determined under a statutory hybrid benefit formula is not greater than a market rate of return.

(ii) Definitions relating to market rate of return. (A) Interest credit. Subject to other rules in this paragraph (d), an interest credit for purposes of this paragraph (d) and section 411(b)(5)(B) means the following adjustments to a participant's accumulated benefit under a statutory hybrid benefit formula, to the extent not conditioned on current service and not made on account of imputed service (as defined in § 1.401(a)(4)-11(d)(3)(ii)(B))—

(1) Any increase or decrease for a period, under the terms of the plan at the beginning of the period, that is calculated by applying a rate of interest or rate of return (including a rate of increase or decrease under an index) to the participant's accumulated benefit (or a portion thereof) as of the beginning of the period; and

(2) Any other increase for a period, under the terms of the plan at the beginning of the period.

(B) Treatment of plan amendments. An increase to a participant's accumulated benefit is not treated as an interest credit to the extent the increase is made as a result of a plan amendment providing for a one-time adjustment to the participant's accumulated benefit. However, a pattern of repeated plan amendments each of which provides for a one-time adjustment to a participant's accumulated benefit will cause such adjustments to be treated as provided on a permanent basis under the terms of the plan. See § 1.411(d)-4, A-1(c)(1).

(C) Interest crediting rate. Except as otherwise provided in this paragraph (d), the interest crediting rate, or effective rate of return, for a period with respect to a participant equals the total amount of interest credits for the period divided by the participant's accumulated benefit at the beginning of the period.

(D) Principal credit. For purposes of this paragraph (d), a principal credit means any increase to a participant's accumulated benefit under a statutory hybrid benefit formula that is not an interest credit. Thus, for example, a principal credit includes an increase to a participant's accumulated benefit to the extent the increase is conditioned on current service or made on account of imputed service. As a result, a principal credit includes an increase to the value of an accumulated percentage of the participant's final average compensation. For indexed benefits described in paragraph (b)(2) of this section, a principal credit includes an increase to the participant's accrued benefit other than an increase provided by indexing. In addition, pursuant to the rule in paragraph (d)(1)(ii)(B) of this section, a principal credit generally includes an increase to a participant's accumulated benefit to the extent the increase is made as a result of a plan amendment providing for a one-time adjustment to the participant's accumulated benefit. As a result, a principal credit includes an opening hypothetical account balance or opening accumulated percentage of the participant's final average compensation, as described in paragraph (c)(3) of this section.

(iii) Market rate of return for single rates. Except as otherwise provided in this paragraph (d)(1), an interest crediting rate is not in excess of a market rate of return only if the plan terms provide that the interest credit for each plan year is determined using one of the following specified interest crediting rates:

(A) The interest rate on long-term investment grade corporate bonds (as described in paragraph (d)(3) of this section).

(B) An interest rate that, under paragraph (d)(4) of this section, is deemed to be not in excess of the interest rate described in paragraph (d)(3) of this section.

(C) A rate of return that, under paragraph (d)(5) of this section, is not in excess of a market rate of return.

(iv) Timing and other rules related to interest crediting rate. (A) In general. A plan that provides interest credits must specify how the plan determines interest credits and must specify how and when interest credits are credited. The plan must specify the method for determining interest credits in accordance with the requirements of paragraph (d)(1)(iv)(B) of this section, the frequency of interest crediting in accordance with the requirements of paragraph (d)(1)(iv)(C) of this section, and the treatment of interest credits on distributed amounts, as well as other debits and credits during the period, in accordance with the rules of paragraph (d)(1)(iv)(D) of this section. See paragraph (e) of this section for additional rules that apply to changes in the interest crediting rate.

(B) Methods to determine interest credits. A plan that is using any specified interest crediting rate can determine interest credits for each current interest crediting period based on the effective periodic interest crediting rate that applies over the period. Alternatively, a plan that is using one of the interest crediting rates described in paragraph (d)(3) or (d)(4) of this section can determine interest credits for a stability period based on the interest crediting rate for a specified lookback month with respect to that stability period. For purposes of the preceding sentence, the stability period and lookback month must satisfy the rules for selecting the stability period and lookback month under § 1.417(e)-1(d)(4), although the interest crediting rate can be any one of the rates in paragraph (d)(3) or (d)(4) of this section and the stability period and lookback month need not be the same as those used under the plan for purposes of section 417(e)(3).

(C) Frequency of interest crediting. Interest credits under a plan must be provided on an annual or more frequent periodic basis and interest credits for each interest crediting period must be credited as of the end of the period. If a plan provides for the crediting of interest more frequently than annually (for example, daily, monthly or quarterly) based on one of the annual interest rates described in paragraph (d)(3) or (d)(4) of this section, then the plan generally provides an above market rate of return unless each periodic interest credit is determined using an interest crediting rate that is no greater than a pro rata portion of the applicable annual interest crediting rate. However, a plan that credits interest daily based on one of the annual interest rates described in paragraph (d)(3) or (d)(4) of this section is not treated as providing an above market rate of return merely because the plan determines each daily interest credit using a daily interest crediting rate that is 1/360 of the applicable annual interest crediting rate. In addition, interest credits determined, under the terms of a plan, based on one of the annual interest rates described in paragraph (d)(3) or (d)(4) of this section are not treated as creating an effective rate of return that is in excess of a market rate of return merely because an otherwise permissible interest crediting rate for a plan year is compounded more frequently than annually. Thus, for example, if a plan's terms provide for interest to be credited monthly and for the interest crediting rate to be equal to the interest rate on long-term investment grade corporate bonds (as described in paragraph (d)(3) of this section) and the applicable annual rate on these bonds for the plan year is 6 percent, then the accumulated benefit at the beginning of each month could be increased as a result of interest credits by as much as 0.5 percent per month during the plan year without resulting in an interest crediting rate that is in excess of a market rate of return.

(D) Debits and credits during the interest crediting period. [Reserved].

(v) Lesser rates. An interest crediting rate is not in excess of a market rate of return if the rate can never be in excess of a particular rate that is described in paragraph (d)(1)(iii) of this section. Thus, for example, an interest crediting rate that always equals the rate described in paragraph (d)(3) of this section minus 200 basis points is not in excess of a market rate of return because it can never be in excess of the rate described in paragraph (d)(3) of this section. Similarly, an interest crediting rate that always equals the lesser of the yield on 30-year Treasury bonds and a fixed 6 percent interest rate is not in excess of a market rate of return because it can never be in excess of the yield on 30-year Treasury bonds.

(vi) Greater-of rates. If a statutory hybrid plan determines an interest credit by applying the greater of 2 or more different rates to the accumulated benefit, the effective interest crediting rate is not in excess of a market rate of return only if each of the different rates would separately satisfy the requirements of this paragraph (d) and the requirements of paragraph (d)(6) of this section are also satisfied.

(vii) Blended rates. A statutory hybrid plan does not provide an effective interest crediting rate that is in excess of a market rate of return merely because the plan determines an interest credit by applying different rates to different predetermined portions of the accumulated benefit, provided each rate would separately satisfy the requirements of this paragraph (d) if the rate applied to the entire accumulated benefit.

*(2) Preservation of capital requirement.* (i) General rule. A statutory hybrid plan satisfies the requirements of section 411(b)(1)(H) only if the plan provides that the participant's benefit under the statutory hybrid benefit formula determined as of the participant's annuity starting date is no less than the benefit based on the sum of all principal credits (as described in paragraph (d)(1)(ii)(D) of this section) credited under the plan to the participant as of that date (including principal credits that were credited before the applicable statutory effective date of paragraph (f)(1) of this section).

(ii) Application to multiple annuity starting dates. [Reserved].

(iii) Exception for variable annuity benefit formulas. See paragraph (b)(2)(iii)(B) of this section for an exception to this paragraph (d)(2).

*(3) Long-term investment grade corporate bonds.* For purposes of this paragraph (d), the rate of interest on long-term investment grade corporate bonds means the third segment rate described in section 417(e)(3)(D) or 430(h)(2)(C)(iii) (determined with or without regard to the transition rules of section 417(e)(3)(D)(ii) or 430(h)(2)(G)). However, for plan years beginning prior to January 1, 2008, the rate of interest on long-term investment grade corporate bonds means the rate described in section 412(b)(5)(B)(ii)(II) prior to amendment by the Pension Protection Act of 2006, Public Law 109-280 (120 Stat. 780) (PPA '06).

*(4) Safe harbor rates of interest.* (i) In general. This paragraph (d)(4) identifies interest rates that are deemed to be not in excess of the interest rate described in paragraph (d)(3) of this section. The Commissioner may, in guidance of general applicability, specify additional interest crediting rates that are deemed to be not in excess of the rate described in paragraph (d)(3) of this section. See § 601.601(d)(2)(ii)(b).

(ii) Rates based on bonds with margins. (A) In general. An interest crediting rate is deemed to be not in excess of the interest rate described in paragraph (d)(3) of this section if the rate is equal to the sum of any of the following rates of interest for bonds and the associated margin for that interest rate:

| Interest rate bond index | Associated margin |
|---|---|
| The discount rate on 3-month Treasury Bills. | 175 basis points. |
| The discount rate on 12-month or shorter Treasury Bills. | 150 basis points. |
| The yield on 1-year Treasury Constant Maturities. | 100 basis points. |
| The yield on 3-year or shorter Treasury bonds. | 50 basis points. |
| The yield on 7-year or shorter Treasury bonds. | 25 basis points. |
| The yield on 30-year or shorter Treasury bonds. | 0 basis points. |
| The first segment rate | 0 basis points. |
| The second segment rate | 0 basis points. |

(B) Rule of application. For purposes of this paragraph (d)(4), the first and second segment rates mean the first and second segment rates described in section 417(e)(3)(D) or 430(h)(2)(C), determined with or without regard to the transition rules of section 417(e)(3)(D)(ii) or 430(h)(2)(G).

(iii) Eligible cost-of-living indices. An interest crediting rate is deemed to be not in excess of the interest rate described in paragraph (d)(3) of this section if the rate is adjusted no less frequently than annually and is equal to the rate of increase with respect to an eligible cost-of-living index described in § 1.401(a)(9)-6, A-14(b), except that, for purposes of this paragraph (d)(4)(iii), the eligible cost-of-living index described in § 1.401(a)(9)-6, A-14(b)(2) is increased by 300 basis points.

(iv) Fixed rate of interest. [Reserved].

*(5) Other rates of return.* (i) General rule. This paragraph (d)(5) sets forth additional methods for determining an interest crediting rate that is not in excess of a market rate of return.

(ii) Actual rate of return on plan assets. In the case of indexed benefits described in paragraph (b)(2) of this section, an interest crediting rate equal to the actual rate of return on the aggregate assets of the plan, including both positive returns and negative returns, is not in excess of a market rate of return if the plan's assets are diversified so as to minimize the volatility of returns. This requirement that plan assets be diversified so as to minimize the volatility of returns does not require greater diversification than is required under section 404(a)(1)(C) of Title I of the Employee Retirement Income Security Act of 1974, Public Law 93-406 (88 Stat. 829 (1974)) with respect to defined benefit pension plans.

(iii) Annuity contract rates. The rate of return on the annuity contract for the employee issued by an insurance company licensed under the laws of a State is not in excess of a market rate of return. However, this paragraph (d)(5)(iii) does not apply if the Commissioner determines that the annuity contract has been structured to provide an interest crediting rate that is in excess of a market rate of return.

(iv) Rate of return on certain RICs. [Reserved].

*(6) Combinations of rates of return.* (i) In general. A plan that determines interest credits based, in whole or in part, on the greater of two or more different interest crediting rates provides an effective interest crediting rate in excess of a market rate of return unless the combination of rates is described in paragraph (d)(6)(ii), (d)(6)(iii), (e)(3)(iii), or (e)(4) of this section. However, a plan is not treated as providing the greater of two or more interest crediting rates merely because the plan satisfies the requirements of paragraph (d)(2) of this section. In addition, a plan is not treated as providing the greater of two or more interest crediting rates merely because a rate of return described in paragraph (d)(5)(iii) of this section is itself based on the greater of two or more rates.

(ii) Annual or more frequent floor applied to bond-based rates. [Reserved].

(iii) Cumulative floor applied to equity-based or bond-based rates. [Reserved].

**(e) Other rules regarding market rates of return.** *(1) In general.* This paragraph (e) sets forth additional rules regarding the application of the market rate of return requirement with respect to benefits determined under a statutory hybrid benefit formula.

*(2) Plan termination.* [Reserved].

*(3) Rules relating to section 411(d)(6).* (i) General rule. The right to interest credits in the future that are not conditioned on future service constitutes a section 411(d)(6) protected benefit (as defined in § 1.411(d)-3(g)(14)). Thus, to the extent that benefits have accrued under the terms of a statutory hybrid plan that entitle the participant to future interest credits, an amendment to the plan to change the interest crediting rate must satisfy section 411(d)(6) if the revised rate under any circumstances could result in interest credits that are smaller as of any date after the applicable amendment date (within the meaning of § 1.411(d)-3(g)(4)) than the interest credits that would be provided without regard to the amendment. For additional rules, see § 1.411(d)-3(b). Paragraphs (e)(3)(ii) and (e)(3)(iii) of this section set forth special rules that apply regarding the interaction of section 411(d)(6) and changes to a plan's interest crediting rate. The Commissioner may, in guidance of general applicability, prescribe additional rules regarding the interaction of section 411(d)(6) and section 411(b)(5), including changes to a plan's interest crediting rate. See § 601.601(d)(2)(ii)(b).

(ii) Adoption of long-term investment grade corporate bond rate. For purposes of applying section 411(d)(6) and this paragraph (e) to an amendment to change to the interest crediting rate described in paragraph (d)(3) of this section, a plan is not treated as providing interest credits that are smaller as of any date after the applicable amendment date than the interest credits that would be provided using an interest crediting rate described in paragraph (d)(4) of this section merely because the plan credits interest after the applicable amendment date using the interest crediting rate described in paragraph (d)(3) of this section, provided—

(A) The amendment only applies to interest credits to be credited after the effective date of the amendment;

(B) The effective date of the amendment is at least 30 days after adoption of the amendment; and

(C) On the effective date of the amendment, the new interest crediting rate is not lower than the interest crediting rate that would have applied in the absence of the amendment.

(iii) Coordination of section 411(d)(6) and market rate of return limitation. [Reserved].

*(4) Actuarial increases after normal retirement age.* [Reserved].

**(f) Effective/applicability date.** *(1) Statutory effective/applicability dates.* (i) In general. Except as provided in paragraph (f)(1)(iii) of this section, section 411(b)(5) applies for periods beginning on or after June 29, 2005.

(ii) Conversion amendments. The requirements of section 411(b)(5)(B)(ii), 411(b)(5)(B)(iii), and 411(b)(5)(B)(iv) apply to a conversion amendment (as defined in paragraph (c)(4) of this section) that both is adopted on or after June 29, 2005, and takes effect on or after June 29, 2005.

(iii) Market rate of return. (A) Plans in existence on June 29, 2005. (1) In general. In the case of a plan that was in existence on June 29, 2005 (regardless of whether the plan was a statutory hybrid plan on that date), section 411(b)(5)(B)(i) applies to plan years that begin on or after January 1, 2008.

(2) Exception for plan sponsor election. Notwithstanding paragraph (f)(1)(iii)(A)(1) of this section, a plan sponsor of a plan that was in existence on June 29, 2005 (regardless of whether the plan was a statutory hybrid plan on that date) may elect to have the requirements of section 411(a)(13)(B) and section 411(b)(5)(B)(i) apply for any period on or after June 29, 2005, and before the first plan year beginning after December 31, 2007. In accordance with section 1107 of the PPA '06, an employer is permitted to adopt an amendment to make this election as late as the last day of the first plan year that begins on or after January 1, 2009 (January 1, 2011, in the case of a governmental plan as defined in section 414(d)) if the plan operates in accordance with the election.

(B) Plans not in existence on June 29, 2005. In the case of a plan not in existence on June 29, 2005, section 411(b)(5)(B)(i) applies to the plan on and after the later of June 29, 2005, and the date the plan becomes a statutory hybrid plan.

(iv) Collectively bargained plans. (A) In general. Notwithstanding paragraph (f)(1)(iii) of this section, in the case of a collectively bargained plan maintained pursuant to one or more collective bargaining agreements between employee representatives and one or more employers ratified on or before August 17, 2006, the requirements of section 411(b)(5)(B)(i) do not apply to plan years that begin before the earlier of—

(1) The later of—

(i) The date on which the last of those collective bargaining agreements terminates (determined without regard to any extension thereof on or after August 17, 2006); or

(ii) January 1, 2008; or

(2) January 1, 2010.

(B) Treatment of plans with both collectively bargained and non-collectively bargained employees. In the case of a plan with respect to which a collective bargaining agreement applies to some, but not all, of the plan participants, the plan is considered a collectively bargained plan for purposes of this paragraph (f)(1)(iv) if it is considered a collectively bargained plan under the rules of § 1.436-1(a)(5)(ii)(B).

*(2) Effective/applicability date of regulations.* (i) In general.

(A) General effective date. Except as provided in paragraph (f)(2)(i)(B) of this section, this section applies to plan years that begin on or after January 1, 2011.

(B) Special effective date. Paragraphs (d)(1)(iii), (d)(1)(vi), and (d)(6)(i) of this section apply to plan years that begin on or after January 1, 2012.

(ii) Conversion amendments. With respect to a conversion amendment (within the meaning of paragraph (c)(4) of this section), where the effective date of the conversion amendment (as defined in paragraph (c)(4)(vi) of this section) is on or after the statutory effective date set forth in paragraph (f)(1)(ii) of this section, the requirements of paragraph (c)(2) of this section apply only to a participant who has an hour of service on or after the regulatory effective date set forth in paragraph (f)(2)(i) of this section.

(iii) Reliance before regulatory effective date. For the periods after the statutory effective date set forth in paragraph (f)(1) of this section and before the regulatory effective date set forth in paragraph (f)(2)(i) of this section, the safe harbor and other relief of section 411(b)(5) apply and the market rate of return and other requirements of section 411(b)(5) must be satisfied. During these periods, a plan is permitted to rely on the provisions of this section for purposes of applying the relief and satisfying the requirements of section 411(b)(5).

---

T.D. 9505, 10/18/2010.

---

PAR. 4. Section 1.411(b)(5)-1 is amended by:

1. Revising paragraph (c)(3)(iii).

2. Adding Example 8 to paragraph (c)(5).

3. Revising paragraphs (d)(1)(iv)(D), (d)(2)(ii), (d)(4)(iv), (d)(5)(ii), (d)(5)(iv), (d)(6)(ii), (d)(6)(iii), (e)(2), (e)(3)(iii), (e)(4), and (f)(2)(i)(B).

The revisions and addition read as follows:

**Proposed § 1.411(b)(5)-1 Reduction in rate of benefit accrual under a defined benefit plan.** [*For Preamble, see ¶ 153,191*]

* * * * *

**(c)** * * *

*(3)* * * *

(iii) Comparison of benefits at effective date of conversion amendment. (A) In general. A plan satisfies the requirements of this paragraph (c)(3)(iii) with respect to a participant only if an opening hypothetical account balance is established to replicate the pre-conversion benefit and the requirements of paragraphs (c)(3)(iii)(B) through (c)(3)(iii)(G) of this section are each satisfied.

(B) Single-sum payment. At the annuity starting date, the participant elects to receive payment in the form of a single-sum distribution equal to the sum of the then-current balance of the hypothetical account used to replicate the pre-conversion benefit and the benefit attributable to post-conversion service under the post-conversion benefit formula.

(C) Not less than pre-conversion benefit. In accordance with section 411(d)(6), the aggregate benefit payable at the annuity starting date after the effective date of the conversion amendment is not less than the benefit described in paragraph (c)(2)(i)(A) of this section.

(D) Form of pre-conversion benefit. The plan, as in effect immediately prior to the effective date of the conversion amendment, either did not provide a single-sum payment option (for benefits that cannot be immediately distributed under section 411(a)(11)) or provided a single-sum payment option that was based solely on the present value of the benefit payable at normal retirement age (or at date of benefit commencement, if later), and which was not based on the present value of the benefit payable commencing at any date prior to normal retirement age.

(E) Minimum opening account balance. The plan provides for the opening hypothetical account balance under paragraph (c)(3)(i) of this section to be established in accordance with rules under which the amount of this opening balance will not be less than the present value, determined in accordance with section 417(e), of the participant's accrued benefit under the plan immediately prior to the effective date of the conversion amendment.

(F) Interest credits. (1) Requirement as of effective date of conversion amendment. As of the effective date of the conversion amendment, the interest crediting rate under the plan is an interest crediting rate described in paragraph (d)(3) or (d)(4) of this section. In addition, as of that date, the value of the index used to determine the interest crediting rate under the plan is at least as great for every participant or beneficiary as the interest rate that was used pursuant to paragraph (c)(3)(iii)(E) of this section to determine the opening hypothetical account balance. This requirement is satisfied, for example, if each participant's opening hypothetical account balance is determined using the applicable interest rate and applicable mortality table under section 417(e)(3), the interest crediting rate under the plan is the third segment rate, and, at the effective date of the conversion amendment, the third segment rate is the highest of the three segment rates.

(2) Requirement for later interest crediting rate changes. If, subsequent to the effective date of the conversion amendment, the interest crediting rate changes (whether by plan amendment or otherwise) with respect to a participant who was a participant at the time of the effective date of the conversion amendment from a particular interest crediting rate described in paragraph (d)(3) or (d)(4) of this section to a different interest crediting rate that is not in all cases at least as great as the prior interest crediting rate under the plan, then the new interest crediting rate does not apply to the existing hypothetical account balance as of the effective date of the change in interest crediting rates (or, if the plan created a subaccount consisting of the opening hypothetical account balance and interest credits on that subaccount, then the new interest crediting rate does not apply to the subaccount).

(G) Death benefits. The plan either—

(1) Provides a death benefit after the effective date of the conversion amendment which has a present value that is at all times at least equal to the then-current balance of the hypothetical account used to replicate the pre-conversion benefit; or

(2) Applied no pre-retirement mortality decrement in establishing the opening hypothetical account balance under paragraph (c)(3)(iii)(E) of this section.

* * * * *

*(5)* * * *

*Example (8)*. (i) Facts where plan establishes opening hypothetical account balance under paragraph (c)(3)(iii) of this section. Employer O sponsors Plan F, a defined benefit plan that provides an accumulated benefit, payable as a straight life annuity commencing at age 65 (which is Plan F's normal retirement age), based on a percentage of highest average compensation times the participant's years of service. Plan F permits any participant who has had a severance from employment to elect payment in the following optional forms of benefit (with spousal consent if applicable), with any payment not made in a straight life annuity converted to an equivalent form based on reasonable actuarial assumptions: A straight life annuity; and a 50 percent, 75 percent, or 100 percent joint and survivor annuity. The payment of benefits may commence at any time after attainment of age 55, with an actuarial reduction if the commencement is before normal retirement age. In addition, the plan offers a single-sum payment after attainment of age 55 equal to the present value of the normal retirement benefit using the applicable interest rate and mortality table under section 417(e)(3) in effect under the terms of the plan on the annuity starting date. (These facts are the same as those in paragraph (i) of Example 1.)

(ii) Facts relating to the conversion amendment and establishment of opening balance. On January 1, 2012, Plan F is amended to eliminate future accruals under the highest average compensation benefit formula and to base future benefit accruals on a hypothetical account balance. As of January 1, 2012, the plan establishes an opening hypothetical account balance for each individual who was a participant in the plan on December 31, 2011, equal to the present value of the participant's accumulated benefits, payable as a straight life annuity commencing at age 65, based on the actuarial assumptions then applicable under section 417(e)(3). New participants begin with a hypothetical account balance of zero on their date of participation. For service on or after January 1, 2012, each participant's hypothetical account balance is credited monthly with a pay credit equal to a specified percentage of the participant's compensation during the month and also with interest based on the third segment rate described in section 430(h)(2)(C)(iii). With respect to benefits under the hypothetical account balance, a participant is permitted to elect (with spousal consent) payment in the same generalized optional forms of benefit (even though different actuarial factors apply) as under the terms of the plan in effect before January 1, 2012, and also as a single-sum distribution. The plan provides that in no event will the benefit payable be less than the benefits attributable to service before January 1, 2012, to be determined under the terms of the plan as in effect immediately before the effective date of the amendment. In the event of death prior to the annuity starting date, the plan provides a death benefit equal to the hypothetical account balance (and allows a surviving spouse to elect payment in the form of an actuarially equivalent life annuity).

(iii) Conclusion. Plan F satisfies the requirements of paragraph (c)(3)(iii) of this section for participants who elect to receive payment in the form of a single-sum distribution equal to the hypothetical account balance in accordance with the requirements of paragraph (c)(3)(iii)(B) of this section for the following reasons. First, Plan F satisfies the requirements of paragraph (c)(3)(iii)(C) of this section because the benefit payable can never be less than the pre-conversion benefit, in accordance with the requirements of section 411(d)(6). Second, Plan F satisfies the requirements of paragraph (c)(3)(iii)(D) of this section because prior to conversion it provided for a single-sum payment option that was based solely on the present value of the benefit payable at normal retirement age. Third, Plan F satisfies the requirements of paragraph (c)(3)(iii)(E) of this section because the amount of the opening balance is not less than the present value of the participant's accrued benefit under the plan immediately prior to the effective date of the conversion amendment, as determined in accordance with section 417(e). Fourth, Plan F satisfies the requirements of paragraph (c)(3)(iii)(F) of this section because it provides for interest credits that are described in paragraph (d)(3) of this section on the opening balance and the interest credits are reasonably expected to be no lower than the interest rate used to determine the opening balance. This is the case because interest is credited at least annually after the effective date of the conversion amendment and the interest rate used to establish the opening balance (which is based on the first, second, and third segment rates described in section 430(h)(2)(C) referenced under section 417(e)(3)) is not greater than the interest rate applicable under the third segment rate described in section 430(h)(2)(C)(iii) which the plan uses to determine interest for all future periods after the effective date of the conversion amendment. Fifth, Plan F satisfies the requirements of paragraph (c)(3)(iii)(G) of this section because it provides a death benefit after the effective date of the conversion amendment which has a present value that is at all times at least equal to the hypothetical account balance at the date of death.

* * * * *

**(d)** * * *

*(1)* * * *

(iv) * * *

(D) Debits and credits during the interest crediting period. A plan is not treated as failing to meet the requirements of this paragraph (d) merely because the plan does not provide for interest credits on amounts distributed prior to the end of the interest crediting period. Furthermore, a plan is not treated as failing to meet the requirements of this paragraph (d) merely because the plan calculates increases or decreases to the participant's accumulated benefit by applying a rate of interest or rate of return (including a rate of increase or decrease under an index) to the participant's adjusted accumulated benefit (or portion thereof) for the period. For this purpose, the participant's adjusted accumulated benefit equals the participant's accumulated benefit as of the beginning of the period, adjusted for debits and credits (other than interest credits) made to the accumulated benefit prior to the end of the interest crediting period, with appropriate weighting for those debits and credits based on their timing within the period. For plans that calculate increases or decreases to the participant's accumulated benefit by applying a rate of interest or rate of return to the participant's adjusted accumulated benefit (or portion thereof) for the period, interest credits include these increases and decreases, to the extent provided under the terms of the plan at the beginning of the period and to the extent not conditioned on current service and not made on account of imputed service (as defined in § 1.401(a)(4)-11(d)(3)(ii)(B)), and the interest crediting rate with respect to a participant equals the total amount of interest credits for the period divided by the participant's adjusted accumulated benefit for the period.

* * * * *

*(2)* * * *

(ii) Application to multiple annuity starting dates. (A) In general. Paragraph (d)(2)(i) of this section applies only at an annuity starting date, within the meaning of § 1.401(a)-20, A-10(b), on which a distribution of the participant's entire benefit under the plan's statutory hybrid benefit formula as of that date commences. For a participant who has more than one annuity starting date, paragraph (d)(2)(ii)(B) of this section provides rules for the application of paragraph (d)(2)(i) of this section, taking into account prior distributions. If the comparison under paragraph (d)(2)(ii)(B) of this section results in the sum of principal credits exceeding the sum of the amounts described in paragraphs (d)(2)(ii)(B)(1) through (d)(2)(ii)(B)(3) of this section, then the participant's benefit to be distributed at the current annuity starting date is increased by an amount equal to the excess.

(B) Comparison to reflect prior distributions. For a participant who has more than one annuity starting date, the sum of all principal credits credited to the participant under the plan, as of the current annuity starting date, is compared to the sum of—

(1) The participant's benefit as of the current annuity starting date;

(2) The amount of the offset to the participant's benefit under the statutory hybrid benefit formula that is attributable to any prior distribution of the participant's benefit under that formula; and

(3) The amount of any increase to the participant's benefit as a result of the application of paragraph (d)(2)(i) of this section to a prior distribution.

* * * * *

*(4)* * * *

(iv) Fixed rate of interest. An annual interest crediting rate equal to a fixed 5 percent is deemed to be not in excess of the interest rate described in paragraph (d)(3) of this section.

* * * * *

*(5)* * * *

(ii) Actual rate of return on plan assets. An interest crediting rate equal to the actual rate of return on the aggregate assets of the plan, including both positive returns and negative returns, is not in excess of a market rate of return if the plan's assets are diversified so as to minimize the volatility of returns. This requirement that plan assets be diversified so as to minimize the volatility of returns does not require greater diversification than is required under section 404(a)(1)(C) of Title I of the Employee Retirement Income Security Act of 1974, Public Law 93-406 (88 Stat. 829 (1974)) with respect to defined benefit pension plans.

* * * * *

(iv) Rate of return on certain RICs. An interest crediting rate is not in excess of a market rate of return if it is equal to the rate of return on a regulated investment company (RIC), as defined in section 851, that is reasonably expected to be not significantly more volatile than the broad United States equities market or a similarly broad international equities market. For example, a RIC that has most of its assets invested in securities of issuers (including other RICs) concentrated in an industry sector or a country other than the United States, that uses leverage, or that has significant investment in derivative financial products, for the purpose of achieving returns that amplify the returns of an unleveraged investment, generally would not meet this requirement. Thus, a RIC that has most of its investments concentrated in the semiconductor industry or that uses leverage in order to provide a rate of return that is twice the rate of return on the Standard & Poor's 500 index (S&P 500) would not meet this requirement. On the other hand, a RIC whose investments track the rate of return on the S&P 500, a broad-based "small-cap" index (such as the Russell 2000 index), or a broad-based international equities index would meet this requirement.

* * * * *

*(6)* * * *

(ii) Annual or more frequent floor applied to bond-based rates. An interest crediting rate under a plan does not fail to be described in paragraph (d)(3) or (d)(4) of this section for an interest crediting period merely because the plan provides that the interest crediting rate for that interest crediting period equals the greater of—

(A) An interest crediting rate described in paragraph (d)(3) or (d)(4) of this section; and

(B) An annual interest rate of 4 percent (or a pro rata portion of an annual interest rate of 4 percent for plans that provide interest credits more frequently than annually).

(iii) Cumulative floor applied to equity-based or bond-based rates. (A) In general. A plan that determines interest credits under a statutory hybrid benefit formula using a particular interest crediting rate described in paragraph (d)(3), (d)(4), or (d)(5) of this section (or an interest crediting rate that can never be in excess of a particular interest crediting rate described in paragraph (d)(3), (d)(4), or (d)(5) of this section) does not provide an effective interest crediting rate in excess of a market rate of return merely because the plan provides that the participant's benefit under the statutory hybrid benefit formula determined as of the participant's annuity starting date is equal to the greater of—

(1) The benefit determined using the interest crediting rate; and

(2) The benefit determined as if the plan had used a fixed annual interest crediting rate equal to 3 percent (or a lower rate) for all principal credits that are made during the guarantee period (minimum guarantee amount).

(B) Guarantee period defined. The guarantee period is the prospective period which begins on the date on which the cumulative floor described in this paragraph (d)(6)(iii) begins to apply to the participant's benefit and which ends on the date on which that cumulative floor ceases to apply to the participant's benefit.

(C) Application to multiple annuity starting dates. The determination under paragraph (d)(6)(iii)(A) of this section is made only at an annuity starting date, within the meaning of § 1.401(a)-20, A-10(b), on which a distribution of the participant's entire benefit under the plan's statutory hybrid benefit formula as of that date commences. For a participant who has more than one annuity starting date, paragraph (d)(6)(iii)(D) of this section provides rules for the application of paragraph (d)(6)(iii)(A) of this section, taking into account any prior distributions. If the comparison under paragraph (d)(6)(iii)(D) of this section results in the minimum guarantee amount exceeding the sum of the amounts described in paragraphs (d)(6)(iii)(D)(1) through (d)(6)(iii)(D)(3) of this section, then the participant's benefit to be distributed at the current annuity starting date is increased by an amount equal to the excess.

(D) Comparison to reflect prior distributions. For a participant who has more than one annuity starting date, the minimum guarantee amount (described in paragraph (d)(6)(iii)(A)(2) of this section), as of the current annuity starting date, is compared to the sum of—

(1) The participant's benefit, as of the current annuity starting date, to which a minimum guaranteed rate described in paragraph (d)(6)(iii)(A)(2) of this section applies;

(2) The amount of the offset to the participant's benefit under the statutory hybrid benefit formula that is attributable to any prior distribution of the participant's benefit under that formula and to which a minimum guaranteed rate described in paragraph (d)(6)(iii)(A)(2) of this section applied, together with interest at that minimum guaranteed rate annually from the prior annuity starting date to the current annuity starting date; and

(3) The amount of any increase to the participant's benefit as a result of the application of paragraph (d)(6)(iii)(A) of this section to any prior distribution, together with interest annually at the minimum guaranteed rate that applied to the prior distribution from the prior annuity starting date to the current annuity starting date.

(E) Application to portion of participant's benefit. A cumulative floor described in this paragraph (d)(6)(iii) may be applied to a portion of a participant's benefit, provided the requirements of this paragraph (d)(6)(iii) are satisfied with respect to that portion of the benefit. If a cumulative floor described in this paragraph (d)(6)(iii) applies to a portion of a participant's benefit, only the principal credits that are attributable to that portion of the participant's benefit are taken into account in determining the amount of the guarantee described in paragraph (d)(6)(iii)(A)(2) of this section.

* * * * *

**(e)** * * *

*(2) Plan termination.* (i) In general. (A) Interest crediting rates. If the interest crediting rate used to determine a participant's accumulated benefit (or a portion thereof) has been a variable rate during the interest crediting periods in the 5-year period ending on the plan termination date (including any case in which the rate was not the same fixed rate during all such periods), then a statutory hybrid plan is treated as meeting the requirements of section 411(b)(5)(B)(i) and paragraph (d)(1) of this section only if the terms of the plan satisfy the requirements of paragraph (e)(2)(ii) of this section. See regulations of the Pension Benefit Guaranty Corporation for additional rules that apply when a pension plan is terminated.

(B) Annuity conversion factors. A statutory hybrid plan is treated as meeting the requirements of section 411(b)(5)(B)(i) and paragraph (d)(1) of this section only if the terms of the plan provide that the interest rate and mortality table (including tabular adjustment factors) used on and after plan termination for purposes of determining the amount of any benefit under the plan payable in the form of an annuity commencing at or after normal retirement age are the interest rate and mortality table specified under the plan for that purpose as of the termination date, except that if the interest rate is a variable rate (as described in paragraph (e)(2)(i) of this section), then the interest rate for that purpose is determined pursuant to the rules of paragraph (e)(2)(ii) of this section.

(ii) Interest crediting rates that are variable. (A) General rule. Subject to the other rules in this paragraph (e)(2), a plan satisfies this paragraph (e)(2)(ii) only if the terms of the plan provide that, on the plan termination date, if the interest crediting rate used to determine a participant's accumulated benefit has been a variable rate as described in paragraph (e)(2)(i) of this section, then the interest crediting rate used to determine the participant's accumulated benefit under the plan after the date of plan termination is equal to the average of the interest crediting rates used under the plan during the 5-year period ending on the plan termination date. For this purpose, an interest crediting rate is used under the plan if the rate applied under the terms of the plan during an interest crediting period for which the interest crediting date is within the 5-year period ending on the plan termination date and the average is determined as the arithmetic average of the rates used, with each rate adjusted to reflect the length of the interest crediting period and the average rate expressed as an annual rate.

(B) Variable interest crediting rates that are based on interest rates. With respect to an interest crediting rate that was a variable interest rate described in paragraph (d)(3) or (d)(4) of this section (taking into account the rules of paragraph (d)(6)(ii) of this section), a variable interest rate that can never be in excess of a rate described in paragraph (d)(3) or (d)(4) of this section, or a fixed interest rate that has not been the same rate during the entire 5-year period ending on the plan termination date, the actual interest rate that applied under the plan for the interest crediting period is used for purposes of determining the average interest crediting rate. For this purpose, the rate that applied for the interest crediting period takes into account minimums, maximums, and other reductions that applied in the period, other than cumulative floors under paragraph (d)(6)(iii) of this section.

(C) Variable interest crediting rates that are other rates of return. With respect to any interest crediting rate not described in paragraph (e)(2)(ii)(B) of this section (that is, a variable rate described in paragraph (d)(5) of this section), the interest crediting rate that applied for the interest crediting period for purposes of determining the average interest crediting rate is deemed to be equal to the third segment rate under section 430(h)(2)(C)(iii) for the last calendar month ending before the beginning of the interest crediting period, as adjusted to account for any minimums or maximums that applied in the period (other than cumulative floors under paragraph (d)(6)(iii) of this section), but without regard to other reductions that applied in the period. Thus, for example, if the actual interest crediting rate in an interest crediting period was equal to the rate of return on plan assets, but not greater than 5 percent, then for purposes of determining the plan's average interest crediting rate, the interest crediting rate for that interest crediting period would be deemed to equal the lesser of the applicable third segment rate for the period and 5 percent. However, if the actual interest crediting rate in an interest crediting period was equal to the rate of return on plan assets minus 200 basis points, then for purposes of determining the plan's average interest crediting rate, the interest crediting rate for that interest crediting period would be deemed to equal the third segment rate.

(iii) Rules of application. (A) Section 411(d)(6) protected benefits. In general, for purposes of determining the average interest crediting rate under paragraph (e)(2)(ii) of this section, the interest crediting rate that applied for each interest crediting period is the ongoing interest crediting rate that was specified under the plan in that period, without regard to any section 411(d)(6) protected benefit using an interest crediting rate that applied under the plan prior to amendment. However, if, at the end of the last interest crediting period prior to plan termination, the participant's accumulated benefit is based on a section 411(d)(6) protected benefit that results from a prior amendment to change the interest crediting rate applicable under the plan, then, for purposes of determining the average interest crediting rate under paragraph (e)(2)(ii) of this section, the pre-amendment interest crediting rate is treated as having applied for each interest crediting period after the date of the interest crediting rate change.

(B) Weighted averages. If the plan determines the interest credit in any interest crediting period by applying different rates to different predetermined portions of the accumulated benefit under paragraph (d)(1)(vii) of this section, then, for purposes of determining the average interest crediting rate under paragraph (e)(2)(ii) of this section, the interest crediting rate that applied for the interest crediting period is the weighted average of the relevant interest rates that apply, under the rules of paragraph (e)(2)(ii) of this section, to each portion of the accumulated benefit.

(C) Participants with less than five years of interest credits upon plan termination. If the plan provided for interest credits for any interest crediting period in which, pursuant to the terms of the plan, the individual was not eligible to receive interest credits (because the individual was not a participant or beneficiary in the relevant interest crediting period or otherwise), then, for purposes of determining the individual's average interest crediting rate under paragraph (e)(2)(ii) of this section, the individual is treated as though the individual received interest credits in that period using the interest crediting rate that applied in that period under the terms of the plan to a similarly situated participant or beneficiary who was eligible to receive interest credits. However, if, under the terms of the plan, the individual was not eligible to receive any interest credits during the entire 5-year period ending on the plan termination date, then the rules under paragraph (e)(2)(ii) do not apply to determine the individual's benefit after plan termination.

(iv) Examples. The following examples illustrate the rules of this paragraph (e)(2). In each case, it is assumed that the plan is terminated in a standard termination.

*Example (1).* (i) Facts. Plan A is a defined benefit plan with a calendar plan year that expresses each participant's accumulated benefit in the form of a hypothetical account balance to which principal credits are made at the end of each calendar quarter and to which interest is credited at the end of each calendar quarter based on the balance at the beginning of the quarter. Interest credits under Plan A are based on a rate of interest fixed at the beginning of each plan year equal to the third segment rate for the preceding December, except that the plan used the rate of interest on 30-year Treasury bonds (instead of the third segment rate) for plan years before 2012. The plan is terminated on March 3, 2016. The third segment rate credited under Plan A from January 1, 2012, through December 31, 2015, is assumed to be: 6 percent annually for each of the four quarters in 2015 (1.5 percent quarterly); 6.5 percent annually for each of the four quarters in 2014 (1.625 percent quarterly); 6 percent annually for each of the four quarters in 2013 (1.5 percent quarterly); and 5.5 percent annually for each of the four quarters in 2012 (1.375 percent quarterly). The rate of interest on 30-year Treasury bonds credited under Plan A for each of the four quarters in 2011 is assumed to be 4.4 percent annually (1.1 percent quarterly).

(ii) Conclusion. Pursuant to paragraph (e)(2)(ii)(B) of this section, the interest crediting rate used to determine accrued benefits under the plan on and after the date of plan termination is 5.68 percent. This is determined by calculating the average quarterly rate of 1.42 percent (the sum of 1.5 percent times 4, 1.625 times 4, 1.5 times 4, 1.375 times 4, and 1.1 percent times 4, divided by the 20 quarters that end in the 5-year period from March 4, 2011 to March 3, 2016) and multiplying such rate by 4 to determine the average annual rate.

*Example (2).* (i) Facts. The facts are the same as Example 1, except that Participant B commenced participation in Plan A on April 17, 2013.

(ii) Conclusion. Pursuant to paragraph (e)(2)(iii)(C) of this section, the interest crediting rate used to determine Participant B's accrued benefits under Plan A on and after the date of plan termination is 5.68 percent, which is the same rate that would have applied to Participant B if Participant B had participated in the plan during the 5-year period preceding the date of plan termination, as described in Example 1.

*Example (3).* (i) Facts. Plan C is a defined benefit plan with a calendar plan year that expresses each participant's accumulated benefit in the form of a hypothetical account balance to which principal credits are made at the end of each calendar year and to which interest is credited at the end of each calendar year based on the balance at the end of the preceding year. The plan is terminated on January 27, 2014. The plan's interest crediting rate for each calendar year during the entire 5-year period ending on the plan termination date is equal to (A) 50 percent of the greater of the rate of interest on 3-month Treasury Bills for the preceding December and an annual rate of 4 percent, plus (B) 50 percent of the rate of return on plan assets. The rate of interest on 3-month Treasury Bills credited under Plan C is assumed to be: 3.4 percent for 2013; 4 percent for 2012; 4.5 percent for 2011; 3.5 percent for 2010; and 4.2 percent for 2009. Each of these rates applied under Plan C for interest credited during this period for purposes of the interest credits described in clause (A) of this paragraph (i), except that the 4 percent minimum rate applied for 2013 and 2010. For purposes of the interest credits described in clause (B) of this paragraph (i), the rate of interest on the third segment rate in the prior years (based on the rate for the preceding December) is assumed to be: 6 percent for 2013; 6.5 percent for 2012; 6 percent for 2011; 5.5 percent for 2010; and 6 percent for 2009.

(ii) Conclusion. Pursuant to paragraph (e)(2)(ii) of this section, the interest crediting rate used to determine accrued benefits under the plan on and after the date of plan termination is 5.07 percent. This number is equal to the sum of 50 percent of 4.14 percent (which is the sum of 4 percent, 4 percent, 4.5 percent, 4 percent, and 4.2 percent, divided by 5), and 50 percent of 6 percent (which is the average third segment rate for the 5 interest crediting periods ending within the 5-year period).

*Example (4).* (i) Facts. The facts are the same as in Example 3, except that the plan had credited interest before January 1, 2012, using the rate of return on a RIC and was amended effective January 1, 2012, to base interest credits for all plan years after 2011 on the interest rate formula described in Example 3(i). In order to comply with section 411(d)(6), the plan provides that, for each participant or beneficiary who was a participant on December 31, 2011, the benefits at any date are based on either the ongoing hypothetical account balance on that date (which is based on the December 31, 2011 balance, with interest credited thereafter at the rate described in the first sentence of Example 3(i) and taking principal credits after 2011 into account) or a special hypothetical account balance (the pre-2012 balance) on that date, whichever balance is greater. For each participant, the pre-2012 balance is a hypothetical account balance equal to the participant's December 31, 2011, balance, with interest credited thereafter at the RIC rate of return, but with no principal credits after 2011. There are 10 participants for whom his or her pre-2012 balance exceeded his or her ongoing hypothetical account balance at the end of 2013.

(ii) Conclusion. Since Plan C credited interest prior to 2012 using the rate of return on a RIC (a rate not described in paragraph (d)(3) or (d)(4) of this section), for purposes of determining the average interest crediting rate upon plan termination, the interest crediting rate used to determine accrued benefits under Plan C for all participants during those periods (for the calendar years 2009, 2010, and 2011) is deemed to be equal to the third segment rate for the preceding December. In addition, since the pre-2012 balances exceeded the ongoing hypothetical account balance for 10 participants in the last interest crediting period prior to plan termination, for purposes of determining the average interest crediting rate upon plan termination, the interest crediting rate used to determine accrued benefits under Plan C for 2012 and 2013 for those participants is deemed to be equal to the third segment rate for the month of December preceding 2012 and the month of December preceding 2013, respectively. For all other participants, for purposes of determining the average interest crediting rate upon plan termination, the interest crediting rate used to determine accrued benefits under Plan C for 2012 and 2013 is based on the ongoing interest crediting rate (the formula described in Example 3).

*(3)* * * *

(iii) Coordination of section 411(d)(6) and market rate of return limitation. (A) In general. An amendment to a statutory hybrid plan that preserves a section 411(d)(6) protected benefit is subject to the rules under paragraph (d) of this section relating to market rate of return. However, in the case of an amendment to change a plan's interest crediting rate for periods after the applicable amendment date from one interest crediting rate (the old rate) that satisfies the requirements of paragraph (d) of this section to another interest crediting rate (the new rate) that satisfies the requirements of paragraph (d) of this section, the plan's effective interest crediting rate is not in excess of a market rate of return for purposes of paragraph (d) of this section merely because the plan provides for the benefit of any participant who is benefiting under the plan (within the meaning of § 1.410(b)-3(a)) on the applicable amendment date to never be less than what it would be if the old rate had continued but without taking into account any principal credits (as defined in paragraph (d)(1)(ii)(D) of this section) after the applicable amendment date.

(B) Multiple amendments. A pattern of repeated plan amendments each of which provides for a prospective change in the plan's interest crediting rate with respect to the benefit as of the applicable amendment date will be treated as resulting in the ongoing plan terms providing that the interest crediting rate equals the greater of each of the interest crediting rates, so that the rule in paragraph (e)(3)(iii)(A) of this section would not apply. See § 1.411(d)-4, A-1(c)(1).

*(4) Actuarial increases after normal retirement age.* A statutory hybrid plan is not treated as providing an effective interest crediting rate that is in excess of a market rate of return for purposes of paragraph (d) of this section merely because the plan provides that the participant's benefit, as of each annuity starting date after normal retirement age, is equal to the greater of—

(i) The benefit determined using an interest crediting rate that is not in excess of a market rate of return under paragraph (d) of this section; and

(ii) The benefit that satisfies the requirements of section 411(a)(2).

* * * * *

**(f)** * * *

*(2)* * * *

(i) * * *

(B) Special effective date. Paragraphs (c)(3)(iii), (d)(1)(iii), (d)(1)(iv)(D), (d)(1)(vi), (d)(2)(ii), (d)(4)(iv), (d)(5)(iv), (d)(6), (e)(2), (e)(3)(iii), and (e)(4) of this section apply to plan years that begin on or after January 1, 2012.

* * * * *

### § 1.411(c)-1 Allocation of accrued benefits between employer and employee contributions.

***Caution:*** The Treasury has not yet amended Reg § 1.411(c)-1 to reflect changes made by P.L. 101-239, P.L. 100-203.

**(a) Accrued benefit derived from employer contributions.** For purposes of section 411 and the regulations thereunder, under section 411(c)(1), an employee's accrued benefit derived from employer contributions under a plan as of any applicable date is the excess, if any, of—

*(1)* The total accrued benefit under the plan provided for the employee as of such date, over

*(2)* The accrued benefit provided for the employee, derived from contributions made by the employee under the plan as of such date.

For computation of accrued benefit derived from employee contributions to a defined contribution plan or from voluntary employee contributions to a defined benefit plan, see paragraph (b) of this section. For computation of accrued benefit derived from mandatory employee contributions to a defined benefit plan, see paragraph (c) of this section.

**(b) Accrued benefit derived from employee contribution to defined contribution plan, etc.** For purposes of section 411 and the regulations thereunder, under section 411(c)(2)(A) the accrued benefit derived from employee contributions to a defined contribution plan is determined under paragraph (b)(1) or (2) of this section, whichever applies. Under section 411(d)(5), the accrued benefit derived from voluntary employee contributions to a defined benefit plan is determined under paragraph (b)(1) of this section.

*(1) Separate accounts maintained.* If a separate account is maintained with respect to an employee's contributions and all income, expenses, gains, and losses attributable thereto, the accrued benefit determined under this subparagraph as of any applicable date is the balance of such account as of such date.

*(2) Separate accounts not maintained.* If a separate account is not maintained with respect to an employee's contributions and the income, expenses, gains, and losses attributable thereto, the accrued benefit determined under this subparagraph is the employee's total accrued benefit determined under the plan multiplied by a fraction—

(i) The numerator of which is the total amount of the employee's contributions under the plan less withdrawals, and

(ii) The denominator of which is the sum of (A) the amount described in paragraph (b)(2)(i) of this section, and (B) the total contributions made under the plan by the employer on behalf of the employee less withdrawals.

For purposes of this subparagraph, contributions include all amounts which are contributed to the plan even if such amounts are used to provide ancillary benefits, such as incidental life insurance, health insurance, or death benefits, and withdrawals include only amounts distributed to the employee and do not reflect the cost of any death benefits under the plan.

**(c) Accrued benefit derived from mandatory employee contributions to a defined benefit plan.** *(1) General rule.* In the case of a defined benefit plan (as defined in section 414(j)) the accrued benefit derived from contributions made by an employee under the plan as of any applicable date is an annual benefit, in the form of a single life annuity (without ancillary benefits) commencing at normal retirement age, equal to the amount of the employee's accumulated contributions (determined under paragraph (c)(3) of this section) multiplied by the appropriate conversion factor (determined under paragraph (c)(2) of this section). Paragraph (e) of this section provides rules for actuarial adjustments where the benefit is to be determined in a form other than the form described in this paragraph.

*(2) Appropriate conversion factor.* For purposes of this paragraph, the term "appropriate conversion factor" means the factor necessary to convert an amount equal to the accumulated contributions to a single life annuity (without ancillary benefits) commencing at normal retirement age and shall be 10 percent for a normal retirement age of 65 years. For other normal retirement ages the appropriate conversion factor shall be the factor as determined by the Commissioner.

*(3) Accumulated contributions.* For purposes of section 411(c) and this section, the term "accumulated contributions" means the total of—

(i) All mandatory contributions made by the employee (determined under paragraph (c)(4) of this section),

(ii) Interest (if any) on such contributions, computed at the rate provided by the plan to the end of the last plan year to which section 411(a)(2) does not apply (by reason of the applicable effective date), and

(iii) Interest on the sum of the amounts determined under paragraphs (c)(3)(i) and (ii) of this section compounded annually at the rate of 5 percent per annum from the beginning of the first plan year to which section 411(a)(2) applies (by reason of the applicable effective date) to the date on which the employee would attain normal retirement age.

For example, if under section 1017 of the Employee Retirement Income Security Act of 1974, section 411(a)(2) of the Code applies for plan years beginning after December 31, 1975, and for plan years beginning before 1975, the plan provided for 3 percent interest on employee contributions, an employee's accumulated contributions would be computed by crediting interest at the rate provided by the plan (3 percent) for plan years beginning before 1976 and by crediting interest at the rate of 5 percent (or another rate prescribed under section 411(c)(2)(D)) thereafter, Section 1017 of the Employee Retirement Income Security Act of 1974 and § 1.411(a)-2 provide the effective dates for the application of section 411(A)(2).

*(4) Mandatory contributions.* For purposes of section 411(c) and this section the term "mandatory contributions" means amounts contributed to the plan by the employee which are required as a condition of his employment, as a condition of his participation in the plan, or as a condition of obtaining benefits (or additional benefits) under the plan attributable to employer contributions. For example, if the benefit derived from employer contributions depends upon a specified level of employee contributions, employee contributions up to that level would be treated as mandatory contributions. Mandatory contributions, otherwise satisfying the requirements of this subparagraph, include amounts contributed to the plan which are used to provide ancillary benefits such as incidental life insurance, health insurance, or death benefits.

**(d) Limitation on accrued benefit.** The accrued benefit derived from mandatory employee contributions under a defined benefit plan (determined under paragraph (c) of this section) shall not exceed the greater of—

*(1)* The accrued benefit of the employee under the plan, or

*(2)* The accrued benefit derived from employee contributions determined without regard to any interest under section 411(c)(2)(C)(ii) and (iii) and under paragraphs (c)(3)(ii) and (iii) of this section.

**(e) Actuarial adjustments for defined benefit plans.** *(1) Accrued benefit.* In the case of a defined benefit plan (as defined in section 414(j)) if an employee's accrued benefit is to be determined as an amount other than an annual benefit commencing at normal retirement age, such benefit (determined under section 411(c)(1) and paragraph (a) of this section) shall be the actuarial equivalent of such benefit, as determined by the Commissioner.

*(2) Accrued benefit derived from employee contributions.* In the case of a defined benefit plan (as defined in section 414(j)) if the accrued benefit derived from mandatory contributions made by an employee is to be determined with respect to a benefit other than an annual benefit in the form of a single life annuity (without ancillary benefits) commencing at normal retirement age, such benefit shall be the actuarial equivalent of such benefit (determined under section 411(c)(2)(B) and paragraph (c) of this section) as determined by the Commissioner.

**(f) Suspension of benefits, etc.** *(1) Suspensions.* No adjustment to an accrued benefit is required on account of any suspension of benefits if such suspension is permitted under section 203(a)(3)(B) of the Employee Retirement Income Security Act of 1974 (88 Stat. 855) (Code section 411(a)(3)(B)).

*(2) Employment after retirement.* No actuarial adjustment to an accrued benefit is required on account of employment after normal retirement age. For example, if a plan with a normal retirement age of 65 provides a benefit of $400 a month payable at age 65, the same $400 benefit (with no upward adjustment) could be paid to an employee who retires at age 68.

---

T.D. 7501, 8/22/77.

---

PAR. 2. Section 1.411(c)-1 is amended by:

1. Revising paragraphs (c)(1), (c)(2), (c)(3), (c)(5) and (c)(6).

2. Revising paragraph (d).

3. Adding paragraph (g).

The additions and revisions read as follows:

**Proposed § 1.411(c)-1 Allocation of accrued benefits between employer and employee contributions.** [*For Preamble, see ¶ 151,705*]

* * * * *

**(c) Accrued benefit derived from mandatory employee contributions to a defined benefit plan.** *(1) General rule.*

In the case of a defined benefit plan (as defined in section 414(j)), the accrued benefit derived from contributions made by an employee under the plan as of any applicable date in the form of an annual benefit commencing at normal retirement age and nondecreasing for the life of the participant is equal to the amount of the employee's accumulated contributions (determined under paragraph (c)(3) of this section) divided by the appropriate conversion factor with respect to that form of benefit (determined under paragraph (c)(2) of this section). Paragraph (e) of this section provides rules for actuarial adjustments where the benefit is to be determined in a form other than the form described in this paragraph (c)(1).

*(2) Appropriate conversion factor.* For purposes of this paragraph, with respect to a form of annual benefit commencing at normal retirement age described in paragraph (c)(1), the term appropriate conversion factor means the present value of an annuity in the form of that annual benefit commencing at normal retirement age at a rate of $1 per year, computed using an interest rate and mortality table which would be used under the plan under section 417(e)(3) and § 1.417(e)-1T (as of the determination date).

*(3) Accumulated contributions.* For purposes of section 411(c) and this section, the term accumulated contributions means the total of—

(i) All mandatory contributions made by the employee (determined under paragraph (c)(4) of this section);

(ii) Interest (if any) on such contributions, computed at the rate provided by the plan to the end of the last plan year to which section 411(a)(2) does not apply (by reason of the applicable effective dates);

(iii) Interest on the sum of the amounts determined under paragraphs (c)(3)(i) and (ii) of this section compounded annually at the rate of 5 percent per annum from the beginning of the first plan year to which section 411(a)(2) applies (by reason of the applicable effective date) to the beginning of the first plan year beginning after December 31, 1987;

(iv) Interest on the sum of the amounts determined under paragraphs (c)(3)(i) through (iii) of this section compounded annually at 120 percent of the Federal mid-term rate(s) (as in effect under section 1274(d) of the Internal Revenue Code for the first month of a plan year) for the period beginning with the first plan year beginning after December 31, 1987 and ending on the determination date; and

(v) Interest on the sum of the amounts determined under paragraphs (c)(3)(i) through (iv) of this section compounded annually, using an interest rate which would be used under the plan under section 417(e)(3) and § 1.417(e)-1T (as of the determination date), from the determination date to the date on which the employee would attain normal retirement age.

* * * * *

*(5) Determination date.* (i) For purposes of section 411(c) and this section, in a case in which a participant will receive his or her entire accrued benefit derived from employee contributions in any one of the forms described in paragraph (c)(5)(ii), the term determination date means the date on which distribution of such benefit commences. Alternatively, in such a case, the plan may provide that the determination date is the annuity starting date with respect to that benefit, as defined in § 1.401(a)-20, Q&A-10.

(ii) Paragraph (c)(5)(i) applies to the following forms: an annuity that is substantially nonincreasing (e.g., an annuity that is nonincreasing except for automatic increases to reflect increases in the consumer price index), substantially nonincreasing installment payments for a fixed number of years, or a single sum distribution.

(iii) In a case in which a participant will receive a distribution that is not described in paragraph (c)(5)(i), the determination date will be as provided by the Commissioner.

*(6) Examples.* (i) Facts. (A) In the following examples, Employer X maintains a qualified defined benefit plan that required mandatory employee contributions for 1987 and prior years, but not for years after 1987. The plan year is the calendar year. The plan provides for a normal retirement age of 65 and for 100 percent vesting in the employer-derived portion of a participant's accrued benefit after 5 years of service.

(B) The terms of the plan provide that the normal form of benefit is a level monthly amount commencing at normal retirement age and payable for the life of the participant. A plan participant who elects not to receive benefits in the form of the qualified joint and survivor annuity provided by the plan may elect to receive a single-sum distribution of the present value of his or her accrued benefit upon termination of employment.

(C) As of January 1, 1995, the plan was amended to provide that, for purposes of computing actuarially equivalent benefits, the single sum is calculated using the unisex version of the 1983 GAM mortality table (as provided in Revenue Ruling 95-6 (1995-1 C.B. 80)), and interest at the rate equal to the annual rate of interest on 30-year Treasury securities for the first calendar month preceding the first day of the plan year during which the annuity starting date occurs.

(D) Under the plan, employee contributions are accumulated at 3 percent interest for plan years beginning before 1976, 5 percent interest for plan years beginning after 1975 and before 1988, and interest at 120 percent of the Federal mid-term rate (as in effect under section 1274(d) for the first month of the plan year) for plan years beginning after 1987 until the determination date. Under the plan, the determination date is defined as the annuity starting date. For the period from the determination date until the date on which the employee attains normal retirement age, interest is credited at the rate which would be used under the plan under section 417(e)(3) as of the determination date.

(E) A, an unmarried participant, terminates employment with X on January 1, 1997 at age 56 with 15 years of service. As of December 31, 1987, A's total accumulated mandatory employee contributions to the plan, including interest compounded annually at 5 percent for plan years beginning after 1975 and before 1988, equaled $3,021. A receives his or her accrued benefit in the form of an annual single life annuity commencing at normal retirement age. A's annuity starting date is January 1, 2006, and therefore the determination date is January 1, 2006.

(ii) Annuity at normal retirement age—determination of employee-derived and total plan vested accrued benefit.

*Example (1).* For purposes of this example, it is assumed that A's total accrued benefit under the plan in the normal form of benefit commencing at normal retirement age is $2,949 per year. A's benefit, as of January 1, 2006, would be determined as follows:

(A) Determine A's total accrued benefit in the form of an annual single life annuity commencing at normal retirement age under the plan's formula ($2,949 per year payable at age 65).

(B) Determine A's accumulated contributions with interest to January 1, 1997. As of December 31, 1987, A's accumulated contributions with interest under the plan provisions were $3,021. A's employee contributions are accumulated from December 31, 1987 to January 1, 1997 using 120 percent of the Federal mid-term rate under section 1274(d). This rate is 10.61 percent for 1988, 11.11 percent for 1989, 9.57 percent for 1990, 9.78 percent for 1991, 8.10 percent for 1992, 7.63 percent for 1993, 6.40 percent for 1994, and 9.54 percent for 1995. It is assumed for purposes of this example that 120 percent of the Federal mid-term rate is 7.00 percent for each year between 1996 and 2006, and that the 30-year Treasury rate for December 2005 is 8.00 percent. Thus, A's contributions accumulated to January 1, 1997, equal $6,480.

(C) Determine A's accumulated contributions with interest to normal retirement age (January 1, 2006) using, for the 1996 plan year and for years until normal retirement age, 120 percent of the Federal mid-term rate under section 1274(d), which is assumed to be 7.00 percent ($11,913).

(D) Determine the accrued annual annuity benefit derived from A's contributions by dividing A's accumulated contributions determined in paragraph (C) of this Example 1 by the plan's appropriate conversion factor. The plan's appropriate conversion factor at age 65 is 9.196, and the accrued benefit derived from A's contributions would be $11,913 ÷ 9.196 = $1,295.

(E) Determine the accrued benefit derived from employer contributions as the excess, if any, of the employee's accrued benefit under the plan over the accrued benefit derived from employee contributions ($2,949 − $1,295 = $1,654 per year).

(F) Determine the vested percentage of the accrued benefit derived from employer contributions under the plan's vesting schedule (100 percent).

(G) Determine the vested accrued benefit derived from employer contributions by multiplying the accrued benefit derived from employer contributions by the vested percentage ($1,654 × 100 percent = $1,654 per year).

(H) Determine A's vested accrued benefit in the form of an annual single life annuity commencing at normal retirement age by adding the accrued benefit derived from employee contributions and the vested accrued benefit derived from employer contributions, the sum of paragraphs (D) and (G) of this Example 1. ($1,295 + $1,654 = $2,949 per year).

*Example (2).* This example assumes the same facts as Example 1 except that A's total accrued benefit under the plan in the normal form of benefit commencing at normal retirement age is $1,000 per year. A's benefit, as of January 1, 2006, would be determined as follows:

(A) Determine A's total accrued benefit in the form of an annual single life annuity commencing at normal retirement age under the plan's formula ($1,000 per year payable at age 65).

(B) Determine A's accumulated contributions with interest to January 1, 1997 ($6,480 from paragraph (B) of Example 1).

(C) Determine A's accumulated contributions with interest to normal retirement age (January 1, 2006)($11,913 from paragraph (C) of Example 1).

(D) Determine the accrued annual annuity benefit derived from A's contributions by dividing A's accumulated contributions determined in paragraph (C) of this Example 2 by the plan's appropriate conversion factor ($1,295 from paragraph (D) of Example 1).

(E) Determine the accrued benefit derived from employer contributions as the excess, if any, of the employee's accrued benefit under the plan over the accrued benefit derived from employee contributions. Because the accrued benefit derived from employee contributions ($1,295) is greater than the employee's accrued benefit under the plan ($1,000), the accrued benefit derived from employer contributions is zero, and A's vested accrued benefit in the form of an annual single life annuity commencing at normal retirement age is $1,295 per year.

**(d) Delegation to Commissioner.** The Commissioner may prescribe additional guidance on calculating the accrued benefit derived from employee contributions under a defined benefit plan through publication in the Internal Revenue Bulletin of revenue rulings, notices, or other documents (see § 601.601(d)(2) of this chapter).

**(e)** * * *

**(f)** * * *

**(g) Effective date.** Paragraphs (c)(1), (c)(2), (c)(3), (c)(5), (c)(6) and (d) of this section are effective for plan years beginning on or after January 1, 1997.

PAR. 6. Section 1.411(c)-1 is amended by revising paragraph (f)(2) to read as follows:

**Proposed § 1.411(c)-1 Allocation of accrued benefits between employer and employee contributions.** [*For Preamble, see ¶ 151,113*]

* * * * *

**(f) Suspension of benefits, etc.** * * *

*(2) Employment after retirement after retirement.* Except as permitted by paragraph (f)(1) of this section, a defined benefit plan must make an actuarial adjustment to an accrued benefit the payment of which is deferred past normal retirement age. See, also, section 411(b)(1)(H) (relating to continued accruals after normal retirement age) and § 1.411(b)-2.

**§ 1.411(d)-1 Coordination of vesting and discrimination requirements. [Reserved]**

PAR. 2.

Paragraph (c)(2) of § 1.411(d)-1, as set forth in the notice of proposed rulemaking published in the FEDERAL REGISTER for April 9, 1980 (45 FR 24202) is modified to read as follows:

**Proposed § 1.411(d)-1 Coordination of vesting and discrimination requirements.** [*For Preamble, see ¶ 150,597*]

* * * * *

**(c) Discriminatory vesting.** * * *

*(2) Test for discriminatory vesting.* The determination of whether there is, or there is reason to believe there will be, discriminatory vesting shall be made on the basis of the facts and circumstances of each case. A reasonable disparity between the vested benefits paid to or accrued by the prohibited group and the vested benefits paid to or accrued by other employees will not result in a finding that there is discriminatory vesting.

**Proposed § 1.411(d)-1 Coordination of vesting and discrimination requirements.** [*For Preamble, see ¶ 150,571*]

***Caution:*** The Treasury has not yet amended Reg § 1.411(d)-1 to reflect changes made by P.L. 101-239, P.L. 99-514.

**(a) General rule.** A plan which satisfies the requirements of section 411(a)(2) shall be treated as satisfying any vesting schedule requirements resulting from the application of section 401(a)(4) unless the plan is discriminatory within the meaning of section 411(d)(1) and this section. A plan is discriminatory if there is a pattern of abuse or there is discriminatory vesting as determined under paragraphs (b) and (c) of this section, respectively. Under section 401(a)(4), a plan which discriminates in favor of employees who are officers, shareholders, or highly compensated (hereinafter referred to as "prohibited group"), is not a qualified plan under section 401(a).

**(b) Pattern of abuse.** *(1) Definition.* A plan is discriminatory under section 411(d)(1)(A) and shall not be considered to satisfy the requirements of section 401(a)(4) if there has been a pattern of abuse under the plan tending to discriminate in favor of the prohibited group (hereinafter referred to as "pattern of abuse").

*(2) Test for pattern of abuse.* The determination of whether there has been a pattern of abuse shall be made on the basis of the facts and circumstances of each case. An example of a pattern of abuse is the systematic dismissal of employees before their accrued benefits vest.

**(c) Discriminatory vesting.** *(1) Definition.* A plan is discriminatory under section 411(d)(1)(B) and shall not be considered to satisfy the requirements of section 401(a)(4) if there have been, or there is reason to believe there will be, an accrual of benefits or forfeitures tending to discriminate in favor of the prohibited group by operation of the vesting schedule (hereinafter referred to as "discriminatory vesting").

*(2) Test for discriminatory vesting.* Unless paragraph (d) applies, the determination of whether there is, or there is reason to believe there will be, discriminatory vesting shall be made on the basis of the facts and circumstances of each case. An unfavorable comparison based on one of the following factors does not require a finding that there is discriminatory vesting. Factors which are relevant to this determination include, but are not limited to, comparisons between the prohibited group and all other employees covered by the plan of:

(i) The employment turnover rate. The term "employment turnover rate" means the annual rate of turnover for employees.

(ii) The average percentage of vesting of each employee currently employed by the employer maintaining the plan.

(iii) The average percentage of vesting of each employee whose employment is terminated. For purposes of this subparagraph, a "termination of employment" occurs when the employee leaves by reason of a quit, discharge, retirement, or any other means.

(iv) The average number of years remaining for each employee until that employee becomes fully vested.

(v) In the case of a plan amendment which increases the length of service required for any particular level of vesting, the percentage of employees satisfying the new length of service requirement at the time it becomes effective.

**(d) Safe harbor test.** *(1) General rule.* A plan whose vesting schedule satisfies the requirements of subparagraph (2) or (3) of this paragraph shall be deemed not to be discriminatory under paragraph (c) of this section.

*(2) Three year rule.* A plan satisfies the requirements of this subparagraph if any employee who has completed 3 years of service has a 100% nonforfeitable right to the accrued benefit derived from employer contributions.

*(3) Ten year rule.* A plan satisfies the requirements of this subparagraph if any employee who has completed 10 years of service has a 100% nonforfeitable right to the accrued benefit derived from employer contributions, and the sum of the 10 relevant percentages of the employee's nonforfeitable rights equals or exceeds 700. The relevant percentages to be added are the employee's vested percentage (if any) prior to the completion of the first year of service, and the vested percentages after the completion of each of the first 9 years of service.

*(4) Determination of years of service.* For purposes of this paragraph, the term "years of service" means years of service required to be taken into account for purposes of section 411(a)(2), determined without regard to subparagraphs (A), (B), and (C) of section 411(a)(4).

*(5) Examples.* The rules provided by this paragraph are illustrated by the following examples:

*Example (1).* (i) Plan A provides that years of service for purposes of vesting are calculated under section 411(a)(2) without regard to subparagraphs (A), (B), and (C) of section 411(a)(4). Under the plan, an employee is 100% vested in the accrued benefit derived from employer contributions after three years of service.

(ii) The vesting schedule of Plan A can be illustrated by the following table:

| Completed years of service | Nonforfeitable percentage |
|---|---|
| Less than 1 | 0 |
| 1 but less than 2 | 0 |
| 2 but less than 3 | 0 |
| 3 but less than 4 | 100 |
| 4 but less than 5 | 100 |
| 5 but less than 6 | 100 |
| 6 but less than 7 | 100 |
| 7 but less than 8 | 100 |
| 8 but less than 9 | 100 |
| 9 but less than 10 | 100 |
| Total | 700 |

(iii) Plan A satisfies the requirements of subparagraph (2) of this paragraph because an employee is 100% vested after three years of service. Plan A also satisfies the requirements of subparagraph (3) of this paragraph because the sum of the 10 relevant percentages equals 700 and an employee is 100% vested after 10 years of service. Therefore, Plan A is deemed to be nondiscriminatory under paragraph (c) of this section.

*Example (2).* (i) Plan B provides that years of service for purposes of vesting are calculated under section 411(a)(2), without regard to subparagraphs (A), (B), and (C) of section 411(a)(4). Under the plan, an employee is 20% vested after one year of service, 40% after two years, 60% after three years, 80% after four years, and 100% after five years.

(ii) The vesting schedule of Plan B can be illustrated by the following table:

| Completed years of service | Nonforfeitable percentage |
|---|---|
| Less than 1 | 0 |
| 1 but less than 2 | 20 |
| 2 but less than 3 | 40 |
| 3 but less than 4 | 60 |
| 4 but less than 5 | 80 |
| 5 but less than 6 | 100 |
| 6 but less than 7 | 100 |
| 7 but less than 8 | 100 |
| 8 but less than 9 | 100 |
| 9 but less than 10 | 100 |
| Total | 700 |

(iii) Plan B does not satisfy the requirements of subparagraph (2) of this paragraph because an employee is not 100% vested after 3 years of service. However, Plan B satisfies the requirements of subparagraph (3) of this paragraph because the sum of the 10 relevant percentages equals 700 and an employee is 100% vested after 10 years of service. Therefore, Plan B is deemed to be nondiscriminatory under paragraph (c) of this section.

*Example (3).* (i) Plan C provides that years of service for purposes of vesting are calculated under section 411(a)(2), with regard to subparagraphs (A), (B), and (C) of section 411(a)(4). Under the plan, an employee's right to the accrued benefit derived from employer contributions vest as provided in section 411(a)(2)(A).

(ii) The vesting schedule of Plan C can be illustrated by the following table:

| Completed years of service | Nonforfeitable percentage |
|---|---|
| Less than 1 | 0 |
| 1 but less than 2 | 0 |
| 2 but less than 3 | 0 |
| 3 but less than 4 | 0 |
| 4 but less than 5 | 0 |
| 5 but less than 6 | 0 |
| 6 but less than 7 | 0 |
| 7 but less than 8 | 0 |
| 8 but less than 9 | 0 |
| 9 but less than 10 | 0 |
| 10 or more | 100 |

(iii) Plan C does not meet the requirements of subparagraph (2) of this paragraph because an employee is not 100% vested after 3 years of service. Plan C does not meet the requirements of subparagraph (3) of this paragraph because the sum of the 10 relevant percentages does not equal 700, although an employee is 100% vested after 10 years of service. Also, Plan C fails to meet the requirements of subparagraph (4) of this paragraph because an employee's service for vesting purposes is calculated using all of the subparagraphs of section 411(a)(4) instead of disregarding subparagraphs (A), (B), and (C) thereof.

(iv) Even though Plan C does not satisfy the requirements of subparagraph (2) or (3) of this paragraph, it may be found to be nondiscriminatory under paragraph (c) of this section if it satisfies the facts and circumstances test set forth in paragraph (c)(2) of this section.

**(e) Defined benefit plans.** A defined benefit plan which satisfies the benefit accrual requirements of section 411(b) shall still be subject to the nondiscrimination requirements of section 401(a)(4) with regard to its benefit accrual rates. Thus, even though a plan satisfies the section 411(b) requirements, the plan may still be discriminatory under section 401(a)(4) with respect to its benefit accruals.

**(f) Effective date.** This section shall apply to plan years beginning 30 days after the publication of this section in the FEDERAL REGISTER as a Treasury decision.

**§ 1.411(d)-2 Termination or partial termination; discontinuance of contributions.**

**(a) General rule.** *(1) Required nonforfeitability.* A plan is not a qualified plan (and a trust forming a part of such plan is not a qualified trust) unless the plan provides that—

(i) Upon the termination or partial termination of the plan, or

(ii) In addition, in the case of a plan to which section 412 (relating to minimum funding standards) does not apply, upon the complete discontinuance of contributions under the plan,

the rights of each affected employee to benefits accrued to the date of such termination or partial termination (or, in the case of a plan to which section 412 does not apply, discontinuance), to the extent funded, or the rights of each employee to the amounts credited to his account at such time, are nonforfeitable (within the meaning of § 1.411(a)-(4)).

*(2) Required allocation.* (i) A plan is not a qualified plan (and a trust forming a part of such plan is not a qualified trust) unless the plan provides for the allocation of any previously unallocated funds to the employees covered by the plan upon the termination or partial termination of the plan (or, in the case of a plan to which section 412 does not apply, upon the complete discontinuance of contributions under the plan). Such provision may be incorporated in the plan at its inception or by an amendment made prior to the termination or partial termination of the plan or the discontinuance of contributions thereunder. In the case of a defined contribution plan under which unallocated forfeitures are held in a suspense account in order to satisfy the requirements of section 415, this subdivision shall not require such plan to provide for allocations from the suspense account to the extent that such allocations would result in annual additions to participants' accounts in excess of amounts permitted under section 415 for the year for which such allocations would be made.

(ii) Any provision for the allocation of unallocated funds which is found by the Secretary of Labor or the Pension Benefit Guaranty Corporation (whichever is appropriate) to satisfy the requirements of section 4044 or section 403(d)(1) of the Employee Retirement Income Security Act of 1974 is acceptable if it specifies the method to be used and does not conflict with the provisions of section 401(a)(4) of the Internal Revenue Code of 1954 and the regulations thereunder. Any allocation of funds required by paragraph (1), (2), (3), or (4)(A) of section 4044(a) of such Act shall be deemed not to result in discrimination prohibited by section 401(a)(4) of the Code (see, however, paragraph (e) of this section). Notwithstanding the preceding sentence, in the case of a plan which establishes subclasses or categories pursuant to section 4044(b)(6) of such Act, the allocation of funds by the use of such subclasses or categories shall not be deemed not to result in discrimination prohibited by the Code. The allocation of unallocated funds may be in cash or in the form of other benefits provided under the plan. However, the allocation of the funds contributed by the employer among the employees need not necessarily benefit all the employees covered by the plan.

(iii) Paragraph (a)(2)(i) and (ii) of this section do not require the allocation of amounts to the account of any employee if such amounts are not required to be used to satisfy the liabilities with respect to employees and their beneficiaries under the plan (see section 401(a)(2)).

**(b) Partial termination.** *(1) General rule.* Whether or not a partial termination of a qualified plan occurs (and the time of such event) shall be determined by the Commissioner with regard to all the facts and circumstances in a particular case. Such facts and circumstances include: the exclusion, by reason of a plan amendment or severance by the employer, of a group of employees who have previously been covered by the plan; and plan amendments which adversely affect the rights of employees to vest in benefits under the plan.

*(2) Special rule.* If a defined benefit plan ceases or decreases future benefit accruals under the plan, a partial termination shall be deemed to occur if, as a result of such cessation or decrease, a potential reversion to the employer, or employers, maintaining the plan (determined as of the date such cessation or decrease is adopted) is created or increased. If no such reversion is created or increased, a partial termination shall be deemed not to occur by reason of such cessation or decrease. However, the Commissioner may determine that a partial termination of such a plan occurs pursuant to subparagraph (1) of this paragraph for reasons other than such cessation or decrease.

*(3) Effect of partial termination.* If a termination of a qualified plan occurs, the provisions of section 411(d)(3) apply only to the part of the plan that is terminated.

**(c) Termination.** *(1) Application.* This paragraph applies to a plan other than a plan described in section 411(e)(1) (relating to governmental, certain church plans, etc.).

*(2) Plans subject to termination insurance.* For purposes of this section, a plan to which title IV of the Employee Retirement Income Security Act of 1974 applies is considered terminated on a particular date if, as of that date—

(i) The plan is voluntarily terminated by the plan administrator under section 4041 of the Employee Retirement Income Security Act of 1974, or

(ii) The Pension Benefit Guaranty Corporation terminates the plan under section 4042 of the Employee Retirement Income Security Act of 1974.

For purposes of this subparagraph, the particular date of termination shall be the date of termination determined under section 4048 of such Act.

*(3) Other plans.* In the case of a plan not described in paragraph (c)(2) of this section, a plan is considered terminated on a particular date if, as of that date, the plan is voluntarily terminated by the employer, or employers, maintaining the plan.

**(d) Complete discontinuance.** *(1) General rule.* For purposes of this section, a complete discontinuance of contributions under the plan is contrasted with a suspension of contributions under the plan which is merely a temporary cessation of contributions by the employer. A complete discontinuance of contributions may occur although some amounts are contributed by the employer under the plan if such amounts are not substantial enough to reflect the intent on the part of the employer to continue to maintain the plan. The determination of whether a complete discontinuance of contributions under the plan has occurred will be made with regard to all the facts and circumstances in the particular case, and without regard to the amount of any contributions made under the plan by employees. Among the factors to be considered in determining whether a suspension constitutes a discontinuance are:

(i) Whether the employer may merely be calling an actual discontinuance of contributions a suspension of such contributions in order to avoid the requirement of full vesting as in the case of a discontinuance, or for any other reason;

(ii) Whether contributions are recurring and substantial; and

(iii) Whether there is any reasonable probability that the lack of contributions will continue indefinitely.

*(2) Time of discontinuance.* In any case in which a suspension of a profit-sharing plan maintained by a single employer is considered a discontinuance, the discontinuance becomes effective not later than the last day of the taxable year of the employer following the last taxable year of such employer for which a substantial contribution was made under the profit-sharing plan. In the case of a profit-sharing plan maintained by more than one employer, the discontinuance becomes effective not later than the last day of the plan year following the plan year within which any employer made a substantial contribution under the plan.

**(e) Contributions or benefits which remains forfeitable.** Under section 411(d)(2) and (3), section 411(a) and this section do not apply to plan benefits which may not be provided for designated employees in the event of early termination of the plan under provisions of the plan adopted pursuant to regulations prescribed by the Secretary or his delegate to preclude the discrimination prohibited by section 401(a)(4). Accordingly, in such a case, plan benefits may be required to be reallocated without regard to this section. See § 1.401-4(c).

---

T.D. 7501, 8/22/77.

---

### § 1.411(d)-3 Section 411(d)(6) protected benefits.

***Caution:*** The Treasury has not yet amended Reg § 1.411(d)-3 to reflect changes made by P.L. 103-465.

**(a) Protection of accrued benefits.** *(1) General rule.* Under section 411(d)(6)(A), a plan is not a qualified plan (and a trust forming a part of such plan is not a qualified trust) if a plan amendment decreases the accrued benefit of any plan participant, except as provided in section 412(d)(2) (section 412(c)(8) for plan years beginning before January 1, 2008), section 4281 of the Employee Retirement Income Security Act of 1974 as amended (ERISA), or other applicable law (see, for example, sections 418D and 418E of the Internal Revenue Code, and section 1107 of the Pension Protection Act of 2006, Public Law 109-280 (120 Stat. 780, 1063)). For purposes of this section, a plan amendment includes any changes to the terms of a plan, including changes resulting from a merger, consolidation, or transfer (as defined in section 414(l)) or a plan termination. The protection of section 411(d)(6) applies to a participant's entire accrued benefit under the plan as of the applicable amendment date, without regard to whether the entire accrued benefit was accrued before a participant's severance from employment or whether any portion was the result of an increase in the accrued benefit of the participant pursuant to a plan amendment adopted after the participant's severance from employment.

*(2) Plan provisions taken into account.* (i) Direct or indirect reduction in accrued benefit. For purposes of determining whether a participant's accrued benefit is decreased, all of the amendments to the provisions of a plan affecting, di-

rectly or indirectly, the computation of accrued benefits are taken into account. Plan provisions indirectly affecting the computation of accrued benefits include, for example, provisions relating to years of service and compensation.

(ii) Amendments effective with the same applicable amendment date. In determining whether a reduction in a participant's accrued benefit has occurred, all plan amendments with the same applicable amendment date are treated as one amendment. Thus, if two amendments have the same applicable amendment date and one amendment, standing alone, increases participants' accrued benefits and the other amendment, standing alone, decreases participants' accrued benefits, the amendments are treated as one amendment and will only violate section 411(d)(6) if, for any participant, the net effect is to decrease participants' accrued benefit as of that applicable amendment date.

(iii) Multiple amendments. (A) General rule. A plan amendment violates the requirements of section 411(d)(6) if it is one of a series of plan amendments that, when taken together, have the effect of reducing or eliminating a section 411(d)(6) protected benefit in a manner that would be prohibited by section 411(d)(6) if accomplished through a single amendment.

(B) Determination of the time period for combining plan amendments. For purposes of applying the rule in paragraph (a)(2)(iii)(A) of this section, generally only plan amendments adopted within a 3-year period are taken into account.

*(3) Application of section 411(a) nonforfeitability provisions with respect to section 411(d)(6) protected benefits.* (i) In general. The rules of this paragraph (a) apply to a plan amendment that decreases a participant's accrued benefits, or otherwise places greater restrictions or conditions on a participant's rights to section 411(d)(6) protected benefits, even if the amendment merely adds a restriction or condition that is permitted under the vesting rules in section 411(a)(3) through (11). However, such an amendment does not violate section 411(d)(6) to the extent it applies with respect to benefits that accrue after the applicable amendment date. See section 411(a)(10) and § 1.411(a)-8 for additional rules relating to changes in a plan's vesting schedule.

(ii) Exception for changes in a plan's vesting computation period. Notwithstanding paragraph (a)(3)(i) of this section, a plan amendment that satisfies the applicable requirements under 29 CFR 2530.203-2(c) (rules relating to vesting computation periods) does not fail to satisfy the requirements of section 411(d)(6) merely because the plan amendment changes the plan's vesting computation period.

*(4) Examples.* The following examples illustrate the application of this paragraph (a):

*Example (1).* (i) Facts. Plan A provides an annual benefit of 2% of career average pay times years of service commencing at normal retirement age (age 65). Plan A is amended on November 1, 2006, effective as of January 1, 2007, to provide for an annual benefit of 1.3% of final pay times years of service, with final pay computed as the average of a participant's highest 3 consecutive years of compensation. As of January 1, 2007, Participant M has 16 years of service, M's career average pay is $37,500, and the average of M's highest 3 consecutive years of compensation is $67,308. Thus, Participant M's accrued benefit as of the applicable amendment date is increased from $12,000 per year at normal retirement age (2% times $37,500 times 16 years of service) to $14,000 per year at normal retirement age (1.3% times $67,308 times 16 years of service). As of January 1, 2007, Participant N has 6 years of service, N's career average pay is $50,000, and the average of N's highest 3 consecutive years of compensation is $51,282. Participant N's accrued benefit as of the applicable amendment date is decreased from $6,000 per year at normal retirement age (2% times $50,000 times 6 years of service) to $4,000 per year at normal retirement age (1.3% times $51,282 times 6 years of service).

(ii) Conclusion. While the plan amendment increases the accrued benefit of Participant M, the plan amendment fails to satisfy the requirements of section 411(d)(6)(A) because the amendment decreases the accrued benefit of Participant N below the level of the accrued benefit of Participant N immediately before the applicable amendment date.

*Example (2).* (i) Facts. The facts are the same as Example 1, except that Plan A includes a provision under which Participant N's accrued benefit cannot be less than what it was immediately before the applicable amendment date (so that Participant N's accrued benefit could not be less than $6,000 per year at normal retirement age).

(ii) Conclusion. The amendment does not violate the requirements of section 411(d)(6)(A) with respect to Participant M (whose accrued benefit has been increased) or with respect to Participant N (although Participant N would not accrue any benefits until the point in time at which the new formula amount would exceed the amount payable under the minimum provision, approximately 3 years after the amendment becomes effective).

*Example (3).* (i) Facts. Employer N maintains Plan C, a qualified defined benefit plan under which an employee becomes a participant upon completion of 1 year of service and is vested in 100% of the employer-derived accrued benefit upon completion of 5 years of service. Plan C provides that a former employee's years of service prior to a break in service will be reinstated upon completion of 1 year of service after being rehired. Plan C has participants who have fewer than 5 years of service and who are accordingly 0% vested in their employer-derived accrued benefits. On December 31, 2007, effective January 1, 2008, Plan C is amended, in accordance with section 411(a)(6)(D), to provide that any nonvested participant who has at least 5 consecutive 1-year breaks in service and whose number of consecutive 1-year breaks in service exceeds his or her number of years of service before the breaks will have his or her pre-break service disregarded in determining vesting under the plan.

(ii) Conclusion. Under paragraph (a)(3) of this section, the plan amendment does not satisfy the requirements of this paragraph (a), and thus violates section 411(d)(6), because the amendment places greater restrictions or conditions on the rights to section 411(d)(6) protected benefits, as of January 1, 2008, for participants who have fewer than 5 years of service, by restricting the ability of those participants to receive further vesting protections on benefits accrued as of that date.

*Example (4).* (i) Facts. (A) Employer O sponsors Plan D, a qualified profit sharing plan under which each employee has a nonforfeitable right to a percentage of his or her employer-derived accrued benefit based on the following table:

| Completed years of service | Nonforfeitable percentage |
|---|---|
| Fewer than 3 | 0 |
| 3 | 20 |
| 4 | 40 |
| 5 | 60 |
| 6 | 80 |
| 7 | 100 |

(B) In January 2006, Employer O acquires Company X, which maintains Plan E, a qualified profit sharing plan under which each employee who has completed 5 years of service has a nonforfeitable right to 100% of the employer-derived accrued benefit. In 2007, Plan E is merged into Plan D. On the effective date for the merger, Plan D is amended to provide that the vesting schedule for participants of Plan E is the 7-year graded vesting schedule of Plan D. In accordance with section 411(a)(10)(A), the plan amendment provides that any participant of Plan E who had completed 5 years of service prior to the amendment is fully vested. In addition, as required under section 411(a)(10)(B), the amendment provides that any participant in Plan E who has at least 3 years of service prior to the amendment is permitted to make an irrevocable election to have the vesting of his or her nonforfeitable right to the employer-derived accrued benefit determined under either the 5-year cliff vesting schedule or the 7-year graded vesting schedule. Participant G, who has an account balance of $10,000 on the applicable amendment date, is a participant in Plan E with 2 years of service as of the applicable amendment date. As of the date of the merger, Participant G's nonforfeitable right to G's employer-derived accrued benefit is 0% under both the 7-year graded vesting schedule of Plan D and the 5-year cliff vesting schedule of Plan E.

(ii) Conclusion. Under paragraph (a)(3) of this section, the plan amendment does not satisfy the requirements of this paragraph (a) and violates section 411(d)(6), because the amendment places greater restrictions or conditions on the rights to section 411(d)(6) protected benefits with respect to G and any participant who has fewer than 5 years of service and who elected (or was made subject to) the new vesting schedule. A method of avoiding a section 411 (d)(6) violation with respect to account balances attributable to benefits accrued as of the applicable amendment date and earnings thereon would be for Plan D to provide for the vested percentage of G and each other participant in Plan E to be no less than the greater of the vesting percentages under the two vesting schedules (for example, for G and each other participant in Plan E to be 20% vested upon completion of 3 years of service, 40% vested upon completion of 4 years of service, and fully vested upon completion of 5 years of service) for those account balances and earnings.

**(b) Protection of section 411(d)(6)(B) protected benefits.** *(1) General rule.* (i) Prohibition against plan amendments eliminating or reducing section 411(d)(6)(B) protected benefits. Except as provided in this section, a plan is treated as decreasing an accrued benefit if it is amended to eliminate or reduce a section 411(d)(6)(B) protected benefit as defined in paragraph (g)(15) of this section. This paragraph (b)(1) applies to participants who satisfy (either before or after the plan amendment) the preamendment conditions for a section 411(d)(6)(B) protected benefit.

(ii) Contingent benefits. The rules of paragraph (b)(1)(i) of this section apply to participants who satisfy (either before or after the plan amendment) the preamendment conditions for the section 411(d)(6)(B) protected benefit even if the condition on which the eligibility for the section 411(d)(6)(B) protected benefit depends is an unpredictable contingent event (e.g., a plant shutdown).

(iii) Application of general rules in paragraph (a) of this section to section 411(d)(6)(B) protected benefits. For purposes of determining whether a participant's section 411(d)(6)(B) protected benefit is eliminated or reduced, the rules of paragraph (a) of this section apply to section 411(d)(6)(B) protected benefits in the same manner as they apply to accrued benefits described in section 411(d)(6)(A). As an example of the application of paragraph (a)(2)(ii) of this section to section 411(d)(6)(B) protected benefits, if there are two amendments with the same applicable amendment date and one amendment increases accrued benefits and the other amendment decreases the early retirement factors that are used to determine the early retirement annuity, the amendments are treated as one amendment and only violate section 411(d)(6) if, after the two amendments, the net dollar amount of any early retirement annuity with respect to the accrued benefit of any participant as of the applicable amendment date is lower than it would have been without the two amendments. As an example of the application of paragraph (a)(2)(iii) of this section to section 411(d)(6)(B) protected benefits, a series of amendments made within a 3-year period that, when taken together, have the effect of reducing or eliminating early retirement benefits or retirement-type subsidies in a manner that adversely affects the rights of any participant in a more than de minimis manner violates section 411(d)(6)(B) even if each amendment would be permissible pursuant to paragraphs (c), (d), or (f) of this section.

*(2) Permissible elimination of section 411(d)(6)(B) protected benefits.* (i) In general. A plan is permitted to be amended to eliminate a section 411(d)(6)(B) protected benefit if the elimination is in accordance with this section or § 1.411(d)-4.

(ii) Increases in payment amounts do not eliminate an optional form of benefit. An amendment is not treated as eliminating an optional form of benefit or eliminating or reducing an early retirement benefit or retirement-type subsidy under the plan, if, effective after the plan amendment, there is another optional form of benefit available to the participant under the plan that is of inherently equal or greater value (within the meaning of § 1.401(a)(4)-4(d)(4)(i)(A)). Thus, for example, a change in the method of calculating a joint and survivor annuity from using a 90% adjustment factor on account of the survivorship payment at particular ages for a participant and a spouse to using a 91% adjustment factor at the same ages is not treated as an elimination of an optional form of benefit. Similarly, a plan that offers a subsidized qualified joint and survivor annuity option for married participants under which the amount payable during the participant's lifetime is not less than the amount payable under the plan's straight life annuity is permitted to be amended to eliminate the straight life annuity option for married participants.

*(3) Permissible elimination of benefits that are not section 411(d)(6) protected benefits.* (i) In general. Section 411(d)(6) does not provide protection for benefits that are ancillary benefits, other rights and features, or any other benefits that are not described in section 411(d)(6). See § 1.411(d)-4, Q&A-1(d). However, a plan may not be amended to recharacterize a retirement-type benefit as an ancillary benefit. Thus, for example, a plan amendment to recharacterize any portion of an early retirement subsidy as a social secur-

ity supplement that is an ancillary benefit violates section 411(d)(6).

(ii) No protection for future benefit accruals. Section 411(d)(6) only protects benefits that accrue before the applicable amendment date. Thus, a plan is permitted to be amended to eliminate or reduce an early retirement benefit, a retirement-type subsidy, or an optional form of benefit with respect to benefits that accrue after the applicable amendment date without violating section 411(d)(6). However, section 4980F(e) of the Internal Revenue Code and section 204(h) of ERISA require notice of an amendment to an applicable pension plan that either provides for a significant reduction in the rate of future benefit accrual or that eliminates or significantly reduces an early retirement benefit or a retirement-type subsidy. See § 54.4980F-1 of this chapter generally, and see § 54.4980F-1, Q&A-7(b) and Q&A-8(c) of this chapter, with respect to the circumstances under which such notice is required for a reduction in an early retirement benefit or retirement-type subsidy.

*(4) Examples.* The following examples illustrate the application of this paragraph (b):

*Example (1).* (i) Facts involving amendments to an early retirement subsidy. Plan A provides an annual benefit of 2% of career average pay times years of service commencing at normal retirement age (age 65). Plan A is amended on November 1, 2006, effective as of January 1, 2007, to provide for an annual benefit of 1.3% of final pay times years of service, with final pay computed as the average of a participant's highest 3 consecutive years of compensation. Participant M is age 50, M has 16 years of service, M's career average pay is $37,500, and the average of M's highest 3 consecutive years of compensation is $67,308. Thus, M's accrued benefit as of the effective date of the amendment is increased from $12,000 per year at normal retirement age (2% times $37,500 times 16 years of service) to $14,000 per year at normal retirement age (1.3% times $67,308 times 16 years of service). (These facts are similar to the facts in Example 1 in paragraph (a)(4) of this section.) Before the amendment, Plan A permitted a former employee to commence distribution of benefits as early as age 55 and, for a participant with at least 15 years of service, actuarially reduced the amount payable in the form of a straight life annuity commencing before normal retirement age by 3% per year from age 60 to age 65 and by 7% per year from age 55 through age 59. Thus, before the amendment, the amount of M's early retirement benefit that would be payable for commencement at age 55 was $6,000 per year ($12,000 per year minus 3% for 5 years and minus 7% for 5 more years). The amendment also alters the actuarial reduction factor so that, for a participant with at least 15 years of service, the amount payable in a straight life annuity commencing before normal retirement age is reduced by 6% per year. As a result, the amount of M's early retirement benefit at age 55 becomes $5,600 per year after the amendment ($14,000 minus 6% for 10 years).

(ii) Conclusion. The straight life annuity payable under Plan A at age 55 is an optional form of benefit that includes an early retirement subsidy. The plan amendment fails to satisfy the requirements of section 411(d)(6)(B) because the amendment decreases the optional form of benefit payable to Participant M below the level that Participant M was entitled to receive immediately before the effective date of the amendment. If instead Plan A had included a provision under which M's straight life annuity payable at any age could be not be less than what it was immediately before the amendment (so that M's straight life annuity payable at age 55 could not be less than $6,000 per year), then the amendment would not fail to satisfy the requirements of section 411(d)(6)(B) with respect to M's straight life annuity payable at age 55 (although the straight life annuity payable to M at age 55 would not increase until the point in time at which the new formula amount with the new actuarial reduction factors exceeds the amount payable under the minimum provision, approximately 14 months after the amendment becomes effective).

*Example (2).* (i) Facts involving plant shutdown benefits. Plan B permits participants who have a severance from employment before normal retirement age (age 65) to commence distributions at any time after age 55 with the amount payable to be actuarially reduced using reasonable actuarial assumptions regarding interest and mortality specified in the plan, but provides that the annual reduction for any participant who has at least 20 years of service and who has a severance from employment after age 55 is only 3% per year (which is a smaller reduction than would apply under reasonable actuarial reductions). Plan B also provides 2 plant shutdown benefits to participants who have a severance of employment as a result of a plant shutdown. First, the favorable 3% per year actuarial reduction applies for commencement of benefits after age 55 and before age 65 for any participant who has at least 10 years of service and who has a severance from employment as a result of a plant shutdown. Second, all participants who have at least 20 years of service and who have a severance from employment after age 55 (and before normal retirement age at age 65) as a result of a plant shutdown will receive supplemental payments. Under the supplemental payments, an additional amount equal to the participant's estimated old-age insurance benefit under the Social Security Act is payable until age 65. The supplemental payments are not a QSUPP, as defined in § 1.401(a)(4)-12, because the plan's terms do not state that the supplement is treated as an early retirement benefit that is protected under section 411(d)(6).

(ii) Conclusion with respect to plant shutdown benefits. The benefits payable with the 3% annual reduction are retirement-type benefits. The excess of the actuarial present value of the early retirement benefit using the 3% annual reduction over the actuarial present value of the normal retirement benefit is a retirement-type subsidy and the right to receive payments of the benefit at age 55 is an early retirement benefit. These conclusions apply not only with respect to the rights that apply to participants who have at least 20 years of service, but also to participants with at least 10 years of service who have a severance from employment as a result of a plant shutdown. Thus, the right to receive benefits based on a 3% annual reduction for participants with at least 10 years of service at the time of a plant shutdown is an early retirement benefit that provides a retirement-type subsidy and is a section 411(d)(6)(B) protected benefit (even though no plant shutdown has occurred). Therefore, a plan amendment cannot eliminate this benefit with respect to benefits accrued before the applicable amendment date, even before the occurrence of the plant shutdown. Because the plan provides that the supplemental payments cannot exceed the OASDI benefit under the Social Security Act, the supplemental payments constitute a social security supplement (but not a QSUPP as defined in § 1.401(a)(4)-12), which is an ancillary benefit that is not a section 411(d)(6)(B) protected benefit and accordingly is not taken into account in determining whether a prohibited reduction has occurred.

*Example (3).* (i) Facts. Plan C, a multiemployer defined benefit plan in which participation is limited to electricians in the construction industry, provides that a participant may elect to commence distributions only if the participant is not currently employed by a participating employer and provides that, if the participant has a specified number of years of service and attains a specified age, the distribution is without any actuarial reduction for commencement before normal retirement age. Since the plan's inception, Plan C has provided for suspension of pension benefits during periods of disqualifying employment (ERISA section 203(a)(3)(B) service). Before 2007, the plan defined disqualifying employment to include any job as an electrician in the particular industry and geographic location to which Plan C applies. This definition of disqualifying employment did not cover a job as an electrician supervisor. In 2005, Participant E, having rendered the specified number of years of service and attained the specified age to retire with a fully subsidized early retirement benefit, retires from E's job as an electrician with Employer Y and starts a position with Employer Z as an electrician supervisor. Employer Z is not a participating employer in Plan C but is an employer in the same industry and geographic location as Employer Y. When E left service with Employer Y, E's position as an electrician supervisor was not disqualifying employment for purposes of Plan C's suspension of pension benefit provision, and E elected to commence benefit payments in 2005. In 2006, effective January 1, 2007, Plan C is amended to expand the definition of disqualifying employment to include any job (including supervisory positions) as an electrician in the same industry and geographic location to which Plan C applies. The plan's definition of disqualifying employment satisfies the requirements of section 411(a)(3)(B). On January 1, 2007, E's pension benefits are suspended because of E's disqualifying employment as an electrician supervisor.

(ii) Conclusion. Under paragraphs (a)(3) and (b)(1) of this section, the 2007 plan amendment violates section 411(d)(6), because the amendment places greater restrictions or conditions on a participant's rights to section 411(d)(6) protected benefits to the extent it applies with respect to benefits that accrued before January 1, 2007. The result would be the same even if the amendment did not apply to former employees and instead applied only to participants who were actively employed at the time of the applicable amendment.

**(c) Permissible elimination of optional forms of benefit that are redundant.** *(1) General rule.* Except as otherwise provided in paragraph (c)(5) of this section, a plan is permitted to be amended to eliminate an optional form of benefit for a participant with respect to benefits accrued before the applicable amendment date if—

(i) The optional form of benefit is redundant with respect to a retained optional form of benefit, within the meaning of paragraph (c)(2) of this section;

(ii) The plan amendment is not applicable with respect to an optional form of benefit with an annuity commencement date that is earlier than the number of days in the maximum QJSA explanation period (as defined in paragraph (g)(9) of this section) after the date the amendment is adopted; and

(iii) The requirements of paragraph (e) of this section are satisfied in any case in which either:

(A) The retained optional form of benefit for the participant does not commence on the same annuity commencement date as the optional form of benefit that is being eliminated; or

(B) As of the date the amendment is adopted, the actuarial present value of the retained optional form of benefit for the participant is less than the actuarial present value of the optional form of benefit that is being eliminated.

*(2) Similar types of optional forms of benefit are redundant.* (i) General rule. An optional form of benefit is redundant with respect to a retained optional form of benefit if, after the amendment becomes applicable—

(A) There is a retained optional form of benefit available to the participant that is in the same family of optional forms of benefit, within the meaning of paragraphs (c)(3) and (4) of this section, as the optional form of benefit being eliminated; and

(B) The participant's rights with respect to the retained optional form of benefit are not subject to materially greater restrictions (such as conditions relating to eligibility, restrictions on a participant's ability to designate the person who is entitled to benefits following the participant's death, or restrictions on a participant's right to receive an in-kind distribution) than applied to the optional form of benefit being eliminated.

(ii) Special rule for core options. An optional form of benefit that is a core option as defined in paragraph (g)(5) of this section may not be eliminated as a redundant benefit under the rules of this paragraph (c) unless the retained optional form of benefit and the eliminated core option are identical except for differences described in paragraph (c)(3)(ii) of this section. Thus, for example, a particular 10-year term certain and life annuity may not be eliminated by plan amendment unless the retained optional form of benefit is another 10-year term certain and life annuity.

*(3) Family of optional forms of benefit.* (i) In general. Paragraph (c)(4) of this section describes certain families of optional forms of benefits. Not every optional form of benefit that is offered under a plan necessarily fits within a family of optional forms of benefit as described in paragraph (c)(4) of this section. Each optional form of benefit that is not included in any particular family of optional forms of benefit listed in paragraph (c)(4) of this section is in a separate family of optional forms of benefit with other optional forms of benefit that would be identical to that optional form of benefit but for differences that are disregarded under paragraph (c)(3)(ii) of this section.

(ii) Certain differences among optional forms of benefit. (A) Differences in actuarial factors and annuity starting dates. The determination of whether two optional forms of benefit are within a family of optional forms of benefit is made without regard to actuarial factors or annuity starting dates. Thus, any optional forms of benefit that are part of the same generalized optional form (within the meaning of paragraph (g)(8) of this section) are in the same family of optional forms of benefit. For example, if a plan has a single-sum distribution option for some participants that is calculated using a 5% interest rate and a specific mortality table (but no less than the minimum present value as determined under section 417(e)) and another single-sum distribution option for other participants that is calculated using the applicable interest rate as defined in section 417(e)(3)(A)(ii)(II) and the applicable mortality table as defined in section 417(e)(3)(A)(ii)(I), both single-sum distribution options are part of the same generalized optional form and thus in the same family of optional forms of benefit under the rules of paragraph (c)(3)(i) of this section. However, differences in actuarial factors and annuity starting dates are taken into account for purposes of the requirements in paragraph (e)(3) of this section.

(B) Differences in pop-up provisions and cash refund features for joint and contingent options. The determination of whether two optional forms of benefit are within a family of optional forms of benefit relating to joint and contingent families (as described in paragraph (c)(4)(i) and (ii) of this section) is made without regard to the following features—

(1) Pop-up provisions (under which payments increase upon the death of the beneficiary or another event that causes the beneficiary not to be entitled to a survivor annuity);

(2) Cash refund features (under which payment is provided upon the death of the last annuitant in an amount that is not greater than the excess of the present value of the annuity at the annuity starting date over the total of payments before the death of the last annuitant); or

(3) Term-certain provisions for optional forms of benefit within a joint and contingent family.

(C) Differences in social security leveling features, refund of employee contributions features, and retroactive annuity starting date features. The determination of whether 2 optional forms of benefit are within a family of optional forms of benefit is made without regard to social security leveling features, refund of employee contributions features, or retroactive annuity starting date features. But see paragraph (c)(5) of this section for special rules relating to social security leveling, refund of employee contributions, and retroactive annuity starting date features in optional forms of benefit.

*(4) List of families.* The following are families of optional forms of benefit for purposes of this paragraph (c):

(i) Joint and contingent options with continuation percentages of 50% to 100%. An optional form of benefit is within the 50% or more joint and contingent family if it provides a life annuity to the participant and a survivor annuity to an individual that is at least 50% and no more than 100% of the annuity payable during the joint lives of the participant and the participant's survivor.

(ii) Joint and contingent options with continuation percentages less than 50%. An optional form of benefit is within the less than 50% joint and contingent family if it provides a life annuity to the participant and a survivor annuity to an individual that is less than 50% of the annuity payable during the joint lives of the participant and the participant's survivor.

(iii) Term certain and life annuity options with a term of 10 years or less. An optional form of benefit is within the 10 years or less term certain and life family if it is a life annuity with a guarantee that payments will continue to the participant's beneficiary for the remainder of a fixed period that is 10 years or less if the participant dies before the end of the fixed period.

(iv) Term certain and life annuity options with a term longer than 10 years. An optional form of benefit is within the longer than 10 years term certain and life family if it is a life annuity with a guarantee that payments will continue to the participant's beneficiary for the remainder of a fixed period that is in excess of 10 years if the participant dies before the end of the fixed period.

(v) Level installment payment options over a period of 10 years or less. An optional form of benefit is within the 10 years or less installment family if it provides for substantially level payments to the participant for a fixed period of at least 2 years and not in excess of 10 years with a guarantee that payments will continue to the participant's beneficiary for the remainder of the fixed period if the participant dies before the end of the fixed period.

(vi) Level installment payment options over a period of more than 10 years. An optional form of benefit is within the more than 10 years installment family if it provides for substantially level payments to the participant for a fixed period that is in excess of 10 years with a guarantee that payments will continue to the participant's beneficiary for the remainder of the fixed period if the participant dies before the end of the fixed period.

*(5) Special rules for certain features included in optional forms of benefit.* For purposes of applying this paragraph (c), to the extent an optional form of benefit that is being eliminated includes either a social security leveling feature or a refund of employee contributions feature, the retained optional form of benefit must also include that feature, and, to the extent that the optional form of benefit that is being eliminated does not include a social security leveling feature or a refund of employee contributions feature, the retained optional form of benefit must not include that feature. For purposes of applying this paragraph (c), to the extent an optional form of benefit that is being eliminated does not include a retroactive annuity starting date feature, the retained optional form of benefit must not include the feature.

*(6) Separate application of redundancy rules for bifurcated benefits.* If a plan permits the participant to make different distribution elections with respect to two or more separate portions of the participant's benefit, the rules of this paragraph (c) are permitted to be applied separately to each such portion of the participant's benefit as if that portion were the participant's entire benefit. Thus, for example, if one set of distribution elections applies to a portion of the participant's accrued benefit and another set of distribution elections applies to the other portion of the participant's accrued benefit, then with respect to one portion of the participant's benefit, the determination of whether any optional form of benefit is within a family of optional forms of benefit is permitted to be made disregarding elections that apply to the other portion of the participant's benefit. Similarly, if a participant can elect to receive any portion of the accrued benefit in a single sum and the remainder pursuant to a set of distribution elections, the rules of this paragraph (c) are permitted to be applied separately to the set of distribution elections that apply to the portion of the participant's accrued benefit that is not payable in a single sum (for example, for the portion of a participant's benefit that is not paid in a single sum, the determination of whether any optional form of benefit is within a family of optional forms of benefit is permitted to be made disregarding the fact that the other portion of the participant's benefit is paid in a single sum).

**(d) Permissible elimination of noncore optional forms of benefit where core options are offered.** *(1) General rule.* Except as otherwise provided in paragraph (d)(2) of this section, a plan is permitted to be amended to eliminate an optional form of benefit for a participant with respect to benefits accrued before the applicable amendment date if—

(i) After the amendment becomes applicable, each of the core options described in paragraph (g)(5) of this section is available to the participant with respect to benefits accrued before and after the amendment;

(ii) The plan amendment is not applicable with respect to an optional form of benefit with an annuity commencement date that is earlier than 4 years after the date the amendment is adopted; and

(iii) The requirements of paragraph (e) of this section are satisfied in any case in which either:

(A) One or more of the core options are not available commencing on the same annuity commencement date as the optional form of benefit that is being eliminated; or

(B) As of the date the amendment is adopted, the actuarial present value of the benefit payable under any core option with the same annuity commencement date is less than the actuarial present value of benefits payable under the optional form of benefit that is being eliminated.

*(2) Special rules.* (i) Treatment of certain features included in optional forms of benefit. For purposes of applying this paragraph (d), to the extent an optional form of benefit that is being eliminated includes either a social security leveling feature or a refund of employee contributions feature, at least one of the core options must also be available with that feature, and, to the extent that the optional form of benefit that is being eliminated does not include a social security leveling feature or a refund of employee contributions feature, each of the core options must be available without that feature. For purposes of applying this paragraph (d), to the extent an optional form of benefit that is being eliminated does not include a retroactive annuity starting date feature, each of the core options must be available without that feature.

(ii) Eliminating the most valuable option for a participant with a short life expectancy. For purposes of applying this paragraph (d), if the most valuable option for a participant with a short life expectancy (as defined in paragraph (g)(5)(iii) of this section) is eliminated, then, after the plan amendment, an optional form of benefit that is identical, except for differences described in paragraph (c)(3)(ii) of this section, must be available to the participant. However, such a plan amendment cannot eliminate a refund of employee contributions feature from the most valuable option for a participant with a short life expectancy.

(iii) Single-sum distributions. A plan amendment is not treated as satisfying this paragraph (d) if it eliminates an optional form of benefit that includes a single-sum distribution that applies with respect to at least 25% of the participant's accrued benefit as of the date the optional form of benefit is eliminated. But see § 1.411(d)-4, Q&A-2(b)(2)(v), relating to involuntary single-sum distributions for benefits with a present value not in excess of the maximum dollar amount in section 411(a)(11).

(iv) Application of multiple amendment rule to core option rule. Notwithstanding paragraph (a)(2)(iii)(B) of this section, if a plan is amended to eliminate an optional form of benefit using the core options rule in this paragraph (d), then the employer must wait 3 years after the first annuity commencement date for which the optional form of benefit is no longer available before making any changes to the core options offered under the plan (other than a change that is not treated as an elimination under paragraph (b)(2)(ii) of this section). Thus, for example, if a plan amendment eliminates an optional form of benefit for a participant using the core options rule under this paragraph (d), with an adoption date of January 1, 2006 and an effective date of January 1, 2010, the plan would not be permitted to be amended to make changes to the core options offered under the plan (and the core options would continue to apply with respect to the participant's accrued benefit) until January 1, 2013.

(v) Special rule for joint and contingent annuity core option. If a plan offers joint and contingent annuities under which a participant is entitled to a life annuity with a survivor annuity for the individual designated by the participant (including a non-spousal contingent annuitant) with continuation percentage options of both 50% and 100% (after adjustments permitted under paragraph (g)(5)(ii) of this section to comply with applicable law), the plan is permitted to treat both of these options as core options for purposes of this paragraph (d), in lieu of a 75% joint and contingent annuity. Thus, such a plan is permitted to use the rules of this paragraph (d) if the plan satisfies all of the requirements of this paragraph (d) (taking into account the modification rule in paragraph (g)(5)(ii) of this section) other than the requirement of offering a 75% joint and contingent annuity as described in paragraph (g)(5)(i)(B) of this section.

**(e) Permissible plan amendments under paragraphs (c) and (d) eliminating or reducing section 411(d)(6)(B) protected benefits that are burdensome and of de minimis value.** *(1) In general.* A plan amendment that, pursuant to paragraph (c)(1)(iii) or (d)(1)(iii) of this section, is required to satisfy this paragraph (e) satisfies this paragraph (e) if—

(i) The amendment eliminates section 411(d)(6)(B) protected benefits that create significant burdens or complexities for the plan and its participants as described in paragraph (e)(2) of this section; and

(ii) The amendment does not adversely affect the rights of any participant in a more than de minimis manner as described in paragraph (e)(3) of this section.

*(2) Plan amendments eliminating section 411(d)(6)(B) protected benefits that create significant burdens and complexities.* (i) Facts and circumstances analysis. (A) In general. The determination of whether a plan amendment eliminates section 411(d)(6)(B) protected benefits that create significant burdens or complexities for the plan and its participants is based on facts and circumstances.

(B) Early retirement benefits. In the case of an amendment that eliminates an early retirement benefit, relevant factors include whether the annuity starting dates under the plan considered in the aggregate are burdensome or complex (e.g., the number of categories of early retirement benefits, whether the terms and conditions applicable to the plan's early retirement benefits are difficult to summarize in a manner that is concise and readily understandable to the average plan participant, and whether those different early retirement benefits were added to the plan as a result of a plan merger, transfer, or consolidation), and whether the effect of the plan amendment is to reduce the number of categories of early retirement benefits.

(C) Retirement-type subsidies and actuarial factors. In the case of a plan amendment eliminating a retirement-type subsidy or changing the actuarial factors used to determine optional forms of benefit, relevant factors include whether the actuarial factors used for determining optional forms of benefit available under the plan considered in the aggregate are burdensome or complex (e.g., the number of different retirement-type subsidies and other actuarial factors available under the plan, whether the terms and conditions applicable to the plan's retirement-type subsidies are difficult to summarize in a manner that is concise and readily understandable to the average plan participant, whether the plan is eliminating one or more generalized optional forms, whether the plan is replacing a complex optional form of benefit that contains a retirement-type subsidy with a simpler form, and whether the different retirement-type subsidies and other actuarial factors were added to the plan as a result of a plan merger, transfer, or consolidation), and whether the effect of the plan amendment is to reduce the number of categories of retirement-type subsidies or other actuarial factors.

(D) Example. The following example illustrates the application of this paragraph (e)(2)(i):

*Example.* (i) Facts. Plan A is a defined benefit plan under which employees may select a distribution in the form of a straight life annuity, a straight life annuity with cost-of-living increases, a 50% qualified joint and survivor annuity with a pop-up provision, or a 10-year term certain and life annuity. On January 15, 2007, Plan A is amended, effective June 1, 2007, to eliminate the 50% qualified joint and survivor annuity with a pop-up provision as described in paragraph (c)(3)(ii)(B)(1) of this section and replace it with a 50% qualified joint and survivor annuity without the pop-up provision (and using the same actuarial factor).

(ii) Conclusion. Plan A satisfies the requirements of paragraph (e)(2)(i)(B) of this section because, based on the relevant facts and circumstances (e.g., the amendment replaces a complex optional form of benefit with a simpler form), the amendment eliminates section 411(d)(6)(B) protected benefits that create significant burdens and complexities. Accordingly, the plan amendment is permitted to eliminate the pop-up provision, provided that the plan amendment satisfies all the other applicable requirements in paragraph (c) or (d) of this section. For example, the plan amendment must not eliminate the most valuable option for a participant with a short life expectancy (as defined in paragraph (g)(5)(iii) of this section) and the plan amendment must not adversely affect the rights of any participant in a more than de minimis manner, taking into account the actuarial factors for the joint and survivor annuity with the pop-up provision and the joint and survivor annuity without the pop-up provision, as described in paragraph (e)(3) of this section.

(ii) Presumptions for certain amendments. (A) Presumption for amendments eliminating certain annuity starting dates. If the annuity starting dates under the plan considered in the aggregate are burdensome or complex, then elimination of any one of the annuity starting dates is presumed to eliminate section 411(d)(6)(B) protected benefits that create significant burdens or complexities for the plan and its participants. However, if the effect of a plan amendment with respect to a set of optional forms of benefit is merely to substitute one set of annuity starting dates for another set of annuity starting dates, without any reduction in the number of different annuity starting dates, then the plan amendment does not satisfy the requirements of this paragraph (e)(2).

(B) Presumption for amendments changing certain actuarial factors. If the actuarial factors used for determining benefit distributions available under a generalized optional form considered in the aggregate are burdensome or complex, then replacing some of the actuarial factors for the generalized optional form is presumed to eliminate section 411(d)(6)(B) protected benefits that create significant burdens or complexities for the plan and its participants. However, if the effect is merely to substitute one set of actuarial factors for another set of actuarial factors, without any reduction in the number of different actuarial factors or the complexity of those factors, then the plan amendment does not satisfy the requirements of this paragraph (e)(2) unless the change of actuarial factors is merely to replace one or more of the plan's actuarial factors for determining optional forms of benefit with new actuarial factors that are more accurate (e.g., reflecting more recent mortality experience or more recent market rates of interest).

(iii) Restrictions against creating burdens or complexities. See paragraphs (a)(2)(iii) and (b)(1)(iii) of this section for general rules applicable to multiple amendments. In accordance with these rules, a plan amendment does not eliminate a section 411(d)(6)(B) protected benefit that creates burdens and complexities for a plan and its participants if, less than 3 years earlier, a plan was previously amended to add another retirement-type subsidy in order to facilitate the elimination of the original retirement-type subsidy, even if the elimination of the other subsidy would not adversely affect the rights of any plan participant in a more than de minimis manner as provided in paragraph (e)(3) of this section.

*(3) Elimination of early retirement benefits or retirement-type subsidies that are de minimis.* (i) Rules for retained optional forms of benefit under paragraph (c) of this section. For purposes of paragraph (c) of this section, the elimination of an optional form of benefit does not adversely affect the rights of any participant in a more than de minimis manner if—

(A) The retained optional form of benefit described in paragraph (c) of this section has substantially the same annuity commencement date as the optional form of benefit that is being eliminated, as described in paragraph (e)(4) of this section; and

(B) Either the actuarial present value of the benefit payable in the optional form of benefit that is being eliminated does not exceed the actuarial present value of the benefit payable in the retained optional form of benefit by more than a de minimis amount, as described in paragraph (e)(5) of this section, or the amendment satisfies the requirements of paragraph (e)(6) of this section relating to a delayed effective date.

(ii) Rules for core options under paragraph (d) of this section. For purposes of paragraph (d) of this section, the elimination of an optional form of benefit does not adversely affect the rights of any participant in a more than de minimis manner if, with respect to each of the core options—

(A) The core option is available after the amendment with substantially the same annuity commencement date as the optional form of benefit that is being eliminated, as described in paragraph (e)(4) of this section; and

(B) Either the actuarial present value of the benefit payable in the optional form of benefit that is being eliminated does not exceed the actuarial present value of the benefit payable under the core option by more than a de minimis amount, as described in paragraph (e)(5) of this section, or the amendment satisfies the requirements of paragraph (e)(6) of this section.

*(4) Definition of substantially the same annuity starting dates.* For purposes of applying paragraphs (e)(3)(i)(A) and (ii)(A) of this section, annuity starting dates are considered substantially the same if they are within 6 months of each other.

*(5) Definition of de minimis difference in actuarial present value.* For purposes of applying paragraph (e)(3)(i)(B) and (ii)(B) of this section, a difference in actuarial present value between the optional form of benefit being eliminated and the retained optional form of benefit or core option is not more than a de minimis amount if, as of the date the amendment is adopted, the difference between the actuarial present value of the eliminated optional form of benefit and the actuarial present value of the retained optional form of benefit or core option is not more than the greater of—

(i) 2% of the present value of the retirement-type subsidy (if any) under the eliminated optional form of benefit prior to the amendment; or

(ii) 1% of the greater of the participant's compensation (as defined in section 415(c)(3)) for the prior plan year or the participant's average compensation for his or her high 3 years (within the meaning of section 415(b)(1)(B) and (b)(3)).

*(6) Delayed effective date.* (i) General rule. For purposes of applying paragraph (e)(3)(i)(B) and (ii)(B) of this section, an amendment that eliminates an optional form of benefit satisfies the requirements of this paragraph (e)(6) if the elimination of the optional form of benefit is not applicable to any annuity commencement date before the end of the expected transition period for that optional form of benefit.

(ii) Determination of expected transition period. (A) General rule. The expected transition period for a plan amendment eliminating an optional form of benefit is the period that begins when the amendment is adopted and ends when it is reasonable to expect, with respect to a section 411(d)(6)(B) protected benefit (i.e., not taking into account benefits that accrue in the future), that the form being eliminated would be subsumed by another optional form of benefit after taking into account expected future benefit accruals.

(B) Determination of expected transition period using conservative actuarial assumptions. The expected transition period for a plan amendment eliminating an optional form of benefit must be determined in accordance with actuarial assumptions that are reasonable at the time of the amendment and that are conservative (i.e., reasonable actuarial assumptions that are likely to result in the longest period of time until the eliminated optional form of benefit would be subsumed). For this purpose, actuarial assumptions are not treated as conservative unless they include assumptions that a participant's compensation will not increase and that future benefit accruals will not exceed accruals in recent periods.

(C) Effect of subsequent amendments reducing future benefit accruals on the expected transition period. If, during the expected transition period for a plan amendment eliminating an optional form of benefit, the plan is subsequently amended to reduce the rate of future benefit accrual (or otherwise to lengthen the expected transition period), thus that subsequent plan amendment must provide that the elimination of the optional form of benefit is void or must provide for the effective date for elimination of the optional form of benefit to be further extended to a new expected transition period that satisfies this paragraph (e)(6) taking into account the subsequent amendment.

(iii) Applicability of the delayed effective date rule limited to employees who continue to accrue benefits through the end of expected transition period. An amendment eliminating an optional form of benefit under this paragraph (e)(6) must be limited to participants who continue to accrue benefits under the plan through the end of the expected transition period. Thus, for example, the plan amendment may not apply to any participant who has a severance from employment during the expected transition period.

(iv) Special rule for section 204(h) notice. See § 54.4980F-1(b), Q&A-8(c) of this chapter for a special rule relating to this paragraph (e)(6).

**(f) Utilization test.** *(1) General rule.* A plan is permitted to be amended to eliminate all of the optional forms of benefit that comprise a generalized optional form (as defined in paragraph (g)(8) of this section) for a participant with respect to benefits accrued before the applicable amendment date if--

(i) None of the optional forms of benefit being eliminated is a core option, within the meaning of paragraph (g)(5) of this section;

(ii) The plan amendment is not applicable with respect to an optional form of benefit with an annuity commencement date that is earlier than the number of days in the maximum Qualified Joint and Survivor Annuity explanation period (as defined in paragraph (g)(9) of this section) after the date the amendment is adopted;

(iii) During the look-back period--

(A) The generalized optional form has been available to at least the applicable number of participants who are taken into account under paragraph (f)(3) and (4) of this section; and

(B) No participant has elected any optional form of benefit that is part of the generalized optional form with an annuity commencement date that is within the look-back period.

*(2) Look-back period.* (i) In general. For purposes of this paragraph (f), the look-back period is the period that includes--

(A) The portion of the plan year in which such plan amendment is adopted that precedes the date of adoption (the pre-adoption period); and

(B) The 2 plan years immediately preceding the pre-adoption period.

(ii) Special look-back period rules. (A) 12-month plan year. In the look-back period, at least 1 of the plan years must be a 12-month plan year.

(B) Permitted 3-month exclusion in the pre-adoption period. A plan is permitted to exclude from the look-back period the calendar month in which the amendment is adopted and the preceding 1 or 2 calendar months to the extent those preceding months are contained within the pre-adoption period.

(C) Permission to extend the look-back period. In order to have a look-back period that satisfies the minimum applicable number of participants requirement in paragraph (f)(1)(iii)(A) of this section, the look-back period described in paragraph (f)(2)(i)(B) of this section is permitted to be expanded, so as to include the 3, 4, or 5 plan years immediately preceding the plan year in which the amendment is adopted. Thus, in determining the look-back period, a plan is permitted to substitute the 3, 4, or 5 plan years immediately preceding the pre-adoption period for the 2 plan years described in paragraph (f)(2)(i)(B) of this section. However, if a plan does not satisfy the minimum applicable number of participants requirement of paragraph (f)(1)(iii)(A) of this section using the pre-adoption period and the immediately preceding 5 plan years, the plan is not permitted to be amended in accordance with the utilization test in this paragraph (f).

*(3) Participants taken into account.* A participant is taken into account for purposes of this paragraph (f) only if the participant was eligible to elect to commence payment of an optional form of benefit that is part of the generalized optional form being eliminated with an annuity commencement date that is within the look-back period. However, a participant is not taken into account if the participant--

(i) Did not elect any optional form of benefit with an annuity commencement date that was within the look-back period;

(ii) Elected an optional form of benefit that included a single-sum distribution that applied with respect to at least 25% of the participant's accrued benefit;

(iii) Elected an optional form of benefit that was only available during a limited period of time and that contained a retirement-type subsidy where the subsidy that is part of the generalized optional form being eliminated was not extended to any optional form of benefit with the same annuity commencement date; or

(iv) Elected an optional form of benefit with an annuity commencement date that was more than 10 years before normal retirement age.

*(4) Determining the applicable number of participants.* For purposes of applying the rules in this paragraph (f), the applicable number of participants is 50 participants. However, notwithstanding paragraph (f)(3)(ii) of this section, a plan is permitted to take into account any participant who elected an optional form of benefit that included a single-sum distribution that applied with respect to at least 25% of the participant's accrued benefit, but only if the applicable number of participants is increased to 1,000 participants.

*(5) Default elections.* For purposes of this paragraph (f), an election includes the payment of an optional form of benefit that applies in the absence of an affirmative election.

**(g) Definitions and use of terms.** The definitions in this paragraph (g) apply for purposes of this section.

*(1) Actuarial present value.* The term actuarial present value means actuarial present value (within the meaning of § 1.401(a)(4)-12) determined using reasonable actuarial assumptions.

*(2) Ancillary benefit.* The term ancillary benefit means—

(i) A social security supplement under a defined benefit plan (other than a QSUPP as defined in § 1.401(a)(4)-12);

(ii) A benefit payable under a defined benefit plan in the event of disability (to the extent that the benefit exceeds the benefit otherwise payable), but only if the total benefit payable in the event of disability does not exceed the maximum qualified disability benefit, as defined in section 411(a)(9);

(iii) A life insurance benefit;

(iv) A medical benefit described in section 401(h);

(v) A death benefit under a defined benefit plan other than a death benefit which is a part of an optional form of benefit; or

(vi) A plant shutdown benefit or other similar benefit in a defined benefit plan that does not continue past retirement age and does not affect the payment of the accrued benefit, but only to the extent that such plant shutdown benefit, or other similar benefit (if any), is permitted in a qualified pension plan (see § 1.401-1(b)(1)(i)).

*(3) Annuity commencement date.* The term annuity commencement date generally means the annuity starting date, except that, in the case of a retroactive annuity starting date under section 417(a)(7), annuity commencement date means the date of the first payment of benefits pursuant to a participant election of a retroactive annuity starting date, as defined in § 1.417(e)-1(b)(3)(iv).

*(4) Applicable amendment date.* The term applicable amendment date, with respect to a plan amendment, means the later of the effective date of the amendment or the date the amendment is adopted.

*(5) Core options.* (i) General rule. With respect to a plan, the term core options means—

(A) A straight life annuity generalized optional form under which the participant is entitled to a level life annuity with no benefit payable after the participant's death;

(B) A 75% joint and contingent annuity generalized optional form under which the participant is entitled to a life annuity with a survivor annuity for any individual designated by the participant (including a non-spousal contingent annuitant) that is 75% of the amount payable during the participant's life (but see paragraph (d)(2)(v) of this section for a special rule relating to the joint and contingent annuity core option);

(C) A 10-year term certain and life annuity generalized optional form under which the participant is entitled to a life annuity with a guarantee that payments will continue to any person designated by the participant for the remainder of a fixed period of 10 years if the participant dies before the end of the 10-year period; and

(D) The most valuable option for a participant with a short life expectancy (as defined in paragraph (g)(5)(iii) of this section).

(ii) Modification of core options to satisfy other requirements. An annuity does not fail to be a core option (e.g., a joint and contingent annuity described in paragraph (g)(5)(i)(B) of this section or a 10-year term certain and life annuity described in paragraph (g)(5)(i)(C) of this section) as a result of differences to comply with applicable law, such as limitations on death benefits to comply with the incidental benefit requirement of § 1.401-1(b)(1)(i) or on account of the spousal consent rules of section 417.

(iii) Most valuable option for a participant with a short life expectancy. (A) General definition. Except as provided in paragraph (g)(5)(iii)(B) of this section, most valuable option for a participant with a short life expectancy means, for an annuity starting date, the optional form of benefit that is reasonably expected to result in payments that have the largest actuarial present value in the case of a participant who dies shortly after the annuity starting date, taking into account both payments due to the participant prior to the participant's death and any payments due after the participant's death. For this purpose, a plan is permitted to assume that the spouse of the participant is the same age as the participant. In addition, a plan is permitted to assume that the optional form of benefit that is the most valuable option for a participant with a short life expectancy when the participant is age 70½ also is the most valuable option for a participant with a short life expectancy at all older ages, and that the most valuable option for a participant with a short life expectancy at age 55 is the most valuable option for a participant with a short life expectancy at all younger ages.

(B) Safe harbor hierarchy. (1) A plan is permitted to treat a single-sum distribution option with an actuarial present value that is not less than the actuarial present value of any optional form of benefit eliminated by the plan amendment as the most valuable option for a participant with a short life expectancy for all of a participant's annuity starting dates if such single-sum distribution option is available at all such dates, without regard to whether the option was available before the plan amendment.

(2) If the plan before the amendment does not offer a single-sum distribution option as described in paragraph (g)(5)(iii)(B)(1) of this section, a plan is permitted to treat a joint and contingent annuity with a continuation percentage that is at least 75% and that is at least as great as the highest continuation percentage available before the amendment as the most valuable option for a participant with a short life

expectancy for all of a participant's annuity starting dates if such joint and contingent annuity is available at all such dates, without regard to whether the option was available before the plan amendment.

(3) If the plan before the amendment offers neither a single-sum distribution option as described in paragraph (g)(5)(iii)(B)(1) of this section nor a joint and contingent annuity with a continuation percentage as described in paragraph (g)(5)(iii)(B)(2) of this section, a plan is permitted to treat a term certain and life annuity with a term certain period no less than 15 years as the most valuable option for a participant with a short life expectancy for each annuity starting date if such 15-year term certain and life annuity is available at all annuity starting dates, without regard to whether the option was available before the plan amendment.

*(6) Definitions of types of section 411(d)(6)(B) protected benefits.*

(i) Early retirement benefit. The term early retirement benefit means the right, under the terms of a plan, to commence distribution of a retirement-type benefit at a particular date after severance from employment with the employer and before normal retirement age. Different early retirement benefits result from differences in terms relating to timing.

(ii) Optional form of benefit. (A) In general. The term optional form of benefit means a distribution alternative (including the normal form of benefit) that is available under the plan with respect to an accrued benefit or a distribution alternative with respect to a retirement-type benefit. Different optional forms of benefit exist if a distribution alternative is not payable on substantially the same terms as another distribution alternative. The relevant terms include all terms affecting the value of the optional form, such as the method of benefit calculation and the actuarial factors or assumptions used to determine the amount distributed. Thus, for example, different optional forms of benefit may result from differences in terms relating to the payment schedule, timing, commencement, medium of distribution (e.g., in cash or in kind), election rights, differences in eligibility requirements, or the portion of the benefit to which the distribution alternative applies. Likewise, differences in the normal retirement ages of employees or in the form in which the accrued benefit of employees is payable at normal retirement age under a plan are taken into account in determining whether a distribution alternative constitutes one or more optional forms of benefit.

(B) Death benefits. If a death benefit is payable after the annuity starting date for a specific optional form of benefit and the same death benefit would not be provided if another optional form of benefit were elected by a participant, then that death benefit is part of the specific optional form of benefit and is thus protected under section 411(d)(6). A death benefit is not treated as part of a specific optional form of benefit merely because the same benefit is not provided to a participant who has received his or her entire accrued benefit prior to death. For example, a $5,000 death benefit that is payable to all participants except any participant who has received his or her accrued benefit in a single-sum distribution is not part of a specific optional form of benefit.

(iii) Retirement-type benefit. The term retirement-type benefit means—

(A) The payment of a distribution alternative with respect to an accrued benefit; or

(B) The payment of any other benefit under a defined benefit plan (including a QSUPP as defined in § 1.401(a)(4)-12) that is permitted to be in a qualified pension plan, continues after retirement, and is not an ancillary benefit.

(iv) Retirement-type subsidy. The term retirement-type subsidy means the excess, if any, of the actuarial present value of a retirement-type benefit over the actuarial present value of the accrued benefit commencing at normal retirement age or at actual commencement date, if later, with both such actuarial present values determined as of the date the retirement-type benefit commences. Examples of retirement-type subsidies include a subsidized early retirement benefit and a subsidized qualified joint and survivor annuity.

(v) Subsidized early retirement benefit or early retirement subsidy. The terms subsidized early retirement benefit or early retirement subsidy mean the right, under the terms of a plan, to commence distribution of a retirement-type benefit at a particular date after severance from employment with the employer and before normal retirement age where the actuarial present value of the optional forms of benefit available to the participant under the plan at that annuity starting date exceeds the actuarial present value of the accrued benefit commencing at normal retirement age (with such actuarial present values determined as of the annuity starting date). Thus, an early retirement subsidy is an early retirement benefit that provides a retirement-type subsidy.

*(7) Eliminate; elimination; reduce; reduction.* The terms eliminate or elimination when used in connection with a section 411(d)(6)(B) protected benefit mean to eliminate or the elimination of an optional form of benefit or an early retirement benefit and to reduce or a reduction in a retirement-type subsidy. The terms reduce or reduction when used in connection with a retirement-type subsidy mean to reduce or a reduction in the amount of the subsidy. For purposes of this section, an elimination includes a reduction and a reduction includes an elimination.

*(8) Generalized optional form.* The term generalized optional form means a group of optional forms of benefit that are identical except for differences due to the actuarial factors that are used to determine the amount of the distributions under those optional forms of benefit and the annuity starting dates.

*(9) Maximum QJSA explanation period.* The term maximum QJSA explanation period means the maximum number of days before an annuity starting date for a qualified joint and survivor annuity for which a written explanation relating to the qualified joint and survivor annuity would satisfy the timing requirements of section 417(a)(3) and § 1.417(e)-1(b)(3)(ii).

*(10) Other right and feature.* The term other right or feature has the meaning set forth at § 1.401(a)(4)-4(e)(3)(ii).

*(11) Refund of employee contributions feature.* The term refund of employee contributions features means a feature with respect to an optional form of benefit that provides for employee contributions and interest thereon to be paid in a single sum at the annuity starting date with the remainder to be paid in another form beginning on that date.

*(12) Retirement; retirement age.* For purposes of this section, the date of retirement means the annuity starting date. Thus, retirement age means a participant's age at the annuity starting date.

*(13) Retroactive annuity starting date feature.* The term retroactive annuity starting date feature means a feature with respect to an optional form of benefit under which the annuity starting date for the distribution occurs on or before the

date the written explanation required by section 417(a)(3) is provided to the participant.

*(14) Section 411(d)(6) protected benefit.* The term section 411(d)(6) protected benefit means the accrued benefit of a participant as of the applicable amendment date described in section 411(d)(6)(A) and any section 411(d)(6)(B) protected benefit.

*(15) Section 411(d)(6)(B) protected benefit.* The term section 411(d)(6)(B) protected benefit means the portion of an early retirement benefit, a retirement-type subsidy, or an optional form of benefit attributable to benefits accrued before the applicable amendment date.

*(16) Social security leveling feature.* The term social security leveling feature means a feature with respect to an optional form of benefit commencing prior to a participant's expected commencement of social security benefits that provides for a temporary period of higher payments which is designed to result in an approximately level amount of income when the participant's estimated old age benefits from Social Security are taken into account.

**(h) Examples.** The following examples illustrate the application of paragraphs (c) through (g) of this section:

*Example (1).* (i) Facts involving elimination of optional forms of benefit as redundant. Plan C is a defined benefit plan under which employees may elect to commence distributions at any time after the later of termination of employment or attainment of age 55. At each potential annuity commencement date, Plan C permits employees to select, with spousal consent where required, a straight life annuity or any of a number of actuarially equivalent alternative forms of payment, including a straight life annuity with cost-of-living increases and a joint and contingent annuity with the participant having the right to select any beneficiary and any continuation percentage from 1% to 100%, subject to modification to the extent necessary to satisfy the requirements of the incidental benefit requirement of § 1.401-1(b)(1)(i). The amount of any alternative payment is determined as the actuarial equivalent of the straight life annuity payable at the same age using reasonable actuarial assumptions. On June 2, 2006, Plan C is amended to delete all continuation percentages for joint and contingent options other than 25%, 50%, 75%, or 100%, effective with respect to annuity commencement dates that are on or after January 1, 2007.

(ii) Conclusion. (A) Categorization of family members under the redundancy rule. The optional forms of benefit described in paragraph (i) of this Example 1 are members of 4 families: a straight life annuity; a straight life annuity with cost-of-living increases; joint and contingent options with continuation percentages of less than 50%; and joint and contingent options with continuation percentages of 50% or more. The amendment does not affect either of the first 2 families, but affects the 2 families relating to joint and contingent options.

(B) Conclusion for elimination of optional forms of benefit as redundant. The amendment satisfies the requirements of paragraph (c) of this section. First, the eliminated optional forms of benefit are redundant with respect to the retained optional forms of benefit because each eliminated joint and contingent annuity option with a continuation percentage of less than 50% is redundant with respect to the 25% continuation option and each eliminated joint and contingent annuity option with a continuation percentage of 50% or higher is redundant with respect to any one of the retained 50%, 75%, or 100% continuation options. In addition, to the extent that the optional form of benefit that is being eliminated does not include a social security leveling feature, return of employee contribution feature, or retroactive annuity starting date feature, the retained optional form of benefit does not include that feature. Second, the amendment is not effective with respect to annuity commencement dates before September 1, 2006, as required under paragraph (c)(1)(ii) of this section. Third, the plan amendment does not eliminate any available core option, including the most valuable option for a participant with a short life expectancy, treating a joint and contingent annuity with a 100% continuation percentage as this optional form of benefit pursuant to paragraph (g)(5)(iii)(B)(2) of this section. Finally, the amendment need not satisfy the requirements of paragraph (e) of this section because the retained optional forms of benefit are available on the same annuity commencement dates and have the same actuarial present value as the optional forms of benefit that are being eliminated.

*Example (2).* (i) Facts involving elimination of optional forms of benefit as redundant if additional restrictions are imposed. The facts are the same as Example 1, except that the plan amendment also restricts the class of beneficiaries that may be elected under the 4 retained joint and contingent annuities to the employee's spouse.

(ii) Conclusion. The amendment fails to satisfy the requirements of paragraph (c)(2)(i)(B) of this section because the retained joint and contingent annuities have materially greater restrictions on the beneficiary designation than did the eliminated joint and contingent annuities. Thus, the joint and contingent annuities being eliminated are not redundant with respect to the retained joint and contingent annuities. In addition, the amendment fails to satisfy the requirements of the core option rules in paragraph (d) of this section because the amendment fails to be limited to annuity commencement dates that are at least 4 years after the date the amendment is adopted, the amendment fails to include the core option in paragraph (g)(5)(i)(B) of this section because the participant does not have the right to designate any beneficiary, and the amendment fails to include the core option described in paragraph (g)(5)(i)(C) of this section because the plan does not provide a 10-year term certain and life annuity.

*Example (3).* (i) Facts involving elimination of a social security leveling feature and a period certain annuity as redundant. Plan D is a defined benefit plan under which participants may elect to commence distributions in the following actuarially equivalent forms, with spousal consent if applicable: a straight life annuity; a 50%, 75%, or 100% joint and contingent annuity; a 5-year, 10-year, or a 15-year term certain and life annuity; and an installment refund annuity (i.e., an optional form of benefit that provides a period certain, the duration of which is based on the participant's age), with the participant having the right to select any beneficiary. In addition, each annuity offered under the plan, if payable to a participant who is less than age 65, is available both with and without a social security leveling feature. The social security leveling feature provides for an assumed commencement of social security benefits at any age selected by the participant between age 62 and 65. Plan D is amended on June 2, 2006, effective as of January 1, 2007, to eliminate the installment refund form of benefit and to restrict the social security leveling feature to an assumed social security commencement age of 65.

(ii) Conclusion. The amendment satisfies the requirements of paragraph (c) of this section. First, the installment refund annuity option is redundant with respect to the 15-year certain and life annuity (except for advanced ages where, because of shorter life expectancies, the installment refund annuity option is redundant with respect to the 5-year certain and life annuity and also redundant with respect to the 10-year certain and life annuity). Second, with respect to restricting the social security leveling feature to an assumed social security commencement age of 65, under paragraph (c)(3)(ii)(C) of this section, straight life annuities with social security leveling features that have different social security commencement ages are treated as members of the same family as straight life annuities without social security leveling features. To the extent an optional form of benefit that is being eliminated includes a social security leveling feature, the retained optional form of benefit must also include that feature, but it is permitted to have a different assumed age for commencement of social security benefits. Third, to the extent that the optional form of benefit that is being eliminated does not include a social security leveling feature, a return of employee contribution feature, or retroactive annuity starting date feature, the retained optional form of benefit must not include that feature. Fourth, the plan amendment does not eliminate any available core option, including the most valuable option for a participant with a short life expectancy, treating a joint and contingent annuity with a 100% continuation percentage as this optional form of benefit pursuant to paragraph (g)(5)(iii)(B)(2) of this section. Fifth, the amendment is not effective with respect to annuity commencement dates before September 1, 2006, as required under paragraph (c)(1)(ii) of this section. The amendment need not satisfy the requirements of paragraph (e) of this section because the retained optional forms of benefit are available on the same annuity commencement dates and have the same actuarial present value as the optional forms of benefit that are being eliminated.

*Example (4).* (i) Facts involving elimination of noncore options. Employer N sponsors Plan E, a defined benefit plan that permits every participant to elect payment in the following actuarially equivalent optional forms of benefit (Plan E's uniformly available options), with spousal consent if applicable: a straight life annuity; a 50%, 75%, or 100% joint and contingent annuity with no restrictions on designation of beneficiaries; and a 5-, 10-, or 15-year term certain and life annuity. In addition, each can be elected in conjunction with a social security leveling feature, with the participant permitted to select a social security commencement age from age 62 to age 67. None of Plan E's uniformly available options include a single-sum distribution. The plan has been in existence for over 30 years, during which time Employer N has acquired a large number of other businesses, including merging over 20 defined benefit plans of acquired entities into Plan E. Many of the merged plans offered optional forms of benefit that were not among Plan E's uniformly available options, including some plans funded through insurance products, often offering all of the insurance annuities that the insurance carrier offers, and with some of the merged plans offering single-sum distributions. In particular, under the XYZ acquisition that occurred in 1990, the XYZ acquired plan offered a single-sum distribution option that was frozen at the time of the acquisition. On April 1, 2006, each single-sum distribution option applies to less than 25% of the XYZ participants' accrued benefits. Employer N has generally, but not uniformly, followed the practice of limiting the optional forms of benefit for an acquired unit to an employee's service before the date of the merger, and has uniformly followed this practice with respect to each of the early retirement subsidies in the acquired unit's plan. As a result, as of April 1, 2007, Plan E includes a large number of generalized optional forms which are not members of families of optional forms of benefit identified in paragraph (c)(4) of this section, but there are no participants who are entitled to any early retirement subsidies because any subsidies have been subsumed by the actuarially reduced accrued benefit. Plan E is amended in April of 2007 to eliminate all of the optional forms of benefit that Plan E offers other than Plan E's uniformly available options, except that the amendment does not eliminate any single-sum distribution option except with respect to XYZ participants and permits any commencement date that was permitted under Plan E before the amendment. Plan E also eliminates the single-sum distribution option for XYZ participants. Further, each of Plan E's uniformly available options has an actuarial present value that is not less than the actuarial present value of any optional form of benefit offered before the amendment. The amendment is effective with respect to annuity commencement dates that are on or after May 1, 2011.

(ii) Conclusion. The amendment satisfies the requirements of paragraph (d) of this section. First, Plan E, as amended, does not eliminate any single-sum distribution option as provided in paragraph (d)(2)(iii) of this section except for single-sum distribution options that apply to less than 25% of a plan participant's accrued benefit as of the date the option is eliminated (May 1, 2011). Second, Plan E, as amended, includes each of the core options as defined in paragraph (g)(5) of this section, including offering the most valuable option for a participant with a short life expectancy (treating the 100% joint and contingent annuity as this benefit, under paragraph (g)(5)(iii)(B)(2) of this section). The 100% joint and contingent annuity option (and not the grandfathered single-sum distribution option) is the most valuable option for a participant with a short life expectancy because the grandfathered single-sum distribution option is not available with respect to a participant's entire accrued benefit. In addition, as required under paragraph (d)(2) of this section, to the extent an optional form of benefit that is being eliminated includes either a social security leveling feature or a refund of employee contributions feature, at least one of the core options is available with that feature and, to the extent that the optional form of benefit that is being eliminated does not include a social security leveling feature or a refund of employee contributions feature, each of the core options is available without that feature. Third, the amendment is not effective with respect to annuity commencement dates that are less than 4 years after the date the amendment is adopted. Finally, the amendment need not satisfy the requirements of paragraph (e) of this section because the retained optional forms of benefit are available on the same annuity commencement date and have the same actuarial present value as the optional forms of benefit that are being eliminated. The conclusion that the amendment satisfies the requirements of paragraph (d) of this section assumes that no amendments are made to change the core options before May 1, 2014.

*Example (5).* (i) Facts involving reductions in actuarial present value. (A) Plan F is a defined benefit plan providing an accrued benefit of 1% of the average of a participant's highest 3 consecutive years' pay times years of service, payable as a straight life annuity beginning at the normal retirement age at age 65. Plan F permits employees to elect to commence actuarially reduced distributions at any time after the later of termination of employment or attainment of age 55. At each potential annuity commencement date, Plan F permits employees to select, with spousal consent, either a straight life annuity, a joint and contingent annuity with the participant having the right to select any beneficiary and a continuation percentage of 50%, 66⅔%, 75%, or 100%, or a 10-year certain and life annuity with the participant having the right to select any beneficiary, subject to modification to the extent necessary to satisfy the requirements of the incidental benefit requirement of § 1.401-1(b)(1)(i). The amount of any joint and contingent annuity and the 10-year certain and life annuity is determined as the actuarial equivalent of the straight life annuity payable at the same age using reasonable actuarial assumptions. The plan covers employees at 4 divisions, one of which, Division X, was acquired on January 1, 1999. The plan provides for distributions before normal retirement age to be actuarially reduced, but, if a participant retires after attainment of age 55 and completion of 10 years of service, the applicable early retirement reduction factor is 3% per year for the years between age 65 and 62 and 6% per year for the ages from 62 to 55 for all employees at any division, except for employees who were in Division X on January 1, 1999, for whom the early retirement reduction factor for retirement after age 55 and 10 years of service is 5% for each year before age 65. On June 2, 2006, effective January 1, 2007, Plan F is amended to change the early retirement reduction factors for all employees of Division X to be the same as for other employees, effective with respect to annuity commencement dates that are on or after January 1, 2008, but only with respect to participants who are employees on or after January 1, 2008 and only if Plan F continues accruals at the current rate through January 1, 2008 (or the effective date of the change in reduction factors is delayed to reflect the change in the accrual rate). For purposes of this Example 5, it is assumed that an actuarially equivalent early retirement factor would have a reduction shown in column 4 of the following table, which compares the reduction factors for Division X before and after the amendment:

| Age<br>1 | Old division X factor (as a %)<br>2 | New factor (as a %)<br>3 | Actuarially equivalent factor (as a %)<br>4 | Column 3 minus column 2<br>5 |
|---|---|---|---|---|
| 65 | NA | NA | NA | NA |
| 64 | 95 | 97 | 91.1 | +2 |
| 63 | 90 | 94 | 83.2 | +4 |
| 62 | 85 | 91 | 76.1 | +5 |
| 61 | 80 | 85 | 69.8 | +5 |
| 60 | 75 | 79 | 64.1 | +4 |
| 59 | 70 | 73 | 59.0 | +3 |
| 58 | 65 | 67 | 54.3 | +2 |
| 57 | 60 | 61 | 50.1 | +1 |
| 56 | 55 | 55 | 46.3 | 0 |
| 55 | 50 | 49 | 42.8 | -1 |

(B) On January 1, 2007, the employee with the largest number of years of service is Employee E, who is age 54 and has 20 years of service. For 2006, Employee E's compensation is $80,000 and E's highest 3 consecutive years of pay on January 1, 2007 is $75,000. Employee E's accrued benefit as of the January 1, 2007 effective date of the amendment is a life annuity of $15,000 per year at normal retirement age (1% times $75,000 times 20 years of service) and E's early retirement benefit commencing at age 55 has a present value of $91,397 as of January 1, 2007. It is assumed for purposes of this example that the longest expected transition period for any active employee does not exceed 5 months (20 years and 5 months, times 1% times 49% exceeds 20 years times 1% times 50%). Finally, it is assumed for purposes of this example that the amendment reduces optional forms of benefit which are burdensome or complex.

(ii) Conclusion concerning application of section 411(d)(6)(B). The amendment reducing the early retirement factors has the effect of eliminating the existing optional forms of benefit (where the amount of the benefit is based on preamendment early retirement factors in any case where the new factors result in a smaller amount payable) and adding new optional forms of benefit (where the amount of benefit is based on the different early retirement factors). Accordingly, the elimination must satisfy the requirements of paragraph (c) or (d) of this section if the amount payable at any date is less than would have been payable under the plan before the amendment.

(iii) Conclusion concerning application of redundancy rules. The amendment satisfies the requirements of paragraph (c)(1)(i) and (ii) of this section (see paragraphs (iv) through (vi) of this Example 5 below for the requirements of paragraph (c)(1)(iii) of this section). First, with respect to each eliminated optional form of benefit (i.e., with respect to each optional form of benefit with the Old Division X Factor), after the amendment there is a retained optional form of benefit that is in the same family of optional forms of benefit (i.e., the optional form of benefit with the New Factor). Second, the amendment is not effective with respect to annuity commencement dates that are less than the time period required under paragraph (c)(1)(ii) of this section. Third, to the extent that the plan amendment eliminates the most valuable option for a participant with a short life expectancy, the retained optional form of benefit is identical except for differences in actuarial factors.

(iv) Conclusion concerning application of the requirements under paragraph (e) of this section. The plan amendment must satisfy the requirements of paragraph (e) of this section because, as of the December 2, 2006 adoption date, the actuarial present value of the early retirement subsidy is less than the actuarial present value of the early retirement subsidy being eliminated. The plan amendment satisfies the requirements under paragraph (e)(1)(i) and (2) of this section because the amendment eliminates optional forms of benefit that create significant burdens or complexities for the plan and its participants. See below for the de minimis requirement under paragraph (e)(1)(ii) and (3) of this section.

(v) Conclusion concerning application of de minimis rules under paragraph (e)(5) of this section. In order to satisfy the requirements under paragraph (e)(1)(ii) and (3) of this section, the amendment must satisfy the requirements of either paragraph (e)(5) or paragraph (e)(6) of this section. The amendment does not satisfy the requirements of paragraph (e)(5) of this section because the reduction in the actuarial present value is more than a de minimis amount under paragraph (e)(5) of this section. For example, for Employee E, the amount of the joint and contingent annuity payable at age 55 is reduced from $7,500 (50% of $15,000) to $7,350 (49% of $15,000) and the reduction in present value as a result of the amendment is $1,828 ($91,397–$89,569). In this case, the retirement-type subsidy at age 55 is the excess of the present value of the 50% early retirement benefit over the present value of the deferred payment of the accrued benefit, or $13,921 ($97,269– $83,348) and the present value at age 54 of the retirement-type subsidy is $13,081. The reduction in present value is more than the greater of 2% of the present value of the retirement-type subsidy and 1% of E's compensation because the reduction in present value exceeds $800 (the greater of $262, which is 2% of the present value of the retirement-type subsidy for the benefit being eliminated, and $800, which is 1% of E's compensation of $80,000).

(vi) Conclusion involving application of de minimis rules under paragraph (e)(6) of this section relating to expected transition period. The amendment satisfies the requirements of paragraph (e)(6) of this section and, thus, satisfies the requirements of paragraph (c) of this section, including the requirement in paragraph (c)(1)(iii) of this section that paragraph (e) of this section be satisfied. First, as assumed under the facts above, the amendment reduces optional forms of benefit that are burdensome or complex. Second, the plan amendment is not effective for annuity commencement dates before January 1, 2008, and that date is not earlier than the longest expected transition period for any participant in Plan F on the date of the amendment. Third, the amendment does not apply to any participant who has a severance from employment during the transition period. If, however, a later plan amendment reduces accruals under Plan F, the initial plan amendment will no longer satisfy the requirements of paragraph (e)(6) of this section (and must be voided) unless, as part of the later amendment, the expected transition period is extended to reflect the reduction in accruals under Plan F.

*Example (6).* (i) Facts involving elimination of noncore options using utilization test. (A) In general. Plan G is a calendar year defined benefit plan under which participants may elect to commence distributions after termination of employment in the following actuarially equivalent forms, with spousal consent, if applicable: a straight life annuity; a 50%, 75%, or 100% joint and contingent annuity; or a 5-year, 10-year, or a 15-year term certain and life annuity. A participant is permitted to elect a single-sum distribution if the present value of the participant's nonforfeitable accrued benefit is not greater than $5,000. The annuities offered under the plan are generally available both with and without a social security leveling feature. The social security leveling feature provides for an assumed commencement of social security benefits at any age selected by the participant between the ages of 62 and 67. Under Plan G, the normal retirement age is defined as age 65.

(B) Utilization test. In 2007, the plan sponsor of Plan G, after reviewing participants' benefit elections, determines that, during the period from January 1, 2005, through June 30, 2007, no participant has elected a 5-year term certain and life annuity with a social security leveling option. During that period, Plan G has made the 5-year term certain and life annuity with a social security leveling option available to 142 participants who were at least age 55 and who elected optional forms of benefit with an annuity commencement dates during that period. In addition, during that period, 20 of the 142 participants elected a single-sum distribution and there was no retirement-type subsidy available for a limited period of time. Plan G, in accordance with paragraph (f)(1) of this section, is amended on September 15, 2007, effective as of January 1, 2008, to eliminate all 5-year term certain and life annuities with a social security leveling option for all annuity commencement dates on or after January 1, 2008.

(ii) Conclusion. The amendment satisfies the requirements of paragraph (f) of this section. First, the 5-year term certain and life annuity with a social security leveling option is not a core option as defined in paragraph (g)(5) of this section. Second, the plan amendment is not applicable with respect to an optional form of benefit with an annuity commencement date that is earlier than the number of days in the maximum QJSA explanation period after the date the amendment is adopted. Third, the 5-year term certain and life annuity with a social security leveling option has been available to at least 50 participants who are taken into account for purposes of paragraph (f) of this section during the look-back period. Fourth, during the look-back period, no participant elected any optional form that is part of the generalized optional form being eliminated (for example, the 5-year term and life annuity with a social security leveling option).

**(i) [Reserved].**

**(j) Effective dates.** *(1) General effective date.* Except as otherwise provided in this paragraph (j), the rules of this section apply to amendments adopted on or after August 12, 2005.

*(2) Effective date for rules relating to contingent event benefits.* Paragraph (b)(1)(ii) of this section applies to amendments adopted after December 31, 2005.

*(3) Effective dates for rules relating to section 411(a) nonforfeitability provisions.* (i) Application of suspension of benefit rules to section 411(d)(6) protected benefits. With respect to a plan amendment that places greater restrictions or conditions on a participant's rights to section 411(d)(6) protected benefits by adding or modifying a plan provision relating to suspension of benefit payments during a period of employment or reemployment, the rules provided in paragraph (a)(3) of this section apply to periods beginning on or after June 7, 2004.

(ii) Application of section 411(a) nonforfeitability provisions to section 411(d)(6) protected benefits. With respect to a plan amendment that places greater restrictions or conditions on a participant's rights to section 411(d)(6) protected benefits other than a plan amendment described in paragraph (j)(3)(i) of this section, the rules provided in paragraph (a)(3) of this section apply to plan amendments adopted after August 9, 2006.

*(4) Effective date for change to redundancy rule regarding bifurcation of benefits.* The rules provided in paragraph (c)(6) of this section are applicable for amendments adopted after August 9, 2006.

*(5) Effective date for rules relating to utilization test.* The rules provided in paragraph (f) of this section are applicable for amendments adopted after December 31, 2006.

T.D. 7501, 8/22/77, amend T.D. 8038, 7/18/85, T.D. 8219, 8/19/88, T.D. 9219, 8/11/2005, T.D. 9280, 8/8/2006, T.D. 9472, 11/23/2009.

### § 1.411(d)-4 Section 411(d)(6) protected benefits.

***Caution:*** The Treasury has not yet amended Reg § 1.411(d)-4 to reflect changes made by P.L. 103-465.

Q-1. What are "section 411(d)(6) protected benefits"?

A-1. **(a) In general.** The term "section 411(d)(6) protected benefit" includes any benefit that is described in one or more of the following categories—

*(1)* benefits described in section 411(d)(6)(A),

*(2)* Early retirement benefits (as defined in § 1.411(d)-3(g)(6)(i)) and retirement-type subsidies (as defined in § 1.411(d)-3(g)(6)(iv)), and

*(3)* optional forms of benefit described in section 411(d)(6)(B)(ii).

Such benefits, to the extent they have accrued, are subject to the protection of section 411(d)(6) and, where applicable, the definitely determinable requirement of section 401(a) (including section 401(a)(25)) and cannot, therefore, be reduced, eliminated, or made subject to employer discretion except to the extent permitted by regulations.

**(b) Optional forms of benefit.** *(1) In general.* The term optional form of benefit has the same meaning as in § 1.411(d)-3(g)(6)(ii). Under this definition, different optional forms of benefit exist if a distribution alternative is not payable on substantially the same terms as another distribution alternative. Thus, for example, different optional forms of benefit may result from differences in terms relating to the payment schedule, timing, commencement, medium of distribution (e.g., in cash or in kind), election rights, differences in eligibility requirements, or the portion of the benefit to which the distribution alternative applies.

*(2) Examples.* The following examples illustrate the meaning of the term "optional form of benefit." Other issues, such as the requirement that the optional forms satisfy section 401(a)(4), are not addressed in these examples and no inferences are intended with respect to such requirements. Assume that the distribution forms, including those not described in these examples, provided under the plan in each of the following examples are identical in all respects not described.

*Example (1).* A plan permits each participant to receive his benefit under the plan as a single sum distribution; a level monthly distribution schedule over 15 years; a single life annuity; a joint and 50 percent survivor annuity; a joint and 75 percent survivor annuity; a joint and 50 percent survivor annuity with a benefit increase for the participant if the beneficiary dies before a specified date; and joint and 50 percent survivor annuity with a 10 year certain feature. Each of these benefit distribution options is an optional form of benefit (without regard to whether the values of these options are actuarially equivalent).

*Example (2).* A plan permits each participant who is employed by division A to receive his benefit in a single sum distribution payable upon termination from employment and each participant who is employed by division B in a single sum distribution payable upon termination from employment on or after the attainment of age 50. This plan provides two single sum optional forms of benefit.

*Example (3).* A plan permits each participant to receive his benefit in a single life annuity that commences in the month after the participant's termination from employment or in a single life annuity that commences upon the completion of five consecutive one year breaks in service. These are two optional forms of benefit.

*Example (4).* A profit-sharing plan permits each participant who is employed by division A to receive an in-service distribution upon the satisfaction of objective criteria set forth in the plan designed to determine whether the participant has a heavy and immediate financial need, and each participant who is employed by division B to receive an in-service distribution upon the satisfaction of objective criteria set forth in the plan designed to determine whether the participant has a heavy and immediate financial need attributable to extraordinary medical expenses. These in-service distribution options are two optional forms of benefits.

*Example (5).* A profit-sharing plan permits each participant who is employed by division A to receive an in-service distribution up to $5,000 and each participant who is employed by division B to receive an in-service distribution of up to his total benefit. These in-service distribution options differ as to the portion of the accrued benefit that may be distributed in a particular form and are, therefore, two optional forms of benefit.

*Example (6).* A profit-sharing plan provides for a single sum distribution on termination of employment. The plan is amended in 1991 to eliminate the single sum optional form of benefit with respect to benefits accrued after the date of amendment. This single sum optional form of benefit continues to be a single optional form of benefit although, over time, the percentage of various employees' accrued benefits that are potentially payable under this single sum may vary because the form is only available with respect to benefits accrued up to and including the date of the amendment.

*Example (7).* A profit-sharing plan permits each participant to receive a single sum distribution of his benefit in cash or in the form of a specified class of employer stock. This plan provides two single sum distribution optional forms of benefit.

*Example (8).* A stock bonus plan permits each participant to receive a single sum distribution of his benefit in cash or in the form of the property in which such participant's benefit was invested prior to the distribution. This plan's single sum distribution option provides two optional forms of benefit.

*Example (9).* A defined benefit plan provides for an early retirement benefit payable upon termination of employment after attainment of age 55 and either after ten years of service or, if earlier, upon plan termination to employees of Division A and provides for an identical early retirement benefit payable on the same terms with the exception of payment on plan termination to employees of Division B. The plan provides for two optional forms of benefit.

*Example (10).* A profit-sharing plan provides for loans secured by an employee's account balance. In the event of default on such a loan, there is an execution on such account balances. Such execution is a distribution of the employee's accrued benefits under the plan. A distribution of an accrued benefit contingent on default under a plan loan secured by such accrued benefits is an optional form of benefit under the plan.

**(c) Plan terms.** *(1) General rule.* Generally, benefits described in section 411(d)(6)(A), early retirement benefits, retirement-type subsidies, and optional forms of benefit are section 411(d)(6) protected benefits only if they are provided under the terms of a plan. However, if an employer establishes a pattern of repeated plan amendments providing for similar benefits in similar situations for substantially consecutive, limited periods of time, such benefits will be treated as provided under the terms of the plan, without regard to the limited periods of time, to the extent necessary to carry out the purposes of section 411(d)(6) and, where applicable, the definitely determinable requirement of section 401(a), including section 401(a)(25). A pattern of repeated plan amendments providing that a particular optional form of benefit is available to certain named employees for a limited period of time is within the scope of this rule and may result in such optional form of benefit being treated as provided under the terms of the plan to all employees covered under the plan without regard to the limited period of time and the limited group of named employees.

*(2) Effective date.* The provisions of paragraph (c)(1) of this Q&A-1 are effective as of July 11, 1988. Thus, patterns or repeated plan amendments adopted and effective before July 11, 1988 will be disregarded in determining whether such amendments have created an ongoing optional form of benefit under the plan.

**(d) Benefits that are not section 411(d)(6) protected benefits.** The following benefits are examples of items that are not section 411(d)(6) protected benefits: (1) ancillary life insurance protection; (2) accident or health insurance benefits; (3) social security supplements described in section 411(a)(9), except qualified social security supplements as defined in § 1.401(a)(4)-12; (4) the availability of loans (other than the distribution of an employee's accrued benefit upon default under a loan); (5) the right to make after-tax employee contributions or elective deferrals described in section 402(g)(3); (6) the right to direct investments; (7) the right to a particular form of investment (e.g., investment in employer stock or securities or investment in certain types of securities, commercial paper, or other investment media); (8) the allocation dates for contributions, forfeitures, and earnings, the time for making contributions (but not the conditions for receiving an allocation of contributions or forfeitures for a plan year after such conditions have been satisfied), and the valuation dates for account balances; (9) administrative procedures for distributing benefits, such as provisions relating to the particular dates on which notices are given and by which elections must be made; and (10) rights that derive from administrative and operational provisions, such as mechanical procedures for allocating investment experience among accounts in defined contribution plans.

Q-2. To what extent may section 411(d)(6) protected benefits under a plan be reduced or eliminated?

A-2. **(a) Reduction or elimination of section 411(d)(6) protected benefits.** *(1) In general.* A plan is not permitted to be amended to eliminate or reduce a section 411(d)(6) protected benefit that has already accrued, except as provided in § 1.411(d)-3 or this section. This is generally the case even if such elimination or reduction is contingent upon the employee's consent. However, a plan may be amended to eliminate or reduce section 411(d)(6) protected benefits with respect to benefits not yet accrued as of the later of the amendment's adoption date or effective date without violating section 411(d)(6).

*(2) Selection of optional forms of benefit.* (i) General rule. A plan may treat a participant as receiving his entire nonforfeitable accrued benefit under the plan if the participant receives his benefit in an optional form of benefit in an amount determined under the plan that is at least the actuarial equivalent of the employee's nonforfeitable accrued benefit payable at normal retirement age under the plan. This is true even though the participant could have elected to receive an optional form of benefit with a greater actuarial value than the value of the optional form received, such as an optional form including retirement-type subsidies, and without regard to whether such other, more valuable optional form could have commenced immediately or could have become available only upon the employee's future satisfaction of specified eligibility conditions.

(ii) Election of an optional form. Except as provided in paragraph (a)(2)(iii) of this Q&A-2, a plan does not violate section 411(d)(6) merely because an employee's election to receive a portion of his nonforfeitable accrued benefit in one optional form of benefit precludes the employee from receiving that portion of his benefit in another optional form of benefit. Such employee retains all 411(d)(6) protected rights with respect to the entire portion of such employee's nonforfeitable accrued benefit for which no distribution election was made. For purposes of this rule, an elective transfer of an otherwise distributable benefit is treated as the selection of an optional form of benefit. See Q&A-3 of this section.

(iii) Buy-back rule. Notwithstanding paragraph (a)(2)(ii) of this Q&A-2, an employee who received a distribution of his nonforfeitable benefit from a plan that is required to provide a repayment opportunity to such employee if he returns to service within the applicable period pursuant to the requirements of section 411(a)(7) and who, upon subsequent reemployment, repays the full amount of such distribution in accordance with section 411(a)(7)(C) must be reinstated in the full array of section 411(d)(6) protected benefits that existed with respect to such benefit prior to distribution.

(iv) *Examples.* The rules in this paragraph (a)(2) can be illustrated by the following examples:

*Example (1).* Defined benefit plan X provides, among its optional forms of benefit, for a subsidized early retirement benefit payable in the form of an annuity and available to employees who terminate from employment on or after their 55th birthdays. In addition plan X provides for a single sum distribution available on termination from employment or termination of the plan. The single sum distribution is determined on the basis of the present value of the accrued normal retirement benefit and does not take the early retirement subsidy into account. Plan X is terminated December 31, 1991. Employees U, age 47, V, age 55, and W, age 47, all continue in the service of the employer. Employees X, age 47, Y, age 55 and Z, age 47, terminate from employment with the employer during 1991. Employees U and V elect to take the single sum optional form of distribution at the time of plan termination. Employees X and Y elect to take the single sum distribution on termination from employment with the employer. The elimination of the subsidized early retirement benefit with respect to employees U, V, X and Y does not result in a violation of section 411(d)(6). This is the result even though employees U and X had not yet satisfied the conditions for the subsidized early retirement benefit. Because employees W and Z have not selected an optional form of benefit, they continue to have a 411(d)(6) protected right to the full array of section 411(d)(6) protected benefits provided under the plan, including the single sum distribution form and the subsidized early retirement benefit.

*Example (2).* A partially vested employee receives a single sum distribution of the present value of his entire nonforfeitable benefit on account of separation from service under a defined benefit plan providing for a repayment provision. Upon reemployment with the employer such employee makes repayment in the required amount in accordance with section 411(a)(7). Such employee may, upon subsequent termination of employment, elect to take such repaid benefits in any optional form provided under the plan as of the time of the employee's initial separation from service. If the plan was amended prior to such repayment, to eliminate the single sum optional form of benefit with respect to benefits accrued after the date of the amendment, such participant has a 411(d)(6) protected right to take distribution of the repaid benefit in the form of a single sum distribution.

*(3) Certain transactions.* (i) Plan mergers and benefit transfers. The prohibition against the reduction or elimination of section 411(d)(6) protected benefits already accrued applies to plan mergers, spinoffs, transfers, and transactions amending or having the effect of amending a plan or plans to transfer plan benefits. Thus, for example, if plan A, a profit-sharing plan that provides for distribution of plan benefits in annual installments over ten or twenty years, is merged with plan B, a profit-sharing plan that provides for distribution of plan benefits in annual installments over life expectancy at time of retirement, the merged plan must retain the ten or twenty year installment option for participants with respect to benefits already accrued under plan A as of the merger and the installments over life expectancy for participants with benefits already accrued under plan B. Similarly, for example, if an employee's benefit under a defined contribution plan is transferred to another defined contribution plan (whether or not of the same employer), the optional forms of benefit available with respect to the employee's benefit accrued under the transferor plan may not be eliminated or reduced except as otherwise permitted under this regulation. See Q&A-3 of this section with respect to the transfer of benefits between and among defined benefit and defined contribution plans.

(ii) Annuity contracts. (A) General rule. The right of a participant to receive a benefit in the form of cash payments from the plan and the right of a participant to receive that benefit in the form of the distribution of an annuity contract that provides for cash payments that are identical in all respects to the cash payments from the plan except with respect to the source of the payments are not separate optional forms of benefit. Therefore, for example, if a plan includes an optional form of benefit under which benefits are distributed in the medium of an annuity contract that provides for cash payments, that optional form of benefit may be modified by a plan amendment that substitutes cash payments from the plan for the annuity contract, where those cash payments from the plan are identical to the cash payments payable from the annuity contract in all respects except with respect to the source of the payments. The protection provided by section 411(d)(6) may not be avoided by the use of annuity contracts. Thus, section 411(d)(6) protected benefits already accrued may not be eliminated or reduced merely because a plan uses annuity contracts to provide such benefits, without regard to whether the plan, a participant, or a beneficiary of a participant holds the contract or whether such annuity contracts are purchased as a result of the termination of the plan. However, to the extent that an annuity contract constitutes payment of benefits in a particular optional form elected by the participant, the plan does not violate section 411(d)(6) merely because it provides that other optional forms are no longer available with respect to such participant. See paragraph (a)(2) of this Q&A-2.

(B) Examples. The provisions of this paragraph (a)(3)(ii) can be illustrated by the following examples:

*Example (1).* A profit-sharing plan that is being terminated satisfies section 411(d)(6) only if the plan makes available to participants annuity contracts that provide for all section 411(d)(6) protected benefits under the plan that may not otherwise be reduced or eliminated pursuant to this Q&A-2. Thus, if such a plan provided for a single sum distribution upon attainment of early retirement age, and a provision for payment in the form of 10 equal annual installments, the plan would satisfy section 411(d)(6) only if the participants had the opportunity to elect to have their benefits provided under an annuity contract that provided for the same single sum distribution upon the attainment of the participant's early retirement age and the same 10 year installment optional form of benefit.

*Example (2).* A defined benefit plan permits each participant who separates from service on or after age 62 to receive a qualified joint and survivor annuity or a single life annuity commencing 45 days after termination from employment. For a participant who separates from service before age 62, payments under these optional forms of benefit commence 45 days after the participant's 62nd birthday. Under the plan, a participant is to elect among these optional forms of benefit during the 90-day period preceding the annuity starting date. However, during such period, a participant may defer both benefit commencement and the election of a particular benefit form to any later date, subject to section 401(a)(9). In January 1990, the employer decides to terminate the plan as of July 1, 1990. The plan will fail to satisfy section 411(d)(6) unless the optional forms of benefit provided under the plan are preserved under the annuity contract purchased on plan termination. Thus, such annuity contract must provide a participant the same optional benefit commencement rights that the plan provided. In addition, such contract must provide the same election rights with respect to such benefit options. This is the case even if, for example, in conjunction with the termination, the employer amended the plan to permit participants to elect a qualified joint and survivor annuity, single life annuity, or single sum distribution commencing on July 1, 1990.

*(4) Benefits payable to a spouse or beneficiary.* Section 411(d)(6) protected benefits may not be eliminated merely because they are payable with respect to a spouse or other beneficiary.

**(b) Section 411(d)(6) protected benefits that may be eliminated or reduced only as permitted by the Commissioner.** *(1) In general.* The Commissioner may, consistent with the provisions of this section, provide for the elimination or reduction of section 411(d)(6) protected benefits that have already accrued only to the extent that such elimination or reduction does not result in the loss to plan participants of either a valuable right or an employer-subsidized optional form of benefit where a similar optional form of benefit with a comparable subsidy is not provided or to the extent such elimination or reduction is necessary to permit compliance with other requirements of section 401(a) (e.g., sections 401(a)(4), 401(a)(9) and 415). The Commissioner may exercise this authority only through the publication of revenue rulings, notices, and other documents of general applicability.

*(2) Section 411(d)(6) protected benefits that may be eliminated or reduced.* The elimination or reduction of certain section 411(d)(6) protected benefits that have already accrued in the following situations does not violate section 411(d)(6). The rules with respect to permissible eliminations and reductions provided in this paragraph (b)(2) generally are effective January 30, 1986; however, the rules of paragraphs (b)(2)(iii) (A) and (B) and (b)(2)(viii) of this Q&A-2 are effective for plan amendments that are adopted and effective on or after September 6, 2000. These exceptions create no inference with respect to whether any other applicable requirements are satisfied (for example, requirements imposed by section 401(a)(9) and section 401(a)(14)).

(i) Change in statutory requirement. A plan may be amended to eliminate or reduce a section 411(d)(6) protected benefit if the following three requirements are met: the amendment constitutes timely compliance with a change in law affecting plan qualification; there is an exercise of section 7805(b) relief by the Commissioner; and the elimination or reduction is made only to the extent necessary to enable the plan to continue to satisfy the requirements for qualified plans. In general, the elimination or reduction of a section 411(d)(6) protected benefit will not be treated as necessary if it is possible through other modifications to the plan (e.g., by expanding the availability of an optional form of benefit to additional employees) to satisfy the applicable qualification requirement.

(ii) Joint and survivor annuity. A plan that provides a range of three or more actuarially equivalent joint and survivor annuity options may be amended to eliminate any of such options, other than the options with the largest and smallest optional survivor payment percentages, even if the effect of such amendment is to change which of the options is the qualified joint and survivor annuity under section 417. Thus, for example, if a money purchase pension plan provides three joint and survivor annuity options with survivor payments of 50%, 75% and 100%, respectively, that are uniform with respect to age and are actuarially equivalent, then the employer may eliminate the option with the 75% survivor payment, even if this option had been the qualified joint and survivor annuity under the plan.

(iii) In-kind distributions. (A) In-kind distributions payable under defined contribution plans in the form of marketable securities other than employer securities. If a defined contribution plan includes an optional form of benefit under which benefits are distributed in the form of marketable securities, other than securities of the employer, that optional form of benefit may be modified by a plan amendment that substitutes cash for the marketable securities as the medium of distribution. For purposes of this paragraph (b)(2)(iii)(A) and paragraph (b)(2)(iii)(B) of this Q&A-2, the term marketable securities means marketable securities as defined in section 731(c)(2), and the term securities of the employer means securities of the employer as defined in section 402(e)(4)(E)(ii).

(B) Amendments to defined contribution plans to specify medium of distribution. If a defined contribution plan includes an optional form of benefit under which benefits are distributable to a participant in a medium other than cash, the plan may be amended to limit the types of property in which distributions may be made to the participant to the types of property specified in the amendment. For this purpose, the types of property specified in the amendment must include all types of property (other than marketable securities that are not securities of the employer) that are allocated to the participant's account on the effective date of the amendment and in which the participant would be able to receive a distribution immediately before the effective date of the amendment if a distributable event occurred. In addition, a plan amendment may provide that the participant's right to receive a distribution in the form of specified types of property is limited to the property allocated to the participant's account at the time of distribution that consists of property of those specified types.

(C) In-kind distributions after plan termination. If a plan includes an optional form of benefit under which benefits are distributed in specified property, that optional form of benefit may be modified for distributions after plan termination by substituting cash for the specified property as the medium of distribution to the extent that, on plan termination, an employee has the opportunity to receive the optional form of benefit in the form of the specified property. This exception is not available, however, if the employer that maintains the terminating plan also maintains another plan that provides an optional form of benefit under which benefits are distributed in the specified property.

(D) Examples. The following examples illustrate the application of this paragraph (b)(2)(iii):

*Example (1).* (i) An employer maintains a profit-sharing plan under which participants may direct the investment of their accounts. One investment option available to participants is a fund invested in common stock of the employer. The plan provides that the participant has the right to a distribution in the form of cash upon termination of employment. In addition, the plan provides that, to the extent a participant's account is invested in the employer stock fund, the participant may receive an in-kind distribution of employer stock upon termination of employment. On October 18, 2000, the plan is amended, effective on January 1, 2001, to remove the fund invested in employer common stock as an investment option under the plan and to provide for the stock held in the fund to be sold. The amendment permits participants to elect how the sale proceeds are to be reallocated among the remaining investment options, and provides for amounts not so reallocated as of January 1, 2001, to be allocated to a specified investment option.

(ii) The plan does not fail to satisfy section 411(d)(6) solely on account of the plan amendment relating to the elimination of the employer stock investment option, which is not a section 411(d)(6) protected benefit. See paragraph (d)(7) of Q&A-1 of this section. Moreover, because the plan did not provide for distributions of employer securities except to the extent participants' accounts were invested in the employer stock fund, the plan is not required operationally to offer distributions of employer securities following the amendment. In addition, the plan would not fail to satisfy section 411(d)(6) on account of a further plan amendment, effective after the plan has ceased to provide for an employer stock fund investment option (and participants' accounts have ceased to be invested in employer securities), to eliminate the right to a distribution in the form of employer stock. See paragraph (b)(2)(iii)(B) of this Q&A-2.

*Example (2).* (i) An employer maintains a profit-sharing plan under which a participant, upon termination of employment, may elect to receive benefits in a single-sum distribution either in cash or in kind. The plan's investments are limited to a fund invested in employer stock, a fund invested in XYZ mutual funds (which are marketable securities), and a fund invested in shares of PQR limited partnership (which are not marketable securities).

(ii) The following alternative plan amendments would not cause the plan to fail to satisfy section 411(d)(6):

(A) A plan amendment that limits non-cash distributions to a participant on termination of employment to a distribution of employer stock and shares of PQR limited partnership. See paragraph (b)(2)(iii)(A) of this Q&A-2.

(B) A plan amendment that limits non-cash distributions to a participant on termination of employment to a distribution of employer stock and shares of PQR limited partnership, and that also provides that only participants with employer stock allocated to their accounts as of the effective date of the amendment have the right to distributions in the form of employer stock, and that only participants with shares of PQR limited partnership allocated to their accounts as of the effective date of the amendment have the right to distributions in the form of shares of PQR limited partnership. To comply with the plan amendment, the plan administrator retains a list of participants with employer stock allocated to their accounts as of the effective date of the amendment, and a list of participants with shares of PQR limited partnership allocated to their accounts as of the effective date of the amendment. See paragraphs (b)(2)(iii) (A) and (B) of this Q&A-2.

(C) A plan amendment that limits non-cash distributions to a participant on termination of employment to a distribution of employer stock and shares of PQR limited partnership to the extent that those assets are allocated to the participant's account at the time of the distribution. See paragraphs (b)(2)(iii) (A) and (B) of this Q&A-2.

(D) A plan amendment that limits non-cash distributions to a participant on termination of employment to a distribution of employer stock and shares of PQR limited partnership, and that provides that only participants with employer stock allocated to their accounts as of the effective date of the amendment have the right to distributions in the form of employer stock, and that only participants with shares of PQR limited partnership allocated to their accounts as of the effective date of the amendment have the right to distributions in the form of shares of PQR limited partnership, and that further provides that the distribution of that stock or those shares is available only to the extent that those assets are allocated to those participants' accounts at the time of the distribution. To comply with the plan amendment, the plan administrator retains a list of participants with employer stock allocated to their accounts as of the effective date of the amendment, and a list of participants with shares of PQR limited partnership allocated to their accounts as of the effective date of the amendment. See paragraphs (b)(2)(iii) (A) and (B) of this Q&A-2.

*Example (3).* (i) An employer maintains a stock bonus plan under which a participant, upon termination of employment, may elect to receive benefits in a single-sum distribution in employer stock. This is the only plan maintained by the employer under which distributions in employer stock are available. The employer decides to terminate the stock bonus plan.

(ii) If the plan makes available a single-sum distribution in employer stock on plan termination, the plan will not fail to satisfy section 411(d)(6) solely because the optional form of benefit providing a single-sum distribution in employer stock on termination of employment is modified to provide that such distribution is available only in cash. See paragraph (b)(2)(iii)(C) of this Q&A-2.

(iv) Coordination with diversification requirement. A tax credit employee stock ownership plan (as defined in section 409(a)) or an employee stock ownership plan (as defined in section 4975(e)(7)) may be amended to provide that a distribution is not available in employer securities to the extent that an employee elects to diversify benefits pursuant to section 401(a)(28).

(v) Involuntary distributions. A plan may be amended to provide for the involuntary distribution of an employee's benefit to the extent such involuntary distribution is permitted under sections 411(a)(11) and 417(e). Thus, for example, an involuntary distribution provision may be amended to require that an employee who terminates from employment with the employer receive a single sum distribution in the event that the present value of the employee's benefit is not more than $1,750, by substituting the cash-out limit in effect under § 1.411(a)-11(c)(3)(ii) for $3,500, without violating section 411(d)(6). In addition, for example, the employer may amend the plan to reduce the involuntary distribution threshold from the cash-out limit in effect under § 1.411(a)-11(c)(3)(ii) to any lower amount and to eliminate the involuntary single sum option for employees with benefits between the cash-out limit in effect under § 1.411(a)-11(c)(3)(ii) and such lower amount without violating section 411(d)(6). This rule does not permit a plan provision permitting employer discretion with respect to optional forms of benefit for employees the present value of whose benefit is less than the cash-out limit in effect under § 1.411(a)-11(c)(3)(ii).

(vi) Distribution exception for certain profit-sharing plans. (A) In general. If a defined contribution plan that is not subject to section 412 and does not provide for an annuity option is terminated, the plan may be amended to provide for the distribution of a participant's accrued benefit upon termination in a single sum optional form without the participant's consent. The preceding sentence does not apply if the employer maintains any other defined contribution plan (other than an employee stock ownership plan as defined in section 4975(e)(7)).

(B) Examples. The provisions of this paragraph (b)(2)(vi) can be illustrated by the following examples:

*Example (1).* Employer X maintains a defined contribution plan that is not subject to section 412. The plan provides for distribution in the form of equal installments over five years or equal installments over twenty years. X maintains no other defined contribution plans. X terminates its defined contribution plan after amending the plan to provide for the distribution of all participants' accrued benefits in the form of single sum distributions, without obtaining participant consent. Pursuant to the rule in this paragraph (b)(2)(iv), this amendment does not violate the requirements of section 411(d)(6).

*Example (2).* Corporations X and Y are members of controlled group employer XY. Both X and Y maintain defined contribution plans. X's plan, which is not subject to section 412, covers only employees working for X. Y's plan, which is subject to section 412, covers only employees working for Y. X terminates its defined contribution plan. Because employer XY maintains another defined contribution plan, plan X may not provide for the distribution of participants' accrued benefits upon termination without a participants' consent.

(vii) Distribution of benefits on default of loans. Notwithstanding that the distribution of benefits arising from an execution on an account balance used to secure a loan on which there has been a default is an optional form of benefit, a plan may be amended to eliminate or change a provision for loans, even if such loans would be secured by an employee's account balance.

(viii) Provisions for transfer of benefits between and among defined contribution plans and defined benefit plans of the employer. A plan may be amended to eliminate provisions permitting the transfer of benefits between and among defined contribution plans and defined benefit plans.

(ix) De minimis change in the timing of an optional form of benefit. A plan may be amended to modify an optional form of benefit by changing the timing of the availability of such optional form if, after the change, the optional form is available at a time that is within two months of the time such optional form was available before the amendment. To the extent the optional form of benefit is available prior to termination of employment, six months may be substituted for two months in the prior sentence. Thus, for example, a plan that makes in-service distributions available to employees once every month may be amended to make such in-service distributions available only once every six months. This exception to section 411(d)(6) relates only to the timing of the availability of the optional form of benefit. Other aspects of an optional form of benefit may not be modified and the value of such optional form may not be reduced merely because of an amendment permitted by this exception.

(x) Amendment of hardship distribution standards. A qualified cash or deferred arrangement that permits hardship distributions under § 1.401(k)-1(d)(3) may be amended to specify or modify nondiscriminatory and objective standards for determining the existence of an immediate and heavy financial need, the amount necessary to meet the need, or other conditions relating to eligibility to receive a hardship distribution. For example, a plan will not be treated as violating section 411(d)(6) merely because it is amended to specify or modify the resources an employee must exhaust to qualify for a hardship distribution or to require employees to provide additional statements or representations to establish the existence of a hardship. A qualified cash or deferred arrangement may also be amended to eliminate hardship distributions. The provisions of this paragraph also apply to profit-sharing or stock bonus plans that permit hardship distributions, whether or not the hardship distributions are limited to those described in § 1.401(k)-1(d)(3).

(xi) Section 415 benefit limitations. Accrued benefits under a plan as of the first day of the first limitation year beginning after December 31, 1986, that exceed the benefit limitations under section 415(b) or (e) effective on the first day of the plan's first limitation year beginning after December 31, 1986, because of a change in the terms and conditions of the plan made after May 5, 1986, or the establishment of a plan after that date, may be reduced to the level permitted under section 415(b) or (e).

**(c) Multiple amendments. (1) General rule.** A plan amendment violates the requirements of section 411(d)(6) if it is one of a series of plan amendments that, when taken together, have the effect of reducing or eliminating a section 411(d)(6) protected benefit in a manner that would be prohibited by section 411(d)(6) if accomplished through a single amendment.

**(2) Determination of time period for combining plan amendments.** For purposes of paragraph (c)(1) of this Q&A-2, generally only plan amendments adopted within a 3-year period are taken into account. But see Q&A-1(c)(1) of this section for rules relating to repeated plan amendments.

**(d) ESOP and stock bonus plan exception.** *(1) In general.* Subject to the limitations in paragraph (d)(2) of this Q&A-2, a tax credit employee stock ownership plan (as defined in section 409(a)) or an employee stock ownership plan (as defined in section 4975(e)(7)) will not be treated as violating the requirements of section 411(d)(6) merely because of any of the circumstances described in paragraphs (d)(1)(i) through (d)(1)(iv) of this Q&A-2. In addition, a stock bonus plan that is not an employee stock ownership plan will not be treated as violating the requirements of section 411(d)(6) merely because of any of the circumstances described in paragraphs (d)(1)(ii) and (d)(1)(iv) of this Q&A-2.

(i) Single sum or installment optional forms of benefit. The employer eliminates, or retains the discretion to eliminate, with respect to all participants, a single sum optional form or installment optional form with respect to benefits that are subject to section 409(h)(1)(B), provided such elimination or retention of discretion is consistent with the distribution and payment requirements otherwise applicable to such plans (e.g., those required by section 409).

(ii) Employer becomes substantially employee-owned or is an S corporation. The employer eliminates, or retains the discretion to eliminate, with respect to all participants, optional forms of benefit by substituting cash distributions for distributions in the form of employer stock with respect to benefits subject to section 409(h) in the circumstances described in paragraph (d)(1)(ii)(A) or (B) of this Q&A-2, but only if the employer otherwise meets the requirements of section 409(h)(2)—

(A) The employer becomes substantially employee-owned; or

(B) For taxable years of the employer beginning after December 31, 1997, the employer is an S corporation as defined in section 1361.

(iii) Employer securities become readily tradable. The employer eliminates, or retains the discretion to eliminate, with respect to all participants, in cases in which the employer securities become readily tradable, optional forms of benefit by substituting distributions in the form of employer securities for distributions in cash with respect to benefits that are subject to section 409(h).

(iv) Employer securities cease to be readily tradable or certain sales. The employer eliminates, or retains the discretion to eliminate, with respect to all participants, optional forms of benefit by substituting cash distributions for distributions in the form of employer stock with respect to benefits that are subject to section 409(h) in the following circumstances:

(A) The employer stock ceases to be readily tradable;

(B) The employer stock continues to be readily tradable but there is a sale of substantially all of the stock of the employer or a sale of substantially all of the assets of a trade or business of the employer and, in either situation, the purchasing employer continues to maintain the plan.

In the situation described in paragraph (d)(1)(iv)(B) of this Q&A-2, the employer may also substitute distributions in the purchasing employer's stock for distributions in the form of employer stock of the predecessor employer.

*(2) Limitations on ESOP and stock bonus plan exceptions.* (i) Nondiscrimination requirement. Plan amendments and the retention and exercise of discretion permitted under the exceptions in paragraph (d)(1) must meet the nondiscrimination requirements of section 401(a)(4).

(ii) ESOP investment requirement. Except as provided in paragraph (d)(2)(iii) of this Q&A-2, benefits provided by employee stock ownership plans will not be eligible for the exceptions in paragraph (d)(1) of this Q&A-2 unless the benefits have been held in a tax credit employee stock ownership plan (as defined in section 409 (a)) or an employee stock ownership plan (as defined in section 4975 (e)(7)) subject to section 409 (h) for the five-year period prior to the exercise of employer discretion or any amendment affecting such benefits and permitted under paragraph (d)(1) of this Q&A-2. For purposes of the preceding sentence, if benefits held under an employee stock ownership plan are transferred to a plan that is an employee stock ownership plan at the time of transfer, then the consecutive periods under the transferor and transferee employee stock ownership plans may be aggregated for purposes of meeting the five-year requirement. If the benefits are held in an employee stock ownership plan throughout the entire period of their existence, and such total period of existence is less than five years, then such lesser period may be substituted for the five year requirement.

*(3) Effective date.* The provisions of this paragraph (d) are effective beginning with the first day of the first plan year commencing on or after January 1, 1989. Prior to this effective date the reduction or elimination of a section 411(d)(6) protected benefit by a tax credit employee stock ownership plan (as defined in section 409(a)) or an employee stock ownership plan (as defined in section 4975(e)(7)) will not be treated as violating the requirements of section 411(d)(6) if such reduction or elimination reflects a reasonable interpretation of the statutory language of section 411(d)(6)(C).

*(4) Additional exceptions and requirements.* The Commissioner may, in revenue rulings, notices or other documents of general applicability, prescribe such additional rules and exceptions, consistent with the purposes of this section, as may be necessary or appropriate.

**(e) Permitted plan amendments affecting alternative forms of payment under defined contribution plans. (1) General rule.** A defined contribution plan does not violate the requirements of section 411(d)(6) merely because the plan is amended to eliminate or restrict the ability of a participant to receive payment of accrued benefits under a particular optional form of benefit for distributions with annuity starting dates after the date the amendment is adopted if, after the plan amendment is effective with respect to the participant, the alternative forms of payment available to the participant include payment in a single-sum distribution form that is otherwise identical to the optional form of benefit that is being eliminated or restricted.

**(2) Otherwise identical single-sum distribution.** For purposes of this paragraph (e), a single-sum distribution form is otherwise identical to an optional form of benefit that is eliminated or restricted pursuant to paragraph (e)(1) of this Q&A-2 only if the single-sum distribution form is identical in all respects to the eliminated or restricted optional form of benefit (or would be identical except that it provides greater rights to the participant) except with respect to the timing of payments after commencement. For example, a single-sum distribution form is not otherwise identical to a specified installment form of benefit if the single-sum distribution form is not available for distribution on the date on which the installment form would have been available for commencement, is not available in the same medium of distribution as the installment form, or imposes any condition of eligibility that did not apply to the installment form. However, an otherwise identical distribution form need not retain rights or features of the optional form of benefit that is eliminated or restricted to the extent that those rights or features would not be protected from elimination or restriction under section 411(d)(6) or this section.

**(3) Example.** The following example illustrates the application of this paragraph (e):

*Example.* (i) P is a participant in Plan M, a qualified profit-sharing plan with a calendar plan year that is invested in mutual funds. The distribution forms available to P under Plan M include a distribution of P's vested account balance under Plan M in the form of distribution of various annuity contract forms (including a single life annuity and a joint and survivor annuity). The annuity payments under the annuity contract forms begin as of the first day of the month following P's severance from employment (or as of the first day of any subsequent month, subject to the requirements of section 401(a)(9)). P has not previously elected payment of benefits in the form of a life annuity, and Plan M is not a direct or indirect transferee of any plan that is a defined benefit plan or a defined contribution plan that is subject to section 412. Distributions on the death of a participant are made in accordance with plan provisions that comply with section 401(a)(11)(B)(iii)(I). On September 2, 2005, Plan M is amended so that, effective for payments that begin on or after November 1, 2005, P is no longer entitled to any distribution in the form of the distribution of an annuity contract. However, after the amendment is effective, P is entitled to receive a single-sum cash distribution of P's vested account balance under Plan M payable as of the first day of the month following P's severance from employment (or as of the first day of any subsequent month, subject to the requirements of section 401(a)(9)).

(ii) Plan M does not violate the requirements of section 411(d)(6) (or section 401(a)(11)) merely because, as of November 1, 2005, the plan amendment has eliminated P's option to receive a distribution in any of the various annuity contract forms previously available.

**(4) Effective date.** This paragraph (e) is applicable on January 25, 2005.

Q-3. Does the transfer of benefits between and among defined benefit plans and defined contribution plans (or similar transactions) violate the requirements of section 411(d)(6)?

A-3. **(a) Transfers and similar transactions.** *(1) General rule.* Section 411(d)(6) protected benefits may not be eliminated by reason of transfer or any transaction amending or having the effect of amending a plan or plans to transfer benefits. Thus, for example, except as otherwise provided in this section, an employer who maintains a money purchase pension plan that provides for a single sum optional form of benefit may not establish another plan that does not provide for this optional form of benefit and transfer participants' account balances to such new plan.

*(2) Defined benefit feature and separate account feature.* The defined benefit feature of an employee's benefit under a defined benefit plan and the separate account feature of an employee's benefit under a defined contribution plan are section 411(d)(6) protected benefits. Thus, for example, the elimination of the defined benefit feature of an employee's benefit under a defined benefit plan, through transfer of benefits from a defined benefit plan to a defined contribution plan or plans, will violate section 411(d)(6).

*(3) Waiver prohibition.*

In general, except as provided in paragraph (b) of this Q&A-3, a participant may not elect to waive section 411(d)(6) protected benefits. Thus, for example, the elimination of the defined benefit feature of a participant's benefit under a defined benefit plan by reason of a transfer of such benefits to a defined contribution plan pursuant to a participant election, at a time when the benefit is not distributable to the participant, violates section 411(d)(6).

*(4) Direct rollovers.* A direct rollover described in Q&A-3 of § 1.401(a)(31)-1 that is paid to a qualified plan is not a transfer of assets and liabilities that must satisfy the requirements of section 414(l), and is not a transfer of benefits for purposes of applying the requirements under section 411(d)(6) and paragraph (a)(1) of this Q&A-3. Therefore, for example, if such a direct rollover is made to another qualified plan, the receiving plan is not required to provide, with respect to amounts paid to it in a direct rollover, the same

optional forms of benefit that were provided under the plan that made the direct rollover. See § 1.401(a)(31)-1, Q&A-14.

**(b) Elective transfers of benefits between defined contribution plans.** *(1) General rule.* A transfer of a participant's entire benefit between qualified defined contribution plans (other than any direct rollover described in Q&A-3 of § 1.401(a)(31)-1) that results in the elimination or reduction of section 411(d)(6) protected benefits does not violate section 411(d)(6) if the following requirements are met—

(i) Voluntary election. The plan from which the benefits are transferred must provide that the transfer is conditioned upon a voluntary, fully-informed election by the participant to transfer the participant's entire benefit to the other qualified defined contribution plan. As an alternative to the transfer, the participant must be offered the opportunity to retain the participant's section 411(d)(6) protected benefits under the plan (or, if the plan is terminating, to receive any optional form of benefit for which the participant is eligible under the plan as required by section 411(d)(6)).

(ii) Types of plans to which transfers may be made. To the extent the benefits are transferred from a money purchase pension plan, the transferee plan must be a money purchase pension plan. To the extent the benefits being transferred are part of a qualified cash or deferred arrangement under section 401(k), the benefits must be transferred to a qualified cash or deferred arrangement under section 401(k). To the extent the benefits being transferred are part of an employee stock ownership plan as defined in section 4975(e)(7), the benefits must be transferred to another employee stock ownership plan. Benefits transferred from a profit-sharing plan other than from a qualified cash or deferred arrangement, or from a stock bonus plan other than an employee stock ownership plan, may be transferred to any type of defined contribution plan.

(iii) Circumstances under which transfers may be made. The transfer must be made either in connection with an asset or stock acquisition, merger, or other similar transaction involving a change in employer of the employees of a trade or business (i.e., an acquisition or disposition within the meaning of § 1.410(b)-2(f)) or in connection with the participant's change in employment status to an employment status with respect to which the participant is not entitled to additional allocations under the transferor plan.

*(2) Applicable qualification requirements.* A transfer described in this paragraph (b) is a transfer of assets or liabilities within the meaning of section 414(l)(1) and, thus, must satisfy the requirements of section 414(l). In addition, this paragraph (b) only provides relief under section 411(d)(6); a transfer described in this paragraph must satisfy all other applicable qualification requirements. Thus, for example, if the survivor annuity requirements of sections 401(a)(11) and 417 apply to the plan from which the benefits are transferred, as described in this paragraph (b), but do not otherwise apply to the receiving plan, the requirements of sections 401(a)(11) and 417 must be met with respect to the transferred benefits under the receiving plan. In addition, the vesting provisions under the receiving plan must satisfy the requirements of section 411(a)(10) with respect to the amounts transferred.

**(3) Status of elective transfer as other right or feature.** A right to a transfer of benefits from a plan pursuant to the elective transfer rules of this paragraph (b) is an other right or feature within the meaning of § 1.401(a)(4)-4(e)(3), the availability of which is subject to the nondiscrimination requirements of section 401(a)(4) and § 1.401(a)(4)-4. However, for purposes of applying the rules of § 1.401(a)(4)-4, the following conditions are to be disregarded in determining the employees to whom the other right or feature is available—

(i) A condition restricting the availability of the transfer to benefits of participants who are transferred to a different employer in connection with a specified asset or stock disposition, merger, or other similar transaction involving a change in employer of the employees of a trade or business (i.e., a disposition within the meaning of § 1.410(b)-2(f)), or in connection with any such disposition, merger, or other similar transaction.

(ii) A condition restricting the availability of the transfer to benefits of participants who have a change in employment status to an employment status with respect to which the participant is not entitled to additional allocations under the transferor plan.

**(c) Elective transfers of certain distributable benefits between qualified plans.** *(1) In general.* A transfer of a participant's benefits between qualified plans that results in the elimination or reduction of section 411(d)(6) protected benefits does not violate section 411(d)(6) if—

(i) The transfer occurs at a time at which the participant's benefits are distributable (within the meaning of paragraph (c)(3) of this Q&A-3);

(ii) For a transfer that occurs on or after January 1, 2002, the transfer occurs at a time at which the participant is not eligible to receive an immediate distribution of the participant's entire nonforfeitable accrued benefit in a single-sum distribution that would consist entirely of an eligible rollover distribution within the meaning of section 401(a)(31)(C);

(iii) The voluntary election requirements of paragraph (b)(1)(i) of this Q&A-3 are met;

(iv) The participant is fully vested in the transferred benefit in the transferee plan;

(v) In the case of a transfer from a defined contribution plan to a defined benefit plan, the defined benefit plan provides a minimum benefit, for each participant whose benefits are transferred, equal to the benefit, expressed as an annuity payable at normal retirement age, that is derived solely on the basis of the amount transferred with respect to such participant; and

(vi) The amount of the benefit transferred, together with the amount of any contemporaneous section 401(a)(31) direct rollover to the transferee plan, equals the entire nonforfeitable accrued benefit under the transferor plan of the participant whose benefit is being transferred, calculated to be at least the greater of the single-sum distribution provided for under the plan for which the participant is eligible (if any) or the present value of the participant's accrued benefit payable at normal retirement age (calculated by using interest and mortality assumptions that satisfy the requirements of section 417(e) and subject to the limitations imposed by section 415).

*(2) Treatment of transfer.* (i) In general. A transfer of benefits pursuant to this paragraph (c) generally is treated as a distribution for purposes of section 401(a). For example, the transfer is subject to the cash-out rules of section 411(a)(7), the early termination requirements of section 411(d)(2), and the survivor annuity requirements of sections 401(a)(11) and 417. A transfer pursuant to the elective transfer rules of this paragraph (c) is not treated as a distribution for purposes of the minimum distribution requirements of section 401(a)(9).

(ii) Status of elective transfer as optional form of benefit. A right to a transfer of benefits from a plan pursuant to the elective transfer rules of this paragraph (c) is an optional form of benefit under section 411(d)(6), the availability of which is subject to the nondiscrimination requirements of section 401(a)(4) and § 1.401(a)(4)-4.

*(3) Distributable benefits.* For purposes of paragraph (c)(1)(i) of this Q&A-3, a participant's benefits are distributable on a particular date if, on that date, the participant is eligible, under the terms of the plan from which the benefits are transferred, to receive an immediate distribution of these benefits (e.g., in the form of an immediately commencing annuity) from that plan under provisions of the plan not inconsistent with section 401(a).

**(d) Effective date.** This Q&A-3 is applicable for transfers made on or after September 6, 2000.

Q-4. May a plan provide that the employer may, through the exercise of discretion, deny a participant a section 411(d)(6) protected benefit for which the participant is otherwise eligible?

A-4. **(a) In general.** Except as provided in paragraph (d) of Q&A-2 of this section with respect to certain employee stock ownership plans, a plan that permits the employer, either directly or indirectly, through the exercise of discretion, to deny a participant a section 411(d)(6) protected benefit provided under the plan for which the participant is otherwise eligible (but for the employer's exercise of discretion) violates the requirements of section 411(d)(6). A plan provision that makes a section 411(d)(6) protected benefit available only to those employees as the employer may designate is within the scope of this prohibition. Thus, for example, a plan provision under which only employees who are designated by the employer are eligible to receive a subsidized early retirement benefit constitutes an impermissible provision under section 411(d)(6). In addition, a pension plan that permits employer discretion to deny the availability of a section 411(d)(6) protected benefit violates the definitely determinable requirement of section 401(a), including section 401(a)(25). See § 1.401-1(b)(1)(i). This is the result even if the plan specifically limits the employer's discretion to choosing among section 411(d)(6) protected benefits, including optional forms of benefit, that are actuarially equivalent. In addition, the provisions of sections 411(a)(11) and 417(e) that allow a plan to make involuntary distributions of certain amounts are not excepted from this limitation on employer discretion. Thus, for example, a plan may not permit employer discretion with respect to whether benefits will be distributed involuntarily in the event that the present value of the employee's benefit is not more than the cash-out limit in effect under § 1.411(a)-11(c)(3)(ii) within the meaning of sections 411(a)(11) and 417(e). (An exception is provided for such provisions with respect to the nondiscrimination requirements of section 401(a)(4). See § 1.401(a)(4)-4(b)(2)(ii)(C).)

**(b)** Exception for administrative discretion. A plan may permit limited discretion with respect to the ministerial or mechanical administration of the plan, including the application of objective plan criteria specifically set forth in the plan. Such plan provisions do not violate the requirements of section 411(d)(6) or the definitely determinable requirement of section 401(a), including section 401(a)(25). For example, these requirements are not violated by the following provisions that permit limited administrative discretion:

*(1)* Commencement of benefit payments as soon as administratively feasible after a stated date or event;

*(2)* Employer authority to determine whether objective criteria specified in the plan (e.g., objective criteria designed to identify those employees with a heavy and immediate financial need or objective criteria designed to determine whether an employee has a permanent and total disability) have been satisfied; and

*(3)* Employer authority to determine, pursuant to specific guidelines set forth in the plan, whether the participant or spouse is dead or cannot be located.

Q-5. When will the exercise of discretion by some person or persons, other than the employer, be treated as employer discretion?

A-5. For purposes of applying the rules of this section and § 1.401(a)-4, the term "employer" includes plan administrator, fiduciary, trustee, actuary, independent third party, and other persons. Thus, if a plan permits any person, other than the participant (and other than the participant's spouse), the discretion to deny or limit the availability of a section 411(d)(6) protected benefit for which the employee is otherwise eligible under the plan (but for the exercise of such discretion), such plan violates the requirements of sections 401(a), including section 411(d)(6) and, where applicable, the definitely determinable requirement of section 401(a), including section 401(a)(25).

Q-6. May a plan condition the availability of a section 411(d)(6) protected benefit on the satisfaction of objective conditions that are specifically set forth in the plan?

A-6. **(a) Certain objective conditions permissible.** (1) In general. The availability of a section 411(d)(6) protected benefit may be limited to employees who satisfy certain objective conditions provided the conditions are ascertainable, clearly set forth in the plan and not subject to the employer's discretion except to the extent reasonably necessary to determine whether the objective conditions have been met. Also, the availability of the section 411(d)(6) protected benefit must meet the nondiscrimination requirements of section 401(a)(4). See § 1.401(a)-4.

*(2)* Examples of permissible conditions. The following examples illustrate of permissible objective conditions: a plan may deny a single sum distribution form to employees for whom life insurance is not available at standard rates as defined under the terms of the plan at the time the single sum distribution would otherwise be payable; a plan may provide that a single sum distribution is available only if the employee is in extreme financial need as defined under the terms of the plan at the time the single sum distribution would otherwise be payable; a plan my condition the availability of a single sum distribution on the execution of a covenant not to compete, provided that objective conditions with respect to the terms of such covenant and the employees and circumstances requiring execution of such covenant are set forth in the plan.

**(b)** Conditions based on factors within employer's discretion generally impermissible. A plan may not limit the availability of section 411(d)(6) protected benefits permitted under the plan on objective conditions that are within the employer's discretion. For example, the availability of section 411(d)(6) protected benefits in a plan may not be conditioned on a determination with respect to the level of the plan's funded status, because the amount of plan funding is within the employer's discretion. However, for example, although conditions based on the plan's funded status are impermissible, a plan may limit the availability of a section 411(d)(6) protected benefit (e.g., a single sum distribution) in an objective manner, such as the following:

*(1)* Single sum distributions of $25,000 and less are available without limit; and

*(2)* Single sum distributions in excess of $25,000 are available for a year only to the extent that the total amount of such single sum distributions for the year is not greater than $5,000,000; and

*(3)* An objective and nondiscriminatory method for determining which particular single sum distributions will not be available during a year in order for the $5,000,000 limit to be satisfied is set forth in the plan.

Q-7. May a plan be amended to add employer discretion or conditions restricting the availability of a section 411(d)(6) protected benefit?

A-7. No. The addition of employer discretion or objective conditions with respect to a section 411(d)(6) protected benefit that has already accrued violates section 411(d)(6). Also, the addition of conditions (whether or not objective) or any change to existing conditions with respect to section 411(d)(6) protected benefits that results in any further restriction violates section 411(d)(6). However, the addition of objective conditions to a section 411(d)(6) protected benefit may be made with respect to benefits accrued after the later of the adoption or effective date of the amendment. In addition, objective conditions may be imposed on section 411(d)(6) protected benefits accrued as of the date of an amendment where permitted under the transitional rules of § 1.401(a)-4 Q&A-5 and Q&A-8 of this section. Finally, objective conditions may be imposed on section 411(d)(6) protected benefits to the extent permitted by the permissible benefit cutback provisions of Q&A-2 of this section.

Q-8. If a plan contains an impermissible employer discretion provision with respect to a section 411(d)(6) protected benefit, what acceptable alternative exist for amending the plan without violating the requirements of section 411(d)(6)?

A-8. **(a) In general.** The following rules apply for purposes of making necessary amendments to existing plans (as defined in Q&A-9 of this section) that contain discretion provisions with respect to the availability of section 411(d)(6) protected benefits that violate the requirements of section 401(a), including sections 401(a)(25) and 411(d)(6), and this section. These transitional rules are provided under the authority of section 411(d)(6) and section 7805(b).

**(b) Transitional alternatives.** If the availability of an optional forms of benefit, early or late retirement benefit, or retirement-type subsidy under an existing plan is conditioned on the exercise of employer discretion, the plan must be amended either to eliminate the optional form of benefit, early or late retirement benefit, or retirement-type subsidy to make such benefit available to all participants without limitation, or to apply objective and nondiscriminatory conditions to the availability of the optional form of benefit, early or later retirement benefit, or retirement-type subsidy. See paragraph (d) of this Q& A-8 for rules limiting the period during which section 411(d)(6) protected benefits may be eliminated or reduced under this paragraph.

**(c) Compliance and amendment date provisions.** *(1) Operational compliance requirement.* On or before the applicable effect date for the plan (as determined under Q&A-9 of this section), the plan sponsor must select one of the alternatives permitted under paragraph (b) of the Q&A-8 with respect to each affected section 411(d)(6) protected benefit and the plan must be operated in accordance with this selection. This is an operational requirement and does not require a plan amendment prior to the period set forth in paragraph (c)(2) of this Q&A-8. There are no special reporting requirements under the Code or this section with respect to this selection.

*(2) Deferred amendment date.* If paragraph (c)(1) of this Q&A-8 is satisfied, a plan amendment conforming the plan to the particular alternative selected under paragraph (b) of this Q&A-8 must be adopted within the time period permitted for amending plans in order to meet the requirements of section 410(b) as amended by TRA '86. The plan amendment to conform the plan to these regulations may be made at an earlier date. Such conforming amendment must be consistent with the sponsor's selection as reflected by plan practice during the period from the effective date to the date the amendment is adopted. Thus, for example, if any existing calendar year noncollectively bargained defined benefit plan does a single sum distribution option that is subject to employer discretion as of August 1, 1986, and such employer makes one or more single sum distributions available on or after January 1, 1989 and before the effective date by which plan amendment is required pursuant to this section, then such employer may not adopt a plan amendment eliminating the single sum distribution, but rather must adopt an amendment eliminating the discretion provision. Any objective conditions that are adopted as part of such amendment must not be inconsistent with the plan practice for the applicable period prior to the amendment. A conforming amendment under this paragraph (c)(2) must be made with respect to each section 411(d)(6) protected benefit for which such amendment is required and must be retroactive to the applicable effective date.

**(d) Limitation on transitional alternatives.** The transitional alternatives permitting the elimination or reduction of section 411(d)(6) protected benefits are only permissible until the applicable effective date for the plan (see Q&A-9 of this section). After the applicable effective date, any amendment (other than one permitted under paragraph (c)(2) of this Q& A-8) that eliminates or reduces a section 411(d)(6) protected benefit or imposes new objective conditions on the availability of such benefit will fail to qualify for the exception to section 411(d)(6) provided in this Q&A-8. This is the case without regard to whether the section 411(d)(6) protected benefit is subject to employer discretion.

Q-9. What are the applicable effective date rules for purposes of this section?

A-9. **(a) General effective date.** Except as otherwise provided in this section, the provisions of this section are effective January 30, 1986.

**(b) New plans.** *(1) In general.* Unless otherwise provided in paragraph (b)(2) of this Q&A-9, plans that are either adopted or made effective on or after August 1, 1986, are "new plans". With respect to such new plans, this section is effective August 1, 1986. This effective date is applicable to such plans whether or not they are collectively bargained.

*(2) Exception with respect to certain new plans.* Plans that are new plans as defined in paragraph (b)(1) of this Q&A-9; under which the availability of a section 411(d)(6) protected benefit is subject to employer discretion; and that receive a favorable determination letter that covered such plan provisions with respect to an application submitted prior to July 11, 1988, will be treated as existing plans with respect to such section 411(d)(6) protected benefit for purposes of the transitional rules of this section. Thus, such plans are eligible for the compliance and amendment alternatives set forth in the transitional rule in Q&A-8 of this section.

**(c) Existing plans.** (i) In general. Plans, including plans that are adoptions of master or prototype plans, that are both adopted and in effect prior to August 1, 1986, are "existing plans" for purposes of this section. In addition, a plan that is established after July 31, 1986, but before January 1, 1989, as an initial adoption of a master or prototype plan for which a favorable opinion letter was issued by the Service after July 16, 1985 and before January 1, 1989, will be deemed to be an existing plan for purposes of this section. See sections 4.01 and 4.02 of Rev. Proc. 84-23, 1984-1 C.B. 457, 459, for the definitions of master prototype plans. However, if such plan ceases to be covered under an opinion letter of the type described above, as a result of amendment of the plan or adoption of a new plan, prior to the first day of the first plan year beginning on or after January 1, 1989, then the effective date for such plan will be determined as though the plan were a new plan initially adopted as of the date of such amendment or adoption of a new plan. Finally, new plans described in paragraph (b)(2) of this Q&A-9 are treated as existing plans with respect to certain section 411(d)(6) protected benefits. Subject to the limitations in paragraph (c) of this Q&A-9, the effective dates set forth in paragraphs (c)(2), (c)(3), and (c)(4) of this Q&A-9 apply to these existing plans for purposes of this section:

*(2)* Existing noncollectively bargained plans. With respect to existing plans other than collectively bargained plans this section is effective for the first day of the first plan year commencing on or after January 1, 1989.

*(3)* Existing collectively bargained plans. With respect to existing collectively bargained plans this section is effective for the later of the first day of the first plan year commencing on or after January 1, 1989, or the first day of the first plan year that the requirements of section 410(b) as amended by TRA '86 apply to such plan.

*(4)* Existing master and prototype plans. With respect to existing plans that are adoptions of master or prototype plans the effective date will be the first day of the first plan year commencing on or after January 1, 1989.

**(d) Delayed effective date not applicable to new alternatives or conditions.** *(1) In general.* The delayed effective dates in paragraphs (c)(2) and (c)(3) of this Q&A-9 for existing plans are only applicable with respect to a section 411(d)(6) protected benefit if both the section 411(d)(6) protected benefit and the condition providing employer discretion as to the availability of such benefit are both adopted and in effect prior to August 1, 1986. If the preceding sentence is not satisfied with respect to a particular section 411(d)(6) protected benefit, this section is effective with respect to such section 411(d)(6) protected benefit as if the plan were a new plan.

*(2)* Addition of discretion on or after January 30, 1986. The delayed effective dates in paragraphs (c)(2) and (c)(3) of this Q&A-9 are not available with respect to any section 411(d)(6) protected benefit if the section 411(d)(6) protected benefit was provided for in the plan prior to January 30, 1986, and the availability of such benefit was made subject to the exercise of employer discretion on or after January 30, 1986. If the conditions set forth in this paragraph are not satisfied with respect to a particular section 411(d)(6) protected benefit, this section is effective with respect to such section 411(d)(6) protected benefit as if the plan were a new plan. A limited exception is provided with respect to existing plans that provided a particular section 411(d)(6) protected benefit prior to January 30, 1986, and then amended the plan after January 30, 1986, and before August 1, 1986, to add a provision for employer discretion with respect to the availability of such benefit. Such plans are required to have been amended retroactively by December 31, 1987, to remove such provision for employer discretion, and, if the benefit made subject to such discretion was subsequently eliminated, the plan is required to have been further amended, by the same date, to retroactively reinstate the benefit.

*(3)* Exception for certain amendments covered by a favorable determination letter. If an amendment adding a section 411(d)(6) protected benefit subject to employer discretion was adopted or made effective after August 1, 1986, and the plan receives a favorable determination letter covering such provision with respect to an application for such letter made prior to July 11, 1988, then the effective date for purposes of amending such provision under the transitional rules is the applicable effective date determined under the rules with respect to existing plans.

**(e) Transitional rule effective date.** The transitional rule provided in Q&A-8 of this section is effective January 30, 1986.

Q-10. If a plan provides for an age 70½ distribution option that commences prior to retirement from employment with the employer maintaining the plan, to what extent may the plan be amended to eliminate this distribution option?

A-10. **(a) In general.** The right to commence benefit distributions in a particular form and at a particular time prior to retirement from employment with the employer maintaining the plan is a separate optional form of benefit within the meaning of section 411(d)(6)(B) and Q&A-1 of this section, even if the plan provision creating this right was included in the plan solely to comply with section 401(a)(9), as in effect for years before January 1, 1997. Therefore, except as otherwise provided in paragraph (b) of this Q&A-10 or any other Q&A in this section, a plan amendment violates section 411(d)(6) if it eliminates an age 70½ distribution option (within the meaning of paragraph (c) of this Q&A-10) to the extent that it applies to benefits accrued as of the later of the adoption date or effective date of the amendment.

**(b) Permitted elimination of age 70½ distribution option.** An amendment of a plan will not violate the requirements of section 411(d)(6) merely because the amendment eliminates an age 70½ distribution option to the extent that the option provides for distribution to an employee prior to retirement from employment with the employer maintaining the plan, provided that—

*(1)* The amendment eliminating this optional form of benefit applies only to benefits with respect to employees who attain age 70½ in or after a calendar year, specified in the amendment, that begins after the later of—

(i) December 31, 1998; or

(ii) The adoption date of the amendment;

*(2)* The plan does not, except to the extent required by section 401(a)(9), preclude an employee who retires after the calendar year in which the employee attains age 70½ from receiving benefits in any of the same optional forms of benefit (except for the difference in the timing of the commencement of payments) that would have been available had the employee retired in the calendar year in which the employee attained age 70½; and

*(3)* The amendment is adopted no later than—

(i) The last day of the remedial amendment period that applies to the plan for changes under the Small Business Job Protection Act of 1996 (110 Stat. 1755); or

(ii) Solely in the case of a plan maintained pursuant to one or more collective bargaining agreements between employee representatives and one or more employers ratified before September 3, 1998, the last day of the twelfth month beginning after the date on which the last of such collective bargaining agreements terminates (determined without regard to any extension thereof on or after September 3, 1998), if later than the date described in paragraph (b)(3)(i) of this Q&A-10. For purposes of this paragraph (b)(3)(ii), the rules of § 1.410(b)-10(a)(2) apply for purposes of determining whether a plan is maintained pursuant to one or more collective bargaining agreements, except that September 3, 1998 is substituted for March 1, 1986, as the date before which the collective bargaining agreements must be ratified.

**(c) Age 70½ distribution option.** For purposes of this Q&A-10, an age 70½ distribution option is an optional form of benefit under which benefits payable in a particular distribution form (including any modifications that may be elected after benefit commencement) commence at a time during the period that begins on or after January 1 of the calendar year in which an employee attains age 70½ and ends April 1 of the immediately following calendar year.

**(d) Examples.** The provisions of this Q&A-10 are illustrated by the following examples:

*Example (1).* Plan A, a defined benefit plan, provides each participant with a qualified joint and survivor annuity (QJSA) that is available at any time after the later of age 65 or retirement. However, in accordance with section 401(a)(9) as in effect prior to January 1, 1997, Plan A provides that if an employee does not retire by the end of the calendar year in which the employee attains age 70½, then the QJSA commences on the following April 1. On October 1, 1998, Plan A is amended to provide that, for an employee who is not a 5-percent owner and who attains age 70½ after 1998, benefits may not commence before the employee retires but must commence no later than the April 1 following the later of the calendar year in which the employee retires or the calendar year in which the employee attains age 70½. This amendment satisfies this Q&A-10 and does not violate section 411(d)(6).

*Example (2).* Plan B, a money purchase pension plan, provides each participant with a choice of a QJSA or a single sum distribution commencing at any time after the later of age 65 or retirement. In addition, in accordance with section 401(a)(9) as in effect prior to January 1, 1997, Plan B provides that benefits will commence in the form of a QJSA on April 1 following the calendar year in which the employee attains age 70½, except that, with spousal consent, a participant may elect to receive annual installment payments equal to the minimum amount necessary to satisfy section 401(a)(9) (calculated in accordance with a method specified in the plan) until retirement, at which time a participant may choose between a QJSA and a single sum distribution (with spousal consent). On June 30, 1998, Plan B is amended to provide that, for an employee who is not a 5-percent owner and who attains age 70½ after 1998, benefits may not commence prior to retirement but benefits must commence no later than April 1 after the later of the calendar year in which the employee retires or the calendar year in which the employee attains age 70½. The amendment further provides that the option described above to receive annual installment payments prior to retirement will not be available under the plan to an employee who is not a 5-percent owner and who attains age 70½ after 1998. This amendment satisfies this Q&A-10 and does not violate section 411(d)(6).

*Example (3).* Plan C, a profit-sharing plan, contains two distribution provisions. Under the first provision, in any year after an employee attains age 59½, the employee may elect a distribution of any specified amount not exceeding the balance of the employee's account. In addition, the plan provides a section 401(a)(9) override provision under which, if, during any year following the year that the employee attains age 70½, the employee does not elect an amount at least equal to the minimum amount necessary to satisfy section 401(a)(9) (calculated in accordance with a method specified in the plan), Plan C will distribute the difference by December 31 of that year (or for the year the employee attains age 70½, by April 1 of the following year). On December 31, 1996, Plan C is amended to provide that, for an employee other than an employee who is a 5-percent owner in the year the employee attains age 70½, in applying the section 401(a)(9) override provision, the later of the year of retirement or year of attainment of age 70½, is substituted for the year of attainment of age 70½. After the amendment, Plan C still permits each employee to elect to receive the same amount as was available before the amendment. Because this amendment does not eliminate an optional form of benefit, the amendment does not violate section 411(d)(6). Accordingly, the amendment is not required to satisfy the conditions of paragraph (b) of this Q&A-10.

**(e) Effective date.** This Q&A-10 applies to amendments adopted and effective after June 5, 1998.

Q-11. To what extent may a plan amendment that is made pursuant to the Taxpayer Relief Act of 1997 (TRA '97) (Public Law 105-34, 111 Stat. 788), reduce or eliminate section 411(d)(6) protected benefits?

A-11. A plan amendment does not violate the requirements of section 411(d)(6) merely because the plan amendment reduces or eliminates section 411(d)(6) protected benefits as of the effective date of the plan amendment, provided that—

**(a)** The plan amendment is made pursuant to an amendment made by title XV, or subtitle H of title X, of TRA '97; and

**(b)** The plan amendment is adopted no later than the last day of any remedial amendment period that applies to the plan pursuant to §§ 1.401(b)-1 and 1.401(b)-1T for changes under TRA '97.

Q-12. Is there a transition period during which a plan is permitted to eliminate a right to in-service distributions in connection with an amendment to ensure that the plan's normal retirement age satisfies the requirements of § 1.401(a)-1(b)(2)?

A-12. **(a)** In general. A plan amendment that changes the normal retirement age under the plan to a later normal retirement age pursuant to § 1.401(a)-1(b)(2) does not violate section 411(d)(6) merely because it eliminates a right to an in-service distribution prior to the amended normal retirement age. However, this paragraph does not provide relief from any other applicable requirements; for example, this relief does not permit the amendment to violate section 411(a)(9) (requiring that the normal retirement benefit not be less than the greater of any early retirement benefit payable under the plan or the benefit under the plan commencing at normal retirement age), section 411(a)(10) (if the amendment changes the plan's vesting rules), section 411(d)(6) (other than elimination of the right to an in-service distribution prior to the amended normal retirement age), or section 4980F (relating to an amendment that reduces the rate of future benefit accrual). This paragraph only applies to a plan amendment that is adopted after May 22, 2007 and on or before the last day of the applicable remedial amendment period under § 1.401(b)-1 with respect to the requirements of § 1.401(a)-1(b)(2) and (3).

**(b)**Example. The following example illustrates the application of this section:

*Example.* (i) Facts. (A) Plan A is a defined benefit plan intended to be qualified under section 401(a). Plan A is maintained by a calendar year taxpayer and has a normal retirement age that is age 45. For employees who cease employment before normal retirement age with a vested benefit, Plan A permits benefits to commence at any date after the attainment of normal retirement age through attainment of age 70½ and provides for benefits to be actuarially increased to the extent they commence after normal retirement age. For employees who continue employment after attainment of normal retirement age, Plan A provides for benefits to continue to accrue and permits benefits to commence at any time, with an actuarial increase in benefits to apply to the extent benefits do not commence after normal retirement age. Age 45 is an age that is earlier than the earliest age that is reasonably representative of the typical retirement age for the industry in which the covered workforce is employed.

(B) On February 18, 2008, Plan A is amended, effective May 22, 2007, to change its normal retirement age to the later of age 65 or the fifth anniversary of participation in the plan. The amendment provides full vesting for any participating employee who is employed on May 21, 2007, and who terminates employment on or after attaining age 45. The amendment provides employees who cease employment before the revised normal retirement age and who are entitled to a vested benefit with the right to be able to commence benefits at any date from age 45 to age 70½. The plan amendment also revises the plan's benefit accrual formula so that the benefit for prior service (payable commencing at the revised normal retirement age or any other age after age 45) is not less than would have applied under the plan's formula before the amendment (also payable commencing at the corresponding dates), based on the benefit accrued on May 21, 2007, and provides for service thereafter to have the same rate of future benefit accrual. Thus, for any participant employed on May 21, 2007, with respect to benefits accrued for service after May 21, 2007, the amount payable under the plan (as amended) at any benefit commencement date after age 45 is the same amount that would have been payable at that benefit commencement date under the plan prior to amendment. The plan amendment also eliminates the right to an in-service distribution between age 45 and the revised normal retirement age. Plan A has been operated since May 22, 2007, in conformity with the amendment adopted on February 18, 2008.

(ii) Conclusion. The plan amendment does not violate section 411(d)(6). Although the amendment eliminates the right to commence benefits in-service between age 45 and the revised normal retirement age, the amendment is made before the last day of the remedial amendment period applicable to the plan under § 1.401(b)-1 with respect to the requirements of § 1.401(a)-1(b)(2) and (3), and therefore the amendment is permitted under paragraph (a) of this A-12. Further, the amendment does not result in a reduction in any benefit for service after May 22, 2007.

Thus, the amendment does not result in a reduction in any benefit for future service, and advance notice of a significant reduction in the rate of future benefit accrual is not required under section 4980F.

---

T.D. 8212, 7/8/88, amend T.D. 8357, 8/8/91, T.D. 8360, 9/12/91, T.D. 8581, 12/22/94, T.D. 8769, 6/4/98, T.D. 8781, 9/3/98, T.D. 8794, 12/18/98, T.D. 8806, 1/7/99, T.D. 8891, 7/18/2000, T.D. 8900, 8/31/2000, T.D. 9169, 12/28/2004, T.D. 9176, 1/24/2005, T.D. 9219, 8/11/2005, T.D. 9325, 5/21/2007.

---

### § 1.411(d)-5 Class year plans; plan years beginning after October 22, 1986.

***Caution:*** The Treasury has not yet amended Reg § 1.411(d)-5 to reflect changes made by P.L. 101-239.

**(a) Plan years beginning prior to 1989.** *(1)* The requirements of section 411(a)(2) shall be treated as satisfied in the case of a class-year plan if such plan provides that 100 percent of each employee's right to or derived from the contributions of the employer on the employee's behalf with respect to any plan year is nonforfeitable not later than when such participant was performing services for the employer as of the close of each of 5 plan years (whether or not consecutive) after the plan year for which the contributions were made.

*(2)* For purposes of paragraph (a)(1) of this section if—

(i) Any contributions are made on behalf of a participant with respect to any plan year, and

(ii) Before such participant meets the requirements of paragraph (a)(1) of this section, such participant was not performing services for the employer as of the close of each of any 5 consecutive plan years after such plan year, then the plan may provide that the participant forfeits any right to or derived from the contributions made with respect to such plan year.

*(3)* This paragraph (a) applies to contributions made for plan years beginning after October 22, 1986.

**(b) Plan years beginning after 1988.** *(1)* The special class year vesting rule in section 411(d)(4) was repealed by section 1113(b) of the Tax Reform Act of 1986 (1986 Act). The repeal is generally effective for plan years beginning after December 31, 1988. See section 1111(e) of the 1986 Act for a special effective date rule applicable to certain plans maintained pursuant to collective bargaining agreements.

*(2)* (i) This subparagraph (2) provides a special rule for class year plans that were in compliance with section 411(d)(4) immediately before the first plan year beginning after section 411(d)(4) is repealed. These plans are not required to retroactively compute years of service under the general section 411(a)(2) rules. Instead, a participant must receive a year of service for each such prior plan year if the employee was performing services on the last day of such year. Similarly, if the participant was not performing services on the last day of such years, the participant will be treated as if a one-year break-in-service occurred for such plan year. This subdivision (i) applies to plan years to which this section applies.

(ii) In the case of a plan year to which § 1.411(d)-3 applied, a class year plan must compute years of service and breaks in service in a manner consistent with the rules in this paragraph (b)(2)(i), giving appropriate regard to the statutory changes made to section 411(d)(4).

---

T.D. 8219, 8/19/88.

---

### Proposed § 1.412(a)-1 General scope of minimum funding standard requirements. [*For Preamble, see ¶ 150,781*]

***Caution:*** The Treasury has not yet amended Reg § 1.412(a)-1 to reflect changes made by P.L. 100-203, P.L. 98-369.

**(a) General rule.** Section 412 of the Code provides minimum funding requirements for plans that include a trust qualified under section 401(a) and for plans that meet the requirements of section 403(a) or section 405(a). Generally, such plans include defined benefit pension plans, money purchase plans (including target benefit plans), qualified annuity plans, and qualified bond purchase plans. The minimum funding requirements continue to apply to any plan that was qualified under, or was determined to have met the requirements of, these sections for any plan year beginning on or after the effective date described in paragraph (d) of this section for the plan. Also, under section 302 of the Employee Retirement Income Security Act of 1974 ("ERISA"), the minimum funding requirements apply to employee pension benefit plans described in section 301(a) of that Act. The regulations prescribed under this section and the following sections with respect to section 412 also apply for purposes of sections 302 and 305 of ERISA. These topics are among those discussed in the following sections: maintenance of a funding standard account (including rules for combining and offsetting amounts to be amortized, rules for computing interest on amounts charged and credited to the account, rules relating to the treatment of gains and losses, and rules relating to retroactive changes in the funding standard account required by the Commissioner), § 1.412(b)-1; amortization of experience gains in connection with group deferred annuity contracts, § 1.412(b)-2; funding standard account adjustments for plan mergers and spinoffs, § 1.412(b)-3; plan terminations, § 1.412(b)-4; election of the alternative amortization method of funding, § 1.412(b)-5; determinations to be made under funding method, § 1.412(c)(1)-1; shortfall method, § 1.412(c)(1)-2; valuation of plan assets and reasonable valuation methods, § 1.412(c)(2)-1; bond valuation election, § 1.412(c)(2)-2; reasonable funding methods, § 1.412(c)(3)-1 and -2; certain changes in accrued liability, § 1.412(c)(4)-1; changes in funding method or plan year, § 1.412(c)(5)-1; full funding and the full funding limitation, § 1.412(c)(6)-1 and § 1.412(c)(7)-1; retroactive plan amendment, § 1.412(c)(8)-1; frequency of actuarial valuations, § 1.412(c)(9)-1; time for making contributions to satisfy section 412, § 1.412(c)(10)-1; and maintenance of an alternative funding standard account, § 1.412(g)-1.

**(b) Exceptions.** See section 412(h) for a list of plans not subject to the requirements of section 412. These excepted plans include profit-sharing or stock bonus plans; certain insurance contract, government, and church plans; and certain plans that do not provide for employer contributions.

**(c) Failure to meet minimum funding standards.** A plan fails to meet the minimum funding standards for a plan year if, as of the end of that plan year, there is an accumulated funding deficiency as defined in section 412(a) and § 54.4971-1(d). See regulations under section 4971 for rules relating to taxes for failure to meet the minimum funding standards.

**(d) Effective date.** *(1) In general.* Unless otherwise provided, this section and the following sections providing regulations under section 412 apply to any plan year to which section 412 applies. For a plan in existence on January 1, 1974, section 412 generally applies to plan years beginning in 1976. However, this time is extended by special transitional rules under section 1017(c)(2) of ERISA for such existing plans under collective bargaining agreements. For a plan not in existence on January 1, 1974, section 412 generally applies for plan years beginning after September 2, 1974.

*(2) Date when plan is in existence.* See § 1.410(a)-2(c) for rules concerning the date when a plan is considered to be in existence.

*(3) Early application of section 412.* See § 1.410(a)-2(d) for rules permitting plans in existence on January 1, 1974, to elect to have section 412, as well as other provisions added by section 1013 of ERISA, apply to plan year beginning after September 4, 1974, and before the effective date of the provision otherwise applicable to the plan.

*(4) Transitional rule.* The regulations issued under sections § 1.412(b)-1, § 1.412(b)-3, § 1.412(b)-4, § 1.412(c)(2)-2, § 1.412(c)(4)-1, § 1.412(c)(5)-1, § 1.412(c)(6)-1, § 1.412(c)(7)-1, § 1.412(c)(8)-1, § 1.412(c)(9)-1, § 1.412(c)(10)-1, and § 1.412(g)-1, unless otherwise indicated, are effective with respect to a particular plan when section 412 first applies to that plan. However, for plan years beginning on or before date 60 days after publication of these regulations as a Treasury Decision in the FEDERAL REGISTER, the plan may rely on the prior published position of the Internal Revenue Service with respect to the application of section 412. Other effective dates are included in § 1.412(b)-2, § 1.412(c)(1)-2, § 1.412(c)(2)-1, § 1.412(c)(3)-2, and § 1.412(i)-1.

**Proposed § 1.412(b)-1 Funding standard account.** [*For Preamble, see ¶ 150,781*]

***Caution:*** The Treasury has not yet amended Reg § 1.412(b)-1 to reflect changes made by P.L. 105-34, P.L. 100-203.

**(a) General rule.** Generally, for each single plan subject to the minimum funding standards there must be maintained a funding standard account as prescribed by section 412(b). (See § 1.414(l)-1(b)(1) for definition of "single plan".) Such an account for a money purchase pension plan reflects charges for contributions required under the plan, credits for amounts contributed, and charges and credits for amortization bases described in paragraph (b)(3) of this section.

**(b) Definitions and special rules.** *(1) Accounting date.* (i) In general. Each charge or credit to the funding standard account is charged or credited as of an accounting date. The accounting date for an item depends on the nature of the item and must be consistent with the computation of the amount of that item.

(ii) Specific accounting dates. The accounting date for each individual charge for normal cost or any charge or credit for the amortization of an amortization base is the date as of which the charge or credit is computed as due during the plan year. The last day of the plan year is the accounting date for any credit described in section 412(b)(3)(C). The first day of the plan year is the accounting date for any credit described in section 412(b)(3)(D) or for any accumulated funding deficiency or credit balance existing as of the end of the prior plan year. The accounting date for each contribution is the date the contribution is made or, if made during the period described in section 412(c)(10), the last day of the plan year. Further any contribution made must be credited as of the accounting date.

*(2) Valuation rate.* The term "valuation rate" means the assumed interest rate used to value plan liabilities.

*(3) Amortization base.* For purposes of this section, the term "amortization base" means any amount established under section 412(b)(2)(B), (C), or (D) to be amortized as a charge to the funding standard account, under section 412(b)(3)(B) to be amortized as a credit to the funding standard account, any other base resulting from a combination of offset of bases or any shortfall gain or loss base under § 1.412(c)(1)-2. Any base required by the Commissioner to be established pursuant to an approved change in funding

method is also an amortization base. Each amortization base established under one of the provisions enumerated above with respect to a particular year is referred to as an "individual base".

*(4) Amortization period.* The amortization period for a base is the period of years stated in section 412(b)(2) or (3) over which a particular base is to be amortized. See § 1.412(c)(1)-2(g)(2) and (h)(2) for amortization periods under the shortfall method. See section 412(b)(2) and (3) for amortization periods for bases described in those sections. See paragraph (d) of this section for amortization periods of bases resulting from a combination or offset of bases. If the number of years in the amortization period is not an integer, the charge or credit in the last year will not be for the entire amortization amount but will be for the outstanding balance of the base at the time of the charge or credit.

*(5) Outstanding balance.* The outstanding balance of a base as of the end of a plan year equals the difference between two amounts:

(i) The first amount is the outstanding balance of the base as of the beginning of the plan year (or, if later, the date as of which the base is required to be established) increased by interest at the valuation rate.

(ii) The second amount is the charge (or credit) for that year for the base increased by interest at the valuation rate.

For purposes of testing the basic funding formula in § 1.412(c)(3)-1(b)(1) the outstanding balance of amortizable bases must be computed as of the valuation date (the same date as of which the present value of future benefits and the present value of normal costs over the future working lifetime of participants are determined), rather than as of the end of the plan year. In testing the basic funding formula, the outstanding balance as of a valuation date equals the difference between two amounts. The first amount is the outstanding balance as of the preceding valuation date (or, if later, the date as of which the base is required to be established) increased by interest at the valuation rate. The second amount is the charge (or credit) for the plan year preceding the plan year to which the current valuation refers increased by interest at the evaluation rate.

*(6) Remaining amortization period.* The remaining amortization period for an amortization base is the difference between the amortization period and the number of years (including whole and fractional years) for which the base has been reduced by charging or crediting the funding standard account, as the case may be, with the amortization payment for each year.

*(7) Amortization amount.* The amortization amount is the amount of the charge or credit to the funding standard account required with respect to an amortization base for a plan year.

*(8) True and absolute values.* See § 1.404(a)-14(b)(4) for a definition of the terms "true value" and "absolute value."

*(9) Immediate gain type funding method.* A funding method is an immediate gain type method if, under the method—

(i) The accrued liability may be determined solely from the computations with respect to the liabilities;

(ii) The accrued liability is an integral part of the funding method; and

(iii) The accrued liability is the excess of the present value, as of any valuation date, of the projected future benefit costs for all plan participants and beneficiaries over the present value of future contributions for the normal cost of all current plan participants.

Examples of the immediate gain type of funding method are the unit credit method, the entry-age normal cost method, and the individual level premium method.

*(10) Spread gain type funding method.* A funding method is a spread gain type method if it is not an immediate gain type method. Examples of the spread gain type of funding method are the aggregate cost method, the frozen initial liability cost method, and the attained age normal cost method.

*(11) Actual unfunded liability for immediate gain funding methods.* (i) In general. For a funding method of the immediate gain type, the actual unfunded liability as of any valuation date is the excess, if any, of the accrued liability over the actuarial value of assets as of that date.

(ii) Accrued liability. The accrued liability is equal to the present value of future normal costs. Generally, for purposes of computing costs for a plan year and gains and losses for a plan year, the normal cost for the plan year to which the valuation refers is considered to be a future normal cost and is not included in the accrued liability.

(iii) Actuarial value of assets. The value of assets must be determined in a manner consistent with section 412(c)(2) of the Code and § 1.412(c)(2)-1. Furthermore, for purposes of computing costs for a plan year and gains and losses for a plan year, the assets must be treated in a manner that is consistent with the method of calculation of the accrued liability. If, in determining the accrued liability, the normal cost for the plan year to which the valuation refers is treated as a future normal cost, then the assets used to compute the unfunded accrued liability should not include contributions that are credited to the funding standard account for the plan year to which the valuation refers or for any plan year thereafter.

*(12) Actual unfunded liability for spread gain funding methods.* For a funding method of the spread gain type that maintains an unfunded liability, the actual unfunded liability equals the expected unfunded liability.

*(13) Expected unfunded liability.* The expected unfunded liability as of any valuation date is determined as:

(i) The actual unfunded liability as of the prior valuation date increased with interest at the valuation rate to this later valuation date, plus;

(ii) Normal costs representing accrued liabilities that were not included in determining the accrued liability as of the prior valuation date (i.e., such costs were considered future normal costs as of the prior valuation date) but that are included (i.e., are not considered future normal costs) in determining the accrued liability as of this later valuation date, plus interest at the valuation rate from the date as of which the normal costs were assumed payable to this valuation date, minus

(iii) The amount considered contributed by the employer to or under the plan for the plan year that was not included in the calculation of the actual unfunded liability as of the prior valuation date and was included in the calculation of the actual unfunded liability as of this later valuation date, plus interest at the valuation rate from the date on which the contribution was made if made during the plan year, or under section 412(C)(10) was deemed to have been made if made after the plan year, to this later valuation date.

*(14) Plan year to which a valuation refers.* The plan year for which the funding standard account is charged with the first normal cost determined by a valuation is the plan year

to which the valuation refers. See also § 1.412(c)(9)-1(b) concerning the date of a valuation.

**(c) Establishment and maintenance of amortization bases.** *(1) Immediate gain type funding methods.* Under a plan using an immediate gain type funding method, a new amortization base must be established to reflect each change in unfunded past service liability arising from a plan amendment, net experience gain or loss, and change in unfunded past service liability arising from a change in funding method or actuarial assumptions.

*(2) Spread gain type funding methods.* (i) In general. Under a plan using a spread gain type funding method, amortization bases may be established to reflect changes in unfunded past service liability arising from plan amendments or changes in actuarial assumptions. Alternatively, these changes in unfunded liability may be reflected in the normal cost. Whether these changes are reflected in amortization bases or in the normal cost is part of the funding method. Thus, any change from past practice constitutes a change in funding method and must be approved under section 412(c)(5). Furthermore, the method must treat increases and decreases due to any type of event consistently.

(ii) Experience gain or loss. An amortization base may not be established to reflect a net experience gain or loss under a plan using a spread gain type funding method.

*(3) Special amortization bases.* Any amortization base established to amortize a waived funding deficiency under section 412(b)(2)(C) must continue to be maintained regardless of the type of funding method used by the plan. Also see § 1.412(b)-1(d)(1).

**(d) Combining and offsetting amounts to be amortized.** *(1) In general.* Under section 412(b)(4), individual bases, with the exception of bases under section 412(b)(2)(C), may be combined and offset to form a single base. This single base is computed under the provisions of paragraph (d) that follow. However, any number of amortization bases having the same remaining amortization period may be combined and offset simply by adding the outstanding balances of the individual bases, using true rather than absolute values, without regard to the computations under paragraph (d) of this section that follow. Bases under section 412(b)(2)(C) may not be combined with any bases not established under section 412(b)(2)(C).

*(2) Combine outstanding balances of bases for changes and for credits.* Except as provided in subparagraph (1), the outstanding balances of any individual bases established for the purpose of charging the funding standard account may be combined as of any date by adding the outstanding balance of each base to be combined as of that date. Likewise, the outstanding balances of any bases for crediting the account may be combined.

*(3) Determine remaining amortization period of each combined base.* The remaining amortization period of a combined base is determined as follows:

(i) Add the amortization amounts, based on the same mode of payment, for the individual bases being combined. Amortization amounts are of the same mode of payment if they are charged or credited on the same day of the plan year, or on the same days if charged or credited in installments during the plan year.

(ii) Divide the outstanding balance of the combined base by the combined amortization amount determined under subdivision (i).

(iii) Compute the period of years for which the amount determined under subdivision (ii) provides an annuity certain of $1 per year at the valuation rate. This number, the remaining amortization period, must be computed in terms of fractional years, if necessary. Standard present value tables may be used together with linear interpolation.

(iv) As an alternative, the amortization period may be rounded to the next lowest integer (if charge bases) or next highest integer (if credit bases) and the amortization amount must then be recomputed by dividing the outstanding balance of the combined base by the present value of an annuity certain of $1 per year at the valuation rate for the rounded amortization period.

*(4) Offset.* Combined bases may be offset only if all charge and credit bases have been combined (except those that may not be combined pursuant to subparagraph (1)). The combined charge base and the combined credit base are offset by subtracting the lesser outstanding balance from the greater outstanding balance. The difference between these two outstanding balances is amortized over the remaining amortization period for the greater of the two outstanding balances, whether for charges or for credits. The amortization amount (charge or credit) for this offset base is the level amount payable for each plan year to reduce the outstanding balance of the base to zero over the remaining amortization period at the valuation rate. However, see paragraph (d)(3)(iv) of this section concerning an alternative method of computing the remaining amortization period.

*(5) Example.* The principles of paragraph (d) of this section are illustrated by the following example:

*Example.* Assume that at the beginning of a plan year the actuary for a plan decides to combine and offset the amortization bases as reflected in the plan's funding standard account. No funding deficiency of the plan has been waived. All amortization amounts are due at the end of the plan year. The valuation rate is 5 percent. Based on pertinent information from the plan records, all amortization bases, A and B for charges and C and D for credits, are combined and offset as follows:

| Base | Outstanding balance (beginning of year) | Amortization amount (due end of year) | Remaining amortization period |
|---|---|---|---|
| (i) Individual bases: | | | |
| A | $165,468 | $10,000 | 36 |
| B | 8,863 | 1,000 | 12 |
| C | (4,153) | (500) | 11 |
| D | (30,745) | (2,000) | 30 |
| (ii) Combined bases: | | | |
| AB | $174,331 | $11,000 | 32.23 |
| CD | (34,898) | (2,500) | 24.53 |
| (iii) Offset base: | | | |
| ABCD | $139,433 | $8,798 | 32.23 |

(iv) The outstanding balances of the charge and credit bases were combined in step (ii) by adding the outstanding balances of the like bases (165,468 + 8,863 = 174,331 and 4,153 + 30,745 = 34,898). The charge and credit base amortization amounts were similarly computed (10,000 + 1,000 = 11,000 and 500 + 2,000 = 2,500). The remaining amortization periods were derived from standard present value tables and linear interpolation as the amount having a present value at the 5 percent valuation rate for a $1 per year annuity certain equal to the ratio of the outstanding balance to the amortization amount.

(v) The combined bases were offset in step (iii) by subtracting base CD from AB to obtain the $139,433 outstanding balance, using the 32.23 remaining amortization period for base AB, and computing the $8,798 amortization amount as the level annual amount necessary to amortize the base fully over 32.23 years. (Alternatively, the amortization period may be rounded to 32 years. The amortization charge corresponding to that amortization period is $8,823.)

**(e) Interest.** *(1) General rule.* The funding standard account is charged or credited with interest at the valuation rate for the time between the accounting date for the item giving rise to the interest charge or credit and the end of the plan year.

*(2) Change of interest rate.* A change of the assumed interest rate under a plan does not affect the outstanding balance or the remaining amortization period of any existing base. However, the amortization amount for each base is increased to reflect an increase in interest and decreased to reflect a decrease in interest so that the present value of future amortization amounts equals the outstanding balance of the base. This change is made in addition to creating any new base required by § 1.412(b)-1(c).

**(f) Gains and losses.** *(1) Amortization requirements.* (i) Immediate gain type funding method. A plan that uses an immediate gain type of funding method separately amortizes experience gains and losses over the period prescribed in section 412(b) (2)(B)(iv) and (3)(B)(ii). The first year of the amortization of an experience gain or loss determined as of a particular valuation date is the plan year to which the valuation refers.

(ii) Spread gain type funding method. A plan that uses a spread gain type of funding method spreads experience gains and losses over future periods as a part of the plan's normal cost. These gains and losses are reflected in the amount charged to the funding standard account under section 412(b)(2)(A) and are not separately amortized.

*(2) Amount of experience gain or loss.* (i) In general. For an immediate gain type of funding method the experience gain determined as of a valuation date is the excess of the expected unfunded liability described in § 1.412(b)-1(b)(13) over the actual unfunded liability described in § 1.412(b)-1(b)(11). The experience loss is the excess of the actual unfunded liability described in § 1.412(b)-1(b)(11) over the expected unfunded liability described in § 1.412(b)-1(b)(13).

(ii) Special rule. Paragraph (f)(2)(ii) of this section applies to an immediate gain funding method if there are no other amortization charges (under section 412(b)(2)(B), (C), or (D)) or credits (under section 412(b)(3)(B)) for the first plan year in which the loss will be amortized. The experience loss as of the valuation date is the sum of—

(A) The actual unfunded liability as of the valuation date, plus

(B) Any credit balance (or minus any funding deficiency) in the funding standard account as of the first day of the first plan year in which the loss will be amortized adjusted with interest at the valuation rate to the valuation date.

**(g) Certain retroactive changes required by Commissioner.** Under section 412(c)(3), all costs liabilities, rates of interest, and other factors under the plan must be determined on the basis of actuarial assumptions and methods which, in the aggregate, are reasonable. Assumptions and methods are established in the first Schedule B (Form 5500) that is filed with respect to a plan year and may not be changed for that plan year. However, upon a determination by the Commissioner that the actuarial assumptions and methods used by a plan are not reasonable in the aggregate, the Commissioner may require certain retroactive adjustments to the funding standard account of the plan. The funding standard account must reflect these changes as required by the Commissioner.

**(h) Reasonable actuarial assumptions.** *(1) In general.* The determination whether actuarial assumptions are reasonable in the aggregate is generally based upon the experience under the plan, unless it is established that past experience is not likely to recur and thus is not a good indication of future experience. In addition, assumptions may be considered unreasonable in the circumstances described in paragraphs (h)(2)-(4) of this section.

*(2) Non counterbalancing assumptions.* Assumptions may be considered unreasonable if an assumption used by the plan is not yet reflected in the experience of the plan, is not reasonable under the circumstances of the plan, and is not counterbalanced by another assumption. For example, in a plan with one participant who has not yet attained the normal retirement age, an assumption of an unreasonable annuity purchase rate at normal retirement age may cause assumptions to be unreasonable in the aggregate. In contrast, an unreasonable annuity purchase rate could be counterbalanced by a change in the plan interest rate.

*(3) Inconsistent with benefit structure.* Assumptions may be unreasonable if use of an assumption is inconsistent with the benefit structure of the plan. For example, a plan which provides benefits not based on compensation may not assume a salary increase if it spreads the present value of future normal costs over the present value of future compensation.

*(4) Inconsistent assumptions.* Assumptions may be considered unreasonable in the aggregate if one plan assumption is inconsistent with other assumptions used by the plan. For example, an assumption which projects benefits based on a salary increase of 5-percent per year may cause assumptions to be unreasonable in the aggregate in a plan which spreads normal costs over future years' compensation using an assumption of 8-percent annual compensation increases.

### § 1.412(b)-2 Amortization of experience gains in connection with certain group deferred annuity contracts.

***Caution:*** The Treasury has not yet amended Reg § 1.412(b)-2 to reflect changes made by P.L. 109-432, P.L. 100-203.

**(a) Experience gain treatment.** Dividends, rate credits, and credits for forfeitures arising in a plan described in paragraph (b) of this section are experience gains described in section 412(b)(3)(B)(ii) (relating to the amortization of experience gains.)

**(b) Plan.** A plan is described in this paragraph (b) if—

*(1)* The plan is funded solely through a group deferred annuity contract,

*(2)* The annual single premium required under the contract for the purchase of the benefits accruing during the plan year is treated as the normal cost of the plan for that year, and

*(3)* The amount necessary to pay in equal annual installments, over the appropriate amortization period, an amount equal to the single premium necessary to provide all past service benefits not initially funded, together with interest thereon, is treated as the annual amortization amount determined under section 412(b)(2)(B)(i), (ii) or (iii).

**(c) Effective date.** This section applies for the first plan year to which section 412 applies that begins after May 22, 1981.

T.D. 7764, 1/19/81.

**Proposed § 1.412(b)-3 Funding standard account adjustments for plan mergers and spinoffs. [Reserved]** [*For Preamble, see ¶ 150,781*]

**Proposed § 1.412(b)-4 Plan termination and plan years of less than twelve months.** [*For Preamble, see ¶ 150,781*]

***Caution:*** The Treasury has not yet amended Reg § 1.412(b)-4 to reflect changes made by P.L. 105-34, P.L. 100-203.

**(a) General rules.** The minimum funding standard under section 412 applies to a plan until the end of the plan year in which the plan terminates. Therefore, the funding standard account (or the alternative funding standard account, as the case may be) must be maintained until the end of the plan year in which the plan terminates even though the plan terminates before the last day of the plan year.

**(b) Defined benefit plans.** In the case of a defined benefit plan, the charges and credits to the funding standard account are adjusted ratably to reflect the portion of the plan year before the day of plan termination. Similarly, annual charges and credits to the funding standard account are adjusted for a short plan year. However, this ratable adjustment is not made for charges described in section 412(b)(2)(C), credits under section 412(b)(3)(A), (C) and (D), for interest charges and credits under section 412(b)(5), and for credits under section 412(c)(6).

**(c) Money purchase pension plans** *(1) General rule for termination.* In the case of a money purchase pension plan, the minimum funding standard requires the funding standard account to be charged with the entire amount of any contribution due on or before the date of plan termination. However, it does not require a charge for contributions due after that date.

*(2) General rule for short plan year.* In the case of a money purchase pension plan, the minimum funding standard requires the funding standard account to be charged with the entire amount of any contribution due as of a date within a short plan year.

*(3) Due date of contributions.* For purposes of paragraphs (c)(1) and (2) of this section, a contribution is due as of the earlier of—

(i) The date specified in the plan, or

(ii) The date as of which the contribution is required to be allocated.

*(4) Date for allocation of contribution.* For purposes of paragraph (c)(3)(ii) of this section, a contribution is required to be allocated as of a date if all the requirements for the allocation have been satisfied as of that date.

**(d) Date of plan termination.** *(1) Title IV plans.* In the case of a plan subject to Title IV of ERISA, the date of plan termination is generally the date described in section 4048 of ERISA. However, if that date precedes the tenth day after the date on which notice of intent to terminate is filed, and if any contributions made or required by Code section 412 to avoid an accumulated funding deficiency for the period ending on such tenth day would increase any participant's benefits upon termination (taking benefits guaranteed by the Pension Benefit Guaranty Corporation into account), the date of termination will be the tenth day after the date on which notice of intent to terminate is filed.

*(2) Other plans.* In the case of a plan not subject to Title IV of ERISA, the date of plan termination occurs no earlier than the date on which the actions necessary to effect the plan termination are taken. The determination of this date is based on the facts and circumstances of each case.

**(e) Partial terminations.** This section does not apply to a partial plan termination within the meaning of section 411(d)(3)(A).

**(f) Funding excise taxes.** See § 54.4971-3(d) of the Pension Excise Tax Regulations (26 CFR Part 54) for the effect of plan termination on an employer's liability for taxes imposed by section 4971(a) and (b).

**§ 1.412(b)-5 Election of the alternative amortization method of funding.**

***Caution:*** The Treasury has not yet amended Reg § 1.412(b)-5 to reflect changes made by P.L. 109-432, P.L. 101-239, P.L. 100-203.

**(a) Alternative amortization method in general.** Section 1013(d) of the Employee Retirement Income Security Act of 1974 provides an alternative method which may be used by certain multiemployer plans (as defined in section 414(f)) which were in existence on January 1, 1974, for funding certain unfunded past service liability. The multiemployer plans which may elect to use this alternative method are those plans (1) under which, on January 1, 1974, contributions were based on a percentage of pay, (2) which use actuarial assumptions with respect to pay that are reasonably related to past and projected experience, and (3) which use rates of interest that are determined on the basis of reasonable actuarial assumptions. The unfunded past service liability to which this method applies is that amount existing as of the date 12 months after the date on which section 412 first applies to the plan. The alternative method allows the plan to fund this liability over a period of 40 plan years by charging the funding standard account with an equal annual percentage of the aggregate pay of all participants in the plan instead of the level dollar charges required under section 412(b)(2)(B). Paragraphs (b), (c), (d) and (e) of this section contain procedural rules for electing this alternative method.

**(b) Election procedure.** To elect the alternative amortization method, a multiemployer plan must attach a statement to the annual report required under section 6058(a) for the plan year for which the election is made, stating that the alternative method for funding unfunded past service liability is being adopted. Advance approval from the Internal Revenue Service is not required. The alternative method must be adopted on or before the last day prescribed for filing the annual report corresponding to the last plan year beginning before January 1, 1982.

**(c) Charges to which the alternative amortization method is applicable.** Once elected, the alternative amortization method is applicable to the unfunded past service liability existing as of the date 12 months after the date on which section 412 first applies to the plan. This results in charges to the funding standard account which are in lieu of—

*(1)* Charges required under clause (i) of section 412(b)(2)(B), and

*(2)* Charges required under clause (iii) of section 412(b)(2)(B) if the plan amendments referred to in such clause result in a net increase in the unfunded past service liability existing as of the date 12 months after the date on

which section 412 first applies to the plan. Such charges generally will arise only with respect to plan amendments adopted in the first plan year to which section 412 applies.

If the election is made on an annual report corresponding to a plan year after the first plan year to which section 412 applies, recomputation of the contributions due in the prior years (to which section 412 applied) will be necessary.

**(d) Limitation.** The sum of the charges described in this paragraph may not be less than the interest on the unfunded past service liabilities described in section 412(b)(2)(B)(i) and (iii), determined as of the date 12 months after the date on which section 412 first applies to the plan.

**(e) Reporting requirements.** Each annual report required by section 6058(a) and periodic report of the actuary required by section 6059 must include all additional information relevant to the use of the alternative amortization method as may be required by the applicable forms and the instructions for such forms.

---

T.D. 7702, 6/12/80.

---

**§ 11.412(c)-7 Election to treat certain retroactive plan amendments as made on the first day of the plan year.**

**(a) General rule.** Under section 412(c)(8), a plan administrator may elect to have any amendment which is adopted after the close of the plan year to which it applies deemed to have been made on the first day of such plan year if the amendment—

*(1)* Is adopted no later than 2 and one-half months after the close of such plan year (or, in the case of a multiemployer plan, no later than 2 years after the close of such plan year),

*(2)* Does not reduce the accrued benefit of any participant determined as of the beginning of such plan year, and

*(3)* Does not reduce the accrued benefit of any participant determined as of the time of adoption of the amendment, or, if it does so reduce such accrued benefit, it is shown that the plan administrator filed a notice with the Secretary of Labor notifying him of the amendment, and—

(i) The Secretary of Labor approved the amendment, or

(ii) The Secretary of Labor failed to disapprove the amendment within 90 days after the date on which the notice was filed.

**(b) Time and manner of making election.** *(1)* The election under section 412(c)(8) shall be made by the plan administrator by a statement of election described in subparagraph (3) of this paragraph, attached to the annual return relating to minimum funding standards required to be filed under section 6058 with respect to the plan year to which the election relates.

*(2)* In the event that an amendment to which paragraph (a) of this section applies is adopted after the filing of the annual return required under section 6058, the plan administrator may make the election under section 412(c)(8) by attaching a statement of election, described in paragraph (b)(3)of this section, to a copy of such annual return, and filing such copy no later than the time allowed for the filing of such returns under section 6058. (In the case of multiemployer plans, such copy may be filed within a 24 month period beginning with the date prescribed for the filing of such returns.)

*(3)* The statement of election filed by or on behalf of the plan administrator shall—

(i) State the date of the close of the first plan year to which the amendment applies and the date on which the amendment was adopted;

(ii) Contain a statement that the amendment does not reduce the accrued benefit of any participant determined as of the beginning of the plan year preceding the plan year in which the amendment is adopted; and

(iii) Contain either—

(A) A statement that the amendment does not reduce the accrued benefit of any participant determined as of the time of adoption of such amendment, or

(B) A copy of the notice filed with the Secretary of Labor under section 412(c)(8) and a statement that either the Secretary of Labor has approved the amendment or he has failed to act within 90 days after notification of the amendment.

---

T.D. 7338, 12/26/74.

---

PAR. 7. The Temporary Regulations under the Employee Retirement Income Security Act of 1974, 26 CFR Part 11, are amended by removing the following sections: § 11.412(c)-7, § 11.412(c)-11, and § 11.412(c)-12.

**Proposed § 11.412(c)-7 [Removed]** [*For Preamble, see ¶ 150,781*]

**§ 11.412(c)-11 Election with respect to bonds.**

***Caution:*** The Treasury has not yet amended Reg § 11.412(c)-11 to reflect changes made by P.L. 100-203.

**(a) In general.** Section 412(c)(2)(B) provides that, at the election of the administrator of a plan which includes a trust qualified under section 401(a) or of a plan which satisfies the requirements of section 403(a) or section 405(a), the value of a bond or other evidence of indebtedness which is held by the plan and which is not in default as to principal or interest may be determined on an amortized basis running from initial cost at purchase to the amount payable at maturity (or, in the case of a bond which is callable prior to maturity, the earliest call date). So long as this election is in effect, the value of any such evidence of indebtedness shall, for purposes of section 412, be determined on such an amortized basis rather than on a method taking into account fair market value as described in section 412(c)(2)(A).

**(b) Manner of making election.** The election to value evidences of indebtedness in accordance with paragraph (a) of this section shall be made by a statement to that effect attached to and filed as a part of the annual return of the plan required under section 6058 of the Code.

**(c) Effect of election.** The election provided by section 412(c)(2)(B), once made, will affect the valuation of all evidences of indebtedness, not in default as to principal or interest, which are held by the plan for the plan year for which the election is made and any evidences of indebtedness which are subsequently acquired by the plan. The value of any evidence of indebtedness which is in default as of the valuation date for the plan year must be determined on the basis of any reasonable actuarial method of valuation which takes into account fair market value in accordance with section 412(c)(2)(A) and must continue to be so valued until the indebtedness is no longer in default.

**(d) Consent to revoke required.** *(1) In general.* An election made in accordance with paragraph (a) of this section may be revoked only if consent to revoke the election is obtained from the Secretary or his delegate.

*(2) Manner of obtaining permission for revocation. [Reserved].*

T.D. 7335, 12/19/74.

**Proposed § 11.412(c)-11 [Removed]** [*For Preamble, see ¶ 150,781*]

**§ 11.412(c)-12 Extension of time to make contributions to satisfy requirements of section 412.**

***Caution:*** The Treasury has not yet amended Reg § 11.412(c)-12 to reflect changes made by P.L. 100-203.

**(a) In general.** Section 412(c)(10) of the Internal Revenue Code of 1954 provides that for purposes of section 412 a contribution for a plan year made after the end of such plan year but not later than two and one-half months after the last day of such plan year shall be deemed to have been made on such last day. Section 412(c)(10) further provides that the two and one-half month period may be extended for not more than six months under regulations.

**(b) Six month extension of two and one-half month period.** *(1)* For purposes of section 412 a contribution for a plan year to which section 412 applies that is made not more than eight and one-half months after the end of such plan year shall be deemed to have been made on the last day of such year.

*(2)* The rules of this section relating to the time a contribution to a plan is deemed made for purposes of the minimum funding standard under section 412 are independent from the rules contained in section 404(a)(6) relating to the time a contribution to a plan is deemed made for purposes of claiming a deduction for such contribution under section 404.

T.D. 7439, 10/21/76.

**Proposed § 11.412(c)-12 [Removed]** [*For Preamble, see ¶ 150,781*]

**§ 1.412(c)(1)-1 Determinations to be made under funding method—terms defined.**

***Caution:*** The Treasury has not yet amended Reg § 1.412(c)(1)-1 to reflect changes made by P.L. 109-432.

**(a) Actuarial cost method and funding method.** Section 3(31) of the Employee Retirement Income Security Act of 1974 ("ERISA") provides certain acceptable (and unacceptable) actuarial cost methods which may (or may not) be used by employee plans. The term "funding method" when used in section 412 has the same meaning as the term "actuarial cost method" in section 3(31) of ERISA. For shortfall method for certain collectively bargained plans, see § 1.412(c)(1)-2; for principles applicable to funding methods in general, see regulations under section 412(c)(3).

**(b) Computations included in funding method.** The funding method of a plan includes not only the overall funding method used by the plan but also each specific method of computation used in applying the overall method. However, the choice of which actuarial assumptions are appropriate to the overall method or to the specific method of computation is not a part of the funding method. For example, the decision to use or not to use a mortality factor in the funding method of a plan is not a part of such funding method. Similarly, the specific mortality rate determined to be applicable to a particular plan year is not part of the funding method. See section 412(c)(5) for the requirement of approval to change the funding method used by a plan.

T.D. 7499, 8/3/77, amend T.D. 7733, 11/13/80.

**§ 1.412(c)(1)-2 Shortfall method.**

***Caution:*** The Treasury has not yet amended Reg § 1.412(c)(1)-2 to reflect changes made by P.L. 109-432, P.L. 105-34.

**(a) In general.** *(1) Shortfall method.* The shortfall method is a funding method that adapts a plan's underlying funding method for purposes of section 412. As such, the use of the shortfall method is subject to section 412(c)(3). A plan described in paragraph (a)(2) of this section may elect to determine the charges to the funding standard account required by section 412(b) under the shortfall method. These charges are computed on the basis of an estimated number of units of service or production (for which a certain amount per unit is to be charged). The difference between the net amount charged under this method and the net amount that otherwise would have been charged under section 412 for the same period is a shortfall loss (gain) and is to be amortized over certain subsequent plan years.

*(2) Eligibility for use of shortfall.* No plan may use the shortfall method unless—

(i) The plan is a collectively bargained plan described in section 413(a), and

(ii) Contributions to the plan are made at a rate specified under the terms of a legally binding agreement applicable to the plan.

For purposes of this section, a plan maintained by a labor organization which is exempt from tax under section 501(c)(5) is treated as a collectively bargained plan and the governing rules of the organization (such as its constitution, bylaws, or other document that can be altered only through action of a convention of the organization) are treated as a collectively bargained agreement.

**(b) Computation and effect of net shortfall charge.** *(1) In general.* The "net shortfall charge" to the funding standard account under the shortfall method is the product of (i) the estimated unit charge described in paragraph (c) of this section that applies for a particular plan year, multiplied by (ii) the actual number of base units (for example, units of service or production) which occurred during that plan year. When the shortfall method is used, the net shortfall charge is a substitute for the specific charges and credits to the funding standard account described in section 412(b)(2) and (3)(B).

*(2) Example.* Paragraph (b)(1) of this section may be illustrated by the following example:

*Example.* A pension plan uses the calendar year as the plan year and the shortfall method. Its estimated unit charge applicable to 1980 is 80 cents per hour of covered employment. During 1980, there were 125,000 hours of covered employment. The net shortfall charge for the plan year is \$100,000, (i.e., 125,000 × \$.80) regardless of the amount which would be charged and credited to the funding standard account under section 412(b)(2) and (3)(B) had the shortfall method not applied. The funding standard account for 1980 will be separately credited for the amount considered contributed for the plan year under section 412(b)(3)(A). The other items which may be credited, if applicable, are a waived funding deficiency and the alternative minimum funding standard credit adjustment under section

412(b)(3)(C) and (D) because these items are not credits under section 412(b)(3)(B).

*(3) Plans with more than one contract, contribution rate, employer, or benefit level.* (i) General rule. A single plan with more than one contract, contribution rate, employer, or benefit level may compute a separate net shortfall charge for each contract, contribution rate, each employer, or each benefit level. The sum of these charges is the plan's total net shortfall charge, under § 1.412(c)(1)-1(b), the use of separate computations would be a specific method of computation used in applying the overall funding method. See also paragraph (f)(5) of this section.

(ii) Single valuation. Only one actuarial valuation shall for the single plan on each actuarial valuation date.

(iii) Reasonableness test. The specific method of computation of the net shortfall charge must be reasonable, determined in the light of the facts and circumstances.

**(c) Estimated unit charge.** The estimated unit charge is the annual computation charge described in paragraph (d) of this section divided by the estimated base units of service or production described in paragraph (e) of this section.

**(d) Annual computation charge.** The annual computation charge for a plan year is the sum of the following amounts:

*(1)* The net charges and credits which, but for using the shortfall method, would be made under section 412(b)(2) and (b)(3)(B).

*(2)* The amount described in paragraph (g)(3) of this section, if applicable, for amortization of shortfall gain or loss.

**(e) Estimated base units.** *(1) In general.* The estimated base units are the expected units of service or production for a plan year (hours, days, tons, dollars of compensation, etc.), determined as of the base unit estimation date for that plan year under paragraph (f) of this section. This estimate must be based on the past experience of the plan and the reasonable expectations of the plan for the plan year. The specific type of unit used must be described in the statement of funding method for the plan year. (See paragraph (i)(3) of this section for reporting requirements.)

*(2) Reasonable expectations.* The reasonableness of expectations used under paragraph (e)(1) of this section is determined under the facts and circumstances of the plan for each plan year as of the relevant base unit estimation date. Expectations will be considered unreasonable if, for example, they do not reflect a consistent and substantial decline or growth in actual base units that has occurred over the course of recent years and that is likely to continue beyond the base unit estimation date. This determination of reasonableness is independent of determinations made under section 412(c)(3) of the reasonableness of actuarial assumptions.

**(f) Base unit estimation date.** *(1) In general.* The base unit estimation date for the current plan year is determined under this paragraph (f). This date shall be an actuarial valuation date no earlier than the last actuarial valuation date occurring at least one year before the earliest date any current collectively bargained agreement in existence during the plan year came into effect.

*(2) Four-month rule.* For purposes of this paragraph (f), a current collectively bargained agreement is one in effect during at least four months of the current plan year.

*(3) Effective date of agreement.* For purposes of this paragraph (f), a collectively bargained agreement shall be deemed to have come into effect on the effective date of the agreement containing the currently effective provision for contributions to the plan or the benefits provided under the plan.

*(4) Long-term contract rule.* The effective date of a collectively bargained agreement shall be deemed not to occur prior to the first day of the third plan year preceding the current year.

*(5) Special rule for plans computing separate net shortfall charge.* A plan that computes a separate net shortfall charge for each contract, contribution rate, employer, or benefit level under paragraph (b)(3) of this section shall determine the base unit estimation date for each separate charge without regard to any collectively bargained agreement that does not relate to that contract, contribution rate, employer, or benefit level. If a collective bargaining agreement requiring contributions by a certain employer, or prescribing a certain benefit level, is in effect on December 31, 1980, the preceding sentence shall not apply to the computation of a separate net shortfall charge for that employer or benefit level until the earlier of—

(i) The first plan year beginning after the date on which expires the collective bargaining agreement requiring contributions by that employer (or the last collective bargaining agreement relating to that benefit level), or

(ii) The first plan year beginning after December 31, 1983.

*(6) Example.* The rules contained in paragraph (f) of this section are illustrated by the following table. In the table, "V" signifies actuarial valuation date (January 1 in each case shown); "B" signifies beginning of a contract; and "E" signifies end of a contract. The table shows the resulting earliest base unit estimation date with respect to the following assumed items:

**COMPUTATION OF EARLIEST BASE UNIT ESTIMATION DATE**

*Plan year (calendar year basis)*

| Example | 1973 | 1974 | 1975 | 1976 | 1977 | 1978 | 1979 | 1980 | 1981 | 1982 | 1983 | 1984 |
|---|---|---|---|---|---|---|---|---|---|---|---|---|
| Plan A | V | | | V | | | V | | | V | | |
| Contract 1 | | | E/B | | | E/B | | E/B | | | | E/B |
| Base unit estimation date[1] | | | | 1973 | 1973 | 1973 | 1976 | 1976 | 1979 | 1979 | 1979 | 1979 |
| Plan B | V | | | V | | | V | | | V | | |
| Contract 2 | | No Contract | | B* | | E/B | | | | E/B* | | |
| Contract 3 | E/B | | | E/B* | | | E/B* | | | E/B | | |
| Base unit estimation date[1] | | | | 1973 | 1973 | 1973 | 1976 | 1976 | 1979 | 1979 | 1979 | 1979 |

| | | | | | | | | | | | | |
|---|---|---|---|---|---|---|---|---|---|---|---|---|
| Plan C | V | V | V | V | V | V | V | V | V | V | V | V |
| Contract 4 | | | E/B | | | E/B* | | | | E/B | | |
| Contract 5 | | | E/B | | | E/B* | | | | | E/B | |
| Base unit estimation date[1] | | | | 1974 | 1974 | 1977 | 1977 | 1977 | 1977 | 1978 | 1979 | 1981 |

[1] The base unit estimation date may be on or any time after the actuarial valuation date in the year indicated on this line.

* Denotees that a prior contract ends and a new contract begins prior to the fifth month of a plan year.

**(g) Amortization of shortfall gain or loss.** *(1) Definition.* The shortfall gain for a plan is the excess for the plan year of—

(i) The net shortfall charge computed under paragraph (b) of this section over

(ii) The annual computation charge described in paragraph (d) of this section.

The shortfall loss for a plan is the excess for the plan year of the annual computation charge over the net shortfall charge.

*(2) Shortfall amortization period.* (i) First year. The plan year in which the amortization of a shortfall gain or loss must begin is the earlier of two years: the fifth plan year following the plan year in which the shortfall gain or loss arose, or the first plan year beginning after the latest scheduled expiration date of a collectively bargained agreement in effect with respect to the plan during the plan year in which the shortfall gain or loss arose. For purposes of this subparagraph, a contract expiring on the last day of a plan year shall be deemed to be renewed on such last day for the same period of years as the contract that succeeds the expiring contract.

(ii) Last year. The plan year in which the amortization of a shortfall gain or loss must end is the 15th plan year following the plan year in which the shortfall gain or loss arose. For a multiemployer plan described in section 414(f), the amortization must end with the 20th plan year instead of the 15th.

*(3) Annual amortization amount.* The shortfall gain or loss must be amortized in equal annual installments. The total amount to be amortized must be adjusted for interest at the rate used for determining the plan's normal cost.

*(4) Shortfall gain or loss under spread gain type of funding method.* (i) In general. A spread gain type of funding method spreads experience gains and losses over future periods as part of a plan's normal cost. (Examples of spread gain types of funding methods are the aggregate cost method, the frozen initial liability method, and the attained age normal method.) However, a shortfall gain or loss is not an experience gain or loss. Therefore, a plan using a spread gain type of funding method together with the shortfall method must amortize shortfall gains and losses and otherwise meet the requirements of paragraph (g) of this section.

(ii) Asset adjustment for aggregate method. A plan using the shortfall method with the aggregate cost method of funding must adjust its plan assets for a shortfall gain or loss in calculating normal cost. The unamortized portion of any shortfall gain is subtracted from plan assets. The unamortized portion of any shortfall loss is added to plan assets.

*(5) Reconciliation of shortfall gain or loss with funding standard account.* At the beginning of each year, the actual unfunded liability under the method used by the plan must equal the outstanding balance of all amortization bases, including bases for shortfall gains and losses, less the credit balance under the funding standard account at the end of the prior year.

*(6) Example.* This paragraph is illustrated by the following examples:

*Example (1).* A multiemployer plan described in section 414(f) is maintained with the calendar year as the plan year and uses the shortfall method. The plan uses the frozen initial liability funding method. A five percent interest assumption is used by the plan, with payments computed as of the first day of each plan year for all items. The expiration dates of contracts in effect during plan years 1976, 1977, and 1978 are such that the amortization of gains or losses for each year must begin in the fifth following plan year. The assumed plan costs and estimated base units for selected years, and the computations under this section which follow from such assumptions are shown in the following table. In the table, "*" denotes an assumed item. The remaining figures have been calculated on the basis of these assumptions.

**(a) Computation of Net Shortfall Charge and Shortfall Gain or Loss**

| Plan year | 1976 | 1977 | 1978 |
|---|---|---|---|
| 1. Normal cost* | $100,000 | $100,000 | $100,000 |
| 2. Amortization of unfunded liability* | 50,000 | 50,000 | 50,000 |
| 3. Total annual computation charges | $150,000 | $150,000 | $150,000 |
| 4. Estimated base units* | 100,000 | 100,000 | 100,000 |
| 5. Estimated unit charge (line 3 ÷ line 4) | $ 1.50 | $ 1.50 | $ 1.50 |
| 6. Actual units during year* | 80,000 | 90,000 | 110,000 |
| 7. Net shortfall charge for year (line 5 × line 6) | $120,000 | $135,000 | $165,000 |
| 8. Shortfall (gain) or loss (line 3 – line 7) | $ 30,000 | $ 15,000 | ($ 15,000) |

**(b) Annual Amortization Amount**

| | | | |
|---|---|---|---|
| 9. Year of shortfall gain or loss | 1976 | 1977 | 1998 |
| 10. First year of amortization | 1981 | 1982 | 1983 |
| 11. Last year of amortization | 1996 | 1997 | 1998 |
| 12. (Gain) or loss adjusted for interest to year amortization begins (1/1/76 to 1/1/81, etc.) | $ 39,299 | $ 10,144 | ($ 19,144) |
| 13. Annual amortization (16 years) | $ 3,364 | $ 1,682 | ($ 1,682) |

**(c) Computation of Net Shortfall Charges for Selected Years (Including Shortfall Amortization)**

| Plan year | 1981 | 1982 | 1983 |
|---|---|---|---|
| 14. Normal cost* | $120,000 | $125,000 | $130,000 |
| 15. Amortization of unfunded liability* | 50,000 | 50,000 | 50,000 |

| | | | |
|---|---|---|---|
| 16. Shortfall amortization (see line 13) from: | | | |
| 1976 | 3,364 | 3,364 | 3,364 |
| 1977 | ....... | 1,682 | 1,682 |
| 1978 | ....... | ....... | (1,682) |
| 17. Total annual computation charges | $173,364 | $180,046 | $183,364 |
| 18. Estimated base units* | 110,000 | 110,000 | 110,000 |
| 19. Estimated unit charge (line 17 ÷ line 18) | $ 1,576 | $ 1,637 | $ 1,667 |
| 20. Actual units during year* | 105,000 | 110,000 | 105,000 |
| 21. Net shortfall charge for year (line 19 × line 20) | $165,480 | $180,070 | $175,035 |
| 22. Shortfall (gain) loss (line 17 − line 21) | $ 7,884 | ($ 24) | $ 8,329 |

The amounts in line 22 will be amortized beginning 1986, 1987, and 1988, respectively. The $24 gain in 1982 results from rounding the estimated unit charge.

*Example (2).* Assume the facts in Example (1). Also assume that the plan uses the frozen initial liability funding method, that the unfunded liability as of January 1, 1976 (corresponding to a 40-year charge of $50,000 due at the beginning of the year) is $900,850, and that actual contributions at the rate of $1.75 per unit are paid at mid-year in 1976.

**(a) Computation of the Unfunded Liability as of December 31, 1976**

| | |
|---|---|
| 1. Unfunded liability as of 1/1/76 | $900,850 |
| 2. Normal cost (that used in the calculation of the total annual computation charges) | 100,000 |
| 3. Interest at 5% due on items 1 and 2 | 50,043 |
| 4. Contribution with interest: $1.75 × 80,000 × 1.025 (actual contribution rate times actual base units times interest adjustment from mid–year) | 143,500 |
| 5. Unfunded liability as of 12/31/76: item 1 + item 2 + item 3 − item 4 | 907,393 |

**(b) Computation of the Outstanding Balance of the Bases as of December 31, 1976**

| | |
|---|---|
| 1. Original base: ($900,850 − $50,000) × 1.05 | $893,393 |
| 2. Shortfall loss $30,000 × 1.05 | 31,500 |
| 3. Total | 924,893 |

**(c) Computation of the Credit Balance as of December 31,1976**

| | |
|---|---|
| 1. Net shortfall charge (Sec. 1.412 (c) (1)-2 (b)) adjusted for interest: $120,000 × 1.05 | $126,000 |
| 2. Actual contributions with interest | 143,500 |
| 3. Credit balance as of 12/31/76: item 2 − item 1 | 17,500 |

(d) Reconciliation of computations. As of January 1, 1977, the unfunded liability ($907,393) equals the outstanding balance of the bases minus the credit balance ($924,893 − $17,500 = $907,393).

**(h) Amortization of experience gain or loss.** *(1) General rule.* In the case of a plan using an immediate gain type of funding method, an experience gain or loss shall be amortized pursuant to section 412(b)(2)(B)(iv) or (b)(3)(B)(ii). (Examples of the immediate gain type of funding method are the unit credit method, the entry age normal cost method, and the individual level premium cost method.) For purposes of this section, a shortfall gain or loss is not an experience gain or loss. The amount of the experience gain or loss must be adjusted for interest at the rate used for determining the plan's normal cost.

*(2) Experience amortization period under shortfall method.* (1) First year. The plan year in which the amortization of an experience gain or loss must begin in the case of a plan using the shortfall method is the earlier of two years: the fifth plan year following the plan year in which the experience gain or loss arose, or the first plan year beginning after the last scheduled expiration date of a contract in effect during the plan year in which the experience gain or loss arose. For purposes of this subparagraph a contract expiring on the last day of the plan year shall be deemed to be renewed on such last day for the same period of years as the contract that succeeds the expiring contract.

(ii) Last year. The plan year in which the amortization of an experience gain or loss must end in the case of a plan using the shortfall method is the 15th plan year following the plan year in which the experience gain or loss arose. For a multi-employer plan described in section 414(f), the amortization must end with the 20th plan year instead of the 15th.

*(3) Use of annual computation charge in determining experience gain or loss.* In the case of a plan using an immediate gain type of funding method, an experience gain or loss is the difference between the expected unfunded liability and the actual unfunded liability under the plan. The expected unfunded liability as of the end of a plan year equals the actual unfunded liability as of the beginning of the year plus normal cost, minus contributions, all adjusted for interest. If the plan adopts the shortfall method, the expected unfunded liability is computed by using the normal cost applicable for the plan year in determining the annual computation charge under paragraph (d) of this section. The same normal cost is used in computing the unfunded liability under the frozen initial liability funding method.

*(4) Example.* This paragraph is illustrated by the following example:

*Example.* Assume the facts in Example (2) from paragraph (g)(6) of this section, except that the entry age normal funding method is used. Also assume that as of December 31, 1976, the actual unfunded liability is $900,000.

**(a) Computation of Expected Unfunded Liability**

| | |
|---|---|
| 1. Actual unfunded liability as of 1/1/76 | $900,850 |
| 2. Normal cost portion of annual computation charge as of 1/1/76 | 100,000 |
| 3. Interest at 5% due on items 1 and 2 | 50,043 |
| 4. Contribution received with interest: $1.75 × 80,000 × 1.025 (actual contribution rate times actual base units times interest adjustment at mid–year) | 143,500 |
| 5. Expected unfunded liability as of 12/31/76 (item 1 + item 2 + item 3 − item 4) | 907,393 |

**(b) Computation of Gain or Loss**

| | |
|---|---|
| 1. Expected unfunded liability as of 12/31/76 | $907,393 |
| 2. Actual unfunded liability as of 12/31/76 | 900,000 |
| 3. Gain (or loss) (item 1 − item 2) | 7,393 |

**(i) Election procedure.** *(1) In general.* To elect the shortfall method, a collectively bargained plan must attach a statement to the annual report required under section 6058(a) for the first plan year to which it is applied. The statement shall state that the shortfall method is adopted, beginning with the plan year covered by such report. Advance approval from the Internal Revenue Service is not required if the shortfall method is first adopted on or before the later of—

(i) The first plan year to which section 412 applies or

(ii) The last plan year commencing before December 31, 1981.

However, approval must be received pursuant to section 412(c)(5) prior to the adoption of the shortfall method at a later time, or the discontinuance of such method, once adopted.

*(2) Use of specific computation method.* A specific method of computation under the shortfall method is described in paragraph (b)(3) of this section, regarding the treatment of more than one contract, employer, or benefit level under the plan. This specific method may be adopted with respect to any plan year to which the shortfall method applies. Approval from the Commissioner must be received under section 412(c)(5) prior to the adoption of this specific computation method for a plan year subsequent to the first plan year to which the shortfall method applies, or prior to the discontinuance of a specific computation method, once adopted.

*(3) Reporting requirements.* Each annual report required by section 6058(a) and periodic report of the actuary required by section 6059 must include all additional information relevant to the use of the shortfall method as may be required by the applicable forms and the instructions for such forms.

**(j) Transitional rule.** In lieu of paragraphs (g)(2) and (h)(2) of this section relating to the amortization period for shortfall and experience gains and losses, for gains and losses arising in plan years beginning before January 1, 1981, a plan may rely on the prior published position of the Internal Revenue Service with respect to the amortization period for shortfall and experience gains and losses.

**(k) Supersession.** This section and § 1.412(c)(1)-1 supersede §§ 11.412(c)(1)-1 and (c)(1)-2 of the Temporary Income Tax Regulations Under the Employee Retirement Income Security Act of 1974.

---

T.D. 7499, 8/3/77, amend T.D. 7733, 11/13/80.

---

### § 1.412(c)(1)-3 Applying the minimum funding requirements to restored plans.

***Caution:*** The Treasury has not yet amended Reg § 1.412(c)(1)-3 to reflect changes made by P.L. 109-432, P.L. 107-147, P.L. 105-34.

**(a) In general.** *(1) Restoration method.* The restoration method is a funding method that adapts the underlying funding method of section 412 in the case of certain plans that are or have been terminated and are later restored by the Pension Benefit Guaranty Corporation (PBGC). The normal operation of the funding standard account, and all other provisions of section 412 and the regulations thereunder, are unchanged except as provided in this § 1.412(c)(1)-3. Under the restoration method, the PBGC shall determine a restoration payment schedule, extending over no more than 30 years, that replaces all charges and credits to the funding standard account attributable to pre-restoration amortization bases. The restoration payment schedule is determined on the basis of an actuarial valuation of the accrued liability of the plan on the initial post-restoration valuation date less the actuarial value of the plan assets on that date. The initial post-restoration valuation date is the date of the valuation that falls in the first plan year beginning on or after the date of the restoration order.

*(2) Applicability of restoration method.* A plan must use the restoration method if, and only if—

(i) The plan is being or has been terminated pursuant to section 4041(c) or section 4042 of the Employee Retirement Income Security Act of 1974 (ERISA); and

(ii) The plan has been restored by the PBGC pursuant to its authority under section 4047 of ERISA.

**(b) Computation and effect of the initial restoration amortization base.** *(1) In general.* The initial restoration amortization base is determined under the underlying funding method used by the plan. When the plan uses a spread gain funding method that does not maintain an unfunded liability, the plan must change either to an immediate gain method that directly calculates an accrued liability or to a spread gain method that maintains an unfunded liability. A plan may adopt any cost method that satisfies this requirement and that is acceptable under section 412 and the regulations thereunder, provided that the plan administrator follows the procedures established by the Commissioner for changes in funding methods. The initial restoration amortization base is determined using the valuation for the plan year in which the initial post-restoration valuation date falls. The initial restoration amortization base equals the accrued liability with respect to plan benefit liabilities returned by the PBGC less the value of the plan assets returned by the PBGC. The initial restoration amortization base replaces all prior amortization bases including those under section 412(b)(2)(B), (C), and (D) and under section 412(b)(3)(B). Any base resulting from a change in funding method, including a change required under this paragraph, is treated as a prior amortization base within the meaning of this paragraph (b). Any accumulated funding deficiency or credit balance in the funding standard account is set equal to zero when the initial restoration amortization base is established.

*(2) Example.* The following example illustrates the provisions of this paragraph (b):

*Example.* A pension plan uses the calendar year as its plan year, makes its annual periodic valuation as of January 1, and uses the unit credit actuarial cost method for funding purposes. The plan is in the process of being terminated. By order of the PBGC the plan is restored as of July 1, 1991. The initial post-restoration valuation date is January 1, 1992, and a restoration payment schedule order is issued on October 31, 1992. If, as of January 1, 1992, the accrued liability of the plan is $1,000,000 and the value of the plan assets is $200,000, the initial restoration amortization base is $800,000.

**(c) Establishment of a restoration payment schedule.** *(1) Certification requirement.* When the PBGC establishes a restoration payment schedule, the Executive Director of the PBGC must certify to the PBGC's Board of Directors, and to the Internal Revenue Service, that the PBGC has reviewed the funding of the plan, the financial condition of the plan sponsor and its controlled group members, the payments required under the restoration payment schedule (taking into account the availability of deferrals authorized under paragraph (c)(4) of this section), and any other factor that the PBGC deems relevant, and, based on that review, determines that it is in the best interests of participants and beneficiaries of the plan and the pension insurance program that the restored plan not be reterminated.

*(2) Requirements for restoration payment schedule.* (i) Amortization of base over period of no more than 30 years. The restoration payment schedule must be prescribed in an order requiring the employer to make stated contributions to

the plan sufficient to amortize the initial restoration amortization base over a period extending not more than 30 years after the initial post-restoration valuation date (the restoration payment period). Payments included in the restoration payment schedule order are charged to the funding standard account of the plan at the end of each plan year in accordance with paragraph (d) of this section. The restoration payment schedule must provide for total charges that are sufficient to amortize the entire amount of the initial restoration amortization base by the end of the restoration payment period. The scheduled charges need not be in level amounts, but the present value of the prescribed charges on the initial post-restoration valuation date, computed with interest at the valuation rate, must equal the initial restoration amortization base.

(ii) Minimum annual charge. The restoration payment schedule must prescribe annual charges that are sufficient to prevent the outstanding balance of the initial restoration amortization base from exceeding whichever of the following amounts is applicable—

(A) During the first 10 plan years on the restoration payment schedule, the amount of the initial restoration amortization base on the date the base was established; or

(B) During plan years 11 through 20 on the restoration payment schedule, the maximum permitted outstanding balance of the initial restoration amortization base at the end of the tenth plan year, as calculated under paragraph (c)(2)(iii) of this section; or

(C) During plan years 21 through the end of the restoration payment schedule, the maximum permitted outstanding balance of the initial restoration amortization base at the end of the twentieth plan year, as calculated under paragraph (c)(2)(iii) of this section.

(iii) Interim amortization requirements. The restoration payment schedule must provide for sufficient periodic charges so that the outstanding balance of the initial restoration amortization base at the end of the tenth plan year and at the end of the twentieth plan year of the restoration payment period will not be larger than the outstanding balance that would have remained at the end of the tenth plan year and at the end of the twentieth plan year, respectively, if the initial restoration amortization base had been amortized in level annual amounts over the restoration payment period at the valuation rate.

*(3) Amendments to the restoration payment schedule.* The order establishing the restoration payment schedule may be amended by the PBGC from time to time with respect to any remaining payments, provided that no amendment may extend the restoration payment period beyond 30 years from the initial post-restoration valuation date, and provided further that the restoration payment schedule, as amended, satisfies the requirements of paragraph (c)(2) of this section.

*(4) Deferral of minimum scheduled annual payment amounts.* (i) Authority to grant deferral. Not later than 2½ months following the end of the plan year, the PBGC may grant a deferral of the charges required in the restoration payment schedule for that plan year if the requirements in paragraph (c)(4)(ii) of this section are satisfied. The PBGC may require the plan sponsor and its controlled group members to provide security to the plan as a condition to granting a deferral.

(ii) Determination of business hardship. Before granting a deferral under this paragraph (c)(4), the PBGC must make a determination that the granting of the deferral is in the best interests of plan participants and the plan termination insurance system, and that the plan sponsor and its controlled group members are unable to make the scheduled restoration payments without experiencing temporary substantial business hardship. In making these determinations, the factors the PBGC shall consider, include, but are not limited to, the following—

(A) Whether the plan sponsor and its controlled group members are operating at an economic loss;

(B) Whether there is substantial unemployment or underemployment in the trades or businesses of the plan sponsor and its controlled group members;

(C) Whether the sales and profits of the industry or industries are depressed or declining; and

(D) Whether it is reasonable to expect that the plan termination insurance system will suffer a greater loss if the plan is terminated than if it is continued as a restored plan.

(iii) Amount of deferral. The amount of the deferral for any particular plan year may not exceed the lesser of the amount that would have been required to be contributed under the restoration payment schedule for that year or interest at the valuation rate on the outstanding balance of the initial restoration amortization base for that year. An amortization payment for a deferral granted for a prior plan year may not be deferred. No deferral may extend the overall restoration payment period beyond 30 years.

(iv) Modification of payment schedule. The restoration payment schedule must be adjusted to reflect any deferral granted for a plan year in the manner prescribed in this paragraph (c). The charge otherwise specified in the schedule is reduced by the amount of any deferral. The charges under the restoration payment schedule for the subsequent plan years are increased by the amounts in paragraph (c)(4)(v) of this section.

(v) Amortization of deferred amount. The amount of any deferral granted by the PBGC for any plan year must be amortized in level amounts over five years or such shorter period as may be prescribed by the PBGC, at the valuation rate, beginning with the plan year following the year of the deferral.

(vi) Number of deferrals permitted. The PBGC may not grant more than five deferrals of the minimum scheduled payments as required by this section during the restoration payment period and no more than three of these deferrals may be granted during the first ten years of that period.

(vii) Deferrals override minimum annual charges and interim amortization requirements. In determining the minimum annual charge under paragraph (c)(2)(ii) of this section and in applying the interim amortization requirements of paragraph (c)(2)(iii) of this section, the unamortized balances of any deferrals granted by the PBGC under this paragraph shall be added to the outstanding balance of the initial restoration amortization base otherwise allowable.

**(d) Charging the scheduled restoration payments to the funding standard account.** In addition to any other charges and credits prescribed in the normal operation of the funding standard account under section 412, the amount of each payment specified in the restoration payment schedule shall be charged against the funding standard account of the plan for the plan year to which that payment is attributed in the restoration payment schedule. To the extent that the restoration payment schedule provides for payments before the end of the plan year, the annual charge to the funding standard account attributable to the restoration payment schedule is equal to the sum of the periodic payments for the plan year accumulated with interest at the valuation rate to the last day of the plan year.

**(e) Changes in actuarial assumptions or methods.** The plan administrator must notify the PBGC of any changes in the actuarial assumptions or methods used by the plan. Upon notification of any such change, the PBGC may make any changes to the restoration payment schedule that it deems appropriate.

**(f) Change to restoration method.** A plan that has been restored must use the restoration method until the initial restoration amortization base has been fully amortized. The use of this method does not require prior approval from the Commissioner. A plan using the restoration method must compute the charges to the funding standard account to amortize the initial restoration amortization base in accordance with the order of the PBGC and in accordance with this section.

**(g) Deficit reduction contribution.** *(1) Calculation of deficit reduction contribution.* For any plan using the restoration method, the deficit reduction contribution under section 412(l)(2) is equal to the sum of—

(i) The unfunded section 412(l) restoration liability amount; plus

(ii) The unfunded new liability amount.

*(2) Unfunded section 412(l) restoration liability amount.* The unfunded section 412(l) restoration liability amount is the amount necessary to amortize fully the unfunded section 412(l) restoration liability in installments, as prescribed by the PBGC, over not more than 30 years. The annual amount need not be level, but at all times the present value of the future amortization charges prescribed under the restoration payment schedule, at the current liability interest rate, must equal the outstanding balance of the unfunded section 412(l) restoration liability and the schedule must provide that at the end of no more than 30 years the entire amount of the unfunded section 412(l) restoration liability base will have been fully amortized. The schedule prescribed for amortization of the unfunded section 412(l) restoration liability must comply with the requirements imposed in paragraph (c) of this section on the restoration payment schedule, except as provided in paragraph (g)(7) of this section and except that the maximum permitted outstanding balance of the unfunded section 412(l) restoration liability at the end of the tenth plan year must not be greater than the outstanding balance of the section 412(l) restoration liability that would have remained at the end of the tenth plan year if the unfunded section 412(l) restoration liability had been amortized in level amounts over the restoration payment period at the actual current liability interest rate for each year, increased by the current liability interest rate differential as defined under paragraph (g)(7) of this section. The unfunded section 412(l) restoration liability amount for the tenth plan year otherwise prescribed under the restoration payment schedule is increased by any outstanding current liability interest rate differential. By issuing an appropriate order, the PBGC may permit the outstanding current liability interest rate differential to be amortized over the tenth through the fourteenth plan years. If the PBGC permits the amortization of the outstanding current liability interest rate differential, then the unfunded section 412(l) restoration liability amount for each year to which an amortization payment is attributed under the order shall be increased by such payment. The outstanding balance otherwise required by paragraph (g)(2) of this section is increased by the outstanding balance, if any, of the base resulting from the amortization of the current liability interest rate differential. The PBGC may amend the amortization schedule for the unfunded section 412(l) restoration liability subject to the limits on amendments to the amortization schedule prescribed for the initial restoration amortization base.

*(3) Establishment of unfunded section 412(l) restoration liability.* In the plan year in which the initial post-restoration valuation date falls, the unfunded section 412(l) restoration liability is equal to the unfunded current liability of the plan.

*(4) Unfunded new liability amount.* In the case of a plan using the restoration method, the unfunded new liability amount is the applicable percentage, as defined in section 412(l)(4)(C), of the unfunded new liability determined under paragraph (g)(5) of this section.

*(5) Unfunded new liability.* The unfunded new liability of a plan using the restoration method is the excess, if any, of the unfunded current liability of the plan, within the meaning of section 412(l)(8)(A) for the plan year (determined without taking into account any unpredictable contingent event benefits, even if the event has occurred) over the outstanding balance of the unfunded section 412(l) restoration liability determined under paragraph (g)(3) of this section.

*(6) Offset of amortization charges.* The amounts charged to the funding standard account pursuant to the restoration payment schedule in order to amortize the initial restoration base, as described in paragraph (d) of this section, must be offset against the deficit reduction contribution in paragraph (g)(1) of this section along with any other applicable amounts provided in section 412(l)(1)(A)(ii).

*(7) Interest rate differential.* During the first 10 plan years after the initial post-restoration valuation date, the restoration payment schedule must prescribe an unfunded section 412(l) restoration liability amount for each plan year that is sufficient to prevent the outstanding balance of the unfunded section 412(l) restoration liability from exceeding the initial amount of the unfunded section 412(l) restoration liability increased by the current liability interest rate differential. The current liability interest rate differential at any point during the first ten years of the restoration payment period is the excess, if any, of the outstanding balance of the unfunded section 412(l) restoration liability determined using the actual current liability interest rate for each year, taking into account the charges described in paragraph (d) of this section, over the outstanding balance of the unfunded section 412(l) restoration liability determined using the lowest, for each year, of the initial current liability interest rate, the current liability interest rate for the computation year, and the valuation interest rate, taking into account the charges described in paragraph (d) of this section.

**(h) Election of the alternative minimum funding standard.** A plan using the restoration method may not elect the alternative minimum funding standard under section 412(g).

**(i) Funding review by the PBGC.** The PBGC must review the funding of any plan using the restoration method at least once in each plan year. As a result of a funding review, the PBGC may amend the restoration payment schedule as provided in paragraph (c)(3) of this section. As part of the funding review, the Executive Director of the PBGC must certify to the PBGC's Board of Directors, and to the Internal Revenue Service, that the PBGC has reviewed the funding of the plan, the financial condition of the plan sponsor and its controlled group members, the payments required under the restoration payment schedule (taking into account the availability of deferrals authorized under paragraph (c)(4) of this section), and any other factor that the PBGC deems relevant, and, based on that review, determines that it is in the best interests of participants and beneficiaries of the plan and the pension insurance program that the restored plan not be reterminated.

T.D. 8494, 10/21/93.

### § 1.412(c)(1)-3T Applying the minimum funding requirements to restored plans (temporary).

***Caution:*** The Treasury has not yet amended Reg § 1.412(c)(1)-3T to reflect changes made by P.L. 109-432, P.L. 105-34.

• ***Caution:*** Under Code Sec. 7805, temporary regulations expire within three years of the date of issuance. This temporary regulation was issued on 10/22/90.

**(a) In general.** *(1) Restoration method.* The restoration method is a funding method that adapts the underlying funding method of section 412 in the case of certain plans that are or have been terminated and are later restored by the Pension Benefit Guaranty Corporation. The normal operation of the funding standard account, and all other provisions of section 412 and the regulations thereunder, are unchanged except as provided in this § 1.412(c)(1)-3T. Under the restoration method, the Pension Benefit Guaranty Corporation shall determine a restoration payment schedule, extending over no more than 30 years, that replaces all charges and credits to the funding standard account attributable to pre-restoration amortization bases. The restoration payment schedule is determined on the basis of an actuarial valuation of the accrued liability of the plan on the initial post-restoration valuation date less the actuarial value of the plan assets on that date. The initial post-restoration valuation date is the date of the first valuation that falls in the first plan year beginning on or after the later of October 23, 1990, or the date of the restoration order.

*(2) Applicability of restoration method.* A plan must use the restoration method if, and only if:

(i) The plan is being or has been terminated pursuant to section 4041(c) or section 4042 of the Employee Retirement Income Security Act of 1974 (ERISA), and

(ii) The plan has been restored by the Pension Benefit Guaranty Corporation pursuant to its authority under section 4047 of ERISA.

**(b) Computation and effect of the initial restoration amortization base.** *(1) In general.* The initial restoration amortization base is determined under the underlying funding method used by the plan. When the plan uses a spread gain funding method that does not maintain an unfunded liability, the plan must change either to an immediate gain method that directly calculates an accrued liability or to a spread gain method that maintains an unfunded liability. A plan may adopt any cost method that satisfies this requirement and that is acceptable under section 412 and the regulations thereunder, provided that the plan follows the procedures established by the Commissioner for changes in funding methods. The initial restoration amortization base is determined using the valuation for the plan year in which the initial post-restoration valuation date falls. The initial restoration amortization base equals the accrued liability with respect to plan benefit liabilities returned by the Pension Benefit Guaranty Corporation less the value of the plan assets returned by the Pension Benefit Guaranty Corporation. The initial restoration amortization base replaces all prior amortization bases including those under subparagraphs (B), (C), and (D) of section 412(b)(2) and under subparagraph (B) of section 412(b)(3). Any base resulting from a change in funding method is treated as a prior amortization base within the meaning of this paragraph (b). Any accumulated funding deficiency or credit balance in the funding standard account is set equal to zero when the initial restoration amortization base is established.

*(2) Example.* A pension plan uses the calendar year as its plan year, makes its annual periodic valuation as of January 1, and uses the unit credit actuarial cost method for funding purposes. The plan is in the process of being terminated. By order of the Pension Benefit Guaranty Corporation the plan is restored as of July 1, 1991, and a restoration payment schedule order issued on October 31, 1992. The initial post-restoration valuation date is January 1, 1993. If, as of that date, the accrued liability of the plan is $1,000,000 and the value of the plan assets is $200,000, the initial restoration amortization base is $800,000.

**(c) Establishment of a restoration payment schedule.** *(1) Certification requirement.* When the PBGC establishes a restoration payment schedule, the Executive Director of the PBGC must certify to the Corporation's Board of Directors, and to the Internal Revenue Service, that the Corporation has reviewed the funding of the plan, the financial condition of the plan sponsor and its controlled group members, the payments required under the restoration payment schedule (taking into account the availability of deferrals authorized under paragraph (c)(4) of this section), and any other factor that the Corporation deems relevant, and, based on that review, determines that it is in the best interests of participants and beneficiaries of the plan and the pension insurance program that the restored plan not be reterminated.

*(2) Requirements for restoration payment schedule.* (i) Amortization of base over period of no more than 30 years. The restoration payment schedule must be prescribed in an order requiring the employer to make stated contributions to the plan sufficient to amortize the initial restoration amortization base over a period extending not more than 30 years after the initial post-restoration valuation date (the restoration payment period). The restoration payment schedule must be sufficient to amortize the entire amount of the initial restoration amortization base by the end of the restoration payment period. The scheduled charges need not be in level amounts, but the present value of the prescribed charges on the initial post-restoration valuation date, computed with interest at the valuation rate, must equal the initial restoration amortization base.

(ii) Minimum annual charge. The restoration payment schedule must require annual charges that are sufficient to prevent the outstanding balance of the initial restoration amortization base from exceeding whichever of the following amounts is applicable:

(A) During the first 10 plan years on the restoration payment schedule, the amount of the initial restoration amortization base on the date the base was established, or

(B) During plan years 11 through 20 on the restoration payment schedule, the maximum permitted outstanding balance of the initial restoration amortization base at the end of the tenth plan year, as calculated under paragraph (c)(2)(iii) below, or

(C) During plan years 21 through the end of the restoration payment schedule, the maximum permitted outstanding balance of the initial restoration amortization base at the end of the twentieth plan year, as calculated under paragraph (c)(2)(iii) below.

(iii) Interim amortization requirements. The restoration payment schedule must provide for sufficient periodic charges so that the outstanding balance of the initial restoration amortization base at the end of the tenth plan year and at the end of the twentieth plan year of the restoration payment period will not be larger than the outstanding balance that would have remained at the end of the tenth plan year and at the end of the twentieth plan year, respectively, if the initial restoration amortization base had been amortized in level amounts over the restoration payment period at the valuation rate.

*(3) Amendments to the restoration payment schedule.* The order establishing the restoration payment schedule may be amended by the Pension Benefit Guaranty Corporation from time to time with respect to any remaining payments, provided that no amendment may extend the restoration payment period beyond 30 years from the initial post-restoration valuation date, and provided further that the restoration payment schedule, as amended, satisfies the requirements of paragraph (c)(2) of this section.

*(4) Deferral of minimum scheduled annual payment amounts.* (i) Authority to grant deferral. Not later than 2½ months following the end of the plan year, the Pension Benefit Guaranty Corporation may grant a deferral of the charges required in the restoration payment schedule for that plan year if the requirements in paragraph (c)(4)(ii) of this section are satisfied. The Pension Benefit Guaranty Corporation may require the plan sponsor and its controlled group members to provide security to the plan as a condition to granting a deferral.

(ii) Determination of business hardship. Before granting a deferral under this paragraph (c)(4), the Pension Benefit Guaranty Corporation must make a determination that the granting of the deferral is in the best interests of plan participants and the plan termination insurance system, and that the plan sponsor and its controlled group members are unable to make the scheduled restoration payments without experiencing temporary substantial business hardship. In making these determinations, the factors the Pension Benefit Guaranty Corporation shall consider, include, but are not limited to, the following:

(A) Whether the plan sponsor and its controlled group members are operating at an economic loss,

(B) Whether there is substantial unemployment or underemployment in the trades or businesses of the plan sponsor and its controlled group members,

(C) Whether the sales and profits of the industry or industries are depressed or declining, and

(D) Whether it is reasonable to expect that the plan termination insurance system will suffer a greater loss if the plan is terminated than if it is continued as a restored plan.

(iii) Amount of deferral. The amount of the deferral for any particular plan year may not exceed the lesser of the amount that would have been required to be contributed under the restoration payment schedule for that year or interest on the outstanding balance of the initial restoration amortization base for that year. An amortization payment for a deferral granted for a prior plan year may not be deferred. No deferral may extend the overall restoration payment period beyond 30 years.

(iv) Modification of payment schedule. The restoration payment schedule must be adjusted to reflect any deferral granted for a plan year in the manner prescribed in this paragraph (c). The charge otherwise specified in the schedule is reduced by the amount of any deferral. The charges under the restoration payment schedule for the subsequent plan years are increased by the amounts in paragraph (c)(4)(v) of this section.

(v) Amortization of deferred amount. The amount of any deferral granted by the Pension Benefit Guaranty Corporation for any plan year must be amortized in level amounts over five years or such shorter period as may be prescribed by the Pension Benefit Guaranty Corporation, at the valuation rate, beginning with the plan year following the year of the deferral.

(vi) Number of deferrals permitted. The Pension Benefit Guaranty Corporation may not grant more than five deferrals of the minimum scheduled payments as required by this section during the restoration payment period and no more than three of these deferrals may be granted during the first ten years of that period.

**(d) Charging the scheduled restoration charges to the funding standard account.** In addition to any other charges and credits prescribed in the normal operation of the funding standard account under section 412, the amount of each charge specified in the restoration payment schedule shall be charged against the funding standard account of the plan for the plan year to which that payment is attributed in the restoration payment schedule.

**(e) Changes in actuarial assumptions.** If changes in actuarial assumptions increase or decrease the charges that would be required to amortize the outstanding balance of the initial restoration amortization base over the remaining years of the restoration payment schedule, the plan must notify the Pension Benefit Guaranty Corporation of the changes so that it may make appropriate changes to the restoration payment schedule.

**(f) Change to restoration method.** A plan that has been restored must use the restoration method until the initial restoration amortization base has been fully amortized. The use of this method does not require prior approval from the Commissioner. A plan using the restoration method must compute the charges and credits to the initial restoration amortization base in accordance with the order of the Pension Benefit Guaranty Corporation and in accordance with this section.

**(g) Deficit reduction contribution.** *(1) Calculation of deficit reduction contribution.* For any plan using the restoration method, the deficit reduction contribution under section 412(l)(2) is equal to the sum of—

(i) the unfunded section 412(l) restoration liability amount, plus

(ii) the unfunded new liability amount.

*(2) Unfunded section 412(l) restoration liability amount.* The unfunded section 412(l) restoration liability amount is the amount necessary to amortize fully the unfunded section 412(l) restoration liability in installments, as prescribed by the Pension Benefit Guaranty Corporation, over not more than 30 years. The annual amount need not be level, but at all times the present value of the future amortization charges under the restoration payment schedule, at the current liability interest rate, must equal the outstanding balance of the unfunded section 412(l) restoration liability and the schedule must provide that at the end of no more than 30 years the entire amount of the unfunded section 412(l) restoration liability base will have been fully amortized. The schedule prescribed for amortization of the unfunded section 412(l) resto-

ration liability must comply with the requirements imposed in paragraph (c) of this section on the restoration payment schedule, except as provided in paragraph (g)(7) of this section and except that the maximum permitted outstanding balance of the unfunded section 412(l) restoration liability at the end of the tenth plan year must not be greater than the outstanding balance of the section 412(l) restoration liability that would have remained at the end of the tenth plan year if the unfunded section 412(l) restoration liability had been amortized in level amounts over the restoration payment period at the current liability interest rate, increased by the current liability interest rate differential as defined under paragraph (g)(7) of this section. The Pension Benefit Guaranty Corporation may amend the amortization schedule for the unfunded section 412(l) restoration liability subject to the limits on amendments to the amortization schedule prescribed for the initial restoration amortization base.

*(3) Establishment of unfunded section 412(l) restoration liability.* In the plan year in which the initial post-restoration valuation date falls, the unfunded section 412(l) restoration liability is equal to the unfunded current liability of the plan.

*(4) Unfunded new liability amount.* In the case of a plan using the restoration method, the unfunded new liability amount is the applicable percentage, as defined in section 412(l)(4)(C), of the unfunded new liability determined under paragraph (g)(5) of this section.

*(5) Unfunded new liability.* The unfunded new liability of a plan using the restoration method is the unfunded current liability of the plan for the plan year less the outstanding balance of the unfunded section 412(l) restoration liability determined under paragraph (g)(3) of this section and less any unpredictable contingent event benefit liabilities (without regard to whether or not the event has occurred).

*(6) Offset of amortization charges.* The charges specified in the restoration payment schedule to amortize the initial restoration amortization base, must be offset against the deficit reduction contribution in paragraph (g)(1) of this section along with any other applicable amounts provided in section 412(l)(1)(A)(ii).

*(7) Interest rate differential.* During the first 10 plan years after the initial post-restoration valuation date, the unfunded section 412(l) restoration liability amount for the plan as determined for purposes of this section must be sufficient to prevent the outstanding balance of the unfunded section 412(l) restoration liability from exceeding the initial amount of the unfunded section 412(l) restoration liability increased by the current liability interest rate differential. The current liability interest rate differential at any point during the first ten years of the restoration payment period is the excess if any of the accumulated interest on the unfunded section 412(l) restoration liability computed at the current liability interest rate over the accumulated interest on the unfunded section 412(l) restoration liability computed at the least of the valuation rate, the current liability interest rate and, current liability interest rate for the plan year in which the initial post restoration valuation date falls. The current liability interest rate differential is charged to the funding standard account at the end of the tenth plan year, but the Pension Benefit Guaranty Corporation may, as part of the restoration payment schedule order, or a modification to that order, direct that the charging of this amount must be spread over not more than 5 years, beginning with the eleventh plan year.

**(h) Election of the alternative minimum funding standard.** A plan using the restoration method may not elect the alternative minimum funding standard under section 412(g).

**(i) Funding review by the Pension Benefit Guaranty Corporation.** The Pension Benefit Guaranty Corporation must review the funding of any plan using the restoration method at least once in each plan year. As a result of a funding review, the Pension Benefit Guaranty Corporation may amend the restoration payment schedule as provided in paragraph (c)(3) of this section. As part of the funding review, the Executive Director of the PBGC must certify to the Corporation's Board of Directors, and to the Internal Revenue Service, that the Corporation has reviewed the funding of the plan, the financial condition of the plan sponsor and its controlled group members, the payments required under the restoration payment schedule (taking into account the availability of deferrals authorized under paragraph (c)(4) of this section), and any other factor that the Corporation deems relevant, and, based on that review, determines that it is in the best interests of participants and beneficiaries of the plan and the pension insurance program that the restored plan not be reterminated.

T.D. 8317, 10/22/90.

### § 1.412(c)(2)-1 Valuation of plan assets; reasonable actuarial valuation methods.

***Caution:*** The Treasury has not yet amended Reg § 1.412(c)(2)-1 to reflect changes made by P.L. 109-432, P.L. 107-16, P.L. 100-203.

**(a) Introduction.** *(1) In general.* This section prescribes rules for valuing plan assets under an actuarial valuation method which satisfies the requirements of section 412(c)(2)(A). An actuarial valuation method is a funding method within the meaning of section 412(c)(3) and the regulations thereunder. Therefore, certain changes affecting the actuarial valuation method are identified in this section as changes in a plan's funding method.

*(2) Exception for certain bonds, etc.* The rules of this section do not apply to bonds or other evidences of indebtedness for which the election described in section 412(c)(2)(B) has been made, nor are such assets counted in applying paragraphs (b) or (c) of this section. Also, an election under section 412(c)(2)(B) is not a change in funding method within the meaning of section 412(c)(5).

*(3) Money purchase pension plan.* A money purchase pension plan must value assets for the purpose of satisfying the requirements of section 412(c)(2)(A) solely on the basis of their fair market value (under paragraph (c) of this section).

*(4) Defined benefit plans.* (i) To satisfy the requirements of section 412(c)(2)(A), an actuarial method valuing assets of a defined benefit plan must meet the requirements of paragraph (b) of this section.

(ii) In general, the purpose of paragraph (b) of this section is to permit use of reasonable actuarial valuation methods designed to mitigate short-run changes in the fair market value of plan assets. The funding of plan benefits and the charges and credits to the funding standard account required by section 412 are generally based upon the assumption that the defined benefit plan will be continued by the employer. Thus, short-run changes in the value of plan assets presumably will offset one another in the long term. Accordingly, in the determination of the amount required to be contributed under section 412 it is generally not necessary to recognize fully each change in fair market value of the assets in the period in which it occurs.

(iii) The asset valuation rules contained in paragraph (b) produce a "smoothing" effect. Thus, investment performance, including appreciation or depreciation in the market value of the assets occurring in each plan year, may be recognized gradually over several plan years. This "smooth- effect which results, for example, from amortizing experience losses and gains over 15 or 20 years under section 412(b)(2)(B)(iv) and (3)(B)(ii).

**(b) Asset valuation method requirements.** *(1) Consistent basis.* (i) The actuarial asset valuation method must be applied on a consistent basis. Any change in meeting the requirements of this paragraph (b) is a change in funding method subject to section 412(c)(5).

(ii) A method may satisfy the consistency requirement even though computations are based only on the period elapsed since the adoption of the method or on asset values occurring during that period.

*(2) Statement of plan's method.* The method of determining the actuarial value (but not fair market value) of the assets must be specified in the plan's actuarial report (required under section 6059). The method must be described in sufficient detail so that another actuary employing the method described would arrive at a reasonably similar result. Whether a deviation from the stated actuarial valuation method is a change in funding method is to be determined in accordance with section 412(c)(5) and the regulations thereunder. A deviation to include a type of asset not previously held by the plan would not be a change in funding method.

*(3) Consistent valuation dates.* The same day or days (such as the first or the last day of a plan year) must be used for all purposes to value the plan's assets for each plan year, or portion of plan year, for which a valuation is made. For purposes of this section, each such day is a valuation date. A change in the day or days used is a change in funding method.

*(4) Reflect fair market value.* The valuation method must take into account fair market value by making use of the—

(i) Fair market value (determined under paragraph (c) of this section), or

(ii) Average value (determined under paragraph (b)(7) of this section) of the plan's assets as of the applicable asset valuation date. This is done either directly in the computation of their actuarial value or indirectly in the computation of upper or lower limits placed on that value.

*(5) Results above and below fair market or average value.* A method will not satisfy the requirements of this paragraph (b) if it is designed to produce a result which will be consistently above or below the values described in paragraph (b)(4)(i) and (ii). However, a method designed to produce a result which consistently falls between fair market value and average value will satisfy this requirement. See Example (5) in paragraph (b)(9) of this section for an illustration of a method described in the preceding sentence.

*(6) Corridor limits.* (i) Regardless of how the method reflects fair market value under paragraph (b)(4), the method must result in an actuarial value of the plan's assets which is not less than a minimum amount and not more than a maximum amount. The minimum amount is the lesser of 80 percent of the current fair market value of plan assets as of the applicable asset valuation date or 85 percent of the average value (as described in subparagraph (7)) of plan assets as of that date. The maximum amount is the greater of 120 percent of the current fair market value of plan assets as of the applicable asset valuation date or 115 percent of the average value of plan assets as of that date.

(ii) Under a plan's method, a preliminary computation of the expected actuarial value may fall outside the prescribed corridor. A method meets the requirements of paragraph (b)(6)(i) of this section is such a case only by adjusting the expected actuarial value to the nearest corridor limit applicable under the method. A plan may use an actuarial valuation method with a narrower corridor than the general corridor required under paragraph (b)(6)(i). The adjustment to the nearest corridor limit of such a method for purposes of this subdivision (ii) would be determined by the narrower corridor stated in the description of the plan's method.

*(7) Average value.* The average value of plan assets is computed by—

(i) Determining the fair market value of plan assets at least annually,

(ii) Adding the current fair market value of the assets (as of the applicable valuation date) and their adjusted values (as described in paragraph (b)(8) of this section) for a stated period not to exceed the five most recent plan years (including the current year), and

(iii) Dividing this sum by the number of values (including the current fair market value) considered in computing the sum described in subdivision (ii).

*(8) Adjusted value.* (i) the adjusted value of plan assets for a prior valuation date is their fair market value on that date with certain positive and negative adjustments. These adjustments reflect changes that occur between the prior asset valuation date and the current valuation date. However, no adjustment is made for increases or decreases in the total value of plan assets that result from the purchase, sale, or exchange of plan assets or from the receipt of payment on a debt obligation held by the plan.

(ii) In determining the adjusted value of plan assets for a prior valuation date, there is added to the fair market value of the plan assets of that date the sum of all additions to the plan assets since that date, excluding appreciation in the fair market value of the assets. The additions would include, for example, any contribution to the plan; any interest or dividend paid to the plan; and any asset not taken into account in a prior valuation of assets, but taken into account for the current year, in computing the fair market value of plan assets under paragraph (c) of this section.

(iii) In determining the adjusted value of plan assets for a prior valuation date, there is subtracted from the fair market value of the plan assets on that date the sum of all reductions in plan assets since that date, excluding depreciation in the fair market value of the assets. The reductions would include, for example, any benefit paid from plan assets; any expense paid from plan assets; and any asset taken into account in a prior valuation of assets but not taken into account for the current year, in computing the fair market value of plan assets under paragraph (c) of this section.

*(9) Examples.* This paragraph (b) may be illustrated by the following examples. In each example, assume that the pension plan uses a consistent actuarial method of valuing its assets within the meaning of paragraph (b)(1), (2), and (3) of this section.

*Example (1).* Plan A considers the value of its assets to be initial cost, increased by an assumed rate of growth of X percent annually. Under the circumstances, the X-percent factor used by the plan is a reasonable assumption. Thus, this method is not designed to produce results consistently above or below fair market value as prohibited by paragraph (b)(5) of this section. Also, the method requires that the actuarial value be adjusted as required to fall within the corridor under paragraph (b)(6) and (7) of this section. Therefore, the method reflects fair market value as required by paragraph (b)(4) of this section.

*Example (2).* Plan B computes the actuarial value of its assets as follows: It determines the fair market value of the plan assets. Then the fair market value is adjusted to the extent necessary to make the actuarial value fall within a "5 percent" corridor. This corridor is plus or minus 5 percent of the following amount: the fair market value of the assets at the beginning of the valuation period plus an assumed annual growth of 4 percent with adjustments for contributions and benefit payments during the period. This method reflects fair market value in a manner prescribed by paragraph (b)(4) of this section. If the 4 percent factor used by the plan is a reasonable assumption, this method is not designed to produce results consistently above or below fair market value, and thus it satisfies paragraph (b)(5). However, this method is unacceptable because in some instances it may result in an actuarial value outside the corridor described in paragraph (b)(6) of this section. This method would be permitted if a second corridor were imposed which would adjust the value of the total plan assets to the corridor limits as required by paragraph (b)(6).

*Example (3).* Plan C values its assets by multiplying their fair market value by an index number. The use of the index results in the hypothetical average value that plan assets present on the valuation date would have had if they had been held during the current and four preceding years, and had appreciated or depreciated at the actual yield rates including appreciation and depreciation experienced by the plan during that period. However, the method requires an adjustment to the extent necessary to bring the resulting actuarial value of the assets inside the corridor described in the statement of the plan's actuarial valuation method. In this case, the stated corridor is 90 to 110 percent of fair market value, a corridor narrower than that described in paragraph (b)(7) of this section. This method is permitted.

*Example (4).* Plan D values its assets by multiplying their fair market value by 95 percent. Although the method reflects fair market value and the results of this method will always be within the required corridor, it is not acceptable because it will consistently result in a value less than fair market value.

*Example (5).* Plan E values its assets by using a five-year average method with appropriate adjustments for the period. Under the particular method used by Plan E, assets are not valued below 80 percent of fair market value or above 100 percent of fair market value. If the average produces a value that exceeds 100 percent of fair market value, the excess between 100 and 120 percent is recorded in a "value reserve account." In years after one in which the average exceeds 100 percent of fair market value, amounts are subtracted from this account and added, to the extent necessary, to raise the value produced by the average for that year to 100 percent of fair market value. This method is permitted because it reflects fair market value under paragraph (b)(4) of this section by appropriately computing an average value, it satisfies paragraph (b)(5) by producing a result that falls consistently between fair market value and average value, and it properly reflects the corridor described in paragraph (b)(7).

*Example (6).* All assets of Plan F are invested in a trust fund and the plan year is the calendar year. The actuarial value is determined by averaging fair market value over 4 years. An actuarial valuation is performed as of December 31, 1988.

(i) The average value as of December 31, 1988, is computed as follows:

| | 1986 | | 1987 | | 1988 | |
|---|---|---|---|---|---|---|
| Fair market value: Jan. 1 | | $150,000 | | $196,500 | | $238,000 |
| Contributions | $65,000 | | $62,000 | | $66,000 | |
| Benefit payments | (22,000) | | (24,000) | | (25,000) | |
| Expenses | (6,500) | | (7,000) | | (7,500) | |
| Interest and dividends | 8,000 | 44,500 | 7,500 | 38,500 | 7,000 | 40,500 |
| Net realized gains (losses) | | (2,000) | 6,000 | (8,000) | | |
| Balancing item[1] | | 4,000 | (3,000) | (42,000) | | |
| Fair market value: Dec. 31 | | 196,500 | 238,000 | 228,000 | | |

[1] This equals the increase (decrease) in unrealized appreciation

| Adjusted values | 1985 | 1986 | 1987 | 1988 |
|---|---|---|---|---|
| Fair market value: Dec. 31 | $150,000 | $196,500 | $238,000 | $228,000 |
| Net adjustments: | | | | |
| 1988 | 40,500 | 40,500 | 40,500 | |
| 1987 | 38,500 | 38,500 | | |
| 1986 | 44,500 | | | |
| Total | 273,500 | 275,500 | 278,500 | 228,000 |

Average value: 1988 = $273,500 + $275,500 + $278,500 + $228,000 ÷ 4 = $263,875

(ii) Plan F properly determines an average value under paragraph (b)(7) of this section for use as an actuarial value. Therefore, the valuation method meets the requirements of this section.

*Example (7).* Plan G computes the actuarial value of the plan assets as follows: The current fair market value of the plan assets is averaged with the most recent prior adjusted actuarial value. This average value is adjusted up or down toward the current fair market value by 20 percent of the difference between it and the current fair market value of the assets. This value is further adjusted to the extent necessary to fall within the corridor described in the statement of the plan's actuarial valuation method. The lower end of the corridor is the lesser of 80 percent of the fair market value of the plan assets or 85 percent of the average value of the plan assets. The higher end of the corridor is the greater of 120 percent of the fair market value of plan assets or 115 percent of the average value of plan assets. Average value for purposes of the corridor is determined under paragraph (b)(7) of this section. Assuming the numerical data of Example (6), the application of the corridor is as follows. The actuarial asset value as of December 31, 1988, must not be less than $182,400 (80 percent of current fair market value, $228,000) nor greater than $303,456 (115 percent of average value, 263,875). This method is permitted because it reflects fair market value in a manner permitted by paragraph (b)(4) of this section, it produces an actuarial value which is neither consistently above nor consistently below fair market or average value to satisfy paragraph (b)(5), and it is appropriately limited by the corridor described in paragraph (b)(6).

**(c) Fair market value of assets.** *(1) General rules.* Except as otherwise provided in this paragraph (c), the fair market value of a plan's assets for purposes of this section is the price at which the property would change hands between a willing buyer and a willing seller, neither being under any compulsion to buy or sell and both having reasonable knowledge of relevant facts.

*(2) [Reserved]*

**(d) Methods for taking into account the fair market value of certain agreements.[Reserved]**

**(e) Effective date and transition rules.** *(1) Effective date.* This section 412, or section 302 of the Employee Retirement Income Security Act of 1974, applies.

*(2) Special rule for certain plan years.* For plan years beginning prior to November 12, 1980, the amounts required to be determined under section 412 may be computed on the basis of any reasonable actuarial method of asset valuation which takes into account the fair market value of the plan's assets, even if the method does not meet all of the requirements of paragraphs (a) through (c) of this section.

*(3) Plan years beginning on or after November 12, 1980.* Paragraphs (a) through (c) of this section apply beginning with the first valuation of plan assets made for a plan year to which section 412 applies that begins on or after November 12, 1980. The statement of the plan's actuarial asset valuation method required by paragraph (b)(2) of this section must be included with the plan's actuarial report for that year, in addition to any subsequent reports.

*(4) Effect of change of asset valuation method.* A plan which is required to change its asset valuation method to comply with paragraphs (a) through (c) of this section must make the change no later than the time when the plan is first required to comply with this section under paragraph (e)(3). A method of adjustment must be used to take account of any difference in the actuarial value of the plan's assets based on the old and new valuation methods. The plan may use either—

(i) A method of adjustment described in paragraph (e)(5) or (e)(6) of this section without prior approval by the Commissioner, or

(ii) Any other method of adjustment if the Commissioner gives prior approval under section 412(c)(5).

*(5) Retroactive recomputation method.* (i) Under this method of adjustment, the plan recomputes the balance of the funding standard account as of the beginning of the first plan year for which it uses its new asset valuation method to comply with paragraphs (a) through (c) of this section. This new balance is recomputed by retroactively applying the plan's new method as of the first day of the first plan year to which section 412 applies.

(ii) Beginning with the first plan year for which it uses its new method, the plan computes the normal cost and amortization charges and credits to the funding standard account based on the retroactive application of its new method as of the first day of the first plan year to which section 412 applies.

(iii) If the recomputed aggregate charges exceed the recomputed aggregate credits to the funding standard account as of the end of the first plan year for which the plan uses its new method, an additional contribution to the plan may be necessary to avoid an accumulated funding deficiency in that year. The use of the retroactive recomputation method may also result in an accumulated funding deficiency for years prior to that first year. In such cases, the rules of section 412(c)(10), relating to the time when certain contributions are deemed to have been made, apply.

*(6) Prospective gain or loss adjustment method.* (i) Under this method of adjustment the plan values its assets under its new method no later than the valuation date for the first plan year beginning after (the publication date of this section).

(ii) Regardless of the type of funding method used by a plan, the difference in the value of the assets under the old and the new asset valuation methods may be treated as arising from an experience loss or gain; or alternatively it may be treated as arising from a change in actuarial assumptions.

(iii) The treatment of this difference as an experience gain or loss or as a change in actuarial assumptions must be consistent with the treatment of such gains, losses, or changes under the funding method used by the plan. Thus, if a plan uses a spread gain type funding method other than the aggregate cost method, the difference in the value of assets under the old and the new asset valuation methods may be either amortized or spread over future periods as a part of normal cost. Examples of this type of funding method are the frozen initial liability cost method and the attained age normal cost method. With an aggregate method, the difference in the value of assets under the old and the new asset valuation methods must be spread over future periods as a part of normal cost.

---

T.D. 7734, 11/10/80.

---

**Proposed § 1.412(c)(2)-2 Bond valuation election.** [*For Preamble, see ¶ 150,781*]

**(a) Scope of election.** *(1) In general.* The election described in section 412(c)(2)(B) with respect to bonds generally applies to all bond and evidence of indebtedness including those acquired by merger. The election applies only to defined benefit plans. A defined contribution plan must value bonds and other evidences of indebtedness on the basis of fair market value.

*(2) Exception.* The election does not apply to bonds or evidences of indebtedness at any time that they are in default as to principal or interest.

*(3) Convertible debt.* For purposes of this section, a debt instrument which is convertible into an equity security and acquired after [the date 90 days after the date on which § 1.412(c)(2)-2 is adopted as a Treasury Decision] is treated as an evidence of indebtedness until the conversion occurs.

**(b) Effect of election.** *(1) In general.* The effect of the election is that bonds and other evidences of indebtedness included among the plan assets are valued on an amortized basis rather than on a fair market value basis.

*(2) Amount amortized.* (i) In general. The amount amortized with respect to a bond or other evidence of indebtedness is generally the difference between its initial costs when acquired by the plan and its redemption value at the end of the amortization period. In the case of a bond or other evidence of indebtedness that was acquired by the plan in a plan year before the plan year for which the election was made, the amortized value for each year must be determined as though the election had always been in effect with respect to the bond or other evidence of indebtedness.

(ii) Spinoffs. The amount amortized after a spinoff is based on the initial cost to the plan which acquired the bond or other evidence of indebtedness and not the value to the plan after the spinoff.

(iii) Mergers. The amount amortized after a merger is based on the cost to the plan which first elected to value the bonds and other evidences of indebtedness on an amortized basis. In the case of a bond or other evidence of indebtedness that was acquired by any merging plan before the election was first made with respect to the bond or other evidence of indebtedness, the premium or discount shall be amortized as provided in paragraph (b)(2)(i).

*(3) Amortization period.* The amortization period is the time from the date on which the plan acquires the bond or other evidence of indebtedness of its maturity date (or, in the case of a debt instrument that is callable prior to maturity, the earliest call date).

**(c) Effect of default.** Once the election is made, it applies to each debt instrument held or acquired that is not in default as to principal or interest. While in default, the instrument is subject to the fair market value requirements of section 412(c)(2)(A).

**(d) Manner of making election.** The plan administrator makes the election by preparing a statement that the election described in section 412(c)(2)(B) is being made and by filing the statement attached to the annual return required under section 6058 for the first plan year for which the election is to apply.

**(e) Revocation of election.** *(1) Effect.* Once consent to the revocation of the election is obtained as prescribed in paragraph (e)(2) of this section, all plan assets are valued under section 412(c)(2)(A).

*(2) Consent.* Consent for the revocation of the election must be obtained in the manner prescribed by the Commissioner for obtaining permission to change funding methods under section 412(c)(5) and § 1.412(c)(5)-1.

*(3) Mergers.* A plan which has acquired a bond or other evidence of indebtedness by merger must obtain the consent of the Commissioner to value bonds and other evidences of indebtedness on a basis other than amortized value if an election under section 412(c)(2)(B) with respect to the asset acquired had been made prior to the merger.

### § 1.412(c)(3)-1 Reasonable funding methods.

> ***Caution:*** The Treasury has not yet amended Reg § 1.412(c)(3)-1 to reflect changes made by P.L. 109-432, P.L. 105-34, P.L. 103-465, P.L. 100-203.

**(a) Introduction.** *(1) In general.* This section prescribes rules for determining whether or not, in the case of an ongoing plan, a funding method is reasonable for purposes of section 412(c)(3). A method is unreasonable only if it is found to be inconsistent with a rule prescribed in this section. The term "reasonable funding method" under this section has the same meaning as the term "acceptable actuarial cost method" under section 3(31) of the Employee Retirement Income Security Act of 1974 (ERISA).

*(2) Computations included in method.* See § 1.412(c)(1)-1(b) for a discussion of matters that are, and are not, included in the funding method of a plan.

*(3) Plans using shortfall.* The shortfall method is a method of determining charges to the funding standard account by adapting the underlying funding method of certain collectively bargained plans in the manner described in § 1.412(c)(1)-2. As such, the shortfall method is a funding method. The underlying method of a plan that uses the shortfall method must be a reasonable funding method under this section. The rules contained in this section, relating to cost under a reasonable funding method, apply in the shortfall method to the annual computation charge under § 1.412(c)(1)-2(d).

*(4) Scope of funding method.* Except for the shortfall method, a reasonable funding method is applied to the computation of—

(i) The normal cost of a plan for a plan year; and, if applicable,

(ii) The bases established under section 412(b)(2)(B), (C), and (D), and (3) (B) ("amortizable bases").

**(b) General rules for reasonable funding methods.** *(1) Basic funding formula.* At any time, except as provided by the Commissioner, the present value of future benefits under a reasonable funding method must equal the sum of the following amounts:

(i) The present value of normal costs (taking into account future mandatory employee contributions, within the meaning of section 411(c)(2)(C), in the case of a contributory plan) over the future working lifetime of participants;

(ii) The sum of the unamortized portions of amortizable bases, if any, treating credit bases under section 412(b)(3)(B) as negative numbers; and

(iii) The plan assets, decreased by a credit balance (and increased by a debit balance) in the funding standard account under section 412(b).

*(2) Normal cost.* Normal cost under a reasonable funding method must be expressed as—

(i) A level dollar amount, or a level percentage of pay, that is computed from year to year on either an individual basis or an aggregate basis; or

(ii) An amount equal to the present value of benefits accruing under the method for a particular plan year.

*(3) Application to shortfall.* Paragraph (b)(2) will not fail to be satisfied merely because an amount described in (i) or (ii) is expressed as permitted under the shortfall method.

**(c) Additional requirements.** *(1) Inclusion of all liabilities.* Under a reasonable funding method, all liabilities of the plan for benefits, whether vested or not, must be taken into account.

*(2) Production of experience gains and losses.* If each actuarial assumption is exactly realized under a reasonable funding method, no experience gains or losses are produced.

*(3) Plan population.* (i) In general. Under a reasonable funding method, the plan population must include three classes of individuals: participants currently employed in the service of the employer; former participants who either terminated service with the employer, or retired, under the plan; and all other individuals currently entitled to benefits under

the plan. See § 1.412(c)(3)-1(d)(2) for rules concerning anticipated future participants.

(ii) Limited exclusion for certain recent participants. Under a reasonable funding method, certain individuals may be excluded from the first class of individuals described in paragraph (c)(3)(i) of this section unless otherwise provided by the Commissioner. The excludable individuals are participants who would be excluded from participation by the minimum age or service requirement of section 410 but who, under the terms of the plan, participate immediately upon entering the service of the employer.

(iii) Special exclusion for "rule of parity" cases. Under a reasonable funding method, certain individuals may be excluded from the second class of individuals described in paragraph (c)(3)(i) of this section. The excludable individuals are those former participants who have terminated service with the employer without vested benefits and whose service might be taken into account in future years because the "rule of parity" of section 411(a)(6)(D) does not permit that service to be disregarded. However if the plan's experience as to separated employees' returning to service has been such that the exclusion described in this subparagraph would be unreasonable, the exclusion would no longer apply.

*(4) Use of salary scale.* (i) General acceptability. The use of a salary scale assumption is not inappropriate merely because of the funding method with which it is used. Therefore, in determining whether actuarial assumptions are reasonable, a salary scale will not be considered to be prohibited merely because a particular funding method is being used.

(ii) Projection to appropriate salary. Under a reasonable funding method, salary scales reflected in projected benefits must be the expected salary on which benefits would be based under the plan at the age when the receipt of benefits is expected to begin.

*(5) Treatment of allocable items.* Under a reasonable funding method that allocates assets to individual participants to determine costs, the allocation of assets among participants must be reasonable. An initial allocation of assets among participants will be considered reasonable only if it is in proportion to related liabilities. However, the Commissioner may determine, based on the facts and circumstances, that it is unreasonable to continue to allocate assets on this basis beyond the initial year. Under a reasonable funding method that allocates liabilities among different elements of past and future service, the allocation of liabilities must be reasonable.

**(d) Prohibited considerations under a reasonable funding method.** *(1) Anticipated benefit changes.* (i) In general. Except as otherwise provided by the Commissioner, a reasonable funding method does not anticipate changes in plan benefits that become effective, whether or not retroactively, in a future plan year or that become effective after the first day of, but during, a current plan year.

(ii) Exception for collectively bargained plans. A collectively bargained plan described in section 413(a) may on a consistent basis anticipate benefit increases scheduled to take effect during the term of the collective-bargaining agreement applicable to the plan. A plan's treatment of benefit increases scheduled in a collective bargaining agreement is part of its funding method. Accordingly, a change in a plan's treatment of such benefit increases (for example, ignoring anticipated increases after taking them into account) is a change of funding method.

*(2) Anticipated future participants.* A reasonable funding method must not anticipate the affiliation with the plan of future participants not employed in the service of the employer on the plan valuation date. However, a reasonable funding method may anticipate the affiliation with the plan of current employees who have not satisfied the participation requirements of the plan.

**(e) Special rules for certain funding methods.** *(1) Applicability of special rules.* Paragraph (e) of this section applies to a funding method that determines normal cost under paragraph (b)(2)(ii) of this section.

*(2) Use of salary scale.* For rules relating to use of a salary scale assumption, see paragraph (c)(4) of this section.

*(3) Allocation of liabilities.* In determining a plan's normal cost and accrued liability for a particular plan year, the projected benefits of the plan must be allocated between past years and future years. Except in the case of a career average pay plan, this allocation must be in proportion to the applicable rates of benefit accrual under the plan. Thus, the allocation to past years is effected by multiplying the projected benefit by a fraction. The numerator of the fraction is the participant's credited years of service. The denominator is the participant's total credited years of service at the anticipated benefit commencement date. Adjustments are made to account for changes in the rate of benefit accrual. An allocation based on compensation is not permitted. In the case of a career average pay plan, an allocation between past and future service benefits must be reasonable.

**(f) Treatment of ancillary benefit costs.** *(1) General rule.* Under a reasonable funding method, except as otherwise provided by this paragraph (f), ancillary benefit costs must be computed by using the same method used to compute retirement benefit costs under a plan.

*(2) Ancillary benefit defined.* For purposes of this paragraph an ancillary benefit is a benefit that is paid as a result of a specified event which—

(i) Occurs not later than a participant's separation from service, and

(ii) Was detrimental to the participant's health.

Thus, for example, benefits payable if a participant dies or becomes disabled prior to separation from service are ancillary benefits because the events giving rise to the benefits are detrimental to the participant's health. However, an early retirement benefit, a social security supplement (as defined in § 1.411(a)-7(c)(4)(ii)), and the vesting of plan benefits (even if more rapid than is required by section 411) are not ancillary benefits because those benefits do not result from an event which is detrimental to the participant's health.

*(3) Exception for certain insurance contracts.* Under a reasonable funding method, regardless of the method used to compute retirement benefit costs, the cost of an ancillary benefit may equal the premium paid for that benefit under an insurance contract if—

(i) The ancillary benefit is provided under the contract, and

(ii) The benefit is guaranteed under the contract.

*(4) Exception for 1-year term funding and other approved methods.[Reserved]*

*(5) Section 401(h) benefits.* Section 412 does not apply to benefits that are described in section 401(h) and for which a separate account is maintained.

**(g) Examples.** The principles of this section are illustrated by the following examples:

*Example (1).* Assume that a plan, using funding method A, is in its first year. No contributions have been made to the plan, other than a nominal contribution to establish a corpus for the plan's trust. There is no past service liability, and the normal cost is a constant percentage of an annually determined amount. The constant percentage is 99 percent, and the annually determined amount is the excess of the present value of future benefits over plan assets. The present value of future benefits is $10,000. Under paragraph (b)(1) of this section, the present value of future benefits must equal the present value of future normal costs plus plan assets. (No amortizable bases exist, nor are there credit or debit balances.) Under method A, the present value of future normal costs would equal the sum of a series of annually decreasing amounts. Because of the constant percentage factor, the present value of future normal costs over the years can never equal $10,000, the present value of future benefits. In effect, then, assets under method A can never equal the present value of future benefits if all assumptions are exactly realized. Therefore, method A is not a reasonable funding method.

*Example (2).* Assume that a plan, using funding method B, determines normal cost by computing the present value of benefits expected to be accrued under the plan by the end of 10 years after the valuation date and adding to this the present value of benefits expected to be paid within these 10 years. Plan assets are subtracted from the sum of the two present value amounts. The difference then is divided by the present value of salaries projected over the 10 years. Under paragraph (c)(1) of this section, all liabilities of a plan must be taken into account. Because method B takes into account only benefits paid or accrued by the end of 10 years, it is not a reasonable funding method.

*Example (3).* Assume that a plan, using funding method C, determines normal cost as a constant percentage of compensation. (This percentage is determined as follows: The excess of projected benefits over accrued benefits is computed. Then the present value of this excess is divided by the present value of future salaries.) However, the accrued liability is computed each year as the present value of accrued benefits. (This computation does not reflect normal cost as a constant percentage of compensation. Thus, normal cost under the plan does not link accrued liabilities under the plan for consecutive years as would be the case, for example, under a unit credit cost method.) In determining gains and losses, method C compares the actual unfunded liability (the accrued liability less assets) with the expected unfunded liability (the sum of the actual unfunded liability in the previous year and the normal cost for the previous year less the contribution made for the previous year, all adjusted for interest). Under paragraph (c)(2) of this section, if actuarial assumptions are exactly realized, experience gains and losses must not be produced. Under method C, the use of a constant percentage in computing normal cost (and the expected unfunded liability) coupled with the manner of computing the accrued liability (and the actual unfunded liability) generally produces gains in the earlier years and losses in the later years if each actuarial assumption is exactly realized. Therefore, method C is not a reasonable funding method.

*Example (4).* Assume that a plan, using funding method D, bases benefits on final average pay. Under method D, the past service liability on any date equals the present value of the accrued benefit on that date based on compensation as of that date. The normal cost for any year equals the present value of a certain amount. That amount is the excess of the projected accrued benefit as of the end of the year over the actual accrued benefit at the beginning of the year. Accrued benefits, projected as of the end of a year, reflect a 1-year salary projection. Under paragraph (c)(4) of this section, salary scales reflected in projected benefits must project salaries to the salary on which benefits would be based under the plan at the age when the receipt of benefits under the plan is expected to begin. Because the plan is not a career average pay plan and compensation is projected only 1 year, method D is not a reasonable funding method. (Under paragraph (c)(4) of this section, the use of a salary scale assumption could be required with a unit credit method if, without the use of a salary scale, assumptions in the aggregate are unreasonable.)

*Example (5).* Assume that a plan, using method E, a unit credit funding method, calculates a participant's accrued benefit according to the following formula: 2 percent of final salary for the first 10 years of service and 1 percent of final salary for the years of service in excess of 10. Under the plan, no employee may be credited with more than 25 years of service. The actuarial assumptions for the valuation include a salary scale of 5 percent per year. For a participant at age 40 with 15 years of service, a current salary of $20,000 and a normal retirement age of 65, the accrued liability for the retirement benefit is the present value of an annuity of $16,932 per year, commencing at age 65. The $16,932 is calculated as follows:

$$\$20,000 \times 3.3864 \times 35\% \times \frac{(10 \times 2) + (5 \times 1)}{(10 \times 2) - (15 \times 1) - (15 \times 0)}$$

(3.3864 is 1.05 raised to the 25th power; the 25th power reflects the difference between normal retirement age and attained age (65 – 40).)

Salary under this method is projected to the age when the receipt of benefits is expected to begin. Therefore, method E meets the requirement of paragraph (c)(4) of this section. Also, the allocation of benefits under method E between past and future years of service meets the requirements of paragraph (e)(3) of this section.

*Example (6).* Assume that a plan that has two participants and that previously used the unit credit cost method wishes to change the funding method at the beginning of the plan year to funding method F, a modification of the aggregate cost method. The modification involves determining normal cost for each of the two participants under the plan. Therefore, it requires an allocation of assets to each participant for valuation purposes. The actuary proposes to allocate the assets on hand at the beginning of the plan year of the change in funding method in proportion to the accrued liabilities calculated under the unit credit cost method. The relevant results of the calculations are shown below:

| | Employees | | |
|---|---|---|---|
| | M | N | Totals |
| Accrued Liabilities (unit credit method): | | | |
| Dollar amount . . . . . . . . . . . . . . | 15,670 | 906 | 16,576 |
| Per cent of total . . . . . . . . . . . . . | 94.53 | 5.47 | 100.00 |
| Assets: | | | |
| Dollar amount . . . . . . . . . . . . . . | 7,835 | 453 | 8,288 |
| per cent of total . . . . . . . . . . . . . | 94.53 | 5.47 | 100.00 |

The proposed allocation in proportion to the accrued liabilities under the unit credit cost method satisfies the requirements of paragraph (c)(5) of this section at the beginning of the first plan year for which the new method is used.

*Example (7).* The facts are the same as in Example (6). However, the actuary proposes to allocate all the assets to employee M, the older employee. Method F, under these facts, is not an acceptable funding method because the allocation is not in proportion to related liabilities as required under paragraph (c)(5) of this section.

T.D. 7746, 12/29/80.

### § 1.412(c)(3)-2 Effective dates and transitional rules relating to reasonable funding methods.

***Caution:*** The Treasury has not yet amended Reg § 1.412(c)(3)-2 to reflect changes made by P.L. 109-432, P.L. 100-203.

**(a) Introduction.** This section prescribes effective dates for rules relating to reasonable funding methods, under section 412(c)(3) and § 1.412(c)(3)-1. Also, this section sets forth rules concerning adjustments to a plan's funding standard account that are necessitated by a change in funding method, and a provision setting forth procedural requirements for use of an optional phase-in of required changes.

**(b) Effective date.** *(1) General rule.* Except as otherwise provided by subparagraph (2) of this paragraph, § 1.412(c)(3)-1 applies to any valuation of a plan's liabilities (within the meaning of section 412(c)(9)) as of a date after April 30, 1981.

*(2) Exception.* If a collective bargaining agreement which determines contributions to a plan is in effect on April 30, 1981, then § 1.412(c)(3)-1 applies to any valuation of that plan's liabilities as of a date after the earlier of the date on which the last such collective bargaining agreement expires or April 30, 1984.

*(3) Transitional rule.* The reasonableness of a funding method used in making a valuation of a plan's liability as of a date before the effective date determined under subparagraph (1) or (2) of this paragraph is determined on the basis of such published guidance as was available on the date as of which the valuation was made.

**(c) Change of funding method without approval.** *(1) In general.* A plan that is required to change its funding method to comply with § 1.412(c)(3)-1 is not required to submit the change of funding method for approval as otherwise required by section 412(c)(5). However, this change must be described on Form 5500, Schedule B for the plan year with respect to which the change is first effective.

*(2) Amortization base.* An amortization base must be established in the plan year of the change in method equal to the change in the unfunded liability due to the change (where both unfunded liabilities are based on the same actuarial assumptions). Such a base must be amortized over 30 years in determining the charges or credits to the funding standard account, unless the Commissioner upon application permits amortization over a shorter period.

**(d) Phase-in of additional funding required by new method.** *(1) In general.* A plan that is required to change its funding method to comply with § 1.412(c)(3)-1 may elect to charge and credit the funding standard account as provided in this paragraph. An election under this paragraph shall be irrevocable.

*(2) Credit in year of change.* In the plan year of the change in method the funding standard account may be credited with an amount not in excess of 0.8 multiplied by the excess (if any) of—

(i) The normal cost under the new method plus the amortization charge (or minus the amortization credit) computed as described in § 1.412(c)(3)-2(c)(2), over

(ii) The normal cost under the prior method, for the plan year of the change in method.

*(3) Credits in the next three years.* In the three years following the year of the change the funding standard account may be credited with an amount not in excess of 0.6, 0.4, and 0.2 respectively in the first, second, and third years, multiplied by either of the following amounts, computed as of the last day of the year of credit—

(i) The excess described in § 1.412(c)(3)-2(d)(2) multiplied by a fraction (not greater than 1), the numerator of which is the number of participants in the year of the credit and the denominator of which is the number of participants in the year of the change, or, at the option of the plan,

(ii) The excess (if any) in the year of credit of—

(A) The net charge to the funding standard account based on the new method, over

(B) The net charge to the funding standing account based on the prior method.

*(4) Computational rules.* For purposes of the calculation described in § 1.412(c)(3)-2(d)(3)(ii), the net charge is the excess of charges under section 412(b)(2)(A) and (B) over the credits under section 412(b)(3)(B) (including the charge or credit described in § 1.412(c)(3)-2(c)) which would be required using the actuarial assumptions and plan benefit structure in effect on the last day of the plan year of change.

*(5) Fifteen-year amortization of credits.* The funding standard account shall be charged with 15-year amortization of each credit described in § 1.412(c)(3)-2(d)(2) and (3) beginning in the year following each such credit.

*(6) Manner of election.* An election under this paragraph shall be made by the claiming of the credits described in § 1.412(c)(3)-2(d)(2) and (3) on Schedule B to Form 5500 and by filing such other information as may be required by the Commissioner.

**(e) Effect on shortfall method.** The charges and credits described in this section apply in the shortfall method to the annual computation charge described in § 1.412(c)(1)-2(d). The amounts described in § 1.412(c)(3)-2(d) shall be determined before the application of the shortfall method.

T.D. 7746, 12/29/80.

### Proposed § 1.412(c)(4)-1 Certain changes in accrued liability. [*For Preamble, see ¶ 150,781*]

***Caution:*** The Treasury has not yet amended Reg § 1.412(c)(4)-1 to reflect changes made by P.L. 105-34.

**(a) In general.** In the case of immediate gain type funding methods, section 412(c)(4) treats certain increases and decreases in the accrued liability under a plan as an experience gain or loss. Plans using a spread gain type of funding method will reflect the gain or loss in determining the normal cost under the plan. Under section 412(b)(2) and (3), plans which are valued using a funding method of the immediate gain type will amortize the amount treated as an experience gain or loss in equal amounts over the period described in section 412(b). See § 1.412(b)-1(b)(9) and (10) for examples of spread gain type and immediate gain type funding methods.

**(b) Applicable changes.** A change treated as an experience gain or loss under section 412(c)(4) includes an increase or decrease in accrued liability caused by:

*(1)* A change in benefits under the Social Security Act,

*(2)* A change in other retirement benefits created under Federal or State law,

*(3)* A change in the definition of "wages" under section 3121, or

*(4)* A change in the amount of wages under section 3121 that are taken into account for purposes of section 401(a)(5) and the regulations thereunder.

**Proposed § 1.412(c)(5)-1 Change in plan year or funding method.** [*For Preamble, see ¶ 150,781*]

Approval given under section 412(c)(5) authorizes a change in plan year or funding method. Written requests for approval are to be submitted, as directed by the Commissioner, to Commissioner of Internal Revenue, Attention: OP:E:A:P, 1111 Constitution Avenue, N.W., Washington, D.C. 20224. Such a request must be submitted before the close of the plan year for which the change is to be effective unless an extension of time for filing the request is granted.

**Proposed § 1.412(c)(6)-1 Full funding and full funding limitation.** [*For Preamble, see ¶ 150,781*]

***Caution:*** The Treasury has not yet amended Reg § 1.412(c)(6)-1 to reflect changes made by P.L. 103-465, P.L. 100-203.

**(a) In general.** This section provides rules relating to full funding and the full funding limitation under section 412(c)(6) and (7). The full funding limitation for a plan year is the excess, if any, of the accrued liability under the plan plus the normal cost for the plan year over the value of the plan's assets.

**(b) Valuation.** *(1) Timing rule.* For purposes of this section, assets and accrued liabilities are to be valued at the usual time used by the plan for valuations.

*(2) Interest adjustments.* If the valuation is performed before the end of the plan year, the assets and accrued liabilities (including normal cost) are projected to the end of the plan year. The projection is based on the valuation rate.

**(c) Calculation of accrued liability.** The accrued liability of a plan is determined under the funding method used by the plan. However, if the funding method used by the plan is not an immediate gain method and, thus, does not directly calculate an accrued liability, the calculation of the accrued liability is made under the entry age normal funding method.

**(d) Calculation of normal cost.** In general, the normal cost is the normal cost determined under the funding method used by the plan. However, if under paragraph (c) accrued liability is calculated under the entry age normal cost method, then the normal cost is also calculated under the entry age normal cost method.

**(e) Calculation of assets.** The value of plan assets used to determine the full funding limitation is the lesser of the fair market value of the assets or the actuarial value of the assets, if different. The value of plan assets must be reduced by any credit balance existing on the first day of the plan year.

**(f) Effect of full funding on deduction limits.** See § 1.404(a)-14(k) for provisions relating to the effect of the full funding limitation on the maximum deductible contribution limitations and 10-year amortization bases under section 404(a).

**(g) Effect of the full funding limitation on the funding standard account.** *(1) General rule.* If, as of the end of any plan year, the accumulated funding deficiency (calculated without regard to any credit balance for the plan year or any contributions made for that plan year) exceeds the full funding limitation of section 412(c)(7) calculated as of the valuation date and projected, if necessary, to the end of the plan year, then the following adjustments are made:

(i) The amount of such excess is credited to the funding standard account for that plan year.

(ii) As of the end of that plan year, all the amounts described in paragraphs (2)(B), (C), (D), and (3)(B) of section 412(b) which are required to be amortized shall be considered to be amortized shall be considered fully amortized.

*(2) Example.* The principles of section 412(c)(6) and of paragraph (e) of this section are illustrated in the following example:

*Example.* Assume that a single employer plan is established on January 1, 1976, with a calendar plan year. The funding method is the accrued benefit cost method (unit credit method), the interest assumption is 5 percent, and both the normal cost and the amortization charges and credits are calculated on the basis of payment at the beginning of the year. The annual charge to the funding standard account due to the amortization (over 30 years) of the initial past service liability is $200, and the annual credit due to the amortization (over 15 years) of a 1979 experience gain is $10. A valuation is performed as of January 1, 1985, to determine costs for the 1985 plan year. There was a credit balance of $100 in the funding standard account on December 31, 1984. As of January 1, 1985, plan assets (determined in accordance with section 412(c)(7)(B) and reduced by the $100 credit balance as of January 1, 1985) were $10,400; the accrued liability under the plan was $10,000; the normal cost (for the 1985 plan year) was $1,200; and the 1985 employer contribution (made as of January 1, 1985) was $1,000. The accumulated funding deficiency (calculated ignoring the credit balance and employer contribution) as of December 31, 1985, is $1,459.50, determined as the excess of charges of $1,470 ($1,200 normal cost, plus $200 amortization charge, plus $70 interest) over the credits of $10.50 ($10 amortization credit, plus $.50 interest). The full funding limitation as of the valuation date (January 1, 1985) is $800, determined as the excess of the sum of the accrued liability ($10,000) plus normal cost ($1,200) over the adjusted plan assets ($10,400). The value of this $800 as of the end of the year (i.e., December 31, 1985) is $800 plus $40 interest, or $840.00. The excess, as of the end of the 1985 plan year, of the accumulated funding deficiency over the full funding limitation is thus $1,459.50 minus $840.00, or $619.50. The funding standard account is charged and credited as follows:

| | | |
|---|---|---|
| Charges: | | |
| Normal cost | $1,200.00 | |
| Amortization charge | 200.00 | |
| interest | 70.00 | |
| Total | | $1,470.00 |
| Credits: | | |
| Credit balance | 100.00 | |
| Contribution | 1,000.00 | |
| Amortization credit | 10.00 | |
| interest | 55.50 | |
| Sec. 412(c)(6) credit | 619.50 | |
| Total | | 1,785.00 |
| Credit balance December 31, 1985 | | 315.00 |

**Proposed § 1.412(c)(7)-1 Full funding limitation.** [*For Preamble, see ¶ 150,781*]

See § 1.412(c)(6)-1 for rules relating both to full funding under section 412(c)(6) and to the full funding limitation under section 412(c)(7).

**Proposed § 1.412(c)(8)-1 Election to treat certain retroactive plan amendments as made on first day of a plan year.** [*For Preamble, see ¶ 150,781*]

The function of the Secretary of Labor described in section 412(c)(8) was transferred to the Secretary of Treasury as of December 31, 1978, by Reorganization Plan No. 4 of 1978, 1979-1 C.B. 480. Therefore, the material described in section 412(c)(8) now must be filed as directed by the Secretary of the Treasury.

**Proposed § 1.412(c)(9)-1 Frequency of actuarial valuations.** [*For Preamble, see ¶ 150,781*]

***Caution:*** The Treasury has not yet amended Reg § 1.412(c)(9)-1 to reflect changes made by P.L. 107-147.

**(a) Required valuation.** Section 412(c)(9) requires an actuarial valuation not less frequently than once every three years. Paragraph (b) of this section provides general rules for performing valuations. Paragraph (d) describes certain situations in which the Commissioner may require an actuarial valuation more frequently than once every three years. These rules may be waived at the discretion of the Commissioner and do not apply to multiemployer plans within the meaning of section 414(f).

**(b) General rules for valuations.** *(1) Date of valuation.* Except as provided by the Commissioner, the valuation must be as of a date within the plan year to which the valuation refers or within the one month prior to that year. All assets and liabilities must be valued as of the same date. The valuation must use data as of the valuation date; it is not permissible to use adjusted date from a prior or subsequent year.

*(2) Use of prior valuations.* A plan may not use a valuation for any subsequent plan year if that valuation was not also used for the year to which it refers. Also, a prior valuation may not be used if the plan has used any subsequent valuation for another plan year.

**(c) Funding standard account rules for years when there is no valuation.** *(1) Amortization of bases.* After an amortization base is established, the amortization amount of that base is charged or credited in each plan year, whether or not a valuation is performed for the year, until the outstanding balance of the base is zero. However, see § 1.412(c)(6)-1 for rules for years after a full funding limitation credit and § 1.412(b)-1 for combining and offsetting bases.

*(2) Normal cost.* If valuations are performed less frequently than every year, then any valuation computes the normal cost for the year to which the valuation refers and for subsequent years until another valuation applies. In those subsequent years, the normal cost is—

(i) If the funding method computes normal cost as a level dollar amount, the same dollar amount as for the year to which the valuation refers;

(ii) If the funding method computes normal cost as a level percentage of pay, the same percentage of current pay as for the year to which the valuation refers, or

(iii) If the funding method computes normal cost as an amount equal to the present value of benefits accruing under the method for the year, under any reasonable method.

The rules in subdivisions (i) and (ii) apply whether the funding method computes normal cost on either an individual or an aggregate basis.

**(d) Situations when more frequent valuations are required.** *(1) Amendments increasing actuarial costs.* (i) General rule. A valuation is required for any plan year when a plan amendment first increases the actuarial costs of a plan. For this purpose, actuarial costs consist of the plan's normal cost under section 412(b)(2)(A), amortization charges under section 412(b)(2)(B), and amortization credits under section 412(b)(3)(B).

(ii) Exception. No valuation will be required under paragraph (d)(1)(i) of this section if two conditions are met: first, the plan actuary estimates that the cost increase attributable to the amendment is less than 5 percent of the actuarial cost determined without regard to the amendment; and second, the actuary files a signed statement to that effect with the annual return required under section 6058 for the year of the amendment.

*(2) Certain changes in number of participants.* (i) General rule. A valuation is required for a plan year when the actual number of plan participants that would be considered in the current valuation differs from the number of participants that were considered in the prior valuation by more than 20 percent of that number.

(ii) Exception. Notwithstanding subdivision (i), no valuation will be required merely because of a change in the number of estimated participants under a plan that determines normal cost as a level percentage of payroll (on either an individual or aggregate basis) or as a level dollar amount per individual.

(iii) Plans using shortfall method. No valuation will be required merely because of a change in the number of estimated participants under a plan which uses the shortfall method described in § 1.412(c)(1)-2. However, a valuation is required for a plan year if the estimated units of service or production ("estimated base units" under § 1.412(c)(1)-2(e)) for the prior plan year exceeds the actual number of units of service or production for that plan year by more than 20 percent.

*(3) Change in actuarial funding method or assumptions.* A valuation is required for any plan year with respect to which a change in the funding method or actuarial assumptions of a plan is made.

*(4) Mergers and spinoffs.* (i) General rule. A valuation is required for any plan year in which a plan merger or spinoff occurs.

(ii) Safe harbor for mergers. In the case of a merger, no valuation will be required under paragraph (d)(4) of this section if the de minimis rule in § 1.414(l)-1(h) is satisfied.

(iii) Safe harbor for spinoffs. In the case of a spinoff, no valuation will be required under paragraph (d)(4) of this section if the present value of all the benefits being spun off from the plan during the plan year is less than 3 percent of the plan's assets as of the beginning of the year.

*(5) Change in average age of participants.* (i) General rule. A valuation is required for any plan year with respect to which the average age of plan participants changes significantly, within the meaning of subdivisions (ii) and (iii), from the average age of plan participants at the last valuation.

(ii) Rule for large plans. For a plan with 100 or more participants, an increase or decrease in average age of more than two years is a significant change.

(iii) Rule for small plans. For a plan with fewer than 100 participants, an increase or decrease in average age of more than four years is a significant change.

*(6) Alternative minimum funding standard account.* A valuation is required for each year for which the plan uses the alternative minimum funding standard account.

*(7) Deductibility considerations.* A valuation is required when it appears that the full funding limitation has been reached for purposes of determining the maximum deductible contribution limitations of section 404(a).

*(8) Other situations.* The Commissioner may require valuations in other situations as the facts and circumstances warrant.

**Proposed § 1.412(c)(10)-1 Time for making contributions to satisfy section 412.** [*For Preamble, see ¶ 150,781*]

***Caution:*** The Treasury has not yet amended Reg § 1.412(c)(10)-1 to reflect changes made by P.L. 100-203.

**(a) General rule.** Under section 412(c)(10), a contribution made after the end of a plan year but no later than two and one-half months after the end of that year is deemed to have been made on the last day of that year.

**(b) Extension of general rule.** *(1) Plan years ending before [90 days after publication date of final regulations].* For plan years ending before [90 days after publication of final regulations], for purposes of section 412 a contribution for such a plan year that is made not later than eight and one-half months after the end of that plan year is deemed to have been made on the last day of that year.

*(2) Plan years ending on or after [90 days after publication of final regulations].* (i) Transitional rule. The two and one-half month period provided in section 412(c)(10) and § 1.410(c)(10)-1(a) is extended for each of the first three plan years ending after [90 days after publication of final regulations]. For the first plan year ending after [90 days after publication of final regulations], a contribution made not later than eight and one-half months after the end of that plan year is deemed to have been made on the last day of that year. For the second year, the two and one-half month period is extended to six and one-half months, and for the third year, the two and one-half month period is extended to four and one-half months.

(ii) Extensions of general and transitional periods. The time for making contributions under the general rule described in paragraph (a) and transitional rule of paragraph (b)(2)(i) of this section may be extended to a date not beyond eight and one-half months after the end of the plan year. Extensions of the two and one-half month period and transitional years' periods are granted on an individual basis by the Commissioner. A request for extension should be submitted to the Commissioner of Internal Revenue, 1111 Constitution Avenue, NW., Washington, D.C. 20224 (Attention OP:E:A).

**(c) Effect on section 404.** The rules of this section, relating to the timing of contributions for purposes of section 412, operate independently from the rules under section 404(a)(6), relating to the timing of contributions for purposes of claiming a deduction under section 404.

**Proposed § 1.412(g)-1 Alternative maximum funding standard account.** [*For Preamble, see ¶ 150,781*]

**(a) In general.** A plan that maintains an alternative minimum funding standard account ("ASA") for any plan year under section 412(g) must satisfy the requirements of this section. To use the ASA, a plan must use a funding method that requires contributions for all years that are not less than those required under the entry age normal cost method of funding. A funding method does not affect the actual cost of plan benefits but only the incidence of contributions in different years. Thus, any funding method that requires a contribution in one year that exceeds that required by the entry age normal method (EAN) for that year must require a lesser contribution in another year. Hence, only a plan which uses the EAN cost method may use the ASA.

**(b) Special rules.** *(1) Dual accounting.* While maintaining an ASA, a plan must maintain the funding standard account under section 412(b) for each plan year.

*(2) Change of method.* For any plan year, the choice of whether to use the ASA is independent of whether the ASA or funding standard account was used in the prior year. Any change from the choice made in the prior year does not require approval of the Commissioner. Further, a plan which has filed for a plan year the actuarial report described in section 6059(b) using the ASA to determine its minimum funding requirement may change to use the funding standard account to determine the funding requirement for that year. However, a plan may not switch to the ASA for a plan year after having filed the actuarial report for that year using the funding standard account.

*(3) PBGC valuation.* In determining charges and credits to the ASA under paragraphs (b) and (c) of this section (other than the amount in paragraph (c)(2)(i)), a plan must value its assets and liabilities on a termination basis as provided in regulations issued by the Pension Benefit Guaranty Corporation (PBGC) under sections 4041 and 4062 of the Employee Retirement Income Security Act of 1974 ("ERISA") for plans placed in trusteeship by PBGC.

*(4) Cumulative nature of account.* When the ASA is used for a plan year after a plan year for which the ASA was not used, the credit balance and charge balance as of the first day of the year equal zero. However, during any continuous period of years for which the ASA is used, the credit or charge balance as of the end of any ASA year are carried forward as beginning balances in the next ASA year.

**(c) Charges.** *(1) In general.* The ASA is charged with the amounts described in paragraph (c) of this section.

*(2) Normal cost.* The ASA is charged with the normal cost of the plan for a plan year. This amount is the normal cost for that plan year computed—

(i) Under the method of funding and actuarial assumptions used for purposes of maintaining the plan's funding standard account or, if less,

(ii) As the present value of benefits expected, on a termination basis, to accrue during the plan year.

*(3) Unfunded accrued benefits.* The ASA is charged with the unfunded accrued benefits of the plan for a plan year. This amount is the excess of—

(i) The present value of accrued benefits under the plan, determined as of the valuation date for the plan year, over

(ii) The fair market value of plan assets, determined as of the valuation date for the plan year.

Because fair market value is used, any election to value evidences of indebtedness at amortized value does not apply in computing this value.

*(4) Credit balance from prior plan year.* The ASA is charged as of the first day of a plan year with any ASA credit balance carried forward from the prior plan year.

*(5) Interest.* The ASA is charge with interest on the amounts charged to the ASA under paragraph (b)(2), (b)(3) and (b)(4) of this section, as generally prescribed for the funding standard account under § 1.412(b)-1(e).

**(d) Credits.** *(1) In general.* The ASA is credited with the amounts described in paragraph (d) of this section.

*(2) Employer contributions.* The ASA is credited with the amount of contributions made by the employer to the plan for the plan year.

*(3) Interest.* The ASA is credited with the interest on the amount credited under paragraph (d)(2) of this section, determined as of the end of the plan year as generally prescribed for the funding standard account under § 1.412(b)-1(e).

**§ 1.412(i)-1 Certain insurance contract plans.**

> ***Caution:*** The Treasury has not yet amended Reg § 1.412(i)-1 to reflect changes made by P.L. 109-432.

**(a) In general.** Under section 412(h)(2) of the Internal Revenue Code of 1954, as added by section 1013(a) of the Employee Retirement Income Security Act of 1974 (88 Stat 914) (hereinafter referred to as "the Act"), an insurance contract plan described in section 412(i) for a plan year is not subject to the minimum funding requirements of section 412 for that plan year. Consequently, if an individual or group insurance contract plan satisfies all of the requirements of paragraph (b)(2) or (c)(2) of this section, whichever are applicable, for the plan year, the plan is not subject to the requirements of section 412 for that plan year. The effective date for section 412 of the Code is determined under section 1017 of the Act. In general, in the case of a plan which was not in existence on January 1, 1974, this section applies for plan years beginning after September 2, 1974, and in the case of a plan in existence on January 1, 1974, to plan years beginning after December 31, 1975.

**(b) Individual insurance contract plans.** *(1)* An individual insurance contract plan is described in section 412(i) during a plan year if the plan satisfies the requirements of paragraph (b)(2) of this section for the plan year.

*(2)* The requirements of this paragraph are:

(i) The plan must be funded exclusively by the purchase from an insurance company or companies (licensed under the law of a State or the District of Columbia to do business with the plan) of individual annuity or individual insurance contracts, or a combination thereof. The purchase may be made either directly by the employer or through the use of a custodial account or trust. A plan shall not be considered to be funded otherwise than exclusively by the purchase of individual annuity or individual insurance contracts merely because the employer makes a payment necessary to comply with the provisions of section 411(c)(2) (relating to accrued benefit from employee contributions).

(ii) The individual annuity or individual insurance contracts issued under the plan must provide for level annual, or more frequent, premium payments to be paid under the plan for the period commencing with the date each individual participating in the plan became a participant and ending not later than the normal retirement age for that individual or, if earlier, the date the individual ceases his participation in the plan. Premium payments may be considered to be level even though items such as experience gains and dividends are applied against premiums. In the case of an increase in benefits, the contracts must provide for level annual payments with respect to such increase to be paid for the period commencing at the time the increase becomes effective. If payment commences on the first payment date under the contract occurring after the date an individual becomes a participant or after the effective date of an increase in benefits, the requirements of this subdivision will be satisfied even though payment does not commence on the date on which the individual's participation commenced or on the effective date of the benefit increase, whichever is applicable. If an individual accrues benefits after his normal retirement age, the requirements of this subdivision are satisfied if payment is made at the time such benefits accrue. If the provisions required by this subdivision are set forth in a separate agreement with the issuer of the individual contracts, they need not be included in the individual contracts.

(iii) The benefits provided by the plan for each individual participant must be equal to the benefits provided under his individual contracts at his normal retirement age under the plan provisions.

(iv) The benefits provided by the plan for each individual participant must be guaranteed by the life insurance company, described in paragraph (b)(2)(i) of this section, issuing the individual contracts to the extent premiums have been paid.

(v) Except as provided in the following sentence, all premiums payable for the plan year, and for all prior plan years, under the insurance or annuity contracts must have been paid before lapse. If the lapse has occurred during the plan year, the requirements of this subdivision will be considered to have been met if reinstatement of the insurance policy, under which the individual insurance contracts are issued, occurs during the year of the lapse and before distribution is made or benefits commence to any participant whose benefits are reduced because of the lapse.

(vi) No rights under the individual contracts may have been subject to a security interest at any time during the plan year. This subdivision shall not apply to contracts which have been distributed to participants if the security interest is created after the date of distribution.

(vii) No policy loans, including loans to individual participants, on any of the individual contracts may be outstanding at any time during the plan year. This subdivision shall not apply to contracts which have been distributed to participants if the loan is made after the date of distribution. An application of funds by the issuer to pay premiums due under the contracts shall be deemed not to be a policy loan if the amount of the funds so applied, and interest thereon, is repaid during the plan year in which the funds are applied and before distribution is made or benefits commence to any participant whose benefits are reduced because of such application.

**(c) Group insurance contract plans.** *(1)* A group insurance contract plan is described in section 412(i) during a plan year if the plan satisfies the requirements of subparagraph (2) for the plan year.

*(2)* The requirements of this subparagraph are:

(i) The plan must be funded exclusively by the purchase from an insurance company or companies, described in paragraph (b)(2)(i) of this section, of group annuity or group insurance contracts, or a combination thereof. The purchase may be made either directly by the employer or through the use of a custodial account or trust. A plan shall not be considered to be funded otherwise than exclusively by the purchase of group annuity or group insurance contracts merely because the employer makes a payment necessary to comply with the provisions of section 411(c)(2) (relating to accrued benefit derived from employee contributions).

(ii) In the case of a plan funded by a group insurance contract or a group annuity contract the requirements of paragraph (b)(2)(ii) of this section must be satisfied by the group contract issued under the plan. Thus, for example, each individual participant's benefits under the group contract must be provided for by level annual, or more frequent, payments equivalent to the payments required to satisfy such paragraph. The requirements of this subdivision will not be satisfied if benefits for any individual are not provided for by level payments made on his behalf under the group contract.

(iii) The group annuity or group insurance contract must satisfy the requirements of clauses (iii), (iv), (v), and (vii) of paragraph (b)(2). Thus, for example, each participant's benefits provided by the plan must be equal to his benefits provided under the group contract at his normal retirement age.

(iv) (A) If the plan is funded by a group annuity contract, the value of the benefits guaranteed by the insurance company issuing the contract under the plan with respect to each participant under the contract must not be less than the value of such benefits which the cash surrender value would provide for that participant under any individual annuity contract plan satisfying the requirements of paragraph (b) and approved for sale in the State where the principal office of the plan is located.

(B) If the plan is funded by a group insurance contract, the value of the benefits guaranteed by the insurance company issuing the contract under the plan with respect to each participate under the contract must not be less than the value of such benefits which the cash surrender value would provide for that participant under any individual insurance contract plan satisfying the requirements of paragraph (b) and approved for sale in the State where the principal office of the plan is located.

(v) Under the group annuity or group insurance contract, premiums or other consideration received by the insurance company (and, if a custodial account or trust is used, the custodian or trustee thereof) must be allocated to purchase individual benefits for participants under the plan. A plan which maintains unallocated funds in an auxiliary trust fund or which provides that an insurance company will maintain unallocated funds in a separate account, such as a group deposit administration contract, does not satisfy the requirements of this subdivision.

**(d) Combination of plans.** A plan which is funded by a combination of individual contracts and a group contract shall be treated as a plan described in section 412(i) for the plan year if the combination, in the aggregate, satisfies the requirements of this section for the plan year.

T.D. 7706, 7/15/80.

## § 1.412(l)(7)-1 Mortality tables used to determine current liability.

***Caution:*** The Treasury has not yet amended Reg § 1.412(l)(7)-1 to reflect changes made by P.L. 109-432.

**(a) In general.** The mortality tables set forth in paragraph (d) of this section are to be used in determining current liability under section 412(l)(7) for participants and beneficiaries (other than disabled participants) for plan years beginning in 2007. For plan years beginning on or after January 1, 2008, the mortality tables described in section 430(h)(3)(A) are to be used in determining current liability under section 412(l)(7) for participants and beneficiaries (other than disabled participants).

**(b) Separate tables for annuitants and nonannuitants.** The separate tables for annuitants and nonannuitants are used unless the plan applies the optional combined table pursuant to paragraph (c) of this section. If these separate tables are used, the nonannuitant mortality table is applied to determine the probability of survival for a nonannuitant for the period before the nonannuitant is projected to commence receiving benefits. The annuitant mortality table is applied to determine the present value of benefits for each annuitant, and for each nonannuitant for the period after which the nonannuitant is projected to commence receiving benefits. For purposes of this section, an annuitant means a plan participant who has commenced receiving benefits and a nonannuitant means a plan participant who has not yet commenced receiving benefits (e.g., an active employee or a terminated vested participant). Thus, for example, with respect to a 45-year-old active participant who is projected to commence receiving an annuity at age 55, current liability would be determined using the nonannuitant mortality table for the period before the participant attains age 55 (i.e., so that the probability of an active male participant living from age 45 to the age of 55 for the table that applies in plan years beginning in 2007 is 98.59%) and the annuitant mortality table for the period ages 55 and above. Similarly, if a 45-year-old terminated vested participant is projected to commence an annuity at age 65, current liability would be determined using the nonannuitant mortality table for the period before the participant attains age 65 and the annuitant mortality table for ages 65 and above. For purposes of this section, a participant whose benefit has partially commenced is treated as an annuitant with respect to the portion of the benefit which has commenced and a nonannuitant with respect to the balance of the benefit.

**(c) Optional combined tables.** As an alternative to the separate tables specified for annuitants and nonannuitants as described in paragraph (b) of this section, the optional combined table, which applies the same mortality rates to both annuitants and nonannuitants, can be used.

**(d) Mortality tables for 2007.** As set forth in paragraph (a) of this section, the following tables are to be used for determining current liability for plan years beginning during 2007 in accordance with the rules of this section.

| Age | Male | | | Female | | |
|---|---|---|---|---|---|---|
| | Non-annuitant table | Annuitant table | Optional combined for small plans | Non-annuitant table | Annuitant table | Optional combined for small plans |
| 1 | 0.000408 | 0.000408 | 0.000408 | 0.000366 | 0.000366 | 0.000366 |
| 2 | 0.000276 | 0.000276 | 0.000276 | 0.000239 | 0.000239 | 0.000239 |
| 3 | 0.000229 | 0.000229 | 0.000229 | 0.000178 | 0.000178 | 0.000178 |
| 4 | 0.000178 | 0.000178 | 0.000178 | 0.000133 | 0.000133 | 0.000133 |
| 5 | 0.000163 | 0.000163 | 0.000163 | 0.000121 | 0.000121 | 0.000121 |
| 6 | 0.000156 | 0.000156 | 0.000156 | 0.000113 | 0.000113 | 0.000113 |
| 7 | 0.000150 | 0.000150 | 0.000150 | 0.000106 | 0.000106 | 0.000106 |
| 8 | 0.000138 | 0.000138 | 0.000138 | 0.000094 | 0.000094 | 0.000094 |
| 9 | 0.000134 | 0.000134 | 0.000134 | 0.000090 | 0.000090 | 0.000090 |
| 10 | 0.000136 | 0.000136 | 0.000136 | 0.000090 | 0.000090 | 0.000090 |
| 11 | 0.000140 | 0.000140 | 0.000140 | 0.000092 | 0.000092 | 0.000092 |
| 12 | 0.000146 | 0.000146 | 0.000146 | 0.000095 | 0.000095 | 0.000095 |
| 13 | 0.000154 | 0.000154 | 0.000154 | 0.000099 | 0.000099 | 0.000099 |
| 14 | 0.000167 | 0.000167 | 0.000167 | 0.000109 | 0.000109 | 0.000109 |
| 15 | 0.000176 | 0.000176 | 0.000176 | 0.000119 | 0.000119 | 0.000119 |
| 16 | 0.000186 | 0.000186 | 0.000186 | 0.000127 | 0.000127 | 0.000127 |
| 17 | 0.000197 | 0.000197 | 0.000197 | 0.000135 | 0.000135 | 0.000135 |
| 18 | 0.000207 | 0.000207 | 0.000207 | 0.000138 | 0.000138 | 0.000138 |
| 19 | 0.000217 | 0.000217 | 0.000217 | 0.000136 | 0.000136 | 0.000136 |
| 20 | 0.000226 | 0.000226 | 0.000226 | 0.000134 | 0.000134 | 0.000134 |
| 21 | 0.000239 | 0.000239 | 0.000239 | 0.000132 | 0.000132 | 0.000132 |
| 22 | 0.000251 | 0.000251 | 0.000251 | 0.000133 | 0.000133 | 0.000133 |
| 23 | 0.000267 | 0.000267 | 0.000267 | 0.000138 | 0.000138 | 0.000138 |
| 24 | 0.000282 | 0.000282 | 0.000282 | 0.000144 | 0.000144 | 0.000144 |
| 25 | 0.000301 | 0.000301 | 0.000301 | 0.000152 | 0.000152 | 0.000152 |
| 26 | 0.000331 | 0.000331 | 0.000331 | 0.000164 | 0.000164 | 0.000164 |
| 27 | 0.000342 | 0.000342 | 0.000342 | 0.000171 | 0.000171 | 0.000171 |
| 28 | 0.000352 | 0.000352 | 0.000352 | 0.000180 | 0.000180 | 0.000180 |
| 29 | 0.000369 | 0.000369 | 0.000369 | 0.000190 | 0.000190 | 0.000190 |
| 30 | 0.000398 | 0.000398 | 0.000398 | 0.000212 | 0.000212 | 0.000212 |
| 31 | 0.000447 | 0.000447 | 0.000447 | 0.000257 | 0.000257 | 0.000257 |
| 32 | 0.000503 | 0.000503 | 0.000503 | 0.000293 | 0.000293 | 0.000293 |
| 33 | 0.000565 | 0.000565 | 0.000565 | 0.000323 | 0.000323 | 0.000323 |
| 34 | 0.000629 | 0.000629 | 0.000629 | 0.000349 | 0.000349 | 0.000349 |
| 35 | 0.000692 | 0.000692 | 0.000692 | 0.000372 | 0.000372 | 0.000372 |
| 36 | 0.000753 | 0.000753 | 0.000753 | 0.000394 | 0.000394 | 0.000394 |
| 37 | 0.000810 | 0.000810 | 0.000810 | 0.000415 | 0.000415 | 0.000415 |
| 38 | 0.000844 | 0.000844 | 0.000844 | 0.000439 | 0.000439 | 0.000439 |
| 39 | 0.000875 | 0.000875 | 0.000875 | 0.000465 | 0.000465 | 0.000465 |
| 40 | 0.000904 | 0.000904 | 0.000904 | 0.000506 | 0.000506 | 0.000506 |
| 41 | 0.000936 | 0.000963 | 0.000936 | 0.000555 | 0.000555 | 0.000555 |
| 42 | 0.000974 | 0.001081 | 0.000975 | 0.000611 | 0.000611 | 0.000611 |
| 43 | 0.001018 | 0.001258 | 0.001021 | 0.000672 | 0.000672 | 0.000672 |
| 44 | 0.001071 | 0.001493 | 0.001079 | 0.000738 | 0.000738 | 0.000738 |
| 45 | 0.001131 | 0.001788 | 0.001146 | 0.000788 | 0.000791 | 0.000788 |
| 46 | 0.001185 | 0.002142 | 0.001211 | 0.000839 | 0.000896 | 0.000840 |
| 47 | 0.001244 | 0.002554 | 0.001286 | 0.000889 | 0.001054 | 0.000893 |
| 48 | 0.001304 | 0.003026 | 0.001366 | 0.000962 | 0.001265 | 0.000972 |
| 49 | 0.001368 | 0.003557 | 0.001457 | 0.001039 | 0.001528 | 0.001059 |
| 50 | 0.001434 | 0.004146 | 0.001557 | 0.001149 | 0.001844 | 0.001184 |
| 51 | 0.001500 | 0.004226 | 0.001636 | 0.001272 | 0.001962 | 0.001312 |
| 52 | 0.001570 | 0.004254 | 0.001754 | 0.001442 | 0.002173 | 0.001496 |
| 53 | 0.001681 | 0.004312 | 0.001932 | 0.001637 | 0.002445 | 0.001714 |
| 54 | 0.001803 | 0.004369 | 0.002134 | 0.001861 | 0.002771 | 0.001969 |
| 55 | 0.001986 | 0.004514 | 0.002508 | 0.002117 | 0.003155 | 0.002314 |
| 56 | 0.002217 | 0.004749 | 0.003020 | 0.002414 | 0.003608 | 0.002755 |
| 57 | 0.002488 | 0.005069 | 0.003464 | 0.002696 | 0.004088 | 0.003170 |
| 58 | 0.002803 | 0.005501 | 0.003990 | 0.002947 | 0.004588 | 0.003583 |
| 59 | 0.003095 | 0.005972 | 0.004529 | 0.003223 | 0.005156 | 0.004066 |
| 60 | 0.003421 | 0.006539 | 0.005177 | 0.003521 | 0.005780 | 0.004640 |
| 61 | 0.003860 | 0.007284 | 0.006030 | 0.003838 | 0.006450 | 0.005354 |
| 62 | 0.004244 | 0.008024 | 0.006929 | 0.004170 | 0.007168 | 0.006148 |

| | | | | | | |
|---|---|---|---|---|---|---|
| 63 | 0.004746 | 0.008989 | 0.008099 | 0.004513 | 0.007932 | 0.007084 |
| 64 | 0.005154 | 0.009947 | 0.009159 | 0.004862 | 0.008758 | 0.007996 |
| 65 | 0.005553 | 0.011015 | 0.010377 | 0.005213 | 0.009662 | 0.009018 |
| 66 | 0.006073 | 0.012379 | 0.011951 | 0.005559 | 0.010640 | 0.010192 |
| 67 | 0.006447 | 0.013705 | 0.013349 | 0.005896 | 0.011690 | 0.011323 |
| 68 | 0.006650 | 0.014940 | 0.014641 | 0.006220 | 0.012838 | 0.012522 |
| 69 | 0.006974 | 0.016504 | 0.016231 | 0.006528 | 0.014126 | 0.013843 |
| 70 | 0.007115 | 0.017971 | 0.017689 | 0.006818 | 0.015607 | 0.015309 |
| 71 | 0.008002 | 0.019884 | 0.019606 | 0.007450 | 0.017078 | 0.016784 |
| 72 | 0.009777 | 0.022078 | 0.021822 | 0.008714 | 0.018995 | 0.018716 |
| 73 | 0.012439 | 0.024592 | 0.024371 | 0.010610 | 0.020819 | 0.020577 |
| 74 | 0.015988 | 0.027435 | 0.027256 | 0.013139 | 0.023074 | 0.022872 |
| 75 | 0.020425 | 0.031057 | 0.030919 | 0.016299 | 0.025117 | 0.024967 |
| 76 | 0.025749 | 0.034615 | 0.034523 | 0.020092 | 0.027673 | 0.027570 |
| 77 | 0.031961 | 0.039054 | 0.038999 | 0.024516 | 0.030911 | 0.030846 |
| 78 | 0.039059 | 0.044018 | 0.043992 | 0.029573 | 0.034074 | 0.034043 |
| 79 | 0.047046 | 0.049617 | 0.049610 | 0.035261 | 0.037618 | 0.037610 |
| 80 | 0.055919 | 0.055919 | 0.055919 | 0.041582 | 0.041582 | 0.041582 |
| 81 | 0.063476 | 0.063476 | 0.063476 | 0.046024 | 0.046024 | 0.046024 |
| 82 | 0.071926 | 0.071926 | 0.071926 | 0.051021 | 0.051021 | 0.051021 |
| 83 | 0.080176 | 0.080176 | 0.080176 | 0.056651 | 0.056651 | 0.056651 |
| 84 | 0.090433 | 0.090433 | 0.090433 | 0.063006 | 0.063006 | 0.063006 |
| 85 | 0.100383 | 0.100383 | 0.100383 | 0.071188 | 0.071188 | 0.071188 |
| 86 | 0.111295 | 0.111295 | 0.111295 | 0.080522 | 0.080522 | 0.080522 |
| 87 | 0.125051 | 0.125051 | 0.125051 | 0.091080 | 0.091080 | 0.091080 |
| 88 | 0.140385 | 0.140385 | 0.140385 | 0.101448 | 0.101448 | 0.101448 |
| 89 | 0.155142 | 0.155142 | 0.155142 | 0.114246 | 0.114246 | 0.114246 |
| 90 | 0.173400 | 0.173400 | 0.173400 | 0.126258 | 0.126258 | 0.126258 |
| 91 | 0.188868 | 0.188868 | 0.188868 | 0.138648 | 0.138648 | 0.138648 |
| 92 | 0.207683 | 0.207683 | 0.207683 | 0.151126 | 0.151126 | 0.151126 |
| 93 | 0.224037 | 0.224037 | 0.224037 | 0.165722 | 0.165722 | 0.165722 |
| 94 | 0.240367 | 0.240367 | 0.240367 | 0.177747 | 0.177747 | 0.177747 |
| 95 | 0.260098 | 0.260098 | 0.260098 | 0.189133 | 0.189133 | 0.189133 |
| 96 | 0.276058 | 0.276058 | 0.276058 | 0.199703 | 0.199703 | 0.199703 |
| 97 | 0.291564 | 0.291564 | 0.291564 | 0.212246 | 0.212246 | 0.212246 |
| 98 | 0.310910 | 0.310910 | 0.310910 | 0.220832 | 0.220832 | 0.220832 |
| 99 | 0.325614 | 0.325614 | 0.325614 | 0.228169 | 0.228169 | 0.228169 |
| 100 | 0.339763 | 0.339763 | 0.339763 | 0.234164 | 0.234164 | 0.234164 |
| 101 | 0.358628 | 0.358628 | 0.358628 | 0.244834 | 0.244834 | 0.244834 |
| 102 | 0.371685 | 0.371685 | 0.371685 | 0.254498 | 0.254498 | 0.254498 |
| 103 | 0.383040 | 0.383040 | 0.383040 | 0.266044 | 0.266044 | 0.266044 |
| 104 | 0.392003 | 0.392003 | 0.392003 | 0.279055 | 0.279055 | 0.279055 |
| 105 | 0.397886 | 0.397886 | 0.397886 | 0.293116 | 0.293116 | 0.293116 |
| 106 | 0.400000 | 0.400000 | 0.400000 | 0.307811 | 0.307811 | 0.307811 |
| 107 | 0.400000 | 0.400000 | 0.400000 | 0.322725 | 0.322725 | 0.322725 |
| 108 | 0.400000 | 0.400000 | 0.400000 | 0.337441 | 0.337441 | 0.337441 |
| 109 | 0.400000 | 0.400000 | 0.400000 | 0.351544 | 0.351544 | 0.351544 |
| 110 | 0.400000 | 0.400000 | 0.400000 | 0.364617 | 0.364617 | 0.364617 |
| 111 | 0.400000 | 0.400000 | 0.400000 | 0.376246 | 0.376246 | 0.376246 |
| 112 | 0.400000 | 0.400000 | 0.400000 | 0.386015 | 0.386015 | 0.386015 |
| 113 | 0.400000 | 0.400000 | 0.400000 | 0.393507 | 0.393507 | 0.393507 |
| 114 | 0.400000 | 0.400000 | 0.400000 | 0.398308 | 0.398308 | 0.398308 |
| 115 | 0.400000 | 0.400000 | 0.400000 | 0.400000 | 0.400000 | 0.400000 |
| 116 | 0.400000 | 0.400000 | 0.400000 | 0.400000 | 0.400000 | 0.400000 |
| 117 | 0.400000 | 0.400000 | 0.400000 | 0.400000 | 0.400000 | 0.400000 |
| 118 | 0.400000 | 0.400000 | 0.400000 | 0.400000 | 0.400000 | 0.400000 |
| 119 | 0.400000 | 0.400000 | 0.400000 | 0.400000 | 0.400000 | 0.400000 |
| 120 | 1.000000 | 1.000000 | 1.000000 | 1.000000 | 1.000000 | 1.000000 |

**(e) Effective date.** This section applies for plan years beginning on or after January 1, 2007.

T.D. 9310, 2/1/2007.

**§ 1.413-1 Special rules for collectively bargained plans.**

***Caution:*** The Treasury has not yet amended Reg § 1.413-1 to reflect changes made by P.L. 100-647.

**(a) Application of section 413(b) to certain collectively bargained plans.** *(1) In general.* Section 413(b) sets forth special rules applicable to certain pension, profit-sharing, and stock bonus plans (and each trust which is a part of such a plan), hereinafter referred to as "section 413(b) plans", described in paragraph (a)(2) of this section. Notwithstanding any other provision of the Code, a section 413(b) plan is subject to the special rules of section 413(b)(1) through (8) and paragraphs (b) through (i) of this section.

*(2) Requirements.* Section 413(b) applies to a plan (and each trust which is a part of such plan) if the plan is a single plan which is maintained pursuant to one or more agreements which the Secretary of Labor finds to be a collective bargaining agreement between employee representatives and one or more employers. A plan which provides benefits for employees of more than one employer is considered a single plan subject to the requirements of section 413(b) and this section if the plan is considered a single plan for purposes of applying section 414(l) (see § 1.414(l)-1(b)(1)). For purposes of determining whether one or more plans (or agreements) are a single plan, under sections 413(a) and 414(l), it is irrelevant that there are in form two or more separate plans (or agreements). For example, a single plan will be considered to exist where agreements are entered into separately by a national labor organization (or one or more local units of such organization), on one hand, and individual employers, on the other hand, if the plan is considered a single plan for purposes of applying section 414(l).

*(3) Additional rules and effective dates.* (i) If a plan is a section 413(b) plan at a relevant time, the rules of section 413(b) and this section apply, and the rules of section 413(c) and § 1.413-2 do not apply to the plan.

(ii) The qualification of a section 413(b) plan, at any relevant time, under section 401(a), 403(a), or 405(a), as modified by sections 413(b) and this section, is determined with respect to all employers maintaining the plan. Consequently, the failure by one employer maintaining the plan (or by the plan itself) to satisfy an applicable qualification requirement will result in the disqualification of the plan for all employers maintaining the plan.

(iii) Except as otherwise provided, section 413(a) and (b) of this section apply to a plan for plan years beginning after December 31, 1953.

**(b) Participation.** Section 410 and the regulations thereunder shall be applied as if all employees of each of the employers who are parties to the collective-bargaining agreement and all such employees who are subject to the same benefit computation formula under the plan were employed by a single employer.

**(c) Discrimination, etc.** *(1) General rule.* Section 401(a)(4) (relating to prohibited discrimination) and section 411(d)(3) (relating to vesting required on termination, partial termination, or discontinuance of contributions) shall be applied as if all the participants in the plan, who are subject to the same benefit computation formula and who are employed by employers who are parties to the collective bargaining agreement, are employed by a single employer.

*(2) Application of discrimination rules.* Under section 401(a)(4) and the regulations thereunder a plan is not qualified unless the contributions or benefits provided under the plan do not discriminate in favor of officers, shareholders or highly compensated employees (hereinafter referred to collectively as "the prohibited group"). The presence or absence of such discrimination under a plan to which this section applies at any time shall not be determined on an employer-by-employer basis, but rather by testing separately each group of employees who are subject to the same benefit computation formula to determine if there is discrimination within such group. Consequently, discrimination in contributions or benefits among two or more different groups or among employees in different groups covered by the plan may be present without causing the plan to be disqualified. However, the presence of prohibited discrimination within one such group will result in the disqualification of the plan for all groups. Section 401(a)(4) and the regulations thereunder provide rules relating to the determination of which employees are members of the prohibited group and to the determination of discrimination in contributions or benefits which are applicable to a plan to which this section applies. The determination of whether or not an individual employee is a highly compensated employee shall be based on the relationship of the compensation of the employee to the compensation of all the other employees of all employers who are maintaining the plan and have employees covered under the same benefit computation formula, whether or not such other employees are covered by the plan or are covered under the same benefit computation formula, rather than to the compensation of all the other employees of the employer of such individual employee.

*(3) Application of termination, etc. rules.* Section 411(d)(3) and the regulations thereunder (relating to vesting required in the case of a termination, partial termination, or complete discontinuance of contributions) apply to a plan subject to the provisions of this section. The requirements of section 411(d)(3) shall be applied as if all participants in the plan who are subject to the same benefit computation formula and who are employed by employers who are parties to the collective bargaining agreement are employed by a single employer. The determination of whether or not there is a termination, partial termination, or complete discontinuance of contributions shall be made separately for each such group of participants who are treated as employed by a single employer. Consequently, if there are two or more groups of participants, a termination, partial termination, or complete discontinuance can take place under a plan with respect to one group of participants but not with respect to another such group of participants or for the entire plan. See § 1.411(d)-2 for rules prescribed under section 411(d)(3).

*(4) Effective dates and transitional rules.* (i) Section 413(b)(2) and this paragraph apply to a plan for plan years beginning after December 31, 1953.

(ii) In applying the rules of this paragraph to a plan for plan years to which section 411 does not apply, section 401(a)(7) (as in effect on September 1, 1974) shall be substituted for section 411(d)(3). See § 1.401-6 for rules prescribed under section 401(a)(7) as in effect on September 1, 1974. See § 1.411(a)-2 for the effective dates of section 411.

*(5) Examples.* The provisions of this paragraph are illustrated by the following examples:

*Example (1).* Plan A is a defined benefit plan subject to the provisions of this section and covers two groups of participants, local unions 1 and 2. Each local union has negotiated its own bargaining agreement with employers X, Y, and Z to provide its own benefit computation formula. The following table indicates the composition of the plan A participants:

| | Employer X | Employer Y | Employer Z | Total |
|---|---|---|---|---|
| Local union 1 . . | 20 | 10 | 70 | 100 |
| Local union 2 . . | 30 | 70 | 100 | 200 |

Under the rules of subparagraph (2) of this paragraph, the determination of whether contributions or benefits provided under the plan discriminate in favor of the prohibited group is made by applying the rules of section 401(a)(4) separately to participants who are members of local union 1 and local union 2. Thus, plan A will satisfy the qualification requirements of section 401(a)(4) if, within local union 1 and local union 2, respectively, plan benefits do not discriminate in favor of participants who are prohibited group employees within local union 1 and local union 2. Under the rules of subparagraph (2) of this paragraph, the determination under section 401(a)(4) of whether or not any individual employee, included within the 300 participants in plan A, is a highly compensated employee is based on the relationship of the compensation of such individual employee to the compensation of all the employees of Employers X, Y, and Z, whether or not such employees are participants in plan A. Thus, if there are 20 participants who are prohibited group employees within the 100 participants of local union 1, discrimination is determined by comparing the benefits of the 20 prohibited group participants to the benefits of the other 80 participants within local union 1. The same comparison would have to be made for the local union 2 participants between the prohibited group participants and the other participants in local union 2. Discrimination in benefits, if any, between the participants in local union 1 and local union 2, or among the employees of X, Y, and Z, would not affect the qualification of plan A under section 401(a)(4).

*Example (2).* Assume the same facts as in example (1). Employer X withdraws from the plan. Under subparagraph (3) of this paragraph, whether or not as a result of the withdrawal there is a partial termination under section 411(d)(3) is to be determined by applying the requirements of such section separately to the local union 1 and local union 2 participants. See § 1.411(d)-2 for the requirements relating to partial terminations. The application of such requirements raises the following possibilities with respect to the plan: (1) A partial termination as to local union 1, (2) a partial termination as to local union 2, (3) a partial termination as to both local unions 1 and 2, or (4) no partial termination for either local union.

*Example (3).* Assume the same facts as in example (1). Plan A is amended to cease future benefit accruals under the plan for local union 1 participants. Under subparagraph (3) of the paragraph, whether or not as a result of the cessation there is a partial termination under section 411(d)(3) is to be determined by applying the requirements of such section separately to the local union 1 and local union 2 participants.

*Example (4).* Plan A is a defined benefit plan that provides for two normal retirement benefits, X and 2X. A participant receives benefit X if the collective bargaining agreement covering his employment provides for a contribution rate, M. If such agreement provides for a contribution rate of N, the participant receives benefit 2X. Benefit X and benefit 2X constitute separate benefit computation formulas.

*Example (5).* Plan B is a defined benefit plan that provides for a normal retirement benefit, X. Benefit X is provided for all plan participants even though there are two collective bargaining agreements providing for different contribution rates, M and N. Plan B has a single benefit computation formula, even though there are two contribution rates.

**(d) Exclusive benefit.** Under section 401(a), a plan is not qualified unless the plan is for the exclusive benefit of the employees (and their beneficiaries) of the employer establishing and maintaining the plan. Other qualification requirements under section 401(a) require the application of the exclusive benefit rule (for example, section 401(a)(2), which precludes diversion of plan assets). For purposes of applying the requirements of section 401(a) in determining whether a plan subject to this section is, with respect to each employer establishing and maintaining the plan, for the exclusive benefit of its employees (and their beneficiaries), all of the employees participating in the plan shall be treated as employees of each such employer. Thus, for example, contributions by employer A to a plan subject to this section could be allocated to employees of other employers maintaining the plan without violating the requirements of section 401(a)(2), because all the employees participating in the plan are deemed to be employees of A.

**(e) Vesting.** Section 411 (other than section 411(d)(3) relating to termination or partial termination; discontinuance of contributions) and the regulations thereunder shall be applied as if all employers who have been parties to the collective-bargaining agreement constituted a single employer. The application of any rules with respect to breaks in service under section 411 shall be made under regulations prescribed by the Secretary of Labor. Thus, for example, all the hours which an employee worked for each employer in a collectively-bargained plan would be aggregated in computing the employee's hours of service under the plan. See also 29 CFR Part 2530 (Department of Labor regulations relating to minimum standards for employee pension benefit plans).

**(f) through (h) [Reserved].**

**(i) Employees of labor unions.** *(1) General rule.* For purposes of section 413(b) and this section, employees of employee representatives shall be treated as employees of an employer establishing and maintaining a plan to which section 413(b) and this section apply if, with respect to the employees of such representatives, the plan satisfies the nondiscrimination requirements of section 401(a)(4) (determined without regard to section 413(b)(2)) and the minimum participation and coverage requirements of section 410 (determined without regard to section 413(b)(1)). For purposes of the preceding sentence, the plan and any affiliated employee health or welfare plan shall be deemed to be an employee representative. If employees of employee representatives, the plan, or an affiliated employee health or welfare plan are covered by the plan and are not treated as employees of an employer establishing and maintaining the plan under the provisions of this paragraph, the plan fails to satisfy the qualification requirements of section 401(a). In addition, in order for such a plan to be qualified, the plan must satisfy the requirements of section 413(b) (1) and (2), relating to participation and discrimination, respectively; see paragraphs (b) and (c) of this section. For purposes of this paragraph, an affiliated health or welfare plan is a health or welfare plan that is maintained under the same collective bargaining agreement or agreements, and that covers the same membership.

*(2) Effective dates and transitional rules.* (i) Section 413(b)(8) and this paragraph apply to a plan for plan years beginning after December 31, 1953.

(ii) In applying the rules of this paragraph to a plan for plan years to which section 410 does not apply, section

401(a)(3) (as in effect on September 1, 1974) shall be substituted for section 410. See § 1.401-3 for rules prescribed under section 401(a)(3) as in effect on September 1, 1974. See § 1.410(a)-2 for the effective dates of section 410.

*(3) Examples.* The provisions of this paragraph are illustrated by the following examples:

*Example (1).* Plan A is a defined benefit plan, maintained pursuant to a collective bargaining agreement between employers, X, Y, and Z and labor union, L, which covers members of L employed by X, Y, and Z. In 1978, plan A is amended to cover, under the same benefit formula, all five employees of L who have satisfied the minimum age and service requirements of the plans (age 25 and 1 year of service). Assume that plan A is subject to section 413(b) and satisfies the requirements of section 413(b)(1) and (2). Assume further that with respect to employees of L, plan A (i) satisfies the nondiscrimination requirements of section 401(a)(4), (ii) meets the minimum participation requirements of section 410(a), and (iii) meets the minimum coverage requirements of section 410(b)(1)(A). Under the rules of subparagraph (1) of this paragraph, because such requirements are all satisfied, the employees of L are treated as employees of an employer establishing and maintaining plan A.

*Example (2).* Assume the same facts as example (1), except that plan A is amended to cover only one of the five employees of L, none of whom is covered by any other plan. Assume further that, under plan A, L does not satisfy the minimum percentage coverage requirement of section 410(b)(1)(A) with respect to employees of L. Assume further that the compensation of the one L employee who is covered by the plan is such that he is highly compensated relative to the four employees of L not covered by the plan. Consequently, L does not satisfy the minimum coverage requirements of section 410(b)(1)(B), with respect to employees of L. Under the rules of subparagraph (1) of this paragraph, the employees of L cannot be treated as employees of an employer establishing and maintaining the A plan because such coverage requirements are not satisfied by L. Consequently, the A plan fails to satisfy the qualification requirements of section 401(a).

---

T.D. 7501, 8/22/77, amend T.D. 7508, 9/14/77, T.D. 7654, 11/8/79.

---

PAR. 5. The Income Tax Regulations, 26 CFR Part 1, are further amended by adding new paragraphs (f) and (g) of § 1.413-1 to read as follows:

**Proposed § 1.413-1 Special rules for collectively bargained plans.** [*For Preamble, see ¶ 150,781*]

* * * * *

**(f) Minimum funding standard.** The minimum funding standard for a collectively bargained plan shall be determined as if all participants in the plan were employed by a single employer.

**(g) Liability for funding tax.** See § 54.4971-3 of the Pension Excise Tax Regulations, 26 CFR Part 54, for rules under section 413(b)(6), relating to liability for excise tax on failure to meet minimum funding standards with respect to collectively bargained plans.

* * * * *

**§ 1.413-2 Special rules for plans maintained by more than one employer.**

***Caution:*** The Treasury has not yet amended Reg § 1.413-2 to reflect changes made by P.L. 100-647.

**(a) Application of section 413(c).** *(1) In general.* Section 413(c) describes certain plans (and each trust which is a part of any such plan) hereinafter referred to as "section 413(c) plans." A plan (and each trust which is a part of such plan) is deemed to be a section 413(c) plan if it is described in subparagraph (2) of this paragraph. Notwithstanding any other provision of the code (not specifically in conflict with the special rules hereinafter mentioned), a section 413(c) plan is subject to the special rules of section 413(c)(1) through (6) and paragraphs (b) through (g) of this section.

*(2) Section 413(c) plan.* A plan (and each trust which is a part of such plan) is a section 413(c) plan if—

(i) The plan is a single plan, within the meaning of section 413(a) and § 1.413-1(a)(2), and

(ii) The plan is maintained by more than one employer.

For purposes of subdivision (ii) of this subparagraph, the number of employers maintaining the plan is determined by treating any employers described in section 414(b) (relating to a controlled group of corporations) or any employers described in section 414(c) (relating to trades or businesses under common control), whichever is applicable, as if such employers are a single employer. See § 1.411(a)-5(b)(3) for rules relating to the time when an employer maintains a plan. A master or prototype plan is not a section 413(c) plan unless such a plan is described in this subparagraph.

Similarly, the mere fact that a plan, or plans, utilizes a common trust fund or otherwise pools plan assets for investment purposes does not, by itself, result in a particular plan being treated as a section 413(c) plan.

*(3) Additional rules.* (i) If a plan is a collectively bargained plan described in § 1.413-1(a), the rules of section 413(c) and this section do not apply, and the rules of section 413(b) and § 1.413-1 do apply to the plan.

(ii) The special rules of section 413(b)(1) and § 1.413-1(b) relating to the application of section 410, other than the rules of section 410(a), do not apply to a section 413(c) plan. Thus, for example, the minimum coverage requirements of section 410(b) are generally applied to a section 413(c) plan on an employer-by-employer basis, taking into account the generally applicable rules such as section 401(a)(5) and section 414 (b) and (c).

(iii) The special rules of section 413(b)(2) and § 1.413-1(c) (relating to (A) section 401(a)(4) and prohibited discrimination, and (B) 411(d)(3) and vesting required on termination, partial termination, or discontinuance of contributions) do not apply to a section 413(c) plan. Thus, for example, the determination of whether or not there is a termination, within the meaning of section 411(d)(3), of a section 413(c) plan is made solely by reference to the rules of sections 411(d)(3) and 413(c)(3).

(iv) The qualification of a section 413(c) plan, at any relevant time, under section 401(a), 403(a) or 405(a), as modified by section 413(c) and this section, is determined with respect to all employers maintaining the section 413(c) plan. Consequently, the failure by one employer maintaining the plan (or by the plan itself) to satisfy an applicable qualification requirement will result in the disqualification of the section 413(c) plan for all employers maintaining the plan.

*(4) Effective dates.* Except as otherwise provided, section 413(c) and this section apply to a plan for plan years beginning after December 31, 1953.

**(b) Participation.** Section 410(a) and the regulations thereunder shall be applied as if all employees of each of the employees who maintain the plan were employed by a single employer.

**(c) Exclusive benefit.** In the case of a plan subject to this section, the exclusive benefit requirements of section 401(a) shall be applied to the plan in the same manner as under section 413(b)(3) and § 1.413-1(d).

**(d) Vesting.** Section 411 and the regulations thereunder shall be applied as if all employers who maintain the plan constituted a single employer. The application of any rules with respect to breaks in service under section 411 shall be made under regulations prescribed by the Secretary of Labor. Thus, for example, all the hours which an employee worked for each employer maintaining the plan would be aggregated in computing the employee's hours of service under the plan. See also 29 CFR Part 2530 (Department of Labor regulations relating to minimum standards for employee pension benefit plans).

---

T.D. 7501, 8/22/77, amend T.D. 7508, 9/14/77, T.D. 7654, 11/8/79.

---

PAR. 6. The Income Tax Regulations, 26 CFR Part 1, are further amended by adding new paragraphs (e) and (f) of § 1.413-2 to read as follows:

**Proposed § 1.413-2 Special rules for plans maintained by more than one employer.** [*For Preamble, see ¶ 150,781*]

* * * * *

**(e) Minimum funding standard.** The minimum funding standard for a plan maintained by more than one employer shall be determined as if all participants in the plan were employed by a single employer.

**(f) Liability for funding tax.** See § 54.4971-3 of the Pension Excise Tax Regulations, 26 CFR Part 54, for rules under section 413(c)(5), relating to liability for excise tax on failure to meet minimum funding standards with respect to plans maintained by more than one employer.

**§ 1.414(b)-1 Controlled group of corporations.**

***Caution:*** The Treasury has not yet amended Reg § 1.414(b)-1 to reflect changes made by P.L. 101-239.

**(a) Definition of controlled group of corporations.** For purposes of this section, the term "controlled group of corporations" has the same meaning as is assigned to the term in section 1563(a) and the regulations thereunder, except that (1) the term "controlled group of corporations" shall not include an "insurance group" described in section 1563(a)(4), and (2) section 1563(e)(3)(C) (relating to stock owned by certain employees' trusts) shall not apply. For purposes of this section, the term "members of a controlled group" means two or more corporations connected through stock ownership described in section 1563(a)(1), (2), or (3), whether or not such corporations are "component members of a controlled group" within the meaning of section 1563(b). Two or more corporations are members of a controlled group at any time such corporations meet the requirements of section 1563(a) (as modified by this paragraph). For purposes of this section, if a corporation is a member of more than one controlled group of corporations, such corporation shall be treated as a member of each controlled group.

**(b) Single plan adopted by two or more members.** If two or more members of a controlled group of corporations adopt a single plan for a plan year, then the minimum funding standard provided in section 412, the tax imposed by section 4971, and the applicable limitations provided by section 404(a) shall be determined as if such members were a single employer. In such a case, the amount of such items and the allocable portion attributable to each member shall be determined in the manner provided in regulations under sections 412, 4971, and 404(a).

**(c) Cross reference.** For rules relating to the application of sections 401, 408(k), 410, 411, 415, and 416 with respect to two or more trades or businesses which are under common control, see section 414(c) and the regulations thereunder.

---

T.D. 8179, 3/1/88.

---

**§ 1.414(c)-1 Commonly controlled trades or businesses.**

For purposes of applying the provisions of sections 401 (relating to qualified pension, profit-sharing, and stock bonus plans), 408(k) (relating to simplified employee pensions), 410 (relating to minimum participation standards), 411 (relating to minimum vesting standards), 415 (relating to limitations on benefits and contributions under qualified plans), and 416 (relating to top-heavy plans), all employees of two or more trades or businesses under common control within the meaning of § 1.414(c)-2 for any period shall be treated as employed by a single employer. See sections 401, 408(k), 410, 411, 415, and 416 and the regulations thereunder for rules relating to employees of trades or businesses which are under common control. See § 1.414(c)-5 for effective date.

---

T.D. 8179, 3/1/88.

---

**§ 1.414(c)-2 Two or more trades or businesses under common control.**

**(a) In general.** For purposes of this section, the term "two or more trades or businesses under common control" means any group of trades or businesses which is either a "parent-subsidiary group of trades or businesses under common control" as defined in paragraph (b) of this section, a "brother-sister group of trades or businesses under common control" as defined in paragraph (c) of this section, or a "combined group of trades or businesses under common control" as defined in paragraph (d) of this section. For purposes of this section and §§ 1.414(c)-3 and 1.414(c)-4, the term "organization" means a sole proprietorship, a partnership (as defined in section 7701(a)(2)), a trust, an estate, or a corporation.

**(b) Parent-subsidiary group of trades or businesses under common control.** *(1) In general.* The term "parent-subsidiary group of trades or businesses under common control" means one or more chains of organizations conducting trades or businesses connected through ownership of a controlling interest with a common parent organization if—

(i) A controlling interest in each of the organizations, except the common parent organization, is owned (directly and with the application of § 1.414(c)-4(b)(1), relating to options) by one or more of the other organizations; and

(ii) The common parent organization owns (directly and with the application of § 1.414(c)-4(b)(1), relating to options) a controlling interest in at least one of the other organizations, excluding, in computing such controlling interest, any direct ownership interest by such other organizations.

*(2) Controlling interest defined.* (i) Controlling interest. For purposes of paragraphs (b) and (c) of this section, the phrase "controlling interest" means:

(A) In the case of an organization which is a corporation, ownership of stock possessing at least 80 percent of total combined voting power of all classes of stock entitled to vote of such corporation or at least 80 percent of the total value of shares of all classes of stock of such corporation;

(B) In the case of an organization which is a trust or estate, ownership of an actuarial interest of at least 80 percent of such trust or estate;

(C) In the case of an organization which is a partnership, ownership of at least 80 percent of the profits interest or capital interest of such partnership; and

(D) In the case of an organization which is a sole proprietorship, ownership of such sole proprietorship.

(ii) Actuarial interest. For purposes of this section, the actuarial interest of each beneficiary of trust or estate shall be determined by assuming the maximum exercise of discretion by the fiduciary in favor of such beneficiary. The factors and methods prescribed in § 20.2031-7 or, for certain prior periods, § 20.2031-7A (Estate Tax Regulations) for use in ascertaining the value of an interest in property for estate tax purposes shall be used for purposes of this subdivision in determining a beneficiary's actuarial interest.

**(c) Brother-sister group of trades or businesses under common control.** *(1) In general.* The term "brother-sister group of trades or businesses under common control" means two or more organizations conducting trades or businesses if (i) the same five or fewer persons who are individuals, estates, or trusts own (directly and with the application of § 1.414(c)-4) a controlling interest in each organization, and (ii) taking into account the ownership of each such person only to the extent such ownership is identical with respect to each such organization, such persons are in effective control of each organization. The five or fewer persons whose ownership is considered for purposes of the controlling interest requirement for each organization must be the same persons whose ownership is considered for purposes of the effective control requirement.

*(2) Effective control defined.* For purposes of this paragraph, persons are in "effective control" of an organization if—

(i) In the case of an organization which is a corporation, such persons own stock possessing more than 50 percent of the total combined voting power of all classes of stock entitled to vote or more than 50 percent of the total value of shares of all classes of stock of such corporation;

(ii) In the case of an organization which is a trust or estate, such persons own an aggregate actuarial interest of more than 50 percent of such trust or estate;

(iii) In the case of an organization which is a partnership, such persons own an aggregate of more than 50 percent of the profits interest or capital interest of such partnership; and

(iv) In the case of an organization which is a sole proprietorship, one of such persons owns such sole proprietorship.

**(d) Combined group of trades or businesses under common control.** The term "combined group of trades or businesses under common control" means any group of three or more organizations, if (1) each such organization is a member of either a parent-subsidiary group of trades or businesses under common control or a brother-sister group of trades or businesses under common control, and (2) at least one such organization is the common parent organization of a parent-subsidiary group of trades or businesses under common control and is also a member of a brother-sister group of trades or businesses under common control.

**(e) Examples.** The definitions of parent-subsidiary group of trades or businesses under common control, brother-sister group of trades or businesses under common control, and combined group of trades or businesses under common control may be illustrated by the following examples.

*Example (1).* (a) The ABC partnership owns stock possessing 80 percent of the total combined voting power of all classes of stock entitled to voting of S corporation. ABC partnership is the common parent of a parent-subsidiary group of trades or businesses under common control consisting of the ABC partnership and S Corporation.

(b) Assume the same facts as in (a) and assume further that S owns 80 percent of the profits interest in the DEF Partnership. The ABC Partnership is the common parent of a parent-subsidiary group of trades or businesses under common control consisting of the ABC Partnership, S Corporation, and the DEF Partnership. The result would be the same if the ABC Partnership, rather than S, owned 80 percent of the profits interest in the DEF Partnership.

*Example (2).* L Corporation owns 80 percent of the only class of stock of T Corporation, and T, in turn, owns 40 percent of the capital interest in the GHI Partnership. L also owns 80 percent of the only class of stock of N Corporation and N, in turn, owns 40 percent of the capital interest in the GHI Partnership. L is the common parent of a parent-subsidiary group of trades or businesses under common control consisting of L Corporation, T Corporation, N Corporation, and the GHI Partnership.

*Example (3).* ABC Partnership owns 75 percent of the only class of stock of X and Y Corporations; X owns all the remaining stock of Y, and Y owns all the remaining stock of X. Since interorganization ownership is excluded (that is, treated as not outstanding) for purposes of determining whether ABC owns a controlling interest of at least one of the other organizations, ABC is treated as the owner of stock possessing 100 percent of the voting power and value of all classes of stock of X and of Y for purposes of paragraph (b)(1)(ii) of this section. Therefore, ABC is the common parent of a parent-subsidiary group of trades or businesses under common control consisting of the ABC Partnership, X Corporation, and Y Corporation.

*Example (4).* Unrelated individuals A, B, C, D, E, and F own an interest in sole proprietorship A, a capital interest in the GHI Partnership, and stock of corporations M, W, X, Y, and Z (each of which has only one class of stock outstanding) in the following proportions:

**Organizations**

| Individuals | A | GHI | M | W | X | Y | Z |
|---|---|---|---|---|---|---|---|
| A ....... | 100% | 50% | 100% | 60% | 40% | 20% | 60% |
| B ....... | — | 40% | — | 15% | 40% | 50% | 30% |
| C ....... | — | — | — | — | 10% | 10% | 10% |
| D ....... | — | — | — | 25% | — | 20% | — |
| E........ | — | 10% | — | — | 10% | — | — |
| | 100% | 100% | 100% | 100% | 100% | 100% | 100% |

Under these facts the following four brother-sister groups of trades or businesses under common control exist: GHI, X and Z; X, Y, and Z; W and Y; A and M. In the case of GHI, X, and Z, for example, A and B together have effective control of each organization because their combined identical ownership of GHI, X and Z is greater than 50%. (A's identical ownership of GHI, X and Z is 40% because A owns at least a 40% interest in each organization. B's identical ownership of GHI, X and Z is 30% because B owns at least a 30% interest in each organization.) A and B (the persons whose ownership is considered for purposes of the effective control requirement) together own a controlling interest in each organization because they own at least 80% of the capital interest of partnership GHI and at least 80% of the total combined voting power of corporations X and Z. Therefore, GHI, X and Z comprise a brother-sister group of trades or businesses under common control. Y is not a member of this group because neither the effective control requirement nor the 80% controlling interest requirement are met. (The effective control requirement is not met because A's and B's combined identical ownership in GHI, X, Y and Z (20% for A and 30% for B) does not exceed 50%. The 80% controlling interest test is not met because A and B together only own 70% of the total combined voting power of the stock of Y.) A and M are not members of this group because B owns no interest in either organization and A's ownership of GHI, X and Z, considered alone, is less than 80%.

*Example (5).* The outstanding stock of corporations U and V, which have only one class of stock outstanding, is owned by the following unrelated individuals:

**Corporations**

| Individuals | U (percent) | V (percent) |
|---|---|---|
| A .................... | 12 | 12 |
| B .................... | 12 | 12 |
| C .................... | 12 | 12 |
| D .................... | 12 | 12 |
| E .................... | 13 | 13 |
| F .................... | 13 | 13 |
| G .................... | 13 | 13 |
| H .................... | 13 | 13 |
| | 100 | 100 |

Any group of five of the shareholders will own more than 50 percent of the stock in each corporation, in identical holdings. However, U and V are not members of a brother-sister group of trades or businesses under common control because at least 80 percent of the stock of each corporation is not owned by the same five or fewer persons.

*Example (6).* A, an individual, owns a controlling interest in ABC Partnership and DEF Partnership. ABC, in turn, owns a controlling interest in X Corporation. Since ABC, DEF, and X are each members of either a parent-subsidiary group or a brother-sister group of trades or businesses under common control, and ABC is the common parent of a parent-subsidiary group of trades or businesses under common control consisting of ABC and X, and also a member of a brother-sister group of trades or businesses under common control consisting of ABC and DEF, ABC Partnership, DEF Partnership, and X Corporation are members of the same combined group of trades or businesses under common control.

T.D. 8179, 3/1/88, amend T.D. 8540, 6/9/94.

### § 1.414(c)-3 Exclusion of certain interests or stock in determining control.

**(a) In general.** For purposes of § 1.414(c)-2(b)(2)(i) and (c)(2), the term "interest" and the term "stock" do not include an interest which is treated as not outstanding under paragraph (b) of this section in the case of a parent-subsidiary group of trades or businesses under common control or under paragraph (c) of this section in the case of a brother-sister group of trades or businesses under common control. In addition, the term "stock" does not include treasury stock or nonvoting stock which is limited and preferred as to dividends. For definitions of certain terms used in this section, see paragraph (d) of this section.

**(b) Parent-subsidiary group of trades or businesses under common control.** *(1) In general.* If an organization (hereinafter in this section referred to as "parent organization") owns (within the meaning of paragraph (b)(2) of this section)—

(i) In the case of a corporation, 50 percent or more of the total combined voting power of all classes of stock entitled to vote or 50 percent or more of the total value of shares of all classes of stock of such corporation.

(ii) In the case of a trust or an estate, an actuarial interest (within the meaning of § 1.414(c)-2(b)(2)(ii)) of 50 percent or more of such trust or estate, and

(iii) In the case of a partnership, 50 percent or more of the profits or capital interest of such partnership, then for purposes of determining whether the parent organization or such other organization (hereinafter in this section referred to as "subsidiary organization") is a member of a parent-subsidiary group of trades or businesses under common control, an interest in such subsidiary organization excluded under paragraph (b)(3), (4), (5), or (6) of this section shall be treated as not outstanding.

*(2) Ownership.* For purposes of paragraph (b)(1) of this section, a parent organization shall be considered to own an interest in or stock of another organization which it owns directly or indirectly with the application of § 1.414(c)-4(b)(1) and—

(i) In the case of a parent organization which is a partnership, a trust, or an estate, with the application of paragraphs (b)(2), (3), and (4) of § 1.414(c)-4, and

(ii) In the case of a parent organization which is a corporation, with the application of § 1.414(c)-4(b)(4).

*(3) Plan of deferred compensation.* An interest which is an interest in or stock of the subsidiary organization held by a trust which is part of a plan of deferred compensation (within the meaning of section 406(a)(3) and the regulations thereunder) for the benefit of the employees of the parent organization or the subsidiary organization shall be excluded.

*(4) Principal owners, officers, etc.* An interest which is an interest in or stock of the subsidiary organization owned (directly and with the application of § 1.414(c)-4) by an individual who is a principal owner, officer, partner, or fiduciary of the parent organization shall be excluded.

*(5) Employees.* An interest which is an interest in or stock of the subsidiary organization owned (directly and with the application of § 1.414(c)-4) by an employee of the subsidiary organization shall be excluded if such interest or such stock is subject to conditions which substantially restrict or limit the employee's right (or if the employee constructively owns such interest or such stock, the direct or record owner's right) to dispose of such interest or such stock and which run in favor of the parent or subsidiary organization.

*(6) Controlled exempt organization.* An interest which is an interest in or stock of the subsidiary organization shall be excluded if owned (directly and with the application of § 1.414(c)-4) by an organization (other than the parent organization):

(i) To which section 501 (relating to certain educational and charitable organizations which are exempt from tax) applies, and

(ii) Which is controlled directly or indirectly (within the meaning of paragraph (d)(7) of this section) by the parent organization or subsidiary organization, by an individual, estate, or trust that is a principal owner of the parent organization, by an officer, partner, or fiduciary of the parent organization, or by any combination thereof.

**(c) Brother-sister group of trades or businesses under common control.** *(1) In general.* If five or fewer persons (hereinafter in this section referred to as "common owners") who are individuals, estates, or trusts own (directly and with the application of § 1.414(c)-4)—

(i) In the case of a corporation, 50 percent or more of the total combined voting power of all classes of stock entitled to vote or 50 percent or more of the total value of shares of all classes of stock of such corporation,

(ii) In the case of a trust or an estate, an actuarial interest (within the meaning of § 1.414(c)-2(b)(2)(ii)) of 50 percent or more of such trust or estate, and

(iii) In the case of a partnership, 50 percent or more of the profits or capital interest of such partnership, then for purposes of determining whether such organization is a member of a brother-sister group of trades or businesses under common control, an interest in such organization excluded under paragraph (c)(2), (3), or (4) of this section shall be treated as not outstanding.

*(2) Exempt employees' trust.* An interest which is an interest in or stock of such organization held by an employees' trust described in section 401(a) which is exempt from tax under section 501(a) shall be excluded if such trust is for the benefit of the employees of such organization.

*(3) Employees.* An interest which is an interest in or stock of such organization owned (directly and with the application of § 1.414(c)-4) by an employee of such organization shall be excluded if such interest or stock is subject to conditions which run in favor of a common owner of such organization or in favor of such organization and which substantially restrict or limit the employee's right (or if the employee constructively owns such interest or stock, the direct or record owner's right) to dispose of such interest or stock.

*(4) Controlled exempt organization.* An interest which is an interest in or stock of such organization shall be excluded if owned (directly and with the application of § 1.414(c)-4) by an organization:

(i) To which section 501(c)(3) (relating to certain educational and charitable organizations which are exempt from tax) applies, and

(ii) Which is controlled directly or indirectly (within the meaning of paragraph (d)(7) of this section) by such organization, by an individual, estate, or trust that is a principal owner of such organization, by an officer, partner, or fiduciary of such organization, or by any combination thereof.

**(d) Definitions.** *(1) Employee.* For purposes of this section, the term "employee" has the same meaning such term is given in section 3306(i) of the Code (relating to definitions for purposes of the Federal Unemployment Tax Act).

*(2) Principal owner.* For purposes of this section, the term "principal owner" means a person who owns (directly and with the application of § 1.414(c)-4)—

(i) In the case of a corporation, 5 percent or more of the total combined voting power of all classes of stock entitled to vote in such corporation or 5 percent of more of the total value of shares of all classes of stock of such corporation;

(ii) In the case of a trust or estate, an actuarial interest of 5 percent or more of such trust or estate; or

(iii) In the case of a partnership, 5 percent or more of the profits or capital interest of such partnership.

*(3) Officer.* For purposes of this section, the term "officer" includes the president, vice-presidents, general manager, treasurer, secretary, and comptroller of a corporation, and any other person who performs duties corresponding to those normally performed by persons occupying such positions.

*(4) Partner.* For purposes of this section, the term "partner" means any person defined in section 7701(a)(2) (relating to definitions of partner).

*(5) Fiduciary.* For purposes of this section and § 1.414(c)-4, the term "fiduciary" has the same meaning as such term is given in section 7701(a)(6) and the regulations thereunder.

*(6) Substantial conditions.* (i) In general. For purposes of this section, an interest in or stock of an organization is subject to conditions which substantially restrict or limit the right to dispose of such interest or stock and which run in favor of another person if the condition extends directly or indirectly to such person preferential rights with respect to the acquisition of the direct owner's (or the record owner's) interest or stock. For a condition to be in favor of another person it is not necessary that such person be extended a discriminatory concession with respect to price. A right of first refusal with respect to an interest or stock in favor of another person is a condition which substantially restricts or limits the direct or record owner's right of disposition which runs in favor of such person. Further, any legally enforceable condition which prohibits the direct or record owner from

disposing of his or her interest or stock without the consent of another person will be considered to be a substantial limitation running in favor of such person.

(ii) Special rule. For purposes of paragraph (c)(3) of this section only, if a condition which restricts or limits an employee's right (or direct or record owner's right) to dispose of his or her interest or stock also applies to the interest or stock in such organization held by a common owner pursuant to a bona fide reciprocal purchase arrangement, such condition shall not be treated as a substantial limitation or restriction. An example of a reciprocal purchase arrangement is an agreement whereby a common owner and the employee are given a right of first refusal with respect to stock of the employer corporation owned by the other party. If, however, the agreement also provides that the common owner has the right to purchase the stock of the employer corporation owned by the employee in the event the corporation should discharge the employee for reasonable cause, the purchase arrangement would not be reciprocal within the meaning of this subdivision.

*(7) Control.* For purposes of paragraphs (b)(6) and (c)(4) of this section, the term "control" means control in fact. The determination of whether there exists control in fact will depend upon all of the facts and circumstances of each case, without regard to whether such control is legally enforceable and irrespective of the method by which such control is exercised or exercisable.

**(e) Examples.** The provisions of this section may be illustrated by the following examples:

*Example (1).* ABC Partnership owns 70 percent of the capital interest and of the profits interest in the DEF Partnership. The remaining capital interest and profits interest in DEF is owned as follows: 4 percent by A (a general partner in ABC), and 26 percent by D (a limited partner in ABC). ABC satisfies the 50-percent capital interest or profits interest ownership requirement of paragraph (b)(1)(iii) of this section with respect to DEF. Since A and D are partners of ABC, under paragraph (b)(4) of this section the capital and profits interests in DEF owned by A and D are treated as not outstanding for purposes of determining whether ABC and DEF are members of a parent-subsidiary group of trades or businesses under common control under § 1.414(c)-2(b). Thus, ABC is considered to own 100 percent (70 ÷ 70) of the capital interest and profits interest in DEF. Accordingly, ABC and DEF are members of a parent-subsidiary group of trades or businesses under common control.

*Example (2).* Assume the same facts as in example (1) and assume further that A owns 15 shares of the 100 shares of the only class of stock of S Corporation and DEF Partnership owns 75 shares of such stock. ABC satisfies the 50 percent stock requirement of paragraph (b)(1)(i) of this section with respect to S since ABC is considered as owning 52.5 percent (70 percent × 75 percent) of the S stock with the application of § 1.414(c)-4(b)(2). Since A is a partner of ABC, the S stock owned by A is treated as not outstanding for purposes of determining whether S is a member of a parent-subsidiary group of trades or businesses under common control. Thus, DEF Partnership is considered to own stock possessing 88.2 percent (75 ÷ 85) of the voting power and value of the S stock. Accordingly, ABC Partnership, DEF Partnership, and S Corporation are members of a parent-subsidiary group of trades or businesses under common control.

*Example (3).* ABC Partnership owns 60 percent of the only class of stock of Corporation Y. D, the president of Y, owns the remaining 40 percent of the stock of Y. D has agreed that if she offers her stock in Y for sale she will first offer the stock to ABC at a price equal to the fair market value of the stock on the first date the stock is offered for sale. Since D is an employee of Y within the meaning of section 3306(i) of the Code and her stock in Y is subject to a condition which substantially restricts or limits her right to dispose of such stock and runs in favor of ABC Partnership, under paragraph (b)(5) of this section such stock is treated as not outstanding for purposes of determining whether ABC and Y are members of a parent-subsidiary group of trades or businesses under common control. Thus, ABC Partnership is considered to own stock possessing 100 percent of the voting power and value of the stock of Y. Accordingly, ABC Partnership and Y Corporation are members of a parent-subsidiary group of trades or businesses under common control. The result would be the same if D's husband, instead of D, owned directly the 40 percent stock interest in Y and such stock was subject to a right of first refusal running in favor of ABC Partnership.

**(f) Exception.** *(1) In general.* If an interest in an organization (including stock of a corporation) is owned by a person directly or with the application of the rules of paragraph (b) of § 1.414(c)-4 and such ownership results in the membership of that organization in a group of two or more trades or businesses under common control for any period, then the interest will not be treated as an excluded interest under paragraph (b) or (c) of this section if the result of applying such provisions is that the organization is not a member of a group of two or more trades or businesses under common control for the period.

*(2) Example.* The provisions of this paragraph may be illustrated by the following example:

*Example.* Corporation P owns directly 50 of the 100 shares of the only class of stock of corporation S. A, an officer of P, owns directly 30 shares of S stock which P has an option to acquire. If, under paragraph (b)(4) of this section, the 30 shares owned directly by A are treated as not outstanding, P would be treated as owning stock possessing only 71 percent (50/70) of the total voting power and value of S stock, and S should not be a member of a parent-subsidiary group of trades or businesses under common control. However, because the 30 shares owned by A that P has an option to purchase are considered as owned by P under paragraph (b)(2) of this section, and that ownership plus P's direct ownership of 50 shares result in S's membership in a parent-subsidiary group of trades or businesses under common control for 1985, the provisions of this paragraph apply. Therefore, A's stock is not treated as an excluded interest and S is a member of a parent-subsidiary group consisting of P and S.

T.D. 8179, 3/1/88.

### § 1.414(c)-4 Rules for determining ownership.

**(a) In general.** In determining the ownership of an interest in an organization for purposes of § 1.414(c)-2 and § 1.414(c)-3, the constructive ownership rules of paragraph (b) of this section shall apply, subject to the operating rules contained in paragraph (c). For purposes of this section the term "interest" means: in the case of a corporation, stock; in the case of a trust or estate, an actuarial interest; in the case of a partnership, an interest in the profits or capital; and in the case of a sole proprietorship, the proprietorship.

**(b) Constructive ownership.** *(1) Options.* If a person has an option to acquire any outstanding interest in an organization, such interest shall be considered as owned by such person. For this purpose, an option to acquire an option, and each one of a series of such options shall be considered as an option to acquire such interest.

*(2) Attribution from partnerships.* (i) General. An interest owned, directly or indirectly, by or for a partnership shall be considered as owned by any partner having an interest of 5 percent or more in either the profits or capital of the partnership in proportion to such partner's interest in the profits or capital, whichever such proportion is greater.

(ii) Example. The provisions of paragraph (b)(2)(i) of this section may be illustrated by the following example:

*Example.* A, B, and C, unrelated individuals, are partners in the ABC Partnership. The partners' interest in the capital and profits of ABC are as follows:

| Partner | Capital (In percent) | Profits (In percent) |
|---|---|---|
| A | 36 | 25 |
| B | 60 | 71 |
| C | 4 | 4 |

The ABC Partnership owns the entire outstanding stock (100 shares) of X Corporation. Under paragraph (b)(2)(i) of this section, A is considered to own the stock of X owned by the partnership in proportion to his interest in capital (36 percent) or profits (25 percent), whichever such proportion is greater. Therefore, A is considered to own 36 shares of X stock. Since B has a greater interest in the profits of the partnership than in the capital, B is considered to own X stock in proportion to his interest in such profits. Therefore, B is considered to own 71 shares of X stock. Since C does not have an interest of 5 percent or more in either the capital or profits of ABC, he is not considered to own any shares of X stock.

*(3) Attribution from estates and trusts.* (i) In general. An interest in an organization (hereinafter called an "organization interest") owned, directly or indirectly, by or for an estate or trust shall be considered as owned by any beneficiary of such estate or trust who has an actuarial interest of 5 percent or more in such organization interest, to the extent of such actuarial interest. For purposes of this subparagraph, the actuarial interest of each beneficiary shall be determined by assuming the maximum exercise of discretion by the fiduciary in favor of such beneficiary and the maximum use of the organization interest to satisfy the beneficiary's rights. A beneficiary of an estate or trust who cannot under any circumstances receive any part of an organization interest held by the estate or trust, including the proceeds from the disposition thereof, or the income therefrom, does not have an actuarial interest in such organization interest. Thus, where stock owned by a decedent's estate has been specifically bequeathed to certain beneficiaries and the remainder of the estate has been specifically bequeathed to other beneficiaries, the stock is attributable only to the beneficiaries to whom it is specifically bequeathed. Similarly a remainderman of a trust who cannot under any circumstances receive any interest in the stock of a corporation which is a part of the corpus of the trust (including any accumulated income therefrom or the proceeds from a disposition thereof) does not have an actuarial interest in such stock. However, an income beneficiary of a trust does have an actuarial interest in stock if he has any right to the income from such stock even though under the terms of the trust instrument such stock can never be distributed to him. The factors and methods prescribed in § 20.2031-7 or, for certain prior periods, § 20.2031-7A (Estate Tax Regulations) for use in ascertaining the value of an interest in property for estate tax purposes shall be used for purposes of this subdivision in determining a beneficiary's actuarial interest in an organization interest owned directly or indirectly by or for an estate or trust.

(ii) Special rules for estates. (A) For purposes of this paragraph (b)(3) with respect to an estate, property of a decedent shall be considered as owned by his or her estate if such property is subject to administration by the executor or administrator for the purposes of paying claims against the estate and expenses of administration notwithstanding that, under local law, legal title to such property vests in the decedent's heirs, legatees or devisees immediately upon death.

(B) For purposes of this paragraph (b)(3) with respect to an estate, the term "beneficiary" includes any person entitled to receive property of a decedent pursuant to a will or pursuant to laws of descent and distribution.

(C) For purposes of this paragraph (b)(3) with respect to an estate, a person shall no longer be considered a beneficiary of an estate when all the property to which he or she is entitled has been received by him or her, when he or she no longer has a claim against the estate arising out of having been a beneficiary, and when there is only a remote possibility that it will be necessary for the estate to seek the return of property from him or her or to seek payment from him or her by contribution or otherwise to satisfy claims against the estate or expenses of administration.

(iii) Grantor trusts, etc. An interest owned, directly or indirectly, by or for any portion of a trust of which a person is considered the owner under subpart E, part I, subchapter J of the Code (relating to grantors and others treated as substantial owners) is considered as owned by such person.

*(4) Attribution from corporations.* (i) General. An interest owned, directly or indirectly, by or for a corporation shall be considered as owned by any person who owns (directly and, in the case of a parent-subsidiary group of trades or businesses under common control, with the application of paragraph (b)(1) of this section, or in the case of a brother-sister group of trades or business under common control, with the application of this section), 5 percent or more in value of the stock in that proportion which the value of the stock which such person so owns bears to the total value of all the stock in such corporation.

(ii) Example. The provisions of paragraph (b)(4)(i) of this section may be illustrated by the following example:

*Example.* B, an individual, owns 60 of the 100 shares of the only class of outstanding stock of corporation P. C, an individual, owns 4 shares of the P stock, and corporation X owns 36 shares of the P stock. Corporation P owns, directly and indirectly, 50 shares of the stock of corporation S. Under this subparagraph, B is considered to own 30 shares of the S stock ($60/100 \times 50$), and X is considered to own 18 shares of S stock ($36/100 \times 50$). Since C does not own 5 percent or more in the value of P stock, he is not considered as owning any of the S stock owned by P. If in this example, C's wife had owned directly 1 share of the P stock, C and his wife would each be considered as owning 5 shares of the P stock, and therefore C and his wife would be considered as owning 2.5 shares of the S stock ($5/100 \times 50$).

*(5) Spouse.* (i) General rule. Except as provided in paragraph (b)(5)(ii) of this section, an individual shall be considered to own an interest owned, directly or indirectly, by or for his or her spouse, other than a spouse who is legally separated from the individual under a decree of divorce,

whether interlocutory or final, or a decree of separate maintenance.

(ii) Exception. An individual shall not be considered to own an interest in an organization owned, directly or indirectly, by or for his or her spouse on any day of a taxable year of such organization, provided that each of the following conditions are satisfied with respect to such taxable year:

(A) Such individual does not, at any time during such taxable year, own directly any interest in such organization;

(B) Such individual is not a member of the board of directors, a fiduciary, or an employee of such organization and does not participate in the management of such organization at any time during such taxable year;

(C) Not more than 50 percent of such organization's gross income for such taxable year was derived from royalties, rents, dividends, interest, and annuities; and

(D) Such interest in such organization is not, at any time during such taxable year, subject to conditions which substantially restrict or limit the spouse's right to dispose of such interest and which run in favor of the individual or the individual's children who have not attained the age of 21 years. The principles of § 1.414(c)-3(d)(6)(i) shall apply in determining whether a condition is a condition described in the preceding sentence.

(iii) Definitions. For purposes of paragraph (b)(5)(ii)(C) of this section, the gross income of an organization shall be determined under section 61 and the regulations thereunder. The terms "interest", "royalties", "rents", "dividends", and "annuities" shall have the same meaning such terms are given for purposes of section 1244(c) and § 1.1244(c)-1(e)(1).

*(6) Children, grandchildren, parents, and grandparents.* (i) Children and parents. An individual shall be considered to own an interest owned, directly or indirectly, by or for the individual's children who have not attained the age of 21 years, and if the individual has not attained the age of 21 years, an interest owned, directly or indirectly, by or for the individual's parents.

(ii) Children, grandchildren, parents, and grandparents. If an individual is in effective control (within the meaning of § 1.414(c)-2(c)(2)), directly and with the application of the rules of this paragraph without regard to this subdivision, of an organization, then such individual shall be considered to own an interest in such organization owned, directly or indirectly, by or for the individual's parents, grandparents, grandchildren, and children who have attained the age of 21 years.

(iii) Adopted children. For purposes of this section, a legally adopted child of an individual shall be treated as a child of such individual.

(iv) Example. The provisions of this subparagraph (6) may be illustrated by the following example:

*Example.* (A) Facts. Individual F owns directly 40 percent of the profits interest of the DEF Partnership. His son, M, 20 years of age, owns directly 30 percent of the profits interest of DEF, and his son, A, 30 years of age, owns directly 20 percent of the profits interest of DEF. The 10 percent remaining of the profits interest and 100 percent of the capital interest of DEF is owned by an unrelated person.

(B) F's ownership. F owns 40 percent of the profits interest in DEF directly and is considered to own the 30 percent profits interest owned directly by M. Since, for purposes of the effective control test contained in paragraph (b)(6)(ii) of this section, F is treated as owning 70 percent of the profits interest of DEF, F is also considered as owning the 20 percent profits interest of DEF owned by his adult son, A. Accordingly, F is considered as owning a total of 90 percent of the profits interest in DEF.

(C) M's ownership. Minor son, M. owns 30 percent of the profits interest in DEF directly, and is considered to own the 40 percent profits interest owned directly by his father, F. However, M is not considered to own the 20 percent profits interest of DEF owned directly by his brother, A, and constructively by F because an interest constructively owned by F by reason of family attribution is not considered as owned by him for purposes of making another member of his family the constructive owner of such interest. (See paragraph (c)(2) of this section.) Accordingly, M is considered as owning a total of 70 percent of the profits interest of the DEF Partnership.

(D) A's ownership. Adult son, A, owns 20 percent of the profits interest in DEF directly. Since, for purposes of determining whether A effectively controls DEF under paragraph (b)(6)(ii) of this section, A is treated as owning only the percentage of profits interest he owns directly, he does not satisfy the condition precedent for the attribution of the DEF profits interest from his father. Accordingly, A is considered as owning only the 20 percent profits interest in DEF which he owns directly.

**(c) Operating rules.** *(1) In general.* Except as provided in paragraph (c)(2) of this section, an interest constructively owned by a person by reason of the application of paragraph (b)(1), (2), (3), (4), (5), or (6) of this section shall, for the purposes of applying such paragraph, be treated as actually owned by such person.

*(2) Members of family.* An interest constructively owned by an individual by reason of the application of paragraph (b)(5) or (6) of this section shall not be treated as owned by such individual for purposes of again applying such subparagraphs in order to make another the constructive owner of such interest.

*(3) Precedence of option attribution.* For purposes of this section, if an interest may be considered as owned under paragraph (b)(1) of this section (relating to option attribution) and under any other subparagraph of paragraph (b) of this section, such interest shall be considered as owned by such person under paragraph (b)(1) of this section.

*(4) Examples.* The provisions of this paragraph may be illustrated by the following examples:

*Example (1).* A, 30 years of age, has a 90 percent interest in the capital and profits of DEF Partnership. DEF owns all the outstanding stock of corporation X and X owns 60 shares of the 100 outstanding shares of corporation Y. Under paragraph (c)(1) of this section, the 60 shares of Y constructively owned by DEF by reason of paragraph (b)(4) of this section are treated as actually owned by DEF for purposes of applying paragraph (b)(2) of this section. Therefore, A is considered as owning 54 shares of the Y stock (90 percent of 60 shares).

*Example (2).* Assume the same facts as in example (1). Assume further that B, who is 20 years of age and the brother of A, directly owns 40 shares of Y stock. Although the stock of Y owned by B is considered as owned by C (the father of A and B) under paragraph (b)(6)(i) of this section, under paragraph (c)(2) of this section such stock may not be treated as owned by C for purposes of applying paragraph (b)(6)(ii) of this section in order to make A the constructive owner of such stock.

*Example (3).* Assume the same facts as in example (2), and further assume that C has an option to acquire the 40 shares of Y stock owned by his son, B. The rule contained in paragraph (c)(2) of this section does not prevent the reattribution of such 40 shares to A because, under paragraph (c)(3) of this section, C is considered as owning the 40 shares by reason of option attribution and not by reason of family attribution. Therefore, since A is in effective control of Y under paragraph (b)(6)(ii) of this section, the 40 shares of Y stock constructively owned by C are reattributed to A. A is considered as owning a total of 94 shares of Y stock.

T.D. 8179, 3/1/88, amend T.D. 8540, 6/9/94.

## § 1.414(c)-5 Certain tax-exempt organizations.

**(a) Application.** This section applies to an organization that is exempt from tax under section 501(a). The rules of this section only apply for purposes of determining when entities are treated as the same employer for purposes of section 414(b), (c), (m), and (o) (including the sections referred to in section 414(b), (c), (m), (o), and (t)), and are in addition to the rules otherwise applicable under section 414(b), (c), (m), and (o) for determining when entities are treated as the same employer. Except to the extent set forth in paragraphs (d), (e), and (f) of this section, this section does not apply to any church, as defined in section 3121(w)(3)(A), or any qualified church-controlled organization, as defined in section 3121(w)(3)(B).

**(b) General rule.** In the case of an organization that is exempt from tax under section 501(a) (an exempt organization) whose employees participate in a plan, the employer with respect to that plan includes the exempt organization whose employees participate in the plan and any other organization that is under common control with that exempt organization. For this purpose, common control exists between an exempt organization and another organization if at least 80 percent of the directors or trustees of one organization are either representatives of, or directly or indirectly controlled by, the other organization. A trustee or director is treated as a representative of another exempt organization if he or she also is a trustee, director, agent, or employee of the other exempt organization. A trustee or director is controlled by another organization if the other organization has the general power to remove such trustee or director and designate a new trustee or director. Whether a person has the power to remove or designate a trustee or director is based on facts and circumstances. To illustrate the rules of this paragraph (b), if exempt organization A has the power to appoint at least 80 percent of the trustees of exempt organization B (which is the owner of the outstanding shares of corporation C, which is not an exempt organization) and to control at least 80 percent of the directors of exempt organization D, then, under this paragraph (b) and § 1.414(b)-1, entities A, B, C, and D are treated as the same employer with respect to any plan maintained by A, B, C, or D for purposes of the sections referenced in section 414(b), (c), (m), (o), and (t).

**(c) Permissive aggregation with entities having a common exempt purpose.** *(1) General rule.* For purposes of this section, exempt organizations that maintain a plan to which section 414(c) applies that covers one or more employees from each organization may treat themselves as under common control for purposes of section 414(c) (and, thus, as a single employer for all purposes for which section 414(c) applies) if each of the organizations regularly coordinates their day-to-day exempt activities. For example, an entity that provides a type of emergency relief within one geographic region and another exempt organization that provides that type of emergency relief within another geographic region may treat themselves as under common control if they have a single plan covering employees of both entities and regularly coordinate their day-to-day exempt activities. Similarly, a hospital that is an exempt organization and another exempt organization with which it coordinates the delivery of medical services or medical research may treat themselves as under common control if there is a single plan covering employees of the hospital and employees of the other exempt organization and the coordination is a regular part of their day-to-day exempt activities.

*(2) Authority to permit aggregation.* (i) For determining when entities are treated as the same employer under section 414(b), (c), (m), and (o), the Commissioner may issue rules of general applicability, in revenue rulings, notices, or other guidance published in the Internal Revenue Bulletin (see § 601.601(d)(2)(ii)(b) of this chapter), permitting other types of combinations of entities that include exempt organizations to elect to be treated as under common control for one or more specified purposes if-

(A) There are substantial business reasons for maintaining each entity in a separate trust, corporation, or other form; and

(B) Such treatment would be consistent with the anti-abuse standards in paragraph (f) of this section.

(ii) For example, this authority might be exercised in any situation in which the organizations are so integrated in their operations as to effectively constitute a single coordinated employer for purposes of section 414(b), (c), (m), and (o), including common employee benefit plans.

**(d) Permissive disaggregation between qualified church controlled organizations and other entities.** In the case of a church plan (as defined in section 414(e)) to which contributions are made by more than one common law entity, any employer may apply paragraphs (b) and (c) of this section to those entities that are not a church (as defined in section 403(b)(12)(B) and § 1.403(b) 2) separately from those entities that are churches. For example, in the case of a group of entities consisting of a church (as defined in section 3121(w)(3)(A)), a secondary school (that is treated as a church under § 1.403(b) 2), and several nursing homes each of which receives more than 25 percent of its support from fees paid by residents (so that none of them is a qualified church-controlled organization under § 1.403(b) 2 and section 3121(w)(3)(B)), the nursing homes may treat themselves as being under common control with each other, but not as being under common control with the church and the school, even though the nursing homes would be under common control with the school and the church under paragraph (b) of this section.

**(e) Application to certain church entities under section 3121(w)(3).** [Reserved].

**(f) Anti-abuse rule.** In any case in which the Commissioner determines that the structure of one or more exempt organizations (which may include an exempt organization and an entity that is not exempt from income tax) or the positions taken by those organizations has the effect of avoiding or evading any requirements imposed under section 401(a), 403(b), or 457(b), or any applicable section (as defined in section 414(t)), or any other provision for which section 414(c) applies, the Commissioner may treat an entity as under common control with the exempt organization.

**(g) Examples.** The provisions of this section are illustrated by the following examples:

*Example (1).* (i) Facts. Organization A is a tax-exempt organization under section 501(c)(3) which owns 80% or more of the total value of all classes of stock of corporation B, which is a for profit organization.

(ii) Conclusion. Under paragraph (a) of this section, this section does not alter the rules of section 414(b) and (c), so that organization A and corporation B are under common control under § 1.414(c)-2(b).

*Example (2).* (i) Facts. Organization M is a hospital which is a tax-exempt organization under section 501(c)(3) and organization N is a medical clinic which is also a tax-exempt organization under section 501(c)(3). N is located in a city and M is located in a nearby suburb. There is a history of regular coordination of day-to-day activities between M and N, including periodic transfers of staff, coordination of staff training, common sources of income, and coordination of budget and operational goals. A single section 403(b) plan covers professional and staff employees of both the hospital and the medical clinic. While a number of members of the board of directors of M are also on the board of directors of N, there is less than 80% overlap in board membership. Both organizations have approximately the same percentage of employees who are highly compensated and have appropriate business reasons for being maintained in separate entities.

(ii) Conclusion. M and N are not under common control under this section, but, under paragraph (c) of this section, may chose to treat themselves as under common control, assuming both of them act in a manner that is consistent with that choice for purposes of § 1.403(b)-5(a), sections 401(a), 403(b), and 457(b), and any other applicable section (as defined in section 414(t)), or any other provision for which section 414(c) applies.

*Example (3).* (i) Facts. Organizations O and P are each tax-exempt organizations under section 501(c)(3). Each organization maintains a qualified plan for it employees, but one of the plans would not satisfy section 410(b) (or section 401(a)(4)) if the organizations were under common control. The two organizations are closely related and, while the organizations have several trustees in common, the common trustees constitute fewer than 80 percent of the trustees of either organization. Organization O has the power to remove any of the trustees of P and to select the slate of replacement nominees.

(ii) Conclusion. Under these facts, pursuant to paragraphs (b) and (f) of this section, the Commissioner treats the entities as under common control.

**(h) Applicable date.** This section applies for plan years beginning after December 31, 2008.

T.D. 9340, 7/23/2007.

### § 1.414(c)-6 Effective date.

**(a) General rule.** Except as provided in paragraph (b), (c), (e), or (f) of this section, the provisions of § 1.414(b)-1 and §§ 1.414(c)-1 through 1.414(c)-4 shall apply for plan years beginning after September 2, 1974.

**(b) Existing plans.** In the case of a plan in existence on January 1, 1974, unless paragraph (c) of this section applies, the provisions of § 1.414(b)-1 and §§ 1.414(c)-1 through 1.414(c)-4 shall apply for plan years beginning after December 31, 1975. For definition of the term "existing plan", see § 1.410(a)-2(c).

**(c) Existing plans electing new provisions.** In the case of a plan in existence on January 1, 1974, for which the plan administrator makes an election under § 1.410(a)-2(d), the provisions of § 1.414(b)-1 and §§ 1.414(c)-1 through 1.414(c)-4 shall apply to the plan years elected under § 1.410(a)-2(d).

**(d) Application.** For purposes of the Employee Retirement Income Security Act of 1974, the provisions of § 1.414(b)-1 and §§ 1.414(c)-1 through 1.414(c)-4 do not apply for any period of time before the plan years described in paragraph (a), (b), or (c) of this section, whichever is applicable.

**(e) Special rule.** Notwithstanding paragraph (a), (b), or (c) of this section, § 1.414(c)-3(f) is effective April 1, 1988.

**(f) Transitional rule.** *(1) In general.* The amendments made by T.D. 8179 apply to the plan years or period described in paragraphs (a), (b), or (c) of this section, whichever is applicable.

*(2) Exception.* In the case of a plan year or period beginning before March 2, 1988, if an organization—

(i) Is a member of a brother-sister group of trades or businesses under common control under § 11.414(c)-2(c), as in effect before removal by T.D. 8179 ("old group"), for such plan year or period, and

(ii) Is not such a member for such plan year or period because of the amendments made by such Treasury decision,

such member (whether or not a corporation) nevertheless will be treated as a member of such old group for purposes of section 414(c) for that plan year or period to the extent provided in § 1.1563-1(d)(2). Also, such member will be treated as a member of an old group for all purposes of the Code for such plan year or period if all the organizations (whether or not corporations) that are members of the old group meet all the requirements of § 1.1563-1(d)(3) with respect to such plan year or period.

T.D. 8179, 3/1/88, amend T.D. 9340, 7/23/2007.

### § 1.414(e)-1 Definition of church plan.

***Caution:*** The Treasury has not yet amended Reg § 1.414(e)-1 to reflect changes made by P.L. 105-34.

**(a) General rule.** For the purposes of part I of subchapter D of chapter 1 of the Code and the regulations thereunder, the term "church plan" means a plan established and at all times maintained for its employees by a church or by a convention or association of churches (hereinafter included within the term "church") which is exempt from tax under section 501(a), provided that such plan meets the requirements of paragraphs (b) and (if applicable) (c) of this section. If at any time during its existence a plan is not a church plan because of a failure to meet the requirements set forth in this section, it cannot thereafter become a church plan.

**(b) Unrelated businesses.** *(1) In general.* A plan is not a church plan unless it is established and maintained primarily for the benefit of employees (or their beneficiaries) who are not employed in connection with one or more unrelated trades or businesses (within the meaning of section 513).

*(2) Establishment or maintenance of a plan primarily for persons not employed in connection with one or more unrelated trades or businesses.* (i) (A) A plan, other than a plan in existence on September 2, 1974, is established primarily for the benefit of employees (or their beneficiaries) who are

not employed in connection with one or more unrelated trades or businesses if on the date the plan is established the number of employees employed in connection with the unrelated trades or businesses eligible to participate in the plan is less than 50 percent of the total number of employees of the church eligible to participate in the plan.

(B) A plan in existence on September 2, 1974, is to be considered established as a plan primarily for the benefit of employees (or their beneficiaries) who are not employed in connection with one or more unrelated trades or businesses if it meets the requirements of both paragraphs (b)(2)(ii)(A) and (B) (if applicable) in either of its first 2 plan years ending after September 2, 1974.

(ii) For plan years ending after September 2, 1974, a plan will be considered maintained primarily for the benefit of employees of a church who are not employed in connection with one or more unrelated trades or businesses if in 4 out of 5 of its most recently completed plan years—

(A) Less than 50 percent of the persons participating in the plan (at any time during the plan year) consist of and in the same year

(B) Less than 50 percent of the total compensation paid by the employer during the plan year (if benefits or contributions are a function of compensation) to employees participating in the plan is paid to,

employees employed in connection with an unrelated trade or business. The determination that the plan is not a church plan will apply to the second year (within a 5 year period) for which the plan fails to meet paragraph (b)(2)(ii)(A) or (B) (if applicable) and to all plan years thereafter unless, taking into consideration all of the facts and circumstances as described in paragraph (b)(2)(iii) of this section, the plan is still considered to be a church plan. A plan that has not completed 5 plan years ending after September 2, 1974, shall be considered maintained primarily for the benefit of employees not employed in connection with an unrelated trade or business unless it fails to meet paragraphs (b)(2)(ii)(A) and (B) in at least 2 such plan years.

(iii) Even though a plan does not meet the provisions of paragraph (b)(2)(ii) of this section, it nonetheless will be considered maintained primarily for the benefit of employees who are not employed in connection with one or more unrelated trades or businesses if the church maintaining the plan can demonstrate that based on all of the facts and circumstances such is the case. Among the facts and circumstances to be considered in evaluating each case are:

(A) The margin by which the plan fails to meet the provisions of paragraph (b)(2)(ii) of this section, and

(B) Whether the failure to meet such provisions was due to a reasonable mistake as to what constituted an unrelated trade or business or whether a particular person or group of persons were employed in connection with one or more unrelated trades or businesses.

(iv) For purposes of this section, an employee will be considered eligible to participate in a plan if such employee is a participant in the plan or could be a participant in the plan upon making mandatory employee contributions to the plan.

*(3) Employment in connection with one or more unrelated trades or businesses.* An employee is employed in connection with one or more unrelated trades or businesses of a church if a majority of such employee's duties and responsibilities in the employ of the church are directly or indirectly related to the carrying on of such trades or businesses. Although an employee's duties and responsibilities may be insignificant with respect to any one unrelated trade or business, such employee will nonetheless be considered as employed in connection with one or more unrelated trades or businesses if such employee's duties and responsibilities with respect to all of the unrelated trades or businesses of the church represent a majority of the total of such person's duties and responsibilities in the employ of the church.

**(c) Plans of two or more employers.** The term "church plan" does not include a plan which, during the plan year, is maintained by two or more employers unless—

*(1)* Each of the employers is a church that is exempt from tax under section 501(a), and

*(2)* With respect to the employees of each employer, the plan meets the provisions of paragraph (b)(2)(ii) of this section or would be determined to be a church plan based on all the facts and circumstances described in paragraph (b)(2)(iii) of this section. Thus, if with respect to a single employer the plan fails to meet any provision of this paragraph, the entire plan ceases to be a church plan unless that employer ceases maintaining the plan for all plan years beginning after the plan year in which it receives a final notification from the Internal Revenue Service that it does not meet the provisions of this paragraph. If the employer does cease maintaining the plan in accordance with this paragraph, the fact that the employer formerly did maintain the plan will not prevent the plan from being a church plan for prior years.

**(d) Special rule.** *(1)* Notwithstanding paragraph (c)(1) of this section, a plan maintained by a church and one or more agencies of such church for the employees of such church and of such agency or agencies, that is in existence on January 1, 1974, shall be treated as a church plan for plan years ending after September 2, 1974, and beginning before January 1, 1983, provided that the plan is described in paragraph (c) of this section without regard to paragraph (c)(1) of this section, and the plan is not maintained by an agency which did not maintain the plan on January 1, 1974.

*(2)* For the purposes of section 414(e) and this section, an agency of a church means an organization which is exempt from tax under section 501 and which is either controlled by, or associated with, a church. For example, an organization, a majority of whose officers or directors are appointed by a church's governing board or by officials of a church, is controlled by a church within the meaning of this paragraph. An organization is associated with a church if it shares common religious bonds and convictions with that church.

**(e) Religious orders and religious organizations.** For the purpose of this section the term "church" includes a religious order or a religious organization if such order or organization (1) is an integral part of a church, and (2) is engaged in carrying out the functions of a church, whether as a civil law corporation or otherwise.

**(f) Separately incorporated fiduciaries.** A plan which otherwise meets the provisions of this section shall not lose its status as a church plan because of the fact that it is administered by a separately incorporated fiduciary such as a pension board or a bank.

**(g) Cross reference.** *(1)* For rules relating to treatment of church plans, see section 410(c), 411(e), 412(h), 4975(g), and the regulations thereunder.

*(2)* For rules relating to church plan elections, see section 410(d) and the regulations thereunder.

---

T.D. 7688, 3/28/80.

---

## § 1.414(f)-1 Definition of multiemployer plan.

**(a) General rule.** For purposes of part 1 of subchapter D of chapter 1 of the Code and the regulations thereunder, a plan is a multiemployer plan for a plan year if all of the following requirements are satisfied:

*(1) Number of contributing employers.* More than one employer is required by the plan instrument or other agreement to contribute (or to have contributions made on its behalf) to the plan for the plan year.

*(2) Collective bargaining agreement.* The plan is maintained for the plan year pursuant to one or more collective bargaining agreements between employee representatives and more than one employer.

*(3) Amount of contributions.* Except as provided by paragraph (c) of this section (relating to the special rule for contributions exceeding 50 percent), the amount of contributions made under the plan for the plan year by or on behalf of each employer is less than 50 percent of the total amount of contributions made under the plan for such plan year by or on behalf of all employers.

*(4) Benefits.* The plan provides that the amount of benefits payable with respect to each employee participating in the plan is determined without regard to whether or not his employer continues as a member of the plan. If benefits accrued as a result of the participant's service with his employer during a period before such employer was a member of the plan, this requirement does not apply to the amount of those benefits, except that this requirement does apply to the amount of those benefits (i) which are accrued benefits derived from employee contributions, or (ii) which are accrued under a plan maintained by an employer prior to the time such employer became a member of the plan to which the requirements of this paragraph (a) are applied.

*(5) Other requirements.* The plan satisfies such other requirements as the Secretary of Labor by regulations prescribes under the authority of section 414(f)(1)(E) of the Code and section 3(37) of the Employee Retirement Income Security Act of 1974 (Pub. L. 93-406, 88 Stat. 839). See 29 CFR 2510.3-37.

**(b) Special rules.** *(1) Amount of contributions.* For purposes of paragraphs (a)(3) and (c) of this section, the amount of contributions made under the plan for the plan year by or on behalf of each employer shall be the sum of such contributions made on or before the last day of the plan year. For purposes of determining whether contributions are made on or before the last day of the plan year, the rule of section 412(c)(10) and the regulations thereunder (relating to the treatment of certain contributions made after the last day of the plan year as made on such last day) shall apply.

*(2) Benefits.* (i) For purposes of paragraph (a)(4) of this section, certain benefit amounts are treated as accrued as a result of the participant's service with an employer during a period before such employer was a member of the plan. The amount of such a benefit so treated is the difference (if any) between two calculated amounts. The first calculated amount is the participant's total accrued benefit calculated under the plan as of the date the employer ceased to be a member of the plan. The second calculated amount is the participant's accrued benefit calculated without regard to his service with such employer during the period before such employer was a member of the plan. However, under a special limitation, this difference may not exceed the benefit a participant accrued from service before his employer became a member of the plan. For purposes of this limitation, this benefit is the benefit accrued as of the date the employer ceases to be a member of the plan. An employer shall be deemed to be a member of the plan in a plan year if the employer is required by the plan instrument or other agreement to contribute (or to have contributions made on its behalf) to the plan for such plan year or if an employee of the employer accrues a benefit, on account of service with the employer during such plan year, under the plan for that plan year.

(ii) The provisions of paragraphs (a)(4) and (b)(2)(i) of this section are illustrated by the following example:

*Example.* On January 1, 1976, employer W became a member of the noncontributory XYZ pension plan which uses the calendar year as the plan year. W did not maintain any plan prior to that date. The plan provided for benefits of $4 per month per year of service (including service with W before January 1, 1976). On January 1, 1980, following adoption of a new collective bargaining agreement, the benefits were increased to $12 per month per year of service for all years of service (including service with W before January 1, 1976). On January 1, 1991, W ceased to be a member of the plan.

A, an employee of W, had 15 years of service before January 1, 1976, 4 years of service between January 1, 1976, and December 31, 1979, and 11 years of service between January 1, 1980, and December 31, 1990. On December 31, 1990, A's accrued benefit was $360 per month ($12 per month x 30). On January 1, 1991, the portion of A's accrued benefit retained and the portion forfeited under the terms of the XYZ pension plan were determined as follows:

| Years | Monthly accrued benefit retained | Monthly accrued benefit |
|---|---|---|
| Before Jan. 1, 1976 | | $12 × 15 years = $180 |
| Jan. 1, 1976 to Dec. 31, 1979 | $ 4 × 4 years = $16 | $ 8 × 4 years = $32 |
| Jan. 1, 1980 to Dec. 31, 1990 | $12 × 11 years = $132 | |
| Total | $ 148 | $ 212 |

The XYZ plan does not satisfy the requirements of paragraphs (a)(4) and (b)(2)(i) of this section because no benefit can be forfeited with respect to service after W began participating in the plan. Thus, the maximum accrued benefit that may be forfeited is $180 per month (the accrued benefit with respect to A's service prior to January 1, 1976). Therefore, in order for the plan to meet the requirements of paragraphs (a)(4) and (b)(2)(i) of this section, the plan must provide for A's accrued benefit after W ceased to be a member of the plan to be at least $180 per month ($360 per month total accrued benefit less $180 per month benefit accrued for service prior to W's membership in the plan).

(iii) For purposes of paragraphs (a)(4) and (b)(2) of this section, if an employer for a period employs two or more individuals who, solely by reason of their employment, are participants in the plan and who do not belong to the same collective bargaining unit, the dates on which the employer became and ceased to be a member of the plan shall be determined separately on a class basis for individuals who belong to separate collective bargaining units, as separate classes, and for individuals who do not belong to a collective bargaining unit, as a further single separate class. Thus, such dates shall be determined with respect to individuals as a class who belong to the same collective bargaining unit (or who do not belong to a collective bargaining unit) without consideration of the employment by the employer of, or the participation in the plan by, other individuals (who do not belong to such collective bargaining unit and who may belong to another collective bargaining unit) or whether the employer is a member of the plan with respect to such other individuals. In no event, however, may service not attributable to service with a particular collective bargaining unit be disregarded under paragraphs (a)(4) and (b)(2) of this section merely because the employer ceases to maintain the plan with respect to such unit. Thus, for example, paragraphs (a)(4) and (b)(2) of this section do not permit the disregard of a period of service of an individual belonging to a collective bargaining unit prior to the time the employer became a member of the plan with respect to such unit to the extent that, during such period of service, the individual belonged to another collective bargaining unit with respect to which the employer was a member of the plan.

*(3) Controlled groups.* For purposes of section 414(f) and this section, all corporations which are members of a controlled group of corporations (within the meaning of section 1563(a) and the regulations thereunder, but determined without regard to section 1563(e)(3)(C) and the regulations thereunder) are deemed to be one employer.

**(c) Contributions exceeding 50 percent.** If a plan was a multiemployer plan as defined in this section for any plan year (including plan years ending prior to September 3, 1974), "75 percent" shall be substituted for "50 percent" in applying paragraph (a)(3) of this section for subsequent plan years until the first plan year following a plan year in which the amount contributed by or on behalf of one employer is 75 percent or more of the total amount of contributions made under the plan for that plan year by or on behalf of all of the employers making contributions. In such case "75 percent" shall not again be substituted for "50 percent" until the plan has met the requirements of paragraph (a) of this section (determined without regard to this paragraph) for one plan year.

**(d) Examples.** The application of this section is illustrated by the following examples. For purposes of these examples, assume that the plan meets the requirements of paragraphs (a)(1), (2), (4), and (5) of this section for each plan year.

*Example (1).* On January 1, 1970, U, V, and W, three employers none of which is a member of a controlled group of corporations with any of the other two employers, establish a plan with a plan year corresponding to the calendar year. U, V, and W each contribute less than one-half of the total contributions made under the plan for each of the years 1970, 1971, and 1972. For the years 1973, 1974, and 1975, U contributes 70 percent and V and W each contribute 15 percent of the total contributions made under the plan for each year. The plan is a multiemployer plan under section 414(f) and this section for 1975 because no employer has contributed 75 percent or more of the total amount contributed for each of the plan years subsequent to 1972.

*Example (2).* (i) First plan year. On January 1, 1975, X, Y, and Z, three employers none of which is a member of a controlled group of corporations with any of the other two employers, establish a plan with a plan year corresponding to the calendar year. X, Y, and Z each contribute less than one-half of the total contributions made under the plan for 1975. The plan is a multiemployer plan for 1975 because it meets the 50 percent contribution requirement of paragraph (a)(3) of this section.

(ii) Second plan year. For the second plan year, 1976, X contributes 70 percent and Y and Z each contribute 15 percent of the total contributions made under the plan. The plan is a multiemployer plan for 1976 because it was a multiemployer plan for the preceding plan year and satisfies the 75 percent contribution requirement of paragraph (c) of this section.

(iii) Third plan year. For the third plan year, 1977, X contributes 80 percent and Y and Z each contribute 10 percent of the total contributions made under the plan. The plan is not a multiemployer plan for 1977 because it fails to satisfy the 75 percent contribution requirement of paragraph (c) of this section.

(iv) Fourth plan year. For the fourth plan year, 1978, Y contributes 60 percent and X and Z each contribute 20 percent of the total contributions made under the plan. The 75 percent contribution requirement of paragraph (c) of this section does not apply. The plan is not a multiemployer plan for 1978 because it fails to satisfy the 50 percent contribution requirement of paragraph (a)(3) of this section.

(v) Fifth plan year. For the fifth plan year, 1979, X, Y, and Z each contribute less than one-half of the total contributions made under the plan. The 75 percent contribution requirement of paragraph (c) of this section does not apply. The plan is a multiemployer plan for 1979 because it again meets the 50 percent contribution requirement of paragraph (a)(3) of this section.

(vi) Sixth plan year. For the sixth plan year, 1980, the plan will continue to be a multiemployer plan, provided that no employer contributes 75 percent or more of the total amount of contributions made under the plan for the plan year.

**(e) Retention of records.** *(1)* For plan years ending prior to September 3, 1974, a plan may be required to furnish proof that it met the requirements of section 414(f) and this section for each plan year ending prior to that date to the extent necessary to show the applicability of the 75 percent test provided in paragraph (c) of this section.

*(2)* For plan years ending after September 2, 1974, a plan may be required to furnish proof that it met the requirements of section 414(f) and this section for 6 immediately preceding plan years.

T.D. 7552, 7/11/78.

### § 1.414(g)-1 Definition of plan administrator.

**(a) In general.** For purposes of part I of subchapter D of chapter 1 of the Code and the regulations thereunder, if the instrument under which the plan is operated for a plan year specifically designates a person as plan administrator of the plan, such person is the plan administrator of the plan for the plan year. In the absence of a person so designated as the plan administrator of the plan by the instrument under which the plan is operated, the plan administrator of the plan for the plan year is the person described in paragraphs (b)(1), (2), or (3) of this section (whichever applies).

**(b) Plan administrator not specifically designated.** If no person is specifically designated as the plan administrator of the plan for a plan year by the instrument under which the plan is established or operated, the plan administrator of the plan for such year is the person determined under the following rules:

*(1) Single employer.* In the case of a plan maintained by a single employer, the employer is the plan administrator.

*(2) Employee organization.* In the case of a plan maintained by an employee organization, the employee organization is the plan administrator.

*(3) Group representing the parties.* In the case of a plan maintained by two or more employers, or jointly by one or more employers and one or more employee organizations, the association, committee, joint board of trustees, or other similar group of representatives of the parties who maintain the plan as the case may be, is the plan administrator.

*(4) Person in control of assets.* In any case where a plan administrator may not be determined by application of paragraphs (a) and (b)(1), (2) and (3) of this section, the plan administrator is the person or persons actually responsible, whether or not under the terms of the plan, for the control, disposition, or management of the cash or property received by or contributed to the plan, irrespective of whether such control, disposition, or management is exercised directly by such person or persons or indirectly through an agent or trustee designated by such person or persons.

T.D. 7618, 5/10/79.

### § 1.414(l)-1 Mergers and consolidations of plans or transfers of plan assets.

**(a) In general.** *(1) Scope of the regulations.* Sections 401(a)(12) and 414(l) apply only to plans to which section 411 applies without regard to section 411(e)(2). Thus, for example, these sections do not apply to a governmental plan within the meaning of section 414(d); a church plan, within the meaning of section 414(e), for which there has not been made the election under section 410(d) to have the participation, vesting, funding, etc. requirements apply; or a plan which at no time after September 2, 1974, provided for employer contributions.

*(2) General rule.* Under section 414(l),

(i) A trust which forms a part of a plan will not constitute a qualified trust under section 401, and

(ii) A plan will not be treated as being qualified under section 403(a) and 405(a), unless, in the case of a merger or consolidation (as defined in paragraph (b)(2) of this section), or a transfer of assets or liabilities (as defined in paragraph (b)(3) of this section), the following condition is satisfied. This condition requires that each participant receive benefits on a termination basis (as defined in paragraph (b)(5) of this section) from the plan immediately after the merger, consolidation or transfer which are equal to or greater than the benefits the participant would receive on a termination basis immediately before the merger, consolidation, or transfer.

**(b) Definitions.** For purposes of this section:

*(1) Single plan.* A plan is a "single plan" if and only if, on an ongoing basis, all of the plan assets are available to pay benefits to employees who are covered by the plan and their beneficiaries. . . . For purposes of the preceding sentence, all the assets of a plan will not fail to be available to provide all the benefits of a plan merely because the plan is funded in part or in whole with allocated insurance instruments. A plan will not fail to be a single plan merely because of the following:

(i) The plan has several distinct benefit structures which apply either to the same or different participants,

(ii) The plan has several plan documents,

(iii) Several employers, whether or not affiliated, contribute to the plan,

(iv) The assets of the plan are invested in several trusts or annuity contracts, or

(v) Separate accounting is maintained for purposes of cost allocation but not for purposes of providing benefits under the plan.

However, more than one plan will exist if a portion of the plan assets is not available to pay some of the benefits. This will be so even if each plan has the same benefit structure or plan document, or if all or part of the assets are invested in one trust with separate accounting with respect to each plan.

*(2) Merger or consolidation.* The terms "merger" or "consolidation" means the combining of two or more plans into a single plan. A merger or consolidation will not occur merely because one or more corporations undergo a reorganization (whether or not taxable). Furthermore, a merger or consolidation will not occur if two plans are not combined into a single plan, such as by using one trust which limits the availability of assets of one plan to provide benefits to participants and beneficiaries of only that plan.

*(3) Transfer of assets or liabilities.* A "transfer of assets or liabilities" occurs when there is a diminution of assets or liabilities with respect to one plan and the acquisition of these assets or the assumption of these liabilities by another plan. For example, the shifting of assets or liabilities pursuant to a reciprocity agreement between two plans in which one plan assumes liabilities of another plan is a transfer of assets or liabilities. However, the shifting of assets between several funding media used for a single plan (such as between trusts, between annuity contracts, or between trusts and annuity contracts) is not a transfer of assets or liabilities.

*(4) Spinoff.* The term "spinoff" means the splitting of a single plan into two or more plans.

*(5) Benefits on a termination basis.* (i) The term "benefits on a termination basis" means the benefits that would be provided exclusively by the plan assets pursuant to section 4044 of the Employee Retirement Income Security Act of 1974 ("ERISA") and the regulations thereunder if the plan terminated. Thus, the term does not include benefits that are guaranteed by the Pension Benefit Guaranty Corporation, but not provided by the plan assets.

(ii) For purposes of determining the benefits on a termination basis, the allocation of assets to various priority categories under section 4044 of ERISA must be made on the basis of reasonable actuarial assumptions. The assumptions used by the Pension Benefit Guaranty Corporation as of the date of the merger or spinoff are deemed reasonable for this purpose.

(iii) If a change in the benefit structure of plan in conjunction with a merger, consolidation, or transfer of assets or liabilities alters the benefits on a termination basis, the change should be designated, at the time the merger, consolidation, or transfer occurs, to be effective either immediately before or immediately after that occurrence. In the event that no designation is made, the change in the benefit structure will be deemed to occur immediately after the merger, consolidation, or transfer of assets or liabilities.

*(6) Lower funded plan.* (i) The term "lower funded plan" generally means the plan which, immediately prior to the merger, would have its assets exhausted in a higher priority category than the other plan.

(ii) Where two plans, immediately prior to the merger, would have their assets exhausted in the same priority category of section 4044 of ERISA in the event of termination, the lower funded plan is the one in which the assets would satisfy a lesser proportion of the liability allocated to that priority category.

*(7) Priority category.* The term "priority category" means the category of benefits described in each paragraph of section 4044(a) of ERISA. References to higher or highest priority categories refer to those priority categories which receive the first allocation of asserts, i.e. the lowest paragraph numbers in section 4044(a).

*(8) Separate accounting of assets.* The term "separate accounting of assets" means the maintenance of an asset account with respect to a given group of participants which is:

(i) Credited with contributions made to the plan on behalf of the participants and with its allocable share of investment income, if any, and

(ii) Charged with benefits paid to the participants, and with its allocable share of investment losses or expenses.

*(9) Present value of accrued benefit.* For purposes of this section, the present value of an accrued benefit must be determined on the basis of reasonable actuarial assumptions. For this purpose, the assumptions used by the Pension Benefit Guaranty Corporation as of the date of the merger or spinoff are deemed reasonable.

*(10) Valuation of plan assets.* In determining the value of a plan's assets, the standards set forth in regulations prescribed by the Pension Benefit Guaranty Corporation (29 CFR Part 2611) shall be applied.

*(11) Date of merger or spinoff.* The actual date of a merger or spinoff shall be determined on the basis of the facts and circumstances of the particular situation. For purposes of this determination, the following factors, none of which is necessarily controlling, are relevant:

(i) The date on which the affected employees stop accruing benefits under one plan and begin coverage and benefit accruals under another plan.

(ii) The date as of which the amount of assets to be eventually transferred is calculated.

(iii) If the merger or spinoff agreement provides that interest is to accrue from a certain date to the date of actual transfer, the date from which such interest will accrue.

**(c) Application of section 414(l).** *(1) Two or more plans.* (i) Section 414(l) does not apply unless more than a single plan is involved. It also does not apply unless at least a single plan assumes liabilities from another plan or obtains assets from another plan (as in a merger or spinoff). For purposes of section 414(l), a transfer of assets or liabilities will not be deemed to occur merely because a defined contribution plan is amended to become a defined benefit plan. This rule will apply even if, under the facts and circumstances of a particular case, a termination of the defined contribution plan will be considered to have occurred for purposes of other provisions of the Code.

(ii) The requirements of this subparagraph may be illustrated as follows:

*Example.* After acquiring Corporation B, Corporation A amends Corporation B's defined benefit plan (Plan B) to provide the same benefits as Corporation A's defined benefit plan (Plan A). The assets of Plan B are transferred to the trust containing the assets of Plan A in such a manner that the assets of each plan: (1) are separately accounted for, and (2) are not available to pay benefits of the other plan. Because of condition (2) there are still two plans and, therefore, a merger did not occur. As a result, section 414(l) does not apply. If at some later date Corporation A were to sell Corporation B and transfer the assets of Plan B that were separately accounted for to another trust or to an annuity contract solely for the purpose of providing Plan B's benefits, this transfer would also not involve section 414(l). This is so because Plan B was a separate plan before the entire transaction and because no plan assumed liabilities or obtained assets from another plan. If, on the other hand, Corporation A merged Plan A and Plan B at the time of the acquisition of Corporation B by deleting condition (2) above, then section 414(l) would apply both to the merger of Plan A and Plan B and to the spinoff of Plan B from the merged plan. The spinoff would have to satisfy the requirements of paragraph (n) of this section, even if the assets attributable to Plan A and Plan B were separately account for in order to allocate funding costs.

*(2) Multiemployer plans.* Except to the extent provided by regulations of the Pension Benefit Guaranty Corporation, section 414(l) does not apply to any transaction to the extent that participants either before or after that transaction are covered under a multiemployer plan within the meaning of section 414(f). Until these regulations are issued, section 414(l) does not apply to any of the following situations:

(i) A multiemployer plan is split into two or more plans, one or more of which are not multiemployer plans, or

(ii) A single employer plan is merged into a multiemployer plan.

Therefore, if some (but not all) of the participants in a single employer plan become participants in a multiemployer plan under an agreement in which the multiemployer plan assumes all the liabilities of the single employer plan with respect to these participants and in which some or all of the assets of the single employer plan are transferred to the multiemployer plan, section 414(l) applies, but only with respect to the participants in the single employer plan who did not transfer to the multiemployer plan.

**(d) Merger of defined contribution plans.** In the case of a merger of two or more defined contribution plans, the requirements of section 414(l) will be satisfied if all of the following conditions are met:

*(1)* The sum of the account balances in each plan equals the fair market value (determined as of the date of the merger) of the entire plan assets.

*(2)* The assets of each plan are combined to form the assets of the plan as merged.

*(3)* Immediately after the merger, each participant in the plan as merged has an account balance equal to the sum of the account balances the participant had in the plans immediately prior to merger.

**(e) Merger of defined benefit plans.** *(1) General rule.* Section 414(l) compares the benefits on a termination basis before and after the merger. If the sum of the assets of all plans is not less than the sum of the present values of the accrued benefit (whether or not vested) of all plans, the requirements of section 414(l) will be satisfied merely by combining the assets and preserving each participant's accrued benefits. This is so because all the accrued benefits of the plan as merged are provided on a termination basis by the plan as merged. However, if the sum of the assets of all plans is less than the sum of the present values of the accrued benefits (whether or not vested) in all plans, the accrued benefits in the plan as merged are not provided on a termination basis.

*(2) Special schedule of benefits.* Generally, for some participants, the benefits provided on a termination basis for the plan as merged would be different from the benefits provided on a termination basis in the plans prior to merger if the assets were merely combined and if each participant retained his accrued benefit. Some participants would, therefore, receive greater benefits on a termination basis as a result of the merger and some other participants would receive smaller benefits. Accordingly, the requirements of section 414(l) would not be satisfied unless the distribution on termination were modified in some manner to prevent any participant from receiving smaller benefits on a termination basis as a result of the merger. This is accomplished through modifying the application of section 4044 of ERISA by inserting a special schedule of benefits.

**(f) Operational rules for the special schedule.** The application of section 4044 of ERISA as modified by the schedule of benefits is accomplished by the following steps:

*(1)* Section 4044 is applied in the plan as merged through the priority categories fully satisfied by the assets of the lower funded plan immediately prior to the merger.

*(2)* The assets in the plan as merged are then allocated to the next priority category as a percentage of the value of the benefits that would otherwise be allocated to that priority category. That percentage is the ratio of (i) the assets allocated to the first priority category not fully satisfied by the lower funded plan immediately prior to the merger to (ii) the assets that would have been allocated had that priority category been fully satisfied.

*(3)* A schedule of benefits is formed listing participants and scheduled accrued benefits. The scheduled accrued benefit is the excess of the benefits provided on a termination basis with respect to any participant from the plans immediately prior to the merger, over the benefits provided on a termination basis in subparagraphs (1) and (2) of this paragraph immediately after the merger. After allocating the assets in accordance with subparagraph (2) of this paragraph, the assets are allocated to the schedule of benefits as follows:

(i) First the assets are allocated to the scheduled benefits to the extent that the participant would have benefits provided in subparagraph (4) of this paragraph if there were no scheduled benefits.

(ii) Then the assets are allocated to the scheduled benefits to the extent that the participant would have benefits provided pursuant to subparagraph (5) of this paragraph if there were no scheduled benefits.

These assets should be allocated first to those scheduled benefits that are in the highest priority category under section 4044.

*(4)* The assets are then allocated to those benefits in the priority category described in subparagraph (2) of this paragraph with respect to which assets were not allocated. This allocation is made to the extent that these benefits are not associated with benefits in the schedule.

*(5)* Finally, the assets are allocated in accordance with section 4044 with respect to priority categories lower than the priority category described in subparagraph (4) of this paragraph. This allocation is made to the extent that these benefits are not associated with benefits in the schedule.

**(g) Successive mergers.** *(1) In general.* In the case of a current merger of a defined benefit plan with another defined benefit plan which as a result of a previous merger has a special schedule, the rules of paragraphs (e) and (f) of this section apply as if the schedule were considered a category described in section 4044 of ERISA. Thus, a second schedule may be formed as a result of the current merger. The second schedule will be inserted in the priority category of section 4044 described in paragraph (f)(2) of this section as of the date of the current merger. This priority category may be higher, lower, or within the schedule of benefits existing on account of a previous merger. If this priority schedule is inserted within a schedule of benefits, a new single schedule of benefits replacing the old schedule of benefits would in effect be created.

*(2) Allocation of assets.* Assets in the new schedule of benefits are allocated as follows:

(i) First to the benefits remaining in the old schedule to the extent that there are assets immediately prior to the second merger to satisfy the original benefits.

(ii) Then to the benefits provided on a termination basis from the plans immediately prior to the second merger to the extent that they are not provided before the schedule after the second merger or in subdivision (i) of this subparagraph.

(iii) Then to benefits remaining in the original schedule not included in subdivision (i) of this subparagraph.

**(h) De minimis rule for merger of defined benefit plan.** *(1) In general.* In the case of a merger of a defined benefit plan ("smaller plan") whose liabilities (*i.e.,* the present value of accrued benefits, whether or not vested) are less than 3 percent of the assets of another defined benefit plan ("larger plan") as of at least one day in the larger plan's plan year in which the merger of the two plans occurs, section 414(l) will be deemed to be satisfied if the following condition is met. The condition requires that a special schedule of benefits (consisting of all the benefits that would be provided by the smaller plan on a termination basis just prior to the merger) be payable in a priority category higher than the highest priority category in section 4044 of ERISA. Assets will be allocated to that schedule in accordance with the allocation of assets to scheduled benefits in paragraph (f)(3) of this section.

*(2) Application to a series of mergers.* In the case of a series of such mergers in a given plan year of the larger plan, the rule described in subparagraph (1) of this paragraph will apply only if the sum of the liabilities (whether or not vested) assumed by the larger plan are less than 3 percent of the assets of the larger plan as of at least one day in the plan year of the larger plan in which the mergers occurred.

*(3) Application to a merger occurring over more than one plan year.* In the case of a merger of a smaller plan or a portion thereof with a larger plan designed to occur in steps over more than one plan year of the larger plan, the entire transaction will be deemed to occur in the plan year of the larger plan which contains the first of these steps.

*(4) Liabilities of the smaller plan.* For purposes of subparagraphs (2) and (3) of this paragraph, mergers satisfying paragraphs (e), (f) or (g) of this section will be ignored in determining the sum of the liabilities assumed by the larger plan.

**(i) Data maintenance.** *(1) Alternative to the special schedule.* In the case of a merger which would require the creation of a special schedule in order to satisfy section 414(l), the schedule need not be created at the time of the merger if data sufficient to create the schedule is maintained. The schedule would only have to be created in the event of a subsequent plan termination or a subsequent spinoff. In that case the schedule must be determined as of the date of the merger.

(2) *Required data.* The data that must be maintained depends on the plan, and care should be taken to ensure that all necessary data is maintained. Furthermore, in order to take advantage of the data maintenance alternative provided in this paragraph, an enrolled actuary must certify to the plan administrator that each element of data necessary to determine the schedule as of the date of the merger is maintained. This certification must be based either upon the enrolled actuary's independent examination of the data, or upon his reliance, which under the circumstances of the particular situation must be reasonable, upon a written statement of the plan administrator concerning what data is actually being maintained.

**(j) Five year rule.** *(1) Limitation on the required use of the special schedule.* A plan will not fail to satisfy the requirements of section 414(l) merely because the effects of the special schedule created pursuant to paragraphs (e)(2) or (h) of this section are ignored 5 years after the date of a merger. Furthermore, the date maintained pursuant to paragraph (i) of this section need not be maintained for more than 5 years after the merger, if the plan does not have a spinoff or a termination within 5 years.

(2) *Illustration.* If Plans A and B merge to form Plan AB and if Plan AB mergers with Plan C 3 years later to form Plan ABC and if Plan ABC terminates 4 years later, the data relating to the merger of Plans A and B need not be maintained for more than 5 years after the merger of Plans A and B. In addition, after 5 years have elapsed after the merger of Plans A and B, the effect of any special schedule created by the merger of Plans A and B on the schedule created by the merger of Plans AB and C may be ignored in determining the later schedule.

**(k) Examples.** The provisions of paragraphs (e) through (j) of this section may be illustrated by the following examples:

*Example (1).* Plan A, whose assets are $220,000, is to be merged with Plan B, whose assets are $200,000. Plan A has three employees. Plan B has two employees. If Plans A and B were to terminate just prior to the merger, the benefits provided on a termination basis would be as follows:

**Plan A**

| | (1) | | | (2) | | | (3) | (4) | | |
|---|---|---|---|---|---|---|---|---|---|---|
| | Annual accrued benefits | | | Present value of accrued benefits | | | Fair market value of assets allocated to priority category | Benefits on a termination basis | | |
| Priority category of sec. 4044 of ERISA: | $EE_1$ | $EE_2$ | $EE_3$ | $EE_1$ | $EE_2$ | $EE_3$ | | $EE_1$ | $EE_2$ | $EE_3$ |
| 3 .......... | $10,000 | | | $120,000 | | | $120,000 | $10,000 | | |
| 4 .......... | 2,000 | $4,000 | | 24,000 | $44,000 | | 68,000 | 2,000 | $4,000 | |
| 5 .......... | | 3,000 | $4,000 | | 33,000 | $40,000 | 32,000 | | 1,315* | $1,753** |
| 6 .......... | | | 1,000 | | | 10,000 | | | | |
| Total ..... | | | | | | | 220,000 | 12,000 | 5,315 | 1,753 |

$$* \; 3{,}000 \times \frac{\$32{,}000}{\$73{,}000}$$

$$** \; \$4{,}000 \times \frac{\$32{,}000}{\$73{,}000}$$

i.e. Accrued benefit ×

$$\frac{\text{Assets available for priority category 5}}{\text{Total present value of accrued benefits in category 5}}$$

**Plan B**

| | $EE_4$ | $EE_5$ | $EE_4$ | $EE_5$ | | $EE_4$ | $EE_5$ |
|---|---|---|---|---|---|---|---|
| 3 .......... | $15,000 | | $195,000 | | $195,000 | $15,000 | |
| 4 .......... | | $5,000 | | $50,000 | 5,000 | | $ 500* |
| 5 .......... | | 8,000 | | 80,000 | | | |
| Total ..... | | | | | $200,000 | $15,000 | $ 500 |

$$*5{,}000 \times \frac{\$5{,}000}{\$50{,}000}$$

Because Plan B's assets are exhausted in a higher priority category than Plan A's assets, Plan B is the lower funded plan. A schedule will, therefore, be inserted in Priority Category 4 of the plan as merged after providing 10% of the benefits provided in category 4, i.e. the ratio of $5,000 assets in Plan B allocated to category 4 to the $50,000 liability in category 4. The schedule would be constructed as follows:

| | (1) Benefits on a termination basis before merger | (2) Benefits provided from priority categories higher than category 4 | (3) 10 percent of benefits provided in priority category 4 | (4) Benefits provided before schedule (2) + (3) | (5) Schedule of benefits (1) − (4) |
|---|---|---|---|---|---|
| EE: | | | | | |
| 1 . . . . . . . . . . . . . . | $12,000 | $10,000 | $200 | $10,200 | $1,800 |
| 2 . . . . . . . . . . . . . . | 5,315 | | 400 | 400 | 4,195 |
| 3 . . . . . . . . . . . . . . | 1,753 | | | | 1,753 |
| 4 . . . . . . . . . . . . . . | 15,000 | 15,000 | | 15,000 | |
| 5 . . . . . . . . . . . . . . | 500 | | 500 | 500 | |

*Example (2).* The facts are the same as in Example (1). The plan, however, terminates one year later. Furthermore no employee has accrued additional benefits during the year except that the $2,000 benefit of $EE_1$ that was originally in category 4 is now in category 3. The assets would be allocated to the priority categories to the extent that there are assets to cover the following benefits.

| Priority termination category | $EE_1$ | $EE_2$ | $EE_3$ | $EE_4$ | $EE_5$ |
|---|---|---|---|---|---|
| 3 . . . . . . . . . . . . . . . . . . . . . . . . . . . . . . . . . . . . . . . . | $12,000 | | | $15,000 | |
| 10 pct of 4 . . . . . . . . . . . . . . . . . . . . . . . . . . . . . . . . . . . | | $ 400 | | | |
| Schedule of benefits included in balance of category 4 . . . . . . . . . . . . . . . . . . | | 3,600 | | | |
| Schedule of benefits included in category 5 . . . . . . . . . . . . . . . . . . . . . . . . . . | | 1,315 | $1,753 | | |
| Schedule of benefits included in category 6 . . . . . . . . . . . . . . . . . . . . . . . . . . | | | | | |
| Balance of category 4 not included in schedule . . . . . . . . . . . . . . . . . . . . . . . | | | | | 4,500 |
| Balance of category 5 not included in schedule . . . . . . . . . . . . . . . . . . . . . . . | | 1,685 | 2,247 | | 8,000 |
| Balance of category 6 not included in schedule . . . . . . . . . . . . . . . . . . . . . . . | | | 1,000 | | |

**(l) Merger of defined benefit and defined contribution plan.** In the case of a merger of a defined benefit plan with a defined contribution plan, one of the plans before the merger should be converted into the other type of plan (*i.e.*, the defined benefit converted into a defined contribution or the defined contribution converted into a defined benefit) and either paragraph (d) or paragraphs (e) through (j) of this section, whichever is appropriate, should be applied.

**(m) Spinoff of a defined contribution plan.** In the case of a spinoff of a defined contribution plan, the requirements of section 414(l) will be satisfied if after the spinoff—

*(1)* The sum of the account balances for each of the participants in the resulting plans equals the account balance of the participant in the plan before the spinoff, and

*(2)* The assets in each of the plans immediately after the spinoff equals the sum of the account balances for all participants in that plan.

**(n) Spinoff of a defined benefit plan.** *(1) General rule.* In the case of a spinoff of a defined benefit plan, the requirements of section 414(l) will be satisfied if—

(i) All of the accrued benefits of each participant are allocated to only one of the spun off plans, and

(ii) The value of the assets allocated to each of the spun off plans is not less than the sum of the present value of the benefits on a termination basis in the plan before the spin off for all participants in that spun off plan.

*(2) De minimis rule.* In the case of a spin off the requirements of section 414(l) will be deemed to be satisfied if the value of the assets spun off—

(i) Equals the present value of the accrued benefits spun off (whether or not vested), and

(ii) In conjunction with other assets spun off during the plan year in which the spinoff occurs in accordance with this subparagraph, is less than 3 percent of the assets as of at least one day in that year.

Spinoffs occurring in previous or subsequent plan years are ignored if they are not part of a single spinoff designed to occur in steps over more than one plan year.

*(3) Special temporary rule.* In the case of a defined benefit plan maintained for different groups of employees, which is a single plan (as defined in paragraph (b)(1) of this section) and under which there has been separate accounting of assets for each group, a spinoff of the plan on or before July 1, 1978, into a separate plan for each group will be deemed to satisfy section 414(l) if—

(i) All the liabilities with respect to each group of employees are allocated to a separate plan for that group of employees, and

(ii) The assets that are separately accounted for with respect to each group of employees are allocated to the separate plan for that group of employees.

For purposes of this subparagraph, a separate accounting of assets will not be considered to have occurred to the extent that the assets allocated to each single plan are determined by an historical re-creation of benefits, contributions, investment gains, etc.

**(o) Transfers of assets or liabilities.** Any transfer of assets or liabilities will for purposes of section 414(l) be considered as a combination of separate mergers and spinoffs using the rules of paragraphs (d), (e) through (j), (l), (m), or (n) of this section, whichever is appropriate. Thus, for example, if in accordance with the transfer of one or more employees, a block of assets and liabilities are transferred from Plan A to Plan B, each of which is a defined benefit plan, the transaction will be considered as a spinoff from Plan A and a merger of one of the spinoff plans with Plan B. The spinoff and merger described in the previous sentence would be subject to the requirements of paragraphs (n) and (e) through (j) of this section respectively.

**(p) Effective date.** The provisions of this section apply to mergers, consolidations and transfers of assets or liabilities which occur after September 2, 1974.

---

T.D. 7638, 8/16/79.

---

**Proposed § 1.414(m)-1 Affiliated service groups.** [*For Preamble, see ¶ 150,825*]

***Caution:*** The Treasury has not yet amended Reg § 1.414(m)-1 to reflect changes made by P.L. 99-514, P.L. 97-248.

**(a) In general.** Section 414(m) provides rules that require, in some circumstances, employees of separate organizations to be treated as if they were employed by a single employer for purposes of certain employee benefit requirements. For other rules requiring aggregation of employees of different organizations, see section 414(b) (relating to controlled groups of corporations) and section 414(c) (relating to trades or businesses under common control). If aggregation is required under either of the preceding provisions and also under section 414(m), the requirements with respect to all of the applicable provisions must be satisfied.

**(b) Aggregation.** Except as provided in paragraph (c), all the employees of the members of an affiliated service group shall be treated as if they were employed by a single employer for purposes of the employee benefit requirements listed in § 1.414(m)-3.

**(c) Aggregation not required.** Pursuant to the authority contained in section 414(m)(1), a corporation, other than a professional service corporation, shall not be treated as a First Service Organization (see § 1.414(m)-2 for purposes of section 414(m)(2)(A). Also, a special rule is provided in § 1.414(m)-2(c)(4) for determining ownership under section 414(m)(2)(B). For purposes of this paragraph, a professional service corporation is a corporation that is organized under state law for the principal purpose of providing professional services and has at least one shareholder who is licensed or otherwise legally authorized to render the type of services for which the corporation is organized. " Professional services" means the services performed by certified or other public accountants, actuaries, architects, attorneys, chiropodists, chiropractors, medical doctors, dentists, professional engineers, optometrists, osteopaths, podiatrists, psychologists, and veterinarians. The Commissioner may expand the list of services in the preceding sentence. However, no such expansion will be effective with respect to any organization until the first day of the first plan year beginning at least 180 days after the publication of such change.

**Proposed § 1.414(m)-2 Definitions.** [*For Preamble, see ¶ 150,825*]

***Caution:*** The Treasury has not yet amended Reg § 1.414(m)-2 to reflect changes made by P.L. 99-514, P.L. 97-248.

**(a) Affiliated service group.** "Affiliated service group" means a group consisting of a service organization (First Service Organization) and

*(1)* One or more A Organizations described in paragraph (b), or

*(2)* One or more B Organizations described in paragraph (c), or

*(3)* One or more A Organizations described in paragraph (b) and one or more B Organizations described in paragraph (c).

**(b) A Organizations.** *(1) General rule.* A service organization is an A Organization if it:

(i) Is a partner or shareholder in the First Service Organization (regardless of the percentage interest it owns in the First Service Organization but determined with regard to the constructive ownership rules of paragraph (d)); and

(ii) Regularly performs services for the First Service Organization, or is regularly associated with the First Service Organization in performing services for third persons.

It is not necessary that any of the employees of the organization directly perform services for the First Service Organization; it is sufficient that the organization is regularly associated with the First Service Organization in performing services for third persons.

*(2) Regularly performs services for.* The determination of whether a service organization regularly performs services for the First Service Organization or is regularly associated with the First Service Organization in performing services for third persons shall be made on the basis of the facts and circumstances. One factor that is relevant in making this determination is the amount of the earned income that the organization derives from performing services for the First Service Organization, or from performing services for third persons in association with the First Service Organization.

*(3) Examples.* The provisions of this paragraph may be illustrated by the following examples.

*Example (1).* A Organization. (i) Attorney N is incorporated, and the corporation is a partner in a law firm. Attorney N and his corporation are regularly associated with the law firm in performing services for third persons.

(ii) Considering the law firm as a First Service Organization, the corporation is an A Organization because it is a partner in the law firm and it is regularly associated with the law firm in performing services for third persons. Accordingly, the corporation and the law firm constitute an affiliated service group.

*Example (2).* Corporation. (i) Corporation F is a service organization that is a shareholder in Corporation G, another service organization. F regularly provides services for G. Neither corporation is a professional service corporation within the meaning of subsection (1)(c).

(ii) Neither corporation may be considered a First Service Organization for purposes of this paragraph and, thus, aggregation will not be required by operation of the A Organization test. However, G or F may be treated as a First Service Organization and the other organization may be a B Organization under the rules of subsection (2)(c).

*Example (3).* Regularly associated with. (i) R, S & T is a law partnership with offices in numerous cities. The office in the city of D is incorporated, and the corporation is a partner in the law firm. All of the employees of the corporation work directly for the corporation, and none of them work directly for any of the other offices of the law firm.

(ii) Considering the law firm as a First Service Organization, the corporation is an A Organization because it is a partner in the First Service Organization and is regularly associated with the law firm in performing services for third persons. Accordingly, the corporation and the law firm constitute an affiliated service group.

**(c) B Organizations.** *(1) General rule.* An organization is a B Organization if:

(i) A significant portion of the business of the organization is the performance of services for the First Service Organization, for one or more A Organizations determined with respect to the First Service Organization, or for both.

(ii) Those services are of a type historically performed by employees in the service field of the First Service Organization or the A Organizations, and

(iii) Ten percent or more of the interests in the organization is held, in the aggregate, by persons who are designated group members (as defined in subparagraph (4)) of the First Service Organization or of the A Organizations, determined using the constructive ownership rules of paragraph (d).

*(2) Significant portion.* (i) General rule. Except as provided in paragraphs (c)(2)(ii) and (iii), the determination of whether providing services for the First Service Organization, for one or more A Organizations, or for both, is a significant portion of the business of an organization will be based on the facts and circumstances. Wherever it appears in this paragraph (c)(2), "one or more A organizations" means one or more A organizations determined with respect to the First Service Organization.

(ii) Service Receipts safe harbor. The performance of services for the First Service Organizations, for one or more A Organizations, or for both, will not be considered a significant portion of the business of an organization if the Service Receipts Percentage is less than five percent.

(iii) Total Receipts threshold test. The performance of services for the First Service Organization, for one or more A Organizations, or for both, will be considered a significant portion of the business of an organization if the Total Receipts Percentage is ten percent or more.

(iv) Service Receipts Percentage. The Service Receipts Percentage is the ratio of the gross receipts of the organization derived from performing services for the First Service Organization, for one or more A Organizations, or for both, to the total gross receipts of the organization derived from performing services. This ratio is the greater of the ratio for the year for which the determination is being made or for the three year period including that year and the two preceding years (or the period of the organization's existence, if less).

(v) Total Receipts Percentage. The Total Receipts Percentage is calculated in the same manner as the Service Receipts Percentage, except that gross receipts in the denominator are determined without regard to whether they were derived from performing services.

*(3) Historically performed.* Services will be considered of a type historically performed by employees in a particular service field if it was not unusual for the services to be performed by employees of organizations in that service field (in the United States) on December 13, 1980.

*(4) Designated group.* (i) Definition. "Designated group" members are the officers, the highly compensated employees, and the common owners of an organization (as defined in paragraph (c)(4)(ii)). However, even though a person is not a common owner, the interests the person holds in the potential B Organization will be taken into account if the person is an officer or a highly compensated employee of the First Service Organization or of an A Organization.

(ii) Common owner. A person who is an owner of a First Service Organization or of an A Organization is a common owner if at least three percent of the interests in the organization is, in the aggregate, held by persons who are owners of the potential B organization (determined using the constructive ownership rules of paragraph (d)).

*(5) Owner.* The term "owner" includes organizations that have an ownership interest described in paragraph (e).

*(6) Aggregation of ownership interests.* It is not necessary that a single designated group member of the First Service Organization or of an A Organization own ten percent or more of the interests, determined using the constructive ownership rules of paragraph (d), in the organization for the organization to be a B Organization. It is sufficient that the sum of the interests, determined using the constructive ownership rules of paragraph (d), held by all of the designated group members of the First Service Organization, and the designated group members of the A Organizations, is ten percent or more of the interests in the organizations.

*(7) Non-service organization.* An organization may be a B Organization even though it does not quality as a service organization under paragraph (f).

*(8) Examples.* The provisions of this paragraph may be illustrated by the following examples.

*Example (1).* B Organization. (i) R is a service organization that has 11 partners. Each partner of R owns one percent of the stock in Corporation D. The corporation provides services to the partnership of a type historically performed by employees in the service field of the partnership. A significant portion of the business of the corporation consists of providing services to the partnership.

(ii) Considering the partnership as a First Service Organization, the corporation is a B organization because a significant portion of the business of the corporation is the performance of services for the partnership of a type historically performed by employees in the service field of the partnership, and more than ten percent of the interests in the corporation is held, in the aggregate, by the designated group members (consisting of the 11 common owners of the partnership). Accordingly, the corporation and the partnership constitute an affiliated service group.

(iii) A similar result would be obtained if no more than 8 percent of the 11 percent ownership in Corporation D were held by highly compensated employees of R who were not owners of R (even though no one group of the three preceding groups held 10 percent or more of the stock of Corporation D).

*Example (2).* Other aggregation rules. (i) C, an individual, is a 60 percent partner in D, a service organization, and regularly performs services for D. C is also an 80 percent partner in F. A significant portion of the gross receipts of F are derived from providing services to D of a type historically performed by employees in the service field of D.

(ii) Viewing D as a First Service Organization, F is a B Organization because a significant portion of gross receipts of F are derived from performing services for D of a type historically performed by employees in that service field, and more than ten percent of the interests in F is held by the designated group member C (who is a common owner of D). Accordingly, D and F constitute an affiliated service group. Additionally, the employees of D and F are aggregated under the rules of section 414(c). Thus, any plan maintained by a member of the affiliated service group must satisfy the aggregation rules of sections 414(c) and 414(m).

*Example (3).* Common owner. (i) Corporation T is a service organization. The sole function of Corporation W is to provide services to Corporation T of a type historically performed by employees in the service field of Corporation T.

Individual C owns all of the stock of Corporation W and two percent of the stock of Corporation T. C is not an officer or a highly compensated employee of Corporation T.

(ii) Considering Corporation T as a First Service Organization, Corporation W is not a B Organization because it is not 10 percent owned by designated group members. Because C owns less than 3 percent of Corporation T, C is not a common owner of T.

*Example (4).* B Organization. (i) Individual M owns one-third of an employee benefit consulting firm. M also owns one-third of an insurance agency. A significant portion of the business of the consulting firm consists of assisting the insurance agency in developing employee benefit packages for sale to third persons and providing services to the insurance company in connection with employee benefit programs sold to other clients of the insurance agency. Additionally, the consulting firm frequently provides services to clients who have purchased insurance arrangements from the insurance company for the employee benefit plans they maintain. The insurance company frequently refers clients to the consulting firm to assist them in the design of their employee benefit plans. The percentage of the total gross receipts of the consulting firm that represent gross receipts from the performance of these services for the insurance agency is 20 percent.

(ii) Considering the insurance agency as a First Service Organization, the consulting firm is a B Organization because a significant portion of the business of the consulting firm (as determined under the Total Receipts Percentage Test) is the performance of services for the insurance agency of a type historically performed by employees in the service field of insurance, and more than 10 percent of the interests in the consulting firm is held by owners of the insurance agency. Thus, the insurance agency and the consulting form constitute an affiliated service group.

*Example (5).* B Organization. (i) Attorney T is incorporated, and the corporation is a 6% shareholder in a law firm (which is also incorporated). All of the work of Corporation T is performed for the law firm.

(ii) Under the principles of section 267(c), T is deemed to own the shares of the law firm owned by T Corporation. Thus, T is a common owner of the law firm. Considering the law firm as a First Service Organization, Corporation T is a B Organization because a significant portion of the business of Corporation T consists of performing services for the law firm of a type historically performed by employees, and 100 percent of Corporation T is owned by a common owner of the law firm.

*Example (6).* Significant portion. (i) The income of Corporation X is derived from both performing services and other business activities. The amount of its receipts derived from performing services for, and its total receipts derived from, Corporation Z and the total for all other customers is set forth below:

| Origin of income | | Corporation Z | All customers |
|---|---|---|---|
| Year 1 | Services | $ 4 | $100 |
| | Total | — | 120 |
| Year 2 | Services | 9 | 150 |
| | Total | — | 180 |
| Year 3 | Services | 42 | 200 |
| | Total | — | 240 |

(ii) In year 1 (the first year of existence of Corporation X), the Services Receipts Percentage for Corporation X (for its business with Corporation Z) is less than five percent ($4/$100, or 4%). Thus performing services for Corporation Z will not be considered a significant portion of the business of Corporation X.

(iii) In year 2, the Service Receipts Percentage is the greater of the ratio for that year ($9/$150, or 6%) or for years 1 and 2 combined ($13/$250, or 5.2%), which is six percent. The Total Receipts Percentage is the greater of the ratio for that year ($9/$180, or 5%) or for years 1 and 2 combined ($13/$300, or 4.3%), which if five percent. Because the Services Receipts Percentage is greater than five percent and the Total Receipts Percentage is less than ten percent, whether performing services for Corporation Z constitutes a significant portion of the business of Corporation X is determined by the facts and circumstances.

(iv) In year 3, the Services Receipts Percentage is the greater of the ratio for that year ($42/$200, or 21%) or for years 1, 2, and 3 combined ($55/$450, or 12.2%), which is 21 percent. The Total Receipts Percentage is the greater of the ratio for that year ($42/$240, or 17.5%) or for years 1, 2, and 3 combined ($55/$540, or 10.1%), which is 17.5 percent. Because the Total Receipts Percentage is greater than ten percent and the Services Receipts Percentage is not less than five percent, a significant portion of the business of Corporation X is considered to be the performance of services for Corporation Z.

**(d) Ownership.** *(1) Constructive ownership.* Except as otherwise provided in the regulations under section 414(m), the principles of section 267(c) (relating to constructive ownership of stock) shall apply in determining ownership for purposes of section 414(m). Accordingly, the rules of section 267(c) shall apply to partnership interests as well as to stock.

*(2) Qualified plans.* In determining ownership for purposes of section 414(m), an individual's interest under a plan that qualifies under section 401(a) will be taken into account.

*(3) Special rules.* For purposes of section 414(m):

(i) Stock or partnership interests owned, directly or indirectly, by or for a corporation, partnership, estate, or trust shall be considered as being owned proportionately by or for its shareholders, partners, or beneficiaries;

(ii) An individual shall be considered as owning the stock or partnership interests owned, directly or indirectly, by or for his family;

(iii) An individual owning (otherwise than by the application of paragraph (d)(3)(ii)) any stock in a corporation or interest in a partnership shall be considered as owning the stock or partnership interests owned, directly or indirectly, by or for his partner;

(iv) The family of an individual shall include only his brothers and sisters (whether by the whole or half blood), spouse, ancestors, and lineal descendants; and

(v) Stock or partnership interests constructively owned by a person by reason of the application of paragraph (d)(3)(i) shall, for the purpose of applying paragraph (d)(3)(i), (ii), or (iii), be treated as actually owned by such person, but stock or partnership interests constructively owned by an individual by reason of the application of paragraph (d) (3)(ii) or (iii) shall not be treated as owned by him for the purpose of again applying either of such subdivisions in order to make another the constructive owner of such stock or partnership interests.

*(4) Examples.* The provisions of this paragraph may be illustrated by the following examples.

*Example (1).* Constructive ownership. (i) Individual K is incorporated as K Corporation, and K Corporation is a partner in a management consulting firm K & F. K regularly performs services for the management consulting firm K & F. The secretarial services for the consulting firm are performed by Corporation M. A significant portion of the business of the secretarial corporation, M, consists of providing services to the consulting firm. All of the stock of the secretarial corporation, M, is owned by individual K.

(ii) Considering the consulting firm as a First Service Organization, Corporation K is an A Organization because it is a partner in the consulting firm and regularly performs services for the firm or is regularly associated with the firm in performing services for third persons.

(iii) Under the principles of section 267(c), individual K is deemed to own the partnership interest in the consulting firm that is held by K Corporation. Thus, K is considered to be an owner of the consulting firm.

(iv) Considering the consulting firm as a First Service Organization, the secretarial corporation is a B Organization because a significant portion of its business consists of performing services for the consulting firm or for Corporation K of a type historically performed by employees in the service field of management consulting, and at least ten percent of the interests in the secretarial corporation, M, is held by individual K, an owner of the consulting firm.

*Example (2).* Constructive ownership. (i) J is the office manager and highly compensated employee of an accounting partnership H & H. The secretarial services for the partnership are provided by Corporation W. J owns fifty percent of the stock of the secretarial corporation. A significant portion of the business of the secretarial corporation consists of providing services to the partnership.

(ii) Considering the partnership as a First Service Organization, the secretarial corporation is a B Organization because a significant portion of the business of the secretarial corporation is the performance of services for the partnership of a type historically performed by employees of accounting firms, and more than ten percent of the interests in the corporation is held by a highly compensated employee of the partnership.

(iii) Under the principles of section 267(c), the result would be the same for example, if the stock were held (instead of by J) by the spouse of J, the children of J, the parents or grandparents of J, a trust for the benefit of J's children, or by a combination of such relatives.

*Example (3).* Qualified plan. (i) T is the chief executive officer of W Corporation, which is a consulting firm. T is also a participant in the W Corporation Profit-Sharing Plan, which qualifies under section 401(a). T's account balance in the plan is $150,000, and it consists of 25 percent of the stock of X Corporation. The sole function of X Corporation is to provide secretarial services to W Corporation.

(ii) Considering W Corporation as a First Service Organization, X Corporation is a B Organization because a significant portion of the business of X Corporation consists of providing secretarial services to W Corporation, secretarial services are of a type historically performed by employees in the field of consulting, and 25 percent of the stock of X Corporation is considered to be owned by T, a highly compensated employee of W Corporation, using the principles of section 267(c). Accordingly, W Corporation and X Corporation constitute an affiliated service group.

**(e) Organization.** *(1) General rule.* The term "organization" includes a sole proprietorship, partnership, corporation, or any other type of entity regardless of its ownership format.

*(2) Special rule. [Reserved]*

**(f) Service organization.** *(1) Non-capital intensive organizations.* The principal business of an organization will be considered the performance of services if capital is not a material income-producing factor for the organization, even though the organization is not engaged in a field listed in paragraph (f)(2). Whether capital is a material income-producing factor must be determined by reference to all the facts and circumstances of each case. In general, capital is a material income-producing factor if a substantial portion of the gross income of the business is attributable to the employment of capital in the business, as reflected, for example, by a substantial investment in inventories, plant, machinery, or other equipment. Additionally, capital is a material income-producing factor for banks and similar institutions. However, capital is not a material income-producing factor if the gross income of the business consists principally of fees, commissions, or other compensation for personal services performed by an individual.

*(2) Specific fields.* Regardless of whether paragraph (f)(1) applies, an organization engaged in any one or more of the following fields is a service organization:

(i) Health;

(ii) Law;

(iii) Engineering;

(iv) Architecture;

(v) Accounting;

(vi) Actuarial science;

(vii) Performing arts;

(viii) Consulting; and

(ix) Insurance.

Notwithstanding the preceding sentence, an organization will not be considered to be performing services merely because it is engaged in the manufacture or sale of equipment or supplies used in the above fields, or merely because it is engaged in performing research or publishing in the above fields. An organization will not be considered to be a service organization under this paragraph (f)(2) merely because an employee provides one of the enumerated services to the organization or to other employees of the organization unless the organization is also engaged in the performance of the same services for third parties.

*(3) Other organizations.* Organizations engaged in performing services and that are not described in paragraph (f)(1) or (2) shall not be considered to be service organizations. The Commissioner may expand the list of fields contained in paragraph (f)(2). However, no such expansion will be effective until the first day of the first plan year beginning at least 180 days after the publication of such change.

*(4) Exempted organizations.* The Commissioner may determine that certain organizations, or types of organizations, should not be considered as subject to the requirements of section 414(m), even though the organizations are described in paragraph (f)(1) or (2).

**(g) Multiple affiliated service groups.** *(1) Multiple First Service Organizations.* Two or more affiliated service groups will not be aggregated simply because an organization is an A Organization or a B Organization with respect to each affiliated service group.

*(2) Multiple A or B Organizations.* If an organization is a First Service Organization with respect to two or more A Organizations or two or more B Organizations, or both, all of the organizations shall be considered to constitute a single affiliated service group.

*(3)* The provisions of this paragraph may be illustrated by the following examples.

*Example (1).* Multiple First Service Organizations. (i) Corporation P provides secretarial service to numerous dentists in a medical building, each of whom maintains his own separate unincorporated practice. Dentist T owns 20 percent of the secretarial corporation and accounts for 20 percent of its gross receipts. Dentist W owns 25 percent of the corporation and accounts for 25 percent of its gross receipts.

(ii) Considering Dentist T as a First Service Organization, the secretarial corporation, P, is a B Organization because 20 percent of the gross receipts of the corporation are derived from performing services for Dentist T of a type historically performed by employees of dentists, and 20 percent of the interests in the corporation is owned by Dentist T. Accordingly, Dentist T and the corporation constitute an affiliated service group.

(iii) Considering Dentist W as a First Service Organization, the secretarial corporation, P, is a B Organization, because 25 percent of the gross receipts of the corporation are derived from performing services for Dentist W of a type historically performed by employees of dentists, and 25 percent of the interests in the corporation is owned by Dentist W. Accordingly, Dentist W and the corporation constitute an affiliated service group. However, this affiliated service group does not include Dentist T even though the secretarial corporation, P, is a B Organization with respect to both dentists. Thus, there are two affiliated service groups.

*Example (2).* Multiple B Organizations. (i) Doctor N is incorporated as Corporation N. Secretarial services are provided to Corporation N by Corporation Q. Corporation N owns 20 percent of the interests in the secretarial corporation and provides 20 percent of its gross receipts. Nursing services are provided to Corporation N by Corporation R. Corporation N owns 25 percent of the interests in the nursing corporation and provides 25 percent of its gross receipts.

(ii) Considering Corporation N as a First Service Organization, the secretarial corporation, Q, is a B Organization because 20 percent of the gross receipts of the secretarial corporation, Q, are derived from performing services for Corporation N of a type historically performed by employees of doctors, and 20 percent of the secretarial corporation is owned by the owner of Corporation N. Accordingly, Corporation N and the secretarial corporation, Q, constitute an affiliated service group.

(iii) Considering Corporation N as a First Service Organization, the nursing corporation, R, is a B Organization because 25 percent of the gross receipts of the nursing corporation, R, are derived from performing services for Corporation N of a type historically performed by employees of doctors, and 25 percent of the nursing corporation is owned by the owner of Corporation N. Accordingly, Corporation N and the nursing corporation constitute an affiliated service group.

(iv) For purposes of section 414(m), there will be considered to be one affiliated service group consisting of Corporation N, the secretarial corporation, Q, and the nursing corporation, R.

**Proposed § 1.414(m)-3 Employee benefit requirements.**
[*For Preamble, see ¶ 150,825*]

***Caution:*** The Treasury has not yet amended Reg § 1.414(m)-3 to reflect changes made by P.L. 99-514, P.L. 97-248.

**(a) Employee benefit requirements affected.** All of the employees of the members of an affiliated service group shall be treated as employed by a single employer for purposes of the following employee benefit requirements:

*(1)* Sections 401(a)(3) and 410 (relating to minimum participation requirements);

*(2)* Section 401(a)(4) (requiring that contributions or benefits do not discriminate in favor of employees who are officers, shareholders, or highly compensated);

*(3)* Sections 401(a)(7) and 411 (relating to minimum vesting standards);

*(4)* Sections 401(a)(16) and 415 (relating to limitations on contributions and benefits);

*(5)* Section 408(k) (relating to simplified employee pensions);

*(6)* Section 105(h) (relating to self-insured medical reimbursement plans);

*(7)* Section 125 (relating to cafeteria plans); and

*(8)* Pursuant to the authority granted in section 414(m)(6), section 401(a)(10) (relating to plans providing contributions or benefits to owner-employees).

**(b) Special requirements.** If a plan maintained by a member of an affiliated service group covers an employee described in section 401(c)(1) (self-employed individual), an owner-employee within the meaning of section 401(c)(3), or a shareholder-employee within the meaning of section 1379(d), the plan must also satisfy the following requirements to the extent they apply:

*(1)* Section 401(a)(9) (relating to special distribution requirements for plans benefiting self-employed individuals);

*(2)* Section 401(a)(10) (relating to special requirements for plans benefiting owner-employees);

*(3)* Section 401(a)(17) (relating to a limitation on the compensation base of plans benefiting self-employed individuals or shareholder-employees); and

*(4)* Section 401(a)(18) (relating to special requirements for defined benefit plans benefiting self-employed individuals or shareholder-employees).

Pursuant to the authority granted in section 414(m)(6), a plan that covers a self-employed individual, an owner-employee, or a shareholder-employee will be subject to the preceding requirements, even though that individual is not employed by the member of the affiliated service group maintaining the plan. These requirements apply only if the earned income of the self-employed individual or owner-employee or the compensation received as a shareholder- employee is taken into account in computing contributions or benefits under the plan.

**(c) Multiple employer plans.** *(1) General rule.* If a plan maintained by a member of an affiliated service group covers an individual who is not an employee of that member, but who is an employee of another member of that affiliated service group, the plan will be considered to be maintained by the member that does employ that individual. Thus, the plan will be considered to be maintained by more than one employer for purposes of section 413(c)(2) (relating to the exclusive benefit rule), (4) (relating to funding), (5) (relating to liability for funding tax), and (6) (relating to deductions).

Therefore, a member of an affiliated service group may deduct contributions on behalf of individuals who are not employees of that member, if the individuals are employed by another member of that affiliated service group.

*(2) Special rule.* The multiple employer plan rule contained in paragraph (c)(1) shall not apply in the case of a controlled group of corporations (as described in section 414(b)) or a group of trades or businesses under common control (as described in section 414(c)).

**(d) Discrimination.** In testing for discrimination under section 401(a)(4) (requiring that contributions or benefits do not discriminate in favor of employees who are officers, shareholders, or highly compensated), all of the compensation paid to an employee must be considered in determining the contributions or benefits under a plan maintained by a member of an affiliated service group, without regard to the percentage of the organization employing the individual owned by the member maintaining the plan.

**(e) Example.** The provisions of this section may be illustrated by the following example.

*(1)* T is incorporated and Corporation T is a partner in a service organization. Corporation T employs only its sole shareholder and maintains a retirement plan. W and Z, the other partners in the service organization, are not incorporated. Each partner has a one-third interest in the service organization. The partnership has eight common law employees.

*(2)* Considering the partnership as a First Service Organization, Corporation T is an A Organization because it is a partner in the First Service Organization and regularly performs services for the partnership or is regularly associated with the partnership in performing services for third persons. Accordingly, the partnership and Corporation T constitute an affiliated service group.

*(3)* If the retirement plan maintained by Corporation T covers any of the common law employees of the partnership, it will be benefiting individuals who are not employees of the member of the affiliated service group maintaining the plan (Corporation T). As such, the plan will be considered to be maintained by more than one employer, and will be subject to the rules of section 413(c)(2), (4), (5), and (6) and the regulations thereunder. Thus, contributions by Corporation T on behalf of these individuals will not fail to be deductible under section 404 merely because they are not employees of Corporation T. In testing for discrimination under section 401(a)(4), all of the compensation paid to the employees of the partnership must be taken into account in determining their contributions or benefits under the plan, without regard to the percentage of the partnership owned by Corporation T.

*(4)* If the plan maintained by Corporation T covers partners W and Z, the plan must also satisfy the requirements listed in paragraph (b), to the extent they are applicable.

**Proposed § 1.414(m)-4 Effective dates.** [*For Preamble, see ¶ 150,825*]

**(a) Effective dates.** *(1) New plans.* In the case of a plan that was not in existence on November 30, 1980, section 414(m) and the regulations thereunder apply to plan years ending after November 30, 1980.

*(2) Existing plans.* In the case of a plan in existence on November 30, 1980, section 414(m) and the regulations thereunder shall apply to plan years beginning after November 30, 1980.

**(b) Frozen plans.** *(1) Defined contribution plans.* In the case of a defined contribution plan inexistence on November 30, 1980, that fails to satisfy the requirements of section 401(a) solely because of the application of section 414(m), the trust shall be treated as continuing to satisfy the requirements of section 401(a) after the effective date of section 414(m) if the plan is terminated and all amounts are distributed to the participants within 180 days after the latest of:

(i) [The date of the publication of this regulation in the FEDERAL REGISTER as a Treasury decision],

(ii) The date on which notice of the final determination with respect to a request for a determination letter is issued by the Internal Revenue Service, such request is withdrawn, or such request is finally disposed of by the Internal Revenue Service, provided the request for a determination letter was pending on [the date of the publication of this regulation in the FEDERAL REGISTER as a Treasury decision] or, in the case of a request for a determination letter on the plan termination, was made within 60 days after [the date of the publication of this regulation in the Federal Register as a Treasury decision].

(iii) If a petition is timely filed with the United States Tax Court for a declaratory judgment under section 7476 with respect to the final determination (or the failure of the Internal Revenue Service to make a final determination) in response to such request, the date on which the decision of the United States Tax Court in such proceeding becomes final.

*(2) Defined benefit plans.* In the case of a defined benefit plan in existence on November 30, 1980, that fails to satisfy the requirements of section 401(a) solely because of the application of section 414(m), the trust shall be treated as continuing to satisfy the requirements of section 414(m) if the plan is terminated within 180 days after the latest of the dates determined in a manner consistent with paragraph (b)(1). However, deductions for contributions to the plan for plan years after the effective date of section 414(m) are limited to those necessary to satisfy the minimum funding standards of section 412.

**Proposed § 1.414(o)-1 Avoidance of employee benefit requirements through the use of separate organizations, employee leasing, or other arrangements.** [*For Preamble, see ¶ 151,095*]

**(a) In general.** *(1)* Pursuant to section 414(o), this section provides rules, in addition to the rules contained in sections 414(m) and 414(n) and the regulations thereunder, to prevent the avoidance of any employee benefit requirement listed in either § 1.414(m)-3 or § 1.414(n)-3, through the use of separate organizations, employee leasing, or other arrangements.

*(2)* For the definition of the terms "person" and "leased employee," see § 1.414(n)-1(b). For the definition of the term "organization," see § 1.414(m)-5(a)(2). For the definition of the terms "management functions" and "management activities or services," see § 1.414(m)-5(c).

*(3)* For purposes of this section, the term "plan" means a stock bonus, pension, or profit-sharing plan qualified under section 401(a) or a simplified employee pension under section 408(k).

*(4)* For purposes of this section, the term "employee" includes a "self-employed individual" as defined in section 401(c)(1).

*(5)* For purposes of this section, the term "maintained," when used in the context of a plan maintained by any person, means "maintained at any time."

*(6)* For purposes of this section, services performed for a person other than as an employee of such person means services performed directly or indirectly for such person.

**(b) Services performed by leased owners.** *(1) In general.* (i) If an individual is a leased owner with respect to a recipient, then for purposes of determining whether any qualified plan actually maintained by the recipient and whether any qualified plan maintained by a leasing organization in which the leased owner is a participant (or in which the leased owner has or had an accrued benefit) satisfies the employee benefit requirements of section 1.414(n)-3(a) (except for paragraph (a)(6) of that section) for a plan year, the leased owner's interest in the leasing organization's qualified plan attributable to services performed by the leased owner for the recipient is to be treated as provided under a separate qualified plan maintained by the recipient covering only the leased owner and the leased owner is to be treated as an employee of the recipient. If a separate qualified plan is treated as maintained by the recipient with respect to a leased owner and such leased owner also participates in a qualified plan actually maintained by the recipient, the leased owner's interest in the leasing organization's qualified plan attributable to the leased owner's performance of services for the recipient that is treated as provided to the leased owner under a separate qualified plan of the recipient is to be treated as provided to the leased owner under the qualified plan actually maintained by the recipient for purposes of determining whether such qualified plan satisfies the applicable employee benefit requirements. If either the separate qualified plan for the leased owner that is treated as maintained by the recipient or any qualified plan that is actually maintained by the recipient fails to satisfy any of the applicable employee benefit requirements, then except as provided in paragraphs (b)(1)(ii) and (b)(1)(iii) of this section, the following qualified plans shall be treated as not satisfying such requirements: any qualified plan actually maintained by the recipient in which the leased owner is a participant (or has or had an accrued benefit) and any qualified plan that is actually maintained by a leasing organization in which the leased owner has an interest that is attributable to the leased owner's performance of services for the recipient.

(ii) The Commissioner will not apply paragraph (b)(1)(i) of this section so as to disqualify a plan actually maintained by a recipient unless the Commissioner determines that, taking into account all the facts and circumstances, the disqualification of a leasing organization's plan would be ineffective as a means of securing compliance with the applicable employee benefit requirements. For example, it may be appropriate to disqualify the recipient's plan where a leasing organization's plan was terminated or substantial assets were removed therefrom in a year for which the statute of limitations has run with respect to the employer, employee, or trust.

(iii) If pursuant to paragraph (b)(1)(i) of this section, more than one leasing organization plan is subject to disqualification and at least one of the plans would not be disqualified if another plan or plans were disqualified first, all affected plan sponsors may, by agreement, elect the plan or plans subject to disqualification, provided that such election is not inconsistent with the purposes of this paragraph (b), such as where the plan or plans elected were terminated or substantial assets were removed therefrom in a year for which the statute of limitations has run with respect to the employer, employee, or trust. In the absence of such an election, the Commissioner, taking into account all the facts and circumstances, shall have the discretion to determine which plan or plans shall be disqualified.

*(2) Leased owner.* (i) For purposes of this paragraph (b), an individual is a "leased owner" with respect to a recipient if during the plan year of a plan maintained by a leasing organization the individual (A) performs any services for a recipient other than as an employee of the recipient and (B) is, at the time such services are performed, a five-percent owner of the recipient. The fact that an individual may also perform services as an employee of the recipient does not affect his status as a leased owner. If an individual becomes a leased owner with respect to a recipient, such individual is from that point on always to be considered a leased owner with respect to the recipient, notwithstanding anything in this paragraph (b) to the contrary, even if subsequently all services performed by the individual for the recipient are performed as an employee of the recipient.

(ii) Except as provided in paragraph (b)(2)(iii) of this section, and notwithstanding the first sentence of paragraph (b)(2)(i) of this section to the contrary, an individual is not a leased owner with respect to a recipient for purposes of a plan year of a plan maintained by a leasing organization if, during each calendar year containing at least one day of such plan year, less than 25 percent of his total hours actually worked for substantial compensation are for all recipients with respect to which he is a leased owner (but for the application of this paragraph (b)(2)(ii)) and less than 25 percent of his total compensation is derived from performing services for all such recipients. For purposes of this paragraph (b)(2)(ii), performing services for the recipient includes services performed as an employee of the recipient and in any other capacity. For purposes of this paragraph (b)(2)(ii), the term "compensation" means (A) with respect to services performed as a common-law employee, compensation reportable on Form W-2, and (B) with respect to services performed other than as a common-law employee, earned income as defined in section 401(c)(2). See section 414(s) for the definition of "compensation" for years beginning after December 31, 1986.

(iii) Paragraph (b)(2)(ii) of this section does not apply to an individual who (A) is a leased owner with respect to a recipient pursuant to the application of the first sentence of paragraph (b)(2)(i) of this section, and (B) performs professional services (as defined in § 1.414(m)-1(c)) for the recipient, whether or not as an employee of the recipient, during the plan year of the plan maintained by the leasing organization, of the same type as the professional services performed by the recipient for third parties.

*(3) Recipient.* For purposes of this paragraph (b), the term "recipient" has the same meaning as in paragraphs (b)(2) and (b)(6) of § 1.414(n)-1, except that "leased owner" is substituted for "leased employee."

*(4) Leasing organization.* For purposes of this paragraph (b), the term "leasing organization" has the same meaning as in § 1.414(n)-1(b)(1), except that "leased owner" is substituted for "leased employee" and that "or provided" is added after "provides."

*(5) Five-percent owner.* For purposes of this paragraph (b), an individual is a five-percent owner of a recipient if such individual is a 5-percent owner (as defined in section 416(i)) of any person included in the recipient.

*(6) Contributions, benefit, etc., provided to a leased owner.* For purposes of this paragraph (b), a leased owner's interest in a leasing organization (as defined in § 1.414(n)-2(b)(1)(ii) and in a leasing organization's qualified plan (as

defined in § 1.414(n)-2(b)(1)(i)), to the extent attributable to services for the recipient by the leased owner, is, for purposes of the applicable employee benefit requirements, treated as provided by the recipient or under a plan of the recipient. For rules relating to the application of this requirement, see paragraph (b)(2) of § 1.414(n)-2.

*(7) Effect on employee rules.* To the extent that a leased owner performs services for a recipient other than in the capacity of an employee, a leased owner is not an employee of the recipient and may not be actually covered by a plan of the recipient. Such leased owner may, however, qualify as a leased employee under section 414(n) and the regulations thereunder.

**(c)** through (k)(1) withdrawn 4/27/93.

*(2)* The provisions of paragraph (b) of this section are effective for tax years of recipients beginning after December 31, 1983. Therefore, the provisions of paragraph (b) apply to plan years beginning during and after the first tax year of a recipient beginning after December 31, 1983. For purposes of applying paragraph (b) of this section to plan years beginning during and after the first tax year of a recipient beginning after December 31, 1983, contributions, forfeitures and benefits provided during any plan year beginning prior to the first tax year of a recipient beginning after December 31, 1983, shall be taken into account if they would have been taken into account had paragraph (b) been effective for such prior plan year.

*(3)* [Withdrawn 4/27/93].

*(4)* [Withdrawn 4/27/93].

* * * * *

### § 1.414(q)-1 Highly compensated employee.

***Caution:*** The Treasury has not yet amended Reg § 1.414(q)-1 to reflect changes made by P.L. 104-188.

Q&A-1 through Q&A-8: [Reserved] See § 1.414(q)-1T, Q&A-1 through Q&A-8 for further guidance.

Q-9. How is the top-paid group determined?

A-9. **(a) [Reserved]** See § 1.414(q)-1T, Q&A-9(a) for further guidance.

**(b) Number of employees in the top-paid group.** *(1) Exclusions.* The number of employees who are in the top-paid group for a year is equal to 20 percent of the total number of active employees of the employer for such year. However, solely for purposes of determining the total number of active employees in the top-paid group for a year, the employees described in § 1.414(q)-1T, A-9(b)(1)(i), (ii) and (iii)(B) are disregarded. Paragraph (g) of this A-9 provides rules for determining those employees who are excluded for purposes of applying section 414(r)(2)(A), relating to the 50-employee requirement applicable to a qualified separate line of business.

(i) through (iii) [Reserved] See § 1.414(q)-1T, Q&A-9(b)(1)(i) through (iii) for further guidance.

*(2) Alternative exclusion provisions.* (i) and (ii) [Reserved] See § 1.414(q)-1T, Q&A-9(b)(2)(i) and (ii) for further guidance.

(iii) Method of election. The elections in this paragraph (b)(2) must be provided for in all plans of the employer and must be uniform and consistent with respect to all situations in which the section 414(q) definition is applicable to the employer. Thus, with respect to all plan years beginning in the same calendar year, the employer must apply the test uniformly for purposes of determining its top-paid group with respect to all its qualified plans and employee benefit plans. If either election is changed during the determination year, no recalculation of the look-back year based on the new election is required, provided the change in election does not result in discrimination in operation.

**(c) through (f) [Reserved]** See § 1.414(q)-1T, Q&A-9(c) through (f) for further guidance.

**(g) Excluded employees under section 414(r)(2)(A).** *(1) In general.* This paragraph (g) provides the rules for determining which employees are excluded employees for purposes of applying section 414(r)(2)(A), relating to the 50-employee requirement applicable to a qualified separate line of business.

*(2) Excluded employees.* (i) Age and service exclusion. All employees are excluded who are described in § 1.414(q)-1T, A-9(b)(1)(i) (relating to exclusions based on age or service). For this purpose, the rules in § 1.414(q)-1T, A-9(e) and (f) (relating respectively to the 17½-hour rule and the 6-month rule) apply. However, the election in § 1.414(q)-1T, A-9(b)(2)(i) (permitting the employer to elect reduced minimum age or service requirements) does not apply.

(ii) Nonresident alien exclusion. All employees are excluded who are described in § 1.414(q)-1T, A-9(b)(1)(ii) (relating to the exclusion of nonresident aliens with no U.S.-source income from the employer).

(iii) Inclusion of employees covered under a collective bargaining agreement. All employees are included who are described in § 1.414(q)-1T, A-9(b)(1)(iii)(A) (relating to employees covered under a collective bargaining agreement) and who are not otherwise described in paragraph (g)(2)(i) or (ii) of this A-9. For this purpose, the exclusion in § 1.414(q)-1T, A-9(b)(1)(iii)(B) and the related election in § 1.414(q)-1T, A-9(b)(2)(ii) do not apply.

*(3) Applicable period.* The determination of which employees are excluded employees is made on the basis of the testing year specified in the regulations under section 414(r) and not on the basis of the determination year or the look-back year under section 414(q).

**(h) Effective date.** The provisions of this A-9 apply to plan years and testing years beginning on or after January 1, 1994.

Q&A-10 through Q&A-15: [Reserved] See § 1.414(q)-1T, Q&A-10 through Q&A-15 for further guidance.

T.D. 8548, 6/23/94.

### § 1.414(q)-1T Highly compensated employee (temporary).

***Caution:*** The Treasury has not yet amended Reg § 1.414(q)-1T to reflect changes made by P.L. 104-188.

The following questions and answers relate to the definition of "highly compensated employee" provided in section 414(q). The definitions and rules provided in these questions and answers are provided solely for purposes of determining the group of highly compensated employees.

**Table of contents.**

Q&A-5 Definition of separation year.

Q&A-6 Definition of employer.

Q&A-7 Definition of employee.

Q&A-8 Definition of 5-percent owner.

Q&A-9 Definition of top-paid group.

Q&A-10 Definition of officer and rules on inclusion of officers in highly compensated group.

Q&A-11 Rules with respect to family aggregation.

Q&A-12 Definition of family member.

Q&A-13 Definition of compensation.

Q&A-14 Rules with respect to the relevant determination periods.

Q&A-15 Transition rule applicable to plan years beginning in 1987 and 1988 for certain employers that have plans that must comply with the provisions of section 401(k)(3) or 401(m)(2).

Q-1. To what employee benefit plans and statutory provisions is the definition of highly compensated employee contained in section 414(q) applicable?

A-1. **(a) In general.** This definition is applicable to statutory provisions that incorporate the definition by reference.

**(b) Qualified retirement plans.** *(1) In general.* Generally, this definition is incorporated in many of the nondiscrimination requirements applicable to pension, profit-sharing, and stock bonus plans qualified under section 401(a). See, e.g., the nondiscrimination provisions of sections 401(a)(4) and (5), 401(k)(3), 401(l), 401(m), 406(b), 407(b), 408(k), 410(b) and 411(d)(1). The definition is also incorporated by certain other provisions with respect to such plans, including the aggregation rules of section 414(m) and section 4975 (tax on prohibited transactions).

*(2) Not applicable where not incorporated by reference.* This definition is not applicable to qualified plan provisions that do not incorporate it. See, e.g., section 415 (limitations on contributions and benefits), with the exception of section 415(c)(3)(C) and 415(c)(6) (special rules for permanent and total disability and employee stock ownership plans respectively).

**(c) Other employee benefit plans or arrangements.** This definition is incorporated by various sections relating to employee benefit provisions. See, e.g., section 89 (certain other employee benefit plans), section 106 (accident and health plans), 117(d) (qualified tuition reduction), section 125 (cafeteria plans), section 129 (dependent care assistance programs), section 132 (certain fringe benefits), section 274 (certain entertainment, etc. expenses), section 423(b) (employee stock purchase plan provisions), section 501(c)(17) and (18) (certain exempt trusts providing benefits to employees), and section 505 (certain exempt organizations or trusts providing benefits to individuals). See the respective sections for the applicable effective dates.

**(d) ERISA.** This definition is not determinative with respect to any provisions of Title I of the Employee Retirement Income Security Act of 1974 (ERISA), unless it is explicitly incorporated by reference (e.g., section 408(b)(1)(B)).

Q-2. Who is a highly compensated employee?

A-2. The group of employees (including former employees) who are highly compensated employees consists of both highly compensated active employees (see A-3 of this § 1.414(q)-1T) and highly compensated former employees (see A-4 of this § 1.414(q)-1T). In many circumstances, highly compensated active employees and highly compensated former employees are considered separately in applying the provisions for which the definition of highly compensated employees in section 414(q) is applicable. Specific rules with respect to the treatment of highly compensated active employees and highly compensated former employees will be provided in the regulations with respect to the sections to which the definition of highly compensated employees is applicable.

Q-3. Who is a highly compensated active employee?

A-3. **(a) General rule.** For purposes of the year for which the determination is being made (the determination year), a highly compensated active employee is any employee who, with respect to the employer, performs services during the determination year and is described in any one or more of the following groups applicable with respect to the look-back year calculation and/or determination year calculation for such determination year. See A-14 for rules relating to the periods for which the look-back year calculation and determination year calculation are to be made.

*(1) Look-back year calculation.*

(i) 5-percent owner. The employee is a 5-percent owner at any time during the look-back year (i.e., generally, the 12-month period immediately preceding the determination year; see A-14. (See A-8 of this § 1.414(q)-1T.)

(ii) Compensation above $75,000. The employee receives compensation in excess of $75,000 during the look-back year.

(iii) Compensation above $50,000 and top-paid group. The employee receives compensation in excess of $50,000 during the look-back year and is a member of the top-paid group for the look-back year. (See A-9 of this § 1.414(q)-1T).

(iv) Officer. The employee is an "includible officer" during the look-back year. (See A-10 of this § 1.414(q)-1T.)

*(2) Determination year calculation.*

(i) 5-percent owner. The employee is a 5-percent owner at any time during the determination year. (See A-8 of this § 1.414(q)-1T.)

(ii) Top-100 employees. The employee is both (A) described in paragraph (a)(1)(i), (ii) and/or (iv) of this A-3, when such paragraphs are modified to substitute the determination year for the look-back year, and (B) one of the 100 employees who receive the most compensation from the employer during the determination year.

**(b) Rounding and tie-breaking rules.** In making the look-back year and determination year calculations for a determination year, it may be necessary for an employer to adopt a rule for rounding calculations (e.g., in determining the number of employees in the top-paid group). In addition, it may be necessary to adopt a rule breaking ties among two or more employees (e.g., in identifying those particular employees who are in the top-paid group or who are among the 100 most highly compensated employees). In such cases, the employer may adopt any rounding or tie-breaking rules it desires, so long as such rules are reasonable, nondiscriminatory, and uniformly and consistently applied.

**(c) Adjustments to dollar thresholds.** *(1) Indexing of dollar thresholds.* The dollar amounts in paragraph (a)(1)(i) and (ii) of this A-3 are indexed at the same time and in the same manner as the section 415(b)(1)(A) dollar limitation for defined benefit plans.

*(2) Applicable dollar threshold.* The applicable dollar amount for a particular determination year or look-back year is the dollar amount for the calendar year in which such de-

termination year or look-back year begins. Thus, the dollar amount for purposes of determining the highly compensated active employees for a particular look-back year is based on the calendar year in which such look-back year begins, not the calendar year in which such look-back year ends or in which the determination year with respect to such look-back year begins.

**(d) Employees described in more than one group.** An individual who is a highly compensated active employee for a determination year, by reason of being described in one group in paragraph (a) of this A-3, under either the look-back year calculation or the determination year calculation, is not disregarded in determining whether another individual is a highly compensated active employee by reason of being described in another group under paragraph (a). For example, an individual who is a highly compensated active employee for a determination year, by reason of being a 5-percent owner during such year, who receives compensation in excess of $50,000 during both the look-back year and the determination year, is taken into account in determining the group of employees who are highly compensated active employees for such determination year by reason of receiving more than $50,000, and being in the top-paid group under either or both the look-back year calculation or determination year calculation for such determination year.

**(e) Examples.** The following examples, in which the determination year and look-back year are the calendar year, are illustrative of the rules in paragraph (a) of this A-3. For purposes of these examples, the threshold dollar amounts in paragraph (a)(1)(ii) and (iii) of this A-3 are not increased pursuant to paragraph (c) of this A-3.

*Example (1).* Employee A, who is not at any time a 5-percent owner, an officer, or a member of the top-100 within the meaning of paragraph (a)(1)(i), or (iv), or (a)(2)(i) or (ii), but who was a member of the top-paid group for each year, is included in or excluded from the highly compensated groups as specified below for the following years:

| Year | Compensation | Status | Comments |
|---|---|---|---|
| 1986 | $45,000 | N/A | Although prior to 414(g) effective date, 1986 constitutes the look–back year for purposes of determining the highly compensated group for the 1987 determination year. |
| 1987 | 80,000 | Excl | Excluded because A was not an employee described in paragraph (a)(1)(ii) or (iii) of this A-3 for the look–back year (1986). |
| 1988 | 80,000 | Incl | Included because A was an employee described in paragraph (a)(1)(ii) or (iii) of this A-3 for the look–back year (1987). |
| 1989 | 45,000 | Incl | Included because A was an employee described in paragraph (a)(1)(ii) or (iii) of this A-3 for the look–back year (1988). |
| 1990 | 45,000 | Excl | Excluded because A was not an employee described in paragraph (a)(1)(ii) or (iii) of this A-3 for the look–back year (1989). |

*Example (2).* Assuming the same facts as those given in Example (1), except that A is a member of the top-100 employees within the meaning of paragraph (a)(2)(ii) of this A-3 for the 1987 year and 1990 year, the results are as follows:

| Year | Compensation | Status | Comments |
|---|---|---|---|
| 1986 | $45,000 | N/A | Although prior to 414(g) effective date, 1986 constitutes the look–back year for purposes of determining the highly compensated group for the 1987 determination year. |
| 1987 | 80,000 | Incl | Included because A was an employee described in paragraph (a)(1)(ii) or (iii) of this A-3 for the determination year (1987) and was described in paragraph (a)(2)(ii) of this A-3 in that year. |
| 1988 | 80,000 | Incl | Included because A was an employee described in paragraph (a)(1)(ii) or (iii) of this A-3 for the look–back year (1987). |
| 1989 | 45,000 | Incl | Included because A was an employee described in paragraph (a)(1)(ii) or (iii) of this A-3 for the look–back year (1988). |
| 1990 | 45,000 | Excl | Excluded even though in top 100 employees during 1990 determination year because A was not an employee described in paragraph (a)(1)(ii) or (iii) of this A-3 for the look–back year (1989) or for the determination year (1990). |

Q-4. Who is a highly compensated former employee?

A-4. **(a) General rule.** Except to the extent provided in paragraph (d) of this A-4, a highly compensated former employee for a determination year is any former employee who, with respect to the employer, had a separation year (as defined in A-5 of this § 1.414(q)-1T) prior to the determination year and was a highly compensated active employee as defined in A-3 of this § 1.414(q)-1T for either such employee's separation year or any determination year ending on or after the employee's 55th birthday. Thus, for example, an employee who is a highly compensated active employee for such employee's separation year, by reason of receiving over $75,000 during the look-back year, is a highly compensated former employee for determination years after such employee's separation year.

**(b) Special rule for employees who perform no services for the employer in the determination year.** For purposes of this rule, employees who perform no services for an employer during a determination year are treated as former employees. Thus, for example, an employee who performed no services for the employer during a determination year, by reason of a leave of absence during such year, is treated as a former employee for such year.

**(c) Dollar amounts for pre-1987 determination years.** For determination years beginning before January 1, 1987, the dollar amounts in paragraph (a)(1)(B) and (C) of A-2 of this § 1.414(q)-1T are $75,000 and $50,000 respectively.

**(d) Special rule for employees who separated from service before January 1, 1987.** *(1) Election of special rule.* Employers may elect to apply paragraph (d)(2) of this A-4 in lieu of paragraph (a) of this A-4 in determining whether former employees who separated from service prior to January 1, 1987, are highly compensated former employees. If this election is made with respect to any qualified plan, it must be provided for in the plan. If the employer makes this election with respect to any employee benefit plan, such election must be used uniformly for all purposes for which the section 414(q) definition is applicable. The election, once made, cannot be changed without the consent of the Commissioner.

*(2) Special definition of highly compensated former employee.* A highly compensated former employee includes any former employee who separated from service with the employer prior to January 1, 1987, and was described in any one or more of the following groups during either the employee's separation year (or the year preceding such separation year) or any year ending on or after such individual's 55th birthday (or the last year ending before such employee's 55th birthday):

(i) 5-percent owner. The employee was a 5-percent owner of the employer at any time during the year.

(ii) Compensation amount. The employee received compensation is excess of $50,000 during the year.

The determinations provided for in this paragraph (b)(2) may be made on the basis of the calendar year, the plan year, or any other twelve month period selected by the employer and applied on a reasonable and consistent basis.

**(e) Rules with respect to former employees.** *(1) In general.* For specific provisions with respect to the treatment of former employees and of highly compensated former employees, refer to the rules with respect to which the section 414(q) definition of highly compensated employee is applicable.

*(2) Former employees excluded in determining top-paid group, top-100 employees and includible officers.* Former employees are not included in the top-paid group, the group of the top-100 employees, or the group of includible officers for purposes of applying section 414(q) to active employees. In addition, former employees are not counted as employees for purposes of determining the number of employees in the top-paid group.

Q-5. What is a separation year for purposes of section 414(q)?

A-5. **(a) Separation year.** *(1) In general.* The separation year generally is the determination year during which the employee separates from service with the employer. For purposes of this rule, an employee who performs no services for the employer during a determination year will be treated as having separated from service with the employer in the year in which such employee last performed services for the employer. Thus, for example, an employee who performs no services for the employer by reason of being on a leave of absence throughout the determination year is considered to have separated from service with the employer in the year in which such employee last performed services prior to beginning the leave of absence.

*(2) Deemed separation.* An employee who performs services for the employer during a determination year may be deemed to have separated from service with the employer during such year pursuant to the rules in paragraph (a)(3) of this A-5. Such deemed separation year is relevant for purposes of determining whether such employee is a highly compensated former employee after such employee actually separates from service, not for purposes of identifying such employee as either an active or former employee. Because employees to whom the provisions of paragraph (a)(2) of this A-5 apply are still performing services for the employer during the determination year, they are treated as active employees. Thus, for example, an employee who has a deemed separation year in 1989, a year during which he was a highly compensated employee, who continues to work for the employer until he retires from employment in 1995, is an active employee of the employer until 1995 and is either highly compensated or not highly compensated for any determination year during such period based on the rules with respect to highly compensated active employees. For determination years after the year of such employee's retirement, such employee is a highly compensated former employee because such employee was a highly compensated active employee for the deemed separation year.

*(3) Deemed separation year.* An employee will be deemed to have a separation year if, in a determination year prior to attainment of age 55, the employee receives compensation in an amount less than 50% of the employee's average annual compensation for the three consecutive calendar years preceding such determination year during which the employee received the greatest amount of compensation from the employer (or the total period of the employee's service with the employer, if less).

*(4) Leave of absence.* The deemed separation rules contained in paragraph (a)(2) and (3) of this A-5 apply without regard to whether the reduction in compensation occurs on account of a leave of absence.

**(b) Deemed resumption of employment.** An employee who is treated as having a deemed separation year by reason of the provisions of paragraph (a) of this A-5 will not be treated as a highly compensated former employee (by reason of such deemed separation year) after such employee actually separates from service with the employer if, after such deemed separation year, and before the year of actual separation; such employee's services for and compensation from the employer for a determination year increase significantly so that such employee is treated as having a deemed resumption of employment. The determination of whether an employee who has incurred a deemed separation year has an increase in services and compensation sufficient to result in a deemed resumption of employment will be made on the basis of all the surrounding facts and circumstances pertaining to each individual case. At a minimum, there must be an increase in compensation from the employer to the extent that such compensation would not result in a deemed separation year under the tests in paragraph (a)(2) of this A-5 using the same three-year period taken into account in such paragraph.

**(c) Examples.** Paragraphs (a) and (b) of this A-5 are illustrated by the following examples based on calendar years. For purposes of these examples the threshold dollar amounts in A-5(a) of this § 1.414(q)-1T have not been increased pursuant to A-5(b) of this § 1.414(q)-1T.

*Example (1).* Assume that in 1990 A is a highly compensated employee of X by reason of having earned more than $75,000 during the 1989 look-back year. In 1987, 1988 and 1989, A's years of greatest compensation received from X, A received $76,000, $80,000 and $79,000 respectively. In February of 1990, A received $30,000 in compensation. Because A's compensation during the 1990 determination year is less than 50% of A's average annual compensation from

X during A's high three prior determination years, A is deemed to have a separation year during the 1990 determination year pursuant to the provisions of paragraph (a) of this A-5. Since A is a highly compensated employee for X in 1990, A's deemed separation year, A will be treated as a highly compensated former employee after A actually separates from service with the employer unless A experiences a deemed resumption of employment within the meaning of paragraph (b) of this A-5.

*Example (2).* Assume that in 1990 A is a highly compensated employee by reason of having been an officer (with annual compensation in excess of the section 415(c)(1)(A) dollar limitation) during the 1989 look-back year. A's compensation from X during 1990 is $37,000. A's average compensation from X for the three-year period ending with or within January, 1990, was $60,000. A's compensation during the 1990 determination year is not less than 50% of the compensation earned during the test period. Therefore, A is not deemed to have a separation year under paragraph (a)(2)(i) of this A-5.

*Example (3).* Assume that in 1990 C is 35 and a highly compensated employee of Z for the reasons given in Example (1) with the same compensation set forth in that example. During 1990, C leaves C's 40 hour a week position as director of the actuarial division of Z and starts working as an actuary for the same division, producing actuarial reports approximately 15 to 20 hours a week, approximately half of these hours at home. C contemplates returning to full-time employment with Z when C's child enters school. During the 1990 determination year, C's compensation is less than 50% of C's compensation during her high three preceding determination years. Therefore, C has a deemed separation year during the 1990 determination year. In 1991 C commences working 32 hours a week for X at X's place of business and receives compensation in an amount equal to 80 percent of her average annual compensation during her high three prior determination years. The C's increased compensation, considered in conjunction with the reasons for the reduction in service, the nature and extent of the services performed before and after the reduction in services, and the lack of proximity of C's age to age 55 at the time of the reduction are sufficient to establish that C has a deemed resumption of employment within the meaning of paragraph (b) of this A-5. Therefore, when C separates from service with the employer, C will not be treated as a highly compensated former employee by reason of C's deemed separation year in 1990.

Q-6. Who is the employer?

A-6. **(a) Aggregation of certain entities.** The employer is the entity employing the employees and includes all other entities aggregated with such employing entity under the aggregation requirements of section 414(b), (c), (m) and (o). Thus, the following entities must be taken into account as a single employer for purposes of determining the employees who are "highly compensated employees" within the meaning of section 414(q):

*(1)* All corporations that are members of a controlled group of corporations (as defined in section 414(b)) that includes the employing entity.

*(2)* All trades or businesses (whether or not incorporated) that are under common control (as defined in section 414(c)) which group includes the employing entity.

*(3)* All organizations (whether or not incorporated) that are members of an affiliated service group (as defined in section 414(m)) that includes the employing entity.

*(4)* Any other entities required to be aggregated with the employing entity pursuant to section 414(o) and the regulations thereunder.

**(b) Priority of aggregation provisions.** The aggregation requirements of paragraph (a) of this A-6 and of A-7(b) of this section with respect to leased employees are applied before the application of any of the other provisions of section 414(q) and this section.

**(c) Line of business rules.** The section 414(r) rules with respect to separate lines of business are not applicable in determining the group of highly compensated employees.

Q-7. Who is an employee for purposes of section 414(q)?

A-7. **(a) General rule.** Except as provided in paragraph (b) of this A-7, the term "employee" for purposes of section 414(q) refers to individuals who perform services for the employer and are either common-law employees of the employer or self-employed individuals who are treated as employees pursuant to section 401(c)(1). This rule with respect to the inclusion of certain self-employed individuals in the group of highly compensated employees is applicable whether or not such individuals are eligible to participate in the plan or benefit arrangement being tested.

**(b) Leased employees.** *(1) In general.* The term "employee" includes a leased employee who is treated as an employee of the recipient pursuant to the provisions of section 414(n)(2) or 414(o)(2). Employees that an employer treats as leased employees under section 414(n), pursuant to the requirements of section 414(o), are considered to be leased employees for purposes of this rule.

*(2) Safe-harbor exception.* For purposes of qualified retirement plans, if an employee who would be a leased employee within the meaning of section 414(n)(2) is covered in a safe-harbor plan described in section 414(n)(5) (a qualified money purchase pension plan maintained by the leasing organization), and not otherwise covered under a qualified retirement plan of the employer, then such employee is excluded from the term "employee" unless the employer elects to include such employee pursuant to the provisions of paragraph (4) of this paragraph (b).

*(3) Other employee benefit plans.* The exception in paragraph (b)(2) of this A-7 is not applicable to the determination of the highly compensated employee group for purposes of the sections enumerated in section 414(n)(3)(C). Thus, for example, a leased employee covered by a safe-harbor plan is considered to be an employee in applying the nondiscrimination provisions of section 89 to statutory benefit plans. Consequently, an employer with leased employees covered in a safe-harbor plan may have 2 groups of highly compensated employees, one with respect to its retirement plans and another with respect to its statutory benefit plans.

*(4) Election with respect to leased employee exclusion.* An employer may elect to include the employees excepted under the provisions of paragraph (b)(2) of this A-7 in determining the highly compensated group with respect to an employer's retirement plans. Thus, for example, by electing to forego the exception in paragraph (b)(2) of this A-7, an employer may achieve more uniform highly compensated employee groups for purposes of its retirement plans and welfare benefit plans. The election to include such employees must be made on a reasonable and consistent basis and must be provided for in the plan.

Q-8. Who is a 5-percent owner of the employer?

A-8. An employee is a 5-percent owner of the employer for a particular year if, at any time during such year, such employee is a 5-percent owner as defined in section 416(i)(B)(i) and § 1.416-1 A T-17&18. Thus, if the employer is a corporation, a 5-percent owner is any employee who owns (or is considered as owning within the meaning of section 318) more than 5 percent of the value of the outstanding stock of the corporation or stock possessing more than 5 percent of the total combined voting power of all stock of the corporation. If the employer is not a corporation, a 5-percent owner is any employee who owns more than 5 percent of the capital or profits interest in the employer. The rules of subsections (b), (c), and (m) of section 414 do not apply for purposes of determining who is a 5-percent owner. Thus, for example, an individual who is a 5-percent owner of a subsidiary corporation that is part of a controlled group of corporations within the meaning of section 414(b) is treated as a 5-percent owner for purposes of these rules.

Q-9. How is the "top-paid group" determined?

A-9. **(a) General rule.** An employee is in the top-paid group of employees for a particular year if such employee is in the group consisting of the top 20 percent of the employer's employees when ranked on the basis of compensation received from the employer during such year. The identification of the particular employees who are in the top-paid group for a year involves a two-step procedure:

*(1)* The determination of the number of employees that corresponds to 20 percent of the employer's employees, and

*(2)* The identification of the particular employees who are among the number of employees who receive the most compensation during this year. Employees who perform no services for the employer during a year are not included in making either of these determinations for such year.

**(b) Number of employees in the top-paid group.** *(1) Exclusions. [Reserved] See § 1.414(q)-1, Q&A-9(b)(1) for further information.*

(i) Age and service exclusion. The following employees are excluded on the basis of age or service absent an election by the employer pursuant to the rules in paragraph (b)(2) of this A-9:

(A) Employees who have not completed 6 months of service by the end of such year. For purposes of this paragraph (A), an employee's service in the immediately preceding year is added to service in the current year in determining whether the exclusion is applicable with respect to a particular employee in the current year. For example, given a plan with a calendar determination year, if employee A commences work August 1, 1989, and terminates employment May 31, 1990, A may be excluded under this paragraph (b)(1)(i)(A) in 1989 because A completed only 5 months of service by December 31, 1989. However, A cannot be excluded pursuant to this rule in 1990 because A has completed 10 months of service, for purposes of this rule, by the end of 1990.

(B) Employees who normally work less than 17½ hours per week as defined in paragraph (d) of this A-9 for such year.

(C) Employees who normally work during less than 6 months during any year as defined in paragraph (e) of this A-9 for such year.

(D) Employees who have not had their 21st birthdays by the end of such year.

(ii) Nonresident alien exclusion. Employees who are nonresident aliens and who receive no earned income (within the meaning of section 911(d)(2)) from the employer that constitutes income from sources within the United States (within the meaning of section 861(a)(3)) are excluded.

(iii) Collective bargaining exclusion. (A) In general. Except as provided in paragraph (B) of this paragraph (b)(1)(iii), employees who are included in a unit of employees covered by an agreement that the Secretary of Labor finds to be a collective bargaining agreement between employee representatives and the employer, which agreement satisfies section 7701(a)(46) and § 301.7701-17T (Temporary), are included in determining the number of employees in the top-paid group.

(B) Percentage exclusion provision. If 90 percent or more of the employees of the employer are covered under collective bargaining agreements that the Secretary of Labor finds to be collective bargaining agreements between employee representatives and the employer which agreements satisfy section 7701(a)(46) and § 301.7701-17T (Temporary), and the plan being tested covers only employees who are not covered under such agreements, then the employees who are covered under such collective bargaining agreements are not counted in determining the number of noncollective bargaining employees who will be included in the top-paid group for purposes of testing such plan. In addition, such employees are not included in the top-paid group for such purposes. Thus, if the conditions of this paragraph (b)(1)(iii)(B) are satisfied, a separate calculation is required to determine the number and identity of noncollective bargaining employees who will be highly compensated employees by reason of receiving over $50,000 and being in the top-paid group of employees for purposes of testing those plans that cover only noncollective bargaining employees.

*(2) Alternative exclusion provisions.* (i) Age and service exclusion election. An employer may elect, on a consistent and uniform basis, to modify the permissible exclusions set forth in paragraph (b)(1)(i)(A), (B), (C), and (D) of this A-9 by substituting any shorter period of service or lower age than that specified in such paragraph. These exclusions may be modified to substitute a zero service or age requirement.

(ii) Election not to apply percentage exclusion provision. An employer may elect not to exclude employees under the rules in paragraph (b)(1)(iii)(B) of this A-9.

(iii) Method of election. [Reserved] See § 1.414(q)-1, Q&A-9(b)(2)(iii) for further information.

**(c) Identification of top-paid group members.** With the exception of the paragraph (b)(1)(iii) of this A-9 exclusion for certain employees covered by collective bargaining agreements, the exclusions in paragraph (b)(1) of this A-9 are not applicable for purposes of identifying the particular employees in the top-paid group. Thus, for example, even if an employee who normally works for less than 17½ hours is excluded in determining the number of employees in the top-paid group such employee may be a member of the top-paid group. Similarly, if during a determination year, employee A receives over $75,000 and is one of the top-100 employees ranked by compensation, then employee A is a highly compensated active employee for such determination year. This is true even though employee A has worked less than six months and thus may be excluded in determining the number of persons in the top-paid group for the determination year.

**(d) Example.** Paragraphs (b) and (c) of this A-9 are illustrated by the following example:

*Example.* Employer X has 200 active employees during the 1989 determination year, 100 of whom normally work less than 17½ hours per week during such year and 80 of whom normally work less than 15 hours per week during such year. X elects to exclude all employees who normally work less than 15 hours per week in determining the number of employees in the top-paid group. Thus, X excludes 80 employees in determining the number of employees in the top-paid group. X's top-paid group for the 1989 determination year consists of 20% of 120 or 24 employees. All 200 of X's employees must then be ranked in order by compensation received during the year, and the 24 employees X paid the greatest amount of compensation during the year are top-paid employees with respect to X for the 1989 determination year.

**(e) 17½ hour rule.** *(1) In general.* The determination of whether an employee normally works less than 17½ hours per week is made independently for each year based on the rules in paragraph (e)(2) and (3) of this A-9. In making this determination, weeks during which the employee did not work for the employer are not considered. Thus, for example, if an employee normally works twenty hours a week for twenty-five weeks during the fall and winter school quarters, 10 hours a week for the 12 week spring quarter, and does not work for the employer during the three-month summer quarter, such employee is treated as normally working more than 17½ hours per week under the rule of this paragraph (e).

*(2) Deemed above 17½.* An employee who works 17½ hours a week or more, for more than fifty percent of the total weeks worked by such employee during the year, is deemed to normally work more than 17½ hours a week for purposes of this rule.

*(3) Deemed below 17½.* An employee who works less than 17½ hours a week for fifty percent or more of the total weeks worked by such employee during the year is deemed to normally work less than 17½ hours a week for purposes of this rule.

*(4) Application.* The determination provided for in paragraph (e)(1), (2), and (3) of this A-9 may be made separately with respect to each employee, or on the basis of groups of employees who fall within particular job categories as established by the employer on a reasonable basis. For example, under the rule of this paragraph (e)(4) an employer may exclude all office cleaning personnel if, for the year in question, the employees performing this function normally work less than 17½ hours a week. This is true even though one or more employees within this group normally work in excess of 17½ hours. The election to make this determination on the basis of individuals or groups is operational and does not require a plan provision.

*(5) Application based on groups.* (i) Groups of employees who perform the same job are not required to be considered as one category for purposes of the rule in paragraph (e)(4) of this A-9. Thus, for example, an employer supermarket may determine its highly compensated employees by excluding part-time grocery checkers if such personnel normally work less than 17½ hours a week while continuing to include full-time personnel performing this function. In general, 80 percent of the positions within a particular job category must be filled by employees who normally work less than 17½ hours a week before any employees may be excluded under this rule on the basis of their membership in that job category.

(ii) Alternatively, an employer may exclude employees who are members of a particular job category if the median number of hours of service credited to employees in that category during a determination or look-back year is 500 or less.

**(f) 6-month rule.** *(1) In general.* The determination of whether employees normally work during not more than 6 months in any year is made on the basis of the facts and circumstances of the particular employer as evidenced by the employer's customary experience in the years preceding the determination year. An employee who works on one day during a month is deemed to have worked during that month.

*(2) Application of prior year experience.* In making the determination under this paragraph (f), the experience for years immediately preceding the determination year will generally be weighed more heavily than that of earlier years. However, this emphasis on more recent years is not appropriate if the data for a particular year reflects unusual circumstances. For example, if fishermen working for employer X worked 9 months in 1987 and 1988, 8 months in 1989, and then, because of abnormal ice conditions, worked only 5 months in 1990, such fishermen could not be excluded under this rule in 1990. Furthermore, the data with respect to 1990 would not be weighed more heavily in making a determination with respect to subsequent years.

*(3) Individual or group basis.* This determination may be made separately with respect to each employee or on the basis of groups of employees who fall within particular job categories in the manner set forth in paragraph (e)(4) of this A-8.

Q-10. For purposes of determining the group of highly compensated employees, which employees are officers and which officers must be included in the highly compensated group?

A-10. **(a) In general.** Subject to the limitations set forth in paragraph (b) of this A-10 and the top-100 employee rule set forth in A-2, an employee is an includible officer for purposes of this section and is a member of the group of highly compensated employees if such employee is an officer of the employer (within the meaning of section 416(i) and § 1.416-1 A-T 13 & A-T 15) at any time during the determination year or look-back year and receives compensation during such year that is greater than 150 percent of the dollar limitation in effect under section 415(c)(1)(A) for the calendar year in which the determination or look-back year begins. In addition, an officer who does not meet the 415(c)(1)(A) dollar limitation requirement may be an includible officer based on the minimum inclusion rules set forth in paragraph (c) of this A-10.

**(b) Maximum limitation.** *(1) In general.* Nor more than 50 employees (or, if lesser, the greater of 3 employees or 10 percent of the employees without regard to any exclusions) shall be treated as officers for purposes of this provision in determining the group of highly compensated employees for any determination year or look-back year.

*(2) Total number of employees.* The total number of employees for purposes of the limitation in this paragraph (b) is the number of employees the employer has during the particular determination year or look-back year. For purposes of this A-10, employees include only those individuals who perform services for the employer during the determination or look-back year. The exclusions applicable for purposes of determining the number of employees in the top-paid group are not applicable for purposes of the limitations in this paragraph (b).

*(3) Inclusion ranking.* If the number of the employer's officers who satisfy paragraph (a) of this A-10 during either

the determination year or the look-back year exceeds the limitation under this paragraph (b), then the officers who will be considered as includible officers for purposes of this rule are those who receive the greatest compensation from the employer during such determination or look-back year. The definition of compensation in A-13 is to be used for this purpose.

**(c) Minimum inclusion rule.** This paragraph (c) is applicable when no officer of the employer satisfies the compensation requirements of paragraph (a) of this A-10 during either a determination year or look-back year. In such case, the highest paid officer of the employer for such year is treated as a highly compensated employee by reason of being an officer, without regard to the amount of compensation paid to such officer in relation to the section 415(c)(1)(A) dollar amount for the year. This is true whether or not such employee is also a highly compensated employee on any other basis. Thus, for example, if no officer of employer X meets the compensation requirements of paragraph (a) of this A-10 during the 1989 look-back year, and employee A is both the highest paid officer during such year and a 5-percent owner, employee A is treated as an includible officer satisfying the minimum inclusion rules of this paragraph.

**(d) Separate application.** The maximum and minimum officer inclusion rules of paragraphs (b) and (c) of this A-10 apply separately with respect to the determination year calculation and the look-back year calculation. Thus, for example, if no officer of employer X receives compensation above the threshold amount in paragraph (a) of this A-10 during either the determination year or look-back year, application of the minimum inclusion rule would result in the officer of employer X who received the greatest compensation during the look-back year being treated as a highly compensated employee and, in addition, the officer of employer X who receives the most compensation during the determination year would be included in the highly compensated group if such officer is also in the top-100 employees of employer X for such year. Thus, two officers may be treated as highly compensated active employees for a determination year by reason of the provisions of the minimum inclusion rule.

Q-11. To what extent must family members who are employed by the same employer be aggregated for purposes of section 414(q)?

A-11. **(a) Family aggregation.** *(1) In general.* Aggregation is required with respect to an employee who is, during a particular determination year or look-back year, a family member (as defined in A-12) of either (i) a 5-percent owner who is an active or former employee or (ii) a highly compensated employee who is one of the ten most highly compensated employees ranked on the basis of compensation paid by the employer during such year.

*(2) Aggregation of contributions or benefits.* As prescribed in regulations under the provisions to which section 414(q) is applicable, a family member and a 5-percent owner or top-10 highly compensated employee aggregated under this rule are generally treated as a single employee receiving an amount of compensation and a plan contribution or benefit that is based on the compensation, contributions, and benefits of such family member and 5-percent owner or top-10 highly compensated employee.

**(b) Exclusion status irrelevant.** Family members are subject to this aggregation rule whether or not they fall within the categories of employees that may be excluded for purposes of determining the number of employees in the top-paid group and whether or not they are highly compensated employees when considered separately.

**(c) Order of determination.** *(1) Determination of highly compensated employees.* The determination of which employees are highly compensated employees and which highly compensated employees are among the ten most highly compensated employees in making the look-back year calculation or the determination year calculation for a determination year will be made prior to the application of the rules in paragraph (a) of this A-11.

*(2) Determination of top-paid group and top-100 employees.* The determination of the number and identity of employees in the top-paid group under the look-back year calculation or the determination year calculation for a determination year and the identity of individuals in the top-100 employees under the determination year calculation for a determination year is made prior to application of the rules in paragraph (a) of this A-11.

**(d) Determination period.** The rules under paragraph (a) of this A-11 apply separately to the determination year and the look-back year. Thus, assuming there are no 5-percent owners, if employees A, B, C, D, E, F, G, H, I and J are the top 10 highly compensated employees in the 1988 look-back year, and employees F, G, H, I, J, K, L, M, N and O are the top 10 highly compensated employees in the 1989 determination year, then family aggregation would be required with respect to all fifteen of such employees (i.e., employees A, B, C, D, E, F, G, H, I, J, K, L, M, N, and O).

Q-12. Which individuals are family members for purposes of the aggregation rules in section 414(a)(6)(A) and A-11?

A-12. **(a) Definition of family member.** Individuals who are family members for purposes of these provisions include, with respect to any employee or former employee, such employee's or former employee's spouse and lineal ascendants or descendants and the spouses of such lineal ascendants and descendants. In determining whether an individual is a family member with respect to an employee or former employee, legal adoptions shall be taken into account.

**(b) Test period.** If an individual is a family member with respect to an employee or former employee on any day during the year, such individual is treated as a family member for the entire year. Thus, for example, if an individual is a family member with respect to an employee on the first day of a year, such individual continues to be a family member with respect to such employee throughout the year even though their relationship changes as a result of death or divorce.

Q-13. How is "compensation" determined for purposes of determining the group of "highly compensated employees."

A-13. **(a) In general.** For purposes of section 414(q), the term "compensation" means compensation within the meaning of section 415(c)(3) without regard to sections 125, 402(a)(8), and 402(h)(1)(B) and, in the case of employer contributions made pursuant to a salary reduction agreement, without regard to section 403(b). Thus, compensation includes elective or salary reduction contributions to a cafeteria plan, cash or deferred arrangement or tax-sheltered annuity.

**(b) Determination period.** For purposes of determining the group of highly compensated employees, compensation must be calculated on the basis of the applicable period for the determination year and look-back year respectively.

**(c) Compensation taken into account.** Only compensation received by an employee during the determination year or during the look-back year is considered in determining whether such employee is a highly compensated active employee under either the look-back year calculation or determination year calculation for such determination year. Thus, compensation is not annualized for purposes of determining an employee's compensation in the determination year or the look-back year in applying the rules of paragraph (a) of this A-13.

Q-14. What periods must be used for determining who is a highly compensated employee for a determination year?

A-14. **(a) Determination year and look-back year.** *(1) In general.* For purposes of determining the group of highly compensated employees for a determination year, the determination year calculation is made on the basis of the applicable year of the plan or other entity for which a determination is being made and the look-back year calculation is made on the basis of the twelve month period immediately preceding such year. Thus, in testing plans X and Y of an employer, if plan X has a calendar year plan year and plan Y has a July 1 to June 30 plan year, the determination year calculation and look-back year calculation for plan X must be made on the basis of the calendar year. Similarly, the determination year calculation and look-back year calculation for plan Y must be made on the basis of the July 1 to June 30 year.

*(2) Applicable year.* For purposes of this A-14, the applicable year is the plan year of the qualified plan or other employee benefit arrangement to which the definition of highly compensated employees is applicable as defined in the written plan document or otherwise identified in regulations pursuant to sections to which the definition of highly compensated employees is applicable. To the extent that the definition of highly compensated employees is applicable to entities of other arrangements that do not have an otherwise identified plan year, then either the calendar year of the employer's fiscal year may be treated as the plan year.

*(3) Look-back year.* The look-back year is never less than a twelve month period.

**(b) Calendar year calculation election.** *(1) In general.* An employer may elect to make the look-back year calculation for a determination year on the basis of the calendar year ending with or within the applicable determination year (or, in the case of a determination year that is shorter than twelve months, the calendar year ending with or within the twelve-month period ending with the end of the applicable determination year). In such case, the employer must make the determination year calculation for the determination year on the basis of the period (if any) by which the applicable determination year extends beyond such calendar year (i.e., the lag period). If the applicable year for which the determination is being made is the calendar year, the employer still may elect to make the calendar year calculation election under this A-14(b). In such case, the look-back year calculation is made on the basis of the calendar year determination year and, because there is no lag period, a separate determination year calculation under A-3(a)(2) of this § 1.414(q)-1 is not required.

*(2) Lag period calculation.* In making the determination year calculation under A-3(a)(2) of this § 1.414(q)-1 on the basis of the lag period, the dollar amounts applicable under A-3(a)(1)(B) and (C) of this § 1.414(q)-1 are to be adjusted by multiplying such dollar amounts by a fraction, the numerator of which is the number of calendar months that are included in the lag period and the denominator of which is twelve.

*(3) Determination of active employees.* An employee will be considered an active employee for purposes of a determination year for which the calendar year calculation election is in effect so long as such employee performs services for the employer during the applicable year for which the determination is being made. This is the case even if such employee does not perform services for the employer during the lag-period for such determination year.

*(4) Election requirement.* If the employer elects to make the calendar year calculation election with respect to one plan, entity, or arrangement, such election must apply with respect to all plans, entities, and arrangements of the employer. In addition, such election must be provided for in the plan.

**(c) Change in applicable years.** Where there is a change in the applicable year for which a determination is being made with respect to a plan entity, or other arrangement that is not subject to the calendar year calculation election, the look-back year calculation for the short applicable year is to be made on the basis of the twelve month period preceding the short applicable year (i.e., generally, the old applicable year) and the determination year calculation for the short applicable year is to be made on the basis of the short applicable year. In addition, the dollar amounts under A-3(a)(1)(B) and (C) are to be adjusted for such determination year calculation as if the short applicable year were a lag period under paragraph (b)(2) of this A-14.

**(d) Example.** The following examples illustrate the rules of this A-14:

*Example (1).* Employer X has a single plan (Plan A) with an April 1 to March 31 plan year. Employer X makes no election to use the calendar year for the determination period. Therefore, in determining the group of highly compensated employees for the April 1, 1988 to March 31, 1990 plan year, the determination year is the plan year ending March 31, 1990 and the look-back year is the plan year ending March 31, 1989.

*Example (2).* Assume the same facts given above. With respect to the plan year beginning in 1990, employer X elects to use the calendar year for the determination period. Therefore, in determining the group of highly compensated employees for the April 1, 1990 to March 31, 1991 plan year, the lag-period determination year is the period from January 1, 1991, through March 31, 1991, and the applicable look-back year is the 1990 calendar year.

*Example (3).* Employer Y has a single plan (Plan B) with a calendar plan year. With respect to the plan year beginning in 1990, employer Y elects to make the look-back year calculation for the 1990 determination year on the basis of the calendar year ending with or within the 1990 determination year. Because employer Y's determination year is the 1990 calendar year there is no lag period and employer Y determines the group of highly compensated employees for purposes of the 1990 calendar plan year on the basis of such plan year alone.

Q-15. Is there any transition rule in determining the group of highly compensated employees for 1987 and 1988?

A-15. **(a) In general.** Solely for purposes of section 401(k)(3) and (m)(2) and solely for twelve-month plan years beginning in 1987 and 1988, an eligible employer may elect to define the group of highly compensated employees as the group consisting of 5-percent owners of the employer at any time during the plan year and employees who receive compensation in excess of $50,000 during the plan year. This rule would apply in lieu of the look-back year calculation and determination year calculation otherwise applicable under A-3(a) of this § 1.44(q)-1. In addition, an eligible employer may elect to make the determinations permitted under this transition rule on the basis of the calendar year ending in the plan year and the period by which such plan year extends beyond such calendar year, in accordance with the rules of A-14(b), in lieu of making the determinations under this transition rule on the basis of the plan year for which the determinations are being made.

**(b) Eligible employers.** An employer is an eligible employer under this A-15 if such employer satisfies both of the following requirements:

*(1)* The employer does not maintain any top-heavy plan within the meaning of section 416 at any time during 1987 and 1988; and

*(2)* Under each plan of the employer to which section 401(k)(3) or 401(m)(2) is applicable, the group of eligible employees that comprises the highest 25% of eligible employees ranked on the basis of compensation includes at least one employee whose compensation is $50,000 or below. This requirement must be met separately with respect to each such plan of the employer.

**(c) Uniformity requirement.** An eligible employer may not make the election under paragraph (a) of this A-15 unless the election applies to all of the plans maintained by the employer to which section 401(k)(3) or 401(m)(2) applies.

**(d) Election requirements.** This election is operational and does not require a plan provision.

---

T.D. 8173, 2/18/88, amend T.D. 8334, 1/31/91, T.D. 8548, 6/23/94.

---

### § 1.414(r)-0 Table of contents.

**(a) In general.** Sections 1.414(r)-1 through 1.414(r)-11 provide rules for determining whether an employer is treated as operating qualified separate lines of business under section 414(r) of the Internal Revenue Code of 1986 as added to the Code by section 1115(a) of the Tax Reform Act of 1986 (Pub. L. No. 99-514), as well as rules for applying the requirements of sections 410(b), 401(a)(26), and 129(d)(8) separately with respect to the employees of each qualified separate line of business of an employer. Paragraph (b) of this section contains a listing of the headings of §§ 1.414(r)-1 through 1.414(r)-11. Paragraph (c) of this section provides a flowchart showing how the major provisions of §§ 1.414(r)-1 through 1.414(r)-6 are applied.

**(b) Table of contents.** The following is a listing of the headings of §§ 1.414(r)-1 through 1.414(r)-11.

(b) Separate organization and operation.

(1) In general.

(2) Separate organizational unit.

(3) Separate financial accountability.

(4) Separate employee workforce.

(5) Separate management.

(c) Supplementary rules.

(1) In general.

(2) Determination of separate employee workforce.

(3) Determination of separate management.

(4) Employees taken into account.

(5) Services taken into account.

(i) Provision of services to a separate line of business.

(ii) Period for which services are provided.

(iii) Optional rule for employees who change status.

(A) In general.

(B) Change in employee's status.

(6) Examples of the separate employee workforce requirement.

(7) Examples of the separate management requirement.

(d) Optional rule for vertically integrated lines of business.

(1) In general.

(2) Requirements.

(3) Optional rule.

(i) Treatment of employees.

(ii) Purposes for which optional rule applies.

(4) Examples.

*§ 1.414(r)-4 Qualified separate line of business—fifty-employee and notice requirements.*

(a) In general.

(b) Fifty-employee requirement.

(c) Notice requirement.

(1) General rule.

(2) Effect of notice.

*§ 1.414(r)-5 Qualified separate line of business—administrative scrutiny requirement— safe harbors.*

(a) In general.

(b) Statutory safe harbor.

(1) General rule.

(2) Highly compensated employee percentage ratio.

(3) Employees taken into account.

(4) Ten-percent exception.

(5) Determination based on preceding testing year.

(6) Examples.

(c) Safe harbor for separate lines of business in different industries.

(1) In general.

(2) Optional rule for foreign operations.

(3) Establishment of industry categories.

(4) Examples.

(d) Safe harbor for separate lines of business that are acquired through certain mergers and acquisitions.

(1) General rule.

(2) Employees taken into account.

(3) Transition period.

(4) Examples.

(e) Safe harbor for separate lines of business reported as industry segments.

(1) In general.

(2) Reported as an industry segment in conformity with Form 10-K or Form 20-F.

(3) Timely filing of Form 10-K or 20-F.

(4) Examples.

(f) Safe harbor for separate lines of business that provide same average benefits as other separate lines of business.

(1) General rule.

(2) Separate lines of business benefiting disproportionate number of nonhighly compensated employees.

(i) Applicability of safe harbor.

(ii) Requirement.

(3) Separate lines of business benefiting disproportionate number of highly compensated employees.

(i) Applicability of safe harbor.

(ii) Requirement.

(4) Employees taken into account.

(5) Example.

(g) Safe harbor for separate lines of business that provide minimum or maximum benefits.

(1) In general.

(2) Minimum benefit required.

(i) Applicability.

(ii) Requirement.

(iii) Defined benefit minimum.

(A) In general.

(B) Normal form and equivalent benefits.

(C) Compensation definition.

(D) Average compensation requirement.

(E) Special rules.

(iv) Defined contribution minimum.

(A) In general.

(B) Modified allocation definition for averaging.

(3) Maximum benefit permitted.

(i) Applicability.

(ii) Requirement.

(iii) Defined benefit maximum.

(A) In general.

(B) Determination of defined benefit maximum.

(C) Adjustment for different compensation definitions.

(D) Adjustment for certain subsidies.

(iv) Defined contribution maximum.

(4) Duplication of benefits or contributions.

(i) Plans of the same type.

(ii) Plans of different types.

(iii) Special rule for floor-offset arrangements.

(5) Certain contingency provisions ignored.

(6) Employees taken into account.

*§ 1.414(r)-6 Qualified separate line of business—administrative scrutiny requirement— individual determinations.*

(a) In general.
(b) Authority to establish procedures.

*§ 1.414(r)-7 Determination of the employees of an employer's qualified separate lines of business.*

(a) Introduction.
(1) In general.
(2) Purposes for which this section applies.
(b) Assignment procedure.
(1) In general.
(2) Assignment for the first testing day.
(3) Assignment of new employees for subsequent testing days.
(4) Special rule for employers using annual option under section 410(b).
(c) Assignment and allocation of residual shared employees.
(1) In general.
(2) Dominant line of business method of allocation.
(i) In general.
(ii) Dominant line of business.
(iii) Employee assignment percentage.
(A) Determination of percentage.
(B) Employees taken into account.
(iv) Option to apply reduced percentage.
(v) Examples.
(3) Pro-rata method of allocation.
(i) In general.
(ii) Allocation procedure.
(iii) Examples.
(4) HCE percentage ratio method of allocation.
(i) In general.
(ii) Highly compensated employee percentage assignment ratio.
(iii) Allocation procedure.
(5) Small group method.
(i) In general.
(ii) Size of group.
(iii) Composition of qualified separate line of business.
(iv) Reasonable allocation.

*§ 1.414(r)-8 Separate application of section 410(b).*

(a) General rule.
(b) Rules of separate application.
(1) In general.
(2) Satisfaction of section 410(b)(5)(B) on an employer-wide basis.
(i) General rule.
(ii) Application of facts and circumstances requirements under nondiscriminatory classification test.
(iii) Modification of unsafe harbor percentage for plans satisfying ratio percentage test at 90 percent level.
(A) General rule.
(B) Facts and circumstances alternative.
(3) Satisfaction of section 410(b) on a qualified-separate-line-of-business basis.
(4) Examples.
(c) Coordination of section 401(a)(4) with section 410(b).
(1) General rule.
(2) Examples.
(d) Supplementary rules.
(1) In general.
(2) Definition of plan.
(3) Employees of a qualified separate line of business.
(4) Consequences of failure.

*§ 1.414(r)-9 Separate application of section 401(a)(26).*

(a) General rule.
(b) Requirements applicable to a plan.
(c) Supplementary rules.
(1) In general.
(2) Definition of plan.
(3) Employees of a qualified separate line of business.
(4) Consequences of failure.

*§ 1.414(r)-10 Separate application of section 129(d)(8). [Reserved]*

*§ 1.414(r)-11 Definitions and special rules.*

(a) In general.
(b) Definitions.
(1) In general.
(2) Substantial-service employee.
(3) Top-paid employee.
(4) Residual shared employee.
(5) Testing year.
(6) Testing day.
(7) First testing day.
(8) Section 401(a)(26) testing day.
(c) Averaging rules.
(1) In general.
(2) Specified provisions.
(3) Averaging of large fluctuations not permitted.
(4) Consistency requirements.

(c) Flowchart. The following is a flowchart showing how the major provisions of §§ 1.414(r)-1 through 1.414(r)-6 are applied.

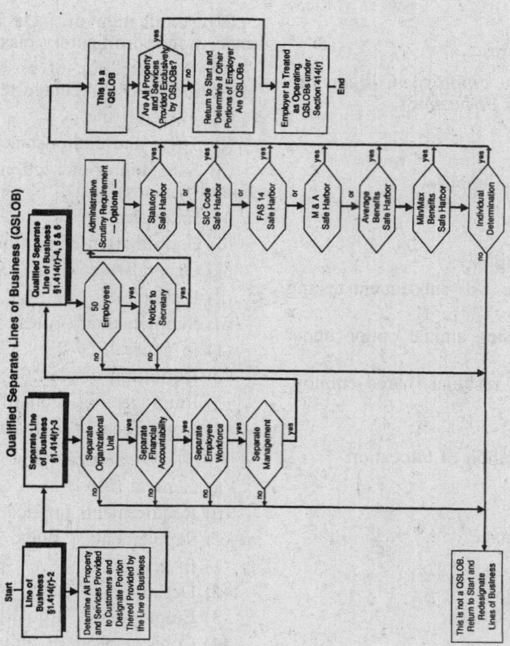


T.D. 8376, 12/2/91, amend T.D. 8548, 6/23/94.

### § 1.414(r)-1 Requirements applicable to qualified separate lines of business.

**(a) In general.** Section 414(r) prescribes the conditions under which an employer is treated as operating qualified separate lines of business. If an employer is treated as operating qualified separate lines of business under section 414(r), certain requirements under the Code may be applied separately with respect to the employees of each qualified separate line of business. These requirements are limited to the minimum coverage requirements of section 410(b) (including the nondiscrimination requirements of section 401(a)(4)), the minimum participation requirements of section 401(a)(26), and the 55-percent average benefits test of section 129(d)(8). This section provides the exclusive rules for determining whether an employer is treated as operating qualified separate lines of business under section 414(r), as well as rules for applying the requirements of sections 410(b), 401(a)(26), and 129(d)(8) separately with respect to the employees of a qualified separate line of business.

**(b) Conditions under which an employer is treated as operating qualified separate lines of business.** *(1) In general.* An employer is treated as operating qualified separate lines of business under section 414(r) only if all property and services provided by the employer to its customers are provided exclusively by qualified separate lines of business. Thus, once an employer has determined its qualified separate lines of business under paragraph (b)(2) of this section, no portion of the employer may remain that is not included in a qualified separate line of business. In addition, once the employer has determined the employees of its qualified separate lines of business under paragraph (b)(3) of this section, every employee must be treated as an employee of a qualified separate line of business, and no employee may be treated as an employee of more than one qualified separate line of business.

*(2) Qualified separate line of business.* (i) In general. A qualified separate line of business is a portion of the employer that is a line of business within the meaning of paragraph (b)(2)(ii) of this section, that is also a separate line of business within the meaning of paragraph (b)(2)(iii) of this section, and, finally, that satisfies the requirements of section 414(r)(2) in accordance with paragraph (b)(2)(iv) of this section.

(ii) Line of business. A line of business is a portion of an employer that is identified by the property or services it provides to customers of the employer. For this purpose, the employer is permitted to determine the lines of business it operates by designating the property and services that each of its lines of business provides to customers of the employer. Rules for determining an employer's lines of business are provided in § 1.414(r)-2.

(iii) Separate line of business. A separate line of business is a line of business that is organized and operated separately from the remainder of the employer. The determination of whether a line of business is organized and operated separately from the remainder of the employer is made on the basis of objective criteria. These criteria generally require that the line of business be organized into one or more separate organizational units (e.g., corporations, partnerships, or divisions), that the line of business constitute one or more distinct profit centers within the employer, and that no more than a moderate overlap exist between the employee workforce and management employed by the line of business and those employed by the remainder of the employer. Rules for determining whether a line of business is organized and operated separately from the remainder of the employer and thus constitutes a separate line of business are provided in § 1.414(r)-3. These rules include an optional rule for vertically integrated lines of business.

(iv) Qualified separate line of business. (A) In general. A qualified separate line of business must satisfy the three statutory requirements in section 414(r)(2). A separate line of business that satisfies these three statutory requirements in accordance with paragraphs (b)(2)(iv)(B) through (b)(2)(iv)(D) of this section constitutes a qualified separate line of business.

(B) Fifty-employee requirement. Under section 414(r)(2)(A), a separate line of business must have at least 50 employees. Rules for determining whether this requirement is satisfied are provided in § 1.414(r)-4(b).

(C) Notice requirement. Under section 414(r)(2)(B), the employer must notify the Secretary that it treats itself as operating qualified separate lines of business under section 414(r) for purposes of applying the requirements of section 410(b), 401(a)(26), or 129(d)(8) separately with respect to the employees of the separate line of business. Rules and procedures for complying with this requirement are provided in § 1.414(r)-(c).

(D) Requirement of administrative scrutiny. Under section 414(r)(2)(C), a separate line of business must pass administrative scrutiny. A separate line of business may satisfy this requirement in one of two ways. First, a separate line of business that satisfies any of the safe harbors in § 1.414(r)-5 satisfies the requirement of administrative scrutiny. These safe harbors implement the statutory safe harbor of section 414(r)(3) as well as the guidelines prescribed under section 414(r)(2)(C). Second, a separate line of business that does not satisfy any of the safe harbors in § 1.414(r)-5 nonetheless satisfies the requirement of administrative scrutiny if the employer requests and receives an individual determination from the Commissioner that the separate line of business satisfies the requirement of administrative scrutiny. Rules and procedures applicable to requesting and receiving an individual determination are provided in § 1.414(r)-6. A separate line of business is permitted to satisfy the requirement of administrative scrutiny in any manner permitted under this paragraph (b)(2)(iv)(D), regardless of how any other separate line of business of the employer satisfies the requirement.

*(3) Determining the employees of a qualified separate line of business.* In order to apply certain provisions under these regulations, it is necessary to determine the employees of a qualified separate line of business. For these purposes, the employees of a qualified separate line of business consist of all employees who are substantial-service employees with respect to the qualified separate line of business, and all other employees who are assigned to the qualified separate line of business. Rules for making these determinations are provided in § 1.414(r)-7. These rules apply solely for the purposes specified in these regulations (see § 1.414(r)-7(a)(2) for a comprehensive listing of these purposes). These rules do not apply for any other purpose (e.g., the determination under § 1.414(r)-3 of whether a line of business is organized and operated separately from the remainder of the employer).

**(c) Separate application of certain Code requirements to employees of a qualified separate line of business.** *(1) In general.* If an employer is treated as operating qualified separate lines of business under section 414(r) in accordance with paragraph (b) of this section, the requirements of sections 410(b), 401(a)(26), and 129(d)(8) may be applied separately with respect to the employees of each qualified separate line of business. Paragraphs (c)(2) through (c)(4) of this section provide for the separate application of these requirements. In general, the requirements of a Code section are applied separately with respect to the employees of a qualified separate line of business by treating those employees as if they were the only employees of the employer. Paragraph (c)(5) of this section prescribes the limited conditions under which other Code requirements may be applied separately with respect to the employees of a qualified separate line of business.

*(2) Separate application of section 410(b).* (i) General rule. Except as provided in paragraph (c)(2)(ii) of this section, an employer is permitted to apply the requirements of section 410(b) separately with respect to the employees of each qualified separate line of business operated by the employer only if the employer does so with respect to all its plans, all its employees, and all its qualified separate lines of business. For this purpose, the requirements of section 410(b) encompass the requirements of section 401(a)(4) (including, but not limited to, the permitted disparity rules of section 401(l), the actual deferral percentage test of section 401(k)(3) and the actual contribution percentage test of section 401(m)(2)). Rules for applying section 410(b) separately with respect to the employees of a qualified separate line of business are provided in § 1.414(r)-8. An employer may apply the rules of section 414(r) for purposes of section 410(b) even if it does not apply the rules of section 414(r) for purposes of section 401(a)(26).

(ii) Special rule for employer-wide plans. Notwithstanding paragraph (c)(2)(i) of this section, an employer that is treated as operating qualified separate lines of business for purposes of section 410(b) in accordance with paragraph (b) of this section may apply the requirements of section 410(b) on an employer-wide rather than a qualified-separate-line-of-business basis with respect to any plan (within the meaning of § 1.414(r)-8(d)(2), but without regard to the mandatory disaggregation rule of § 1.410(b)-7(c)(4) for portions of a plan that benefit employees of different qualified separate lines of business) that benefits a group of employees that satisfies the percentage test of section 410(b)(1)(A)(i.e., benefits at least 70 percent of the employer's nonexcludable nonhighly compensated employees). If section 401(a)(4) requires that a group of employees under the plan described in the preceding sentence satisfy section 410(b) for purposes of satisfying section 401(a)(4), the percentage test of section 410(b)(1)(A) must be satisfied by each such group of employees. See § 1.414(r)-8(c). The rules of this paragraph (c)(2)(ii) are illustrated by the following example.

*Example.* Employer A maintains a single profit-sharing plan, Plan W, and three pension plans, Plans X, Y and Z, each benefiting employees of a different one of Employer A's three qualified separate lines of business. Contributions to the profit-sharing plan are made pursuant to a cash or deferred arrangement in which all employees of Employer A are eligible to participate. Assume that, as a result, Plan W satisfies the requirements to be tested under this paragraph (c)(2)(ii). None of the pension plans benefits more than 70 percent of the nonexcludable nonhighly compensated employees of Employer A. Employer A is treated as operating qualified separate lines of business for purposes of applying section 410(b) to its qualified plans. The requirements of sections 410(b) and 401(a)(4) must therefore be applied to Plans X, Y and Z separately with respect to the employees of each of the three qualified separate line of business operated by Employer A. Since Plan W benefits at least 70 percent of the nonexcludable nonhighly compensated employees of Employer A, however, the requirements of sections

410(b) and 401(a)(4)(including section 401(k)) may be applied to Plan W on an employer-wide basis.

*(3) Separate application of section 401(a)(26).* (i) General rule. Except as provided in paragraph (c)(3)(ii) of this section, an employer is permitted to apply the requirements of section 401(a)(26) separately with respect to the employees of each qualified separate line of business operated by the employer only if the employer does so with respect to all its plans, all its employees, and all its qualified separate lines of business. Rules for applying the requirements of section 401(a)(26) separately with respect to the employees of a qualified separate line of business are provided in § 1.414(r)-9. An employer may apply the rules of section 414(r) for purposes of section 401(a)(26) even if it does not apply the rules of section 414(r) for purposes of section 410(b).

(ii) Special rule for employer-wide plans. Notwithstanding the first sentence of paragraph (c)(3)(i) of this section, an employer that is treated as operating qualified separate lines of business in accordance with paragraph (b) of this section for purposes of both sections 410(b) and 401(a)(26) may apply the requirements of section 401(a)(26) on an employer-wide rather than a qualified-separate-line-of-business basis with respect to any plan (within the meaning of § 1.414(r)-9(c)(2), but without regard to the mandatory disaggregation rule of § 1.401(a)(26)-2(d)(1)(iv) for portions of a plan that benefit employees of different qualified separate lines of business), but only if the special rule for employer-wide plans in paragraph (c)(2)(ii) of this section is applied to the same plan for the same plan year.

*(4) Separate application of section 129(d)(8).[Reserved]*

*(5) Separate application of other Code requirements.* Under no circumstance may the requirements of any section of the Code (other than a section described in paragraphs (c)(2) through (c)(4) of this section) be applied separately with respect to the employees of a qualified separate line of business unless the section specifically cross-references, or is specifically cross-referenced by, section 414(r). The Code sections whose requirements may not be applied separately with respect to the employees of a qualified separate line of business include, but are not limited to, sections 79(d)(3), 105(h), 117(d)(3), 120(c)(2), 125(g)(3), 127(b)(2), 129(d)(3), 132, 195, 401(a)(3) (as in effect on September 1, 1974), 414(g)(4), 501(c)(17)(A)(ii), 501(c)(17)(B)(iii), 501(c)(18)(B), and 505(b)(1)(A).

**(d) Application of requirements.** *(1) In general.* The requirements of paragraphs (b) and (c) of this section must be applied in accordance with the rules in this paragraph (d).

*(2) Interpretation.* The provisions of this section and of §§ 1.414(r)-2 through 1.414(r)-11 are to be interpreted in a reasonable manner consistent with the purpose of section 414(r) to recognize an employer's operation of qualified separate lines of business for bona fide business reasons and not for reasons of evading the requirements of any section of the Code, including sections 410(b), 401(a)(26), and 129(d)(8). See section 414(r)(1) and (r)(7). Thus, for example, an employer is not permitted to apply these regulations in a manner that may literally comply with the other provisions of this section and of §§ 1.414(r)-2 through 1.414(r)-11, but that does not reflect the employer's operation of qualified separate lines of business for bona fide business reasons.

*(3) Separate operating units.* No additional requirements beyond those provided in these regulations apply to a separate operating unit. Thus, a separate operating unit that satisfies the requirements of paragraph (b)(2) of this section is deemed to satisfy the geographic separation requirement of section 414(r)(7) and accordingly is treated as a qualified separate line of business for all purposes under this section, including the separate application of section 401(a)(26).

*(4) Certain mergers and acquisitions.* A portion of an employer that is acquired in a transaction described in section 410(b)(6)(C) and § 1.410(b)-2(f) (i.e., an asset or stock acquisition, merger, or other similar transaction involving a change in the employer of the employees of a trade or business) is deemed to satisfy the requirements to be a qualified separate line of business, other than the 50-employee requirement and the notice requirement of paragraphs (b)(2)(iv)(B) and (b)(2)(iv)(C) of this section, respectively. In addition, the acquired employees are not taken into account, and the property and services provided by the acquired portion to customers of the employer are disregarded, for purposes of determining whether the employer's remaining lines of business satisfy the requirements of §§ 1.414(r)-3 through 1.414(r)-6. The rules in this paragraph (d)(4) apply only for those testing years with first testing days that fall within the transition period described in section 410(b)(6)(C). For this purpose, the transition period described in section 410(b)(6)(C) lasts only for so long as the conditions in that section are satisfied. For the definition of "first testing day," see § 1.414(r)-11(b)(7). See § 1.414(r)-5(d)(4), Example 1, for an example of the application of the rule in this paragraph (d)(4). See also § 1.414(r)-5(d) for an administrative scrutiny safe harbor applicable to certain separate lines of business acquired in a transaction described in this section.

*(5) Governmental and tax-exempt employers.* (i) General rule. Except as provided in paragraph (d)(5)(ii) of this section, the rules of this section are applicable in determining whether section 401(a)(26) is satisfied by a plan maintained by an employer that is exempt from tax under Subtitle A of the Internal Revenue Code (including a governmental plan within the meaning of section 414(d)). Similarly, except as provided in paragraph (d)(5)(ii) of this section, the rules of this section are applicable in determining whether section 410(b) is satisfied by a plan that is subject to section 410(b) (including by virtue of § 1.410(b)-2(e)) and is maintained by an employer that is exempt from tax under Subtitle A of the Internal Revenue Code (including a governmental plan within the meaning of section 414(d)).

(ii) Additional rules. [Reserved]

*(6) Testing year basis of application.* (i) Section 414(r). Whether an employer is treated as operating qualified separate lines of business under section 414(r) in accordance with paragraph (b) of this section is determined on a year-by-year basis with respect to the testing year. It is therefore possible for an employer to satisfy paragraph (b) of this section for one testing year and to fail to satisfy it for another testing year. It is also possible for an employer to satisfy paragraph (b) of this section for two testing years but to have designated its lines of business differently in each of those two testing years. In determining whether an employer satisfies paragraph (b) of this section for a testing year, the requirements of that paragraph are applied solely with respect to the testing year. Thus, all property and services provided by the employer to its customers during the testing year must be provided exclusively by portions of the employer that for the testing year constitute qualified separate lines of business. Furthermore, each employee of the employer must respectively be treated as an employee of one and only one of those qualified separate lines of business for all purposes with respect to the testing year.

(ii) Sections 410(b), 401(a)(26), and 129(d)(8). For purposes of paragraph (c) of this section, relating to the separate application of sections 410(b), 401(a)(26), and 129(d)(8) to the employees of a qualified separate line of business, the determination whether an employer operates qualified separate lines of business in accordance with paragraph (b) of this section for a testing year generally applies for all plan years beginning in the testing year. Rules for the separate application of sections 410(b), 401(a)(26), and 129(d)(8) are respectively provided in §§ 1.414(r)-8, 1.414(r)-9, and 1.414(r)-10.

*(7) Averaging rules.* The employer is permitted to apply certain provisions of these regulations on the basis of a consecutive-year average (not to exceed five consecutive years) under the averaging rules of § 1.414(r)-11(c).

*(8) Definitions.* In applying the provisions of this section and of §§ 1.414(r)-2 through 1.414(r)-11, the definitions in §§ 1.414(r)-11(b) and 1.410(b)-9 govern, unless otherwise provided.

*(9) Effective date.* (i) General rule. The provisions of this section and of §§ 1.414(r)-2 through 1.414(r)-11 apply to plan years and testing years beginning on or after January 1, 1994 (or January 1, 1996, in the case of plans maintained by organizations exempt from income taxation under section 501(a), including plans subject to section 403(b)(12)(A)(i) (nonelective plans)).

(ii) Reasonable compliance. (A) In general. With respect to plan years beginning before the date on which the Commissioner begins issuing determinations under section 414(r)(2)(C), and on or after the first day of the first plan year to which section 414(r) applies under section 1112(a) of the Tax Reform Act of 1986, an employer is treated as operating qualified separate lines of business if the employer reasonably determines that it meets the requirements of section 414(r) (other than the requirement of administrative scrutiny under section 414(r)(2)(C)).

(B) Determination of reasonable compliance. Whether an employer reasonably determines that it meets the requirements of section 414(r) generally will be determined on the basis of all relevant facts and circumstances, including the extent to which the employer has resolved unclear issues in its favor. For the period described in paragraph (d)(9)(ii)(A) of this section, the Internal Revenue Service will consider the employer's compliance with the terms of these final regulations (other than the requirement of administrative scrutiny under paragraph (b)(2)(iv)(D) of this section) to constitute a reasonable determination that the employer meets the requirements of section 414(r) (other than the requirement of administrative scrutiny under section 414(r)(2)(C)).

(C) Effect on other plans. If an employer sponsors a plan that has a plan year beginning within the period described in paragraph (d)(9)(ii)(A) of this section, the employer's reasonable determination of its qualified separate lines of business for the testing year in which that plan year begins, and the allocation of employees to those qualified separate lines of business, must also be used for purposes of applying § 1.414(r)-8 and § 1.414(r)-9 for plan years that begin in that testing year but after the end of the period described in paragraph (d)(9)(ii)(A) of this section.

**(e) Additional rules.** The Commissioner may, in revenue rulings, notices, and other guidance of general applicability, provide any additional rules that may be necessary or appropriate in applying the qualified separate line of business requirements of section 414(r). These additional rules may include, for example, new safe harbors in § 1.414(r)-5.

T.D. 8376, 12/2/91, amend T.D. 8548, 6/23/94.

### § 1.414(r)-2 Line of business.

**(a) General rule.** A line of business is a portion of an employer that is identified by the property or services it provides to customers of the employer. For this purpose, an employer is permitted to determine its lines of business by designating the property or services that each of its lines of business provides to customers of the employer. Paragraph (b) of this section explains how an employer determines its lines of business for a testing year. Paragraph (c) of this section provides examples illustrating the application of this section.

**(b) Employer determination of its lines of business.** *(1) In general.* An employer determines its lines of business for a testing year first by identifying all the property and services it provides to its customers during the testing year, and then by designating which portion of the property and services is provided by each of its lines of business.

*(2) Property and services provided to customers.* (i) In general. Property, whether real or personal, tangible or intangible, is provided by an employer to a customer if the employer provides the property to or on behalf of the customer for consideration. Similarly, services are provided by an employer to a customer if the employer renders the services to or on behalf of the customer for consideration. An individual item of property or service is taken into account under this paragraph (b)(2) only if the employer provides the item to a person other than the employer in the ordinary course of a trade or business conducted by the employer and the person to whom the employer provides the item is acting in the capacity of a customer of the employer. A type of tangible property is deemed to be provided to customers of the employer for purposes of this section if, with respect to a business that produces or manufactures that type of tangible property, the employer satisfies the special rule in § 1.414(r)-3(d)(2)(iii)(B) for vertically integrated businesses.

(ii) Timing of provision of property or services. Generally an employer determines its lines of business on the basis of the property and services it provides to its customers for consideration during the testing year. However, it is not necessary both that property or services actually be provided, and that consideration for the property or services actually be paid, during the current testing year. For an employer to be considered to provide property or services to customers for consideration during a testing year under this paragraph (b)(2), it is sufficient that the property or services actually be provided to customers during the testing year, the consideration actually be paid during the testing year, or the employer actually incur significant costs during the testing year associated with the provision of the property or services to a specified customer or specified customers.

*(3) Employer designation.* (i) In general. Once the employer has identified all the property and services it provides to its customers during the testing year under paragraph (b)(2) of this section, the employer determines its lines of business for the testing year by designating which portion of those property and services is provided by each of its lines of business. For this purpose, the employer must apportion all the property and services identified under paragraph (b)(2) of this section among its lines of business. An employer generally is not required to designate its lines of business for the testing year in the same manner as it designates its lines of business for any other testing year.

(ii) Ability to combine unrelated types of property or services in a single line of business. For purposes of this paragraph (b)(3), there is no requirement that a line of business provide only one type of property or service, or only related types of property or services. Nor is there any requirement that a line of business provide solely property or solely services. Thus, the employer is permitted to combine in a single line of business dissimilar types of property or services that are otherwise unrelated to one another.

(iii) Ability to separate related types of property or services into two or more lines of business. For purposes of this paragraph (b)(3), there is no requirement that all property or services of related types or the same type be provided by a single line of business. Thus, the employer is permitted to designate two or more lines of business that provide related types of property or services, or the same type of property or service. An employer might designate two or more lines of business that provide property or services of related types or the same type, for example, where the lines of business manufacture, prepare, or provide the property or services in different geographic areas (e.g., in different regions of the country or the world), or at different levels in the chain of commercial distribution (e.g., wholesale versus retail), or in different types of transactions (e.g., sale versus lease), or for different types of customers (e.g., governmental versus private), or subject to different legal constraints (e.g., regulated versus unregulated), or if the lines of business have developed differently (e.g., one line of business was acquired while another line of business developed internally). Notwithstanding the foregoing, an employer is not permitted to designate two or more lines of business that provide property or services of related types or the same type, if the employer's designation is unreasonable. An employer's designation would be unreasonable, for example, if the designation separated two types of property or services in different lines of business, but the employer did not provide those types of property or services separately from one another to its customers. Similarly, an employer's designation would be unreasonable if it separated two types of property or services in different lines of business, but the provision of one type of property or service was merely ancillary or incidental to, or regularly associated with, the provision of the other type of property or service. See generally § 1.414(r)-1(d)(2) (requiring an employer's operation of qualified separate lines of business to be for bona fide business reasons).

(iv) Affiliated service groups. An employer is not permitted to designate its lines of business in a manner that results in separating employees of an affiliated service group (within the meaning of section 414(m)) from other employees of the employer. See section 414(r)(8).

**(c) Examples.** *(1) In general.* Paragraphs (c)(2) and (c)(3) of this section provide examples that illustrate the application of this section.

*(2) Examples illustrating employer designation.* The following examples illustrate the application of paragraph (b)(3) of this section relating to an employer's designation of the property or services provided to customers by each of its lines of business.

*Example (1).* Employer A is a domestic conglomerate engaged in the manufacture and sale of consumer food and beverage products and the provision of data processing services to private industry. Employer A provides no other property or services to its customers. Pursuant to paragraph (b)(3) of this section, Employer A apportions all the property and services it provides to its customers among three lines of business, one providing all its consumer food products, a second providing all its consumer beverage products, and a third providing all its data processing services. Employer A has three lines of business for purposes of this section.

*Example (2).* The facts are the same as in Example 1, except that Employer A determines that neither the consumer food products line of business nor the consumer beverage products line of business would satisfy the separateness criteria of § 1.414(r)-3 for recognition as a separate line of business. Accordingly, pursuant to paragraph (b)(3) of this section, Employer A apportions all the property and services it provides to its customers between only two lines of business, one providing all its consumer food and beverage products, and a second providing all its data processing services. Employer A has two lines of business for purposes of this section.

*Example (3).* The facts are the same as in Example 2, except that Employer A also owns and operates a regional commuter airline, a professional basketball team, a pharmaceutical manufacturer, and a leather tanning company. Pursuant to paragraph (b)(3) of this section, Employer A apportions all the property and services it provides to its customers among three lines of business, one providing all its consumer food and beverage products, a second providing all its data processing services, and a third providing all the other property and services provided to customers through Employer A's regional commuter airline, professional basketball team, pharmaceutical manufacturer, and leather tanning company. Even though the third line of business includes dissimilar types of property and services that are otherwise unrelated to one another, paragraph (b)(3)(ii) of this section permits Employer A to combine these property and services in a single line of business. Employer A has three lines of business for purposes of this section.

*Example (4).* The facts are the same as in Example 2, except that Employer A has recently acquired Corporation L, whose only product is a well-known brand of gourmet ice cream. Although Employer A manufactures and sells other ice cream products, it does not manufacture or market the newly acquired brand of gourmet ice cream except through Corporation L. Pursuant to paragraph (b)(3) of this section, Employer A apportions all the property and services it provides to its customers among three lines of business, one providing only the newly acquired brand of gourmet ice cream, a second providing all its other consumer food and beverage products (including the other ice cream products manufactured and sold by Employer A), and a third providing all its data processing services. Even though the gourmet ice cream line of business provides the same type of property as the consumer food and beverage line of business (i.e., ice cream), paragraph (b)(3)(iii) of this section permits Employer A to separate its ice cream products between two different lines of business. Employer A has three lines of business for purposes of this section.

*Example (5).* The facts are the same as in Example 2, except that Employer A operates the data processing services portion of its business in two separate subsidiaries, one serving customers in the eastern half of the United States and the other serving customers in the western half of the United States. Pursuant to paragraph (b)(3) of this section, Employer A apportions all the property and services it provides to its customers among three lines of business, one providing all its consumer food and beverage products, a second providing data processing services to customers in the eastern half of the United States, and a third providing data processing services to customers in the western half of the United

States. Even though the second and third lines of business provide the same type of service (i.e., data processing services), paragraph (b)(3)(iii) of this section permits Employer A to separate its data processing services into two lines of business. Employer A has three lines of business for purposes of this section.

*Example (6).* Employer B is a diversified engineering firm offering civil, chemical, and aeronautical engineering services to government and private industry. Employer B provides no other property or services to its customers. Employer B operates the aeronautical engineering services portion of its business as two separate divisions, one serving federal government customers and the other serving customers in private industry. Pursuant to paragraph (b)(3) of this section, Employer B apportions all the property and services it provides to its customers among four lines of business, one providing all its civil engineering services, a second providing all its chemical engineering services, a third providing aeronautical engineering services to federal government customers, and a fourth providing aeronautical engineering services to customers in private industry. Even though the third and fourth lines of business include the same type of service (i.e., aeronautical engineering services), paragraph (b)(3)(iii) of this section permits Employer B to separate its aeronautical engineering services into two lines of business. Employer B has four lines of business for purposes of this section.

*Example (7).* Among its other business activities, Employer C manufactures industrial diesel generators. At no additional cost to its buyers, Employer C warrants the proper functioning of its diesel generators for a one-year period following sale. Pursuant to its warranty, Employer C provides labor and parts to repair or replace any components that malfunction within the one-year warranty period. Because Employer C does not provide the industrial diesel generators, on the one hand, and the warranty repair services and replacement parts, on the other hand, separately from one another to its customers, under paragraph (b)(3)(iii) of this section it would be unreasonable for Employer C to separate these property and services in different lines of business.

*Example (8).* Among its other business activities, Employer D leases office photo-copying equipment. Employer D also provides photo-copying supplies and repair services to its lessees for a separate charge. Employer D generally does not provide such supplies and repair services to persons other than its lessees. Lessees of Employer D's equipment are permitted to use photo-copying supplies and repair services from suppliers other than Employer D. Because the provision of the photo-copying supplies and repair services are merely ancillary or incidental to the provision of the leased photo-copiers, under paragraph (b)(3)(iii) of this section it would be unreasonable for Employer D to separate these property and services in different lines of business.

*Example (9).* Employer E operates a medical clinic. The employees of the clinic include physicians, nurses, and laboratory technicians, all of whom participate in providing medical and related services to patients of the clinic. Under paragraph (b)(3)(iii) of this section, it would be unreasonable for Employer E to separate the services of the physicians, nurses, and laboratory technicians in different lines of business.

*Example (10).* Employer F is a law firm. The employees of the firm include lawyers, paralegals, and secretaries, all of whom participate in rendering legal and related services to clients of the firm. Under paragraph (b)(3)(iii) of this section, it would be unreasonable for Employer F to separate the services of the lawyers, paralegals, and secretaries in different lines of business.

*Example (11).* Employer G is a management consulting firm. The employees of the firm include management consultants, secretaries, and other support staff personnel, all of whom participate in rendering management consulting and related services to clients of the firm. Under paragraph (b)(3)(iii) of this section, it would be unreasonable for Employer G to separate the services of the management consultants, secretaries, and other support staff personnel in different lines of business.

*(3) Examples illustrating property and services provided to customers.* The following examples illustrate the application of paragraph (b)(2) of this section relating to property and services provided to customers of the employer.

*Example (1).* Employer H operates several dairy farms and dairy product processing plants. The dairy farms provide part of their output of milk and milk by-products to Employer H's dairy product processing plants and also sell part to retail distributors unrelated to Employer H. The dairy farms' provision of milk and milk by-products to Employer H's dairy product processing plants does not constitute the provision of property or services to customers of Employer H because the milk and milk by-products are not provided to a person other than employer H. However, the dairy farms' provision of milk and milk by-products to independent retail distributors does constitute the provision of property or services to customers of Employer H under paragraph (b)(2) of this section.

*Example (2).* The facts are the same as in Example 1, except that the dairy farms provide their entire output of milk and milk by-products to Employer H's dairy product processing plants. The dairy farms' provision of milk and milk by-products to the dairy product processing plants generally does not constitute the provision of property or services to customers of Employer H because the milk and milk by-products are not provided to a person other than Employer H. However, paragraph (b)(2)(i) of this section provides a special rule for vertically integrated businesses that satisfy § 1.414(r)-3(d)(2)(iii)(B). If § 1.414(r)-3(d)(2)(iii)(B) is satisfied, then, under the special rule of paragraph (b)(2)(i) of this section, the milk and milk by-products are deemed to be provided to customers of Employer H.

*Example (3).* Among its other business activities, Employer J manufactures automobiles. Employer J operates a cafeteria at one of its automobile manufacturing facilities. The cafeteria is intended primarily for use by employees of Employer J, but non-employees are not prohibited from using the cafeteria. The cafeteria charges the same prices to employees and non-employees. Under paragraph (b)(2) of this section, the provision of cafeteria services to employees of Employer J does not constitute the provision of property or services to customers of Employer J, because the cafeteria services are provided to the employees in their capacity as employees of Employer J and not as customers of Employer J.

*Example (4).* Employer K sells books and periodicals to members of the public and provides telecommunications services to private industry. Employer K periodically acquires and disposes of businesses in both asset and stock transactions. In addition, for its own investment purposes, Employer K acquires and disposes of corporate and other securities. Under paragraph (b)(2) of this section, the sale by Employer K of businesses and investment securities does not constitute the provision of property or services to customers of Employer K, because the sales are not made in the ordinary course of a trade or business conducted by Employer K. However, the sale of published materials and the provision of telecommunications services to persons unrelated to Employer K does constitute the provision of property or services to customers of Employer K.

*Example (5).* Employer L is active in the financial services industry. Subsidiary 1 of Employer L is a brokerage firm that is regulated as a broker-dealer under applicable federal and state law. In its capacity as a dealer, Subsidiary 1 holds in its own inventory securities of unrelated corporations and regularly sells these securities to unrelated persons. Under paragraph (b)(2) of this section, the sale by Subsidiary 1 of the securities to unrelated persons constitutes the provision of property or services to customers of Employer L, because the sales are made in the ordinary course of Subsidiary 1's trade or business as a broker-dealer.

*Example (6).* The facts are the same as in Example 5. Subsidiary 2 of Employer L is an insurance company that is regulated under applicable state insurance laws. In managing its investments, Subsidiary 2 regularly makes use of the brokerage services of Subsidiary 1 (which Subsidiary 1 regularly provides to unrelated persons as well). Under paragraph (b)(2) of this section, Subsidiary 1's provision of brokerage services to Subsidiary 2 does not constitute the provision of property or services to customers of Employer L, because the brokerage services are not provided to a person other than Employer L. However, Subsidiary 1's provision of brokerage services to unrelated persons does constitute the provision of property or services to customers of Employer L.

*Example (7).* Employer M is a shipbuilder. In a testing year, Employer M enters into a contract with a customer to construct a new cargo ship for delivery two years later. Employer M incurs significant costs designing and planning for the production of the new ship during the testing year, but receives no payments from the customer during that year. Under paragraph (b)(2) of this section, Employer M is treated as providing the cargo ship to the customer during the testing year.

*Example (8).* The facts are the same as in Example 7, except that, pursuant to a request from the customer, Employer M also incurred significant costs developing a prototype and submitting a bid on the new cargo ship in the prior testing year, and that these costs were not reimbursed by the customer. Under paragraph (b)(2) of this section, Employer M is also treated as providing the cargo ship to the customer in the prior testing year.

---

T.D. 8376, 12/2/91, amend T.D. 8548, 6/23/94.

---

### § 1.414(r)-3 Separate line of business.

**(a) General rule.** A separate line of business is a line of business (as determined under § 1.414(r)-2) that is organized and operated separately from the remainder of the employer. Paragraph (b) of this section sets forth the rules for determining whether a line of business is organized and operated separately from the remainder of the employer. Paragraph (c) of this section provides certain supplementary rules necessary to apply the requirements of paragraph (b) of this section, as well as examples illustrating the application of those requirements. Paragraph (d) of this section provides an optional rule for lines of business that are vertically integrated.

**(b) Separate organization and operation.** *(1) In general.* A line of business is organized and operated separately from the remainder of the employer for a testing year only if it satisfies all the requirements of paragraphs (b)(2) through (b)(5) of this section for the testing year.

*(2) Separate organizational unit.* The line of business must be formally organized as a separate organizational unit or group of separate organizational units within the employer. For this purpose, an organizational unit is a corporation, partnership, division, or other unit having a similar degree of organizational formality. This requirement must be satisfied on every day of the testing year.

*(3) Separate financial accountability.* The line of business must be a separate profit center or group of separate profit centers within the employer. This requirement must be satisfied on every day of the testing year. In addition, the employer must maintain books and records that provide separate revenue and expense information that is used for internal planning and control with respect to each profit center comprising the line of business.

*(4) Separate employee workforce.* The line of business must have its own separate employee workforce. A line of business has its own separate workforce only if at least 90 percent of the employees who provide services to the line of business, and who are not substantial-service employees with respect to any other line of business, are substantial-service employees with respect to the line of business.

*(5) Separate management.* The line of business must have its own separate management. A line of business has its own separate management only if at least 80 percent of the employees who are top-paid employees with respect to the line of business are substantial-service employees with respect to the line of business. See paragraph (c)(3) of this section to determine how the percentage in the preceding sentence is calculated for the testing year.

**(c) Supplementary rules.** *(1) In general.* This paragraph (c) provides certain supplementary rules necessary to apply the requirements of paragraph (b) of this section, as well as examples illustrating the application of those requirements.

*(2) Determination of separate employee workforce.* The percentage in paragraph (b)(4) of this section is the fraction (expressed as a percentage)—

(i) The numerator of which is the number of substantial-service employees with respect to the line of business within the meaning of § 1.414(r)-11(b)(2); and

(ii) The denominator of which is the total number of employees who provide services to the line of business within the meaning of paragraph (c)(5) of this section and who are not substantial-service employees with respect to any other line of business.

*(3) Determination of separate management.* The percentage in paragraph (b)(5) of this section is the fraction (expressed as a percentage)—

(i) The numerator of which is the number of employees who are both top-paid employees and substantial-service employees with respect to the line of business within the meaning of § 1.414(r)-11(b)(3) and (2), respectively; and

(ii) The denominator of which is the total number of top-paid employees with respect to the line of business within the meaning of § 1.414(r)-11(b)(3).

*(4) Employees taken into account.* For purposes of applying this paragraph (c), only employees who are employees on the first testing day are taken into account. For this purpose, there are no excludable employees except nonresident aliens described in section 410(b)(3)(C). Consequently, all other employees who are employees on the first testing day are taken into account, including collectively bargained em-

ployees. For the definition of first testing day, see § 1.414(r)-11(b)(7).

*(5) Services taken into account.* (i) Provision of services to a line of business. An employee provides services to a line of business if more than a negligible portion of the employee's services contributes to providing the property or services provided by the line of business to customers of the employer. All of the services of each employee who provides services to the employer contribute, whether directly or indirectly, to the provision of property or services to customers of the employer, and therefore each employee who provides services to the employer must be treated as providing more than a negligible portion of the employee's services to one or more lines of business operated by the employer.

(ii) Period for which services are provided. Only services performed by an employee during the testing year that contribute to providing the property or services provided by a line of business to customers are taken into account. An employee's services during the testing year are considered to contribute to providing the property or services provided by a line of business to customers of the employer if—

(A) The employee's services during the testing year contribute to providing such property or services to customers of the employer during the testing year; or

(B) It is reasonably anticipated that the employee's services during the testing year will contribute to providing such property and services to customers of the employer after the close of the testing year.

(iii) Optional rule for employees who change status. (A) In general. Solely for purposes of the separateness rules of this section and the assignment rules of § 1.414(r)-7, if an employee changes status as described in paragraph (c)(5)(iii)(B) of this section, an employer may, for up to three consecutive testing years after the base year (within the meaning of paragraph (c)(5)(iii)(B)(1) or (2) of this section), treat the employee as providing the same level of service to its lines of business as the employee provided in the base year.

(B) Change in employee's status. An employee changes status as described in this paragraph (c)(5)(iii)(B) if—

(1) For a testing year (the base year), the employee was a substantial-service employee with respect to a qualified separate line of business of the employer (prior line of business) and, for the immediately succeeding testing year, the employee is not a substantial-service employee with respect to that prior line of business; or

(2) For a testing year (the base year), the employee was a residual shared employee and, for the immediately succeeding testing year, the employee is a substantial-service employee with respect to a qualified separate line of business.

*(6) Examples of the separate employee workforce requirement.* The following examples illustrate the application of the separate employee workforce requirement in paragraph (b)(4) of this section and the supplementary rules of this paragraph (c). Unless otherwise specified, it is assumed that the employees and their services described in these examples are taken into account under paragraphs (c)(4) and (5) of this section for the testing year. Unless otherwise specified, it is assumed that the employees and their services described in these examples are taken into account under paragraphs (c)(4) and (5) of this section for the testing year and that the employer does not use the option under § 1.414(r)-11(b)(2) to treat employees who provide less than 75 percent of their services to a line of business as substantial-service employees with respect to the line of business.

*Example (1).* Employer A operates three lines of business as determined under § 1.414(r)-2. One of Employer A's lines of business manufactures and sells tires and other automotive products. Employee M is a tire press operator in Employer A's tire factory. Employee N is the manager of the tire factory. Under these facts, the services of Employees M and N contribute to providing tires to customers of Employer A. Both employees therefore provide services to Employer A's tire and automotive products line of business within the meaning of paragraph (c)(5) of this section.

*Example (2).* The facts are the same as in Example 1. In addition, none of the services of Employees M and N that contribute to providing property or services to customers contribute to providing any property or service other than tires to customers of Employer A. Under these facts, Employees M and N provide at least 75 percent of their respective services to Employer A's tire and automotive products line of business. Therefore Employees M and N are substantial-service employees with respect to Employer A's tire and automotive products line of business within the meaning of § 1.414(r)-11(b)(2), and do not provide any services within the meaning of paragraph (c)(5) of this section to any of Employer A's other lines of business. Moreover, because Employees M and N provide at least 75 percent of their services to Employer A's tire and automotive products line of business and are substantial-service employees with respect to that line, they are disregarded in applying paragraph (b)(4) of this section to any other line of business, even if they provide services to the other line.

*Example (3).* The facts are the same as in Example 2. Employer A's second line of business manufactures and sells construction machinery, and Employer A's third line of business manufactures and sells agricultural equipment. As part of these lines of business, Employer A operates a construction machinery factory and an agricultural equipment factory on the same site as the tire factory described in Example 2. Employer A's facilities at the site include a health clinic and a fitness center that serve the employees of the construction machinery factory, the agricultural equipment factory, and the tire factory. Employee O is a nurse in the health clinic, and Employee P is a fitness instructor in the fitness center. Both employees therefore provide services within the meaning of paragraph (c)(5) of this section to Employer A's tire and automotive products line of business, construction machinery line of business, and agricultural equipment line of business. In addition, under these facts, Employer A determines that approximately 33 percent of the services of Employees O and P are provided to each of Employer A's three lines of business. As a result, neither Employee O or P provide at least 75 percent of their respective services to any of Employer A's lines of business. Therefore, Employees O and P are not substantial-service employees with respect to any of Employer A's three lines of business within the meaning of § 1.414(r)-11(b)(2).

*Example (4).* The facts are the same as in Example 3. Employee Q is the president and chief executive officer of Employer A and is responsible for reviewing the performance of all Employer A's lines of business. Under these facts, the services of Employee Q contributes to providing property and services to customers of each of Employer A's three lines of business. Employee Q therefore provides services to each of these three lines of business. Employer A determines that Employee Q provides the following percentages of his services to Employer A's three lines of business: tire and automotive products - 40 percent; construction machinery - 40 percent, and agricultural equipment - 20 percent. Employee Q does not provide at least 75 percent of his services to any of Employer A's lines of business. Therefore, Employee Q is not a substantial-service employee with respect to any of Employer A's three lines of business within the meaning of § 1.414(r)-11(b)(2).

*Example (5).* The facts are the same as in Example 4, except that Employer A also owns 75 percent of Corporation X. Corporation X is not treated as part of Employer A within the meaning of § 1.410(b)-9. Employee R is an accountant in the accounting department of Employer A. Employee R devotes all of his time to maintaining the accounting books and records of the tire and automotive products line of business of Employer A and the accounting books and records of Corporation X. Employer A determines that Employee R provides 40 percent of his services directly to the tire and automotive products line of business. Employer A also determines that Employee R provides the following percentages of the remainder of Employee R's services (i.e., his provision of services of maintaining the accounting books and records of Corporation X) indirectly to Employer A's three lines of business by virtue of the services he provides to Corporation X: tire and automotive products - 25 percent; construction machinery - 20 percent, and agricultural equipment - 15 percent. Therefore, Employee R provides 65 percent of his services to the tire and automotive products line of business of Employer A (i.e., 40 percent directly and 25 percent indirectly). Under the definition of substantial-service employee in § 1.414(r)-11(b)(2), Employer A may treat Employee R as a substantial-service employee with respect to the tire and automotive products line of business because Employee R provides at least 50 percent of his services to that line. In that case, Employee R would be disregarded in applying paragraph (b)(4) of this section to the construction machinery and agricultural equipment lines of business.

*Example (6).* The facts are the same as in Example 5. Employee S is a lawyer in the legal department located at the headquarters who devotes all her time to product liability suits filed against the construction machinery line of business. Under these facts, the services of Employee S contribute to providing property and services to customers of Employer A in the construction machinery line of business, and therefore Employee S provides services to that line of business. Because Employee S's services do not contribute to providing property or services in any other of Employer A's lines of business within the meaning of paragraph (c)(5) of this section, Employee S provides more than 75 percent of her services to the construction machinery line of business and therefore is a substantial-service employee with respect to Employer A's construction machinery line of business within the meaning of § 1.414(r)-11(b)(2).

*Example (7).* The facts are the same as in Example 6. Employer A also maintains a separate facility that houses a centralized procurement, marketing, and billing operation for all of its lines of business. None of the procurement, marketing, or billing employees specializes in any particular line of business. Under these facts, the services of the procurement, marketing, and billing employees contribute to providing property and services to customers of Employer A in each of Employer A's three lines of business. Employer A determines that each of the procurement, marketing, and billing employees provides approximately an equal proportion of their services to each of Employer A's three lines of business. These employees therefore provide services to all of Employer A's lines of business within the meaning of paragraph (c)(5) of this section. However, none of them provides at least 75 percent of his services to any line of business. Therefore, these employees are not substantial-service employees with respect to any of Employer A's three lines of business within the meaning of § 1.414(r)-11(b)(2).

*Example (8).* The facts are the same as in Example 7. Employee T works for the construction machinery line of business. During the testing year, he is temporarily detailed to the agricultural equipment line of business. His temporary detail lasts for one week, after which he returns to his regular duties with the construction machinery line of business. Under these facts, Employee T does not provide more than a negligible portion of his services during the testing year to the agricultural equipment line of business. Accordingly, Employee T does not provide services to the agricultural equipment line of business within the meaning of paragraph (c)(5) of this section. In addition, because Employee T provides at least 75 percent of his services to the construction machinery line of business, Employee T is a substantial-service employee with respect to Employer A's agricultural equipment line of business within the meaning of § 1.414(r)-11(b)(2).

*Example (9).* The facts are the same as in Example 8, except that, during the testing year but before the first testing day, Employee T retires from employment with Employer A. Under paragraph (c)(5)(ii) of this section, Employee T is not taken into account in determining whether Employer A's construction machinery line of business has its own separate employee workforce within the meaning of paragraph (b)(4) of this section.

*Example (10).* Employer B is a multinational controlled group of corporations that engages in the exploration, production, refining, and marketing of petrochemical products. Employer B operates two lines of business as determined under § 1.414(r)-2. The first line of business (the "exploration, production, and refining line of business") provides lubricating oil, gasoline, and other petrochemical products to wholesale customers of Employer B as well as to the second line of business. The wholesale customers of Employer B include independent jobbers, independent franchisees that operate retail filling stations under Employer B's trademark and tradename, as well as chemical and plastics manufacturers. The second line of business (the "retail marketing line of business") provides lubricating oil and gasoline products to retail customers of Employer B through filling stations owned and operated by Employer B. Employee U is an attendant at a filling station owned and operated by Employer B. Employee U performs no other services for Employer B. Under these facts, Employee U provides at least 75 percent of his services to Employer B's retail marketing line of business and therefore is a substantial-service employee with respect to that line of business within the meaning of § 1.414(r)-11(b)(2), and does not provide any services within the meaning of paragraph (c)(5) of this section to any of Employer B's other lines of business.

*Example (11).* The facts are the same as in Example 10. Employer B operates a refinery that produces lubricating oil, gasoline, and other petrochemical products. Employee V is an operating engineer at the refinery who is involved at a stage in the refining process before lubricating oil and gasoline products have been separated form other types of petrochemical products. Employee V performs no other services for Employer B. Under these facts, Employee V's services contribute to providing property and services to customers of Employer B in both the exploration, production, and refining line of business and the retail marketing line of business. Employee V therefore provides services to both lines of business within the meaning of paragraph (c)(5) of this section. See paragraph (d) of this section, however, for an optional rule for vertically integrated lines of business.

*Example (12).* The facts are the same as in Example 11. Employee W is a petroleum engineer who conducts geological studies of potential future drilling sites. Although Employee W's services during the testing year will not contribute to providing lubricating oil, gasoline, and other petrochemical products to customers of Employer B during the testing year, it is reasonably anticipated (in accordance with paragraph (c)(5)(ii)(B) of this section) that her services during the testing year will contribute to providing such products to customers of Employer B after the close of the testing year. Under these facts, Employee W provides her services to both of Employer B's lines of business within the meaning of paragraph (c)(5) of this section.

*(7) Examples of the separate management requirement.* The following examples illustrate the application of the separate management requirement in paragraph (b)(5) of this section and the supplementary rules of this paragraph (c). Unless otherwise specified, it is assumed that employees who provide services to a line of business are not substantial-service employees with respect to any other line of business and that, in determining the top-paid employees with respect to a line of business, the employer is using the option under § 1.414(r)-11(b)(3) to disregard all employees who provide less than 25 percent of their services to that line of business.

*Example (1).* (a) Employer C operates three lines of business as determined under § 1.414(r)-2. One of its lines of business is the operation of a chain of athletic equipment and apparel stores. Of Employer C's total workforce, 12,000 employees provide more than a negligible amount of the services they provide to Employer C to the athletic equipment and apparel stores line of business, within the meaning of paragraph (c)(5) of this section. Of the 1,200 employees who constitute the top ten percent by compensation of those 12,000 employees, 930 are substantial-service employees with respect to that line of business. Because 930 is 77.5 percent of 1,200, less than 80 percent of the top-paid employees with respect to the line of business are substantial-service employees with respect to that line of business. Therefore, Employer C's athletic equipment and apparel stores line of business does not have its own separate management under paragraph (b)(5) of this section.

(b) Assume that, in determining the top-paid employees with respect to the athletic equipment and apparel stores line of business, Employer C chooses to disregard all employees who provide less than 25 percent of their services to the line of business as permitted under the definition in § 1.414(r)-11(b)(3). Of the 12,000 employees who provide more than a negligible amount of their services to the athletic equipment and apparel stores line of business, 10,000 provide at least 25 percent of their services to that line. Of the 1,000 employees who constitute the top ten percent by compensation of those 10,000 employees, 930 are substantial-service employees with respect to the athletic equipment and apparel stores line of business. Because 930 is 93 percent of 1,000, at least 80 percent of the top-paid employees with respect to the line of business are substantial-service employees with respect to that line of business. Therefore, Employer C's athletic equipment and apparel stores line of business has its own separate management and satisfies the requirement of paragraph (b)(5) of this section.

*Example (2).* The facts are the same as in Example 1. Employee X is a vice president of the accounting department located at the headquarters, who devotes all of his time supervising the staff of Employer C's accounting department. Employer C determines that 10 percent of Employee X's services contribute to providing property and services to customers of Employer C's athletic equipment and apparel stores line of business and 45 percent of Employee X's services contribute to providing property and services to customers to each of Employer C's other two lines of business. Because Employee X does not provide at least 25 percent of his services to Employer C's athletic equipment and apparel stores line of business, Employee X is not one of the 10,000 employees described in Example 1 and therefore cannot be a top-paid employee within the meaning of § 1.414(r)-11(b)(3) with respect to the athletic equipment and apparel stores line of business. Therefore, Employee X is not taken into account in determining whether the athletic equipment and apparel stores line of business satisfies the separate management requirement of paragraph (b)(5) of this section.

*Example (3).* The facts are the same as in Example 2 except that Employee X provides 60 percent of his services to Employer C's second line of business, an athletic equipment factory, and 30 percent of his service to Employer C's third line of business, a fast-food chain. Because Employee X provides at least 50 percent of his services to the athletic equipment factory line of business, Employer C chooses to treat him as a substantial-service employee with respect to that line of business, as permitted under § 1.414(r)-11(b)(2). Thus, Employee X is taken into account as a substantial-service employee with respect to the athletic equipment factory line of business and is disregarded in applying the separate workforce and separate management requirements under paragraphs (b)(4) and (5) to the fast-food chain line of business.

*Example (4).* Employer D operates four lines of business as determined under § 1.414(r)-2. One of its lines of business is a machine tool shop. Sixty of Employer D's employees provide at least 25 percent of their services to the machine tool shop line of business. Of the six employees who constitute the top 10 percent by compensation of those 60 employees, four are substantial-service employees with respect to the line of business. Because four is 67 percent of six, 80 percent of the top-paid employees with respect to the machine tool shop line of business are not substantial-service employees with respect to that line of business. Therefore the machine tool shop line of business does not satisfy the separate management requirement of paragraph (b)(5) of this section.

*Example (5).* The facts are the same as in Example 4, except that, in addition, another of Employer D's lines of business is an automotive repair shop, and 80 of Employer D's employees provide at least 25 percent of their services to that line of business. Employer D combines the machine shop line of business with the automotive repair shop line of business and treats them as a single line of business. As a result, Employer D has three lines of business as determined under § 1.414(r)-2. Assume that 150 of employer D's employees provide more than 25 percent of their services to the machine tool shop/automotive repair shop line of business within the meaning of paragraph (c)(5) of this section. Of the 15 employees who constitute the top 10 percent by compensation of these 150 employees, 12 are substantial-service employees with respect to that line of business. Because 12 is 80 percent of 15, at least 80 percent of the top-paid employees with respect to the machine tool shop/automotive repair shop line of business are substantial-service employees with respect to that line of business. Therefore, the machine tool shop/automotive repair shop line of business satisfies the separate management requirement of paragraph (b)(5) of this section.

**(d) Optional rule for vertically integrated lines of business.** *(1) In general.* If two lines of business satisfy the requirements of this paragraph (d) with respect to a type of property or service for a testing year, the employer is permitted to apply the optional rule in this paragraph (d) for the testing year.

*(2) Requirements.* Two lines of business satisfy the requirements of this paragraph (d) with respect to a type of property or service only if—

(i) One of the lines of business (the upstream line of business) provides a type of property or service to the other line of business (the downstream line of business);

(ii) The downstream line of business either—

(A) Uses, consumes, or substantially modifies the property or service in the course of itself providing property or services to customers of the employer; or

(B) Provides the same property or service to customers of the employer at a different level in the chain of commercial distribution from the upstream line of business (e.g., retail versus wholesale); and

(iii) The upstream line of business either—

(A) Provides the same type of property or service to customers of the employer, and at least 25 percent of the total number of units of the same type of property or service provided by the upstream line of business to all persons (including customers of the employer, the downstream line of business, and all other lines of business of the employer) are provided to customers of the employer by the upstream line of business, when measured on a uniform basis; or

(B) Provides to the downstream line of business property consisting primarily of a type of tangible property (i.e., goods, not services) that it produces or manufactures, and some entities outside the employer's controlled group that are engaged in a similar business as the upstream line of business provide the same type of tangible property to unrelated customers (i.e., customers outside those entities' respective controlled groups).

*(3) Optional rule.* (i) Treatment of employees. For purposes of determining the lines of business to which an employee provides services under paragraph (c)(5) of this section, an employee is not treated as providing services to the downstream line of business if—

(A) The employee is considered to provide services to the downstream line of business under paragraph (c)(5) of this section (applied without regard to the optional rule in this paragraph (d)); and

(B) The employee is so considered solely because the employee's services contribute to providing the property or service from the upstream line of business to the downstream line of business.

(ii) Purposes for which optional rule applies. If an employer applies the optional rule in this paragraph (d), the treatment specified in paragraphs (d)(3)(i)(A) and (B) of this section applies for all the following purposes and only for the following purposes—

(A) The separate employee workforce and separate management requirements of paragraphs (b)(4) and (b)(5) of this section;

(B) The 50-employee requirement of § 1.414(r)-4(b); and

(C) The determination of the employees of a qualified separate line of business under § 1.414(r)-7.

*(4) Examples.* The following examples illustrate the application of the optional rule in this paragraph (d).

*Example (1).* Employer E operates two lines of business as determined under § 1.414(r)-2, one engaged in upholstery textile manufacturing and the other in furniture manufacturing. During the testing year, the upholstery textile line of business provides its entire output of upholstery textiles to the furniture line of business. The furniture line of business uses the upholstery textiles in the manufacture of upholstered furniture for sale to customers of Employer E. The furniture line of business thus substantially modifies the upholstery textiles provided to it by the upholstery textile line of business in providing upholstered furniture products to customers of Employer E. In addition, although the upholstery textile line of business does not provide upholstery textiles to customers of Employer E, some entities engaged in upholstery textile manufacturing provide upholstery textiles to customers outside their controlled groups. Under these facts, Employer E's two lines of business satisfy the requirements of this paragraph (d) with respect to upholstery textiles for the testing year.

*Example (2).* Employer B is a multinational controlled group of corporations that engages in the exploration, production, refining, and marketing of petrochemical products. See Example 10 under paragraph (c)(7) of this section. Employer B operates two lines of business as determined under § 1.414(r)-2. The first line of business ("the exploration, production, and refining line of business") provides lubricating oil, gasoline, and other petrochemical products to wholesale customers of Employer B as well as the second line of business. The wholesale customers of Employer B include independent jobbers, independent franchisees that operate retail filling stations under Employer B's trademark and tradename, as well as chemical and plastics manufacturers. The second line of business (the "retail marketing line of business") provides lubricating oil and gasoline products to retail customers of Employer B through filling stations owned and operated by Employer B. During the testing year, the exploration, production, and refining line of business provides 25,000 gallons of lubricating oil, 100,000 gallons of unleaded and 150,000 gallons of leaded gasoline to the retail marketing line of business, and 75,000 gallons of lubricating oil, 500,000 gallons of unleaded gasoline and 15,000 gallons of leaded gasoline to wholesale customers of Employer B. Thus, the exploration, production, and refining line of business provides 75 percent of its output of lubricating oil during the testing year to wholesale customers of Employer B. In addition, because unleaded and leaded gasoline is the same type of property (i.e., gasoline), the exploration, production, and refining line of business provides 67 percent of its output of gasoline products during the testing year to wholesale customers of Employer B. Furthermore, the retail line of business provides lubricating oil and gasoline products to customers of Employer B at different levels in the chain of commercial distribution than the exploration, production, and refining line of business. Under these facts, Employer B's two lines of business satisfy the requirements of this paragraph (d) with respect to both lubricating oil and gasoline products for the testing year.

*Example (3).* The facts are the same as in Example 2. Employer B operates a refinery that produces lubricating oil, gasoline, and other petrochemical products. Employee V is an operating engineer at the refinery who is involved at a stage in the refining process before lubricating oil and gasoline products have been separated from other types of petrochemical products. Employee V performs no other services for Employer B. Absent application of the optional rule in this paragraph (d), Employee V would be considered to provide services to both of Employer B's lines of business. See Example 11 under paragraph (c)(7) of this section. However, because Employee V's services to the retail marketing line of business contribute solely to providing lubricating oil and gasoline products from the exploration, production, and refining line of business to the retail marketing line of business, under the optional rule in paragraph (d)(3)(i) of this section Employee V is not treated as providing services to the retail marketing line of business.

*Example (4).* The facts are the same as in Example 3. Employee W is a petroleum engineer who conducts geological studies of potential future drilling sites. Employee W performs no other services for Employer B. Absent application of the optional rule in this paragraph (d), Employee W would be considered to provide services to both of Employer B's lines of business. See Example 12 under paragraph (c)(7) of this section. However, because Employee W's services to the retail marketing line of business contribute solely to providing lubricating oil and gasoline products from the exploration, production, and refining line of business to the retail marketing line of business, under the optional rule in paragraph (d)(3)(i) of this section Employee W is not treated as providing services to the retail marketing line of business.

*Example (5).* The facts are the same as in Example 4. Employee Y is a vice president in Employer B's home office. As part of his senior management responsibilities, Employee Y helps to set the rate of production at Employer B's refineries in the United States and also helps to set the price charged at the pump at the retail filling stations owned and operated by Employer B in this country. Absent application of the optional rule in this paragraph (d), Employee X would be considered to provide services to both of Employer B's lines of business within the meaning of paragraph (c)(5) of this section for purposes of satisfying the separate workforce requirement of paragraph (b)(4) of this section. Because Employee X helps to set the price charged at the pump by Employer B's retail marketing line of business, Employee X's services to the retail marketing line of business are not limited to contributing solely to providing lubricating oil and gasoline products from the exploration, production, and refining line of business to the retail marketing line of business, as required under paragraph (d)(3)(i)(B) of this section. Accordingly, even though Employer B's two lines of business satisfy the requirements of this paragraph (d) with respect to both lubricating oil and gasoline products for the testing year, and even though Employer B applies the optional rule in this paragraph (d), Employee X is still considered to provide services to both of Employer B's lines of business.

T.D. 8376, 12/2/91, amend T.D. 8548, 6/23/94.

## § 1.414(r)-4 Qualified separate line of business—fifty-employee and notice requirements.

**(a) In general.** This section sets forth the rules for determining whether a separate line of business (as determined under § 1.414(r)-3) satisfies the 50-employee and notice requirements of § 1.414(r)-1(b)(2)(iv)(B) and (C), respectively.

**(b) Fifty-employee requirement.** A separate line of business satisfies the 50-employee requirement of § 1.414(r)-1(b)(2)(iv)(B) for a testing year only if on each day of the testing year there are at least 50 employees who provide services to the separate line of business for the testing year and do not provide services to any other separate line of business of the employer for the testing year within the meaning of § 1.414(r)-3(c)(5). For this purpose, all employees of the employer are taken into account (including collectively bargained employees), except employees described in § 1.414(q)-1, Q&A-9(g) (i.e., the same employees, subject to certain modifications, who are excluded in determining the number of employees in the top-paid group under section 414(q)(4)).

**(c) Notice requirement.** *(1) General rule.* A separate line of business satisfies the notice requirement of § 1.414(r)-1(b)(2)(iv)(C) for a testing year only if the employer notifies the Secretary that it treats itself as operating qualified separate lines of business for the testing year in accordance with § 1.414(r)-1(b). The employer's notice for the testing year must specify each of the qualified separate lines of business operated by the employer and the section or sections of the Code to be applied on a qualified-separate-line-of-business basis. See § 1.414(r)-1(c). The employer's notice must take the form, must be filed at the time and the place, and must contain any additional information prescribed by the Commissioner in revenue procedures, notices, or other guidance of general applicability. No other notice, whether actual or constructive, satisfies the requirement of this paragraph (c).

*(2) Effect of notice.* Once an employer has provided the notice prescribed in this paragraph (c) for a testing year, and the time for filing the notice for the testing year has expired without its being modified, withdrawn, or revoked, the employer is deemed to have irrevocably elected to apply the requirements of the section or sections of the Code specified in the notice separately with respect to the employees of each qualified separate line of business specified in the notice for all plan years that begin in the testing year. The Commissioner may, in revenue procedures, notices, or other guidance of general applicability, provide for exceptions to the rule in this paragraph (c)(2) as well as for the effect that will be given to the employer's notice for purposes of any future testing year.

T.D. 8376, 12/2/91, amend T.D. 8548, 6/23/94.

## § 1.414(r)-5 Qualified separate line of business—administrative scrutiny requirement—safe harbors.

**(a) In general.** A separate line of business (as determined under § 1.414(r)-3) satisfies the administrative scrutiny requirement of § 1.414(r)-1(b)(2)(iv)(D) for a testing year if the separate line of business satisfies any of the safe harbors in paragraphs (b) through (g) of this section for the testing year. The safe harbor in paragraph (b) of this section implements the statutory safe harbor of section 414(r)(3). The safe harbors in paragraphs (c) through (g) of this section constitute the guidelines provided for under section 414(r)(2)(C). A separate line of business that does not satisfy any of the safe harbors in this section nonetheless satisfies the requirement of administrative scrutiny if the employer requests and receives an individual determination from the Commissioner under § 1.414(r)-6 that the separate line of business satisfies the requirement of administrative scrutiny.

**(b) Statutory safe harbor.** *(1) General rule.* A separate line of business satisfies the safe harbor in this paragraph (b) for the testing year only if the highly compensated employee percentage ratio of the separate line of business is—

(i) At least 50 percent; and

(ii) No more than 200 percent.

*(2) Highly compensated employee percentage ratio.* For purposes of this paragraph (b), the highly compensated employee percentage ratio of a separate line of business is the fraction (expressed as a percentage), the numerator of which is the percentage of the employees of the separate line of business who are highly compensated employees, and the denominator of which is the percentage of all employees of the employer who are highly compensated employees.

*(3) Employees taken into account.* For purposes of this paragraph (b), the employees taken into account are the same employees who are taken into account for purposes of applying section 410(b) with respect to the first testing day. For this purpose, employees described in section 410(b)(3) and (b)(4) are excluded. However, section 410(b)(4) is applied with reference to the lowest minimum age requirement applicable under any plan of the employer, and with reference to the lowest service requirement applicable under any plan of the employer, as if all the plans were a single plan under § 1.410(b)-6(b)(2). The employees of the separate line of business are determined by applying § 1.414(r)-7 to the employees taken into account under this paragraph (b)(3). An employee is treated as a highly compensated employee for purposes of this paragraph (b) if the employee is treated as a highly compensated employee for purposes of applying section 410(b) with respect to the first testing day. For the definition of "first testing day," see § 1.414(r)-11(b)(7).

*(4) Ten-percent exception.* A separate line of business is deemed to satisfy paragraph (b)(1)(i) of this section for the testing year if at least 10 percent of all highly compensated employees of the employer provide services to the separate line of business during the testing year and do not provide services to any other separate line of business of the employer during the testing year within the meaning of § 1.414(r)-3(c)(5).

*(5) Determination based on preceding testing year.* A separate line of business that satisfied this safe harbor for the immediately preceding testing year (without taking into account the special rule in this paragraph (b)(5)) is deemed to satisfy the safe harbor for the current testing year. The preceding sentence applies to a separate line of business only if the employer designated the same line of business in the immediately preceding testing year as in the current testing year and either—

(i) The highly compensated employee percentage ratio of the separate line of business for the current testing year does not deviate by more than 10 percent (not 10 percentage points) from the highly compensated employee percentage ratio of the separate line of business for the immediately preceding testing year; or

(ii) No more than five percent of the employees of the separate line of business for the current testing year were employees of a different separate line of business for the immediately preceding testing year, and no more than five percent of the employees of the separate line of business for the immediately preceding testing year are employees of a different separate line of business for the current testing year.

*(6) Examples.* The following examples illustrate the application of the safe harbor in this paragraph (b).

*Example (1).* (i) Employer A operates three separate lines of business as determined under § 1.414(r)-3, that respectively consist of a railroad, an insurance company, and a newspaper. Employer A employs a total of 400 employees, 100 of whom are highly compensated employees. Thus, the percentage of all employees of Employer A who are highly compensated employees is 25 percent. After applying § 1.414(r)-7, the distribution of highly and nonhighly compensated employees among Employer A's separate lines of business is as follows:

| | Employer-Wide | Railroad | Insurance Company | Newspaper |
|---|---|---|---|---|
| Number of Employees | 400 | 100 | 150 | 150 |
| Number of HCEs | 100 | 20 | 50 | 30 |
| Number of Non-HCEs | 300 | 80 | 100 | 120 |
| HCE Percentage | 25% (100/400) | 20% (20/100) | 33% (50/150) | 20% (30/150) |
| HCE Percentage Ratio | N/A | 80% (20%/25%) | 133% (33%/25%) | 80% (20%/25%) |

(ii) Because the highly compensated employee percentage ratio of each separate line of business is at least 50 percent and no more than 200 percent, each of Employer A's separate lines of business satisfies the requirements of the safe harbor in this paragraph (b).

*Example (2).* (i) Employer B operates three separate lines of business as determined under § 1.414(r)-3, that respectively consist of a dairy products manufacturer, a candy manufacturer, and a chain of housewares stores. Employer B employs a total of 1,000 employees, 100 of whom are highly compensated employees. Thus, the percentage of all employees of Employer B who are highly compensated employees is 10 percent. After applying § 1.414(r)-7, the distribution of highly and nonhighly compensated employees among Employer B's separate lines of business is as follows:

| | Employer-Wide | Dairy Products | Candy | Housewares Stores |
|---|---|---|---|---|
| Number of Employees | 1,000 | 200 | 500 | 300 |
| Number of HCEs | 100 | 5 | 50 | 45 |
| Number of Non-HCEs | 900 | 195 | 450 | 255 |
| HCE Percentage | 10% (100/1,000) | 2.5% (5,200) | 10% (50/500) | 15% (45/300) |
| HCE Percentage Ratio | N/A | 25% (2.5%/10%) | 100% (10%/10%) | 150% (15%/10%) |

(ii) Because the highly compensated employee percentage ratio for the dairy products line of business is less than 50 percent, it does not satisfy the requirements of the statutory safe harbor in this paragraph (b). However, because Employer B's other two separate lines of business (candy manufacturing and housewares stores) each has a highly compensated employee percentage ratio that is no less than 50 percent and no greater than 200 percent, they each satisfy the statutory safe harbor in this paragraph (b).

*Example (3).* (i) The facts are the same as in Example 2, except that Employer B operates only two separate lines of business as determined under § 1.414(r)-3, one consisting of the dairy products manufacturer and the candy manufacturer, and the other consisting of the chain of housewares stores. After applying § 1.414(r)-7, the distribution of highly and nonhighly compensated employees among Employer B's separate lines of business is as follows:

| | Employer-Wide | Candy/Dairy Products | Housewares Stores |
|---|---|---|---|
| Number of Employees | 1,000 | 700 | 300 |
| Number of HCEs | 100 | 55 | 45 |
| Number of Non-HCEs | 900 | 645 | 255 |
| HCE Percentage | 10% (100/1,000) | 7.9% (55/700) | 15% (45/300) |
| HCE Percentage Ratio | N/A | 79% (7.9%/10%) | 150% (15%/10%) |

(ii) Because the highly compensated employee percentage ratio for both of Employer B's separate lines of business is at least 50 percent and no more than 200 percent, they each satisfy the requirements of the statutory safe harbor in this paragraph (b).

**(c) Safe harbor for separate lines of business in different industries.** *(1) In general.* A separate line of business satisfies the safe harbor in this paragraph (c) for the testing year if it is in a different industry or industries from every other separate line of business of the employer. For this purpose, a separate line of business is in a different industry or industries from every other separate line of business of the employer only if—

(i) The property or services provided to customers of the employer by the separate line of business (as designated by the employer for the testing year under § 1.414(r)-2) fall exclusively within one or more industry categories established by the Commissioner for purposes of this paragraph (c); and

(ii) None of the property or services provided to customers of the employer by any of the employer's other separate lines of business (as designated by the employer for the testing year under § 1.414(r)-2) falls within the same industry category or categories.

*(2) Optional rule for foreign operations.* For purposes of satisfying this paragraph (c), an employer is permitted to disregard any property or services provided to customers of the employer during the testing year by a foreign corporation or foreign partnership (as defined in section 7701(a)(5)), to the extent that income from the provision of the property or services is not effectively connected with the conduct of the trade or business within the United States within the meaning of section 864(c). Thus, for example, an employer is permitted to take into account only property and services provided to customers of the employer by its domestic subsidiaries and property and services provided by its foreign subsidiaries that generate income effectively connected with the conduct of a trade or business within the United States in determining whether the property or services provided to customers of the employer by a separate line of business fall exclusively within one or more industry categories and also whether the property or services provided by any other separate line of business fall within the same industry category or categories.

*(3) Establishment of industry categories.* The Commissioner shall, by revenue procedure or other guidance of general applicability, establish industry categories for purposes of this paragraph (c).

*(4) Examples.* The following examples illustrate the application of the safe harbor in this paragraph (c). For purposes of these examples, it is assumed that, pursuant to paragraph (c)(3) of this section, the Commissioner has established the following industry categories (among others): transportation equipment and services; banking, insurance, and finance; machinery and electronics; and entertainment, sports, and hotels.

*Example (1).* Among its other business activities, Employer C operates a commercial airline that constitutes a separate line of business under § 1.414(r)-3. In addition, no other separate line of business of Employer C provides to customers of Employer C any property or services in the transportation equipment and services industry category. Under these facts, the separate line of business described in this example satisfies the safe harbor in this paragraph (c).

*Example (2).* The facts are the same as in Example 1, except that Employer C also operates a trucking company that constitutes another separate line of business of Employer C under § 1.414(r)-3. Because the commercial airline and the trucking company both provide to customers of Employer C services in the transportation equipment and services industry category, neither separate line of business satisfies the safe harbor in this paragraph (c).

*Example (3).* Among its other business activities, Employer D operates a commercial bank and a luxury hotel that together constitute a single separate line of business under § 1.414(r)-3. No other separate line of business of Employer D provides to customers of Employer D property or services in either the banking, insurance, or financial industry category, or the entertainment, sports, or hotel industry category. Under these facts, the separate line of business described in this example satisfies the safe harbor in this paragraph (c).

*Example (4).* The facts are the same as in Example 3, except that Employer D also manufactures computers in the United States and abroad. Employer D apportions its computer operations by designating these operations between two separate lines of business, one consisting of its domestic operations located in the United States and the second consisting of its foreign operations by a foreign subsidiary. Because both lines of business provide property and services in the machinery and electronics industry category to customers of Employer D, neither separate line of business would satisfy the safe harbor in this paragraph (c). However, pursuant to the optional rule in paragraph (c)(2) of this section, Employer D disregards the property and services provided by its foreign computer subsidiary. As a result, no other separate line of business of Employer D provides to customers of Employer D any property or services in the machinery and electronics industry category. Under these facts, Employer D's domestic computer operations separate line of business satisfies the safe harbor in this paragraph (c).

**(d) Safe harbor for separate lines of business that are acquired through certain mergers and acquisitions.** *(1) General rule.* A portion of the employer that is acquired through a transaction described in section 410(b)(6)(C) and § 1.410(b)-2(f) (i.e., an asset or stock acquisition, merger, or other similar transaction involving a change in the employer of the employees of a trade or business) (the "acquired line of business") satisfies the safe harbor in this paragraph (d) for each testing year in the transition period provided in paragraph (d)(3) of this section if each of the following requirements is satisfied—

(i) For each testing year within the transition period the employer designates the acquired line of business as a line of business within the meaning of § 1.414(r)-2;

(ii) On the first testing day in each testing year in the transition period:

(A) The acquired line business constitutes a separate line of business within the meaning of § 1.414(r)-3 (taking into account § 1.414(r)-1(d)(4));

(B) No more than 10 percent of the employees who are substantial-service employees with respect to the acquired line of business were substantial-service employees with respect to a different separate line of business for the immediately preceding testing year; and

(C) No more than 10 percent of the employees who were substantial-service employees with respect to the acquired line of business for the immediately preceding testing year are substantial-service employees with respect to a different separate line of business in the respective testing year.

(iii) If the transaction described in paragraph (d)(1) of this section occurs after the first testing day in a testing year, the determinations required by paragraphs (d)(1)(ii)(B) and (C) of this section with respect to that testing year are made as of the date of the transaction.

*(2) Employees taken into account.* For purposes of this paragraph (d), the employees taken into account are the same employees who are taken into account for purposes of applying section 410(b) with respect to the first testing day. For this purpose, employees described in section 410(b)(3) and (b)(4) are excluded. However, section 410(b)(4) is applied with reference to the lowest minimum age requirement, and with reference to the lowest service requirement applicable under any plan of the employer that benefits employees of the separate line of business, as if all the plans were a single plan under § 1.410(b)-6(b)(2). The employees of the separate line of business are determined by applying § 1.414(r)-7 to the employees taken into account under this paragraph (d)(2).

*(3) Transition period.* The transition period for purposes of this safe harbor is the period that begins with the first testing year beginning after the date that the transaction described in paragraph (d)(1) of this section occurs. The employer is permitted, but not required, to extend the transition period to include one, two, or three of the testing years immediately succeeding that first testing year.

*(4) Examples.* The following examples illustrate the application of the safe harbor in this paragraph (d).

*Example (1).* Employer E is treated as operating three qualified separate lines of business pursuant to § 1.414(r)-1(b). In 1996, Employer E acquires a company that employs 4,000 employees who manufacture and sell pharmaceutical supplies, and designates that portion as a line of business under § 1.414(r)-2. Under § 1.414(r)-1(d)(4), the pharmaceutical supplies line of business is deemed to satisfy the requirements to be a qualified separate line of business (other than the 50-employee and notice requirements) for testing year 1996. In addition, the determination of whether Employer E's remaining three lines of business constitute qualified separate lines of business for testing year 1996 is made without taking into account the acquired employees and by disregarding the property and services provided to customers of Employer E by the pharmaceutical supplies line of business.

*Example (2).* The facts are the same as in Example 1 except that, by the first testing day in 1997 (Transition Year 1), there are 300 additional substantial-service employees with respect to the pharmaceutical supplies line of business, increasing the total number to 4,300. Of those 300 employees, 250 were substantial-service employees with respect to a different separate line of business for testing year 1996 and 50 are new hires. Assume that, on the first testing day in Transition Year 1, the pharmaceutical supplies line of business satisfies the requirements of § 1.414(r)-3 (taking into account § 1.414(r)-1(d)(4)) and therefore constitutes a separate line of business. Because 250 is 6 percent of 4,300, no more than ten percent of the employees who are substantial-service employees with respect to the pharmaceutical supplies line of business were substantial-service employees with respect to a different separate line of business for the immediately preceding testing year. The 50 newly hired employees are disregarded in making this determination. Under these facts, the pharmaceutical supplies separate line of business satisfies the safe harbor in this paragraph (d) for Transition Year 1.

*Example (3).* The facts are the same as in Example 2, except that, before the first day of the next testing year ("Transition Year 2"), Employer E permanently transfers 200 of the 4,300 employees who were substantial-service employees with respect to the pharmaceutical line of business on the first testing day in Transition Year 1 to a different line of business and does not hire any additional employees for the pharmaceutical supplies line of business. Therefore, by the first testing day in Transition Year 2, the number of employees who are substantial-service employees with respect to the pharmaceutical line of business of Employer E has decreased from 4,300 to 4,100. Assume that, on that first testing day in Transition Year 2, the pharmaceutical supplies line of business constitutes a separate line of business within the meaning of § 1.414(r)-3. Because 200 is approximately 5 percent of 4,300, no more than 10 percent of the employees who were substantial-service employees of the pharmaceutical line of business for Transition Year 1 are not substantial-service employees of the pharmaceutical line of business in Transition Year 2. Under these facts, the pharmaceutical supplies separate line of business continues to satisfy the safe harbor in this paragraph (d) for Transition Year 2.

**(e) Safe harbor for separate lines of business reported as industry segments.** *(1) In general.* A separate line of business satisfies the safe harbor in this paragraph (e) for the testing year if, for the employer's fiscal year ending latest in the testing year, the separate line of business is reported as one or more industry segments on its annual report required to be filed in conformity with either—

(i) Form 10-K, Annual Report Pursuant to Section 13 or 15(d) of the Securities Exchange Act of 1934 ("Form 10-K"); or

(ii) Form 20-F, Annual Report Pursuant to Section 13(a) or 15(d) of the Securities Exchange Act of 1934 with Item 18 financials ("Form 20-F"),

and the employer timely files either the Form 10-K or Form 20-F with the Securities and Exchange Commission ("SEC").

*(2) Reported as an industry segment in conformity with Form 10-K or Form 20-F.* For purposes of this paragraph (e), a separate line of business is reported as one or more industry segments in conformity with either Form 10-K or Form 20-F only if—

(i) The separate line of business consists of one or more industry segments within the meaning of paragraphs 10(a), 11(b), and 12 through 14 of the Statement of Financial Accounting Standards No. 14, Financial Reporting for Segments of a Business Enterprise ("FAS 14"); and

(ii) The property or services provided to customers of the employer by the separate line of business (as designated by the employer for the testing year under § 1.414(r)-2) is identical to the property or services provided to customers of the employer by the industry segment or segments (as determined under paragraphs 10(a), 11(b), and 12 through 14 of FAS 14).

*(3) Timely filing of Form 10-K or Form 20-F.* For purposes of this paragraph (e), a Form 10-K or Form 20-F is timely filed with the SEC if it is filed within the required period as provided under 17 C.F.R. § 240.12b-25(b)(2)(ii). Therefore, the required period for timely filing of the Form 10-K is the 90-day period after the end of the fiscal year covered by the annual report (including the 15-day extension), and the required period for timely filing of the Form 20-F is the six month period after the end of the fiscal year covered by the annual report (including the 15-day extension).

*(4) Examples.* The following examples illustrate the application of the safe harbor in this paragraph (e).

*Example (1).* Among its other business activities, Employer F operates a bearing manufacturing firm that constitutes a separate line of business under § 1.414(r)-3. Employer F is required to file an annual Form 10-K with the SEC. On its timely filed Form 10-K, Employer F reports its bearing manufacturing operations as an industry segment in accordance of FAS 14 (as determined under paragraphs 10(a), 11(b), and 12 through 14 of FAS 14). The group of bearing products provided by the separate line of business (as designated by Employer F under § 1.414(r)-2) is identical to the group of bearing products provided by the industry segment (as determined under paragraphs 10(a), 11(b), and 12 through 14 of FAS 14). Under these facts, the separate line of business described in this example satisfies the safe harbor in this paragraph (e).

*Example (2).* The facts are the same as in Example 1, except that Employer F has apportioned its bearing manufacturing operations between two separate lines of business as determined under § 1.414(r)-3, one engaged in the manufacture of bearings for use in the automotive industry, and a second engaged in the manufacture of bearings for use in the aerospace industry. Because neither separate line of business provides a group of property or services to customers of Employer F that is identical to the group of bearing products provided by the industry segment reported on Employer F's annual Form 10-K, neither separate line of business described in this example satisfies the safe harbor in this paragraph (e).

**(f) Safe harbor for separate lines of business that provide the same average benefits as other separate lines of business.** *(1) General rule.* A separate line of business satisfies the safe harbor in this paragraph (f) for the testing year only if the level of benefits provided to employees of the separate line of business satisfies paragraph (f)(2) or (f)(3) of this section, whichever is applicable.

*(2) Separate lines of business with a disproportionate number of nonhighly compensated employees.* (i) Applicability of safe harbor. This paragraph (f)(2) applies to a separate line of business that for the testing year has a highly compensated employee percentage ratio of less than 50 percent (as determined under paragraph (b)(2) of this section).

(ii) Requirement. A separate line of business satisfies this paragraph (f)(2) only if the actual benefit percentage of the group of nonhighly compensated employees of the separate line of business for the testing period that ends with or within the testing year is at least as great as the actual benefit percentage of the group of all other nonhighly compensated employees of the employer for the same testing period. See § 1.410(b)-5(c) and (d)(3)(ii) for the definitions of actual benefit percentage and testing period, respectively. In determining actual benefit percentages for purposes of this paragraph (f)(2)(ii), the special rule in § 1.410(b)-5(e)(3) (permitting an employer to determine employee benefit percentages separately for defined contribution and defined benefit plans) may not be used.

*(3) Separate lines of business with a disproportionate number of highly compensated employees.* (i) Applicability of safe harbor. This paragraph (f)(3) applies to a separate line of business that for the testing year has a highly com-

pensated employee percentage ratio of more than 200 percent (as determined under paragraph (b)(2) of this section).

(ii) Requirement. A separate line of business satisfies this paragraph (f)(3) only if the actual benefit percentage of the group of highly compensated employees of the separate line of business for the testing period that ends with or within the testing year is no greater than the actual benefit percentage of the group of all other highly compensated employees of the employer for the same testing period. See § 1.410(b)-5(c) and (d)(3)(ii) for the definitions of actual benefit percentage and testing period, respectively. In determining actual benefit percentages for purposes of this paragraph (f)(3)(ii), the special rule in § 1.410(b)-5(e)(3) (permitting an employer to determine employee benefit percentages separately for defined contribution and defined benefit plans) may not be used.

*(4) Employees taken into account.* An employee of a separate line of business (as determined under § 1.414(r)-7) is taken into account for a testing period for purposes of this paragraph (f) only if the employee is an employee of the separate line of business on the first testing day, and would not be an excludable employee for purposes of applying the average benefit percentage test of § 1.410(b)-5 to a plan for a plan year included in that testing period. In determining whether an employee is an excludable employee for purposes of the average benefit percentage test, the employer is assumed not to be operating qualified separate lines of business under § 1.414(r)-1(b). An employee is treated as a highly compensated employee for purposes of this paragraph (f) if the employee is treated as a highly compensated employee for purposes of applying section 410(b) on the first testing day. See § 1.414(r)-11(b)(7) for the definition of "first testing day".

*(5) Example.* The rules of this paragraph (f) are illustrated by the following example.

*Example.* (i) Employer G is treated as operating two separate lines of business, Line 1 and Line 2, in accordance with § 1.414(r)-1(b). Employer G maintains three qualified plans. Plan A is a calendar-year profit-sharing plan that benefits all employees of Employer G. Plan B is a defined benefit plan with a plan year ending March 31 that benefits all employees of Line 1. Plan C is a defined benefit plan with a plan year ending November 30 that benefits all employees of Line 2.

(ii) In 1995, Line 1 has a highly compensated employee percentage ratio of 25 percent. Employer G's first testing day is March 31. After applying the rules of § 1.414(r)-7, the nonhighly compensated employees of Line 1 and Line 2 on March 31, 1995, are N1-N80 and N81-N100, respectively. N1 is an excludable employee under § 1.410(b)-6 for purposes of the average benefit percentage test during the testing period that includes the plan years of Plans A, B, and C that end in 1995 (the "1995 testing period"), and would therefore not be taken into account in determining whether any of those plans satisfied the average benefit percentage test of § 1.410(b)-5 for plan years included in that testing period, because N1 does not satisfy the minimum age and service conditions under any plan of the employer. All other employees of Line 1 and Line 2 on March 31, 1995, are nonexcludable employees for purposes of the average benefit percentage test during the 1995 testing period.

(iii) In order for Line 1 to satisfy the requirements of this paragraph (f) for 1995, the actual benefit percentage of N2-N80 for the 1995 testing period under Plans A, B and C must be at least as great as the actual benefit percentage of N81-N100 for the same testing period under the same plans. N1 is not taken into account because N1 is an excludable employees for purposes of the average benefit percentage test for the 1995 testing period. Any other employees who were taken into account for purposes of the average benefit percentage test for the 1995 testing period are excluded because they are not employees of Line 1 or Line 2 on March 31, 1995.

**(g) Safe harbor for separate lines of business that provide minimum or maximum benefits.** *(1) In general.* A separate line of business satisfies the safe harbor in this paragraph (g) for the testing year only if the level of benefits provided to employees of the separate line of business satisfies paragraph (g)(2) or (g)(3) of this section, whichever is applicable. For this purpose, the level of benefits is determined with respect to all qualified plans of the employer that benefit employees of the separate line of business for plan years that begin in the testing year.

*(2) Minimum benefit required.* (i) Applicability. This paragraph (g)(2) applies to a separate line of business that for the testing year has a highly compensated employee percentage ratio of less than 50 percent (as determined under paragraph (b)(2) of this section).

(ii) Requirement. A separate line of business satisfies this paragraph (g)(2) only if one of the following requirements is satisfied—

(A) At least 80 percent of all nonhighly compensated employees of the separate line of business either accrue a benefit for the plan year that equals or exceeds the defined benefit minimum in paragraph (g)(2)(iii) of this section, receive an allocation for the plan year that equals or exceeds the defined contribution minimum in paragraph (g)(2)(iv) of this section, or accrue a benefit and receive an allocation that together equal or exceed the combined plan minimum in paragraph (g)(4) of this section. The defined benefit minimum must be provided in a defined benefit plan, and the defined contribution minimum must be provided in a defined contribution plan.

(B) The separate line of business would satisfy the requirements of paragraph (g)(2)(ii)(A) of this section if the 80 percent threshold were reduced to 60 percent, and the average of the accrual rates or allocation rates of all nonhighly compensated employees in the separate line of business equals or exceeds the minimum amount described for each individual employee in paragraph (g)(2)(ii)(A) of this section.

(iii) Defined benefit minimum. (A) In general. The benefit plan with a plan year ending March 31 that benefits defined benefit minimum for a plan year is the employer-derived accrual that would result in a normal accrual rate for the plan year equal to 0.75 percent of compensation. For purposes of this paragraph (g)(2)(iii), the normal accrual rate is the percentage (not less than 0) determined by subtracting the employee's normalized accrued benefit as of the end of the prior plan year (expressed as a percentage of average annual compensation as of the end of the prior plan year) from the employee's normalized accrued benefit as of the end of the plan year (expressed as a percentage of average annual compensation as of the end of the plan year).

(B) Normal form and equivalent benefits. The benefit that is tested for purposes of this paragraph (g)(2)(iii) is the accrued retirement benefit commencing at normal retirement age. If the normal form of benefit for a plan being tested is other than a straight life annuity beginning at a normal retirement age of 65, the benefit must be normalized (within the meaning of § 1.401(a)(4)-12) to a straight life annuity commencing at age 65. No adjustment is permitted for early retirement benefits or for any ancillary benefit, including disability benefits.

(C) Compensation definition. The underlying definition of compensation used for purposes of determining accrual rates under this paragraph (g)(2)(iii) must be a definition of compensation that automatically satisfies section 414(s) without a test for nondiscrimination (see § 1.414(s)-1(c)).

(D) Average compensation requirement. For purposes of determining accrual rates, compensation must be average annual compensation within the meaning of § 1.401(a)(4)-3(e)(2) determined using a five year averaging period. The compensation history to be taken into account are all years beginning with the first year in which the employee benefits under the plan, and ending with the last plan year in which the employee participates in the plan. However, a plan may disregard in a reasonable and consistent manner: years before the effective date of these regulations as set forth in § 1.414(r)-1(d)(9)(i), years more than 10 years preceding the current plan year, and years for which the employer does not use this paragraph (g)(2) to satisfy this safe harbor with respect to the separate line of business. If a plan provides a defined benefit minimum that uses three consecutive years (in lieu of five) for calculating average annual compensation, the 0.75 percent annual accrual rate in paragraph (g)(2)(iii)(A) of this section is multiplied by 93.3 percent, resulting in a normal accrual rate equal to 0.70 percent. If a plan provides a defined benefit minimum that uses more than five consecutive years for calculating average annual compensation or the plan is an accumulation plan as defined in § 1.401(a)(4)-12, the 0.75 percent annual accrual rate in paragraph (g)(2)(iii)(A) of this section is multiplied by 133.3 percent, resulting in a normal accrual rate equal to 1.0 percent.

(E) Special rules. The special rules of § 1.401(a)(4)-3(f) apply for purposes of determining whether a benefit accrual satisfies the minimum benefit requirement. For example, benefits may be determined on other than a plan year basis as permitted by § 1.401(a)(4)-3(f)(6). A plan described in section 412(i) may be used to provide the defined benefit minimum described in this paragraph (g)(2). In such case, the rules in § 1.416-1, M-17, apply to such a plan. For purposes of this paragraph (g)(2)(iii) an employee is treated as accruing a benefit equal to the minimum benefit in paragraph (g)(2)(iii)(A) of this section if the reason that the employee does not accrue such a benefit is either—

(1) The application of a plan provision that applies uniformly to all employees in the plan and limits the service used for purposes of benefit accrual to a specified maximum no less than 25 years, or

(2) The employee has attained normal retirement age and fails to accrue a benefit solely because of the provisions of section 411(b)(1)(H)(iii) regarding adjustments for delayed retirement.

(iv) Defined contribution minimum. (A) In general. The defined contribution minimum for a plan year is an allocation that results in an allocation rate for the plan year (within the meaning of § 1.401(a)(4)-2(c)) equal to three percent of an employee's plan year compensation. Plan year compensation must be based on a definition of compensation that automatically satisfies section 414(s) without a test for nondiscrimination (see § 1.414(s)-1(c)). For this purpose, allocations that are taken into account do not include matching contributions described in § 1.401(m)-1(a)(2), elective contributions described in § 1.401(k)-6, any adjustment in allocation rates permitted under section 401(l) or imputed disparity under § 1.401(a)(4)-7.

(B) Modified allocation definition for averaging. For purposes of determining whether the average allocation rates for all nonhighly compensated employees of the separate line of business satisfy the minimum benefit requirement in paragraph (g)(2)(ii)(B) of this section, matching contributions described in § 1.401(m)-1(a)(2) are treated as employer allocations.

*(3) Maximum benefit permitted.* (i) Applicability. This paragraph (g)(3) applies to a separate line of business that for the testing year has a highly compensated employee percentage ratio that exceeds 200 percent (as determined under paragraph (b)(2) of this section).

(ii) Requirement. A separate line of business satisfies this paragraph (g)(3) only if one of the following requirements is satisfied—

(A) No highly compensated employee of the separate line of business accrues a benefit for the plan year that results in an accrual rate that exceeds the defined benefit maximum in paragraph (g)(3)(iii) of this section, receives an allocation that exceeds the defined contribution maximum in paragraph (g)(3)(iv) of this section, or accrues a benefit and receives an allocation that together exceed the combined plan maximum in paragraph (g)(4) of this section. All benefits provided by qualified defined benefit plans are subject to the defined benefit maximum, and all benefits provided by qualified defined contribution plans are subject to the defined contribution maximum.

(B) The average of the accrual rates or allocation rates of all highly compensated employees of the separate line of business is no more than 80 percent of the maximum amount described for any individual employee in paragraph (g)(3)(ii)(A) of this section.

(iii) Defined benefit maximum. (A) In general. The defined benefit maximum is the employer-derived accrued benefit that would result from calculating a normal accrual rate equal to 2.5 percent of compensation.

(B) Determination of defined benefit maximum. The accrual rate used for the defined benefit maximum is determined in the same manner as the normal accrual rate used for the defined benefit minimum is determined under paragraph (g)(2)(iii) of this section, except as provided below. Thus, a defined benefit plan may provide, in addition to the defined benefit maximum, any benefit the value of which is not taken into account under paragraph (g)(2)(iii) of this section. For example, a plan may provide qualified disability benefits described in section 411(a)(9) or ancillary benefits described in § 1.401(a)(4)-4(e)(2).

(C) Adjustment for different compensation definitions. If a plan subject to the defined benefit maximum determines accrual rates by using three consecutive years (in lieu of five) for purposes of determining average annual compensation, the 2.5 percent annual accrual rate in paragraph (g)(3)(iii)(B) of this section is multiplied by 93.3 percent, resulting in a maximum accrual rate equal to 2.33 percent. Compensation may be less inclusive than the compensation described in paragraph (g)(2)(iii)(C) of this section. However, no adjustment is made to the maximum normal accrual rate because of the use of a definition of compensation that is less inclusive than the compensation described in paragraph (g)(2)(iii)(C) of this section. In addition, no adjustment is made to the maximum normal accrual rate because the plan uses more than five consecutive years for calculating average annual compensation or the plan is an accumulation plan as defined in § 1.401(a)(4)-12.

(D) Adjustment for certain subsidies. If the plan provides subsidized optional forms of benefit, the accrual rate for purposes of this paragraph (g)(3) must be determined by taking those subsidies into account. An optional form of benefit is considered subsidized if the normalized optional form of benefit is larger than the normalized normal retirement benefit under the plan. In the case of a plan with subsidized optional forms, the determination of accrual rate for the plan year under paragraph (g)(2)(iii)(A) of this section is the percentage (not less than 0) determined by subtracting the largest of the sums of the employee's normalized QJSAs and QSUPPs determined for each age under § 1.401(a)(4)-3(d)(1)(ii) as of the end of the prior plan year (expressed as a percentage of average annual compensation as of the end of the prior plan year) from the largest of the sums of the employee's normalized QJSAs and QSUPPs determined for each age under § 1.401(a)(4)-3(d)(1)(ii) as of the end of the plan year (expressed as a percentage of average annual compensation as of the end of the plan year).

(iv) Defined contribution maximum. The defined contribution maximum is an allocation that results in an allocation rate for the plan year (within the meaning of § 1.401(a)(4)-2(c)) equal to 10 percent of an employee's plan year compensation. Compensation may be less inclusive than the compensation described in paragraph (g)(2)(iv)(A) of this section. However, no adjustment is made to the defined contribution maximum because of the use of a definition of compensation that is less inclusive than the compensation described in paragraph (g)(2)(iv)(A) of this section. For this purpose, allocations that are taken into account do not include elective contributions described in § 1.401(k)-6, any adjustment in allocation rates permitted under section 401(l) or imputed disparity under § 1.401(a)(4)-7 but do include employer matching contributions under § 1.401(m)-1(f)(12).

*(4) Duplication of benefits or contributions.* (i) Plans of the same type. In the case of an employee who benefits under more than one defined benefit plan, the defined benefit minimum required or the defined benefit maximum permitted under this paragraph (g) is determined by reference to the employee's aggregate employer-provided benefit under all qualified defined benefit plans of the employer. In the case of an employee who benefits under more than one defined contribution plan, the defined contribution minimum required or the defined contribution maximum permitted under this paragraph (g) is determined by reference to the employee's aggregate employer-provided allocations under all qualified defined contribution plans of the employer.

(ii) Plans of different types. In the case of an employee who benefits under both a defined benefit plan and a defined contribution plan, a percentage of the minimum benefit required or the maximum benefit permitted under this paragraph (g) may be provided in each type of plan as long as the combined percentage equals at least 100 percent in the case of the minimum benefit required and does not exceed 100 percent in the case of the maximum benefit permitted. Thus, for example, if a highly compensated employee benefits under both types of plans and accrues an aggregate adjusted normal accrual rate equal to 1.25 percent of average annual compensation under all defined benefit plans of the employer (i.e., 50 percent of the defined benefit maximum described in paragraph (g)(3)(iii) of this section), in order to comply with the maximum benefit safe harbor, the employee may not receive an aggregate allocation under all defined contribution plans of the employer in excess of five percent of plan year compensation (i.e., 50 percent of the defined contribution maximum described in paragraph (g)(3)(iv) of this section).

(iii) Special rule for floor-offset arrangements. In the case of a floor-offset arrangement (as described in § 1.401(a)(4)-8(d)), the minimum or maximum benefit rules are applied to each plan as if the other plan did not exist. Thus, the defined benefit plan must provide at least 100 percent of the defined benefit minimum (or no more than 100 percent of the defined benefit maximum) based on the gross benefit prior to offset, and the defined contribution plan must provide at least 100 percent of the defined contribution minimum (or no more than 100 percent of the defined contribution maximum).

*(5) Certain contingency provisions ignored.* For purposes of this paragraph (g), an employee's accrual or allocation rate is determined without regard to any minimum benefit or any maximum benefit limitation that is applicable to the employee only if the separate line of business fails otherwise to satisfy the requirement of administrative scrutiny.

*(6) Employees taken into account.* For purposes of this paragraph (g), an employee is taken into account if the employee is taken into account for purposes of applying section 410(b) with respect to any testing day for the testing year. For this purpose, employees described in section 410(b)(3) and (b)(4) are excluded. However, section 410(b)(4) is applied with reference to the lowest minimum age requirement applicable, and with reference to the lowest service requirement applicable under any plan of the employer that benefits employees of the separate line of business, as if all the plans were a single plan under § 1.410(b)-6(b)(2). For purposes of the minimum benefit requirement of paragraph (g)(2) of this section, section 410(b)(4) may be applied with reference to the lowest minimum age requirement, and with reference to the lowest minimum service requirement, applicable under any plan of the employer that benefits highly compensated employees of the separate line of business, as if all the plans were a single plan under § 1.410(b)-6(b)(2), or, if no plan of the employer benefits highly compensated employees of the separate line of business, with reference to the greatest age and service requirements permitted under section 410(a)(1)(A). The employees of the separate line of business are determined by applying § 1.414(r)-7 to the employees taken into account under this paragraph (g)(6). An employee is treated as a highly compensated employee for purposes of this paragraph (g) if the employee is treated as a highly compensated employee for purposes of applying section 410(b) on any testing day for the testing year. For the definition of "testing day," see § 1.414(r)-11(b)(6).

T.D. 8376, 12/2/91, amend T.D. 8548, 6/23/94, T.D. 9169, 12/28/2004.

### § 1.414(r)-6 Qualified separate line of business—administrative scrutiny requirement—individual determinations.

**(a) In general.** A separate line of business (as determined under § 1.414(r)-3) that does not satisfy any of the safe harbors in § 1.414(r)-5 for a testing year nonetheless satisfies the administrative scrutiny requirement of § 1.414(r)-1(b)(2)(iv)(D) if the employer requests and receives from the Commissioner an individual determination under this section that the separate line of business satisfies the requirement of administrative scrutiny for the testing year. This section implements the individual determinations provided for under section 414(r)(2)(C). The Commissioner shall issue such an individual determination only when it is consistent with the purpose of section 414(r), taking into account the nondiscrimination requirements of sections 401(a)(4) and 410(b). Paragraph (b) of this section authorizes the Commissioner to establish procedures for requesting and granting individual determinations.

**(b) Authority to establish procedures.** The Commissioner may, in revenue rulings and procedures, notices, and other guidance, published in the Internal Revenue Bulletin (see § 601.601(d)(2)(ii)(b) of this chapter), provide any additional guidance that may be necessary or appropriate for requesting and granting individual determinations under this section. For example, such guidance may specify the circumstances in which an employer may request an individual determination and factors to be taken into account in deciding whether to grant a favorable individual determination. In addition, such guidance may describe situations that automatically fail the administrative scrutiny requirement.

T.D. 8376, 12/2/91, amend T.D. 8548, 6/23/94.

**§ 1.414(r)-7 Determination of the employees of an employer's qualified separate lines of business.**

**(a) Introduction.** *(1) In general.* This section provides the rules for determining the employees of each qualified separate line of business operated by an employer. Paragraph (a)(2) of this section lists the specific provisions of the regulations for which these rules apply. Paragraph (b) of this section provides the procedure for assigning the employees of the employer among the qualified separate lines of business of the employer and for determining the day or days on which such assignments must be made. Under this procedure, each employee (i.e., a substantial-service employee or a residual shared employee as defined in § 1.414(r)-11(b)(2) and (4)) is assigned to a single qualified separate line of business in a consistent manner for all purposes listed in paragraph (a)(2) of this section with respect to the testing year and plan years beginning within the testing year. Paragraph (c) of this section provides methods for allocating residual shared employees among qualified separated lines of business.

*(2) Purposes for which this section applies.* This section applies solely for purposes of determining whether—

(i) A separate line of business satisfies the statutory safe harbor of § 1.414(r)-5(b) for a testing year (see § 1.414(r)-5(b)(3) for the employees taken into account for this purpose);

(ii) A separate line of business satisfies the merger and acquisition safe harbor of § 1.414(r)-5(d) for a testing year (see § 1.414(r)-5(d)(2) for the employees taken into account for this purpose);

(iii) A separate line of business satisfies the average benefits safe harbor of § 1.414(r)-5(f) for a testing year (see § 1.414(r)-5(f)(4) for the employees taken into account for this purpose);

(iv) A separate line of business satisfies the minimum or maximum benefits safe harbor of § 1.414(r)-5(g) for a testing year (see § 1.414(r)-5(g)(6) for the employees taken into account for this purpose);

(v) A plan of the employer satisfies sections 410(b) and 401(a)(4) for a plan year (see § 1.414(r)-8(d)(3) for the employees taken into account for this purpose); or

(vi) A plan of the employer satisfies section 401(a)(26) for a plan year (see § 1.414(r)-9(c)(3) for the employees taken into account for this purpose).

**(b) Assignment procedure.** *(1) In general.* To apply the provisions listed in paragraph (a)(2) of this section with respect to a testing year or plan year, as the case may be, each of the employees taken into account under that provision must be assigned to a qualified separate line of business of the employer on one or more testing days (or section 401(a)(26) testing days) during the year. The first day for which this assignment procedure is required for a testing year is the first testing day. See § 1.414(r)-11(b)(6), (7) and (8) (definitions of "testing day", "first testing day" and "section 401(a)(26) testing day"). Section 1.414(r)-8 may require that the assignment procedure be repeated for testing days that fall after the first testing day (including testing days that fall after the close of the testing year in a plan year that begins in the testing year). Accordingly, new employees may be taken into account for the first time on these later testing days who were not taken into account on the first testing day. Section 1.414(r)-9 may have the same effect with respect to section 401(a)(26) testing days that fall after the first testing day.

*(2) Assignment for the first testing day.* The employees taken into account under a provision described in paragraph (a)(2) of this section with respect to the first testing day for a testing year are assigned among the employer's qualified separate lines of business by applying the following procedure to each of those employees—

(i) An employee who is a substantial-service employee with respect to a qualified separate line of business within the meaning of § 1.414(r)-11(b)(2) must be assigned to that qualified separate line of business;

(ii) An employee who is a residual shared employee within the meaning of § 1.414(r)-11(b)(4) must be assigned to a qualified separate line of business under paragraph (c) of this section.

Each employee assigned to a qualified separate line of business under paragraph (b)(2)(i) of this section or this paragraph (b)(2)(ii) remains assigned to the same qualified separate line of business for all purposes with respect to the testing year listed in paragraph (a)(2) of this section and for all plan years beginning in that testing year. Once an employee is assigned to a qualified separate line of business with respect to a particular testing day or section 401(a)(26) testing day, that employee remains assigned to that qualified separate line of business after the employee terminates employment. However, after the employee terminates employment, that employee will in most cases not be taken into account with respect to a subsequent testing day or section 401(a)(26) testing day for purposes of applying one or more of the provisions in paragraph (a)(2) of this section.

*(3) Assignment of new employees for subsequent testing days.* After the first testing day for the testing year, the employees taken into account under a provision described in paragraph (a)(2) of this section with respect to a subsequent testing day (or a section 401(a)(26) testing day) for the testing year may include one or more employees who previously have not been assigned to a qualified separate line of business for any purpose listed in paragraph (a)(2) of this section with respect to the testing year. An employee may not previously have been assigned to a qualified separate line of business for any purpose with respect to the testing year if, for example, the employee has just been hired or has just become a nonexcludable employee. Previously unassigned employees are assigned among the employer's qualified separate lines of business by applying the procedure in paragraph (b)(2) of this section to those employees. In determining whether an employee who is not employed by the employer

during the testing year is a substantial-service or a residual shared employee with respect to a qualified separate line of business, § 1.414(r)-3(c)(5) is applied with reference to services performed by the employee during a period in the immediately succeeding testing year that are reasonably representative of the employee's services for the employer.

*(4) Special rule for employers using annual option under section 410(b).* Notwithstanding the fact that paragraphs (b)(1) through (b)(3) of this section generally only require employees to be assigned on testing days beginning with the first testing day, if a plan is tested under section 410(b) using the annual option of § 1.410(b)-8(a)(4) (including for purposes of the average benefit percentage test), employees must be assigned on every day of the plan year of that plan for purposes of this paragraph (b). Thus, all employees who provide services at any time during the plan year of a plan that is tested using the annual option of § 1.410(b)-8(a)(4) must be assigned to a line of business even if they terminate employment before the first testing day within the meaning of § 1.414(r)-11(b)(7) of the testing year in which the plan year begins.

**(c) Assignment and allocation of residual shared employees.** *(1) In general.* All residual shared employees must be allocated among an employer's qualified separate lines of business under one of the allocation methods provided in paragraphs (c)(2) through (5) of this section. An employer is permitted to select which method of allocation to apply for the testing year to residual shared employees. However, the same allocation method must be used for all of the employer's residual shared employees and for all purposes listed in paragraph (a)(2) of this section with respect to the testing year.

*(2) Dominant line of business method of allocation.* (i) In general. Under the method of allocation in this paragraph (c)(2), all residual shared employees are allocated to the employer's dominant line of business. This method does not apply unless the employer has a dominant line of business within the meaning of paragraph (c)(2)(ii) or paragraph (c)(2)(iv) of this section. If an employer has more than one dominant line of business under this paragraph (c), the employer must select which qualified separate lines of business is its dominant line of business.

(ii) Dominant line of business. An employer's dominant line of business is that qualified separate line of business that has an employee assignment percentage of at least 50 percent.

(iii) Employee assignment percentage. (A) Determination of percentage. The employee assignment percentage of a qualified separate line of business is the fraction (expressed as a percentage)—

(1) The numerator of which is the number of substantial-service employees with respect to the qualified separate line of business who are assigned to that line of business under paragraph (b) of this section; and

(2) The denominator of which is the total number of substantial-service employees who are assigned to all qualified separate lines of business of the employer under paragraph (b) of this section.

(B) Employees taken into account. The employee assignment percentage is calculated solely with respect to employees who are taken into account for purposes of satisfying section 410(b) with respect to the first testing day. Therefore, this percentage is calculated only once for all purposes with respect to a testing year. The employees described in section 410(b)(3) and (4) are excluded. However, section 410(b)(4) is applied with reference to the lowest minimum age requirement applicable under any plan of the employer, and with reference to the lowest service requirement applicable under any plan of the employer, as if all the plans were a single plan under § 1.410(b)-6(b)(2).

(iv) Option to apply reduced percentage. An employer is permitted to determine whether it has a dominant line of business by substituting 25 percent for 50 percent in paragraph (c)(2)(ii) of this section. This option is available for a testing year only if the qualified separate line of business satisfies one of the following requirements:

(A) The qualified separate line of business accounts for at least 60 percent of the employer's gross revenues for the employer's latest fiscal year ending in the testing year.

(B) The employee assignment percentage of the qualified separate line of business would be at least 60 percent if collectively bargained employees were taken into account.

(C) Each qualified separate line of business of the employer satisfies the statutory safe harbor of § 1.414(r)-5(b), the average benefits safe harbor of § 1.414(r)-5(f), or the minimum or maximum benefits safe harbor of § 1.414(r)-5(g). Whether a qualified separate line of business satisfies one of these safe harbors is determined after the application of this section, including the assignment of all residual shared employees under this paragraph (c)(2).

(D) The employee assignment percentage of the qualified separate line of business is at least twice the employee assignment percentages of each of the employer's other qualified separate lines of business.

(v) Examples. The following examples illustrate the application of the method of allocation in this paragraph (c)(2).

*Example (1).* (i) Employer A operates four qualified separate lines of business as determined under § 1.414(r)-1(b) for the testing year, consisting of a software developer, a health food products supplier, a real estate developer, and a ski equipment manufacturer. In applying this section for the first testing day with respect to the testing year, Employer A determines that it has a total of 21,000 employees, of whom 10,000 are substantial-service employees not excludable under section 410(b)(3) or (b)(4). Pursuant to paragraph (b) of this section, these 10,000 employees are assigned among Employer A's qualified separate lines of business as follows:

| | Software Developer | Health Food | Real Estate | Ski Equipment |
|---|---|---|---|---|
| Substantial-Service Employees | 2,500 | 1,000 | 2,500 | 4,000 |
| Percentage Assigned to QSLOB | 25% | 10% | 25% | 40% |

(ii) Under these facts, Employer A is not permitted to apply the method of allocation in paragraph (c)(2)(ii) of this section, because none of its qualified separate lines of business satisfies the 50 percent requirement in paragraph (c)(3)(ii) of this section.

*Example (2).* The facts are the same as in Example 1, except that, after allocating all residual shared employees to the ski equipment line of business, the software, ski equipment and health food supplier lines of business each would satisfy the statutory safe harbor of § 1.414(r)-5(b), and that the real estate development line of business would satisfy the minimum or maximum benefits safe harbor of § 1.414(r)-5(g). Under these facts, Employer A is permitted to apply the method of allocation in this paragraph (c)(2) to allocate all its residual shared employees to the ski equipment line of business, because the employee assignment percentage of the ski equipment line of business exceeds 25 percent and each qualified separate line of business satisfies either the statutory safe harbor of § 1.414(r)-5(b) or the minimum or maximum benefits safe harbor of § 1.414(r)-5(g).

*Example (3).* (i) The facts are the same as in Example 1, except that, Employer A chooses not to satisfy the minimum or maximum benefits safe harbor of § 1.414(r)-5(g). Instead, Employer A combines the real estate developer and ski equipment manufacturer into a single line of business. As a result, Employer A has three qualified separate lines of business as determined under § 1.414(r)-1(b). Assume that no residual shared employee becomes a substantial-service employee as a result of the new combination. Employer A's substantial-service employees are assigned among Employer A's qualified separate lines of business as follows:

| | Software Developer | Health Food | Real Estate/ Ski Equipment |
|---|---|---|---|
| Substantial-Service Employees | 2,500 | 1,000 | 6,500 |
| Percentage Assigned to QSLOB | 25% | 10% | 65% |

(ii) Under these facts, Employer A is permitted to apply the method of allocation in this paragraph (c)(2) to allocate all its residual shared employees to the combined real estate development and ski equipment manufacturing line of business, because more than 50 percent of Employer A's substantial-service employees that are taken into account for the first testing day are assigned to that qualified separate line of business.

*Example (4).* (i) The facts are the same as in Example 1, except that, of the remaining 11,000 employees of Employer A, 10,000 employees are substantial-service employees who are collectively bargained employees. Pursuant to paragraph (b) of this section, the 10,000 substantial-service employees and the 10,000 substantial-service employees who are collectively bargained employees are assigned among Employer A's qualified separate lines of business as follows:

| | Software Developer | Health Food | Real Estate | Ski Equipment |
|---|---|---|---|---|
| Substantial–Service Employees | 2,500 | 1,000 | 2,500 | 4,000 |
| Percentage of total substantial–service employees assigned to QSLOB | 25% | 10% | 25% | 40% |
| Substantial–Service Employees (including collectively bargained employees) | 2,500 | 1,000 | 2,500 | 14,000 |
| Percentage of total employees (including collectively bargained employees) assigned to QSLOB | 12.5% | 5% | 12.5% | 70% |

(ii) Thus, the ski equipment line of business satisfies the 25-percent threshold in paragraph (c)(2)(iv) of this section. In addition, the ski equipment's percentage of substantial-service employees is at least 60 percent when taking into account substantial-service employees who are collectively bargained employees and therefore satisfies the requirement under paragraph (c)(2)(iv)(B) of this section. Under these facts, Employer A is permitted to apply the method of allocation in this paragraph (c)(2) to allocate all its residual shared employees to the ski equipment line of business.

*(3) Pro-rata method of allocation.* (i) In general. Under the method of allocation in this paragraph (c)(3), all residual shared employees are allocated among an employer's qualified separate lines of business in proportion to the employee assignment percentage of each qualified separate line of business, as determined under paragraph (c)(2)(iii) of this section.

(ii) Allocation procedure. The procedure for allocating residual shared employees under the method in this paragraph (c)(3) is as follows—

(A) The number of highly compensated residual shared employees who are allocated to each qualified separate line of business is equal to the product determined by multiplying the total number of highly compensated residual shared employees of the employer by the employee assignment percentage determined with respect to the qualified separate line of business under paragraph (c)(3)(i) of this section;

(B) The number of nonhighly compensated residual shared employees who are allocated to each qualified separate line of business is equal to the product determined by multiplying the total number of nonhighly compensated residual shared employees of the employer by the employee assignment percentage determined with respect to the qualified separate line of business under paragraph (c)(3)(i) of this section;

(C) For purposes of this procedure, the employer is permitted to determine which highly compensated residual shared employees and which nonhighly compensated residual shared employees are allocated to each qualified separate line of business, provided that the required number of highly and nonhighly compensated residual shared employees are allocated to each qualified separate line of business.

(iii) Examples. The following example illustrates the application of the method of allocation in this paragraph (c)(3).

*Example (1).* The facts are the same as in Example 1 under paragraph (c)(2)(v) of this section except that there are no additional residual shared employees after the first testing day. Of Employer A's 1,000 residual shared employees, 800 are highly compensated employees and 200 are nonhighly compensated employees. Employer A applies the pro-rata method of allocation in this paragraph (c)(3). Under these facts, the 1,000 residual shared employees are allocated among Employer A's qualified separate lines of business as follows:

| | Software Developer | Health Food | Real Estate | Ski Equipment |
|---|---|---|---|---|
| Substantial-Service Employees | 2,500 | 1,000 | 2,500 | 4,000 |
| Percentage Assigned to QSLOB ("employee assignment percentage") | 25% | 10% | 25% | 40% |
| Residual Shared HCEs Allocated to QSLOB | 200<br>(25% × 800) | 80<br>(10% × 800) | 200<br>(25% × 800) | 320<br>(40% × 800) |
| Residual Shared NHCEs Allocated to QSLOB | 50<br>(25% × 200) | 20<br>(10% × 200) | 50<br>(25% × 200) | 80<br>(40% × 200) |

*(4) HCE percentage ratio method of allocation.* (i) In general. Under the method of allocation in this paragraph (c)(4), all residual shared employees are allocated among an employer's qualified separate lines of business according to the highly compensated employee percentage assignment ratio of each qualified separate line of business.

(ii) Highly compensated employee percentage assignment ratio. For purposes of this paragraph (c)(4), the highly compensated employee percentage assignment ratio of a qualified separate line of business is the fraction (expressed as a percentage)—

(A) The numerator of which is the percentage of all employees who have previously been assigned to the qualified separate line of business under this section with respect to the testing year who are highly compensated employees; and

(B) The denominator of which is the percentage of all employees who have previously been assigned to any qualified separate line of business under this section with respect to the testing year who are highly compensated employees.

Thus, the highly compensated employee percentage assignment ratio of each of the employer's qualified separate lines of business is recalculated each time a residual shared employee is allocated to a qualified separate line of business under this paragraph (c)(4).

(iii) Allocation procedure. The procedure for allocating all residual shared employees under the method in this paragraph (c)(4) is as follows—

(A) If there are any qualified separate lines of business with a highly compensated employee percentage assignment ratio of less than 50 percent (as determined immediately before the employee is allocated to a qualified separate line of business), the highly compensated residual shared employee must be allocated to one of these qualified separate lines of business;

(B) If there are any qualified separate lines of business with a highly compensated employee percentage assignment ratio greater than 200 percent (as determined immediately before the employee is allocated to a qualified separate line of business), the nonhighly compensated residual shared employee must be allocated to one of these qualified separate lines of business;

(C) If there are no qualified separate lines of business with a highly compensated employee percentage assignment ratio less than 50 percent, a highly compensated residual shared employee may be allocated to any qualified separate line of business with a highly compensated employee percentage assignment ratio of no more than 200 percent, provided that the employee's allocation to the qualified separate line of business does not cause its highly compensated employee percentage assignment ratio to exceed 200 percent (as determined immediately after the employee is allocated to the qualified separate line of business);

(D) If there are no qualified separate lines of business with a highly compensated employee percentage assignment ratio greater than 200 percent, a nonhighly compensated residual shared employee may be allocated to any qualified separate line of business with a highly compensated employee percentage assignment ratio of no less than 50 percent, provided that the employee's allocation to the qualified separate line of business does not cause its highly compensated employee percentage assignment ratio to fall below 50 percent (as determined immediately after the employee is allocated to the qualified separate line of business);

(E) For purposes of this procedure, the employer is permitted to determine which highly compensated residual shared employees and which nonhighly compensated residual shared employees are allocated to each qualified separate line of business, provided that the requirements of this paragraph (c)(4)(iii) are satisfied.

*(5) Small group method.* (i) In general. Under the method of allocation provided for in this paragraph (c)(5), each residual shared employee is allocated to a qualified separate line of business chosen by the employer. This method does not apply unless all of the requirements of paragraphs (c)(5)(ii), (iii), and (iv) of this section are satisfied.

(ii) Size of group. The total number of the employer's residual shared employees allocated under this paragraph (c) must not exceed three percent of all of the employer's employees. For this purpose, the employer's employees include only those employees taken into account under paragraph (c)(2)(iii)(B) of this section.

(iii) Composition of qualified separate line of business. The qualified separate line of business to which the residual shared employee is allocated must have an employee assignment percentage under paragraph (c)(2)(iii) of this section of at least ten percent. In addition, the qualified separate line of business to which the residual shared employee is allocated must satisfy the statutory safe harbor under § 1.414(r)-5(b) after the employee is so allocated.

(iv) Reasonable allocation. The allocation of residual shared employees under the small group method provided for in this paragraph (c)(5) must be reasonable. Reasonable allocations generally include allocations that are based on the level of services that the residual shared employees provide to the employer's qualified separate lines of business, the similar treatment of similarly-situated residual shared employees, and other bona fide business criteria; in contrast, an allocation that is designed to maximize benefits for select employees is not considered a reasonable allocation. For example, allocation of all residual shared employees who work in the same department, or at the same location, to the same qualified separate line of business would be an indication of reasonableness. However, allocation of a group of similarly-situated residual shared employees to a qualified separate line of business for which they provide minimal services might not be considered reasonable. In addition, the allocation of the professional employees of a department to one qualified separate line of business and the allocation of the support staff of the same department to a different qualified separate line of business would not be reasonable.

---

T.D. 8376, 12/2/91, amend T.D. 8548, 6/23/94.

---

### § 1.414(r)-8 Separate application of section 410(b).

**(a) General rule.** If an employer is treated as operating qualified separate lines of business for purposes of section 410(b) in accordance with § 1.414(r)-1(b) for a testing year, the requirements of section 410(b) must be applied in accordance with this section separately with respect to the employees of each qualified separate line of business for purposes of testing all plans of the employer for plan years that begin in the testing year (other than a plan tested under the special rule for employer-wide plans in § 1.414(r)-1(c)(2)(ii) for such a plan year). Conversely, if an employer is not treated as operating qualified separate lines of business for purposes of section 410(b) in accordance with § 1.414(r)-1(b) for a testing year, the requirements of section 410(b) must be applied on an employer-wide basis for purposes of testing all plans of the employer for plan years that begin in the testing year. See § 1.414(r)-1(c)(2) and (d)(6). Paragraph (b) of this section explains how the requirements of section 410(b) are applied separately with respect to the employees of a qualified separate line of business for purposes of testing a plan. Paragraph (c) of this section explains the coordination between sections 410(b) and 401(a)(4). Paragraph (d) of this section provides certain supplementary rules necessary for the application of this section.

**(b) Rules of separate application.** *(1) In general.* If the requirements of section 410(b) are applied separately with respect to the employees of each qualified separate line of business operated by the employer for a testing year, a plan (other than a plan that is tested under the special rule for employer-wide plans in § 1.414(r)-1(c)(2)(ii) for a plan year) satisfies the requirements of section 410(b) only if—

(i) The plan satisfies section 410(b)(5)(B) on an employer-wide basis; and

(ii) The plan satisfies section 410(b) on a qualified-separate-line-of-business basis.

*(2) Satisfaction of section 410(b)(5)(B) on an employer-wide basis.* (i) General rule. Section 410(b)(5)(B) provides that a plan is not permitted to be tested separately with respect to the employees of a qualified separate line of business unless the plan benefits a classification of employees found by the Secretary to be nondiscriminatory. A plan satisfies this requirement only if the plan satisfies either the ratio percentage test of § 1.410(b)-2(b)(2) or the nondiscriminatory classification test of § 1.410(b)-4 (without regard to the average benefit percentage test of § 1.410(b)-5), taking into account the other applicable provisions of §§ 1.410(b)-1 through 1.410(b)-10. For this purpose, the nonexcludable employees of the employer taken into account in testing the plan under section 410(b) are determined under § 1.410(b)-6, without regard to the exclusion in § 1.410(b)-6(e) for employees of other qualified separate lines of business of the employer. Thus, in testing a plan separately with respect to the employees of one qualified separate line of business under this paragraph (b)(2), the otherwise nonexcludable employees of the employer's other qualified separate lines of business are not treated as excludable employees. However, under the definition of "plan" in paragraph (d)(2) of this

section, these employees are not treated as benefiting under the plan for purposes of applying this paragraph (b)(2).

(ii) Application of facts and circumstances requirements under nondiscriminatory classification test. The fact that an employer has satisfied the qualified-separate-line-of-business requirements in §§ 1.414(r)-1 through 1.414(r)-7 is taken into account in determining whether a classification of employees benefiting under a plan that falls between the safe and unsafe harbors satisfies § 1.410(b)-4(c)(3) (facts and circumstances requirements). Except in unusual circumstances, this fact will be determinative.

(iii) Modification of unsafe harbor percentage for plans satisfying ratio percentage test at 90 percent level. (A) General rule. If a plan benefits a group of employees for a plan year that would satisfy the ratio percentage test of § 1.410(b)-2(b)(2) on a qualified-separate-line-of-business basis under paragraph (b)(3) of this section if the percentage in § 1.410(b)-2(b)(2) were increased to 90 percent, the unsafe harbor percentage in § 1.410(b)-4(c)(4)(ii) for the plan is reduced by five percentage points (not five percent) for the plan year and is applied without regard to the requirement that the unsafe harbor percentage not be less than 20 percent. Thus, if the requirements of this paragraph (b)(2)(iii)(A) are satisfied, the unsafe harbor percentage in § 1.410(b)-4(c)(4)(ii) is treated as 35 percent, reduced by ¾ of a percentage point for each whole percentage point by which the nonhighly compensated employee concentration percentage exceeds 60 percent.

(B) Facts and circumstances alternative. If a plan satisfies the requirements of paragraph (b)(2)(iii)(A) of this section, but has a ratio percentage on an employer-wide basis that falls below the unsafe harbor percentage determined under paragraph (b)(2)(iii)(A) of this section, the plan nonetheless is deemed to satisfy section 410(b)(5)(B) on an employer-wide basis if the Commissioner determines that, on the basis of all of the relevant facts and circumstances, the plan benefits such employees as qualify under a classification of employees that does not discriminate in favor of highly compensated employees.

*(3) Satisfaction of section 410(b) on a qualified-separate-line-of-business basis.* A plan satisfies section 410(b) on a qualified-separate-line-of-business basis only if the plan satisfies either the ratio percentage test of § 1.410(b)-2(b)(2) or the average benefit test of § 1.410(b)-2(b)(3) (including the nondiscriminatory classification test of § 1.410(b)-4 and the average benefit percentage test of § 1.410(b)-5), taking into account the other applicable provisions of §§ 1.410(b)-1 through 1.410(b)-10. For this purpose, the nonexcludable employees of the employer taken into account in testing the plan under section 410(b) are determined under § 1.410(b)-6, taking into account the exclusion in § 1.410(b)-6(e) for employees of other qualified separate lines of business of the employer. Thus, in testing a plan separately with respect to the employees of one qualified separate line of business under this paragraph (b)(3), all employees of the employer's other qualified separate lines of business are treated as excludable employees.

*(4) Examples.* The following examples illustrate the application of this paragraph (b).

*Example (1).* (i) Employer A is treated as operating qualified separate lines of business for purposes of section 410(b) in accordance with § 1.414(r)-1(b) for the 1994 testing year with respect to all of its plans. Employer A operates two qualified separate lines of business as determined under § 1.414(r)-1(b)(2), Line 1 and Line 2. Employer A maintains only two plans, Plan X which benefits solely employees of Line 1, and Plan Y which benefits solely employees of Line 2. In testing Plan X under section 410(b) with respect to the first testing day for the plan year of Plan X beginning in the 1994 testing year, it is determined that Employer A has 2,100 nonexcludable employees, of whom 100 are highly compensated employees and 2,000 are nonhighly compensated employees. After applying § 1.414(r)-7 to these employees, 50 of the highly compensated employees and 100 of the nonhighly compensated employees are treated as employees of Line 2, and the remaining 50 highly compensated employees and the remaining 1,900 nonhighly compensated employees are treated as employees of Line 1.

(ii) All of the highly compensated employees and 1,300 of the nonhighly compensated employees who are treated as employees of Line 1 benefit under Plan X. Thus, on an employer-wide basis, Plan X benefits 50 percent of all Employer A's highly compensated employees (50 out of 100) and 65 percent of all Employer A's nonhighly compensated employees (1,300 out of 2,000). Plan X consequently has a ratio percentage determined on an employer-wide-basis of 130 percent (65% ÷ 50%), see § 1.410(b)-9, and could satisfy section 410(b) under the ratio percentage test of § 1.410(b)-2(b)(2) if that section were applied on an employer-wide basis without regard to the provisions of this paragraph (b). Under paragraph (a) of this section, however, the requirements of section 410(b) must be applied separately with respect to the employees of each qualified separate line of business operated by Employer A for all plans of Employer A for plan years that begin in the 1994 testing year. This rule does not apply to plans tested under the special rule for employer-wide plans in § 1.414(r)-1(c)(2)(ii). Plan X benefits only 65 percent of the nonhighly compensated employees of Employer A, however, and therefore cannot satisfy the 70 percent requirement necessary to be tested under that rule. As a result, for the plan year of Plan X beginning in the 1994 testing year, Plan X is not permitted to satisfy section 410(b) on an employer-wide basis and, instead, is only permitted to satisfy section 410(b) separately with respect to the employees of each qualified separate line of business operated by Employer A, in accordance with paragraphs (b)(2) and (b)(3) of this section.

*Example (2).* The facts are the same as in Example 1. All of the 50 highly compensated employees treated as employees of Line 2 benefit under Plan Y, and 80 of the 100 nonhighly compensated employees treated as employees of Line 2 benefit under Plan Y. Thus, Plan Y benefits 50 percent of all Employer A's highly compensated employees (50 out of 100) and only 4 percent of all Employer A's nonhighly compensated employees (80 out of 2,000). Thus, while Plan Y has a ratio percentage of 80 percent (80% ÷ 100%) on a qualified-separate-line-of-business basis, it has a ratio percentage of only 8 percent (4% ÷ 50%) on an employer-wide basis. See § 1.410(b)-9. Under § 1.410(b)-4(c)(4)(iii), the nonhighly compensated employee concentration percentage is 2,000/2,100 or 95 percent. Because 8 percent is less than 20 percent (the unsafe harbor percentage applicable to Employer A under § 1.410(b)-4(c)(4)(ii)), Plan Y does not satisfy the nondiscriminatory classification test of § 1.410(b)-4 on an employer-wide basis. Nor does Plan Y satisfy the ratio percentage test of § 1.410(b)-2(b)(2) on an employer-wide basis, since 8 percent is less than 70 percent. Under these facts, Plan Y does not satisfy section 410(b)(5)(B) on an employer-wide basis in accordance with paragraph (b)(2) of this section for the plan year of Plan Y beginning in the 1994 testing year, and therefore fails to satisfy section 410(b) for that year. This is true even though Plan Y satisfies section 410(b) on a qualified-separate-line-of-business basis in accordance with paragraph (b)(3) of this section.

*Example (3).* The facts are the same as in Example 2, except that all of the employees treated as employees of Line 2 benefit under Plan Y. Thus, Plan Y benefits 50 percent of all of Employer A's highly compensated employees (50 out of 100) and 5 percent of all of Employer A's nonhighly compensated employees (100 out of 2,000). Plan Y therefore has a ratio percentage of 100 percent (100% ÷ 100%) on a qualified-separate-line-of-business basis and a ratio percentage of 10 percent (5% ÷ 50%) on an employer-wide basis. Because Plan Y has a ratio percentage of at least 90 percent on a qualified-separate-line-of-business basis, a reduced unsafe harbor percentage applies to Plan Y under paragraph (b)(2)(iii)(A) of this section. The reduced unsafe harbor percentage applicable to Plan Y is 8.75 percent because Employer A's nonhighly compensated employee concentration percentage is 95 percent. Plan Y's employer-wide ratio percentage of 10 percent therefore exceeds the unsafe harbor percentage. Plan Y thus satisfies section 410(b)(5)(B) on an employer-wide basis in accordance with paragraph (b)(2) of this section for the plan year of Plan Y beginning in the 1994 testing year. Plan Y also satisfies section 410(b) on a qualified-separate-line-of-business basis in accordance with paragraph (b)(3) of this section.

*Example (4).* The facts are the same as in Example 3, except that Employer A's total nonexcludable nonhighly compensated employees are 2,500 (rather than 2,000), of whom 100 are treated as employees of Line 2 and of whom 90 benefit under Plan Y. Plan Y has a ratio percentage of 90 percent (90% ÷ 100%) on a qualified-separate-line-of-business basis, and Employer A's nonhighly compensated employee concentration percentage is 2,500/2,600 or 96 percent. Thus, the reduced unsafe harbor percentage applicable to Plan Y under paragraph (b)(2)(iii)(A) of this section is 8 percent. Plan Y benefits 50 percent of all of Employer A's highly compensated employees (50 out of 100) and 3.6 percent of all of Employer A's nonhighly compensated employees (90 out of 2,500). Plan Y therefore has a ratio percentage of only 7.2 percent (3.6% ÷ 50%) on an employer-wide basis, which falls below the reduced unsafe harbor percentage of 8 percent. Nonetheless, under paragraph (b)(2)(iii)(B) of this section, Plan Y will be deemed to satisfy section 410(b)(5)(B) on an employer-wide basis if the Commissioner determines that, on the basis of all of the relevant facts and circumstances, the plan benefits such employees as qualify under a classification of employees that does not discriminate in favor of highly compensated employees.

*Example (5).* (i) The facts are the same as in Example 1, except that Plan X benefits only 950 of the employees of Line 1. Assume Plan X satisfies the reasonable classification requirement of § 1.410(b)-4(b) on an employer-wide basis. Plan X benefits 50 percent of all Employer A's highly compensated employees (50 out of 100) and 47.5 percent of all Employer A's nonhighly compensated employees (950 out of 2,000). Plan X consequently has a ratio percentage determined on an employer-wide basis of 95 percent (47.5% ÷ 50%), see § 1.410(b)-9, and thus satisfies section 410(b)(5)(B) on an employer-wide basis.

(ii) Plan X has a ratio percentage determined on a qualified-separate-line-of-business basis of 50 percent (50% ÷ 100%). Because 50 percent is less than 70 percent, Plan X must satisfy the nondiscriminatory classification test of § 1.410(b)-4 and the average benefit percentage test of § 1.410(b)-5 on a qualified-separate-line-of-business basis in order to satisfy the other requirements of section 410(b). Plan X satisfies the nondiscriminatory classification requirement of § 1.410(b)-4(c) on a qualified-separate-line-of-business because its ratio percentage determined on a qualified-separate-line-of-business basis is more than 22.25 percent, the safe harbor percentage applicable to Line 1 under § 1.410(b)-4(c)(4)(i). Because Plan X satisfies the reasonable classification requirement of § 1.410(b)-4(b) on an employer-wide basis, it is also deemed to satisfy this requirement on a qualified-separate-line-of-business basis. See § 1.410(b)-7(c)(5). In determining whether Plan X satisfies the average benefit percentage test of § 1.410(b)-5, only Plan X and only employees of Line 1 are taken into account. See §§ 1.410(b)-6(e) and 1.410(b)-7(e).

*Example (6).* The facts are the same as in Example 2, except that, prior to the 1994 testing year, Employer A merges Plan X and Plan Y so that they form a single plan within the meaning of section 414(l). Under the definition of "plan" in paragraph (d)(2) of this section, however, the portion of the newly merged plan that benefits employees of Line 2 (former Plan Y) is still treated as a separate plan from the portion of the newly merged plan that benefits employees of Line 1 (former Plan X). The portion of the newly merged plan that benefits employees of Line 2 (former Plan Y) fails to satisfy section 410(b) for the reasons stated in Example 2. Under these facts, because the portion of the newly merged plan that benefits employees of Line 2 fails to satisfy section 410(b), the entire newly merged plan fails to satisfy section 410(b) for the plan year of the newly merged plan that begins in the 1994 testing year. See paragraph (d)(5) of this section.

**(c) Coordination of section 401(a)(4) with section 410(b).** *(1) General rule.* For purposes of these regulations, the requirements of section 410(b) encompass the requirements of section 401(a)(4) (including, but not limited to, the permitted disparity rules of section 401(l), the actual deferral percentage test of section 401(k)(3), and the actual contribution percentage test of section 401(m)(2)). Therefore, if the requirements of section 410(b) are applied separately with respect to the employees of each qualified separate line of business of an employer for purposes of testing one or more plans of the employer for plan years that begin in a testing year, the requirements of section 401(a)(4) must also be applied separately with respect to the employees of the same qualified separate lines of business for purposes of testing the same plans for the same plan years. Furthermore, if section 401(a)(4) requires that a group of employees under the plan satisfy section 410(b) for purposes of satisfying section 401(a)(4), section 410(b) must be applied for this purpose in the same manner provided in paragraph (b) of this section. See, for example, §§ 1.401(a)(4)-2(c)(1) and 1.401(a)(4)-3(c)(1) (requiring each rate group of employees under a plan to satisfy section 410(b)), § 1.401(a)(4)-4(b) (requiring the group of employees to whom each benefit, right, or feature is currently available under a plan to satisfy section 410(b)), and § 1.401(a)(4)-9(c)(1) (requiring the group of employees included in each component plan into which a plan is restructured to satisfy section 410(b)). Thus, the group of employees must satisfy section 410(b)(5)(B) on an employer-wide basis in accordance with paragraph (b)(2) of this section and also must satisfy section 410(b) on a qualified-separate-line-of-business basis in accordance with paragraph (b)(3) of this section, in both cases as if the group of employees were the only employees benefiting under the plan.

*(2) Examples.* The following examples illustrate the application of the rule in this paragraph (c).

*Example (1).* Employer B is treated as operating qualified separate lines of business for purposes of section 410(b) in accordance with § 1.414(r)-1(b) for the 1993 testing year. Employer B operates two qualified separate lines of business as determined under § 1.414(r)-1(b)(2), Line 1 and Line 2. Employer B maintains Plan Z, which benefits employees in both Line 1 and Line 2. Under the definition of "plan" in paragraph (d)(2) of this section, the portion of Plan Z that benefits employees of Line 1 is treated as a separate plan from the portion of Plan Z that benefits employees of Line 2. Under this paragraph (c), this result applies for purposes of both section 410(b) and section 401(a)(4).

*Example (2).* The facts are the same as in Example 1, except that Plan Z benefits solely employees of Line 1. In testing Plan Z under section 401(a)(4) for the plan year of Plan Z beginning in the 1993 testing year, Employer B restructures Plan Z into several component plans (within the meaning of § 1.401(a)(4)-9(c)). Under § 1.401(a)(4)-9(c)(1), each of these component plans is required to satisfy section 410(b). This paragraph (c) requires that each of the component plans be tested separately with respect to the employees of each qualified separate line of business operated by Employer B. This testing must be done in accordance with paragraph (b) of this section. Consequently, each component plan must satisfy section 410(b)(5)(B) on an employer-wide basis in accordance with paragraph (b)(2) of this section and must also satisfy section 410(b) on a qualified-separate-line-of-business basis in accordance with paragraph (b)(3) of this section.

*Example (3).* The facts are the same as in Example 1, except that Plan Z is a profit-sharing plan, and contributions to Plan Z are made pursuant to cash or deferred arrangement in which all employees of Employer B are eligible to participate. Assume that, as a result, Plan Z satisfies the requirements to be tested under the special rule for employer-wide plans in § 1.414(r)-1(c)(2)(ii). Under these facts, the requirements of sections 410(b), 401(a)(4) and 401(k), including the actual deferral percentage test of section 401(k)(3) and § 1.401(k)-1(b), would generally be required to be applied separately to the portions of Plan Z that benefit the employees of Line 1 and Line 2, respectively. However, if Plan Z is tested under the special rule in § 1.414(r)-1(c)(2)(ii), these requirements must be applied on an employer-wide basis.

**(d) Supplementary rules.** *(1) In general.* This paragraph (d) provides certain supplementary rules necessary for the application of this section.

*(2) Definition of plan.* For purposes of this section, the term "plan" means a plan within the meaning of § 1.410(b)-7(a) and (b), after application of the mandatory disaggregation rules of § 1.410(b)-7(c) (including the mandatory disaggregation rule for portions of a plan that benefit employees of different qualified separate lines of business) and the permissive aggregation rules of § 1.410(b)-7(d). Thus, for purposes of this section, the portion of a plan that benefits employees of one qualified separate line of business is treated as a separate plan from the other portions of the same plan that benefit employees of other qualified separate lines of business of the employer, unless the plan is tested under the special rule for employer-wide plans in § 1.414(r)-1(c)(2)(ii) for the plan year.

*(3) Employees of a qualified separate line of business.* For purposes of applying paragraph (b) of this section with respect to a testing day, the employees of each qualified separate line of business of the employer are determined by applying § 1.414(r)-7 to the employees of the employer otherwise taken into account under section 410(b) for the testing day. For purposes of applying paragraph (c) of this section with respect to a testing day, the employees of each qualified separate line of business of the employer are determined by applying § 1.414(r)-7 to the employees of the employer otherwise taken into account under section 401(a)(4) for the testing day. For the definition of "testing day," see § 1.414(r)-11(b)(6).

*(4) Consequences of failure.* If a plan fails to satisfy either paragraph (b)(2), (b)(3), or (c)(1) of this section, the plan (and any plan of which it constitutes a portion) fails to satisfy section 401(a). However, this failure alone does not cause the employer to fail to be treated as operating qualified separate lines of business in accordance with § 1.414(r)-1(b), unless the employer is relying on benefits provided under the plan to satisfy the minimum benefit portion of the safe harbor in § 1.414(r)-5(g)(2) with respect to at least one of its qualified separate lines of business.

T.D. 8376, 12/2/91, amend T.D. 8548, 6/23/94.

## § 1.414(r)-9 Separate application of section 401(a)(26).

***Caution:*** The Treasury has not yet amended Reg § 1.414(r)-9 to reflect changes made by P.L. 104-188.

**(a) General rule.** If an employer is treated as operating qualified separate lines of business for purposes of section 401(a)(26) in accordance with § 1.414(r)-1(b) for a testing year, the requirements of section 401(a)(26) must be applied separately with respect to the employees of each qualified separate line of business for purposes of testing all plans of the employer for plan years that begin in the testing year (other than a plan tested under the special rule for employer-wide plans in § 1.414(r)-1(c)(3)(ii) for such a plan year). Conversely, if an employer is not treated as operating qualified separate lines of business for purposes of section 401(a)(26) in accordance with § 1.414(r)-1(b) for a testing year, the requirements of section 401(a)(26) must be applied on an employer-wide basis for purposes of testing all plans of the employer for plan years that begin in the testing year. See § 1.414(r)-1(c)(3) and (d)(6). Paragraph (b) of this section explains how the requirements of section 401(a)(26) are applied separately with respect to the employees of a qualified separate line of business for purposes of testing a plan. Paragraph (c) of this section provides certain supplementary rules necessary for the application of this section.

**(b) Requirements applicable to a plan.** If the requirements of section 401(a)(26) are applied separately with respect to the employees of a qualified separate line of business for a testing year, a plan (other than a plan that is tested under the special rule for employer-wide plans in § 1.414(r)-1(c)(3)(ii) for a plan year) satisfies section 401(a)(26) only if it satisfies the requirements of §§ 1.401(a)(26)-1 through 1.401(a)(26)-9 on a qualified-separate-line-of-business basis. For this purpose, the nonexcludable employees of the employer taken into account in testing the plan under section 401(a)(26) are determined under § 1.401(a)(26)-6(b), taking into account the exclusion in § 1.401(a)(26)-6(b)(8) for employees of other qualified separate lines of business of the employer. Thus, in testing a plan separately with respect to the employees of one qualified separate line of business under this paragraph (b), all employees of the employer's other qualified separate lines of business are treated as excludable employees.

**(c) Supplementary rules.** *(1) In general.* This paragraph (c) provides certain supplementary rules necessary for the application of this section.

*(2) Definition of plan.* For purposes of this section, the term "plan" means a plan within the meaning of § 1.401(a)(26)-2(c) and (d), including the mandatory disaggregation rule of § 1.401(a)(26)-2(d)(6) for portions of a plan that benefit employees of different qualified separate lines of business. Thus, for purposes of this section, the portion of a plan that benefits employees of one qualified separate line of business is treated as a separate plan from the other portions of the same plan that benefit employees of other qualified separate lines of business of the employer, unless the plan is tested under the special rule for employer-wide plans in § 1.414(r)-1(c)(3)(ii) for the plan year.

*(3) Employees of a qualified separate line of business.* For purposes of applying paragraph (b)(2) of this section with respect to a section 401(a)(26) testing day, the employees of each qualified separate line of business of the employer are determined by applying § 1.414(r)-7 to the employees of the employer otherwise taken into account under section 401(a)(26) for the section 401(a)(26) testing day. For the definition of "section 401(a)(26) testing day," see § 1.414(r)-11(b)(8).

*(4) Consequences of failure.* If a plan fails to satisfy paragraph (b)(2) of this section, the plan (and any plan of which it constitutes a portion) fails to satisfy section 401(a). However, this failure alone would not cause the employer to fail to be treated as operating qualified separate lines of business in accordance with § 1.414(r)-1(b), unless the employer is relying on benefits provided under the plan to satisfy the minimum benefit portion of the safe harbor in § 1.414(r)-5(g)(2) with respect to at least one of its qualified separate lines of business.

T.D. 8376, 12/2/91.

### § 1.414(r)-10 Separate application of section 129(d)(8). [Reserved]

### § 1.414(r)-11 Definitions and special rules.

**(a) In general.** This section contains certain definitions and special rules applicable under these regulations. Paragraph (b) of this section provides certain definitions that apply for purposes of these regulations. Paragraph (c) of this section provides averaging rules under which certain provisions of these regulations may be applied on the basis of a two-year or a three-year average.

**(b) Definitions.** *(1) In general.* In applying the provisions of this section and of §§ 1.414(r)-1 through 1.414(r)-10, unless otherwise provided, the definitions in this paragraph (b) govern in addition to the definitions in § 1.410(b)-9.

*(2) Substantial-service employee.* An employee is a substantial-service employee with respect to a line of business for a testing year if at least 75 percent of the employee's services are provided to that line of business for that testing year within the meaning of § 1.414(r)-3(c)(5). In addition, if an employee provides at least 50% and less than 75% of the employee's services to a line of business for the testing year within the meaning of § 1.414(r)-3(c)(5), the employer may treat that employee as a substantial-service employee with respect to that line of business provided the employee is so treated for all purposes of these regulations. The employer may choose such treatment separately with respect to each employee.

*(3) Top-paid employee.* Generally, an employee is a top-paid employee with respect to a line of business for a testing year if the employee is among the top 10 percent by compensation of those employees who provide services to that line of business for that testing year within the meaning of § 1.414(r)-3(c)(5) and who are not substantial-service employees within the meaning of paragraph (b)(2) of this section with respect to any other line of business. In addition, in determining the group of top-paid employees, the employer may choose to disregard all employees who provide less than 25 percent of their services to the line of business. For purposes of this paragraph (b)(3), an employee's compensation is the compensation used to determine the employee's status as a highly or nonhighly compensated employee under section 414(q) for purposes of applying section 410(b) with respect to the first testing day. For this purpose, only compensation received during the determination year (within the meaning of § 1.414(q)-1T, Q&A-13) is taken into account. See § 1.414(r)-3(c)(7) for examples of the determination of top-paid employee.

*(4) Residual shared employee.* An employee is a residual shared employee for a testing year if the employee is not a substantial-service employee with respect to any line of business for the testing year.

*(5) Testing year.* The term "testing year" means the calendar year.

*(6) Testing day.* The term "testing day" means any day on which § 1.410(b)-8(a)(1) requires any plan (within the meaning of § 1.414(r)-8(d)(2)) of the employer actually to satisfy section 410(b) with respect to a plan year that begins in the testing year. Thus, if a plan is required to satisfy section 410(b) on one day within each quarter of the plan year under the quarterly testing option of § 1.410(b)-8(a)(3), each of those four days is a testing day. Similarly, if a plan is required to satisfy section 410(b) on every day of the plan year under the daily testing option of § 1.410(b)-8(a)(2), every day of the plan year is a testing day.

*(7) First testing day.* The term "first testing day" means the testing day that occurs earliest in time of all the testing days under all plans of the employer with respect to the testing year. If a plan is tested under the annual testing option of § 1.410(b)-8(a)(4) (other than for purposes of the average benefit percentage test of § 1.410(b)-5) for a plan year that begins in a testing year, then, solely for purposes of determining the first testing day in a testing year, the employer may treat any day in the plan year as a testing day, provided that the coverage of each plan of the employer on the day selected is reasonably representative of the coverage of the plan over the entire plan year. The first testing day with respect to a testing year must fall within that testing year.

*(8) Section 401(a)(26) testing day.* The term "section 401(a)(26) testing day" means any day on which § 1.401(a)(26)-7(a) or (b) requires any plan of the employer actually to satisfy section 401(a)(26) with respect to a plan year that begins in the testing year. In no event may a section 401(a)(26) testing day with respect to a testing year fall before the first testing day for that testing year. For purposes of this paragraph (b)(8), the term "plan" has the same meaning as in § 1.414(r)-9(c)(2).

**(c) Averaging rules.** *(1) In general.* The provisions specified in this paragraph (c) are permitted to be applied based on the average of the percentages for the current testing year and the consecutive testing years (not to exceed four consecutive testing years) immediately preceding the current testing year.

*(2) Specified provisions.* The provisions specified in this paragraph (c) are—

(i) The 90-percent separate employee workforce requirement of § 1.414(r)-3(b)(4);

(ii) The 80-percent separate management requirement of § 1.414(r)-3(b)(5);

(iii) The 25-percent provision-to-customers requirement of § 1.414(r)-3(d)(2)(iii);

(iv) The minimum and maximum highly compensated employee percentage ratios under the statutory safe harbor of § 1.414(r)-5(b)(1)(i) and (ii) (50 percent and 200 percent, respectively), but not the 10-percent exception in § 1.414(r)-5(b)(4);

(v) The employee assignment percentage applied for purposes of the dominant line of business method of allocating residual shared employees under § 1.414(r)-7(c)(2) and the pro-rata method for allocating residual shared employees under § 1.414(r)-7(c)(3).

*(3) Averaging of large fluctuations not permitted.* A provision is not permitted to be applied based on an average determined under this paragraph (c) if the percentage for any testing year taken into account in calculating the average falls below a minimum percentage, or exceeds a maximum percentage, by more than 10 percent (not 10 percentage points) of the respective minimum or maximum percentage. Thus, for example, the statutory safe harbor of § 1.414(r)-5(b) is not permitted to be applied based on an average determined under this paragraph (c) if the percentage for any testing year taken into account in calculating the average falls below 45 percent (which is 10 percent below the 50-percent minimum) or exceeds 220 percent (which is 10 percent above the 200-percent maximum).

*(4) Consistency requirements.* A provision is permitted to be applied on an averaging basis under this paragraph (c) regardless of how any other provision is applied, except in the case of the separate employee workforce and separate management requirements of § 1.414(r)-3(b)(4) and (5), which each must be applied on the same basis as the other. A provision is also permitted to be applied on an averaging basis under this paragraph (c) for a testing year, regardless of how the provision is applied for any other testing year. However, once a provision is applied on an averaging basis under this paragraph (c) for a testing year, it must be applied on the same basis to all the employer's lines of business to which the provision is applied for the testing year. The percentage for a preceding testing year may be taken into account under this paragraph (c) only if—

(i) The employer calculates the percentage for the preceding testing year in the same manner as the employer calculates the percentage for the current testing year;

(ii) The employer is treated as operating qualified separate lines of business in accordance with § 1.414(r)-1(b) for the preceding testing year; and

(iii) The employer designated the same lines of business in the preceding testing year as in the current testing year.

T.D. 8376, 12/2/91, amend T.D. 8548, 6/23/94.

## § 1.414(s)-1 Definition of compensation.

***Caution:*** The Treasury has not yet amended Reg § 1.414(s)-1 to reflect changes made by P.L. 104-188.

**(a) Introduction.** *(1) In general.* Section 414(s) and this section provide rules for defining compensation for purposes of applying any provision that specifically refers to section 414(s) or this section. For example, section 414(s) is referred to in many of the nondiscrimination provisions applicable to pension, profit-sharing, and stock bonus plans qualified under section 401(a). In accordance with section 414(s)(1), this section defines compensation as compensation within the meaning of section 415(c)(3). It also implements the election provided in section 414(s)(2) to treat certain deferrals as compensation and exercises the authority granted to the Secretary in section 414(s)(3) to prescribe alternative nondiscriminatory definitions of compensation.

*(2) Limitations on scope of section 414(s).* Section 414(s) and this section do not apply unless a provision specifically refers to section 414(s) or this section. For example, even though a definition of compensation permitted under section 414(s) must be used in determining whether the contributions or benefits under a pension, profit-sharing, or stock bonus plan satisfy a certain applicable provision (such as section 401(a)(4)), except as otherwise specified, the plan is not required to use a definition of compensation that satisfies section 414(s) in calculating the amount of contributions or benefits actually provided under the plan.

*(3) Overview.* Paragraph (b) of this section provides rules of general application that govern a definition of compensation that satisfies section 414(s). Paragraph (c) of this section contains specific definitions of compensation that satisfy section 414(s) without satisfying any additional nondiscrimination requirement under section 414(s). Paragraph (d) of this section provides rules permitting the use of alternative definitions of compensation that satisfy section 414(s) as long as the nondiscrimination requirement and other requirements described in paragraph (d) of this section are satisfied. Paragraphs (e) and (f) of this section provides special rules permitting the use of rate of compensation, or prior-employer compensation or imputed compensation, rather than actual compensation, under a definition of compensation that satisfies section 414(s). Paragraph (g) of this section provides other special rules, including a special rule for determining the compensation of a self-employed individual under an alternative definition of compensation. Paragraph (h) of this section provides definitions for certain terms used in this section.

**(b) Rules of general application.** *(1) Use of a definition.* Any definition of compensation that satisfies section 414(s) may be used when a provision explicitly refers to section 414(s) unless the reference or this section specifically indicates otherwise.

*(2) Consistency rule.* (i) General rule. A definition of compensation selected by an employer for use in satisfying an applicable provision must be used consistently to define the compensation of all employees taken into account in satisfying the requirements of the applicable provision for the determination period. For example, although any definition of compensation that satisfies section 414(s) may be used for section 401(a)(4) purposes, the same definition of compensation generally must be used consistently to define the compensation of all employees taken into account in determining whether a plan satisfies section 401(a)(4). Furthermore, a different definition of compensation that satisfies section 414(s) is permitted to be used to determine whether another plan maintained by the same employer separately satisfies the requirements of section 401(a)(4). Although a definition of compensation must be used consistently, an employer may change its definition of compensation for a subsequent determination period with respect to the applicable provision.

Rules provided under any applicable provision may modify the consistency requirements of this paragraph (b)(2).

(ii) Scope of consistency rule. Compensation will not fail to be defined consistently for a group of employees merely because some employees do not receive one or more of the types of compensation included in the definition. For example, a definition of compensation that includes salary, regular or scheduled pay, overtime, and specified types of bonuses will not fail to define compensation consistently merely because only salaried employees receive salary and these specified types of bonuses and only hourly employees receive regular or scheduled pay and overtime.

*(3) Self-employed individuals.* Notwithstanding paragraph (b)(1) of this section, self-employed individuals' compensation can only be determined under paragraph (c)(2) of this section (with or without the modification permitted by paragraph (c)(4) of this section or a modification permitted by paragraph (c)(5) of this section) or by using an equivalent alternative compensation amount determined in accordance with paragraph (g)(1) of this section. These limitations on self-employed individuals do not affect their common-law employees. Thus, the compensation of common-law employees of a partnership or sole proprietorship may be defined using an alternative definition, provided the definition otherwise satisfies paragraph (c)(3), (d), (e), or (f) of this section. If an alternative definition of compensation under paragraph (c)(3), (d), (e), or (f) of this section is used for other employees to satisfy an applicable provision, the consistency requirement is only met if paragraph (g) of this section is used for the self-employed individuals.

**(c) Specific definitions of compensation that satisfy section 414(s).** *(1) General rules.* The definitions of compensation provided in paragraphs (c)(2) and (c)(3) of this section satisfy section 414(s) and need not satisfy any additional requirements under section 414(s). Paragraph (c)(2) of this section describes definitions of compensation within the meaning of section 415(c)(3). Paragraph (c)(3) of this section provides a safe harbor alternative definition that excludes certain additional items of compensation. Paragraph (c)(4) of this section permits any definition provided in paragraph (c)(2) or (c)(3) of this section to include certain types of elective contributions and deferred compensation. Paragraph (c)(5) of this section permits certain modifications to a definition otherwise provided under this paragraph (c).

*(2) Compensation within the meaning of section 415(c)(3).* A definition of compensation that includes all compensation within the meaning of section 415(c)(3) and excludes all other compensation satisfies section 414(s). Sections 1.415(c)-2(b) and (c) provide rules for determining items of compensation included in and excluded from compensation within the meaning of section 415(c)(3). In addition, section 414(s) is satisfied by the safe harbor definitions provided in § 1.415(c)-2(d)(2), (d)(3) and (d)(4) and any additional definitions of compensation prescribed by the Commission under the authority provided in § 1.415(c)-2(d)(1) that are treated as satisfying section 415(c)(3).

*(3) Safe harbor alternative definition.* Under the safe harbor alternative definition in this paragraph (c)(3), compensation is compensation as defined in paragraph (c)(2) of this section, reduced by all of the following items (even if includible in gross income): reimbursements or other expense allowances, fringe benefits (cash and noncash), moving expenses, deferred compensation, and welfare benefits.

*(4) Inclusion of certain deferrals in compensation.* Any definition of compensation provided in paragraph (c)(2) or (c)(3) of this section satisfies section 414(s) even though it is modified to include all of the following types of elective contributions and all of the following types of deferred compensation—

(i) Elective contributions that are made by the employer on behalf of its employees that are not includible in gross income under section 125, section 402(e)(3), section 402(h), and section 403(b);

(ii) Compensation deferred under an eligible deferred compensation plan within the meaning of section 457(b) (deferred compensation plans of state and local governments and tax-exempt organizations); and

(iii) Employee contributions (under governmental plans) described in section 414(h)(2) that are picked up by the employing unit and thus are treated as employer contributions.

*(5) Exclusions applicable solely to highly compensated employees.* Any definition of compensation that satisfies paragraph (c)(2) or (c)(3) of this section, with or without the modification permitted by paragraph (c)(4) of this section, may be modified to exclude any portion of the compensation of some or all of the employer's highly compensated employees (including, for example, any one or more of the types of elective contributions or deferred compensation described in paragraph (c)(4) of this section).

**(d) Alternative definitions of compensation that satisfy section 414(s).** *(1) General rule.* In addition to the definitions provided in paragraph (c) of this section, any definition of compensation satisfies section 414(s) with respect to employees (other than self-employed individuals treated as employees under section 401(c)(1)) if the definition of compensation does not by design favor highly compensated employees, is reasonable within the meaning of paragraph (d)(2) of this section, and satisfies the nondiscrimination requirement in paragraph (d)(3) of this section.

*(2) Reasonable definition of compensation.* (i) General rule. An alternative definition of compensation under this paragraph (d) is reasonable under section 414(s) if it is a definition of compensation provided in paragraph (c) of this section, modified to exclude all or any portion of one or more of the types of compensation described in paragraph (d)(2)(ii) of this section. See paragraph (e) of this section, however, for special rules that permit definitions of compensation based on employees' rates of compensation and paragraph (f) of this section for special rules that permit definitions of compensation that include prior-employer compensation or imputed compensation.

(ii) Items that may be excluded. A reasonable definition of compensation is permitted to exclude, on a consistent basis, all or any portion of irregular or additional compensation, including (but not limited to) one or more of the following: any type of additional compensation for employees working outside their regularly scheduled tour of duty (such as overtime pay, premiums for shift differential, and call-in premiums), bonuses, or any one or more of the types of compensation excluded under the safe harbor alternative definition in paragraph (c)(3) of this section. Whether a type of compensation is irregular or additional is determined based on all the relevant facts and circumstances. A reasonable definition is also permitted to include, on a consistent basis, all or any portion of the types of elective contributions or deferred compensation described in paragraph (c)(4) of this section and, thus, need not include all those types of elective contributions or deferred compensation as otherwise required under paragraph (c)(4) of this section.

(iii) Limits on the amount excluded from compensation. A definition of compensation is not reasonable if it provides that each employee's compensation is a specified portion of the employee's compensation measured for the otherwise applicable determination period under another definition. For example, a definition of compensation that specifically limits each employee's compensation for a determination period to 95 percent of the employee's compensation using a definition provided in paragraph (c) of this section is not reasonable. Similarly, a definition of compensation that limits each employee's compensation used to satisfy an applicable provision with a 12-month determination period to compensation under a definition provided in paragraph (c) of this section for one month is not a reasonable definition of compensation. However, a definition of compensation is not unreasonable merely because it excludes all compensation in excess of a specified dollar amount.

*(3) Nondiscrimination requirement.* (i) In general. An alternative definition of compensation under this paragraph (d) is nondiscriminatory under section 414(s) for a determination period if the average percentage of total compensation included under the alternative definition of compensation for an employer's highly compensated employees as a group for the determination period does not exceed by more than a de minimis amount the average percentage of total compensation included under the alternative definition for the employer's nonhighly compensated employees as a group.

(ii) Total compensation. (A) General rule. For purposes of this paragraph (d)(3), total compensation must be determined using a definition of compensation provided in paragraph (c)(2) of this section, either with or without the modification permitted by paragraph (c)(4) of this section. Thus, total compensation does not include prior-employer compensation or imputed compensation described in paragraph (f)(1) of this section (including imputed compensation for a period during which an employee performs services for another employer). Total compensation taken into account for each employee (including, if added, the elective contributions and deferred compensation described in paragraph (c)(4) of this section) may not exceed the annual compensation limit of section 401(a)(17).

(B) Alternative definitions with exclusions applicable solely to highly compensated employees. If an alternative definition of compensation contains a provision that excludes amounts from compensation and, as described in paragraph (c)(5) of this section, the provision only applies in defining the compensation of some highly compensated employees, then, for purposes of this paragraph (d)(3), the total compensation of any highly compensated employee subject to the provision must be reduced by any amount excluded from the employee's compensation as a result of the provision. However, if the provision applies consistently in defining the compensation of all highly compensated employees, this adjustment to total compensation is not required.

(iii) Employees taken into account. (A) General rule. In applying the requirement of this paragraph (d)(3), the employees taken into account are the same employees taken into account in satisfying the requirements of the applicable provision for the determination period. For example, in determining whether a plan satisfies section 401(a)(4), an alternative definition must satisfy this paragraph (d)(3) taking into account all employees who benefit under the plan for the plan year (within the meaning of § 1.410(b)-3(a)). If an employer is using the same alternative definition of compensation to determine whether more than one separate plan satisfies section 401(a)(4), the employer is permitted to take into account all the employees who benefit under all of those plans for the plan year in determining whether the alternative definition of compensation being used satisfies this paragraph (d)(3).

(B) Exclusion of self-employed individuals. In applying the requirement of this paragraph (d)(3), self-employed individuals are disregarded.

(C) Certain employees disregarded. If an employee's total compensation for the determination period, determined under paragraph (d)(3)(ii) and (d)(3)(vi)(B) of this section, is zero, the employee is disregarded in determining whether the nondiscrimination requirement of paragraph (d)(3) of this section is satisfied for that determination period. For example, an employee who does not receive any actual compensation during a determination period because the employee is on unpaid leave of absence for the entire period, but who is credited with imputed compensation described in paragraph (f)(1) of this section, is disregarded in determining whether the nondiscrimination requirement of this paragraph (d)(3) is satisfied for that determination period.

(iv) Calculation of average percentages. (A) General rule. To determine the average percentages described in paragraph (d)(3)(i) of this section, an individual compensation percentage must be calculated for each employee in a group, and then the average of the separately calculated compensation percentages for each employee in the group must be determined. The individual compensation percentage for an employee is calculated by dividing the amount of the employee's compensation that is included under the alternative definition by the amount of the employee's total compensation.

(B) Other reasonable methods. Notwithstanding paragraph (d)(3)(iv)(A) of this section, any other reasonable method is permitted to be used to determine the average percentages described in paragraph (d)(3)(i) of this section for either or both of the groups (i.e., highly compensated employees and nonhighly compensated employees), provided that the method cannot reasonably be expected to create a significant variance from the average percentage for that group determined using the individual-percentage method provided in paragraph (d)(3)(iv)(A) of this section. The same method is not required to be used for calculating the two average percentages. For example, to determine the average percentage for nonhighly compensated employees as a group, an employer may calculate an aggregate compensation percentage by dividing the aggregate amount of compensation of nonhighly compensated employees that is included under the alternative definition by the aggregate amount of total compensation of nonhighly compensated employees, provided the resulting percentage is not reasonably expected to vary significantly from the average percentage produced using the individual-percentage method provided in paragraph (d)(3)(iv)(A) of this section because of the extra weight given employees with higher compensation.

(v) Facts and circumstances determination. The determination of whether the average percentage of total compensation included for the employer's highly compensated employees as a group for a determination period exceeds by more than a de minimis amount the average percentage of total compensation included for the employer's nonhighly compensated employees as a group is based on all the relevant facts and circumstances. The differences between the percentages for prior determination periods may be considered in determining whether the amount of the difference between the percentages is more than de minimis. In addition, an isolated instance of a more than de minimis difference between the compensation percentages that is due to an extraordinary unforeseeable event (such as overtime payments to employees of a public utility due to a major hurricane) will be disregarded if the amount of the difference in prior determination periods was de minimis.

(vi) Special rules for definitions of compensation based on rate of compensation or that include prior-employer or imputed compensation. (A) Special rule for determining compensation included under an alternative definition. If an alternative definition uses rate of compensation or includes prior-employer compensation or imputed compensation, the amount of each employee's compensation for a determination period that is treated as included under the alternative definition for purposes of determining the average percentages for the nondiscrimination requirement (i.e. the amount used in the numerator) must not be more than 100 percent of the employee's total compensation for that period, determined under paragraph (d)(3)(ii) and (d)(3)(vi)(B) of this section. This limit on the amount of compensation treated as included under the alternative definition applies even if the amount of compensation actually credited to the employee for the determination period under the definition and, thus, used as compensation within the meaning of section 414(s), exceeds the employee's total compensation for the period.

(B) Special rule for determining total compensation. If an alternative definition uses rate of compensation or includes prior-employer compensation or imputed compensation, each employee's total compensation for purposes of determining the average percentages for the nondiscrimination requirement (i.e. the amount used in the denominator) must include all the types of elective contributions and deferred compensation described in paragraph (c)(4) of this section.

**(e) Rate of compensation.** *(1) General rule.* A definition of compensation satisfies section 414(s) as a reasonable definition of compensation even though it defines the amount of each employee's basic or regular compensation using the employee's basic or regular rate of compensation rather than using the employee's actual basic or regular compensation from the employer if the definition satisfies the requirements specified in paragraph (e)(3) of this section and otherwise satisfies the requirements of paragraph (d) of this section, including the nondiscrimination test in paragraph (d)(3) of this section. For this purpose, the employee's rate of compensation must be determined using an hourly pay scale, weekly salary, or similar unit of basic or regular compensation applicable to the employee. A definition will not fail to satisfy the requirements of this paragraph (e) merely because it defines compensation as including each employee's basic or regular compensation, the amount of which is determined using each employee's basic or regular rate of compensation, plus actual amounts of irregular or additional compensation, such as overtime or bonuses. In addition, a definition of compensation will not fail to satisfy section 414(s) merely because it defines compensation for each employee as the greater of the employee's actual compensation, the amount of which is determined using a definition that would otherwise satisfy paragraph (c) or (d)(2) of this section, or the employee's basic or regular compensation, the amount of which is determined using the employee's basic or regular rate of compensation.

*(2) Not applicable to certain contributions.* This paragraph (e) does not apply to a definition of compensation used in determining whether elective deferrals (as defined in section 402(g)(3)), matching contributions (as defined in section 401(m)(4)), or employee contributions subject to section 401(m) satisfy any applicable provision. Thus, for example, a definition of compensation that defines compensation based on each employee's basic or regular rate of compensation may not be used to measure compensation for purposes of determining if a qualified cash or deferred arrangement satisfies the actual deferral percentage test in section 401(k)(3).

*(3) Requirements for definitions of compensation based on rate of compensation.* (i) Benefit determination. The definition of compensation must actually be used to calculate the benefits, contributions, or other amounts, that are subject to the applicable provision. For example, a definition of compensation that defines compensation based on each employee's basic or regular rate of compensation may not be used to determine whether a plan satisfies section 401(a)(4) unless the benefits, contributions, or other amounts for each employee in the plan are determined using that definition of compensation.

(ii) Period for determining compensation. The amount of each employee's basic or regular compensation for the determination period must be determined using the employee's basic or regular rate of compensation as of a designated date in the determination period. For example, if the determination period is a calendar year, this requirement would be satisfied if the amount of each employee's basic or regular compensation for the calendar year is determined using the employee's basic or regular rate of compensation as of January 1 of the calendar year. Alternatively, the amount of each employee's basic or regular compensation for a determination period can be the sum of the amounts separately determined for shorter specified periods (e.g., weeks or months) within the determination period provided the amount of each employee's basic or regular compensation for each specified period is determined using the employee's basic or regular rate of compensation as of a designated date within the specified period.

(iii) Dates for determining rate of compensation. One or more dates may be used to determine employees' rates of compensation for a determination period or specified period provided that, if the same date is not used for all employees, the dates selected are designed to determine the rates of compensation for that period on a consistent basis for all employees taken into account for the determination period. For example, if annual compensation increases are provided to different groups of employees on different dates during the year, it would be consistent to choose a different date for each group in order to include the annual increase in the employees' rates of compensation for the determination period. In addition, the date or dates selected, by themselves, must not cause the portion of total compensation included to vary significantly among employees.

(iv) Periods without compensation or with reduced compensation. An employee's compensation may generally only be determined using the employee's rate of compensation for employment periods during which the employer actually compensates the employee. However, if an employee terminates employment or otherwise stops performing services (such as for a leave of absence, lay off or similar event) either without compensation or with reduced compensation during a determination period, the employer may continue to credit the employee with compensation based on the employee's rate of compensation for a period of up to 31 days after the event, but not beyond the end of the determination period. Paragraph (f) of this section contains special rules for crediting imputed compensation for periods extending beyond 31 days during which an employee is not compensated or an employee's compensation is reduced. See also the definition of Section 414(s) compensation in § 1.401(a)(4)-12 that, for purposes of satisfying section 401(a)(4), permits adjustments to compensation to reflect the equivalent of full-time compensation to the extent necessary to satisfy the requirements of 29 CFR 2530.204-2(d) (regarding double proration of service and compensation).

**(f) Prior-employer compensation and imputed compensation.** *(1) General rule.* Solely for purposes of determining whether a defined benefit plan, as defined in § 1.410(b)-9, satisfies section 401(a)(4) or 410(b), an alternative definition that includes prior-employer compensation or imputed compensation satisfies section 414(s) as a reasonable alternative definition if the definition satisfies the requirements specified in paragraphs (f)(2) and (3) of this section. For this purpose, prior-employer compensation is compensation from an employer other than the employer (determined at the time that the compensation is paid) maintaining the plan that is credited for periods prior to the employee's employment with the employer maintaining the plan and during which the employee performed services for the other employer. For this purpose, imputed compensation is compensation credited for periods after an employee has commenced or recommenced participation in a plan while the employee is not compensated by the employer maintaining the plan or is compensated at a reduced rate by that employer because the employee is not performing services as an employee for the employer (including a period in which the employee performs services for another employer, e.g., a joint venture) or because the employee has a reduced work schedule.

*(2) Requirements for definitions of compensation crediting prior-employer compensation or imputed compensation.* (i) General requirement. The definition must otherwise be described in paragraph (c) of this section or must otherwise satisfy the requirements of paragraph (d) or (e) of this section for alternative definitions of compensation, including the nondiscrimination requirement in paragraph (d)(3) of this section.

(ii) Benefit determination. A definition of compensation that credits prior-employer compensation or imputed compensation must actually be used to calculate the benefits under the plan. For example, the definition may not be used to determine whether a defined benefit plan satisfies section 401(a)(4) unless the benefits for each employee in the plan are determined using that definition of compensation.

(iii) Provision applied to all similarly-situated employees. A provision in a plan's definition of compensation crediting prior-employer compensation or imputed compensation must apply on the same terms to all similarly-situated employees in the plan. The criteria for determining whether employees are similarly situated for this purpose are the same as the criteria for determining whether a plan provision crediting pre-participation or imputed service satisfies the requirements of § 1.401(a)(4)-11(d)(3)(iii)(A).

(iv) Legitimate business purpose. There must be a legitimate business purpose, based on all of the relevant facts and circumstances, for crediting prior-employer compensation or imputed compensation to an employee for the period being credited. The standard for determining whether crediting prior-employer compensation or imputed compensation satisfies this requirement is the same as the standard for determining whether crediting pre-participation or imputed service under a plan satisfies the requirements of § 1.401(a)(4)-11(d)(3)(iii)(B) and whether crediting imputed service satisfies the additional requirements of § 1.401(a)(4)-11(d)(3)(iv)(A). However, if the legitimate business reason for crediting imputed compensation relates to the services the employee is performing for another employer and the reason satisfies the standard in § 1.401(a)(4)-11(d)(3)(iii)(B), the additional requirements of § 1.401(a)(4)-11(d)(3)(iv)(A) are deemed to be satisfied. For example, if an employee becomes employed by another employer as a result of a merger, acquisition or similar transaction with the other employer and imputed compensation is credited to the employee while the employee is performing services for the other employer, the crediting of imputed compensation to the employee satisfies the standard in § 1.401(a)(4)-11(d)(3)(iii)(B). Thus, under that example, crediting the imputed compensation to the employee is deemed to satisfy the additional requirements of § 1.401(a)(4)-11(d)(3)(iv)(A), even if the employee is not performing those services under an arrangement that provides an ongoing business benefit to the employer maintaining the plan.

(v) No significant discrimination. Based on all of the relevant facts and circumstances, crediting prior-employer compensation or imputed compensation must not by design or in operation discriminate significantly in favor of highly compensated employees. The standard for determining whether crediting prior-employer compensation or imputed compensation satisfies this requirement is the same as the standard for determining whether crediting pre-participation or imputed service satisfies the requirement in § 1.401(a)(4)-11(d)(3)(iii)(C) and whether crediting imputed service satisfies the additional requirement of § 1.401(a)(4)-11(d)(3)(iv)(B).

*(3) Reasonable method.* (i) General rule. Any reasonable method may be used to determine the amount of prior-employer compensation or imputed compensation provided that the requirements of paragraph (f)(3)(ii) or (iii) of this section are satisfied, whichever is applicable.

(ii) Requirements for prior-employer compensation. Prior-employer compensation credited to an employee for a period that an employee is performing services for another employer must be compensation for the employee from the other employer (or be based on the employee's basic or regular rate of compensation from the other employer) for that period. In addition, prior employer compensation credited to an employee must not exceed the amount of compensation from the other employer that would have been included under the definition of compensation in effect for that period for compensation from the employer maintaining the plan. Reasonable assumptions may be made in determining the amount of compensation received from another employer for a period that would have been included under the definition of compensation in effect for that period for compensation from the employer maintaining the plan.

(iii) Requirements for imputed compensation. (A) General rule. The amount of imputed compensation credited to an employee during any period, when combined with the amount of any actual compensation being included, must not exceed an amount that, based on all of the relevant facts and circumstances, is reasonably representative of the amount of compensation that the employee would have received and that would have been included under the definition of compensation in effect for the period if the employee had continued to perform services for the employer during that period at the same level as the employee was performing before the employee stopped performing services or changed to a reduced work schedule. The relevant facts and circumstances include the compensation that the employee was receiving immediately before the employee stopped performing services or changed to a reduced work schedule, and, if applicable, the rate of compensation in effect while the employee is not performing services or has a reduced work schedule that is applicable to the employee's specific job grade immediately before the change occurred.

(B) Imputed compensation from another employer. Imputed compensation credited for a period that an employee is performing services for another employer is deemed to satisfy paragraph (f)(3)(iii)(A) of this section if the amount of compensation credited satisfies the requirements of paragraph (f)(3)(ii) of this section for prior-employer compensation. Thus, for example, the amount of imputed compensation credited to an employee for a period that the employee is performing services for another employer is deemed to satisfy paragraph (f)(3)(iii)(A) of this section if the amount credited is compensation for the employee from the other employer (or is based on the employee's basic or regular rate of compensation from the other employer) for that period, and the amount credited does not exceed the compensation from the other employer that would be included for the employee under the definition of compensation in effect for that period for compensation from the employer maintaining the plan.

*(4) Special nondiscrimination rule for safe harbor definitions.* If a definition of compensation crediting prior-employer or imputed compensation is otherwise described in paragraph (c) of this section, and the prior-employer compensation or imputed compensation credited satisfies the requirements of paragraphs (f)(1), (2), and (3) of this section, then the definition is deemed to satisfy paragraph (d) of this section (i.e., it is deemed to be nondiscriminatory).

**(g) Special rules.** *(1) Self-employed individuals.* (i) General rule. If an alternative definition of compensation under paragraph (c)(3), (d), (e), or (f) of this section is used to satisfy an applicable provision, an equivalent alternative compensation amount must be determined for any self-employed individual who is in the group of employees for whom paragraph (b) of this section requires a single definition of compensation to be used. This equivalent alternative compensation amount is determined by multiplying the self-employed individual's total earned income (as defined in section 401(c)(2)) for the determination period by the percentage of total compensation (as defined in paragraph (d)(3)(ii) of this section) included under the alternative definition for the employer's nonhighly compensated common-law employees as a group (determined in a manner consistent with the rules in paragraph (d)(3)(iii) of this section and, if applicable, paragraph (d)(3)(vi) of this section) Thus, for purposes of this determination, highly compensated common-law employees must be disregarded. This equivalent alternative compensation amount will be treated as the self-employed individual's compensation under the alternative definition of compensation for the determination period.

(ii) Inclusion of elective contributions. If the alternative definition of compensation includes any types of elective contributions described in paragraph (c)(4) of this section, the self-employed individual's earned income for this determination must be increased by the amount of elective contributions made by the employer on behalf of the self-employed individual, and the definition of total compensation for this determination must include all the types of elective contributions described in paragraph (c)(4) of this section made by the employer on behalf of common-law employees (other than highly compensated employees).

(iii) Reductions in equivalent alternative compensation amount applicable only to highly compensated employees. An alternative definition of compensation may provide that compensation under the alternative definition for some or all self-employed individuals who are highly compensated employees is a specified portion of, rather than equal to, the equivalent compensation amount determined under paragraph (g)(1)(i).

*(2) Leased employees. [Reserved]*

**(h) Definitions.** The following definitions apply for purposes of this section:

*(1) Applicable provision.* Applicable provision means a provision that specifically refers to section 414(s) or this section.

*(2) Determination period.* Determination period means a period during which the amount of compensation is measured for use in determining whether the requirements of an applicable provision are satisfied. If no period is provided under the applicable provision for measuring compensation, the determination period is the period for which the applicable provision must be satisfied. The applicable provision may provide additional rules concerning the determination period to be used for satisfying the nondiscrimination requirement in paragraph (d) of this section.

*(3) Employee.* Employee means employee within the meaning of § 1.410(b)-9.

*(4) Highly compensated employee.* Highly compensated employee means highly compensated employee within the meaning of § 1.410(b)-9.

*(5) Nonhighly compensated employee.* Nonhighly compensated employee means nonhighly compensated employee within the meaning of § 1.410(b)-9.

*(6) Self-employed individual.* Self-employed individual means self-employed individual within the meaning of section 401(c)(1).

**(i) Additional rules.** The Commissioner may in revenue rulings, notices, and other guidance of general applicability provide additional rules for defining compensation within the meaning of section 414(s), including additional definitions of compensation that satisfy section 414(s).

**(j) Effective date and transition rules.** *(1) Statutory effective date.* Section 414(s) applies to years beginning on or after January 1, 1987.

*(2) Regulatory effective date.* (i) In general. Except as otherwise provided in paragraph (j)(2)(ii) of this section, § 1.414(s)-1(a) through (i) apply to years beginning on or after January 1, 1994.

(ii) Plans of tax-exempt organizations. In the case of a plan maintained by an organization that is exempt from income taxation pursuant to section 501(a), including plans subject to section 403(b)(12)(A)(i) (nonelective plans), § 1.414(s)-1(a) through (i) apply to plan years beginning on or after January 1, 1996.

*(3) Compliance during transition period.* For plan years beginning before the effective date of these regulations, as set forth in paragraph (j)(2) of this section, and on or after the statutory effective date as set forth in paragraph (j)(1) of this section, a plan must be operated in accordance with a reasonable, good faith interpretation of section 414(s). Whether a plan is operated in accordance with a reasonable, good faith interpretation of section 414(s) will generally be determined based on all relevant facts and circumstances, including the extent to which an employer has resolved unclear issues in its favor. A plan will be deemed to be operated in accordance with a reasonable, good faith interpretation of section 414(s)(1) and (2) if it is operated in accordance with the terms of § 1.414(s)-1(a) through (i). For years beginning on or after the statutory effective date and

before the effective date of these regulations, a definition of compensation is also deemed to satisfy section 414(s) as an alternative method of determining compensation under section 414(s)(3) if the definition satisfies the requirements of § 1.414(s)-1(a) through (i) or if the definition satisfies the prior regulation provisions of § 1.414(s)-1T. (See § 1.414(s)-1T as contained in the CFR edition revised as of April 1, 1991.) In addition, for those transition years, a definition of compensation is deemed to satisfy section 414(s) as an alternative method of determining compensation under section 414(s)(3) if, based on all the relevant facts and circumstances in effect for the year, use of the definition does not cause discrimination in favor of highly compensated employees.

T.D. 8361, 9/12/91, amend T.D. 8488, 9/1/93, T.D. 9319, 4/4/2007.

### § 1.414(v)-1 Catch-up contributions.

**(a) Catch-up contributions.** *(1) General rule.* An applicable employer plan shall not be treated as failing to meet any requirement of the Internal Revenue Code solely because the plan permits a catch-up eligible participant to make catch-up contributions in accordance with section 414(v) and this section. With respect to an applicable employer plan, catch-up contributions are elective deferrals made by a catch-up eligible participant that exceed any of the applicable limits set forth in paragraph (b) of this section and that are treated under the applicable employer plan as catch-up contributions, but only to the extent they do not exceed the catch-up contribution limit described in paragraph (c) of this section (determined in accordance with the special rules for employers that maintain multiple applicable employer plans in paragraph (f) of this section, if applicable). To the extent provided under paragraph (d) of this section, catch-up contributions are disregarded for purposes of various statutory limits. In addition, unless otherwise provided in paragraph (e) of this section, all catch-up eligible participants of the employer must be provided the opportunity to make catch-up contributions in order for an applicable employer plan to comply with the universal availability requirement of section 414(v)(4). The definitions in paragraph (g) of this section apply for purposes of this section and § 1.402(g)-2.

*(2) Treatment as elective deferrals.* Except as specifically provided in this section, elective deferrals treated as catch-up contributions remain subject to statutory and regulatory rules otherwise applicable to elective deferrals. For example, catch-up contributions under an applicable employer plan that is a section 401(k) plan are subject to the distribution and vesting restrictions of section 401(k)(2)(B) and (C). In addition, the plan is permitted to provide a single election for catch-up eligible participants, with the determination of whether elective deferrals are catch-up contributions being made under the terms of the plan.

*(3) Coordination with section 457(b)(3).* In the case of an applicable employer plan that is a section 457 eligible governmental plan, the catch-up contributions permitted under this section shall not apply to a catch-up eligible participant for any taxable year for which a higher limitation applies to such participant under section 457(b)(3). For additional guidance, see regulations under section 457.

**(b) Elective deferrals that exceed an applicable limit.** *(1) Applicable limits.* An applicable limit for purposes of determining catch-up contributions for a catch-up eligible participant is any of the following:

(i) Statutory limit. A statutory limit is a limit on elective deferrals or annual additions permitted to be made (without regard to section 414(v) and this section) with respect to an employee for a year provided in section 401(a)(30), 402(h), 403(b), 408, 415(c), or 457(b)(2) (without regard to section 457(b)(3)), as applicable.

(ii) Employer-provided limit. An employer-provided limit is any limit on the elective deferrals an employee is permitted to make (without regard to section 414(v) and this section) that is contained in the terms of the plan, but which is not required under the Internal Revenue Code. Thus, for example, if, in accordance with the terms of the plan, highly compensated employees are limited to a deferral percentage of 10% of compensation, this limit is an employer-provided limit that is an applicable limit with respect to the highly compensated employees.

(iii) Actual deferral percentage (ADP) limit. In the case of a section 401(k) plan that would fail the ADP test of section 401(k)(3) if it did not correct under section 401(k)(8), the ADP limit is the highest amount of elective deferrals that can be retained in the plan by any highly compensated employee under the rules of section 401(k)(8)(C) (without regard to paragraph (d)(2)(iii) of this section). In the case of a simplified employee pension (SEP) with a salary reduction arrangement (within the meaning of section 408(k)(6)) that would fail the requirements of section 408(k)(6)(A)(iii) if it did not correct in accordance with section 408(k)(6)(C), the ADP limit is the highest amount of elective deferrals that can be made by any highly compensated employee under the rules of section 408(k)(6) (without regard to paragraph (d)(2)(iii) of this section).

*(2) Contributions in excess of applicable limit.* (i) Plan year limits. (A) General rule. Except as provided in paragraph (b)(2)(ii) of this section, the amount of elective deferrals in excess of an applicable limit is determined as of the end of the plan year by comparing the total elective deferrals for the plan year with the applicable limit for the plan year. In addition, except as provided in paragraph (b)(2)(i)(B) of this section, in the case of a plan that provides for separate employer-provided limits on elective deferrals for separate portions of plan compensation within the plan year, the applicable limit for the plan year is the sum of the dollar amounts of the limits for the separate portions. For example, if a plan sets a deferral percentage limit for each payroll period, the applicable limit for the plan year is the sum of the dollar amounts of the limits for the payroll periods.

(B) Alternative method for determining employer-provided limit. (1) General rule. If the plan limits elective deferrals for separate portions of the plan year, then, solely for purposes of determining the amount that is in excess of an employer-provided limit, the plan is permitted to provide that the applicable limit for the plan year is the product of the employee's plan year compensation and the time-weighted average of the deferral percentage limits, rather than determining the employer-provided limit as the sum of the limits for the separate portions of the year. Thus, for example, if, in accordance with the terms of the plan, highly compensated employees are limited to 8% of compensation during the first half of the plan year and 10% of compensation for the second half of the plan year, the plan is permitted to provide that the applicable limit for a highly compensated employee is 9% of the employee's plan year compensation.

(2) Alternative definition of compensation permitted. A plan using the alternative method in this paragraph (b)(2)(i)(B) is permitted to provide that the applicable limit for the plan year is determined as the product of the catch-up eligible participant's compensation used for purposes of the ADP test and the time-weighted average of the deferral

percentage limits. The alternative calculation in this paragraph (b)(2)(i)(B)(2) is available regardless of whether the deferral percentage limits change during the plan year.

(ii) Other year limit. In the case of an applicable limit that is applied on the basis of a year other than the plan year (e.g., the calendar-year limit on elective deferrals under section 401(a)(30)), the determination of whether elective deferrals are in excess of the applicable limit is made on the basis of such other year.

**(c) Catch-up contribution limit.** *(1) General rule.* Elective deferrals with respect to a catch-up eligible participant in excess of an applicable limit under paragraph (b) of this section are treated as catch-up contributions under this section as of a date within a taxable year only to the extent that such elective deferrals do not exceed the catch-up contribution limit described in paragraphs (c)(1) and (2) of this section, reduced by elective deferrals previously treated as catch-up contributions for the taxable year, determined in accordance with paragraph (c)(3) of this section. The catch-up contribution limit for a taxable year is generally the applicable dollar catch-up limit for such taxable year, as set forth in paragraph (c)(2) of this section. However, an elective deferral is not treated as a catch-up contribution to the extent that the elective deferral, when added to all other elective deferrals for the taxable year under any applicable employer plan of the employer, exceeds the participant's compensation (determined in accordance with section 415(c)(3)) for the taxable year. See also paragraph (f) of this section for special rules for employees who participate in more than one applicable employer plan maintained by the employer.

*(2) Applicable dollar catch-up limit.* (i) In general. The applicable dollar catch-up limit for an applicable employer plan, other than a plan described in section 401(k)(11) or 408(p), is determined under the following table:

| For taxable years beginning in | Applicable dollar catch-up limit |
|---|---|
| 2002 | $1,000 |
| 2003 | 2,000 |
| 2004 | 3,000 |
| 2005 | 4,000 |
| 2006 | 5,000 |

(ii) SIMPLE plans. The applicable dollar catch-up limit for a SIMPLE 401(k) plan described in section 401(k)(11) or a SIMPLE IRA plan as described in section 408(p) is determined under the following table:

| For taxable years beginning in | Applicable dollar catch-up limit |
|---|---|
| 2002 | $ 500 |
| 2003 | 1,000 |
| 2004 | 1,500 |
| 2005 | 2,000 |
| 2006 | 2,500 |

(iii) Cost of living adjustments. For taxable years beginning after 2006, the applicable dollar catch-up limit is the applicable dollar catch-up limit for 2006 described in paragraph (c)(2)(i) or (ii) of this section increased at the same time and in the same manner as adjustments under section 415(d), except that the base period shall be the calendar quarter beginning July 1, 2005, and any increase that is not a multiple of $500 shall be rounded to the next lower multiple of $500.

*(3) Timing rules.* For purposes of determining the maximum amount of permitted catch-up contributions for a catch-up eligible participant, the determination of whether an elective deferral is a catch-up contribution is made as of the last day of the plan year (or in the case of section 415, as of the last day of the limitation year), except that, with respect to elective deferrals in excess of an applicable limit that is tested on the basis of the taxable year or calendar year (e.g., the section 401(a)(30) limit on elective deferrals), the determination of whether such elective deferrals are treated as catch-up contributions is made at the time they are deferred.

**(d) Treatment of catch-up contributions.** *(1) Contributions not taken into account for certain limits.* Catch-up contributions are not taken into account in applying the limits of section 401(a)(30), 402(h), 403(b), 408, 415(c), or 457(b)(2) (determined without regard to section 457(b)(3)) to other contributions or benefits under an applicable employer plan or any other plan of the employer.

*(2) Contributions not taken into account in application of ADP test.* (i) Calculation of ADR. Elective deferrals that are treated as catch-up contributions pursuant to paragraph (c) of this section with respect to a section 401(k) plan because they exceed a statutory or employer-provided limit described in paragraph (b)(1)(i) or (ii) of this section, respectively, are subtracted from the catch-up eligible participant's elective deferrals for the plan year for purposes of determining the actual deferral ratio (ADR) (as defined in regulations under section 401(k)) of a catch-up eligible participant. Similarly, elective deferrals that are treated as catch-up contributions pursuant to paragraph (c) of this section with respect to a SEP because they exceed a statutory or employer-provided limit described in paragraph (b)(1)(i) or (ii) of this section, respectively, are subtracted from the catch-up eligible participant's elective deferrals for the plan year for purposes of determining the deferral percentage under section 408(k)(6)(D) of a catch-up eligible participant.

(ii) Adjustment of elective deferrals for correction purposes. For purposes of the correction of excess contributions in accordance with section 401(k)(8)(C), elective deferrals under the plan treated as catch-up contributions for the plan year and not taken into account in the ADP test under paragraph (d)(2)(i) of this section are subtracted from the catch-up eligible participant's elective deferrals under the plan for the plan year.

(iii) Excess contributions treated as catch-up contributions. A section 401(k) plan that satisfies the ADP test of section 401(k)(3) through correction under section 401(k)(8) must retain any elective deferrals that are treated as catch-up contributions pursuant to paragraph (c) of this section because they exceed the ADP limit in paragraph (b)(1)(iii) of this section. In addition, a section 401(k) plan is not treated as failing to satisfy section 401(k)(8) merely because elective deferrals described in the preceding sentence are not distributed or recharacterized as employee contributions. Similarly, a SEP is not treated as failing to satisfy section 408(k)(6)(A)(iii) merely because catch-up contributions are not treated as excess contributions with respect to a catch-up eligible participant under the rules of section 408(k)(6)(C). Notwithstanding the fact that elective deferrals described in this paragraph (d)(2)(iii) are not distributed, such elective deferrals are still considered to be excess contributions under section 401(k)(8), and accordingly, matching contributions with respect to such elective deferrals are permitted to be forfeited under the rules of section 411(a)(3)(G).

*(3) Contributions not taken into account for other nondiscrimination purposes.* (i) Application for top-heavy. Catch-up

contributions with respect to the current plan year are not taken into account for purposes of section 416. However, catch-up contributions for prior years are taken into account for purposes of section 416. Thus, catch-up contributions for prior years are included in the account balances that are used in determining whether the plan is top-heavy under section 416(g).

(ii) Application for section 410(b). Catch-up contributions with respect to the current plan year are not taken into account for purposes of section 410(b). Thus, catch-up contributions are not taken into account in determining the average benefit percentage under § 1.410(b)-5 for the year if benefit percentages are determined based on current year contributions. However, catch-up contributions for prior years are taken into account for purposes of section 410(b). Thus, catch-up contributions for prior years would be included in the account balances that are used in determining the average benefit percentage if allocations for prior years are taken into account.

*(4) Availability of catch-up contributions.* An applicable employer plan does not violate § 1.401(a)(4)-4 merely because the group of employees for whom catch-up contributions are currently available (i.e., the catch-up eligible participants) is not a group of employees that would satisfy section 410(b) (without regard to § 1.410(b)-5). In addition, a catch-up eligible participant is not treated as having a right to a different rate of allocation of matching contributions merely because an otherwise nondiscriminatory schedule of matching rates is applied to elective deferrals that include catch-up contributions. The rules in this paragraph (d)(4) also apply for purposes of satisfying the requirements of section 403(b)(12).

**(e) Universal availability requirement.** *(1) General rule.* (i) Effective opportunity. An applicable employer plan that offers catch-up contributions and that is otherwise subject to section 401(a)(4) (including a plan that is subject to section 401(a)(4) pursuant to section 403(b)(12)) will not satisfy the requirements of section 401(a)(4) unless all catch-up eligible participants who participate under any applicable employer plan maintained by the employer are provided with an effective opportunity to make the same dollar amount of catch-up contributions. A plan fails to provide an effective opportunity to make catch-up contributions if it has an applicable limit (e.g., an employer-provided limit) that applies to a catch-up eligible participant and does not permit the participant to make elective deferrals in excess of that limit. An applicable employer plan does not fail to satisfy the universal availability requirement of this paragraph (e) solely because an employer-provided limit does not apply to all employees or different limits apply to different groups of employees under paragraph (b)(2)(i) of this section. However, a plan may not provide lower employer-provided limits for catch-up eligible participants.

(ii) Certain practices permitted. (A) Proration of limit. An applicable employer plan does not fail to satisfy the universal availability requirement of this paragraph (e) merely because the plan allows participants to defer an amount equal to a specified percentage of compensation for each payroll period and for each payroll period permits each catch-up eligible participant to defer a pro-rata share of the applicable dollar catch-up limit in addition to that amount.

(B) Cash availability. An applicable employer plan does not fail to satisfy the universal availability requirement of this paragraph (e) merely because it restricts the elective deferrals of any employee (including a catch-up eligible participant) to amounts available after other withholding from the employee's pay (e.g., after deduction of all applicable income and employment taxes). For this purpose, an employer limit of 75% of compensation or higher will be treated as limiting employees to amounts available after other withholdings.

*(2) Certain employees disregarded.* An applicable employer plan does not fail to satisfy the universal availability requirement of this paragraph (e) merely because employees described in section 410(b)(3) (e.g., collectively bargained employees) are not provided the opportunity to make catch-up contributions.

*(3) Exception for certain plans.* An applicable employer plan does not fail to satisfy the universal availability requirement of this paragraph (e) merely because another applicable employer plan that is a section 457 eligible governmental plan does not provide for catch-up contributions to the extent set forth in section 414(v)(6)(C) and paragraph (a)(3) of this section.

*(4) Exception for section 410(b)(6)(C)(ii) period.* If an applicable employer plan satisfies the universal availability requirement of this paragraph (e) before an acquisition or disposition described in § 1.410(b)-2(f) and would fail to satisfy the universal availability requirement of this paragraph (e) merely because of such event, then the applicable employer plan shall continue to be treated as satisfying this paragraph (e) through the end of the period determined under section 410(b)(6)(C)(ii).

**(f) Special rules for an employer that sponsors multiple plans.** *(1) General rule.* For purposes of paragraph (c) of this section, all applicable employer plans, other than section 457 eligible governmental plans, maintained by the same employer are treated as one plan and all section 457 eligible governmental plans maintained by the same employer are treated as one plan. Thus, the total amount of catch-up contributions under all applicable employer plans of an employer (other than section 457 eligible governmental plans) is limited to the applicable dollar catch-up limit for the taxable year, and the total amount of catch-up contributions for all section 457 eligible governmental plans of an employer is limited to the applicable dollar catch-up limit for the taxable year.

*(2) Coordination of employer-provided limits.* An applicable employer plan is permitted to allow a catch-up eligible participant to defer amounts in excess of an employer-provided limit under that plan without regard to whether elective deferrals made by the participant have been treated as catch-up contributions for the taxable year under another applicable employer plan aggregated with such plan under this paragraph (f). However, to the extent elective deferrals under another plan maintained by the employer have already been treated as catch-up contributions during the taxable year, the elective deferrals under the plan may be treated as catch-up contributions only up to the amount remaining under the catch-up limit for the year. Any other elective deferrals that exceed the employer-provided limit may not be treated as catch-up contributions and must satisfy the otherwise applicable nondiscrimination rules. For example, the right to make contributions in excess of the employer-provided limit is another right or feature which must satisfy § 1.401(a)(4)-4 to the extent that the contributions are not catch-up contributions. Also, contributions in excess of the employer provided limit are taken into account under the ADP test to the extent they are not catch-up contributions.

*(3) Allocation rules.* If a catch-up eligible participant makes additional elective deferrals in excess of an applicable

limit under paragraph (b)(1) of this section under more than one applicable employer plan that is aggregated under the rules of this paragraph (f), the applicable employer plan under which elective deferrals in excess of an applicable limit are treated as catch-up contributions is permitted to be determined in any manner that is not inconsistent with the manner in which such amounts were actually deferred under the plan.

**(g) Definitions.** *(1) Applicable employer plan.* The term applicable employer plan means a section 401(k) plan, a SIMPLE IRA plan as defined in section 408(p), a simplified employee pension plan as defined in section 408(k) (SEP), a plan or contract that satisfies the requirements of section 403(b), or a section 457 eligible governmental plan.

*(2) Elective deferral.* The term elective deferral means an elective deferral within the meaning of section 402(g)(3) or any contribution to a section 457 eligible governmental plan.

*(3) Catch-up eligible participant.* An employee is a catch-up eligible participant for a taxable year if—

(i) The employee is eligible to make elective deferrals under an applicable employer plan (without regard to section 414(v) or this section); and

(ii) The employee's 50th or higher birthday would occur before the end of the employee's taxable year.

*(4) Other definitions.* (i) The terms employer, employee, section 401(k) plan, and highly compensated employee have the meanings provided in § 1.410(b)-9.

(ii) The term section 457 eligible governmental plan means an eligible deferred compensation plan described in section 457(b) that is established and maintained by an eligible employer described in section 457(e)(1)(A).

**(h) Examples.** The following examples illustrate the application of this section. For purposes of these examples, the limit under section 401(a)(30) is $15,000 and the applicable dollar catch-up limit is $5,000 and, except as specifically provided, the plan year is the calendar year. In addition, it is assumed that the participant's elective deferrals under all plans of the employer do not exceed the participant's section 415(c)(3) compensation, that the taxable year of the participant is the calendar year and that any correction pursuant to section 401(k)(8) is made through distribution of excess contributions. The examples are as follows:

*Example (1).* (i) Participant A is eligible to make elective deferrals under a section 401(k) plan, Plan P. Plan P does not limit elective deferrals except as necessary to comply with sections 401(a)(30) and 415. In 2006, Participant A is 55 years old. Plan P also provides that a catch-up eligible participant is permitted to defer amounts in excess of the section 401(a)(30) limit up to the applicable dollar catch-up limit for the year. Participant A defers $18,000 during 2006.

(ii) Participant A's elective deferrals in excess of the section 401(a)(30) limit ($3,000) do not exceed the applicable dollar catch-up limit for 2006 ($5,000). Under paragraph (a)(1) of this section, the $3,000 is a catch-up contribution and, pursuant to paragraph (d)(2)(i) of this section, it is not taken into account in determining Participant A's ADR for purposes of section 401(k)(3).

*Example (2).* (i) Participants B and C, who are highly compensated employees each earning $120,000, are eligible to make elective deferrals under a section 401(k) plan, Plan Q. Plan Q limits elective deferrals as necessary to comply with section 401(a)(30) and 415, and also provides that no highly compensated employee may make an elective deferral at a rate that exceeds 10% of compensation. However, Plan Q also provides that a catch-up eligible participant is permitted to defer amounts in excess of 10% during the plan year up to the applicable dollar catch-up limit for the year. In 2006, Participants B and C are both 55 years old and, pursuant to the catch-up provision in Plan Q, both elect to defer 10% of compensation plus a pro-rata portion of the $5,000 applicable dollar catch-up limit for 2006. Participant B continues this election in effect for the entire year, for a total elective contribution for the year of $17,000. However, in July 2006, after deferring $8,500, Participant C discontinues making elective deferrals.

(ii) Once Participant B's elective deferrals for the year exceed the section 401(a)(30) limit ($15,000), subsequent elective deferrals are treated as catch-up contributions as they are deferred, provided that such elective deferrals do not exceed the catch-up contribution limit for the taxable year. Since the $2,000 in elective deferrals made after Participant B reaches the section 402(g) limit for the calendar year does not exceed the applicable dollar catch-up limit for 2006, the entire $2,000 is treated as a catch-up contribution.

(iii) As of the last day of the plan year, Participant B has exceeded the employer-provided limit of 10% (10% of $120,000 or $12,000 for Participant B) by an additional $3,000. Since the additional $3,000 in elective deferrals does not exceed the $5,000 applicable dollar catch-up limit for 2006, reduced by the $2,000 in elective deferrals previously treated as catch-up contributions, the entire $3,000 of elective deferrals is treated as a catch-up contribution.

(iv) In determining Participant B's ADR, the $5,000 of catch-up contributions are subtracted from Participant B's elective deferrals for the plan year under paragraph (d)(2)(i) of this section. Accordingly, Participant B's ADR is 10% ($12,000/$120,000). In addition, for purposes of applying the rules of section 401(k)(8), Participant B is treated as having elective deferrals of $12,000.

(v) Participant C's elective deferrals for the year do not exceed an applicable limit for the plan year. Accordingly, Participant C's $8,500 of elective deferrals must be taken into account in determining Participant C's ADR for purposes of section 401(k)(3).

*Example (3).* (i) The facts are the same as in Example 2, except that Plan Q is amended to change the maximum permitted deferral percentage for highly compensated employees to 7%, effective for deferrals after April 1, 2006. Participant B, who has earned $40,000 in the first 3 months of the year and has been deferring at a rate of 10% of compensation plus a pro-rata portion of the $5,000 applicable dollar catch-up limit for 2006, reduces the 10% of pay deferral rate to 7% for the remaining 9 months of the year (while continuing to defer a pro-rata portion of the $5,000 applicable dollar catch-up limit for 2006). During those 9 months, Participant B earns $80,000. Thus, Participant B's total elective deferrals for the year are $14,600 ($4,000 for the first 3 months of the year plus $5,600 for the last 9 months of the year plus an additional $5,000 throughout the year).

(ii) The employer-provided limit for Participant B for the plan year is $9,600 ($4,000 for the first 3 months of the year, plus $5,600 for the last 9 months of the year). Accordingly, Participant B's elective deferrals for the year that are in excess of the employer-provided limit are $5,000 (the excess of $14,600 over $9,600), which does not exceed the applicable dollar catch-up limit of $5,000.

(iii) Alternatively, Plan Q may provide that the employer-provided limit is determined as the time-weighted average of the different deferral percentage limits over the course of the year. In this case, the time-weighted average limit is 7.75% for all participants, and the applicable limit for Participant B is 7.75% of $120,000, or $9,300. Accordingly, Participant B's elective deferrals for the year that are in excess of the employer-provided limit are $5,300 (the excess of $14,600 over $9,300). Since the amount of Participant B's elective deferrals in excess of the employer-provided limit ($5,300) exceeds the applicable dollar catch-up limit for the taxable year, only $5,000 of Participant B's elective deferrals may be treated as catch-up contributions. In determining Participant B's actual deferral ratio, the $5,000 of catch-up contributions are subtracted from Participant B's elective deferrals for the plan year under paragraph (d)(2)(i) of this section. Accordingly, Participant B's actual deferral ratio is 8% ($9,600/ $120,000). In addition, for purposes of applying the rules of section 401(k)(8), Participant B is treated as having elective deferrals of $9,600.

*Example (4).* (i) The facts are the same as in Example 1. In addition to Participant A, Participant D is a highly compensated employee who is eligible to make elective deferrals under Plan P. During 2006, Participant D, who is 60 years old, elects to defer $14,000.

(ii) The ADP test is run for Plan P (after excluding the $3,000 in catch-up contributions from Participant A's elective deferrals), but Plan P needs to take corrective action in order to pass the ADP test. After applying the rules of section 401(k)(8)(C) to allocate the total excess contributions determined under section 401(k)(8)(B), the maximum deferrals which may be retained by any highly compensated employee in Plan P is $12,500.

(iii) Pursuant to paragraph (b)(1)(iii) of this section, the ADP limit under Plan P of $12,500 is an applicable limit. Accordingly, $1,500 of Participant D's elective deferrals exceed the applicable limit. Similarly, $2,500 of Participant A's elective deferrals (other than the $3,000 of elective deferrals treated as catch-up contributions because they exceed the section 401(a)(30) limit) exceed the applicable limit.

(iv) The $1,500 of Participant D's elective deferrals that exceed the applicable limit are less than the applicable dollar catch-up limit and are treated as catch-up contributions. Pursuant to paragraph (d)(2)(iii) of this section, Plan P must retain Participant D's $1,500 in elective deferrals and Plan P is not treated as failing to satisfy section 401(k)(8) merely because the elective deferrals are not distributed to Participant D.

(v) The $2,500 of Participant A's elective deferrals that exceed the applicable limit are greater than the portion of the applicable dollar catch-up limit ($2,000) that remains after treating the $3,000 of elective deferrals in excess of the section 401(a)(30) limit as catch-up contributions. Accordingly, $2,000 of Participant A's elective deferrals are treated as catch-up contributions. Pursuant to paragraph (d)(2)(iii) of this section, Plan P must retain Participant A's $2,000 in elective deferrals and Plan P is not treated as failing to satisfy section 401(k)(8) merely because the elective deferrals are not distributed to Participant A. However, $500 of Participant A's elective deferrals cannot be treated as catch-up contributions and must be distributed to Participant A in order to satisfy section 401(k)(8).

*Example (5).* (i) Participant E is a highly compensated employee who is a catch-up eligible participant under a section 401(k) plan, Plan R, with a plan year ending October 31, 2006. Plan R does not limit elective deferrals except as necessary to comply with section 401(a)(30) and section 415. Plan R permits all catch-up eligible participants to defer an additional amount equal to the applicable dollar catch-up limit for the year ($5,000) in excess of the section 401(a)(30) limit. Participant E did not exceed the section 401(a)(30) limit in 2005 and did not exceed the ADP limit for the plan year ending October 31, 2005. Participant E made $3,200 of deferrals in the period November 1, 2005 through December 31, 2005 and an additional $16,000 of deferrals in the first 10 months of 2006, for a total of $19,200 in elective deferrals for the plan year.

(ii) Once Participant E's elective deferrals for the calendar year 2006 exceed $15,000, subsequent elective deferrals are treated as catch-up contributions at the time they are deferred, provided that such elective deferrals do not exceed the applicable dollar catch-up limit for the taxable year. Since the $1,000 in elective deferrals made after Participant E reaches the section 402(g) limit for the calendar year does not exceed the applicable dollar catch-up limit for 2006, the entire $1,000 is a catch-up contribution. Pursuant to paragraph (d)(2)(i) of this section, $1,000 is subtracted from Participant E's $19,200 in elective deferrals for the plan year ending October 31, 2006 in determining Participant E's ADR for that plan year.

(iii) The ADP test is run for Plan R (after excluding the $1,000 in elective deferrals in excess of the section 401(a)(30) limit), but Plan R needs to take corrective action in order to pass the ADP test. After applying the rules of section 401(k)(8)(C) to allocate the total excess contributions determined under section 401(k)(8)(C), the maximum deferrals that may be retained by any highly compensated employee under Plan R for the plan year ending October 31, 2006 (the ADP limit) is $14,800.

(iv) Under paragraph (d)(2)(ii) of this section, elective deferrals that exceed the section 401(a)(30) limit under Plan R are also subtracted from Participant E's elective deferrals under Plan R for purposes of applying the rules of section 401(k)(8). Accordingly, for purposes of correcting the failed ADP test, Participant E is treated as having contributed $18,200 of elective deferrals in Plan R. The amount of elective deferrals that would have to be distributed to Participant E in order to satisfy section 401(k)(8)(C) is $3,400 ($18,200 minus $14,800), which is less than the excess of the applicable dollar catch-up limit ($5,000) over the elective deferrals previously treated as catch-up contributions under Plan R for the taxable year ($1,000). Under paragraph (d)(2)(iii) of this section, Plan R must retain Participant E's $3,400 in elective deferrals and is not treated as failing to satisfy section 401(k)(8) merely because the elective deferrals are not distributed to Participant E.

(v) Even though Participant E's elective deferrals for the calendar year 2006 have exceeded the section 401(a)(30) limit, Participant E can continue to make elective deferrals during the last 2 months of the calendar year, since Participant E's catch-up contributions for the taxable year are not taken into account in applying the section 401(a)(30) limit for 2006. Thus, Participant E can make an additional contribution of $3,400 ($15,000 minus ($16,000 minus $4,400)) without exceeding the section 401(a)(30) for the calendar year and without regard to any additional catch-up contributions. In addition, Participant E may make additional catch-up contributions of $600 (the $5,000 applicable dollar catch-up limit for 2006, reduced by the $4,400 ($1,000 plus $3,400) of elective deferrals previously treated as catch-up contributions during the taxable year). The $600 of catch-up contributions will not be taken into account in the ADP test for the plan year ending October 31, 2007.

*Example (6).* (i) The facts are the same as in Example 5, except that Participant E exceeded the section 401(a)(30) limit for 2005 by $1,300 prior to October 31, 2005, and made $600 of elective deferrals in the period November 1, 2005, through December 31, 2005 (which were catch-up contributions for 2005). Thus, Participant E made $16,600 of elective deferrals for the plan year ending October 31, 2006.

(ii) Once Participant E's elective deferrals for the calendar year 2006 exceed $15,000, subsequent elective deferrals are treated as catch-up contributions as they are deferred, provided that such elective deferrals do not exceed the applicable dollar catch-up limit for the taxable year. Since the $1,000 in elective deferrals made after Participant E reaches the section 402(g) limit for calendar year 2006 does not exceed the applicable dollar catch-up limit for 2006, the entire $1,000 is a catch-up contribution. Pursuant to paragraph (d)(2)(i) of this section, $1,000 is subtracted from Participant E's elective deferrals in determining Participant E's ADR for the plan year ending October 31, 2006. In addition, the $600 of catch-up contributions from the period November 1, 2005 to December 31, 2005 are subtracted from Participant E's elective deferrals in determining Participant E's ADR. Thus, the total elective deferrals taken into account in determining Participant E's ADR for the plan year ending October 31, 2006, is $15,000 ($16,600 in elective deferrals for the current plan year, less $1,600 in catch-up contributions).

(iii) The ADP test is run for Plan R (after excluding the $1,600 in elective deferrals in excess of the section 401(a)(30) limit), but Plan R needs to take corrective action in order to pass the ADP test. After applying the rules of section 401(k)(8)(C) to allocate the total excess contributions determined under section 401(k)(8)(C), the maximum deferrals that may be retained by any highly compensated employee under Plan R (the ADP limit) is $14,800.

(iv) Under paragraph (d)(2)(ii) of this section, elective deferrals that exceed the section 401(a)(30) limit under Plan R are also subtracted from Participant E's elective deferrals under Plan R for purposes of applying the rules of section 401(k)(8). Accordingly, for purposes of correcting the failed ADP test, Participant E is treated as having contributed $15,000 of elective deferrals in Plan R. The amount of elective deferrals that would have to be distributed to Participant E in order to satisfy section 401(k)(8)(C) is $200 ($15,000 minus $14,800), which is less than the excess of the applicable dollar catch-up limit ($5,000) over the elective deferrals previously treated as catch-up contributions under Plan R for the taxable year ($1,000). Under paragraph (d)(2)(iii) of this section, Plan R must retain Participant E's $200 in elective deferrals and is not treated as failing to satisfy section 401(k)(8) merely because the elective deferrals are not distributed to Participant E.

(v) Even though Participant E's elective deferrals for calendar year 2006 have exceeded the section 401(a)(30) limit, Participant E can continue to make elective deferrals during the last 2 months of the calendar year, since Participant E's catch-up contributions for the taxable year are not taken into account in applying the section 401(a)(30) limit for 2006. Thus Participant E can make an additional contribution of $200 ($15,000 minus ($16,000 minus $1,200)) without exceeding the section 401(a)(30) for the calendar year and without regard to any additional catch-up contributions. In addition, Participant E may make additional catch-up contributions of $3,800 (the $5,000 applicable dollar catch-up limit for 2006, reduced by the $1,200 ($1,000 plus $200) of elective deferrals previously treated as catch-up contributions during the taxable year). The $3,800 of catch-up contributions will not be taken into account in the ADP test for the plan year ending October 31, 2007.

*Example (7).* (i) Participant F, who is 58 years old, is a highly compensated employee who earns $100,000 per year. Participant F participates in a section 401(k) plan, Plan S, for the first 6 months of the year and then transfers to another section 401(k) plan, Plan T, sponsored by the same employer, for the second 6 months of the year. Plan S limits highly compensated employees' elective deferrals to 6% of compensation for the period of participation, but permits catch-up eligible participants to defer amounts in excess of 6% during the plan year, up to the applicable dollar catch-up limit for the year. Plan T limits highly compensated employees' elective deferrals to 8% of compensation for the period of participation, but permits catch-up eligible participants to defer amounts in excess of 8% during the plan year, up to the applicable dollar catch-up limit for the year. Participant F earned $50,000 in the first 6 months of the year and deferred $6,000 under Plan S. Participant F also deferred $6,500 under Plan T.

(ii) As of the last day of the plan year, Participant F has $3,000 in elective deferrals under Plan S that exceed the employer-provided limit of $3,000. Under Plan T, Participant F has $2,500 in elective deferrals that exceed the employer-provided limit of $4,000. The total amount of elective deferrals in excess of employer-provided limits, $5,500, exceeds the applicable dollar catch-up limit by $500. Accordingly, $500 of the elective deferrals in excess of the employer-provided limits are not catch-up contributions and are treated as regular elective deferrals (and are taken into account in the ADP test). The determination of which elective deferrals in excess of an applicable limit are treated as catch-up contributions is permitted to be made in any manner that is not inconsistent with the manner in which such amounts were actually deferred under Plan S and Plan T.

*Example (8).* (i) Employer X sponsors Plan P, which provides for matching contributions equal to 50% of elective deferrals that do not exceed 10% of compensation. Elective deferrals for highly compensated employees are limited, on a payroll-by-payroll basis, to 10% of compensation. Employer X pays employees on a monthly basis. Plan P also provides that elective contributions are limited in accordance with section 401(a)(30) and other applicable statutory limits. Plan P also provides for catch-up contributions. Under Plan P, for purposes of calculating the amount to be treated as catch-up contributions (and to be excluded from the ADP test), amounts in excess of the 10% limit for highly compensated employees are determined at the end of the plan year based on compensation used for purposes of ADP testing (testing compensation), a definition of compensation that is different from the definition used under the plan for purposes of calculating elective deferrals and matching contributions during the plan year (deferral compensation).

(ii) Participant A, a highly compensated employee, is a catch-up eligible participant under Plan P with deferral compensation of $10,000 per monthly payroll period. Participant A defers 10% per payroll period for the first 10 months of the year, and is allocated a matching contribution each payroll period of $500. In addition, Participant A defers an additional $4,000 during the first 10 months of the year. Participant A then reduces deferrals during the last 2 months of the year to 5% of compensation. Participant A is allocated a matching contribution of $250 for each of the last 2 months of the plan year. For the plan year, Participant A has $15,000 in elective deferrals and $5,500 in matching contributions.

(iii) A's testing compensation is $118,000. At the end of the plan year, based on 10% of testing compensation, or $11,800, Plan P determines that A has $3,200 in deferrals that exceed the 10% employer provided limit. Plan P excludes $3,200 from ADP testing and calculates A's ADR as $11,800 divided by $118,000, or 10%. Although A has not been allocated a matching contribution equal to 50% of $11,800, because Plan P provides that matching contributions are calculated based on elective deferrals during a payroll period as a percentage of deferral compensation, Plan P is not required to allocate an additional $400 of matching contributions to A.

**(i) Effective date.** *(1) Statutory effective date.* Section 414(v) applies to contributions in taxable years beginning on or after January 1, 2002.

*(2) Regulatory effective date.* Paragraphs (a) through (h) of this section apply to contributions in taxable years beginning on or after January 1, 2004.

T.D. 9072, 7/7/2003.

### § 1.414(w)-1 Permissible Withdrawals From Eligible Automatic Contribution Arrangements.

**(a) Overview.** Section 414(w) provides rules under which certain employees are permitted to elect to make a withdrawal of default elective contributions from an eligible automatic contribution arrangement. This section sets forth the rules applicable to permissible withdrawals from an eligible automatic contribution arrangement within the meaning of section 414(w). Paragraph (b) of this section defines an eligible automatic contribution arrangement. Paragraph (c) of this section describes a permissible withdrawal and addresses which employees are eligible to elect a withdrawal, the timing of the withdrawal election, and the amount of the withdrawal. Paragraph (d) of this section describes the tax and other consequences of the withdrawal. Paragraph (e) of this section includes the definitions applicable to this section.

**(b) Eligible automatic contribution arrangement.** *(1) In general.* An eligible automatic contribution arrangement is an automatic contribution arrangement under an applicable employer plan that is intended to be an eligible automatic contribution arrangement for the plan year and that satisfies the uniformity requirement under paragraph (b)(2) of this section, and the notice requirement under paragraph (b)(3) of this section. An eligible automatic contribution arrangement need not cover all employees who are eligible to elect to have contributions made on their behalf under the applicable employer plan.

*(2) Uniformity requirement.* (i) In general. An eligible automatic contribution arrangement must provide that the default elective contribution is a uniform percentage of compensation.

(ii) Exception to uniform percentage requirement. An arrangement does not violate the uniformity requirement of paragraph (b)(2)(i) of this section merely because the percentage varies in a manner that is permitted under § 1.401(k)-3(j)(2)(iii), except that the rule of § 1.401(k)-3(j)(2)(iii)(B) is applied without regard to whether the arrangement is intended to be a qualified automatic contribution arrangement.

(iii) Rules of application. For purposes of this paragraph (b)(2), all automatic contribution arrangements that are intended to be eligible automatic contribution arrangements within a plan (or within the disaggregated plan under § 1.410(b)-7, in the case of a plan subject to section 410(b)) are aggregated. Thus, for example, if a single plan within the meaning of section 414(l) covering employees in two separate divisions has two different automatic contribution arrangements that are intended to be eligible automatic contributions arrangements, the two automatic contribution arrangements can constitute eligible automatic contribution arrangements only if the default elective contributions under the arrangements are the same percentage of compensation. However, if the different automatic contribution arrangements cover employees in portions of the plan that are mandatorily disaggregated under the rules of section 410(b), then there is no requirement to aggregate those automatic contribution arrangements under the uniformity requirements of this paragraph (b)(2).

*(3) Notice requirement.* (i) General rule. The notice requirement of this paragraph (b)(3) is satisfied for a plan year if each covered employee is given notice of the employee's rights and obligations under the arrangement. The notice must be sufficiently accurate and comprehensive to apprise the employee of such rights and obligations, and be written in a manner calculated to be understood by the average employee to whom the arrangement applies. The notice must be in writing; however, see § 1.401(a)-21 for rules permitting the use of electronic media to provide applicable notices.

(ii) Content requirement. The notice must include the provisions found in § 1.401(k)-3(d)(2)(ii) to the extent those provisions apply to the arrangement. A notice is not considered sufficiently accurate and comprehensive unless the notice accurately describes—

(A) The level of the default elective contributions which will be made on the employee's behalf if the employee does not make an affirmative election;

(B) The employee's rights to elect not to have default elective contributions made to the plan on his or her behalf or to have a different percentage of compensation or different amount of contribution made to the plan on his or her behalf;

(C) How contributions made under the arrangement will be invested in the absence of any investment election by the employee; and

(D) The employee's rights to make a permissible withdrawal, if applicable, and the procedures to elect such a withdrawal.

(iii) Timing. (A) General rule. The timing requirement of this paragraph (b)(3)(iii) is satisfied if the notice is provided within a reasonable period before the beginning of each plan year or, in the plan year the employee is first eligible to make a cash or deferred election (or first becomes covered under the automatic contribution arrangement as a result of a change in employment status), within a reasonable period before the employee becomes a covered employee. In addition, a notice satisfies the timing requirements of paragraph (b)(3) of this section only if it is provided sufficiently early so that the employee has a reasonable period of time after receipt of the notice in order to make the election described under paragraph (e)(2)(i) or (e)(2)(ii) of this section.

(B) Deemed satisfaction of timing requirement. The timing requirement of this paragraph (b)(3)(iii) is satisfied if at least 30 days (and no more than 90 days) before the beginning of each plan year, the notice is given to each employee covered under the automatic contribution arrangement for the plan year. In the case of an employee who does not receive the notice within the period described in the previous sentence because the employee becomes eligible to make a cash or deferred election (or becomes covered under the automatic contribution arrangement as a result of a change in employment status) after the 90th day before the beginning of the plan year, the timing requirement is deemed to be satisfied if the notice is provided no more than 90 days before the employee becomes eligible to make a cash or deferred election (or becomes covered under the automatic contribution arrangement as a result of a change in employment status), and no later than the date that affords the employee a reasonable period of time after receipt of the notice to make the election described under paragraph (e)(2)(i) or (e)(2)(ii) of this section. If it is not practicable for the notice to be provided on or before the date specified in the plan that an employee becomes eligible to make a cash or deferred election, the notice will nonetheless be treated as provided timely if it is provided as soon as practicable after that date and the employee is permitted to elect to defer from all types of compensation that may be deferred under the plan earned beginning on that date.

**(c) Permissible withdrawal.** *(1) In general.* If the plan so provides, any employee who has default elective contributions made under the eligible automatic contribution arrangement may elect to make a withdrawal of such contributions (and earnings attributable thereto) in accordance with the requirements of this paragraph (c). An applicable employer plan that includes an eligible automatic contribution arrangement will not fail to satisfy the prohibition on in-service withdrawals under section 401(k)(2)(B), 403(b)(7), 403(b)(11), or 457(d)(1) merely because it permits withdrawals that satisfy the timing requirement of paragraph (c)(2) of this section and the amount requirement of paragraph (c)(3) of this section.

*(2) Timing.* (i) Last date to make election. A covered employee's election to withdraw default elective contributions must be made no later than 90 days after the date of the first default elective contribution under the eligible automatic contribution arrangement and must be effective no later than the date set forth in paragraph (c)(2)(iii) of this section. A plan is permitted to set an earlier deadline for making this election, but if a plan provides that a covered employee may withdraw default elective contributions, then the election period for the covered employee must be at least 30 days.

(ii) Determination of date of first default elective contribution. For purposes of this paragraph (c)(2), the date of the first default elective contribution is the date that the compensation that is subject to the cash or deferred election would otherwise have been included in gross income.

(iii) Latest effective date of the election. The effective date of an election described in this paragraph (c)(2) cannot be after the earlier of—

(A) The pay date for the second payroll period that begins after the date the election is made; and

(B) The first pay date that occurs at least 30 days after the election is made.

(iv) Special rules. (A) Treatment of periods without default elective contributions. For purposes of determining the date of the first default elective contribution under the eligible automatic contribution arrangement, a plan is permitted to treat an employee who for an entire plan year did not have default elective contributions made under the eligible automatic contribution arrangement as if the employee had not had such contributions for any prior plan year as well.

(B) Treatment relating to aggregation of arrangements. The determination of whether an election is made no later than 90 days after the date of the first default elective contribution under the eligible automatic contribution arrangement must take into account any other eligible automatic contribution arrangement that is required to be aggregated with the eligible automatic contribution arrangement under the rules of paragraph (b)(2)(iii) of this section.

*(3) Amount and timing of distributions.* (i) In general. A distribution satisfies the requirement of this paragraph (c)(3) if the distribution is equal to the amount of default elective contributions made under the eligible automatic contribution arrangement through the effective date of the election described in paragraph (c)(2) of this section (adjusted for allocable gains and losses to the date of distribution). If default elective contributions are separately accounted for in the participant's account, the amount of the distribution will be the total amount in that account. However, if default elective contributions are not separately accounted for under the plan, the amount of the allocable gains and losses will be determined under rules similar to those provided under § 1.401(k)-2(b)(2)(iv) for the distribution of excess contributions.

(ii) Fees. The distribution amount as determined under this paragraph (c)(3) may be reduced by any generally applicable fees. However, the plan may not charge a higher fee for a distribution under section 414(w) than would apply to any other distributions of cash.

(iii) Date of distribution. The distribution must be made in accordance with the plan's ordinary timing procedures for processing distributions and making distributions.

**(d) Consequences of the withdrawal.** *(1) Income tax consequences.* (i) Year of inclusion. The amount of the withdrawal is includible in the eligible employee's gross income for the taxable year in which the distribution is made. However, any portion of the distribution consisting of designated Roth contributions is not included in an employee's gross income a second time. The portion of the withdrawal that is treated as an investment in the contract is determined without regard to any plan contributions other than those distributed as a withdrawal of default elective contributions.

(ii) No additional tax on early distributions from qualified retirement plans. The withdrawal is not subject to the additional tax under section 72(t).

(iii) Reporting. The amount of the withdrawal is reported on Form 1099-R, "Distributions From Pensions, Annuities, Retirement or Profit-Sharing Plans, IRAs, Insurance Contracts, etc.," as described in the applicable instructions.

(iv) Disregarded for purposes of section 402(g). The amount of the withdrawal is not taken into account in determining the limitation on elective deferrals under section 402(g).

*(2) Forfeiture of matching contributions.* In the case of any withdrawal made under paragraph (c) of this section, employer matching contributions with respect to the amount withdrawn that have been allocated to the participant's account (adjusted for allocable gains and losses) must be forfeited. A plan is permitted to provide that employer matching contributions will not be made with respect to any withdrawal made under paragraph (c) of this section if the withdrawal has been made prior to the date as of which the match would otherwise be allocated.

*(3) Consent rules.* A withdrawal made under paragraph (c) of this section may be made without regard to any notice or consent otherwise required under section 401(a)(11) or 417.

**(e) Definitions.** Unless indicated otherwise, the following definitions apply for purposes of section 414(w) and this section.

*(1) Applicable employer plan.* An applicable employer plan means a plan that—

(i) Is qualified under section 401(a);

(ii) Satisfies the requirements of section 403(b);

(iii) Is a section 457(b) eligible governmental plan described in § 1.457-2(f);

(iv) Is a simplified employee pension the terms of which provide for a salary reduction arrangement described in section 408(k)(6); or

(v) Is a SIMPLE described in section 408(p).

*(2) Automatic contribution arrangement.* An automatic contribution arrangement means an arrangement that provides for a cash or deferred election and which specifies that, in the absence of a covered employee's affirmative election, a default election applies under which the employee is treated as having elected to have default elective contributions made on his or her behalf under the plan. The default election begins to apply with respect to an eligible employee no earlier than a reasonable period of time after receipt of the notice describing the automatic contribution arrangement. This default election ceases to apply with respect to an eligible employee for periods of time with respect to which the employee has an affirmative election that is currently in effect to—

(i) Not have any default elective contributions made on his or her behalf; or

(ii) Have contributions made in a different amount or percentage of compensation.

*(3) Covered employee.* Covered employee means an employee who is covered under the automatic contribution arrangement, determined under the terms of the plan. A plan must provide whether an employee who makes an affirmative election remains a covered employee. If a plan provides that an employee who makes an affirmative election described in paragraph (e)(2)(i) or (e)(2)(ii) of this section remains a covered employee, then the employee must continue to receive the notice described in paragraph (b)(3) of this section and the plan may be eligible for the excise tax relief with respect to excess amounts distributed within 6 months after the end of the plan year under section 4979(f)(1). Such an employee will also have the default election reapply if the plan provides that the employee's prior affirmative election no longer remains in effect and the employee does not make a new affirmative election.

*(4) Default elective contributions.* Default elective contributions means the contributions that are made at a specified level or amount under an automatic contribution arrangement in the absence of a covered employee's affirmative election that are—

(i) Contributions described in section 402(g)(3); or

(ii) Contributions made to an eligible governmental plan within the meaning of § 1.457-2(f) that would be elective contributions if they were made under a qualified plan.

**(f) Effective/applicability date.** *(1) Statutory effective date.* Section 414(w) applies to plan years beginning on or after January 1, 2008.

*(2) Regulatory effective date.* This section applies to plan years beginning on or after January 1, 2010. For plan years that begin in 2008, a plan must operate in accordance with a good faith interpretation of section 414(w). For this purpose, a plan that operates in accordance with this section will be treated as operating in accordance with a good faith interpretation of section 414(w).

---

T.D. 9447, 2/23/2009.

---

PAR. 6. Section 1.415-1 is amended by removing paragraph (c) and paragraph (f)(3).

**Proposed § 1.415-1 [Amended]** [*For Preamble, see ¶ 150,933*]

PAR. 7. Section 1.415-2 is amended by removing paragraph (b)(8).

**Proposed § 1.415-2 [Amended]** [*For Preamble, see ¶ 150,933*]

PAR. 8. Section 1.415-6 is amended by:

*(1)* Revising paragraph (b)(3) to read as set forth below, (2) removing paragraph (b)(7)(iv), and (3) adding a new paragraph (b)(8) to read as set forth below.

**Proposed § 1.415-6 Limitation for defined contribution plans.** [*For Preamble, see ¶ 150,933*]

* * * * *

**(b) Annual additions.** * * *

*(3) Employee contributions.* For purposes of subparagraph (1)(ii) of this paragraph, the term "annual additions" includes, to the extent employee contributions would otherwise be taken into account under this section as an annual addition, mandatory employee contributions (as defined in section 411(c)(2)(C) and the regulations thereunder) as well as voluntary employee contributions. The term "annual additions" does not include—

(i) Rollover contributions (as defined in section 402(a)(5), 403(a)(4), 403(b)(8), 405(d)(3), 408(d)(3) and 409(b)(3)(C)),

(ii) Repayments of loans made to a participant from the plan,

(iii) Repayments of amounts described in section 411(a)(7)(B) (in accordance with section 411(a)(7)(C)) and section 411(a)(3)(D) (see § 1.411(a)(7)(d)(6)(iii)(B)),

(iv) The direct transfer of employee contributions from one qualified plan to another,

(v) Employee contributions to a simplified employee pension allowable as a deduction under section 219(a), or

(vi) Deductible employee contributions within the meaning of section 72(o)(5).

However, the Commissioner may in an appropriate case, considering all of the facts and circumstances, treat transactions between the plan and the employee or certain allocations to participants' accounts as giving rise to annual additions.

* * * * *

*(8) Qualified voluntary employee contributions.* This subparagraph provides rules for qualified voluntary employee contributions that are eligible for the deduction under section 219(a). This subparagraph is applicable only if the total of such contributions for the year is not in excess of $2,000. If such contributions are not deductible under section 219, and result in an annual addition that causes the section 415 limits to be exceeded, they will not be treated as annual additions to the extent that the portion of the contribution exceeding the limitation (and earnings thereon) is returned to the employee as soon as administratively feasible after the employer knows or has reason to know that such contributions are not deductible employee contributions within the meaning of section 72(o)(5).

* * * * *

PAR. 9. Section 1.415-7 is amended by:

(1) Removing paragraph (c)(2)(iii), (2) redesignating paragraph (c)(2)(iv) as paragraph (c)(2)(iii), and (3) removing paragraph (i).

**Proposed § 1.415-7 [Amended]** [*For Preamble, see ¶ 150,933*]

PAR. 12. Section 1.415-8 is amended by adding at the end thereof new paragraph (i).

**Proposed § 1.415-8 Combining and aggregating plans.** [*For Preamble, see ¶ 150,703*]

* * * * *

**(i) Special aggregation rule for simplified employee pension.** For purposes of section 415 and this section, any contribution made by an employer to a simplified employee pension (as defined in section 408(k)) of an individual for a calendar year shall be treated as an employer contribution to a defined contribution plan maintained by that employer. This paragraph shall apply to taxable years beginning after December 31, 1980.

PAR. 3. Paragraph (c) of § 1.415-8 is amended by adding "or by an affiliated service group (within the meaning of section 414(m)" before the words "is deemed maintained."

**Proposed § 1.415-8 [Amended]** [*For Preamble, see ¶ 150,825*]

**§ 1.415(a)-1 General rules with respect to limitations on benefits and contributions under qualified plans.**

**(a) Trusts.** Under sections 415 and 401(a)(16), a trust that forms part of a pension, profit-sharing, or stock bonus plan will not be qualified under section 401(a) if any of the following conditions exists:

*(1)* In the case of a defined benefit plan, the annual benefit with respect to any participant for any limitation year exceeds the limitations of section 415(b) and § 1.415(b)-1.

*(2)* In the case of a defined contribution plan, the annual additions credited with respect to any participant for any limitation year exceed the limitations of section 415(c) and § 1.415(c)-1.

*(3)* The trust has been disqualified under section 415(g) and § 1.415(g)-1 for any year.

**(b) Certain annuities and accounts.** *(1) In general.* Under section 415, an employee annuity plan described in section 403(a), an annuity contract described in section 403(b), or a simplified employee pension described in section 408(k) will not be considered to be described in the otherwise applicable section if any of the following conditions exists:

(i) The annual benefit under a defined benefit plan with respect to any participant for any limitation year exceeds the limitations of section 415(b) and § 1.415(b)-1.

(ii) The contributions and other additions credited under a defined contribution plan with respect to any participant for any limitation year exceed the limitations of section 415(c) and § 1.415(c)-1.

(iii) The employee annuity plan, annuity contract, or simplified employee pension has been disqualified under section 415(g) and § 1.415(g)-1 for any year.

*(2) Special rule for section 403(b) annuity contracts.* If the contributions and other additions under an annuity contract that otherwise satisfies the requirements of section 403(b) exceed the limitations of section 415(c) and § 1.415(c)-1 with respect to any participant for any limitation year (regardless of whether the annuity contract is a defined contribution plan or a defined benefit plan), then the portion of the contract that includes such excess annual addition fails to be a section 403(b) annuity contract, and the remaining portion of the contract is a section 403(b) annuity contract. However, the status of the remaining portion of the contract as a section 403(b) annuity contract is not retained unless, for the year of the excess and each year thereafter, the issuer of the contract maintains separate accounts for each such portion. In addition, if the benefit under an annuity contract that is a defined benefit plan and that otherwise satisfies the requirements of section 403(b) exceeds the limitations of section 415(b) and § 1.415(b)-1 with respect to any participant for any limitation year, then the contract fails to be a section 403(b) annuity contract.

*(3) Section 403(b) annuity contract.* For purposes of section 415 and regulations promulgated under section 415, the term section 403(b) annuity contract includes arrangements that are treated as annuity contracts for purposes of section 403(b). Thus, such term includes custodial accounts described in section 403(b)(7) and retirement income accounts described in section 403(b)(9).

**(c) Regulations.** *(1) In general.* This section provides general rules regarding the application of section 415. For further rules regarding the application of section 415, see—

(i) Section 1.415(b)-1 (for general rules regarding the limits applicable to defined benefit plans);

(ii) Section 1.415(b)-2 (for special rules for defined benefit plans where a participant has multiple annuity starting dates);

(iii) Section 1.415(c)-1 (for general rules regarding the limits applicable to defined contribution plans);

(iv) Section 1.415(c)-2 (for rules regarding the definition of compensation for purposes of section 415);

(v) Section 1.415(d)-1 (for rules regarding cost-of-living adjustments to the various limits of section 415);

(vi) Section 1.415(f)-1 (for rules for aggregating plans for purposes of section 415);

(vii) Section 1.415(g)-1 (for rules regarding disqualification of plans that fail to satisfy the requirements of section 415); and

(viii) Section 1.415(j)-1 (for rules regarding limitation years).

*(2) Cross references to special rules for section 403(b) annuity contracts.* For special rules relating to section 403(b) annuity contracts, see—

(i) Section 1.415(c)-2(g)(1) and (3) (relating to the definition of compensation for section 403(b) annuity contracts);

(ii) Section 1.415(f)-1(f) (relating to rules for section 403(b) annuity contracts for purposes of aggregating plans);

(iii) Section 1.415(g)-1(b)(3)(iv)(C) (regarding disqualification of a section 403(b) annuity contract aggregated with a qualified defined contribution plan if the aggregated plans exceed the limitations of section 415(c));

(iv) Section 1.415(g)-1(c) (relating to the plan year for section 403(b) annuity contracts); and

(v) Section 1.415(j)-1(e) (relating to the limitation year for section 403(b) annuity contracts).

*(3) Cross references to special rules for governmental plans.* For special rules relating to governmental plans, see—

(i) Paragraph (f)(4) of this section (regarding permissive service credits);

(ii) Paragraph (g)(2) of this section (providing a delayed effective date for governmental plans);

(iii) Section 1.415(b)-1(a)(6)(i) (providing an exception from the compensation-based limit of section 415(b)(1)(B) for governmental plans);

(iv) Section 1.415(b)-1(a)(7)(ii) (regarding a special limitation for certain governmental plans making an election during 1990);

(v) Section 1.415(b)-1(b)(4) (regarding qualified governmental excess benefit arrangements);

(vi) Section 1.415(b)-1(d)(3) and (4) (regarding age adjustments to the dollar limit of section 415(b)(1)(A) for employees of police and fire departments and members of the Armed Forces of the United States, and for survivor and disability benefits);

(vii) Section 1.415(b)-1(g)(3) (regarding adjustments to applicable limitations for years of participation, and adjustments to applicable limitations for years of service for survivor and disability benefits under governmental plans);

(viii) Section 1.415(c)-1(b)(2)(ii) and (3)(iii) (regarding amounts not treated as annual additions under governmental plans); and

(ix) Section 1.415(c)-2(e)(5) (providing an alternative rule for inclusion of compensation after a severance from employment for governmental plans).

*(4) Cross references to special rules for multiemployer plans.* For special rules relating to multiemployer plans as defined in section 414(f), see—

(i) Paragraph (e) of this section (regarding benefits or contributions taken into account where a plan is maintained by more than one employer);

(ii) Paragraph (f)(5)(ii) of this section (providing a special definition of severance from employment for multiemployer plans);

(iii) Section 1.415(b)-1(a)(6)(ii) (providing an exception from the compensation-based limit for multiemployer plans);

(iv) Section 1.415(b)-1(f)(3) (regarding the application of the minimum $10,000 limitation on benefits in the case of a multiemployer plan);

(v) Section 1.415(f)-1(g) (providing special rules for aggregating multiemployer plans with other plans); and

(vi) Section 1.415(g)-1(b)(3)(ii) (regarding plan disqualification rules where a multiemployer plan is aggregated with a plan that is not a multiemployer plan and the aggregated plans exceed the limitations of section 415).

*(5) Cross references to special rules for plans that are not subject to the requirements of section 411.* For special rules relating to plans that are not subject to the requirements of section 411, see—

(i) Paragraph (d)(1) of this section and § 1.415(b)-1(a)(7)(iii) (providing that the rule limiting accruals to the section 415(b) limits does not apply to plans that are not subject to the requirements of section 411); and

(ii) Section 1.415(b)-1(b)(2)(iii) (providing rules for applying the section 411(c) factors in determining the annual benefit attributable to employee contributions for plans that are not subject to the requirements of section 411).

*(6) Cross references to special rules for plans maintained by churches.* For special rules relating to plans maintained by churches as defined in section 3121(w)(3)(A), see §§ 1.415(b)-1(a)(6)(iv) and 1.415(b)-1(a)(7)(iv) (providing an exception from the compensation-based limit for participants who have never been a highly compensated employee of the church).

**(d) Plan provisions.** *(1) In general.* Although no specific plan provision is required under section 415 in order for a plan to establish or maintain its qualification, the plan provisions must preclude the possibility that any distribution under a defined benefit plan or annual addition under a defined contribution plan will exceed the limitations of section 415. In addition, a defined benefit plan that is subject to the requirements of section 411 must preclude the possibility that any accrual under the plan will exceed the limitations of section 415. A defined benefit plan may include provisions that automatically freeze or reduce the rate of benefit accrual (or limit the benefit payable in the case of a plan that is not subject to the requirements of section 411), and a defined contribution plan may include provisions that automatically limit the annual addition to a level necessary to prevent the limitations of section 415 from being exceeded with respect to any participant. For rules relating to this type of plan provision and the definitely determinable benefit requirement for pension plans, see § 1.401(a)-1(b)(1)(iii). Because § 1.401(a)-1(b)(1)(iii) requires that the operation of such a provision preclude discretion by the employer, if two defined benefit plans that are aggregated under the rules of section 415(f) would otherwise provide for aggregate benefits that might exceed the limits of section 415(b), the plan provisions must specify (without involving employer discretion) how benefits will be limited to prevent a violation of section 415(b).

*(2) Special rule for profit-sharing and stock bonus plans.* A provision of a profit-sharing or stock bonus plan that automatically freezes or reduces the amount of annual additions to ensure that the limitations of section 415 will not be exceeded must comply with the requirement set forth in § 1.401-1(b)(1)(ii) or (iii) (as applicable) that such plans provide a definite predetermined formula for allocating the contributions made to the plan among the participants. If the operation of a provision that automatically freezes or reduces the amount of annual additions to ensure that the limitations of section 415 are not exceeded does not involve discretionary action on the part of the employer, the definite predetermined allocation formula requirement is not violated by the provision. If the operation of such a provision involves discretionary action on the part of the employer, the definite predetermined allocation formula requirement is violated. For example, if two profit-sharing plans of one employer otherwise provide for aggregate contributions which may exceed the limits of section 415(c), the plan provisions must specify (without involving employer discretion) under which plan contributions and allocations will be reduced to prevent an excess annual addition and how the reduction will occur.

*(3) Incorporation by reference.* (i) In general. A plan is permitted to incorporate by reference the limitations of section 415, and will not fail to meet the definitely determinable benefit requirement or the definite predetermined allocation formula requirement, whichever applies to the plan, merely because it incorporates the limits of section 415 by reference.

(ii) Section 415 can be applied in more than one manner, but a statutory or regulatory default rule exists. Where a provision of section 415 is permitted to be applied in more than one manner but is to be applied in a specified manner in the absence of contrary plan provisions (in other words, a default rule exists), if a plan incorporates the limitations of section 415 by reference with respect to that provision of section 415 and does not specifically vary from the default rule, then the default rule applies. With respect to a provision of section 415 for which a default rule exists, if the limitations of section 415 are to be applied in a manner other than using the default rule, the plan must specify the manner in which the limitation is to be applied in addition to generally incorporating the limitations of section 415 by reference. For example, if a plan generally incorporates the limitations of section 415 by reference and does not restrict the accrued benefits to which the amendments to section 415(b)(2)(E) made by the Uruguay Round Agreements Act of 1994, Public Law 103-465 (108 Stat. 4809) (GATT), apply (as permitted by Q&A-12 of Rev. Rul. 98-1 (1998-1 CB 249) (see § 601.601(d)(2) of this chapter), which reflects the amendments to section 767 of GATT made by section 1449 of the Small Business Job Protection Act of 1996, Public Law 104-188 (110 Stat. 1755)), then the amendments to section 415(b)(2)(E) made by GATT apply to all benefits under the plan.

(iii) Section 415 can be applied in more than one manner with no statutory or regulatory default. If a limitation of section 415 may be applied in more than one manner, and if there is no governing principle pursuant to which that limitation is applied in the absence of contrary plan provisions, then the plan must specify the manner in which the limitation is to be applied in addition to generally incorporating the limitations of section 415 by reference. For example, if an employer maintains two profit-sharing plans, and if any participant participates in more than one such plan, then both plans must specify (in a consistent manner) under which of the employer's two profit-sharing plans annual additions must be reduced if aggregate annual additions would otherwise exceed the limitations of section 415(c)).

(iv) Former requirements. A plan is not permitted to incorporate by reference formerly applicable requirements of section 415 that are no longer in force (such as the limits of former section 415(e)).

(v) Cost-of-living adjustments. (A) In general. A plan is permitted to incorporate by reference the annual adjustments to the limitations of section 415 that are made pursuant to section 415(d). See § 1.415(d)-1 for additional rules relating to cost-of-living adjustments under section 415(d).

(B) Cost-of-living adjustments not included in accrued benefit until effective. Notwithstanding that a plan incorporates the increases to the applicable limits under section 415(d) by reference, the accrued benefit of a participant for purposes of section 411 and any amount payable to a participant for purposes of § 1.415(b)-1(a)(1) are not permitted to reflect increases pursuant to the annual increase under section 415(d) of the dollar limitation described in section 415(b)(1)(A) or the compensation limit described in section 415(b)(1)(B) for any period before the annual increase becomes effective. See § 1.415(d)-1(a)(3) for rules relating to when the annual adjustments to the dollar and compensation limitations are effective. A plan amendment does not violate the requirements of section 411(d)(6) merely because it eliminates the incorporation by reference of the increases under section 415(d) with respect to increases that have not yet occurred.

(C) Application of increase in defined benefit dollar limit to participants who have incurred a severance from employment or commenced receiving benefits. If a plan incorporates by reference the annual adjustments to the limitations of section 415 pursuant to this paragraph (d)(3)(v), the plan will be treated as applying the section 415(d) cost-of-living adjustments to the maximum extent permitted under the safe harbor described in § 1.415(d)-1(a)(5), except to the extent provided in this paragraph (d)(3)(v)(C). Thus, such a plan is not subject to the requirements of § 1.415(b)-1(b)(1)(iii) (providing special rules for determining the annual benefit of an employee in the case of multiple annuity starting dates) with respect to benefit increases that result solely from an increase in the section 415(b) limits pursuant to section 415(d). If a plan incorporates by reference the annual adjustments to the limitations of section 415 pursuant to this paragraph (d)(3)(v), the annual increase under section 415(d) of the dollar limitation described in section 415(b)(1)(A) does not apply with respect to a participant if the increase is effective after the participant's severance from employment with the employer maintaining the plan (or, if earlier, after the annuity starting date in the case of a participant who has commenced receiving benefits), unless the plan specifies that this annual increase applies. Similarly, if a plan incorporates by reference the annual adjustments to the limitations of section 415 pursuant to this paragraph (d)(3)(v), the annual increase under section 415(d) of the compensation-based limitation described in section 415(b)(1)(B) does not apply with respect to a participant for increases that are effective after the participant's severance from employment with the employer maintaining the plan (or, if earlier, after the annuity starting date in the case of a participant who has commenced receiving benefits), unless the plan specifies that this annual increase applies.

(D) Treatment of cost-of-living adjustments for funding and deduction purposes. In general, the annual increase under section 415(d) of the dollar limitation described in section 415(b)(1)(A) and the compensation limitation described in section 415(b)(1)(B) is treated as a plan amendment, regardless of whether the plan reflects the increase automatically through operation of plan provisions in accordance with this paragraph (d)(3)(v) or the plan is amended to reflect the increase (pursuant to § 1.415(d)-1(a)(5)). However, where a plan reflects the annual increase under section 415(d) of the dollar limitation described in section 415(b)(1)(A) or the compensation limitation described in section 415(b)(1)(B) automatically through operation of plan provisions pursuant to this paragraph (d)(3)(v), the funding method for the plan is permitted to provide for this annual increase to be treated as an experience loss for purposes of applying sections 404, 412, and 431.

**(e) Rules for plans maintained by more than one employer.** Except as provided in § 1.415(f)-1(g)(2)(i) (regarding aggregation of multiemployer plans with plans other than multiemployer plans), for purposes of applying the limitations of section 415 with respect to a participant in a plan maintained by more than one employer, benefits and contributions attributable to such participant from all of the employers maintaining the plan must be taken into account. Furthermore, in applying the limitations of section 415 with respect to a participant in such a plan, the total compensation received by the participant from all of the employers maintaining the plan is taken into account under the plan, unless the plan specifies otherwise.

**(f) Special rules.** *(1) Affiliated employers.* Pursuant to section 414(b) and § 1.414(b)-1, all employees of all corporations that are members of a controlled group of corporations (within the meaning of section 1563(a), as modified by section 1563(f)(5), and determined without regard to section 1563(a)(4) and (e)(3)(C)) are treated as employed by a single employer for purposes of section 415. Similarly, pursuant to section 414(c) and regulations promulgated under section

414(c), all employees of trades or businesses that are under common control are treated as employed by a single employer. Thus, any defined benefit plan or defined contribution plan maintained by any member of a controlled group of corporations (within the meaning of section 414(b)) or by any trade or business (whether or not incorporated) that is part of a group of trades or businesses that are under common control (within the meaning of section 414(c)) is deemed maintained by all such members or such trades or businesses. Pursuant to section 415(h), for purposes of section 415, sections 414(b) and 414(c) are applied by using the phrase "more than 50 percent" instead of the phrase "at least 80 percent" each place the latter phrase appears in section 1563(a)(1) and in the regulations under section 414(c) (except for purposes of determining whether two or more organizations are a brother-sister group of trades or businesses under common control under the rules in § 1.414(c)-2(c)).

*(2) Affiliated service groups.* Any defined benefit plan or defined contribution plan maintained by any member of an affiliated service group (within the meaning of section 414(m)) is deemed maintained by all members of that affiliated service group.

*(3) Leased employees.* (i) In general. Pursuant to section 414(n), except as provided in paragraph (f)(3)(ii) of this section, with respect to any person (referred to as the recipient) for whom a leased employee (within the meaning of section 414(n)(2)) performs services, the leased employee is treated as an employee of the recipient, but contributions or benefits provided by the leasing organization that are attributable to services performed for the recipient are treated as provided under a plan maintained by the recipient.

(ii) Exception for leased employees covered by safe harbor plans. Pursuant to section 414(n)(5), the rule of paragraph (f)(3)(i) of this section does not apply to a leased employee with respect to services performed for a recipient if—

(A) The leased employee is covered by a plan that is maintained by the leasing organization and that meets the requirements of section 414(n)(5)(B); and

(B) Leased employees (determined without regard to this paragraph (f)(3)(ii)) do not constitute more than 20 percent of the recipient's nonhighly compensated workforce.

*(4) Permissive service credit under governmental plans.* See section 415(n) for rules regarding the application of the limitations of sections 415(b) and (c) where a participant makes contributions (including a transfer described in section 403(b)(13) or section 457(e)(17)) to a defined benefit governmental plan to purchase permissive service credit under the plan.

*(5) Definition of severance from employment.* (i) General rule. For purposes of this section and §§ 1.415(b)-1, 1.415(b)-2, 1.415(c)-1, 1.415(c)-2, 1.415(d)-1, 1.415(f)-1, 1.415(g)-1, and 1.415(j)-1, whether an employee has a severance from employment with the employer that maintains a plan is determined in the same manner as under § 1.401(k)-1(d)(2) except that, for purposes of determining the employer of an employee, the modifications provided under section 415(h) (described in paragraph (f)(1) of this section) to the employer aggregation rules apply. Thus, an employee has a severance from employment when the employee ceases to be an employee of the employer maintaining the plan, and an employee does not have a severance from employment if, in connection with a change of employment, the employee's new employer maintains such plan with respect to the employee. The determination of whether an employee ceases to be an employee of the employer maintaining the plan is based on all of the relevant facts and circumstances.

(ii) Multiemployer plans. A participant in a multiemployer plan (within the meaning of section 414(f)) is not treated as having incurred a severance from employment with the employer maintaining the multiemployer plan for purposes of this section and §§ 1.415(b)-1, 1.415(b)-2, 1.415(c)-1, 1.415(c)-2, 1.415(d)-1, 1.415(f)-1, 1.415(g)-1, and 1.415(j)-1 if the participant continues to be an employee of another employer maintaining the multiemployer plan.

*(6) Qualified domestic relations orders.* A benefit provided to an alternate payee (as defined in section 414(p)(8)) of a participant pursuant to a qualified domestic relations order (as defined in section 414(p)(1)(A)) is treated as if it were provided to the participant for purposes of applying the limitations of section 415. See § 1.401(a)-13(g)(4)(iv).

*(7) Effect on other requirements.* Except as provided in § 1.417(e)-1(d)(1), the application of section 415 does not relieve a plan from the obligation to satisfy other applicable qualification requirements. Accordingly, the terms of the plan must provide for the plan to satisfy section 415 as well as all other applicable requirements. For example, if a defined benefit plan has a normal retirement age of 62, and if a participant's benefit remains unchanged between the ages of 62 and 65 because of the application of the section 415(b)(1)(A) dollar limit, the plan satisfies the requirements of section 411 only if the plan either commences distribution of the participant's benefit at normal retirement age (without regard to severance from employment) or provides for a suspension of benefits at normal retirement age that satisfies the requirements of section 411(a)(3)(B) and 29 CFR 2530.203-3. Similarly, if the increase to a participant's benefit under a defined benefit plan in a year after the participant has attained normal retirement age is less than the actuarial increase to the participant's previously accrued benefit because of the application of the section 415(b)(1)(B) compensation limitation (which is not adjusted for commencement after age 65), the plan satisfies the requirements of section 411 only if the plan either commences distribution of the participant's benefit at normal retirement age (without regard to severance from employment) or provides for a suspension of benefits at normal retirement age that satisfies the requirements of section 411(a)(3)(B) and 29 CFR 2530.203-3.

**(g) Effective date.** *(1) General rule.* Except as otherwise provided, this section and §§ 1.415(b)-1, 1.415(c)-1, 1.415(c)-2, 1.415(d)-1, 1.415(f)-1, 1.415(g)-1, and 1.415(j)-1 apply to limitation years beginning on or after July 1, 2007.

*(2) Governmental plans.* In the case of a governmental plan as defined in section 414(d), this section and §§ 1.415(b)-1, 1.415(c)-1, 1.415(c)-2, 1.415(d)-1, 1.415(f)-1, 1.415(g)-1, and 1.415(j)-1 apply to limitation years that begin more than 90 days after the close of the first regular legislative session of the legislative body with authority to amend the plan that begins on or after July 1, 2007. A governmental plan is permitted to apply the provisions of this section and §§ 1.415(b)-1, 1.415(c)-1, 1.415(c)-2, 1.415(d)-1, 1.415(f)-1, 1.415(g)-1, and 1.415(j)-1 to limitation years beginning on or after July 1, 2007, provided the plan applies all the applicable provisions of this section and §§ 1.415(b)-1, 1.415(c)-1, 1.415(c)-2, 1.415(d)-1, 1.415(f)-1, 1.415(g)-1, and 1.415(j)-1 for such limitation years.

*(3) Option to apply regulations earlier.* A plan may apply the rules in § 1.415(c)-2(e) regarding post-severance compensation payments for limitation years prior to the effective date described in paragraphs (g)(1) and (2) of this section.

This early application affects the rules relating to the definition of compensation in § 1.401(k)-1(e)(8) and § 1.457-4(d).

*(4) Grandfather rule for preexisting benefits.* A defined benefit plan is considered to satisfy the limitations of section 415(b) for a participant with respect to benefits accrued or payable under the plan as of the end of the limitation year that is immediately prior to the effective date of final regulations under this section and §§ 1.415(b)-1, 1.415(c)-1, 1.415(c)-2, 1.415(d)-1, 1.415(f)-1, 1.415(g)-1, and 1.415(j)-1 (as provided under paragraph (g)(1) or (2) of this section) pursuant to plan provisions (including plan provisions relating to the plan's limitation year) that were both adopted and in effect before April 5,2007, but only if such plan provisions meet the applicable requirements of statutory provisions, regulations, and other published guidance relating to section 415 in effect immediately before the effective date of final regulations under this section and §§ 1.415(b)-1, 1.415(c)-1, 1.415(c)-2, 1.415(d)-1, 1.415(f)-1, 1.415(g)-1, and 1.415(j)-1 (as provided under paragraph (g)(1) or (2) of this section). Plan provisions will not be treated as failing to satisfy these requirements merely because the plan has not been amended to reflect changes to section 415(b) made by the Pension Funding Equity Act of 2004, Public Law 108-218 (118 Stat. 596), and the Pension Protection Act of 2006, Public Law 109-280 (120 Stat. 780). In addition, plan provisions will not be treated as failing to satisfy these requirements merely because the plan's definition of compensation for a limitation year that is used for purposes of applying the limitations of section 415(b)(1)(B) reflects compensation for a plan year that is in excess of the limitation under section 401(a)(17) that applies to that plan year. If benefits under a plan are accrued after the applicable effective date under paragraph (g)(1) or (2) of this section, then the sum of the benefits grandfathered under the first sentence of this paragraph (g)(4) and benefits accrued after the applicable effective date must satisfy the requirements of section 415, taking into account the requirements of this section and §§ 1.415(b)-1, 1.415(c)-1, 1.415(c)-2, 1.415(d)-1, 1.415(f)-1, 1.415(g)-1, and 1.415(j)-1.

---

T.D. 9319, 4/4/2007.

---

### § 1.415(b)-1 Limitations for defined benefit plans.

**(a) General rules.** *(1) Maximum limitations.* Except as otherwise provided under this section, a defined benefit plan fails to satisfy the requirements of section 415(a) for a limitation year if, during the limitation year, either the annual benefit (as defined in paragraph (b)(1)(i) of this section) accrued by a participant (whether or not the benefit is vested) or the annual benefit payable to a participant at any time under the plan exceeds the lesser of—

(i) $160,000 (as adjusted pursuant to section 415(d), § 1.415(d)-1(a), and this section); or

(ii) 100 percent of the participant's average compensation for the period of the participant's high-3 years of service (as adjusted pursuant to section 415(d), § 1.415(d)-1(a), and this section).

*(2) Defined benefit plan.* For purposes of section 415 and regulations promulgated under section 415, a defined benefit plan is any plan, contract, or account to which section 415 applies pursuant to § 1.415(a)-1(a) or (b) (or any portion thereof) that is not a defined contribution plan within the meaning of § 1.415(c)-1(a)(2). In addition, a section 403(b) annuity contract that is not described in section 414(i) is treated as a defined benefit plan for purposes of section 415 and regulations promulgated under section 415.

*(3) Plan provisions.* As required in § 1.415(a)-1(d)(1), in order to satisfy the limitations on benefits under this section, the plan provisions (including the provisions of any annuity) must preclude the possibility that any annual benefit exceeding these limitations will be accrued (except as provided in paragraph (a)(7)(iii) of this section), distributed, or otherwise payable in any optional form of benefit (including the normal form of benefit) at any time (from the plan, from an annuity contract that will make distributions to the participant on behalf of the plan, or from an annuity contract that has been distributed under the plan). Thus, for example, a plan that is subject to the requirements of section 411 will fail to satisfy the limitations of this section if the plan does not contain terms that preclude the possibility that any annual benefit exceeding these limitations will be accrued or payable in any optional form of benefit (including the normal form of benefit) at any time, even though no participant has actually accrued a benefit in excess of these limitations.

*(4) Adjustments to dollar limitation for commencement before age 62 or after age 65.* The age-adjusted section 415(b)(1)(A) dollar limit computed pursuant to paragraph (d) or (e) of this section is used in place of the dollar limitation described in section 415(b)(1)(A) and paragraph (a)(1)(i) of this section in the case of a benefit with an annuity starting date that occurs before the participant attains age 62 or after the participant attains age 65.

*(5) Average compensation for period of high-3 years of service.* (i) In general. Except as otherwise provided in this paragraph (a)(5), for purposes of applying the limitation on benefits described in this section, the period of a participant's high-3 years of service is the period of 3 consecutive calendar years (taking into account the rule in paragraph (a)(5)(iii) of this section) during which the employee had the greatest aggregate compensation (as defined in § 1.415(c)-2) from the employer, and the average compensation for the period of a participant's high-3 years of service is determined by dividing the aggregate compensation for this period by 3. For purposes of this paragraph (a)(5), in determining a participant's high-3 years of service, the plan may use any 12-month period to determine a year of service instead of the calendar year, provided that it is uniformly and consistently applied in a manner that is specified under the terms of the plan. As provided under § 1.415(c)-2(f), because a plan is not permitted to base benefits on compensation in excess of the limitation under section 401(a)(17), a plan's definition of compensation for a year that is used for purposes of applying the limitations of section 415 is not permitted to reflect compensation for a year that is in excess of the limitation under section 401(a)(17) that applies to that year. See §§ 1.401(a)(17)-1(a)(3)(i) and 1.401(a)(17)-1(b)(3)(ii) for rules regarding the effective date of increases in the section 401(a)(17) compensation limitation for a plan year and for a 12-month period other than the plan year.

(ii) Short periods of service. For a participant who is employed with an employer for less than 3 consecutive years, the period of the participant's high-3 years of service is the actual number of consecutive years of service (including fractions of years, but not less than one year). In such a case, the limitation of section 415(b)(1)(B) of 100 percent of the participant's average compensation for the period of the participant's high-3 years of service is computed by dividing the participant's compensation during the participant's longest consecutive period of service by the number of years in that period (including fractions of years, but not less than one year). The rule in paragraph (a)(5)(iii) of this section is used for purposes of determining a participant's consecutive years of service.

(iii) Break in service. In the case of a participant who has had a severance from employment with an employer that maintains the plan and who is subsequently rehired by the employer, the period of the participant's high-3 years of service is calculated by excluding all years for which the participant performs no services for and receives no compensation from the employer maintaining the plan (referred to as the break period), and by treating the year of service immediately prior to and the year of service immediately after the break period as if such years of service were consecutive. See § 1.415(d)-1(a)(2)(iii) for a special rule for determining a rehired participant's section 415(b)(1)(B) compensation limit in the case of a plan that adjusts the compensation limit for limitation years after the limitation year in which the participant incurs a severance from employment.

(iv) Examples. For purposes of these examples, except as otherwise stated, the plan year and the limitation year are the calendar year, and the plan uses the calendar year for purposes of determining the period of high-3 years of service. In addition, except as otherwise stated, it is assumed that the plan's normal retirement age is 65, and all participants discussed in these examples have at least ten years of service with the employer and at least ten years of participation in the plan at issue. It is also assumed that none of the plans in the examples are governmental plans. The following examples illustrate the rules of this paragraph (a)(5):

*Example (1).* (i) Facts. Plan A, which was established on January 1, 2008, covers Participant M, who was hired on January 1, 1990. Participant M's compensation (as defined in § 1.415(c)-2) from the employer maintaining the plan is $140,000 each year for 1990 through 1992, is $120,000 each year for 1993 through 2007, and is $165,000 for 2008 and 2009. Assume that for Plan A's 2008 and 2009 limitation years, the section 415(b)(1)(A) age-adjusted dollar limit for M is $185,000 and $190,000, respectively, prior to the reduction of the age-adjusted dollar limit pursuant to paragraph (g)(1) of this section (which requires a reduction in the dollar limit if a participant has less than 10 years of participation in the plan).

(ii) Conclusion. As of the end of the 2008 limitation year, the period of M's high-3 consecutive years of service runs from January 1, 1990, through December 31, 1992, and M's average compensation for this period is $140,000. Thus, the limitation under section 415(b)(1)(B) for the 2008 limitation year is $140,000. As of the end of the 2009 limitation year, the period of M's high-3 consecutive years of service runs from January 1, 2007, through December 31, 2009, and M's average compensation for this period is $150,000. Thus, the limitation under section 415(b)(1)(B) for the 2009 limitation year is $150,000.

*Example (2).* (i) Facts. Participant N is a participant in Plan B. N's compensation for 2008, 2009, and 2010 is $300,000 for each year. N's average compensation for the period of N's high-3 years of service (determined before the application of section 401(a)(17)) is $300,000, based on N's compensation for 2008, 2009, and 2010. For all years before 2008, Participant N's compensation was less than the then-applicable section 401(a)(17) limit. On January 1, 2011, N commences receiving benefits from Plan B at the age of 75, 10 years after attaining N's normal retirement age under Plan B, when the age-adjusted section 415(b)(1)(A) dollar limit for benefits commencing at that age is $293,453.

(ii) Conclusion. Pursuant to § 1.415(c)-2(f) and section 401(a)(17), Plan B is not permitted to provide for a definition of compensation that includes compensation for a year that is in excess of the limitation under section 401(a)(17) that applies to that year. Accordingly, the limitation under section 415(b)(1)(B) based on N's average compensation for the period of N's high three years of service must not reflect compensation for a year that is in excess of the limitation under section 401(a)(17) that applies to that year. Thus, if the limitation under section 401(a)(17) for years beginning in 2008, 2009, and 2010 is $230,000, $235,000, and $240,000, respectively, then the limitation under section 415(b)(1)(B) based on N's average compensation for the period of N's high three years of service is $235,000.

*Example (3).* (i) Facts. The facts are the same as in Example 2, except that N commences receiving benefits from Plan B on January 1, 2008, at the age of 75, 10 years after attaining N's normal retirement age under Plan B. In addition, N's period of high three years of service is from January 1, 2003, through December 31, 2005, and N's average compensation for this period is $300,000. The section 401(a)(17) limits for 2003, 2004 and 2005 are $200,000, $205,000, and $210,000, respectively. As of December 31, 2007, pursuant to plan provisions adopted and in effect on January 1, 2007, N's accrued benefit under Plan B, payable in the form of a straight life annuity, actuarially adjusted to reflect commencement 10 years after normal retirement age, is $300,000. Plan B has not been amended during 2007, and that as of December 31, 2007, Plan B satisfied all of the requirements of section 415(b) with respect to N's accrued benefit, pursuant to statutory provisions, regulations, and other published guidance in effect immediately before the limitation year beginning on January 1, 2008.

(ii) Conclusion. Under § 1.415(a)-1(g)(4), Plan B is considered to satisfy the section 415(b)(1)(B) compensation limit with respect to N's benefit payable at age 75 of $300,000 (which N accrued prior to January 1, 2008), for limitation years beginning after December 31, 2007. This is because § 1.415(a)-1(g)(4) provides that plan provisions will not be treated as failing to satisfy the requirements of section 415(b)(1)(B) merely because the plan's definition of compensation that is used for purposes of applying the limitations of section 415(b)(1)(B) reflects compensation in excess of the section 401(a)(17) limitation for limitation years beginning before January 1, 2008. N, however, cannot accrue any additional benefits under Plan B for limitation years beginning after December 31, 2007, until N's section 415(b)(1)(B) compensation limit, as limited by § 1.415(c)-2(f) and section 401(a)(17), increases above $300,000.

*Example (4).* (i) Facts. Participant O participates in Plan C, maintained by Employer X. Plan C does not adjust a participant's section 415(b)(1)(B) compensation limit for limitation years after the limitation year in which the participant incurs a severance from employment. Prior to separating from employment with X in 2010, O's average compensation for O's period of high-3 years of service is $50,000, based on O's compensation for 2007, 2008, and 2009, which was $50,000 for each year. O's compensation for 2010 was $45,000. O's compensation is $0 for 2011. In 2012, O is rehired by X and resumes participation in Plan C. O's compensation in 2012 is $45,000, and is $70,000 in 2013.

(ii) Conclusion. As of the end of the 2013 limitation year, O's average compensation for O's period of high-3 years of service is $53,333, based on O's compensation in 2010, 2012, and 2013. See paragraph (a)(5)(iii) of this section.

*Example (5).* (i) Facts. The facts are the same as in Example 4, except that, in accordance with § 1.415(a)-1(d)(3)(v), Plan C incorporates by reference section 415(d) adjustments to a participant's section 415(b)(1)(B) compensation limit for limitation years after the limitation year in which the participant incurs a severance from employment. Assume that the annual adjustment factor described in § 1.415(d)-1(a)(2)(ii) for 2011 through 2013 is 1.03 for each year. Thus, disregarding O's rehire by X, O's average compensation for O's period of high-3 years of service for the 2013 limitation year is equal to $54,636 ($50,000 * 1.03 * 1.03 * 1.03).

(ii) Conclusion. Under § 1.415(d)-1(a)(2)(iii), O's average compensation for O's period of high-3 years of service for the 2013 limitation year is $54,636.

*(6) Exceptions from compensation limit.* The limit under paragraph (a)(1)(ii) of this section (100 percent of the participant's average compensation for the participant's high-3 years of service) does not apply to—

(i) A governmental plan (as defined in section 414(d));

(ii) A multiemployer plan (as defined in section 414(f));

(iii) A collectively bargained plan that is described in section 415(b)(7); or

(iv) A participant in a plan maintained by an organization described in section 3121(w)(3)(A) who has never been a highly compensated employee (within the meaning of section 414(q)) of the organization.

*(7) Special rules.* (i) Total benefits not in excess of $10,000. See section 415(b)(4) and paragraph (f) of this section for an exception from the limits of section 415(b)(1) and paragraph (a)(1) of this section with respect to retirement benefits that do not exceed $10,000 for the limitation year.

(ii) Governmental plans electing during 1990. For a special limitation applicable to certain governmental plans electing the application of this rule during the first plan year beginning after December 31, 1989, see section 415(b)(10).

(iii) Defined benefit plans not subject to the requirements of section 411. In the case of a defined benefit plan that is not subject to the requirements of section 411, the limitations described in this paragraph (a) are not required to be applied to the annual benefit accrued by a participant before the benefit is payable. However, such a defined benefit plan is subject to the limitations described in this paragraph (a) with respect to the annual benefit payable to a participant at any time under the plan.

(iv) Application of compensation limitation exception to a church employee who becomes a highly compensated employee. (A) In general. If a participant who was described in paragraph (a)(6)(iv) of this section for a prior limitation year later becomes a highly compensated employee (within the meaning of section 414(q)) of the organization that maintains the defined benefit plan, the plan is not treated as failing to satisfy the compensation-based limitation described in paragraph (a)(1)(ii) of this section with respect to the participant if the requirements of paragraph (a)(7)(iv)(B) of this section are satisfied with respect to the participant.

(B) Limitation on accruals. The requirements of this paragraph (a)(7)(iv)(B) are satisfied with respect to a participant if no plan amendments increasing the participant's benefits are adopted during the limitation year in which the participant first becomes a highly compensated employee (within the meaning of section 414(q)) of the organization that maintains the plan, and there is no increase in the participant's accrued benefit derived from employer contributions (including increases as a result of increased compensation or service) in subsequent limitation years.

**(b) Annual benefit.** *(1) In general.* (i) Definition of annual benefit. (A) Straight life annuities. For purposes of this section and § 1.415(b)-2, the term annual benefit means a benefit that is payable in the form of a straight life annuity. A straight life annuity means an annuity payable in equal installments for the life of the participant that terminates upon the participant's death. Examples of benefits that are not in the form of a straight life annuity include an annuity with a post-retirement death benefit and an annuity providing a guaranteed number of payments. If a benefit is payable in the form of a straight life annuity, no adjustment is made to the benefit to account for differences in the timing of payments during a year (for example, no adjustment is made on account of the annuity being payable in annual or monthly installments).

(B) Other benefit forms. With respect to a benefit payable in a form other than a straight life annuity, the annual benefit is determined as the straight life annuity payable on the first day of each month that is actuarially equivalent to the benefit payable in such other form, determined under the rules of paragraph (c) of this section.

(ii) Rules for determination of annual benefit. The annual benefit does not include the annual benefit attributable to either employee contributions or rollover contributions (as described in sections 401(a)(31), 402(c)(1), 403(a)(4), 403(b)(8), 408(d)(3), and 457(e)(16)), determined pursuant to the rules of paragraph (b)(2) of this section. The treatment of transferred benefits is determined under the rules of paragraph (b)(3) of this section. Paragraph (b)(4) of this section discusses the treatment of qualified governmental excess benefit arrangements.

(iii) Determination of annual benefit in the case of multiple annuity starting dates. (A) General rule. If a participant has or will have distributions commencing at more than one annuity starting date, then the limitations of section 415 must be satisfied as of each of the annuity starting dates, taking into account the benefits that have been or will be provided at all of the annuity starting dates. This will happen, for example, where benefit distributions to a participant have previously commenced under a plan that is aggregated for purposes of section 415 with a plan under which the participant receives current accruals. In determining the annual benefit for such a participant as of a particular annuity starting date, the plan must actuarially adjust the past and future distributions with respect to the benefits that commenced at the other annuity starting dates. For limitation years to which § 1.415(b)-2 applies, these adjustments must be made using the rules of § 1.415(b)-2. For purposes of this paragraph (b)(1)(iii) and § 1.415(b)-2, the determination of whether a new annuity starting date has occurred is made without regard to the rule of § 1.401(a)-20, Q&A-10(d) (under which the commencement of certain distributions may not give rise to a new annuity starting date).

(B) Scope of multiple annuity starting date rules. The rules provided in this paragraph (b)(1)(iii) and § 1.415(b)-2 apply for purposes of determining the annual benefit of a participant where a new distribution election is effective during the current limitation year with respect to a distribution that previously commenced. The rules of this paragraph (b)(1)(iii) and § 1.415(b)-2 also apply for determining the annual benefit of a participant for purposes of applying the limitations of section 415(b) and this section where benefit payments are increased as a result of plan terms or a plan amendment applying a cost-of-living adjustment or similar benefit increase, unless the increase is described in paragraph (b)(1)(iii)(C) of this section.

(C) Safe harbors for certain benefit increases. An increase to benefit payments as a result of plan terms or a plan amendment applying a cost-of-living adjustment or similar benefit increase is described in this paragraph (b)(1)(iii)(C) if the increase—

(1) Has previously been accounted for as part of the annual benefit under the rules of paragraph (c) of this section;

(2) Is not required to be accounted for as part of the annual benefit, pursuant to the exception for certain automatic benefit increase features under paragraph (c)(5) of this section;

(3) Is pursuant to a plan provision that automatically incorporates section 415(d) cost-of-living adjustments under § 1.415(a)-1(d)(3)(v); or

(4) Complies with one of the safe harbors described in § 1.415(d)-1(a)(5) or (6) (providing safe harbors for annual and other periodic adjustments to distributions).

*(2) Determination of annual benefit attributable to employee contributions and rollover contributions.* (i) In general. If employee contributions (other than contributions described in paragraph (b)(2)(ii) of this section) or rollover contributions are made to the plan, the annual benefit attributable to these contributions is determined as provided in this paragraph (b)(2).

(ii) Certain employee contributions disregarded. For purposes of this paragraph (b)(2), the following are not treated as employee contributions:

(A) Contributions that are picked up by a governmental employer as provided under section 414(h)(2).

(B) Repayment of any loan made to a participant from the plan.

(C) Repayment of a previously distributed amount as described in section 411(a)(7)(B) in accordance with section 411(a)(7)(C).

(D) Repayment of a withdrawal of employee contributions as provided under section 411(a)(3)(D).

(E) Repayments that would have been described in paragraph (b)(2)(ii)(C) or (b)(2)(ii)(D) of this section except that the plan does not restrict the timing of repayments to the maximum extent permitted by section 411(a).

(iii) Annual benefit attributable to mandatory employee contributions. In the case of mandatory employee contributions as defined in section 411(c)(2)(C) and § 1.411(c)-1(c)(4) (or contributions that would be mandatory employee contributions if section 411 applied to the plan), the annual benefit attributable to those contributions is determined by applying the factors applicable to mandatory employee contributions as described in section 411(c)(2)(B) and (C) and regulations promulgated under section 411 to those contributions to determine the amount of a straight life annuity commencing at the annuity starting date, regardless of whether the requirements of sections 411 and 417 apply to that plan. For purposes of applying such factors to a plan that is not subject to the requirements of section 411, the applicable effective date of section 411(a)(2) (which is used under § 1.411(c)-1(c)(3) to determine the beginning date from which statutorily specified interest must be credited to mandatory employee contributions) must be determined as if section 411 applied to the plan, and in determining the annual benefit that is actuarially equivalent to these accumulated contributions, the plan must determine the interest rate that would have been required under section 417(e)(3) as if section 417 applied to the plan. See § 1.415(c)-1(a)(2)(ii)(B) and (b)(3) for rules regarding treatment of mandatory employee contributions to a defined benefit plan as annual additions under a defined contribution plan.

(iv) Voluntary employee contributions. If voluntary employee contributions are made to the plan, the portion of the plan to which voluntary employee contributions are made is treated as a defined contribution plan pursuant to section 414(k) and, accordingly, is a defined contribution plan pursuant to § 1.415(c)-1(a)(2)(i). Accordingly, the portion of a plan to which voluntary employee contributions are made is not a defined benefit plan within the meaning of paragraph (a)(2) of this section and is not taken into account in determining the annual benefit under the portion of the plan that is a defined benefit plan.

(v) Annual benefit attributable to rollover contributions. The annual benefit attributable to rollover contributions from an eligible retirement plan, as defined in section 402(c)(8)(B) (for example, a contribution received pursuant to a direct rollover under section 401(a)(31)(A)), is determined in the same manner as the annual benefit attributable to mandatory employee contributions if the plan provides for a benefit derived from the rollover contribution (other than a benefit derived from a separate account to be maintained with respect to the rollover contribution and actual earnings and losses thereon). Thus, in the case of rollover contributions from a defined contribution plan to a defined benefit plan to provide an annuity distribution, the annual benefit attributable to those rollover contributions for purposes of section 415(b) is determined by applying the rules of section 411(c) as described in paragraph (b)(2)(iii) of this section, regardless of the assumptions used to compute the annuity distribution under the plan and regardless of whether the plan is subject to the requirements of sections 411 and 417. Accordingly, in such a case, if the plan uses more favorable factors than those specified in section 411(c) to determine the amount of annuity payments arising from rollover contributions, the annual benefit under the plan would reflect the excess of those annuity payments over the amounts that would be payable using the factors specified in section 411(c). See § 1.415(c)-1(b)(3)(i) for rules excluding rollover contributions maintained in a separate account that is treated as a defined contribution plan pursuant to section 414(k) from annual additions to a defined contribution plan.

*(3) Treatment of transferred benefits.* (i) In general. (A) Treatment of transferor plan if transferred benefits are aggregated with transferor plan. Except as provided in paragraph (b)(3)(ii) of this section, when there has been a transfer of benefits from one defined benefit plan to another plan, to the extent the benefits transferred to the transferee plan are otherwise required to be taken into account pursuant to section 415(f) and § 1.415(f)-1 in determining whether the transferor plan satisfies the limitations of section 415(b) for a limitation year, the transferred benefits are not treated as being provided under the transferor plan. This will occur, for example, if the employer sponsoring the transferor plan and the employer sponsoring the transferee plan are in the same controlled group within the meaning of section 414(b).

(B) Treatment of transferor plan if transferred benefits are not aggregated with transferor plan. Except as provided in paragraph (b)(3)(ii) of this section, when there has been a transfer of benefits from one defined benefit plan to another plan, to the extent the benefits transferred to the transferee plan are not otherwise required to be taken into account pursuant to section 415(f) and § 1.415(f)-1 in determining whether the transferor plan satisfies the limitations of section 415(b) for a limitation year, the transferred benefits are treated by the transferor plan as if such benefits were provided under annuities purchased to provide benefits under a plan that must be aggregated with the transferor plan and that terminated immediately prior to the transfer with sufficient assets to pay all benefit liabilities under the plan, in accordance with the rules of paragraph (b)(5)(i) of this section. This will occur, for example, in the case of a transfer of benefits between defined benefit plans maintained by employers that are not required to be aggregated under sections 414(b) and (c) (as modified by section 415(h)) or sections 414(m).

(C) Treatment of transferee plan. Except as provided in paragraph (b)(3)(ii) of this section, where there has been a transfer of benefits from one defined benefit plan to another defined benefit plan, the transferee plan must take into account the transferred benefits in determining whether it satisfies the limitations of section 415(b).

(ii) Elective transfer of distributable benefit. Where, as described in § 1.411(d)-4, Q&A-3(c) (permitting certain elective transfers of distributable benefits), a distributable benefit is transferred to a defined benefit plan from either a defined contribution plan or a defined benefit plan, the amount transferred is treated as a benefit paid from the transferor plan, and the annual benefit provided by the transferee defined benefit plan does not include the annual benefit attributable to the amount transferred (determined as if the transferred amount were a rollover contribution subject to the rules of paragraph (b)(2)(v) of this section). The rule in the preceding sentence applies regardless of whether the requirements of section 411 apply to the plan and, in the case of a transfer from a defined contribution plan that is not subject to the requirements of section 411 (such as a governmental plan) to a defined benefit plan, the rule applies even if the participant's benefits are not distributable from the defined contribution plan at the time of the transfer.

*(4) Treatment of qualified governmental excess benefit arrangements.* Pursuant to section 415(m), in determining whether a governmental plan (as defined in section 414(d)) meets the requirements of this section, the annual benefit does not include benefits provided under a qualified governmental excess benefit arrangement, as defined in section 415(m)(3). Thus, the limitation of section 415(b) does not apply to benefits to the extent the benefits are provided under a qualified governmental excess benefit arrangement.

*(5) Treatment of benefits provided under a terminated plan.* (i) Terminated plan with sufficient assets. If a defined benefit plan is terminated with sufficient assets for the payment of the benefit liabilities of all plan participants and a participant in the plan has not yet commenced benefits under the plan, for purposes of satisfying section 415(b) with respect to the participant, all other defined benefit plans maintained by the employer that maintained the terminated plan are required to take into account the benefits provided pursuant to the annuities purchased to provide benefits under the terminated plan at each possible annuity starting date. In such a case, see paragraph (b)(1)(iii) of this section for rules regarding the determination of a participant's annual benefit if the participant commences receiving benefits under the terminated plan.

(ii) Terminated plan with insufficient assets. If a defined benefit plan is terminated and there are not sufficient assets for the payment of the benefit liabilities of all plan participants, for purposes of satisfying section 415(b) with respect to a participant, all other defined benefit plans maintained by the employer that maintained the terminated plan are required to take into account the benefits that are actually provided to the participant under the terminated plan. For example, in the case of a plan that is subject to Title IV of the Employee Retirement Income Security Act of 1974 (88 Stat. 829), Public Law 93-406 (ERISA), and that terminates with insufficient assets for the payment of the benefit liabilities of all plan participants, all other defined benefit plans maintained by the employer that maintained the terminating plan must take into account benefits that are paid by the Pension Benefit Guaranty Corporation. In such a case, see paragraph (b)(1)(iii) of this section for rules regarding the determination of a participant's annual benefit if the participant commences receiving benefits under the terminated plan.

(iii) Other guidance. The Commissioner may provide guidance regarding the rules applicable to terminated plans (and plans that are deemed to have been terminated pursuant to paragraph (b)(3)(i)(B) of this section) in revenue rulings, notices, and other guidance published in the Internal Revenue Bulletin. See § 601.601(d) of this chapter.

**(c) Adjustment to form of benefit for forms other than a straight life annuity.** *(1) In general.* This paragraph (c) provides rules for adjusting a form of benefit other than a straight life annuity to an actuarially equivalent straight life annuity beginning at the same time for purposes of determining the annual benefit described in paragraph (b) of this section. Paragraph (c)(2) of this section describes how to adjust a benefit paid in a form to which section 417(e)(3) does not apply. Paragraph (c)(3) of this section describes how to adjust a benefit paid in a form to which section 417(e)(3) applies. Paragraph (c)(4) of this section describes benefit forms for which no adjustment is required. Paragraph (c)(5) of this section provides an exception from the requirements of this paragraph (c) with respect to certain automatic benefit increase features. Paragraph (c)(6) of this section sets forth examples illustrating the application of this paragraph (c). The Commissioner may, in revenue rulings, notices, or other guidance published in the Internal Revenue Bulletin set forth simplified methods for adjusting a form of benefit other than a straight life annuity to an actuarially equivalent straight life annuity beginning at the same time for purposes of determining the annual benefit described in paragraph (b) of this section. See § 601.601(d)(2) of this chapter.

*(2) Benefits paid in a form to which section 417(e)(3) does not apply.* For a benefit paid in a form to which section 417(e)(3) does not apply, the actuarially equivalent straight life annuity benefit is the greater of—

(i) The annual amount of the straight life annuity (if any) payable to the participant under the plan commencing at the same annuity starting date as the form of benefit payable to the participant; or

(ii) The annual amount of the straight life annuity commencing at the same annuity starting date that has the same actuarial present value as the form of benefit payable to the participant, computed using a 5 percent interest assumption and the applicable mortality table described in § 1.417(e)-1(d)(2) for that annuity starting date.

*(3) Benefits paid in a form to which section 417(e)(3) applies.* (i) In general. Except as otherwise provided in this paragraph (c)(3), for a benefit paid in a form to which section 417(e)(3) applies, the actuarially equivalent straight life annuity benefit is the greatest of:

(A) The annual amount of the straight life annuity commencing at the annuity starting date that has the same actuarial present value as the particular form of benefit payable, computed using the interest rate and mortality table, or tabular factor, specified in the plan for actuarial equivalence;

(B) The annual amount of the straight life annuity commencing at the annuity starting date that has the same actuarial present value as the particular form of benefit payable, computed using a 5.5 percent interest assumption and the applicable mortality table for the distribution under § 1.417(e)-1(d)(2); or

(C) The annual amount of the straight life annuity commencing at the annuity starting date that has the same actuarial present value as the particular form of benefit payable (computed using the applicable interest rate for the distribution under § 1.417(e)-1(d)(3) and the applicable mortality table for the distribution under § 1.417(e)-1(d)(2)), divided by 1.05.

(ii) Special rule for distributions in plan years beginning in 2004 and 2005. For a distribution to which section 417(e)(3) applies and which has an annuity starting date occurring in plan years beginning in 2004 or 2005, except as provided in section 101(d)(3) of the Pension Funding Equity Act of 2004, Public Law 108-218 (118 Stat. 596), the actuarially equivalent straight life annuity benefit is the greater of—

(A) The annual amount of the straight life annuity commencing at the annuity starting date that has the same actuarial present value as the particular form of benefit payable, computed using the interest rate and mortality table, or tabular factor, specified in the plan for actuarial equivalence; or

(B) The annual amount of the straight life annuity commencing at the annuity starting date that has the same actuarial present value as the particular form of benefit payable, computed using a 5.5 percent interest assumption and the applicable mortality table for the distribution under § 1.417(e)-1(d)(2).

*(4) Certain benefit forms for which no adjustment is required.* (i) In general. For purposes of the adjustments described in this paragraph (c), the following benefits are not taken into account:

(A) Survivor benefits payable to a surviving spouse under a qualified joint and survivor annuity (as defined in section 417(b)) to the extent that such benefits would not be payable if the participant's benefit were not paid in the form of a qualified joint and survivor annuity.

(B) Ancillary benefits that are not directly related to retirement benefits, such as preretirement disability benefits not in excess of the qualified disability benefit, preretirement incidental death benefits (including a qualified preretirement survivor annuity), and post-retirement medical benefits.

(ii) Rules of application. (A) Social security supplements. Although a social security supplement described in section 411(a)(9) and § 1.411(a)-7(c)(4) may be an ancillary benefit, it is included in determining the annual benefit because it is payable upon retirement and therefore is directly related to retirement income benefits.

(B) Qualified joint and survivor annuities combined with other distributions. If benefits are paid partly in the form of a qualified joint and survivor annuity (QJSA) and partly in some other form (such as a single-sum distribution), the rule of paragraph (c)(4)(i)(A) of this section (under which survivor benefits are not included in determining the annual benefit) applies to the survivor annuity payments under the portion of the benefit that is paid in the form of a QJSA.

*(5) Exception for certain automatic benefit increase features.* (i) General rule. Notwithstanding paragraph (b)(1)(i)(B) of this section, no adjustment is required to a benefit that is paid in a form that is not a straight life annuity to take into account the inclusion in that form of an automatic benefit increase feature, as described in paragraph (c)(5)(ii) of this section, if:

(A) The benefit is paid in a form to which section 417(e)(3) does not apply.

(B) The plan satisfies the requirements of paragraph (c)(5)(iii) of this section.

(ii) Definition of automatic benefit increase feature. An automatic benefit increase feature is included in a form of benefit if that form provides for automatic, periodic increases to the benefits paid in that form, such as a form of benefit that automatically increases the benefit paid under that form annually according to a specified percentage or objective index, or a form of benefit that automatically increases the benefit paid in that form to share favorable investment returns on plan assets.

(iii) Requirements. A plan satisfies the requirements of this paragraph (c)(5)(iii) with respect to a form of benefit that includes an automatic benefit increase feature if the form of benefit without regard to the automatic benefit increase feature satisfies the requirements of section 415(b) and this section, and the plan provides that in no event will the amount payable to the participant under the form of benefit in any limitation year be greater than the section 415(b) limit applicable at the annuity starting date (which is the lesser of the age-adjusted section 415(b)(1)(A) dollar limit described in paragraph (a)(1)(i) of this section or the section 415(b)(1)(B) compensation limit described in paragraph (a)(1)(ii) of this section), as increased in subsequent years pursuant to section 415(d) and § 1.415(d)-1. If the form of benefit without regard to the automatic benefit increase feature is not a straight life annuity, then the preceding sentence is applied by reducing the section 415(b) limit applicable at the annuity starting date to an actuarially equivalent amount (determined using the assumptions specified in paragraph (c)(2)(ii) of this section) that takes into account the death benefits under the form of benefit (other than the survivor portion of a QJSA).

*(6) Examples.* The following examples illustrate the provisions of this paragraph (c). For purposes of these examples, except as otherwise stated, actuarial equivalence under the plan is determined using a 5 percent interest assumption and the mortality table that applies under section 417(e)(3) as of January 1, 2003. It is assumed for purposes of these examples that the interest rate that applies under section 417(e)(3) and § 1.417(e)-1(d)(3) for relevant time periods is 5.25 percent and that the mortality table that applies under section 417(e)(3) and § 1.417(e)-1(d)(2) for relevant time periods is the mortality table that applies under section 417(e)(3) as of January 1, 2003. In addition, it is assumed that all participants discussed in these examples have at least ten years of service with the employer and at least ten years of participation in the plan at issue, all payments other than a payment of a single sum are made monthly, on the first day of each calendar month, and each plan's normal retirement age is 65. The examples are as follows:

*Example (1).* (i) Facts. Plan A provides a single-sum distribution determined as the actuarial present value of the straight life annuity payable at the actual retirement date. Plan A provides that a participant's single sum is determined as the greater of the present value determined using the otherwise applicable actuarial assumptions of the plan and the present value determined using the applicable interest rate and the applicable mortality table for the distribution under section 417(e)(3). In accordance with § 1.417(e)-1(d)(1), Plan A also provides that the single sum is not less than the actuarial present value of the accrued benefit payable at normal retirement age, determined using the applicable interest rate and the applicable mortality table under section 417(e)(3) and § 1.417(e)-1(d). Participant M retires at age 65 with a benefit under the plan formula (and before the application of section 415) of $152,619 and elects to receive a distribution in the form of a single sum. Under the plan and before the application of section 415, the amount of the single sum is $1,800,002 (which is based on the 5 percent interest rate and applicable mortality table as of January 1, 2003, since that present value is greater than the present value that would have been determined using the applicable interest rate (5.25 percent) and the applicable mortality table (the January 1, 2003, table) for the distribution under section 417(e)(3)).

(ii) Conclusion. For purposes of this section, the annual benefit is the greatest of the annual amount of the actuarially equivalent straight life annuity commencing at the same age (determined using the plan's actuarial factors), the annual amount of the actuarially equivalent straight life annuity commencing at the same age (determined using a 5.5 percent interest assumption and the applicable mortality table for the distribution under § 1.417(e)-1(d)(2)), and the annual amount of the actuarially equivalent straight life annuity commencing at the same age (determined using the applicable interest rate and applicable mortality table for the distribution under §§ 1.417(e)-1(d)(2) and (d)(3)) divided by 1.05. Based on the factors used in the plan to determine the actuarially equivalent lump sum (in this case, an interest rate of 5 percent and the applicable mortality table as of January 1, 2003), $1,800,002 payable as a single sum is actuarially equivalent to an immediate straight life annuity at age 65 of $152,619. A single sum payment of $1,800,002 is actuarially equivalent to an immediate straight life annuity at age 65 of $159,105, using a 5.5 percent interest assumption and the applicable mortality table under § 1.417(e)-1(d)(2). Based on the applicable interest rate and the applicable mortality table for the distribution under §§ 1.417(e)-1(d)(2) and (d)(3), $1,800,002 payable as a single sum is actuarially equivalent to an immediate straight life annuity at age 65 of $155,853. $148,432 is the result when this annual amount is divided by 1.05. With respect to the single-sum distribution, M's annual benefit for purposes of section 415(b) is equal to the greatest of the three resulting amounts ($152,619, $159,105, and $148,432), or $159,105.

*Example (2).* (i) Facts. The facts are the same as in Example 1, except that Participant M elects to receive his benefit in the form of a 10-year certain and life annuity. Applying the plan's actuarial equivalence factors, the benefit payable in this form is $146,100.

(ii) Conclusion. Since the form of benefit elected by M is a form of benefit to which section 417(e)(3) does not apply, the annual benefit for purposes of this section is the greater of the annual amount of the plan's straight life annuity commencing at the same age or the annual amount of the actuarially equivalent straight life annuity commencing at the same age, determined using a 5 percent interest rate and the applicable mortality table described in § 1.417(e)-1(d)(2) for that annuity starting date. In this case, the straight life annuity payable under the plan commencing at the same age is $152,619. Because the plan's factors for actuarial equivalence in this case are the same standardized actuarial factors required to be applied to determine the actuarially equivalent straight life annuity, the actuarially equivalent straight life annuity using the required standardized factors is also $152,619. With respect to the 10-year certain and life annuity distribution, M's annual benefit is equal to the greater of the two resulting amounts ($152,619 and $152,619), or $152,619.

*Example (3).* (i) Facts. The facts are the same as in Example 1. Participant M retires at age 62 with a benefit under the plan (before the application of section 415) of $100,000 (after application of the plan's early retirement factors) and a Social Security supplement of $10,000 per year payable until age 65. N chooses to receive the accrued benefit in the form of a straight life annuity. The Plan has no provisions under which the actuarial value of the Social Security supplement can be paid as a level annuity for life.

(ii) Conclusion. Because the form of benefit elected by M is a form of benefit to which section 417(e)(3) does not apply and because the plan does not provide for a straight life annuity beginning at age 62, the annual benefit for purposes of this section is the annual amount of the straight life annuity commencing at age 62 that is actuarially equivalent to the distribution stream of $110,000 for three years and $100,000 thereafter, where actuarial equivalence is determined using a 5 percent interest rate and the applicable mortality table described in § 1.417(e)-1(d)(2) for the annuity starting date. In this case, the actuarially equivalent straight life annuity is $102,180. Accordingly, with respect to this distribution stream, N's annual benefit is equal to $102,180. The results are the same without regard to whether the Social Security supplement is a QSUPP (as defined in § 1.401(a)(4)-12).

*Example (4).* (i) Facts. Plan B is a defined benefit plan that provides a benefit equal to 100 percent of a participant's average compensation for the period of the participant's high-3 years of service, payable as a straight life annuity. For a married participant who does not elect another form of benefit, the benefit is payable in the form of a joint and 100 percent survivor annuity benefit that is a QJSA within the meaning of section 417 and that is reduced from the straight life annuity. For purposes of determining the amount of this QJSA, the plan provides that the reduction is only half of the reduction that would normally apply under the actuarial assumptions specified in the plan for determining actuarial equivalence of optional forms. The plan also provides that a married participant can elect to receive the plan benefits as a straight life annuity, or in the form of a single sum distribution that is the actuarial equivalent of the joint and 100 percent survivor annuity determined using the applicable interest rate and the applicable mortality table under section 417(e)(3) and § 1.417(e)-1(d). Participant O elects, with spousal consent, a single-sum distribution.

(ii) Conclusion. The special rule that disregards the value of the survivor portion of a QJSA set forth in paragraph (c)(4)(i) of this section only applies to a benefit that is payable in the form of a qualified joint and survivor annuity. Any other form of benefit must be adjusted to a straight life annuity in accordance with paragraph (c)(1) of this section. Accordingly, because the benefit payable under the plan in the form of a single-sum distribution is actuarially equivalent to a straight life annuity that is greater than 100 percent of a participant's average compensation for the period of the participant's high-3 years of service, the limitation of section 415(b)(1)(B) has been exceeded.

*Example (5).* (i) Facts. Plan C is a defined benefit plan that provides an option to receive the benefit in the form of a joint and 100 percent survivor annuity with a 10-year certain feature, where the survivor beneficiary is the participant's spouse.

(ii) Conclusion. Since this form of benefit is not subject to section 417(e)(3), for a participant at age 65, the annual benefit with respect to the joint and 100 percent survivor annuity with a 10-year certain feature is determined for purposes of this section as the greater of the annual amount of the straight life annuity payable to the participant under the plan at age 65 (if any), or the annual amount of the straight life annuity commencing at age 65 that has the same actuarial present value as the joint and 100 percent survivor annuity with a 10-year certain feature (but excluding the survivor annuity payments pursuant to paragraph (c)(4)(i)(A) of this section), computing using a 5 percent interest assumption and the applicable mortality table described in § 1.417(e)-1(d)(2) for the annuity starting date. This latter amount is equal to the product of the annual payments under this optional form of benefit and the factor that provides for actuarial equivalence between a straight life annuity and a 10-year certain and life annuity (with no annuity for the survivor) computed using a 5 percent interest rate and the applicable mortality table described in § 1.417(e)-1(d)(2) for the annuity starting date.

*Example (6).* (i) Facts. Plan E provides a benefit at age 65 of a straight life annuity equal to the lesser of 90 percent of the participant's average compensation for the period of the participant's high-3 years of service and $148,500. Upon retirement at age 65, the optional forms of benefit available to a participant include payment of a QJSA with annual payments equal to 50 percent of the annual payments under the straight life annuity, along with a single-sum distribution that is actuarially equivalent (determined as the greater of the single sum calculated using a 5 percent interest assumption and the section 417(e)(3)(A)(ii)(I) mortality table in effect on January 1, 2003, and the single sum calculated using the section 417(e)(3)(A)(ii)(II) applicable interest rate and the section 417(e)(3)(A)(ii)(I) applicable mortality table for the distribution) to 50 percent of the annual payments under the straight life annuity. Participant Q retires at age 65. Q's average compensation for the period of Q's high-3 years of service is $100,000. Q elects to receive a distribution in the optional form of benefit described above, under which the annual payments under the QJSA are $45,000 and the single-sum distribution is equal to $530,734. Q's spouse is 3 years younger than Q.

(ii) Determination of annual benefit. Q's annual benefit under Plan E for purposes of section 415(b) is determined as the sum of the annual benefit attributable to the QJSA portion of the distribution and the annual benefit attributable to the single-sum portion of the distribution.

(iii) Annual benefit attributable to QJSA portion. Because survivor benefits are not taken into account in determining the annual benefit attributable to the QJSA portion of the distribution, the annual benefit attributable to the QJSA portion of the distribution is determined as if that distribution were a straight life annuity of $45,000 per year commencing at age 65. Thus, no form adjustment is needed to determine the annual benefit attributable to the QJSA portion of the distribution, and the annual benefit attributable to the QJSA portion of the benefit is $45,000.

(iv) Annual benefit attributable to single sum portion. The annual benefit attributable to the single sum portion of the distribution is determined as the greatest of the annual amount of the actuarially equivalent straight life annuity commencing at the same age (determined using the plan's actuarial factors), the annual amount of the actuarially equivalent straight life annuity commencing at the same age (determined using a 5.5 percent interest assumption and the applicable mortality table under § 1.417(e)-1(d)(2) for the distribution), and the annual amount of the actuarially equivalent straight life annuity commencing at the same age (determined using the applicable interest rate and applicable mortality table under section 417(e)(3) and §§ 1.417(e)-1(d)(2) and (d)(3) for the distribution) divided by 1.05. With respect to the single-sum distribution, the annual amount of the actuarially equivalent straight life annuity commencing at the same age determined using the plan's actuarial factors is equal to $45,954. The annual amount of the actuarially equivalent straight life annuity commencing at the same age determined using a 5.5 percent interest assumption and the applicable mortality table under § 1.417(e)-1(d)(2) for the distribution is $46,912. The actuarially equivalent straight life annuity commencing at the same age determined using the applicable interest rate and the applicable mortality table under section 417(e)(3) and §§ 1.417(e)-1(d)(2) and (d)(3) for the distribution is equal to $45,954. This amount divided by 1.05 is equal to $43,766. Thus, the annual benefit attributable to the single sum portion of the benefit is $46,912.

(v) Conclusion. Q's annual benefit under the optional form of benefit for purposes of section 415(b) is equal to the sum of the annual benefit attributable to the QJSA portion of the distribution and the annual benefit attributable to the single sum portion of the distribution, or $91,912. Because Q's average compensation for the period of Q's high-3 years of service is $100,000, the distribution satisfies the compensation limit of section 415(b)(1)(B).

*Example (7).* (i) Facts. Plan D is a defined benefit plan with a normal retirement age of 65. The normal retirement benefit under Plan D (and the only life annuity available under Plan D) is a life annuity with a fixed increase of 2 percent per year. The increase applies to the benefit provided in the prior year and is thus compounded. The plan provides that the benefit is limited to the lesser of 84 percent of the participant's average compensation for the period of the participant's high-3 years of service or 84 percent of the age-adjusted section 415(b)(1)(A) dollar limit (which is assumed to be $180,000 at age 65). Plan D does not incorporate the section 415(d) cost-of-living adjustments to the section 415(b) limits for limitation years following the limitation year in which a participant incurs a severance from employment. Participant P's retires at age 65, at which time P's average compensation for the period of P's high-3 years of service is $165,000. Under Plan D, P commences receiving benefits in the form of a life annuity of $138,600 with a fixed increase of 2 percent per year.

(ii) Conclusion. Because Plan D does not provide for a straight life annuity and the form of benefit is not subject to section 417(e)(3), P's annual benefit for purposes of section 415(b) is the annual amount of the straight life annuity, commencing at age 65, that is actuarially equivalent to the distribution stream of $138,600 with a fixed increase of 2 percent per year, where actuarial equivalence is determined using a 5 percent interest rate and the applicable mortality table for the distribution under section 417(e)(3) and § 1.417(e)-1(d)(2). In order to satisfy the requirements of section 415 and this section, this annual benefit must not exceed 100 percent of the average compensation for the period of the participant's high-3 years of service, or $165,000. Using a 5 percent interest rate and the section 417(e)(3) applicable mortality table for the distribution, the actuarially equivalent straight life annuity is $165,453, which exceeds

$165,000. Accordingly, the plan fails to satisfy the compensation-based limitation of section 415(b)(1)(B).

*Example (8).* (i) Facts. The facts are the same as in Example 7, except that Plan D incorporates by reference the section 415(d) cost-of-living adjustments to the section 415(b) limits as described in § 1.415(a)-1(d)(3)(v) and Plan D provides that the benefit is limited to the applicable section 415(b) limit. Under Plan D, P commences receiving benefits at age 65 in the form of a life annuity of $138,221 with a fixed increase of 2 percent per year.

(ii) Conclusion. Because Plan D does not provide for a straight life annuity and the form of benefit is not subject to section 417(e)(3), P's annual benefit for purposes of section 415(b) is the annual amount of the straight life annuity, commencing at age 65, that is actuarially equivalent to the distribution stream of $138,221 with a fixed increase of 2 percent per year, where actuarial equivalence is determined using a 5 percent interest rate and the applicable mortality table for P's annuity starting date under section 417(e)(3) and § 1.417(e)-1(d)(2). In order to satisfy the requirements of section 415(b) and this section, this annual benefit must not exceed 100 percent of P's average compensation for the period of P's high-3 years of service, or $165,000. Using a 5 percent interest rate and the section 417(e)(3) applicable mortality table for the distribution, the actuarially equivalent straight life annuity is $165,000, which does not exceed $165,000. Accordingly, the plan satisfies the compensation-based limitation of section 415(b)(1)(B).

(iii) Section 415(d) adjustments. In addition to the fixed 2 percent per year automatic increase, P's benefit will be increased in limitation years following the limitation year in which P retires in accordance with the plan provisions that incorporate by reference the section 415(d) cost-of-living adjustments to the section 415(b) limits (or, if Plan D did not incorporate by reference the section 415(d) adjustments, P's benefit may be increased pursuant to plan amendments that comply with the safe harbors provided in § 1.415(d)-1(a)(5) or (6)), and such increases will not cause P's benefit to violate the requirements of section 415(b). For example, if in a later limitation year the applicable section 415(b) limit is increased by 3 percent pursuant to section 415(d) and § 1.415(d)-1, P's benefit payable under Plan D will be increased by both the fixed automatic 2 percent per year increase and by the 3 percent section 415(d) cost-of-living adjustment. The effect of the combined increases may result in P's benefits for a year exceeding the then applicable dollar limit under section 415(b), but the plan will not violate section 415(b).

*Example (9).* (i) Facts. The facts are the same as in Example 7, except that the plan provides that benefits are limited to the lesser of 100 percent of the participant's average compensation for the period of the participant's high-3 years of service or 100 percent of the age-adjusted section 415(b)(1)(A) dollar limit. Assume that P retires at age 65 with a benefit in the form of a life annuity of $165,000 per year with a fixed increase of 2 percent per year. Additionally, assume that Plan D incorporates by reference the section 415(d) cost-of-living adjustments to the section 415(b) limits as described in § 1.415(a)-1(d)(3)(v) and the plan provides pursuant to paragraph (c)(5) of this section that in no event will a benefit payable from the plan, as increased by the fixed increase of 2 percent per year, be greater than the section 415(b) limit applicable as of the annuity starting date for the benefit (increased pursuant to the rules of section 415(d) and § 1.415(d)-1).

(ii) Conclusion. The benefit payable to P at age 65 is not required to be adjusted to take into account the fixed increase of 2 percent per year. This is because the benefit payable to P satisfies the requirements of section 415(b) without regard to the fixed increase of 2 percent per year, and pursuant to paragraph (c)(5) of this section, the plan provides that the benefit payable to P, as increased by the fixed increase of 2 percent per year, will never be greater than the section 415(b) limit applicable as of P's annuity starting date (increased in subsequent limitation years pursuant to the rules of section 415(d) and § 1.415(d)-1).

(iii) Section 415(d) adjustments. In addition to the fixed 2 percent per year automatic increase, P's benefit will be increased in limitation years following the limitation year in which P retires in accordance with the plan provisions that incorporate by reference the section 415(d) cost-of-living adjustments to the section 415(b) limits (or, if Plan D did not incorporate by reference the section 415(d) adjustments, P's benefit may be increased pursuant to plan amendments that comply with the safe harbors provided in § 1.415(d)-1(a)(5) or (6)), and such increases will not cause P's benefit to violate the requirements of section 415(b). However, pursuant to paragraph (c)(5)(iii) of this section, P's benefit during any limitation year, as increased by the 2 percent per year automatic increase feature and any plan provisions that incorporate by reference the section 415(d) cost-of-living adjustments or any plan amendments that increase P's benefits, cannot exceed the then applicable section 415(b) limit (as increased pursuant to section 415(d) and § 1.415(d)-1).

*Example (10).* (i) Facts. Employer T maintains a defined benefit plan. Under the terms of the plan, all benefits in pay status (other than single sum payments) are adjusted upwards or downwards annually depending on an annual comparison of actual return on plan assets and an assumed interest rate of 4 percent. Thus, the plan does not offer a straight life annuity form of benefit, and the plan must determine for purposes of applying the section 415(b) limits the actuarially equivalent straight life annuity for benefits provided under the plan.

(ii) Conclusion. Benefits under the plan are paid in a form to which section 417(e)(3) does not apply. In determining the actuarially equivalent straight life annuity of benefits that are subject to the annual investment performance adjustment, the plan must assume a 5 percent return on plan assets. See paragraph (c)(2) of this section. Therefore, in determining the actuarially equivalent straight life annuity, the plan must assume that the form of benefit payable under the plan will be an annuity that increases annually by a factor equal to 1.05 divided by 1.04. This increasing annuity is then converted to an actuarially equivalent straight life annuity under paragraph (c)(2) of this section using a 5 percent interest rate and the applicable mortality table described in § 1.417(e)-1(d)(2) for the relevant annuity starting date.

*Example (11).* (i) Facts. R is a participant in a defined benefit plan maintained by R's employer. Under the terms of the plan, R must make contributions to the plan in a stated amount to accrue benefits derived from employer contributions.

(ii) Conclusion. R's contributions are mandatory employee contributions within the meaning of section 411(c)(2)(C) and, thus, the annual benefit attributable to these contributions is not taken into account for purposes of testing the annual benefit derived from employer contributions against the applicable limitation on benefits. However, these contributions are treated as contributions to a defined contribution plan maintained by R's employer for purposes of section 415(c). See § 1.415(c)-1(a)(2)(ii)(B). Accordingly, with respect to the current limitation year, the limitation on benefits (as described in paragraph (a)(1) of this section) is applicable to the annual benefit attributable to employer contributions to the defined benefit plan, and the limitation on contributions and other additions (as described in § 1.415(c)-1) is applicable to the portion of the plan treated as a defined contribution plan, which consists of R's mandatory contributions. These same limitations would also apply if, instead of providing for mandatory employee contributions, the plan permitted voluntary employee contributions, because the portion of the plan attributable to voluntary employee contributions and earnings thereon is treated as a defined contribution plan maintained by the employer pursuant to section 414(k), and thus is not subject to the limitations of section 415(b).

*Example (12).* (i) Facts. V is a participant in a defined benefit plan maintained by V's employer. Under the terms of the plan, V must make contributions to the plan in a stated amount to accrue benefits derived from employer contributions. V's contributions are mandatory employee contributions within the meaning of section 411(c)(2)(C). Thus, the annual benefit attributable to these contributions is not taken into account for purposes of testing the annual benefit derived from employer contributions against the applicable limitation on benefits. V terminates employment and receives a distribution from the plan that includes V's mandatory employee contributions. Subsequently, V resumes employment with the employer maintaining the plan. V recommences participation in the plan and repays the prior distribution from the plan (including the portion of the distribution that included V's prior mandatory employee contributions to the plan) with reasonable interest.

(ii) Conclusion. In determining V's annual benefit under the plan for purposes of applying the limitations of section 415(b), no portion of V's repayment of the prior distribution is treated as employee contributions. See paragraphs (b)(2)(ii)(C), (D) and (E) of this section. However, V's annual benefit under the plan is determined by excluding the portion of the annual benefit attributable to V's employee contributions to the plan made both prior to the first distribution and during V's subsequent recommencement of plan participation.

**(d) Adjustment to section 415(b)(1)(A) dollar limit for commencement before age 62.** *(1) General rule.* (i) Calculation using statutory factors. For a distribution with an annuity starting date that occurs before the participant attains the age of 62, the age-adjusted section 415(b)(1)(A) dollar limit generally is determined as the actuarial equivalent of the annual amount of a straight life annuity commencing at the annuity starting date that has the same actuarial present value as a deferred straight life annuity commencing at age 62, where annual payments under the straight life annuity commencing at age 62 are equal to the dollar limitation of section 415(b)(1)(A) (as adjusted pursuant to section 415(d) and § 1.415(d)-1 for the limitation year), and where the actuarially equivalent straight life annuity is computed using a 5 percent interest rate and the applicable mortality table under § 1.417(e)-1(d)(2) that is effective for that annuity starting date (and expressing the participant's age based on completed calendar months as of the annuity starting date). However, if the plan has an immediately commencing straight life annuity payable both at age 62 and the age of benefit commencement, then the age-adjusted section 415(b)(1)(A) dollar limit is equal to the lesser of—

(A) The limit as otherwise determined under this paragraph (d)(1)(i); and

(B) The amount determined under paragraph (d)(1)(ii) of this section.

(ii) Calculation using plan factors. The amount determined under this paragraph (d)(1)(ii) is equal to the section 415(b)(1)(A) dollar limit (as adjusted pursuant to section 415(d) and § 1.415(d)-1 for the limitation year) multiplied by the ratio of the annual amount of the immediately commencing straight life annuity under the plan to the annual amount of the straight life annuity under the plan commencing at age 62, with both annual amounts determined without applying the rules of section 415.

*(2) Mortality adjustments.* (i) In general. For purposes of determining the actuarially equivalent amount described in paragraph (d)(1)(i) of this section, to the extent that a forfeiture does not occur upon the participant's death before the annuity starting date, no adjustment is made to reflect the probability of the participant's death between the annuity starting date and the participant's attainment of age 62, unless the plan provides for such an adjustment. To the extent that a forfeiture occurs upon the participant's death before the annuity starting date, an adjustment must be made to reflect the probability of the participant's death between the annuity starting date and the participant's attainment of age 62.

(ii) No forfeiture deemed to occur where qualified preretirement survivor annuity payable. For purposes of paragraphs (d)(2)(i) and (e)(2)(i) of this section, a plan is permitted to treat no forfeiture as occurring upon a participant's death if the plan does not charge participants for providing a qualified preretirement survivor annuity (QPSA) (as defined in section 417(c)) on the participant's death, but only if the plan applies this treatment both for adjustments before age 62 and adjustments after age 65. Thus, in such a case, the plan is permitted to provide that, in computing the adjusted dollar limitation under section 415(b)(1)(A), no adjustment is made to reflect the probability of a participant's death after the annuity starting date and before age 62 or after age 65 and before the annuity starting date.

*(3) Exception for certain participants of certain governmental plans.* Pursuant to section 415(b)(2)(G) and (H), no age adjustment is made to the dollar limit for commencement before age 62 for any qualified participant. For this purpose, a qualified participant is a participant in a defined benefit plan that is maintained by a state, Indian tribal government (as defined in section 7701(a)(40)), or any political subdivision of a state or Indian tribal government with respect to whom the service taken into account in determining the amount of the benefit under the defined benefit plan includes at least 15 years of service of the participant—

(i) As a full-time employee of any police department or fire department that is organized and operated by the state, Indian tribal government, or political subdivision maintaining such defined benefit plan to provide police protection, firefighting services, or emergency medical services for any area within the jurisdiction of such state, Indian tribal government, or political subdivision; or

(ii) As a member of the Armed Forces of the United States.

*(4) Exception for survivor and disability benefits under governmental plans.* Pursuant to section 415(b)(2)(I), no age adjustment is made to the dollar limit for commencement before age 62 for a distribution from a governmental plan (as defined in section 414(d)) on account of the participant's

becoming disabled by reason of personal injuries or sickness, or as a result of the death of the participant.

*(5) Special rule for commercial airline pilots.* Pursuant to section 415(b)(9), no age adjustment is made to the dollar limit for early commencement on or after age 60 for a participant if—

(i) The participant is a commercial airline pilot;

(ii) The participant separates from service upon or after attaining age 60; and

(iii) As of the time of the participant's retirement, regulations prescribed by the Federal Aviation Administration require an individual to separate from service as a commercial airline pilot after attaining any age occurring on or after age 60 and before age 62.

*(6) No decrease in age-adjusted section 415(b)(1)(A) dollar limit on account of age or service.* Notwithstanding any other provision of this paragraph (d), the age-adjusted section 415(b)(1)(A) dollar limit applicable to a participant does not decrease on account of an increase in age or the performance of additional service.

*(7) Examples.* The following examples illustrate the application of this paragraph (d). For purposes of these examples, it is assumed that the dollar limitation under section 415(b)(1)(A) for all relevant years is $180,000, that the normal form of benefit under the plan is a straight life annuity payable beginning at age 65, and that all payments other than a payment of a single sum are made monthly, on the first day of each calendar month. The examples are as follows:

*Example (1).* (i) Plan A provides that early retirement benefits are determined by reducing the accrued benefit by 4 percent for each year that the early retirement age is less than age 65. Participant M retires at age 60 with exactly 30 years of service with a benefit (prior to the application of section 415) in the form of a straight life annuity of $100,000 payable at age 65, and is permitted to elect to commence benefits at any time between M's retirement and M's attainment of age 65. For example, M can elect to commence benefits at age 60 in the amount of $80,000, can wait until age 62 and commence benefits in the amount of $88,000, or can wait until age 65 and commence benefits in the amount of $100,000. Plan A provides a QPSA to all married participants without charge. Plan A provides (consistent with paragraph (d)(2)(ii) of this section) that, for purposes of adjusting the dollar limitation under section 415(b)(1)(A) for commencement before age 62 or after age 65, no forfeiture is treated as occurring upon a participant's death before retirement and, therefore, in computing the adjusted dollar limitation under section 415(b)(1)(A), no adjustment is made to reflect the probability of a participant's death after the annuity starting date and before age 62 or after age 65 and before the annuity starting date.

(ii) The age-adjusted section 415(b)(1)(A) dollar limit that applies for commencement of M's benefit at age 60 is the lesser of the section 415(b)(1)(A) dollar limit multiplied by the ratio of the annuity payable at age 60 to the annuity payable at age 62, or the straight life annuity payable at age 60 that is actuarially equivalent, using 5 percent interest and the applicable mortality table effective for that annuity starting date under section 417(e)(3)(A)(ii)(I) and § 1.417(e)-1(d)(2), to the deferred annuity payable at age 62 of $180,000 per year. In this case, the age-adjusted section 415(b)(1)(A) dollar limit at age 60 is $156,229 (the lesser of $163,636 ($180,000* $80,000/$88,000) and $156,229 (the straight life annuity at age 60 that is actuarially equivalent to a deferred annuity of $180,000 commencing at age 62, determined using 5 percent interest and the applicable mortality table, without a mortality decrement for the period between 60 and 62)).

*Example (2).* (i) The facts are the same as in Example 1, except that participant M elects to retire at age 60, 6 months, and 21 days.

(ii) Under paragraph (d)(1)(i) of this section, M is treated as age 60 and 6 months (or, age 60.5). Absent the rule provided in paragraph (d)(6) of this section, the age-adjusted section 415(b)(1)(A) dollar limit that applies for commencement of M's benefit at age 60.5 is the lesser of the section 415(b)(1)(A) dollar limit multiplied by the ratio of the annuity payable at age 60.5 to the annuity payable at age 62, or the straight life annuity payable at age 60.5 that is actuarially equivalent, using 5 percent interest and the applicable mortality table for that annuity starting date under section 417(e)(3)(A)(ii)(I) and § 1.417(e)-1(d)(2), to the deferred annuity payable at age 62 of $180,000 per year. The age-adjusted section 415(b)(1)(A) dollar limit at age 60.5 is $161,769 (the lesser of $167,727 ($180,000* $82,000/$88,000) and $161,769 (the straight life annuity at age 60.5 that is actuarially equivalent to a deferred annuity of $180,000 commencing at age 62, determined using 5 percent interest and the applicable mortality table, without a mortality decrement for the period between 60.5 and 62).

*Example (3).* (i) The facts are the same as in Example 1, except the plan provides that, if a participant has 30 or more years of service, no reduction applies for benefits commencing at age 62 and later.

(ii) Absent the rule provided in paragraph (d)(6) of this section, the age-adjusted section 415(b)(1)(A) dollar limit that applies for commencement of M's benefit at age 60 is the lesser of the section 415(b)(1)(A) dollar limit multiplied by the ratio of the annuity payable at age 60 to the annuity payable at age 62, or the straight life annuity payable at age 60 that is actuarially equivalent, using 5 percent interest and the applicable mortality table for that annuity starting date under section 417(e)(3)(A)(ii)(I) and § 1.417(e)-1(d)(2), to the deferred annuity payable at age 62 of $180,000 per year. In this case, because M has 30 years of service and would be eligible for the unreduced early retirement benefit at age 62, the age-adjusted section 415(b)(1)(A) dollar limit at age 60 would be $144,000 (the lesser of $144,000 ($180,000* $80,000/$100,000) and $156,229 (the straight life annuity at age 60 that is actuarially equivalent to a deferred annuity of $180,000 commencing at age 62, determined using 5 percent interest and the applicable mortality table, without a mortality decrement for the period between 60 and 62)).

(ii) However, at age 59 11/12 with 29 11/12 years of service, the age-adjusted section 415(b)(1)(A) dollar limit for M is $155,311 (the lesser of $162,955 ($180,000* $79,667/$88,000) and $155,311 (the straight life annuity at age 59 11/12 that is actuarially equivalent to a deferred annuity of $180,000 commencing at age 62, determined using 5 percent interest and the applicable mortality table, without a mortality decrement for the period between 59 and 62). Thus, after applying the rule provided in paragraph (d)(6) of this section, the age-adjusted section 415(b)(1)(A) dollar limit that applies for commencement of M's benefit at age 60 is $155,311.

*Example (4).* (i) The facts are the same as in Example 1, except that the plan provides that, if a participant has 30 or more years of service, then no reduction is made in early retirement benefits if the early retirement age is at least age 62 and, in the case of an early retirement age before age 62, the early retirement benefit is determined by reducing the accrued benefit by 4 percent for each year that the early retirement age is less than age 62.

(ii) The age-adjusted section 415(b)(1)(A) dollar limit that applies for commencement of M's benefit at age 60 is the lesser of the section 415(b)(1)(A) dollar limit multiplied by the ratio of the annuity payable at age 60 to the annuity payable at age 62, or the straight life annuity payable at age 60 that is actuarially equivalent, using 5 percent interest and the applicable mortality table for that annuity starting date under section 417(e)(3)(A)(ii)(I) and § 1.417(e)-1(d)(2), to the deferred annuity payable at age 62 of $180,000 per year. In this case, because M has 30 years of service and would be eligible for the unreduced early retirement benefit at age 62, the age-adjusted section 415(b)(1)(A) dollar limit at age 60 is $156,229 (the lesser of $165,600 ($180,000* $92,000/$100,000) and $156,229 (the straight life annuity at age 60 that is actuarially equivalent to a deferred annuity of $180,000 commencing at age 62, determined using 5 percent interest and the applicable mortality table, without a mortality decrement for the period between 60 and 62)).

*Example (5).* (i) The facts are the same as in Example 1, except that Participant M chooses to receive benefits in the form of a 10-year certain and life annuity under which payments are 97 percent of the periodic payments that would be made under the immediately commencing straight life annuity. Annual payments to M are 97 percent of $80,000, or $77,600. Additionally, M's average compensation for the period of M's high-3 years of service is $120,000. As in Example 1, the age-adjusted section 415(b)(1)(A) dollar limit at age 60 is $156,229.

(ii) In the case of a form of benefit to which section 417(e)(3) does not apply, the annual benefit for purposes of this section is the greater of the annual amount of the plan's straight life annuity commencing at the same age or the annual amount of the actuarially equivalent straight life annuity commencing at the same age, determined using a 5 percent interest rate and the applicable mortality table for that annuity starting date under section 417(e)(3)(A)(ii)(I) and § 1.417(e)-1(d)(2). In this case, the straight life annuity payable under the plan commencing at the same age is $80,000. The annual amount of the straight life annuity that is actuarially equivalent to the $77,600 benefit payable as a 10-year certain and life annuity is determined by applying the required standardized factors (a 5 percent interest assumption and the applicable mortality under section 417(e)(3)(A)(ii)(I) and § 1.417(e)-1(d)(2), and is $79,416. With respect to the 10-year certain and life annuity commencing at age 62, M's annual benefit is equal to the greater of the two resulting amounts ($80,000 and $79,416), or $80,000. Because M's annual benefit is less than the age-adjusted section 415(b)(1)(A) dollar limit and is less than the section 415(b)(1)(B) compensation limit, M's benefit satisfies section 415.

*Example (6).* (i) Participant O is a full-time civilian employee of the Harbor Police Division of the State of X Port Authority. The Harbor Police Division provides police protection services. O performs clerical services for the Harbor Police Division. O is a participant in the defined benefit plan that is maintained by the State of X with respect to whom the years of service taken into account in determining the amount of the benefit under the plan includes 10 years of service working for the Harbor Police Division and 5 years of service as a member of the Armed Forces of the United States.

(ii) For a distribution with an annuity starting date that occurs before O attains the age of 62, there is no age adjustment to the section 415(b)(1)(A) dollar limit.

*Example (7).* (i) Participant R is a full-time employee of the Emergency Medical Service Department of County Y (which is not a part of a police or fire department) who performs services as a driver of an ambulance. R is a participant in the defined benefit plan that is maintained by County Y with respect to whom the years of service taken into account in determining the amount of the benefit under the plan includes 15 years of service working for County Y. R does not have service credit for time in the Armed Forces of the United States.

(ii) The age adjustments to the limitations of section 415(b)(1)(A) pursuant to section 415(b)(2)(C) and (D) will apply if R commences receiving a distribution at an age to which either of those adjustments applies.

**(e) Adjustment to section 415(b)(1)(A) dollar limit for commencement after age 65.** *(1) General rule.* (i) Calculation using statutory factors. For a distribution with an annuity starting date that occurs after the participant attains the age of 65, the age-adjusted section 415(b)(1)(A) dollar limit generally is determined as the actuarial equivalent of the annual amount of a straight life annuity commencing at the annuity starting date that has the same actuarial present value as a straight life annuity commencing at age 65, where annual payments under the straight life annuity commencing at age 65 are equal to the dollar limitation of section 415(b)(1)(A) (as adjusted pursuant to section 415(d) and § 1.415(d)-1 for the limitation year), and where the actuarially equivalent straight life annuity is computed using a 5 percent interest rate and the applicable mortality table under § 1.417(e)-1(d)(2) that is effective for that annuity starting date (and expressing the participant's age based on completed calendar months as of the annuity starting date). However, if the plan has an immediately commencing straight life annuity payable as of the annuity starting date and an immediately commencing straight life annuity payable at age 65, then the age-adjusted section 415(b)(1)(A) dollar limit is equal to the lesser of—

(A) The limit as otherwise determined under this paragraph (e)(1)(i); and

(B) The amount determined under paragraph (e)(1)(ii) of this section.

(ii) Calculation using plan factors. The amount determined under this paragraph (e)(1)(ii) is equal to the section 415(b)(1)(A) dollar limit (as adjusted pursuant to section 415(d) and § 1.415(d)-1 for the limitation year) multiplied by the adjustment ratio described in paragraph (e)(2)(i) of this section.

*(2) Adjustment ratio.* (i) General rule. For purposes of applying the rule of paragraph (e)(1)(ii) of this section, the adjustment ratio is equal to the ratio of the annual amount of the adjusted immediately commencing straight life annuity under the plan described in paragraph (e)(2)(ii) of this section to the adjusted age 65 straight life annuity described in paragraph (e)(2)(iii) of this section.

(ii) Adjusted immediately commencing straight life annuity. The adjusted immediately commencing straight life annuity that is used for purposes of paragraph (e)(2)(i) of this section is the annual amount of the immediately commencing straight life annuity payable to the participant, computed disregarding the participant's accruals after age 65 but including actuarial adjustments even if those actuarial adjustments are applied to offset accruals. For this purpose, the annual amount of the immediately commencing straight life annuity is determined without applying the rules of section 415.

(iii) Adjusted age 65 straight life annuity. The adjusted age 65 straight life annuity that is used for purposes of paragraph (e)(2)(i) of this section is the annual amount of the straight life annuity that would be payable under the plan to a hypothetical participant who is 65 years old and has the same accrued benefit (with no actuarial increases for commencement after age 65) as the participant receiving the distribution (determined disregarding the participant's accruals after age 65 and without applying the rules of section 415).

*(3) Mortality adjustments.* (i) In general. For purposes of determining the actuarially equivalent amount described in paragraph (e)(1)(i) of this section, to the extent that a forfeiture does not occur upon the participant's death before the annuity starting date, no adjustment is made to reflect the probability of the participant's death between the participant's attainment of age 65 and the annuity starting date. To the extent that a forfeiture occurs upon the participant's death before the annuity starting date, an adjustment must be made to reflect the probability of the participant's death between the participant's attainment of age 65 and the annuity starting date.

(ii) No forfeiture deemed to occur where QPSA payable. See paragraph (d)(2)(ii) of this section for a rule deeming no forfeiture to occur if the plan does not charge participants for providing a QPSA on the participant's death.

*(4) Examples.* The following examples illustrate the application of this paragraph (e):

*Example (1).* (i) Plan A provides that monthly benefits payable upon commencement after normal retirement age (which is age 65) are increased by 0.5 percent for each month of delay in commencement after attainment of normal retirement age. Plan A provides a QPSA to all married participants without charge. Plan A provides (consistent with paragraph (d)(2)(ii) of this section) that, for purposes of adjusting the dollar limitation under section 415(b)(1)(A) for commencement before age 62 or after age 65, no adjustment is made to reflect the probability of a participant's death between the annuity starting date and the participant's attainment of age 62 or between the age of 65 and the annuity starting date. The normal form of benefit under Plan A is a straight life annuity commencing at age 65. Plan A does not provide additional benefit accruals once a participant is credited with 30 years of service. Participant M was credited with 30 years of service under Plan A when M attained age 65. M retires at age 70 on January 1, 2008, with a benefit (prior to the application of section 415) that is payable monthly in the form of a straight life annuity of $195,000, which reflects the actuarial increase of 30 percent applied to the accrued benefit of $150,000. It is assumed that all payments under Plan A, other than a payment of a single sum, are made monthly, on the first day of each calendar month. It is also assumed that the dollar limit in 2008 is $185,000.

(ii) The age-adjusted section 415(b)(1)(A) dollar limit at age 70 is the lesser of the section 415(b)(1)(A) dollar limit multiplied by the ratio of the adjusted immediately commencing straight life annuity payable at age 70 (computed disregarding the rules of section 415 and accruals after age 65, but including actuarial adjustments) to the adjusted age 65 straight life annuity (computed disregarding the rules of section 415 and any accruals after age 65), or the straight life annuity payable at age 70 that is actuarially equivalent, using 5 percent interest and the applicable mortality table for that annuity starting date under section 417(e)(3)(A)(ii)(I) and § 1.417(e)-1(d)(2), to the straight life annuity payable at age 65, where annual payments under the straight life annuity payable at age 65 are equal to the dollar limitation of section 415(b)(1)(A). In this case, the age-adjusted section 415(b)(1)(A) dollar limit at age 70 is $240,500 (the lesser of $240,500 ($185,000* $195,000/$150,000) and $271,444 (the straight life annuity at age 70 that is actuarially equivalent to an annuity of $185,000 commencing at age 65, determined using 5 percent interest and the applicable mortality table, without a mortality decrement for the period between 65 and 70)).

*Example (2).* (i) The facts are the same as in Example 1, except that Plan A does not limit benefit accruals to 30 years of credited service, and thus M accrues benefits between ages 65 and 70.

(ii) Since M's accruals after attaining age 65 are disregarded for purposes of determining the age-adjusted section 415(b)(1)(A) dollar limit applicable to M at age 70, the result is the same as in Example 1.

*Example (3).* (i) The facts are the same as in Example 1, except that Plan A does not limit benefit accruals to 30 years of credited service. However, benefit accruals after an employee has reached normal retirement age (age 65), are offset by the actuarial increase that the plan provides for commencement of benefits after normal retirement age.

(ii) The result is the same as in Example 1, even if the actuarial increases for post-age 65 benefit commencement provided under Plan A do or do not fully offset M's benefit accruals after attaining age 65. This is because benefit accruals after age 65 are disregarded for purposes of determining the age-adjusted section 415(b)(1)(A) dollar limit applicable to M after age 65.

**(f) Total annual payments not in excess of $10,000.** *(1) In general.* Pursuant to section 415(b)(4), the annual benefit (without regard to the age at which benefits commence) payable with respect to a participant under any defined benefit plan is not considered to exceed the limitations on benefits described in section 415(b)(1) and in paragraph (a)(1) of this section if—

(i) The benefits (other than benefits not taken into account in the computation of the annual benefit under the rules of paragraph (b) or (c) of this section) payable with respect to the participant under the plan and all other defined benefit plans of the employer do not in the aggregate exceed $10,000 (as adjusted under paragraph (g) of this section) for the limitation year, or for any prior limitation year; and

(ii) The employer (or a predecessor employer) has not at any time maintained a defined contribution plan in which the participant participated.

*(2) Computation of benefits for purposes of applying the $10,000 amount.* For purposes of paragraph (f)(1)(i) of this section, the benefits payable with respect to the participant under a plan for a limitation year reflect all amounts payable under the plan for the limitation year (other than benefits not taken into account in the computation of the annual benefit under the rules of paragraph (b) or (c) of this section), and are not adjusted for form of benefit or commencement date.

*(3) Special rule with respect to participants in multiemployer plans.* The special $10,000 exception set forth in paragraph (f)(1) of this section applies to a participant in a multiemployer plan described in section 414(f) without regard to whether that participant ever participated in one or more other plans maintained by an employer who also maintains

the multiemployer plan, provided that none of such other plans were maintained as a result of collective bargaining involving the same employee representative as the multiemployer plan.

*(4) Special rule with respect to employee contributions.* Notwithstanding §§ 1.415(c)-1(a)(2)(ii)(B) and 1.415(c)-1(b)(3), mandatory employee contributions under a defined benefit plan described in paragraph (b)(2)(iii) of this section are not considered a separate defined contribution plan maintained by the employer for purposes of paragraph (f)(1)(ii) of this section. Thus, the special dollar limitation provided for in this paragraph (f) applies to a contributory defined benefit plan. Similarly, for purposes of this paragraph (f), an individual medical account under section 401(h) or an account for postretirement medical benefits established pursuant to section 419A(d)(1) is not considered a separate defined contribution plan maintained by the employer.

*(5) Examples.* The application of this paragraph (f) may be illustrated by the following examples. For purposes of these examples, it is assumed that each participant has 10 years of participation in the plan and service with the employer. The examples are as follows:

*Example (1).* (i) B is a participant in a defined benefit plan maintained by X Corporation, which provides for a benefit payable in the form of a straight life annuity beginning at age 65. B's average compensation for the period of B's high-3 years of service is $6,000. The plan does not provide for mandatory employee contributions, and at no time has B been a participant in a defined contribution plan maintained by X. With respect to the current limitation year, B's benefit under the plan (before the application of section 415) is $9,500.

(ii) Because annual payments under B's benefit do not exceed $10,000, and because B has at no time participated in a defined contribution plan maintained by X, the benefits payable under the plan are not considered to exceed the limitation on benefits otherwise applicable to B ($6,000).

(iii) This result would remain the same even if, under the terms of the plan, B's benefit of $9,500 were payable at age 60, or if the plan provided for mandatory employee contributions.

*Example (2).* (i) The facts are the same as in Example 1, except that the plan provides for a benefit payable in the form of a life annuity with a 10-year certain feature with annual payments of $9,500. Assume that, after the adjustment described in paragraph (c) of this section, B's actuarially equivalent straight life annuity (which is the annual benefit used for demonstrating compliance with section 415) for the current limitation year is $10,400.

(ii) For purposes of applying the special rule provided in this paragraph for total benefits not in excess of $10,000, there is no adjustment required if the retirement benefit payable under the plan is not in the form of a straight life annuity. Therefore, because B's retirement benefit does not exceed $10,000, B may receive the full $9,500 benefit without the otherwise applicable benefit limitations of this section being exceeded.

*Example (3).* (i) The facts are the same as in Example 1, except that the plan provides for a benefit payable in the form of a single sum and the amount of the single sum that is the actuarial equivalent of the straight life annuity payable to B ($9,500 annually), determined in accordance with the rules of section 417(e)(3) and § 1.417(e)-1(d), is $95,000.

(ii) Because the amount payable to B for the limitation year would exceed $10,000, the rule of this paragraph (f) does not provide an exception from the generally applicable limits of section 415(b)(1) for the single-sum distribution. Thus, the otherwise applicable limits apply to the single-sum distribution, and a single-sum distribution of $95,000 would not satisfy the requirements of section 415(b). Limiting the single-sum distribution to $60,000 (the present value of the annuity that complies with the compensation-based limitation of section 415(b)(1)(B)) in order to satisfy section 415 would be an impermissible forfeiture under the requirements of section 411(a). Accordingly, the plan should not provide for a single-sum distribution in these circumstances.

**(g) Special rule for participation or service of less than 10 years.** *(1) Proration of dollar limit based on years of participation.* (i) In general. Pursuant to section 415(b)(5)(A), where a participant has less than 10 years of participation in the plan, the dollar limit described in paragraph (a)(1)(i) of this section (as adjusted pursuant to section 415(d), § 1.415(d)-1, and paragraphs (d) and (e) of this section) is reduced by multiplying the otherwise applicable limitation by a fraction—

(A) The numerator of which is the number of years of participation in the plan (or 1, if greater); and

(B) The denominator of which is 10.

(ii) Years of participation. The following rules apply for purposes of determining a participant's years of participation for purposes of this paragraph (g)(1)—

(A) A participant is credited with a year of participation (computed to fractional parts of a year) for each accrual computation period for which the participant is credited with at least the number of hours of service (or period of service if the elapsed time method is used for benefit accrual purposes) required under the terms of the plan in order to accrue a benefit for the accrual computation period, and the participant is included as a plan participant under the eligibility provisions of the plan for at least one day of the accrual computation period. If these two conditions are met, the portion of a year of participation credited to the participant is equal to the amount of benefit accrual service credited to the participant for such accrual computation period. For example, if under the terms of a plan, a participant receives 1/10 of a year of benefit accrual service for an accrual computation period for each 200 hours of service, and the participant is credited with 1,000 hours of service for the period, the participant is credited with 1/2 a year of participation for purposes of section 415(b)(5)(A) and this paragraph (g)(1).

(B) A participant who is permanently and totally disabled within the meaning of section 415(c)(3)(C)(i) for an accrual computation period is credited with a year of participation with respect to that period for purposes of section 415(b)(5)(A) and this paragraph (g)(1).

(C) For a participant to receive a year of participation (or part thereof) for an accrual computation period for purposes of section 415(b)(5)(A) and this paragraph (g)(1), the plan must be established no later than the last day of such accrual computation period.

(D) No more than one year of participation may be credited for any 12-month period for purposes of section 415(b)(5)(A) and this paragraph (g)(1).

*(2) Proration of compensation limit and special rule for total annual payments less than $10,000 based on years of service.* (i) In general. Pursuant to section 415(b)(5)(B), where a participant has less than 10 years of service with the employer, the compensation limit described in paragraph (a)(1)(ii) of this section and the $10,000 amount under the

special rule for small annual payments under paragraph (f) of this section are reduced by multiplying the otherwise applicable limitation by a fraction—

(A) The numerator of which is the number of years of service with the employer (or 1, if greater); and

(B) The denominator of which is 10.

(ii) Years of service. (A) In general. For purposes of applying this paragraph (g)(2), years of service must be determined on a reasonable and consistent basis. A plan is considered to be determining years of service on a reasonable and consistent basis for this purpose if, subject to the limits of paragraph (g)(2)(ii)(B) of this section, a participant is credited with a year of service (computed to fractional parts of a year) for each accrual computation period for which the participant is credited with at least the number of hours of service (or period of service if the elapsed time method is used for benefit accrual purposes) required under the terms of the plan in order to accrue a benefit for the accrual computation period.

(B) Rules of application. No more than one year of service may be credited for any 12-month period for purposes of section 415(b)(5)(B). In addition, only the participant's service with the employer or a predecessor employer (as defined in § 1.415(f)-1(c)) may be taken into account in determining the participant's years of service for this purpose. Thus, if an employer does not maintain a former employer's plan, a participant's service with the former employer may be taken into account in determining the participant's years of service for purposes of this paragraph (g)(2) only if the former employer is a predecessor employer with respect to the employer pursuant to § 1.415(f)-1(c)(2) (which defines predecessor employer to include, under certain circumstances, a former entity that antedates the employer).

(C) Period of disability. Notwithstanding the rules of paragraph (g)(2)(ii)(B) of this section, a plan is permitted to provide that a participant who is permanently and totally disabled within the meaning of section 415(c)(3)(C)(i) for an accrual computation period is credited with service with respect to that period for purposes of section 415(b)(5)(B).

*(3) Exception for survivor and disability benefits under governmental plans.* The requirements of this paragraph (g) (regarding participation or service of less than 10 years) do not apply to a distribution from a governmental plan (as defined in section 414(d)) on account of the participant's becoming disabled by reason of personal injuries or sickness, or as a result of the death of the participant.

*(4) Examples.* The provisions of this paragraph (g) may be illustrated by the following examples:

*Example (1).* (i) C begins employment with Employer A on January 1, 2005, at the age of 58. Employer A maintains only a noncontributory defined benefit plan which provides for a straight life annuity beginning at age 65 and uses the calendar year for the limitation and plan year. Employer A has never maintained a defined contribution plan. C becomes a participant in Employer A's plan on January 1, 2006, and works through December 31, 2011, when C is age 65. C begins to receive benefits under the plan in 2012. C's average compensation for the period of C's high-3 years of service is $40,000. Furthermore, under the terms of Employer A's plan, for purposes of computing C's nonforfeitable percentage in C's accrued benefit derived from employer contributions, C has only 7 years of service with Employer A (2005-2011).

(ii) Because C has only 7 years of service with Employer A at the time he begins to receive benefits under the plan, the maximum permissible annual benefit payable with respect to C is $28,000 ($40,000 multiplied by 7/10).

*Example (2).* (i) The facts are the same as in Example 1, except that C's average compensation for the period of his high-3 years of service is $8,000.

(ii) Because C has only 7 years of service with Employer A at the time he begins to receive benefits, the maximum benefit payable with respect to C would be reduced to $5,600 ($8,000 multiplied by 7/10). However, the special rule for total benefits not in excess of $10,000, provided in paragraph (f) of this section, is applicable in this case. Accordingly, C may receive an annual benefit of $7,000 ($10,000 multiplied by 7/10) without the benefit limitations of this section being exceeded.

*Example (3).* (i) Employer B maintains a defined benefit plan. Benefits under the plan are computed based on months of service rather than years of service. Accordingly, for purposes of applying the reduction based on years of service less than 10 to the limitations under section 415(b), the plan provides that the otherwise applicable limitation is multiplied by a fraction, the numerator of which is the number of completed months of service with the employer (but not less than 12 months), and the denominator of which is 120. The plan further provides that months of service are computed in the same manner for this purpose as for purposes of computing plan benefits.

(ii) The manner in which the plan applies the reduction based on years of service less than 10 to the limitations under section 415(b) is consistent with the requirements of this paragraph (g).

*Example (4).* (i) G begins employment with Employer D on January 1, 2003, at the age of 58. Employer D maintains a noncontributory defined benefit plan which provides for a straight life annuity beginning at age 65 and uses the calendar year for the limitation and plan year. G becomes a participant in Employer D's plan on January 1, 2004, and works through December 31, 2009, when G is age 65. G performs sufficient service to be credited with a year of service under the plan for each year during 2003 through 2009 (although G is not credited with a year of service for 2003 because G is not yet a plan participant). G begins to receive benefits under the plan during 2010. The plan's accrual computation period is the plan year. The plan provides that, for purposes of applying the rules of section 415(b)(5)(B), a participant is credited with a year of service (computed to fractional parts of a year) for each plan year for which the participant is credited with sufficient service to accrue a benefit for the plan year. G's average compensation for the period of G's high-3 years of service is $200,000. It is assumed for purposes of this example that the dollar limitation of section 415(b)(1)(A) for limitation years ending in 2010 is $195,000.

(ii) G has 7 years of service and 6 years of participation in the plan at the time G begins to receive benefits under the plan. Accordingly, the limitation under section 415(b)(1)(B) based on G's average compensation for the period of G's high-3 years of service that applies pursuant to the adjustment required under section 415(b)(5)(B) is $140,000 ($200,000 multiplied by 7/10), and the dollar limitation under section 415(b)(1)(A) that applies to G pursuant to the adjustment required under section 415(b)(5)(A) is $117,000 ($195,000 multiplied by 6/10).

**(h) Retirement Protection Act of 1994 transition rules.** For special rules affecting the actuarial adjustment for form of benefit under paragraph (c) of this section and the adjustment to the dollar limit for early or late commencement under paragraphs (d) and (e) of this section for certain plans adopted and in effect before December 8, 1994, see section 767(d)(3)(A) of the Uruguay Round Agreements Act of 1994, Public Law 103-465 (108 Stat. 4809) as amended by section 1449(a) of the Small Business Job Protection Act of 1996, Public Law 104-188 (110 Stat. 1755). The Commissioner may provide guidance regarding these special rules in revenue rulings, notices, and other guidance published in the Internal Revenue Bulletin. See § 601.601(d) of this chapter.

T.D. 9319, 4/4/2007.

**§ 1.415(b)-2 [Reserved] Multiple annuity starting dates.**

T.D. 9319, 4/4/2007.

**§ 1.415(c)-1 Limitations for defined contribution plans.**

**(a) General rules.** *(1) Maximum limitations.* Under section 415(c) and this section, to satisfy the provisions of section 415(a) for any limitation year, except as provided by paragraph (a)(3) of this section, the annual additions (as defined in paragraph (b) of this section) credited to the account of a participant in a defined contribution plan for the limitation year must not exceed the lesser of—

(i) $40,000 (adjusted pursuant to section 415(d) and § 1.415(d)-1(b)); or

(ii) 100 percent of the participant's compensation (as defined in § 1.415(c)-2 for the limitation year.

*(2) Defined contribution plan.* (i) Definition. For purposes of section 415 and regulations promulgated under section 415, the term defined contribution plan means a defined contribution plan within the meaning of section 414(i) (including the portion of a plan treated as a defined contribution plan under the rules of section 414(k)) that is—

(A) A plan described in section 401(a) which includes a trust which is exempt from tax under section 501(a);

(B) An annuity plan described in section 403(a); or

(C) A simplified employee pension described in section 408(k).

(ii) Additional plans treated as defined contribution plans. (A) In general. Contributions to the types of arrangements described in paragraphs (a)(2)(ii)(B) through (D) of this section are treated as contributions to defined contribution plans for purposes of section 415 and regulations promulgated under section 415.

(B) Employee contributions to a defined benefit plan. Mandatory employee contributions (as defined in section 411(c)(2)(C) and § 1.411(c)-1(c)(4), regardless of whether the plan is subject to the requirements of section 411) to a defined benefit plan are treated as contributions to a defined contribution plan. For this purpose, contributions that are picked up by the employer as described in section 414(h)(2) are not considered employee contributions.

(C) Individual medical benefit accounts under section 401(h). Pursuant to section 415(l)(1), contributions allocated to any individual medical benefit account which is part of a pension or annuity plan established pursuant to section 401(h) are treated as contributions to a defined contribution plan.

(D) Post-retirement medical accounts for key employees. Pursuant to section 419A(d)(2), amounts attributable to medical benefits allocated to an account established for a key employee (any employee who, at any time during the plan year or any preceding plan year, is or was a key employee as defined in section 416(i)) pursuant to section 419A(d)(1) are treated as contributions to a defined contribution plan.

(iii) Section 403(b) annuity contracts. Annual additions under an annuity contract described in section 403(b) are treated as annual additions under a defined contribution plan for purposes of this section.

*(3) Alternative contribution limitations.* (i) Church plans. For alternative contribution limitations relating to church plans, see paragraph (d) of this section.

(ii) Special rules for medical benefits. For additional rules relating to certain medical benefits, see paragraph (e) of this section.

(iii) Employee stock ownership plans. For additional rules relating to employee stock ownership plans, see paragraph (f) of this section.

**(b) Annual additions.** *(1) In general.* (i) General definition. The term annual addition means, for purposes of this section, the sum, credited to a participant's account for any limitation year, of—

(A) Employer contributions;

(B) Employee contributions; and

(C) Forfeitures.

(ii) Certain excess amounts treated as annual additions. Contributions do not fail to be annual additions merely because they are excess contributions (as described in section 401(k)(8)(B)) or excess aggregate contributions (as described in section 401(m)(6)(B)), or merely because excess contributions or excess aggregate contributions are corrected through distribution.

(iii) Direct transfers. The direct transfer of a benefit or employee contributions from a qualified plan to a defined contribution plan does not give rise to an annual addition.

(iv) Reinvested employee stock ownership plan dividends. The reinvestment of dividends on employer securities under an employee stock ownership plan pursuant to section 404(k)(2)(A)(iii)(II) does not give rise to an annual addition.

*(2) Employer contributions.* (i) Amounts treated as an annual addition. For purposes of paragraph (b)(1)(i)(A) of this section, the term annual addition includes employer contributions credited to the participant's account for the limitation year and other allocations described in paragraph (b)(4) of this section that are made during the limitation year. See paragraph (b)(6) of this section for timing rules applicable to annual additions with respect to employer contributions.

(ii) Amounts not treated as annual additions. (A) Certain restorations of accrued benefits. The restoration of an employee's accrued benefit by the employer in accordance with section 411(a)(3)(D) or section 411(a)(7)(C) or resulting from the repayment of cashouts (as described in section 415(k)(3)) under a governmental plan (as defined in section 414(d)) is not considered an annual addition for the limitation year in which the restoration occurs. This treatment of a restoration of an employee's accrued benefit as not giving rise to an annual addition applies regardless of whether the plan restricts the timing of repayments to the maximum extent allowed by section 411(a).

(B) Catch-up contributions. A catch-up contribution made in accordance with section 414(v) and § 1.414(v)-1 does not give rise to an annual addition.

(C) Restorative payments. A restorative payment that is allocated to a participant's account does not give rise to an annual addition for any limitation year. For this purpose, restorative payments are payments made to restore losses to a plan resulting from actions by a fiduciary for which there is reasonable risk of liability for breach of a fiduciary duty under Title I of the Employee Retirement Income Security Act of 1974 (88 Stat. 829), Public Law 93-406 (ERISA) or under other applicable federal or state law, where plan participants who are similarly situated are treated similarly with respect to the payments. Generally, payments to a defined contribution plan are restorative payments only if the payments are made in order to restore some or all of the plan's losses due to an action (or a failure to act) that creates a reasonable risk of liability for such a breach of fiduciary duty (other than a breach of fiduciary duty arising from failure to remit contributions to the plan). This includes payments to a plan made pursuant to a Department of Labor order, the Department of Labor's Voluntary Fiduciary Correction Program, or a court-approved settlement, to restore losses to a qualified defined contribution plan on account of the breach of fiduciary duty (other than a breach of fiduciary duty arising from failure to remit contributions to the plan). Payments made to a plan to make up for losses due merely to market fluctuations and other payments that are not made on account of a reasonable risk of liability for breach of a fiduciary duty under Title I of ERISA are not restorative payments and generally constitute contributions that give rise to annual additions under paragraph (b)(4) of this section.

(D) Excess deferrals. Excess deferrals that are distributed in accordance with § 1.402(g)-1(e)(2) or (3) do not give rise to annual additions.

*(3) Employee contributions.* For purposes of paragraph (b)(1)(i)(B) of this section, the term annual addition includes mandatory employee contributions (as defined in section 411(c)(2)(C) and regulations promulgated under section 411) as well as voluntary employee contributions. The term annual addition does not include—

(i) Rollover contributions (as described in sections 401(a)(31), 402(c)(1), 403(a)(4), 403(b)(8), 408(d)(3), and 457(e)(16));

(ii) Repayments of loans made to a participant from the plan;

(iii) Repayments of amounts described in section 411(a)(7)(B) (in accordance with section 411(a)(7)(C)) and section 411(a)(3)(D) or repayment of contributions to a governmental plan (as defined in section 414(d)) as described in section 415(k)(3);

(iv) Repayments that would have been described in paragraph (b)(3)(iii) of this section except that the plan does not restrict the timing of repayments to the maximum extent permitted by section 411(a); or

(v) Employee contributions to a qualified cost of living arrangement within the meaning of section 415(k)(2)(B).

*(4) Transactions with plan.* The Commissioner may in an appropriate case, considering all of the facts and circumstances, treat transactions between the plan and the employer, transactions between the plan and the employee, or certain allocations to participants' accounts as giving rise to annual additions. Further, where an employee or employer transfers assets to a plan in exchange for consideration that is less than the fair market value of the assets transferred to the plan, there is an annual addition in the amount of the difference between the value of the assets transferred and the consideration. A transaction described in this paragraph (b)(4) may constitute a prohibited transaction with the meaning of section 4975(c)(1).

*(5) Contributions other than cash.* For purposes of this paragraph (b), a contribution by the employer or employee of property rather than cash is considered to be a contribution in an amount equal to the fair market value of the property on the date the contribution is made. For this purpose, the fair market value is the price at which the property would change hands between a willing buyer and a willing seller, neither being under any compulsion to buy or to sell and both having reasonable knowledge of relevant facts. In addition, a contribution described in this paragraph (b)(5) may constitute a prohibited transaction within the meaning of section 4975(c)(1).

*(6) Timing rules.* (i) In general.

(A) Date of allocation. For purposes of this paragraph (b), an annual addition is credited to the account of a participant for a particular limitation year if it is allocated to the participant's account under the terms of the plan as of any date within that limitation year. Similarly, an annual addition that is made pursuant to a corrective amendment that complies with the requirements of § 1.401(a)(4)-11(g) is credited to the account of a participant for a particular limitation year if it is allocated to the participant's account under the terms of the corrective amendment as of any date within that limitation year. However, if the allocation of an annual addition is dependent upon the satisfaction of a condition (such as continued employment or the occurrence of an event) that has not been satisfied by the date as of which the annual addition is allocated under the terms of the plan, then the annual addition is considered allocated for purposes of this paragraph (b) as of the date the condition is satisfied.

(B) Date of employer contributions. For purposes of this paragraph (b), employer contributions are not treated as credited to a participant's account for a particular limitation year unless the contributions are actually made to the plan no later than 30 days after the end of the period described in section 404(a)(6) applicable to the taxable year with or within which the particular limitation year ends. If, however, contributions are made by an employer exempt from Federal income tax (including a governmental employer), the contributions must be made to the plan no later than the 15th day of the tenth calendar month following the end of the calendar year or fiscal year (as applicable, depending on the basis on which the employer keeps its books) with or within which the particular limitation year ends. If contributions are made to a plan after the end of the period during which contributions can be made and treated as credited to a participant's account for a particular limitation year, allocations attributable to those contributions are treated as credited to the participant's account for the limitation year during which those contributions are made.

(C) Date of employee contributions. For purposes of this paragraph (b), employee contributions, whether voluntary or mandatory, are not treated as credited to a participant's account for a particular limitation year unless the contributions are actually made to the plan no later than 30 days after the close of that limitation year.

(D) Date for forfeitures. A forfeiture is treated as an annual addition for the limitation year that contains the date as of which it is allocated to a participant's account as a forfeiture.

(E) Treatment of elective contributions as plan assets. The extent to which elective contributions constitute plan assets for purposes of the prohibited transaction provisions of section 4975 and Title I of ERISA, is determined in accordance with regulations and rulings issued by the Department of Labor. See 29 CFR 2510.3-102.

(ii) Special timing rules. (A) Corrective contributions. For purposes of this section, if, in a particular limitation year, an employer allocates an amount to a participant's account because of an erroneous forfeiture in a prior limitation year, or because of an erroneous failure to allocate amounts in a prior limitation year, the corrective allocation will not be considered an annual addition with respect to the participant for that particular limitation year, but will be considered an annual addition for the prior limitation year to which it relates. An example of a situation in which an employer contribution might occur under the circumstances described in the preceding sentence is a retroactive crediting of service for an employee under 29 CFR 2530.200b-2(a)(3) in accordance with an award of back pay. For purposes of this paragraph (b)(6)(ii), if the amount so contributed in the particular limitation year takes into account actual investment gains attributable to the period subsequent to the year to which the contribution relates, the portion of the total contribution that consists of such gains is not considered as an annual addition for any limitation year.

(B) Contributions for accumulated funding deficiencies and previously waived contributions. (1) Accumulated funding deficiency. In the case of a defined contribution plan to which the rules of section 412 apply, a contribution made to reduce an accumulated funding deficiency will be treated as if it were timely made for purposes of determining the limitation year in which the annual additions arising from the contribution are made, but only if the contribution is allocated to those participants who would have received an annual addition if the contribution had been timely made.

(2) Previously waived contributions. In the case of a defined contribution plan to which the rules of section 412 apply and for which there has been a waiver of the minimum funding standard in a prior limitation year in accordance with section 412(d), that portion of an employer contribution in a subsequent limitation year which, if not for the waiver, would have otherwise been required in the prior limitation year under section 412(a) will be treated as if it were timely made (without regard to the funding waiver) for purposes of determining the limitation year in which the annual additions arising from the contribution are made, but only if the contribution is allocated to those participants who would have received an annual addition if the contribution had been timely made (without regard to the funding waiver).

(3) Interest. For purposes of determining the amount of the annual addition under paragraphs (b)(6)(ii)(B)(1) and (2) of this section, a reasonable amount of interest paid by the employer is disregarded. However, any interest paid by the employer that is in excess of a reasonable amount, as determined by the Commissioner, is taken into account as an annual addition for the limitation year during which the contribution is made.

(C) Simplified employee pensions. For purposes of this paragraph (b), amounts contributed to a simplified employee pension described in section 408(k) are treated as allocated to the individual's account as of the last day of the limitation year ending with or within the taxable year for which the contribution is made.

(D) Treatment of certain contributions made pursuant to veterans' reemployment rights. If, in a particular limitation year, an employer contributes an amount to an employee's account with respect to a prior limitation year and such contribution is required by reason of such employee's rights under chapter 43 of title 38, United States Code, resulting from qualified military service, as specified in section 414(u)(1), then such contribution is not considered an annual addition with respect to the employee for that particular limitation year in which the contribution is made, but, in accordance with section 414(u)(1)(B), is considered an annual addition for the limitation year to which the contribution relates.

**(c) Examples.** The following examples illustrate the rules of paragraphs (a) and (b) of this section:

*Example (1).* (i) P is a participant in a qualified profit-sharing plan maintained by his employer, ABC Corporation. The limitation year for the plan is the calendar year. P's compensation (as defined in § 1.415(c)-2) for the current limitation year is $30,000.

(ii) Because the compensation limitation described in section 415(c)(1)(B) applicable to P for the current limitation year is lower than the dollar limitation described in section 415(c)(1)(A), the maximum annual addition which can be allocated to P's account for the current limitation year is $30,000 (100 percent of $30,000).

*Example (2).* (i) The facts are the same as in Example 1, except that P's compensation for the current limitation year is $140,000.

(ii) The maximum amount of annual additions that may be allocated to P's account in the current limitation year is the lesser of $140,000 (100 percent of P's compensation) or the dollar limitation of section 415(c)(1)(A) as in effect as of January 1 of the calendar year in which the current limitation year ends. If, for example, the dollar limitation of section 415(c)(1)(A) in effect as of January 1 of the calendar year in which the current limitation year ends is $45,000, then the maximum annual addition that can be allocated to P's account for the current limitation year is $45,000.

*Example (3).* (i) Employer N maintains a qualified profit-sharing plan that uses the calendar year as its plan year and its limitation year. N's taxable year is a fiscal year beginning June 1 and ending May 31. Under the terms of the profit-sharing plan maintained by N, employer contributions are made to the plan two months after the close of N's taxable year and are allocated as of the last day of the plan year ending within the taxable year (and are not dependent on the satisfaction of a condition). Thus, employer contributions for the 2008 calendar year limitation year are made on July 31, 2009 (the date that is two months after the close of N's taxable year ending May 31, 2009) and are allocated as of December 31, 2008.

(ii) Because the employer contributions are actually made to the plan no later than 30 days after the end of the period described in section 404(a)(6) with respect to N's taxable year ending May 31, 2009, the contributions will be considered annual additions for the 2008 calendar year limitation year.

*Example (4).* (i) The facts are the same as in Example 3, except that the plan year for the profit-sharing plan maintained by N is the 12-month period beginning on February 1 and ending on January 31. The limitation year continues to be the calendar year. Under the terms of the plan, an employer contribution which is made to the plan on July 31, 2009, is allocated to participants' accounts as of January 31, 2009.

(ii) Because the last day of the plan year is in the 2009 calendar year limitation year, and because, under the terms of the plan, employer contributions are allocated to participants' accounts as of the last day of the plan year, the contributions are considered annual additions for the 2009 calendar year limitation year.

*Example (5).* (i) XYZ Corporation maintains a profit-sharing plan to which a participant may make voluntary employee contributions for any year not to exceed 10 percent of the participant's compensation for the year. The plan permits a participant to make retroactive make-up contributions for any year for which the participant contributed less than 10 percent of compensation. XYZ uses the calendar year as the plan year and the limitation year. Under the terms of the plan, voluntary employee contributions are credited to a participant's account for a particular limitation year if such contributions are allocated to the participant's account as of any date within that limitation year. Participant A's compensation is as follows—

| Limitation year | Compensation |
|---|---|
| 2008 .................... | $30,000 |
| 2009 .................... | $32,000 |
| 2010 .................... | $34,000 |
| 2011 .................... | $36,000 |

(ii) Participant A makes no voluntary employee contributions during limitation years 2008, 2009, and 2010. On October 1, 2011, participant A makes a voluntary employee contribution of $13,200 (10 percent of A's aggregate compensation for limitation years 2008, 2009, 2010, and 2011 of $132,000). Under the terms of the plan, $3,000 of this 2011 contribution is allocated to A's account as of limitation year 2008; $3,200 is allocated to A's account of limitation year 2009; $3,400 is allocated to A's account as of limitation year 2010, and $3,600 is allocated to A's account as of limitation year 2011.

(iii) Under the rule set forth in paragraph (b)(6)(i)(C) of this section, employee contributions will not be considered credited to a participant's account for a particular limitation year for section 415 purposes unless the contributions are actually made to the plan no later than 30 days after the close of that limitation year. Thus, A's voluntary employee contribution of $13,200 made on October 1, 2011, would be considered as credited to A's account only for the 2011 calendar year limitation year, notwithstanding the plan provisions.

**(d) Special rules relating to church plans.** *(1) Alternative contribution limitation.* (i) In general. Pursuant to section 415(c)(7)(A), notwithstanding the general rule of paragraph (a)(1) of this section, additions for a section 403(b) annuity contract for a year with respect to a participant who is an employee of a church or a convention or association of churches, including an organization described in section 414(e)(3)(B)(ii), when expressed as an annual addition to such participant's account, are treated as not exceeding the limitation of paragraph (a)(1) of this section if such annual additions for the year are not in excess of $10,000.

(ii) $40,000 aggregate limitation. With respect to any participant, the total amount of annual additions that are in excess of the limitation of paragraph (a)(1) of this section but, pursuant to the rule of paragraph (d)(1)(i) of this section, are treated as not exceeding that limitation (taking into account the rule of paragraph (d)(3) of this section) cannot exceed $40,000. Thus, the aggregate of annual additions for all limitation years that would exceed the limitation of this section but for this paragraph (d)(1) is limited to $40,000.

*(2) Years of service taken into account for duly ordained, commissioned, or licensed ministers or lay employees.* For purposes of this paragraph (d)—

(i) All years of service by an individual as an employee of a church, or a convention or association of churches, including an organization described in section 414(e)(3)(B)(ii), are considered as years of service for one employer; and

(ii) All amounts contributed for annuity contracts by each such church (or convention or association of churches) during such years for the employee are considered to have been contributed by one employer.

*(3) Foreign missionaries.* Pursuant to section 415(c)(7)(C), in the case of any individual described in paragraph (d)(1) of this section performing any services for the church outside the United States during the limitation year, additions for an annuity contract under section 403(b) for any year are not treated as exceeding the limitation of paragraph (a)(1) of this section if such annual additions for the year do not exceed $3,000. The preceding sentence shall not apply with respect to any taxable year to any individual whose adjusted gross income for such taxable year (determined separately and without regard to community property law) exceeds $17,000.

*(4) Church, convention or association of churches.* For purposes of this paragraph (d), the terms "church" and "convention or association of churches" have the same meaning as when used in section 414(e).

*(5) Examples.* The following examples illustrate the rules of this paragraph (d):

*Example (1).* (i) E is an employee of ABC Church earning $7,000 during each calendar year. E participates in a section 403(b) annuity contract maintained by ABC Church beginning in the year 2008. E's taxable year is the calendar year, and the limitation year for the plan coincides with the calendar year. ABC Church contributes $10,000 to be allocated to E's account under the plan for the year 2008.

(ii) Under paragraph (d)(1) of this section, this allocation is treated as not violating the limits established in paragraph (a)(1) of this section because it does not exceed $10,000. Moreover, since an annual addition of $10,000 would otherwise exceed the limitation of paragraph (a)(1) of this section by $3,000, $3,000 is counted toward the aggregate limitation specified in paragraph (d)(1)(ii) of this section for year 2008. Accordingly, ABC Church may make such allocations for 13 years (for example, for years 2008 through 2020) without exceeding the aggregate limitation of $40,000 specified in paragraph (d) of this section. For the fourteenth year, ABC Church could allocate only $8,000 to E's account (the sum of the $7,000 limitation computed under paragraph (a)(1)(ii) of this section and the remaining $1,000 of the $40,000 aggregate limitation under paragraph (d)(1)(ii) of this section on annual additions in excess of the limits under paragraph (a)(1) of this section).

*Example (2).* (i) F is an employee of XYZ Church and F's taxable year is the calendar year. F earns $2,000 during each calendar year for services he provides to XYZ Church, all of which are performed outside the United States during each calendar year. F participates in a section 403(b) annuity contract maintained by ABC Church beginning in the year 2008. The limitation year for the plan coincides with the calendar year. ABC Church contributes $10,000 to be allocated to F's account under the plan for the year 2008. F's adjusted gross income for each taxable year (determined separately and without regard to community property law) does not exceed $17,000.

(ii) Under paragraph (d)(1) of this section, this allocation is treated as not violating the limits established in paragraph (a)(1) of this section because it does not exceed $10,000. Moreover, since an annual addition of $10,000 would otherwise exceed the limitation of paragraph (a)(1) of this section by $7,000 (the excess of $10,000 over the greater of the $2,000 compensation limitation under section 415(c)(1)(B) or the $3,000 section 415(c)(7)(C) amount), XYZ Church may make such allocations for 5 years (for example, for years 2008 through 2012) without exceeding the aggregate limitation of $40,000 specified in paragraph (d) of this section. In year 2013, XYZ church may contribute $8,000 to be allocated to F's account under the plan (the sum of the $3,000 limitation computed under paragraph (d)(3) of this section and the remaining $5,000 of the $40,000 aggregate limitation under paragraph (d)(1)(ii) of this section on annual additions in excess of the limits under paragraph (a)(1) of this section). For years after 2013, pursuant to paragraph (d)(3) of this section, XYZ Church could allocate $3,000 per year to F's account.

**(e) Special rules for medical benefits.** The limit under paragraph (a)(1)(ii) of this section (100 percent of the participant's compensation for the limitation year) does not apply to—

*(1)* An individual medical benefit account (as defined in section 415(l)); or

*(2)* A post-retirement medical benefits account for a key employee (as defined in section 419A(d)(1)).

**(f) Special rules for employee stock ownership plans.** *(1) In general.* Special rules apply to employee stock ownership plans, as provided in paragraphs (f)(2) through (f)(4) of this section.

*(2) Determination of annual additions for leveraged employee stock ownership plans.* (i) In general. Except as provided in this paragraph (f) of this section, in the case of an employee stock ownership plan to which an exempt loan as described in § 54.4975-7(b) of this chapter has been made, the amount of employer contributions that is considered an annual addition for the limitation year is calculated with respect to employer contributions of both principal and interest used to repay that exempt loan for the limitation year.

(ii) Employer stock that has decreased in value. A plan may provide that, in lieu of computing annual additions in accordance with paragraph (f)(2)(i) of this section, annual additions with respect to a loan repayment described in paragraph (f)(2)(i) of this section are determined as the fair market value of shares released from the suspense account on account of the repayment and allocated to participants for the limitation year if that amount is less than the amount determined in accordance with paragraph (f)(2)(i) of this section.

*(3) Exclusions from annual additions for certain employee stock ownership plans that allocate to a broad range of participants.* (i) General rule. Pursuant to section 415(c)(6), in the case of an employee stock ownership plan (as described in section 4975(e)(7)) that meets the requirements of paragraph (f)(3)(ii) of this section for a limitation year, the limitations imposed by this section do not apply to—

(A) Forfeitures of employer securities (within the meaning of section 409(l)) under such an employee stock ownership plan if such securities were acquired with the proceeds of a loan (as described in section 404(a)(9)(A)); or

(B) Employer contributions to such an employee stock ownership plan which are deductible under section 404(a)(9)(B) and charged against the participant's account.

(ii) Employee stock ownership plans to which the special exclusion applies. An employee stock ownership plan meets the requirements of this paragraph (f)(3)(ii) for a limitation year if no more than one-third of the employer contributions for the limitation year that are deductible under section 404(a)(9) are allocated to highly compensated employees (within the meaning of section 414(q)).

*(4) Gratuitous transfers under section 664(g)(1).* The amount of any qualified gratuitous transfer (as defined in section 664(g)(1)) allocated to a participant for any limitation year is not taken into account in determining whether any other annual addition exceeds the limitations imposed by this section, but only if the amount of the qualified gratuitous transfer does not exceed the limitations imposed by section 415.

T.D. 9319, 4/4/2007.

### § 1.415(c)-2 Compensation.

**(a) General definition.** Except as otherwise provided in this section, compensation from the employer within the meaning of section 415(c)(3), which is used for purposes of section 415 and regulations promulgated under section 415, means all items of remuneration described in paragraph (b) of this section, but excludes the items of remuneration described in paragraph (c) of this section. Paragraph (d) of this section provides safe harbor definitions of compensation that are permitted to be provided in a plan in lieu of the generally applicable definition of compensation. Paragraph (e) of this section provides timing rules relating to compensation. Paragraph (f) of this section provides rules regarding the application of the rules of section 401(a)(17) to the definition of compensation for purposes of section 415. Paragraph (g) of this section provides special rules relating to the determination of compensation, including rules for determining compensation for a section 403(b) annuity contract, rules for determining the compensation of employees of controlled groups or affiliated service groups, rules for disabled employees, rules relating to foreign compensation, rules regarding deemed section 125 compensation, rules for employees in qualified military service, and rules relating to back pay.

**(b) Items includible as compensation.** For purposes of applying the limitations of section 415, except as otherwise provided in this section, the term compensation means remuneration for services of the following types—

*(1)* The employee's wages, salaries, fees for professional services, and other amounts received (without regard to whether or not an amount is paid in cash) for personal services actually rendered in the course of employment with the employer maintaining the plan, to the extent that the amounts are includible in gross income (or to the extent amounts would have been received and includible in gross income but for an election under section 125(a), 132(f)(4), 402(e)(3), 402(h)(1)(B), 402(k), or 457(b)). These amounts include, but are not limited to, commissions paid to salespersons, compensation for services on the basis of a percentage of profits, commissions on insurance premiums, tips, bonuses, fringe benefits, and reimbursements or other expense allowances under a nonaccountable plan as described in § 1.62-2(c).

*(2)* In the case of an employee who is an employee within the meaning of section 401(c)(1) and regulations promulgated under section 401(c)(1), the employee's earned income (as described in section 401(c)(2) and regulations promulgated under section 401(c)(2)), plus amounts deferred at the election of the employee that would be includible in gross

income but for the rules of section 402(e)(3), 402(h)(1)(B), 402(k), or 457(b).

*(3)* Amounts described in section 104(a)(3), 105(a), or 105(h), but only to the extent that these amounts are includible in the gross income of the employee.

*(4)* Amounts paid or reimbursed by the employer for moving expenses incurred by an employee, but only to the extent that at the time of the payment it is reasonable to believe that these amounts are not deductible by the employee under section 217.

*(5)* The value of a nonstatutory option (which is an option other than a statutory option as defined in § 1.421-1(b)) granted to an employee by the employer, but only to the extent that the value of the option is includible in the gross income of the employee for the taxable year in which granted.

*(6)* The amount includible in the gross income of an employee upon making the election described in section 83(b).

*(7)* Amounts that are includible in the gross income of an employee under the rules of section 409A or section 457(f)(1)(A) or because the amounts are constructively received by the employee.

**(c) Items not includible as compensation.** The term compensation does not include—

*(1)* Contributions (other than elective contributions described in section 402(e)(3), section 408(k)(6), section 408(p)(2)(A)(i), or section 457(b)) made by the employer to a plan of deferred compensation (including a simplified employee pension described in section 408(k) or a simple retirement account described in section 408(p), and whether or not qualified) to the extent that the contributions are not includible in the gross income of the employee for the taxable year in which contributed. In addition, any distributions from a plan of deferred compensation (whether or not qualified) are not considered as compensation for section 415 purposes, regardless of whether such amounts are includible in the gross income of the employee when distributed. However, if the plan so provides, any amounts received by an employee pursuant to a nonqualified unfunded deferred compensation plan are permitted to be considered as compensation for section 415 purposes in the year the amounts are actually received, but only to the extent such amounts are includible in the employee's gross income.

*(2)* Amounts realized from the exercise of a nonstatutory option (which is an option other than a statutory option as defined in § 1.421-1(b)), or when restricted stock or other property held by an employee either becomes freely transferable or is no longer subject to a substantial risk of forfeiture (see section 83 and regulations promulgated under section 83).

*(3)* Amounts realized from the sale, exchange, or other disposition of stock acquired under a statutory stock option (as defined in § 1.421-1(b)).

*(4)* Other amounts that receive special tax benefits, such as premiums for group-term life insurance (but only to the extent that the premiums are not includible in the gross income of the employee and are not salary reduction amounts that are described in section 125).

*(5)* Other items of remuneration that are similar to any of the items listed in paragraphs (c)(1) through (c)(4) of this section.

**(d) Safe harbor rules with respect to plan's definition of compensation.** *(1) In general.* Paragraphs (d)(2) through (4) of this section contain safe harbor definitions of compensation that are automatically considered to satisfy section 415(c)(3) if specified in the plan. The Commissioner may, in revenue rulings, notices, and other guidance of general applicability published in the Internal Revenue Bulletin (see § 601.601(d)(2) of this chapter), provide additional definitions of compensation that are treated as satisfying section 415(c)(3).

*(2) Simplified compensation.* The safe harbor definition of compensation under this paragraph (d)(2) includes only those items specified in paragraph (b)(1) or (2) of this section and excludes all those items listed in paragraph (c) of this section.

*(3) Section 3401(a) wages.* The safe harbor definition of compensation under this paragraph (d)(3) includes wages within the meaning of section 3401(a) (for purposes of income tax withholding at the source), plus amounts that would be included in wages but for an election under section 125(a), 132(f)(4), 402(e)(3), 402(h)(1)(B), 402(k), or 457(b). However, any rules that limit the remuneration included in wages based on the nature or location of the employment or the services performed (such as the exception for agricultural labor in section 3401(a)(2)) are disregarded for this purpose.

*(4) Information required to be reported under sections 6041, 6051 and 6052.* The safe harbor definition of compensation under this paragraph (d)(4) includes amounts that are compensation under the safe harbor definition of paragraph (d)(3) of this section, plus all other payments of compensation to an employee by his employer (in the course of the employer's trade or business) for which the employer is required to furnish the employee a written statement under sections 6041(d), 6051(a)(3), and 6052. See §§ 1.6041-1(a), 1.6041-2(a)(1), 1.6052-1, and 1.6052-2, and also see § 31.6051-1(a)(1)(i)(C) of this chapter. This safe harbor definition of compensation may be modified to exclude amounts paid or reimbursed by the employer for moving expenses incurred by an employee, but only to the extent that, at the time of the payment, it is reasonable to believe that these amounts are deductible by the employee under section 217.

**(e) Timing rules.** *(1) In general.* (i) Payment during the limitation year. Except as otherwise provided in this paragraph (e), in order to be taken into account for a limitation year, compensation within the meaning of section 415(c)(3) must be actually paid or made available to an employee (or, if earlier, includible in the gross income of the employee) within the limitation year. For this purpose, compensation is treated as paid on a date if it is actually paid on that date or it would have been paid on that date but for an election under section 125, 132(f)(4), 401(k), 403(b), 408(k), 408(p)(2)(A)(i), or 457(b).

(ii) Payment prior to severance from employment. Except as otherwise provided in this paragraph (e), in order to be taken into account for a limitation year, compensation within the meaning of section 415(c)(3) must be paid or treated as paid to the employee (in accordance with the rules of paragraph (e)(1)(i) of this section) prior to the employee's severance from employment with the employer maintaining the plan See § 1.415(a)-1(f)(5) for the definition of severance from employment.

*(2) Certain minor timing differences.* Notwithstanding the provisions of paragraph (e)(1)(i) of this section, a plan may provide that compensation for a limitation year includes amounts earned during that limitation year but not paid during that limitation year solely because of the timing of pay periods and pay dates if—

(i) These amounts are paid during the first few weeks of the next limitation year;

(ii) The amounts are included on a uniform and consistent basis with respect to all similarly situated employees; and

(iii) No compensation is included in more than one limitation year.

*(3) Compensation paid after severance from employment.* (i) In general. Any compensation described in paragraph (e)(3)(ii) of this section does not fail to be compensation (within the meaning of section 415(c)(3)) pursuant to the rule of paragraph (e)(1)(ii) of this section merely because it is paid after the employee's severance from employment with the employer maintaining the plan, provided the compensation is paid by the later of 2½ months after severance from employment with the employer maintaining the plan or the end of the limitation year that includes the date of severance from employment with the employer maintaining the plan. In addition, the plan may provide that amounts described in paragraph (e)(3)(iii) of this section are included in compensation (within the meaning of section 415(c)(3)) if—

(A) Those amounts are paid by the later of 2½ months after severance from employment with the employer maintaining the plan or the end of the limitation year that includes the date of severance from employment with the employer maintaining the plan; and

(B) Those amounts would have been included in the definition of compensation if they were paid prior to the employee's severance from employment with the employer maintaining the plan.

(ii) Regular pay after severance from employment. An amount is described in this paragraph (e)(3)(ii) if—

(A) The payment is regular compensation for services during the employee's regular working hours, or compensation for services outside the employee's regular working hours (such as overtime or shift differential), commissions, bonuses, or other similar payments; and

(B) The payment would have been paid to the employee prior to a severance from employment if the employee had continued in employment with the employer.

(iii) Leave cashouts and deferred compensation. An amount is described in this paragraph (e)(3)(iii) if the amount is either—

(A) Payment for unused accrued bona fide sick, vacation, or other leave, but only if the employee would have been able to use the leave if employment had continued; or

(B) Received by an employee pursuant to a nonqualified unfunded deferred compensation plan, but only if the payment would have been paid to the employee at the same time if the employee had continued in employment with the employer and only to the extent that the payment is includible in the employee's gross income.

(iv) Other post-severance payments. Any payment that is not described in paragraph (e)(3)(ii) or (iii) of this section is not considered compensation under paragraph (e)(3)(i) of this section if paid after severance from employment with the employer maintaining the plan, even if it is paid within the time period described in paragraph (e)(3)(i) of this section. Thus, compensation does not include severance pay, or parachute payments within the meaning of section 280G(b)(2), if they are paid after severance from employment with the employer maintaining the plan, and does not include post-severance payments under a nonqualified unfunded deferred compensation plan unless the payments would have been paid at that time without regard to the severance from employment.

*(4) Salary continuation payments for military service and disabled participants.* The rule of paragraph (e)(1)(ii) of this section does not apply to payments to an individual who does not currently perform services for the employer by reason of qualified military service (as that term is used in section 414(u)(1)) to the extent those payments do not exceed the amounts the individual would have received if the individual had continued to perform services for the employer rather than entering qualified military service, but only if the plan so provides. In addition, the rule of paragraph (e)(1)(ii) of this section does not apply to compensation paid to a participant who is permanently and totally disabled (as defined in section 22(e)(3)) if the conditions set forth in paragraph (g)(4)(ii)(A) of this section are satisfied (applied by substituting a continuation of compensation for the continuation of contributions), but only if the plan so provides.

*(5) Special rule for governmental plans.* For purposes of applying the rules of paragraph (e)(3) of this section, a governmental plan (as defined in section 414(d)) may provide for the substitution of the calendar year in which the severance from employment with the employer maintaining the plan occurs for the limitation year in which the severance from employment with the employer maintaining the plan occurs.

*(6) Examples.* The provisions of this paragraph (e) are illustrated by the following examples:

*Example (1).* (i) Facts. Participant A was a common law employee of Employer X, performing services as a script writer for Employer X from January 1, 2005 to December 31, 2005. Pursuant to a collective bargaining agreement, Employer X, Employer Y and Employer Z maintain and contribute to Plan T, a multiemployer plan (as defined in section 414(f)) in which Participant A participates. Under the collective bargaining agreement, Participant A is entitled to residual payments whenever television shows that Participant A wrote are re-used commercially (These residual payments constitute compensation described in paragraph (b) of this section and do not constitute compensation described in paragraph (c) of this section.). In the year 2008, Participant A receives residual payments from Employer X for television programs using the scripts that Participant A wrote in the year 2005 that were rebroadcast in the year 2008. In the years 2006, 2007, and 2008, Participant A was a common law employee of Employer Y, and did not perform any services for Employer X.

(ii) Conclusion. The residual payments received from Employer X by Participant A in the year 2008 are compensation for purposes of section 415(c)(3). The payments are not treated as made after severance from employment because Plan T is a multiemployer plan (as defined in section 414(f)) and Participant A continues to be employed by an employer maintaining Plan T.

*Example (2).* (i) Facts. The facts are the same as in Example 1, except that Participant A: ceased employment with Employer Y in the year 2006; subsequently moved away from the area in which A formerly worked; performs no services as an employee for any employer; and commenced receiving distributions under Plan T in March, 2006.

(ii) Conclusion. Based on the facts and circumstances, A has ceased employment with any employer maintaining Plan T. Pursuant to paragraph (e)(1)(ii) of this section, compensation must be paid prior to an employee's severance from employment with the employer maintaining the plan. Accordingly, the residual payments received by Participant A in the year 2008 are not compensation for purposes of section 415(c)(3).

**(f) Interaction with section 401(a)(17).** Because a plan may not base allocations (in the case of a defined contribution plan) or benefits (in the case of a defined benefit plan) on compensation in excess of the limitation under section 401(a)(17), a plan's definition of compensation for a year that is used for purposes of applying the limitations of section 415 is not permitted to reflect compensation for a year that is in excess of the limitation under section 401(a)(17) that applies to that year. See §§ 1.401(a)(17)-1(a)(3)(i) and 1.401(a)(17)-1(b)(3)(ii) for rules regarding the effective date of increases in the section 401(a)(17) compensation limitation for a plan year and for a 12-month period other than the plan year.

**(g) Special rules.** *(1) Compensation for section 403(b) annuity contract.* In the case of an annuity contract described in section 403(b), the term participant's compensation means the participant's includible compensation determined under section 403(b)(3). Accordingly, the rules for determining a participant's compensation pursuant to section 415(c)(3) (other than section 415(c)(3)(E)) and this section do not apply to a section 403(b) annuity contract.

*(2) Employees of controlled groups of corporations, etc.* In the case of an employee of two or more corporations which are members of a controlled group of corporations (as defined in section 414(b) as modified by section 415(h)), the term compensation for such employee includes compensation from all employers that are members of the group, regardless of whether the employee's particular employer has a qualified plan. This special rule is also applicable to an employee of two or more trades or businesses (whether or not incorporated) that are under common control (as defined in section 414(c) as modified by section 415(h)), to an employee of two or more members of an affiliated service group as defined in section 414(m), and to an employee of two or more members of any group of employers who must be aggregated and treated as one employer pursuant to section 414(o).

*(3) Aggregation of section 403(b) annuity with qualified plan of controlled employer.* If a section 403(b) annuity contract is aggregated with a qualified plan of a controlled employer in accordance with § 1.415(f)-1(f)(2), then, in applying the limitations of section 415(c) in connection with the aggregation of the section 403(b) annuity with a qualified plan, the total compensation from both employers is permitted to be taken into account.

*(4) Permanent and total disability of defined contribution plan participant.* (i) In general. Pursuant to section 415(c)(3)(C), if the conditions set forth in paragraph (g)(4)(ii) of this section are satisfied, then, in the case of a participant in any defined contribution plan who is permanently and totally disabled (as defined in section 22(e)(3)), the participant's compensation means the compensation the participant would have received for the year if the participant was paid at the rate of compensation paid immediately before becoming permanently and totally disabled, if such compensation is greater than the participant's compensation determined without regard to this paragraph (g)(4).

(ii) Conditions for deemed disability compensation. The rule of paragraph (g)(4)(i) of this section applies only if the following conditions are satisfied—

(A) Either the participant is not a highly compensated employee (as defined in section 414(q)) immediately before becoming disabled, or the plan provides for the continuation of contributions on behalf of all participants who are permanently and totally disabled for a fixed or determinable period;

(B) The plan provides that the rule of this paragraph (g)(4) (treating certain amounts as compensation for a disabled participant) applies with respect to the participant; and

(C) Contributions made with respect to amounts treated as compensation under this paragraph (g)(4) are nonforfeitable when made.

*(5) Foreign compensation, etc.* (i) In general. Amounts paid to an individual as compensation for services do not fail to be treated as compensation under paragraphs (b)(1) and (2) of this section (and are not excluded from the definition of compensation pursuant to paragraph (c)(4) of this section) merely because those amounts are not includible in the individual's gross income on account of the location of the services. Similarly, compensation for services do not fail to be treated as compensation under paragraphs (b)(1) and (2) of this section (and are not excluded from the definition of compensation pursuant to paragraph (c)(4) of this section) merely because those amounts are paid by an employer with respect to which all compensation paid to the participant by such employer is excluded from gross income. Thus, for example, the determination of whether an amount is treated as compensation under paragraph (b)(1) or (2) of this section is made without regard to the exclusions from gross income under sections 872, 893, 894, 911, 931, and 933.

(ii) Exclusion of non-participant compensation by the plan. With respect to a nonresident alien who is not a participant in a plan, the plan may provide that the compensation described in paragraph (g)(5)(i) of this section is not treated as compensation for purposes of paragraphs (b)(1) and (b)(2) of this section to the extent the compensation is excludable from gross income and is not effectively connected with the conduct of a trade or business within the United States, but only if the plan applies this rule uniformly to all such employees. For purposes of this paragraph (g)(5)(ii), nonresident alien has the same meaning as in section 7701(b)(1)(B).

*(6) Deemed section 125 compensation.* (i) General rule. A plan is permitted to provide that deemed section 125 compensation (as defined in paragraph (g)(6)(ii) of this section) is compensation within the meaning of section 415(c)(3), but only if the plan applies this rule uniformly to all employees with respect to whom amounts subject to section 125 are included in compensation.

(ii) Definition of deemed section 125 compensation. Deemed section 125 compensation is an amount that is excludable from the income of the participant under section 106 that is not available to the participant in cash in lieu of group health coverage under a section 125 arrangement solely because that participant is not able to certify that the participant has other health coverage. Under this definition, amounts are deemed section 125 compensation only if the employer does not otherwise request or collect information regarding the participant's other health coverage as part of the enrollment process for the health plan.

*(7) Employees in qualified military service.* See section 414(u)(7) for special rules regarding compensation of employees who are in qualified military service within the meaning of section 414(u)(5).

*(8) Back pay.* Payments awarded by an administrative agency or court or pursuant to a bona fide agreement by an employer to compensate an employee for lost wages are

compensation within the meaning of section 415(c)(3) for the limitation year to which the back pay relates, but only to the extent such payments represent wages and compensation that would otherwise be included in compensation under this section.

T.D. 9319, 4/4/2007.

### § 1.415(d)-1 Cost of living adjustments.

**(a) Defined benefit plans.** *(1) Dollar limitation.* (i) Determination of adjusted limit. Under section 415(d)(1)(A), the dollar limitation described in section 415(b)(1)(A) applicable to defined benefit plans is adjusted annually to take into account increases in the cost of living. The adjustment of the dollar limitation is made by multiplying the adjustment factor for the year, as described in paragraph (a)(1)(ii)(A) of this section, by $160,000, and rounding the result in accordance with paragraph (a)(1)(iii) of this section. The adjusted dollar limitation is prescribed by the Commissioner and published in the Internal Revenue Bulletin. See § 601.601(d)(2) of this chapter.

(ii) Determination of adjustment factor. (A) Adjustment factor. The adjustment factor for a calendar year is equal to a fraction, the numerator of which is the value of the applicable index for the calendar quarter ending September 30 of the preceding calendar year, and the denominator of which is the value of such index for the base period. The applicable index is determined consistent with the procedures used to adjust benefit amounts under section 215(i)(2)(A) of the Social Security Act, Public Law 92-336 (86 Stat. 406), as amended. If, however, the value of that fraction is less than one for a calendar year, then the adjustment factor for the calendar year is equal to one.

(B) Base period. For the purpose of adjusting the dollar limitation pursuant to paragraph (a)(1)(ii)(A) of this section, the base period is the calendar quarter beginning July 1, 2001.

(iii) Rounding. Any increase in the $160,000 amount specified in section 415(b)(1)(A) which is not a multiple of $5,000 is rounded to the next lowest multiple of $5,000.

*(2) Average compensation for high-3 years of service limitation.* (i) Determination of adjusted limit. Under section 415(d)(1)(B), with regard to participants who have had a severance from employment with the employer maintaining the plan, the compensation limitation described in section 415(b)(1)(B) is permitted to be adjusted annually to take into account increases in the cost of living. For any limitation year beginning after the severance occurs, the adjustment of the compensation limitation is made by multiplying the annual adjustment factor (as defined in paragraph (a)(2)(ii) of this section) by the compensation limitation applicable to the participant in the prior limitation year. The annual adjustment factor is prescribed by the Commissioner and published in the Internal Revenue Bulletin. See § 601.601(d)(2) of this chapter.

(ii) Annual adjustment factor. The annual adjustment factor for a calendar year is equal to a fraction, the numerator of which is the value of the applicable index for the calendar quarter ending September 30 of the preceding calendar year, and the denominator of which is the value of such index for the calendar quarter ending September 30 of the calendar year prior to that preceding calendar year. The applicable index is determined consistent with the procedures used to adjust benefit amounts under section 215(i)(2)(A) of the Social Security Act. If the value of the fraction described in the first sentence of this paragraph (a)(2)(ii) is less than one for a calendar year, then the adjustment factor for the calendar year is equal to one. In such a case, the annual adjustment factor for future calendar years will be determined in accordance with revenue rulings, notices, or other published guidance prescribed by the Commissioner and published in the Internal Revenue Bulletin. See § 601.601(d)(2) of this chapter.

(iii) Special rule for rehired employees. If, after having a severance from employment with the employer maintaining the plan, an employee is rehired by the employer maintaining the plan, the employee's compensation limit under section 415(b)(1)(B) is the greater of—

(A) 100 percent of the participant's average compensation for the period of the participant's high-3 years of service, as determined prior to the employee's severance from employment with the employer maintaining the plan, as adjusted pursuant to paragraph (a)(2)(i) of this section (if the plan so provides); or

(B) 100 percent of the participant's average compensation for the period of the participant's high-3 years of service, with the period of the participant's high-3 years of service determined pursuant to § 1.415(b)-1(a)(5)(iii).

*(3) Effective date of adjustment.* The adjusted dollar limitation applicable to defined benefit plans and the adjusted compensation limit applicable to a participant are effective as of January 1 of each calendar year and apply with respect to limitation years ending with or within that calendar year. However, benefit payments (and, in the case of plans that are subject to the requirements of section 411, accrued benefits for a limitation year) cannot exceed the currently applicable dollar limitation or compensation limitation (as in effect before the January 1 adjustment) prior to January 1. Thus, where there is an increase in the limitation under section 415(b)(1), any increase in a participant's benefits associated with the limitation increase is permitted to occur as of a date no earlier than January 1 of the calendar year for which the increase in the limitation is effective, and can only be applied for payments due on or after January 1 of such calendar year. For example, assume that a participant in a defined benefit plan is currently receiving a benefit in the form of a straight life annuity, payable monthly, in an amount equal to the section 415(b)(1)(A) dollar limit, and the defined benefit plan has a limitation year that runs from July 1 to June 30. If the plan is amended to reflect the section 415(d) increase to the section 415(b)(1)(A) dollar limit that is effective as of January 1, 2009, the associated increase in the participant's monthly benefit payments is only effective for payments due on or after January 1, 2009, and the participant's benefit cannot be increased to reflect the section 415(d) increase that is effective January 1, 2009, with respect to any monthly payment due prior to January 1, 2009.

*(4) Application of adjusted figure.* (i) In general. If the dollar limitation of section 415(b)(1)(A) or the compensation limitation of section 415(b)(1)(B) is adjusted pursuant to section 415(d) for a limitation year, the adjustment is applied as provided in this paragraph (a)(4).

(ii) Application of adjusted limitations to benefits that have not commenced. An adjustment to the dollar limitation of section 415(b)(1)(A) is permitted to be applied to a participant who has not commenced benefits before the date on which the adjustment is effective. Annual adjustments to the compensation limit of section 415(b)(1)(B) as described in paragraph (a)(2) of this section are permitted to be made for all limitation years that begin after the participant's severance from employment, and apply to distributions that commence after the effective dates of such adjustments. However, no adjustment to the compensation limit of section 415(b)(1)(B) is made for any limitation year that begins on or before the date of the participant's severance from employment with the employer maintaining the plan.

(iii) Application of adjusted dollar limitation to remaining payments under benefits that have commenced. With respect to a distribution of accrued benefits that commenced before the date on which an adjustment to the section 415(b)(1)(A) dollar limitation is effective, a plan is permitted to apply the adjusted limitations to that distribution, but only to the extent that benefits have not been paid. Thus, for example, a plan cannot provide that the adjusted dollar limitation applies to a participant who has previously received the entire plan benefit in a single-sum distribution. However, a plan can provide for an increase in benefits to a participant who accrues additional benefits under the plan that could have been accrued without regard to the adjustment of the dollar limitation (including benefits that accrue as a result of a plan amendment) on or after the effective date of the adjusted limitation.

(iv) Manner of adjustment for benefits that have commenced. If a plan is amended to increase benefits payable under the plan in accordance with paragraphs (a)(5) or (a)(6) of this section (or the plan is treated as applying paragraph (a)(5) of this section because the plan incorporates the section 415(d) cost-of-living adjustments automatically by reference pursuant to § 1.415(a)-1(d)(3)(v)), or if benefits payable under the plan are increased pursuant to a form of benefit that is described in § 1.415(b)-1(c)(5), then the distribution as increased will be treated as continuing to satisfy the requirements of section 415(b). If benefits payable under a plan are increased in a manner other than as described in the preceding sentence, the plan must satisfy the requirements of § 1.415(b)-1(b)(1)(iii), treating the commencement of the additional benefit as the commencement of a new distribution that gives rise to a new annuity starting date.

*(5) Safe harbor for annual adjustments to distributions.* An amendment to a plan to incorporate adjustments to the section 415(b) limits that increases a distribution that has previously commenced is described in this paragraph (a)(5) if—

(i) The employee has received one or more distributions that satisfy the requirements of section 415(b) before the date the adjustment to the applicable limits is effective (as determined under paragraph (a)(3) of this section);

(ii) The increased distribution is solely as a result of the amendment of the plan to reflect the adjustment to the applicable limits pursuant to section 415(d); and

(iii) The amounts payable to the employee on and after the effective date of the adjustment (as determined under paragraph (a)(3) of this section) are not greater than the amounts that would otherwise be payable without regard to the adjustment, multiplied by a fraction determined for the limitation year, the numerator of which is the limitation under section 415(b) (which is the lesser of the applicable dollar limitation under section 415(b)(1)(A), as adjusted for age at commencement, and the applicable compensation-based limitation under section 415(b)(1)(B)) in effect with respect to the distribution taking into account the section 415(d) adjustment, and the denominator of which is the limitation under section 415(b) in effect for the distribution immediately before the adjustment.

*(6) Safe harbor for periodic adjustments to distributions.* (i) General rule. An amendment to a plan that increases a distribution that has previously commenced is made using the safe harbor methodology of this paragraph (a)(6) if—

(A) The employee has received one or more distributions that satisfy the requirements of section 415(b) before the date on which the increase is effective; and

(B) The amounts payable to the employee on and after the effective date of the increase are not greater than the amounts that would otherwise be payable without regard to the increase, multiplied by the cumulative adjustment fraction.

(ii) Cumulative adjustment fraction. The cumulative adjustment fraction for purposes of this paragraph (a)(6) is equal to the product of all of the fractions described in paragraph (a)(5)(iii) of this section that would have applied after benefits commence if the plan had been amended each year to incorporate the section 415(d) adjustments to the applicable section 415(b) limits and had otherwise satisfied the safe harbor methodology described in paragraph (a)(5) of this section. For purposes of the preceding sentence, if for the limitation year for which the increase to the section 415(b)(1)(A) dollar limitation pursuant to section 611(a)(1)(A) of the Economic Growth and Tax Relief Reconciliation Act of 2001 (115 Stat. 38), Public Law 107-16 (EGTRRA), is first effective (generally, the first limitation year beginning after December 31, 2001), the section 415(b)(1)(A) dollar limit applicable to a participant is less than the section 415(b)(1)(B) compensation limit for the participant, then the fraction described in paragraph (a)(5)(iii) of this section for that limitation year is 1.0.

*(7) Examples.* The following examples illustrate the application of this paragraph (a):

*Example (1).* (i) X is a participant in a qualified defined benefit plan maintained by X's employer. The plan has a calendar year limitation year. Under the terms of the plan, X is entitled to a benefit consisting of a straight life annuity equal to 100 percent of X's average compensation for the period of X's high-3 years of service. X's average compensation for the period of X's high-3 years of service is $50,000. X incurs a severance from employment with the employer maintaining the plan on October 3, 2007, at age 65 with a nonforfeitable right to the accrued benefit after more than 10 years of participation in the plan. X begins to receive annual benefit payments (payable monthly) of $50,000, commencing on November 1, 2007. The dollar limitation for the 2007 limitation year (as adjusted pursuant to section 415(d)) is $180,000. Assume that the dollar limitation for the 2008 limitation year (as adjusted pursuant to section 415(d)) is $185,000 and the annual adjustment factor for adjusting the compensation limitation of section 415(b)(1)(B) for the 2008 limitation year is 1.0334. Effective January 1, 2008, the plan is amended to incorporate these adjustments to the dollar and compensation limitations, and accordingly, X's annual benefit payment is increased, effective for payments due on or after January 1, 2008. Prior to the plan amendment incorporating the application of the adjusted dollar and compensation limitations, X has received one or more distributions that satisfy the requirements of section 415(b). In addition, the adjustment to X's annual benefit payments is solely on account of the plan amendment incorporating the adjusted limitations.

(ii) For the limitation year beginning January 1, 2008, the dollar limit applicable to X under section 415(b)(1)(A) is $185,000, and the compensation limit applicable to X under section 415(b)(1)(B) is $51,670 ($50,000 multiplied by the annual adjustment factor of 1.0334). Accordingly, the adjustment to X's benefit satisfies the safe harbor for cost-of-living adjustments under paragraph (a)(5) of this section if, after the adjustment, X's benefit payable in the 2008 limitation year is no greater than $50,000 multiplied by $51,670 (X's section 415(b) limitation for 2008)/$50,000 (X's section 415(b) limitation for 2007).

*Example (2).* (i) The facts are the same as in Example 1, except that X's average compensation for the period of X's high-3 consecutive years of service is $200,000. Consequently, X's annual benefit payments commencing on November 1, 2007, are limited to $180,000.

(ii) For the limitation year beginning January 1, 2008, the dollar limit applicable to X under section 415(b)(1)(A) is $185,000, and the compensation limit applicable to X under section 415(b)(1)(B) is $206,680 ($200,000 multiplied by the annual adjustment factor of 1.0334). Accordingly, the adjustment to X's benefit satisfies the safe harbor for cost-of-living adjustments under paragraph (a)(5) of this section if, after the adjustment, X's benefit payable in 2008 is no greater than $180,000 multiplied by $185,000 (X's section 415(b) limitation for 2008)/$180,000 (X's section 415(b) limitation for 2007).

*Example (3).* (i) X is a participant in Plan T, a qualified defined benefit plan maintained by X's employer. In the year 2008, X receives a single-sum distribution of X's entire accrued benefit under the plan. At the time that X receives the single-sum distribution, X's accrued benefit under Plan T is limited by the section 415(b)(1)(A) age-adjusted dollar limit. X accrues no further benefits under Plan T after X receives the single-sum distribution. In the 2009 limitation year, pursuant to section 415(d) and § 1.415(d)-1, the section 415(b)(1)(A) dollar limit is increased.

(ii) In the 2009 limitation year, Plan T may not provide additional benefits to X on account of the increase in the section 415(b)(1)(A) dollar limit pursuant to section 415(d) and § 1.415(d)-1.

*Example (4).* (i) X is a participant in Plan T, a qualified defined benefit plan maintained by X's employer, Employer S. Plan T has a calendar limitation year. In 2008, X incurs a severance from employment with Employer S and X commences receiving distributions from Plan T in the form of a single life annuity in an annual amount of $30,000. At the time that X commences receiving distributions from Plan T, X's accrued benefit under Plan T is limited by the section 415(b)(1)(B) compensation limit. In 2009, the annual adjustment factor described in paragraph (a)(2) of this section (which is the factor for adjusting the compensation limit described in section 415(b)(1)(B)) is 1.03. Employer S amends Plan T, effective as of January 1, 2009, to increase the annual benefit of all participants who, prior to January 1, 2009, incurred a severance from employment with Employer S and who have commenced receiving benefits from Plan T by a factor of 1.015. Assume that for limitation years prior to 2009, X's distributions from Plan T satisfy the requirements of section 415(b).

(ii) The increase in X's annual benefit pursuant to the amendment effective January 1, 2009, is within the safe harbor described in paragraph (a)(6) of this section. This is because the amount payable to X under Plan T for the 2009 limitation year and limitation years thereafter (as increased by the amendment effective January 1, 2009) is not greater than the product of the amount payable to X under Plan T for such limitation years (as determined without regard to the amendment increasing X's benefit effective January 1, 2009) and the cumulative adjustment fraction (which, in X's case, is 1.03). Thus, X's annual benefit, as increased by the amendment, is not determined pursuant to the rules of § 1.415(b)-1(b)(1)(iii).

*Example (5).* (i) Participant P participated in Plan A, maintained by Employer M, for more than 10 years. Plan A uses a calendar year limitation year and Plan A automatically adjusts a participant's section 415(b)(1)(B) compensation limit for limitation years after the limitation year in which the participant incurs a severance from employment as described in § 1.415(a)-1(d)(3)(v). Prior to separating from employment with M in 2010, P's average compensation for P's period of high-3 years while a participant in Plan A is $50,000, based on P's compensation for 2007, 2008, and 2009, which was $50,000 for each year. P's compensation for year 2010 was $45,000. In year 2012, P is rehired by M and resumes participation in Plan A. P's compensation in year 2012 is $45,000, and is $70,000 in year 2013. Assume that the annual adjustment factor described in § 1.415(d)-1(a)(2)(ii) for the limitation years 2011 through 2013 is 1.03 for each year. Thus, disregarding P's rehire by M, P's average compensation for P's period of high-3 years while a participant in Plan A for the 2013 limitation year would be equal to $54,636 (or 1.03 * 1.03 * 1.03 * $50,000). See § 1.415(b)-1(a)(5)(iii).

(ii) Under § 1.415(d)-1(a)(2)(iii), P's average compensation for P's period of high-3 years while a participant in Plan A for the 2013 limitation year is $54,636.

**(b) Defined contribution plans.** *(1) In general.* Under section 415(d)(1)(C), the dollar limitation described in section 415(c)(1)(A) is adjusted annually to take into account increases in the cost of living. The adjusted dollar limitation is prescribed by the Commissioner and published in the Internal Revenue Bulletin. See § 601.601(d)(2) of this chapter.

*(2) Determination of adjusted limit.* (i) Base period. The base period taken into account for purposes of adjusting the dollar limitation pursuant to paragraph (b)(2)(ii) of this section is the calendar quarter beginning July 1, 2001.

(ii) Method of adjustment. (A) In general. The dollar limitation is adjusted with respect to a calendar year based on the increase in the applicable index for the calendar quarter ending September 30 of the preceding calendar year over such index for the base period. Adjustment procedures similar to the procedures used to adjust benefit amounts under section 215(i)(2)(A) of the Social Security Act will be used.

(B) Rounding. Any increase in the $40,000 amount specified in section 415(c)(1)(A) which is not a multiple of $1,000 shall be rounded to the next lowest multiple of $1,000.

(iii) Effective date of adjustment. The adjusted dollar limitation applicable to defined contribution plans is effective as of January 1 of each calendar year and applies with respect to limitation years ending with or within that calendar year. Annual additions for a limitation year cannot exceed the currently applicable dollar limitation (as in effect before the January 1 adjustment) prior to January 1. However, after a January 1 adjustment is made, annual additions for the entire limitation year are permitted to reflect the dollar limitation as adjusted on January 1.

**(c) Application of rounding rules to other cost-of-living adjustments.** Pursuant to section 415(d)(4)(A), the $5,000 rounding methodology of paragraph (a)(1)(iii) of this section is used for purposes of any provision of chapter 1 of subtitle A of the Internal Revenue Code that provides for adjustments in accordance with section 415(d), except to the extent provided by that provision. Thus, the $5,000 rounding methodology of paragraph (a)(1)(iii) of this section is used for purposes of—

*(1)* Determining the level of compensation specified in section 414(q)(1)(B) that is used to determine whether an employee is a highly compensated employee;

*(2)* Calculating the amounts used pursuant to section 409(o)(1)(C) to determine the maximum period over which distributions from an employee stock ownership plan may be made without participant consent; and

*(3)* Determining the levels of compensation specified in § 1.61-21(f)(5)(i) and (iii) used in determining whether an employee is a control employee of a nongovernmental employer for purposes of the commuting valuation rule of § 1.61-21(f).

**(d) Implementation of cost-of-living adjustments.** A plan is permitted to be amended to reflect any of the adjustments described in this section at any time after those limitations become applicable. Alternatively, a plan is permitted to incorporate by reference any of the adjustments described in this section in accordance with the rules of § 1.415(a)-1(d)(3)(v). Because the accrued benefit of a participant can reflect increases in the applicable limitations only after those increases become effective, a pattern of repeated plan amendments increasing annual benefits to reflect the increases in the section 415(b) limitations pursuant to section 415(d) does not result in any protection under section 411(d)(6) for future increases to reflect increases in the section 415(b) limitations pursuant to § 1.411(d)-4, Q&A-1(c)(1). Thus, a plan does not violate the requirements of section 411(d)(6) merely because the plan has been amended annually for a number of years to increase annual benefits to reflect the increases in the section 415(b) limitations pursuant to section 415(d) and subsequently is not amended to reflect later increases in the section 415(b) limitations.

---

T.D. 9319, 4/4/2007.

---

### § 1.415(f)-1 Aggregating plans.

**(a) In general.** Except as provided in paragraph (g) of this section (regarding multiemployer plans), and taking into account the rules of paragraph (b)(2) (regarding the break-up of affiliated employers and affiliated service groups), paragraph (c) (regarding predecessor employers), and paragraph (d)(1) (regarding nonduplication rules) of this section, section 415(f) and this section require that for purposes of applying the limitations of sections 415(b) and (c) applicable to a participant for a particular limitation year—

*(1)* All defined benefit plans (without regard to whether a plan has been terminated) ever maintained by the employer (or a predecessor employer within the meaning of paragraphs (c)(1) and (c)(2) of this section) under which the participant has accrued a benefit are treated as one defined benefit plan;

*(2)* All defined contribution plans (without regard to whether a plan has been terminated) ever maintained by the employer (or a predecessor employer within the meaning of paragraphs (c)(1) and (c)(2) of this section) under which the participant receives annual additions are treated as one defined contribution plan; and

*(3)* All section 403(b) annuity contracts purchased by an employer (including plans purchased through salary reduction contributions) for the participant are treated as one section 403(b) annuity contract.

**(b) Affiliated employers, affiliated service groups, and leased employees.** *(1) General rule.* See § 1.415(a)-1(f)(1) and (2) for rules regarding aggregation of employers in the case of affiliated employers and affiliated service groups. See § 1.415(a)-1(f)(3) for rules regarding the treatment of leased employees.

*(2) Special rule in the case of the break-up of an affiliated employer or an affiliated service group.* (i) In general. A formerly affiliated plan of an employer is taken into account for purposes of applying paragraph (a) of this section to the employer, but the formerly affiliated plan is treated as if it had terminated immediately prior to the cessation of affiliation with sufficient assets to pay benefit liabilities under the plan, and had purchased annuities to provide plan benefits. See § 1.415(b)-1(b)(5)(i) for rules determining annual benefits under a terminated defined benefit plan under which annuities are purchased to provide plan benefits.

(ii) Definitions. For purposes of this paragraph (b)(2), a formerly affiliated plan of an employer is a plan that, immediately prior to the cessation of affiliation, was actually maintained by one or more of the entities that constitute the employer (as determined under the employer affiliation rules described in § 1.415(a)-1(f)(1) and (2)), and immediately after the cessation of affiliation, is not actually maintained by any of the entities that constitute the employer (as determined under the employer affiliation rules described in § 1.415(a)-1(f)(1) and (2)). For purposes of this paragraph (b)(2), a cessation of affiliation means the event that causes an entity to no longer be aggregated with one or more other entities as a single employer under the employer affiliation rules described in § 1.415(a)-1(f)(1) and (2) (such as the sale of a subsidiary outside a controlled group), or that causes a plan to not actually be maintained by any of the entities that constitute the employer under the employer affiliation rules of § 1.415(a)-1(f)(1) and (2) (such as a transfer of plan sponsorship outside of a controlled group).

**(c) Predecessor employer.** *(1) Where plan is maintained by successor.* For purposes of section 415 and regulations promulgated under section 415, a former employer is a predecessor employer with respect to a participant in a plan maintained by an employer if the employer maintains a plan under which the participant had accrued a benefit while performing services for the former employer (for example, the employer assumed sponsorship of the former employer's plan, or the employer's plan received a transfer of benefits from the former employer's plan), but only if that benefit is provided under the plan maintained by the employer. In such a case, in applying the limitations of section 415 to a participant in a plan maintained by the employer, paragraph (a) of this section requires the plan to take into account benefits provided to the participant under plans that are maintained by the predecessor employer and that are not maintained by the employer. For this purpose, the formerly affiliated plan rules in paragraph (b)(2) of this section apply as if the employer and predecessor employer constituted a single employer under the rules described in § 1.415(a)-1(f)(1) and (2) immediately prior to the cessation of affiliation (and as if they constituted two, unrelated employers under the rules described in § 1.415(a)-1(f)(1) and (2) immediately after the cessation of affiliation) and cessation of affiliation was the event that gives rise to the predecessor employer relationship, such as a transfer of benefits or plan sponsorship.

*(2) Where plan is not maintained by successor.* With respect to an employer of a participant, a former entity that antedates the employer is a predecessor employer with respect to the participant if, under the facts and circumstances, the employer constitutes a continuation of all or a portion of

the trade or business of the former entity. This will occur, for example, where formation of the employer constitutes a mere formal or technical change in the employment relationship and continuity otherwise exists in the substance and administration of the business operations of the former entity and the employer.

**(d) Special rules.** *(1) Nonduplication.* In applying the limitations of section 415 to a plan maintained by an employer, if the plan is aggregated with another plan pursuant to the aggregation rules of paragraph (a) of this section, a participant's benefits are not counted more than once in determining the participant's aggregate annual benefit or annual additions. For example, if a defined benefit plan is treated as if it terminated immediately prior to a cessation of affiliation under paragraph (b)(2) of this section, the plans maintained by the employer (as determined after the cessation of affiliation) that actually maintains the plan do not double count the annual benefit provided under the plan by aggregating under paragraph (a) of this section both the participant's annual benefit provided under the plan and the participant's annual benefit under the plan as a formerly affiliated plan (which is a plan that the employers formerly affiliated with the employer must take into account as a terminated plan under the rules of paragraph (b)(2) of this section). Instead, the plans maintained by the employer include the annual benefit provided to the participant under the actual plan that the employer maintains. Similarly, if a defined benefit plan maintained by an employer (the transferee plan) receives a transfer of benefits from a defined benefit plan maintained by a predecessor employer (the transferor plan) and the transfer is described in § 1.415(b)-1(b)(3)(i)(B) (which requires the transferred benefits to be treated by the transferor plan as if the benefits were provided under a plan that must be aggregated with the transferor plan that terminated immediately prior to the transfer), the transferee plan does not double count the transferred benefits under paragraph (a) of this section by taking into account both the actual benefit provided under the transferee plan and the benefit provided under the deemed terminated plan that the predecessor employer is treated as maintaining (and that otherwise would have to be taken into account by the transferee plan under the predecessor employer aggregation rules of paragraph (a) of this section). Instead, the transferee plan takes into account the transferred benefits that are actually provided under transferee plan (see § 1.415(b)-1(b)(3)(i)(C)) and, pursuant to paragraph (c)(1) of this section, any nontransferred benefits provided under plans maintained by the predecessor employer with respect to a participant whose benefits have been transferred to the transferee plan.

*(2) Determination of years of participation for multiple plans.* If two or more defined benefit plans are aggregated under section 415(f) and this section for a particular limitation year, in applying the reduction for participation of less than ten years (as described in section 415(b)(5)(A)) to the dollar limitation under section 415(b)(1)(A), time periods that are counted as years of participation under any of the plans are counted in computing the limitation of the aggregated plans under this section.

*(3) Determination of years of service for multiple plans.* If two or more defined benefit plans are aggregated under section 415(f) and this section for a particular limitation year, in applying the reduction for service of less than ten years (as described in section 415(b)(5)(B)) to the compensation limitation under section 415(b)(1)(B), time periods that are counted as years of service under any of the plans are counted in computing the limitation of the aggregated plans under this section.

**(e) Previously unaggregated plans.** *(1) In general.* This paragraph (e) provides rules for those situations in which two or more existing plans, which previously were not required to be aggregated pursuant to section 415(f) and this section, are aggregated during a particular limitation year and, as a result, the limitations of section 415(b) or (c) are exceeded for that limitation year. Paragraph (e)(2) of this section provides rules for defined contribution plans that are first required to be aggregated pursuant to section 415(f) and this section in a plan year. Paragraph (e)(3) of this section provides rules for defined benefit plans that are first required to be aggregated pursuant to section 415(f) and this section, and for defined benefit plans under which a participant's benefit is frozen following aggregation. *(2) Defined contribution plans.* Two or more defined contribution plans that are not required to be aggregated pursuant to section 415(f) and this section as of the first day of a limitation year do not fail to satisfy the requirements of section 415 with respect to a participant for the limitation year merely because they are aggregated later in that limitation year, provided that no annual additions are credited to the participant's account after the date on which the plans are required to be aggregated.

*(3) Defined benefit plans.* (i) First year of aggregation. Two or more defined benefit plans that are not required to be aggregated pursuant to section 415(f) and this section as of the first day of a limitation year do not fail to satisfy the requirements of section 415 for the limitation year merely because they are aggregated later in that limitation year, provided that no plan amendments increasing benefits with respect to the participant under either plan are made after the occurrence of the event causing the plan to be aggregated.

(ii) All years of aggregation in which accrued benefits are frozen. Two or more defined benefit plans that are required to be aggregated pursuant to section 415(f) and this section during a limitation year subsequent to the limitation year during which the plans were first aggregated do not fail to satisfy the requirements of section 415 with respect to a participant for the limitation year merely because they are aggregated if there have been no increases in the participant's accrued benefit derived from employer contributions (including increases as a result of increased compensation or service) under any of the plans within the period during which the plans have been aggregated.

**(f) Section 403(b) annuity contracts.** *(1) In general.* In the case of a section 403(b) annuity contract, except as provided in paragraph (f)(2) of this section, the participant on whose behalf the annuity contract is purchased is considered for purposes of section 415 to have exclusive control of the annuity contract. Accordingly, except as provided in paragraph (f)(2) of this section, the participant, and not the participant's employer who purchased the section 403(b) annuity contract, is deemed to maintain the annuity contract, and such a section 403(b) annuity contract is not aggregated with a qualified plan that is maintained by the participant's employer.

*(2) Special rules under which the employer is deemed to maintain the annuity contract.* (i) In general. Where a participant on whose behalf a section 403(b) annuity contract is purchased is in control of any employer for a limitation year as defined in paragraph (f)(2)(ii) of this section (regardless of whether the employer controlled by the participant is the employer maintaining the section 403(b) annuity contract), the annuity contract for the benefit of the participant is treated as a defined contribution plan maintained by both the

controlled employer and the participant for that limitation year. Accordingly, where a participant on whose behalf a section 403(b) annuity contract is purchased is in control of any employer for a limitation year, the section 403(b) annuity contract is aggregated with all other defined contribution plans maintained by that employer. In addition, in such a case, the section 403(b) annuity contract is aggregated with all other defined contribution plans maintained by the employee or any other employer that is controlled by the employee. Thus, for example, if a doctor is employed by a non-profit hospital to which section 501(c)(3) applies and which provides him with a section 403(b) annuity contract, and the doctor also maintains a private practice as a shareholder owning more than 50 percent of a professional corporation, then any qualified defined contribution plan of the professional corporation must be aggregated with the section 403(b) annuity contract for purposes of applying the limitations of section 415(c) and § 1.415(c)-1. For purposes of this paragraph (f)(2), it is immaterial whether the section 403(b) annuity contract is purchased as a result of a salary reduction agreement between the employer and the participant.

(ii) Determination of when a participant is in control of an employer. For purposes of paragraph (f)(2)(i) of this section, a participant is in control of an employer for a limitation year if, pursuant to § 1.415(a)-1(f)(1) and (2), a plan maintained by that employer would have to be aggregated with a plan maintained by an employer that is 100 percent owned by the participant. Thus, for example, if a participant owns 60 percent of the common stock of a corporation, the participant is considered to be in control of that employer for purposes of applying paragraph (f)(2)(i) of this section.

*(3) Aggregation of section 403(b) annuity with qualified plan of controlled employer.* If a section 403(b) annuity contract is aggregated with a qualified plan of a controlled employer in accordance with paragraph (f)(2) of this section, the plans must satisfy the limitations of section 415(c) both separately and on an aggregate basis. In applying separately the limitations of section 415 to the qualified plan and to the section 403(b) annuity contract, compensation from the controlled employer may not be aggregated with compensation from the employer purchasing the section 403(b) annuity contract (that is, without regard to § 1.415(c)-2(g)(3)).

**(g) Multiemployer plans.** *(1) Multiemployer plan aggregated with another multiemployer plan.* Pursuant to section 415(f)(3)(B), multiemployer plans, as defined in section 414(f), are not aggregated with other multiemployer plans for purposes of applying the limits of section 415.

*(2) Multiemployer plan aggregated with other plan.* (i) Aggregation only for benefits provided by the employer. Notwithstanding the rule of § 1.415(a)-1(e), a multiemployer plan, as defined in section 414(f), is permitted to provide that only the benefits under that multiemployer plan that are provided by an employer are aggregated with benefits under plans maintained by that employer that are not multiemployer plans. If the multiemployer plan so provides, then, where an employer maintains both a plan which is not a multiemployer plan and a multiemployer plan, only the benefits under the multiemployer plan that are provided by the employer are aggregated with benefits under the employer's plans other than multiemployer plans (in lieu of including benefits provided by all employers under the multiemployer plan pursuant to the generally applicable rule of § 1.415(a)-1(e)).

(ii) Exception from aggregation for purposes of applying section 415(b)(1)(B) compensation limit. Pursuant to section 415(f)(3)(A), a multiemployer plan, as defined in section 414(f), is not aggregated with any other plan that is not a multiemployer plan for purposes of applying the compensation limit of section 415(b)(1)(B) and § 1.415(b)-1(a)(1)(ii).

**(h) Special rules for aggregating certain plans, etc.** If a plan, annuity contract or arrangement is subject to a special limitation in addition to, or instead of, the regular limitations described in section 415(b) or (c), and is aggregated under this section with a plan which is subject only to the regular section 415(b) or (c) limitations, the following rules apply:

*(1)* Each plan, annuity contract or arrangement which is subject to a special limitation must meet its own applicable limitation and each plan subject to the regular limitations of section 415 must meet its applicable limitation.

*(2)* The limitation for the aggregated plans is the larger of the applicable limitations for the separate plans.

**(i) [Reserved.]**

**(j) Examples. The following examples illustrate the rules of this section.** Except to the extent otherwise stated in an example, each entity is not and has never been affiliated with another entity under the employer affiliation rules of § 1.415(a)-1(f)(1) and (2), each entity has never maintained a qualified plan (other than the plans specifically mentioned in the example), and the limitation year for each qualified plan is the calendar year.

*Example (1).* (i) Facts. M was formerly an employee of ABC Corporation and is currently an employee of XYZ Corporation. ABC maintains a qualified defined benefit plan (Plan ABC) and a qualified defined contribution plan in which M participates and XYZ maintains a qualified defined benefit plan (Plan XYZ) and a qualified defined contribution plan in which M participates. ABC Corporation owns 60 percent of XYZ Corporation.

(ii) Treatment as a single employer. ABC Corporation and XYZ Corporation are members of a controlled group of corporations within the meaning of section 414(b) as modified by section 415(h). Because ABC Corporation and XYZ Corporation are members of a controlled group of corporations within the meaning of section 414(b) as modified by section 415(h), M is treated as being employed by a single employer under § 1.415(a)-1(f)(1).

(iii) Plan aggregation. Under paragraph (a)(1) of this section, the sum of M's annual benefit under Plan ABC and M's annual benefit under Plan XYZ is not permitted to exceed the limitations of section 415(b) and § 1.415(b)-1; and, under paragraph (a)(2) of this section, the sum of the annual additions to M's account under the defined contribution plans maintained by ABC and XYZ may not exceed the limitations of section 415(c) and § 1.415(c)-1. For purposes of determining the limitations of section 415(b) and § 1.415(b)-1 for the aggregated plans, a year of service for either employer is considered as a year of service for purposes of § 1.415(b)-1(g)(2) (phase-in rules for the compensation limit) and a year of participation under either plan is considered as a year of participation for purposes of § 1.415(b)-1(g)(1) (phase-in rules for the dollar limit).

*Example (2).* (i) Facts. The facts are the same as in Example 1, except that ABC Corporation and XYZ Corporation do not maintain defined contribution plans. In addition, Participant O was formerly an employee of ABC Corporation and is currently an employee of XYZ Corporation. Participant O has an accrued benefit under the ABC Plan, but Participant O has no accrued benefit under the XYZ Plan. Effective January 1, 2010, ABC Corporation sells all of its shares of stock of XYZ Corporation to an unaffiliated entity,

LMN Corporation (the 2010 stock sale). After the 2010 stock sale, XYZ Corporation continues to maintain Plan XYZ. LMN Corporation maintains a qualified defined benefit plan (Plan LMN). After the 2010 stock sale, M begins to accrue benefits under Plan LMN, but O does not participate in Plan LMN.

(ii) Affiliated employer status of the corporations. Immediately after the 2010 stock sale, ABC Corporation and XYZ Corporation are no longer members of a controlled group of corporations under section 414(b) (as modified by section 414(h)) and accordingly are no longer treated as a single employer under the employer affiliation rules of § 1.415(a)-1(f)(1). Immediately after the 2010 stock sale, LMN Corporation and XYZ Corporation are members of a controlled group of corporations under section 414(b) (as modified by section 414(h)) and accordingly are treated as a single employer under the employer affiliation rules of § 1.415(a)-1(f)(1).

(iii) Treatment of plans maintained by ABC Corporation after the 2010 stock sale. Under § 1.415(a)-1(f)(1), any plan maintained by any member of a controlled group of corporations is deemed maintained by all members of the controlled group, and paragraph (a)(1) of this section requires that, for purposes of applying the limitations of section 415(b), all defined benefit plans ever maintained by an employer (as determined under the affiliation rules of § 1.415(a)-1(f)(1) and (2)) are treated as one defined benefit plan. Therefore, defined benefit plans maintained by ABC Corporation must take into account the annual benefit of a participant provided under Plan XYZ in applying the limitations of section 415(b) to the participant because Plan XYZ is a plan that had once been maintained by ABC Corporation. However, beginning with the 2010 limitation year, the aggregation of the annual benefit accrued by a participant under Plan XYZ for purposes of testing defined benefit plans maintained by ABC Corporation is limited to the annual benefit accrued by the participant under Plan XYZ immediately prior to the 2010 stock sale. This is because paragraph (b)(2)(i) of this section provides that a formerly affiliated plan of an employer is treated as if it had terminated immediately prior to the cessation of affiliation with sufficient assets to pay benefit liabilities under the plan, and had purchased annuities to provide plan benefits. The 2010 stock sale is a cessation of affiliation under paragraph (b)(2)(ii) of this section because this event caused XYZ Corporation to no longer be affiliated with ABC Corporation under the employer affiliation rules of § 1.415(a)-1(f)(1) and (2). Immediately after the 2010 stock sale, Plan XYZ is a formerly affiliated plan with respect to ABC Corporation under paragraph (b)(2)(ii) of this section because immediately prior to the cessation of affiliation, Plan XYZ was actually maintained by XYZ Corporation (which together with ABC Corporation constituted a single employer under the employer affiliation rules of § 1.415(a)-1(f)(1) and (2)), and immediately after the cessation of affiliation, Plan XYZ is not actually maintained by ABC Corporation or any other entity affiliated with it.

(iv) Application of rules to Participants M and O with respect to plans maintained by ABC Corporation after the 2010 stock sale. In applying the limitations of section 415(b) to Participant M for the 2010 limitation year and later limitation years, Plan ABC must take into account the annual benefit provided under Plan ABC to Participant M and the annual benefit provided under Plan XYZ to Participant M, but treating Plan XYZ as if it had terminated immediately prior to the 2010 stock sale with sufficient assets to pay benefit liabilities under the plan, and had purchased annuities to provide plan benefits. The aggregation of Plan XYZ with Plan ABC is irrelevant for purposes of Participant O because Participant O does not have any accrued benefit under Plan XYZ (as determined prior to the 2010 stock sale).

(v) Treatment of plans maintained by LMN Corporation and XYZ Corporation after the 2010 stock sale. Under § 1.415(a)-1(f)(1) and paragraph (a)(1) of this section, when applying the limitations of section 415(b) to a participant under Plans LMN and XYZ for the 2010 limitation year and later years, the annual benefit provided to the participant under Plans LMN, XYZ and ABC must be aggregated. Benefits under Plan ABC must be included in this aggregation because XYZ Corporation is deemed to have once maintained Plan ABC pursuant to § 1.415(a)-1(f)(1), and since LMN Corporation and XYZ Corporation constitute a single employer under § 1.415(a)-1(f)(1), paragraph (a)(1) of this section requires the aggregation of all defined benefit plans ever maintained by LMN Corporation and XYZ Corporation. However, in performing this aggregation, a participant's annual benefit under Plan ABC is limited to the annual benefit accrued by the participant immediately prior to the 2010 stock sale. This is because, pursuant to paragraph (b)(2)(i) of this section, Plan ABC is a formerly affiliated plan of LMN Corporation and XYZ Corporation.

(vi) Application of rules to Participants M and O with respect to plans maintained by LMN Corporation and XYZ Corporation after the 2010 stock sale. In applying the limitation of section 415(b) to Participant M for the 2010 limitation year and later limitation years, Plan LMN and Plan XYZ must take into account the annual benefit provided under Plans LMN and XYZ to Participant M and the annual benefit provided under Plan ABC to Participant M as if Plan ABC had terminated immediately prior to the 2010 stock sale with sufficient assets to pay benefit liabilities under the plan, and had purchased annuities to provide plan benefits. Participant O does not have an accrued benefit under Plan LMN or Plan XYZ, so the aggregation of Plan ABC with Plans LMN and XYZ is currently irrelevant with respect to Participant O. However, if Participant O were to ever participate in Plans LMN or XYZ after the 2010 stock sale, Participant O's annual benefit under Plan ABC (determined as if Plan ABC terminated immediately prior to the 2010 stock sale) would have to be aggregated with any annual benefit that Participant O accrues under Plan LMN or Plan XYZ.

(vii) Application of nonduplication rule. In applying paragraph (a)(1) of this section to plans maintained by ABC Corporation after 2010 stock sale, plans maintained by ABC Corporation do not take into account the deemed termination of Plan ABC since ABC Corporation maintains Plan ABC after the cessation of affiliation. Similarly, in applying paragraph (a)(1) of this section to plans maintained by LMN Corporation and XYZ Corporation after the 2010 stock sale, plans maintained by LMN Corporation and XYZ Corporation do not take into account the deemed termination of Plan XYZ since XYZ Corporation maintains Plan XYZ after the cessation of affiliation. See paragraph (d)(1) of this section.

*Example (3).* (i) Facts. The facts are the same as in Example 2, except that on January 1, 2009, Plan ABC transfers Participant M's benefit to Plan XYZ.

(ii) Treatment of plans maintained by ABC Corporation. Pursuant to § 1.415(b)-1(b)(3)(i)(A), M's benefit that is transferred from Plan ABC to Plan XYZ is not treated as being provided under Plan ABC for the limitation year in which the transfer occurs (2009). This is because M's transferred benefit is otherwise required to be taken into account by Plan ABC for the 2009 limitation year since Plan XYZ must be aggregated with Plan ABC pursuant to paragraph (a)(1) of this section. This result does not change for the 2010 limitation year and later limitation years, where pursuant to paragraph (b)(2)(i) of this section, Plan XYZ becomes a formerly affiliated plan with respect to ABC Corporation due to the 2010 stock sale. Under paragraph (b)(2)(i) of this section, Plan XYZ (the formerly affiliated plan) is treated from the perspective of plans maintained by ABC Corporation (Plan ABC) as if Plan XYZ terminated immediately prior to the 2010 stock sale with sufficient assets to pay benefit liabilities under the plan, and had purchased annuities to provide plan benefits. However, the pre-2010 stock sale benefits of Plan XYZ include the January 1, 2009, transfer of Participant M's benefit. Thus, in the 2010 limitation year, M's transferred benefit is still otherwise required to be taken into account by Plan ABC on account of the aggregation of Plan XYZ with Plan ABC pursuant to paragraph (a)(1) of this section, and therefore the transferred benefit is not treated as being provided by Plan ABC.

(iii) Treatment of plans maintained by LMN Corporation and XYZ Corporation. Pursuant to § 1.415(b)-1(b)(3)(i)(C), Participant M's benefit that is transferred to Plan XYZ from Plan ABC must be treated as provided under Plan XYZ for purposes of applying the limitations of section 415 to Plan XYZ with respect to Participant M for the limitation year in which the transfer occurs and later years. This result does not change on account of the 2010 stock sale. When applying the limitation of section 415 to Plans LMN and XYZ for the 2010 limitation year and later years, Plans LMN and XYZ must aggregate the annual benefit provided to a participant under each plan along with the participant's benefit under Plan ABC pursuant to § 1.415(a)-1(f)(1) and paragraph (a)(1) of this section. However, under paragraph (b)(2)(i) of this section, for the 2010 limitation year and later years, this aggregation of M's Plan ABC benefit only includes the annual benefit attributable to a participant's accrued benefit under Plan ABC immediately prior to the 2010 stock sale, which (due to the 2009 transfer) is zero.

*Example (4).* (i) Facts. The facts are the same as in Example 2, except that on January 1, 2011, Plan ABC transfers Participant M's benefit to Plan XYZ.

(ii) Treatment of plans maintained by ABC Corporation for the 2011 limitation year and later years. Pursuant to § 1.415(b)-1(b)(3)(i)(B), M's benefit that is transferred from Plan ABC to Plan XYZ during the 2011 limitation year is treated by Plan ABC for the 2011 limitation year and later years as if the transferred benefit were provided under a plan that must be aggregated with Plan ABC that terminated immediately prior to the transfer with sufficient assets to pay benefit liabilities under the plan, and had purchased annuities to provide plan benefits. This is because M's transferred benefit is not otherwise required to be taken into account by Plan ABC for the 2011 limitation year and later years pursuant to paragraphs (a)(1) and (b)(2)(i) of this section. While Plan ABC must take into account Participant M's annual benefit under Plan XYZ under paragraph (a)(1) of this section, Participant M's annual benefit for this purpose is limited under paragraph (b)(2)(i) of this section to M's accrued benefit under Plan XYZ immediately prior to the 2010 stock sale, and Participant M's pre-2010 stock sale accrued benefit under Plan XYZ excludes the 2011 transfer.

(iii) Treatment of plans maintained by LMN Corporation and XYZ Corporation for the 2011 limitation year and later years. Pursuant to § 1.415(b)-1(b)(3)(i)(C), Participant M's benefit that is transferred to Plan XYZ from Plan ABC must be treated as provided under Plan XYZ for purposes of applying the limitations of section 415 to Plan XYZ with respect to Participant M for the limitation year in which the transfer occurs and later years. In applying the limitations of section 415(b) to Plans LMN and XYZ with respect to Participant M for the 2010 limitation year and later years, the annual benefit of Participant M under Plans ABC, LMN, and XYZ must be aggregated pursuant to § 1.415(a)-1(f)(1) and paragraph (a)(1) of this section, but for this purpose, Participant M's benefit under Plan ABC is treated as if it were provided under a plan that terminated immediately prior to the cessation of affiliation of ABC Corporation and XYZ Corporation with sufficient assets to pay benefit liabilities under the plan, and had purchased an annuity to provide Participant M's benefits. (See paragraph (b)(2)(i) of this section and Example 2.) In applying the limitations of section 415(b) to Plans LMN and XYZ with respect to Participant M for the 2011 limitation year and later years, the annual benefit of Participant M under Plans ABC, LMN, and XYZ still must be aggregated pursuant to § 1.415(a)-1(f)(1) and paragraph (a)(1) of this section. However, beginning with the 2011 limitation year, ABC Corporation is a predecessor employer with respect to LMN Corporation and XYZ Corporation with respect to Participant M on account of the transfer of benefits from Plan ABC to Plan XYZ, pursuant to paragraph (c)(1) of this section. Therefore, Plans LMN and XYZ must take into account benefits that Participant M accrued under Plan ABC after the January 1, 2010, cessation of affiliation of ABC Corporation and XYZ Corporation that were not transferred to Plan XYZ on January 1, 2011, pursuant to paragraphs (c)(1) and (d)(1) of this section. Since all of Participant M's benefit in Plan ABC is transferred to Plan XYZ on January 1, 2011, Participant M's annual benefit from Plan ABC for purposes of aggregating Plan ABC with Plans LMN and XYZ is zero.

*Example (5).* (i) Facts. The facts are the same as in Example 2, except that instead of the 2010 stock sale, XYZ Corporation sells some of its operating assets to LMN Corporation (and, under the facts and circumstances, the sale does not result in XYZ Corporation constituting a predecessor employer of LMN Corporation under the rules of paragraph (c)(2) of this section), and in connection with the asset sale, LMN Corporation assumes sponsorship of Plan XYZ in place of XYZ Corporation, effective January 1, 2010.

(ii) Treatment of plans maintained by ABC Corporation and XYZ Corporation. Pursuant to paragraph (a)(1) of this section, all defined benefit plans ever maintained by ABC Corporation and XYZ Corporation must be aggregated as a single defined benefit plan for purposes of applying the limitations of section 415(b). However, for purposes of determining the annual benefit under Plan XYZ for the 2010 limitation year and later years, the aggregation of a participant's benefit under Plan XYZ is limited to the participant's annual benefit accrued immediately prior to the January 1, 2010, transfer of sponsorship of Plan XYZ. This is because paragraph (b)(2)(i) of this section provides that a formerly affiliated plan of an employer is treated as if it were a plan that terminated immediately prior to the cessation of affiliation with sufficient assets to pay benefit liabilities under the plan, and had purchased annuities to provide plan benefits. The January 1, 2010, transfer of sponsorship of Plan XYZ is a cessation of affiliation under paragraph (b)(2)(ii) of this section because this event causes Plan XYZ to no longer actually be maintained by either ABC Corporation or XYZ Corporation. Effective immediately after the January 1, 2010, transfer of sponsorship, Plan XYZ is a formerly affiliated plan with respect to ABC Corporation and XYZ Corporation under paragraph (b)(2)(ii) of this section because immediately prior to the cessation of affiliation, Plan XYZ was actually maintained by XYZ Corporation, and immediately after the cessation of affiliation, Plan XYZ is not actually maintained by either XYZ Corporation or ABC Corporation. Therefore, in applying the limitation of section 415(b) to Participant M for the 2010 limitation year and later limitation years, Plan ABC must take into account the annual benefit provided under Plan ABC to Participant M and the annual benefit provided under Plan XYZ to Participant M as if Plan XYZ had terminated immediately prior to the 2010 stock sale with sufficient assets to pay benefit liabilities under the plan, and had purchased annuities to provide plan benefits. The aggregation of Plan XYZ with Plan ABC is irrelevant for purposes of Participant O because Participant O does not have any accrued benefit under Plan XYZ (as determined prior to the 2010 transfer of sponsorship).

(iii) Treatment of plans maintained by LMN Corporation. Under paragraph (a)(1) of this section, all defined benefit plans ever maintained by LMN Corporation or a predecessor employer must be aggregated as a single plan for purposes of applying the limitations of section 415(b). ABC Corporation and XYZ Corporation constitute a predecessor employer pursuant to paragraph (c)(1) of this section with respect to the participants who participate in Plan XYZ on the date of the transfer of sponsorship of Plan XYZ (the transferred participants) from XYZ Corporation to LMN Corporation, such as Participant M. This is because, effective with the January 1, 2010, transfer of sponsorship, LMN Corporation maintains a plan (Plan XYZ) under which the participants accrued a benefit while performing services for XYZ Corporation (which is in turn affiliated with ABC Corporation under § 1.415(a)-1(f)(1)) and such benefits are provided under a plan maintained by LMN Corporation. Therefore, for the 2010 limitation year and later years, the annual benefit under Plan ABC of the transferred participants (such as Participant M) must be aggregated with the annual benefit provided to such participants under Plans XYZ and LMN for purposes of determining whether Plan LMN or Plan XYZ satisfies the limitations of section 415(b). However, the aggregation of the transferred participants' Plan ABC annual benefits is limited to the annual benefit accrued under Plan ABC immediately prior to January 1, 2010, transfer of sponsorship. This is because, pursuant to paragraph (c)(1) of this section, Plan ABC is treated from the perspective of plans maintained by LMN Corporation as if Plan ABC had terminated immediately prior to the transfer of sponsorship of Plan ABC to LMN Corporation with sufficient assets to pay benefit liabilities under the plan, and had purchased annuities to provide plan benefits. ABC Corporation and XYZ Corporation do not constitute a predecessor employer with respect to Participant O. Thus, if Participant O is a participant in Plan LMN or becomes a participant in Plan XYZ after the 2010 transfer of sponsorship, neither plan aggregates Participant O's Plan ABC benefits for purposes of satisfying section 415(b). In applying paragraph (a)(1) of this section to a participant, plans maintained by LMN Corporation do not double count the participant's annual benefit. See paragraph (d)(1) of this section. Thus, such plans do not aggregate the annual benefit provided under Plan XYZ with the annual benefit from the deemed termination of Plan XYZ that LMN Corporation's predecessor employer (which is ABC and XYZ Corporations) must take into account in applying paragraph (a)(1) of this section, and instead consider the annual benefit actually provided under Plan XYZ.

*Example (6).* (i) Facts. N is employed by a hospital which purchases an annuity contract described in section 403(b) on N's behalf for the current limitation year. N is in control of the hospital within the meaning of section 414(b) or (c), as modified by section 415(h). The hospital also maintains a qualified defined contribution plan during the current limitation year in which N participates.

(ii) Conclusion. Under section 415(k)(4), the hospital, as well as N, is considered to maintain the annuity contract. Accordingly, for N the sum of the annual additions under the qualified defined contribution plan and the annuity contract must satisfy the limitations of section 415(c) and § 1.415(c)-1.

*Example (7).* (i) Facts. The facts are the same as in Example 6, except that instead of being in control of the hospital, N is the 100 percent owner of a professional corporation P, which maintains a qualified defined contribution plan in which N participates.

(ii) Conclusion. Under section 415(k)(4), the professional corporation, as well as N, is considered to maintain the annuity contract. Accordingly, the sum of the annual additions under the qualified defined contribution plan maintained by professional corporation P and the annuity contract must satisfy the limitations of section 415(c) and § 1.415(c)-1. See § 1.415(g)-1(b)(3)(iv)(C)(2) for an example of the treatment of a contribution to a section 403(b) annuity contract that exceeds the limits of section 415(c) by reason of the aggregation required by this section.

*Example (8).* (i) Facts. J is an employee of two corporations, N and M, each of which has employed J for more than 10 years. N and M are not required to be aggregated pursuant to section 415(f) and this section. Each corporation has a qualified defined benefit plan in which J has participated for more than 10 years. Each plan provides a benefit which is equal to 75 percent of a participant's average compensation for the period of the participant's high-3 years of service and is payable in the form of a straight life annuity beginning at age 65. J's average compensation for the period of his high-3 years of service from each corporation is $160,000. In July 2008, N Corporation becomes a wholly owned subsidiary of M Corporation.

(ii) Plan aggregation analysis. As a result of the acquisition of N Corporation by M Corporation, J is treated as being employed by a single employer under section 414(b). Therefore, because section 415(f)(1)(A) requires that all defined benefit plans of an employer be treated as one defined benefit plan, the two plans must be aggregated for purposes of applying the limitations of section 415. However, under paragraph (e)(3)(i) of this section, since the plans were not aggregated as of the first day of the 2008 limitation year (January 1, 2008), they will not be considered aggregated until the limitation year beginning January 1, 2009, provided that no plan amendment increasing benefits with respect to participant J is made after the acquisition of N by M.

(iii) Application to Participant J. J has a total benefit under the two plans of $240,000, which, as a result of the plan aggregation, is in excess of the section 415(b) limit. However, under paragraph (e)(3)(ii) of this section, the limitations of section 415(b) and § 1.415(b)-1 applicable to J may be exceeded in this situation without plan disqualification so long as J's accrued benefit derived from employer contributions is not increased (that is, J's accrued benefit does not increase on account of increased compensation, service, participation, or other accruals) during the period within which the limitations are being exceeded.

*Example (9).* (i) Facts. A, age 30, owns all of the stock of X Corporation and also owns 10 percent of the stock of Z Corporation. F, A's father, directly owns 75 percent of the stock of Z Corporation. Both corporations have qualified defined contribution plans in which A participates. A's compensation (within the meaning of § 1.415(c)-2) for 2008 is $20,000 from Z Corporation and $150,000 from X Corporation. During the period January 1, 2008 through June 30, 2008, annual additions of $20,000 are credited to A's account under the plan of Z Corporation, while annual additions of $40,000 are credited to A's account under the plan of X Corporation. In both instances, the amount of annual additions represent the maximum allowable under section 415(c) and § 1.415(c)-1. On July 15, 2008, F dies, and A inherits all of F's stock in Z in 2008.

(ii) Conclusion. As of July 15, 2008, A is considered to be in control of X and Z Corporations, and the two plans must be aggregated for purposes of applying the limitations of section 415. However, even though A's total annual additions for 2008 are $60,000, the limitations of section 415(c) and § 1.415(c)-1 are not violated for 2008, provided no annual additions are credited to A's accounts after July 15, 2008 (the date that A is first in control of Z) for the remainder of the 2008 limitation year.

*Example (10).* (i) Facts. P is a key employee of employer XYZ who participates in a qualified defined contribution plan (Plan X). P is also provided post-retirement medical benefits, and XYZ has taken into account a reserve for those benefits under section 419A(c)(2). In the 2008 limitation year, P's compensation is $30,000 and P's annual additions under Plan X are $5,000. Pursuant to section 419A(d), a separate account is maintained for P, and that account is credited with an allocation of $32,000 for the 2008 limitation year. It is assumed that the section 415(c)(1)(A) dollar limit for 2008 is $46,000.

(ii) Separate testing analysis. Under paragraph (h)(1) of this section, Plan X and the individual medical account must separately satisfy the requirements of section 415(c), taking into account any special limit applicable to that arrangement. In this case, the contributions to Plan X separately satisfy the limitations of section 415(c). While the individual medical account is treated as a defined contribution plan subject to the rules of section 415(c), it is not subject to the 100 percent of compensation limit of section 415(c)(1)(B), so the contributions to that account satisfy the limitations of section 415(c).

(iii) Aggregation analysis. The sum of the annual additions under Plan X and the amounts contributed to the separate account on P's behalf must satisfy the requirements of section 415(c). Under paragraph (h)(2) of this section, the limit applicable to the aggregated plan is equal to the greater of the limits applicable to the separate plans. In this case, the limit applicable to the medical account is $46,000 (which is greater than the limit of $30,000 applicable to the qualified plan), so the limit that applies to the aggregated plan is $46,000, and the aggregated plan satisfies the requirements of section 415.

---

T.D. 9319, 4/4/2007.

---

### § 1.415(g)-1 Disqualification of plans and trusts.

**(a) Disqualification of plans.** *(1) In general.* Under section 415(g) and this section, with respect to a particular limitation year, a plan (and the trust forming part of the plan) is disqualified in accordance with the rules provided in paragraph (b) of this section, if the conditions described in paragraph (a)(2) or (a)(3) of this section apply. For purposes of this paragraph (a), the determination of whether a plan or a group of aggregated plans exceeds the limitations imposed by section 415 for a particular limitation year is, except as otherwise provided, made by taking into account the aggregation of plan rules provided in section 415(f) and § 1.414(f)-1.

*(2) Defined contribution plans.* A plan is disqualified in accordance with the rules provided in paragraph (b) of this section if annual additions (as defined in § 1.415(c)-1(b)) with respect to the account of any participant in a defined contribution plan maintained by the employer exceed the limitations of section 415(c) and § 1.415(c)-1.

*(3) Defined benefit plans.* A plan is disqualified in accordance with the rules provided in paragraph (b) of this section if the annual benefit (as defined in § 1.415(b)-1(b)(1)) of a participant in a defined benefit plan maintained by the employer exceeds the limitations of section 415(b) and § 1.415(b)-1.

**(b) Rules for disqualification of plans and trusts.** *(1) In general.* If any plan (including a trust which forms part of such plan) is disqualified for a particular limitation year under the rules set forth in this paragraph (b), then the disqualification is effective as of the first day of the first plan year containing any portion of the particular limitation year.

*(2) Single plan.* In the case of a single qualified defined benefit plan (determined without regard to section 415(f) and § 1.415(f)-1) maintained by the employer that provides an annual benefit (as defined in § 1.415(b)-1(b)(1)) in excess of the limitations of section 415(b) and § 1.415(b)-1 for any particular limitation year, such plan is disqualified in that limitation year. Similarly, if the employer only maintains a single defined contribution plan (determined without regard to section 415(f) and § 1.415(f)-1) under which annual additions (as defined in § 1.415(c)-1(b)) allocated to the account of any participant exceed the limitations of section 415(c) and § 1.415(c)-1 for any particular limitation year, such plan is also disqualified in that limitation year.

*(3) Multiple plans.* (i) In general. If the limitations of section 415(b) and § 1.415(b)-1, or section 415(c) and § 1.415(c)-1, are exceeded for a particular limitation year with respect to any participant solely because of the application of the aggregation rules of section 415(f)(1) and § 1.415(f)-1 (taking into account the rules of § 1.415(a)-1(f)), then one or more of the plans is disqualified in accordance with the ordering rules set forth in paragraph (b)(3)(ii) of this section, applied in accordance with the rules of application set forth in paragraph (b)(3)(iii) of this section, subject to the special rules set forth in paragraph (b)(3)(iv) of this section, until, without regard to annual benefits or annual additions under the disqualified plan or plans, the remaining plans satisfy the applicable limitations of section 415.

(ii) Ordering rules. (A) Disqualification of ongoing plans other than multiemployer plans. If there are two or more plans that have not been terminated at any time including the last day of the particular limitation year, and if one or more of those plans is a multiemployer plan described in section 414(f), then one or more of the plans (as needed to satisfy the limitations of section 415) that has not been terminated and is not a multiemployer plan is disqualified in that limitation year. For purposes of the preceding sentence, the determination of whether a plan is a multiemployer plan described in section 414(f) is made as of the last day of the particular limitation year.

(B) Disqualification of ongoing multiemployer plans. If, after the application of paragraph (b)(3)(ii)(A) of this section, there are two or more plans and one or more of the plans has been terminated at any time including the last day of the particular limitation year, then one or more of the plans (as needed to satisfy the applicable limitations of section 415) that has not been so terminated (regardless of whether the plan is a multiemployer plan described in section 414(f)) is disqualified in that limitation year.

(iii) Rules of application. (A) Employer elects which plan is disqualified. If there are two or more plans of an employer within a group of plans one or more of which is to be disqualified pursuant to paragraph (b)(3)(ii)(A) or (B) of this section, then the employer may elect, in a manner determined by the Commissioner, which plan or plans are disqualified. If those two or more plans are involved because of the application of § 1.415(a)-1(f), the employers involved may elect, in a manner determined by the Commissioner, which plan or plans are disqualified. However, the election described in the preceding sentence is not effective unless made by all of those employers.

(B) Commissioner determines which plan is disqualified. If the election described in paragraph (b)(3)(iii)(A) of this section is not made with respect to the two plans described in paragraph (b)(3)(iii)(A) of this section, then the Commissioner, taking into account all of the facts and circumstances, has the discretion to determine the plan that is disqualified in the particular limitation year. In making this determination, some of the factors that will be taken into account include, but are not limited to, the number of participants in each plan, the amount of benefits provided on an overall basis by each plan, and the extent to which benefits are distributed or retained in each plan.

(iv) Special rules. (A) Simplified employee pensions. If there are two or more plans one or more of which is to be disqualified pursuant to paragraph (b)(3)(ii)(A) or (B) of this section, and if one of the plans is a simplified employee pension (as defined in section 408(k)), then the simplified employee pension is not disqualified until all of the other plans have been disqualified. However, if one of the plans has been terminated, then the simplified employee pension is disqualified before the terminated plan. For purposes of this paragraph (b)(3)(iv)(A), the disqualification of a simplified employee pension means that the simplified employee pension is no longer described under section 408(k).

(B) Aggregating medical accounts with defined contribution plans. In the event that aggregating a medical account described in § 1.415(c)-1(a)(2)(ii)(C) or (D) and a defined contribution plan other than such a medical account causes the limitations of section 415(c) and § 1.415(c)-1 applicable to a participant to be exceeded for a particular limitation year, the defined contribution plan other than the medical account is disqualified for the limitation year.

(C) Aggregating section 403(b) annuity contract and qualified defined contribution plan. (1) In general. In the event that aggregating a section 403(b) annuity contract and a qualified defined contribution plan under the provisions of section 415(f)(1)(B) causes the limitations of section 415(c) and § 1.415(c)-1 applicable to a participant under the aggregated defined contribution plans to be exceeded for a particular limitation year, the excess of the contributions to the annuity contract plus the annual additions to the qualified plan over such limitations is attributed to the annuity contract and therefore includable in the gross income of the participant for the taxable year with or within which that limitation year ends. See § 1.415(a)-1(b)(2) for rules regarding the treatment of a contribution to a section 403(b) annuity contract that exceeds the limitations of section 415.

(2) Example. The following example illustrates the application of this paragraph (b)(3)(iv)(C). It is assumed for purposes of this example that the dollar limitation under section 415(c)(1)(A) that applies for all relevant limitation years is $45,000. The example is as follows:

*Example.* (i) N is employed by a hospital which purchases an annuity contract described in section 403(b) on N's behalf for the current limitation year. N is also the 100 percent owner of a professional corporation P that maintains a qualified defined contribution plan during the current limitation year in which N participates. (The facts of this example are the same as in § 1.415(f)-1(j) Example 7.) N's compensation (within the meaning of § 1.415(c)-2) from the hospital for the current limitation year is $150,000. For the current limitation year, the hospital contributes $30,000 for the section 403(b) annuity contract on N's behalf, which is within the limitations applicable to N under the annuity contract (specifically, the limit under the annuity contract is $45,000)). Professional corporation P also contributes $20,000 to the qualified defined contribution plan on N's behalf for the current limitation year (which represents the only annual additions allocated to N's account under the plan for such year), which is within the $45,000 limitation of section 415(c)(1) applicable to N under the plan.

(ii) Under section 415(k)(4), the professional corporation, as well as N, is considered to maintain the annuity contract. Accordingly, the sum of the annual additions under the qualified defined contribution plan maintained by professional corporation P and the annuity contract must satisfy the limitations of section 415(c) and § 1.415(c)-1.

(iii) Because the total aggregate contributions ($50,000) exceed the section 415(c) limitation applicable to N ($45,000), $5,000 of the $30,000 contributed to the section 403(b) annuity contract is considered an excess contribution and therefore currently includable in N's gross income. The contract continues to be a section 403(b) annuity contract only if, for the current limitation year and all years thereafter, the issuer of the contract maintains separate accounts for each portion attributable to such excess contributions. See §§ 1.415(a)-1(b)(2).

**(c) Plan year for certain annuity contracts and individual retirement plans.** For purposes of this section, unless the plan under which the annuity contract or individual retirement plan is provided specifies that a different twelve-month period is considered to be the plan year—

*(1)* An annuity contract described in section 403(b) is considered to have a plan year coinciding with the taxable year of the individual on whose behalf the contract has been purchased; and

*(2)* A simplified employee pension described in section 408(k) is considered to have a plan year coinciding with the year under the plan that is used pursuant to section 408(k)(7)(C).

T.D. 9319, 4/4/2007.

**§ 1.415(j)-1 Limitation year.**

**(a) In general.** Unless the terms of a plan provide otherwise, the limitation year, with respect to any qualified plan maintained by the employer, is the calendar year.

**(b) Alternative limitation year election.** The terms of a plan may provide for the use of any other consecutive twelve month period as the limitation year. This includes a fiscal year with an annual period varying from 52 to 53 weeks, so long as the fiscal year satisfies the requirements of section 441(f). A plan may only provide for one limitation year regardless of the number or identity of the employers maintaining the plan.

**(c) Multiple limitation years.** *(1) In general.* Where an employer maintains more than one qualified plan, those plans may provide for different limitation years. The rule described in this paragraph (c) also applies to a controlled group of employers (within the meaning of section 414(b) or (c), as modified by section 415(h)). If the plans of an employer (or a controlled group of employers whose plans are aggregated) have different limitation years, section 415 is applied in accordance with the rule of paragraphs (c)(2) and (3) of this section.

*(2) Testing rule for defined contribution plans.* If a participant is credited with annual additions in only one defined contribution plan, in determining whether the requirements of section 415(c) are satisfied, only the limitation year applicable to that plan is considered. However, if a participant is credited with annual additions in more than one defined contribution plan, each such plan satisfies the requirements of section 415(c) only if the limitations of section 415(c) are satisfied with respect to amounts that are annual additions for the limitation year with respect to the participant under the plan, plus amounts credited to the participant's account under all other plans required to be aggregated with the plan pursuant to section 415(f) and § 1.415(f)-1 that would have been considered annual additions for the limitation year under the plan if they had been credited under the plan rather than an aggregated plan.

*(3) Testing rule for defined benefit plans.* If a participant has participated in only one defined benefit plan, in determining whether the requirements of section 415(b) are satisfied, only the limitation year applicable to that plan is considered. However, if a participant has participated in more than one defined benefit plan, a plan satisfies the requirements of section 415(b) only if the annual benefit under all plans required to be aggregated pursuant to section 415(f) and § 1.415(f)-1 for the limitation year of that plan with respect to the participant satisfy the applicable limitations of section 415(b). Thus, for example, the dollar limitation of section 415(b)(1)(A) applicable to the limitation year for each plan must be applied to annual benefits under all aggregated plans to determine whether the plan satisfies the requirements of section 415(b).

**(d) Change of limitation year.** *(1) In general.* Once established, the limitation year may be changed only by amending the plan. Any change in the limitation year must be a change to a 12-month period commencing with any day within the current limitation year. For purposes of this section, the limitations of section 415 are to be applied in the normal manner to the new limitation year.

*(2) Application to short limitation period.* Where there is a change of limitation year, the limitations of section 415 are to be separately applied to a limitation period which begins with the first day of the current limitation year and which ends on the day before the first day of the first limitation year for which the change is effective. In the case of a defined contribution plan, the dollar limitation with respect to this limitation period is determined by multiplying the applicable dollar limitation for the calendar year in which the limitation period ends by a fraction, the numerator of which is the number of months (including any fractional parts of a month) in the limitation period, and the denominator of which is 12. In the case of a defined benefit plan, no adjustment is made to the section 415(b) limitations to reflect a short limitation period.

*(3) Deemed change of limitation year.* If a defined contribution plan is terminated effective as of a date other than the last day of the plan's limitation year, the plan is treated for purposes of this section as if the plan was amended to change its limitation year. Thus, the rules of this paragraph (d) apply to the terminating plan's final limitation year.

**(e) Limitation year for individuals on whose behalf section 403(b) annuity contracts have been purchased.** The limitation year of an individual on whose behalf a section 403(b) annuity contract has been purchased by an employer is determined in the following manner.

*(1)* If the individual is not in control of any employer (within the meaning of § 1.415(f)-1(f)(2)(ii)), the limitation year is the calendar year. However, the individual may elect to change the limitation year to another twelve-month period. To do this, the individual must attach a statement to his or her income tax return filed for the taxable year in which the change is made. Any change in the limitation year must comply with the rules set forth in paragraph (d) of this section.

*(2)* If the individual is in control of an employer (within the meaning of § 1.415(f)-1(f)(2)(ii)), the limitation year is the limitation year of that employer.

**(f) Limitation year for individuals on whose behalf individual retirement plans are maintained.** The limitation year of an individual on whose behalf an individual retirement plan (within the meaning of section 7701(a)(37)) is maintained is determined in the manner described in paragraph (e) of this section.

**(g) Examples.** The following examples illustrate the application of this section:

*Example (1).* (i) Participant M is employed by both Employer A and Employer B, each of which maintains a qualified defined contribution plan. M participates in both of these plans. The limitation year for Employer A's plan is January 1 through December 31, and the limitation year for Employer B's plan is April 1 through March 31. Employer A and Employer B are both corporations, and Corporation X owns 100 percent of the stock of Employer A and Employer B.

(ii) The two plans in which M participates are required under section 415(f) to be aggregated for purposes of applying the limitations of section 415(c) to annual additions made with respect to M. Thus, for example, for the limitation year of Employer A's plan that begins January 1, 2008, annual additions with respect to M that are subject to the limitations of section 415(c) include both amounts that are annual additions with respect to M under Employer A's plan for the period beginning January 1, 2008, and ending December 31, 2008, and amounts contributed to Employer B's plan with respect to M that would have been considered annual additions for the period beginning January 1, 2008, and ending December 31, 2008, under Employer A's plan if those amounts had instead been contributed to Employer A's plan.

*Example (2).* In 2008, an employer with a qualified defined contribution plan using the calendar year as the limitation year elects to change the limitation year to a period beginning July 1 and ending June 30. Because of this change, the plan must satisfy the limitations of section 415(c) for the limitation period beginning January 1, 2008, and ending June 30, 2008. In applying the limitations of section 415(c) to this limitation period, the amount of compensation taken into account may only include compensation for this period. Furthermore, the dollar limitation for this period is the otherwise applicable dollar limitation for calendar year 2008, multiplied by 6/12.

T.D. 9319, 4/4/2007.

### § 1.416-1 Questions and answers on top-heavy plans.

***Caution:*** The Treasury has not yet amended Reg § 1.416-1 to reflect changes made by P.L. 107-147, P.L. 107-16, P.L. 104-188, P.L. 100-647, P.L. 99-514.

The following questions and answers relate to special rules for top-heavy plans under section 416 of the Internal Revenue Code of 1954, as added by section 240 of the Tax Equity and Fiscal Responsibility Act of 1982 (Pub. L. 97-248) (TEFRA), and amended by sections 524 and 713(f) of the Tax Reform Act of 1984 (Pub. L. 98-369):

TABLE OF CONTENTS



G. GENERAL PROVISIONS

*G-1 Q.* What requirement plans are subject to the top-heavy rules added to the Code by the Tax Equity and Fiscal Responsibility Act and amended by the Tax Reform Act of 1984?

A. All stock bonus, pension, or profit-sharing plans intended to qualify under section 401(a), annuity contracts described in section 403(a), and simplified employee pensions described in section 408(k) are subject to the new top-heavy rules added to the Code by the Tax Equity and Fiscal Responsibility Act and amended by the Tax Reform Act ("TRA") of 1984.

*G-2 Q.* Is a multiple employer plan subject to the top-heavy requirements of section 416?

A. A multiple employer plan is subject to the requirements of section 416, but only with respect to each individual employer. Thus, if twelve employers contribute to a multiple employer plan and the accrued benefits for the key employees of one employer exceed 60 percent of the accrued benefits of all employees for such employer, the plan is top-heavy with respect to that employer. A failure by the multiple employer plan to satisfy section 416 with respect to the employees of such employer means that all employers are maintaining a plan that is not a qualified plan.

*G-3 Q.* As of what date must plan amendments to comply with top-heavy rules be effective?

A. Amendments required to comply with the top-heavy rules must be effective as of the first day of the first plan year which begins after 1983. See § 1.401(b)-1 for the date by which such amendments must be adopted.

T. TOP-HEAVINESS DETERMINATIONS

*T-1 Q.* What factors must be considered in determining whether a plan is top-heavy?

A. (a) In order to determine whether a plan is top-heavy for a plan year, it is necessary to determine which employers will be treated as a single employer for purposes of section 416; what the determination date is for the plan year; which employees are or formerly were key employees; which former employees have not performed any service for the employer maintaining the plan at any time during the five-year period ending on the determination date; which plans of such employers are required or permitted to be aggregated to determine top-heavy status; and the present value of the accrued benefits (including distributions made during the plan year containing the determination date and the four preceding plan years) of key employees, former key employees, and non-key employees.

(b) All employers that are aggregated under section 414(b), (c), and (m) must be taken into account as a single employer for the plan year in question, and those employees in all plans maintained by the employers that are aggregated must be categorized as key employees, as former key employees, or as non-key employees. See Question and Answer T-12 for the determination of which employees are or were key employees. All plans maintained by the employers in which a key employee participates, and certain other plans, must then be aggregated (the required aggregation group). See Question and Answer T-6 for rules concerning required aggregation. Other plans may in some cases be aggregated with the required aggregation group. See Question and Answer T-7 for rules concerning such permissive aggregation.

(c) Once aggregated, all plans that are required to be aggregated will either be top-heavy or not top-heavy, depending upon whether the aggregation group is top-heavy. A plan or aggregation group will be considered top-heavy if the sum of the present value of the accrued benefits for key employees is more than 60 percent of the sum of the present value of accrued benefits of all employees.

(d) Except as otherwise stated, for purposes of section 416(g), an employee is an individual currently or formerly employed by an employer. Former key employees are non-key employees and are excluded entirely from the calculation to determine top-heaviness. In all cases, the present value of accrued benefits includes distributions made during the plan year containing the determination date and the preceding four plan years. See Questions and Answers T-24 and T-25 for rules concerning the account balances and present value of accrued benefits. For plan years beginning after December 31, 1984, the accrued benefit of an employee who has not performed any service for the employer maintaining the plan at any time during the five-year period ending on the determination date is excluded from the calculation to determine top-heaviness. However, if an employee performs no services for five years and then performs services, such employee's total accrued benefit is included in the calculation for top-heaviness.

*T-2 Q.* To what extent are multiemployer plans and multiple employer plans to which an employer makes contributions on behalf of its employees treated as plans of that employer for top-heavy purposes?

A. Multiemployer plans described in section 414(f) and multiple employer plans described in section 413(c) to which an employer makes contributions on behalf of its employees are treated as plans of that employer to the extent that benefits under the plan are provided to employees of the employer because of service with that employer.

*T-3 Q.* Must a collectively-bargained plan be aggregated with other plans of the employer to determine whether some or all of the employer's plans are top-heavy?

A. A collectively-bargained plan that includes a key employee of an employer must be included in the required aggregation group for that employer. See Question and Answer T-6 for rules concerning required aggregation. A collectively-bargained plan that does not include a key employee may be included in a permissive aggregation group. See Question and Answer T-7 for rules concerning permissive aggregation. However, the special rules in section 416(b), (c), or (d) applicable to top-heavy plans do not apply with respect to any employee included in a unit of employees covered by an agreement which the Secretary of Labor finds to be a collective-bargaining agreement between employee representatives and one or more employers if there is evidence that retirement benefits were the subject of good faith bargaining between such employee representatives and such employer or employers. In determining whether there is a collective-bargaining agreement between employee representatives and one or more employers, the additional condition of section 7701(a)(46) must be satisfied after March 31, 1984.

*T-4 Q.* How is a terminated plan treated for purposes of the top-heavy rules?

A. A terminated plan is treated like any other plan for purposes of the top-heavy rules. For purposes of section 416, a terminated plan is one that has been formally terminated, has ceased crediting service for benefit accruals and vesting, and has been or is distributing all plan assets to participants or their beneficiaries as soon as administratively feasible. Such a plan must be aggregated with other plans of the employer if it was maintained within the last five years ending on the determination date for the plan year in question and would, but for the fact that it terminated, be part of a required aggregation group for such plan year. Distributions which have taken place within the five years ending on the determination date must be accounted for in accordance with section 416(g)(3). No additional vesting, benefit accruals or contributions must be provided for participants in a terminated plan.

*T-5 Q.* How are frozen plans treated for purposes of the top-heavy rules?

A. For purposes of section 416, a frozen plan is one in which benefit accruals have ceased but all assets have not been distributed to participants or their beneficiaries. Such plans are treated, for purposes of the top-heavy rules, as any non-frozen plan. That is, such plans must provide minimum contributions or benefit accruals, limit the amount of compensation which can be taken into account in providing benefits, and provide top-heavy vesting. A frozen defined contribution plan may not be required to provide additional contributions because of the rule in section 416(c)(2)(B).

*T-6 Q.* What is a required aggregation group?

A. For purposes of determining whether the plans of an employer are top-heavy for a particular plan year, the required aggregation group includes each plan of the employer in which a key employee participates in the plan year containing the determination date, or any of the four preceding plan years. In addition, each other plan of the employer which, during this period, enables any plan in which a key employee participates to meet the requirements of section 401(a)(4) or 410 is part of the required aggregation group. This concept may be illustrated by the following examples:

*Example (1).* An employer maintains two plans. Key employees participate in one plan, but not in the other. If the plan containing key employees independently satisfies the coverage and non-discrimination rules of sections 410 and 401(a)(4), it may be tested independently to determine whether it is top-heavy. Also, the plan not covering key employees would not be part of a required aggregation group and would not need to be tested to determine whether it is top-heavy. However, if the plan containing key employees satisfies the coverage requirements of section 410(b) or the nondiscrimination requirements of section 401(a) (4) only when it is considered together with the other plan in accordance with § 1.410(b)-1(d)(3), the plan not covering key employees would be part of the required aggregation group.

*Example (2).* A sole proprietor terminated a Keogh plan in 1981. In 1982, the sole proprietor incorporated and established a corporate plan with a calendar-year plan year. For purposes of determining whether the corporate plan is top-heavy for its 1984 plan year, the terminated Keogh plan and the corporate plan would be part of a required aggregation group. The sole proprietor and the corporation would be treated as a single employer under section 414(c). Under Question and Answer T-4, the terminated plan would be aggregated with the corporate plan because it was maintained within the five-year period ending on the determination date for the 1984 plan year and because, but for the fact that it terminated, it would be aggregated with the corporate plan because it covered a key employee.

*T-7 Q.* What is a permissive aggregation group?

A. A permissive aggregation group consists of plans of the employer that are required to be aggregated, plus one or more plans of the employer that are not part of a required aggregation group but that satisfy the requirements of sections 401(a)(4) and 410 when considered together with the required aggregation group. This concept may be illustrated by the following examples:

*Example (1).* (a) An employer maintains two plans: 1. Plan A covers key employees and independently satisfies the requirements of sections 410 and 401(a)(4).

2. Plan B covers no key employees. It also independently satisfies the requirements of sections 410 and 401(a)(4).

(b) As indicated in Question and Answer T-6, Plan B is not required to be aggregated with Plan A. Further, if Plan B provided contributions or benefits that were not at least comparable to the contributions or benefits provided under Plan A, then Plan B could not be permissively aggregated with Plan A because the contributions and benefits would discriminate if the two plans were considered as a unit. However, if the benefits or contributions under Plan B were comparable to those under Plan A, the two plans would be permitted to be aggregated to determine whether or not the group consisting of both plans is top-heavy. If Plan A and Plan B are permitted to be aggregated, and if the permissive aggregation group is not top-heavy, then neither Plan A nor Plan B would be considered top-heavy.

*Example (2).* (a) Employer W maintains two plans. 1. Plan C covers salaried employees and independently satisfies the requirements of sections 410 and 401(a)(4).

2. Plan D covers employees who are included in a unit of employees covered by an agreement which the Secretary of Labor has found to be a collective-bargaining agreement between employee representatives and the employer and retirement benefits were bargained for between employee representatives and the employer.

(b) The fact that Plan D is a collectively bargained plan does not necessarily mean that it may be permissively aggregated with Plan C. In order to be permissively aggregated with Plan C, Plan D must provide contributions or benefits with respect to service with Employer W that are at least comparable to the contributions or benefits provided under Plan C.

*T-8 Q.* May an employer permissively aggregate multiemployer plans, multiple employer plans and simplified employee pension plans to which the employer contributes with a plan covering key employees or a required aggregated group?

A. Yes. Multiemployer plans, multiple employer plans and simplified employee pensions to which an employer makes contributions may be permissively aggregated with a plan covering key employees or with a required aggregation group if the contributions or benefits provided under the multiemployer plan, multiple employer plan or simplified employee pension by the employer are comparable to the contributions or benefits provided under the plan covering key employees or the plans in the required aggregation group. In making this determination, only the employer's contribution to the simplified employee pension may be used.

*T-9 Q.* What plans will be treated as top-heavy if they are part of a required aggregation group that is top-heavy?

A. In the case of plans that are required to be aggregated, each plan in the required aggregation group will be top-heavy if the group is top-heavy. No plan in the required aggregation group will be top-heavy if the group is not top-heavy.

*T-10 Q.* If a required aggregation group is top-heavy, and one plan of the group satisfies the requirements of sections 416(b), (c), and (d), may other plans in the group include provisions which do not satisfy sections 416(b), (c) and (d)?

A. No. Each plan in a required aggregation group is top-heavy if the group is top-heavy. Thus, each plan must contain provisions satisfying the requirements of sections 416(b) and (d). If all the plans are defined contribution plans, only one plan need satisfy the requirements of section 416(c)(2) with respect to any non-key employee who participates in more than one of the plans. If all the plans are defined benefit plans, only one plan need satisfy the requirements of section 416(c)(1) with respect to any non-key employee who participates in more than one of the plans. However, in the case of non-key employees who do not participate in more than one plan, each plan must separately provide the applicable minimum contribution or benefit with respect to each such employee. See Question and Answer M-12 in the case of employees who are covered under both a defined benefit and a defined contribution plan.

*T-11 Q.* What plans will be treated as top-heavy if a permissive aggregation group is top-heavy?

A. If a permissive aggregation group is top-heavy, only those plans that are part of the required aggregation group will be subject to the requirements of section 416(b), (c) and (d). Plans that are not part of the required aggregation group will not be subject to these requirements. Thus, if an employer wishes to demonstrate that the plans maintained by the employer are not top-heavy, the employer need consider only the required aggregation group. If, after considering the required aggregation group, it is determined that the plans are not top-heavy, the requirements of section 416(b), (c) and (d) will not apply to any of the plans. If, on the other hand, the plans required to be aggregated are top-heavy, the employer may wish to determine whether there are any plans that may be permissively aggregated to demonstrate that the plans are not top-heavy. Assuming that there are plans that are eligible for permissive aggregation, the employer may take these plans into consideration. If, after taking such plans into consideration, the net result is that the entire group is not top-heavy, the top-heavy requirements do not apply to any plan in the group.

*T-12 Q.* For purposes of determining whether a plan is top-heavy for a plan year, who is a key employee?

A. Under section 416(i)(1), a key employee is any employee (including any deceased employee) who at any time during the plan year containing the determination date for the plan year in question or the four preceding plan years (including plan years before 1984) is:

1. An officer of the employer having annual compensation from the employer for a plan year greater than 150 percent of the dollar limitation in effect under section 415(c)(1)(A) for the calendar year in which such plan year ends (see Questions and Answers T-13, T-14, and T-15),

2. One of the ten employees having annual compensation from the employer for a plan year greater than the dollar limitation in effect under section 415(c)(1)(A) for the calendar year in which such plan year ends and owning (or considered as owning within the meaning of section 318) both more than a ½ percent interest and the largest interests in the employer (see Question and Answer T-19),

3. A 5-percent owner of the employer, or

4. A 1-percent owner of the employer having annual compensation from the employer for a plan year more than $150,000 (see Questions and Answers T-16 and T-21).

An individual may be considered a key employee in a plan year for more than one reason. For example, an individual may be both an officer and one of the ten largest owners. However, in testing whether a plan or group is top-heavy, an individual's accrued benefit is counted only once. The terms key employee, former key employee, and non-key employee include the beneficiaries of such individuals. This Question and Answer is illustrated by the following examples:

*Example (1).* An employer maintains a calendar-year plan. An individual who was an employee of the employer and a 5-percent owner of the employer in 1986 was neither an employee nor an owner in 1987 or thereafter. Even though the individual is no longer an employee or owner of the employer, the individual would be treated as a key employee for purposes of determining whether the plan is top-heavy for each plan year through the 1991 plan year. However, for purposes of determining whether the plan is top-heavy for the 1992 plan year and for subsequent plan years, the individual would be treated as a former key employee.

*Example (2).* The facts are the same as in example (1), except that the individual died in early 1987 and his total benefit under the plan was distributed to his beneficiary in 1987. Such distribution would be treated as the accrued benefit of the individual for each year through the 1991 plan year. However, such individual would be treated as a former key employee for purposes of determining whether the plan is top-heavy for the 1992 plan year and for subsequent plan years. The conclusions are not affected by whether the beneficiary of the individual is a non-key employee or a key employee of the employer.

*T-13 Q.* For purposes of defining a key employee, who is an officer?

A. Whether an individual is an officer shall be determined upon the basis of all the facts, including, for example, the source of his authority, the term for which elected or appointed, and the nature and extent of his duties. Generally, the term officer means an administrative executive who is in regular and continued service. The term officer implies continuity of service and excludes those employed for a special and single transaction. An employee who merely has the title of an officer but not the authority of an officer is not considered an officer for purposes of the key employee test. Similarly, an employee who does not have the title of an officer but has the authority of an officer is an officer for purposes of the key employee test. In the case of one or more employers treated as a single employer under sections 414(b), (c), or (m), whether or not an individual is an officer shall be determined based upon his responsibilities with respect to the employer or employers for which he is directly employed, and not with respect to the controlled group of corporations, employers under common control or affiliated service group. A partner of a partnership will not be treated as an officer for purposes of the key employee test merely because he owns a capital or profits interest in the partnership, exercises his voting rights as a partner, and may, for limited purposes, be authorized and does in fact act as an agent of the partnership.

*T-14 Q.* For purposes of determining whether a plan is top-heavy for a plan year, how many officers must be taken into account?

A. There is no minimum number of officers that must be taken into account. Only individuals who are in fact officers within the meaning of Question and Answer T-13 must be considered. For example, a corporation with only one officer and two employees would have only one officer for purposes of section 416(i)(1)(A)(i). After aggregating all employees (including leased employees within the meaning of section 414(n)) of employers required to be aggregated under section 414(b), (c) or (m), there is a maximum limit to the number of officers that are to be taken into account as officers for the entire group of employers that are so aggregated. The number of employees an employer (including all employers required to be aggregated under section 414(b), (c), or (m)) has for the plan year containing the determination date is the greatest number of employees it had during that plan year or any of the four preceding plan years. For purposes of this Question and Answer, employees include only those individuals who perform services for the employer during a plan year. If the number of employees (including part-time employees) of all the employers aggregated under section 414(b), (c) or (m) is less than 30 employees, no more than three individuals shall be treated as key employees for the plan year containing the determination date by reason of being officers. If the number of employees of all organizations aggregated under section 414(b), (c) or (m) is greater than 30 but less than 500, no more than 10% of the number of employees will be treated as key employees by reason of being officers. (If 10% of the number of employees is not an integer, the maximum number of individuals to be treated as key employees by reason of being officers shall be increased to the next integer). If the number of employees of employers aggregated under section 414(b), (c) and (m) exceeds 500, no more than 50 employees are to be considered as key employees by reason of being officers. This limited number of officers is comprised of the individual officers, selected from the group of all individuals who were officers in the plan year containing the determination date or any one of the four preceding plan years, who had annual plan year compensation (in the officer year) in excess of 150 percent of the dollar limitation in effect under section 415(c)(1)(A) for the calendar year in which the plan year ends and who had the largest annual plan-year compensation in that five-year period. (The definition of compensation contained in Question and Answer T-21 is to be used for this purpose.) In determining the officers of an employer, an employee who is an officer shall be counted as an officer for key employee purposes without regard to whether the employee is a key employee for any other reason. However, in testing whether the plan(s) is top-heavy, an individual's present value of accrued benefits is counted only once.

*Example.* A company is testing to see if its plan is top-heavy for the 1985 plan year. In each year from 1980 through 1984 it has more than 500 employees. Assume that (1) because of rapid turnover among officers, the individuals who are officers each year are different from the individuals who are officers in any preceding year, and (2) the annual plan year compensation of each officer exceeds 150 percent of the dollar limitation in effect under section 415(c)(1)(A) for the calendar year in which the plan year ends. Under the limitations, only a total of 50 individuals would be considered to be key employees by virtue of being officers in testing for top-heaviness for the 1985 plan year. Further, the 50 individuals considered as key employees under this test would be determined by selecting the 50 out of 250 individuals (50 different officers each year) who had the highest annual plan-year compensation during the 1980–1984 period (while officers).

*T-15 Q.* For purposes of section 416, do organizations other than corporations have officers?

A. Yes. For purposes of the top-heavy rules, sole proprietorships, partnerships, associations, trusts, and labor organizations may have officers. This rule is effective for purposes of determining whether a plan is top-heavy for plan years which begin after February 28, 1985.

*T-16 Q.* Who is a 1-percent owner of the employer?

A.

(a) If the employer is a corporation, a 1-percent owner is any employee who owns (or is considered as owning within the meaning of section 318) more than 1 percent of the value of the outstanding stock of the corporation or stock possessing more than 1 percent of the total combined voting power of all stock of the corporation. If the employer is not a corporation, a 1-percent owner is any employee who owns more than 1 percent of the capital or profits interest in the employer. The rules of subsections (b), (c), and (m) of section 414 do not apply for purposes of determining who is a 1-percent owner.

(For purposes of determining who is a 1-percent owner, 5-percent owner, or top-ten owner, value means fair market value taking into account all facts and circumstances.

*T-17 Q.* Who is a 5-percent owner of the employer?

A. If the employer is a corporation, a 5-percent owner is any employee who owns (or is considered as owning within the meaning of section 318) more than 5 percent of the value of the outstanding stock of the corporation or stock possessing more than 5 percent of the total combined voting power of all stock of the corporation. If the employer is not a corporation, a 5-percent owner is any employee who owns more than 5 percent of the capital or profits interest in the employer. The rules of subsections (b), (c), and (m) of section 414 do not apply for purposes of determining who is a 5-percent owner.

*T-18 Q.* How do the rules of section 318 apply for purposes of determining ownership in an entity other than a corporation?

A. For purposes of determining ownership is an entity other than a corporation, the rules of section 318 apply in a manner similar to the way in which they apply for purposes of determining ownership in a corporation. For non-corporate interests, capital or profits interest must be substituted for stock.

*T-19 Q.* Which employees will be considered one of the top ten owners?

A. (a) For purposes of determining whether a plan is top-heavy for a plan year, the top ten owners are the ten employees who (1) own (or are considered as owning within the meaning of section 318) during the plan year containing the determination date or any of the four preceding plan years both more than a ½ percent ownership interest in value and the largest percentage ownership interests in value of any of the employers required to be aggregated under section 414(b), (c), or (m), and (2) have during the plan year of ownership annual plan year compensation from the employer more than the limitation in effect under section 415(c)(1)(A) for the calendar year in which such plan year ends. The five years for which the test is made will be referred to as the "testing period." An employee whose annual plan year compensation exceeds the section 415(c)(1)(A) limit in effect for the calendar year in which a plan year in the testing period ends who has an ownership interest greater than ½ percent in that plan year is considered to be one of the top ten owners unless at least ten other employees own a greater interest in the employer during any year of the testing period and have annual plan year compensation during such plan year of ownership greater than the section 415(c)(1)(A) limit in effect for the calendar year in which such plan year ends. Ownership each plan year is determined on the basis of percentage of ownership interest in total ownership value and not dollar amounts. Thus, an employee whose stock interest is valued at 15 percent of the total stock value of a corporation in year one that was worth $15,000 is ranked higher than an employee whose stock interest is valued at 5 percent of the total stock value of the same corporation in year three which is now worth $50,000.

(b) If an employee's ownership interest changes during a plan year, his ownership interest for the year is the largest interest owned at any time during the year. If two employees have the same ownership interest in the employer during the testing period, the employee having the largest annual compensation from the employer for the plan year during any part of which that ownership interest existed shall be treated as having a larger interest. Thus, if 25 employees each own 4 percent in value of the employer during the testing period, the 10 employees with the largest single plan year compensation during this period will be considered the top ten owners. For purposes of this Question and Answer, compensation has the meaning set forth in Question and Answer T-21. This Question and Answer is illustrated by the following examples:

*Example (1).* Corporation K maintains a calendar year defined contribution plan. On January 1, 1986, Corporation K has five owners who owned the following value percentages of K stock: A = 50%, B = 20%, C = 15%, D = 10%, and E = 5%. On June 30, 1987, the five owners of Corporation K sold all of their shares of stock. The new owners and their respective ownership percentages were: F = 40%, G = 30%, H = 10%, I = 10%, and J = 10%. Assume that, for 1986, A, B, C, D, and E had annual compensation from Corporation K greater than the section 415(c)(1)(A) limit and that, for 1987, F, G, H, I, and J also had compensation from Corporation K greater than the section 415(c)(1)(A) limit. For purposes of determining whether the plan is top-heavy for the 1991 plan year, the top ten owners will include A, B, C, D, E, F, G, H, I, and J because no 10 individuals during the testing period, 1986–1990, had a greater ownership interest than these individuals.

*Example (2).* Assume the same facts in *Example 1,* except that on June 1, 1988, F, G, H, I, and J sold their interests to new owners, K, L, M, N, and O. K, L, M, N, and O owned, respectively, 30%, 30%, 30%, 5% and 5% of the value of the shares of X. Assume also that for 1988 K, L, M, N, and O earned more than the section 415(c)(1)(A) limitation. For purposes of determining whether the plan is top-heavy for the 1991 plan year, the top ten owners will include: A, B, F, K, G, L, M, and C because these eight individuals owned the highest value percentages of the Corporation K stock. Since D, H, I, and J owned equal 10% interests in value, the two employees of this group who had the largest annual plan year compensation during the plan years of their ownership will be the last 2 top ten owners.

*T-20 Q.* For purposes of determining whether an employee is a key employee under section 416(i)(1)(A), what aggregation rules apply?

A. In the case of ownership percentages, each employer that would otherwise be aggregated under section 414(b), (c) and (m) is treated as a separate employer. (See section 416(i)(1)(C).) However, for purposes of determining whether an individual has compensation of $150,000, or whether an individual is a key employee by reason of being an officer or a top ten owner, compensation from each entity required to be aggregated under sections 414(b), (c) and (m) is taken into account. These rules may be illustrated by the following example:

*Example.* An individual owns two percent of the value of a professional corporation, which in turn owns a ¹⁄₁₀th of 1 percent interest in a partnership. The entities must be aggregated in accordance with section 414(m). The individual performs services for the professional corporation and for the partnership. The individual receives compensation of $125,000 from the professional corporation and $26,000 from the partnership. The individual is considered to be a key employee with respect to the employer that comprises both the professional corporation and the partnership because he has a two percent interest in the professional corporation and because his combined compensation from both the professional corporation and the partnership is more than $150,000.

*T-21 Q.*For purposes of testing whether an individual has compensation of more than $150,000, what definition of compensation must be used?

A. The definition of compensation to be used is the definition in § 1.415(c)-2, however, compensation must be determined for a plan year, not a limitation year. Alternatively, compensation that would be stated on an employee's Form W-2, "Wage and Tax Statement," for the calendar year that ends with or within the plan year may be used, although amounts that would have been stated on the employee's Form W-2 but for an election under section 125, 132(f)(4), 401(k), 403(b), 408(k), 408(p)(2)(A)(i), or 457(b) must be included. A plan must use the same definition of compensation for all top-heavy plan purposes for which the definition in this Q and A must be used.

*T-22 Q.* In the case of an employer who maintains a single plan, when must the determination whether the plan is top-heavy be made?

A. Whether a plan is top-heavy for a particular plan year is determined as of the determination date for such plan year. The determination date with respect to a plan year is defined in section 416(g)(4)(C) as (1) the last day of the preceding plan year, or (2) in the case of the first plan year, the last day of such plan year. Distributions made and the present value of accrued benefits are generally determined as of the determination date. (See Questions and Answers T-24 and T-25 for more specific rules.)

*T-23 Q.* In the case of an aggregation group, when must the determination whether the group is top-heavy be made?

A. When two or more plans constitute an aggregation group in accordance with section 416(g)(2), the following procedures are used to determine whether the plans are top-heavy for a particular plan year. First, the present value of the accrued benefits (including distributions for key employees and all employees) is determined separately for each plan as of each plan's determination date. The plans are then aggregated by adding together the results for each plan as of the determination dates for such plans that fall within the same calendar year. The combined results will indicate whether or not the plans so aggregated are top-heavy. These rules may be illustrated by the following example:

*Example.* An employer maintains Plan A and Plan B, each containing a key employee. Plan A's plan year commences July 1 and ends June 30. Plan B's plan year is the calendar year. For Plan A's plan year commencing July 1, 1984, the determination date is June 30, 1984. For Plan B's plan year in 1985, the determination date is December 31, 1984. These plans are required to be aggregated. For each of these plans as of their respective determination dates, the present value of the accrued benefits for key employees and all employees are separately determined. The two determination dates, June 30, 1984, and December 31, 1984, fall within the same calendar year. Accordingly, the present values of accrued benefits as of each of these determination dates are combined for purposes of determining whether the group is top-heavy. If, after combining the two present values, the total results show that the group is top-heavy, Plan A will be top-heavy for the plan year commencing July 1, 1984, and Plan B will be top-heavy for the 1985 calendar year.

*T-24 Q.* How is the present value of an accrued benefit determined in a defined contribution plan?

A. The present value of accrued benefits as of the determination date for any individual is the sum of (a) the account balance as of the most recent valuation date occurring within a 12-month period ending on the determination date, and (b) an adjustment for contributions due as of the determination date. In the case of a plan not subject to the minimum funding requirements of section 412, the adjustment in (b) is generally the amount of any contributions actually made after the valuation date but on or before the determination date. However, in the first plan year of the plan, the adjustment in (b) should also reflect the amount of any contributions made after the determination date that are allocated as of a date in that first plan year. In the case of a plan that is subject to the minimum funding requirements, the account balance in (a) should include contributions that would be allocated as of a date not later than the determination date, even though those amounts are not yet required to be contributed. Thus, the account balance will include contributions waived in prior years as reflected in the adjusted account balance and contributions not paid that resulted in a funding deficiency. The adjusted account balance is described in Rev. Rul. 78-223, 1978-1 C.B. 125. Also, the adjustment in (b) should reflect the amount of any contribution actually made (or due to be made) after the valuation date but before the expiration of the extended payment period in section 412(c)(10).

*T-25. Q.* How is the present value of an accrued benefit determined in a defined benefit plan?

A. The present value of an accrued benefit as of a determination date must be determined as of the most recent valuation date which is within a 12-month period ending on the determination date. In the first plan year of a plan, the accrued benefit for a current employee must be determined either (i) as if the individual terminated service as of the determination date or (ii) as if the individual terminated service as of the valuation date, but taking into account the estimated accrued benefit as of the determination date. For the second plan year of a plan, the accrued benefit taken into account for a current participant must not be less than the accrued benefit taken into account for the first plan year unless the difference is attributable to using an estimate of the accrued benefit as of the determination date for the first plan year and using the actual accrued benefit as of the determination date for the second plan year. For any other plan year, the accrued benefit for a current employee must be determined as if the individual terminated service as of such valuation date. For this purpose, the valuation date must be the same valuation date for computing plan costs for minimum funding, regardless of whether a valuation is performed that year.

*T-26. Q.* What actuarial assumptions are used for determining the present value of accrued benefits for defined benefit plans?

A.

(a) There are no specific prescribed actuarial assumptions that must be used for determining the present value of accrued benefits. The assumptions used must be reasonable and need not relate to the actual plan and investment experience. The assumptions need not be the same as those used for minimum funding purposes or for purposes of determining the actuarial equivalence of optional benefits under the plan. The accrued benefit for each current employee is computed as if the employee voluntarily terminated service as of the valuation date. The present value must be computed using an interest and a post-retirement mortality assumption. Pre-retirement mortality and future increases in cost of living (but not in the maximum dollar amount permitted by section 415) may also be assumed. However, assumptions as to future withdrawals or future salary increases may not be used. In the case of a plan providing a qualified joint and survivor annuity within the meaning of section 401(a)(11) as a normal form of benefit, for purposes of determining the present value of the accrued benefit, the spouse of the participant may be assumed to be the same age as the participant.

(b) Except in the case where the plan provides for a nonproportional subsidy, the present value should reflect a benefit payable commencing at normal retirement age (or attained age, if later). Thus, benefits not relating to retirement benefits, such as pre-retirement death and disability benefits and post-retirement medical benefits, must not be taken into account. Further, subsidized early retirement benefits and subsidized benefit options must not be taken into account unless they are nonproportional subsidies. See Question and Answer T-27.

(c) Where the plan provides for a nonproportional subsidy, the benefit should be assumed to commence at the age at which the benefit is most valuable. In the case of two or more defined benefit plans which are being tested for determining whether an aggregation group is top-heavy, the actuarial assumptions used for all plans within the group must be the same. Any assumptions which reflect a reasonable mortality experience and an interest rate not less than five percent or greater than six percent will be considered as reasonable. Plans, however, are not required to use an interest rate in this range.

*T-27 Q.* In determining the present value of accrued benefits in a defined benefit plan, what standards are applied toward determining whether a subsidy is nonproportional?

A. A subsidy is nonproportional unless the subsidy applies to a group of employees that would independently satisfy the requirements of section 410(b). If two or more plans are considered as a unit for comparability purposes under § 1.410(b)-1(d)(3), subsidies may be necessary in both plans or else the subsidy may be nonproportional. Thus, for example, in the case of a plan which provides an early retirement benefit after age 55 and 20 years of service equal to the normal retirement benefit without actuarial reduction and if the employees who may conceivably reach age 55 with 20 years of service would, as a group, satisfy the requirements of section 410(b), that subsidy is proportional. However, in contrast, consider a plan that provides an early retirement benefit that is the actuarial equivalent of the normal retirement benefit. In determining the early retirement benefit, the plan imposes the section 415 limits only on the early retirement benefit (not on the normal retirement benefit before applying the early retirement reduction factors). In such a plan, a participant with a normal retirement benefit (before limitation by section 415) in excess of the section 415 limits will receive a subsidized early retirement benefit, whereas a participant with a lower normal retirement benefit will not. Thus, such a benefit would be a nonproportional subsidy if the group of individuals who are limited by the limitations under section 415 do not, by themselves, constitute a cross section of employees that could satisfy section 410(b).

*T-28 Q.* For purposes of determining the present value of accrued benefits in either a defined benefit or defined contribution plan, are the accrued benefits attributable to employee contributions considered to be part of the accrued benefits?

A. The accrued benefits attributable to employee contributions are considered to be part of the accrued benefits without regard to whether such contributions are mandatory or voluntary. However, the amounts attributable to deductible employee contributions (as defined in section 72(o)(5)(A)) are not considered to be part of the accrued benefits.

*T-29 Q.* How are plans described in section 401(k) treated for purposes of the top-heavy rules?

A. No special top-heavy rules are provided for plans described in section 401(k), except a transitional rule. For plan years beginning after December 31, 1984, amounts which an employee elects to defer are treated as employer contributions for purposes of determining minimum required contributions under section 416(c)(2). However, for plan years beginning prior to January 1, 1985, amounts which an employee elects to have contributed to a plan described in section 401(k) are not treated as employer contributions for these purposes. A plan described in section 401(k) which is top-heavy must provide minimum contributions by the employer and limit the amount of compensation which can be taken into account in providing benefits under the plan.

*T-30 Q.* What distributions are added to the present value of accrued benefits in determining whether a plan is top-heavy for a particular plan year?

A. Under section 416(g)(3)(A), distributions made within the plan year that includes the determination date and within the four preceding plan years are added to the present value of accrued benefits of key employees and non-key employees in testing for top-heaviness. However, in the case of distributions made after the valuation date and prior to the determination date, such distributions are not included as distributions in section 416(g)(3)(A) to the extent that such distributions are included in the present value of the accrued benefits as of the valuation date. In the case of the distribution of an annuity contract, the amount of such distribution is deemed to be the current actuarial value of the contract, determined on the date of the distribution. Certain distributions that are rolled over by the employee are not included as distributions. See Question and Answer T-32. A distribution will not fail to be considered in determining the present value of accrued benefits merely because it was made before the effective date of section 416. For purposes of this question and answer, distributions mean all distributions made by a plan, including all distributions of employee contributions made during and before the plan year.

*T-31 Q.* Are benefits paid on account of death treated as distributions for purposes of section 416(g)(3)?

A. Benefits paid on account of death are treated as distributions for purposes of section 416(g)(3) to the extent such benefits do not exceed the present value of accrued benefits existing immediately prior to death; benefits paid on account of death are not treated as distributions for purposes of section 416(g)(3) to the extent such benefits exceed the present value of accrued benefits existing immediately prior to death. The distribution from a defined contribution plan (including the cash value of life insurance policies) of a participant's account balance on account of death will be treated as a distribution for purposes of section 416(g)(3).

*T-32 Q.* How are rollovers and plan-to-plan transfers treated in testing whether a plan is top-heavy?

A. The rules for handling rollovers and transfers depend upon whether they are unrelated (both initiated by the employee and made from a plan maintained by one employer to a plan maintained by another employer) or related (a rollover or transfer either not initiated by the employee or made to a plan maintained by the same employer). Generally, a rollover or transfer made incident to a merger or consolidation of two or more plans or the division of a single plan into two or more plans will not be treated as being initiated by the employee. The fact that the employer initiated the distribution does not mean that the rollover was not initiated by the employee. For purposes of determining whether two employers are to be treated as the same employer, all employers aggregated under section 414(b), (c) or (m) are treated as the same employer. In the case of unrelated rollovers and transfers, (1) the plan making the distribution or transfer is to count the distribution as a distribution under section 416(g)(3), and (2) the plan accepting the rollover or transfer is not to consider the rollover or transfer as part of the accrued benefit if such rollover or transfer was accepted after December 31, 1983, but is to consider it as part of the accrued benefit if such rollover or transfer was accepted prior to January 1, 1984. In the case of related rollovers and transfers, the plan making the distribution or transfer is not to count the distribution or transfer under section 416(g)(3) and the plan accepting the rollover or transfer counts the rollover or transfer in the present value of the accrued benefits. Rules for related rollovers and transfers do not depend on whether the rollover or transfer was accepted prior to January 1, 1984.

*T-33 Q.* How are the aggregate defined benefit and defined contribution limits under section 415(e) affected by the top-heavy rules?

A. Section 416(h) modifies the aggregate limits in section 415(e) for super top-heavy plans and for top-heavy plans that are not super top-heavy but do not provide for an additional minimum contribution or benefit. A plan is a super top-heavy plan if the present value of accrued benefits for key employees exceeds 90% of the present value of the accrued benefits for all employees. In the case of a top-heavy aggregation group, the test is applied to all plans in the group as a whole. These present values are computed using the same rules as are used for determining whether the plan is top-heavy. In the case of a super top-heavy plan, in computing the denominators of the defined benefit and defined contribution fractions under section 415(e), a factor of 1.0 is used instead of 1.25 for all employees. In the case of a top-heavy plan that is not super top-heavy, the same rule applies unless each non-key employee who is entitled to a minimum contribution or benefit receives an additional minimum contribution or benefit. In the case of a defined benefit plan, the additional minimum benefit is one percentage point (up to a maximum of ten percentage points) for each year of service described in Question and Answer M-2 of the participant's average compensation for the years described in Question and Answer M-2. In the case of a defined contribution plan, the additional minimum contribution is one percent of the participant's compensation. If a plan does not provide the applicable additional one percent minimum or if a plan is super top-heavy, the factor of 1.25 may be used for an individual only if there are both no further accruals for that individual under any defined benefit plan and no further annual additions for that individual under any defined contribution plan until the combined fraction satisfies the rules of section 415(e) using the 1.0 factor for that individual. The rules contained in this Question and Answer apply for each limitation year that contains any portion of a plan year for which the plan is top-heavy. This Question and Answer may be illustrated by the following example:

*Example.* A Corporation maintains a profit-sharing plan and a defined benefit plan, and these plans constitute a required aggregation group. Both plans use the calendar year for the plan year and the limitation year under section 415. The plans were determined to be top-heavy for plan year 1986. The plans use the 1.25 factor under section 415(e), and non-key employees covered by both the profit-sharing and the defined benefit plan accrue, under the defined benefit plan, 3% of compensation for each year of service (up to a maximum of 30%). The plans become super top-heavy for the 1990 plan year. In order to satisfy section 415, no further accruals and no further annual additions may take place for any employee covered by both plans until the combined defined benefit-defined contribution fraction for such employee is less than 1.0, using the 1.0 factor in place of 1.25.

*T-34 Q.* May plans be permissively aggregated to avoid being super top-heavy?

A. Yes, plans may be permissively aggregated to avoid being super top-heavy.

*T-35 Q.* What provisions must be contained in a plan to comply with the top-heavy requirements?

A. Section 401(a)(10)(B) provides that a plan will qualify only if it contains provisions which will take effect if the plan becomes top-heavy and which meet the requirements of section 416. See Questions and Answers T-39 and T-40 for rules on what provisions must be included. Under section 401(a)(10)(B)(ii), regulations may waive this requirement for some plans. See Question and Answer T-38 for a description of plans that need not include such provisions.

*T-36 Q.* For an employer who has no employee who has participated or is eligible to participate in both a defined benefit and defined contribution plan (or a simplified employee pension, "SEP") of that employer, what provisions must be in the plan(s) to comply with the top-heavy requirements?

A.

(a) If the defined benefit plan has no participants who are or could be participants in a defined contribution plan of the employer (or vice versa), the defined benefit plan (or defined contribution plan) need not include provisions describing the defined benefit or defined contribution fractions for purposes of section 415 and, thus, the plan need not contain provisions to determine whether the plan is super top-heavy or to change any plan provisions if the plan becomes super top-heavy. Furthermore, if the plan contains a single benefit structure that satisfies the requirements of section 416(b), (c), and (d) for each plan year without regard to whether the plan is top-heavy for such year, the plan need not include separate provisions to determine whether the plan is top-heavy or that apply if the plan is top-heavy. If the plan's single benefit structure does not assure that section 416(b), (c), and (d) will be satisfied in all cases, then the plan must include three types of provisions.

(b) First, the plan must contain provisions describing how to determine whether the plan is top-heavy. These provisions must include (1) the criteria for determining which employees are key employees (or non-key employees), (2) in the case of a defined benefit plan, the actuarial assumptions and benefits considered to determine the present value of accrued benefits, (3) a description of how the top-heavy ratio is computed, (4) a description of what plans (or types of plans) will be aggregated in testing whether the plan is top-heavy, and (5) a definition of the determination date and the valuation date applicable to the determination date. These determinations must be based on standards that are uniformly and consistently applied and that satisfy the rules set forth in section 416 and these Questions and Answers. The provisions in (1) and (3) above may be incorporated in the plan by reference to the applicable sections of the Internal Revenue Code without adversely affecting the qualification of the plan. However, the plan must state the definition of compensation for purposes of determining who is a key employee.

(c) Second, the plan must specifically contain the following provisions that will become effective if the plan becomes top-heavy: vesting that satisfies the minimum vesting requirements of section 416(b), benefits that will not be less than the minimum benefits set forth in section 416(c), and the compensation limitation described in section 416(d). The compensation limitation described in section 416(d) may be incorporated by reference. If a plan always meets the requirements of either section 416(b), (c) or (d), the plan need not include additional provisions to meet any such requirements.

(d) Third, the plan must include provisions insuring that any change in the plan's benefit structure (including vesting schedules) resulting from a change in the plan's top-heavy status will not violate section 411(a)(10). Thus, if a plan ceases being top-heavy, certain restrictions apply with respect to the change in the applicable vesting schedule.

*T-37 Q.* For an employer who maintains or has maintained both a defined benefit and a defined contribution plan (or a simplified employee pension, "SEP") and some participants do or could participate in both types of plan, what provisions must be in the plans to comply with the top-heavy requirements?

A. If an employer maintains (or has maintained) both a defined benefit plan and a defined contribution plan (or SEP), and the plans have or could have participants who participate in both types of plans, then the plans must contain more provisions than those described in Question and Answer T-36. First, the plans may exclude rules to determine whether the plan is top-heavy (or to apply when the plan is top-heavy) only if both plans contain a single benefit structure that satisfies sections 416(b), (c), and (d) without regard to whether the plans are top-heavy. Second, unless the plans always satisfy the requirements of section 415(e) using the 1.0 factor in the defined benefit and defined contribution fractions as described in section 416(h)(i), the plans must include provisions similar to those in Question and Answer T-36 (for top-heavy) to determine whether the plan is super top-heavy and to satisfy section 416(h) if it is.

*T-38 Q.* Are any plans exempted from including top-heavy provisions?

A. Section 401(a)(10)(B) exempts governmental plans (as defined in section 414(d)) from the top-heavy requirements and provides that regulations may exempt certain plans from including the top-heavy provisions. A plan need not include any top-heavy provisions if the plan: (1) is not top-heavy, and (2) covers only employees who are included in a unit of employees covered by a collective-bargaining agreement (if retirement benefits were the subject of good faith bargaining) or employees of employee representatives. The requirement set forth in section 7701(a)(46) must be met before an agreement will be considered a collective-bargaining agreement after March 31, 1984.

*T-39 Q.* Must ratios be computed each year to determine whether a plan is top-heavy?

A. No. In order to administer the plan, the plan administrator must know whether the plan is top-heavy. However, precise top-heavy ratios need not be computed every year. If, on examination, the Internal Revenue Service requests a demonstration as to whether the plan is top-heavy (or super top-heavy; see Question and Answer T-33) the employer must demonstrate to the Service's satisfaction that the plan is not operating in violation of section 401(a)(10)(B). For purposes of any demonstration, the employer may use computations that are not precisely in accordance with this section but which mathematically prove that the plan is not top-heavy. For example, if the employer determined the present value of accrued benefits for key employees in a simplified manner which overstated that value, determined the present value for non-key employees in a simplified manner which understated that value, and the ratio of the key employee present value divided by the sum of the present values was less than 60 percent, the plan would not be considered top-heavy. This would be a sufficient demonstration because the simplified fraction could be shown to be greater than the exact fraction and, thus, the exact fraction must also be less than 60 percent.

Several methods that may be used to simplify the determinations are indicated below.

(1) If the top-heavy ratio, computed considering all the key employees and only some of the non-key employees, is less than 60 percent, then it is not necessary to accumulate employee data on the remaining non-key employees. Inclusion of additional non-key employees would only further decrease the ratio.

(2) If the number of key employees is known but the identity of the key employees is not known (i.e. if the only key employees are officers and the limit on officers is applicable), the numerator may be determined by using a hypothetical "worst case" basis. Thus, in the case of a defined benefit plan, if the numerator of the top-heavy ratio were determined assuming each key employee's present value of accrued benefits were equal to the maximum section 415 benefits at the age that would maximize such present value, that assumption would only overstate the present value of accrued benefits for key employees. Thus, if that ratio is less than 60 percent, the plan is not top-heavy and accurate data on the key employees need not be collected.

(3) If the employer has available present value of accrued benefit computations for key and non-key employees in a defined benefit plan, and these values differ from those that would be produced under Question and Answer T-25 only by inclusion of a withdrawal assumption, the present value for the key employees (but not the non-key employees) may be adjusted to a "worst case" value by dividing by the lowest possible probability of not withdrawing from plan participation before normal retirement age. If the top-heavy ratio based on this inflated key employee value is less than 60 percent, the present value need not be recomputed without the withdrawal assumption. The methods set forth in this answer may also be used to determine whether a plan is super top-heavy by inserting "90%" for "60%" in the appropriate places.

*T-40 Q.* Will a plan fail to qualify if it provides that the $200,000 maximum amount of annual compensation taken into account under section 416(d) for any plan year that the plan is top-heavy may be automatically increased in accordance with regulations under section 416?

A. No.

*T-41 Q.* If a plan provides benefits based on compensation in excess of $200,000 and the plan becomes top-heavy, must any accrued benefits attributable to this excess compensation be eliminated?

A. No. For any year that a plan is top-heavy, section 416(d) provides that compensation in excess of $200,000 must not be taken into account. However, a top-heavy plan may continue to provide for any benefits attributable to compensation in excess of $200,000 to the extent such benefits were accrued before the plan was top-heavy. Furthermore, section 411(d)(6) will be violated if any individual's pre-top-heavy benefit is reduced by either (1) a plan amendment adding the $200,000 restriction, or (2) an automatic change in the plan benefits structure imposing the $200,000 restriction due to the plan's becoming top-heavy.

*T-42 Q.* Under a top-heavy defined benefit plan, are the requirements of section 416(d) satisfied if the annual compensation of an employee taken into account to determine plan benefits is limited to the amount currently described in section 416(d) for years during which the plan is top-heavy but higher compensation is taken into account for years before the plan became top-heavy?

A. No. For the top-heavy plan to meet the requirements of section 416(d), compensation for all years, including years before the plan became top-heavy, that is taken into account to determine plan benefits must not exceed the amount currently described in section 416(d). However, if the accrued benefit as of the end of the last plan year before the plan became top-heavy (ignoring any plan amendments after that date) is greater than the accrued benefit determined by limiting compensation in accordance with section 416(d), that higher accrued benefit as of the end of the last plan year before the plan became top-heavy must not be reduced. Providing such higher accrued benefit will not cause the plan to violate section 416(d).

*T-43 Q.* What happens to an individual who has ceased employment before a plan becomes top-heavy?

A. If an individual has ceased employment before a plan becomes top-heavy, such individual would not be required to receive any additional benefit accruals, contributions, or vesting, unless the individual returned to employment with the employer. See Questions and Answers V-3, M-4, and M-10. In addition, if the individual is receiving benefits based on annual compensation greater than $200,000, such benefits cannot be decreased.

V. Vesting Rules for Top-Heavy Plans

*V-1 Q.* What vesting must be provided under a top-heavy plan?

A. Under section 416(b), the accrued benefits attributable to employer contributions must be nonforfeitable in accordance with one of two statutory standards. Either such accrued benefits must be nonforfeitable after 3 years of service or the nonforfeitable portion of accrued benefits must be at least 20 percent after 2 years of service, 40 percent after 3 years of service, 60 percent after 4 years of service, 80 percent after 5 years of service, and 100 percent after 6 years of service. The accrued benefits attributable to employer contributions has the same meaning as under section 411(c) of the Code. As under section 411(a), the accrued benefits attributable to employee contributions must be nonforfeitable at all times.

*V-2 Q.* What service must be counted in determining vesting requirements?

A. All service required to be counted under section 411(a) must be counted for these purposes. All service permitted to be disregarded under section 411(a)(4) may similarly be disregarded under the schedules of section 416(b).

*V-3 Q.* What benefits must be subject to the minimum vesting schedule of section 416(b)?

A. All accrued benefits within the meaning of section 411(a)(7) must be subject to the minimum vesting schedule. These accrued benefits include benefits accrued before the effective date of section 416 and benefits accrued before a plan becomes top-heavy. However, when a plan becomes top-heavy, the accrued benefits of any employee who does not have an hour of service after the plan becomes top-heavy are not required to be subject to the minimum vesting schedule. Accrued benefits which have been forfeited before a plan becomes top-heavy need not vest when a plan becomes top-heavy.

*V-4 Q.* May a top-heavy plan provide a minimum eligibility requirement of the later of age 21 or the completion of 3 years of service and provide that all benefits are nonforfeitable when accrued?

A. Yes. For plan years which begin after December 31, 1984, a top-heavy plan may provide a minimum eligibility requirement of the later of age 21, or the completion of 3 years of service, and provide that all benefits are nonforfeitable when accrued. For plan years which begin before January 1, 1985, "25" may be substituted for "21" in the preceding sentence.

*V-5 Q.* What does nonforfeitable mean?

A. In general, nonforfeitable has the same meaning as in section 411(a). However, the minimum benefits required under section 416 (to the extent required to be nonforfeitable under section 416(b)) may not be forfeited under section 411(a)(3)(B) or (D). Thus, if benefits are suspended (ceased) during a period of reemployment, the benefit payable upon the subsequent resumption of payments must be actuarially increased to reflect the nonpayment of benefits during such period of re-employment.

*V-6 Q.* Will a class-year plan automatically satisfy the minimum vesting requirements in section 416(b) if it provides that contributions with respect to any plan year become nonforfeitable no later than the end of the third plan year following the plan year for which the contribution was made?

A. No. Although this vesting schedule is similar to the 3-year minimum vesting schedule permitted by section 416(b)(1)(A), it does not satisfy that minimum. The 3-year vesting schedule in section 416(b)(1)(A) requires that, after completion of 3 years of service, the entire accrued benefit of a participant be nonforfeitable. Under the class-year vesting schedule described above, a portion of a participant's accrued benefit (that portion attributable to contributions for the prior 3 years) is forfeitable regardless of the participant's years of service.

*V-7 Q.* When a top-heavy plan ceases to be top-heavy, may the vesting schedule be altered to a vesting schedule permitted without regard to section 416?

A. When a top-heavy plan ceases to be top-heavy, the vesting schedule may be changed to one that would otherwise be permitted. However, in changing the vesting schedule, the rules described in section 411(a)(10) apply. Thus, the nonforfeitable percentage of the accrued benefit before the plan ceased to be top-heavy must not be reduced; also, any employee with five or more years of service must be given the option of remaining under the prior (i.e., top-heavy) vesting schedule.

M. Minimum Benefits under Top-heavy Plans

*M-1 Q.* Which employees must receive minimum contributions or benefits in a top-heavy plan?

A. Generally, every non-key employee who is a participant in a top-heavy plan must receive minimum contributions or benefits under such plan. However, see Questions and Answers M-4 and M-10 for certain exceptions. Different minimums apply for defined benefit and defined contribution plans.

*M-2 Q.* What is the defined benefit minimum?

A. (a) The defined benefit minimum requires that the accrued benefit at any point in time must equal at least the product of (i) an employee's average annual compensation for the period of consecutive years (not exceeding five) when the employee had the highest aggregate compensation from the employer and (ii) the lesser of 2% per year of service with the employer or 20%.

(b) For purposes of the defined benefit minimum, years of service with the employer are generally determined under the rules of section 411(a)(4), (5) and (6). However, a plan may disregard any year of service if the plan was not top-heavy for any plan year ending during such year of service, or if the year of service was completed in a plan year beginning before January 1, 1984.

(c) In determining the average annual compensation for a period of consecutive years during which the employee had the largest aggregate compensation, years for which the employee did not earn a year of service under the rules of section 411(a)(4), (5), and (6) are to be disregarded. Thus, if an employee has received compensation from the employer during years one two, and three, and for each of these years the employee earned a year of service, then the employee's average annual compensation is determined by dividing the employee's aggregate compensation for these three years by three. If the employee fails to earn a year of service in the next year, but does earn a year of service in the fifth year, the employee's average annual compensation is calculated by dividing the employee's aggregate compensation for years one, two, three, and five by four. The compensation required to be taken into account is the compensation described in Question and Answer T-21. In addition, compensation received for years ending in plan years beginning before January 1, 1984, and compensation received for years beginning after the close of the last plan year in which the plan is top-heavy may be disregarded.

(d) The defined benefit minimum is expressed as a life annuity (with no ancillary benefits) commencing at normal retirement age. Thus, if post-retirement death benefits are also provided, the 2% minimum annuity benefit may be adjusted. (See Question and Answer M-3.) The 2% minimum annuity benefit may not be adjusted due to the provision of pre-retirement ancillary benefits. Normal retirement age has the same meaning as under section 411(a)(8).

(e) Any accruals of employer-derived benefits, whether or not attributable to years for which the plan is top-heavy, may be used to satisfy the defined benefit minimums. Thus, if a non-key employee had already accrued a benefit of 20 percent of final average pay at the time the plan became top-heavy, no additional minimum accruals are required (although the accrued benefit would increase as final average pay increased). Accrued benefits attributable to employee contributions must be ignored. Accrued benefits attributable to employer and employee contributions have the same meaning as under section 411(c).

*M-3 Q.* What defined benefit minimum must be received if an employee receives a benefit in a form other than a single life annuity or a benefit other than at normal retirement age?

A. If the form of benefit is other than a single life annuity, the employee must receive an amount that is the actuarial equivalent of the minimum single life annuity benefit. If the benefit commences at a date other than at normal retirement age, the employee must receive at least an amount that is the actuarial equivalent of the minimum single life annuity benefit commencing at normal retirement age. Thus, the employee may receive a lower benefit if the benefit commences before the normal retirement age and the employee must receive a higher benefit if the benefit commences after the normal retirement age. No specific actuarial assumptions are mandated providing different actuarial equivalents. However, the assumptions must be reasonable.

*M-4 Q.* Which employees must accrue a minimum benefit in a top-heavy defined benefit plan?

A. Each non-key employee who is a participant in a top-heavy defined benefit plan and who has at least one thousand hours of service (or equivalent service as determined under Department of Labor regulations, 29 CFR 2530.200b-3) for an accrual computation period must accrue a minimum benefit in a top-heavy defined benefit plan for that accrual computation period. If the accrual computation period does not coincide with the plan year, a minimum benefit must be provided, if required, for both accrual periods within the top-heavy plan year. For a top-heavy plan that does not base accruals on accrual computation periods, minimum benefits must be credited for all periods of service required to be credited for benefit accrual. (See § 1.410(a)-7). A non-key employee may not fail to accrue a minimum benefit merely because the employee was not employed on a specified date. Similarly, a non-key employee may not fail to accrue a minimum benefit because either (1) an employee is excluded from participation (or accrues no benefit) merely because the employee's compensation is less than a stated amount, or (2) the employee is excluded from participation (or accrues no benefit) merely because of a failure to make mandatory employee contributions.

*M-5 Q.* Would the defined benefit minimum be satisfied if the plan provides a normal retirement benefit equal to the greater of the plan's projected formula or the projected minimum benefit and if benefits accrue in accordance with the fractional rule described in section 411(b)(1)(C)?

A. No. The fact that this fractional rule would not satisfy the defined benefit minimum may be illustrated by the following example. Consider a non-key employee, age 25, entering a top-heavy plan in which the projected minimum for the employee is greater than the projected minimum for the employee is greater than the projected benefit under the normal formula. Under the fractional rule, the employee's accrued benefit ten years later at age 35 would be 5% (20% × (10/40)). Under section 416, the employee's minimum accrued benefit after ten years of service must be at least 20%. Thus, because the 5% benefit is less than the 20% benefit required under section 416, such benefit would not satisfy the required minimum.

*M-6 Q.* What benefit must an employer provide in a top-heavy defined benefit employee pay-all plan?

A. The defined benefit minimum in an employee pay-all top-heavy plan is the same as that for a plan which has employer contributions. That is, the employer must provide the benefits specified in Question and Answer M-2.

*M-7 Q.* What is the defined contribution minimum?

A. The sum of the contributions and forfeitures allocated to the account of any non-key employee who is a participant in a top-heavy defined contribution plan must equal at least 3% of such employee's compensation (see Question and Answer T-21 for the definition of compensation) for that plan year or for the calendar year ending within the plan year. However, a lower minimum is permissible where the largest contribution made or required to be made for key employees is less than 3%. The preceding sentence does not apply to any plan required to be included in an aggregation group if such plan enables a defined benefit plan required to be included in such group to meet the requirements of section 401(a)(4) or 410. The contribution made or required to be made on behalf of any key employee is equal to the ratio of the sum of the contributions made or required to be made and forfeitures allocated for such key employee divided by the compensation (not in excess of $200,000) for such key employee. Thus, the defined contribution minimum that must be provided for any non-key employee for a top-heavy plan year is the largest percentage of compensation (not in excess of $200,000) provided on behalf of any key employee for that plan year (if the largest percentage of compensation provided on behalf of any key employee for that plan year is less than 3%).

*M-8 Q.* If an employer maintains two top-heavy defined contribution plans, must both plans provide the defined contribution minimum for each non-key employee who is a participant in both plans?

A. No. If one of the plans provides the defined contribution minimum for each non-key employee who participates in both plans, the other plan need not provide an additional contribution for such employees. However, the other plan must provide the vesting required by section 416(b) and must limit compensation (based on all compensation from all aggregated employers) in providing benefits as required by section 416(d).

*M-9 Q.* In the case of the waiver of minimum funding standards of section 412(d), how does section 416 treat the defined contribution minimum?

A. For purposes of determining the contribution that is required to be made on behalf of a key employee, a waiver of the minimum funding requirements is disregarded. Thus, if a defined contribution plan receives a waiver of the minimum funding requirement, and if the minimum contribution required under the plan without regard to the waiver exceeds 3%, the exception described in Question and Answer M-7 does not apply even though no key employee receives a contribution in excess of 3% and even though the amount required to be contributed on behalf of the key employee has been waived. Also, a waiver of the minimum funding requirements will not alter the requirements of section 416. Thus, in the case of the top-heavy defined contribution plan in which the non-key employee must receive an allocation, a waiver of the minimum funding requirements may eliminate a funding violation and such waiver will preclude a violation under section 416 even though the required contribution is not made. However, the adjusted account balance (as described in Rev. Rul. 78-223, 1978-1 C.B. 125) of the non-key employees must reflect the required minimum contribution even though such contribution was not made.

*M-10 Q.* Which employees must receive the defined contribution minimum?

A. Those non-key employees who are participants in a top-heavy defined contribution plan who have not separated from service by the end of the plan year must receive the defined contribution minimum. Non-key employees who have become participants but who subsequently fail to complete 1,000 hours of service (or the equivalent) for an accrual computation period must receive the defined contribution minimum. A non-key employee may not fail to receive a defined contribution minimum because either (1) the employee is excluded from participation (or accrues no benefit) merely because the employee's compensation is less than a stated amount, or (2) the employee is excluded from participation (or accrues no benefit) merely because of a failure to make mandatory employee contributions or, in the case of a cash or deferred arrangement, elective contributions.

*M-11 Q.* May either the defined benefit minimum or the defined contribution minimum be integrated with social security?

A. No.

*M-12 Q.* What minimum contribution or benefit must be received by a non-key employee who participates in a top-heavy plan?

A. In the case of an employer maintaining only one plan, if such plan is a defined benefit plan, each non-key employee covered by that plan must receive the defined benefit minimum. If such plan is a defined contribution plan (including a target benefit plan), each non-key employee covered by the plan must receive the defined contribution minimum. In the case of an employer who maintains more than one plan, employees covered under only the defined benefit plan must receive the defined benefit minimum. Employees covered under only the defined contribution plan must receive the defined contribution minimum. In the case of employees covered under both defined benefit and defined contribution plans, the rules are more complicated. Section 416(f) precludes, in the case of employees covered under both defined benefit and defined contribution plans, either required duplication or inappropriate omission. Therefore, such employees need not receive both the defined benefit and the defined contribution minimums.

There are four safe harbor rules a plan may use in determining which minimum must be provided to a non-key employee who is covered by both defined benefit and defined contribution plans. Since the defined benefit minimums are generally more valuable, if each employee covered under both a top-heavy defined benefit plan and a top-heavy defined contribution plan receives the defined benefit minimum, the defined benefit and defined contribution minimums will be satisfied. Another approach that may be used is a floor offset approach (see Rev. Rul. 76-259, 1976-2 C.B. 111) under which the defined benefit minimum is provided in the defined benefit plan and is offset by the benefits provided under the defined contribution plan. Another approach that may be used in the case of employees covered under both defined benefit and defined contribution plans is to prove, using a comparability analysis (see Rev. Rul. 81-202, 1981-2 C.B. 93) that the plans are providing benefits at least equal to the defined benefit minimum. Finally, in order to preclude the cost of providing the defined benefit minimum alone, the complexity of a floor offset plan and the annual fluctuation of a comparability analysis, a safe haven minimum defined contribution is being provided. If the contributions and forfeitures under the defined contribution plan equal 5% of compensation for each plan year the plan is top-heavy, such minimum will be presumed to satisfy the section 416 minimums.

*M-13 Q.* An employer maintains a defined benefit plan and a profit-sharing plan. Both plans are top-heavy and are members of a required aggregation group. In order to meet the minimum contribution/minimum benefit requirements, the employer decides to contribute 5% of compensation to the profit-sharing plan. What happens if for a particular plan year there are no profits out of which to make contributions to the profit-sharing plan?

A. In this particular situation, in order to satisfy the requirements of section 416(c), the employer must provide the defined contribution minimum, 5% of compensation. This rule is an exception to the general rule that an employer cannot make a contribution to a profit-sharing plan if there are no profits. Alternatively, the employer may provide the defined benefit minimum for this year.

*M-14 Q.* What minimum contribution or benefit must be received by a non-key employee when he is covered under both a defined benefit plan and defined contribution plan (both of which are top-heavy) of an employer and the employer desires to use a factor of 1.25 in computing the denominators of the defined benefit and defined contribution fractions under section 415(e)?

A. In this particular situation, the employer may use one of the four rules set forth in Question and Answer M-12, subject to the following modifications. The defined benefit minimum must be increased by one percentage point (up to a maximum of ten percentage points) for each year of service described in Question and Answer M-2 of the participant's average compensation for the years described in Question and Answer M-2. The defined contribution minimum is increased to 7½ percent of compensation. If the floor offset or comparability analysis approach is used, the defined benefit minimum must be increased by one percentage point (up to a maximum of ten percentage points) for each year of service described in Question and Answer M-2 of the participant's average compensation for the years described in Question and Answer M-2.

*M-15 Q.* May an employer use a different method each year to meet the requirements of Question and Answer M-12 or Question and Answer M-14 without amending the plans each year?

A. No. An employer must set forth in the plan document the method he will use to meet the requirements of Question and Answer M-12 or M-14, as the case may be. If an employer desires to change the method, the plan document must be amended.

*M-16 Q.* Will target benefit plans be treated as defined benefit or defined contribution plans for purposes of the top-heavy rules?

A. Target benefit plans will be treated as defined contribution plans for purposes of the top-heavy rules.

*M-17 Q.* Can a plan described in section 412(i) (funded exclusively by level premium insurance contracts) also satisfy the minimum benefit requirements of section 416?

A. The accrued benefits provided for a non-key employee under most level premium insurance contracts might not provide a benefit satisfying the defined benefit minimum because of the lower cash values in early years under most level premium insurance contracts, and because such contracts normally provide for level premiums until normal retirement age. However, a plan will not be considered to violate the requirements of section 412(i) merely because it funds certain benefits through either an auxiliary fund or deferred annuity contracts, if the following conditions are met:

(1) The targeted benefit at normal retirement age under the level premium insurance contract is determined, taking into account the defined benefit minimum that would be required assuming the current top-heavy (or non top-heavy) status of the plan continues until normal retirement age; and

(2) The benefits provided by the auxiliary fund or deferred annuity contracts do not exceed the excess of the defined benefit minimum benefits over the benefits provided by the level premium insurance contract.

If the above conditions are satisfied, then the plan is still exempt from the minimum funding requirements under section 412 and may still utilize the special accrued benefit rule in section 411(b)(1)(F) subject to the following modifications: Although the portion of the plan funded by the level premium annuity contract is exempt from the minimum funding requirements, the portion funded by an auxiliary fund is subject to those requirements. (Thus, a funding standard account must be maintained and a Schedule B must be filed with the annual report). The accrued benefit for any participant may be determined using the rule in section 411(b)(1)(F) but must not be less than the defined benefit minimum.

*M-18 Q.* May qualified nonelective contributions described in section 401(m)(4)(C) be treated as employer contributions for purposes of the minimum contribution or benefit requirement of section 416?

A. Yes. This is the case even if the qualified nonelective contributions are taken into account under the actual deferral percentage test of § 1.401(k)-1(b)(2) or under the actual contribution percentage test of § 1.401(m)-1(b).

*M-19 Q.* May matching contributions described in section 401(m)(4)(A) be treated as employer contributions for purposes of the minimum contribution or benefit requirement of section 416?

A. Matching contributions allocated to key employees are treated as employer contributions for purposes of determining the minimum contribution or benefit under section 416. However, if a plan uses contributions allocated to employees other than key employees on the basis of employee contributions or elective contributions to satisfy the minimum contribution requirement, these contributions are not treated as matching contributions for purposes of applying the requirements of sections 401(k) and 401(m) for plan years beginning after December 31, 1988. Thus these contributions must meet the nondiscrimination requirements of section 401(a)(4) without regard to section 401(m). See § 1.401(m)-1(f)(12)(iii).

*M-20 Q.* May elective contributions be treated as employer contributions for purposes of satisfying the minimum contribution or benefit requirement of section 416(c)(2)?

A. Elective contributions on behalf of key employees are taken into account in determining the minimum required contribution under section 416(c)(2). However, elective contributions on behalf of employees other than key employees may not be treated as employer contributions for purposes of the minimum contribution or benefit requirement of section 416. See section 401(k)(4)(C) and the regulations thereunder. This Question and Answer is effective for plan years beginning after December 31, 1988.

T.D. 7997, 12/27/84, amend T.D. 8357, 8/8/91, T.D. 9319, 4/4/2007.

## § 1.417(a)(3)-1 Required explanation of qualified joint and survivor annuity and qualified preretirement survivor annuity.

**(a) Written explanation requirement.** *(1) General rule.* A plan meets the survivor annuity requirements of section 401(a)(11) only if the plan meets the requirements of section 417(a)(3) and this section regarding the written explanation required to be provided a participant with respect to a QJSA or a QPSA. A written explanation required to be provided to a participant with respect to either a QJSA or a QPSA under section 417(a)(3) and this section is referred to in this section as a section 417(a)(3) explanation. See § 1.401(a)-20, Q&A-37, for exceptions to the written explanation requirement in the case of a fully subsidized QPSA or QJSA, and § 1.401(a)-20, Q&A-38, for the definition of a fully subsidized QPSA or QJSA.

*(2) Time for providing section 417(a)(3) explanation.* (i) QJSA explanation. See § 1.417(e)-1(b)(3)(ii) for rules governing the timing of the QJSA explanation.

(ii) QPSA explanation. See § 1.401(a)-20, Q&A-35, for rules governing the timing of the QPSA explanation.

*(3) Required method for providing section 417(a)(3) explanation.* A section 417(a)(3) explanation must be a written explanation. First class mail to the last known address of the participant is an acceptable delivery method for a section 417(a)(3) explanation. Likewise, hand delivery is acceptable. However, the posting of the explanation is not considered provision of the section 417(a)(3) explanation. But see

§ 1.401(a)-21 of this chapter for rules permitting the use of electronic media to provide applicable notices to recipients with respect to retirement plans.

*(4) Understandability.* A section 417(a)(3) explanation must be written in a manner calculated to be understood by the average participant.

**(b) Required content of section 417(a)(3) explanation.** *(1) Content of QPSA explanation.* The QPSA explanation must contain a general description of the QPSA, the circumstances under which it will be paid if elected, the availability of the election of the QPSA, and, except as provided in paragraph (d)(3) of this section, a description of the financial effect of the election of the QPSA on the participant's benefits (i.e., an estimate of the reduction to the participant's estimated normal retirement benefit that would result from an election of the QPSA).

*(2) Content of QJSA explanation.* The QJSA explanation must satisfy either paragraph (c) or paragraph (d) of this section. Under paragraph (c) of this section, the QJSA explanation must contain certain specific information relating to the benefits available under the plan to the particular participant. Alternatively, under paragraph (d) of this section, the QJSA explanation can contain generally applicable information in lieu of specific participant information, provided that the participant has the right to request additional information regarding the participant's benefits under the plan.

**(c) Participant-specific information required to be provided.** *(1) In general.* A QJSA explanation satisfies this paragraph (c) if it provides the following information with respect to each of the optional forms of benefit presently available to the participant (i.e., optional forms of benefit for which the QJSA explanation applies that have an annuity starting date after the providing of the QJSA explanation and optional forms of benefit with retroactive annuity starting dates that are available with payments commencing at that same time)—

(i) A description of the optional form of benefit;

(ii) A description of the eligibility conditions for the optional form of benefit;

(iii) A description of the financial effect of electing the optional form of benefit (i.e., the amounts and timing of payments to the participant under the form of benefit during the participant's lifetime, and the amounts and timing of payments after the death of the participant);

(iv) In the case of a defined benefit plan, a description of the relative value of the optional form of benefit compared to the value of the QJSA, in the manner described in paragraph (c)(2) of this section; and

(v) A description of any other material features of the optional form of benefit.

*(2) Requirement for numerical comparison of relative values.* (i) In general. The description of the relative value of an optional form of benefit compared to the value of the QJSA under paragraph (c)(1)(iv) of this section must be expressed to the participant in a manner that provides a meaningful comparison of the relative economic values of the two forms of benefit without the participant having to make calculations using interest or mortality assumptions. Thus, in performing the calculations necessary to make this comparison, the benefits under one or both optional forms of benefit must be converted, taking into account the time value of money and life expectancies, so that the values of both optional forms of benefit are expressed in the same form. For example, such a comparison may be expressed to the participant using any of the following techniques—

(A) Expressing the actuarial present value of the optional form of benefit as a percentage or factor of the actuarial present value of the QJSA;

(B) Stating the amount of the annuity that is the actuarial equivalent of the optional form of benefit and that is payable at the same time and under the same conditions as the QJSA; or

(C) Stating the actuarial present value of both the optional form of benefit and the QJSA.

(ii) Use of one form for both married and unmarried individuals. (A) In general. Under the rules of this paragraph (c)(2)(ii), in lieu of providing different QJSA explanations for married and unmarried individuals, the plan may provide a QJSA explanation to an individual that does not vary based on the participant's marital status. Except as specifically provided in this section, any reference in this section to comparing the relative value of an optional form of benefit to the value of the QJSA may be satisfied using the substitution permitted under paragraph (c)(2)(ii)(B) or (C) of this section.

(B) Substitution of single life annuity for married individual. For a married participant, in lieu of comparing the value of each optional form of benefit presently available to the participant to the value of the QJSA, the plan can compare the value of each optional form of benefit (including the QJSA) to the value of a QJSA for an unmarried participant (i.e., a single life annuity), but only if that same single life annuity is available to that married participant.

(C) Substitution of joint and survivor annuity for unmarried individual. For an unmarried participant, in lieu of comparing the value of each optional form of benefit presently available to the participant to the value of the QJSA for that individual (which is a single life annuity), the plan can compare the value of each optional form of benefit (including the single life annuity) to the value of the joint and survivor annuity that is the QJSA for a married participant, but only if that same joint and survivor annuity is available to that unmarried participant.

(iii) Simplified presentations permitted. (A) Grouping of certain optional forms. Two or more optional forms of benefit that have approximately the same value may be grouped for purposes of a required numerical comparison described in this paragraph (c)(2). For this purpose, two or more optional forms of benefit have approximately the same value if none of those optional forms of benefit vary in relative value in comparison to the value of the QJSA by more than 5 percentage points when the relative value comparison is made by expressing the actuarial present value of each of those optional forms of benefit as a percentage of the actuarial present value of the QJSA. For such a group of optional forms of benefit, the requirement relating to disclosing the relative value of each optional form of benefit compared to the value of the QJSA can be satisfied by disclosing the relative value of any one of the optional forms in the group compared to the value of the QJSA, and disclosing that the other optional forms of benefit in the group are of approximately the same value. If a single-sum distribution is included in such a group of optional forms of benefit, the single-sum distribution must be the distribution form that is used for purposes of this comparison.

(B) Representative relative value for grouped optional forms. If, in accordance with paragraph (c)(2)(iii)(A) of this section, two or more optional forms of benefits are grouped, the relative values for all of the optional forms of benefit in the group can be stated using a representative relative value as the approximate relative value for the entire group. For this purpose, a representative relative value is any relative value that is not less than the relative value of the member of the group of optional forms of benefit with the lowest relative value and is not greater than the relative value of the member of that group with the highest relative value when measured on a consistent basis. For example, if three grouped optional forms have relative values of 87.5 percent, 89 percent, and 91 percent of the value of the QJSA, all three optional forms can be treated as having a relative value of approximately 90 percent of the value of the QJSA. As required under paragraph (c)(2)(iii)(A) of this section, if a single-sum distribution is included in the group of optional forms of benefit, the 90 percent relative factor of the value of the QJSA must be disclosed as the approximate relative value of the single sum, and the other forms can be described as having the same approximate value as the single sum.

(C) Special rule for optional forms of benefit that are close in value to the QJSA. The relative value of all optional forms of benefit that have an actuarial present value that is at least 95% of the actuarial present value of the QJSA and no greater than 105% of the actuarial present value of the QJSA is permitted to be described by stating that those optional forms of benefit are approximately equal in value to the QJSA, or that all of those forms of benefit and the QJSA are approximately equal in value.

(iv) Actuarial assumptions used to determine relative values. For the purpose of providing a numerical comparison of the value of an optional form of benefit to the value of the immediately commencing QJSA under this paragraph (c)(2), the following rules apply—

(A) If an optional form of benefit is subject to the requirements of section 417(e)(3) and § 1.417(e)-1(d), any comparison of the value of the optional form of benefit to the value of the QJSA must be made using the applicable mortality table and the applicable interest rate as defined in § 1.417(e)-1(d)(2) and (3) (or, at the option of the plan, another reasonable interest rate and reasonable mortality table used under the plan to calculate the amount payable under the optional form of benefit); and

(B) All other optional forms of benefit payable to the participant must be compared with the QJSA using a single set of interest and mortality assumptions that are reasonable and that are applied uniformly with respect to all such optional forms payable to the participant (regardless of whether those assumptions are actually used under the plan for purposes of determining benefit payments). For this purpose, the reasonableness of interest and mortality assumptions is determined without regard to the circumstances of the individual participant. In addition, the applicable mortality table and the applicable interest rate as defined in § 1.417(e)-1(d)(2) and (3) are considered reasonable actuarial assumptions for this purpose and thus are permitted (but not required) to be used.

(v) Required disclosure of assumptions. (A) Explanation of concept of relative value. The notice must provide an explanation of the concept of relative value, communicating that the relative value comparison is intended to allow the participant to compare the total value of distributions paid in different forms, that the relative value comparison is made by converting the value of the optional forms of benefit presently available to a common form (such as the QJSA or a single-sum distribution), and that this conversion uses interest and life expectancy assumptions. The explanation of relative value must include a general statement that all comparisons provided are based on average life expectancies, and that the relative value of payments ultimately made under an annuity optional form of benefit will depend on actual longevity.

(B) Disclosure of assumptions. A required numerical comparison of the value of the optional form of benefit to the value of the QJSA under this paragraph (c)(2) is required to include a disclosure of the interest rate that is used to develop the comparison. If all optional forms of benefit are permitted to be grouped under paragraph (c)(2)(iii)(A) of this section, then the requirement of this paragraph (c)(2)(v)(B) does not apply for any optional form of benefit not subject to the requirements of section 417(e)(3) and § 1.417(e)-1(d)(3).

(C) Offer to provide actuarial assumptions. If the plan does not disclose the actuarial assumptions used to calculate the numerical comparison required under paragraph (c)(2) of this section, then, the notice must be accompanied by a statement that includes an offer to provide, upon the participant's request, the actuarial assumptions used to calculate the relative value of optional forms of benefit under the plan.

*(3) Permitted estimates of financial effect and relative value.* (i) General rule. For purposes of providing a description of the financial effect of the distribution forms available to a participant as required under paragraph (c)(1)(iii) of this section, and for purposes of providing a description of the relative value of an optional form of benefit compared to the value of the QJSA for a participant as required under paragraph (c)(1)(iv) of this section, the plan is permitted to provide reasonable estimates (e.g., estimates based on data as of an earlier date than the annuity starting date, a reasonable assumption for the age of the participant's spouse, or, in the case of a defined contribution plan, reasonable estimates of amounts that would be payable under a purchased annuity contract), including reasonable estimates of the applicable interest rate under section 417(e)(3).

(ii) Right to more precise calculation. If a QJSA notice uses a reasonable estimate under paragraph (c)(3)(i) of this section, the QJSA explanation must identify the estimate and explain that the plan will, upon the request of the participant, provide a more precise calculation and the plan must provide the participant with a more precise calculation if so requested. Thus, for example, if a plan provides an estimate of the amount of the QJSA that is based on a reasonable assumption concerning the age of the participant's spouse, the participant can request a calculation that takes into account the actual age of the spouse, as provided by the participant.

(iii) Revision of prior information. If a more precise calculation described in paragraph (c)(3)(ii) of this section materially changes the relative value of an optional form compared to the value of the QJSA, the revised relative value of that optional form must be disclosed, regardless of whether the financial effect of selecting the optional form is affected by the more precise calculation. For example, if a participant provides a plan with the age of the participant's spouse and that information materially changes the relative value of an optional form of benefit (such as a single sum) compared to the value of the QJSA, then the revised relative value of the optional form of benefit and the value of the QJSA must be disclosed, regardless of whether the amount of the payment under that optional form of benefit is affected by the more precise calculation.

*(4) Special rules for disclosure of financial effect for defined contribution plans.* For a written explanation provided by a defined contribution plan, a description of financial effect required by paragraph (c)(1)(iii) of this section with respect to an annuity form of benefit must include a statement that the annuity will be provided by purchasing an annuity contract from an insurance company with the participant's account balance under the plan. If the description of the financial effect of the optional form of benefit is provided using estimates rather than by assuring that an insurer is able to provide the amount disclosed to the participant, the written explanation must also disclose this fact.

*(5) Simplified presentations of financial effect and relative value to enhance clarity for participants.* (i) In general. This paragraph (c)(5) permits certain simplified presentations of financial effect and relative value of optional forms of benefit to permit more useful presentations of information to be provided to participants in certain cases in which a plan offers a range of optional forms of benefit. Paragraph (c)(5)(ii) of this section permits simplified presentations of financial effect and relative value for a plan that offers a significant number of substantially similar optional forms of benefit. Paragraph (c)(5)(iii) of this section permits simplified presentations of financial effect and relative value for a plan that permits the participant to make separate benefit elections with respect to parts of a benefit.

(ii) Disclosure for plans offering a significant number of substantially similar optional forms of benefit. (A) In general. If a plan offers a significant number of substantially similar optional forms of benefit within the meaning of paragraph (c)(5)(ii)(B) of this section and disclosing the financial effect and relative value of each such optional form of benefit would provide a level of detail that could be overwhelming rather than helpful to participants, then the financial effect and relative value of those optional forms of benefit can be disclosed by disclosing the relative value and financial effect of a representative range of examples of those optional forms of benefit as described in paragraph (c)(5)(ii)(C) of this section if the requirements of paragraph (c)(5)(ii)(D) of this section (relating to additional information available upon request) are satisfied.

(B) Substantially similar optional forms of benefit. For purposes of this paragraph (c)(5)(ii), optional forms of benefit are substantially similar if those optional forms of benefit are identical except for a particular feature or features (with associated adjustment factors) and the feature or features vary linearly. For example, if a plan offers joint and survivor annuity options with survivor payments available in every whole number percentage between 50% and 100%, those joint and survivor annuity options are substantially similar optional forms of benefit. Similarly, if a participant is entitled under the plan to receive a particular form of benefit with an annuity starting date that is the first day of any month beginning three years before commencement of a distribution and ending on the date of commencement of the distribution, those forms of benefit are substantially similar optional forms of benefit.

(C) Representative range of examples. A range of examples with respect to substantially similar optional forms of benefit as permitted under this paragraph (c)(5) is representative only if it includes examples illustrating the financial effect and relative value of the optional forms of benefit that reflect each varying feature at both extremes of its linear range, plus at least one example illustrating the financial effect and relative value of the optional forms of benefit that reflects each varying feature at an intermediate point. However, if one intermediate example is insufficient to illustrate the pattern of variation in relative value with respect to a varying feature, examples sufficient to illustrate such pattern must be provided. Thus, for example, if a plan offers joint and survivor annuity options with survivor payments available in every whole number percentage between 50% and 100%, and if all such optional forms of benefit would be permitted to be disclosed as approximately equal in value as described in paragraph (c)(5)(ii)(B) of this section, the plan could satisfy the requirement to disclose the financial effect and relative value of a representative range of examples of those optional forms of benefit by disclosing the financial effect and relative value with respect to the joint and 50% survivor annuity, the joint and 75% survivor annuity, and the joint and 100% survivor annuity.

(D) Requirement to provide information with respect to other optional forms of benefit upon request. If a QJSA explanation discloses the financial effect and relative value of substantially similar optional forms of benefit by disclosing the financial effect and relative value of a representative range of examples in accordance with this paragraph (c)(5)(ii), the QJSA explanation must explain that the plan will, upon the request of the participant, disclose the financial effect and relative value of any particular optional form of benefit from among the substantially similar optional forms of benefit and the plan must provide the participant with the financial effect and relative value of any such optional form of benefit if the participant so requests.

(iii) Separate presentations permitted for elections that apply to parts of a benefit. If the plan permits the participant to make separate benefit elections with respect to two or more portions of the participant's benefit, the description of the financial effect and relative values of optional forms of benefit can be made separately for each such portion of the benefit, rather than for each optional form of benefit (i.e., each combination of possible elections).

**(d) Substitution of generally applicable information for participant information in the section 417(a)(3) explanation.** *(1) Forms of benefit available.* In lieu of providing the information required under paragraphs (c)(1)(i) through (v) of this section for each optional form of benefit presently available to the participant as described in paragraph (c) of this section, the QJSA explanation may contain the information required under paragraphs (c)(1)(i) through (v) of this section for the QJSA and each other optional form of benefit generally available under the plan, along with a reference to where a participant may readily obtain the information required under paragraphs (c)(1)(i) through (v) of this section for any other optional forms of benefit that are presently available to the participant.

*(2) Financial effect and comparison of relative values.* (i) General rule. In lieu of providing a statement of the financial effect of electing an optional form of benefit as required under paragraph (c)(1)(iii) of this section, or a comparison of relative values as required under paragraph (c)(1)(iv) of this section, based on the actual age and benefit of the participant, the QJSA explanation is permitted to include a chart (or other comparable device) showing the financial effect and relative value of optional forms of benefit in a series of examples specifying the amount of the optional form of benefit payable to a hypothetical participant at a representative range of ages and the comparison of relative values at those same representative ages. Each example in this chart must show the financial effect of electing the optional form of benefit pursuant to the rules of paragraph (c)(1)(iii) of this section, and a comparison of the relative value of the op-

tional form of benefit to the value of the QJSA pursuant to the rules of paragraph (c)(2) of this section, using reasonable assumptions for the age of the hypothetical participant's spouse and any other variables that affect the financial effect, or relative value, of the optional form of benefit. The requirement to show the financial effect of electing an optional form can be satisfied through the use of other methods (e.g., expressing the amount of the optional form as a percentage or a factor of the amount payable under the normal form of benefit), provided that the method provides sufficient information so that a participant can determine the amount of benefits payable in the optional form. The chart (or other comparable device) must be accompanied by the disclosures described in paragraph (c)(2)(v) of this section explaining the concept of relative value and disclosing certain interest assumptions. In addition, the chart (or other comparable device) must be accompanied by a general statement describing the effect of significant variations between the assumed ages or other variables on the financial effect of electing the optional form of benefit and the comparison of the relative value of the optional form of benefit to the value of the QJSA.

(ii) Actual benefit must be disclosed. The generalized notice described in this paragraph (d)(2) will satisfy the requirements of paragraph (b)(2) of this section only if the notice includes either the amount payable to the participant under the normal form of benefit or the amount payable to the participant under the normal form of benefit adjusted for immediate commencement. For this purpose, the normal form of benefit is the form under which payments due to the participant under the plan are expressed under the plan, prior to adjustments for form of benefit. For example, assuming that a plan's benefit accrual formula is expressed as a straight life annuity, the generalized notice must provide the amount of either the straight life annuity commencing at normal retirement age or the straight life annuity commencing immediately. Reasonable estimates of the type described in paragraph (c)(3)(i) of this section may be used to determine the amount payable to the participant under the normal form of benefit for purposes of this paragraph (d)(2)(ii) if the requirements of paragraphs (c)(3)(ii) and (iii) of this section are satisfied with respect to those estimates.

(iii) Ability to request additional information. The generalized notice described in this paragraph (d)(2) must be accompanied by a statement that includes an offer to provide, upon the participant's request, a statement of financial effect and a comparison of relative values that is specific to the participant for any presently available optional form of benefit, and a description of how a participant may obtain this additional information.

*(3) Financial effect of QPSA election.* In lieu of providing a specific description of the financial effect of the QPSA election, the QPSA explanation may provide a general description of the financial effect of the election. Thus, for example, the description can be in the form of a chart showing the reduction to a hypothetical participant's normal retirement benefit at a representative range of participant ages as a result of the QPSA election (using a reasonable assumption for the age of the hypothetical participant's spouse relative to the age of the hypothetical participant). In addition, this chart must be accompanied by a statement that includes an offer to provide, upon the participant's request, an estimate of the reduction to the participant's estimated normal retirement benefit, and a description of how a participant may obtain this additional information.

*(4) Additional information required to be furnished at the participant's request.* The generalized notice described in paragraph (d)(2) of this section must be accompanied by a statement that includes an offer to provide, upon the participant's request, information described in this paragraph (d)(4)(i) and (ii), and a description of how a participant may obtain this additional information.

(i) Explanation of QJSA. If, as permitted under paragraphs (d)(1) and (2) of this section, the content of a QJSA explanation does not include all the items described in paragraph (c) of this section, then, upon a participant's request for any of the information required under paragraphs (c)(1)(i) through (v) of this section for one or more presently available optional forms (including a request for all optional forms presently available to the participant), the plan must furnish the information required under paragraphs (c)(1)(i) through (v) of this section with respect to those optional forms. Thus, with respect to those optional forms of benefit, the participant must receive a QJSA explanation specific to the participant that is based on the participant's actual age and benefit. In addition, the plan must comply with paragraph (c)(3)(iii) of this section. Further, if as permitted under paragraph (c)(2)(v)(B) of this section, the plan does not disclose the actuarial assumptions used to calculate the numerical comparison required under paragraph (c)(2) of this section, then, upon request, the plan must provide the actuarial assumptions used to calculate the relative value of optional forms of benefit under the plan.

(ii) Explanation of QPSA. If, as permitted under paragraph (d)(3) of this section, the content of a QPSA explanation does not include all the items described in paragraph (b)(1) of this section, then, upon a participant's request, the plan must furnish an estimate of the reduction to the participant's estimated normal retirement benefit that would result from a QPSA election.

*(5)* Use of participant-specific information in generalized notice. A QJSA explanation does not fail to satisfy the requirements of this paragraph (d) merely because it contains an item of participant-specific information in place of the corresponding generally applicable information.

**(e) Examples.** The following examples illustrate the application of this section. Solely for purposes of these examples, the applicable interest rate that applies to any distribution that is subject to the rules of section 417(e)(3) is assumed to be 5½ percent, and the applicable mortality table under section 417(e)(3) and § 1.417(e)-1(d)(2) is assumed to be the table that applies as of January 1, 2003. In addition, solely for purposes of these examples, assume that a plan which determines actuarial equivalence using 6 percent interest and the applicable mortality table under section 417(e)(3) and § 1.417(e)-1(d)(2) that applies as of January 1, 1995, is using reasonable actuarial assumptions. The examples are as follows:

*Example (1).* (i) Participant M participates in Plan A, a qualified defined benefit plan. Under Plan A, the QJSA is a joint and 100 percent survivor annuity, which is actuarially equivalent to the single life annuity determined using 6 percent interest and the section 417(e)(3) applicable mortality table that applies as of January 1, 1995. On October 1, 2004, M will terminate employment at age 55. When M terminates employment, M will be eligible to elect an unreduced early retirement benefit, payable as either a single life annuity or the QJSA. M will also be eligible to elect a single-sum distribution equal to the actuarial present value of the single life annuity payable at normal retirement age (age 65), determined using the applicable mortality table and the applicable interest rate under section 417(e)(3).

(ii) Consistent with paragraph (c) of this section, Participant M is provided with a QJSA explanation that describes the single life annuity, the QJSA, and single-sum distribution options under the plan, and any eligibility conditions associated with these options. Participant M is married when the explanation is provided. The explanation indicates that, if Participant M commenced benefits at age 55 and had a spouse age 55, the monthly benefit under an immediately commencing single life annuity is $3,000, the monthly benefit under the QJSA is estimated to be 89.96 percent of the monthly benefit under the immediately commencing single life annuity or $2,699, and the single sum is estimated to be 74.7645 times the monthly benefit under the immediately commencing single life annuity or $224,293.

(iii) The QJSA explanation indicates that the single life annuity and the QJSA are of approximately the same value, but that the single-sum option is equivalent in value to a monthly benefit under the QJSA of $1,215. (This amount is 45 percent of the value of the QJSA at age 55 ($1,215 divided by 89.96 percent of $3,000 equals 45 percent).) The explanation states that the relative value comparison converts the value of the single life annuity and the single-sum options to the value of each if paid in the form of the QJSA and that this conversion uses interest and life expectancy assumptions. The explanation specifies that the calculations relating to the single-sum distribution were prepared using 5.5 percent interest and average life expectancy, that the other calculations were prepared using a 6 percent interest rate and that the relative value of actual annuity payments for an individual can vary depending on how long the individual and spouse live. The explanation notes that the calculation of the QJSA assumed that the spouse was age 55, that the amount of the QJSA will depend on the actual age of the spouse (for example, annuity payments will be significantly lower if the spouse is significantly younger than the participant), and that the amount of the single-sum payment will depend on the interest rates that apply when the participant actually takes a distribution. The explanation also includes an offer to provide a more precise calculation to the participant taking into account the spouse's actual age.

(iv) In accordance with paragraph (c)(3)(ii) of this section, Participant M requests a more precise calculation of the financial effect of choosing a QJSA taking into account that Participant M's spouse is 50 years of age. Using the actual age of Participant M's spouse, Plan A determines that the monthly payments under the QJSA are 87.62 percent of the monthly payments under the single life annuity, or $2,628.60 per month, and provides this information to M. Plan A is not required to provide an updated calculation of the relative value of the single sum because the value of single sum continues to be 45 percent of the value of the QJSA.

*Example (2).* (i) The facts are the same as in Example 1, except that the comparison of the relative values of optional forms of benefit to the value of the QJSA is not expressed as a percentage of the actuarial present value of the QJSA, but instead is expressed by disclosing the actuarial present values of the optional forms and the QJSA. In addition, the Plan uses the applicable interest rate and the applicable mortality table under section 417(e)(3) for all comparison purposes.

(ii) Accordingly, the QJSA explanation indicates that the QJSA has an actuarial present value of $498,089, while the single-sum payment has an actuarial present value of $224,293 (i.e. the amount of the single sum is $224,293) and that the single life annuity is approximately equal in value to the QJSA. The explanation states that the relative value comparison converts the value of single life annuity and the QJSA into an amount payable in the form of the single-sum option (even though a single-sum distribution in that amount is not available under the plan) and that this conversion uses interest and life expectancy assumptions. The explanation specifies that the calculations were prepared using 5.5 percent interest and average life expectancy, and that the relative value of actual annuity payments for an individual can vary depending on how long the individual and spouse live. The explanation notes that the calculation of the QJSA assumed that the spouse was age 55, that the amount of the QJSA will depend on the actual age of the spouse (for example, annuity payments will be significantly lower if the spouse is significantly younger than the participant), and that the amount of the single-sum payment will depend on the interest rates that apply when the participant actually takes a distribution. The explanation also includes an offer to provide a more precise calculation to the participant taking into account the spouse's actual age.

*Example (3).* (i) The facts are the same as in Example 1, except that, in lieu of providing information specific to Participant M in the QJSA notice as set forth in paragraph (c) of this section, Plan A satisfies the QJSA explanation requirement in accordance with paragraph (d)(2) of this section by providing M with a statement that M's monthly benefit under an immediately commencing single life annuity (which is the normal form of benefit under Plan A, adjusted for immediate commencement) is $3,000, along with the following chart. The chart shows the financial effect of electing each optional form of benefit for a hypothetical participant with a $1,000 benefit and a spouse who is the same age as the participant. Instead of showing the relative value of these optional forms of benefit compared to the value of the QJSA, the chart shows the relative value of these optional forms of benefit compared to the value of the single life annuity. Separate charts are provided for ages 55, 60, and 65 as follows:

**Age 55 Commencement**

| Optional form | Amount of distribution per $1,000 of immediate single life annuity | Relative value |
|---|---|---|
| Life Annuity | $1,000 per month | n/a. |
| QJSA (Joint and 100 percent survivor annuity). | $900 per month ($900 per month for survivor annuity). | Approximately the same value as the Life Annuity. |
| Lump sum | $74,764 | Approximately 45 percent of the value of the Life Annuity. |

**Age 60 Commencement**

| Optional form | Amount of distribution per $1,000 of immediate single life annuity | Relative value |
|---|---|---|
| Life Annuity | $1,000 per month | n/a. |
| QJSA (Joint and 100 percent survivor annuity). | $878 per month ($878 per month for survivor annuity). | Approximately the same value as the Life Annuity. |
| Lump sum | $99,792 | Approximately 66 percent of the value of the Life Annuity. |

**Age 65 Commencement**

| Optional form | Amount of distribution per $1,000 of immediate single life annuity | Relative value |
|---|---|---|
| Life Annuity | $1,000 per month | n/a. |
| QJSA (Joint and 100 percent survivor annuity). | $852 per month ($852 per month for survivor annuity). | Approximately the same value as the Life Annuity. |
| Lump sum | $135,759 | Approximately the same value as the Life Annuity. |

(ii) In accordance with paragraph (d)(4)(i) of this section, when Participant M requests specific information regarding the amounts payable under the QJSA, the joint and 100 percent survivor annuity, and the single-sum distribution and provides the age of M's spouse, Plan A determines that M's QJSA is $2,628.60 per month and the single-sum distribution is $224,293. The actuarial present value of the QJSA (determined using the 5.5 percent interest and the section 417(e)(3) applicable mortality table) is $498,896 and the actuarial present value of the single life annuity is $497,876. Accordingly, the specific information discloses that the single-sum distribution has a value that is 45 percent of the value of the single life annuity available to M on October 1, 2004. In accordance with paragraph (c)(2)(iii)(C) of this section, the QJSA notice provides that the QJSA is of approximately the same value as the single life annuity.

*Example (4).* (i) The facts are the same as in Example 1, except that under Plan A, the single-sum distribution is determined as the actuarial present value of the immediately commencing single life annuity. In addition, Plan A provides a joint and 75 percent survivor annuity that is reduced from the single life annuity and that is the QJSA under Plan A. For purposes of determining the amount of the QJSA, if the participant is married the reduction is only half of the reduction that would normally apply under the actuarial assumptions specified in Plan A for determining actuarial equivalence of optional forms.

(ii) In lieu of providing information specific to Participant M in the QJSA notice as set forth in paragraph (c) of this section, Plan A satisfies the QJSA explanation requirement in accordance with paragraph (d)(2) of this section by providing M with a statement that M's monthly benefit under an immediately commencing single life annuity (which is the normal form of benefit under Plan A, adjusted for immediate commencement) is $3,000, along with the following chart showing the financial effect and the relative value of the optional forms of benefit compared to the QJSA for a hypothetical participant with a $1,000 benefit and a spouse who is three years younger than the participant. For each optional form generally available under the plan, the chart shows the financial effect and the relative value, using the grouping rules of paragraph (c)(2)(iii) of this section. Separate charts are provided for ages 55, 60, and 65, as follows:

**Age 55 Commencement**

| Optional form | Amount of distribution per $1,000 of immediate single life annuity | Relative value |
|---|---|---|
| Life Annuity | $1,000 per month | Approximately the same value as the QJSA. |
| QJSA (joint and 75 percent survivor annuity for a participant who is married). | $956 per month ($717 per month for survivor annuity). | n/a. |
| Joint and 100 percent survivor annuity. | $886 per month ($886 per month for survivor annuity). | Approximately the same value as the QJSA. |
| Lump sum | $165,959 | Approximately the same value as the QJSA. |

**Age 60 Commencement**

| Optional form | Amount of distribution per $1,000 of immediate single life annuity | Relative value |
|---|---|---|
| Life Annuity | $1,000 per month | Approximately 94 percent of the value of the QJSA. |
| QJSA (joint and 75 percent survivor annuity for a participant who is married). | $945 per month ($709 per month for survivor annuity). | n/a. |
| Joint and 100 percent survivor annuity. | $859 per month ($859 per month for survivor annuity). | Approximately 94 percent of the value of the QJSA. |
| Lump sum | $151,691 | Approximately the same value as the QJSA. |

**Age 65 Commencement**

| Optional form | Amount of distribution per $1,000 of immediate single life annuity | Relative value |
|---|---|---|
| Life Annuity | $1,000 per month | Approximately 93 percent of the value of the QJSA. |
| QJSA (joint and 75 percent survivor annuity for a participant who is married). | $932 per month ($699 per month for survivor annuity). | n/a. |
| Joint and 100 percent survivor annuity. | $828 per month ($828 per month for survivor annuity). | Approximately 93 percent of the value of the QJSA. |
| Lump sum | $135,759 | Approximately 93 percent of the value of the QJSA. |

(iii) The chart disclosing the financial effect and relative value of the optional forms specifies that the calculations were prepared assuming that the spouse is three years younger than the participant, that the calculations relating to the single-sum distribution were prepared using 5.5 percent interest and average life expectancy, that the other calculations were prepared using a 6 percent interest rate, and that the relative value of actual payments for an individual can vary depending on how long the individual and spouse live. The explanation states that the relative value comparison converts the single life annuity, the joint and 100 percent survivor annuity, and the single-sum options to value of each if paid in the form of the QJSA and that this conversion uses interest and life expectancy assumptions. The explanation notes that the calculation of the QJSA depends on the actual age of the spouse (for example, annuity payments will be significantly lower if the spouse is significantly younger than the participant), and that the amount of the single-sum payment will depend on the interest rates that apply when the participant actually takes a distribution. The explanation also includes an offer to provide a calculation specific to the participant upon request, and an offer to provide mortality tables used in preparing calculations upon request.

(iv) In accordance with paragraph (d)(4)(i) of this section, Participant M requests specific information regarding the amounts payable under the QJSA, the joint and 100 percent survivor annuity, and the single sum.

(v) Based on the information about the age of Participant M's spouse, Plan A determines that M's QJSA is $2,856.30 per month, the joint and 100 percent survivor annuity is $2,628.60 per month, and the single sum is $497,876. The actuarial present value of the QJSA (determined using the 5.5 percent interest and the section 417(e)(3) applicable mortality table, the actuarial assumptions required under section 417) is $525,091. Accordingly, the value of the single-sum distribution available to M on October 1, 2004, is 94.8 percent of the actuarial present value of the QJSA. In addition, the actuarial present value of the life annuity and the 100 percent joint and survivor annuity are 95.0 percent of the actuarial present value of the QJSA.

(vi) Plan A provides M with a QJSA explanation that incorporates these more precise calculations of the financial effect and relative value of the optional forms for which M requested information.

**(f) Effective date.** *(1) General effective date for QJSA explanations.* (i) In general. Except as otherwise provided in this paragraph (f), this section applies to a QJSA explanation with respect to any distribution with an annuity starting date that is on or after February 1, 2006.

(ii) Reasonable, good faith transition rule. Except with respect to any portion of a QJSA explanation that is subject to the earlier effective date rule of paragraph (f)(2) of this section, a reasonable, good faith effort to comply with these regulations will be deemed to satisfy the requirements of these regulations for QJSA explanations provided before January 1, 2007, with respect to distributions with annuity starting dates that are on or after February 1, 2006. For this purpose, a reasonable, good faith effort to comply with these regulations includes substantial compliance with § 1.417(a)(3)-1 as it appeared in 26 CFR part 1 revised April 1, 2004.

*(2) Special effective date for certain QJSA explanations.* (i) Application to QJSA explanations with respect to certain optional forms that are less valuable than the QJSA. This section also applies to a QJSA explanation with respect to any distribution with an annuity starting date that is on or after October 1, 2004, and before February 1, 2006, if the actuarial present value of any optional form of benefit that is subject to the requirements of section 417(e)(3) is less than the actuarial present value (as determined under § 1.417(e)-1(d)) of the QJSA. For purposes of this paragraph (f)(2)(i), the actuarial present value of an optional form is treated as not less than the actuarial present value of the QJSA if—

(A) Using the applicable interest rate and applicable mortality table under § 1.417(e)-1(d)(2) and (3), the actuarial present value of that optional form is not less than the actuarial present value of the QJSA for an unmarried participant; and

(B) Using reasonable actuarial assumptions, the actuarial present value of the QJSA for an unmarried participant is not less than the actuarial present value of the QJSA for a married participant.

(ii) Requirement to disclose differences in value for certain optional forms. A QJSA explanation with respect to any distribution with an annuity starting date that is on or after October 1, 2004, and before February 1, 2006, is only required to be provided under this section with respect to—

(A) An optional form of benefit that is subject to the requirements of section 417(e)(3) and that has an actuarial present value that is less than the actuarial present value of the QJSA (as described in paragraph (f)(2)(i) of this section); and

(B) The QJSA (determined without application of paragraph (c)(2)(ii) of this section).

(iii) Application to QJSA explanations with respect to optional forms that are approximately equal in value to the QJSA. Paragraph (c)(2)(iii)(C) of this section, relating to disclosures of optional forms of benefit that are permitted to be described as approximately equal in value to the QJSA, is not applicable to a QJSA explanation provided before January 1, 2007. However, § 1.417(a)(3)-1(c)(2)(iii)(C), as it appeared in 26 CFR part 1 revised April 1, 2004, applies to a QJSA explanation with respect to any distribution with an annuity starting date that is on or after October 1, 2004, and that is provided before January 1, 2007.

*(3) Annuity starting date.* For purposes of paragraphs (f)(1) and (2) of this section, in the case of a retroactive annuity starting date under section 417(a)(7), as described in § 1.417(e)-1(b)(3)(vi), the date of commencement of the actual payments based on the retroactive annuity starting date is substituted for the annuity starting date.

*(4) Effective date for QPSA explanations.* This section applies to any QPSA explanation provided on or after July 1, 2004.

---

T.D. 9099, 12/16/2003, amend T.D. 9256, 3/23/2006, T.D. 9294, 10/19/2006.

---

**§ 1.417(e)-1 Restrictions and valuations of distributions from plans subject to sections 401(a)(11) and 417.**

***Caution:*** The Treasury has not yet amended Reg § 1.417(e)-1 to reflect changes made by P.L. 109-280, P.L. 107-147, P.L. 105-34.

**(a) Scope.** *(1) In general.* A plan does not satisfy the requirements of sections 401(a)(11) and 417 unless it satisfies the consent requirements, the determination of present value requirements and the other requirements set forth in this section. See section 401(a)(11) and § 1.401(a)-20 for other rules regarding the survivor annuity requirements.

*(2) Additional requirements.* See § 1.411(a)-(11) for other rules applicable to the consent requirements.

*(3) Accrued benefit.* The definition of "accrued benefit" in § 1.411(a)-(11) applies when that term is used in this section.

**(b) Consent, etc. requirements.** *(1) General rule.* Generally plans may not commence the distribution of any portion of a participant's accrued benefit in any form unless the applicable consent requirements are satisfied. No consent of the participant or spouse is needed for distribution of a QJSA or QPSA after the benefit is no longer immediately distributable (after the participant attains (or would have attained if not dead) the later of normal retirement age (as defined in section 411(a)(8)) or age 62). No consent of the spouse is needed for distribution of a QJSA at any time. After the participant's death, a benefit may be paid to a nonspouse beneficiary without the beneficiary's consent. A distribution cannot be made at any time in a form other than a QJSA unless such QJSA has been waived by the participant and such waiver has been consented to by the spouse. A QJSA is an annuity that commences immediately. Thus, for example, a plan may not offer a participant separating from service at age 45 a choice only between a single sum distribution at separation of service and a joint and survivor annuity that satisfies all the requirements of a QJSA except that it commences at normal retirement age rather than immediately. To satisfy this section, the plan must also offer a QJSA (i.e., an annuity that satisfies all the requirements for a QJSA including the requirement that it commences immediately).

*(2) Consent.* (i) Written consent of the participant and, if the participant is married at the annuity starting date and the benefit is to be paid in a form other than a QJSA, the participant's spouse (or, if either the participant or the spouse has died, the survivor) is required before the commencement of the distribution of any part of an accrued benefit if the present value of the nonforfeitable benefit is greater than the cash-out limit in effect under § 1.411(a)-11(c)(3)(ii). No consent is valid unless the participant has received a general description of the material features, and an explanation of the relative values of, the optional forms of benefit available under the plan in a manner which would satisfy the notice requirements of section 417(a)(3). See § 1.417(a)(3)-1. No consent is required before the annuity starting date if the present value of the nonforfeitable benefit is not more than the cash-out limit in effect under § 1.411(a)-11(c)(3)(ii). After the annuity starting date, consent is required for the immediate distribution of the present value of the accrued benefit being distributed in any form, including a qualified joint and survivor annuity or a qualified preretirement survivor annuity, regardless of the amount of such present value.

(ii) In determining the present value of any nonforfeitable accrued benefit, a defined benefit plan is limited by the interest rate restriction as set forth in paragraph (d) of this section.

(iii) Paragraph (b)(2)(i) of this section applies to distributions made on or after October 17, 2000. For distributions prior to October 17, 2000, § 1.417(e)-1(b)(2)(i) in effect prior to October 17, 2000 (as contained in 26 CFR part 1 revised as of April 1, 2000) applies.

*(3) Time of consent.* (i) Written consent of the participant and the participant's spouse to the distribution must be made not more than 90 days before the annuity starting date, and, except as otherwise provided in paragraphs (b)(3)(iii) and (b)(3)(iv) of this section, no later than the annuity starting date.

(ii) A plan must provide participants with the written explanation of the QJSA required by section 417(a)(3) no less than 30 days and no more than 90 days before the annuity starting date, except as provided in paragraph (b)(3)(iv) of this section regarding retroactive annuity starting dates. However, if the participant, after having received the written explanation of the QJSA, affirmatively elects a form of distribution and the spouse consents to that form of distribution (if necessary), a plan will not fail to satisfy the requirements of section 417(a) merely because the written explanation was provided to the participant less than 30 days before the annuity starting date, provided that the following conditions are met:

(A) The plan administrator provides information to the participant clearly indicating that (in accordance with the first sentence of this paragraph (b)(3)(ii)) the participant has a right to at least 30 days to consider whether to waive the QJSA and consent to a form of distribution other than a QJSA.

(B) The participant is permitted to revoke an affirmative distribution election at least until the annuity starting date, or, if later, at any time prior to the expiration of the 7-day period that begins the day after the explanation of the QJSA is provided to the participant.

(C) The annuity starting date is after the date that the explanation of the QJSA is provided to the participant.

(D) Distribution in accordance with the affirmative election does not commence before the expiration of the 7-day period that begins the day after the explanation of the QJSA is provided to the participant.

(iii) The plan may permit the annuity starting date to be before the date that any affirmative distribution election is made by the participant (and before the date that distribution is permitted to commence under paragraph (b)(3)(ii)(D) of this section), provided that, except as otherwise provided in paragraph (b)(3)(vii) of this section regarding administrative delay, distributions commence not more than 90 days after the explanation of the QJSA is provided.

(iv) Retroactive annuity starting dates. (A) Notwithstanding the requirements of paragraphs (b)(3)(i) and (ii) of this section, pursuant to section 417(a)(7), a defined benefit plan is permitted to provide benefits based on a retroactive annuity starting date if the requirements described in paragraph (b)(3)(v) of this section are satisfied. A defined benefit plan is not required to provide for retroactive annuity starting dates. If a plan does provide for a retroactive annuity starting date, it may impose conditions on the availability of a retroactive annuity starting date in addition to those imposed by paragraph (b)(3)(v) of this section, provided that imposition of those additional conditions does not violate any of the rules applicable to qualified plans. For example, a plan that includes a single sum payment as a benefit option may limit the election of a retroactive annuity starting date to those participants who do not elect the single sum payment. A defined contribution plan is not permitted to have a retroactive annuity starting date.

(B) For purposes of this section, a "retroactive annuity starting date" is an annuity starting date affirmatively elected by a participant that occurs on or before the date the written explanation required by section 417(a)(3) is provided to the participant. In order for a plan to treat a participant as having elected a retroactive annuity starting date, future periodic payments with respect to a participant who elects a retroactive annuity starting date must be the same as the future periodic payments, if any, that would have been paid with respect to the participant had payments actually commenced on the retroactive annuity starting date. The participant must receive a make-up payment to reflect any missed payment or payments for the period from the retroactive annuity starting date to the date of the actual make-up payment (with an appropriate adjustment for interest from the date the missed payment or payments would have been made to the date of the actual make-up payment). Thus, the benefit determined as of the retroactive annuity starting date must satisfy the requirements of sections 417(e)(3), if applicable, and section 415 with the applicable interest rate and applicable mortality table determined as of that date. Similarly, a participant is not permitted to elect a retroactive annuity starting date that precedes the date upon which the participant could have otherwise started receiving benefits (e.g., in the case of an ongoing plan, the earlier of the participant's termination of employment or the participant's normal retirement age) under the terms of the plan in effect as of the retroactive annuity starting date. A plan does not fail to treat a participant as having elected a retroactive annuity starting date as described in this paragraph (b)(3)(iv)(B) merely because the distributions are adjusted to the extent necessary to satisfy the requirements of paragraph (b)(3)(v)(B) and (C) of this section relating to sections 415 and 417(e)(3).

(C) If the participant's spouse as of the retroactive annuity starting date would not be the participant's spouse determined as if the date distributions commence was the participant's annuity starting date, consent of that former spouse is not needed to waive the QJSA with respect to the retroactive annuity starting date, unless otherwise provided under a qualified domestic relations order (as defined in section 414(p)).

(D) A distribution payable pursuant to a retroactive annuity starting date election is treated as excepted from the present value requirements of paragraph (d) of this section under paragraph (d)(6) of this section if the distribution form would have been described in paragraph (d)(6) of this section had the distribution actually commenced on the retroactive annuity starting date. Similarly, annuity payments that otherwise satisfy the requirements of a QJSA under section 417(b) will not fail to be treated as a QJSA for purposes of section 415(b)(2)(B) merely because a retroactive annuity starting date is elected and a make-up payment is made. Also, for purposes of section 72(t)(2)(A)(iv), a distribution that would otherwise be one of a series of substantially equal periodic payments will be treated as one of a series of substantially equal periodic payments notwithstanding the distribution of a make-up payment provided for in paragraph (b)(3)(iv)(B) of this section.

(E) The following example illustrates the application of paragraph (b)(3)(iv)(D) of this section:

*Example.* Under the terms of a defined benefit plan, participant A is entitled to a QJSA with a monthly payment of $1,500 beginning as of his annuity starting date. Due to administrative error, the QJSA explanation is provided to A after the annuity starting date. After receiving the QJSA explanation A elects a retroactive annuity starting date. Pursuant to this election, A begins to receive a monthly payment of $1,500 and also receives a make-up payment of $10,000. Under these circumstances the monthly payments may be treated as a QJSA for purposes of section 415(b)(2)(B). In addition, the monthly payments of $1,500 and the make-up payment of $10,000 may be treated as part of as series of substantially equal periodic payments for purpose of section 72(t)(2)(A)(iv).

(v) Requirements applicable to retroactive annuity starting dates. A distribution is permitted to have a retroactive annuity starting date with respect to a participant's benefit only if the following requirements are met:

(A) The participant's spouse (including an alternate payee who is treated as the spouse under a qualified domestic relations order (QDRO), as defined in section 414(p)), determined as if the date distributions commence were the participant's annuity starting date, consents to the distribution in a manner that would satisfy the requirements of section 417(a)(2). The spousal consent requirement of this paragraph (b)(3)(v)(A) is satisfied if such spouse consents to the distribution under paragraph (b)(2)(i) of this section. The spousal consent requirement of this paragraph (b)(3)(v)(A) does not apply if the amount of such spouse's survivor annuity payments under the retroactive annuity starting date election is no less than the amount that the survivor payments to such spouse would have been under an optional form of benefit that would satisfy the requirements to be a QJSA under section 417(b) and that has an annuity starting date after the date that the explanation was provided.

(B) The distribution (including appropriate interest adjustments) provided based on the retroactive annuity starting date would satisfy the requirements of section 415 if the date the distribution commences is substituted for the annuity starting date for all purposes, including for purposes of determining the applicable interest rate and the applicable mortality table. However, in the case of a form of benefit that would have been excepted from the present value requirements of paragraph (d) of this section under paragraph (d)(6) of this section if the distribution had actually commenced on the retroactive annuity starting date, the requirement to apply section 415 as of the date distribution commences set forth in this paragraph (b)(3)(v)(B) does not apply if the date distribution commences is twelve months or less from the retroactive annuity starting date.

(C) In the case of a form of benefit that would have been subject to section 417(e)(3) and paragraph (d) of this section if distributions had commenced as of the retroactive annuity starting date, the distribution is no less than the benefit produced by applying the applicable interest rate and the applicable mortality table determined as of the date the distribution commences to the annuity form that corresponds to the annuity form that was used to determine the benefit amount as of the retroactive annuity starting date. Thus, for example, if a distribution paid pursuant to an election of a retroactive annuity starting date is a single-sum distribution that is based on the present value of the straight life annuity payable at normal retirement age, then the amount of the distribution must be no less than the present value of the annuity payable at normal retirement age, determined as of the distribution date using the applicable mortality table and applicable interest rate that apply as of the distribution date. Likewise, if a distribution paid pursuant to an election of a retroactive annuity starting date is a single-sum distribution that is based on the present value of the early retirement annuity payable as of the retroactive annuity starting date, then the amount of the distribution must be no less than the present value of the early retirement annuity payable as of the distribution date, determined as of the distribution date using the applicable mortality table and applicable interest rate that apply as of the distribution date.

(vi) Timing of notice and consent requirements in the case of retroactive annuity starting dates. In the case of a retroactive annuity starting date, the date of the first actual payment of benefits based on the retroactive annuity starting date is substituted for the annuity starting date for purposes of satisfying the timing requirements for giving consent and providing an explanation of the QJSA provided in paragraphs (b)(3)(i) and (ii) of this section, except that the substitution does not apply for purposes of paragraph (b)(3)(iii) of this section. Thus, the written explanation required by section 417(a)(3)(A) must generally be provided no less than 30 days and no more than 90 days before the date of the first payment of benefits and the election to receive the distribution must be made after the written explanation is provided and on or before the date of the first payment. Similarly, the written explanation may also be provided less than 30 days prior to the first payment of benefits if the requirements of paragraph (b)(3)(ii) of this section would be satisfied if the date of the first payment is substituted for the annuity starting date.

(vii) Administrative delay. A plan will not fail to satisfy the 90-day timing requirements of paragraphs (b)(3)(iii) and (vi) of this section merely because, due solely to administrative delay, a distribution commences more than 90 days after the written explanation of the QJSA is provided to the participant.

(viii) The following example illustrates the provisions of this paragraph (b)(3):

*Example.* Employee E, a married participant in a defined benefit plan who has terminated employment, is provided with the explanation of the QJSA on November 28.

Employee E elects (with spousal consent) on December 2 to waive the QJSA and receive an immediate distribution in the form of a single life annuity. The plan may permit Employee E to receive payments with an annuity starting date of December 1, provided that the first payment is made no earlier than December 6 and the participant does not revoke the election before that date. The plan can make the remaining monthly payments on the first day of each month thereafter in accordance with its regular payment schedule.

(ix) The additional rules of this paragraph (b)(3) concerning the notice and consent requirements of section 417 apply to distributions on or after September 22, 1995. For distributions before September 22, 1995, the additional rules concerning the notice and consent requirements of section 417 in § 1.417(e)-1(b)(3) in effect prior to September 22, 1995 (see § 1.417(e)-1 (b)(3) in 26 CFR Part 1 revised as of April 1, 1995) apply.

*(4) Delegation to Commissioner.* The Commissioner, in revenue rulings, notices, and other guidance published in the Internal Revenue Bulletin, may modify, or provide additional guidance with respect to, the notice and consent requirements of this section. See § 601.601(d)(2)(ii)(b) of this chapter.

**(c) Permitted distributions.** A plan may not require that a participant or surviving spouse begin to receive benefits without satisfying paragraph (b) of this section while such benefits are immediately distributable, (see paragraph (b)(1) of this section). Once benefits are no longer immediately distributable, all benefits that the plan requires to begin must be provided in the form of a QJSA and QPSA unless the applicable written explanation, election and consent requirements of section 417 are satisfied.

**(d) Present value requirement.** *(1) General rule.* A defined benefit plan must provide that the present value of any accrued benefit and the amount (subject to sections 411(c)(3) and 415) of any distribution, including a single sum, must not be less than the amount calculated using the applicable interest rate described in paragraph (d)(3) of this section (determined for the month described in paragraph (d)(4) of this section) and the applicable mortality table described in paragraph (d)(2) of this section. The present value of any optional form of benefit cannot be less than the present value of the normal retirement benefit determined in accordance with the preceding sentence.

The same rules used for the plan under this paragraph (d) must also be used to compute the present value of the benefit for purposes of determining whether consent for a distribution is required under paragraph (b) of this section.

*(2) Applicable mortality table.* The applicable mortality table is the mortality table based on the prevailing commissioners' standard table (described in section 807(d)(5)(A)) used to determine reserves for group annuity contracts issued on the date as of which present value is being determined (without regard to any other subparagraph of section 807(d)(5)), that is prescribed by the Commissioner in revenue rulings, notices, or other guidance published in the Internal Revenue Bulletin (see § 601.601(d)(2)(ii)(b) of this chapter). The Commissioner may prescribe rules that apply in the case of a change to the prevailing commissioners' standard table (described in section 807(d)(5)(A)) used to determine reserves for group annuity contracts, in revenue rulings, notices, or other guidance published in the Internal Revenue Bulletin (see § 601.601(d)(2)(ii)(b) of this chapter).

*(3) Applicable interest rate.* (i) General rule. The applicable interest rate for a month is the annual interest rate on 30-year Treasury securities as specified by the Commissioner for that month in revenue rulings, notices or other guidance published in the Internal Revenue Bulletin (see § 601.601(d)(2)(ii)(b) of this chapter).

(ii) Example. This example illustrates the rules of this paragraph (d)(3):

*Example.* Plan A is a calendar year plan. For its 1995 plan year, Plan A provides that the applicable mortality table is the table described in Rev. Rul. 95-6 (1995-1 C.B. 80), and that the applicable interest rate is the annual interest rate on 30-year Treasury securities as specified by the Commissioner for the first full calendar month preceding the calendar month that contains the annuity starting date. Participant P is age 65 in January 1995, which is the month that contains P's annuity starting date. P has an accrued benefit payable monthly of $1,000 and has elected to receive a distribution in the form of a single sum in January 1995. The annual interest rate on 30-year Treasury securities as published by the Commissioner for December 1994 is 7.87 percent. To satisfy the requirements of section 417(e)(3) and this paragraph (d), the single sum received by P may not be less than $111,351.

*(4) Time for determining interest rate.* (i) General rule. Except as provided in paragraph (d)(4)(iv) or (v) of this section, the applicable interest rate to be used for a distribution is the rate determined under paragraph (d)(3) of this section for the applicable lookback month. The applicable lookback month for a distribution is the lookback month (as described in paragraph (d)(4)(iii) of this section) for the month (or other longer stability period described in paragraph (d)(4)(ii) of this section) that contains the annuity starting date for the distribution. The time and method for determining the applicable interest rate for each participant's distribution must be determined in a consistent manner that is applied uniformly to all participants in the plan.

(ii) Stability period. A plan must specify the period for which the applicable interest rate remains constant. This stability period may be one calendar month, one plan quarter, one calendar quarter, one plan year, or one calendar year.

(iii) Lookback month. A plan must specify the lookback month that is used to determine the applicable interest rate. The lookback month may be the first, second, third, fourth, or fifth full calendar month preceding the first day of the stability period.

(iv) Permitted average interest rate. A plan may apply the rules of paragraph (d)(4)(i) of this section by substituting a permitted average interest rate with respect to the plan's stability period for the rate determined under paragraph (d)(3) of this section for the applicable lookback month for the stability period. For this purpose, a permitted average interest rate with respect to a stability period is an interest rate that is computed by averaging the applicable interest rates determined under paragraph (d)(3) of this section for two or more consecutive months from among the first, second, third, fourth, and fifth calendar months preceding the first day of the stability period. For this paragraph (d)(4)(iv) to apply, a plan must specify the manner in which the permitted average interest rate is computed.

(v) Additional determination dates. The Commissioner may prescribe, in revenue rulings, notices or other guidance published in the Internal Revenue Bulletin (see § 601.601(d)(2)(ii)(b)), other times that a plan may provide for determining the applicable interest rate.

(vi) Example. This example illustrates the rules of this paragraph (d)(4):

*Example.* Employer X maintains Plan A, a calendar year plan. Employer X wishes to amend Plan A so that the applicable interest rate will remain fixed for each plan quarter, and so that the applicable interest rate for distributions made during each plan quarter can be determined approximately 80 days before the beginning of the plan quarter. To comply with the provisions of this paragraph (d)(4), Plan A is amended to provide that the applicable interest rate is the annual interest rate on 30-year Treasury securities as specified by the Commissioner for the fourth calendar month preceding the first day of the plan quarter during which the annuity starting date occurs.

*(5) Use of alternative interest rate and mortality table.* If a plan provides for use of an interest rate or mortality table other than the applicable interest rate or the applicable mortality table, the plan must provide that a participant's benefit must be at least as great as the benefit produced by using the applicable interest rate and the applicable mortality table. For example, if a plan provides for use of an interest rate of 7% and the UP-1984 Mortality Table (see § 1.401(a)(4)-12, Standard mortality table) in calculating single-sum distributions, the plan must provide that any single-sum distribution is calculated as the greater of the single-sum benefit calculated using 7% and the UP-1984 Mortality Table and the single-sum benefit calculated using the applicable interest rate and the applicable mortality table.

*(6) Exceptions.* This paragraph (d) (other than the provisions relating to section 411(d)(6) requirements in paragraph (d)(10) of this section) does not apply to the amount of a distribution paid in the form of an annual benefit that—

(i) Does not decrease during the life of the participant, or, in the case of a QPSA, the life of the participant's spouse; or

(ii) Decreases during the life of the participant merely because of—

(A) The death of the survivor annuitant (but only if the reduction is to a level not below 50% of the annual benefit payable before the death of the survivor annuitant); or

(B) The cessation or reduction of Social Security supplements or qualified disability benefits (as defined in section 411(a)(9)).

*(7) Defined contribution plans.* Because the accrued benefit under a defined contribution plan equals the account balance, a defined contribution plan is not subject to the re-

quirements of this paragraph (d), even though it is subject to section 401(a)(11).

*(8) Effective date.* (i) In general. This paragraph (d) is effective for distributions with annuity starting dates in plan years beginning after December 31, 1994.

(ii) Optional delayed effective date of Retirement Protection Act of 1994 (RPA '94)(108 Stat. 5012) rules for plans adopted and in effect before December 8, 1994. For a plan adopted and in effect before December 8, 1994, the application of the rules relating to the applicable mortality table and applicable interest rate under paragraphs (d)(2) through (4) of this section is delayed to the extent provided in this paragraph (d)(8)(ii), if the plan provisions in effect on December 7, 1994, met the requirements of section 417(e)(3) and § 1.417(e)-1(d) as in effect on December 7, 1994 (as contained in 26 CFR part 1 revised April 1, 1995). In the case of a distribution from such a plan with an annuity starting date that precedes the optional delayed effective date described in paragraph (d)(8)(iv) of this section, and that precedes the first day of the first plan year beginning after December 31, 1999, the rules of paragraph (d)(9) of this section (which generally apply to distributions with annuity starting dates in plan years beginning before January 1, 1995) apply in lieu of the rules of paragraphs (d)(2) through (4) of this section. The interest rate under the rules of paragraph (d)(9) of this section is determined under the provisions of the plan as in effect on December 7, 1994, reflecting the interest rate or rates published by the Pension Benefit Guaranty Corporation (PBGC) and the provisions of the plan for determining the date on which the interest rate is fixed. The above described interest rate or rates published by the PBGC are those determined by the PBGC (for the date determined under those plan provisions) pursuant to the methodology under the regulations of the PBGC for determining the present value of a lump sum distribution on plan termination under 29 CFR part 2619 that were in effect on September 1, 1993 (as contained in 29 CFR part 2619 revised July 1, 1994).

(iii) Optional accelerated effective date of RPA '94 rules. This paragraph (d) is also effective for a distribution with an annuity starting date after December 7, 1994, during a plan year beginning before January 1, 1995, if the employer elects, on or before the annuity starting date, to make the rules of this paragraph (d) effective with respect to the plan as of the optional accelerated effective date described in paragraph (d)(8)(iv) of this section. An employer is treated as making this election by making the plan amendments described in paragraph (d)(8)(iv) of this section.

(iv) Determination of delayed or accelerated effective date by plan amendment adopting RPA '94 rules. The optional delayed effective date of paragraph (d)(8)(ii) of this section, or the optional accelerated effective date of paragraph (d)(8)(iii) of this section, whichever is applicable, is the date plan amendments applying both the applicable mortality table of paragraph (d)(2) of this section and the applicable interest rate of paragraph (d)(3) of this section are adopted or, if later, are made effective.

*(9) Plan years beginning before January 1, 1995.* (i) Interest rate. (A) For distributions made in plan years beginning after December 31, 1986, and before January 1, 1995, the following interest rate described in paragraph (d)(9)(i)(A)(1) or (2) of this section, whichever applies, is substituted for the applicable interest rate for purposes of this section—

(1) The rate or rates that would be used by the PBGC for a trusteed single-employer plan to value the participant's (or beneficiary's) vested benefit (PBGC interest rate) if the present value of such benefit does not exceed $25,000; or

(2) 120 percent of the PBGC interest rate, as determined in accordance with paragraph (d)(9)(i)(A)(1) of this section, if such present value exceeds $25,000. In no event shall the present value determined by use of 120 percent of the PBGC interest rate result in a present value less than $25,000.

(B) The PBGC interest rate may be a series of interest rates for any given date. For example, the PBGC interest rate for immediate annuities for November 1994 is 6%, and the PBGC interest rates for the deferral period for that month are as follows: 5.25% for the first 7 years of the deferral period, 4% for the following 8 years of the deferral period, and 4% for the remainder of the deferral period. For November 1994, 120 percent of the PBGC interest rate is 7.2% (1.2 times 6%) for an immediate annuity, 6.3% (1.2 times 5.25%) for the first 7 years of the deferral period, 4.8% (1.2 times 4%) for the following 8 years of the deferral period, and 4.8% (1.2 times 4%) for the remainder of the deferral period. The PBGC interest rates are the interest rates that would be used (as of the date of the distribution) by the PBGC for purposes of determining the present value of that benefit upon termination of an insufficient trusteed single employer plan. Except as otherwise provided by the Commissioner, the PBGC interest rates are determined by PBGC regulations. See subpart B of 29 CFR part 4044 for the applicable PBGC rates.

(ii) Time for determining interest rate. (A) Except as provided in paragraph (d)(9)(ii)(B) of this section, the PBGC interest rate or rates are determined on either the annuity starting date or the first day of the plan year that contains the annuity starting date. The plan must provide which date is applicable.

(B) The plan may provide for the use of any other time for determining the PBGC interest rate or rates provided that such time is not more than 120 days before the annuity starting date if such time is determined in a consistent manner and is applied uniformly to all participants.

(C) The Commissioner may, in revenue rulings, notices or other guidance published in the Internal Revenue Bulletin (see § 601.601(d)(2)(ii)(b), prescribe other times for determining the PBGC interest rate or rates.

(iii) No applicable mortality table. In the case of a distribution to which this paragraph (d)(9) applies, the rules of this paragraph (d) are applied without regard to the applicable mortality table described in paragraph (d)(2) of this section.

*(10) Relationship with section 411(d)(6).* (i) In general. A plan amendment that changes the interest rate, the time for determining the interest rate, or the mortality assumptions used for the purposes described in paragraph (d)(1) of this section is subject to section 411(d)(6). But see § 1.411(d)-4, Q&A-2(b)(2)(v) (regarding plan amendments relating to involuntary distributions). In addition, a plan amendment that changes the interest rate or the mortality assumptions used for the purposes described in paragraph (d)(1) of this section merely to eliminate use of the interest rate described in paragraph (d)(3) or paragraph (d)(9) of this section, or the applicable mortality table, with respect to a distribution form described in paragraph (d)(6) of this section, for distributions with annuity starting dates occurring after a specified date that is after the amendment is adopted, does not violate the requirements of section 411(d)(6) if the amendment is adopted on or before the last day of the last plan year ending before January 1, 2000.

(ii) Section 411(d)(6) relief for change in time for determining interest rate. Notwithstanding the general rule of paragraph (d)(10)(i) of this section, if a plan amendment changes the time for determining the applicable interest rate (including an indirect change as a result of a change in plan year), the amendment will not be treated as reducing accrued benefits in violation of section 411(d)(6) merely on account of this change if the conditions of this paragraph (d)(10)(ii) are satisfied. If the plan amendment is effective on or after the adoption date, any distribution for which the annuity starting date occurs in the one-year period commencing at the time the amendment is effective must be determined using the interest rate provided under the plan determined at either the date for determining the interest rate before the amendment or the date for determining the interest rate after the amendment, whichever results in the larger distribution. If the plan amendment is adopted retroactively (that is, the amendment is effective prior to the adoption date), the plan must use the interest rate determination date resulting in the larger distribution for the period beginning with the effective date and ending one year after the adoption date.

(iii) Section 411(d)(6) relief for plan amendments pursuant to changes to section 417 made by RPA '94 providing for statutory interest rate determination date. Notwithstanding the general rule of paragraph (d)(10)(i) of this section, except as provided in paragraph (d)(10)(vi)(B) of this section, a participant's accrued benefit is not considered to be reduced in violation of section 411(d)(6) merely because of a plan amendment that changes any interest rate or mortality assumption used to calculate the present value of a participant's benefit under the plan, if the following conditions are satisfied—

(A) The amendment replaces the PBGC interest rate (or an interest rate or rates based on the PBGC interest rate) as the interest rate used under the plan in determining the present value of a participant's benefit under this paragraph (d); and

(B) After the amendment is effective, the present value of a participant's benefit under the plan cannot be less than the amount calculated using the applicable mortality table and the applicable interest rate for the first full calendar month preceding the calendar month that contains the annuity starting date.

(iv) Section 411(d)(6) relief for plan amendments pursuant to changes to section 417 made by RPA '94 providing for prior determination date or up to two months earlier. Notwithstanding the general rule of paragraph (d)(10)(i) of this section, except as provided in paragraph (d)(10)(vi)(B) of this section, a participant's accrued benefit is not considered to be reduced in violation of section 411(d)(6) merely because of a plan amendment that changes any interest rate or mortality assumption used to calculate the present value of a participant's benefit under the plan, if the following conditions are satisfied—

(A) The amendment replaces the PBGC interest rate (or an interest rate or rates based on the PBGC interest rate) as the interest rate used under the plan in determining the present value of a participant's benefit under this paragraph (d); and

(B) After the amendment is effective, the present value of a participant's benefit under the plan cannot be less than the amount calculated using the applicable mortality table and the applicable interest rate, but only if the applicable interest rate is the annual interest rate on 30-year Treasury securities for the calendar month that contains the date as of which the PBGC interest rate (or an interest rate or rates based on the PBGC interest rate) was determined immediately before the amendment, or for one of the two calendar months immediately preceding such month.

(v) Section 411(d)(6) relief for plan amendments pursuant to changes to section 417 made by RPA '94 providing for other interest rate determination date. Notwithstanding the general rule of paragraph (d)(10)(i) of this section, except as provided in paragraph (d)(10)(vi)(B) of this section, a participant's accrued benefit is not considered to be reduced in violation of section 411(d)(6) merely because of a plan amendment that changes any interest rate or mortality assumption used to calculate the present value of a participant's benefit under the plan, if the following conditions are satisfied—

(A) The amendment replaces the PBGC interest rate (or an interest rate or rates based on the PBGC interest rate) as the interest rate used under the plan in determining the present value of a participant's benefit under this paragraph (d);

(B) After the amendment is effective, the present value of a participant's benefit under the plan cannot be less than the amount calculated using the applicable mortality table and the applicable interest rate; and

(C) The plan amendment satisfies either the condition of paragraph (d)(10)(ii) of this section (determined using the interest rate provided under the terms of the plan after the effective date of the amendment) or the special early transition interest rate rule of paragraph (d)(10)(vi)(C) of this section.

(vi) Special rules. (A) Provision of temporary additional benefits. A plan amendment described in paragraph (d)(10)(iii), (iv), or (v) of this section is not considered to reduce a participant's accrued benefit in violation of section 411(d)(6) even if the plan amendment provides for temporary additional benefits to accommodate a more gradual transition from the plan's old interest rate to the new rules.

(B) Replacement of non-PBGC interest rate. The section 411(d)(6) relief provided in paragraphs (d)(10)(iii) through (v) of this section does not apply to a plan amendment that replaces an interest rate other than the PBGC interest rate (or an interest rate or rates based on the PBGC interest rate) as an interest rate used under the plan in determining the present value of a participant's benefit under this paragraph (d). Thus, the accrued benefit determined using that interest rate and the associated mortality table is protected under section 411(d)(6). For purposes of this paragraph (d), an interest rate is based on the PBGC interest rate if the interest rate is defined as a specified percentage of the PBGC interest rate, the PBGC interest rate minus a specified number of basis points, or an average of such interest rates over a specified period.

(C) Special early transition interest rate rule for paragraph (d)(10)(v). A plan amendment satisfies the special rule of this paragraph (d)(10)(vi)(C) if any distribution for which the annuity starting date occurs in the one-year period commencing at the time the plan amendment is effective is determined using whichever of the following two interest rates results in the larger distribution—

(1) The interest rate as provided under the terms of the plan after the effective date of the amendment, but determined at a date that is either one month or two months (as specified in the plan) before the date for determining the interest rate used under the terms of the plan before the amendment; or

(2) The interest rate as provided under the terms of the plan after the effective date of the amendment, determined at

the date for determining the interest rate after the amendment.

(vii) Examples. The provisions of this paragraph (d)(10) are illustrated by the following examples:

*Example (1).* On December 31, 1994, Plan A provided that all single-sum distributions were to be calculated using the UP-1984 Mortality Table and 100% of the PBGC interest rate for the date of distribution. On January 4, 1995, and effective on February 1, 1995, Plan A was amended to provide that all single-sum distributions are calculated using the applicable mortality table and the annual interest rate on 30-year Treasury securities for the first full calendar month preceding the calendar month that contains the annuity starting date. Pursuant to paragraph (d)(10)(iii) of this section, this amendment of Plan A is not considered to reduce the accrued benefit of any participant in violation of section 411(d)(6).

*Example (2).* On December 31, 1994, Plan B provided that all single-sum distributions were to be calculated using the UP-1984 Mortality Table and an interest rate equal to the lesser of 100% of the PBGC interest rate for the date of distribution, or 6%. On January 4, 1995, and effective on February 1, 1995, Plan B was amended to provide that all single-sum distributions are calculated using the applicable mortality table and the annual interest rate on 30-year Treasury securities for the second full calendar month preceding the calendar month that contains the annuity starting date. Pursuant to paragraph (d)(10)(iv) of this section, this amendment of Plan B is not considered to reduce the accrued benefit of any participant in violation of section 411(d)(6) merely because of the replacement of the PBGC interest rate. However, under paragraph (d)(10)(vi)(B) of this section, the section 411(d)(6) relief provided in paragraphs (d)(10)(iii) through (v) of this section does not apply to a plan amendment that replaces an interest rate other than the PBGC interest rate (or a rate based on the PBGC interest rate). Therefore, pursuant to paragraph (d)(10)(vi)(B) of this section, to satisfy the requirements of section 411(d)(6), the plan must provide that the single-sum distribution payable to any participant must be no less than the single-sum distribution calculated using the UP-1984 Mortality Table and an interest rate of 6%, based on the participant's benefits under the plan accrued through January 31, 1995, and based on the participant's age at the annuity starting date.

*Example (3).* On December 31, 1994, Plan C, a calendar year plan, provided that all single sum distributions were to be calculated using the UP-1984 Mortality Table and an interest rate equal to the PBGC interest rate for January 1 of the plan year. On March 1, 1995, and effective on July 1, 1995, Plan C was amended to provide that all single-sum distributions are calculated using the applicable mortality table and the annual interest rate on 30-year Treasury securities for August of the year before the plan year that contains the annuity starting date. The plan amendment provides that each distribution with an annuity starting date after June 30, 1995, and before July 1, 1996, is calculated using the 30-year Treasury rate for August of the year before the plan year that contains the annuity starting date, or the 30-year Treasury rate for January of the plan year that contains the annuity starting date, whichever produces the larger benefit. Pursuant to paragraph (d)(10)(v) of this section, the amendment of Plan C is not considered to have reduced the accrued benefit of any participant in violation of section 411(d)(6).

*Example (4).* (a) Employer X maintains Plan D, a calendar year plan. As of December 7, 1994, Plan D provided for single-sum distributions to be calculated using the PBGC interest rate as of the annuity starting date for distributions not greater than $25,000, and 120% of that interest rate (but not an interest rate producing a present value less than $25,000) for distributions over $25,000. Employer X wishes to delay the effective date of the RPA '94 rules for a year, and to provide for an extended transition from the use of the PBGC interest rate to the new applicable interest rate under section 417(e)(3). On December 1, 1995, and effective on January 1, 1996, Employer X amends Plan D to provide that single-sum distributions are determined as the sum of—

(i) The single-sum distribution calculated based on the applicable mortality table and the annual interest rate on 30-year Treasury securities for the first full calendar month preceding the calendar month that contains the annuity starting date; and

(ii) A transition amount.

(b) The amendment provides that the transition amount for distributions in the years 1996-99 is a transition percentage of the excess, if any, of the amount that the single-sum distribution would have been under the plan provisions in effect prior to this amendment over the amount of the single sum described in paragraph (a)(i) of this Example 4. The transition percentages are 80% for 1996, decreasing to 60% for 1997, 40% for 1998 and 20% for 1999. The amendment also provides that the transition amount is zero for plan years beginning on or after the year 2000. Pursuant to paragraphs (d)(10)(iii) and (vi)(A) of this section, the amendment of Plan D is not considered to have reduced the accrued benefit of any participant in violation of section 411(d)(6).

*Example (5).* On December 31, 1994, Plan E, a calendar year plan, provided that all single sum distributions were to be calculated using the UP-1984 Mortality Table and an interest rate equal to the PBGC interest rate for January 1 of the plan year. On March 1, 1995, and effective on July 1, 1995, Plan E was amended to provide that all single-sum distributions are calculated using the applicable mortality table and the annual interest rate on 30-year Treasury securities for August of the year before the plan year that contains the annuity starting date. The plan amendment provides that each distribution with an annuity starting date after June 30, 1995, and before July 1, 1996, is calculated using the 30-year Treasury rate for August of the year before the plan year that contains the annuity starting date, or the 30-year Treasury rate for November of the plan year preceding the plan year that contains the annuity starting date, whichever produces the larger benefit. Pursuant to paragraphs (d)(10)(v) and (vi)(C) of this section, the amendment of Plan E is not considered to have reduced the accrued benefit of any participant in violation of section 411(d)(6).

**(e) Special rules for annuity contracts.** *(1) General rule.* Any annuity contract purchased by a plan subject to section 401(a)(11) and distributed to or owned by a participant must provide that benefits under the contract are provided in accordance with the applicable consent, present value, and other requirements of sections 401(a)(11) and 417 applicable to the plan.

**(f) Effective dates.** *(1) Annuity contracts.* (i) Paragraph (e) of this section does not apply to contracts distributed to or owned by a participant prior to September 17, 1985, unless additional contributions are made under the plan by the employer with respect to such contracts.

(ii) In the case of a contract owned by the employer or distributed to or owned by a participant prior to the first plan year beginning after December 31, 1988, paragraph (e) of this section shall be satisfied if the annuity contracts described therein satisfy the requirements in §§ 1.401(a)-11T and 1.417(e)-1T. The preceding sentence shall not apply if additional contributions are made under the plan by the employer with respect to such contracts on or after the beginning of the first plan year beginning after December 31, 1988.

*(2) Interest rates.* (i) A plan that uses the PBGC immediate interest rate as required by § 1.417(e)-1T(e) for distributions commencing in plan years beginning before January 1, 1987, shall be deemed to satisfy paragraph (d) of this section for such years.

(ii) For a special exception to the requirements of section 411(d)(6) for certain plan amendments that incorporate applicable interest rates, see section 1139(d)(2) of the Tax Reform Act of 1986.

*(3) Other effective dates and transitional rules.* (i) Except as otherwise provided, a plan will be treated as satisfying sections 401(a)(11) and 417 for plan years beginning before the first plan year that the requirements of section 410(b) as amended by TRA 86 apply to such plan, if the plan satisfied the requirements in §§ 1.401(a)-11T and 1.417(e)-1T.

(ii) See § 1.401(a)-20 for other effective dates and transitional rules that apply to plans subject to sections 401(a)(11) and 417.

T.D. 8219, 8/19/88, amend T.D. 8591, 4/4/95, T.D. 8620, 9/15/95, T.D. 8768, 4/3/98, T.D. 8794, 12/18/98, T.D. 8796, 12/17/98, T.D. 8891, 7/18/2000, T.D. 9076, 7/15/2003, T.D. 9099, 12/16/2003.

PAR. 2. For each entry listed in the "Location" column, remove the language in the "Remove" column and add the language in the "Add" column in its place.

PAR. 2. For each entry listed in the "Location" column, remove the language in the "Remove" column and add the language in the "Add" column in its place.

PAR. 2. For each entry listed in the "Location" column, remove the language in the "Remove" column and add the language in the "Add" column in its place.

PAR. 2. For each entry listed in the "Location" column, remove the language in the "Remove" column and add the language in the "Add" column in its place.

PAR. 2. For each entry listed in the "Location" column, remove the language in the "Remove" column and add the language in the "Add" column in its place.

**Proposed § 1.417(e)-1** [*For Preamble, see ¶ 153,065*]

| Location | Remove | Add |
|---|---|---|
| 1.401(a)-13(g)(4)(ii), first sentence | 90 days | 180 days. |
| 1.401(a)-20, A-4, third sentence | 90 days | 180 days. |
| 1.401(a)-20, A-10(a), fifth and sixth sentences. | 90 days | 180 days. |
| 1.401(a)-20, A-16, sixth sentence. | 90 days | 180 days. |
| 1.401(a)-20, A-24(a)(1), fifth sentence. | 90 days | 180 days. |
| 1.402(f)-1, A-2(a), first sentence. | 90 days | 180 days. |
| 1.411(a)-11(c)(2)(ii) | 90 days | 180 days. |
| 1.411(a)-11(c)(2)(iii)(A), first sentence. | 90 days | 180 days. |
| 1.417(e)-1(b)(3)(i) | 90 days | 180 days. |
| 1.417(e)-1(b)(3)(ii), first sentence. | 90 days | 180 days. |
| 1.417(e)-1(b)(3)(iii) | 90 days | 180 days. |
| 1.417(e)-1(b)(3)(vi), second sentence. | 90 days | 180 days. |
| 1.417(e)-1(b)(3)(vii) | 90 days | 180 days. |
| 1.417(e)-1(b)(3)(vii) | 90-day | 180-day. |

### § 1.417(e)-1T Restrictions and valuations of distributions from plans subject to sections 401(a)(11) and 417 (temporary).

• ***Caution:*** Under Code Sec. 7805, temporary regulations expire within three years of the date of issuance. This temporary regulation was issued on 4/4/95.

***Caution:*** The Treasury has not yet amended Reg § 1.417(e)-1T to reflect changes made by P.L. 104-188.

**(a) [Reserved].**

**(b) Consent, etc. requirements.** *(1) General rule.* [Reserved]

*(2) Consent.* [Reserved]

**(c) [Reserved]**

**(d)** For rules regarding the present value of a participant's accrued benefit and related matters, see § 1.417(e)-1(d).

T.D. 8591, 4/4/95, amend T.D. 8620, 9/15/95, T.D. 8768, 4/3/98, T.D. 8796, 12/17/98.

### § 1.419-1T Treatment of welfare benefit funds (temporary).

Q-1. What does section 419 of the Internal Revenue Code provide?

A-1. Section 419 prescribes limitations upon deductions for contributions paid or accrued with respect to a welfare benefit fund. Under section 419(a) and (b), an employer's contributions to a welfare benefit fund are not deductible under section 162 (relating to trade or business expenses) or section 212 (relating to expenses for production of income) but, if the requirements of section 162 or 212 are otherwise met, are deductible under section 419 for the taxable year of the employer in which paid to the extent of the welfare benefit fund's qualified cost (within the meaning of section 419(c)(1)) for the taxable year of the fund that relates to such taxable year of the employer. Under section 419(g), section 419 and this section shall also apply to the deduction by a taxpayer of contributions with respect to a fund that would be a welfare benefit fund but for the fact that there is no employer-employee relationship between the person providing the services and the person for whom the services are provided. Contributions paid to a welfare benefit fund after section 419 becomes effective with respect to such contributions are deemed to relate, first, to amounts accrued and deducted (but not paid) by the employer with respect to such fund before section 419 becomes effective with respect to such contributions and thus shall not be treated as satisfying the payment requirement of section 419. See paragraph (b) of Q&A-5 for special deduction limits applicable to employer contributions to welfare benefit funds with excess reserves.

Q-2. When do the deduction rules of section 419, as enacted by the Tax Reform Act of 1984, become effective?

A-2. (a) Section 419 generally applies to contributions paid or accrued with respect to a welfare benefit fund after December 31, 1985, in taxable years of employers ending after that date. See Q&A-9 of this regulation for special rules relating to the deduction limit for the first taxable year of a fiscal year employer ending after December 31, 1985.

(b) In the case of a welfare benefit fund which is part of a plan maintained pursuant to one or more collective bargaining agreements (1) between employee representatives and one or more employers, and (2) that are in effect on July 1, 1985 (or ratified on or before such date), section 419 shall not apply to contributions paid or accrued in taxable years beginning before the termination of the last of the collective bargaining agreements pursuant to which the plan is maintained (determined without regard to any extension thereof agreed to after July 1, 1985). For purposes of the preceding sentence, any plan amendment made pursuant to a collective bargaining agreement relating to the plan which amends the plan solely to conform to any requirement added under section 511 of the Tax Reform Act of 1984 (i.e., requirements under sections 419, 419A, 512(a)(3)(E), and 4976) shall not be treated as a termination of such collective bargaining agreement. See § 1.419A-2T for special rules relating to the application of section 419 to collectively bargained welfare benefit funds.

(c) Notwithstanding paragraphs (a) and (b), section 419 applies to any contribution of a facility to a welfare benefit fund (or other contribution, such as cash, which is used to acquire, construct, or improve such a facility) after June 22, 1984, unless such facility is placed in service by the fund before January 1, 1987, and either (1) is acquired or improved by the fund (or contributed to the fund) pursuant to a binding contract in effect on June 22, 1984, and at all times thereafter, or (2) the construction of which was begun by or for the welfare benefit fund before June 22, 1984. See Q&A-11 of this regulation for special rules relating to the application of section 419 to the contribution of a facility to a welfare benefit fund (and to the contribution of other amounts, such as cash, used to acquire, construct, or improve such a facility) before section 419 generally becomes effective with respect to contributions to the fund.

Q-3. What is a "welfare benefit fund" under section 419?

A-3. (a) A "welfare benefit fund" is any fund which is part of a plan, or method or arrangement, of an employer and through which the employer provides welfare benefits to employees or their beneficiaries. For purposes of this section, the term "welfare benefit" includes any benefit other than a benefit with respect to which the employer's deduction is governed by section 83(h), section 404 (determined without regard to section 404(b)(2)), section 404A, or section 463.

(b) Under section 419(e)(3)(A) and (B), the term "fund" includes any organization described in section 501(c) (7), (9), (17) or (20), and any trust, corporation, or other organization not exempt from tax imposed by chapter 1, subtitle A, of the Internal Revenue Code. Thus, a taxable trust or taxable corporation that is maintained for the purpose of providing welfare benefits to an employer's employees is a "welfare benefit fund."

(c) Section 419(e)(3)(C) also provides that the term "fund" includes, to the extent provided in regulations, any account held for an employer by any person. Pending the issuance of further guidance, only the following accounts, and arrangements that effectively constitute accounts, as described below, are "funds" within section 419(e)(3)(C).

A retired lives reserve or a premium stabilization reserve maintained by an insurance company is a "fund," or part of a "fund," if it is maintained for a particular employer and the employer has the right to have any amount in the reserve applied against its future years' benefit costs or insurance premiums. Also, if an employer makes a payment to an insurance company under an "administrative services only" arrangement with respect to which the life insurance company maintains a separate account to provide benefits, then the arrangement would be considered to be a "fund." Finally, an insurance or premium arrangement between an employer and an insurance company is a "fund" if, under the arrangement, the employer has a right to a refund, credit, or additional benefits (including upon termination of the arrangement) based on the benefit or claims experience, administrative cost experience, or investment experience attributable to such employer. However, an arrangement with an insurance company is not a "fund" under the previous sentence merely because the employer's premium for a renewal year reflects the employer's own experience for an earlier year if the arrangement is both cancellable by the insurance company and cancellable by the employer as of the end of any policy year and, upon cancellation by either of the parties, neither of the parties can receive a refund or additional amounts or benefits and neither of the parties can incur a residual liability beyond the end of the policy year (other than, in the case of the insurer, to provide benefits with respect to claims incurred before cancellation). The determination whether either of the parties can receive a refund or additional amounts or benefits or can incur a residual liability upon cancellation of an arrangement will be made by examining both the contractual rights and obligations of the parties under the arrangement and the actual practice of the insurance company (and other insurance companies) with respect to other employers upon cancellation of similar arrangements. Similarly, a disability income policy does not constitute a "fund" under the preceding provisions merely because, under the policy, an employer pays an annual premium so that employees who became disabled in such year may receive benefit payments for the duration of the disability.

Q-4. For purposes of determining the section 419 limit on the employer's deduction for contributions to the fund for a taxable year of the employer, which taxable year of the welfare benefit fund is related to the taxable year of the employer?

A-4. The amount of an employer's deduction for contributions to a welfare benefit fund for a taxable year of the employer is limited to the "qualified cost" of the welfare benefit fund for the taxable year of the fund that is related to such taxable year of the employer. The taxable year of the welfare benefit fund that ends with or within the taxable year of the employer is the taxable year of the fund that is related to the taxable year of the employer. Thus, for example, if an employer has a calendar taxable year and it makes contributions to a fund having a taxable year ending June 30, the "qualified cost" of the fund for the taxable year of the fund ending on June 30, 1986, applies to limit the employer's deduction for contributions to the fund in the employer's 1986 taxable year. In the case of employer contributions paid directly to an account or arrangement with an insurance company that is treated as a welfare benefit fund for the purposes of section 419, the policy year will be treated as the taxable year of the fund. See Q&A-7 of this regulation for special section 419 rules relating to the coordination of taxable years for the taxable year of the employer in which a welfare benefit fund is established and for the next following taxable year of the employer.

Q-5. What is the "qualified cost" of a welfare benefit fund for a taxable year under section 419?

A-5. (a) Under section 419(c), the "qualified cost" of a welfare benefit fund for a taxable year of the fund is the sum of: (1) The "qualified direct cost" of such fund for such taxable year of the fund, and (2) the amount that may be added to the qualified asset account for such taxable year of the fund to the extent that such addition does not result in a total amount of such account as of the end of such taxable year of the fund that exceeds the applicable account limit under section 419A(c). However, in calculating the qualified cost of a welfare benefit fund for a taxable year of the fund, this sum is reduced by the fund's "after-tax income" (as defined in section 419(c)(4)) for such taxable year of the fund. Also, the qualified cost of a welfare benefit fund is reduced further under the provisions of paragraph (b) of this Q&A.

(b)(1) Pursuant to section 419A(i), notwithstanding section 419 and § 1.419-1T, contributions to a welfare benefit fund during any taxable year of the employer beginning after December 31, 1985, shall not be deductible for such taxable year to the extent that such contributions result in the total amount in the fund as of the end of the last taxable year of the fund ending with or within such taxable year of the employer exceeding the account limit applicable to such taxable year of the fund (as adjusted under section 419A(f)(7)). Solely for purposes of this subparagraph, (i) contributions paid to a welfare benefit fund during the taxable year of the employer but after the end of the last taxable year of the fund that relates to such taxable year of the employer, and (ii) contributions accrued with respect to a welfare benefit fund during the taxable year of the employer or during any prior taxable year of the employer (but not actually paid to such fund on or before the end of a taxable year of the employer) and deducted by the employer for such or any prior taxable year of the employer, shall be treated as an amount in the fund as of the end of the last taxable year of the fund that relates to the taxable year of the employer. Contributions that are not deductible under this subparagraph are in excess of the qualified cost of the welfare benefit fund for the taxable year of the fund that relates to the taxable year of the employer and thus are treated as contributed to the fund on the first day of the employer's next taxable year.

(2) Paragraph (b)(1) of this section shall not apply to contributions with respect to a collectively bargained welfare benefit fund within the meaning of § 1.419A-2T. In addition, paragraph (b)(1) of this section shall not apply to any taxable year of an employer beginning after the end of the earlier of the following taxable years: (i) the first taxable year of the employer beginning after December 31, 1985, for which the employer's deduction limit under section 419 (after the application of paragraph (b)(1) of this section) is at least equal to the qualified direct cost of the fund for the taxable year (or years) of the fund that relates to such first taxable year of the employer, or (ii) the first taxable year of the employer beginning after December 31, 1985, with or within which ends the first taxable year of the fund with respect to which the total amount in the fund as of the end of such taxable year of the fund does not exceed the account limit for such taxable year of the fund (as adjusted under section 419A(f)(7)).

(3) For example, assume an employer with a taxable year ending June 30 and a welfare benefit fund with a taxable year ending January 31. During its taxable year ending June 30, 1987, the employer contributes $250,000 to the fund, and during the remaining portion of its taxable year ending June 30, 1987, the employer contributes $200,000. The qualified direct cost of the fund for its taxable year ending January 31, 1987, is $500,000, the account limit applicable to such taxable year (after the adjustment under section 419A(f)(7)) is $750,000, and the total amount in the fund as of January 31, 1987, is $800,000. Before the application of this paragraph, the employer may deduct the entire $450,000 contribution for its taxable year ending June 30, 1987. However, under this paragraph, the excess of (i) the sum of the total amount in the fund as of January 31, 1987 ($800,000), and employer contributions to the fund after January 31, 1987, and on or before June 30, 1987 ($200,000), over (ii) the account limit applicable to the fund for its taxable year ending January 31, 1987 ($750,000), is $250,000. Thus, under this paragraph, only $200,000 of the $450,000 contribution the employer made during its taxable year ending June 30, 1987, is deductible for such taxable year. If the excess were $450,000 or greater, no portion of the $450,000 contribution would be deductible by the employer for its taxable year ending June 30, 1987. Such nondeductible contributions are in excess of the fund's qualified cost for the taxable year related to the employer's taxable year and thus are deemed to be contributed on the first day of the employer's next taxable year.

(c) See Q&A-7 of this regulation for special rules relating to the calculation of the qualified cost of a welfare benefit fund for an Initial Fund Year and an Overlap Fund Year (as defined in Q&A-7). See Q&A-11 of this regulation for special rules relating to the application of section 419 to the contribution to a welfare benefit fund of a facility (and to the contribution of other amounts, such as cash, used to acquire, construct, or improve a facility) before section 419 generally becomes effective with respect to contributions to the fund. See § 1.419A-2T for special rules relating to certain collectively bargained welfare benefit funds.

Q-6. What is the "qualified direct cost" of a welfare benefit fund under section 419(c)(3)?

A-6. (a) Under section 419(c)(3), the "qualified direct cost" of a welfare benefit fund for any taxable year of the fund is the aggregate amount which would have been allowable as a deduction to the employer for benefits provided by such fund during such year (including insurance coverage for such year) if (1) such benefits were provided directly by the employer and (2) the employer used the cash receipts and disbursements method of accounting and had the same taxable year as the fund. In this regard, a benefit is treated as provided when such benefit would be includible in the gross income of the employee if provided directly by the employer (or would be so includible but for a provision of chapter 1, subtitle A, of the Internal Revenue Code excluding it from gross income). Thus, for example, if a calendar year welfare benefit fund pays an insurance company in July 1986 the full premium for coverage of its current employees under a term health insurance policy for the twelve month period ending June 30, 1987, the insurance coverage will be treated as provided by the fund over such twelve month period. Accordingly, only the portion of the premium for coverage during 1986 will be treated as a "qualified direct cost" of the fund for 1986; the remaining portion of the premium will be treated as a "qualified direct cost" of the fund for 1987. The "qualified direct cost" for a taxable year of the fund includes the administrative expenses incurred by the welfare benefit fund in delivering the benefits for such year.

(b) If, in a taxable year of a welfare benefit fund, the fund holds an asset with a useful life extending substantially beyond the end of the taxable year (e.g., buildings, vehicles, tangible assets, and licenses) and, for such taxable year of the fund, the asset is used in the provision of welfare benefits to employees, the "qualified direct cost" of the fund for such taxable year of the fund includes the amount that would have been allowable to the employer as a deduction under the applicable Code provisions (e.g., sections 168 and 179) with respect to the portion of the asset used in the provision of welfare benefits for such year if the employer had acquired and placed in service the asset at the same time the fund received and placed in service the asset, and the employer had the same taxable year as the fund. This rule applies regardless of whether the fund received the asset through a contribution of the asset by the employer or through an acquisition or the construction by the fund of the asset. For example, assume that in 1986 a calendar year employer contributes recovery property under section 168(c) to a welfare benefit fund with a calendar taxable year to be used in the provision of welfare benefits. The employer will be treated as having sold the property in such year and thus will recognize gain to the extent that the fair market value of the property exceeds the employer's adjusted basis in the property. In this regard, see section 1239(d). Also, the employer will be treated as having made a contribution to the fund in such year equal to the fair market value of the property. Finally, the qualified direct cost of the welfare benefit fund for 1986 will include the amount that the employer could have deducted in 1986 with respect to the portion of the property used in the provision of welfare benefits if the employer had acquired the property in 1986 and had placed the property in service when the fund actually placed the property in service. Similarly, for example, assume that in 1986 a welfare benefit fund purchases and places in service a facility to be used in the provision of welfare benefits. The qualified direct cost of the fund for 1986 will include the amount that the employer could have deducted with respect to such facility if the employer had purchased and placed in service the facility at the same time that the fund purchased and placed in service the facility.

(c) The qualified direct cost of a welfare benefit fund does not include expenditures by the fund that would not have been deductible if they had been made directly by the employer. For example, a fund's purchase of land in a year for an employee recreational facility will not be treated as a qualified direct cost because, if made directly by the employer, the purchase would not have been deductible under section 263. See also sections 264 and 274.

(d) Notwithstanding the preceding paragraphs, the qualified direct cost of a welfare benefit fund with respect to that portion of a child care facility used in the provision of welfare benefits for a year will include the amount that would have been allowable to the employer as a deduction for the year under a straight-line depreciation schedule for a period of 60 months beginning with the month in which the facility is placed in service under rules similar to those provided for section 188 property under § 1.188-1(a). For purposes of this section, a "child care facility" is tangible property of a character subject to depreciation that is located in the United States and specifically used as an integral part of a "qualified child care center facility" within the meaning of § 1.188-1(d)(4).

(e) See Q&A-7 of this regulation for special section 419 rules relating to the calculation of the qualified direct cost of a welfare benefit fund for an Initial Fund Year and an Overlap Fund Year (as defined in Q&A-7). See Q&A-11 of this regulation for special rules relating to the contribution to a welfare benefit fund of a facility (and to the contribution of other amounts, such as cash, used to acquire, construct, or improve a facility) before section 419 generally becomes effective with respect to contributions to the fund.

Q-7. What special rules apply for purposes of determining the section 419 limit on the employer's deduction for contributions to a welfare benefit fund for the taxable year of the employer in which the fund is established and for the next following taxable year of the employer?

A-7. (a) If the taxable year of a welfare benefit fund is the same as the taxable year of the employer, there are no special rules that apply for purposes of determining the section 419 limit on an employer's deduction for contributions to the fund for either the taxable year of the employer in which the fund is established or the next following taxable year of the employer. However, if the taxable year of a welfare benefit fund is different from the taxable year of the employer, the general section 419 rules are modified by the special rules set forth below for purposes of determining the section 419 deduction limit for the taxable year of the employer in which a fund is established and for the next following taxable year of the employer.

(b) If a welfare benefit fund is established after December 31, 1985, during a taxable year of an employer and either (i) the first taxable year of the fund ends after the close of such taxable year of the employer, or (ii) the first taxable year of the fund is six months or less and ends before the close of such taxable year of the employer and the second taxable year of the fund begins before and ends after the close of such taxable year of the employer, the taxable year of the fund that contains the closing day of such taxable year of the employer will be treated as an "Overlap Fund Year." For purposes of determining the limit on the employer's deduction for contributions to a welfare benefit fund for the taxable year of the employer in which the fund was established, the period between the beginning of the fund's Overlap Fund Year and the end of the employer's taxable year in which the Overlap Fund Year began will be treated as a taxable year of the fund ("Initial Fund Year").

(c) The qualified cost of a welfare benefit fund for its Initial Fund Year will be equal to the qualified direct cost of the fund for such Initial Fund Year. The qualified cost of a fund for its Overlap Fund Year will be determined under the general rules of Q&A-5 of this regulation and section 419(c), with the exception that such qualified cost will be reduced by the employer contributions made during the Initial Fund Year and deductible by the employer for the taxable year of the employer in which the Overlap Fund Year of the fund begins.

(d) Assume that an employer with a calendar taxable year establishes on July 1, 1986, a welfare benefit fund with a taxable year ending on June 30. The fund's first taxable year from July 1, 1986, to June 30, 1987, is an Overlap Fund Year. The employer contributes $1,000 to the fund during its taxable year ending December 31, 1986 (i.e., during the period between July 1, 1986, and December 31, 1986, which is also the Initial Fund Year) and another $1,500 to the fund during its taxable year ending December 31, 1987. Assume further that the qualified direct cost of the fund for the Initial Fund Year is $900 and that the qualified cost for the Overlap Fund Year is $2,500 (prior to the reduction required by paragraph (c) of this Q&A). Under the special rules of paragraphs (b) and (c), the employer may deduct $900 for its taxable year ending on December 31, 1986, and $1,600 for its taxable year ending on December 31, 1987. If the qualified direct cost of the fund for the Initial Fund Year had been $1,050 and the qualified cost for the Overlap Fund Year had been $2,500 (prior to the reduction required by paragraph (c) of this Q&A), the employer's deduction for its taxable year ending December 31, 1986, would have been $1,000 and its deduction for its taxable year ending December 31, 1987, would have been $1,500.

(e) Assume that an employer with a calendar taxable year establishes on March 1, 1986, a welfare benefit fund with a taxable year ending June 30. Thus, the fund has a short first taxable year ending June 30, 1986, an Overlap Fund Year from July 1, 1986, until June 30, 1987, and an ongoing June 30 taxable year. The employer contributes $1,750 to the fund during the employer's taxable year ending December 31, 1986—$750 during the short first taxable year of the fund and $1,000 during the Initial Fund Year (i.e., the period between July 1, 1986, and December 31, 1986)—and $1,500 to the fund during its taxable year ending December 31, 1987. Assume that the qualified cost of the fund for the short first taxable year of the fund is $800, the qualified direct cost for the Initial Fund Year is $900, and the qualified cost for the Overlap Fund Year is $2,500 (prior to the reduction required by paragraph (c) of this Q&A). Under the special rules of paragraphs (b) and (c), the employer may deduct $1,700 for its taxable year ending December 31, 1986, and $1,550 for its taxable year ending December 31, 1987.

Q-8. How does section 419 treat an employer's contribution with respect to a welfare benefit fund in excess of the applicable deduction limit for a taxable year of the employer?

A-8. (a) If an employer makes contributions to a welfare benefit fund in a taxable year of the employer and such contributions (when combined with prior contributions that are deemed under the rule of this Q&A and section 419(d) to have been made in such taxable year) exceed the section 419 deduction limit for such taxable year of the employer, the excess amounts are deemed to be contributed to the fund on the first day of the next taxable year of the employer. Such deemed contributions are combined with amounts actually contributed by the employer to the fund during the next taxable year and may be deductible for such year, subject to the otherwise applicable section 419 deduction limit for such year.

(b) Contributions to a welfare benefit fund on or before December 31, 1985, that were not deductible by the employer for any taxable year of the employer ending on or before December 31, 1985, or for the first taxable year of the employer ending after December 31, 1985, as pre-1986 contributions (see Q&A-9 of this regulation) are deemed to be contributed to the fund on January 1, 1986, However, see Q&A-11 of this regulation for special rules relating to the contribution to a welfare benefit fund of amounts (such as cash) used to acquire, construct, or improve a facility before section 419 generally becomes effective with respect to contributions to the fund. Generally, such contributions (to the extent that they were made after June 22, 1984 and on or before December 31, 1985) are treated as nondeductible pre-1986 contributions and are deemed to be contributed in the form of a facility at the same time as when the facility is placed in service by the fund.

Q-9. How does an employer with a fiscal taxable year calculate its deduction limit for contributions with respect to a welfare benefit fund for the first taxable year of the employer ending after December 31, 1985?

A-9. (a) If the first taxable year of an employer ending after December 31, 1985 (or, if applicable under paragraph (b) of Q&A-2 of this section, the first taxable year of an employer beginning after termination of the last of the collective bargaining agreements pursuant to which the fund is maintained) is a fiscal year, the employer's deduction for such taxable year for contributions to a welfare benefit fund that is not a collectively bargained welfare benefit fund under § 1.419A-2T is limited to the greater of the following two amounts: (1) The contributions paid to the fund during such first taxable year up to the qualified cost of the welfare benefit fund for the taxable year of the fund that relates to such taxable year of the employer, and (2) the contributions paid to the fund during the 1985 portion of such first taxable year of the employer ("the pre-1986 contributions") to the extent that such pre-1986 contributions are deductible under the rules governing the deduction of such contributions before section 419 generally becomes effective (including the rules set forth in Q&A-10 of this regulation, modified for purposes of this Q&A-9 by substituting "December 31, 1986" for "December 31, 1985" in paragraph (c)). See Q&A-11 of this regulation for special rules relating to the contribution to a welfare benefit fund of a facility (and to the contribution of other amounts, such as cash, used to acquire, construct, or improve such a facility) before section 419 generally becomes effective with respect to contributions to such fund.

(b) For example, assume that an employer with a taxable year ending June 30, contributes to a welfare benefit fund with a taxable year ending January 31. This employer contributes $1,000 to the fund between July 1, 1985, and December 31, 1985, and an additional $500 to the fund between January 1, 1986, and June 30, 1986. Assume further that the qualified direct cost of the fund for the taxable year of the fund ending January 31, 1986, is $500 and that the qualified cost for such taxable year is $800. Under the deduction rule set forth above, the employer's deduction for its taxable year ending June 30, 1986, is the greater of two amounts: (1) The contributions made during such full taxable year ($1,500) up to the qualified cost of the fund with respect to such taxable year ($800), and (2) the pre-1986 contributions ($1,000) to the extent that such pre-1986 contributions are deductible under the pre-section 419 rules. In determining the extent to which the pre-1986 contributions are deductible under the pre-section 419 rules, the rules contained in Q&A-10 apply as though December 31, 1985, in paragraph (c) were December 31, 1986. Assuming that only $875 is deductible under the pre-section 419 rules, because $875 is greater than $800, this employer may deduct $875 for its first taxable year ending after December 31, 1985. This full $875 deduction for 1985 is deemed to consist entirely of pre-1986 contributions.

Q-10. How do the rules of sections 263, 446(b), 461(a), and 461(h) apply in determining whether contributions with respect to a welfare benefit fund are deductible for a taxable year?

A-10. (a) Both before and after the effective date of section 419 (see Q&A-2 of this regulation), an employer is allowed a deduction for taxable year for contributions paid or accrued with respect to a "welfare benefit fund" (as defined in Q&A-3 of this regulation and section 419(e)) only to the extent that such contributions satisfy the requirements of section 162 or 212. These requirements must be satisfied after the effective date of section 419 because 419 requires that (among other requirements) contributions to a welfare benefit fund satisfy the requirements of section 162 or 212.

(b) Except as provided in paragraphs (c) and (d), in determining the extent to which contributions paid or accrued with respect to welfare benefit fund satisfy the requirements of section 162 or 212 for a taxable year (both before and after section 419 generally becomes effective with respect to such contributions), the rules of sections 263, 446(b), 461(a) (including the rules that relate to the creation of an asset with a useful life extending substantially beyond the close of the taxable year), and 461(h) (to the extent that such section is effective with respect to such contributions) are are generally applicable.

(c) Notwithstanding paragraph (b), under the authority of section 7805(b), the rules of sections 263, 446(b), and 461(a) shall not be applied in determining the extent to which an employer's contribution with respect to a welfare benefit fund is deductible under section 162 or 212 with respect to any taxable year of the employer ending on or before December 31, 1985, to the extent that, for such taxable year, (1) the contribution was made pursuant to a bona fide collective bargaining agreement requiring fixed and determinable contributions to a collectively bargained welfare benefit fund (as defined in § 1.419A-2T), or (2) the contribution was not in excess of the amount deductible under the principles of Revenue Rulings 69-382, 1969-2 C.B. 28; 69-478, 1969-2 C.B. 29; and 73-599, 1973-2 C.B. 40, modified as appropriate for benefits for active employees.

(d) Notwithstanding paragraph (b), in determining the extent to which contributions paid or accrued with respect to a welfare benefit fund are deductible under section 419, the rules of sections 263, 446(b), and 461(a) will be treated as having been satisfied to the extent that such contributions satisfy the otherwise applicable rules of section 419. Thus, for example, contributions to a welfare benefit fund will not fail to be deductible under section 419 merely because they create an asset with a useful life extending substantially beyond the close of the taxable year if such contributions satisfy the otherwise applicable requirements of section 419.

(e) In determining the extent to which contributions with respect to a welfare benefit fund satisfy the requirements of section 461(h) for any taxable year for which section 461(h) is effective, pursuant to the authority under section 461(h)(2), economic performance occurs as contributions to the welfare benefit fund are made. Solely for purposes of section 461(h), in the case of an employer's taxable year ending on or after July 18, 1984, and on or before March 21, 1986, contributions made to the welfare benefit fund after the end of such taxable year and on or before March 21, 1986 shall be deemed to have been made on the last day of such taxable year.

Q-11. What special section 419 rules apply to the payment or accrual with respect to a welfare benefit fund of a facility (and the payment or accrual of other amounts, such as cash, used to acquire, construct, or improve such a facility)?

A-11. (a)(1) In the case of an employer's payment or accrual with respect to a welfare benefit fund after June 22, 1984, and on or before December 31, 1985 (or, if applicable under paragraph (b) of Q&A-2 of this regulation, before section 419 generally becomes effective with respect to contributions to such fund), of a facility, the rules of section 419, § 1.419-1T, and § 1.419A-2T generally apply to determine the extent to which such contribution is deductible by the employer for its taxable year of contribution. For this purpose, however, the facility is to be treated as the only contribution made to the fund and the qualified cost of the fund for the taxable year of the fund in which the facility was contributed is to be equal to the qualified direct cost directly attributable to the facility (as determined under Q&A-6 of this regulation). Also, for this purpose, the welfare benefit fund to which the facility was contributed may not be aggregated with any other fund. For purposes of this Q& A, "facility" means any tangible asset with a useful life extending substantially beyond the end of the taxable year (e.g., vehicles, buildings) and any intangible asset (e.g., licenses) related to a tangible asset, whether or not such asset is used in the provision of welfare benefits. See, however, paragraph (c) of Q&A-2 of this regulation for a binding contract exception.

(2) For example, assume that an employer and a welfare benefit fund each has a calendar taxable year and that, during 1985, the employer contributes to the fund $200,000 in cash and a facility with a fair market value of $100,000. Such facility is used in the provision of welfare benefits under the fund. The employer is treated as having sold the facility in such year and thus will recognize gain to the extent that the fair market value of the facility exceeds the employer's adjusted basis in the facility. In this regard, see section 1239(d). The extent to which the facility contribution is deductible by the employer for its 1985 taxable year is determined as though it were the only contribution made by the employer to the fund during such year and the qualified cost of the fund for the taxable year of the fund in which the contribution was made (i.e., the 1985 taxable year) were equal to the amount that would have been allowable to the employer as a deduction for such year under the applicable Code provisions with respect to the portion of the facility used in the provision of welfare benefits for such year if the employer had placed in service the facility at the time the fund placed in service the facility and if the employer had the same taxable year as the fund. If, under these assumptions, the employer would have been allowed a $10,000 deduction with respect to the facility for the 1985 taxable year, the fund's qualified cost for its 1985 taxable year would be only $10,000. Thus, only $10,000 of the $100,000 facility contribution would be deductible by the employer for its 1985 taxable year (i.e., the taxable year of the employer with or within which the applicable taxable year of the fund ends). However, in determining the extent to which the $200,000 in cash is deductible by the employer for its 1985 taxable year, the $100,000 facility is not to be disregarded. Thus, if under the applicable pre-section 419 rules the employer is allowed for 1985 a total deduction of only $175,000, the employer would be permitted a deduction for 1985 of $175,000 ($10,000 with respect to the facility and $165,000 of the cash contribution). The nondeductible portion of the cash contribution is to be treated as contributed to the fund on the first day of the next taxable year of the employer. If under the applicable pre-section 419 rules the employer were allowed a total deduction of $300,000 for 1985, the employer would be permitted a deduction for 1985 of

only $210,000 ($10,000 with respect to the facility and the full $200,000 cash contribution).

(3) For example, assume that an employer has a June 30 taxable year and maintains a welfare benefit fund with a taxable year ending January 31. During the 1985 portion of its taxable year ending June 30, 1986, the employer contributes $50,000 in cash and a facility with a fair market value of $100,000; and during the 1986 portion of such taxable year, the employer contributes another $75,000 in cash to the fund. The facility is used in the provision of welfare benefits under the fund. Under the rules of Q&A-9 of this regulation, the employer's deduction for its June 30, 1986, taxable year is limited to the greater of the following two amounts: (i) The contributions paid to the fund during such taxable year ($225,000) up to the qualified cost of the fund for the taxable year of the fund ending January 31, 1986, and (ii) the contributions paid to the fund during the 1985 portion of the employer's taxable year ending June 30, 1986 ("the pre-1986 contributions") ($150,000) to the extent that such pre-1986 contributions are deductible under the rules governing the deduction of such contributions before section 419 is generally effective with respect to the fund. For purposes of this rule, the contribution of the facility on or before December 31, 1985, is to be treated as a pre-1986 contribution and the rules of section 419 and this Q&A are to be treated as rules governing the deduction of such contribution before section 419 generally becomes effective with respect to the fund. Thus, in determining the extent to which the facility is deductible as a pre-1986 contribution under the rules before section 419 generally becomes effective, the facility is treated as the only contribution to the welfare benefit fund and the qualified cost of such fund for the taxable year of the fund in which the facility was contributed is the amount that would have been allowable to the employer as a deduction with respect to the portion of the facility used in the provision of welfare benefits if the employer had placed in service the facility at the same time that the fund placed in service the facility and the employer's taxable year ended on January 31, 1986.

(b)(1) The preceding rules shall also apply for purposes of determining when and the extent to which an employer may deduct contributions or other items and amounts after June 22, 1984 and on or before December 31, 1985 (or, if applicable under paragraph (b) of Q&A-2 of this regulation, before section 419 generally becomes effective with respect to contributions to the fund) that are not facilities (e.g., cash contributions) to a welfare benefit fund that are used by the fund to acquire, construct, or improve a facility. The most recent non-facility contributions made to a welfare benefit fund before the facility in question is placed in service by the fund (up to the fair market value of the facility at such time) are to be treated as used by the fund for the acquisition, construction, or improvement (as the case may be) of such facility. To the extent that contributions before such a facility is placed in service are not at least equal to the value of the facility at such time, contributions after such date (up to the value of the facility at the time it is placed in service) are treated as used for acquisition, construction, or improvement of the facility. Such non-facility contributions, to the extent that they were made after June 22, 1984, and on or before December 31, 1985 (or, if applicable under paragraph (b) of Q&A-2 of this regulation, before section 419 generally becomes effective with respect to contributions to the fund), are not deductible by the employer as non-facility contributions for any year. Instead, the employer is permitted a deduction with respect to such contributions only under the rules of this Q&A as though the employer had contributed a facility to the fund at the same time that the fund placed in service the facility in question and, at such time, the facility had a fair market value equal to the total of such non-facility contributions.

(2) For example, assume that an employer and a welfare benefit fund each has a calendar taxable year and during 1985 the fund acquired and placed in service a facility with a fair market value of $100,000 to be used in the provision of welfare benefits. Further, during July 1984 the employer contributed $150,000 in cash to the fund and, during the portion of 1985, before the facility was placed in service by the fund, the employer contributed another $75,000 in cash to the fund; during the remaining portion of 1985, the employer contributed $125,000 in cash. The facility is used in the provision of welfare benefits under the fund. Because $25,000 of the employer's 1984 contribution is treated under this rule as used for the acquisition of a facility, such $25,000 is not deductible by the employer for 1984. For purposes of determining the employer's deduction for 1985, the employer will be treated as having contributed $125,000 in cash and a facility with a fair market value of $100,000. The employer's deduction for its 1985 taxable year will be determined under the rules relating to the contribution of a facility after June 22, 1984, and on or before December 31, 1985.

(3) For example, assume that an employer and a welfare benefit fund each has a calendar taxable year and during 1986 the fund placed in service a facility with a fair market value of $100,000 to be used in the provision of welfare benefits. During 1985, the employer contributed $125,000 in cash to the fund. During the portion of 1986 before the facility was placed in service, the employer contributed $60,000 in cash, and during the remaining portion of 1986, the employer contributed another $75,000 in cash. The facility is used in the provision of welfare benefits under the fund. Because $40,000 of its 1985 cash contribution is treated under this rule as used for the acquisition of the facility, such $40,000 is not deductible by the employer for 1985. For purposes of determining the employer's deduction for 1986, the employer will be treated as though it had contributed a $40,000 facility to the fund at the time the fund placed the facility in service.

(c) For purposes of calculating the "existing excess reserve amount" under Q&A-1 of § 1.419A-1T and the "existing reserves for post-retirement medical or life insurance benefits" under Q&A-4 of § 1.512(a)-5T (but not the exempt function income under Q&A-3 of § 1.512(a)-5T), the amount set aside as of any applicable date is to be reduced to the extent that contributions originally included in such amount are subsequently treated under this Q&A as used for the acquisition, construction, or improvement of an asset excluded from the calculation of the total amount set aside under paragraph (b) of § 1.512(a)-5T (or would be so treated under this Q&A if it applied to such asset). The reduction required under this paragraph applies for purposes of calculating the "existing excess reserve amount" and the "existing reserves for post-retirement medical or life insurance benefits" for all taxable years of the welfare benefit fund.

---

T.D. 8073, 1/29/86.

---

**§ 1.419A-1T Qualified asset account limitation of additions to account (temporary).**

Q-1. What does the transition rule under section 419A(f)(7) provide?

A-1. Section 419A(f)(7) provides that, in the case of a welfare benefit fund that was in existence on July 18, 1984, the account limit (as determined under section 419A(c)) for each of the first four taxable years of the fund that relate to taxable years of the employer ending after December 31, 1985 (or, if applicable under paragraph (b) of Q&A-2 of § 1.419-1T, taxable years of the employer beginning after the termination of the last of the collective bargaining agreements pursuant to which the plan is maintained) shall be increased by the following percentages of the "existing excess reserve amount":

| | Percent |
|---|---|
| First taxable year | 80 |
| Second taxable year | 60 |
| Third taxable year | 40 |
| Fourth taxable year | 20 |

For purposes of this section, the "existing excess reserve amount" for any taxable year of a fund is the excess of (a) the assets actually set aside for purposes described in section 419A(a) at the close of the first taxable year of the fund ending after July 18, 1984 (calculated in the manner set forth in Q&A-3 of § 1.512(a)-3T, and adjusted under paragraph (c) of Q&A-11 of § 1.419-1T), reduced by employer contributions to the fund before the close of such first taxable year to the extent that such contributions are not deductible for the taxable year of the employer with or within which such taxable year of the fund ends and for any prior taxable year of the employer, over (b) the account limit which would have applied to the taxable year of the fund for which the excess is being computed (without regard to this transition rule). A welfare benefit fund is treated as in existence on July 18, 1984, for purposes of this transition rule only if amounts were actually set aside in such fund on such date to provide welfare benefits enumerated under section 419A.

T.D. 8073, 1/29/86.

### § 1.419A-2T Qualified asset account limitation for collectively bargained funds (temporary).

Q-1. What account limits apply to welfare benefit funds that are maintained pursuant to a collective bargaining agreement?

A-1. Contributions to a welfare benefit fund maintained pursuant to one or more collective bargaining agreements and the reserves of such a fund generally are subject to the rules of sections 419, 419A, and 512. However, neither contributions to nor reserves of such a collectively bargained welfare benefit fund shall be treated as exceeding the otherwise applicable limits of section 419(b), 419A(b), or 512(a)(3)(E) until the earlier of: (i) The date on which the last of the collective bargaining agreements relating to the fund in effect on, or ratified on or before, the date of issuance of final regulations concerning such limits for collectively bargained welfare benefit funds terminates (determined without regard to any extension thereof agreed to after the date of issuance of such final regulations), or (ii) the date 3 years after the issuance of such final regulations.

Q-2. What is a welfare benefit fund maintained pursuant to a collective bargaining agreement for purposes of Q&A-1?

A-2. *(1)* For purposes of Q&A-1, a collectively bargained welfare benefit fund is a welfare benefit fund that is maintained pursuant to an agreement which the Secretary of Labor determines to be a collective bargaining agreement and which meets the requirements of the Secretary of the Treasury as set forth in paragraph 2 below.

(2) Notwithstanding a determination by the Secretary of Labor that an agreement is a collective bargaining agreement, a welfare benefit fund is considered to be maintained pursuant to a collective bargaining agreement only if the benefits provided through the fund were the subject of arms-length negotiations between employee representatives and one or more employers, and if such agreement between employee representatives and one or more employers satisfies section 7701(a)(46) of the Code. Moreover, the circumstances surrounding a collective bargaining agreement must evidence good faith bargaining between adverse parties over the welfare benefits to be provided through the fund. Finally, a welfare benefit fund is not considered to be maintained pursuant to a collective bargaining agreement unless at least 50 percent of the employees eligible to receive benefits under the fund are covered by the collective bargaining agreement.

(3) In the case of a collectively bargained welfare benefit fund, only the portion of the fund (as determined under allocation rules to be provided by the Commissioner) attributable to employees covered by a collective bargaining agreement, and from which benefits for such employees are provided, is considered to be maintained pursuant to a collective bargaining agreement.

(4) Notwithstanding the preceding paragraphs and pending the issuance of regulations setting account limits for collectively bargained welfare benefit funds, a welfare benefit fund will not be treated as a collectively bargained welfare benefit fund for purposes of Q&A-1 if and when, after July 1, 1985, the number of employees who are not covered by a collective bargaining agreement and are eligible to receive benefits under the fund increases by reason of an amendment, merger, or other action of the employer or the fund. In addition, pending the issuance of such regulations, for purposes of applying the 50 percent test of paragraph (2) to a welfare benefit fund that is not in existence on July 1, 1985, "90 percent" shall be substituted for "50 percent".

T.D. 8034, 7/1/85.

### § 1.419A(f)(6)-1 Exception for 10 or more employer plan.

**(a) Requirements.** *(1) In general.* Sections 419 and 419A do not apply in the case of a welfare benefit fund that is part of a 10 or more employer plan described in section 419A(f)(6). A plan is a 10 or more employer plan described in section 419A(f)(6) only if it is a single plan—

(i) To which more than one employer contributes;

(ii) To which no employer normally contributes more than 10 percent of the total contributions contributed under the plan by all employers;

(iii) That does not maintain an experience-rating arrangement with respect to any individual employer; and

(iv) That satisfies the requirements of paragraph (a)(2) of this section.

*(2) Compliance information.* A plan satisfies the requirements of this paragraph (a)(2) if the plan is maintained pursuant to a written document that requires the plan administrator to maintain records sufficient for the Commissioner or any participating employer to readily verify that the plan satisfies the requirements of section 419A(f)(6) and this section and that provides the Commissioner and each participating employer (or a person acting on the participating employer's

behalf) with the right, upon written request to the plan administrator, to inspect and copy all such records. See § 1.414(g)-1 for the definition of plan administrator.

*(3) Application of rules.* (i) In general. The requirements described in paragraph (a)(1) and (2) of this section must be satisfied both in form and in operation.

(ii) Arrangement is considered in its entirety. The determination of whether a plan is a 10 or more employer plan described in section 419A(f)(6) is based on the totality of the arrangement and all related facts and circumstances, including any related insurance contracts. Accordingly, all agreements and understandings (including promotional materials and policy illustrations) and the terms of any insurance contract will be taken into account in determining whether the requirements are satisfied in form and in operation.

**(b) Experience-rating arrangements.** *(1) General rule.* A plan maintains an experience-rating arrangement with respect to an individual employer and thus does not satisfy the requirement of paragraph (a)(1)(iii) of this section if, with respect to that employer, there is any period for which the relationship of contributions under the plan to the benefits or other amounts payable under the plan (the cost of coverage) is or can be expected to be based, in whole or in part, on the benefits experience or overall experience (or a proxy for either type of experience) of that employer or one or more employees of that employer. For purposes of this paragraph (b)(1), an employer's contributions include all contributions made by or on behalf of the employer or the employer's employees. See paragraph (d) of this section for the definitions of benefits experience, overall experience, and benefits or other amounts payable. The rules of this paragraph (b) apply under all circumstances, including employer withdrawals and plan terminations.

*(2) Adjustment of contributions.* An example of a plan that maintains an experience-rating arrangement with respect to an individual employer is a plan that entitles an employer to (or for which the employer can expect) a reduction in future contributions if that employer's overall experience is positive. Similarly, a plan maintains an experience-rating arrangement with respect to an individual employer where an employer can expect its future contributions to be increased if the employer's overall experience is negative. A plan also maintains an experience-rating arrangement with respect to an individual employer where an employer is entitled to receive (or can expect to receive) a rebate of all or a portion of its contributions if that employer's overall experience is positive or, conversely, where an employer is liable to make additional contributions if its overall experience is negative.

*(3) Adjustment of benefits.* An example of a plan that maintains an experience-rating arrangement with respect to an individual employer is a plan under which benefits for an employer's employees are (or can be expected to be) increased if that employer's overall experience is positive or, conversely, under which benefits are (or can be expected to be) decreased if that employer's overall experience is negative. A plan also maintains an experience-rating arrangement with respect to an individual employer if benefits for an employer's employees are limited by reference, directly or indirectly, to the overall experience of the employer (rather than having all the plan assets available to provide the benefits).

*(4) Special rules.* (i) Treatment of insurance contracts. (A) In general. For purposes of this section, insurance contracts under the arrangement will be treated as assets of the fund. Accordingly, the value of the insurance contracts (including non-guaranteed elements) is included in the value of the fund, and amounts paid between the fund and the insurance company are disregarded, except to the extent they generate gains or losses as described in paragraph (b)(4)(i)(C) of this section.

(B) Payments to and from an insurance company. Payments from a participating employer or its employees to an insurance company pursuant to insurance contracts under the arrangement will be treated as contributions made to the fund, and amounts paid under the arrangement from an insurance company will be treated as payments from the fund.

(C) Gains and losses from insurance contracts. As of any date, if the sum of the benefits paid by the insurer and the value of the insurance contract (including non-guaranteed elements) is greater than the cumulative premiums paid to the insurer, the excess is treated as a gain to the fund. As of any date, if the cumulative premiums paid to the insurer are greater than the sum of the benefits paid by the insurer and the value of the insurance contract (including non-guaranteed elements), the excess is treated as a loss to the fund.

(ii) Treatment of flexible contribution arrangements. Solely for purposes of determining the cost of coverage under a plan, if contributions for any period can vary with respect to a benefit package, the Commissioner may treat the employer as contributing the minimum amount that would maintain the coverage for that period.

(iii) Experience rating by group of employers or group of employees. A plan will not be treated as maintaining an experience-rating arrangement with respect to an individual employer merely because the cost of coverage under the plan with respect to the employer is based, in whole or in part, on the benefits experience or the overall experience (or a proxy for either type of experience) of a rating group, provided that no employer normally contributes more than 10 percent of all contributions with respect to that rating group. For this purpose, a rating group means a group of participating employers that includes the employer or a group of employees covered under the plan that includes one or more employees of the employer.

(iv) Family members, etc. For purposes of this section, contributions with respect to an employee include contributions with respect to any other person (e.g., a family member) who may be covered by reason of the employee's coverage under the plan and amounts provided with respect to an employee include amounts provided with respect to such a person.

(v) Leased employees. In the case of an employer that is the recipient of services performed by a leased employee described in section 414(n)(2) who participates in the plan, the leased employee is treated as an employee of the recipient and contributions made by the leasing organization attributable to service performed with the recipient are treated as made by the recipient.

**(c) Characteristics indicating a plan is not a 10 or more employer plan.** *(1) In general.* The presence of any of the characteristics described in paragraphs (c)(2) through (c)(6) of this section generally indicates that the plan is not a 10 or more employer plan described in section 419A(f)(6). Accordingly, unless established to the satisfaction of the Commissioner that the plan satisfies the requirements of section 419A(f)(6) and this section, a plan having any of the following characteristics is not a 10 or more employer plan described in section 419A(f)(6). A plan's lack of all the following characteristics does not create any inference that the plan is a 10 or more employer plan described in section 419A(f)(6).

*(2) Allocation of plan assets.* Assets of the plan or fund are allocated to a specific employer or employers through separate accounting of contributions and expenditures for individual employers, or otherwise.

*(3) Differential pricing.* The amount charged under the plan is not the same for all the participating employers, and those differences are not merely reflective of differences in current risk or rating factors that are commonly taken into account in manual rates used by insurers (such as current age, gender, geographic locale, number of covered dependents, and benefit terms) for the particular benefit or benefits being provided.

*(4) No fixed welfare benefit package.* The plan does not provide for fixed welfare benefits for a fixed coverage period for a fixed cost, within the meaning of paragraph (d)(5) of this section.

*(5) Unreasonably high cost.* The plan provides for fixed welfare benefits for a fixed coverage period for a fixed cost, but that cost is unreasonably high for the covered risk for the plan as a whole.

*(6) Nonstandard benefit triggers.* Benefits or other amounts payable can be paid, distributed, transferred, or otherwise provided from a fund that is part of the plan by reason of any event other than the illness, personal injury, or death of an employee or family member, or the employee's involuntary separation from employment. Thus, for example, a plan exhibits this characteristic if the plan provides for the payment of benefits or the distribution of an insurance contract to an employer's employees on the occasion of the employer's withdrawal from the plan. A plan will not be treated as having the characteristic described in this paragraph merely because, upon cessation of participation in the plan, an employee is provided with the right to convert coverage under a group life insurance contract to coverage under an individual life insurance contract without demonstrating evidence of insurability, but only if there is no additional economic value associated with the conversion right.

**(d) Definitions.** For purposes of this section:

*(1) Benefits or other amounts payable.* The term benefits or other amounts payable includes all amounts that are payable or distributable (or that will be otherwise provided) directly or indirectly to employers, to employees or their beneficiaries, or to another fund as a result of a spinoff or transfer, and without regard to whether payable or distributable as welfare benefits, cash, dividends, rebates of contributions, property, promises to pay, or otherwise.

*(2) Benefits experience.* The benefits experience of an employer (or of an employee or a group of employers or employees) means the benefits and other amounts incurred, paid, or distributed (or otherwise provided) directly or indirectly, including to another fund as a result of a spinoff or transfer, with respect to the employer (or employee or group of employers or employees), and without regard to whether provided as welfare benefits, cash, dividends, credits, rebates of contributions, property, promises to pay, or otherwise.

*(3) Overall experience.* (i) Employer's overall experience. The term overall experience means, with respect to an employer (or group of employers), the balance that would have accumulated in a welfare benefit fund if that employer (or those employers) were the only employer (or employers) providing welfare benefits under the plan. Thus, the overall experience is credited with the sum of the contributions under the plan with respect to that employer (or group of employers), less the benefits and other amounts paid or distributed (or otherwise provided) with respect to that employer (or group of employers) or the employees of that employer (or group of employers), and adjusted for gain or loss from insurance contracts (as described in paragraph (b)(4)(i) of this section), investment return, and expenses. Overall experience as of any date may be either a positive or a negative number.

(ii) Employee's overall experience. The term overall experience means, with respect to an employee (or group of employees, whether or not employed by the same employer), the balance that would have accumulated in a welfare benefit fund if the employee (or group of employees) were the only employee (or employees) being provided welfare benefits under the plan. Thus, the overall experience is credited with the sum of the contributions under the plan with respect to that employee (or group of employees), less the benefits and other amounts paid or distributed (or otherwise provided) with respect to that employee (or group of employees), and adjusted for gain or loss from insurance contracts (as described in paragraph (b)(4)(i) of this section), investment return, and expenses. Overall experience as of any date may be either a positive or a negative number.

*(4) Employer.* The term employer means the employer whose employees are participating in the plan and those employers required to be aggregated with the employer under section 414(b), (c), or (m).

*(5) Fixed welfare benefit package.* (i) In general. A plan provides for fixed welfare benefits for a fixed coverage period for a fixed cost, if it—

(A) Defines one or more welfare benefits, each of which has a fixed amount that does not depend on the amount or type of assets held by the fund;

(B) Specifies fixed contributions to provide for those welfare benefits; and

(C) Specifies a coverage period during which the plan agrees to provide specified welfare benefits, subject to the payment of the specified contributions by the employer.

(ii) Treatment of actuarial gains or losses. A plan will not be treated as failing to provide for fixed welfare benefits for a fixed coverage period for a fixed cost merely because the plan does not pay the promised benefits (or requires all participating employers to make proportionate additional contributions based on the fund's shortfall) when there are insufficient assets under the plan to pay the promised benefits. Similarly, a plan will not be treated as failing to provide for fixed welfare benefits for a fixed coverage period for a fixed cost merely because the plan provides a period of extended coverage after the end of the coverage period with respect to employees of all participating employers at no cost to the employers (or provides a proportionate refund of contributions to all participating employers) because of the plan-wide favorable actuarial experience during the coverage period.

**(e) Maintenance of records.** The plan administrator of a plan that is intended to be a 10 or more employer plan described in section 419A(f)(6) shall maintain permanent records and other documentary evidence sufficient to substantiate that the plan satisfies the requirements of section 419A(f)(6) and this section. (See § 1.414(g)-1 for the definition of plan administrator.)

**(f) Examples.** The provisions of paragraph (c) of this section and the provisions of section 419A(f)(6) and this section relating to experience-rating arrangements may be illustrated by the following examples. Unless stated otherwise, it should be assumed that any life insurance contract described in an example is non-participating and has no value other than the value of the policy's current life insurance protection plus its cash value, and that no employer normally contributes more than 10 percent of the total contributions contributed under the plan by all employers. Paragraph (ii) of each example applies the characteristics listed in paragraph (c) of this section to the facts described in that example. Paragraphs (iii) and (iv) of each example analyze the facts described in the example to determine whether the plan maintains experience-rating arrangements with respect to individual employers. Paragraphs (iii) and (iv) of each example illustrate only the meaning of experience-rating arrangements. No inference should be drawn from these examples about whether these plans are otherwise described in section 419A(f)(6) or about the applicability or nonapplicability of any other Internal Revenue Code provision that may limit or deny the deduction of contributions to the arrangements. Further, no inference should be drawn from the examples concerning the tax treatment of employees as a result of the employer contributions or the provision of the benefits. The examples are as follows:

*Example (1).* (i) An arrangement provides welfare benefits to employees of participating employers. Each year a participating employer is required to contribute an amount equal to the claims and other expenses expected with respect to that employer for the year (based on current age, gender, geographic locale, number of participating employees, benefit terms, and other risk or rating factors commonly taken into account in manual rates used by insurers for the benefits being provided), multiplied by the ratio of actual claims with respect to that employer for the previous year over the expected claims with respect to that employer for the previous year.

(ii) This arrangement exhibits at least one of the characteristics listed in paragraph (c) of this section generally indicating that an arrangement is not a 10 or more employer plan described in section 419A(f)(6). Differential pricing exists under this arrangement because the amount charged under the plan is not the same for all the participating employers, and those differences are not merely reflective of differences in current risk or rating factors that are commonly taken into account in manual rates used by insurers for the particular benefit or benefits being provided.

(iii) This arrangement does not satisfy the requirements of section 419A(f)(6) and this section because, at a minimum, the requirement of paragraph (a)(1)(iii) of this section is not satisfied. Under the arrangement, an employer's cost of coverage for each year is based, in part, on that employer's benefits experience (i.e., the benefits and other amounts provided in the past with respect to one or more employees of that employer). Accordingly, pursuant to paragraph (b)(1) of this section, the arrangement maintains experience-rating arrangements with respect to individual employers.

*Example (2).* (i) The facts are the same as in Example 1, except that the amount charged to an employer each year is equal to claims and other expenses expected with respect to that employer for the year (determined the same as in Example 1), multiplied by the ratio of actual claims for the previous year (determined on a plan-wide basis) over the expected claims for the previous year (determined on a plan-wide basis).

(ii) Based on the limited facts described above, this arrangement exhibits none of the characteristics listed in paragraph (c) of this section generally indicating that an arrangement is not a 10 or more employer plan described in section 419A(f)(6). Unlike the arrangement discussed in Example 1, there is no differential pricing under the arrangement because the only differences in the amounts charged to the employers are solely reflective of differences in current risk or rating factors that are commonly taken into account in manual rates used by insurers for the particular benefit or benefits being provided.

(iii) Nothing in the facts described in this Example 2 indicates that the arrangement maintains experience-rating arrangements prohibited under section 419A(f)(6) and this section. An employer's cost of coverage under the arrangement is based, in part, on the benefits experience of that employer (as well as of all the other participating employers). However, pursuant to paragraph (b)(4)(iii) of this section, the arrangement will not be treated as maintaining experience-rating arrangements with respect to the individual employers merely because the employers' cost of coverage is based on the benefits experience of a group of employees eligible under the plan, provided no employer normally contributes more than 10 percent of all contributions with respect to the rating group that includes the employees of an individual employer. Under the arrangement described in this Example 2, the rating group includes all the participating employers (or all of their employees), and no employer normally contributes more than 10 percent of the contributions made under the arrangement by all the employers. Accordingly, absent other facts, the arrangement will not be treated as maintaining experience-rating arrangements with respect to individual employers.

*Example (3).* (i) Arrangement A provides welfare benefits to employees of participating employers. Each year an employer is required to contribute an amount equal to the claims and other expenses expected with respect to that employer for the year (based on current risk or rating factors commonly taken into account in manual rates used by insurers for the benefits being provided), adjusted based on the employer's notional account. An employer's notional account is determined as follows. The account is credited with the sum of the employer's contributions previously paid under the plan less the benefit claims for that employer's employees. The notional account is further increased by a fixed five percent investment return (regardless of the actual investment return earned on the funds). If an employer's notional account is positive, the employer's contributions are reduced by a specified percentage of the notional account. If an employer's notional account is negative, the employer's contributions are increased by a specified percentage of the notional account.

(ii) Arrangement A exhibits at least two of the characteristics listed in paragraph (c) of this section generally indicating that an arrangement is not a 10 or more employer plan described in section 419A(f)(6). First, assets under the plan are allocated to specific employers. Second, differential pricing exists because the amount charged under the plan is not the same for all the participating employers, and those differences are not merely reflective of differences in current risk or rating factors that are commonly taken into account in manual rates used by insurers for the particular benefit or benefits being provided.

(iii) Arrangement A does not satisfy the requirements of section 419A(f)(6) and this section because, at a minimum, the requirement of paragraph (a)(1)(iii) of this section is not satisfied. Under the arrangement, a participating employer's cost of coverage for each year is based on a proxy for that employer's overall experience. An employer's overall experience, as that term is defined in paragraph (d)(3) of this section, includes the balance that would have accumulated in the fund if that employer's employees were the only employees being provided benefits under the plan. Under that definition, the overall experience is credited with the sum of the contributions paid under the plan by or on behalf of that employer less the benefits or other amounts provided to with respect to that employer's employees, and adjusted for gain or loss from insurance contracts, expenses, and investment return. Under the formula used by the arrangement in this example to determine employer contributions, expenses are disregarded and a fixed investment return of five percent is used instead of actual investment return. The disregard of expenses and substitution of the fixed investment return for the actual investment return merely results in an employer's notional account that is a proxy for the overall experience of that employer. Accordingly, the arrangement maintains experience-rating arrangements with respect to individual employers.

*Example (4).* (i) Under Arrangement B, death benefits are provided for eligible employees of each participating employer. Individual level premium whole life insurance policies are purchased to provide the death benefits. Each policy has a face amount equal to the death benefit payable with respect to the individual employee. Each year, a participating employer is charged an amount equal to the level premiums payable with respect to the employees of that employer. One participating employer, F, has an employee, P, whose coverage under the arrangement commenced at the beginning of 2000, when P was age 50. P is covered under the arrangement for $1 million of death benefits, and a life insurance policy with a face amount of $1 million has been purchased on P's life. The level annual premium on the policy is $23,000. At the beginning of 2005, when P is age 55, the $23,000 premium amount has been paid for five years and the policy, which continues to have a face amount of $1 million, has a cash value of $92,000. Another employer, G, has an employee, R, who is also 55 years old at the beginning of 2005 and is covered under Arrangement B for $1 million, for which a level premium life insurance policy with a face amount of $1 million has been purchased. However, R did not become covered under Arrangement B until the beginning of 2005. Because R's coverage began at age 55, the level annual premium charged for the policy on R's life is $30,000, or $7,000 more than the premiums payable on the policy in effect on P's life. Employer F is charged $23,000 and employer G is charged $30,000 for the death benefit for employees P and R, respectively. Assume that employees P and R are the only covered employees of their respective employers and that they are identical with respect to current risk and rating factors that are commonly taken into account in manual rates used by insurers for death benefits.

(ii) Arrangement B exhibits at least three of the characteristics listed in paragraph (c) of this section generally indicating that an arrangement is not a 10 or more employer plan described in section 419A(f)(6). First, assets of the plan are effectively allocated to specific employers. Second, there is differential pricing under the arrangement. That is, the amount charged under the plan during the year for a specific amount of death benefit coverage is not the same for all the employers (employer F is charged $23,000 each year for $1 million of death benefit coverage while employer G is charged $30,000 each year for the same coverage), and the difference is not merely reflective of differences in current risk or rating factors that are commonly taken into account in manual rates used by insurers for the death benefit being provided. (The differences in amounts charged are attributable to differences in issue age and not to differences in current risk or rating factors, as employees P and R are the same age). Third, during the early years of the arrangement, the amounts charged are unreasonably high for the covered risk for the plan as a whole.

(iii) Arrangement B does not satisfy the requirements of section 419A(f)(6) and this section because, at a minimum, the requirement of paragraph (a)(1)(iii) of this section is not satisfied. Arrangement B maintains experience-rating arrangements with respect to individual employers because the cost of coverage for each year for any employer participating in the arrangement is based on a proxy for the overall experience of that employer. Under Arrangement B, employer F's cost of coverage for 2005 is $23,000 for $1 million of coverage. The $92,000 cash value at the beginning of 2005 in the policy insuring P's life is a proxy for employer F's overall experience. (The $92,000 is essentially the balance that would have accumulated in the fund if employer F were the only employer providing welfare benefits under Arrangement B.) Further, the $23,000 charged to F for the $1 million of coverage in 2005 is based on the $92,000 since, in the absence of the $92,000, employer F would have been charged $30,000 for P's $1 million death benefit coverage. (Note that the conclusion that the $92,000 balance is the basis for the lower premium charged to employer F is consistent with the fact that a $92,000 balance, if converted to a life annuity using the same actuarial assumptions as were used to calculate the cash value amount, would be sufficient to provide for annual annuity payments of $7,000 for the life of P—an amount equal to the $7,000 difference from the premium charged in 2005 to employer G for the $1 million of coverage on employee R's life.) Thus, F's cost of coverage for 2005 is based on a proxy for F's overall experience. Accordingly, Arrangement B maintains an experience-rating arrangement with respect to employer F.

(iv) Arrangement B also maintains an experience-rating arrangement with respect to employer G because it can be expected that each year G will be charged $30,000 for the $1 million of coverage on R's life. Each year, G's cost of coverage will reflect G's prior contributions and allocable earnings, so that G's cost of coverage will be based on a proxy for G's overall experience. Accordingly, Arrangement B maintains an experience-rating arrangement with respect to employer G. Similarly, Arrangement B maintains an experience-rating arrangement with respect to each other participating employer. Accordingly, Arrangement B maintains experience-rating arrangements with respect to individual employers. This would also be the result if Arrangement B maintained an experience-rating arrangement with respect to only one individual employer.

*Example (5).* (i) The facts are the same as in Example 4 except that the death benefits are provided under 10-year level term life insurance policies. One participating employer, H, has an employee, M, whose coverage under the arrangement commenced at the beginning of 2000, when M was age 35. M is covered under the arrangement for $1 million of death benefits, and a 10-year level term life insurance policy with a face amount of $1 million has been purchased on M's life. The level annual premium on the policy for the first 10 years is $700. At the beginning of 2007, when M is age 42, the $700 premium amount has been paid for seven years. Another employer, J, has an employee, N, who is also 42 years old at the beginning of 2007 and is covered under the arrangement for $1 million, for which a 10-year level term life insurance policy with a face amount of $1 million has been purchased. However, N did not become covered under the arrangement until the beginning of 2007. Because N's coverage began at age 42, the 10-year level term premium charged for the policy on N's life is $1,100, or $400 more than the premiums then payable on the policy in effect on M's life. Neither the policy on employee M nor the policy on employee N has any cash value at any point during its term. Assume that employees M and N are the only covered employees of their respective employers and that they are identical with respect to any current risk and rating factors that are commonly taken into account in manual rates used by insurers for the death benefit being provided.

(ii) Based on the facts described in this Example 5, this arrangement exhibits at least two of the characteristics listed in paragraph (c) of this section generally indicating that an arrangement is not a 10 or more employer plan described in section 419A(f)(6). First, for the same reasons as described in paragraph (ii) of Example 4, there is differential pricing under the arrangement. Second, assets of the plan are effectively allocated to specific employers. This is the case even though the insurance policies used by employers H and J have no accessible cash value.

(iii) The facts described in this Example 5 indicate that the arrangement does not satisfy the requirements of section 419A(f)(6) and this section because, at a minimum, the requirement of paragraph (a)(1)(iii) of this section is not satisfied. This arrangement maintains experience-rating arrangements with respect to individual employers because the cost of coverage for each year for any employer participating in the arrangement is based on a proxy for the overall experience of that employer. Under this arrangement employer H's cost of coverage in 2007 is $700 for $1 million of coverage. Although the policy insuring M's life has no cash value accessible to employer H, the accumulation of the excesses of the amounts paid by employer H on behalf of employee M over each year's underlying mortality and expense charges for providing life insurance coverage to employee M provide economic value to employer H (i.e., the ability to purchase future coverage on M's life at a premium that is less than the underlying mortality and expense charges as those underlying charges increase with M's increasing age). Thus, H's cost of coverage for 2007 is based on a proxy for H's overall experience. Accordingly, this arrangement maintains an experience-rating arrangement with respect to employer H.

(iv) This arrangement also maintains an experience-rating arrangement with respect to employer J because it can be expected that for each of the next nine years J will be charged $1,100 for the $1 million of coverage on N's life. Each year, J's cost of coverage will reflect J's prior contributions, so that J's cost of coverage will be based on a proxy for J's overall experience. Accordingly, this arrangement maintains an experience-rating arrangement with respect to employer J. Similarly, this arrangement maintains an experiencing-rating arrangement with respect to each other participating employer. Accordingly, this arrangement maintains experience-rating arrangements with respect to individual employers. This would also be the result if this arrangement maintained an experience-rating arrangement with respect to only one individual employer.

*Example (6).* (i) Under Arrangement C, death benefits are provided for eligible employees of each participating employer. Flexible premium universal life insurance policies are purchased to provide the death benefits. Each policy has a face amount equal to the death benefit payable with respect to the individual employee. Each participating employer can make any contributions to the arrangement provided that the amount paid for each employee is at least the amount needed to prevent the lapse of the policy. The amount needed to prevent the lapse of the universal life insurance policy is the excess, if any, of the mortality and expense charges for the year over the policy balance. All contributions made by an employer are paid as premiums to the universal life insurance policies purchased on the lives of the covered employees of that employer. Participating employers S and V each have a 50-year-old employee covered under Arrangement C for death benefits of $1 million, which is the face amount of the respective universal life insurance policies on the lives of the employees. In the first year of coverage employer S makes a contribution of $23,000 (the amount of a level premium) while employer V contributes only $6,000, which is the amount of the mortality and expense charges for the first year. At the beginning of year two, the balance in employer S's policy (including earnings) is $18,000, but the balance in V's policy is zero. Although S is not required to contribute anything in the second year of coverage, S contributes an additional $15,000 in the second year. Employer V contributes $7,000 in the second year.

(ii) Arrangement C exhibits at least two of the characteristics listed in paragraph (c) of this section generally indicating that an arrangement is not a 10 or more employer plan described in section 419A(f)(6). First, assets of the plan are effectively allocated to specific employers. Second, the arrangement does not provide for fixed welfare benefits for a fixed coverage period for a fixed cost.

(iii) Arrangement C does not satisfy the requirements of section 419A(f)(6) and this section because, at a minimum, the requirement of paragraph (a)(1)(iii) of this section is not satisfied. Arrangement C maintains experience-rating arrangements with respect to individual employers because the cost of coverage of an employer participating in the arrangement is based on a proxy for the overall experience of that employer. Pursuant to paragraph (b)(4)(ii) of this section (concerning treatment of flexible contribution arrangements), solely for purposes of determining an employer's cost of coverage, the Commissioner may treat an employer as contributing the minimum amount needed to maintain the coverage. Applying this treatment, H's cost of coverage for the first year of coverage under Arrangement C is $6,000 for $1 million of death benefit coverage, but for the second year it is zero for the same amount of coverage because that is the minimum amount needed to keep the insurance policy from lapsing. Employer H's overall experience at the beginning of the second year of coverage is $18,000, because that is the balance that would have accumulated in the fund if H were the only employer providing benefits under Arrangement C. (The special rule of paragraph (b)(4)(ii) of this section only applies to determine cost of coverage; it does not apply in determining overall experience.) The $18,000 balance in the policy insuring the life of employer H's employee is a proxy for H's overall experience. Employer H can choose not to make any contributions in the second year of coverage due to the $18,000 policy balance. Thus, H's cost of coverage for the second year is based on a proxy for H's overall experience. Accordingly, Arrangement C maintains an experience-rating arrangement with respect to employer H.

(iv) Arrangement C also maintains an experience-rating arrangement with respect to employer J because in each year J can contribute more than the amount needed to prevent a lapse of the policy on the life of its employee and can expect that its cost of coverage for subsequent years will reflect its prior contributions and allocable earnings. Accordingly, Arrangement C maintains an experience-rating arrangement with respect to employer J.

*Example (7).* (i) Arrangement D provides death benefits for eligible employees of each participating employer. Each employer can choose to provide a death benefit of either one, two, or three times the annual compensation of the covered employees. Under Arrangement D, the death benefit is payable only if the employee dies while employed by the employer. If an employee terminates employment with the employer or if the employer withdraws from the arrangement, the death benefit is no longer payable, no refund or other credit is payable to the employer or to the employees, and no policy or other property is transferrable to the employer or the employees. Furthermore, the employees are not provided with any right under Arrangement D to coverage under any other arrangement, nor with any right to purchase or to convert to an individual insurance policy, other than any conversion rights the employees may have in accordance with state law (and which provide no additional economic benefit). Arrangement D determines the amount required to be contributed by each employer for each month of coverage by aggregating the amount required to be contributed for each covered employee of the employer. The amount required to be contributed for each covered employee is determined by multiplying the amount of the death benefit coverage (in thousands) for the employee by five-year age bracket rates in a table specified by the plan, which is used uniformly for all covered employees of all participating employers. The rates in the specified table do not exceed the rates set forth in Table I of § 1.79-3(d)(2), and differences in the rates in the table are merely reflective of differences in mortality risk for the various age brackets. The rates in the table are not based in whole or in part on the experience of the employers participating in Arrangement D. Arrangement D uses the amount contributed by each employer to purchase one-year term insurance coverage on the lives of the covered employees with a face amount equal to the death benefit provided by the plan. No employer is entitled to any rebates or refunds provided under the insurance contract.

(ii) Arrangement D does not exhibit any of the characteristics listed in paragraph (c) of this section generally indicating that an arrangement is not a 10 or more employer plan described in section 419A(f)(6). Under Arrangement D, assets are not allocated to a specific employer or employers. Differences in the amounts charged to the employers are solely reflective of differences in risk or rating factors that are commonly taken into account in manual rates used by insurers for the particular benefit or benefits being provided. The arrangement provides for fixed welfare benefits for a fixed coverage period for a fixed cost, within the meaning of paragraph (d)(5) of this section. The cost charged under the arrangement is not unreasonably high for the covered risk of the plan as a whole. Finally, benefits and other amounts payable can be paid, distributed, transferred, or otherwise made available only by reason of the death of the employee, so that there is no nonstandard benefit trigger under the arrangement.

(iii) Nothing in the facts of this Example 7 indicates that Arrangement D fails to satisfy the requirements of section 419A(f)(6) or this section by reason of maintaining experience-rating arrangements with respect to individual employers. Based solely on the facts described above, Arrangement D does not maintain an experience rating-arrangement with respect to any individual employer because for each participating employer there is no period for which the employer's cost of coverage under the arrangement is based, in whole or in part, on either the benefits experience or the overall experience (or a proxy for either type of experience) of that employer or its employees.

*Example (8).* (i) The facts are the same as in Example 7, except that under the arrangement, any refund or rebate provided under that year's insurance contract is allocated among all the employers participating in the arrangement in proportion to their contributions, and is used to reduce the employers' contributions for the next year.

(ii) This arrangement exhibits at least one of the characteristics listed in paragraph (c) of this section generally indicating that an arrangement is not a 10 or more employer plan described in section 419A(f)(6). The arrangement includes nonstandard benefit triggers because amounts are made available to an employer by reason of the insurer providing a refund or rebate to the plan, an event that is other than the illness, personal injury, or death of an employee or family member, or an employee's involuntary separation from employment.

(iii) Based on the limited and specific facts described in this Example 8, an employer participating in this arrangement should be able to establish to the satisfaction of the Commissioner that the plan does not maintain experience-rating arrangements with respect to individual employers. A participating employer's cost of coverage is the relationship of its contributions to the death benefit coverage or other amounts payable with respect to that employer, including the employer's portion of the insurance company rebate and refund amounts. The rebate and refund amounts are allocated to an employer based on that employer's contribution for the prior year. However, even though an employer's overall experience includes its past contributions, contributions alone are not a proxy for an employer's overall experience under the particular facts described in this Example 8. As a result, a participating employer's cost of coverage under the arrangement for each year (or any other period) is not based on that employer's benefits experience or its overall experience (or a proxy for either type of experience), except as follows: If the total of the insurance company refund or rebate amounts is a proxy for the overall experience of all participating employers, a participating employer's cost of coverage will be based in part on that employer's overall experience (or a proxy therefor) by reason of that employer's overall experience being a portion of the overall experience of all participating employers. Under the special rule of paragraph (b)(2)(iii) of this section, however, that fact alone will not cause the arrangement to be treated as maintaining an experience-rating arrangement with respect to an individual employer because no employer normally contributes more than 10 percent of the total contributions under the plan by all employers (the rating group). Accordingly, the arrangement will not be treated as maintaining experience-rating arrangements with respect to individual employers.

*Example (9).* (i) Arrangement E provides medical benefits for covered employees of 90 participating employers. The level of medical benefits is determined by a schedule set forth in the trust document and does not vary by employer. Other than any rights an employee may have to COBRA continuation coverage, the medical benefits cease when an employee terminates employment with the employer. If an employer withdraws from the arrangement, there is no refund of any contributions and there is no transfer of anything of value to employees of the withdrawing employer, to the withdrawing employer, or to another plan or arrangement maintained by the withdrawing employer. Arrangement E determines the amount required to be contributed by each employer for each year of coverage, and the aggregate amounts charged are not unreasonably high for the covered risk for the plan as a whole. To determine the amount to be contributed for each employer, Arrangement E classifies an employer based on the employer's location. These geographic areas are not changed once established under the arrangement. The amount charged for the coverage under the arrangement to the employers in a geographic area is determined from a rate-setting manual based on the benefit package and geographic area, and differences in the rates in the manual are merely reflective of current differences in those risk or rating factors. The rates in the rate-setting manual are not based in whole or in part on the experience of the employers participating in Arrangement E.

(ii) Arrangement E does not exhibit any of the characteristics listed in paragraph (c) of this section generally indicating that an arrangement is not a 10 or more employer plan described in section 419A(f)(6). Although the amounts charged under the arrangement to an employer in one geographic area can be expected to differ from those charged to an employer in another geographic area, the differences are merely reflective of differences in current risk or rating factors that are commonly taken into account in manual rates used by insurers for medical benefits.

(iii) Nothing in the facts of this Example 9 indicates that Arrangement E fails to satisfy the requirements of section 419A(f)(6) or this section by reason of maintaining experience-rating arrangements with respect to individual employers. Based solely on the facts described above, Arrangement E does not maintain an experience rating-arrangement with respect to any individual employer because for each participating employer there is no period for which the employer's cost of coverage under the arrangement is based, in whole or in part, on either the benefits experience or the overall experience (or a proxy for either type of experience) of that employer or its employees.

*Example (10).* (i) The facts are the same as in Example 9, except that the amount charged for the coverage under the arrangement to the employers in a geographic area is initially determined from a rate-setting manual based on the benefit package and then adjusted to reflect the claims experience of the employers in that classification as a whole. The arrangement does not have any geographic area classification for which one of the employers in the classification normally contributes more than 10 percent of the contributions made by all the employers in that classification.

(ii) This arrangement exhibits at least one of the characteristics listed in paragraph (c) of this section generally indicating that an arrangement is not a 10 or more employer plan described in section 419A(f)(6). There is differential pricing under the arrangement because the amounts charged to an employer in one geographic area can be expected to differ from those charged to an employer in another geographic area, and the differences are not merely reflective of current risk or rating factors that are commonly taken into account in manual rates used by insurers for medical benefits.

(iii) Based on the facts described in this Example 10, an employer participating in this arrangement should be able to establish to the satisfaction of the Commissioner that the plan does not maintain experience-rating arrangements with respect to individual employers even though there is differential pricing. Although an employer's cost of coverage for each year is based, in part, on its benefits experience (as well as the benefits experience of the other employers in its geographic area), that does not result in experience-rating arrangements with respect to any individual employer because the employers in each geographic area are a rating group and no employer normally contributes more than 10 percent of the contributions made by all the employers in its rating group. (See paragraph (b)(4)(iii) of this section.)

*Example (11).* (i) The facts of Arrangement F are the same as those described in Example 10, except that K, an employer in one of Arrangement F's geographic areas, normally contributes more than 10 percent of the contributions made by the employers in that geographic area.

(ii) For the same reasons as described in Example 10, Arrangement F results in differential pricing.

(iii) Arrangement F does not satisfy the requirements of section 419A(f)(6) and this section because, at a minimum, the requirement of paragraph (a)(1)(iii) of this section is not satisfied. An employer's cost of coverage for each year is based, in part, on its benefits experience (as well as the benefits experience of the other employers in its geographic area) and the special rule for experience-rating by a rating group does not apply to Arrangement F because employer K normally contributes more than 10 percent of the contributions made by the employers in its rating group. Accordingly, Arrangement F maintains experience-rating arrangements with respect to individual employers.

*Example (12).* (i) The facts of Arrangement G are the same as those described in Example 10, except for the way that the arrangement classifies the employers. Under Arrangement G, the experience of each employer for the prior year is reviewed and then the employer is assigned to one of three classifications (low cost, intermediate cost, or high cost) based on the ratio of actual claims with respect to that employer to expected claims with respect to that employer. No employer in any classification normally contributes more than 10 percent of the contributions of all employers in that classification.

(ii) For the same reasons as described in Example 10, Arrangement G results in differential pricing.

(iii) Arrangement G does not satisfy the requirements of section 419A(f)(6) and this section because, at a minimum, the requirement of paragraph (a)(1)(iii) of this section is not satisfied. The special rule in paragraph (b)(4)(iii) of this section for rating groups can prevent a plan from being treated as maintaining experience-rating arrangements with respect to individual employers if the mere use of a rating group is the only reason a plan would be so treated. Under Arrangement G, however, an employer's cost of coverage for each year is based on the employer's benefits experience in two ways: the employer's benefits experience is part of the benefits experience of a rating group that is otherwise permitted under the special rule of paragraph (b)(4)(iii) of this section, and the employer's benefits experience is considered annually in redetermining the rating group to which the employer is assigned. Accordingly, Arrangement G maintains experience-rating arrangements with respect to individual employers.

*Example (13).* (i) Arrangement H provides a death benefit equal to a multiple of one, two, or three times compensation as elected by the participating employer for all of its covered employees. Universal life insurance contracts are purchased on the lives of the covered employees. The face amount of each contract is the amount of the death benefit payable upon the death of the covered employee. Under the arrangement, each employer is charged annually an amount equal to 200 percent of the mortality and expense charges under the contracts for that year covering the lives of the covered employees of that employer. Arrangement H pays the amount charged each employer to the insurance company. Thus, the insurance company receives an amount equal to 200 percent of the mortality and expense charges under the policies. The excess amounts charged and paid to the insurance company increase the policy value of the universal life insurance contracts. When an employer ceases to participate in Arrangement H, the insurance policies are distributed to each of the covered employees of the withdrawing employer.

(ii) Arrangement H exhibits at least three of the characteristics listed in paragraph (c) of this section generally indicating that an arrangement is not a 10 or more employer plan described in section 419A(f)(6). First, assets are effectively allocated to specific employers. Second, because the amount of the withdrawal benefit (i.e., the value of the life insurance policies to be distributed) is unknown, the arrangement does not provide for fixed welfare benefits for a fixed coverage period for a fixed cost. Finally, Arrangement H includes nonstandard benefit triggers because amounts can be distributed under the arrangement for a reason other than the illness, personal injury, or death of an employee or family member, or an employee's involuntary separation from employment.

(iii) Arrangement H does not satisfy the requirements of section 419A(f)(6) and this section because, at a minimum, the requirement of paragraph (a)(1)(iii) of this section is not satisfied. Pursuant to paragraph (b)(1) of this section, the prohibition against maintaining experience-rating arrangements applies under all circumstances, including employer withdrawals. Arrangement H maintains experience-rating arrangements with respect to individual employers because the cost of coverage for a participating employer is based on a proxy for the overall experience of that employer. Under Arrangement H, the contributions of a participating employer are fixed. The benefits or other amounts payable with respect to an employer include the value of the life insurance policies that are distributable to the employees of that employer upon the withdrawal of that employer from the plan. Thus, the cost of coverage for any period of an employer's participation in Arrangement H is the relationship between the fixed contributions for that period and the variable benefits payable under the arrangement. The value of those variable benefits depends on the value of the policies that would be distributed if the employer were to withdraw at the end of the period. (Each year the insurance policies to be distributed to the employees in the event of the employer's withdrawal will increase in value due to the premium amounts paid on the policy in excess of current mortality and expense charges.) For reasons similar to those discussed above in Example 6, the aggregate value of the life insurance policies on the lives of an employer's employees is a proxy for that employer's overall experience. Thus, a participating's employer's cost of coverage for any period is based on a proxy for the overall experience of that employer. Accordingly, Arrangement H maintains experience-rating arrangements with respect to individual employers.

(iv) The result would be the same if, rather than distributing the policies, Arrangement H distributed cash amounts equal to the cash values of the policies. The result would also be the same if the distribution of policies or cash values is triggered by employees terminating their employment rather than by employers ceasing to participate in the arrangement.

*Example (14).* (i) (1) The facts of Arrangement J are the same as those described in Example 13 for Arrangement H, except that—

(A) Arrangement J purchases a special term insurance policy on the life of each covered employee with a face amount equal to the death benefit payable upon the death of the covered employee; and

(B) there is no benefit distributable upon an employer's withdrawal.

(2) The special term policy includes a rider that extends the term protection for a period of time beyond the term provided on the policy's face. The length of the extended term is not guaranteed, but is based on the excess of premiums over mortality and expense charges during the period of original term protection, increased by any investment return credited to the policies.

(ii) Arrangement J exhibits two of the characteristics listed in paragraph (c) of this section generally indicating that an arrangement is not a 10 or more employer plan described in section 419A(f)(6). First, assets of the plan are effectively allocated to specific employers. Second, the plan does not provide for fixed welfare benefits for a fixed coverage period for a fixed cost because the coverage period is not fixed.

(iii) Arrangement J does not satisfy the requirements of section 419A(f)(6) and this section because, at a minimum, the requirement of paragraph (a)(1)(iii) of this section is not satisfied. Arrangement J maintains experience-rating arrangements with respect to individual employers because the cost of coverage for a participating employer is based on a proxy for the overall experience of that employer. Under Arrangement J, the contributions of a participating employer are fixed. The benefits or other amounts payable with respect to an employer are the one-, two-, or three-times-compensation death benefit for each employee of the employer for the current year, plus the extended term protection coverage for future years. Thus, for any period extending to or beyond the end of the original term of one or more of the policies on the lives of an employer's employees, the employer's cost of coverage is the relationship between the fixed contributions for that period and the variable benefits payable under the arrangement. The value of those variable benefits depends on the aggregate value of the policies insuring the employer's employees (i.e., the total of the premiums paid on the policies by Arrangement J to the insurance company, reduced by the mortality and expense charges that were needed to provide the original term protection, and increased by any investment return credited to the policies). The aggregate value of the policies insuring an employer's employees is, at any time, a proxy for the employer's overall experience. Thus, a participating employer's cost of coverage for any period described above is based on a proxy for the overall experience of that employer. Accordingly, Arrangement J maintains experience-rating arrangements with respect to individual employers.

*Example (15).* (i) Arrangement K provides a death benefit to employees of participating employers equal to a specified multiple of compensation. Under the arrangement, a flexible-premium universal life insurance policy is purchased on the life of each covered employee in the amount of that employee's death benefit. Each policy has a face amount equal to the employee's death benefit under the arrangement. Each participating employer is charged annually with the aggregate amount (if any) needed to maintain the policies covering the lives of its employees. However, each employer is permitted to make additional contributions to the arrangement and, upon doing so, the additional contributions are paid to the insurance company and allocated to one or more contracts covering the lives of the employer's employees. In the event that any policy covering the life of an employee would lapse in the absence of new contributions from that employee's employer, and if at the same time there are policies covering the lives of other employees of the employer that have cash values in excess of the amounts needed to prevent their lapse, the employer has the option of reducing its otherwise-required contribution by amounts withdrawn from those other policies.

(ii) Arrangement K exhibits at least two of the characteristics listed in paragraph (c) of this section generally indicating that an arrangement is not a 10 or more employer plan described in section 419A(f)(6). First, assets of the plan are allocated to specific employers. Second, because the plan allows an employer to choose to contribute an amount that is different than that contributed by another employer for the same benefit, the amount charged under the plan is not the same for all participating employers (and the differences in the amounts are not merely reflective of differences in current risk or rating factors that are commonly taken into account in manual rates used by insurers for the particular benefit or benefits being provided), resulting in differential pricing.

(iii) Arrangement K does not satisfy the requirements of section 419A(f)(6) and this section because, at a minimum, the requirement of paragraph (a)(1)(iii) of this section is not satisfied. Arrangement K maintains experience-rating arrangements with respect to individual employers because the cost of coverage for any employer participating in the arrangement is based on a proxy for the overall experience of that employer. Under Arrangement K the benefits with respect to an employer for any year are a fixed amount. For purposes of determining the employer's cost of coverage for that year, the Commissioner may treat the employer's contribution under the special rule of paragraph (b)(4)(ii) of this section (concerning treatment of flexible contribution\arrangements) as being the minimum contribution amount needed to maintain the universal life policies with respect to that employer for the death benefit coverage for that year. Because the employer has the option to prevent the lapse of one policy by having amounts withdrawn from other policies, that minimum contribution amount will be based in part on the aggregate value of the policies on the lives of that employer's employees. That aggregate value is a proxy for the employer's overall experience. Accordingly, Arrangement K maintains experience-rating arrangements with respect to individual employers.

**(g) Effective date.** *(1) In general.* Except as set forth in paragraph (g)(2) of this section, this section applies to contributions paid or incurred in taxable years of an employer beginning on or after July 11, 2002.

*(2) Compliance information and recordkeeping.* Paragraphs (a)(1)(iv), (a)(2), and (e) of this section apply for taxable years of a welfare benefit fund beginning after July 17, 2003.

---

T.D. 9079, 7/16/2003.

---

### § 1.420-1 Significant reduction in retiree health coverage during the cost maintenance period.

***Caution:*** The Treasury has not yet amended Reg § 1.420-1 to reflect changes made by P.L. 108-357.

**(a) In general.** Notwithstanding section 420(c)(3)(A), the minimum cost requirements of section 420(c)(3) are not met if the employer significantly reduces retiree health coverage during the cost maintenance period.

**(b) Significant reduction.** *(1) In general.* An employer significantly reduces retiree health coverage during the cost maintenance period if, for any taxable year beginning on or after January 1, 2002, that is included in the cost maintenance period, either—

(i) The employer-initiated reduction percentage for that taxable year exceeds 10 percent; or

(ii) The sum of the employer-initiated reduction percentages for that taxable year and all prior taxable years during the cost maintenance period exceeds 20 percent.

*(2) Employer-initiated reduction percentage.* The employer-initiated reduction percentage for any taxable year is the fraction B/A, expressed as a percentage, where:

A = The total number of individuals (retired employees plus their spouses plus their dependents) receiving coverage for applicable health benefits as of the day before the first day of the taxable year.

B = The total number of individuals included in A whose coverage for applicable health benefits ended during the taxable year by reason of employer action.

*(3) Special rules for taxable years beginning before January 1, 2002.* The following rules apply for purposes of computing the amount in paragraph (b)(1)(ii) of this section if any portion of the cost maintenance period precedes the first day of the first taxable year beginning on or after January 1, 2002—

(i) Aggregation of taxable years. The portion of the cost maintenance period that precedes the first day of the first taxable year beginning on or after January 1, 2002 (the initial period) is treated as a single taxable year and the employer-initiated reduction percentage for the initial period is computed as set forth in paragraph (b)(2) of this section, except that the words "initial period" apply instead of "taxable year."

(ii) Loss of coverage. If coverage for applicable health benefits for an individual ends by reason of employer action at any time during the initial period, an employer may treat that coverage as not having ended if the employer restores coverage for applicable health benefits to that individual by the end of the initial period.

*(4) Employer action.* (i) General rule. For purposes of paragraph (b)(2) of this section, an individual's coverage for applicable health benefits ends during a taxable year by reason of employer action, if on any day within the taxable year, the individual's eligibility for applicable health benefits ends as a result of a plan amendment or any other action of the employer (e.g., the sale of all or part of the employer's business) that, in conjunction with the plan terms, has the effect of ending the individual's eligibility. An employer action is taken into account for this purpose regardless of when the employer action actually occurs (e.g., the date the plan amendment is executed), except that employer actions occurring before the later of December 18, 1999, and the date that is 5 years before the start of the cost maintenance period are disregarded.

(ii) Special rule. Notwithstanding paragraph (b)(4)(i) of this section, coverage for an individual will not be treated as having ended by reason of employer action merely because such coverage ends under the terms of the plan if those terms were adopted contemporaneously with the provision under which the individual became eligible for retiree health coverage. This paragraph (b)(4)(ii) does not apply with respect to plan terms adopted contemporaneously with a plan amendment that restores coverage for applicable health benefits before the end of the initial period in accordance with paragraph (b)(3)(ii) of this section.

(iii) Sale transactions. If a purchaser provides coverage for retiree health benefits to one or more individuals whose coverage ends by reason of a sale of all or part of the employer's business, the employer may treat the coverage of those individuals as not having ended by reason of employer action. In such a case, for the remainder of the year of the sale and future taxable years of the cost maintenance period—

(A) For purposes of computing the applicable employer cost under section 420(c)(3), those individuals are treated as individuals to whom coverage for applicable health benefits was provided (for as long as the purchaser provides retiree health coverage to them), and any amounts expended by the purchaser of the business to provide for health benefits for those individuals are treated as paid by the employer;

(B) For purposes of determining whether a subsequent termination of coverage is by reason of employer action under this paragraph (b)(4), the purchaser is treated as the employer. However, the special rule in paragraph (b)(4)(ii) of this section applies only to the extent that any terms of the plan maintained by the purchaser that have the effect of ending retiree health coverage for an individual are the same as terms of the plan maintained by the employer that were adopted contemporaneously with the provision under which the individual became eligible for retiree health coverage under the plan maintained by the employer.

**(c) Definitions.** The following definitions apply for purposes of this section:

*(1) Applicable health benefits.* Applicable health benefits means applicable health benefits as defined in section 420(e)(1)(C).

*(2) Cost maintenance period.* Cost maintenance period means the cost maintenance period as defined in section 420(c)(3)(D).

*(3) Sale.* A sale of all or part of an employer's business means a sale or other transfer in connection with which the employees of a trade or business of the employer become employees of another person. In the case of such a transfer, the term purchaser means a transferee of the trade or business.

**(d) Examples.** The following examples illustrate the application of this section:

*Example (1).* (i) Employer W maintains a defined benefit pension plan that includes a 401(h) account and permits qualified transfers that satisfy section 420. The number of individuals receiving coverage for applicable health benefits as of the day before the first day of Year 1 is 100. In Year 1, Employer W makes a qualified transfer under section 420. There is no change in the number of individuals receiving health benefits during Year 1. As of the last day of Year 2, applicable health benefits are provided to 99 individuals, because 2 individuals became eligible for coverage due to retirement and 3 individuals died in Year 2. During Year 3, Employer W amends its health plan to eliminate coverage for 5 individuals, 1 new retiree becomes eligible for coverage and an additional 3 individuals are no longer covered due to their own decision to drop coverage. Thus, as of the last day of Year 3, applicable health benefits are provided to 92 individuals. During Year 4, Employer W amends its health plan to eliminate coverage under its health plan for 8 more individuals, so that as of the last day of Year 4, applicable health benefits are provided to 84 individuals. During Year 5, Employer W amends its health plan to eliminate coverage for 8 more individuals.

(ii) There is no significant reduction in retiree health coverage in either Year 1 or Year 2, because there is no reduction in health coverage as a result of employer action in those years.

(iii) There is no significant reduction in Year 3. The number of individuals whose health coverage ended during Year 3 by reason of employer action (amendment of the plan) is 5. Since the number of individuals receiving coverage for applicable health benefits as of the last day of Year 2 is 99, the employer-initiated reduction percentage for Year 3 is 5.05 percent (5/99), which is less than the 10 percent annual limit.

(iv) There is no significant reduction in Year 4. The number of individuals whose health coverage ended during Year 4 by reason of employer action is 8. Since the number of individuals receiving coverage for applicable health benefits as of the last day of Year 3 is 92, the employer-initiated reduction percentage for Year 4 is 8.70 percent (8/92), which is less than the 10 percent annual limit. The sum of the employer-initiated reduction percentages for Year 3 and Year 4 is 13.75 percent, which is less than the 20 percent cumulative limit.

(v) In Year 5, there is a significant reduction under paragraph (b)(1)(ii) of this section. The number of individuals whose health coverage ended during Year 5 by reason of employer action (amendment of the plan) is 8. Since the number of individuals receiving coverage for applicable health benefits as of the last day of Year 4 is 84, the employer-initiated reduction percentage for Year 5 is 9.52 percent (8/84), which is less than the 10 percent annual limit. However, the sum of the employer-initiated reduction percentages for Year 3, Year 4, and Year 5 is 5.05 percent + 8.70 percent + 9.52 percent = 23.27 percent, which exceeds the 20 percent cumulative limit.

*Example (2).* (i) Employer X, a calendar year taxpayer, maintains a defined benefit pension plan that includes a 401(h) account and permits qualified transfers that satisfy section 420. X also provides lifetime health benefits to employees who retire from Division A as a result of a plant shutdown, no health benefits to employees who retire from Division B, and lifetime health benefits to all employees who retire from Division C. In 2000, X amends its health plan to provide coverage for employees who retire from Division B as a result of a plant shutdown, but only for the 2-year period coinciding with their severance pay. Also in 2000, X amends the health plan to provide that employees who retire from Division A as a result of a plant shutdown receive health coverage only for the 2-year period coinciding with their severance pay. A plant shutdown that affects Division A and Division B employees occurs in 2000. The number of individuals receiving coverage for applicable health benefits as of the last day of 2001 is 200. In 2002, Employer X makes a qualified transfer under section 420. As of the last day of 2002, applicable health benefits are provided to 170 individuals, because the 2-year period of benefits ends for 10 employees who retired from Division A and 20 employees who retired from Division B as a result of the plant shutdown that occurred in 2000.

(ii) There is no significant reduction in retiree health coverage in 2002. Coverage for the 10 retirees from Division A who lose coverage as a result of the end of the 2-year period is treated as having ended by reason of employer action, because coverage for those Division A retirees ended by reason of a plan amendment made after December 17, 1999. However, the terms of the health plan that limit coverage for employees who retired from Division B as a result of the 2000 plant shutdown (to the 2-year period) were adopted contemporaneously with the provision under which those employees became eligible for retiree coverage under the health plan. Accordingly, under the rule provided in paragraph (b)(4)(ii) of this section, coverage for those 20 retirees from Division B is not treated as having ended by reason of employer action. Thus, the number of individuals whose health benefits ended by reason of employer action in 2002 is 10. Since the number of individuals receiving coverage for applicable health benefits as of the last day of 2001 is 200, the employer-initiated reduction percentage for 2002 is 5 percent (10/200), which is less than the 10 percent annual limit.

**(e) Regulatory effective date.** This section is applicable to transfers of excess pension assets occurring on or after December 18, 1999.

T.D. 8948, 6/14/2001.

## § 1.421-1 Meaning and use of certain terms.

**(a) Option.** *(1)* For purposes of this section and §§ 1.421-2 through 1.424-1, the term "option" means the right or privilege of an individual to purchase stock from a corporation by virtue of an offer of the corporation continuing for a stated period of time, whether or not irrevocable, to sell such stock at a price determined under paragraph (e) of this section, such individual being under no obligation to purchase. The individual who has such right or privilege is referred to as the optionee and the corporation offering to sell stock under such an arrangement is referred to as the optionor. While no particular form of words is necessary, the option must express, among other things, an offer to sell at the option price, the maximum number of shares purchasable under the option, and the period of time during which the offer remains open. The term option includes a warrant that meets the requirements of this paragraph (a)(1).

*(2)* An option may be granted as part of or in conjunction with an employee stock purchase plan or subscription contract. See section 423.

*(3)* An option must be in writing (in paper or electronic form), provided that such writing is adequate to establish an option right or privilege that is enforceable under applicable law.

**(b) Statutory options.** *(1)* The term statutory option, for purposes of this section and §§ 1.421-2 through 1.424-1, means an incentive stock option, as defined in § 1.422-2(a), or an option granted under an employee stock purchase plan, as defined in § 1.423-2.

*(2)* An option qualifies as a statutory option only if the option is not transferable (other than by will or by the laws of descent and distribution) by the individual to whom the option was granted, and is exercisable, during the lifetime of such individual, only by such individual. See §§ 1.422-2(a)(2)(v) and 1.423-2(j). Accordingly, an option which is transferable or transferred by the individual to whom the option is granted during such individual's lifetime, or is exercisable during such individual's lifetime by another person, is not a statutory option. However, if the option or the plan under which the option was granted contains a provision permitting the individual to designate the person who may exercise the option after such individual's death, neither such provision, nor a designation pursuant to such provision, disqualifies the option as a statutory option. A pledge of the stock purchasable under an option as security for a loan that is used to pay the option price does not cause the option to violate the nontransferability requirements of this paragraph (b). Also, the transfer of an option to a trust does not disqualify the option as a statutory option if, under section 671 and applicable State law, the individual is considered the sole beneficial owner of the option while it is held in the trust. If an option is transferred incident to divorce (within the meaning of section 1041) or pursuant to a domestic relations order, the option does not qualify as a statutory option as of the day of such transfer. For the treatment of nonstatutory options, see § 1.83-7.

*(3)* (i) The determination of whether an option is a statutory option is made as of the date such option is granted. An option which is a statutory option when granted does not lose its character as such an option by reason of subsequent events, and an option which is not a statutory option when granted does not become such an option by reason of subsequent events. See, however, paragraph (e) of § 1.424-1, relating to modification, extension, or renewal of an option. For rules concerning options that are not statutory options, see § 1.83-7.

(ii) The application of this subparagraph may be illustrated by the following examples:

*Example (1).* X Corporation is a subsidiary of S Corporation which, in turn, is a subsidiary of P Corporation. On June 1, 2004, P grants to an employee of P a statutory option to purchase a share of stock of X. On January 1, 2005, S sells a portion of the X stock which it owns to an unrelated corporation and, as of that date, X ceases to be a subsidiary of S. On May 1, 2005, while still employed by P, the employee exercises his option to purchase a share of X stock. Because X was a subsidiary of P on the date of the grant of the statutory option, the option does not fail to be a statutory option even though X ceases to be a subsidiary of P.

*Example (2).* Assume P grants an option to an employee under the same facts as in example (1) above, except that on June 1, 2004, X is not a subsidiary of either S or P. Such option is not a statutory option on June 1, 2004. On January 1, 2005, S purchases from an unrelated corporation a sufficient number of shares of X stock to make X, as of that date, a subsidiary of S. On May 1, 2005, while still employed by P, the employee exercises his option to purchase a share of X stock. Because X was not a subsidiary of S or P on the date of the grant of the option, the option is not a statutory option even though X later becomes a subsidiary of P. See §§ 1.422-2(a)(2) and 1.423-2(b).

**(c) Time and date of granting option.** *(1)* For purposes of this section and §§ 1.421-2 through 1.424-1, the language "the date of the granting of the option" and "the time such option is granted," and similar phrases refer to the date or time when the granting corporation completes the corporate action constituting an offer of stock for sale to an individual under the terms and conditions of a statutory option. Except as set forth in § 1.423-2(h)(2), a corporate action constituting an offer of stock for sale is not considered complete until the date on which the maximum number of shares that can be purchased under the option and the minimum option price are fixed or determinable.

*(2)* If the corporation imposes conditions on the granting of an option (as distinguished from conditions governing the exercise of the option), such conditions shall be given effect in accordance with the intent of the corporation. However, under section 424(i), if the grant of an option is subject to approval by stockholders, the date of grant of the option shall be determined as if the option had not been subject to such approval. A condition which does not require corporate

action, such as the approval of, or registration with, some regulatory or governmental agency, for example, a stock exchange or the Securities and Exchange Commission, is ordinarily considered a condition upon the exercise of the option unless the corporate action clearly indicates that the option is not to be granted until such condition is satisfied. If an option is granted to an individual upon the condition that such individual will become an employee of the corporation granting the option or of a related corporation, such option is not granted prior to the date the individual becomes such an employee.

*(3)* In general, conditions imposed upon the exercise of an option will not operate to make ineffective the granting of the option. For example, on June 1, 2004, the A Corporation grants to X, an employee, an option to purchase 5,000 shares of the corporation's stock, exercisable by X on or after June 1, 2005, provided he is employed by the corporation on June 1, 2005, and provided that A's profits during the fiscal year preceding the year of exercise exceed $200,000. Such an option is granted to X on June 1, 2004, and will be treated as outstanding as of such date.

**(d) Stock and voting stock.** *(1)* For purposes of this section and §§ 1.421-2 through 1.424-1, the term stock means capital stock of any class, including voting or nonvoting common or preferred stock. Except as otherwise provided, the term includes both treasury stock and stock of original issue. Special classes of stock authorized to be issued to and held by employees are within the scope of the term stock as used in such sections, provided such stock otherwise possesses the rights and characteristics of capital stock.

*(2)* For purposes of determining what constitutes voting stock in ascertaining whether a plan has been approved by stockholders under § 1.422-2(b) or 1.423-2(c) or whether the limitations pertaining to voting power contained in §§ 1.422-2(f) and 1.423-2(d) have been met, stock which does not have voting rights until the happening of an event, such as the default in the payment of dividends on preferred stock, is not voting stock until the happening of the specified event. Generally, stock which does not possess a general voting power, and may vote only on particular questions, is not voting stock. However, if such stock is entitled to vote on whether a stock option plan may be adopted, it is voting stock.

*(3)* In general, for purposes of this section and §§ 1.421-2 through 1.424-1, ownership interests other than capital stock are considered stock.

**(e) Option price.** *(1)* For purposes of this section and §§ 1.421-2 through 1.424-1, the term option price, price paid under the option, or exercise price means the consideration in cash or property which, pursuant to the terms of the option, is the price at which the stock subject to the option is purchased. The term option price does not include any amounts paid as interest under a deferred payment arrangement or treated as interest.

*(2)* Any reasonable valuation method may be used to determine whether, at the time the option is granted, the option price satisfies the pricing requirements of sections 422(b)(4), 422(c)(5), 422(c)(7), and 423(b)(6) with respect to the stock subject to the option. Such methods include, for example, the valuation method described in § 20.2031-2 of this chapter (Estate Tax Regulations).

**(f) Exercise.** For purposes of this section and §§ 1.421-2 through 1.424-1, the term "exercise", when used in reference to an option, means the act of acceptance by the optionee of the offer to sell contained in the option. In general, the time of exercise is the time when there is a sale or a contract to sell between the corporation and the individual. A promise to pay the option price does not constitute an exercise of the option unless the optionee is subject to personal liability on such promise. An agreement or undertaking by the employee to make payments under a stock purchase plan does not constitute the exercise of an option to the extent the payments made remain subject to withdrawal by or refund to the employee.

**(g) Transfer.** For purposes of this section and §§ 1.421-2 through 1.424-1, the term "transfer", when used in reference to the transfer to an individual of a share of stock pursuant to his exercise of a statutory option, means the transfer of ownership of such share, or the transfer of substantially all the rights of ownership. Such transfer must, within a reasonable time, be evidenced on the books of the corporation. For purposes of section 422, a transfer may occur even if a share of stock is subject to a substantial risk of forfeiture or is not otherwise transferable immediately after the date of exercise. See § 1.422-1(b)(3) Example 2. A transfer does not fail to occur merely because, under the terms of the arrangement, the individual may not dispose of the share for a specified period of time, or the share is subject to a right of first refusal or a right to reacquire the share at the share's fair market value at the time of sale.

**(h) Employment relationship.** *(1)* An option is a statutory option only if, at the time the option is granted, the optionee is an employee of the corporation granting the option, or a related corporation of such corporation. If the option has been assumed or a new option has been substituted in its place under § 1.424-1(a), the optionee must, at the time of such substitution or assumption, be an employee (or a former employee within the 3-month period following termination of the employment relationship) of the corporation so substituting or assuming the option, or a related corporation of such corporation. The determination of whether the optionee is an employee at the time the option is granted (or at the time of the substitution or assumption under § 1.424-1(a)) is made in accordance with section 3401(c) and the regulations thereunder. As to the granting of an option conditioned upon employment, see paragraph (c)(2) of this section. A statutory option must be granted for a reason connected with the individual's employment by the corporation or by its related corporation.

*(2)* In addition, § 1.421-2(a) is applicable to the transfer of a share pursuant to the exercise of the statutory option only if the optionee is, at all times during the period beginning with the date of the granting of such option and ending on the day 3 months before the date of such exercise, an employee of either the corporation granting such option, a related corporation of such corporation, or a corporation (or a related corporation of such corporation) substituting or assuming a stock option in a transaction to which § 1.424-1(a) applies. For purposes of the preceding sentence, the employment relationship is treated as continuing intact while the individual is on military leave, sick leave, or other bona fide leave of absence (such as temporary employment by the Government) if the period of such leave does not exceed 3 months, or if longer, so long as the individual's right to reemployment with the corporation granting the option (or a related corporation of such corporation) or a corporation (or a related corporation of such corporation) substituting or assuming a stock option in a transaction to which § 1.424-1(a) applies, is provided either by statute or by contract. If the period of leave exceeds 3 months and the individual's right to reemployment is not provided either by statute or by con-

tract, the employment relationship is deemed to terminate on the first day immediately following such three-month period. Thus, if the option is not exercised before such deemed termination of employment, § 1.421-2(a) applies to the transfer of a share pursuant to an exercise of the option only if the exercise occurs within 3 months from the date the employment relationship is deemed terminated.

*(3)* For purposes of determining whether an individual meets the requirements of this paragraph, the term "employer corporation", as used in section 424(e) and (f), shall be read as "grantor corporation" or "corporation issuing or assuming a stock option in a transaction to which section 424(a) is applicable", as the case may be. For purposes of the employment requirement, a corporation employing an optionee is considered a related corporation if it was a parent or subsidiary of the corporation granting the option or substituting or assuming the option during the entire portion of the requisite period of employment during which it was the employer of such optionee.

*(4)* The application of this paragraph may be illustrated by the following examples:

*Example (1).* On June 1, 2004, X Corporation granted a statutory option to A, an employee of X Corporation, to purchase a share of X stock. On February 1, 2005, X sold the plant where A was employed to M Corporation, an unrelated corporation, and A was employed by M. If A exercises his statutory option on June 1, 2005, section 421 is not applicable to such exercise, because on June 1, 2005, A is not employed by the corporation which granted the option or by a related corporation of such corporation, nor was he employed by any of such corporations within 3 months before June 1, 2005.

*Example (2).* Assume the facts to be the same as in example (1), except that when A was employed by M Corporation, the option to purchase X stock was terminated and was replaced by an option to buy M stock in such circumstances that M Corporation is treated as a corporation substituting an option under section 424(a). If A exercises the option to purchase the share of M stock on June 1, 2005, section 421 is applicable to the transfer of the M stock because, at all times during the period beginning with the date of grant of the X option and ending with the date of exercise of the M option, A was an employee of the corporation granting the option or substituting or assuming the option under § 1.424-1(a).

*Example (3).* E is an employee of P Corporation. On June 1, 2004, P grants E a statutory option to purchase a share of P stock. On June 1, 2005, P acquires 100 percent of the stock of S Corporation; on such date S becomes a subsidiary of P. On July 1, 2005, E ceases to be employed by P and becomes employed by S. On October 10, 2005, while still employed by S, E exercises his option to buy P stock. Since E was at all times during the requisite period of employment an employee of either P, the corporation granting the option, or S, a subsidiary of the grantor during the period in which such corporation was E's employer, section 421 is applicable to the exercise of the option.

*Example (4).* Assume the same facts as in example (3) except assume that at the time E became an employee of S Corporation, S assumed E's option to purchase P stock under section 424(a). Section 421 is applicable to E's exercise of his option to buy P stock.

*Example (5).* M Corporation grants a statutory option to E, an employee of such corporation. E is an officer in a reserve Air Force unit. E goes on military leave with his unit for 3 weeks. Regardless of whether E is an employee of M within the meaning of section 3401(c) and the regulations thereunder during such 3-week period, E's employment relationship with M is treated as uninterrupted during the period of E's military leave.

*Example (6).* Assume the same facts as in example (5) and assume further that E's active duty status is extended indefinitely, but that E has a right to reemployment with M or a related corporation on the termination of any military duty E may be required to serve. E exercises his M option while on active military duty. Irrespective of whether E is an employee of M or a related corporation within the meaning of section 3401(c) and the regulations thereunder at the time of such exercise or within 3 months before such exercise, section 421 applies to such exercise.

*Example (7).* X Corporation grants an incentive option to A, an employee of X Corporation, whose employment contract provides that in the event of illness, A's right to reemployment with X, or a related corporation of X, will continue for 1 year after the time A becomes unable to perform his duties for X. A falls ill for 90 days. For purposes of section 422(a)(2), A's employment relationship with X will be treated as uninterrupted during the 90-day period. If A's incapacity extends beyond 90 days, then, for purposes of section 422(a)(2), A's employment relationship with X will be treated as continuing uninterrupted until A's reemployment rights terminate. Under section 422(a)(2), A has 3 months in which to exercise his an incentive option after his employment relationship with X (and related corporations) is deemed terminated.

**(i) Additional definitions.** *(1) Corporation.* For purposes of this section and §§ 1.421-2 through 1.424-1, the term corporation has the meaning prescribed by section 7701(a)(3) and § 301.7701-2(b) of this chapter. For example, a corporation for purposes of the preceding sentence includes an S corporation (as defined in section 1361), a foreign corporation (as defined in section 7701(a)(5)), and a limited liability company that is treated as a corporation for all Federal tax purposes.

*(2) Parent corporation and subsidiary corporation.* For the definition of the terms parent corporation (and parent) and subsidiary corporation (and subsidiary), for purposes of this section and §§ 1.421-2 through 1.424-1, see § 1.424-1(f)(i) and (ii), respectively. Related corporation as used in this section and in §§ 1.421-2 through 1.424-1 means either a parent corporation or subsidiary corporation.

**(j) Effective/applicability date.** *(1) In general.* Except for paragraph (c)(1) of this section, the regulations under this section are effective on August 3, 2004. Paragraph (c)(1) of this section is effective on November 17, 2009. Paragraph (c)(1) of this section applies to statutory options granted on or after January 1, 2010.

*(2) Reliance and transition period.* For statutory options granted on or before June 9, 2003, taxpayers may rely on the 1984 proposed regulations LR-279-81 (49 FR 4504), the 2003 proposed regulations REG-122917-02 (68 FR 34344), or this section until the earlier of January 1, 2006, or the first regularly scheduled stockholders meeting of the granting corporation occurring 6 months after August 3, 2004. For statutory options granted after June 9, 2003, and before the earlier of January 1, 2006, or the first regularly scheduled stockholders meeting of the granting corporation occurring at least 6 months after August 3, 2004, taxpayers may rely on either REG-122917-02 or this section. Taxpayers may not rely on LR-279-81 or REG-122917-02 after Decem-

ber 31, 2005. Reliance on LR-279-81, REG-122917-02, or this section must be in its entirety, and all statutory options granted during the reliance period must be treated consistently.

T.D. 6887, 6/23/66, amend T.D. 6975, 10/2/68, T.D. 7554, 7/21/78, T.D. 9144, 8/2/2004, T.D. 9471, 11/16/2009.

### § 1.421-2 General rules.

*Caution:* The Treasury has not yet amended Reg § 1.421-2 to reflect changes made by P.L. 108-357.

**(a) Effect of qualifying transfer.** *(1)* If a share of stock is transferred to an individual pursuant to the individual's exercise of a statutory option, and if the requirements of § 1.422-1(a) (relating to incentive stock options) or § 1.423-1(a) (relating to employee stock purchase plans) whichever is applicable, are met, then—

(i) No income results under section 83 at the time of the transfer of such share to the individual upon the exercise of the option with respect to such share;

(ii) No deduction under sections 83(h) or 162 or the regulations thereunder (relating to trade or business expenses) is allowable at any time with respect to the share so transferred; and

(iii) No amount other than the price paid under the option is considered as received by the employer corporation, a related corporation of such corporation, or a corporation substituting or assuming a stock option in a transaction to which § 1.424-1(a) (relating to corporate reorganizations, liquidations, etc.) applies, for the share so transferred.

*(2)* For the purpose of this paragraph, each share of stock transferred pursuant to a statutory option is treated separately. For example, if an individual, while employed by a corporation granting him a statutory option, exercises the option with respect to part of the stock covered by the option, and if such individual exercises the balance of the option more than three months after leaving such employment, the application of section 421 to the stock obtained upon the earlier exercise of the option is not affected by the fact that the income taxes of the employer and the individual with respect to the stock obtained upon the later exercise of the option are not determined under section 421.

**(b) Effect of disqualifying disposition.** *(1)* (i) The disposition (as defined in § 1.424-1(c)) of a share of stock acquired by the exercise of a statutory option before the expiration of the applicable holding periods as determined under § 1.422-1(a) or 1.423-1(a) is a disqualifying disposition and makes paragraph (a) of this section inapplicable to the transfer of such share. See section 83(a) to determine the amount includible on a disqualifying disposition. The income attributable to such transfer (determined without reduction for any brokerage fees or other costs paid in connection with the disposition) is treated by the individual as compensation income received in the taxable year in which such disqualifying disposition occurs. A deduction attributable to such transfer is allowable, to the extent otherwise allowable under section 162, for the taxable year in which such disqualifying disposition occurs to the employer corporation, or a related corporation of such corporation, or a corporation substituting or assuming an option in a transaction to which § 1.424-1(a) applies. Additionally, the amount allowed as a deduction must be determined as if the requirements of section 83(h) and § 1.83-6(a) apply. No amount is treated as income, and no amount is allowed as a deduction, for any taxable year other than the taxable year in which the disqualifying disposition occurs. If the amount realized on the disposition exceeds (or is less than) the sum of the amount paid for the share and the amount of compensation income recognized as a result of such disposition, the extent to which the difference is treated as gain (or loss) is determined under the rules of section 302 or 1001, as applicable.

(ii) The following examples illustrate the principles of this paragraph (b):

*Example (1).* On June 1, 2006, X Corporation grants an incentive stock option to A, an employee of X, entitling A to purchase 100 shares of X stock at $10 per share. On August 1, 2006, A exercises the option when the fair market value of X stock is $20 per share, and 100 shares of X stock are transferred to A on that date. On December 15, 2007, A sells the stock for $20 per share. Because A disposed of the stock before June 2, 2008, A did not satisfy the holding period requirements of § 1.422-1(a). Under paragraph (b)(1)(i) of this section, A therefore made a disqualifying disposition of the stock. Thus, paragraph (a) of this section is inapplicable to the transfer of the shares, and A must include the compensation income attributable to the transfer of the shares in gross income in the year of the disqualifying disposition. The amount of compensation income A must include in income is $1,000 ($2,000, the fair market value of X stock on transfer less $1,000, the exercise price per share). If the requirements of § 83(h) and § 1.83-6(a) are satisfied and otherwise allowable under section162, X is allowed a deduction of $1,000 for its taxable year in which the disqualifying disposition occurs.

*Example (2).* Y Corporation grants an incentive stock option for 100 shares of its stock to E, an employee of Y. The option has an exercise price of $10 per share. E exercises the option and is transferred the shares when the fair market value of a share of Y stock is $30. Before the applicable holding periods are met, Y redeems the shares for $70 per share. Because the holding period requirements of § 1.422-1(a) are not met, the redemption of the shares is a disqualifying disposition of the shares. Under paragraph (b)(1)(i) of this section, A made a disqualifying disposition of the stock. Thus, paragraph (a) of this section is inapplicable to the transfer of the shares, and E must include the compensation income attributable to the transfer of the shares in gross income in the year of the disqualifying disposition. The amount of compensation income that E must include in income is $2,000 ($3,000, the fair market value of Y stock on transfer, less $1,000, the exercise price paid by E). The character of the additional gain that is includible in E's income as a result of the redemption is determined under the rules of section 302. If the requirements of § 83(h) and § 1.83-6(a) are satisfied and otherwise allowable under section 162, Y is allowed a deduction for the taxable year in which the disqualifying disposition occurs for the compensation income of $2,000. Y is not allowed a deduction for the additional gain includible in E's income as a result of the redemption.

*(2)* If an optionee transfers stock acquired through the optionee's exercise of a statutory option prior to the expiration of the applicable holding periods, paragraph (a) of this section continues to apply to the transfer of the stock pursuant to the exercise of the option if such transfer is not a disposition of the stock as defined in § 1.424-1(c) (for example, a transfer from a decedent to the decedent's estate or a transfer by bequest or inheritance). Similarly, a subsequent transfer by the executor, administrator, heir, or legatee is not a disqualifying disposition by the decedent. If a statutory option is exercised by the estate of the optionee or by a person who

acquired the option by bequest or inheritance or by reason of the death of such optionee, see paragraph (c) of this section. If a statutory option is exercised by the individual to whom the option was granted and the individual dies before the expiration of the holding periods, see paragraph (d) of this section.

*(3)* For special rules relating to the disqualifying disposition of a share of stock acquired by exercise of an incentive stock option, see §§ 1.422-5(b)(2) and 1.424-1(c)(3).

**(c) Exercise by estate.** *(1)* 1) If a statutory option is exercised by the estate of the individual to whom the option was granted (or by any person who acquired such option by bequest or inheritance or by reason of the death of such individual), paragraph (a) of this section applies to the transfer of stock pursuant to such exercise in the same manner as if the option had been exercised by the deceased optionee. Consequently, neither the estate nor such person is required to include any amount in gross income as a result of a transfer of stock pursuant to the exercise of the option. Paragraph (a) of this section applies even if the executor, administrator, or such person disposes of the stock so acquired before the expiration of the applicable holding periods as determined under § 1.422-1(a) or 1.423-1(a). This special rule does not affect the applicability of section 423(c), relating to the estate's or other qualifying person's recognition of compensation income, or section 1222, relating to what constitutes a short-term and long-term capital gain or loss. Paragraph (a) of this section also applies even if the executor, administrator, or such person does not exercise the option within three months after the death of the individual or is not employed as described in § 1.421-1(h), either when the option is exercised or at any time. However, paragraph (a) of this section does not apply to a transfer of shares pursuant to an exercise of the option by the estate or by such person unless the individual met the employment requirements described in § 1.421-1(h) either at the time of the individual's death or within three months before such time (or, if applicable, within the period described in § 1.422-1(a)(3)). Additionally, paragraph (a) of this section does not apply if the option is exercised by a person other than the executor or administrator, or other than a person who acquired the option by bequest or inheritance or by reason of the death of such deceased individual. For example, if the option is sold by the estate, paragraph (a) of this section does not apply to the transfer of stock pursuant to an exercise of the option by the buyer, but if the option is distributed by the administrator to an heir as part of the estate, paragraph (a) of this section applies to the transfer of stock pursuant to an exercise of the option by such heir.

*(2)* Any transfer by the estate, whether a sale, a distribution of assets, or otherwise, of the stock acquired by its exercise of the option under this paragraph is a disposition of the stock for purposes of section 423(c). Therefore, if section 423(c), is applicable, the estate must include an amount as compensation in its gross income. Similarly, if section 423(c) is applicable in case of an exercise of the option under this paragraph by a person who acquired the option by bequest or inheritance or by reason of the death of the individual to whom the option was granted, there must be included in the gross income of such person an amount as compensation, either when such person disposes of the stock, or when he dies owning the stock.

*(3)* (i) If, under section 423(c), an amount is required to be included in the gross income of the estate or of such person, the estate or such person shall be allowed a deduction as a result of the inclusion of the value of the option in the estate of the individual to whom the option was granted. Such deduction shall be computed under section 691(c) by treating the option as an item of gross income in respect of a decedent under section 691 and by treating the amount required to be included in gross income under section 423(c), as an amount included in gross income under section 691 in respect of such item of gross income. No such deduction shall be allowable with respect to any amount other than an amount includible under section 423(c). For the rules relating to the computation of a deduction under section 691(c), see § 1.691(c)-1.

(ii) The application of subdivision (i) may be illustrated by the following example:

*Example.* On June 1, 2004, E was granted an option under an employee stock purchase plan to purchase for $85 one share of the stock of his employer. On such day, the fair market value of such stock was $100 per share. E died on February 1, 2006, without having exercised such option. The option was, however, exercisable by his estate, and for purposes of the estate tax was valued at $30. On March 1, 2006, the estate exercised the option, and on March 15, 2006, sold for $150 the share of stock so acquired. For its taxable year including March 15, 2006, the estate is required by sections 421(c)(1)(B) and 423(c) to include in its gross income as compensation the amount of $15. During such taxable year, no amounts of income were properly paid, credited, or distributable to the beneficiaries of the estate. However, under section 421(c)(2), the estate is entitled to a deduction determined in the following manner. E's estate includes no other items of income in respect of a decedent referred to in section 691(a), and no deductions referred to in section 691(b), so that the value for estate tax purposes of the option, $30, is also the net value of all items of income in respect of the decedent. The estate tax attributable to the inclusion of the option in the estate of E is $10. Since $15, the amount includible in gross income by reason of sections 421(c)(1)(B) and 423(c), is less than the value for estate tax purposes of the option, only 15⁄30 of the estate tax attributable to the inclusion of the option in the estate is deductible; that is, 15⁄30 of $10, or $5. No deduction under section 421(c)(2) is allowable with respect to any capital gain.

*(4)* (i) (a) In the case of the death of an optionee, the basis of any share of stock acquired by the exercise of an option under this paragraph, determined under section 1011, shall be increased by an amount equal to the portion of the basis of the option attributable to such share. For example, if a statutory option to acquire 10 shares of stock has a basis of $100, the basis of one share acquired by a partial exercise of the option, determined under section 1011, would be increased by 1⁄10th of $100, or $10. The option acquires a basis, determined under section 1014(a), only if the transfer of the share pursuant to the exercise of such option qualifies for the special tax treatment provided by section 421(a). To the extent the option is so exercised, in whole or in part, it will acquire a basis equal to its fair market value at the date of the employee's death or, if an election is made under section 2032, its value at its applicable valuation date. In certain cases, the basis of the share is subject to the adjustments provided by (b) and (c) of this subdivision, but such adjustments are only applicable in the case of an option which is subject to section 423(c).

(b) If the amount which would have been includible in gross income under section 423(c) had the employee exercised the option on the date of his death and held the share at the time of his death exceeds the amount which is includible in gross income under such section, the basis of the share, determined under (a) of this subdivision, shall be reduced by such excess. For example, if $15 would have been includible in the gross income of the employee had he exercised the option and held such share at the time of his death, and only $10 is includible under section 423(c), the basis of the share, determined under (a) of this subdivision, would be reduced by $5. For purposes of determining the amount which would have been includible in gross income under section 423(c), if the employee had exercised the option and held such share at the time of his death, the amount which would have been paid for the share shall be computed as if the option had been exercised on the date the employee died.

(c) If the amount includible in gross income under section 423(c), exceeds the portion of the basis of the option attributable to the share, the basis of the share, determined under (a) of this subdivision, shall be increased by such excess. Thus, if $15 is includible in gross income under such section, and the basis of the option with respect to the share is $10, the basis of the share, determined under (a) of this subdivision, will be increased by $5.

(ii) If a statutory option is not exercised by the estate of the individual to whom the option was granted, or by the person who acquired such option by bequest or inheritance or by reason of the death of such individual, the option shall be considered to be property which constitutes a right to receive an item of income in respect of a decedent to which the rules of sections 691 and 1014(c) apply.

(iii) The application of this subparagraph may be illustrated by the following examples:

*Example (1).* On June 1, 2005, the X Corporation granted to E, an employee, an option under its employee stock purchase plan to purchase a share of X Corporation stock for $85. The fair market value of X Corporation stock on such date was $100 per share. On June 1, 2006, E died. The fair market value of X Corporation stock on such date exceeded $100 per share and the fair market value of the option on the applicable valuation date was $35. On August 1, 2006,, the estate of E exercised the option and sold the share of X Corporation stock at a time when the fair market value of the share was $120. The basis of the share is $120 (the $85 paid for the stock plus the $35 basis of the option). When the share is sold for $120, the estate is required to include $15 in its gross income as compensation. Since $15 would have been includible in E's gross income if he had exercised the option and held such share at the time of his death, paragraph (c)(4)(i)(b) of this section does not apply. Moreover, since the $15 includible in the gross income of the estate does not exceed the basis of the option ($35), paragraph (c)(4)(i)(c) of this section does not apply. Since the basis of the stock and the sale price are the same, no gain or loss is realized by the estate on the disposition of the share.

*Example (2).* Assume the same facts as in Example 1, except that the fair market value of the share of stock at the time of its sale was $90. The basis of the share, determined under paragraph (c)(4)(i)(a) of this section, is $120 (the $85 paid for the stock plus the $35 basis of the option). When the share is sold for $90, the estate is required to include $5 in its gross income as compensation. If the employee had exercised the option and held the share at the time of his death, $15 would have been includible in gross income as compensation for the taxable year ending with his death. Since such amount exceeds by $10 the amount which the estate is required to include in its gross income, paragraph (c)(4)(i)(b) of this section applies, and the basis of the share ($120), determined under paragraph (c)(4)(i)(a) of this section is reduced by $10. Accordingly, the basis is $110, and a capital loss of $20 is realized on the disposition of the share.

*Example (3).* Assume the same facts as in Example 1, except that the fair market value of the option on the applicable valuation date was $5, and that the fair market value of X Corporation stock on the date the employee died did not exceed $100. The basis of the share, determined under paragraph (c)(4)(i)(a) of this section, is $90 (the $85 paid for the stock plus the $5 basis of the option). When the share is sold for $120, the estate is required to include $15 in its gross income as compensation. Since such amount exceeds by $10 the basis of the option, paragraph (c)(4)(i)(c) of this section applies, and the basis of the share ($90), determined under paragraph (c)(4)(i)(a) of this section, is increased by $10. Accordingly, the basis is $100 and a capital gain of $20 is realized on the disposition of the share.

*Example (4).* Assume the same facts as in Example 1, except that on June 1, 2006, the date the employee died, the fair market value of X Corporation stock was $98, and that on June 1, 2007, the alternate valuation date, the fair market value of the stock had declined substantially, and the fair market value of the option was $5. On August 1, 2007, the estate of E exercised the option and sold the share when its fair market value was $92. The basis of the share, determined under paragraph (c)(4)(i)(a) of this section, is $90 (the $85 paid for the stock plus the $5 basis of the option). When the share is sold for $92, the estate is required to include $7 in its gross income as compensation. Since $13 would have been includible in E's gross income if he had exercised the option and held such share at the time of his death, paragraph (c)(4)(i)(b) of this section applies, and the basis of the share ($90), determined under paragraph (c)(4)(i)(a) of this section, is reduced by $6 to $84. Furthermore, since the $7 that the estate is required to include in its gross income when the share is sold for $92 exceeds by $2 the basis of the option, paragraph (c)(4)(i)(c) of this section applies, and the basis of the share ($84), determined under paragraph (c)(4)(i)(a) of this section and paragraph (c)(4)(i)(b) of this section, is increased by $2. Accordingly, the basis is $86 and a capital gain of $6 is realized on the disposition of the share.

**(d) Option exercised by the individual to whom the option was granted if the individual dies before expiration of the applicable holding periods.** If a statutory option is exercised by the individual to whom the option was granted and such individual dies before the expiration of the applicable holding periods as determined under § 1.422-1(a) or 1.423-1(a), paragraph (a) of this section does not become inapplicable if the executor or administrator of the estate of such individual, or any person who acquired such stock by bequest or inheritance or by reason of the death of such individual, disposes of such stock before the expiration of such applicable holding periods. This rule does not affect the applicability of section 423(c), relating to the individual's recognition of compensation income, or section 1222, relating to what constitutes a short-term and long-term capital gain or loss.

**(e) Incorporation by reference.** Any requirement that an option expressly contain or state a prescribed limitation or term will be considered met if such limitation or term is set forth in a statutory option plan and is incorporated by reference by the option. Thus, if a statutory option plan expressly provides that no option granted thereunder shall be exercisable after five years from the date of grant, and if an option granted thereunder expressly provides that the option is granted subject to the terms and limitations of such plan, the option will be regarded as being, by its terms, not exercisable after the expiration of 5 years from the date such option is granted.

**(f) Effective date.** *(1) In general.* These regulations are effective on August 3, 2004.

*(2) Reliance and transition period.* For statutory options granted on or before June 9, 2003, taxpayers may rely on the 1984 proposed regulations LR-279-81 (49 FR 4504), the 2003 proposed regulations REG-122917-02 (68 FR 34344), or this section until the earlier of January 1, 2006, or the first regularly scheduled stockholders meeting of the granting corporation occurring 6 months after August 3, 2004. For statutory options granted after June 9, 2003, and before the earlier of January 1, 2006, or the first regularly scheduled stockholders meeting of the granting corporation at least 6 months after August 3, 2004, taxpayers may rely on either REG-122917-02 or section. Taxpayers may not rely on LR-279-81 or REG-122917-02 after December 31, 2005. Reliance on LR-279-81, REG-122917-02, or this section must be in its entirety, and all statutory options granted during the reliance period must be treated consistently.

---

T.D. 6887, 6/23/66, amend T.D. 9144, 8/2/2004.

---

PAR. 4. Section 1.421-7 is amended by revising paragraphs (b)(1), (b)(2), (d), (e)(1), (e)(2), and (h)(2) to read as follows:

**Proposed § 1.421-7 Meaning and use of certain terms.**
[*For Preamble, see ¶ 150,935*]

* * * * *

• ***Caution:*** This Notice of Proposed Rulemaking was finalized by TD 9144, 8/2/2004. For statutory options granted on or before June 9, 2003, taxpayers may rely on any of these three sets of regs, in their entirety: (i) proposed regs issued in '84 (reproduced below); (ii) proposed regs issued on June 9, 2003; or (iii) final regs-until the earlier of (a) Jan. 1, 2006, or (b) the first regularly scheduled stockholders meeting of the granting corporation occurring at least six months after Aug. 3, 2004.

**(b) Statutory options.** *(1)* The term " statutory option", used for purposes of convenience hereinafter in this section and in §§ 1.421-8 through 1.425-1, means a qualified stock option, as defined by section 422(b) and § 1.422-2; an incentive stock option, as defined by section 422A(b) and § 1.422A-2; an option granted under an employee stock purchase plan, as defined by section and 423(b) § 1.423-2; and a restricted stock option, as defined in section 424(b) and § 1.424-2.

*(2)* An option may qualify as a statutory option only if the option is not transferable (other than by will or by the laws of descent and distribution) by the individual to whom it is granted, and is exercisable, during the lifetime of such individual, only by him. See sections 422(b)(6), 422A(b)(5), 423(b)(9), and 424(b)(2). Accordingly, an option which is transferable by the individual to whom it is granted during his lifetime, or is exercisable during such individual's lifetime by another person, is not a statutory option. However, in case the option or the plan under which the option was granted contains a provision permitting the individual to whom the option was granted to designate the person who may exercise the option after his death, neither such provision, nor a designation pursuant to such provision, disqualifies the option as a statutory option.

* * * * *

**(d) Stock and voting stock.** For purposes of sections 421 through 425, the term "stock" means capital stock of any class, including voting or nonvoting common or preferred stock. Except as otherwise provided, the term includes both treasury stock and stock of original issue. Special classes of stock authorized to be issued to and held by employees are within the scope of the term "stock" as used in such sections, provided such stock otherwise possesses the rights and characteristics of capital stock. For purposes of determining what constitutes voting stock in ascertaining whether a plan has been approved by stockholders or whether the limitations pertaining to voting power contained in sections 422(b)(7), 422A(b)(6), 423(b)(3) and 424(b)(3) and the regulations thereunder have been met, stock which does not have voting rights until the happening of an event, such as the default in the payment of dividends on preferred stock, is not voting stock until the happening of the specified event. Moreover, stock which does not possess a general voting power, and may vote only on particular questions, is not voting stock. However, if such stock is entitled to vote on whether a stock option plan is to be adopted, it is voting stock for the purpose of ascertaining whether the plan has been approved by the shareholders.

**(e) Option price.** *(1)* For purposes of sections 421 through 425, the term "option price" or "price paid under the option" means the consideration if money or other property which, pursuant to the terms of the option, is the price at which the stock subject to the option is purchased. The term "option price" does not include amounts paid as interest under a deferred payment arrangement or treated as unstated interest under section 483 and the regulations thereunder. Thus, for example, section 483 is applicable in determining whether the pricing requirements of section 422(b)(4), 422A(b)(4) and (c)(8), 423(b)(6), 424(b)(1), or 424(c) are met and is applicable in determining the basis of any stock acquired pursuant to the exercise of a statutory option. However, with respect to statutory options granted prior to January 1, 1965, the determination of whether the applicable pricing requirements are met shall be made without regard to section 483, but section 483 shall be taken into consideration in determining basis for purposes of determining gain or loss.

*(2)* In the case of a statutory option, any reasonable valuation method may be used for the purpose of determining whether at the time the option is granted the option price satisfies the pricing requirements of section 442(b)(4) (relating to qualified stock options), section 422A(b)(4) and (c)(8) (relating to incentive stock options), section 423(b)(6) (relating to employee stock purchase plans), or section 424(b)(1) (relating to restricted stock options), whichever is applicable, with respect to the stock subject to the option. Such methods include the valuation methods described in § 20.2031-2 of this chapter (Estate Tax Regulations).

* * * * *

**(h) Employment relationship.** * * *

*(2)* In order to qualify for the special tax treatment of section 421, in addition to meeting the requirements of subparagraph (1) of this paragraph, an individual exercising a qualified stock option, an incentive stock option, or an option

granted under an employee stock purchase plan must, at all times during the period beginning with the date of the granting of such option and ending at the time of such exercise or on the day 3 months before the date of such exercise, be an employee of either the corporation granting such option, a related corporation of such corporation, or a corporation or a related corporation of such corporation issuing or assuming a stock option in a transaction to which section 425(a) applies. For this pur- pose, the employment relationship in respect of an option granted in accordance with the requirements of subparagraph (1) of this paragraph will be treated as continuing intact while the individual is on military, sick leave or other bona fide leave of absence (such as temporary employment by the Government) if the period of such leave does not exceed 90 days, or, if longer, so long as the individual's right to reemployment with the corporation granting the option (or a related corporation of such corporation, or a corporation, or a related corporation of such corporation issuing or assuming a stock option in a transaction to which section 425(a) applies) is guaranteed either by statute or by contract. Where the period of leave exceeds 90 days and where the individual's right to reemployment is not guaranteed either by statute or by contract, the employment relationship will be deemed to have terminated on the 91st day of such leave.

* * * * *

PAR. 5. Section 1.421-8 is amended by revising paragraphs (a)(1), (b)(1), and (b)(2), adding new paragraph (b)(4), and revising paragraphs (c)(1) and (d) to read as follows:

**Proposed § 1.421-8 General rules.** [*For Preamble, see ¶ 150,935*]

• ***Caution:*** This Notice of Proposed Rulemaking was finalized by TD 9144, 8/2/2004. For statutory options granted on or before June 9, 2003, taxpayers may rely on any of these three sets of regs, in their entirety: (i) proposed regs issued in '84 (reproduced below); (ii) proposed regs issued on June 9, 2003; or (iii) final regs-until the earlier of (a) Jan. 1, 2006, or (b) the first regularly scheduled stockholders meeting of the granting corporation occurring at least six months after Aug. 3, 2004.

**(a) Effect of qualifying transfer.** *(1)* If a share of stock is transferred to an individual pursuant to his exercise of a statutory option, and if the requirements of section 422(a) (relating to qualified stock options), section 422A(a) (relating to incentive stock options) section 423(a) (relating to employee stock purchase plans), or section 424(a) (relating to restricted stock option), whichever is applicable, are met, then—

(i) Except as provided in section 422(c)(1) (relating to exercise of option when price is less than value of stock), and paragraph (e)(2) of § 1.422-2, no income shall result at the time of the transfer of such share to the individual upon his exercise of the option with respect to such share;

(ii) No deduction under section 162 or the regulations thereunder (relating to trade or business expenses) shall be allowable at any time to the employer corporation, a related corporation of such corporation, or a corporation issuing or assuming a stock option in a transaction to which section 425(a) and paragraph (a) of § 1.425-1 (relating to corporate reorganizations, liquidations, etc.) applies, with respect to the share so transferred; and

(iii) No amount other than the price paid under the option shall be considered as received by any of such corporations for the share so transferred.

* * * * *

**(b) Effect of disqualifying disposition.** *(1)* The disposition of a share of stock, acquired by the exercise of a statutory option before the expiration of the applicable holding period as determined under section 422(a)(1), 422A(a)(1), 423(a)(1), or 424(a)(1), makes section 421 inapplicable to the transfer of such share. The income attributable to such transfer shall be treated by the individual as income received in the taxable year in which such disposition occurs. Similarly, a deduction under section 162 attributable to the transfer of the share of stock pursuant to the exercise of the option shall be allowable for the taxable year in which such disposition occurs to the employer corporation, its parent or subsidiary corporation or a corporation issuing or assuming a stock option in a transaction to which section 425(a) applies. In such cases, no amount shall be treated as income, and no amount shall be allowed as a deduction, for any taxable year other than the taxable year in which the disposition occurs. If the stock was transferred pursuant to the exercise of the option in a taxable year other than the taxable year or the disposition, the amount of the deduction shall be determined as if the employee had been paid compensation at the time provided in paragraph (d) of § 1.421-6.

*(2)* Section 421 is not made inapplicable by a transfer before the expiration of the applicable holding period as determined under section 422(a)(1), 422A(a)(1), 423(a)(1), or 424(a)(1), if such transfer is not a disposition of the stock as defined in section 425(c) and paragraph (c) of § 1.425-1, for example, a transfer from the decendent to his estate or a transfer by bequest or inheritance. Similarly, a disposition by the executor, administrator, heir, or legatee is not a disposition by the decedent. In case a statutory option is exercised by the estate of the individual to whom the option was granted, or by a person who acquired the option by bequest or inheritance or by reason of the death of such individual, see paragraph (c) of this section.

* * * * *

*(4)* For special rules relating to a disqualifying disposition of a share of stock acquired by exercise of an incentive stock option, see paragraph (b) of § 1.422A-1.

**(c) Exercise by estate.** *(1)* If a statutory option is exercised by the estate of the individual to whom the option was granted, or by any person who acquired such option by bequest or inheritance or by reason of the death of such individual, section 421(a) applies to such exercise in the same manner as if such option had been exercised by such deceased individual. Consequently, except as provided by section 422(c)(1) and paragraph (e)(2) of § 1.422-2, neither the estate nor such person is required to include any amount in gross income as a result of a transfer of stock pursuant to such exercise of the option. Nor does section 421(a) become inapplicable if such executor, administrator, or person disposes of the stock so acquired before the expiration of the applicable holding period as determined under section 422(a)(1), 422A(a)(1), 423(a)(1), or 424(a)(1). This special rule does not affect the applicability of section 1222, relating to what constitutes a short-term and long-term capital gain or loss. The executor, administrator, or such person need not exercise the option within three months after the death of the individual to whom the option was granted for section 421(a) to be applicable. However, the exercise of the option must be pursuant to the terms of the option, and any change in the terms of the option is subject to the rules of paragraph (e) of § 1.425-1, relating to the modification, extension, or renewal of the option. Section 421(a) is applicable even though such executor, administrator, or person is not employed by the corporation granting the option, or a related corporation, either when the option is exercised or at any time. However, section 421(a) is not applicable to an exercise of the option by the estate or by such person, unless the individual to whom the option was granted met the employment requirements of section 422(a)(2), 422A(a)(2), 423(a)(2), or 424(a)(2), whichever is applicable, either at the time of his death or within three months before such time. If the option is exercised by a person other than the executor or administrator, or other than a person who acquired the option by bequest or inheritance or by reason of the death of such deceased individual, section 421(a) is not applicable to the exercise. For example, if the option is sold by the estate, section 421(a) does not apply to an exercise of the option by such buyer; but if the option is distributed by the administrator to an heir as part of the estate, section 421(a) is applicable to an exercise of the option by such heir.

* * * * *

**(d) Exercise by deceased employee during lifetime.** If a statutory option is exercised by an individual to whom the option was granted and the individual dies before the expiration of the applicable holding period as determined under section 422(a)(1), 422A(a)(1), 423(a)(1), or 424(a)(1), section 421(a) does not become inapplicable if the executor or administrator of the estate of such individual, or any person who acquired such stock by bequest or inheritance or by reason of the death of such individual, disposes of such stock before the expiration of such applicable holding period. This rule does not affect the applicability of section 1222, relating to what constitutes a short-term and long-term capital gain or loss.

* * * * *

### § 1.422-1 Incentive stock options; general rules.

**(a) Applicability of section 421(a).** *(1)* (i) Section 1.421-2(a) applies to the transfer of a share of stock to an individual pursuant to the individual's exercise of an incentive stock option if the following conditions are satisfied—

(A) The individual makes no disposition of such share before the later of the expiration of the 2-year period from the date of grant of the option pursuant to which such share was transferred, or the expiration of the 1-year period from the date of transfer of such share to the individual; and

(B) At all times during the period beginning on the date of grant of the option and ending on the day 3 months before the date of exercise, the individual was an employee of either the corporation granting the option, a related corporation of such corporation, or a corporation (or a related corporation of such corporation) substituting or assuming a stock option in a transaction to which § 1.424-1(a) applies.

(ii) For rules relating to the disposition of shares of stock acquired pursuant to the exercise of a statutory option, see § 1.424-1(c). For rules relating to the requisite employment relationship, see § 1.421-1(h).

*(2)* (i) The holding period requirement of section 422(a)(1), described in paragraph (a)(1)(i)(A) of this section, does not apply to the transfer of shares by an insolvent individual described in this paragraph (a)(2). If an insolvent individual holds a share of stock acquired pursuant to the individual's exercise of an incentive stock option, and if such share is transferred to a trustee, receiver, or other similar fiduciary in any proceeding under the Bankruptcy Act or any other similar insolvency proceeding, neither such transfer, nor any other transfer of such share for the benefit of the individual's creditors in such proceeding is a disposition of such share for purposes of this paragraph (a). For purposes of this paragraph (a)(2), an individual is insolvent only if the individual's liabilities exceed the individual's assets or the individual is unable to satisfy the individual's liabilities as they become due. See section 422(c)(3).

(ii) A transfer by the trustee or other fiduciary that is not treated as a disposition for purposes of this paragraph (a) may be a sale or exchange for purposes of recognizing capital gain or loss with respect to the share transferred. For example, if the trustee transfers the share to a creditor in an insolvency proceeding, capital gain or loss must be recognized by the insolvent individual to the extent of the difference between the amount realized from such transfer and the adjusted basis of such share.

(iii) If any transfer by the trustee or other fiduciary (other than a transfer back to the insolvent individual) is not for the exclusive benefit of the creditors in an insolvency proceeding, then whether such transfer is a disposition of the share by the individual for purposes of this paragraph (a) is determined under § 1.424-1(c). Similarly, if the trustee or other fiduciary transfers the share back to the insolvent individual, any subsequent transfer of the share by such individual which is not made in respect of the insolvency proceeding may be a disposition of the share for purposes of this paragraph (a).

*(3)* If the employee exercising an option ceased employment because of permanent and total disability, within the meaning of section 22(e)(3), 1 year is used instead of 3 months in the employment period requirement of paragraph (a)(1)(i)(B) of this section.

**(b) Failure to satisfy holding period requirements.** *(1) General rule.* For general rules concerning a disqualifying disposition of a share of stock acquired pursuant to the exercise of an incentive stock option, see § 1.421-2(b)(1).

*(2)* (i) Special rule. If an individual makes a disqualifying disposition of a share of stock acquired by the exercise of an incentive stock option, and if such disposition is a sale or exchange with respect to which a loss (if sustained) would be recognized to the individual, then, under this paragraph (b)(2)(i), the amount includible (determined without reduction for brokerage fees or other costs paid in connection with the disposition) in the gross income of such individual, and deductible from the income of the employer corporation (or a related corporation of such corporation, or of a corporation substituting or assuming the option in a transaction to which § 1.424-1(a) applies) as compensation attributable to the exercise of such option, shall not exceed the excess (if any) of the amount realized on such sale or exchange over the adjusted basis of such share. Subject to the special rule provided by this paragraph (b)(2)(i), the amount of compensation attributable to the exercise of the option is determined under section 83(a); see § 1.421-2(b)(1)(i).

(ii) Limitation to special rule. The special rule described in paragraph (b)(2)(i) of this section does not apply if the disposition is a sale or exchange with respect to which a loss (if sustained) would not be recognized by the individual. Thus, for example, if a disqualifying disposition is a sale described in section 1091 (relating to loss from wash sales of stock or securities), a gift (or any other transaction which is not at arm's length), or a sale described in section 267(a)(1) (relating to sales between related persons), the special rule described in paragraph (b)(2)(i) of this section does not apply because a loss sustained in any such transaction would not be recognized.

*(3) Examples.* The following examples illustrate the principles of this paragraph (b):

*Example (1).* Disqualifying disposition of vested stock. On June 1, 2006, X Corporation grants an incentive stock option to A, an employee of X Corporation, entitling A to purchase one share of X Corporation stock. On August 1, 2006, A exercises the option, and the share of X Corporation stock is transferred to A on that date. The option price is $100 (the fair market value of a share of X Corporation stock on June 1, 2006), and the fair market value of a share of X Corporation stock on August 1, 2006 (the date of transfer) is $200. The share transferred to A is transferable and not subject to a substantial risk of forfeiture. A makes a disqualifying disposition by selling the share on June 1, 2007, for $250. The amount of compensation attributable to A's exercise is $100 (the difference between the fair market value of the share at the date of transfer, $200, and the amount paid for the share, $100). Because the amount realized ($250) is greater than the value of the share at transfer ($200), paragraph (b)(2)(i) of this section does not apply and thus does not affect the amount includible as compensation in A's gross income and deductible by X. A must include in gross income for the taxable year in which the sale occurred $100 as compensation and $50 as capital gain ($250, the amount realized from the sale, less A's basis of $200 (the $100 paid for the share plus the $100 increase in basis resulting from the inclusion of that amount in A's gross income as compensation attributable to the exercise of the option)). If the requirements of section 83(h) and § 1.83-6(a) are satisfied and the deduction is otherwise allowable under section 162, for its taxable year in which the disqualifying disposition occurs, X Corporation is allowed a deduction of $100 for compensation attributable to A's exercise of the incentive stock option.

*Example (2).* Disqualifying disposition of unvested stock. Assume the same facts as in Example 1, except that the share of X Corporation stock received by A is subject to a substantial risk of forfeiture and not transferable for a period of six months after such exercise. Assume further that the fair market value of X Corporation stock is $225 on February 1, 2007, the date on which the six-month restriction lapses. Because section 83 does not apply for ordinary income tax purposes on the date of exercise, A cannot make an effective section 83(b) election at that time (although such an election is permissible for alternative minimum tax purposes). Additionally, at the time of the disposition, section 422 and Sec. 1.422-1a) no longer apply, and thus, section 83(a) is used to measure the consequences of the disposition and the holding period for capital gain purposes begin on the vesting date, six months after exercise. The amount of compensation attributable to A's exercise of the option and disqualifying disposition of the share is $125 (the difference between the fair market value of the share on the date that the restriction lapsed, $225, and the amount paid for the share, $100). Because the amount realized ($225) is greater than the value of the share at transfer ($200), paragraph (b)(2)(i) of this section does not apply and thus does not affect the amount includible as compensation in A's gross income and deductible by X. A must include $125 of compensation income and $25 of capital gain in gross income for the taxable year in which the disposition occurs ($250, the amount realized from the sale, less A's basis of $225 (the $100 paid for the share plus the $125 increase in basis resulting from the inclusion of that amount of compensation in A's gross income)). If the requirements of section 83(h) and § 1.83-6(a) are satisfied and the deduction is otherwise allowable under section 162, for its taxable year in which the disqualifying disposition occurs, X Corporation is allowed a deduction of $125 for the compensation attributable to A's exercise of the option.

*Example (3).* (i) Disqualifying disposition and application of special rule. Assume the same facts as in Example 1, except that A sells the share for $150 to M.

(ii) If the sale to M is a disposition that meets the requirements of paragraph (b)(2)(i) of this section, instead of $100 which otherwise would have been includible as compensation under § 1.83-7, under paragraph (b)(2)(i) of this section, A must include only $50 (the excess of the amount realized on such sale, $150, over the adjusted basis of the share, $100) in gross income as compensation attributable to the exercise of the incentive stock option. Because A's basis for the share is $150 (the $100 which A paid for the share, plus the $50 increase in basis resulting from the inclusion of that amount in A's gross income as compensation attributable to the exercise of the option), A realizes no capital gain or loss as a result of the sale. If the requirements of section 83(h) and § 1.83-6(a) are satisfied and the deduction is otherwise allowable under section 162, for its taxable year in which the disqualifying disposition occurs, X Corporation is allowed a deduction of $50 for the compensation attributable to A's exercise of the option and disqualifying disposition of the share.

(iii) Assume the same facts as in paragraph (i) of this Example 3, except that 10 days after the sale to M, A purchases substantially identical stock. Because under section 1091(a) a loss (if it were sustained on the sale) would not be recognized on the sale, under paragraph (b)(2)(ii) of this section, the special rule described in paragraph (b)(2)(i) of this section does not apply. A must include $100 (the difference between the fair market value of the share on the date of transfer, $200, and the amount paid for the share, $100) in gross income as compensation attributable to the exercise of the option for the taxable year in which the disqualifying disposition occurred. A recognizes no capital gain or loss on the transaction. If the requirements of section 83(h) and § 1.83-6(a) are satisfied and the deduction is otherwise allowable under section 162, for its taxable year in which the disqualifying disposition occurs X Corporation is allowed a $100 deduction for compensation attributable to A's exercise of the option and disqualifying disposition of the share.

(iv) Assume the same facts as in paragraph (ii) of this Example 3, except that A sells the share for $50. Under paragraph (b)(2)(i) of this section, A is not required to include any amount in gross income as compensation attributable to the exercise of the option. A is allowed a capital loss of $50 (the difference between the amount realized on the sale, $50, and the adjusted basis of the share, $100). X Corporation is not allowed any deduction attributable to A's exercise of the option and disqualifying disposition of the share.

**(c) Failure to satisfy employment requirement.** Section 1.421-2(a) does not apply to the transfer of a share of stock pursuant to the exercise of an incentive stock option if the employment requirement, as determined under paragraph (a)(1)(i)(B) of this section, is not met at the time of the exercise of such option. Consequently, the effects of such a transfer are determined under the rules of § 1.83-7. For rules relating to the employment relationship, see § 1.421-1(h).

T.D. 9144, 8/2/2004.

### § 1.422-2 Incentive stock options defined.

**(a) Incentive stock option defined.** *(1) In general.* The term incentive stock option means an option that meets the requirements of paragraph (a)(2) of this section on the date of grant. An incentive stock option is also subject to the $100,000 limitation described in § 1.422-4. An incentive stock option may contain a number of permissible provisions that do not affect the status of the option as an incentive stock option. See § 1.422-5 for rules relating to permissible provisions of an incentive stock option.

*(2) Option requirements.* To qualify as an incentive stock option under this section, an option must be granted to an individual in connection with the individual's employment by the corporation granting such option (or by a related corporation as defined in § 1.421-1(i)(2)), and granted only for stock of any of such corporations. In addition, the option must meet all of the following requirements—

(i) It must be granted pursuant to a plan that meets the requirements described in paragraph (b) of this section;

(ii) It must be granted within 10 years from the date of the adoption of the plan or the date such plan is approved by the stockholders, whichever is earlier (see paragraph (c) of this section);

(iii) It must not be exercisable after the expiration of 10 years from the date of grant (see paragraph (d) of this section);

(iv) It must provide that the option price per share is not less than the fair market value of the share on the date of grant (see paragraph (e) of this section);

(v) By its terms, it must not be transferrable by the individual to whom the option is granted other than by will or the laws of descent and distribution, and must be exercisable, during such individual's lifetime, only by such individual (see §§ 1.421-1(b)(2) and 1.421-2(c)); and

(vi) Except as provided in paragraph (f) of this section, it must be granted to an individual who, at the time the option is granted, does not own stock possessing more than 10 percent of the total combined voting power of all classes of stock of the corporation employing such individual or of any related corporation of such corporation.

*(3) Amendment of option terms.* Except as otherwise provided in § 1.424-1, the amendment of the terms of an incentive stock option may cause it to cease to be an option described in this section. If the terms of an option that has lost its status as an incentive stock option are subsequently changed with the intent to re-qualify the option as an incentive stock option, such change results in the grant of a new option on the date of the change. See § 1.424-1(e).

*(4) Terms provide option not an incentive stock option.* If the terms of an option, when granted, provide that it will not be treated as an incentive stock option, such option is not treated as an incentive stock option.

**(b) Option plan.** *(1) In general.* An incentive stock option must be granted pursuant to a plan that meets the requirements of this paragraph (b). The authority to grant other stock options or other stock-based awards pursuant to the plan, where the exercise of such other options or awards does not affect the exercise of incentive stock options granted pursuant to the plan, does not disqualify such incentive stock options. The plan must be in writing or electronic form, provided that such writing or electronic form is adequate to establish the terms of the plan. See § 1.422-5 for rules relating to permissible provisions of an incentive stock option.

*(2) Stockholder approval.* (i) The plan required by this paragraph (b) must be approved by the stockholders of the corporation granting the incentive stock option within 12 months before or after the date such plan is adopted. Ordinarily, a plan is adopted when it is approved by the granting corporation's board of directors, and the date of the board's action is the reference point for determining whether stockholder approval occurs within the applicable 24-month period. However, if the board's action is subject to a condition (such as stockholder approval) or the happening of a particular event, the plan is adopted on the date the condition is met or the event occurs, unless the board's resolution fixes the date of approval as the date of the board's action.

(ii) For purposes of paragraph (b)(2)(i) of this section, the stockholder approval must comply with the rules described in § 1.422-3.

(iii) The provisions relating to the maximum aggregate number of shares to be issued under the plan (described in paragraph (b)(3) of this section) and the employees (or class or classes of employees) eligible to receive options under the plan (described in paragraph (b)(4) of this section) are the only provisions of a stock option plan that, if changed, must be re-approved by stockholders for purposes of section 422(b)(1). Any increase in the maximum aggregate number of shares that may be issued under the plan (other than an increase merely reflecting a change in the number of outstanding shares, such as a stock dividend or stock split), or change in the designation of the employees (or class or classes of employees) eligible to receive options under the plan is considered the adoption of a new plan requiring stockholder approval within the prescribed 24-month period. In addition, a change in the granting corporation or the stock available for purchase or award under the plan is considered the adoption of a new plan requiring new stockholder approval within the prescribed 24-month period. Any other changes in the terms of an incentive stock option plan are not considered the adoption of a new plan and, thus, do not require stockholder approval.

*(3) Maximum aggregate number of shares.* (i) The plan required by this paragraph (b) must designate the maximum aggregate number of shares that may be issued under the plan through incentive stock options. If nonstatutory options or other stock-based awards may be granted, the plan may separately designate terms for each type of option or other stock-based awards and designate the maximum number of shares that may be issued under such option or other stock-based awards. Unless otherwise specified, all terms of the plan apply to all options and other stock-based awards that may be granted under the plan.

(ii) A plan that merely provides that the number of shares that may be issued as incentive stock options under such plan may not exceed a stated percentage of the shares outstanding at the time of each offering or grant under such plan does not satisfy the requirement that the plan state the maximum aggregate number of shares that may be issued under the plan. However, the maximum aggregate number of shares that may be issued under the plan may be stated in terms of a percentage of the authorized, issued, or outstanding shares at the date of the adoption of the plan. The plan may specify that the maximum aggregate number of shares available for grants under the plan may increase annually by a specified percentage of the authorized, issued, or outstanding shares at the date of the adoption of the plan. A plan which provides that the maximum aggregate number of shares that may be issued as incentive stock options under the plan may change based on any other specified circumstances satisfies the requirements of this paragraph (b)(3) only if the stockholders approve an immediately determinable maximum aggregate number of shares that may be issued under the plan in any event.

(iii) It is permissible for the plan to provide that, shares purchasable under the plan may be supplied to the plan through acquisitions of stock on the open market; shares purchased under the plan and forfeited back to the plan; shares surrendered in payment of the exercise price of an option; shares withheld for payment of applicable employment taxes and/or withholding obligations resulting from the exercise of an option.

(iv) If there is more than one plan under which incentive stock options may be granted and stockholders of the granting corporation merely approve a maximum aggregate number of shares that are available for issuance under such plans, the stockholder approval requirements described in paragraph (b)(2) of this section are not satisfied. A separate maximum aggregate number of shares available for issuance pursuant to incentive stock options must be approved for each plan.

*(4) Designation of employees.* The plan described in this paragraph (b), as adopted and approved, must indicate the employees (or class or classes of employees) eligible to receive the options or other stock-based awards to be granted under the plan. This requirement is satisfied by a general designation of the employees (or the class or classes of employees) eligible to receive options or other stock-based awards under the plan. Designations such as "key employees of the grantor corporation"; "all salaried employees of the grantor corporation and its subsidiaries, including subsidiaries which become such after adoption of the plan;" or "all employees of the corporation" meet this requirement. This requirement is considered satisfied even though the board of directors, another group, or an individual is given the authority to select the particular employees who are to receive options or other stock-based awards from a described class and to determine the number of shares to be optioned or granted to each such employee. If individuals other than employees may be granted options or other stock-based awards under the plan, the plan must separately designate the employees or classes of employees eligible to receive incentive stock options.

*(5) Conflicting option terms.* An option on stock available for purchase or grant under the plan is treated as having been granted pursuant to a plan even if the terms of the option conflict with the terms of the plan, unless such option is granted to an employee who is ineligible to receive options under the plan, options have been granted on stock in excess of the aggregate number of shares which may be issued under the plan, or the option provides otherwise.

*(6)* The following examples illustrate the principles of this paragraph (b):

*Example (1).* Stockholder approval. (i) S Corporation is a subsidiary of P Corporation, a publicly traded corporation. On January 1, 2006, S adopts a plan under which incentive stock options for S stock are granted to S employees.

(ii) To meet the requirements of paragraph (b)(2) of this section, the plan must be approved by the stockholders of S (in this case, P) within 12 months before or after January 1, 2006.

(iii) Assume the same facts as in paragraph (i) of this Example 1, except that the plan was adopted on January 1, 2010. Assume further that the plan was approved by the stockholders of S (in this case, P) on March 1, 2010. On January 1, 2012, S changes the plan to provide that incentive stock options for P stock will be granted to S employees under the plan. Because there is a change in the stock available for grant under the plan, the change is considered the adoption of a new plan that must be approved by the stockholder of S (in this case, P) within 12 months before or after January 1, 2012.

*Example (2).* Stockholder approval. (i) Assume the same facts as in paragraph (i) of Example 1, except that on March 15, 2007, P completely disposes of its interest in S. Thereafter, S continues to grant options for S stock to S employees under the plan.

(ii) The new S options are granted under a plan that meets the stockholder approval requirements of paragraph (b)(2) of this section without regard to whether S seeks approval of the plan from the stockholders of S after P disposes of its interest in S.

(iii) Assume the same facts as in paragraph (i) of this Example 2, except that under the plan as adopted on January 1, 2006, only options for P stock are granted to S employees. Assume further that after P disposes of its interest in S, S changes the plan to provide for the grant of options for S stock to S employees. Because there is a change in the stock available for purchase or grant under the plan, under paragraph (b)(2)(iii) of this section, the stockholders of S must approve the plan within 12 months before or after the change to the plan to meet the stockholder approval requirements of paragraph (b) of this section.

*Example (3).* Stockholder approval. (i) Corporation X maintains a plan under which incentive stock options may be granted to all eligible employees. Corporation Y does not maintain an incentive stock option plan. On May 15, 2006, Corporation X and Corporation Y consolidate under state law to form one corporation. The new corporation will be named Corporation Y. The consolidation agreement describes the Corporation X plan, including the maximum aggregate number of shares available for issuance pursuant to incentive stock options after the consolidation and the employees eligible to receive options under the plan. Additionally, the consolidation agreement states that the plan will be continued by Corporation Y after the consolidation and incentive stock options will be issued by Corporation Y. The consolidation agreement is unanimously approved by the shareholders of Corporations X and Y on May 1, 2006. Corporation Y assumes the plan formerly maintained by Corporation X and continues to grant options under the plan to all eligible employees.

(ii) Because there is a change in the granting corporation (from Corporation X to Corporation Y), under paragraph (b)(2)(iii) of this section, Corporation Y is considered to have adopted a new plan. Because the plan is fully described in the consolidation agreement, including the maximum aggregate number of shares available for issuance pursuant to incentive stock options and employees eligible to receive options under the plan, the approval of the consolidation agreement by the shareholders constitutes approval of the plan. Thus, the shareholder approval of the consolidation agreement satisfies the shareholder approval requirements of paragraph (b)(2) of this section, and the plan is considered to be adopted by Corporation Y and approved by its shareholders on May 1, 2006.

*Example (4).* Maximum aggregate number of shares. X Corporation maintains a plan under which statutory options and nonstatutory options may be granted. The plan designates the number of shares that may be used for incentive stock options. Because the maximum aggregate number of shares that will be used for incentive stock options is designated in the plan, the requirements of paragraph (b)(3) of this section are satisfied.

*Example (5).* Maximum aggregate number of shares. Y Corporation adopts an incentive stock option plan on November 1, 2006. On that date, there are two million outstanding shares of Y Corporation stock. The plan provides that the maximum aggregate number of shares that may be issued under the plan may not exceed 15% of the outstanding number of shares of Y Corporation on November 1, 2006. Because the maximum aggregate number of shares that may be issued under the plan is designated in the plan, the requirements of paragraph (b)(3) of this section are met.

*Example (6).* Maximum aggregate number of shares. (i) B Corporation adopts an incentive stock option plan on March 15, 2005. The plan provides that the maximum aggregate number of shares available for issuance under the plan is 50,000, increased on each anniversary date of the adoption of the plan by 5 percent of the then-outstanding shares.

(ii) Because the maximum aggregate number of shares is not designated under the plan, the requirements of paragraph (b)(3) of this section are not met.

(iii) Assume the same facts as in paragraph (i) of this Example 6, except that the plan provides that the maximum aggregate number of shares available under the plan is the lesser of (a) 50,000 shares, increased each anniversary date of the adoption of the plan by 5 percent of the then-outstanding shares, or (b) 200,000 shares. Because the maximum aggregate number of shares that may be issued under the plan is designated as the lesser of one of two numbers, one of which provides an immediately determinable maximum aggregate number of shares that may be issued under the plan in any event, the requirements of paragraph (b)(3) of this section are met.

**(c) Duration of option grants under the plan.** An incentive stock option must be granted within 10 years from the date that the plan under which it is granted is adopted or the date such plan is approved by the stockholders, whichever is earlier. To grant incentive stock options after the expiration of the 10-year period, a new plan must be adopted and approved.

**(d) Period for exercising options.** An incentive stock option, by its terms, must not be exercisable after the expiration of 10 years from the date such option is granted, or 5 years from the date such option is granted to an employee described in paragraph (f) of this section. An option that does not contain such a provision when granted is not an incentive stock option.

**(e) Option price.** *(1)* Except as provided by paragraph (e)(2) of this section, the option price of an incentive stock option must not be less than the fair market value of the stock subject to the option at the time the option is granted. The option price may be determined in any reasonable manner, including the valuation methods permitted under § 20.2031-2 of this chapter, so long as the minimum price possible under the terms of the option is not less than the fair market value of the stock on the date of grant. For general rules relating to the option price, see § 1.421-1(e). For rules relating to the determination of when an option is granted, see § 1.421-1(c).

*(2)* (i) If a share of stock is transferred to an individual pursuant to the exercise of an option which fails to qualify as an incentive stock option merely because there was a failure of an attempt, made in good faith, to meet the option price requirements of paragraph (e)(1) of this section, the requirements of such paragraph are considered to have been met. Whether there was a good-faith attempt to set the option price at not less than the fair market value of the stock subject to the option at the time the option was granted depends on the relevant facts and circumstances.

(ii) For publicly held stock that is actively traded on an established market at the time the option is granted, determining the fair market value of such stock by the appropriate method described in § 20.2031-2 of this chapter establishes that a good-faith attempt to meet the option price requirements of this paragraph (e) was made.

(iii) For non-publicly traded stock, if it is demonstrated, for example, that the fair market value of the stock at the date of grant was based upon an average of the fair market values as of such date set forth in the opinions of completely independent and well-qualified experts, such a demonstration generally establishes that there was a good-faith attempt to meet the option price requirements of this paragraph (e). The optionee's status as a majority or minority stockholder may be taken into consideration.

(iv) Regardless of whether the stock offered under an option is publicly traded, a good-faith attempt to meet the option price requirements of this paragraph (e) is not demonstrated unless the fair market value of the stock on the date of grant is determined with regard to nonlapse restrictions (as defined in § 1.83-3(h)) and without regard to lapse restrictions (as defined in § 1.83-3(i)).

(v) Amounts treated as interest and amounts paid as interest under a deferred payment arrangement are not includible as part of the option price. See § 1.421-1(e)(1). An attempt to set the option price at not less than fair market value is not regarded as made in good faith where an adjustment of the option price to reflect amounts treated as interest results in the option price being lower than the fair market value on which the option price was based.

*(3)* Notwithstanding that the option price requirements of paragraphs (e)(1) and (2) of this section are satisfied by an option granted to an employee whose stock ownership exceeds the limitation provided by paragraph (f) of this section, such option is not an incentive stock option when granted unless it also complies with paragraph (f) of this section. If the option, when granted, does not comply with the requirements described in paragraph (f) of this section, such option can never become an incentive stock option, even if the employee's stock ownership does not exceed the limitation of paragraph (f) of this section when such option is exercised.

**(f) Options granted to certain stockholders.** *(1)* If, immediately before an option is granted, an individual owns (or is treated as owning) stock possessing more than 10 percent of the total combined voting power of all classes of stock of the corporation employing the optionee or of any related corporation of such corporation, then an option granted to such individual cannot qualify as an incentive stock option unless the option price is at least 110 percent of the stock's fair market value on the date of grant and such option by its terms is not exercisable after the expiration of 5 years from the date of grant. For purposes of determining the minimum option price for purposes of this paragraph (f), the rules described in paragraph (e)(2) of this section, relating to the good-faith determination of the option price, do not apply.

*(2)* For purposes of determining the stock ownership of the optionee, the stock attribution rules of § 1.424-1(d) apply. Stock that the optionee may purchase under outstanding options is not treated as stock owned by the individual. The determination of the percentage of the total combined voting power of all classes of stock of the employer corporation (or of its related corporations) that is owned by the optionee is made with respect to each such corporation in the related group by comparing the voting power of the shares owned (or treated as owned) by the optionee to the aggregate voting power of all shares of each such corporation actually issued and outstanding immediately before the grant of the option to the optionee. The aggregate voting power of all shares actually issued and outstanding immediately before the grant of the option does not include the voting power of treasury shares or shares authorized for issue under outstanding options held by the individual or any other person.

*(3) Examples.* The rules of this paragraph (f) are illustrated by the following examples:

*Example (1).* (i) E, an employee of M Corporation, owns 15,000 shares of M Corporation common stock, which is the only class of stock outstanding. M has 100,000 shares of its common stock outstanding. On January 1, 2005, when the fair market value of M stock is $100, E is granted an option with an option price of $100 and an exercise period of 10 years from the date of grant.

(ii) Because E owns stock possessing more than 10 percent of the total combined voting power of all classes of M Corporation stock, M cannot grant an incentive stock option to E unless the option is granted at an option price of at least 110 percent of the fair market value of the stock subject to the option and the option, by its terms, expires no later than 5 years from its date of grant. The option granted to E fails to meet the option-price and term requirements described in paragraph (f)(1) of this section and, thus, the option is not an incentive stock option.

(iii) Assume the same facts as in paragraph (i) of this Example 1, except that E's father and brother each owns 7,500 shares of M Corporation stock, and E owns no M stock in E's own name. Because under the attribution rules of § 1.424-1(d), E is treated as owning stock held by E's parents and siblings, M cannot grant an incentive stock option to E unless the option price is at least 110 percent of the fair market value of the stock subject to the option, and the option, by its terms, expires no later than 5 years from the date of grant.

*Example (2).* Assume the same facts as in paragraph (i) of this Example 1. Assume further that M is a subsidiary of P Corporation. Regardless of whether E owns any P stock and the number of P shares outstanding, if P Corporation grants an option to E which purports to be an incentive stock option, but which fails to meet the 110-percent-option-price and 5-year-term requirements, the option is not an incentive stock option because E owns more than 10 percent of the total combined voting power of all classes of stock of a related corporation of P Corporation (i.e., M Corporation). An individual who owns (or is treated as owning) stock in excess of the ownership specified in paragraph (f)(1) of this section, in any corporation in a group of corporations consisting of the employer corporation and its related corporations, cannot be granted an incentive stock option by any corporation in the group unless such option meets the 110-percent-option-price and 5-year-term requirements of paragraph (f)(1) of this section.

*Example (3).* (i) F is an employee of R Corporation. R has only one class of stock, of which 100,000 shares are issued and outstanding. F owns no stock in R Corporation or any related corporation of R Corporation. On January 1, 2005, R grants a 10-year incentive stock option to F to purchase 50,000 shares of R stock at $3 per share, the fair market value of R stock on the date of grant of the option. On April 1, 2005, F exercises half of the January option and receives 25,000 shares of R stock that previously were not outstanding. On July 1, 2005, R grants a second 50,000 share option to F which purports to be an incentive stock option. The terms of the July option are identical to the terms of the January option, except that the option price is $3.25 per share, which is the fair market value of R stock on the date of grant of the July option.

(ii) Because F does not own more than 10% of the total combined voting power of all classes of stock of R Corporation or any related corporation on the date of the grant of the January option and the pricing requirements of paragraph (e) of this section are satisfied on the date of grant of such option, the unexercised portion of the January option remains an incentive stock option regardless of the changes in F's percentage of stock ownership in R after the date of grant. However, the July option is not an incentive stock option because, on the date that it is granted, F owns 20 percent (25,000 shares owned by F divided by 125,000 shares of R stock issued and outstanding) of the total combined voting power of all classes of R Corporation stock and, thus the pricing requirements of paragraph (f)(1) of this section are not met.

(iii) Assume the same facts as in paragraph (i) of this Example 3 except that the partial exercise of the January incentive stock option on April 1, 2003, is for only 10,000 shares. Under these circumstances, the July option is an incentive stock option, because, on the date of grant of the July option, F does not own more than 10 percent of the total combined voting power (10,000 shares owned by F divided by 110,000 shares of R issued and outstanding) of all classes of R Corporation stock.

T.D. 9144, 8/2/2004, amend T.D. 9471, 11/16/2009.

## § 1.422-3 Stockholder approval of incentive stock option plans.

This section addresses the stockholder approval of incentive stock option plans required by section 422(b)(1) of the Internal Revenue Code. (Section 422 was added to the Code as section 422A by section 251 of the Economic Recovery Tax Act of 1981, and was redesignated as section 422 by section 11801 of the Omnibus Budget Reconciliation Act of 1990.) The approval of stockholders must comply with all applicable provisions of the corporate charter, bylaws, and applicable State law prescribing the method and degree of stockholder approval required for the issuance of corporate stock or options. If the applicable State law does not prescribe a method and degree of stockholder approval in such cases an incentive stock option plan must be approved:

**(a)** By a majority of the votes cast at a duly held stockholders' meeting at which a quorum representing a majority of all outstanding voting stock is, either in person or by proxy, present and voting on the plan; or

**(b)** By a method and in a degree that would be treated as adequate under applicable State law in the case of an action requiring stockholder approval (i.e., an action on which stockholders would be entitled to vote if the action were taken at a duly held stockholders' meeting).

T.D. 8374, 11/29/91, amend T.D. 9144, 8/2/2004.

**§ 1.422-4 $100,000 limitation for incentive stock options.**

**(a) $100,000 per year limitation.** *(1) General rule.* An option that otherwise qualifies as an incentive stock option nevertheless fails to be an incentive stock option to the extent that the $100,000 limitation described in paragraph (a)(2) of this section is exceeded.

*(2) $100,000 per year limitation.* To the extent that the aggregate fair market value of stock with respect to which an incentive stock option (determined without regard to this section) is exercisable for the first time by any individual during any calendar year (under all plans of the employer corporation and related corporations) exceeds $100,000, such option is treated as a nonstatutory option. See § 1.83-7 for rules applicable to nonstatutory options.

**(b) Application.** To determine whether the limitation described in paragraph (a)(2) of this section has been exceeded, the following rules apply:

*(1)* An option that does not meet the requirements of § 1.422-2 when granted (including an option which, when granted, contains terms providing that it will not be treated as an incentive stock option) is disregarded. See § 1.422-2(a)(4).

*(2)* The fair market value of stock is determined as of the date of grant of the option for such stock.

*(3)* Except as otherwise provided in paragraph (b)(4) of this section, options are taken into account in the order in which they are granted.

*(4)* For purposes of this section, an option is considered to be first exercisable during a calendar year if the option will become exercisable at any time during the year assuming that any condition on the optionee's ability to exercise the option related to the performance of services is satisfied. If the optionee's ability to exercise the option in the year is subject to an acceleration provision, then the option is considered first exercisable in the calendar year in which the acceleration provision is triggered. After an acceleration provision is triggered, the options subject to such provision are then taken into account in accordance with paragraph (b)(3) of this section for purposes of applying the limitation described in paragraph (a)(2) of this section to all options first exercisable during a calendar year. However, because an acceleration provision is not taken into account prior to its triggering, an incentive stock option that becomes exercisable for the first time during a calendar year by operation of such a provision does not affect the application of the $100,000 limitation with respect to any option (or portion thereof) exercised prior to such acceleration. For purposes of this paragraph (b)(4), an acceleration provision includes, for example, a provision that accelerates the exercisability of an option on a change in ownership or control or a provision that conditions exercisability on the attainment of a performance goal. See paragraph (d), Example 4 of this section.

*(5)* (i) An option (or portion thereof) is disregarded if, prior to the calendar year during which it would otherwise have become exercisable for the first time, the option (or portion thereof) is modified and thereafter ceases to be an incentive stock option described in § 1.422-2, is canceled, or is transferred in violation of § 1.421-1(b)(2).

(ii) If an option (or portion thereof) is modified, canceled, or transferred at any other time, such option (or portion thereof) is treated as outstanding according to its original terms until the end of the calendar year during which it would otherwise have become exercisable for the first time.

*(6)* A disqualifying disposition has no effect on the determination of whether an option exceeds the $100,000 limitation.

**(c) Bifurcation.** *(1) Options.* The application of the rules described in paragraph (b) of this section may result in an option being treated, in part, as an incentive stock option and, in part, as a nonstatutory option. See § 1.83-7 for the treatment of nonstatutory options.

*(2) Stock.* A corporation may issue a separate certificate for incentive option stock or designate such stock as incentive stock option stock in the corporation's transfer records or plan records. In such a case, the issuance of separate certificates or designation in the corporation's transfer records or plan records is not a modification under § 1.424-1(e). In the absence of such an issuance or designation, shares are treated as first purchased under an incentive stock option to the extent of the $100,000 limitation, and the excess shares are treated as purchased under a nonstatutory option. See § 1.83-7 for the treatment of nonstatutory options.

**(d) Examples.** The following examples illustrate the principles of this section. In each of the following examples E is an employee of X Corporation. The examples are as follows:

*Example (1).* General rule. Effective January 1, 2004, X Corporation adopts a plan under which incentive stock options may be granted to its employees. On January 1, 2004, and each succeeding January 1 through January 1, 2013, E is granted immediately exercisable options for X Corporation stock with a fair market value of $100,000 determined on the date of grant. The options qualify as incentive stock options (determined without regard to this section). On January 1, 2014, E exercises all of the options. Because the $100,000 limitation has not been exceeded during any calendar year, all of the options are treated as incentive stock options.

*Example (2).* Order of grant. X Corporation is a parent corporation of Y Corporation, which is a parent corporation of Z Corporation. Each corporation has adopted its own separate plan, under which an employee of any member of the corporate group may be granted options for stock of any member of the group. On January 1, 2004, X Corporation grants E an incentive stock option (determined without regard to this section) for stock of Y Corporation with a fair market value of $100,000 on the date of grant. On December 31, 2004, Y Corporation grants E an incentive stock option (determined without regard to this section) for stock of Z Corporation with a fair market value of $75,000 as of the date of grant. Both of the options are immediately exercisable. For purposes of this section, options are taken into account in the order in which granted using the fair market value of stock as of the date on the option is granted. During calendar year 2004, the aggregate fair market value of stock with respect to which E's options are exercisable for the first time exceeds $100,000. Therefore, the option for Y Corporation stock is treated as an incentive stock option, and the option for Z Corporation stock is treated as a nonstatutory option.

*Example (3).* Acceleration provision. (i) In 2004, X Corporation grants E three incentive stock options (determined without regard to this section) to acquire stock with an aggregate fair market value of $150,000 on the date of grant. The dates of grant, the fair market value of the stock (as of the applicable date of grant) with respect to which the options are exercisable, and the years in which the options are first exercisable (without regard to acceleration provisions) are as follows:

| | Date of grant | Fair market value of stock | First exercisable |
|---|---|---|---|
| Option 1 . . . . . . . . . . . . . . . . . . . . . . . . | April 1, 2004 . . . | $60,000 | 2004 |
| Option 2 . . . . . . . . . . . . . . . . . . . . . . . . | May 1, 2004 . . . . | 50,000 | 2006 |
| Option 3 . . . . . . . . . . . . . . . . . . . . . . . . | June 1, 2004 . . . . | 40,000 | 2004 |

(ii) In July of 2004, a change in control of X Corporation occurs, and, under the terms of its option plan, all outstanding options become immediately exercisable. Under the rules of this section, Option 1 is treated as an incentive stock option in its entirety; Option 2 exceeds the $100,000 aggregate fair market value limitation for calendar year 2004 by $10,000 (Option 1's $60,000 + Option 2's $50,000 = $110,000) and is, therefore, bifurcated into an incentive stock option for stock with a fair market value of $40,000 as of the date of grant and a nonstatutory option for stock with a fair market value of $10,000 as of the date of grant. Option 3 is treated as a nonstatutory option in its entirety.

*Example (4).* Exercise of option and acceleration provision. (i) In 2004, X Corporation grants E three incentive stock options (determined without regard to this section) to acquire stock with an aggregate fair market value of $120,000 on the date of grant. The dates of grant, the fair market value of the stock (as of the applicable date of grant) with respect to which the options are exercisable, and the years in which the options are first exercisable (without regard to acceleration provisions) are as follows:

| | Date of grant | Fair market value of stock | First exercisable |
|---|---|---|---|
| Option 1 . . . . . . . . . . . . . . . . . . . . . . . . | April 1, 2004 . . . | $60,000 | 2005 |
| Option 2 . . . . . . . . . . . . . . . . . . . . . . . . | May 1, 2004 . . . . | 40,000 | 2006 |
| Option 3 . . . . . . . . . . . . . . . . . . . . . . . . | June 1, 2004 . . . . | 20,000 | 2005 |

(ii) On June 1, 2005, E exercises Option 3. At the time of exercise of Option 3, the fair market value of X stock (at the time of grant) with respect to which options held by E are first exercisable in 2005 does not exceed $100,000. On September 1, 2005, a change of control of X Corporation occurs, and, under the terms of its option plan, Option 2 becomes immediately exercisable. Under the rules of this section, because E's exercise of Option 3 occurs before the change of control and the effects of an acceleration provision are not taken into account until it is triggered, Option 3 is treated as an incentive stock option in its entirety. Option 1 is treated as an incentive stock option in its entirety. Option 2 is bifurcated into an incentive stock option for stock with a fair market value of $20,000 on the date of grant and a nonstatutory option for stock with a fair market value of $20,000 on the date of grant because it exceeds the $100,000 limitation for 2003 by $20,000 (Option 1 for $60,000 + Option 3 for $20,000 + Option 2 for $40,000 = $120,000).

(iii) Assume the same facts as in paragraph (ii) of this Example 4, except that the change of control occurs on May 1, 2005. Because options are taken into account in the order in which they are granted, Option 1 and Option 2 are treated as incentive stock options in their entirety. Because the exercise of Option 3 (on June 1, 2005) takes place after the acceleration provision is triggered, Option 3 is treated as a nonstatutory option in its entirety.

*Example (5).* Cancellation of option. (i) In 2004, X Corporation grants E three incentive stock options (determined without regard to this section) to acquire stock with an aggregate fair market value of $140,000 as of the date of grant. The dates of grant, the fair market value of the stock (as of the applicable date of grant) with respect to which the options are exercisable, and the years in which the options are first exercisable (without regard to acceleration provisions) are as follows:

| | Date of grant | Fair market value of stock | First exercisable |
|---|---|---|---|
| Option 1 . . . . . . . . . . . . . . . . . . . . . . . . | April 1, 2004 . . . | $60,000 | 2005 |
| Option 2 . . . . . . . . . . . . . . . . . . . . . . . . | May 1, 2004 . . . . | 40,000 | 2005 |
| Option 3 . . . . . . . . . . . . . . . . . . . . . . . . | June 1, 2004 . . . . | 40,000 | 2005 |

(ii) On December 31, 2004, Option 2 is canceled. Because Option 2 is canceled before the calendar year during which it would have become exercisable for the first time, it is disregarded. As a result, Option 1 and Option 3 are treated as incentive stock options in their entirety.

(iii) Assume the same facts as in paragraph (ii) of this Example 5, except that Option 2 is canceled on January 1, 2005. Because Option 2 is not canceled prior to the calendar year during which it would have become exercisable for the first time (2005), it is treated as an outstanding option for purposes of determining whether the $100,000 limitation for 2005 has been exceeded. Because options are taken into account in the order in which granted, Option 1 is treated as an incentive stock option in its entirety. Because Option 3 exceeds the $100,000 limitation by $40,000 (Option 1 for $60,000 + Option 2 for $40,000 + Option 3 for $40,000 = $140,000), it is treated as a nonstatutory option in its entirety.

(iv) Assume the same facts as in paragraph (i) of this Example 5, except that on January 1, 2005, E exercises Option 2 and immediately sells the stock in a disqualifying disposition. A disqualifying disposition has no effect on the determination of whether the underlying option is considered outstanding during the calendar year during which it is first exercisable. Because options are taken into account in the order in which granted, Option 1 is treated as an incentive stock option in its entirety. Because Option 3 exceeds the $100,000 limitation by $40,000 (Option 1 for $60,000 + Option 2 for $40,000 + Option 3 for $40,000 = $140,000), it is treated as a nonstatutory option in its entirety.

*Example (6).* Designation of stock. On January 1, 2004, X grants E an immediately exercisable incentive stock option (determined without regard to this section) to acquire X stock with a fair market value of $150,000 on that date. Under the rules of this section, the option is bifurcated and treated as an incentive stock option for X stock with a fair market value of $100,000 and a nonstatutory option for X stock with a fair market value of $50,000. In these circumstances, X may designate the stock that is treated as stock acquired pursuant to the exercise of an incentive stock option by issuing a separate certificate (or certificates) for $100,000 of stock and identifying such certificates as Incentive Stock Option Stock in its transfer records. In the absence of such a designation (or a designation in the corporation's transfer records or the plan records) shares with a fair market value of $100,000 are deemed purchased first under an incentive stock option, and shares with a fair market value of $50,000 are deemed purchased under a nonstatutory option.

---

T.D. 9144, 8/2/2004.

---

## § 1.422-5 Permissible provisions.

**(a) General rule.** An option that otherwise qualifies as an incentive stock option does not fail to be an incentive stock option merely because such option contains one or more of the provisions described in paragraphs (b), (c), and (d) of this section.

**(b) Cashless exercise.** *(1)* An option does not fail to be an incentive stock option merely because the optionee may exercise the option with previously acquired stock of the corporation that granted the option or stock of the corporation whose stock is being offered for purchase under the option. For special rules relating to the use of statutory option stock to pay the option price of an incentive stock option, see § 1.424-1(c)(3).

*(2)* All shares acquired through the exercise of an incentive stock option are individually subject to the holding period requirements described in § 1.422-1(a) and the disqualifying disposition rules of § 1.422-1(b), regardless of whether the option is exercised with previously acquired stock of the corporation that granted the option or stock of the corporation whose stock is being offered for purchase under the option. If an incentive stock option is exercised with such shares, and the exercise results in the basis allocation described in paragraph (b)(3) of this section, the optionee's disqualifying disposition of any of the stock acquired through such exercise is treated as a disqualifying disposition of the shares with the lowest basis.

*(3)* If the exercise of an incentive stock option with previously acquired shares is comprised in part of an exchange to which section 1036 (and so much of section 1031 as relates to section 1036) applies, then:

(i) The optionee's basis in the incentive stock option shares received in the section 1036 exchange is the same as the optionee's basis in the shares surrendered in the exchange, increased, if applicable, by any amount included in gross income as compensation pursuant to sections 421 through 424 or section 83. Except for purposes of § 1.422-1(a), the holding period of the shares is determined under section 1223. For purposes of § 1.422-1 and sections 421(b) and 83 and the regulations thereunder, the amount paid for the shares purchased under the option is the fair market value of the shares surrendered on the date of the exchange.

(ii) The optionee's basis in the incentive stock option shares not received pursuant to the section 1036 exchange is zero. For all purposes, the holding period of such shares begins as of the date that such shares are transferred to the optionee. For purposes of § 1.422-1(b) and sections 421(b) and 83 and the regulations thereunder, the amount paid for the shares is considered to be zero.

**(c) Additional compensation.** An option does not fail to be an incentive stock option merely because the optionee has the right to receive additional compensation, in cash or property, when the option is exercised, provided such additional compensation is includible in income under section 61 or section 83. The amount of such additional compensation may be determined in any manner, including by reference to the fair market value of the stock at the time of exercise or to the option price.

**(d) Option subject to a condition.**

*(1)* An option does not fail to be an incentive stock option merely because the option is subject to a condition, or grants a right, that is not inconsistent with the requirements of §§ 1.422-2 and 1.422-4.

*(2)* An option that includes an alternative right is not an incentive stock option if the requirements of § 1.422-2 are effectively avoided by the exercise of the alternative right. For example, an alternative right extending the option term beyond ten years, setting an option price below fair market value, or permitting transferability prevents an option from qualifying as an incentive stock option. If either of two options can be exercised, but not both, each such option is a disqualifying alternative right with respect to the other, even though one or both options would individually satisfy the requirements of §§ 1.422-2, 1.422-4, and this section.

*(3)* An alternative right to receive a taxable payment of cash and/ or property in exchange for the cancellation or surrender of the option does not disqualify the option as an incentive stock option if the right is exercisable only when the then fair market value of the stock exceeds the exercise price of the option and the option is otherwise exercisable, the right is transferable only when the option is otherwise transferable, and the exercise of the right has economic and tax consequences no more favorable than the exercise of the option followed by an immediate sale of the stock. For this purpose, the exercise of the alternative right does not have the same economic and tax consequences if the payment exceeds the difference between the then fair market value of the stock and the exercise price of the option.

**(e) Examples.** The principles of this section are illustrated by the following examples:

*Example (1).* On June 1, 2004, X Corporation grants an incentive stock option to A, an employee of X Corporation, entitling A to purchase 100 shares of X Corporation common stock at $10 per share. The option provides that A may exercise the option with previously acquired shares of X Corporation common stock. X Corporation has only one class of common stock outstanding. Under the rules of section 83, the shares transferable to A through the exercise of the option are transferable and not subject to a substantial risk of forfeiture. On June 1, 2005, when the fair market value of an X Corporation share is $25, A uses 40 shares of X Corporation common stock, which A had purchased on the open market on June 1, 2002, for $5 per share, to pay the full option price. After exercising the option, A owns 100 shares of incentive stock option stock. Under section 1036 (and so much of section 1031 as relates to section 1036), 40 of the shares have a $200 aggregate carryover basis (the $5 purchase price x 40 shares) and a three-year holding period for purposes of determining capital gain, and 60 of the shares have a zero basis and a holding period beginning on June 1, 2005, for purposes of determining capital gain. All 100 shares have a holding period beginning on June 1, 2005, for purposes of determining whether the holding period requirements of § 1.422-1(a) are met.

*Example (2).* Assume the same facts as in Example 1. Assume further that, on September 1, 2005, A sells 75 of the shares that A acquired through exercise of the incentive stock option for $30 per share. Because the holding period requirements were not satisfied, A made a disqualifying disposition of the 75 shares on September 1, 2005. Under the rules of paragraphs (b)(2) and (b)(3) of this section, A has sold all 60 of the non-section-1036 shares and 15 of the 40 section-1036 shares. Therefore, under paragraph (b)(3) of this section and section 83(a), the amount of compensation attributable to A's exercise of the option and subsequent disqualifying disposition of 75 shares is $1,500 (the difference between the fair market value of the stock on the date of transfer, $1,875 (75 shares at $25 per share), and the amount paid for the stock, $375 (60 shares at $0 per share plus 15 shares at $25 per share)). In addition, A must recognize a capital gain of $675, which consists of $375 ($450, the amount realized from the sale of 15 shares, less A's basis of $75) plus $300 ($1,800, the amount realized from the sale of 60 shares, less A's basis of $1,500 resulting from the inclusion of that amount in income as compensation). Accordingly, A must include in gross income for the taxable year in which the sale occurs $1,500 as compensation and $675 as capital gain. For its taxable year in which the disqualifying disposition occurs, if otherwise allowable under section 162 and if the requirements of § 1.83-6(a) are met, X Corporation is allowed a deduction of $1,500 for the compensation paid to A.

*Example (3).* Assume the same facts as in Example 2, except that, instead of selling the 75 shares of incentive stock option stock on September 1, 2005, A uses those shares to exercise a second incentive stock option. The second option was granted to A by X Corporation on January 1, 2005, entitling A to purchase 100 shares of X Corporation common stock at $22.50 per share. As in Example 2, A has made a disqualifying disposition of the 75 shares of stock pursuant to § 1.424-1(c). Under paragraph (b) of this section, A has disposed of all 60 of the non-section-1036 shares and 15 of the 40 section-1036 shares. Therefore, pursuant to paragraph (b)(3) of this section and section 83(a), the amount of compensation attributable to A's exercise of the first option and subsequent disqualifying disposition of 75 shares is $1,500 (the difference between the fair market value of the stock on the date of transfer, $1,875 (75 shares at $25 per share), and the amount paid for the stock, $375 (60 shares at $0 per share plus 15 shares at $25 per share)). Unlike Example 2, A does not recognize any capital gain as a result of exercising the second option because, for all purposes other than the determination of whether the exercise is a disposition pursuant to section 424(c), the exercise is considered an exchange to which section 1036 applies. Accordingly, A must include in gross income for the taxable year in which the disqualifying disposition occurs $1,500 as compensation. If the requirements of § 83(h) and § 1.83-6(a) are satisfied and the deduction is otherwise allowable under section 162, for its taxable year in which the disqualifying disposition occurs, X Corporation is allowed a deduction of $1,500 for the compensation paid to A. After exercising the second option, A owns a total of 125 shares of incentive stock option stock. Under section 1036 (and so much of section 1031 as relates to section 1036), the 100 "new" shares of incentive stock option stock have the following bases and holding periods: 15 shares have a $75 carryover basis and a three-year-and-three-month holding period for purposes of determining capital gain, 60 shares have a $1,500 basis resulting from the inclusion of that amount in income as compensation and a three-month holding period for purposes of determining capital gain, and 25 shares have a zero basis and a holding period beginning on September 1, 2005, for purposes of determining capital gain. All 100 shares have a holding period beginning on September 1, 2005, for purposes of determining whether the holding period requirements of § 1.422-1(a) are met.

*Example (4).* Assume the same facts as in Example 2, except that, instead of selling the 75 shares of incentive stock option stock on September 1, 2005, A uses those shares to exercise a nonstatutory option. The nonstatutory option was granted to A by X Corporation on January 1, 2005, entitling A to purchase 100 shares of X Corporation common stock at $22.50 per share. Unlike Example 3, A has not made a disqualifying disposition of the 75 shares of stock. After exercising the nonstatutory option, A owns a total of 100 shares of incentive stock option stock and 25 shares of nonstatutory stock option stock. Under section 1036 (and so much of section 1031 as relates to section 1036), the 75 new shares of incentive stock option stock have the same basis and holding period as the 75 old shares used to exercise the nonstatutory option. The additional 25 shares of stock received upon exercise of the nonstatutory option are taxed under the rules of section 83(a). Accordingly, A must include in gross income for the taxable year in which the transfer of such shares occurs $750 (25 shares at $30 per share) as compensation. A's basis in such shares is the same as the amount included in gross income. For its taxable year in which the transfer occurs, X Corporation is allowed a deduction of $750 for the compensation paid to A to the extent the requirements of section 83(h) and § 1.83-6(a) are satisfied and the deduction is otherwise allowable under section 162.

*Example (5).* Assume the same facts in Example 1, except that the shares transferred pursuant to the exercise of the incentive stock option are subject to a substantial risk of forfeiture and not transferable (substantially nonvested) for a period of six months after such transfer. Assume further that the shares that A uses to exercise the incentive stock option are similarly restricted. Such shares were transferred to A on January 1, 2005, through A's exercise of a nonstatutory stock option which was granted to A on January 1, 2004. A paid $5 per share for the stock when its fair market value was $22.50 per share. A did not file a section 83(b) election to include the $700 spread (the difference between the option price and the fair market value of the stock on date of exercise of the nonstatutory option) in gross income as compensation. After exercising the incentive stock option with the 40 substantially-nonvested shares, A owns 100 shares of substantially-nonvested incentive stock option stock. Section 1036 (and so much of section 1031 as relates to section 1036) applies to the 40 shares exchanged in exercise of the incentive stock option. However, pursuant to section 83(g), the stock received in such exchange, because it is incentive stock option stock, is not subject to restrictions and conditions substantially similar to those to which the stock given in such exchange was subject. For purposes of section 83(a) and § 1.83-1(b)(1), therefore, A has disposed of the 40 shares of substantially-nonvested stock on June 1, 2005, and must include in gross income as compensation $800 (the difference between the amount realized upon such disposition, $1,000, and the amount paid for the stock, $200). Accordingly, 40 shares of the incentive stock option stock have a $1,000 basis (the $200 original basis plus the $800 included in income as compensation) and 60 shares of the incentive stock option stock have a zero basis. For its taxable year in which the disposition of the substantially-nonvested stock occurs, X Corporation is allowed a deduction of $800 for the compensation paid to A, provided the requirements of section 83(h) and § 1.83-6(a) are satisfied and the deduction is otherwise allowable under section 162.

**(f) Effective/applicability date.** *(1) In general.* Except for § 1.422-2(b)(6) Example 1 (iii), the regulations under this section are effective on August 3, 2004. Section 1.422-2(b)(6) Example 1 (iii) is effective on November 17, 2009. Section 1.422-2(b)(6) Example 1 (iii) applies to statutory options granted on or after January 1, 2010.

*(2) Reliance and transition period.* For statutory options granted on or before June 9, 2003, taxpayers may rely on the 1984 proposed regulations LR-279-81 (49 FR 4504), the 2003 proposed regulations REG-122917-02 (68 FR 34344), or this section until the earlier of January 1, 2006, or the first regularly scheduled stockholders meeting of the granting corporation occurring 6 months after August 3, 2004. For statutory options granted after June 9, 2003, and before the earlier of January 1, 2006, or the first regularly scheduled stockholders meeting of the granting corporation occurring at least 6 months after August 3, 2004, taxpayers may rely on either REG-122917-02 or this section. Taxpayers may not rely on LR-279-81 or REG-122917-02 after December 31, 2005. Reliance on LR-279-81, REG-122917-02, or this section must be in its entirety, and all statutory options granted during the reliance period must be treated consistently.

T.D. 9144, 8/2/2004, amend T.D. 9471, 11/16/2009.

**Proposed § 1.422A-1 Incentive stock options—general rules.** [*For Preamble, see ¶ 150,935*]

• ***Caution:*** This Notice of Proposed Rulemaking was finalized by TD 9144, 8/2/2004. For statutory options granted on or before June 9, 2003, taxpayers may rely on any of these three sets of regs, in their entirety: (i) proposed regs issued in '84 (reproduced below); (ii) proposed regs issued on June 9, 2003; or (iii) final regs-until the earlier of (a) Jan. 1, 2006, or (b) the first regularly scheduled stockholders meeting of the granting corporation occurring at least six months after Aug. 3, 2004.

***Caution:*** The Treasury has not yet amended Reg § 1.422A-1 to reflect changes made by P.L. 101-508, P.L. 99-514.

**(a) Applicability of section 421(a).** *(1)* (i) Section 421(a) applies with respect to the transfer of a share of stock to an individual pursuant to the exercise of an incentive stock option if the following conditions are satisfied—

(A) The individual makes no disposition of such share before the later of the expiration of the 2-year period beginning on the day of the grant of the option pursuant to which such share was transferred, or the expiration of the 1-year period beginning on the day of the transfer of such share, and

(B) At all times during the period beginning on the day of the grant of the option and ending on the day 3 months before the date of such exercise, the individual was an employee of either the corporation granting the option, a related corporation of such corporation, or a corporation (or a related corporation of such corporation) issuing or assuming a stock option in a transaction to which section 425(a) applies.

(ii) For rules relating to the disposition of shares of stock, see paragraph (c) of § 1.425-1. For rules relating to the requisite employment relationship, see paragraph (h) of § 1.421.7.

*(2)* (i) The holding period requirement of section 422A(a)(1), set forth in paragraph (a)(1)(i)(A) of this section, does not apply to certain transfers by insolvent individuals. If an insolvent individual holds a share of stock acquired pursuant to the exercise of an incentive stock option, and if such share is transferred to a trustee, receiver, or other similar fiduciary in any proceeding under the Bankruptcy Act or any other similar insolvency proceeding, neither such transfer, nor any other transfer of such share for the benefit of the insolvent individual's creditors in such proceeding shall constitute a disposition of such share for the purpose of section 422A(a)(1). For the purpose of this paragraph (a)(2) an individual is an insolvent only if his liabilities exceed his assets, or if the individual is unable to satisfy his liabilities as they become due.

(ii) A transfer by the trustee or other fiduciary that is not treated as a disposition for the purpose of section 422A(a)(1) may be a sale or exchange for purposes of recognizing capital gain or loss with respect to the share transferred. For example, if the trustee transfers the share to a creditor in the insolvency proceeding in complete or partial satisfaction of such creditor's claim against the insolvent individual, capital gain or loss must be recognized by the insolvent individual to the extent of the difference between the amount realized from such transfer and the adjusted basis of such share. To the extent any transfer by the trustee or other fiduciary (other than a transfer back to the insolvent individual) is not for the exclusive benefit of the creditors in the insolvency proceeding, such transfer will be treated as a disposition for purposes of section 422A(a)(1). Similarly, if the trustee or other fiduciary transfers the share back to the insolvent individual, any subsequent disposition of the share which is not made in respect of the insolvency proceeding and for the exclusive benefit of the creditors in such proceeding will be treated as a disposition for purposes of section 422A(a)(1).

*(3)* If the employee exercising an option ceased employment because of permanent and total disability within the meaning of either section 37(e)(3) or section 105(d)(4), 1 year is substituted for 3 months in the employment period requirement of section 422A(a)(2) and paragraph (a)(1)(i)(B) of this section.

**(b) Failure to satisfy holding period requirement.** *(1)* A disqualifying disposition of a share of stock acquired by the exercise of an incentive stock option (i.e., a disposition before the expiration of the holding periods as determined under section 422A(a)(1) and paragraph (a)(1)(i)(A) of this section) makes section 421(a) inapplicable to the transfer of such share. Pursuant to section 421(b), the income attributable to such transfer shall be treated by the individual as income received in the taxable year in which such disqualifying disposition occurs. Similarly, a deduction under section 162 attributable to the transfer of the share of stock pursuant to the exercise of the option shall be allowable for the taxable year in which such disqualifying disposition occurs to the employer corporation (or to a corporation issuing or assuming the option in a transaction to which section 425(a) applies). In such cases, no amount shall be treated as income, and no amount shall be allowed as a deduction, for any taxable year other than the taxable year in which the disqualifying disposition occurs. Except as provided by section 421(b) and paragraph (b) of this section, the effects of a disqualifying disposition shall be determined pursuant to section 83 and the regulations thereunder.

*(2)* If an individual makes a disqualifying disposition of a share of stock acquired by the exercise of an incentive stock option, and if such disposition is a sale or exchange with respect to which a loss (if sustained) would be recognized to the individual, then, under section 422A(c)(2), the amount includible in the gross income of such individual, and deductible from the income of the employer corporation (or of a corporation issuing or assuming the option in a transaction to which section 425(a) applies) as compensation attributable to the exercise of such option, shall not exceed the excess (if any) of the amount realized on such sale or exchange over the adjusted basis of such share. Thus, the limitation does not apply when the disqualifying disposition is a sale described in section 1091 (relating to loss from wash sales of stock or securities), a gift, or a sale described in section 267(a)(1) (relating to sales between related persons), since a loss sustained in any such transaction would not be recognized. Subject to the limitation provided by section 422A(c)(2) and this paragraph (b)(2), the amount of compensation attributable to the exercise of the option is determined under § 1.83-7.

*(3)* The application of this paragraph may be illustrated by the following examples:

*Example (1).* On June 1, 1982, X Corporation grants an incentive stock option to A, an employee of X Corporation, entitling A to purchase one share of X Corporation stock. On August 1, 1982, A exercises the option and the share of X Corporation stock is transferred to A on that date. In order to meet the holding period requirements of section 422A(a)(1), A must not dispose of the share acquired by exercise of the incentive stock option before June 1, 1984.

*Example (2).* Assume the same facts as in example (1) except that A exercises the option on June 1, 1983, and the share of X Corporation stock is transferred to A on June 10, 1983. In order to meet the holding period requirements of section 422A(a)(1). A must not dispose of the share acquired by exercise of the incentive stock option before June 10, 1984.

*Example (3).* Assume the same facts as in example (1) and assume further that the option price was $100, the fair market value of X Corporation stock on June 1, 1982, and that the fair market value of X Corporation stock was $200 on August 1, 1982, the date of exercise. Assume further that the share of X Corporation stock transferred to A was transferable and not subject to a substantial risk of forfeiture. A makes a disqualifying disposition by selling the share on June 1, 1983, for $250. Under section 83(a) and paragraph (a) of § 1.83-7 (relating to options to which section 421 does not apply) the amount of compensation attributable to A's exercise is $100 (the difference between the fair market value of the share at the date of exercise, $200, and the amount paid for the share, $100). Because the amount realized, $250 is greater than the value of the stock at exercise, section 422A(c)(2) does not apply and thus does not affect the amount includible as compensation in A's gross income and deductible by X. A must include in gross income for the taxable year in which the sale occurred $100 as compensation and $50 as capital gain ($250, the amount realized from the sale, less A's basis of $200 (the $100 paid for the share plus the $100 increase in basis resulting from the inclusion of that amount in A's gross income as compensation attributable to the exercise of the option)). For its taxable year in which the disqualifying disposition occurs, X Corporation is allowed a deduction of $100 for compensation attributable to A's exercise of the incentive stock option provided the withholding requirements of § 1.83-6 are met.

*Example (4).* Assume the same facts as in example (3), except that A sells the share for $150. Under section 422A(c)(2), A must include only $50 (the excess of the amount realized on such sale, $150, over the adjusted basis of the share, $100) in gross income as compensation attributable to the exercise of the incentive stock option instead of the $100 which otherwise would have been includible as compensation under section 83(a). A realizes no capital gain or loss as a result of the sale, since A's basis for the share is $150 (the $100 which A paid for the share, plus the $50 increase in basis resulting from the inclusion of that amount in A's gross income as compensation attributable to the exercise of the option). For its taxable year in which the disqualifying disposition occurs, X Corporation is allowed a deduction of $50 for compensation attributable to A's exercise of the stock option provided the withholding requirements of § 1.83-6 are met.

*Example (5).* Assumes the same facts as in example (3), except that A sells the share for $50. The limitation of section 422A(c)(2) applies and A is not required to include any amount in gross income as compensation attributable to the exercise of the incentive stock option. A is allowed a capital loss of $50 (the difference between the amount realized on the sale, $50, and the adjusted basis of the share, $100). X Corporation is not allowed any deduction for compensation attributable to A's exercise of the incentive stock option and disqualifying disposition.

*Example (6).* Assume the same facts as in example (4) except that A sells the share to A's son for $150. Under section 267, a loss sustained in such a sale would not be recognized. Therefore, the limitation of section 422A(c)(2) does not apply. Accordingly, under section 83(a). A must include $100 (the difference between the fair market value of the share at date of exercise, $200, and the amount paid for the share, $100) in gross income as compensation attributable to the exercise of the incentive stock option in the taxable year in which the disqualifying disposition occurred. A will recognize no capital gain or loss on the transaction. X Corporation will be allowed a $100 deduction for compensation paid to A in its taxable year in which the disqualifying disposition occurred provided the withholding requirements of § 1.83-6 are met.

*Example (7).* Assume the same facts as in example (4), except assume that, as a result of the failure of a good-faith attempt to set the option price at the fair market value of X Corporation stock on the date of grant, the option price was set at $90 instead of $100. The requirement that the option price be not less than the fair market value of the stock at the time such option is granted, shall be considered to have been met pursuant to section 422A(c)(1). Upon sale of the share, A will include $60 (the excess of the amount realized on such sale, $150, over the adjusted basis of the share, $90) in gross income as compensation attributable to the exercise of the incentive stock option, in the taxable year in which the disqualifying disposition occurs. A will have no capital gain or loss as a result of such sale. Under section 422A(c)(2), X Corporation will be allowed a deduction of $60 as compensation attributable to A's exercise, in the taxable year of A's disqualifying disposition, provided the withholding requirements of § 1.83-6 are met.

*Example (8).* Assume the same facts as in example (3), except that the share of X Corporation stock transferred to A is subject to a substantial risk of forfeiture and not transferable for a period of six months after such transfer. Assume further that the fair market value of X Corporation stock was $225 on February 1, 1983, the date the six-month restriction lapsed. Under section 83(a) and paragraph (a) of § 1.83-7, the amount of compensation attributable to A's exercise of the option and subsequent disqualifying disposition is $125 (the difference between the fair market value of the share on the date the restriction lapsed, $225, and the amount paid for the share, $100). A must include in gross income for the taxable year in which the sale occurred $125 as compensation and $25 as capital gain ($250, the amount realized from the sale, less A's basis of $225 (the $100 paid for the share plus the $125 increase in basis resulting from the inclusion of that amount in A's gross income as compensation attributable to the exercise of the option)). For its taxable year in which the disqualifying disposition occurs, X Corporation is allowed a deduction of $125 for compensation attributable to A's exercise of the option provided the withholding requirements of § 1.83-6 are met.

**(c) Failure to satisfy employment requirement.** Section 421 does not apply to the transfer of a share of stock acquired by the exercise of an incentive stock option if the employment requirement as determined under section 422A(a)(2) and paragraph (a)(1)(i)(B) of this section is not met at the time of transfer. Consequently, the effects of such a transfer shall be determined pursuant to section 83 and the regulations thereunder.

## Proposed § 1.422A-2 Incentive stock options defined.

*[For Preamble, see ¶ 150,935]*

• ***Caution:*** This Notice of Proposed Rulemaking was finalized by TD 9144, 8/2/2004. For statutory options granted on or before June 9, 2003, taxpayers may rely on any of these three sets of regs, in their entirety: (i) proposed regs issued in '84 (reproduced below); (ii) proposed regs issued on June 9, 2003; or (iii) final regs-until the earlier of (a) Jan. 1, 2006, or (b) the first regularly scheduled stockholders meeting of the granting corporation occurring at least six months after Aug. 3, 2004.

***Caution:*** The Treasury has not yet amended Reg § 1.422A-2 to reflect changes made by P.L. 101-508, P.L. 99-514.

**(a) Incentive stock option defined.** *(1)* (i) In general, the term "incentive stock option" means an option that meets the requirements of section 422A(b) and this section at the time of grant and that is granted to an individual after August 13, 1981. In addition, certain stock options granted to an individual after December 31, 1975, that were not incentive stock options at the time of grant, may be converted into incentive stock options. See § 1.422A-3 for special rules relating to such options. Section 422A(b)(1) requires that an incentive stock option be granted pursuant to a plan which meets certain requirements. See paragraph (b) of this section. Section 422A(b)(2) provides that in order for an option to be an incentive stock option it must be granted within 10 years of the adoption of the plan or the date of stockholder approval, whichever is earlier. See paragraph (c) of this section. In order to grant incentive stock options after the expiration of such 10-year period, a new plan must be adopted and approved. Such new plan may retain all of the terms of the old plan or may include new terms. Paragraphs (3), (4), (5), and (7) of section 422A(b) establish certain requirements which must be met by the terms of an incentive stock option. An option which, when granted, does not by its terms meet these requirements cannot be an incentive stock option. See paragraphs (d), (e), (f), and (g) of this section. However, an amendment of the terms of an option at any time to permit such option to meet the requirement of section 422A(b)(5) will be given retroactive effect. See section 425(h)(3)(B) and paragraph (e)(5)(iii) of § 1.425-1. Section 422A(b)(6) generally bars the grant of an incentive stock option to any employee whose stock ownership exceeds the limits provided by such section. An option granted to an employee whose stock ownership exceeds such limits cannot be an incentive stock option unless the special rule of section 422A(c)(8) applies. See paragraph (h) of this section. Section 422A(b)(8) bars the grant of an incentive stock option to any employee whose annual grants of incentive stock options exceed the limits provided by such section. An option granted to an employee whose annual grants exceed such limits cannot be an incentive stock option. See paragraph (b)(4) of this section. Section 422A(c)(5) provides that an incentive stock option may contain a number of permissible provisions that will not affect the option's status as an incentive stock option. See paragraph (i) of this section.

(ii) Whether a particular option is an incentive stock option is determined at the time such option is granted. Accordingly, except as otherwise specifically provided by sections 421 through 425 and the regulations thereunder, events subsequent to the grant of an option cannot affect the status of the option. For example, an option which is granted at a fair market value option price to an employee whose stock ownership exceeds the limitation provided by section 422A(b)(6) is not an incentive stock option when granted and can never become an incentive stock option, even if the individual's stock ownership is within the limitation at the time such option is exercised.

(iii) Except as otherwise specifically provided by sections 421 through 425 and the regulations thereunder, an incentive stock option must meet the requirements of section 422A(b) and this section at all times during the period beginning on the date of the granting of the option and ending on the date of the exercise or expiration of the option. Accordingly, such requirements must be met even during periods when section 421(a) would not apply to the transfer of stock on exercise of the option. For example, an option which provides that the sequential exercise restriction of section 422A(b)(7) will cease to have effect 3 months and a day after an optionee terminates employment is not an incentive stock option when granted and can never become an incentive stock option.

(iv) An option granted after April 9, 1984, which meets the requirements of section 422A(b) and this section at the time of grant is an incentive stock option irrespective of any option or plan labeling to the contrary.

*(2)* Section 422A and this section do not apply to an option which is a restricted or qualified stock option.

**(b) Option plan.** *(1)* An incentive stock option must be granted pursuant to a written plan which meets the requirements of section 422A(b) and this paragraph (b). The authority to grant other stock options or rights pursuant to the plan, where the exercise of such other options or rights does not affect the exercise of incentive stock options granted pursuant to the plan, will not disqualify such incentive stock options.

*(2)* The plan required by section 422A must be approved by the stockholders of the granting corporation within 12 months before or after the date such plan is adopted. Ordinarily, a plan is adopted when approved by the board of directors and the date of such board action will be the reference point for determining whether stockholder approval occurs within the 12-month period. However, if the board's action is subject to a condition, such as stockholder approval, or the happening of a particular event, the plan is adopted on the date the condition is met or the event occurs, unless the board's resolution fixes the date of approval as the date of the board's action. The approval of stockholders must comply with all applicable provisions of the corporate charter, bylaws and applicable State law prescribing the method and degree of stockholder approval required for the granting of incentive stock options. Absent any such prescribed method and degree of stockholder approval, an incentive stock option plan must be approved by a simple majority vote of stockholders, voting either in person or by proxy, at a duly held stockholders' meeting.

*(3)* (i) The plan required by section 422A must designate the aggregate number of shares which may be issued under the plan and the employees or class of employees eligible to receive options under the plan. Unless otherwise specified, the terms designated shall apply to all options that may be granted under the plan, including options other than incentive stock options. If options other than incentive stock options may be granted, the plan may separately designate terms for each type of option. If individuals other than employees may be granted options, the plan must separately designate the employees or class of employees eligible to receive incentive stock options.

(ii) A plan which merely provides that the number of shares which may be issued under options shall not exceed a stated percentage of the shares outstanding at the time of each offering or grant under the plan will not satisfy the requirement that the plan state the aggregate number of shares which may be issued under the plan. However, the maximum number of shares which may be issued under the plan may be stated in terms of a percentage of either the authorized, issued or outstanding shares at the date of the adoption of the plan.

(iii) The requirement that the plan as adopted and approved must indicate the class of employees (or the employees) eligible to receive options will be considered satisfied by a general designation of the class of employees eligible to receive options under the plan. Thus, such designations as "key employees of the grantor corporation," "all salaried employees of the grantor corporation and its subsidiaries, including subsidiaries which become such after adoption of the plan" or "all employees of the corporation" will meet this requirement. Moreover, this requirement will be considered satisfied although the board of directors or another group is given authority to select the particular employees who are to receive options from a described class and to determine the number of shares to be optioned to each such employee.

(iv) The provisions relating to the aggregate number of shares to be issued under the plan and the class of employees (or the employees) eligible to receive options under the plan are the only provisions of a stock option plan which require stockholder approval for purposes of section 422A(b)(1). Any increase in the aggregate number of shares which may be issued under the plan (other than an increase merely reflecting in change in capitalization such as a stock dividend or stock split), or change in the designation of the employees or class of employees eligible to receive options under the plan will be considered as the adoption of a new plan requiring stockholder approval within the prescribed 12-month period. Any other changes in the terms of an incentive stock option plan are not considered the adoption of a new plan.

An option intended by the grantor corporation to be an incentive stock option will be treated as having been granted pursuant to a plan notwithstanding that the terms of the option conflict with terms of the plan unless such option is granted to an employee not eligible to receive options under the plan or options have been granted on stock in excess of the aggregate number of shares which may be issued under the plan.

*(4)* (i) The plan required by section 422A must, by its terms, provide that the aggregate fair market value (determined at the time of grant of the option) of stock for which an employee may be granted incentive stock options in any calendar year after 1980, under all such plans of the employer corporation (or its parent or subsidiary corporations, or a predecessor corporation (as defined in paragraph (f)(2) of this section) of any such corporation), shall not exceed $100,000 plus any unused limit carryover to such year.

(ii) The unused limit carryover is an amount determined for a calendar year after 1980 equal to one-half of the amount by which $100,000 exceeds the aggregate fair market value (determined at the time of grant of the option) of stock for which an employee was granted incentive stock options in such calendar year. The unused limit carryover for a calendar year may be applied to each of the 3 succeeding calendar years, reduced each calendar year by the amount of such carryover which was used in a prior calendar year. For purposes of this paragraph, the amount of incentive stock options granted during any calendar year shall be treated as first using up the $100,000 limit for such calendar year, and then any unused limit carryover to such calendar year in the order in which the carryovers arose.

(iii) Amounts may be a carried over from calendar years after 1980 whether or not the granting corporation had an incentive stock option plan in effect for the year of the unused limit carryover, provided that the individual was employed by such corporation (or its parent or subsidiary corporations, or a predecessor corporation (as defined in paragraph (f)(2) of this section) of any such corporation) for some part of such year.

(iv) If an option intended to be an incentive stock option is granted to an employee, but such option gives the employee the right to buy stock in excess of the amount permitted by this paragraph (b)(4), no portion of such option is an incentive stock option. However, if the amount permitted has been exceeded because there was a failure of an attempt, made in good faith, to meet the option price requirements of section 422A(b)(4) and paragraph (e)(1) of this section, the requirements of this paragraph (b)(4) shall be considered to have been met. To determine whether there was a good-faith attempt to meet the option price requirements of section 422A(b)(4) and paragraph (e)(1) of this section, see paragraph (e)(2)(ii) of this section.

**(c) Duration of option grants under the plan.** An incentive stock option must be granted within 10 years from the date the plan required by section 422A is adopted, or the date such plan is approved by the stockholders, whichever is earlier.

**(d) Period for exercising options.** An incentive stock option by its terms must not be exercisable after the expiration of 10 years from the date the option is granted. An option which does not contain such a provision when granted cannot be an incentive stock option.

**(e) Option price.** *(1)* Except as provided by section 422A(c)(1) and paragraph (e)(2) of this section, the option price of an incentive stock option must not be less than the fair market value of the stock subject to the option at the time the option is granted. For general rules relating to the option price, see paragraph (e) of § 1.421-7. For rules relating to the determination of when an option is granted, see paragraph (c) of § 1.421-7. The option price may be determined in any manner so long as the minimum price possible under the terms of the option cannot be less than the fair market value of the stock at the date of grant.

*(2)* (i) Under section 422A(c)(1), if a share of stock is transferred to an individual pursuant to the exercise of an option which would fail to qualify as an incentive stock option because there was a failure of an attempt, made in good faith, to meet the requirements of section 422A(b)(4) and paragraph (e)(1) of this section, the requirements of such section and paragraph shall be considered to have been met.

(ii) Whether there was a good-faith attempt to set the option price at not less than the fair market value of the stock subject to the option at the time the option was granted depends on the facts and circumstances surrounding the case. For example, in the case of a publicly held stock that was actively traded in an established market at the time the option was granted, determining the fair market value of such stock by any reasonable method using market quotations would establish that a good-faith attempt to meet the requirements of section 422A(b)(4) and this paragraph was made. On the other hand, in the case of a stock which is not publicly traded, it it is shown, for example, that the fair market value of the stock at the date of grant was based upon an average of the fair market values as of such date set forth in the opinions of completely independent and well-qualified experts, such a showing will establish that there was a good-faith attempt to meet the requirements of section 422A(b)(4) and this paragraph. However, amounts treated as unstated interest under section 483 and the regulations thereunder, and amounts paid as interest under a deferred payment arrangement are not includible as part of the " option price." See paragraph (e)(1) of § 1.421-7. An attempt to set the option price at not less than fair market value will not be regarded as made in good faith where an adjustment of the option price to allow for the application of section 483 results in the option price being lower than the fair market value on which the option price was based.

**(f) Prior outstanding options.** *(1)* (i) Section 422A(b)(7) provides that an incentive stock option must, by its terms, not be exercisable while there is outstanding any incentive stock option which was granted, before the granting of the new incentive stock option, to the individual to purchase stock in the employer corporation, or in a corporation which, at the time of the granting of the new incentive stock option, is a parent or subsidiary corporation of the employer corporation, or a predecessor corporation of any of such corporations. Thus, in general, under section 422A(b)(7), an incentive stock option must not be exercisable until all incentive stock options which were previously granted to the individual by the grantor corporation, or by related or predecessor corporations, have been exercised in full or have expired solely by reason of the lapse of time. The limitation of section 422A(b)(7) applies irrespective of whether the transfer of stock pursuant to such prior outstanding incentive stock options can qualify for the special tax treatment of section 421. The exercisability of an incentive stock option is not affected by options which are not incentive stock options.

(ii) The restriction imposed by section 422A(b)(7) must be set forth in the terms of the option unless the individual in fact has no prior outstanding incentive stock options to purchase stock of the grantor corporation, a related corporation, or a predecessor corporation of any of such corporations at the time the new incentive stock option is granted. An option which incorporates by reference the provision of a plan containing the restrictions required by section 422A(b)(7) will be treated as an option which by its terms sets forth such restrictions. Except as provided by this paragraph (f)(2)(ii), an option which does not contain the restriction imposed by section 422A(b)(7), either expressly or incorporated by reference, cannot be an incentive stock option, irrespective of whether such restriction is in fact complied with at the time the option is exercised and irrespective of whether the plan under which the option is granted contains the restriction required by section 422A(b)(7).

(iii) For purposes of section 422A(b)(7) and this paragraph (f), options granted or exercised on the same day are considered simultaneously granted or exercised.

*(2)* For purposes of section 422A(b)(7) and this paragraph (f), the term " predecessor corporation" means a corporation which was a party to a transaction described in section 425(a) (or which would be so described if a substitution or assumption under such section had been effected) with the grantor corporation, or a corporation which, at the time the new incentive stock option is granted, is a related corporation of the grantor corporation, or a predecessor corporation of any of such corporations.

*(3)* Except as is otherwise provided by this paragraph (f)(3), for purposes of section 422A(b)(7), an incentive stock option is treated as outstanding according to its original terms until such option is exercised in full or expires by reason of the lapse of time. Thus, for example, if an option outstanding according to its terms for 10 years is revised to shorten to 1 year the period during which it may be exercised, such option is treated as outstanding for 10 years from the original date of grant for purposes of section 422A(b)(7),

notwithstanding the revision. If any portion of such an option is not exercised, such portion will be treated as outstanding until the expiration of the maximum period during which such portion, according to the terms of the option when granted, could have been exercised under any circumstances. An incentive stock option previously held by an individual and replaced in a transaction to which section 425(a) applies will not thereafter be treated as outstanding. However, if an incentive stock option is modified and under section 425(h) such modification is considered as the granting of a new option (even though for other purposes only one option is regarded as being in existence), the original incentive stock option continues for the purposes of section 422A(b)(7) to be outstanding, and may prevent an exercise of the new incentive stock option until the original option has, by its original terms, expired.

*(4)* The application of this paragraph may be illustrated by the following examples:

*Example (1).* S Corporation is a subsidiary of P Corporation. In 1982 E was an employee of S Corporation and was granted an incentive stock option by S to buy S stock. In June of 1983 E left S and became an employee of X Corporation, where he was granted an incentive stock option to purchase X stock. X Corporation is neither a related nor predecessor corporation of P or S. On June 1, 1984, E leaves X to become an employee of P Corporation, and on such date E is granted an incentive stock option by P to purchase P stock. Both E's incentive stock option on S stock and his incentive stock option on X stock are outstanding on June 1, 1984. In order to meet the requirements of section 422A(b)(7), E's incentive stock option on P stock must, by its terms, not be exercisable until E's incentive stock option on S stock is exercised in full or expires solely by reason of the lapse of time. This requirement must be met even though at the time E's incentive stock option on P stock is granted. E's incentive stock option on S stock no longer qualifies for the special tax treatment or section 421.

*Example (2).* E is an employee of P Corporation. E holds an incentive stock option granted June 1, 1982, and an incentive stock option granted June 1, 1983. Both options were granted to him by P to purchase P stock. E has been granted no other incentive stock options by P, a related corporation, or a predecessor corporation of any of such corporations. On November 30, 1984, P cancels E's 1982 incentive stock option and in exchange therefore issues a new incentive stock option to E. Assume that each incentive stock option runs 10 years from grant. The 1982 incentive stock option, according to its terms when granted, would have expired solely by reason of the lapse of time at the close of business on May 31, 1982. Under section 422A(b)(7) and (c)(7), E's 1982 incentive stock option is treated as outstanding according to its original terms when granted, and E cannot exercise any of his incentive stock options until June 1, 1992 (the first day after the expiration of the original period for which E's 1982 incentive stock option was granted). On June 1, 1992, E's 1983 incentive stock option will be fully exercisable. E's 1984 incentive stock option will not be exercisable until after the full exercise or expiration of E's 1983 incentive stock option.

*Example (3).* Assume the same facts as in example (2). On June 1, 1986, P Corporation sells all of its assets to M Corporation, and on such date E becomes an employee of M Corporation. Assume further that M Corporation substitutes new options to purchase M stock for those options held by E in a transaction to which section 425(a) applies. For purposes of section 422A(b)(7), each M Corporation option received by E in substitution for a P Corporation option will be treated as outstanding to the same extent and in the same manner as the P option which it replaces. Thus, none of the M options received by E in substitution for his P options may be exercisable before June 1, 1992, and the M option issued in substitution for E's 1984 P option may be exercisable only after the full exercise or expiration of the M option issued in substitution for E's 1983 P option. If, in 1987, E is granted another incentive stock option by M Corporation, such option may be exercisable only after the full exercise or expiration of the incentive stock options granted by M to E in 1986 in substitution for E's options to purchase P stock. The options to purchase P stock which were replaced by M in the transaction to which section 425(a) applied will not be treated as outstanding for any purposes under section 422A(b)(7).

*Example (4).* Assume the same facts as in example (3) except assume that M does not effect a substitution or assumption of E's P Corporation incentive stock options under section 425(a). Although P is neither a parent nor subsidiary of M, for purposes of section 422A(b)(7), P is a predecessor corporation of M Corporation. Accordingly, any incentive stock options granted to E by M (or its parent or subsidiary corporations, or a predecessor corporation of any of such corporations) must, by their terms, not be exercisable until the expiration of the option periods for all of E's incentive stock options granted to E by P Corporation.

*Example (5).* F is an employee of N Corporation. On January 1, 1982, N granted an incentive stock option to F to purchase 100 shares of N Corporation stock at a price of $100 per share. The option is exercisable in installments as follows: 20 shares on or after June 1, 1983; another 40 shares on or after June 1, 1984; and the last 40 shares on or after June 1, 1985. Under section 422A(c)(7), the entire option is treated as being outstanding as of the January 1, 1982 date of grant. Thus, under the facts given, any incentive stock options granted to F after January 1, 1982, may not be exercised until the full exercise or expiration of all installments of F's January 1, 1982 incentive stock option.

*Example (6).* F is an employee of N Corporation. On January 1, 1982, N grants F an incentive stock option to purchase 100 shares of N Corporation stock at a price of $100 a share at any time prior to January 1, 1992. The stock is then selling at $100 a share. On January 1, 1983, when the stock was selling at $95 a shares, N modified the option to permit F to purchase 100 shares of N Corporation stock at a price of $95 a share and to exercise the option at any time prior to January 1, 1993. Under section 425(n) N's modification is treated as the granting of a new option to F. Although for other purposes F, after the modification, has one option to purchase 100 shares of N Corporation stock at a price of $95 a share at any time prior to January 1, 1993, for purposes of section 422A(b)(7), F is regarded as having two options. Thus, F may not exercise the modified option until January 1, 1992, because until that date the original option is regarded as outstanding. If the option period had not been extended, F would never have been able to exercise the modified option because of the limitation of section 422A(b)(7) and the existence, for the purposes of that section, of a prior outstanding option having the same expiration date as the new option.

**(g) Restriction on transferability.** An incentive stock option, by its terms, must not be transferable by the individual to whom it is granted otherwise than by will or the laws of descent and distribution, and, during the lifetime of such individual, must not be exercisable by any other person. For general rules relating to the restriction on transferability required by section 422A(b)(5), see paragraph (b)(2) of § 1.421-7 and paragraph (c) of § 1.421-8. For a limited exception to the requirement of section 422A(b)(5), see section 425(h)(3).

**(h) Options granted to certain shareholders.** *(1)* (i) Except as provided in paragraph (h)(2) of this section, an option is not an incentive stock option if, immediately before such option is granted, the optionee owns stock possessing more than 10 percent of the total combined voting power of all classes of stock either of the employer corporation or of its parent or subsidiary corporation. In applying the limitation of section 422A(b)(6), the rules of section 425(d) (relating to attribution of stock ownership) shall apply in determining the stock ownership of the individual, and stock that the individual may purchase under outstanding options shall not be treated as stock owned by the individual.

(ii) The determination of the percentage of the total combined voting power of all classes of stock of the employer corporation (or of its parent or subsidiary corporations) that is owned by the individual is made with respect to each such corporation in the related group by comparing the voting power of the shares owned (or treated as owned) by the individual to the aggregate voting power of all shares actually issued and outstanding immediately before the grant of the option to such individual. The aggregate voting power of all shares actually issued and outstanding immediately before the grant of the option does not include the voting power of treasury shares or shares authorized for issue under outstanding options held by the individual or any other person.

*(2)* Paragraph (h)(1) of this section does not apply to an option if the time such option is granted the option price is at least 110 percent of the fair market value at such time of the stock subject to the option and such option by its terms is not exercisable after the expiration of 5 years from the date such option is granted. The rules of paragraph (e)(2) of this section relating to option price shall not apply to the determination of the minimum option price for purposes of this paragraph (h)(2).

*(3)* The application of this paragraph may be illustrated by the following examples:

*Example (1).* E, an employee of M Corporation, owns 15,000 shares of the common stock of M Corporation, the only class of M stock outstanding. M has 100,000 shares of its common stock outstanding. Since E owns stock comprising more than 10 percent of the total combined voting power of all classes of M Corporation stock, M cannot grant an incentive stock option to E unless such option is granted at an option price of at least 110 percent of the fair market value of the stock subject to the option and such option would expire no later than 5 years from its date of grant. An option is granted to E which purports to be an incentive stock option but which fails to meet the above option-price and term requirements. Such option is not an incentive stock option and is, therefore, subject to section 83(a). If E's father and brother each owned 7,500 shares of M Corporation stock, and E owned no M stock in E's own name, the result in this case would be the same, since under section 425(d) a person is treated as owning stock held by parents and siblings.

*Example (2).* Assume the same facts as in example (1) and assume further that M is a subsidiary corporation of P Corporation. Irrespective of whether E owns any P stock and irrespective of the number of P shares outstanding, an option granted to E by P Corporation which purports to be an incentive stock option, but which fails to meet the 110-percent-option-price and 5-year-term requirements, is not an incentive stock option. This results from E's ownership of more than 10 percent of the total combined voting power of all classes of stock of a subsidiary of P Corporation (i.e., M Corporation). Thus, an individual who owns (or is treated as owning) stock in excess of the limitation of section 422A(b)(6), in any corporation in a group of corporations consisting of the employer corporation and its parent and subsidiary corporations, cannot receive an incentive stock option from any corporation in the group unless such option meets the 110-percent-option-price and 5-year-term requirements of section 422A(b)(6).

*Example (3).* F is an employee of R Corporation. R has only one class of stock, of which 100,000 shares are issued and outstanding. F owns no stock in R Corporation or in any parent or subsidiary of R Corporation or in any parent or subsidiary of R Corporation for purposes of section 422A(b)(6). On January 1, 1983, R grants a 10-year incentive stock option to F to purchase 50,000 shares of R stock at $1 per share, the fair market value of R stock on the date of grant of the option. On April 1, 1983, F exercises half of the January option and receives 25,000 shares of R stock. On July 1, 1983, R grants a second 50,000 share option to F which purports to be an incentive stock option. All of the terms of the July option are identical to the terms of the January option, including an option price of $1 per share, the fair market value of R stock on the date of grant of the second option. Pursuant to section 422A(b)(6), the July option is not an incentive stock option because on the date such option was granted F owned 20 percent (25,000 shares owned by F divided by 125,000 shares of R stock issued and outstanding) of the total combined voting power of all classes of R Corporation stock. The unexercised portion of the January option, because it was an incentive stock option on the date it was granted, remains an incentive stock option regardless of changes in the employee's percentage of stock ownership after grant of the option.

*Example (4).* Assume the same facts as in example (3) except that the partial exercise of the January incentive stock option on April 1, 1983, was for only 10,000 shares. Under these circumstances, the July option is an incentive stock option because on the date such option was granted, F did not own more than 10 percent of the total combined voting power of all classes of R Corporation stock.

**(i) Permissible provisions.** *(1)* (i) Pursuant to section 422A(c)(5)(A), an option which otherwise meets the requirements of section 422A(b) and this section will be an incentive stock option even if the employee has the right to exercise the option with previously acquired stock of the corporation which granted the option. For special rules relating to the transfer of statutory option stock as payment in connection with the exercise of an incentive stock option, see section 425(c) and the regulations thereunder.

(ii) All stock transferred pursuant to the exercise of an incentive stock option is subject to the holding period requirements of section 422A(a)(1) and paragraph (a) of § 1.422A-1, and the disqualifying disposition rules of section 421(b) and paragraph (b) of § 1.422A-1, regardless of whether such option is exercised with previously acquired stock of the corporation which granted the option. If an incentive stock option is exercised with previously acquired stock of the corporation which granted the option, and such exercise results in the basis allocation described in paragraph (i)(1)(iii) of this section, a disqualifying disposition of stock transferred pursuant to such exercise will be a disqualifying disposition of the stock with the lowest basis.

(iii) If the exercise of an incentive stock option with previously acquired stock of the corporation which granted the option is comprised in part an exchange to which section 1036 (and so much of section 1031 as relates to section 1036) applies, then—

(A) The employee's basis in the incentive stock option stock transferred pursuant to the section 1036 exchange shall be the same as the employee's basis in the stock exchanged increased, if applicable, by any amount included in gross income as compensation pursuant to either sections 421 through 425 or section 83. Except for purposes of section 422A(a)(1) and paragraph (a) of § 1.422A-1, the holding period of the stock shall be determined pursuant to section 1223. For purposes of section 421(b), paragraph (b) of § 1.422A-1, and section 83 and the regulations thereunder, the amount paid for the stock shall be the fair market value of such stock on the date of the exchange.

(B) The employee's basis in the incentive stock option stock not transferred pursuant to the section 1036 exchange shall be zero. For all purposes, the holding period of the stock shall begin as of the date such stock is transferred. For purposes of section 421(b), paragraph (b) of § 1.422A-1, and section 83 and the regulations thereunder, the amount paid for the stock shall be zero.

*(2)* Pursuant to section 422A(c)(5)(B), an option which otherwise meets the requirements of section 422A(b) and this section will be an incentive stock option even if the employee has the right to receive additional compensation, whether in cash or other property, at the time the option is exercised, provided such additional compensation is includible in income under the provisions of sections 61 and 83. The additional compensation may be determined in any manner including by reference to the fair market value of the stock at the time of exercise, or by reference to the option price.

*(3)* (i) Pursuant to section 422A(c)(5)(C), an option which otherwise meets the requirements of section 422A(b) and this section will be an incentive stock option even if the option is subject to a condition, or grants a right, not inconsistent with the requirements of section 422A(b) and this section.

(ii) An option that includes an alternative right is not an incentive stock option if the requirements of section 422A(b) and this section may be avoided by exercise of the alternative right. For example, an alternative right extending the option term beyond ten years, setting a price below fair market value, permitting transferability, or allowing nonsequential exercise, will prevent an option from qualifying as an incentive stock option. If either of two options can be exercised, but not both, each such option is a disqualifying alternative right with respect to the other even though one or both options would individually satisfy the requirements of section 422A(b) and this section.

(iii) An alternative right to receive a taxable payment of cash and/or other property in exchange for the cancellation or surrender of the option does not disqualify the option as an incentive stock option if the right is exercisable only when the then fair market value of the stock exceeds the exercise price of the option and the option is otherwise exercisable, the right is transferable only when the option is otherwise transferable, and the exercise of the right has the same economic and tax consequences as the exercise of the option followed by an immediate sale of the stock. For this purpose, the exercise of the alternative right does not have the same economic and tax consequences if the payment exceeds the difference between the then fair market value of the stock and the exercise price of the option. If the above conditions have been met, the exercise of the alternative right will be considered to be the exercise of the option for purposes of the sequencing provisions of section 422A(b)(7).

(iv) Section 425(h)(1) shall not apply to the amendment of an alternative right described in paragraph (i)(3)(iii) of this section in order to conform the terms of the alternative right to the technical requirements of such paragraph. This paragraph (iv) shall apply only to options granted after August 13, 1981, and before January 21, 1982, that are amended before [insert date 60 days after this document is published in the FEDERAL REGISTER as final regulations].

*(4)* The application of this paragraph may be illustrated by the following examples:

*Example (1).* On June 1, 1984, X Corporation grants an incentive stock option to A, an employee of X Corporation, entitling A to purchase 100 shares of X Corporation common stock at $10 per share. The option provides that A may exercise the option with previously acquired X Corporation common stock. X Corporation has only one class of common stock outstanding. The stock transferable to A pursuant to the exercise of the incentive stock option is transferable and not subject to a substantial risk of forfeiture. On June 1, 1985, when the fair market value of X Corporation stock is $25 per share, A exercises the option and the 100 shares are transferred to A on that date. To exercise the option, A transferred to X Corporation 40 shares of X Corporation common stock that A had purchased on the open market on June 1, 1982, for $5 per share. After exercising the option, A owns 100 shares of incentive stock option stock. Pursuant to section 1036 (and so much of section 1031 as relates to section 1036), 40 shares have a $200 carryover basis and a three-year holding period, and 60 shares have a zero basis and a holding period beginning June 1, 1985.

*Example (2).* Assume the same facts as in example (1) and assume further that A sells 75 shares of the incentive stock option stock on September 1, 1985, for $30 per share. On that date, A has made a disqualifying disposition of the 75 shares of stock. Pursuant to paragraph (i)(1)(ii) of this section, A has sold all 60 of the non-section-1036 shares and 15 of the 40 section-1036 shares. Therefore, pursuant to paragraph (i)(1)(iii) of this section and section 83(a), the amount of compensation attributable to A's exercise of the option and subsequent disqualifying disposition of 75 shares is $1,500 (the difference between the fair market value of the stock on the date of exercise, $1,875 (75 shares at $25 per share), and the amount paid for the stock, $375 (60 shares at $0 per share plus 15 shares at $25 per share)). In addition, A must recognize a long-term capital gain of $375 ($450, the amount realized from the sale of 15 shares, less A's basis of $75), and a short-term capital gain of $300 ($1,800, the amount realized from the sale of 60 shares, less A's basis of $1,500 resulting from the inclusion of that amount in income as compensation). Accordingly, A must include in gross income for the taxable year in which the sale occurs $1,500 as compensation, $375 as long-term capital gain, and $300 as short-term capital gain. For its taxable year in which the disqualifying disposition occurs, X Corporation is allowed a deduction of $1,500 for compensation paid to A provided the withholding requirements of § 1.83-6 are met.

*Example (3).* Assume the same facts as in example (2), except that instead of selling the 75 shares of incentive stock option stock on September 1, 1985, A uses those shares to exercise a second incentive stock option. The second option was granted to A by X Corporation on January 1, 1985, entitling A to purchase 100 shares of X Corporation common stock at $22.50 per share. As in example (2), A has made a disqualifying disposition of the 75 shares of stock. Pursuant to paragraph (i)(1)(ii) of this section, A has disposed of all 60 of the non-section-1036 shares and 15 of the 40 section-1036 shares. Therefore, pursuant to paragraph (i)(1)(iii) of this section and section 83(a), the amount of compensation attributable to A's exercise of the first option and subsequent disqualifying disposition of 75 shares is $1,500 (the difference between the fair market value of the stock on the date of exercise, $1,875 (75 shares at $25 per share), and the amount paid for the stock, $375 (60 shares at $0 per share plus 15 shares at $25 per share)). Unlike example (2), A does not recognize any capital gain as a result of exercising the second option because, for all purposes other than the determination of whether the exercise is a disposition pursuant to section 425(c), such exercise is an exchange to which section 1036 applies. Accordingly, A must include in gross income for the taxable year in which the disqualifying disposition occurs $1,500 as compensation. For its taxable year in which the disqualifying disposition occurs, X Corporation is allowed a deduction of $1,500 for compensation paid to A provided the withholding requirements of § 1.83-6 are met. After exercising the second option, A owns a total of 125 shares of incentive stock option stock. Pursuant to section 1036 (and so much of section 1031 as relates to section 1036), the 100 "new" shares of incentive stock option stock have the following bases and holding periods: 15 shares have a $74 carryover basis and a three-year-and-three-month holding period, 60 shares have a $1,500 basis resulting from the inclusion of that amount in income as compensation and a three-month holding period, and 25 shares have a zero basis and a holding period beginning September 1, 1985.

*Example (4).* Assume the same facts as in example (2), except that instead of selling the 75 shares of incentive stock option stock on September 1, 1985, A uses those shares to exercise a non-statutory stock option. The nonstatutory stock option was granted to A by X Corporation on January 1, 1985, entitling A to purchase 100 shares of X Corporation common stock at $22.50 per share. Unlike example (3), A has not made a disqualifying disposition of the 75 shares of stock. After exercising the non-statutory stock option, A owns a total of 100 shares of incentive stock option stock and 25 shares of non-statutory stock option stock. Pursuant to section 1036 (and so much of section 1031 as relates to section 1036), the 75 "new" shares of incentive stock option stock have the same basis and holding period as the 75 "old" shares used to exercise the non-statutory stock option. The additional 25 shares of stock received upon exercise of the nonstatutory stock option are compensation for services pursuant to section 83(a). Accordingly, A must include in gross income for the taxable year in which the transfer of such shares occurs $750 (25 shares at $30 per share) as compensation. A's basis in such shares is the same as the amount included in gross income. For its taxable year in which the transfer occurs, X Corporation is allowed a deduction of $750 for compensation paid to A provided the withholding requirements of § 1.83-6 are met.

*Example (5).* Assume the same facts in example (1), except that the stock transferred pursuant to the exercise of the incentive stock option is subject to a substantial risk of forfeiture and not transferable for a period of six months after such transfer. Assume further that the shares that A uses to exercise the incentive stock option are similarly restricted. Such shares were transferred to A on January 1, 1985, pursuant to the exercise of a non-statutory stock option granted to A on January 1, 1984. A paid $5 per share for the stock when its fair market value was $22.50 per share, A did not file a section 83(b) election to include the $700 spread (the difference between the option price and the fair market value of the stock on date of exercise of the option) in gross income as compensation. After exercising the incentive stock option with the 40 shares of restricted stock, A owns 100 shares of restricted incentive stock option stock. Section 1036 (and so much of section 1031 as relates to section 1036) applies to the 40 shares exchanged in exercise of the incentive stock option. However, pursuant to section 83(g), the stock received in such exchange, because it is incentive stock option stock, is not subject to restrictions and conditions substantially similar to those to which the stock given in such exchange was subject. For purposes of section 83(a) and § 1.83-1(b)(1), therefore, A has disposed of the 40 shares of restricted stock on June 1, 1985, and must include in gross income as compensation $800 (the difference between the amount realized upon such disposition, $1,000, and the amount paid for the stock, $200). Accordingly, 40 shares of the incentive stock option stock have a $1,000 basis (the $200 original basis plus the $800 included in income as compensation) and 60 shares of the incentive stock option stock have a zero basis. For its taxable year in which the disposition of the restricted stock occurs, X Corporation is allowed a deduction of $800 for compensation paid to A provided the withholding requirements of § 1.83-6 are met.

### Proposed § 1.422A-3 Incentive stock option transitional rules. [*For Preamble, see ¶ 150,935*]

• ***Caution:*** This Notice of Proposed Rulemaking was finalized by TD 9144, 8/2/2004. For statutory options granted on or before June 9, 2003, taxpayers may rely on any of these three sets of regs, in their entirety: (i) proposed regs issued in '84 (reproduced below); (ii) proposed regs issued on June 9, 2003; or (iii) final regs-until the earlier of (a) Jan. 1, 2006, or (b) the first regularly scheduled stockholders meeting of the granting corporation occurring at least six months after Aug. 3, 2004.

***Caution:*** The Treasury has not yet amended Reg § 1.422A-3 to reflect changes made by P.L. 101-508, P.L. 99-514.

**(a) In general.** *(1)* This section provides special rules pursuant to section 251(c) of the Economic Recovery Tax Act of 1981 (95 Stat. 172) for converting stock options into incentive stock options. These special rules apply to stock options granted after December 31, 1975, and either exercised on or after January 1, 1981, or outstanding on such date, if such stock options—

(i) Were granted prior to January 1, 1981;

(ii) Were exercised before January 21, 1982 and did not meet the requirements of section 422A(b) and § 1.422A-2 at the time of exercise;

(iii) Did not meet the requirements of section 422A(b) and § 1.422A-2 when granted and were outstanding on August 13, 1981; or

(iv) Were granted after December 31, 1980, and before August 14, 1981, and otherwise met the requirements of section 422A(b) and § 1.422A-2 when granted.

*(2)* Stock options granted before January 1, 1981, may be converted into incentive stock options, but only if the corporation that granted such options makes an election under paragraph (b) of this section. The aggregate fair market value of stock the options for which may be converted into incentive stock options by such an election is subject to an annual and a cumulative restriction. Such aggregate fair market value (determined as of the time the options were granted) may not exceed $50,000 per employee for options granted in any calendar year and $200,000 per employee for all options granted in the 5-year period ending December 31, 1980.

*(3)* Stock options that were exercised before January 21, 1982, and that did not meet certain requirements of section 422A(b) and § 1.422A-2 at the time of exercise may be converted into incentive stock options if the requirements of paragraph (c)(3) of this section are met.

*(4)* Stock options that did not meet the requirements of section 422A(b) and § 1.422-2 when granted and that were outstanding on August 13, 1981, may be converted into incentive stock options in accordance with paragraph (d) of this section. Section 425(h)(1) (relating to the modification of statutory stock options) shall not apply to any change in the terms of an option (or the terms of the plan under which the option was granted) or shareholder approval of such a change required to convert such option into an incentive stock option if such change or shareholder approval occurs on or before August 13, 1982.

*(5)* Stock options that were granted after December 31, 1980, and before August 14, 1981, are incentive stock options if they otherwise meet the requirements of section 422A(b) and § 1.422A-2 when granted. No election is necessary to convert such options into incentive stock options.

**(b) Election procedure and requirements.** *(1)* A corporation may make only one election to convert stock options granted before 1981 into incentive stock options and such election must include all options granted by the corporation before 1981 that are to be converted into incentive stock options. Thus, a corporation that makes an election with respect to certain options granted before 1981 may not make any subsequent election with respect to other options granted before 1981. An election shall be made by attaching an election statement to the granting corporation's income tax return either for the first taxable year during which an incentive stock option (including an option treated as an incentive stock option by reason of the election or the other provisions of this section) is exercised, or for any prior taxable year. An election shall be made no later than the due date (taking extensions into account) of the income tax return. If such due date occurs before August 14, 1982, the granting corporation will be permitted to make the election at any time prior to August 14, 1982, on an election statement attached to an amended return. In any event, no election will be permitted after the due date (taking extensions into account) of the income tax return for the taxable year including December 31, 1982. The election statement must—

(i) Contain the name, address, and taxpayer identification number of the corporation;

(ii) Identify the election as an election under section 251(c)(1)(B) of the Economic Recovery Tax Act of 1981; and

(iii) Specify, by employee, the options to which the election applies and state, for each such option, the date of original grant (and, if applicable, date of most recent modification) and total exercise price (i.e., the total number of shares subject to the option multiplied by the price per share).

All options to which the election applies must meet the section 422A qualification requirements (other than the requirement of securing stockholder approval) at the time the election statement is filed.

*(2)* In its election under this paragraph, a corporation may generally select any eligible option (or portion of such option). The selection is, however, subject to the $50,000 annual and $200,000 cumulative limits applicable to each employee, and also subject to any existing plan requirements relating to who must be benefited under such plan as among different classes of employees. Eligible options (or portions of such options) may be selected on an option-by-option basis and/or an employee-by-employee basis. If only a portion of an option is selected and such portion is not exercised prior to January 21, 1982, the option must be amended prior to the exercise of such portion so as to clearly identify it as an incentive stock option. Whenever such a dual option is exercised, separate stock certificates must be issued (or reissued). See § 1.422A-3(c)(3)(iv) for the deadlines for amending options.

**(c) Eligibility issues: Pre-enactment modifications, dollar limitations.** *(1)* An option is not eligible for incentive stock option conversion unless it was originally granted after December 31, 1975. A modification, extension, or renewal on or after January 1, 1976, of an option originally granted prior to that date, will not make such option eligible for conversion into an incentive stock option, regardless of whether the option as so modified, extended, or renewed would be treated as newly granted within the meaning of section 425(h).

*(2)* An amendment to an otherwise eligible option (or plan) prior to August 13, 1981, will be subject to the rules of section 425(h). If, pursuant to section 425(h), the amendment is a modification, extension, or renewal or the option, such amendment shall be considered as the grant of a new option. Such an option is not eligible for conversion into incentive stock option unless the option (and plan) comply with the section 422A qualification requirements. Since the option will be considered to have been granted on the date it was amended, the option price cannot be less than the fair market value of the stock on that date. If the option price is less than the fair market value of the stock on the date the option was amended, the corporation may qualify the option by adjusting the option price, so long as such adjustment occurs prior to the earliest of the exercise of the option, the date of the election under paragraph (b) of this section (if applicable), or August 14, 1982. If the corporation wishes to retain the original grant price (and grant date) of the option, the corporation may do so by rescinding the amendment, so long as such rescission occurs prior to the earliest of the exercise of the option, the date of the election under paragraph (b) of this section (if applicable), or August 14, 1982. If only a portion of an option is to become an incentive stock option, the adjustment of the option price or the rescission of the amendment need apply only to that portion. If an amendment is rescinded as to only a portion of an option so as to restore the original date of grant for that portion, the balance of the option is not eligible for conversion into an incentive stock option. For example, in the case of a $100,000 option granted in 1978 and amended in 1980, the corporation could not rescind the modification as to only half of the option, and then elect to convert into incentive stock options both the $50,000 portion of the option treated as granted in 1978 and the $50,000 portion of the option treated as granted in 1980.

*(3)* (i) Except as provided in this paragraph (c)(3), and option is eligible for incentive stock option conversion only if, at the time of exercise, such option (and its plan) conform to all of the section 422A qualification requirements and the transitional rule limitations. It is not possible to amend an exercised option retroactively to correct nonconforming or missing terms, or to rescind an improper exercise.

(ii) An option exercised prior to January 21, 1982, may be converted into an incentive stock option even if the option does not contain the sequential exercise restriction required by section 422A(b)(7). Incentive stock option conversion will be available, however, only if the employee in fact had no prior outstanding incentive stock options at the time the option in question was exercised. An option exercised on or after January 21, 1982, without containing the sequential exercise restriction may not be converted into an incentive stock option unless the employee in fact had no prior outstanding incentive stock options at the time the option in question was granted. In order to identify prior outstanding incentive stock options it will be necessary to take into account all options elected or amended to become incentive stock options and all options granted as incentive stock options.

(iii) An option granted after 1980 and exercised prior to January 21, 1982, may be converted into an incentive stock option even if the plan does not contain at the time of exercise the $100,000 annual plus carryover limit required by section 422A(b)(8). Incentive stock option conversion will be available, however, only for exercised amounts that do not exceed such limit. Where the limit has been exceeded, separate stock certificates must be issued (or reissued) no later than March 15, 1982. An option exercised on or after January 21, 1982, and before the plan has been amended to include the $100,000 annual plus carryover limit, may not be converted into an incentive stock option. Incentive stock option conversion is not available for such an option regardless of whether the limit is exceeded. An option exercised on or after January 21, 1982, and after the plan has been amended to include the $100,000 annual plus carryover limit, may not be converted into an incentive stock option where such limit has been exceeded. An option in excess of the limit must be amended, before it is exercised, so as clearly to identify that portion of the option intended to become an incentive stock option. Upon exercise of the option, separate stock certificates must be issued. An amended option that was required by its original terms to be exercised in full, must still be required to be exercised in full after it is amended.

(iv) An option granted before 1981 and exercised prior to January 21, 1982, may be converted into an incentive stock option even if the $50,000 annual limit or the $200,000 cumulative limit of paragraph (a)(2) of this section was exceeded. Incentive stock option conversion will be available, however, only for exercised amounts that do not exceed such limits. If either limit has been exceeded, separate stock certificates must be issued (or re-issued) no later than March 15, 1982. An option exercised on or after January 21, 1982, where either the $50,000 annual limit or the $200,000 cumulative limit was exceeded, may not be converted into an incentive stock option. An option in excess of such limits must be amended, before it is exercised, so as clearly to identify that portion of the option intended to become an incentive stock option. Upon exercise of the option, separate stock certificates must be issued. An amended option that was required by its original terms to be exercised in full, must still be required to be exercised in full after it is amended.

*(4)* The $50,000 annual and the $200,000 cumulative limits apply only to options granted prior to 1981 that are converted into incentive stock options by reason of an election under paragraph (b) of this section. Additionally, the limits relate only to the year of grant of an option, not the year in which an option vests (as in the case of an installment option) or the year of exercise. Unlike the $100,000 annual limit for options granted after 1980, the $50,000 annual limit does not incorporate an unused limit carryover from prior years. Both the $50,000 and the $200,000 limits apply to the fair market value of the stock at the time the options are granted, not to the option price of the options granted. Thus, in the case of an employee who is a 10 percent stockholder, an election would be permitted with respect to an option to purchase $50,000 worth of stock at an option price of $55,000. The requirement that options for which the election is made not exceed the $50,000 annual limit and the $200,000 cumulative limit will be deemed to have been satisfied if, at the time of grant, there was a good-faith attempt to value the stock accurately even if such valuation should subsequently prove to be in error.

**(d) Required option and plan amendments.** *(1)* The transitional rule waives the applicability of section 425(h) with respect to amendments of an option or a plan that are necessary to meet the minimum qualification requirements of section 422A. An amendment to add, modify, or delete a permissible term that is not necessary to meet such minimum qualification requirements does not fall within the waiver of section 425(h).

*(2)* The transitional rule waives the applicability of section 425(h) with respect to option and plan amendments only with respect to options outstanding on August 13, 1981. An option granted after August 31, 1981, and amended prior to exercise so as to qualify it as an incentive stock option, does not fall within the waiver of section 425(h). Such an option, therefore, will be treated as having been granted on the date it was amended. Consequently, the option price cannot be less that the fair market value of the stock as of the date of amendment. The option as originally granted, since it was not an incentive stock option at that time, will not be treated as still outstanding for purposes of the sequential exercise restriction of section 422A(b)(7).

*(3)* Amendments to an option plan, so as to meet the qualification requirements of section 422A, will apply to previously granted and outstanding options only if such amendments, by their terms, are clearly intended to have retroactive effect. Even if such amendments are intended to have retroactive effect, they need not apply to all previously granted options.

*(4)* The grant of an incentive stock option in exchange for the cancellation of an outstanding nonincentive stock option will not violate either the qualification requirements of section 422A or the transitional rules, provided the outstanding option is cancelled prior to the grant of the incentive stock option. The cancelled option will not be treated as still outstanding for purposes of the sequential exercise restriction of section 422A(b)(7).

**(e) Stockholder approval issues.** *(1)* If an option plan received stockholder approval within 12 months before or after the date such plan was originally adopted and it is amended so as to qualify it as an incentive stock option plan, new stockholder approval will be required only if the original plan either did not specify the aggregate number of shares which may be issued under the plan or did not identify the employees or class of employees eligible to receive options under the plan, or if either of such terms is modified. The amendment of an option plan to add the $100,000 annual plus carryover limit, applicable to incentive stock options granted after 1980, will not require new stockholder approval.

*(2)* If a plan never received stockholder approval, or did not receive such approval within 12 months before or after such plan was adopted, the plan will qualify as an incentive stock option plan if stockholder approval is obtained prior to August 14, 1982, but only if an option granted pursuant to the plan was outstanding on August 13, 1981, and such option is to become an incentive stock option. If no option granted pursuant to the plan was outstanding on August 13, 1981, or no option outstanding on August 13, 1981, is to become an incentive stock option, the plan must be re-adopted by the granting corporation and, if necessary, amended to meet the qualification requirements of section 422A. Stockholder approval must be obtained within 12 months before or after the plan is re-adopted. Consequently, any option granted after August 13, 1981, and before the date the plan is re-adopted, that is to become an incentive stock option will be treated as having been granted on the date of re-adoption of the plan. The option price of such an option, therefore, cannot be less than the fair market value of the stock as of the date of re-adoption of the plan. The option as originally granted, since it was not an incentive stock option at that time, will not be treated as still outstanding for purposes of the sequential exercise restriction of section 422A(b)(7).

*(3)* If an option was granted pursuant to no plan at all and such option was outstanding on August 13, 1981, a plan may be adopted and stockholder approval obtained in order to qualify the option as an incentive stock option. The adoption of an incentive stock option plan and the obtaining of stockholder approval will be treated as amendments permitted under the transitional rules if they occur prior to August 14, 1982.

*(4)* Options granted under a plan that must be approved by stockholders to qualify as an incentive stock option plan and outstanding on August 13, 1981, are eligible to become incentive stock options even if they are exercised prior to the obtaining of stockholder approval provided stockholder approval is obtained before August 14, 1982.

*(5)* If, pursuant to paragraph (e) of this section, new stockholder approval is required in order to qualify a plan as an incentive stock option plan, see paragraph (b)(2) of § 1.422A-2 for the prescribed method and degree of stockholder approval.

**(f) Sequential exercise issues.** *(1)* The original grant dates (or later grant dates for options with pre-enactment modifications) of options that are converted into incentive stock options will determine the sequencing order for purposes of the sequential exercise restriction of section 422A(b)(7). For example, in the case of options granted in 1977, 1978, and 1979, assume that in 1980 the 1978 option was amended to add a term beneficial to the employee. Such an amendment would be a modification under the rules of section 425(h) and would cause the option to be treated as newly granted in 1980. If the 1977, 1978 (as modified), and 1979 options are converted into incentive stock options, the sequencing order would be as follows: the 1977 option must be exercised first, the 1979 option second, and the 1978 option (as modified) third.

*(2)* Options granted prior to 1981 that are converted into incentive stock options must be exercised prior to the exercise of any incentive stock options granted after 1980. For example, assume that an option granted and exercised during January of 1982 automatically qualifies, by its terms, as an incentive stock option. During February of 1982, the employer elected to convert an option granted to the employee during 1978 into an incentive stock option. For purposes of this section only, such an election will retroactively disqualify the 1982 option as an incentive stock option. If the 1982 option is to qualify as an incentive stock option, it cannot be exercised prior to the exercise or expiration of all incentive stock options previously granted and outstanding on the date the 1982 option was granted. When the 1982 option was granted during January of 1982, the 1978 option was already granted and outstanding for purposes of the sequential exercise restriction of section 422A(b)(7).

*(3)* The existence (or exercise) of stock options that are not converted into incentive stock options will not prevent the exercise of an incentive stock option because of the sequential exercise restriction of section 422A(b)(7). However, if an option that is converted into an incentive stock option contains other sequencing restrictions, the option will continue to be burdened by such restrictions. The deletion of such sequencing restrictions is not an amendment necessary in order to qualify the option as an incentive stock option. Consequently, the rules of section 425(h) would apply to such an amendment.

### § 1.423-1 Applicability of section 421(a).

***Caution:*** The Treasury has not yet amended Reg § 1.423-1 to reflect changes made by P.L. 98-369.

**(a) General rule.** Subject to the provisions of section 423(c) and § 1.423-2(k), the special rules of income tax treatment provided in section 421(a) apply with respect to the transfer of a share of stock to an individual pursuant to the individual's exercise of an option granted under an employee stock purchase plan, as defined in § 1.423-2, if the following conditions are satisfied—

*(1)* The individual makes no disposition of such share before the later of the expiration of the two-year period from the date of the grant of the option pursuant to which such share was transferred or the expiration of the one-year period from the date of transfer of such share to the individual; and

*(2)* At all times during the period beginning on the date of the grant of the option and ending on the day three months before the date of exercise, the individual was an employee of the corporation granting the option, a related corporation, or a corporation (or a related corporation) substituting or assuming the stock option in a transaction to which section 424(a) applies.

**(b) Cross-references.** For rules relating to the requisite employment relationship, see § 1.421-1(h). For rules relating to the effect of a disqualifying disposition, see section 421(b) and § 1.421-2(b). For the definition of the term "disposition," see section 424(c) and § 1.424-1(c). For the definition of the term "related corporation," see § 1.421-1(i).

**(c) Effective/applicability date.** The regulations under this section are effective on November 17, 2009. The regulations under this section apply to options granted under an employee stock purchase plan on or after January 1, 2010.

---

T.D. 6887, 6/23/66, amend T.D. 7728, 10/31/80, T.D. 9144, 8/2/2004, T.D. 9471, 11/16/2009.

---

### § 1.423-2 Employee stock purchase plan defined.

**(a) In general.** *(1)* The term "employee stock purchase plan" means a plan that meets the requirements of paragraphs (a)(2) and (a)(3) of this section. If the terms of the plan do not satisfy the requirements of paragraph (a)(3) of this section, then such requirements may be satisfied by the terms of an offering made under the plan. However, where the requirements of paragraph (a)(3) of this section are satisfied by the terms of an offering, such requirements will be treated as satisfied only with respect to options exercised under that offering. One or more offerings may be made under an employee stock purchase plan. Offerings may be consecutive or overlapping, and the terms of each offering need not be identical provided the terms of the plan and the offering together satisfy the requirements of paragraphs (a)(2) and (a)(3) of this section. The plan and the terms of an offering must be in writing or electronic form, provided that such writing or electronic form is adequate to establish the terms of the plan or offering, as applicable.

*(2)* To satisfy the requirements of this paragraph (a)(2) and § 1.423-1, the plan must meet both of the following requirements—

(i) The plan must provide that options can be granted only to employees of the employer corporation or of a related corporation (as defined in paragraph (i) of § 1.421-1) to purchase stock in any such corporation (see paragraph (b) of this section); and

(ii) The plan must be approved by the stockholders of the granting corporation within 12 months before or after the date the plan is adopted (see paragraph (c) of this section).

*(3)* To satisfy the requirements of this paragraph (a)(3) and § 1.423-1, the terms of the plan or offering must meet all of the following requirements—

(i) An employee cannot be granted an option if, immediately after the option is granted, the employee owns stock possessing 5 percent or more of the total combined voting power or value of all classes of stock of the employer corporation or of a related corporation (see paragraph (d) of this section);

(ii) Options must be granted to all employees of any corporation whose employees are granted any options by reason of their employment by the corporation (see paragraph (e) of this section);

(iii) All employees granted options must have the same rights and privileges (see paragraph (f) of this section);

(iv) The option price cannot be less than the lesser of—

(A) An amount equal to 85 percent of the fair market value of the stock at the time the option is granted, or

(B) An amount not less than 85 percent of the fair market value of the stock at the time the option is exercised (see paragraph (g) of this section).

(v) Options cannot be exercised after the expiration of—

(A) Five years from the date the option is granted if, under the terms of such plan, the option price cannot be less than 85 percent of the fair market value of the stock at the time the option is exercised, or

(B) Twenty-seven months from the date the option is granted, if the option price is not determined in the manner described in paragraph (a)(3)(v)(A) of this section (see paragraph (h) of this section).

(vi) No employee may be granted an option that permits the employee's rights to purchase stock under all employee stock purchase plans of the employer corporation and its related corporations to accrue at a rate that exceeds $25,000 of fair market value of the stock (determined at the time the option is granted) for each calendar year in which the option is outstanding at any time (see paragraph (i) of this section); and

(vii) Options are not transferable by the optionee other than by will or the laws of descent and distribution, and are exercisable, during the lifetime of the optionee, only by the optionee (see paragraph (j) of this section).

*(4)* The determination of whether a particular option is an option granted under an employee stock purchase plan is made at the time the option is granted. If the terms of an option are inconsistent with the terms of the employee stock purchase plan or the offering under the plan pursuant to which the option is granted, the option will not be treated as granted under an employee stock purchase plan. If an option with terms that are inconsistent with the terms of the plan or an offering under the plan is granted to an employee who is entitled to the grant of an option under the terms of the plan or offering, and the employee is not granted an option under the offering that qualifies as an option granted under an employee stock purchase plan, the offering will not meet the requirements of paragraph (e) of this section. Accordingly, none of the options granted under the offering will be eligible for the special tax treatment of section 421. However, if an option with terms that are inconsistent with the terms of the plan or an offering under the plan is granted to an individual who is not entitled to the grant of an option under the terms of the plan or offering, the option will not be treated as an option granted under an employee stock purchase plan but the grant of the option will not disqualify the options granted under the plan or offering. If, at the time of grant, an option qualifies as an option granted under an employee stock purchase plan, but after the time of grant one or more of the requirements of paragraph (a)(3) of this section is not satisfied with respect to the option, the option will not be treated as granted under an employee stock purchase plan but this failure to comply with the terms of the option will not disqualify the other options granted under the plan or offering.

*(5)* Examples. The following examples illustrate the principles of paragraph (a):

*Example (1).* Corporation A operates an employee stock purchase plan under which options for A stock are granted to employees of A. The terms of an offering provide that the option price will be 90 percent of the fair market value of A stock on the date of exercise. A grants an option under the offering to Employee Z, an employee of A. The terms of the option provide that the option price will be 85 percent of the fair market value of A stock on the date of exercise. Because the terms of Z's option are inconsistent with the terms of the offering, the option granted to Z will not be treated as an option granted under the employee stock purchase plan. Further, unless Z is granted an option under the offering that qualifies as an option granted under the employee stock purchase plan, the offering will not meet the requirements of paragraph (e) of this section and none of the options granted under the offering will be eligible for the special tax treatment of section 421.

*Example (2).* Corporation B operates an employee stock purchase plan that provides that options for B stock may only be granted to employees of B. Under the terms of the plan, options may not be granted to consultants and other non-employees. B grants an option to Consultant Y, a consultant of B. Because Y is ineligible to receive an option under the plan because Y is not an employee, the grant of the option to Y is inconsistent with the terms of the plan and the option granted to Y will not be treated as an option granted under the employee stock purchase plan. However, the grant of the option to Y will not disqualify the options granted under the plan or any offering because Y was not entitled to the grant of an option under the plan.

*Example (3).* Corporation C operates an employee stock purchase plan under which options for C stock are granted to employees of C. C grants an option pursuant to an offering under the plan to Employee X, an employee of C who is a highly compensated employee. The terms of the employee stock purchase plan exclude highly compensated employees from participation in the plan. Because X is ineligible to receive an option under the plan by reason of X's exclusion from participation in the plan, the option granted to X will not be treated as an option granted under the employee stock purchase plan. However, the grant of the option to X will not disqualify the options granted under the plan or offering because X was not entitled to the grant of an option under the plan.

*Example (4).* Corporation D operates an employee stock purchase plan under which options for D stock are granted to employees of D. D grants an option pursuant to an offering under the plan to Employee W, an employee of D. The terms of the option provide that the option price will be 90 percent of the fair market value of D stock on the date of exercise. On the date of exercise, W pays only 85 percent of the fair market value of D stock. Because the terms of W's option are not satisfied, the option granted to W will not be treated as an option granted under the employee stock purchase plan. However, the failure to comply with the terms of the option granted to W will not disqualify the options granted under the plan or offering.

**(b) Options restricted to employees.** An employee stock purchase plan must provide that options can be granted only to employees of the employer corporation (or employees of its related corporations) to purchase stock in the employer corporation (or one of its related corporations). If such a provision is not included in the terms of the plan, the plan will not be an employee stock purchase plan and options granted under the plan will not qualify for the special tax treatment of section 421. For rules relating to the employment requirement, see § 1.421-1(h).

**(c) Stockholder approval.** *(1)* An employee stock purchase plan must be approved by the stockholders of the granting corporation within 12 months before or after the date such plan is adopted. The approval of the stockholders must comply with all applicable provisions of the corporate charter and bylaws and of applicable State law prescribing the method and degree of stockholder approval required for the issuance of corporate stock or options. If the applicable State law does not prescribe a method and degree of stockholder approval, then an employee stock purchase plan must be approved—

(i) By a majority of the votes cast at a duly held stockholder's meeting at which a quorum representing a majority of all outstanding voting stock is, either in person or by proxy, present and voting on the plan; or

(ii) By a method and in a degree that would be treated as adequate under applicable State law in the case of an action requiring stockholder approval (such as, an action on which stockholders would be entitled to vote if the action were taken at a duly held stockholders' meeting).

*(2)* For purposes of the stockholder approval required by this paragraph (c), ordinarily, a plan is adopted when it is approved by the granting corporation's board of directors, and the date of the board's action is the reference point for determining whether stockholder approval occurs within the applicable 24-month period. However, if the board's action is subject to a condition (such as stockholder approval) or the happening of a particular event, the plan is adopted on the date the condition is met or the event occurs, unless the board's resolution fixes the date of adoption as the date of the board's action.

*(3)* An employee stock purchase plan, as adopted and approved, must designate the maximum aggregate number of shares that may be issued under the plan, and the corporations or class of corporations whose employees may be offered options under the plan. A plan that merely provides that the number of shares that may be issued under the plan may not exceed a stated percentage of the shares outstanding at the time of each offering or grant under the plan does not satisfy the requirements of this paragraph (c)(3). However, the maximum aggregate number of shares that may be issued under the plan may be stated in terms of a percentage of the authorized, issued, or outstanding shares on the date of the adoption of the plan. The plan may specify that the maximum aggregate number of shares available for grants under the plan may increase annually by a specified percentage of the authorized, issued, or outstanding shares on the date of the adoption of the plan. A plan that provides that the maximum aggregate number of shares that may be issued as options under the plan may change based on any other specific circumstances satisfies the requirements of this paragraph only if the stockholders approve an immediately determinable maximum number of shares that may be issued under the plan in any event. If there is more than one employee stock purchase plan under which options may be granted and stockholders of the granting corporation merely approve a maximum aggregate number of shares that are available for issuance under the plans, the stockholder approval requirements described in paragraph (c)(1) of this section are not satisfied. A separate maximum aggregate number of shares available for issuance pursuant to options must be specified and approved for each plan.

*(4)* Once an employee stock purchase plan is approved by the stockholders of the granting corporation, the plan need not be reapproved by the stockholders of the granting corporation unless the plan is amended or changed in a manner that is considered the adoption of a new plan, in which case the plan must be reapproved within the prescribed 24-month period. Any increase in the aggregate number of shares that may be issued under the plan (other than an increase merely reflecting a change in the number of outstanding shares, such as a stock dividend or stock split) will be considered the adoption of a new plan requiring stockholder approval within the prescribed 24-month period. Similarly, a change in the designation of corporations whose employees may be offered options under the plan will be considered the adoption of a new plan requiring stockholder approval within the prescribed 24-month period unless the plan provides that designations of participating corporations may be made from time to time from among a group consisting of the granting corporation and its related corporations. The group from among which such changes and designations are permitted without additional stockholder approval may include corporations having become parents or subsidiaries of the granting corporation after the adoption and approval of the plan. In addition, a change in the granting corporation or the stock available for purchase under the plan will be considered the adoption of a new plan requiring stockholder approval within the prescribed 24-month period. Any other changes in the terms of an employee stock purchase plan are not con-

sidered the adoption of a new plan and, thus, do not require stockholder approval.

*(5)* Examples. The following examples illustrate the principles of this paragraph (c):

*Example (1).* (i) Corporation E is a subsidiary of Corporation F, a publicly traded corporation. On January 1, 2010, E adopts an employee stock purchase plan under which options for E stock are granted to E employees.

(ii) To meet the requirements of paragraph (c)(1) of this section, the plan must be approved by the stockholders of E (in this case, F) within 12 months before or after January 1, 2010.

(iii) Assume the same facts as in paragraph (i) of this Example 1, except that the plan was approved by the stockholders of E (in this case, F) on March 1, 2010. On January 1, 2012, E changes the plan to provide that options for F stock will be granted to E employees under the plan. Because there is a change in the stock available for grant under the plan, under paragraph (c)(4) of this section, the change is considered the adoption of a new plan that must be approved by the stockholders of E (in this case, F) within 12 months before or after January 1, 2012.

*Example (2).* (i) Assume the same facts as in paragraph (i) of Example 1, except that on March 15, 2011, F completely disposes of its interest in E. Thereafter, E continues to grant options for E stock to E employees under the plan.

(ii) The new E options are granted under a plan that meets the stockholder approval requirements of paragraph (c)(1) of this section without regard to whether E seeks approval of the plan from the stockholders of E after F disposes of its interest in E.

(iii) Assume the same facts as in paragraph (i) of this Example 2, except that under the plan as adopted on January 1, 2010, only options for F stock are granted to E employees. Assume further that, after F disposes of its interest in E, E changes the plan to provide for the grant of options for E stock to E employees. Because there is a change in the stock available for purchase or grant under the plan, under paragraph (c)(4) of this section, the stockholders of E must approve the plan within 12 months before or after the change to the plan to meet the stockholder approval requirements of paragraph (c) of this section.

*Example (3).* (i) Corporation G maintains an employee stock purchase plan providing options for G stock. Corporation H does not maintain an employee stock purchase plan. On May 15, 2010, G and H consolidate under State law to form one corporation. The new corporation is named Corporation H. The consolidation agreement describes the G plan, including the maximum aggregate number of shares available for issuance under the plan after the consolidation. Additionally, the consolidation agreement states that the plan will be continued by H after the consolidation. The consolidation agreement is approved by the stockholders of G and H on May 1, 2010. H assumes the plan formerly maintained by G and continues to grant options under the plan to all eligible employees, but the options are for H stock.

(ii) Because there is a change in the granting corporation (from G to H) and the stock available for purchase, under paragraph (c)(4) of this section, H is considered to have adopted a new plan. Because the plan is fully described in the consolidation agreement, including the maximum aggregate number of shares available for issuance under the plan, the approval of the consolidation agreement by the stockholders constitutes approval of the plan. Thus, the stockholder approval of the consolidation agreement satisfies the stockholder approval requirements of paragraph (c)(1) of this section, and the plan is considered to be adopted by H and approved by its stockholders on May 1, 2010.

*Example (4).* Corporation I adopts an employee stock purchase plan on November 1, 2010. On that date, there are two million shares of I stock outstanding. The plan provides that the maximum aggregate number of shares that may be issued under the plan may not exceed 15 percent of the number of shares of I stock outstanding on November 1, 2010. Because the maximum aggregate number of shares that may be issued under the plan is designated in the plan, the requirements of paragraph (c)(3) of this section are met.

*Example (5).* (i) Corporation J adopts an employee stock purchase plan on March 15, 2010. The plan provides that the maximum aggregate number of shares of J stock available for issuance under the plan is 50,000, increased on each anniversary date of the adoption of the plan by 5 percent of the then outstanding shares. Because the maximum aggregate number of shares is not designated under the plan, the requirements of paragraph (c)(3) of this section are not met.

(ii) Assume the same facts as in paragraph (i) of this Example 5, except that the plan provides that the maximum aggregate number of shares available under the plan is the lesser of (a) 50,000 shares, increased each anniversary date of the adoption of the plan by 5 percent of the then-outstanding shares, or (b) 200,000 shares. Because the maximum aggregate number of shares that may be issued under the plan is designated as the lesser of two numbers, one of which provides an immediately determinable maximum aggregate number of shares that may be issued under the plan in any event, the requirements of paragraph (c)(3) of this section are met.

**(d) Options granted to certain shareholders.** *(1)* An employee stock purchase plan or offering must, by its terms, provide that an employee cannot be granted an option if the employee, immediately after the option is granted, owns stock possessing 5 percent or more of the total combined voting power or value of all classes of stock of the employer corporation or a related corporation. In determining whether the stock ownership of an employee equals or exceeds this 5 percent limit, the rules of section 424(d) (relating to attribution of stock ownership) shall apply, and stock that the employee may purchase under outstanding options (whether or not the options qualify for the special tax treatment afforded by section 421(a)) shall be treated as stock owned by the employee. An option is outstanding for purposes of this paragraph (d) although under its terms it may be exercised only in installments or after the expiration of a fixed period of time. If an option is granted to an employee whose stock ownership (as determined under this paragraph (d)) exceeds the limitation set forth in this paragraph (d), no portion of the option will be treated as having been granted under an employee stock purchase plan.

*(2)* The determination of the percentage of the total combined voting power or value of all classes of stock of the employer corporation (or a related corporation) that is owned by the employee is made by comparing the voting power or value of the shares owned (or treated as owned) by the employee to the aggregate voting power or value of all shares actually issued and outstanding immediately after the grant of the option to the employee. The aggregate voting power or value of all shares actually issued and outstanding immediately after the grant of the option does not include the voting power or value of treasury shares or shares authorized for issue under outstanding options held by the employee or any other person.

*(3)* Examples. The following examples illustrate the principles of this paragraph (d):

*Example (1).* Employee V, an employee of Corporation K, owns 6,000 shares of K common stock, the only class of K stock outstanding. K has 100,000 shares of its common stock outstanding. Because V owns 6 percent of the combined voting power or value of all classes of K stock, K cannot grant an option to V under K's employee stock purchase plan. If V's father and brother each owned 3,000 shares of K stock and V did not own any K stock, then the result would be the same because, under section 424(d), an individual is treated as owning stock held by the person's father and brother. Similarly, the result would be the same if, instead of actually owning 6,000 shares, V merely held an option on 6,000 shares of K stock, irrespective of whether the transfer of stock under the option could qualify for the special tax treatment of section 421, because this paragraph (d) provides that stock the employee may purchase under outstanding options is treated as stock owned by such employee.

*Example (2).* Assume the same facts as in Example 1, except that K is a 50 percent subsidiary corporation of Corporation L. Irrespective of whether V owns any L stock, V cannot receive an option from L under L's employee stock purchase plan because he owns 5 percent of the total combined voting power of all classes of stock of a subsidiary of L, in this example, K. An employee who owns (or is treated as owning) stock in excess of the limitation of this paragraph (d), in any corporation in a group of related corporations, consisting of a parent and its subsidiary corporations, cannot receive an option under an employee stock purchase plan from any corporation in the group.

*Example (3).* Employee U is an employee of Corporation M. M has only one class of stock, of which 100,000 shares are issued and outstanding. Assuming U does not own (and is not treated as owning) any stock in M or in any related corporation of M, M may grant an option to U under its employee stock purchase plan for 4,999 shares, because immediately after the grant of the option, U would not own 5 percent or more of the combined voting power or value of all classes of M stock actually issued and outstanding at such time. The 4,999 shares that U would be treated as owning under this paragraph (d) would not be added to the 100,000 shares actually issued and outstanding immediately after the grant for purposes of determining whether U's stock ownership exceeds the limitation of this paragraph (d).

*Example (4).* Assume the same facts as in Example 3 but instead of an option for 4,999 shares, M grants U an option, purportedly under its employee stock purchase plan, for 5,000 shares. No portion of this option will be treated as granted under an employee stock purchase plan because U's stock ownership exceeds the limitation of this paragraph (d).

**(e) Employees covered by plan.** *(1)* Subject to the provisions of this paragraph (e) and the limitations of paragraphs (d), (f) and (i) of this section, an employee stock purchase plan or offering must, by its terms, provide that options are to be granted to all employees of any corporation whose employees are granted any of such options by reason of their employment by that corporation, except that one or more of the following categories of employees may be excluded from the coverage of the plan or offering—

(i) Employees who have been employed less than two years;

(ii) Employees whose customary employment is 20 hours or less per week;

(iii) Employees whose customary employment is for not more than five months in any calendar year; and

(iv) Highly compensated employees (within the meaning of section 414(q)).

*(2)* A plan or offering does not fail to satisfy the coverage provision of paragraph (e)(1) of this section in the following circumstances—

(i) The plan or offering excludes employees who have completed a shorter period of service or whose customary employment is for fewer hours per week or fewer months in a calendar year than is specified in paragraphs (e)(1)(i), (ii) and (iii) of this section, provided the exclusion is applied in an identical manner to all employees of every corporation whose employees are granted options under the plan or offering.

(ii) The plan or offering excludes highly compensated employees (within the meaning of section 414(q)) with compensation above a certain level or who are officers or subject to the disclosure requirements of section 16(a) of the Securities Exchange Act of 1934, provided the exclusion is applied in an identical manner to all highly compensated employees of every corporation whose employees are granted options under the plan or offering.

*(3)* Notwithstanding paragraph (e)(1) of this section, employees who are citizens or residents of a foreign jurisdiction (without regard to whether they are also citizens of the United States or resident aliens (within the meaning of section 7701(b)(1)(A))) may be excluded from the coverage of an employee stock purchase plan or offering under the following circumstances—

(i) The grant of an option under the plan or offering to a citizen or resident of the foreign jurisdiction is prohibited under the laws of such jurisdiction; or

(ii) Compliance with the laws of the foreign jurisdiction would cause the plan or offering to violate the requirements of section 423.

*(4)* No option granted under a plan or offering that excludes from participation any employees, other than those who may be excluded under this paragraph (e), and those barred from participation by reason of paragraphs (d), (f) and (i) of this section, can be regarded as having been granted under an employee stock purchase plan. If an option is not granted to any employee who is entitled to the grant of an option under the terms of the plan or offering, none of the options granted under such offering will be treated as having been granted under an employee stock purchase plan. However, a plan that, by its terms, permits all eligible employees to elect to participate in an offering will not violate the requirements of this paragraph solely because eligible employees who elect not to participate in the offering are not granted options pursuant to such offering.

*(5)* For purposes of this paragraph (e), the existence of the employment relationship between an individual and the corporation participating under the plan will be determined under § 1.421-1(h).

*(6)* Examples. The following examples illustrate the principles of this paragraph (e):

*Example (1).* Corporation N has a stock purchase plan that meets all the requirements of paragraphs (a)(2) and (a)(3) of this section except that options are not required to be granted to employees whose weekly rate of pay is less than $1,000. As a matter of corporate practice, however, N grants options under its plan to all employees, irrespective of their weekly rate of pay. Even though N's plan is operated in compliance with the requirements of this paragraph (e), N's plan is not an employee stock purchase plan because the terms of the plan exclude a category of employees that is not permitted under this paragraph (e).

*Example (2).* Assume the same facts as in Example 1, except that the first offering under N's plan provides that options will be granted to all employees of N. The terms of the first offering will be treated as part of the terms of N's plan, but only for purposes of the first offering. Because the terms of the first offering satisfy the requirements of this paragraph (e), stock transferred pursuant to options exercised under the first offering will be treated as stock transferred pursuant to the exercise of options granted under an employee stock purchase plan for purposes of section 421.

*Example (3).* Corporation O has a stock purchase plan that excludes from participation all employees who have been employed less than one year. Assuming all other requirements of paragraphs (a)(2) and (a)(3) of this section are satisfied, O's plan qualifies as an employee stock purchase plan under section 423.

*Example (4).* Corporation P has a stock purchase plan that excludes from participation clerical employees who have been employed less than two years. However, non-clerical employees with less than two years of service are permitted to participate in the plan. P's plan is not an employee stock purchase plan because the exclusion of employees who have been employed less than two years applies only to certain employees of P and is not applied in an identical manner to all employees of P. If, instead, P's plan excludes from participation all employees (both clerical and non-clerical) who have been employed less than two years, then P's plan would qualify as an employee stock purchase plan under section 423 assuming all other requirements of paragraphs (a)(2) and (a)(3) of this section are satisfied.

*Example (5).* Corporation Q has a stock purchase plan that excludes from participation all officers who are highly compensated employees (within the meaning of section 414(q)). Assuming all other requirements of paragraphs (a)(2) and (a)(3) of this section are satisfied, Q's plan qualifies as an employee stock purchase plan under section 423.

*Example (6).* Corporation R maintains an employee stock purchase plan that excludes from participation all highly compensated employees (within the meaning of section 414(q)), except highly compensated employees who are officers of R. R's plan is not an employee stock purchase plan because the exclusion of all highly compensated employees except highly compensated employees who are officers of R is not a permissible exclusion under paragraph (e)(2)(ii) of this section.

*Example (7).* Corporation S is the parent corporation of Subsidiary YY and Subsidiary ZZ. S maintains an employee stock purchase plan with both YY and ZZ participating in the same offering under the plan. Under the terms of the offering under the plan, all employees of YY and ZZ are permitted to participate in the plan with the exception of ZZ's highly compensated employees with annual compensation greater than $300,000. None of the options granted under the offering will be considered granted under an employee stock purchase plan because the exclusion of highly compensated employees with annual compensation greater than $300,000 is not applied in an identical manner to all employees of YY and ZZ granted options in the same offering.

*Example (8).* Assume the same facts as in Example 7, except that Corporation S establishes separate offerings under the plan for YY and ZZ. Under the terms of the separate offering for YY, all employees of YY are permitted to participate in the plan. Under the terms of the separate offering established for ZZ, all employees of ZZ are permitted to participate in the plan with the exception of ZZ's highly compensated employees with annual compensation greater than $300,000. The options granted under the separate offering for YY will be considered granted under an employee stock purchase plan. Further, the options granted under the separate offering for ZZ will be considered granted under an employee stock purchase plan because the exclusion of highly compensated employees with annual compensation greater than $300,000 is applied in an identical manner to all employees of ZZ granted options in the same offering.

*Example (9).* The laws of Country A require that options granted to residents of Country A be transferable during the lifetime of the option recipient. Corporation T has a stock purchase plan that excludes residents of Country A from participation in the plan. Because compliance with the laws of Country A would cause options granted to residents of Country A to violate paragraph (j) of this section, T may exclude residents of Country A from participation in the plan. Assuming all other requirements of paragraph (a)(2) of this section are satisfied, T's plan qualifies as an employee stock purchase plan under section 423.

**(f) Equal rights and privileges.** *(1)* Except as otherwise provided in paragraphs (f)(2) through (f)(6) of this section, an employee stock purchase plan or offering must, by its terms, provide that all employees granted options under the plan or offering shall have the same rights and privileges. Thus, the provisions applying to one option under an offering (such as the provisions relating to the method of payment for the stock and the determination of the purchase price per share) must apply to all other options under the offering in the same manner. If all the options granted under a plan or offering do not, by their terms, give the respective optionees the same rights and privileges, none of the options will be treated as having been granted under an employee stock purchase plan for purposes of section 421.

*(2)* The requirements of this paragraph (f) do not prevent the maximum amount of stock that an employee may purchase from being determined on the basis of a uniform relationship to the total compensation, or the basic or regular rate of compensation, of all employees.

*(3)* A plan or offering will not fail to satisfy the requirements of this paragraph (f) because the plan or offering provides that no employee may purchase more than a maximum amount of stock fixed under the plan or offering.

*(4)* A plan or offering will not fail to satisfy the requirements of this paragraph (f) if, in order to comply with the laws of a foreign jurisdiction, the terms of an option granted under a plan or offering to citizens or residents of such foreign jurisdiction (without regard to whether they are also citizens of the United States or resident aliens (within the meaning of section 7701(b)(1)(A))) are less favorable than the terms of options granted under the same plan or offering to employees resident in the United States.

*(5)* (i) Except as provided in this paragraph and paragraph (f)(5)(ii) of this section, a plan or offering permitting one or more employees to carry forward amounts that were withheld but not applied toward the purchase of stock under an earlier plan or offering and apply the amounts towards the purchase of additional stock under a subsequent plan or offering will be a violation of the equal rights and privileges under paragraph (f)(1) of this section. However, the carry forward of amounts withheld but not applied toward the

purchase of stock under an earlier plan or offering will not violate the equal rights and privileges requirement of paragraph (f)(1) of this section, if all other employees participating in the current plan or offering are permitted to make direct payments toward the purchase of shares under a subsequent plan or offering in an amount equal to the excess of the greatest amount which any employee is allowed to carry forward from an earlier plan or offering over the amount, if any, the employee will carry forward from an earlier plan or offering.

(ii) A plan or offering will not fail to satisfy the requirements of this section merely because employees are permitted to carry forward amounts representing a fractional share, that were withheld but not applied toward the purchase of stock under an earlier plan or offering and apply the amounts toward the purchase of additional stock under a subsequent plan or offering.

*(6)* Paragraph (f) does not prohibit the delaying of the grant of an option to any employee who is barred from being granted an option solely by reason of the employee's failing to meet a minimum service requirement set forth in paragraph (e)(1) of this section until the employee meets such requirement.

*(7)* Examples. The following examples illustrate the principles of this paragraph (f):

*Example (1).* Corporation U has an employee stock purchase plan that provides that the maximum amount of stock that each employee may purchase under the offering is one share for each $100 of annual gross pay. The plan meets the requirements of this paragraph (f).

*Example (2).* Corporation V has an employee stock purchase plan that provides that the maximum amount of stock that each employee may purchase under the offering is one share for each $100 of annual gross pay up to and including $10,000, and two shares for each $100 of annual gross pay in excess of $10,000. The plan will not meet the requirements of this paragraph (f) because the amount of stock that may be purchased under the plan is not based on a uniform relationship to the total compensation of all employees.

*Example (3).* Corporation W has an employee stock purchase plan that provides that options to purchase stock in an amount equal to ten percent of an employee's annual salary at a price equal to 85 percent of the fair market value on the first day of the offering will be granted to all employees other than those who have been employed less than 18 months. In addition, the plan provides that employees who have not yet met the minimum service requirements on the first day of the offering will be granted similar options on the date the 18 month service requirement has been attained. The plan meets the requirements of this paragraph (f).

*Example (4).* Corporation X is the parent corporation of Subsidiary AA, Subsidiary BB and Subsidiary CC. X maintains an employee stock purchase plan with AA, BB and CC participating in the same offering under the plan. Under the terms of the offering under the plan, options to purchase stock at a price equal to 90 percent of the fair market value at the time the option is exercised will be granted to all employees. Certain employees of AA are residents of Country B. The laws of Country B provide that options granted to employees who are residents of Country B must have a purchase price not less than 95 percent of the fair market value at the time the option is exercised. The plan will not fail to satisfy the requirements of this paragraph (f) merely because the residents of Country B are granted options under the plan to purchase stock at a price equal to 95 percent of the fair market value at the time the option is exercised.

*Example (5).* Assume the same facts as in Example 4, except that Corporation X establishes two separate offerings under the plan: A separate offering for the employees of AA and a separate offering for the employees of BB and CC. Under the separate offering for the employees of BB and CC, options are granted to all employees with an exercise price equal to 90 percent of the fair market value at the time the option is exercised. Under the separate offering for the employees of AA, options are granted to all employees with an exercise price equal to 95 percent of the fair market value at the time the option is exercised. The plan does not violate the equal rights and privileges requirement of this paragraph (f) merely because the exercise price of options granted under one offering is less than the exercise price of options granted under a separate offering.

*Example (6).* Corporation Y maintains an employee stock purchase plan. Employee T is employed by Y. T is granted an option under the current offering to purchase a maximum of 100 shares of Y stock at an option price equal to 85 percent of the fair market value of the stock at exercise. The plan permits the carry forward of withheld but unused amounts from an earlier offering. Prior to the exercise date, $2000 of T's salary has been withheld and is available to be applied toward the purchase of Y stock. On the exercise date, the fair market value of Y stock is $20 per share. T is able to purchase 100 shares of Y stock at $17 per share for an aggregate purchase price of $1700. T can carry forward $300 to the subsequent offering. Each employee in the subsequent offering other than T will be permitted to make direct payments toward the purchase of shares under the subsequent offering in a maximum amount of $300 less any amount the employee has carried forward from an earlier offering. The plan does not violate the equal rights and privileges requirement of this paragraph (f).

**(g) Option price.** *(1)* An employee stock purchase plan or offering must, by its terms, provide that the option price will not be less than the lesser of—

(i) An amount equal to 85 percent of the fair market value of the stock at the time the option is granted, or

(ii) An amount that under the terms of the option may not be less than 85 percent of the fair market value of the stock at the time the option is exercised.

*(2)* For purposes of determining the option price, the fair market value of the stock may be determined in any reasonable manner, including the valuation methods permitted under § 20.2031-2. However, the option price must meet the minimum pricing requirements of this paragraph (g). For general rules relating to the option price, see § 1.421-1(e). For rules relating to the determination of when an option is granted, see §§ 1.421-1(c) and 1.423-2(h)(2). Any option that does not meet the minimum pricing requirements of this paragraph (g) will not be treated as an option granted under an employee stock purchase plan irrespective of whether the plan or offering satisfies those requirements. If an option that does not meet the minimum pricing requirements is granted to an employee who is entitled to the grant of an option under the terms of the plan or offering, and the employee is not granted an option under such offering that qualifies as an option granted under an employee stock purchase plan, the offering will not meet the requirements of paragraph (e) of this section. Accordingly, none of the options granted under the offering will be eligible for the special tax treatment of section 421.

*(3)* The option price may be stated either as a percentage or as a dollar amount. If the option price is stated as a dollar amount, then the requirement of this paragraph (g) can only be met by a plan or offering in which the price is fixed at not less than 85 percent of the fair market value of the stock at the time the option is granted. If the fixed price is less than 85 percent of the fair market value of the stock at grant, then the option cannot meet the requirement of this paragraph (g) even if a decline in the fair market value of the stock results in such fixed price being not less than 85 percent of the fair market value of the stock at the time the option is exercised, because that result was not certain to occur under the terms of the option.

*(4)* Examples. The following examples illustrate the principles of this paragraph (g):

*Example (1).* Corporation Z has an employee stock purchase plan that provides that the option price will be 85 percent of the fair market value of the stock on the first day of the offering (which is the date of grant in this case), or 85 percent of the fair market value of the stock at exercise, whichever amount is the lesser. Upon the exercise of an option issued under Z's plan, Z agrees to accept an option price that is less than the minimum amount allowable under the terms of such plan. Notwithstanding that the option was issued under an employee stock purchase plan, the transfer of stock pursuant to the exercise of such option does not satisfy the requirement of this paragraph (g) and cannot qualify for the special tax treatment of section 421.

*Example (2).* Corporation AA has an employee stock purchase plan that provides that the option price is set at 85 percent of the fair market value of AA stock at exercise, but not less than $80 per share. On the first day of the offering (which is the date of grant in this case), the fair market value of AA stock is $100 per share. The option satisfies the requirement of this paragraph (g), and can qualify for the special tax treatment of section 421.

*Example (3).* Assume the same facts as in Example 2, except that the option price is set at 85 percent of the fair market value of AA stock at exercise, but not more than $80 per share. This option cannot satisfy the requirement of this paragraph (g) irrespective of whether, at the time the option is exercised, 85 percent of the fair market value of AA stock is $80 or less.

**(h) Option period.** *(1)* An employee stock purchase plan or offering must, by its terms, provide that options granted under the plan cannot be exercised after the expiration of 27 months from the date of grant unless, under the terms of the plan or offering, the option price is not less than 85 percent of the fair market value of the stock at the time of the exercise of the option. If the option price is not less than 85 percent of the fair market value of the stock at the time the option is exercised, then the option period provided under the plan must not exceed five years from the date of grant. If the requirements of this paragraph (h) are not met by the terms of the plan or offering, then options issued under such plan or offering will not be treated as options granted under an employee stock purchase plan irrespective of whether the options, by their terms, are exercisable beyond the period allowable under this paragraph (h). An option that provides that the option price is not less than 85 percent of the fair market value of the stock at exercise may have an option period of 5 years irrespective of whether the fair market value of the stock at exercise is more or less than the fair market value of the stock at grant. However, if the option provides that the option price is 85 percent of the fair market value of the stock at exercise, but not more than some other fixed amount determined in accordance with the provisions of paragraph (g) of this section, then irrespective of the price paid on exercise, the option period must not be more than 27 months.

*(2)* Section 1.421-1(c) provides that, for purposes of §§ 1.421-1 through 1.424-1, the language "the date of the granting of the option" and the "time such option is granted," and similar phrases refer to the date or time when the granting corporation completes the corporate action constituting an offer of stock for sale to an individual under the terms and conditions of a statutory option. With respect to options granted under an employee stock purchase plan, the principles of § 1.421-1(c) shall be applied without regard to the requirement that the minimum option price must be fixed or determinable in order for the corporate action constituting an offer of stock to be considered complete.

*(3)* The date of grant will be the first day of an offering if the terms of an employee stock purchase plan or offering designate a maximum number of shares that may be purchased by each employee during the offering. Similarly, the date of grant will be the first day of an offering if the terms of the plan or offering require the application of a formula to establish, on the first day of the offering, the maximum number of shares that may be purchased by each employee during the offering. It is not required that an employee stock purchase plan or offering designate a maximum number of shares that may be purchased by each employee during the offering or incorporate a formula to establish a maximum number of shares that may be purchased by each employee during the offering. If the maximum number of shares that can be purchased under an option is not fixed or determinable until the date the option is exercised, then the date of exercise will be the date of grant of the option.

*(4)* Examples. The following examples illustrate the principles of this paragraph (h):

*Example (1).* (i) Corporation BB has an employee stock purchase plan that provides that the option price will be the lesser of 85 percent of the fair market value of the stock on the first day of an offering or 85 percent of the fair market value of the stock on the last day of the offering. Options are exercised on the last day of the offering. One million shares of BB stock are reserved for issuance under the plan. The plan provides that no employee may be permitted to purchase stock under the plan at a rate that exceeds $25,000 in fair market value of the BB stock (determined on the date of grant) for each calendar year during which an option granted to the employee is outstanding. The terms of each option granted under an offering provide that a maximum of 500 shares may be purchased by the option recipient during the offering. Because the maximum number of shares that can be purchased under the option is fixed and determinable on the first day of the offering, the date of grant for the option is the first day of the offering.

(ii) Assume the same facts as in paragraph (i) of Example 1, except that BB's plan excludes all employees who have been employed less than 18 months. The plan provides that employees who have not yet met the minimum service requirements on the first day of an offering will be granted an option on the date the 18-month service requirement has been attained. With respect to those employees who have been employed less than 18 months on the first day of an offering, the date of grant for the option is the date the 18-month service requirement has been attained.

*Example (2).* Assume the same facts as in paragraph (i) of Example 1, except that the terms of each option granted do not provide that a maximum of 500 shares may be purchased by the option recipient during the offering. Notwithstanding the fixed number of shares reserved for issuance under the plan and the $25,000 limitation set forth in the plan, the maximum number of shares that can be purchased under the option is not fixed or determinable until the last day of the offering when the option is exercised. Therefore the date of grant for the option is the last day of the offering when the option is exercised.

*Example (3).* Corporation CC has an employee stock purchase plan that provides that the option price will be 85 percent of the fair market value of the stock on the last day of the offering. Options are exercised on the last day of the offering. Each offering under the plan begins on January 1 and ends on December 31 of the same calendar year. The terms of each option granted under an offering provide that the maximum number of shares that may be purchased by any employee during the offering equals $25,000 divided by the fair market value of the stock on the first day of the offering. The maximum number of shares that can be purchased under the option is fixed and determinable on the first day of the offering and therefore the date of grant for the option is the first day of the offering.

*Example (4).* Assume the same facts as in Example 3 except that the terms of each option granted under an offering provide that the maximum number of shares that may be purchased by any employee during the offering equals 10 percent of the employee's annual salary (determined as of January 1 of the year in which the offering commences) divided by the fair market value of the stock on the first day of the offering. The maximum number of shares that can be purchased under the option is fixed and determinable on the first day of the offering and therefore the date of grant for the option is the first day of the offering.

**(i) Annual $25,000 limitation.** *(1)* An employee stock purchase plan or offering must, by its terms, provide that no employee may be permitted to purchase stock under all the employee stock purchase plans of the employer corporation and its related corporations at a rate that exceeds $25,000 in fair market value of the stock (determined at the time the option is granted) for each calendar year in which any option granted to the employee is outstanding at any time. In applying the foregoing limitation—

(i) The right to purchase stock under an option accrues when the option (or any portion thereof) first becomes exercisable during the calendar year;

(ii) The right to purchase stock under an option accrues at the rate provided in the option, but in no case may such rate exceed $25,000 of fair market value of such stock (determined at the time such option is granted) for any one calendar year; and

(iii) A right to purchase stock that has accrued under one option granted pursuant to the plan may not be carried over to any other option.

*(2)* If an option is granted under an employee stock purchase plan that satisfies the requirement of this paragraph (i), but the option gives the optionee the right to buy stock in excess of the maximum rate allowable under this paragraph (i), then no portion of the option will be treated as having been granted under an employee stock purchase plan. Furthermore, if the option was granted to an employee entitled to the grant of an option under the terms of the plan or offering, and the employee is not granted an option under the offering that qualifies as an option granted under an employee stock purchase plan, then the offering will not meet the requirements of paragraph (e) of this section. Accordingly, none of the options granted under the offering will be eligible for the special tax treatment of section 421.

*(3)* The limitation of this paragraph (i) applies only to options granted under employee stock purchase plans and does not limit the amount of stock that an employee may purchase under incentive stock options (as defined in section 422(b)) or any other stock options except those to which section 423 applies. Stock purchased under options to which section 423 does not apply will not limit the amount that an employee may purchase under an employee stock purchase plan, except for purposes of the 5-percent stock ownership provision of paragraph (d) of this section.

*(4)* Under the limitation of this paragraph (i), an employee may purchase up to $25,000 of stock (based on the fair market value of the stock at the time the option was granted) in each calendar year during which an option granted to the employee under an employee stock purchase plan is outstanding. Alternatively, an employee may purchase more than $25,000 of stock (based on the fair market value of such stock at the time the option was granted) in a calendar year, so long as the total amount of stock that the employee purchases does not exceed $25,000 in fair market value of the stock (determined at the time the option was granted) for each calendar year in which any option was outstanding. If, in any calendar year, the employee holds two or more outstanding options granted under employee stock purchase plans of the employer corporation, or a related corporation, then the employee's purchases of stock attributable to that year under all options granted under employee stock purchase plans must not exceed $25,000 in fair market value of the stock (determined at the time the options were granted). Under an employee stock purchase plan, an employee may not purchase stock in anticipation that the option will be outstanding in some future year. Thus, the employee may purchase only the amount of stock that does not exceed the limitation of this paragraph (i) for the year of the purchase and for preceding years during which the option was outstanding. Thus, the amount of stock that may be purchased under an option depends on the number of years in which the option is actually outstanding. The amount of stock that may be purchased under an employee stock purchase plan may not be increased by reason of the failure to grant an option in an earlier year under such plan, or by reason of the failure to exercise an earlier option. For example, if an option is granted to an individual and expires without having been exercised at all, then the failure to exercise the option does not increase the amount of stock which such individual may be permitted to purchase under an option granted in a year following the year of such expiration. If an option granted under an employee stock purchase plan is outstanding in more than one calendar year, then stock purchased pursuant to the exercise of such an option will be applied first, to the extent allowable under this paragraph (i), against the $25,000 limitation for the earliest year in which the option was outstanding, then, against the $25,000 limitation for each succeeding year, in order.

*(5)* Examples. The following examples illustrate the principles of this paragraph (i):

*Example (1).* Assume that Corporation DD maintains an employee stock purchase plan and that Employee S is employed by DD. On June 1, 2010, DD grants S an option under the plan to purchase a total of 750 shares of DD stock at $85 per share. On that date, the fair market value of DD stock is $100 per share. The option provides that it may be exercised at any time but cannot be exercised after May 31,

2012. Under this paragraph (i), the option must not permit S to purchase more than 250 shares of DD stock during the calendar year 2010, because 250 shares are equal to $25,000 in fair market value of DD stock determined at the time of grant. During the calendar year 2011, S may purchase under the option an amount of DD stock equal to the difference between $50,000 in fair market value of DD stock (determined at the time the option was granted) and the fair market value of DD stock (determined at the time of grant of the option) purchased during the year 2010. During the calendar year 2012, S may purchase an amount of DD stock equal to the difference between $75,000 in fair market value of the stock (determined at the time of grant of the option) and the total amount of the fair market value of the stock (determined at the time of grant of the option) purchased under the option during the calendar years 2010 and 2011. S may purchase $25,000 of stock for the year 2010, and $25,000 of stock for the year 2012, although the option was outstanding for only a part of each of such years. However, S may not be granted another option under an employee stock purchase plan of DD or a related corporation to purchase stock of DD or a related corporation during the calendar years 2010, 2011, and 2012, so long as the option granted June 1, 2010, is outstanding.

*Example (2).* Assume the same facts as in Example 1, except that the option granted to S in 2010 is terminated in 2011 without any part of the option having been exercised, and that subsequent to the termination and during 2011, S is granted another option under DD's employee stock purchase plan. Under that option, S may be permitted to purchase $25,000 of stock for 2011. The failure of S to exercise the option granted to S in 2010, does not increase the amount of stock that S may be permitted to purchase under the option granted to S in 2011.

*Example (3).* Assume the same facts as in Example 1, except that, on May 31, 2012, S exercised the option granted to S in 2010, and purchased 600 shares of DD stock. Five hundred shares, the maximum amount of stock that could have been purchased in 2011, under the option, are treated as having been purchased for the years 2010 and 2011. Only 100 shares of the stock are treated as having been purchased for 2012. After S's exercise of the option on May 31, 2012, S is granted another option under DD's employee stock purchase plan. S may be permitted under the new option to purchase for 2012 stock having a fair market value of no more than $15,000 at the time the new option is granted.

*Example (4).* Corporation EE maintains an employee stock purchase plan and Employee R is employed by EE. On August 1, 2010, EE grants R an option under the plan to purchase 150 shares of EE stock at $85 per share during each of the calendar years 2010, 2011, and 2012. On that date, the fair market value of EE stock is $100 per share. The option provides that it may be exercised at any time during years 2010, 2011, and 2012. Because this option permits R to purchase only $15,000 of EE's stock for each year the option is outstanding, R could be granted another option by EE, or by a related corporation, in year 2010, permitting R to purchase an additional $10,000 of stock during each of the calendar years 2010, 2011, and 2012.

*Example (5).* Corporation FF maintains an employee stock purchase plan and Employee Q is employed by FF. On September 1, 2010, FF grants Q an option under the plan that will be automatically exercised on August 31, 2011, and August 31, 2012. The terms of the option provide that no more than 150 shares may be purchased on each date that the option is automatically exercised. On August 31, 2011, Q may purchase under the option an amount of FF stock equal to $50,000 in fair market value of FF stock (determined at the time the option was granted). On August 31, 2012, Q may purchase under the option an amount of FF stock equal to the difference between $75,000 in fair market value of FF stock (determined at the time the option was granted) and the fair market value of FF stock (determined at the time of grant of the option ) purchased during year 2011.

**(j) Restriction on transferability.** An employee stock purchase plan or offering must, by its terms, provide that options granted under the plan are not transferable by the optionee other than by will or the laws of descent and distribution, and must be exercisable, during the optionee's lifetime, only by the optionee. For general rules relating to the restriction on transferability required by this paragraph (j), see § 1.421-1(b)(2). For a limited exception to the requirement of this paragraph (j), see section 424(h)(3).

**(k) Special rule where option price is between 85 percent and 100 percent of value of stock.** *(1)* (i) If all the conditions necessary for the application of section 421(a) exist, this paragraph (k) provides additional rules that are applicable in cases where, at the time the option is granted, the option price per share is less than 100 percent (but not less than 85 percent) of the fair market value of the share. In that case, upon the disposition of the share by the employee after the expiration of the two-year and the one-year holding periods, or upon the employee's death while owning the share (whether occurring before or after the expiration of such periods), there shall be included in the employee's gross income as compensation (and not as gain upon the sale or exchange of a capital asset) the lesser of—

(A) The amount, if any, by which the price paid under the option was exceeded by the fair market value of the share at the time the option was granted, or

(B) The amount, if any, by which the price paid under the option was exceeded by the fair market value of the share at the time of such disposition or death.

(ii) For purposes of applying the rules of this paragraph (k), if the option price is not fixed or determinable at the time the option is granted, the option price will be computed as if the option had been exercised at such time. The amount of compensation resulting from the application of this paragraph (k) shall be included in the employee's gross income for the taxable year in which the disposition occurs, or for the taxable year closing with the employee's death, whichever event results in the application of this paragraph (k).

(iii) The application of the special rules provided in this paragraph (k) shall not affect the rules provided in section 421(a) with respect to the employee exercising the option, the employer corporation, or a related corporation. Thus, notwithstanding the inclusion of an amount as compensation in the gross income of an employee, as provided in this paragraph (k), no income results to the employee at the time the stock is transferred to the employee, and no deduction under section 162 is allowable at any time to the employer corporation or a related corporation with respect to such amount.

(iv) If, during the employee's lifetime, the employee exercises an option granted under an employee stock purchase plan, but the employee dies before the stock is transferred to the employee pursuant to the exercise of the option, then for the purpose of sections 421 and 423, on the employee's death, the stock is deemed to be transferred immediately to the employee, and immediately thereafter, the employee is deemed to have transferred the stock to the employee's executor, administrator, trustee, beneficiary by operation of law, heir, or legatee, as the case may be.

*(2)* If the special rules provided in this paragraph (k) are applicable to the disposition of a share of stock by an employee, then the basis of the share in the employee's hands at the time of the disposition, determined under section 1011, shall be increased by an amount equal to the amount includible as compensation in the employee's gross income under this paragraph (k). However, the basis of a share of stock acquired after the death of an employee by the exercise of an option granted to the employee under an employee stock purchase plan shall be determined in accordance with the rules of section 421(c) and § 1.421-2(c). If the special rules provided in this paragraph (k) are applicable to a share of stock upon the death of an employee, then the basis of the share in the hands of the estate or the person receiving the stock by bequest or inheritance shall be determined under section 1014, and shall not be increased by reason of the inclusion upon the decedent's death of any amount in the decedent's gross income under this paragraph (k). See Example (9) of this paragraph (k) with respect to the determination of basis of the share in the hands of a surviving joint owner.

*(3)* Examples. The following examples illustrate the principles of this paragraph (k):

*Example (1).* On June 1, 2010, Corporation GG grants to Employee P, an employee of GG, an option under GG's employee stock purchase plan to purchase a share of GG stock for $85. The fair market value of GG stock on such date is $100 per share. On June 1, 2011, P exercises the option and on that date GG transfers the share of stock to P. On January 1, 2013, P sells the share for $150, its fair market value on that date. P's income tax return is filed on the basis of the calendar year. The income tax consequences to P and GG are as follows—

(i) Compensation in the amount of $15 is includible in P's gross income for the year 2013, the year of the disposition of the share. The $15 represents the difference between the option price ($85) and the fair market value of the share on the date the option was granted ($100), because the value is less than the fair market value of the share on the date of disposition ($150). For the purpose of computing P's gain or loss on the sale of the share, P's cost basis of $85 is increased by $15, the amount includible in P's gross income as compensation. Thus, P's basis for the share is $100. Because the share was sold for $150, P realizes a gain of $50, which is treated as long-term capital gain; and

(ii) GG is not entitled to any deduction under section 162 at any time with respect to the share transferred to P.

*Example (2).* Assume the same facts as in Example 1, except that P sells the share of GG stock on January 1, 2014, for $75, its fair market value on that date. Because $75 is less than the option price ($85), no amount in respect of the sale is includible as compensation in P's gross income for the year 2014. P's basis for determining gain or loss on the sale is $85. Because P sold the share for $75, P realized a loss of $10 on the sale that is treated as a long-term capital loss.

*Example (3).* Assume the same facts as in Example 1, except that the option provides that the option price shall be 90 percent of the fair market value of the stock on the day the option is exercised. On June 1, 2011, when the option is exercised, the fair market value of the stock is $120 per share so that P pays $108 for the share of the stock. Compensation in the amount of $10 is includible in P's gross income for the year 2013, the year of the disposition of the share. This is determined in the following manner: The excess of the fair market value of the stock at the time of the disposition ($150) over the price paid for the share ($108) is $42; and the excess of the fair market value of the stock at the time the option was granted ($100) over the option price, computed as if the option had been exercised at such time ($90), is $10. Accordingly, $10, the lesser, is includible in gross income. In this situation, P's cost basis of $108 is increased by $10, the amount includible in P's gross income as compensation. Thus, P's basis for the share is $118. Because the share was sold for $150, P realizes a gain of $32 that is treated as long-term capital gain.

*Example (4).* Assume the same facts as in Example 1, except that the option provides that the option price shall be the lesser of 95 percent of the fair market value of the stock on the first day of the offering period and 95 percent of the fair market value of the stock on the day the option is exercised. On June 1, 2011, when the option is exercised, the fair market value of the stock is $120 per share. P pays $95 for the share of the stock. Compensation in the amount of $5 is includible in P's gross income for the year 2013, the year of the disposition of the share. This is determined in the following manner: The excess of the fair market value of the stock at the time of the disposition ($150) over the price paid for the share ($95) is $55; and the excess of the fair market value of the stock at the time the option was granted ($100) over the option price, computed as if the option had been exercised at such time ($95), is $5. Accordingly, $5, the lesser, is includible in gross income. In this situation, P's cost basis of $95 is increased by $5, the amount includible in P's gross income as compensation. Thus, P's basis for the share is $100. Because the share was sold for $150, P realizes a gain of $50 that is treated as long-term capital gain.

*Example (5).* Assume the same facts as in Example 1, except that instead of selling the share on January 1, 2013, P makes a gift of the share on that day. In that case $15 is includible as compensation in P's gross income for 2013. P's cost basis of $85 is increased by $15, the amount includible in P's gross income as compensation. Thus, P's basis for the share is $100, which becomes the donee's basis, as of the time of the gift, for determining gain or loss.

*Example (6).* Assume the same facts as in Example 2, except that instead of selling the share on January 1, 2014, P makes a gift of the share on that date. Because the fair market value of the share on that day ($75) is less than the option price ($85), no amount in respect of the disposition by way of gift is includible as compensation in P's gross income for 2014. P's basis for the share is $85, which becomes the donee's basis, as of the time of the gift, for the purpose of determining gain. The donee's basis for the purpose of determining loss, determined under section 1015(a), is $75 (fair market value of the share at the date of gift).

*Example (7).* Assume the same facts as in Example 1, except that after acquiring the share of stock on June 1, 2011, P dies on August 1, 2012, at which time the share has a fair market value of $150. Compensation in the amount of $15 is includible in P's gross income for the taxable year closing with P's death, $15 being the difference between the option price ($85) and the fair market value of the share when the option was granted ($100), because such value is less than the fair market value at date of death ($150). The basis of the share in the hands of P's estate is determined under section 1014 without regard to the $15 includible in the decedent's gross income.

*Example (8).* Assume the same facts as in Example 7, except that P dies on August 1, 2011, at which time the share has a fair market value of $150. Although P's death occurred within one year after the transfer of the share to P, the income tax consequences are the same as in Example 7.

*Example (9).* Assume the same facts as in Example 1, except that the share of stock was issued in the names of P and P's spouse jointly with right of survivorship, and that P and P's spouse sold the share on June 15, 2012, for $150, its fair market value on that date. Compensation in the amount of $15 is includible in P's gross income for the year 2012, the year of the disposition of the share. The basis of the share in the hands of P and P's spouse for the purpose of determining gain or loss on the sale is $100, that is, the cost of $85 increased by the amount of $15 includible as compensation in P's gross income. The gain of $50 on the sale is treated as long-term capital gain, and is divided equally between P and P's spouse.

*Example (10).* Assume the same facts as in Example 1, except that the share of stock was issued in the names of P and P's spouse jointly with right of survivorship, and that P predeceased P's spouse on August 1, 2012, at which time the share had a fair market value of $150. Compensation in the amount of $15 is includible in P's gross income for the taxable year closing with his death. See Example 7. The basis of the share in the hands of P's spouse as survivor is determined under section 1014 without regard to the $15 includible in the decedent's gross income.

*Example (11).* Assume the same facts as in Example 10, except that P's spouse predeceased P on July 1, 2012. Section 423(c) does not apply in respect of the death of P's spouse. Upon the subsequent death of P on August 1, 2012, the income tax consequences in respect of P's taxable year closing with the date of P's death, and in respect of the basis of the share in the hands of P's estate, are the same as in Example 7. If P had sold the share on July 15, 2012 (after the death of P's spouse), for $150, its fair market value at that time, the income tax consequences would be the same as in Example 1.

**(l) Effective/applicability date.** The regulations under this section are effective on November 17, 2009. The regulations under this section apply to options granted under an employee stock purchase plan on or after January 1, 2010.

---

T.D. 6887, 6/23/66, amend T.D. 7645, 9/27/79, T.D. 7728, 10/31/80, T.D. 8235, 12/1/88, T.D. 9144, 8/2/2004, T.D. 9471, 11/16/2009.

---

### § 1.424-1 Definitions and special rules applicable to statutory options.

***Caution:*** The Treasury has not yet amended Reg § 1.424-1 to reflect changes made by P.L. 101-508.

**(a) Substitutions and assumptions of options.** *(1) In general.* (i) This paragraph (a) provides rules under which an eligible corporation (as defined in paragraph (a)(2) of this section) may, by reason of a corporate transaction (as defined in paragraph (a)(3) of this section), substitute a new statutory option (new option) for an outstanding statutory option (old option) or assume an old option without such substitution or assumption being considered a modification of the old option. For the definition of modification, see paragraph (e) of this section.

(ii) For purposes of §§ 1.421-1 through 1.424-1, the phrase "substituting or assuming a stock option in a transaction to which section 424 applies," "substituting or assuming a stock option in a transaction to which § 1.424-1(a) applies," and similar phrases means a substitution of a new option for an old option or an assumption of an old option that meets the requirements of this paragraph (a). For a substitution or assumption to qualify under this paragraph (a), the substitution or assumption must meet all of the requirements described in paragraphs (a)(4) and (a)(5) of this section.

*(2) Eligible corporation.* For purposes of this paragraph (a), the term eligible corporation means a corporation that is the employer of the optionee or a related corporation of such corporation. For purposes of this paragraph (a), the determination of whether a corporation is the employer of the optionee or a related corporation of such corporation is based upon all of the relevant facts and circumstances existing immediately after the corporate transaction. See § 1.421-1(h) for rules concerning the employment relationship.

*(3) Corporate transaction.* For purposes of this paragraph (a), the term corporate transaction includes—

(i) A corporate merger, consolidation, acquisition of property or stock, separation, reorganization, or liquidation;

(ii) A distribution (excluding an ordinary dividend or a stock split or stock dividend described in § 1.424-1(e)(4)(v)) or change in the terms or number of outstanding shares of such corporation; and

(iii) Such other corporate events prescribed by the Commissioner in published guidance.

*(4) By reason of.* (i) For a change in an option or issuance of a new option to qualify as a substitution or assumption under this paragraph (a), the change must be made by an eligible corporation (as defined in paragraph (a)(2) of this section) and occur by reason of a corporate transaction (as defined in paragraph (a)(3) of this section).

(ii) Generally, a change in an option or issuance of a new option is considered to be by reason of a corporate transaction, unless the relevant facts and circumstances demonstrate that such change or issuance is made for reasons unrelated to such corporate transaction. For example, a change in an option or issuance of a new option will be considered to be made for reasons unrelated to a corporate transaction if there is an unreasonable delay between the corporate transaction and such change in the option or issuance of a new option, or if the corporate transaction serves no substantial corporate business purpose independent of the change in options. Similarly, a change in the number or price of shares purchasable under an option merely to reflect market fluctuations in the price of the stock purchasable under an option is not by reason of a corporate transaction.

(iii) A change in an option or issuance of a new option is by reason of a distribution or change in the terms or number of the outstanding shares of a corporation (as described in paragraph (a)(3)(ii) of this section) only if the option as changed, or the new option issued, is an option on the same stock as under the old option (or if such class of stock is eliminated in the change in capital structure, on other stock of the same corporation).

*(5) Other requirements.* For a change in an option or issuance of a new option to qualify as a substitution or assumption under this paragraph (a), all of the requirements described in this paragraph (a)(5) must be met.

(i) In the case of an issuance of a new option (or a portion thereof) in exchange for an old option (or portion thereof), the optionee's rights under the old option (or portion thereof) must be canceled, and the optionee must lose all rights under the old option (or portion thereof). There cannot be a substitution of a new option for an old option within the meaning of this paragraph (a) if the optionee may exercise both the old option and the new option. It is not necessary to have a complete substitution of a new option for the old option. However, any portion of such option which is not substituted or assumed in a transaction to which this paragraph (a) applies is an outstanding option to purchase stock or, to the extent paragraph (e) of this section applies, a modified option.

(ii) The excess of the aggregate fair market value of the shares subject to the new or assumed option immediately after the change in the option or issuance of a new option over the aggregate option price of such shares must not exceed the excess of the aggregate fair market value of all shares subject to the old option (or portion thereof) immediately before the change in the option or issuance of a new option over the aggregate option price of such shares.

(iii) On a share by share comparison, the ratio of the option price to the fair market value of the shares subject to the option immediately after the change in the option or issuance of a new option must not be more favorable to the optionee than the ratio of the option price to the fair market value of the stock subject to the old option (or portion thereof) immediately before the change in the option or issuance of a new option. The number of shares subject to the new or assumed option may be adjusted to compensate for any change in the aggregate spread between the aggregate option price and the aggregate fair market value of the shares subject to the option immediately after the change in the option or issuance of the new option as compared to the aggregate spread between the option price and the aggregate fair market value of the shares subject to the option immediately before the change in the option or issuance of the new option.

(iv) The new or assumed option must contain all terms of the old option, except to the extent such terms are rendered inoperative by reason of the corporate transaction.

(v) The new option or assumed option must not give the optionee additional benefits that the optionee did not have under the old option.

*(6) Obligation to substitute or assume not necessary.* For a change in the option or issuance of a new option to meet the requirements of this paragraph (a), it is not necessary to show that the corporation changing an option or issuing a new option is under any obligation to do so. In fact, this paragraph (a) may apply even when the option that is being replaced or assumed expressly provides that it will terminate upon the occurrence of certain corporate transactions. However, this paragraph (a) cannot be applied to revive a statutory option which, for reasons not related to the corporate transaction, expires before it can properly be replaced or assumed under this paragraph (a).

*(7) Issuance of stock without meeting the requirements of this paragraph (a).* A change in the terms of an option resulting in a modification of such option occurs if an optionee's new employer (or a related corporation of the new employer) issues its stock (or stock of a related corporation) upon exercise of such option without satisfying all of the requirements described in paragraphs (a)(4) and (5) of this section.

*(8) Date of grant.* For purposes of applying the rules of this paragraph (a), a substitution or assumption is considered to occur on the date that the optionee would, but for this paragraph (a), be considered to have been granted the option that the eligible corporation is substituting or assuming. A substitution or an assumption that occurs by reason of a corporate transaction may occur before or after the corporate transaction.

*(9)* Any reasonable methods may be used to determine the fair market value of the stock subject to the option immediately before the assumption or substitution and the fair market value of the stock subject to the option immediately after the assumption or substitution. Such methods include the valuation methods described in § 20.2031-2 of this chapter (the Estate Tax Regulations). In the case of stock listed on a stock exchange, the fair market value may be based on the last sale before and the first sale after the assumption or substitution if such sales clearly reflect the fair market value of the stock, or may be based upon an average selling price during a longer period, such as the day or week before, and the day or week after, the assumption or substitution. If the stocks are not listed, or if they are newly issued, it will be reasonable to base the determination on experience over even longer periods. In the case of a merger, consolidation, or other reorganization which is arrived at by arm's-length negotiations, the fair market value of the stocks subject to the option before and after the assumption or substitution may be based upon the values assigned to the stock for purposes of the reorganization. For example, if in the case of a merger the parties treat each share of the merged company as being equal in value to a share of the surviving company, it will be reasonable to assume that the stocks are of equal value so that the substituted option may permit the employee to purchase at the same price one share of the surviving company for each share he could have purchased of the merged company.

*(10) Examples.* The principles of this paragraph (a) are illustrated by the following examples:

*Example (1).* Eligible corporation. X Corporation acquires a new subsidiary, Y Corporation, and transfers some of its employees to Y. Y Corporation wishes to grant to its new employees and to the employees of X Corporation new options for Y shares in exchange for old options for X shares that were previously granted by X Corporation. Because Y Corporation is an employer with respect to its own employees and a related corporation of X Corporation, Y Corporation is an eligible corporation under paragraph (a)(2) of this section with respect to both the employees of X and Y Corporations.

*Example (2).* Corporate transaction. (i) On January 1, 2004, Z Corporation grants E, an employee of Z, an option to acquire 100 shares of Z common stock. At the time of grant, the fair market value of Z common stock is $200 per share. E's option price is $200 per share. On July 1, 2005, when the fair market value of Z common stock is $400, Z declares a stock dividend of preferred stock distributed on common stock that causes the fair market value of Z common stock to decrease to $200 per share. On the same day, Z grants to E a new option to acquire 200 shares of Z common stock in exchange for E's old option. The new option has an exercise price of $100 per share.

(ii) A stock dividend other than that described in § 1.424-1(e)(4)(v) is a corporate transaction under paragraph (a)(3)(ii) of this section. Generally, the issuance of a new option is considered to be by reason of a corporate transaction. None of the facts in this Example 2 indicate that the new option is not issued by reason of the stock dividend. In addition, the new option is issued on the same stock as the old option. Thus, the substitution occurs by reason of the corporate transaction. Assuming the other requirements of this section are met, the issuance of the new option is a substitution that meets the requirements of this paragraph (a) and is not a modification of the option.

(iii) Assume the same facts as in paragraph (i) of this Example 2. Assume further that on December 1, 2005, Z declares an ordinary cash dividend. On the same day, Z grants E a new option to acquire Z stock in substitution for E's old option. Under paragraph (a)(3)(ii) of this section, an ordinary cash dividend is not a corporate transaction. Thus, the exchange of the new option for the old option does not meet the requirements of this paragraph (a) and is a modification of the option.

*Example (3).* Corporate transaction. On March 15, 2004, A Corporation grants E, an employee of A, an option to acquire 100 shares of A stock at $50 per share, the fair market value of A stock on the date of grant. On May 2, 2005, A Corporation transfers several employees, including E, to B Corporation, a related corporation. B Corporation arranges to purchase some assets from A on the same day as E's transfer to B. Such purchase is without a substantial business purpose independent of making the exchange of E's old options for the new options appear to be by reason of a corporate transaction. The following day, B Corporation grants to E, one of its new employees, an option to acquire shares of B stock in exchange for the old option held by E to acquire A stock. Under paragraph (a)(3)(i) of this section, the purchase of assets is a corporate transaction. Generally, the substitution of an option is considered to occur by reason of a corporate transaction. However, in this case, the relevant facts and circumstances demonstrate that the issuance of the new option in exchange for the old option occurred by reason of the change in E's employer rather than a corporate transaction and that the sale of assets is without a substantial corporate business purpose independent of the change in the options. Thus, the exchange of the new option for the old option is not by reason of a corporate transaction that meets the requirements of this paragraph (a) and is a modification of the old option.

*Example (4).* Corporate transaction. (i) E, an employee of Corporation A, holds an option to acquire 100 shares of Corporation A stock. On September 1, 2006, Corporation A has one class of stock outstanding and declares a stock dividend of one share of common stock for each outstanding share of common stock. The rights associated with the common stock issued as a dividend are the same as the rights under existing shares of stock. In connection with the stock dividend, E's option is exchanged for an option to acquire 200 shares of Corporation A stock. The per-share exercise price is equal to one half of the per-share exercise price of the original option. The stock dividend merely changes the number of shares of Corporation A outstanding and effects no other change to the stock of Corporation A. The option is proportionally adjusted and the aggregate exercise price remains the same and therefore satisfies the requirements described in § 1.424-1(e)(4)(v).

(ii) The stock dividend is not a corporate transaction under paragraph (a)(3) of this section, and the declaration of the stock dividend is not a modification of the old option under paragraph (a) of this section. Pursuant to § 1.424-1(e)(4)(v), the exercise price of the old option may be adjusted proportionally with the change in the number of outstanding shares of Corporation A such that the ratio of the aggregate exercise price of the option to the number of shares covered by the option is the same both before and after the stock dividend. The adjustment of E's option is not treated as a modification of the option.

*Example (5).* Additional benefit. On June 1, 2004, P Corporation acquires 100 percent of the shares of S Corporation and issues a new option to purchase P shares in exchange for an old option to purchase S shares that is held by E, an employee of S. On the date of the exchange, E's old option is exercisable for 3 more years, and, after the exchange, E's new option is exercisable for 5 years. Because the new option is exercisable for an additional period of time beyond the time allowed under the old option, the effect of the exchange of the new option for the old option is to give E an additional benefit that E did not enjoy under the old option. Thus, the requirements of paragraph (a)(5) of this section are not met, and this paragraph (a) does not apply to the exchange of the new option for the old option. Therefore, the exchange is a modification of the old options.

*Example (6).* Spread and ratio tests. E is an employee of S Corporation. E holds an old option that was granted to E by S to purchase 60 shares of S at $12 per share. On June 1, 2005, S Corporation is merged into P Corporation, and on such date P issues a new option to purchase P shares in exchange for E's old option to purchase S shares. Immediately before the exchange, the fair market value of an S share is $32; immediately after the exchange, the fair market value of a P share is $24. The new option entitles E to buy P shares at $9 per share. Because, on a share-by-share comparison, the ratio of the new option price ($9 per share) to the fair market value of a P share immediately after the exchange ($24 per share) is not more favorable to E than the ratio of the old option price ($12 per share) to the fair market value of an S share immediately before the exchange ($32 per share) ($9/24 = 12/32$), the requirements of paragraph (a)(5)(iii) of this section are met. The number of shares subject to E's option to purchase P stock is set at 80. Because the excess of the aggregate fair market value over the aggregate option price of the shares subject to E's new option to purchase P stock, $1,200 (80 x $24 minus 80 x $9), is not greater than the excess of the aggregate fair market value over the aggregate option price of the shares subject to E's old option to purchase S stock, $1,200 (60 x $32 minus 60 x $12), the requirements of paragraph (a)(5)(ii) of this section are met.

*Example (7).* Ratio test and partial substitution. Assume the same facts as in Example 6, except that the fair market value of an S share immediately before the exchange of the new option for the old option is $8, that the option price is $10 per share, and that the fair market value of a P share immediately after the exchange is $12. P sets the new option price at $15 per share. Because, on a share-by-share comparison, the ratio of the new option price ($15 per share) to the fair market value of a P share immediately after the exchange ($12) is not more favorable to E than the ratio of the old option price ($10 per share) to the fair market value of an S share immediately before the substitution ($8 per share) ($15/12 = 10/8$), the requirements of paragraph (a)(5)(iii) of this section are met. Assume further that the number of shares subject to E's P option is set at 20, as compared to 60 shares under E's old option to buy S stock. Immediately after the exchange, 2 shares of P are worth $24, which is what 3 shares of S were worth immediately before the exchange (2 x $12 = 3 x $8). Thus, to achieve a complete substitution of a new option for E's old option, E would need to receive a new option to purchase 40 shares of P (i.e., 2 shares of P for each 3 shares of S that E could have purchased under the old option ($2/3 = 40/60$). Because E's new option is for only 20 shares of P, P has replaced only ½ of E's old option, and the other ½ is still outstanding.

*Example (8).* Partial substitution. X Corporation forms a new corporation, Y Corporation, by a transfer of certain assets and, in a spin-off, distributes the shares of Y Corporation to the stockholders of X Corporation. E, an employee of X Corporation, is thereafter an employee of Y. Y wishes to substitute a new option to purchase some of its stock for E's old option to purchase 100 shares of X. E's old option to purchase shares of X, at $50 a share, was granted when the fair market value of an X share was $50, and an X share was worth $100 just before the distribution of the Y shares to X's stockholders. Immediately after the spin-off, which is also the time of the substitution, each share of X and each share of Y is worth $50. Based on these facts, a new option to purchase 200 shares of Y at an option price of $25 per share could be granted to E in complete substitution of E's old option. In the alternative, it would also be permissible in connection with the spin off, to grant E a new option to purchase 100 shares of Y, at an option price of $25 per share, and for E to retain an option to purchase 100 shares of X under the old option, with the option price adjusted to $25. However, because X is no longer a related corporation with respect to Y, E must exercise the option for 100 shares of X within three months from the date of the spin off for the option to be treated as a statutory option. See § 1.421-1(h). It would also be permissible to grant E a new option to purchase 100 shares of Y, at an option price of $25 per share, in substitution for E's right to purchase 50 of the shares under the old option.

*Example (9).* Stockholder approval requirements. (i) X Corporation, a publicly traded corporation, adopts an incentive stock option plan that meets the requirements of § 1.422-2. Under the plan, options to acquire X stock are granted to X employees. X Corporation is acquired by Y Corporation and becomes a subsidiary corporation of Y Corporation. After the acquisition, X employees remain employees of X. In connection with the acquisition, Y Corporation substitutes new options to acquire Y stock for the old options to acquire X stock previously granted to the employees of X. As a result of this substitution, on exercise of the new options, X employees receive Y Corporation stock.

(ii) Because the requirements of § 1.422-2 were met on the date of grant, the substitution of the new Y options for the old X options does not require new stockholder approval. If the other requirements of paragraphs (a)(4) and (5) of this section are met, the issuance of new options for Y stock in exchange for the old options for X stock meets the requirements of this paragraph (a) and is not a modification of the old options.

(iii) Assume the same facts as in paragraphs (i) and (ii) of this Example 9. Assume further that as part of the acquisition, X amends its plan to allow future grants under the plan to be grants to acquire Y stock. Because the amendment of the plan to allow options on a different stock is considered the adoption of a new plan under § 1.422-2(b)(2)(iii), the stockholders of X (in this case, Y) must approve the plan within 12 months before or after the date of the amendment of the plan. If the stockholders of X (in this case, Y) timely approve the plan, the future grants to acquire Y stock will be incentive stock options (assuming the other requirements of § 1.422-2 have been met).

*Example (10).* Modification. X Corporation merges into Y Corporation. Y Corporation retains employees of X who hold old options to acquire X Corporation stock. When the former employees of X exercise the old options, Y Corporation issues Y stock to the former employees of X. Under paragraph (a)(7) of this section, because Y issues its stock on exercise of the old options for X stock, there is a change in the terms of the old options for X stock. Thus, the issuance of Y stock on exercise of the old options is a modification of the old options.

*Example (11).* Eligible corporation. (i) D Corporation grants an option to acquire 100 shares of D Corporation stock to E, an employee of D Corporation. S Corporation is a subsidiary of D Corporation. On March 1, 2005, D Corporation spins off S Corporation. E remains an employee of D Corporation. In connection with the spin off, D Corporation substitutes a new option to acquire D Corporation stock and a new option to acquire S Corporation stock for the old option in a manner that meets the requirements of paragraph (a) of this section.

(ii) The substitution of the new option to acquire S and D stock for the old option to acquire D stock is not a modification of the old option. However, because S is no longer a related corporation with respect to D Corporation, E must exercise the option for S stock within three months from March 1, 2005, for the option to be treated as a statutory option. See § 1.421-1(h).

(iii) Assume the same facts as in paragraph (i) of this Example 11 except that E's employment with D Corporation is terminated on February 20, 2005. The substitution of the new option to acquire S and D stock for the old option to acquire D stock is not a modification of the old option. However, because the employment relationship between E and D Corporation terminated on February 20, 2005, E must exercise the option for the D and S stock within three months from February 20, 2005, for the option to be treated as a statutory option. See § 1.421-1(h).

**(b) Acquisition of new stock.** *(1)* Section 424(b) provides that the rules provided by sections 421 through 424 which are applicable with respect to stock transferred to an individual upon his exercise of an option, shall likewise be applicable with respect to stock acquired by a distribution or an exchange to which section 305, 354, 355, 356, or 1036 (or so much of section 1031 as relates to section 1036) applies. Stock so acquired shall, for purposes of section 421 through 424, be considered as having been transferred to the individual upon his exercise of the option. A similar rule shall be applied in the case of a series of such acquisitions. With respect to such acquisitions, section 424(b) does not make inapplicable any of the provisions of section 305, 354, 355, 356, or 1036 (or so much of section 1031 as relates to section 1036).

*(2)* The application of this paragraph may be illustrated by the following example:

*Example.* If, with respect to stock transferred pursuant to the timely exercise of a statutory option, there is a distribution of new stock to which section 305(a) is applicable, and if there is a disposition of such new stock before the expiration of the applicable holding period required with respect to the stock originally acquired pursuant to the exercise of such option, such disposition makes section 421 inapplicable to the transfer of the original stock pursuant to the exercise of the option to the extent that the disposition effects a reduction of the individual's total interest in the old and new stock. However, if the new stock, as well as the old stock, is not disposed of before the expiration of the holding period required with respect to the original stock acquired pursuant to the exercise of the option, the special tax treatment provided by section 421 is applicable to both the original shares and the shares acquired by virtue of the distribution to which section 305(a) applies.

**(c) Disposition of stock.** *(1)* For purposes of sections 421 through 424, the term "disposition of stock" includes a sale, exchange, gift, or any transfer of legal title, but does not include—

(i) A transfer from a decedent to his estate or a transfer by bequest or inheritance; or

(ii) An exchange to which is applicable section 354, 355, 356, or 1036 (or so much of section 1031 as relates to section 1036); or

(iii) A mere pledge or hypothecation. However, a disposition of the stock pursuant to a pledge or hypothecation is a disposition by the individual, even though the making of the pledge or hypothecation is not such a disposition.

(iv) A transfer between spouses or incident to divorce (described in section 1041(a)). The special tax treatment of § 1.421-2(a) with respect to the transferred stock applies to the transferee. However, see § 1.421-1(b)(2) for the treatment of the transfer of a statutory option incident to divorce.

*(2)* A share of stock acquired by an individual pursuant to the exercise of a statutory option is not considered disposed of by the individual if such share is taken in the name of the individual and another person jointly with right of survivorship, or is subsequently transferred into such joint ownership, or is retransferred from such joint ownership to the sole ownership of the individual. However, any termination of such joint ownership (other than a termination effected by the death of a joint owner) is a disposition of such share, except to the extent the individual reacquires ownership of the share. For example, if such individual and his joint owner transfer such share to another person, the individual has made a disposition of such share. Likewise, if a share of stock held in the joint names of such individual and another person is transferred to the name of such other person, there is a disposition of such share by the individual. If an individual exercises a statutory option and a share of stock is transferred to another or is transferred to such individual in his name as trustee for another, the individual has made a disposition of such share. However, a termination of joint ownership resulting from the death of one of the owners is not a disposition of such share. For determination of basis in the hands of the survivor where joint ownership is terminated by the death of one of the owners, see section 1014.

*(3)* If an optionee exercises an incentive stock option with statutory option stock and the applicable holding period requirements (under § 1.422-1(a) or § 1.423-1(a)) with respect to such statutory option stock are not met before such transfer, then sections 354, 355, 356, or 1036 (or so much of 1031 as relates to 1036) do not apply to determine whether there is a disposition of those shares. Therefore, there is a disposition of the statutory option stock, and the special tax treatment of § 1.421-2(a) does not apply to such stock.

*(4)* The application of this paragraph may be illustrated by the following examples:

*Example (1).* On June 1, 2004, the X Corporation grants to E, an employee, a statutory option to purchase 100 shares of X Corporation stock at $100 per share, the fair market value of X Corporation stock on that date. On June 1, 2005, while employed by X Corporation, E exercises the option in full and pays X Corporation $10,000, and on that day X Corporation transfers to E 100 shares of its stock having a fair market value of $12,000. Before June 1, 2006, E makes no disposition of the 100 shares so purchased. E realizes no income on June 1, 2005, with respect to the transfer to him of the 100 shares of X Corporation stock. X Corporation is not entitled to any deduction at any time with respect to its transfer to E of the stock. E's basis for such 100 shares is $10,000.

*Example (2).* Assume the same facts as in example (1), except assume that on August 1, 2006, three years and two months after the transfer of the shares to him, E sells the 100 shares of X Corporation stock for $13,000 which is the fair market value of the stock on that date. For the taxable year in which the sale occurs, E realizes a gain of $3,000 ($13,000 minus E's basis of $10,000), which is treated as capital gain.

*Example (3).* Assume the same facts as in example (2), except assume that on August 1, 2006, E makes a gift of the 100 shares of Y Corporation stock to his son. Such disposition results in no realization of gain to E either for the taxable year in which the option is exercised or the taxable year in which the gift is made. E's basis of $10,000 becomes the donee's basis for determining gain or loss.

*Example (4).* Assume the same facts as in example (1), except assume that on May 1, 2006, E sells the 100 shares of X Corporation stock for $13,000. The special rules of section 421(a) are not applicable to the transfer of the stock by X Corporation to E, because disposition of the stock was made by E within two years from the date the options were granted and within one year of the date that the shares were transferred to him.

*Example (5).* Assume the same facts as in example (1), except assume that E dies on September 1, 2005, owning the 100 shares of X Corporation stock acquired by him pursuant to his exercise on June 1, 2005, of the statutory option. On the date of death, the fair market value of the stock is $12,500. No income is realized by E by reason of the transfer of the 100 shares to his estate. If the stock is valued as of the date of E's death for estate tax purposes, the basis of the 100 shares in the hands of the executor is $12,500.

*Example (6).* Assume the same facts as in example (1), except assume that on June 1, 2005, when the option is exercised by E the 100 shares are transferred by X to E and his wife W, as joint owners with right of survivorship, and that E dies on July 1, 2005. Neither the transfer into joint ownership nor the termination of such joint ownership by E's death is a disposition. Because E has made no disqualifying disposition of the shares, section 421(a) is applicable and E realizes no compensation income at death with respect to the shares even though he held the stock less than 2 years after the transfer of the shares to him pursuant to his exercise of the option. § 1.421-2(b)(2).

*Example (7).* On January 1, 2004, X Corporation grants to E, an employee of X Corporation, an incentive stock option to purchase 100 shares of X Corporation stock at $100 per share (the fair market value of an X Corporation share on that date). On January 1, 2005, when the fair market value of a share of X Corporation stock is $200, E exercises half of the option, pays X Corporation $5,000 in cash, and is transferred 50 shares of X Corporation stock with an aggregate fair market value of $10,000. E makes no disposition of the shares before January 2, 2006. Under § 1.421-2(a), no income is recognized by E on the transfer of shares pursuant to the exercise of the incentive stock option, and X Corporation is not entitled to any deduction at any time with respect to its transfer of the shares to E. E's basis in the shares is $5,000.

*Example (8).* Assume the same facts as in Example 7, except that on December 1, 2005, one year and 11 months after the grant of the option and 11 months after the transfer of the 50 shares to E, E uses 25 of those shares, with a fair market value of $5,000, to pay for the remaining 50 shares purchasable under the option. On that day, X Corporation transfers 50 of its shares, with an aggregate fair market value of $10,000, to E. Because E disposed of the 25 shares before the expiration of the applicable holding periods, § 1.421-2(a) does not apply to the January 1, 2005, transfer of the 25 shares used by E to exercise the remainder of the option. As a result of the disqualifying disposition of the 25 shares, E recognizes compensation income under the rules of § 1.421-2(b).

*Example (9).* On January 1, 2005, X Corporation grants an incentive stock option to E, an employee of X Corporation. The exercise price of the option is $10 per share. On June 1, 2005, when the fair market value of an X Corporation share is $20, E exercises the option and purchases 5 shares with an aggregate fair market value of $100. On January 1, 2006, when the fair market value of an X Corporation share is $50, X Corporation is acquired by Y Corporation in a section 368(a)(1)(A) reorganization. As part of the acquisition, all X Corporation shares are converted into Y Corporation shares. After the conversion, if an optionee holds a fractional share of Y Corporation stock, Y Corporation will purchase the fractional share for cash equal to its fair market value. After applying the conversion formula to the shares held by E, E has 10½ Y Corporation shares. Y Corporation purchases E's one-half share for $25, the fair market value of one-half of a Y Corporation share on the conversion date. Because E sells the one-half share prior to expiration of the holding periods described in § 1.422-1(a), the sale is a disqualifying disposition of the one-half share. Thus, in 2006, E must recognize compensation income of $5 (one-half of the fair market value of an X Corporation share on the date of exercise of the option, or $10, less one-half of the exercise price per share, or $5). For purposes of computing any additional gain, E's basis in the one-half share increases to $10 (reflecting the $5 included in income as compensation). E recognizes an additional gain of $15 ($25, the fair market value of the one-half share, less $10, the basis in such share). The extent to which the additional $15 of gain is treated as a redemption of Y Corporation stock is determined under section 302.

**(d) Attribution of stock ownership.** To determine the amount of stock owned by an individual for purposes of applying the percentage limitations relating to certain stockholders described in §§ 1.422-2(f) and 1.423-2(d), shares of the employer corporation or of a related corporation that are owned (directly or indirectly) by or for the individual's brothers and sisters (whether by the whole or half blood), spouse, ancestors, and lineal descendants, are considered to be owned by the individual. Also, for such purposes, if a domestic or foreign corporation, partnership, estate, or trust owns (directly or indirectly) shares of the employer corporation or of a related corporation, the shares are considered to be owned proportionately by or for the stockholders, partners, or beneficiaries of the corporation, partnership, estate, or trust. The extent to which stock held by the optionee as a trustee of a voting trust is considered owned by the optionee is determined under all of the facts and circumstances.

**(e) Modification, extension, or renewal of option.** *(1)* This paragraph (e) provides rules for determining whether a share of stock transferred to an individual upon the individual's exercise of an option after the terms of the option have been changed is transferred pursuant to the exercise of a statutory option.

*(2)* Any modification, extension, or renewal of the terms of an option to purchase shares is considered the granting of a new option. The new option may or may not be a statutory option. To determine the date of grant of the new option for purposes of section 422 or 423, see § 1.421-1(c).

*(3)* If section 423(c) applies to an option then, in case of a modification, extension, or renewal of an option, the highest of the following values shall be considered to be the fair market value of the stock at the time of the granting of such option for purposes of applying the rules of sections 423(b)(6),—

(i) The fair market value on the date of the original granting of the option,

(ii) The fair market value on the date of the making of such modification, extension, or renewal, or

(iii) The fair market value at the time of the making of any intervening modification, extension, or renewal.

*(4)* (i) For purposes of §§ 1.421-1 through 1.424-1 the term modification means any change in the terms of the option (or change in the terms of the plan pursuant to which the option was granted or in the terms of any other agreement governing the arrangement) that gives the optionee additional benefits under the option regardless of whether the optionee in fact benefits from the change in terms. In contrast, for example, a change in the terms of the option shortening the period during which the option is exercisable is not a modification. However, a change providing an extension of the period during which an option may be exercised (such as after termination of employment) or a change providing an alternative to the exercise of the option (such as a stock appreciation right) is a modification regardless of whether the optionee in fact benefits from such extension or alternative right. Similarly, a change providing an additional benefit upon exercise of the option (such as the payment of a cash bonus) or a change providing more favorable terms for payment for the stock purchased under the option (such as the right to tender previously acquired stock) is a modification.

(ii) If an option is not immediately exercisable in full, a change in the terms of the option to accelerate the time at which the option (or any portion thereof) may be exercised is not a modification for purposes of this section. Additionally, no modification occurs if a provision accelerating the time when an option may first be exercised is removed prior to the year in which it would otherwise be triggered. For example, if an acceleration provision is timely removed to avoid exceeding the $100,000 limitation described in § 1.422-4, a modification of the option does not occur.

(iii) A change to an option which provides, either by its terms or in substance, that the optionee may receive an additional benefit under the option at the future discretion of the grantor, is a modification at the time that the option is changed to provide such discretion. In addition, the exercise of discretion to provide an additional benefit is a modification of the option. However, it is not a modification for the grantor to exercise discretion specifically reserved under an option with respect to the payment of a cash bonus at the time of exercise, the availability of a loan at exercise, the right to tender previously acquired stock for the stock purchasable under the option, or the payment of employment taxes and/or required withholding taxes resulting from the exercise of a statutory option. An option is not modified merely because an optionee is offered a change in the terms of an option if the change to the option is not made. An offer to change the terms of an option that remains open less than 30 days is not a modification of the option. However, if an offer to change the terms of an option remains outstanding for 30 days or more, there is a modification of the option as of the date the offer to change the option is made.

(iv) A change in the terms of the stock purchasable under the option that increases the value of the stock is a modification of such option, except to the extent that a new option is substituted for such option by reason of the change in the terms of the stock in accordance with paragraph (a) of this section.

(v) If an option is amended solely to increase the number of shares subject to the option, the increase is not considered a modification of the option but is treated as the grant of a new option for the additional shares. Notwithstanding the previous sentence, if the exercise price and number of shares subject to an option are proportionally adjusted to reflect a stock split (including a reverse stock split) or stock dividend, and the only effect of the stock split or stock dividend is to increase (or decrease) on a pro rata basis the number of shares owned by each shareholder of the class of stock subject to the option, then the option is not modified if it is proportionally adjusted to reflect the stock split or stock dividend and the aggregate exercise price of the option is not less than the aggregate exercise price before the stock split or stock dividend.

(vi) Any change in the terms of an option made in an attempt to qualify the option as a statutory option grants additional benefits to the optionee and is, therefore, a modification.

(vii) An extension of an option refers to the granting by the corporation to the optionee of an additional period of time within which to exercise the option beyond the time originally prescribed. A renewal of an option is the granting by the corporation of the same rights or privileges contained in the original option on the same terms and conditions. The rules of this paragraph apply as well to successive modifications, extensions, and renewals.

(viii) Any inadvertent change to the terms of an option (or change in the terms of the plan pursuant to which the option was granted or in the terms of any other agreement governing the arrangement) that is treated as a modification under this paragraph (e) is not considered a modification of the option to the extent the change in the terms of the option is removed by the earlier of the date the option is exercised or the last day of the calendar year during which such change occurred. Thus, for example, if the terms of an option are inadvertently changed on March 1 to extend the exercise period and the change is removed on November 1, then if the option is not exercised prior to November 1, the option is not considered modified under this paragraph (e).

*(5)* A statutory option may, as a result of a modification, extension, or renewal, thereafter cease to be a statutory option, or any option may, by modification, extension, or renewal, thereafter become a statutory option.

*(6)* [Reserved.]

*(7)* The application of this paragraph may be illustrated by the following examples:

*Example (1).* On June 1, 2004, the X Corporation grants to an employee an option under X's employee stock purchase plan to purchase 100 shares of the stock of X Corporation at $90 per share, such option to be exercised on or before June 1, 2006. At the time the option is granted, the fair market value of the X Corporation stock is $100 per share. On February 1, 2005, before the employee exercises the option, X Corporation modifies the option to provide that the price at which the employee may purchase the stock shall be $80 per share. On February 1, 2005, the fair market value of the X Corporation stock is $90 per share. Under section 424(h), the X Corporation is deemed to have granted an option to the employee on February 1, 2005. Such option shall be treated as an option to purchase at $80 per share 100 shares of stock having a fair market value of $100 per share, that is, the higher of the fair market value of the stock on June 1, 2004, or on February 1, 2005. Because the requirements of § 1.424-1(e)(3) and § 1.423-2(g) have not been met, the exercise of such option by the employee after February 1, 2005, is not the exercise of a statutory option.

*Example (2).* On June 1, 2004, the X Corporation grants to an employee an option under X's employee stock purchase plan to purchase 100 shares of X Corporation stock at $90 per share, exercisable after December 31, 2005, and on or before June 1, 2006. On June 1, 2004, the fair market value of X Corporation's stock is $100 per share. On February 1, 2005, X Corporation modifies the option to provide that the option shall be exercisable on or before September 1, 2006. On February 1, 2005, the fair market value of X Corporation stock is $110 per share. Under section 424(h), X Corporation is deemed to have granted an option to the employee on February 1, 2005, to purchase at $90 per share 100 shares of stock having a fair market value of $110 per share, that is, the higher of the fair market value of the stock on June 1, 2004, or on February 1, 2005. Because the requirements of § 1.424-1(e)(3) and § 1.423-2(g) have not been met, the exercise of such option by the employee is not the exercise of a statutory option.

*Example (3).* The facts are the same as in example (1), except that the employee exercised the option to the extent of 50 shares on January 15, 2005, before the date of the modification of the option. Any exercise of the option after February 1, 2005, the date of the modification, is not the exercise of a statutory option. See example (1) in this subparagraph. The exercise of the option on January 15, 2005, pursuant to which 50 shares were acquired, is the exercise of a statutory option.

**(f) Definitions.** The following definitions apply for purposes of §§ 1.421-1 through 1.424-1:

*(1) Parent corporation.* The term parent corporation, or parent, means any corporation (other than the employer corporation) in an unbroken chain of corporations ending with the employer corporation if, at the time of the granting of the option, each of the corporations other than the employer corporation owns stock possessing 50 percent or more of the total combined voting power of all classes of stock in one of the other corporations in such chain.

*(2) Subsidiary corporation.* The term subsidiary corporation, or subsidiary, means any corporation (other than the employer corporation) in an unbroken chain of corporations beginning with the employer corporation if, at the time of the granting of the option, each of the corporations other than the last corporation in an unbroken chain owns stock possessing 50 percent or more of the total combined voting power of all classes of stock in one of the other corporations in such chain.

**(g) Effective/applicability date.** *(1) In general.* Except for § 1.424-1(a)(10) Example 9 (iii), the regulations under this section are effective on August 3, 2004. Section 1.424-1(a)(10) Example 9 (iii) is effective on November 17, 2009. Section 1.424-1(a)(10) Example 9 (iii) applies to statutory options granted on or after January 1, 2010.

*(2) Reliance and transition period.* For statutory options granted on or before June 9, 2003, taxpayers may rely on the 1984 proposed regulations LR-279-81 (49 FR 4504), the

2003 proposed regulations REG-122917-02 (68 FR 34344), or this section until the earlier of January 1, 2006, or the first regularly scheduled stockholders meeting of the granting corporation occurring 6 months after August 3, 2004. For statutory options granted after June 9, 2003, and before the earlier of January 1, 2006, or the first regularly scheduled stockholders meeting of the granting corporation occurring at least 6 months after August 3, 2004, taxpayers may rely on either REG-122917-02 or this section. Taxpayers may not rely on LR-279-81 or REG-122917-02 after December 31, 2005. Reliance on LR-279-81, REG-122917-02, or this section must be in its entirety, and all statutory options granted during the reliance period must be treated consistently.

---

T.D. 6887, 6/23/66, amend T.D. 9144, 8/2/2004, T.D. 9471, 11/16/2009.

---

PAR. 6. Section 1.425-1 is amended by revising paragraph (a)(6), redesignating paragraph (c)(3) as paragraph (c)(4) and revising paragraph (c)(4), adding new paragraph (c)(3), and revising paragraphs (d), (e)(1), (e)(5)(i) and (iii) and (e)(6) to read as follows:

**Proposed § 1.425-1 Definitions and special rules applicable to statutory options.** [*For Preamble, see ¶ 150,935*]

• ***Caution:*** This Notice of Proposed Rulemaking was finalized by TD 9144, 8/2/2004. For statutory options granted on or before June 9, 2003, taxpayers may rely on any of these three sets of regs, in their entirety: (i) proposed regs issued in '84 (reproduced below); (ii) proposed regs issued on June 9, 2003; or (iii) final regs-until the earlier of (a) Jan. 1, 2006, or (b) the first regularly scheduled stockholders meeting of the granting corporation occurring at least six months after Aug. 3, 2004.

***Caution:*** The Treasury has not yet amended Reg § 1.425-1 to reflect changes made by P.L. 101-508.

**(a) Corporate reorganizations, liquidations, etc.** * * *

*(6)* In order to have a substitution of an option under section 425(a) the optionee must, in connection with the corporate transaction, lose his rights under the old option. There cannot be a substitution of a new option for an old option within the meaning of section 425(a) if it is contemplated that the optionee may exercise both the old option and the new option. It is not necessary, however, to have a complete substitution of a new option for the old option. However, if the old option was a qualified, incentive, or restricted stock option, any portion of such option which is not substituted or assumed in a transaction to which section 425(a) applies will be treated as an outstanding option to purchase stock of a predecessor corporation of the new employer or grantor corporation. See section 422(b)(5) and (c)(2) and paragraph (f) of § 1.422-2, and section 422A(b)(7) and (c)(7) and paragraph (f) of § 1.422A-2. For example, assume that X Corporation forms a new corporation, Y Corporation, by a transfer of certain assets and distributes the stock of Y Corporation to the shareholders of X Corporation. Assume further that E, an employee of X Corporation, is thereafter an employee of both X Corporation and Y Corporation. Y Corporation wishes to substitute an option to purchase some of its stock for the statutory option which E has entitling him to purchase 100 shares of the stock of X Corporation. The option to purchase the stock of X Corporation, at $50 a share, was granted when the stock had a fair market value of $50 a share, and the stock was worth $100 a share just before the distribution of the new corporation's stock to the shareholders of X Corporation. The stock of X Corporation and of Y Corporation is worth $50 a share just after such distribution, which also is the time of the substitution. On these facts an option to purchase 200 shares of stock of Y Corporation at $25 a share could be given to the employee in complete substitution for the old option. It would also be permissible to give the employee an option to purchase 100 shares of stock of Y Corporation at $25 a share in substitution for his right to purchase 50 of the shares covered by the old option. However, if the option to purchase X stock was a qualified, incentive, or restricted stock option, then to the extent the old option is not assumed or a new option issued in substitution therefor in a transaction to which section 425(a) applies, such old option will be treated as an outstanding option under either section 422(c)(2) for purposes of section 422(b)(5), or section 422A(c)(7) for purposes of section 422A(b)(7). See paragraph (f) of § 1.422-2 and paragraph (f) of § 1.422A-2.

* * * * *

**(c) Disposition of stock.** * * *

*(3)* (i) If there is a transfer of statutory option stock in connection with the exercise of any incentive stock option, and the applicable holding period requirements (under section 422(a)(1), 422A(a)(1), 423(a)(1), or 424(a)(1)) are not met before such transfer, then no section referred to in paragraph (c)(1)(ii) of this section shall apply to such transfer for purposes of determining whether there has been a disposition of such stock.

(ii) For purposes of this paragraph (c)(3), the term "statutory option stock" means any stock acquired through the exercise of a qualified stock option, an incentive stock option, an option granted under an employee stock purchase plan, or a restricted stock option.

(iii) This paragraph (c)(3) applies only with respect to transfers of statutory option stock in connection with the exercise of an incentive stock option occurring after March 15, 1982.

*(4)* * * *

*Example (7).* On January 1, 1982, the X Corporation grants to E, an employee, an incentive stock option to purchase 100 shares of X Corporation stock at $100 per share, the fair market value of X Corporation stock on that date. According to the terms of the option, E can exercise the option by using previously acquired X Corporation stock. On January 1, 1983, while employed by X Corporation, E exercises part of the option and pays X Corporation $5,000 in cash. On that day, X Corporation transfers to E 50 shares of its stock having a fair market value of $6,000. Before January 1, 1984, E makes no disposition of the 50 shares so purchased. E realizes no income with respect to the transfer of the 50 shares of X Corporation stock on January 1, 1983. X Corporation is not entitled to any deduction at any time with respect to its transfer to E of the stock. E's basis for such 50 shares is $5,000.

*Example (8).* Assume the same facts as in example (7), except assume that on December 1, 1983, one year and 11 months after the grant of the incentive stock option and 11 months after the transfer of the 50 shares, E transfers 25 of the shares, having a fair market value of $5,000, to X Corporation as payment for the balance of the incentive stock option still outstanding. On that day, X Corporation transfers to E 50 shares of its stock having a fair market value of $10,000. The special rules of section 421(a) are not applicable to the transfer of 25 of the shares transferred on January 1, 1983, because disposition of such shares was made by E within two years of grant of the option and one year of exercise of the option.

**(d) Attribution of stock ownership.** Section 425(d) provides that in determining the amount of stock owned by an individual for purposes of applying the percentage limitations of section 422(b)(7), 422A(b)(6), 423(b)(3), and 424(b)(3), stock of the employer corporation or of a related corporation which is owned (directly or indirectly) by or for such individual's brothers and sisters (whether by the whole or half blood), spouse, ancestors, and lineal descendants, shall be considered as owned by such individual. Also, for such purpose, if a domestic or foreign corporation, partnership, estate, or trust owns (directly or indirectly) stock of the employer corporation or of its parent or subsidiary, such stock shall be considered as being owned proportionately by or for the shareholders, partners, or beneficiaries of the corporation, partnership, estate, or trust.

**(e) Modification, extension, or renewal of option.** *(1)* Section 425(h) provides the rules for determining whether a share of stock transferred to an individual upon his exercise of an option, after the terms thereof have been modified, extended, or renewed, is transferred pursuant to the exercise of a statutory option. Such rules and the rules of this section are applicable to modifications, extensions, or renewals (or to changes which are not treated as modifications) of an option in any taxable year of the optionee which begins after December 31, 1963, except that section 425(h)(1) and this paragraph shall not apply to any change made before January 1, 1965, in the terms of an option granted after December 31, 1963, to permit such option to meet the requirements of section 422(b)(3), (4), or (5), and the regulations thereunder. See paragraphs (d), (e), and (f), of § 1.422-2, relating to period for exercising options, option price, and prior outstanding options, respectively, in the case of qualified stock options. In addition, section 425(h)(1) and this paragraph shall not apply to any change made after August 13, 1981, and before August 14, 1982, in the terms of an option granted after December 31, 1975, and outstanding on August 13, 1981, necessary to permit such option to meet the requirements of section 422A and the regulations thereunder. See § 1.422A-3 for special rules relating to the conversion of existing options into incentive stock options.

* * * * *

*(5)* (i) The time or date when an option is modified, extended, or renewed shall be determined, insofar as applicable, in accordance with the rules governing determination of the time or date of granting an option provided in paragraph (c) of § 1.421-7. For purposes of sections 421 through 425, the term "modification" means any change in the terms of the option (or change in the terms of the plan pursuant to which the option was granted) which gives the optionee additional benefits under the option regardless of whether the optionee in fact benefits from the change in the terms. For example, a change in the terms of the option, which shortens the period during which the option is exercisable, is not a modification. However, any one of the following changes is a modification: A change which provides more favorable terms for payment for the stock purchased under the option, such as the right to tender previously acquired stock; a change which provides an extension of the period during which an option may be exercised, such as after termination of employment; a change which provides an additional benefit upon exercise of the option, such as the payment of a cash bonus; and a change which provides an alternatives to the exercise of the option, such as a stock appreciation right. Finally, a change which provides, either by its terms or in substance, that the optionee may receive an additional benefit under the option at the future discretion of the grantor, is a modification both at the time the option is changed and at the time the benefit is actually granted. Where an option is amended solely to increase the number of shares subject to the option, such increase shall not be considered as a modification of the option, but shall be treated as the grant of a new option for the additional shares.

* * * * *

(iii) Any change in the terms of an option for the purpose of qualifying the option as a statutory option grants additional benefits and, therefore, is a modification. However, if the terms of an option are changed to provide that the optionee cannot transfer the option except by will or by the laws of descent and distribution in order to meet the requirements of section 422(b)(6), 422A(b)(5), 423(b)(9), or 424(b)(2), such change is not a modification, provided that in any case where the purpose of the change is to meet the requirements of section 424(b)(2) the option is at the same time changed so that it is not exercisable after the expiration of ten years from the date the option was granted. Where an option is not immediately exercisable in full, a change in the terms of such option to accelerate the time at which the option (or any portion thereof) may be exercised is not a modification for purposes of section 425(h) and this section. A modification results where an option is revised to insert the language required by section 422(c)(6)(B).

* * * * *

*(6)* A statutory option may, as a result of a modification, extension, or renewal, thereafter cease to be a statutory option, or any option may, by modification, extension, or renewal, thereafter become a statutory option. Moreover, a qualified option after a modification may not be exercisable in accordance with its terms because of the requirements of section 422(b)(5) and section 422(c)(6). See paragraph (f)(3)(i) of § 1.422-2 and examples (8) and (9) of paragraph (f)(4) of § 1.422-2. Similarly, an incentive stock option after a modification may not be exercisable in accordance with its terms because of section 422A(b)(7). See paragraph (f)(3) of § 1.422A-2 and example (6) of paragraph (f)(4) of § 1.422A-2.

* * * * *

**Proposed § 1.430(a)-1 Determination of minimum required contribution.** [*For Preamble, see ¶ 152,985*]

***Caution:*** The Treasury has not yet amended Reg § 1.430(a)-1 to reflect changes made by P.L. 111-192.

**(a) In general.** *(1) Overview.* This section sets forth rules for determining a plan's minimum required contribution for a plan year under section 430(a). Section 430 and this section apply to single employer defined benefit plans (including multiple employer plans as defined in section 413(c)) that are subject to section 412 but do not apply to multiemployer plans (as defined in section 414(f)). Paragraph (b) of this section defines a plan's minimum required contribution for a plan year. Paragraph (c) of this section provides rules for determining shortfall amortization installments. Paragraph (d) of this section provides rules for determining waiver amortization installments. Paragraph (e) of this section provides for early deemed amortization of shortfall and waiver amortization bases for fully funded plans. Paragraph (f) of this section provides definitions that apply for purposes of this section. Paragraph (g) of this section provides examples that illustrate the application of this section. Paragraph (h) of this section provides effective/applicability dates and transition rules.

*(2) Special rules for multiple employer plans.* In the case of a multiple employer plan to which section 413(c)(4)(A) applies, the rules of section 430 and this section are applied separately for each employer under the plan, as if each employer maintained a separate plan. Thus, the minimum required contribution is computed separately for each employer under such a multiple employer plan. In the case of a multiple employer plan to which section 413(c)(4)(A) does not apply (that is, a plan described in section 413(c)(4)(B) that has not made the election for section 413(c)(4)(A) to apply), the rules of section 430 and this section are applied as if all participants in the plan were employed by a single employer.

**(b) Definition of minimum required contribution.** *(1) In general.* In the case of a defined benefit plan that is not a multiemployer plan (within the meaning of section 414(f)), except as offset under section 430(f) and § 1.430(f)-1, the minimum required contribution for a plan year is determined as the applicable amount determined under paragraph (b)(2) of this section or paragraph (b)(3) of this section, reduced by the amount of any funding waiver under section 412(c) that is granted for the plan year. See paragraph (b)(4) of this section for special rules for a plan maintained by a commercial passenger airline (or other eligible employer) for which an election under section 402 of the Pension Protection Act of 2006, Public Law 109-280 (120 Stat. 780) (PPA '06), has been made, and see section 430(j) and § 1.430(j)-1 for rules regarding the required interest adjustment for a contribution that is paid on a date other than the valuation date for the plan year.

*(2) Plan assets less than funding target.* (i) General rule. For any plan year in which the value of plan assets of the plan (as reduced to reflect the subtraction of certain funding balances as provided under § 1.430(f)-1(c), but not below zero) is less than the funding target of the plan for the plan year, the minimum required contribution for that plan year is equal to the sum of—

(A) The target normal cost of the plan for the plan year;

(B) The total (not less than zero) of the shortfall amortization installments determined with respect to the shortfall amortization bases for the plan year and each of the 6 preceding plan years as described in paragraph (c) of this section; and

(C) The total of the waiver amortization installments determined with respect to the waiver amortization bases for each of the 5 preceding plan years as described in paragraph (d) of this section.

(ii) Special rule for short plan years. (A) Proration of amortization installments. In determining the minimum required contribution in the case of a plan year that is shorter than 12 months (and is not a 52-week plan year of a plan that uses a 52-53 week plan year), the shortfall amortization installments and waiver amortization installments that are taken into account under paragraphs (b)(2)(i)(B) and (C) of this section are determined by multiplying the amount of those installments that would be taken into account for a 12-month plan year by a fraction, the numerator of which is the duration of the short plan year and the denominator of which is 1 year.

(B) Effect on subsequent years. In plan years after the short plan year, installments with respect to a shortfall amortization base (or waiver amortization base) continue to be taken into account under paragraphs (b)(2)(i)(B) and (C) of this section until the total amount of those installments, as originally determined to be paid over 7 years (or 5 years in the case of waiver amortization installments), has been taken into account. Thus, for example, in the case of a plan that has a short plan year, an additional partial installment will be taken into account under paragraphs (b)(2)(i)(B) and (C) of this section during the plan year after the end of the original amortization period in an amount determined so that the total of the amortization installments (including the prorated installment payable for the short plan year and the additional partial installment) is equal to the total amount of the amortization installments as originally determined. Similarly, in the case of a plan that has a short plan year, the total number of plan years required to take into account the full amount of installments will exceed 7 plan years (or 5 plan years in the case of waiver amortization installments), and, accordingly, the number of preceding plan years taken into account in paragraphs (b)(2)(i)(B) and (C) of this section is correspondingly increased so that the total amount of the amortization installments as originally determined is taken into account. In addition, for plan years beginning after the close of the short plan year, the shortfall amortization installments and waiver amortization installments that are taken into account under paragraphs (b)(2)(i)(B) and (C) of this section are assumed to be paid on the valuation date for the new plan year (rather than on the valuation date for the short plan year and preceding plan years).

*(3) Plan assets equal or exceed funding target.* For any plan year in which the value of plan assets (as reduced to reflect the subtraction of certain funding balances as provided under § 1.430(f)-1(c), but not below zero) equals or exceeds the funding target of the plan for the plan year, the minimum required contribution for that plan year is equal to the target normal cost of the plan for the plan year reduced (but not below zero) by that excess.

*(4) Special rules for commercial passenger airlines.* (i) In general. This paragraph (b)(4) provides special rules for a plan maintained by a commercial passenger airline (or an employer whose principal business is providing catering services to a commercial passenger airline) for which an election under section 402 of PPA '06 has been made.

(ii) Frozen plans. (A) Determinations during 17-year amortization period. If an election described in section 402(a)(1) of PPA '06 applies for the plan year with respect to an eligible plan described in section 402(c)(1) of PPA '06, then the plan's minimum required contribution for purposes of section 430 of the Code for the plan year is equal to the amount necessary to amortize (at an interest rate of 8.85 percent) the unfunded liability of the plan in equal installments over the remaining amortization period. For this purpose, the unfunded liability means the excess of the accrued liability under the plan determined using the unit credit funding method and an interest rate of 8.85 percent over the fair market value of assets, and the remaining amortization period is the 17-plan-year period beginning with the first plan year for which the election was made, reduced by 1 year for each plan year after the first plan year for which the election was made. In addition, the section 430(f)(3) election to apply funding balances against the minimum required contribution does not apply to a plan to which the election described in section 402(a)(1) of PPA '06 applies for the plan year.

(B) Determinations following 17-year amortization period. If an election described in section 402(a)(1) of PPA '06 applied to the plan for any preceding plan year but does not apply for the current plan year, then the plan's minimum required contribution for purposes of section 430 of the Code for the plan year is determined without regard to that election. For the first plan year for which that election no longer applies to the plan, any prefunding balance or funding standard carryover balance is reduced to zero.

(iii) Other plans of commercial passenger airlines. If an election described in section 402(a)(2) of PPA '06 has been made for an eligible plan described in section 402(c)(1) of PPA '06, then the minimum required contribution for purposes of section 430 is determined under generally applicable rules, except that the shortfall amortization base for the first plan year for which section 430 applies to the plan is amortized over 10 years (rather than over 7 years as provided in paragraph (c)(1) of this section) in accordance with § 1.430(h)(2)-1(e) and (f) using the interest rates that apply for the first plan year for which section 430 applies to the plan. In such a case, the shortfall amortization installments with respect to the shortfall amortization base for that plan year will continue to be included in determining the minimum required contribution for 10 years rather than 7 years. See also § 1.430(h)(2)-1(b)(6) for a special rule for determining the funding target in the case of a plan for which an election under section 402(a)(2) of PPA '06 has been made.

**(c) Shortfall amortization installments.** *(1) In general.* For purposes of this section, the shortfall amortization installments with respect to a shortfall amortization base established for a plan year are the annual amounts necessary to amortize that shortfall amortization base in level annual installments over the 7-year period beginning with that plan year. See § 1.430(h)(2)-1(e) and (f) for rules regarding interest rates used for determining shortfall amortization installments and the date within each plan year on which the installments are assumed to be paid. The shortfall amortization installments are determined using the interest rates that apply for the plan year for which the shortfall amortization base is established and are not redetermined in subsequent plan years to reflect changes in interest rates under section 430(h)(2) for those subsequent plan years. *(2) Shortfall amortization base.* (i) In general. For purposes of this section, unless the value of plan assets (as reduced to reflect the subtraction of certain funding balances as provided under § 1.430(f)-1(c)(2), but not below zero) is equal to or greater than the funding target of the plan for the plan year, a shortfall amortization base is established for the plan year equal to—

(A) The funding shortfall of the plan for the plan year; minus

(B) The amount attributable to future installments determined under paragraph (c)(2)(ii) of this section.

(ii) Amount attributable to future installments. The amount attributable to future installments is equal to the sum of the present values (determined in accordance with § 1.430(h)(2)-1(e) and (f) using the interest rates that apply for the current plan year) of—

(A) The shortfall amortization installments that have been determined for the plan year and any succeeding plan year with respect to the shortfall amortization bases of the plan for any plan year preceding the plan year; and

(B) The waiver amortization installments that have been determined for the plan year and any succeeding plan year with respect to the waiver amortization bases of the plan for any plan year preceding the plan year.

(iii) Transition rule. See paragraph (h)(4) of this section for a transition rule under which only a portion of the funding target is taken into account in determining whether a shortfall amortization base is established under this paragraph (c)(2).

**(d) Waiver amortization installments.** *(1) In general.* For purposes of this section, the waiver amortization installments with respect to a waiver amortization base established for a plan year are the annual amounts necessary to amortize that waiver amortization base in level annual installments over the 5-year period beginning with the following plan year. See § 1.430(h)(2)-1(e) and (f) for rules regarding interest rates used for determining waiver amortization installments and the date within each plan year on which the installments are assumed to be paid. The waiver amortization installments established with respect to a waiver amortization base are determined using the interest rates that apply for the plan year for which the waiver is granted (even though the first installment with respect to the waiver amortization base is not due until the subsequent plan year) and are not redetermined in subsequent plan years to reflect changes in interest rates under section 430(h)(2) for those subsequent plan years.

*(2) Waiver amortization base.* (i) In general. For purposes of this section, a waiver amortization base is established for each plan year for which a waiver of the minimum funding standard has been granted in accordance with section 412(c). The amount of the waiver amortization base is equal to the amount of the minimum required contribution waived (or the waived funding deficiency) for the plan year.

(ii) Transition rule. See paragraph (h)(3) of this section for the treatment of funding waivers granted for plan years beginning before 2008.

**(e) Early deemed amortization upon attainment of funding target.** In any case in which the funding shortfall of a plan for a plan year is zero—

*(1)* The shortfall amortization bases for all preceding plan years (and all shortfall amortization installments determined with respect to those shortfall amortization bases) are reduced to zero; and

*(2)* The waiver amortization bases for all preceding plan years (and all waiver amortization installments determined with respect to such bases) are reduced to zero.

**(f) Definitions.** *(1) In general.* The definitions set forth in this paragraph (f) apply for purposes of this section.

*(2) Funding shortfall.* The term funding shortfall means the excess (if any) of—

(i) The funding target of the plan for a plan year; over

(ii) The value of plan assets for the plan year (as reduced to reflect the subtraction of the funding standard carryover balance and prefunding balance to the extent provided under § 1.430(f)-1(c), but not below zero).

*(3) Funding target.* The term funding target means the plan's funding target for a plan year determined under § 1.430(d)-1(b)(2), § 1.430(i)-1(c), or § 1.430(i)-1(e)(1), whichever applies to the plan for the plan year.

*(4) Target normal cost.* The term target normal cost means the plan's target normal cost for a plan year determined under § 1.430(d)-1(b)(1), § 1.430(i)-1(d), or § 1.430(i)-1(e)(2), whichever applies to the plan for the plan year.

**(g) Examples.** The following examples illustrate the rules of this section. Unless otherwise indicated, these examples are based on the following assumptions: the plan is subject to section 430 starting in 2008; the plan year is the calendar year; the valuation date is January 1; and the plan's funding standard carryover balance is $0.

*Example (1).* (i) Plan A has a funding target of $2,500,000 and assets totaling $1,800,000 as of January 1, 2008. The 2008 actuarial valuation is performed using the 24-month average segment rates applicable for September 2007 (determined without regard to the transitional rule of section 430(h)(2)(G)).

(ii) A $700,000 shortfall amortization base is established for 2008, which is equal to the $2,500,000 funding target less $1,800,000 of assets.

(iii) With respect to this shortfall amortization base of $700,000, there is a shortfall amortization installment of $116,852 (which is equal to the $700,000 shortfall amortization base amortized over 7 years) for each year from 2008 through 2014. The amount of this shortfall amortization installment is determined by discounting the first five installments using the first segment interest rate of 5.26%, and by discounting the sixth and seventh installments using the second segment rate of 5.82%.

*Example (2).* (i) The facts are the same as in Example 1, except that the plan was granted a funding waiver of $300,000 in 2006, as of December 31, 2006. The valuation interest rate for the January 1, 2007, actuarial valuation is 8.50% (which exceeds 150% of the applicable federal mid-term rate).

(ii) The waiver amortization installment for the plan year beginning January 1, 2007, is $70,166, which is equal to the $300,000 funding waiver base amortized over 5 years at the valuation interest rate of 8.50%.

(iii) As of January 1, 2008, the present value of the remaining waiver amortization installments is $260,318, which is determined by discounting the remaining four waiver amortization installments of $70,166 to January 1, 2008, using the first segment rate of 5.26%. See paragraph (h)(3) of this section.

(iv) A $439,682 shortfall amortization base is established for 2008, which is equal to the $2,500,000 funding target, less $1,800,000 of assets, less $260,318 (which is the present value of the remaining waiver amortization installments).

(v) With respect to this shortfall amortization base of $439,682, there is a shortfall amortization installment of $73,397 (which is equal to the $439,682 shortfall amortization base amortized over 7 years) for each year from 2008 through 2014.

*Example (3).* (i) The facts are the same as in Example 2. Plan A has a $100,000 target normal cost for the 2008 plan year and was granted a funding waiver for 2008 to the largest extent permitted under section 412(c).

(ii) The minimum required contribution is $243,563 as of January 1, 2008. This is equal to the $100,000 target normal cost, plus the $70,166 waiver amortization installment from the 2006 waiver, plus the $73,397 January 1, 2008, shortfall amortization installment.

(iii) In accordance with section 412(c)(1)(C), the portion of the minimum required contribution attributable to the amortization of the 2006 funding waiver cannot be waived. Therefore, the maximum amount of the January 1, 2008, minimum required contribution that can be waived is $173,397.

(iv) In accordance with paragraph (d) of this section, a waiver amortization base of $173,397 is established as of January 1, 2008, to be amortized over 5 years beginning with the 2009 plan year. Although the waiver amortization installments for the 2008 funding waiver are not included in the minimum required contribution until 2009, the amount of those installments is determined based on the interest rates used for the 2008 plan year.

(v) The waiver amortization installments are calculated using the first segment interest rate of 5.26% for the first four installments (calculated as of January 1, 2009, through January 1, 2012) and the second segment interest rate of 5.82% for the final installment payable as of January 1, 2013. Accordingly, the waiver amortization installments that are payable beginning January 1, 2009, are $40,530 each.

*Example (4).* (i) The facts are the same as in Example 3. As of January 1, 2009, Plan A has a funding target of $2,750,000 and assets totaling $1,900,000. The 2009 actuarial valuation is performed using the 24-month average segment rates applicable for September 2008 (determined without regard to the transitional rule of section 430(h)(2)(G)). For the 2009 plan year, the first segment rate is equal to 5.50%, the second segment rate is equal to 6.00%, and the third segment rate is equal to 6.50%.

(ii) As of January 1, 2009, the present value of the remaining three waiver amortization installments with respect to the 2006 waiver is $199,715, which is determined using the first segment rate of 5.50%.

(iii) As of January 1, 2009, the present value of the remaining five waiver amortization installments with respect to the 2008 waiver is $182,594, which is determined using the first segment rate of 5.50%.

(iv) As of January 1, 2009, the present value of the remaining six shortfall amortization installments with respect to the 2008 shortfall amortization base is $385,511, which is determined using the first segment rate of 5.50% for the first five installments and the second segment rate of 6.00% for the sixth installment.

(v) A shortfall amortization base of $82,180 is established for 2009, which is equal to the $2,750,000 funding target, less $1,900,000 of assets, less $199,715 (the present value of the remaining waiver amortization installments with respect to the 2006 waiver), less $182,594 (the present value of the remaining waiver amortization installments with respect to the 2008 waiver), less $385,511 (the present value of the remaining installments with respect to the 2008 shortfall amortization base).

(vi) With respect to this shortfall amortization base of $82,180, there is a shortfall amortization installment of $13,795 (which is equal to the $82,180 shortfall amortization base amortized over 7 years) for each year from 2009 through 2015.

*Example (5).* (i) The facts are the same as in Example 4, except that Plan A has assets totaling $2,000,000 as of January 1, 2009. Plan A has a target normal cost of $110,000 as of January 1, 2009.

(ii) A shortfall amortization base of -$17,820 is established for 2009, which is equal to the $2,750,000 funding target, less $2,000,000 of assets, less $199,715 (the present value of the remaining installments with respect to the 2006 waiver), less $182,594 (the present value of the remaining installments with respect to the 2008 waiver), less $385,511 (the present value of the remaining installments with respect to the 2008 shortfall amortization base).

(iii) The shortfall amortization installment for the 2009 shortfall amortization base is -$2,991, which is equal to the -$17,820 shortfall amortization base amortized over 7 years. The first five shortfall amortization installments are discounted using the first segment rate of 5.50% and the sixth and seventh shortfall amortization installments are discounted using the second segment rate of 6.00%.

(iv) The minimum required contribution for the 2009 plan year is $291,102. This is equal to the target normal cost of $110,000 plus the shortfall amortization charge of $70,406 (that is, $73,397 minus $2,991) plus the waiver amortization charge of $110,696 (that is, $70,166 plus $40,530).

*Example (6).* (i) The facts are the same as in Example 5, except that Plan A has assets totaling $2,800,000 as of January 1, 2009.

(ii) Because the assets of $2,800,000 exceed the funding target of $2,750,000 as of January 1, 2009, no new shortfall amortization base is established under paragraph (c)(2) of this section.

(iii) Furthermore, under paragraph (e) of this section, all shortfall amortization bases and waiver amortization bases (and all shortfall amortization installments and waiver amortization installments associated with those bases) are reduced to zero as of January 1, 2009.

(iv) The minimum required contribution for the 2009 plan year is $60,000, which is equal to the $110,000 target normal cost less the excess of the assets over the funding target ($2,800,000 minus $2,750,000).

*Example (7).* (i) The actuarial valuation for Plan B as of January 1, 2008, based on a 12-month plan year, determines a target normal cost of $110,000 and a shortfall amortization installment for 2008 of $185,000. The plan year for Plan B is changed to April 1 through March 31, effective April 1, 2008, resulting in a short plan year beginning January 1, 2008, and ending March 31, 2008.

(ii) The target normal cost for the short plan year is redetermined in order to reflect the fact that there is a short plan year. An actuarial valuation shows that the target normal cost is $25,000 for the short plan year based on the accruals for that short plan year (determined in accordance with 29 CFR § 2530.204-2(e)).

(iii) In accordance with paragraph (b)(2)(ii)(A) of this section, the shortfall amortization base is prorated to reflect the three months covered by the short plan year. Accordingly, the shortfall amortization installment for the short plan year is $46,250 (that is, $185,000 multiplied by 3/12).

(iv) The total minimum required contribution for the short plan year (without offset for any carryover balance as of January 1, 2008) is $71,250 (that is, the sum of the target normal cost of $25,000 plus the shortfall amortization installment of $46,250).

*Example (8).* (i) The facts are the same as in Example 7. The first segment rate for the plan year beginning April 1, 2008, is 5.30%, and the second segment rate is 5.80%.

(ii) The present value of the remaining shortfall amortization installments with respect to the January 1, 2008, shortfall amortization base is equal to $1,074,937. This is determined by discounting the remaining installments (6 full-year installments due April 1, 2008 through April 1, 2013, and a final 9-month installment due April 1, 2014) using the first segment rate of 5.30% for the first five installments and the second segment rate of 5.80% for the remaining installments.

**(h) Effective/applicability dates and transition rules.** *(1) In general.* Section 430 generally applies to plan years beginning on or after January 1, 2008. In general, this section applies to plan years beginning on or after January 1, 2009. However, plans are permitted to apply this section in determining the minimum required contribution for plan years beginning in 2008.

*(2) Plans with delayed effective date.* In the case of a plan for which the effective date of section 430 is delayed in accordance with sections 104 through 106 of PPA '06, this section applies to plan years beginning on or after the date section 430 first applies with respect to the plan.

*(3) Treatment of pre-2008 funding waivers.* In the case of a plan that has received a funding waiver under section 412 for a plan year for which section 430 was not yet effective with respect to the plan, the waiver is treated as giving rise to a waiver amortization base and the amortization charges with respect to that funding waiver are treated as waiver amortization installments as described in paragraph (d) of this section. With respect to such a preexisting funding waiver, the amount of the waiver amortization installment is equal to the amortization charge with respect to that waiver determined using the interest rate or rates that applied for the pre-effective plan year.

*(4) Transition rule for determining whether shortfall amortization base is established.* (i) In general. Except as provided in paragraphs (h)(4)(iii) and (iv) of this section, in the case of plan years beginning after 2007 and before 2011, only the applicable percentage of the funding target is taken into account in determining whether a shortfall amortization base is established for the plan year under paragraph (c)(2) of this section.

(ii) Applicable percentage. For purposes of paragraph (h)(4)(i) of this section, the applicable percentage is determined in accordance with the following table:

| Calendar year in which the plan year begins | Applicable percentage |
|---|---|
| 2008 | 92 |
| 2009 | 94 |
| 2010 | 96 |

(iii) Transition rule not available if funding falls below applicable percentage. The transition rule of paragraph (h)(4)(i) of this section does not apply with respect to any plan year beginning after 2008 if a shortfall amortization base was required to be established under paragraph (c)(2) of this section for any preceding year.

(iv) Transition rule not available for new plans or deficit reduction plans. The transition rule of paragraph (h)(4)(i) of this section does not apply to a plan—

(A) That was not in effect for a plan year beginning in 2007; or

(B) That was subject to section 412(l) for the pre-effective plan year, determined after the application of sections 412(l)(6) and (9) (regardless of whether the deficit reduction contribution for the pre-effective plan year was equal to zero).

(v) Pre-effective plan year. For purposes of this section, the pre-effective plan year for a plan is the last plan year beginning before section 430 applies to the plan. Thus, except for plans with a delayed effective date under paragraph (h)(2) of this section, the pre-effective plan year for a plan is the last plan year beginning before January 1, 2008.

**§ 1.430(d)-1 Determination of target normal cost and funding target.**

**(a) In general.** *(1) Overview.* This section sets forth rules for determining a plan's target normal cost and funding target under sections 430(b) and 430(d), including guidance relating to the rules regarding actuarial assumptions under sections 430(h)(1), 430(h)(4), and 430(h)(5). Section 430 and this section apply to single employer defined benefit plans (including multiple employer plans as defined in section 413(c)) that are subject to section 412, but do not apply to multiemployer plans (as defined in section 414(f)). For further guidance on actuarial assumptions, see § 1.430(h)(2)-1 (relating to interest rates) and §§ 1.430(h)(3)-1 and 1.430(h)(3)-2 (relating to mortality tables). See also § 1.430(i)-1 for the determination of the funding target and the target normal cost for a plan that is in at-risk status.

*(2) Organization of regulation.* Paragraph (b) of this section sets forth certain definitions that apply for purposes of section 430. Paragraph (c) of this section provides rules regarding which benefits are taken into account in determining a plan's target normal cost and funding target. Paragraph (d) of this section sets forth the rules regarding the plan provisions that are taken into account in making these determinations, and paragraph (e) of this section provides rules on the plan population that is taken into account for this purpose. Paragraph (f) of this section provides rules relating to the actuarial assumptions and the plan's funding method that are used to determine present values. Paragraph (g) of this section contains effective/ applicability dates and transition rules.

*(3) Special rules for multiple employer plans.* In the case of a multiple employer plan to which section 413(c)(4)(A) applies, the rules of section 430 and this section are applied separately for each employer under the plan, as if each employer maintained a separate plan. Thus, the plan's funding target and target normal cost are computed separately for each employer under such a multiple employer plan. In the case of a multiple employer plan to which section 413(c)(4)(A) does not apply (that is, a plan described in section 413(c)(4)(B) that has not made the election for section 413(c)(4)(A) to apply), the rules of section 430 and this section are applied as if all participants in the plan were employed by a single employer.

**(b) Definitions.** *(1) Target normal cost.* (i) In general. For a plan that is not in at-risk status under section 430(i) for a plan year, subject to the adjustments described in paragraph (b)(1)(iii) of this section, the target normal cost of the plan for the plan year is the present value (determined as of the valuation date) of all benefits under the plan that accrue during, are earned during, or are otherwise allocated to service for the plan year under the applicable rules of this section, including paragraph (c)(1)(ii)(B), (C), or (D) of this section. See § 1.430(i)-1(d) and (e)(2) for the determination of the target normal cost for a plan that is in at-risk status.

(ii) Benefits allocated to a plan year. The benefits that accrue, are earned, or are otherwise allocated to service for the plan year are based on the actual benefits accrued, earned, or otherwise allocated to service for the plan year through the valuation date and benefits expected to accrue, be earned, or be otherwise allocated to service for the plan year for the period from the valuation date through the end of the plan year. The benefits that are allocated to the plan year under the rules of paragraph (c) of this section include any increase in benefits during the plan year that is attributable to increases in compensation for the current plan year even if that increase in benefits is with respect to benefits attributable to service performed in a preceding plan year. In addition, the benefits that are allocated to the plan year under the rules of paragraph (c) of this section include any increase in benefits during the plan year that arises on account of mandatory employee contributions (within the meaning of § 1.411(c)-1(c)(4)) that are made during the plan year.

(iii) Special adjustments— (A) In general. The target normal cost of the plan for the plan year (determined under paragraph (b)(1)(i) of this section) is adjusted (not below zero) by adding the amount of plan-related expenses expected to be paid from plan assets during the plan year and subtracting the amount of mandatory employee contributions (within the meaning of § 1.411(c)-1(c)(4)) that are expected to be made during the plan year.

(B) Plan-related expenses. [Reserved]

*(2) Funding target.* For a plan that is not in at-risk status under section 430(i) for a plan year, the funding target of the plan for the plan year is the present value (determined as of the valuation date) of all benefits under the plan that have been accrued, earned, or otherwise allocated to years of service prior to the first day of the plan year under the applicable rules of this section, including paragraph (c)(1)(ii)(B), (C), or (D) of this section. See § 1.430(i)-1(c) and (e)(1) for the determination of the funding target for a plan that is in at-risk status.

*(3) Funding target attainment percentage.* (i) In general. Except as otherwise provided in this paragraph (b)(3), the funding target attainment percentage of a plan for a plan year is a fraction (expressed as a percentage)—

(A) The numerator of which is the value of plan assets for the plan year (determined under the rules of § 1.430(g)-1) after subtraction of the prefunding balance and the funding standard carryover balance under section 430(f)(4)(B) and § 1.430(f)-1(c); and

(B) The denominator of which is the funding target of the plan for the plan year (determined without regard to the at-risk rules of section 430(i) and § 1.430(i)-1).

(ii) Determination of funding target attainment percentage for plans with delayed effective dates. If section 430 does not apply for purposes of determining the plan's minimum required contribution for a plan year that begins on or after January 1, 2008 (as is the case for a plan described in section 104, 105, or 106 of the Pension Protection Act of 2006 (PPA '06), Public Law 109-280 (120 Stat. 780)), then the funding target attainment percentage is determined for that plan year in accordance with the rules of paragraph (b)(3)(i) of this section in the same manner as for a plan to which section 430 applies to determine the plan's minimum required contribution, except that the value of plan assets that forms the numerator under paragraph (b)(3)(i)(A) of this section is determined without subtraction of the funding standard carryover balance or the credit balance under the funding standard account.

(iii) Special rule for plans with zero funding target. If the funding target of the plan is equal to zero for a plan year, then the funding target attainment percentage under this paragraph (b)(3) is equal to 100 percent for the plan year.

*(4) Present value.* The present value of a benefit (including a portion of a benefit) with respect to a participant that is taken into account under the rules of paragraph (c) of this section is determined as of the valuation date by multiplying the amount of that benefit by the probability that the benefit will be paid at a future date and then discounting the resulting product using the appropriate interest rate under § 1.430(h)(2)-1. The probability that the benefit will be paid with respect to the participant at such future date is determined using the actuarial assumptions that satisfy the standards of paragraph (f) of this section as to the probability of future service, advancement in age, and other events (such as death, disability, termination of employment, and selection of optional form of benefit) that affect whether the participant or beneficiary will be eligible for the benefit and whether the benefit will be paid at that future date.

**(c) Benefits taken into account.** *(1) In general.* (i) Benefits earned or accrued. The benefits taken into account in determining the target normal cost and the funding target under paragraph (b) of this section are all benefits earned or accrued under the plan that have not yet been paid as of the valuation date, including retirement-type and ancillary benefits (within the meaning of § 1.411(d)-3(g)). The benefits taken into account are based on the participant's or beneficiary's status (such as active employee, vested or partially vested terminated employee, or disabled participant) as of the valuation date, and those benefits are allocated to the funding target or the target normal cost under paragraph (c)(1)(ii) of this section.

(ii) Allocation of benefits— (A) In general. To the extent that the amount of a participant's benefit that is expected to be paid is a function of the accrued benefit, the allocation of the benefit for purposes of determining the funding target and the target normal cost is made using the rules of paragraph (c)(1)(ii)(B) of this section. To the extent that the amount of a participant's benefit that is expected to be paid is not a function of the accrued benefit, but is a function of the participant's years of service (or is the excess of a function of the participant's years of service over a function of the participant's accrued benefit), the allocation of the benefit for purposes of determining the funding target and the target normal cost is made using the rules of paragraph (c)(1)(ii)(C) of this section. To the extent that the amount of a participant's benefit that is expected to be paid is not allocated under the rules of paragraph (c)(1)(ii)(B) or (C) of this section, the allocation of the benefit for purposes of determining the funding target and the target normal cost is made using the rules of paragraph (c)(1)(ii)(D) of this section.

(B) Benefits that are based on accrued benefits. If the allocation of the benefit for purposes of determining the funding target and the target normal cost is made under this paragraph (c)(1)(ii)(B), then the portion of a participant's benefit that is taken into account in the funding target for a plan year is determined by applying the function to the accrued benefit as of the first day of the plan year, and the portion of the benefit that is taken into account in determining the target normal cost for the plan year is determined by applying that function to the increase in the accrued benefit during the plan year. For example, a benefit that is assumed to be payable at a particular early retirement age in the amount of 90 percent of the accrued benefit is taken into account in the funding target in the amount of 90 percent of the accrued benefit as of the beginning of the plan year, and that benefit is taken into account in the target normal cost in the amount of 90 percent of the increase in the accrued benefit during the plan year.

(C) Benefits that are based on service. If the allocation of the benefit for purposes of determining the funding target and the target normal cost is made under this paragraph (c)(1)(ii)(C), then the portion of a participant's benefit that is taken into account in determining the funding target for a plan year is determined by applying the function to the participant's years of service as of the first day of the plan year, and the portion of the benefit that is taken into account in determining the target normal cost for the plan year is determined by applying that function to the increase in the participant's years of service during the plan year. For example, if a plan provides a post-retirement death benefit of $500 per year of service, then the funding target is determined based on a death benefit of $500 multiplied by a participant's years of service at the beginning of the year, and if the participant earns or is expected to earn a full year of service during the plan year, the target normal cost is based on the additional $500 in death benefits attributable to that additional year of service.

(D) Other benefits. If the allocation of the benefit for purposes of determining the funding target and the target normal cost is made under this paragraph (c)(1)(ii)(D), then the portion of a participant's benefit that is taken into account in determining the funding target for a plan year is equal to the total benefit multiplied by the ratio of the participant's years of service as of the first day of the plan year to the years of service the participant will have at the time of the event that causes the benefit to be payable (whether the benefit is expected to be paid at the time of that decrement or at a future time), and the portion of the benefit that is taken into account in determining the target normal cost for the plan year is the increase in the proportionate benefit attributable to the increase in the participant's years of service during the plan year. For example, if a plan provides a Social Security supplement for a participant who retires after 30 years of service that is equal to a participant's Social Security benefit, the funding target with respect to the benefit payable beginning at a particular age (which reflects the probability of retirement at that age) is determined based on the projected Social Security benefit payable at the particular age multiplied by a fraction, the numerator of which is the participant's years of service as of the first day of the plan year and the denominator of which is the participant's projected years of service at the particular age. In such a case, if the participant earns or is expected to earn a full year of service during the plan year, the target normal cost is determined based on the projected Social Security benefit payable at the particular age multiplied by a fraction, the numerator of which is one and the denominator of which is the participant's projected years of service at the particular age.

(iii) Application of section 436 limitations to funding target and target normal cost determination— (A) Effect of limitation on unpredictable contingent event benefits. The determination of the funding target and the target normal cost of a plan for a plan year must take into account any limitation on unpredictable contingent event benefits under section 436(b) with respect to unpredictable contingent events which occurred before the valuation date, but must not take into account anticipated funding-based limitations on unpredictable contingent event benefits under section 436(b) with respect to unpredictable contingent events which are expected to occur on or after the valuation date.

(B) Effect of limitation on applicability of plan amendments. See paragraph (d) of this section for rules regarding the treatment of plan amendments that take effect during the plan year taking into account the restrictions under section 436(c).

(C) Effect of limitation on prohibited payments. The determination of the funding target and the target normal cost of a plan for a plan year must take into account any limitation on prohibited payments under section 436(d) with respect to any annuity starting date that was before the valuation date, but must not take into account any limitation on prohibited payments under section 436(d) for any annuity starting date on or after the valuation date (however, the determination must take into account benefit distributions under plan provisions that allow new annuity starting dates with respect to distributions that were limited under section 436(d)).

(D) Effect of limitation on benefit accruals. Except as otherwise provided in this paragraph (c)(1)(iii)(D), the determination of the funding target of a plan for a plan year must take into account any limitation on benefit accruals under section 436(e) applicable before the valuation date. However, if the plan terms provide for the automatic restoration of benefit accruals as permitted under § 1.436-1(a)(4)(ii)(B), and the restoration of benefits as of the valuation date will not be treated as resulting from a plan amendment under the rules of § 1.436-1(c)(3) (because the period of limitation as of the valuation date does not exceed 12 months and the adjusted funding target attainment percentage for the plan would not be less than 60 percent taking into account the restored benefit accruals), then the determination of the funding target of a plan for a plan year must not take into account the limitation on benefit accruals under section 436(e) for that period. The determination of the target normal cost of a plan for a plan year must not take into account any limitation on benefit accruals under section 436(e). Thus, if an employer wishes to take a plan freeze into account in determining the target normal cost, the plan must be specifically amended to cease accruals.

(iv) Effect of other limitations of benefits— (A) Liquidity shortfalls. The determination of the funding target and the target normal cost of a plan for a plan year must take into account any restrictions on payments under section 401(a)(32) on account of a liquidity shortfall (as defined in section 430(j)(4)) for periods preceding the valuation date. The determination of the funding target and the target normal cost must not take into account any restrictions on payments under section 401(a)(32) on account of a liquidity shortfall or possible liquidity shortfall for any period on or after the valuation date.

(B) High 25 limitation. The determination of the funding target and the target normal cost of a plan for a plan year must take into account any restrictions on payments under § 1.401(a)(4)-5(b) to highly compensated employees to the extent that benefits were not paid or will not be paid because of a limitation that applied prior to the valuation date. If a benefit that was otherwise restricted was paid prior to the valuation date but with suitable security (such as an escrow account) provided to the plan in the event of a plan termination, the benefit is treated as distributed for purposes of section 430 and this section. Accordingly, the funding target does not include any liability for the benefit and the plan assets do not include the security. The determination of the funding target and the target normal cost of a plan for a plan year must not take into account any restrictions on payments under § 1.401(a)(4)-5(b) to highly compensated employees that are anticipated with respect to annuity starting dates on or after the valuation date on account of the funded status of the plan.

*(2) Benefits provided by insurance.* (i) General rule. A plan generally is required to reflect in the plan's funding target and target normal cost the liability for benefits that are funded through insurance contracts held by the plan, and to include the corresponding insurance contracts in plan assets. Paragraph (c)(2)(ii) of this section sets forth an alternative to this general approach. A plan's treatment of benefits funded through insurance contracts pursuant to this paragraph (c)(2) is part of the plan's funding method. Accordingly, that treatment can be changed only with the consent of the Commissioner. (ii) Separate funding of insured benefits. As an alternative to the treatment described in paragraph (c)(2)(i) of this section, in the case of benefits that are funded through insurance contracts, the liability for benefits provided under such contracts is permitted to be excluded from the plan's funding target and target normal cost, provided that the corresponding insurance contracts are excluded from plan assets. This treatment is only available with respect to insurance purchased from an insurance company licensed under the laws of a State and only to the extent that a participant's or beneficiary's right to receive those benefits is an irrevocable contractual right under the insurance contracts, based on premiums paid to the insurance company prior to the valuation date. For example, in the case of a retired participant receiving benefits from an annuity contract in pay status under which no premiums are required on or after the valuation date, the liability for benefits provided by the contract is permitted to be excluded from the plan's funding target provided that the value of the contract is also excluded from the value of plan assets. Similarly, in the case of an active or deferred vested participant whose benefits are funded by a life insurance or annuity contract under which further premiums are required on or after the valuation date, the liability for benefits, if any, that would be paid from the contract if no further premiums were to be paid (for example, if the contract were to go on reduced paid-up status) is permitted to be excluded from the plan's funding target and target normal cost, provided that the value of the contract is excluded from the value of plan assets. By contrast, if the plan trustee can surrender a contract to the insurer for its cash value, then the participant's or beneficiary's right to receive those benefits is not an irrevocable contractual right and, therefore, the liability for benefits provided under the contract must be taken into account in determining the plan's funding target and target normal cost and the contracts cannot be excluded from plan assets.

**(c) Plan provisions taken into account.** *(1) General rule.* (i) Plan provisions adopted by valuation date. Except as otherwise provided in this paragraph (d), a plan's funding target and target normal cost for a plan year are determined based on plan provisions that are adopted no later than the valuation date for the plan year and that take effect on or before the last day of the plan year. For example, in the case of a plan amendment adopted on or before the valuation date for the plan year that has an effective date occurring in the current plan year, the plan amendment is taken into account in determining the funding target and the target normal cost for the current plan year if it is permitted to take effect under the rules of section 436(c) for the current plan year, but the amendment is not taken into account for the current plan year if it does not take effect until a future plan year.

(ii) Plan provisions adopted after valuation date. If a plan administrator makes the election described in section 412(d)(2) with respect to a plan amendment, then the plan amendment is treated as having been adopted on the first day of the plan year for purposes of this paragraph (d). Section 412(d)(2) applies to any plan amendment adopted no later than 2½ months after the close of the plan year, including an amendment adopted during the plan year. Thus, if an amendment is adopted after the valuation date for a plan year (and no later than 2½ months after the close of the plan year), but takes effect by the last day of the plan year, the amendment is taken into account in determining the plan's funding target and target normal cost for the plan year if the plan administrator makes the election described in section 412(d)(2) with respect to such amendment.

(iii) Determination of when an amendment takes effect. For purposes of this paragraph (d)(1), the determination of whether an amendment that increases benefits takes effect and when it takes effect is determined in accordance with the rules of section 436(c) and § 1.436-1(c)(5). For purposes of this paragraph (d)(1), in the case of an amendment that decreases benefits, the amendment takes effect under a plan on the first date on which the benefits of any individual who is or could be a participant or beneficiary under the plan would be less than those benefits would be under the pre-amendment plan provisions if the individual were on that date to satisfy the applicable conditions for the benefits. In either case, the determination of when an amendment takes effect is unaffected by an election under section 412(d)(2).

*(2) Special rule for certain amendments increasing liabilities.* In the case of a plan amendment that is not required to be taken into account under the rules of paragraph (d)(1) of this section because it is adopted after the valuation date for the plan year, the plan amendment must be taken into account in determining a plan's funding target and target normal cost for the plan year if the plan amendment—

(i) Takes effect by the last day of the plan year;

(ii) Increases the liabilities of the plan by reason of increases in benefits, establishment of new benefits, changing the rate of benefit accrual, or changing the rate at which benefits become nonforfeitable; and

(iii) Would not be permitted to take effect under the rules of section 436(c) if those rules were applied—

(A) By treating the increase in the target normal cost for the plan year attributable to the amendment (and all other amendments that must be taken into account solely because of the application of the rules in this paragraph (d)(2)) as if the increase were an increase in the funding target for the plan year; and

(B) By taking into account all unpredictable contingent event benefits permitted to be paid for unpredictable contingent events that occurred during the current plan year and all plan amendments that took effect in the current plan year (including all amendments to which this paragraph (d)(2) applies for the plan year).

*(3) Allocation of benefits attributable to plan amendments.* If a plan amendment is taken into account for a plan year under the rules of this paragraph (d), then the allocation of benefits that is used to determine the funding target and the target normal cost for that plan year is based on the plan as amended. Thus, if an amendment that is taken into account for a plan year increases a participant's accrued benefit for service prior to the beginning of the plan year, then the present value of that increase is included in the funding target for the plan year.

**(e) Plan population taken into account.** *(1) In general.* In making any determination of the funding target or target normal cost under paragraph (b) of this section, the plan population is determined as of the valuation date. The plan population must include three classes of individuals— (i) Participants currently employed in the service of the employer;

(ii) Participants who are retired under the plan or who are otherwise no longer employed in the service of the employer; and

(iii) All other individuals currently entitled to benefits under the plan. *(2) Assumption regarding rehiring of former employees.* (i) Special exclusion for "rule of parity" cases. Certain individuals may be excluded from the class of individuals described in paragraph (e)(1)(ii) of this section. The excludable individuals are those former employees who, prior to the valuation date for the plan year, have terminated service with the employer without vested benefits and whose service might be taken into account in future years because the "rule of parity" of section 411(a)(6)(D) does not permit that service to be disregarded. However, if the plan's experience as to separated employees returning to service has been such that the exclusion described in this paragraph (e)(2) would be unreasonable, then no such exclusion is permitted.

(ii) Application to partially vested participants. Whether former employees who are terminated with partially vested benefits are assumed to return to service is determined under the same rules that apply to former employees without vested benefits under paragraph (e)(2)(i) of this section.

*(3)* Anticipated future participants. In making any determination of the funding target or target normal cost under paragraph (b) of this section, the actuarial assumptions and funding method used for the plan must not anticipate the affiliation with the plan of future participants not employed in the service of the employer on the plan's valuation date. However, any such determination may anticipate the affiliation with the plan of current employees who have not yet satisfied the participation (age and service) requirements of the plan as of the valuation date.

**(f) Actuarial assumptions and funding method used in determination of present value.** *(1) Selection of actuarial assumptions and funding method*— (i) General rules. The determination of any present value or other computation under section 430 and this section must be made on the basis of actuarial assumptions and a funding method. Except as otherwise specifically provided (for example, in § 1.430(h)(2)-1(b)(6) or section 4006(a)(3)(E)(iv) of the Employee Retirement Income Security Act of 1974, as amended (ERISA)), the same actuarial assumptions and funding method must be used for all computations under sections 430 and 436. For example, the actuarial assumptions and the funding method used in making a certification of the adjusted funding target attainment percentage for a plan year must be the same as those disclosed on the actuarial report under section 6059 (Schedule SB, "Single-Employer Defined Benefit Plan Actuarial Information" of Form 5500, "Annual Return/Report of Employee Benefit Plan").

(ii) Changes in actuarial assumptions and funding method. Actuarial assumptions established for a plan year cannot subsequently be changed for that plan year unless the Commissioner determines that the assumptions that were used are unreasonable. Similarly, a funding method established for a plan year cannot subsequently be changed for that plan year unless the Commissioner determines that the use of that funding method for that plan year is impermissible.

(iii) Procedures for establishing actuarial assumptions and funding method. For purposes of this paragraph (f)(1), in the case of a plan for which an actuarial report under section 6059 (Schedule SB of Form 5500) is required to be filed for a plan year, actuarial assumptions and the funding method are established by the filing of the actuarial report if it is filed no later than the due date (with extensions) for the report. In the case of a plan for which an actuarial report for a plan year is not required to be filed, actuarial assumptions and the funding method are established by the delivery of the completed report to the employer if it is delivered no later than what would be the due date (with extensions) for filing the actuarial report were such a filing required. If the actuarial report is not filed or delivered by the applicable date described in the two preceding sentences, then the same actuarial assumptions (such as the same interest rate and mortality table elections) and funding method as were used for the preceding plan year apply for all computations under sections 430 and 436 for the current plan year, unless the Commissioner permits or requires other actuarial assumptions or another funding method permitted under section 430 to be used for the current plan year.

(iv) Scope of funding method. A plan's funding method includes not only the overall funding method used by the plan but also each specific method of computation used in applying the overall method. However, the choice of which actuarial assumptions are appropriate to the overall method or to the specific method of computation is not a part of the funding method. The assumed earnings rate used for purposes of determining the actuarial value of assets under section 430(g)(3)(B) is treated as an actuarial assumption, rather than as part of the funding method.

*(2) Interest and mortality rates.* Section 430(h)(2) and § 1.430(h)(2)-1 set forth the interest rates, and section 430(h)(3) and §§ 1.430(h)(3)-1 and 1.430(h)(3)-2 set forth the mortality tables, that must be used for purposes of determining any present value under this section. However, notwithstanding the requirement to use the mortality tables, in the case of a plan which has fewer than 100 participants and beneficiaries who are not in pay status, the actuarial assumptions may assume no pre-retirement mortality, but only if that assumption would be a reasonable assumption.

*(3) Other assumptions.* In the case of actuarial assumptions other than those specified in sections 430(h)(2), 430(h)(3), and 430(i), each of those actuarial assumptions must be reasonable (taking into account the experience of the plan and reasonable expectations). In addition, the actuarial assumptions (other than those specified in sections 430(h)(2), 430(h)(3), and 430(i)) must, in combination, offer the plan's enrolled actuary's best estimate of anticipated experience under the plan based on information determined as of the valuation date. See paragraph (f)(4)(iii) of this section for special rules for determining the present value of a single-sum and similar distributions.

*(4) Probability of benefit payments in single sum or other optional forms* (i) In general. This paragraph (f)(4) provides rules relating to the probability that benefit payments will be paid as single sums or other optional forms under a plan and the impact of that probability on the determination of the present value of those benefit payments under section 430.

(ii) General rules of application. Any determination of present value or any other computation under this section must take into account—

(A) The probability that future benefit payments under the plan will be made in the form of any optional form of benefit provided under the plan (including single-sum distributions), determined on the basis of the plan's experience and other related assumptions, in accordance with paragraph (f)(3) of this section; and

(B) Any difference in the present value of future benefit payments that results from the use of actuarial assumptions in determining the amount of benefit payments in any such optional form of benefit that are different from those prescribed by section 430(h).

(iii) Single-sum and similar distributions— (A) Distributions using section 417(e) assumptions. In the case of a distribution that is subject to section 417(e)(3) and that is determined using the applicable interest rates and applicable mortality table under section 417(e)(3), for purposes of applying paragraph (f)(4)(ii) of this section, the computation of the present value of that distribution is treated as having taken into account any difference in present value that results from the use of actuarial assumptions that are different from those prescribed by section 430(h) (as required under paragraph (f)(4)(ii)(B) of this section) if and only if the present value of the distribution is determined in accordance with this paragraph (f)(4)(iii).

(B) Substitution of annuity form. Except as otherwise provided in this paragraph (f)(4)(iii), the present value of a distribution is determined in accordance with this paragraph (f)(4)(iii) if that present value is determined as the present value, using special actuarial assumptions, of the annuity (either the deferred or immediate annuity) which is used under the plan to determine the amount of the distribution. Under these special assumptions, for the period beginning with the expected annuity starting date for the distribution, the current applicable mortality table under section 417(e)(3) that would apply to a distribution with an annuity starting date occurring on the valuation date is substituted for the mortality table under section 430(h)(3) that would otherwise be used. In addition, under these special assumptions, the valuation interest rates under section 430(h)(2) are used for purposes of discounting the projected annuity payments from their expected payment dates to the valuation date (as opposed to the interest rates under section 417(e)(3) which the plan uses to determine the amount of the benefit).

(C) Optional application of generational mortality and phase-in of interest rates. In determining the present value of a distribution under this paragraph (f)(4)(iii), if a plan uses the generational mortality tables under § 1.430(h)(3)-1(a)(4) or § 1.430(h)(3)-2, the plan is permitted to use a 50-50 male-female blend of the annuitant mortality rates under the § 1.430(h)(3)-1(a)(4) generational mortality tables in lieu of the applicable mortality table under section 417(e)(3) that would apply to a distribution with an annuity starting date occurring on the valuation date. Similarly, a plan is permitted to make adjustments to the interest rates in order to reflect differences between the phase-in of the section 430(h)(2) segment rates under section 430(h)(2)(G) and the adjustments to the segment rates under section 417(e)(3)(D)(iii).

(D) Distributions subject to section 417(e)(3) using other assumptions. In the case of a distribution that is subject to section 417(e)(3) but that is determined on a basis other than using the applicable interest rates and the applicable mortality table under section 417(e)(3), for purposes of applying paragraph (f)(4)(ii)(B) of this section, the computation of present value must take into account the extent to which the present value of the distribution is different from the present value determined using the rules of paragraph (f)(4)(iii)(B) of this section, based on actuarial assumptions that satisfy the requirements of paragraph (f)(3) of this section. If the plan provides that the amount of the benefit is based on a comparison of the section 417(e)(3) benefit (that is, the benefit determined using the applicable interest rates and the applicable mortality table under section 417(e)(3)) with another benefit determined using some other basis, then paragraph (f)(4)(ii)(B) of this section is applied as of the valuation date by comparing the present value of the section 417(e)(3) benefit determined under the rules of paragraph (f)(4)(iii)(B) of this section with the present value of the other benefit. The rule of this paragraph (f)(4)(iii)(D) applies, for example, where a distribution that is subject to section 417(e)(3) is determined as the greater of the benefit determined using the applicable interest rates and the applicable mortality table under section 417(e)(3) and the benefit determined using some other basis, or where the amount of a distribution that is subject to section 417(e)(3) is determined using an interest rate other than the applicable interest rates as required under section 415(b)(2)(E)(ii) (see § 1.417(e)-1(d)(1)).

*(5) Distributions from applicable defined benefit plans under section 411(a)(13)(C).* (i) In general. In the case of an applicable defined benefit plan described in section 411(a)(13)(C), if the amount of a future distribution is based on an interest adjustment applied to the current accumulated benefit, then the amount of that distribution is determined by projecting the future interest credits or equivalent amount under the plan's interest crediting rules using actuarial assumptions that satisfy the requirements of paragraph (f)(3) of this section. Thus, if a plan provides for a single-sum distribution equal to the balance of a participant's hypothetical account under a cash balance plan, then the amount of that future distribution is equal to the projected account balance at the expected date of payment determined using actuarial assumptions that satisfy the requirements of paragraph (f)(3) of this section.

(ii) Annuity distributions— (A) General rule. In the case of an applicable defined benefit plan described in section 411(a)(13)(C), if the amount of an annuity distribution is based on either the balance of a hypothetical account maintained for a participant or the accumulated percentage of a participant's final average compensation, then the amount of that annuity distribution is calculated by converting the projected account balance (or accumulated percentage of final average compensation), in accordance with paragraph (f)(5)(i) of this section, to an annuity by applying the plan's annuity conversion provisions using the rules of this paragraph (f)(5)(ii).

(B) Use of current annuity factors. Except as otherwise provided in paragraph (f)(5)(ii)(C) of this section, if the plan bases the conversion of the projected account balance (or accumulated percentage of final average compensation) to an annuity using the applicable interest rates and applicable mortality table under section 417(e)(3), then the amount of the annuity distribution is determined by dividing the projected account balance (or accumulated percentage of final average compensation) by an annuity factor corresponding to the assumed form of payment using, for the period beginning with the annuity starting date, the current applicable mortality table under section 417(e)(3) that would apply to a distribution with an annuity starting date occurring on the valuation date (in lieu of the mortality table under section 430(h)(3) that would otherwise be used) and the valuation interest rates under section 430(h)(2) (as opposed to the interest rates under section 417(e)(3) which the plan uses to determine the amount of the annuity).

(C) Optional application of generational mortality and phase-in of segment rates. In determining the amount of an annuity distribution under paragraph (f)(5)(ii)(B) of this section, a plan is permitted to apply the options described in paragraph (f)(4)(iii)(C) of this section.

(D) Distributions using assumptions other than assumptions under section 417(e)(3). In applying this paragraph (f)(5)(ii), in the case of a plan that determines an annuity using a basis other than the applicable interest rates and applicable mortality table under section 417(e)(3), the amount of the annuity distribution must be based on actuarial assumptions that satisfy the requirements of paragraph (f)(3) of this section.

*(6) Unpredictable contingent event benefits.* Any determination of present value or any other computation under this section must take into account, based on information as of the valuation date, the probability that future benefits (or increased benefits) will become payable under the plan due to the occurrence of an unpredictable contingent event (as described in § 1.436-1(j)(9)). For this purpose, this probability with respect to an unpredictable contingent event may be assumed to be zero if there is not more than a de minimis likelihood that the unpredictable contingent event will occur.

*(7) Reasonable techniques permitted.* (i) Determination of benefits to be paid during the plan year. Any reasonable technique can be used to determine the present value of the benefits expected to be paid during a plan year, based on the interest rates and mortality assumptions applicable for the plan year. For example, the present value of a monthly retirement annuity payable at the beginning of each month can be determined—

(A) Using the standard actuarial approximation that reflects 13/ 24ths of the discounted expected payments for the year as of the beginning of the year and 11/24ths of the discounted expected payments for the year as of the end of the year;

(B) By assuming a uniform distribution of death during the year; or

(C) By assuming that the payment is made in the middle of the year.

(ii) Determination of target normal cost. In the case of a participant for whom there is a less than 100 percent probability that the participant will terminate employment during the plan year, for purposes of determining the benefits expected to accrue, be earned, or otherwise allocated to service during the plan year which are used to determine the target normal cost, it is permissible to assume the participant will not terminate during the plan year, unless using this method of calculation would be unreasonable.

*(8) Approval of significant changes in actuarial assumptions for large plans.*

(i) In general. Except as otherwise provided in paragraph (f)(8)(iii) of this section, any actuarial assumptions used to determine the funding target of a plan for a plan year during which the plan is described in paragraph (f)(8)(ii) of this section cannot be changed from the actuarial assumptions that were used for the preceding plan year without the approval of the Commissioner if the changes in assumptions result in a decrease in the plan's funding shortfall (within the meaning of section 430(c)(4)) for the current plan year (disregarding the effect on the plan's funding shortfall resulting from changes in interest and mortality assumptions under sections 430(h)(2) and (h)(3)) that either exceeds $50,000,000, or exceeds $5,000,000 and is 5 percent or more of the funding target of the plan before such change.

(ii) Affected plans. A plan is described in this paragraph (f)(8)(ii) for a plan year if—

(A) The plan is a defined benefit plan (other than a multiemployer plan) to which Title IV of ERISA applies; and

(B) The aggregate unfunded vested benefits used to determine variable-rate premiums for the plan year (as determined under section 4006(a)(3)(E)(iii) of ERISA) of the plan and all other plans maintained by the contributing sponsors (as defined in section 4001(a)(13) of ERISA) and members of such sponsors' controlled groups (as defined in section 4001(a)(14) of ERISA) which are covered by Title IV of ERISA (disregarding multiemployer plans and disregarding plans with no unfunded vested benefits) exceed $50,000,000.

(iii) Automatic approval to resume use of previously used assumptions upon exiting at-risk status during phase-in. A plan that is not in at-risk status for the current plan year and that was in at-risk status for the prior plan year (but not for a period of 5 or more consecutive plan years) is granted automatic approval to use the actuarial assumptions that were applied before the plan entered at-risk status and that were used in combination with the required at-risk assumptions during the period the plan was in at-risk status.

*(9)* Examples. The following examples illustrate the rules of this section. Unless otherwise indicated, these examples are based on the following assumptions: The normal retirement age is 65, the minimum required contribution for the plan is determined under the rules of section 430 starting in 2008, the plan year is the calendar year, the valuation date is January 1, no plan-related expenses are paid or expected to be paid from plan assets, and the plan does not provide for mandatory employee contributions. The examples are as follows:

*Example (1).* (i) Plan P provides an accrued benefit equal to 1.0% of a participant's highest 3-year average compensation for each year of service. Plan P provides that an early retirement benefit can be received at age 60 equal to the participant's accrued benefit reduced by 0.5% per month for early commencement. On January 1, 2010, Participant A is age 60 and has 12 years of past service. Participant A's compensation for the years 2007 through 2009 was $47,000, $50,000, and $52,000, respectively. Participant A's rate of compensation at December 31, 2009, is $54,000 and A's rate of compensation for 2010 is assumed not to increase at any point during 2010. Decrements are applied at the beginning of the plan year.

(ii) Participant A's annual accrued benefit as of January 1, 2010, is $5,960 [0.01 x 12 x ($47,000 + $50,000 + $52,000) / 3]. Participant A's expected benefit accrual for 2010 is $800 [0.01 x 13 x ($50,000 + $52,000 + $54,000) / 3 - $5,960], to the extent that Participant A is expected to continue in employment for the full 2010 plan year.

(iii) Because the early retirement benefit is a function of the participant's accrued benefit, the allocation of the benefit for purposes of determining the target normal cost and funding target is made under paragraph (c)(1)(ii)(B) of this section. Accordingly, for Participant A, the early retirement benefit that is taken into account with respect to the decrement at age 60 when determining the 2010 funding target is $4,172 [$5,960 accrued benefit x (1 - 0.005 x 60 months)]. The expected accrual of the early retirement benefit during 2010 that is taken into account for Participant A with respect to the decrement at age 60 when determining the 2010 target normal cost is zero, because in this example the age-60 decrement would be applied as of January 1, 2010, before Participant A would earn any additional benefits. (But see paragraph (f)(7)(ii) of this section for an alternative approach for determining the expected accrual with respect to the decrement at age 60.)

(iv) The early retirement benefit for Participant A with respect to the decrement at age 61 that is taken into account in determining the funding target for the 2010 plan year is $4,529.60 [$5,960 accrued benefit x (1 - 0.005 x 48 months)]. The portion of the early retirement benefit that is taken into account for Participant A with respect to the decrement at age 61 that is taken into account in determining the target normal cost for the 2010 plan year is $608 [$800 expected annual accrual x (1 - 0.005 x 48 months)].

*Example (2).* (i) The facts are the same as in Example 1. In addition, the plan offers a $500 temporary monthly supplement to participants who complete 15 years of service and retire from active employment after attaining age 60. The temporary supplement is payable until the participant turns age 62. In addition, the supplement is limited so that it does not exceed the participant's Social Security benefit payable at age 62. On January 1, 2010, Participant B is age 55 and has 20 years of past service, and Participant C is age 60 and has 14 years of past service. For Participants B and C, the projected Social Security benefit is greater than $500 per month.

(ii) Because the temporary supplement is not a function of the participant's accrued benefit or service, the allocation of the benefit for purposes of determining the target normal cost and funding target is made under paragraph (c)(1)(ii)(D) of this section. The portion of the annual temporary supplement for Participant B with respect to the early retirement decrement occurring at age 60 that is taken into account in determining the funding target for the 2010 plan year is $4,800 [($500 x 12 months) x 20 years of past service / 25 years of service at assumed early retirement age]. The portion of the annual temporary supplement for Participant B with respect to the early retirement decrement occurring at age 61 that is taken into account in determining the funding target for the 2010 plan year is $4,615 [($500 x 12 months) x 20 years of past service / 26 years of service at assumed early retirement age]. In each case, the allocable portion of the benefit is assumed to be payable until age 62 (or the participant's death, if earlier).

(iii) For Participant B, the portion of the annual temporary supplement with respect to the early retirement decrement occurring at age 60 that is taken into account in determining the target normal cost for the 2010 plan year is $240 [($500 x 12 months) x 1 year of service expected to be earned during the plan year / 25 years of service at assumed early retirement age]. The portion of the annual temporary supplement with respect to the early retirement decrement occurring at age 61 that is taken into account in determining the target normal cost for the 2010 plan year is $230.77 [($500 x 12 months) x 1 year of service expected to be earned during the plan year / 26 years of service at assumed early retirement age]. The present value of these amounts reflects a payment period beginning with the decrement at age 60 or 61, as applicable, until age 62 (or assumed death, if earlier).

(iv) For Participant C, the portion of the annual temporary supplement with respect to the early retirement decrement occurring at age 61 (when the participant is first eligible for the benefit) that is taken into account in determining the funding target for the 2010 plan year is $5,600 [($500 x 12 months) x 14 years of past service / 15 years of service at assumed early retirement age]. The present value of this amount reflects a payment period beginning with the decrement at age 61 until age 62 (or death if earlier).

*Example (3).* (i) The facts are the same as in Example 1. The plan also provides a single-sum death benefit (in addition to the qualified pre-retirement spouse's benefit) equal to the greater of the participant's annual accrued benefit at the time of death, or $10,000. The benefit is limited as necessary to ensure that the plan meets the incidental death benefit requirements of section 401(a).

(ii) The determination of the portion of the death benefit that is taken into account in determining the target normal cost and funding target is made under paragraph (c)(1)(ii)(B) of this section to the extent that it is a function of the participant's accrued benefit and under paragraph (c)(1)(ii)(D) of this section to the extent that it relates to the part of the death benefit that is not a function of the participant's accrued benefit.

(iii) The portion of the single-sum death benefit corresponding to the accrued benefit, or $5,960, is taken into account when determining the 2010 funding target for Participant A.

(iv) The excess of the death benefit over Participant A's accrued benefit is $4,040 (that is, $10,000 - $5,960). Because this part of the death benefit is not a function of the participant's accrued benefit nor is it a function of service, the determination of the corresponding portion of the death benefit taken into account in determining the target normal cost and funding target for 2010 is made under paragraph (c)(1)(ii)(D) of this section. For example, for Participant A, the portion of this benefit with respect to the death decrement occurring at age 64 that is taken into account for purposes of determining the funding target for the 2010 plan year is $3,030 ($4,040 x 12 years of past service / 16 years of service at assumed age of death).

(v) The total single-sum death benefit for Participant A with respect to the death decrement at age 64 that is taken into account in determining the funding target for the 2010 plan year is $8,990 ($5,960 + $3,030).

(vi) Similarly, the portion of the single-sum death benefit for Participant A that is taken into account in determining the target normal cost for the 2010 plan year is equal to the sum of the expected increase in the accrued benefit during 2010, and the expected change in the allocable portion of the excess death benefit attributable to service during 2010 as determined in accordance with paragraph (c)(1)(ii)(D) of this section. As described in Example 1, the expected increase in Participant A's accrued benefit during 2010 is $800, to the extent that Participant A is expected to continue in employment for the full 2010 plan year.

(vii) At the end of 2010, Participant A's accrued benefit is expected to be $6,760 ($5,960 + $800). The excess portion of the single-sum death benefit to be allocated in accordance with paragraph (c)(1)(ii)(D) of this section is $3,240 ($10,000 - $6,760), and the allocable portion of the excess benefit for Participant A as of December 31, 2010, with respect to the death decrement at age 64, is $2,632.50 ($3,240 x 13 years of service as of December 31, 2010 / 16 years of service at assumed age of death). The change in the allocable portion of Participant A's excess death benefit due to an additional year of service, with respect to the death decrement at age 64, is a decrease of $397.50. Therefore, the target normal cost for the 2010 plan year attributable to Participant A, with respect to the death decrement at age 64, will reflect a single-sum death benefit of $402.50 ($800 expected increase in Participant A's accrued benefit minus a $397.50 expected decrease in the allocable portion of the death benefit in excess of the accrued benefit).

*Example (4).* (i) The facts are the same as in Example 3, except that the plan provides a single-sum death benefit equal to the greater of the present value of the qualified pre-retirement survivor annuity or 100 times the amount of the participant's monthly retirement benefit with service projected to normal retirement age. The valuation is based on the assumption that all surviving spouses choose to receive their benefit in the form of a single sum. For Participant A, the value of the qualified pre-retirement survivor annuity is less than 100 times Participant A's projected monthly retirement benefit.

(ii) The allocation of the death benefit that is a function of Participant A's accrued benefit is based on service and compensation to the first day of the plan year for purposes of determining the funding target, and the allocation of the death benefit that is a function of the increase in Participant A's accrued benefit during the plan year for purposes of determining the target normal cost is made in accordance with paragraph (c)(1)(ii)(B) of this section. As described in Example 1, Participant A's accrued benefit based on service and compensation as of January 1, 2010, is $5,960, or $496.67 per month. Accordingly, the portion of the single-sum death benefit corresponding to the accrued benefit, or $49,667 (100 times $496.67), is taken into account when determining the 2010 funding target for Participant A.

(iii) In addition, the funding target and the target normal cost reflect a portion of Participant A's death benefit in excess of the amount based on Participant A's accrued benefit. Based on Participant A's average compensation as of the first day of the plan year, Participant A's accrued benefit with service projected to normal retirement is $8,443 [.01 x 17 years of service at age 65 x ($47,000 + $50,000 + $52,000) / 3], or $703.61 per month. The corresponding death benefit is $70,361.

(iv) The excess of the death benefit over Participant A's accrued benefit as of January 1, 2010, is $20,694 (that is, $70,361 - $49,667). Because this part of the death benefit is not a function of Participant A's accrued benefit or service, the portion that is taken into account in determining the funding target is determined under paragraph (c)(1)(ii)(D) of this section. For Participant A, the portion of this benefit with respect to the death decrement occurring at age 64 that is taken into account when determining the funding target for the 2010 plan year is $15,521 ($20,694 x 12 years of past service / 16 years of service at assumed age of death). The total single-sum death benefit for Participant A with respect to the death decrement at age 64 reflected in the funding target for the 2010 plan year is $65,188 ($49,667 + $15,521).

(v) Similarly, the portion of the single-sum death benefit for Participant A that is taken into account when determining the target normal cost for 2010 is equal to the sum of the death benefit based on the expected increase in the accrued benefit during 2010 and the expected change in the allocable portion of the excess death benefit attributable to service during 2010 as determined in accordance with paragraph (c)(1)(ii)(D) of this section.

(vi) At the end of 2010, Participant A's accrued benefit is expected to be $6,760 ($5,960 + $800), or $563.33 per month, and the associated death benefit is $56,333. The expected increase in the amount of the death benefit attributable to the increase in Participant A's accrued benefit is therefore $6,666 ($56,333 - $49,667).

(vii) Participant A's projected accrued benefit at normal retirement based on average compensation as of the end of 2010 is $8,840 [.01 x 17 years of service at age 65 x ($50,000 + $52,000 + $54,000) / 3], or $736.67 per month. The corresponding death benefit is $73,667. The excess portion of the single-sum death benefit to be allocated in accordance with paragraph (c)(1)(ii)(D) of this section is $17,334 ($73,667 - $56,333), and the allocable portion of the excess benefit for Participant A as of December 31, 2010, with respect to the death decrement at age 64, is $14,084 ($17,334 x 13 years of service as of December 31, 2010 / 16 years of service at assumed age of death).

(viii) The change in the allocable portion of Participant A's excess death benefit during 2010, with respect to the death decrement at age 64, is a decrease of $1,437 ($14,084 - $15,521). Therefore, the target normal cost for the 2010 plan year attributable to Participant A, with respect to the death decrement at age 64, will reflect a single-sum death benefit of $5,229 ($6,666 expected increase in Participant A's death benefit based on the expected increase in the accrued benefit, minus an expected decrease of $1,437 in the amount of the death benefit in excess of the amount attributable to the accrued benefit).

*Example (5).* (i) The facts are the same as in Example 1. In addition, the plan provides a disability benefit to participants who become disabled after completing 15 years of service. The disability benefit is payable at normal retirement age or an earlier date if elected by a participant. For purposes of calculating the disability benefit, service continues to accrue until normal retirement age (unless recovery or commencement of retirement benefits occurs earlier). Further, compensation is deemed to continue at the same rate as when the disability began.

(ii) Participant A will be eligible for the disability benefit at age 63 after completion of 15 years of service. Participant A's annual disability benefit at normal retirement age is $9,180 (that is, 1% of highest 3-year average compensation of $54,000 multiplied by 17 years of deemed service at normal retirement age).

(iii) The portion of the disability benefit based on the participant's accrued benefit as of the valuation date that is taken into account in determining the target normal cost and funding target is determined in accordance with paragraph (c)(1)(ii)(B) of this section. Accordingly, the portion of the disability benefit corresponding to Participant A's accrued benefit as of January 1, 2010, or $5,960, is taken into account when determining the 2010 funding target.

(iv) The excess of Participant A's disability benefit over the accrued benefit as of January 1, 2010, is $3,220 ($9,180 - $5,960). Because this portion of the disability benefit is not based on Participant A's accrued benefit or service, the portion that is taken into account in determining the funding target is determined under paragraph (c)(1)(ii)(D) of this section. The portion of Participant A's excess disability benefit with respect to the disability decrement occurring at age 63 that is taken into account when determining the 2010 funding target is $2,576 [$3,220 x (12 years of past service / 15 years of service at assumed date of disability)]. The total disability benefit for Participant A, with respect to the disability decrement occurring at age 63, that is taken into account in determining the funding target for the 2010 plan year is $8,536 ($5,960 + $2,576).

(v) The portion of Participant A's disability benefit with respect to the disability decrement occurring at age 64 that is taken into account when determining the 2010 funding target is $8,375 [$5,960 + $3,220 x (12 years of past service / 16 years of service at assumed date of disability)].

(vi) If in fact Participant A becomes disabled at age 63, the funding target will reflect the full disability benefit to which Participant A will be entitled at normal retirement age, based on service projected to normal retirement age (17 years) and final average compensation reflecting compensation projected to normal retirement age at the rate Participant A was earning at the time of disablement.

*Example (6).* (i) The facts are the same as in Example 5, except that the disability benefit is based on the accrued benefit calculated using service and compensation earned to the date of disability.

(ii) Because the disability benefit is a function of the participant's accrued benefit, the portion of Participant A's disability benefit that is taken into account when determining the funding target for the 2010 plan year is Participant A's annual accrued benefit as of January 1, 2010, or $5,960, as determined in Example 1. This amount is taken into account for both the disability decrement occurring at age 63 and the disability decrement occurring at age 64.

(iii) Similarly, the benefit accrual for Participant A with respect to the disability decrements occurring at age 63 and age 64 that is taken into account when determining the target normal cost for the 2010 plan year is equal to Participant A's expected benefit accrual for 2010 determined in Example 1, or $800.

*Example (7).* (i) Retiree D, a participant in Plan P, is a male age 72 and is receiving a $100 monthly straight life annuity. The 2009 actuarial valuation is performed using the segment rates applicable for September 2008 (determined without regard to the transition rule of section 430(h)(2)(G)), and the 2009 annuitant and nonannuitant (male and female) mortality tables (published in Notice 2008-85). See § 601.601(d)(2) relating to objectives and standards for publishing regulations, revenue rulings and revenue procedures in the Internal Revenue Bulletin.

(ii) The present value of Retiree D's straight life annuity on the valuation date is $10,535.79. This is equal to the sum of: $5,029.99, which is the present value of payments expected to be made during the first 5 years, using the first segment interest rate of 5.07%; $5,322.26, which is the present value of payments expected to be made during the next 15 years, using the second segment interest rate of 6.09%; and $183.54, which is the present value of payments expected to be made after 20 years, using the third segment interest rate of 6.56%.

*Example (8).* (i) The facts are the same as in Example 7. Plan P does not provide for early retirement benefits or single-sum distributions. The actuary assumes that no participants terminate employment prior to age 50 (other than by death), there is a 5% probability of withdrawal at age 50, and that those participants who withdraw receive a deferred annuity starting at age 65. Participant E is a male age 46 on January 1, 2009, and has an annual accrued benefit of $23,000 beginning at age 65.

(ii) Before taking into account the 5% probability of withdrawal, the funding target associated with Participant E's assumed age 50 withdrawal benefit in the 2009 actuarial valuation is $68,396.75. This is equal to the sum of: $6,925.29, which is the present value of payments expected to be made during the year the participant turns age 65 (the 20th year after the valuation date), using the second segment interest rate of 6.09%; and $61,471.46, which is the present value of payments expected to be made after the 20th year, using the third segment interest rate of 6.56%.

(iii) Taking the 5% probability of withdrawal into account, the funding target for the 2009 plan year associated with Participant E's assumed age 50 withdrawal benefit is $3,419.84 ($68,396.75 x 5%).

*Example (9).* (i) The facts are the same as in Example 8, except the plan offers a single-sum distribution payable at normal retirement age (age 65) determined based on the applicable interest rates and the applicable mortality table under section 417(e)(3). The actuary assumes that 70% of the participants will elect a single sum upon retirement and the remaining 30% will elect a straight life annuity.

(ii) Before taking into account the 5% probability of withdrawal or the 70% probability of electing a single-sum payment, the portion of the 2009 funding target that is attributable to Participant E's assumed single-sum payment, deferred to age 65, is $70,052.30. This is calculated in the same manner as the present value of annuity payments, except that, for the period after the annuity starting date, the 2009 applicable mortality rates are substituted for the 2009 male annuitant mortality rates. This portion of the funding target for the 2009 plan year is equal to the sum of: $6,929.00, which is the present value of annuity payments expected to be made between age 65 and 66 (during the 20th year after the valuation date), using the second segment interest rate of 6.09%; and $63,123.30, which is the present value of annuity payments expected to be made after the 20th year following the valuation date, using the third segment interest rate of 6.56%. These present value amounts reflect the 2009 male nonannuitant mortality rates prior to the assumed commencement of benefits at age 65 and the 100% probability of retiring at age 65.

(iii) Taking the 5% probability of withdrawal and the 70% probability of electing a single-sum payment into account, the portion of the 2009 funding target attributable to Participant E's assumed single-sum payment based on withdrawal at age 50 is $2,451.83 ($70,052.30 x 5% x 70%). After taking into account the 5% probability of withdrawal and the 30% probability of electing a straight life annuity, the portion of the 2009 funding target that is attributable to Participant E's assumed straight life annuity (based on assumed withdrawal at age 50), deferred to age 65, is equal to 30% of the result obtained in Example 8.

*Example (10).* (i) The facts are the same as in Example 9, except the plan offers an immediate single sum upon withdrawal at age 50 determined based on the applicable interest rates and the applicable mortality table under section 417(e)(3). The actuary assumes that 70% of the participants will elect to receive a single-sum distribution upon withdrawal.

(ii) Before taking into account the 5% probability of withdrawal and the 70% probability of electing a single-sum payment, the portion of the funding target for the 2009 plan year that is attributable to Participant E's assumed single-sum payment based on withdrawal at age 50 is $68,908.39. This is calculated in the same manner as the present value of annuity payments, except that the 2009 applicable mortality rates are substituted for the 2009 male annuitant and nonannuitant mortality rates after the annuity starting date. This portion of the 2009 funding target is equal to the sum of $6,815.85, which is the present value of annuity payments expected to be made between age 65 and 66 (during the 20th year after the valuation date), using the second segment interest rate of 6.09%, and $62,092.54, which is the present value of annuity payments expected to be made after the 20th year following the valuation date, using the third segment interest rate of 6.56%. These present value amounts reflect the 2009 male nonannuitant mortality rates prior to the assumed single-sum distribution age of 50.

(iii) Applying the 5% probability of withdrawal at age 50 and the 70% probability of electing a single-sum payment, the portion of the funding target for the 2009 plan year that is attributable to Participant E's assumed single-sum payment (based on withdrawal at age 50) is $2,411.79 ($68,908.39 x 5% x 70%).

*Example (11).* (i) The facts are the same as in Example 8, except that the plan sponsor elects under section 430(h)(2)(D)(ii) to use the monthly corporate bond yield curve instead of segment rates. The enrolled actuary assumes payments are made monthly throughout the year and uses the interest rate from the middle of the monthly corporate bond yield curve because this mid-year yield rate most closely matches the average timing of benefits paid. In accordance with § 1.430(h)(2)-1(e)(4), the applicable monthly corporate bond yield curve is the yield curve derived from December 2008 rates.

(ii) Before taking into account the 5% probability of withdrawal, the funding target associated with Participant E's assumed age 50 withdrawal benefit in the 2009 actuarial valuation is $67,394.12. This reflects the sum of each year's expected payments, discounted at the yield rates described in paragraph (i) of this Example 11, as shown below:

| Age | Maturity | Yield rate | Present value |
|---|---|---|---|
| 65 .... | 19.5 .... | 6.97% .... | $5,897.88 |
| 66 .... | 20.5 .... | 6.90% .... | 5,524.69 |
| 67 .... | 21.5 .... | 6.84% .... | 5,164.63 |
| 68 and over .... | Varies .... | Varies .... | 50,806.92 |
| Total .... | .... | .... | 67,394.12 |

(iii) Applying the 5% probability of withdrawal, the portion of the funding target for the 2009 plan year attributable to Participant E's assumed withdrawal at age 50 is $3,369.71 ($67,394.12 x 5%).

*Example (12).* (i) The facts are the same as in Example 10, except that the plan determines the amount of the immediate single-sum distribution upon withdrawal at age 50 based on the applicable interest rates under section 417(e)(3) or an interest rate of 6.25%, whichever produces the higher amount. The applicable mortality table under section 417(e)(3) is used for both calculations.

(ii) Before taking into account the 5% probability of withdrawal and the 70% probability of electing a single-sum payment, the present value of Participant E's single-sum distribution as of January 1, 2009, using an interest rate of 6.25%, based on withdrawal at age 50, is $77,391.88. This amount is determined by calculating the projected single-sum distribution at age 50 using the applicable mortality rate under section 417(e)(3) and an interest rate of 6.25%, or $94,789.10, and discounting the result to the January 1, 2009, valuation date using the first segment rate of 5.07% (because the single-sum distribution is assumed to be paid 4 years after the valuation date) and the male non-annuitant mortality rates for 2009.

(iii) Before taking into account the 5% probability of withdrawal and the 70% probability of electing a single-sum payment, the present value as of January 1, 2009, of Participant E's age-50 single-sum distribution using the applicable interest rates and applicable mortality table under section 417(e)(3) is $68,908.39, as developed in Example 10. Corresponding to plan provisions, the present value reflected in the funding target is the larger of this amount or the present value of the amount based on a 6.25% interest rate, or $77,391.88.

(iv) Applying the 5% probability of withdrawal at age 50 and the 70% probability of electing a single-sum payment, the portion of the funding target for the 2009 plan year that is attributable to Participant E's assumed single-sum payment (based on withdrawal at age 50) is $2,708.72 ($77,391.88 x 5% x 70%).

*Example (13).* (i) Plan Q is a cash balance plan that permits an immediate payment of a single sum equal to the participant's hypothetical account balance upon termination of employment. Plan Q's terms provide that the hypothetical account is credited with interest at a market-related rate, based on a specified index. The January 1, 2009, actuarial valuation is performed using the 24-month average segment rates applicable for September 2008 (determined without regard to the transition rule of section 430(h)(2)(G)). Participant F is a male age 61 on January 1, 2009, and has a hypothetical account balance equal to $150,000 on that date. In the 2009 actuarial valuation, the enrolled actuary assumes that the hypothetical account balances will increase with annual interest credits of 7% until the participant commences receiving his or her benefit, corresponding to the actuary's best estimate of future interest rates credited under the terms of the plan. The actuary also assumes that all participants will retire on the first day of the plan year in which they attain age 65 (that is, no participant will terminate employment prior to age 65 other than by death), and that 100% of participants will elect a single sum upon retirement.

(ii) Participant F's hypothetical account balance projected to January 1, 2013 (the plan year in which F attains age 65) is $196,619.40 based on the assumed annual interest crediting rate of 7%. The funding target for the 2009 plan year attributable to Participant F's benefit at age 65 is $158,525.81, which is calculated by discounting the projected hypothetical account balance of $196,619.40 using the first segment rate of 5.07% and the male non-annuitant mortality rates.

*Example (14).* (i) The facts are the same as in Example 13, except that the actuary assumes that 10% of the participants will choose to collect their benefits in the form of a straight life annuity. The plan provides that the participant's account balance at retirement is converted to an annuity using the applicable interest rates and applicable mortality table under section 417(e)(3).

(ii) Participant F's hypothetical account balance projected to January 1, 2013 (the plan year in which F attains age 65) is $196,619.40, as outlined in Example 13. This amount is converted to an annuity payable commencing at age 65 by dividing the projected account balance by an annuity factor based on the applicable mortality table for 2009 under section 417(e)(3) (corresponding to the valuation date) and the interest rates used for the valuation. The resulting annuity factor is 10.8321, reflecting one year of interest at the first segment rate (5.07%) corresponding to the first year of the expected annuity payments (the fifth year after the valuation date), 15 years of interest at the second segment rate (6.09%) and all remaining years at the third segment rate (6.56%). The projected future annuity is therefore $196,619.40 divided by 10.8321, or $18,151.55 per year.

(iii) Before taking into account the 10% probability that the participant will elect to take the distribution in the form of a lifetime annuity, the funding target associated with the future annuity payout for Participant F is $149,120.41. This is equal to the sum of $14,242.79, which is the present value of the annuity payment expected to made during the year the participant turns age 65 (the 5th year after the valuation date), using the first segment interest rate of 5.07%; $116,321.72, which is the present value of payments expected to be made during the 6th through the 20th years following the valuation date, using the second segment interest rate of 6.09%; and $18,555.90, which is the present value of payments expected to be made after the 20th year following the valuation date, using the third segment interest rate of 6.56%.

(iv) Applying the 10% probability of electing a lifetime annuity, the portion of the 2009 funding target attributable to Participant F's assumed lifetime annuity payable at age 65 is $14,912.04. The portion of the 2009 funding target attributable to Participant F's assumed single-sum payment is 90% of the result obtained in Example 13.

*Example (15).* (i) Plan H provides a monthly benefit of $50 times service for all participants. Plan H has a funding target of $1,000,000 and an actuarial value of assets of $810,000 as of January 1, 2010. No annuity contracts have been purchased, and Plan H has no funding standard carryover balance or prefunding balance as of January 1, 2010. The enrolled actuary certifies that the January 1, 2010, AFTAP is 81%. Effective July 1, 2010, Plan H is amended on June 14, 2010, to increase the plan's monthly benefit to $55 for years of service earned on or after July 1, 2010. The present value of the increase in plan benefits during 2010 (reflecting benefit accruals attributable to the six months between July 1, 2010, and December 31, 2010) is $25,000.

(ii) The amendment increases benefits for future service only, and so the funding target is unaffected. Since section 436(c) only restricts plan amendments that increase plan liabilities, the plan amendment can take effect.

(iii) If the $25,000 present value of the increase in plan benefits during 2010 were included in Plan H's funding target of $1,000,000, the total would be $1,025,000, and the AFTAP would be 79.02% (that is, $810,000/$1,025,000). Since this is less than 80%, the amendment would not have been permitted to take effect if the 2010 increase were included in the funding target instead of target normal cost.

(iv) Because the amendment was adopted after the January 1, 2010, valuation date, the plan sponsor would generally have the option of deciding whether to reflect this amendment in the January 1, 2010, valuation or defer recognition of the amendment to the January 1, 2011, valuation. However, under paragraph (d)(2) of this section, because the plan amendment would not have been permitted to take effect under the provisions of section 436 if the increase in the target normal cost for the plan year had been taken into account in the funding target, the actuary must take into account the amendment in the January 1, 2010, valuation for purposes of section 430. Thus, the target normal cost for the plan year includes the $25,000 that results from the plan amendment.

**(g) Effective/applicability dates and transition rules.** *(1) Statutory effective date/applicability date* (i) In general. Section 430 generally applies to plan years beginning on or after January 1, 2008. The applicability of section 430 for purposes of determining the minimum required contribution is delayed for certain plans in accordance with sections 104 through 106 of PPA '06.

(ii) Applicability of special adjustments. The special adjustments of paragraph (b)(1)(iii) of this section (relating to adjustments to the target normal cost for plan-related expenses and mandatory employee contributions) apply to plan years beginning after December 31, 2008. In addition, a plan sponsor may elect to make the special adjustments of paragraph (b)(1)(iii) of this section for a plan year beginning in 2008. This election must take into account both adjustments described in paragraph (b)(1)(iii) of this section. This election is subject to the same rules that apply to an election to add an amount to the plan's prefunding balance pursuant to § 1.430(f)-1(f), and it must be made in the same manner as the election made under § 1.430(f)-1(f). Thus, the election can be made no later than the last day for making the minimum required contribution for the plan year to which the election relates.

*(2) Effective date/applicability date of regulations.* This section applies to plan years beginning on or after January 1, 2010, regardless of whether section 430 applies to determine the minimum required contribution for the plan year. For plan years beginning before January 1, 2010, plans are permitted to rely on the provisions set forth in this section for purposes of satisfying the requirements of section 430.

*(3) Approval for changes in funding method.* (i) 2008 plan year. Any changes in a plan's funding method that are made for the first plan year beginning in 2008 that are not inconsistent with the requirements of section 430 are treated as having been approved by the Commissioner and do not require the Commissioner's specific prior approval.

(ii) Application of this section— (A) First plan year for which regulations are effective. Except as otherwise provided in paragraph (g)(3)(ii)(B) of this section, any change in a plan's funding method for the first plan year that begins on or after January 1, 2010, is treated as having been approved by the Commissioner and does not require the Commissioner's specific prior approval.

(B) Optional earlier application of regulations. For the first plan year that a plan applies all the provisions of this section, §§ 1.430(f)-1, 1.430(g)-1, 1.430(i)-1, and 1.436-1, any change in a plan's funding method for that plan year is treated as having been approved by the Commissioner and does not require the Commissioner's specific prior approval. For example, if the change in funding method includes a change in the valuation software, the change in the valuation software is treated as having been approved by the Commissioner and does not require the Commissioner's specific prior approval. If that plan year begins before January 1, 2010, the automatic approval for a change in funding method under paragraph (g)(3)(ii)(A) of this section does not apply to the plan.

(C) Special rule for changes in allocation. Any change in a plan's funding method for a plan year earlier than the first plan year beginning on or after January 1, 2010, that is necessary to apply the rules of paragraph (c)(1)(ii) of this section is treated as having been approved by the Commissioner and does not require the Commissioner's specific prior approval.

(iii) First plan year for which section 430 applies to determine minimum funding. For a plan for which the minimum required contribution is not determined under section 430 for the first plan year that begins on or after January 1, 2008, pursuant to sections 104 through 106 of PPA '06, any change in a plan's funding method for the first plan year to which section 430 applies to determine the plan's minimum required contribution is treated as having been approved by the Commissioner and does not require the Commissioner's specific prior approval.

*(4) Approval for changes in actuarial assumptions.* The Commissioner's specific prior approval is not required with respect to any actuarial assumptions that are adopted for the first plan year for which section 430 applies to determine the minimum required contribution for the plan and that are not inconsistent with the requirements of section 430.

*(5) Transition rule for determining funding target attainment percentage for the 2007 plan year.* (i) In general. For purposes of the first plan year beginning on or after January 1, 2008, the funding target attainment percentage for the plan's prior plan year (the 2007 plan year) is determined as the fraction (expressed as a percentage), the numerator of which is the value of plan assets determined under paragraph (g)(5)(ii) of this section, and the denominator of which is the plan's current liability determined pursuant to section 412(l)(7) (as in effect prior to amendment by PPA '06) as of the valuation date for the 2007 plan year.

(ii) Determination of value of plan assets— (A) In general. The value of plan assets for the 2007 plan year under this paragraph (g)(5)(ii)(A) is determined as the value of plan assets as described in paragraph (g)(5)(ii)(B) of this section, reduced by the plan's funding standard account credit balance for the 2007 plan year as described in paragraph (g)(5)(iii)(A) of this section except to the extent provided in paragraph (g)(5)(iii)(B) of this section.

(B) Value of plan assets. The value of plan assets for the 2007 plan year under this paragraph (g)(5)(ii)(B) is determined under section 412(c)(2) as in effect for the 2007 plan year, except that the value of plan assets prior to subtracting the plan's funding standard account credit balance described in paragraph (g)(5)(iii)(A) of this section must be adjusted so that it is neither less than 90 percent of the fair market value of plan assets nor greater than 110 percent of the fair market value of plan assets on the valuation date for that plan year. If the value of plan assets prior to adjustment under this paragraph (g)(5)(ii)(B) is less than 90 percent of the fair market value of plan assets on the valuation date, then the value of plan assets under this paragraph (g)(5)(ii)(B) is equal to 90 percent of the fair market value of plan assets. If the value of plan assets determined under this paragraph (g)(5)(ii)(B) is greater than 110 percent of the fair market value of plan assets on the valuation date, then the value of plan assets under this paragraph (g)(5)(ii)(B) is equal to 110 percent of the fair market value of plan assets.

(iii) Subtraction of credit balance— (A) In general. If a plan has a funding standard account credit balance as of the valuation date for the 2007 plan year, then, except as described in paragraph (g)(5)(iii)(B) of this section, that balance is subtracted from the value of plan assets described in paragraph (g)(5)(ii)(B) of this section as of that valuation date to determine the value of plan assets for the 2007 plan year. However, the value of plan assets is not reduced below zero. (B) Effect of funding standard carryover balance reduction for the 2008 plan year. Notwithstanding the rules of paragraph (g)(5)(iii)(A) of this section, for the first plan year beginning in 2008, if the employer has made an election to reduce some or all of the funding standard carryover balance as of the first day of that year in accordance with § 1.430(f)-1(e), then the present value (determined as of the valuation date for the 2007 plan year using the valuation interest rate for that 2007 plan year) of the amount so reduced is not treated as part of the funding standard account credit balance when that balance is subtracted from the value of plan assets pursuant to paragraph (g)(5)(iii)(A) of this section.

---

T.D. 9467, 10/07/2009.

---

## § 1.430(f)-1 Effect of prefunding balance and funding standard carryover balance.

**(a) In general.** *(1) Overview.* This section provides rules relating to the application of prefunding and funding standard carryover balances under section 430(f). Section 430 and this section apply to single employer defined benefit plans (including multiple employer plans) that are subject to section 412, but do not apply to multiemployer plans (as defined in section 414(f)). Paragraph (b) of this section sets forth rules regarding a plan's prefunding balance and a plan sponsor's election to maintain a funding standard carryover balance. Paragraph (c) of this section provides rules under which those balances must be subtracted from plan assets. Paragraph (d) of this section describes a plan sponsor's election to use those balances to offset the minimum required contribution. Paragraph (e) of this section describes a plan sponsor's election to reduce those balances (which will affect the determination of the value of plan assets for purposes of sections 430 and 436). Paragraph (f) of this section sets forth rules regarding elections under this section. Paragraph (g) of this section contains examples. Paragraph (h) of this section contains effective/applicability dates and transition rules.

*(2) Special rules for multiple employer plans.* In the case of a multiple employer plan to which section 413(c)(4)(A) applies, the rules of this section are applied separately for each employer under the plan, as if each employer maintained a separate plan. Thus, each employer under such a multiple employer plan may have a separate funding standard carryover balance and a prefunding balance for the plan. In the case of a multiple employer plan to which section 413(c)(4)(A) does not apply (that is, a plan described in section 413(c)(4)(B) that has not made the election for section 413(c)(4)(A) to apply), the rules of this section are applied as if all participants in the plan were employed by a single employer.

**(b) Maintenance of balances.** *(1) Prefunding balance.* (i) In general. A plan sponsor is permitted to elect to maintain a prefunding balance for a plan. A prefunding balance maintained for a plan consists of a beginning balance of zero, increased by the amount of excess contributions to the extent the employer elects to do so as described in paragraph (b)(1)(ii) of this section, and decreased to the extent provided in paragraph (b)(1)(iii) of this section. The plan sponsor's initial election to add to the prefunding balance under paragraph (b)(1)(ii) of this section constitutes an election to maintain a prefunding balance. The prefunding balance is adjusted further for investment return and interest as provided in paragraphs (b)(3) and (b)(4) of this section.

(ii) Increases— (A) In general. If the plan sponsor of a plan elects to add to the plan's prefunding balance, as of the first day of a plan year following the first effective plan year for the plan, the prefunding balance is increased by the amount so elected by the plan sponsor for the plan year. The amount added to the prefunding balance cannot exceed the present value of the excess contributions for the preceding plan year determined under paragraph (b)(1)(ii)(B) of this section, increased for interest in accordance with paragraph (b)(1)(iv)(A) of this section.

(B) Present value of excess contribution. The present value of the excess contribution for the preceding plan year is the excess, if any, of—

(1) The present value (determined under the rules of paragraph (b)(1)(iv)(B) of this section) of the employer contributions (other than contributions to avoid or terminate benefit limitations described in § 1.436-1(f)(2)) to the plan for such preceding plan year; over

(2) The minimum required contribution for such preceding plan year.

(C) Treatment of unpaid minimum required contributions. For purposes of this paragraph (b)(1)(ii), a contribution made during a plan year to correct an unpaid minimum required contribution (within the meaning of section 4971(c)(4)) for a prior plan year is not treated as a contribution for the current plan year.

(iii) Decreases. As of the first day of each plan year, the prefunding balance of a plan is decreased (but not below zero) by the sum of—

(A) Any amount of the prefunding balance that was used under paragraph (d) of this section to offset the minimum required contribution of the plan for the preceding plan year; and

(B) Any reduction in the prefunding balance under paragraph (e) of this section for the plan year.

(iv) Adjustments for interest— (A) Adjustment of excess contribution. The present value of the excess contribution for the preceding year (as determined under paragraph (b)(1)(ii)(B) of this section) is increased for interest accruing for the period between the valuation date for the preceding plan year and the first day of the current plan year. For this purpose, interest is determined by using the plan's effective interest rate under section 430(h)(2)(A) for the preceding plan year, except to the extent provided in paragraph (b)(3)(iii) of this section.

(B) Determination of present value. The present value of the contributions described in paragraph (b)(1)(ii)(B)(1) of this section is determined as of the valuation date for the preceding plan year, using the plan's effective interest rate under section 430(h)(2)(A) for the preceding plan year.

*(2) Funding standard carryover balance.* (i) In general. A funding standard carryover balance is automatically established for a plan that had a positive balance in the funding standard account under section 412(b) (as in effect prior to amendment by the Pension Protection Act of 2006 (PPA '06), Public Law 109-280 (120 Stat. 780)) as of the end of the pre-effective plan year for the plan. The funding standard carryover balance as of the beginning of the first effective plan year for the plan is the positive balance in the funding

standard account under section 412(b) (as in effect prior to amendment by PPA '06) as of the end of the pre-effective plan year for the plan. After that date, the funding standard carryover balance is decreased to the extent provided in paragraph (b)(2)(ii) of this section and adjusted further for investment return and interest as provided in paragraphs (b)(3) and (b)(4) of this section.

(ii) Decreases. As of the first day of each plan year, the funding standard carryover balance of a plan is decreased (but not below zero) by the sum of—

(A) Any amount of the funding standard carryover balance that was used under paragraph (d) of this section to offset the minimum required contribution of the plan for the preceding plan year; and

(B) Any reduction in the funding standard carryover balance under paragraph (e) of this section for the plan year.

*(3) Adjustments for investment experience.* (i) In general. A plan's prefunding balance under paragraph (b)(1) of this section and a plan's funding standard carryover balance under paragraph (b)(2) of this section as of the first day of a plan year must be adjusted to reflect the actual rate of return on plan assets for the preceding plan year. For this purpose, the actual rate of return on plan assets for the preceding plan year is determined on the basis of fair market value and must take into account the amount and timing of all contributions, distributions, and other plan payments made during that period.

(ii) Ordering rules for adjustments. In general, the adjustment for actual rate of return on plan assets is applied to the balance after any reduction of prefunding and funding standard carryover balances for that preceding plan year under paragraph (e) of this section and after subtracting amounts used to offset the minimum required contribution for the preceding plan year pursuant to paragraph (d) of this section. However, see paragraph (d)(1)(ii)(D) of this section for a special ordering rule when adjusting for investment experience.

(iii) Special rule for excess contributions attributable to use of funding balances. Notwithstanding paragraph (b)(1)(iv)(A) of this section, to the extent that a contribution is included in the present value of excess contributions solely because the minimum required contribution has been offset under paragraph (d) of this section, the contribution is adjusted for investment experience under the rules of this paragraph (b)(3).

*(4) Valuation date other than the first day of the plan year* (i) In general. If a plan's valuation date is not the first day of the plan year, then, solely for purposes of applying paragraphs (c), (d), and (e) of this section, the plan's prefunding and funding standard carryover balances (if any) determined under this paragraph (b) are increased from the first day of the plan year to the valuation date using the plan's effective interest rate under section 430(h)(2)(A) for the plan year.

(ii) Special rule for adjustments for investment experience. In the case of a plan with a valuation date that is not the first day of the plan year, for purposes of applying the subtraction under paragraph (b)(3)(ii) of this section for amounts used to offset the minimum required contribution for the preceding plan year and the decreases under paragraphs (b)(1)(iii) and (b)(2)(ii) of this section, the amount of the prefunding balance or funding standard carryover balance that is used to offset the minimum required contribution under paragraph (d) of this section or reduced under paragraph (e) of this section is discounted from the valuation date to the first day of the plan year using the effective interest rate under section 430(h)(2)(A) for the plan year.

*(5) Special rule for quarterly contributions.* (i) Quarterly contributions due on or after the valuation date. For purposes of applying a prefunding balance or funding standard carryover balance to required installments described in section 430(j)(3) that are due on or after the valuation date for the plan year for which they are due, the respective balances are increased from the beginning of the year to the date of the election (using the plan's effective interest rate for the plan year) to determine the amount available to offset the required quarterly installment. The amounts used to offset required quarterly installments are then discounted from that date to the first day of the plan year for purposes of the subtraction under paragraph (b)(3)(ii) of this section and the decreases under paragraphs (b)(1)(iii) and (b)(2)(ii) of this section, using the effective interest rate for the plan year. However, see paragraph (d)(1)(i)(B) of this section for a special rule regarding late quarterly installments when determining the amount that is used to offset the minimum required contribution for the plan year. (ii) Quarterly contributions due before the valuation date. ]Reserved.]

**(c) Effect of balances on the value of plan assets.**

*(1) In general.* In the case of any plan with a prefunding balance or a funding standard carryover balance, the amount of those balances is subtracted from the value of plan assets for purposes of sections 430 and 436, except as otherwise provided in paragraphs (c)(2), (c)(3), and (d)(3) of this section and § 1.436-1(j)(1)(ii)(B).

*(2) Subtraction of balances in determining new shortfall amortization base.* (i) Prefunding balance. For purposes of determining whether a plan is exempt from the requirement to establish a new shortfall amortization base under section 430(c)(5), the amount of the prefunding balance is subtracted from the value of plan assets only if an election under paragraph (d) of this section to use the prefunding balance to offset the minimum required contribution is made for the plan year.

(ii) Funding standard carryover balance. For purposes of determining whether a plan is exempt from the requirement to establish a new shortfall amortization base under section 430(c)(5), the funding standard carryover balance is not subtracted from the value of plan assets regardless of whether any portion of either the funding standard carryover balance or the prefunding balance is used to offset the minimum required contribution for the plan year under paragraph (d) of this section.

*(3)* Special rule for certain binding agreements with PBGC. If there is in effect for a plan year a binding written agreement with the Pension Benefit Guaranty Corporation (PBGC) which provides that all or a portion of the prefunding balance or funding standard carryover balance (or both balances) is not available to offset the minimum required contribution for a plan year, that specified amount is not subtracted from the value of plan assets for purposes of determining the funding shortfall under section 430(c)(4). For example, if a plan has no prefunding balance and a $20 million funding standard carryover balance, a PBGC agreement provides that $5 million of a plan's funding standard carryover balance is unavailable to offset the minimum required contribution for a plan year, and the plan's assets are $100 million, then the value of plan assets for purposes of determining the funding shortfall under section 430(c)(4) is reduced by $15 million ($20 million less $5 million) to $85

million. For purposes of this paragraph (c)(3), an agreement with the PBGC is taken into account with respect to a plan year only if the agreement was executed prior to the valuation date for the plan year.

**(d) Election to apply balances against minimum required contribution.** *(1) In general.* (i) Amount of offset to minimum required contribution— (A) Effect of use of balances. Subject to the limitations provided in this paragraph (d), in the case of any plan year with respect to which the plan sponsor elects to use all or a portion of the prefunding balance or the funding standard carryover balance to offset the minimum required contribution for the plan year, the minimum required contribution for the plan year (determined after taking into account any waiver under section 412(c)) is offset as of the valuation date for the plan year by the amount so used.

(B) Special rule for late quarterly contributions— (1) Quarterly contributions due on or after the valuation date. Notwithstanding paragraph (d)(1)(i)(A) of this section, if the plan sponsor elects to use all or a portion of the prefunding balance or the funding standard carryover balance to satisfy a required installment under section 430(j)(3) that is due on or after the valuation date, the amount used to offset the minimum required contribution for the plan year is the portion of the balance so used, discounted in accordance with the rules of paragraph (b)(5) of this section, unless the date of the election is after the due date of the required installment. If the election to use all or a portion of the prefunding balance or the funding standard carryover balance to satisfy the required installments under section 430(j)(3) is made after the due date for the required installment, then the amount used to offset the minimum required contribution for the plan year is the portion of the balance so used, discounted from the date of the election to the due date of the required installment at the effective interest rate plus 5 percentage points, and then further discounted from the installment due date to the valuation date at the effective interest rate. For example, if a quarterly installment of $20,250 is due on April 15 for a calendar year plan with a valuation date on January 1 and an effective interest rate of 6 percent, and the installment is satisfied by an election to apply the funding standard carryover balance that is made on July 1 (2½; months after the April 15 due date), then the amount used to offset the minimum required contribution under this paragraph (d)(1)(i) is $19,481 (that is, $20,250 / $1.11^{(2.5/12)}$ / $1.06^{(3.2/12)}$). However, the amount by which the funding standard carryover balance is reduced under paragraph (b)(2)(ii) of this section is $19,669 (that is, $20,250 / $1.06^{(6/12)}$).

(2) Quarterly contributions due before the valuation date. [Reserved.]

(ii) Maximum amount of available balances and coordination of elections— (A) General requirement to follow chronology. In general, the amount of prefunding and funding standard carryover balances that may be used to offset the minimum required contribution for a plan year must take into account any decrease in those balances which results from a prior election either to use the prefunding balance or funding standard carryover balance under section 430(f)(3) and this paragraph (d) or to reduce those balances under section 430(f)(5) and paragraph (e) of this section (including deemed elections under section 436(f)(3) and § 1.436-1(a)(5)). For example, for a calendar plan year with a January 1 valuation date, a deemed election under section 436(f)(3) and § 1.436-1(a)(5) on April 1, 2010 (the first day of the 4th month of the plan year) will reduce the available prefunding balance or funding standard carryover balance that can be used with respect to an election made after April 1, 2010.

(B) Exception to chronological rule. Notwithstanding the general rule of paragraph (d)(1)(ii)(A) of this section, all elections under section 430(f)(5) and paragraph (e) of this section to reduce the prefunding balance or funding standard carryover balance for the current plan year (including deemed elections under section 436(f)(3) and § 1.436-1(a)(5)) are deemed to occur on the valuation date for the plan year and before any election under section 430(f)(3) and this paragraph (d) to offset the minimum required contribution for the current plan year. Accordingly, if an election to use the prefunding balance or funding standard carryover balance to offset the minimum required contribution for the plan year (including an election to satisfy the quarterly contribution requirement) has been made prior to the election to reduce the prefunding balance or funding standard carryover balance, then the amount available for use to offset the otherwise applicable minimum required contribution for the plan year under this paragraph (d) will be retroactively reduced. However, an election to reduce a prefunding balance or funding standard carryover balance for a plan year does not affect a prior election to use a prefunding balance or funding standard carryover balance to offset a minimum required contribution for a prior plan year.

(C) Investment experience. In addition to reflecting any decrease in the prefunding balance or the funding standard carryover balance which results from a prior election for the previous year either to use the prefunding balance or funding standard carryover balance under section 430(f)(3) and this paragraph (d) to offset the minimum required contribution for such prior plan year or to reduce those balances under section 430(f)(5) and paragraph (e) of this section (including deemed elections under section 436(f)(3) and § 1.436-1(a)(5)), the prior plan year's prefunding and funding standard carryover balances must be adjusted under the rules of paragraph (b)(3) of this section for investment experience for that prior plan year before determining the amount of those balances available for such an election for the current plan year.

(D) Special rule for current year elections that are made before prior year elections. This paragraph (d)(1)(ii)(D) sets forth a special rule that applies if, for the current plan year, a plan sponsor makes an election under this paragraph (d) or paragraph (e) of this section (including a deemed election under section 436(f)(3) and § 1.436-1(a)(5)), and then subsequently makes an election under this paragraph (d) to offset the minimum required contribution for the prior plan year. This special rule applies solely for purposes of determining the amount of prefunding and funding standard carryover balances available for that subsequent election. Under this special rule, in lieu of decreasing the funding standard carryover balance or prefunding balance as of the valuation date for the current year to take into account the current year election, the funding standard carryover balance or prefunding balance as of the valuation date for the prior plan year is decreased by the amount of the prior year equivalent of the current year election. The prior year equivalent of the current year election is determined by dividing the amount of the current year election (as of the first day of the current plan year) by a number equal to 1 plus the rate of investment return for the prior plan year determined under paragraph (b)(3) of this section. If this paragraph (d)(1)(ii)(D) applies for a plan year, then the funding standard carryover balance and prefunding balance are nonetheless adjusted in accordance with the rules of paragraph (b) of this section, after the application of the rules of this paragraph (d)(1)(ii)(D). Thus, the amount used to offset the minimum required contribution for the earlier plan year is subtracted from the prefunding balance or funding standard carryover balance as of the valuation date for that year prior to the adjustment for investment return under paragraph (b)(3) of this section for that plan year, and the amount by which the prefunding balance or funding standard carryover balance is decreased for the second year is based on the elections made for the second year.

*(2)* Requirement to use funding standard carryover balance before prefunding balance. To the extent that a plan has a funding standard carryover balance greater than zero, no amount of the plan's prefunding balance may be used to offset the minimum required contribution. Thus, a plan's funding standard carryover balance must be exhausted before the plan's prefunding balance may be applied under paragraph (d)(1) of this section to offset the minimum required contribution.

*(3) Limitation for underfunded plans.* (i) In general. An election to use the prefunding balance or funding standard carryover balance to offset the minimum required contribution under this paragraph (d) is not available for a plan year if the plan's prior plan year funding ratio is less than 80 percent. For purposes of this paragraph (d)(3), except as otherwise provided in this paragraph (d)(3) or paragraph (h)(3) of this section, the plan's prior plan year funding ratio is the fraction (expressed as a percentage)—

(A) The numerator of which is the value of plan assets on the valuation date for the preceding plan year, reduced by the amount of any prefunding balance (but not the amount of any funding standard carryover balance); and

(B) The denominator of which is the funding target of the plan for the preceding plan year (determined without regard to the at-risk rules of section 430(i)(1)).

(ii) Special rule for second year of a new plan with no past service. In the case of a new plan that was neither the result of a merger nor involved in a spinoff, if the prior plan year was the first year of the plan and the funding target for the prior plan year was zero, then the plan's prior plan year funding ratio is deemed to be 80 percent for purposes of this paragraph (d)(3).

(iii) Special rule for plans that are the result of a merger. [Reserved]

(iv) Special rules for plans that are involved in a spinoff. [Reserved]

**(e) Election to reduce balances.** *(1) In general.* A plan sponsor may make an election for a plan year to reduce any portion of a plan's prefunding and funding standard carryover balances under this paragraph (e). If such an election is made, the amount of those balances that must be subtracted from the value of plan assets pursuant to paragraph (c)(1) of this section will be smaller and, accordingly, the value of plan assets taken into account for purposes of sections 430 and 436 will be larger. Thus, this election to reduce a plan's prefunding and funding standard carryover balances is taken into account in the determination of the value of plan assets for the plan year and applies for all purposes under sections 430 and 436, including for purposes of determining the plan's prior plan year funding ratio under paragraph (d)(3) of this section for the following plan year. See also section 436(f)(3) and § 1.436-1(a)(5) for a rule under which the plan sponsor is deemed to make the election described in this paragraph (e). The rules of paragraph (d)(1)(ii) of this section also apply for purposes of determining the maximum amount of prefunding balance or funding standard carryover balance that is available for an election under this paragraph (e).

*(2) Requirement to reduce funding standard carryover balance before prefunding balance.* To the extent that a plan has a funding standard carryover balance greater than zero, no election under paragraph (e)(1) of this section is permitted to be made that reduces the plan's prefunding balance. Thus, a plan must exhaust its funding standard carryover balance before it is permitted to make an election under paragraph (e)(1) of this section with respect to its prefunding balance.

**(f) Elections.** *(1) Method of making elections.* (i) In general. Any election under this section by the plan sponsor must be made by providing written notification of the election to the plan's enrolled actuary and the plan administrator. The written notification must set forth the relevant details of the election, including the specific dollar amount involved in the election (except as provided in paragraph (f)(1)(ii) of this section). Thus, except as provided in paragraph (f)(1)(ii) of this section, a conditional or formula-based election generally does not satisfy the requirements of this paragraph (f).

(ii) Standing elections to increase or use balances. A plan sponsor may provide a standing election in writing to the plan's enrolled actuary to use the funding standard carryover balance and the prefunding balance to offset the minimum required contribution for the plan year to the extent needed to avoid an unpaid minimum required contribution under section 4971(c)(4) taking into account any contributions that are or are not made. In addition, a plan sponsor may provide a standing election in writing to the plan's enrolled actuary to add the maximum amount possible each year to the prefunding balance. Any election made pursuant to a standing election under this paragraph (f)(1)(ii) is deemed to occur on the last day available to make the election for the plan year as provided under paragraph (f)(2)(i) of this section. Any standing election under this paragraph (f)(1)(ii) remains in effect for the plan with respect to the enrolled actuary named in the election, unless—

(A) The standing election is revoked under the rules of paragraph (f)(3) of this section; or

(B) The enrolled actuary who signs the actuarial report under section 6059 (Schedule SB, "Single-Employer Defined Benefit Plan Actuarial Information" of Form 5500, "Annual Return/Report of Employee Benefit Plan") for the plan for the plan year is not the enrolled actuary named in the standing election.

*(2) Timing of elections.* (i) General rule. Except as otherwise provided in paragraph (f)(2)(ii) or (iii) of this section, any election under this section with respect to a plan year must be made no later than the last date for making the minimum required contribution for the plan year as described in section 430(j)(1). For this purpose, an election to add to the prefunding balance relates to the plan year for which excess contributions were made. For example, an election to add to the prefunding balance as of the first day of the plan year that begins on January 1, 2010 (in an amount not in excess of the present value of the excess contribution as of the valuation date in 2009, adjusted for interest under the rules of paragraph (b)(1)(ii) of this section), must be made no later than September 15, 2010, even though the election is reported on the 2010 Schedule SB of Form 5500, which is not due until 2011. Except for the standing elections covered by paragraph (f)(1)(ii) of this section, an election under this section may not be made prior to the first day of the plan year to which the election relates.

(ii) Special rule for standing election revoked by a change in enrolled actuary. If there is a change in enrolled actuary for the plan year which would result in a revocation of the standing election under the rule of paragraph (f)(1)(ii)(B) of this section, then the plan sponsor may reinstate the revoked standing election by providing a replacement to the new enrolled actuary by the due date of the Schedule SB of Form 5500.

(iii) Election to reduce balances. Any election under paragraph (e) of this section to reduce the prefunding balance or funding standard carryover balance for a plan year (for example, in order to avoid or terminate a benefit restriction under section 436) must be made by the end of the plan year to which the election relates.

(iv) Earlier elections. This paragraph (f)(2) sets forth the latest date that an election can be made. A plan sponsor is permitted to make an earlier election, and in certain circumstances may need to make such an election in order to timely satisfy a quarterly contribution requirement under section 430(j)(3).

*(3) Irrevocability of elections.* (i) In general. Except as otherwise provided in this paragraph (f)(3), a plan sponsor's election under this section with respect to the plan's prefunding balance or funding standard carryover balance is irrevocable (and must be unconditional). A standing election by the plan sponsor may be revoked by providing written notification of the revocation to the plan's enrolled actuary and the plan administrator on or before the date the corresponding election is deemed to occur pursuant to paragraph (f)(1)(ii) of this section.

(ii) Exception for certain elections. An election to use the prefunding balance or funding standard carryover balance to offset the minimum required contribution for a plan year (including an election to satisfy the quarterly contribution requirements for a plan year) is permitted to be revoked to the extent the amount the plan sponsor elected to use to offset the minimum contribution requirements (including an election used to satisfy the quarterly contribution requirements) exceeds the minimum required contribution for a plan year (determined without regard to the election under paragraph (d) of this section) if and only if the election is revoked by providing written notification of the revocation to the plan's enrolled actuary and the plan administrator by the deadline set forth in paragraph (f)(3)(iii) of this section. If no such revocation is made, then, under paragraph (b) of this section, the funding standard carryover balance or prefunding balance is decreased by the entire amount that the plan sponsor elected to use to offset the minimum required contribution for a plan year (including an election to satisfy the quarterly contribution requirements for a plan year).

(iii) Deadline for revoking election. The deadline for revoking the election described in paragraph (f)(3)(ii) of this section is generally the end of the plan year. However, for plans with a valuation date other than the first day of the plan year, the deadline for the revocation is the deadline for contributions for the plan year as described in section 430(j)(1). In addition, for the first plan year beginning in 2008, the deadline for the revocation for all plans is deferred to the due date (including extensions) of the Schedule SB, "Single-Employer Defined Benefit Plan Actuarial Information" of Form 5500, "Annual Return/Report of Employee Benefit Plan".

*(4) Plan sponsor.* (i) In general. For purposes of the elections described in this section, except as otherwise provided in paragraph (f)(4)(ii) of this section, any reference to the plan sponsor means the employer or employers responsible for making contributions to or under the plan.

(ii) Certain multiple employer plans. For purposes of the elections described in this section, in the case of plans that are multiple employer plans to which section 413(c)(4)(A) does not apply, any reference to the plan sponsor means the plan administrator within the meaning of section 414(g).

**(g) Examples.** The following examples illustrate the rules of this section:

*Example (1).* (i) Plan P is a defined benefit plan with a plan year that is the calendar year and a valuation date of January 1. The funding standard carryover balance of Plan P is $25,000 and the prefunding balance is zero as of the beginning of the 2010 plan year. The sponsor of Plan P, Sponsor S, does not elect to use any portion of the balance to offset the minimum required contribution for 2010 pursuant to paragraph (d)(1) of this section, or to reduce any portion of the funding standard carryover balance prior to the determination of the value of plan assets for 2010, pursuant to paragraph (e)(1) of this section. The actual rate of return on Plan P's assets for 2010 is 2%. Plan P's effective interest rate for 2010 is 6%. The minimum required contribution for Plan P under section 430 for 2010 is $100,000, and no quarterly installments are required for Plan P for the 2010 plan year. As of January 1, 2010, the value of plan assets is $1,100,000 and the funding target is $1,000,000. Therefore, the prior plan year funding ratio for Plan P for 2010, as determined under paragraph (d)(3) of this section, is 110%.

(i) Sponsor S makes a contribution to Plan P of $150,000 on December 1, 2010, for the 2010 plan year and makes no other contributions for the 2010 plan year. Because this contribution was made on a date other than the valuation date for the 2010 plan year, the contribution must be adjusted to reflect interest that would otherwise have accrued between the valuation date and the date of the contribution, at the effective interest rate for the 2010 plan year. The amount of the contribution after adjustment is $142,198, determined as $150,000 discounted for 11 months of compound interest at an effective annual interest rate of 6%.

(iii) The excess of employer contributions for 2010 over the minimum required contribution for 2010, as of the valuation date, is $42,198 ($142,198 less $100,000). Accordingly, the increase in Plan P's prefunding balance as of January 1, 2011, cannot exceed $44,730 (which is the present value of the excess contribution of $42,198 adjusted for 12 months of interest at an effective interest rate of 6%).

(iv) Plan P's funding standard carryover balance as of January 1, 2011, is $25,500 (which is the funding standard carryover balance as of January 1, 2010, adjusted for investment experience during 2010 at a rate of 2%).

*Example (2).* (i) The facts are the same as in Example 1, except that the contribution of $150,000 is made on February 1, 2011, for the 2010 plan year.

(ii) The amount of the contribution after adjustment is $140,824, which is determined as $150,000 discounted for 13 months of interest at an effective interest rate of 6%. Accordingly, the increase in Plan P's prefunding balance as of January 1, 2011, cannot exceed $43,273 (which is the present value of the excess contribution of $40,824 adjusted for 12 months of interest at an effective interest rate of 6%).

(iii) Plan P's funding standard carryover balance as of January 1, 2011, is $25,500, as developed in Example 1 of this section. If Sponsor S elects to increase the prefunding balance as of January 1, 2011, by the present value of the excess contribution adjusted for interest, or $43,273, the total of the funding standard carryover balance and prefunding balance as of January 1, 2011, is $68,773.

*Example (3).* (i) The facts are the same as in Example 1, except that Sponsor S contributes $90,539 to Plan P on February 1, 2011, for the 2010 plan year and makes no other contributions to Plan P for the 2010 plan year. In addition, on February 1, 2011, Sponsor S elects to use $15,000 of the funding standard carryover balance to offset P's minimum required contribution for 2010, pursuant to paragraph (d)(1) of this section. This is permitted because Plan P's prior-year funding ratio determined under paragraph (d)(3) of this section is 110%, and is therefore not less than 80%.

(ii) Because the contribution was made on a date other than the valuation date for the 2010 plan year, the contribution must be adjusted to reflect interest that would otherwise have accrued between the valuation date and the date of the contribution, at the effective interest rate for the 2010 plan year. The amount of the contribution after adjustment is $85,000, determined as $90,539 discounted for 13 months of compound interest at an effective interest rate of 6%. The adjusted contribution of $85,000 plus the $15,000 of the funding standard carryover balance used to offset the minimum required contribution equals the minimum required contribution for the 2010 plan year of $100,000. Therefore, no excess contributions are available to increase the prefunding balance, and the prefunding balance as of January 1, 2011, remains zero.

(iii) The funding standard carryover balance as of January 1, 2011, is adjusted for investment experience during the 2010 plan year, in accordance with paragraph (b)(3) of this section. The amount of the adjustment is $200, determined as the actual rate of return on plan assets for 2010 as applied to the 2010 funding standard carryover balance after reduction for the amount of that balance used under paragraph (d)(1) of this section (that is, $25,000 less $15,000, multiplied by the actual rate of return of 2%).

(iv) The funding standard carryover balance, as of January 1, 2011, is $10,200, determined as the 2010 funding standard carryover balance less the amount used to offset the 2010 minimum required contribution, adjusted for investment experience during the 2010 year ($25,000 less $15,000 plus $200).

*Example (4).* (i) The facts are the same as in Example 3, except that Sponsor S contributes $150,000 (instead of $90,539) to Plan P on February 1, 2011, for the 2010 plan year.

(ii) Because the contribution was made on a date other than the valuation date for the 2010 plan year, the contribution must be adjusted to reflect interest that would otherwise have accrued between the valuation date and the date of the contribution, at the effective interest rate for the 2010 plan year. The amount of the contribution after adjustment is $140,824, determined as $150,000 discounted for 13 months of interest at an effective interest rate of 6%.

(iii) Because Sponsor S elected to use $15,000 of the funding standard carryover balance to offset the minimum required contribution for 2010 of $100,000, the cash contribution requirement for 2010, adjusted with interest to January 1, 2010, is $85,000. The adjusted contribution of $140,824 exceeds this amount by $55,824. Of this amount, $15,000 exceeds the minimum required contribution only because of Sponsor S's election to use the funding standard carryover balance to offset the minimum required contribution as provided in paragraph (d)(1) of this section. The remaining $40,824 ($140,824 minus $100,000) results from cash contributions made in excess of the minimum required contribution before offset by the funding standard carryover balance.

(iv) The portion of the excess contribution resulting solely because the minimum required contribution was offset by a portion of the funding standard carryover balance is adjusted for investment experience during 2009, pursuant to paragraph (b)(3)(iii) of this section. Accordingly, this portion of the present value of the excess contribution adjusted for interest as of January 1, 2011, is $15,300 ($15,000 adjusted for investment experience during 2010 at a rate of 2%).

(v) The excess contribution resulting from cash contributions in excess of the minimum required contribution before offset by the funding standard carryover balance is adjusted for interest at the effective interest rate for 2010, pursuant to paragraph (b)(1)(iv)(A) of this section. Accordingly, this portion of the present value of the excess contribution adjusted for interest as of January 1, 2011, is $43,273 ($40,824 increased by the effective interest rate of 6%). The increase in Plan P's prefunding balance as of January 1, 2011, cannot exceed the total present value of the excess contribution adjusted for interest of $58, 573 ($15,300 plus $43,273).

(vi) The funding standard carryover balance as of January 1, 2011, is $10,200, determined as the 2010 funding standard carryover balance less the $15,000 used to offset the 2010 minimum required contribution, adjusted for investment experience during the 2010 plan year as developed in Example 3 ($25,000 less $15,000 plus $200).

(vii) Sponsor S elects to increase the prefunding balance by the maximum amount of the present value of the excess contribution adjusted for interest of $58,573, resulting in a total of the funding standard carryover balance and the prefunding balance as of January 1, 2011, of $68,773, the same amount as that developed in Example 2.

*Example (5).* (i) Plan Q is a defined benefit plan with a plan year that is the calendar year and a valuation date of July 1. The funding standard carryover balance of Plan Q is $50,000 as of January 1, 2010, the beginning of the 2010 plan year. The prefunding balance of Plan Q as of the beginning of the 2010 plan year is $0. The actual rate of return on Plan Q's assets for 2010 is 10%. Plan Q's effective interest rate for 2010 is 6.25%. The funding ratio for Plan Q for 2009 (the prior plan year funding ratio with respect to 2010, as determined under paragraph (d)(3) of this section) is 85%, which is not less than 80%. The minimum required contribution for Plan Q for 2010 is $200,000. Sponsor T makes a contribution to Plan Q of $190,000 on July 1, 2010, for the 2010 plan year, and makes no other contributions for the 2010 plan year. Sponsor T elects to use $10,000 of the funding standard carryover balance to offset Plan Q's minimum required contribution in 2010.

(ii) Pursuant to paragraph (b)(4) of this section, the funding standard carryover balance is increased to $51,539 as of July 1, 2010 (that is, an increase to reflect 6 months of interest at an effective interest rate of 6.25%) for the purpose of adjusting plan assets under paragraph (c) of this section, and for applying any election to use or reduce Plan Q's funding standard carryover balance under paragraph (d) or (e) of this section. However, Sponsor T does not elect in 2010 to reduce any portion of the funding standard carryover balance pursuant to paragraph (e) of this section. The funding standard carryover balance ($51,539) is subtracted from the value of plan assets, as of July 1, 2010, prior to the determination of the minimum funding contribution, and $51,539 is the maximum amount that may applied against the minimum required contribution.

(iii) The value of the funding standard carryover balance as of January 1, 2011, is determined by first discounting the amount used to offset the minimum required contribution for 2010 from July 1, 2010, to January 1, 2010, using the effective interest rate of 6.25%, and subtracting the discounted amount from the January 1, 2010, funding standard carryover balance. The resulting amount is adjusted for investment experience to January 1, 2011, using a rate equal to the actual rate of return on plan assets of 10% during 2010. Thus, the $10,000 used to offset Plan Q's minimum required contribution as of July 1, 2010, is discounted for 6 months of interest, at an effective interest rate of 6.25%, to obtain an amount of $9,701 as of January 1, 2010. The remaining funding standard carryover balance as of January 1, 2010, solely for purposes of determining the adjustment for investment experience during 2010, is $40,299 ($50,000--$9,701), and the adjustment for investment experience is $4,030 ($40,299 x 10%). The value of the funding standard carryover balance as of January 1, 2011, is $44,329 (that is, $50,000 - $9,701 + $4,030).

*Example (6).* (i) The facts are the same as in Example 5, except that Sponsor T contributes $200,000 on July 1, 2010, for the 2010 plan year.

(ii) The cash contribution required for 2010, after offsetting the minimum required contribution by $10,000 of the funding standard carryover balance in accordance with T's election, is $190,000. The difference, or $10,000, must be adjusted to January 1, 2011, to determine the maximum amount that can be added to the prefunding balance as of that date.

(iii) The excess contribution is first adjusted to January 1, 2010, by discounting for 6 months of interest using the effective interest rate for 2010 of 6.25%. This results in an excess contribution of $9,701 ($10,000 / 1.0625 \0.5\). Because this amount is an excess contribution solely because of Sponsor T's election to offset the minimum required contribution for 2010 by a portion of the funding standard carryover balance, the amount is then adjusted for investment experience during 2010 at a rate of 10%, in accordance with paragraph (b)(3)(iii) of this section, for a present value of the excess contribution adjusted for interest of $10,671 ($9,701 x 1.10) as of January 1, 2011.

*Example (7).* (i) The facts are the same as in Example 4. Plan P's effective interest rate for 2011 is 6.5%, and the rate of return on investments during 2011 is 7%. All required quarterly installments for the 2011 plan year were made by the applicable due dates. On February 1, 2012, Sponsor S elects to use $50,000 of Plan P's prefunding and funding standard carryover balances to offset the minimum required contribution for the 2011 plan year. On April 15, 2012, Sponsor S elects to use Plan P's prefunding and funding standard carryover balances to offset the 2012 minimum required contribution by $20,000, in accordance with paragraph (d) of this section, in order to offset the required quarterly installment then due.

(ii) When adjusting Plan P's prefunding and funding standard carryover balances to reflect Sponsor S's election to use them to offset the 2011 minimum required contribution, the remaining $10,200 in the funding standard carryover balance as of January 1, 2011, must be used before any portion of the prefunding balance. The prefunding balance is reduced by the remaining $39,800 ($50,000 total election minus $10,200 from the funding standard carryover balance).

(iii) The amount available for Sponsor S's election to use Plan P's prefunding and funding standard carryover balances to offset the 2012 minimum required contribution is determined by reducing the January 1, 2011, prefunding and funding standard carryover balances to reflect the election to use the prefunding and funding standard carryover balances to offset the 2011 minimum required contribution, and by adjusting the resulting amount to January 1, 2012, using the rate of investment return for Plan P during 2011. Accordingly, the available amount in Plan P's funding standard carryover balance as of January 1, 2012, is zero. The available amount in Plan P's prefunding balance as of January 1, 2012, is $20,087 ($58,573 minus $39,800, increased by 7%). Therefore, Sponsor S has $20,087 available to offset the minimum required contribution for the 2012 plan year.

*Example (8).* (i) The facts are the same as in Example 7, except that based on the enrolled actuary's certification of the AFTAP on July 1, 2012, Sponsor S is deemed to elect to reduce the January 1, 2012, prefunding balance by $15,000 under section 436(f)(3).

(ii) In accordance with paragraph (d)(1)(ii)(B) of this section, the deemed election to reduce the prefunding balance is deemed to occur on the first day of the plan year, and before the date of any election to offset the minimum required contribution for the 2012 plan year. The deemed election does not affect Sponsor S's election to offset the 2011 minimum contribution because that election was made on February 1, 2012, before the date of the deemed election, July 1, 2012.

(iii) As shown in Example 7, the available prefunding balance as of January 1, 2012, after reflecting the February 1, 2012, election to offset the 2011 minimum required contribution but before reflecting the April 15, 2012, election to offset the 2012 minimum required contribution, is $20,087. Adjusting this amount to reflect the deemed election to reduce the prefunding balance by $15,000 leaves a balance of $5,087 available to offset the minimum required contribution for 2012.

(iv) The portion of the quarterly installment due April 15, 2012 that was not covered by the remaining $5,087 prefunding balance is considered unpaid retroactive to April 15, 2012.

*Example (9).* (i) The facts are the same as in Example 8, except that Sponsor S does not make the election to offset the 2011 minimum required contribution until August 1, 2012, and the deemed election as of July 1, 2012, reduces Plan P's prefunding and funding standard carryover balances as of January 1, 2012, by $68,500. Sponsor S does not elect to use Plan P's prefunding and funding standard carryover balances to offset the 2012 minimum contribution.

(ii) In accordance with paragraph (d)(1)(ii)(A) of this section, the July 1, 2012, deemed election to reduce Plan P's prefunding and funding standard carryover balances must be taken into account before determining the amount available to offset the 2011 minimum required contribution because the election to offset the 2011 minimum required contribution was made after the date of the deemed election, July 1, 2012.

(iii) Pursuant to paragraph (d)(1)(ii)(C) of this section, the January 1, 2011, prefunding and funding standard carryover balances are adjusted to January 1, 2012, using Plan P's rate of investment return for 2011 of 7%. This results in an available funding standard carryover balance of $10,914 ($10,200 x 1.07) and an available prefunding balance of $62,673 (58,573 x 1.07) as of January 1, 2012.

(iv) Paragraph (d)(2) of this section requires that the funding standard carryover balance must be used before reducing Plan P's prefunding balance. Accordingly, the funding standard carryover balance is eliminated, and the prefunding balance is reduced by the remaining $57,586 ($68,500 - $10,914), resulting in an available prefunding balance of $5,087 ($62,673 - $57,586) as of January 1, 2012.

(v) In accordance with paragraph (d)(1)(ii)(D) of this section, the remaining balance is adjusted to January 1, 2011, to determine the amount available to offset the 2011 minimum required contribution. This adjustment is done by dividing the remaining balance by 1 plus the rate of investment return for 2011. Accordingly, the amount available to offset the 2011 minimum required contribution is $4,754 ($5,087 / 1.07).

(vi) If the plan sponsor elects to use the $4,754 available balance to offset the 2011 minimum required contribution, the funding standard carryover balance as of January 1, 2012 (prior to the deemed reduction under section 436(f)(3)) is $5,827 ($10,200 less $4,754, plus $381 for investment experience at a rate of 7%). The prefunding balance as of January 1, 2012 (prior to the deemed reduction under section 436(f)(3)) is $62,673 (that is, $58,573 x 1.07). The deemed election to reduce Plan P's balance is first applied to eliminate the funding standard carryover balance, and the remaining $62,673 ($68,500 less $5,827) reduces the January 1, 2012, prefunding balance to zero.

*Example (10).* (i) Plan V is a defined benefit plan with a plan year that is the calendar year and a valuation date of December 31. The valuation is based on the fair market value of plan assets, which amounts to $1,000,000 as of December 31, 2010, before any adjustments. As of January 1, 2010, Plan V's funding standard carryover balance is $0 and its prefunding balance is $125,000. Plan V's effective interest rate for 2010 is 5.5%. The enrolled actuary's certification of AFTAP for 2010 on March 31, 2010, results in a deemed reduction of $15,000 in the plan's prefunding balance as of January 1, 2010. Plan V's sponsor elected to use the prefunding balance to offset any portion of the minimum required contribution for 2010 not covered by cash contributions.

(ii) In accordance with paragraph (b)(4)(i) of this section, the amount of the prefunding balance subtracted from plan assets is increased from the first day of the plan year to the valuation date using the effective interest rate of 5.5% for 2009. Accordingly, the prefunding balance used for this purpose is $116,050 [($125,000 - $15,000 deemed reduction) x 1.055].

(iii) The fair market value of plan assets used for the December 31, 2010, valuation is $883,950 ($1,000,000 - $116,050).

*Example (11).* (i) The facts are the same as in Example 10. The minimum contribution for Plan V for the 2010 plan year is $45,000; no quarterly installments are required for Plan V for 2010. Plan V's sponsor makes a contribution of $20,000 for the 2010 plan year on July 1, 2011. The actual rate of return on assets for Plan V during 2010 is 10%.

(ii) The contribution of $20,000 is discounted to December 31, 2010, using the effective interest rate of 5.5% to determine the remaining balance of the 2010 minimum required contribution. Accordingly, the contribution is adjusted to $19,472 ($20,000 / 1.055 \0.5\) as of December 31, 2010, and the balance of the minimum required contribution is $25,528 ($45,000 - $19,472). This balance will be covered by the plan sponsor's election to use the prefunding balance to offset any portion of the minimum required contribution not covered by cash contributions.

(iii) Under section (b)(4)(ii) of this section, the amount used to offset the 2010 minimum required contribution for the purpose of adjusting the prefunding balance is discounted to January 1, 2010, using the effective interest rate for 2010. This amount is calculated as $24,197 ($25,528 / 1.055).

(iv) The prefunding balance as of January 1, 2011, is reduced by the deemed election of $15,000 and the discounted amount used to offset the 2010 minimum required contribution ($24,197), and adjusted for investment experience for 2010 using the actual rate of return of 10%. Accordingly, the prefunding balance as of January 1, 2011 is $94,383 [($125,000 - $15,000 - $24,197) x 1.10].

*Example (12).* (i) The facts are the same as in Example 11, except that the enrolled actuary's certification of the AFTAP as of March 31, 2011, results in a deemed reduction of the prefunding balance as of January 1, 2011, of $75,000.

(ii) Under paragraph (d)(1)(ii) of this section, the deemed reduction of the prefunding balance is applied before the election to use the prefunding balance to offset the balance of the minimum required contribution for 2010. To determine the amount of the prefunding balance available to cover the remaining minimum required contribution for 2010, the deemed reduction is adjusted for investment experience to January 1, 2010, using the actual rate of return of 10% for 2010. Accordingly, the adjusted deemed reduction is $68,182 ($75,000 / 1.10) and the available prefunding balance as of January 1, 2010, is $41,818 ($125,000 - $15,000 adjusted deemed reduction for 2010 - $68,182 adjusted deemed reduction for 2011).

(iii) This amount is then adjusted to December 31, 2010, using the effective interest rate of 5.5%. The amount of the prefunding balance available to offset the 2009 minimum required contribution as of December 31, 2010, is $44,118 ($41,818 x 1.055). This amount is larger than the election made by Plan V's sponsor to offset the minimum required contribution for 2010 ($25,528) and so the election remains valid.

**(h) Effective/applicability date and transition rules.** *(1) Statutory effective date/applicability date.* Section 430 generally applies to plan years beginning on or after January 1, 2008. The applicability of section 430 for purposes of determining the minimum required contribution is delayed for certain plans in accordance with sections 104 through 106 of PPA '06.

*(2) Effective date/applicability date of regulations.* This section applies to plan years beginning on or after January 1, 2010. For plan years beginning before January 1, 2010, plans are permitted to rely on the provisions set forth in this section for purposes of satisfying the requirements of section 430.

*(3) Special lookback rule for 2007 plan year's funding ratio.* (i) Plan assets. For purposes of determining a plan's prior plan year funding ratio under paragraph (d)(3) of this section with respect to the first plan year beginning on or after January 1, 2008, the value of plan assets on the valuation date of the preceding plan year (the "2007 plan year") is determined under section 412(c)(2) as in effect for the 2007 plan year, except that, for this purpose—

(A) If the value of plan assets is less than 90 percent of the fair market value of plan assets for the 2007 plan year on that date, such value is considered to be 90 percent of the fair market value; and

(B) If the value of plan assets is greater than 110 percent of the fair market value of plan assets for the 2007 plan year on that date, such value is considered to be 110 percent of the fair market value.

(ii) Funding target. For purposes of determining a plan's prior plan year funding ratio under paragraph (d)(3) of this section with respect to the first plan year beginning on or after January 1, 2008, the funding target of the plan for the preceding plan year is equal to the plan's current liability under section 412(l)(7) (as in effect prior to amendment by PPA '06) on the valuation date for the 2007 plan year.

(iii) Special rules for new plans, mergers, and spinoffs. In the case of a plan described in paragraph (d)(3)(ii), (d)(3)(iii), or (d)(3)(iv) of this section, the plan's prior plan year funding ratio with respect to the first plan year beginning on or after January 1, 2008 is determined using rules similar to the rules of paragraphs (d)(3)(ii), (d)(3)(iii), and (d)(3)(iv) of this section.

*(4) First effective plan year.* For purposes of this section, the term first effective plan year means the first plan year beginning on or after the date section 430 applies for purposes of determining the minimum required contribution for the plan.

*(5) Pre-effective plan year.* For purposes of this section, the term pre-effective plan year means the plan year immediately preceding the first effective plan year.

T.D. 9467, 10/07/2009.

## § 1.430(g)-1 Valuation date and valuation of plan assets.

**(a) In general.** *(1) Overview.* This section provides rules relating to a plan's valuation date and the valuation of a plan's assets for a plan year under section 430(g). Section 430 and this section apply to single employer defined benefit plans (including multiple employer plans as defined in section 413(c)) that are subject to the rules of section 412, but do not apply to multiemployer plans (as defined in section 414(f)). Paragraph (b) of this section describes valuation date rules. Paragraph (c) of this section describes rules regarding the determination of the asset value for purposes of a plan's actuarial valuation. Paragraph (d) of this section contains rules for taking employer contributions into account in the determination of the value of plan assets. Paragraph (e) of this section contains examples. Paragraph (f) of this section sets forth effective/applicability dates and transition rules.

*(2) Special rules for multiple employer plans.* In the case of a multiple employer plan to which section 413(c)(4)(A) applies, the rules of section 430 and this section are applied separately for each employer under the plan as if each employer maintained a separate plan. Thus, in such a case, the value of plan assets is determined separately for each employer under the plan. In the case of a multiple employer plan to which section 413(c)(4)(A) does not apply (that is, a plan described in section 413(c)(4)(B) that has not made the election for section 413(c)(4)(A) to apply), the rules of section 430 and this section are applied as if all participants in the plan were employed by a single employer.

**(b) Valuation date.** *(1) In general.* The determination of the funding target, target normal cost, and value of plan assets for a plan year is made as of the valuation date for that plan year. Except as otherwise provided in paragraph (b)(2) of this section, the valuation date for any plan year is the first day of the plan year.

*(2) Exception for small plans.* (i) In general. If, on each day during the preceding plan year, a plan had 100 or fewer participants determined by applying the rules of § 1.430(d)-1(e)(1) and (2) (including active and inactive participants and all other individuals entitled to future benefits), then the plan may designate any day during the plan year as its valuation date for that plan year and succeeding plan years. For purposes of this paragraph (b)(2)(i), all defined benefit plans (other than multiemployer plans as defined in section 414(f)) maintained by an employer are treated as one plan, but only participants with respect to that employer are taken into account.

(ii) Employer determination. For purposes of this paragraph (b)(2), the employer includes all members of the employer's controlled group determined pursuant to section 414(b), (c), (m), and (o) and includes any predecessor of the employer that, during the prior year, employed any employees of the employer who are covered by the plan.

(iii) Application of exception in first plan year. In the case of the first plan year of any plan, the exception for small plans under paragraph (b)(2)(i) of this section is applied by taking into account the number of participants that the plan is reasonably expected to have on each day during the first plan year.

(iv) Valuation date is part of funding method. The selection of a plan's valuation date is part of the plan's funding method and, accordingly, may only be changed with the consent of the Commissioner. A change of a plan's valuation date that is required by section 430 is treated as having been approved by the Commissioner and does not require the Commissioner's prior specific approval. Thus, if a plan that ceases to be eligible for the small plan exception under this paragraph (b)(2) for a plan year because the number of participants exceeded 100 in the prior plan year, then the resulting change in the valuation date to the first day of the plan year is automatically approved by the Commissioner.

**(c) Determination of asset value.** *(1) In general.* (i) General use of fair market value. Except as otherwise provided in this paragraph (c), the value of plan assets for purposes of section 430 is equal to the fair market value of plan assets on the valuation date. Prior year contributions made after the valuation date and current year contributions made before the valuation date are taken into account to the extent provided in paragraph (d) of this section.

(ii) Fair market value. The fair market value of an asset is determined as the price at which the asset would change hands between a willing buyer and a willing seller, neither being under any compulsion to buy or sell and both having reasonable knowledge of relevant facts. Except as otherwise provided by the Commissioner, any guidance on the valuation of insurance contracts under Subchapter D of Chapter 1 the Internal Revenue Code applies for purposes of this paragraph (c)(1)(ii).

*(2) Averaging of fair market values.* (i) In general. Subject to the plan asset corridor rules of paragraph (c)(2)(iii) of this section, a plan is permitted to determine the value of plan assets on the valuation date as the average of the fair market value of assets on the valuation date and the adjusted fair market value of assets determined for one or more earlier determination dates (adjusted using the method described in paragraph (c)(2)(ii) of this section). The method of determining the value of assets is part of the plan's funding method and, accordingly, may only be changed with the consent of the Commissioner.

(ii) Adjusted fair market value— (A) Determination dates. The period of time between each determination date (treating the valuation date as a determination date) must be equal and that period of time cannot exceed 12 months. In addition, the earliest determination date with respect to a plan year cannot be earlier than the last day of the 25th month before the valuation date of the plan year (or a similar period in the case of a valuation date that is not the first day of a month). In a typical situation, the earlier determination dates will be the two immediately preceding valuation dates. However, these rules also permit the use of more frequent determination dates. For example, monthly or quarterly determination dates may be used.

(B) Adjustments for contributions and distributions. The adjusted fair market value of plan assets for a prior determination date is the fair market value of plan assets on that date, increased for contributions included in the plan's asset balance on the valuation date that were not included in the plan's asset balance on the earlier determination date, reduced for benefits and all other amounts paid from plan assets during the period beginning with the prior determination date and ending immediately before the valuation date, and adjusted for expected earnings as described in paragraph (c)(2)(ii)(D) of this section. For this purpose, the fair market value of assets as of a determination date includes any contribution for a plan year that ends with or prior to the determination date that is receivable as of the determination date (but only if the contribution is actually made within 8½ months after the end of the applicable plan year). If the contribution that is receivable as of the determination date is for a plan year beginning on or after January 1, 2008, then only the present value as of the determination date (determined using the effective interest rate under section 430(h)(2)(A) for the plan year for which the contribution is made) is included in the fair market value of assets.

(C) Treatment of spin-offs and plan-to-plan transfers. For purposes of determining the adjusted fair market value of plan assets, assets spun-off from a plan as a result of a spin-off described in § 1.414(l)-1(b)(4) are treated as an amount paid from plan assets. Except as otherwise provided by the Commissioner, for purposes of determining the adjusted fair market value of plan assets, assets that are added to a plan as a result of a plan-to-plan transfer described in § 1.414(l)-1(b)(3) are treated in the same manner as contributions.

(D) Adjustments for expected earnings. [Reserved]

(E) Assumed rate of return. [Reserved]

(F) Limitation on the assumed rate of return for periods within plan years for which the three segment rates were used. [Reserved]

(G) Limitation on the assumed rate of return for periods within plan years for which the full yield curve was used. [Reserved]

(iii) Restriction to 90-110 percent corridor— (A) In general. This paragraph (c)(2)(iii) provides rules for applying the 90 to 110 percent corridor set forth in section 430(g)(3)(B)(iii). The rules for accounting for contribution receipts under paragraphs (d)(1) and (d)(2) of this section are applied prior to the application of the 90 to 110 percent corridor under this paragraph (c)(2)(iii).

(B) Asset value less than 90 percent of fair market value. If the value of plan assets determined under paragraph (c)(2)(i) of this section is less than 90 percent of the fair market value of plan assets, then the value of plan assets under this paragraph (c)(2) is equal to 90 percent of the fair market value of plan assets.

(C) Asset value greater than 110 percent of fair market value. If the value of plan assets determined under paragraph (c)(2)(i) of this section is greater than 110 percent of the fair market value of plan assets, then the value of plan assets under this paragraph (c)(2) is equal to 110 percent of the fair market value of plan assets.

*(3) Qualified transfers to health benefit accounts.* In the case of a qualified transfer (as defined in section 420), any assets so transferred are not treated as plan assets for purposes of section 430 and this section.

**(d) Accounting for contribution receipts.** *(1) Prior year contributions.* (i) In general. For purposes of determining the value of plan assets under paragraph (c) of this section, if an employer makes a contribution to the plan after the valuation date for the current plan year and the contribution is for an earlier plan year, then the present value of the contribution determined as of that valuation date is taken into account as an asset of the plan as of the valuation date, but only if the contribution is made before the deadline for contributions as described in section 430(j)(1) for the plan year immediately preceding the current plan year. For this purpose, the present value is determined using the effective interest rate under section 430(h)(2)(A) for the plan year for which the contribution is made. (ii) Special rule for contributions for the 2007 plan year— (A) Timely contributions. Notwithstanding paragraph (d)(1)(i) of this section, if the employer makes a contribution to the plan after the valuation date for the first plan year that begins on or after January 1, 2008, and the contribution is for the immediately preceding plan year and is made by the deadline for contributions for that preceding plan year under section 412(c)(10) (as in effect before amendment by the Pension Protection Act of 2006 (PPA '06), Public Law 109-280 (120 Stat. 780)), then the contribution is taken into account as a plan asset under paragraph (d)(1)(i) of this section without applying any present value discount.

(B) Late contributions. If a contribution is for the plan year that immediately precedes the first plan year that begins on or after January 1, 2008, and is not described in paragraph (d)(1)(ii)(A) of this section, then the rules of paragraph (d)(1)(i) apply to the contribution except that the present value is determined using the valuation interest rate under section 412(c)(2) for that plan year.

(iii) Ordering rules. For purposes of this paragraph (d)(1), the ordering rules of section 4971(c)(4)(B) apply for purposes of determining the plan year for which a contribution is made.

*(2) Current year contributions made before valuation date.* In the case of a plan with a valuation date that is not the first day of the plan year, for purposes of determining the value of plan assets under paragraph (c) of this section, if an employer makes a contribution for a plan year before that year's valuation date, that contribution (and any interest on the contribution for the period between the contribution date and the valuation date, determined using the effective interest rate under section 430(h)(2)(A) for the plan year) must be subtracted from plan assets in determining the value of plan assets as of the valuation date. If the result of this subtraction is a number less than zero, the value of plan assets as of the valuation date is equal to zero.

**(e) Examples.** [Reserved]

**(f) Effective/applicability dates and transition rules.** *(1) Statutory effective date/applicability date.* Section 430 generally applies to plan years beginning on or after January 1, 2008. The applicability of section 430 for purposes of determining the minimum required contribution is delayed for certain plans in accordance with sections 104 through 106 of PPA '06.

*(2) Effective date/applicability date of regulations.* (i) In general. This section applies to plan years beginning on or after January 1, 2010, regardless of whether section 430 applies to determine the minimum required contribution for the plan year. For plan years beginning before January 1, 2010, plans are permitted to rely on the provisions set forth in this section for purposes of satisfying the requirements of section 430.

(ii) Permission to use averaging for 2008. For purposes of determining the actuarial value of assets for a plan year beginning during 2008 using the averaging rules of paragraph (c)(2) of this section, a plan is permitted to apply an assumed earnings rate of zero under paragraph (c)(2)(ii)(E) of this section (even if zero is not the actuary's best estimate of the anticipated annual rate of return on plan assets).

*(3) Approval for changes in the valuation date and valuation method.* Any change in a plan's valuation date or asset valuation method that satisfies the rules of this section and is made for either the first plan year beginning in 2008, the first plan year beginning in 2009, or the first plan year beginning in 2010 is treated as having been approved by the Commissioner and does not require the Commissioner's specific prior approval. In addition, a change in a plan's valuation date or asset valuation method for the first plan year to which section 430 applies to determine the plan's minimum required contribution (even if that plan year begins after December 31, 2010) that satisfies the rules of this section is treated as having been approved by the Commissioner and does not require the Commissioner's specific prior approval.

---

T.D. 9467, 10/07/2009.

---

### § 1.430(h)(2)-1 Interest rates used to determine present value.

**(a) In general.** *(1) Overview.* This section provides rules relating to the interest rates to be applied for a plan year under section 430(h)(2). Section 430(h)(2) and this section apply to single employer defined benefit plans (including multiple employer plans as defined in section 413(c)) that are subject to section 412 but do not apply to multiemployer plans (as defined in section 414(f)). Paragraph (b) of this section describes how the segment interest rates are used for a plan year. Paragraph (c) of this section describes those segment rates. Paragraph (d) of this section describes the monthly corporate bond yield curve that is used to develop the segment rates. Paragraph (e) of this section describes certain elections that are permitted to be made under this section. Paragraph (f) of this section describes other rules related to interest rates. Paragraph (g) of this section contains examples. Paragraph (h) of this section contains effective/applicability dates and transition rules.

*(2) Special rules for multiple employer plans.* In the case of a multiple employer plan to which section 413(c)(4)(A) applies, the rules of section 430 and this section are applied separately for each employer under the plan as if each employer maintained a separate plan. Thus, each employer under such a multiple employer plan may make elections with respect to the interest rate rules under this section that are independent of the elections of other employers under the plan. In the case of a multiple employer plan to which section 413(c)(4)(A) does not apply (that is, a plan described in section 413(c)(4)(B) that has not made the election for section 413(c)(4)(A) to apply), the rules of section 430 and this section are applied as if all participants in the plan were employed by a single employer.

**(b) Interest rates for determining plan liabilities.** *(1) In general.* The interest rates used in determining the present value of the benefits that are included in the target normal cost and the funding target for the plan for a plan year are determined as set forth in this paragraph (b).

*(2) Benefits payable within 5 years.* (i) Plans with valuation dates at the beginning of the plan year. If the valuation date is the first day of the plan year, in the case of benefits expected to be payable during the 5-year period beginning on the valuation date for the plan year, the interest rate used in determining the present value of the benefits that are included in the target normal cost and the funding target for the plan is the first segment rate with respect to the applicable month, as described in paragraph (c)(2)(i) of this section.

(ii) Plans with valuation dates other than the first day of the plan year. [Reserved]

*(3) Benefits payable after 5 years and within 20 years.* In the case of benefits expected to be payable during the 15-year period beginning after the end of the period described in paragraph (b)(2) of this section, the interest rate used in determining the present value of the benefits that are included in the target normal cost and the funding target for the plan is the second segment rate with respect to the applicable month, as described in paragraph (c)(2)(ii) of this section.

*(4) Benefits payable after 20 years.* In the case of benefits expected to be payable after the period described in paragraph (b)(3) of this section, the interest rate used in determining the present value of the benefits that are included in the target normal cost and the funding target for the plan is the third segment rate with respect to the applicable month, as described in paragraph (c)(2)(iii) of this section.

*(5) Applicable month.* Except as otherwise provided in paragraph (e) of this section, the term applicable month for purposes of this paragraph (b) means the month that includes the valuation date of the plan for the plan year.

*(6) Special rule for certain airlines.* (i) In general. Pursuant to section 6615 of the U.S. Troop Readiness, Veterans' Care, Katrina Recovery, and Iraq Accountability Appropriations Act, 2007, Public Law 110-28 (121 Stat. 112), for a plan sponsor that makes the election described in section 402(a)(2) of the Pension Protection Act of 2006 (PPA '06), Public Law 109-280 (120 Stat. 780), the interest rate required to be used to determine the plan's funding target for each of the 10 years under that election is 8.25 percent (rather than the segment rates otherwise described in this paragraph (b) or the full yield curve as permitted under paragraph (e)(4) of this section).

(ii) Special interest rate not applicable for other purposes. The special interest rate described in paragraph (b)(6)(i) of this section does not apply for other purposes such as the determination of the plan's target normal cost.

**(c) Segment rates.** *(1) Overview.* This paragraph (c) sets forth rules for determining the first, second, and third segment rates for purposes of paragraph (b) of this section. The first, second, and third segment rates are set forth in revenue rulings, notices, or other guidance published in the Internal Revenue Bulletin. See § 601.601(d)(2) relating to objectives and standards for publishing regulations, revenue rulings and revenue procedures in the Internal Revenue Bulletin. See paragraph (h)(4) of this section for a transition rule under which the definition of the segment rates is modified for plan years beginning in 2008 and 2009.

*(1) Definition of segment rates.* (i) First segment rate. For purposes of this section, except as otherwise provided under the transition rule of paragraph (h)(4) of this section, the first segment rate is, with respect to any month, the single rate of interest determined by the Commissioner on the basis of the average of the monthly corporate bond yield curves (described in paragraph (d) of this section) for the 24-month period ending with the month preceding that month, taking into account only the first 5 years of each of those yield curves.

(ii) Second segment rate. For purposes of this section, except as otherwise provided under the transition rule of paragraph (h)(4) of this section, the second segment rate is, with respect to any month, the single rate of interest determined by the Commissioner on the basis of the average of the monthly corporate bond yield curves (described in paragraph (d) of this section) for the 24-month period ending with the month preceding that month, taking into account only the portion of each of those yield curves corresponding to the 15-year period that follows the end of the 5-year period described in paragraph (c)(2)(i) of this section.

(iii) Third segment rate. For purposes of this section, except as otherwise provided under the transition rule of paragraph (h)(4) of this section, the third segment rate is, with respect to any month, the single rate of interest determined by the Commissioner on the basis of the average of the monthly corporate bond yield curves (described in paragraph (d) of this section) for the 24-month period ending with the month preceding that month, taking into account only the portion of each of those yield curves corresponding to the 40-year period that follows the end of the 15-year period described in paragraph (c)(2)(ii) of this section.

**(d) Monthly corporate bond yield curve.** *(1) In general.* For purposes of this section, the monthly corporate bond yield curve is, with respect to any month, a yield curve that is prescribed by the Commissioner for that month based on yields for that month on investment grade corporate bonds with varying maturities that are in the top three quality levels available.

*(2) Determination and publication of yield curve.* A description of the methodology for determining the monthly corporate bond yield curve is provided in guidance issued by the Commissioner that is published in the Internal Revenue Bulletin. The yield curve for a month will be set forth in revenue rulings, notices, or other guidance published in the Internal Revenue Bulletin. See § 601.601(d)(2) relating to objectives and standards for publishing regulations, revenue rulings and revenue procedures in the Internal Revenue Bulletin.

**(e) Elections.** *(1) In general.* This paragraph (e) describes elections for a plan year that a plan sponsor can make to use alternative interest rates under this section. Any election under this paragraph (e) must be made by providing written notification of the election to the plan's enrolled actuary. Any election in this paragraph (e) may be adopted for a plan year without obtaining the consent of the Commissioner, but, once adopted, that election will apply for that plan year and all future plan years and may be changed only with the consent of the Commissioner.

*(2) Election for alternative applicable month.* As an alternative to defining the applicable month as the month that includes the valuation date for the plan year, a plan sponsor that is using segment rates as provided under paragraph (b) of this section may elect to use one of the 4 months preceding that month as the applicable month.

*(3) Election not to apply transition rule.* The plan sponsor may elect not to apply the transition rule in paragraph (h)(4) of this section.

*(4) Election to use full yield curve.* (i) In general. For purposes of determining the plan's funding target and target normal cost, and for all other purposes under section 430 (including the determination of shortfall amortization installments, waiver installments, and the present values of those installments as described in paragraph (f)(2) of this section), the plan sponsor may elect to use interest rates under the monthly corporate bond yield curve described in paragraph (d) of this section for the month preceding the month that includes the valuation date in lieu of the segment rates determined under paragraph (c) of this section. In order to address the timing of benefit payments during a year, reasonable approximations are permitted to be used to value benefit payments that are expected to be made during a plan year.

(ii) Reasonable techniques permitted. In the case of a plan sponsor using the monthly corporate bond yield curve under this paragraph (e)(4), if with respect to a decrement the benefit is only expected to be paid for one-half of a year (because the decrement was assumed to occur in the middle of the year), the interest rate for that year can be determined as if the benefit were being paid for the entire year. See § 1.430(d)-1(f)(7) for additional reasonable techniques that can be used in determining present value.

*(5) Plan sponsor.* For purposes of the elections described in this section, any reference to the plan sponsor generally means the employer or employers responsible for making contributions to or under the plan. In the case of plans that are multiple employer plans to which section 413(c)(4)(A) does not apply, any reference to the plan sponsor means the plan administrator within the meaning of section 414(g).

**(f) Interest rates used for other purposes.** *(1) Effective interest rate.* (i) In general. Except as otherwise provided in paragraph (f)(2) of this section, the effective interest rate determined under section 430(h)(2)(A) for the plan year is the single interest rate that, if used to determine the present value of the benefits that are taken into account in determining the plan's funding target for the plan year, would result in an amount equal to the plan's funding target determined for the plan year under section 430(d) as described in § 1.430(d)-1(b)(2) (without regard to calculations for plans in at-risk status under section 430(i)).

(ii) Zero funding target. If, for the plan year, the plan's funding target is equal to zero, then the effective interest rate determined under section 430(h)(2)(A) for the plan year is the single interest rate that, if used to determine the present value of the benefits that are taken into account in determining the plan's target normal cost for the plan year, would result in an amount equal to the plan's target normal cost determined for the plan year under section 430(b) as described in § 1.430(d)-1(b)(1) (without regard to calculations for plans in at-risk status under section 430(i)).

*(2) Interest rates used for determining shortfall amortization installments and waiver amortization installments.* The interest rates used to determine the amount of shortfall amortization installments and waiver amortization installments and the present value of those installments are determined based on the dates those installments are assumed to be paid, using the same timing rules that apply in determining target normal cost as described in paragraph (b) of this section. Thus, for a plan that uses the segment rates described in paragraph (c) of this section, the first segment rate applies to

the installments assumed to be paid during the first 5-year period beginning on the valuation date for the plan year, and the second segment rate applies to the installments assumed to be paid during the subsequent 15-year period. For purposes of this paragraph (f)(2), the shortfall amortization installments for a plan year are assumed to be paid on the valuation date for that plan year. For example, for a plan that uses the segment rates described in paragraph (c) of this section, the shortfall amortization installment for the fifth plan year following the current plan year (the sixth installment) is assumed to be paid on the valuation date for that year so that such shortfall amortization installment will be determined using the second segment rate.

**(g) Examples.** The following examples illustrate the rules of this section:

*Example (1).* (i) The January 1, 2009, valuation of Plan P is performed using the segment rates applicable for September 2008 (determined without regard to the transition rule of section 430(h)(2)(G)), and the 2009 annuitant and nonannuitant (male and female) mortality tables as published in Notice 2008-85. See § 601.601(d)(2) relating to objectives and standards for publishing regulations, revenue rulings and revenue procedures in the Internal Revenue Bulletin. Plan P provides for early retirement benefits as early as age 50, and offers a single-sum distribution payable immediately at retirement. The single-sum payment is equal to the present value of the participant's accrued benefit, based on the applicable interest rates and the applicable mortality table under section 417(e)(3). Participant E is the only participant in the plan, and is a male age 46 as of January 1, 2009, with an annual accrued benefit of $23,000 payable beginning at age 65. The actuary assumes a 100% probability that Participant E will terminate at age 50 and will elect to receive his benefit in the form of a single-sum payment.

(ii) Plan P's funding target is $68,908 as of January 1, 2009. This figure is based on the male nonannuitant rates for ages prior to age 50, the applicable mortality rates under section 417(e)(3) for ages 50 and later, and segment interest rates of 5.07% for the first 5 years after the valuation date, 6.09% for the next 15 years, and 6.56% for periods more than 20 years after the valuation date. (See § 1.430(d)-1(f)(9), Example 10, for additional details.)

(iii) The present value of Participant E's benefits as of January 1, 2009, is $68,908 if a single interest rate of 6.52805% is substituted for the segment interest rates but all other assumptions remain the same. Thus (rounded), the effective interest rate for Plan P is 6.53% for 2009.

*Example (2).* (i) The facts are the same as for Example 1, except that Plan P offers a single-sum distribution equal to the present value of the accrued benefit based on the applicable interest rates under section 417(e)(3) or an interest rate of 6.25%, whichever produces the higher amount. The applicable mortality table under section 417(e)(3) is used for both calculations.

(ii) The present value of Participant E's age-50 single-sum distribution as of January 1, 2009 (when Participant E is age 46) is $77,392. This amount is determined by calculating the projected single-sum distribution at age 50 using the applicable mortality table under section 417(e)(3) and an interest rate of 6.25%, and discounting the result to January 1, 2009, using the first segment rate of 5.07% and male nonannuitant mortality rates for 2009. Because this amount is larger than the present value of Participant E's single-sum payment based on the applicable interest rates under section 417(e)(3) (that is, $68,908), the funding target for Plan P is $77,392 as of January 1, 2009. (See § 1.430(d)-1(f)(9), Example 12 for additional details.)

(iii) The effective interest rate is the single interest rate that will produce the same funding target if substituted for the segment interest rates keeping all other assumptions the same, including the fixed interest rate used by the plan to determine single-sum payments. The only segment interest rate used to develop the funding target of $77,392 was the first segment rate of 5.07%. Therefore, considering only this calculation, the single interest rate that would produce the same funding target would be 5.07%.

(iv) However, the effective interest rate must also reflect the fact that the single-sum payment under Plan P is equal to the greater of the present value of Participant E's accrued benefit based on the fixed rate of 6.25% or the applicable interest rates under section 417(e)(3). If the single rate of 5.07% is substituted for the segment rates used to calculate the present value of the single-sum payment based on the applicable interest rates, the resulting funding target would be higher than $77,392.

(v) Using a single interest rate of 6.0771%, the January 1, 2009, present value of Participant E's single-sum payment based on the applicable interest rates is $77,392, and the present value of Participant E's single sum payment based on the plan's interest rate of 6.25% is $74,494. Plan P's funding target is the larger of the two, or $77,392, which is the same as the funding target based on the segment interest rates used for the 2009 valuation. Therefore, Plan P's effective interest rate for 2009 (rounded) is 6.08%.

**(h) Effective/applicability dates and transition rules.** *(1) Statutory effective date/applicability date.* Section 430 generally applies to plan years beginning on or after January 1, 2008. The applicability of section 430 for purposes of determining the minimum required contribution is delayed for certain plans in accordance with sections 104 through 106 of PPA'06.

*(2) Effective date/applicability date of regulations.* This section applies to plan years beginning on or after January 1, 2010, regardless of whether section 430 applies to determine the minimum required contribution for the plan year. For plan years beginning before January 1, 2010, plans are permitted to rely on the provisions set forth in this section for purposes of satisfying the requirements of section 430.

*(3) Approval for changes in interest rate.* Any change to an election under paragraph (e) of this section that is made for the first plan year beginning in 2009 or the first plan year beginning in 2010 is treated as having been approved by the Commissioner and does not require the Commissioner's specific prior approval.

*(4) Transition rule.* (i) In general. Notwithstanding the general rules for determination of segment rates under paragraph (c)(2) of this section, for plan years beginning in 2008 or 2009, the first, second, or third segment rate for a plan with respect to any month is equal to the sum of—

(A) The product of that rate for that month determined without regard to this paragraph (h)(4), multiplied by the applicable percentage; and

(B) The product of the weighted average interest rate determined under the rules of paragraph (h)(4)(iii) of this section, multiplied by a percentage equal to 100 percent minus the applicable percentage.

(ii) Applicable percentage. For purposes of this paragraph (h)(4), the applicable percentage is 33\1/3\ percent for plan years beginning in 2008 and 66\2/3\ percent for plan years beginning in 2009.

(iii) Weighted average interest rate. The weighted average interest rate for purposes of paragraph (h)(4)(i)(B) of this section is the weighted average interest rate under section 412(b)(5)(B)(ii)(II) (as that provision was in effect for plan years beginning in 2007) as of—

(A) The month which contains the first day of the plan year;

(B) The month which contains the valuation date (if the applicable month is determined under paragraph (b)(5) of this section); or

(C) The applicable month (if the applicable month is determined under paragraph (e)(2) of this section).

(iv) New plans ineligible. The transition rule of this paragraph (h)(4) does not apply if the first plan year of the plan begins on or after January 1, 2008.

T.D. 9467, 10/07/2009.

### § 1.430(h)(3)-1 Mortality tables used to determine present value.

**(a) Basis for mortality tables.** *(1) In general.* This section sets forth rules for the mortality tables to be used in determining present value or making any computation under section 430. Generally applicable mortality tables for participants and beneficiaries are set forth in this section pursuant to section 430(h)(3)(A). In lieu of using the mortality tables provided under this section with respect to participants and beneficiaries, plan-specific substitute mortality tables are permitted to be used for this purpose pursuant to section 430(h)(3)(C) provided that the requirements of § 1.430(h)(3)-2 are satisfied. Mortality tables that may be used with respect to disabled individuals are to be provided in guidance published in the Internal Revenue Bulletin. See § 601.601(d)(2)(ii)(b) of this chapter.

*(2) Static tables or generational tables permitted.* The generally applicable mortality tables provided under section 430(h)(3)(A) are the static tables described in paragraph (a)(3) of this section and the generational mortality tables described in paragraph (a)(4) of this section. A plan is permitted to use either of those sets of mortality tables with respect to participants and beneficiaries pursuant to this section.

*(3) Static tables.* The static mortality tables that are permitted to be used pursuant to paragraph (a)(2) of this section are updated annually to reflect expected improvements in mortality experience as described in paragraph (c)(2) of this section. Static mortality tables that are to be used with respect to valuation dates occurring during 2008 are provided in paragraph (e) of this section. The mortality tables to be used with respect to valuation dates occurring in later years are to be provided in guidance published in the Internal Revenue Bulletin. See § 601.601(d)(2)(ii)(b) of this chapter.

*(4) Generational mortality tables.* (i) In general. The generational mortality tables that are permitted to be used pursuant to paragraph (a)(2) of this section are determined pursuant to this paragraph (a)(4) using the base mortality tables and projection factors set forth in paragraph (d) of this section. Under the generational mortality tables, the probability of an individual's death at a particular age is determined as the individual's base mortality rate (that is, the applicable mortality rate from the table set forth in paragraph (d) of this section for the age for which the probability of death is being determined) multiplied by the mortality improvement factor. The mortality improvement factor is equal to (1-projection factor for that age)\n\, where n is equal to the projection period. For this purpose, the projection period is the number of years between 2000 and the year for which the probability of death is being determined.

(ii) Examples of calculation. As an example of the use of generational mortality tables under paragraph (a)(4)(i) of this section, for purposes of determining the probability of death at age 54 for a male annuitant born in 1974, the base mortality rate is .005797, the projection factor is .020, and the projection period (the period from the year 2000 until the year the participant will attain age 54) is 28 years, so that the mortality improvement factor is .567976, and the probability of death at age 54 is .003293. Similarly, under these generational mortality tables, the probability of death at age 55 for the same male annuitant would be determined by using the base mortality rate and projection factor at age 55, and a projection period of 29 years (the period from the year 2000 until the year the participant will attain age 55). Thus, the base mortality rate is .005905, the projection factor is .019, so that the mortality improvement factor is .573325 ((1-.019)\29\), and the probability of death at age 55 is .003385 (.573325 times .005905). Because these generational mortality tables reflect expected improvements in mortality experience, no periodic updates are needed.

**(b) Use of the tables.** *(1) Separate tables for annuitants and nonannuitants.* (i) In general. Separate tables are provided for use for annuitants and nonannuitants. The nonannuitant mortality table is applied to determine the probability of survival for a nonannuitant for the period before the nonannuitant is projected to commence receiving benefits. The annuitant mortality table is applied to determine the present value of benefits for each annuitant, and for each nonannuitant for the period beginning when the nonannuitant is projected to commence receiving benefits. For purposes of this section, an annuitant means a plan participant who has commenced receiving benefits and a nonannuitant means a plan participant who has not yet commenced receiving benefits (for example, an active employee or a terminated vested participant). A participant whose benefit has partially commenced is treated as an annuitant with respect to the portion of the benefit which has commenced and a nonannuitant with respect to the balance of the benefit. In addition, for any period in which an annuitant is projected to be receiving benefits, any beneficiary with respect to that annuitant is also treated as an annuitant for purposes of this paragraph (b)(1).

(ii) Examples of calculation. As an example of the use of separate annuitant and nonannuitant tables under paragraph (b)(1)(i) of this section, with respect to a 45-year-old active participant who is projected to commence receiving an annuity at age 55, the funding target would be determined using the nonannuitant mortality table for the period before the participant attains age 55 (so that, if the static mortality tables are used pursuant to paragraph (a)(3) of this section, the probability of an active male participant living from age 45 to age 55 using the table that applies for a plan year beginning in 2008 is 98.61%) and the annuitant mortality table for the period ages 55 and above. Similarly, if a 45-year-old terminated vested participant is projected to commence an annuity at age 65, the funding target would be determined using the nonannuitant mortality table for the period before the participant attains age 65 and the annuitant mortality table for ages 65 and above.

*(2) Small plan tables.* If static mortality tables are used pursuant to paragraph (a)(3) of this section, as an alternative

to the separate static tables specified for annuitants and nonannuitants pursuant to paragraph (b)(1) of this section, a combined static table that applies the same mortality rates to both annuitants and nonannuitants is permitted to be used for a small plan. For this purpose, a small plan is defined as a plan with 500 or fewer participants (including both active and inactive participants) on the valuation date.

**(c) Construction of static tables.** *(1) Source of basic rates.* The static mortality tables that are used pursuant to paragraph (a)(3) of this section are based on the base mortality tables set forth in paragraph (d) of this section.

*(2) Projected mortality improvements.* The mortality rates under the base mortality tables are projected to improve using the projection factors provided in Projection Scale AA, as set forth in paragraph (d) of this section. Using these projection factors, the mortality rate for an individual at each age is determined as the individual's base mortality rate (that is, the applicable base mortality rate from the table set forth in paragraph (d) of this section for the individual at that age) multiplied by the mortality improvement factor. The mortality improvement factor is equal to (1-projection factor for that age)\n\, where n is equal to the projection period. The annuitant mortality rates for a plan year are determined using a projection period that runs from the calendar year 2000 until 7 years after the calendar year that contains the valuation date for the plan year. The nonannuitant mortality rates for a plan year are determined using a projection period that runs from the calendar year 2000 until 15 years after the calendar year that contains the valuation date for the plan year. Thus, for example, for a plan year with a January 1, 2012, valuation date, the annuitant mortality rates are determined using a projection period that runs from 2000 until 2019 (19 years) and the nonannuitant mortality rates are determined using a projection period that runs from 2000 until 2027 (27 years).

*(3) Construction of combined tables for small plans.* The combined mortality tables that are permitted to be used for small plans pursuant to paragraph (b)(2) of this section are constructed from the separate nonannuitant and annuitant tables using the weighting factors for small plans that are set forth in paragraph (d) of this section. The weighting factors are applied to develop these mortality tables using the following equation: Combined mortality rate = [nonannuitant rate *\ (1-weighting factor)] + [annuitant rate *\ weighting factor].

**(d) Base mortality tables and projection factors.** The following base mortality tables and projection factors are used to determine generational mortality tables for purposes of determining present value or making any computation under section 430 as set forth in paragraph (a)(4) of this section. In addition, the following base mortality tables and projection factors are used to determine the static mortality tables that are used for purposes of determining present value or making any computation under section 430 as set forth in paragraphs (a)(3) and (c) of this section. See § 1.430(h)(3)-2(c)(3) for rules regarding the required use of the projection factors set forth in this paragraph (d) in connection with a plan-specific substitute mortality table.

| Age | Male Base non-annuitant mortality rates (year 2000) | Male Base annuitant mortality rates (year 2000) | Male Scale AA projection factors | Male Weighting factors for small plans | Female Base non-annuitant mortality rates (year 2000) | Female Base annuitant mortality rates (year 2000) | Female Scale AA projection factors | Female Weighting factors for small plans |
|---|---|---|---|---|---|---|---|---|
| 1 ........ | 0.000637 | 0.000637 | 0.020 | .... | 0.000571 | 0.000571 | 0.020 | .... |
| 2 ........ | 0.000430 | 0.000430 | 0.020 | .... | 0.000372 | 0.000372 | 0.020 | .... |
| 3 ........ | 0.000357 | 0.000357 | 0.020 | .... | 0.000278 | 0.000278 | 0.020 | .... |
| 4 ........ | 0.000278 | 0.000278 | 0.020 | .... | 0.000208 | 0.000208 | 0.020 | .... |
| 5 ........ | 0.000255 | 0.000255 | 0.020 | .... | 0.000188 | 0.000188 | 0.020 | .... |
| 6 ........ | 0.000244 | 0.000244 | 0.020 | .... | 0.000176 | 0.000176 | 0.020 | .... |
| 7 ........ | 0.000234 | 0.000234 | 0.020 | .... | 0.000165 | 0.000165 | 0.020 | .... |
| 8 ........ | 0.000216 | 0.000216 | 0.020 | .... | 0.000147 | 0.000147 | 0.020 | .... |
| 9 ........ | 0.000209 | 0.000209 | 0.020 | .... | 0.000140 | 0.000140 | 0.020 | .... |
| 10 ....... | 0.000212 | 0.000212 | 0.020 | .... | 0.000141 | 0.000141 | 0.020 | .... |
| 11 ....... | 0.000219 | 0.000219 | 0.020 | .... | 0.000143 | 0.000143 | 0.020 | .... |
| 12 ....... | 0.000228 | 0.000228 | 0.020 | .... | 0.000148 | 0.000148 | 0.020 | .... |
| 13 ....... | 0.000240 | 0.000240 | 0.020 | .... | 0.000155 | 0.000155 | 0.020 | .... |
| 14 ....... | 0.000254 | 0.000254 | 0.019 | .... | 0.000162 | 0.000162 | 0.018 | .... |
| 15 ....... | 0.000269 | 0.000269 | 0.019 | .... | 0.000170 | 0.000170 | 0.016 | .... |
| 16 ....... | 0.000284 | 0.000284 | 0.019 | .... | 0.000177 | 0.000177 | 0.015 | .... |
| 17 ....... | 0.000301 | 0.000301 | 0.019 | .... | 0.000184 | 0.000184 | 0.014 | .... |
| 18 ....... | 0.000316 | 0.000316 | 0.019 | .... | 0.000188 | 0.000188 | 0.014 | .... |
| 19 ....... | 0.000331 | 0.000331 | 0.019 | .... | 0.000190 | 0.000190 | 0.015 | .... |
| 20 ....... | 0.000345 | 0.000345 | 0.019 | .... | 0.000191 | 0.000191 | 0.016 | .... |
| 21 ....... | 0.000357 | 0.000357 | 0.018 | .... | 0.000192 | 0.000192 | 0.017 | .... |
| 22 ....... | 0.000366 | 0.000366 | 0.017 | .... | 0.000194 | 0.000194 | 0.017 | .... |
| 23 ....... | 0.000373 | 0.000373 | 0.015 | .... | 0.000197 | 0.000197 | 0.016 | .... |
| 24 ....... | 0.000376 | 0.000376 | 0.013 | .... | 0.000201 | 0.000201 | 0.015 | .... |
| 25 ....... | 0.000376 | 0.000376 | 0.010 | .... | 0.000207 | 0.000207 | 0.014 | .... |
| 26 ....... | 0.000378 | 0.000378 | 0.006 | .... | 0.000214 | 0.000214 | 0.012 | .... |
| 27 ....... | 0.000382 | 0.000382 | 0.005 | .... | 0.000223 | 0.000223 | 0.012 | .... |
| 28 ....... | 0.000393 | 0.000393 | 0.005 | .... | 0.000235 | 0.000235 | 0.012 | .... |
| 29 ....... | 0.000412 | 0.000412 | 0.005 | .... | 0.000248 | 0.000248 | 0.012 | .... |
| 30 ....... | 0.000444 | 0.000444 | 0.005 | .... | 0.000264 | 0.000264 | 0.010 | .... |

| | | | | | | | | |
|---|---|---|---|---|---|---|---|---|
| 31 ........ | 0.000499 | 0.000499 | 0.005 | .... | 0.000307 | 0.000307 | 0.008 | .... |
| 32 ........ | 0.000562 | 0.000562 | 0.005 | .... | 0.000350 | 0.000350 | 0.008 | .... |
| 33 ........ | 0.000631 | 0.000631 | 0.005 | .... | 0.000394 | 0.000394 | 0.009 | .... |
| 34 ........ | 0.000702 | 0.000702 | 0.005 | .... | 0.000435 | 0.000435 | 0.010 | .... |
| 35 ........ | 0.000773 | 0.000773 | 0.005 | .... | 0.000475 | 0.000475 | 0.011 | .... |
| 36 ........ | 0.000841 | 0.000841 | 0.005 | .... | 0.000514 | 0.000514 | 0.012 | .... |
| 37 ........ | 0.000904 | 0.000904 | 0.005 | .... | 0.000554 | 0.000554 | 0.013 | .... |
| 38 ........ | 0.000964 | 0.000964 | 0.006 | .... | 0.000598 | 0.000598 | 0.014 | .... |
| 39 ........ | 0.001021 | 0.001021 | 0.007 | .... | 0.000648 | 0.000648 | 0.015 | .... |
| 40 ........ | 0.001079 | 0.001079 | 0.008 | .... | 0.000706 | 0.000706 | 0.015 | .... |
| 41 ........ | 0.001142 | 0.001157 | 0.009 | 0.0045 | 0.000774 | 0.000774 | 0.015 | .... |
| 42 ........ | 0.001215 | 0.001312 | 0.010 | 0.0091 | 0.000852 | 0.000852 | 0.015 | .... |
| 43 ........ | 0.001299 | 0.001545 | 0.011 | 0.0136 | 0.000937 | 0.000937 | 0.015 | .... |
| 44 ........ | 0.001397 | 0.001855 | 0.012 | 0.0181 | 0.001029 | 0.001029 | 0.015 | .... |
| 45 ........ | 0.001508 | 0.002243 | 0.013 | 0.0226 | 0.001124 | 0.001124 | 0.016 | 0.0084 |
| 46 ........ | 0.001616 | 0.002709 | 0.014 | 0.0272 | 0.001223 | 0.001223 | 0.017 | 0.0167 |
| 47 ........ | 0.001734 | 0.003252 | 0.015 | 0.0317 | 0.001326 | 0.001335 | 0.018 | 0.0251 |
| 48 ........ | 0.001860 | 0.003873 | 0.016 | 0.0362 | 0.001434 | 0.001559 | 0.018 | 0.0335 |
| 49 ........ | 0.001995 | 0.004571 | 0.017 | 0.0407 | 0.001550 | 0.001896 | 0.018 | 0.0419 |
| 50 ........ | 0.002138 | 0.005347 | 0.018 | 0.0453 | 0.001676 | 0.002344 | 0.017 | 0.0502 |
| 51 ........ | 0.002288 | 0.005528 | 0.019 | 0.0498 | 0.001814 | 0.002459 | 0.016 | 0.0586 |
| 52 ........ | 0.002448 | 0.005644 | 0.020 | 0.0686 | 0.001967 | 0.002647 | 0.014 | 0.0744 |
| 53 ........ | 0.002621 | 0.005722 | 0.020 | 0.0953 | 0.002135 | 0.002895 | 0.012 | 0.0947 |
| 54 ........ | 0.002812 | 0.005797 | 0.020 | 0.1288 | 0.002321 | 0.003190 | 0.010 | 0.1189 |
| 55 ........ | 0.003029 | 0.005905 | 0.019 | 0.2066 | 0.002526 | 0.003531 | 0.008 | 0.1897 |
| 56 ........ | 0.003306 | 0.006124 | 0.018 | 0.3173 | 0.002756 | 0.003925 | 0.006 | 0.2857 |
| 57 ........ | 0.003628 | 0.006444 | 0.017 | 0.3780 | 0.003010 | 0.004385 | 0.005 | 0.3403 |
| 58 ........ | 0.003997 | 0.006895 | 0.016 | 0.4401 | 0.003291 | 0.004921 | 0.005 | 0.3878 |
| 59 ........ | 0.004414 | 0.007485 | 0.016 | 0.4986 | 0.003599 | 0.005531 | 0.005 | 0.4360 |
| 60 ........ | 0.004878 | 0.008196 | 0.016 | 0.5633 | 0.003931 | 0.006200 | 0.005 | 0.4954 |
| 61 ........ | 0.005382 | 0.009001 | 0.015 | 0.6338 | 0.004285 | 0.006919 | 0.005 | 0.5805 |
| 62 ........ | 0.005918 | 0.009915 | 0.015 | 0.7103 | 0.004656 | 0.007689 | 0.005 | 0.6598 |
| 63 ........ | 0.006472 | 0.010951 | 0.014 | 0.7902 | 0.005039 | 0.008509 | 0.005 | 0.7520 |
| 64 ........ | 0.007028 | 0.012117 | 0.014 | 0.8355 | 0.005429 | 0.009395 | 0.005 | 0.8043 |
| 65 ........ | 0.007573 | 0.013419 | 0.014 | 0.8832 | 0.005821 | 0.010364 | 0.005 | 0.8552 |
| 66 ........ | 0.008099 | 0.014868 | 0.013 | 0.9321 | 0.006207 | 0.011413 | 0.005 | 0.9118 |
| 67 ........ | 0.008598 | 0.016460 | 0.013 | 0.9510 | 0.006583 | 0.012540 | 0.005 | 0.9367 |
| 68 ........ | 0.009069 | 0.018200 | 0.014 | 0.9639 | 0.006945 | 0.013771 | 0.005 | 0.9523 |
| 69 ........ | 0.009510 | 0.020105 | 0.014 | 0.9714 | 0.007289 | 0.015153 | 0.005 | 0.9627 |
| 70 ........ | 0.009922 | 0.022206 | 0.015 | 0.9740 | 0.007613 | 0.016742 | 0.005 | 0.9661 |
| 71 ........ | 0.010912 | 0.024570 | 0.015 | 0.9766 | 0.008309 | 0.018579 | 0.006 | 0.9695 |
| 72 ........ | 0.012892 | 0.027281 | 0.015 | 0.9792 | 0.009700 | 0.020665 | 0.006 | 0.9729 |
| 73 ........ | 0.015862 | 0.030387 | 0.015 | 0.9818 | 0.011787 | 0.022970 | 0.007 | 0.9763 |
| 74 ........ | 0.019821 | 0.033900 | 0.015 | 0.9844 | 0.014570 | 0.025458 | 0.007 | 0.9797 |
| 75 ........ | 0.024771 | 0.037834 | 0.014 | 0.9870 | 0.018049 | 0.028106 | 0.008 | 0.9830 |
| 76 ........ | 0.030710 | 0.042169 | 0.014 | 0.9896 | 0.022224 | 0.030966 | 0.008 | 0.9864 |
| 77 ........ | 0.037640 | 0.046906 | 0.013 | 0.9922 | 0.027094 | 0.034105 | 0.007 | 0.9898 |
| 78 ........ | 0.045559 | 0.052123 | 0.012 | 0.9948 | 0.032660 | 0.037595 | 0.007 | 0.9932 |
| 79 ........ | 0.054469 | 0.057927 | 0.011 | 0.9974 | 0.038922 | 0.041506 | 0.007 | 0.9966 |
| 80 ........ | 0.064368 | 0.064368 | 0.010 | 1.0000 | 0.045879 | 0.045879 | 0.007 | 1.0000 |
| 81 ........ | 0.072041 | 0.072041 | 0.009 | 1.0000 | 0.050780 | 0.050780 | 0.007 | 1.0000 |
| 82 ........ | 0.080486 | 0.080486 | 0.008 | 1.0000 | 0.056294 | 0.056294 | 0.007 | 1.0000 |
| 83 ........ | 0.089718 | 0.089718 | 0.008 | 1.0000 | 0.062506 | 0.062506 | 0.007 | 1.0000 |
| 84 ........ | 0.099779 | 0.099779 | 0.007 | 1.0000 | 0.069517 | 0.069517 | 0.007 | 1.0000 |
| 85 ........ | 0.110757 | 0.110757 | 0.007 | 1.0000 | 0.077446 | 0.077446 | 0.006 | 1.0000 |
| 86 ........ | 0.122797 | 0.122797 | 0.007 | 1.0000 | 0.086376 | 0.086376 | 0.005 | 1.0000 |
| 87 ........ | 0.136043 | 0.136043 | 0.006 | 1.0000 | 0.096337 | 0.096337 | 0.004 | 1.0000 |
| 88 ........ | 0.150590 | 0.150590 | 0.005 | 1.0000 | 0.107303 | 0.107303 | 0.004 | 1.0000 |
| 89 ........ | 0.166420 | 0.166420 | 0.005 | 1.0000 | 0.119154 | 0.119154 | 0.003 | 1.0000 |
| 90 ........ | 0.183408 | 0.183408 | 0.004 | 1.0000 | 0.131682 | 0.131682 | 0.003 | 1.0000 |
| 91 ........ | 0.199769 | 0.199769 | 0.004 | 1.0000 | 0.144604 | 0.144604 | 0.003 | 1.0000 |
| 92 ........ | 0.216605 | 0.216605 | 0.003 | 1.0000 | 0.157618 | 0.157618 | 0.003 | 1.0000 |
| 93 ........ | 0.233662 | 0.233662 | 0.003 | 1.0000 | 0.170433 | 0.170433 | 0.002 | 1.0000 |
| 94 ........ | 0.250693 | 0.250693 | 0.003 | 1.0000 | 0.182799 | 0.182799 | 0.002 | 1.0000 |
| 95 ........ | 0.267491 | 0.267491 | 0.002 | 1.0000 | 0.194509 | 0.194509 | 0.002 | 1.0000 |
| 96 ........ | 0.283905 | 0.283905 | 0.002 | 1.0000 | 0.205379 | 0.205379 | 0.002 | 1.0000 |
| 97 ........ | 0.299852 | 0.299852 | 0.002 | 1.0000 | 0.215240 | 0.215240 | 0.001 | 1.0000 |

| | | | | | | | | |
|---|---|---|---|---|---|---|---|---|
| 98 ........ | 0.315296 | 0.315296 | 0.001 | 1.0000 | 0.223947 | 0.223947 | 0.001 | 1.0000 |
| 99 ........ | 0.330207 | 0.330207 | 0.001 | 1.0000 | 0.231387 | 0.231387 | 0.001 | 1.0000 |
| 100 ....... | 0.344556 | 0.344556 | 0.001 | 1.0000 | 0.237467 | 0.237467 | 0.001 | 1.0000 |
| 101 ....... | 0.358628 | 0.358628 | 0.000 | 1.0000 | 0.244834 | 0.244834 | 0.000 | 1.0000 |
| 102 ....... | 0.371685 | 0.371685 | 0.000 | 1.0000 | 0.254498 | 0.254498 | 0.000 | 1.0000 |
| 103 ....... | 0.383040 | 0.383040 | 0.000 | 1.0000 | 0.266044 | 0.266044 | 0.000 | 1.0000 |
| 104 ....... | 0.392003 | 0.392003 | 0.000 | 1.0000 | 0.279055 | 0.279055 | 0.000 | 1.0000 |
| 105 ....... | 0.397886 | 0.397886 | 0.000 | 1.0000 | 0.293116 | 0.293116 | 0.000 | 1.0000 |
| 106 ....... | 0.400000 | 0.400000 | 0.000 | 1.0000 | 0.307811 | 0.307811 | 0.000 | 1.0000 |
| 107 ....... | 0.400000 | 0.400000 | 0.000 | 1.0000 | 0.322725 | 0.322725 | 0.000 | 1.0000 |
| 108 ....... | 0.400000 | 0.400000 | 0.000 | 1.0000 | 0.337441 | 0.337441 | 0.000 | 1.0000 |
| 109 ....... | 0.400000 | 0.400000 | 0.000 | 1.0000 | 0.351544 | 0.351544 | 0.000 | 1.0000 |
| 110 ....... | 0.400000 | 0.400000 | 0.000 | 1.0000 | 0.364617 | 0.364617 | 0.000 | 1.0000 |
| 111 ....... | 0.400000 | 0.400000 | 0.000 | 1.0000 | 0.376246 | 0.376246 | 0.000 | 1.0000 |
| 112 ....... | 0.400000 | 0.400000 | 0.000 | 1.0000 | 0.386015 | 0.386015 | 0.000 | 1.0000 |
| 113 ....... | 0.400000 | 0.400000 | 0.000 | 1.0000 | 0.393507 | 0.393507 | 0.000 | 1.0000 |
| 114 ....... | 0.400000 | 0.400000 | 0.000 | 1.0000 | 0.398308 | 0.398308 | 0.000 | 1.0000 |
| 115 ....... | 0.400000 | 0.400000 | 0.000 | 1.0000 | 0.400000 | 0.400000 | 0.000 | 1.0000 |
| 116 ....... | 0.400000 | 0.400000 | 0.000 | 1.0000 | 0.400000 | 0.400000 | 0.000 | 1.0000 |
| 117 ....... | 0.400000 | 0.400000 | 0.000 | 1.0000 | 0.400000 | 0.400000 | 0.000 | 1.0000 |
| 118 ....... | 0.400000 | 0.400000 | 0.000 | 1.0000 | 0.400000 | 0.400000 | 0.000 | 1.0000 |
| 119 ....... | 0.400000 | 0.400000 | 0.000 | 1.0000 | 0.400000 | 0.400000 | 0.000 | 1.0000 |
| 120 ....... | 1.000000 | 1.000000 | 0.000 | 1.0000 | 1.000000 | 1.000000 | 0.000 | 1.0000 |

**(e) Static mortality tables with respect to valuation dates occurring during 2008.** The following static mortality tables are used pursuant to paragraph (a)(3) of this section for determining present value or making any computation under section 430 with respect to valuation dates occurring during 2008.

| Age | Male Non-annuitant mortality rates | Male Annuitant mortality rates | Male Optional combined table for small plans | Female Non-annuitant mortality rates | Female Annuitant mortality rates | Female Optional combined table for small plans |
|---|---|---|---|---|---|---|
| 1............ | 0.000400 | 0.000400 | 0.000400 | 0.000359 | 0.000359 | 0.000359 |
| 2............ | 0.000270 | 0.000270 | 0.000270 | 0.000234 | 0.000234 | 0.000234 |
| 3............ | 0.000224 | 0.000224 | 0.000224 | 0.000175 | 0.000175 | 0.000175 |
| 4............ | 0.000175 | 0.000175 | 0.000175 | 0.000131 | 0.000131 | 0.000131 |
| 5............ | 0.000160 | 0.000160 | 0.000160 | 0.000118 | 0.000118 | 0.000118 |
| 6............ | 0.000153 | 0.000153 | 0.000153 | 0.000111 | 0.000111 | 0.000111 |
| 7............ | 0.000147 | 0.000147 | 0.000147 | 0.000104 | 0.000104 | 0.000104 |
| 8............ | 0.000136 | 0.000136 | 0.000136 | 0.000092 | 0.000092 | 0.000092 |
| 9............ | 0.000131 | 0.000131 | 0.000131 | 0.000088 | 0.000088 | 0.000088 |
| 10........... | 0.000133 | 0.000133 | 0.000133 | 0.000089 | 0.000089 | 0.000089 |
| 11........... | 0.000138 | 0.000138 | 0.000138 | 0.000090 | 0.000090 | 0.000090 |
| 12........... | 0.000143 | 0.000143 | 0.000143 | 0.000093 | 0.000093 | 0.000093 |
| 13........... | 0.000151 | 0.000151 | 0.000151 | 0.000097 | 0.000097 | 0.000097 |
| 14........... | 0.000163 | 0.000163 | 0.000163 | 0.000107 | 0.000107 | 0.000107 |
| 15........... | 0.000173 | 0.000173 | 0.000173 | 0.000117 | 0.000117 | 0.000117 |
| 16........... | 0.000183 | 0.000183 | 0.000183 | 0.000125 | 0.000125 | 0.000125 |
| 17........... | 0.000194 | 0.000194 | 0.000194 | 0.000133 | 0.000133 | 0.000133 |
| 18........... | 0.000203 | 0.000203 | 0.000203 | 0.000136 | 0.000136 | 0.000136 |
| 19........... | 0.000213 | 0.000213 | 0.000213 | 0.000134 | 0.000134 | 0.000134 |
| 20........... | 0.000222 | 0.000222 | 0.000222 | 0.000132 | 0.000132 | 0.000132 |
| 21........... | 0.000235 | 0.000235 | 0.000235 | 0.000129 | 0.000129 | 0.000129 |
| 22........... | 0.000247 | 0.000247 | 0.000247 | 0.000131 | 0.000131 | 0.000131 |
| 23........... | 0.000263 | 0.000263 | 0.000263 | 0.000136 | 0.000136 | 0.000136 |
| 24........... | 0.000278 | 0.000278 | 0.000278 | 0.000142 | 0.000142 | 0.000142 |
| 25........... | 0.000298 | 0.000298 | 0.000298 | 0.000150 | 0.000150 | 0.000150 |
| 26........... | 0.000329 | 0.000329 | 0.000329 | 0.000162 | 0.000162 | 0.000162 |
| 27........... | 0.000340 | 0.000340 | 0.000340 | 0.000169 | 0.000169 | 0.000169 |
| 28........... | 0.000350 | 0.000350 | 0.000350 | 0.000178 | 0.000178 | 0.000178 |
| 29........... | 0.000367 | 0.000367 | 0.000367 | 0.000188 | 0.000188 | 0.000188 |
| 30........... | 0.000396 | 0.000396 | 0.000396 | 0.000210 | 0.000210 | 0.000210 |
| 31........... | 0.000445 | 0.000445 | 0.000445 | 0.000255 | 0.000255 | 0.000255 |
| 32........... | 0.000501 | 0.000501 | 0.000501 | 0.000291 | 0.000291 | 0.000291 |
| 33........... | 0.000562 | 0.000562 | 0.000562 | 0.000320 | 0.000320 | 0.000320 |

| | | | | | | |
|---|---|---|---|---|---|---|
| 34 | 0.000626 | 0.000626 | 0.000626 | 0.000345 | 0.000345 | 0.000345 |
| 35 | 0.000689 | 0.000689 | 0.000689 | 0.000368 | 0.000368 | 0.000368 |
| 36 | 0.000749 | 0.000749 | 0.000749 | 0.000389 | 0.000389 | 0.000389 |
| 37 | 0.000806 | 0.000806 | 0.000806 | 0.000410 | 0.000410 | 0.000410 |
| 38 | 0.000839 | 0.000839 | 0.000839 | 0.000432 | 0.000432 | 0.000432 |
| 39 | 0.000869 | 0.000869 | 0.000869 | 0.000458 | 0.000458 | 0.000458 |
| 40 | 0.000897 | 0.000897 | 0.000897 | 0.000499 | 0.000499 | 0.000499 |
| 41 | 0.000928 | 0.000955 | 0.000928 | 0.000547 | 0.000547 | 0.000547 |
| 42 | 0.000964 | 0.001070 | 0.000965 | 0.000602 | 0.000602 | 0.000602 |
| 43 | 0.001007 | 0.001243 | 0.001010 | 0.000662 | 0.000662 | 0.000662 |
| 44 | 0.001058 | 0.001474 | 0.001066 | 0.000727 | 0.000727 | 0.000727 |
| 45 | 0.001116 | 0.001763 | 0.001131 | 0.000776 | 0.000779 | 0.000776 |
| 46 | 0.001168 | 0.002109 | 0.001194 | 0.000824 | 0.000882 | 0.000825 |
| 47 | 0.001225 | 0.002513 | 0.001266 | 0.000873 | 0.001037 | 0.000877 |
| 48 | 0.001284 | 0.002975 | 0.001345 | 0.000944 | 0.001244 | 0.000954 |
| 49 | 0.001345 | 0.003495 | 0.001433 | 0.001021 | 0.001502 | 0.001041 |
| 50 | 0.001408 | 0.004072 | 0.001529 | 0.001130 | 0.001812 | 0.001164 |
| 51 | 0.001472 | 0.004146 | 0.001605 | 0.001252 | 0.001931 | 0.001292 |
| 52 | 0.001538 | 0.004168 | 0.001718 | 0.001422 | 0.002142 | 0.001476 |
| 53 | 0.001647 | 0.004226 | 0.001893 | 0.001617 | 0.002415 | 0.001693 |
| 54 | 0.001767 | 0.004281 | 0.002091 | 0.001842 | 0.002744 | 0.001949 |
| 55 | 0.001948 | 0.004428 | 0.002460 | 0.002100 | 0.003130 | 0.002295 |
| 56 | 0.002177 | 0.004663 | 0.002966 | 0.002400 | 0.003586 | 0.002739 |
| 57 | 0.002446 | 0.004983 | 0.003405 | 0.002682 | 0.004067 | 0.003153 |
| 58 | 0.002758 | 0.005413 | 0.003926 | 0.002933 | 0.004565 | 0.003566 |
| 59 | 0.003046 | 0.005876 | 0.004457 | 0.003207 | 0.005130 | 0.004045 |
| 60 | 0.003366 | 0.006435 | 0.005095 | 0.003503 | 0.005751 | 0.004617 |
| 61 | 0.003802 | 0.007175 | 0.005940 | 0.003818 | 0.006418 | 0.005327 |
| 62 | 0.004180 | 0.007904 | 0.006825 | 0.004149 | 0.007132 | 0.006117 |
| 63 | 0.004680 | 0.008864 | 0.007986 | 0.004490 | 0.007893 | 0.007049 |
| 64 | 0.005082 | 0.009807 | 0.009030 | 0.004838 | 0.008715 | 0.007956 |
| 65 | 0.005476 | 0.010861 | 0.010232 | 0.005187 | 0.009613 | 0.008972 |
| 66 | 0.005994 | 0.012218 | 0.011795 | 0.005531 | 0.010586 | 0.010140 |
| 67 | 0.006363 | 0.013527 | 0.013176 | 0.005866 | 0.011632 | 0.011267 |
| 68 | 0.006557 | 0.014731 | 0.014436 | 0.006189 | 0.012774 | 0.012460 |
| 69 | 0.006876 | 0.016273 | 0.016004 | 0.006495 | 0.014055 | 0.013773 |
| 70 | 0.007009 | 0.017702 | 0.017424 | 0.006784 | 0.015529 | 0.015233 |
| 71 | 0.007888 | 0.019586 | 0.019312 | 0.007411 | 0.016975 | 0.016683 |
| 72 | 0.009646 | 0.021747 | 0.021495 | 0.008666 | 0.018881 | 0.018604 |
| 73 | 0.012283 | 0.024223 | 0.024006 | 0.010548 | 0.020673 | 0.020433 |
| 74 | 0.015799 | 0.027024 | 0.026849 | 0.013058 | 0.022912 | 0.022712 |
| 75 | 0.020195 | 0.030622 | 0.030486 | 0.016195 | 0.024916 | 0.024768 |
| 76 | 0.025470 | 0.034131 | 0.034041 | 0.019959 | 0.027451 | 0.027349 |
| 77 | 0.031624 | 0.038547 | 0.038493 | 0.024351 | 0.030694 | 0.030629 |
| 78 | 0.038657 | 0.043489 | 0.043464 | 0.029370 | 0.033835 | 0.033805 |
| 79 | 0.046569 | 0.049071 | 0.049064 | 0.035017 | 0.037355 | 0.037347 |
| 80 | 0.055360 | 0.055360 | 0.055360 | 0.041291 | 0.041291 | 0.041291 |
| 81 | 0.062905 | 0.062905 | 0.062905 | 0.045702 | 0.045702 | 0.045702 |
| 82 | 0.071350 | 0.071350 | 0.071350 | 0.050664 | 0.050664 | 0.050664 |
| 83 | 0.079534 | 0.079534 | 0.079534 | 0.056255 | 0.056255 | 0.056255 |
| 84 | 0.089800 | 0.089800 | 0.089800 | 0.062565 | 0.062565 | 0.062565 |
| 85 | 0.099680 | 0.099680 | 0.099680 | 0.070761 | 0.070761 | 0.070761 |
| 86 | 0.110516 | 0.110516 | 0.110516 | 0.080120 | 0.080120 | 0.080120 |
| 87 | 0.124300 | 0.124300 | 0.124300 | 0.090716 | 0.090716 | 0.090716 |
| 88 | 0.139683 | 0.139683 | 0.139683 | 0.101042 | 0.101042 | 0.101042 |
| 89 | 0.154366 | 0.154366 | 0.154366 | 0.113903 | 0.113903 | 0.113903 |
| 90 | 0.172706 | 0.172706 | 0.172706 | 0.125879 | 0.125879 | 0.125879 |
| 91 | 0.188113 | 0.188113 | 0.188113 | 0.138232 | 0.138232 | 0.138232 |
| 92 | 0.207060 | 0.207060 | 0.207060 | 0.150672 | 0.150672 | 0.150672 |
| 93 | 0.223365 | 0.223365 | 0.223365 | 0.165391 | 0.165391 | 0.165391 |
| 94 | 0.239646 | 0.239646 | 0.239646 | 0.177391 | 0.177391 | 0.177391 |
| 95 | 0.259578 | 0.259578 | 0.259578 | 0.188755 | 0.188755 | 0.188755 |
| 96 | 0.275506 | 0.275506 | 0.275506 | 0.199303 | 0.199303 | 0.199303 |
| 97 | 0.290981 | 0.290981 | 0.290981 | 0.212034 | 0.212034 | 0.212034 |
| 98 | 0.310600 | 0.310600 | 0.310600 | 0.220611 | 0.220611 | 0.220611 |
| 99 | 0.325288 | 0.325288 | 0.325288 | 0.227940 | 0.227940 | 0.227940 |
| 100 | 0.339424 | 0.339424 | 0.339424 | 0.233930 | 0.233930 | 0.233930 |

| | | | | | | |
|---|---|---|---|---|---|---|
| 101 . . . . . . . . . . | 0.358628 | 0.358628 | 0.358628 | 0.244834 | 0.244834 | 0.244834 |
| 102 . . . . . . . . . . | 0.371685 | 0.371685 | 0.371685 | 0.254498 | 0.254498 | 0.254498 |
| 103 . . . . . . . . . . | 0.383040 | 0.383040 | 0.383040 | 0.266044 | 0.266044 | 0.266044 |
| 104 . . . . . . . . . . | 0.392003 | 0.392003 | 0.392003 | 0.279055 | 0.279055 | 0.279055 |
| 105 . . . . . . . . . . | 0.397886 | 0.397886 | 0.397886 | 0.293116 | 0.293116 | 0.293116 |
| 106 . . . . . . . . . . | 0.400000 | 0.400000 | 0.400000 | 0.307811 | 0.307811 | 0.307811 |
| 107 . . . . . . . . . . | 0.400000 | 0.400000 | 0.400000 | 0.322725 | 0.322725 | 0.322725 |
| 108 . . . . . . . . . . | 0.400000 | 0.400000 | 0.400000 | 0.337441 | 0.337441 | 0.337441 |
| 109 . . . . . . . . . . | 0.400000 | 0.400000 | 0.400000 | 0.351544 | 0.351544 | 0.351544 |
| 110 . . . . . . . . . . | 0.400000 | 0.400000 | 0.400000 | 0.364617 | 0.364617 | 0.364617 |
| 111 . . . . . . . . . . | 0.400000 | 0.400000 | 0.400000 | 0.376246 | 0.376246 | 0.376246 |
| 112 . . . . . . . . . . | 0.400000 | 0.400000 | 0.400000 | 0.386015 | 0.386015 | 0.386015 |
| 113 . . . . . . . . . . | 0.400000 | 0.400000 | 0.400000 | 0.393507 | 0.393507 | 0.393507 |
| 114 . . . . . . . . . . | 0.400000 | 0.400000 | 0.400000 | 0.398308 | 0.398308 | 0.398308 |
| 115 . . . . . . . . . . | 0.400000 | 0.400000 | 0.400000 | 0.400000 | 0.400000 | 0.400000 |
| 116 . . . . . . . . . . | 0.400000 | 0.400000 | 0.400000 | 0.400000 | 0.400000 | 0.400000 |
| 117 . . . . . . . . . . | 0.400000 | 0.400000 | 0.400000 | 0.400000 | 0.400000 | 0.400000 |
| 118 . . . . . . . . . . | 0.400000 | 0.400000 | 0.400000 | 0.400000 | 0.400000 | 0.400000 |
| 119 . . . . . . . . . . | 0.400000 | 0.400000 | 0.400000 | 0.400000 | 0.400000 | 0.400000 |
| 120 . . . . . . . . . . | 1.000000 | 1.000000 | 1.000000 | 1.000000 | 1.000000 | 1.000000 |

**(f) Effective/Applicability date.** This section applies for plan years beginning on or after January 1, 2008.

T.D. 9419, 7/31/2008.

### § 1.430(h)(3)-2 Plan-specific substitute mortality tables used to determine present value.

**(a) In general.** This section sets forth rules for the use of substitute mortality tables under section 430(h)(3)(C) in determining any present value or making any computation under section 430 in accordance with § 1.430(h)(3)-1(a)(1). In order to use substitute mortality tables, a plan sponsor must obtain approval to use substitute mortality tables for the plan in accordance with the procedures set forth in paragraph (b) of this section. Paragraph (c) of this section sets forth rules for the development of substitute mortality tables, including guidelines for determining whether a plan has sufficient credible mortality experience to use substitute mortality tables. Paragraph (d) of this section sets forth special rules regarding the use of substitute mortality tables. The Commissioner may, in revenue rulings and procedures, notices or other guidance published in the Internal Revenue Bulletin (see § 601.601(d)(2)(ii)(b) of this chapter), provide additional guidance regarding approval and use of substitute mortality tables under section 430(h)(3)(C) and related matters.

**(b) Procedures for obtaining approval to use substitute mortality tables.** *(1) Written request to use substitute mortality tables.* (i) General requirements. In order to use substitute mortality tables, a plan sponsor must submit a written request to the Commissioner that demonstrates that those substitute mortality tables meet the requirements of section 430(h)(3)(C) and this section. This request must state the first plan year and the term of years (not more than 10) that the tables are requested to be used.

(ii) Time for written request.

(A) In general. Except as provided in this paragraph (b)(1)(ii), substitute mortality tables cannot be used for a plan year unless the plan sponsor submits the written request described in paragraph (b)(1)(i) of this section at least 7 months prior to the first day of the first plan year for which the substitute mortality tables are to apply.

(B) Special rule for requests submitted on or before October 1, 2007. Notwithstanding the rule of paragraph (b)(1)(ii)(A) of this section, the timing of the written request described in paragraph (b)(1)(i) of this section does not prevent a plan from using substitute mortality tables for a plan year provided that the written request is submitted no later than October 1, 2007.

(C) Special rule for requests submitted on or before October 1, 2008, with respect to plan years beginning during 2009. Notwithstanding the rule of paragraph (b)(1)(ii)(A) of this section, the timing of the written request described in paragraph (b)(1)(i) of this section does not prevent a plan from using substitute mortality tables for a plan year that begins during 2009 provided that the written request is submitted no later than October 1, 2008.

*(2) Commissioner's review of request.* (i) In general. During the 180-day period that begins on the date the plan sponsor submits a request to use substitute mortality tables for a plan pursuant to this section, the Commissioner will determine whether the request to use substitute mortality tables satisfies the requirements of this section (including any published guidance issued pursuant to paragraph (a) of this section), and will either approve or deny the request. The Commissioner will deny a request if the request fails to meet the requirements of this section or if the Commissioner determines that a substitute mortality table does not sufficiently reflect the mortality experience of the applicable plan population.

(ii) Request for additional information. The Commissioner may request additional information with respect to the submission. Failure to provide that information on a timely basis constitutes grounds for denial of the request.

(iii) Deemed approval. Except as provided in paragraph (b)(2)(iv) of this section, if the Commissioner does not issue a denial within the 180-day review period, the request is deemed to have been approved.

(iv) Extension of time permitted. The Commissioner and a plan sponsor may, before the expiration of the 180-day review period, agree in writing to extend that period, provided that any such agreement also specifies any revisions in the plan sponsor's request, including any change in the requested term of use of the substitute mortality tables.

**(c) Development of substitute mortality tables.** *(1) Mortality experience requirements.* (i) In general. Substitute mortality tables must reflect the actual mortality experience of the pension plan for which the tables are to be used and that mortality experience must be credible mortality experience as described in paragraph (c)(1)(ii) of this section. Separate mortality tables must be established for each gender under the plan, and a substitute mortality table is permitted to be established for a gender only if the plan has credible mortality experience with respect to that gender.

(ii) Credible mortality experience. There is credible mortality experience for a gender within a plan if and only if, over the period covered by the experience study described in paragraph (c)(2)(ii) of this section, there are at least 1,000 deaths within that gender.

(iii) Gender without credible mortality experience. (A) In general. If, for the first year for which a plan uses substitute mortality tables, one gender has credible mortality experience but the other gender does not have credible mortality experience, the substitute mortality tables are used for the gender that does have credible mortality experience and the mortality tables under § 1.430(h)(3)-1 are used for the gender that does not have credible mortality experience. For a subsequent plan year, the plan sponsor may continue to use substitute mortality tables for the gender with credible mortality experience without using substitute mortality tables for the other gender only if the other gender continues to lack credible mortality experience for that subsequent plan year.

(B) Demonstration of lack of credible mortality experience for a gender. In general, in order to demonstrate that a gender within a plan does not have credible mortality experience for a plan year, the demonstration that the gender population within the plan has fewer than 1,000 deaths over a 4-year period must be made using a 4-year period that ends less than 3 years before the first day of that plan year. For example, if a plan uses substitute mortality tables based on credible mortality experience obtained over a 4-year experience study period for its male population and the standard mortality tables under § 1.430(h)(3)-1 for its female population, there must be a demonstration that the plan's female population does not have at least 1,000 deaths in a 4-year period that ends less than 3 years before the first day of that plan year. However, if the experience study period described in paragraph (c)(2)(ii)(A) of this section exceeds 4 years, then in order to demonstrate that a gender within a plan does not have credible mortality experience for a plan year, the mortality experience of that population must be analyzed over a period that is the same length as the experience study on which the substitute mortality tables are based and that ends less than 3 years before the first day of that plan year.

(iv) Disabled individuals. Under section 430(h)(3)(D), separate mortality tables are permitted to be used for certain disabled individuals. If such separate mortality tables are used for those disabled individuals, then those individuals are disregarded for all purposes under this section. Thus, if the mortality tables under section 430(h)(3)(D) are used for disabled individuals under a plan, mortality experience with respect to those individuals must be excluded in developing mortality rates for substitute mortality tables under this section.

*(2) Base table and base year.* (i) In general. Development of a substitute mortality table under this section requires creation of a base table and identification of a base year under this paragraph (c)(2). The base table and base year are then used to determine a substitute mortality table under paragraph (c)(3) of this section.

(ii) Experience study and base table requirements. (A) In general. The base table for a plan population must be developed from an experience study of the mortality experience of that plan population that generates amounts-weighted mortality rates based on experience data for the plan that is collected over an experience study period. The minimum length of the experience study period is 2 years. The maximum length of the experience study period is 5 years, but can be extended by the Commissioner in revenue rulings, notices, or other guidance published in the Internal Revenue Bulletin (see § 601.601(d)(2)(ii)(b) of this chapter). The last day of the final year reflected in the experience data must be less than 3 years before the first day of the first plan year for which the substitute mortality tables are to apply. For example, if July 1, 2009, is the first day of the first plan year for which the substitute mortality tables will be used, then an experience study using calendar year data must include data collected for a period that ends no earlier than December 31, 2006.

(B) Amounts-weighted mortality rates. The amounts-weighted mortality rate for an age is equal to the quotient determined by dividing the sum of the accrued benefits (or payable benefits, in the case of individuals in pay status) for all individuals at that age at the beginning of the year who died during the year, by the sum of the accrued benefits (or payable benefits, in the case of individuals in pay status) for all individuals at that age at the beginning of the year, with appropriate adjustments for individuals who left the relevant plan population during the year for reasons other than death. Because amounts-weighted mortality rates for a plan cannot be determined without accrued (or payable) benefits, the mortality experience study used to develop a base table cannot include periods before the plan was established.

(C) Grouping of ages. Amounts-weighted mortality rates may be derived from amounts-weighted mortality rates for age groups: The Commissioner, in revenue rulings, notices, or other guidance published in the Internal Revenue Bulletin (see § 601.601(d)(2)(ii)(b) of this chapter), may specify grouping rules (for example, 5-year age groups, except for extreme ages such as ages above 100 or below 20) and methods for developing amounts-weighted mortality rates for individual ages from amounts-weighted mortality rates initially determined for each age group.

(D) Base table construction. The base tables must be constructed from the amounts-weighted mortality rates determined in paragraph (c)(2)(ii)(B) of this section. The base tables must be constructed either directly through graduation of the amounts-weighted mortality rates or indirectly by applying a level percentage to the applicable mortality table set forth in § 1.430(h)(3)-1, provided that the adjusted table sufficiently reflects the mortality experience of the plan. The Commissioner also may permit the use of other recognized mortality tables in the construction of base tables, applying a similar mortality experience standard.

(iii) Base year requirements. The base year is the calendar year that contains the day before the midpoint of the experience study period. If the base table is constructed by applying a level percentage to a table set forth in § 1.430(h)(3)-1, then the percentage must be applied to the table under § 1.430(h)(3)-1 after it has been projected to the base year using Projection Scale AA, as set forth in § 1.430(h)(3)-1(d). Thus, for example, if the base year of the mortality experience study is 2005, the applicable base (year 2000) mortality rates must be projected 5 years prior to determining the level percentage to be applied to the applicable projected base (year 2000) mortality rates.

(iv) Change in number of individuals covered by table. Experience data cannot be used to develop a base table if the number of individuals in the population covered by the table (for example, the male annuitant population) as of the last day of the plan year before the year the request to use substitute mortality tables is made, compared to the average number of individuals in that population over the years covered by the experience study on which the substitute mortality tables are based, reflects a difference of 20 percent or more, unless it is demonstrated to the satisfaction of the Commissioner that the experience data is accurately predictive of future mortality of that plan population (taking into account the effect of the change in individuals) after appropriate adjustments to the data are made (for example, excluding data from individuals with respect to a spun-off portion of the plan). For this purpose, a reasonable estimate of the number of individuals in the population covered by the table may be used, such as the estimated number of participants and beneficiaries used for purposes of the PBGC Form 1-ES.

*(3) Determination of substitute mortality tables.* (i) In general. A plan's substitute mortality tables must be generational mortality tables. Substitute mortality tables are determined using the base mortality tables developed pursuant to paragraph (c)(2) of this section and the projection factors provided in Projection Scale AA, as set forth in § 1.430(h)(3)-1(d). Under the generational mortality tables, the probability of an individual's death at a particular age is determined as the individual's base mortality rate (that is, the applicable mortality rate from the base mortality table for the age for which the probability of death is being determined) multiplied by the mortality improvement factor. The mortality improvement factor is equal to (1-projection factor for that age)n, where n is equal to the projection period (the number of years between the base year for the base mortality table and the calendar year in which the individual attains the age for which the probability of death is being determined).

(ii) Example of calculation. As an example of the use of generational mortality tables under paragraph (c)(3)(i) of this section, if approved substitute mortality tables are based on data collected during 2005 and 2006, the base year would be 2005 because 2005 would be the year that contains the day before the midpoint of the experience study period. If the tables show a base mortality rate of .006000 for male annuitants at age 54, the probability of death at age 54 for a male annuitant born in 1974 would be determined using the base mortality rate of .006000, the age-54 projection factor of .020 (pursuant to the Scale AA Projection Factors set forth in § 1.430(h)(3)-1(d)) and a projection period of 23 years. The projection period is the number of years between the base year of 2005 and the calendar year in which the individual reaches age 54. Accordingly, the mortality improvement factor would be .628347 and the probability of death at age 54 would be .003770.

*(4) Separate tables for specified populations.* (i) In general. Except as provided in this paragraph (c)(4), separate substitute mortality tables are permitted to be used for separate populations within a gender under a plan only if—

(A) All individuals of that gender in the plan are divided into separate populations;

(B) Each separate population has credible mortality experience as provided in paragraph (c)(4)(iii) of this section; and

(C) The separate substitute mortality table for each separate population is developed using mortality experience data for that population.

(ii) Annuitant and nonannuitant separate populations. Notwithstanding paragraph (c)(4)(i)(B) of this section, substitute mortality tables for separate populations of annuitants and nonannuitants within a gender may be used even if only one of those separate populations has credible mortality experience. Similarly, if separate populations that satisfy paragraph (c)(4)(i)(B) of this section are established, then any of those populations may be further subdivided into separate annuitant and nonannuitant subpopulations, provided that at least one of the two resulting subpopulations has credible mortality experience. The standard mortality tables under § 1.430(h)(3)-1 are used for a resulting subpopulation that does not have credible mortality experience. For example, in the case of a plan that has credible mortality experience for both its male hourly and salaried individuals, if the male salaried annuitant population has credible mortality experience, the plan may use substitute mortality tables with respect to that population even if the standard mortality tables under § 1.430(h)(3)-1 are used for the male salaried nonannuitant population (because that nonannuitant population does not have credible mortality experience).

(iii) Credible mortality experience for separate populations. In determining whether a separate population within a gender has credible mortality experience, the requirements of paragraph (c)(1)(ii) of this section must be satisfied but, in applying that paragraph (c)(1)(ii), the separate population should be substituted for the particular gender. In demonstrating that an annuitant or nonannuitant population within a gender or within a separate population does not have credible mortality experience, the requirements of paragraph (c)(1)(iii) of this section must be satisfied but, in applying that paragraph, the annuitant (or nonannuitant) population should be substituted for the particular gender.

**(d) Special rules.** *(1) All plans in controlled group must use substitute mortality tables.* (i) In general. Except as otherwise provided in this paragraph (d)(1), substitute mortality tables are permitted to be used for a plan for a plan year only if, for that plan year (or any portion of that plan year), substitute mortality tables are also approved and used for each other pension plan subject to the requirements of section 430 that is maintained by the sponsor and by each member of the plan sponsor's controlled group. For purposes of this section, the term controlled group means any group treated as a single employer under paragraph (b), (c), (m), or (o) of section 414.

(ii) Plans without credible experience. (A) In general. For the first year for which a plan uses substitute mortality tables, the use of substitute mortality tables for the plan is not prohibited merely because another plan described in paragraph (d)(1)(i) of this section cannot use substitute mortality tables because neither the males nor the females under that other plan have credible mortality experience for a plan year. For each subsequent plan year, the plan sponsor may continue to use substitute mortality tables for the plan with credible mortality experience without using substitute mortality tables for the other plan only if neither the males nor the females under that other plan have credible mortality experience for that subsequent plan year.

(B) Analysis of mortality experience. For each plan year in which a plan uses substitute mortality tables, in order to demonstrate that the male and female populations of another plan maintained by the plan sponsor (or by a member of the plan sponsor's controlled group) do not have credible mortality experience, the requirements of paragraph (c)(1)(iii)(B) of this section must be satisfied for that plan year. Thus, a plan is not prohibited from using substitute mortality tables for a plan year merely because another plan in the controlled group of the plan sponsor does not have at least 1,000 male deaths and does not have at least 1,000 female deaths in a 4-year period (or a period that is the length of the experience study period if the experience study period under paragraph (c)(2)(ii)(A) of this section is longer than 4 years) that ends less than 3 years before the first day of that plan year.

(iii) Newly affiliated plans not using substitute mortality tables. (A) In general. The use of substitute mortality tables for a plan is not prohibited merely because a newly affiliated plan does not use substitute mortality tables, but only through the last day of the plan year of the plan using substitute mortality tables that contains the last day of the period described in section 410(b)(6)(C)(ii) for either the newly affiliated plan or the plan using substitute mortality tables, whichever is later. Thus, for the following plan year, the mortality tables prescribed under § 1.430(h)(3)-1 apply with respect to the plan (and all other plans within the plan sponsor's controlled group, including the newly affiliated plan) unless—

(1) Approval to use substitute mortality tables has been obtained with respect to the newly affiliated plan pursuant to paragraph (b)(1) of this section; or

(2) The newly affiliated plan cannot use substitute mortality tables because neither the males nor the females under the plan have credible mortality experience as described in paragraph (c)(1)(ii) of this section (as determined in accordance with the rules of paragraph (d)(1)(iv) of this section).

(B) Definition of newly affiliated plan. For purposes of this section, a plan is treated as a newly affiliated plan if it becomes maintained by the plan sponsor (or by a member of the plan sponsor's controlled group) in connection with a merger, acquisition, or similar transaction described in § 1.410(b)-2(f). A plan also is treated as a newly affiliated plan for purposes of this section if the plan is established in connection with a transfer of assets and liabilities from another employer's plan in connection with a merger, acquisition, or similar transaction described in § 1.410(b)-2(f).

(iv) Demonstration of credible mortality experience for newly affiliated plan. (A) In general. In general, in the case of a newly affiliated plan described in paragraph (d)(1)(iii) of this section, the demonstration of whether credible mortality experience exists for the plan for a plan year may be made by either including or excluding mortality experience data for the period prior to the date the plan becomes maintained by a member of the new plan sponsor's controlled group. If a plan sponsor excludes mortality experience data for the period prior to the date the plan becomes maintained within the new plan sponsor's controlled group, the exclusion must apply for all populations within the plan.

(B) Demonstration of credible mortality experience. Regardless of whether mortality experience data for the period prior to the date a newly affiliated plan becomes maintained within the new plan sponsor's controlled group is included or excluded for a plan year, the provisions of this section, including the demonstration of credible mortality experience in accordance with paragraph (c)(1)(ii) of this section, must be satisfied before substitute mortality tables may be used with respect to the plan. Thus, for example, the plan must meet the rule in paragraph (c)(2)(ii)(A) of this section that the base table be based on mortality experience data for the plan over a 2-year or longer consecutive period that ends less than 3 years before the first day of the plan year for which substitute mortality tables will be used.

(C) Demonstration of lack of credible mortality experience. In the case of a newly affiliated plan described in paragraph (d)(1)(iii) of this section, in order to demonstrate a lack of credible mortality experience with respect to a gender for a plan year, the rules of paragraph (c)(1)(iii)(B) of this section generally will apply. However, a special rule applies if the plan's mortality experience demonstration for a plan year is made by excluding mortality experience for the period prior to the date the plan becomes maintained by a member of the new plan sponsor's controlled group. In such a case, an employer is permitted to demonstrate a plan's lack of credible mortality experience using an experience study period of less than four years, provided that the experience study period begins with the date the plan becomes maintained within the sponsor's controlled group and ends not more than one year and one day before the first day of the plan year with respect to which the lack of credible mortality experience demonstration is made.

(D) Example. The following example illustrates the application of this paragraph (d)(1):

*Example.* (i) Employer A is a corporation and maintains Plan M, which has a calendar year plan year and has obtained approval to use substitute mortality tables for 10 years beginning with the plan year that begins on January 1, 2009. Employer B is a corporation and maintains Plan N, which does not use substitute mortality tables and has a calendar year plan year. On July 1, 2010, Employer A acquires 100% of the stock of Employer B.

(ii) Pursuant to paragraph (d)(1)(iii) of this section, the maintenance of Plan N within the controlled group that maintains Plan M does not impair the use of substitute mortality tables by Plan M through the end of the plan year that ends on December 31, 2011.

(iii) Pursuant to paragraph (d)(1)(iii) of this section, beginning with the plan year that begins on January 1, 2012, Plan M continues to use substitute mortality tables only if either Plan N obtains approval to use substitute mortality tables or Employer A can demonstrate that Plan N does not have credible mortality experience. Pursuant to paragraph (d)(1)(iv)(C) of this section, Employer A is permitted to either exclude mortality experience date for the period of time before July 1, 2010 (the date Plan N became maintained with Employer A's controlled group), or include that mortality experience data for purposes of demonstrating that Plan N does not have credible mortality experience. Thus, if there is an experience study that shows that the male and female populations of Plan N each do not have 1,000 deaths during the period from July 1, 2010, through December 31, 2010, then the maintenance of Plan N within the Employer A's controlled group does not impair Plan M's use of substitute mortality tables for Plan M's 2012 plan year.

(iv) For Plan M's 2013 plan year, pursuant to paragraph (d)(1)(iv)(C) of this section, the maintenance of Plan N within Employer A's controlled group does not impair Plan M's use of substitute mortality tables if there is an experience study that shows that the male and female populations of Plan N each do not have 1,000 deaths during the period from July 1, 2010, through December 31, 2011.

*(2) Duration of use of tables.* Except as provided in paragraph (d)(4) of this section, substitute mortality tables are used with respect to a plan for the term of consecutive plan years specified in the plan sponsor's written request to use such tables under paragraph (b)(1) of this section and approved by the Commissioner, or such shorter period prescribed by the Commissioner in the approval to use substi-

tute mortality tables. Following the end of such term of use, or following any early termination of use described in paragraph (d)(4) of this section, the mortality tables specified in § 1.430(h)(3)-1 apply with respect to the plan unless approval under paragraph (b)(1) of this section has been received by the plan sponsor to use substitute mortality tables for a further term.

*(3) Aggregation.* (i) Permissive aggregation of plans. In order for a plan sponsor to use a set of substitute mortality tables with respect to two or more plans, the rules of this section are applied by treating those plans as a single plan. In such a case, the substitute mortality tables must be used for the aggregated plans and must be based on data collected with respect to those aggregated plans.

(ii) Required aggregation of plans. In general, plans are not required to be aggregated for purposes of applying the rules of this section. However, for purposes of this section, a plan is required to be aggregated with any plan that was previously spun off from that plan for purposes of this section if the Commissioner determines that one purpose of the spinoff is to avoid the use of substitute mortality tables for any of the plans that were involved in the spinoff.

*(4) Early termination of use of tables.* (i) General rule. A plan's substitute mortality tables cannot be used as of the earliest of—

(A) The plan year in which the plan fails to satisfy the requirements of paragraph (c)(1) of this section (regarding credible mortality experience requirements and demonstrations);

(B) The plan year in which the plan fails to satisfy the requirements of paragraph (d)(1) of this section (regarding use of substitute mortality tables by controlled group members);

(C) The second plan year following the plan year in which there is a significant change in individuals covered by the plan as described in paragraph (d)(4)(ii) of this section;

(D) The plan year following the plan year in which a substitute mortality table used for a plan population is no longer accurately predictive of future mortality of that population, as determined by the Commissioner or as certified by the plan's actuary to the satisfaction of the Commissioner; or

(E) The date specified in guidance published in the Internal Revenue Bulletin (see § 601.601(d)(2)(ii)(b) of this chapter) pursuant to a replacement of mortality tables specified under section 430(h)(3)(A) and § 1.430(h)(3)-1 (other than annual updates to the static mortality tables issued pursuant to § 1.430(h)(3)-1(a)(3)).

(ii) Significant change in coverage. (A) Change in coverage from time of experience study. For purposes of applying the rules of paragraph (d)(4)(i)(C) of this section, a significant change in the individuals covered by a substitute mortality table occurs if there is an increase or decrease in the number of individuals of at least 20 percent compared to the average number of individuals in that population over the years covered by the experience study on which the substitute mortality tables are based. However, a change in coverage is not treated as significant if the plan's actuary certifies in writing to the satisfaction of the Commissioner that the substitute mortality tables used for the plan population continue to be accurately predictive of future mortality of that population (taking into account the effect of the change in the population).

(B) Change in coverage from time of certification. For purposes of applying the rules of paragraph (d)(4)(i)(C) of this section, a significant change in the individuals covered by a substitute mortality table occurs if there is an increase or decrease in the number of individuals covered by a substitute mortality table of at least 20 percent compared to the number of individuals in a plan year for which a certification described in paragraph (d)(4)(ii)(A) of this section was made on account of a prior change in coverage. However, a change in coverage is not treated as significant if the plan's actuary certifies in writing to the satisfaction of the Commissioner that the substitute mortality tables used by the plan with respect to the covered population continue to be accurately predictive of future mortality of that population (taking into account the effect of the change in the plan population).

**(e) Effective/Applicability date.** This section applies for plan years beginning on or after January 1, 2009.

T.D. 9419, 7/31/2008.

### § 1.430(i)-1 Special rules for plans in at-risk status.

**(a) In general.** *(1) Overview.* This section provides special rules related to determining the funding target and making other computations for certain defined benefit plans that are in at-risk status for the plan year. Section 430(i) and this section apply to single employer defined benefit plans (including multiple employer plans) but do not apply to multiemployer plans (as defined in section 414(f)). Paragraph (b) of this section describes rules for determining whether a plan is in at-risk status for a plan year, including the determination of a plan's funding target attainment percentage and at-risk funding target attainment percentage. Paragraph (c) of this section describes the funding target for a plan in at-risk status. Paragraph (d) of this section describes the target normal cost for a plan in at-risk status. Paragraph (e) of this section describes rules regarding how the funding target and the target normal cost are determined for a plan that has been in at-risk status for fewer than 5 consecutive plan years. Paragraph (f) of this section sets forth effective/applicability dates and transition rules.

*(2) Special rules for multiple employer plans.* In the case of a multiple employer plan to which section 413(c)(4)(A) applies, the rules of section 430 and this section are applied separately for each employer under the plan, as if each employer maintained a separate plan. For example, at-risk status is determined separately for each employer under such a multiple employer plan. In the case of a multiple employer plan to which section 413(c)(4)(A) does not apply (that is, a plan described in section 413(c)(4)(B) that has not made the election for section 413(c)(4)(A) to apply), the rules of section 430 and this section are applied as if all participants in the plan were employed by a single employer.

**(b) Determination of at-risk status of a plan.** *(1) General rule.* Except as otherwise provided in this section, a plan is in at-risk status for a plan year if—

(i) The funding target attainment percentage for the preceding plan year (determined under paragraph (b)(3) of this section) is less than 80 percent; and

(ii) The at-risk funding target attainment percentage for the preceding plan year (determined under paragraph (b)(4) of this section) is less than 70 percent.

*(2) Small plan exception.* If, on each day during the preceding plan year, a plan had 500 or fewer participants (including both active and inactive participants), determined in accordance with the same rules that apply for purposes of § 1.430(g)-1(b)(2)(ii), then the plan is not treated as being in at-risk status for the plan year.

*(3) Funding target attainment percentage.* For purposes of this section, except as otherwise provided in paragraph (b)(5) of this section, the funding target attainment percentage of a plan for a plan year is the funding target attainment percentage as defined in § 1.430(d)-1(b)(3).

*(4) At-risk funding target attainment percentage.* Except as otherwise provided in paragraph (b)(5) of this section, the at-risk funding target attainment percentage of a plan for a plan year is a fraction (expressed as a percentage)—

(i) The numerator of which is the value of plan assets for the plan year after subtraction of the prefunding balance and the funding standard carryover balance under section 430(f)(4)(B); and

(ii) The denominator of which is the at-risk funding target of the plan for the plan year (determined under paragraph (c) of this section, but without regard to the loading factor imposed under paragraph (c)(2)(ii) of this section).

*(5) Special rules.* (i) Special rule for new plans. Except as otherwise provided in paragraph (b)(5)(iii) of this section, in the case of a new plan that was neither the result of a merger nor involved in a spinoff, the funding target attainment percentage under paragraph (b)(3) of this section and the at-risk funding target attainment percentage under paragraph (b)(4) of this section are equal to 100 percent for years before the plan exists.

(ii) Special rule for plans with zero funding target. Except as otherwise provided in paragraph (b)(5)(iii) of this section, if the funding target of the plan is equal to zero for a plan year, then the funding target attainment percentage under paragraph (b)(3) of this section and the at-risk funding target attainment percentage under paragraph (b)(4) of this section are equal to 100 percent for that plan year.

(iii) Exception when plan has predecessor plan that was in at-risk status. [Reserved]

(iv) Special rules for plans that are the result of a merger. [Reserved]

(v) Special rules for plans that are involved in a spinoff. [Reserved]

*(6) Special rule for determining at-risk status of plans of specified automobile manufacturers.* See section 430(i)(4)(C) for special rules for determining the at-risk status of plans of specified automobile and automobile parts manufacturers.

**(c) Funding target for plans in at-risk status.** *(1) In general.* If the plan has been in at-risk status for 5 consecutive years, including the current plan year, then the funding target for the plan is the at-risk funding target determined under paragraph (c)(2) of this section. See paragraph (e) of this section for the determination of the funding target where the plan is in at-risk status for the plan year but was not in at-risk status for one or more of the 4 preceding plan years.

*(2) At-risk funding target.* (i) Use of modified actuarial assumptions. Except as otherwise provided in this paragraph (c)(2), the at-risk funding target of the plan under this paragraph (c)(2) for the plan year is equal to the present value of all benefits accrued or earned under the plan as of the beginning of the plan year, as determined in accordance with § 1.430(d)-1 but using the additional actuarial assumptions described in paragraph (c)(3) of this section.

(ii) Funding target includes load. The at-risk funding target is increased by the sum of—

(A) $700 multiplied by the number of participants in the plan (including active participants, inactive participants, and beneficiaries); plus

(B) Four percent of the funding target (determined under § 1.430(d)-1(b)(2) as if the plan was not in at-risk status) of the plan for the plan year.

(iii) Minimum amount. Notwithstanding any otherwise applicable provisions of this section, the at-risk funding target of a plan for a plan year is not less than the plan's funding target for the plan year determined without regard to this section.

*(3) Additional actuarial assumptions.* (i) In general. The actuarial assumptions used to determine a plan's at-risk funding target for a plan year are the actuarial assumptions that are applied under section 430, with the modifications described in this paragraph (c)(3).

(ii) Special retirement age assumption— (A) Participants eligible to retire and collect benefits within 11 years. Subject to paragraph (c)(3)(ii)(B) of this section, if a participant would be eligible to commence an immediate distribution by the end of the 10th plan year after the current plan year (that is, the end of the 11th plan year beginning with the current plan year), that participant is assumed to commence an immediate distribution at the earliest retirement age under the plan, or, if later, at the end of the current plan year. The rule of this paragraph (c)(3)(ii)(A) does not affect the application of plan assumptions regarding an employee's termination of employment prior to the employee's earliest retirement age.

(B) Participants otherwise assumed to retire immediately. The special retirement age assumption of paragraph (c)(3)(ii)(A) of this section does not apply to a participant to the extent the participant is otherwise assumed to commence benefits during the current plan year under the actuarial assumptions for the plan. For example, if generally applicable retirement assumptions would provide for a 25 percent probability that a participant will commence benefits during the current plan year, the special retirement age assumption of paragraph (c)(3)(ii)(A) of this section requires the plan's enrolled actuary to assume a 75 percent probability that the participant will commence benefits at the end of the plan year.

(C) Definition of earliest retirement date. For purposes of this paragraph (c)(3)(ii), a plan's earliest retirement date for an employee is the earliest date on which the employee can commence receiving an immediate distribution of a fully vested benefit under the plan. See § 1.401(a)-20, Q&A-17(b).

(iii) Requirement to assume most valuable benefit. All participants and beneficiaries who are assumed to retire on a particular date are assumed to elect the optional form of benefit available under the plan that would result in the highest present value of benefits commencing at that date.

(iv) Reasonable techniques permitted. The plan's actuary is permitted to use reasonable techniques in determining the actuarial assumptions that are required to be used pursuant to this paragraph (c)(3). For example, the plan's actuary is permitted to use reasonable assumptions in determining the optional form of benefit under the plan that would result in the highest present value of benefits for this purpose.

**(d) Target normal cost of plans in at-risk status.** *(1) General rule.* If the plan has been in at-risk status for 5 consecutive years, including the current plan year, then the target normal cost for the plan is the at-risk target normal cost determined under paragraph (d)(2) of this section. See paragraph (e) of this section for the determination of the target normal cost where the plan is in at-risk status for the plan year but was not in at-risk status for one or more of the 4 preceding plan years.

*(2) At-risk target normal cost.* (i) Use of modified actuarial assumptions— (A) In general. Except as otherwise provided in this paragraph (d)(2), the at-risk target normal cost of a plan for the plan year is equal to the present value (determined as of the valuation date) of all benefits that accrue during, are earned during, or are otherwise allocated to service in the plan year, as determined in accordance with § 1.430(d)-1 but using the additional actuarial assumptions described in paragraph (c)(3) of this section.

(B) Special adjustments. The target normal cost of the plan for the plan year (determined under paragraph (d)(2)(i)(A) of this section) is adjusted (not below zero) by adding the amount of plan-related expenses expected to be paid from plan assets during the plan year and subtracting the amount of any mandatory employee contributions expected to be made during the plan year.

(C) Plan-related expenses. For purposes of this paragraph (d)(2), plan-related expenses are determined using the rules of § 1.430(d)-1(b)(1)(iii)(B).

(ii) Loading factor. The at-risk target normal cost is increased by a loading factor equal to 4 percent of the present value (determined as of the valuation date) of all benefits under the plan that accrue, are earned, or are otherwise allocated to service for the plan year under the applicable rules of § 1.430(d)-1(c)(1)(ii)(B), (C), or (D), determined as if the plan were not in at-risk status.

(iii) Minimum amount. The at-risk target normal cost of a plan for a plan year is not less than the plan's target normal cost determined without regard to section 430(i) and this section.

**(e) Transition between applicable funding targets and applicable target normal costs** *(1) Funding target.* If a plan that is in at-risk status for the plan year has not been in at-risk status for one or more of the preceding 4 plan years, the plan's funding target for the plan year is determined as the sum of—

(i) The funding target determined without regard to section 430(i) and this section; plus

(ii) The phase-in percentage for the plan year multiplied by the excess of—

(A) The at-risk funding target determined under paragraph (c)(2) of this section (determined taking into account paragraph (e)(4) of this section); over

(B) The funding target determined without regard to section 430(i) and this section.

*(2) Target normal cost.* If a plan that is in at-risk status for the plan year has not been in at-risk status for one or more of the preceding 4 plan years, the plan's target normal cost for the plan year is determined as the sum of—

(i) The target normal cost determined without regard to section 430(i) and this section; plus

(ii) The phase-in percentage for the plan year multiplied by the excess of—

(A) The at-risk target normal cost determined under paragraph (d)(2) of this section (determined taking into account paragraph (e)(4) of this section); over

(B) The target normal cost determined without regard to section 430(i) and this section.

*(3) Phase-in percentage.* For purposes of this paragraph (e), the phase-in percentage is 20 percent multiplied by the number of consecutive plan years that the plan has been in at-risk status (including the current plan year) and not taking into account years before the first effective plan year for a plan.

*(4) Transition funding target and target normal cost determined without load.* Notwithstanding paragraph (c)(2)(ii) of this section, if a plan has not been in at-risk status for 2 or more of the preceding 4 plan years (not taking into account years before the first effective plan year for a plan), then the plan's at-risk funding target that is used for purposes of paragraph (e)(1)(ii)(A) of this section (to calculate the plan's funding target where the plan has been in at-risk status for fewer than 5 plan years) is determined without regard to the loading factor set forth in paragraph (c)(2)(ii) of this section. Similarly, if a plan has not been in at-risk status for 2 or more of the preceding 4 plan years (not taking into account years before the first effective plan year for a plan), then the plan's at-risk target normal cost that is used for purposes of paragraph (e)(2)(ii)(A) of this section (to calculate the plan's target normal cost where the plan has been in at-risk status for fewer than 5 plan years) is determined without regard to the loading factor set forth in paragraph (d)(2)(ii) of this section.

**(f) Effective/applicability dates and transition rules.** *(1) Statutory effective date/applicability date.* (i) General rule. Section 430 generally applies to plan years beginning on or after January 1, 2008. The applicability of section 430 for purposes of determining the minimum required contribution is delayed for certain plans in accordance with sections 104 through 106 of the Pension Protection Act of 2006 (PPA '06), Public Law 109-280 (120 Stat. 780).

(ii) Applicability of special adjustments to target normal cost. The special adjustments of paragraph (d)(2)(i)(B) of this section (relating to adjustments to the target normal cost for plan-related expenses and mandatory employee contributions) apply to plan years beginning after December 31, 2008. In addition, a plan sponsor may elect to make the special adjustments of paragraph (d)(2)(i)(B) of this section for plan years beginning in 2008. This election is made in the same manner and is subject to the same rules as an election to add an amount to the plan's prefunding balance pursuant to § 1.430(f)-1(f). Thus, the election can be made no later than the last day for making the minimum required contribution for the plan year to which the election relates.

*(2) Effective date/applicability date of regulations.* This section applies to plan years beginning on or after January 1, 2010. For plan years beginning before January 1, 2010, plans are permitted to rely on the provisions set forth in this section for purposes of satisfying the requirements of section 430.

*(3) First effective plan year.* For purposes of this section, the first effective plan year for a plan is the first plan year to which section 430 applies to the plan for purposes of determining the minimum required contribution.

*(4) Transition rule for determining at-risk status.* In the case of plan years beginning in 2008, 2009, and 2010, paragraph (b)(1)(i) of this section is applied by substituting the following percentages for "80 percent"—

(i) 65 percent in the case of 2008;

(ii) 70 percent in the case of 2009; and

(iii) 75 percent in the case of 2010.

---

T.D. 9467, 10/07/2009.

---

**Proposed § 1.430(j)-1 Payment of minimum required contributions.** [*For Preamble, see ¶ 152,985*]

**(a) In general.** *(1) Overview.* This section provides rules related to the payment of minimum required contributions, including the payment of quarterly contributions. Section 430(j) and this section apply to single employer defined benefit plans (including multiple employer plans as defined in section 413(c)) but do not apply to multiemployer plans (as defined in section 414(f)). Paragraph (b) of this section describes the general timing requirement for minimum required contributions. Paragraph (c) of this section describes the accelerated quarterly contribution schedule for plans with a funding shortfall in the preceding plan year. Paragraph (d) of this section provides rules regarding liquidity requirements. Paragraph (e) of this section provides definitions. Paragraph (f) of this section provides examples that illustrate the rules of this section. Paragraph (g) of this section sets forth effective/applicability dates and transition rules.

*(2) Special rules for multiple employer plans.* In the case of a multiple employer plan to which section 413(c)(4)(A) applies, the rules of section 430 and this section are applied separately for each employer under the plan, as if each employer maintained a separate plan. Thus, for example, required quarterly contributions are determined separately for each employer under such a multiple employer plan. In the case of a multiple employer plan to which section 413(c)(4)(A) does not apply (that is, a plan described in section 413(c)(4)(B) that has not made the election for section 413(c)(4)(A) to apply), the rules of section 430 and this section are applied as if all participants in the plan were employed by a single employer.

*(3) Applicability of section 430(j) to plans of commercial passenger airlines.* (i) In general. Except as otherwise provided in this section, the rules of section 430(j) and this section apply to a plan for which an election described in section 402 of the Pension Protection Act of 2006, Public Law 109-280 (120 Stat. 780) (PPA '06), has been made in the same manner as those rules apply to any other plan subject to section 430.

(ii) Special rules for plans for which election was made pursuant to section 402(a)(1) of PPA '06. For purposes of applying the rules of section 430(j) and this section to a plan with respect to which the election under section 402(a)(1) of PPA 06 has been made, the effective interest rate for the plan is deemed to be 8.85% during the period for which the election applies. In addition, see paragraph (e)(4)(ii) of this section for a special determination of the funding shortfall for a plan for which the election in section 402(a)(1) of PPA '06 has been made.

**(b) General timing requirement for minimum required contributions.** *(1) Earliest date for contributions.* A payment of the minimum required contribution under section 430 for a plan year can be made no earlier than the first day of the plan year.

*(2) Deadline for contributions.* The deadline for any payment of any minimum required contribution for a plan year is 8½ months after the close of the plan year. See section 4971 and the regulations thereunder regarding an excise tax that applies with respect to minimum required contributions not paid by this deadline. See also section 430(k) of the Code and section 101(d) of the Employee Retirement Income Security Act of 1974 (ERISA), 29 U.S.C. 1021(d), for additional rules that apply in the case of a failure to pay minimum required contributions by this deadline.

*(3) Adjustment for interest.* Any payment of the minimum required contribution under section 430 for a plan year that is made on a date other than the valuation date for that plan year is adjusted for interest accruing for the period between the valuation date and the payment date, at the effective interest rate for the plan for that plan year determined pursuant to § 1.430(h)(2)-1(f)(1). The direction of the adjustment depends on whether the contribution is paid before or after the valuation date for the plan year. If the contribution is paid after the valuation date for the plan year, the contribution is discounted to the valuation date using the plan's effective interest rate. By contrast, if the contribution is paid before the valuation date for the plan year (which could only occur in the case of a small plan described in section 430(g)(2)(B)), the contribution is increased for interest using the plan's effective interest rate.

**(c) Accelerated quarterly contribution schedule for underfunded plans.** *(1) In general.* (i) Plan subject to quarterly contribution requirement. In any case in which the plan has a funding shortfall for the preceding plan year, the employer maintaining the plan shall make the required installments described in paragraph (c)(3) of this section by the due dates described in paragraph (c)(4) of this section.

(ii) Satisfaction of installments through use of funding balances. In the case of a plan that is subject to the quarterly contribution requirement under this paragraph (c), if the plan sponsor makes an election to use the plan's prefunding balance or funding standard carryover balance under section 430(f), then the plan sponsor is treated as satisfying the obligation to make a required installment under paragraph (c)(1)(i) of this section on the date of the election to the extent of the amount elected, as adjusted with interest. This interest adjustment is made at the plan's effective interest rate under section 430(h)(2)(A) for the plan year from the valuation date through the due date of the installment.

(iii) Consequences of failure to make quarterly contribution. (A) Interest adjustment. If the full amount of a required installment is not paid by the due date for that installment, then an increased rate of interest applies in adjusting the payment to the valuation date. This increased rate of interest is equal to the rate otherwise used under paragraph (b) of this section plus 5 percentage points, and applies with respect to the underpayment of the required installment (determined pursuant to paragraph (c)(2) of this section) for the period of time that begins on the due date for the required installment and that ends on the date on which payment is made.

(B) Application to required installments due before the valuation date. The modified interest rate described in paragraph (c)(1)(iii)(A) of this section only applies to a required installment that is due on or after the valuation date for the plan year. See paragraph (c)(6) of this section for rules that apply to required installments that are due before the valuation date for the plan year.

(C) Additional consequences. See section 430(k) of the Code and section 101(d) of ERISA for examples of additional consequences of failure to make quarterly contributions.

*(2) Determination of underpayment.* (i) Underpayment for a quarter. For purposes of this section, the amount of the underpayment with respect to a required installment for a quarter is equal to the excess of—

(A) The required installment; over

(B) The amount (if any) of the installment contributed to or under the plan on or before the due date for the installment.

(ii) Order of crediting contributions. For purposes of this section, contributions are first credited against the earliest unpaid required installments.

*(3) Amount of required installment.* (i) In general. For purposes of this section, the amount of any required installment is equal to 25% of the required annual payment described in paragraph (c)(3)(ii) of this section.

(ii) Required annual payment. The required annual payment is equal to the lesser of—

(A) 90% of the minimum required contribution under section 430 for the plan year; or

(B) 100% of the minimum required contribution under section 430 (determined without regard to any funding waiver under section 412) for the preceding plan year.

(iii) Treatment of funding balances. For purposes of paragraph (c)(3)(ii) of this section, the minimum required contribution for a plan year is determined without regard to the use of the prefunding balance or funding standard carryover balance in the current year or any prior year. However, see paragraph (c)(1)(ii) of this section regarding a plan sponsor's election to use the plan's prefunding balance or funding standard carryover balance in the current year for the payment of quarterly installments.

*(4) Due dates for installments.* For purposes of this section, there is a required installment for each quarter of the plan year. The due dates for the four required quarterly installments with respect to a full plan year are set forth in the following table:

| Installment | Due date |
|---|---|
| First quarter's installment | 15th day of 4th plan month. |
| Second quarter's installment | 15th day of 7th plan month. |
| Third quarter's installment | 15th day of 10th plan month. |
| Fourth quarter's installment | 15th day after the close of the plan year. |

*(5) Special rules for short plan years.* (i) In general. In the case of a short plan year, the rules of this paragraph (c) are modified as provided in this paragraph (c)(5).

(ii) Current plan year is short plan year. (A) Amount of required annual payment. In determining the required annual payment pursuant to paragraph (c)(3)(ii) of this section for a short plan year, the amount otherwise determined under paragraph (c)(3)(ii)(B) (based on the prior year's minimum required contribution) is multiplied by a fraction, the numerator of which is the duration of the short plan year and the denominator of which is 1 year.

(B) Number and due dates of installments. If the plan has a short plan year, then an installment is due 15 days after the close of that short plan year. In addition, an installment is required for each due date determined under paragraph (c)(4) of this section that falls within the short plan year. Thus, for example, if the short plan year ends before the 15th day of the 4th plan month of the plan year, there will be only one installment for that short plan year, and that installment will be due on the 15th day after the close of the short plan year.

(C) Amount of installments. The amount of each installment required to be paid for the short plan year is equal to the required annual payment determined pursuant to paragraph (c)(3)(ii) of this section (as modified by paragraph (c)(5)(ii)(A) of this section) divided by the number of installments determined pursuant to paragraph (c)(5)(ii)(B) of this section.

(iii) Prior plan year is short plan year. If the prior plan year is a short plan year, then the rule of paragraph (c)(3)(ii)(B) regarding the use of 100% of the prior year's minimum required contribution in determining the required annual payment does not apply. Accordingly, in such a case, the required annual payment is equal to 90% of the minimum required contribution under section 430 for the current plan year.

*(6) Special rule for plans with valuation dates after the first day of the plan year.* [Reserved]

**(d) Liquidity requirement in connection with quarterly contributions.** *(1) In general.* (i) Requirement to make additional quarterly contributions. Except as provided in paragraphs (d)(1)(ii) and (iii) of this section, if a plan is subject to the requirement to make quarterly contributions under paragraph (c) of this section, then the plan is treated as failing to pay the full amount of a required installment for a quarter to the extent that the value of the liquid assets contributed after the close of that quarter and on or before the due date for the installment is less than the liquidity shortfall for that quarter.

(ii) Limitation on increase. The amount by which any required installment is increased by reason of paragraph (d)(1)(i) of this section cannot exceed the amount that, when added to prior required installments for the plan year, would increase the funding target attainment percentage of the plan for the plan year (taking into account the expected increase in the funding target due to benefits accruing or earned during the plan year) to 100%.

(iii) Small plan exception. The liquidity requirement of this paragraph (d) does not apply to a small plan that is described in § 1.430(g)-1(b)(2).

*(2) Period of underpayment.* (i) General rule. For purposes of applying the additional 5 percentage point interest adjustment pursuant to paragraph (c)(1)(iii) of this section, the liquidity increment with respect to a quarter as described in paragraph (d)(2)(ii) of this section continues to be treated as unpaid until the close of the quarter in which the due date for that installment occurs without regard to when that portion is paid. However, for purposes of adjusting the contribution to the valuation date at the effective interest rate under paragraph (b)(3) of this section, the adjustment is made from the contribution date (rather than the close of the quarter).

(ii) Liquidity increment. For purposes of this paragraph (d), the liquidity increment with respect to a quarter is the portion of the required installment for that quarter that is treated as not paid solely by reason of paragraph (d)(1)(i) of this section.

(iii) Ordering rule. If the employer makes a contribution for a quarter that, after application of paragraph (c)(2)(ii) of this section, is less than the total amount needed to satisfy the requirements of paragraph (c) of this section as increased by this paragraph (d) for a quarter, then the contribution is first attributed toward satisfying the requirements of paragraph (c) of this section (without regard to this paragraph (d)) and then to the liquidity increment.

*(3) Consequences of failure to pay liquidity shortfall.* See section 4971(f) for an excise tax on the failure to pay a liquidity shortfall. See also section 206(e) of ERISA.

**(e) Definitions.** *(1) In general.* The definitions set forth in this paragraph (e) apply for purposes of this section.

*(2) Adjusted disbursements.* The term adjusted disbursements means disbursements from the plan reduced by the product of—

(i) The plan's funding target attainment percentage determined under section 430(d)(2) for the plan year; and

(ii) The sum of the purchases of annuities and payments of single sums.

*(3) Disbursements from the plan.* The term disbursements from the plan means all disbursements from the trust, including purchases of annuities, payments of single sums and other benefits, and administrative expenses.

*(4) Funding shortfall.* (i) In general. The term funding shortfall means the excess (if any) of—

(A) The funding target of the plan for a plan year; over

(B) The value of plan assets for the plan year (as reduced to reflect the subtraction of certain funding balances as provided under § 1.430(f)-1(c), but not below zero).

(ii) Special rule for plans of commercial passenger airlines. In the case of a plan year for which an election described in section 402(a)(1) of PPA '06 is in effect, the term funding shortfall means the unfunded liability for that plan year determined under § 1.430(a)-1(b)(4)(ii).

(iii) Special rule for first effective plan year. See paragraph (g)(5)(ii) of this section for a calculation of the funding shortfall for the plan's pre-effective plan year.

(iv) Special rule for plan spinoffs and mergers. [Reserved]

*(5) Liquid assets.* (i) In general. The term liquid assets means cash, marketable securities, and other assets described in this paragraph (e)(5)(i). For this purpose, marketable securities include financial instruments such as stocks and other equity interests, evidences of indebtedness (including certificates of deposit), options, futures contracts, and other derivatives, for which there is a liquid financial market, and other interests in entities (such as partnerships, trusts, or regulated investment companies) for which there is a liquid financial market. For purposes of the preceding sentence, a liquid financial market is an established financial market described in § 1.1092(d)-1(b) (other than an interbank market or an interdealer market described in § 1.1092(d)-1(b)(1)(v) and (vi), respectively). Any security that is issued or guaranteed by the government of the United States or an agency or instrumentality thereof for which there is an established financial market described in § 1.1092(d)-1(b) is a marketable security. Finally, any financial instrument or other interest in an entity that, under its terms, contains a right by which the instrument or other interest may immediately be redeemed, exchanged, or converted into cash or a marketable security, is a marketable security, provided there are no restrictions on the exercise of that right.

(ii) Insurance and annuity contracts. Other assets that are treated as liquid assets of a plan are insurance, annuity, or other contracts issued by an insurance company that is licensed to do business under the laws of any State, but only if the insurance, annuity, or other contract—

(A) Would be treated as a marketable security under paragraph (e)(5)(i) of this section if it were a financial instrument;

(B) Provides for substantially equal monthly disbursements to the extent provided in paragraph (e)(5)(iii) of this section; or

(C) Is benefit responsive within the meaning of paragraph (e)(5)(iv) of this section.

(iii) Insurance and annuity contracts providing for substantially equal periodic payments. If the contract provides for substantially equal monthly disbursements (for example, an annuity contract in pay status), the only portion of the contract that may be treated as liquid assets for a quarter is the amount equal to 36 times the monthly disbursement (in the month containing the last day of the quarter) which is available under the terms of the contract, provided there are no restrictions (within the meaning of paragraph (e)(5)(v) of this section) on the disbursements.

(iv) Benefit responsive insurance and annuity contracts. A contract is considered benefit responsive if, under applicable law and contractual provisions, the plan has the right to receive disbursements from the contract in order to pay plan benefits for any participant in the plan, without restrictions (within the meaning of paragraph (e)(5)(v) of this section).

(v) Restrictions. For purposes of paragraphs (e)(5)(iii) and (iv) of this section, a restriction on a redemption, exchange or conversion right, or a restriction on a disbursement, may result not only from applicable law or contractual provisions, but also from rehabilitation, conservatorship, receivership, insolvency, bankruptcy or similar proceedings.

*(6) Liquidity shortfall.* (i) In general. The term liquidity shortfall means, with respect to any required installment, an amount equal to the excess (as of the last day of the quarter for which that installment is made) of—

(A) The base amount with respect to the quarter, over

(B) The value (as of the last day of the quarter) of the plan's liquid assets.

(ii) Base amount. (A) In general. For purposes of this paragraph (e)(6)(ii), the term base amount means, with respect to any quarter, an amount equal to 3 times the sum of the adjusted disbursements from the plan for the 12 months ending on the last day of such quarter.

(B) Special rule. If the generally applicable base amount for a quarter determined under paragraph (e)(6)(ii)(A) of this section exceeds an amount equal to 2 times the sum of the adjusted disbursements from the plan for the 36 months ending on the last day of the quarter and the enrolled actuary for the plan certifies to the satisfaction of the Commissioner that such excess is the result of nonrecurring circumstances, the base amount with respect to that quarter is determined without regard to amounts related to those nonrecurring circumstances.

*(7) Plan month.* (i) Plan year begins on the first day of a calendar month. For a plan year that begins with the first day of a calendar month, the term plan month means any calendar month that begins during the plan year.

(ii) Plan year begins on a date other than the first day of a calendar month. For a plan year that begins on a date other than the first day of a calendar month, the first day of each plan month is the day of the calendar month that corresponds to the day of the calendar month that is the first day of the plan year. Thus, for example, if the first day of a plan year is January 15, then a plan month starts on the 15th of each calendar month. However, if a calendar month does not contain a day that corresponds to the day of the calendar month which is the first day of the plan year (for example, if a calendar month has only 30 days and the first day of the plan year is the 31st day of a calendar month), then the first day of the plan month that begins during that calendar month is the last day of that calendar month.

*(8) Quarter.* The term quarter means, with respect to any required installment, the 3-plan-month period preceding the plan month in which the due date for that installment occurs.

*(9) Short plan year.* The term short plan year means a plan year that is shorter than 12 months (and is not a 52-week plan year of a plan that uses a 52-53 week plan year).

**(f) Examples.** The following examples illustrate the rules of this section.

*Example (1).* (i) Plan A has a calendar year plan year and a January 1 valuation date. Plan A has a funding standard carryover balance of $15,000 as of January 1, 2008, and the plan's funding ratio for 2007 (determined using the transition rule in § 1.430(f)-1(h)(5)) was over 80%. The minimum required contribution for Plan A (prior to any offset for the carryover balance) is $100,000 for 2008 and is $125,000 for 2009. The effective interest rate for the 2009 plan year is 5.90%. Plan A is subject to the quarterly contribution requirements for 2008.

(ii) The required annual payment for 2009 is equal to the lesser of (a) 100% of the 2008 minimum required contribution ($100,000) or (b) 90% of the 2009 minimum required contribution (90% of $125,000, or $112,500). Therefore, each required quarterly installment for 2009 is 25% of $100,000, or $25,000.

(iii) Installments of $25,000 each are due by April 15, 2009, July 15, 2009, October 15, 2009, and January 15, 2010. The final contribution for the 2009 plan year is due by September 15, 2010. The amount of this contribution is equal to $125,000, less the contributions made prior to that date, with all contributions adjusted to the valuation date using the effective interest rate for the 2009 plan year. If the plan sponsor makes each required quarterly installment on the date due, the remaining amount due is determined as follows:

(A) The contribution paid April 15, 2009, is adjusted by discounting the contribution amount for 3 ½ months at the effective interest rate ($25,000 / 1.0590 (3.5[sol]12) = $24,585).

(B) The contribution paid July 15, 2009, is discounted for 6½ months at the effective interest rate ($25,000 / 1.0590 (6.5[sol]12) = $24,236).

(C) The contribution paid October 15, 2009, is discounted for 9½ months at the effective interest rate ($25,000 / 1.0590 (9.5[sol]12) = $23,891).

(D) The contribution paid January 15, 2010, is discounted for 12½ months at the effective interest rate ($25,000 / 1.0590 (12.5[sol]12) = $23,551).

(E) The sum of the above contributions for the 2009 plan year paid through January 15, 2010, adjusted for interest to the valuation date, is $96,263. The remaining amount due for the 2009 plan year is $125,000 minus $96,263, or $28,737, as of January 1, 2009.

(iv) If the final contribution is made on September 15, 2010, the remaining amount due must be increased for interest at the plan's effective interest rate for the 20½ months between January 1, 2009, and September 15, 2010 (so that when it is discounted with interest for those 20½ months the resulting amount will equal $28,737). Therefore, the remaining contribution made on September 15, 2010, is $28,737 x 1.0590 (20.5[sol]12) = $31,694.

*Example (2).* (i) The facts are the same as in Example 1, except that the plan sponsor elects to use the $15,000 carryover balance as of January 1, 2008, to offset the minimum required contribution for the 2008 plan year. The plan sponsor makes a contribution on January 1, 2008, of $85,000, which satisfies the minimum contribution requirement for 2008.

(ii) The required quarterly installment for 2009 is unaffected by the plan sponsor's election to offset the minimum required contribution by the carryover balance for 2008. Therefore, the required annual payment is $100,000 (determined as the lesser of (a) 100% of $100,000 or (b) 90% of $125,000) and the amount of each required quarterly installment for 2009 is 25% of the required annual payment, or $25,000.

*Example (3).* (i) The facts are the same as in Example 1. Plan A's funding standard carryover balance has increased to $17,000 as of January 1, 2009, based on the actual rate of return of plan assets for the 2008 plan year. Plan A's funding ratio for 2008 (determined under § 1.430(f)-1(d)(3)) is over 80%. On April 13, 2009, the plan sponsor elects to use the entire amount of the carryover balance to offset the minimum required contribution for 2009.

(ii) The plan sponsor's election to use the carryover balance to offset the minimum required contribution is treated as satisfying the requirement to make a required installment to the extent of the amount elected, adjusted with interest. This adjustment is made at the plan's effective interest rate for the 2009 plan year, and applies for the period between January 1, 2009, and April 15, 2009. Therefore, the $17,000 carryover balance as of January 1, 2009, offsets $17,000 x 1.0590 (3.5[sol]12) or $17,287 of the $25,000 quarterly contribution installment due April 15, 2009, and the remaining contribution due on April 15, 2009, is $25,000 minus $17,287, or $7,713.

(iii) The interest adjustments in paragraph (ii) of this Example 3 are based on the effective interest rate even if that rate is not determined by the time that the quarterly contribution is due. If the plan's effective interest rate for the plan year has not been determined at the time that the quarterly contribution is due, the actual amount of the required installment satisfied by the use of the carryover balance is determined after the effective interest rate is determined. If the extent to which the carryover balance satisfies the installment requirement is overestimated and the result is the full amount of the required quarterly installment is not paid by the due date, the plan is subject to the consequences for late or unpaid quarterly contributions as described in paragraph (c)(1)(iii) of this section.

*Example (4).* (i) The facts are the same as in Example 3. The plan sponsor makes a contribution of $7,713 (which is equal to the remaining portion of the first required quarterly installment) on April 15, 2009. For the 2009 plan year, the plan sponsor makes another contribution of $200,000 on June 30, 2009. No further contributions are made for the 2009 plan year.

(ii) The contributions made for the 2009 plan year are adjusted to the valuation date using the plan's effective interest rate for the 2009 plan year. The contribution paid April 15, 2009, is discounted for the 3½ months between January 1, 2009, and the date of payment, using the effective interest rate of 5.90% ($7,713/ 1.0590 (3.5[sol]12) = $7,585). The contribution paid June 30, 2009, is discounted for 6 months using the effective interest rate ($200,000/1.0590 (6[sol]12)

= $194,349), for a total interest-adjusted contribution of $201,934.

(iii) The minimum required contribution for 2009 (prior to any offset for the carryover balance) is $125,000 and, under § 1.430(f)-1(b)(1)(ii)(B), this amount is used to determine the interest-adjusted excess contribution. Accordingly, the interest-adjusted excess contribution for 2009 is $201,934 minus $125,000, or $76,934, increased for interest to January 1, 2010, using the effective interest rate for 2009 of 5.90%. Thus, the interest-adjusted excess contribution as of January 1, 2010, is $76,934 multiplied by 1.059, or $81,473. All or a portion of this amount may be credited to the prefunding balance at the election of the plan sponsor.

*Example (5).* (i) The facts are the same as in Example 3. The plan sponsor pays the required quarterly installment of $7,713 on April 15, 2009, and installments of $25,000 each on July 15, 2009, and October 15, 2009. However, only $10,000 of the installment due on January 15, 2010, is paid. No additional contributions are made until the final contribution for the plan year of $55,000 is paid on September 15, 2010.

(ii) The 2009 Schedule SB shows that the contributions for the plan year exceed the minimum required contribution. This is determined by comparing the minimum required contribution of $108,000 ($125,000 offset by $17,000 for the amount of carryover balance used) and the interest-adjusted contributions made for the 2009 plan year, developed as shown below:

(A) The contribution paid April 15, 2009, is adjusted by discounting the contribution amount for 3½ months at the effective interest rate ($7,713 / 1.0590 (3.5[sol]12) = $7,585).

(B) The contribution paid July 15, 2009, is discounted for 6½ months at the effective interest rate ($25,000 / 1.0590 (6.5[sol]12) = $24,236).

(C) The contribution paid October 15, 2009, is discounted for 9½ months at the effective interest rate ($25,000 / 1.0590 (9.5[sol]12) = $23,891).

(D) The contribution paid January 15, 2010, is discounted for 12½ months at the effective interest rate ($10,000 / 1.0590 (12.5[sol]12) = $9,420).

(E) Pursuant to paragraph (c)(1)(iii)(A) of this section, the adjustment for interest on the $15,000 underpayment of the quarterly installment due January 15, 2010, is increased by 5 percentage points for the 8-month period of underpayment (January 15, 2010, through September 15, 2010). Accordingly, $15,000 of the contribution paid on September 15, 2010, is discounted using a rate of 10.90% for 8 months and at the 5.90% effective interest rate for the remaining 12½ months between the quarterly contribution due date of January 15, 2010, and the valuation date of January 1, 2009. This portion of the September 15, 2010, contribution results in an adjusted amount of $13,189 as of January 1, 2009 ($15,000 / 1.1090 (8[sol]12) / 1.0590 (12.5[sol]12)).

(F) The remaining $40,000 of the contribution paid on September 15, 2010, is discounted using the effective interest rate of 5.90% for the 20½-month period between the date of payment and the valuation date. This portion of the payment is therefore adjusted to $36,268 as of the valuation date (that is, $40,000 / 1.0590 (20.5[sol]12)).

(G) The sum of the above contributions for the 2009 plan year paid through January 15, 2010, adjusted for interest to the valuation date, is $114,589. This is greater than the minimum required contribution for the 2009 plan year of $108,000.

*Example (6).* (i) The facts are the same as in Example 5, except that the plan sponsor does not make a contribution on September 15, 2010. Another contribution is not made until December 15, 2010.

(ii) The 2009 Schedule SB shows an unpaid minimum required contribution of $42,868 as of January 1, 2009. This is equal to the difference between the minimum required contribution of $108,000 ($125,000 offset by $17,000 for the amount of carryover balance used) and $65,132 (the interest-adjusted contributions made for the 2009 plan year before the 8½ month deadline, as illustrated in paragraphs (ii)(A) through (ii)(D) of Example 5).

*Example (7).* (i) The facts are the same as in Example 1, except that the plan year is changed to an August 1-July 31 plan year effective August 1, 2009. This results in a short plan year beginning January 1, 2009, and ending July 31, 2009. The minimum required contribution for the 7-month period covered by the plan year is calculated as $72,917 in accordance with § 1.430(a)-1(b)(2)(ii).

(ii) As provided in paragraph (c)(5) of this section, a required installment is due 15 days after the close of the short plan year (August 15, 2009), and required installments are also due on the regularly scheduled due dates for quarterly installments that occur within the short plan year (April 15, 2009, and July 15, 2009).

(iii) The required installments are determined based on the lesser of (a) 90% of the minimum required contribution for the short plan year ending July 31, 2009 (90% of $72,917, or $65,625) or (b) 7/12 of 100% of the 2008 minimum required contribution ($100,000 x 7/12, or $58,333). The required installments are thus based on $58,333 since that is the smaller amount.

(iv) The amount of each required installment is determined by dividing the amount determined in paragraph (iii) of this Example 7 by the number of required installments for the short plan year. This calculation results in required installments of $19,444 each (that is, $58,333 divided by 3 installments).

(v) The deadline for the remaining payment is 8½ months after the end of the short plan year, or April 15, 2010. If the plan sponsor pays the minimum required amount at each installment date, does not elect to offset any amounts by any carryover or prefunding balance, and makes a final payment on April 15, 2010, then the remaining payment is $17,429, determined as follows:

(A) The contribution paid April 15, 2009, is adjusted by discounting the contribution amount for 3½ months at the effective interest rate ($19,444 / 1.0590 (3.5[sol]12) = $19,122).

(B) The contribution paid July 15, 2009, is discounted for 6½ months at the effective interest rate ($19,444 / 1.0590 (6.5[sol]12) = $18,850).

(C) The contribution paid August 15, 2009, is discounted for 7½ months at the effective interest rate ($19,444 / 1.0590 (7.5[sol]12) = $18,760).

(D) The sum of the above contributions for the 2009 plan year paid through August 15, 2009, adjusted for interest to the valuation date, is $56,732. The remaining amount paid April 15, 2010, for the 2009 plan year is ($72,917 - $56,732) x 1.059 (15.5[sol]12) = $17,429.

*Example (8).* (i) Plan B has an August 10 to August 9 plan year. Quarterly installments are required for the plan year that begins August 10, 2009.

(ii) For the plan year that begins on August 10, 2009, a plan month begins on the 10th day of each calendar month. Accordingly, the due dates for the required installments for that plan year are November 24, 2009, February 24, 2010, May 24, 2010, and August 24, 2010. The deadline for the final contribution for the plan year is April 24, 2011.

*Example (9).* (i) Plan C has a calendar-year plan year and is not a small plan described in section 430(g)(2)(B). Plan C is subject to the requirement to pay quarterly contributions under paragraph (c) of this section for the 2009 plan year. The valuation date for Plan C is January 1, and Plan C's funding target attainment percentage ("FTAP") is 85% as of January 1, 2009. Before taking the liquidity requirement of paragraph (d) of this section into account, quarterly contributions are required for the 2009 plan year in the amount of $50,000 each. During the 12-month period ending March 31, 2009, periodic annuity payments of $350,000 and lump sum payments of $200,000 were made by Plan C. None of these payments were due to nonrecurring circumstances. In addition, administrative expenses of $100,000 were paid from the plan trust. The market value of Plan C's assets is $1,500,000 as of March 31, 2008, of which $1,300,000 is in liquid assets. The amount needed to increase the plan's FTAP (including the expected increase in the funding target due to benefits accruing or earned during the plan year) to 100% is $500,000.

(ii) The amount of the adjusted disbursements from Plan C for the 12-month period ending March 31, 2009, is calculated as the sum of the annuity benefits, lump sum payments, and administrative expenses paid during the 12-month period, reduced by the product of the lump sum payments and the plan's FTAP. This results in adjusted disbursements for the period of $480,000 (that is, $350,000 plus $200,000 plus $100,000, reduced by 85% of $200,000 in lump sum payments).

(iii) The base amount is calculated in accordance with paragraph (e)(6)(ii) of this section as three times the adjusted disbursements determined in paragraph (ii) of this Example 9, or $1,440,000.

(iv) The liquidity shortfall is the difference between the base amount of $1,440,000 determined in paragraph (iii) of this Example 9 and the $1,300,000 in liquid assets as of March 31, 2008, or $140,000. The quarterly contribution due on April 15, 2009, is therefore $140,000, since this amount is larger than the $50,000 quarterly contribution requirement otherwise applicable but less than the $500,000 needed to increase the plan's FTAP (including the expected increase in the funding target due to benefits accruing or earned during the plan year) to 100%. The liquidity increment is $90,000.

(v) Note that any contributions made through March 31, 2009, are included in Plan C's assets as of March 31, 2009, and would therefore not be applied toward satisfying the liquidity shortfall contribution requirement due April 15, 2009. Similarly, any funding standard carryover balance or prefunding balance as of January 1, 2009, cannot be applied to offset the liquidity shortfall contribution requirement. Only contributions made in cash or other liquid assets made after March 31, 2009, and by April 15, 2009, can be used to timely satisfy this requirement.

*Example (10).* (i) The facts are the same as in Example 9. The plan sponsor makes a contribution of $30,000 on April 15, 2009, and makes an additional contribution of $110,000 on April 30, 2009. The effective interest rate for Plan C for the 2009 plan year is 5.90%.

(ii) The contribution paid on April 15, 2009, is applied first to the portion of the quarterly contribution that is required under paragraph (c) of this section (that is, the portion not attributable to the liquidity shortfall contribution). This results in an underpayment of this portion of the quarterly contribution due April 15, 2009, of $20,000 (that is, $50,000 minus $30,000). In accordance with paragraph (c)(1)(iii)(A) of this section, the interest rate used to adjust this portion of the late quarterly contribution is increased by 5 percentage points for the ½ month period of underpayment. Accordingly, $20,000 of the April 15, 2009, contribution is adjusted to the January 1, 2009, valuation date using an interest rate of 10.90% for the ½ month between the April 15, 2009, due date and the April 30, 2009, payment date, and by 5.90% for the 3½ month period between January 1, 2009, and the April 15, 2009, due date. This portion results in an interest-adjusted contribution of $19,584 as of January 1, 2009 ($20,000 / 1.1090 (0.5[sol]12) / 1.059 (3.5[sol]12)).

(iii) Under paragraph (d)(2) of this section, the interest rate used to adjust the portion of the underpayment attributable to the liquidity shortfall contribution is increased by 5 percentage points, and the contribution is treated as unpaid until the close of the quarter in which the due date occurs. Therefore, even though the full amount of the liquidity shortfall was paid by April 30, 2009, the increase in the interest rate is applied as if the late liquidity shortfall contribution was not made until June 30, 2009, 2½ months after the contribution was due.

(iv) However, in accordance with paragraph (d)(2) of this section, each payment is discounted for interest based on the date of the actual payment, despite the fact that the 5-percentage-point increase in the interest rate is calculated as if the payment was not made until the end of the quarter. Therefore, the portion of the underpayment due to the liquidity increment ($140,000 minus the $50,000 quarterly contribution requirement otherwise required, or $90,000) is adjusted for interest for the 4-month period between the January 1, 2009, valuation date and the April 30, 2009, date of payment. An interest rate of 10.90% is used for 2½ months (corresponding to the period between the April 15, 2009, due date and June 30, 2009, the end of the quarter in which the payment was due), and Plan C's effective interest rate for the 2009 plan year (5.90%) is used for the remaining 1½ months. Therefore, the portion of the April 30, 2009, contribution attributable to the liquidity increment is adjusted to $87,452 as of January 1, 2009 ($90,000 / 1.1090 (2.5[sol]12) / 1.0590 (1.5[sol]12)).

*Example (11).* (i) The facts are the same as in Example 10, except that the plan sponsor does not make the second contribution of $110,000 until July 15, 2009.

(ii) The July 15, 2009, contribution is adjusted for interest for a total of 6½ months for the period between January 1, 2009, and the payment date of July 15, 2009. In accordance with paragraph (d)(2) of this section, the 5-percentage-point increase in the interest rate used to adjust the portion of the contribution attributable to the unpaid liquidity shortfall contribution is applied as if the contribution was made at the end of the quarter in which the payment was due. Therefore, the interest adjustment for the $90,000 attributable to the late liquidity shortfall contribution uses an interest rate of 10.90% for the 2½-month period corresponding to the period between the April 15, 2009, due date and June 30, 2009, the end of the quarter in which the payment was due, and the effective interest rate of 5.90% for the remaining 4 months.

(iii) The liquidity shortfall is recalculated as of June 30, 2009, and the larger of the resulting amount or the $50,000 quarterly contribution otherwise applicable is due on July 15, 2009. This amount is required to be paid in addition to the unpaid liquidity shortfall contribution due April 15, 2009. Note that the amount of liquid assets as of June 30, 2009 is smaller than it would have been had the April 15, 2009, liquidity shortfall payment been made. Therefore, the fact that the April 15, 2009, liquidity shortfall payment was not made before June 30, 2009, means that the plan sponsor is required to contribute more than the amount needed to increase the liquid assets to the base amount as of June 30, 2009. However, in accordance with paragraph (d)(1)(ii) of this section, the total amount of the required installments (including those due but not paid) is limited so that it is no larger than the amount that would increase the plan's FTAP (taking into account the expected increase in the funding target due to benefits accruing or earned during the plan year) to 100%.

*Example (12).* (i) Plan D, which is a small plan described in section 430(g)(2)(B), has a calendar year plan year and a valuation date of December 31. The quarterly required installments for the 2009 plan year are $30,000 each and each of the required installments is paid on the due date. The effective interest rate for Plan D for the 2009 plan year is 5.90%.

(ii) The total contributions made for the plan year and before the valuation date, adjusted with interest to the valuation date, equal $92,402. This is developed as shown below:

(A) The contribution paid April 15, 2009, is adjusted by increasing the contribution amount for 8½ months at the effective interest rate ($30,000 x 1.0590 (8.5[sol]12) = $31,243).

(B) The contribution paid July 15, 2009, is increased for 5½ months at the effective interest rate ($30,000 x 1.0590 (5.5[sol]12) = $30,799).

(C) The contribution paid October 15, 2009, is increased for 2½ months at the effective interest rate ($30,000 x 1.0590 (2.5[sol]12) = $30,360).

(iii) Pursuant to § 1.430(g)-1(d)(2), the interest-adjusted value of the contributions for the 2009 plan year that are made before the valuation date is subtracted from the December 31, 2009, plan assets in determining the value of plan assets for the December 31, 2009 actuarial valuation.

**(g) Effective/applicability dates and transition rules.** *(1) In general.* Section 430 generally applies to plan years beginning on or after January 1, 2008. In general, this section applies to plan years beginning on or after January 1, 2009. However, plans are permitted to apply this section in applying the rules of section 430(j) for plan years beginning in 2008.

*(2) Plans with delayed effective date.* In the case of a plan for which the effective date of section 430 is delayed in accordance with sections 104 through 106 of PPA '06, this section applies to plan years beginning on or after the first day of the first effective plan year.

*(3) First effective plan year.* For purposes of this section, the first effective plan year for a plan is the first plan year for which section 430 applies to the plan.

*(4) Pre-effective plan year.* For purposes of this section, the pre-effective plan year for a plan is the last plan year before the first effective plan year. Thus, except for plans with a delayed effective date under paragraph (g)(2) of this section, the pre-effective plan year for a plan is the last plan year beginning before January 1, 2008.

*(5) Special rules relating to first effective plan year.* (i) Determination of minimum required contribution for pre-effective plan year. In the case of the plan's first effective plan year, the minimum required contribution for the preceding plan year for purposes of paragraph (c)(3)(ii)(B) of this section is equal to the minimum required contribution under section 412 for the pre-effective plan year (determined without regard to any funding waiver under section 412), which is determined as of the last day of the pre-effective plan year and is determined without regard to the use of the plan's credit balance.

(ii) Determination of funding shortfall for pre-effective plan year. [Reserved]

**§ 1.431(c)(6)-1 Mortality tables used to determine current liability.**

**(a) Mortality tables used to determine current liability.** The mortality assumptions that apply to a defined benefit plan for the plan year pursuant to section 430(h)(3)(A) and § 1.430(h)(3)-1(a)(2) are used to determine a multiemployer plan's current liability for purposes of applying the rules of section 431(c)(6). A multiemployer plan is permitted to apply either the static mortality tables used pursuant to § 1.430(h)(3)-1(a)(3) or generational mortality tables used pursuant to § 1.430(h)(3)-1(a)(4) for this purpose. However, for this purpose, a multiemployer plan is not permitted to use substitute mortality tables under § 1.430(h)(3)-2.

**(b) Effective/applicability date.** This section applies for plan years beginning on or after January 1, 2008.

T.D. 9419, 7/31/2008.

**Proposed § 1.432(a)-1 General rules relating to section 432.** [*For Preamble, see ¶ 152,975*]

**(a) In general.** *(1) Overview.* This section provides rules relating to multiemployer plans (within the meaning of section 414(f)) that are in endangered status or critical status under section 432. Section 432 and this section only apply to multiemployer plans that are in effect on July 16, 2006. Paragraph (b) of this section sets forth definitions of terms that apply for purposes of section 432. Paragraph (c) of this section sets forth special rules for plans described in section 404(c) and for the treatment of nonbargained participation.

*(2) Plans in endangered status.* (i) Plan sponsor must adopt funding improvement plan. If a plan is in endangered status, the plan sponsor must adopt and implement a funding improvement plan that satisfies the requirements of section 432(c).

(ii) Restrictions applicable to plans in endangered status. If a plan is in endangered status, the plan and plan sponsor must satisfy the requirements of section 432(d)(1) during the funding plan adoption period specified in section 432(c)(8).

(iii) Restrictions applicable after the adoption of funding improvement plan. In the case of a plan that is in endangered status after adoption of the funding improvement plan, the plan and the plan sponsor must satisfy the requirements of section 432(d)(2) until the end of the funding improvement period.

*(3) Plans in critical status.* (i) Plan sponsor must adopt rehabilitation plan. If a plan is in critical status, the plan sponsor must adopt and implement a rehabilitation plan that satisfies the requirements of section 432(e).

(ii) Restrictions applicable to plans in critical status. If a plan is in critical status, the plan and the plan sponsor must satisfy the requirements of section 432(f)(4) during the rehabilitation plan adoption period as defined in section 432(e)(5). The plan must also apply the restrictions on single sum and other accelerated benefits set forth in paragraph (a)(3)(iii) of this section.

(iii) Restrictions on single sums and other accelerated benefits—

(A) In general. A plan in critical status is required to provide that, effective on the date the notice of certification of the plan's critical status for the initial critical year under § 1.432(b)-1(e) is sent, no payment in excess of the monthly amount payable under a single life annuity (plus any social security supplements described in the last sentence of section 411(a)(9)), and no payment for the purchase of an irrevocable commitment from an insurer to pay benefits, may be made except as provided in section 432(f)(2). A plan amendment that provides for these restrictions does not violate section 411(d)(6).

(B) Exceptions. Pursuant to section 432(f)(2)(B), the restrictions under this paragraph (a)(3)(iii) do not apply to a benefit which under section 411(a)(11) may be immediately distributed without the consent of the participant or to any makeup payment in the case of a retroactive annuity starting date or any similar payment of benefits owed with respect to a prior period.

(C) [Reserved.]

(D) Correction of erroneous restrictions. If the notice described in § 1.432(b)-1(e) has been sent and the restrictions provided under this paragraph (a)(3)(iii) have been applied, and it is later determined that the restrictions should not have been applied, then the plan must correct any benefit payments that were restricted in error. Thus, for example, if pursuant to section 212(e)(2) of the Pension Protection Act of 2006, Public Law 109-280, 120 Stat. 780 the enrolled actuary for the plan certified that it was reasonably expected that the plan would be in critical status with respect to the first plan year beginning after 2007, and the notice described in § 1.432(b)-1(e)(3)(i) was sent, but the plan is not later certified to be in critical status for that plan year, then the plan must correct any benefit payments that were restricted after the notice was sent. Similarly, if the enrolled actuary for the plan certified that it was reasonably expected that the plan would be in critical status with respect to the first plan year beginning after 2007, and the notice described in § 1.432(b)-1(e)(3)(i) was sent before the first day of that plan year, the restriction on benefits under section 432(f)(2) first applies beginning on the first day of the first plan year beginning after 2007. If the plan restricts benefits before that date, then the plan must correct any improperly restricted benefits.

(iv) Restrictions applicable after the adoption of rehabilitation plan. In the case of a plan that is in critical status after the adoption of the rehabilitation plan, the plan and the plan sponsor must satisfy the requirements of section 432(f)(1) until the end of the rehabilitation period.

**(b) Definitions.** The following definitions apply for purposes of section 432 and the regulations:

*(1) Accumulated funding deficiency.* The term accumulated funding deficiency has the same meaning as the term accumulated funding deficiency under section 431(a).

*(2) Active participant.* The term active participant means a participant who is in covered service under the plan.

*(3) Bargaining party.* Except as provided in paragraph (c)(1) of this section, the term bargaining party means an employer who has an obligation to contribute under the plan and an employee organization which, for purposes of collective bargaining, represents plan participants employed by an employer which has an obligation to contribute under the plan.

*(4) Benefit commencement date.* The term benefit commencement date means the annuity starting date (or in the case of a retroactive annuity starting date, the date on which benefit payments begin).

*(5) Critical status.* A multiemployer plan is in critical status if the plan meets one of the tests set forth in § 1.432(b)-1(c).

*(6) Endangered status.* A plan is in endangered status if the plan meets one of the tests set forth in § 1.432(b)-1(b).

*(7) Funded percentage.* The term funded percentage means a fraction (expressed as a percentage) the numerator of which is the actuarial value of the plan's assets as determined under section 431(c)(2) and the denominator of which is the accrued liability of the plan, determined using the actuarial assumptions described in section 431(c)(3) and the unit credit funding method.

*(8) Funding improvement period for endangered or seriously endangered plans.* The term funding improvement period means the period that begins on the first day of the first plan year beginning after the earlier of the second anniversary of the date of the adoption of the funding improvement plan, or the expiration of the collective bargaining agreements that are in effect on the due date for the actuarial certification of endangered status for the initial endangered year and which cover, as of such due date, at least 75 percent of the active participants in the plan. The funding improvement period ends on the last day of the 10th year (15 years for seriously endangered plans, except as provided in section 432(c)(5)) after it begins or, if earlier, the date of the change in status described in section 432(c)(4)(C).

*(9) Funding plan adoption period.* The term funding plan adoption period means the period that begins on the date of the actuarial certification for the initial endangered year and ends on the day before the first day of the funding improvement period.

*(10) Inactive participant.* The term inactive participant means—

(i) A participant who is not an active participant,

(ii) A beneficiary under the plan, or

(iii) An alternate payee under the plan.

*(11) Initial critical year.* The term initial critical year means the first year for which the enrolled actuary for the plan has certified that the plan is or will be in critical status. If a plan is in critical status in one year, emerges from critical status in a subsequent year and then returns to critical status, the year of reentry into critical status is treated as the initial critical year with respect to subsequent years.

*(12) Initial endangered year.* The term initial endangered year means the first year for which the enrolled actuary for the plan has certified that the plan is in endangered status. If a plan is in endangered status in one year, changes from endangered status in a subsequent year and then returns to endangered status, the year of reentry into endangered status is treated as the initial endangered year with respect to subsequent years.

*(13) Nonbargained participant.* The term nonbargained participant means a participant in the plan whose participa-

tion is other than pursuant to a collective bargaining agreement within the meaning of section 7701(a)(46). A participant will not be treated as a nonbargained participant merely because the participant is no longer covered by the collective bargaining agreement solely as a result of retirement or severance from employment.

*(14) Obligation to contribute.* The term obligation to contribute means an obligation to contribute arising under one or more collective bargaining (or related) agreements or as a result of a duty under applicable labor-management relations law.

*(15) Plan sponsor.* Except as provided in paragraph (c)(1) of this section, the term plan sponsor means the association, committee, joint board of trustees, or other similar group of representatives of the parties who establish or maintain the plan.

*(16) Rehabilitation period.* The term rehabilitation period means the period that begins on the first day of the first plan year beginning after the earlier of the second anniversary of the date of the adoption of the rehabilitation plan, or the expiration of the collective bargaining agreements that are in effect on the due date for the actuarial certification of critical status for the initial critical year and which cover, as of such due date, at least 75 percent of the active participants in the plan. The rehabilitation period ends on the last day of the 10th year after it begins or, if earlier, the plan year preceding the plan year in which the plan has emerged from critical status as described in section 432(e)(4)(B).

*(17) Rehabilitation plan adoption period.* The term rehabilitation plan adoption period means the period that begins on the date of the actuarial certification for the initial critical year and ends on the day before the first day of the rehabilitation period.

*(18) Seriously endangered status.* A plan is in seriously endangered status if the plan is in endangered status and is described in both § 1.432(b)-1(b)(2) and (3).

**(c) Special rules.** *(1) Plan described in section 404(c).* In the case of a plan described in section 404(c), or a continuation of such a plan, the association of employers that is the employer settlor of the plan is treated as a bargaining party and is treated as the plan sponsor for purposes of section 432.

*(2) Plans covering both bargained and nonbargained participants.* In the case of an employer that contributes to a plan with respect to both employees who are covered by one or more collective bargaining agreements and employees who are nonbargained participants, if the plan is in endangered status or critical status, benefits of and contributions for the nonbargained participants (including surcharges on those contributions) are determined as if those nonbargained participants were covered under the employer's collective bargaining agreement in effect when the plan entered endangered or critical status that is the first to expire.

*(3) Plans covering nonbargained participants only.* In the case of an employer that contributes to a multiemployer plan only with respect to employees who are not covered by a collective bargaining agreement, section 432 and the regulations thereunder are applied as if the employer were the bargaining party, and its participation agreement with the plan were a collective bargaining agreement with a term ending on the first day of the plan year beginning after the employer is provided the schedules described in sections 432(c) and (e).

**(d) Effective/applicability date.** These regulations apply to plan years ending after March 18, 2008, but only with respect to plan years that begin on or after January 1, 2008.

**Proposed § 1.432(b)-1 Determination of status and adoption of a plan.** [*For Preamble, see ¶ 152,975*]

**(a) In general.** This section provides rules relating to multiemployer plans (within the meaning of section 414(f)) that are in endangered status or critical status under section 432. Section 432 and this section only apply to multiemployer plans that are in effect on July 16, 2006. Paragraph (b) of this section sets forth the factors for determining whether a plan is in endangered status. Paragraph (c) of this section sets forth the factors for determining whether a plan is in critical status. Paragraph (d) sets forth the requirements for the annual certification by the plan's enrolled actuary. Paragraph (e) of this section describes the notice to employees that is required for plans that are in endangered or critical status.

**(b) Determination of endangered status.** *(1) In general.* A plan is in endangered status for a plan year if, as determined by the enrolled actuary for the plan, the plan is not in critical status for the plan year and if, as of the beginning of the plan year, the plan is described either in paragraph (b)(2) of this section or paragraph (b)(3) of this section. The enrolled actuary's determination of whether a plan is in endangered status is made under the rules of paragraph (d)(5) of this section.

*(2) Endangered status based on funding percentage.* A plan is described in this paragraph (b)(2) for a plan year if the plan's funded percentage for such plan year is less than 80 percent.

*(3) Endangered status based on projection of funding deficiency.* A plan is described in this paragraph (b)(3) for a plan year if the plan has an accumulated funding deficiency for such plan year (or is projected to have such an accumulated funding deficiency for any of the 6 succeeding plan years), taking into account any extension of amortization periods under section 431(d).

**(c) Critical Status.** *(1) In general.* A multiemployer plan is in critical status for a plan year if, as determined by the enrolled actuary for the plan, the plan is described in one or more of paragraphs (c)(2) through (c)(6) of this section as of the beginning of the plan year. The enrolled actuary's determination of critical status must be made in accordance with the rules of paragraph (d)(5) of this section. Notwithstanding paragraph (d)(5)(iii) of this section, for purposes of applying the critical status tests described in paragraphs (c)(2) and (c)(5) of this section, the actuary must assume that the terms of all collective bargaining agreements pursuant to which the plan is maintained for the current plan year continue in effect for succeeding plan years.

*(2) Critical status based on 6-year projection of benefit payments.* A plan is described in this paragraph (c)(2) if the funded percentage of the plan is less than 65 percent, and the present value of all nonforfeitable benefits projected to be payable under the plan during the current plan year and each of the 6 succeeding plan years (plus administrative expenses for such plan years) is greater than the sum of—

(i) The fair market value of plan assets, plus

(ii) The present value of the reasonably anticipated employer contributions for the current plan year and the 6 succeeding plan years.

*(3) Critical status based on short term funding deficiency.* A plan is described in this paragraph (c)(3) if—

(i) The plan has an accumulated funding deficiency for the current plan year, not taking into account any extension of amortization periods under section 431(d), or

(ii) The plan is projected to have an accumulated funding deficiency for any of the 3 succeeding plan years (4 succeeding plan years if the funded percentage of the plan is 65 percent or less), not taking into account any extension of amortization periods under section 431(d).

*(4) Critical status based on contributions less than normal cost plus interest.* A plan is described in this paragraph (c)(4) if—

(i) The present value of the reasonably anticipated employer and employee contributions for the current plan year is less than the sum of—

(A) The plan's normal cost (determined under the unit credit funding method), and

(B) Interest (determined at the rate used for determining costs under the plan) on the excess if any of—

(1) The accrued liability of the plan (determined using the actuarial assumptions described in section 431(c)(3) and the unit credit funding method) over

(2) The actuarial value of assets determined under section 431(c)(2),

(ii) The present value, as of the beginning of the current plan year, of nonforfeitable benefits of inactive participants is greater than the present value of nonforfeitable benefits of active participants, and

(iii) The plan has an accumulated funding deficiency for the current plan year (or is projected to have such a deficiency for any of the 4 succeeding plan years), not taking into account any extension of amortization periods under section 431(d).

*(5) Critical status based on 4-year projection of benefit payments.* A plan is described in this paragraph (c)(5) if the present value of all benefits projected to be payable under the plan during the current plan year or any of the 4 succeeding plan years (plus administrative expenses for such plan years) is greater than the sum of—

(i) The fair market value of plan assets, plus

(ii) The present value of the reasonably anticipated employer contributions for the current plan year and each of the 4 succeeding plan years.

*(6) Critical status based on failure to meet emergence criteria.* A plan is described in this paragraph (c)(6) if—

(i) The plan was in critical status for the immediately preceding plan year, and

(ii) The enrolled actuary for the plan has certified that the plan is projected to have an accumulated funding deficiency for the plan year or any of the 9 succeeding plan years, without regard to the use of the shortfall funding method but taking into account any extensions of the amortization periods under section 431(d).

**(d) Annual certification by the plan's enrolled actuary.** *(1) In general.* Not later than the 90th day of each plan year of a multiemployer plan, the enrolled actuary for the plan must certify to the Secretary of the Treasury and to the plan sponsor—

(i) Whether or not the plan is in endangered status for such plan year;

(ii) Whether or not the plan is or will be in critical status for such plan year, and

(iii) In the case of a plan which is in a funding improvement or rehabilitation period, whether or not the plan is making the scheduled progress in meeting the requirements of its funding improvement or rehabilitation plan.

*(2) Transmittal of certification.* (i) Transmittal to the plan sponsor. The certification of plan status described in paragraph (d)(1) must be submitted to the plan sponsor at the address stated by the plan sponsor on their Annual Report (Form 5500) or such other address as the plan sponsor may designate in writing for receipt of this certification.

(ii) Transmittal to the Secretary of the Treasury. Except as provided in guidance of general applicability to be published in the Internal Revenue Bulletin, the annual certification of plan status described in paragraph (d)(1) must be transmitted to the Secretary of the Treasury by mailing the certification to: Internal Revenue Service, Employee Plans Compliance Unit, Group 7602 (SE:TEGE:EP), Room 1700— 17th Floor, 230 S. Dearborn Street, Chicago, IL 60604.

*(3) Content of annual certification.* (i) In general. The annual certification must contain the information described in this paragraph (d)(3). The Secretary may add to or otherwise modify the requirements in this paragraph (d)(3) in guidance of general applicability to be published in the Internal Revenue Bulletin.

(ii) Plan identification. The annual certification must include the name of the plan; the plan number; the name, address, and telephone number of the plan sponsor; and the plan year for which the certification is being made.

(iii) Enrolled actuary identification. The annual certification must include the name, address and telephone number of the enrolled actuary signing the certification; the actuary's enrollment identification number; the actuary's signature, and the date of the signature.

(iv) Information on plan status. The annual certification must state whether the plan is in endangered status (which includes seriously endangered status); critical status, or neither endangered nor critical status.

(v) Information on scheduled progress. If the annual certification is made with respect to a plan year that is within the plan's funding improvement period or rehabilitation period arising from a prior certification of endangered or critical status, the actuary must also certify whether or not the plan is making scheduled progress in meeting the requirements of its funding improvement or rehabilitation plan.

*(4) Penalty for failure to secure timely actuarial certification.* A failure of a plan's actuary to certify the plan's status under this paragraph (d) by the date specified in paragraph (d)(1) of this section is treated as a failure or refusal by the plan administrator to file the annual report required to be filed with the Secretary of Labor under section 101(b)(4) of the Employee Retirement Income Security Act of 1974.

*(5) Actuarial projections of assets and liabilities.* (i) In general. In making the determinations and projections under section 432(b) and this section, the enrolled actuary for the plan must make projections required for the current and succeeding plan years of the current value of the assets of the plan and the present value of all liabilities to participants and beneficiaries under the plan for the current plan year as of the beginning of such year. These projections must be based on reasonable actuarial estimates, assumptions, and methods in accordance with section 431(c)(3) and that offer the actuary's best estimate of anticipated experience under the plan. Notwithstanding the previous sentence, the actuary is permitted to rely on the plan sponsor's projection of activity in the industry provided under paragraph (d)(5)(iii) of this section.

The projected present value of liabilities as of the beginning of such year must be determined based on the most recent information reported on the most recent of either—

(A) The actuarial statement required under section 103(d) of the Employee Retirement Income Security Act of 1974 that has been filed with respect to the most recent year, or

(B) The actuarial valuation for the preceding plan year.

(ii) Determinations of future contributions. Any actuarial projection of plan assets shall assume either—

(A) Reasonably anticipated employer contributions for the current and succeeding plan years, assuming that the terms of the one or more collective bargaining agreements pursuant to which the plan is maintained for the current plan year continue in effect for succeeding plan years, or

(B) That employer contributions for the most recent plan year will continue indefinitely, but only if the enrolled actuary for the plan determines there have been no significant demographic changes that would make such assumption unreasonable.

(iii) Projected industry activity. The plan sponsor shall provide any necessary projection of activity in the industry, including future covered employment, to the plan actuary. For this purpose, the plan sponsor must act reasonably and in good faith.

*(6) Treatment of amortization extensions under section 412(e).* For purposes of section 432, if the plan received an extension of any amortization period under section 412(e), the extension is treated the same as an extension under section 431(d). Thus, such an extension is not taken into account in determining whether a plan has or will have an accumulated funding deficiency under paragraph (c)(3) and (c)(4) of this section, but it is taken into account in determining whether a plan has or will have an accumulated funding deficiency under paragraph (b)(3) of this section.

**(e) Notice of endangered or critical status.** *(1) In general.* In any case in which the enrolled actuary for the plan certifies that a multiemployer plan is or will be in endangered or critical status for a plan year, the plan sponsor must, not later than 30 days after the date of the certification, provide notification of the endangered or critical status to the participants and beneficiaries, the bargaining parties, the Pension Benefit Guaranty Corporation, and the Secretary of Labor.

*(2) Plans in critical status.* If it is certified that a multiemployer plan is or will be in critical status for a plan year, the plan sponsor must include in the notice an explanation of the possibility that adjustable benefits (as defined in section 432(e)(8)) may be reduced, and such reductions may apply to participants and beneficiaries whose benefit commencement date is on or after the date such notice is provided for the first plan year in which the plan is in critical status. If the plan provides benefits that are restricted under section 432(f)(2), the notice must also include an explanation that the plan cannot pay single sums and similar benefits described in section 432(f)(2) that are greater than the monthly amount due under a single life annuity. A plan sponsor that sends the model notice issued by the Secretary of Labor pursuant to section 432(b)(3)(D)(iii) satisfies this requirement.

*(3) Transition rules.* (i) Early notice permitted. If, after August 17, 2006, the enrolled actuary for the plan certifies that a plan is reasonably expected to be in critical status with respect to the first plan year beginning after 2007, then the notice described in this paragraph (e) may be provided before the date the actuary certifies the plan is in critical status for that plan year. The ability to provide early notice does not extend the otherwise applicable deadline for providing the notice under paragraph (e)(1) of this section.

(ii) Reformation of prior notice. If notice has been provided prior to the date required under paragraph (e)(1) of this section, but the notice did not include all of the information described in paragraph (e)(2) of this section, then that notice will not satisfy the requirements for notice under section 432(b)(3)(D). Accordingly, the restrictions under section 432(f)(2) will not apply as a result of the issuance of such a notice. However, if prior to the date notice is required to be provided under paragraph (e)(1) of this section additional notice is provided that includes all of the information required under paragraph (e)(2) of this section, then the notice requirements of section 432(b)(3)(D) are satisfied as of the date of that additional notice and the restrictions of section 432(f)(2) will apply beginning on that date. In such a case, the date of the earlier notice will still apply for purposes of section 432(e)(8)(A)(ii) provided that the earlier notice included all of the information required under section 432(b)(3)(D)(ii).

**(f) Effective applicability date.** These regulations apply to plan years ending after [INSERT DATE OF PUBLICATION OF THESE REGULATIONS IN THE FEDERAL REGISTER] but only with respect to plan years that begin on or after January 1, 2008.

**§ 1.436-0 Table of contents.**

This section contains a listing of the major headings of § 1.436-1.

(5) Right to delay commencement.

(6) Plan alternative for special optional forms.

(7) Exception for distributions permitted without consent of the participant under section 411(a)(11).

(e) Limitation on benefit accruals for plans with severe funding shortfalls.

(1) In general.

(2) Exemption if section 436 contribution is made.

(3) Special rule under section 203 of the Worker, Retiree, and Employer Recovery Act of 2008. [Reserved]

(f) Methods to avoid or terminate benefit limitations.

(1) In general.

(2) Current year contributions to avoid or terminate benefit limitations.

(3) Security to increase adjusted funding target attainment percentage.

(4) Examples.

(g) Rules of operation for periods prior to and after certification.

(1) In general.

(2) Periods prior to certification during which a presumption applies.

(3) Periods prior to certification during which no presumption applies.

(4) Modification of the presumed AFTAP.

(5) Periods after certification of AFTAP.

(6) Examples.

(h) Presumed underfunding for purposes of benefit limitations.

(1) Presumption of continued underfunding.

(2) Presumption of underfunding beginning on first day of 4th month for certain underfunded plans.

(3) Presumption of underfunding beginning on first day of 10th month.

(4) Certification of AFTAP.

(5) Examples of rules of paragraphs (h)(1), (h)(2), and (h)(3) of this section.

(6) Examples of application of paragraph (h)(4) of this section.

(i) [Reserved]

(j) Definitions.

(1) Adjusted funding target attainment percentage.

(2) Annuity starting date.

(3) First effective plan year.

(4) Funding target.

(5) Prior year adjusted funding target attainment percentage.

(6) Prohibited payment.

(7) Section 436 contributions.

(8) Section 436 measurement date.

(9) Unpredictable contingent event.

(10) Examples.

(k) Effective/applicability dates.

(1) Statutory effective date.

(2) Collectively bargained plan exception.

(9) Effective date/applicability date of regulations.

---

T.D. 9467, 10/07/2009.

---

### § 1.436-1 Limits on benefits and benefit accruals under single employer defined benefit plans.

**(a) General rules.** *(1) Qualification requirement.* Section 401(a)(29) provides that a defined benefit pension plan that is subject to section 412 and that is not a multiemployer plan (within the meaning of section 414(f)) is a qualified plan only if it satisfies the requirements of section 436. This section provides rules relating to funding-based limitations on certain benefits under section 436, and the requirements of section 436 are satisfied only if the plan meets the requirements of this section beginning with the plan's first effective plan year. This section applies to single employer defined benefit plans (including multiple employer plans), but does not apply to multiemployer plans.

*(2) Organization of the regulation.* Paragraph (b) of this section describes limitations on shutdown benefits and other unpredictable contingent event benefits. Paragraph (c) of this section describes limitations on plan amendments increasing liabilities. Paragraph (d) of this section describes limitations on prohibited payments. Paragraph (e) of this section describes limitations on benefit accruals. Paragraph (f) of this section provides rules relating to methods to avoid or terminate benefit limitations. Paragraph (g) of this section provides rules for the operation of the plan in relation to benefit limitations under section 436. Paragraph (h) of this section describes related presumptions regarding underfunding that apply for purposes of the benefit limitations under section 436 and requirements relating to certifications. Paragraph (j) of this section contains definitions. Paragraph (k) of this section contains effective/applicability date provisions.

*(3) Special rules for certain plans.* (i) New plans. The limitations described in paragraphs (b), (c), and (e) of this section do not apply to a plan for the first 5 plan years of the plan. Except as otherwise provided by the Commissioner in guidance of general applicability, plan years of the plan include the following (in addition to plan years during which the plan was maintained by the employer or plan sponsor):

(A) Plan years when the plan was maintained by a predecessor employer within the meaning of § 1.415(f)-1(c)(1).

(B) Plan years of another defined benefit plan maintained by a predecessor employer within the meaning of § 1.415(f)-1(c)(2) within the preceding five years if any participants in the plan participated in that other defined benefit plan (even if the plan maintained by the employer is not the plan that was maintained by the predecessor employer).

(C) Plan years of another defined benefit plan maintained by the employer within the preceding five years if any participants in the plan participated in that other defined benefit plan.

(ii) Application of section 436 after termination of a plan— (A) In general. Except as otherwise provided in paragraph (a)(3)(ii)(B) of this section, any section 436 limitations in effect immediately before the termination of a plan do not cease to apply thereafter.

(B) Exception for payments pursuant to plan termination. The limitations under section 436(d) and paragraph (d) of this section do not apply to prohibited payments (within the meaning of paragraph (j)(6) of this section) that are made to carry out the termination of a plan in accordance with applicable law. For example, a plan sponsor's purchase of an irrevocable commitment from an insurer to pay benefit liabilities in connection with the standard termination of a plan in accordance with section 4041(b)(3) of the Employee Retirement Income Security Act of 1974, as amended (ERISA), and in accordance with 29 CFR 4041.28, does not violate section 436(d) or this section.

(iii) Multiple employer plans. In the case of a multiple employer plan to which section 413(c)(4)(A) applies, this section applies separately with respect to each employer under the plan, as if each employer maintained a separate plan. Thus, the benefit limitations under section 436 and this section could apply differently to participants who are employees of different employers under such a multiple employer plan. In the case of a multiple employer plan to which section 413(c)(4)(A) does not apply (that is, a plan described in section 413(c)(4)(B) that has not made the election for section 413(c)(4)(A) to apply), this section applies as if all participants in the plan were employed by a single employer.

*(4) Treatment of plan as of close of prohibited or cessation period.* (i) Application to prohibited payments and accruals— (A) Resumption of prohibited payments. If a limitation on prohibited payments under paragraph (d) of this section applied to a plan as of a section 436 measurement date (as defined in paragraph (j)(8) of this section), but that limit no longer applies to the plan as of a later section 436 measurement date, then the limitation on prohibited payments under the plan does not apply to benefits with annuity starting dates (as defined in paragraph (j)(2) of this section) that are on or after that later section 436 measurement date. Any amendment to eliminate an optional form of benefit that contains a prohibited payment with respect to an annuity starting date during a period in which the limitations of section 436(d) and paragraph (d) of this section do not apply to the plan is subject to the rules of section 411(d)(6).

(B) Resumption of benefit accruals. If a limitation on benefit accruals under paragraph (e) of this section applied to a plan as of a section 436 measurement date, but that limit no longer applies to the plan as of a later section 436 measurement date, then that limitation does not apply to benefit accruals that are based on service on or after that later section 436 measurement date, except to the extent that the plan provides that benefit accruals will not resume when the limitation ceases to apply. The plan must comply with the rules relating to partial years of participation and the prohibition on double proration under Department of Labor regulation 29 CFR 2530.204-2(c) and (d). (ii) Restoration of options and missed benefit accruals— (A) Option to amend plan. A plan is permitted to be amended to provide participants who had an annuity starting date within a period during which a limitation under paragraph (d) of this section applied to the plan with the opportunity to make a new election under which the form of benefit previously elected is modified, subject to applicable qualification requirements. A participant who makes such a new election is treated as having a new annuity starting date under sections 415 and 417. Similarly, a plan is permitted to be amended to provide that any benefit accruals which were limited under the rules of paragraph (e) of this section are credited under the plan when the limitation no longer applies, subject to applicable qualification requirements. Any such plan amendment with respect to a new annuity starting date or crediting of benefit accruals is subject to the requirements of section 436(c) and paragraph (c) of this section.

(B) Automatic plan provisions. A plan is permitted to provide that participants who had an annuity starting date within a period during which a limitation under paragraph (d) of this section applied to the plan will be provided with the opportunity to have a new annuity starting date (which would constitute a new annuity starting date under sections 415 and 417) under which the form of benefit previously elected may be modified, subject to applicable qualification requirements, once the limitations of paragraph (d) of this section cease to apply. In addition, subject to the rules of paragraph (c)(3) of this section, a plan is permitted to provide for the automatic restoration of benefit accruals that had been limited under section 436(e) as of the section 436 measurement date that the limitation ceases to apply.

(iii) Shutdown and other unpredictable contingent event benefits. If unpredictable contingent event benefits with respect to an unpredictable contingent event that occurs during the plan year are not permitted to be paid after the occurrence of the event because of the limitations of section 436(b) and paragraph (b) of this section, but are permitted to be paid later in the plan year as a result of additional contributions under paragraph (f)(2) of this section or pursuant to the enrolled actuary's certification of the adjusted funding target attainment percentage for the plan year that meets the requirements of paragraph (g)(5)(ii)(B) of this section, then those unpredictable contingent event benefits must automatically become payable, retroactive to the period those benefits would have been payable under the terms of the plan (other than plan terms implementing the requirements of section 436(b)). If the benefits do not become payable during the plan year in accordance with the preceding sentence, then the plan is treated as if it does not provide for those benefits. However, all or any portion of those benefits can be restored pursuant to a plan amendment that meets the requirements of section 436(c) and paragraph (c) of this section and other applicable qualification requirements.

(iv) Treatment of plan amendments that do not take effect. If a plan amendment does not take effect as of the effective date of the amendment because of the limitations of section 436(c) and paragraph (c) of this section, but is permitted to take effect later in the plan year as a result of additional contributions under paragraph (f)(2) of this section or pursuant to the enrolled actuary's certification of the adjusted funding target attainment percentage for the plan year that meets the requirements of paragraph (g)(5)(ii)(C) of this section, then the plan amendment must automatically take effect as of the first day of the plan year (or, if later, the original effective date of the amendment). If the plan amendment cannot take effect during the plan year, then it must be treated as if it were never adopted, unless the plan amendment provides otherwise.

(v) Example. The following example illustrates the rules of this paragraph (a)(4):

*Example (1).* (i) Plan T is a non-collectively bargained defined benefit plan with a plan year that is the calendar year and a valuation date of January 1. As of January 1, 2011, Plan T does not have a funding standard carryover balance or a prefunding balance. Plan T's sponsor is not in bankruptcy. Beginning January 1, 2011, Plan T is subject to the restriction on prohibited payments under paragraph (d)(3) of this section based on a presumed adjusted funding target attainment percentage (AFTAP) of 75%.

(ii) U is a participant in Plan T. Participant U retires on February 1, 2011, and elects to receive benefits in the form of a single sum. Plan T may pay only a portion (generally, 50%) of the prohibited payment. Accordingly, U elects in accordance with paragraph (d)(3)(ii) of this section to receive 50% of U's benefit in a single sum (up to the 2011 PBGC maximum benefit guarantee amount described in paragraph (d)(3)(iii)(C) of this section) and the remainder as an immediately commencing straight life annuity.

(iii) On March 1, 2011, the enrolled actuary for the Plan certifies that the AFTAP for 2011 is 80%. Accordingly, beginning March 1, 2011, Plan T is no longer subject to the restriction under paragraph (d)(3) of this section.

(iv) Effective March 1, 2011, Plan T is amended to provide that a participant whose benefits were restricted under paragraph (d)(3) of this section with respect to an annuity starting date between January 1, 2011, and February 28, 2011, may elect, within a specified period on or after March 1, 2011, a new annuity starting date and receive the remainder of his or her pension benefits in an accelerated form of payment. Plan T's enrolled actuary determines that the AFTAP, taking into account the amendment, would still be 80%. The amendment is permitted to take effect because Plan T would have an AFTAP of 80% taking into account the amendment and is therefore neither subject to the restriction on plan amendments in paragraph (c) of this section nor the restrictions on prohibited payments under paragraphs (d)(1) and (d)(3) of this section. Accordingly, Participant U may elect, within the specified period and subject to otherwise applicable qualification rules, including spousal consent, to receive the remainder of U's benefits in the form of a single sum on or after March 1, 2011.

*(5) Deemed election to reduce funding balances.* (i) Limitations on accelerated benefit payments. If a benefit limitation under paragraph (d)(1) or (d)(3) of this section would (but for this paragraph (a)(5)) apply to a plan, the employer is treated as having made an election under section 430(f) to reduce the prefunding balance or funding standard carryover balance by such amount as is necessary for the adjusted funding target attainment percentage to be at the applicable threshold (60 or 80 percent, as the case may be) in order for the benefit limitation not to apply to the plan. The determination of whether a benefit limitation under paragraph (d) of this section would apply to a plan is based on whether the plan provides for an optional form of benefit that would be limited under section 436(d) and is not based on whether any participant elects payment of benefits in such a form.

(ii) Other limitations for collectively bargained plans— (A) General rule. In the case of a collectively bargained plan to which a benefit limitation under paragraph (b), (c), or (e) of this section would (but for this paragraph (a)(5)) apply, the employer is treated as having made an election under section 430(f) to reduce the prefunding balance or funding standard carryover balance by such amount as is necessary for the adjusted funding target attainment percentage to be at the applicable threshold (60 or 80 percent, as the case may be) in order for the benefit limitation not to apply to the plan, taking into account the adjustments described in paragraph (g)(2)(iii)(A), (g)(3)(ii)(A), or (g)(5)(i)(B) of this section, whichever applies.

(B) Collectively bargained plans. A plan is considered a collectively bargained plan for purposes of this paragraph (a)(5)(ii) if—

(1) At least 50 percent of the employees benefiting under the plan (within the meaning of § 1.410(b)-3(a)) are members of collective bargaining units for which the benefit levels under the plan are specified under a collective bargaining agreement; or

(2) At least 25 percent of the participants in the plan are members of collective bargaining units for which the benefit levels under the plan are specified under a collective bargaining agreement.

(iii) Exception for insufficient funding balances— (A) In general. Paragraphs (a)(5)(i) and (a)(5)(ii) of this section apply with respect to a benefit limitation for any plan year only if the application of those paragraphs would result in the corresponding benefit limitation not applying for such plan year. Thus, if the plan's prefunding and funding standard carryover balances were reduced to zero and the resulting increase in plan assets taken into account would still not increase the plan's adjusted funding target attainment percentage enough to reach the threshold percentage applicable to the benefit limitation, the deemed election to reduce those balances pursuant to paragraph (a)(5)(i) or (a)(5)(ii) of this section does not apply.

(B) Presumed adjusted funding target attainment percentage less than 60 percent. During any period when a plan is presumed to have an adjusted funding target attainment percentage of less than 60 percent as a result of paragraph (h)(3) of this section, the plan is treated as if the prefunding balance and the funding standard carryover balance are insufficient to increase the adjusted funding target attainment percentage to the threshold percentage of 60 percent. Accordingly, the deemed election to reduce those balances pursuant to paragraphs (a)(5)(i) and (a)(5)(ii) of this section does not apply to the plan.

(iv) Other rules— (A) Date of deemed election. If an election is deemed to be made pursuant to this paragraph (a)(5), then the plan sponsor is treated as having made that election on the date as of which the applicable benefit limitation would otherwise apply.

(B) Coordination with section 436 contributions. The determination of whether one of the benefit limitations described in paragraph (a)(5)(ii)(A) of this section would otherwise apply is made without regard to any contribution described in paragraph (f)(2) of this section. Thus, the requirement to reduce the prefunding balance or funding standard carryover balance under paragraph (a)(5)(ii) of this section cannot be avoided through the use of a section 436 contribution.

(C) Coordination with elections to offset minimum required contribution. See § 1.430(f)-1(d)(1)(ii) for rules on the coordination of elections to offset the minimum required contribution and the deemed election to reduce the prefunding and funding standard carryover balances under this paragraph (a)(5).

(v) Example. The following example illustrates the rules of this paragraph (a)(5):

*Example (1).* (i) Plan W is a collectively bargained, single employer defined benefit plan sponsored by Sponsor X, with a plan year that is the calendar year and a valuation date of January 1.

(ii) The enrolled actuary for Plan W issues a certification on March 1, 2010, that the 2010 AFTAP is 81%. Sponsor X adopts an amendment on March 25, 2010, to increase benefits under a formula based on participant compensation, with an effective date of May 1, 2010. (Because the formula is based on compensation, the exception in paragraph (c)(4)(i) of this section does not apply.) The plan's enrolled actuary determines that the plan's AFTAP for 2010 would be 75% if the benefits attributable to the plan amendment were taken into account in determining the funding target.

(iii) Because the AFTAP would be below the 80% threshold if the benefits attributable to the plan amendment were taken into account in determining the funding target, Sponsor X is deemed pursuant to paragraph (a)(5)(ii) of this section to have made an election to reduce Plan W's prefunding and funding standard carryover balances by the amount necessary for the AFTAP to reach the 80% threshold (reflecting the increase in funding target attributable to the plan amendment), provided that the amount of those balances is sufficient for this purpose.

(iv) If the deemed election described in paragraph (iii) of this example occurs, the plan amendment takes effect on its effective date (May 1, 2010). See paragraph (f) of this section for other methods to avoid or terminate benefit limitations (where, for example, the amount necessary for a benefit limitation not to apply for a plan year exceeds the sum of the prefunding balance and the funding standard carryover balance).

*(6) Notice requirements.* See section 101(j) of ERISA for rules requiring the plan administrator of a single employer plan to provide a written notice to participants and beneficiaries within 30 days after certain specified dates, which depend on whether the plan has become subject to a restriction described in the ERISA provisions that are parallel to Internal Revenue Code sections 436(b), 436(d), and 436(e) (ERISA sections 206(g)(1), 206(g)(3), and 206(g)(4), respectively).

**(b) Limitation on shutdown benefits and other unpredictable contingent event benefits.** *(1) In general.* Except as otherwise provided in this paragraph (b), a plan satisfies section 436(b) and this paragraph (b) only if it provides that unpredictable contingent event benefits with respect to any unpredictable contingent events occurring during a plan year will not be paid if the adjusted funding target attainment percentage for the plan year is—

(i) Less than 60 percent; or

(ii) 60 percent or more, but would be less than 60 percent if the adjusted funding target attainment percentage were redetermined applying an actuarial assumption that the likelihood of occurrence of the unpredictable contingent event during the plan year is 100 percent.

*(2) Exemption if section 436 contribution is made.* The prohibition on payment of unpredictable contingent event benefits under paragraph (b)(1) of this section ceases to apply with respect to benefits attributable to an unpredictable contingent event occurring during the plan year upon payment by the plan sponsor of the contribution described in paragraph (f)(2)(iii) of this section with respect to that event. If the prior sentence applies with respect to an unpredictable contingent event, then all benefits with respect to the unpredictable contingent event must be paid, including benefits for periods prior to the contribution. See paragraph (f) of this section for additional rules.

*(3) Rules of application.* (i) Participant-by-participant application. The limitations of section 436(b) and this paragraph (b) apply on a participant-by-participant basis. Thus, whether payment or commencement of an unpredictable contingent event benefit under a plan is restricted with respect to a participant is determined based on whether the participant satisfies the plan's eligibility requirements (other than the attainment of any age, performance of any service, receipt or derivation of any compensation, or the occurrence of death or disability) for such a benefit in a plan year in which the limitations of section 436(b) and this paragraph (b) apply.

(ii) Multiple contingencies. In the case of a plan that provides for a benefit that depends upon the occurrence of more than one unpredictable contingent event with respect to a participant, the unpredictable contingent event for purposes of section 436(b) and this paragraph (b) occurs upon the last to occur of those unpredictable contingent events.

(iii) Cessation of benefits. Cessation of a benefit under a plan upon the occurrence of a specified event is not an unpredictable contingent event for purposes of section 436(b) and this paragraph (b). Thus, section 436(b) and this paragraph (b) do not prohibit provisions of a plan that provide for cessation, suspension, or reduction of any benefits upon occurrence of any event. However, upon any subsequent recommencement of benefits (including any restoration of benefits), the rules of section 436 and this section will apply.

*(4) Prior unpredictable contingent event.* Unpredictable contingent event benefits attributable to an unpredictable contingent event that occurred within a period during which no limitation under this paragraph (b) applied to the plan are not affected by the limitation described in this paragraph (b) as it applies in a subsequent period. For example, if a plant shutdown occurs in 2010 and the plan's funded status is such that benefits contingent upon that plant shutdown are not subject to the limitation described in this paragraph (b) for that calendar plan year, this paragraph (b) does not apply to restrict payment of those benefits even if another plant shutdown occurs in 2012 that results in the restriction of benefits that are contingent upon that later plant shutdown under this paragraph (b) (where the plan's adjusted funding target attainment percentage for 2012 would be less than 60 percent taking into account the liability attributable to those shutdown benefits).

**(c) Limitations on plan amendments increasing liability for benefits.** *(1) In general.* Except as otherwise provided in this paragraph (c), a plan satisfies section 436(c) and this paragraph (c) only if the plan provides that no amendment to the plan that has the effect of increasing liabilities of the plan by reason of increases in benefits, establishment of new benefits, changing the rate of benefit accrual, or changing the rate at which benefits become nonforfeitable will take effect in a plan year if the adjusted funding target attainment percentage for the plan year is—

(i) Less than 80 percent; or

(ii) 80 percent or more, but would be less than 80 percent if the benefits attributable to the amendment were taken into account in determining the adjusted funding target attainment percentage.

*(2) Exemption if section 436 contribution is made.* (i) General rule. The limitations on plan amendments in paragraph (c)(1) of this section cease to apply with respect to an amendment upon payment by the plan sponsor of the contribution described in paragraph (f)(2)(iv) of this section, so that the amendment is permitted to take effect as of the later of the first day of the plan year or the effective date of the amendment. See paragraph (f) of this section for additional rules.

(ii) Amendments that do not increase funding target. If the amount of the contribution described in paragraph (f)(2)(iv) of this section is $0 (because the amendment increases benefits solely for future periods), the amendment is permitted to take effect without regard to this paragraph (c). However, see § 1.430(d)-1(d)(2) for a rule that requires such an amendment to be taken into account in determining the funding target and the target normal cost in certain situations.

*(3) Rules of application regarding pre-existing plan provisions.* If a plan contains a provision that provides for the automatic restoration of benefit accruals that were not permitted to accrue because of the application of section 436(e) and paragraph (e) of this section, the restoration of those ac-

cruals is generally treated as a plan amendment that is subject to section 436(c). However, such a provision is permitted to take effect without regard to the limits of section 436(c) and this paragraph (c) if—

(i) The continuous period of the limitation is 12 months or less; and

(ii) The plan's enrolled actuary certifies that the adjusted funding target attainment percentage for the plan would not be less than 60 percent taking into account the restored benefit accruals for the prior plan year.

*(4) Exceptions.* (i) Benefit increases based on compensation— (A) In general. In accordance with section 436(c)(3), section 436(c) and this paragraph (c) do not apply to any amendment that provides for an increase in benefits under a formula that is not based on a participant's compensation, but only if the rate of increase in benefits does not exceed the contemporaneous rate of increase in average wages of participants covered by the amendment. The determination of the rate of increase in average wages is made by taking into consideration the net increase in average wages from the period of time beginning with the effective date of the most recent benefit increase applicable to all of those participants who are covered by the current amendment and ending on the effective date of the current amendment.

(B) Application to participants who are not currently employed. If an amendment applies to both currently employed participants and other participants, all participants to whom the amendment applies are included in determining the increase in average wages of the participants covered by the amendment for purposes of this paragraph (c)(4)(i). For this purpose, participants who are not employees at any time during the period from the effective date of the most recent earlier benefit increase applicable to all of the participants who are covered by the current amendment and ending on the effective date of the current amendment are treated as having no increase or decrease in wages for the period after severance from employment.

(C) Separate amendments for different plan populations. In lieu of a single amendment that applies to both currently employed participants and other participants as described in paragraph (c)(4)(i)(B) of this section, the employer can adopt multiple amendments--such as one that increases benefits for participants currently employed on the effective date of the current amendment and another one that increases benefits for other participants. In that case, the two amendments are considered separately in determining the increase in average wages, and the exception in this paragraph (c)(4)(i) applies separately to each amendment. Thus, the increase in benefits for currently employed participants takes effect if it satisfies the exception under this paragraph (c)(4), but the amendment increasing benefits for other participants who received no increase in wages from the employer during the period over which the increase in average wages is separately subject to the rules of this paragraph (c) without regard to the rules of this paragraph (c)(4).

(ii) Plan provisions providing for accelerated vesting. To the extent that any amendment provides for (or any pre-existing plan provision results in) a mandatory increase in the vesting of benefits under the Code or ERISA (such as vesting rate increases pursuant to statute, plan termination amendments or partial terminations under section 411(d)(3), and vesting increases required by the rules for top-heavy plans under section 416), that amendment (or pre-existing plan provision) does not constitute an amendment that changes the rate at which benefits become nonforfeitable for purposes of section 436(c) and this paragraph (c). However, this paragraph (c)(4)(ii) applies only to the extent the increase in vesting is necessary to enable the plan to continue to satisfy the requirements for qualified plans.

(iii) Authority for additional exceptions. The Commissioner may, in guidance of general applicability, issue additional rules under which other amendments to a plan are not treated as amendments to which section 436(c) and this paragraph (c) apply. See § 601.601(d)(2) relating to objectives and standards for publishing regulations, revenue rulings and revenue procedures in the Internal Revenue Bulletin.

*(5) Rule for determining when an amendment takes effect.* For purposes of section 436(c) and this paragraph (c), in the case of an amendment that increases benefits, the amendment takes effect under a plan on the first date on which any individual who is or could be a participant or beneficiary under the plan would obtain a legal right to the increased benefit if the individual were on that date to satisfy the applicable requirements for entitlement to the benefit (such as the attainment of any age, performance of any service, receipt or derivation of any compensation, or the occurrence of death, disability, or severance from employment).

*(6) Treatment of mergers, consolidations, and transfers of plan assets into a plan.* [Reserved]

**(d) Limitations on prohibited payments.** *(1) AFTAP less than 60 percent.* A plan satisfies the requirements of section 436(d)(1) and this paragraph (d)(1) only if the plan provides that, if the plan's adjusted funding target attainment percentage for a plan year is less than 60 percent, a participant or beneficiary is not permitted to elect an optional form of benefit that includes a prohibited payment, and the plan will not pay any prohibited payment, with an annuity starting date on or after the applicable section 436 measurement date.

*(2) Bankruptcy.* A plan satisfies the requirements of section 436(d)(2) and this paragraph (d)(2) only if the plan provides that a participant or beneficiary is not permitted to elect an optional form of benefit that includes a prohibited payment, and the plan will not pay any prohibited payment, with an annuity starting date that occurs during any period in which the plan sponsor is a debtor in a case under title 11, United States Code, or similar Federal or State law, except for payments made within a plan year with an annuity starting date that occurs on or after the date on which the enrolled actuary of the plan certifies that the plan's adjusted funding target attainment percentage for that plan year is not less than 100 percent.

*(3) Limited payment if AFTAP at least 60 percent but less than 80 percent.* (i) In general. A plan satisfies the requirements of section 436(d)(3) and this paragraph (d)(3) only if the plan provides that, in any case in which the plan's adjusted funding target attainment percentage for a plan year is 60 percent or more but is less than 80 percent, a participant or beneficiary is not permitted to elect the payment of an optional form of benefit that includes a prohibited payment, and the plan will not pay any prohibited payment, with an annuity starting date on or after the applicable section 436 measurement date, unless the present value, determined in accordance with section 417(e)(3), of the portion of the benefit that is being paid in a prohibited payment (which portion is determined under paragraph (d)(3)(iii)(B) of this section) does not exceed the lesser of—

(A) 50 percent of the present value (determined in accordance with section 417(e)(3)) of the benefit payable in the optional form of benefit that includes the prohibited payment; or

(B) 100 percent of the PBGC maximum benefit guarantee amount described in paragraph (d)(3)(iii)(C) of this section.

(ii) Bifurcation if optional form unavailable— (A) Requirement to offer bifurcation. If an optional form of benefit that is otherwise available under the terms of the plan is not available as of the annuity starting date because of the application of paragraph (d)(3)(i) of this section, then the plan must permit the participant or beneficiary to elect to—

(1) Receive the unrestricted portion of that optional form of benefit (determined under the rules of paragraph (d)(3)(iii)(D) of this section) at that annuity starting date, determined by treating the unrestricted portion of the benefit as if it were the participant's or beneficiary's entire benefit under the plan;

(2) Commence benefits with respect to the participant's or beneficiary's entire benefit under the plan in any other optional form of benefit available under the plan at the same annuity starting date that satisfies paragraph (d)(3)(i) of this section; or

(3) Defer commencement of the payments to the extent described in paragraph (d)(5) of this section.

(B) Rules relating to bifurcation. If the participant or beneficiary elects payment of the unrestricted portion of the benefit as described in paragraph (d)(3)(ii)(A)(1) of this section, then the plan must permit the participant or beneficiary to elect payment of the remainder of the participant's or beneficiary's benefits under the plan in any optional form of benefit at that annuity starting date otherwise available under the plan that would not have included a prohibited payment if that optional form applied to the entire benefit of the participant or beneficiary. The rules of § 1.417(e)-1 are applied separately to the separate optional forms for the unrestricted portion of the benefit and the remainder of the benefit (the restricted portion).

(C) Plan alternative that anticipates election of payment that includes a prohibited payment. With respect to an optional form of benefit that includes a prohibited payment and that is not permitted to be paid under paragraph (d)(3)(i) of this section, for which no additional information from the participant or beneficiary (such as information regarding a social security leveling optional form of benefit) is needed to make that determination, rather than wait for the participant or beneficiary to elect such optional form of benefit, a plan is permitted to provide for separate elections with respect to the restricted and unrestricted portions of that optional form of benefit. However, the rule in the preceding sentence applies only if—

(1) The plan applies the rule to all such optional forms; and

(2) The plan identifies the option that the bifurcation election replaces.

(iii) Definitions applicable to limited payment option—

(A) In general. The definitions in this paragraph (d)(3)(iii) apply for purposes of this paragraph (d)(3).

(B) Portion of benefit being paid in a prohibited payment. If a benefit is being paid in an optional form for which any of the payments is greater than the amount payable under a straight life annuity to the participant or beneficiary (plus any social security supplements described in the last sentence of section 411(a)(9) payable to the participant or beneficiary) with the same annuity starting date, then the portion of the benefit that is being paid in a prohibited payment is the excess of each payment over the smallest payment during the participant's lifetime under the optional form of benefit (treating a period after the annuity starting date and during the participant's lifetime in which no payments are made as a payment of zero).

(C) PBGC maximum benefit guarantee amount. The PBGC maximum benefit guarantee amount described in this paragraph (d)(3)(iii)(C) is the present value (determined under guidance prescribed by the Pension Benefit Guaranty Corporation, using the interest and mortality assumptions under section 417(e)) of the maximum benefit guarantee with respect to a participant (based on the participant's age or the beneficiary's age at the annuity starting date) under section 4022 of ERISA for the year in which the annuity starting date occurs.

(D) Unrestricted portion of the benefit— (1) General rule. Except as otherwise provided in this paragraph (d)(3)(iii)(D), the unrestricted portion of the benefit with respect to any optional form of benefit is 50 percent of the amount payable under the optional form of benefit.

(2) Special rule for forms which include social security leveling or a refund of employee contributions. For an optional form of benefit that is a prohibited payment on account of a social security leveling feature (as defined in § 1.411(d)-3(g)(16)) or a refund of employee contributions feature (as defined in § 1.411(d)-3(g)(11)), the unrestricted portion of the benefit is the optional form of benefit that would apply if the participant's or beneficiary's accrued benefit were 50 percent smaller.

(3) Limited to PBGC maximum benefit guarantee amount. After the application of the preceding rules of this paragraph (d)(3)(iii)(D), the unrestricted portion of the benefit with respect to the optional form of benefit is reduced, to the extent necessary, so that the present value (determined in accordance with section 417(e)) of the unrestricted portion of that optional form of benefit does not exceed the PBGC maximum benefit guarantee amount (described in paragraph (d)(3)(iii)(C) of this section).

(iv) Other rules— (A) One time application. A plan satisfies the requirements of this paragraph (d)(3) only if the plan provides that, in the case of a participant with respect to whom a prohibited payment (or series of prohibited payments under a single optional form of benefit) is made pursuant to paragraph (d)(3)(i) or (ii) of this section, no additional prohibited payment may be made with respect to that participant during any period of consecutive plan years for which prohibited payments are limited under this paragraph (d).

(B) Treatment of beneficiaries. For purposes of this paragraph (d)(3), benefits provided with respect to a participant and any beneficiary of the participant (including an alternate payee, as defined in section 414(p)(8)) are aggregated. If the only benefits paid under the plan with respect to the participant are death benefits payable to the beneficiary, then paragraph (d)(3)(iii)(B) of this section is applied by substituting the lifetime of the beneficiary for the lifetime of the participant. If the accrued benefit of a participant is allocated to such an alternate payee and one or more other persons, then the unrestricted amount under paragraph (d)(3)(iii)(D) of this section is allocated among such persons in the same manner as the accrued benefit is allocated, unless a qualified domestic relations order (as defined in section 414(p)(1)(A)) with respect to the participant or the alternate payee provides otherwise. See paragraphs (j)(2)(ii) and (j)(6)(ii) of this section for other special rules relating to beneficiaries.

(C) Treatment of annuity purchases and plan transfers. This paragraph (d)(3)(iv)(C) applies for purposes of applying paragraphs (d)(3)(i) and (iii)(D) of this section. In the case of a prohibited payment described in paragraph (j)(6)(i)(B) of this section (relating to purchase from an insurer), the present value of the portion of the benefit that is being paid in a prohibited payment is the cost to the plan of the irrevocable commitment and, in the case of a prohibited payment described in paragraph (j)(6)(i)(C) of this section (relating to certain plan transfers), the present value of the portion of the benefit that is being paid in a prohibited payment is the present value of the liabilities transferred (determined in accordance with section 414(l)). In addition, the present value of the accrued benefit is substituted for the present value of the benefit payable in the optional form of benefit that includes the prohibited payment in paragraph (d)(3)(i)(A) of this section. (Further, see § 1.411(d)-4, A-2(a)(3)(ii), for a rule under section 411(d)(6) that applies to an optional form of benefit that includes a prohibited payment described in paragraph (j)(6)(i)(B) of this section.)

(v) Examples. The following examples illustrate the rules of this paragraph (d)(3):

*Example (1).* (i) Plan A has a plan year that is the calendar year, and is subject to the restriction on prohibited payments under paragraph (d)(3) of this section for the 2010 plan year. Participant P is not married, and retires at age 65 during 2010, while the restriction under paragraph (d)(3) of this section applies to Plan A. P's accrued benefit is $10,000 per month, payable commencing at age 65 as a straight life annuity. Plan A provides for an optional single-sum payment (subject to the restrictions under section 436) equal to the present value of the participant's accrued benefit using actuarial assumptions under section 417(e). P's single-sum payment, determined without regard to this paragraph (d), is calculated to be $1,416,000, payable at age 65.

(ii) The PBGC guaranteed monthly benefit for a straight life annuity payable at age 65 in 2010 (for purposes of this example) is assumed to be $4,500. The PBGC maximum benefit guarantee amount at age 65 is assumed to be $637,200 for 2010.

(iii) Because Participant P retires during a period when the restriction in paragraph (d)(3) of this section applies to Plan A, only a portion of the benefit can be paid in the form of a single sum. P elects a single-sum payment. Because a single-sum payment is a prohibited payment, a determination must be made whether the payment can be paid under paragraph (d)(3)(i) of this section. In this case, because the present value of the portion of Participant P's benefit that is being paid in a prohibited payment exceeds the lesser of 50% of the benefit or the PBGC maximum benefit guarantee amount, it cannot be paid under paragraph (d)(3)(i) of this section. Accordingly, the maximum single sum that P can receive is $637,200 (that is, the lesser of 50% of $1,416,000 or $637,200).

(iv) Pursuant to paragraph (d)(3)(ii) of this section, Plan A must offer P the option to bifurcate the benefit into unrestricted and restricted portions. The unrestricted portion is a monthly straight life annuity of $4,500, which can be paid in a single sum of $637,200. If P elects to receive the unrestricted portion of the benefit in the form of a single sum, then, with respect to the $5,500 restricted portion, Plan A must permit P to elect any form of benefit that would otherwise be permitted with respect to the full $10,000 and that is not a prohibited payment. Alternatively, Plan A may provide that P is permitted to elect to defer commencement of the restricted portion, subject to applicable qualification rules.

*Example (2).* (i) The facts are the same as in Example 1. In addition, Plan A provides an optional form of payment (subject to any benefit restrictions under section 436) that consists of a partial payment equal to the total return of employee contributions to the plan accumulated with interest, with an annuity payment for the remainder of the participant's benefit.

(ii) Participant Q is not married, and retires at age 65 during 2010, while Plan A is subject to the restriction under paragraph (d)(3) of this section. Participant Q has an accrued benefit equal to a straight life annuity of $3,000 per month. Under the optional form described in paragraph (i) of this Example 2, Q may elect a partial payment of $99,120 (representing the return of employee contributions accumulated with interest), plus a straight life annuity of $2,300 per month. The present value of Participant Q's accrued benefit, using actuarial assumptions under section 417(e), is $424,800.

(iii) Because the present value of the portion of Q's benefit that is being paid in a prohibited payment ($99,120) does not exceed the lesser of 50% of the present value of benefits (50% of $424,800) or 100% of the PBGC maximum benefit guarantee amount ($637,200 at age 65 for 2010), the optional form described in paragraph (i) of this Example 2 is permitted to be paid under paragraph (d)(3)(i) of this section.

*Example (3).* (i) The facts are the same as in Example 1. In addition, Plan A provides an optional form of payment under a social security leveling option (subject to any benefit restrictions under section 436) that consists of an increased temporary benefit payable until age 62, with reduced payments beginning at age 62. The benefit is structured so that the combination of the participant's pension benefit and Social Security benefit provides an approximately level income for the participant's lifetime. The PBGC maximum benefit guarantee amount at age 55 is assumed to be $362,776 for 2010.

(ii) Participant R retires at age 55 in 2010 and is eligible to receive a level lifetime annuity of $1,200 per month beginning immediately. Instead, Participant R elects to receive a benefit under the social security leveling optional form of payment. Participant R's Social Security benefit payable at age 62 is projected, under the terms specified in Plan A, to be $1,500 per month. The Plan A adjustment factor for the social security leveling option using the minimum present value requirements of section 417(e)(3) is .590 at age 55. Therefore, Participant R's benefit payable from age 55 to age 62 is $2,085 per month ($1,200 + .590 x $1,500), and the benefit payable for Participant's lifetime, beginning after age 62, is $585 per month ($2,085-$1,500).

(iii) Because the optional form provides some payments which are greater than payments described in paragraph (j)(6)(i)(A) of this section ($1,200), the portion of the benefit that is being paid in a prohibited payment is $1,500 per month which is payable from age 55 to age 62. Using the applicable interest and mortality rates under section 417(e) as in effect for Plan A at the time the benefit commences, the present value of a temporary benefit of $1,500 per month ($2,085-$585) payable from age 55 to age 62 is $106,417, and the present value of the entire benefit (a temporary benefit of $2,085 per month payable from age 55 to age 62 plus a deferred lifetime benefit of $585 commencing at age 62) is $207,468.

(iv) Because $106,417 is more than 50% of $207,468 (and because 50% of Participant R's benefit is less than $362,776, which is the PBGC maximum guaranteed benefit amount at age 55 for 2010), Participant R can only receive 50% of the benefit in the form of the social security leveling option. Pursuant to paragraph (d)(3)(ii) of this section, Plan A must offer Participant R the option to bifurcate the benefit into unrestricted and restricted portions. Participant R elects to receive the restricted portion of the early retirement benefit as a level lifetime annuity of $600 commencing at age 55.

(v) Participant R elects to receive the unrestricted portion of the early retirement benefit in the social security leveling form of payment. This portion of the benefit is determined under the social security leveling form of payment as if Participant R's benefit was one-half of the early retirement benefit, or $600. However, using a monthly level lifetime benefit of $600 and a monthly social security benefit of $1,500, Participant R would have a negative benefit after age 62 ($600 + .590 x $1,500 is only $1,485; offsetting $1,500 at age 62 would produce a negative amount). Plan A provides that in this situation, the benefit under the social security leveling option is an actuarially equivalent monthly annuity payable until age 62, with zero payable thereafter. Using the actuarial equivalence factor of .590 at age 55, the plan administrator determines that the unrestricted portion of Participant R's benefit is $1,463 per month, payable from age 55 to age 62 ($600 + .590 x $1,463 = $1,463 payable until age 62; $1,463-$1,463 = zero payable after age 62).

(vi) Combining the unrestricted and restricted portions of the benefit, Participant R will receive a total of $2,063 per month from age 55 to age 62 ($1,463 from the unrestricted portion of the benefit plus $600 from the restricted portion of the benefit), and $600 per month beginning at age 62 (zero from the unrestricted portion of the benefit plus $600 from the restricted portion of the benefit).

*(4) Exception for cessation of benefit accruals.* This paragraph (d) does not apply to a plan for a plan year if the terms of the plan, as in effect for the period beginning on September 1, 2005, provided for no benefit accruals with respect to any participants. If a plan that is described in this paragraph (d)(4) provides for benefit accruals during any time on or after September 1, 2005 (treating benefit increases pursuant to a plan amendment as benefit accruals), this paragraph (d)(4) ceases to apply for the plan as of the date any benefits accrue under the plan (or the date the amendment takes effect). For example, the exception in this paragraph (d)(4) does not apply to a plan after the plan increases benefits to take into account increases in the limitations under section 415(b) on or after September 1, 2005.

*(5) Right to delay commencement.* If a participant or beneficiary requests a distribution in an optional form of benefit that includes a prohibited payment that is not permitted to be paid under paragraph (d)(1), (d)(2), or (d)(3) of this section, the participant retains the right to delay commencement of benefits in accordance with the terms of the plan and applicable qualification requirements (such as sections 411(a)(11) and 401(a)(9)).

*(6) Plan alternative for special optional forms.* A plan is permitted to offer optional forms of benefit that are solely available during the period in which paragraph (d)(1), (d)(2), or (d)(3) of this section applies to limit prohibited payments under the plan. For example, a plan may permit participants or beneficiaries who commence benefits during the period in which paragraph (d)(1) of this section (or paragraph (d)(2) of this section) applies to limit prohibited payments under the plan to elect, within a specified period after the date on which that paragraph ceases to apply to limit prohibited payments under the plan, to receive the remaining benefit in the form of a single-sum payment equal to the present value of the remaining benefit, but only to the extent then permitted under this paragraph (d). As another example, during a period when paragraph (d)(3) of this section applies to a plan, the plan may permit participants and beneficiaries to elect payment in an optional form of benefit that provides for the current payment of the unrestricted portion of the benefit, with a delayed commencement for the restricted portion of the benefit (subject to other applicable qualification requirements, such as sections 411(a)(11) and 401(a)(9)), or may satisfy paragraph (d)(3)(i) of this section by permitting participants and beneficiaries to elect an optional form of benefit that combines an unsubsidized single-sum payment for over 50 percent of the accrued benefit with a subsidized early retirement life annuity for the remainder of the accrued benefit. Any such optional forms must satisfy this paragraph (d) and applicable qualification requirements, including satisfaction of section 417(e) and section 415 (at each annuity starting date).

*(7) Exception for distributions permitted without consent of the participant under section 411(a)(11).* [Reserved]

**(e) Limitation on benefit accruals for plans with severe funding shortfalls.** *(1) In general.* Except as otherwise provided in this paragraph (e), a plan satisfies the requirements of section 436(e) and this paragraph (e) only if it provides that, in any case in which the plan's adjusted funding target attainment percentage for a plan year is less than 60 percent, benefit accruals under the plan will cease as of the applicable section 436 measurement date. If a plan is required to cease benefit accruals under this paragraph (e), then the plan is not permitted to be amended in a manner that would increase the liabilities of the plan by reason of an increase in benefits or establishment of new benefits. The preceding sentence applies regardless of whether an amendment would otherwise be permissible under paragraph (c)(2) or (c)(3) of this section.

*(2) Exemption if section 436 contribution is made.* The prohibition on additional benefit accruals under a plan described in paragraph (e)(1) of this section ceases to apply with respect to a plan year, effective as of the first day of the plan year, upon payment by the plan sponsor of the contribution described in paragraph (f)(2)(v) of this section. See paragraph (f) of this section for additional rules.

*(3) Special rule under section 203 of the Worker, Retiree, and Employer Recovery Act of 2008.* "Reserved"

**(f) Methods to avoid or terminate benefit limitations.** *(1) In general.* This paragraph (f) sets forth rules relating to employer contributions and other methods to avoid or terminate the application of section 436 limitations under a plan for a plan year. In general, there are four methods a plan sponsor may utilize to avoid or terminate one or more of the benefit limitations under this section for a plan year. Two of these methods (where the plan sponsor elects to reduce the prefunding balance or funding standard carryover balance and where the plan sponsor makes additional contributions under section 430 for the prior plan year within the time period provided by section 430(j)(1) that are not added to the prefunding balance) involve increasing the amount of plan assets which are taken into account in determining the adjusted funding target attainment percentage. The other two methods (making a contribution that is specifically designated as a current year contribution to avoid or terminate application of a benefit limitation under paragraph (b), (c), or (e) of this section, and providing security under section 436(f)(1)) are described in paragraphs (f)(2) and (f)(3) of this section, respectively.

*(2) Current year contributions to avoid or terminate benefit limitations.* (i) General rules— (A) Amount of contribution— (1) In general. This paragraph (f)(2) sets forth rules regarding contributions to avoid or terminate the application of section 436 limitations under a plan for a plan year that apply to unpredictable contingent event benefits, plan amendments that increase liabilities for benefits, and benefit accruals.

(2) Interest adjustment. Any contribution made by a plan sponsor pursuant to this paragraph (f)(2) on a date other than the valuation date for the plan year must be adjusted with interest at the plan's effective interest rate under section 430(h)(2)(A) for the plan year. If the plan's effective interest rate for the plan year has not been determined at the time of the contribution, then this interest adjustment must be made using the highest of the three segment rates as applicable for the plan year under section 430(h)(2)(C). In such a case, if the effective interest rate for the plan year under section 430(h)(2)(A) is subsequently determined to be less than that highest rate, the excess is recharacterized as an employer contribution taken into account under section 430 for the current plan year.

(B) Timing requirement for section 436 contributions. Any contribution described in this paragraph (f)(2) must be paid before the unpredictable contingent event benefits are permitted to be paid, the plan amendment is permitted to take effect, or the benefit accruals are permitted to resume. In addition, any contribution described in this paragraph (f)(2) must be paid during the plan year.

(C) Prefunding balance or funding standard carryover balance may not be used. No prefunding balance or funding standard carryover balance under section 430(f) may be used as a contribution described in this paragraph (f)(2). However, a plan sponsor is permitted to elect to reduce the funding standard carryover balance or the prefunding balance in order to increase the adjusted funding target attainment percentage for a plan year. See paragraph (a)(5) of this section for a rule mandating such a reduction in certain situations.

(ii) Section 436 contributions separate from minimum required contributions— (A) In general. The contributions described in this paragraph (f)(2) are contributions described in sections 436(b)(2), 436(c)(2), and 436(e)(2), and are separate from any minimum required contributions under section 430. Thus, if a plan sponsor makes a contribution described in this paragraph (f)(2) for a plan year but does not make the minimum required contribution for the plan year, the plan fails to satisfy the minimum funding requirements under section 430 for the plan year. In addition, a contribution described in this paragraph (f)(2) is disregarded in determining the maximum addition to the prefunding balance under section 430(f)(6) and § 1.430(f)-1(b)(1)(ii).

(B) Designation requirement. Any contribution made by a plan sponsor pursuant to this paragraph (f)(2) must be designated as such at the time the contribution is used to avoid or terminate the limitations under this paragraph (f)(2), including designation of the benefits or amendments to which the limits do not apply because of the contribution. Except as specifically provided in paragraph (f)(2)(i)(A)(2), (g) or (h) of this section, such a contribution cannot be subsequently recharacterized with respect to any plan year as a contribution to satisfy a minimum required contribution obligation, or otherwise. The designation must be made in accordance with the rules and procedures that otherwise apply to elections under § 1.430(f)-1(f) with respect to the prefunding and funding standard carryover balances.

(C) Requirement to recertify AFTAP. If the plan's enrolled actuary has already certified the adjusted funding target attainment percentage for the plan year, a plan sponsor is treated as making the contribution described in paragraph (f)(2)(iii)(B), (f)(2)(iv)(B), or (f)(2)(v) of this section for the plan year only after the plan's enrolled actuary certifies an updated adjusted funding target attainment percentage for the plan year that takes into account the increased liability for the unpredictable contingent event benefits, the plan amendments, or restored accruals, and the associated section 436 contribution, under the rules of paragraph (h)(4)(v) of this section. See also paragraph (g)(4)(i) of this section for a requirement to modify the presumed adjusted funding target attainment percentage to take the liability for the unpredictable contingent event benefits or plan amendments, and the associated section 436 contribution, into account (if the contribution described in paragraph (f)(2)(iii)(B), (f)(2)(iv)(B), or (f)(2)(v) of this section is made before the plan's enrolled actuary certifies the adjusted funding target attainment percentage for the plan year).

(iii) Contribution for unpredictable contingent event benefits. In the case of a contribution to avoid or terminate the application of the limitation on benefits attributable to an unpredictable contingent event under section 436(b)—

(A) In the event that the adjusted funding target attainment percentage for the plan year determined without taking into account the liability attributable to the unpredictable contingent event benefits is less than 60 percent, the amount of the contribution under section 436(b)(2) is equal to the amount of the increase in the funding target of the plan for the plan year if the benefits attributable to the unpredictable contingent event were included in the determination of the funding target.

(B) In the event that the adjusted funding target attainment percentage for the plan year determined without taking into account the liability attributable to the unpredictable contingent event benefits is 60 percent or more, the amount of the contribution under section 436(b)(2) is the amount that would be sufficient to result in an adjusted funding target attainment percentage for the plan year of 60 percent if the contribution (and any prior section 436 contributions made for the plan year) were included as part of the plan assets and the funding target were to take into account the adjustments described in paragraph (g)(2)(iii)(A), (g)(3)(ii)(A), or (g)(5)(i)(B) of this section, whichever applies.

(iv) Contribution for plan amendments increasing liability for benefits. In the case of a contribution to avoid or terminate the application of the limitation on benefits attributable to a plan amendment under section 436(c)—

(A) In the event that the adjusted funding target attainment percentage for the plan year determined without taking into account the liability attributable to the plan amendment is less than 80 percent, the amount of the contribution under section 436(c)(2) is equal to the amount of the increase in the funding target of the plan for the plan year if the liabilities attributable to the amendment were included in the determination of the funding target.

(B) In the event that the adjusted funding target attainment percentage for the plan year determined without taking into account the liability attributable to the plan amendment is 80 percent or more, the amount of the contribution under section 436(c)(2) is the amount that would be sufficient to result in an adjusted funding target attainment percentage for the plan year of 80 percent if the contribution (and any prior section 436 contributions made for the plan year) were included as part of the plan assets and the funding target were to take into account the adjustments described in paragraph (g)(2)(iii)(A), (g)(3)(ii)(A), or (g)(5)(i)(B) of this section, whichever applies.

(v) Contribution required for continued benefit accruals. In the case of a contribution to avoid or terminate the application of the limitation on accruals under section 436(e), the amount of the contribution under section 436(e)(2) is equal to the amount sufficient to result in an adjusted funding target attainment percentage for the plan year of 60 percent if the contribution (and any prior section 436 contributions made for the plan year) were included as part of the plan assets and the funding target were to take into account the adjustments described in paragraph (g)(2)(iii)(A) or (g)(5)(i)(B) of this section, whichever applies.

*(3) Security to increase adjusted funding target attainment percentage.* (i) In general. For purposes of avoiding benefit limitations under section 436, a plan sponsor may provide security in the form described in paragraph (f)(3)(ii) of this section. In such a case, the adjusted funding target attainment percentage for the plan year is determined by treating as an asset of the plan any security provided by a plan sponsor by the valuation date for the plan year in a form meeting the requirements of paragraph (f)(3)(ii) of this section. However, this security is not taken into account as a plan asset for any other purpose, including section 430.

(ii) Form of security. The forms of security permitted under paragraph (f)(3)(i) of this section are limited to—

(A) A bond issued by a corporate surety company that is an acceptable surety for purposes of section 412 of ERISA; or

(B) Cash, or United States obligations which mature in 3 years or less, held in escrow by a bank or an insurance company.

(iii) Enforcement. Any form of security provided under paragraph (f)(3)(i) of this section must provide—

(A) That it will be paid to the plan upon the earliest of—

(1) The plan termination date as defined in section 4048 of ERISA;

(2) If there is a failure to make a payment of the minimum required contribution for any plan year beginning after the security is provided, the due date for the payment under section 430(j)(1) or 430(j)(3); or

(3) If the plan's adjusted funding target attainment percentage is less than 60 percent (without regard to any security provided under this paragraph (f)(3)) for a consecutive period of 7 plan years, the valuation date for the last plan year in the 7-year period; and

(B) That the plan administrator must notify the surety, bank, or insurance company that issued or holds the security of any event described in paragraph (f)(3)(iii)(A) of this section within 10 days of its occurrence.

(iv) Release of security. The form of security is permitted to provide that it will be released (and any amounts thereunder will be refunded to the plan sponsor together with any interest accrued thereon) as provided in the agreement governing the security, but such release is not permitted until the plan's enrolled actuary has certified that the plan's adjusted funding target attainment percentage for a plan year is at least 90 percent (without regard to any security provided under this paragraph (f)(3)) or until replacement security has been provided in accordance with paragraph (f)(3)(vi) of this section.

(v) Contribution of security to plan. Any security provided under this paragraph (f)(3) that is subsequently turned over to the plan (whether pursuant to the enforcement mechanism of paragraph (f)(3)(iii) of this section or after its release under paragraph (f)(3)(iv) of this section) is treated as a contribution by the plan sponsor taken into account under section 430 when contributed and, if turned over pursuant to paragraph (f)(3)(iii) of this section, is not a contribution under paragraph (f)(2) of this section.

(vi) Replacement security. If security has been provided to a plan pursuant to this paragraph (f)(3), the plan sponsor may provide new security to the plan and subsequently or simultaneously have the original security released, but only if—

(A) The new security is in a form that satisfies the requirements of paragraph (f)(3)(ii) of this section;

(B) The amount of the new security is no less than the amount of the original security, determined at the time the original security is released; and

(C) The period described in paragraph (f)(3)(iii)(A)(3) of this section with respect to the new security is the same as the period that applied under that paragraph to the original security.

*(4) Examples.* The following examples illustrate the rules of this paragraph (f):

*Example (1).* (i) Plan Z is a non-collectively bargained defined benefit plan with a plan year that is the calendar year and a valuation date of January 1. Plan Z's sponsor is not in bankruptcy, and Plan Z did not purchase any annuities in 2009 or 2010. As of January 1, 2011, Plan Z does not have a funding standard carryover balance or a prefunding balance, and is not in at-risk status. As of that date, Plan Z has plan assets (and adjusted plan assets) of $2,000,000 and a funding target (and an adjusted funding target) of $2,550,000. On March 1, 2011, the enrolled actuary for the plan certifies that the AFTAP as of January 1, 2011, is 78.43%. The effective interest rate for Plan Z for the 2011 plan year is 5.5%.

(ii) On May 1, 2011, the plan sponsor amends Plan Z to increase benefits. The enrolled actuary for the plan determines that the present value, as of January 1, 2011, of the increase in the funding target due to the amendment is $400,000. Because the AFTAP prior to the plan amendment is less than 80%, Plan Z is subject to the restriction on plan amendments in paragraph (c) of this section, and the amendment cannot take effect unless the employer utilizes one of the methods described in paragraph (f) of this section to avoid benefit limitations.

(iii) In order for the amendment to be permitted to take effect, the plan sponsor makes a contribution described in paragraph (f)(2) of this section. Because the AFTAP prior to the amendment was less than 80%, the provisions of paragraph (f)(2)(iv)(A) of this section apply. The amount of the contribution as of January 1, 2011, needed to avoid the restriction on plan amendments under paragraph (c) of this section is equal to the amount of the increase in funding target attributable to the amendment, or $400,000. Under the provisions of paragraph (f)(2)(iv)(A) of this section, this contribution is required even though, if the contribution were included as part of the plan assets and the liabilities attributable to the plan amendment were included in the funding target, the AFTAP would be 81.36% (that is, adjusted plan assets of $2,000,000 plus the contribution of $400,000 as of January 1, 2011; divided by the adjusted funding target of

$2,550,000 increased to reflect the additional $400,000 in the funding target attributable to the plan amendment).

(iv) However, because the contribution is not paid until May 1, 2011, the necessary contribution amount must be adjusted to reflect interest from the valuation date to the date of the contribution, at Plan Z's effective interest rate for the 2011 plan year. The amount of the required contribution after adjustment is $407,203, determined as $400,000 increased for 4 months of compound interest at an effective annual interest rate of 5.5%.

(v) A contribution of $407,203 is made on May 1, 2011, and is designated as a contribution under paragraph (f)(2) of this section with respect to the May 1, 2011, plan amendment. Accordingly, the contribution is not applied toward minimum funding requirements under section 430, and is not eligible for inclusion in the prefunding balance under § 1.430(f)-1(b)(1). Since this contribution meets the requirements of paragraph (f)(2) of this section, the plan amendment takes effect in accordance with its terms.

*Example (2).* (i) The facts are the same as in Example 1, except that the plan is in at-risk status under section 430(i). The funding target determined under section 430(i) is $2,600,000, and the funding target determined without regard to section 430(i) is $2,550,000.

(ii) On May 1, 2011, the plan sponsor amends Plan Z to increase benefits. The plan's enrolled actuary determines that the present value as of January 1, 2011 of the increase in the funding target due to the amendment (taking into account the at-risk status of the plan) is $440,000. Because the AFTAP prior to the plan amendment is 78.43% (determined taking into account the at-risk status of Plan Z), Plan Z is subject to the restriction on plan amendments in paragraph (c) of this section, and the amendment cannot take effect unless the employer utilizes one of the methods described in this paragraph (f) to avoid benefit limitations.

(iii) In order for this amendment to be permitted to take effect, the plan sponsor makes a contribution described in paragraph (f)(2) of this section. Because the AFTAP prior to the amendment was less than 80%, the provisions of paragraph (f)(2)(iv)(A) of this section apply. The amount of the contribution as of January 1, 2011, needed to avoid the restriction on plan amendments under paragraph (c) of this section is equal to the amount of the increase in funding target attributable to the amendment, or $440,000. Under the provisions of paragraph (f)(2)(iv)(A) of this section, this contribution is required even though, if the contribution were included as part of the plan assets and the liability attributable to the plan amendment were included in the funding target, the AFTAP would exceed 80%.

(iv) However, because the contribution is not paid until May 1, 2011, the necessary contribution amount must be adjusted to reflect interest from the valuation date to the date of the contribution, at Plan Z's effective interest rate for the 2011 plan year. The amount of the required contribution after adjustment is $447,923, determined as $440,000 increased for 4 months of compound interest at an effective annual interest rate of 5.5%.

(v) A contribution of $447,923 is made on May 1, 2011, and is designated as a contribution under paragraph (f)(2) of this section with respect to the May 1, 2011, plan amendment. Accordingly, the contribution is not applied toward minimum funding requirements under section 430, and is not eligible for inclusion in the prefunding balance under § 1.430(f)-1(b)(1). Since this contribution meets the requirements of paragraph (f)(2) of this section, the plan amendment takes effect in accordance with its terms.

*Example (3).* (i) The facts are the same as in Example 1, except that the enrolled actuary for the plan does not issue the certification of the 2011 AFTAP until September 1, 2011. Prior to October 1, 2010, the enrolled actuary had certified the 2010 AFTAP to be 82%. Other than this amendment, no other amendment or unpredictable contingent event has occurred that requires a recertification. As of May 1, 2011, the plan's effective interest rate for the 2011 plan year has not yet been determined. The highest of the three segment rates applicable to the 2011 plan year under section 430(h)(2)(C) is 6%.

(ii) Because the enrolled actuary has not certified the actual AFTAP as of January 1, 2011, and the amendment is scheduled to take effect after April 1, 2011, the rules of paragraph (h)(2)(iii) of this section apply. Accordingly, the AFTAP for 2011 (prior to reflecting the effect of the amendment) is presumed to be 10 percentage points lower than the 2010 AFTAP, or 72%. Because this presumed AFTAP is less than 80%, the restriction on plan amendments in paragraph (c) of this section applies, and the plan amendment cannot take effect.

(iii) In order to allow the plan amendment to take effect, the plan sponsor decides to make a contribution under paragraph (f)(2) of this section on May 1, 2011. Because the presumed AFTAP was less than 80% prior to reflecting the plan amendment, the rules of paragraph (f)(2)(iv)(A) of this section apply, and the amount of the contribution under section 436(c)(2) is the amount of the increase in the funding target for the year if the plan amendment were included in the determination of the funding target. Accordingly, an additional contribution of $400,000 is required as of January 1, 2011, to avoid the restriction on plan amendments under paragraph (c) of this section.

(iv) However, since the contribution is not made until May 1, 2011, the amount of the required contribution must be adjusted to reflect interest from the valuation date to the date of the contribution. Since the effective interest rate has not yet been determined, the interest adjustment is based on the highest of the three segment rates applicable for the 2011 plan year under section 430(h)(2)(C), or 6%. The amount of the required contribution after adjustment is $407,845, determined as $400,000 increased for 4 months of compound interest at the highest segment interest rate for 2011, or 6%.

(v) A contribution of $407,845 is made on May 1, 2011, and is designated as a contribution under paragraph (f)(2) of this section with respect to the May 1, 2011, plan amendment. Accordingly, the contribution is not applied toward minimum funding requirements under section 430, and is not eligible for inclusion in the prefunding balance under § 1.430(f)-1(b)(1). Since this contribution meets the requirements of paragraph (f)(2) of this section, the plan amendment takes effect in accordance with its terms.

(vi) After the plan's effective interest rate for 2011 has been determined to be 5.5%, the amount of excess interest previously contributed is recharacterized as an employer contribution taken into account under section 430 for 2011 (because that rate for the year is less than 6%).

**(g) Rules of operation for periods prior to and after certification.** *(1) In general.* Section 436(h) and paragraph (h) of this section set forth a series of presumptions that apply before the enrolled actuary for a plan issues a certification of the plan's adjusted funding target attainment percentage for the plan year. This paragraph (g) sets forth rules for the application of limitations under sections 436(b), 436(c), 436(d), and 436(e) prior to and during the period those presumptions apply to the plan, and describes the interaction of those presumptions with plan operations after the plan's enrolled actuary has issued a certification of the plan's adjusted funding target attainment percentage for the plan year. Paragraph (g)(2) of this section sets forth rules that apply to periods during which a presumption under section 436(h) and paragraph (h) of this section applies. Paragraph (g)(3) of this section sets forth rules that apply to periods during which no presumptions under section 436(h) and paragraph (h) of this section apply but which are prior to the enrolled actuary's certification of the plan's adjusted funding target attainment percentage for the plan year. Paragraph (g)(4) of this section sets forth rules for modifying the plan's presumed adjusted funding target attainment percentage in certain situations. Paragraph (g)(5) of this section sets forth rules that apply after the enrolled actuary's certification of the plan's adjusted funding target attainment percentage for a plan year. Paragraph (g)(6) of this section sets forth examples illustrating the rules in this paragraph (g).

*(2) Periods prior to certification during which a presumption applies.* (i) Plan must follow presumptions. A plan must provide that, for any period during which a presumption under section 436(h) and paragraph (h)(1), (2), or (3) of this section applies to the plan, the limitations applicable under section 436 and paragraphs (b), (c), (d), and (e) of this section are applied to the plan as if the adjusted funding target attainment percentage for the year were the presumed adjusted funding target attainment percentage determined under the rules of section 436(h) and paragraph (h)(1), (2), or (3) of this section, as applicable, updated to take into account certain unpredictable contingent event benefits and plan amendments in accordance with section 436 and the rules of this paragraph (g).

(ii) Determination of amount of reduction in balances—(A) In general. During the period described in this paragraph (g)(2), the rules of paragraph (a)(5) of this section (relating to the deemed election to reduce the funding standard carryover balance and the prefunding balance) must be applied based on the presumed adjusted funding target attainment percentage. This paragraph (g)(2)(ii) provides rules for the determination of the reduction that applies as of the first day of the plan year, and, in certain circumstances, that applies later in the plan year. Paragraph (g)(2)(iii) of this section provides additional rules that apply with respect to unpredictable contingent event benefits or plan amendments, which rules must be applied prior to the application of paragraph (g)(2)(iv) of this section relating to section 436 contributions. The reapplication of the rules under this paragraph (g)(2) regarding the deemed election in paragraph (a)(5) of this section may require an additional reduction in the prefunding and funding standard carryover balances if the amount of the reduction in those balances that is necessary to reach the applicable threshold to avoid the application of a section 436 limitation exceeds the amount that was initially reduced. Prior reductions of the prefunding and funding standard carryover balances continue to apply.

(B) Reduction in balances at the first day of plan year—(1) Plans with a certified AFTAP for the prior plan year. If section 436(h)(1) and paragraph (h)(1) of this section apply to determine the presumed adjusted funding target attainment percentage as of the first day of the current plan year based on the plan's enrolled actuary certification of the adjusted funding target attainment percentage for the prior plan year made during that prior plan year, then, in order to determine the amount of the reduction (if any) in the funding standard carryover balance and prefunding balance under this paragraph (g)(2)(ii), a presumed adjusted funding target must be established as of the first day of the plan year, and that amount is then compared to the interim value of adjusted plan assets as of that date. For this purpose, the interim value of adjusted plan assets is equal to the value of adjusted plan assets (within the meaning of paragraph (j)(1)(ii) of this section) as of the first day of the plan year, determined without regard to future contributions and future elections with respect to the plan's prefunding and funding standard carryover balances under section 430(f) (for example, elections to add to the prefunding balance for the prior plan year, elections to use the prefunding and funding standard carryover balances to offset the minimum required contribution for a year, and elections (including deemed elections under paragraph (a)(5) of this section) to reduce the prefunding and funding standard carryover balances for the current plan year), and the presumed adjusted funding target is equal to the interim value of adjusted plan assets for the plan year divided by the presumed adjusted funding target attainment percentage. As provided in § 1.430(f)-1(e)(1), the rules of § 1.430(f)-1(d)(1)(ii) apply for purposes of determining the amount of the prefunding balance or the funding standard carryover balance that is available for reduction.

(2) Plans with presumed AFTAP deemed under 60 percent. If paragraph (g)(2)(ii)(B)(1) of this section does not apply to the plan for a plan year and the last day of the plan year is on or after the first day of the 10th month of the plan year, such that the presumed adjusted funding target attainment percentage for the prior plan year is conclusively presumed to be less than 60 percent under section 436(h)(2) and paragraph (h)(3) of this section, then no reduction in the funding standard carryover balance and prefunding balance is required under this paragraph (g)(2)(ii)(B). However, see paragraph (g)(2)(iv)(A) of this section for rules for determining the amount of a section 436 contribution that would permit unpredictable contingent event benefits to be paid in such a case.

(3) Treatment of short plan years. If paragraph (g)(2)(ii)(B)(1) of this section does not apply to the plan for a plan year but the last day of the plan year is before the first day of the 10th month of the plan year, such that section 436(h)(2) and paragraph (h)(3) of this section did not apply for that plan year, then paragraph (g)(2)(ii)(B)(1) of this section must be applied as of the first day of the next plan year based on the presumed adjusted funding target attainment percentage as of that last day of the prior short plan year.

(C) Change in presumed AFTAP later in the plan year. If the presumed adjusted funding target attainment percentage for the plan year changes during the year, the rules regarding the deemed election to reduce the prefunding and funding standard carryover balances described in paragraph (a)(5) of this section must be reapplied based on the new presumed adjusted funding target attainment percentage. This will typically occur on the first day of the 4th month of a plan year, but could happen at a different date if the enrolled actuary certifies the adjusted funding target attainment percentage for the prior plan year during the current plan year. In order to determine the amount of any reduction in the prefunding and funding standard carryover balances that would apply in such a situation, a new presumed adjusted funding target must be established, which is then compared to the updated interim value of adjusted plan assets. For this purpose, the updated interim value of adjusted plan assets for the plan year is determined as the interim value of adjusted plan assets as of the first day of the plan year updated to take into account contributions for the prior plan year and section 430(f) elections with respect to the plan's prefunding and funding standard carryover balances made before the date of the change in the presumed adjusted funding target attainment percentage, and the new presumed adjusted funding target is equal to the updated interim value of adjusted plan assets divided by the new presumed adjusted funding target attainment percentage.

(D) Plans funded below the threshold. If, after application of paragraph (g)(2)(ii)(B) and (C) of this section, the presumed adjusted funding target attainment percentage under this paragraph (g)(2)(ii) is less than the 60 percent threshold under section 436(e), then no benefit accruals are permitted under the plan unless the plan sponsor makes a section 436 contribution as provided in paragraph (g)(2)(iv)(A) of this section. See paragraph (g)(5)(ii) of this section for rules that apply on and after the date the enrolled actuary for the plan issues a certification of the adjusted funding target attainment percentage of the plan for the current plan year.

(iii) Calculation of inclusive presumed AFTAP for application to unpredictable contingent event benefits and plan amendments— (A) Requirement to calculate inclusive presumed AFTAP. For purposes of applying the limitations under paragraphs (b) and (c) of this section during the period described in this paragraph (g)(2), an inclusive presumed adjusted funding target attainment percentage must be calculated. The inclusive presumed adjusted funding target attainment percentage is the ratio (expressed as a percentage) of the interim value of adjusted plan assets (updated to take into account contributions for the prior plan year, any prior section 436 contributions made for the plan year to the extent not previously taken into account in the interim value of adjusted plan assets for the plan year, and section 430(f) elections with respect to the plan's prefunding and funding standard carryover balances made before the date of the unpredictable contingent event or the date the plan amendment would take effect) to the inclusive presumed adjusted funding target. The inclusive presumed adjusted funding target is calculated as the presumed adjusted funding target determined under paragraph (g)(2)(ii)(B) or (C) of this section, increased to take into account—

(1) The unpredictable contingent event benefits or plan amendment;

(2) Any unpredictable contingent event benefits that are permitted to be paid as a result of any unpredictable contingent event that occurred, or plan amendment that has taken effect, in the prior plan year to the extent not taken into account in the prior plan year adjusted funding target attainment percentage; and

(3) Any other unpredictable contingent event benefits that are permitted to be paid as a result of any unpredictable contingent event that occurred, or plan amendment that has taken effect, in the current plan year to the extent not previously taken into account in the presumed adjusted funding target for the plan year.

(B) Mandatory reduction for collectively bargained plans. During the period described in this paragraph (g)(2), the rules of paragraph (a)(5)(ii) of this section (relating to the deemed election to reduce the funding standard carryover balance and the prefunding balance) must be applied by treating the inclusive presumed adjusted funding target attainment percentage determined under this paragraph (g)(2)(iii) as if it were the adjusted funding target attainment percentage.

(C) Optional reduction for plans that are not collectively bargained plans. A plan sponsor of a plan that is not a collectively bargained plan (and, thus, is not required to reduce the funding standard carryover balance and the prefunding balance under the rules of paragraph (a)(5)(ii) of this section) is permitted to elect to reduce those balances in order to increase the updated interim value of adjusted plan assets that is used to determine the inclusive presumed adjusted funding target attainment percentage under this paragraph (g)(2)(iii).

(D) Plans funded below the threshold. If, after application of paragraph (g)(2)(iii)(B) and (C) of this section, the inclusive presumed adjusted funding target attainment percentage determined under this paragraph (g)(2)(iii) is less than the applicable threshold under section 436(b) or 436(c), then the plan is not permitted to provide any benefits attributable to the unpredictable contingent event, nor is the plan amendment permitted to take effect, unless the plan sponsor makes a section 436 contribution as provided in paragraph (g)(2)(iv) of this section. See paragraph (g)(5)(ii) of this section for rules that apply on and after the date the enrolled actuary for the plan issues a certification of the adjusted funding target attainment percentage of the plan for the current plan year.

(E) Plans funded at or above the threshold. If, after application of paragraph (g)(2)(iii)(B) or (C) of this section, the inclusive presumed adjusted funding target attainment percentage is greater than or equal to the applicable threshold under section 436(b) or 436(c), then the plan is not permitted to limit the payment of unpredictable contingent event benefits described in paragraph (b) of this section, nor is the plan permitted to restrict a plan amendment increasing benefit liabilities described in paragraph (c) of this section from taking effect, based on an expectation that the limitations under paragraph (b) or (c) of this section will apply following the enrolled actuary's certification of the adjusted funding target attainment percentage for the plan year.

(iv) Section 436 contributions (A) Plans with presumed AFTAP below 60 percent— (1) Unpredictable contingent event benefits. If the presumed adjusted funding target attainment percentage for a plan is less than 60 percent, then unpredictable contingent event benefits are permitted to be paid as a result of an unpredictable contingent event occurring during the period described in this paragraph (g)(2) if the plan sponsor makes the section 436 contribution described in paragraph (f)(2)(iii)(A) of this section.

(2) Plan amendments. If the presumed adjusted funding target attainment percentage for a plan is less than 60 percent, then no plan amendment increasing plan liabilities is permitted to take effect during the period described in this paragraph (g)(2). See paragraph (e)(1) of this section.

(3) Benefit accruals. If the presumed adjusted funding target attainment percentage for a plan year of less than 60 percent is determined based on the plan's enrolled actuary certification of the adjusted funding target attainment percentage for the prior plan year made during that prior plan year (as opposed to being presumed to be less than 60 percent under the rules of section 436(h)(2) and paragraph (h)(3) of this section because the actuary has not certified the adjusted funding target attainment percentage for the prior plan year before the first day of the 10th month of the prior plan year), then benefits are permitted to accrue if the plan sponsor makes a section 436 contribution in the amount neces-

sary to bring the ratio of the updated interim value of adjusted plan assets to the presumed adjusted funding target up to 60 percent, as described in paragraph (f)(2)(v) of this section.

(B) Plan amendments for plans with presumed AFTAP below 80 percent. If the presumed adjusted funding target attainment percentage for a plan is less than 80 percent, but is not less than 60 percent, then a plan amendment increasing plan liabilities is permitted to take effect during the period described in this paragraph (g)(2) if the plan sponsor makes a section 436 contribution described in paragraph (f)(2)(iv)(A) of this section.

(C) Contributions required to reach threshold. If a plan is described in paragraph (g)(2)(iii)(D) of this section and neither paragraph (g)(2)(iv)(A) nor (B) of this section apply to the plan, then unpredictable contingent event benefits are permitted to be paid or the plan amendment is permitted to become effective during the period this paragraph (g)(2) applies to the plan only if the plan sponsor makes a section 436 contribution in the amount necessary to bring the ratio of the updated interim value of adjusted plan assets to the inclusive presumed adjusted funding target up to the applicable threshold under section 436(b) or (c), as described in paragraph (f)(2)(iii)(B) or (f)(2)(iv)(B) of this section. This paragraph (g)(2)(iv)(C) applies, for example, if an unpredictable contingent event occurs in the case of a plan with a presumed adjusted funding target attainment percentage of more than 60 percent where taking into account the unpredictable contingent event benefit in the inclusive presumed adjusted funding target would cause the ratio of the interim value of adjusted plan assets to the inclusive presumed adjusted funding target to be less than 60 percent.

(v) Bankruptcy of plan sponsor. Pursuant to section 436(d)(2), during any period in which the plan sponsor of a plan is a debtor in a case under title 11, United States Code, or any similar Federal or State law (as described in paragraph (d)(2) of this section), no prohibited payment within the meaning of paragraph (j)(6) of this section may be paid if the plan's enrolled actuary has not yet certified the plan's adjusted funding target attainment percentage for the plan year to be at least 100 percent. Thus, the presumption rules of paragraph (h) of this section do not apply for purposes of section 436(d)(2) and this paragraph (g)(2)(v).

*(3) Periods prior to certification during which no presumption applies.* (i) Prohibited payments and benefit accruals. If no presumptions under section 436(h) apply to a plan during a period and the plan's enrolled actuary has not yet issued the certification of the plan's actual adjusted funding target attainment percentage for the plan year, the plan is not permitted to limit prohibited payments under paragraph (d) of this section or the accrual of benefits under paragraph (e) of this section based on an expectation that those paragraphs will apply to the plan once an actuarial certification is issued. However, see paragraph (g)(2)(v) of this section for a restriction on prohibited payments during any period in which the plan sponsor of a plan is a debtor in a case under title 11, United States Code, or any similar Federal or State law.

(i) Unpredictable contingent event benefits and plan amendments increasing benefit liability— (A) In general. If no presumptions under section 436(h) apply to a plan during a period and the plan's enrolled actuary has not yet issued a certification of the plan's adjusted funding target attainment percentage for the plan year, the limitations on unpredictable contingent event benefits under paragraph (b) of this section and plan amendments increasing benefit liabilities under paragraph (c) of this section must be applied during that period by following the rules of paragraphs (g)(2)(iii) of this section, based on the inclusive presumed adjusted funding target determined using the prior plan year adjusted funding target attainment percentage. Thus, whether unpredictable contingent event benefits are permitted to be paid or a plan amendment is permitted to take effect during a plan year is determined by calculating the ratio of the interim value of adjusted plan assets to the inclusive presumed adjusted funding target, where the inclusive presumed adjusted funding target is determined by dividing the interim value of adjusted plan assets by the prior plan year adjusted funding target attainment percentage and then adding the adjustments described in paragraphs (g)(2)(iii)(A)(1), (2) and (3) of this section. If, after application of paragraphs (g)(2)(iii)(B) and (C) of this section, that ratio is less than the applicable threshold under section 436(b) or 436(c), then the plan is not permitted to provide any benefits attributable to the unpredictable contingent event, nor is the plan amendment permitted to take effect, unless the plan sponsor makes the contribution described in paragraph (g)(2)(iv)(C) of this section.

(B) Recharacterization of contributions made to avoid benefit limitations. In any case where, pursuant to paragraph (g)(3)(ii)(A) of this section, the plan sponsor makes section 436 contributions to avoid the application of the applicable benefit limitation, to the extent those contributions would not be needed to permit the payment of the unpredictable contingent event benefits or for the plan amendment to go into effect based on a subsequent certification of the adjusted funding target attainment percentage for the current plan year that takes into account the increase in the liability attributable to the unpredictable contingent event benefits or plan amendment, the excess section 436 contributions are recharacterized as employer contributions taken into account under section 430 for the current plan year.

*(4) Modification of the presumed AFTAP.* (i) Section 436 contributions. If, in accordance with the rules of paragraph (g)(2)(iv) of this section, unpredictable contingent event benefits are permitted to be paid, or a plan amendment takes effect, during the plan year because the plan sponsor makes a contribution described in paragraph (f)(2)(iii)(B) or (f)(2)(iv)(B) of this section, then the presumed adjusted funding target must be adjusted to reflect any increase in the funding target attributable to the unpredictable contingent event benefits or the plan amendment and the interim value of plan assets must be increased by the present value of the contribution. Similarly, if benefit accruals are permitted to resume in a plan year because the plan sponsor makes the contribution described in paragraph (f)(2)(v) of this section, then the presumed adjusted funding target must be adjusted to reflect any increase in the funding target attributable to the benefit accruals for the prior plan year and the interim value of adjusted plan assets must be increased by the present value of the contribution. The adjustment to the presumed adjusted funding target is made as of the date of the contribution, and that date is a section 436 measurement date.

(ii) Modification of the presumed AFTAP for reduction in balances. If a plan's funding standard carryover balance or prefunding balance is reduced under the rules of paragraph (g)(2) or (g)(3) of this section, then the presumed adjusted funding target attainment percentage for the plan year is increased to reflect the higher interim value of adjusted plan assets resulting from the reduction in the funding standard carryover balance or prefunding balance. The date of the event that causes the reduction is a section 436 measurement date.

*(5) Periods after certification of AFTAP.* (i) Plan must follow certified AFTAP— (A) In general. The rules of paragraphs (g)(2) and (g)(3) of this section no longer apply for a plan year on and after the date the enrolled actuary for the plan issues a certification of the adjusted funding target attainment percentage of the plan for the current plan year, provided that the certification is issued before the first day of the 10th month of the plan year. For example, the plan must provide that the limitations on prohibited payments apply for distributions with annuity starting dates on and after the date of that certification using the certified adjusted funding target attainment percentage of the plan for the plan year. Similarly, the plan must provide that any prohibition on accruals under paragraph (e) of this section as a result of the enrolled actuary's certification that the adjusted funding target attainment percentage of the plan for the plan year is less than 60 percent is effective as of the date of the certification and that any prohibition on accruals ceases to be effective on the date the enrolled actuary issues a certification that the adjusted funding target attainment percentage of the plan for the plan year is at least 60 percent.

(B) Unpredictable contingent events and plan amendments. In the case of a plan that has been issued a certification of the plan's adjusted funding target attainment percentage for a plan year by the plan's enrolled actuary, the plan sponsor must comply with the requirements of paragraphs (b) and (c) of this section for an unpredictable contingent event that occurs or a plan amendment that takes effect on or after the date of the enrolled actuary's certification. Thus, the plan administrator must determine if the adjusted funding target attainment percentage would be at or above the applicable threshold if it were modified to take into account—

(1) The unpredictable contingent event or plan amendment;

(2) Any other unpredictable contingent event benefits that were permitted to be paid as a result of any unpredictable contingent event that occurred, and any other plan amendment that took effect, earlier during the plan year to the extent not taken into account in the certified adjusted funding target attainment percentage for the plan year; and

(3) Any earlier section 436 contributions made for the plan year to the extent those contributions were not taken into account in the certified adjusted funding target attainment percentage.

(C) Application of rule for deemed election to reduce funding balances. After the adjusted funding target attainment percentage for a plan year is certified by the plan's enrolled actuary, the deemed election to reduce the prefunding and funding standard carryover balances under paragraph (a)(5) of this section must be reapplied based on the actual funding target for the year (provided the certification is issued before the first day of the 10th month of the plan year). The reapplication of the rules under this paragraph (g)(5) regarding the deemed election in paragraph (a)(5) of this section may require an additional reduction in the prefunding and funding standard carryover balances if the amount of the reduction in the prefunding and funding standard carryover balances that is necessary to reach the applicable threshold to avoid the application of a section 436 limitation exceeds the amount that was initially reduced. Prior reductions of the prefunding and funding standard carryover balances continue to apply.

(ii) Applicability to prior periods— (A) In general. Except as otherwise provided in this paragraph (g)(5)(ii), the enrolled actuary's certification of the adjusted funding target attainment percentage for the plan for the plan year does not affect prior periods. For example, the certification does not affect the application of the limitation under paragraph (d) of this section for distributions with annuity starting dates before the certification or the application of the limitation under paragraph (e) of this section prior to the date of that certification. See paragraph (a)(4) of this section for rules relating to the period of time after benefits cease to be limited. Except as otherwise provided in this paragraph (g)(5)(ii), the enrolled actuary's certification of the adjusted funding target attainment percentage for the plan for the plan year does not affect the application of the limitation under paragraph (b) or (c) of this section to unpredictable contingent event benefits, or a plan amendment that increases the liability for benefits, where the unpredictable contingent event occurs or the amendment takes effect during the periods to which paragraphs (g)(2) and (g)(3) of this section apply.

(B) Special rule for unpredictable contingent event benefits. If a plan does not pay benefits attributable to an unpredictable contingent event because of the application of paragraph (g)(2)(iii)(D) or (g)(3)(ii)(A) of this section, then the plan must pay the benefits attributable to that event that were not previously paid if such benefits would be permitted under the rules of section 436 based on a certified adjusted funding target attainment percentage for the plan year that takes into account the increase in the funding target that would be attributable to those unpredictable contingent event benefits.

(C) Special rule for plan amendments that increase liability. If a plan amendment does not take effect because of the application of paragraph (g)(2)(iii)(D) or (g)(3)(ii)(A) of this section, the plan amendment must go into effect if it would be permitted under the rules of section 436 based on a certified actual adjusted funding target attainment percentage for the plan year that takes into account the increase in the funding target attributable to the plan amendment, unless the plan amendment provides otherwise.

(D) Ordering rule for multiple unpredictable contingent events or plan amendments. [Reserved]

*(6) Examples.* The following examples illustrate the rules of this paragraph (g). Unless otherwise indicated, these examples are based on the following facts: each plan has a plan year that is the calendar year and a valuation date of January 1; section 436 applies to the plan beginning in 2008; the plan has no funding standard carryover balance; the plan sponsor is not in bankruptcy; no annuity purchases have been made from the plan; and the plan offers a lump sum form of payment. No plan is in at-risk status for the years discussed in the examples. The examples read as follows:

*Example (1).* (i) The plan's certified AFTAP as of January 1, 2010, is 75%. As of January 1, 2011, Plan A has assets of $3,300,000 and a prefunding balance of $300,000. Beginning on January 1, 2011, Plan A's AFTAP for 2011 is presumed to be 75%, under the rules of paragraph (h) of this section and based on the certified AFTAP for 2010.

(ii) Based on Plan A's presumed AFTAP of 75%, Plan A would continue to be subject to the restriction on prohibited payments in paragraph (d)(3) of this section as of January 1, 2011. However, under the provisions of paragraph (a)(5) of this section, if the prefunding balance is large enough, Plan A's sponsor is deemed to elect to reduce the prefunding balance to the extent needed to avoid this restriction.

(iii) The amount needed to avoid the restriction in paragraph (d)(3) of this section is determined by comparing the presumed adjusted funding target for Plan A with the interim value of adjusted plan assets as of the valuation date. The interim value of adjusted plan assets for Plan A is $3,000,000 (that is, the asset value of $3,300,000 reduced by the prefunding balance of $300,000). The presumed adjusted funding target for Plan A is the interim value of the adjusted plan assets divided by the presumed AFTAP, or $4,000,000 (that is, $3,000,000 divided by 75%).

(iv) In order to avoid the restriction on prohibited payments in paragraph (d)(3) of this section, Plan A's presumed AFTAP must be increased to 80%. This requires an increase in Plan A's adjusted plan assets of $200,000 (that is, 80% of the presumed adjusted funding target of $4,000,000, minus the interim value of the adjusted plan assets of $3,000,000). Plan A's prefunding balance as of January 1, 2011, is reduced by $200,000 under the deemed election provisions of paragraph (a)(5) of this section. Accordingly, Plan A's prefunding balance is $100,000 (that is, $300,000 minus $200,000) and the interim value of adjusted plan assets is increased to $3,200,000 (that is, $3,300,000 minus the reduced prefunding balance of $100,000). Pursuant to paragraph (g)(4)(ii) of this section, the presumed adjusted funding target attainment percentage for Plan A is redetermined as 80% and Plan A must pay the full amount of the accelerated benefit distributions elected by participants with an annuity starting date of January 1, 2011, or later.

*Example (2).* (i) The facts are the same as in Example 1. As of April 1, 2011, the enrolled actuary for Plan A has not certified the 2011 AFTAP. Therefore, beginning April 1, 2011, Plan A's AFTAP is presumed to be reduced by 10 percentage points to 70%, in accordance with paragraph (h)(2) of this section. Under the provisions of paragraph (g)(2)(ii)(B) of this section, the deemed election to reduce the prefunding and funding standard carryover balances described in paragraph (a)(5) of this section must be reapplied based on the new presumed AFTAP.

(ii) In accordance with paragraph (g)(2)(ii)(C) of this section, a new presumed adjusted funding target must be determined based on the new presumed AFTAP and must be compared to an updated interim value of adjusted plan assets. The new presumed adjusted funding target is $3,200,000 divided by the new presumed AFTAP of 70%, or $4,571,429.

(iii) In order to avoid the restriction on prohibited payments in paragraph (d)(3) of this section, Plan A's presumed AFTAP must be increased to 80%. This requires an additional increase in Plan A's adjusted plan assets of $457,143 (that is, 80% of the new presumed adjusted funding target of $4,571,429, minus the updated interim value of the adjusted plan assets of $3,200,000 reflecting the deemed reduction in Plan A's prefunding balance).

(iv) Plan A's remaining prefunding balance as of January 1, 2011, is only $100,000, which is not enough to avoid the restriction on prohibited payments under paragraph (d)(3) of this section. Accordingly, unless Plan A's sponsor utilizes one of the methods described in paragraph (f) of this section to avoid the restriction, Plan A is subject to the restriction on prohibited payments in paragraph (d)(3) of this section and cannot pay accelerated benefit distributions elected by participants with an annuity starting date of April 1, 2011, or later.

(v) Plan A's prefunding balance remains at $100,000 because, under paragraph (a)(5)(iii) of this section, the deemed reduction rules do not apply if the prefunding balance is not large enough to increase the adjusted value of plan assets enough to avoid the restriction. However, the earlier deemed reduction of $200,000 continues to apply because all elections (including deemed elections) to reduce a plan's funding standard carryover balance or prefunding balance are irrevocable and must be unconditional in accordance with paragraph (g)(2)(ii)(A) of this section.

*Example (3).* (i) The facts are the same as in Example 1. On July 1, 2011, the enrolled actuary for Plan A calculates the actual adjusted funding target as $3,700,000 as of January 1, 2011. Therefore, the 2011 AFTAP would have been 81.08% without reducing the prefunding balance (that is, plan assets of $3,300,000 minus the prefunding balance of $300,000, divided by the adjusted funding target of $3,700,000), and Plan A would not have been subject to the restrictions under paragraph (d)(3) of this section.

(ii) However, paragraph (g)(5)(i)(C) of this section requires that any prior reductions in the prefunding or funding standard carryover balances continue to apply, and so Plan A's prefunding balance remains at the reduced amount of $100,000 as of January 1, 2011. The enrolled actuary certifies that the 2011 AFTAP is 86.49% (that is, plan assets of $3,300,000 reduced by the prefunding balance of $100,000, divided by the adjusted funding target of $3,700,000).

*Example (4).* (i) Plan B is a collectively bargained plan with assets of $2,500,000 and a prefunding balance of $150,000 as of January 1, 2011. On August 14, 2010, the enrolled actuary for Plan B certified the AFTAP for 2010 to be 83%. No unpredictable contingent events giving rise to unpredictable contingent event benefits occurred during 2010 and no plan amendments took effect in 2010 that were not taken into account in the certified AFTAP.

(ii) On January 10, 2011, Plan B's sponsor amends the plan to increase benefits effective on February 1, 2011. The amendment would increase Plan B's funding target by $350,000. Under the rules of paragraph (g)(3) of this section, the determination of whether the amendment is permitted to take effect is based on a comparison of the inclusive presumed adjusted funding target with the updated interim value of adjusted plan assets.

(iii) Plan B's interim value of adjusted plan assets as of the valuation date is $2,350,000 (that is, $2,500,000 minus the prefunding balance of $150,000). Prior to reflecting the amendment, Plan B's presumed adjusted funding target as of January 1, 2011, is $2,831,325, which is equal to the interim value of adjusted plan assets as of the valuation date of $2,350,000, divided by the presumed AFTAP of 83%. Increasing Plan B's presumed adjusted funding target by $350,000 to reflect the amendment results in an inclusive presumed adjusted funding target of $3,181,325 and would result in a presumed AFTAP of 73.87% (that is, the interim value of adjusted plan assets as of the valuation date of $2,350,000 divided by the inclusive presumed adjusted funding target of $3,181,325).

(iv) Because Plan B's presumed AFTAP was over 80% prior to taking the amendment into account but would be less than 80% if the amendment were taken into account, section 436(c) and paragraph (c) of this section prohibit the plan amendment from taking effect unless the adjusted plan assets are increased so that the inclusive presumed AFTAP would be increased to 80%. This would require an additional amount of $195,060 (that is, 80% of the inclusive presumed adjusted funding target of $3,181,325 less the interim value of adjusted plan assets of $2,350,000).

(v) Plan B's prefunding balance of $150,000 is not large enough for Plan B to avoid the restriction on plan amendments, and therefore the deemed election to reduce the prefunding balance under paragraph (a)(5) of this section does not apply, and the amendment cannot take effect unless the plan sponsor makes a contribution described in paragraph (f)(2) of this section.

*Example (5).* (i) The facts are the same as in Example 4, except that Plan B's sponsor decides to make a contribution on February 1, 2011, to avoid the benefit limitation as provided in paragraph (f)(2) of this section. As of February 1, 2011, Plan B's effective interest rate for the 2011 plan year has not yet been determined. Pursuant to paragraph (f)(2)(i)(A)(2) of this section, Plan B's effective interest rate for 2011 is treated as 6.25%, which is the largest of the three segment interest rates applicable to the 2011 plan year, as provided in paragraph (f)(2)(i)(A)(2) of this section.

(ii) The amount of the contribution as of January 1, 2011, needed to avoid the restriction on plan amendments under paragraph (c) of this section is $195,060. However, because the contribution is not paid until February 1, 2011, the necessary contribution amount must be adjusted to reflect interest that would otherwise have accrued between the valuation date and the date of the contribution, at Plan B's effective interest rate for the 2011 plan year. The amount of the required contribution after adjustment is $196,048, determined as $195,060 increased for one month of compound interest at an effective annual interest rate of 6.25%.

(iii) In accordance with paragraph (g)(4)(i) of this section, the inclusive presumed AFTAP as of February 1, 2011, is 80 percent.

*Example (6).* (i) The facts are the same as in Example 5. As of April 1, 2011, the enrolled actuary for the plan has not certified the 2011 AFTAP. Beginning April 1, 2011, Plan A's presumed AFTAP is equal to be 70%, 10 percentage points lower than the inclusive presumed AFTAP as of February 1, 2011, in accordance with paragraphs (g)(2)(iii)(A) and (h)(2) of this section. On July 1, 2011, the enrolled actuary for the plan calculates the actual adjusted funding target, prior to taking the plan amendment into account, as $2,700,000, and determines the actual effective interest rate for 2011 to be 5.25%. On this basis, the actual AFTAP for 2011 (prior to taking the amendment into account) as 87.04% (that is, adjusted assets of $2,350,000 divided by the adjusted funding target of $2,700,000). Reflecting the $350,000 increase in funding target due to the plan amendment would increase the adjusted funding target to $3,050,000 and would decrease Plan B's AFTAP to 77.05%.

(ii) Based on the calculated adjusted funding target, the amount that was necessary to avoid the benefit restriction under paragraph (c) of this section was $90,000 (that is, 80% of the adjusted funding target reflecting the plan amendment (or $3,050,000), minus the adjusted value of plan assets of $2,350,000). This amount must be adjusted for interest between the valuation date and the date the contribution was made using the effective interest rate for Plan B. Therefore, the amount required on the payment date of February 1, 2011, was $90,385 (that is, $90,000 adjusted for compound interest for one month at Plan B's effective interest rate of 5.25% per year).

(iii) Under paragraph (g)(3)(ii)(B) of this section, the contribution made on February 1, 2011, is recharacterized as an employer contribution under section 430 to the extent that it exceeded the amount necessary to avoid application of the restriction on plan amendments under paragraph (c) of this section. Therefore, $105,663 (that is, the $196,048 actual contribution paid on February 1, 2011, minus the $90,385 required contribution based on the actual AFTAP) is recharacterized as an employer contribution under section 430 for the 2011 plan year. As such, it may be applied toward the minimum required contribution for 2011, or the plan sponsor can elect to credit the contribution to Plan B's prefunding balance to the extent that the contributions for the 2011 plan year exceed the minimum required contribution.

(iv) This recharacterization applied only because the 436 contribution was made during a period prior to the certification of Plan B's actual AFTAP for 2011 and during which no presumption applied (that is, when section 436 is applied based on the 2010 AFTAP, which was high enough that no restrictions applied for 2010). If the contribution had been made during a time when the presumptions applied (for instance, after April 1, 2011, when the presumed AFTAP was under 80%) then the only portion of the 436 contribution that would be recharacterized as an employer contribution under section 430 would be the portion of the interest adjustment attributable to the difference between the highest segment rate (6.25%) and the plan's actual effective interest rate (5.25%), in accordance with paragraph (f)(2)(i)(A)(2) of this section.

(v) After reflecting the plan amendment and the present value of the portion of the section 436 contribution that is not recharacterized as an employer contribution under section 430, the adjusted assets as of January 1, 2011, for purposes of section 436 are $2,440,000 ($2,350,000 plus $90,000) and the inclusive adjusted funding target is $3,050,000. Accordingly, the enrolled actuary certifies the inclusive AFTAP for 2011 as 80% ($2,440,00 / $3,050,000). Note that assets for section 430 purposes are not increased to reflect the section 436 contribution as of January 1, 2011.

*Example (7).* (i) The facts are the same as in Example 6, except that on July 1, 2011, the enrolled actuary for Plan B calculates the actual adjusted funding target (before reflecting the plan amendment) as $3,000,000 and certifies the actual AFTAP as 78.33% prior to reflecting the plan amendment (that is, adjusted plan assets of $2,350,000 divided by the actual adjusted funding target of $3,000,000). Based on the provisions of paragraph (c) of this section, because the AFTAP prior to reflecting the amendment is less than 80%, the contribution required to avoid the restriction on plan amendments would have been the amount equal to the increase in funding target due to the plan amendment, or $350,000.

(ii) However, according to paragraph (g)(5)(ii)(A) of this section, the enrolled actuary's certification of the 2011 AFTAP does not affect the application of the limitation under paragraph (c) of this section to the amendment, because the amendment to Plan B took effect prior to the date of the certification. Therefore, it is not necessary for Plan B's sponsor to contribute an additional amount in order for the plan amendment to remain in effect regardless of the extent to which the certified AFTAP for the plan year is less than the presumed inclusive AFTAP.

**(h) Presumed underfunding for purposes of benefit limitations.** *(1) Presumption of continued underfunding.* (i) In general. This paragraph (h)(1) applies to a plan for a plan year if a limitation under paragraph (b), (c), (d), or (e) of this section applied to the plan on the last day of the preceding plan year. If this paragraph (h)(1) applies to a plan, the first day of the plan year is a section 436 measurement date and the presumed adjusted funding target attainment percentage for the plan is the percentage under paragraph (h)(1)(ii) or (iii) of this section, whichever applies to the plan, beginning on that first day of the plan year and ending on the date specified in paragraph (h)(1)(iv) of this section.

(ii) Rule where preceding year certification issued during preceding year— (A) General rule. In any case in which the plan's enrolled actuary has issued a certification under paragraph (h)(4) of this section of the adjusted funding target attainment percentage for the plan year preceding the current plan year before the first day of the current plan year, the presumed adjusted funding target attainment percentage of the plan for the current plan year is equal to the prior plan year adjusted funding target attainment percentage until it is changed under paragraph (h)(1)(iv) of this section.

(B) Special rule for late certifications. If the certification of the adjusted funding target attainment percentage for the prior plan year occurred after the first day of the 10th month of that prior plan year, the plan is treated as if no such certification was made, unless the certification took into account the effect of any unpredictable contingent event benefits that are permitted to be paid based on unpredictable contingent events that occurred, and any plan amendments that became effective, during the prior plan year but before the certification (and any associated section 436 contributions).

(iii) No certification for preceding year issued during preceding year— (A) Deemed percentage continues. In any case in which the plan's enrolled actuary has not issued a certification under paragraph (h)(4) of this section of the adjusted funding target attainment percentage of the plan for the plan year preceding the current plan year during that prior plan year, the presumed adjusted funding target attainment percentage of the plan for the current plan year is equal to the presumed adjusted funding target attainment percentage that applied on the last day of the preceding plan year until the presumed adjusted funding target attainment percentage is changed under paragraph (h)(1)(iii)(B) or (h)(1)(iv) of this section. Thus, if the prior plan year was a 12-month plan year (so that the last day of the plan year was after the first day of the 10th month of the plan year and the rules of section 436(h)(2) and paragraph (h)(3) of this section applied to the plan for that plan year), then the presumed adjusted funding target attainment percentage for the current plan year is presumed to be less than 60 percent. By contrast, if the prior plan year was less than 9 months, the presumed adjusted funding target attainment percentage for the current plan year is the presumed adjusted funding target attainment percentage at the last day of the preceding plan year.

(B) Enrolled actuary's certification in following year. In any case in which the plan's enrolled actuary has issued the certification under paragraph (h)(4) of this section of the adjusted funding target attainment percentage of the plan for the plan year preceding the current plan year on or after the first day of the current plan year, the date of that prior plan year certification is a new section 436 measurement date for the current plan year. In such a case, the presumed adjusted funding target attainment percentage for the current plan year is equal to the prior plan year adjusted funding target attainment percentage (reduced by 10 percentage points if paragraph (h)(2)(iv) of this section applies to the plan) until it is changed under paragraph (h)(1)(iv) of this section. The rules of paragraph (h)(1)(ii)(B) of this section apply for purposes of determining whether the enrolled actuary has issued a certification of the adjusted funding target attainment percentage for the prior plan year during the current plan year.

(iv) Duration of use of presumed adjusted funding target attainment percentage. If this paragraph (h)(1) applies to a plan for a plan year, the presumed adjusted funding target attainment percentage determined under this paragraph (h)(1) applies until the earliest of—

(A) The first day of the 4th month of the plan year if paragraph (h)(2) of this section applies;

(B) The first day of the 10th month of the plan year if paragraph (h)(3) of this section applies;

(C) The date of a change in the presumed adjusted funding target attainment percentage under paragraph (g)(4) of this section; or

(D) The date the enrolled actuary issues a certification under paragraph (h)(4) of this section of the adjusted funding target attainment percentage for the plan year.

*(2) Presumption of underfunding beginning on first day of 4th month for certain underfunded plans.* (i) In general. This paragraph (h)(2) applies to a plan for a plan year if—

(A) The enrolled actuary for the plan has not issued a certification of the adjusted funding target attainment percentage for the plan year before the first day of the 4th month of the plan year; and

(B) The plan's adjusted funding target attainment percentage for the preceding plan year was either—

(1) At least 60 percent but less than 70 percent; or

(2) At least 80 percent but less than 90 percent.

(ii) Special rule for first plan year a plan is subject to section 436. This paragraph (h)(2) also applies to a plan for the first effective plan year if—

(A) The enrolled actuary for the plan has not issued a certification of the adjusted funding target attainment percentage for the plan year before the first day of the 4th month of the plan year; and

(B) The prior plan year adjusted funding target attainment percentage is at least 70 percent but less than 80 percent.

(iii) Presumed adjusted funding target attainment percentage. If this paragraph (h)(2) applies to a plan for a plan year and the date of the enrolled actuary's certification of the adjusted funding target attainment percentage under paragraph (h)(4) of this section for the prior plan year (taking into account the special rules for late certifications under paragraph (h)(1)(ii)(B) of this section) occurred before the first day of the 4th month of the current plan year, then, commencing on the first day of the 4th month of the current plan year—

(A) The presumed adjusted funding target attainment percentage of the plan for the plan year is reduced by 10 percentage points; and

(B) The first day of the 4th month of the plan year is a section 436 measurement date.

(iv) Certification for prior plan year. If this paragraph (h)(2) applies to a plan and the date of the enrolled actuary's certification of the adjusted funding target attainment percentage under paragraph (h)(4) of this section for the prior plan year (taking into account the rules for late certifications under paragraph (h)(1)(ii)(B) of this section) occurs on or after the first day of the 4th month of the current plan year, then, commencing on the date of that prior plan year certification—

(A) The presumed adjusted funding target attainment percentage of the plan for the current plan year is equal to 10 percentage points less than the prior plan year adjusted funding target attainment percentage; and

(B) The date of the prior plan year certification is a section 436 measurement date.

(v) Duration of use of presumed adjusted funding target attainment percentage. If this paragraph (h)(2) applies to a plan for a plan year, the presumed adjusted funding target attainment percentage determined under this paragraph (h)(2) applies until the earliest of—

(A) The first day of the 10th month of the plan year if paragraph (h)(3) of this section applies;

(B) The date of a change in the presumed adjusted funding target attainment percentage under paragraph (g)(4) of this section; or

(C) The date the enrolled actuary issues a certification under paragraph (h)(4) of this section of the adjusted funding target attainment percentage for the plan year.

*(3)* Presumption of underfunding beginning on first day of 10th month. In any case in which no certification of the specific adjusted funding target attainment percentage for the current plan year under paragraph (h)(4) of this section is made with respect to the plan before the first day of the 10th month of the plan year, then, commencing on the first day of the 10th month of the current plan year—

(i) The presumed adjusted funding target attainment percentage of the plan for the plan year is presumed to be less than 60 percent; and

(ii) The first day of the 10th month of the plan year is a section 436 measurement date.

*(4) Certification of AFTAP.* (i) Rules generally applicable to certifications— (A) In general. The enrolled actuary's certification referred to in this section must be made in writing, must be signed and dated to show the date of the signature, must be provided to the plan administrator, and, except as otherwise provided in paragraph (h)(4)(ii) of this section, must certify the plan's adjusted funding target attainment percentage for the plan year. Except in the case of a range certification described in paragraph (h)(4)(ii) of this section, the certification must set forth the value of plan assets, the prefunding balance, the funding standard carryover balance, the value of the funding target used in the determination, the aggregate amount of annuity purchases included in the adjusted value of plan assets and the adjusted funding target, the unpredictable contingent event benefits permitted to be paid for unpredictable contingent events that occurred during the current plan year that were taken into account for the current plan year (including any associated section 436 contributions), the plan amendments that took effect in the current plan year that were taken into account for the current plan year (including any associated section 436 contributions), any benefit accruals that were restored for the plan year (including any section 436 contributions), and any other relevant factors. The actuarial assumptions and funding methods used in the calculation for the certification must be the actuarial assumptions and funding methods used for the plan for purposes of determining the minimum required contributions under section 430 for the plan year. (B) Determination of plan assets. For purposes of making any determination of the adjusted funding target attainment percentage under this section, the determination is not permitted to include in plan assets contributions that have not been made to the plan by the certification date. Thus, the enrolled actuary's certification of the adjusted funding target attainment percentage for a plan year cannot take into account contributions that are expected to be made after the certification date. Notwithstanding the foregoing, for plan years beginning before January 1, 2009, the enrolled actuary's certification of the adjusted funding target attainment percentage is permitted to take into account employer contributions for the prior plan year that are reasonably expected to be made for that prior plan year but have not been contributed by the date of the enrolled actuary's certification. See paragraphs (h)(4)(iii) and (v) of this section for rules relating to changes in the certified percentage.

(ii) Special rules for certification within range— (A) In general. Under this paragraph (h)(4)(ii), the plan's enrolled actuary is permitted to certify during a plan year that the plan's adjusted funding target attainment percentage for that plan year either is less than 60 percent, is 60 percent or higher (but is less than 80 percent), is 80 percent or higher, or is 100 percent or higher. If the enrolled actuary has issued such a range certification for a plan year and the enrolled actuary subsequently issues a certification of the specific adjusted funding target attainment percentage for the plan before the end of that plan year, then the certification of the specific adjusted funding target attainment percentage is treated as a change in the applicable percentage to which paragraph (h)(4)(iii) of this section applies.

(B) Effect of range certification before certification of specific percentage. If a plan's enrolled actuary issues a range certification pursuant to this paragraph (h)(4)(ii), then, for purposes of this section (including application of the limitations of sections 436(b) and (c), contributions described in sections 436(b)(2), 436(c)(2), and 436(e)(2), and the mandatory reduction of the prefunding and funding standard carryover balances under paragraph (a)(5) of this section), the plan is treated as having a certified percentage at the smallest value within the applicable range until a certification of the plan's specific adjusted funding target attainment percentage for the plan year has been issued under paragraph (h)(4)(i) of this section. However, if the plan's enrolled actuary has issued a range certification for the plan year but does not issue a certification of the specific adjusted funding target attainment percentage for the plan by the last day of that plan year, the adjusted funding target attainment percentage for the plan is retroactively deemed to be less than 60 percent as of the first day of the 10th month of the plan year.

(C) Effect of range certification on and after certification of specific percentage. Once the certification of the specific adjusted funding target attainment percentage is issued by the plan's enrolled actuary, the certified percentage applies for all purposes of this section on and after the date of that certification. If the plan sponsor made section 436 contributions to avoid application of a benefit limitation during the period a range certification was in effect, those section 436 contributions are recharacterized as employer contributions under section 430 to the extent the contributions exceed the amount necessary to avoid application of a limitation based on the specific adjusted funding target attainment percentage as certified by the plan's enrolled actuary on or before the last day of the plan year.

(iii) Change of certified percentage— (A) Application of new percentage. If the enrolled actuary for the plan provides a certification of the adjusted funding target attainment percentage of the plan for the plan year under this paragraph (h)(4) (including a range certification) and that certified percentage is superseded by a subsequent determination of the adjusted funding target attainment percentage for that plan year, then, except to the extent provided in paragraph (h)(4)(iv)(B) of this section, that later percentage must be applied for the portion of the plan year beginning on the date of the earlier certification. The subsequent determination could be the correction of a prior incorrect certification or it could be an update of a prior correct certification to take into account subsequent facts under the rules of paragraph (h)(4)(v) of this section. The implications of such a change depend on whether the change is a material change or an immaterial change. See paragraph (h)(4)(iv) of this section.

(B) Material change. A change in a plan's certified adjusted funding target attainment percentage constitutes a material change for a plan year if plan operations with respect to benefits that are addressed by section 436, taking into account any actual contributions and elections under section 430(f) made by the plan sponsor based on the prior certified percentage, would have been different based on the subsequent determination of the plan's adjusted funding target attainment percentage for the plan year. A change in a plan's adjusted funding target attainment percentage for a plan year can be a material change even if the only impact of the change occurs in the following plan year under the rules for determining the presumed adjusted funding target attainment percentage in that following year.

(C) Immaterial change. In general, an immaterial change is any change in an adjusted funding target attainment percentage for a plan year that is not a material change. In addition, subject to the requirement to recertify the adjusted funding target attainment percentage in paragraph (h)(4)(v)(B) of this section, a change in adjusted funding target attainment percentage is deemed to be an immaterial change if it merely reflects a change in the funding target for the plan year or the value of the adjusted plan assets after the date of the enrolled actuary's certification resulting from—

(1) Additional contributions for the preceding year that are made by the plan sponsor;

(2) The plan sponsor's election to reduce the prefunding balance or funding standard carryover balance;

(3) The plan sponsor's election to apply the prefunding balance or funding standard carryover balance to offset the prior plan year's minimum required contribution;

(4) A change in funding method or actuarial assumptions, where such change required actual approval of the Commissioner (rather than deemed approval);

(5) Unpredictable contingent event benefits which are permitted to be paid because the employer makes the section 436 contribution described in paragraph (f)(2)(iii)(A) of this section;

(6) Unpredictable contingent event benefits which are permitted to be paid because the plan's enrolled actuary determines that the increase in the funding target attributable to the occurrence of the unpredictable contingent event would not cause the plan's adjusted funding target attainment percentage to fall below 60 percent;

(7) A plan amendment which takes effect because the employer makes the section 436 contribution described in paragraph (f)(2)(iv)(A) of this section, the liability for which was not taken into account in the certification of the adjusted funding target attainment percentage; or

(8) A plan amendment which takes effect because the plan's enrolled actuary determines that the increase in the funding target attributable to the plan amendment would not cause the plan's adjusted funding target attainment percentage to fall below 80 percent, the liability for which was not taken into account in the certification of the adjusted funding target attainment percentage.

(iv) Effect of change in percentage— (A) Material change. In the case of a material change, if the plan's prior operations were in accordance with the prior certification of the adjusted funding target attainment percentage for the plan year (rather than the actual adjusted funding target attainment percentage for the plan year), then the plan will not have satisfied the requirements of section 401(a)(29) and section 436. Even if the plan's prior operations were in accordance with the subsequent certification of the adjusted funding target attainment percentage, the plan will not have satisfied the qualification requirements of section 401(a) because the plan will not have been operated in accordance with its terms during the period of time the prior certification applied. In addition, in the case of a material change, the rules requiring application of a presumed adjusted funding target attainment percentage under paragraphs (h)(1) through (h)(3) of this section continue to apply from and after the date of the prior certification until the date of the subsequent certification.

(B) Immaterial change. An immaterial change in the adjusted funding target attainment percentage applies prospectively only and does not change the inapplicability of the presumptions under paragraphs (h)(1), (2), and (3) of this section prior to the date of the later certification.

(v) Rules relating to updated certification— (A) In general. This paragraph (h)(4)(v) sets forth rules relating to updates of an actuary's certification of the plan's adjusted funding target attainment percentage for a plan year. Paragraphs (h)(4)(v)(B) and (D) of this section require that an updated adjusted funding target attainment percentage be certified in certain situations. Even if the updated adjusted funding target attainment percentage is not required to be certified, plan administrators may request that the actuary prepare an updated certification of the adjusted funding target attainment percentage, as described in paragraphs (h)(4)(v)(C) and (E) of this section. Any updated adjusted funding target attainment percentage determined under this paragraph (h)(4)(v) will apply beginning as of the date of the event that gave rise to the need for the update which is a section 436 measurement date. Thus, pursuant to this paragraph (h)(4)(v), the updated funding target attainment percentage applies thereafter for all purposes of section 436, including application with respect to unpredictable contingent events occurring on or after the measurement date (but not for unpredictable contingent events that occurred before such measurement date or for benefits with annuity starting dates before that measurement date). The updated adjusted funding target attainment percentage will continue to apply for the remainder of the plan year and will be used for the presumed adjusted funding target attainment percentage for the next plan year, unless there is a later updated certification of adjusted funding target attainment percentage for the plan year.

(B) Requirement to recertify AFTAP if plan sponsor contributes to threshold. If, during the plan year, unpredictable contingent event benefits are permitted to be paid, a plan amendment takes effect, or benefits are permitted to accrue because the plan sponsor makes a contribution described in paragraph (f)(2)(iii)(B), (f)(2)(iv)(B), or (f)(2)(v) of this section, then, in accordance with paragraph (f)(2)(ii)(C) of this section, the plan's enrolled actuary must issue an updated certification of the adjusted funding target attainment percentage that takes into account such contribution as well as the liability for unpredictable contingent event benefits that are permitted to be paid, plan amendments that take effect during the plan year, and restored benefits.

(C) Optional recertification of AFTAP after other unpredictable contingent event or plan amendment. Except as provided in paragraph (h)(4)(v)(D) of this section, if, during a plan year, unpredictable contingent event benefits are permitted to be paid, or a plan amendment takes effect, because either the plan sponsor makes a contribution described in paragraph (f)(2)(iii)(A) or (f)(2)(iv)(A) of this section, or the plan's enrolled actuary determines that the increase in the funding target attributable to the occurrence of the unpredictable contingent event or the plan amendment would not cause the plan's adjusted funding target attainment percentage to fall below the applicable 60 percent or 80 percent threshold (taking into account the occurrence of all previous unpredictable contingent event benefits and plan amendments to the extent not already reflected in the certified adjusted funding target attainment percentage for the plan year (or update)), then the plan administrator may request that the plan actuary issue an updated certification of the adjusted funding target attainment percentage that takes into account the unpredictable contingent event benefits or plan amendments and any associated section 436 contribution.

(D) Requirement to recertify AFTAP after deemed immaterial change. If a change in the adjusted funding target attainment percentage as a result of one of the items listed in paragraph (h)(4)(iii)(C) of this section would be a material change, then the change is treated as an immaterial change only if the plan's enrolled actuary recertifies the adjusted funding target attainment percentage for the plan year as soon as practicable after the event that gives rise to the change.

(E) Optional recertification after other immaterial change. If a change in the adjusted funding target attainment percentage is immaterial, then the plan administrator may request that the plan actuary issue an updated certification of the adjusted funding target attainment percentage that takes into account the unpredictable contingent event benefits or plan amendments and any associated section 436 contribution.

*(5) Examples of rules of paragraphs (h)(1), (h)(2), and (h)(3) of this section.* The following examples illustrate the rules of paragraphs (h)(1), (h)(2), and (h)(3) of this section. Unless otherwise indicated, the examples in this section are based on the information in this paragraph (h)(5). Each plan is a non-collectively bargained defined benefit plan with a plan year that is the calendar year and a valuation date of January 1. The plan year is subject to section 436 in 2008. The plan does not have a funding standard carryover balance or a prefunding balance as of any of the dates mentioned, and the plan sponsor does not elect to utilize any of the methods in paragraph (f) of this section to avoid applicable benefit restrictions. No range certification under paragraph (h)(4) of this section has been issued. The plan sponsor is not in bankruptcy. The examples read as follows:

*Example (1).* (i) On July 15, 2010, the adjusted funding target attainment percentage ("AFTAP") for Plan T for 2010 is certified to be 65%. Based on this AFTAP, Plan T is subject to the restriction on prohibited payments in paragraph (d)(3) of this section for the remainder of 2010.

(ii) Beginning January 1, 2011, Plan T's AFTAP for 2011 is presumed to be equal to the AFTAP for 2010, or 65%, under the provisions of paragraph (h)(1)(ii) of this section. Accordingly, the restriction on prohibited payments in paragraph (d)(3) of this section continues to apply.

(iii) On March 1, 2011, the enrolled actuary for the plan certifies that the actual AFTAP for 2011 is 80%. Therefore, beginning March 1, 2011, Plan T is no longer subject to the restriction under paragraph (d)(3) of this section, and so Plan T resumes paying the full amount of any prohibited payments elected by participants with an annuity starting date of March 1, 2011, or later.

*Example (2).* (i) The facts are the same as in Example 1, except that the enrolled actuary for the plan does not certify the AFTAP for 2011 until June 1, 2011, when it is certified to be 66%.

(ii) Beginning January 1, 2011, Plan T's AFTAP for 2011 is presumed to be equal to the AFTAP for 2010, or 65%, under the provisions of paragraph (h)(1)(ii) of this section. Accordingly, the restriction on prohibited payments in paragraph (d)(3) of this section continues to apply.

(iii) Pursuant to paragraph (h)(2)(iv) of this section, beginning April 1, 2011, the AFTAP for 2011 is presumed to be 55% (10 percentage points less than the AFTAP for 2010). Plan T is subject to the restriction on prohibited payments under paragraph (d)(1) of this section for annuity starting dates on or after April 1, 2011. In addition, Plan T is subject to the restriction on unpredictable contingent event benefits under paragraph (b) of this section for unpredictable contingent events occurring on or after April 1, 2011 and benefits are required to be frozen on and after April 1, 2011 under paragraph (e) of this section.

(iv) Once the enrolled actuary for the plan certifies that the AFTAP for 2011 for Plan T is 66%, Plan T is no longer subject to the restriction under paragraph (d)(1) of this section, but it is subject to the restriction under paragraph (d)(3) of this section. Plan T must resume paying prohibited payments, as restricted under paragraph (d)(3) of this section, for participants who elect benefits in accelerated forms of payment and who have an annuity starting date of June 1, 2011, or later. In addition, Plan T must provide benefits for any unpredictable contingent event occurring on or after January 1, 2011, to the extent permitted under paragraph (b) of this section. Similarly, Plan T is no longer subject to the restriction on benefit accruals under paragraph (e) of this section, and benefit accruals resume under Plan T beginning June 1, 2011, unless Plan T provides otherwise.

*Example (3).* (i) The facts are the same as in Example 1, except that the enrolled actuary for the plan does not certify the 2011 AFTAP until November 15, 2011. Beginning October 1, 2011, Plan T is conclusively presumed to have an AFTAP of less than 60%, in accordance with the provisions of paragraph (h)(3) of this section. Accordingly, Plan T is subject to the restrictions in paragraphs (b), (d)(1), and (e) of this section commencing on October 1, 2011.

(ii) On November 15, 2011, the enrolled actuary for the plan certifies that the AFTAP for 2011 is 72%. However, because the certification occurred after September 30, 2011, the certification does not constitute a new section 436 measurement date, and Plan T continues to be subject to the restrictions on unpredictable contingent event benefits, prohibited payments, and benefit accruals under paragraphs (b), (d)(1), and (e) of this section.

(iii) Beginning January 1, 2012, the 2012 AFTAP for Plan T is presumed to be equal to the 2011 AFTAP of 72%. Because the presumed 2012 AFTAP is between 70% and 80% and, therefore, paragraph (h)(2) of this section (which provides for a 10 percentage point reduction in a plan's AFTAP in certain cases) will not apply, the presumed AFTAP will remain at 72% until the plan's enrolled actuary certifies the AFTAP for 2012 or until paragraph (h)(3) of this section applies on the first day of the 10th month of the plan year. Because the presumed AFTAP is 72%, Plan T is no longer subject to the restrictions on prohibited payments under paragraph (d)(1) of this section, and Plan T must provide benefits for any unpredictable contingent event occurring on or after January 1, 2012, to the extent permitted under paragraph (b) of this section and must resume paying prohibited payments, as restricted under paragraph (d)(3) of this section, that are elected by participants with annuity starting dates on or after January 1, 2012. Similarly, Plan T is no longer subject to the restriction on benefit accruals under paragraph (e) of this section, and benefit accruals resume under Plan T beginning January 1, 2012, unless Plan T provides otherwise.

*Example (4).* (i) The facts are the same as in Example 3, except that the enrolled actuary for the plan does not issue a certification of the AFTAP for 2011 for Plan T until February 1, 2012.

(ii) Beginning on January 1, 2012, the presumptions in paragraph (h)(1)(iii) of this section apply for the 2012 plan year. Because the enrolled actuary for the plan has not certified the AFTAP for 2011, the presumed AFTAP as of October 1, 2011, continues to apply for the period beginning January 1, 2012. Therefore, the AFTAP as of January 1, 2012, is presumed to be less than 60%, and Plan T continues to be subject to the restrictions on unpredictable contingent event benefits under paragraph (b) of this section, prohibited payments under paragraph (d)(1) of this section, and benefit accruals under paragraph (e) of this section.

(iii) On February 1, 2012, the enrolled actuary for the plan certifies that the AFTAP for 2011 for Plan T is 65%. Because the enrolled actuary for the plan has not issued a certification of the AFTAP for 2012, the provisions of paragraph (h)(1)(iii)(B) of this section apply. Accordingly, the certification date for the 2011 AFTAP (February 1, 2012) is a section 436 measurement date and 65% is the presumed AFTAP for 2012 beginning on that date.

(iv) Because the presumed AFTAP is over 60% but less than 80%, the full restriction on prohibited payments under paragraph (d)(1) of this section no longer applies; however, the partial restriction on prohibited payments under paragraph (d)(3) of this section applies beginning on February 1, 2012. Therefore, Plan T must pay a portion of the prohibited payments elected by participants with annuity starting dates on or after February 1, 2012. Furthermore, based on the presumed AFTAP of 65%, the restriction on unpredictable contingent event benefits under paragraph (b) of this section ceases to apply for events occurring on or after February 1, 2012, to the extent permitted under paragraph (b) of this section and the restriction on benefit accruals under paragraph (e) of this section no longer applies so that, unless Plan T provides otherwise, benefit accruals will resume as of February 1, 2012.

*Example (5).* (i) The facts are the same as in Example 3, except that the enrolled actuary for the plan does not issue a certification of the actual AFTAP for Plan T as of January 1, 2011, until May 1, 2012.

(ii) Beginning on January 1, 2012, the presumptions in paragraph (h)(1)(iii) of this section apply for the 2012 plan year. Because the enrolled actuary for the plan has not certified the actual AFTAP as of January 1, 2011, the presumed AFTAP as of October 1, 2011, continues to apply for the period beginning January 1, 2012. Therefore, the AFTAP as of January 1, 2012, is presumed to be less than 60%, and Plan T continues to be subject to the restrictions on unpredictable contingent event benefits under paragraph (b) of this section, on prohibited payments under paragraph (d)(1) of this section, and on benefit accruals under paragraph (e) of this section.

(iii) Since the enrolled actuary for the plan has not issued a certification of the actual AFTAP as of January 1, 2011, the rules of paragraph (h)(1)(iii) of this section apply beginning April 1, 2012, and the AFTAP is presumed to remain less than 60%. Plan T continues to be subject to the restrictions on unpredictable contingent event benefits under paragraph (b) of this section, on prohibited payments under paragraph (d)(1) of this section, and on benefit accruals under paragraph (e) of this section.

(iv) On May 1, 2012, the enrolled actuary for the plan certifies that the actual AFTAP for 2011 for Plan T is 65%. Because the enrolled actuary for the plan has not issued a certification of the actual AFTAP as of January 1, 2012, the provisions of paragraph (h)(2)(iv) of this section apply. Accordingly, on May 1, 2012, the 2012 AFTAP is presumed to be 10 percentage points less than the 2011 AFTAP, or 55%, so that the restrictions under paragraphs (b), (d), and (e) of this section continue to apply.

*Example (6).* (i) The enrolled actuary for Plan V certifies the plan's AFTAP for 2010 to be 69%. Based on this AFTAP, Plan V is subject to the restriction in paragraph (d)(3) of this section, and can only pay a portion (generally 50%) of the prohibited payments otherwise due to plan participants who commence benefits while the restriction is in effect. The enrolled actuary for the plan does not issue a certification of the AFTAP for 2011 until June 1, 2011.

(i) Beginning January 1, 2011, Plan V's 2011 AFTAP is presumed to be equal to the 2010 AFTAP, or 69%, under the provisions of paragraph (h)(1)(ii) of this section. Accordingly, the restriction on prohibited payments in paragraph (d)(3) of this section continues to apply from January 1, 2011, through March 31, 2011, and Plan T may only pay a portion of the prohibited payments otherwise due to participants who commence benefit payments during this period.

(iii) Beginning April 1, 2011, the provisions of paragraph (h)(2)(ii) of this section apply. Under those provisions, the AFTAP beginning April 1, 2011, is presumed to be 10 percentage points lower than the presumed 2011 AFTAP, or 59%. Because Plan V's presumed AFTAP for 2011 is less than 60%, the restrictions on unpredictable contingent event benefits under paragraph (b) of this section, on the payment of accelerated benefit distributions under paragraph (d)(1) of this section, and on benefit accruals under paragraph (e) of this section apply. Accordingly, Plan V cannot pay any unpredictable contingent event benefits for events occurring on or after April 1, 2011, or prohibited payments to participants with an annuity starting date on or after April 1, 2011, and benefit accruals cease as of April 1, 2011.

(iv) On June 1, 2011, Plan V's enrolled actuary certifies that the plan's AFTAP for 2011 is 71%. Therefore, the restrictions on unpredictable contingent event benefits, prohibited payments, and benefit accruals in paragraphs (b), (d)(1), and (e) of this section no longer apply, but the partial restriction on benefit payments in paragraph (d)(3) of this section does apply. Accordingly, Plan V begins paying unpredictable contingent event benefits for events occurring on or after January 1, 2011, to the extent permitted under paragraph (b) of this section and a portion of the prohibited payments elected by participants with an annuity starting date on or after June 1, 2011. Benefit accruals previously restricted under paragraph (e) of this section resume effective June 1, 2011, unless Plan V provides otherwise.

(v) Participants who were not able to elect an accelerated form of payment during the period from April 1, 2011, through May 31, 2011, would be able to elect a new annuity starting date with a partial distribution of accelerated benefits effective June 1, 2011, if Plan V contained a preexisting provision permitting such an election after the restriction in paragraph (d)(1) of this section no longer applies. This is permitted because, under paragraph (a)(4)(ii)(B) of this section, a preexisting provision of this type is not considered a plan amendment and is therefore not subject to the plan amendment restriction in paragraph (c) of this section even though Plan V's AFTAP for 2011 is less than 80%.

(vi) Benefit accruals for the period beginning April 1, 2011, through May 31, 2011, would be automatically restored if Plan V contained a preexisting provision to retroactively restore benefit accruals restricted under paragraph (e) of this section after the restriction no longer applies. This is permitted because under paragraph (a)(4)(ii)(B) of this section, a preexisting provision of this type is not considered to be a plan amendment and is therefore not subject to the plan amendment restriction in paragraph (c) of this section even though Plan V's AFTAP for 2011 is less than 80%, because the period of the restriction did not exceed 12 months.

*(6) Examples of rules of paragraph (h)(4) of this section.* The following examples illustrate the rules of paragraph (h)(4) of this section:

*Example (1).* (i) Plan Y is a non-collectively bargained defined benefit plan with a plan year that is the calendar year and a valuation date of January 1. Plan Y does not have a funding standard carryover balance or a prefunding balance. Plan Y's sponsor is not in bankruptcy. In June of 2010, the actual AFTAP for 2010 for Plan Y is certified as 65%. On the last day of the 2010 plan year, Plan Y is subject to the restrictions in paragraph (d)(3) of this section.

(ii) The enrolled actuary for the plan issues a range certification on March 21, 2011, certifying that the AFTAP for 2011 is at least 60% and less than 80%. Because the certification was issued before the first day of the 4th month of the plan year, the 10 percentage point reduction in the presumed AFTAP under paragraph (h)(2) of this section does not apply. In addition, because the enrolled actuary for the plan has certified that the AFTAP is within this range, Plan Y is not subject to the full restriction on accelerated benefit payments in paragraph (d)(1) of this section or the restriction on benefit accruals under paragraph (e) of this section.

(iii) On August 1, 2011, the enrolled actuary for the plan certifies that the actual AFTAP as of January 1, 2011, is 75.86%. This AFTAP falls within the previously certified range. Thus, the change is immaterial under paragraph (h)(4)(iii) of this section and the new certification does not change the applicability or inapplicability of the restrictions in this section.

*Example (2).* (i) The facts are the same as in Example 1, except that the plan sponsor makes an additional contribution for the 2010 plan year on September 1, 2011, that is not added to the prefunding balance. Reflecting this contribution, the enrolled actuary for the plan issues a revised certification stating that the AFTAP for 2011 is 81%, and Plan Y is no longer subject to the restriction on accelerated benefit payments under paragraph (d)(3) of this section on that date.

(ii) Although the revised certification changes the applicability of the restriction under paragraph (d)(3) of this section, the change is not a material change under paragraph (h)(4)(iii)(C)(1) of this section because the AFTAP changed only because of additional contributions for the preceding year made by the plan sponsor after the date of the enrolled actuary's initial certification.

**(i) [Reserved]**

**(j) Definitions.** For purposes of this section—

*(1) Adjusted funding target attainment percentage.* (i) In general. Except as otherwise provided in this paragraph (j)(1), the adjusted funding target attainment percentage for a plan year is the fraction (expressed as a percentage)—

(A) The numerator of which is the adjusted plan assets for the plan year described in paragraph (j)(1)(ii) of this section; and

(B) The denominator of which is the adjusted funding target for the plan year described in paragraph (j)(1)(iii) of this section.

(ii) Adjusted plan assets— (A) General rule. The adjusted plan assets for a plan year is generally determined by—

(1) Subtracting the plan's funding standard carryover balance and prefunding balance as of the valuation date from the value of plan assets for the plan year under section 430(g) (but treating the resulting value as zero if it is below zero); and

(2) Increasing the resulting value by the aggregate amount of purchases of annuities for participants and beneficiaries (other than participants who, at the time of the purchase, were highly compensated employees as defined in section 414(q), which definition includes highly compensated former employees under § 1.414(q)-1T, Q&A-4) which were made by the plan during the preceding 2 plan years, to the extent not included in plan assets for purposes of section 430.

(B) Special rule for plans that are fully funded without regard to subtraction of funding balances from plan assets. If for a plan year the value of plan assets determined without subtracting the funding standard carryover balance and the prefunding balance is not less than 100 percent of the plan's funding target determined under section 430 without regard to section 430(i), then the adjusted value of plan assets used in the calculation of the adjusted funding target attainment percentage for the plan year is determined without subtracting the plan's funding standard carryover balance and prefunding balance from the value of plan assets for the plan year.

(C) Special rule for plans with section 436 contributions. If an employer makes a contribution described in paragraph (f)(2) of this section after the valuation date in order to avoid or terminate limitations under section 436, then the present value of that contribution (determined using the effective interest rate under section 430(h)(2)(A) for the plan year) is permitted to be added to the plan assets as of the valuation date for purposes of determining or redetermining the adjusted funding target attainment percentage for a plan year, but only if the liability for the benefits, amendment, or accruals that would have been limited (but for the contribution) is included in determining the adjusted funding target for the plan year.

(D) Transition rule. Paragraph (j)(1)(ii)(B) of this section is applied to plan years beginning after 2007 and before 2011 by substituting for "100 percent" the applicable percentage determined in accordance with the following table:

| In the case of a plan year beginning in calendar year: | The applicable percentage is: |
|---|---|
| 2008 . . . . | 92 |
| 2009 . . . . | 94 |
| 2010 . . . . | 96 |

(E) Limitation on transition rule. Paragraph (j)(1)(ii)(D) of this section does not apply with respect to the current plan year unless, for each plan year beginning after December 31, 2007, and before the current plan year, the value of plan assets determined without subtracting the funding standard carryover balance and the prefunding balance is not less than the product of—

(1) The applicable percentage determined under paragraph (j)(1)(ii)(D) of this section for that plan year; and

(2) The funding target (determined without regard to the at-risk rules of section 430(i)) for that plan year.

(iii) Adjusted funding target— (A) In general. Except as otherwise provided in this paragraph (j)(1)(iii), the adjusted funding target equals the funding target for the plan year, determined in accordance with the rules set forth in § 1.430(d)-1, but without regard to the at-risk rules under section 430(i), increased by the aggregate amount of purchases of annuities that were added to assets for purposes of determining the plan's adjusted plan assets under paragraph (j)(1)(ii)(A)(2) of this section. The definition of adjusted funding target for a plan maintained by a commercial airline for which the plan sponsor has made the election described in section 402(a)(1) of Pension Protection Act of 2006 (PPA '06), Public Law 109-280 (120 Stat. 780), is the same as if it did not make such an election.

(B) Adjusted funding target after updated certification. After the plan's enrolled actuary prepares an updated certification of the adjusted funding target attainment percentage under paragraph (h)(4)(v) of this section, the adjusted funding target will also be updated to reflect unpredictable contingent event benefits and plan amendments not already taken into account.

(iv) Plans with zero adjusted funding target. If the adjusted funding target for the plan year is zero, then the adjusted funding target attainment percentage for the plan year is 100 percent.

(v) Plans with end of year valuation dates. [Reserved]

(vi) Special rule for plans that are the result of a merger. [Reserved]

(vii) Special rule for plans that are involved in a spinoff. [Reserved]

*(2) Annuity starting date.* (i) General rule. The term annuity starting date means, as applicable—

(A) The first day of the first period for which an amount is payable as an annuity as described in section 417(f)(2)(A)(i);

(B) In the case of a benefit not payable in the form of an annuity, the annuity starting date is the annuity starting date for the qualified joint and survivor annuity that is payable under the plan at the same time as the benefit that is not payable as an annuity;

(C) In the case of an amount payable under a retroactive annuity starting date, the benefit commencement date (instead of the date determined under paragraphs (j)(2)(i)(A) and (B) of this section);

(D) The date of the purchase of an irrevocable commitment from an insurer to pay benefits under the plan; and

(E) The date of any transfer to another plan described in paragraph (j)(6)(i)(C) of this section.

(ii) Special rule for beneficiaries. If a participant commences benefits at an annuity starting date (as defined in paragraph (j)(2)(i) of this section) and, after the death of the participant, payments continue to a beneficiary, the annuity starting date for the payments to the participant constitutes the annuity starting date for payments to the beneficiary, except that a new annuity starting date occurs (determined by applying paragraph (j)(2)(i)(A), (B), and (C) of this section to the payments to the beneficiary) if the amounts payable to all beneficiaries of the participant in the aggregate at any future date can exceed the monthly amount that would have been paid to the participant had he or she not died.

*(3) First effective plan year.* The first effective plan year for a plan is the first plan year to which section 436 applies to the plan under paragraph (k)(1) or (k)(2) of this section.

*(4)* Funding target. In general, the funding target means the funding target under § 1.430(d)-1, without regard to the at-risk rules under section 430(i) and § 1.430(i)-1. However, solely for purposes of sections 436(b)(2)(A) and (c)(2)(A), the funding target means the funding target under § 1.430(i)-1 if the plan is in at-risk status for the plan year.

*(5)* Prior plan year adjusted funding target attainment percentage— (i) In general. Except as otherwise provided in this paragraph (j)(5), the prior plan year adjusted funding target attainment percentage is the adjusted funding target attainment percentage determined under paragraph (j)(1) of this section for the immediately preceding plan year.

(ii) Special rules— (A) Special rule for new plans. In the case of a plan established during the plan year that was not the result of a merger or spinoff, the adjusted funding target attainment percentage is equal to 100 percent for plan years before the plan was established. Except as otherwise provided in paragraph (j)(5)(ii)(B) of this section, a plan that has a predecessor plan in accordance with § 1.415(f)-1(c) is not a plan established during the plan year under this paragraph (j)(5)(ii)(A). Instead, if the plan has a predecessor plan, the adjusted funding target attainment percentage for the prior plan year is the adjusted funding target attainment percentage for the prior plan year for the predecessor plan (and that predecessor plan's adjusted funding target attainment percentage is treated as equal to 100 percent on any date on which it is terminated, other than in a distress termination).

(B) Special rules for plans that are the result of a merger. [Reserved]

(C) Special rules for plans that are involved in a spinoff. [Reserved]

(iii) Special rules for 2007 plan year— (A) General determination of 2007 adjusted funding target attainment percentage. In the case of the first plan year beginning in 2008, except as otherwise provided in this paragraph (j)(5), the adjusted funding target attainment percentage for the immediately preceding plan year (the 2007 plan year) is determined as the fraction (expressed as a percentage)—

(1) The numerator of which is the value of plan assets determined under paragraph (j)(5)(iii)(B) of this section increased by the aggregate amount of purchases of annuities for participants and beneficiaries (other than participants who, at the time of the purchase, were highly compensated employees as defined in section 414(q), which definition includes highly compensated former employees under § 1.414(q)-1T, Q&A-4 which were made by the plan during the preceding 2 plan years, to the extent not included in plan assets under section 412(c)(2) (as in effect prior to amendment by PPA '06); and

(2) The denominator of which is the plan's current liability determined pursuant to section 412(l)(7) (as in effect prior to amendment by PPA '06) on the valuation date for the 2007 plan year increased by the aggregate amount of purchases of annuities that were added to the plan assets under the rules of paragraph (j)(5)(iii)(A)(1) of this section.

(B) General determination of value of plan assets— (1) In general. The value of plan assets for purposes of this paragraph (j)(5)(iii) is determined under section 412(c)(2) as in effect for the 2007 plan year, except that the value of plan assets prior to subtracting the plan's funding standard account credit balance described in paragraph (j)(5)(iii)(B)(2) of this section must be adjusted so that the value of plan assets is neither less than 90 percent of the fair market value of plan assets nor greater than 110 percent of the fair market value of plan assets on the valuation date for that plan year.

(2) Subtraction of credit balance. If a plan has a funding standard account credit balance as of the valuation date for the 2007 plan year, that balance is subtracted from the value of plan assets described in paragraph (j)(5)(iii)(B)(1) of this section as of that valuation date. However, the subtraction does not apply if the value of plan assets prior to adjustment under paragraph (j)(5)(iii)(B)(1) of this section is greater than or equal to 90 percent of the plan's current liability as of the valuation date for the 2007 plan year.

(3) Effect of funding standard carryover balance reduction for 2007 plan year. Notwithstanding paragraph (j)(5)(iii)(B)(2) of this section, if, for the first plan year beginning in 2008, the employer has made an election to reduce some or all of the funding standard carryover balance as of the first day of that year in accordance with § 1.430(f)-1(e), then the present value (determined as of the valuation date for the 2007 plan year using the valuation interest rate for that plan year) of the amount so reduced is not treated as part of the funding standard account credit balance when that balance is subtracted from the asset value under paragraph (j)(5)(iii)(B)(2) of this section.

(C) Plan with end-of-year valuation date. With respect to the first plan year beginning in 2008, if the plan had a valuation date under section 412 that was the last day of the plan year for each of the plan years beginning in 2006 and 2007, the adjusted funding target attainment percentage for the 2007 plan year may be determined as the fraction (expressed as a percentage)—

(1) The numerator of which is the value of plan assets determined under paragraph (j)(5)(iii)(D) of this section increased by the aggregate amount of purchases of annuities for participants and beneficiaries (other than participants who, at the time of the purchase, were highly compensated employees as defined in section 414(q), which definition includes highly compensated former employees under § 1.414(q)-1T, Q&A-4 which were made by the plan during the preceding 2 plan years, to the extent not included in plan assets under section 412(c)(2) (as in effect prior to amendment by PPA '06); and

(2) The denominator of which is the plan's current liability determined pursuant to section 412(l)(7) (as in effect prior to amendment by PPA '06) on the valuation date for the second plan year that begins before 2008 (the 2006 plan year), including the increase in current liability for the 2006 plan year, increased by the aggregate amount of purchases of annuities that were added to the plan assets under the rules of paragraph (j)(5)(iii)(C)(1) of this section.

(D) Special asset determinations for 2006 adjusted funding target attainment percentage— (1) General rule. If the adjusted funding target attainment percentage for the 2007 plan year is determined under the rules of paragraph (j)(5)(iii)(C) of this section, then the value of plan assets is determined as the value of plan assets under section 412(c)(2) as in effect for the 2006 plan year, adjusted as provided in this paragraph (j)(5)(iii)(D).

(2) Inclusion of contributions for 2006. Contributions made for the 2006 plan year are taken into account in determining the value of plan assets, regardless of whether those contributions are made during the plan year or after the end of the plan year and within the period specified under section 412(c)(10) (as in effect prior to amendment by PPA '06).

(3) Restriction to 90-110 percent corridor. The value of plan assets taking into account the amount of contributions made for the 2006 plan year is increased or decreased, as necessary, so that it is neither less than 90 percent of the fair market value of plan assets nor greater than 110 percent of the fair market value of plan assets on the valuation date for the 2006 plan year (taking into account assets attributable to contributions for the 2006 plan year).

(4) Subtraction of credit balance. The plan's funding standard account credit balance as of the end of the 2006 plan year is generally subtracted from the value of plan assets determined after application of paragraph (j)(5)(iii)(D)(3) of this section. However, this subtraction does not apply if the value of plan assets is greater than or equal to 90 percent of the plan's current liability determined under section 412(l)(7) (as in effect prior to amendment by PPA '06) on the valuation date for the 2006 plan year.

(E) Special rules for mergers and spinoffs. Rules similar to the rules of paragraph (j)(5)(ii) of this section apply for purposes of determining the adjusted funding target attainment percentage for the 2007 plan year in the case of a newly established plan, a plan that is the result of a merger of two plans, or a plan that is in involved in a spinoff.

*(6) Prohibited payment.* (i) General rule. The term prohibited payment means—

(A) Any payment for a month that is in excess of the monthly amount paid under a straight life annuity (plus any social security supplements described in the last sentence of section 411(a)(9)) to a participant or beneficiary whose annuity starting date occurs during any period that a limitation under paragraph (d) of this section is in effect;

(B) Any payment for the purchase of an irrevocable commitment from an insurer to pay benefits;

(C) Any transfer of assets and liabilities to another plan maintained by the same employer (or by any member of the employer's controlled group) that is made in order to avoid or terminate the application of section 436 benefit limitations; and

(D) Any other amount that is identified as a prohibited payment by the Commissioner in revenue rulings and procedures, notices, and other guidance published in the Internal Revenue Bulletin (see § 601.601(d)(2) relating to objectives and standards for publishing regulations, revenue rulings and revenue procedures in the Internal Revenue Bulletin).

(ii) Special rule for beneficiaries. In the case of a beneficiary that is not an individual, the amount that is a prohibited payment is determined by substituting for the amount in paragraph (j)(1)(i)(A) of this section the monthly amount payable in installments over 240 months that is actuarially equivalent to the benefit payable to the beneficiary.

*(7)* Section 436 contributions. Section 436 contributions are the contributions described in paragraph (f)(2) of this section that are made in order to avoid the application of section 436 limitations under a plan for a plan year.

*(8)* Section 436 measurement date. A section 436 measurement date is the date that is used to determine when the limitations of sections 436(d) and 436(e) apply or cease to apply, and is also used for calculations with respect to applying the limitations of paragraphs (b) and (c) of this section. See paragraphs (h)(1)(i), (h)(2)(iii)(B), (h)(2)(iv)(B), and (h)(3)(i) of this section regarding section 436 measurement dates that result from application of the presumptions under paragraph (h) of this section.

*(9)* Unpredictable contingent event. An unpredictable contingent event benefit means any benefit or increase in benefits to the extent the benefit or increase would not be payable but for the occurrence of an unpredictable contingent event. For this purpose, an unpredictable contingent event means a plant shutdown (whether full or partial) or similar event, or an event (including the absence of an event) other than the attainment of any age, performance of any service, receipt or derivation of any compensation, or the occurrence of death or disability. For example, if a plan provides for an unreduced early retirement benefit upon the occurrence of an event other than the attainment of any age, performance of any service, receipt or derivation of any compensation, or the occurrence of death or disability, then that unreduced early retirement benefit is an unpredictable contingent event benefit to the extent of any portion of the benefit that would not be payable but for the occurrence of the event, even if the remainder of the benefit is payable without regard to the occurrence of the event. Similarly, if a plan includes a benefit payable upon the presence (including the absence) of circumstances specified in the plan (other than the attainment of any age, performance of any service, receipt or derivation of any compensation, or the occurrence of death or disability), but not upon a severance from employment that does not include those circumstances, that benefit is an unpredictable contingent event benefit.

*(10)* Examples. The following examples illustrate the rules of this paragraph (j):

*Example (1).* (i) Plan S is a non-collectively bargained defined benefit plan with a plan year that is the calendar year and a valuation date of January 1. The first effective plan year is 2008. Plan S is not in at-risk status for 2008.

(i) As of January 1, 2008, Plan S has a value of plan assets (equal to the market value of assets) of $2,100,000 and a funding standard carryover balance of $200,000. During 2006, assets from Plan S were used to purchase a total of $100,000 in annuities for employees other than highly compensated employees. No annuities were purchased during 2007. On May 1, 2008, the enrolled actuary for the plan determines that the funding target as of January 1, 2008, is $2,500,000.

(iii) The adjusted value of assets for Plan S as of January 1, 2008, is $2,000,000 (that is, plan assets of $2,100,000, plus annuity purchases of $100,000, and minus the funding standard carryover balance of $200,000). The adjusted funding target is $2,600,000 (that is, the funding target of $2,500,000, increased by the annuity purchases of $100,000).

(iv) Based on the above adjusted plan assets and adjusted funding target, the adjusted funding target attainment percentage (AFTAP) as of January 1, 2008, would be 76.92%. Since the AFTAP is less than 80% but is at least 60%, Plan S is subject to the restrictions in paragraph (d)(3) of this section.

*Example (2).* (i) The facts are the same as in Example 1, except that it is reasonable to expect that the plan sponsor will make a contribution of $80,000 to Plan S for the 2007 plan year by September 15, 2008. This amount is in excess of the minimum required contribution for 2007. The plan sponsor elects to reduce the funding standard carryover balance by $80,000.

(ii) Because it is reasonable to expect that the $80,000 will be contributed by the plan sponsor, that amount is taken into account when the enrolled actuary certifies the 2008 AFTAP under the special rule in paragraph (h)(4)(i)(B) of this section for plan years beginning before 2009. Accordingly, the enrolled actuary for the plan certifies the 2008 AFTAP as 80% (that is, adjusted plan assets of $2,080,000, reflecting the $80,000 in contributions receivable, divided by the adjusted funding target of $2,600,000).

(iii) The ability to take contributions into account before they are actually paid to the plan is available only for plan years beginning before 2009. Furthermore, if the employer does not actually make the contribution and the difference between the incorrect certification and the corrected AFTAP constitutes a material change, the plan will have violated section 401(a)(29) or will not have been operated in accordance with its terms.

*Example (3).* (i) Plan R is a defined benefit plan with a plan year that is the calendar year and a valuation date of January 1. Section 436 applies to Plan R for 2008. The valuation interest rate for the 2007 plan year for Plan R is 7%. The fair market value of assets of Plan R as of January 1, 2007, is $1,000,000. The actuarial value of assets of Plan R as of January 1, 2007, is $1,200,000. The current liability of Plan R as of January 1, 2007, is $1,500,000. The funding standard account credit balance as of January 1, 2007, is $80,000. The funding standard carryover balance of Plan R is $50,000 as of the beginning of the 2008 plan year. The sponsor of Plan R, Sponsor T, elects in 2008 to reduce the funding standard carryover balance in accordance with § 1.430(f)-1 by $45,000. No annuities were purchased using plan assets during 2005 or 2006.

(i) Pursuant to paragraph (j)(5)(iii)(B)(1) of this section, the asset value used to determine the AFTAP for the 2007 plan year is limited to 110% of the fair market value of assets on January 1, 2007, or $1,100,000 (110% of $1,000,000).

(iii) Pursuant to paragraph (j)(5)(iii)(B)(2) of this section, the funding standard account credit balance as of January 1, 2007, is subtracted from the asset value used to determine the AFTAP for the 2007 plan year. However, pursuant to paragraph (j)(5)(iii)(B)(3) of this section, the present value of the amount by which Sponsor T elected to reduce the funding standard carryover balance in 2008 is not subtracted.

(iv) The present value, determined at an interest rate of 7%, of the $45,000 reduction in the funding standard carryover balance elected by Sponsor T in 2008 is $42,056. Thus, $42,056 is not subtracted from the 2007 plan year asset value. Accordingly, the funding standard account credit balance that is subtracted from the 2007 plan year asset value is $37,944 (that is, $80,000 less $42,056).

(v) Thus, the asset value that is used to determine the FTAP for the 2007 plan year is $1,100,000 less $37,944, or $1,062,056. Accordingly, for purposes of this section, the FTAP for the 2007 plan year for Plan R is 70.8% (that is, $1,062,056 divided by $1,500,000).

*Example (4).* (i) Plan T is a non-collectively bargained defined benefit plan that was established prior to 2007. Plan T has a plan year that is the calendar year and a valuation date of January 1. The first effective plan year is 2008; the plan met the conditions of paragraph (j)(1)(ii)(E) of this section for 2008. As of January 1, 2009, Plan T has a value of plan assets (equal to the market value of assets) of $3,000,000, a funding standard carryover balance of $150,000, and a prefunding balance of $50,000. During 2007 and 2008, assets from Plan T were used to purchase a total of $400,000 in annuities for employees other than highly compensated employees. The funding target for Plan T (without regard to the at-risk rules of section 430(i)) is $3,200,000 as of January 1, 2009.

(ii) The plan's funding status is calculated in accordance with paragraph (j)(1)(ii)(B) of this section to determine whether the special rule for fully-funded plans applies to Plan T. Accordingly, the value of plan assets determined without subtracting the funding standard carryover balance and the prefunding balance is 93.75% of the plan's funding target ($3,000,000 / $3,200,000). The applicable transitional percentage in paragraph (j)(1)(ii)(D) of this section is 94% for 2009. Because the percentage calculated above is less than 94%, the transition rule does not apply to Plan T.

(iii) Accordingly, the January 1, 2009, AFTAP for Plan T is calculated without reflecting the special rule in paragraph (j)(1)(ii)(B) of this section. The AFTAP as of January 1, 2009, is calculated by dividing the adjusted assets by the adjusted funding target. For this purpose, the value of assets is increased by the annuities purchased for nonhighly compensated employees during 2007 and 2008, and decreased by the funding standard carryover balance and the prefunding balance as of January 1, 2009, resulting in an adjusted asset value of $3,200,000 (that is, $3,000,000 + $400,000-$150,000-$50,000). The funding target is increased by the annuities purchased for nonhighly compensated employees during 2007 and 2008, resulting in an adjusted funding target of $3,600,000 (that is, $3,200,000 + $400,000). The AFTAP for Plan T for 2009 is therefore $3,200,000 / $3,600,000, or 88.89%.

**(k) Effective/applicability dates.** *(1) Statutory effective date.* Section 436 generally applies to plan years beginning on or after January 1, 2008. The applicability of section 436 for purposes of determining the minimum required contribution is delayed for certain plans in accordance with sections 104 through 106 of PPA '06.

*(2) Collectively bargained plan exception.* (i) In general. In the case of a collectively bargained plan that is maintained pursuant to one or more collective bargaining agreements between employee representatives and one or more employers ratified before January 1, 2008, section 436 does not apply to plan years beginning before the earlier of—

(A) January 1, 2010; or

(B) The later of—

(1) The date on which the last such collective bargaining agreement relating to the plan terminates (determined without regard to any extension thereof agreed to after August 17, 2006); or

(2) The first day of the first plan year to which section 436 would (but for this paragraph (k)(2)) apply.

(ii) Treatment of certain plan amendments. For purposes of this paragraph (k)(2), any plan amendment made pursuant to a collective bargaining agreement relating to the plan which amends the plan solely to conform to any requirement added by section 436 is not treated as a termination of the collective bargaining agreement.

(ii) Treatment of plans with both collectively bargained and non-collectively bargained employees. In the case of a plan with respect to which a collective bargaining agreement applies to some, but not all, of the plan participants, the plan is considered a collectively bargained plan for purposes of this paragraph (k)(2) if it is considered a collectively bargained plan under the rules of paragraph (a)(5)(ii)(B) of this section.

*(3) Effective date/applicability date of regulations.* This section applies to plan years beginning on or after January 1, 2010. For plan years beginning before January 1, 2010, plans are permitted to rely on the provisions set forth in this section for purposes of satisfying the requirements of section 436.

---

T.D. 9467, 10/07/2009.

---

### § 1.441-0 Table of contents.

This section lists the captions contained in § 1.441-1 through 1.441-4 as follows:

---

T.D. 8996, 5/16/2002.

---

### § 1.441-1 Period for computation of taxable income.

***Caution:*** The Treasury has not yet amended Reg § 1.441-1 to reflect changes made by P.L. 108-357.

**(a) Computation of taxable income.** *(1) In general.* Taxable income must be computed and a return must be made for a period known as the taxable year. For rules relating to methods of accounting, the taxable year for which items of gross income are included and deductions are taken, inventories, and adjustments, see parts II and III (section 446 and following), subchapter E, chapter 1 of the Internal Revenue Code, and the regulations thereunder.

*(2) Length of taxable year.* Except as otherwise provided in the Internal Revenue Code and the regulations thereunder (e.g., § 1.441-2 regarding 52-53-week taxable years), a taxable year may not cover a period of more than 12 calendar months.

**(b) General rules and definitions.** The general rules and definitions in this paragraph (b) apply for purposes of sections 441 and 442 and the regulations thereunder.

*(1) Taxable year.* Taxable year means—

(i) The period for which a return is made, if a return is made for a period of less than 12 months (short period). See section 443 and the regulations thereunder;

(ii) Except as provided in paragraph (b)(1)(i) of this section, the taxpayer's required taxable year (as defined in paragraph (b)(2) of this section), if applicable;

(iii) Except as provided in paragraphs (b)(1)(i) and (ii) of this section, the taxpayer's annual accounting period (as defined in paragraph (b)(3) of this section), if it is a calendar year or a fiscal year; or

(iv) Except as provided in paragraphs (b)(1)(i) and (ii) of this section, the calendar year, if the taxpayer keeps no books, does not have an annual accounting period, or has an annual accounting period that does not qualify as a fiscal year.

*(2) Required taxable year.* (i) In general. Certain taxpayers must use the particular taxable year that is required under the Internal Revenue Code and the regulations thereunder (the required taxable year). For example, the required taxable year is—

(A) In the case of a foreign sales corporation or domestic international sales corporation, the taxable year determined under section 441(h) and § 1.921-1T(a)(11), (b)(4), and (b)(6);

(B) In the case of a personal service corporation (PSC), the taxable year determined under section 441(i) and § 1.441-3;

(C) In the case of a nuclear decommissioning fund, the taxable year determined under § 1.468A-4(c)(1);

(D) In the case of a designated settlement fund or a qualified settlement fund, the taxable year determined under § 1.468B-2(j);

(E) In the case of a common trust fund, the taxable year determined under section 584(i);

(F) In the case of certain trusts, the taxable year determined under section 644;

(G) In the case of a partnership, the taxable year determined under section 706 and § 1.706-1;

(H) In the case of an insurance company, the taxable year determined under section 843 and § 1.1502-76(a)(2);

(I) In the case of a real estate investment trust, the taxable year determined under section 859;

(J) In the case of a real estate mortgage investment conduit, the taxable year determined under section 860D(a)(5) and § 1.860D-1(b)(6);

(K) In the case of a specified foreign corporation, the taxable year determined under section 898(c)(1)(A);

(L) In the case of an S corporation, the taxable year determined under section 1378 and § 1.1378-1; or

(M) In the case of a member of an affiliated group that makes a consolidated return, the taxable year determined under § 1.1502-76.

(ii) Exceptions. Notwithstanding paragraph (b)(2)(i) of this section, the following taxpayers may have a taxable year other than their required taxable year:

(A) 52-53-week taxable years. Certain taxpayers may elect to use a 52-53-week taxable year that ends with reference to their required taxable year. See, for example, §§ 1.441-3 (PSCs), 1.706-1 (partnerships), 1.1378-1 (S corporations), and 1.1502-76(a)(1) (members of a consolidated group).

(B) Partnerships, S corporations, and PSCs. A partnership, S corporation, or PSC may use a taxable year other than its required taxable year if the taxpayer elects to use a taxable year other than its required taxable year under section 444, elects a 52-53-week taxable year that ends with reference to its required taxable year as provided in paragraph (b)(2)(ii)(A) of this section or to a taxable year elected under section 444, or establishes a business purpose to the satisfaction of the Commissioner under section 442 (such as a grandfathered fiscal year).

(C) Specified foreign corporations. A specified foreign corporation (as defined in section 898(b)) may use a taxable year other than its required taxable year if it elects a 52-53-week taxable year that ends with reference to its required taxable year as provided in paragraph (b)(2)(ii)(A) of this section or makes a one-month deferral election under section 898(c)(1)(B).

*(3) Annual accounting period.* Annual accounting period means the annual period (calendar year or fiscal year) on the basis of which the taxpayer regularly computes its income in keeping its books.

*(4) Calendar year.* Calendar year means a period of 12 consecutive months ending on December 31. A taxpayer who has not established a fiscal year must make its return on the basis of a calendar year.

*(5) Fiscal year.* (i) Definition. Fiscal year means—

(A) A period of 12 consecutive months ending on the last day of any month other than December; or

(B) A 52-53-week taxable year, if such period has been elected by the taxpayer. See § 1.441-2.

(ii) Recognition. A fiscal year will be recognized only if the books of the taxpayer are kept in accordance with such fiscal year.

*(6) Grandfathered fiscal year.* Grandfathered fiscal year means a fiscal year (other than a year that resulted in a three month or less deferral of income) that a partnership or an S corporation received permission to use on or after July 1, 1974, by a letter ruling (i.e., not by automatic approval).

*(7) Books.* Books include the taxpayer's regular books of account and such other records and data as may be necessary to support the entries on the taxpayer's books and on the taxpayer's return, as for example, a reconciliation of any difference between such books and the taxpayer's return. Records that are sufficient to reflect income adequately and clearly on the basis of an annual accounting period will be regarded as the keeping of books. See section 6001 and the regulations thereunder for rules relating to the keeping of books and records.

*(8) Taxpayer.* Taxpayer has the same meaning as the term person as defined in section 7701(a)(1) (e.g., an individual, trust, estate, partnership, association, or corporation) rather than the meaning of the term taxpayer as defined in section 7701(a)(14) (any person subject to tax).

**(c) Adoption of taxable year.** *(1) In general.* Except as provided in paragraph (c)(2) of this section, a new taxpayer may adopt any taxable year that satisfies the requirements of section 441 and the regulations thereunder without the approval of the Commissioner. A taxable year of a new taxpayer is adopted by filing its first Federal income tax return using that taxable year. The filing of an application for automatic extension of time to file a Federal income tax return (e.g., Form 7004, "Application for Automatic Extension of Time To File Corporation Income Tax Return"), the filing of an application for an employer identification number (i.e., Form SS-4, "Application for Employer Identification Number"), or the payment of estimated taxes, for a particular taxable year do not constitute an adoption of that taxable year.

*(2) Approval required.* (i) Taxpayers with required taxable years. A newly-formed partnership, S corporation, or PSC that wants to adopt a taxable year other than its required taxable year, a taxable year elected under section 444, or a 52-

53-week taxable year that ends with reference to its required taxable year or a taxable year elected under section 444 must establish a business purpose and obtain the approval of the Commissioner under section 442.

(ii) Taxpayers without books. A taxpayer that must use a calendar year under section 441(g) and paragraph (f) of this section may not adopt a fiscal year without obtaining the approval of the Commissioner.

**(d) Retention of taxable year.** In certain cases, a partnership, S corporation, electing S corporation, or PSC will be required to change its taxable year unless it obtains the approval of the Commissioner under section 442, or makes an election under section 444, to retain its current taxable year. For example, a corporation using a June 30 fiscal year that either becomes a PSC or elects to be an S corporation and, as a result, is required to use the calendar year under section 441(i) or 1378, respectively, must obtain the approval of the Commissioner to retain its current fiscal year. Similarly, a partnership using a taxable year that corresponds to its required taxable year must obtain the approval of the Commissioner to retain such taxable year if its required taxable year changes as a result of a change in ownership. However, a partnership that previously established a business purpose to the satisfaction of the Commissioner to use a taxable year is not required to obtain the approval of the Commissioner if its required taxable year changes as a result of a change in ownership.

**(e) Change of taxable year.** Once a taxpayer has adopted a taxable year, such taxable year must be used in computing taxable income and making returns for all subsequent years unless the taxpayer obtains approval from the Commissioner to make a change or the taxpayer is otherwise authorized to change without the approval of the Commissioner under the Internal Revenue Code (e.g., section 444 or 859) or the regulations thereunder.

**(f) Obtaining approval of the Commissioner or making a section 444 election.** See § 1.442-1(b) for procedures for obtaining approval of the Commissioner (automatically or otherwise) to adopt, change, or retain an annual accounting period. See §§ 1.444-1T and 1.444-2T for qualifications, and 1.444-3T for procedures, for making an election under section 444.

---

T.D. 8996, 5/16/2002.

---

PAR. 2. Section 1.441-1 is amended as follows:

1.a. Paragraph (b)(1) is revised;

b. A new sentence is added at the end of paragraph (b)(3);

c. A new sentence is added at the end of paragraph (b)(4); and

2. A new paragraph (h) is added immediately after paragraph (g).

The revised and added provisions read as follows:

**Proposed § 1.441-1 Period for computation of taxable income.** [*For Preamble, see ¶ 151,083*]

* * * * *

**(b) Taxable year.** *(1)* The term "taxable year" means—

(i) The taxpayer's annual accounting period, if it is a calendar year or a fiscal year (within the meaning of paragraph (e) of this section);

(ii) The calendar year, if section 441(g) (relating to taxpayers who keep no books or have no accounting period) applies:

(iii) The period for which the return is made, if the return is made under section 443 for a period of less than 12 months, referred to as a "short period"; or

(iv) In the case of a FSC, a small FSC or a DISC filing a return for a period of at least 12 months, the period determined under section 441(h) and paragraph (h) of this section.

* * * * *

*(3)* * * * For rules applicable to the adoption of a taxable year by a FSC or a DISC, see paragraph (h) of this section.

* * * * *

*(4)* * * * For rules applicable to a change of taxable year by a FSC or a DISC, see paragraph (h) of this section.

* * * * *

**(h) Taxable year of FSCs and DISCs.** *(1) In general.* (i) The taxable year of any FSC, or of any DISC established after December 31, 1984, shall be the same taxable year as the taxable year of the FSC's or DISC's principal shareholder (as defined in paragraph (h)(2) of this section). In addition, any domestic corporation which was a DISC on or at any time before December 31, 1984, and which elects to be treated as a DISC for any taxable year beginning after December 31, 1984, must adopt the same taxable year as its principal shareholder. For purposes of this section, the term "FSC" includes a small FSC as defined in section 922(b).

(ii) The corporation shall (without being required to obtain the consent of the Commissioner, and without filing Form 1128, Application for Change in Accounting Period) adopt the taxable year of its principal shareholder by ending the corporation's first taxable year for which it elects to be treated as a FSC or a DISC on the last day of the principal shareholder's taxable year, and the corporation shall file its return for such first taxable year and for succeeding taxable years on that basis. If the principal shareholder's annual accounting period is a 52-53 week year under section 441(f), the FSC or DISC shall also adopt such 52-53 week year as the taxable year.

*(2) Principal shareholder.* (i) General rule. The "principal shareholder" of a FSC or DISC is the shareholder (or group of shareholders having the same taxable year) who has the highest percentage of voting power in the FSC or DISC. If the principal shareholder of the DISC or FSC is a pass-through entity, such as an S corporation, a partnership, a trust or an estate, the DISC or FSC shall adopt the taxable year of the pass-through entity without regard to the taxable year of the pass-through entity without regard to the taxable year of the pass-through entity's shareholders, partners or beneficiaries.

(ii) Voting power. (A) In the case of a FSC, "voting power" is determined on the basis of the total combined voting power of all classes of stock in the corporation entitled to vote.

(B) In the case of a DISC, "voting power" is determined on the basis of the one class of stock that the DISC is permitted to issue under section 992(a)(1)(C).

(iii) More than one principal shareholder. If two or more shareholders, or groups of shareholders, have the highest percentage of voting power in the FSC or DISC and have different taxable years, such FSC or DISC shall conform its taxable year (in the manner prescribed in paragraph (h)(1)(ii) of this section) to the taxable year of any one of such shareholders or groups, and only the shareholder or group shall be considered the principal shareholder for purposes of this paragraph (h).

*(3) Subsequent changes in FSC's or DISC's accounting period.* (i) General rule. Except as provided in this paragraph (h)(3), a FSC or a DISC shall not change its taxable year.

(ii) Principal shareholder changes its taxable year. If the principal shareholder of a FSC or a DISC changes its taxable year, the FSC or DISC shall also change its accounting period to conform to the principal shareholder's new taxable year, including using the same short period to effect such change. The Commissioner will not grant consent, under section 442, to a request for change in the principal shareholder's taxable year unless the FSC or DISC also agrees to make and makes the same change in its annual accounting period.

(iii) New principal shareholder. This paragraph (h)(3)(iii) is effective for changes of ownership described in subparagraphs (A) and (B) of this paragraph (h)(3)(iii) which occur (insert date 30 days after date this document is published in the Federal Register as a Treasury Decision]. For such changes in ownership occurring before such date, see 26 CFR 1.921-1T(b)(6) (Revised as of April 1, 1985). If (A) the voting power of the principal shareholder in the FSC or DISC is reduced by 10 or more percentage points, and (B) immediately after such reduction such shareholder is no longer a principal shareholder of the FSC or DISC, the FSC or DISC shall change its annual accounting period to that of the new principal shareholder in the manner prescribed by section 442 and the regulations thereunder. The short period required for the FSC or DISC to effect such change shall end on the last day of the new principal shareholder's taxable year within which the change in ownership occurs. For example, assume that in 1985 a FSC or DISC adopts the calendar year to conform to the annual accounting period of its sole shareholder, and that on March 1, 1987, a new shareholder having a fiscal year ending on June 30 becomes the principal shareholder by acquiring 60 percent of the total voting power of the stock of the FSC or DISC. The short period required to change the FSC's or DISC's annual accounting period shall be the period beginning January 1, 1987, and ending June 30, 1987. If, however, the new principal shareholder's taxable year were the fiscal year ending January 31, then the short period required for the FSC or DISC to change its annual accounting period shall be the period beginning January 1, 1988, and ending January 31, 1988. The change in the FSC's or DISC's annual accounting period shall be made in accordance with section 442 and the regulations thereunder.

* * * * *

PAR. 2. Section 1.441-1T is amended by adding paragraph (b)(1)(ii)(I) to read as follows:

**Proposed § 1.441-1T Period for computation of taxable income (temporary).** [*For Preamble, see ¶ 151,485*]

* * * * *

**(b)** * * *

*(1)* * * *

(ii) * * *

(I) In the case of any controlled foreign corporation or foreign personal holding company that is a specified foreign corporation, within the meaning of section 898 and § 1.898-2, the applicable rules are contained in section 898 and the regulations under that section.

* * * * *

**§ 1.441-2 Election of taxable year consisting of 52-53 weeks.**

***Caution:*** The Treasury has not yet amended Reg § 1.441-2 to reflect changes made by P.L. 108-357.

**(a) In general.** *(1) Election.* An eligible taxpayer may elect to compute its taxable income on the basis of a fiscal year that—

(i) Varies from 52 to 53 weeks;

(ii) Ends always on the same day of the week; and

(iii) Ends always on—

(A) Whatever date this same day of the week last occurs in a calendar month; or

(B) Whatever date this same day of the week falls that is the nearest to the last day of the calendar month.

*(2) Effect.* In the case of a taxable year described in paragraph (a)(1)(iii)(A) of this section, the year will always end within the month and may end on the last day of the month, or as many as six days before the end of the month. In the case of a taxable year described in paragraph (a)(1)(iii)(B) of this section, the year may end on the last day of the month, or as many as three days before or three days after the last day of the month.

*(3) Eligible taxpayer.* A taxpayer is eligible to elect a 52-53-week taxable year if such fiscal year would otherwise satisfy the requirements of section 441 and the regulations thereunder. For example, a taxpayer that is required to use a calendar year under § 1.441-1(b)(2)(i)(D) is not an eligible taxpayer.

*(4) Example.* The provisions of this paragraph (a) are illustrated by the following example:

*Example.* If the taxpayer elects a taxable year ending always on the last Saturday in November, then for the year 2001, the taxable year would end on November 24, 2001. On the other hand, if the taxpayer had elected a taxable year ending always on the Saturday nearest to the end of November, then for the year 2001, the taxable year would end on December 1, 2001.

**(b) Procedures to elect a 52-53-week taxable year.** *(1) Adoption of a 52-53-week taxable year.* (i) In general. A new eligible taxpayer elects a 52-53-week taxable year by adopting such year in accordance with § 1.441-1(c). A newly-formed partnership, S corporation or personal service corporation (PSC) may adopt a 52-53-week taxable year without the approval of the Commissioner if such year ends with reference to either the taxpayer's required taxable year (as defined in § 1.441-1(b)(2)) or the taxable year elected under section 444. See §§ 1.441-3, 1.706-1, and 1.1378-1. Similarly, a newly-formed specified foreign corporation (as defined in section 898(b)) may adopt a 52-53-week taxable year if such year ends with reference to the taxpayer's required taxable year, or, if the one-month deferral election under section 898(c)(1)(B) is made, with reference to the month immediately preceding the required taxable year. See §§ 1.1502-76(a)(1) for special rules regarding subsidiaries adopting 52-53-week taxable years.

(ii) Filing requirement. A taxpayer adopting a 52-53-week taxable year must file with its Federal income tax return for its first taxable year a statement containing the following information—

(A) The calendar month with reference to which the 52-53-week taxable year ends;

(B) The day of the week on which the 52-53-week taxable year always will end; and

(C) Whether the 52-53-week taxable year will always end on the date on which that day of the week last occurs in the calendar month, or on the date on which that day of the week falls that is nearest to the last day of that calendar month.

*(2) Change to (or from) a 52-53-week taxable year.* (i) In general. An election of a 52-53-week taxable year by an existing eligible taxpayer with an established taxable year is treated as a change in annual accounting period that requires the approval of the Commissioner in accordance with § 1.442-1. Thus, a taxpayer must obtain approval to change from its current taxable year to a 52-53-week taxable year, even if such 52-53-week taxable year ends with reference to the same calendar month. Similarly, a taxpayer must obtain approval to change from a 52-53-week taxable year, or to change from one 52-53-week taxable year to another 52-53-week taxable year. However, a taxpayer may obtain approval for 52-53-week taxable year changes automatically to the extent provided in administrative procedures published by the Commissioner. See § 1.442-1(b) for procedures for obtaining such approval.

(ii) Special rules for the short period required to effect the change. If a change to or from a 52-53-week taxable year results in a short period (within the meaning of § 1.443-1(a)) of 359 days or more, or six days or less, the tax computation under § 1.443-1(b) does not apply. If the short period is 359 days or more, it is treated as a full taxable year. If the short period is six days or less, such short period is not a separate taxable year but instead is added to and deemed a part of the following taxable year. (In the case of a change to or from a 52-53-week taxable year not involving a change of the month with reference to which the taxable year ends, the tax computation under § 1.443-1(b) does not apply because the short period will always be 359 days or more, or six days or less.) In the case of a short period which is more than six days and less than 359 days, taxable income for the short period is placed on an annual basis for purposes of § 1.443-1(b) by multiplying such income by 365 and dividing the result by the number of days in the short period. In such case, the tax for the short period is the same part of the tax computed on such income placed on an annual basis as the number of days in the short period is of 365 days (unless § 1.443-1(b)(2), relating to the alternative tax computation, applies). For an adjustment in deduction for personal exemption, see § 1.443-1(b)(1)(v).

*(3) Examples.* The following examples illustrate paragraph (b)(2)(ii) of this section:

*Example (1).* A taxpayer having a fiscal year ending April 30, obtains approval to change to a 52-53-week taxable year ending the last Saturday in April for taxable years beginning after April 30, 2001. This change involves a short period of 362 days, from May 1, 2001, to April 27, 2002, inclusive. Because the change results in a short period of 359 days or more, it is not placed on an annual basis and is treated as a full taxable year.

*Example (2).* Assume the same conditions as Example 1, except that the taxpayer changes for taxable years beginning after April 30, 2002, to a taxable year ending on the Thursday nearest to April 30. This change results in a short period of two days, May 1 to May 2, 2002. Because the short period is less than seven days, tax is not separately computed. This short period is added to and deemed part of the following 52-53-week taxable year, which would otherwise begin on May 3, 2002, and end on May 1, 2003.

**(c) Application of effective dates.** *(1) In general.* Except as provided in paragraph (c)(3) of this section, for purposes of determining the effective date (e.g., of legislative, regulatory, or administrative changes) or the applicability of any provision of the internal revenue laws that is expressed in terms of taxable years beginning, including, or ending with reference to the first or last day of a specified calendar month, a 52-53-week taxable year is deemed to begin on the first day of the calendar month nearest to the first day of the 52-53-week taxable year, and is deemed to end or close on the last day of the calendar month nearest to the last day of the 52-53-week taxable year, as the case may be. Examples of provisions of this title, the applicability of which is expressed in terms referred to in the preceding sentence, include the provisions relating to the time for filing returns and other documents, paying tax, or performing other acts, and the provisions of part II, subchapter B, chapter 6 (section 1561 and following) relating to surtax exemptions of certain controlled corporations.

*(2) Examples.* The provisions of paragraph (c)(1) of this section may be illustrated by the following examples:

*Example (1).* Assume that an income tax provision is applicable to taxable years beginning on or after January 1, 2001. For that purpose, a 52-53-week taxable year beginning on any day within the period December 26, 2000, to January 4, 2001, inclusive, is treated as beginning on January 1, 2001.

*Example (2).* Assume that an income tax provision requires that a return must be filed on or before the 15th day of the third month following the close of the taxable year. For that purpose, a 52-53-week taxable year ending on any day during the period May 25 to June 3, inclusive, is treated as ending on May 31, the last day of the month ending nearest to the last day of the taxable year, and the return, therefore, must be made on or before August 15.

*Example (3).* Assume that a revenue procedure requires the performance of an act by the taxpayer within the first 90 days of the taxable year, by the 75th day of the taxable year, or, alternately, by the last day of the taxable year. The taxpayer employs a 52-53-week taxable year that ends always on the Saturday closest to the last day of December. These requirements are not expressed in terms of taxable years beginning, including, or ending with reference to the first or last day of a specified calendar month, and are accordingly outside the scope of the rule stated in § 1.441-2(c)(1). Accordingly, the taxpayer must perform the required act by the 90th, 75th, or last day, respectively, of its taxable year.

*Example (4).* X, a corporation created on January 1, 2001, elects a 52-53-week taxable year ending on the Friday nearest the end of December. Thus, X's first taxable year begins on Monday, January 1, 2001, and ends on Friday, December 28, 2001; its next taxable year begins on Saturday, December 29, 2001, and ends on Friday, January 3, 2003; and its next taxable year begins on Saturday, January 4, 2003, and ends on Friday, January 2, 2004. For purposes of applying the provisions of Part II, subchapter B, chapter 6 of the Internal Revenue Code, X's first taxable year is deemed to end on December 31, 2001; its next taxable year is deemed to begin on January 1, 2002, and end on December 31, 2002, and its next taxable year is deemed to begin on January 1, 2003, and end on December 31, 2003. Accordingly, each such taxable year is treated as including one and only one December 31st.

*(3) Changes in tax rates.* If a change in the rate of tax is effective during a 52-53-week taxable year (other than on the first day of such year as determined under paragraph (c)(1) of this section), the tax for the 52-53-week taxable year must be computed in accordance with section 15, relating to effect of changes, and the regulations thereunder. For the purpose of the computation under section 15, the determination of the number of days in the period before the change, and in the period on and after the change, is to be made without regard to the provisions of paragraph (b)(1) of this paragraph.

*(4) Examples.* The provisions of paragraph (c)(3) of this section may be illustrated by the following examples:

*Example (1).* Assume a change in the rate of tax is effective for taxable years beginning after June 30, 2002. For a 52-53-week taxable year beginning on Friday, November 2, 2001, the tax must be computed on the basis of the old rates for the actual number of days from November 2, 2001, to June 30, 2002, inclusive, and on the basis of the new rates for the actual number of days from July 1, 2002, to Thursday, October 31, 2002, inclusive.

*Example (2).* Assume a change in the rate of tax is effective for taxable years beginning after June 30, 2001. For this purpose, a 52-53-week taxable year beginning on any of the days from June 25 to July 4, inclusive, is treated as beginning on July 1. Therefore, no computation under section 15 will be required for such year because of the change in rate.

**(d) Computation of taxable income.** The principles of section 451, relating to the taxable year for inclusion of items of gross income, and section 461, relating to the taxable year for taking deductions, generally are applicable to 52-53-week taxable years. Thus, except as otherwise provided, all items of income and deduction must be determined on the basis of a 52-53-week taxable year. However, a taxpayer may determine particular items as though the 52-53-week taxable year were a taxable year consisting of 12 calendar months, provided that practice is consistently followed by the taxpayer and clearly reflects income. For example, an allowance for depreciation or amortization may be determined on the basis of a 52-53-week taxable year, or as though the 52-53-week taxable year is a taxable year consisting of 12 calendar months, provided the taxpayer consistently follows that practice with respect to all depreciable or amortizable items.

**(e) Treatment of taxable years ending with reference to the same calendar month.** *(1) Pass-through entities.* If a pass-through entity (as defined in paragraph (e)(3)(i) of this section) or an owner of a pass-through entity (as defined in paragraph (e)(3)(ii) of this section), or both, use a 52-53-week taxable year and the taxable year of the pass-through entity and the owner end with reference to the same calendar month, then, for purposes of determining the taxable year in which items of income, gain, loss, deductions, or credits from the pass-through entity are taken into account by the owner of the pass-through, the owner's taxable year will be deemed to end on the last day of the pass-through's taxable year. Thus, if the taxable year of a partnership and a partner end with reference to the same calendar month, then for purposes of determining the taxable year in which that partner takes into account items described in section 702 and items that are deductible by the partnership (including items described in section 707(c)) and includible in the income of that partner, that partner's taxable year will be deemed to end on the last day of the partnership's taxable year. Similarly, if the taxable year of an S corporation and a shareholder end with reference to the same calendar month, then for purposes of determining the taxable year in which that shareholder takes into account items described in section 1366(a) and items that are deductible by the S corporation and includible in the income of that shareholder, that shareholder's taxable year will be deemed to end on the last day of the S corporation's taxable year.

*(2) Personal service corporations and employee-owners.* If the taxable year of a PSC (within the meaning of § 1.441-3(c)) and an employee-owner (within the meaning of § 1.441-3(g)) end with reference to the same calendar month, then for purposes of determining the taxable year in which an employee-owner takes into account items that are deductible by the PSC and includible in the income of the employee-owner, the employee-owner's taxable year will be deemed to end on the last day of the PSC's taxable year.

*(3) Definitions.* (i) Pass-through entity. For purposes of this section, a pass-through entity means a partnership, S corporation, trust, estate, closely-held real estate investment trust (within the meaning of section 6655(e)(5)(B)), common trust fund (within the meaning of section 584(i)), controlled foreign corporation (within the meaning of section 957), foreign personal holding company (within the meaning of section 552), or passive foreign investment company that is a qualified electing fund (within the meaning of section 1295).

(ii) Owner of a pass-through entity. For purposes of this section, an owner of a pass-through entity generally means a taxpayer that owns an interest in, or stock of, a pass-through entity. For example, an owner of a pass-through entity includes a partner in a partnership, a shareholder of an S corporation, a beneficiary of a trust or an estate, an owner of a closely-held real estate investment trust (within the meaning of section 6655(e)(5)(A)), a participant in a common trust fund, a U.S. shareholder (as defined in section 951(b)) of a controlled foreign corporation, a U.S. shareholder (as defined in section 551(a)) of a foreign personal holding company, or a U.S. person that holds stock in a passive foreign investment company that is a qualified electing fund with respect to that shareholder.

*(4) Examples.* The provisions of paragraph (e)(2) of this section may be illustrated by the following examples:

*Example (1).* ABC Partnership uses a 52-53-week taxable year that ends on the Wednesday nearest to December 31, and its partners, A, B, and C, are individual calendar year taxpayers. Assume that, for ABC's taxable year ending January 3, 2001, each partner's distributive share of ABC's taxable income is $10,000. Under section 706(a) and paragraph (e)(1) of this section, for the taxable year ending December 31, 2000, A, B, and C each must include $10,000 in income with respect to the ABC year ending January 3, 2001. Similarly, if ABC makes a guaranteed payment to A on January 2, 2001, A must include the payment in income for A's taxable year ending December 31, 2000.

*Example (2).* X, a PSC, uses a 52-53-week taxable year that ends on the Wednesday nearest to December 31, and all of the employee-owners of X are individual calendar year taxpayers. Assume that, for its taxable year ending January 3, 2001, X pays a bonus of $10,000 to each employee-owner on January 2, 2001. Under paragraph (e)(2) of this section, each employee-owner must include its bonus in income for the taxable year ending December 31, 2000.

*(5) Transition rule.* In the case of an owner of a pass-through entity (other than the owner of a partnership or S corporation) that is required by this paragraph (e) to include in income for its first taxable year ending on or after May 17, 2002 amounts attributable to two taxable years of a pass-

through entity, the amount that otherwise would be required to be included in income for such first taxable year by reason of this paragraph (e) should be included in income ratably over the four-taxable-year period beginning with such first taxable year under principles similar to § 1.702-3T, unless the owner of the pass-through entity elects to include all such income in its first taxable year ending on or after May 17, 2002.

T.D. 8996, 5/16/2002.

**§ 1.441-3 Taxable year of a personal service corporation.**

**(a) Taxable year.** *(1) Required taxable year.* Except as provided in paragraph (a)(2) of this section, the taxable year of a personal service corporation (PSC) (as defined in paragraph (c) of this section) must be the calendar year.

*(2) Exceptions.* A PSC may have a taxable year other than its required taxable year (i.e., a fiscal year) if it makes an election under section 444, elects to use a 52-53-week taxable year that ends with reference to the calendar year or a taxable year elected under section 444, or establishes a business purpose for such fiscal year and obtains the approval of the Commissioner under section 442.

**(b) Adoption, change, or retention of taxable year.** *(1) Adoption of taxable year.* A PSC may adopt, in accordance with § 1.441-1(c), the calendar year, a taxable year elected under section 444, or a 52-53-week taxable year ending with reference to the calendar year or a taxable year elected under section 444 without the approval of the Commissioner. See § 1.441-1. A PSC that wants to adopt any other taxable year must establish a business purpose and obtain the approval of the Commissioner under section 442.

*(2) Change in taxable year.* A PSC that wants to change its taxable year must obtain the approval of the Commissioner under section 442 or make an election under section 444. However, a PSC may obtain automatic approval for certain changes, including a change to the calendar year or to a 52-53-week taxable year ending with reference to the calendar year, pursuant to administrative procedures published by the Commissioner.

*(3) Retention of taxable year.* In certain cases, a PSC will be required to change its taxable year unless it obtains the approval of the Commissioner under section 442, or makes an election under section 444, to retain its current taxable year. For example, a corporation using a June 30 fiscal year that becomes a PSC and, as a result, is required to use the calendar year must obtain the approval of the Commissioner to retain its current fiscal year.

*(4) Procedures for obtaining approval or making a section 444 election.* See § 1.442-1(b) for procedures to obtain the approval of the Commissioner (automatically or otherwise) to adopt, change, or retain a taxable year. See §§ 1.444-1T and 1.444-2T for qualifications, and 1.444-3T for procedures, for making an election under section 444.

*(5) Examples.* The provisions of paragraph (b)(4) of this section may be illustrated by the following examples:

*Example (1).* X, whose taxable year ends on January 31, 2001, becomes a PSC for its taxable year beginning February 1, 2001, and does not obtain the approval of the Commissioner for using a fiscal year. Thus, for taxable years ending before February 1, 2001, this section does not apply with respect to X. For its taxable year beginning on February 1, 2001, however, X will be required to comply with paragraph (a) of this section. Thus, unless X obtains approval of the Commissioner to use a January 31 taxable year, or makes a section 444 election, X will be required to change its taxable year to the calendar year under paragraph (b) of this section by using a short taxable year that begins on February 1, 2001, and ends on December 31, 2001. Under paragraph (b)(1) of this section, X may obtain automatic approval to change its taxable year to a calendar year. See § 1.442-1(b).

*Example (2).* Assume the same facts as in Example 1, except that X desires to change to a 52-53-week taxable year ending with reference to the month of December. Under paragraph (b)(1) of this section X may obtain automatic approval to make the change. See § 1.442-1(b).

**(c) Personal service corporation defined.** *(1) In general.* For purposes of this section and section 442, a taxpayer is a PSC for a taxable year only if—

(i) The taxpayer is a C corporation (as defined in section 1361(a)(2)) for the taxable year;

(ii) The principal activity of the taxpayer during the testing period is the performance of personal services;

(iii) During the testing period, those services are substantially performed by employee-owners (as defined in paragraph (g) of this section); and

(iv) Employee-owners own (as determined under the attribution rules of section 318, except that the language "any" applies instead of "50 percent" in section 318(a)(2)(C)) more than 10 percent of the fair market value of the outstanding stock in the taxpayer on the last day of the testing period.

*(2) Testing period.* (i) In general. Except as otherwise provided in paragraph (c)(2)(ii) of this section, the testing period for any taxable year is the immediately preceding taxable year.

(ii) New corporations. The testing period for a taxpayer's first taxable year is the period beginning on the first day of that taxable year and ending on the earlier of—

(A) The last day of that taxable year; or

(B) The last day of the calendar year in which that taxable year begins.

*(3) Examples.* The provisions of paragraph (c)(2)(ii) of this section may be illustrated by the following examples:

*Example (1).* Corporation A's first taxable year begins on June 1, 2001, and A desires to use a September 30 taxable year. However, if A is a personal service corporation, it must obtain the Commissioner's approval to use a September 30 taxable year. Pursuant to paragraph (c)(2)(ii) of this section, A's testing period for its first taxable year beginning June 1, 2001, is the period June 1, 2001 through September 30, 2001. Thus, if, based upon such testing period, A is a personal service corporation, A must obtain the Commissioner's permission to use a September 30 taxable year.

*Example (2).* The facts are the same as in Example 1, except that A desires to use a March 31 taxable year. Pursuant to paragraph (c)(2)(ii) of this section, A's testing period for its first taxable year beginning June 1, 2001, is the period June 1, 2001, through December 31, 2001. Thus, if, based upon such testing period, A is a personal service corporation, A must obtain the Commissioner's permission to use a March 31 taxable year.

**(d) Performance of personal services.** *(1) Activities described in section 448(d)(2)(A).* For purposes of this section, any activity of the taxpayer described in section 448(d)(2)(A) or the regulations thereunder will be treated as the performance of personal services. Therefore, any activity of the taxpayer that involves the performance of services in the fields of health, law, engineering, architecture, accounting, actuarial science, performing arts, or consulting (as such fields are defined in § 1.448-1T) will be treated as the performance of personal services for purposes of this section.

*(2) Activities not described in section 448(d)(2)(A).* For purposes of this section, any activity of the taxpayer not described in section 448(d)(2)(A) or the regulations thereunder will not be treated as the performance of personal services.

**(e) Principal activity.** *(1) General rule.* For purposes of this section, the principal activity of a corporation for any testing period will be the performance of personal services if the cost of the corporation's compensation (the compensation cost) for such testing period that is attributable to its activities that are treated as the performance of personal services within the meaning of paragraph (d) of this section (i.e., the total compensation for personal service activities) exceeds 50 percent of the corporation's total compensation cost for such testing period.

*(2) Compensation cost.* (i) Amounts included. For purposes of this section, the compensation cost of a corporation for a taxable year is equal to the sum of the following amounts allowable as a deduction, allocated to a long-term contract, or otherwise chargeable to a capital account by the corporation during such taxable year—

(A) Wages and salaries; and

(B) Any other amounts, attributable to services performed for or on behalf of the corporation by a person who is an employee of the corporation (including an owner of the corporation who is treated as an employee under paragraph (g)(2) of this section) during the testing period. Such amounts include, but are not limited to, amounts attributable to deferred compensation, commissions, bonuses, compensation includible in income under section 83, compensation for services based on a percentage of profits, and the cost of providing fringe benefits that are includible in income.

(ii) Amounts excluded. Notwithstanding paragraph (e)(2)(i) of this section, compensation cost does not include amounts attributable to a plan qualified under section 401(a) or 403(a), or to a simplified employee pension plan defined in section 408(k).

*(3) Attribution of compensation cost to personal service activity.* (i) Employees involved only in the performance of personal services. The compensation cost for employees involved only in the performance of activities that are treated as personal services under paragraph (d) of this section, or employees involved only in supporting the work of such employees, are considered to be attributable to the corporation's personal service activity.

(ii) Employees involved only in activities that are not treated as the performance of personal services. The compensation cost for employees involved only in the performance of activities that are not treated as personal services under paragraph (d) of this section, or for employees involved only in supporting the work of such employees, are not considered to be attributable to the corporation's personal service activity.

(iii) Other employees. The compensation cost for any employee who is not described in either paragraph (e)(3)(i) or (ii) of this section (a mixed-activity employee) is allocated as follows—

(A) Compensation cost attributable to personal service activity. That portion of the compensation cost for a mixed activity employee that is attributable to the corporation's personal service activity equals the compensation cost for that employee multiplied by the percentage of the total time worked for the corporation by that employee during the year that is attributable to activities of the corporation that are treated as the performance of personal services under paragraph (d) of this section. That percentage is to be determined by the taxpayer in any reasonable and consistent manner. Time logs are not required unless maintained for other purposes;

(B) Compensation cost not attributable to personal service activity. That portion of the compensation cost for a mixed activity employee that is not considered to be attributable to the corporation's personal service activity is the compensation cost for that employee less the amount determined in paragraph (e)(3)(iii)(A) of this section.

**(f) Services substantially performed by employee-owners.** *(1) General rule.* Personal services are substantially performed during the testing period by employee-owners of the corporation if more than 20 percent of the corporation's compensation cost for that period attributable to its activities that are treated as the performance of personal services within the meaning of paragraph (d) of this section (i.e., the total compensation for personal service activities) is attributable to personal services performed by employee-owners.

*(2) Compensation cost attributable to personal services.* For purposes of paragraph (f)(1) of this section—

(i) The corporation's compensation cost attributable to its activities that are treated as the performance of personal services is determined under paragraph (e)(3) of this section; and

(ii) The portion of the amount determined under paragraph (f)(2)(i) of this section that is attributable to personal services performed by employee-owners is to be determined by the taxpayer in any reasonable and consistent manner.

*(3) Examples.* The provisions of this paragraph (f) may be illustrated by the following examples:

*Example (1).* For its taxable year beginning February 1, 2001, Corp A's testing period is the taxable year ending January 31, 2000. During that testing period, A's only activity was the performance of personal services. The total compensation cost of A (including compensation cost attributable to employee-owners) for the testing period was $1,000,000. The total compensation cost attributable to employee-owners of A for the testing period was $210,000. Pursuant to paragraph (f)(1) of this section, the employee-owners of A substantially performed the personal services of A during the testing period because the compensation cost of A's employee-owners was more than 20 percent of the total compensation cost for all of A's employees (including employee-owners).

*Example (2).* Corp B has the same facts as corporation A in Example 1, except that during the taxable year ending January 31, 2001, B also participated in an activity that would not be characterized as the performance of personal services under this section. The total compensation cost of B (including compensation cost attributable to employee-owners) for the testing period was $1,500,000 ($1,000,000 attributable to B's personal service activity and $500,000 attributable to B's other activity). The total compensation cost attributable to employee-owners of B for the testing period was $250,000 ($210,000 attributable to B's personal service activity and $40,000 attributable to B's other activity). Pursuant to paragraph (f)(1) of this section, the employee-owners of B substantially performed the personal services of B during the testing period because more than 20 percent of

B's compensation cost during the testing period attributable to its personal service activities was attributable to personal services performed by employee-owners ($210,000).

**(g) Employee-owner defined.** *(1) General rule.* For purposes of this section, a person is an employee-owner of a corporation for a testing period if—

(i) The person is an employee of the corporation on any day of the testing period; and

(ii) The person owns any outstanding stock of the corporation on any day of the testing period.

*(2) Special rule for independent contractors who are owners.* Any person who is an owner of the corporation within the meaning of paragraph (g)(1)(ii) of this section and who performs personal services for, or on behalf of, the corporation is treated as an employee for purposes of this section, even if the legal form of that person's relationship to the corporation is such that the person would be considered an independent contractor for other purposes.

**(h) Special rules for affiliated groups filing consolidated returns.** *(1) In general.* For purposes of applying this section to the members of an affiliated group of corporations filing a consolidated return for the taxable year—

(i) The members of the affiliated group are treated as a single corporation;

(ii) The employees of the members of the affiliated group are treated as employees of such single corporation; and

(iii) All of the stock of the members of the affiliated group that is not owned by any other member of the affiliated group is treated as the outstanding stock of that corporation.

*(2) Examples.* The provisions of this paragraph (h) may be illustrated by the following examples:

*Example (1).* The affiliated group AB, consisting of corporation A and its wholly owned subsidiary B, filed a consolidated Federal income tax return for the taxable year ending January 31, 2001, and AB is attempting to determine whether it is affected by this section for its taxable year beginning February 1, 2001. During the testing period (i.e., the taxable year ending January 31, 2001), A did not perform personal services. However, B's only activity was the performance of personal services. On the last day of the testing period, employees of A did not own any stock in A. However, some of B's employees own stock in A. In the aggregate, B's employees own 9 percent of A's stock on the last day of the testing period. Pursuant to paragraph (h)(1) of this section, this section is effectively applied on a consolidated basis to members of an affiliated group filing a consolidated Federal income tax return. Because the only employee-owners of AB are the employees of B, and because B's employees do not own more than 10 percent of AB on the last day of the testing period, AB is not a PSC subject to the provisions of this section. Thus, AB is not required to determine on a consolidated basis whether, during the testing period, its principal activity is the providing of personal services, or the personal services are substantially performed by employee-owners.

*Example (2).* The facts are the same as in Example 1, except that on the last day of the testing period A owns only 80 percent of B. The remaining 20 percent of B is owned by employees of B. The fair market value of A, including its 80 percent interest in B, as of the last day of the testing period, is $1,000,000. In addition, the fair market value of the 20 percent interest in B owned by B's employees is $50,000 as of the last day of the testing period. Pursuant to paragraphs (c)(1)(iv) and (h)(1) of this section, AB must determine whether the employee-owners of A and B (i.e., B's employees) own more than 10 percent of the fair market value of A and B as of the last day of the testing period. Because the $140,000 [($1,000,000 × .09) + $50,000] fair market value of the stock held by B's employees is greater than 10 percent of the aggregate fair market value of A and B as of the last day of the testing period, or $105,000 [$1,000,000 + $50,000 × .10], AB may be subject to this section if, on a consolidated basis during the testing period, the principal activity of AB is the performance of personal services and the personal services are substantially performed by employee-owners.

T.D. 8996, 5/16/2002.

**§ 1.441-4 Effective date.**

Sections 1.441-0 through 1.441-3 are applicable for taxable years ending on or after May 17, 2002.

T.D. 8996, 5/16/2002.

**§ 1.442-1 Change of annual accounting period.**

**(a) Approval of the Commissioner.** A taxpayer that has adopted an annual accounting period (as defined in § 1.441-1(b)(3)) as its taxable year generally must continue to use that annual accounting period in computing its taxable income and for making its Federal income tax returns. If the taxpayer wants to change its annual accounting period and use a new taxable year, it must obtain the approval of the Commissioner, unless it is otherwise authorized to change without the approval of the Commissioner under either the Internal Revenue Code (e.g., section 444 and section 859) or the regulations thereunder (e.g., paragraph (c) of this section). In addition, as described in §§ 1.441-1(c) and (d), a partnership, S corporation, electing S corporation, or personal service corporation (PSC) generally is required to secure the approval of the Commissioner to adopt or retain an annual accounting period other than its required taxable year. The manner of obtaining approval from the Commissioner to adopt, change, or retain an annual accounting period is provided in paragraph (b) of this section. However, special rules for obtaining approval may be provided in other sections.

**(b) Obtaining approval.** *(1) Time and manner for requesting approval.* In order to secure the approval of the Commissioner to adopt, change, or retain an annual accounting period, a taxpayer must file an application, generally on Form 1128, "Application To Adopt, Change, or Retain a Tax Year," with the Commissioner within such time and in such manner as is provided in administrative procedures published by the Commissioner.

*(2) General requirements for approval.* An adoption, change, or retention in annual accounting period will be approved where the taxpayer establishes a business purpose for the requested annual accounting period and agrees to the Commissioner's prescribed terms, conditions, and adjustments for effecting the adoption, change, or retention. In determining whether a taxpayer has established a business purpose and which terms, conditions, and adjustments will be required, consideration will be given to all the facts and circumstances relating to the adoption, change, or retention, including the tax consequences resulting therefrom. Generally, the requirement of a business purpose will be satisfied, and adjustments to neutralize any tax consequences will not be required, if the requested annual accounting period coincides with the taxpayer's required taxable year (as defined in

§ 1.441-1(b)(2)), ownership taxable year, or natural business year. In the case of a partnership, S corporation, electing S corporation, or PSC, deferral of income to partners, shareholders, or employee-owners will not be treated as a business purpose.

*(3) Administrative procedures.* The Commissioner will prescribe administrative procedures under which a taxpayer may be permitted to adopt, change, or retain an annual accounting period. These administrative procedures will describe the business purpose requirements (including an ownership taxable year and a natural business year) and the terms, conditions, and adjustments necessary to obtain approval. Such terms, conditions, and adjustments may include adjustments necessary to neutralize the tax effects of a substantial distortion of income that would otherwise result from the requested annual accounting period including: a deferral of a substantial portion of the taxpayer's income, or shifting of a substantial portion of deductions, from one taxable year to another; a similar deferral or shifting in the case of any other person, such as a beneficiary in an estate; the creation of a short period in which there is a substantial net operating loss, capital loss, or credit (including a general business credit); or the creation of a short period in which there is a substantial amount of income to offset an expiring net operating loss, capital loss, or credit. See, for example, Rev. Proc. 2002-39, 2002-22 I.R.B., procedures for obtaining the Commissioner's prior approval of an adoption, change, or retention in annual accounting period through application to the national office; Rev. Proc. 2002-37, 2002-22 I.R.B., automatic approval procedures for certain corporations; Rev. Proc. 2002-38, 2002-22 I.R.B., automatic approval procedures for partnerships, S corporations, electing S corporations, and PSCs; and Rev. Proc. 66-50, 1966-2 C.B. 1260, automatic approval procedures for individuals. For availability of Revenue Procedures and Notices, see § 601.601(d)(2) of this chapter.

*(4) Taxpayers to whom section 441(g) applies.* If section 441(g) and § 1.441-1(b)(1)(iv) apply to a taxpayer, the adoption of a fiscal year is treated as a change in the taxpayer's annual accounting period under section 442. Therefore, that fiscal year can become the taxpayer's taxable year only with the approval of the Commissioner. In addition to any other terms and conditions that may apply to such a change, the taxpayer must establish and maintain books that adequately and clearly reflect income for the short period involved in the change and for the fiscal year proposed.

**(c) Special rule for change of annual accounting period by subsidiary corporation.** A subsidiary corporation that is required to change its annual accounting period under § 1.1502-76, relating to the taxable year of members of an affiliated group that file a consolidated return, does not need to obtain the approval of the Commissioner or file an application on Form 1128 with respect to that change.

**(d) Special rule for newly married couples.** *(1)* A newly married husband or wife may obtain automatic approval under this paragraph (d) to change his or her annual accounting period in order to use the annual accounting period of the other spouse so that a joint return may be filed for the first or second taxable year of that spouse ending after the date of marriage. Such automatic approval will be granted only if the newly married husband or wife adopting the annual accounting period of the other spouse files a Federal income tax return for the short period required by that change on or before the 15th day of the 4th month following the close of the short period. See section 443 and the regulations thereunder. If the due date for any such short-period return occurs before the date of marriage, the first taxable year of the other spouse ending after the date of marriage cannot be adopted under this paragraph (d). The short-period return must contain a statement at the top of page one of the return that it is filed under the authority of this paragraph (d). The newly married husband or wife need not file Form 1128 with respect to a change described in this paragraph (d). For a change of annual accounting period by a husband or wife that does not qualify under this paragraph (d), see paragraph (b) of this section.

*(2)* The provisions of this paragraph (d) may be illustrated by the following example:

*Example.* H & W marry on September 25, 2001. H is on a fiscal year ending June 30, and W is on a calendar year. H wishes to change to a calendar year in order to file joint returns with W. W's first taxable year after marriage ends on December 31, 2001. H may not change to a calendar year for 2001 since, under this paragraph (d), he would have had to file a return for the short period from July 1 to December 31, 2000, by April 16, 2001. Since the date of marriage occurred subsequent to this due date, the return could not be filed under this paragraph (d). Therefore, H cannot change to a calendar year for 2001. However, H may change to a calendar year for 2002 by filing a return under this paragraph (d) by April 15, 2002, for the short period from July 1 to December 31, 2001. If H files such a return, H and W may file a joint return for calendar year 2002 (which is W's second taxable year ending after the date of marriage).

**(e) Effective date.** The rules of this section are applicable for taxable years ending on or after May 17, 2002.

---

T.D. 6226, 2/27/57, amend T.D. 6432, 12/18/59, T.D. 6614, 10/12/62, T.D. 7235, 12/27/72, T.D. 7244, 12/29/72, T.D. 7286, 9/26/73, T.D. 7323, 9/24/74, T.D. 7470, 2/28/77, T.D. 7767, 2/3/81, T.D. 7936, 1/17/84, T.D. 8123, 2/4/87, T.D. 8996, 5/16/2002.

---

PAR. 3. Section 1.442-1 is amended by adding a sentence to the end of paragraphs (a)(1), (b)(3) and (c)(5), to read as follows:

**Proposed § 1.442-1 Change of annual accounting period.**
[*For Preamble, see ¶ 151,485*]

**(a)** * * *

*(1)* * * * For special rules relating to controlled foreign corporations and foreign personal holding companies that are specified foreign corporations, within the meaning of section 898 and § 1.898-2, see section 898 and the regulations under that section.

* * * * *

**(b)** * * *

*(3)* * * * For special rules relating to controlled foreign corporations and foreign personal holding companies that are specified foreign corporations, within the meaning of section 898 and § 1.898-2, see section 898 and the regulations under that section.

* * * * *

**(c)** * * *

*(5)* * * * For special rules relating to controlled foreign corporations and foreign personal holding companies that are specified foreign corporations, within the meaning of section 898 and § 1.898-2, see section 898 and the regulations under that section.

* * * * *

PAR. 4. Section 1.442-2T is amended by adding paragraph (a)(9) to read as follows:

**Proposed § 1.442-2T Special limitations on certain changes of annual accounting period (Temporary).** [*For Preamble, see ¶ 151,485*]

**(a)** * * *

*(9)* Any specified foreign corporation, within the meaning of section 898 and § 1.898-2, that is required to change its taxable year to the required year under section 898 and the regulations under that section.

* * * * *

**§ 1.443-1 Returns for periods of less than 12 months.**

**(a) Returns for short period.** A return for a short period, that is, for a taxable year consisting of a period of less than 12 months, shall be made under any of the following circumstances:

*(1) Change of annual accounting period.* In the case of a change in the annual accounting period of a taxpayer, a separate return must be filed for the short period of less than 12 months beginning with the day following the close of the old taxable year and ending with the day preceding the first day of the new taxable year. However, such a return is not required for a short period of six days or less, or 359 days or more, resulting from a change from or to a 52– 53-week taxable year. See section 441(f) and § 1.441-2. The computation of the tax for a short period required to effect a change of annual accounting period is described in paragraph (b) of this section. In general, a return for a short period resulting from a change of annual accounting period shall be filed and the tax paid within the time prescribed for filing a return for a taxable year of 12 months ending on the last day of the short period. For rules applicable to a subsidiary corporation which becomes a member of an affiliated group which files a consolidated return, see § 1.1502-76.

*(2) Taxpayer not in existence for entire taxable year.* If a taxpayer is not in existence for the entire taxable year, a return is required for the short period during which the taxpayer was in existence. For example, a corporation organized on August 1 and adopting the calendar year as its annual accounting period is required to file a return for the short period from August 1 to December 31, and returns for each calendar year thereafter. Similarly, a dissolving corporation which files its returns for the calendar year is required to file a return for the short period from January 1 to the date it goes out of existence. Income for the short period is not required to be annualized if the taxpayer is not in existence for the entire taxable year, and, in the case of a taxpayer other than a corporation, the deduction under section 151 for personal exemptions (or deductions in lieu thereof) need not be reduced under section 443(c). In general, the requirements with respect to the filing of returns and the payment of tax for a short period where the taxpayer has not been in existence for the entire taxable year are the same as for the filing of a return and the payment of tax for a taxable year of 12 months ending on the last day of the short period. Although the return of a decedent is a return for the short period beginning with the first day of his last taxable year and ending with the date of his death, the filing of a return and the payment of tax for a decedent may be made as though the decedent had lived throughout his last taxable year.

**(b) Computation of tax for short period on change of annual accounting period.** *(1) General rule.* (i) If a return is made for a short period resulting from a change of annual accounting period, the taxable income for the short period shall be placed on an annual basis by multiplying such income by 12 and dividing the result by the number of months in the short period. Unless section 443(b)(2) and subparagraph (2) of this paragraph apply, the tax for the short period shall be the same part of the tax computed on the annual basis as the number of months in the short period is of 12 months.

(ii) If a return is made for a short period of more than 6 days, but less than 359 days, resulting from a change from or to a 52– 53-week taxable year, the taxable income for the short period shall be annualized and the tax computed on a daily basis, as provided in section 441(f)(2)(B)(iii) and § 1.441-2(b)(2)(ii).

(iii) For method of computation of income for a short period in the case of a subsidiary corporation required to change its annual accounting period to conform to that of its parent, see § 1.1502-76(b).

(iv) An individual taxpayer making a return for a short period resulting from a change of annual accounting period is not allowed to take the standard deduction provided in section 141 in computing his taxable income for the short period. See section 142(b)(3).

(v) In computing the taxable income of a taxpayer other than a corporation for a short period (which income is to be annualized in order to determine the tax under section 443(b)(1)), the personal exemptions allowed individuals under section 151 (and any deductions allowed other taxpayers in lieu thereof, such as the deduction under section 642(b)) shall be reduced to an amount which bears the same ratio to the full amount of the exemptions as the number of months in the short period bears to 12. In the case of the taxable income for a short period resulting from a change from or to a 52– 53-week taxable year to which section 441(f)(2)(B)(iii) applies, the computation required by the preceding sentence shall be made on a daily basis, that is, the deduction for personal exemptions (or any deduction in lieu thereof) shall be reduced to an amount which bears the same ratio to the full deduction as the number of days in the short period bears to 365.

(vi) If the amount of a credit against the tax (for example, the credits allowable under section 34 (for dividends received on or before December 31, 1964), and 35 (for partially tax-exempt interest)) is dependent upon the amount of any item of income or deduction, such credit shall be computed upon the amount of the item annualized separately in accordance with the foregoing rules. The credit so computed shall be treated as a credit against the tax computed on the basis of the annualized taxable income. In any case in which a limitation on the amount of a credit is based upon taxable income, taxable income shall mean the taxable income computed on the annualized basis.

(vii) The provisions of this subparagraph may be illustrated by the following examples:

*Example (1).* A taxpayer with one dependent who has been granted permission under section 442 to change his annual accounting period files a return for the short period of 10 months ending October 31, 1956. He has income and deductions as follows:

**Income**

| | | |
|---|---|---|
| Interest income | | $10,000.00 |
| Partially tax-exempt interest with respect to which a credit is allowable under section 35 | | 500.00 |
| Dividends to which sections 34 and 116 are applicable | | 750.00 |
| | | 11,250.00 |

**Deductions**

| | | | |
|---|---|---|---|
| Real estate taxes | | | 200.00 |
| 2 personal exemptions at $600 on an annual basis | | | 1,200.00 |
| The tax for the 10-month period is computed as follows: | | | |
| Total income as above | | | $11,250.00 |
| Less: | | | |
| Exclusion for dividends received | | $ 50.00 | |
| 2 personal exemptions ($1,200 × 10/12) | | 1,000.00 | |
| Real estate taxes | | 200.00 | |
| | | | 1,250.00 |
| Taxable income for 10-month period before annualizing | | | 10,000.00 |
| Taxable income annualized (10,000 × 12/10) | | | 12,000.00 |
| Tax on $12,000 before credits | | | 3,400.00 |
| Deduct credits: | | | |
| Dividends received for 10-month period | $750.00 | | |
| Less: Excluded portion | 50.00 | | |
| Included in gross income | 700.00 | | |
| Dividend income annualized ($700 × 12/10) | 840.00 | | |
| Credit (4 percent of $840) | | $ 33.60 | |
| Partially tax-exempt interest included in gross income for 10-month period | 500.00 | | |
| Partially tax-exempt interest (annualized) ($500 × 12/10) | 600.00 | | |
| Credit (3 percent of $600) | | 18.00 | |
| | | | 51.60 |
| Tax on $12,000 (after credits) | | | 3,348.40 |
| Tax for 10-month period ($3,348.40 × 10/12) | | | 2,790.33 |

*Example (2).* The X Corporation makes a return for the one-month period ending September 30, 1956, because of a change in annual accounting period permitted under section 442. Income and expenses for the short period are as follows:

| | | |
|---|---|---|
| Gross operating income | | $126,000 |
| Business expenses | | 130,000 |
| Net loss from operations | | (4,000) |
| Dividends received from taxable domestic corporations | | $ 30,000 |
| Gross income for short period before annualizing | | 26,000 |
| Dividends received deduction (85 percent of $30,000, but not in excess of 85 percent of $26,000) | | 22,100 |
| Taxable income for short period before annualizing | | 3,900 |
| Taxable income annualized ($3,900 × 12) | | $ 46,800 |
| Tax on annual basis: | | |
| $46,800 at 52 percent | $24,336 | |
| Less surtax exemption | 5,500 | |
| | | 18,836 |
| Tax for 1-month period ($18,836 × 1/12) | | 1,570 |

*Example (3).* The Y Corporation makes a return for the six-month period ending June 30, 1957, because of a change in annual accounting period permitted under section 442. Income for the short period is as follows:

| | | |
|---|---|---|
| Taxable income exclusive of net long-term capital gain | | $ 40,000 |
| Net long-term capital gain | | 10,000 |
| Taxable income for short period before annualizing | | 50,000 |
| Taxable income annualized ($50,000 × 12/6) | | 100,000 |

**Regular Tax Computation**

| | | |
|---|---|---|
| Taxable income annualized | | 100,000 |
| Tax on annual basis: | | |
| $100,000 at 52 percent | $52,000 | |
| Less surtax exemption | 5,500 | |
| | | 46,500 |
| Tax for 6-month period ($46,500 × 6/12) | | 23,250 |

**Alternative Tax Computation**

| | |
|---|---|
| Taxable income annualized | $100,000 |
| Less annualized capital gain ($10,000 × 12/6) | 20,000 |
| Annualized taxable income subject to partial tax | 80,000 |

**Partial Tax On Annual Basis**

| | | |
|---|---|---|
| $80,000 at 52 percent | $41,600 | |
| Less surtax exemption | 5,500 | |
| | | 36,100 |
| 25 percent of annualized capital gain ($20,000) | | 5,000 |

| | |
|---|---|
| Alternative tax on annual basis .......... | 41,100 |
| Alternative tax for 6-month period ($41,100 × 6/12) .................................... | 20,550 |

Since the alternative tax of $20,550 is less than the tax computed in the regular manner ($23,250), the corporation's tax for the 6-month short period is $20,550.

*(2) Exception: computation based on 12-month period.* (i) A taxpayer whose tax would otherwise be computed under section 443(b)(1) (or section 441(f)(2)(B)(iii) in the case of certain changes from or to a 52–53-week taxable year) for the short period resulting from a change of annual accounting period may apply to the district director to have his tax computed under the provisions of section 443(b)(2) and this subparagraph. If such application is made, as provided in subdivision (v) of this subparagraph, and if the taxpayer establishes the amount of his taxable income for the 12-month period described in subdivision (ii) of this subparagraph, then the tax for the short period shall be the greater of the following—

(a) An amount which bears the same ratio to the tax computed on the taxable income which the taxpayer has established for the 12-month period as the taxable income computed on the basis of the short period bears to the taxable income for such 12-month period; or

(b) The tax computed on the taxable income for the short period without placing the taxable income on an annual basis.

However, if the tax computed under section 443(b)(2) and this subparagraph is not less than the tax for the short period computed under section 443(b)(1) (or section 441(f)(2)(B)(iii) in the case of certain changes from or to a 52–53-week taxable year), then section 443(b)(2) and this subparagraph do not apply.

(ii) The term "12-month period" referred to in subdivision (i) of this subparagraph means the 12-month period beginning on the first day of the short period. However, if the taxpayer is not in existence at the end of such 12-month period, or if the taxpayer is a corporation which has disposed of substantially all of its assets before the end of such 12-month period, the term "12-month period" means the 12-month period ending at the close of the last day of the short period. For the purposes of the preceding sentence, a corporation which has ceased business and distributed so much of the assets used in its business that it cannot resume its customary operations with the remaining assets, will be considered to have disposed of substantially all of its assets. In the case of a change from a 52–53-week taxable year, the term "12-month period" means the period of 52 or 53 weeks (depending on the taxpayer's 52–53-week taxable year) beginning on the first day of the short period.

(iii) (a) The taxable income for the 12-month period is computed under the same provisions of law as are applicable to the short period and is computed as if the 12-month period were an actual annual accounting period of the taxpayer. All items which fall in such 12-month period must be included even if they are extraordinary in amount or of an unusual nature. If the taxpayer is a member of a partnership, his taxable income for the 12-month period shall include his distributive share of partnership income for any taxable year of the partnership ending within or with such 12-month period, but no amount shall be included with respect to a taxable year of the partnership ending before or after such 12-month period. If any other item partially applicable to such 12-month period can be determined only at the end of a taxable year which includes only part of the 12-month period, the taxpayer, subject to review by the Commissioner, shall apportion such item to the 12-month period in such manner as will most clearly reflect income for the 12-month period.

(b) In the case of a taxpayer permitted or required to use inventories, the cost of goods sold during a part of the 12-month period included in a taxable year shall be considered, unless a more exact determination is available, as such part of the cost of goods sold during the entire taxable year as the gross receipts from sales for such part of the 12-month period is of the gross receipts from sales for the entire taxable year. For example, the 12-month period of a corporation engaged in the sale of merchandise, which has a short period from January 1, 1956, to September 30, 1956, is the calendar year 1956. The three-month period, October 1, 1956, to December 31, 1956, is part of the taxpayer's taxable year ending September 30, 1957. The cost of goods sold during the three-month period, October 1, 1956, to December 31, 1956, is such part of the cost of goods sold during the entire fiscal year ending September 30, 1957, as the gross receipts from sales for such three-month period are of the gross receipts from sales for the entire fiscal year.

(c) The Commissioner may, in granting permission to a taxpayer to change his annual accounting period, require, as a condition to permitting the change, that the taxpayer must take a closing inventory upon the last day of the 12-month period if he wishes to obtain the benefits of section 443(b)(2). Such closing inventory will be used only for the purposes of section 443(b)(2), and the taxpayer will not be required to use such inventory in computing the taxable income for the taxable year in which such inventory is taken.

(iv) The provisions of this subparagraph may be illustrated by the following examples:

*Example (1).* The taxpayer in example (1) under paragraph (b)(1)(vii) of this section establishes his taxable income for the 12-month period from January 1, 1956, to December 31, 1956. The taxpayer has a short period of 10 months, from January 1, 1956, to October 31, 1956. The taxpayer files an application in accordance with subdivision (v) of this subparagraph to compute his tax under section 443(b)(2). The taxpayer's income and deductions for the 12-month period, as so established, follow:

**Income**

| | |
|---|---|
| Interest income .............................. | $11,000 |
| Partially tax-exempt interest with respect to which a credit is allowable under section 35 ......... | 600 |
| Dividends to which sections 34 and 116 are applicable .............................. | 850 |
| | 12,450 |

**Deductions**

| | |
|---|---|
| Real estate taxes .............................. | 200 |
| 2 personal exemptions at $600 ................ | 1,200 |

**Tax Computation For Short Period Under Section 443(b)(2)(A)(i)**

| | | |
|---|---|---|
| Total income as above .............................. | | $12,450 |
| Less: | | |
| Exclusion for dividends received ...... | $ 50 | |
| Personal exemptions .................. | 1,200 | |
| Deduction for taxes ................. | 200 | |
| | | 1,450 |
| Taxable income for 12-month period ...... | | 11,000 |

| | | |
|---|---|---|
| Tax before credits | | 3,020 |
| Credit for partially tax-exempt interest (3 percent of $600) | $ 18 | |
| Credit for dividends received (4 percent of ($850 – 50)) | 32 | |
| | | 50 |
| Tax under section 443(b)(2)(A)(i) for 12-month period | | 2,970 |
| Taxable income for 10-month short period from example (1) of paragraph (b)(1)(vii) of this section before annualizing | | 10,000 |
| Tax for short period under section 443(b)(2)(A)(i) ($2,970 × $10,000 (taxable income for short period)/$11,000 (taxable income for 12-month period)) | | 2,700 |

**Tax Computation For Short Period Under Section 443(b)(2)(A)(ii)**

| | | |
|---|---|---|
| Total income for 10-month short period | | $11,250 |
| Less: | | |
| Exclusion for dividends received | | $ 50 |
| 2 personal exemptions | | 1,200 |
| Real estate taxes | | 200 |
| | | 1,450 |
| Taxable income for short period without annualizing and without proration of personal exemptions | | 9,800 |
| Tax before credits | | 2,572 |
| Less credits: | | |
| Partially tax-exempt interest (3 percent of $500) | $ 15 | |
| Dividends received (4 percent of ($750 – 50)) | 28 | |
| | | $ 43 |
| Tax for short period under section 443(b)(2)(A)(ii) | | 2,529 |

The tax of $2,700 computed under section 443(b)(2)(A)(i) is greater than the tax of $2,529, computed under section 443(b)(2)(A)(ii), and is, therefore, the tax under section 443(b)(2). Since the tax of $2,700 (computed under section 443(b)(2)) is less than the tax of $2,790.33 (computed under section 443(b)(1)) on the annualized income of the short period (see example (1) of paragraph (b)(1)(vii) of this section), the taxpayer's tax for the 10-month short period is $2,700.

*Example (2).* Assume the same facts as in example (1) of this subdivision, except that, during the month of November 1956, the taxpayer suffered a casualty loss of $5,000. The tax computation for the short period under section 443(b)(2) would be as follows:

**Tax Computation For Short Period Under Section 443(b)(2)(A)(i)**

| | | |
|---|---|---|
| Taxable income for 12-month period from example (1) | | $11,000 |
| Less: Casualty loss | | 5,000 |
| Taxable income for 12-month period | | 6,000 |
| Tax before credits | 1,360 | |
| Credits from example (1) | 50 | |
| Tax under section 443(b)(2)(A)(i) for 12-month period | | 1,310 |
| Tax for short period ($1,310 × $10,000/$6,000) under section 443(b)(2)(A)(i) | | 2,183 |

**Tax Computation For Short Period Under Section 443(b)(2)(A)(ii)**

| | | |
|---|---|---|
| Total income for the short period | | $11,250 |
| Less: | | |
| Exclusion for dividends received | $ 50 | |
| 2 personal exemptions | 1,200 | |
| Real estate taxes | 200 | |
| | | 1,450 |
| Taxable income for short period without annualizing and without proration of personal exemptions | | 9,800 |
| Tax before credits | | 2,572 |
| Less credits: | | |
| Partially tax-exempt interest (3 percent of $500) | $ 15 | |
| Dividends received (4 percent of $750 – 50)) | 28 | |
| | | 43 |
| Tax for short period under section 443(b)(2)(A)(ii) | | 2,529 |

The tax of $2,529, computed under section 443(b)(2)(A)(ii) is greater than the tax of $2,183 computed under section 443(b)(2)(A)(i) and is, therefore, the tax under section 443(b)(2). Since this tax is less than the tax of $2,790.33, computed under section 443(b)(1) (see example (1) of paragraph (b)(1)(vii) of this section), the taxpayer's tax for the 10-month short period is $2,529.

(v) (a) A taxpayer who wishes to compute his tax for a short period resulting from a change of annual accounting period under section 443(b)(2) must make an application therefor. Except as provided in (b) of this subdivision, the taxpayer shall first file his return for the short period and compute his tax under section 443(b)(1). The application for the benefits of section 443(b)(2) shall subsequently be made in the form of a claim for credit or refund. The claim shall set forth the computation of the taxable income and the tax thereon for the 12-month period and must be filed not later than the time (including extensions) prescribed for filing the return for the taxpayer's first taxable year which ends on or after the day which is 12 months after the beginning of the short period. For example, assume that a taxpayer changes his annual accounting period from the calendar year to a fiscal year ending September 30, and files a return for the short period from January 1, 1956, to September 30, 1956. His application for the benefits of section 443(b)(2) must be filed not later than the time prescribed for filing his return for his first taxable year which ends on or after the last day of December, 1956, the twelfth month after the beginning of the short period. Thus, the taxpayer must file his application not later than the time prescribed for filing the return for his fiscal year ending September 30, 1957. If he obtains an extension of time for filing the return for such fiscal year, he may file his application during the period of such extension. If the district director determines that the taxpayer has established the amount of his taxable income for the 12-month period, any excess of the tax paid for the short period over the tax computed under section 443(b)(2) will be credited or refunded to the taxpayer in the same manner as in the case of an overpayment.

(b) If at the time the return for the short period is filed, the taxpayer is able to determine that the 12-month period ending with the close of the short period (see section

443(b)(2)(B)(ii) and subparagraph (2)(ii) of this paragraph) will be used in the computations under section 443(b)(2), then the tax on the return for the short period may be determined under the provisions of section 443(b)(2). In such case, a return covering the 12-month period shall be attached to the return for the short period as a part thereof, and the return and attachment will then be considered as an application for the benefits of section 443(b)(2).

**(c) Adjustment in deduction for personal exemption.** For adjustment in the deduction for personal exemptions in computing the tax for a short period resulting from a change of annual accounting period under section 443(b)(1) (or under section 441(f)(2)(B)(iii) in the case of certain changes from or to a 52–53-week taxable year), see paragraph (b)(1)(v) of this section.

**(d) Adjustment in exclusion for computing minimum tax for tax preferences.** *(1)* If a return is made for a short period on account of any of the reasons specified in subsection (a) of section 443, the $30,000 amount specified in section 56 (relating to minimum tax for tax preferences), modified as provided by section 58 and the regulations thereunder, shall be reduced to the amount which bears the same ratio to such specified amount as the number of days in the short period bears to 365.

*(2) Example.* The provisions of this paragraph may be illustrated by the following example:

*Example.* A taxpayer who is an unmarried individual has been granted permission under section 442 to change his annual accounting period files a return for the short period of 4 months ending April 30, 1970. The $30,000 amount specified in section 56 is reduced as follows:

120/365 × $30,000 =
$9,835.89.

**(e) Cross references.** For inapplicability of section 443(b) and paragraph (b) of this section in computing—

*(1)* Accumulated earnings tax, see section 536 and the regulations thereunder;

*(2)* Personal holding company tax, see section 546 and the regulations thereunder;

*(3)* Undistributed foreign personal holding company income, see section 557 and the regulations thereunder;

*(4)* The taxable income of a regulated investment company, see section 852(b)(2)(E) and the regulations thereunder; and

*(5)* The taxable income of a real estate investment trust, see section 857(b)(2)(C) and the regulations thereunder.

T.D. 6226, 2/27/57, amend T.D. 6598, 4/25/62, T.D. 6777, 12/15/64, T.D. 7244, 12/29/72, T.D. 7564, 9/11/78, T.D. 7575, 12/15/78, T.D. 7767, 2/3/81, T.D. 8996, 5/16/2002.

PAR. 2. In the list below, for each section indicated in the left column, remove the old language in the middle column and add the new language in the right column.

| Affected Section | Remove | Add |
|---|---|---|
| 1.46-1(p)(2)(iv) | paragraph (b)(1) of § 1.441-2 | § 1.441-2 |
| 1.48-3(d)(1)(iii) | paragraph (b)(1) of § 1.441-2 | § 1.441-2 |
| 1.280H-1T(a), last sentence | § 1.441-4T(d) | § 1.441-3(c) |
| 1.443-1(b)(1)(ii) | and paragraph (c)(5) of § 1.441-2 | and § 1.441-1(b)(2)(ii). |
| 1.444-1T(a)(1), first sentence | § 1.444-4T(d) | § 1.441-3(c) |
| 1.444-2T(a), last sentence | § 1.441-4T(d) | § 1.441-3(c) |
| 1.448-1(h)(2)(ii)(B)(1) | § 1.441-2T(b)(1) | § 1.441-2(c) |
| 1.469-1(h)(4)(ii)(D) | § 1.441-4T(f) | § 1.441-3(e) |
| 1.469-1T(g)(2)(i) | § 1.441-4T(d) | § 1.441-2 |
| 1.1561-1(c)(2) | See paragraph (b)(1) of § 1.441-2 | See § 1.441-2 |
| 1.6654-2(a), concluding text | paragraph (b) of § 1.441-2 | § 1.441-2(c) |
| 1.6655-2(a)(4), first sentence | paragraph (b) of § 1.441-2 | § 1.441-1(b) |

**Proposed § 1.443-1** [*For Preamble, see ¶ 152,177*]

• ***Caution:*** This Notice of Proposed Rulemaking was partially finalized by T.D. 8996, issued on 5/16/2002. Proposed regulation §§ 1.46-1, 1.48-3, 1.280H-1T, 1.443-1, 1.444-1T, 1.444-2T, 1.448-1, 1.469-1, 1.469-1T, 1.898-4, 1.1561-1, 1.6654-2, 1.6655-2 and 301.7701(b)-6 remains in effect.

**§ 1.444-0T Table of contents (temporary).**

This section lists the captions that appear in the temporary regulations under section 444.

(ii) Duration of section 444 election.

(3) Section 444 election not required for certain years.

(4) Required taxable year.

(5) Termination of section 444 election.

(i) In general.

(ii) Effective date of termination.

(iii) Example.

(iv) Special rule for entity that liquidates or is sold prior to making a section 444 election, required return, or required payment.

(6) Re-activating certain S elections.

(i) Certain corporations electing S status that did not make a back-up calendar year request.

(ii) Certain corporations that revoked their S status.

(iii) Procedures for re-activating an S election.

(iv) Examples.

(b) Limitation on taxable years that may be elected.

(1) General rule.

(2) Changes in taxable year.

(i) In general.

(ii) Special rule for certain existing corporations electing S status.

(iii) Deferral period of the taxable year that is being changed.

(iv) Examples.

(3) Special rule for entities retaining 1986 taxable year.

(4) Deferral period.

(i) Retentions of taxable year.

(ii) Adoptions of and changes in taxable year.

(A) In general.

(B) Special rule.

(C) Examples.

(5) Miscellaneous rules.

(i) Special rule for determining the taxable year of a corporation electing S status.

(ii) Special procedure for cases where an income tax return is superseded.

(A) In general.

(B) Procedure for superseding return.

(iii) Anti-abuse rule.

(iv) Special rules for partial months and 52-53-week taxable years.

(c) Effective date.

(d) Examples.

(1) Changes in taxable year.

(2) Special rule for entities retaining their 1986 taxable year.

*§ 1.444-2T Tiered structure (temporary).*

(a) General rule.

(b) Definition of a member of a tiered structure.

(1) In general.

(2) Deferral entity.

(i) In general.

(ii) Grantor trusts.

(3) Anti-abuse rule.

(c) De minimis rules.

(1) In general.

(2) Downstream de minimis rule.

(i) General rule.

(ii) Definition of testing period.

(iii) Definition of adjusted taxable income.

(A) Partnership.

(B) S corporation.

(C) Personal service corporation.

(iv) Special rules.

(A) Pro-forma rule.

(B) Reasonable estimates allowed.

(C) Newly formed deferral entities.

(1) Newly formed deferral entities.

(2) Newly formed partnership, S corporation, or personal service corporation desiring to make a section 444 election.

(3) Upstream de minimis rule.

(d) Date for determining the existence of a tiered structure.

(1) General rule.

(2) Special rule for taxable years beginning in 1987.

(e) Same taxable year exception.

(1) In general.

(2) Definition of tiered structure.

(i) General rule.

(ii) Special flow-through rule for downstream controlled partnerships.

(3) Determining the taxable year of a partnership or S corporation.

(4) Special rule for 52-53-week taxable years.

(5) Interaction with de minimis rules.

(i) Downstream de minimis rule.

(A) In general.

(B) Special rule for members of a tiered structure directly owned by a downstream controlled partnership.

(ii) Upstream de minimis rule.

(f) Examples.

(g) Effective date.

*§ 1.444-3T Manner and time of making section 444 election (temporary).*

(a) In general.

(b) Manner and time of making election.

(1) General rule.

(2) Special extension of time for making an election.

(3) Corporation electing to be an S corporation.

(i) In general.

(ii) Examples.

(4) Back-up section 444 election.

(i) General rule.

(ii) Procedures for making a back-up section 444 election.

(iii) Procedures for activating a back-up section 444 election.

(A) Partnerships and S corporations.

(1) In general.

T.D. 8205, 5/24/88.

### § 1.444-1T Election to use a taxable year other than the required taxable year (temporary).

**(a) General rules.** *(1) Year other than required year.* Except as otherwise provided in this section and § 1.444-2T, a partnership, S corporation, or personal service corporation (as defined in § 1.441-3(c)) may make or continue an election (a "section 444 election") to have a taxable year other than its required taxable year. See paragraph (b) of this section for limitations on the taxable year that may be elected. See § 1.444-2T for rules that generally prohibit a partnership, S corporation, or personal service corporation that is a member of a tiered structure from making or continuing a section 444 election. See § 1.444-3T for rules explaining how and when to make a section 444 election.

*(2) Effect of section 444 election.* (i) In general. A partnership or S corporation that makes or continues a section 444 election shall file returns and make payments as required by §§ 1.7519-1T and 1.7519-2T. A personal service corporation that makes or continues a section 444 election is subject to the deduction limitation of § 1.280H-1T.

(ii) Duration of section 444 election. A section 444 election shall remain in effect until the election is terminated pursuant to paragraph (a) (5) of this section.

*(3) Section 444 election not required for certain years.* A partnership, S corporation, or personal service corporation is not required to make a section 444 election to use—

(i) A taxable year for which such entity establishes a business purpose to the satisfaction of the Commissioner *(i.e.*, approved under section 4 or 6 of Rev. Proc. 87-32, 1987-28 I.R.B. 14, or any successor revenue ruling or revenue procedure), or

(ii) A taxable year that is a "grandfathered fiscal year," within the meaning of section 5.01(2) of Rev. Proc. 87-32 or any successor revenue ruling or revenue procedure.

Although a partnership, S corporation or personal service corporation qualifies to use a taxable year described in paragraph (a) (3) (i) or (ii) of this section, such entity may, if otherwise qualified, make a section 444 election to use a different taxable year. Thus, for example, assume that a personal service corporation that historically used a January 31 taxable year established to the satisfaction of the Commissioner, under section 6 of Rev. Proc. 87-32, a business purpose to use a September 30 taxable year for its taxable year beginning February 1, 1987. Pursuant to this paragraph (a) (3), such personal service corporation may use a September 30 taxable year without making a section 444 election. However, the corporation may, if otherwise qualified, make a section 444 election to use a year ending other than September 30 for its taxable year beginning February 1, 1987.

*(4) Required taxable year.* For purposes of this section, the term "required taxable year" means the taxable year determined under section 706 (b), 1378, or 441 (i) without taking into account any taxable year which is allowable either—

(i) By reason of business purpose *(i.e.*, approved under section 4 or 6 of Rev. Proc. 87-32 or any successor revenue ruling or procedure), or

(ii) As a "grandfathered fiscal year" within the meaning of section 5.01(2) of Rev. Proc. 87-32, or any successor revenue ruling or procedure.

*(5) Termination of section 444 election.* (i) In general. A section 444 election is terminated when—

(A) A partnership, S corporation, or personal service corporation changes to its required taxable year; or

(B) A partnership, S corporation, or personal service corporation liquidates (including a deemed liquidation of a partnership under § 1.708-1(b)(1)(iv)); or

(C) A partnership, S corporation, or personal service corporation willfully fails to comply with the requirements of section 7519 or 280H, whichever is applicable; or

(D) A partnership, S corporation, or personal service corporation becomes a member of a tiered structure (within the meaning of § 1.444-2T), unless it is a partnership or S corporation that meets the same taxable year exception under § 1.444-2T(e); or

(E) An S corporation's S election is terminated; or

(F) A personal service corporation ceases to be a personal service corporation.

However, if a personal service corporation, that has a section 444 election in effect, elects to be an S corporation, the S corporation may continue the section 444 election of the personal service corporation. Similarly, if an S corporation that has a section 444 election in effect terminates its S election and immediately becomes a personal service corporation, the personal service corporation may continue the section 444 election of the S corporation. If a section 444 election is terminated under this paragraph (a) (5), the partnership, S corporation, or personal service corporation may not make another section 444 election for any taxable year.

(ii) Effective date of termination. A termination of a section 444 election shall be effective—

(A) In the case of a change to the required year, on the first day of the short year caused by the change;

(B) In the case of a liquidating entity, on the date the liquidation is completed for tax purposes;

(C) In the case of willful failure to comply, on the first day of the taxable year (determined as if a section 444 election had never been made) determined in the discretion of the District Director;

(D) In the case of membership in a tiered structure, on the first day of the taxable year in which the entity is considered to be a member of a tiered structure, or such other taxable year determined in the discretion of the District Director;

(E) In the case of termination of S status, on the first day of the taxable year for which S status no longer exists;

(F) In the case of a personal service corporation that changes status, on the first day of the taxable year, for which the entity is no longer a personal service corporation.

In the case of a termination under this paragraph (a)(5) that results in a short taxable year, an income tax return is required for the short period. In order to allow the Service to process the affected income tax return in an efficient manner, a partnership, S corporation, or personal service corporation that files such a short period return should type or legibly print at the top of the first page of the income tax return for the short taxable year— "SECTION 444 ELECTION TERMINATED." In addition, a personal service corporation that changes its taxable year to the required taxable year is required to annualize its income for the short period.

(iii) Example. The provisions of paragraph (a)(5)(ii) of this section may be illustrated by the following example.

*Example.* Assume a partnership that is 100 percent owned, at all times, by calendar year individuals has historically used a June 30 taxable year. Also assume the partnership makes a valid section 444 election to retain a year ending June 30 for its taxable year beginning July 1, 1987. However, for its taxable year beginning July 1, 1988, the partnership changes to a calendar year, its required year. Based on these facts, the partnership's section 444 election is terminated on July 1, 1988, and the partnership must file a short period return for the period July 1, 1988 - December 31, 1988. Furthermore, pursuant to § 1.702-3T(a)(1), the partners in such partnership are not entitled to a 4-year spread with respect to partnership items of income and expense for the taxable year beginning July 1, 1988 and ending December 31, 1988.

(iv) Special rule for entity that liquidates or is sold prior to making a section 444 election, required return, or required payment. A partnership, S corporation, or personal service corporation that is liquidated or sold for tax purposes before a section 444 election, required return, or required payment is made for a particular year may, nevertheless, make or continue a section 444 election, if otherwise qualified. (See §§ 1.7519-2T(a)(2) and 1.7519-1T (a) (3), respectively, for a description of the required return and a definition of the term "required payment.") However, the partnership, S corporation, or personal service corporation (or a trustee or agent thereof) must comply with the requirements for making or continuing a section 444 election. Thus, if applicable, required payments must be made and a subsequent claim for refund must be made in accordance with § 1.7519-2T(a)(6). The following examples illustrate the application of this paragraph (a)(5)(iv).

*Example (1).* Assume an existing S corporation historically used a June 30 taxable year and desires to make a section 444 election for its taxable year beginning July 1, 1987. Assume further that the S corporation is liquidated for tax purposes on February 15, 1988. If otherwise qualified, the S corporation (or a trustee or agent thereof) may make a section 444 election to have a taxable year beginning July 1, 1987, and ending February 15, 1988. However, if the S corporation makes a section 444 election, it must comply with the requirements for making a section 444 election, including making required payments.

*Example (2).* The facts are the same as in example (1), except that instead of liquidating on February 15, 1988, the shareholders of the S corporation sell their stock to a corporation on February 15, 1988. Thus, the corporation's S election is terminated on February 15, 1988. If otherwise qualified, the corporation may make a section 444 election to have a taxable year beginning July 1, 1987, and ending February 14, 1988.

*Example (3).* The facts are the same as in example (2), except that the new shareholders are individuals. Furthermore, the corporation's S election is not terminated. Based on these facts, the S corporation, if otherwise qualified, may make a section 444 election to retain a year ending June 30 for its taxable year beginning July 1, 1987. Furthermore, the S corporation may, if otherwise qualified, continue its section 444 election for subsequent taxable years.

*(6) Re-activating certain S elections.* (i) Certain corporations electing S status that did not make a back-up calendar year request. If a corporation that timely filed Form 2553, Election by a Small Business Corporation, effective for its first taxable year beginning in 1987—

(A) Requested a fiscal year based on business purpose,

(B) Did not agree to use a calendar year in the event its business purpose request was denied, and

(C) Such business purpose request is denied or withdrawn, such corporation may retroactively re-activate its S election by making a valid section 444 election for its first taxable year beginning in 1987 and complying with the procedures in paragraph (a)(6)(iii) of this section.

(ii) Certain corporations that revoked their S status. If a corporation that used a fiscal year revoked its S election (pursuant to section 1362(d)(1)) for its first taxable year beginning in 1987, such corporation may retroactively re-activate its S election *(i.e.,* rescind its revocation) by making a valid section 444 election for its first taxable year beginning in 1987 and complying with the procedures in paragraph (a)(6)(iii) of this section.

(iii) Procedures for re-activating an S election. A corporation re-activating its S election pursuant to paragraph (a) (6) (i) or (ii) of this section must—

(A) Obtain the consents of all shareholders who have owned stock in the corporation since the first day of the first taxable year of the corporation beginning after December 31, 1986,

(B) Include the following statement at the top of the first page of the corporation's Form 1120S for its first taxable year beginning in 1987—"SECTION 444 ELECTION—RE-ACTIVATES S STATUS," and

(C) Include the following statement with Form 1120S—"RE-ACTIVATION CONSENTED TO BY ALL SHAREHOLDERS WHO HAVE OWNED STOCK AT ANY TIME SINCE THE FIRST DAY OF THE FIRST TAXABLE YEAR OF THIS CORPORATION BEGINNING AFTER DECEMBER 31, 1986."

(iv) Examples. The provisions of this paragraph (a) (6) may be illustrated by the following examples.

*Example (1).* Assume a corporation historically used a June 30 taxable year and such corporation timely filed Form 2553, Election by a Small Business Corporation, to be effective for its taxable year beginning July 1, 1987. On its Form 2553, the corporation requested permission to retain its June 30 taxable year based on business purpose. However, the corporation did not agree to use a calendar year in the event its business purpose request was denied. On April 1, 1988, the Internal Revenue Service notified the corporation that its business purpose request was denied and therefore the corporation's S election was not effective. Pursuant to paragraph (a)(6)(i) of this section, the corporation may re-activate its S election by making a valid section 444 election and complying with the procedures in paragraph (a)(6)(iii) of this section.

*Example (2).* The facts are the same as in example (1), except that as of Jul 26 1988 the Internal Revenue Service has not yet determined whether the corporation has a valid business purpose to retain a June 30 taxable year. Based on these facts, the corporation may, if otherwise qualified, make a back-up section 444 election as provided in § 1.444-3T(b)(4). If the corporation's business purpose request is subsequently denied, the corporation should follow the procedures in § 1.444-3T (b)(4)(iii) for activating a back-up section 444 election rather than the procedures provided in this paragraph (a)(6) for re-activating an S election.

*Example (3).* Assume a corporation has historically been an S corporation with a March 31 taxable year. However, for its taxable year beginning April 1, 1987, the corporation revoked its S election pursuant to section 1362(d)(1). Pursuant to paragraph (a)(6)(ii) of this section, such corporation may retroactively rescind its S election revocation by making a valid section 444 election for its taxable year beginning April 1, 1987, and complying with the procedures provided in paragraph (a)(6)(iii) of this section. If the corporation retroactively rescinds its S revocation, the corporation shall file a Form 1120S for its taxable year beginning April 1, 1987.

**(b) Limitation on taxable years that may be elected.** *(1) General rule.* Except as provided in paragraphs (b)(2) and (3) of this section, a section 444 election may be made only if the deferral period (as defined in paragraph (b)(4) of this section) of the taxable year to be elected is not longer than three months.

*(2) Changes in taxable year.* (i) In general. In the case of a partnership, S corporation, or personal service corporation changing its taxable year, such entity may make a section 444 election only if the deferral period of the taxable year to be elected is not longer than the shorter of—

(A) Three months, or

(B) The deferral period of the taxable year that is being changed, as defined in paragraph (b)(2)(iii) of this section.

(ii) Special rule for certain existing corporations electing S status. If a corporation with a taxable year other than the calendar year—

(A) Elected after September 18, 1986, and before January 1, 1988, under section 1362 of the Code to be an S corporation, and

(B) Elected to have the calendar year as the taxable year of the S corporation,

then, for taxable years beginning before 1989, paragraph (b)(2)(i)(i) of this section shall be applied by taking into account the deferral period of the last taxable year of the corporation prior to electing to be an S corporation, rather than the deferral period of the taxable year that is being changed. Thus, the provisions of the preceding sentence do not apply to a corporation that elected to be an S corporation for its first taxable year.

(iii) Deferral period of the taxable year that is being changed. For purposes of paragraph (b)(2)(i)(B) of this section, the phrase "deferral period of the taxable year that is being changed" means the deferral period of the taxable year immediately preceding the taxable year for which the taxpayer desires to make a section 444 election. Furthermore, the deferral period of such year will be determined by using the required taxable year of the taxable year for which the taxpayer desires to make a section 444 election. For example, assume P, a partnership that has historically used a March 31 taxable year, desires to change to a September 30 taxable year by making a section 444 election for its taxable year beginning April 1, 1987. Furthermore, assume that pursuant to paragraph (a)(4) of this section, P's required taxable year for the taxable year beginning April 1, 1987 is a year ending December 31. Based on these facts, the deferral period of the taxable year being changed is nine months (the period from March 31 to December 31).

(iv) Examples. See paragraph (d)(1) of this section for examples that illustrate the provisions of this paragraph (b)(2).

*(3) Special rule for entities retaining 1986 taxable year.* Notwithstanding paragraph (b) (2) of this section, a partnership, S corporation, or personal service corporation may, for its first taxable year beginning after December 31, 1986, if otherwise qualified, make a section 444 election to have a taxable year that is the same as the entity's last taxable year beginning in 1986. See paragraph (d)(2) of this section for examples that illustrate the provisions of this paragraph (b)(3).

*(4) Deferral period.* (i) Retentions of taxable year. For a partnership, S corporation, or personal service corporation that desires to retain its taxable year by making a section 444 election, the term "deferral period" means the months between the beginning of such year and the close of the first required taxable year (as defined in paragraph (a)(4) of this section). The following example illustrates the application of this paragraph (b)(4)(i).

*Example.* AB partnership has historically used a taxable year ending July 31. AB desires to retain its July 31 taxable year by making a section 444 election for its taxable year beginning August 1, 1987. Calendar year individuals, A and B, each own 50 percent of the profits and capital of AB; thus, under paragraph (a)(4) of this section AB's required taxable year is the year ending December 31. Pursuant to this paragraph (b)(4)(i), if AB desires to retain its year ending July 31, the deferral period is five months (the months between July 31 and December 31).

(ii) Adoptions of and changes in taxable year. (A) In general. For a partnership, S corporation, or personal service corporation that desires to adopt or change its taxable year by making a section 444 election, the term "deferral period" means the months that occur after the end of the taxable year desired under section 444 and before the close of the required taxable year.

(B) Special rule. If a partnership, S corporation or personal service corporation is using the required taxable year as its taxable year, the deferral period is deemed to be zero.

(C) Examples. The provisions of this paragraph (b)(4)(ii) may be illustrated by the following examples.

*Example (1).* Assume that CD partnership has historically used the calendar year and that CD's required taxable year is the calendar year. Under the special rule provided in paragraph (b)(4)(ii) (B) of this section, CD's deferral period is zero. See paragraph (b)(2)(i) of this section for rules that preclude CD from making a section 444 election to change its taxable year.

*Example (2).* E, a newly formed partnership, began operations on December 1, 1987, and is owned by calendar year individuals. E desires to make a section 444 election to adopt a September 30 taxable year. E's required taxable year is December 31. Pursuant to paragraph (b)(4)(ii) of this section, E's deferral period for the taxable year beginning December 1, 1987, is three months (the number of months between September 30 and December 31).

*Example (3).* Assume that F, a personal service corporation, has historically used a June 30 taxable year. F desires to make a section 444 election to change to an August 31 taxable year, effective for its taxable year beginning July 1, 1987. For purposes of determining the availability of a section 444 election for changing to the taxable year ending

August 31, the deferral period of an August 31 taxable year is four months (the number of months between August 31 and December 31). The deferral period for F's existing June 30 taxable year is six months (the number of months between June 30 and December 31). Pursuant to § 1.444-1T (b) (2) (i), F may not make a section 444 election to change to an August 31 taxable year.

*(5) Miscellaneous rules.* (i) Special rule for determining the taxable year of a corporation electing S status. For purposes of this section, and only for purposes of this section, a corporation that elected to be an S corporation for a taxable year beginning in 1987 or 1988 and which elected to be an S corporation prior to Sep 26, 1988 will not be considered to have adopted or changed its taxable year by virtue of information included on Form 2553, Election by a Small Business Corporation. See example (8) in paragraph (d) of this section.

(ii) Special procedure for cases where an income tax return is superseded. (A) In general. In the case of a partnership, S corporation, or personal service corporation that filed an income tax return for its first taxable year beginning after December 31, 1986, but subsequently makes a section 444 election that would result in a different year end for such taxable year, the income tax return filed pursuant to the section 444 election will supersede the original return. However, any payments of income tax made with respect to such superseded return will be credited to the taxpayer's superseding return and the taxpayer may file a claim for refund for such payments. See examples (5) and (7) in paragraph (d)(2) of this section.

(B) Procedure for superseding return. In order to allow the Service to process the affected income tax returns in an efficient manner, a partnership, S corporation, or personal service corporation that desires to supersede an income tax return in accordance with paragraph (b)(5)(ii)(A) of this section, should type or legibly print at the top of the first page of the income tax return for the taxable year elected—"SECTION 444 ELECTION—SUPERSEDES PRIOR RETURN."

(iii) Anti-abuse rule. If an existing partnership, S corporation or personal service corporation ("predecessor entities" ), or the owners thereof, transfer assets to a related party and the principal purpose of such transfer is to—

(A) Create a deferral period greater than the deferral period of the predecessor entity's taxable year, or

(B) Make a section 444 election following the termination of the predecessor entity's section 444 election,

then such transfer will be disregarded for purposes of section 444 and this section, even if the deferral created by such change is effectively eliminated by a required payment (within the meaning of section 7519) or deferral of a deduction (to a personal service corporation under section 280H). The following example illustrates the application of this paragraph (b) (5) (iii).

*Example.* Assume that P1 is a partnership that historically used the calendar year and is owned by calendar year partners. Assume that P1 desires to make a section 444 election to change to a September year for the taxable year beginning January 1, 1988. P1 may not make a section 444 election to change taxable years under section 444 (b)(2) because its current deferral period is zero. Assume further that P1 transfers a substantial portion of its assets to a newly-formed partnership (P2), which is owned by the partners of P1. Absent paragraph (b)(5)(iii) of this section, P2 could, if otherwise qualified, make a section 444 election under paragraph (b) (1) of this section to use a taxable year with a three month or less deferral period *(i.e.,* a September 30, October 31, or November 30 taxable year). However, if the principal purpose of the asset transfer was to create a one-, two-, or three-month deferral period by P2 making a section 444 election, the section 444 election shall not be given effect, even if the deferral would be effectively eliminated by P2 making a required payment under section 7519.

(iv) Special rules for partial months and 52-53-week taxable years. Except as otherwise provided in § 1.280H-1T (c)(2)(i)(A), for purposes of this section and §§ 1.7519-1T, 1.7519-2T and 1.280H-1T—

(A) A month of less than 16 days is disregarded, and a month of more than 15 days is treated as a full month; and

(B) A 52-53-week taxable year with reference to the end of a particular month will be considered to be the same as a taxable year ending with reference to the last day of such month.

**(c) Effective date.** This section is effective for taxable years beginning after December 31, 1986.

**(d) Examples.** *(1) Changes in taxable year.* The following examples illustrate the provisions of paragraph (b)(2) of this section.

*Example (1).* A is a personal service corporation that historically used a June 30 taxable year. A desires to make a section 444 election to change to an August 31 taxable year, effective with its taxable year beginning July 1, 1987. Under paragraph (b)(4)(ii) of this section, the deferral period of the taxable year to be elected is four months (the number of months between August 31 and December 31). Furthermore, the deferral period of the taxable year that is being changed is six months (the number of months between June 30 and December 31). Pursuant to paragraph (b)(2)(i) of this section, a taxpayer may, if otherwise qualified, make a section 444 election to change to a taxable year only if the deferral period of the taxable year to be elected is not longer than the shorter of three months or the deferral period of the taxable year being changed. Since the deferral period of the taxable year to be elected (August 31) is greater than three months, A may not make a section 444 election to change to the taxable year ending August 31. However, since the deferral period of the taxable year that is being changed is three months or more, A may, if otherwise qualified, make a section 444 election to change to a year ending September 30, 1987 (three-month deferral period), a year ending October 31, 1987 (two-month deferral period), or a year ending November 30, 1987 (one-month deferral period). In addition, instead of making a section 444 election to change its taxable year, A could, if otherwise qualified, make a section 444 election to retain its June year end, pursuant to paragraph (b)(3) of this section.

*Example (2).* B, a corporation that historically used an August 31 taxable year, elected on November 1, 1986 to be an S corporation for its taxable year beginning September 1, 1986. As a condition to having the S election accepted, B agreed on Form 2553 to use a calendar year. Pursuant to the general effective date provided in paragraph (c) of this section, B may not make a section 444 election for its taxable year beginning in 1986. Thus, B must file a short period income tax return for the period September 1 to December 31, 1986.

*Example (3).* The facts are the same as in example (2), except that B desires to make a section 444 election for its taxable year beginning January 1, 1987. Absent paragraph (b)(2)(ii) of this section, B would not be allowed to change its taxable year because the deferral period of the taxable year being changed (*i.e.,* the calendar year) is zero. However, pursuant to the special rule provided in paragraph (b)(2)(ii) of this section, B shall apply paragraph (b)(2)(i) of this section by taking into account the deferral period of the last taxable year of B prior to B's election to be an S corporation (four months), rather than the deferral period of B's taxable year that is being changed (zero months). Thus, if otherwise qualified, B may make a section 444 election to change to a taxable year ending September 30, October 31, or November 30, for its taxable year beginning January 1, 1987.

*Example (4).* The facts are the same as in example (3), except that B files a calendar year income tax return for 1987 rather than making a section 444 election. However, for its taxable year beginning January 1, 1988, B desires to change its taxable year by making a section 444 election. Given that the special rule provided in paragraph (b)(2)(ii) of this section applies to section 444 elections made in taxable years beginning before 1989, B may, if otherwise qualified, make a section 444 election to change to a taxable year ending September 30, October 31, or November 30 for its taxable year beginning January 1, 1988.

*Example (5).* C, a corporation that historically used a June 30 taxable year, elected on December 15, 1986 to be an S corporation for its taxable year beginning July 1, 1987. As a condition to having the S election accepted, C agreed on Form 2553 to use a calendar year. Although pursuant to paragraph (b)(3) of this section, C would, if otherwise qualified, be allowed to retain its June 30 taxable year, C desires to change to a September 30 taxable year by making a section 444 election. Pursuant to paragraph (b) (2) of this section, a taxpayer may, if otherwise qualified, make a section 444 election to change to a taxable year only if the deferral period of the taxable year to be elected is not longer than the shorter of three months or the deferral period of the taxable year being changed. Given these facts, the deferral period of the taxable year to be elected is 3 months (September 30 to December 31) while the deferral period of the taxable year being changed is 6 months (June 30 to December 31). Thus, C may, if otherwise qualified, change to a September 30 taxable year for its taxable year beginning July 1, 1987, by making a section 444 election. The fact that C agreed on Form 2553 to use a calendar year is not relevant.

*Example (6).* D, a corporation that historically used a March 31 taxable year, elects on June 1, 1988 to be an S corporation for its taxable year beginning April 1, 1988. D desires to change to a June 30 taxable year by making a section 444 election for its taxable year beginning April 1, 1988. Pursuant to paragraph (b)(2)(i) of this section, D may not change to a June 30 taxable year because such year would have a deferral period greater than 3 months. However, if otherwise qualified, D may make a section 444 election to change to a taxable year ending September 30, October 31, or November 30 for its taxable year beginning April 1, 1988.

*Example (7).* E, a corporation that began operations on November 1, 1986, elected to be an S corporation on December 15, 1986, for its taxable year beginning November 1, 1986. E filed a short period income tax return for the period November 1 to December 31, 1986. E desires to change to a September 30 taxable year by making a section 444 election for its taxable year beginning January 1, 1987. Although E elected to be an S corporation after September 18, 1986, and before January 1, 1988, paragraph (b)(2)(ii) of this section does not apply to E since E was not a C corporation prior to electing S status. Thus, E may not change its taxable year for the taxable year beginning January 1, 1987, by making a section 444 election.

*Example (8).* The facts are the same as in example (7), except that E began operations on April 15, 1987, and elected to be an S corporation on June 1, 1987, for its taxable year beginning April 15, 1987. As a condition to being an S corporation, E agreed on Form 2553 to use a calendar year. E desires to make a section 444 election to use a year ending September 30 for its taxable year beginning April 15, 1987. Pursuant to paragraph (b)(5)(i) of this section, E's agreement to use a calendar year on Form 2553 does not mean that E has adopted a calendar year. Thus, E's desire to make a section 444 election to use a September 30 taxable year will not be considered a change in taxable year and thus paragraph (b)(2) of this section will not apply. Instead, E will be subject to paragraph (b)(1) of this section. Since a September 30 taxable year would result in only a three-month deferral period (September 30 to December 31), E may, if otherwise qualified, make a section 444 election to use a year ending September 30 for its taxable year beginning April 15, 1987.

*(2) Special rule for entities retaining their 1986 taxable year.* The following examples illustrate the provisions of paragraph (b)(3) of this section.

*Example (1).* F, an S corporation that elected to be an S corporation several years ago, has historically used a June 30 taxable year. F desires to retain its June 30 taxable year by making a section 444 election for its taxable year beginning July 1, 1987. Pursuant to paragraph (b)(4)(i) of this section, the deferral period of the taxable year being retained is 6 months (June 30 to December 31, F's required taxable year). Absent the special rule provided in paragraph (b)(3) of this section, F would be subject to the general rule provided in paragraph (b)(1) of this section which limits the deferral period of the taxable year elected to three months or less. However, pursuant to paragraph (b)(3) of this section, F may, if otherwise qualified, make a section 444 election to retain its year ending June 30 for its taxable year beginning July 1, 1987.

*Example (2).* The facts are the same as in example (1), except that F received permission from the Commissioner to change its taxable year to the calendar year, and filed a short period income tax return for the period July 1 to December 31, 1986. F desires to make a section 444 election to use a year ending June 30 for its taxable year beginning January 1, 1987. Given that F had a December 31 taxable year for its last taxable year beginning in 1986, the special rule provided in paragraph (b)(3) of this section does not allow F to use a June 30 taxable year for its taxable year beginning January 1, 1987. Furthermore, pursuant to paragraph (b)(2)(i) of this section, F is not allowed to change its taxable year from December 31 to June 30 because the deferral period of the taxable year being changed is zero months.

*Example (3).* G, a corporation that historically used an August 31 taxable year, elected be an S corporation on November 15, 1986, for its taxable year beginning September 1, 1986. As a condition to obtaining S status, G agreed to use a calendar year. Thus, G filed its first S corporation return for the period September 1 to December 31, 1986. G desires to make a section 444 election to use a year ending August 31 for its taxable year beginning January 1, 1987. Since G's last taxable year beginning in 1986 was a calendar year, G cannot use paragraph (b) (3) of this section, relating to retentions of taxable years, to elect an August 31 taxable year. Thus, G is subject to paragraph (b)(2)(i) of this section, relating to changes in taxable year. Although G, if otherwise qualified, may use the special rule provided in paragraph (b)(2)(ii) of this section, G may only change from its current taxable year *(i.e.,* the calendar year) to a taxable year that has no more than a three-month deferral period *(i.e.,* September 30, October 31, or November 30).

*Example (4).* The facts are the same as in example (3), except that G elected to be an S corporation for its taxable year beginning September 1, 1987, rather than its taxable year beginning September 1, 1986. As a condition to making its S election, G agreed, on Form 2553, to use the calendar year. However, G has not yet filed a short period income tax return for the period September 1 to December 31, 1987. Given these facts, paragraph (b)(3) of this section would allow G, if otherwise qualified, to make a section 444 election to retain an August 31 taxable year for its taxable year beginning September 1, 1987.

*Example (5).* The facts are the same as in example (4), except that G has already filed a short period income tax return for the period September 1 to December 31, 1987. Pursuant to paragraph (b)(5)(ii)(a) of this section, G may supersede the return it filed for the period September 1 to December 31, 1987. Thus, pursuant to paragraph (b)(3) of this section, G may, if otherwise qualified, make a section 444 election to retain an August 31 taxable year for the taxable year beginning September 1, 1987. In addition, G should follow the special procedures set forth in paragraph (b)(5)(ii)(B) of this section.

*Example (6).* H, a corporation that historically used a May 31 taxable year, elects to be an S corporation on June 15, 1988 for its taxable year beginning June 1, 1988. H desires to make a section 444 election to use a taxable year other than the calendar year. Since the taxable year in issue is not H's first taxable year beginning after December 31, 1986, H may not use the special rule provided in paragraph (b)(3)(i) and thus may not retain its May 31 year. However, H may, if otherwise qualified, make a section 444 election under paragraph (b)(2)(i) of this section, to change to a taxable year that has no more than a three-month deferral period *(i.e.,* September 30, October 31, or November 30) for its taxable year beginning June 1, 1988.

*Example (7).* I is a partnership that has historically used a calendar year. Sixty percent of the profits and capital of I are owned by Q, a corporation (that is neither an S corporation nor a personal service corporation) that has a June 30 taxable year, and 40 percent of the profits and capital are owned by R, a calendar year individual. Since the partner that has more than a fifty percent interest in I has a June 30 taxable year, I's required taxable year is June 30. Accordingly, I filed an income tax return for the period January 1 to June 30, 1987. Based on these facts, I may, pursuant to paragraph (b)(5)(ii)(A) of this section, disregard the income tax return filed for the period January 1 to June 30, 1987. Thus, if otherwise qualified, I may make a section 444 election under paragraph (b) (2) (i) of this section to use a calendar year for its taxable year beginning January 1, 1987. If I makes such a section 444 election, I should follow the special procedures set forth in paragraph (b)(5)(ii) (B) of this section.

---

T.D. 8205, 5/24/88, amend T.D. 8996, 5/16/2002.

---

PAR. 2. In the list below, for each section indicated in the left column, remove the old language in the middle column and add the new language in the right column.

| Affected Section | Remove | Add |
|---|---|---|
| 1.46-1(p)(2)(iv) | paragraph (b)(1) of § 1.441-2 | § 1.441-2 |
| 1.48-3(d)(1)(iii) | paragraph (b)(1) of § 1.441-2 | § 1.441-2 |
| 1.280H-1T(a), last sentence | § 1.441-4T(d) | § 1.441-3(c) |
| 1.443-1(b)(1)(ii) | and paragraph (c)(5) of § 1.441-2 | and § 1.441-1(b)(2)(ii). |
| 1.444-1T(a)(1), first sentence | § 1.444-4T(d) | § 1.441-3(c) |
| 1.444-2T(a), last sentence | § 1.441-4T(d) | § 1.441-3(c) |
| 1.448-1(h)(2)(ii)(B)(1) | § 1.441-2T(b)(1) | § 1.441-2(c) |
| 1.469-1(h)(4)(ii)(D) | § 1.441-4T(f) | § 1.441-3(e) |
| 1.469-1T(g)(2)(i) | § 1.441-4T(d) | § 1.441-2 |
| 1.1561-1(c)(2) | See paragraph (b)(1) of § 1.441-2 | See § 1.441-2 |
| 1.6654-2(a), concluding text | paragraph (b) of § 1.441-2 | § 1.441-2(c) |
| 1.6655-2(a)(4), first sentence | paragraph (b) of § 1.441-2 | § 1.441-1(b) |

**Proposed § 1.444-1T** [*For Preamble, see ¶ 152,177*]

• ***Caution:*** This Notice of Proposed Rulemaking was partially finalized by T.D. 8996, issued on 5/16/2002. Proposed regulation §§ 1.46-1, 1.48-3, 1.280H-1T, 1.443-1, 1.444-1T, 1.444-2T, 1.448-1, 1.469-1, 1.469-1T, 1.898-4, 1.1561-1, 1.6654-2, 1.6655-2 and 301.7701(b)-6 remains in effect.

### § 1.444-2T Tiered structure (temporary).

**(a) General rule.** Except as provided in paragraph (e) of this section, no section 444 election shall be made or continued with respect to a partnership, S corporation, or personal service corporation that is a member of a tiered structure on the date specified in paragraph (d) of this section. For purposes of this section, the term "personal service corporation" means a personal service corporation as defined in § 1.441-3(c).

**(b) Definition of a member of a tiered structure.** *(1) In general.* A partnership, S corporation, or personal service corporation is considered a member of a tiered structure if—

(i) The partnership, S corporation, or personal service corporation directly owns any portion of a deferral entity, or

(ii) A deferral entity directly owns any portion of the partnership, S corporation, or personal service corporation.

However, see paragraph (c) of this section for certain de minimis rules, and see paragraph (b)(3) of this section for an anti-abuse rule. In addition, for purposes of this section, a beneficiary of a trust shall be considered to own an interest in the trust.

*(2) Deferral entity.* (i) In general. For purposes of this section, the term "deferral entity" means an entity that is a partnership, S corporation, personal service corporation, or trust. In the case of an affiliated group of corporations filing a consolidated income tax return that is treated as a personal service corporation pursuant to § 1.441-4T (i), such affiliated group is considered to be a single deferral entity.

(ii) Grantor trusts. The term "deferral entity" does not include a trust (or a portion of a trust) which is treated as owned by the grantor or beneficiary under Subpart E, part I, subchapter J, chapter 1, of the Code (relating to grantor trusts), including a trust that is treated as a grantor trust pursuant to section 1361(d)(1)(A) of the Code (relating to qualified subchapter S trusts). Thus, any taxpayer treated under subpart E as owning a portion of a trust shall be treated as owning the assets of the trust attributable to that ownership. The following examples illustrate the provisions of this paragraph (b)(2)(ii).

*Example (1).* A, an individual, is the sole beneficiary of T. T is a trust that owns 50 percent of the profits and capital of X, a partnership that desires to make a section 444 election. Furthermore, pursuant to Subpart E, Part I, subchapter J, chapter 1 of the Code, A is treated as an owner of X. Based upon these facts, T is not a deferral entity and 50 percent of X is considered to be directly owned by A.

*Example (2).* The facts are the same as in example (1), except that A is a personal service corporation rather than an individual. Given these facts, 50 percent of X is considered to be directly owned by A, a deferral entity. Thus, X is considered to be a member of a tiered structure.

*(3) Anti-abuse rule.* Notwithstanding paragraph (b)(1) of this section, a partnership, S corporation, or personal service corporation is considered a member of a tiered structure if the partnership, S corporation, personal service corporation, or related taxpayers have organized or reorganized their ownership structure or operations for the principal purpose of obtaining a significant unintended tax benefit from making or continuing a section 444 election. For purposes of the preceding sentence, a significant unintended tax benefit results when a partnership, S corporation, or personal service corporation makes a section 444 election and, as a result, a taxpayer (not limited to the entity making the election) obtains a significant deferral of income substantially all of which is not eliminated by a required payment under section 7519. See examples (15) through (19) in paragraph (f) of this section.

**(c) De minimis rules.** *(1) In general.* For rules relating to a de minimis exception to paragraph (b)(1)(i) of this section (the "downstream de minimis rule"), see paragraph (c)(2) of this section. For rules relating to a de minimis exception to paragraph (b)(1)(ii) of this section (the "upstream de minimis rule"), see paragraph (c)(3) of this section. For rules relating to the interaction of the de minimis rules provided in this paragraph (c) and the "same taxable year exception" provided in paragraph (e) of this section, see paragraph (e)(5) of this section.

*(2) Downstream de minimis rule.* (i) General rule. If a partnership, S corporation, or personal service corporation directly owns any portion of one or more deferral entities as of the date specified in paragraph (d) of this section, such ownership is disregarded for purposes of paragraph (b)(1)(i) of this section if, in the aggregate, all such deferral entities accounted for—

(A) Not more than 5 percent of the partnership's, S corporation's, or personal service corporation's adjusted taxable income for the testing period ("5 percent adjusted taxable income test"), or

(B) Not more than 2 percent of the partnership's, S corporation's, or personal service corporation's gross income for the testing period ("2 percent gross income test"). See section 702(c) for rules relating to the determination of gross income of a partner in a partnership.

See examples (3) through (5) in paragraph (f) of this section.

(ii) Definition of testing period. For purposes of this paragraph (c)(2), the term "testing period" means the taxable year that ends immediately prior to the taxable year for which the partnership, S corporation, or personal service corporation desires to make or continue a section 444 election. However, see the special rules provided in paragraph (c)(2)(iv) of this section for certain special cases (*e.g.*, the partnership, S corporation, personal service corporation or deferral entity was not in existence during the entire testing period). The following example illustrates the application of this paragraph (c)(2)(ii).

*Example.* A partnership desires to make a section 444 election for its taxable year beginning November 1, 1987. The testing period for purposes of determining whether deferral entities owned by such partnership are de minimis under paragraph (c)(2) of this section is the taxable year ending October 31, 1987. If either the partnership or the deferral entities were not in existence for the entire taxable year ending October 1, 1987, see the special rules provided in paragraph (c)(2)(iv) of this section.

(iii) Definition of adjusted taxable income. (A) Partnership. In the case of a partnership, adjusted taxable income for purposes of paragraph (c)(2) of this section is an amount equal to the sum of the—

(1) Aggregate amount of the partnership items described in section 702(a) (other than credits and tax-exempt income),

(2) Applicable payments defined in section 7519(d)(3) that are deducted in determining the amount described in paragraph (c)(2)(iii)(A)(1) of this section, and

(3) Guaranteed payments defined in section 707(c) that are deducted in determining the amount described in paragraph (c)(2)(iii)(A)(1) of this section and are not otherwise included in paragraph (c)(2)(iii)(A)(2) of this section. For purposes of determining the aggregate amount of partnership

items under paragraph (c)(2)(iii)(A)(1) of this section, deductions and losses are treated as negative income. Thus, for example, if under section 702(a) a partnership has $1,000 of ordinary taxable income, $500 of specially allocated deductions, and $300 of capital loss, the partnership's aggregate amount of partnership items under paragraph (c)(2)(iii)(A)(1) of this section is $200 ($1,000 – $500 – $300).

(B) S corporation. In the case of an S corporation, adjusted taxable income for purposes of paragraph (c)(2) of this section is an amount equal to the sum of the—

(1) Aggregate amount of the S corporation items described in section 1366(a) (other than credits and tax-exempt income), and

(2) Applicable payments defined in section 7519(d)(3) that are deducted in determining the amount described in paragraph (c)(2)(iii)(B)(1) of this section.

For purposes of determining the aggregate amount of S corporation items under paragraph (c)(2)(iii)(B)(1) of this section, deductions and losses are treated as negative income. Thus, for example, if under section 1366(a) an S corporation has $2,000 of ordinary taxable income, $1,000 of deductions described in section 1366(a)(1)(A) of the Code, and $500 of capital loss, the S corporation's aggregate amount of S corporation items under paragraph (c)(2)(iii)(B)(1) of this section is $500 ($2,000 $1,000 – $500).

(C) Personal service corporation. In the case of a personal service corporation, adjusted taxable income for purposes of paragraph (c)(2) of this section is an amount equal to the sum of the—

(1) Taxable income of the personal service corporation, and

(2) Applicable amounts defined in section 280H(f)(1) that are deducted in determining the amount described in paragraph (c)(2)(iii)(C)(1) of this section.

(iv) Special rules. (A) Pro-forma rule. Except as provided in paragraph (c)(iv)(C)(2) of this section, if a partnership, S corporation, or personal service corporation directly owns any interest in a deferral entity as of the date specified in paragraph (d) of this section and such ownership interest is different in amount from the partnership's, S corporation's, or personal service corporation's interest on any day during the testing period, the 5 percent adjusted taxable income test and the 2 percent gross income test must be applied on a pro-forma basis *(i.e.,* adjusted taxable income and gross income must be calculated for the testing period assuming that the partnership, S corporation, or personal service corporation owned the same interest in the deferral entity that it owned as of the date specified in paragraph (d) of this section). The following example illustrates the application of this paragraph (c)(2)(iv)(A).

*Example.* A personal service corporation desiring to make a section 444 election for its taxable year beginning October 1, 1987, acquires a 25 percent ownership interest in a partnership on or after October 1, 1987. Furthermore, the partnership has been in existence for several years. The personal service corporation must modify its calculations of the 5 percent adjusted taxable income test and the 2 percent gross income test for the testing period ended September 30, 1987, by assuming that the personal service corporation owned 25 percent of the partnership during such testing period and the personal service corporation's adjusted taxable income and gross income were correspondingly adjusted.

(B) Reasonable estimates allowed. If the information necessary to complete the pro-forma calculation described in paragraph (c)(2)(iv)(A) of this section is not readily available, the partnership, S corporation, or personal service corporation may make a reasonable estimate of such information.

(C) Newly formed entities. (1) Newly formed deferral entities. If a partnership, S corporation, or personal service corporation owns any portion of a deferral entity on the date specified in paragraph (d) of this section and such deferral entity was not in existence during the entire testing period (hereinafter referred to as a "newly formed deferral entity"), both the 5 percent adjusted taxable income test and the 2 percent gross income test are modified as follows. First, the partnership, S corporation, or personal service corporation shall calculate the percentage of its adjusted taxable income or gross income that is attributable to deferral entities, excluding newly formed deferral entities. Second, the partnership, S corporation, or personal service corporation shall calculate (on the date specified in paragraph (d) of this section) the percentage of the tax basis of its assets that are attributable to its tax basis with respect to its ownership interests in all newly formed deferral entities. If the sum of the two percentages is 5 percent or less, the deferral entities are considered de minimis and are disregarded for purposes of paragraph (b)(1)(i) of this section. If the sum of the two percentages is greater than 5 percent, the deferral entities do not qualify for the de minimis rule provided in paragraph (c)(2) of this section and thus the partnership, S corporation, or personal service corporation is considered to be a member of a tiered structure for purposes of this section.

(2) Newly formed partnership, S corporation, or personal service corporation desiring to make a section 444 election. If a partnership, S corporation, or personal service corporation desires to make a section 444 election for the first taxable year of its existence, the 5 percent adjusted taxable income test and the 2 percent gross income test are replaced by a 5 percent of assets test. Thus, if on the date specified in paragraph (d) of this section, 5 percent or less of the assets (measured by reference to the tax basis of the assets) of the newly formed partnership, S corporation, or personal service corporation are attributable to the tax basis with respect to its ownership interests in the deferral entities, the deferral entities will be considered de minimis and will be disregarded for purposes of paragraph (b)(1)(i) of this section.

(3) Upstream de minimis rule. If a partnership, S corporation or personal service corporation is directly owned by one or more deferral entities as of the date specified in paragraph (d) of this section, such ownership is disregarded for purposes of paragraph (b)(1)(ii) of this section if on the date specified in paragraph (d) of this section the deferral entities directly own, in the aggregate, 5 percent or less of—

(i) An interest in the current profits of the partnership, or

(ii) The stock (measured by value) of the S corporation or personal service corporation.

See examples (6) and (7) in paragraph (f) of this section.

**(d) Date for determining the existence of a tiered structure.** *(1) General rule.* For purposes of paragraph (a) of this section, a partnership, S corporation, or personal service corporation will be considered a member of a tiered structure for a particular taxable year if the partnership, S corporation, or personal service corporation is a member of a tiered structure on the last day of the required taxable year (as defined in section 444(e) of the Code) ending within such year. If a particular taxable year does not include the last day of the required taxable year for such year, the partnership, S corporation, or personal service corporation will not be considered a member of a tiered structure for such year. The following examples illustrate the application of this paragraph (d)(1).

*Example (1).* Assume that a newly formed partnership whose first taxable year begins November 1, 1988, desires to adopt a September 30 taxable year by making a section 444 election. Furthermore, assume that for its taxable year beginning November 1, 1988, the partnership's required taxable year is December 31. If the partnership is a member of a tiered structure on December 31, 1988, it will not be eligible to make a section 444 election for a taxable year beginning November 1, 1988, and ending September 30, 1989.

*Example (2).* Assume an S corporation that historically used a June 30 taxable year desires to make a section 444 election to change to a year ending September 30 for its taxable year beginning July 1, 1987. If the S corporation can make the section 444 election, it will have a short taxable year beginning July 1, 1987, and ending September 30, 1987. Given these facts, the short taxable year beginning July 1, 1987, does not include the last day of the S corporation's required taxable year for such year (i.e., December 31, 1987). Thus, pursuant to paragraph (d)(1) of this section, the S corporation will not be considered a member of a tiered structure for its taxable year beginning July 1, 1987, and ending September 30, 1987.

*(2) Special rule for taxable years beginning in 1987.* For purposes of paragraph (a) of this section, a partnership, S corporation, or personal service corporation will not be considered a member of a tiered structure for a taxable year beginning in 1987 if the partnership, S corporation, or personal service corporation is not a member of a tiered structure on the day the partnership, S corporation, or personal service corporation timely files its section 444 election for such year. The following examples illustrate the application of this paragraph (d)(2).

*Example (1).* Assume that a partnership desires to retain a June 30 taxable year by making a section 444 election for its taxable year beginning July 1, 1987. Furthermore, assume that the partnership's required taxable year for such year is December 31 and that the partnership was a member of a tiered structure on such date. Also assume that the partnership was not a member of a tiered structure as of the date it timely filed its section 444 election for its taxable year beginning July 1, 1987. Based upon the special rule provided in this paragraph (d)(2), the partnership will not be considered a member of a tiered structure for its taxable year beginning July 1, 1987.

*Example (2).* Assume the same facts as in example (1), except that the partnership was a member of a tiered structure on the date it filed its section 444 election for its taxable year beginning July 1, 1987, but was not a member of a tiered structure on December 31, 1987. Paragraph (d)(1) of this section would still apply and thus the partnership would not be considered part of a tiered structure for its taxable year beginning July 1, 1987. However, the partnership would be considered a member of a tiered structure for its taxable year beginning July 1, 1988, if the partnership was a member of a tiered structure on December 31, 1988.

**(e) Same taxable year exception.** *(1) In general.* Although a partnership or S corporation is a member of a tiered structure as of the date specified in paragraph (d) of this section, the partnership or S corporation may make or continue a section 444 election if the tiered structure (as defined in paragraph (e)(2) of this section) consists entirely of partnerships or S corporations (or both), all of which have the same taxable year as determined under paragraph (e)(3) of this section. However, see paragraph (e)(5) of this section for the interaction of the de minimis rules provided in paragraph (c) of this section with the same taxable year exception. For purposes of this paragraph (e), two or more entities are considered to have the same taxable year if their taxable years end on the same day, even though they begin on different days. See examples (8) through (14) in paragraph (f) of this section.

*(2) Definition of tiered structure.* (i) General rule. For purposes of the same taxable year exception, the members of a tiered structure are defined to include the following entities—

(A) The partnership or S corporation that desires to qualify for the same taxable year exception,

(B) A deferral entity (or entities) directly owned (in whole or in part) by the partnership or S corporation that desires to qualify for the same taxable year exception,

(C) A deferral entity (or entities) directly owning any portion of the partnership or S corporation that desires to qualify for the same taxable year exception, and

(D) A deferral entity (or entities) directly owned (in whole or in part) by a "downstream controlled partnership," as defined in paragraph (e)(2)(ii) of this section.

(ii) Special flow-through rule for downstream controlled partnerships. If more than 50 percent of a partnership's profits and capital are owned by a partnership or S corporation that desires to qualify for the same taxable year exception, such owned partnership is considered a downstream controlled partnership for purposes of paragraph (e)(2)(i) of this section. Furthermore, if more than 50 percent of a partnership's profits and capital are owned by a downstream controlled partnership, such owned partnership is considered a downstream controlled partnership for purposes of paragraph (e)(2)(i) of this section.

*(3) Determining the taxable year of a partnership or S corporation.* The taxable year of a partnership or S corporation to be taken into account for purposes of paragraph (e)(1) of this section is the taxable year ending with or prior to the date specified in paragraph (d) of this section. Furthermore, the determination of such taxable year will take into consideration any section 444 elections made by the partnership or S corporation. See examples (10) and (11) in paragraph (f) of this section.

*(4) Special rule for 52-53-week taxable years.* For purposes of this paragraph (e), a 52-53-week taxable year with reference to the end of a particular month will be considered to be the same as a taxable year ending with reference to the last day of such month.

*(5) Interaction with de minimis rules.* (i) Downstream de minimis rule. (A) In general. If a partnership or S corporation that desires to make or continue a section 444 election is a member of a tiered structure (as defined in paragraph (e)(2) of this section) and directly owns any member (or members) of the tiered structure with a taxable year different from the taxable year of the partnership or S corporation, such ownership is disregarded for purposes of the same taxable year exception of paragraph (e)(1) of this section provided that, in the aggregate, the de minimis rule of paragraph (c)(2) of this section is satisfied with respect to such owned member (or members). The following example illustrates the application of this paragraph (e)(5)(i)(A).

*Example.* P, a partnership with a June 30 taxable year, owns 60 percent of P1, another partnership with a June 30 taxable year. P also owns 1 percent of P2 and P3, calendar year partnerships. If, in the aggregate, P's ownership interests in P2 and P3 are considered de minimis under paragraph (c)(2) of this section, P meets the same taxable year exception and may make a section 444 election to retain its June 30 taxable year.

(B) Special rule for members of a tiered structure directly owned by a downstream controlled partnership. For purposes of paragraph (e)(5)(i)(A) of this section, a partnership or S corporation desiring to make or continue a section 444 election is considered to directly own any member of the tiered structure (as defined in paragraph (e)(2) of this section) directly owned by a downstream controlled partnership (as defined in paragraph (e)(2)(ii) of this section). The adjusted taxable income or gross income of the partnership or S corporation that is attributable to a member of a tiered structure directly owned by a downstream controlled partnership equals the adjusted taxable income or gross income of such member multiplied by the partnership's or S corporation's indirect ownership percentage of such member. The following example illustrates the application of this paragraph (e)(5)(i)(B).

*Example.* P, a partnership, desires to retain its June 30 taxable year by making a section 444 election. However, as of the date specified in paragraph (d) of this section, P owns 75 percent of P1, a June 30 partnership, and P1 owns 40 percent of P2, a calendar year partnership. P also owns 25 percent of P3, a calendar year partnership. Pursuant to paragraphs (e)(5)(i)(A) and (B) of this section, P may only qualify to use the same taxable year exception if, in the aggregate, P2 and P3 are de minimis with respect to P. Pursuant to paragraph (e)(5)(i)(B) of this section, P's adjusted taxable income or gross income attributable to P2 equals 30 percent (75 percent times 40 percent) of P2's adjusted taxable income or gross income.

(ii) Upstream de minimis rule. If a partnership or S corporation that desires to make or continue a section 444 election is a member of a tiered structure (as defined in paragraph (e)(2) of this section) and is owned directly by a member (or members) of the tiered structure with taxable years different from the taxable year of the partnership or S corporation, such ownership is disregarded for purposes of the same taxable year exception of paragraph (e)(1) of this section provided that, in the aggregate, the de minimis rule of paragraph (c)(3) of this section is satisfied with respect to such owning member (or members). See example (12) of paragraph (f) of this section.

**(f) Examples.** The provisions of this section may be illustrated by the following examples.

*Example (1).* A, a partnership, desires to make or continue a section 444 election. However, on the date specified in paragraph (d) of this section, A is owned by a combination of individuals and S corporations. The S corporations are deferral entities, as defined in paragraph (b)(2) of this section. Thus, pursuant to paragraph (b)(1)(ii) of this section, A will be a member of a tiered structure unless under paragraph (c)(3) of this section, the S corporations, in the aggregate, own a de minimis portion of A. If the S corporations' ownership in A is not considered de minimis under paragraph (c)(3) of this section, A is a member of a tiered structure and will be allowed to make or continue a section 444 election only if it meets the same taxable year exception provided in paragraph (e) of this section.

*Example (2).* B, a partnership, desires to make or continue a section 444 election. However, on the date specified in paragraph (d) of this section, B is a partner in two partnerships, B1 and B2. B1 and B2 are deferral entities, as defined in paragraph (b)(2) of this section. Thus, under paragraph (b)(1)(i) of this section, B will be a member of a tiered structure unless B's aggregate ownership interests in B1 and B2 are considered de minimis under paragraph (c)(2) of this section. If B is a member of a tiered structure on the date specified in paragraph (d) of this section, B will be allowed to make or continue a section 444 election only if it meets the same taxable year exception provided in paragraph (e) of this section.

*Example (3).* C, a partnership with a September 30 taxable year, is 100 percent owned by calendar year individuals. C desires to make a section 444 election for its taxable year beginning October 1, 1987. However, on the date specified in paragraph (d) of this section, C owns a 1 percent interest in C1, a partnership. C does not own any other interest in a deferral entity. For the taxable year ended September 30, 1987, 10 percent of C's adjusted taxable income (as defined in paragraph (c)(2)(iii) of this section) was attributable to C's partnership interest in C1. Furthermore, 4 percent of C's gross income for the taxable year ended September 30, 1987, was attributable to C's partnership interest in C1. Under paragraph (c)(2) of this section, C's partnership interest in C1 is not de minimis because during the testing period more than 5 percent of C's adjusted taxable income is attributable to C1 and more than 2 percent of C's gross income is attributable to C1. Thus, C is a member of a tiered structure for its taxable year beginning October 1, 1987.

*Example (4).* The facts are the same as example (3), except that for the taxable year ended September 30, 1987, only 2 percent of C's adjusted taxable income was attributable to C1. Under paragraph (c)(2) of this section, C's partnership interest in C1 is considered de minimis for purposes of determining whether C is a member of a tiered structure because not more than 5 percent of C's adjusted taxable income during the testing period is attributable to C1. Thus, C is not a member of a tiered structure for its taxable year beginning October 1, 1987.

*Example (5).* The facts are the same as example (4), except that in addition to owning C1, C also owns 15 percent of C2, another partnership. For the taxable year ended September 30, 1987, 2 percent of C's adjusted taxable income is attributable to C1 and an additional 4 percent is attributable to C2. Furthermore, for the taxable year ended September 30, 1987, 4 percent of C's gross income is attributable to C1 while 3 percent is attributable to C2. Under paragraph (c)(2) of this section, C1 and C2 must be aggregated for purposes of determining whether C meets either the 5 percent adjusted taxable income test or the 2 percent gross income test. Since C's adjusted taxable income attributable to C1 and C2 is 6 percent (2 percent + 4 percent) and C's gross income attributable to C1 and C2 is 7 percent (4 percent + 3 percent), C does not meet the downstream de minimis rule provided in paragraph (c)(2) of this section. Thus, C is a member of a tiered structure for its taxable year beginning October 1, 1987.

*Example (6).* The facts are the same as example (3), except that instead of determining whether C is part of a tiered structure, the issue is whether C1 is part of a tiered structure. In addition, assume that on the date specified in paragraph (d) of this section, the remaining 99 percent of C1 is owned by calendar year individuals and C1 does not own an interest in any deferral entity. Although C in Example (3) was considered to be a part of a tiered structure by virtue of its ownership interest in C1, C1 must be tested separately to determine whether it is part of a tiered structure. Since C's interest in C1 is 5 percent or less, C's interest in C1 is de minimis with respect to C1. See paragraph (c) (3) of this section. Thus, based upon these facts, C1 is not part of a tiered structure.

*Example (7).* The facts are the same as example (6), except that the remaining 99 percent of C1 is owned 94 percent by calendar year individuals and 5 percent by C3, another partnership. Thus, deferral entities own 6 percent of C1 (1 percent owned by C and 5 percent owned by C3). Under paragraph (c)(3) of this section, deferral entities own more than a de minimis interest *(i.e.,* 5 percent) of C1, and thus C1 is part of a tiered structure.

*Example (8).* D, a partnership with a September 30 taxable year, desires to make a section 444 election for its taxable year beginning October 1, 1987. On December 31, 1987, and the date D plans to file its section 444 election, D is 10 percent owned by D1, a personal service corporation with a September 30 taxable year, and 90 percent owned by calendar year individuals. Furthermore, D1 will retain its September 30 taxable year because it previously established a business purpose for such year. Since D is owned in part by D1, a personal service corporation, and the ownership interest is not de minimis under paragraph (c)(3) of this section, D is considered a member of a tiered structure for its taxable year beginning October 1, 1987. Furthermore, although D and D1 have the same taxable year, D does not qualify for the same taxable year exception provided in paragraph (e) of this section because D1 is a personal service corporation rather than a partnership or S corporation. Thus, pursuant to paragraph (a) of this section, D may not make a section 444 election for its taxable year beginning October 1, 1987.

*Example (9).* The facts are the same as example (8), except that D1 is a partnership rather than a personal service corporation. Based upon these facts, D qualifies for the same taxable year exception provided in paragraph (e) of this section. Thus, D may make a section 444 election for its taxable year beginning October 1, 1987.

*Example (10).* The facts are the same as example (9), except that D1 has not established a business purpose for a September 30 taxable year. In addition, D1 does not desire to make a section 444 election and, under section 706(b), D1 will be required to change to a calendar year for its taxable year beginning October 1, 1987. Pursuant to paragraph (e)(3) of this section, D and D1 do not have the same taxable year for purposes of the same taxable year exception provided in paragraph (e) of this section. Thus, D may not make a section 444 election for its taxable year beginning October 1, 1987.

*Example (11).* The facts are the same as example (8), except that D1 is a partnership with a March 31 taxable year. Furthermore, for its taxable year beginning April 1, 1987, D1 will change to a September 30 taxable year by making a section 444 election. Pursuant to paragraph (e) (3) of this section, D1 is considered to have a September 30 taxable year for purposes of determining whether D qualifies for the same taxable year exception provided in paragraph (e) of this section. Since both D and D1 will have the same taxable year as of the date specified in paragraph (d) of this section, D may make a section 444 election for its taxable year beginning October 1, 1987.

*Example (12).* The facts are the same as example (11), except that instead of the remaining 90 percent of D being owned by calendar year individuals, it is owned 86 percent by individuals and 4 percent by D2, a calendar year partnership. Thus, D, a September 30 partnership, is 10 percent owned by D1, a September 30 partnership, 86 percent owned by calendar year individuals, and 4 percent owned by D2, a calendar year partnership. Under paragraph (e)(5)(ii) of this section, D2's ownership interest in D is considered de minimis for purposes of the same taxable year exception. Since D2's ownership interest in D is considered de minimis, it is disregarded for purposes of determining whether D qualifies for the same taxable year exception provided in paragraph (e) of this section. Thus, since both D and D1 will have the same taxable year as of the date specified in paragraph (d) of this section, D may make a section 444 election for its taxable year beginning October 1, 1987.

*Example (13).* E, a partnership with a June 30 taxable year, desires to make a section 444 election for its taxable year beginning July 1, 1987. On the date specified in paragraph (d) of this section, E is 100 percent owned by calendar year individuals; E owns 99 percent of the profits and capital of E1, a partnership with a June 30 taxable year; and E1 owns 30 percent of the profits and capital of E2, a partnership with a September 30 taxable year. E owns no other deferral entities. Pursuant to paragraph (b)(1)(i) of this section, E is considered to be a member of a tiered structure. Furthermore, pursuant to paragraph (e) of this section, E does not qualify for the same taxable year exception because E2 does not have the same taxable year as E and E1.

*Example (14).* The facts are the same as example (13), except that E owns only 49 percent (rather than 99 percent) of the profits and capital of E1. Pursuant to paragraph (e) of this section, E qualifies for the same taxable year exception because E and E1 have the same taxable year. Pursuant to paragraph (e) of this section, E1's ownership interest in E2 is disregarded since E does not own more than 50 percent of E1's profits and capital.

*Example (15).* Prior to consideration of the anti-abuse rule provided in paragraph (b)(3) of this section, H, a partnership that commenced operations on October 1, 1987, is eligible to make a section 444 election for its taxable year beginning October 1, 1987. Although H may obtain a significant deferral of income substantially all of which is not eliminated by a required payment under section 7519 (since there will be no required payment for H's first taxable year), the anti-abuse rule of paragraph (b)(3) will not apply unless the principal purpose of organizing H was the attainment of a significant deferral of income that would result from making a section 444 election.

*Example (16).* F, a partnership with a January 31 taxable year, desires to make a section 444 election to retain its January 31 taxable year for the taxable year beginning February 1, 1987. F is 100 percent owned by calendar year individuals. Prior to the date specified in paragraph (d) of this section, F contributes substantially all of its assets to F1, a partnership, in exchange for a 51 percent interest in F1. The remaining 49 percent of F1 is owned by the calendar year individuals owning 100 percent of F. If F is allowed to make a section 444 election to retain its January 31 taxable year, F1's required taxable year will be January 31 since a majority of F1's partners use a January 31 taxable year (see § 1.706-3T). F's principal purpose for creating F1 and contributing its assets to F1 is to obtain an 11-month deferral on 49 percent of the income previously earned by F and now earned by F1. Pursuant to paragraph (b)(3) of this section, F is not allowed to make a section 444 election for its taxable year beginning February 1, 1987.

*Example (17).* The facts are the same as in example (16), except that F does not create F1 and contribute its assets to F1 until immediately after F makes it section 444 election for the taxable year beginning February 1, 1987. Thus, F is allowed to make a section 444 election for its taxable year beginning February 1, 1987. However, pursuant to paragraph (b)(3) of this section, F will have its section 444 election terminated for subsequent years unless the tax deferral inherent in the structure is eliminated *(e.g.,* F1 is liquidated or the individual owners of F contribute their interests in F1 to F) prior to the date specified in paragraph (d) of this section for subsequent taxable years beginning on or after February 1, 1988.

*Example (18).* The facts are the same as in example (16), except that F1 is 99 percent owned by F and none of the individual owners of F own any portion of F1. Furthermore, F obtained no tax benefit from creating and contributing assets to F1. Given these facts paragraph (b)(3) of this section does not apply and thus, F may make a section 444 election for its taxable year beginning February 1, 1987.

*Example (19).* G, a partnership with an October 31 taxable year, desires to retain its October 31 taxable year for its taxable year beginning November 1, 1987. However, as of December 31, 1987, G owns a 30 percent interest in G1, a calendar year partnership. G owns no other deferral entity, and G is 100 percent owned by calendar year individuals. Furthermore, G's interest in G1 does not meet the de minimis rule provided in paragraph (c)(3) of this section. Thus, in order to avoid being a tiered structure, G sells its interest in G1 to an unrelated third party prior to the date G timely makes it section 444 election for its taxable year beginning November 1, 1987. Although the sale of G1 allows G to qualify to make a section 444 election, and therefore to obtain a significant tax benefit, such benefit is not unintended. Thus, paragraph (b)(3) of this section does not apply, and G may make a section 444 election for its taxable year beginning November 1, 1987.

**(g) Effective date.** This section is effective for taxable years beginning after December 31, 1986.

T.D. 8205, 5/24/88, amend T.D. 8996, 5/16/2002.

PAR. 2. In the list below, for each section indicated in the left column, remove the old language in the middle column and add the new language in the right column.

| Affected Section | Remove | Add |
|---|---|---|
| 1.46-1(p)(2)(iv) | paragraph (b)(1) of § 1.441-2 | § 1.441-2 |
| 1.48-3(d)(1)(iii) | paragraph (b)(1) of § 1.441-2 | § 1.441-2 |
| 1.280H-1T(a), last sentence | § 1.441-4T(d) | § 1.441-3(c) |
| 1.443-1(b)(1)(ii) | and paragraph (c)(5) of § 1.441-2 | and § 1.441-1(b)(2)(ii). |
| 1.444-1T(a)(1), first sentence | § 1.444-4T(d) | § 1.441-3(c) |
| 1.444-2T(a), last sentence | § 1.441-4T(d) | § 1.441-3(c) |
| 1.448-1(h)(2)(ii)(B)(1) | § 1.441-2T(b)(1) | § 1.441-2(c) |
| 1.469-1(h)(4)(ii)(D) | § 1.441-4T(f) | § 1.441-3(e) |
| 1.469-1T(g)(2)(i) | § 1.441-4T(d) | § 1.441-2 |
| 1.1561-1(c)(2) | See paragraph (b)(1) of § 1.441-2 | See § 1.441-2 |
| 1.6654-2(a), concluding text | paragraph (b) of § 1.441-2 | § 1.441-2(c) |
| 1.6655-2(a)(4), first sentence | paragraph (b) of § 1.441-2 | § 1.441-1(b) |

PAR. 2. In the list below, for each section indicated in the left column, remove the old language in the middle column and add the new language in the right column.

| Affected Section | Remove | Add |
|---|---|---|
| 1.46-1(p)(2)(iv) | paragraph (b)(1) of § 1.441-2 | § 1.441-2 |
| 1.48-3(d)(1)(iii) | paragraph (b)(1) of § 1.441-2 | § 1.441-2 |
| 1.280H-1T(a), last sentence | § 1.441-4T(d) | § 1.441-3(c) |
| 1.443-1(b)(1)(ii) | and paragraph (c)(5) of § 1.441-2 | and § 1.441-1(b)(2)(ii). |
| 1.444-1T(a)(1), first sentence | § 1.444-4T(d) | § 1.441-3(c) |
| 1.444-2T(a), last sentence | § 1.441-4T(d) | § 1.441-3(c) |
| 1.448-1(h)(2)(ii)(B)(1) | § 1.441-2T(b)(1) | § 1.441-2(c) |

| | | |
|---|---|---|
| 1.469-1(h)(4)(ii)(D) | § 1.441-4T(f) | § 1.441-3(e) |
| 1.469-1T(g)(2)(i) | § 1.441-4T(d) | § 1.441-2 |
| 1.1561-1(c)(2) | See paragraph (b)(1) of § 1.441-2 | See § 1.441-2 |
| 1.6654-2(a), concluding text | paragraph (b) of § 1.441-2 | § 1.441-2(c) |
| 1.6655-2(a)(4), first sentence | paragraph (b) of § 1.441-2 | § 1.441-1(b) |

PAR. 2. In the list below, for each section indicated in the left column, remove the old language in the middle column and add the new language in the right column.

| Affected Section | Remove | Add |
|---|---|---|
| 1.46-1(p)(2)(iv) | paragraph (b)(1) of § 1.441-2 | § 1.441-2 |
| 1.48-3(d)(1)(iii) | paragraph (b)(1) of § 1.441-2 | § 1.441-2 |
| 1.280H-1T(a), last sentence | § 1.441-4T(d) | § 1.441-3(c) |
| 1.443-1(b)(1)(ii) | and paragraph (c)(5) of § 1.441-2 | and § 1.441-1(b)(2)(ii). |
| 1.444-1T(a)(1), first sentence | § 1.444-4T(d) | § 1.441-3(c) |
| 1.444-2T(a), last sentence | § 1.441-4T(d) | § 1.441-3(c) |
| 1.448-1(h)(2)(ii)(B)(1) | § 1.441-2T(b)(1) | § 1.441-2(c) |
| 1.469-1(h)(4)(ii)(D) | § 1.441-4T(f) | § 1.441-3(e) |
| 1.469-1T(g)(2)(i) | § 1.441-4T(d) | § 1.441-2 |
| 1.1561-1(c)(2) | See paragraph (b)(1) of § 1.441-2 | See § 1.441-2 |
| 1.6654-2(a), concluding text | paragraph (b) of § 1.441-2 | § 1.441-2(c) |
| 1.6655-2(a)(4), first sentence | paragraph (b) of § 1.441-2 | § 1.441-1(b) |

PAR. 2. In the list below, for each section indicated in the left column, remove the old language in the middle column and add the new language in the right column.

| Affected Section | Remove | Add |
|---|---|---|
| 1.46-1(p)(2)(iv) | paragraph (b)(1) of § 1.441-2 | § 1.441-2 |
| 1.48-3(d)(1)(iii) | paragraph (b)(1) of § 1.441-2 | § 1.441-2 |
| 1.280H-1T(a), last sentence | § 1.441-4T(d) | § 1.441-3(c) |
| 1.443-1(b)(1)(ii) | and paragraph (c)(5) of § 1.441-2 | and § 1.441-1(b)(2)(ii). |
| 1.444-1T(a)(1), first sentence | § 1.444-4T(d) | § 1.441-3(c) |
| 1.444-2T(a), last sentence | § 1.441-4T(d) | § 1.441-3(c) |
| 1.448-1(h)(2)(ii)(B)(1) | § 1.441-2T(b)(1) | § 1.441-2(c) |
| 1.469-1(h)(4)(ii)(D) | § 1.441-4T(f) | § 1.441-3(e) |
| 1.469-1T(g)(2)(i) | § 1.441-4T(d) | § 1.441-2 |
| 1.1561-1(c)(2) | See paragraph (b)(1) of § 1.441-2 | See § 1.441-2 |
| 1.6654-2(a), concluding text | paragraph (b) of § 1.441-2 | § 1.441-2(c) |

| | | |
|---|---|---|
| 1.6655-2(a)(4), first sentence | paragraph (b) of § 1.441-2 | § 1.441-1(b) |

PAR. 2. In the list below, for each section indicated in the left column, remove the old language in the middle column and add the new language in the right column.

| Affected Section | Remove | Add |
|---|---|---|
| 1.46-1(p)(2)(iv) | paragraph (b)(1) of § 1.441-2 | § 1.441-2 |
| 1.48-3(d)(1)(iii) | paragraph (b)(1) of § 1.441-2 | § 1.441-2 |
| 1.280H-1T(a), last sentence | § 1.441-4T(d) | § 1.441-3(c) |
| 1.443-1(b)(1)(ii) | and paragraph (c)(5) of § 1.441-2 | and § 1.441-1(b)(2)(ii). |
| 1.444-1T(a)(1), first sentence | § 1.444-4T(d) | § 1.441-3(c) |
| 1.444-2T(a), last sentence | § 1.441-4T(d) | § 1.441-3(c) |
| 1.448-1(h)(2)(ii)(B)(1) | § 1.441-2T(b)(1) | § 1.441-2(c) |
| 1.469-1(h)(4)(ii)(D) | § 1.441-4T(f) | § 1.441-3(e) |
| 1.469-1T(g)(2)(i) | § 1.441-4T(d) | § 1.441-2 |
| 1.1561-1(c)(2) | See paragraph (b)(1) of § 1.441-2 | See § 1.441-2 |
| 1.6654-2(a), concluding text | paragraph (b) of § 1.441-2 | § 1.441-2(c) |
| 1.6655-2(a)(4), first sentence | paragraph (b) of § 1.441-2 | § 1.441-1(b) |

PAR. 2. In the list below, for each section indicated in the left column, remove the old language in the middle column and add the new language in the right column.

| Affected Section | Remove | Add |
|---|---|---|
| 1.46-1(p)(2)(iv) | paragraph (b)(1) of § 1.441-2 | § 1.441-2 |
| 1.48-3(d)(1)(iii) | paragraph (b)(1) of § 1.441-2 | § 1.441-2 |
| 1.280H-1T(a), last sentence | § 1.441-4T(d) | § 1.441-3(c) |
| 1.443-1(b)(1)(ii) | and paragraph (c)(5) of § 1.441-2 | and § 1.441-1(b)(2)(ii). |
| 1.444-1T(a)(1), first sentence | § 1.444-4T(d) | § 1.441-3(c) |
| 1.444-2T(a), last sentence | § 1.441-4T(d) | § 1.441-3(c) |
| 1.448-1(h)(2)(ii)(B)(1) | § 1.441-2T(b)(1) | § 1.441-2(c) |
| 1.469-1(h)(4)(ii)(D) | § 1.441-4T(f) | § 1.441-3(e) |
| 1.469-1T(g)(2)(i) | § 1.441-4T(d) | § 1.441-2 |
| 1.1561-1(c)(2) | See paragraph (b)(1) of § 1.441-2 | See § 1.441-2 |
| 1.6654-2(a), concluding text | paragraph (b) of § 1.441-2 | § 1.441-2(c) |
| 1.6655-2(a)(4), first sentence | paragraph (b) of § 1.441-2 | § 1.441-1(b) |

PAR. 2. In the list below, for each section indicated in the left column, remove the old language in the middle column and add the new language in the right column.

| Affected Section | Remove | Add |
|---|---|---|
| 1.46-1(p)(2)(iv) | paragraph (b)(1) of § 1.441-2 | § 1.441-2 |
| 1.48-3(d)(1)(iii) | paragraph (b)(1) of § 1.441-2 | § 1.441-2 |
| 1.280H-1T(a), last sentence | § 1.441-4T(d) | § 1.441-3(c) |
| 1.443-1(b)(1)(ii) | and paragraph (c)(5) of § 1.441-2 | and § 1.441-1(b)(2)(ii). |
| 1.444-1T(a)(1), first sentence | § 1.444-4T(d) | § 1.441-3(c) |
| 1.444-2T(a), last sentence | § 1.441-4T(d) | § 1.441-3(c) |
| 1.448-1(h)(2)(ii)(B)(1) | § 1.441-2T(b)(1) | § 1.441-2(c) |
| 1.469-1(h)(4)(ii)(D) | § 1.441-4T(f) | § 1.441-3(e) |
| 1.469-1T(g)(2)(i) | § 1.441-4T(d) | § 1.441-2 |
| 1.1561-1(c)(2) | See paragraph (b)(1) of § 1.441-2 | See § 1.441-2 |
| 1.6654-2(a), concluding text | paragraph (b) of § 1.441-2 | § 1.441-2(c) |
| 1.6655-2(a)(4), first sentence | paragraph (b) of § 1.441-2 | § 1.441-1(b) |

PAR. 2. In the list below, for each section indicated in the left column, remove the old language in the middle column and add the new language in the right column.


| Affected Section | Remove | Add |
|---|---|---|
| 1.46-1(p)(2)(iv) | paragraph (b)(1) of § 1.441-2 | § 1.441-2 |
| 1.48-3(d)(1)(iii) | paragraph (b)(1) of § 1.441-2 | § 1.441-2 |
| 1.280H-1T(a), last sentence | § 1.441-4T(d) | § 1.441-3(c) |
| 1.443-1(b)(1)(ii) | and paragraph (c)(5) of § 1.441-2 | and § 1.441-1(b)(2)(ii). |
| 1.444-1T(a)(1), first sentence | § 1.444-4T(d) | § 1.441-3(c) |
| 1.444-2T(a), last sentence | § 1.441-4T(d) | § 1.441-3(c) |
| 1.448-1(h)(2)(ii)(B)(1) | § 1.441-2T(b)(1) | § 1.441-2(c) |
| 1.469-1(h)(4)(ii)(D) | § 1.441-4T(f) | § 1.441-3(e) |
| 1.469-1T(g)(2)(i) | § 1.441-4T(d) | § 1.441-2 |
| 1.1561-1(c)(2) | See paragraph (b)(1) of § 1.441-2 | See § 1.441-2 |
| 1.6654-2(a), concluding text | paragraph (b) of § 1.441-2 | § 1.441-2(c) |
| 1.6655-2(a)(4), first sentence | paragraph (b) of § 1.441-2 | § 1.441-1(b) |

PAR. 2. In the list below, for each section indicated in the left column, remove the old language in the middle column and add the new language in the right column.

| Affected Section | Remove | Add |
|---|---|---|
| 1.46-1(p)(2)(iv) | paragraph (b)(1) of § 1.441-2 | § 1.441-2 |
| 1.48-3(d)(1)(iii) | paragraph (b)(1) of § 1.441-2 | § 1.441-2 |
| 1.280H-1T(a), last sentence | § 1.441-4T(d) | § 1.441-3(c) |
| 1.443-1(b)(1)(ii) | and paragraph (c)(5) of § 1.441-2 | and § 1.441-1(b)(2)(ii). |
| 1.444-1T(a)(1), first sentence | § 1.444-4T(d) | § 1.441-3(c) |
| 1.444-2T(a), last sentence | § 1.441-4T(d) | § 1.441-3(c) |
| 1.448-1(h)(2)(ii)(B)(1) | § 1.441-2T(b)(1) | § 1.441-2(c) |
| 1.469-1(h)(4)(ii)(D) | § 1.441-4T(f) | § 1.441-3(e) |
| 1.469-1T(g)(2)(i) | § 1.441-4T(d) | § 1.441-2 |
| 1.1561-1(c)(2) | See paragraph (b)(1) of § 1.441-2 | See § 1.441-2 |
| 1.6654-2(a), concluding text | paragraph (b) of § 1.441-2 | § 1.441-2(c) |
| 1.6655-2(a)(4), first sentence | paragraph (b) of § 1.441-2 | § 1.441-1(b) |

PAR. 2. In the list below, for each section indicated in the left column, remove the old language in the middle column and add the new language in the right column.

| Affected Section | Remove | Add |
|---|---|---|
| 1.46-1(p)(2)(iv) | paragraph (b)(1) of § 1.441-2 | § 1.441-2 |
| 1.48-3(d)(1)(iii) | paragraph (b)(1) of § 1.441-2 | § 1.441-2 |
| 1.280H-1T(a), last sentence | § 1.441-4T(d) | § 1.441-3(c) |
| 1.443-1(b)(1)(ii) | and paragraph (c)(5) of § 1.441-2 | and § 1.441-1(b)(2)(ii). |
| 1.444-1T(a)(1), first sentence | § 1.444-4T(d) | § 1.441-3(c) |
| 1.444-2T(a), last sentence | § 1.441-4T(d) | § 1.441-3(c) |
| 1.448-1(h)(2)(ii)(B)(1) | § 1.441-2T(b)(1) | § 1.441-2(c) |
| 1.469-1(h)(4)(ii)(D) | § 1.441-4T(f) | § 1.441-3(e) |
| 1.469-1T(g)(2)(i) | § 1.441-4T(d) | § 1.441-2 |
| 1.1561-1(c)(2) | See paragraph (b)(1) of § 1.441-2 | See § 1.441-2 |
| 1.6654-2(a), concluding text | paragraph (b) of § 1.441-2 | § 1.441-2(c) |
| 1.6655-2(a)(4), first sentence | paragraph (b) of § 1.441-2 | § 1.441-1(b) |

PAR. 2. In the list below, for each section indicated in the left column, remove the old language in the middle column and add the new language in the right column.

| Affected Section | Remove | Add |
|---|---|---|
| 1.46-1(p)(2)(iv) | paragraph (b)(1) of § 1.441-2 | § 1.441-2 |
| 1.48-3(d)(1)(iii) | paragraph (b)(1) of § 1.441-2 | § 1.441-2 |
| 1.280H-1T(a), last sentence | § 1.441-4T(d) | § 1.441-3(c) |
| 1.443-1(b)(1)(ii) | and paragraph (c)(5) of § 1.441-2 | and § 1.441-1(b)(2)(ii). |
| 1.444-1T(a)(1), first sentence | § 1.444-4T(d) | § 1.441-3(c) |
| 1.444-2T(a), last sentence | § 1.441-4T(d) | § 1.441-3(c) |
| 1.448-1(h)(2)(ii)(B)(1) | § 1.441-2T(b)(1) | § 1.441-2(c) |
| 1.469-1(h)(4)(ii)(D) | § 1.441-4T(f) | § 1.441-3(e) |
| 1.469-1T(g)(2)(i) | § 1.441-4T(d) | § 1.441-2 |
| 1.1561-1(c)(2) | See paragraph (b)(1) of § 1.441-2 | See § 1.441-2 |
| 1.6654-2(a), concluding text | paragraph (b) of § 1.441-2 | § 1.441-2(c) |
| 1.6655-2(a)(4), first sentence | paragraph (b) of § 1.441-2 | § 1.441-1(b) |

PAR. 2. In the list below, for each section indicated in the left column, remove the old language in the middle column and add the new language in the right column.


| Affected Section | Remove | Add |
|---|---|---|
| 1.46-1(p)(2)(iv) | paragraph (b)(1) of § 1.441-2 | § 1.441-2 |
| 1.48-3(d)(1)(iii) | paragraph (b)(1) of § 1.441-2 | § 1.441-2 |
| 1.280H-1T(a), last sentence | § 1.441-4T(d) | § 1.441-3(c) |
| 1.443-1(b)(1)(ii) | and paragraph (c)(5) of § 1.441-2 | and § 1.441-1(b)(2)(ii). |
| 1.444-1T(a)(1), first sentence | § 1.444-4T(d) | § 1.441-3(c) |
| 1.444-2T(a), last sentence | § 1.441-4T(d) | § 1.441-3(c) |
| 1.448-1(h)(2)(ii)(B)(1) | § 1.441-2T(b)(1) | § 1.441-2(c) |
| 1.469-1(h)(4)(ii)(D) | § 1.441-4T(f) | § 1.441-3(e) |
| 1.469-1T(g)(2)(i) | § 1.441-4T(d) | § 1.441-2 |
| 1.1561-1(c)(2) | See paragraph (b)(1) of § 1.441-2 | See § 1.441-2 |
| 1.6654-2(a), concluding text | paragraph (b) of § 1.441-2 | § 1.441-2(c) |
| 1.6655-2(a)(4), first sentence | paragraph (b) of § 1.441-2 | § 1.441-1(b) |

PAR. 2. In the list below, for each section indicated in the left column, remove the old language in the middle column and add the new language in the right column.

| Affected Section | Remove | Add |
|---|---|---|
| 1.46-1(p)(2)(iv) | paragraph (b)(1) of § 1.441-2 | § 1.441-2 |
| 1.48-3(d)(1)(iii) | paragraph (b)(1) of § 1.441-2 | § 1.441-2 |
| 1.280H-1T(a), last sentence | § 1.441-4T(d) | § 1.441-3(c) |
| 1.443-1(b)(1)(ii) | and paragraph (c)(5) of § 1.441-2 | and § 1.441-1(b)(2)(ii). |
| 1.444-1T(a)(1), first sentence | § 1.444-4T(d) | § 1.441-3(c) |
| 1.444-2T(a), last sentence | § 1.441-4T(d) | § 1.441-3(c) |
| 1.448-1(h)(2)(ii)(B)(1) | § 1.441-2T(b)(1) | § 1.441-2(c) |
| 1.469-1(h)(4)(ii)(D) | § 1.441-4T(f) | § 1.441-3(e) |
| 1.469-1T(g)(2)(i) | § 1.441-4T(d) | § 1.441-2 |
| 1.1561-1(c)(2) | See paragraph (b)(1) of § 1.441-2 | See § 1.441-2 |
| 1.6654-2(a), concluding text | paragraph (b) of § 1.441-2 | § 1.441-2(c) |
| 1.6655-2(a)(4), first sentence | paragraph (b) of § 1.441-2 | § 1.441-1(b) |

**Proposed § 1.444-2T** [*For Preamble, see ¶ 152,177*]

• ***Caution:*** This Notice of Proposed Rulemaking was partially finalized by T.D. 8996, issued on 5/16/2002. Proposed regulation §§ 1.46-1, 1.48-3, 1.280H-1T, 1.443-1, 1.444-1T, 1.444-2T, 1.448-1, 1.469-1, 1.469-1T, 1.898-4, 1.1561-1, 1.6654-2, 1.6655-2 and 301.7701(b)-6 remains in effect.

**§ 1.444-3T Manner and time of making section 444 election (temporary).**

**(a) In general.** A section 444 election shall be made in the manner and at the time provided in this section.

**(b) Manner and time of making election.** *(1) General rule.* A section 444 election shall be made by filing a properly prepared Form 8716, "Election to Have a Tax Year Other Than a Required Tax Year," with the Service Center indicated by the instructions to Form 8716. Except as provided in paragraphs (b)(2) and (4) of this section, Form 8716 must be filed by the earlier of—

(i) The 15th day of the fifth month following the month that includes the first day of the taxable year for which the election will first be effective, or

(ii) The due date (without regard to extensions) of the income tax return resulting from the section 444 election.

In addition, a copy of Form 8716 must be attached to Form 1065 or Form 1120 series form, whichever is applicable, for the first taxable year for which the section 444 election is made. Form 8716 shall be signed by any person who is authorized to sign Form 1065 or Form 1120 series form, whichever is applicable. (See sections 6062 and 6063, relating to the signing of returns). The provisions of this paragraph (b)(1) may be illustrated by the following examples.

*Example (1).* A, a partnership that began operations on September 10, 1988, is qualified to make a section 444 election to use a September 30 taxable year for its taxable year beginning September 10, 1988. Pursuant to paragraph (b)(1) of this section, A must file Form 8716 by the earlier of the 15th day of the fifth month following the month that includes the first day of the taxable year for which the election will first be effective *(i.e.,* February 15, 1989) or the due date (without regard to extensions) of the partnership's tax return for the period September 10, 1988 to September 30, 1988 *(i.e.,* January 15, 1989). Thus, A must file Form 8716 by January 15, 1989.

*Example (2).* The facts are the same as in example (1), except that A began operations on October 20, 1988. Based upon these facts, A must file Form 8716 by March 15, 1989, the 15th day of the fifth month following the month that includes the first day of the taxable year for which the election will first be effective.

*Example (3).* B is a corporation that first becomes a personal service corporation for its taxable year beginning September 1, 1988. B qualifies to make a section 444 election to use a September 30 taxable year for its taxable year beginning September 1, 1988. Pursuant to this paragraph (b)(1), B must file Form 8716 by December 15, 1988, the due date of the income tax return for the short period September 1 to September 30, 1988.

*(2) Special extension of time for making an election.* If, pursuant to paragraph (b)(1) of this section, the due date for filing Form 8716 is prior to July 26, 1988, such date is extended to July 26, 1988. The provisions of this paragraph (b)(2) may be illustrated by the following examples.

*Example (1).* B, a partnership that historically used a June 30 taxable year, is qualified to make a section 444 election to retain a June 30 taxable year for its taxable year beginning July 1, 1987. Absent paragraph (b)(2) of this section, B would be required to file Form 8716 by December 15, 1987. However, pursuant to paragraph (b)(2) of this section, B's due date for filing Form 8716 is extended to July 26, 1988.

*Example (2).* C, a partnership that began operations on January 20, 1988, is qualified to make a section 444 election to use a year ending September 30 for its taxable year beginning January 20, 1988. Absent paragraph (b)(2) of this section, C is required to file Form 8716 by June 15, 1988 (the 15th day of the fifth month following the month that includes the first day of the taxable year for which the election will first be effective). However, pursuant to paragraph (b)(2) of this section, the due date for filing Form 8716 is July 26, 1988.

*(3) Corporation electing to be an S corporation.* (i) In general. A corporation electing to be an S corporation is subject to the same time and manner rules for filing Form 8716 as any other taxpayer making a section 444 election. Thus, a corporation electing to be an S corporation that desires to make a section 444 election is not required to file Form 8716 with its Form 2553, "Election by a Small Business Corporation." However, a corporation electing to be an S corporation after Sep 26 1988, is required to state on Form 2553 its intention to—

(A) Make a section 444 election, if qualified, or

(B) Make a "back-up section 444 election" as described in paragraph (b) (4) of this section. If a corporation electing to be an S corporation fails to state either of the above intentions, the District Director may, at his discretion, disregard any section 444 election for such taxpayer.

(ii) Examples. The provisions of this paragraph (b)(3) may be illustrated by the following examples.

*Example (1).* D is a corporation that commences operations on October 1, 1988, and elects to be an S corporation for its taxable year beginning October 1, 1988. All of D's shareholders use the calendar year as their taxable year. D desires to adopt a September 30 taxable year. D does not believe it has a business purpose for a September 30 taxable year and thus it must make a section 444 election to use such year. Based on these facts, D must, pursuant to the instructions to Form 2553, state on Form 2553 that, if qualified, it will make a section 444 election to adopt a year ending September 30 for its taxable year beginning October 1, 1988. If D is qualified *(i.e.,* D is not a member of a tiered structure on December 31, 1988) to make a section 444 election for its taxable year beginning October 1, 1988, D must file Form 8716 by March 15, 1989. If D ultimately is not qualified to make a section 444 election for its taxable year beginning October 1, 1988, D's election to be an S corporation will not be effective unless, pursuant to the instructions to Form 2553, D made a back-up calendar year election *(i.e.,* an election to adopt the calendar year in the event D ultimately is not qualified to make a section 444 election for such year).

*Example (2).* The facts are the same as in example (1), except that D believes it can establish, to the satisfaction of the Commissioner, a business purpose for adopting a September 30 taxable year. However, D desires to make a "back-up section 444 election" (see paragraph (b)(4) of this section) in the event that the Commissioner does not grant permission to adopt a September 30 taxable year based upon business purpose. Based on these facts, D must, pursuant to the instructions to Form 2553, state on Form 2553 its intention, if qualified, to make a back-up section 444 election to adopt a September 30 taxable year. If, by March 15, 1989, D has not received permission to adopt a September 30 taxable year and D is qualified to make a section 444 election, D must make a back-up election in accordance with paragraph (b)(4) of this section.

*(4) Back-up section 444 election.* (i) General rule. A taxpayer that has requested (or is planning to request) permission to use a particular taxable year based upon business purpose, may, if otherwise qualified, file a section 444 election (referred to as a "back-up section 444 election"). If the Commissioner subsequently denies the business purpose request, the taxpayer will, if otherwise qualified, be required to activate the back-up section 444 election. See examples (1) and (2) in paragraph (b)(4)(iv) of this section.

(ii) Procedures for making a back-up section 444 election. In addition to following the general rules provided in this section, a taxpayer making a back-up section 444 election should, in order to allow the Service to process the affected returns in an efficient manner, type or legibly print the words "BACK-UP ELECTION" at the top of Form 8716, "Election to Have a Tax Year Other Than a Required Tax Year." However, if such Form 8716 is filed on or after the date a Form 1128, Application for Change in Accounting Period, is filed with respect to a period that begins on the same date, the words "FORM 1128 BACK-UP ELECTION" should be typed or legibly printed at the top of Form 8716.

(iii) Procedures for activating a back-up section 444 election. (A) Partnerships and S corporations. (1) In general. A back-up section 444 election made by a partnership or S corporation is activated by filing the return required in § 1.7519-2T (a)(2)(i) and making the payment required in § 1.7519-1T. The due date for filing such return and payment will be the later of—

(i) The due dates provided in § 1.7519-2T, or

(ii) 60 days from the date the Commissioner denies the business purpose request.

However, interest will be assessed (at the rate provided in section 6621 (a)(2)) on any required payment made after the due date (without regard to any extension for a back-up election) provided in § 1.7519-2T(a)(4)(i) or (a)(4)(ii), whichever is applicable, for such payment. Interest will be calculated from such due date to the date such amount is actually paid. Interest assessed under this paragraph will be separate from any required payments. Thus, interest will not be subject to refund under § 1.7519-2T.

(2) Special rule if Form 720 used to satisfy return requirement. If, pursuant to § 1.7519-2T(a)(3), a partnership or S corporation must use Form 720, "Quarterly Federal Excise Tax Return," to satisfy the return requirement of § 1.7519-2T(a)(2), then in addition to following the general rules provided in § 1.7519-2T, the partnership or S corporation must type or legibly print the words "ACTIVATING BACK-UP ELECTION" on the top of Form 720. A partnership or S corporation that would otherwise file a Form 720 on or before the date specified in paragraph (b)(4)(iii)(A)(1) of this section may satisfy the return requirement by including the necessary information on such Form 720. Alternatively, such partnership or S corporation may file an additional Form 720 *(i.e.,* a Form 720 separate from the Form 720 it would otherwise file). Thus, for example, if the due date for activating an S corporation's back-up election is November 15, 1988, and the S corporation must file a Form 720 by October 31, 1988, to report manufacturers excise tax for the third quarter of 1988, the S corporation may use that Form 720 to activate its back-up election. Alternatively, the S corporation may file its regular Form 720 that is due October 31, 1988, and file an additional Form 720 by November 15, 1988, activating its back-up election.

(B) Personal service corporations. A back-up section 444 election made by a personal service corporation is activated by filing Form 8716 with the personal service corporation's original or amended income tax return for the taxable year in which the election is first effective, and typing or legibly printing the words—"ACTIVATING BACK-UP ELECTION" on the top of such income tax return.

(iv) Examples. The provisions of this paragraph (b)(4) may be illustrated by the following examples. Also see example (2) in paragraph (b)(3) of this section.

*Example (1).* E, a partnership that historically used a June 30 taxable year, requested (pursuant to section 6 of Rev. Proc. 87-32, 1987-28 I.R.B. 14) permission from the Commissioner to retain a June 30 taxable year for its taxable year beginning July 1, 1987. Furthermore, E is qualified to make a section 444 election to retain a June 30 taxable year for its taxable year beginning July 1, 1987. However, as of the date specified in paragraph (b)(2) of this section, the Commissioner has not determined whether E has a valid business purpose for retaining its June 30 taxable year. Based on these facts, E may, by the date specified in paragraph (b)(2) of this section, make a back-up section 444 election to retain its June 30 taxable year.

*Example (2).* The facts are the same as in example (1). In addition, on August 12, 1988, the Internal Revenue Service notifies E that its business purpose request is denied. E asks for reconsideration of the Service's decision, and the Service sustains the original denial on September 30, 1988. Based on these facts, E must activate its back-up section 444 election within 60 days after September 30, 1988.

*Example (3).* The facts are the same as in example (1), except that E desires to make a section 444 election to use a year ending September 30 for its taxable year beginning July 1, 1987. Although E qualifies to make a section 444 election to retain its June 30 taxable year, E may make a back-up section 444 election for a September 30 taxable year.

**(c) Administrative relief.** *(1) Extension of time to file income tax returns.* (i) Automatic extension. If a partnership, S corporation, or personal service corporation makes a section 444 election (or does not make a section 444 election, either because it is ineligible or because it decides not to make the election, and therefore changes to its required taxable year) for its first taxable year beginning after December 31, 1986, the due date for filing its income tax return for such year shall be the later of—

(A) The due date established under—

(1) Section 6072, in the case of Form 1065,

(2) § 1.6037-1(b), in the case of Form 1120S,

(3) Section 6072(b), in the case of other Form 1120 series form; or

(B) August 15, 1988.

The words "SECTION 444 RETURN" should, in order to allow the Service to process the affected returns in an efficient manner, be typed or legibly printed at the top of the Form 1065 or Form 1120 series form, whichever is applicable, filed under this paragraph (c)(1)(i).

(ii) Additional extensions. If the due date of the income tax return for the first taxable year beginning after December 31, 1986, extended as provided in paragraph (c)(1)(i)(B) of this section, occurs before the date that is 6 months after the date specified in paragraph (c)(1)(i) (A) of this section, the partnership, S corporation, or personal service corporation may request an additional extension or extensions of time (up to 6 months after the date specified in paragraph (c)(1)(i)(A) of this section) to file its income tax return for such first taxable year. The request must be made by the later of the date specified in paragraph (c)(1)(i)(A) or (c)(1)(i)(B) of this section and must be made on Form 7004, "Application for Automatic Extension of Time To File Corporation Income Tax Return", or Form 2758, "Application for Extension of Time to File U.S. Partnership, Fiduciary, and Certain Other Returns," whichever is applicable, in accordance with the form and its instructions. In addition, the following words should be typed or legibly printed at the top of the form— "SECTION 444 REQUEST FOR ADDITIONAL EXTENSION."

(iii) Examples. The provisions of paragraph (c) (1) of this section may be illustrated by the following examples.

*Example (1).* G, a partnership that historically used a January 31 taxable year, makes a section 444 election to retain such year for its taxable year beginning February 1, 1987. Absent paragraph (c)(1)(i) of this section, G's Form 1065 for the taxable year ending January 31, 1988, is due on or before May 15, 1988. However, if G types or legibly prints "SECTION 444 RETURN" at the top of Form 1065 for such year paragraph (c)(1)(i) of this section automatically extends the due date of such return to August 15, 1988.

*Example (2).* The facts are the same as in example (1), except that G desires to extend the due date of its income tax return for the year ending January 31, 1988, to a date beyond August 15, 1988. Pursuant to paragraph (c)(1)(ii) of this section, G may extend such return to November 15, 1988 *(i.e.,* the date that is up to 6 months after May 15, 1988, the normal due date of the return). However, in order to obtain this additional extension, G must file Form 2758 pursuant to paragraph (c)(1)(i) of this section on or before August 15, 1988.

*Example (3).* H, a partnership that historically used a May 31 taxable year, makes a section 444 election to use a year ending September 30 for its taxable year beginning on June 1, 1987. Absent paragraph (c)(1)(i) of this section, H's Form 1065 for the taxable year beginning June 1, 1987, and ending September 30, 1987, is due on or before January 15, 1988. However, if H types or legibly prints "SECTION 444 RETURN" at the top of Form 1065 for such year, paragraph (c)(1)(i) of this section automatically extends the due date of such return to August 15, 1988.

*Example (4).* The facts are the same as in example (3), except H desires to further extend *(i.e.,* extend beyond August 15, 1988) the due date of its income tax return for its taxable year beginning June 1, 1987, and ending September 30, 1987. Since August 15, 1988, is 6 months or more after the due date (without extensions) of such return, paragraph (c)(1)(ii) of this section prevents H from further extending the time for filing such return.

*Example (5).* I, a partnership that historically used a June 30 taxable year, considered making a section 444 election to retain such taxable year, but eventually decided to change to a December 31 taxable year (I's required taxable year). Absent paragraph (c)(1)(i) of this section, I's Form 1065 for the taxable year beginning July 1, 1987, and ending December 31, 1987, is due on or before April 15, 1988. Pursuant to paragraph (c)(1)(i) of this section, if I types or legibly prints "SECTION 444 RETURN" at the top of Form 1065 for such year, paragraph (c)(1)(i) of this section automatically extends the due date of such return to August 15, 1988. In addition, I may further extend such return pursuant to paragraph (c)(1)(ii) of this section.

*(2) No penalty for certain late payments.* (i) In general. In the case of a personal service corporation or S corporation described in paragraph (c)(1)(i) of this section, no penalty under section 6651 (a)(2) will be imposed for failure to pay income tax (if any) for the first taxable year beginning after December 31, 1986, but only for the period beginning with the last date for payment and ending with the later of the

date specified in paragraph (c)(1)(i) or paragraph (c)(1)(ii) of this section.

(ii) Example. The provisions of paragraph (c)(2)(i) of this section may be illustrated by the following example.

*Example.* J, a personal service corporation that historically used a January 31 taxable year, makes a section 444 election to retain such year for its taxable year beginning February 1, 1987. The last date (without extension) for payment of J's income tax (if any) for its taxable year beginning February 1, 1987, is April 15, 1988. However, under paragraph (c)(2)(i) of this section, no penalty under section 6651(a)(2) will be imposed on any underpayment of income tax for the period beginning April 15, 1988 and ending August 15, 1988.

**(d) Effective date.** This section is effective for taxable years beginning after December 31, 1986.

T.D. 8205, 5/24/88.

### § 1.444-4 Tiered structure.

**(a) Electing small business trusts.** For purposes of § 1.444-2T, solely with respect to an S corporation shareholder, the term deferral entity does not include a trust that is treated as an electing small business trust under section 1361(e). An S corporation with an electing small business trust as a shareholder may make an election under section 444. This paragraph is applicable to taxable years beginning on and after December 29, 2000; however, taxpayers may voluntarily apply it to taxable years of S corporations beginning after December 31, 1996.

**(b) Certain tax-exempt trusts.** For purposes of § 1.444-2T, solely with respect to an S corporation shareholder, the term deferral entity does not include a trust that is described in section 401(a) or 501(c)(3), and is exempt from taxation under section 501(a). An S corporation with a trust as a shareholder that is described in section 401(a) or section 501(c)(3), and is exempt from taxation under section 501(a) may make an election under section 444. This paragraph is applicable to taxable years beginning on and after December 29, 2000; however taxpayers may voluntarily apply it to taxable years of S corporations beginning after December 31, 1997.

**(c) Certain terminations disregarded.** *(1) In general.* An S corporation that is described in this paragraph (c)(1) may request that a termination of its election under section 444 be disregarded, and that the S corporation be permitted to resume use of the year it previously elected under section 444, by following the procedures of paragraph (c)(2) of this section. An S corporation is described in this paragraph if the S corporation is otherwise qualified to make a section 444 election, and its previous election was terminated under § 1.444-2T(a) solely because—

(i) In the case of a taxable year beginning after December 31, 1996, a trust that is treated as an electing small business trust became a shareholder of such S corporation; or

(ii) In the case of a taxable year beginning after December 31, 1997, a trust that is described in section 401(a) or 501(c)(3), and is exempt from taxation under section 501(a) became a shareholder of such S corporation.

*(2) Procedure.* (i) In general. An S corporation described in paragraph (c)(1) of this section that wishes to make the request described in paragraph (c)(1) of this section must do so by filing Form 8716, "Election To Have a Tax Year Other Than a Required Tax Year," and typing or printing legibly at the top of such form— "CONTINUATION OF SECTION 444 ELECTION UNDER § 1.444-4." In order to assist the Internal Revenue Service in updating the S corporation's account, on Line 5 the Box "Changing to" should be checked. Additionally, the election month indicated must be the last month of the S corporation's previously elected section 444 election year, and the effective year indicated must end in 2002.

(ii) Time and place for filing Form 8716. Such form must be filed on or before October 15, 2002, with the service center where the S corporation's returns of tax (Forms 1120S) are filed. In addition, a copy of the Form 8716 should be attached to the S corporation's short period Federal income tax return for the first election year beginning on or after January 1, 2002.

*(3) Effect of request.* (i) Taxable years beginning on or after January 1, 2002. An S corporation described in paragraph (c)(1) of this section that requests, in accordance with this paragraph, that a termination of its election under section 444 be disregarded will be permitted to resume use of the year it previously elected under section 444, commencing with its first taxable year beginning on or after January 1, 2002. Such S corporation will be required to file a return under § 1.7519-2T for each taxable year beginning on or after January 1, 2002. No payment under section 7519 will be due with respect to the first taxable year beginning on or after January 1, 2002. However, a required payment will be due on or before May 15, 2003, with respect to such S corporation's second continued section 444 election year that begins in calendar year 2002.

(ii) Taxable years beginning prior to January 1, 2002. An S corporation described in paragraph (c)(1) of this section that requests, in accordance with this paragraph, that a termination of its election under section 444 be disregarded will not be required to amend any prior Federal income tax returns, make any required payments under section 7519, or file any returns under § 1.7519-2T, with respect to taxable years beginning on or after the date the termination of its section 444 election was effective and prior to January 1, 2002.

(iii) Section 7519: required payments and returns. The Internal Revenue Service waives any requirement for an S corporation described in paragraph (c)(1) of this section to file the federal tax returns and make any required payments under section 7519 for years prior to the taxable year of continuation as described in paragraph (c)(3)(i) of this section, if for such years the S corporation filed its federal income tax returns on the basis of its required taxable year.

T.D. 8994, 5/13/2002.

### § 1.446-1 General rule for methods of accounting.

***Caution:*** The Treasury has not yet amended Reg § 1.446-1 to reflect changes made by P.L. 110-246.

**(a) General rule.** *(1)* Section 446(a) provides that taxable income shall be computed under the method of accounting on the basis of which a taxpayer regularly computes his income in keeping his books. The term "method of accounting" includes not only the over-all method of accounting of the taxpayer but also the accounting treatment of any item. Examples of such over-all methods are the cash receipts and disbursements method, an accrual method, combinations of such methods, and combinations of the foregoing with various methods provided for the accounting treatment of special items. These methods of accounting for special items include the accounting treatment prescribed for research and experimental expenditures, soil and water conservation expenditures, depreciation, net operating losses, etc. Except for deviations permitted or required by such special accounting treatment, taxable income shall be computed under the method of accounting on the basis of which the taxpayer regularly computes his income in keeping his books. For requirement respecting the adoption or change of accounting method, see section 446(e) and paragraph (e) of this section.

*(2)* It is recognized that no uniform method of accounting can be prescribed for all taxpayers. Each taxpayer shall adopt such forms and systems as are, in his judgment, best suited to his needs. However, no method of accounting is acceptable unless, in the opinion of the Commissioner, it clearly reflects income. A method of accounting which reflects the consistent application of generally accepted accounting principles in a particular trade or business in accordance with accepted conditions or practices in that trade or business will ordinarily be regarded as clearly reflecting income, provided all items of gross income and expense are treated consistently from year to year.

*(3)* Items of gross income and expenditures which are elements in the computation of taxable income need not be in the form of cash. It is sufficient that such items can be valued in terms of money. For general rules relating to the taxable year for inclusion of income and for taking deductions, see sections 451 and 461, and the regulations thereunder.

*(4)* Each taxpayer is required to make a return of his taxable income for each taxable year and must maintain such accounting records as will enable him to file a correct return. See section 6001 and the regulations thereunder. Accounting records include the taxpayer's regular books of account and such other records and data as may be necessary to support the entries on his books of account and on his return, as for example, a reconciliation of any differences between such books and his return. The following are among the essential features that must be considered in maintaining such records:

(i) In all cases in which the production, purchase, or sale of merchandise of any kind is an income-producing factor, merchandise on hand (including finished goods, work in process, raw materials, and supplies) at the beginning and end of the year shall be taken into account in computing the taxable income of the year. (For rules relating to computation of inventories, see sections 263A, 471, and 472 and the regulations thereunder.)

(ii) Expenditures made during the year shall be properly classified as between capital and expense. For example, expenditures for such items as plant and equipment, which have a useful life extending substantially beyond the taxable year, shall be charged to a capital account and not to an expense account.

(iii) In any case in which there is allowable with respect to an asset a deduction for depreciation, amortization, or depletion, any expenditures (other than ordinary repairs) made to restore the asset or prolong its useful life shall be added to the asset account or charged against the appropriate reserve.

**(b) Exceptions.** *(1)* If the taxpayer does not regularly employ a method of accounting which clearly reflects his income, the computation of taxable income shall be made in a manner which, in the opinion of the Commissioner, does clearly reflect income.

*(2)* A taxpayer whose sole source of income is wages need not keep formal books in order to have an accounting method. Tax returns, copies thereof, or other records may be sufficient to establish the use of the method of accounting used in the preparation of the taxpayer's income tax returns.

**(c) Permissible methods.** *(1) In general.* Subject to the provisions of paragraphs (a) and (b) of this section, a taxpayer may compute his taxable income under any of the following methods of accounting:

(i) Cash receipts and disbursements method. Generally, under the cash receipts and disbursements method in the computation of taxable income, all items which constitute gross income (whether in the form of cash, property, or services) are to be included for the taxable year in which actually or constructively received. Expenditures are to be deducted for the taxable year in which actually made. For rules relating to constructive receipt, see § 1.451-2. For treatment of an expenditure attributable to more than one taxable year, see section 461(a) and paragraph (a)(1) of § 1.461-1.

(ii) Accrual method. (A) Generally, under an accrual method, income is to be included for the taxable year when all the events have occurred that fix the right to receive the income and the amount of the income can be determined with reasonable accuracy. Under such a method, a liability is incurred, and generally is taken into account for Federal income tax purposes, in the taxable year in which all the events have occurred that establish the fact of the liability, the amount of the liability can be determined with reasonable accuracy, and economic performance has occurred with respect to the liability. (See paragraph (a)(2)(iii)(A) of § 1.461-1 for examples of liabilities that may not be taken into account until after the taxable year incurred, and see §§ 1.461-4 through 1.461-6 for rules relating to economic performance.) Applicable provisions of the Code, the Income Tax Regulations, and other guidance published by the Secretary prescribe the manner in which a liability that has been incurred is taken into account. For example, section 162 provides that a deductible liability generally is taken into account in the taxable year incurred through a deduction from gross income. As a further example, under section 263 or 263A, a liability that relates to the creation of an asset having a useful life extending substantially beyond the close of the taxable year is taken into account in the taxable year incurred through capitalization (within the meaning of § 1.263A-1(c)(3)), and may later affect the computation of taxable income through depreciation or otherwise over a period including subsequent taxable years, in accordance with applicable Internal Revenue Code sections and related guidance.

(B) The term "liability" includes any item allowable as a deduction, cost, or expense for Federal income tax purposes. In addition to allowable deductions, the term includes any amount otherwise allowable as a capitalized cost, as a cost taken into account in computing cost of goods sold, as a cost allocable to a long-term contract, or as any other cost or expense. Thus, for example, an amount that a taxpayer expends or will expend for capital improvements to property must be incurred before the taxpayer may take the amount into account in computing its basis in the property. The term "liability" is not limited to items for which a legal obligation to pay exists at the time of payment. Thus, for example, amounts prepaid for goods or services and amounts paid without a legal obligation to do so may not be taken into account by an accrual basis taxpayer any earlier than the taxable year in which those amounts are incurred.

(C) No method of accounting is acceptable unless, in the opinion of the Commissioner, it clearly reflects income. The method used by the taxpayer in determining when income is to be accounted for will generally be acceptable if it accords with generally accepted accounting principles, is consistently used by the taxpayer from year to year, and is consistent with the Income Tax Regulations. For example, a taxpayer engaged in a manufacturing business may account for sales of the taxpayer's product when the goods are shipped, when the product is delivered or accepted, or when title to the goods passes to the customers, whether or not billed, depending on the method regularly employed in keeping the taxpayer's books.

(iii) Other permissible methods. Special methods of accounting are described elsewhere in chapter 1 of the Code and the regulations thereunder. For example, see the following sections and the regulations thereunder: Sections 61 and 162, relating to the crop method of accounting; section 453, relating to the installment method; section 460, relating to the long-term contract methods. In addition, special methods of accounting for particular items of income and expense are provided under other sections of chapter 1. For example, see section 174, relating to research and experimental expenditures, and section 175, relating to soil and water conservation expenditures.

(iv) Combinations of the foregoing methods. (a) In accordance with the following rules, any combination of the foregoing methods of accounting will be permitted in connection with a trade or business if such combination clearly reflects income and is consistently used. Where a combination of methods of accounting includes any special methods, such as those referred to in subdivision (iii) of this subparagraph, the taxpayer must comply with the requirements relating to such special methods. A taxpayer using an accrual method of accounting with respect to purchases and sales may use the cash method in computing all other items of income and expense. However, a taxpayer who uses the cash method of accounting in computing gross income from his trade or business shall use the cash method in computing expenses of such trade or business. Similarly, a taxpayer who uses an accrual method of accounting in computing business expenses shall use an accrual method in computing items affecting gross income from his trade or business.

(b) A taxpayer using one method of accounting in computing items of income and deductions of his trade or business may compute other items of income and deductions not connected with his trade or business under a different method of accounting.

*(2) Special rules.* (i) In any case in which it is necessary to use an inventory the accrual method of accounting must be used with regard to purchases and sales unless otherwise authorized under subdivision (ii) of this subparagraph.

(ii) No method of accounting will be regarded as clearly reflecting income unless all items of gross profit and deductions are treated with consistency from year to year. The Commissioner may authorize a taxpayer to adopt or change to a method of accounting permitted by this chapter although the method is not specifically described in the regulations in this part if, in the opinion of the Commissioner, income is clearly reflected by the use of such method. Further, the Commissioner may authorize a taxpayer to continue the use of a method of accounting consistently used by the taxpayer, even though not specifically authorized by the regulations in this part, if, in the opinion of the Commissioner, income is clearly reflected by the use of such method. See section 446(a) and paragraph (a) of this section, which require that taxable income shall be computed under the method of accounting on the basis of which the taxpayer regularly computes his income in keeping his books, and section 446(e) and paragraph (e) of this section, which require the prior approval of the Commissioner in the case of changes in accounting method.

(iii) The timing rules of § 1.1502-13 are a method of accounting for intercompany transactions (as defined in § 1.1502-13(b)(1)(i)), to be applied by each member of a consolidated group in addition to the member's other methods of accounting. See § 1.1502-13(a)(3)(i). This paragraph (c)(2)(iii) is applicable to consolidated return years beginning on or after November 7, 2001.

**(d) Taxpayer engaged in more than one business.** *(1)* Where a taxpayer has two or more separate and distinct trades or businesses, a different method of accounting may be used for each trade or business, provided the method used for each trade or business clearly reflects the income of that particular trade or business. For example, a taxpayer may account for the operations of a personal service business on the cash receipts and disbursements method and of a manufacturing business on an accrual method, provided such businesses are separate and distinct and the methods used for each clearly reflect income. The method first used in accounting for business income and deductions in connection with each trade or business, as evidenced in the taxpayer's income tax return in which such income or deductions are first reported, must be consistently followed thereafter.

*(2)* No trade or business will be considered separate and distinct for purposes of this paragraph unless a complete and separable set of books and records is kept for such trade or business.

*(3)* If, by reason of maintaining different methods of accounting, there is a creation or shifting of profits or losses between the trades or businesses of the taxpayer (for example, through inventory adjustments, sales, purchases, or expenses) so that income of the taxpayer is not clearly reflected, the trades or businesses of the taxpayer will not be considered to be separate and distinct.

**(e) Requirement respecting the adoption or change of accounting method.** *(1)* A taxpayer filing his first return may adopt any permissible method of accounting in computing taxable income for the taxable year covered by such return. See section 446(c) and paragraph (c) of this section for permissible methods. Moreover, a taxpayer may adopt any permissible method of accounting in connection with each separate and distinct trade or business, the income from which is reported for the first time. See section 446(d) and paragraph (d) of this section. See also section 446(a) and paragraph (a) of this section.

*(2)* (i) Except as otherwise expressly provided in chapter 1 of the Code and the regulations thereunder, a taxpayer who changes the method of accounting employed in keeping his books shall, before computing his income upon such new method for purposes of taxation, secure the consent of the Commissioner. Consent must be secured whether or not such method is proper or is permitted under the Internal Revenue Code or the regulations thereunder.

(ii) (a) A change in the method of accounting includes a change in the overall plan of accounting for gross income or deductions or a change in the treatment of any material item used in such overall plan. Although a method of accounting may exist under this definition without the necessity of a pattern of consistent treatment of an item, in most instances a method of accounting is not established for an item without such consistent treatment. A material item is any item that involves the proper time for the inclusion of the item in income or the taking of a deduction. Changes in method of accounting include a change from the cash receipts and disbursement method to an accrual method, or vice versa, a change involving the method or basis used in the valuation of inventories (see sections 471 and 472 and the regulations under sections 471 and 472), a change from the cash or accrual method to a long-term contract method, or vice versa (see § 1.460-4), certain changes in computing depreciation or amortization (see paragraph (e)(2)(ii)(d) of this section), a change involving the adoption, use or discontinuance of any other specialized method of computing taxable income, such as the crop method, and a change where the Internal Revenue Code and regulations under the Internal Revenue Code specifically require that the consent of the Commissioner must be obtained before adopting such a change.

(b) A change in method of accounting does not include correction of mathematical or posting errors, or errors in the computation of tax liability (such as errors in computation of the foreign tax credit, net operating loss, percentage depletion, or investment credit). Also, a change in method of accounting does not include adjustment of any item of income or deduction that does not involve the proper time for the inclusion of the item of income or the taking of a deduction. For example, corrections of items that are deducted as interest or salary, but that are in fact payments of dividends, and of items that are deducted as business expenses, but that are in fact personal expenses, are not changes in method of accounting. In addition, a change in the method of accounting does not include an adjustment with respect to the addition to a reserve for bad debts. Although such adjustment may involve the question of the proper time for the taking of a deduction, such items are traditionally corrected by adjustment in the current and future years. For the treatment of the adjustment of the addition to a bad debt reserve (for example, for banks under section 585 of the Internal Revenue Code), see the regulations under section 166 of the Internal Revenue Code. A change in the method of accounting also does not include a change in treatment resulting from a change in underlying facts. For further guidance on changes involving depreciable or amortizable assets, see paragraph (e)(2)(ii)(d) of this section and § 1.1016-3(h).

(c) A change in an overall plan or system of identifying or valuing items in inventory is a change in method of accounting. Also a change in the treatment of any material item used in the overall plan for identifying or valuing items in inventory is a change in method of accounting.

(d) Changes involving depreciable or amortizable assets. (1) Scope. This paragraph (e)(2)(ii)(d) applies to property subject to section 167, 168, 197, 14001, 1400L(c), to section 168 prior to its amendment by the Tax Reform Act of 1986 (100 Stat. 2121) (former section 168), or to an additional first year depreciation deduction provision of the Internal Revenue Code (for example, section 168(k), 1400L(b), or 1400N(d)).

(2) Changes in depreciation or amortization that are a change in method of accounting. Except as provided in paragraph (e)(2)(ii)(d)(3) of this section, a change in the treatment of an asset from nondepreciable or nonamortizable to depreciable or amortizable, or vice versa, is a change in method of accounting. Additionally, a correction to require depreciation or amortization in lieu of a deduction for the cost of depreciable or amortizable assets that had been consistently treated as an expense in the year of purchase, or vice versa, is a change in method of accounting. Further, except as provided in paragraph (e)(2)(ii)(d)(3) of this section, the following changes in computing depreciation or amortization are a change in method of accounting:

(i) A change in the depreciation or amortization method, period of recovery, or convention of a depreciable or amortizable asset.

(ii) A change from not claiming to claiming the additional first year depreciation deduction provided by, for example, section 168(k), 1400L(b), or 1400N(d), for, and the resulting change to the amount otherwise allowable as a depreciation deduction for the remaining adjusted depreciable basis (or similar basis) of, depreciable property that qualifies for the additional first year depreciation deduction (for example, qualified property, 50-percent bonus depreciation property, qualified New York Liberty Zone property, or qualified Gulf Opportunity Zone property), provided the taxpayer did not make the election out of the additional first year depreciation deduction (or did not make a deemed election out of the additional first year depreciation deduction; for further guidance, for example, see Rev. Proc. 2002-33 (2002-1 C.B. 963), Rev. Proc. 2003-50 (2003-2 C.B. 119), Notice 2006-77 (2006-40 I.R.B. 590), and § 601.601(d)(2)(ii)(b) of this chapter) for the class of property in which the depreciable property that qualifies for the additional first year depreciation deduction (for example, qualified property, 50-percent bonus depreciation property, qualified New York Liberty Zone property, or qualified Gulf Opportunity Zone property) is included:

(iii) A change from claiming the 30-percent additional first year depreciation deduction to claiming the 50-percent additional first year depreciation deduction for depreciable property that qualifies for the 50-percent additional first year depreciation deduction, provided the property is not included in any class of property for which the taxpayer elected the 30-percent, instead of the 50-percent, additional first year depreciation deduction (for example, 50-percent bonus depreciation property or qualified Gulf Opportunity Zone property), or a change from claiming the 50-percent additional first year depreciation deduction to claiming the 30-percent additional first year depreciation deduction for depreciable property that qualifies for the 30-percent additional first year depreciation deduction, including property that is included in a class of property for which the taxpayer elected the 30-percent, instead of the 50-percent, additional first year depreciation deduction (for example, qualified property or qualified New York Liberty Zone property), and the resulting change to the amount otherwise allowable as a depreciation deduction for the property's remaining adjusted depreciable basis (or similar basis). This paragraph (e)(2)(ii)(d)(2)(iii) does not apply if a taxpayer is making a late election or revoking a timely valid election under the applicable additional first year depreciation deduction provision of the Internal Revenue Code (for example, section 168(k), 1400L(b), or 1400N(d)) (see paragraph (e)(2)(ii)(d)(3)(iii) of this section).

(iv) A change from claiming to not claiming the additional first year depreciation deduction for an asset that does not qualify for the additional first year depreciation deduction, including an asset that is included in a class of property for which the taxpayer elected not to claim any additional first year depreciation deduction (for example, an asset that is not qualified property, 50-percent bonus depreciation property, qualified New York Liberty Zone property, or qualified Gulf Opportunity Zone property), and the resulting change to the amount otherwise allowable as a depreciation deduction for the property's depreciable basis.

(v) A change in salvage value to zero for a depreciable or amortizable asset for which the salvage value is expressly treated as zero by the Internal Revenue Code (for example, section 168(b)(4)), the regulations under the Internal Revenue Code (for example, § 1.197-2(f)(1)(ii)), or other guidance published in the Internal Revenue Bulletin.

(vi) A change in the accounting for depreciable or amortizable assets from a single asset account to a multiple asset account (pooling), or vice versa, or from one type of multiple asset account (pooling) to a different type of multiple asset account (pooling).

(vii) For depreciable or amortizable assets that are mass assets accounted for in multiple asset accounts or pools, a change in the method of identifying which assets have been disposed. For purposes of this paragraph (e)(2)(ii)(d)(2)(vii), the term mass assets means a mass or group of individual items of depreciable or amortizable assets that are not necessarily homogeneous, each of which is minor in value relative to the total value of the mass or group, numerous in quantity, usually accounted for only on a total dollar or quantity basis, with respect to which separate identification is impracticable, and placed in service in the same taxable year.

(viii) Any other change in depreciation or amortization as the Secretary may designate by publication in the Federal Register or in the Internal Revenue Bulletin (see § 601.601(d)(2) of this chapter).

(3) Changes in depreciation or amortization that are not a change in method of accounting. Section 1.446-1(e)(2)(ii)(b) applies to determine whether a change in depreciation or amortization is not a change in method of accounting. Further, the following changes in depreciation or amortization are not a change in method of accounting:

(i) Useful life. An adjustment in the useful life of a depreciable or amortizable asset for which depreciation is determined under section 167 (other than under section 168, section 14001, section 1400L(c), former section 168, or an additional first year depreciation deduction provision of the Internal Revenue Code (for example, section 168(k), 1400L(b), or 1400N(d))) is not a change in method of accounting. This paragraph (e)(2)(ii)(d)(3)(i) does not apply if a taxpayer is changing to or from a useful life (or recovery period or amortization period) that is specifically assigned by the Internal Revenue Code (for example, section 167(f)(1), section 168(c), section 168(g)(2) or (3), section 197), the regulations under the Internal Revenue Code, or other guidance published in the Internal Revenue Bulletin and, therefore, such change is a change in method of accounting (unless paragraph (e)(2)(ii)(d)(3)(v) of this section applies). See paragraph (e)(2)(ii)(d)(5)(iv) of this section for determining the taxable year in which to correct an adjustment in useful life that is not a change in method of accounting.

(ii) Change in use. A change in computing depreciation or amortization allowances in the taxable year in which the use of an asset changes in the hands of the same taxpayer is not a change in method of accounting.

(iii) Elections. Generally, the making of a late depreciation or amortization election or the revocation of a timely valid depreciation or amortization election is not a change in method of accounting, except as otherwise expressly provided by the Internal Revenue Code, the regulations under the Internal Revenue Code, or other guidance published in the Internal Revenue Bulletin. This paragraph (e)(2)(ii)(d)(3)(iii) also applies to making a late election or revoking a timely valid election made under section 13261(g)(2) or (3) of the Revenue Reconciliation Act of 1993 (107 Stat. 312, 540) (relating to amortizable section 197 intangibles). A taxpayer may request consent to make a late election or revoke a timely valid election by submitting a request for a private letter ruling. For making or revoking an election under section 179 of the Internal Revenue Code, see section 179(c) and § 1.179-5.

(iv) Salvage value. Except as provided under paragraph (e)(2)(ii)(d)(2)(v) of this section, a change in salvage value of a depreciable or amortizable asset is not treated as a change in method of accounting.

(v) Placed-in-service date. Except as otherwise expressly provided by the Internal Revenue Code, the regulations under the Internal Revenue Code, or other guidance published in the Internal Revenue Bulletin, any change in the placed-in-service date of a depreciable or amortizable asset is not treated as a change in method of accounting. For example, if a taxpayer changes the placed-in-service date of a depreciable or amortizable asset because the taxpayer incorrectly determined the date on which the asset was placed in service, such a change is a change in the placed-in-service date of the asset and, therefore, is not a change in method of accounting. However, if a taxpayer incorrectly determines that a depreciable or amortizable asset is nondepreciable property and later changes the treatment of the asset to depreciable property, such a change is not a change in the placed-in-service date of the asset and, therefore, is a change in method of accounting under paragraph (e)(2)(ii)(d)(2) of this section. Further, a change in the convention of a depreciable or amortizable asset is not a change in the placed-in-service date of the asset and, therefore, is a change in method of accounting under paragraph (e)(2)(ii)(d)(2)(i) of this section. See paragraph (e)(2)(ii)(d)(5)(v) of this section for determining the taxable year in which to make a change in the placed-in-service date of a depreciable or amortizable asset that is not a change in method of accounting.

(vi) Any other change in depreciation or amortization as the Secretary may designate by publication in the Federal Register or in the Internal Revenue Bulletin (see § 601.601(d)(2) of this chapter).

(4) Item being changed. For purposes of a change in depreciation or amortization to which this paragraph (e)(2)(ii)(d) applies, the item being changed generally is the depreciation treatment of each individual depreciable or amortizable asset. However, the item is the depreciation treatment of each vintage account with respect to a depreciable asset for which depreciation is determined under § 1.167(a)-11 (class life asset depreciation range (CLADR) property). Similarly, the item is the depreciable treatment of each general asset account with respect to a depreciable asset for which general asset account treatment has been elected under section 168(i)(4) or the item is the depreciation treatment of each mass asset account with respect to a depreciable asset for which mass asset account treatment has been elected under former section 168(d)(2)(A). Further, a change in computing depreciation or amortization under section 167 (other than under section 168, section 14001, section 1400L(c), former section 168, or an additional first year depreciation deduction provision of the Internal Revenue Code (for example, section 168(k), 1400L(b), or 1400N(d))) is permitted only with respect to all assets in a particular account (as defined in § 1.167(a)-7) or vintage account.

(5) Special rules. For purposes of a change in depreciation or amortization to which this paragraph (e)(2)(ii)(d) applies—

(i) Declining balance method to the straight line method for MACRS property. For tangible, depreciable property subject to section 168 (MACRS property) that is depreciated using the 200-percent or 150-percent declining balance method of depreciation under section 168(b)(1) or (2), a taxpayer may change without the consent of the Commissioner from the declining balance method of depreciation to the straight line method of depreciation in the first taxable year in which the use of the straight line method with respect to the adjusted depreciable basis of the MACRS property as of the beginning of that year will yield a depreciation allowance that is greater than the depreciation allowance yielded by the use of the declining balance method. When the change is made, the adjusted depreciable basis of the MACRS property as of the beginning of the taxable year is recovered through annual depreciation allowances over the remaining recovery period (for further guidance, see section 6.06 of Rev. Proc. 87-57 (1987-2 C.B. 687) and § 601.601(d)(2)(ii)(b) of this chapter).

(ii) Depreciation method changes for section 167 property. For a depreciable or amortizable asset for which depreciation is determined under section 167 (other than under section 168, section 14001, section 1400L(c), former section 168, or an additional first year depreciation deduction provision of the Internal Revenue Code (for example, section 168(k), 1400L(b), or 1400N(d))), see § 1.167(e)-1(b), (c), and (d) for the changes in depreciation method that are permitted to be made without the consent of the Commissioner. For CLADR property, see § 1.167(a)-11(c)(1)(iii) for the changes in depreciation method for CLADR property that are permitted to be made without the consent of the Commissioner. Further, see § 1.167(a)-11(b)(4)(iii)(c) for how to correct an incorrect classification or characterization of CLADR property.

(iii) Section 481 adjustment. Except as otherwise expressly provided by the Internal Revenue Code, the regulations under the Internal Revenue Code, or other guidance published in the Internal Revenue Bulletin, no section 481 adjustment is required or permitted for a change from one permissible method of computing depreciation or amortization to another permissible method of computing depreciation or amortization for an asset because this change is implemented by either a cut-off method (for further guidance, for example, see section 2.06 of Rev. Proc. 97-27 (1997-1 C.B. 680), section 2.06 of Rev. Proc. 2002-9 (2002-1 C.B. 327), and § 601.601(d)(2)(ii)(b) of this chapter) or a modified cut-off method (under which the adjusted depreciable basis of the asset as of the beginning of the year of change is recovered using the new permissible method of accounting), as appropriate. However, a change from an impermissible method of computing depreciation or amortization to a permissible method of computing depreciation or amortization for an asset results in a section 481 adjustment. Similarly, a change in the treatment of an asset from nondepreciable or nonamortizable to depreciable or amortizable (or vice versa) or a change in the treatment of an asset from expensing to depreciating (or vice versa) results in a section 481 adjustment.

(iv) Change in useful life. This paragraph (e)(2)(ii)(d)(5)(iv) applies to an adjustment in the useful life of a depreciable or amortizable asset for which depreciation is determined under section 167 (other than under section 168, section 14001, section 1400L(c), former section 168, or an additional first year depreciation deduction provision of the Internal Revenue Code (for example, section 168(k), 1400L(b), or 1400N(d))) and that is not a change in method of accounting under paragraph (e)(2)(ii)(d) of this section. For this adjustment in useful life, no section 481 adjustment is required or permitted. The adjustment in useful life, whether initiated by the Internal Revenue Service (IRS) or a taxpayer, is corrected by adjustments in the taxable year in which the conditions known to exist at the end of that taxable year changed thereby resulting in a redetermination of the useful life under § 1.167(a)-1(b) (or if the period of limitation for assessment under section 6501(a) has expired for that taxable year, in the first succeeding taxable year open under the period of limitation for assessment), and in subsequent taxable years. In other situations (for example, the useful life is incorrectly determined in the placed-in-service year), the adjustment in the useful life, whether initiated by the IRS or a taxpayer, may be corrected by adjustments in the earliest taxable year open under the period of limitation for assessment under section 6501(a) or the earliest taxable year under examination by the IRS but in no event earlier than the placed-in-service year of the asset, and in subsequent taxable years. However, if a taxpayer initiates the correction in useful life, in lieu of filing amended Federal tax returns (for example, because the conditions known to exist at the end of a prior taxable year changed thereby resulting in a redetermination of the useful life under § 1.167(a)-1(b)), the taxpayer may correct the adjustment in useful life by adjustments in the current and subsequent taxable years.

(v) Change in placed-in-service date. This paragraph (e)(2)(ii)(d)(5)(v) applies to a change in the placed-in-service date of a depreciable or amortizable asset that is not a change in method of accounting under paragraph (e)(2)(ii)(d) of this section. For this change in placed-in-service date, no section 481 adjustment is required or permitted. The change in placed-in-service date, whether initiated by the IRS or a taxpayer, may be corrected by adjustments in the earliest taxable year open under the period of limitation for assessment under section 6501(a) or the earliest taxable year under examination by the IRS but in no event earlier than the placed-in-service year of the asset, and in subsequent taxable years. However, if a taxpayer initiates the change in placed-in-service date, in lieu of filing amended Federal tax returns, the taxpayer may. correct the placed-in-service date by adjustments in the current and subsequent taxable years.

(iii) Examples. The rules of this paragraph (e) are illustrated by the following examples:

*Example (1).* Although the sale of merchandise is an income producing factor, and therefore inventories are required, a taxpayer in the retail jewelry business reports his income on the cash receipts and disbursements method of accounting. A change from the cash receipts and disbursements method of accounting to the accrual method of accounting is a change in the overall plan of accounting and thus is a change in method of accounting.

*Example (2).* A taxpayer in the wholesale dry goods business computes its income and expenses on the accrual method of accounting and files its Federal income tax returns on such basis except for real estate taxes which have been reported on the cash receipts and disbursements method of accounting. A change in the treatment of real estate taxes from the cash receipts and disbursements method to the accrual method is a change in method of accounting because such change is a change in the treatment of a material item within his overall accounting practice.

*Example (3).* A taxpayer in the wholesale dry goods business computes its income and expenses on the accrual method of accounting and files its Federal income tax returns on such basis. Vacation pay has been deducted in the year in which paid because the taxpayer did not have a completely vested vacation pay plan, and, therefore, the liability for payment did not accrue until that year. Subsequently, the taxpayer adopts a completely vested vacation pay plan that changes its year for accruing the deduction from the year in which payment is made to the year in which the liability to make the payment now arises. The change for the year of deduction of the vacation pay plan is not a change in method of accounting but results, instead, because the underlying facts (that is, the type of vacation pay plan) have changed.

*Example (4).* From 1968 through 1970, a taxpayer has fairly allocated indirect overhead costs to the value of inventories on a fixed percentage of direct costs. If the ratio of indirect overhead costs to direct costs increases in 1971, a change in the underlying facts has occurred. Accordingly, an increase in the percentage in 1971 to fairly reflect the increase in the relative level of indirect overhead costs is not a change in method of accounting but is a change in treatment resulting from a change in the underlying facts.

*Example (5).* A taxpayer values inventories at cost. A change in the basis for valuation of inventories from cost to the lower of cost or market is a change in an overall practice of valuing items in inventory. The change, therefore, is a change in method of accounting for inventories.

*Example (6).* A taxpayer in the manufacturing business has for many taxable years valued its inventories at cost. However, cost has been improperly computed since no overhead costs have been included in valuing the inventories at cost. The failure to allocate an appropriate portion of overhead to the value of inventories is contrary to the requirement of the Internal Revenue Code and the regulations under the Internal Revenue Code. A change requiring appropriate allocation of overhead is a change in method of accounting because it involves a change in the treatment of a material item used in the overall practice of identifying or valuing items in inventory.

*Example (7).* A taxpayer has for many taxable years valued certain inventories by a method which provides for deducting 20 percent of the cost of the inventory items in determining the final inventory valuation. The 20 percent adjustment is taken as a "reserve for price changes." Although this method is not a proper method of valuing inventories under the Internal Revenue Code or the regulations under the Internal Revenue Code, it involves the treatment of a material item used in the overall practice of valuing inventory. A change in such practice or procedure is a change of method of accounting for inventories.

*Example (8).* A taxpayer has always used a base stock system of accounting for inventories. Under this system a constant price is applied to an assumed constant normal quantity of goods in stock. The base stock system is an overall plan of accounting for inventories which is not recognized as a proper method of accounting for inventories under the regulations. A change in this practice is, nevertheless, a change of method of accounting for inventories.

*Example (9).* In 2003, A1, a calendar year taxpayer engaged in the trade or business of manufacturing knitted goods, purchased and placed in service a building and its components at a total cost of $10,000,000 for use in its manufacturing operations. A1 classified the $10,000,000 as nonresidential real property under section 168(e). A1 elected not to deduct the additional first year depreciation provided by section 168(k) on its 2003 Federal tax return. As a result, on its 2003, 2004, and 2005 Federal tax returns, A1 depreciated the $10,000,000 under the general depreciation system of section 168(a), using the straight line method of depreciation, a 39-year recovery period, and the mid-month convention. In 2006, A1 completes a cost segregation study on the building and its components and identifies items that cost a total of $1,500,000 as section 1245 property. As a result, the $1,500,000 should have been classified in 2003 as 5-year property under section 168(e) and depreciated on A1's 2003, 2004, and 2005 Federal tax returns under the general depreciation system, using the 200-percent declining balance method of depreciation, a 5-year recovery period, and the half-year convention. Pursuant to paragraph (e)(2)(ii)(d)(2)(i) of this section, A1's change to this depreciation method, recovery period, and convention is a change in method of accounting. This method change results in a section 481 adjustment. The useful life exception under paragraph (e)(2)(ii)(d)(3)(i) of this section does not apply because the assets are depreciated under section 168.

*Example (10).* In 2003, B, a calendar year taxpayer, purchased and placed in service new equipment at a total cost of $1,000,000 for use in its plant located outside the United States. The equipment is 15-year property under section 168(e) with a class life of 20 years. The equipment is required to be depreciated under the alternative depreciation system of section 168(g). However, B incorrectly depreciated the equipment under the general depreciation system of section 168(a), using the 150-percent declining balance method, a 15-year recovery period, and the half-year convention. In 2010, the IRS examines B's 2007 Federal income tax return and changes the depreciation of the equipment to the alternative depreciation system, using the straight line method of depreciation, a 20-year recovery period, and the half-year convention. Pursuant to paragraph (e)(2)(ii)(d)(2)(i) of this section, this change in depreciation method and recovery period made by the IRS is a change in method of accounting. This method change results in a section 481 adjustment. The useful life exception under paragraph (e)(2)(ii)(d)(3)(i) of this section does not apply because the assets are depreciated under section 168.

*Example (11).* In May 2003, C, a calendar year taxpayer, purchased and placed in service equipment for use in its trade or business. C never held this equipment for sale. However, C incorrectly treated the equipment as inventory on its 2003 and 2004 Federal tax returns. In 2005, C realizes that the equipment should have been treated as a depreciable asset. Pursuant to paragraph (e)(2)(ii)(d)(2) of this section, C's change in the treatment of the equipment from inventory to a depreciable asset is a change in method of accounting. This method change results in a section 481 adjustment.

*Example (12).* Since 2003, D, a calendar year taxpayer, has used the distribution fee period method to amortize distributor commissions and, under that method, established pools to account for the distributor commissions (for further guidance, see Rev. Proc. 2000-38 (2000-2 C.B. 310) and § 601.601(d)(2)(ii)(b) of this chapter). A change in the accounting of distributor commissions under the distribution fee period method from pooling to single asset accounting is a change in method of accounting pursuant to paragraph (e)(2)(ii)(d)(2)(vi) of this section. This method change results in no section 481 adjustment because the change is from one permissible method to another permissible method.

*Example (13).* Since 2003, E, a calendar year taxpayer, has accounted for items of MACRS property that are mass assets in pools. Each pool includes only the mass assets that are placed in service by E in the same taxable year. E is able to identify the cost basis of each asset in each pool. None of the pools are general asset accounts under section 168(i)(4) and the regulations under section 168(i)(4). E identified any dispositions of these mass assets by specific identification. Because of changes in E's recordkeeping in 2006, it is impracticable for E to continue to identify disposed mass assets using specific identification. As a result, E wants to change to a first-in, first-out method under which the mass assets disposed of in a taxable year are deemed to be from the pool with the earliest placed-in-service year in existence as of the beginning of the taxable year of each disposition. Pursuant to paragraph (e)(2)(ii)(d)(2)(vii) of this section, this change is a change in method of accounting. This method change results in no section 481 adjustment because the change is from one permissible method to another permissible method.

*Example (14).* In August 2003, F, a calendar year taxpayer, purchased and placed in service a copier for use in its trade or business. F incorrectly classified the copier as 7-year property under section 168(e), F elected not to deduct the additional first year depreciation provided by section 168(k) on its 2003 Federal tax return. As a result, on its 2003 and 2004 Federal tax returns, F depreciated the copier under the general depreciation system of section 168(a), using the 200-percent declining balance method of depreciation, a 7-year recovery period, and the half-year convention. In 2005, F realizes that the copier is 5-year property and should have been depreciated on its 2003 and 2004 Federal tax returns under the general depreciation system using a 5-year recovery period rather than a 7-year recovery period. Pursuant to paragraph (e)(2)(ii)(d)(2)(i) of this section, F's change in recovery period from 7 to 5 years is a change in method of accounting. This method change results in a section 481 adjustment. The useful life exception under paragraph (e)(2)(ii)(d)(3)(i) of this section does not apply because the copier is depreciated under section 168.

*Example (15).* In 2004, G, a calendar year taxpayer, purchased and placed in service an intangible asset that is not an amortizable section 197 intangible and that is not described in section 167(f). G amortized the cost of the intangible asset under section 167(a) using the straight line method of depreciation and a determinable useful life of 13 years. The safe harbor useful life of 15 or 25 years under § 1.167(a)-3(b) does not apply to the intangible asset. In 2008, because of changing conditions, G changes the remaining useful life of the intangible asset to 2 years. Pursuant to paragraph (e)(2)(ii)(d)(3)(i) of this section, G's change in useful life is not a change in method of accounting because the intangible asset is depreciated under section 167 and G is not changing to or from a useful life that is specifically assigned by the Internal Revenue Code, the regulations under the Internal Revenue Code, or other guidance published in the Internal Revenue Bulletin.

*Example (16).* In July 2003, H, a calendar year taxpayer, purchased and placed in service "off-the-shelf" computer software and a new computer. The cost of the new computer and computer software are separately stated. H incorrectly included the cost of this software as part of the cost of the computer, which is 5-year property under section 168(e). On its 2003 Federal tax return, H elected to depreciate its 5-year property placed in service in 2003 under the alternative depreciation system of section 168(g) and H elected not to deduct the additional first year depreciation provided by section 168(k). The class life for a computer is 5 years. As a result, because H included the cost of the computer software as part of the cost of the computer hardware, H depreciated the cost of the software under the alternative depreciation system, using the straight line method of depreciation, a 5-year recovery period, and the half-year convention. In 2005, H realizes that the cost of the software should have been amortized under section 167(f)(1), using the straight line method of depreciation, a 36-month useful life, and a monthly convention. H's change from 5-years to 36-months is a change in method of accounting because H is changing to a useful life that is specifically assigned by section 167(f)(1). The change in convention from the half-year to the monthly convention also is a change in method of accounting. Both changes result in a section 481 adjustment.

*Example (17).* On May 1, 2003, 12, a calendar year taxpayer, purchased and placed in service new equipment at a total cost of $500,000 for use in its business. The equipment is 5-year property under section 168(e) with a class life of 9 years and is qualified property under section 168(k)(2). I2 did not place in service any other depreciable property in 2003. Section 168(g)(1)(A) through (D) do not apply to the equipment. I2 intended to elect the alternative depreciation system under section 168(g) for 5-year property placed in service in 2003. However, I2 did not make the election. Instead, I2 deducted on its 2003 Federal tax return the 30-percent additional first year depreciation attributable to the equipment and, on its 2003 and 2004 Federal tax returns, depreciated the remaining adjusted depreciable basis of the equipment under the general depreciation system under 168(a), using the 200-percent declining balance method, a 5-year recovery period, and the half-year convention. In 2005, I2 realizes its failure to make the alternative depreciation system election in 2003 and files a Form 3115, "Application for Change in Accounting Method," to change its method of depreciating the remaining adjusted depreciable basis of the 2003 equipment to the alternative depreciation system. Because this equipment is not required to be depreciated under the alternative depreciation system, I2 is attempting to make an election under section 168(g)(7). However, this election must be made in the taxable year in which the equipment is placed in service (2003) and, consequently, I2 is attempting to make a late election under section 168(g)(7). Accordingly, I2's change to the alternative depreciation system is not a change in accounting method pursuant to paragraph (e)(2)(ii)(d)(3)(iii) of this section. Instead, 12 must submit a request for a private letter ruling under § 301.9100-3 of this chapter, requesting an extension of time to make the alternative depreciation system election on its 2003 Federal tax return.

*Example (18).* On December 1, 2004, J, a calendar year taxpayer, purchased and placed in service 20 previously-owned adding machines. For the 2004 taxable year, J incorrectly classified the adding machines as items in its "suspense" account for financial and tax accounting purposes. Assets in this suspense account are not depreciated until reclassified to a depreciable fixed asset account. In January 2006, J realizes that the cost of the adding machines is still in the suspense account and reclassifies such cost to the appropriate depreciable fixed asset account. As a result, on its 2004 and 2005 Federal tax returns, J did not depreciate the cost of the adding machines. Pursuant to paragraph (e)(2)(ii)(d)(2) of this section, J's change in the treatment of the adding machines from nondepreciable assets to depreciable assets is a change in method of accounting. The placed-in-service date exception under paragraph (e)(2)(ii)(d)(3)(v) of this section does not apply because the adding machines were incorrectly classified in a nondepreciable suspense account. This method change results in a section 481 adjustment.

*Example (19).* In December 2003, K, a calendar year taxpayer, purchased and placed in service equipment for use in its trade or business. However, K did not receive the invoice for this equipment until January 2004. As a result, K classified the equipment on its fixed asset records as being placed in service in January 2004. On its 2004 and 2005 Federal tax returns, K depreciated the cost of the equipment. In 2006, K realizes that the equipment was actually placed in service during the 2003 taxable year and, therefore, depreciation should have began in the 2003 taxable year instead of the 2004 taxable year. Pursuant to paragraph (e)(2)(ii)(d)(3)(v) of this section, K's change in the placed-in-service date of the equipment is not a change in method of accounting.

*(3)* (i) Except as otherwise provided under the authority of paragraph (e)(3)(ii) of this section, to secure the Commissioner's consent to a taxpayer's change in method of accounting the taxpayer must file an application on Form 3115 with the Commissioner during the taxable year in which the taxpayer desires to make the change in method of accounting. To the extent applicable, the taxpayer must furnish all information requested on the Form 3115. This information includes all classes of items that will be treated differently under the new method of accounting, any amounts that will be duplicated or omitted as a result of the proposed change, and the taxpayer's computation of any adjustments necessary to prevent such duplications or omissions. The Commissioner may require such other information as may be necessary to determine whether the proposed change will be permitted. Permission to change a taxpayer's method of accounting will not be granted unless the taxpayer agrees to the Commissioner's prescribed terms and conditions for effecting the change, including the taxable year or years in which any adjustment necessary to prevent amounts from being duplicated or omitted is to be taken into account. See section 481 and the regulations thereunder, relating to certain adjustments resulting from accounting method changes, and section 472 and the regulations thereunder, relating to adjustments for changes to and from the last-in, first-out inventory method. For any Form 3115 filed on or after May 15, 1997, see § 1.446-1T(e)(3)(i)(B).

(ii) Notwithstanding the provisions of paragraph (e)(3)(i) of this section, the Commissioner may prescribe administrative procedures under which taxpayers will be permitted to change their method of accounting. The administrative procedures shall prescribe those terms and conditions necessary to obtain the Commissioner's consent to effect the change and to prevent amounts from being duplicated or omitted. The terms and conditions that may be prescribed by the Commissioner may include terms and conditions that require the change in method of accounting to be effected on a cut-off basis or by an adjustment under section 481(a) to be taken into account in the taxable year or years prescribed by the Commissioner.

(iii) This paragraph (e)(3) applies to Forms 3115 filed on or after December 31, 1997. For other Forms 3115, see § 1.446-1(e)(3) in effect prior to December 31, 1997 (§ 1.446-1(e)(3) as contained in the 26 CFR part 1 edition revised as of April 1, 1997).

*(4) Effective date.* (i) In general. Except as provided in paragraphs (e)(3)(iii) and (e)(4)(ii) of this section, paragraph (e) of this section applies on or after December 30, 2003. For the applicability of regulations before December 30, 2003, see § 1.446-1(e) in effect prior to December 30, 2003 (§ 1.446-1(e) as contained in 26 CFR part 1 edition revised as of April 1, 2003).

(ii) Changes involving depreciable or amortizable assets. With respect to paragraph (e)(2)(ii)(d) of this section, paragraph (e)(2)(iii) Examples 9 through 19 of this section, and the language "certain changes in computing depreciation or amortization (see paragraph (e)(2)(ii)(d) of this section)" in the last sentence of paragraph (e)(2)(ii)(a) of this section—

(A) For any change in depreciation or amortization that is a change in method of accounting, this section applies to such a change in method of accounting made by a taxpayer for a depreciable or amortizable asset placed in service by the taxpayer in a taxable year ending on or after December 30, 2003; and

(B) For any change in depreciation or amortization that is not a change in method of accounting, this section applies to such a change made by a taxpayer for a depreciable or amortizable asset placed in service by the taxpayer in a taxable year ending on or after December 30, 2003.

---

T.D. 6282, 12/24/57, amend T.D. 6584, 12/20/61, T.D. 7073, 11/17/70, T.D. 7285, 9/14/73, T.D. 8067, 12/30/85, T.D. 8131, 3/24/87, T.D. 8408, 4/9/92, T.D. 8482, 8/6/93, T.D. 8608, 8/4/95, T.D. 8719, 5/14/97, T.D. 8742, 12/30/97, T.D. 8929, 1/10/2001, T.D. 9025, 12/13/2002, T.D. 9105, 12/30/2003, T.D. 9307, 12/22/2006.

---

PAR. 2. In § 1.446-1, paragraph (c)(2)(iii) is added to read as follows:

**Proposed § 1.446-1 General rule for methods of accounting.** [*For Preamble, see ¶ 151,953*]

* * * * *

**(c)** * * *

*(2)* * * *

(iii) Section 475 is the exclusive authority on which a taxpayer may rely to use the mark-to-market method of accounting for nonfinancial customer paper, as defined in section 475(c)(4)(B). Thus, except to the extent provided in § 1.475(c)-2(d), the mark-to-market method of accounting is not a permissible method of accounting for nonfinancial customer paper. In addition, the lower-of-cost-or-market method of accounting is not a permissible method of accounting for these assets. See § 1.471-12. This paragraph (c)(2)(iii) applies to all tax years ending on or after January 28, 1999.

* * * * *

PAR. 5. Section 1.446-1 is amended by:

1. Revising the first sentence in paragraph (e)(3)(i) and adding a new second sentence.

2. Revising the first sentence in paragraph (e)(4)(i).

3. Adding paragraph (e)(4)(iii).

The revisions and addition read as follows:

**Proposed § 1.446-1 General rule for methods of accounting.** [*For Preamble, see ¶ 152,935*]

* * * * *

**(e)** * * *

*(3)* * * * (i) Except as otherwise provided under the authority of paragraph (e)(3)(ii) of this section, to secure the Commissioner's consent to a taxpayer's change in method of accounting, the taxpayer generally must file an application on Form 3115 with the Commissioner during the taxable year in which the taxpayer desires to make the change in method of accounting. See §§ 1.381(c)(4)-1(d)(2) and 1.381(c)(5)-1(d)(2) for rules allowing additional time, in some circumstances, for the filing of an application on Form 3115 with respect to a transaction to which section 381(a) applies.

* * * * *

*(4)* * * * (i) In general. Except as provided in paragraphs (e)(3)(iii), (e)(4)(ii) and (e)(4)(iii) of this section,

paragraph (e) of this section applies on or after December 30, 2003.

* * * * *

(iii) Effective/applicability date for paragraph (e)(3)(i). The rules of paragraph (e)(3)(i) of this section apply to corporate reorganizations and tax-free liquidations described in section 381(a) that occur on or after the date of publication of the Treasury decision adopting these rules as final regulations in the Federal Register.

**§ 1.446-2 Method of accounting for interest.**

**(a) Applicability.** *(1) In general.* This section provides rules for determining the amount of interest that accrues during and accrual period (other than interest described in paragraph (a)(2) of this section) and for determining the portion of a payment that consists of accrued interest. For purposes of this section, interest includes original issue discount and amounts treated as interest (whether stated or unstated) in any lending or deferred payment transaction. Accrued interest determined under this section is taken into account by a taxpayer under the taxpayer's regular method of accounting (e.g., an accrual method or the cash receipts and disbursements method). Application of an exception described in paragraph (a)(2) of this section to one party to a transaction does not affect the application of this section to any other party to the transaction.

*(2) Exceptions.* (i) Interest included or deducted under certain other provisions. This section does not apply to interest that is taken into account under—

(A) Sections 1272(a), 1275, and 163(e) (income and deductions relating to original issue discount);

(B) Section 467(a)(2) (certain payments for the use of property or services);

(C) Sections 1276 through 1278 (market discount);

(D) Sections 1281 through 1283 (discount on certain short-term obligations);

(E) Section 7872(a) (certain loans with below-market interest rates); or

(F) Section 1.1272-3 (an election by a holder to treat all interest on a debt instrument as original issue discount).

(ii) De minimis original issue discount. This section does not apply to de minimis original issue discount (other than de minimis original issue discount treated as qualified stated interest) as determined under § 1.1273-1(d). See § 1.163-7 for the treatment of de minimis original issue discount by the issuer and §§ 1.1273-1(d) and 1.1272-3 for the treatment of de minimis original issue discount by the holder.

**(b) Accrual of qualified stated interest.** Qualified stated interest (as defined in § 1.1273-1(c)) accrues ratably over the accrual period (or periods) to which it is attributable and accrues at the stated rate for the period (or periods).

**(c) Accrual of interest other than qualified stated interest.** Subject to the modifications in paragraph (d) of this section, the amount of interest (other than qualified stated interest) that accrues for any accrual period is determined under rules similar to those in the regulations under sections 1272 and 1275 for the accrual of original issue discount. The preceding sentence applies regardless of any contrary formula agreed to by the parties.

**(d) Modifications.** *(1) Issue price.* The issue price of the loan or contract is equal to—

(i) In the case of a contract for the safe or exchange of property to which section 483 applies, the amount described in § 1.483-2(a)(1)(i) or (ii), whichever is applicable;

(ii) In the case of a contract for the sale or exchange of property to which section 483 does not apply, the stated principal amount; or

(iii) In any other case, the amount loaned.

*(2) Principal payments that are not deferred payments.* In the case of a contract to which section 483 applies, principal payments that are not deferred payments are ignored for purposes of determining yield and adjusted issue price.

**(e) Allocation of interest to payments.** *(1) In general.* Except as provided in paragraphs (e)(2), (e)(3) and (e)(4) of this section, each payment under a loan (other than payments of additional interest or similar charges provided with respect to amounts that are not paid when due) is treated as a payment of interest to the extent of the accrued and unpaid interest determined under paragraphs (b) and (c) of this section as of the date the payment becomes due.

*(2) Special rule for points deductible under section 461(g)(2).* If a payment of points is deductible by the borrower under section 461(g)(2), the payment is treated by the borrower as a payment of interest.

*(3) Allocation respected in certain small transactions.[Reserved]*

*(4) Pro rata prepayments.* Accrued but unpaid interest is allocated to a pro rata prepayment under rules similar to those for allocating accrued but unpaid original issue discount to a pro rata prepayment under § 1.1275-2(f). For purposes of the preceding sentence, a pro rata prepayment is a payment that is made prior to maturity that—

(i) Is not made pursuant to the contract's payment schedule; and

(ii) Results in a substantially pro rata reduction of each payment remaining to be paid on the contract.

**(f) Aggregation rule.** For purposes of this section, all contracts calling for deferred payments arising from the same transaction (or a series of related transactions) are treated as a single contract. This rule, however, generally only applies to contracts involving a single borrower and a single lender.

**(g) Debt instruments denominated in a currency other than the U.S. dollar.** This section applies to a debt instrument that provides for all payments denominated in, or determined by reference to, the functional currency of the taxpayer or qualified business unit of the taxpayer (even if that currency is other than the U.S. dollar). See § 1.988-2(b) to determine interest income or expense for debt instruments that provide for payments denominated in, or determined by reference to, a nonfunctional currency.

**(h) Example.** The following example illustrates the rules of this section.

*Example.* Allocation of unstated interest to deferred payments.

(i) Facts. On July 1, 1996, A sells his personal residence to B for a stated purchase price of $1,297,143.66. The property is not personal use property (within the meaning of section 1275(b)(3)) in the hands of B. Under the loan agreement, B is required to make two installment payments of $648,571.83 each, the first due on June 30, 1998, and the second due on June 30, 2000. Both A and B use the cash receipts and disbursements method of accounting and use a calendar year for their taxable year.

(ii) Amount of unstated interest. Under section 483, the agreement does not provide for adequate stated interest. Thus, the loan's yield is the test rate of interest determined under § 1.483-3. Assume that both A and B use annual accrual periods and that the test rate of interest is 9.2 percent, compounded annually. Under § 1.483-2, the present value of the deferred payments is $1,000,000. Thus, thee agreement has unstated interest of $297,143.66.

(iii) First two accrual periods. Under paragraph (d)(1) of this section, the issue price at the beginning of the first accrual period is $1,000,000 (the amount described in § 1.483-2(a)(1)(i)). Under paragraph (c) of this section, the amount of interest that accrues for the first accrual period is $92,000 ($1,000,000 × .092) and the amount of interest that accrues for the second accrual period is $100,464 ($1,092,000 × .092). Thus, $192,464 of interest has accrued as of the end of the second accrual period. Under paragraph (e)(1) of this section, the $648,571.83 payment made on June 30, 1998, is treated first as a payment of interest to the extent of $192,464. The remainder of the payment ($456,107.83) is treated as a payment of principal. Both A and B take the payment of interest ($192,464) into account in 1998.

(iv) Second two accrual periods. The adjusted issue price at the beginning of the third accrual period is $543,892.17 ($1,092,000 + $100,464 − $648,571.83). The amount of interest that accrues for the third accrual period is $50,038.08 ($543,892.17 × .092) and the amount of interest that accrues for the final accrual period is $54,641.58, the excess of the amount payable at maturity ($648,571.83), over the adjusted issue price at the beginning of the accrual period ($593,930.25). As of the date the second payment becomes due, $104,679.66 of interest has accrued. Thus, of the $648,571.83 payment made on June 30, 2000, $104,679.66 is treated as interest and $543,892.17 is treated as principal. Both A and B take the payment of interest ($104,679.66) into account in 2000.

**(i) [Reserved]**

**(j) Effective date.** This section applies to debt instruments issued on or after April 4, 1994, and to lending transactions, sales, and exchanges that occur on or after April 4, 1994. Taxpayers, however, may rely on this section for debt instruments issued after December 21, 1992, and before April 4, 1994, and for lending transactions, sales, and exchanges that occur after December 21, 1992, and before April 4, 1994.

---

T.D. 8517, 1/27/94.

---

PAR. 3. Section 1.446-2, as proposed on April 8, 1986 (51 FR 12031), is revised to read as follows:

**Proposed § 1.446-2 Method of accounting for interest.**
[*For Preamble, see ¶ 151,457*]

• ***Caution:*** Prop regs §§ 1.163-7, 1.483-1, 1.483-2, 1.483-3, 1.1001-1, 1.1012-1, 1.1271-1, 1.1272-1, 1.1272-2, 1.1272-3, 1.1273-1, 1.1273-2, 1.1274-1, 1.1274-2, 1.1274-3, 1.1274-4, 1.1274-5, 1/1274A-1, 1.1275-1, 1.1275-2, 1.1275-3 and 1.1275-5 were finalized by T.D. 8517, 1/27/94. Prop regs § 1.446-2(e)(3) remains proposed.

* * * * *

**(e) Allocation of interest to payments.**

* * * * *

*(3) Allocation respected in certain small transactions.* (i) In general. If the aggregate amount of interest and principal payable under a contract does not exceed $250,000 and sec tion 483 does not apply to the loan, an express allocation of the payments between interest and principal by the parties is respected. Similarly, if section 483 applies to a contract under which the aggregate amount payable does not exceed $250,000, but does not apply to a party to the contract (as, for example, in the case of an obligor under a debt instru ment given in consideration for the sale or exchange of per sonal use property), an express allocation of the payments between interest and principal by the parties is respected for purposes of determining the tax liability of the party not sub ject to section 483.

(ii) Prepaid interest. The amount of interest allocated to any payment under this paragraph (e)(3) is treated as prepaid interest to the extent the amount exceeds—

(A) The aggregate amount of accrued interest as of the date the payment becomes due; reduced (but not below zero) by

(B) The aggregate amount of interest allocated to prior payments under this paragraph (e)(3).

(iii) Accounting for prepaid interest. Prepaid interest must be included in income by a lender when received, regardless of the lender's method of accounting. Except as otherwise provided in section 461(g)(2), prepaid interest is not deducti ble before such interest accrues (as determined under para graph (c) of this section).

* * * * *

**§ 1.446-3 Notional principal contracts.**

**(a) Table of contents.** This paragraph (a) lists captioned paragraphs contained in § 1.446-3.

*§ 1.446-3 Notional principal contracts.*

(i) In general.

(ii) General rule for swaps.

(iii) Alternative methods for swaps.

(A) Prepaid swaps.

(B) Other nonperiodic swap payments.

(iv) General rule for caps and floors.

(v) Alternative methods for caps and floors that hedge debt instruments.

(A) Prepaid caps and floors.

(B) Other caps and floors.

(C) Special method for collars.

(vi) Additional methods.

(3) Term of extendible or terminable contracts.

(4) Examples.

(g) Special rules.

(1) Disguised notional principal contracts.

(2) Hedged notional principal contracts.

(3) Options and forwards to enter into notional principal contracts.

(4) Swaps with significant nonperiodic payments.

(5) Caps and floors that are significantly in-the-money. [Reserved]

(6) Examples.

(h) Termination payments.

(1) Definition.

(2) Taxable year of inclusion and deduction by original parties.

(3) Taxable year of inclusion and deduction by assignees.

(4) Special rules.

(i) Assignment of one leg of a contract.

(ii) Substance over form.

(5) Examples.

(i) Anti-abuse rule.

(j) Effective date.

**(b) Purpose.** The purpose of this section is to enable the clear reflection of the income and deductions from notional principal contracts by prescribing accounting methods that reflect the economic substance of such contracts.

**(c) Definitions and scope.** *(1) Notional principal contract.* (i) In general. A notional principal contract is a financial instrument that provides for the payment of amounts by one party to another at specified intervals calculated by reference to a specified index upon a notional principal amount in exchange for specified consideration or a promise to pay similar amounts. An agreement between a taxpayer and a qualified business unit (as defined in section 989(a)) of the taxpayer, or among qualified business units of the same taxpayer, is not a notional principal contract because a taxpayer cannot enter into a contract with itself. Notional principal contracts governed by this section include interest rate swaps, currency swaps, basis swaps, interest rate caps, interest rate floors, commodity swaps, equity swaps, equity index swaps, and similar agreements. A collar is not itself a notional principal contract, but certain caps and floors that comprise a collar may be treated as a single notional principal contract under paragraph (f)(2)(v)(C) of this section. A contract may be a notional principal contract governed by this section even though the term of the contract is subject to termination or extension. Each confirmation under a master agreement to enter into agreements governed by this section is treated as a separate notional principal contract.

(ii) Excluded contracts. A contract described in section 1256(b), a futures contract, a forward contract, and an option are not notional principal contracts. An instrument or contract that constitutes indebtedness under general principles of Federal income tax law is not a notional principal contract. An option or forward contract that entitles or obligates a person to enter into a notional principal contract is not a notional principal contract, but payments made under such an option or forward contract may be governed by paragraph (g)(3) of this section.

(iii) Transactions within section 475. To the extent that the rules provided in paragraphs (e) and (f) of this section are inconsistent with the rules that apply to any notional principal contract that is governed by section 475 and regulations thereunder, the rules of section 475 and the regulations thereunder govern.

(iv) Transactions within section 988. To the extent that the rules provided in this section are inconsistent with the rules that apply to any notional principal contract that is also a section 988 transaction or that is integrated with other property or debt pursuant to section 988(d), the rules of section 988 and the regulations thereunder govern.

*(2) Specified index.* A specified index is—

(i) A fixed rate, price, or amount;

(ii) A fixed rate, price, or amount applicable in one or more specified periods followed by one or more different fixed rates, prices, or amounts applicable in other periods;

(iii) An index that is based on objective financial information (as defined in paragraph (c)(4)(ii) of this section); and

(iv) An interest rate index that is regularly used in normal lending transactions between a party to the contract and unrelated persons.

*(3) Notional principal amount.* For purposes of this section, a notional principal amount is any specified amount of money or property that, when multiplied by a specified index, measures a party's rights and obligations under the contract, but is not borrowed or loaned between the parties as part of the contract. The notional principal amount may vary over the term of the contract, provided that it is set in advance or varies based on objective financial information (as defined in paragraph (c)(4)(ii) of this section).

*(4) Special definitions.* (i) Related person and party to the contract. A related person is a person related (within the meaning of section 267(b) or 707(b)(1)) to one of the parties to the notional principal contract or a member of the same consolidated group (as defined in § 1.1502-1(h)) as one of the parties to the contract. For purposes of this paragraph (c), a related person is considered to be a party to the contract.

(ii) Objective financial information. For purposes of this paragraph (c), objective financial information is any current, objectively determinable financial or economic information that is not within the control of any of the parties to the contract and is not unique to one of the parties' circumstances (such as one party's dividends, profits, or the value of its stock). Thus, for example, a notional principal amount may be based on a broadly-based equity index or the outstanding balance of a pool of mortgages, but not on the value of a party's stock.

(iii) Dealer in notional principal contracts. A dealer in notional principal contracts is a person who regularly offers to enter into, assume, offset, assign, or otherwise terminate positions in notional principal contracts with customers in the ordinary course of a trade or business.

**(d) Taxable year of inclusion and deduction.** For all purposes of the Code, the net income or net deduction from a notional principal contract for a taxable year is included in or deducted from gross income for that taxable year. The net income or net deduction from a notional principal contract for a taxable year equals the total of all of the periodic payments that are recognized from that contract for the taxable year under paragraph (e) of this section and all of the nonperiodic payments that are recognized from that contract for the taxable year under paragraph (f) of this section.

**(e) Periodic payments.** *(1) Definition.* Periodic payments are payments made or received pursuant to a notional principal contract that are payable at intervals of one year or less during the entire term of the contract (including any extension periods provided for in the contract), that are based on a specified index described in paragraph (c)(2)(i), (iii), or (iv) of this section (appropriately adjusted for the length of the interval), and that are based on either a single notional principal amount or a notional principal amount that varies over the term of the contract in the same proportion as the notional principal amount that measures the other party's payments. Payments to purchase or sell a cap or a floor, however, are not periodic payments.

*(2) Recognition rules.* (i) In general. All taxpayers, regardless of their method of accounting, must recognize the ratable daily portion of a periodic payment for the taxable year to which that portion relates.

(ii) Rate set in arrears. If the amount of a periodic payment is not determinable at the end of a taxable year because the value of the specified index is not fixed until a date that occurs after the end of the taxable year, the ratable daily portion of a periodic payment that relates to that taxable year is generally based on the specified index that would have applied if the specified index were fixed as of the last day of the taxable year. If a taxpayer determines that the value of the specified index as of the last day of the taxable year does not provide a reasonable estimate of the specified index that will apply when the payment is fixed, the taxpayer may use a reasonable estimate of the specified index each year, provided that the taxpayer (and any related person that is a party to the contract) uses the same method to make the estimate consistently from year to year and uses the same estimate for purposes of all financial reports to equity holders and creditors. The taxpayer's treatment of notional principal contracts with substantially similar specified indices will be considered in determining whether the taxpayer's estimate of the specified index is reasonable. Any difference between the amount that is recognized under this paragraph (e)(2)(ii) and the corresponding portion of the actual payment that becomes fixed under the contract is taken into account as an adjustment to the net income or net deduction from the notional principal contract for the taxable year during which the payment becomes fixed.

(iii) Notional principal amount set in arrears. Rules similar to the rules of paragraph (e)(2)(ii) of this section apply if the amount of a periodic payment is not determinable at the end of a taxable year because the notional principal amount is not fixed until a date that occurs after the end of the taxable year.

*(3) Examples.* The following examples illustrate the application of paragraph (e) of this section.

*Example (1).* Accrual of periodic swap payments.

(a) On April 1, 1995, A enters into a contract with unrelated counterparty B under which, for a term of five years, A is obligated to make a payment to B each April 1, beginning April 1, 1996, in an amount equal to the London Interbank Offered Rate (LIBOR), as determined on the immediately preceding April 1, multiplied by a notional principal amount of $100 million. Under the contract, B is obligated to make a payment to A each April 1, beginning April 1, 1996, in an amount equal to 8% multiplied by the same notional principal amount. A and B are calendar year taxpayers that use the accrual method of accounting. On April 1, 1995, LIBOR is 7.80%.

(b) This contract is a notional principal contract as defined by paragraph (c)(1) of this section, and both LIBOR and a fixed interest rate of 8% are specified indices under paragraph (c)(2) of this section. All of the payments to be made by A and B are periodic payments under paragraph (e)(1) of this section because each party's payments are based on a specified index described in paragraphs (c)(2)(iii) and (c)(2)(i) of this section, respectively, are payable at periodic intervals of one year or less throughout the term of the contract, and are based on a single notional principal amount.

(c) Under the terms of the swap agreement, on April 1, 1996, B is obligated to make a payment to A of $8,000,000 (8% × $100,000,000) and A is obligated to make a payment to B of $7,800,000 (7.80% × $100,000,000). Under paragraph (e)(2)(i) of this section, the ratable daily portions for 1995 are the amounts of these periodic payments that are attributable to A's and B's taxable year ending December 31, 1995. The ratable daily portion of the 8% fixed leg is $6,010,929 (275 days/366 days × $8,000,000), and the ratable daily portion of the floating leg is $5,860,656 (275 days/366 days × $7,800,000). The net amount for the taxable year is the difference between the ratable daily portions of the two periodic payments, or $150,273 ($6,010,929 − $5,860,656). Accordingly, A has net income of $150,273 from this swap for 1995, and B has a corresponding net deduction of $150,273.

(d) The $49,727 unrecognized balance of the $200,000 net periodic payment that is made on April 1, 1996, is included in A's and B's net income or net deduction from the contract for 1996.

(e) If the parties had entered into the contract on February 1, 1995, the result would not change because no portion of either party's obligation to make a payment under the swap relates to the period prior to April 1, 1995. Consequently, under paragraph (e)(2) of this section, neither party would accrue any income or deduction from the swap for the period from February 1, 1995, through March 31, 1995.

*Example (2).* Accrual of periodic swap payments by cash method taxpayer.

(a) On April 1, 1995, C enters into a contract with unrelated counterparty D under which, for a period of five years, C is obligated to make a fixed payment to D each April 1, beginning April 1, 1996, in an amount equal to 8% multiplied by a notional principal amount of $100 million. D is obligated to make semi-annual payments to C each April 1 and October 1, beginning October 1, 1995, in an amount equal to one-half of the LIBOR amount as of the first day of the preceding 6-month period multiplied by the notional principal amount. The payments are to be calculated using a 30/360 day convention. C is a calendar year taxpayer that uses the accrual method of accounting. D is a calendar year taxpayer that uses the cash receipts and disbursements method of accounting. LIBOR is 7.80% on April 1, 1995, and 7.46% on October 1, 1995.

(b) This contract is a notional principal contract as defined by paragraph (c)(1) of this section, and LIBOR and the fixed interest rate of 8% are each specified indices under paragraph (c)(2) of this section. All of the payments to be made by C and D are periodic payments under paragraph (e)(1) of this section because they are each based on appropriate specified indices, are payable at periodic intervals of one year or less throughout the term of the contract, and are based on a single notional principal amount.

(c) Under the terms of the swap agreement, D pays C $3,900,000 (0.5 × 7.8% × $100,000,000) on October 1, 1995. In addition, D is obligated to pay C $3,730,000 (0.5 × 7.46% × $100,000,000) on April 1, 1996. C is obligated to pay D $8,000,000 on April 1, 1996. Under paragraph (e)(2)(i) of this section, C's and D's ratable daily portions for 1995 are the amounts of the periodic payments that are attributable to their taxable year ending December 31, 1995. The ratable daily portion of the 8% fixed leg is $6,000,000 (270 days/360 days × $8,000,000), and the ratable daily portion of the floating leg is $5,765,000 ($3,900,000 + (90 days/180 days × $3,730,000)). Thus, C's net deduction from the contract for 1995 is $235,000 ($6,000,000 – $5,765,000) and D reports $235,000 of net income from the contract for 1995.

(d) The net unrecognized balance of $135,000 ($2,000,000 balance of the fixed leg – $1,865,000 balance of the floating leg) is included in C's and D's net income or net deduction from the contract for 1996.

*Example (3).* Accrual of swap payments on index set in arrears.

(a) The facts are the same as in Example 1, except that A's obligation to make payments based upon LIBOR is determined by reference to LIBOR on the day each payment is due. LIBOR is 8.25% on December 31, 1995, and 8.16% on April 1, 1996.

(b) On December 31, 1995, the amount that A is obligated to pay B is not known because it will not become fixed until April 1, 1996. Under paragraph (e)(2)(ii) of this section, the ratable daily portion of the periodic payment from A to B for 1995 is based on the value of LIBOR on December 31, 1995 (unless A or B determines that the value of LIBOR on that day does not reasonably estimate the value of the specified index). Thus, the ratable daily portion of the floating leg is $6,198,770 (275 days/366 days × 8.25% × $100,000,000), while the ratable daily portion of the fixed leg is $6,010,929 (275 days/366 days × $8,000,000). The net amount for 1995 on this swap is $187,841 ($6,198,770 – $6,010,929). Accordingly, B has $187,841 of net income from the swap in 1995, and A has a net deduction of $187,841.

(c) On April 1, 1996, A makes a net payment to B of $160,000 ($8,160,000 payment on the floating leg – $8,000,000 payment on the fixed leg). For purposes of determining their net income or net deduction from this contract for the year ended December 31, 1996, B and A must adjust the net income and net deduction they recognized in 1995 by $67,623 (275 days/366 days × ($8,250,000 presumed payment on the floating leg – $8,160,000 actual payment on the floating leg)).

**(f) Nonperiodic payments.** *(1) Definition.* A nonperiodic payment is any payment made or received with respect to a notional principal contract that is not a periodic payment (as defined in paragraph (e)(1) of this section) or a termination payment (as defined in paragraph (h) of this section). Examples of nonperiodic payments are the premium for a cap or floor agreement (even if it is paid in installments), the payment for an off-market swap agreement, the prepayment of part or all of one leg of a swap, and the premium for an option to enter into a swap if and when the option is exercised.

*(2) Recognition rules.* (i) In general. All taxpayers, regardless of their method of accounting, must recognize the ratable daily portion of a nonperiodic payment for the taxable year to which that portion relates. Generally, a nonperiodic payment must be recognized over the term of a notional principal contract in a manner that reflects the economic substance of the contract.

(ii) General rule for swaps. A nonperiodic payment that relates to a swap must be recognized over the term of the contract by allocating it in accordance with the forward rates (or, in the case of a commodity, the forward prices) of a series of cash-settled forward contracts that reflect the specified index and the notional principal amount. For purposes of this allocation, the forward rates or prices used to determine the amount of the nonperiodic payment will be respected, if reasonable. See paragraph (f)(4) Example 7 of this section.

(iii) Alternative methods for swaps. Solely for purposes of determining the timing of income and deductions, a nonperiodic payment made or received with respect to a swap may be allocated to each period of the swap contract using one of the methods described in this paragraph (f)(2)(iii). The alternative methods may not be used by a dealer in notional principal contracts (as defined in paragraph (c)(4)(iii) of this section) for swaps entered into or acquired in its capacity as a dealer.

(A) Prepaid swaps. An upfront payment on a swap may be amortized by assuming that the nonperiodic payment represents the present value of a series of equal payments made throughout the term of the swap contract (the level payment method), adjusted as appropriate to take account of increases or decreases in the notional principal amount. The discount rate used in this calculation must be the rate (or rates) used by the parties to determine the amount of the nonperiodic payment. If that rate is not readily ascertainable, the discount rate used must be a rate that is reasonable under the circumstances. Under this method, an upfront payment is allocated by dividing each equal payment into its principal recovery and time value components. The principal recovery components of the equal payments are treated as periodic payments that are deemed to be made on each of the dates that the swap contract provides for periodic payments by the payor of the nonperiodic payment or, if none, on each of the dates that the swap contract provides for periodic payments by the recipient of the nonperiodic payment. The time value component is needed to compute the amortization of the nonperiodic payment, but is otherwise disregarded. See paragraph (f)(4) Example 5 of this section.

(B) Other nonperiodic swap payments. Nonperiodic payments on a swap other than an upfront payment may be amortized by treating the contract as if it provided for a single upfront payment (equal to the present value of the nonperiodic payments) and a loan between the parties. The discount rate (or rates) used in determining the deemed upfront payment and the time value component of the deemed loan is the same as the rate (or rates) used in the level payment method. The single upfront payment is then amortized under the level payment method described in paragraph (f)(2)(iii)(A) of this section. The time value component of the loan is not treated as interest, but, together with the amortized amount of the deemed upfront payment, is recognized as a periodic payment. See paragraph (f)(4) Example 6 of this section. If both parties make nonperiodic payments, this calculation is done separately for the nonperiodic payments made by each party.

(iv) General rule for caps and floors. A payment to purchase or sell a cap or floor must be recognized over the term of the agreement by allocating it in accordance with the prices of a series of cash-settled option contracts that reflect the specified index and the notional principal amount. For purposes of this allocation, the option pricing used by the parties to determine the total amount paid for the cap or floor will be respected, if reasonable. Only the portion of the purchase price that is allocable to the option contract or contracts that expire during a particular period is recognized for that period. Thus, under this paragraph (f)(2)(iv), straight-line or accelerated amortization of a cap premium is generally not permitted. See paragraph (f)(4) Examples 1 and 2 of this section.

(v) Alternative methods for caps and floors that hedge debt instruments. Solely for purposes of determining the timing of income and deductions, if a cap or floor is entered into primarily to reduce risk with respect to a specific debt instrument or group of debt instruments held or issued by the taxpayer, the taxpayer may amortize a payment to purchase or sell the cap or floor using the methods described in this paragraph (f)(2)(v), adjusted as appropriate to take account of increases or decreases in the notional principal amount. The alternative methods may not be used by a dealer in notional principal contracts (as defined in paragraph (c)(4)(iii) of this section) for caps or floors entered into or acquired in its capacity as a dealer.

(A) Prepaid caps and floors. A premium paid upfront for a cap or a floor may be amortized using the "level payment method" described in paragraph (f)(2)(iii)(A) of this section. See paragraph (f)(4) Example 3 of this section.

(B) Other caps and floors. Nonperiodic payments on a cap or floor other than an upfront payment are amortized by treating the contract as if it provided for a single upfront payment (equal to the present value of the nonperiodic payments) and a loan between the parties as described in paragraph (f)(2)(iii)(B) of this section. Under the level payment method, a cap or floor premium paid in level annual installments over the term of the contract is effectively included or deducted from income ratably, in accordance with the level payments. See paragraph (f)(4) Example 4 of this section.

(C) Special method for collars. A taxpayer may also treat a cap and a floor that comprise a collar as a single notional principal contract and may amortize the net nonperiodic payment to enter into the cap and floor over the term of the collar in accordance with the methods prescribed in this paragraph (f)(2)(v).

(vi) Additional methods. The Commissioner may, by a revenue ruling or a revenue procedure published in the Internal Revenue Bulletin, provide alternative methods for allocating nonperiodic payments that relate to a notional principal contract to each year of the contract. See § 601.601(d)(2)(ii)(b) of this chapter.

*(3) Term of extendible or terminable contracts.* For purposes of this paragraph (f), the term of a notional principal contract that is subject to extension or termination is the reasonably expected term of the contract.

*(4) Examples.* The following examples illustrate the application of paragraph (f) of this section.

*Example (1).* Cap premium amortized using general rule. (a) On January 1, 1995, when LIBOR is 8%, F pays unrelated party E $600,000 for a contract that obligates E to make a payment to F each quarter equal to one-quarter of the excess, if any, of three-month LIBOR over 9% with respect to a notional principal amount of $25 million. Both E and F are calendar year taxpayers. E provides F with a schedule of allocable premium amounts indicating that the cap was priced according to a reasonable variation of the Black-Scholes option pricing formula and that the total premium is allocable to the following periods:

| | Pricing allocation |
|---|---|
| 1995 | $ 55,000 |
| 1996 | 225,000 |
| 1997 | 320,000 |
| | $600,000 |

(b) This contract is a notional principal contract as defined by paragraph (c)(1) of this section, and LIBOR is a specified index under paragraph (c)(2)(iii) of this section. Any payments made by E to F are periodic payments under paragraph (e)(1) of this section because they are payable at periodic intervals of one year or less throughout the term of the contract, are based on an appropriate specified index, and are based on a single notional principal amount. The $600,000 cap premium paid by F to E is a nonperiodic payment as defined in paragraph (f)(1) of this section.

(c) The Black-Scholes model is recognized in the financial industry as a standard technique for pricing interest rate cap agreements. Therefore, because E has used a reasonable option pricing model, the schedule generated by E is consistent with the economic substance of the cap, and may be used by both E and F for calculating their ratable daily portions of the cap premium. Under paragraph (f)(2)(iv) of this section, E recognizes the ratable daily portion of the cap premium as income, and F recognizes the ratable daily portion of the cap premium as a deduction based on the pricing schedule. Thus, E and F account for the contract as follows:

| | Ratable daily portion |
|---|---|
| 1995 | $ 55,000 |
| 1996 | 225,000 |
| 1997 | 320,000 |
| | $600,000 |

(d) Any periodic payments under the cap agreement (that is, payments that E makes to F because LIBOR exceeds 9%) are included in the parties' net income or net deduction from the contract in accordance with paragraph (e)(2) of this section.

*Example (2).* Cap premium allocated to proper period.

(a) The facts are the same as in Example 1, except that the cap is purchased by F on November 1, 1994. The first determination date under the cap agreement is January 31, 1995 (the last day of the first quarter to which the contract relates). LIBOR is 9.1% on December 31, 1994, and is 9.15% on January 31, 1995.

(b) E and F recognize $9,192 (61 days/365 days × $55,000) as the ratable daily portion of the nonperiodic payment for 1994, and include that amount in their net income or net deduction from the contract for 1994. If E's pricing model allocated the cap premium to each quarter covered by the contract, the ratable daily portion would be 61 days/92 days times the premium allocated to the first quarter.

(c) Under paragraph (e)(2)(ii) of this section, E and F calculate the payments using LIBOR as of December 31, 1994.

F recognizes as income the ratable daily portion of the presumed payment, or $4,144 (61 days/92 days × .25 × .001 × $25,000,000). Thus, E reports $5,048 of net income from the contract for 1994 ($9,192 – $4,144), and F reports a net deduction from the contract of $5,048.

(d) On January 31, 1995, E pays F $9,375 (.25 × .0015 × $25,000,000) under the terms of the cap agreement. For purposes of determining their net income or net deduction from this contract for the year ended December 31, 1995, E and F must adjust their respective net income and net deduction from the cap by $2,072 (61 days/92 days × ($9,375 actual payment under the cap on January 31, 1995 – $6,250 presumed payment under the cap on December 31, 1994)).

*Example (3)*. Cap premium amortized using alternative method.

(a) The facts are the same as in Example 1, except that the cap provides for annual payments by E and is entered into by F primarily to reduce risk with respect to a debt instrument issued by F. F elects to amortize the cap premium using the alternative level payment method provided under paragraph (f)(2)(v)(A) of this section. Under that method, F amortizes the cap premium by assuming that the $600,000 is repaid in 3 equal annual payments of $241,269, assuming a discount rate of 10%. Each payment is divided into a time value component and a principal component, which are set out below.

| | Level Payment | Time Value Component | Principal component |
|---|---|---|---|
| 1995 | $241,269 | $ 60,000 | $181,269 |
| 1996 | 241,269 | 41,873 | 199,396 |
| 1997 | 241,269 | 21,934 | 219,335 |
| | $723,807 | $123,807 | $600,000 |

(b) The net of the ratable daily portions of the principal component and the payments, if any, received from E comprise F's annual net income or net deduction from the cap. The time value components are needed only to compute the ratable daily portions of the cap premium, and are otherwise disregarded.

*Example (4)*. Cap premium paid in level installments and amortized using alternative method.

(a) The facts are the same as in Example 3, except that F agrees to pay for the cap in three level installments of $241,269 (a total of $723,807) on December 31, 1995, 1996, and 1997. The present value of three payments of $241,269, discounted at 10%, is $600,000. For purposes of amortizing the cap premium under the alternative method provided in paragraph (f)(2)(v)(B) of this section, F is treated as paying $600,000 for the cap on January 1, 1995, and borrowing $600,000 from E that will be repaid in three annual installments of $241,269. The time value component of the loan is computed as follows:

| | Loan Balance | Time Value Component | Principal Component |
|---|---|---|---|
| 1995 | $600,000 | $ 60,000 | $181,269 |
| 1996 | 418,731 | 41,873 | 199,396 |
| 1997 | 219,335 | 21,934 | 219,335 |
| | | $123,807 | $600,000 |

(b) F is treated as making periodic payments equal to the amortized principal components from a $600,000 cap paid in advance (as described in Example 3), increased by the time value components of the $600,000 loan, which totals $241,269 each year. The time value components of the $600,000 loan are included in the periodic payments made by F, but are not characterized as interest income or expense. The effect of the alternative method in this situation is to allow F to amortize the cap premium in level installments, the same way it is paid. The net of the ratable daily portions of F's deemed periodic payments and the payments, if any, received from E comprise F's annual net income or net deduction from the cap.

*Example (5)*. Upfront interest rate swap payment amortized using alternative method.

(a) On January 1, 1995, G enters into an interest rate swap agreement with unrelated counterparty H under which, for a term of five years, G is obligated to make annual payments at 11% and H is obligated to make annual payments at LIBOR on a notional principal amount of $100 million. At the time G and H enter into this swap agreement, the rate for similar on-market swaps is LIBOR to 10%. To compensate for this difference, on January 1, 1995, H pays G a yield adjustment fee of $3,790,786. G provides H with information that indicates that the amount of the yield adjustment fee was determined as the present value, at 10% compounded annually, of five annual payments of $1,000,000 (1% × $100,000,000). G and H are calendar year taxpayers.

(b) This contract is a notional principal contract as defined by paragraph (c)(1) of this section. The yield adjustment fee is a nonperiodic payment as defined in paragraph (f)(1) of this section.

(c) Under the alternative method described in paragraph (f)(2)(iii)(A) of this section, the yield adjustment fee is recognized over the life of the agreement by assuming that the $3,790,786 is repaid in five level payments. Assuming a constant yield to maturity and annual compounding at 10%, the ratable daily portions are computed as follows:

| | Level Payment | Time Value Component | Principal component |
|---|---|---|---|
| 1995 | $1,000,000 | $ 379,079 | $ 620,921 |
| 1996 | 1,000,000 | 316,987 | 683,013 |
| 1997 | 1,000,000 | 248,685 | 751,315 |
| 1998 | 1,000,000 | 173,554 | 826,446 |
| 1999 | 1,000,000 | 90,909 | 909,091 |
| | $5,000,000 | $1,209,214 | $3,790,786 |

(d) G also makes swap payments to H at 11%, while H makes swap payments to G based on LIBOR. The net of the ratable daily portions of the 11% payments by G, the LIBOR payments by H, and the principal component of the yield adjustment fee paid by H determines the annual net income or net deduction from the contract for both G and H. The time value components are needed only to compute the ratable daily portions of the yield adjustment fee paid by H, and are otherwise disregarded.

*Example (6)*. Backloaded interest rate swap payment amortized using alternative method.

(a) The facts are the same as in Example 5, but H agrees to pay G a yield adjustment fee of $6,105,100 on December 31, 1999. Under the alternative method in paragraph (f)(2)(iii)(B) of this section, H is treated as paying a yield adjustment fee of $3,790,786 (the present value of $6,105,100, discounted at a 10% rate with annual compounding) on January 1, 1995. Solely for timing purposes, H is treated as borrowing $3,790,786 from G. Assuming annual compounding at 10%, the time value component is computed as follows:

| | Loan Balance | Time Value Component | Principal Component |
|---|---|---|---|
| 1995 | $3,790,786 | $ 379,079 | $ -0- |
| 1996 | 4,169,865 | 416,987 | -0- |
| 1997 | 4,586,852 | 458,685 | -0- |
| 1998 | 5,045,537 | 504,554 | -0- |
| 1999 | 5,550,091 | 555,009 | 6,105,100 |

(b) The amortization of H's yield adjustment fee is equal to the amortization of a yield adjustment fee of $3,790,786 paid in advance (as described in Example 5), increased by the time value component of the $3,790,786 deemed loan from G to H. Thus, the amount of H's yield adjustment fee that is allocated to 1995 is $1,000,000 ($620,921 + $379,079). The time value components of the $3,790,786 loan are included in the periodic payments paid by H, but are not characterized as interest income or expense. The net of the ratable daily portions of the 11% swap payments by G, and the LIBOR payments by H, added to the principal components from Example 5 and the time value components from this Example 6, determines the annual net income or net deduction from the contract for both G and H.

*Example (7).* Nonperiodic payment on a commodity swap amortized under general rule.

(a) On January 1, 1995, I enters into a commodity swap agreement with unrelated counterparty J under which, for a term of three years, I is obligated to make annual payments based on a fixed price of $2.35 per bushel times a notional amount of 100,000 bushels of corn and J is obligated to make annual payments equal to the spot price times the same notional amount. Assume that on January 1, 1995, the price of a one year forward for corn is $2.40 per bushel, of a two year forward $2.55 per bushel, and of a 3 year forward $2.75 per bushel. To compensate for the below-market fixed price provided in the swap agreement, I pays J $53,530 for entering into the swap. I and J are calendar year taxpayers.

(b) This contract is a notional principal contract as defined by paragraph (c)(1) of this section, and $2.35 and the spot price of corn are specified indices under paragraphs (c)(2)(i) and (iii) of this section, respectively. The $53,530 payment is a nonperiodic payment as defined by paragraph (f)(1) of this section.

(c) Assuming that I does not use the alternative methods provided under paragraph (f)(2)(iii) of this section, paragraph (f)(2)(ii) of this section requires that I recognize the nonperiodic payment over the term of the agreement by allocating the payment to each forward contract in accordance with the forward price of corn. Solely for timing purposes, I treats the $53,530 nonperiodic payment as a loan that J will repay in three installments of $5,000, $20,000, and $40,000, the expected payouts on the in-the-money forward contracts. With annual compounding at 8%, the ratable daily portions are computed as follows:

| | Expected Forward Payment | Time Value Component | Principal Component |
|---|---|---|---|
| 1995 | $ 5,000 | $ 4,282 | $ 718 |
| 1996 | 20,000 | 4,225 | 15,775 |
| 1997 | 40,000 | 2,963 | 37,037 |
| | $65,000 | $11,470 | $53,530 |

(d) The ratable daily portion of the principal component is added to I's periodic payments in computing its net income or net deduction from the notional principal contract for each taxable year. The time value components are needed only to compute the principal components, and are otherwise disregarded.

**(g) Special rules.** *(1) Disguised notional principal contracts.* The Commissioner may recharacterize all or part of a transaction (or series of transactions) if the effect of the transaction (or series of transactions) is to avoid the application of this section.

*(2) Hedged notional principal contracts.* If a taxpayer, either directly or through a related person (as defined in paragraph (c)(4)(i) of this section), reduces risk with respect to a notional principal contract by purchasing, selling, or otherwise entering into other notional principal contracts, futures, forwards, options, or other financial contracts (other than debt instruments), the taxpayer may not use the alternative methods provided in paragraphs (f)(2)(iii) and (v) of this section. Moreover, where such positions are entered into to avoid the appropriate timing or character of income from the contracts taken together, the Commissioner may require that amounts paid to or received by the taxpayer under the notional principal contract be treated in a manner that is consistent with the economic substance of the transaction as a whole.

*(3) Options and forwards to enter into notional principal contracts.* An option or forward contract that entitles or obligates a person to enter into a notional principal contract is subject to the general rules of taxation for options or forward contracts. Any payment with respect to the option or forward contract is treated as a nonperiodic payment for the underlying notional principal contract under the rules of paragraphs (f) and (g)(4) or (g)(5) of this section if and when the underlying notional principal contract is entered into.

*(4) Swaps with significant nonperiodic payments.* A swap with significant nonperiodic payments is treated as two separate transactions consisting of an on-market, level payment swap and a loan. The loan must be accounted for by the parties to the contract independently of the swap. The time value component associated with the loan is not included in the net income or net deduction from the swap under paragraph (d) of this section, but is recognized as interest for all purposes of the Internal Revenue Code. See paragraph (g)(6) Example 3 of this section. For purposes of section 956, the Commissioner may treat any nonperiodic swap payment, whether or not it is significant, as one or more loans.

*(5) Caps and floors that are significantly in-the-money.[Reserved]*

*(6) Examples.* The following examples illustrate the application of paragraph (g) of this section.

*Example (1).* Cap hedged with options.

(a) On January 1, 1995, K sells to unrelated counterparty L three cash settlement European-style put options on Eurodollar time deposits with a strike rate of 9%. The options have exercise dates of January 1, 1996, January 1, 1997, and January 1, 1998, respectively. If LIBOR exceeds 9% on any of the exercise dates, L will be entitled, by exercising the relevant option, to receive from K an amount that corresponds to the excess of LIBOR over 9% times $25 million. L pays K $650,000 for the three options. Furthermore, K is related to F, the cap purchaser in paragraph (f)(4) Example 1 of this section.

(b) K's option agreements with L reduce risk with respect to F's cap agreement with E. Accordingly, under paragraph (g)(2) of this section, F cannot use the alternative methods provided in paragraph (f)(2)(v) of this section to amortize the premium paid under the cap agreement. F must amortize the cap premium it paid in accordance with paragraph (f)(2)(iv) of this section.

(c) The method that E may use to account for its agreement with F is not affected by the application of paragraph (g)(2) of this section to F.

*Example (2).* Nonperiodic payment that is not significant.

(a) On January 1, 1995, G enters into an interest rate swap agreement with unrelated counterparty H under which, for a term of five years, G is obligated to make annual payments at 11% and H is obligated to make annual payments at LIBOR on a notional principal amount of $100 million. At the time G and H enter into this swap agreement, the rate for similar on-market swaps is LIBOR to 10%. To compensate for this difference, on January 1, 1995, H pays G a yield adjustment fee of $3,790,786. G provides H with information that indicates that the amount of the yield adjustment fee was determined as the present value, at 10% compounded annually, of five annual payments of $1,000,000 (1% × $100,000,000). G and H are calendar year taxpayers. (These facts are the same as in paragraph (f)(4) Example 5 of this section.)

(b) In this situation, the yield adjustment fee of $3,790,786 is not a significant nonperiodic payment within the meaning of paragraph (g)(4) of this section, in light of the amount of the fee in proportion to the present value of the total amount of fixed payments due under the contract. Accordingly, no portion of the swap is recharacterized as a loan for purposes of this section.

*Example (3).* Significant nonperiodic payment.

(a) On January 1, 1995, unrelated parties M and N enter into an interest rate swap contract. Under the terms of the contract, N agrees to make five annual payments to M equal to LIBOR times a notional principal amount of $100 million. In return, M agrees to pay N 6% of $100 million annually, plus $15,163,147 on January 1, 1995. At the time M and N enter into this swap agreement the rate for similar on-market swaps is LIBOR to 10%, and N provides M with information that the amount of the initial payment was determined as the present value, at 10% compounded annually, of five annual payments from M to N of $4,000,000 (4% of $100,000,000).

(b) Although the parties have characterized this transaction as an interest rate swap, the $15,163,147 payment from M to N is significant when compared to the present value of the total fixed payments due under the contract. Accordingly, under paragraph (g)(4) of this section, the transaction is recharacterized as consisting of both a $15,163,147 loan from M to N that N repays in installments over the term of the agreement, and an interest rate swap between M and N in which M immediately pays the installment payments on the loan back to N as part of its fixed payments on the swap in exchange for the LIBOR payments by N.

(c) The yield adjustment fee is recognized over the life of the agreement by treating the $15,163,147 as a loan that will be repaid with level payments over five years. Assuming a constant yield to maturity and annual compounding at 10%, M and N account for the principal and interest on the loan as follows:

| | Level Payment | Interest Component | Principal Component |
|---|---|---|---|
| 1995 | $ 4,000,000 | $ 1,516,315 | $ 2,483,685 |
| 1996 | $ 4,000,000 | 1,267,946 | 2,732,054 |
| 1997 | 4,000,000 | 994,741 | 3,005,259 |
| 1998 | 4,000,000 | 694,215 | 3,305,785 |
| 1999 | 4,000,000 | 363,636 | 3,636,364 |
| | $20,000,000 | $ 4,836,853 | $15,163,147 |

(d) M recognizes interest income, and N claims an interest deduction, each taxable year equal to the interest component of the deemed installment payments on the loan. These interest amounts are not included in the parties' net income or net deduction from the swap contract under paragraph (d) of this section. The principal components are needed only to compute the interest component of the level payment for the following period, and do not otherwise affect the parties' net income or net deduction from this contract.

(e) N also makes swap payments to M based on LIBOR, and receives swap payments from M at a fixed rate that is equal to the sum of the stated fixed rate and the rate calculated by dividing the deemed level annual payments on the loan by the notional principal amount. Thus, the fixed rate on this swap is 10%, which is the sum of the stated rate of 6% and the rate calculated by dividing the annual loan payment of $4,000,000 by the notional principal amount of $100,000,000, or 4%. Using the methods provided in paragraph (e)(2) of this section, the swap payments from M to N of $10,000,000 (10% of $100,000,000) and the LIBOR swap payments from N to M are included in the parties' net income or net deduction from the contract for each taxable year.

*Example (4).* Swaps recharacterized as a loan.

(a) The facts are the same as in Example 3, except that on January 1, 1995, N also enters into an interest rate swap agreement with unrelated counterparty O under which, for a term of five years, N is obligated to make annual payments at 12% and O is obligated to make annual payments at LIBOR on a notional principal amount of $100 million. At the time N and O enter into this swap agreement, the rate for similar on-market swaps is LIBOR to 10%. To compensate for this difference, O pays N an upfront yield adjustment fee of $7,581,574. This yield adjustment fee equals the present value, at 10% compounded annually, of five annual payments of $2,000,000 (2% of $100,000,000).

(b) In substance, these two interest rate swaps are the equivalent of a fixed rate borrowing by N of $22,744,721 ($15,163,147 from M plus $7,581,574 from O). Under paragraph (g)(2) of this section, if these positions were entered into to avoid interest character on a net loan position, the Commissioner may recharacterize the swaps as a loan which N will repay with interest in five annual installments of $6,000,000 each (the difference between the 12% N pays under the swap with O and the 6% N receives under the swap with M, multiplied by the $100,000,000 notional principal amount).

(c) N recognizes no net income or net deduction from these contracts under paragraph (d) of this section because, as to N, there is no notional principal contract income or expense. However, the recharacterization of N's separate transactions as a loan has no effect on the way M and O must each account for their notional principal contracts under paragraphs (d) through (g) of this section.

**(h) Termination payments.** *(1) Definition.* A payment made or received to extinguish or assign all or a proportionate part of the remaining rights and obligations of any party under a notional principal contract is a termination payment to the party making the termination payment and the party receiving the payment. A termination payment includes a payment made between the original parties to the contract (an extinguishment), a payment made between one party to the contract and a third party (an assignment), and any gain or loss realized on the exchange of one notional principal contract for another. Where one party assigns its remaining rights and obligations to a third party, the original nonassigning counterparty realizes gain or loss if the assignment results in a deemed exchange of contracts and a realization event under section 1001.

*(2) Taxable year of inclusion and deduction by original parties.* Except as otherwise provided (for example, in section 453, section 1092, or § 1.446-4), a party to a notional principal contract recognizes a termination payment in the year the contract is extinguished, assigned, or exchanged. When the termination payment is recognized, the party also recognizes any other payments that have been made or received pursuant to the notional principal contract, but that have not been recognized under paragraph (d) of this section. If only a proportionate part of a party's rights and obligations is extinguished, assigned, or exchanged, then only that proportion of the unrecognized payments is recognized under the previous sentence.

*(3) Taxable year of inclusion and deduction by assignees.* A termination payment made or received by an assignee pursuant to an assignment of a notional principal contract is recognized by the assignee under the rules of paragraphs (f) and (g)(4) or (g)(5) of this section as a nonperiodic payment for the notional principal contract that is in effect after the assignment.

*(4) Special rules.* (i) Assignment of one leg of a contract. A payment is not a termination payment if it is made or received by a party in exchange for assigning all or a portion of one leg of a notional principal contract at a time when a substantially proportionate amount of the other leg remains unperformed and unassigned. The payment is either an amount loaned, an amount borrowed, or a nonperiodic payment, depending on the economic substance of the transaction to each party. This paragraph (h)(4)(i) applies whether or not the original notional principal contract is terminated as a result of the assignment.

(ii) Substance over form. Any economic benefit that is given or received by a taxpayer in lieu of a termination payment is a termination payment.

*(5) Examples.* The following examples illustrate the application of this paragraph (h). The contracts in the examples are not hedging transactions as defined in § 1.1221-2(b), and all of the examples assume that no loss-deferral rules apply.

*Example (1).* Termination by extinguishment.

(a) On January 1, 1995, P enters into an interest rate swap agreement with unrelated counterparty Q under which, for a term of seven years, P is obligated to make annual payments based on 10% and Q is obligated to make semi-annual payments based on LIBOR and a notional principal amount of $100 million. P and Q are both calendar year taxpayers. On January 1, 1997, when the fixed rate on a comparable LIBOR swap has fallen to 9.5%, P pays Q $1,895,393 to terminate the swap.

(b) The payment from P to Q extinguishes the swap contract and is a termination payment, as defined in paragraph (h)(1) of this section, for both parties. Accordingly, under paragraph (h)(2) of this section, P recognizes a loss of $1,895,393 in 1997 and Q recognizes $1,895,393 of gain in 1997.

*Example (2).* Termination by assignment.

(a) The facts are the same as in Example 1, except that on January 1, 1997, P pays unrelated party R $1,895,393 to assume all of P's rights and obligations under the swap with Q. In return for this payment, R agrees to pay 10% of $100 million annually to Q and to receive LIBOR payments from Q for the remaining five years of the swap.

(b) The payment from P to R terminates P's interest in the swap contract with Q and is a termination payment, as defined in paragraph (h)(1) of this section, for P. Under paragraph (h)(2) of this section, P recognizes a loss of $1,895,393 in 1997. Whether Q also has a termination payment with respect to the payment from P to R is determined under section 1001.

(c) Under paragraph (h)(3) of this section, the assignment payment that R receives from P is a nonperiodic payment for an interest rate swap. Because the assignment payment is not a significant nonperiodic payment within the meaning of paragraph (g)(1) of this section, R amortizes the $1,895,393 over the five year term of the swap agreement under paragraph (f)(2) of this section.

*Example (3).* Assignment of swap with yield adjustment fee.

(a) The facts are the same as in Example 2, except that on January 1, 1995, Q paid P a yield adjustment fee to enter into the seven year interest rate swap. In accordance with paragraph (f)(2) of this section, P and Q included the ratable daily portions of that nonperiodic payment in their net income or net deduction from the contract for 1995 and 1996. On January 1, 1997, $300,000 of the nonperiodic payment has not yet been recognized by P and Q.

(b) Under paragraph (h)(2) of this section, P recognizes a loss of $1,595,393 ($1,895,393 – $300,000) in 1997. R accounts for the termination payment in the same way it did in Example 2; the existence of an unamortized payment with respect to the original swap has no effect on R.

*Example (4).* Assignment of one leg of a swap.

(a) On January 1, 1995, S enters into an interest rate swap agreement with unrelated counterparty T under which, for a term of five years, S will make annual payments at 10% and T will make annual payments at LIBOR on a notional principal amount of $50 million. On January 1, 1996, unrelated party U pays T $15,849,327 for the right to receive the four remaining $5,000,000 payments from S. Under the terms of the agreement between S and T, S is notified of this assignment, and S is contractually bound thereafter to make its payments to U on the appropriate payment dates. S's obligation to pay U is conditioned on T making its LIBOR payment to S on the appropriate payment dates.

(b) Because T has assigned to U its rights to the fixed rate payments, but not its floating rate obligations under the notional principal contract, U's payment to T is not a termination payment as defined in paragraph (h)(1) of this section, but is covered by paragraph (h)(4)(i) of this section. The economic substance of the transaction between T and U is a loan that does not affect the way that S and T account for the notional principal contract under this section.

**(i) Anti-abuse rule.** If a taxpayer enters into a transaction with a principal purpose of applying the rules of this section to produce a material distortion of income, the Commissioner may depart from the rules of this section as necessary to reflect the appropriate timing of income and deductions from the transaction.

**(j) Effective date.** These regulations are effective for notional principal contracts entered into on or after December 13, 1993.

T.D. 8491, 10/8/93, amend T.D. 8554, 7/13/94.

PAR. 4. Section 1.446-3 is amended by:

1. Revising the introductory text of paragraph (a) and the table of contents in paragraph (a).
2. Adding paragraph (c)(5).
3. Revising paragraphs (d), (f)(2)(i), (f)(2)(iii)(A), and (g)(4).
4. Redesignating the text of paragraph (g)(6) as paragraph (g)(7).
5. Adding new paragraph (g)(6).
6. Amending the newly designated text of paragraph (g)(7) by:

(a) Revising the heading for Example 3.

(b) Adding Example 5 through Example 9.

7. Revising paragraphs (i) and (j).

The revisions and additions read as follows:

**Proposed § 1.446-3 Notional principal contracts.** [*For Preamble, see ¶ 152,497*]

**(a) Table of contents.** This paragraph (a) lists captioned paragraphs contained in this section.

*§ 1.446-3 Notional principal contracts.*

(2) Scope of election.

(3) Determination of fair market value.

(i) Determination based on readily ascertainable value.

(ii) Determination based on value used for financial statements.

(iii) Determination based on counterparty's mark-to-market value.

(iv) Determination based on value used in determining net asset value.

(4) Requirements for use of financial statement values. [Reserved]

(5) Notional principal contracts accruing interest on significant nonperiodic payments.

(i) General rule.

(ii) Special rules for significant contingent nonperiodic payments.

(iii) Nonapplicability to regulated investment companies.

(6) Election.

(j) Effective dates.

(1) General rule.

(2) Exception.

* * * * *

**(c)** * * *

*(5) Risk-free interest rate and determination date.* (i) Risk-free interest rate. The risk-free interest rate is the applicable Federal rate determined in accordance with section 1274(d)(1) for a determination date and the period remaining in the term of the contract on the determination date.

(ii) Determination date. A determination date is the commencement date of the swap, each redetermination date as defined in paragraph (g)(6)(ii) of this section, and each special redetermination date as defined in paragraph (g)(6)(iv)(B) of this section.

**(d) Taxable year of inclusion and deduction; adjustment of gain or loss.** *(1) Inclusion and deduction.* For all purposes of the Internal Revenue Code, the net income or net deduction from a notional principal contract for a taxable year is taken into account for that taxable year. The net income or net deduction from a notional principal contract for a taxable year equals the total of all of the periodic payments that are recognized from that contract for the taxable year under paragraph (e) of this section, all of the nonperiodic payments that are recognized from that contract for the taxable year under paragraph (f) of this section, and the mark-to-market income inclusions and deductions recognized from that contract under paragraph (i) of this section.

*(2) Adjustment of gain or loss.* Proper adjustment shall be made in the amount of any gain or loss realized on a sale, exchange, or termination of a notional principal contract for inclusions or deductions pursuant to paragraphs (d)(1) and (g)(4) of this section and for payments or receipts with respect to the notional principal contract.

* * * * *

**(f)** * * *

*(2) Recognition rules.* (i) In general. All taxpayers, regardless of their method of accounting, must recognize the ratable daily portion of a nonperiodic payment for the taxable year to which that portion relates. Generally, a nonperiodic payment must be recognized over the term of a notional principal contract in a manner that reflects the economic substance of the contract. See paragraph (g)(6) of this section for additional rules for contingent nonperiodic payments.

* * * * *

(iii) * * *

(A) Prepaid swaps. An upfront payment on a swap may be amortized by assuming that the nonperiodic payment represents the present value of a series of equal payments made throughout the term of the swap contract (the level payment method), adjusted as appropriate to take account of increases or decreases in the notional principal amount. The discount rate used in this calculation must be the rate (or rates) used by the parties to determine the amount of the nonperiodic payment. If that rate is not readily ascertainable, the discount rate used must be a rate that is reasonable under the circumstances. Under this method, an upfront payment is allocated by dividing each equal payment into its principal recovery and time value components. The principal recovery components of the equal payments are treated as periodic payments that are deemed to be made on each of the dates that the swap contract provides for periodic payments by the payor of the nonperiodic payment or, if none, on each of the dates that the swap contract provides for periodic payments by the recipient of the nonperiodic payment. The sum of the principal recovery components equals the amount of the upfront payment. The time value component is used to compute the amortization of the nonperiodic payment but is otherwise disregarded. See paragraph (f)(4) Example 5 of this section.

* * * * *

**(g)** * * *

*(4) Swaps with significant nonperiodic payments.* The parties to a swap with one or more significant nonperiodic payments must treat the contract as two or more separate transactions consisting of an on-market swap and one or more loans. The parties must account for the loans separately from the swap. The payments associated with the on-market swap are included in the net income or net deduction from the swap under paragraph (d) of this section. The time value components associated with the loans are not included in the net income or net deduction from the swap under paragraph (d) of this section but are recognized as interest for all purposes of the Internal Revenue Code. The on-market swap must result in recognition of the payments associated with the swap in a manner that complies with the principles set forth in paragraph (f)(2)(i) of this section. See paragraph (g)(7) Example 3 of this section for a situation in which the on-market swap payments for a party making a significant nonperiodic upfront payment will be level payments that may be constructed through a combination of the actual payments on the swap and level payments computed under the level payment method provided by paragraph (f)(2)(iii)(A) of this section. In certain cases, a swap with significant nonperiodic payments other than an upfront payment may be treated as if the swap provided for a series of level payment loan advances having a present value equal to the present value of the nonperiodic payments, with the amount of each loan advance being immediately returned as a level payment on the swap. See paragraph (g)(7) Example 5 of this section. For purposes of section 956, the Commissioner may treat any nonperiodic swap payment, whether or not it is significant, as one or more loans.

* * * * *

*(6) Notional principal contracts with contingent nonperiodic payments.* (i) Definitions. (A) Noncontingent nonperiodic payments. A noncontingent nonperiodic payment is a

nonperiodic payment that either is fixed on or before the end of the taxable year in which a contract commences or is equal to the sum of amounts that would be periodic payments if they are paid when they become fixed (including amounts determined as interest accruals).

(B) Contingent nonperiodic payments. A contingent nonperiodic payment is any nonperiodic payment other than a noncontingent nonperiodic payment.

(ii) Noncontingent swap method. Under the noncontingent swap method, a taxpayer, regardless of its method of accounting, recognizes each contingent nonperiodic payment with respect to a notional principal contract by determining the projected amount of the payment and by applying to that projected amount the level payment method described in paragraphs (f)(2)(iii)(A) and (B) of this section. The projected amount of a contingent nonperiodic payment is the reasonably expected amount of the payment, which is determined by using one of the methods described in paragraph (g)(6)(iii) of this section and by using the risk-free interest rate in applying the level payment method. On each successive anniversary date for the notional principal contract (a redetermination date) and each special redetermination date (as defined in paragraph (g)(6)(iv)(B) of this section), the taxpayer must redetermine the projected amount of each contingent nonperiodic payment, reapply the level payment method as provided in paragraph (g)(6)(iv) of this section, and make the adjustments specified in paragraph (g)(6)(v) of this section. If paragraph (g)(4) of this section applies to the notional principal contract, redeterminations and adjustments must also be made to account for the time value components of the transaction as interest in accordance with that paragraph. Except for contingent nonperiodic payments governed by paragraph (g)(6)(iv)(B) of this section, in the taxable year in which a contingent payment is made or received, the parties must make appropriate adjustments to the amount of income or deductions attributable to the notional principal contract for any differences between projected and actual contingent nonperiodic payments as provided in paragraph (g)(6)(vi) of this section.

(iii) Determining projected amount of contingent payment. (A) Payment based on actively traded futures or forward contracts. If a contingent nonperiodic payment is determined under the contract by reference to the value of a specified index on a designated future date, the projected amount of the payment may be determined on the basis of the future value for the specified index in actively traded futures or forward contracts, if any, providing for delivery or settlement on the designated future date. If no actively traded contract exists for the designated future date, a determination from the future values for the specified index in actively traded futures or forward contracts, if any, providing for delivery or settlement on dates within three months of the designated future date may be used.

(B) Payment based on extrapolation from current market prices. If a contingent nonperiodic payment is determined under the contract by reference to the value of a specified index on a designated future date, the projected amount of the payment may be determined on the basis of the current value of the specified index as established by objective financial information adjusted to convert the current value to a future value for the specified index on the designated future date. The current value is converted to a future value by adding to the current value an amount equal to the accrual of interest on the current value under a constant yield method at the risk-free interest rate with appropriate compounding and by making appropriate adjustments for expected cash payments on the property underlying the specified index.

(C) Payment based on reasonable estimate. If the methods provided in paragraphs (g)(6)(iii)(A) and (B) of this section do not result in a reasonable estimate of the amount of the contingent payment, the taxpayer must use another method that does result in a reasonable estimate of the amount of the contingent payment and that is based on objective financial information.

(iv) Redeterminations of projected payments and level payment amounts. (A) General rule. On each redetermination date, the taxpayer must redetermine the projected amount using current values on the redetermination date and the same method that was used on the commencement date of the notional principal contract, and must reapply the level payment method as of the commencement date of the notional principal contract on the basis of the new projected payment amount and the risk-free interest rate in effect on the redetermination date.

(B) Special rule for fixed but deferred contingent nonperiodic payments. If a contingent nonperiodic payment is fixed more than six months before it is due, and if the date the payment is fixed is in a different taxable year from the date the payment is due, the date on which the payment is fixed is a special redetermination date. As of that date, the taxpayer must treat the fixed amount as the projected amount for that contingent nonperiodic payment and apply paragraphs (g)(6)(iv) and (v) of this section as if the special redetermination date were a redetermination date.

(v) Adjustments following redeterminations. Following each redetermination of projected payments and level payment amounts, the taxpayer must apply the new schedule of level payments for purposes of determining amounts to be recognized in the current and subsequent taxable years with respect to the contingent nonperiodic payments. Any difference between the amounts recognized in prior taxable years and the amounts that would have been recognized in those years had the new level payment schedule been in effect for those years is taken into account as additional payments or receipts with respect to the contract ratably over the one-year period beginning with the redetermination date and, to the extent attributable to a difference in the interest amounts calculated under paragraph (g)(4) of this section, is recognized as interest for all purposes of the Internal Revenue Code.

(vi) Adjustments for differences between projected and actual payments. Any difference between the amounts taken into account under paragraph (f) and this paragraph (g)(6) on the one hand and the amount of the actual payment under the contract on the other hand is taken into account as an adjustment to the net income or net deduction from the notional principal contract for the taxable year during which the payment occurs, and not as an adjustment to interest income or expense.

(vii) Recordkeeping requirements. The books and records maintained by a taxpayer must contain a description of the method used to determine the projected amount of a contingent payment, projected payment schedules, any adjustments following redeterminations, and any adjustments for differences between projected and actual contingent payments.

*(7)* * * *

*Example (3).* Upfront significant nonperiodic payment. * * *

* * * * *

*Example (5).* Backloaded significant nonperiodic payment. (i) On January 1, 2003, unrelated parties P and Q enter into an interest rate swap contract. Under the terms of the contract, P agrees to make five annual payments to Q equal to LIBOR times a notional principal amount of $100,000,000. In return, Q agrees to pay P 6% of $100,000,000 annually, plus $24,420,400 on December 31, 2007. At the time P and Q enter into this swap agreement the rate for similar on-market swaps is LIBOR to 10%. Assume that on January 1, 2003, the risk-free rate is 10%.

(ii) The $24,420,400 payment from Q to P is significant when compared to the present value of the total payments due from Q under the contract. Accordingly, pursuant to paragraph (g)(4) of this section, the transaction is recharacterized as two separate transactions. First, P is treated as paying to Q a series of $4,000,000 level payment loan advances. The present value of the level payment loan advances equals the present value of $24,420,400, the significant nonperiodic payment. Stated differently, the sum of the level payment loan advances and accrued interest on those advances equals the significant nonperiodic payment.

(iii) Next, Q is treated as using each loan advance to fund five annual level swap payments of $4,000,000. The level payment loan advances and accrued interest on the advances computed with annual compounding at 10% are as follows:

| | Level payment | Accrued interest |
|---|---|---|
| 2003 | $4,000,000 | $0 |
| 2004 | 4,000,000 | 400,000 |
| 2005 | 4,000,000 | 840,000 |
| 2006 | 4,000,000 | 1,324,000 |
| 2007 | 4,000,000 | 1,856,400 |
| | $20,000,000 | $4,420,400 |

(iv) P recognizes interest income, and Q accrues interest expense, each taxable year equal to the interest accruals on the deemed level payment loan advances. These interest amounts are not included in the parties' net income or net deduction from the swap contract under paragraph (d) of this section.

(v) The level payment amounts of $4,000,000 are taken into account in determining the parties' net income and deductions on the swap pursuant to paragraph (d) of this section.

*Example (6).* Contingent nonperiodic payment on an equity swap. (i) On January 1, 2005, unrelated parties V and W enter into an equity swap contract. Under the terms of the contract, V agrees to make three annual payments to W equal to 1-year LIBOR times a notional principal amount of $50,000,000. In return, W agrees to make a single payment on December 31, 2007, equal to the appreciation, if any, of a $50,000,000 investment in a basket of equity securities over the term of the swap. V is obligated to make a single payment on December 31, 2007, equal to the depreciation, if any, in the same $50,000,000 investment in the basket of equity securities. Assume that on January 1, 2005, 1-year LIBOR is 9.5%, and the risk-free rate is 10.0%.

(ii) This contract is a notional principal contract as defined in paragraph (c)(1) of this section. The annual LIBOR-based payments from V to W are periodic payments and the single payment on December 31, 2007, is a contingent nonperiodic payment.

(iii) Pursuant to the method described in (g)(6)(iii)(B) of this section, the parties determine that the projected amount of the contingent nonperiodic payment that W will pay V on December 31, 2007, is $16,550,000. The present value of this projected fixed payment is significant when compared to the present value of the total payments due from W under the contract. Accordingly, pursuant to paragraph (g)(4) of this section, the transaction is recharacterized as two separate transactions.

(iv) As a preliminary step, using the risk-free rate of 10.0% as the discount rate, the parties determine the level payment amounts that have a present value equal to the present value of $16,550,000, the projected significant nonperiodic payment. Stated differently, the sum of the level payment amounts and accrued interest at 10.0% on those amounts must equal the projected significant nonperiodic payment. The level payment amounts thus determined are $5,000,000.

(v) Next, V is treated as paying to W a series of $5,000,000 loan advances.

(vi) Then, W is treated as using each loan advance to fund one of the three annual level swap payments of $5,000,000. The level payment loan advances and accrued interest on the advances computed with annual compounding at 10.0% are as follows:

| | Level payment | Accrued interest |
|---|---|---|
| 2005 | $5,000,000 | $0 |
| 2006 | 5,000,000 | 500,000 |
| 2007 | 5,000,000 | 1,050,000 |
| | $15,000,000 | $1,550,000 |

(vii) No interest amount is taken into account for the contract year 2005.

(viii) The level payment amount of $5,000,000 is taken into account for the contract year 2005 in determining the parties' net income and deductions on the swap pursuant to paragraph (d) of this section.

(ix) For the contract year 2005, V makes a swap payment to W equal to 1-year LIBOR at 9.5% times $50,000,000, or $4,750,000, and W is deemed to make a swap payment to V equal to the annual level payment of $5,000,000. The net of the ratable daily portions of these payments determines the annual net income or deduction from the contract for both V and W.

*Example (7).* Initial Adjustment. (i) The terms of the equity swap agreement are the same as in Example 6. In addition, assume that on January 1, 2006, the first redetermination date, 1-year LIBOR is 10.0%, and the risk-free rate is 10.5%. On that date, the parties redetermine the projected amount of the contingent nonperiodic payment using current values in effect on that date. Under the method described in (g)(6)(iii)(B) of this section, the parties determine that the reprojected amount of the contingent nonperiodic payment that W will pay V on December 31, 2007, is $23,261,500. The present value as of January 1, 2005, of this projected fixed payment is significant when compared to the present value of the total payments due from W under the contract. Accordingly, pursuant to paragraph (g)(4) of this section, the transaction is recharacterized as two separate transactions.

(ii) The parties use the redetermined projected amount of $23,261,500, to reapply the method provided by paragraph (g)(4) of this section effective as of the commencement date of the swap. As a preliminary step, using the risk-free rate of 10.5% as the discount rate, the parties determine the level payment amounts that have a present value equal to the present value of $23,261,500, the reprojected significant nonperiodic payment. Stated differently, the sum of the level payment amounts and accrued interest at 10.5% on those amounts must equal the reprojected significant nonperiodic payment. The level payment amounts thus determined are $6,993,784.

(iii) Next, V is treated as paying to W a series of $6,993,784 loan advances.

(iv) Then, W is treated as using each loan advance to fund one of the three annual level swap payments of $6,993,784. The level payment loan advances and accrued interest on the advances computed with annual compounding at 10.5%, are as follows:

| | Level payment | Accrued interest |
|---|---|---|
| 2005 . . . . . . . . . . . . . | $6,993,784 | $0 |
| 2006 . . . . . . . . . . . . . | 6,993,784 | 734,347 |
| 2007 . . . . . . . . . . . . . | 6,993,784 | 1,545,801 |
| | $20,981,352 | $2,280,148 |

(v) For the contract year 2006, V recognizes interest income, and W accrues interest expense equal to the accrued interest of $734,347 on the deemed level payment loan advance. These interest amounts are not included in the parties' net income or net deduction from the swap contract under paragraph (d) of this section.

(vi) The level payment amount of $6,993,784 is taken into account for the contract year 2006 in determining the parties' net income and deductions on the swap pursuant to paragraph (d) of this section.

(vii) The parties also take into account for the contract year 2006 the difference between the amount recognized for 2005 and the amount that would have been recognized in 2005 had the new level payment schedule in this Example 7 been in effect in 2005. Thus, for purposes of paragraph (d) of this section, W is treated as making a swap payment, and V is treated as receiving a swap payment of $1,993,784 ($6,993,784-$5,000,000) for purposes of paragraph (d) of this section.

(viii) For the contract year 2006, V makes a swap payment to W equal to 1-year LIBOR at 10.0% times $50,000,000, or $5,000,000, and W is deemed to make a swap payment to V equal to the annual level payment of $6,993,784 and the adjustment amount of $1,993,784. The net of the ratable daily portions of these payments determines the annual net income or deduction from the contract for both V and W.

*Example (8).* Subsequent Adjustment. (i) The terms of the equity swap agreement are the same as in Example 7. In addition, assume that on January 1, 2007, the second redetermination date, 1-year LIBOR is 11.0%, and the risk-free rate is also 11.0%. On that date, the parties redetermine the projected amount of the contingent nonperiodic payment using current values in effect on that date. The parties determine that the reprojected amount of the contingent nonperiodic payment that W will pay V on December 31, 2007, is $11,050,000. The present value as of January 1, 2005, of this projected fixed payment is significant when compared to the present value of the total payments due from W under the contract. Accordingly, pursuant to paragraph (g)(4) of this section, the transaction is recharacterized as two separate transactions.

(ii) The parties use the redetermined projected amount of $11,050,000, to reapply the method provided by paragraph (g)(4) effective as of the commencement date of the swap. As a preliminary step, using the risk-free rate of 11.0% as the discount rate, the parties determine the level payment amounts that have a present value equal to the present value of $11,050,000, the reprojected significant nonperiodic payment. Stated differently, the sum of the level payment amounts and accrued interest at 11.0% on those amounts must equal the reprojected significant nonperiodic payment. The level payment amounts thus determined are $3,306,304.

(iii) Next, V is treated as paying to W a series of $3,306,304 loan advances.

(iv) Then, W is treated as using each loan advance to fund one of the three annual level swap payments of $3,306,304. The level payment loan advances and accrued interest on the loan advances computed with annual compounding at 11.0% are as follows:

| | Level payment | Accrued interest |
|---|---|---|
| 2005 . . . . . . . . . . . . . | $3,306,304 | $0 |
| 2006 . . . . . . . . . . . . . | 3,306,304 | 363,693 |
| 2007 . . . . . . . . . . . . . | 3,306,304 | 767,393 |
| | $9,918,912 | $1,131,086 |

(v) For 2007, V recognizes interest income, and W accrues interest expense equal to the $767,393 accrued interest amount for 2007 on the deemed loan advances. In addition, V has a net interest expense item and W has a net interest income item equal to $370,654 ($734,347-$363,693), the difference between the interest accrual taken into account for 2006 and the amount that would have been taken into account for 2006 had the new level payment schedule in this Example 8 been in effect for 2006. As a result, V has net interest income and W has net interest expense in the amount of $396,739 for 2007. These interest amounts are not included in the parties' net income or net deduction from the swap contract under paragraph (d) of this section.

(vi) The level payment amount of $3,306,304 is taken into account for the contract year 2007 in determining the parties' net income and deductions on the swap pursuant to paragraph (d) of this section.

(vii) For 2007, the parties also take into account for 2007 the difference between the amounts previously recognized for 2005 and 2006 and the amounts that would have been recognized for those years had the new level payment schedule in this Example 8 been in effect in 2005 and 2006. The amounts previously recognized were: a total of $6,993,784 for 2005, which is the sum of $5,000,000 (in 2005) and $1,993,784 (in 2006), and a total of $6,993,784 for 2006 (in 2006). The adjustment amount, therefore, equals two times $3,687,480 ($6,993,784-$3,306,304), or $7,374,960. This amount is taken into account as a payment for purposes of paragraph (d) of this section.

(viii) For the contract year 2007, V makes a swap payment to W equal to 1-year LIBOR at 11.0% times $50,000,000, or $5,500,000. W is deemed to make a swap payment to V equal to the annual level payment for 2007 of $3,306,304, and V is deemed to make a swap payment to W equal to the adjustment amount of $7,374,960. The net of the ratable daily portions of these payments determines the annual net income or deduction from the contract for both V and W.

*Example (9).* Adjustment for actual payment. (i) The terms of the equity swap agreement are the same as in Example 8. In addition, on December 31, 2007, W makes a payment to V of $25,000,000, an amount equal to the appreciation of a $50,000,000 investment in the basket of equity securities.

(ii) For 2007, $13,950,000, the difference between $25,000,000 and $11,050,000, the projected amount of the contingent payment as of January 1, 2007, is taken into account as an adjustment to the parties' net income or deductions for each party's taxable year that contains December 31, 2007, pursuant to paragraph (d) of this section.

*   *   *   *   *

**(i) Election to mark to market.** A taxpayer may elect to mark to market notional principal contracts providing for nonperiodic payments. The rules of paragraphs (f) (other than (f)(2)(i)), (g)(6)(ii) through (vii), and (h) of this section do not apply to contracts to which this paragraph (i) applies. See paragraph (i)(5) of this section for rules respecting interest accruals under paragraph (g)(4) of this section for contracts providing for significant nonperiodic payments to which this paragraph (i) applies.

*(1) General rule.* In the case of any contract held at the close of the taxable year to which this paragraph (i) applies, the taxpayer shall determine income inclusions and deductions by reference to the gain or loss that would be realized if the contract were sold for its fair market value on the last business day of the taxable year. Proper adjustment shall be made in the amount of any gain or loss subsequently realized (or calculated) for the income inclusions and deductions taken into account by reason of this paragraph (i)(1) as provided in paragraph (d)(2) of this section.

*(2) Scope of election.* The election provided by this paragraph is available for notional principal contracts that are—

(i) Of a type that is actively traded within the meaning of § 1.1092(d)-1(c) (determined without regard to the limitation in § 1.1092(d)-1(c)(2));

(ii) Marked to market by the taxpayer for purposes of determining the taxpayer's financial income provided the taxpayer satisfies the requirements in paragraph (i)(4) of this section;

(iii) Subject to an agreement by a party to the contract that is subject to section 475 to supply to the taxpayer the value that it uses in applying section 475(a)(2); or

(iv) Marked to market by a regulated investment company described in section 1296(e)(2).

*(3) Determination of fair market value.* For purposes of paragraph (i)(1) of this section, fair market value is determined by applying the rules set forth in paragraphs (i)(3)(i) through (iv) of this section.

(i) Determination based on readily ascertainable value. For a contract described in paragraph (i)(2)(i) of this section, fair market value is determined based on the mean between the bid and asked prices quoted for the contract on an established financial market as defined in § 1.1092(d)-1(b)(1), or, if bid and asked prices are not available, comparable prices determined on the basis of recent price quotations described in § 1.1092(d)-1(b)(2).

(ii) Determination based on value used for financial statements. For a contract described in paragraph (i)(2)(ii) of this section that is not described in paragraph (i)(2)(i) of this section, fair market value is the value used by the taxpayer for purposes of preparing its financial statements under paragraph (i)(4) of this section.

(iii) Determination based on counterparty's mark-to-market value. For a contract described in paragraph (i)(2)(iii) of this section that is not described in paragraph (i)(2)(i) of this section, fair market value is the mark-to-market value provided by a counterparty as being the value the counterparty used for purposes of section 475(a)(2).

(iv) Determination based on value used in determining net asset value. Notwithstanding paragraphs (i)(3)(i) through (iii) of this section, for a contract described in paragraph (i)(2)(iv) of this section, fair market value is the value used by the taxpayer in determining its net asset value.

*(4) Requirements for use of financial statement values.* [Reserved].

*(5) Notional principal contracts accruing interest on significant nonperiodic payments.* (i) General rule. If a notional principal contract that is marked to market under this paragraph (i) provides for one or more significant nonperiodic payments, paragraph (g)(4) of this section applies to the contract (computed with regard to the rule in paragraph (i)(5)(ii) of this section). Proper adjustment shall be made in the amount of any income inclusions or deductions recognized under paragraph (i)(1) of this section to take into account amounts recognized as interest under paragraph (g)(4) of this section and the payment or receipt of the nonperiodic payment or payments.

(ii) Special rules for significant contingent nonperiodic payments. In the case of a contract providing for a significant contingent nonperiodic payment, the projected amount of the payment is determined by applying one of the methods described in paragraph (g)(6)(iii) of this section or by applying the deemed equivalent value method described in this paragraph (i)(5)(ii). The amount of the payment is not redetermined except as provided in paragraph (g)(6)(iv)(B) of this section. The deemed equivalent value method may be applied if the contract fixes the timing and amount of all of the payments under the contract, except for a sole significant contingent nonperiodic payment. Under the deemed equivalent value method, the amount of the significant contingent nonperiodic payment is the amount that, as of the date the terms of the contract are fixed, causes the present value of all of the payments by the taxpayer to equal the present value of all of the payments of the counterparty to the contract. The present value of each payment of the contract is determined by applying the risk-free interest rate.

(iii) Nonapplicability to regulated investment companies. Paragraphs (i)(5)(i) and (ii) of this section do not apply to a regulated investment company described in paragraph (i)(2)(iv) of this section that makes an election under paragraph (i) of this section.

*(6) Election.* An election to apply this paragraph (i) must be made with respect to all notional principal contracts described in paragraph (i)(2) of this section to which the taxpayer is a party. The election must be made in the time and manner prescribed by the Commissioner and is effective for the taxable year for which made and all subsequent taxable years, unless revoked with the consent of the Commissioner.

**(j) Effective dates.** *(1) General rule.* Except as provided in paragraph (j)(2) of this section, this section is applicable for notional principal contracts entered into on or after December 13, 1993.

*(2) Exception.* Paragraphs (g)(6) (other than (g)(6)(i)) and (i) of this section are applicable for notional principal contracts entered into on or after 30 days after the date a Treasury decision based on these proposed regulations is published in the Federal Register.

**Proposed § 1.446-3 Notional principal contracts.** [*For Preamble, see ¶ 151,289*]

• *Caution:* This Notice of Proposed Rulemaking was partially finalized by TD 8491, 10/14/93.

**(a) Table of contents.** This paragraph (a) lists captioned paragraphs contained in §§ 1.446-3 and 1.446-4, proposed regulations under section 446 of the Internal Revenue Code.

*§ 1.446-3 Notional Principal Contracts*



*§ 1.446-4 Mark-to-Market Election for Dealers and Traders of Derivative Financial Instruments.*



**(b) Purpose.** This section is intended to clearly reflect the income and deductions from notional principal contracts by prescribing accounting methods that reflect the economic substance of such contracts.

**(c) Definitions and scope.** *(1) Notional principal contract.* (i) In general. A notional principal contract is a financial instrument that provides for the payment of amounts by one party to another at specified intervals calculated by reference to a specified index upon a notional principal amount in exchange *31355 for specified consideration or a promise to pay similar amounts. An agreement between a taxpayer and a qualified business unit (as defined in section 989(a)) of the taxpayer, or among qualified business units of the same taxpayer, is not a notional principal contract because a taxpayer can not enter into a contract with itself.

(ii) Notional principal contracts governed by this section. Notional principal contracts governed by this section include interest rate swaps, basis swaps, interest rate caps, interest rate floors, commodity swaps, equity swaps, total return swaps, equity index swaps, and similar agreements. Each confirmation under a master agreement to enter into agreements governed by this section is treated as a separate notional principal contract. A contract described in section 1256(b) is not a notional principal contract. A contract under which neither party's obligations are determined by reference to a variable specified index is not a notional principal contract. An option or forward contract that entitles or obligates a person to enter into, extend, cancel, or change the terms of a notional principal contract is not a notional principal contract, but payments made under such an option or forward contract may be governed by paragraph (e)(5) of this section.

(iii) Section 988 transactions. To the extent that the timing rules provided in this section are inconsistent with the rules that apply to any notional principal contract that is also a section 988 transaction, as defined in § 1.988-1T(a), the rules of section 988 and the regulations thereunder govern.

*(2) Specified index.* The term specified index refers to:

(i) A single fixed interest rate, price, or amount;

(ii) An interest rate that is made known publicly and offered currently to unrelated borrowers in private lending transactions by a financial institution;

(iii) An interest rate that reflects an average (based on a statistically significant sample) of current yields on a class of publicly traded debt instruments;

(iv) A price or index of prices of publicly traded stock, securities, commodities, or other publicly traded property;

(v) An amount or index of amounts that reflects the total return on one or more publicly traded stocks or securities;

(vi) An interest rate, price, index, or amount that is more or less than a specified index by a constant number of percentage or basis points, dollars, or other units in which the specified index is measured;

(vii) An interest rate, price, index, or amount that is expressed as a fixed multiple of a specified index;

(viii) Any other interest rate, price, index, or amount that is designated by the Commissioner in a revenue ruling, revenue procedure, or other administrative pronouncement published in the Internal Revenue Bulletin; and

(ix) an amount that is arrived at through any average or combination of paragraphs (c)(2) (i) through (viii) of this section.

*(3) Notional principal amount.* For purposes of this section, a notional principal amount is any specified amount of money or property that, when multiplied by a specified index, measures the parties' rights and obligations under a contract. The notional principal amount serves only as a reference for determining the amount of payments to be made under the contract and is not actually borrowed or loaned between the parties.

**(d) Description of common notional principal contracts.** *(1) Swap.* A swap is a notional principal contract that generally involves one party making periodic payments of a fixed amount and the other party (often referred to as the counterparty) making periodic payments based on a variable specified index. Both parties' payments are determined by reference to the same notional principal amount. The payments by one party to a swap contract may be made on different dates than the payments by the counterparty. If the parties' payments are made on the same date, the swap contract may provide for the payments to be offset, so that only the net amount is paid by one party to the other.

*(2) Interest rate swap.* An interest rate swap is a swap in which the notional principal amount is expressed in dollars and the specified index is an interest rate or interest rate index.

*(3) Commodity swap.* A commodity swap is a swap in which the notional principal amount is expressed in units of a commodity and the specified index is a commodity price or commodity price index. Typically, one party agrees to make periodic payments equal to a specified fixed price (e.g., an average of the forward prices at the time the swap contract is entered into) times the notional principal amount, and the counterparty agrees to make periodic payments equal to a specified index (e.g., the spot price on specified dates in the future) times the notional principal amount.

*(4) Basis swap.* A basis swap or floating swap is an interest rate swap in which the parties agree to swap payments based on one variable specified index multiplied by a notional principal amount for payments based on another variable specified index multiplied by the notional principal amount.

*(5) Cap.* A cap is a notional principal contract which generally involves an initial cash payment by one party to a counterparty in exchange for an agreement by the counterparty to make cash payments at specified future dates equal to the product of a notional principal amount and the excess, if any, of a specified index over a fixed interest rate, price, or amount (the cap rate).

*(6) Interest rate cap.* An interest rate cap is a cap in which the notional principal amount is expressed in dollars and the specified index is an interest rate or interest rate index.

*(7) Floor.* A floor is a notional principal contract which generally involves an initial cash payment by one party to a counterparty in exchange for an agreement by the counterparty to make cash payments at specified future dates equal to the product of a notional principal amount and the excess, if any, of a fixed interest rate, price, or amount (the floor rate) over a specified index.

*(8) Interest rate floor.* An interest rate floor is a floor in which the notional principal amount is expressed in dollars and the specified index is an interest rate or interest rate index.

*(9) Collar.* A cap and floor can be combined to create a collar. In a collar transaction a party purchases a cap and simultaneously sells a floor, or purchases a floor and simultaneously sells a cap. Ordinarily, the cap and the floor are based on the same notional principal amount and specified index.

**(e) Taxable year of inclusion and deduction.** *(1) Net income or deduction from a notional principal contract for the taxable year.* The net income or deduction from a notional principal contract for a taxable year is included in or deducted from gross income for that taxable year. The net income or deduction from a notional principal contract for a taxable year equals the total of all of the periodic payments that are recognized from that contract for the taxable year under paragraph (e)(2) of this section and all of the nonperiodic payments that are recognized from that contract for the taxable year under paragraph (e)(3) of this section. No portion of a payment by a party is recognized prior to the first year to which any portion of a payment by the counterparty relates.

*(2) Periodic payments.* (i) Definition. (A) In general. Periodic payments are payments made or received pursuant to a notional principal contract that are payable at fixed periodic intervals of one year or less during the entire term of the contract, and the amounts of which are based on a single specified index. Payments made to acquire a cap or a floor are not periodic payments.

(B) Short or long first or last intervals. Payments made or received pursuant to a notional principal contract do not fail to be periodic payments solely because the interval that precedes the first or last payment under the contract is shorter than, or no more than 90 days longer than, the fixed periodic interval between each of the other payments under the contract.

(ii) Recognition rules. (A) In general. All taxpayers, regardless of their method of accounting, must recognize the ratable daily portion of a periodic payment for the taxable year to which that portion relates. Any amount that is recognized under this paragraph (e)(2)(ii)(A) is included in or deducted from the taxpayer's gross income as provided in paragraph (e)(1) of this section.

(B) Rate set in arrears. If the amount of a periodic payment is not determinable at the end of a taxable year because the value of the specified index is not fixed until a date that occurs after the end of the taxable year, the ratable daily portion of a periodic payment that relates to that taxable year must be based on the specified index that would have applied if the value of the specified index were fixed as of the last day of the taxable year. Any difference that arises due to a change in the specified index between the last day of the taxable year and a date the payment becomes fixed under the contract is taken into account as an adjustment to the income or deduction from the notional principal contract for the taxable year during which the payment becomes fixed.

(iii) Examples. The following examples illustrate the application of paragraphs (e)(1) and (e)(2) of this section.

*Example (1).* (a) On April 1, 1992, A enters into a contract with unrelated counterparty B under which, for a term of five years, A is obligated to make a payment to B each April 1, beginning April 1, 1993, in an amount equal to the London Interbank Offered Rate ("LIBOR"), as determined on the immediately preceding April 1, multiplied by a notional principal amount of $100 million. Under the contract, B is obligated to make a payment to A each April 1, beginning April 1, 1993, in an amount equal to 8% multiplied by the same notional principal amount. A and B are calendar year taxpayers that use the accrual method of accounting. On April 1, 1992, LIBOR is 7.80%.

(b) This contract is a notional principal contract as defined by paragraph (c)(1) of this section and an interest rate swap as described in paragraph (d)(2) of this section. LIBOR and a fixed interest rate of 8% are each specified indices under paragraph (c)(2) of this section. All of the payments to be made by A and B are periodic payments under paragraph (e)(2)(i) of this section because they are each based on a single specified index and are payable at fixed periodic intervals of one year or less throughout the term of the contract.

(c) Under the terms of the swap agreement, on April 1, 1993, B is obligated to make payment to A of $8,000,000 (8%x$100,000,000) and A is obligated to make a payment to B of $7,800,000 (7.80%x$100,000,000). Under paragraph (e)(2)(ii) of this section, the ratable daily portions for 1992 are the amounts of these periodic payments that are attributable to A and B's taxable year ending December 31, 1992. The ratable daily portion of the 8% fixed leg is $6,027,397 (275 days/365 daysx$8,000,000), and the ratable daily portion of the floating leg is $5,876,712 (275 days/365 daysx$7,800,000). The net amount for the taxable year is the difference between the ratable daily portions of the two periodic payments, or $150,685 ($6,027,397-$5,876,712). Accordingly, A has net income of $150,685 from this swap for 1992, and B has a corresponding net deduction of $150,685.

(d) The $49,315 unrecognized balance of the $200,000 net periodic payments that are made on April 1, 1993, will be included in A's and B's net income or deduction from the contract for 1993. (e) If the parties had entered into the contract on February 1, 1992, the result would not change because no portion of either party's obligation to make a payment under the swap relates to the period prior to April 1, 1992. Consequently, under the rules of paragraph (e)(1) of this section, neither party would accrue any income or deduction from the swap for the period from February 1, 1992, through March 31, 1992.

*Example (2).* (a) On April 1, 1992, C enters into a contract with unrelated counterparty D under which, for a period of five years, C is obligated to make a fixed payment to D each April 1, beginning April 1, 1993, in an amount equal to 8% multiplied by a notional principal amount of $100 million. D is obligated to make semi-annual payments to C each April 1 and October 1, beginning October 1, 1992, in an amount equal to one-half of the LIBOR amount as of the first day of the preceding 6-month period multiplied by the notional principal amount. C is a calendar year taxpayer that uses the accrual method of accounting. D is a calendar year taxpayer that uses the cash receipts and disbursements method of accounting. LIBOR is 7.80% on April 1, 1992, and 7.46% on October 1, 1992.

(b) This contract is a notional principal contract as defined by paragraph (c)(1) of this section and an interest rate swap as described in paragraph (d)(2) of this section. LIBOR and a fixed interest rate of 8% are each specified indices under paragraph (c)(2) of this section. All of the payments to be made by C and D are periodic payments under paragraph (e)(2)(i) of this section because they are each based on a single specified index and are payable at fixed periodic intervals of one year or less throughout the term of the contract.

(c) Under the terms of the swap agreement, D pays C $3,900,000 (.5x7.8%x $100,000,000) on October 1, 1992. In addition, D is obligated to pay C $3,730,000 (.5x7.46%$100,000,000) on April 1, 1993. C is obligated to pay D $8,000,000 on April 1, 1993. Under paragraph (e)(2)(ii) of this section, C's and D's ratable daily portions for 1992 are the amounts of the periodic payments that are attributable to their taxable year ending December 31, 1992. The ratable daily portion of the 8% fixed leg is $6,027,397 (275 days/365 days x $8,000,000), and the ratable daily portion of the floating leg is $5,785,495 ($3,900,000+(92 days/182 daysx$3,730,000)). Thus, C's net deduction from the contract for 1992 is $241,902 ($6,027,397-$5,785,495) and D reports $241,902 of net income from the contract for 1992.

(d) The $1,972,603 unrecognized balance of the fixed leg and the $1,844,506 unrecognized balance of the floating leg will be included in C's net income or deduction from the contract for 1993.

*Example (3).* (a) The facts are the same as in Example 1, except that A's obligation to make payments based upon LIBOR is determined by reference to LIBOR on the day each payment is due. LIBOR is 8.25% on December 31, 1992, and 8.16% on April 1, 1993.

(b) On December 31, 1992, the amount that A is obligated to pay B is not known because it will not become fixed until April 1, 1993. Under paragraph (e)(2)(ii)(B) of this section, the ratable daily portion of the periodic payment from A to B for 1992 is based on the value of LIBOR on December 31, 1992. Thus, the ratable daily portion of the floating leg is $6,215,753 (275 days/365daysx8.25%x$100,000,000) while the ratable daily portion of the fixed leg is $6,027,397 (275 days/365 daysx$8,000,000). The net amount for 1992 on this swap is $188,356 ($6,215,753-$6,027,397). Accordingly, B has $188,356 of net income from the swap in 1992, and A has a net deduction of $188,356.

(c) On April 1, 1993, A makes a net payment to B of $160,000 ($8,160,000 payment on the floating leg--$8,000,000 payment on the fixed leg). For purposes of determining their net income or deduction from this contract for the year ended December 31, 1993, B and A must adjust the net income and deduction they recognized in 1992 by $67,808 (275 days/365 daysx($8,250,000 presumed payment on the floating leg--$8,160,000 actual payment on the floating leg)).

*(3) Nonperiodic payments.* (i) Definition. A nonperiodic payment is any payment made or received pursuant to a notional principal contract that is not a periodic payment (as defined in paragraph (e)(2)(i) of this section) or a termination payment (as defined in paragraph (e)(6)(i) of this section). Examples of nonperiodic payments are *31357 the

premium for a cap or floor agreement (even if it is paid in installments), the yield adjustment fee for an off-market interest rate swap agreement, and the premium for an option to enter into a swap if and when the option is exercised.

(ii) Recognition rules. (A) In general. All taxpayers, regardless of their method of accounting, must recognize the ratable daily portion of a nonperiodic payment for the taxable year to which that portion relates. Except as provided in paragraph (e)(4) of this section, any amount that is recognized under this paragraph (e)(3)(ii) is included in or deducted from the taxpayer's gross income as provided in paragraph (e)(1) of this section. A nonperiodic payment must be recognized over the term of a notional principal contract in a manner that reflects the economic substance of the contract. Thus, the timing of income and deductions from the contract depends upon the type of notional principal contract involved and its economic characteristics. Most notional principal contracts resemble other financial instruments, and the amount of a nonperiodic payment made pursuant to the notional principal contract corresponds to the value of those instruments, adjusted to reflect a discount for early payment or a premium for late payment.

(B) Swaps. A nonperiodic payment that relates to a swap must be recognized over the term of the contract by allocating it in accordance with the values of a series of cash-settled forward contracts that reflect the specified index and the notional principal amount. For purposes of this allocation the forward prices, interest rate and compounding method used by the parties to determine the amount of the nonperiodic payment will be respected, if reasonable.

(C) Caps and floors. Any payment that relates to the purchase and sale of a cap or floor must be recognized over the term of the agreement by allocating it in accordance with the values of a series of cash-settled option contracts that reflect the specified index and the notional principal amount. For purposes of this allocation the option pricing used by the parties to determine the total amount paid for the cap or floor will be respected, if reasonable. Only the portion of the purchase price that is allocable to the option contract or contracts that expire during a particular period is recognized for that period. Accordingly, straight-line and accelerated amortization methods are not permissible.

(D) Optional methods for interest rate swaps, caps and floors. (1) Interest rate swaps. A nonperiodic payment made or received with respect to an interest rate swap may be allocated to each period of the swap contract by assuming that the nonperiodic payment represents the present or future value, determined under the constant yield to maturity method, of a series of equal payments made throughout the term of the swap contract (the "level payment constant yield to maturity method"). Under this method, for example, an upfront payment is allocated by dividing each equal payment into its principal recovery and time value components. The principal recovery components of the equal payments are treated as periodic payments that are deemed to be made on each of the dates that the swap contract provides for periodic payments by the payor of the nonperiodic payment or, if none, on each of the dates that the swap contract provides for periodic payments by the recipient of the nonperiodic payment. Generally, the calculation must use semi-annual compounding and a discount rate equal to the overpayment rate established under section 6621(a)(1) on the date the nonperiodic payment is fixed. However, if the parties actually use the level payment constant yield to maturity method to determine the amount of the nonperiodic payment, the calculation may employ the actual interest rate and compounding method used in that determination.

(2) Interest rate caps and floors. The Commissioner may, by a revenue procedure published in the Internal Revenue Bulletin, provide an alternative method for allocating the premium paid or received for interest rate caps and floors to each year of the agreements.

(iii) Examples. The following examples illustrate the application of paragraph (e)(3) of this section.

*Example (1).* (a) On January 1, 1992, when LIBOR is 8%, F pays unrelated party E $600,000 for a contract which obligates E to make a payment to F each quarter equal to one-quarter of the excess, if any, of three-month LIBOR over 9% with respect to a notional principal amount of $25 million. Both E and F are calendar year taxpayers. E provides F with a schedule of allocable premium amounts that indicates the cap was priced according to a variation of the Black-Scholes option pricing formula and that the total premium is allocable to the following periods:

(b) This contract is a notional principal contract as defined by paragraph (c)(1) of this section and an interest rate cap as described in paragraph (d)(6) of this section. LIBOR is a specified index under paragraph (c)(2) of this section. Any payments made by E to F are periodic payments under paragraph (e)(2)(i) of this section because they are payable at fixed periodic intervals of one year or less throughout the term of the contract and are based on a specified index. The $600,000 cap premium paid by F to E is a nonperiodic payment as defined in paragraph (e)(3)(i) of this section.

(c) The Black-Scholes model is recognized in the financial industry as a standard technique for pricing interest rate cap agreements. Therefore, although E has modified the Black-Scholes option pricing model, the schedule generated by E's proprietary Black-Scholes model is consistent with the economic substance of the cap, and may be used by both E and F for calculating their ratable daily portions of the cap premium. E recognizes the ratable daily portion of the cap premium as income, and F recognizes the ratable daily portion of the cap premium as a deduction based on the pricing schedule. Thus, E and F account for the contract as follows:

(d) Any periodic payments under the cap agreement (that is, payments that E makes to F because LIBOR exceeds 9%) are included in the parties' net income or deduction from the contract in accordance with paragraph (e)(2) of this section.

(e) If F had paid E $600,000 to enter into the same cap agreement on November 1, 1991, the ratable daily portions would not change because no portion of the premium paid for the cap relates to the period prior to January 1, 1992. Consequently, under the rules of paragraph (e)(1) of this section, neither party would accrue any income or deduction with respect to the cap for the period from November 1, 1991, through December 31, 1991.

*Example (2).* (a) The facts are the same as in Example 1, except that the cap is purchased by F on November 1, 1992. The first determination date under the cap agreement is January 31, 1993 (the last day of the first quarter to which the contract relates). LIBOR is 9.1% on December 31, 1992, and is 9.15% on January 31, 1993.

(b) E and F recognize $9,192 (61 days/365 days x $55,000) as the ratable daily portion of the nonperiodic payment for 1992, and *31358 include that amount in their net income or deduction from the contract for 1992. If E's pricing model allocates the cap premium to each quarter covered by the contract, the ratable daily portion is 61 days/92 days times the premium allocated to the first quarter.

(c) Because LIBOR exceeds 9% of December 31, 1992, F must recognize as income (and E as a deduction) the ratable daily portion of the presumed payment under paragraph (e)(3)(ii), or $4,143 (61 days/92 daysx.25x.001x$25,000,000). Therefore, E reports $5,049 of net income from the contract for 1992 ($9,192- $4,143), and F reports a net deduction from the contract of $5,049.

(d) On January 31, 1993, E pays F $9,375 (.25x.0015x$25,000,000) under the terms of the cap agreement. For purposes of determining their net income or deduction from this contract for the year ended December 31, 1993, E and F must adjust their respective income and deduction recognized in 1992 from the cap by $2,072 (61 days/92 daysx($9,375 actual payment under the cap - $6,250 presumed payment under the cap)).

*Example (3).*

(a) The facts are the same as in Example 1, except that F agrees to pay E for the cap in three annual installments of $219,335 each, on January 1 of 1992, 1993 and 1994.

(b) Under paragraph (e)(3)(ii)(C) of this section, the cap is presumed to be priced using an option pricing formula that allocates increasing portions of the premium to the later year of the contract. Although E agrees to receive the $600,000 premium for the cap over three years (with interest compounded annually at 10%), rather than at the inception of the contract, E and F must recognize the payments in accordance with the economic substance of a comparable series of option contracts.

(c) First, to determine the cap premium that would have been paid at the beginning of the contract, the installment payments are discounted back using the rate of interest and compounding method that was used by the parties to compute the installments.

(d) Second, the $600,000 cap premium must be recognized by allocating it among the options that comprise the cap contract in accordance with an option pricing model that allocates increasing portions of the premium to the later years of the contract, or under the optional method referred to in paragraph (e)(3)(ii)(D)(2) of this section. In this case E's option pricing model allocates $55,000 to the first year, $225,000 to the second year, and $320,000 to the third year.

(e) Third, the excess of the sum of the installment payments over the $600,000 premium must be recognized by allocating it among the options that comprise the cap contract. That excess represents an additional amount that is paid by F to E for the right to pay installments instead of paying the entire premium at the outset of the contract. In this case, F pays an additional $58,005, the excess of the $658,005 in total installment payments (3x$219,335) over the $600,000 cap premium. Of this additional amount, $38,066 is allocated to 1992 (10% of the unpaid premium, of $600,000-$219,335) and the remainder of $19,939 to 1993 (10% of $380,665+$38,066-$219,335). None of the additional amount is allocated to 1994, because F's final payment to E occurs on January 1, 1994.

(f) E and F report net income or deduction from the contract equal to the net of any periodic payments that E makes to F under the cap agreement, the ratable daily portion of the premium that is recognized under paragraph (d) of this example, and that additional amount that is recognized under paragraph (e) of this example.

*Example (4).*

(a) The facts are the same as in Example 1, except that F views the cap as a wasting asset, composed of a series of options each of which is expected to lose value prior to the year in which it expires. Accordingly, F claims amortization deductions for the cap premium as follows: F reasons that, because it could have purchased a two-year cap at the beginning of 1992 for $280,000 ($55,000+$225,000) instead of a three-year cap for $600,000, $320,000 of the premium ($600,000-$280,000) must be allocable to the first year of the contract.

(b) This is not an acceptable method of allocating the premium to the options that comprise the cap contract because it is inconsistent with the economic substance of the contract. F's conclusion that the options will lose value before they expire is based on an implicit assumption that interest rates will not rise during the term of the cap. If this were true, the cap would be valueless.

(c) F must allocate the premium paid among the options that comprise the cap contract in accordance with an option pricing model that allocates increasing portions of the premium to the later years of the contract, or under the optional method referred to in paragraph (e)(3)(ii)(D)(2) of this section.

*Example (5).*

(a) On January 1, 1992, G enters into an interest rate swap agreement with unrelated counterparty H under which, for a term of five years, G is obligated to make annual payments at 11% and H is obligated to make annual payments at LIBOR on a notional principal amount of $100 million. At the time G and H enter into this swap agreement, the rate for similar on-market swaps is LIBOR to 10%. To compensate for this difference, on January 1, 1992 H pays G a yield adjustment fee of $3,695,897. G provides H with information that indicates that the amount of the yield adjustment fee was determined as the present value, at 11% compounded annually, of five annual payments of $1,000,000 (1%x$100,000,000). G and H are calendar year taxpayers.

(b) This contract is a notional principal contract as defined by paragraph (c)(1) of this section and an interest rate swap as described in paragraph (d)(2) of this section. The yield adjustment fee is a nonperiodic payment as defined in paragraph (e)(3)(i) of this section.

(c) In this case, the parties have actually used the level payment constant yield to maturity method to determine the amount of the yield adjustment fee. Accordingly, under paragraph (e)(3)(ii)(D)(1) of this section, the yield adjustment fee may be recognized over the life of the agreement using the level payment constant yield to maturity method and the discount rate and compounding method used by the parties. With annual compounding at 11%, the ratable daily portions are:

(d) G also makes swap payments to H at 11%, while H makes swap payments to G based on LIBOR. The net of the ratable daily portions of the 11% payments by G, the ratable daily portions of the LIBOR payments by H, and the ratable daily portions of the yield adjustment fee paid by H equals the annual net income or deduction from the contract for both G and H. The time value components are needed to compute the ratable daily portions of the yield adjustment fee paid by H, but do not otherwise affect the parties' method of accounting for this contract.

*Example (6).*

(a) On January 1, 1992, I enters into a commodity swap agreement with unrelated counterpart J under which, for a term of six years, I is obligated to make annual payments based on a fixed price of $22 per barrel times a notional amount of 500,000 barrels of crude oil and J is obligated to make annual payments equal to the spot price times the same notional amount. In addition, on January 1, 1992, I pays J *31359 $1,200,000 for entering into the swap agreement. I and J are calendar year taxpayers.

(b) This contract is a notional principal contract as defined by paragraph (c)(1) of this section and a commodity swap as described in paragraph (d)(3) of this section. The $1,200,000 payment is a nonperiodic payment as defined by paragraph (e)(3)(i) of this section.

(c) Under paragraph (e)(3)(ii)(B) of this section, the nonperiodic payment must be recognized over the term of the agreement by allocating the payment to each forward contract in accordance with the value of each forward contract. In allocating the $1,200,000 payment in accordance with the values of a series of forward contracts, I and J must use the forward prices and interest rates that were used to determine the amount of the payment.

*(4) Special rules.* (i) Compound and disguised notional principal contracts. A financial instrument that is comprised of two or more notional principal contracts, such as a collar or an interest rate swap with a cap on the floating leg, is treated for purposes of this section as two or more separate notional principal contracts. In addition, the Commissioner may recharacterize all or part of a transaction (or series of transactions) if the effect of the transaction (or series of transactions) is to avoid the application of this section.

(ii) Hedged notional principal contracts. A taxpayer that, either directly or through a related party, hedges a notional principal contract by purchasing, selling, or otherwise entering into other notional principal contracts, futures, forwards, options, or other financial instruments may not use the optional methods of paragraph (e)(3)(ii)(D) of this section to amortize any nonperiodic payment made or received with respect to the hedged notional principal contract. Moreover, the Commissioner may require that amounts paid to or received by the taxpayer under the notional principal contract be treated in a manner that is consistent with the economic substance of the transaction as a whole.

(iii) Swaps with significant nonperiodic payments. A swap that involves significant nonperiodic payments is treated as including one or more loans, which must be accounted for by both parties to the contract independently of the swap. For example, a significant upfront payment includes a self-amortizing loan that must be amortized over the term of the agreement using the level payment constant yield to maturity method described in paragraph (e)(3)(ii)(D)(l) of this section. The time value component of the loan is recognized as interest for all purposes of the Code. Interest that is recognized under this paragraph is not included in the net income or loss from the contract under paragraph (e)(1) of this section. For purposes of section 956, the Commissioner may treat any nonperiodic swap payment, whether or not it is significant, as one or more loans.

(iv) Caps and floors that are significantly in-the-money. If, on the date that a cap or floor is entered into, the current value of the specified index in a cap agreement exceeds the cap rate by a significant amount, or the floor rate exceeds the current value of the specified index in a floor agreement by a significant amount, then the cap or floor is treated as including one or more loans. The time value component of a cap or floor that is significantly in-the-money is recognized as interest for all purposes of the Code. For any taxable year during the term of the agreement, this time value component is deemed to be the lesser of:

(A) The ratable daily portion of the cap or floor premium that is recognized for the taxable year under paragraph (e)(3)(ii)(C) of this section, multiplied by the discount rate used by the parties to determine the amount paid for the cap or floor compounded from the date the premium is paid to the earlier of the date such option contracts expire or the end of the taxable year; or

(B) The net income or deduction from the cap or floor for the taxable year under paragraph (e)(1) of this section, computed without regard to this paragraph (e)(4)(iv).

In the case of an interest rate cap or an interest rate floor, a significant amount for purposes of this paragraph (e)(4)(iv) is more than 25 basis points. Interest recognized under this paragraph (e)(4)(iv) is not included in the net income or deduction from the cap or floor under paragraph (e)(1) of this section.

(v) Examples. The following examples illustrate the application of paragraph (e)(4) of this section.

*Example (1).* (a) On January 1, 1992, K sells to unrelated counterparty L three cash settlement European-style put options on Eurodollar time deposits with a strike rate of 9%. The options have exercise dates of January 1, 1993, January 1, 1994, and January 1, 1995, respectively. If LIBOR exceeds 9% on any of the exercise dates, L will be entitled, by exercising the relevant option, to receive from K an amount that corresponds to the excess of LIBOR over 9% times $25 million. L pays K $650,000 for the three options. Furthermore, K is related to F, the cap purchaser in Example 1 under paragraph (e)(3) of this section.

(b) F's cap agreement with E is hedged by K's option agreements with L. Accordingly, under paragraph (e)(4)(ii) of this section, F cannot make use of the optional method contemplated by paragraph (e)(3)(ii)(D)(2) of this section in amortizing the premium paid under the cap agreement. F must amortize the premium paid or received in accordance with the rules of paragraph (e)(3)(ii)(C) of this section.

(c) The method that E may use to account for its agreement with F is not affected by the application of paragraph (e)(4)(ii) of this section to F.

*Example (2).*

(a) The facts are the same as in Example 5 under paragraph (e)(3) of this section.

(b) In this case, the yield adjustment fee of $3,695,897 is not a significant nonperiodic payment within the meaning of paragraph (e)(4)(iii) of this section, in light of the amount of the fee in proportion to the present value of the total amount of fixed payments due under the contract. Accordingly, no portion of the swap is recharacterized as a loan under that paragraph.

*Example (3).*

(a) On January 1, 1992, unrelated parties M and N enter into an interest rate swap contract. Under the terms of the contract, N agrees to make five annual payments to M equal to LIBOR times a notional principal amount of $100 million. In return, M agrees to pay N 6% of $100 million annually, plus $15,163,147 on January 1, 1992. At the time M and N enter into this swap agreement the rate for similar on-market swaps is LIBOR to 10%, and N provides M with information that the amount of the initial payment was determined as the present value, at 10% compounded annually, of five annual payments from M to N of $4,000,000 (4% of $100,000,000).

(b) Although the parties have characterized this transaction as an interest rate swap, the $15,163,147 payment from

M to N is significant when compared to the present value of the total fixed payments due under the contract. Accordingly, under paragraph (e)(4)(iii) of this section, the transaction is recharacterized as consisting of a $15,163,147 loan from M to N that N repays in installments over the term of the agreement, and an interest rate swap between M and N in which M immediately pays the installment payments on the loan back to N as part of its fixed payments on the swap in exchange for the LIBOR payments by N.

(c) The loan is amortized using the level payment constant yield to maturity method; that is, by finding the level payments needed to amortize the $15,163,147 payment over five years. Under paragraph (e)(3)(ii)(D)(1), the level payment may be determined in this case using the parties' discount rate of 10% and annual compounding. M and N account for the principal and interest on the loan as follows: M recognizes interest income, and N claims an interest deduction, each taxable year equal to the interest component of the deemed installment payments on the loan. These interest amounts are not included in the parties' net income or deduction from the contract under paragraph (e)(1) of this section. The principal components are needed to compute the interest component of the level payment for the following period, but do not otherwise affect the parties' income or deductions from this contract.

(d) N also makes swap payments to M based on LIBOR, and receives swap payments from M at a fixed rate that is equal to the sum of the stated fixed rate and the rate calculated by dividing the annuitized annual loan payments by the notional principal amount. Thus, the fixed rate on this swap is 10%, which is the sum of the stated rate of 6% and the rate calculated by dividing the annual loan payment of $4,000,000 by the notional principal amount of $100,000,000, or 4%. Using the methods provided in paragraph (e)(2) of this section, the 10% swap payments from M to N and the LIBOR swap payments from N to M are included in the parties' net income or deduction from the contract for each taxable year.

*Example (4).*

(a) The facts are the same as in Example 3, except that on January 1, 1992, N also enters into an interest rate swap agreement with unrelated counterparty O under which, for a term of five years, N is obligated to make annual payments at 12% and O is obligated to make annual payments at LIBOR on a notional principal amount of $100 million. At the time N and O enter into this swap agreement, the rate for similar on-market swaps is LIBOR to 10%. To compensate for this difference, O pays N an upfront yield adjustment fee of $7,391,794 for this off-market swap agreement. This yield adjustment fee equals the present value, at 11% compounded annually, of five annual payments of $2,000,000 (2% of $100,000,000).

(b) In substance, these two interest rate swaps are the equivalent of a fixed rate borrowing by N of $22,554,941 ($15,163,147 from M plus $7,391,794 from O). Under paragraph (e)(4)(ii) of this section, the Commissioner may recharacterize the swaps as a loan which N will repay with interest in five annual installments of $6,000,000 each (the difference between the 12% N pays under the swap with O and the 6% N receives under the swap with M, multiplied by the $100,000,000 notional principal amount).

(c) N recognizes no net income or deduction from the contract under paragraph (e)(1) of this section because, as to N, there is no notional principal contract income or expense. However, the recharacterization of N's hedged transactions as a loan has no effect on the way M and O must each account for their notional principal contracts under paragraphs (e)(1) through (e)(4) of this section.

*(5) Options and forwards to enter into notional principal contracts.* An option or forward contract that entitles or obligates a person to enter into a notional principal contract is subject to the general rules of taxation for options or forward contracts. Any payment with respect to the option or forward contract is treated as a nonperiodic payment for the underlying notional principal contract under the rules of paragraphs (e)(3) and (e)(4) of this section if and when the underlying notional principal contract is entered into.

*(6) Termination payments.* (i) Definition. A payment, whether made or received, that extinguishes or assigns all or a proportionate part of the rights and obligations of any party under a notional principal contract is a termination payment for all parties to the contract. A termination payment includes a payment made between the original parties to the contract (an extinguishment), and a payment made between one party to the contract and a third party (an assignment).

(ii) Taxable year of inclusion and deduction by original parties. Except as otherwise provided in section 1092 and the regulations thereunder, the parties to a notional principal contract recognize a termination payment that is received or made with respect to that contract in the year of the extinguishment or assignment. Any payments that have been made or received pursuant to a notional principal contract but that have not been recognized under paragraph (e)(2) or (e)(3) of this section are also recognized in the year of the extinguishment or assignment. If only a proportionate part of a party's rights and obligations is extinguished or assigned, then only that proportion of the unrecognized payments is recognized under this paragraph.

(iii) Taxable year of inclusion and deduction by assignees. A termination payment made or received by an assignee pursuant to an assignment of a notional principal contract is recognized by the assignee under the rules of paragraphs (e)(3) and (e)(4) of this section as a nonperiodic payment for the notional principal contract that is in effect after the assignment.

(iv) Substance over form. The Commissioner may treat any economic benefit that is given or received by a taxpayer in lieu of a termination payment as a termination payment. Cf. § 1.988-2T(d)(2)(ii)(B) (realization by offset) and § 1.988-2T(d)(2)(v) (extension of the contract maturity date).

(v) Exception. This paragraph (e)(6) does not apply to any contract that is integrated with other property or debt pursuant to section 988(d) and the regulations thereunder.

(vi) Examples. The following examples illustrate the application of this paragraph (e)(6).

*Example (1).* (a) On January 1, 1992, P enters into an interest rate swap agreement with unrelated counterparty O under which, for a term of seven years, P is obligated to make annual payments based on 10% and O is obligated to make semi-annual payments based on LIBOR and a notional principal amount of $100 million. P and O are both calendar year taxpayers. On January 1, 1994, when the fixed rate on a comparable LIBOR swap has fallen to 9.5%, P pays O $1,895,393 to terminate the swap.

(b) The payment from P to O extinguishes the swap contract and is a termination payment, as defined in paragraph (e)(6)(i) of this section, for both parties. Accordingly, under paragraph (e)(6)(ii) of this section, P recognizes a loss of

$1,895,393 in 1994 and O recognizes $1,895,393 of income or gain in 1994.

*Example (2).* (a) The facts are the same as in Example 1, except that on January 1, 1994, P pays unrelated party R $1,895,393 to assume all of P's rights and obligations under the swap with Q. In return for this payment, R agrees to pay 10% of $100 million annually to Q and to receive LIBOR payments from Q for the remaining five years of the swap.

(b) The payment from P to R terminates P's interest in the swap contract with Q and is a termination payment, as defined in paragraph (e)(6)(i) of this section, for all three parties. Under paragraph (e)(6)(ii) of this section, P recognizes a loss of $1,895,393 in 1994. Under paragraph (e)(6)(ii) of this section, Q recognizes $1,895,393 of income or gain in 1994 and is permitted to amortize its resulting $1,895,393 of basis in the interest rate swap over the remaining five year term of the swap agreement, using a method prescribed for amortizing nonperiodic swap payments under paragraph (e)(3)(ii) of this section.

(c) Under paragraph (e)(6)(iii) of this section, the assignment payment that R receives from P is a nonperiodic payment for an interest rate swap. Because the assignment payment is not a significant nonperiodic payment within the meaning of paragraph (e)(4)(iii) of this section, R amortizes the $1,895,393 over the five year term of the swap agreement in accordance with paragraph (e)(3)(ii) of this section.

*Example (3).* (a) The facts are the same as in Example 2, except that on January 1, 1992, Q pays P a yield adjustment fee to enter into the seven year interest rate swap. In accordance with paragraph (e)(3)(ii) of this section, P and Q included the ratable daily portions of that nonperiodic payment in their net income or deduction from the contract for 1992 and 1993. On January 1, 1994, $300,000 of the nonperiodic payment has not yet been recognized by P and Q.

(b) Under paragraph (e)(6)(ii) of this section, P recognizes a loss of $1,595,393 ($1,895,393-$300,000) in 1994 and Q recognizes $1,595,393 of income or gain in 1994. R accounts for the termination payment in the same way it did in Example 2; the existence of an unamortized payment with respect to the original swap has no effect on R.

*Example (4).* (a) On January 1, 1992, S enters into an interest rate swap agreement with unrelated counterparty T under which, for a term of five years, S will make annual payments at 10% and T will make annual *31361 payments at LIBOR on a notional principal amount of $50 million. On January 1, 1993, unrelated party U pays T $15,849,327 for the right to receive the four remaining $5,000,000 payments from S. Under the terms of the agreement between S and T, S is notified of this assignment, and S is contractually bound thereafter to make its payments to U on the appropriate payment dates. S's obligation to pay U is conditioned on T making its LIBOR payment to S on the appropriate payment dates.

(b) Because T has assigned to U its rights but not its obligations under the notional principal contract, U's payment to T is not a termination payment as defined in paragraph (e)(6)(i) of this section. The transaction between T and U does not affect the way that S and T account for the notional principal contract under this section.

**(f) Anti-abuse rule.** If:

*(1)* A taxpayer enters into a transaction that is not a customary commercial transaction,

*(2)* Applying the rules of this section to that transaction would produce a material distortion of the taxpayer's income from that transaction, and

*(3)* The taxpayer would not have entered into the transaction but for that material distortion, then the Commissioner may exercise his discretion to depart from the rules of this section as necessary to clearly reflect the income from the transaction.

**(g) Effective date.** These regulations are effective for notional principal contracts entered into after [the date a Treasury Decision based on these proposed regulations is published in the Federal Register].

**§ 1.446-4 Hedging transactions.**

**(a) In general.** Except as provided in this paragraph (a), a hedging transaction as defined in § 1.1221-2(b) (whether or not the character of gain or loss from the transaction is determined under § 1.1221-2) must be accounted for under the rules of this section. To the extent that provisions of any other regulations governing the timing of income, deductions, gain, or loss are inconsistent with the rules of this section, the rules of this section control.

*(1) Trades or businesses excepted.* A taxpayer is not required to account for hedging transactions under the rules of this section for any trade or business in which the cash receipts and disbursements method of accounting is used or in which § 1.471-6 is used for inventory valuations if, for all prior taxable years ending on or after September 30, 1993, the taxpayer met the $5,000,000 gross receipts test of section 448(c) (or would have met that test if the taxpayer were a corporation or partnership). A taxpayer not required to use the rules of this section may nonetheless use a method of accounting that is consistent with these rules.

*(2) Coordination with other sections.* This section does not apply to—

(i) Any position to which section 475(a) applies;

(ii) An integrated transaction subject to § 1.1275-6;

(iii) Any section 988 hedging transaction if the transaction is integrated under § 1.988-5 or if other regulations issued under section 988(d) (or an advance ruling described in § 1.988-5(e)) govern when gain or loss from the transaction is taken into account; or

(iv) The determination of the issuer's yield on an issue of tax-exempt bonds for purposes of the arbitrage restrictions to which § 1.148-4(h) applies.

**(b) Clear reflection of income.** The method of accounting used by a taxpayer for a hedging transaction must clearly reflect income. To clearly reflect income, the method used must reasonably match the timing of income, deduction, gain, or loss from the hedging transaction with the timing of income, deduction, gain, or loss from the item or items being hedged. Taking gains and losses into account in the period in which they are realized may clearly reflect income in the case of certain hedging transactions. For example, where a hedge and the item being hedged are disposed of in the same taxable year, taking realized gain or loss into account on both items in that taxable year may clearly reflect income. In the case of many hedging transactions, however, taking gains and losses into account as they are realized does not result in the matching required by this section.

**(c) Choice of method and consistency.** For any given type of hedging transaction, there may be more than one method of accounting that satisfies the clear reflection requirement of paragraph (b) of this section. A taxpayer is generally permitted to adopt a method of accounting for a particular type of hedging transaction that clearly reflects the taxpayer's income from that type of transaction. See paragraph (e) of this section for requirements and limitations on the taxpayer's choice of method. Different methods of accounting may be used for different types of hedging transactions and for transactions that hedge different types of items. Once a taxpayer adopts a method of accounting, however, that method must be applied consistently and can only be changed with the consent of the Commissioner, as provided by section 446(e) and the regulations and procedures thereunder.

**(d) Recordkeeping requirements.** *(1) In general.* The books and records maintained by a taxpayer must contain a description of the accounting method used for each type of hedging transaction. The description of the method or methods used must be sufficient to show how the clear reflection requirement of paragraph (b) of this section is satisfied.

*(2) Additional identification.* In addition to the identification required by § 1.1221-2(f), the books and records maintained by a taxpayer must contain whatever more specific identification with respect to a transaction is necessary to verify the application of the method of accounting used by the taxpayer for the transaction. This additional identification may relate to the hedging transaction or to the item, items, or aggregate risk being hedged. The additional identification must be made at the time specified in § 1.1221-2(f)(2) and must be made on, and retained as part of, the taxpayer's books and records.

*(3) Transactions in which character of gain or loss is not determined under § 1.1221-2.* A section 988 transaction, as defined in section 988(c)(1), or a qualified fund, as defined in section 988(c)(1)(E)(iii), is subject to the identification and recordkeeping requirements of § 1.1221-2(f). See § 1.1221-2(a)(4).

**(e) Requirements and limitations with respect to hedges of certain assets and liabilities.** In the case of certain hedging transactions, this paragraph (e) provides guidance in determining whether a taxpayer's method of accounting satisfies the clear reflection requirement of paragraph (b) of this section. Even if these rules are satisfied, however, the taxpayer's method, as actually applied to the taxpayer's hedging transactions, must clearly reflect income by meeting the matching requirement of paragraph (b) of this section.

*(1) Hedges of aggregate risk.* (i) In general. The method of accounting used for hedges of aggregate risk must comply with the matching requirements of paragraph (b) of this section. Even though a taxpayer may not be able to associate the hedging transaction with any particular item being hedged, the timing of income, deduction, gain, or loss from the hedging transaction must be matched with the timing of the aggregate income, deduction, gain, or loss from the items being hedged. For example, if a notional principal contract hedges a taxpayer's aggregate risk, taking into account income, deduction, gain, or loss under the provisions of § 1.446-3 may clearly reflect income. See paragraph (e)(5) of this section.

(ii) Mark-and-spread method. The following method may be appropriate for taking into account income, deduction, gain, or loss from hedges of aggregate risk:

(A) The hedging transactions are marked to market at regular intervals for which the taxpayer has the necessary data, but no less frequently than quarterly; and

(B) The income, deduction, gain, or loss attributable to the realization or periodic marking to market of hedging transactions is taken into account over the period for which the hedging transactions are intended to reduce risk. Although the period over which the hedging transactions are intended to reduce risk may change, the period must be reasonable and consistent with the taxpayer's hedging policies and strategies.

*(2) Hedges of items marked to market.* In the case of a transaction that hedges an item that is marked to market under the taxpayer's method of accounting, marking the hedge to market clearly reflects income.

*(3) Hedges of inventory.* (i) In general. If a hedging transaction hedges purchases of inventory, gain or loss on the hedging transaction may be taken into account in the same period that it would be taken into account if the gain or loss were treated as an element of the cost of inventory. Similarly, if a hedging transaction hedges sales of inventory, gain or loss on the hedging transaction may be taken into account in the same period that it would be taken into account if the gain or loss were treated as an element of sales proceeds. If a hedge is associated with a particular purchase or sales transaction, the gain or loss on the hedge may be taken into account when it would be taken into account if it were an element of cost incurred in, or sales proceeds from, that transaction. As with hedges of aggregate risk, however, a taxpayer may not be able to associate hedges of inventory purchases or sales with particular purchase or sales transactions. In order to match the timing of income, deduction, gain, or loss from the hedge with the timing of aggregate income, deduction, gain, or loss from the hedged purchases or sales, it may be appropriate for a taxpayer to account for its hedging transactions in the manner described in paragraph (e)(1)(ii) of this section, except that the gain or loss that is spread to each period is taken into account when it would be if it were an element of cost incurred (purchase hedges), or an element of proceeds from sales made (sales hedges), during that period.

(ii) Alternative methods for certain inventory hedges. In lieu of the method described in paragraph (e)(3)(i) of this section, other simpler, less precise methods may be used in appropriate cases where the clear reflection requirement of paragraph (b) of this section is satisfied. For example:

(A) Taking into account realized gains and losses on both hedges of inventory purchases and hedges of inventory sales when they would be taken into account if the gains and losses were elements of inventory cost in the period realized may clearly reflect income in some situations, but does not clearly reflect income for a taxpayer that uses the last-in, first-out method of accounting for the inventory; and

(B) Marking hedging transactions to market with resulting gain or loss taken into account immediately may clearly reflect income even though the inventory that is being hedged is not marked to market, but only if the inventory is not accounted for under either the last-in, first-out method or the lower-of-cost-or-market method and only if items are held in inventory for short periods of time.

*(4) Hedges of debt instruments.* Gain or loss from a transaction that hedges a debt instrument issued or to be issued by a taxpayer, or a debt instrument held or to be held by a taxpayer, must be accounted for by reference to the terms of the debt instrument and the period or periods to which the hedge relates. A hedge of an instrument that provides for interest to be paid at a fixed rate or a qualified floating rate, for example, generally is accounted for using constant yield principles. Thus, assuming that a fixed rate or qualified floating rate instrument remains outstanding, hedging gain or

loss is taken into account in the same periods in which it would be taken into account if it adjusted the yield of the instrument over the term to which the hedge relates. For example, gain or loss realized on a transaction that hedged an anticipated fixed rate borrowing for its entire term is accounted for, solely for purposes of this section, as if it decreased or increased the issue price of the debt instrument. Similarly, gain or loss realized on a transaction that hedges a contingent payment on a debt instrument subject to § 1.1275-4(c) (a contingent payment debt instrument issued for nonpublicly traded property) is taken into account when the contingent payment is taken into account under § 1.1275-4(c).

*(5) Notional principal contracts.* The rules of § 1.446-3 govern the timing of income and deductions with respect to a notional principal contract unless, because the notional principal contract is part of a hedging transaction, the application of those rules would not result in the matching that is needed to satisfy the clear reflection requirement of paragraph (b) and, as applicable, (e)(4) of this section. For example, if a notional principal contract hedges a debt instrument, the method of accounting for periodic payments described in § 1.446-3(e) and the methods of accounting for nonperiodic payments described in § 1.446-3(f)(2)(iii) and (v) generally clearly reflect the taxpayer's income. The methods described in § 1.446-3(f)(2)(ii) and (iv), however, generally do not clearly reflect the taxpayer's income in that situation.

*(6) Disposition of hedged asset or liability.* If a taxpayer hedges an item and disposes of, or terminates its interest in, the item but does not dispose of or terminate the hedging transaction, the taxpayer must appropriately match the built-in gain or loss on the hedging transaction to the gain or loss on the disposed item. To meet this requirement, the taxpayer may mark the hedge to market on the date it disposes of the hedged item. If the taxpayer intends to dispose of the hedging transaction within a reasonable period, however, it may be appropriate to match the realized gain or loss on the hedging transaction with the gain or loss on the disposed item. If the taxpayer intends to dispose of the hedging transaction within a reasonable period and the hedging transaction is not actually disposed of within that period, the taxpayer must match the gain or loss on the hedge at the end of the reasonable period with the gain or loss on the disposed item. For purposes of this paragraph (e)(6), a reasonable period is generally 7 days.

*(7) Recycled hedges.* If a taxpayer enters into a hedging transaction by recycling a hedge of a particular hedged item to serve as a hedge of a different item, as described in § 1.1221-2(d)(4), the taxpayer must match the built-in gain or loss at the time of the recycling to the gain or loss on the original hedged item, items, or aggregate risk. Income, deduction, gain, or loss attributable to the period after the recycling must be matched to the new hedged item, items, or aggregate risk under the principles of paragraph (b) of this section.

*(8) Unfulfilled anticipatory transactions.* (i) In general. If a taxpayer enters into a hedging transaction to reduce risk with respect to an anticipated asset acquisition, debt issuance, or obligation, and the anticipated transaction is not consummated, any income, deduction, gain, or loss from the hedging transaction is taken into account when realized.

(ii) Consummation of anticipated transaction. A taxpayer consummates a transaction for purposes of paragraph (e)(8)(i) of this section upon the occurrence (within a reasonable interval around the expected time of the anticipated transaction) of either the anticipated transaction or a different but similar transaction for which the hedge serves to reasonably reduce risk.

*(9) Hedging by members of a consolidated group.* (i) General rule: single-entity approach. In general, a member of a consolidated group must account for its hedging transactions as if all of the members were separate divisions of a single corporation. Thus, the timing of the income, deduction, gain, or loss on a hedging transaction must match the timing of income, deduction, gain, or loss from the item or items being hedged. Because all of the members are treated as if they were divisions of a single corporation, intercompany transactions are neither hedging transactions nor hedged items for these purposes.

(ii) Separate-entity election. If a consolidated group makes an election under § 1.1221-2(e)(2), then paragraph (e)(9)(i) of this section does not apply. Thus, in that case, each member of the consolidated group must account for its hedging transactions in a manner that meets the requirements of paragraph (b) of this section. For example, the income, deduction, gain, or loss from intercompany hedging transactions (as defined in § 1.1221-2(e)(2)(ii)) is taken into account under the timing rules of § 1.446-4 rather than under the timing rules of § 1.1502-13.

(iii) Definitions. For definitions of consolidated group, divisions of a single corporation, intercompany transaction, and member, see section 1502 and the regulations thereunder.

(iv) Effective date. This paragraph (e)(9) applies to transactions entered into on or after March 8, 1996.

**(f) Type or character of income and deduction.** The rules of this section govern the timing of income, deduction, gain, or loss on hedging transactions but do not affect the type or character of income, deduction, gain, or loss produced by the transaction. Thus, for example, the rules of paragraph (e)(3) of this section do not affect the computation of cost of goods sold or sales proceeds for a taxpayer that hedges inventory purchases or sales. Similarly, the rules of paragraph (e)(4) of this section do not increase or decrease the interest income or expense of a taxpayer that hedges a debt instrument or a liability.

**(g) Effective date.** This section applies to hedging transactions entered into on or after October 1, 1994.

**(h) Consent to change methods of accounting.** The Commissioner grants consent for a taxpayer to change its methods of accounting for transactions that are entered into on or after October 1, 1994, and that are described in paragraph (a) of this section. This consent is granted only for changes for the taxable year containing October 1, 1994. The taxpayer must describe its new methods of accounting in a statement that is included in its Federal income tax return for that taxable year.

---

T.D. 8554, 7/13/94, amend T.D. 8653, 1/5/96, T.D. 8674, 6/11/96, T.D. 8985, 3/15/2002.

---

**Proposed § 1.446-4 Mark-to-market election for dealers and traders in derivative financial instruments.** [*For Preamble, see ¶ 151,289*]

• ***Caution:*** This Notice of Proposed Rulemaking was partially finalized by TD 8491, 10/14/93.

**(a) Mark-to-market election.** A dealer or trader in derivative financial instruments may elect to account for those instruments on its income tax return at market value. A dealer or trader in derivative financial instruments may elect to account for a derivative financial instrument at market value only if:

*(1)* The dealer or trader purchased or entered into the derivative financial instrument either--(i) In its capacity as a dealer or trader; or (ii) As a hedge of another financial instrument that the dealer or trader holds or intends to hold in its capacity as a dealer or trader;

*(2)* The dealer or trader values all of the derivative financial instruments that it holds in its capacity as a dealer or trader (or as hedges of such instruments) at market for purposes of computing net income or loss on its applicable financial statement (as defined in § 1.56-1(c)), and the dealer or trader uses the same methods of valuing those instruments on its income tax return;

*(3)* The dealer or trader and all persons related to the dealer or trader within the meaning of sections 267(b) and 707(b)(1) account for the securities and commodities that they hold in their capacity as dealers or traders (or as hedges or such securities or commodities) on their income tax returns either on the basis of cost or on the basis of market value, but not at the lower of cost or market value;

*(4)* A description of the methods employed to value each class of derivative financial instruments is attached to the dealer's or trader's income tax return for each year; and

*(5)* The method elected under this section is used consistently in subsequent years, unless another method is authorized by the Commissioner pursuant to a written request under § 1.446-1(e) of the regulations.

**(b) Dealer or trader defined.** For purposes of this section, a dealer or trader in derivative financial instruments is any taxpayer with an established place of business that:

*(1)* Makes a market in derivative financial instruments by regularly and actively offering to enter into, offset, assign, or otherwise terminate positions in these instruments with customers in the ordinary course of its trade or business; or

*(2)* Regularly and actively engages in the frequent and substantial trading of derivative financial instruments for the principal purpose of deriving gains and profits from trading those instruments rather than from periodic income such as dividends, interest, net income from notional principal contracts, or long term appreciation.

**(c) Derivative financial instrument defined.** For purposes of this section, the term "derivative financial instrument" includes options, forward contracts, futures contracts, notional principal contracts, short positions in securities and commodities, and any similar financial instrument.

**(d) Effective date.** This regulation is effective for taxable years ending on or after [the date a Treasury Decision based on these proposed regulations is published in the Federal Register].

**§ 1.446-5 Debt issuance costs.**

**(a) In general.** This section provides rules for allocating debt issuance costs over the term of the debt. For purposes of this section, the term debt issuance costs means those transaction costs incurred by an issuer of debt (that is, a borrower) that are required to be capitalized under § 1.263(a)-5. If these costs are otherwise deductible, they are deductible by the issuer over the term of the debt as determined under paragraph (b) of this section.

**(b) Method of allocating debt issuance costs.** *(1) In general.* Solely for purposes of determining the amount of debt issuance costs that may be deducted in any period, these costs are treated as if they adjusted the yield on the debt. To effect this, the issuer treats the costs as if they decreased the issue price of the debt. See § 1.1273-2 to determine issue price. Thus, debt issuance costs increase or create original issue discount and decrease or eliminate bond issuance premium.

*(2) Original issue discount.* Any resulting original issue discount is taken into account by the issuer under the rules in § 1.163-7, which generally require the use of a constant yield method (as described in § 1.1272-1) to compute how much original issue discount is deductible for a period. However, see § 1.163-7(b) for special rules that apply if the total original issue discount on the debt is de minimis.

*(3) Bond issuance premium.* Any remaining bond issuance premium is taken into account by the issuer under the rules of § 1.163-13, which generally require the use of a constant yield method for purposes of allocating bond issuance premium to accrual periods.

**(c) Examples.** The following examples illustrate the rules of this section:

*Example (1).* (i) On January 1, 2004, X borrows $10,000,000. The principal amount of the loan ($10,000,000) is repayable on December 31, 2008, and payments of interest in the amount of $500,000 are due on December 31 of each year the loan is outstanding. X incurs debt issuance costs of $130,000 to facilitate the borrowing.

(ii) Under § 1.1273-2, the issue price of the loan is $10,000,000. However, under paragraph (b) of this section, X reduces the issue price of the loan by the debt issuance costs of $130,000, resulting in an issue price of $9,870,000. As a result, X treats the loan as having original issue discount in the amount of $130,000 (stated redemption price at maturity of $10,000,000 minus the issue price of $9,870,000). Because this amount of original issue discount is more than the de minimis amount of original issue discount for the loan determined under § 1.1273-1(d) ($125,000 ($10,000,000 × .0025 × 5)), X must allocate the original issue discount to each year based on the constant yield method described in § 1.1272-1(b). See § 1.163-7(a). Based on this method and a yield of 5.30%, compounded annually, the original issue discount is allocable to each year as follows: $23,385 for 2004, $24,625 for 2005, $25,931 for 2006, $27,306 for 2007, and $28,753 for 2008.

*Example (2).* (i) Assume the same facts as in Example 1, except that X incurs debt issuance costs of $120,000 rather than $130,000.

(ii) Under § 1.1273-2, the issue price of the loan is $10,000,000. However, under paragraph (b) of this section, X reduces the issue price of the loan by the debt issuance costs of $120,000, resulting in an issue price of $9,880,000. As a result, X treats the loan as having original issue discount in the amount of $120,000 (stated redemption price at maturity of $10,000,000 minus the issue price of $9,880,000). Because this amount of original issue discount is less than the de minimis amount of original issue discount for the loan determined under § 1.1273-1(d) ($125,000), X does not have to use the constant yield method described in § 1.1272-1(b) to allocate the original issue discount to each year. Instead, under § 1.163-7(b)(2), X can choose to allocate the original issue discount to each year on a straight-line basis over the term of the loan or in proportion to the stated interest payments ($24,000 each year). X also could choose to deduct the original issue discount at maturity of the loan. X makes its choice by reporting the original issue discount in a manner consistent with the method chosen on X's timely filed federal income tax return for 2004. If X wanted to use the constant yield method, based on a yield of 5.279%, compounded annually, the original issue discount is allocable to each year as follows: $21,596 for 2004, $22,736 for 2005, $23,937 for 2006, $25,200 for 2007, and $26,531 for 2008.

**(d) Effective date.** This section applies to debt issuance costs paid or incurred for debt instruments issued on or after December 31, 2003.

**(e) Accounting method changes.** *(1) Consent to change.* An issuer required to change its method of accounting for debt issuance costs to comply with this section must secure the consent of the Commissioner in accordance with the requirements of § 1.446-1(e). Paragraph (e)(2) of this section provides the Commissioner's automatic consent for certain changes.

*(2) Automatic consent.* The Commissioner grants consent for an issuer to change its method of accounting for debt issuance costs incurred for debt instruments issued on or after December 31, 2003. Because this change is made on a cut-off basis, no items of income or deduction are omitted or duplicated and, therefore, no adjustment under section 481 is allowed. The consent granted by this paragraph (e)(2) applies provided—

(i) The change is made to comply with this section;

(ii) The change is made for the first taxable year for which the issuer must account for debt issuance costs under this section; and

(iii) The issuer attaches to its federal income tax return for the taxable year containing the change a statement that it has changed its method of accounting under this section.

T.D. 9107, 12/31/2003.

## § 1.446-6 REMIC inducement fees.

**(a) Purpose.** This section provides specific timing rules for the clear reflection of income from an inducement fee received in connection with becoming the holder of a noneconomic REMIC residual interest. An inducement fee must be included in income over a period reasonably related to the period during which the applicable REMIC is expected to generate taxable income or net loss allocable to the holder of the noneconomic residual interest.

**(b) Definitions.** For purposes of this section:

*(1) Applicable REMIC.* The applicable REMIC is the REMIC that issued the noneconomic residual interest with respect to which the inducement fee is paid.

*(2) Inducement fee.* An inducement fee is the amount paid to induce a person to become the holder of a noneconomic residual interest in an applicable REMIC.

*(3) Noneconomic residual interest.* A REMIC residual interest is a noneconomic residual interest if it is a noneconomic residual interest within the meaning of § 1.860E-1(c)(2).

*(4) Remaining anticipated weighted average life.* The remaining anticipated weighted average life is the anticipated weighted average life determined using the methodology set forth in § 1.860E-1(a)(3)(iv) applied as of the date of acquisition of the noneconomic residual interest.

*(5) REMIC.* The term REMIC has the same meaning in this section as given in § 1.860D-1.

**(c) General rule.** All taxpayers, regardless of their overall method of accounting, must recognize an inducement fee over the remaining expected life of the applicable REMIC in a manner that reasonably reflects, without regard to this paragraph, the after-tax costs and benefits of holding that noneconomic residual interest.

**(d) Special rule on disposition of a residual interest.** If any portion of an inducement fee received with respect to becoming the holder of a noneconomic residual interest in an applicable REMIC has not been recognized in full by the holder as of the time the holder transfers, or otherwise ceases to be the holder for Federal tax purposes of, that residual interest in the applicable REMIC, then the holder must include the unrecognized portion of the inducement fee in income at that time. This rule does not apply to a transaction to which section 381(c)(4) applies.

**(e) Safe harbors.** If inducement fees are recognized in accordance with a method described in this paragraph (e), that method complies with the requirements of paragraph (c) of this section.

*(1) The book method.* Under the book method, an inducement fee is recognized in accordance with the method of accounting, and over the same period, used by the taxpayer for financial reporting purposes (including consolidated financial statements to shareholders, partners, beneficiaries, and other proprietors and for credit purposes), provided that the inducement fee is included in income for financial reporting purposes over a period that is not shorter than the period during which the applicable REMIC is expected to generate taxable income.

*(2) The modified REMIC regulatory method.* Under the modified REMIC regulatory method, the inducement fee is recognized ratably over the remaining anticipated weighted average life of the applicable REMIC as if the inducement fee were unrecognized gain being included in gross income under § 1.860F-2(b)(4)(iii).

*(3) Additional safe harbor methods.* The Commissioner, by revenue ruling or revenue procedure (see § 1.601(d)(2) of this chapter), may provide additional safe harbor methods for recognizing inducement fees relating to noneconomic REMIC residual interests.

**(f) Method of accounting.** The treatment of inducement fees is a method of accounting to which the provisions of sections 446 and 481 and the regulations thereunder apply. A taxpayer is generally permitted to adopt a method of accounting for inducement fees that satisfies the requirements of paragraph (c) of this section. Once a taxpayer adopts a method of accounting for inducement fees, that method must be applied consistently to all inducement fees received in connection with noneconomic REMIC residual interests and may be changed only with the consent of the Commissioner, as provided by section 446(e) and the regulations and procedures thereunder.

**(g) Effective date.** This section is applicable for taxable years ending on or after May 11, 2004.

T.D. 9128, 5/7/2004.

## § 1.448-1 Limitation on the use of the cash receipts and disbursements method of accounting.

**(a) through (f). [Reserved]**

**(g) Treatment of accounting method change and timing rules for section 481(a) adjustment.** *(1) Treatment of change in accounting method.* Notwithstanding any other procedure published prior to January 7, 1991, concerning changes from the cash method, any taxpayer to whom section 448 applies must change its method of accounting in accordance with the provisions of this paragraph (g) and paragraph (h) of this section. In the case of any taxpayer required by this section to change its method of accounting for any taxable year, the change shall be treated as a change initiated by the taxpayer. The adjustments required under section 481(a) with respect to the change in method of accounting of such a taxpayer shall not be reduced by amounts attributable to taxable years preceding the Internal Revenue Code of 1954. Paragraph (h)(2) of this section provides procedures under which a taxpayer may change to an overall accrual method of accounting for the first taxable year the taxpayer is subject to this section ("first section 448 year"). If the taxpayer complies with the provisions of paragraph (h)(2) of this section for its first section 448 year, the change shall be treated as made with the consent of the Commissioner. Paragraph (h)(3) of this section provides procedures under which a taxpayer may change to other than an overall accrual method of accounting for its first section 448 year. Unless the taxpayer complies with the provisions of paragraph (h)(2) or (h)(3) of this section for its first section 448 year, the taxpayer must comply with the provisions of paragraph (h)(4) of this section. See paragraph (h) of this section for rules to effect a change in method of accounting.

*(2) Timing rules for section 481(a) adjustment.* (i) In general. Except as otherwise provided in paragraphs (g)(2)(ii) and (g)(3) of this section, a taxpayer required by this section to change from the cash method must take the net section 481(a) adjustment into account over the section 481(a) adjustment period as determined under the applicable administrative procedures issued under Sec. 1.446-1(e)(3)(ii) for obtaining the Commissioner's consent to a change in accounting method (for example, see Rev. Proc. 2002-9 (2002-1 C.B. 327) and Rev. Proc. 97-27 (1997-1 C.B. 680) (also see Sec. 601.601(d)(2) of this chapter)), provided the taxpayer complies with the provisions of paragraph (h)(2) or (3) of this section for its first section 448 year.

(ii) Hospital timing rules. (A) In general. In the case of a hospital that is required by this section to change from the cash method, the section 481(a) adjustment shall be taken into account ratably (beginning with the year of change) over 10 years, provided the taxpayer complies with the provisions of paragraph (h)(2) or (h)(3) of this section for its first section 448 year.

(B) Definition of hospital. For purposes of paragraph (g) of this section, a hospital is an institution—

(1) Accredited by the Joint Commission on Accreditation of Healthcare Organizations or its predecessor (the JCAHO) (or accredited or approved by a program of the qualified governmental unit in which such institution is located if the Secretary of Health and Human Services has found that the accreditation or comparable approval standards of such qualified governmental unit are essentially equivalent to those of the JCAHO);

(2) Used primarily to provide, by or under the supervision of physicians, to inpatients diagnostic services and therapeutic services for medical diagnosis, treatment, and care of injured, disabled, or sick persons;

(3) Requiring every patient to be under the care and supervision of a physician; and

(4) Providing 24-hour nursing services rendered or supervised by a registered professional nurse and having a licensed practical nurse or registered nurse on duty at all times.

For purposes of this section, an entity need not be owned by or on behalf of a governmental unit or by a section 501(c)(3) organization, or operated by a section 501(c)(3) organization, in order to be considered a hospital. In addition, for purposes of this section, a hospital does not include a rest or nursing home, continuing care facility, daycare center, medical school facility, research laboratory, or ambulatory care facility.

(C) Dual function facilities. With respect to any taxpayer whose operations consist both of a hospital, and other facilities not qualifying as a hospital, the portion of the adjustment required by section 481(a) that is attributable to the hospital shall be taken into account in accordance with the rules of paragraph (g)(2) of this section relating to hospitals. The portion of the adjustment required by section 481(a) that is not attributable to the hospital shall be taken into account in accordance with the rules of paragraph (g)(2) of this section not relating to hospitals.

(iii) Untimely change in method of accounting to comply with this section. Unless a taxpayer (including a hospital and a cooperative) required by this section to change from the cash method complies with the provisions of paragraph (h)(2) or (h)(3) of this section for its first section 448 year within the time prescribed by those paragraphs, the taxpayer must take the section 481(a) adjustment into account under the provisions of any applicable administrative procedure that is prescribed by the Commissioner after January 7, 1991, specifically for purposes of complying with this section. Absent such an administrative procedure, a taxpayer must request a change under § 1.446-1(e)(3) and shall be subject to any terms and conditions (including the year of change) as may be imposed by the Commissioner.

*(3) Special timing rules for section 481(a) adjustment.* (i) (i) Cessation of trade or business. If the taxpayer ceases to engage in the trade or business to which the section 481(a) adjustment relates, or if the taxpayer operating the trade or business terminates existence, and such cessation or termination occurs prior to the expiration of the adjustment period described in paragraph (g)(2)(i) or (ii) of this section, the taxpayer must take into account, in the taxable year of such cessation or termination, the balance of the adjustment not previously taken into account in computing taxable income. For purposes of this paragraph (g)(3)(i), the determination as to whether a taxpayer has ceased to engage in the trade or business to which the section 481(a) adjustment relates, or has terminated its existence, is to be made under the principles of Sec. 1.446-1(e)(3)(ii) and its underlying administrative procedures.

(ii) De minimis rule for a taxpayer other than a cooperative. Notwithstanding paragraph (g)(2)(i) and (ii) of this section, a taxpayer other than a cooperative (within the meaning of section 1381(a)) that is required to change from the cash method by this section may elect to use, in lieu of the adjustment period described in paragraph (g)(2)(i) and (ii) of this section, the adjustment period for de minimis section 481(a) adjustments provided in the applicable administrative procedure issued under Sec. 1.446-1(e)(3)(ii) for obtaining the Commissioner's consent to a change in accounting method. A taxpayer may make an election under this paragraph (g)(3)(ii) only if—

(A) The taxpayer's entire net section 481(a) adjustment (whether positive or negative) is a de minimis amount as determined under the applicable administrative procedure issued under § 1.446-1(e)(3)(ii) for obtaining the Commissioner's consent to a change in accounting method,

(B) The taxpayer complies with the provisions of paragraph (h)(2) or (3) of this section for its first section 448 year,

(C) The return for such year is due (determined with regard to extensions) after December 27, 1993, and

(D) The taxpayer complies with any applicable instructions to Form 3115 that specify the manner of electing the adjustment period for de minimis section 481(a) adjustments.

*(4) Additional rules relating to section 481(a) adjustment.* In addition to the rules set forth in paragraph (g)(2) and (3) of this section, the following rules shall apply in taking the section 481(a) adjustment into account—

(i) Any net operating loss and tax credit carryforwards will be allowed to offset any positive section 481(a) adjustment,

(ii) Any net operating loss arising in the year of change or in any subsequent year that is attributable to a negative section 481(a) adjustment may be carried back to earlier taxable years in accordance with section 172, and

(iii) For purposes of determining estimated income tax payments under sections 6654 and 6655, the section 481(a) adjustment will be recognized in taxable income ratably throughout a taxable year.

*(5) Outstanding section 481(a) adjustment from previous change in method of accounting.* If a taxpayer changed its method of accounting to the cash method for a taxable year prior to the year the taxpayer was required by this section to change from the cash method (the section 448 year), any section 481(a) adjustment from such prior change in method of accounting that is outstanding as of the section 448 year shall be taken into account in accordance with the provisions of this paragraph (g)(5). A taxpayer shall account for any remaining portion of the prior section 481(a) adjustment outstanding as of the section 448 year by continuing to take such remaining portion into account under the provisions and conditions of the prior change in method of accounting, or, at the taxpayer's option, combining or netting the remaining portion of the prior section 481(a) adjustment with the section 481(a) adjustment required under this section, and taking into account under the provisions of this section the resulting net amount of the adjustment. Any taxpayer choosing to combine or net the section 481(a) adjustments as described in the preceding sentence shall indicate such choice on the Form 3115 required to be filed by such taxpayer under the provisions of paragraph (h) of this section.

**(h) Procedures for change in method of accounting.** *(1) Applicability.* Paragraph (h) of this section applies to taxpayers who change from the cash method as required by this section. Paragraph (h) of this section does not apply to a change in accounting method required by any Code section (or regulations thereunder) other than this section.

*(2) Automatic rule for changes to an overall accrual method.* (i) Timely changes in method of accounting. Notwithstanding any other available procedures to change to the accrual method of accounting, a taxpayer to whom paragraph (h) of this section applies who desires to make a change to an overall accrual method for its first section 448 year must make that change under the provisions of this paragraph (h)(2). A taxpayer changing to an overall accrual method under this paragraph (h)(2) must file a current Form 3115 by the time prescribed in paragraph (h)(2)(ii). In addition, the taxpayer must set forth on a statement accompanying the Form 3115 the period over which the section 481(a) adjustment will be taken into account and the basis for such conclusion. Moreover, the taxpayer must type or legibly print the following statement at the top of page 1 of the Form 3115: "Automatic Change to Accrual Method—Section 448." The consent of the Commissioner to the change in method of accounting is granted to taxpayers who change to an overall accrual method under this paragraph (h)(2). See paragraph (g)(2)(i), (g)(2)(ii), or (g)(3) of this section, whichever is applicable, for rules to account for the section 481(a) adjustment.

(ii) Time and manner for filing Form 3115. (A) In general. Except as provided in paragraph (h)(2)(ii)(B) of this section, the Form 3115 required by paragraph (h)(2)(i) must be filed no later than the due date (determined with regard to extensions) of the taxpayer's federal income tax return for the first section 448 year and must be attached to that return.

(B) Extension of filing deadline. Notwithstanding paragraph (h)(2)(ii)(A) of this section, the filing of the Form 3115 required by paragraph (h)(2)(i) shall not be considered late if such Form 3115 is attached to a timely filed amended income tax return for the first section 448 year, provided that—

(1) The taxpayer's first section 448 year is a taxable year that begins (or, pursuant to § 1.441-2(c), is deemed to begin) in 1987, 1988, 1989, or 1990,

(2) The taxpayer has not been contacted for examination, is not before appeals, and is not before a federal court with respect to an income tax issue (each as defined in applicable administrative pronouncements), unless the taxpayer also complies with any requirements for approval in those applicable administrative pronouncements, and

(3) Any amended return required by this paragraph (h)(2)(ii)(B) is filed on or before July 8, 1991.

Filing an amended return under this paragraph (h)(2)(ii)(B) does not extend the time for making any other election. Thus, for example, taxpayers that comply with this section by filing an amended return pursuant to this paragraph (h)(2)(ii)(B) may not elect out of section 448 pursuant to paragraph (i)(2) of this section.

*(3) Changes to a method other than overall accrual method.* (i) In general. A taxpayer to whom paragraph (h) of this section applies who desires to change to a special method of accounting must make that change under the provisions of this paragraph (h)(3), except to the extent other special procedures have been promulgated regarding the special method of accounting. Such a taxpayer includes taxpayers who change to both an accrual method of accounting and a special method of accounting such as a long-term contract method. In order to change an accounting method under this paragraph (h)(3), a taxpayer must submit an application for change in accounting method under the applicable administrative procedures in effect at the time of change, including the applicable procedures regarding the time and place of filing the application for change in method. Moreover, a taxpayer who changes an accounting method under this paragraph (h)(3) must type or legibly print the following statement on the top of page 1 of Form 3115: "Change to a Special Method of Accounting—Section 448." The filing of a Form 3115 by any taxpayer requesting a change of method of accounting under this paragraph (h)(3) for its taxable year beginning in 1987 will not be considered late if the form is filed with the appropriate office of the Internal Revenue Service on or before the later of: the date that is the 180th day of the taxable year of change; or September 14, 1987. If the Commissioner approves the taxpayer's application for change in method of accounting, the timing of the adjustment required under section 481(a), if applicable, will be de-

termined under the provisions of paragraph (g)(2)(i), (g)(2)(ii), or (g)(3) of this section, whichever is applicable. If the Commissioner denies the taxpayer's application for change in accounting method, or if the taxpayer's application is untimely, the taxpayer must change to an overall accrual method of accounting under the provisions of either paragraph (h)(2) or (h)(4) of this section, whichever is applicable.

(ii) Extension of filing deadline. Notwithstanding paragraph (h)(3)(i) of this section, if the events or circumstances which under section 448 disqualify a taxpayer from using the cash method occur after the time prescribed under applicable procedures for filing the Form 3115, the filing of such form shall not be considered late if such form is filed on or before 30 days after the close of the taxable year.

*(4) Untimely change in method of accounting to comply with this section.* Unless a taxpayer to whom paragraph (h) of this section applies complies with the provisions of paragraph (h)(2) or (h)(3) of this section for its first section 448 year, the taxpayer must comply with the requirements of § 1.446-1(e)(3) (including any applicable administrative procedure that is prescribed thereunder after January 7, 1991 specifically for purposes of complying with this section) in order to secure the consent of the Commissioner to change to a method of accounting that is in compliance with the provisions of this section. The taxpayer shall be subject to any terms and conditions (including the year of change) as may be imposed by the Commissioner.

**(i) Effective date.** *(1) In general.* Except as provided in paragraph (i)(2), (3), (4), and (5) of this section, this section applies to any taxable year beginning after December 31, 1986.

*(2) Election out of section 448.* (i) In general. A taxpayer may elect not to have this section apply to any (A) transaction with a related party (within the meaning of section 267(b) of the Internal Revenue Code of 1954, as in effect on October 21, 1986), (B) loan, or (C) lease, if such transaction, loan, or lease was entered into on or before September 25, 1985. Any such election described in the preceding sentence may be made separately with respect to each transaction, loan or lease. For rules relating to the making of such election, see § 301.9100-7T (temporary regulations relating to elections under the Tax Reform Act of 1986). Notwithstanding the provisions of this paragraph (i)(2), the gross receipts attributable to a transaction, loan, or lease described in this paragraph (i)(2) shall be taken into account for purposes of the $5,000,000 gross receipts test described in paragraph (f) of this section.

(ii) Special rules for loans. If the taxpayer makes an election under paragraph (i)(2)(i) of this section with respect to a loan entered into on or before September 25, 1985, the election shall apply only with respect to amounts that are attributable to the loan balance outstanding on September 25, 1985. The election shall not apply to any amounts advanced or lent after September 25, 1985, regardless of whether the loan agreement was entered into on or before such date. Moreover, any payments made on outstanding loan balances after September 25, 1985, shall be deemed to first extinguish loan balances outstanding on September 25, 1985, regardless of any contrary treatment of such loan payments by the borrower and lender.

*(3) Certain contracts entered into before September 25, 1985.* This section does not apply to a contract for the acquisition or transfer of real property or a contract for services related to the acquisition or development of real property if—

(i) The contract was entered into before September 25, 1985; and

(ii) The sole element of the contract which was not performed as of September 25, 1985, was payment for such property or services.

*(4) Transitional rule for paragraphs (g) and (h) of this section.* To the extent the provisions of paragraphs (g) and (h) of this section were not reflected in paragraphs (g) and (h) of § 1.448-1T (as set forth in 26 CFR Part 1 as revised on April 1, 1993), paragraphs (g) and (h) of this section will not be adversely applied to a taxpayer with respect to transactions entered into before December 27, 1993.

*(5) Effective date of paragraph (g)(2)(i).* Paragraph (g)(2)(i) of this section applies to taxable years ending on or after June 16, 2004.

T.D. 8514, 12/23/93, amend T.D. 8996, 5/16/2002, T.D. 9131, 6/15/2004.

PAR. 2. In the list below, for each section indicated in the left column, remove the old language in the middle column and add the new language in the right column.

| Affected Section | Remove | Add |
|---|---|---|
| 1.46-1(p)(2)(iv) | paragraph (b)(1) of § 1.441-2 | § 1.441-2 |
| 1.48-3(d)(1)(iii) | paragraph (b)(1) of § 1.441-2 | § 1.441-2 |
| 1.280H-1T(a), last sentence | § 1.441-4T(d) | § 1.441-3(c) |
| 1.443-1(b)(1)(ii) | and paragraph (c)(5) of § 1.441-2 | and § 1.441-1(b)(2)(ii). |
| 1.444-1T(a)(1), first sentence | § 1.444-4T(d) | § 1.441-3(c) |
| 1.444-2T(a), last sentence | § 1.441-4T(d) | § 1.441-3(c) |
| 1.448-1(h)(2)(ii)(B)(1) | § 1.441-2T(b)(1) | § 1.441-2(c) |
| 1.469-1(h)(4)(ii)(D) | § 1.441-4T(f) | § 1.441-3(e) |
| 1.469-1T(g)(2)(i) | § 1.441-4T(d) | § 1.441-2 |
| 1.1561-1(c)(2) | See paragraph (b)(1) of § 1.441-2 | See § 1.441-2 |

| | | |
|---|---|---|
| 1.6654-2(a), concluding text | paragraph (b) of § 1.441-2 | § 1.441-2(c) |
| 1.6655-2(a)(4), first sentence | paragraph (b) of § 1.441-2 | § 1.441-1(b) |

**Proposed § 1.448-1** [*For Preamble, see ¶ 152,177*]

• ***Caution:*** This Notice of Proposed Rulemaking was partially finalized by T.D. 8996, issued on 5/16/2002. Proposed regulation §§ 1.46-1, 1.48-3, 1.280H-1T, 1.443-1, 1.444-1T, 1.444-2T, 1.448-1, 1.469-1, 1.469-1T, 1.898-4, 1.1561-1, 1.6654-2, 1.6655-2 and 301.7701(b)-6 remains in effect.

**§ 1.448-1T Limitation on the use of the cash receipts and disbursements method of accounting (temporary).**

***Caution:*** The Treasury has not yet amended Reg § 1.448-1T to reflect changes made by P.L. 100-647.

**(a) Limitation on accounting method.** *(1) In general.* This section prescribes regulations under section 448 relating to the limitation on the use of the cash receipts and disbursements method of accounting (the cash method) by certain taxpayers.

*(2) Limitation rule.* Except as otherwise provided in this section, the computation of taxable income using the cash method is prohibited in the case of a—

(i) C corporation,

(ii) Partnership with a C corporation as a partner, or

(iii) Tax shelter.

A partnership is described in paragraph (a)(2)(ii) of this section, if the partnership has a C corporation as a partner at any time during the partnership's taxable year beginning after December 31, 1986.

*(3) Meaning of C corporation.* For purposes of this section, the term "C corporation" includes any corporation that is not an S corporation. For example, a regulated investment company (as defined in section 851) or a real estate investment trust (as defined in section 856) is a C corporation for purposes of this section. In addition, a trust subject to tax under section 511(b) shall be treated, for purposes of this section, as a C corporation, but only with respect to the portion of its activities that constitute an unrelated trade or business. Similarly, for purposes of this section, a corporation that is exempt from federal income taxes under section 501(a) shall be treated as a C corporation only with respect to the portion of its activities that constitute an unrelated trade or business. Moreover, for purposes of determining whether a partnership has a C corporation as a partner, any partnership described in paragraph (a)(2)(ii) of this section is treated as a C corporation. Thus, if partnership ABC has a partner that is a partnership with a C corporation, then, for purposes of this section, partnership ABC is treated as a partnership with a C corporation partner.

*(4) Treatment of a combination of methods.* For purposes of this section, the use of a method of accounting that records some, but not all, items on the cash method shall be considered the use of the cash method. Thus, a C corporation that uses a combination of accounting methods including the use of the cash method is subject to this section.

**(b) Tax shelter defined.** *(1) In general.* For purposes of this section, the term "tax shelter" means any—

(i) Enterprise (other than a C corporation) if at any time (including taxable years beginning before January 1, 1987) interests in such enterprise have been offered for sale in any offering required to be registered with any federal or state agency having the authority to regulate the offering of securities for sale,

(ii) Syndicate (within the meaning of paragraph (b)(3) of this section), or

(iii) Tax shelter within the meaning of section 6662(d)(2)(C).

*(2) Requirement of registration.* For purposes of paragraph (b)(1)(i) of this section, an offering is required to be registered with a federal or state agency if, under the applicable federal or state law, failure to register the offering would result in a violation of the applicable federal or state law (regardless of whether the offering is in fact registered). In addition, an offering is required to be registered with a federal or state agency if, under the applicable federal or state law, failure to file a notice of exemption from registration would result in a violation of the applicable federal or state law (regardless of whether the notice is in fact filed).

*(3) Meaning of syndicate.* For purposes of paragraph (b)(1)(ii) of this section, the term "syndicate" means a partnership or other entity (other than a C corporation) if more than 35 percent of the losses of such entity during the taxable year (for taxable years beginning after December 31, 1986) are allocated to limited partners or limited entrepreneurs. For purposes of this paragraph (b)(3), the term "limited entrepreneur" has the same meaning given such term in section 464(e)(2). In addition, in determining whether an interest in a partnership is held by a limited partner, or an interest in an entity or enterprise is held by a limited entrepreneur, section 464(c)(2) shall apply in the case of the trade or business of farming (as defined in paragraph (d)(2) of this section), and section 1256(e)(3)(C) shall apply in any other case. Moreover, for purposes of this paragraph (b)(3), the losses of a partnership, entity, or enterprise (the enterprise) means the excess of the deductions allowable to the enterprise over the amount of income recognized by such enterprise under the enterprise's method of accounting used for federal income tax purposes (determined without regard to this section). For this purpose, gains or losses from the sale of capital assets or section 1221(2) assets are not taken into account.

*(4) Presumed tax avoidance.* For purposes of paragraph (b)(1)(iii) of this section, marketed arrangements in which persons carrying on farming activities using the services of a common managerial or administrative service will be presumed to have the principal purpose of tax avoidance if such persons use borrowed funds to prepay a substantial portion of their farming expenses (*e.g.,* payment for farm supplies that will not be used or consumed until a taxable year subsequent to the taxable year of payment).

*(5) Taxable year tax shelter must change accounting method.* A partnership, entity, or enterprise that is a tax shel-

ter must change from the cash method for the later of (i) the first taxable year beginning after December 31, 1986, or (ii) the taxable year that such partnership, entity, or enterprise becomes a tax shelter.

**(c) Effect of section 448 on other provisions.** Nothing in section 448 shall have any effect on the application of any other provision of law that would otherwise limit the use of the cash method, and no inference shall be drawn from section 448 with respect to the application of any such provision. For example, nothing in section 448 affects the requirement of section 447 that certain corporations must use an accrual method of accounting in computing taxable income from farming, or the requirement of § 1.446-1(c)(2) that an accrual method be used with regard to purchases and sales of inventory. Similarly, nothing in section 448 affects the authority of the Commissioner under section 446(b) to require the use of an accounting method that clearly reflects income, or the requirement under section 446(e) that a taxpayer secure the consent of the Commissioner before changing its method of accounting. For example, a taxpayer using the cash method may be required to change to an accrual method of accounting under section 446(b) because such method clearly reflects that taxpayer's income, even though the taxpayer is not prohibited by section 448 from using the cash method. Similarly, a taxpayer using an accrual method of accounting that is not prohibited by section 448 from using the cash method may not change to the cash method unless the taxpayer secures the consent of the Commissioner under section 446(e), and, in the opinion of the Commissioner, the use of the cash method clearly reflects that taxpayer's income under section 446(b).

**(d) Exception for farming business.** *(1) In general.* Except in the case of a tax shelter, this section shall not apply to any farming business. A taxpayer engaged in a farming business and a separate nonfarming business is not prohibited by this section from using the cash method with respect to the farming business, even though the taxpayer may be prohibited by this section from using the cash method with respect to the nonfarming business.

*(2) Meaning of farming business.* For purposes of paragraph (d) of this section, the term "farming business" means—

(i) The trade or business of farming as defined in section 263A(e)(4) (including the operation of a nursery or sod farm, or the raising or harvesting of trees bearing fruit, nuts, or other crops, or ornamental trees), or

(ii) The raising, harvesting, or growing of trees described in section 263A(c)(5) (relating to trees raised, harvested, or grown by the taxpayer other than trees described in paragraph (d)(2)(i) of this section).

Thus, for purposes of this section, the term "farming business" includes the raising of timber. For purposes of this section, the term "farming business" does not include the processing of commodities or products beyond those activities normally incident to the growing, raising or harvesting of such products. For example, assume that a C corporation taxpayer is in the business of growing and harvesting wheat and other grains. The taxpayer processes the harvested grains to produce breads, cereals, and similar food products which it sells to customers in the course of its business. Although the taxpayer is in the farming business with respect to the growing and harvesting of grain, the taxpayer is not in the farming business with respect to the processing of such grains to produce food products which the taxpayer sells to customers. Similarly, assume that a taxpayer is in the business of raising poultry or other livestock. The taxpayer uses the livestock in a meat processing operation in which the livestock are slaughtered, processed, and packaged or canned for sale to customers. Although the taxpayer is in the farming business with respect to the raising of livestock, the taxpayer is not in the farming business with respect to the meat processing operation. However, under this section the term "farming business" does include processing activities which are normally incident to the growing, raising or harvesting of agricultural products. For example, assume a taxpayer is in the business of growing fruits and vegetables. When the fruits and vegetables are ready to be harvested, the taxpayer picks, washes, inspects, and packages the fruits and vegetables for sale. Such activities are normally incident to the raising of these crops by farmers. The taxpayer will be considered to be in the business of farming with respect to the growing of fruits and vegetables, and the processing activities incident to the harvest.

**(e) Exception for qualified personal service corporation.** *(1) In general.* Except in the case of a tax shelter, this section does not apply to a qualified personal service corporation.

*(2) Certain treatment for qualified personal service corporation.* For purposes of paragraph (a)(2)(ii) of this section (relating to whether a partnership has a C corporation as a partner), a qualified personal service corporation shall be treated as an individual.

*(3) Meaning of qualified personal service corporation.* For purposes of this section, the term "qualified personal service corporation" means any corporation that meets—

(i) The function test paragraph (e)(4) of this section, and

(ii) The ownership test of paragraph (e)(5) of this section.

*(4) Function test.* (i) In general. A corporation meets the function test if substantially all the corporation's activities for a taxable year involve the performance of services in one or more of the following fields—

(A) Health,

(B) Law,

(C) Engineering (including surveying and mapping),

(D) Architecture,

(E) Accounting,

(F) Actuarial science,

(G) Performing arts, or

(H) Consulting.

Substantially all of the activities of a corporation are involved in the performance of services in any field described in the preceding sentence (a qualifying field), only if 95 percent or more of the time spent by employees of the corporation, serving in their capacity as such, is devoted to the performance of services in a qualifying field. For purposes of determining whether this 95 percent test is satisfied, the performance of any activity incident to the actual performance of services in a qualifying field is considered the performance of services in that field. Activities incident to the performance of services in a qualifying field include the supervision of employees engaged in directly providing services to clients, and the performance of administrative and support services incident to such activities.

(ii) Meaning of services performed in the field of health. For purposes of paragraph (e)(4)(i)(A) of this section, the performance of services in the field of health means the provision of medical services by physicians, nurses, dentists, and other similar healthcare professionals. The performance of services in the field of health does not include the provision of services not directly related to a medical field, even though the services may purportedly relate to the health of the service recipient. For example, the performance of services in the field of health does not include the operation of health clubs or health spas that provide physical exercise or conditioning to their customers.

(iii) Meaning of services performed in the field of performing arts. For purposes of paragraph (e)(4)(i)(G) of this section, the performance of services in the field of the performing arts means the provision of services by actors, actresses, singers, musicians, entertainers, and similar artists in their capacity as such. The performance of services in the field of the performing arts does not include the provision of services by persons who themselves are not performing artists *(e.g.,* persons who may manage or promote such artists, and other persons in a trade or business that relates to the performing arts). Similarly, the performance of services in the field of the performing arts does not include the provision of services by persons who broadcast or otherwise disseminate the performances of such artists to members of the public *(e.g.,* employees of a radio station that broadcasts the performances of musicians and singers). Finally, the performance of services in the field of the performing arts does not include the provision of services by athletes.

(iv) Meaning of services performed in the field of consulting. (A) In general. For purposes of paragraph (e)(4)(i)(H) of this section, the performance of services in the field of consulting means the provision of advice and counsel. The performance of services in the field of consulting does not include the performance of services other than advice and counsel, such as sales or brokerage services, or economically similar services. For purposes of the preceding sentence, the determination of whether a person's services are sales or brokerage services, or economically similar services, shall be based on all the facts and circumstances of that person's business. Such facts and circumstances include, for example, the manner in which the taxpayer is compensated for the services provided *(e.g.,* whether the compensation for the services is contingent upon the consummation of the transaction that the services were intended to effect).

(B) Examples. The following examples illustrate the provisions of paragraph (e)(4)(iv)(A) of this section. The examples do not address all types of services that may or may not qualify as consulting. The determination of whether activities not specifically addressed in the examples qualify as consulting shall be made by comparing the service activities in question to the types of service activities discussed in the examples. With respect to a corporation which performs services which qualify as consulting under this section, and other services which do not qualify as consulting, see paragraph (e)(4)(i) of this section which requires that substantially all of the corporation's activities involve the performance of services in a qualifying field.

*Example (1).* A taxpayer is in the business of providing economic analyses and forecasts of business prospects for its clients. Based on these analyses and forecasts, the taxpayer advises its clients on their business activities. For example, the taxpayer may analyze the economic conditions and outlook for a particular industry which a client is considering entering. The taxpayer will then make recommendations and advise the client on the prospects of entering the industry, as well as on other matters regarding the client's activities in such industry. The taxpayer provides similar services to other clients, involving, for example, economic analyses and evaluations of business prospects in different areas of the United States or in other countries, or economic analyses of overall economic trends and the provision of advice based on these analyses and evaluations. The taxpayer is considered to be engaged in the performance of services in the field of consulting.

*Example (2).* A taxpayer is in the business of providing services that consist of determining a client's electronic data processing needs. The taxpayer will study and examine the client's business, focusing on the types of data and information relevant to the client and the needs of the client's employees for access to this information. The taxpayer will then make recommendations regarding the design and implementation of data processing systems intended to meet the needs of the client. The taxpayer does not, however, provide the client with additional computer programming services distinct from the recommendations made by the taxpayer with respect to the design and implementation of the client's data processing systems. The taxpayer is considered to be engaged in the performance of services in the field of consulting.

*Example (3).* A taxpayer is in the business of providing services that consist of determining a client's management and business structure needs. The taxpayer will study the client's organization, including, for example, the departments assigned to perform specific functions, lines of authority in the managerial hierarchy, personnel hiring, job responsibility, and personnel evaluations and compensation. Based on the study, the taxpayer will then advise the client on changes in the client's management and business structure, including, for example, the restructuring of the client's departmental systems or its lines of managerial authority. The taxpayer is considered to be engaged in the performance of services in the field of consulting.

*Example (4).* A taxpayer is in the business of providing financial planning services. The taxpayer will study a particular client's financial situation, including, for example, the client's present income, savings and investments, and anticipated future economic and financial needs. Based on this study, the taxpayer will then assist the client in making decisions and plans regarding the client's financial activities. Such financial planning includes the design of a personal budget to assist the client in monitoring the client's financial situation, the adoption of investment strategies tailored to the client's needs, and other similar services. The taxpayer is considered to be engaged in the performance of services in the field of consulting.

*Example (5).* A taxpayer is in the business of executing transactions for customers involving various types of securities or commodities generally traded through organized exchanges or other similar networks. The taxpayer provides its clients with economic analyses and forecasts of conditions in various industries and businesses. Based on these analyses, the taxpayer makes recommendations regarding transactions in securities and commodities. Clients place orders with the taxpayer to trade securities or commodities based on the taxpayer's recommendations. The taxpayer's compensation for its services is typically based on the trade orders. The taxpayer is not considered to be engaged in the performance of services in the field of consulting. The taxpayer is engaged in brokerage services. Relevant to this determination is the fact that the compensation of the taxpayer for its services is contingent upon the consummation of the transaction the services were intended to effect (i.e., the execution of trade orders for its clients).

*Example (6).* A taxpayer is in the business of studying a client's needs regarding its data processing facilities and making recommendations to the client regarding the design and implementation of data processing systems. The client will then order computers and other data processing equipment through the taxpayer based on the taxpayer's recommendations. The taxpayer's compensation for its services is typically based on the equipment orders made by the clients. The taxpayer is not considered to be engaged in the performance of services in the field of consulting. The taxpayer is engaged in the performance of sales services. Relevant to this determination is the fact that the compensation of the taxpayer for its services it contingent upon the consummation of the transaction the services were intended to effect (i.e., the execution of equipment orders for its clients).

*Example (7).* A taxpayer is in the business of assisting businesses in meeting their personnel requirements by referring job applicants to employers with hiring needs in a particular area. The taxpayer may be informed by potential employers of their need for job applicants, or, alternatively, the taxpayer may become aware of the client's personnel requirements after the taxpayer studies and examines the client's management and business structure. The taxpayer's compensation for its services is typically based on the job applicants, referred by the taxpayer to the clients, who accept employment positions with the clients. The taxpayer is not considered to be engaged in the performance of services in the field of consulting. The taxpayer is involved in the performance of services economically similar to brokerage services. Relevant to this determination is the fact that the compensation of the taxpayer for its services is contingent upon the consummation of the transaction the services were intended to effect (i.e., the hiring of a job applicant by the client).

*Example (8).* The facts are the same as in example (7), except that the taxpayer's clients are individuals who use the services of the taxpayer to obtain employment positions. The taxpayer is typically compensated by its clients who obtain employment as a result of the taxpayer's services. For the reasons set forth in example (7), the taxpayer is not considered to be engaged in the performance of services in the field of consulting.

*Example (9).* A taxpayer is in the business of assisting clients in placing advertisements for their goods and services. The taxpayer analyzes the conditions and trends in the client's particular industry, and then makes recommendations to the client regarding the types of advertisements which should be placed by the client and the various types of advertising media (e.g., radio, television, magazines, etc.) which should be used by the client. The client will then purchase, through the taxpayer, advertisements in various media based on the taxpayer's recommendations. The taxpayer's compensation for its services is typically based on the particular orders for advertisements which the client makes. The taxpayer is not considered to be engaged in the performance of services in the field of consulting. The taxpayer is engaged in the performance of services economically similar to brokerage services. Relevant to this determination is the fact that the compensation of the taxpayer for its services is contingent upon the consummation of the transaction the services were intended to effect (i.e., the placing of advertisements by clients).

*Example (10).* A taxpayer is in the business of selling insurance (including life and casualty insurance), annuities, and other similar insurance products to various individual and business clients. The taxpayer will study the particular client's financial situation, including, for example, the client's present income, savings and investments, business and personal insurance risks, and anticipated future economic and financial needs. Based on this study, the taxpayer will then make recommendations to the client regarding the desirability of various insurance products. The client will then purchase these various insurance products through the taxpayer. The taxpayer's compensation for its services is typically based on the purchases made by the clients. The taxpayer is not considered to be engaged in the performance of services in the field of consulting. The taxpayer is engaged in the performance of brokerage or sales services. Relevant to this determination is the fact that the compensation of the taxpayer for its services is contingent upon the consummation of the transaction the services were intended to effect (i.e., the purchase of insurance products by its clients).

*(5) Ownership test.* (i) In general. A corporation meets the ownership test, if at all times during the taxable year, substantially all the corporation's stock, by value, is held, directly or indirectly, by—

(A) Employees performing services for such corporation in connection with activities involving a field referred to in paragraph (e)(4) of this section,

(B) Retired employees who had performed such services for such corporation,

(C) The estate of any individual described in paragraph (e)(5)(i)(A) or (B) of this section, or

(D) Any other person who acquired such stock by reason of the death of an individual described in paragraph (e)(5)(i)(A) or (B) of this section, but only for the 2-year period beginning on the date of the death of such individual.

For purposes of this paragraph (e)(5) of this section, the term "substantially all" means an amount equal to or greater than 95 percent.

(ii) Definition of employee. For purposes of the ownership test of this paragraph (e)(5) of this section, a person shall not be considered an employee of a corporation unless the services performed by that person for such corporation, based on the facts and circumstances, are more than de minimis. In addition, a person who is an employee of a corporation shall not be treated as an employee of another corporation merely by reason of the employer corporation and the other corporation being members of the same affiliated group or otherwise related.

(iii) Attribution rules. For purposes of this paragraph (e)(5) of this section, a corporation's stock is considered held indirectly by a person if, and to the extent, such person owns a proportionate interest in a partnership, S corporation, or qualified personal service corporation that owns such stock. No other arrangement or type of ownership shall constitute indirect ownership of a corporation's stock for purposes of this paragraph (e)(5) of this section. Moreover, stock of a corporation held by a trust is considered held by a person if, and to the extent, such person is treated under subpart E, part I, subchapter J, chapter 1 of the Code as the owner of the portion of the trust that consists of such stock.

(iv) Disregard of community property laws. For purposes of this paragraph (e)(5) of this section, community property laws shall be disregarded. Thus, in determining the stock ownership of a corporation, stock owned by a spouse solely by reason of community property laws shall be treated as owned by the other spouse.

(v) Treatment of certain stock plans. For purposes of this paragraph (e)(5) of this section, stock held by a plan described in section 401(a) that is exempt from tax under section 501(a) shall be treated as held by an employee described in paragraph (e)(5)(i)(A) of this section.

(vi) Special election for certain affiliated groups. For purposes of determining whether the stock ownership test of this paragraph (e)(5) of this section has been met, at the election of the common parent of an affiliated group (within the meaning of section 1504(a)), all members of such group shall be treated as one taxpayer if substantially all (within the meaning of paragraph (e)(4)(i) of this section) the activities of all such members (in the aggregate) are in the same field described in paragraph (e)(4)(i)(A)-(H) of this section. For rules relating to the making of the election, see 26 CFR 5h.5 (temporary regulations relating to elections under the Tax Reform Act of 1986).

(vii) Examples. The following examples illustrate the provisions of paragraph (e) of this section:

*Example (1).* (i) X, a Corporation, is engaged in the business of providing accounting services to its clients. These services consist of the preparation of audit and financial statements and the preparation of tax returns. For purposes of section 448, such services consist of the performance of services in the field of accounting. In addition, for purposes of section 448, the supervision of employees directly preparing the statements and returns, and the performance of all administrative and support services incident to such activities (including secretarial, janitorial, purchasing, personnel, security, and payroll services) are the performance of services in the field of accounting.

(ii) In addition, X owns and leases a portion of an office building. For purposes of this section, the following types of activities undertaken by the employees of X shall be considered as the performance of services in a field other than the field of accounting: (A) services directly relating to the leasing activities, e.g., time spent in leasing and maintaining the leased portion of the building; (B) supervision of employees engaged in directly providing services in the leasing activity; and (C) all administrative and support services incurred incident to services described in (A) and (B). The leasing activities of X are considered the performance of services in a field other than the field of accounting, regardless of whether such leasing activities constitute a trade or business under the Code. If the employees of X spend 95% or more of their time in the performance of services in the field of accounting, X satisfies the function test of paragraph (e)(4) of this section.

*Example (2).* Assume that Y, a C corporation, meets the function test of paragraph (e)(4) of this section. Assume further that all the employees of Y are performing services for Y in a qualifying field as defined in paragraph (e)(4) of this section. P, a partnership, owns 40%, by value, of the stock of Y. The remaining 60% of the stock of Y is owned directly by employees of Y. Employees of Y have an aggregate interest of 90% in the capital and profits of P. This, 96% of the stock of Y is held directly, or indirectly, by employees of Y performing services in a qualifying field. Accordingly, Y meets the ownership test of paragraph (e)(5) of this section and is a qualified personal service corporation.

*Example (3).* The facts are the same as in example (2), except that 40% of the stock of Y is owned by Z, a C corporation. The remaining 60% of the stock is owned directly by the employees of Y. Employees of Y own 90% of the stock, by value, of Z. Assume that Z independently qualifies as a personal service corporation. The result is the same as in example (2), i.e., 96% of the stock of Y is held, directly or indirectly, by employees of Y performing services in a qualifying field. Thus, Y is a qualified personal service corporation.

*Example (4).* The facts are the same as in example (3), except that Z does not independently qualify as a personal service corporation. Because Z is not a qualified personal service corporation, the Y stock owned by Z is not treated as being held indirectly by the Z shareholders. Consequently, only 60% of the stock of Y is held, directly or indirectly, by employees of Y. Thus, Y does not meet the ownership test of paragraph (e)(5) of this section, and is not a qualified personal service corporation.

*Example (5).* Assume that W, a C corporation, meets the function test of paragraph (e)(4) of this section. In addition, assume that all the employees of W are performing services for W in a qualifying field. Nominal legal title to 100% of the stock of W is held by employees of W. However, due solely to the operation of community property laws, 20% of the stock of W is held by spouses of such employees who themselves are not employees of W. In determining the ownership of the stock, community property laws are disregarded. Thus, Y meets the ownership test of paragraph (e)(5) of this section, and is a qualified personal service corporation.

*Example (6).* Assume that 90% of the stock of T, a C corporation, is directly owned by the employees of T. Spouses of T's employees directly own 5% of the stock of T. The spouses are not employees of T, and their ownership does not occur solely by operation of community property laws. In addition, 5% of the stock of T is held by trusts (other than a trust described in section 401(a) that is exempt from tax under section 501(a)), the sole beneficiaries of which are employees of T. The employees are not treated as owners of the trusts under subpart E, part I, subchapter J, chapter 1 of the Code. Since a person is not treated as owning the stock of a corporation owned by that person's spouse, or by any portion of a trust that is not treated as owned by such person under subpart E, only 90% of the stock of T is treated as held, directly or indirectly, by employees of T. Thus, T does not meet the ownership test of paragraph (e)(5) of this section, and is not a qualified personal service corporation.

*Example (7).* Assume that Y, a C corporation, directly owns all the stock of three subsidiaries, F, G, and H. Y is a common parent of an affiliated group within the meaning of section 1504(a) consisting of Y, F, G, and H. Y is not engaged in the performance of services in a qualifying field. Instead, Y is a holding company whose activities consist of its ownership and investment in its operating subsidiaries. Substantially all the activities of F involve the performance of services in the field of engineering. In addition, a majority of (but not substantially all) the activities of G involve the performance of services in the field of engineering; the remainder of G's services involve the performance of services in a nonqualifying field. Moreover, a majority of (but not substantially all) the activities of H involve the performance of services in the field of engineering; the remainder of H's activities involve the performance of services in the field of architecture. Nevertheless, substantially all the activities of the group consisting of Y, F, G, and H, in the aggregate, involve the performance of services in the field of engineering. Accordingly, Y elects under paragraph (e)(5)(vi) of this section to be treated as one taxpayer for determining the ownership test of paragraph (e)(5) of this section. Assume that substantially all the stock of Y (by value) is held by employees of F, G, or H who perform services in connection with a qualifying field (engineering or architecture). Thus, for purposes of determining whether any member corporation is a qualified personal service corporation, the ownership test of paragraph (e)(5) of this section has been satisfied. Since F and H satisfy the function test of paragraph (e)(4) of this section, F and H are qualified personal service corporations. However, since Y and G each fail the function test of paragraph (e)(4) of this section, neither corporation is a qualified personal service corporation.

*Example (8).* The facts are the same as in example (7), except that less than substantially all the activities of the group consisting of Y, F, G, and H, in the aggregate, are performed in the field of engineering. Substantially all the activities of the group consisting of Y, F, G, and H, are, in the aggregate, performed in two fields, the fields of engineering and architecture. Y may not elect to have the affiliated group treated as one taxpayer for purposes of determining whether group members meet the ownership test of paragraph (e)(5) of this section. The election is available only if substantially all the activities of the group, in the aggregate, involve the performance of services in only one qualifying field. Moreover, none of the group members are qualified personal service corporations. Y fails the function test of paragraph (e)(4) of this section because less than substantially all the activities of Y are performed in a qualifying field. In addition, F, G, and H fail the ownership test of paragraph (e)(5) of this section because substantially all their stock is owned by Y and not by their employees. The owners of Y are not deemed to indirectly own the stock owned by Y because Y is not a qualified personal service corporation.

*Example (9).* (i) The facts are the same as in example (8), except Y itself satisfies the function tests of paragraph (e)(4) of this section because substantially all the activities of Y involve the performance of services in the field of engineering. In addition, assume that all employees of Y are involved in the performance of services in the field of engineering, and that all such employees own 100% of Y's stock. Moreover, assume that one-third of all the employees of Y are separately employed by F. Similarly, another one-third of the employees of Y are separately employed by G and H, respectively. None of the employees of Y are employed by more than one of Y's subsidiaries. Also, no other persons except the employees of Y are employed by any of the subsidiaries.

(ii) Y is a personal service corporation under section 448 because Y satisfies both the function and the ownership test of paragraphs (e)(4) and (5) of this section. As in example (8), Y is unable to make the election to have the affiliated group treated as one taxpayer for purposes of determining whether group members meet the ownership test of paragraph (e)(5) of this section because less than substantially all the activities, in the aggregate, of the group members are performed in one of the qualifying fields. However, because Y is a personal service corporation, the stock owned by Y is treated as indirectly owned, proportionately, by the owners of Y. Thus, the employees of F are collectively treated as owning one-third of the stock of F, G, and H. The employees of G and H are similarly treated as owning one-third of each subsidiary's stock.

(iii) F, G, and H each fail the ownership test of paragraph (e)(5) of this section because less than substantially all of each corporation's stock is owned by the employees of the respective corporation. Only one-third of each corporation's stock is owned by employees of that corporation. Thus, F, G, and H are not qualified personal service corporations.

*Example (10).* (i) Assume that Y, a C corporation, directly owns all the stock of three subsidiaries, F, G, and Z. Y is a common parent of an affiliated group within the meaning of section 1504(a) consisting of Y, F, and G. Z is a foreign corporation and is excluded from the affiliated group under section 1504. Assume that Y is a holding company whose activities consist of its ownership and investment in its operating subsidiaries. Substantially all the activities of F, G, and Z involve the performance of services in the field of engineering. Assume that employees of Z own one-third of the stock of Y and that none of these employees are also employees of Y, F, or G. In addition, assume that Y elects to be treated as one taxpayer for determining whether group members meet the ownership tests of paragraph (e)(5) of this section. Thus, Y, F, and G are treated as one taxpayer for purposes of the ownership test.

(ii) None of the members of the group are qualified personal service corporations. Y, F, and G fail the ownership test of paragraph (e)(5) of this section because less than substantially all the stock of Y is owned by employees of either Y, F, or G. Moreover, Z fails the ownership test of paragraph (e)(5) of this section because substantially all its stock is owned by Y and not by its employees.

*(6) Application of function and ownership tests.* A corporation that fails the function test of paragraph (e)(4) of this section for any taxable year, or that fails the ownership test of paragraph (e)(5) of this section at any time during any taxable year, shall change from the cash method effective for the year in which the corporation fails to meet the function test or the ownership test. For example, if a personal service corporation fails the function test for taxable year 1987, such corporation must change from the cash method effective for taxable year 1987. A corporation that fails the function or ownership test for a taxable year shall not be treated as a qualified personal service corporation for any part of that taxable year.

**(f) Exception for entities with gross receipts of not more than $5 million.** *(1) In general.* Except in the case of a tax shelter, this section shall not apply to any C corporation or partnership with a C corporation as a partner for any taxable year if, for all prior taxable years beginning after December 31, 1985, such corporation or partnership (or any predecessor thereof) meets the $5,000,000 gross receipts test of paragraph (f)(2) of this section.

*(2) The $5,000,000 gross receipts test.* (i) In general. A corporation meets the $5,000,000 gross receipts test of this paragraph (f)(2) for any prior taxable year if the average annual gross receipts of such corporation for the 3 taxable years (or, if shorter, the taxable years during which such corporation was in existence) ending with such prior taxable year does not exceed $5,000,000. In the case of a C corporation exempt from federal income taxes under section 501(a), or a trust subject to tax under section 511(b) that is treated as a C corporation under paragraph (a)(3) of this section, only gross receipts from the activities of such corporation or trust that constitute unrelated trades or businesses are taken into account in determining whether the $5,000,000 gross receipts test is satisfied. A partnership with a C corporation as a partner meets the $5,000,000 gross receipts test of this paragraph (f)(2) for any prior taxable year if the average annual gross receipts of such partnership for the 3 taxable years (or, if shorter, the taxable years during which such partnership was in existence) ending with such prior year does not exceed $5,000,000. The gross receipts of the corporate partner are not taken into account in determining whether the partnership meets the $5,000,000 gross receipts test.

(ii) Aggregation of gross receipts. For purposes of determining whether the $5,000,000 gross receipts test has been satisfied, all persons treated as a single employer under section 52(a) or (b), or section 414(m) or (o) (or who would be treated as a single employer under such sections if they had employees) shall be treated as one person. Gross receipts attributable to transactions between persons who are treated as a common employer under this paragraph shall not be taken into account in determining whether the $5,000,000 gross receipts test is satisfied.

(iii) Treatment of short taxable year. In the case of any taxable year of less than 12 months (a short taxable year), the gross receipts shall be annualized by (A) multiplying the gross receipts for the short period by 12 and (B) dividing the result by the number of months in the short period.

(iv) Determination of gross receipts. (A) In general. The term "gross receipts" means gross receipts of the taxable year in which such receipts are properly recognized under the taxpayer's accounting method used in that taxable year (determined without regard to this section) for federal income tax purposes. For this purpose, gross receipts include total sales (net of returns and allowances) and all amounts received for services. In addition, gross receipts include any income from investments, and from incidental or outside sources. For example, gross receipts include interest (including original issue discount and tax-exempt interest within the meaning of section 103), dividends, rents, royalties, and annuities, regardless of whether such amounts are derived in the ordinary course of the taxpayer's trade of business. Gross receipts are not reduced by cost of goods sold or by the cost of property sold if such property is described in section 1221(1), (3), (4) or (5). With respect to sales of capital assets as defined in section 1221, or sales of property described in 1221(2) (relating to property used in a trade or business), gross receipts shall be reduced by the taxpayer's adjusted basis in such property. Gross receipts do not include the repayment of a loan or similar instrument *(e.g.,* a repayment of the principal amount of a loan held by a commercial lender). Finally, gross receipts do not include amounts received by the taxpayer with respect to sales tax or other similar state and local taxes if, under the applicable state or local law, the tax is legally imposed on the purchaser of the good or service, and the taxpayer merely collects and remits the tax to the taxing authority. If, in contrast, the tax is imposed on the taxpayer under the applicable law, then gross receipts shall include the amounts received that are allocable to the payment of such tax.

*(3) Examples.* The following examples illustrate the provisions of paragraph (f) of this section:

*Example (1).* X, a calendar year C corporation, was formed on January 1, 1986. Assume that in 1986 X has gross receipts of $15 million. For taxable year 1987, this section applies to X because in 1986, the period during which X was in existence, X has average annual gross receipts of more than $5 million.

*Example (2).* Y, a calendar year C corporation that is not a qualified personal service corporation, has gross receipts of $10 million, $9 million, and $4 million for taxable years 1984, 1985, and 1986, respectively. In taxable year 1986, X has average annual gross receipts for the 3-taxable-year period ending with 1986 of $7.67 million ($10 million + 9 million + 4 million ÷ 3). Thus, for taxable year 1987, this section applies and Y must change from the cash method for such year.

*Example (3).* Z, a C corporation which is not a qualified personal service corporation, has a 5% partnership interest in ZAB partnership, a calendar year cash method taxpayer. All other partners of ZAB partnership are individuals. Z corporation has average annual gross receipts of $100,000 for the 3-taxable-year period ending with 1986 *(i.e.,* 1984, 1985 and 1986). The ZAB partnership has average annual gross receipts of $6 million for the same 3-taxable-year period. Since ZAB fails to meet the $5,000,000 gross receipts test for 1986, this section applies to ZAB for its taxable year beginning January 1, 1987. Accordingly, ZAB must change from the cash method for its 1987 taxable year. The gross receipts of Z corporation are not relevant in determining whether ZAB is subject to this section.

*Example (4).* The facts are the same as in example (3), except that during the 1987 taxable year of ZAB, the Z corporation transfers its partnership interest in ZAB to an individual. Under paragraph (a)(1) of this section, ZAB is treated as a partnership with a C corporation as a partner. Thus, this section requires ZAB to change from the cash method effective for its taxable year 1987. If ZAB later desires to change its method of accounting to the cash method for its taxable year beginning January 1, 1988 (or later), ZAB must comply with all requirements of law, including sections 446(b), 446(e), and 481, to effect the change.

*Example (5).* X, a C corporation that is not a qualified personal service corporation, was formed on January 1, 1986, in a transaction described in section 351. In the transaction, A, an individual, contributed all of the assets and liabilities of B, a trade or business, to X, in return for the receipt of all the outstanding stock of X. Assume that in 1986 X has gross receipts of $4 million. In 1984 and 1985, the gross receipts of B, the trade or business, were $10 million and $7 million respectively. The gross receipts test is applied for the period during which X and its predecessor trade or business were in existence. X has average annual gross receipts for the 3-taxable-year period ending with 1986 of $7 million ($10 million + $7 million + $4 million ÷ 3). Thus, for taxable year 1987, this section applies and X must change from the cash method for such year.

T.D. 8143, 6/12/87, amend T.D. 8329, 1/4/91, T.D. 8514, 12/23/93, T.D. 9174, 1/4/2005.

### § 1.448-2 Nonaccrual of certain amounts by service providers.

**(a) In general.** This section applies to taxpayers qualified to use a nonaccrual-experience method of accounting provided for in section 448(d)(5) with respect to amounts to be received for the performance of services. A taxpayer that satisfies the requirements of this section is not required to accrue any portion of amounts to be received from the performance of services that, on the basis of the taxpayer's experience, and to the extent determined under the computation or formula used by the taxpayer and allowed under this section, will not be collected. Except as otherwise provided in this section, a taxpayer is qualified to use a nonaccrual-experience method of accounting if the taxpayer uses an accrual method of accounting with respect to amounts to be received for the performance of services by the taxpayer and either—

*(1)* The services are in fields referred to in section 448(d)(2)(A) and described in § 1.448-1T(e)(4) (health, law, engineering, architecture, accounting, actuarial science, performing arts, or consulting); or

*(2)* The taxpayer meets the $5 million annual gross receipts test of section 448(c) and § 1.448-1T(f)(2) for all prior taxable years.

**(b) Application of method and treatment as method of accounting.** The rules of section 448(d)(5) and the regulations are applied separately to each taxpayer. For purposes of section 448(d)(5), the term taxpayer has the same meaning as the term person defined in section 7701(a)(1) (rather than the meaning of the term defined in section 7701(a)(14)). The nonaccrual of amounts to be received for the performance of services is a method of accounting (a nonaccrual-experience method). A change to a nonaccrual-experience method, from one nonaccrual-experience method to another nonaccrual-experience method, or to a periodic system (for example, see Notice 88-51 (1988-1 C.B. 535) and § 601.601(d)(2)(ii)(b) of this chapter), is a change in method of accounting to which the provisions of sections 446 and 481 and the regulations apply. See also paragraphs (c)(2)(i), (c)(5), (d)(4), and (e)(3)(i) of this section. Except as provided in other published guidance, a taxpayer who wishes to adopt or change to any nonaccrual-experience method other than one of the safe harbor methods described in paragraph (f) of this section must request and receive advance consent from the Commissioner in accordance with the applicable administrative procedures issued under § 1.446-1(e)(3)(ii) for obtaining the Commissioner's consent.

**(c) Definitions and special rules.** *(1) Accounts receivable.* (i) In general. Accounts receivable include only amounts that are earned by a taxpayer and otherwise recognized in income through the performance of services by the taxpayer. For purposes of determining a taxpayer's nonaccrual-experience under any method provided in this section, amounts described in paragraph (c)(1)(ii) of this section are not taken into account. Except as otherwise provided, for purposes of this section, accounts receivable do not include amounts that are not billed (such as for charitable or pro bono services) or amounts contractually not collectible (such as amounts in excess of a fee schedule agreed to by contract). See paragraph (g) Examples 1 and 2 of this section for examples of this rule.

(ii) Method not available for certain receivables. (A) Amounts not earned and recognized through the performance of services. A nonaccrual-experience method of accounting may not be used with respect to amounts that are not earned by a taxpayer and otherwise recognized in income through the performance of services by the taxpayer. For example, a nonaccrual-experience method may not be used with respect to amounts owed to the taxpayer by reason of the taxpayer's activities with respect to lending money, selling goods, or acquiring accounts receivable or other rights to receive payment from other persons (including persons related to the taxpayer) regardless of whether those persons earned the amounts through the provision of services. However, see paragraph (d)(3) of this section for special rules regarding acquisitions of a trade or business or a unit of a trade or business.

(B) If interest or penalty charged on amounts due. A nonaccrual-experience method of accounting may not be used with respect to amounts due for which interest is required to be paid or for which there is any penalty for failure to timely pay any amounts due. For this purpose, a taxpayer will be treated as charging interest or penalties for late payment if the contract or agreement expressly provides for the charging of interest or penalties for late payment, regardless of the practice of the parties. If the contract or agreement does not expressly provide for the charging of interest or penalties for late payment, the determination of whether the taxpayer charges interest or penalties for late payment will be made based on all of the facts and circumstances of the transaction, and not merely on the characterization by the parties or the treatment of the transaction under state or local law. However, the offering of a discount for early payment of an amount due will not be regarded as the charging of interest or penalties for late payment under this section, if—

(1) The full amount due is otherwise accrued as gross income by the taxpayer at the time the services are provided; and

(2) The discount for early payment is treated as an adjustment to gross income in the year of payment, if payment is received within the time required for allowance of the discount. See paragraph (g) Example 3 of this section for an example of this rule.

*(2) Applicable period.* (i) In general. The applicable period is the number of taxable years on which the taxpayer bases its nonaccrual-experience method. A change in the number of taxable years included in the applicable period is a change in method of accounting to which the procedures of section 446 apply. A change in the inclusion or exclusion of the current taxable year in the applicable period is a change in method of accounting to which the procedures of section 446 apply. A change in the number of taxable years included in the applicable period or the inclusion or exclusion of the current taxable year in the applicable period is made on a cut-off basis.

(ii) Applicable period for safe harbors. For purposes of the safe harbors under paragraph (f) of this section the applicable period may consist of at least three but not more than six of the immediately preceding consecutive taxable years. Alternatively, the applicable period may consist of the current taxable year and at least two but not more than five of the immediately preceding consecutive taxable years. A period shorter than six taxable years is permissible only if the period contains the most recent preceding taxable years and all of the taxable years in the applicable period are consecutive.

*(3) Bad debts.* Bad debts are accounts receivable determined to be uncollectible and charged off.

*(4) Charge-offs.* Amounts charged off include only those amounts that would otherwise be allowable under section 166(a).

*(5) Determination date.* The determination date in safe harbor 2 provided in paragraph (f)(2) of this section is used as a cut-off date for determining all known data to be taken into account in the computation of the taxable year's uncollectible amount. The determination date may not be later than the earlier of the due date, including extensions, for filing the taxpayer's Federal income tax return for that taxable year or the date on which the taxpayer timely files the return for that taxable year. The determination date may be different in each taxable year. However, once a determination date is selected and used for a particular taxable year, it may not be changed for that taxable year. The choice of a determination date is not a method of accounting.

*(6) Recoveries.* Recoveries are amounts previously excluded from income under a nonaccrual-experience method or charged off that the taxpayer recovers.

*(7) Uncollectible amount.* The uncollectible amount is the portion of any account receivable amount due that, under the taxpayer's nonaccrual-experience method, will be not collected.

**(d) Use of experience to estimate uncollectible amounts.** *(1) In general.* In determining the portion of any amount due that, on the basis of experience, will not be collected, a taxpayer may use any nonaccrual-experience method that clearly reflects the taxpayer's nonaccrual-experience. The determination of whether a nonaccrual-experience method clearly reflects the taxpayer's nonaccrual-experience is made in accordance with the rules under paragraph (e) of this section. Alternatively, the taxpayer may use any one of the five safe harbor nonaccrual-experience methods of accounting provided in paragraphs (f)(1) through (f)(5) of this section, which are presumed to clearly reflect a taxpayer's nonaccrual-experience.

*(2) Application to specific accounts receivable.* The nonaccrual-experience method is applied with respect to each account receivable of the taxpayer that is eligible for this method. With respect to a particular account receivable, the taxpayer determines, in the manner prescribed in paragraphs (d)(1) or (f)(1) through (f)(5) of this section (whichever applies), the uncollectible amount. The determination is required to be made only once with respect to each account receivable, regardless of the term of the receivable. The uncollectible amount is not recognized as gross income. Thus, the amount recognized as gross income is the amount that would otherwise be recognized as gross income with respect to the account receivable, less the uncollectible amount. A taxpayer that excludes an amount from income during a taxable year as a result of the taxpayer's use of a nonaccrual-experience method may not deduct in any subsequent taxable year the amount excluded from income. Thus, the taxpayer may not deduct the excluded amount in a subsequent taxable year in which the taxpayer actually determines that the amount is uncollectible and charges it off. If a taxpayer using a nonaccrual-experience method determines that an amount that was not excluded from income is uncollectible and should be charged off (for example, a calendar-year taxpayer determines on November 1st that an account receivable that was originated on May 1st of the same taxable year is uncollectible and should be charged off), the taxpayer may deduct the amount charged off when it is charged off, but must include any subsequent recoveries in income. The reasonableness of a taxpayer's determination that amounts are uncollectible and should be charged off may be considered on examination. See paragraph (g) Example 12 of this section for an example of this rule.

*(3) Acquisitions and dispositions.* (i) Acquisitions. If a taxpayer acquires the major portion of a trade or business of another person (predecessor) or the major portion of a separate unit of a trade or business of a predecessor, then, for purposes of applying this section for any taxable year ending on or after the acquisition, the experience from preceding taxable years of the predecessor attributable to the portion of the trade or business acquired, if available, must be used in determining the taxpayer's experience.

(ii) Dispositions. If a taxpayer disposes of a major portion of a trade or business or the major portion of a separate unit of a trade or business, and the taxpayer furnished the acquiring person the information necessary for the computations required by this section, then, for purposes of applying this section for any taxable year ending on or after the disposition, the experience from preceding taxable years attributable to the portion of the trade or business disposed may not be used in determining the taxpayer's experience.

(iii) Meaning of terms. For the meaning of the terms acquisition, separate unit, and major portion, see paragraph (b) of § 1.52-2. The term acquisition includes an incorporation or a liquidation.

*(4) New taxpayers.* The rules of this paragraph (d)(4) apply to any newly formed taxpayer to which the rules of paragraph (d)(3)(i) of this section do not apply. Any newly formed taxpayer that wants to use a safe harbor nonaccrual-experience method of accounting described in paragraph (f)(1), (f)(2), (f)(3), (f)(4), or (f)(5) of this section applies the methods by using the experience of the actual number of taxable years available in the applicable period. A newly formed taxpayer that wants to use one of the safe harbor nonaccrual-experience methods of accounting described in paragraph (f)(2), (f)(4), or (f)(5) of this section in its first taxable year and does not have any accounts receivable upon formation may not exclude any portion of its year-end accounts receivable from income for its first taxable year. The taxpayer must begin creating its moving average in its second taxable year by tracking the accounts receivable as of the first day of its second taxable year. The use of one of the safe harbor nonaccrual-experience methods of accounting described in paragraph (f)(2), (f)(4), or (f)(5) of this section in a taxpayer's second taxable year in this situation is not a change in method of accounting. Although the taxpayer must maintain the books and records necessary to perform the computations under the adopted safe harbor nonaccrual-experience method, the taxpayer is not required to affirmatively elect the method on its Federal income tax return for its first taxable year.

*(5) Recoveries.* Regardless of the nonaccrual-experience method of accounting used by a taxpayer under this section, the taxpayer must take recoveries into account. If, in a subsequent taxable year, a taxpayer recovers an amount previously excluded from income under a nonaccrual-experience method or charged off, the taxpayer must include the recovered amount in income in that subsequent taxable year. See paragraph (g) Example 13 of this section for an example of this rule.

*(6) Request to exclude taxable years from applicable period.* A period shorter than the applicable period generally is permissible only if the period consists of consecutive taxable years and there is a change in the type of a substantial portion of the outstanding accounts receivable such that the risk of loss is substantially increased. A decline in the general economic conditions in the area, which substantially increases the risk of loss, is a relevant factor in determining whether a shorter period is appropriate. However, approval to use a shorter period will not be granted unless the taxpayer supplies evidence that the accounts receivable outstanding at the close of the taxable years for the shorter period requested are more comparable in nature and risk to accounts receivable outstanding at the close of the current taxable year. A substantial increase in a taxpayer's bad debt experience is not, by itself, sufficient to justify the use of a shorter period. If approval is granted to use a shorter period, the experience for the excluded taxable years may not be used for any subsequent taxable year. A request for approval to exclude the experience of a prior taxable year must be made in accordance with the applicable procedures for requesting a letter ruling and must include a statement of the reasons the experience should be excluded. A request will not be considered unless it is sent to the Commissioner at least 30 days before the close of the first taxable year for which the approval is requested.

*(7) Short taxable years.* A taxpayer with a short taxable year that uses a nonaccrual-experience method that compares accounts receivable balance to total bad debts during the taxable year should make appropriate adjustments.

*(8) Recordkeeping requirements.* (i) A taxpayer using a nonaccrual-experience method of accounting must keep sufficient books and records to establish the amount of any ex-

clusion from gross income under section 448(d)(5) for the taxable year, including books and records demonstrating—

(A) The nature of the taxpayer's nonaccrual-experience method;

(B) Whether, for any particular taxable year, the taxpayer qualifies to use its nonaccrual-experience method (including the self-testing requirements of paragraph (e) of this section (if applicable));

(C) The taxpayer's determination that amounts are uncollectible;

(D) The proper amount that is excludable under the taxpayer's nonaccrual-experience method; and

(E) The taxpayer's determination date under paragraph (c)(5) of this section (if applicable).

(ii) If a taxpayer does not maintain records of the data that are sufficient to establish the amount of any exclusion from gross income under section 448(d)(5) for the taxable year, the Internal Revenue Service may change the taxpayer's method of accounting on examination. See § 1.6001-1 for rules regarding records.

**(e) Requirements for nonaccrual method to clearly reflect experience.** *(1) In general.* A nonaccrual-experience method clearly reflects the taxpayer's experience if the taxpayer's nonaccrual-experience method meets the self-test requirements described in this paragraph (e). If a taxpayer is using one of the safe harbor nonaccrual-experience methods described in paragraphs (f)(1) through (f)(4) of this section, its method is deemed to clearly reflect its experience and is not subject to the self-testing requirements in paragraphs (e)(2) and (e)(3) of this section.

*(2) Requirement to self-test.* (i) In general. A taxpayer using, or desiring to use, a nonaccrual-experience method must self-test its nonaccrual-experience method for its first taxable year for which the taxpayer uses, or desires to use, that nonaccrual-experience method (first-year self-test) and every three taxable years thereafter (three-year self-test). Each self-test must be performed by comparing the uncollectible amount (under the taxpayer's nonaccrual-experience method) with the taxpayer's actual experience. A taxpayer using the safe harbor under paragraph (f)(5) of this section must self-test using the safe harbor comparison method in paragraph (e)(3) of this section.

(ii) First-year self-test. The first-year self-test must be performed by comparing the uncollectible amount with the taxpayer's actual experience for its first taxable year for which the taxpayer uses, or desires to use, that nonaccrual-experience method. If the uncollectible amount for the first-year self-test is less than or equal to the taxpayer's actual experience for its first taxable year for which the taxpayer uses, or desires to use, that nonaccrual-experience method, the taxpayer's nonaccrual-experience method is treated as clearly reflecting its experience for the first taxable year. If, as a result of the first-year self-test, the uncollectible amount for the test period is greater than the taxpayer's actual experience, then—

(A) The taxpayer's nonaccrual-experience method is treated as not clearly reflecting its experience;

(B) The taxpayer is not permitted to use that nonaccrual-experience method in that taxable year; and

(C) The taxpayer must change to (or adopt) for that taxable year either—

(1) Another nonaccrual-experience method that clearly reflects experience, that is, a nonaccrual-experience method that meets the first-year self-test requirement; or

(2) A safe harbor nonaccrual-experience method described in paragraphs (f)(1) through (f)(5) of this section.

(iii) Three-year self-test. (A) In general. The three-year self-test must be performed by comparing the sum of the uncollectible amounts for the current taxable year and prior two taxable years (cumulative uncollectible amount) with the sum of the taxpayer's actual experience for the current taxable year and prior two taxable years (cumulative actual experience amount).

(B) Recapture. If the cumulative uncollectible amount for the test period is greater than the cumulative actual experience amount for the test period, the taxpayer's uncollectible amount is limited to the cumulative actual experience amount for the test period. Any excess of the taxpayer's cumulative uncollectible amount over the taxpayer's cumulative actual nonaccrual-experience amount excluded from income during the test period must be recaptured into income in the third taxable year of the three-year self-test period.

(C) Determination of whether method is permissible or impermissible. If the cumulative uncollectible amount is less than 110 percent of the cumulative actual experience amount, the taxpayer's nonaccrual-experience method is treated as a permissible method and the taxpayer may continue to use its alternative nonaccrual-experience method, subject to the three-year self-test requirement of this paragraph (e)(2)(iii). If the cumulative uncollectible amount is greater than or equal to 110 percent of the cumulative actual experience amount, the taxpayer's nonaccrual-experience method is treated as impermissible in the taxable year subsequent to the three-year self-test year and does not clearly reflect its experience. The taxpayer must change to another nonaccrual-experience method that clearly reflects experience, including, for example, one of the safe harbor nonaccrual-experience methods described in paragraphs (f)(1) through (f)(5) of this section, for the subsequent taxable year. A change in method of accounting from an impermissible method under this paragraph (e)(2)(iii)(C) to a permissible method in the taxable year subsequent to the three-year self-test year is made on a cut-off basis.

(iv) Determination of taxpayer's actual experience. [Reserved.]

*(3) Safe harbor comparison method.* (i) In general. A taxpayer using, or desiring to use, a nonaccrual-experience method under the safe harbor in paragraph (f)(5) of this section must self-test its nonaccrual-experience method for its first taxable year for which the taxpayer uses, or desires to use, that nonaccrual-experience method (first-year self-test) and every three taxable years thereafter (three-year self-test). A nonaccrual-experience method under the safe harbor in paragraph (f)(5) of this section is deemed to clearly reflect experience provided all the requirements of the safe harbor comparison method of this paragraph (e)(3) are met. Each self-test must be performed by comparing the uncollectible amount (under the taxpayer's nonaccrual-experience method) with the uncollectible amount that would have resulted from use of one of the safe harbor methods described in paragraph (f)(1), (f)(2), (f)(3), or (f)(4) of this section. A change from a nonaccrual-experience method that uses the safe harbor comparison method for self-testing to a nonaccrual-experience method that does not use the safe harbor comparison method for self-testing, and vice versa, is a change in method of accounting to which the provisions of sections 446 and 481 and the regulations apply. A change solely to use or discontinue use of the safe harbor comparison method for purposes of determining whether the nonaccrual-experience method

clearly reflects experience must be made on a cut-off basis and without audit protection.

(ii) Requirements to use safe harbor comparison method. (A) First-year self-test. The first-year self-test must be performed by comparing the uncollectible amount with the uncollectible amount determined under any of the safe harbor methods described in paragraph (f)(1), (f)(2), (f)(3), or (f)(4) of this section (safe harbor uncollectible amount) for its first taxable year for which the taxpayer uses, or desires to use, that nonaccrual-experience method. If the uncollectible amount for the first-year self-test is less than or equal to the safe harbor uncollectible amount, then the taxpayer's nonaccrual-experience method is treated as clearly reflecting its experience for the first taxable year. If, as a result of the first-year self-test, the uncollectible amount for the test period is greater than the safe harbor uncollectible amount, then—

(1) The taxpayer's nonaccrual-experience method is treated as not clearly reflecting its experience;

(2) The taxpayer is not permitted to use that nonaccrual-experience method in that taxable year; and

(3) The taxpayer must change to (or adopt) for that taxable year either—

(i) Another nonaccrual-experience method that clearly reflects experience, that is, a nonaccrual-experience method that meets the first-year self-test requirement; or

(ii) A safe harbor nonaccrual-experience method described in paragraphs (f)(1) through (f)(5) of this section.

(B) Three-year self-test. The three-year self-test must be performed by comparing the sum of the uncollectible amounts for the current taxable year and prior two taxable years (cumulative uncollectible amount) with the sum of the uncollectible amount determined under any of the safe harbor methods described in paragraph (f)(1), (f)(2), (f)(3), or (f)(4) of this section for the current taxable year and prior two taxable years (cumulative safe harbor uncollectible amounts). If the cumulative uncollectible amount for the three-year self-test is less than or equal to the cumulative safe harbor uncollectible amount for the test period, then the taxpayer's nonaccrual-experience method is treated as clearly reflecting its experience for the test period and the taxpayer may continue to use that nonaccrual-experience method, subject to a requirement to self-test again after three taxable years. If the cumulative uncollectible amount for the test period is greater than the cumulative safe harbor uncollectible amount for the test period, the taxpayer's uncollectible amount is limited to the cumulative safe harbor uncollectible amount for the test period. Any excess of the taxpayer's cumulative uncollectible amount over the taxpayer's cumulative safe harbor uncollectible amount excluded from income during the test period must be recaptured into income in the third taxable year of the three-year self-test period. If the cumulative uncollectible amount is less than 110 percent of the cumulative safe harbor uncollectible amount, the taxpayer's nonaccrual-experience method is treated as a permissible method and the taxpayer may continue to use its alternative nonaccrual-experience method, subject to the three-year self-test requirement of this paragraph (e)(3)(ii)(B). If the cumulative uncollectible amount is greater than or equal to 110 percent of the cumulative safe harbor uncollectible amount, the taxpayer's nonaccrual-experience method is treated as impermissible in the taxable year subsequent to the three-year self-test year and does not clearly reflect its experience. The taxpayer must change to another nonaccrual-experience method that clearly reflects experience, including, for example, one of the safe harbor nonaccrual-experience methods described in paragraphs (f)(1) through (f)(5) of this section, for the subsequent taxable year. A change in method of accounting from an impermissible method under this paragraph (e)(3)(ii)(B) to a permissible method in the taxable year subsequent to the three-year self-test year is made on a cut-off basis.

*(4) Methods that do not clearly reflect experience.* [Reserved.]

*(5) Contemporaneous documentation.* For purposes of this paragraph (e), including the safe harbor comparison method of paragraph (e)(3) of this section, a taxpayer must document in its books and records, in the taxable year any first-year or three-year self-test is performed, the method used to conduct the self-test, including appropriate documentation and computations that resulted in the determination that the taxpayer's nonaccrual-experience method clearly reflected the taxpayer's nonaccrual-experience for the applicable test period.

**(f) Safe harbors.** *(1) Safe harbor 1: revenue-based moving average method.* A taxpayer may use a nonaccrual-experience method under which the taxpayer determines the uncollectible amount by multiplying its accounts receivable balance at the end of the current taxable year by a percentage (revenue-based moving average percentage). The revenue-based moving average percentage is computed by dividing the total bad debts sustained, adjusted by recoveries received, throughout the applicable period by the total revenue resulting in accounts receivable earned throughout the applicable period. See paragraph (g) Example 4 of this section for an example of this method. Thus, the uncollectible amount under the revenue-based moving average method is computed:

$$\frac{\text{Bad debts sustained, adjusted by recoveries received, during the applicable period}}{\text{Total revenue resulting in accounts receivable during the applicable period}} \times \text{Accounts receivable at end of current taxable year}$$

*(2) Safe harbor 2: actual experience method.* (i) Option A: single determination date. A taxpayer may use a nonaccrual-experience method under which the taxpayer determines the uncollectible amount by multiplying its accounts receivable balance at the end of the current taxable year by a percentage (moving average nonaccrual-experience percentage) and then increasing the resulting amount by 5 percent. See paragraph (g) Example 5 of this section for an example of safe harbor 2 in general, and paragraph (g) Example 6 of this section for an example of the single determination date option of safe harbor 2. The taxpayer's moving average nonaccrual-experience percentage is computed by dividing the total bad debts sustained, adjusted by recoveries that are allocable to the bad debts, by the determination date of the current taxable year related to the taxpayer's accounts receivable balance at the beginning of each taxable year during the applicable period by the sum of the accounts receivable at the beginning of each taxable year during the applicable

period. Thus, the uncollectible amount under Option A of the actual experience method is computed:

$$\frac{\text{Bad debts sustained, adjusted by recoveries received that are allocable to the bad debts, by the determination date of the current taxable year related to the taxpayer's accounts receivable balance at the beginning of each taxable year during the applicable period}}{\text{Sum of accounts receivable at the beginning of each taxable year during the applicable period}} \times \text{Accounts receivable at end of current taxable year} \times 1.05$$

(ii) Option B: multiple determination dates. Alternatively, in computing its bad debts related to the taxpayer's accounts receivable balance at the beginning of each taxable year during the applicable period, a taxpayer may use the original determination date for each taxable year during the applicable period. That is, the taxpayer may use bad debts sustained, adjusted by recoveries received that are allocable to the bad debts, by the determination date of each taxable year during the applicable period rather than the determination date of the current taxable year. See paragraph (g) Example 7 of this section for an example of the multiple determination date option of safe harbor 2. Thus, the uncollectible amount under Option B of the actual experience method is computed:

$$\frac{\text{Sum of, for each taxable year during the applicable period, bad debts sustained, adjusted by recoveries received that are allocable to the bad debts, by that taxable year's determination date and related to the taxpayer's accounts receivable balance at the beginning of the taxable year}}{\text{Sum of accounts receivable at the beginning of each taxable year during the applicable period}} \times \text{Accounts receivable at end of current taxable year} \times 1.05$$

(iii) Tracing of recoveries. (A) In general. Bad debts related to the taxpayer's accounts receivable balance at the beginning of each taxable year during the applicable period must be adjusted by the portion, if any, of recoveries received that are properly allocable to the bad debts.

(B) Specific tracing. If a taxpayer, without undue burden, can trace all recoveries to their corresponding charge-offs, the taxpayer must specifically trace all recoveries.

(C) Recoveries cannot be traced without undue burden. If a taxpayer has any recoveries that cannot, without undue burden, be traced to corresponding charge-offs, the taxpayer may allocate those or all recoveries between charge-offs of amounts in the relevant beginning accounts receivable balances and other charge-offs using an allocation method that is reasonable under all of the facts and circumstances.

(1) Reasonable allocations. An allocation method is reasonable if there is a cause and effect relationship between the allocation base or ratio and the recoveries. A taxpayer may elect to trace recoveries that are traceable and allocate all untraceable recoveries to charge-offs of amounts in the relevant beginning accounts receivable balances. Such an allocation method will be deemed to be reasonable under all the facts and circumstances.

(2) Allocations that are not reasonable. Allocation methods that generally will not be considered reasonable include, for example, methods in which there is not a cause and effect relationship between the allocation base or ratio and methods in which receivables for which the nonaccrual-experience method is not allowed to be used are included in the allocation. See paragraph (c)(1)(ii) of this section for examples of receivables for which the nonaccrual-experience method is not allowed.

*(3) Safe harbor 3: modified Black Motor method.* A taxpayer may use a nonaccrual-experience method under which the taxpayer determines the uncollectible amount by multiplying its accounts receivable balance at the end of the current taxable year by a percentage (modified Black Motor moving average percentage) and then reducing the resulting amount by the bad debts written off during the current taxable year relating to accounts receivable generated during the current taxable year. The modified Black Motor moving average percentage is computed by dividing the total bad debts sustained, adjusted by recoveries received, during the applicable period by the sum of accounts receivable at the end of each taxable year during the applicable period. See paragraph (g) Example 8 of this section for an example of this method. Thus, the uncollectible amount under the modified Black Motor method is computed:

$$\frac{\text{Bad debts sustained, adjusted by recoveries received, during the applicable period}}{\text{Sum of accounts receivable at the end of each taxable year during the applicable period}} \times \text{Accounts receivable at end of current taxable year} - \text{Bad debts written off during the current taxable year relating to accounts receivable generated during the current taxable year}$$

*(4) Safe harbor 4: modified moving average method.* A taxpayer may use a nonaccrual-experience method under which the taxpayer determines the uncollectible amount by multiplying its accounts receivable balance at the end of the current taxable year by a percentage (modified moving average percentage). The modified moving average percentage is computed by dividing the total bad debts sustained, adjusted by recoveries received, during the applicable period other than bad debts that were written off in the same taxable year the related accounts receivable were generated by the sum of accounts receivable at the beginning of each taxable year during the applicable period. See paragraph (g) Example 9

of this section for an example of this method. Thus, the uncollectible amount under the modified moving average method is computed:

$$\frac{\text{(Bad debts sustained, adjusted by recoveries received, during the applicable period} - \text{Bad debts written off in same taxable year accounts receivable generated)}}{\text{Sum of accounts receivable at the beginning of each taxable year during the applicable period}} \times \text{Accounts receivable at end of current taxable year}$$

*(5) Safe harbor 5: alternative nonaccrual-experience method.* A taxpayer may use an alternative nonaccrual-experience method that clearly reflects the taxpayer's actual nonaccrual-experience, provided the taxpayer's alternative nonaccrual-experience method meets the self-test requirements described in paragraph (e)(3) of this section.

**(g) Examples.** The following examples illustrate the provisions of this section. In each example, the taxpayer uses a calendar year for Federal income tax purposes and an accrual method of accounting, does not require the payment of interest or penalties with respect to past due accounts receivable (except in the case of Example 3) and, in the case of Examples 5 through 7, selects an appropriate determination date for each taxable year. The examples are as follows:

*Example (1).* Contractual allowance or adjustment. B, a healthcare provider, performs a medical procedure on individual C, who has health insurance coverage with IC, an insurance company. B bills IC and C for $5,000, B's standard charge for this medical procedure. However, B has a contract with IC that obligates B to accept $3,500 as full payment for the medical procedure if the procedure is provided to a patient insured by IC. Under the contract, only $3,500 of the $5,000 billed by B is legally collectible from IC and C. The remaining $1,500 represents a contractual allowance or contractual adjustment. Under paragraph (c)(1)(i) of this section, the remaining $1,500 is not a contractually collectible amount for purposes of this section and B may not use a nonaccrual-experience method with respect to this portion of the receivable.

*Example (2).* Charitable or pro bono services. D, a law firm, agrees to represent individual E in a legal matter and to provide services to E on a pro bono basis. D normally charges $500 for these services. Because D provides its services to E pro bono, D's services are never billed or intended to result in revenue. Thus, under paragraph (c)(1)(i) of this section, the $500 is not a collectible amount for purposes of this section and D may not use a nonaccrual-experience method with respect to this portion of the receivable.

*Example (3).* Charging interest and/or penalties. Z has two billing methods for the amounts to be received from Z's provision of services described in paragraph (a)(1) of this section. Under one method, for amounts that are more than 90 days past due, Z charges interest at a market rate until the amounts (together with interest) are paid. Under the other billing method, Z charges no interest for amounts past due. Under paragraph (c)(1)(ii) of this section, A may not use a nonaccrual-experience method of accounting with respect to any of the amounts billed under the method that charges interest on amounts that are more than 90 days past due. Z may, however, use the nonaccrual-experience method with respect to the amounts billed under the method that does not charge interest for amounts past due.

*Example (4).* Safe harbor 1: Revenue-based moving average method.

(i) F uses the revenue-based moving average method described in paragraph (f)(1) of this section with an applicable period of six taxable years. F's total accounts receivable and bad debt experience for the 2006 taxable year and the five immediately preceding consecutive taxable years are as follows:

| Taxable year | Total accounts receivable earned during the taxable year | Bad debts adjusted for recoveries |
|---|---|---|
| 2001 | $ 40,000 | $ 5,700 |
| 2002 | 40,000 | 7,200 |
| 2003 | 40,000 | 11,000 |
| 2004 | 60,000 | 10,200 |
| 2005 | 70,000 | 14,000 |
| 2006 | 80,000 | 16,800 |
| Total | $330,000 | $64,900 |

(ii) F's revenue-based moving average percentage is 19.67% ($64,900/$330,000). If $49,300 of accounts receivable remains outstanding as of the close of that taxable year (2006), F's uncollectible amount using the revenue-based moving average safe harbor method is computed by multiplying $49,300 by the revenue-based moving average percentage of 19.67%, or $9,697. Thus, F may exclude $9,697 from gross income for 2006.

*Example (5).* Safe harbor 2: Actual experience method. (i) G is eligible to use a nonaccrual-experience method and wishes to adopt the actual experience method of paragraph (f)(2) of this section. G elects to use a three-year applicable period consisting of the current and two immediately preceding consecutive taxable years. G determines that its actual accounts receivable collection experience is as follows:

| Taxable year | Total A/R balance at beginning of taxable year | Bad debts adjusted for recoveries, related to A/R balance at beginning of taxable year |
|---|---|---|
| 2006 | $1,000,000 | $ 35,000 |
| 2007 | 760,000 | 75,000 |
| 2007 | 1,975,000 | 65,000 |
| Total | $3,735,000 | $175,000 |

(ii) G's ending A/R Balance on December 31, 2008, is $880,000. In 2008, G computes its uncollectible amount by using a three-year moving average under paragraph (f)(2) of this section. G's moving average nonaccrual-experience percentage is 4.7%, determined by dividing the sum of the amount of G's accounts receivable outstanding on January 1 of 2006, 2007, and 2008, that were determined to be bad debts (adjusted for recoveries allocable to the bad debts) on or before the corresponding determination date(s), by the sum of the amount of G's accounts receivable outstanding on January 1 of 2006, 2007, and 2008 ($175,000/$3,735,000 or 4.7%). G's uncollectible amount for 2008 is determined by multiplying this percentage by the balance of G's accounts receivable on December 31, 2008 ($880,000 x 4.7% = $41,360), and increasing this amount by 105% ($41,360 x 105% = $43,428). G may exclude $43,428 from gross income for 2008.

*Example (6).* Safe harbor 2: Single determination date (Option A). H is eligible to use a nonaccrual-experience method and wishes to adopt the actual experience method of paragraph (f)(2) of this section. H elects to use a six-year applicable period consisting of the current and five immediately preceding taxable years. H also elects to use a single determination date in accordance with paragraph (f)(2)(i) of this section. H selects December 31, its taxable year-end, as its determination date. Since H is using a single determination date from the current taxable year, its determination date for the 2001-2006 applicable period is December 31, 2006. H has a $800 charge-off in 2003 of an account receivable in the 2003 beginning accounts receivable balance. In 2005, H has a recovery of $100 which is traceable, without undue burden, to the $800 charge-off in 2003. Since the $100 recovery occurred prior to H's December 31, 2006, determination date, it reduces the amount of H's bad debts in the numerator of the formula for purposes of determining H's moving average nonaccrual-experience percentage. In addition, H must include the $100 recovery in income in 2005 (see paragraph (d)(5) of this section regarding recoveries).

*Example (7).* Safe harbor 2: Multiple determination dates (Option B). The facts are the same as in Example 6, except H elects to use multiple determination dates in accordance with paragraph (f)(2)(ii) of this section. Consequently, H's determination date is December 31, 2001, for its calculations of the portion of the numerator relating to the 2001 taxable year, December 31, 2002, for its calculations of the portion of the numerator relating to the 2002 taxable year, and so on through the final taxable year (2006), which has a determination date of December 31, 2006. Since the $100 recovery did not occur until after December 31, 2003 (the determination date for the 2003 taxable year), it does not reduce the amount of H's bad debts in the numerator of the formula for purposes of determining H's moving average nonaccrual-experience percentage. However, H still must include the $100 recovery in income in 2005 (see paragraph (d)(5) of this section regarding recoveries).

*Example (8).* Safe harbor 3: Modified Black Motor method. (i) J uses the modified Black Motor method described in paragraph (f)(3) of this section and a six-year applicable period. J's total accounts receivable and bad debt experience for the 2006 taxable year and the five immediately preceding consecutive taxable years are as follows:

| Taxable year | Accounts receivable at end of taxable year | Bad debts (adjusted for recoveries) |
|---|---|---|
| 2001 | $130,000 | $ 9,100 |
| 2002 | 140,000 | 7,000 |
| 2003 | 140,000 | 14,000 |
| 2004 | 160,000 | 14,400 |
| 2005 | 170,000 | 20,400 |
| 2006 | 180,000 | 10,800 |
| Total | $920,000 | $75,700 |

(ii) J's modified Black Motor moving average percentage is 8.228% ($75,700/$920,000). If the accounts receivable generated and written off during the current taxable year are $3,600, J's uncollectible amount is $11,210, computed by multiplying J's accounts receivable on December 31, 2006 ($180,000) by the modified Black Motor moving average percentage of 8.228% and reducing the resulting amount by $3,600 (J's accounts receivable generated and written off during the 2006 taxable year). J may exclude $11,210 from gross income for 2006.

*Example (9).* Safe harbor 4: Modified moving average method. (i) The facts are the same as in Example 8, except that the balances represent accounts receivable at the beginning of the taxable year, and J uses the modified moving average method described in paragraph (f)(4) of this section and a six-year applicable period. Furthermore, the accounts receivable that were written off in the same taxable year they were generated, adjusted for recoveries of bad debts during the period are as follows:

| Taxable Year | Accounts receivable written off in same taxable year as generated (adjusted for recoveries) |
|---|---|
| 2001 | $ 3,033 |
| 2002 | 2,333 |
| 2003 | 4,667 |
| 2004 | 4,800 |
| 2005 | 6,800 |
| 2006 | 3,600 |
| Total | $25,233 |

(ii) J's modified moving average percentage is 5.486% (($75,700-$25,233)/$920,000). J's uncollectible amount is $9,875, computed by multiplying J's accounts receivable on December 31, 2006 ($180,000) by the modified moving average percentage of 5.486%. J may exclude $9,875 from gross income for 2006.

*Example (10).* First-year self-test. Beginning in 2006, K is eligible to use a nonaccrual-experience method and wants to adopt an alternative nonaccrual-experience method under paragraph (f)(5) of this section, and consequently is subject to the safe harbor comparison method of self-testing under paragraph (e)(3) of this section. K elects to self-test against safe harbor 1 for purposes of conducting its first-year self-test. K's uncollectible amount for 2006 is $22,000. K's safe harbor uncollectible amount under safe harbor 1 is $21,000. Because K's uncollectible amount for 2006 ($22,000) is greater than the safe harbor uncollectible amount ($21,000), K's alternative nonaccrual-experience method is treated as not clearly reflecting its nonaccrual experience for 2006. Accordingly, K must adopt either another nonaccrual-experience method that clearly reflects experience (subject to the self-testing requirements of paragraph (e)(2)(ii) of this section, or a safe harbor nonaccrual-experience method described in paragraph (f)(1) (revenue-based moving average), (f)(2) (actual experience method), (f)(3) (modified Black Motor method), (f)(4) (modified moving average method) of this section, or another alternative nonaccrual-experience method under paragraph (f)(5) of this section that meets the self-testing requirements of paragraph (e)(3) of this section.

*Example (11).* Three-year self-test. The facts are the same as in Example 10, except that K's safe harbor uncollectible amount under safe harbor 1 for 2006 is also $22,000. Consequently, K meets the first-year self-test requirement and may use its alternative nonaccrual-experience method. Subsequently, K's cumulative uncollectible amount for 2007 through 2009 is $300,000. K's safe harbor uncollectible amount for 2007 through 2009 under its chosen safe harbor method for self-testing (safe harbor 1) is $295,000. Because K's cumulative uncollectible amount for the three-year test period (taxable years 2007 through 2009) is greater than its safe harbor uncollectible amount for the three-year test period ($295,000), under paragraph (e)(3)(ii)(B) of this section, the $5,000 excess of K's cumulative uncollectible amount over K's safe harbor uncollectible amount for the three-year test period must be recaptured into income in 2009 in accordance with paragraph (e)(3)(ii)(B) of this section. Since K's cumulative uncollectible amount for the three-year test period ($300,000) is less than 110% of its safe harbor uncollectible amount ($295,000 x 110% = $324,500), under paragraph (e)(3)(ii)(B) of this section, K may continue to use its alternative nonaccrual-experience method, subject to the three-year self-test requirement.

*Example (12).* Subsequent worthlessness of year-end receivable. The facts are the same as in Example 4, except that one of the accounts receivable outstanding at the end of 2002 was for $8,000, and in 2003, under section 166, the entire amount of this receivable becomes wholly worthless. Because F does not accrue as income $1,573 of this account receivable ($8,000 x .1967) under the nonaccrual-experience method in 2002, under paragraph (d)(2) of this section F may not deduct this portion of the account receivable as a bad debt deduction under section 166 in 2003. F may deduct the remaining balance of the receivable in 2003 as a bad debt deduction under section 166 ($8,000-$1,574 = $6,426).

*Example (13).* Subsequent collection of year-end receivable. The facts are the same as in Example 4. In 2007, F collects in full an account receivable of $1,700 that was outstanding at the end of 2006. Under paragraph (d)(5) of this section, F must recognize additional gross income in 2007 equal to the portion of this receivable that F excluded from gross income in the prior taxable year ($1,700 x .1967 = $334). That amount ($334) is a recovery under paragraph (d)(5) of this section.

**(h) Effective date.** This section is applicable for taxable years ending on or after August 31, 2006.

T.D. 9285, 8/31/2006.

### § 1.451-1 General rule for taxable year of inclusion.

**(a) General rule.** Gains, profits, and income are to be included in gross income for the taxable year in which they are actually or constructively received by the taxpayer unless includible for a different year in accordance with the taxpayer's method of accounting. Under an accrual method of accounting, income is includible in gross income when all the events have occurred which fix the right to receive such income and the amount thereof can be determined with reasonable accuracy. Therefore, under such a method of accounting if, in the case of compensation for services, no determination can be made as to the right to such compensation or the amount thereof until the services are completed, the amount of compensation is ordinarily income for the taxable year in which the determination can be made. Under the cash receipts and disbursements method of accounting, such an amount is includible in gross income when actually or constructively received. Where an amount of income is properly accrued on the basis of a reasonable estimate and the exact amount is subsequently determined, the difference, if any, shall be taken into account for the taxable year in which such determination is made. To the extent that income is attributable to the recovery of bad debts for accounts charged off in prior years, it is includible in the year of recovery in accordance with the taxpayer's method of accounting, regardless of the date when the amounts were charged off. For treatment of bad debts and bad debt recoveries, see sections 166 and 111 and the regulations thereunder. For rules relating to the treatment of amounts received in crop shares, see section 61 and the regulations thereunder. For the year in which a partner must include his distributive share of partnership income, see section 706(a) and paragraph (a) of § 1.706-1. If a taxpayer ascertains that an item should have been included in gross income in a prior taxable year, he should, if within the period of limitation, file an amended return and pay any additional tax due. Similarly, if a taxpayer ascertains that an item was improperly included in gross income in a prior taxable year, he should, if within the period of limitation, file claim for credit or refund of any overpayment of tax arising therefrom.

**(b) Special rule in case of death.** *(1)* A taxpayer's taxable year ends on the date of his death. See section 443(a)(2) and paragraph (a)(2) of § 1.443-1. In computing taxable income for such year, there shall be included only amounts properly includible under the method of accounting used by the taxpayer. However, if the taxpayer used an accrual method of accounting, amounts accrued only by reason of his death shall not be included in computing taxable income for such year. If the taxpayer uses no regular accounting method, only amounts actually or constructively received during such year shall be included. (For rules relating to the inclusion of partnership income in the return of a decedent partner, see subchapter K, chapter 1 of the Code, and the regulations thereunder.)

*(2)* If the decedent owned an installment obligation the income from which was taxable to him under section 453, no income is required to be reported in the return of the decedent by reason of the transmission at death of such obligation. See section 453(d)(3). For the treatment of installment obligations acquired by the decedent's estate or by any person by bequest, devise, or inheritance from the decedent, see section 691(a)(4) and the regulations thereunder.

**(c) Special rule for employee tips.** Tips reported by an employee to his employer in a written statement furnished to the employer pursuant to section 6053(a) shall be included in gross income of the employee for the taxable year in which the written statement is furnished the employer. For provisions relating to the reporting of tips by an employee to his employer, see section 6053 and § 31.6053-1 of this chapter (Employment Tax Regulations).

**(d) Special rule for ratable inclusion of original issue discount.** For ratable inclusion of original issue discount in respect of certain corporate obligations issued after May 27, 1969, see section 1232(a)(3).

**(e) Special rule for inclusion of qualified tax refund effected by allocation.** For rules relating to the inclusion in income of an amount paid by a taxpayer in respect of his liability for a qualified State individual income tax and allocated or reallocated in such a manner as to apply it toward the taxpayer's liability for the Federal income tax, see paragraph (f)(1) of § 301.6361-1 of this chapter (Regulations on Procedure and Administration).

**(f) Timing of income from notional principal contracts.** For the timing of income with respect to notional principal contracts, see § 1.446-3.

**(g) Timing of income from section 467 rental agreements.** For the timing of income with respect to section 467 rental agreements, see section 467 and the regulations thereunder.

---

T.D. 6282, 12/24/57, amend T.D. 7001, 1/17/69, T.D. 7154, 12/27/71, T.D. 7577, 12/19/78, T.D. 8491, 10/8/93, T.D. 8820, 5/17/99.

---

PAR. 9. In paragraph (d) of § 1.451-1 the heading and text are revised to read as follows:

**Proposed § 1.451-1 General rule for taxable year of inclusion.** [*For Preamble, see ¶ 151,065*]

• ***Caution:*** Prop reg § 1.482-2 was finalized by T.D. 8204, 5/20/88. Prop regs §§ 1.163-7, 1.446-2, 1.483-1 through -5, 1.1001-1, 1.1012-1, 1.1271 through -3, 1.1272-1, 1.1273-1, 1.1273-2, 1.1274-1 throught -7, 1.1274A-1, 1.1275-1 through -3, and 1.1275-5 were withdrawn by the Treasury on 12/22/92, 57 Fed. Reg. 67050. Prop reg § 1.1275-4 was superseded by the Treasury on 12/16/94, Fed. Reg. 59, 64884, which was finalized by T.D. 8674, 6/11/96.

* * * * *

**(d) Special rule for inclusion of original issue discount.** For inclusion of original issue discount in respect of certain debt instruments issued after May 27, 1969, see section 1272.

* * * * *

### § 1.451-2 Constructive receipt of income.

**(a) General rule.** Income although not actually reduced to a taxpayer's possession is constructively received by him in the taxable year during which it is credited to his account, set apart for him, or otherwise made available so that he may draw upon it at any time, or so that he could have drawn upon it during the taxable year if notice of intention to withdraw had been given. However, income is not constructively received if the taxpayer's control of its receipt is subject to substantial limitations or restrictions. Thus, if a corporation credits its employees with bonus stock, but the stock is not available to such employees until some future date, the mere crediting on the books of the corporation does not constitute receipt. In the case of interest, dividends, or other earnings (whether or not credited) payable in respect of any deposit or account in a bank, building and loan association, savings and loan association, or similar institution, the following are not substantial limitations or restrictions on the taxpayer's control over the receipt of such earnings:

*(1)* A requirement that the deposit or account, and the earnings thereon, must be withdrawn in multiples of even amounts;

*(2)* The fact that the taxpayer would, by withdrawing the earnings during the taxable year, receive earnings that are not substantially less in comparison with the earnings for the corresponding period to which the taxpayer would be entitled had he left the account on deposit until a later date [for example, if an amount equal to three months' interest must be forfeited upon withdrawal or redemption before maturity of a one year or less certificate of deposit, time deposit, bonus plan, or other deposit arrangement then the earnings payable on premature withdrawal or redemption would be substantially less when compared with the earnings available at maturity);

*(3)* A requirement that the earnings may be withdrawn only upon a withdrawal of all or part of the deposit or account. However, the mere fact that such institutions may pay earnings on withdrawals, total or partial, made during the last three business days of any calendar month ending a regular quarterly or semiannual earnings period at the applicable rate calculated to the end of such calendar month shall not constitute constructive receipt of income by any depositor or account holder in any such institution who has not made a withdrawal during such period;

*(4)* A requirement that a notice of intention to withdraw must be given in advance of the withdrawal. In any case when the rate of earnings payable in respect of such a deposit or account depends on the amount of notice of intention to withdraw that is given, earnings at the maximum rate are constructively received during the taxable year regardless of how long the deposit or account was held during the year or whether, in fact, any notice of intention to withdraw is given during the year. However, if in the taxable year of withdrawal the depositor or account holder receives a lower rate of earnings because he failed to give the required notice of intention to withdraw, he shall be allowed an ordinary loss in such taxable year in an amount equal to the difference between the amount of earnings previously included in gross income and the amount of earnings actually received. See section 165 and the regulations thereunder.

**(b) Examples of constructive receipt.** Amounts payable with respect to interest coupons which have matured and are payable but which have not been cashed are constructively received in the taxable year during which the coupons mature, unless it can be shown that there are no funds available for payment of the interest during such year. Dividends on corporate stock are constructively received when unqualifiedly made subject to the demand of the shareholder. However, if a dividend is declared payable on December 31 and the corporation followed its usual practice of paying the dividends by checks mailed so that the shareholders would not receive them until January of the following year, such dividends are not considered to have been constructively received in December. Generally, the amount of dividends or interest credited on savings bank deposits or to shareholders of organizations such as building and loan associations or co-operative banks is income to the depositors or shareholders for the taxable year when credited. However, if any portion of such dividends or interest is not subject to withdrawal at the time credited, such portion is not constructively received and does not constitute income to the depositor or shareholder until the taxable year in which the portion first may be withdrawn. Accordingly, if, under a bonus or forfeiture plan, a portion of the dividends or interest is accumulated and may not be withdrawn until the maturity of the plan, the crediting of such portion to the account of the shareholder or depositor does not constitute constructive receipt. In this case, such credited portion is income to the depositor or shareholder in the year in which the plan matures. However, in the case of certain deposits made after December 31, 1970, in banks, domestic building and loan associations, and similar financial institutions, the ratable inclusion rules of section 1232(a)(3) apply. See § 1.1232-3A. Accrued interest on unwithdrawn insurance policy dividends is gross income to the taxpayer for the first taxable year during which such interest may be withdrawn by him.

---

T.D. 6282, 12/24/57, amend T.D. 6723, 4/20/64, T.D. 7154, 12/27/71, T.D. 7663, 12/21/79.

---

PAR. 10. Paragraph (b) of § 1.451-2 is amended by removing the eighth and ninth sentences and adding in their place new sentences to read as follows:

**Proposed § 1.451-2 Constructive receipt of income.** [*For Preamble, see ¶ 151,065*]

• ***Caution:*** Prop reg § 1.482-2 was finalized by T.D. 8204, 5/20/88. Prop regs §§ 1.163-7, 1.446-2, 1.483-1 through -5, 1.1001-1, 1.1012-1, 1.1271 through -3, 1.1272-1, 1.1273-1, 1.1273-2, 1.1274-1 throught -7, 1.1274A-1, 1.1275-1 through -3, and 1.1275-5 were withdrawn by the Treasury on 12/22/92, 57 Fed. Reg. 67050. Prop reg § 1.1275-4 was superseded by the Treasury on 12/16/94, Fed. Reg. 59, 64884, which was finalized by T.D. 8674, 6/11/96.

* * * * *

**(b) Examples of constructive receipt.** * * * However, in the case of certain deposits made after December 31, 1970, in banks, domestic building and loan associations, and similar financial institutions, the inclusion rules of section 1272 apply. See §§ 1.1232-3A and 1.1272-1. * * *

**§ 1.451-4 Accounting for redemption of trading stamps and coupons.**

**(a) In general.** *(1) Subtraction from receipts.* If an accrual method taxpayer issues trading stamps or premium coupons with sales, or an accrual method taxpayer is engaged in the business of selling trading stamps or premium coupons, and such stamps or coupons are redeemable by such taxpayer in merchandise, cash, or other property, the taxpayer should, in computing the income from such sales, subtract from gross receipts with respect to sales of such stamps or coupons (or from gross receipts with respect to sales with which trading stamps or coupons are issued) an amount equal to—

(i) The cost to the taxpayer of merchandise, cash, and other property used for redemptions in the taxable year.

(ii) Plus the net addition to the provision for future redemptions during the taxable year (or less the net subtraction from the provision for future redemptions during the taxable year).

*(2) Trading stamp companies.* For purposes of this section, a taxpayer will be considered as being in the business of selling trading stamps or premium coupons if—

(i) The trading stamps or premium coupons sold by him are issued by purchasers to promote the sale of their merchandise or services.

(ii) The principal activity of the trade or business is the sale of such stamps or coupons.

(iii) Such stamps or coupons are redeemable by the taxpayer for a period of at least 1 year from the date of sale, and

(iv) Based on his overall experience, it is estimated that not more than two-thirds of the stamps or coupons sold which it is estimated, pursuant to paragraph (c) of this section, will be ultimately redeemed, will be redeemed within 6 months of the date of sale.

**(b) Computation of the net addition to or subtraction from the provision for future redemptions.** *(1) Determination of the provision for future redemptions.* (i) The provision for future redemptions as of the end of a taxable year is computed by multiplying "estimated future redemptions" (as defined in subdivision (ii) of this subparagraph) by the estimated average cost of redeeming each trading stamp or coupon (computed in accordance with subdivision (iii) of this subparagraph).

(ii) For purposes of this section, the term "estimated future redemptions" as of the end of a taxable year means the number of trading stamps or coupons outstanding as of the end of such year that it is reasonably estimated will ultimately be presented for redemption. Such estimate shall be determined in accordance with the rules contained in paragraph (c) of this section.

(iii) For purposes of this section, the estimated average cost of redeeming each trading stamp or coupon shall be computed by including only the costs to the taxpayer of acquiring the merchandise, cash, or other property needed to redeem such stamps or coupons. The term "the costs to the taxpayer of acquiring the merchandise, cash, or other property needed to redeem such stamps or coupons" includes only the price charged by the seller (less trade or other discounts, except strictly cash discounts approximating a fair interest rate, which may be deducted or not at the option of the taxpayer provided a consistent course is followed) plus transportation or other necessary charges in acquiring possession of the goods. Items such as the costs of advertising, catalogs, operating redemption centers, transporting merchandise or other property from a central warehouse to a branch warehouse (or from a warehouse to a redemption center), and storing the merchandise or other property used to redeem stamps or coupons should not be included in costs of redeeming stamps or premium coupons, but rather should be accounted for in accordance with the provisions of sections 162 and 263.

*(2) Changes in provision for future redemptions.* For purposes of this section, a "net addition to" or "net subtraction from" the provision for future redemptions for a taxable year is computed as follows:

(i) Carry over the provision for future redemptions (if any) as of the end of the preceding taxable year,

(ii) Compute the provision for future redemptions as of the end of the taxable year in accordance with subparagraph (1) of this paragraph, and

(iii) If the amount referred to in subdivision (ii) of this subparagraph exceeds the amount referred to in subdivision (i) of this subparagraph, such excess is the net addition to the provision for future redemptions for the taxable year. On the other hand, if the amount referred to in such subdivision (i) exceeds the amount referred to in such subdivision (ii), such excess is the net subtraction from the provision for future redemptions for the taxable year.

*(3) Example.* The provisions of this paragraph and paragraph (a)(1) of this section may be illustrated by the following example:

*Example.* (a) X Company, a calendar year accrual method taxpayer, is engaged in the business of selling trading stamps to merchants. In 1971, its first year of operation, X sells 10 million stamps at $5 per 1,000; it redeems 3 million stamps for merchandise and cash of an average value of $3 per 1,000 stamps. At the end of 1971 it is estimated (pursuant to paragraph (c) of this section) that a total of 9 million stamps of the 10 million stamps issued in 1971 will eventually be presented for redemption. At this time it is estimated that the average cost of redeeming stamps (as described in subparagraph (1)(iii) of this paragraph) would continue to be $3 per 1,000 stamps. Under these circumstances, X computes its gross income from sales of trading stamps as follows:

| | | |
|---|---|---|
| Gross receipts from sales (10 million stamps at $5 per 1,000) | | $50,000 |
| Less: | | |
| Cost of actual redemptions (3 million stamps at $3 per 1,000) | $9,000 | |
| Provision for future redemptions on December 31, 1971 (9 million stamps - 3 million stamps × $3 per 1,000) | 18,000 | |
| | | 27,000 |
| 1971 gross income from sales of stamps | | 23,000 |

(b) In 1972, X also sells 10 million stamps at $5 per 1,000 stamps. During 1972 X redeems 7 million stamps at an average cost of $3.01 per 1,000 stamps. At the end of 1972 it is determined that the estimated future redemptions (within the meaning of subparagraph (1)(ii) of this paragraph) is 8 million. It is further determined that the estimated average cost of redeeming stamps would continue to be $3.01 per 1,000 stamps. X thus computes its gross income from sales of trading stamps for 1972 a follows:

| | | |
|---|---|---|
| Gross receipts from sales (10 million stamps at $5 per 1,000) | | $50,000 |
| Less: | | |
| Cost of actual redemption (7 million stamps at $3.01 per 1,000) | $21,070 | |
| Plus: | | |
| Provision for future redemptions on Dec. 31, 1972 (8 million stamps at $3.01 per 1,000) | $24,080 | |
| Minus: | | |
| Provision for future redemptions on Dec. 31, 1971 | 18,000 | |

| | | |
|---|---|---|
| Addition to provision for future redemptions | 6,080 | |
| Total cost of redemptions | | 27,150 |
| 1972 Gross income from sales of stamps | | 22,850 |

**(c) Estimated future redemptions.** *(1) In general.* A taxpayer may use any method of determining the estimated future redemptions as of the end of a year so long as—

(i) Such method results in a reasonably accurate estimate of the stamps or coupons outstanding at the end of such year that will ultimately be presented for redemption,

(ii) Such method is used consistently, and

(iii) Such taxpayer complies with the requirements of this paragraph and paragraphs (d) and (e) of this section.

*(2) Utilization of prior redemption experience.* Normally, the estimated future redemptions of a taxpayer shall be determined on the basis of such taxpayer's prior redemption experience. However, if the taxpayer does not have sufficient redemption experience to make a reasonable determination of his "estimated future redemptions," or if because of a change in his mode of operation or other relevant factors the determination cannot reasonably be made completely on the basis of the taxpayer's own experience, the experiences of similarly situated taxpayers may be used to establish an experience factor.

*(3) One method of determining estimated future redemptions.* One permissible method of determining the estimated future redemptions as of the end of the current taxable year is as follows:

(i) Estimate for each preceding taxable year and the current taxable year the number of trading stamps or coupons issued for each such year which will ultimately be presented for redemption.

(ii) Determine the sum of the estimates under subdivision (i) of this subparagraph for each taxable year prior to and including the current taxable year.

(iii) The difference between the sum determined under subdivision (ii) of this subparagraph and the total number of trading stamps or coupons which have already been presented for redemption is the estimated future redemptions as of the end of the current taxable year.

*(4) Determination of an "estimated redemption percentage."* For purposes of applying subparagraph (3)(i) of this paragraph, one permissible method of estimating the number of trading stamps or coupons issued for a taxable year that will ultimately be presented for redemption is to multiply such number of stamps issued for such year by an "estimated redemption percentage." For purposes of this section the term "estimated redemption percentage" for a taxable year means a fraction, the numerator of which is the number of trading stamps or coupons issued during a taxable year that it is reasonably estimated will ultimately be redeemed, and the denominator of which is the number of trading stamps or coupons issued during such year. Consequently, the product of such percentage and the number of stamps issued for such year equals the number of trading stamps or coupons issued for such year that it is estimated will ultimately be redeemed.

*(5) Five-year rule.* (i) One permissible method of determining the "estimated redemption percentage" for a taxable year is to—

(a) Determine the percentage which the total number of stamps or coupons redeemed in the taxable year and the 4 preceding taxable years is of the total number of stamps or coupons issued or sold in such 5 years; and

(b) Multiply such percentage by an appropriate growth factor as determined pursuant to guidelines published by the Commissioner.

(ii) If a taxpayer uses the method described in subdivision (i) of this subparagraph for a taxable year, it will normally be presumed that such taxpayer's "estimated redemption percentage" is reasonably accurate.

*(6) Other methods of determining estimated future redemptions.* (i) If a taxpayer uses a method of determining his "estimated future redemptions" (other than a method which applies the 5-year rule as described in subparagraph (5)(i) of this paragraph) such as a probability sampling technique, the appropriateness of the method (including the appropriateness of the sampling technique, if any) and the accuracy and reliability of the results obtained must, if requested, be demonstrated to the satisfaction of the district director.

(ii) No inference shall be drawn from subdivision (i) of this subparagraph that the use of any method to which such subdivision applies is less acceptable than the method described in subparagraph (5)(i) of this paragraph. Therefore, certain probability sampling techniques used in determining estimated future redemptions may result in reasonably accurate and reliable estimates. Such a sampling technique will be considered appropriate if the sample is—

(a) Taken in accordance with sound statistical sampling principles,

(b) In accordance with such principles, sufficiently broad to produce a reasonably accurate result, and

(c) Taken with sufficient frequency as to produce a reasonably accurate result.

In addition, if the sampling technique is appropriate, the results obtained therefrom in determining estimated future redemptions will be considered accurate and reliable if the evaluation of such results is consistent with sound statistical principles. Ordinarily, samplings and recomputations of the estimated future redemptions will be required annually. However, the facts and circumstances in a particular case may justify such a recomputation being taken less frequently than annually. In addition, the Commissioner may prescribe procedures indicating that samples made to update the results of a sample of stamps redeemed in a prior year need not be the same size as the stamps of such prior year.

**(d) Consistency with financial reporting.** *(1) Estimated future redemptions.* For taxable years beginning after August 22, 1972, the estimated future redemptions must be no greater than the estimate that the taxpayer uses for purposes of all reports (including consolidated financial statements) to shareholders, partners, beneficiaries, other proprietors, and for credit purposes.

*(2) Average cost of redeeming stamps.* For taxable years beginning after August 22, 1972, the estimated average cost of redeeming each stamp or coupon must be no greater than the average cost of redeeming each stamp or coupon (computed in accordance with paragraph (b)(1)(iii) of this section) that the taxpayer uses for purposes of all reports (including consolidated financial statements) to shareholders, partners, beneficiaries, other proprietors, and for credit purposes.

**(e) Information to be furnished with return.** *(1) In general.* For taxable years beginning after August 22, 1972, a taxpayer described in paragraph (a) of this section who uses a method of determining the "estimated future redemptions" other than that described in paragraph (c)(5)(i) of this section shall file a statement with his return showing such information as is necessary to establish the correctness of the amount subtracted from gross receipts in the taxable year.

*(2) Taxpayers using the 5-year rule.* If a taxpayer uses the method of determining estimated future redemptions described in paragraph (c)(5)(i) of this section, he shall file a statement with his return showing, with respect to the taxable year and the 4 preceding taxable years—

(i) The total number of stamps or coupons issued or sold during each year, and

(ii) The total number of stamps or coupons redeemed in each such year.

*(3) Trading stamp companies.* In addition to the information required by subparagraph (1) or (2) of this paragraph, a taxpayer engaged in the trade or business of selling trading stamps or premium coupons shall include with the statement described in subparagraph (1) or (2) of this paragraph such information as may be necessary to satisfy the requirements of paragraph (a)(2)(iv) of this section.

T.D. 6282, 12/24/57, amend T.D. 7201, 8/22/72.

### § 1.451-5 Advance payments for goods and long-term contracts.

**(a) Advance payment defined.** *(1)* For purposes of this section, the term "advance payment" means any amount which is received in a taxable year by a taxpayer using an accrual method of accounting for purchases and sales or a long-term contract method of accounting (described in § 1.451-3), pursuant to, and to be applied against, an agreement:

(i) For the sale or other disposition in a future taxable year of goods held by the taxpayer primarily for sale to customers in the ordinary course of his trade or business, or

(ii) For the building, installing, constructing or manufacturing by the taxpayer of items where the agreement is not completed within such taxable year.

*(2)* For purposes of subparagraph (1) of this paragraph:

(i) The term "agreement" includes (a) a gift certificate that can be redeemed for goods, and (b) an agreement which obligates a taxpayer to perform activities described in subparagraph (1)(i) or (ii) of this paragraph and which also contains an obligation to perform services that are to be performed as an integral part of such activities; and

(ii) Amounts due and payable are considered "received."

*(3)* If a taxpayer (described in subparagraph (1) of this paragraph) receives an amount pursuant to, and to be applied against, an agreement that not only obligates the taxpayer to perform the activities described in subparagraph (1)(i) and (ii) of this paragraph, but also obligates the taxpayer to perform services that are not to be performed as an integral part of such activities, such amount will be treated as an "advance payment" (as defined in subparagraph (1) of this paragraph) only to the extent such amount is properly allocable to the obligation to perform the activities described in subparagraph (1) (i) and (ii) of this paragraph. The portion of the amount not so allocable will not be considered an "advance payment" to which this section applies. If, however, the amount not so allocable is less than 5 percent of the total contract price, such amount will be treated as so allocable except that such treatment can not result in delaying the time at which the taxpayer would otherwise accrue the amounts attributable to the activities described in subparagraph (1) (i) and (ii) of this paragraph.

**(b) Taxable year of inclusion.** *(1) In general.* Advance payments must be included in income either—

(i) In the taxable year of receipt; or

(ii) Except as provided in paragraph (c) of this section.

(a) In the taxable year in which properly accruable under the taxpayer's method of accounting for tax purposes if such method results in including advance payments in gross receipts no later than the time such advance payments are included in gross receipts for purposes of all of his reports (including consolidated financial statements) to shareholders, partners, beneficiaries, other proprietors, and for credit purposes, or

(b) If the taxpayer's method of accounting for purposes of such reports results in advance payments (or any portion of such payments) being included in gross receipts earlier than for tax purposes, in the taxable year in which includible in gross receipts pursuant to his method of accounting for purposes of such reports.

*(2) Examples.* This paragraph may be illustrated by the following examples:

*Example (1).* S, a retailer who uses for tax purposes and for purposes of the reports referred to in subparagraph (1)(ii)(a) of this paragraph, an accrual method of accounting under which it accounts for its sales of goods when the goods are shipped, receives advance payments for such goods. Such advance payments must be included in gross receipts for tax purposes either in the taxable year the payments are received or in the taxable year such goods are shipped (except as provided in paragraph (c) of this section).

*Example (2).* T, a manufacturer of household furniture, is a calendar year taxpayer who uses an accrual method of accounting pursuant to which income is accrued when furniture is shipped for purposes of its financial reports (referred to in subparagraph (1)(ii)(a) of this paragraph) and an accrual method of accounting pursuant to which the income is accrued when furniture is delivered and accepted for tax purposes. See § 1.446-1(c)(1)(ii). In 1974, T receives an advance payment of $8,000 from X with respect to an order of furniture to be manufactured for X for a total price of $20,000. The furniture is shipped to X in December 1974, but it is not delivered to and accepted by X until January 1975. As a result of this contract, T must include the entire advance payment in its gross income for tax purposes in 1974 pursuant to subparagraph (1)(ii)(b) of this paragraph. T must include the remaining $12,000 of the gross contract price in its gross income in 1975 for tax purposes.

*(3) Long-term contracts.* In the case of a taxpayer, accounting for advance payments for tax purposes pursuant to a long-term contract method of accounting under § 1.460-4, or of a taxpayer accounting for advance payments with respect to a long-term contract pursuant to an accrual method of accounting referred to in the succeeding sentence, advance payments shall be included in income in the taxable year in which properly included in gross receipts pursuant to such method of accounting (without regard to the financial reporting requirement contained in subparagraph (1)(ii)(a) or (b) of this paragraph). An accrual method of accounting to which the preceding sentence applies shall consist of any method of accounting under which the income is accrued when, and costs are accumulated until, the subject matter of the contract (or, if the subject matter of the contract consists of more than one item, an item) is shipped, delivered, or accepted.

*(4) Installment method.* The financial reporting requirement of subparagraph (1)(ii)(a) or (b) of this paragraph shall not be construed to prevent the use of the installment method under section 453. See § 1.446-1(c)(1)(ii).

**(c) Exemption for inventoriable goods.** *(1)* (i) If a taxpayer receives an advance payment in a taxable year with respect to an agreement for the sale of goods properly includible in his inventory or with respect to an agreement (such as a gift certificate) which can be satisfied with goods or a type of goods that cannot be identified in such taxable year, and on the last day of such taxable year the taxpayer—

(a) Is accounting for advance payments pursuant to a method described in paragraph (b)(1)(ii) of this section for tax purposes.

(b) Has received "substantial advance payments" (as defined in subparagraph (3) of this paragraph) with respect to such agreement, and

(c) Has on hand (or available to him in such year through his normal source of supply) goods of substantially similar kind and in sufficient quantity to satisfy the agreement in such year,

then all advance payments received with respect to such agreement by the last day of the second taxable year following the year in which such substantial advance payments are received, and not previously included in income in accordance with the taxpayer's accrual method of accounting, must be included in income in such second taxable year.

(ii) If advance payments are required to be included in income in a taxable year solely by reason of subdivision (i) of this subparagraph, the taxpayer must take into account in such taxable year the costs and expenditures included in inventory at the end of such year with respect to such goods (or substantially similar goods) on hand or, if no such goods are on hand by the last day of such second taxable year, the estimated cost of goods necessary to satisfy the agreement.

(iii) Subdivision (ii) of this subparagraph does not apply if the goods or type of goods with respect to which the advance payment is received are not identifiable in the year the advance payments are required to be included in income by reason of subdivision (i) of this subparagraph (for example, where an amount is received for a gift certificate).

*(2)* If subparagraph (1)(i) of this paragraph is applicable to advance payments received with respect to an agreement, any advance payments received with respect to such agreement subsequent to such second taxable year must be included in gross income in the taxable year of receipt. To the extent estimated costs of goods are taken into account in a taxable year pursuant to subparagraph (1)(ii) of this paragraph, such costs may not again be taken into account in another year. In addition, any variance between the costs or estimated costs taken into account pursuant to subparagraph (1)(ii) of this paragraph and the costs actually incurred in fulfilling the taxpayer's obligations under the agreement must be taken into account as an adjustment to the cost of goods sold in the year the taxpayer completes his obligations under such agreement.

*(3)* For purposes of subparagraph (1) of this paragraph, a taxpayer will be considered to have received "substantial advance payments" with respect to an agreement by the last day of a taxable year if the advance payments received with respect to such agreement during such taxable year plus the advance payments received prior to such taxable year pursuant to such agreement, equal or exceed the total costs and expenditures reasonably estimated as includible in inventory with respect to such agreement. Advance payments received in a taxable year with respect to an agreement (such as a gift certificate) under which the goods or type of goods to be sold are not identifiable in such year shall be treated as "substantial advance payments" when received.

*(4)* The application of this paragraph is illustrated by the following example:

*Example.* In 1971, X, a calendar year accrual method taxpayer, enters into a contract for the sale of goods (properly includible in X's inventory) with a total contract price of $100. X estimates that his total inventoriable costs and expenditures for the goods will be $50. X receives the following advance payments with respect to the contract:

| | |
|---|---|
| 1971 | $35 |
| 1972 | 20 |
| 1973 | 15 |
| 1974 | 10 |
| 1975 | 10 |
| 1976 | 10 |

The goods are delivered pursuant to the customer's request in 1977. X's closing inventory for 1972 of the type of goods involved in the contract is sufficient to satisfy the contract. Since advance payments received by the end of 1972 exceed the inventoriable costs X estimates that he will incur, such payments constitute "substantial advance payments." Accordingly, all payments received by the end of 1974, the end of the second taxable year following the taxable year during which "substantial advance payments" are received, are includible in gross income for 1974. Therefore, for taxable year 1974 X must include $80 in his gross income. X must include in his cost of goods sold for 1974 the cost of such goods (or similar goods) on hand or, if no such goods are on hand, the estimated inventoriable costs necessary to satisfy the contract. Since no further deferral is allowable for such contract, X must include in his gross income for the remaining years of the contract, the advance payment received each year. Any variance between estimated costs and the costs actually incurred in fulfilling the contract is to be taken into account in 1977, when the goods are delivered. See paragraph (c)(2) of this section.

**(d) Information schedule.** If a taxpayer accounts for advance payments pursuant to paragraph (b)(1)(ii) of this section, he must attach to his income tax return for each taxable year to which such provision applies an annual information schedule reflecting the total amount of advance payments received in the taxable year, the total amount of advance payments received in prior taxable years which has not been included in gross income before the current taxable year, and the total amount of such payments received in prior taxable years which has been included in gross income for the current taxable year.

**(e) Adoption of method.** *(1)* For taxable years ending on or after December 31, 1969, and before January 1, 1971, a taxpayer (even if he has already filed an income tax return for a taxable year ending within such period) may secure the consent of the Commissioner to change his method of accounting for such year to a method prescribed in paragraph (b)(1)(ii) of this section in the manner prescribed in section 446 and the regulations thereunder, if an application to secure such consent is filed on Form 3115 within 180 days after March 23, 1971.

*(2)* A taxpayer who is already reporting his income in accordance with a method prescribed in paragraph (b)(1)(ii)(a) of this section need not secure the consent of the Commissioner to continue to utilize this method. However, such a taxpayer, for all taxable years ending after March 23, 1971,

must comply with the requirements of paragraphs (b)(1)(ii)(a) (including the financial reporting requirement) and (d) (relating to an annual information schedule) of this section.

**(f) Cessation of taxpayer's liability.** If a taxpayer has adopted a method prescribed in paragraph (b)(1)(ii) of this section, and if in a taxable year the taxpayer dies, ceases to exist in a transaction other than one to which section 381(a) applies, or his liability under the agreement otherwise ends, then so much of the advance payment as was not includible in his gross income in preceding taxable years shall be included in his gross income for such taxable year.

**(g) Special rule for certain transactions concerning natural resources.** A transaction which is treated as creating a mortgage loan pursuant to section 636 and the regulations thereunder rather than as a sale shall not be considered a "sale or other disposition" within the meaning of paragraph (a)(1) of this section. Consequently, any payment received pursuant to such a transaction, which payment would otherwise qualify as an "advance payment", will not be treated as an "advance payment" for purposes of this section.

T.D. 7103, 3/23/71, amend T.D. 7397, 1/14/76, T.D. 8067, 12/30/85, T.D. 8929, 1/10/2001.

## § 1.451-6 Election to include crop insurance proceeds in gross income in the taxable year following the taxable year of destruction or damage.

**(a) In general.** *(1)* For taxable years ending after December 30, 1969, a taxpayer reporting gross income on the cash receipts and disbursements method of accounting may elect to include insurance proceeds received as a result of the destruction of, or damage to, crops in gross income for the taxable year following the taxable year of the destruction or damage, if the taxpayer establishes that, under the taxpayer's normal business practice, the income from those crops would have been included in gross income for any taxable year following the taxable year of the destruction or damage. However, if the taxpayer receives the insurance proceeds in the taxable year following the taxable year of the destruction or damage, the taxpayer shall include the proceeds in gross income for the taxable year of receipt without having to make an election under section 451(d) and this section. For the purposes of this section only, federal payments received as a result of destruction or damage to crops caused by drought, flood, or any other natural disaster, or the inability to plant crops because of such a natural disaster, shall be treated as insurance proceeds received as a result of destruction or damage to crops. The preceding sentence shall apply to payments that are received by the taxpayer after December 31, 1973.

*(2)* In the case of a taxpayer who receives insurance proceeds as a result of the destruction of, or damage to, two or more specific crops, if such proceeds may, under section 451(d) and this section, be included in gross income for the taxable year following the taxable year of such destruction or damage, and if such taxpayer makes an election under section 451(d) and this section with respect to any portion of such proceeds, then such election will be deemed to cover all of such proceeds which are attributable to crops representing a single trade or business under section 446(d). A separate election must be made with respect to insurance proceeds attributable to each crop which represents a separate trade or business under section 446(d).

**(b)** *(1) Time and manner of making election.* The election to include in gross income insurance proceeds received as a result of destruction of, or damage to, the taxpayer's crops in the taxable year following the taxable year of such destruction or damage shall be made by means of a statement attached to the taxpayer's return (or an amended return) for the taxable year of destruction or damage. The statement shall include the name and address of the taxpayer (or his duly authorized representative), and shall set forth the following information:

(i) A declaration that the taxpayer is making an election under section 451(d) and this section;

(ii) Identification of the specific crop or crops destroyed or damaged;

(iii) A declaration that under the taxpayer's normal business practice the income derived from the crops which were destroyed or damaged would have been included in this gross income for a taxable year following the taxable year of such destruction or damage;

(iv) The cause of destruction or damage of crops and the date or dates on which such destruction or damage occurred;

(v).The total amount of payments received from insurance carriers, itemized with respect to each specific crop and with respect to the date each payment was received;

(vi) The name(s) of the insurance carrier or carriers from whom payments were received.

*(2) Scope of election.* Once made, an election under section 451(d) is binding for the taxable year for which made unless the district director consents to a revocation of such election. Requests for consent to revoke an election under section 451(d) shall be made by means of a letter to the district director for the district in which the taxpayer is required to file his return, setting forth the taxpayer's name, address, and identification number, the year for which it is desired to revoke the election, and the reasons therefor.

T.D. 7097, 3/17/71, amend T.D. 7526, 12/23/77, T.D. 8429, 8/25/92.

## § 1.451-7 Election relating to livestock sold on account of drought.

***Caution:*** The Treasury has not yet amended Reg § 1.451-7 to reflect changes made by P.L. 108-357; P.L. 105-34.

**(a) In general.** Section 451(e) provides that for taxable years beginning after December 31, 1975, a taxpayer whose principal trade or business is farming (within the meaning of § 6420(c)(3)) and who reports taxable income on the cash receipts and disbursements method of accounting may elect to defer for one year a certain portion of income. The income which may be deferred is the amount of gain realized during the taxable year from the sale or exchange of that number of livestock sold or exchanged solely on account of a drought which caused an area to be designated as eligible for assistance by the Federal Government (regardless of whether the designation is made by the President or by an agency or department of the Federal Government). That number is equal to the excess of the number of livestock sold or exchanged over the number which would have been sold or exchanged had the taxpayer followed its usual business practices in the absence of such drought. For example, if in the past it has been a taxpayer's practice to sell or exchange annually 400 head of beef cattle but due to qualifying drought conditions 550 head were sold in a given taxable year, only income from the sale of 150 head may qualify for deferral under this section. The election is not available with respect to livestock described in section 1231(b)(3) (relating to cattle, horses (and other livestock) held by the taxpayer for 24 months (12 months) and used for draft, breeding, dairy, or sporting purposes).

**(b) Usual business practice.** The determination of the number of animals which a taxpayer would have sold if it had followed its usual business practice in the absence of drought will be made in light of all the facts and circumstances. In the case of taxpayers who have not established a usual business practice, reliance will be placed upon the usual business practice of similarly situated taxpayers in the same general region as the taxpayer.

**(c) Special rules.** *(1) Connection with drought area.* To qualify under section 451(e) and this section, the livestock need not be raised, and the sale or exchange need not take place, in a drought area. However, the sale or exchange of the livestock must occur solely on account of drought conditions, the existence of which affected the water, grazing, or other requirements of the livestock so as to necessitate their sale or exchange.

*(2) Sale prior to designation of area as eligible for Federal assistance.* The provisions of this section will apply regardless of whether all or a portion of the excess number of animals were sold or exchanged before an area becomes eligible for Federal assistance, so long as the drought which caused such dispositions also caused the area to be designated as eligible for Federal assistance.

**(d) Classifications of livestock with respect to which the election may be made.** The election to have the provisions of section 451(e) apply must be made separately for each broad generic classification of animals (e.g., hogs, sheep, cattle) for which the taxpayer wishes the provisions to apply. Separate elections shall not be made solely by reason of the animals' age, sex, or breed.

**(e) Computation.** *(1) Determination of amount deferred.* The amount of income which may be deferred for a classification of livestock pursuant to this section shall be determined in the following manner. The total amount of income realized from the sale or exchange of all livestock in the classification during the taxable year shall be divided by the total number of all such livestock sold. The resulting quotient shall then be multiplied by the excess number of such livestock sold on account of drought.

*(2) Example.* The provisions of this paragraph may be illustrated by the following example:

*Example.* A, a calendar year taxpayer normally sells 100 head of beef cattle a year. As the result of drought conditions existing during 1976, A sells 135 head during that year. A realizes $35,100 of income from the sale of the 135 head. On August 9, 1976, as a result of the drought, the affected area was declared a disaster area thereby eligible for Federal assistance. The amount of income which A may defer until 1977, presuming the other provisions of this section are met, is determined as follows:

$$\frac{\$35{,}100 \text{ (total income from sales of beef cattle)}}{135 \text{ (total number of beef cattle sold)}} \times 35 \text{ (excess number of beef cattle sold, i.e., } 135 - 100) = \$9{,}100$$

(amount which A may defer until 1977)

**(f) Successive elections.** If a taxpayer makes an election under section 451(e) for successive years, the amount deferred from one year to the next year shall not be deemed to have been received from the sale or exchange of livestock during the later year. In addition, in determining the taxpayer's normal business practice for the later year, earlier years for which an election under section 451(e) was made shall not be considered.

**(g) Time and manner of making election.** The election provided for in this section must be made by the later of (1) the due date for filing the income tax return (determined with regard to any extensions of time granted the taxpayer for filing such return) for the taxable year in which the early sale of livestock occurs, or (2) (the 90th day after the date these regulations are published as a Treasury decision in the FEDERAL REGISTER). The election must be made separately for each taxable year to which it is to apply. It must be made by attaching a statement to the return or an amended return for such taxable year. The statement shall include the name and address of the taxpayer and shall set forth the following information for each classification of livestock for which the election is made:

*(1)* A declaration that the taxpayer is making an election under section 451(e);

*(2)* Evidence of the existence of the drought conditions which forced the early sale or exchange of the livestock and the date, if known, on which an area was designated as eligible for assistance by the Federal Government as a result of the drought conditions;

*(3)* A statement explaining the relationship of the drought area to the taxpayer's early sale or exchange of the livestock;

*(4)* The total number of animals sold in each of the three preceding years;

*(5)* The number of animals which would have been sold in the taxable year had the taxpayer followed its normal business practice in the absence of drought;

*(6)* The total number of animals sold, and the number sold on account of drought, during the taxable year; and

*(7)* A computation, pursuant to paragraph (e) of this section, of the amount of income to be deferred for each such classification.

**(h) Revocation of election.** Once an election under this section is made for a taxable year, it may be revoked only with the approval of the Commissioner.

**(i) Cross reference.** For provisions relating to the involuntary conversion of livestock sold on account of drought see section 1033(e) and the regulations thereunder.

T.D. 7526, 12/23/77.

### § 15A.453-0 Taxable years affected.

**(a) In general.** Except as otherwise provided, the provisions of § 15a.453-1(a) through (e) generally apply to installment method reporting for sales of real property and casual sales of personal property occurring after October 19, 1980. See 26 CFR § 1.453-1 (rev. as of April 1, 1980) for the provisions relating to installment method reporting for sales of real property and casual sales before October 20, 1980 (except as provided in paragraph (b) of this section) and for provisions relating to installment sales by dealers in personal property occurring before October 20, 1980.

**(b) Certain limitations.** The provisions of prior law (section 453(b) of the Internal Revenue Code of 1954, in effect as of October 18, 1980) which required that the buyer receive no more than 30 percent of the selling price in the taxable year of the installment sale and that at least two payments be received shall not apply to reporting for casual installment sales of personal property and installment sales of real property occurring in a taxable year ending after October 19, 1980.

---

T.D. 7768, 1/30/81.

---

Section 1.453-1 is amended by revising paragraph (f) to read as follows:

**Proposed § 1.453-1 Installment method reporting for sales of real property and casual sales of personal property.** [*For Preamble, see ¶ 150,947*]

* * * * *

**(f) Installment obligations received in certain nonrecognition exchanges.** *(1) Exchanges described in section 1031(b).* (i) In general. The provisions of paragraph (f)(1) of this section apply to exchanges described in section 1031(b) ("section 1031(b) exchanges") in which the taxpayer receives as boot (property which is "other property" under section 1031(b)) an installment obligation issued by the other party to the exchange, as well as property with respect to which no gain or loss is recognized ("permitted property" for purposes of paragraph (f)(1) of this section). However, an exchange otherwise described in section 1036 in which the receipt of an installment obligation is treated as a dividend (or would be treated as a dividend if the issuing corporation had adequate earnings and profits) is not a section 1031(b) exchange for purposes of this section.

(ii) Exclusion from payment. Receipt of permitted property will not be considered payment for purposes of paragraph (c) of this section.

(iii) Installment method determinations. In a section 1031(b) exchange, the taxpayer's basis in the property transferred by the taxpayer, including nondeductible expenses of the exchange, will first be allocated to the permitted property received by the taxpayer up to, but not in excess of, the fair market value of such property. If the taxpayer's basis exceeds the fair market value of the permitted property, that excess amount of basis is "excess basis." In making all required installment method determinations, the exchange is treated as if the taxpayer had made an installment sale of appreciated property (with a basis equal to the amount of excess basis) in which the consideration received was the installment obligation and any other boot. In a section 1031(b) exchange, only net qualifying indebtedness is taken into account in determining the amount of qualifying indebtedness (as defined in § 1.453-1A(b)(2)(iv)). For this purpose, net qualifying indebtedness is the excess of—

(A) Liabilities of the taxpayer (or liabilities encumbering the property) assumed or taken subject to by the other party to the exchange as part of the consideration to the taxpayer, over

(B) The sum of any net cash paid (cash paid less any cash received) by the taxpayer in the exchange and any liability assumed or taken subject to by the taxpayer in the exchange.

Therefore, for purposes of installment method determinations, the selling price is the sum of the face value of the installment obligation (reduced by any portion of the obligation characterized as interest by section 483 or 1232), any net qualifying indebtedness, any cash received (in excess of any cash paid) by the taxpayer, and the fair market value of any other boot. The basis is the excess basis. The total contract price is the selling price less any net qualifying indebtedness that does not exceed the excess basis. Finally, payment in the year of exchange includes any net qualifying indebtedness that exceeds the excess basis.

(iv) Examples. The provisions of paragraph (f)(1) of this section are illustrated by the following examples:

*Example (1).* In 1981, A makes a section 1031(b) exchange of real property held for investment (basis $400,000) for permitted property worth $200,000, and an $800,000 installment obligation issued by the other party to the exchange bearing adequate stated interest. Neither the property transferred by A nor the property received in the exchange is mortgaged property. A's basis of $400,000 is allocated first to the permitted property received, up to the fair market value of $200,000. A's excess basis is $200,000 ($400,000 – $200,000). Since the installment obligation is the only boot received by A in the exchange, A's entire excess basis of $200,000 is allocable to it. Under the installment method, the selling price is $800,000 (the face amount of the installment obligation), and the contract price is also $800,000 (selling price less qualifying indebtedness, $800,000 – 0). The gross profit is $600,000 (selling price less excess basis allocated to the installment obligation, $300,000 – $200,000), and the gross profit ratio is 75% ($600,000/$800,000). A recognizes no gain until payments are received on the installment obligation. As A receives payments (exclusive of interest) on the installment obligation, 75% of each payment will be gain attributable to the exchange and 25% of each payment will be recovery of basis. A will hold the permitted property received in the exchange with a basis of $200,000.

*Example (2).* The facts are the same as in example (1), except that in the exchange A receives permitted property worth $200,000, a $600,000 installment obligation, and $200,000 in cash. A is treated as having sold appreciated property (basis equal to the $200,000 excess basis) for $200,000 cash and a $600,000 installment obligation. As in example (1), the contract price and the selling price are $800,000, the gross profit is $600,000, and the gross profit ratio is 75%. Accordingly, A will recognize gain of $150,000 on receipt of the cash (75% of the $200,000 payment). A holds the permitted property with a basis of $200,000.

*Example (3).* The facts are the same as in example (2), except that A does not receive $200,000 in cash. Instead, the property transferred by A in the exchange was subject to a mortgage (meeting the definition of qualifying indebtedness) of $200,000 to which the other party to the exchange took subject. The permitted property received by A in the exchange was not subject to a mortgage. A is treated as having sol appreciated property (basis equal to $200,000 excess basis) for $600,000 cash and $200,000 net relief of mortgage liability. The mortgage liability of which A is deemed relieved ($200,000), reduced by any cash paid by A and any mortgage liability encumbering the like-kind property received by A in the simultaneous exchange ($0), is treated as qualifying indebtedness. Since the qualifying indebtedness ($200,000) does not exceed A's excess basis ($200,000), B's taking subject to such indebtedness does not constitute payment to A in the year of exchange. Under the installment method, the selling price is $800,000 and the total contract price is $600,000 (selling price of $800,000 less $200,000 of qualifying indebtedness that does not exceed A's excess basis). Gross profit is also $600,000 ($800,000 selling price less $200,000 excess basis), and the gross profit ratio is 1

($600,000/$600,000). A recognizes no gain until payments are received on the installment obligation. As A receives payment (exclusive of interest) on the $600,000 installment obligation, the full amount received will be gain attributable to the exchange. A holds the permitted property with a basis of $200,000.

*Example (4).* The facts are the same as in example (2), except that A's basis in the property transferred by A was only $160,000. Since A's basis first must be allocated to permitted property received in the exchange up to the fair market value ($200,000) of that permitted property, there is no excess basis. Accordingly, A will recognize gain equal to the full amount of cash received ($200,000), and will hold the installment obligation at a basis of zero. A will hold the permitted property at a basis of $160,000.

*(2) Certain exchanges described in section 356(a).* (i) In general. The provisions of paragraph (f)(2) of this section apply to exchanges described in section 356(a)(1) ("section 356(a)(1) exchanges") in which the taxpayer receives as boot (property which is "other property" under section 356(a)(1)(B)) an installment obligation issued by qualifying corporation which is not treated as a dividend to the taxpayer. For purposes of section 453(f)(6) and paragraph (f)(2) of this section, any such section 356(a)(1) exchange shall be treated as a disposition of property by the taxpayer to the qualifying corporation and an acquisition of such property by the qualifying corporation from the taxpayer. If section 354 would apply to the exchange but for the receipt of boot, the term "qualifying corporation" means a corporation the stock of which could be received by the taxpayer in the exchange without recognition of gain or loss. If section 355 would apply to the exchange but for the receipt of boot, the term "qualifying corporation" means the distributing corporation (referred to in section 355(a)(1)(A)). Receipt of an installment obligation is treated as a dividend if section 356(a)(2) applies (determined without regard to the presence or absence of accumulated earnings and profits), or if section 356(e) (relating to certain exchanges for section 306 stock) applies to the taxpayer's receipt of the installment obligation.

(ii) Exclusion from payment. Receipt of permitted property shall not be considered payment for purposes of paragraph (c) of this section. For purposes of paragraph (f)(1) of this section, "permitted property" means property, the receipt of which does not result in recognition of gain under section 356(a)(1) (i.e., stock of a qualifying corporation).

(iii) Installment method determinations. Installment method determinations with respect to an installment obligation receive in an exchange to which paragraph (f)(2) of this section applies shall be made in accordance with the rules prescribed in paragraph (f)(1)(iii) of this section. In applying such rules, a section 356(a)(1) exchange shall be treated as a section 1031(b) exchange and permitted property shall mean permitted property described in paragraph (f)(2) of this section.

(iv) Examples. The provisions of paragraph (f)(2) of this section are illustrated by the following examples:

*Example (1).* T corporation and P corporation are unrelated closely held corporations. A owns 10% of the stock of T. A is not related to any other T stockholder or to any P stockholder. S corporation is a wholly-owned subsidiary of P. Pursuant to a plan of reorganization, T merges with and into S. In the merger, the T shares held by A are exchanged for shares of P worth $100,000 and a $300,000 installment obligation (bearing adequate interest) issued by P. In the merger the other stockholders of T exchange their T shares solely for P shares worth, in the aggregate, $3,600,000. The merger is a reorganization described in sections 368(a)(1)(A) and (a)(2)(D), and T, S, and P each is a party to the reorganization under section 368(b). P is a qualifying corporation and A is party to a section 356(a)(1) exchange in which receipt by A of the installment obligation will not be treated as a dividend to A. Because, for purposes of section 453(f)(6), this transaction is treated as a direct exchange between P and A, no gain or loss is recognized by S with respect to the P obligation. Assume A's basis in the T shares exchanged by A was $150,000. A's basis is allocated first to the permitted property (P shares) received, up to the fair market value of $100,000. A's excess basis is $50,000 ($150,000-$100,000). Since the installment obligation is the only boot received by A in the exchange, the entire excess basis of $50,000 is allocable to it. Under the installment method, the contract price is $300,000 (face amount of the installment obligation), the gross profit is $250,000 (contract price less $50,000 excess basis allocated to the installment obligation), and the gross profit ratio is 5/6 ($250,000/$300,000). A recognizes no gain until payments are received on the installment obligation. As A receives payments (exclusive of interest) on the installment obligation, 5/6ths of each payment will be gain attributable to the exchange and 1/6th of each payment will be recovery of basis. A will hold the permitted property (P stock) received in the exchange at a basis of $100,000.

*Example (2).* The facts are the same as in example (1). B, who also owns 10% of the stock of T directly and owns no other stock of T by attribution within the meaning of 318(a), exchanges the T shares in the merger for a $400,000 installment obligation issued by P (bearing adequate interest). Although section 356(a)(1) will not apply to this exchange because B receives no P stock in the transaction and the character of the gain is determined under section 302(a), for purposes of section 453 and paragraph (a) of this section, B is treated as having sold the T shares to P in exchange for P's installment obligation. B will report the installment sale on the installment method unless B elects under paragraph (e) of this section not to report the transaction on the installment method. If, by reason of constructive ownership of T shares under section 318(a) and failure to meet the requirements of section 302(c)(2), the character of the transaction as to B were determined under section 302(d), section 453 would not apply to the exchange by B.

*Example (3).* The facts are the same as in examples (1) and (2), except that the P stock is voting stock and S merges into T in a reorganization described in section 368(a)(2)(E). The results are the same as in examples (1) and (2).

*Example (4).* (i) T Corporation and larger P Corporation are unrelated public corporations the stock of each of which is widely held. A is a stockholder of T. S Corporation is a wholly owned subsidiary of P. On December 31, 1981, pursuant to a plan of reorganization which provides for a "note option" election, T merges with and into S. In the merger, A exercises the note option and the T shares held by A are exchanged for a $30,000 installment obligation (bearing adequate interest) issued by P, 1,000 P shares (worth $10 per share on the date of merger), and a non-negotiable certificate evidencing a right to receive (within 5 years from the date of merger) up to 1,000 additional P shares (plus adequate interest) if certain earnings conditions are satisfied. Neither the installment obligation nor the certificate evidencing the right to receive additional P shares is readily tradable within the meaning of § 1.453-1A(c)(4)(iv)(C). There is a valid business reason for not issuing all of the P shares immediately. Certain of the other T shareholders exercise the note option and exchange their T shares for a similar package. Other T shareholders do not exercise the note option and receive in the merger P shares plus a non-negotiable right to receive up to an equal number of additional P shares (plus adequate interest) within 5 years. In the aggregate, the total outstanding T shares are exchanged for 20% P installment obligations, 40% P shares, and rights to receive an equal number of additional P shares within 5 years. The merger of T into S qualifies as a reorganization under section 368(a)(1)(A) and (a)(2)(D). P is a qualifying corporation, the P shares received and which may subsequently be received by A are permitted property, and the exchange to which A is a party is a section 356(a)(1) exchange.

(ii) Assume A's basis in the T shares exchanged by A was $25,000. A's basis is allocated first to permitted property (P shares) up to fair market value. In the exchange A has received 1,000 P shares (worth $10,000) and may receive up to an additional 1,000 P shares in the future. In allocating A's basis, it is assumed that all contingencies contemplated by the merger agreement will be met or otherwise resolved in a manner that will maximize the consideration A will receive. It is further assumed that each P share, when received, will have a fair market value equal to the fair market value ($10) of a P share at the date of merger. Accordingly, since A may receive a maximum of 2,000 P shares, $20,000 (2,000 × $10) of A's basis will be allocated to the 1,000 P shares A has received ($10 per share) and to A's right to receive up to an additional 1,000 P shares (at $10 per share). A's excess basis of $5,000 ($25,000 – $20,000) is allocated to the $30,000 P installment obligation.

(iii) In 1983 the earnings condition is fully satisfied and A receives an additional 1,000 P shares (plus adequate interest). Each P share held by A has a basis of $10.

(iv) Assume instead that the earnings condition is only party satisfied and, by the close of 1986, A has received only an additional 600 P shares and is not entitled to receive any further P shares. Initially, each P share received by A was assigned a basis of $10. Of A's $25,000 basis in the T shares exchanged, $4,000 ($20,000 initially allocated to P shares received and to be received less $16,000 (1,600 P shares × $10)) now must be accounted for. The $4,000 of remaining basis will be assigned to the P shares then held by A. Thus, if A continues to hold all 1,600 P shares, A's basis in each P share will be increased by $2.50 ($4,000 divided by 1,600 P shares). If A previously sold 800 P shares and retains only 800 P shares, A's basis in each retained P share will be increased by $5 ($4,000 divided by 800 P shares). If A retains no P shares, and if all of the additional 600 P shares were issued to A and sold by A before the final year of the five year earn-out term (i.e., by the end of 1985), A's remaining basis of $4,000 will be added to the basis at which A holds the unpaid portion of the P installment obligation (up to but not in excess of the maximum amount remaining payable under that obligation less A's remaining basis in the installment obligation determined immediately before the addition to basis). If A has previously disposed of the P installment obligation, so that A holds neither P shares nor the P installment obligation to which the remaining $4,000 of A's basis can be allocated, A will be allowed a $4,000 loss in 1986. Similarly, if A continues to hold the P installment obligation but the facts are such that the maximum amount thereafter payable under the obligation is only $3,000 in excess of A's basis in the obligation determined immediately before assignment of A's remaining $4,000 basis, $3,000 of that remaining basis would be assigned to the installment obligation and P would be allowed a $1,000 loss in 1986.

*Example (5).* Pursuant to a plan to acquire all the stock of T corporation, P purchases 90% of the T stock for cash. To acquire the remaining 10% of T stock P creates S corporation and transfers P stock and P's newly issued installment notes to S in exchange for all of S's stock. The P notes are not readily tradable. Thereafter S merges into T, the P stock and P's installment notes are distributed to the T minority shareholders, and the S stock held by P is automatically converted into T stock. Assume that for federal tax purposes the existence of S is disregarded and the transaction is treated as a sale of T stock to P in exchange for P stock and P's installment notes. The minority shareholders will report the gain realized on the receipt of the P installment notes on the installment method unless they elect otherwise. The receipt of P stock will be treated as a payment in the year of sale.

*Example (6).* The facts are the same as example (5) except P transferred only P's installment notes to S and only these notes were distributed to T minority shareholders. As in example (5) the transaction is treated as a sale of T stock to P in exchange for P's installment notes. Each minority shareholder realizing gain on the receipt of the installment notes will report the gain on the installment method unless electing otherwise.

*(3) Other partial recognition exchanges.* (i) In general. The provisions of paragraph (f)(3) of this section apply to exchanges not described in paragraph (f)(1) or (2) of this section in which a taxpayer, in exchange for appreciated property, receives both permitted property (i.e., property with respect to which no gain or loss would be recognized but which, in the hands of the taxpayer, would have as basis for determining gain or loss the same basis in whole or in part as the property exchanged) and boot that includes an installment obligation issued by the other party to the exchange. Ordinarily, the installment method rules set forth in paragraph (f)(1)(ii) and (iii) of this section will apply to an exchange described in paragraph (f)(3) of this section subject to such variations, if any, as may be required under the applicable provisions of the Code.

(ii) Exchanges to which section 351 applies. If a taxpayer receives, in an exchange to which section 351(b) applies (a "section 351(b) exchange"), an installment obligation that is not a security within the meaning of section 351(a), the installment obligation is boot and the stock and securities (within the meaning of section 351(a)) are permitted property (within the meaning of paragraph (f)(1)(ii) of this section). The taxpayer will report the installment obligation on the installment method and any other boot received will treated as a payment made in the year of the exchange. In applying the rules of paragraph (f)(1)(iii) of this section to a section 351(b) exchange the excess basis is the amount, if any, by which the taxpayer's basis in the property transferred (plus and cash transferred) by the taxpayer exceeds the sum of the transferred liabilities which are not treated as money received under section 357 plus the fair market value of permitted property received by the taxpayer. In determining selling price and total contract price, transferred liabilities which are not treated as money received under section 357 shall be disregarded. For purposes of paragraph (f)(3)(ii) of this section, transferred liabilities are liabilities described in section 357(a)(2). Solely for the purpose of applying section 358(a)(1), the taxpayer shall be treated as if the taxpayer elected not to report receipt of the installment obligation on the installment method. Under section 362(a)(1) the corporation's basis in the property received from the taxpayer is the taxpayer's basis in the property increased by the gain recognized by the taxpayer at the time of the exchange.

As the taxpayer recognizes gain on the installment method, the corporation will increase its basis in the property by an amount equal to the amount of gain recognized by the taxpayer.

(iii) Examples. The provisions of paragraph (f)(3) of this section are illustrated by the following examples. In each example, assume that adequate stated interest means both a reasonable rate of interest within the meaning of any applicable regulation promulgated under section 385 and a rate of interest not less than the test rate prescribed in the regulations under section 483, and that the debt to equity ratio of the issuing corporation is a permissible ratio under any applicable regulation promulgated under section 385.

*Example (1).* A owns Blackacre, unimproved real property, with a basis of $300,000. The fair market value of Blackacre is $700,000. Blackacre is encumbered by a long-standing mortgage of $200,000. A transfers Blackacre, subject to the mortgage, to newly organized X corporation. A receives in exchange all of the stock of X, worth $400,000, and a $100,000 installment obligation (bearing adequate stated interest) issued by X. A realizes $400,000 of gain on the exchange. The installment obligation calls for a single payment of the full $100,000 face amount three years following the date of issue. The installment obligation is not a "security" within the meaning of section 351(a), and thus the exchange by A is a transaction described in section 351(b). The installment obligation is boot received by A in the exchange and the X stock is permitted property received by A in exchange. In applying the provisions of paragraph (f)(1)(ii) and (iii) of this section to a section 351(b) exchange, reference is required to section 357(a) under which the $200,000 mortgage liability is not treated as money or other property received by A in the exchange, and to section 358(a)(1) under which the basis of the X stock in the hands of A will be determined. These rules apply as follows: Neither receipt of the X stock nor relief of the mortgage encumbrance is treated as payment to A and thus A will recognize no gain in the year of the exchange. A's basis of $300,000 in Blackacre is reduced by the $200,000 mortgage from which A is deemed relieved in the exchange. The remaining basis of $100,000 is allocated to the X stock (but not in excess of the fair market value of the X stock); since the fair market value of the X stock is $400,000, the basis of the X stock in the hands of A is $100,000. Accordingly, in A's hands the installment obligation has a basis of zero. In the hands of X, the initial basis of Blackacre, determined under section 362(a), is $300,000 (the basis of the property in the hands of A), increased by the amount of gain recognized by A at the time of the transfer ($0)). As A receives payments on the installment obligation and recognizes gain, X's basis in Blackacre will be increased, at that time, in an amount equal to the gain recognized by A. Thus, if the $100,000 installment obligation is paid in full on the third anniversary date, A will recognize gain, of $100,000 (because A's basis in the installment obligation is zero) and X at that time will increase the basis at which it holds Blackacre by $100,000. If in the third year X had sold the property for cash before making payment on the installment obligation, X would recognize a loss of $100,000 when X paid the obligation in that amount to A on the third anniversary date.

*Example (2).* B owns Whiteacre, unencumbered, unimproved real property, with a basis of $250,000. The fair market value of Whiteacre is $300,000. A transfers Whiteacre to newly organized Y corporation in exchange for all of the stock of Y corporation (worth $200,000) and a $100,000 installment obligation (bearing adequate interest). The installment obligation is payable in full on the second anniversary of the date of issue. The installment obligation is not a "security" within the meaning of section 351(a), and thus the transaction is a section 351(b) exchange. Applying the rules summarized in example (1) to the facts of this case, receipt of the installment obligation is not treated as payment to A, $200,000 of A's basis of $250,000 in Whiteacre is allocated to the Y stock (equal to the fair market value of the Y stock), and the excess basis of $50,000 is allocated to the installment obligation. In the hands of Y, the basis of Whiteacre initially is $250,000, and will be increased by $50,000 when the installment obligation is paid and A recognizes gain of $50,000.

*Example (3).* D owns a machine which is unencumbered 5-year recovery property with an adjusted basis of $500,000. The recomputed basis (as defined in section 1245(a)(2)) of the machine in the hands of D is $1 million. The fair market value of the machine also is $1 million. D transfers the machine to newly organized X Corporation, and E, an unrelated individual, simultaneously transfers property worth $1 million to X Corporation. D receives in exchange 400 shares of X common stock worth $400,000, a $400,000 15-year debenture issued by X (worth its face amount), and a $200,000 installment obligation (bearing adequate interest) issued by X. The installment obligation calls for a single payment of the full $200,000 face amount two years following the date of issue. E receives in the exchange 1,000 shares of X common stock worth $1 million. D and E are in control (as defined in section 368(c)) of X immediately after the exchange. The debenture received by D is a "security" within the meaning of section 351(a), but the installment obligation received by D is not a " security" within the meaning of that section and thus the exchange by D is a transaction described in section 351(b). The installment obligation is boot received by D in the exchange and the X stock and X debenture are permitted property received by D in the exchange. Since the aggregate fair market value ($800,000) of the X stock ($400,000) and the X debenture ($400,000) received by D exceeds D's $500,000 adjusted basis in the machine, all of that basis is allocated proportionately among the items of permitted property. This, D will hold the X stock with a basis of $250,000. Since there is no excess basis, in the hands of D the installment obligation has a basis of zero. In the hands of X, the adjusted basis of the machine remains $500,000. When D receives payment from X on the $200,000 installment obligation, D will recognize gain of $200,000, all of which gain will be treated as ordinary income. See sections 1245(a)(1) and 453B(a). At that time, X's adjusted basis in the machine will be increased in an amount equal to the $200,000 gain recognized by D.

*Example (4).* In 1976 H and W purchased Blackacre as their principal residence for $50,000. In 1981 H and W, both of whom are less than 55 years of age, sold Blackacre to A for $90,000: $15,000 cash, A's assumption of the $40,000 mortgage, and A's promise to pay H and W $7,000 (with adequate stated interest) in each of the next 5 years. Within 2 years of the sale of Blackacre, H and W acquire. Whiteacre, an unencumbered property, which will be their principal residence, for $80,000. Of the $40,000 gain that H and W realized upon the sale of Whiteacre, $30,000 will not be recognized pursuant to the provisions of section 1034. Unless H and W elect not to report the transaction on the installment method, they will treat the $10,000 gain to be recognized as the gross profit for purposes of calculating the gross profit ratio. Accordingly the gross profit ratio is ⅕

($10,000 gross profit/$50,000 contract price) and H and W will report as gain $3,000 (1/5 × $15,000) in the year of the sale and $1,400 (1/5 × $7,000) in each of the next five years.

*(4) Installment obligations received as distributions in redemptions of stock pursuant to section 302(a).* If a corporation redeems its stock and the redemption is treated as a distribution in part or full payment in exchange for the stock under section 302(a), then an installment obligation which meets the requirements of section 453 and is distributed in the redemption shall be reported on the installment method unless the taxpayer elects otherwise.

*Example.* A owns 10% of the Stock of X corporation and is not considered as owning (under section 318(a)) any other shares of X corporation. X redeems all of A's X shares and distributes its installment obligation to A in full payment. The reduction is treated as a sale of the X shares by A under section 302(b)(3). A will report any gain realized in the redemption on the installment method unless A elects otherwise.

### § 15a.453-1 Installment method reporting for sales of real property and casual sales of personal property.

***Caution:*** The Treasury has not yet amended Reg § 15a.453-1 to reflect changes made by P.L. 108-27, P.L. 106-170, P.L. 104-203, P.L. 99-514.

**(a) In general.** Unless the taxpayer otherwise elects in the manner prescribed in paragraph (d)(3) of this section, income from a sale of real property or a casual sale of personal property, where any payment is to be received in a taxable year after the year of sale, is to be reported on the installment method.

**(b) Installment sale defined.** *(1) In general.* The term "installment sale" means a disposition of property (except as provided in paragraph (b)(4) of this section) where at least one payment is to be received after the close of the taxable year in which the disposition occurs. The term "installment sale" includes dispositions from which payment is to be received in a lump sum in a taxable year subsequent to the year of sale. For purposes of this paragraph, the taxable year in which payments are to be received is to be determined without regard to section 453(e) (relating to related party sales), section (f)(3) (relating to the definition of a "payment") and section (g) (relating to sales of depreciable property to a spouse or 80-percent-owned entity).

*(2) Installment method defined.* (i) In general. Under the installment method, the amount of any payment which is income to the taxpayer is that portion of the installment payment received in that year which the gross profit realized or to be realized bears to the total contract price (the "gross profit ratio"). See paragraph (c) of this section for rules describing installment method reporting of contingent payment sales.

(ii) Selling price defined. The term "selling price" means the gross selling price without reduction to reflect any existing mortgage or other encumbrance on the property (whether assumed or taken subject to by the buyer) and, for installment sales in taxable years ending after October 19, 1980, without reduction to reflect any selling expenses. Neither interest, whether stated or unstated, nor original issue discount is considered to be a part of the selling price. See paragraph (c) of this section for rules describing installment method reporting of contingent payment sales.

(iii) Contract price defined. The term "contract price" means the total contract price equal to selling price reduced by that portion of any qualifying indebtedness (as defined in paragraph (b)(2)(iv) of this section, assumed or taken subject to by the buyer, which does not exceed the seller's basis in the property (adjusted, for installment sales in taxable years ending after October 19, 1980, to reflect commissions and other selling expenses as provided in paragraph (b)(2)(v) of this section). See paragraph (c) of this section for rules describing installment method reporting of contingent payment sales.

(iv) Qualifying indebtedness. The term "qualifying indebtedness" means a mortgage or other indebtedness encumbering the property and indebtedness, not secured by the property but incurred or assumed by the purchaser incident to the purchaser's acquisition, holding, or operation in the ordinary course of business or investment, of the property. The term "qualifying indebtedness" does not include an obligation of the taxpayer incurred incident to the disposition of the property ( *e.g.,* legal fees relating to the taxpayer's sale of the property) or an obligation functionally unrelated to the acquisition, holding, or operating of the property ( *e.g.,* the taxpayer's medical bill). Any obligation created subsequent to the taxpayer's acquisition of the property and incurred or assumed by the taxpayer or placed as an encumbrance on the property in contemplation of disposition of the property is not qualifying indebtedness if the arrangement results in accelerating recovery of the taxpayer's basis in the installment sale.

(v) Gross profit defined. The term "gross profit" means the selling price less the adjusted basis as defined in section 1011 and the regulations thereunder. For sales in taxable years ending after October 19, 1980, in the case of sales of real property by a person other than a dealer and casual sales of personal property, commissions and other selling expenses shall be added to basis for purposes of determining the proportion of payments which is gross profit attributable to the disposition. Such additions to basis will not be deemed to affect the taxpayer's holding period in the transferred property.

*(3) Payment.* (i) In general. Except as provided in paragraph (e) of this section (relating to purchaser evidences of indebtedness payable on demand or readily tradable), the term "payment" does not include the receipt of evidences of indebtedness of the person acquiring the property ("installment obligation"), whether or not payment of such indebtedness is guaranteed by a third party (including a government agency). For special rules regarding the receipt of an evidence of indebtedness of a transferee of a qualified intermediary, see §§ 1.1031(b)-2(b) and 1.1031(k)-1(j)(2)(iii) of this chapter. A standby letter of credit (as defined in paragraph (b)(3)(iii) of this section) shall be treated as a third party guarantee. Payments include amounts actually or constructively received in the taxable year under an installment obligation. For a special rule regarding a transfer of property to a qualified intermediary followed by the sale of such property by the qualified intermediary, see § 1.1031(k)-1(j)(2)(ii) of this chapter. Receipt of an evidence of indebtedness which is secured directly or indirectly by cash or a cash equivalent, such as a bank certificate of deposit or a treasury note, will be treated as the receipt of payment. For a special rule regarding a transfer of property in exchange for an obligation that is secured by cash or a cash equivalent held in a qualified escrow account or a qualified trust, see § 1.1031(k)-1(j)(2)(i) of this chapter. Payment may be received in cash or other property, including foreign currency, marketable securities, and evidences or indebtedness which are payable on demand or readily tradable. However, for special rules relating to the receipt of certain property with respect to which gain is not recognized, see paragraph (f) of this section (relating to transactions described in sections

351, 356(a) and 1031). Except as provided in § 15A.453-2 of these regulations (relating to distributions of installment obligations in corporate liquidations described in section 337), payment includes receipt of an evidence of indebtedness of a person other than the person acquiring the property from the taxpayer. For purposes of determining the amount of payment received in the taxable year, the amount of qualifying indebtedness (as defined in paragraph (b)(2)(iv) of this section) assumed or taken subject to by the person acquiring the property shall be included only to the extent that it exceeds the basis of the property (determined after adjustment to reflect selling expenses). For purposes of the preceding sentence, an arrangement under which the taxpayer's liability on qualifying indebtedness is eliminated incident to the disposition ( *e.g.,* a novation) shall be treated as an assumption of the qualifying indebtedness. If the taxpayer sells property to a creditor of the taxpayer and indebtedness of the taxpayer is cancelled in consideration of the sale, such cancellation shall be treated as payment. To the extent that cancellation is not in consideration of the sale, see §§ 1.61-12(b)(1) and 1.1001-2(a)(2) relating to discharges of indebtedness. If the taxpayer sells property which is encumbered by a mortgage or other indebtedness on which the taxpayer is not personally liable, and the person acquiring the property is the obligee, the taxpayer shall be treated as having received payment in the amount of such indebtedness.

(ii) Wrap-around mortgage. This paragraph (b)(3)(ii) shall apply generally to any installment sale after March 4, 1981 unless the installment sale was completed before June 1, 1981 pursuant to a written obligation binding on the seller that was executed on or before March 4, 1981. A "wrap-around mortgage" means an agreement in which the buyer initially does not assume and purportedly does not take subject to part or all of the mortgage or other indebtedness encumbering the property ("wrapped indebtedness") and, instead, the buyer issues to the seller an installment obligation the principal amount of which reflects such wrapped indebtedness. Ordinarily, the seller will use payments received on the installment obligation to service the wrapped indebtedness. The wrapped indebtedness shall be deemed to have been taken subject to even though title to the property has not passed in the year of sale and even though the seller remains liable for payments on the wrapped indebtedness. In the hands of the seller, the wrap-around installment obligation shall have a basis equal to the seller's basis in the property which was the subject of the installment sale, increased by the amount of gain recognized in the year of sale, and decreased by the amount of cash and the fair market value of other nonqualifying property received in the year of sale. For purposes of this paragraph (b)(3)(ii), the amount of any indebtedness assumed or taken subject to by the buyer (other than wrapped indebtedness) is to be treated as cash received by the seller in the year of sale. Therefore, except as otherwise required by section 483 or 1232, the gross profit ratio with respect to the wrap-around installment obligation is a fraction, the numerator of which is the face value of the obligation less the taxpayer's basis in the obligation and the denominator of which is the face value of the obligation.

(iii) Standby letter of credit. The term "standby letter of credit" means a non-negotiable, non-transferable (except together with the evidence of indebtedness which it secures) letter of credit, issued by a bank or other financial institution, which serves as a guarantee of the evidence of indebtedness which is secured by the letter of credit. Whether or not the letter of credit explicitly states it is non-negotiable and nontransferable, it will be treated as non-negotiable and nontransferable if applicable local law so provides. The mere right of the secured party (under applicable local law) to transfer the proceeds of a letter of credit shall be disregarded in determining whether the instrument qualifies as a standby letter of credit. A letter of credit is not a standby letter of credit if it may be drawn upon in the absence of default in payment of the underlying evidence of indebtedness.

*(4) Exceptions.* The term "installment sale" does not include, and the provisions of section 453 do not apply to, dispositions of personal property on the installment plan by a person who regularly sells or otherwise disposes of personal property on the installment plan, or to dispositions of personal property of a kind which is required to be included in the inventory of the taxpayer if on hand at the close of the taxable year. See section 453A and the regulations thereunder for rules relating to installment sales by dealers in personal property. A dealer in real property or a farmer who is not required under his method of accounting to maintain inventories may report the gain on the installment method under section 453.

*(5) Examples.* The following examples illustrate installment method reporting under this section:

*Example (1).* In 1980, A, a calendar year taxpayer, sells Blackacre, an unencumbered capital asset in A's hands, to B for $100,000: $10,000 down and the remainder payable in equal annual installments over the next 9 years, together with adequate stated interest. A's basis in Blackacre, exclusive of selling expenses, is $38,000. Selling expenses paid by A are $2,000. Therefore, the gross profit is $60,000 ($100,000 selling price – $40,000 basis inclusive of selling expenses). The gross profit ratio is 3/5 (gross profit of $60,000 divided by $100,000 contract price). Accordingly, $6,000 3/5 of $10,000) of each $10,000 payment received is gain attributable to the sale and $4,000 ($10,000 – $6,000) is recovery of basis. The interest received in addition to principal is ordinary income to A.

*Example (2).* C sells Whiteacre to D for a selling price of $160,000. Whiteacre is encumbered by a longstanding mortgage in the principal amount of $60,000. D will assume or take subject to the $60,000 mortgage and pay the remaining $100,000 in 10 equal annual installments together with adequate stated interest. C's basis in Whiteacre is $90,000. There are no selling expenses. The contract price is $100,000, the $160,000 selling price reduced by the mortgage of $60,000 assumed or taken subject to. Gross profit is $70,000 ($160,000 selling price less C's basis of $90,000). C's gross profit ratio is 7/10 (gross profit of $70,000 divided by $100,000 contract price). Thus, $7,000 (7/10 of $10,000) of each $10,000 annual payment is gain attributable to the sale, and $3,000 ($10,000 – $7,000) is recovery of basis.

*Example (3).* The facts are the same as in example (2), except that C's basis in the land is $40,000. In the year of the sale C is deemed to have received payment of $20,000 ($60,000 – $40,000, the amount by which the mortgage D assumed or took subject to exceeds C's basis). Since basis is fully recovered in the year of sale, the gross profit ratio is 1 ($120,000/$120,000) and C will report 100% of the $20,000 deemed payment in the year of sale and each $10,000 annual payment as gain attributable to the sale.

*Example (4).* E sells Blackacre, an unencumbered capital gain property in E's hands, to F on January 2, 1981. F makes a cash down payment of $500,000 and issues a note to E obliging F to pay an additional $500,000 on the fifth anniversary date. The note does not require a payment of interest. In determining selling price, section 483 will apply to recharacterize as interest a portion of the $500,000 future payment. Assume that under section 483 and the applicable regulations $193,045 is treated as total unstated interest, and the selling price is $806,955 ($1 million less unstated interest). Assuming E's basis (including selling expenses) in Blackacre is $200,000) gross profit is $606,955 ($806,955 – $200,000) and the gross profit ratio is 75.21547%. Accordingly, of the $500,000 cash down payment received by E in 1981, $376,077 (75.21547% of $500,000) is gain attributable to the sale and $123,923 is recovery of basis ($500,000 – $376,077).

*Example (5).* In 1982, G sells to H Blackacre, which is encumbered by a first mortgage with a principal amount of $500,000 and a second mortgage with a principal amount of $400,000 for a selling price of $2 million. G's basis in Blackacre is $700,000. Under the agreement between G and H, passage of title is deferred and H does not assume and purportedly does not take subject to either mortgage in the year of sale. H pays G $200,000 in cash and issues a wrap-around mortgage note with a principal amount of $1,800,000 bearing adequate stated interest. H is deemed to have acquired Blackacre subject to the first and second mortgages (wrapped indebtedness) totalling $900,000. The contract price is $1,300,000 (selling price of $2 million less $700,000 mortgages within the seller's basis assumed or taken subject to). Gross profit is also $1,300,000 (selling price of $2 million less $700,000 basis). Accordingly in the year of sale, the gross profit ratio is 1 ($1,300,000/$1,300,000). Payment in the year of sale is $400,000 ($200,000 cash received plus $200,000 mortgage in excess of basis ($900,000 – $700,000)). Therefore, G recognizes $400,000 gain in the year of sale ($400,000 × 1). In the hands of G the wrap-around installment obligation has a basis of $900,000, equal to G's basis in Blackacre ($700,000) increased by the gain recognized by G in the year of sale ($400,000) reduced by the cash received by G in the year of sale ($200,000). G's gross profit with respect to the note is $900,000 ($1,800,000 face amount less $900,000 basis in the note) and G's contract price with respect to the note is its face amount of $1,800,000. Therefore, the gross profit ratio with respect to the note is ½ ($900,000/$1,800,000).

*Example (6).* The facts are the same as example (5) except that under the terms of the agreement H assumes the $500,000 first mortgage on Blackacre. H does not assume and purportedly does not take subject to the $400,000 second mortgage on Blackacre. The wrap-around installment obligation issued by H to G has a face amount of $1,300,000. The tax results in the year of sale to G are the same as example (5) ($400,000 payment received and gain recognized). In the hands of G, basis in the wrap-around installment obligation is $400,000 ($700,000 basis in Blackacre plus $400,000 gain recognized in the year of sale minus $700,000 ($200,000 cash received and $500,000 treated as cash received as a result of H's assumption of the first mortgage)). G's gross profit with respect to the note is $900,000 ($1,300,000 face amount of the wrap-around installment obligation less $400,000 basis in that note) and G's contract price with respect to the note is its face value of $1,300,000. Therefore, the gross profit ratio with respect to the note is 9/13 ($900,000/$1,300,000).

*Example (7).* A sells the stock of X. corporation to B for a $1 million installment obligation payable in equal annual installments over the next 10 years with adequate stated interest. The installment obligation is secured by a standby letter of credit (within the meaning of paragraph (b)(3)(iii) of this section) issued by M bank. Under the agreement between B and M bank, B is required to maintain a compensating balance in an account B maintains with M bank and is required by the M bank to post additional collateral, which may include cash or a cash equivalent, with M bank. Under neither the standby letter of credit nor any other agreement or arrangement is A granted a direct lien upon or other security interest in such cash or cash equivalent collateral. Receipt of B's installment obligation secured by the standby letter of credit will not be treated as the receipt of payment by A.

*Example (8).* The facts are the same as in example (7) except that the standby letter of credit is in the drawable sum of $600,000. To secure fully its $1 million note issued to A, B deposits in escrow $400,000 in cash and Treasury bills. Under the escrow agreement, upon default in payment of the note A may look directly to the escrowed collateral. Receipt of B's installment obligation will be treated as the receipt payment by A in the sum of $400,000.

**(c) Contingent payment sales.** *(1) In general.* Unless the taxpayer otherwise elects in the manner prescribed in paragraph (d)(3) of this section, contingent payment sales are to be reported on the installment method. As used in this section, the term "contingent payment sale" means a sale or other disposition of property in which the aggregate selling price cannot be determined by the close of the taxable year in which such sale or other disposition occurs.

The term "contingent payment sale" does not include transactions with respect to which the installment obligation represents, under applicable principles of tax law, a retained interest in the property which is the subject of the transaction, an interest in a joint venture or a partnership, an equity interest in a corporation or similar transactions, regardless of the existence of a stated maximum selling price or a fixed payment term. See paragraph (c)(8) of this section, describing the extent to which the regulations under section 385 apply to the determination of whether an installment obligation represents an equity interest in a corporation.

This paragraph prescribes the rules to be applied in allocating the taxpayer's basis (including selling expenses except for selling expenses of dealers in real estate) to payments received and to be received in a contingent payment sale. The rules are designed appropriately to distinguish contingent payment sales for which a maximum selling price is determinable, sales for which a maximum selling price is not determinable but the time over which payments will be received is determinable, and sales for which neither a maximum selling price nor a definite payment term is determinable. In addition, rules are prescribed under which, in appropriate circumstances, the taxpayer will be permitted to recover basis under an income forecast computation.

*(2) Stated maximum selling price.* (i) In general. (A) contingent payment sale will be treated as having a stated maximum selling price if, under the terms of the agreement, the maximum amount of sale proceeds that may be received by the taxpayer can be determined as of the end of the taxable year in which the sale or other disposition occurs. The stated maximum selling price shall be determined by assuming that all of the contingencies contemplated by the agreement are met or otherwise resolved in a manner that will maximize the selling price and accelerate payments to the earliest date or dates permitted under the agreement. Except as provided in paragraph (c)(2)(ii) and (7) of this section (relating to certain payment recomputations), the taxpayer's basis shall be allocated to payments received and to be received under a stated maximum selling price agreement by treating the stated maximum selling price as the selling price for purposes of paragraph (b) of this section. The stated maximum

selling price, as initially determined, shall thereafter be treated as the selling price unless and until that maximum amount is reduced, whether pursuant to the terms of the original agreement, by subsequent amendment, by application of the payment recharacterization rule (described in paragraph (c)(2)(ii) of this section), or by a subsequent supervening event such as bankruptcy of the obligor. When the maximum amount is subsequently reduced, the gross profit ratio will be recomputed with respect to payments received in or after the taxable year in which an event requiring reduction occurs. If, however, application of the foregoing rules in a particular case would substantially and inappropriately accelerate or defer recovery of the taxpayer's basis, a special rule will apply. See paragraph (c)(7) of this section.

(B) The following examples illustrate the provisions of paragraph (e)(2)(i) of this section. In each example, it is assumed that application of the rules illustrated will not substantially and inappropriately defer or accelerate recovery of the taxpayer's basis.

*Example (1).* A sells all of the stock of X corporation to B for $100,000 payable at closing plus an amount equal to 5% of the net profits of X for each of the next nine years, the contingent payments to be made annually together with adequate stated interest. The agreement provides that the maximum amount A may receive, inclusive of the $100,000 down payment but exclusive of interest, shall be $2,000,000. A's basis in the stock of X inclusive of selling expenses, is $200,000. Selling price and contract price are considered to be $2,000,000. Gross profit is $1,800,000, and the gross profit ratio is 9/10 ($1,800,000/$2,000,000). Accordingly, of the $100,000 received by A in the year of sale, $90,000 is reportable as gain attributable to the sale and $10,000 is recovery of basis.

*Example (2).* C owns Blackacre which is encumbered by a long-standing mortgage of $100,000. On January 15, 1981, C sells Blackacre to D under the following payment arrangement: $100,000 in cash on closing; nine equal annual installment payments of $100,000 commencing January 15, 1982; and nine annual payments (the first to be made on March 30, 1982) equal to 5% of the gross annual rental receipts from Blackacre generated during the preceding calendar year. The agreement provides that each deferred payment shall be accompanied by a payment of interest calculated at the rate of 12% per annum and that the maximum amount payable to C under the agreement (exclusive of interest) shall be $2,100,000. The agreement also specifies that D will assume the long-standing mortgage. C's basis (inclusive of selling expenses) in Blackacre is $300,000. Accordingly, selling price is $2,100,000 and contract price is $2,000,000 (selling price of $2,100,000 less the $100,000 mortgage). The gross profit ratio is 9/10 (gross profit of $1,800,000 divided by $2,000,000 contract price). Of the $100,000 cash payment received by C in 1981, $90,000 is gain attributable to the sale of Blackacre and $10,000 is recovery of basis.

(ii) Certain interest recomputations. When interest is stated in the contingent price sale agreement at a rate equal to or greater than the applicable prescribed test rate referred to in § 1.483-1(d)(1)(ii) and such stated interest is payable in addition to the amounts otherwise payable under the agreement, such stated interest is not considered a part of the selling price. In other circumstances ( *i.e.,* section 483 is applicable because no interest is stated or interest is stated below the applicable test rate, or interest is stated under a payment recharacterization provision of the sale agreement), the special rule set forth in this (ii) shall be applied in the initial computation and subsequent recomputations of selling price, contract price, and gross profit ratio. The special rule is referred to in this section as the "price-interest recomputation rule." As used in this section, the term "payment recharacterization" refers to a contractual arrangement under which a computed amount otherwise payable as part of the selling price is denominated an interest payment. The amount of unstated interest determined under section 483 or (if section 483 is inapplicable in the particular case) the amount of interest determined under a payment recharacterization arrangement is collectively referred to in this section as "internal interest" amounts. The price-interest recomputation rule is applicable to any stated maximum selling price agreement which contemplates receipt of internal interest by the taxpayer. Under the rule, stated maximum selling price will be determined as of the end of the taxpayer's taxable year in which the sale or other disposition occurs, taking into account all events which have occurred and are subject to prompt subsequent calculation and verification and assuming that all amounts that may become payable under the agreement will be paid on the earliest date or dates permitted under the agreement. With respect to the year of sale, the amount (if any) of internal interest then shall be determined taking account of the respective components of that calculation. The maximum amount initially calculated, minus the internal interest so determined, is the initial stated maximum selling price under the price-interest recomputation rule. For each subsequent taxable year, stated maximum selling price (and thus selling price, contract price, and gross profit ratio) shall be recomputed, taking into account all events which have occurred and are subject to prompt subsequent calculation and verification and assuming that all amounts that may become payable under the agreement will be paid on the earliest date or dates permitted under the agreement. The redetermined gross profit ratio, adjusted to reflect payments received and gain recognized in prior taxable years, shall be applied to payments received in that taxable year.

(iii) Examples. The following examples illustrate installment method reporting of a contingent payment sale under which there is a stated maximum selling price. In each example, it is assumed that application of the rules described will not substantially and inappropriately defer or accelerate recovery of the taxpayer's basis.

*Example (1).* A owns all of the stock of X corporation with a basis to A of $20 million. On July 1, 1981, A sells the stock of X to B under an agreement calling for fifteen annual payments respectively equal to 5% of the net profits of X earned in the immediately preceding fiscal year beginning with the fiscal year ending March 31, 1982. Each payment is to be made on the following June 15th, commencing June 15, 1982, together with adequate stated interest. The agreement specifies that the maximum amount (exclusive of interest) payable to A shall not exceed $60 million. Since stated interest is payable as an addition to the selling price and the specified rate is not below the section 483 test rate, there is no internal interest under the agreement. The stated maximum selling price is $60 million. The gross profit ratio is 2/3 (gross profit of $40 million divided by $60 million contract price). Thus, if on June 15, 1982, A receives a payment of $3 million (exclusive of interest) under the agreement, in that year A will report $2 million ($3 million × 2/3) as gain attributable to the sale, and $1 million as recovery of basis.

*Example (2).* (i) The facts are the same as in example (1) except that the agreement does not call for the payment of any stated interest but does provide for an initial cash payment of $3 million on July 1, 1981. The maximum amount payable, including the $3 million initial payment, remains

$60 million. Since section 483 will apply to each payment received by A more than one year following the date of sale (section 483 is inapplicable to the contingent payment that will be received on June 15, 1982 since that date is within one year following the July 1, 1981 sale date), the agreement contemplates internal interest and the price-interest recomputation rule is applicable. Under the rule, an initial determination must be made for A's taxable year 1981. On December 31, 1981, the last day of the taxable year, no events with regard to the first fiscal year have occurred which are subject to prompt subsequent calculation and verification because that fiscal year will end March 31, 1982. Under the price-interest recomputation rule, on December 31, 1981 A is required to assume that the maximum amount subsequently payable under the agreement ($57 million, equal to $60 million less the $3 million initial cash payment received by A in 1981) will be paid on the earliest date permissible under the agreement, *i.e.*, on June 15, 1982. Since no part of a payment received on that date would be treated as interest under section 483, the initial stated maximum selling price, applicable to A's 1981 tax calculations, is deemed to be $60 million. Thus, the 1981 gross profit ratio is ⅔ and for the taxable year 1981 A will report $2 million as gain attributable to the sale.

(ii) The net profits of X for its fiscal year ending March 31, 1982 are $120 million. On June 15, 1982 A receives a payment from B equal to 5% of that amount, or $6 million. On December 31, 1982, A knows that the maximum amount he may subsequently receive under the agreement is $51 million, and A is required to assume that this amount will be paid to him on the earliest permissible date, June 15, 1983. Section 483 does not treat as interest any part of the $6 million received by A on June 15, 1982, but section 483 will treat as unstated interest a computed part of the $51 million it is assumed A will receive on June 15, 1983. Assuming that under the tables in the regulations under section 483, it is determined that the principal component of a payment received more than 21 months but less than 27 months after the date of sale is considered to be .82270, $41,957,700 of the presumed $51 million payment will be treated as principal. The balance of $9,042,300 is interest. Accordingly, in A's 1982 tax calculations stated maximum selling price will be $50,957,700, which amount is equal to the stated maximum selling price that was determined in the 1981 tax calculations ($60 million) reduced by the section 483 interest component of the $6 million payment received by A in 1982 ($0) and further reduced by the section 483 interest component of the $51 million presumed payment to be received by A on June 15, 1983 ($9,042,300). Similarly, in determining gross profit for 1982 tax calculations, the gross profit of $40 million determined in the 1981 tax calculations must be reduced by the same section 483 interest amounts, yielding a recomputed gross profit of $30,957,700 ($40,000,000 – $9,042,300). Further, since prior to 1982 A received payment under the agreement (1981 payment of $3 million of which $2 million was profit), the appropriate amounts must be subtracted in the 1982 tax calculation. The total previously received selling price payment of $3 million is subtracted from the recomputed maximum selling price of $50,957,700, yielding an adjusted selling price of $47,957,700. The total previously recognized gain of $2 million is subtracted from the recomputed maximum gross profit of $30,957,700, yielding an adjusted gross profit of $28,957,700. The gross profit percentage applicable to 1982 tax calculations thus is determined to be 60.38175%, equal to the quotient of dividing the adjusted gross profit of $28,957,700 by the adjusted selling price of $47,957,700. Accordingly, of the $6 million received by A in 1982, no part of which is unstated interest under section 483, A will report $3,622,905 (60.38175% of $6 million) as gain attributable to the sale and $2,377,095 ($6,000,000 – $3,622,905) as recovery of basis.

(iii) The net profits of X for its fiscal year ending March 31, 1983 are $200 million. On June 15, 1983 A receives a payment from B equal to $10 million. On December 31, 1983, A knows that the maximum amount he may subsequently receive under the agreement is $41 million, and A is required to assume that this amount will be paid to him on the earliest permissible date, June 15, 1984. Assuming that under the tables in the regulations under section 483 it is determined that the principal component of a payment received more than 33 months but less than 39 months after the date of sale is .74622, $30,595,020 of the presumed $41 million ($51 million – $10 million) payment will be treated as principal and $10,404,980 is interest. Based upon the assumed factor for 21 months but less than 27 months (.82270) $8,227,000 of the $10 million payment is principal and $1,773,000 is interest. Accordingly, in A's 1983 tax calculations stated maximum selling price will be $47,822,020, which amount is equal to the stated maximum selling price determined in the 1981 calculation ($60 million) reduced by the section 483 interest component of the $6 million 1982 payment ($0), the section 483 interest component of the 1983 payment ($1,773,000) and by the section 483 interest component of the presumed $41 million payment to be received in 1984 ($10,404,980). The recomputed gross profit is $27,822,020 ($40 million – $10,404,980 – $1,773,000). The previously reported payments must be deducted for the 1983 calculation. Selling price is reduced to $38,822,020 by subtracting the $3 million 1981 payment and the $6 million 1982 payment ($47,822,020 – $9 million) and gross profit is reduced to $22,199,115 by subtracting the 1981 profit of $2 million and the 1982 profit of $3,622,905 ($27,822,020 – $5,622,905), yielding a gross profit percentage of 57.18176% ($22,199,115/$38,822,020). Accordingly, of the $10 million received in 1983, A will report $1,773,000 as interest under section 483, and of the remaining principal component of $8,227,000, $4,704,343 as gain attributable to the sale ($8,227,000 × 57.18176%) and $3,522,657 ($8,227,000 – $4,704,343) as recovery of basis.

*Example (3).* The facts are the same as in example (2) except that X is a collapsible corporation as defined in section 341(b)(1) and no limitation or exception under section 341(d), (e), or (f) is applicable. Under section 341(a), all of A's gain on the sale will be ordinary income. Accordingly, section 483 will not apply to treat as interest any part of the payments to be received by A under his agreement with B. See section 483(f)(3). Therefore, the price-interest recomputation rule is inapplicable and the tax results to A in each year in which payment is received will be determined in a manner consistent with example (1).

*Example (4).* The facts are the same as in example (2) (maximum amount payable under the agreement $60 million) except that the agreement between A and B contains the following "payment recharacterization" provision:

"Any payment made more than one year after the (July 1, 1981) date of sale shall be composed of an interest element and a principal element, the interest element being computed on the principal element at an interest rate of 9% per annum computed from the date of sale to the date of payment." The results reached in example (2), with respect to the $3 million initial cash payment received by A in 1981 remain the same because, under the payment recharacterization formula, no amount received or assumed to be received prior to July 1, 1982 is treated as interest. The 1982 tax computation method described in example (2) is equally applicable to the $6 million payment received in 1982. However, the adjusted gross profit ratio determined in this example (4) will differ from the ratio determined in example (2). The difference is attributable to the difference between a 9% stated interest rate calculation (in this example (4)) and the compound rate of unstated interest required under section 483 and used in calculating the results in example (2).

*Example (5).* The facts are the same as in example (1). In 1992 X is adjudged a bankrupt and it is determined that, in and after 1992, B will not be required to make any further payments under the agreement, *i.e.*, B's contingent payment obligation held by A now has become worthless. Assume that A previously received aggregate payments (exclusive of interest) of $45 million and out of those payments recovered $15 million of A's total $20 million basis. For 1992 A will report a loss of $5 million attributable to the sale, taken at the time determined to be appropriate under the rules generally applicable to worthless debts.

*Example (6).* (i) C owns all of the stock of Z corporation, a calendar year taxpayer. On July 1, 1981, C sells the stock of Z to D under an agreement calling for payment, each year for the next ten years, of an amount equal to 10% of the net profits of Z earned in the immediately preceding calendar year beginning with the year ending December 31, 1981. Each payment is to be made on the following April 1st, commencing April 1, 1982. In addition, C is to receive a payment of $5 million on closing. The agreement specifies that the maximum amount payable to C, including the $5 million cash payment at closing, is $24 million. The agreement does not call for the payment of any stated interest. Since section 483 will apply to each payment received by C more than one year following the date of sale (section 483 is inapplicable to the payment that will be received on April 1, 1982, since that date is within one year following the July 1, 1981 sale date), the agreement contemplates internal interest and the price interest recomputation rule is applicable. Under that rule, C must make an initial determination for his taxable year 1981.

(ii) On December 31, 1981, the exact amount of Z's 1981 net profit is not known, since it normally takes a number of weeks to compile the relevant information. However, the events which will determine the amount of the payment C will received on April 1, 1982 have already occurred, and the information (Z's 1981 financial statement) will be promptly calculated and verified and will be available prior to the time C's 1981 tax return is timely filed. On March 15, 1982, Z reports net income of $14 million, and on April 1, 1982 D pays C $1.4 million.

(iii) Under the price-interest recomputation rule, C is required to determine the gross profit ratio for the 1981 $5 million payment on the basis of the events which occurred by the close of that taxable year and which are verifiable before the due date of the 1981 return. Because at the end of C's 1981 taxable year all events which will determine the amount of the April 1, 1982 payment have occurred and because the actual facts are known prior to the due date of C's return, C will take those facts into account when calculating the gross profit ratio. Thus, because C knows that the 1982 payment is $1.4 million, C knows that the remaining amount to be recovered under the contract is $17.6 million ($24 million – ($5 million + $1.4 million)). For purposes of this paragraph C must assume that the entire $17.6 million will be paid on the earliest possible date, April 1, 1983. Because section 483 will apply to that payment, and assuming that under the tables in the regulations under section 483 the principal component of a payment received 21 months after the date of sale is considered to be .86384, $15,203,584 of the $17.6 million would be principal and $2,396,416 ($17,600,000 – $15,203,584) would be interest. Therefore C must assume, for purposes of reporting the $5 million payment received in 1981, that the selling price is $21,603,584 calculated as follows:

| | |
|---|---|
| Total selling price | $24,000,000 |
| Interest component of the $17,600,000 payment which C must assume will be made April 1, 1983 | – 2,396,416 |
| Adjusted selling price to be used when reporting the 1981 payment | 21,603,584 |

(iv) Assume that on March 15, 1982, Z reports net income of $15 million for 1982 and that on April 1, 1983 D pays C $1.5 million. Because section 483 will apply to that payment, and assuming that under the tables in the regulations under section 483 the principal component of a payment received 21 months after the date of sale is considered to be .86384, $1,295,760 of the $1,500,000 payment will be principal and $204,240 ($1,500,000 – $1,295,760) will be interest. Because C knows the amount of the 1983 payment when filing the 1982 tax return, C must assume that the remaining amount to be received under the contract, $16.1 million ($24 million – ($5 million + $1.4 million + $1.5 million)), will be received as a lump sum on April 1, 1984. Because section 483 will again apply, and assuming that the principal component of a payment made 34 months after the date of the sale is .74622, $12,014,142 of the $16.1 million would be principal, and $4,085,858 ($16,100,000 – $12,014,142) would be interest. Therefore, C must assume, for purpose of reporting the $1.4 million payment made April 1, 1982, that the adjusted selling price (within the meaning of example (2)) is $14,709,902, calculated as follows:

| | |
|---|---|
| Total selling price | $24,000,000 |
| Interest component of the $1,500,000 payment made April 1, 1983 | – 204,240 |
| Interest component of the $16,100,000 payment which C must assume will be made April 1, 1984 | – 4,085,858 |
| Payment made in 1981 | – 5,000,000 |
| Adjusted selling price for calculations for reporting the 1982 payment | 14,709,902 |

*(3) Fixed period.* (i) In general. When a stated maximum selling price cannot be determined as of the close of the taxable year in which the sale or other disposition occurs, but the maximum period over which payments may be received under the contingent sale price agreement is fixed, the taxpayer's basis (inclusive of selling expenses) shall be allocated to the taxable years in which payment may be received under the agreement in equal annual increments. In making the allocation it is not relevant whether the buyer is required to pay adequate stated interest. However, if the terms of the agreement incorporate an arithmetic component that is not identical for all taxable years, basis shall be allocated among the taxable years to accord with that component unless, taking into account all of the payment terms of the agreement, it is inappropriate to presume that payments under the contract are likely to accord with the variable component. If in any taxable year no payment is received or the amount of payment received (exclusive of interest) is less than the basis allocated to that taxable year, no loss shall be allowed unless

the taxable year is the final payment year under the agreement or unless it is otherwise determined in accordance with the rules generally applicable to worthless debts that the future payment obligation under the agreement has become worthless. When no loss is allowed, the unrecovered portion of basis allocated to the taxable year shall be carried forward to the next succeeding taxable year. If application of the foregoing rules to a particular case would substantially and inappropriately defer or accelerate recovery of the taxpayer's basis, a special rule will apply. See paragraph (c)(7) of this section.

(ii) Examples. The following examples illustrate the rules for recovery of basis in a contingent payment sale in which stated maximum selling price cannot be determined but the period over which payments are to be received under the agreement is fixed. In each case, it is assumed that application of the described rules will not substantially and inappropriately defer or accelerate recovery of the taxpayer's basis.

*Example (1).* A sells Blackacre to B for 10 percent of Blackacre's gross yield for each of the next 5 years. A's basis in Blackacre is $5 million. Since the sales price is indefinite and the maximum selling price is not ascertainable from the terms of the contract, basis is recovered ratably over the period during which payment may be received under the contract. Thus, assuming A receives the payments (exclusive of interest) listed in the following table, A will report the following:

| Year | Payment | Basis Recovered | Gain Attributable To The Sale |
|---|---|---|---|
| 1 | $1,300,000 | $1,000,000 | $300,000 |
| 2 | 1,500,000 | 1,000,000 | 500,000 |
| 3 | 1,400,000 | 1,000,000 | 400,000 |
| 4 | 1,800,000 | 1,000,000 | 800,000 |
| 5 | 2,100,000 | 1,000,000 | 1,100,000 |

*Example (2).* The facts are the same as in example (1), except that the payment in year 1 is only $900,000. Since the installment payment is less than the amount of basis allocated to that year, the unrecovered basis, $100,000, is carried forward to year 2.

| Year | Payment | Basis Recovered | Gain Attributable To The Sale |
|---|---|---|---|
| 1 | $900,000 | $900,000 | ........... |
| 2 | 1,500,000 | 1,100,000 | $400,000 |
| 3 | 1,400,000 | 1,000,000 | 400,000 |
| 4 | 1,800,000 | 1,000,000 | 800,000 |
| 5 | 2,100,000 | 1,000,000 | 1,100,000 |

*Example (3).* C owns all of the stock of X corporation with a basis of $100,000 (inclusive of selling expenses). D purchases the X stock from C and agrees to make four payments computed in accordance with the following formula: 40% of the net profits of X in year 1, 30% in year 2, 20% in year 3, and 10% in year 4. Accordingly, C's basis is allocated as follows: $40,000 to year 1, $30,000 to year 2, $20,000 to year 3, and $10,000 to year 4.

*Example (4).* The facts are the same as in example (3), but the agreement also requires that D make fixed installment payments in accordance with the following schedule: no payment in year 1, $100,000 in year 2, $200,000 in year 3, $300,000 in year 4, and $400,000 in year 5. Thus, while it is reasonable to project that the contingent component of the payments will decrease each year, the fixed component of the payments will increase each year. Accordingly, C is required to allocate $20,000 of basis to each of the taxable years 1 through 5.

*(4) Neither stated maximum selling price nor fixed period.* If the agreement neither specifies a maximum selling price nor limits payments to a fixed period, a question arises whether a sale realistically has occurred or whether, in economic effect, payments received under the agreement are in the nature of rent or royalty income. Arrangements of this sort will be closely scrutinized. If, taking into account all of the pertinent facts, including the nature of the property, the arrangement is determined to qualify as a sale, the taxpayer's basis (including selling expenses) shall be recovered in equal annual increments over a period of 15 years commencing with the date of sale. However, if in any taxable year no payment is received or the amount of payment received (exclusive of interest) is less than basis allocated to the year, no loss shall be allowed unless it is otherwise determined in accordance with the timing rules generally applicable to worthless debts that the future payment obligation under the agreement has become worthless; instead the excess basis shall be reallocated in level amounts over the balance of the 15 year term. Any basis not recovered at the end of the 15th year shall be carried forward to the next succeeding year, and to the extent unrecovered thereafter shall be carried forward from year to year until all basis has been recovered or the future payment obligation is determined to be worthless. The general rule requiring initial level allocation of basis over 15 years shall not apply if the taxpayer can establish to the satisfaction of the Internal Revenue Service that application of the general rule would substantially and inappropriately defer recovery of the taxpayer's basis. See paragraph (c)(7) of this section. If the Service determines that initially allocating basis in level amounts over the first 15 years will substantially and inappropriately accelerate recovery of the taxpayer's basis in early years of that 15-year term, the Service may require that basis be reallocated within the 15-year term but the Service will not require that basis initially be allocated over more than 15 years. See paragraph (c)(7) of this section.

*(5) Foreign currency and other fungible payment units.* (i) In general. An installment sale may call for payment in foreign currency. For federal income tax purposes, foreign currency is property. Because the value of foreign currency will vary over time in relation to the United States dollar, an installment sale requiring payment in foreign currency is a contingent payment sale. However, when the consideration payable under an installment sale agreement is specified in foreign currency, the taxpayer's basis (including selling expenses) shall be recovered in the same manner as basis would have been recovered had the agreement called for payment in United States dollars. This rule is equally applicable to any installment sale in which the agreement specifies that payment shall be made in identified, fungible units of property the value of which will or may vary over time in relation to the dollar *(e.g.,* bushels of wheat or ounces of gold).

(ii) Example. The following example illustrates the provisions of this subparagraph:

*Example.* A sells Blackacre to B for 4 million Swiss francs payable 1 million in year 2 and 3 million in year 3, together with adequate stated interest. A's basis (including selling expenses) in Blackacre is $100,000. Twenty five thousand dollars of A's basis (¼ of total basis) is allocable to the year 2 payment of 1 million Swiss francs and $75,000 of A's basis is allocable to the year 3 payment of 3 million Swiss francs.

*(6) Income forecast method for basis recovery.* (i) In general. The rules for ratable recovery of basis set forth in paragraph (c)(2) through (4) of this section focus on the payment terms of the contingent selling price agreement. Except to the extent contemplated by paragraph (c)(7) of this section (relating to a special rule to prevent substantial distortion of basis recovery), the nature and productivity of the property sold is not independently relevant to the basis to be recovered in any payment year. The special rule for an income forecast method of basis recovery set forth in paragraph (c)(6) of this section recognizes that there are cases in which failure to take account of the nature or productivity of the property sold may be expected to result in distortion of the taxpayer's income over time. Specifically, when the property sold is depreciable property of a type normally eligible for depreciation on the income forecast method, or is depletable property of a type normally eligible for cost depletion in which total future production must be estimated, and payments under the contingent selling price agreement are based upon receipts or units produced by or from the property, the taxpayer's basis may appropriately be recovered by using an income forecast method.

(ii) Availability of method. In lieu of applying the rules set forth in paragraph (c)(2) through (4) of this section, in an appropriate case the taxpayer may elect (on its tax return timely filed for the first year under the contingent payment agreement in which a payment is received) to recover basis using the income forecast method of basis recovery. No special form of election is prescribed. An appropriate case is one meeting the criteria set forth in paragraph (c)(6)(i) of this section in which the property sold is a mineral property, a motion picture film, a television film, or a taped television show. The Internal Revenue Service may from time to time specify other properties of a similar character which, in appropriate circumstances, will be eligible for recovery of basis on the income forecast method. In addition, a taxpayer may seek a ruling from the Service as to whether a specific property qualifies as property of a similar character eligible, in appropriate circumstances, for income forecast recovery of basis.

(iii) Required calculations. The income forecast method requires application of a fraction, the numerator of which is the payment (exclusive of interest) received in the taxable year under a contingent payment agreement, and the denominator of which is the forecast or estimated total payments (exclusive of interest) to be received under the agreement. This fraction is multiplied by the taxpayer's basis in the property sold to determine the basis recovered with respect to the payment received in the taxable year. If in a subsequent year it is found that the income forecast was substantially overestimated or underestimated by reason of circumstances occurring in such subsequent year, an adjustment of the income forecast of such subsequent year shall be made. In such case, the formula for computing recovery of basis would be as follows: payment received in the taxable year (exclusive of interest) divided by the revised estimated total payments (exclusive of interest) then and thereafter to be made under the agreement (the current year's payment and total estimated future payments), multiplied by the taxpayer's unrecovered basis remaining as of the beginning of the taxable year. If the agreement contemplates internal interest (as defined in paragraph (c)(2)(ii) of this section), in making the initial income forecast computation and in making any required subsequent recomputation the amount of internal interest (which shall not be treated as payment under the agreement) shall be calculated by assuming that each future contingent selling price payment will be made in the amount and at the time forecast. The total forecast of estimated payments to be received under the agreement shall be based on the conditions known to exist at the end of the taxable year for which the return is filed. If a subsequent upward or downward revision of this estimate is required, the revision shall be made at the end of the subsequent taxable year based on additional information which became available after the last prior estimate. No loss shall be allowed unless the taxable year is the final payment year under the agreement or unless it is otherwise determined in accordance with the rules generally applicable to the time a debt becomes worthless that the future payment obligation under the agreement has become worthless.

(iv) Examples. The following examples illustrate the income forecast method of basis recovery:

*Example (1).* A sells a television film to B for 5% of annual gross receipts from the exploitation of the film. The film is an ordinary income asset in the hands of A. A reasonably forecasts that total payments to be received under the contingent selling price agreement will be $1,200,000, and that A will be paid $600,000 in year 1, $150,000 in year 2, $300,000 in year 3, $100,000 in year 4, and $50,000 in year 5. A reasonably anticipates no or only insignificant receipts thereafter. A's basis in the film is $100,000. Under the income forecast method, A's basis initially is allocated to the five taxable years of forecasted payment as follows:

| Year | Percentage | Basis |
|---|---|---|
| 1 | 50.00 | $50,000 |
| 2 | 12.50 | 12,500 |
| 3 | 25.00 | 25,000 |
| 4 | 8.33 | 8,333 |
| 5 | 4.17 | 4,167 |

Payments are received and A reports the sale under the installment method as follows:

| Year | Payment Received | Basis Recovered | Gain On Sale |
|---|---|---|---|
| 1 | $600,000 | $50,000 | $550,000 |
| 2 | 150,000 | 12,500 | 137,500 |
| 3 | 300,000 | 25,000 | 275,000 |
| 4 | 100,000 | 8,333 | 91,667 |
| 5 | 50,000 | 4,167 | 45,833 |

*Example (2).* The facts are the same as in example (1), except that in year 2 A receives no payment. In year 3 A receives a payment of $300,000 and reasonably estimates that in subsequent years he will receive total additional payments of only $100,000. In year 2 A will be allowed no loss. At the beginning of year 3 A's unrecovered basis is $50,000. In year 3 A must recompute the applicable basis recovery fraction based upon facts known and forecast as at the end of year 3: year 3 payment of $300,000 divided by estimated current and future payments of $400,000, equaling 75%. Thus, in year 3 A recovers $37,500 (75% of $50,000) of A's previously unrecovered basis.

*(7) Special rule to avoid substantial distortion.* (i) In general. The normal basis recovery rules set forth in paragraph (c) (2) through (4) of this section may, with respect to a particular contingent payment sale, substantially and inappropriately defer or accelerate recovery of the taxpayer's basis.

(ii) Substantial and inappropriate deferral. The taxpayer may use an alternative method of basis recovery if the taxpayer is able to demonstrate prior to the due date of the return including extensions for the taxable year in which the first payment is received, that application of the normal basis recovery rule will substantially and inappropriately defer recovery of basis. To demonstrate that application of the normal basis recovery rule will substantially and inappropriately defer recovery of basis, the taxpayer must show (A) that the alternative method is a reasonable method of ratably recovering basis and, (B) that, under that method, it is reasonable to conclude that over time the taxpayer likely will recover basis at a rate twice as fast as the rate at which basis would have been recovered under the otherwise applicable normal basis recovery rule. The taxpayer must receive a ruling from the Internal Revenue Service before using an alternative method of basis recovery described in paragraph (c)(7)(ii) of this section.

The request for a ruling shall be made in accordance with all applicable procedural rules set forth in the Statement of Procedural Rules (26 CFR Part 601) and any applicable revenue procedures relating to submission of ruling requests. The request shall be submitted to the Commissioner of Internal Revenue, Attention: Assistant Commissioner (Technical), Washington, DC 20224. The taxpayer must file a request for a ruling prior to the due date for the return including extensions. In demonstrating that application of the normal basis recovery rule would substantially and inappropriately defer recovery of the taxpayer's basis, the taxpayer in appropriate circumstances may rely upon contemporaneous or immediate past relevant sales, profit, or other factual data that are subject to verification. The taxpayer ordinarily is not permitted to rely upon projections of future productivity, receipts, profits, or the like. However, in special circumstances a reasonable projection may be acceptable if the projection is based upon a specific event that already has occurred ( *e.g.*, corporate stock has been sold for future payments contingent on profits and an inadequately insured major plant facility of the corporation has been destroyed).

(iii) Substantial and inappropriate acceleration. Notwithstanding the other provisions of this paragraph, the Internal Revenue Service may find that the normal basis recovery rule will substantially and inappropriately accelerate recovery of basis. In such a case, the Service may require an alternate method of basis recovery, unless the taxpayer is able to demonstrate either (A) that the method of basis recovery required by the Service is not a reasonable method of ratable recovery, or (B) that it is not reasonable to conclude that the taxpayer over time is likely to recover basis at a rate twice as fast under the normally applicable basis recovery rule as the rate at which basis would be recovered under the method proposed by the Service. In making such demonstrations the taxpayer may rely in appropriate circumstances upon contemporaneous or immediate past relevant sales, profit, or other factual data subject to verification. In special circumstances a reasonable projection may be acceptable, but only with the consent of the Service, if the projection is based upon a specific event that has already occurred.

(iv) Subsequent recomputation. A contingent payment sale may initially and properly have been reported under the normally applicable basis recovery rule and, during the term of the agreement, circumstances may show that continued reporting on the original method will substantially and inappropriately defer or accelerate recovery of the unrecovered balance of the taxpayer's basis. In this event, the special rule provided in this paragraph is applicable.

(v) Examples. The following examples illustrate the application of the special rule of this paragraph. In examples (1) and (2) it is assumed that rulings consistent with paragraph (c)(7)(ii) of this section have been requested.

*Example (1).* A owns all of the stock of X corporation with a basis of $100,000. A sells the stock of X to B for a cash down payment of $1,800,000 and B's agreement to pay A an amount equal to 1% of the net profits of X in each of the next 10 years (together with adequate stated interest). The agreement further specifies that the maximum amount that may be paid to A (exclusive of interest) shall not exceed $10 million. A is able to demonstrate the current and recent profits of X have approximated $2 million annually, and that there is no reason to anticipate a major increase in the annual profits of X during the next 10 years. One percent of $2 million annual profits is $20,000, a total of $200,000 over 10 years. Under the basis recovery rule normally applicable to a maximum contingent selling price agreement, in the year of sale A would recover $18,000 of A's total $100,000 basis, and would not recover more than a minor part of the balance until the final year under the agreement. On a $2 million selling price ($200,000 plus $1,800,000 down payment), A would recover $90,000 of A's total $100,000 basis in the year of sale and 5% of each payment ($100,000/$2,000,000) received up to a maximum of $10,000 over the next ten years. Since the rate of basis recovery under the demonstrated method is more than twice the rate under the normal rule, A will be permitted to recover $90,000 basis in the year of sale.

*Example (2).* The facts are the same as in example (1) except that no maximum contingent selling price is stated in the agreement. Under the basis recovery rule normally applicable when no maximum amount is stated but the payment term is fixed, in the year of sale and in each subsequent year A would recover approximately $9,100 (1/11 of $100,000) of A's total basis. A will be permitted to recover $90,000 of A's total basis in the year of sale.

*Example (3).* The facts are the same as in example (1) except that A sells the X stock to B on the following terms: 1% of the annual net profits of X in each of the next 10 years and a cash payment of $1,800,000 in the eleventh year, all payments to be made together with adequate stated interest. No maximum contingent selling price is stated. Under the normally applicable basis recovery rule, A would recover 1/11 of A's total $100,000 basis in each of the 11 payment years under the agreement. On the facts (see example (1)), A cannot demonstrate that application of the normal rule would not substantially and inappropriately accelerate recovery of A's basis. Accordingly, A will be allowed to recover only $1,000 of A's total basis in each of the 10 contingent payment years under the agreement, and will recover the $90,000 balance of A's basis in the final year in which the large fixed cash payment will be made.

*(8) Coordination with regulations under section 385.* (i) In general. The regulations under section 385 do not apply to an instrument (as defined in § 1.385-3(c)) providing for a contingent payment of principal (with or without stated interest) issued in connection with a sale or other disposition of property to a corporation if § 1.385-6 (relating to proportionality) does not apply to such instrument (or to a class of instruments which includes such instrument). Thus, such instrument will be treated as stock or indebtedness under applicable principles of law without reference to the regulations under section 385.

*Example (1).* On January 1, 1982, corporation X buys a factory from Y, an independent creditor (within the meaning of § 1.385-6(b)). In exchange for the factory, Y receives $200,000 in cash on January 1, 1982. In addition, on January 1, 1984, Y will receive a payment in the range of $100,000 to $300,000, plus adequate stated interest, depending on the factory's output. Based on these facts, § 1.385-6 does not apply to X's obligation to Y (see § 1.385-6(a)(3)(ii) and the regulations under section 385 doe not apply to X's obligation to Y.

(ii) Examples. The following examples illustrate the application of this paragraph:

*Example (2).* The facts are the same as in example (1), except that the contingent payment due on January 1, 1984 will be in the range of $50,000 to $250,000. In addition, on January 1, 1982, Y receives a $50,000 noninterest-bearing note due absolutely and unconditionally on January 1, 1984. Based on these facts, the $50,000 note is treated as stock or indebtedness under the regulations under section 385.

**(d) Election not to report an installment sale on the installment method.** *(1) In general.* An installment sale is to be reported on the installment method unless the taxpayer elects otherwise in accordance with the rules set forth in paragraph (d)(3) of this section.

*(2) Treatment of an installment sale when a taxpayer elects not to report on the installment method.* (i) In general. A taxpayer who elects not to report an installment sale on the installment method must recognize gain on the sale in accordance with the taxpayer's method of accounting. The fair market value of an installment obligation shall be determined in accordance with paragraph (d)(2)(ii) and (iii) of this section. In making such determination, any provision of contract or local law restricting the transferability of the installment obligation shall be disregarded. Receipt of an installment obligation shall be treated as a receipt of property, in an amount equal to the fair market value of the installment obligation, whether or not such obligation is the equivalent of cash. An installment obligation is considered to be property and is subject to valuation, as provided in paragraph (d)(2)(ii) and (iii) of this section, without regard to whether the obligation is embodied in a note, an executory contract, or any other instrument, or is an oral promise enforceable under local law.

(ii) Fixed amount obligations. (A) A fixed amount obligation means an installment obligation the amount payable under which is fixed. Solely for the purpose of determining whether the amount payable under an installment obligation is fixed, the provisions of section 483 and any "payment recharacterization" arrangement (as defined in paragraph (c)(2)(ii) of this section) shall be disregarded. If the fixed amount payable is stated in identified, fungible units of property the value of which will or may vary over time in relation to the United States dollar *(e.g.,* foreign currency, ounces of gold, or bushels of wheat), such units shall be converted to United States dollars at the rate of exchange or dollar value on the date the installment sale is made. A taxpayer using the cash receipts and disbursements methods of accounting shall treat as an amount realized in the year of sale the fair market value of the installment obligation. In no event will the fair market value of the installment obligation be considered to be less than the fair market value of the property sold (minus any other consideration received by the taxpayer on the sale). A taxpayer using the accrual method of accounting shall treat as an amount realized in the year of sale the total amount payable under the installment obligation. For this purpose, neither interest (whether stated or unstated) nor original issue discount is considered to be part of the amount payable. If the amount payable is otherwise fixed, but because the time over which payments may be made is contingent, a portion of the fixed amount will or may be treated as internal interest (as defined in paragraph (c)(2)(ii) of this section), the amount payable shall be determined by applying the price interest recomputation rule (described in paragraph (c)(2)(ii) of this section). Under no circumstances will an installment sale for a fixed amount obligation be considered an "open" transaction. For purposes of this (ii), remote or incidental contingencies are not to be taken into account.

(B) The following examples illustrate the provisions of paragraph (d)(2) of this section.

*Example (1).* A, an accrual method taxpayer, owns all of the stock of X corporation with a basis of $20 million. On July 1, 1981, A sells the stock of X corporation to B for $60 million payable on June 15, 1992. The agreement also provides that against this fixed amount, B shall make annual prepayments (on June 15) equal to 5% of the net profits of X earned in the immediately preceding fiscal year beginning with the fiscal year ending March 31, 1982. Thus the first prepayment will be made on June 15, 1982. No stated interest is payable under the agreement and thus the unstated interest provisions of section 483 are applicable. Under section 483, no part of any payment made on June 15, 1982 (which is within one year following the July 1, 1981 sale date), will be treated as unstated interest. Under the price interest recomputation rule, it is presumed that the entire $60 million fixed amount will be paid on June 15, 1982. Accordingly, if A elects not to report the transaction on the installment method, in 1981 A must report $60 million as the amount realized on the sale and must report $40 million as gain on the sale in that year.

*Example (2).* The facts are the same as in example (1) except that A uses the cash receipts and disbursements method of accounting. In 1981 A must report as an amount realized on the sale the fair market value of the installment obligation and must report as gain on the sale in 1981 the excess of that amount realized over A's basis of $20 million. In no event will the fair market value of the installment obligation be considered to be less than the fair market value of the stock of X. In determining the fair market value of the installment obligation, any contractual or legal restrictions on the transferability of the installment obligation, and any remote or incidental contingencies otherwise affecting the amount payable or time of payments under the installment obligation, shall be disregarded.

(iii) Contingent payment obligations. Any installment obligation which is not a fixed amount obligation (as defined in paragraph (d)(2)(ii) of this section) is a contingent payment obligation. If an installment obligation contains both a fixed amount component and a contingent payment component, the fixed amount component shall be treated under the rules of paragraph (d)(2)(ii) of this section and the contingent amount component shall be treated under the rules of this (iii). The fair market value of a contingent payment obligation shall be determined by disregarding any restrictions on transfer imposed by agreement or under local law. The fair market value of a contingent payment obligation may be ascertained from, and in no event shall be considered to be less than, the fair market value of the property sold (less the amount of any other consideration received in the sale). Only in those rare and extraordinary cases involving sales for a contingent payment obligation in which the fair market value of the obligation (determinable under the preceding sentences) cannot reasonably be ascertained will the taxpayer be entitled to assert that the transaction is "open." Any such transaction will be carefully scrutinized to determine whether a sale in fact has taken place. A taxpayer using the cash receipts and disbursements method of accounting must report as an amount realized in the year of sale the fair market value of the contingent payment obligation. A taxpayer using the accrual method of accounting must report an amount realized in the year of sale determined in accordance with that method of accounting, but in no event less than the fair market value of the contingent payment obligation.

*(3) Time and manner for making election.* (i) In general. An election under paragraph (d)(1) of this section must be made on or before the due date prescribed by law (including extensions) for filing the taxpayer's return for the taxable year in which the installment sale occurs. The election must be made in the manner prescribed by the appropriate forms for the taxpayer's return for the taxable year of the sale. A taxpayer who reports an amount realized equal to the selling price including the full face amount of any installment obligation on the tax return filed for the taxable year in which the installment sale occurs will be considered to have made an effective election under paragraph (d)(1) of this section. A cash method taxpayer receiving an obligation the fair market value of which is less than the face value must make the election in the manner prescribed by appropriate instructions for the return filed for the taxable year of the sale.

(ii) Election made after the due date. Elections after the time specified in paragraph (d)(3)(i) of this section will be permitted only in those rare circumstances when the Internal Revenue Service concludes that the taxpayer had good cause for failing to make a timely election. A recharacterization of a transaction as a sale in a taxable year subsequent to the taxable year in which the transaction occurred ( *e.g.*, a transaction initially reported as a lease later is determined to have been an installment sale) will not justify a late election. No conditional elections will be permitted. For a special transitional rule relating to certain taxable years for which a return is filed prior to February 19, 1981, see paragraph (d)(5) of this section.

*(4) Revoking an election.* Generally, an election made under paragraph (d)(1) is irrevocable. An election may be revoked only with the consent of the Internal Revenue Service. A revocation is retroactive. A revocation will not be permitted when one of its purposes is the avoidance of federal income taxes, or when the taxable year in which any payment was received has closed. For a special transitional rule relating to certain taxable years for which a return is filed prior to February 19, 1981, see paragraph (d)(5) of this section.

*(5) Transitional rules.* The following transitional rules shall apply with respect to any contingent payment sale made after October 19, 1980 in a taxable year, ending after that date, for which the taxpayer has filed a federal income tax return prior to February 19, 1981. If in such tax return the taxpayer has treated the contingent payment sale under the installment method, consent of the Internal Revenue Service to a late election by the taxpayer not to report the transaction on the installment method will generally be granted if the request for election out of installment method treatment is filed by May 5, 1981. If in such tax return the taxpayer has elected not to report the contingent payment sale under the installment method, consent of the Service to revocation of the election by the taxpayer will generally be granted if the request for revocation is filed by May 5, 1981.

**(e) Purchaser evidences of indebtedness payable on demand or readily tradable.** *(1) Treatment as payment.* (i) In general. A bond or other evidence of indebtedness (hereinafter in this section referred to as an obligation) issued by any person and payable on demand shall be treated as a payment in the year received, not as installment obligations payable in future years. In addition, an obligation issued by a corporation or a government or political subdivision thereof—

(A) With interest coupons attached (whether or not the obligation is readily tradable in an established securities market),

(B) In registered form (other than an obligation issued in registered form which the taxpayer establishes will not be readily tradable in an established securities market), or

(C) In any other form designed to render such obligation readily tradable in an established securities market,

shall be treated as a payment in the year received, not as an installment obligation payable in future years. For purposes of this paragraph, an obligation is to be considered in registered form if it is registered as to principal, interest, or both and if its transfer must be effected by the surrender of the old instrument and either the reissuance by the corporation of the old instrument to the new holder or the issuance by the corporation of a new instrument to the new holder.

(ii) Examples. The rules stated in this paragraph may be illustrated by the following examples:

*Example (1).* On July 1, 1981, A, an individual on the cash method of accounting reporting on a calendar year basis, transferred all of his stock in corporation X (traded on an established securities market and having a fair market value of $1,000,000) to corporation Y in exchange for 250 of Y's registered bonds (which are traded in an over-the-counter-market) each with a principal amount and fair market value of $1,000 (with interest payable at the rate of 12 percent per year), and Y's unsecured promissory note with a principal amount of $750,000. At the time of such exchange A's basis in the X stock is $900,000. The promissory note is payable at the rate of $75,000 annually, due on July 1 of each year following 1981 until the principal balance is paid. The note provides for the payment of interest at the rate of 12 percent per year also payable on July 1 of each year. Under the rule stated in paragraph (e)(1)(i) of this section, the 250 registered bonds of Y are treated as a payment in 1981 in the amount of the value of the bonds, $250,000.

*Example (2).* Assume the same facts as in example (1). Assume further that on July 1, 1982, Y makes its first installment payment to A under the terms of the unsecured promissory note with 75 more of its $1,000 registered bonds. A must include $7,500 (i.e., 10 percent gross profit percentage times $75,000) A's gross income for calendar year 1982. In addition, A includes the interest payment made by Y on July 1 in A's gross income for 1982.

*(2) Amounts treated as payment.* If under paragraph (e)(1) of this section an obligation is treated as a payment in the year received, the amount realized by reason of such payment shall be determined in accordance with the taxpayer's method of accounting. If the taxpayer uses the cash receipts and disbursements method of accounting, the amount realized on such payment is the fair market value of the obligation. If the taxpayer uses the accrual method of accounting, the amount realized on receipt of an obligation payable on demand is the face amount of the obligation, and the amount realized on receipt of an obligation with coupons attached or a readily tradable obligation is the stated redemption price at maturity less any original issue discount (as defined in section 1232(b)(1)) or, if there is no original issue discount, the amount realized is the stated redemption price at maturity appropriately discounted to reflect total unstated interest (as defined in section 483(b)), if any.

*(3) Payable on demand.* An obligation shall be treated as payable on demand only if the obligation is treated as payable on demand under applicable state or local law.

*(4) Designed to be readily tradable in an established securities market.* (i) In general. Obligations issued by a corporation or government or political subdivision thereof will be deemed to be in a form designed to render such obligations readily tradable in an established securities market if—

(A) Steps necessary to create a market for them are taken at the time of issuance (or later, if taken pursuant to an expressed or implied agreement or understanding which existed at the time of issuance),

(B) If they are treated as readily tradable in an established securities market under paragraph (e)(4)(ii) of this section, or

(C) If they are convertible obligations to which paragraph (e)(5) of this section applies.

(ii) Readily tradable in an established securities market. An obligation will be treated as readily tradable in an established securities market if—

(A) The obligation is part of an issue or series of issues which are readily tradable in an established securities market, or

(B) The corporation issuing the obligation has other obligations of a comparable character which are described in paragraph (e)(4)(ii)(A) of this section. For purposes of paragraph (e)(4)(ii)(B) of this section, the determination as to whether there exist obligations of a comparable character depends upon the particular facts and circumstances. Factors to be considered in making such determination include, but are not limited to, substantial similarity with respect to the presence and nature of security for the obligation, the number of obligations issued (or to be issued), the number of holders of such obligation, the principal amount of the obligation, and other relevant factors.

(iii) Readily tradable. For purposes of paragraph (e)(4)(ii)(A) of this section, an obligation shall be treated as readily tradable if it is regularly quoted by brokers or dealers making a market in such obligation or is part of an issue a portion of which is in fact traded in an established securities market.

(iv) Established securities market. For purposes of this paragraph, the term "established securities market" includes (A) a national securities exchange which is registered under section 6 of the Securities Exchange Act of 1934 (15 U.S.C. 78f), (B) an exchange which is exempted from registration under section 5 of the Securities Exchange Act of 1934 (15 U.S.C. 78e) because of the limited volume of transactions, and (c) any over-the-counter market. For purposes of this (iv), an over-the-counter market is reflected by the existence of an interdealer quotation system. An interdealer quotation system is any system of general circulation to brokers and dealers which regularly disseminates quotations of obligations by identified brokers or dealers, other than a quotation sheet prepared and distributed by a broker or dealer in the regular course of business and containing only quotations of such broker or dealer.

(v) Examples. The rules stated in this paragraph may be illustrated by the following examples:

*Example (1).* On June 1, 1982, 25 individuals owning equal interests in a tract of land with a fair market value of $1 million sell the land to corporation Y. The $1 million sales price is represented by 25 bonds issued by Y, each having a face value of $40,000. The bonds are not in registered form and do not have interest coupons attached, and, in addition, are payable in 120 equal installments, each due on the first business day of each month. In addition, the bonds are negotiable and may be assigned by the holder to any other person. However, the bonds are not quoted by any brokers or dealers who deal in corporate bonds, and, furthermore, there are no comparable obligations of Y (determined with reference to the characteristics set forth in paragraph (e)(2) of this section) which are so quoted. Therefore, the bonds are not treated as readily tradable in an established securities market. In addition, under the particular facts and circumstances stated, the bonds will not be considered to be in a form designed to render them readily tradable in an established securities market. The receipt of such bonds by the holder is not treated as a payment for purposes of section 453(f)(4), notwithstanding that they are freely assignable.

*Example (2).* On April 1, 1981, corporation M purchases in a casual sale of personal property a fleet of trucks from corporation N in exchange for M's negotiable notes, not in registered form and without coupons attached. The M notes are comparable to earlier notes issued by M, which notes are quoted in the Eastern Bond section of the National Daily Quotation Sheet, which is an interdealer quotation system. Both issues of notes are unsecured, held by more than 100 holders, have a maturity date of more than 5 years, and were issued for a comparable principal amount. On the basis of these similar characteristics it appears that the latest notes will also be readily tradable. Since an interdealer system reflects an over-the-counter market, the earlier notes are treated as readily tradable in an established securities market. Since the later notes are obligations comparable to the earlier ones, which are treated as readily tradable in an established securities market, the later notes are also treated as readily tradable in an established securities market (whether or not such notes are actually traded).

*(5) Special rule for convertible securities.* (i) General rule. If an obligation contains a right whereby the holder of such obligation may convert it directly or indirectly into another obligation which would be treated as a payment under paragraph (e)(1) of this section or may convert it directly or indirectly into stock which would be treated as readily tradable in an established securities market under paragraph (e)(4) of this section, the convertible obligation shall be considered to be in a form designed to render such obligation readily tradable in an established securities market unless such obligation is convertible only at a substantial discount. In determining whether the stock or obligation into which an obligation is convertible is readily tradable or designed to be readily tradable in an established securities market, the rules stated in paragraph (e)(4) of this section shall apply, and for purposes of such paragraph (e)(4) if such obligation is convertible into stock then the term "stock" shall be substituted for the term "obligation" wherever it appears in such paragraph (e)(4).

(ii) Substantial discount rule. Whether an obligation is convertible at a substantial discount depends upon the particular facts and circumstances. A substantial discount shall be considered to exist if at the time the convertible obligation is issued, the fair market value of the stock or obligation into which the obligation is convertible is less than 80 percent of the fair market value of the obligation (determined by taking into account all relevant factors, including proper discount to reflect the fact that the convertible obligation is not readily tradable in an established securities market and any additional consideration required to be paid by the taxpayer). Also, if a privilege to convert an obligation into stock or an obligation which is readily tradable in an established securities market may not be exercised within a period of one year from the date the obligation is issued, a substantial discount shall be considered to exist.

*(6) Effective date.* The provisions of this paragraph (e) shall apply to sales or other dispositions occurring after May 27, 1969, which are not made pursuant to a binding written contract entered into on or before such date. No inference shall be drawn from this section as to any questions of law concerning the application of section 453 to sales or other dispositions occurring on or before May 27, 1969.

T.D. 7768, 1/30/81, amend T.D. 7788, 9/30/81, T.D. 8535, 4/19/94.

## § 1.453-3 Purchaser evidences of indebtedness payable on demand or readily tradable.

**(a) In general.** A bond or other evidence of indebtedness (hereinafter in this section referred to as an obligation) issued by any person and payable on demand shall not be treated as an evidence of indebtedness of the purchaser in applying section 453(b) to a sale or other disposition of real property or to a casual sale or other casual disposition of personal property. In addition, an obligation issued by a corporation or a government or political subdivision thereof—

*(1)* With interest coupons attached (whether or not the obligation is readily tradable in an established securities market),

*(2)* In registered form (other than an obligation issued in registered form which the taxpayer establishes will not be readily tradable in an established securities market), or

*(3)* In any other form designed to render such obligation readily tradable in an established securities market)

shall not be treated as an evidence of indebtedness of the purchaser in applying section 453(b) to a sale or other disposition of real property or to a casual sale or other casual disposition of personal property. For purposes of this section, an obligation is to be considered in registered form if it is registered as to principal, interest, or both and if its transfer must be effected by the surrender of the old instrument and either the reissuance by the corporation of the old instrument to the new holder or the issuance by the corporation of a new instrument to the new holder.

**(b) Treatment as payment.** If under section 453(b)(3) an obligation is not treated as an evidence of indebtedness of the purchaser, then—

*(1)* For purposes of determining whether the payments received in the taxable year of the sale or other disposition exceed 30 percent of the selling price, and

*(2)* For purposes of returning income on the installment method during the taxable year of the sale or disposition or in a subsequent taxable year, the receipt by the seller of such obligation shall be treated as a payment. The rules stated in this paragraph may be illustrated by the following examples:

*Example (1).* On July 1, 1970, A, an individual on the cash method of accounting reporting on a calendar year basis, transferred all of his stock in corporation X (traded on an established securities market and having a fair market value of $1 million) to corporation Y in exchange for 250 of corporation Y's registered bonds (which are traded in an over-the-counter bond market) each with a principal amount and fair market value of $1,000 (with interest payable at the rate of 8 percent per year), and Y's unsecured promissory note, with a principal amount of $750,000. At the time of such exchange A's basis in the corporation X stock is $900,000. The promissory note is payable at the rate of $75,000 annually, due on July 1, of each year following 1970, until the principal balance is paid. The note provides for the payment of interest at the rate of 10 percent per year also payable on July 1 of each year. Under the rule stated in subparagraph (1) of this paragraph, the 250 registered bonds of corporation Y are treated as a payment for purposes of the 30 percent test described in section 453(b)(2)(A)(ii). The payment on account of the bonds equals 25 percent of the selling price determined as follows:

$$\frac{\text{\$250,000 payment (i.e., 250 of corporation Y's registered bonds each with a principal amount and fair market value of \$1,000).}}{\text{\$1 million selling price (i.e., \$250,000 of corporation Y's registered bonds plus promissory note of \$750,000).}} = 25 \text{ percent.}$$

Since the payments received in the taxable year of the sale do not exceed 30 percent of the selling price and the sales price exceeds $1,000, A may report the income received on the sale of his corporation X stock on the installment method. A elects to report the income on the installment method. The gross profit to be realized when the corporation X stock is fully paid for is 10 percent of the total contract price, computed as follows: $100,000 gross profit (i.e., $1 million contract price less $900,000 basis in corporation X stock) over $1 million contract price. However, since subparagraph (2) of this paragraph also treats the 250 corporation Y registered bonds as a payment for purposes of reporting income, A must include $25,000 (i.e., 10 percent times $250,000) in his gross income for calendar year 1970, the taxable year of the sale.

*Example (2).* Assume the same facts as in example (1). Assume further that on July 1, 1971, corporation Y makes its first installment payment to A under the terms of the unsecured promissory note with 75 more of its $1,000 registered bonds. A must include $7,500 (i.e., 10 percent gross profit percentage times $75,000) in his gross income for calendar year 1971. In addition, A includes the interest payment made by corporation Y on July 1, in his gross income for 1971.

**(c) Payable on demand.** Under section 453(b)(3), an obligation shall be treated as payable on demand only if the obligation is treated as payable on demand under applicable state or local law.

**(d) Designed to be readily tradable in an established securities market.** *(1) In general.* Obligations issued by a corporation or government or political subdivision thereof will be deemed to be in a form designed to render such obligations readily tradable in an established securities market if—

(i) Steps necessary to create a market for them are taken at the time of issuance (or later, if taken pursuant to an expressed or implied agreement or understanding which existed at the time of issuance),

(ii) If they are treated as readily tradable in an established securities market under subparagraph (2) of this paragraph, or

(iii) If they are convertible obligations to which paragraph (e) of this section applies.

*(2) Readily tradable in an established securities market.* An obligation will be treated as readily tradable in an established securities market if—

(i) The obligation is part of an issue or series of issues which are readily tradable in an established securities market, or

(ii) The corporation issuing the obligation has other obligations of a comparable character which are described in subdivision (i) of this subparagraph.

For purposes of subdivision (ii) of this subparagraph, the determination as to whether there exist obligations of a comparable character depends upon the particular facts and circumstances. Factors to be considered in making such determination include, but are not limited to, substantial similarity with respect to the presence and nature of security for the obligation, the number of obligations issued (or to be issued), the number of holders of such obligation, the principal amount of the obligation, and other relevant factors.

*(3) Readily tradable.* For purposes of subparagraph (2)(i) of this paragraph, an obligation shall be treated as readily tradable if it is regularly quoted by brokers or dealers making a market in such obligation or is part of an issue a portion of which is in fact traded in an established securities market.

*(4) Established securities market.* For purposes of this paragraph, the term established securities market includes (i) a national securities exchange which is registered under section 6 of the Securities and Exchange Act of 1934 (15 U.S.C. 78f), (ii) an exchange which is exempted from registration under section 5 of the Securities Exchange Act of 1935 (15 U.S.C. 78e) because of its limited volume of transactions, and (iii) any over-the-counter market. For purposes of this subparagraph, an over-the-counter market is reflected by the existence of an interdealer quotation system. An interdealer quotation system is any system of general circulation to brokers and dealers which regularly disseminates quotations of obligations by identified brokers or dealers, other than a quotation sheet prepared and distributed by a broker or dealer in the regular course of his business and containing only quotations of such broker or dealer.

*(5) Examples.* The rules stated in this paragraph may be illustrated by the following examples:

*Example (1).* On June 1, 1971, 25 individuals owning equal interests in a tract of land with a fair market value of $1 million sell the land to corporation Y. The $1 million sales price is represented by 25 bonds issued by corporation Y each having a face value of $40,000. The bonds are not in registered form and do not have interest coupons attached, and, in addition, are payable in 120 equal installments each due on the first business day of each month. In addition, the bonds are negotiable and may be assigned by the holder to any other person. However, the bonds are not quoted by any brokers or dealers who deal in corporate bonds, and, furthermore, there are no comparable obligations of corporation Y (determined with reference to the characteristics set forth in subparagraph (2) of this paragraph) which are so quoted. Therefore, the bonds are not treated as readily tradable in an established securities market. In addition, under the particular facts and circumstances stated, the bonds will not be considered to be in a form designed to render them readily tradeable in an established securities market. Since the bonds are not in registered form, do not have coupons attached, are not in a form designed to render them readily tradable in an established securities market, the receipt of such bonds by the holder is not treated as a payment for purposes of section 453(b), notwithstanding that they are freely assignable.

*Example (2).* On April 1, 1972, corporation M purchases in a casual sale of personal property a fleet of trucks from corporation N in exchange for corporation M's negotiable notes, not in registered form and without coupons attached. The corporation M notes are comparable to earlier notes issued by corporation M, which notes are quoted in the Eastern Bond section of the National daily quotation sheet, which is an interdealer quotation system. Both issues of notes are unsecured, held by more than 100 holders, have a maturity date of more than 5 years, and were issued for a comparable principal amount. On the basis of these similar characteristics it appears that the latest notes will also be readily tradable. Since an interdealer system reflects an over-the-counter market, the earlier notes are treated as readily tradable in an established securities market. Since the later notes are obligations comparable to the earlier ones, which are treated as readily tradable in an established securities market, the later notes are also treated as readily tradable in an established securities market (whether or not such notes are actually traded).

**(e) Special rule for convertible securities.** *(1) General rule.* For purposes of paragraph (d)(1) of this section, if an obligation contains a right whereby the holder of such obligation may convert it directly or indirectly into another obligation which would be treated as a payment under paragraph (b) of this section or many convert it directly or indirectly into stock which would be treated as readily tradable or designed to be readily tradable in an established securities market under paragraph (d) of this section, the convertible obligation shall be considered to be in a form designed to render such obligation readily tradable in an established securities market unless such obligation is convertible only at a substantial discount. In determining whether the stock or obligation, into which an obligation is convertible, is readily tradable or designed to be readily tradable in an established securities market, the rules stated in paragraph (d) of this section shall apply, and for purposes of such paragraph (d) if such obligation is convertible into stock then the term "stock" shall be substituted for the term "obligation" wherever it appears in such paragraph (d).

*(2) Substantial discount rule.* Whether an obligation is convertible at a substantial discount depends upon the particular facts and circumstances. A substantial discount shall be considered to exist if at the time the convertible obligation is issued, the fair market value of the stock or obligation into which the obligation is convertible is less than 80 percent of the fair market value of the obligation (determined by taking into account all relevant factors, including proper discount to reflect the fact that the convertible obligation is not readily tradable in an established securities market and any additional consideration required to be paid by the taxpayer). Also, if a privilege to convert an obligation into stock or an obligation which is readily tradable in an established securities market may not be exercised within a period of 1 year from the date the obligation is issued, a substantial discount shall be considered to exist.

**(f) Effective date.** The provisions of this section shall apply to sales or other dispositions occurring after May 27, 1969, which are not made pursuant to a binding written contract entered into on or before such date. No inference shall be drawn from this section as to any question of law concerning the application of section 453 to sales or other dispositions occurring on or before May 27, 1969.

T.D. 6314, 9/17/58, amend T.D. 7197, 7/10/72.

### § 1.453-4 Sale of real property involving deferred periodic payments.

***Caution:*** The Treasury has not yet amended Reg § 1.453-4 to reflect changes made by P.L. 96-471.

**(a) In general.** Sales of real property involving deferred payments include (1) agreements of purchase and sale which contemplate that a conveyance is not to be made at the outset, but only after all or a substantial portion of the selling price has been paid, and (2) sales in which there is an immediate transfer of title, the vendor being protected by a mortgage or other lien as to deferred payments.

**(b) Classes of sales.** Such sales, under either paragraph (a)(1) or (2) of this section, fall into two classes when considered with respect to the terms of sale, as follows:

*(1)* Sales of real property may be accounted for on the installment method, that is, sales of real property in which (i) there are no payments during the taxable year of the sale or (ii) the payments in such taxable year (exclusive of evidences of indebtedness of the purchaser) do not exceed 30 percent of the selling price, or

*(2)* Deferred-payment sales of real property in which the payments received in cash or property other than evidences of indebtedness of the purchaser during the taxable year in which the sale is made exceed 30 percent of the selling price.

**(c) Determination of "selling price".** In the sale of mortgaged property the amount of the mortgage, whether the property is merely taken subject to the mortgage or whether the mortgage is assumed by the purchaser, shall, for the purpose of determining whether a sale is on the installment plan, be included as a part of the "selling price"; and for the purpose of determining the payments and the total contract price as those terms are used in section 453, and §§ 1.453-1 through 1.453-7, the amount of such mortgage shall be included only to the extent that it exceeds the basis of the property. The term "payments" does not include amounts received by the vendor in the year of sale from the disposition to a third person of notes given by the vendee as part of the purchase price which are due and payable in subsequent years. Commissions and other selling expenses paid or incurred by the vendor shall not reduce the amount of the payments, the total contract price, or the selling price.

T.D. 6314, 9/17/58.

### § 1.453-5 Sale of real property treated on installment method.

***Caution:*** The Treasury has not yet amended Reg § 1.453-5 to reflect changes made by P.L. 96-471.

**(a) In general.** In any transaction described in paragraph (b)(1) of § 1.453-4, that is, sales of real property in which there are no payments during the year of sale or the payments in that year do not exceed 30 percent of the selling price, the vendor may return as income from each such transaction in any taxable year that proportion of the installment payments actually received in that year which the gross profit (as described in paragraph (b) of § 1.453-1) realized or to be realized when the property is paid for bears to the total contract price. In any case, the sale of each lot or parcel of a subdivided tract must be treated as a separate transaction and gain or loss computed accordingly. (See paragraph (a) of § 1.61-6.)

**(b) Defaults and repossessions.** *(1) Effective date.* This paragraph shall apply only with respect to taxable years beginning before September 3, 1964, in respect of which an election has not been properly made to have the provisions of section 1038 apply. For rules applicable to taxable years beginning after September 2, 1964, and for taxable years beginning after December 31, 1957, to which such an election applies, see §§ 1.1038 through 1.1038-3.

*(2) Gain or loss on reacquisition of property.* If the purchaser of real property on the installment plan defaults in any of his payments, and the vendor returning income on the installment method reacquires the property sold, whether title thereto had been retained by the vendor or transferred to the purchaser, gain or loss for the year in which the reacquisition occurs is to be computed upon any installment obligations of the purchaser which are satisfied or discharged upon the reacquisition or are applied by the vendor to the purchase or bid price of the property. Such gain or loss is to be measured by the difference between the fair market value at the date of reacquisition of the property reacquired (including the fair market value of any fixed improvements placed on the property by the purchaser) and the basis in the hands of the vendor of the obligations of the purchaser which are so satisfied, discharged, or applied, with proper adjustment for any other amounts realized or costs incurred in connection with the reacquisition.

*(3) Fair market value of reacquired property.* If the property reacquired is bid in by the vendor at a foreclosure sale, the fair market value of the property shall be presumed to be the purchase or bid price thereof in the absence of clear and convincing proof to the contrary.

*(4) Basis of obligations.* The basis in the hands of the vendor of the obligations of the purchaser satisfied, discharged, or applied upon the reacquisition of the property will be the excess of the face value of such obligations over an amount equal to the income which would be returnable were the obligations paid in full. For definition of the basis of an installment obligation, see section 453(d)(2) and paragraph (b)(2) of § 1.453-9.

*(5) Bad debt deduction.* No deduction for a bad debt shall in any case be taken on account of any portion of the obligations of the purchaser which are treated by the vendor as not having been satisfied, discharged, or applied upon the reacquisition of the property, unless it is clearly shown that after the property was reacquired the purchaser remained liable for such portion; and in no event shall the amount of the deduction exceed the basis in the hands of the vendor of the portion of the obligations with respect to which the purchaser remained liable after the reacquisition. See section 166 and the regulations thereunder.

*(6) Basis of reacquired property.* If the property reacquired is subsequently sold, the basis for determining gain or loss is the fair market value of the property at the date of reacquisition, including the fair market value of any fixed improvements placed on the property by the purchaser.

T.D. 6314, 9/17/58, amend T.D. 6916, 4/12/67.

### § 1.453-6 Deferred-payment sale of real property not on installment method.

***Caution:*** The Treasury has not yet amended Reg § 1.453-6 to reflect changes made by P.L. 96-471.

**(a) Value of obligations.** *(1)* In transactions included in paragraph (b)(2) of § 1.453-4, that is, sales of real property involving deferred payments in which the payments received during the year of sale exceed 30 percent of the selling price, the obligations of the purchaser received by the vendor are to be considered as an amount realized to the extent of their fair market value in ascertaining the profit or loss from the transaction. Such obligations, however, are not considered in determining whether the payments during the year of sale exceed 30 percent of the selling price.

*(2)* If the obligations received by the vendor have no fair market value, the payments in cash or other property having a fair market value shall be applied against and reduce the basis of the property sold and, if in excess of such basis, shall be taxable to the extent of the excess. Gain or loss is realized when the obligations are disposed of or satisfied, the amount thereof being the difference between the reduced basis as provided in the preceding sentence and the amount realized therefor. Only in rare and extraordinary cases does property have no fair market value.

**(b) Repossession of property where title is retained by vendor.** *(1) Gain or loss on repossession.* If the vendor in sales referred to in paragraph (a) of this section has retained title to the property and the purchaser defaults in any of his payments, and the vendor repossesses the property, the difference between—

(i) The entire amount of the payments actually received on the contract and retained by the vendor plus the fair market value at the time of repossession of fixed improvements placed on the property by the purchaser, and

(ii) The sum of the profits previously returned as income in connection therewith and an amount representing what would have been a proper adjustment for exhaustion, wear and tear, obsolescence, amortization, and depletion of the property during the period the property was in the hands of the purchaser had the sale not been made, will constitute gain or loss, as the case may be, to the vendor for the year in which the property is repossessed.

*(2) Basis of repossessed property.* The basis of the property described in subparagraph (1) of this paragraph in the hands of the vendor will be the original basis at the time of the sale plus the fair market value at the time of repossession of fixed improvements placed on the property by the purchaser, except that, with respect to repossessions occurring after September 18, 1958, the basis of the property shall be reduced by what would have been a proper adjustment for exhaustion, wear and tear, obsolescence, amortization, and depletion of the property during the period the property was in the hands of the purchaser if the sale had not been made.

**(c) Reacquisition of property where title is transferred to purchaser.** *(1) Gain or loss on reacquisition.* If the vendor in sales described in paragraph (a) of this section has previously transferred title to the purchaser, and the purchaser defaults in any of his payments, and the vendor accepts a voluntary reconveyance of the property, in partial or full satisfaction of the unpaid portion of the purchase price, the receipt of the property so reacquired, to the extent of its fair market value at that time, including the fair market value of fixed improvements placed on the property by the purchaser, shall be considered as the receipt of payment on the obligations satisfied. If the fair market value of the property is greater than the basis of the obligations of the purchaser so satisfied (generally, such basis being the fair market value of such obligations previously recognized in computing income), the excess constitutes ordinary income. If the value of such property is less than the basis of such obligations, the difference may be deducted as a bad debt if uncollectible, except that, if the obligations satisfied are securities (as defined in section 165(g)(2)(C)), any gain or loss resulting from the transaction is a capital gain or loss subject to the provisions of sections 1201 through 1241.

*(2) Basis of reacquired property.* If the reacquired property described in subparagraph (1) of this paragraph is subsequently sold, the basis for determining gain or loss is the fair market value of the property at the date of reacquisition, including the fair market value of the fixed improvements placed on the property by the purchaser. See section 166 and the regulations thereunder with respect to property reacquired by the vendor in a foreclosure proceeding.

**(d) Effective date.** Paragraphs (b) and (c) of this section shall apply only with respect to taxable years beginning before September 3, 1964, in respect of which an election has not been properly made to have the provisions of section 1038 apply. For rules applicable to taxable years beginning after September 2, 1964, and for taxable years beginning after December 31, 1957, to which such an election applies, see §§ 1.1038 through 1.1038-3.

---

T.D. 6314, 9/17/58, amend T.D. 6916, 4/12/67.

---

### § 1.453-9 Gain or loss on disposition of installment obligations.

***Caution:*** The Treasury has not yet amended Reg § 1.453-9 to reflect changes made by P.L. 108-27, P.L. 99-514, P.L. 98-369, P.L. 96-471.

**(a) In general.** Subject to the exceptions contained in section 453(d)(4) and paragraph (c) of this section, the entire amount of gain or loss resulting from any disposition or satisfaction of installment obligations, computed in accordance with section 453(d), is recognized in the taxable year of such disposition or satisfaction and shall be considered as resulting from the sale or exchange of the property in respect of which the installment obligation was received by the taxpayer.

**(b) Computation of gain or loss.** *(1)* The amount of gain or loss resulting under paragraph (a) of this section is the difference between the basis of the obligation and (i) the amount realized, in the case of satisfaction at other than face value or in the case of a sale or exchange, or (ii) the fair market value of the obligation at the time of disposition, if such disposition is other than by sale or exchange.

*(2)* The basis of an installment obligation shall be the excess of the face value of the obligation over an amount equal to the income which would be returnable were the obligation satisfied in full.

*(3)* The application of subparagraphs (1) and (2) of this paragraph may be illustrated by the following examples:

*Example (1).* In 1960 the M Corporation sold a piece of unimproved real estate to B for $20,000. The company acquired the property in 1948 at a cost of $10,000. During 1960 the company received $5,000 cash and vendee's notes for the remainder of the selling price, or $15,000, payable in subsequent years. In 1962, before the vendee made any further payments, the company sold the notes for $13,000 in cash. The corporation makes its returns on the calendar year basis. The income to be reported for 1962 is $5,500, computed as follows:

| | | |
|---|---|---|
| Proceeds of sale of notes | | $13,000 |
| Selling price of property | $20,000 | |
| Cost of property | 10,000 | |
| Total profit | 10,000 | |
| Total contract price | 20,000 | |
| Percent of profit, or proportion of each payment returnable as income, $10,000 divided by $20,000, 50 percent. | | |
| Face value of notes | 15,000 | |
| Amount of income returnable were the notes satisfied in full, 50 percent of $15,000 | 7,500 | |
| Basis of obligation—excess of face value of notes over amount of income returnable were the notes satisfied in full | | 7,500 |
| Taxable income to be reported for 1962 | | 5,500 |

*Example (2).* Suppose in example (1) the M Corporation, instead of selling the notes, distributed them in 1962 to its shareholders as a dividend, and at the time of such distribution, the fair market value of the notes was $14,000. The income to be reported for 1962 is $6,500, computed as follows:

| | |
|---|---|
| Fair market value of notes | $14,000 |
| Basis of obligation—excess of face value of notes over amount of income returnable were the notes satisfied in full (computed as in example (1)) | 7,500 |
| Taxable income to be reported for 1962 | 6,500 |

**(c) Disposition from which no gain or loss is recognized.** *(1)* (i) Under section 453(d)(4)(A), no gain or loss shall be recognized to a distributing corporation with respect to the distribution made after November 13, 1966, of installment obligations if (a) the distribution is made pursuant to a plan for the complete liquidation of a subsidiary under section 332, and (b) the basis of such obligations in the hands of the distributee is determined under section 334(b)(1).

(ii) Under section 453(d)(4)(B), no gain or loss shall be recognized to a distributing corporation with respect to the distribution of installment obligations if the distribution is made, pursuant to a plan for the complete liquidation of a corporation which meets the requirements of section 337, under conditions whereby no gain or loss would have been recognized to the corporation had such installment obligations been sold or exchanged on the day of the distribution. The preceding sentence shall not apply to the extent that under section 453(d)(1) gain to the distributing corporation would be considered as gain to which section 341(f)(2), 617(d)(1), 1245(a)(1), 1250(a)(1), 1251(c)(1), 1252(a)(1), or 1254(a)(1) applies, computed under the principles of the regulations under such provisions. See paragraph (d) of § 1.1245-6, paragraph (c)(6) of § 1.1250-1, paragraph (e)(6) of § 1.1251-1, paragraph (d)(3) of § 1.1252-1, and paragraph (d) of § 1.1254-1.

*(2)* Where the Code provides for exceptions to the recognition of gain or loss in the case of certain dispositions, no gain or loss shall result under section 453(d) in the case of a disposition of an installment obligation. Such exceptions include: Certain transfers to corporations under sections 351 and 361; contributions of property to a partnership by a partner under section 721; and distributions by a partnership to a partner under section 731 (except as provided by section 736 and section 751).

*(3)* Any amount received by a person in payment or settlement of an installment obligation acquired in a transaction described in subparagraphs (1) or (2) of this paragraph (other than an amount received by a stockholder with respect to an installment obligation distributed to him pursuant to section 337) shall be considered to have the character it would have had in the hands of the person from whom such installment obligation was acquired.

**(d) Carryover of installment method.** For the treatment of income derived from installment obligations received in transactions to which section 381(a) is applicable, see section 381(c)(8) and the regulations thereunder.

**(e) Installment obligations transmitted at death.** Where installment obligations are transmitted at death, see section 691(a)(4) and the regulations thereunder for the treatment of amounts considered income in respect of a decedent.

**(f) Losses.** See subchapter P (section 1201 and following), chapter 1 of the Code, as to the limitation on capital losses sustained by corporations and the limitation as to both capital gains and capital losses of individuals.

**(g) Disposition of installment obligations to life insurance companies.** *(1)* Notwithstanding the provisions of section 453(d)(4) and paragraph (c) of this section or any provision of subtitle A relating to the nonrecognition of gain, the entire amount of any gain realized on the disposition of an installment obligation by any person, other than a life insurance company (as defined in section 801(a) and paragraph (b) of § 1.801-3), to a life insurance company or to a partnership of which a life insurance company is a partner shall be recognized and treated in accordance with section 453(d)(1) and paragraphs (a) and (b) of this section. If a corporation which is a life insurance company for the taxable year was a corporation which was not a life insurance company for the preceding taxable year, such corporation shall be treated, for purposes of section 453(d)(1) and this paragraph, as having transferred to a life insurance company, on the last day of the preceding taxable year, all installment obligations which it held on such last day. The gain, if any, realized by reason of the installment obligations being so transferred shall be recognized and treated in accordance with section 453(d)(1) and paragraphs (a) and (b) of this section. Similarly, a partnership of which a life insurance company becomes a partner shall be treated, for purposes of section 453(d)(1) and this paragraph, as having transferred to a life insurance company, on the last day of the preceding taxable year of such partnership, all installment obligations which it holds at the time such life insurance company becomes a partner. The gain, if any, realized by reason of the installment obligations being so transferred shall be recognized and treated in accordance with section 453(d)(1) and paragraphs (a) and (b) of this section.

*(2)* The provisions of section 453(d)(5) and subparagraph (1) of this paragraph shall not apply to losses sustained in connection with the disposition of installment obligations to a life insurance company.

*(3)* For the effective date of the provisions of section 453(d)(5) and this paragraph, see paragraph (f) of § 1.453-10.

*(4)* Application of the provisions of this paragraph may be illustrated by the following examples:

*Example (1).* A, an individual, in a transaction to which section 351 applies, transfers in 1961 certain assets, including installment obligations, to a new corporation, X, which qualifies as a life insurance company (as defined in section 801(a)) for the year 1961. A makes his return on the calendar year basis. Section 453(d)(5) provides that the nonrecognition provisions of section 351 will not apply to the installment obligations transferred by A to X Corporation. Therefore, the entire amount of any gain realized by A on the transfer of the installment obligations shall be recognized in 1961, with the amount of any such gain computed in accordance with the provisions of section 453(d)(1) and paragraph (b) of this section.

*Example (2).* The M Corporation did not qualify as a life insurance company (as defined in section 801(a)) for the taxable year 1958. On December 31, 1958, it held $60,000 of installment obligations. The M Corporation qualified as a life insurance company for the taxable year 1959. Accordingly, the M Corporation is treated as having transferred to a life insurance company, on December 31, 1958, the $60,000 of installment obligations it held on such date. The gain, if any, realized by M by reason of such installment obligations being so transferred shall be recognized in the taxable year 1958, with the amount of any such gain computed in accordance with the provisions of section 453(d)(1) and paragraph (b) of this section.

*Example (3).* During its taxable year 1958, none of the partners of the N partnership qualified as a life insurance company (as defined in section 801(a)). The N partnership held $30,000 of installment obligations on December 31, 1958. On July 30, 1959, the O Corporation, a life insurance company (as defined in section 801(a)), became a partner in the partnership. The N partnership held $50,000 of installment obligations on July 30, 1959. Pursuant to section 453(d)(5), the N partnership is treated as having transferred to a life insurance company, on December 31, 1958, the $50,000 of installment obligations is held on July 30, 1959. The gain, if any, realized by the N partnership by reason of such installment obligations being so transferred shall be recognized in the taxable year 1958, with the amount of any such gain computed in accordance with the provisions of section 453(d)(1) and paragraph (b) of this section.

*Example (4).* In 1960, the P Corporation, in a reorganization qualifying under section 368(a), transferred certain assets (including installment obligations) to the R Corporation, a life insurance company as defined in section 801(a). P realized a loss upon the transfer of the installment obligations, which was not recognized under section 361. Pursuant to subparagraph (2) of paragraph (c) of this section, no loss with respect to the transfer of these obligations will be recognized to P under section 453(d)(1).

T.D. 6314, 9/17/58, amend T.D. 6590, 2/12/62, T.D. 6832, 7/6/65, T.D. 7084, 1/7/71, T.D. 7418, 5/6/76, T.D. 8586, 1/9/95.

### § 1.453-10 Effective date.

***Caution:*** The Treasury has not yet amended Reg § 1.453-10 to reflect changes made by P.L. 100-647, P.L. 100-203, P.L. 99-514, P.L. 96-471.

**(a)** Except as provided in this section, the provisions of section 453 and §§ 1.453-1 through 1.453-9 shall apply to taxable years beginning after December 31, 1953, and ending after August 16, 1954.

**(b)** The provisions of paragraphs (a)(2) and (3), (b), and (c) of § 1.453-8 shall apply to taxable years ending after December 17, 1958.

**(c)** Under the provisions of sections 453(b) and 7851(a)(1)(C), section 453(b)(1) and the regulations with respect thereto shall also apply—

*(1)* To a sale or other disposition during a taxable year beginning before January 1, 1954, only if the income was returnable (by reason of section 44(b) of the Internal Revenue Code of 1939) on the basis and in the manner prescribed in section 44(a) of such code.

*(2)* To a sale or other disposition during a taxable year beginning after December 31, 1953, and ending before August 17, 1954, though such taxable year is subject to the provisions of the Internal Revenue Code of 1939.

**(d)** Under the provisions of sections 453(c)(1)(B) and 7851(a)(1)(C), section 453(c) and the regulations with respect thereto shall also apply to taxable years beginning after December 31, 1953, and ending before August 17, 1954, though such taxable years are subject to the provisions of the Internal Revenue Code of 1939.

**(e)** The provisions of paragraph (b)(3) of § 1.453-6 shall apply to repossessions occurring after December 18, 1958.

**(f)** The provisions of section 453(d)(5) and paragraph (g) of § 1.453-9 shall apply to taxable years ending after December 31, 1957, but only as to transfers or other dispositions of installment obligations occurring after such date.

T.D. 6314, 9/17/58, amend T.D. 6590, 2/12/62, T.D. 6682, 10/15/63.

### § 1.453-11 Installment obligations received from a liquidating corporation.

***Caution:*** The Treasury has not yet amended Reg § 1.453-11 to reflect changes made by P.L. 106-170.

**(a) In general.** *(1) Overview.* Except as provided in section 453(h)(1)(C) (relating to installment sales of depreciable property to certain closely related persons), a qualifying shareholder (as defined in paragraph (b) of this section) who receives a qualifying installment obligation (as defined in paragraph (c) of this section) in a liquidation that satisfies section 453(h)(1)(A) treats the receipt of payments in respect of the obligation, rather than the receipt of the obligation itself, as a receipt of payment for the shareholder's stock. The shareholder reports the payments received on the installment method unless the shareholder elects otherwise in accordance with § 15a.453-1(d) of this chapter.

*(2) Coordination with other provisions.* (i) Deemed sale of stock for installment obligation. Except as specifically provided in section 453(h)(1)(C), a qualifying shareholder treats a qualifying installment obligation, for all purposes of the Internal Revenue Code, as if the obligation is received by the shareholder from the person issuing the obligation in exchange for the shareholder's stock in the liquidating corporation. For example, if the stock of a corporation that is liquidating is traded on an established securities market, an installment obligation distributed to a shareholder of the corporation in exchange for the shareholder's stock does not qualify for installment reporting pursuant to section 453(k)(2).

(ii) Special rules to account for the qualifying installment obligation. (A) Issue price. A qualifying installment obligation is treated by a qualifying shareholder as newly issued on the date of the distribution. The issue price of the qualifying installment obligation on that date is equal to the sum of the adjusted issue price of the obligation on the date of the distribution (as determined under § 1.1275-1(b)) and the amount of any qualified stated interest (as defined in § 1.1273-1(c)) that has accrued prior to the distribution but that is not payable until after the distribution. For purposes of the preceding sentence, if the qualifying installment obligation is subject to § 1.446-2 (e.g., a debt instrument that has unstated interest under section 483), the adjusted issue price of the obligation is determined under § 1.446-2(c) and (d).

(B) Variable rate debt instrument. If the qualifying installment obligation is a variable rate debt instrument (as defined in § 1.1275-5), the shareholder uses the equivalent fixed rate debt instrument (within the meaning of § 1.1275-5(e)(3)(ii)) constructed for the qualifying installment obligation as of the date the obligation was issued to the liquidating corporation to determine the accruals of original issue discount, if any, and interest on the obligation.

*(3) Liquidating distributions treated as selling price.* All amounts distributed or treated as distributed to a qualifying shareholder incident to the liquidation, including cash, the issue price of qualifying installment obligations as determined under paragraph (a)(2)(ii)(A) of this section, and the fair market value of other property (including obligations that are not qualifying installment obligations) are considered as having been received by the shareholder as the selling price (as defined in § 15a.453-1(b)(2)(ii) of this chapter) for the shareholder's stock in the liquidating corporation. For the proper method of reporting liquidating distributions received in more than one taxable year of a shareholder, see paragraph (d) of this section. An election not to report on the installment method an installment obligation received in the liquidation applies to all distributions received in the liquidation.

*(4) Assumption of corporate liability by shareholders.* For purposes of this section, if in the course of a liquidation a shareholder assumes secured or unsecured liabilities of the liquidating corporation, or receives property from the corporation subject to such liabilities (including any tax liabilities incurred by the corporation on the distribution), the amount of the liabilities is added to the shareholder's basis in the stock of the liquidating corporation. These additions to basis do not affect the shareholder's holding period for the stock. These liabilities do not reduce the amounts received in computing the selling price.

*(5) Examples.* The provisions of this paragraph (a) are illustrated by the following examples. Except as otherwise provided, assume in each example that A, an individual who is a calendar-year taxpayer, owns all of the stock of T corporation. A's adjusted tax basis in that stock is $100,000. On February 1, 1998, T, an accrual method taxpayer, adopts a plan of complete liquidation that satisfies section 453(h)(1)(A) and immediately sells all of its assets to unrelated B corporation in a single transaction. The examples are as follows:

*Example (1).* (i) The stated purchase price for T's assets is $3,500,000. In consideration for the sale, B makes a down payment of $500,000 and issues a 10-year installment obligation with a stated principal amount of $3,000,000. The obligation provides for interest payments of $150,000 on January 31 of each year, with the total principal amount due at maturity.

(ii) Assume that for purposes of section 1274, the test rate on February 1, 1998, is 8 percent, compounded semi-annually. Also assume that a semi-annual accrual period is used. Under § 1.1274-2, the issue price of the obligation on February 1, 1998, is $2,368,450. Accordingly, the obligation has $631,550 of original issue discount ($3,000,000–$2,368,450). Between February 1 and July 31, $19,738 of original issue discount and $75,000 of qualified stated interest accrue with respect to the obligation and are taken into account by T.

(iii) On July 31, 1998, T distributes the installment obligation to A in exchange for A's stock. No other property is ever distributed to A. On January 31, 1999, A receives the first annual payment of $150,000 from B.

(iv) When the obligation is distributed to A on July 31, 1998, it is treated as if the obligation is received by A in an installment sale of shares directly to B on that date. Under § 1.1275-1(b), the adjusted issue price of the obligation on that date is $2,388,188 (original issue price of $2,368,450 plus accrued original issue discount of $19,738). Accordingly, the issue price of the obligation under paragraph (a)(2)(ii)(A) of this section is $2,463,188, the sum of the adjusted issue price of the obligation on that date ($2,388,188) and the amount of accrued but unpaid qualified stated interest ($75,000).

(v) The selling price and contract price of A's stock in T is $2,463,188, and the gross profit is $2,363,188 ($2,463,188 selling price less A's adjusted tax basis of $100,000). A's gross profit ratio is thus 96 percent (gross profit of $2,363,188 divided by total contract price of $2,463,188).

(vi) Under §§ 1.446-2(e)(1) and 1.1275-2(a), $98,527 of the $150,000 payment is treated as a payment of the interest and original issue discount that accrued on the obligation from July 31, 1998, to January 31, 1999 ($75,000 of qualified stated interest and $23,527 of original issue discount). The balance of the payment ($51,473) is treated as a payment of principal. A's gain recognized in 1999 is $49,414 (96 percent of $51,473).

*Example (2).* (i) T owns Blackacre, unimproved real property, with an adjusted tax basis of $700,000. Blackacre is subject to a mortgage (underlying mortgage) of $1,100,000. A is not personally liable on the underlying mortgage and the T shares held by A are not encumbered by the underlying mortgage. The other assets of T consist of $400,000 of cash and $600,000 of accounts receivable attributable to sales of inventory in the ordinary course of business. The unsecured liabilities of T total $900,000.

(ii) On February 1, 1998, T adopts a plan of complete liquidation complying with section 453(h)(1)(A), and promptly sells Blackacre to B for a 4-year mortgage note (bearing adequate stated interest and otherwise meeting all of the requirements of section 453) in the face amount of $4 million. Under the agreement between T and B, T (or its successor) is to continue to make principal and interest payments on the underlying mortgage. Immediately thereafter, T completes its liquidation by distributing to A its remaining cash of $400,000 (after payment of T's tax liabilities), accounts receivable of $600,000, and the $4 million B note. A assumes T's $900,000 of unsecured liabilities and receives the distributed property subject to the obligation to make payments on the $1,100,000 underlying mortgage. A receives no payments from B on the B note during 1998.

(iii) Unless A elects otherwise, the transaction is reported by A on the installment method. The selling price is $5 million (cash of $400,000, accounts receivable of $600,000, and the B note of $4 million). The total contract price also is $5 million. A's adjusted tax basis in the T shares, initially $100,000, is increased by the $900,000 of unsecured T liabilities assumed by A and by the obligation (subject to which A takes the distributed property) to make payments on the $1,100,000 underlying mortgage on Blackacre, for an aggregate adjusted tax basis of $2,100,000. Accordingly, the gross profit is $2,900,000 (selling price of $5 million less aggregate adjusted tax basis of $2,100,000). The gross profit ratio is 58 percent (gross profit of $2,900,000 divided by the total contract price of $5 million). The 1998 payments to A are $1 million ($400,000 cash plus $600,000 receivables) and A recognizes gain in 1998 of $580,000 (58 percent of $1 million).

(iv) In 1999, A receives payment from B on the B note of $1 million (exclusive of interest). A's gain recognized in 1999 is $580,000 (58 percent of $1 million).

**(b) Qualifying shareholder.** For purposes of this section, *qualifying shareholder* means a shareholder to which, with respect to the liquidating distribution, section 331 applies. For example, a creditor that receives a distribution from a liquidating corporation, in exchange for the creditor's claim, is not a qualifying shareholder as a result of that distribution regardless of whether the liquidation satisfies section 453(h)(1)(A).

**(c) Qualifying installment obligation.** *(1) In general.* For purposes of this section, *qualifying installment obligation* means an installment obligation (other than an evidence of indebtedness described in § 15a.453-1(e) of this chapter, relating to obligations that are payable on demand or are readily tradable) acquired in a sale or exchange of corporate assets by a liquidating corporation during the 12-month period beginning on the date the plan of liquidation is adopted. See paragraph (c)(4) of this section for an exception for installment obligations acquired in respect of certain sales of inventory. Also see paragraph (c)(5) of this section for an exception for installment obligations attributable to sales of certain property that do not generally qualify for installment method treatment.

*(2) Corporate assets.* Except as provided in section 453(h)(1)(C), in paragraph (c)(4) of this section (relating to certain sales of inventory), and in paragraph (c)(5) of this section (relating to certain tax avoidance transactions), the nature of the assets sold by, and the tax consequences to, the selling corporation do not affect whether an installment obligation is a qualifying installment obligation. Thus, for example, the fact that the fair market value of an asset is less than the adjusted basis of that asset in the hands of the corporation; or that the sale of an asset will subject the corporation to depreciation recapture (e.g., under section 1245 or section 1250); or that the assets of a trade or business sold by the corporation for an installment obligation include depreciable property, certain marketable securities, accounts receivable, installment obligations, or cash; or that the distribution of assets to the shareholder is or is not taxable to the corporation under sections 336 and 453B, does not affect whether installment obligations received in exchange for those assets are treated as qualifying installment obligations by the shareholder. However, an obligation received by the corporation in exchange for cash, in a transaction unrelated to a sale or exchange of noncash assets by the corporation, is not treated as a qualifying installment obligation.

*(3) Installment obligations distributed in liquidations described in section 453(h)(1)(E).* (i) In general. In the case of a liquidation to which section 453(h)(1)(E) (relating to certain liquidating subsidiary corporations) applies, a qualifying installment obligation acquired in respect of a sale or exchange by the liquidating subsidiary corporation will be treated as a qualifying installment obligation if distributed by a controlling corporate shareholder (within the meaning of section 368(c)) to a qualifying shareholder. The preceding sentence is applied successively to each controlling corporate shareholder, if any, above the first controlling corporate shareholder.

(ii) Examples. The provisions of this paragraph (c)(3) are illustrated by the following examples:

*Example (1).* (i) A, an individual, owns all of the stock of T corporation, a C corporation. T has an operating division and three wholly-owned subsidiaries, X, Y, and Z. On February 1, 1998, T, Y, and Z all adopt plans of complete liquidation.

(ii) On March 1, 1998, the following sales are made to unrelated purchasers: T sells the assets of its operating division to B for cash and an installment obligation. T sells the stock of X to C for an installment obligation. Y sells all of its assets to D for an installment obligation. Z sells all of its assets to E for cash. The B, C, and D installment obligations bear adequate stated interest and meet the requirements of section 453.

(iii) In June 1998, Y and Z completely liquidate, distributing their respective assets (the D installment obligation and cash) to T. In July 1998, T completely liquidates, distributing to A cash and the installment obligations respectively issued by B, C, and D. The liquidation of T is a liquidation to which section 453(h) applies and the liquidations of Y and Z into T are liquidations to which section 332 applies.

(iv) Because T is in control of Y (within the meaning of section 368(c)), the D obligation acquired by Y is treated as acquired by T pursuant to section 453(h)(1)(E). A is a qualifying shareholder and the installment obligations issued by B, C, and D are qualifying installment obligations. Unless A elects otherwise, A reports the transaction on the installment method as if the cash and installment obligations had been received in an installment sale of the stock of T corporation. Under section 453B(d), no gain or loss is recognized by Y on the distribution of the D installment obligation to T. Under sections 453B(a) and 336, T recognizes gain or loss on the distribution of the B, C, and D installment obligations to A in exchange for A's stock.

*Example (2).* (i) A, a cash-method individual taxpayer, owns all of the stock of P corporation, a C corporation. P owns 30 percent of the stock of Q corporation. The balance of the Q stock is owned by unrelated individuals. On February 1, 1998, P adopts a plan of complete liquidation and sells all of its property, other than its Q stock, to B, an unrelated purchaser for cash and an installment obligation bearing adequate stated interest. On March 1, 1998, Q adopts a plan of complete liquidation and sells all of its property to an unrelated purchaser, C, for cash and installment obligations. Q immediately distributes the cash and installment obligations to its shareholders in completion of its liquidation. Promptly thereafter, P liquidates, distributing to A cash, the B installment obligation, and a C installment obligation that P received in the liquidation of Q.

(ii) In the hands of A, the B installment obligation is a qualifying installment obligation. In the hands of P, the C installment obligation was a qualifying installment obligation. However, in the hands of A, the C installment obligation is not treated as a qualifying installment obligation because P owned only 30 percent of the stock of Q. Because P did not own the requisite 80 percent stock interest in Q, P was not a controlling corporate shareholder of Q (within the meaning of section 368(c)) immediately before the liquidation. Therefore, section 453(h)(1)(E) does not apply. Thus, in the hands of A, the C obligation is considered to be a third-party note (not a purchaser's evidence of indebtedness) and is treated as a payment to A in the year of distribution. Accordingly, for 1998, A reports as payment the cash and the fair market value of the C obligation distributed to A in the liquidation of P.

(iii) Because P held 30 percent of the stock of Q, section 453B(d) is inapplicable to P. Under sections 453B(a) and

336, accordingly, Q recognizes gain or loss on the distribution of the C obligation. P also recognizes gain or loss on the distribution of the B and C installment obligations to A in exchange for A's stock. See sections 453B and 336.

*(4) Installment obligations attributable to certain sales of inventory.* (i) In general. An installment obligation acquired by a corporation in a liquidation that satisfies section 453(h)(1)(A) in respect of a broken lot of inventory is not a qualifying installment obligation. If an installment obligation is acquired in respect of a broken lot of inventory and other assets, only the portion of the installment obligation acquired in respect of the broken lot of inventory is not a qualifying installment obligation. The portion of the installment obligation attributable to other assets is a qualifying installment obligation. For purposes of this section, the term *broken lot of inventory* means inventory property that is sold or exchanged other than in bulk to one person in one transaction involving substantially all of the inventory property attributable to a trade or business of the corporation. See paragraph (c)(4)(ii) of this section for rules for determining what portion of an installment obligation is not a qualifying installment obligation and paragraph (c)(4)(iii) of this section for rules determining the application of payments on an installment obligation only a portion of which is a qualifying installment obligation.

(ii) Rules for determining nonqualifying portion of an installment obligation. If a broken lot of inventory is sold to a purchaser together with other corporate assets for consideration consisting of an installment obligation and either cash, other property, the assumption of (or taking property subject to) corporate liabilities by the purchaser, or some combination thereof, the installment obligation is treated as having been acquired in respect of a broken lot of inventory only to the extent that the fair market value of the broken lot of inventory exceeds the sum of unsecured liabilities assumed by the purchaser, secured liabilities which encumber the broken lot of inventory and are assumed by the purchaser or to which the broken lot of inventory is subject, and the sum of the cash and fair market value of other property received. This rule applies solely for the purpose of determining the portion of the installment obligation (if any) that is attributable to the broken lot of inventory.

(iii) Application of payments. If, by reason of the application of paragraph (c)(4)(ii) of this section, a portion of an installment obligation is not a qualifying installment obligation, then for purposes of determining the amount of gain to be reported by the shareholder under section 453, payments on the obligation (other than payments of qualified stated interest) shall be applied first to the portion of the obligation that is not a qualifying installment obligation.

(iv) Example. The following example illustrates the provisions of this paragraph (c)(4). In this example, assume that all obligations bear adequate stated interest within the meaning of section 1274(c)(2) and that the fair market value of each nonqualifying installment obligation equals its face amount. The example is as follows:

*Example.* (i) P corporation has three operating divisions, X, Y, and Z, each engaged in a separate trade or business, and a minor amount of investment assets. On July 1, 1998, P adopts a plan of complete liquidation that meets the criteria of section 453(h)(1)(A). The following sales are promptly made to purchasers unrelated to P: P sells all of the assets of the X division (including all of the inventory property) to B for $30,000 cash and installment obligations totalling $200,000. P sells substantially all of the inventory property of the Y division to C for a $100,000 installment obligation, and sells all of the other assets of the Y division (excluding cash but including installment receivables previously acquired in the ordinary course of the business of the Y division) to D for a $170,000 installment obligation. P sells ⅓ of the inventory property of the Z division to E for $100,000 cash, ⅓ of the inventory property of the Z division to F for a $100,000 installment obligation, and all of the other assets of the Z division (including the remaining ⅓ of the inventory property worth $100,000) to G for $60,000 cash, a $240,000 installment obligation, and the assumption by G of the liabilities of the Z division. The liabilities assumed by G, which are unsecured liabilities and liabilities encumbering the inventory property acquired by G, aggregate $30,000. Thus, the total purchase price G pays is $330,000.

(ii) P immediately completes its liquidation, distributing the cash and installment obligations, which otherwise meet the requirements of section 453, to A, an individual cash-method taxpayer who is its sole shareholder. In 1999, G makes a payment to A of $100,000 (exclusive of interest) on the $240,000 installment obligation.

(iii) In the hands of A, the installment obligations issued by B, C, and D are qualifying installment obligations because they were timely acquired by P in a sale or exchange of its assets. In addition, the installment obligation issued by C is a qualifying installment obligation because it arose from a sale to one person in one transaction of substantially all of the inventory property of the trade or business engaged in by the Y division.

(iv) The installment obligation issued by F is not a qualifying installment obligation because it is in respect of a broken lot of inventory. A portion of the installment obligation issued by G is a qualifying installment obligation and a portion is not a qualifying installment obligation, determined as follows: G purchased part of the inventory property (with a fair market value of $100,000) and all of the other assets of the Z division by paying cash ($60,000), issuing an installment obligation ($240,000), and assuming liabilities of the Z division ($30,000). The assumed liabilities ($30,000) and cash ($60,000) are attributed first to the inventory property. Therefore, only $10,000 of the $240,000 installment obligation is attributed to inventory property. Accordingly, in the hands of A, the G installment obligation is a qualifying installment obligation to the extent of $230,000, but is not a qualifying installment obligation to the extent of the $10,000 attributable to the inventory property.

(v) In the 1998 liquidation of P, A receives a liquidating distribution as follows:

| Item | Qualifying installment obligations | Cash and other property |
|---|---|---|
| Cash | | $190,000 |
| B note | $200,000 | |
| C note | $100,000 | |
| D note | $170,000 | |
| F note | | $100,000 |
| G note[1] | $230,000 | $10,000 |
| Total | $700,000 | $300,000 |

(vi) Assume that A's adjusted tax basis in the stock of P is $100,000. Under the installment method, A's selling price and the contract price are both $1 million, the gross profit is $900,000 (selling price of $1 million less adjusted tax basis of $100,000), and the gross profit ratio is 90 percent (gross profit of $900,000 divided by the contract price of $1 million). Accordingly, in 1998, A reports gain of $270,000 (90 percent of $300,000 payment in cash and other property). A's adjusted tax basis in each of the qualifying installment obligations is an amount equal to 10 percent of the obligation's respective face amount. A's adjusted tax basis in the F note, a nonqualifying installment obligation, is $100,000, i.e., the fair market value of the note when received by A. A's adjusted tax basis in the G note, a mixed obligation, is $33,000 (10 percent of the $230,000 qualifying installment obligation portion of the note, plus the $10,000 nonqualifying portion of the note).

(vii) With respect to the $100,000 payment received from G in 1999, $10,000 is treated as the recovery of the adjusted tax basis of the nonqualifying portion of the G installment obligation and $9,000 (10 percent of $90,000) is treated as the recovery of the adjusted tax basis of the portion of the note that is a qualifying installment obligation. The remaining $81,000 (90 percent of $90,000) is reported as gain from the sale of A's stock. See paragraph (c)(4)(iii) of this section.

*(5) Installment obligations attributable to sales of certain property.* (i) In general. An installment obligation acquired by a liquidating corporation, to the extent attributable to the sale of property described in paragraph (c)(5)(ii) of this section, is not a qualifying obligation if the corporation is formed or availed of for a principal purpose of avoiding section 453(b)(2) (relating to dealer dispositions and certain other dispositions of personal property), section 453(i) (relating to sales of property subject to recapture), or section 453(k) (relating to dispositions under a revolving credit plan and sales of stock or securities traded on an established securities market) through the use of a party bearing a relationship, either directly or indirectly, described in section 267(b) to any shareholder of the corporation.

(ii) Covered property. Property is described in this paragraph (c)(5)(ii) if, within 12 months before or after the adoption of the plan of liquidation, the property was owned by any shareholder and—

(A) The shareholder regularly sold or otherwise disposed of personal property of the same type on the installment plan or the property is real property that the shareholder held for sale to customers in the ordinary course of a trade or business (provided the property is not described in section 453(l)(2) (relating to certain exceptions to the definition of dealer dispositions));

(B) The sale of the property by the shareholder would result in recapture income (within the meaning of section 453(i)(2)), but only if the amount of the recapture income is equal to or greater than 50 percent of the property's fair market value on the date of the sale by the corporation;

(C) The property is stock or securities that are traded on an established securities market; or

(D) The sale of the property by the shareholder would have been under a revolving credit plan.

(iii) Safe harbor. Paragraph (c)(5)(i) of this section will not apply to the liquidation of a corporation if, on the date the plan of complete liquidation is adopted and thereafter, less than 15 percent of the fair market value of the corporation's assets is attributable to property described in paragraph (c)(5)(ii) of this section.

(iv) Example. The provisions of this paragraph (c)(5) are illustrated by the following example:

*Example.* Ten percent of the fair market value of the assets of T is attributable to stock and securities traded on an established securities market. T owns no other assets described in paragraph (c)(5)(ii) of this section. T, after adopting a plan of complete liquidation, sells all of its stock and securities holdings to C corporation in exchange for an installment obligation bearing adequate stated interest, sells all of its other assets to B corporation for cash, and distributes the cash and installment obligation to its sole shareholder, A, in a complete liquidation that satisfies section 453(h)(1)(A). Because the C installment obligation arose from a sale of publicly traded stock and securities, T cannot report the gain on the sale under the installment method pursuant to section 453(k)(2). In the hands of A, however, the C installment obligation is treated as having arisen out of a sale of the stock of T corporation. In addition, the general rule of paragraph (c)(5)(i) of this section does not apply, even if a principal purpose of the liquidation was the avoidance of section 453(k)(2), because the fair market value of the publicly traded stock and securities is less than 15 percent of the total fair market value of T's assets. Accordingly, section 453(k)(2) does not apply to A, and A may use the installment method to report the gain recognized on the payments it receives in respect of the obligation.

**(d) Liquidating distributions received in more than one taxable year.** If a qualifying shareholder receives liquidating distributions to which this section applies in more than one taxable year, the shareholder must reasonably estimate the gain attributable to distributions received in each taxable year. In allocating basis to calculate the gain for a taxable year, the shareholder must reasonably estimate the anticipated aggregate distributions. For this purpose, the shareholder must take into account distributions and other relevant events or information that the shareholder knows or reasonably could know up to the date on which the federal

1. Face amount $240,000.

income tax return for that year is filed. If the gain for a taxable year is properly taken into account on the basis of a reasonable estimate and the exact amount is subsequently determined the difference, if any, must be taken into account for the taxable year in which the subsequent determination is made. However, the shareholder may file an amended return for the earlier year in lieu of taking the difference into account for the subsequent taxable year.

**(e) Effective date.** This section is applicable to distributions of qualifying installment obligations made on or after January 28, 1998.

T.D. 8762, 1/27/98.

### § 1.453-12 Allocation of unrecaptured section 1250 gain reported on the installment method.

***Caution:*** The Treasury has not yet amended Reg § 1.453-12 to reflect changes made by P.L. 106-170.

**(a) General rule.** Unrecaptured section 1250 gain, as defined in section 1(h)(7), is reported on the installment method if that method otherwise applies under section 453 or 453A and the corresponding regulations. If gain from an installment sale includes unrecaptured section 1250 gain and adjusted net capital gain (as defined in section 1(h)(4)), the unrecaptured section 1250 gain is taken into account before the adjusted net capital gain.

**(b) Installment payments from sales before May 7, 1997.** The amount of unrecaptured section 1250 gain in an installment payment that is properly taken into account after May 6, 1997, from a sale before May 7, 1997, is determined as if, for all payments properly taken into account after the date of sale but before May 7, 1997, unrecaptured section 1250 gain had been taken into account before adjusted net capital gain.

**(c) Installment payments received after May 6, 1997, and on or before August 23, 1999.** If the amount of unrecaptured section 1250 gain in an installment payment that is properly taken into account after May 6, 1997, and on or before August 23, 1999, is less than the amount that would have been taken into account under this section, the lesser amount is used to determine the amount of unrecaptured section 1250 gain that remains to be taken into account.

**(d) Examples.** In each example, the taxpayer, an individual whose taxable year is the calendar year, does not elect out of the installment method. The installment obligation bears adequate stated interest, and the property sold is real property held in a trade or business that qualifies as both section 1231 property and section 1250 property. In all taxable years, the taxpayer's marginal tax rate on ordinary income is 28 percent. The following examples illustrate the rules of this section:

*Example (1).* General rule. This example illustrates the rule of paragraph (a) of this section as follows:

(i) In 1999, A sells property for $10,000, to be paid in ten equal annual installments beginning on December 1, 1999. A originally purchased the property for $5000, held the property for several years, and took straight-line depreciation deductions in the amount of $3000. In each of the years 1999-2008, A has no other capital or section 1231 gains or losses.

(ii) A's adjusted basis at the time of the sale is $2000. Of A's $8000 of section 1231 gain on the sale of the property, $3000 is attributable to prior straight-line depreciation deductions and is unrecaptured section 1250 gain. The gain on each installment payment is $800.

(iii) As illustrated in the table in this paragraph (iii) of this Example 1., A takes into account the unrecaptured section 1250 gain first. Therefore, the gain on A's first three payments, received in 1999, 2000, and 2001, is taxed at 25 percent. Of the $800 of gain on the fourth payment, received in 2002, $600 is taxed at 25 percent and the remaining $200 is taxed at 20 percent. The gain on A's remaining six installment payments is taxed at 20 percent. The table is as follows:

| | 1999 | 2000 | 2001 | 2002 | 2003 | 2004-2008 | Total gain |
|---|---|---|---|---|---|---|---|
| Installment gain | 800 | 800 | 800 | 800 | 800 | 4000 | 8000 |
| Taxed at 25% | 800 | 800 | 800 | 600 | — | — | 3000 |
| Taxed at 20% | — | — | — | 200 | 800 | 4000 | 5000 |
| Remaining to be taxed at 25% | 2200 | 1400 | 600 | — | — | — | — |

*Example (2).* Installment payments from sales prior to May 7, 1997. This example illustrates the rule of paragraph (b) of this section as follows:

(i) The facts are the same as in Example 1 except that A sold the property in 1994, received the first of the ten annual installment payments on December 1, 1994, and had no other capital or section 1231 gains or losses in the years 1994-2003.

(ii) As in Example 1, of A's $8000 of gain on the sale of the property, $3000 was attributable to prior straight-line depreciation deductions and is unrecaptured section 1250 gain.

(iii) As illustrated in the following table, A's first three payments, in 1994, 1995, and 1996, were received before May 7, 1997, and taxed at 28 percent. Under the rule described in paragraph (b) of this section, A determines the allocation of unrecaptured section 1250 gain for each installment payment after May 6, 1997, by taking unrecaptured section 1250 gain into account first, treating the general rule of paragraph (a) of this section as having applied since the time the property was sold, in 1994. Consequently, of the $800 of gain on the fourth payment, received in 1997, $600 is taxed at 25 percent and the remaining $200 is taxed at 20 percent. The gain on A's remaining six installment payments is taxed at 20 percent. The table is as follows:

| | 1994 | 1995 | 1996 | 1997 | 1998 | 1999-2003 | Total gain |
|---|---|---|---|---|---|---|---|
| Installment gain | 800 | 800 | 800 | 800 | 800 | 4000 | 8000 |
| Taxed at 28% | 800 | 800 | 800 | — | — | — | 2400 |
| Taxed at 25% | — | — | — | 600 | — | — | 600 |
| Taxed at 20% | — | — | — | 200 | 800 | 4000 | 5000 |
| Remaining to be taxed at 25% | 2200 | 1400 | 600 | — | — | — | — |

*Example (3).* Effect of section 1231(c) recapture. This example illustrates the rule of paragraph (a) of this section when there are non-recaptured net section 1231 losses, as defined in section 1231(c)(2), from prior years as follows:

(i) The facts are the same as in Example 1, except that in 1999 A has non-recaptured net section 1231 losses from the previous four years of $1000.

(ii) As illustrated in the table in paragraph (iv) of this Example 3, in 1999, all of A's $800 installment gain is recaptured as ordinary income under section 1231(c). Under the rule described in paragraph (a) of this section, for purposes of determining the amount of unrecaptured section 1250 gain remaining to be taken into account, the $800 recaptured as ordinary income under section 1231(c) is treated as reducing unrecaptured section 1250 gain, rather than adjusted net capital gain. Therefore, A has $2200 of unrecaptured section 1250 gain remaining to be taken into account.

(iii) In the year 2000, A's installment gain is taxed at two rates. First, $200 is recaptured as ordinary income under section 1231(c). Second, the remaining $600 of gain on A's year 2000 installment payment is taxed at 25 percent. Because the full $800 of gain reduces unrecaptured section 1250 gain, A has $1400 of unrecaptured section 1250 gain remaining to be taken into account.

(iv) The gain on A's installment payment received in 2001 is taxed at 25 percent. Of the $800 of gain on the fourth payment, received in 2002, $600 is taxed at 25 percent and the remaining $200 is taxed at 20 percent. The gain on A's remaining six installment payments is taxed at 20 percent. The table is as follows:

| | 1999 | 2000 | 2001 | 2002 | 2003 | 2004-2008 | Total gain |
|---|---|---|---|---|---|---|---|
| Installment gain | 800 | 800 | 800 | 800 | 800 | 4000 | 8000 |
| Taxed at ordinary rates under section 1231(c) | 800 | 200 | — | — | — | — | 1000 |
| Taxed at 25% | — | 600 | 800 | 600 | — | — | 2000 |
| Taxed at 20% | — | — | — | 200 | 800 | 4000 | 5000 |
| Remaining non-recaptured net section 1231 losses | 200 | — | — | — | — | — | — |
| Remaining to be taxed at 25% | 2200 | 1400 | 600 | — | — | — | — |

*Example (4).* Effect of a net section 1231 loss. This example illustrates the application of paragraph (a) of this section when there is a net section 1231 loss as follows:

(i) The facts are the same as in Example 1 except that A has section 1231 losses of $1000 in 1999.

(ii) In 1999, A's section 1231 installment gain of $800 does not exceed A's section 1231 losses of $1000. Therefore, A has a net section 1231 loss of $200. As a result, under section 1231(a) all of A's section 1231 gains and losses are treated as ordinary gains and losses. As illustrated in the following table, A's entire $800 of installment gain is ordinary gain. Under the rule described in paragraph (a) of this section, for purposes of determining the amount of unrecaptured section 1250 gain remaining to be taken into account, A's $800 of ordinary section 1231 installment gain in 1999 is treated as reducing unrecaptured section 1250 gain. Therefore, A has $2200 of unrecaptured section 1250 gain remaining to be taken into account.

(iii) In the year 2000, A has $800 of section 1231 installment gain, resulting in a net section 1231 gain of $800. A also has $200 of non-recaptured net section 1231 losses. The $800 gain is taxed at two rates. First, $200 is taxed at ordinary rates under section 1231(c), recapturing the $200 net section 1231 loss sustained in 1999. Second, the remaining $600 of gain on A's year 2000 installment payment is taxed at 25 percent. As in Example 3, the $200 of section 1231(c) gain is treated as reducing unrecaptured section 1250 gain, rather than adjusted net capital gain. Therefore, A has $1400 of unrecaptured section 1250 gain remaining to be taken into account.

(iv) The gain on A's installment payment received in 2001 is taxed at 25 percent, reducing the remaining unrecaptured section 1250 gain to $600. Of the $800 of gain on the fourth payment, received in 2002, $600 is taxed at 25 percent and the remaining $200 is taxed at 20 percent. The gain on A's remaining six installment payments is taxed at 20 percent. The table is as follows:

| | 1999 | 2000 | 2001 | 2002 | 2003 | 2004-2008 | Total gain |
|---|---|---|---|---|---|---|---|
| Installment gain | 800 | 800 | 800 | 800 | 800 | 4000 | 8000 |
| Ordinary gain under section 1231(a) | 800 | — | — | — | — | — | 800 |
| Taxed at ordinary rates under section 1231(c) | — | 200 | — | — | — | — | 200 |
| Taxed at 25% | — | 600 | 800 | 600 | — | — | 2000 |
| Taxed at 20% | — | — | — | 200 | 800 | 400 | 5000 |
| Net section 1231 loss | 200 | — | — | — | — | — | — |
| Remaining to be taxed at 25% | 2200 | 1400 | 600 | — | — | — | — |

**(e) Effective date.** This section applies to installment payments properly taken into account after August 23, 1999.

T.D. 8836, 8/20/99.

### § 1.453A-0 Table of contents.

This section lists the paragraphs and subparagraphs contained in §§ 1.453A-1 through 1.453A-3.

*§ 1.453A-1 Installment method of reporting income by dealers in personal property.*

(a) In general.

(b) Effect of security.

(c) Definition of dealer, sale, and sale on the installment plan.

(d) Installment plans.

(1) Traditional installment plans.

(2) Revolving credit plans.

(e) Installment income of dealers in personal property.

(1) In general.

(2) Gross profit and total contract price.

(3) Carrying changes not included in total contract price.

(f) Other accounting methods.

(g) Records.

(h) Effective date.

*§ 1.453A-2 Treatment of revolving credit plans; taxable years beginning on or before December 31, 1986.*

(a) In general.

(b) Coordination with traditional installment plan.

(c) Revolving credit plans.

(d) Effective date.

*§ 1.453A-3 Requirements for adoption of or change to installment method by dealers in personal property.*

(a) In general.

(b) Time and manner of electing installment method reporting.

(1) Time for election.

(2) Adoption of installation method.

(3) Change to installment method.

(4) Deemed elections.

(c) Consent.

(d) Cut-off method for amounts previously accrued.

(e) Effective date.

T.D. 8270, 11/2/89.

### § 1.453A-1 Installment method of reporting income by dealers on personal property.

**(a) In general.** A dealer (as defined in paragraph (c)(1) of this section) may elect to return the income from the sale of personal property on the installment method if such sale is a sale on the installment plan (as defined in paragraphs (c)(3) and (d) of this section). Under the installment method of accounting, a taxpayer may return as income from installment sales in any taxable year that proportion of the installment payments actually received in that year which the gross profit realized or to be realized when the property is paid for bears to the total contract price. For this purpose, gross profit means sales less cost of goods sold. See paragraph (d) of this section for additional rules relating to the computation of income under the installment method of accounting. In addition, see § 1.453A-2 for rules treating revolving credit plans as installment plans for taxable years beginning on or before December 31, 1986.

**(b) Effect of security.** A dealer may adopt (but is not required to do so) one of the following four ways of protecting against loss in case of default by the purchaser:

*(1)* An agreement that title is to remain in the vendor until performance of the purchaser's part of the transaction is completed;

*(2)* A form of contract in which title is conveyed to the purchaser immediately, but subject to a lien for the unpaid portion of the selling price;

*(3)* A present transfer of title to the purchaser, who at the same time executes a reconveyance in the form of a chattel mortgage to the vendor; or

*(4)* A conveyance to a trustee pending performance of the contract and subject to its provisions.

**(c) Definitions of dealer, sale, and sale on the installment plan.** For purposes of the regulations under section 453A—

*(1)* The term "dealer" means a person who regularly sells or otherwise disposes of personal property on the installment plan;

*(2)* The term "sale" includes sales and other dispositions; and

*(3)* Except as provided in paragraph (d)(2) of this section, the term "sale on the installment plan" means—

(i) A sale of personal property by the taxpayer under any plan for the sale of personal property, which plan, by its terms and conditions, contemplates that each sale under the plan will be paid for in two or more payments; or

(ii) A sale of personal property by the taxpayer under any plan for the sale of personal property—

(A) Which plan, by its terms and conditions, contemplates that such sale will be paid for in two or more payments; and

(B) Which sale is in fact paid for in two or more payments.

**(d) Installment plans.** *(1) Traditional installment plans.* A traditional installment plan usually has the following characteristics:

(i) The execution of a separate installment contract for each sale or disposition of personal property; and

(ii) The retention by the dealer of some type of security interest in such property. Normally, a sale under a traditional installment plan meets the requirements of paragraph (c)(3)(i) of this section.

*(2) Revolving credit plans.* Sales under a revolving credit plan (within the meaning of § 1.453A-2(c)(1))—

(i) Are treated, for taxable years beginning on or before December 31, 1986, as sales on the installment plan to the extent provided in § 1.453A-2, which provides for the application of the requirements of paragraph (c)(3)(ii) of this section to sales under revolving credit plans; and

(ii) Are not treated as sales on the installment plan for taxable years beginning after December 31, 1986.

**(e) Installment income of dealers in personal property.** *(1) In general.* The income from sales on the installment plan of a dealer may be ascertained by treating as income that proportion of the total payments received in the taxable year from sales on the installment plan (such payments being allocated to the year against the sales of which they apply) which the gross profit realized or to be realized on the total sales on the installment plan made during each year bears to the total contract price of all such sales made during that respective year. However, if the dealer demonstrates to the satisfaction of the district director that income from sales on the installment plan is clearly reflected, the income from such sales may be ascertained by treating as income that proportion of the total payments received in the taxable year from sales on the installment plan (such payments being allocated to the year against the sales of which they apply) which either:

(i) The gross profit realized or to be realized on the total credit sales made during each year bears to the total contract price of all credit sales during that respective year, or

(ii) The gross profit realized or to be realized on all sales made during each year bears to the total contract price of all sales made during that respective year.

A dealer who desires to compute income by the installment method shall maintain accounting records in such a manner as to enable an accurate computation to be made by such method in accordance with the provisions of this section, section 446, and § 1.446-1.

*(2) Gross profit and total contract price.* For purposes of paragraph (e)(1) of this section, in computing the gross profit realized or to be realized on the total sales on the installment plan, there shall be included in the total selling price and, thus, in the total contract price of all such sales.

(i) The amount of carrying charges or interest which is determined at the time of each sale and is added to the established cash selling price of such property and is treated as part of the selling price for customer billing purposes, and

(ii) In the case of sales made in taxable years beginning on or after January 1, 1960, the amount of carrying charges or interest determined with respect to such sales which are added contemporaneously with the sale on the books of account of the seller but are treated as periodic service charges for customer billing purposes.

Any change in the amount of the carrying charges or interest in a year subsequent to the sale will not affect the computation of the gross profit for the year of sale but will be taken into account at the time the carrying charges or interest are adjusted. The application of this paragraph (e)(2) to carrying charges or interest described in paragraph (e)(2)(ii) of this section may be illustrated by the following example:

*Example.* X Corporation makes sales on the traditional installment plan. The customer's order specifies that the total price consists of a cash price plus a "time price differential" of 1½ percent per month on the outstanding balance in the customer's account, and the customer is billed in this manner. On its books and for purposes of reporting to stockholders, X Corporation consistently makes the following entries each month when it records its sales. A debit entry is made to accounts receivable (for the total price) and balancing credit entries are made to sales (for the established selling price) and to a reserve account for collection expense (for the amount of the time price differential). In computing the gross profit realized or to be realized on the total sales on the installment plan, the total selling price and, thus, the total contract price for purposes of this paragraph (e) would, with respect to sales made in taxable years beginning on or after January 1, 1960, include the time price differential.

*(3) Carrying charges not included in total contract price.* In the case of sales by dealers in personal property made during taxable years beginning after December 31, 1963, the income from which is returned on the installment method, if the carrying charges or interest with respect to such sales is not included in the total contract price, payments received with respect to such sales shall be treated as applying first against such carrying charges or interest.

**(f) Other accounting methods.** If the vendor chooses as a matter of consistent practice to return the income from installment sales on an accrual method (,) such a course is permissible.

**(g) Records.** In adopting the installment method of accounting the seller must maintain such records as are necessary to clearly reflect income in accordance with this section, section 446 and § 1.446-1.

**(h) Effective date.** This section applies for taxable years beginning after December 31, 1953, and ending after August 16, 1954, but generally does not apply to sales made after December 31, 1987, in taxable years ending after such date. For sales made after December 31, 1987, sales made by a dealer in personal or real property shall not be treated as sales on the installment plan. (However, see section 453(1)(2) for exceptions to this rule.)

T.D. 8270, 11/2/89.

### § 1.453A-2 Treatment of revolving credit plans; taxable years beginning on or before December 31, 1986.

**(a) In general.** If a dealer sells or otherwise disposes of personal property under a revolving credit plan—

*(1)* Such sales will be treated as sales on the installment plan to the extent provided in paragraph (c) of this section;

*(2)* Income from sales treated as sales on the installment plan under paragraph (c) of this section may be returned on the installment method; and

*(3)* Income returned on the installment method is computed in accordance with § 1.453A-1, except that—

(i) The gross profit on such sales is computed without regard to § 1.453A-1(e)(2);

(ii) Under the circumstances described in paragraph (c)(6)(vi) of this section, the taxpayer may, in computing income for a taxable year, treat all such sales as sales made in such taxable year for purposes of applying the gross profit percentage; and

(iii) The rule contained in § 1.453A-1(e)(3) is applied in accordance with paragraph (c)(6)(v) of this section.

**(b) Coordination with traditional installment plan.** A dealer who makes sales of personal property under both a revolving credit plan and a traditional installment plan (1) may elect to report only sales under the traditional installment plan on the installment method, (2) may elect to report only sales under the revolving credit plan on the installment method, or (3) may elect to report both sales under the revolving credit plan and the traditional installment plan on the installment method.

**(c) Revolving credit plans.** *(1)* To the extent provided in this paragraph (c) sales under a revolving credit plan will be treated as sales on the installment plan. The term "revolving credit plan" includes cycle budget accounts, flexible budget accounts, continuous budget accounts, and other similar plans or arrangements for the sale of personal property under which the customer agrees to pay each billing-month (as defined in paragraph (c)(6)(iii) of this section) a part of the outstanding balance of the customer's account. Sales under a revolving credit plan do not constitute sales on the installment plan merely by reason of the fact that the total debt at the end of a billing-month is paid in installments. The terms and conditions of a revolving credit plan do not contemplate that each sale under the plan will be paid for in two or more payments and thus do not meet the requirements of § 1.453A-1(c)(3)(i). In addition, since under a revolving credit plan payments are not generally applied to liquidate any particular sale, and since the terms and conditions of such plan contemplate that account balances may be paid in full or in installments, it is generally impossible to determine that a particular sale under a revolving credit plan is to be or is in fact paid for in installments so as to meet the requirements of § 1.453A-1(c)(3)(ii). However, paragraphs (c)(2) and (3) of this section provides rules under which a certain percentage of charges under a revolving credit plan will be treated as sales on the installment plan. For purposes of arriving at this percentage, these rules, in general, treat as sales on the plan those sales under a revolving installment credit plan: (i) Which are of the type which the terms and conditions of the plan contemplate will be paid for in two or more installments and (ii) Which are charged to accounts on which subsequent payments indicate that such sales are being paid for in two or more installments.

*(2)* (i) The percentage of charges under a revolving credit plan which will be treated as sales on the installment plan shall be computed by making an actual segregation of charges in a probability sample of the revolving credit accounts and by applying the rules contained in paragraph (c)(3) of this section to determine what percentage of charges in the sample is to be treated as sales on the installment plan. (See paragraph (c)(5) of this section for rules to be used if some of the sales under a revolving credit plan are nonpersonal property sales (as defined in paragraph (c)(6)(iv) of this section).) Such segregation shall be made of charges which make up the balances in the sample accounts as of the end of each customer's last billing-month ending within the taxable year. (See paragraph (c)(6)(v) of this section for rules to be used in determining which charges make up the balance of an account.) However, in making such segregation, any account to which a sale is charged during the taxable year on which no payment is credited after the billing-month within which the sale is made (hereinafter called the "billing-month of sale") and on or before the end of the first billing-month ending in the taxpayer's next taxable year shall be disregarded and not taken into account in the determination of what percentage of charges in the sample is to be treated as sales on the installment plan. In order to obtain a probability sample, the accounts shall be selected in accordance with generally accepted probability sampling techniques. The appropriateness of the sampling technique and the accuracy and reliability of the results obtained must, if requested, be demonstrated to the satisfaction of the district director. If the district director is not satisfied that the taxpayer's sample is appropriate or that the results obtained are accurate and reliable, the taxpayer shall recompute the sample percentage or make appropriate adjustments to the original computations in a manner satisfactory to the district director. The taxpayer shall maintain records in sufficient detail to show the method of computing and applying the sample.

(ii) For taxable years ending before January 31, 1964, a taxpayer who has reported for income tax purposes all or a portion of sales under a revolving credit plan as sales on the installment method may apply the percentage obtained for the first taxable year ending on or after such date in determining the percentage of charges under a revolving credit plan for such prior taxable year (or years) which will be treated as sales on the installment plan. However, in computing the percentage to be applied in determining the percentage of charges under a revolving credit plan which will be treated as sales on the installment plan for such prior taxable year (or years), the rule stated in § 1.453A-1(e)(3) shall not apply. See paragraph (c)(6)(v) of this section for rules relating to the application of payments to finance charges for such prior taxable years.

*(3)* For the purpose of determining the percentage described in paragraph (c)(2) of this section, a charge under a revolving credit plan will be treated as a sale on the installment plan only if such charge is a sale (as defined in paragraph (c)(6) of this section) and meets the following requirements:

(i) The sale must be of the type which the terms and conditions of the plan contemplate will be paid for in two or more installments. If the aggregate of sales charged during a billing-month to an account under a revolving credit plan exceeds the required monthly payment, then all sales during such billing-month shall be considered to be of the type which the terms and conditions of such plan contemplate will be paid for in two or more installments. The required monthly payment shall be the amount of the payment which the terms and conditions of the revolving credit contract require the customer to make with respect to a billing-month. If the amount of such payment is not fixed at the date the contract is entered into, but is dependent upon the balance of the account, then such amount shall be the amount that the customer is required to pay (but not including any past-due payments) as shown on the statement either:

(A) For the last billing-month ending within the taxpayer's taxable year or

(B) For the billing-month of sale, whichever method the taxpayer adopts for all accounts. A taxpayer shall not change such method of determining the required monthly payment based upon the balance of the account without obtaining the consent of the district director. In any case where the required monthly payment is not set in accordance with a consistent method used during the entire taxable year, the district director may determine the required monthly payment in accordance with the method used during the major portion of such taxable year if the use of such method is necessary in order to reflect properly the income from sales under a revolving credit plan. The requirements stated in this paragraph (c)(3)(i) may be illustrated by the following examples:

*Example (1).* Under the terms of a revolving credit plan the required monthly payment to be made by customer A is $20. During the billing-month ending in December, sales aggregating $80 are charged to customer A's account, and during the next billing-month, ending in January, sales aggregating $19.95 and finance charges of $.60 are charged to A's account. Since the aggregate of sales charged to customer A's account during the billing-month ending in December ($80) exceeds the required monthly payment ($20), the terms and conditions of the plan contemplate that the sales charged during such billing-month are of the type which will be paid for in two or more installments. Since the aggregate of sales charged to customer A's account during the billing-month ending in January ($19.95) does not exceed the required monthly payment, the sales making up the aggregate of sales in such billing-month are not of the type which the terms and conditions of the plan contemplate will be paid for in two or more installments.

*Example (2).* The terms of a revolving credit plan require a payment of 20 percent of the balance of the customer's account as of the end of the billing-month for which the statement is rendered. A customer makes purchases aggregating $25 in the customer's next to the last billing-month ending within the taxpayer's taxable year, and the balance at the end of that month is $150. At the end of the customer's last billing-month ending within the taxpayer's taxable year, the balance of the account has decreased to $110. If the taxpayer determines the required monthly payment by reference to the payment required on the statement for the last billing-month ending within the taxable year and applies such method consistently to all accounts, then the sales making up the $25 aggregate of sales are of the type which the terms and conditions of the plan contemplate will be paid for in two or more installments. Although such aggregate was less than the $30 payment (20% × $150) required on the statement rendered for the billing-month of sales. It was more than the $22 (20% × $110) that the customer was required to pay on the statement rendered for his last billing-month ending within the taxable year, and thus meets the requirements of this paragraph (c)(3)(i). If, however, the taxpayer determines the required monthly payment by reference to the payment required on the statement for the billing-month of sale, then the sales making up the aggregate of sales during such billing-month do not meet the requirements of this paragraph (c)(3)(i) because such aggregate was less than the $30 payment required on the statement rendered for such month.

(ii) The sale must be charged to an account on which the first payment after the billing-month of sale indicates that the sale is being paid in installments. The first payment after the billing-month of sale indicates that the sale is being paid in installments if, and only if, such payment is an amount which is less than the balance of the account as of the close of the billing-month of sale. For purposes of this paragraph (c)(3)(ii), such balance shall be reduced by any return or allowance credited to the account after the close of the billing-month of sale and before the close of the billing-month within which the first payment after the billing-month of sale is credited to the account, unless the taxpayer demonstrates that the return or allowance was attributable to a charge made in a month subsequent to the billing-month of sale. The requirements stated in this paragraph (c)(3)(ii) may be illustrated by the following examples, in which it is assumed that the taxpayer's annual accounting period ends on January 31.

*Example (1).* Customer A's revolving credit account shows the following sales and payments:

| Month Ending | Aggregate Sales In Month | Payments | Balance |
|---|---|---|---|
| December 20 | $150 | 0 | $150 |
| January 20 | 75 | $ 30 | 195 |
| February 20 | 0 | 195 | 0 |

All sales made in the billing-month ending December 20 meet the requirements of this paragraph (c)(3)(ii) because the first payment on the account after such billing-month ($30) was less than the balance of the account as of the close of such billing-month ($150); and none of the sales made in the billing-month ending January 20 meets the requirements of this paragraph (c)(3)(ii) because the balance of the account as of the end of such billing-month was liquidated in one payment. By application of the rules of paragraph (c)(6)(v) of this section, the balance in the account as of the last billing-month ending in the taxable year ($195) consists of $120 of the $150 of sales made in the billing-month ending December 20 and all of the $75 of sales made in the billing-month ending January 20. Therefore, $120 of the account balance meets the requirements of this paragraph (c)(3)(ii) and $75 does not.

*Example (2).* Customer B's revolving credit account shows the following sales and payments:

| Month Ending | Aggregate Sales In Month | Payments | Balance |
|---|---|---|---|
| December 20 | $ 50 | 0 | $ 50 |
| January 20 | 100 | 0 | 150 |
| February 20 | 0 | $50 | 100 |

None of the sales made in the billing-month ending December 20 meets the requirements of this paragraph (c)(3)(ii) because the first payment credited to the account after such billing-month ($50) is not less than the balance of the account as of the close of such month ($50). All of the sales made in the billing-month ending January 20 meet the requirements of this paragraph (c)(3)(ii) because the first payment after such billing-month ($50) is less than the balance of the account as of the close of such month ($150).

*Example (3).* Customer C's revolving credit account shows the following purchases and credits:

| Month Ending | Item | Charges | Credits | Balance |
|---|---|---|---|---|
| January 20 | Coat | $55 | — | — |
| | Dress | 40 | — | — |
| | Shirt | 5 | — | $100 |
| February 20 | Return | — | $ 5 | — |
| | Payments | — | 95 | 0 |

None of the sales made in the billing-month ending January 20 meets the requirements of this paragraph (c)(3)(ii) because the first payment credited to the account after such billing-month ($95) was equal to the balance of the account as of the end of such billing-month, $95. For this purpose, the balance of $100 is reduced by the $5 return which was credited to the account after the close of the billing-month of sale and before the close of the billing-month within which the first payment after the billing-month of sale is credited.

*(4)* The provisions of paragraphs (c)(2) and (3) of this section may be illustrated by the following examples in which it is assumed that the taxpayer is a dealer whose annual accounting period ends on January 31.

*Example (1).* Customer A's revolving credit ledger account shows the following:

| Month Ending | Aggregate Sales In Month[1] | Returns And Allowances | Payments | Finance Charges | Balance |
|---|---|---|---|---|---|
| January 20 | $15.00 | 0 | 0 | 0 | $15.00 |
| February 20 | 0 | 0 | 0 | $0.15 | 15.15 |

[1] Including sales of personal property and nonpersonal property sales.

For purposes of the segregation provided for in paragraph (c)(2)(i) of this section, customer A's account will be disregarded and not taken into account in the determination of what percentage of charges in the sample is to be treated as sales on the installment plan because no payment was credited to that account after the billing-month of sale and on or before February 20.

*Example (2).* This example is applicable with respect to sales made during taxable years beginning before January 1, 1964. Under the terms of corporation X's revolving credit plan, payments are required in accordance with the following schedule:

| | Required Monthly Payment |
|---|---|
| Unpaid balance: | |
| 0 to $99.99 | $20 |
| $100 to $199.99 | 40 |
| $200 to $299.99 | 60 |

Customer B's revolving credit ledger account for the period beginning on September 21, 1963, and ending February 20, 1964, shows the following:

| Month Ending | Aggregate Sales In Month[1] | Returns And Allowances | Payments | Finance Charges | Balances |
|---|---|---|---|---|---|
| October 20 | $55.00 | 0 | 0 | 0 | $55.00 |
| November 20 | 45.00 | 0 | $20.00 | $0.35 | 80.35 |
| December 20 | 20.00 | 0 | 20.00 | .60 | 80.95 |
| January 20 | 26.00 | $5.00 | 20.00 | .61 | 82.56 |
| February 20 | 0 | 10.00 | 72.56 | 0 | 0 |

[1] Including sales of personal property and nonpersonal property sales.

The three $20 payments and the $5 return or allowance made in the billing-months ending in the taxable year are applied under the rules in paragraph (c)(6)(v) of this section to liquidate the earliest outstanding charges, first to the $55 aggregate of sales in the billing-month ending October 20 and next to $10 of the aggregate of sales made in the billing-month ending November 20. Thus, the balance of the account as of the close of the billing-month ending January 20, $82.56, is made up as follows:

| | |
|---|---|
| Remainder of sales in billing-month ending Nov. 20 ($45 − $10) | $35.00 |
| Finance charges for billing-month ending Nov. 20 | 0.35 |
| Sales for billing-month ending Dec. 20 | 20.00 |
| Finance charge for billing-month ending Dec. 20 | 0.60 |
| Sales for billing-month ending Jan. 20 | 26.00 |
| Finance charge for billing-month ending Jan. 20 | 0.61 |
| Total | 82.56 |

The sales of $35 remaining from the aggregate of sales for the billing-month ending November 20 meet the requirements of paragraph (c)(3)(i) of this section because the aggregate of sales charged during such billing-month ($45) exceeds the required monthly payment ($20), and such sales meet the requirements of paragraph (c)(3)(ii) of this section because the first payment after the billing-month of sale ($20) is an amount less than the balance of the account as of the close of such month ($80.35). Therefore, $35 of sales will be treated as sales on the installment plan. The $20 aggregate of sales charged during the billing-month ending December 20 does not meet the requirements of paragraph (c)(3)(i) of this section because it is in an amount which does not exceed the required monthly payment ($20). (The finance charge of $0.60 added in the billing-month does not enter into the determination of the aggregate of sales for the month because the term "sales" (as defined in paragraph (c)(6)(i) of this section does not include finance charges). The $26 aggregate of sales for the billing-month ending January 20 does not meet the requirements of paragraph (c)(3)(ii) of this section because the first payment after such billing-month ($72.56) was equal to the balance of the account as of the close of such billing-month ($72.56). For this purpose, the balance of $82.56 is reduced by the $10 return or allowance which was credited after the billing-month of sale and before February 20. Thus, of the $82.56 balance of B's account as of the close of the last billing-month ending within corporation X's taxable year, $35 will be treated as sales on the installment plan for purposes of determining the percentage provided for paragraph (c)(2) of this section.

*Example (3).* This example is applicable with respect to sales made during taxable years beginning after December 31, 1963. Assume the facts in example (2), except that Customer B's revolving credit ledger account is for the period beginning on September 21, 1964 and ending February 20, 1965. Since payments received are first used to liquidate any outstanding finance charges under the rule in paragraph (c)(6)(v) of this section, the $20 payment in December liquidated the $0.35 finance charge accrued at the end of the November billing-month and the $20 payment in January liquidated the $0.60 finance charge accrued at the end of the December billing-month. The balance of the three $20 payments ($59.05) and the $5 return or allowance are applied (under the rules in paragraph (c)(6)(v) of this section) to liquidate the earliest outstanding sales, first to the $55 aggregate of sales in the billing-month ending October 20 and next to $9.05 of the aggregate of sales made in the billing-month ending November 20. Thus, the balance of the account as of the close of the billing-month ending January 20, $82.56, is made up as follows:

| | |
|---|---|
| Remainder of sales in billing-month ending Nov. 20 ($45 – $9.05) | $35.95 |
| Sales for billing-month ending Dec. 20 | 20.00 |
| Sales for billing-month ending Jan. 20 | 26.00 |
| Finance charge for billing-month ending Jan. 20 | 0.61 |
| Total | 82.56 |

The sales of $35.95 remaining from the aggregate of sales for the billing-month ending November 20 meet the requirements of paragraph (c)(3)(i) of this section because the aggregate of sales charged during such billing-month ($45) exceeds the required monthly payment ($20), and such sales meet the requirements of paragraph (c)(3)(ii) of this section because the first payment after the billing-month of sale ($20) is an amount less than the balance of the account as of the close of such month ($80.35). Therefore, $35.95 of sales will be treated as sales on the installment plan. The $20 aggregate of sales charged during the billing-month ending December 20 does not meet the requirements of paragraph (c)(3)(i) of this section because it is in an amount which does not exceed the required monthly payment ($20). The $26 aggregate of sales for the billing-month ending January 20 does not meet the requirements of paragraph (c)(3)(ii) of this section because the first payment after such billing-month ($72.56) was equal to the balance of the account as of the close of such billing-month ($72.56). For this purpose, the balance of $82.56 is reduced by the $10 return or allowance which was credited after the billing-month of sale and before February 20. Thus, of the $82.56 balance of B's account as of the close of the last billing-month ending within corporation X's taxable year $35.95 will be treated as sales on the installment plan for purposes of determining the percentage provided for in paragraph (c)(2) of this section.

*(5)* Sales under a revolving credit plan which are nonpersonal property sales (as defined in paragraph (c)(6)(iv) of this section) do not constitute sales on the installment plan. Therefore, the charges under a revolving credit plan must be reduced by the nonpersonal property sales, if any, under such plan, before application of the sample percentage as provided for in paragraph (c)(2)(i) of this section. The taxpayer may treat as the nonpersonal property sales under the plan for the taxable year an amount which bears the same ratio to the total sales under the revolving credit plan made in the taxable year as the total nonpersonal property sales made in such year bears to the total sales made in such year.

*(6)* For purposes of this paragraph (c)—

(i) The term "sales" includes sales of services, such as a charge for watch repair, as well as sales of property, but does not include finance or service charges.

(ii) The term "charges" includes sales of services and property as well as finance or service charges.

(iii) A billing-month is that period of time for which a periodic statement of charges and credits is rendered to a customer.

(iv) The term "nonpersonal property sales" means all sales which are not sales of personal property made by the taxpayer. Thus, sales of a department leased by the taxpayer to another are nonpersonal property sales. Likewise, charges for services rendered by the taxpayer are nonpersonal property sales unless such services are incidental to and rendered contemporaneously with the sale of personal property, in which case such charges shall be considered as constituting part of the selling price of such property.

(v) Except as otherwise provided in this paragraph (c)(6)(v), each payment received from a customer under a revolving credit plan before the close of the last billing-month ending in the taxable year shall be applied to liquidate the earliest outstanding charges under such plan, notwithstanding any rule of law or contract provision to the contrary. For purposes of determining which charges remain in the balance of an account at the end of the last billing-month ending in the taxable year, the taxpayer may apply returns and allowances which are credited before the close of the last billing-month ending in the taxable year either (A) to liquidate or reduce the charge for the specific item so returned or for which an allowance is permitted, or (B) to liquidate or reduce the earliest outstanding charges. The method so selected for applying returns and allowances shall be followed on a consistent basis from year to year unless the district director consents to a change. Additionally, finance or service charges which are computed on the basis of the balance of the account at the end of the previous billing-month (usually reduced by payments during the current billing-month) are accrued at the end of the current billing-month and are therefore considered, for purposes of determining the earliest outstanding charges, as charged to the account after any sales made during the current billing month. However, for purposes of determining which charges remain in the balance of an account at the end of the last billing-month ending in a taxable year which began after December 31, 1963, payments received during such year shall be applied first against any finance or service charges which were outstanding at the time such payment was received. The preceding sentence shall not apply with respect to a computation made for purposes of applying the rule described in paragraph (c)(2)(ii) of this section.

(vi) The taxpayer shall allocate those sales under a revolving credit plan which are treated as sales on the installment plan to the proper year of sale in order to apply the appropriate gross profit percentage as provided for in § 1.453A-1(e). This allocation shall be made on the basis of the percentages of charges treated as sales on the installment plan which are attributable to each taxable year as determined in the sample of accounts described in paragraph (c)(2) of this section. However, if the taxpayer demonstrates to the satisfaction of the district director that income from sales on the installment plan is clearly reflected, all sales may be considered as being made in the taxable year for purposes of applying the gross profit percentage.

*(7)* The provisions of this paragraph (c) may be illustrated by the following example:

*Example.* Corporation X is a dealer and has elected to report on the installment method those sales under its revolving credit plan which may be treated as sales on the installment plan. Corporation X's taxable year ends on January 31, and the total balance of all its revolving credit accounts as of January 31, 1964, is $2,000,000. The total sales made in the taxable year are $10,000,000 of which $500,000 are nonpersonal property sales. The gross profit percentage realized or to be realized on all sales made in the taxable year is 40 percent. The amount of the gross profit contained in the year-end balance of $2,000,000 which may be deferred to succeeding years is computed as follows:

(i) In order to reduce the charges appearing in the year-end balance of revolving credit accounts receivable by the nonpersonal property sales contained therein, corporation X determines the amount of such nonpersonal property sales under the method permitted in paragraph (c)(5) of this section. Corporation X first determines the ratio which total nonpersonal property sales made during the year ($500,000) bears to total sales made during the year ($10,000,000), and then applies the percentage (5 percent) thus obtained to the year-end balance of revolving credit accounts receivable ($2,000,000). The nonpersonal property sales thus determined ($100,000) is subtracted from such year-end balance to obtain the charges under the revolving credit plan appearing in the year-end balance ($1,900,000) to which the sample percentage is to be applied.

(ii) In accordance with generally accepted sampling techniques, the taxpayer selects a probability sample of all revolving credit accounts having balances for billing-months ending in January 1964. The technique employed results in a random selection of accounts with total balances of $100,000.

(iii) Analysis of these sample accounts discloses that of the $100,000 of balances, $10,000 of balances are in accounts on which no payment was credited after a billing-month of sale and on or before the end of the first billing-month ending in the taxable year beginning February 1, 1964. These balances are, therefore, disregarded and not taken into account in the determination of what percentage of sales in the sample is to be treated as sales on the installment plan. Of the remaining $90,000 of balances, the taxpayer determines, by analyzing the ledger cards in the sample, that $63,000 of balances are composed of sales which meet the requirements of paragraphs (c)(3)(i) and (ii) of this section and are thus treated as sales on the installment plan. The remaining $27,000 of balances either did not meet the requirements of paragraphs (c)(3)(i) and (ii) of this section or were not sales (as defined in paragraph (c)(6)(i) of this section). The percentage of charges in the sample treated as sales on the installment plan is, therefore, 70 percent ($63,000 × $90,000).

(iv) The charges in the year-end balance which are to be treated as sales on the installment plan, $1,330,000, are computed by multiplying the charges to which the sample percentage is applied ($1,900,000) by the sample percentage (70 percent).

(v) The deferred gross profit attributable to sales under the revolving credit plan for the taxable year, $532,000, is determined by multiplying the amount treated as sales on the installment plan ($1,330,000), by the gross profit percentage (40 percent). (Corporation X will be able to demonstrate to the satisfaction of the district director that (A) since the gross profit percentage for all sales does not vary materially from the gross profit percentage for all sales made under the revolving credit plan, (B) since only an insubstantial amount of sales included in year-end account balances was made prior to the taxable year, and (C) since the prior year's gross profit percentage does not vary materially from the gross profit percentage for the taxable year, income from sales on the installment plan will be clearly reflected by applying the current year's gross profit percentage for all sales under the revolving credit plan treated as sales on the installment plan.)

**(d) Effective date.** This section applies for taxable years beginning after December 31, 1953, and ending after August 16, 1954, but does not apply for any taxable year beginning after December 31, 1986. For taxable years beginning after December 31, 1986, sales under a revolving credit plan shall not be treated as sales on the installment plan.

T.D. 8270, 11/2/89.

### § 1.453A-3 Requirements for adoption of or change to installment method by dealers in personal property.

**(a) In general.** A dealer (within the meaning of § 1.453A-1(c)(1)) may adopt or change to the installment method for a type or types of sales on the installment plan (within the meaning of § 1.453A-1(c)(3) and (d)) in the manner prescribed in this section. This section applies only to dealers and only with respect to their sales on the installment plan.

**(b) Time and manner of electing installment method reporting.** *(1) Time for election.* An election to adopt or change to the installment method for a type or types of sales must be made on an income tax return for the taxable year of the election, filed on or before the time specified (including extensions thereof) for filing such return.

*(2) Adoption of installment method.* A taxpayer who adopts the installment method for the first taxable year in which sales are made on an installment plan of any kind must indicate in the income tax return for that taxable year that the installment method of accounting is being adopted and specify the type or types of sales included within the election. If a taxpayer in the year of the initial election made only one type of sale on the installment plan, but during a subsequent taxable year makes another type of sale on the installment plan and adopts the installment method for that other type of sale, the taxpayer must indicate in the income tax return for the subsequent year that an election is being made to adopt the installment method of accounting for the additional type of sale.

*(3) Change to installment method.* A taxpayer who changes to the installment method for a particular type or types of sales on the installment plan in accordance with this section must, for each type of sale on the installment plan for which the installment method is to be used, attach a separate statement to the income tax return for the taxable year with respect to which the change is made. Each statement must show the method of accounting used in computing taxable income before the change and the type of sale on the installment plan for which the installment method is being elected.

*(4) Deemed elections.* A dealer (including a person who is a dealer as a result of the recharacterization of transactions as sales) is deemed to have elected the installment method if the dealer treats a sale on the installment plan as a transaction other than a sale and fails to report the full amount of gain in the year of the sale. For example, if a transaction treated by a dealer as a lease is recharacterized by the Internal Revenue Service as a sale on the installment plan, the dealer will be deemed to have elected the installment method assuming the dealer failed to report the full amount of gain in the year of the transaction.

**(c) Consent.** A dealer may adopt or change to the installment method for sales on the installment plan without the consent of the Commissioner. However, a dealer may not change from the installment method to the accrual method of accounting or to any other method of accounting without the consent of the Commissioner.

**(d) Cut-off method for amounts previously accrued.** An election to change to the installment method for a type of sale applies only with respect to sales made on or after the first day of the taxable year of change. Thus, payments received in the taxable year of the change, or in subsequent years, in respect of an installment obligation which arose in a taxable year prior to the taxable year of change are not taken into account on the installment method, but rather must be accounted for under the taxpayer's method of accounting in use in the prior year.

**(e) Effective date.** This section applies to sales by dealers in taxable years ending after October 19, 1980, but generally does not apply to sales made after December 31, 1987. For sales made after December 31, 1987, sales by a dealer in personal or real property shall not be treated as sales on the installment plan. (However, see section 453(l)(2) for certain exceptions to this rule.) For rules relating to sales by dealers in taxable years ending before October 20, 1980, see 26 CFR 1.453-7 and 1.453-8 (rev. as of April 1, 1987).

T.D. 8269, 11/2/89.

### § 1.454-1 Obligations issued at discount.

**(a) Certain non-interest-bearing obligations issued at discount.** *(1) Election to include increase in income currently.* If a taxpayer owns—

(i) A non-interest-bearing obligation issued at a discount and redeemable for fixed amounts increasing at stated intervals (other than an obligation issued by a corporation after May 27, 1969, as to which ratable inclusion of original issue discount is required under section 1232(a)(3)), or

(ii) An obligation of the United States, other than a current income obligation, in which he retains his investment in a matured series E U.S. savings bond, or

(iii) A nontransferable obligation (whether or not a current income obligation) of the United States for which a series E U.S. savings bond was exchanged (whether or not at final maturity) in an exchange upon which gain is not recognized because of section 1037(a) (or so much of section 1031(b) as relates to section 1037),

and if the increase, if any, in redemption price of such obligation described in subdivision (i), (ii), or (iii) of this subparagraph during the taxable year (as described in subparagraph (2) of this paragraph) does not constitute income for such year under the method of accounting used in computing his taxable income, then the taxpayer may, at his election, treat the increase as constituting income for the year in which such increase occurs. If the election is not made and section 1037 (or so much of section 1031 as relates to section 1037) does not apply, the taxpayer shall treat the increase as constituting income for the year in which the obligation is redeemed or disposed of, or finally matures, whichever is earlier. Any such election must be made in the taxpayer's return and may be made for any taxable year. If an election is made with respect to any such obligation described in subdivision (i), (ii), or (iii) of this subparagraph, it shall apply also to all other obligations of the type described in such subdivisions owned by the taxpayer at the beginning of the first taxable year to which the election applies, and to those thereafter acquired by him, and shall be binding for the taxable year for which the return is filed and for all subsequent taxable years, unless the Commissioner permits the taxpayer to change to a different method of reporting income from such obligations. See section 446(e) and paragraph (e) of § 1.446-1, relating to requirement respecting a change of accounting method. Although the election once made is binding upon the taxpayer, it does not apply to a transferee of the taxpayer.

*(2) Amount of increase in case of noninterest-bearing obligations.* In any case in which an election is made under section 454, the amount which accrues in any taxable year to which the election applies is measured by the actual increase in the redemption price occurring in that year. This amount does not accrue ratably between the dates on which the redemption price changes. For example, if two dates on which the redemption price increases (February 1 and August 1) fall within a taxable year and if the redemption price increases in the amount of 50 cents on each such date, the amount accruing in that year would be $1 ($0.50 on February 1 and $0.50 on August 1). If the taxpayer owns a noninterest-bearing obligation of the character described in subdivision (i), (ii), or (iii) of subparagraph (1) of this paragraph acquired prior to the first taxable year to which his election applies, he must also include in gross income for such first taxable year (i) the increase in the redemption price of such obligation occurring between the date of acquisition of the obligation and the first day of such first taxable year and (ii), in a case where a series E bond was exchanged for such obligation, the increase in the redemption price of such series E bond occurring between the date of acquisition of such series E bond and the date of the exchange.

*(3) Amount of increase in case of current income obligations.* If an election is made under section 454 and the taxpayer owns, at the beginning of the first taxable year to which the election applies, a current income obligation of the character described in subparagraph (1)(iii) of this paragraph acquired prior to such taxable year, he must also include in gross income for such first taxable year the increase in the redemption price of the series E bond which was surrendered to the United States in exchange for such current income obligation; the amount of the increase is that occurring between the date of acquisition of the series E bond and the date of the exchange.

*(4) Illustrations.* The application of this paragraph may be illustrated by the following examples:

*Example (1).* Throughout the calendar year 1954, a taxpayer who uses the cash receipts and disbursements method of accounting holds series E U.S. savings bonds having a maturity value of $5,000 and a redemption value at the beginning of the year 1954 of $4,050 and at the end of the year 1954 of $4,150. He purchased the bonds on January 1, 1949, for $3,750, and holds no other obligation of the type described in this section. If the taxpayer exercises the election in his return for the calendar year 1954, he is required to include $400 in taxable income with respect to such bonds. Of this amount, $300 represents the increase in the redemption price before 1954 and $100 represents the increase in the redemption price in 1954. The increases in redemption value occurring in subsequent taxable years are includible in gross income for such taxable years.

*Example (2).* In 1958 B, a taxpayer who uses the cash receipts and disbursements method of accounting and the calendar year as his taxable year, purchased for $7,500 a series E United States savings bond with a face value of $10,000. In 1965, when the stated redemption value of the series E bond is $9,760, B surrenders it to the United States in exchange solely for a $10,000 series H U.S. current income savings bond in an exchange qualifying under section 1037(a), after paying $240 additional consideration. On the exchange of the series E bond for the series H bond in 1965, B realizes a gain of $2,260 ($9,760 less $7,500), none of which is recognized for that year by reason of section

1037(a). B retains the series H bond and redeems it at maturity in 1975 for $10,000, but in 1966 he exercises the election under section 454(a) in his return for that year with respect to five series E bonds he purchased in 1960. B is required to include in gross income for 1966 the increase in redemption price occurring before 1966 and in 1966 with respect to the series E bonds purchased in 1960; he is also required to include in gross income for 1966 the $2,260 increase in redemption price of the series E bond which was exchanged in 1965 for the series H bond.

**(b) Short-term obligations issued on a discount basis.** In the case of obligations of the United States or any of its possessions, or of a State, or Territory, or any political subdivision thereof, or of the District of Columbia, issued on a discount basis and payable without interest at a fixed maturity date not exceeding one year from the date of issue, the amount of discount at which such obligation originally sold does not accrue until the date on which such obligation is redeemed, sold, or, otherwise disposed of. This rule applies regardless of the method of accounting used by the taxpayer. For examples illustrating rules for computation of income from sale or other disposition of certain obligations of the type described in this paragraph, see section 1221 and the regulations thereunder.

**(c) Matured U.S. savings bonds.** *(1) Inclusion of increase in income upon redemption or final maturity.* If a taxpayer (other than a corporation) holds—

(i) A matured series E U.S. savings bond.

(ii) An obligation of the United States, other than a current income obligation, in which he retains his investment in a matured series E U.S. savings bond, or

(iii) A nontransferable obligation (whether or not a current income obligation) of the United States for which a series E U.S. savings bond was exchanged (whether or not at final maturity) in an exchange upon which gain is not recognized because of section 1037(a) (or so much of section 1031(b) as relates to section 1037(a)), the increase in redemption price of the series E bond in excess of the amount paid for such series E bond shall be included in the gross income of such taxpayer for the taxable year in which the obligation described in subdivision (i), (ii), or (iii) of this subparagraph is redeemed or disposed of, or finally matures, whichever is earlier, but only to the extent such increase has not previously been includible in the gross income of such taxpayer or any other taxpayer. If such obligation is partially redeemed before final maturity, or partially disposed of by being partially reissued to another owner, such increase in redemption price shall be included in the gross income of such taxpayer for such taxable year on a basis proportional to the total denomination of obligations redeemed or disposed of. The provisions of section 454(c) and of this subparagraph shall not apply in the case of any taxable year for which the taxpayer's taxable income is computed under an accrual method of accounting or for a taxable year for which an election made by the taxpayer under section 454(a) and paragraph (a) of this section applies. For rules respecting the character of the gain realized upon the disposition or redemption of an obligation described in subdivision (iii) of this subparagraph, see paragraph (b) of § 1.1037-1.

*(2) Illustrations.* The application of this paragraph may be illustrated by the following examples, in which it is assumed that the taxpayer uses the cash receipts and disbursements method of accounting and the calendar year as his taxable year:

*Example (1).* On June 1, 1941, A purchased for $375 a series E U.S. savings bond which was redeemable at maturity (10 years from issue date) for $500. At maturity of the bond, A exercised the option of retaining the matured series E bond for the 10-year extended maturity period. On June 2, 1961, A redeemed the series E bond, at which time the stated redemption value was $674.60. A never elected under section 454(a) to include the annual increase in redemption price in gross income currently. Under section 454(c), A is required to include $299.60 ($674.60 less $375) in gross income for 1961 by reason of his redemption of the bond.

*Example (2).* The facts are the same as in example (2) in paragraph (a)(4) of this section. On redemption of the series H bond received in the exchange qualifying under section 1037(a), B realizes a gain of $2,260, determined as provided in example (5) in paragraph (b)(4) of § 1.1037-1. None of this amount is includible in B's gross income for 1975, such amount having already been includible in his gross income for 1966 because of his election under section 454(a).

*Example (3).* C, who had elected under section 454(a) to include the annual increase in the redemption price of his non-interest-bearing obligations in gross income currently, owned a $1,000 series E U.S. savings bond, which was purchased on October 1, 1949, for $750. C died on February 1, 1955, when the redemption value of the bond was $820. The bond was immediately reissued to D, his only heir, who has not made an election under section 454(a). On January 15, 1960, when the redemption value of the bond is $1,000, D surrenders it to the United States in exchange solely for a $1,000 series H U.S. savings bond in an exchange qualifying under the provisions of section 1037(a). For 1960 D properly does not return any income from the exchange of bonds, although he returns the interest payments on the series H bond for the taxable years in which they are received. On September 1, 1964, prior to maturity of the series H bond, D redeems it for $1,000. For 1964, D must include $180 in gross income under section 454(c) from the redemption of the series H bond, that is, the amount of the increase in the redemption price of the series E bond ($1,000 less $820) occurring between February 1, 1955, and January 15, 1960, the period during which he owned the series E bond.

---

T.D. 6282, 12/24/57, amend T.D. 6935, 11/16/67, T.D. 7154, 12/27/71.

---

PAR. 11. Paragraph (a)(1)(i) of § 1.454-1 is revised to read as follows:

**Proposed § 1.454-1 Obligations issued at discount.** [*For Preamble, see ¶ 151,065*]

• ***Caution:*** Prop reg § 1.482-2 was finalized by T.D. 8204, 5/20/88. Prop regs §§ 1.163-7, 1.446-2, 1.483-1 through -5, 1.1001-1, 1.1012-1, 1.1271 through -3, 1.1272-1, 1.1273-1, 1.1273-2, 1.1274-1 throught -7, 1.1274A-1, 1.1275-1 through -3, and 1.1275-5 were withdrawn by the Treasury on 12/22/92, 57 Fed. Reg. 67050. Prop reg § 1.1275-4 was superseded by the Treasury on 12/16/94, Fed. Reg. 59, 64884, which was finalized by T.D. 8674, 6/11/96.

**(a) Certain non-interest bearing obligations issued at discount.** *(1) Election to include increase in income currently.* If a taxpayer owns—

(i) A non-interest bearing obligation issued at a discount and redeemable for fixed amounts increasing at stated intervals (other than a debt instrument issued after May 27, 1969, as to which inclusion of original issue discount is required under section 1272), or

* * * * *

### § 1.455-1 Treatment of prepaid subscription income.

Effective with respect to taxable years beginning after December 31, 1957, section 455 permits certain taxpayers to elect with respect to a trade or business in connection with which prepaid subscription income is received, to include such income in gross income for the taxable years during which a liability exists to furnish or deliver a newspaper, magazine, or other periodical. If a taxpayer does not elect to treat prepaid subscription income under the provisions of section 455, such income is includible in gross income for the taxable year in which received by the taxpayer, unless under the method or practice of accounting used in computing taxable income such amount is to be properly accounted for as of a different period.

T.D. 6591, 2/26/62.

### § 1.455-2 Scope of election under section 455.

**(a)** If a taxpayer makes an election under section 455 and § 1.455-6 with respect to a trade or business, all prepaid subscription income from such trade or business shall be included in gross income for the taxable years during which the liability exists to furnish or deliver a newspaper, magazine, or other periodical. Such election shall be applicable to all prepaid subscription income received in connection with the trade or business for which the election is made; except that the taxpayer may further elect to include in gross income for the taxable year of receipt (as described in section 455(d)(3) and paragraph (c) of § 1.455-5) the entire amount of any prepaid subscription income if the liability from which it arose is to end within 12 months after the date of receipt, hereinafter sometimes referred to as "within 12 months" election.

**(b)** If the taxpayer is engaged in more than one trade or business in which a liability is incurred to furnish or deliver a newspaper, magazine, or other periodical, a separate election may be made under section 455 with respect to each such trade or business. In addition, a taxpayer may make a separate "within 12 months" election for each separate trade or business for which it has made an election under section 455.

**(c)** An election made under section 455 shall be binding for the first taxable year for which the election is made and for all subsequent taxable years, unless the taxpayer secures the consent of the Commissioner to the revocation of such election. Thus, in any case where the taxpayer has elected a method prescribed by section 455 for the inclusion of prepaid subscription income in gross income, such method of reporting income may not be changed without the prior approval of the Commissioner. In order to secure the Commissioner's consent to the revocation of such election, an application must be filed with the Commissioner in accordance with section 446(e) and the regulations thereunder. For purposes of subtitle A of the Code, the computation of taxable income under an election made under section 455 shall be treated as a method of accounting. For adjustments required by changes in method of accounting, see section 481 and the regulations thereunder.

**(d)** An election made under section 455 shall not apply to any prepaid subscription income received before the first taxable year to which the election applies. For example, Corporation M, which computes its taxable income under an accrual method of accounting and files its income tax returns on the calendar year basis, publishes a monthly magazine and customarily sells subscriptions on a 3-year basis. In 1958 it received $135,000 of 3-year prepaid subscription income for subscriptions beginning during 1958, and in 1959 it received $142,000 of prepaid subscription income for subscriptions beginning after December 31, 1958. In February 1959 it elected, with the consent of the Commissioner, to report its prepaid subscription income under the provisions of section 455 for the year 1959 and subsequent taxable years. The $135,000 received in 1958 from prepaid subscriptions must be included in gross income in full in that year, and no part of such 1958 income shall be allocated to the years 1959, 1960, and 1961 during which M was under a liability to deliver its magazine. The $142,000 received in 1959 from prepaid subscriptions shall be allocated to the years 1959, 1960, 1961, and 1962.

**(e)** No election may be made under section 455 with respect to a trade or business if, in computing taxable income, the cash receipts and disbursements method of accounting is used with respect to such trade or business. However, if the taxpayer is on a "combination" method of accounting under section 446(c)(4) and the regulations thereunder, it may elect the benefits of section 455 if it uses an accrual method of accounting for subscription income.

T.D. 6591, 2/26/62.

### § 1.455-3 Method of allocation.

**(a)** Prepaid subscription income to which section 455 applies shall be included in gross income for the taxable years during which the liability to which the income relates is discharged or is deemed to be discharged on the basis of the taxpayer's experience.

**(b)** For purposes of determining the period or periods over which the liability of the taxpayer extends, and for purposes of allocating prepaid subscription income to such periods, the taxpayer may aggregate similar transactions during the taxable year in any reasonable manner, provided the method of aggregation and allocation is consistently followed.

T.D. 6591, 2/26/62.

### § 1.455-4 Cessation of taxpayer's liability.

**(a)** If a taxpayer has elected to apply the provisions of section 455 to a trade or business in connection with which prepaid subscription income is received, and if its liability to furnish or deliver a newspaper, magazine, or other periodical ends for any reason, then so much of the prepaid subscription income attributable to such liability as was not includible in its gross income under section 455 for preceding taxable years shall be included in its gross income for the taxable year in which such liability ends. A taxpayer's liability may end, for example, because of the cancellation of a subscription. See section 381(a)(4) and the regulations thereunder for the treatment of prepaid subscription income in a transaction to which section 381(a) applies.

**(b)** If a taxpayer who has elected to apply the provisions of section 455 to a trade or business dies or ceases to exist, then so much of the prepaid subscription income attributable to such trade or business which was not includible in its gross income under section 455 for preceding taxable years shall be included in its gross income for the taxable year in which such death or cessation of existence occurs. See section 381(c)(4) and the regulations thereunder for the treatment of prepaid subscription income in a transaction to which section 381(a) applies.

T.D. 6591, 2/26/62.

**§ 1.455-5 Definitions and other rules.**

**(a) Prepaid subscription income.** *(1)* The term "prepaid subscription income" means any amount includible in gross income which is received in connection with, and is directly attributable to, a liability of the taxpayer which extends beyond the close of the taxable year in which such amount is received and which is income from a newspaper, magazine, or other periodical. For example where Corporation X, a publisher of newspapers, magazines, and other periodicals makes sales on a subscription basis and the purchaser pays the subscription price in advance, prepaid subscription income would include the amounts actually received by X in connection with its liability to furnish or deliver the newspaper, magazine, or other periodical.

*(2)* For purposes of section 455, prepaid subscription income does not include amounts received by a taxpayer in connection with sales of subscriptions on a prepaid basis where such taxpayer does not have the liability to furnish or deliver a newspaper, magazine, or other periodical. The provisions of this subparagraph may be illustrated by the following example. Corporation D has a contract with each of several large publishers which grants it the right to sell subscriptions to their periodicals. Corporation D collects the subscription price from the subscribers, retains a portion thereof as its commission and remits the balance to the publishers. The amount retained by Corporation D represents commissions on the sale of subscriptions, and is not prepaid subscription income for purposes of section 455 since the commissions represent compensation for services rendered and are not directly attributable to a liability of Corporation D to furnish or deliver a newspaper, magazine, or other periodical.

**(b) Liability.** The term "liability" means a liability of the taxpayer to furnish or deliver a newspaper, magazine, or other periodical.

**(c) Receipt of prepaid subscription income.** For purposes of section 455, prepaid subscription income shall be treated as received during the taxable year for which it is includible in gross income under section 451, relating to general rule for taxable year of inclusion, without regard to section 455.

**(d) Treatment of prepaid subscription income under an established accounting method.** Notwithstanding the provisions of section 455 and § 1.455-1, any taxpayer who, for taxable years beginning before January 1, 1958, has reported prepaid subscription income for income tax purposes under an established and consistent method or practice of deferring such income may continue to report such income in accordance with such method or practice for all subsequent taxable years to which section 455 applies without making an election under section 455.

T.D. 6591, 2/26/62.

**§ 1.455-6 Time and manner of making election.**

***Caution:*** The Treasury has not yet amended Reg § 1.455-6 to reflect changes made by P.L. 94-455.

**(a) Election without consent.** *(1)* A taxpayer may, without consent, elect to treat prepaid subscription income of a trade or business under section 455 for the first taxable year—

(i) Which begins after December 31, 1957, and

(ii) In which there is received prepaid subscription income from the trade or business for which the election is made.

Such an election shall be made not later than the time prescribed by law for filing the income tax return for such year (including extensions thereof), and shall be made by means of a statement attached to such return.

*(2)* The statement shall indicate that the taxpayer is electing to apply the provisions of section 455 to his trade or business, and shall contain the following information:

(i) The name and a description of the taxpayer's trade or business to which the election is to apply;

(ii) The method of accounting used in such trade or business;

(iii) The total amount of prepaid subscription income from such trade or business for the taxable year;

(iv) The period or periods over which the liability of the taxpayer to furnish or deliver a newspaper, magazine, or other periodical extends;

(v) The amount of prepaid subscription income applicable to each such period; and

(vi) A description of the method used in allocating the prepaid subscription income to each such period.

In any case in which prepaid subscription income is received from more than one trade or business, the statement shall set forth the required information with respect to each trade or business subject to the election.

*(3)* See paragraph (c) of this section for additional information required to be submitted with the statement if the taxpayer also elects to include in gross income for the taxable year of receipt the entire amount of prepaid subscription income attributable to a liability which is to end within 12 months after the date of receipt.

**(b) Election with consent.** A taxpayer may, with the consent of the Commissioner, elect at any time to apply the provisions of section 455 to any trade or business in which it receives prepaid subscription income. The request for such consent shall be in writing, signed by the taxpayer or its authorized representative, and shall be addressed to the Commissioner of Internal Revenue, Attention: T:R:C, Washington 25, D.C. The request must be filed on or before the later of the following dates: (1) 90 days after the beginning of the first taxable year to which the election is to apply or (2) May 28, 1962, and must contain the information described in paragraph (a)(2) of this section. See paragraph (c) of this section for additional information required to be submitted with the requests if the taxpayer also elects to include in gross income for the taxable year of receipt the entire amount of prepaid subscription income attributable to a liability which is to end within 12 months after the date of receipt.

**(c) "Within 12 months" election.** *(1)* A taxpayer who elects to apply the provisions of section 455 to any trade or business may also elect to include in gross income for the taxable year of receipt (as described in section 455(d)(3) and paragraph (c) of § 1.455-5) the entire amount of any prepaid subscription income from such trade or business if the liability from which it arose is to end within 12 months after the date of receipt. Any such election is binding for the first taxable year for which it is effective and for all subsequent taxable years, unless the taxpayer secures permission from the Commissioner to treat such income differently. Application to revoke or change a "within 12 months" election shall be made in accordance with the provisions of section 446(e) and the regulations thereunder.

*(2)* The "within 12 months" election shall be made by including in the statement required by paragraph (a) of this section or the request described in paragraph (b) of this section, whichever is applicable, a declaration that the taxpayer elects to include such income in gross income in the taxable year of receipt, and the amount of such income. If the taxpayer is engaged in more than one trade or business for which the election under section 455 is made, it must include, in such statement or request, a declaration for each trade or business for which it makes the "within 12 months" election. See also paragraph (e) of § 1.455-2.

*(3)* If the taxpayer does not make the "within 12 months" election for its trade or business at the time prescribed for making the election to include prepaid subscription income in gross income for the taxable years during which its liability to furnish or deliver a newspaper, magazine, or other periodical exists for such trade or business, but later wishes to make such election, it must apply for permission from the Commissioner. Such application shall be made in accordance with the provisions of section 446(e) and the regulations thereunder.

T.D. 6591, 2/26/62.

### § 1.456-1 Treatment of prepaid dues income.

Effective for taxable years beginning after December 31, 1960, a taxpayer which is a membership organization (as described in paragraph (c) of § 1.456-5 in connection with its trade or business of rendering services or making available membership privileges may elect under section 456 to include such income in gross income ratably over the taxable years during which its liability (as described in paragraph (b) of § 1.456-5) to render such services or extend such privileges exists, if such liability does not extend over a period of time in excess of 36 months. If the taxpayer does not elect to treat prepaid dues income under section 456, or if such income may not be reported under section 456, as for example, where the income relates to a liability to render services or make available membership privileges which extends beyond 36 months, then such income is includible in gross income for the taxable year in which it is received (as described in paragraph (d) of § 1.456-5).

T.D. 6937, 11/29/67.

### § 1.456-2 Scope of election under section 456.

**(a)** An election made under section 456 and § 1.456-6, shall be applicable to all prepaid dues income received in connection with the trade or business for which the election is made. However, the taxpayer may further elect to include in gross income for the taxable year of receipt the entire amount of any prepaid dues income attributable to a liability extending beyond the close of the taxable year but ending within 12 months after the date of receipt, hereinafter referred to as the "within 12 months" election.

**(b)** If the taxpayer is engaged in more than one trade or business in connection with which prepaid dues income is received, a separate election may be made under section 456 with respect to each such trade or business. In addition, a taxpayer may make a separate "within 12 months" election for each separate trade or business for which it has made an election under section 456.

**(c)** A section 456 election and a "within 12 months" election shall be binding for the first taxable year for which the election is made and for all subsequent taxable years, unless the taxpayer secures the consent of the Commissioner to the revocation of either election. In order to secure the Commissioner's consent to the revocation of the section 456 election or the "within 12 months" election, an application must be filed with the Commissioner in accordance with section 446(e) and the regulations thereunder. However, an application for consent to revoke the section 456 election or the "within 12 months" election in the case of all taxable years which end before November 30, 1967 must be filed on or before February 28, 1968. For purposes of Subtitle A of the Code, the computation of taxable income under an election made under section 456 or under the "within 12 months" election shall be treated as a method of accounting. For adjustments required by changes in method of accounting, see section 481 and the regulations thereunder.

**(d)** Except as provided in section 456(d) and § 1.456-7, an election made under section 456 shall not apply to any prepaid dues income received before the first taxable year to which the election applies. For example, Corporation X, a membership organization which files its income tax returns on a calendar year basis, customarily sells 3-year memberships, payable in advance. In 1961 it received $160,000 of prepaid dues income for 3-year memberships beginning during 1961, and in 1962 it received $185,000 of prepaid dues income for 3-year memberships beginning on January 1, 1962. In March 1962 it elected, with the consent of the Commissioner, to report its prepaid dues income under the provisions of section 456 for the year 1962 and subsequent taxable years. The $160,000 received in 1961 from prepaid dues must be included in gross income in full in that year, and except as provided in section 456(d) and § 1.456-7, no part of such income shall be allocated to the taxable years 1962, 1963, and 1964 during which X was under a liability to make available its membership privileges. The $185,000 received in 1962 from prepaid dues income shall be allocated to the years 1962, 1963, and 1964.

**(e)** No election may be made under section 456 with respect to a trade or business if, in computing taxable income, the cash receipts and disbursements method (or a hybrid thereof) of accounting is used with respect to such trade or business, unless the combination of the section 456 election and the taxpayer's hybrid method of accounting is used with respect to such trade or business, unless the combination of the section 456 election and the taxpayer's hybrid method of accounting does not result in a material distortion of income.

T.D. 6937, 11/29/67.

### § 1.456-3 Method of allocation.

**(a)** Prepaid dues income for which an election has been made under section 456 shall be included in gross income over the period of time during which the liability to render services or make available membership privileges exists. The liability to render the services or make available the membership privileges shall be deemed to exist ratably over the period of time such services are required to be rendered, or such membership privileges are required to be made available. Thus, the prepaid dues income shall be included in gross income ratably over the period of the membership contract. For example, Corporation X, a membership organization, which files its income tax returns on a calendar year basis, elects, for its taxable year beginning January 1, 1961, to report its prepaid dues income in accordance with the provisions of section 456. On March 31, 1961, it sells a 2-year membership for $48 payable in advance, the membership to extend from May 1, 1961, to April 30, 1963. X shall include in its gross income for the taxable year 1961 8/24 of the $48, or $16, and for the taxable year 1962 12/24 of the $48, or $24, and for the taxable year 1963 4/24 of the $48, or $8.

**(b)** For purposes of determining the period or periods over which the liability of the taxpayer exists, and for purposes of allocating prepaid dues income to such periods, the taxpayer may aggregate similar transactions during the taxable year in any reasonable manner, provided the method of aggregation and allocation is consistently followed.

T.D. 6937, 11/29/67.

### § 1.456-4 Cessation of liability or existence.

**(a)** If a taxpayer has elected to apply the provisions of section 456 to a trade or business in connection with which prepaid dues income is received, and if the taxpayer's liability to render services or make available membership privileges ends for any reason, as for example, because of the cancellation of a membership then so much of the prepaid dues income attributable to such liability as was not includible in the taxpayer's gross income under section 456 for preceding taxable years shall be included in gross income for the taxable year in which such liability ends. This paragraph shall not apply to amounts includible in gross income under § 1.456-7.

**(b)** If a taxpayer which has elected to apply the provisions of section 456 ceases to exist, then the prepaid dues income which was not includible in gross income under section 456 for preceding taxable years shall be included in the taxpayer's gross income for the taxable year in which such cessation of existence occurs. This paragraph shall not apply to amounts includible in gross income under § 1.456-7.

**(c)** If a taxpayer is a party to a transaction to which section 381(a) applies and the taxpayer's method of accounting with respect to prepaid dues income is used by the acquiring corporation under the provisions of section 381(c)(4); then neither the liability nor the existence of the taxpayer shall be deemed to have ended or ceased. In such cases see section 381(c)(4) and the regulations thereunder for the treatment of the portion of prepaid dues income which was not included in gross income under section 456 for preceding taxable years.

T.D. 6937, 11/29/67.

### § 1.456-5 Definitions and other rules.

**(a) Prepaid dues income.** *(1)* The term "prepaid dues income" means any amount for membership dues includible in gross income which is received by a membership organization in connection with, and is directly attributable to, a liability of the taxpayer to render services or make available membership privileges over a period of time which extends beyond the close of the taxable year in which such amount is received.

*(2)* For purposes of section 456, prepaid dues income does not include amounts received by a taxpayer in connection with sales of memberships on a prepaid basis where the taxpayer does not have the liability to furnish the services or make available the membership privileges. For example, where a taxpayer has a contract with several membership organizations to sell memberships in such organizations and retains a portion of the amounts received from the sale of such memberships and remits the balance to the membership organizations, the amounts retained by such taxpayer represent commissions and do not constitute prepaid dues income for purposes of section 456.

**(b) Liability.** The term "liability" means a liability of the taxpayer to render services or make available membership privileges over a period of time which does not exceed 36 months. Thus, if during the taxable year a taxpayer sells memberships for more than 36 months and also memberships for 36 months or less, section 456 does not apply to the income from the sale of memberships for more than 36 months. For the purpose of determining the duration of a liability, a bona fide renewal of a membership shall not be considered to be a part of the existing membership.

**(c) Membership organization.** *(1)* The term "membership organization" means a corporation, association, federation, or other similar organization meeting the following requirements:

(i) It is organized without capital stock of any kind,

(ii) Its charter, bylaws, or other written agreement or contract expressly prohibits the distribution of any part of the net earnings directly or indirectly, in money, property, or services, to any member, and

(iii) No part of the net earnings of which is in fact distributed to any member either directly or indirectly, in money, property, or services.

*(2)* For purposes of this paragraph an increase in services or reduction in dues to all members shall generally not be considered distributions of net earnings.

*(3)* If a corporation, association, federation, or other similar organization subsequent to the time it elects to report its prepaid dues income in accordance with the provisions of section 456, (i) issues any kind of capital stock either to any member or nonmember, (ii) amends its charter, bylaws, or other written agreement or contract to permit distributions of its net earnings to any member or, (iii) in fact, distributes any part of its net earnings either in money, property, or services to any member, then immediately after such event the organization shall not be considered a membership organization within the meaning of section 456(e)(3).

**(d) Receipt of prepaid dues income.** For purposes of section 456, prepaid dues income shall be treated as received during the taxable year for which it is includible in gross income under section 451, relating to the general rule for taxable year of inclusion, without regard to section 456.

T.D. 6937, 11/29/67.

### § 1.456-6 Time and manner of making election.

**(a) Election without consent.** A taxpayer may make an election under section 456 without the consent of the Commissioner for the first taxable year beginning after December 31, 1960, in which it receives prepaid dues income in the trade or business for which such election is made. The election must be made not later than the time prescribed by law for filing the income tax return for such year (including extensions thereof). The election must be made by means of a statement attached to such return. In addition, there should be attached a copy of a typical membership contract used by the organization and a copy of its charter, bylaws, or other written agreement or contract of organization or association.

The statement shall indicate that the taxpayer is electing to apply the provisions of section 456 to the trade or business, and shall contain the following information:

*(1)* The taxpayer's name and a description of the trade or business to which the election is to apply.

*(2)* The method of accounting used for prepaid dues income in the trade or business during the first taxable year for which the election is to be effective and during each of 3 preceding taxable years, and if there was a change in the method of accounting for prepaid dues income during such 3-year period, a detailed explanation of such change including the adjustments necessary to prevent duplications or omissions of income.

*(3)* Whether any type of deferral method for prepaid dues income has been used during any of the 3 taxable years preceding the first taxable year for which the election is effective. Where any type of such deferral method has been used during this period, an explanation of the method and a schedule showing the amounts received in each such year and the amounts deferred to each succeeding year.

*(4)* A schedule with appropriate explanations showing:

(i) The total amount of prepaid dues income received in the trade or business in the first taxable year for which the election is effective and the amount of such income to be included in each taxable year in accordance with the election.

(ii) The total amount, if any, of prepayments of dues received in the first taxable year for which the election is effective which are directly attributable to a liability of the taxpayer to render services or make available membership privileges over a period of time in excess of 36 months, and

(iii) The total amount, if any, of prepaid dues income received in the trade or business in—

(a) The taxable year preceding the first taxable year for which the election is effective if all memberships sold by the taxpayer are for periods of 1 year or less,

(b) Each of the 2 taxable years preceding the first taxable year for which the election is effective if any memberships are sold for periods in excess of 1 year but none are sold for periods in excess of 2 years, or

(c) Each of the 3 taxable years preceding the first taxable year for which the election is effective if any memberships are sold for periods in excess of 2 years.

In each case there shall be set forth the amount of such income which would have been includible in each taxable year had the election been effective for the years for which the information is required. In any case in which prepaid dues income is received from more than one trade or business, the statement shall set forth separately the required information with respect to each trade or business for which the election is made. See paragraph (c) of this section for additional information required to be submitted with the statement if the taxpayer also elects to include in gross income for the taxable year of receipt the entire amount of prepaid dues income attributable to a liability which is to end within 12 months after the date of receipt.

**(b) Election with consent.** A taxpayer may elect with the consent of the Commissioner, to apply the provisions of section 456 to any trade or business in which it receives prepaid dues income. The request for such consent shall be in writing, signed by the taxpayer or its authorized representative, and shall be addressed to the Commissioner of Internal Revenue, Washington, D.C. 20224. The request must be filed on or before the later of the following dates: (1) 90 days after the beginning of the first taxable year to which the election is to apply, or (2) February 28, 1968 and should contain the information described in paragraph (a) of this section. See paragraph (c) of this section for additional information required to be submitted with the request if the taxpayer also elects to include in gross income for the taxable year of receipt the entire amount of prepaid dues income attributable to a liability which is to end within 12 months after the date of receipt.

**(c) "Within 12 months" election.** *(1)* The "within 12 months" election shall be made by including in the statement required by paragraph (a) of this section or the request described in paragraph (b) of this section, whichever is applicable, a declaration that the taxpayer elects to include such income in gross income in the taxable year of receipt, and the amount of such income for each taxable year to which the election is to apply which has ended prior to the time such statement or request is filed. If the taxpayer is engaged in more than one trade or business for which the election under section 456 is made, it must include, in such statement or request, a declaration for each trade or business for which it wishes to make the "within 12 months" election.

*(2)* If the taxpayer does not make the "within 12 months" election for a trade or business at the time it makes the election under paragraph (a) or (b) of this section, but later wishes to make such election, it must apply for permission from the Commissioner. Such application shall be made in accordance with the provisions of section 446(e) and § 1.446(e)(3).

---

T.D. 6937, 11/29/67.

---

### § 1.456-7 Transitional rule.

***Caution:*** The Treasury has not yet amended Reg § 1.456-7 to reflect changes made by P.L. 94-455.

**(a)** Under section 456(d)(1), a taxpayer making an election under section 456 shall include in its gross income for the first taxable year to which the election applies and for each of the 2 succeeding taxable years not only that portion of prepaid dues income which is includible in gross income for each such taxable year under section 456(a), but also an additional amount equal to that portion of the total prepaid dues income received in each of the 3 taxable years preceding the first taxable year to which the election applies which would have been includible in gross income for such first taxable year and such 2 succeeding taxable years had the election under section 456 been effective during such 3 preceding taxable years. In computing such additional amounts—

*(1)* In the case of taxpayers who did not include in gross income for the taxable year preceding the first taxable year for which the election is effective, that portion of the prepaid dues income received in such year attributable to a liability which is to end within 12 months after the date of receipt, no effect shall be given to a "within 12 months" election made under paragraph (c) of § 1.456-6, and

*(2)* There shall be taken into account only prepaid dues income arising from a trade or business with respect to which an election is made under section 456 and § 1.456-6.

Section 481 and the regulations thereunder shall have no application to the additional amounts includible in gross income under section 456(d) and this section, but section 481 and the regulations thereunder shall apply to prevent other amounts from being duplicated or omitted.

**(b)** A taxpayer who makes an election with respect to prepaid dues income, and who includes in gross income for any taxable year to which the election applies an additional amount computed under section 456(d)(1) and paragraph (a) of this section, shall be permitted under section 456(d)(2) to deduct for such taxable year and for each of the 4 succeeding taxable years an amount equal to one-fifth of such additional amount, but only to the extent that such additional amount was also included in the taxpayer's gross income for any of the 3 taxable years preceding the first taxable year to which such election applies. The taxpayer shall maintain books and records in sufficient detail to enable the district director to determine upon audit that the additional amounts were included in the taxpayer's gross income for any of the 3 taxable years preceding such first taxable year. If, however, the taxpayer ceases to exist, as described in paragraph (b) of § 1.456-4, and there is included in gross income, under such paragraph, of the year of cessation the entire portion of prepaid dues income not previously includible in gross income under section 456 for preceding taxable years (other than for amounts received prior to the first year for which an election was made), all the amounts not previously deducted under this paragraph shall be permitted as a deduction in the year of cessation of existence.

**(c)** The provisions of this section may be illustrated by the following example:

*Example.* (1) Assume that X Corporation, a membership organization qualified to make the election under section 456, elects to report its prepaid dues income in accordance with the provisions of section 456 for its taxable year ending December 31, 1961. Assume further that X Corporation receives in the middle of each taxable year $3,000 of prepaid dues income in connection with a liability to render services over a 3-year period beginning with the date of receipt. Under section 456(a), X Corporation will report income received in 1961 and subsequent years as follows:

| Year Of Receipt | Total Receipts | 1961 | 1962 | 1963 | 1964 | 1965 | 1966 | 1967 | 1968 |
|---|---|---|---|---|---|---|---|---|---|
| 1961 | $3,000 | $500 | $1,000 | $1,000 | $ 500 | | | | |
| 1962 | 3,000 | | 500 | 1,000 | 1,000 | $ 500 | | | |
| 1963 | 3,000 | | | 500 | 1,000 | 1,000 | $ 500 | | |
| 1964 | 3,000 | | | | 500 | 1,000 | 1,000 | $ 500 | |
| 1965 | 3,000 | | | | | 500 | 1,000 | 1,000 | $ 500 |
| 1966 | 3,000 | | | | | | 500 | 1,000 | 1,000 |
| 1967 | 3,000 | | | | | | | 500 | 1,000 |
| 1968 | 3,000 | | | | | | | | 500 |
| Total reportable under section 456(a) | | $500 | $1,500 | $2,500 | $3,000 | $3,000 | $3,000 | $3,000 | $3,000 |

(2) Under section 456(d)(1), X Corporation must include in its gross income for the first taxable year to which the election applies and for each of the 2 succeeding taxable years, the amounts which would have been included in those years had the election been effective 3 years earlier. If the election had been effective in 1958, the following amounts received in 1958, 1959, and 1960 would have been reported in 1961 and subsequent years:

| Year Of Receipt | Amount Received | Years Of Including Additional Amounts 1961 | 1962 | 1963 |
|---|---|---|---|---|
| 1958 | $3,000 | $500 | | |
| 1959 | 3,000 | 1,000 | $500 | |
| 1960 | 3,000 | 1,000 | 1,000 | $500 |
| Total additional amounts to be included under section 456(d)(1) | | 2,500 | 1,500 | 500 |

(3) Having included the additional amounts as required by section 456(d)(1), and assuming such amounts were actually included in gross income in the 3 taxable years preceding the first taxable year for which the election is effective, X Corporation is entitled to deduct under section 456(d)(2) in the year of inclusion and in each of the succeeding 4 years an amount equal to one-fifth of the amounts included, as follows:

| Year of inclusion | Amount | Years of deduction 1961 | 1962 | 1963 | 1964 | 1965 | 1966 | 1967 |
|---|---|---|---|---|---|---|---|---|
| 1961 ........ | $2,500 | $500 | $500 | $500 | $500 | $500 | | |
| 1962 ........ | 1,500 | | 300 | 300 | 300 | 300 | $300 | |
| 1963 ........ | 500 | | | 100 | 100 | 100 | 100 | $100 |
| Total amount deductible under section 456(d)(2) ........ | | $500 | $800 | $900 | $900 | $900 | $400 | $100 |

(4) The net result of the inclusions under section 456(d)(1) and the deductions under section 456(d)(2) may be summarized as follows:

| | 1961 | 1962 | 1963 | 1964 | 1965 | 1966 | 1967 | 1968 |
|---|---|---|---|---|---|---|---|---|
| Amount includible under section 456(a) ........ | $ 500 | $1,500 | $2,500 | $3,000 | $3,000 | $3,000 | $3,000 | $3,000 |
| Amount includible under section 456(d)(1) ........ | 2,500 | 1,500 | 500 | | | | | |
| Total ........ | $3,000 | $3,000 | $3,000 | $3,000 | $3,000 | $3,000 | $3,000 | $3,000 |
| Amount deductible under section 456(d)(2) ........ | 500 | 800 | 900 | 900 | 900 | 400 | 100 | |
| Net amount reportable under section 456 ........ | $2,500 | $2,200 | $2,100 | $2,100 | $2,100 | $2,600 | $2,900 | $3,000 |

T.D. 6937, 11/29/67.

## § 1.457-1 General overviews of section 457.

***Caution:*** The Treasury has not yet amended Reg § 1.457-1 to reflect changes made by P.L. 100-647.

Section 457 provides rules for nonqualified deferred compensation plans established by eligible employers as defined under § 1.457-2(d). Eligible employers can establish either deferred compensation plans that are eligible plans and that meet the requirements of section 457(b) and §§ 1.457-3 through 1.457-10, or deferred compensation plans or arrangements that do not meet the requirements of section 457(b) and §§ 1.457-3 through 1.457-10 and that are subject to tax treatment under section 457(f) and § 1.457-11.

T.D. 7836, 9/23/82, amend T.D. 9075, 7/10/2003.

## § 1.457-2 Definitions.

***Caution:*** The Treasury has not yet amended Reg § 1.457-2 to reflect changes made by P.L. 101-239, P.L. 100-647.

This section sets forth the definitions that are used under §§ 1.457-1 through 1.457-11.

**(a) Amount(s) deferred.** Amount(s) deferred means the total annual deferrals under an eligible plan in the current and prior years, adjusted for gain or loss. Except as provided at §§ 1.457-4(c)(1)(iii) and 1.457-6(a), amount(s) deferred includes any rollover amount held by an eligible plan as provided under § 1.457-10(e).

**(b) Annual deferral(s).** *(1)* Annual deferral(s) means, with respect to a taxable year, the amount of compensation deferred under an eligible plan, whether by salary reduction or by nonelective employer contribution. The amount of compensation deferred under an eligible plan is taken into account as an annual deferral in the taxable year of the participant in which deferred, or, if later, the year in which the amount of compensation deferred is no longer subject to a substantial risk of forfeiture.

*(2)* If the amount of compensation deferred under the plan during a taxable year is not subject to a substantial risk of forfeiture, the amount taken into account as an annual deferral is not adjusted to reflect gain or loss allocable to the compensation deferred. If, however, the amount of compensation deferred under the plan during the taxable year is subject to a substantial risk of forfeiture, the amount of compensation deferred that is taken into account as an annual deferral in the taxable year in which the substantial risk of forfeiture lapses must be adjusted to reflect gain or loss allocable to the compensation deferred until the substantial risk of forfeiture lapses.

*(3)* If the eligible plan is a defined benefit plan within the meaning of section 414(j), the annual deferral for a taxable year is the present value of the increase during the taxable year of the participant's accrued benefit that is not subject to a substantial risk of forfeiture (disregarding any such increase attributable to prior annual deferrals). For this purpose, present value must be determined using actuarial assumptions and methods that are reasonable (both individually and in the aggregate), as determined by the Commissioner.

*(4)* For purposes solely of applying § 1.457-4 to determine the maximum amount of the annual deferral for a participant for a taxable year under an eligible plan, the maximum amount is reduced by the amount of any deferral for the participant under a plan described at paragraph (k)(4)(i) of this section (relating to certain plans in existence before January 1, 1987) as if that deferral were an annual deferral under another eligible plan of the employer.

**(c) Beneficiary.** Beneficiary means a person who is entitled to benefits in respect of a participant following the participant's death or an alternate payee as described in § 1.457-10(c).

**(d) Catch-up.** Catch-up amount or catch-up limitation for a participant for a taxable year means the annual deferral permitted under section 414(v) (as described in § 1.457-4(c)(2)) or section 457(b)(3) (as described in § 1.457-4(c)(3)) to the extent the amount of the annual deferral for the participant for the taxable year is permitted to exceed the plan ceiling applicable under section 457(b)(2) (as described in § 1.457-4(c)(1)).

**(e) Eligible employer.** Eligible employer means an entity that is a State that establishes a plan or a tax-exempt entity that establishes a plan. The performance of services as an independent contractor for a State or local government or a tax-exempt entity is treated as the performance of services for an eligible employer. The term eligible employer does not include a church as defined in section 3121(w)(3)(A), a qualified church-controlled organization as defined in section 3121(w)(3)(B), or the Federal government or any agency or instrumentality thereof. Thus, for example, a nursing home which is associated with a church, but which is not itself a church (as defined in section 3121(w)(3)(A)) or a qualified church-controlled organization as defined in section 3121(w)(3)(B)), would be an eligible employer if it is a tax-exempt entity as defined in paragraph (m) of this section.

**(f) Eligible plan.** An eligible plan is a plan that meets the requirements of §§ 1.457-3 through 1.457-10 that is established and maintained by an eligible employer. An eligible governmental plan is an eligible plan that is established and maintained by an eligible employer as defined in paragraph (l) of this section. An arrangement does not fail to constitute a single eligible governmental plan merely because the arrangement is funded through more than one trustee, custodian, or insurance carrier. An eligible plan of a tax-exempt entity is an eligible plan that is established and maintained by an eligible employer as defined in paragraph (m) of this section.

**(g) Includible compensation.** Includible compensation of a participant means, with respect to a taxable year, the participant's compensation, as defined in section 415(c)(3), for services performed for the eligible employer. The amount of includible compensation is determined without regard to any community property laws.

**(h) Ineligible plan.** Ineligible plan means a plan established and maintained by an eligible employer that is not maintained in accordance with §§ 1.457-3 through 1.457-10. A plan that is not established by an eligible employer as defined in paragraph (e) of this section is neither an eligible nor an ineligible plan.

**(i) Nonelective employer contribution.** A nonelective employer contribution is a contribution made by an eligible employer for the participant with respect to which the participant does not have the choice to receive the contribution in cash or property. Solely for purposes of section 457 and §§ 1.457-2 through 1.457-11, the term nonelective employer contribution includes employer contributions that would be described in section 401(m) if they were contributions to a qualified plan.

**(j) Participant.** Participant in an eligible plan means an individual who is currently deferring compensation, or who has previously deferred compensation under the plan by salary reduction or by nonelective employer contribution and who has not received a distribution of his or her entire benefit under the eligible plan. Only individuals who perform services for the eligible employer, either as an employee or as an independent contractor, may defer compensation under the eligible plan.

**(k) Plan.** Plan includes any agreement or arrangement between an eligible employer and a participant or participants (including an individual employment agreement) under which the payment of compensation is deferred (whether by salary reduction or by nonelective employer contribution). The following types of plans are not treated as agreements or arrangements under which compensation is deferred: a bona fide vacation leave, sick leave, compensatory time, severance pay, disability pay, or death benefit plan described in section 457(e)(11)(A)(i) and any plan paying length of service awards to bona fide volunteers (and their beneficiaries) on account of qualified services performed by such volunteers as described in section 457(e)(11)(A)(ii). Further, the term plan does not include any of the following (and section 457 and §§ 1.457-2 through 1.457-11 do not apply to any of the following)—

*(1)* Any nonelective deferred compensation under which all individuals (other than those who have not satisfied any applicable initial service requirement) with the same relationship with the eligible employer are covered under the same plan with no individual variations or options under the plan as described in section 457(e)(12), but only to the extent the compensation is attributable to services performed as an independent contractor;

*(2)* An agreement or arrangement described in § 1.457-11(b);

*(3)* Any plan satisfying the conditions in section 1107(c)(4) of the Tax Reform Act of 1986 (100 Stat. 2494) (TRA '86) (relating to certain plans for State judges); and

*(4)* Any of the following plans or arrangements (to which specific transitional statutory exclusions apply)—

(i) A plan or arrangement of a tax-exempt entity in existence prior to January 1, 1987, if the conditions of section 1107(c)(3)(B) of the TRA '86, as amended by amended by section 1011(e)(6) of the Technical and Miscellaneous Revenue Act of 1988 (102 Stat. 3700) (TAMRA), are satisfied (see § 1.457-2(b)(4) for a special rule regarding such plan);

(ii) A collectively bargained nonelective deferred compensation plan in effect on December 31, 1987, if the conditions of section 6064(d)(2) of TAMRA are satisfied;

(iii) Amounts described in section 6064(d)(3) of TAMRA (relating to certain nonelective deferred compensation arrangements in effect before 1989); and

(iv) Any plan satisfying the conditions in section 1107(c)(4) or (5) of TRA '86 (relating to certain plans for certain individuals with respect to which the Service issued guidance before 1977).

**(l) State.** State means a State (treating the District of Columbia as a State as provided under section 7701(a)(10)), a political subdivision of a State, and any agency or instrumentality of a State.

**(m) Tax-exempt entity.** Tax-exempt entity includes any organization exempt from tax under subtitle A of the Internal Revenue Code, except that a governmental unit (including an international governmental organization) is not a tax-exempt entity.

**(n) Trust.** Trust means a trust described under section 457(g) and § 1.457-8. Custodial accounts and contracts described in section 401(f) are treated as trusts under the rules described in § 1.457-8(a)(2).

---

T.D. 7836, 9/23/82, amend T.D. 9075, 7/10/2003.

---

### § 1.457-3 General introduction to eligible plans.

**(a) Compliance in form and operation.** An eligible plan is a written plan established and maintained by an eligible employer that is maintained, in both form and operation, in accordance with the requirements of §§ 1.457-4 through 1.457-10. An eligible plan must contain all the material terms and conditions for benefits under the plan. An eligible plan may contain certain optional features not required for plan eligibility under section 457(b), such as distributions for unforeseeable emergencies, loans, plan-to-plan transfers, additional deferral elections, acceptance of rollovers to the plan, and distributions of smaller accounts to eligible participants. However, except as otherwise specifically provided in §§ 1.457-4 through 1.457-10, if an eligible plan contains any optional provisions, the optional provisions must meet, in both form and operation, the relevant requirements under section 457 and §§ 1.457-2 through 1.457-10.

**(b) Treatment as single plan.** In any case in which multiple plans are used to avoid or evade the requirements of §§ 1.457-4 through 1.457-10, the Commissioner may apply the rules under §§ 1.457-4 through 1.457-10 as if the plans were a single plan. See also § 1.457-4(c)(3)(v) (requiring an eligible employer to have no more than one normal retirement age for each participant under all of the eligible plans it sponsors), the second sentence of § 1.457-4(e)(2) (treating deferrals under all eligible plans under which an individual participates by virtue of his or her relationship with a single employer as a single plan for purposes of determining excess deferrals), and § 1.457-5 (combining annual deferrals under all eligible plans).

T.D. 7836, 9/23/82, amend T.D. 9075, 7/10/2003.

### § 1.457-4 Annual deferrals, deferral limitations, and deferral agreements under eligible plans.

**(a) Taxation of annual deferrals.** Annual deferrals that satisfy the requirements of paragraphs (b) and (c) of this section are excluded from the gross income of a participant in the year deferred or contributed and are not includible in gross income until paid to the participant in the case of an eligible governmental plan, or until paid or otherwise made available to the participant in the case of an eligible plan of a tax-exempt entity. See § 1.457-7.

**(b) Agreement for deferral.** In order to be an eligible plan, the plan must provide that compensation may be deferred for any calendar month by salary reduction only if an agreement providing for the deferral has been entered into before the first day of the month in which the compensation is paid or made available. A new employee may defer compensation payable in the calendar month during which the participant first becomes an employee if an agreement providing for the deferral is entered into on or before the first day on which the participant performs services for the eligible employer. An eligible plan may provide that if a participant enters into an agreement providing for deferral by salary reduction under the plan, the agreement will remain in effect until the participant revokes or alters the terms of the agreement. Nonelective employer contributions are treated as being made under an agreement entered into before the first day of the calendar month.

**(c) Maximum deferral limitations.** *(1) Basic annual limitation.* (i) Except as described in paragraphs (c)(2) and (3) of this section, in order to be an eligible plan, the plan must provide that the annual deferral amount for a taxable year (the plan ceiling) may not exceed the lesser of—

(A) The applicable annual dollar amount specified in section 457(e)(15): $11,000 for 2002; $12,000 for 2003; $13,000 for 2004; $14,000 for 2005; and $15,000 for 2006 and thereafter. After 2006, the $15,000 amount is adjusted for cost-of-living in the manner described in paragraph (c)(4) of this section; or

(B) 100 percent of the participant's includible compensation for the taxable year.

(ii) The amount of annual deferrals permitted by the 100 percent of includible compensation limitation under paragraph (c)(1)(i)(B) of this section is determined under section 457(e)(5) and § 1.457-2(g).

(iii) For purposes of determining the plan ceiling under this paragraph (c), the annual deferral amount does not include any rollover amounts received by the eligible plan under § 1.457-10(e).

(iv) The provisions of this paragraph (c)(1) are illustrated by the following examples:

*Example (1).* (i) Facts. Participant A, who earns $14,000 a year, enters into a salary reduction agreement in 2006 with A's eligible employer and elects to defer $13,000 of A's compensation for that year. A is not eligible for the catch-up described in paragraph (c)(2) or (3) of this section, participates in no other retirement plan, and has no other income exclusions taken into account in computing includible compensation.

(ii) Conclusion. The annual deferral limit for A in 2006 is the lesser of $15,000 or 100 percent of includible compensation, $14,000. A's annual deferral of $13,000 is permitted under the plan because it is not in excess of $14,000 and thus does not exceed 100 percent of A's includible compensation.

*Example (2).* (i) Facts. Assume the same facts as in Example 1, except that A's eligible employer provides an immediately vested, matching employer contribution under the plan for participants who make salary reduction deferrals under A's eligible plan. The matching contribution is equal to 100 percent of elective contributions, but not in excess of 10 percent of compensation (in A's case, $1,400).

(ii) Conclusion. Participant A's annual deferral exceeds the limitations of this paragraph (c)(1). A's maximum deferral limitation in 2006 is $14,000. A's salary reduction deferral of $13,000 combined with A's eligible employer's nonelective employer contribution of $1,400 exceeds the basic annual limitation of this paragraph (c)(1) because A's annual deferrals total $14,400. A has an excess deferral for the taxable year of $400, the amount exceeding A's permitted annual deferral limitation. The $400 excess deferral is treated as described in paragraph (e) of this section.

*Example (3).* (i) Facts. Beginning in year 2002, Eligible Employer X contributes $3,000 per year for five years to B's eligible plan account. B's interest in the account vests in 2006. B has annual compensation of $50,000 in each of the five years 2002 through 2006. B is 41 years old. B is not eligible for the catch-up described in paragraph (c)(2) or (3) of this section, participates in no other retirement plan, and has no other income exclusions taken into account in computing includible compensation. Adjusted for gain or loss, the value of B's benefit when B's interest in the account vests in 2006 is $17,000.

(ii) Conclusion. Under this vesting schedule, $17,000 is taken into account as an annual deferral in 2006. B's annual deferrals under the plan are limited to a maximum of $15,000 in 2006. Thus, the aggregate of the amounts deferred, $17,000, is in excess of B's maximum deferral limitation by $2,000. The $2,000 is treated as an excess deferral described in paragraph (e) of this section.

*(2) Age 50 catch-up.* (i) In general. In accordance with section 414(v) and the regulations thereunder, an eligible governmental plan may provide for catch-up contributions for a participant who is age 50 by the end of the year, provided that such age 50 catch-up contributions do not exceed the catch-up limit under section 414(v)(2) for the taxable year. The maximum amount of age 50 catch-up contributions for a taxable year under section 414(v) is as follows: $1,000 for 2002; $2,000 for 2003; $3,000 for 2004; $4,000 for 2005; and $5,000 for 2006 and thereafter. After 2006, the $5,000 amount is adjusted for cost-of-living. For additional guidance, see regulations under section 414(v).

(ii) Coordination with special section 457 catch-up. In accordance with sections 414(v)(6)(C) and 457(e)(18), the age 50 catch-up described in this paragraph (c)(2) does not apply for any taxable year for which a higher limitation applies under the special section 457 catch-up under paragraph (c)(3) of this section. Thus, for purposes of this paragraph (c)(2)(ii) and paragraph (c)(3) of this section, the special section 457 catch-up under paragraph (c)(3) of this section applies for any taxable year if and only if the plan ceiling taking into account paragraph (c)(1) of this section and the special section 457 catch-up described in paragraph (c)(3) of this section (and disregarding the age 50 catch-up described in this paragraph (c)(2)) is larger than the plan ceiling taking into account paragraph (c)(1) of this section and the age 50 catch-up described in this paragraph (c)(2) (and disregarding the special section 457 catch-up described in paragraph (c)(3) of this section). Thus, if a plan so provides, a participant who is eligible for the age 50 catch-up for a year and for whom the year is also one of the participant's last three taxable years ending before the participant attains normal retirement age is eligible for the larger of—

(A) The plan ceiling under paragraph (c)(1) of this section and the age 50 catch-up described in this paragraph (c)(2) (and disregarding the special section 457 catch-up described in paragraph (c)(3) of this section) or

(B) The plan ceiling under paragraph (c)(1) of this section and the special section 457 catch-up described in paragraph (c)(3) of this section (and disregarding the age 50 catch-up described in this paragraph (c)(2)).

(iii) Examples. The provisions of this paragraph (c)(2) are illustrated by the following examples:

*Example (1).* (i) Facts. Participant C, who is 55, is eligible to participate in an eligible governmental plan in 2006. The plan provides a normal retirement age of 65. The plan provides limitations on annual deferrals up to the maximum permitted under paragraphs (c)(1) and (3) of this section and the age 50 catch-up described in this paragraph (c)(2). For 2006, C will receive compensation of $40,000 from the eligible employer. C desires to defer the maximum amount possible in 2006. The applicable basic dollar limit of paragraph (c)(1)(i)(A) of this section is $15,000 for 2006 and the additional dollar amount permitted under the age 50 catch-up is $5,000 for 2006.

(ii) Conclusion. C is eligible for the age 50 catch-up in 2006 because C is 55 in 2006. However, C is not eligible for the special section 457 catch-up under paragraph (c)(3) of this section in 2006 because 2006 is not one of the last three taxable years ending before C attains normal retirement age. Accordingly, the maximum that C may defer for 2006 is $20,000.

*Example (2).* (i) Facts. The facts are the same as in Example 1, except that, in 2006, C will attain age 62. The maximum amount that C can elect under the special section 457 catch-up under paragraph (c)(3) of this section is $2,000 for 2006.

(ii) Conclusion. The maximum that C may defer for 2006 is $20,000. This is the sum of the basic plan ceiling under paragraph (c)(1) of this section equal to $15,000 and the age 50 catch-up equal to $5,000. The special section 457 catch-up under paragraph (c)(3) of this section is not applicable since it provides a smaller plan ceiling.

*Example (3).* (i) Facts. The facts are the same as in Example 2, except that the maximum additional amount that C can elect under the special section 457 catch-up under paragraph (c)(3) of this section is $7,000 for 2006.

(ii) Conclusion. The maximum that C may defer for 2006 is $22,000. This is the sum of the basic plan ceiling under paragraph (c)(1) of this section equal to $15,000, plus the additional special section 457 catch-up under paragraph (c)(3) of this section equal to $7,000. The additional dollar amount permitted under the age 50 catch-up is not applicable to C for 2006 because it provides a smaller plan ceiling.

*(3) Special section 457 catch-up.* (i) In general. Except as provided in paragraph (c)(2)(ii) of this section, an eligible plan may provide that, for one or more of the participant's last three taxable years ending before the participant attains normal retirement age, the plan ceiling is an amount not in excess of the lesser of—

(A) Twice the dollar amount in effect under paragraph (c)(1)(i)(A) of this section; or

(B) The underutilized limitation determined under paragraph (c)(3)(ii) of this section.

(ii) Underutilized limitation. The underutilized amount determined under this paragraph (c)(3)(ii) is the sum of—

(A) The plan ceiling established under paragraph (c)(1) of this section for the taxable year; plus

(B) The plan ceiling established under paragraph (c)(1) of this section (or under section 457(b)(2) for any year before the applicability date of this section) for any prior taxable year or years, less the amount of annual deferrals under the plan for such prior taxable year or years (disregarding any annual deferrals under the plan permitted under the age 50 catch-up under paragraph (c)(2) of this section).

(iii) Determining underutilized limitation under paragraph (c)(3)(ii)(B) of this section. A prior taxable year is taken into account under paragraph (c)(3)(ii)(B) of this section only if it is a year beginning after December 31, 1978, in which the participant was eligible to participate in the plan, and in which compensation deferred (if any) under the plan during the year was subject to a plan ceiling established under paragraph (c)(1) of this section. This paragraph (c)(3)(iii) is subject to the special rules in paragraph (c)(3)(iv) of this section.

(iv) Special rules concerning application of the coordination limit for years prior to 2002 for purposes of determining the underutilized limitation. (A) General rule. For purposes of determining the underutilized limitation for years prior to 2002, participants remain subject to the rules in effect prior to the repeal of the coordination limitation under section 457(c)(2). Thus, the applicable basic annual limitation under paragraph (c)(1) of this section and the special section 457 catch-up under this paragraph (c)(3) for years in effect prior to 2002 are reduced, for purposes of determining a participant's underutilized amount under a plan, by amounts excluded from the participant's income for any prior taxable year by reason of a nonelective employer contribution, salary reduction or elective contribution under any other eligible section 457(b) plan, or a salary reduction or elective contribution under any 401(k) qualified cash or deferred arrangement, section 402(h)(1)(B) simplified employee pension (SARSEP), section 403(b) annuity contract, and section 408(p) simple retirement account, or under any plan for which a deduction is allowed because of a contribution to an organization described in section 501(c)(18) (pre-2002 coordination plans). Similarly, in applying the section 457(b)(2)(B) limitation for includible compensation for years prior to 2002, the limitation is 33⅓ percent of the participant's compensation includible in gross income.

(B) Coordination limitation applied to participant. For purposes of determining the underutilized limitation for years prior to 2002, the coordination limitation applies to pre-2002 coordination plans of all employers for whom a participant has performed services, whether or not those are plans of the participant's current eligible employer. Thus, for purposes of determining the amount excluded from a participant's gross income in any prior taxable year under paragraph (c)(3)(ii)(B) of this section, the participant's annual deferrals under an eligible plan, and salary reduction or elective deferrals under all other pre-2002 coordination plans, must be determined on an aggregate basis. To the extent that the combined deferrals for years prior to 2002 exceeded the maximum deferral limitations, the amount is treated as an excess deferral under paragraph (e) of this section for those prior years.

(C) Special rule where no annual deferrals under the eligible plan. A participant who, although eligible, did not defer any compensation under the eligible plan in any year before 2002 is not subject to the coordinated deferral limit, even though the participant may have deferred compensation under one of the other pre-2002 coordination plans. An individual is treated as not having deferred compensation under an eligible plan for a prior taxable year if all annual deferrals under the plan are distributed in accordance with paragraph (e) of this section. Thus, to the extent that a participant participated solely in one or more of the other pre-2002 coordination plans during a prior taxable year (and not the eligible plan), the participant is not subject to the coordinated limitation for that prior taxable year. However, the participant is treated as having deferred an amount in a prior taxable year, for purposes of determining the underutilized limitation for that prior taxable year under this paragraph (c)(3)(iv)(C), to the extent of the participant's aggregate salary reduction contributions and elective deferrals under all pre-2002 coordination plans up to the maximum deferral limitations in effect under section 457(b) for that prior taxable year. To the extent an employer did not offer an eligible plan to an individual in a prior given year, no underutilized limitation is available to the individual for that prior year, even if the employee subsequently becomes eligible to participate in an eligible plan of the employer.

(D) Examples. The provisions of this paragraph (c)(3)(iv) are illustrated by the following examples:

*Example (1).* (i) Facts. In 2001 and in years prior to 2001, Participant D earned $50,000 a year and was eligible to participate in both an eligible plan and a section 401(k) plan. However, D had always participated only in the section 401(k) plan and had always deferred the maximum amount possible. For each year before 2002, the maximum amount permitted under section 401(k) exceeded the limitation of paragraph (c)(3)(i) of this section. In 2002, D is in the 3-year period prior to D's attainment of the eligible plan's normal retirement age of 65, and D now wants to participate in the eligible plan and make annual deferrals of up to $30,000 under the plan's special section 457 catch-up provisions.

(ii) Conclusion. Participant D is treated as having no underutilized amount under paragraph (c)(3)(ii)(B) of this section for 2002 for purposes of the catch-up limitation under section 457(b)(3) and paragraph (c)(3) of this section because, in each of the years before 2002, D has deferred an amount equal to or in excess of the limitation of paragraph (c)(3)(i) of this section under all of D's coordinated plans.

*Example (2).* (i) Facts. Assume the same facts as in Example 1, except that D only deferred $2,500 per year under the section 401(k) plan for one year before 2002.

(ii) Conclusion. D is treated as having an underutilized amount under paragraph (c)(3)(ii)(B) of this section for 2002 for purposes of the special section 457 catch-up limitation. This is because D has deferred an amount for prior years that is less than the limitation of paragraph (c)(1)(i) of this section under all of D's coordinated plans.

*Example (3).* (i) Facts. Participant E, who earned $15,000 for 2000, entered into a salary reduction agreement in 2000 with E's eligible employer and elected to defer $3,000 for that year under E's eligible plan. For 2000, E's eligible employer provided an immediately vested, matching employer contribution under the plan for participants who make salary reduction deferrals under E's eligible plan. The matching contribution was equal to 67 percent of elective contributions, but not in excess of 10 percent of compensation before salary reduction deferrals (in E's case, $1,000). For 2000, E was not eligible for any catch-up contribution, participated in no other retirement plan, and had no other income exclusions taken into account in computing taxable compensation.

(ii) Conclusion. Participant E's annual deferral equaled the maximum limitation of section 457(b) for 2000. E's maximum deferral limitation in 2000 was $4,000 because E's includible compensation was $12,000 ($15,000 minus the deferral of $3,000) and the applicable limitation for 2000 was one third of the individual's includible compensation (one-third of $12,000 equals $4,000). E's salary reduction deferral of $3,000 combined with E's eligible employer's matching contribution of $1,000 equals the limitation of section 457(b) for 2000 because E's annual deferrals totaled $4,000. E's underutilized amount for 2000 is zero.

(v) Normal retirement age. (A) General rule. For purposes of the special section 457 catch-up in this paragraph (c)(3), a plan must specify the normal retirement age under the plan. A plan may define normal retirement age as any age that is on or after the earlier of age 65 or the age at which participants have the right to retire and receive, under the basic defined benefit pension plan of the State or tax-exempt entity (or a money purchase pension plan in which the participant also participates if the participant is not eligible to participate in a defined benefit plan), immediate retirement benefits without actuarial or similar reduction because of retirement before some later specified age, and that is not later than age 70½. Alternatively, a plan may provide that a participant is allowed to designate a normal retirement age within these ages. For purposes of the special section 457 catch-up in this paragraph (c)(3), an entity sponsoring more than one eligible plan may not permit a participant to have more than one normal retirement age under the eligible plans it sponsors.

(B) Special rule for eligible plans of qualified police or firefighters. An eligible plan with participants that include qualified police or firefighters as defined under section 415(b)(2)(H)(ii)(I) may designate a normal retirement age for such qualified police or firefighters that is earlier than the earliest normal retirement age designated under the general rule of paragraph (c)(3)(i)(A) of this section, but in no event may the normal retirement age be earlier than age 40. Alternatively, a plan may allow a qualified police or firefighter participant to designate a normal retirement age that is between age 40 and age 70½.

(vi) Examples. The provisions of this paragraph (c)(3) are illustrated by the following examples:

*Example (1).* (i) Facts. Participant F, who will turn 61 on April 1, 2006, becomes eligible to participate in an eligible plan on January 1, 2006. The plan provides a normal retirement age of 65. The plan provides limitations on annual deferrals up to the maximum permitted under paragraphs (c)(1) through (3) of this section. For 2006, F will receive compensation of $40,000 from the eligible employer. F desires to defer the maximum amount possible in 2006. The applicable basic dollar limit of paragraph (c)(1)(i)(A) of this section is $15,000 for 2006 and the additional dollar amount permitted under the age 50 catch-up in paragraph (c)(2) of this section for an individual who is at least age 50 is $5,000 for 2006.

(ii) Conclusion. F is not eligible for the special section 457 catch-up under paragraph (c)(3) of this section in 2006 because 2006 is not one of the last three taxable years ending before F attains normal retirement age. Accordingly, the maximum that F may defer for 2006 is $20,000. See also paragraph (c)(2)(iii) Example 1 of this section.

*Example (2).* (i) Facts. The facts are the same as in Example 1 except that, in 2006, F elects to defer only $2,000 under the plan (rather than the maximum permitted amount of $20,000). In addition, assume that the applicable basic dollar limit of paragraph (c)(1)(i)(A) of this section continues to be $15,000 for 2007 and the additional dollar amount permitted under the age 50 catch-up in paragraph (c)(2) of this section for an individual who is at least age 50 continues to be $5,000 for 2007. In F's taxable year 2007, which is one of the last three taxable years ending before F attains the plan's normal retirement age of 65, F again receives a salary of $40,000 and elects to defer the maximum amount permissible under the plan's catch-up provisions prescribed under paragraph (c) of this section.

(ii) Conclusion. For 2007, which is one of the last three taxable years ending before F attains the plan's normal retirement age of 65, the applicable limit on deferrals for F is the larger of the amount under the special section 457 catch-up or $20,000, which is the basic annual limitation ($15,000) and the age 50 catch-up limit of section 414(v) ($5,000). For 2007, F's special section 457 catch-up amount is the lesser of two times the basic annual limitation ($30,000) or the sum of the basic annual limitation ($15,000) plus the $13,000 underutilized limitation under paragraph (c)(3)(ii) of this section (the $15,000 plan ceiling in 2006, minus the $2,000 contributed for F in 2006), or $28,000. Thus, the maximum amount that F may defer in 2007 is $28,000.

*Example (3).* (i) Facts. The facts are the same as in Examples 1 and 2, except that F does not make any contributions to the plan before 2010. In addition, assume that the applicable basic dollar limitation of paragraph (c)(1)(i)(A) of this section continues to be $15,000 for 2010 and the additional dollar amount permitted under the age 50 catch-up in paragraph (c)(2) of this section for an individual who is at least age 50 continues to be $5,000 for 2010. In F's taxable year 2010, the year in which F attains age 65 (which is the normal retirement age under the plan), F desires to defer the maximum amount possible under the plan. F's compensation for 2010 is again $40,000.

(ii) Conclusion. For 2010, the maximum amount that F may defer is $20,000. The special section 457 catch-up provisions under paragraph (c)(3) of this section are not applicable because 2010 is not a taxable year ending before the year in which F attains normal retirement age.

*(4) Cost-of-living adjustment.* For years beginning after December 31, 2006, the $15,000 dollar limitation in paragraph (c)(1)(i)(A) of this section will be adjusted to take into account increases in the cost-of-living. The adjustment in the dollar limitation is made at the same time and in the same manner as under section 415(d) (relating to qualified plans under section 401(a)), except that the base period is the calendar quarter beginning July 1, 2005 and any increase which is not a multiple of $500 will be rounded to the next lowest multiple of $500.

**(d) Deferrals after severance from employment, including sick, vacation, and back pay under an eligible plan.** *(1) In general.* An eligible plan may provide that a participant who has not had a severance from employment may elect to defer accumulated sick pay, accumulated vacation pay, and back pay under an eligible plan if the requirements of section 457(b) are satisfied. For example, the plan must provide, in accordance with paragraph (b) of this section, that these amounts may be deferred for any calendar month only if an agreement providing for the deferral is entered into before the beginning of the month in which the amounts would otherwise be paid or made available and the participant is an employee on the date the amounts would otherwise be paid or made available. For purposes of section 457, compensation that would otherwise be paid for a payroll period that begins before severance from employment is treated as an amount that would otherwise be paid or made available before an employee has a severance from employment. In addition, deferrals may be made for former employees with respect to compensation described in § 1.415(c)-2(e)(3)(i) (relating to certain compensation paid by the later of 2½ months after severance from employment or the end of the limitation year that includes the date of severance from employment). For this purpose, the calendar year is substituted for the limitation year. In addition, compensation described in § 1.415(c)-2(e)(4), (g)(4), or (g)(7) (relating to compensation paid to participants who are permanently and totally disabled or compensation relating to qualified military service under section 414(u)), provided those amounts represent compensation described in § 1.415(c)-2(e)(3)(i).

*(2) Examples.* The provisions of this paragraph (d) are illustrated by the following examples:

*Example (1).* (i) Facts. Participant G, who is age 62 in year 2007, is an employee who participates in an eligible plan providing a normal retirement age of 65 and a bona fide sick leave and vacation pay program of the eligible employer. Under the terms of G's employer's eligible plan and the sick leave and vacation pay program, G is permitted to make a one-time election to contribute amounts representing accumulated sick pay to the eligible plan. G has a severance from employment on January 12, 2008, at which time G's accumulated sick and vacation pay that is payable on March 15, 2008, totals $12,000. G elects, on February 4, 2008, to have the $12,000 of accumulated sick and vacation pay contributed to the eligible plan.

(ii) Conclusion. Under the terms of the eligible plan and the sick and vacation pay program, G may elect before March 1, 2008, to defer the accumulated sick and vacation pay because the agreement providing for the deferral is entered into before the beginning of the month in which the amount is currently available and the amount is bona fide accumulated sick and vacation pay, as described in § 1.415(c)-2(e)(3)(ii), and that is payable by the later of 2½ months after severance from employment or the end of the calendar year that includes the date of severance from employment by G. Thus, under this section and § 1.415(c)-2(e)(3)(ii), the $12,000 is included in G's includible compensation for purposes of determining G's includible compensation in year 2008.

*Example (2).* (i) Facts. Same facts as in Example 1, except that G's severance from employment is on May 31,

2008, G's $12,000 of accumulated sick and vacation pay is payable on September 15, 2008 (which is by the later of 2½ months after severance from employment or the end of the calendar year that includes the date of severance from employment by G), and G's election to defer the accumulated sick and vacation pay is made before May 1, 2008.

(ii) Conclusion. Under this section and § 1.415(c)-2(e)(3)(ii), the $12,000 is included in G's includible compensation for purposes of determining G's includible compensation in year 2008.

*Example (3).* (i) Facts. Employer X maintains an eligible plan and a vacation leave plan. Under the terms of the vacation leave plan, employees generally accrue three weeks of vacation per year. Up to one week's unused vacation may be carried over from one year to the next, so that in any single year an employee may have a maximum of four weeks' vacation time. At the beginning of each calendar year, under the terms of the eligible plan (which constitutes an agreement providing for the deferral), the value of any unused vacation time from the prior year in excess of one week is automatically contributed to the eligible plan, to the extent of the employee's maximum deferral limitations. Amounts in excess of the maximum deferral limitations are forfeited.

(ii) Conclusion. The value of the unused vacation pay contributed to X's eligible plan pursuant to the terms of the plan and the terms of the vacation leave plan is treated as an annual deferral to the eligible plan for January of the calendar year. No amounts contributed to the eligible plan will be considered made available to a participant in X's eligible plan.

**(e) Excess deferrals under an eligible plan.** *(1) In general.* Any amount deferred under an eligible plan for the taxable year of a participant that exceeds the maximum deferral limitations set forth in paragraphs (c)(1) through (3) of this section, and any amount that exceeds the individual limitation under § 1.457-5, constitutes an excess deferral that is taxable in accordance with § 1.457-11 for that taxable year. Thus, an excess deferral is includible in gross income in the taxable year deferred or, if later, the first taxable year in which there is no substantial risk of forfeiture.

*(2) Excess deferrals under an eligible governmental plan other than as a result of the individual limitation.* In order to be an eligible governmental plan, the plan must provide that any excess deferral resulting from a failure of a plan to apply the limitations of paragraphs (c)(1) through (3) of this section to amounts deferred under the eligible plan (computed without regard to the individual limitation under § 1.457-5) will be distributed to the participant, with allocable net income, as soon as administratively practicable after the plan determines that the amount is an excess deferral. For purposes of determining whether there is an excess deferral resulting from a failure of a plan to apply the limitations of paragraphs (c)(1) through (3) of this section, all plans under which an individual participates by virtue of his or her relationship with a single employer are treated as a single plan (without regard to any differences in funding). An eligible governmental plan does not fail to satisfy the requirements of paragraphs (a) through (d) of this section or §§ 1.457-6 through 1.457-10 (including the distribution rules under § 1.457-6 and the funding rules under § 1.457-8) solely by reason of a distribution made under this paragraph (e)(2). If such excess deferrals are not corrected by distribution under this paragraph (e)(2), the plan will be an ineligible plan under which benefits are taxable in accordance with § 1.457-11.

*(3) Excess deferrals under an eligible plan of a tax-exempt employer other than as a result of the individual limitation.* If a plan of a tax-exempt employer fails to comply with the limitations of paragraphs (c)(1) through (3) of this section, the plan will be an ineligible plan under which benefits are taxable in accordance with § 1.457-11.

However, a plan may distribute to a participant any excess deferrals (and any income allocable to such amount) not later than the first April 15 following the close of the taxable year of the excess deferrals. In such a case, the plan will continue to be treated as an eligible plan. However, any excess deferral is included in the gross income of a participant for the taxable year of the excess deferral. If the excess deferrals are not corrected by distribution under this paragraph (e)(3), the plan is an ineligible plan under which benefits are taxable in accordance with § 1.457-11. For purposes of determining whether there is an excess deferral resulting from a failure of a plan to apply the limitations of paragraphs (c)(1) through (3) of this section, all eligible plans under which an individual participates by virtue of his or her relationship with a single employer are treated as a single plan.

*(4) Excess deferrals arising from application of the individual limitation.* An eligible plan may provide that an excess deferral that is a result solely of a failure to comply with the individual limitation under § 1.457-5 for a taxable year may be distributed to the participant, with allocable net income, as soon as administratively practicable after the plan determines that the amount is an excess deferral. An eligible plan does not fail to satisfy the requirements of paragraphs (a) through (d) of this section or §§ 1.457-6 through 1.457-10 (including the distribution rules under § 1.457-6 and the funding rules under § 1.457-8) solely by reason of a distribution made under this paragraph (e)(4). Although a plan will still maintain eligible status if excess deferrals are not distributed under this paragraph (e)(4), a participant must include the excess amounts in income as provided in paragraph (e)(1) of this section.

*(5) Examples.* The provisions of this paragraph (e) are illustrated by the following examples:

*Example (1).* (i) Facts. In 2006, the eligible plan of State Employer X in which Participant H participates permits a maximum deferral of the lesser of $15,000 or 100 percent of includible compensation. In 2006, H, who has compensation of $28,000, nevertheless defers $16,000 under the eligible plan. Participant H is age 45 and normal retirement age under the plan is age 65. For 2006, the applicable dollar limit under paragraph (c)(1)(i)(A) of this section is $15,000. Employer X discovers the error in January of 2007 when it completes H's 2006 Form W-2 and promptly distributes $1,022 to H (which is the sum of the $1,000 excess and $22 of allocable net income).

(ii) Conclusion. Participant H has deferred $1,000 in excess of the $15,000 limitation provided for under the plan for 2006. The $1,000 excess must be included by H in H's income for 2006. In order to correct the failure and still be an eligible plan, the plan must distribute the excess deferral, with allocable net income, as soon as administratively practicable after determining that the amount exceeds the plan deferral limitations. In this case, $22 of the distribution of $1,022 is included in H's gross income for 2007 (and is not an eligible rollover distribution). If the excess deferral were not distributed, the plan would be an ineligible plan with respect to which benefits are taxable in accordance with § 1.457-11.

*Example (2).* (i) Facts. The facts are the same as in Example 1, except that X uses a number of separate arrangements with different trustees and annuity insurers to permit employees to defer and H elects deferrals under several of the funding arrangements none of which exceeds $15,000 for any individual funding arrangement, but which total $16,000.

(ii) Conclusion. The conclusion is the same as in Example 1.

*Example (3).* (i) Facts. The facts are the same as in Example 1, except that H's deferral under the eligible plan is limited to $11,000 and H also makes a salary reduction contribution of $5,000 to an annuity contract under section 403(b) with the same Employer X.

(ii) Conclusion. H's deferrals are within the plan deferral limitations of Employer X. Because of the repeal of the application of the coordination limitation under former paragraph (2) of section 457(c), H's salary reduction deferrals under the annuity contract are no longer considered in determining H's applicable deferral limits under paragraphs (c)(1) through (3) of this section.

*Example (4).* (i) Facts. The facts are the same as in Example 1, except that H's deferral under the eligible governmental plan is limited to $14,000 and H also makes a deferral of $4,000 to an eligible governmental plan of a different employer. Participant H is age 45 and normal retirement age under both eligible plans is age 65.

(ii) Conclusion. Because of the application of the individual limitation under § 1.457-5, H has an excess deferral of $3,000 (the sum of $14,000 plus $4,000 equals $18,000, which is $3,000 in excess of the dollar limitation of $15,000). The $3,000 excess deferral, with allocable net income, may be distributed from either plan as soon as administratively practicable after determining that the combined amount exceeds the deferral limitations. If the $3,000 excess deferral is not distributed to H, each plan will continue to be an eligible plan, but the $3,000 must be included by H in H's income for 2006.

*Example (5).* (i) Facts. Assume the same facts as in Example 3, except that H's deferral under the eligible governmental plan is limited to $14,000 and H also makes a deferral of $4,000 to an eligible plan of Employer Y, a tax-exempt entity.

(ii) Conclusion. The results are the same as in Example 3, namely, because of the application of the individual limitation under § 1.457-5, H has an excess deferral of $3,000. If the $3,000 excess deferral is not distributed to H, each plan will continue to be an eligible plan, but the $3,000 must be included by H in H's income for 2006.

*Example (6).* (i) Facts. Assume the same facts as in Example 5, except that X is a tax-exempt entity and thus its plan is an eligible plan of a tax-exempt entity.

(ii) Conclusion. The results are the same as in Example 5, namely, because of the application of the individual limitation under § 1.457-5, H has an excess deferral of $3,000. If the $3,000 excess deferral is not distributed to H, each plan will continue to be an eligible plan, but the $3,000 must be included by H into H's income for 2006.

T.D. 7836, 9/23/82, amend T.D. 9075, 7/10/2003, T.D. 9319, 4/4/2007.

### § 1.457-5 Individual limitation for combined annual deferrals under multiple eligible plans.

**(a) General rule.** The individual limitation under section 457(c) and this section equals the basic annual deferral limitation under § 1.457-4(c)(1)(i)(A), plus either the age 50 catch-up amount under § 1.457-4(c)(2), or the special section 457 catch-up amount under § 1.457-4(c)(3), applied by taking into account the combined annual deferral for the participant for any taxable year under all eligible plans. While an eligible plan may include provisions under which it will limit deferrals to meet the individual limitation under section 457(c) and this section, annual deferrals by a participant that exceed the individual limit under section 457(c) and this section (but do not exceed the limits under § 1.457-4(c)) will not cause a plan to lose its eligible status. However, to the extent the combined annual deferrals for a participant for any taxable year exceed the individual limitation under section 457(c) and this section for that year, the amounts are treated as excess deferrals as described in § 1.457-4(e).

**(b) Limitation applied to participant.** The individual limitation in this section applies to eligible plans of all employers for whom a participant has performed services, including both eligible governmental plans and eligible plans of a tax-exempt entity and both eligible plans of the employer and eligible plans of other employers. Thus, for purposes of determining the amount excluded from a participant's gross income in any taxable year (including the underutilized limitation under § 1.457-4 (c)(3)(ii)(B)), the participant's annual deferral under an eligible plan, and the participant's annual deferrals under all other eligible plans, must be determined on an aggregate basis. To the extent that the combined annual deferral amount exceeds the maximum deferral limitation applicable under § 1.457-4 (c)(1)(i)(A), (c)(2), or (c)(3), the amount is treated as an excess deferral under § 1.457-4(e).

**(c) Special rules for catch-up amounts under multiple eligible plans.** For purposes of applying section 457(c) and this section, the special section 457 catch-up under § 1.457-4 (c)(3) is taken into account only to the extent that an annual deferral is made for a participant under an eligible plan as a result of plan provisions permitted under § 1.457-4 (c)(3). In addition, if a participant has annual deferrals under more than one eligible plan and the applicable catch-up amount under § 1.457-4 (c)(2) or (3) is not the same for each such eligible plan for the taxable year, section 457(c) and this section are applied using the catch-up amount under whichever plan has the largest catch-up amount applicable to the participant.

**(d) Examples.** The provisions of this section are illustrated by the following examples:

*Example (1).* (i) Facts. Participant F is age 62 in 2006 and participates in two eligible plans during 2006, Plans J and K, which are each eligible plans of two different governmental entities. Each plan includes provisions allowing the maximum annual deferral permitted under § 1.457-4(c)(1) through (3). For 2006, the underutilized amount under § 1.457-4 (c)(3)(ii)(B) is $20,000 under Plan J and is $40,000 under Plan K. Normal retirement age is age 65 under both plans. Participant F defers $15,000 under each plan. Participant F's includible compensation is in each case in excess of the deferral. Neither plan designates the $15,000 contribution as a catch-up permitted under each plan's special section 457 catch-up provisions.

(ii) Conclusion. For purposes of applying this section to Participant F for 2006, the maximum exclusion is $20,000. This is equal to the sum of $15,000 plus $5,000, which is the age 50 catch-up amount. Thus, F has an excess amount of $10,000 which is treated as an excess deferral for Participant F for 2006 under § 1.457-4(e).

*Example (2).* (i) Facts. Participant E, who will turn 63 on April 1, 2006, participates in four eligible plans during year 2006: Plan W which is an eligible governmental plan; and Plans X, Y, and Z which are each eligible plans of three different tax-exempt entities. For year 2006, the limitation that applies to Participant E under all four plans under § 1.457-4(c)(1)(i)(A) is $15,000. For year 2006, the additional age 50 catch-up limitation that applies to Participant E under all four plans under § 1.457-4(c)(2) is $5,000. Further, for year 2006, different limitations under § 1.457-4(c)(3) and (c)(3)(ii)(B) apply to Participant E under each of these plans, as follows: under Plan W, the underutilized limitation under § 1.457-4(c)(3)(ii)(B) is $7,000; under Plan X, the underutilized limitation under § 1.457-4(c)(3)(ii)(B) is $2,000; under Plan Y, the underutilized limitation under § 1.457-4(c)(3)(ii)(B) is $8,000; and under Plan Z, § 1.457-4(c)(3) is not applicable since normal retirement age is 62 under Plan Z. Participant E's includible compensation is in each case in excess of any applicable deferral.

(ii) Conclusion. For purposes of applying this section to Participant E for year 2006, Participant E could elect to defer $23,000 under Plan Y, which is the maximum deferral limitation under § 1.457-4(c)(1) through (3), and to defer no amount under Plans W, X, and Z. The $23,000 maximum amount is equal to the sum of $15,000 plus $8,000, which is the catch-up amount applicable to Participant E under Plan Y and which is the largest catch-up amount applicable to Participant E under any of the four plans for year 2006. Alternatively, Participant E could instead elect to defer the following combination of amounts: an aggregate total of $15,000 to Plans X, Y, and Z, if no contribution is made to Plan W; an aggregate total of $20,000 to any of the four plans; or $22,000 to Plan W and none to any of the other three plans.

(iii) If the underutilized amount under Plans W, X, and Y for year 2006 were in each case zero (because E had always contributed the maximum amount or E was a new participant) or an amount not in excess of $5,000, the maximum exclusion under this section would be $20,000 for Participant E for year 2006 ($15,000 plus the $5,000 age 50 catch-up amount), which Participant E could contribute to any of the plans.

T.D. 9075, 7/10/2003, amend T.D. 9319, 4/4/2007.

## § 1.457-6 Timing of distributions under eligible plans.

***Caution:*** The Treasury has not yet amended Reg § 1.457-6 to reflect changes made by P.L. 109-432.

**(a) In general.** Except as provided in paragraph (c) of this section (relating to distributions on account of an unforeseeable emergency), paragraph (e) of this section (relating to distributions of small accounts), § 1.457-10(a) (relating to plan terminations), or § 1.457-10(c) (relating to domestic relations orders), amounts deferred under an eligible plan may not be paid to a participant or beneficiary before the participant has a severance from employment with the eligible employer or when the participant attains age 70½, if earlier. For rules relating to loans, see paragraph (f) of this section. This section does not apply to distributions of excess amounts under § 1.457-4(e). However, except to the extent set forth by the Commissioner in revenue rulings, notices, and other guidance published in the Internal Revenue Bulletin (see § 601.601(d) of this chapter), this section applies to amounts held in a separate account for eligible rollover distributions maintained by an eligible governmental plan as described in § 1.457-10(e)(2).

**(b) Severance from employment.** *(1) Employees.* An employee has a severance from employment with the eligible employer if the employee dies, retires, or otherwise has a severance from employment with the eligible employer. See regulations under section 401(k) for additional guidance concerning severance from employment.

*(2) Independent contractors.* (i) In general. An independent contractor is considered to have a severance from employment with the eligible employer upon the expiration of the contract (or in the case of more than one contract, all contracts) under which services are performed for the eligible employer if the expiration constitutes a good-faith and complete termination of the contractual relationship. An expiration does not constitute a good faith and complete termination of the contractual relationship if the eligible employer anticipates a renewal of a contractual relationship or the independent contractor becoming an employee. For this purpose, an eligible employer is considered to anticipate the renewal of the contractual relationship with an independent contractor if it intends to contract again for the services provided under the expired contract, and neither the eligible employer nor the independent contractor has eliminated the independent contractor as a possible provider of services under any such new contract. Further, an eligible employer is considered to intend to contract again for the services provided under an expired contract if the eligible employer's doing so is conditioned only upon incurring a need for the services, the availability of funds, or both.

(ii) Special rule. Notwithstanding paragraph (b)(2)(i) of this section, the plan is considered to satisfy the requirement described in paragraph (a) of this section that no amounts deferred under the plan be paid or made available to the participant before the participant has a severance from employment with the eligible employer if, with respect to amounts payable to a participant who is an independent contractor, an eligible plan provides that—

(A) No amount will be paid to the participant before a date at least 12 months after the day on which the contract expires under which services are performed for the eligible employer (or, in the case of more than one contract, all such contracts expire); and

(B) No amount payable to the participant on that date will be paid to the participant if, after the expiration of the contract (or contracts) and before that date, the participant performs services for the eligible employer as an independent contractor or an employee.

**(c) Rules applicable to distributions for unforeseeable emergencies.** *(1) In general.* An eligible plan may permit a distribution to a participant or beneficiary for an unforeseeable emergency. The distribution must satisfy the requirements of paragraph (c)(2) of this section.

*(2) Requirements.* (i) Unforeseeable emergency defined. An unforeseeable emergency must be defined in the plan as a severe financial hardship of the participant or beneficiary resulting from an illness or accident of the participant or beneficiary, the participant's or beneficiary's spouse, or the participant's or beneficiary's dependent (as defined in section 152, and, for taxable years beginning on or after January 1, 2005, without regard to section 152(b)(1), (b)(2), and (d)(1)(B)); loss of the participant's or beneficiary's property due to casualty (including the need to rebuild a home following damage to a home not otherwise covered by homeowner's insurance, such as damage that is the result of a nat-

ural disaster); or other similar extraordinary and unforeseeable circumstances arising as a result of events beyond the control of the participant or the beneficiary. For example, the imminent foreclosure of or eviction from the participant's or beneficiary's primary residence may constitute an unforeseeable emergency. In addition, the need to pay for medical expenses, including non-refundable deductibles, as well as for the cost of prescription drug medication, may constitute an unforeseeable emergency. Finally, the need to pay for the funeral expenses of a spouse or a dependent (as defined in section 152, and, for taxable years beginning on or after January 1, 2005, without regard to section 152(b)(1), (b)(2), and (d)(1)(B)) of a participant or beneficiary may also constitute an unforeseeable emergency. Except as otherwise specifically provided in this paragraph (c)(2)(i), the purchase of a home and the payment of college tuition are not unforeseeable emergencies under this paragraph (c)(2)(i).

(ii) Unforeseeable emergency distribution standard. Whether a participant or beneficiary is faced with an unforeseeable emergency permitting a distribution under this paragraph (c) is to be determined based on the relevant facts and circumstances of each case, but, in any case, a distribution on account of unforeseeable emergency may not be made to the extent that such emergency is or may be relieved through reimbursement or compensation from insurance or otherwise, by liquidation of the participant's assets, to the extent the liquidation of such assets would not itself cause severe financial hardship, or by cessation of deferrals under the plan.

(iii) Distribution necessary to satisfy emergency need. Distributions because of an unforeseeable emergency must be limited to the amount reasonably necessary to satisfy the emergency need (which may include any amounts necessary to pay for any federal, state, or local income taxes or penalties reasonably anticipated to result from the distribution).

**(d) Minimum required distributions for eligible plans.** In order to be an eligible plan, a plan must meet the distribution requirements of section 457(d)(1) and (2). Under section 457(d)(2), a plan must meet the minimum distribution requirements of section 401(a)(9). See section 401(a)(9) and the regulations thereunder for these requirements. Section 401(a)(9) requires that a plan begin lifetime distributions to a participant no later than April 1 of the calendar year following the later of the calendar year in which the participant attains age 70½ or the calendar year in which the participant retires.

**(e) Distributions of smaller accounts.** *(1) In general.* An eligible plan may provide for a distribution of all or a portion of a participant's benefit if this paragraph (e)(1) is satisfied. This paragraph (e)(1) is satisfied if the participant's total amount deferred (the participant's total account balance) which is not attributable to rollover contributions (as defined in section 411(a)(11)(D)) is not in excess of the dollar limit under section 411(a)(11)(A), no amount has been deferred under the plan by or for the participant during the two-year period ending on the date of the distribution, and there has been no prior distribution under the plan to the participant under this paragraph (e). An eligible plan is not required to permit distributions under this paragraph (e).

*(2) Alternative provisions possible.* Consistent with the provisions of paragraph (e)(1) of this section, a plan may provide that the total amount deferred for a participant or beneficiary will be distributed automatically to the participant or beneficiary if the requirements of paragraph (e)(1) of this section are met. Alternatively, if the requirements of paragraph (e)(1) of this section are met, the plan may provide for the total amount deferred for a participant or beneficiary to be distributed to the participant or beneficiary only if the participant or beneficiary so elects. The plan is permitted to substitute a specified dollar amount that is less than the total amount deferred. In addition, these two alternatives can be combined; for example, a plan could provide for automatic distributions for up to $500, but allow a participant or beneficiary elect a distribution if the total account balance is above $500.

**(f) Loans from eligible plans.** *(1) Eligible plans of tax-exempt entities.* If a participant or beneficiary receives (directly or indirectly) any amount deferred as a loan from an eligible plan of a tax-exempt entity, that amount will be treated as having been paid or made available to the individual as a distribution under the plan, in violation of the distribution requirements of section 457(d).

*(2) Eligible governmental plans.* The determination of whether the availability of a loan, the making of a loan, or a failure to repay a loan made from a trustee (or a person treated as a trustee under section 457(g)) of an eligible governmental plan to a participant or beneficiary is treated as a distribution (directly or indirectly) for purposes of this section, and the determination of whether the availability of the loan, the making of the loan, or a failure to repay the loan is in any other respect a violation of the requirements of section 457(b) and the regulations, depends on the facts and circumstances. Among the facts and circumstances are whether the loan has a fixed repayment schedule and bears a reasonable rate of interest, and whether there are repayment safeguards to which a prudent lender would adhere. Thus, for example, a loan must bear a reasonable rate of interest in order to satisfy the exclusive benefit requirement of section 457(g)(1) and § 1.457-8(a)(1). See also § 1.457-7(b)(3) relating to the application of section 72(p) with respect to the taxation of a loan made under an eligible governmental plan, and § 1.72(p)-1 relating to section 72(p)(2).

*(3) Example.* The provisions of paragraph (f)(2) of this section are illustrated by the following example:

*Example.* (i) Facts. Eligible Plan X of State Y is funded through Trust Z. Plan X permits an employee's account balance under Plan X to be paid in a single sum at severance from employment with State Y. Plan X includes a loan program under which any active employee with a vested account balance may receive a loan from Trust Z. Loans are made pursuant to plan provisions regarding loans that are set forth in the plan under which loans bear a reasonable rate of interest and are secured by the employee's account balance. In order to avoid taxation under § 1.457-7(b)(3) and section 72(p)(1), the plan provisions limit the amount of loans and require loans to be repaid in level installments as required under section 72(p)(2). Participant J's vested account balance under Plan X is $50,000. J receives a loan from Trust Z in the amount of $5,000 on December 1, 2003, to be repaid in level installments made quarterly over the 5-year period ending on November 30, 2008. Participant J makes the required repayments until J has a severance from employment from State Y in 2005 and subsequently fails to repay the outstanding loan balance of $2,250. The $2,250 loan balance is offset against J's $80,000 account balance benefit under Plan X, and J elects to be paid the remaining $77,750 in 2005.

(ii) Conclusion. The making of the loan to J will not be treated as a violation of the requirements of section 457(b) or the regulations. The cancellation of the loan at severance from employment does not cause Plan X to fail to satisfy the requirements for plan eligibility under section 457. In addition, because the loan satisfies the maximum amount and repayment requirements of section 72(p)(2), J is not required to include any amount in income as a result of the loan until 2005, when J has income of $2,250 as a result of the offset (which is a permissible distribution under this section) and income of $77,750 as a result of the distribution made in 2005.

T.D. 9075, 7/10/2003, amend T.D. 9319, 4/4/2007.

**§ 1.457-7 Taxation of distributions under eligible plans.**

**(a) General rules for when amounts are included in gross income.** The rules for determining when an amount deferred under an eligible plan is includible in the gross income of a participant or beneficiary depend on whether the plan is an eligible governmental plan or an eligible plan of a tax-exempt entity. Paragraph (b) of this section sets forth the rules for an eligible governmental plan. Paragraph (c) of this section sets forth the rules for an eligible plan of a tax-exempt entity.

**(b) Amounts included in gross income under an eligible governmental plan.** *(1) Amounts included in gross income in year paid under an eligible governmental plan.* Except as provided in paragraphs (b)(2) and (3) of this section (or in § 1.457-10(c) relating to payments to a spouse or former spouse pursuant to a qualified domestic relations order), amounts deferred under an eligible governmental plan are includible in the gross income of a participant or beneficiary for the taxable year in which paid to the participant or beneficiary under the plan.

*(2) Rollovers to individual retirement arrangements and other eligible retirement plans.* A trustee-to-trustee transfer in accordance with section 401(a)(31) (generally referred to as a direct rollover) from an eligible government plan is not includible in gross income of a participant or beneficiary in the year transferred. In addition, any payment made from an eligible government plan in the form of an eligible rollover distribution (as defined in section 402(c)(4)) is not includible in gross income in the year paid to the extent the payment is transferred to an eligible retirement plan (as defined in section 402(c)(8)(B)) within 60 days, including the transfer to the eligible retirement plan of any property distributed from the eligible governmental plan. For this purpose, the rules of section 402(c)(2) through (7) and (9) apply. Any trustee-to-trustee transfer under this paragraph (b)(2) from an eligible government plan is a distribution that is subject to the distribution requirements of § 1.457-6.

*(3) Amounts taxable under section 72(p)(1).* In accordance with section 72(p), the amount of any loan from an eligible governmental plan to a participant or beneficiary (including any pledge or assignment treated as a loan under section 72(p)(1)(B)) is treated as having been received as a distribution from the plan under section 72(p)(1), except to the extent set forth in section 72(p)(2) (relating to loans that do not exceed a maximum amount and that are repayable in accordance with certain terms) and § 1.72(p)-1. Thus, except to the extent a loan satisfies section 72(p)(2), any amount loaned from an eligible governmental plan to a participant or beneficiary (including any pledge or assignment treated as a loan under section 72(p)(1)(B)) is includible in the gross income of the participant or beneficiary for the taxable year in which the loan is made. See generally § 1.72(p)-1.

*(4) Examples.* The provisions of this paragraph (b) are illustrated by the following examples:

*Example (1).* (i) Facts. Eligible Plan G of a governmental entity permits distribution of benefits in a single sum or in installments of up to 20 years, with such benefits to commence at any date that is after severance from employment (up to the later of severance from employment or the plan's normal retirement age of 65). Effective for participants who have a severance from employment after December 31, 2001, Plan X allows an election—as to both the date on which payments are to begin and the form in which payments are to be made—to be made by the participant at any time that is before the commencement date selected. However, Plan X chooses to require elections to be filed at least 30 days before the commencement date selected in order for Plan X to have enough time to be able to effectuate the election.

(ii) Conclusion. No amounts are included in gross income before actual payments begin. If installment payments begin (and the installment payments are payable over at least 10 years so as not to be eligible rollover distributions), the amount included in gross income for any year is equal to the amount of the installment payment paid during the year.

*Example (2).* (i) Facts. Same facts as in Example 1, except that the same rules are extended to participants who had a severance from employment before January 1, 2002.

(ii) Conclusion. For all participants (that is, both those who have a severance from employment after December 31, 2001, and those who have a severance from employment before January 1, 2002, including those whose benefit payments have commenced before January 1, 2002), no amounts are included in gross income before actual payments begin. If installment payments begin (and the installment payments are payable over at least 10 years so as not to be eligible rollover distributions), the amount included in gross income for any year is equal to the amount of the installment payment paid during the year.

**(c) Amounts included in gross income under an eligible plan of a tax-exempt entity.** *(1) Amounts included in gross income in year paid or made available under an eligible plan of a tax-exempt entity.* Amounts deferred under an eligible plan of a tax-exempt entity are includible in the gross income of a participant or beneficiary for the taxable year in which paid or otherwise made available to the participant or beneficiary under the plan. Thus, amounts deferred under an eligible plan of a tax-exempt entity are includible in the gross income of the participant or beneficiary in the year the amounts are first made available under the terms of the plan, even if the plan has not distributed the amounts deferred. Amounts deferred under an eligible plan of a tax-exempt entity are not considered made available to the participant or beneficiary solely because the participant or beneficiary is permitted to choose among various investments under the plan.

*(2) When amounts deferred are considered to be made available under an eligible plan of a tax-exempt entity.* (i) General rule. Except as provided in paragraphs (c)(2)(ii) through (iv) of this section, amounts deferred under an eligible plan of a tax-exempt entity are considered made available (and, thus, are includible in the gross income of the participant or beneficiary under this paragraph (c)) at the earliest date, on or after severance from employment, on which the plan allows distributions to commence, but in no event later than the date on which distributions must commence pursuant to section 401(a)(9). For example, in the case of a plan that permits distribution to commence on the date that is 60 days after the close of the plan year in which the participant has a severance from employment with the eligible employer, amounts deferred are considered to be made available on that date. However, distributions deferred in ac-

cordance with paragraphs (c)(2)(ii) through (iv) of this section are not considered made available prior to the applicable date under paragraphs (c)(2)(ii) through (iv) of this section. In addition, no portion of a participant or beneficiary's account is treated as made available (and thus currently includible in income) under an eligible plan of a tax-exempt entity merely because the participant or beneficiary under the plan may elect to receive a distribution in any of the following circumstances:

(A) A distribution in the event of an unforeseeable emergency to the extent the distribution is permitted under § 1.457-6(c).

(B) A distribution from an account for which the total amount deferred is not in excess of the dollar limit under section 411(a)(11)(A) to the extent the distribution is permitted under § 1.457-6(e).

(ii) Initial election to defer commencement of distributions. (A) In general. An eligible plan of a tax-exempt entity may provide a period for making an initial election during which the participant or beneficiary may elect, in accordance with the terms of the plan, to defer the payment of some or all of the amounts deferred to a fixed or determinable future time. The period for making this initial election must expire prior to the first time that any such amounts would be considered made available under the plan under paragraph (c)(2)(i) of this section.

(B) Failure to make initial election to defer commencement of distributions. Generally, if no initial election is made by a participant or beneficiary under this paragraph (c)(2)(ii), then the amounts deferred under an eligible plan of a tax-exempt entity are considered made available and taxable to the participant or beneficiary in accordance with paragraph (c)(2)(i) of this section at the earliest time, on or after severance from employment ( but in no event later than the date on which distributions must commence pursuant to section 401(a)(9)), that distribution is permitted to commence under the terms of the plan. However, the plan may provide for a default payment schedule that applies if no election is made. If the plan provides for a default payment schedule, the amounts deferred are includible in the gross income of the participant or beneficiary in the year the amounts deferred are first made available under the terms of the default payment schedule.

(iii) Additional election to defer commencement of distribution. An eligible plan of a tax-exempt entity is permitted to provide that a participant or beneficiary who has made an initial election under paragraph (c)(2)(ii)(A) of this section may make one additional election to defer (but not accelerate) commencement of distributions under the plan before distributions have commenced in accordance with the initial deferral election under paragraph (c)(2)(ii)(A) of this section. Amounts payable to a participant or beneficiary under an eligible plan of a tax-exempt entity are not treated as made available merely because the plan allows the participant to make an additional election under this paragraph (c)(2)(iii). A participant or beneficiary is not precluded from making an additional election to defer commencement of distributions merely because the participant or beneficiary has previously received a distribution under § 1.457-6(c) because of an unforeseeable emergency, has received a distribution of smaller amounts under § 1.457-6(e), has made (and revoked) other deferral or method of payment elections within the initial election period, or is subject to a default payment schedule under which the commencement of benefits is deferred (for example, until a participant is age 65).

(iv) Election as to method of payment. An eligible plan of a tax-exempt entity may provide that an election as to the method of payment under the plan may be made at any time prior to the time the amounts are distributed in accordance with the participant or beneficiary's initial or additional election to defer commencement of distributions under paragraph (c)(2)(ii) or (iii) of this section. Where no method of payment is elected, the entire amount deferred will be includible in the gross income of the participant or beneficiary when the amounts first become made available in accordance with a participant's initial or additional elections to defer under paragraphs (c)(2)(ii) and (iii) of this section, unless the eligible plan provides for a default method of payment (in which case amounts are considered made available and taxable when paid under the terms of the default payment schedule). A method of payment means a distribution or a series of periodic distributions commencing on a date determined in accordance with paragraph (c)(2)(ii) or (iii) of this section.

*(3) Examples.* The provisions of this paragraph (c) are illustrated by the following examples:

*Example (1).* (i) Facts. Eligible Plan X of a tax-exempt entity provides that a participant's total account balance, representing all amounts deferred under the plan, is payable to a participant in a single sum 60 days after severance from employment throughout these examples, unless, during a 30-day period immediately following the severance, the participant elects to receive the single sum payment at a later date (that is not later than the plan's normal retirement age of 65) or elects to receive distribution in 10 annual installments to begin 60 days after severance from employment (or at a later date, if so elected, that is not later than the plan's normal retirement age of 65). On November 13, 2004, K, a calendar year taxpayer, has a severance from employment with the eligible employer. K does not, within the 30-day window period, elect to postpone distributions to a later date or to receive payment in 10 fixed annual installments.

(ii) Conclusion. The single sum payment is payable to K 60 days after the date K has a severance from employment (January 12, 2005), and is includible in the gross income of K in 2005 under section 457(a).

*Example (2).* (i) Facts. The terms of eligible Plan X are the same as described in Example 1. Participant L participates in eligible Plan X. On November 11, 2003, L has a severance from the employment of the eligible employer. On November 24, 2003, L makes an initial deferral election not to receive the single-sum payment payable 60 days after the severance, and instead elects to receive the amounts in 10 annual installments to begin 60 days after severance from employment.

(ii) Conclusion. No portion of L's account is considered made available in 2003 or 2004 before a payment is made and no amount is includible in the gross income of L until distributions commence. The annual installment payable in 2004 will be includible in L's gross income in 2004.

*Example (3).* (i) Facts. The facts are the same as in Example 1, except that eligible Plan X also provides that those participants who are receiving distributions in 10 annual installments may, at any time and without restriction, elect to receive a cash out of all remaining installments. Participant M elects to receive a distribution in 10 annual installments commencing in 2004.

(ii) Conclusion. M's total account balance, representing the total of the amounts deferred under the plan, is considered made available and is includible in M's gross income in 2004.

*Example (4).* (i) Facts. The facts are the same as in Example 3, except that, instead of providing for an unrestricted cashout of remaining payments, the plan provides that participants or beneficiaries who are receiving distributions in 10 annual installments may accelerate the payment of the amount remaining payable to the participant upon the occurrence of an unforeseeable emergency as described in § 1.457-6(c)(1) in an amount not exceeding that described in § 1.457-6(c)(2).

(ii) Conclusion. No amount is considered made available to participant M on account of M's right to accelerate payments upon the occurrence of an unforeseeable emergency.

*Example (5).* (i) Facts. Eligible Plan Y of a tax-exempt entity provides that distributions will commence 60 days after a participant's severance from employment unless the participant elects, within a 30-day window period following severance from employment, to defer distributions to a later date (but no later than the year following the calendar year the participant attains age 70½). The plan provides that a participant who has elected to defer distributions to a later date may make an election as to form of distribution at any time prior to the 30th day before distributions are to commence.

(ii) Conclusion. No amount is considered made available prior to the date distributions are to commence by reason of a participant's right to defer or make an election as to the form of distribution.

*Example (6).* (i) Facts. The facts are the same as in Example 1, except that the plan also permits participants who have made an initial election to defer distribution to make one additional deferral election at any time prior to the date distributions are scheduled to commence. Participant N has a severance from employment at age 50. The next day, during the 30-day period provided in the plan, N elects to receive distribution in the form of 10 annual installment payments beginning at age 55. Two weeks later, within the 30-day window period, N makes a new election permitted under the plan to receive 10 annual installment payments beginning at age 60 (instead of age 55). When N is age 59, N elects under the additional deferral election provisions, to defer distributions until age 65.

(ii) Conclusion. In this example, N's election to defer distributions until age 65 is a valid election. The two elections N makes during the 30-day window period are not additional deferral elections described in paragraph (c)(2)(iii) of this section because they are made before the first permissible payout date under the plan. Therefore, the plan is not precluded from allowing N to make the additional deferral election. However, N can make no further election to defer distributions beyond age 65 (or accelerate distribution before age 65) because this additional deferral election can only be made once.

---

T.D. 9075, 7/10/2003.

---

### § 1.457-8 Funding rules for eligible plans.

**(a) Eligible governmental plans.** *(1) In general.* In order to be an eligible governmental plan, all amounts deferred under the plan, all property and rights purchased with such amounts, and all income attributable to such amounts, property, or rights, must be held in trust for the exclusive benefit of participants and their beneficiaries. A trust described in this paragraph (a) that also meets the requirements of §§ 1.457-3 through 1.457-10 is treated as an organization exempt from tax under section 501(a), and a participant's or beneficiary's interest in amounts in the trust is includible in the gross income of the participants and beneficiaries only to the extent, and at the time, provided for in section 457(a) and §§ 1.457-4 through 1.457-10.

*(2) Trust requirement.* (i) A trust described in this paragraph (a) must be established pursuant to a written agreement that constitutes a valid trust under State law. The terms of the trust must make it impossible, prior to the satisfaction of all liabilities with respect to participants and their beneficiaries, for any part of the assets and income of the trust to be used for, or diverted to, purposes other than for the exclusive benefit of participants and their beneficiaries.

(ii) Amounts deferred under an eligible governmental plan must be transferred to a trust within a period that is not longer than is reasonable for the proper administration of the participant accounts (if any). For purposes of this requirement, the plan may provide for amounts deferred for a participant under the plan to be transferred to the trust within a specified period after the date the amounts would otherwise have been paid to the participant. For example, the plan could provide for amounts deferred under the plan at the election of the participant to be contributed to the trust within 15 business days following the month in which these amounts would otherwise have been paid to the participant.

*(3) Custodial accounts and annuity contracts treated as trusts.* (i) In general. For purposes of the trust requirement of this paragraph (a), custodial accounts and annuity contracts described in section 401(f) that satisfy the requirements of this paragraph (a)(3) are treated as trusts under rules similar to the rules of section 401(f). Therefore, the provisions of § 1.401(f)-1(b) will generally apply to determine whether a custodial account or an annuity contract is treated as a trust. The use of a custodial account or annuity contract as part of an eligible governmental plan does not preclude the use of a trust or another custodial account or annuity contract as part of the same plan, provided that all such vehicles satisfy the requirements of section 457(g)(1) and (3) and paragraphs (a)(1) and (2) of this section and that all assets and income of the plan are held in such vehicles.

(ii) Custodial accounts. (A) In general. A custodial account is treated as a trust, for purposes of section 457(g)(1) and paragraphs (a)(1) and (2) of this section, if the custodian is a bank, as described in section 408(n), or a person who meets the nonbank trustee requirements of paragraph (a)(3)(ii)(B) of this section, and the account meets the requirements of paragraphs (a)(1) and (2) of this section, other than the requirement that it be a trust.

(B) Nonbank trustee status. The custodian of a custodial account may be a person other than a bank only if the person demonstrates to the satisfaction of the Commissioner that the manner in which the person will administer the custodial account will be consistent with the requirements of section 457(g)(1) and (3). To do so, the person must demonstrate that the requirements of § 1.408-2(e)(2) through (6) (relating to nonbank trustees) are met. The written application must be sent to the address prescribed by the Commissioner in the same manner as prescribed under § 1.408-2(e). To the extent that a person has already demonstrated to the satisfaction of the Commissioner that the person satisfies the requirements of § 1.408-2(e) in connection with a qualified trust (or custodial account or annuity contract) under section 401(a), that person is deemed to satisfy the requirements of this paragraph (a)(3)(ii)(B).

(iii) Annuity contracts. An annuity contract is treated as a trust for purposes of section 457(g)(1) and paragraph (a)(1) of this section if the contract is an annuity contract, as defined in section 401(g), that has been issued by an insurance company qualified to do business in the State, and the contract meets the requirements of paragraphs (a)(1) and (2) of this section, other than the requirement that it be a trust. An annuity contract does not include a life, health or accident, property, casualty, or liability insurance contract.

*(4) Combining assets.* [Reserved]

**(b) Eligible plans maintained by tax-exempt entity.** *(1) General rule.* In order to be an eligible plan of a tax-exempt entity, the plan must be unfunded and plan assets must not be set aside for participants or their beneficiaries. Under section 457(b)(6) and this paragraph (b), an eligible plan of a tax-exempt entity must provide that all amounts deferred under the plan, all property and rights to property (including rights as a beneficiary of a contract providing life insurance protection) purchased with such amounts, and all income attributable to such amounts, property, or rights, must remain (until paid or made available to the participant or beneficiary) solely the property and rights of the eligible employer (without being restricted to the provision of benefits under the plan), subject only to the claims of the eligible employer's general creditors.

*(2) Additional requirements.* For purposes of paragraph (b)(1) of this section, the plan must be unfunded regardless of whether or not the amounts were deferred pursuant to a salary reduction agreement between the eligible employer and the participant. Any funding arrangement under an eligible plan of a tax-exempt entity that sets aside assets for the exclusive benefit of participants violates this requirement, and amounts deferred are generally immediately includible in the gross income of plan participants and beneficiaries. Nothing in this paragraph (b) prohibits an eligible plan from permitting participants and their beneficiaries to make an election among different investment options available under the plan, such as an election affecting the investment of the amounts described in paragraph (b)(1) of this section.

T.D. 9075, 7/10/2003.

### § 1.457-9 Effect on eligible plans when not administered in accordance with eligibility requirements.

**(a) Eligible governmental plans.** A plan of a State ceases to be an eligible governmental plan on the first day of the first plan year beginning more than 180 days after the date on which the Commissioner notifies the State in writing that the plan is being administered in a manner that is inconsistent with one or more of the requirements of §§ 1.457-3 through § 1.457-8 or § 1.447-10. However, the plan may correct the plan inconsistencies specified in the written notification before the first day of that plan year and continue to maintain plan eligibility. If a plan ceases to be an eligible governmental plan, amounts subsequently deferred by participants will be includible in income when deferred, or, if later, when the amounts deferred cease to be subject to a substantial risk of forfeiture, as provided at § 1.457-11. Amounts deferred before the date on which the plan ceases to be an eligible governmental plan, and any earnings thereon, will be treated as if the plan continues to be an eligible governmental plan and will not be includible in participant's or beneficiary's gross income until paid to the participant or beneficiary.

**(b) Eligible plans of tax-exempt entities.** A plan of a tax-exempt entity ceases to be an eligible plan on the first day that the plan fails to satisfy one or more of the requirements of §§ 1.457-3 through 1.457-8, or § 1.457-10. See § 1.457-11 for rules regarding the treatment of an ineligible plan.

T.D. 9075, 7/10/2003.

### § 1.457-10 Miscellaneous provisions.

**(a) Plan terminations and frozen plans.** *(1) In general.* An eligible employer may amend its plan to eliminate future deferrals for existing participants or to limit participation to existing participants and employees. An eligible plan may also contain provisions that permit plan termination and permit amounts deferred to be distributed on termination. In order for a plan to be considered terminated, amounts deferred under an eligible plan must be distributed to all plan participants and beneficiaries as soon as administratively practicable after termination of the eligible plan. The mere provision for, and making of, distributions to participants or beneficiaries upon a plan termination will not cause an eligible plan to cease to satisfy the requirements of section 457(b) or the regulations.

*(2) Employers that cease to be eligible employers.* (i) Plan not terminated. An eligible employer that ceases to be an eligible employer may no longer maintain an eligible plan. If the employer was a tax-exempt entity and the plan is not terminated as permitted under paragraph (a)(2)(ii) of this section, the tax consequences to participants and beneficiaries in the previously eligible (unfunded) plan of an ineligible employer are determined in accordance with either section 451 if the employer becomes an entity other than a State or § 1.457-11 if the employer becomes a State. If the employer was a State and the plan is neither terminated as permitted under paragraph (a)(2)(ii) of this section nor transferred to another eligible plan of that State as permitted under paragraph (b) of this section, the tax consequences to participants in the previously eligible governmental plan of an ineligible employer, the assets of which are held in trust pursuant to § 1.457-8(a), are determined in accordance with section 402(b) (section 403(c) in the case of an annuity contract) and the trust is no longer to be treated as a trust that is exempt from tax under section 501(a).

(ii) Plan termination. As an alternative to determining the tax consequences to the plan and participants under paragraph (a)(2)(i) of this section, the employer may terminate the plan and distribute the amounts deferred (and all plan assets) to all plan participants as soon as administratively practicable in accordance with paragraph (a)(1) of this section. Such distribution may include eligible rollover distributions in the case of a plan that was an eligible governmental plan. In addition, if the employer is a State, another alternative to determining the tax consequences under paragraph (a)(2)(i) of this section is to transfer the assets of the eligible governmental plan to an eligible governmental plan of another eligible employer within the same State under the plan-to-plan transfer rules of paragraph (b) of this section.

*(3) Examples.* The provisions of this paragraph (a) are illustrated by the following examples:

*Example (1).* (i) Facts. Employer Y, a corporation that owns a State hospital, sponsors an eligible governmental plan funded through a trust. Employer Y is acquired by a for-profit hospital and Employer Y ceases to be an eligible employer under section 457(e)(1) or § 1.457-2(e). Employer Y terminates the plan and, during the next 6 months, distributes to participants and beneficiaries all amounts deferred that were under the plan.

(ii) Conclusion. The termination and distribution does not cause the plan to fail to be an eligible governmental plan. Amounts that are distributed as eligible rollover distributions may be rolled over to an eligible retirement plan described in section 402(c)(8)(B).

*Example (2).* (i) Facts. The facts are the same as in Example 1, except that Employer Y decides to continue to maintain the plan.

(ii) Conclusion. If Employer Y continues to maintain the plan, the tax consequences to participants and beneficiaries will be determined in accordance with either section 402(b) if the compensation deferred is funded through a trust, section 403(c) if the compensation deferred is funded through annuity contracts, or § 1.457-11 if the compensation deferred is not funded through a trust or annuity contract. In addition, if Employer Y continues to maintain the plan, the trust will no longer be treated as exempt from tax under section 501(a).

*Example (3).* (i) Facts. Employer Z, a corporation that owns a tax-exempt hospital, sponsors an unfunded eligible plan. Employer Z is acquired by a for-profit hospital and is no longer an eligible employer under section 457(e)(1) or § 1.457-2(e). Employer Z terminates the plan and distributes all amounts deferred under the eligible plan to participants and beneficiaries within a one-year period.

(ii) Conclusion. Distributions under the plan are treated as made under an eligible plan of a tax-exempt entity and the distributions of the amounts deferred are includible in the gross income of the participant or beneficiary in the year distributed.

*Example (4).* (i) Facts. The facts are the same as in Example 3, except that Employer Z decides to maintain instead of terminate the plan.

(ii) Conclusion. If Employer Z maintains the plan, the tax consequences to participants and beneficiaries in the plan will thereafter be determined in accordance with section 451.

**(b) Plan-to-plan transfers.** *(1) General rule.* An eligible governmental plan may provide for the transfer of amounts deferred by a participant or beneficiary to another eligible governmental plan if the conditions in paragraphs (b)(2), (3), or (4) of this section are met. An eligible plan of a tax-exempt entity may provide for transfers of amounts deferred by a participant to another eligible plan of a tax-exempt entity if the conditions in paragraph (b)(5) of this section are met. In addition, an eligible governmental plan may accept transfers from another eligible governmental plan as described in the first sentence of this paragraph (b)(1), and an eligible plan of a tax-exempt entity may accept transfers from another eligible plan of a tax-exempt entity as described in the preceding sentence. However, a State may not transfer the assets of its eligible governmental plan to a tax-exempt entity's eligible plan and the plan of a tax-exempt entity may not accept such a transfer. Similarly, a tax-exempt entity may not transfer the assets of its eligible plan to an eligible governmental plan and an eligible governmental plan may not accept such a transfer. In addition, if the conditions in paragraph (b)(4) of this section (relating to permissive past service credit and repayments under section 415) are met, an eligible governmental plan of a State may provide for the transfer of amounts deferred by a participant or beneficiary to a qualified plan (under section 401(a)) maintained by a State. However, a qualified plan may not transfer assets to an eligible governmental plan or to an eligible plan of a tax-exempt entity, and an eligible governmental plan or the plan of a tax-exempt entity may not accept such a transfer.

*(2) Requirements for post-severance plan-to-plan transfers among eligible governmental plans.* A transfer under paragraph (b)(1) of this section from an eligible governmental plan to another eligible governmental plan is permitted if the following conditions are met—

(i) The transferor plan provides for transfers;

(ii) The receiving plan provides for the receipt of transfers;

(iii) The participant or beneficiary whose amounts deferred are being transferred will have an amount deferred immediately after the transfer at least equal to the amount deferred with respect to that participant or beneficiary immediately before the transfer; and

(iv) In the case of a transfer for a participant, the participant has had a severance from employment with the transferring employer and is performing services for the entity maintaining the receiving plan.

*(3) Requirements for plan-to-plan transfers of all plan assets of eligible governmental plan.* A transfer under paragraph (b)(1) of this section from an eligible governmental plan to another eligible governmental plan is permitted if the following conditions are met—

(i) The transfer is from an eligible governmental plan to another eligible governmental plan within the same State;

(ii) All of the assets held by the transferor plan are transferred;

(iii) The transferor plan provides for transfers;

(iv) The receiving plan provides for the receipt of transfers;

(v) The participant or beneficiary whose amounts deferred are being transferred will have an amount deferred immediately after the transfer at least equal to the amount deferred with respect to that participant or beneficiary immediately before the transfer; and

(vi) The participants or beneficiaries whose deferred amounts are being transferred are not eligible for additional annual deferrals in the receiving plan unless they are performing services for the entity maintaining the receiving plan.

*(4) Requirements for plan-to-plan transfers among eligible governmental plans of the same employer.* A transfer under paragraph (b)(1) of this section from an eligible governmental plan to another eligible governmental plan is permitted if the following conditions are met—

(i) The transfer is from an eligible governmental plan to another eligible governmental plan of the same employer (and, for this purpose, the employer is not treated as the same employer if the participant's compensation is paid by a different entity);

(ii) The transferor plan provides for transfers;

(iii) The receiving plan provides for the receipt of transfers;

(iv) The participant or beneficiary whose amounts deferred are being transferred will have an amount deferred immediately after the transfer at least equal to the amount deferred with respect to that participant or beneficiary immediately before the transfer; and

(v) The participant or beneficiary whose deferred amounts are being transferred is not eligible for additional annual deferrals in the receiving plan unless the participant or beneficiary is performing services for the entity maintaining the receiving plan.

*(5) Requirements for post-severance plan-to-plan transfers among eligible plans of tax-exempt entities.* A transfer under paragraph (b)(1) of this section from an eligible plan of a tax-exempt employer to another eligible plan of a tax-exempt employer is permitted if the following conditions are met—

(i) The transferor plan provides for transfers;

(ii) The receiving plan provides for the receipt of transfers;

(iii) The participant or beneficiary whose amounts deferred are being transferred will have an amount deferred immediately after the transfer at least equal to the amount deferred with respect to that participant or beneficiary immediately before the transfer; and

(iv) In the case of a transfer for a participant, the participant has had a severance from employment with the transferring employer and is performing services for the entity maintaining the receiving plan.

*(6) Treatment of amount transferred following a plan-to-plan transfer between eligible plans.* Following a transfer of any amount between eligible plans under paragraphs (b)(1) through (b)(5) of this section—

(i) The transferred amount is subject to the restrictions of § 1.457-6 (relating to when distributions are permitted to be made to a participant under an eligible plan) in the receiving plan in the same manner as if the transferred amount had been originally been deferred under the receiving plan if the participant is performing services for the entity maintaining the receiving plan, and

(ii) In the case of a transfer between eligible plans of tax-exempt entities, except as otherwise determined by the Commissioner, the transferred amount is subject to § 1.457-7(c)(2) (relating to when amounts are considered to be made available under an eligible plan of a tax-exempt entity) in the same manner as if the elections made by the participant or beneficiary under the transferor plan had been made under the receiving plan.

*(7) Examples.* The provisions of paragraphs (b)(1) through (6) of this section are illustrated by the following examples:

*Example (1).* (i) Facts. Participant A, the president of City X's hospital, has accepted a position with another hospital which is a tax-exempt entity. A participates in the eligible governmental plan of City X. A would like to transfer the amounts deferred under City X's eligible governmental plan to the eligible plan of the tax-exempt hospital.

(ii) Conclusion. City X's plan may not transfer A's amounts deferred to the tax-exempt employer's eligible plan. In addition, because the amounts deferred would no longer be held in trust for the exclusive benefit of participants and their beneficiaries, the transfer would violate the exclusive benefit rule of section 457(g) and § 1.457-8(a).

*Example (2).* (i) Facts. County M, located in State S, operates several health clinics and maintains an eligible governmental plan for employees of those clinics. One of the clinics operated by County M is being acquired by a hospital operated by State S, and employees of that clinic will become employees of State S. County M permits those employees to transfer their balances under County M's eligible governmental plan to the eligible governmental plan of State S.

(ii) Conclusion. If the eligible governmental plans of County M and State S provide for the transfer and acceptance of the transfer (and the other requirements of paragraph (b)(1) of this section are satisfied), then the requirements of paragraph (b)(2) of this section are satisfied and, thus, the transfer will not cause either plan to violate the requirements of section 457 or these regulations.

*Example (3).* (i) Facts. City Employer Z, a hospital, sponsors an eligible governmental plan. City Employer Z is located in State B. All of the assets of City Employer Z are being acquired by a tax-exempt hospital. City Employer Z, in accordance with the plan-to-plan transfer rules of paragraph (b) of this section, would like to transfer the total amount of assets deferred under City Employer Z's eligible governmental plan to the acquiring tax-exempt entity's eligible plan.

(ii) Conclusion. City Employer Z may not permit participants to transfer the amounts to the eligible plan of the tax-exempt entity. In addition, because the amounts deferred would no longer be held in trust for the exclusive benefit of participants and their beneficiaries, the transfer would violate the exclusive benefit rule of section 457(g) and § 1.457-8(a).

*Example (4).* (i) Facts. The facts are the same as in Example 3, except that City Employer Z, instead of transferring all of its assets to the eligible plan of the tax-exempt entity, decides to transfer all of the amounts deferred under City Z's eligible governmental plan to the eligible governmental plan of County B in which City Z is located. County B's eligible plan does not cover employees of City Z, but is willing to allow the assets of City Z's plan to be transferred to County B's plan, a related state government entity, also located in State B.

(ii) Conclusion. If City Employer Z's (transferor) eligible governmental plan provides for such transfer and the eligible governmental plan of County B permits the acceptance of such a transfer (and the other requirements of paragraph (b)(1) of this section are satisfied), then the requirements of paragraph (b)(3) of this section are satisfied and, thus, City Employer Z may transfer the total amounts deferred under its eligible governmental plan, prior to termination of that plan, to the eligible governmental plan maintained by County B. However, the participants of City Employer Z whose deferred amounts are being transferred are not eligible to participate in the eligible governmental plan of County B, the receiving plan, unless they are performing services for County B.

*Example (5).* (i) Facts. State C has an eligible governmental plan. Employees of City U in State C are among the eligible employees for State C's plan and City U decides to adopt another eligible governmental plan only for its employees. State C decides to allow employees to elect to transfer all of the amounts deferred for an employee under State C's eligible governmental plan to City U's eligible governmental plan.

(ii) Conclusion. If State C's (transferor) eligible governmental plan provides for such transfer and the eligible governmental plan of City U permits the acceptance of such a transfer (and the other requirements of paragraph (b)(1) of this section are satisfied), then the requirements of paragraph (b)(4) of this section are satisfied and, thus, State C may transfer the total amounts deferred under its eligible governmental plan to the eligible governmental plan maintained by City U.

*(8) Purchase of permissive service credit by plan-to-plan transfers from an eligible governmental plan to a qualified plan.* (i) General rule. An eligible governmental plan of a State may provide for the transfer of amounts deferred by a participant or beneficiary to a defined benefit governmental

plan (as defined in section 414(d)), and no amount shall be includible in gross income by reason of the transfer, if the conditions in paragraph (b)(8)(ii) of this section are met. A transfer under this paragraph (b)(8) is not treated as a distribution for purposes of § 1.457-6. Therefore, such a transfer may be made before severance from employment.

(ii) Conditions for plan-to-plan transfers from an eligible governmental plan to a qualified plan. A transfer may be made under this paragraph (b)(8) only if the transfer is either--

(A) For the purchase of permissive service credit (as defined in section 415(n)(3)(A)) under the receiving defined benefit governmental plan; or

(B) A repayment to which section 415 does not apply by reason of section 415(k)(3).

(iii) Example. The provisions of this paragraph (b)(8) are illustrated by the following example:

*Example.* (i) Facts. Plan X is an eligible governmental plan maintained by County Y for its employees. Plan X provides for distributions only in the event of death, an unforeseeable emergency, or severance from employment with County Y (including retirement from County Y). Plan S is a qualified defined benefit plan maintained by State T for its employees. County Y is within State T. Employee A is an employee of County Y and is a participant in Plan X. Employee A previously was an employee of State T and is still entitled to benefits under Plan S. Plan S includes provisions allowing participants in certain plans, including Plan X, to transfer assets to Plan S for the purchase of service credit under Plan S and does not permit the amount transferred to exceed the amount necessary to fund the benefit resulting from the service credit. Although not required to do so, Plan X allows Employee A to transfer assets to Plan S to provide a service benefit under Plan S.

(ii) Conclusion. The transfer is permitted under this paragraph (b)(8).

**(c) Qualified domestic relations orders under eligible plans.** *(1) General rule.* An eligible plan does not become an ineligible plan described in section 457(f) solely because its administrator or sponsor complies with a qualified domestic relations order as defined in section 414(p), including an order requiring the distribution of the benefits of a participant to an alternate payee in advance of the general rules for eligible plan distributions under § 1.457-6. If a distribution or payment is made from an eligible plan to an alternate payee pursuant to a qualified domestic relations order, rules similar to the rules of section 402(e)(1)(A) shall apply to the distribution or payment.

*(2) Examples.* The provisions of this paragraph (c) are illustrated by the following examples:

*Example (1).* (i) Facts. Participant C and C's spouse D are divorcing. C is employed by State S and is a participant in an eligible plan maintained by State S. C has an account valued at $100,000 under the plan. Pursuant to the divorce, a court issues a qualified domestic relations order on September 1, 2003 that allocates 50 percent of C's $100,000 plan account to D and specifically provides for an immediate distribution to D of D's share within 6 months of the order. Payment is made to D in January of 2004.

(ii) Conclusion. State S's eligible plan does not become an ineligible plan described in section 457(f) and § 1.457-11 solely because its administrator or sponsor complies with the qualified domestic relations order requiring the immediate distribution to D in advance of the general rules for eligible plan distributions under § 1.457-6. In accordance with section 402(e)(1)(A), D (not C) must include the distribution in gross income. The distribution is includible in D's gross income in 2004. If the qualified domestic relations order were to provide for distribution to D at a future date, amounts deferred attributable to D's share will be includible in D's gross income when paid to D.

*Example (2).* (i) Facts. The facts are the same as in Example 1, except that S is a tax-exempt entity, instead of a State.

(ii) Conclusion. State S's eligible plan does not become an ineligible plan described in section 457(f) and § 1.457-11 solely because its administrator or sponsor complies with the qualified domestic relations order requiring the immediate distribution to D in advance of the general rules for eligible plan distributions under § 1.457-6. In accordance with section 402(e)(1)(A), D (not C) must include the distribution in gross income. The distribution is includible in D's gross income in 2004, assuming that the plan did not make the distribution available to D in 2003. If the qualified domestic relations order were to provide for distribution to D at a future date, amounts deferred attributable to D's share would be includible in D's gross income when paid or made available to D.

**(d) Death benefits and life insurance proceeds.** A death benefit plan under section 457(e)(11) is not an eligible plan. In addition, no amount paid or made available under an eligible plan as death benefits or life insurance proceeds is excludable from gross income under section 101.

**(e) Rollovers to eligible governmental plans.** *(1) General rule.* An eligible governmental plan may accept contributions that are eligible rollover distributions (as defined in section 402(c)(4)) made from another eligible retirement plan (as defined in section 402(c)(8)(B)) if the conditions in paragraph (e)(2) of this section are met. Amounts contributed to an eligible governmental plan as eligible rollover distributions are not taken into account for purposes of the annual limit on annual deferrals by a participant in § 1.457-4(c) or § 1.457-5, but are otherwise treated in the same manner as amounts deferred under section 457 for purposes of Sec. § 1.457-3 through 1.457-9 and this section.

*(2) Conditions for rollovers to an eligible governmental plan.* An eligible governmental plan that permits eligible rollover distributions made from another eligible retirement plan to be paid into the eligible governmental plan is required under this paragraph (e)(2) to provide that it will separately account for any eligible rollover distributions it receives. A plan does not fail to satisfy this requirement if it separately accounts for particular types of eligible rollover distributions (for example, if it maintains a separate account for eligible rollover distributions attributable to annual deferrals that were made under other eligible governmental plans and a separate account for amounts attributable to other eligible rollover distributions), but this requirement is not satisfied if any such separate account includes any amount that is not attributable to an eligible rollover distribution.

*(3) Example.* The provisions of this paragraph (e) are illustrated by the following example:

*Example.* (i) Facts. Plan T is an eligible governmental plan that provides that employees who are eligible to participate in Plan T may make rollover contributions to Plan T from amounts distributed to an employee from an eligible retirement plan. An eligible retirement plan is defined in Plan T as another eligible governmental plan, a qualified section 401(a) or 403(a) plan, or a section 403(b) contract, or an individual retirement arrangement (IRA) that holds such amounts. Plan T requires rollover contributions to be paid by the eligible retirement plan directly to Plan T (a direct rollover) or to be paid by the participant within 60 days after the date on which the participant received the amount from the other eligible retirement plan. Plan T does not take rollover contributions into account for purposes of the plan's limits on amounts deferred that conform to § 1.457-4(c). Rollover contributions paid to Plan T are invested in the trust in the same manner as amounts deferred under Plan T and rollover contributions (and earnings thereon) are available for distribution to the participant at the same time and in the same manner as amounts deferred under Plan T. In addition, Plan T provides that, for each participant who makes a rollover contribution to Plan T, the Plan T record-keeper is to establish a separate account for the participant's rollover contributions. The record-keeper calculates earnings and losses for investments held in the rollover account separately from earnings and losses on other amounts held under the plan and calculates disbursements from and payments made to the rollover account separately from disbursements from and payments made to other amounts held under the plan.

(ii) Conclusion. Plan T does not lose its status as an eligible governmental plan as a result of the receipt of rollover contributions. The conclusion would not be different if the Plan T record-keeper were to establish two separate accounts, one of which is for the participant's rollover contributions attributable to annual deferrals that were made under an eligible governmental plan and the other of which is for other rollover contributions.

**(f) Deemed IRAs under eligible governmental plans.** See regulations under section 408(q) for guidance regarding the treatment of separate accounts or annuities as individual retirement plans (IRAs).

T.D. 9075, 7/10/2003, amend T.D. 9319, 4/4/2007.

### § 1.457-11 Tax treatment of participants if plan is not an eligible plan.

**(a) In general.** Under section 457(f), if an eligible employer provides for a deferral of compensation under any agreement or arrangement that is an ineligible plan—

*(1)* Compensation deferred under the agreement or arrangement is includible in the gross income of the participant or beneficiary for the first taxable year in which there is no substantial risk of forfeiture (within the meaning of section 457(f)(3)(B)) of the rights to such compensation;

*(2)* If the compensation deferred is subject to a substantial risk of forfeiture, the amount includible in gross income for the first taxable year in which there is no substantial risk of forfeiture includes earnings thereon to the date on which there is no substantial risk of forfeiture;

*(3)* Earnings credited on the compensation deferred under the agreement or arrangement that are not includible in gross income under paragraph (a)(2) of this section are includible in the gross income of the participant or beneficiary only when paid or made available to the participant or beneficiary, provided that the interest of the participant or beneficiary in any assets (including amounts deferred under the plan) of the entity sponsoring the agreement or arrangement is not senior to the entity's general creditors; and

*(4)* Amounts paid or made available to a participant or beneficiary under the agreement or arrangement are includible in the gross income of the participant or beneficiary under section 72, relating to annuities.

**(b) Exceptions.** Paragraph (a) of this section does not apply with respect to—

*(1)* A plan described in section 401(a) which includes a trust exempt from tax under section 501(a);

*(2)* An annuity plan or contract described in section 403;

*(3)* That portion of any plan which consists of a transfer of property described in section 83;

*(4)* That portion of any plan which consists of a trust to which section 402(b) applies; or

*(5)* A qualified governmental excess benefit arrangement described in section 415(m).

**(c) Amount included in income.** The amount included in gross income on the applicable date under paragraphs (a)(1) and (a)(2) of this section is equal to the present value of the compensation (including earnings to the extent provided in paragraph (a)(2) of this section) on that date. For purposes of applying section 72 on the applicable date under paragraphs (a)(3) and (4) of this section, the participant is treated as having paid investment in the contract (or basis) to the extent that the deferred compensation has been taken into account by the participant in accordance with paragraphs (a)(1) and (a)(2) of this section.

**(d) Coordination of section 457(f) with section 83.** *(1) General rules.* Under paragraph (b)(3) of this section, section 457(f) and paragraph (a) of this section do not apply to that portion of any plan which consists of a transfer of property described in section 83. For this purpose, a transfer of property described in section 83 means a transfer of property to which section 83 applies. Section 457(f) and paragraph (a) of this section do not apply if the date on which there is no substantial risk of forfeiture with respect to compensation deferred under an agreement or arrangement that is not an eligible plan is on or after the date on which there is a transfer of property to which section 83 applies. However, section 457(f) and paragraph (a) of this section apply if the date on which there is no substantial risk of forfeiture with respect to compensation deferred under an agreement or arrangement that is not an eligible plan precedes the date on which there is a transfer of property to which section 83 applies. If deferred compensation payable in property is includible in gross income under section 457(f), then, as provided in section 72, the amount includible in gross income when that property is later transferred or made available to the service provider is the excess of the value of the property at that time over the amount previously included in gross income under section 457(f).

*(2) Examples.* The provisions of this paragraph (d) are illustrated in the following examples:

*Example (1).* (i) Facts. As part of an arrangement for the deferral of compensation, an eligible employer agrees on December 1, 2002 to pay an individual rendering services for the eligible employer a specified dollar amount on January 15, 2005. The arrangement provides for the payment to be made in the form of property having a fair market value equal to the specified dollar amount. The individual's rights to the payment are not subject to a substantial risk of forfeiture (within the meaning of section 457(f)(3)(B)).

(ii) Conclusion. In this Example 1, because there is no substantial risk of forfeiture with respect to the agreement to transfer property in 2005, the present value (as of December 1, 2002) of the payment is includible in the individual's gross income for 2002. Under paragraph (a)(4) of this section, when the payment is made on January 15, 2005, the amount includible in the individual's gross income is equal to the excess of the fair market value of the property when paid, over the amount that was includible in gross income for 2002 (which is the basis allocable to that payment).

*Example (2).* (i) Facts. As part of an arrangement for the deferral of compensation, individuals A and B rendering services for a tax-exempt entity each receive in 2010 property that is subject to a substantial risk of forfeiture (within the meaning of section 457(f)(3)(B) and within the meaning of section 83(c)(1)). Individual A makes an election to include the fair market value of the property in gross income under section 83(b) and individual B does not make this election. The substantial risk of forfeiture for the property transferred to individual A lapses in 2012 and the substantial risk of forfeiture for the property transferred to individual B also lapses in 2012. Thus, the property transferred to individual A is included in A's gross income for 2010 when A makes a section 83(b) election and the property transferred to individual B is included in B's gross income for 2012 when the substantial risk of forfeiture for the property lapses.

(ii) Conclusion. In this Example 2, in each case, the compensation deferred is not subject to section 457(f) or this section because section 83 applies to the transfer of property on or before the date on which there is no substantial risk of forfeiture with respect to compensation deferred under the arrangement.

*Example (3).* (i) Facts. In 2004, Z, a tax-exempt entity, grants an option to acquire property to employee C. The option lacks a readily ascertainable fair market value, within the meaning of section 83(e)(3), has a value on the date of grant equal to $100,000, and is not subject to a substantial risk of forfeiture (within the meaning of section 457(f)(3)(B) and within the meaning of section 83(c)(1)). Z exercises the option in 2012 by paying an exercise price of $75,000 and receives property that has a fair market value (for purposes of section 83) equal to $300,000.

(ii) Conclusion. In this Example 3, under section 83(e)(3), section 83 does not apply to the grant of the option. Accordingly, C has income of $100,000 in 2004 under section 457(f). In 2012, C has income of $125,000, which is the value of the property transferred in 2012, minus the allocable portion of the basis that results from the $100,000 of income in 2004 and the $75,000 exercise price.

*Example (4).* (i) Facts. In 2010, X, a tax-exempt entity, agrees to pay deferred compensation to employee D. The amount payable is $100,000 to be paid 10 years later in 2020. The commitment to make the $100,000 payment is not subject to a substantial risk of forfeiture. In 2010, the present value of the $100,000 is $50,000. In 2018, X transfers to D property having a fair market value (for purposes of section 83) equal to $70,000. The transfer is in partial settlement of the commitment made in 2010 and, at the time of the transfer in 2018, the present value of the commitment is $80,000. In 2020, X pays D the $12,500 that remains due.

(ii) Conclusion. In this Example 4, D has income of $50,000 in 2010. In 2018, D has income of $30,000, which is the amount transferred in 2018, minus the allocable portion of the basis that results from the $50,000 of income in 2010. (Under section 72(e)(2)(B), income is allocated first. The income is equal to $30,000 ($80,000 minus the $50,000 basis), with the result that the allocable portion of the basis is equal to $40,000 ($70,000 minus the $30,000 of income).) In 2020, D has income of $2,500 ($12,500 minus $10,000, which is the excess of the original $50,000 basis over the $40,000 basis allocated to the transfer made in 2018).

T.D. 9075, 7/10/2003.

### § 1.457-12 Effective dates.

**(a) General effective date.** Except as otherwise provided in this section, Sec. § 1.457-1 through 1.457-11 apply for taxable years beginning after December 31, 2001.

**(b) Transition period for eligible plans to comply with EGTRRA.** For taxable years beginning after December 31, 2001, and before January 1, 2004, a plan does not fail to be an eligible plan as a result of requirements imposed by the Economic Growth and Tax Relief Reconciliation Act of 2001 (115 Stat. 385) (EGTRRA) (Public Law 107-16) June 7, 2001, if it is operated in accordance with a reasonable, good faith interpretation of EGTRRA.

**(c) Special rule for distributions from rollover accounts.** The last sentence of § 1.457-6(a) (relating to distributions of amounts held in a separate account for eligible rollover distributions) applies for taxable years beginning after December 31, 2003.

**(d) Special rule for options.** Section 1.457-11(d) does not apply with respect to an option without a readily ascertainable fair market value (within the meaning of section 83(e)(3)) that was granted on or before May 8, 2002.

**(e) Special rule for qualified domestic relations orders.** Section 1.457-10(c) (relating to qualified domestic relations orders) applies for transfers, distributions, and payments made after December 31, 2001.

T.D. 9075, 7/10/2003.

### § 1.458-1 Exclusion for certain returned magazines, paperbacks, or records.

**(a) In general.** *(1) Introduction.* For taxable years beginning after September 30, 1979, section 458 allows accrual basis taxpayers to elect to use a method of accounting that excludes from gross income some or all of the income attributable to qualified sales during the taxable year of magazines, paperbacks, or records, that are returned before the close of the applicable merchandise return period for that taxable year. Any amount so excluded cannot be excluded or deducted from gross income for the taxable year in which the merchandise is returned to the taxpayer. For the taxable year in which the taxpayer first uses this method of accounting, the taxpayer is not allowed to exclude from gross income amounts attributable to merchandise returns received during the taxable year that would have been excluded from gross income for the prior taxable year had the taxpayer used this method of accounting for that prior year. (See paragraph (e) of this section for rules describing how this amount should be taken into account.) The election to use this method of accounting shall be made in accordance with the rules contained in section 458(c) and in § 1.458-2 and this section. A taxpayer that does not elect to use this method of accounting can reduce income for returned merchandise only for the taxable year in which the merchandise is actually returned unsold by the purchaser.

*(2) Effective date.* While this section is generally effective only for taxable years beginning after August 31, 1984, taxpayers may rely on the provisions of paragraphs (a) through (f) of this section in taxable years beginning after September 30, 1979.

**(b) Definitions.** *(1) Magazine.* "Magazine" means a publication, usually paper-backed and sometimes illustrated, that is issued at regular intervals and contains stories, poems, articles, features, etc. This term includes periodicals, but does not include newspapers or volumes of a single publication issued at various intervals. However, volumes of a single publication that are issued at least annually, are related by title or subject matter to a magazine, and would otherwise qualify as a magazine, will be treated as a magazine.

*(2) Paperback.* "Paperback" means a paperback book other than a magazine. Unlike a hardback book, which usually has stiff front and back covers that enclose pages bound to a separate spine, a paperback book is characterized by a flexible outer cover to which the pages of the book are directly affixed.

*(3) Record.* "Record" means a disc, tape, or similar item on which music, spoken or other sounds are recorded. However, the term does not include blank records, tapes, etc., on which it is expected the ultimate purchaser will record. The following items, provided they carry pre-recorded sound, are examples of "records": audio and video cassettes, eight-track tapes, reel-to-reel tapes, cylinders, and flat, compact, and laser discs.

*(4) Qualified sale.* In order for a sale to be considered a qualified sale, both of the following conditions must be met:

(i) The taxpayer must be under a legal obligation (as determined by applicable State law), at the time of sale, to adjust the sales price of the magazine, paperback, or record on account of the purchaser's failure to resell it; and

(ii) The taxpayer must actually adjust the sales price of the magazine, paperback, or record to reflect the purchaser's failure to resell the merchandise. The following are examples of adjustments to the sales price of unsold merchandise: Cash refunds, credits to the account of the purchaser, and repurchases of the merchandise. The adjustment need not be equal to the full amount of the sales price of the item. However, a markdown of the sales price under an agreement whereby the purchaser continues to hold the merchandise for sale or other disposition (other than solely for scrap) does not constitute an adjustment resulting from a failure to resell.

*(5) Merchandise return period.* (i) In general. Unless the taxpayer elects a shorter period, the "merchandise return period" is the period that ends 2 months and 15 days after the close of the taxable year for sales of magazines and 4 months and 15 days after the close of the taxable year for sales of paperbacks and records.

(ii) Election to use shorter period. The taxpayer may select a shorter merchandise return period than the applicable period set forth in paragraph (b)(5)(i) of this section.

(iii) Change in merchandise return period. Any change in the merchandise return period after its initial establishment will be treated as a change in method of accounting.

**(c) Amount of the exclusion.** *(1) In general.* Except as otherwise provided in paragraph (g) of this section, the amount of the gross income exclusion with respect to any qualified sale is equal to the lesser of—

(i) The amount covered by the legal obligation referred to in paragraph (b)(4)(i) of this section; or

(ii) The amount of the adjustment agreed to by the taxpayer before the close of the merchandise return period.

*(2) Price adjustment in excess of legal obligation.* The excess, if any, of the amount described in paragraph (c)(1)(ii) of this section over the amount described in paragraph (c)(1)(i) of this section should be excluded in the taxable year in which it is properly accruable under section 461.

**(d) Return of the merchandise.** *(1) In general.* (i) The exclusion from gross income allowed by section 458 applies with respect to a qualified sale of merchandise only if the seller receives, before the close of the merchandise return period, either—

(A) The physical return of the merchandise; or

(B) Satisfactory evidence that the merchandise has not been and will not be resold (as defined in paragraph (d)(2) of this section).

(ii) For purposes of this paragraph (d), evidence of a return received by an agent of the seller (other than the purchaser who purchased the merchandise from the seller) will be considered to be received by the seller at the time the agent receives the merchandise or evidence.

*(2) Satisfactory evidence.* Evidence that merchandise has not been and will not be resold is satisfactory only if the seller receives—

(i) Physical return of some portion of the merchandise (e.g., covers) provided under either the agreement between the seller and the purchaser or industry practice (such return evidencing the fact that the purchaser has not and will not resell the merchandise); or

(ii) A written statement from the purchaser specifying the quantities of each title not resold, provided either—

(A) The statement contains a representation that the items specified will not be resold by the purchaser; or

(B) The past dealings, if any, between the parties and industry practice indicate that such statement constitutes a promise by the purchaser not to resell the items.

*(3) Retention of evidence.* In the case of a return of merchandise (described in paragraph (d)(1)(i)(A) of this section) or portion thereof (described in paragraph (d)(2)(i) of this section), the seller has no obligation to retain physical evidence of the returned merchandise or portion thereof, provided the seller maintains documentary evidence that describes the quantity of physical items returned to the seller and indicates that the items were returned before the close of the merchandise return period.

**(e) Transitional adjustment.** *(1) In general.* An election to change from some other method of accounting for the return of magazines, paperbacks, or records to the method of accounting described in section 458 is a change in method of accounting that requires a transitional adjustment. Section 458 provides special rules for transitional adjustments that must be taken into account as a result of this change. See paragraph (e)(2) of this section for special rules applicable to magazines and paragraphs (e)(3) and (4) of this section for special rules applicable to paperbacks and records.

*(2) Magazines: 5-year spread of decrease in taxable income.* For taxpayers who have elected to use the method of accounting described in section 458 to account for returned magazines for a taxable year, section 458(d) and this paragraph (e)(2) provide a special rule for taking into account any decrease in taxable income resulting from the adjustment required by section 481(a)(2). Under these provisions, one-fifth of the transitional adjustment must be taken into account in the taxable year of the change and in each of the 4 succeeding taxable years. For example, if the application of section 481(a)(2) would produce a decrease in taxable income of $50 for 1980, the year of change, then $10 (one-fifth of $50) must be taken into account as a decrease in taxable income for 1980, 1981, 1982, 1983, and 1984.

*(3) Suspense account for paperbacks and records.* (i) In general. For taxpayers who have elected to use the method of accounting described in section 458 to account for returned paperbacks and records for a taxable year, section

458(e) provides that, in lieu of applying section 481, an electing taxpayer must establish a separate suspense account for its paperback business and its record business. The initial opening balance of the suspense account is described in paragraph (e)(3)(ii)(A) of this section. An initial adjustment to gross income for the year of election is described in paragraph (e)(3)(ii)(B) of this section. Annual adjustments to the suspense account are described in paragraph (e)(3)(iii)(A) of this section. Gross income adjustments are described in paragraph (e)(3)(iii)(B) of this section. Examples are provided in paragraph (e)(4) of this section. The effect of the suspense account is to defer all, or some part, of the deduction of the transitional adjustment until the taxpayer is no longer engaged in the trade or business of selling paperbacks or records, whichever is applicable.

(ii) Establishing a suspense account. (A) Initial opening balance. To compute the initial opening balance of the suspense account for the first taxable year for which an election is effective, the taxpayer must determine the section 458 amount (as defined in paragraph (e)(3)(ii)(C) of this section) for each of the three preceding taxable years. The initial opening balance of the account is the largest of the section 458 amounts.

(B) Initial year adjustment. If the initial opening balance in the suspense account exceeds the section 458 amount (as defined in paragraph (e)(3)(ii)(C) of this section) for the taxable year immediately preceding the year of election, the excess is included in the taxpayer's gross income for the first taxable year for which the election was made.

(C) Section 458 amount. For purposes of paragraph (e)(3)(ii) of this section, the section 458 amount for a taxable year is the dollar amount of merchandise returns that would have been excluded from gross income under section 458(a) for that taxable year if the section 458 election had been in effect for that taxable year.

(iii) Annual adjustments. (A) Adjustment to the suspense account. Adjustments are made to the suspense account each year to account for fluctuations in merchandise returns. To compute the annual adjustment, the taxpayer must determine the amount to be excluded under the election from gross income under section 458(a) for the taxable year. If the amount is less than the opening balance in the suspense account for the taxable year, the balance in the suspense account is reduced by the difference. Conversely, if the amount is greater than the opening balance in the suspense account for the taxable year, the account is increased by the difference, but not to an amount in excess of the initial opening balance described in paragraph (e)(3)(ii)(A) of this section. Therefore, the balance in the suspense account will never be greater than the initial opening balance in the suspense account determined in paragraph (e)(3)(ii)(A) of this section. However, the balance in the suspense account after adjustments may be less than this initial opening balance in the suspense account.

(B) Gross income adjustments. Adjustments to the suspense account for years subsequent to the year of election also produce adjustments in the taxpayer's gross income. Adjustments which reduce the balance in the suspense account reduce gross income for the year in which the adjustment to the suspense account is made. Adjustments which increase the balance in the suspense account increase gross income for the year in which the adjustment to the suspense account is made.

*(4) Example.* The provisions of paragraph (e)(3) of this section may be illustrated by the following example:

*Example.* (i) X corporation, a paperback distributor, makes a timely section 458 election for its taxable year ending December 31, 1980. If the election had been in effect for the taxable years ending on December 31, 1977, 1978, and 1979, the dollar amounts of the qualifying returns would have been $5, $8, and $6, respectively. The initial opening balance of X's suspense account on January 1, 1980, is $8, the largest of these amounts. Since the initial opening balance ($8), is larger than the qualifying returns for 1979 ($6), the initial adjustment to gross income for 1980 is $2 ($8 – $6).

(ii) X has $5 in qualifying returns for its taxable year ending December 31, 1980. X must reduce its suspense account by $3, which is the excess of the opening balance ($8) over the amount of qualifying returns for the 1980 taxable year ($5). X also reduces its gross income for 1980 by $3. Thus, the net amount excludable from gross income for the 1980 taxable year after taking into account the qualifying returns, the gross income adjustment, and the initial year adjustment is $6 ($3 + $5 – $2).

(iii) X has qualifying returns of $7 for its taxable year ending December 31, 1981. X must increase its suspense account balance by $2, which is the excess of the amount of qualifying returns for 1981 ($7) over X's opening balance in the suspense account ($5). X must also increase its gross income by $2. Thus, the net income excludable from gross income for the 1981 taxable year after taking into account the qualifying returns and the gross income adjustment is $5 ($7 – $2).

(iv) X has qualifying returns of $10 for its taxable year ending December 31, 1982. The opening balance in X's suspense account of $7 will not be increased in excess of the initial opening balance ($8). X must also increase gross income by $1. Thus, the net amount excludable from gross income for the 1982 taxable year is $9 ($10 – $1).

(v) This example is summarized by the following table:

| | Years Ending December 31 | | | | | |
|---|---|---|---|---|---|---|
| | 1977 | 1978 | 1979 | 1980[1] | 1981 | 1982 |
| Facts: | | | | | | |
| Qualifying returns during merchandise return period for the taxable year | $5 | $8 | $6 | $ 5 | $7 | $10 |
| Adjustment to suspense account: | | | | | | |
| Opening balance | ... | ... | .... | $ 8 | $5 | $ 7 |
| Addition to account[2] | ... | ... | .... | ....... | 2 | 1 |
| Reduction to account[3] | ... | ... | ... | (3) | ... | ... |
| Opening balance for next year | ... | ... | ... | $ 5 | $7 | $ 8 |
| Amount excludable from income: | | | | | | |
| Initial year adjustment | ... | ... | .... | $ (2) | ... | ... |
| Amount excludable as qualifying returns in merchandise return period | ... | ... | .... | 5 | $7 | $10 |

| | | | | | | |
|---|---|---|---|---|---|---|
| Adjustment for increase in suspense account | .... | ... | .... | ....... | ([2]) | ([1]) |
| Adjustment for decrease in suspense account | ... | ... | ... | 3 | .... | ... |
| Net amount excludable for the year | .... | ... | .... | $ 6 | $5 | $ 9 |

[1] Year of Change.

[2] Applies when qualifying returns during the merchandise return period exceed the opening balance; the addition is not to cause the suspense account to exceed the initial opening balance.

[3] Applies when qualifying returns during the merchandise return period are less than the opening balance.

**(f) Subchapter C transactions.** *(1) General rule.* If a transfer of substantially all the assets of a trade or business in which paperbacks or records are sold is made to an acquiring corporation, and if the acquiring corporation determines its basis in these assets, in whole or part, with reference to the basis of these assets in the hands of the transferor, then for the purposes of section 458(e) the principles of section 381 and § 1.381(c)(4)-1 will apply. The application of this rule is not limited to the transactions described in section 381(a). Thus, the rule also applies, for example, to transactions described in section 351.

*(2) Special rules.* If, in the case of a transaction described in paragraph (f)(1) of this section, an acquiring corporation acquires assets that were used in a trade or business that was not subject to a section 458 election from a transferor that is owned or controlled directly (or indirectly through a chain of corporations) by the same interests, and if the acquiring corporation uses the acquired assets in a trade or business for which the acquiring corporation later makes an election to use section 458, then the acquiring corporation must establish a suspense account by taking into account not only its own experience but also the transferor's experience when the transferor held the assets in its trade or business. Furthermore, the transferor is not allowed a deduction or exclusion for merchandise returned after the date of the transfer attributable to sales made by the transferor before the date of the transfer. Such returns shall be considered to be received by the acquiring corporation.

*(3) Example.* The provisions of paragraph (f)(2) of this section may be illustrated by the following example.

*Example.* Corporation S, a calendar year taxpayer, is a wholly owned subsidiary of Corporation P, a calendar year taxpayer. On December 31, 1982, S acquires from P substantially all of the assets used in a trade or business in which records are sold. P had not made an election under section 458 with respect to the qualified sale of records made in connection with that trade or business. S makes an election to use section 458 for its taxable year ending December 31, 1983, for the trade or business in which the acquired assets are used. P's qualified record returns within the 4 month and 15 day merchandise return period following the 1980 and 1981 taxable years were $150 and $170, respectively. S's qualified record returns during the merchandise return period following 1982 were $160. S must establish a suspense account by taking into account both P's and S's experience for the 3 immediately preceding taxable years. Thus, the initial opening balance of S's suspense account is $170. S must also make an initial year adjustment of $10 ($170 − $160), which S must include in income for S's taxable year ending December 31, 1983. P is not entitled to a deduction or exclusion for merchandise received after the date of the transfer (December 31, 1982) attributable to sales made by the transferor before the date of transfer. Thus, P is not entitled to a deduction or exclusion for the $160 of merchandise received by S during the first 4 months and 15 days of 1983.

**(g) Adjustment to inventory and cost of goods sold.** *(1)* If a taxpayer makes adjustments to gross receipts for a taxable year under the method of accounting described in section 458, the taxpayer, in determining excludable gross income, is also required to make appropriate correlative adjustments to purchases or closing inventory and to cost of goods sold for the same taxable year. Adjustments are appropriate, for example, where the taxpayer holds the merchandise returned for resale or where the taxpayer is entitled to receive a price adjustment from the person or entity that sold the merchandise to the taxpayer. Cost of goods sold must be properly adjusted in accordance with the provisions of § 1.61-3 which provides, in pertinent part, that gross income derived from a manufacturing or merchandising business equals total sales less cost of goods sold.

*(2)* The provisions of this paragraph (g) may be illustrated by the following examples. These examples do not, however, reflect any required adjustments under paragraph (e)(3) of this section.

*Example (1).* (i) In 1986, P, a publisher, properly elects under section 458 of the Code not to include in its gross income in the year of sale, income attributable to qualified sales of paperback books returned within the specified statutory merchandise return period of 4 months and 15 days. P and D, a distributor, agree that P shall provide D with a full refund for paperback books that D purchases from P and is unable to resell, provided the merchandise is returned to P within four months following the original sale. The agreement constitutes a legal obligation. The agreement provides that D's return of the covers of paperback books within the first four months following their sale constitutes satisfactory evidence that D has not resold and will not resell the paperback books. During P's 1989 taxable year, pursuant to the agreement, P sells D 500 paperback books for $1 each. In 1990, during the merchandise return period, D returns covers from 100 unsold paperback books representing $100 of P's 1989 sales of paperback books. P's cost attributable to the returned books is $25. No adjustment to cost of goods sold is required under paragraph (g)(1) of this section because P is not holding returned merchandise for resale. P's proper amount excluded from its 1989 gross income under section 458 is $100.

(ii) If D returns the paperback books, rather than the covers, to P and these same books are then held by P for resale to other customers, paragraph (g)(1) of this section applies. Under paragraph (g)(1), P is required to decrease its cost of goods sold by $25, the amount of P's cost attributable to the returned merchandise. The proper amount excluded from P's 1989 gross income under section 458 is $75, resulting from adjustments to sales and cost of sales [(100 × $1) − $25].

*Example (2).* (i) In 1986, D a distributor, properly elects under section 458 of the Code not to include in its gross income in the year of sale, income attributable to qualified sales of paperback books returned within the specified statutory merchandise return period of four months and 15 days. D and R, a retailer, agree that D shall provide a full refund for paperback books that R purchases from it and is unable to resell. D and R also have agreed that the merchandise must be returned to D within four months following the original sale. The agreement constitutes a legal obligation. D is similarly entitled to a full refund from P, the publisher, for the same paperback books. In 1990, during the merchandise return period, R returns paperback books to D representing $100 of 1989 sales. D's cost relating to these sales is $50. Under paragraph (g)(1) of this section, D must decrease its costs of goods sold by $50. D's proper amount excluded from its 1989 gross income under section 458 is $50 resulting from adjustments to sales and costs of sales ($100 – $50).

(ii) If D is instead only entitled to a 50 percent refund from P, D is required under paragraph (g)(1) of this section to decrease its costs of goods sold by $25, the amount of refund from P. D's proper amount excluded from its 1989 gross income under section 458 is $75, resulting from adjustments to sales and cost of sales ($100 – $25).

T.D. 8426, 8/25/92.

### § 1.458-2 Manner of and time for making election.

**(a) Scope.** For taxable years beginning after September 30, 1979, section 458 provides a special method of accounting for taxpayers who account for sales of magazines, paperbacks, or records using an accrual method of accounting. In order to use the special method of accounting under section 458, a taxpayer must make an election in the manner prescribed in this section. The election does not require the prior consent of the Internal Revenue Service. The election is effective for the taxable year for which it is made and for all subsequent taxable years, unless the taxpayer secures the prior consent of the Internal Revenue Service to revoke such election.

**(b) Separate election for each trade or business.** An election is made with respect to each trade or business of a taxpayer in connection with which qualified sales (as defined in section 458(b)(5)) of a category of merchandise were made. Magazines, paperbacks, and records are each treated as a separate category of merchandise. If qualified sales of two or more categories of merchandise are made in connection with the same trade or business, then solely for purposes of section 458, each category is treated as a separate trade or business. For example, if a taxpayer makes qualified sales of both magazines and paperbacks in the same trade or business, then solely for purposes of section 458, the qualified sales relating to magazines are considered one trade or business and the qualified sales relating to paperbacks are considered a separate trade or business. Thus, if the taxpayer wishes to account under section 458 for the qualified sales of both magazines and paperbacks, such taxpayer must make a separate election for each category.

**(c) Manner of, and time for, making election.** An election is made under section 458 and this section by filing a statement of election containing the information described in paragraph (d) of this section with the taxpayer's income tax return for first taxable year for which the election is made. The election must be made no later than the time prescribed by law (including extensions) for filing the income tax return for the first taxable year for which the election is made. Thus, the election may not be filed with an amended income tax return after the prescribed date (including extensions) for filing the original return for such year.

**(d) Required information.** The statement of election required by paragraph (c) of this section must indicate that an election is being made under section 458(c) and must set forth the following information:

*(1)* The taxpayer's name, address, and identification number;

*(2)* A description of each trade or business for which an election is made;

*(3)* The first taxable year for which an election is made for each trade or business;

*(4)* The merchandise return period (as defined in section 458(b)(7)) for each trade or business for which an election is made;

*(5)* With respect to an election that applies to magazines, the amount of the adjustment computed under section 481(a) resulting from the change to the method of accounting described in section 458; and

*(6)* With respect to an election that applies to paperbacks or records, the initial opening balance (computed in accordance with section 458(e)) in the suspense account for each trade or business for which an election is made.

The statement of election should be made on a Form 3115 which need contain no information other than that required by this paragraph.

T.D. 7628, 6/8/79, amend T.D. 8426, 8/25/92.

### § 1.460-0 Outline of regulations under section 460.

This section lists the paragraphs contained in § 1.460-1 through § 1.460-6.

*§ 1.460-1 Long-term contracts*

(a) Overview.

(1) In general.

(2) Exceptions to required use of PCM.

(i) Exempt construction contract.

(ii) Qualified ship or residential construction contract.

(b) Terms.

(1) Long-term contract.

(2) Contract for the manufacture, building, installation, or construction of property.

(i) In general.

(ii) De minimis construction activities.

(3) Allocable contract costs.

(4) Related party.

(5) Contracting year.

(6) Completion year.

(7) Contract commencement date.

(8) Incurred..

(9) Independent research and development expenses.

(10) Long-term contract methods of accounting.

(c) Entering into and completing long-term contracts.

(1) In general.

(2) Date contract entered into.

(i) In general.

(ii) Options and change orders.

(3) Date contract completed.

(i) In general.

(ii) Secondary items.

(iii) Subcontracts.

(iv) Final completion and acceptance.

(4) Alternative minimum tax.
(5) Effective date.
(c) Operation of the look-back method.
(1) Overview.
(i) In general.
(ii) Post-completion revenue and expenses.
(A) In general.
(B) Completion.
(C) Discounting of contract price and contract cost adjustments subsequent to completion; election not to discount.
(1) General rule.
(2) Election not to discount.
(3) Year-end discounting convention.
(D) Revenue acceleration rule.
(2) Look-back Step One.
(i) Hypothetical reallocation of income among prior tax years.
(ii) Treatment of estimated future costs in year of completion.
(iii) Interim reestimates not considered.
(iv) Tax years in which income is affected.
(v) Costs incurred prior to contract execution; 10-percent method.
(A) General rule.
(B) Example.
(vi) Amount treated as contract price.
(A) General rule.
(B) Contingencies.
(C) Change orders.
(3) Look-back Step Two: Computation of hypothetical overpayment or underpayment of tax.
(i) In general.
(ii) Redetermination of tax liability.
(iii) Hypothetical underpayment or overpayment.
(iv) Cumulative determination of tax liability.
(v) Years affected by look-back only.
(vi) Definition of tax liability.
(4) Look-back Step Three: Calculation of interest on underpayment or overpayment.
(i) In general.
(ii) Changes in the amount of a loss or credit carryback or carryover.
(iii) Changes in the amount of tax liability that generated a subsequent refund.
(iv) Additional interest due on interest only after tax liability due.
(d) Simplified marginal impact method.
(1) Introduction.
(2) Operation.
(i) In general.
(ii) Applicable tax rate.
(iii) Overpayment ceiling.
(iv) Example.
(3) Anti-abuse rule.
(4) Application.
(i) Required use by certain pass-through entities.
(A) General rule.
(B) Closely held.
(C) Examples.
(D) Domestic contracts.
(1) General rule.
(2) Portion of contract income sourced.
(E) Application to foreign contracts.
(F) Effective date.
(ii) Elective use.
(A) General rule.
(B) Election requirements.
(C) Consolidated group consistency rule.
(e) Delayed reapplication method.
(1) In general.
(2) Time and manner of making election.
(3) Examples.
(f) Look-back reporting.
(1) Procedure.
(2) Treatment of interest on return.
(i) General rule.
(ii) Timing of look-back interest.
(3) Statutes of limitations and compounding of interest on look-back interest.
(g) Mid-contract change in taxpayer.
(1) In general.
(2) Constructive completion transactions.
(3) Step-in-the-shoes transactions.
(i) General rules.
(ii) Application of look-back method to pre-transaction period.
(A) Contract Price.
(B) Method.
(C) Interest accrual period.
(D) Information old taxpayer must provide.
(1) In general.
(2) Special rules for certain pass-through entity transactions.
(iii) Application of look-back method to post-transaction years.
(iv) S corporation elections.
(4) Effective date.
(h) Examples.
(1) Overview.
(2) Step One.
(3) Step Two.
(4) Post-completion adjustments.
(5) Alternative minimum tax.
(6) Credit carryovers.
(7) Net operating losses.
(8) Alternative minimum tax credit.
(9) Period for interest.
(i) [Reserved]
(j) Election not to apply look-back method in de minimis cases.

*§ 1.460-7 Exempt long-term contracts. [Reserved]*

*§ 1.460-8 Changes in method of accounting. [Reserved]*

T.D. 8315, 10/12/90, amend T.D. 8597, 7/12/95, T.D. 8756, 1/12/98, T.D. 8775, 7/1/98, T.D. 8929, 1/10/2001, T.D. 8995, 5/14/2002, T.D. 9137, 7/15/2004.

**§ 1.460-1 Long-term contracts.**

***Caution:*** The Treasury has not yet amended Reg § 1.460-1 to reflect changes made by P.L. 108-357.

**(a) Overview.** *(1) In general.* This section provides rules for determining whether a contract for the manufacture, building, installation, or construction of property is a long-term contract under section 460 and what activities must be accounted for as a single long-term contract. Specific rules for long-term manufacturing and construction contracts are provided in § 2.460-2 and 1.460-3, respectively. A taxpayer generally must determine the income from a long-term contract using the percentage-of-completion method described in § 1.460-4(b) (PCM) and the cost allocation rules described in § 1.460-5(b) or (c). In addition, after a contract subject to the PCM is completed, a taxpayer generally must apply the look-back method described in § 1.460-6 to determine the amount of interest owed on any hypothetical underpayment of tax, or earned on any hypothetical overpayment of tax, attributable to accounting for the long-term contract under the PCM.

*(2) Exceptions to required use of PCM.*

(i) Exempt construction contract. The requirement to use the PCM does not apply to any exempt construction contract described in § 1.460-3(b). Thus, a taxpayer may determine the income from an exempt construction contract using any accounting method permitted by § 1.460-4(c) and, for contracts accounted for using the completed-contract method (CCM), any cost allocation method permitted by § 1.460-5(d). Exempt construction contracts that are not subject to the PCM or CCM are not subject to the cost allocation rules of § 1.460-5 except for the production-period interest rules of § 1.460-5(b)(2)(v). Exempt construction contractors that are large homebuilders described in § 1.460-5(d)(3) must capitalize costs under section 263A. All other exempt construction contractors must account for the cost of construction using the appropriate rules contained in other sections of the Internal Revenue Code or regulations.

(ii) Qualified ship or residential construction contract. The requirement to use the PCM applies only to a portion of a qualified ship contract described in § 1.460-2(d) or residential construction contract described in § 1.460-3(c). A taxpayer generally may determine the income from a qualified ship contract or residential construction contract using the percentage-of-completion/capitalized-cost method (PCCM) described in § 1.460-4(e), but must use a cost allocation method described in § 1.460-5(b) for the entire contract.

**(b) Terms.** *(1) Long-term contract.* A long-term contract generally is any contract for the manufacture, building, installation, or construction of property if the contract is not completed within the contracting year, as defined in paragraph (b)(5) of this section. However, a contract for the manufacture of property is a long-term contract only if it also satisfies either the unique item or 12-month requirements described in § 1.460-2. A contract for the manufacture of personal property is a manufacturing contract. In contrast, a contract for the building, installation, or construction of real property is a construction contract.

*(2) Contract for the manufacture, building, installation, or construction of property.* (i) In general. A contract is a contract for the manufacture, building, installation, or construction of property if the manufacture, building, installation, or construction of property is necessary for the taxpayer's contractual obligations to be fulfilled and if the manufacture, building, installation, or construction of that property has not been completed when the parties enter into the contract. If a taxpayer has to manufacture or construct an item to fulfill its obligations under the contract, the fact that the taxpayer is not required to deliver that item to the customer is not relevant. Whether the customer has title to, control over, or bears the risk of loss from, the property manufactured or constructed by the taxpayer also is not relevant. Furthermore, how the parties characterize their agreement (e.g., as a contract for the sale of property) is not relevant.

(ii) De minimis construction activities. Notwithstanding paragraph (b)(2)(i) of this section, a contract is not a construction contract under section 460 if the contract includes the provision of land by the taxpayer and the estimated total allocable contract costs, as defined in paragraph (b)(3) of this section, attributable to the taxpayer's construction activities are less than 10 percent of the contract's total contract price, as defined in § 1.460-4(b)(4)(i). For the purposes of this paragraph (b)(2)(ii), the allocable contract costs attributable to the taxpayer's construction activities do not include the cost of the land provided to the customer. In addition, a contract's estimated total allocable contract costs include a proportionate share of the estimated cost of any common improvement that benefits the subject matter of the contract if the taxpayer is contractually obligated, or required by law, to construct the common improvement.

*(3) Allocable contract costs.* Allocable contract costs are costs that are allocable to a long-term contract under § 1.460-5.

*(4) Related party.* A related party is a person whose relationship to a taxpayer is described in section 707(b) or 267(b), determined without regard to section 267(f)(1)(A) and determined by replacing "at least 80 percent" with "more than 50 percent" for the purposes of determining the ownership of the stock of a corporation in sections 267(b)(2), (8), (10)(A), and (12).

*(5) Contracting year.* The contracting year is the taxable year in which a taxpayer enters into a contract as described in paragraph (c)(2) of this section.

*(6) Completion year.* The completion year is the taxable year in which a taxpayer completes a contract as described in paragraph (c)(3) of this section.

*(7) Contract commencement date.* The contract commencement date is the date that a taxpayer or related party first incurs any allocable contract costs, such as design and engineering costs, other than expenses attributable to bidding and negotiating activities. Generally, the contract commencement date is relevant in applying § 1.460-6(b)(3) (concerning the de minimis exception to the look-back method under section 460(b)(3)(B)); § 1.460-5(b)(2)(v)(B)(1)(i) (concerning the production period subject to interest allocation); § 1.460-2(d) (concerning qualified ship contracts); and § 1.460-3(b)(1)(ii) (concerning the construction period for exempt construction contracts).

*(8) Incurred.* Incurred has the meaning given in § 1.461-1(a)(2) (concerning the taxable year a liability is incurred under the accrual method of accounting), regardless of a taxpayer's overall method of accounting. See § 1.461-4(d)(2)(ii) for economic performance rules concerning the PCM.

*(9) Independent research and development expenses.* Independent research and development expenses are any ex-

penses incurred in the performance of research or development, except that this term does not include any expenses that are directly attributable to a particular long-term contract in existence when the expenses are incurred and this term does not include any expenses under an agreement to perform research or development.

*(10) Long-term contract methods of accounting.* Long-term contract methods of accounting, which include the PCM, the CCM, the PCCM, and the exempt-contract percentage-of-completion method (EPCM), are methods of accounting that may be used only for long-term contracts.

**(c) Entering into and completing long-term contracts.** *(1) In general.* To determine when a contract is entered into under paragraph (c)(2) of this section and completed under paragraph (c)(3) of this section, a taxpayer must consider all relevant allocable contract costs incurred and activities performed by itself, by related parties on its behalf, and by the customer, that are incident to or necessary for the long-term contract. In addition, to determine whether a contract is completed in the contracting year, the taxpayer may not consider when it expects to complete the contract.

*(2) Date contract entered into.* (i) In general. A taxpayer enters into a contract on the date that the contract binds both the taxpayer and the customer under applicable law, even if the contract is subject to unsatisfied conditions not within the taxpayer's control (such as obtaining financing). If a taxpayer delays entering into a contract for a principal purpose of avoiding section 460, however, the taxpayer will be treated as having entered into a contract not later than the contract commencement date.

(ii) Options and change orders. A taxpayer enters into a new contract on the date that the customer exercises an option or similar provision in a contract if that option or similar provision must be severed from the contract under paragraph (e) of this section. Similarly, a taxpayer enters into a new contract on the date that it accepts a change order or other similar agreement if the change order or other similar agreement must be severed from the contract under paragraph (e) of this section.

*(3) Date contract completed.* (i) In general. A taxpayer's contract is completed upon the earlier of—

(A) Use of the subject matter of the contract by the customer for its intended purpose (other than for testing) and at least 95 percent of the total allocable contract costs attributable to the subject matter have been incurred by the taxpayer; or

(B) Final completion and acceptance of the subject matter of the contract.

(ii) Secondary items. The date a contract accounted for using the CCM is completed is determined without regard to whether one or more secondary items have been used or finally completed and accepted. If any secondary items are incomplete at the end of the taxable year in which the primary subject matter of a contract is completed, the taxpayer must separate the portion of the gross contract price and the allocable contract costs attributable to the incomplete secondary item(s) from the completed contract and account for them using a permissible method of accounting. A permissible method of accounting includes a long-term contract method of accounting only if a separate contract for the secondary item(s) would be a long-term contract, as defined in paragraph (b)(1) of this section.

(iii) Subcontracts. In the case of a subcontract, a subcontractor's customer is the general contractor. Thus, the subject matter of the subcontract is the relevant subject matter under paragraph (c)(3)(i) of this section.

(iv) Final completion and acceptance— (A) In general. Except as otherwise provided in this paragraph (c)(3)(iv), to determine whether final completion and acceptance of the subject matter of a contract have occurred, a taxpayer must consider all relevant facts and circumstances. Nevertheless, a taxpayer may not delay the completion of a contract for the principal purpose of deferring federal income tax.

(B) Contingent compensation. Final completion and acceptance is determined without regard to any contractual term that provides for additional compensation that is contingent on the successful performance of the subject matter of the contract. A taxpayer must account for all contingent compensation that is not includible in total contract price under § 1.460-4(b)(4)(i), or in gross contract price under § 1.460-4(d)(3), using a permissible method of accounting. For application of the look-back method for contracts accounted for using the PCM, see §§ 1.460-6(c)(1)(ii) and (2)(vi).

(C) Assembly or installation. Final completion and acceptance is determined without regard to whether the taxpayer has an obligation to assist or supervise assembly or installation of the subject matter of the contract where the assembly or installation is not performed by the taxpayer or a related party. A taxpayer must account for the gross receipts and costs attributable to such an obligation using a permissible method of accounting, other than a long-term contract method.

(D) Disputes. Final completion and acceptance is determined without regard to whether a dispute exists at the time the taxpayer tenders the subject matter of the contract to the customer. For contracts accounted for using the CCM, see § 1.460-4(d)(4). For application of the look-back method for contracts accounted for using the PCM, see § 1.460-6(c)(1)(ii) and (2)(vi).

**(d) Allocation among activities.** *(1) In general.* Long-term contract methods of accounting apply only to the gross receipts and costs attributable to long-term contract activities. Gross receipts and costs attributable to long-term contract activities means amounts included in total contract price or gross contract price, whichever is applicable, as determined under § 1.460-4, and costs allocable to the contract, as determined under § 1.460-5. Gross receipts and costs attributable to non-long-term contract activities (as defined in paragraph (d)(2) of this section) generally must be taken into account using a permissible method of accounting other than a long-term contract method. See section 446(c) and § 1.446-1(c). However, if the performance of a non-long-term contract activity is incident to or necessary for the manufacture, building, installation, or construction of the subject matter of one or more of the taxpayer's long-term contracts, the gross receipts and costs attributable to that activity must be allocated to the long-term contract(s) benefitted as provided in §§ 1.460-4(b)(4)(i) and 1.460-5(f)(2), respectively. Similarly, if a single long-term contract requires a taxpayer to perform a non-long-term contract activity that is not incident to or necessary for the manufacture, building, installation, or construction of the subject matter of the long-term contract, the gross receipts and costs attributable to that non-long-term contract activity must be separated from the contract and accounted for using a permissible method of accounting other than a long-term contract method. But see paragraph (g) of this section for related party rules.

*(2) Non-long-term contract activity.* Non-long-term contract activity means the performance of an activity other than manufacturing, building, installation, or construction, such as the provision of architectural, design, engineering, and construction management services, and the development or implementation of computer software. In addition, performance under a guaranty, warranty, or maintenance agreement is a non-long-term contract activity that is never incident to or necessary for the manufacture or construction of property under a long-term contract.

**(e) Severing and aggregating contracts.** *(1) In general.* After application of the allocation rules of paragraph (d) of this section, the severing and aggregating rules of this paragraph (e) may be applied by the Commissioner or the taxpayer as necessary to clearly reflect income (e.g., to prevent the unreasonable deferral (or acceleration) of income or the premature recognition (or deferral) of loss). Under the severing and aggregating rules, one agreement may be treated as two or more contracts, and two or more agreements may be treated as one contract. Except as provided in paragraph (e)(3)(ii) of this section, a taxpayer must determine whether to sever an agreement or to aggregate two or more agreements based on the facts and circumstances known at the end of the contracting year.

*(2) Facts and circumstances.* Whether an agreement should be severed, or two or more agreements should be aggregated, depends on the following factors:

(i) Pricing. Independent pricing of items in an agreement is necessary for the agreement to be severed into two or more contracts. In the case of an agreement for similar items, if the price to be paid for the items is determined under different terms or formulas (e.g., if some items are priced under a cost-plus incentive fee arrangement and later items are to be priced under a fixed-price arrangement), then the difference in the pricing terms or formulas indicates that the items are independently priced. Similarly, interdependent pricing of items in separate agreements is necessary for two or more agreements to be aggregated into one contract. A single price negotiation for similar items ordered under one or more agreements indicates that the items are interdependently priced.

(ii) Separate delivery or acceptance. An agreement may not be severed into two or more contracts unless it provides for separate delivery or separate acceptance of items that are the subject matter of the agreement. However, the separate delivery or separate acceptance of items by itself does not necessarily require an agreement to be severed.

(iii) Reasonable businessperson. Two or more agreements to perform manufacturing or construction activities may not be aggregated into one contract unless a reasonable businessperson would not have entered into one of the agreements for the terms agreed upon without also entering into the other agreement(s). Similarly, an agreement to perform manufacturing or construction activities may not be severed into two or more contracts if a reasonable businessperson would not have entered into separate agreements containing terms allocable to each severed contract. Analyzing the reasonable businessperson standard requires an analysis of all the facts and circumstances of the business arrangement between the taxpayer and the customer. For purposes of this paragraph (e)(2)(iii), a taxpayer's expectation that the parties would enter into another agreement, when agreeing to the terms contained in the first agreement, is not relevant.

*(3) Exceptions.* (i) Severance for PCM. A taxpayer may not sever under this paragraph (e) a long-term contract that would be subject to the PCM without obtaining the Commissioner's prior written consent.

(ii) Options and change orders. Except as provided in paragraph (e)(3)(i) of this section, a taxpayer must sever an agreement that increases the number of units to be supplied to the customer, such as through the exercise of an option or the acceptance of a change order, if the agreement provides for separate delivery or separate acceptance of the additional units.

*(4) Statement with return.* If a taxpayer severs an agreement or aggregates two or more agreements under this paragraph (e) during the taxable year, the taxpayer must attach a statement to its original federal income tax return for that year. This statement must contain the following information—

(i) The legend NOTIFICATION OF SEVERANCE OR AGGREGATION UNDER § 1.460-1(e);

(ii) The taxpayer's name; and

(iii) The taxpayer's employer identification number or social security number.

**(f) Classifying contracts.** *(1) In general.* After applying the severing and aggregating rules of paragraph (e) of this section, a taxpayer must determine the classification of a contract (e.g., as a long-term manufacturing contract, long-term construction contract, non-long-term contract) based on all the facts and circumstances known no later than the end of the contracting year. Classification is determined on a contract-by-contract basis. Consequently, a requirement to manufacture a single unique item under a long-term contract will subject all other items in that contract to section 460.

*(2) Hybrid contracts.* (i) In general. A long-term contract that requires a taxpayer to perform both manufacturing and construction activities (hybrid contract) generally must be classified as two contracts, a manufacturing contract and a construction contract. A taxpayer may elect, on a contract-by-contract basis, to classify a hybrid contract as a long-term construction contract if at least 95 percent of the estimated total allocable contract costs are reasonably allocable to construction activities. In addition, a taxpayer may elect, on a contract-by-contract basis, to classify a hybrid contract as a long-term manufacturing contract subject to the PCM.

(ii) Elections. A taxpayer makes an election under this paragraph (f)(2) by using its method of accounting for similar construction contracts or for manufacturing contracts, whichever is applicable, to account for a hybrid contract entered into during the taxable year of the election on its original federal income tax return for the election year. If an electing taxpayer's method is the PCM, the taxpayer also must use the PCM to apply the look-back method under § 1.460-6 and to determine alternative minimum taxable income under § 1.460-4(f).

*(3) Method of accounting.* Except as provided in paragraph (f)(2)(ii) of this section, a taxpayer's method of classifying contracts is a method of accounting under section 446 and, thus, may not be changed without the Commissioner's consent. If a taxpayer's method of classifying contracts is unreasonable, that classification method is an impermissible accounting method.

*(4) Use of estimates.* (i) Estimating length of contract. A taxpayer must use a reasonable estimate of the time required to complete a contract when necessary to classify the contract (e.g., to determine whether the five-year completion rule for qualified ship contracts under § 1.460-2(d), or the two-year completion rule for exempt construction contracts

under § 1.460-3(b), is satisfied, but not to determine whether a contract is completed within the contracting year under paragraph (b)(1) of this section). To be considered reasonable, an estimate of the time required to complete the contract must include anticipated time for delay, rework, change orders, technology or design problems, or other problems that reasonably can be anticipated considering the nature of the contract and prior experience. A contract term that specifies an expected completion or delivery date may be considered evidence that the taxpayer reasonably expects to complete or deliver the subject matter of the contract on or about the date specified, especially if the contract provides bona fide penalties for failing to meet the specified date. If a taxpayer classifies a contract based on a reasonable estimate of completion time, the contract will not be reclassified based on the actual (or another reasonable estimate of) completion time. A taxpayer's estimate of completion time will not be considered unreasonable if a contract is not completed within the estimated time primarily because of unforeseeable factors not within the taxpayer's control, such as third-party litigation, extreme weather conditions, strikes, or delays in securing permits or licenses.

(ii) Estimating allocable contract costs. A taxpayer must use a reasonable estimate of total allocable contract costs when necessary to classify the contract (e.g., to determine whether a contract is a home construction contract under § 1.460-(3)(b)(2)). If a taxpayer classifies a contract based on a reasonable estimate of total allocable contract costs, the contract will not be reclassified based on the actual (or another reasonable estimate of) total allocable contract costs.

**(g) Special rules for activities benefitting long-term contracts of a related party.** *(1) Related party use of PCM.* (i) In general. Except as provided in paragraph (g)(1)(ii) of this section, if a related party and its customer enter into a long-term contract subject to the PCM, and a taxpayer performs any activity that is incident to or necessary for the related party's long-term contract, the taxpayer must account for the gross receipts and costs attributable to this activity using the PCM, even if this activity is not otherwise subject to section 460(a). This type of activity may include, for example, the performance of engineering and design services, and the production of components and subassemblies that are reasonably expected to be used in the production of the subject matter of the related party's contract.

(ii) Exception for components and subassemblies. A taxpayer is not required to use the PCM under this paragraph (g) to account for a component or subassembly that benefits a related party's long-term contract if more than 50 percent of the average annual gross receipts attributable to the sale of this item for the 3-taxable-year-period ending with the contracting year comes from unrelated parties.

*(2) Total contract price.* If a taxpayer is required to use the PCM under paragraph (g)(1)(i) of this section, the total contract price (as defined in § 1.460-4(b)(4)(i)) is the fair market value of the taxpayer's activity that is incident to or necessary for the performance of the related party's long-term contract. The related party also must use the fair market value of the taxpayer's activity as the cost it incurs for the activity. The fair market value of the taxpayer's activity may or may not be the same as the amount the related party pays the taxpayer for that activity.

*(3) Completion factor.* To compute a contract's completion factor (as described in § 1.460-4(b)(5)), the related party must take into account the fair market value of the taxpayer's activity that is incident to or necessary for the performance of the related party's long-term contract when the related party incurs the liability to the taxpayer for the activity, rather than when the taxpayer incurs the costs to perform the activity.

**(h) Effective date.** *(1) In general.* Except as otherwise provided, this section and §§ 1.460-2 through 1.460-5 are applicable for contracts entered into on or after January 11, 2001.

*(2) Change in method of accounting.* Any change in a taxpayer's method of accounting necessary to comply with this section and §§ 1.460-2 through 1.460-5 is a change in method of accounting to which the provisions of section 446 and the regulations thereunder apply. For the first taxable year that includes January 11, 2001, a taxpayer is granted the consent of the Commissioner to change its method of accounting to comply with the provisions of this section and §§ 1.460-2 through 1.460-5 for long-term contracts entered into on or after January 11, 2001. A taxpayer that wants to change its method of accounting under this paragraph (h)(2) must follow the automatic consent procedures in Rev. Proc. 99-49 (1999-52 I.R.B. 725) (see § 601.601(d)(2) of this chapter), except that the scope limitations in section 4.02 of Rev. Proc. 99-49 do not apply. Because a change under this paragraph (h)(2) is made on a cut-off basis, a section 481(a) adjustment is not permitted or required. Moreover, the taxpayer does not receive audit protection under section 7 of Rev. Proc. 99-49 for a change in method of accounting under this paragraph (h)(2). A taxpayer that wants to change its exempt-contract method of accounting is not granted the consent of the Commissioner under this paragraph (h)(2) and must file a Form 3115, "Application for Change in Accounting Method," to obtain consent. See Rev. Proc. 97-27 (1997-1 C.B. 680) (see § 601.601(d)(2) of this chapter).

**(i) [Reserved].**

**(j) Examples.** The following examples illustrate the rules of this section:

*Example (1).* Contract for manufacture of property. B notifies C, an aircraft manufacturer, that it wants to purchase an aircraft of a particular type. At the time C receives the order, C has on hand several partially completed aircraft of this type; however, C does not have any completed aircraft of this type on hand. C and B agree that B will purchase one of these aircraft after it has been completed. C retains title to and risk of loss with respect to the aircraft until the sale takes place. The agreement between C and B is a contract for the manufacture of property under paragraph (b)(2)(i) of this section, even if labeled as a contract for the sale of property, because the manufacture of the aircraft is necessary for C's obligations under the agreement to be fulfilled and the manufacturing was not complete when B and C entered into the agreement.

*Example (2).* De minimis construction activity. C, a master developer whose taxable year ends December 31, owns 5,000 acres of undeveloped land with a cost basis of $5,000,000 and a fair market value of $50,000,000. To obtain permission from the local county government to improve this land, a service road must be constructed on this land to benefit all 5,000 acres. In 2001, C enters into a contract to sell a 1,000-acre parcel of undeveloped land to B, a residential developer, for its fair market value, $10,000,000. In this contract, C agrees to construct a service road running through the land that C is selling to B and through the 4,000 adjacent acres of undeveloped land that C has sold or will sell to other residential developers for its fair market value, $40,000,000. C reasonably estimates that it will incur allocable contract costs of $50,000 (excluding the cost of the land) to construct this service road, which will be owned and maintained by the county. C must reasonably allocate the cost of the service road among the benefitted parcels. The portion of the estimated total allocable contract costs that C allocates to the 1,000-acre parcel being sold to B (based upon its fair market value) is $10,000 ($50,000 x ($10,000,000 $50,000,000)). Construction of the service road is finished in 2002. Because the estimated total allocable contract costs attributable to C's construction activities, $10,000, are less than 10 percent of the contract's total contract price, $10,000,000, C's contract with B is not a construction contract under paragraph (b)(2)(ii) of this section. Thus, C's contract with B is not a long-term contract under paragraph (b)(2)(i) of this section, notwithstanding that construction of the service road is not completed in 2001.

*Example (3).* Completion—customer use. In 2002, C, whose taxable year ends December 31, enters into a contract to construct a building for B. In November of 2003, the building is completed in every respect necessary for its intended use, and B occupies the building. In early December of 2003, B notifies C of some minor deficiencies that need to be corrected, and C agrees to correct them in January 2004. C reasonably estimates that the cost of correcting these deficiencies will be less than five percent of the total allocable contract costs. C's contract is complete under paragraph (c)(3)(i)(A) of this section in 2003 because in that year, B used the building and C had incurred at least 95 percent of the total allocable contract costs attributable to the building. C must use a permissible method of accounting for any deficiency-related costs incurred after 2003.

*Example (4).* Completion—customer use. In 2001, C, whose taxable year ends December 31, agrees to construct a shopping center, which includes an adjoining parking lot, for B. By October 2002, C has finished constructing the retail portion of the shopping center. By December 2002, C has graded the entire parking lot, but has paved only one-fourth of it because inclement weather conditions prevented C from laying asphalt on the remaining three-fourths. In December 2002, B opens the retail portion of the shopping center and the paved portion of the parking lot to the general public. C reasonably estimates that the cost of paving the remaining three-fourths of the parking lot when weather permits will exceed five percent of C's total allocable contract costs. Even though B is using the subject matter of the contract, C's contract is not completed in December 2002 under paragraph (c)(3)(i)(A) of this section because C has not incurred at least 95 percent of the total allocable contract costs attributable to the subject matter.

*Example (5).* Completion—customer use. In 2001, C, whose taxable year ends December 31, agrees to manufacture 100 machines for B. By December 31, 2002, C has delivered 99 of the machines to B. C reasonably estimates that the cost of finishing the related work on the contract will be less than five percent of the total allocable contract costs. C's contract is not complete under paragraph (c)(3)(i)(A) of this section in 2002 because in that year, B is not using the subject matter of the contract (all 100 machines) for its intended purpose.

*Example (6).* Non-long-term contract activity. On January 1, 2001, C, whose taxable year ends December 31, enters into a single long-term contract to design and manufacture a satellite and to develop computer software enabling B to operate the satellite. At the end of 2001, C has not finished manufacturing the satellite. Designing the satellite and developing the computer software are non-long-term contract activities that are incident to and necessary for the taxpayer's manufacturing of the subject matter of a long-term contract because the satellite could not be manufactured without the design and would not operate without the software. Thus, under paragraph (d)(1) of this section, C must allocate these non-long-term contract activities to the long-term contract and account for the gross receipts and costs attributable to designing the satellite and developing computer software using the PCM.

*Example (7).* Non-long-term contract activity. C agrees to manufacture equipment for B under a long-term contract. In a separate contract, C agrees to design the equipment being manufactured for B under the long-term contract. Under paragraph (d)(1) of this section, C must allocate the gross receipts and costs related to the design to the long-term contract because designing the equipment is a non-long-term contract activity that is incident to and necessary for the manufacture of the subject matter of the long-term contract.

*Example (8).* Severance. On January 1, 2001, C, a construction contractor, and B, a real estate investor, enter into an agreement requiring C to build two office buildings in different areas of a large city. The agreement provides that the two office buildings will be completed by C and accepted by B in 2002 and 2003, respectively, and that C will be paid $1,000,000 and $1,500,000 for the two office buildings, respectively. The agreement will provide C with a reasonable profit from the construction of each building. Unless C is required to use the PCM to account for the contract, C is required to sever this contract under paragraph (e)(2) of this section because the buildings are independently priced, the agreement provides for separate delivery and acceptance of the buildings, and, as each building will generate a reasonable profit, a reasonable businessperson would have entered into separate agreements for the terms agreed upon for each building.

*Example (9).* Severance. C, a large construction contractor whose taxable year ends December 31, accounts for its construction contracts using the PCM and has elected to use the 10-percent method described in § 1.460-4(b)(6). In September 2001, C enters into an agreement to construct four buildings in four different cities. The buildings are independently priced and the contract provides a reasonable profit for each of the buildings. In addition, the agreement requires C to complete one building per year in 2002, 2003, 2004, and 2005. As of December 31, 2001, C has incurred 25 percent of the estimated total allocable contract costs attributable to one of the buildings, but only five percent of the estimated total allocable contract costs attributable to all four buildings included in the agreement. C does not request the Commissioner's consent to sever this contract. Using the 10-percent method, C does not take into account any portion of the total contract price or any incurred allocable contract costs attributable to this agreement in 2001. Upon examination of C's 2001 tax return, the Commissioner determines that C entered into one agreement for four buildings rather than four separate agreements each for one building solely to take advantage of the deferral obtained under the 10-percent method. Consequently, to clearly reflect the taxpayer's income, the Commissioner may require C to sever the agreement into four separate contracts under paragraph (e)(2) of this section because the buildings are independently priced, the agreement provides for separate delivery and acceptance of the buildings, and a reasonable businessperson would have entered into separate agreements for these buildings.

*Example (10).* Aggregation. In 2001, C, a shipbuilder, enters into two agreements with the Department of the Navy as the result of a single negotiation. Each agreement obligates

C to manufacture a submarine. Because the submarines are of the same class, their specifications are similar. Because C has never manufactured submarines of this class, however, C anticipates that it will incur substantially higher costs to manufacture the first submarine, to be delivered in 2007, than to manufacture the second submarine, to be delivered in 2010. If the agreements are treated as separate contracts, the first contract probably will produce a substantial loss, while the second contract probably will produce substantial profit. Based upon these facts, aggregation is required under paragraph (e)(2) of this section because the submarines are interdependently priced and a reasonable businessperson would not have entered the first agreement without also entering into the second.

*Example (11).* Aggregation. In 2001, C, a manufacturer of aircraft and related equipment, agrees to manufacture 10 military aircraft for foreign government B and to deliver the aircraft by the end of 2003. When entering into the agreement, C anticipates that it might receive production orders from B over the next 20 years for as many as 300 more of these aircraft. The negotiated contract price reflects C's and B's consideration of the expected total cost of manufacturing the 10 aircraft, the risks and opportunities associated with the agreement, and the additional factors the parties considered relevant. The negotiated price provides a profit on the sale of the 10 aircraft even if C does not receive any additional production orders from B. It is unlikely, however, that C actually would have wanted to manufacture the 10 aircraft but for the expectation that it would receive additional production orders from B. In 2003, B accepts delivery of the 10 aircraft. At that time, B orders an additional 20 aircraft of the same type for delivery in 2007. When negotiating the price for the additional 20 aircraft, C and B consider the fact that the expected unit cost for this production run of 20 aircraft will be lower than the unit cost of the 10 aircraft completed and accepted in 2003, but substantially higher than the expected unit cost of future production runs. Based upon these facts, aggregation is not permitted under paragraph (e)(2) of this section. Because the parties negotiated the prices of both agreements considering only the expected production costs and risks for each agreement standing alone, the terms and conditions agreed upon for the first agreement are independent of the terms and conditions agreed upon for the second agreement. The fact that the agreement to manufacture 10 aircraft provides a profit for C indicates that a reasonable businessperson would have entered into that agreement without entering into the agreement to manufacture the additional 20 aircraft.

*Example (12).* Classification and completion. In 2001, C, whose taxable year ends December 31, agrees to manufacture and install an industrial machine for B. C elects under paragraph (f) of this section to classify the agreement as a long-term manufacturing contract and to account for it using the PCM. The agreement requires C to deliver the machine in August 2003 and to install and test the machine in B's factory. In addition, the agreement requires B to accept the machine when the tests prove that the machine's performance will satisfy the environmental standards set by the Environmental Protection Agency (EPA), even if B has not obtained the required operating permit. Because of technical difficulties, C cannot deliver the machine until December 2003, when B conditionally accepts delivery. C installs the machine in December 2003 and then tests it through February 2004. B accepts the machine in February 2004, but does not obtain the operating permit from the EPA until January 2005. Under paragraph (c)(3)(i)(B) of this section, C's contract is finally completed and accepted in February 2004, even though B does not obtain the operating permit until January 2005, because C completed all its obligations under the contract and B accepted the machine in February 2004.

---

T.D. 8929, 1/10/2001.

---

## § 1.460-2 Long-term manufacturing contracts.

***Caution:*** The Treasury has not yet amended Reg § 1.460-2 to reflect changes made by P.L. 108-357.

**(a) In general.** Section 460 generally requires a taxpayer to determine the income from a long-term manufacturing contract using the percentage-of-completion method described in § 1.460-4(b) (PCM). A contract not completed in the contracting year is a long-term manufacturing contract if it involves the manufacture of personal property that is—

*(1)* A unique item of a type that is not normally carried in the finished goods inventory of the taxpayer; or

*(2)* An item that normally requires more than 12 calendar months to complete (regardless of the duration of the contract or the time to complete a deliverable quantity of the item).

**(b) Unique.** *(1) In general.* Unique means designed for the needs of a specific customer. To determine whether an item is designed for the needs of a specific customer, a taxpayer must consider the extent to which research, development, design, engineering, retooling, and similar activities (customizing activities) are required to manufacture the item and whether the item could be sold to other customers with little or no modification. A contract may require the taxpayer to manufacture more than one unit of a unique item. If a contract requires a taxpayer to manufacture more than one unit of the same item, the taxpayer must determine whether that item is unique by considering the customizing activities that would be needed to produce only the first unit. For the purposes of this paragraph (b), a taxpayer must consider the activities performed on its behalf by a subcontractor.

*(2) Safe harbors.* Notwithstanding paragraph (b)(1) of this section, an item is not unique if it satisfies one or more of the safe harbors in this paragraph (b)(2). If an item does not satisfy one or more safe harbors, the determination of uniqueness will depend on the facts and circumstances. The safe harbors are:

(i) Short production period. An item is not unique if it normally requires 90 days or less to complete. In the case of a contract for multiple units of an item, the item is not unique only if it normally requires 90 days or less to complete each unit of the item in the contract.

(ii) Customized item. An item is not unique if the total allocable contract costs attributable to customizing activities that are incident to or necessary for the manufacture of the item do not exceed 10 percent of the estimated total allocable contract costs allocable to the item. In the case of a contract for multiple units of an item, this comparison must be performed on the first unit of the item and the total allocable contract costs attributable to customizing activities that are incident to or necessary for the manufacture of the first unit of the item must be allocated to that first unit.

(iii) Inventoried item. A unique item ceases to be unique no later than when the taxpayer normally includes similar items in its finished goods inventory.

**(c) Normal time to complete.** *(1) In general.* The amount of time normally required to complete an item is the item's reasonably expected production period, as described in § 1.263A-12, determined at the end of the contracting year. Thus, in general, the expected production period for an item begins when a taxpayer incurs at least five percent of the costs that would be allocable to the item under § 1.460-5 and ends when the item is ready to be held for sale and all reasonably expected production activities are complete. In the case of components that are assembled or reassembled into an item or unit at the customer's facility by the taxpayer's employees or agents, the production period ends when the components are assembled or reassembled into an operable item or unit. To the extent that several distinct activities related to the production of the item are expected to occur simultaneously, the period during which these distinct activities occur is not counted more than once. Furthermore, when determining the normal time to complete an item, a taxpayer is not required to consider activities performed or costs incurred that would not be allocable contract costs under section 460 (e.g., independent research and development expenses (as defined in § 1.460-1(b)(9)) and marketing expenses). Moreover, the time normally required to design and manufacture the first unit of an item for which the taxpayer intends to produce multiple units generally does not indicate the normal time to complete the item.

*(2) Production by related parties.* To determine the time normally required to complete an item, a taxpayer must consider all relevant production activities performed and costs incurred by itself and by related parties, as defined in § 1.460-1(b)(4). For example, if a taxpayer's item requires a component or subassembly manufactured by a related party, the taxpayer must consider the time the related party takes to complete the component or subassembly and, for purposes of determining the beginning of an item's production period, the costs incurred by the related party that are allocable to the component or subassembly. However, if both requirements of the exception for components and subassemblies under § 1.460-1(g)(1)(ii) are satisfied, a taxpayer does not consider the activities performed or the costs incurred by a related party when determining the normal time to complete an item.

**(d) Qualified ship contracts.** A taxpayer may determine the income from a long-term manufacturing contract that is a qualified ship contract using either the PCM or the percentage-of-completion/ capitalized-cost method (PCCM) of accounting described in § 1.460-4(e). A qualified ship contract is any contract entered into after February 28, 1986, to manufacture in the United States not more than 5 seagoing vessels if the vessels will not be manufactured directly or indirectly for the United States Government and if the taxpayer reasonably expects to complete the contract within 5 years of the contract commencement date. Under § 1.460-1(e)(3)(i), a contract to produce more than 5 vessels for which the PCM would be required cannot be severed in order to be classified as a qualified ship contract.

**(e) Examples.** The following examples illustrate the rules of this section:

*Example (1).* Unique item and classification. In December 2001, C enters into a contract with B to design and manufacture a new type of industrial equipment. C reasonably expects the normal production period for this type of equipment to be eight months. Because the new type of industrial equipment requires a substantial amount of research, design, and engineering to produce, C determines that the equipment is a unique item and its contract with B is a long-term contract. After delivering the equipment to B in September 2002, C contracts with B to produce five additional units of that industrial equipment with certain different specifications. These additional units, which also are expected to take eight months to produce, will be delivered to B in 2003. C determines that the research, design, engineering, retooling, and similar customizing costs necessary to produce the five additional units of equipment does not exceed 10 percent of the first unit's share of estimated total allocable contract costs. Consequently, the additional units of equipment satisfy the safe harbor in paragraph (b)(2)(ii) of this section and are not unique items. Although C's contract with B to produce the five additional units is not completed within the contracting year, the contract is not a long-term contract since the additional units of equipment are not unique items and do not normally require more than 12 months to produce. C must classify its second contract with B as a non-long term contract, notwithstanding that it classified the previous contract with B for a similar item as a long-term contract, because the determination of whether a contract is a long-term contract is made on a contract-by-contract basis. A change in classification is not a change in method of accounting because the change in classification results from a change in underlying facts.

*Example (2).* 12-month rule—related party. C manufactures cranes. C purchases one of the crane's components from R, a related party under § 1.460-1(b)(4). Less tn 50 percent of R's gross receipts attributable to the sale of this component comes from sales to unrelated parties; thus, the exception for components and subassemblies under § 1.460-1(g)(1)(ii) is not satisfied. Consequently, C must consider the activities of R as R incurs costs and performs the activities rather than as C incurs a liability to R. The normal time period between the time that both C and R incur five percent of the costs allocable to the crane and the time that R completes the component is five months. C normally requires an additional eight months to complete production of the crane after receiving the integral component from R. C's crane is an item of a type that normally requires more than 12 months to complete under paragraph (c) of this section because the production period from the time that both C and R incur five percent of the costs allocable to the crane until the time that production of the crane is complete is normally 13 months.

*Example (3).* 12-month rule—duration of contract. The facts are the same as in Example 2, except that C enters into a sales contract with B on December 31, 2001 (the last day of C's taxable year), and delivers a completed crane to B on February 1, 2002. C's contract with B is a long-term contract under paragraph (a)(2) of this section because the contract is not completed in the contracting year, 2001, and the crane is an item that normally requires more than 12 calendar months to complete (regardless of the duration of the contract).

*Example (4).* 12-month rule—normal time to complete. The facts are the same as in Example 2, except that C (and R) actually complete B's crane in only 10 calendar months. The contract is a long-term contract because the normal time to complete a crane, not the actual time to complete a crane, is the relevant criterion for determining whether an item is subject to paragraph (a)(2) of this section.

*Example (5).* Normal time to complete. C enters into a multi-unit contract to produce four units of an item. C does not anticipate producing any additional units of the item. C expects to perform the research, design, and development that are directly allocable to the particular item and to produce the first unit in the first 24 months. C reasonably expects the production period for each of the three remaining units will be 3 months. This contract is not a contract that involves the manufacture of an item that normally requires more than 12 months to complete because the normal time to complete the item is 3 months. However, the contract does not satisfy the 90-day safe harbor for unique items because the normal time to complete the first unit of this item exceeds 90 days. Thus, the contract might involve the manufacture of a unique item depending on the facts and circumstances.

T.D. 8929, 1/10/2001.

### § 1.460-3 Long-term construction contracts.

**(a) In general.** Section 460 generally requires a taxpayer to determine the income from a long-term construction contract using the percentage-of-completion method described in § 1.460-4(b) (PCM). A contract not completed in the contracting year is a long-term construction contract if it involves the building, construction, reconstruction, or rehabilitation of real property; the installation of an integral component to real property; or the improvement of real property (collectively referred to as construction). Real property means land, buildings, and inherently permanent structures, as defined in § 1.263A-8(c)(3), such as roadways, dams, and bridges. Real property does not include vessels, offshore drilling platforms, or unsevered natural products of land. An integral component to real property includes property not produced at the site of the real property but intended to be permanently affixed to the real property, such as elevators and central heating and cooling systems. Thus, for example, a contract to install an elevator in a building is a construction contract because a building is real property, but a contract to install an elevator in a ship is not a construction contract because a ship is not real property.

**(b) Exempt construction contracts.** *(1) In general.* The general requirement to use the PCM and the cost allocation rules described in § 1.460-5(b) or (c) does not apply to any long-term construction contract described in this paragraph (b) (exempt construction contract). Exempt construction contract means any—

(i) Home construction contract; and

(ii) Other construction contract that a taxpayer estimates (when entering into the contract) will be completed within 2 years of the contract commencement date, provided the taxpayer satisfies the $10,000,000 gross receipts test described in paragraph (b)(3) of this section.

*(2) Home construction contract.*

(i) In general. A long-term construction contract is a home construction contract if a taxpayer (including a subcontractor working for a general contractor) reasonably expects to attribute 80 percent or more of the estimated total allocable contract costs (including the cost of land, materials, and services), determined as of the close of the contracting year, to the construction of—

(A) Dwelling units, as defined in section 168(e)(2)(A)(ii)(I), contained in buildings containing 4 or fewer dwelling units (including buildings with 4 or fewer dwelling units that also have commercial units); and

(B) Improvements to real property directly related to, and located at the site of, the dwelling units.

(ii) Townhouses and rowhouses. Each townhouse or rowhouse is a separate building.

(iii) Common improvements. A taxpayer includes in the cost of the dwelling units their allocable share of the cost that the taxpayer reasonably expects to incur for any common improvements (e.g., sewers, roads, clubhouses) that benefit the dwelling units and that the taxpayer is contractually obligated, or required by law, to construct within the tract or tracts of land that contain the dwelling units.

(iv) Mixed use costs. If a contract involves the construction of both commercial units and dwelling units within the same building, a taxpayer must allocate the costs among the commercial units and dwelling units using a reasonable method or combination of reasonable methods, such as specific identification, square footage, or fair market value.

*(3) $10,000,000 gross receipts test.*

(i) In general. Except as otherwise provided in paragraphs (b)(3)(ii) and (iii) of this section, the $10,000,000 gross receipts test is satisfied if a taxpayer's (or predecessor's) average annual gross receipts for the 3 taxable years preceding the contracting year do not exceed $10,000,000, as determined using the principles of the gross receipts test for small resellers under § 1.263A-3(b).

(ii) Single employer. To apply the gross receipts test, a taxpayer is not required to aggregate the gross receipts of persons treated as a single employer solely under section 414(m) and any regulations prescribed under section 414.

(iii) Attribution of gross receipts. A taxpayer must aggregate a proportionate share of the construction-related gross receipts of any person that has a five percent or greater interest in the taxpayer. In addition, a taxpayer must aggregate a proportionate share of the construction-related gross receipts of any person in which the taxpayer has a five percent or greater interest. For this purpose, a taxpayer must determine ownership interests as of the first day of the taxpayer's contracting year and must include indirect interests in any corporation, partnership, estate, trust, or sole proprietorship according to principles similar to the constructive ownership rules under sections 1563(e), (f)(2), and (f)(3)(A). However, a taxpayer is not required to aggregate under this paragraph (b)(3)(iii) any construction-related gross receipts required to be aggregated under paragraph (b)(3)(i) of this section.

**(c) Residential construction contracts.** A taxpayer may determine the income from a long-term construction contract that is a residential construction contract using either the PCM or the percentage-of-completion/capitalized-cost method (PCCM) of accounting described in § 1.460-4(e). A residential construction contract is a home construction contract, as defined in paragraph (b)(2) of this section, except that the building or buildings being constructed contain more than 4 dwelling units.

T.D. 8929, 1/10/2001.

PAR. 2. Section 1.460-3 is amended by:

1. Revising paragraph (b)(1)(ii).

2. Redesignating paragraphs (b)(2)(ii), (b)(2)(iii) and (b)(2)(iv) as paragraphs (b)(2)(iii), (b)(2)(iv) and (b)(2)(v), respectively, and revising them.

3. Adding a new paragraph (b)(2)(ii).

The revisions and addition read as follows:

### Proposed § 1.460-3 Long-term construction contracts.

[*For Preamble, see ¶ 153,043*]

* * * * *

**(b)** * * *

*(1)* * * *

(ii) Construction contract, other than a home construction contract, that a taxpayer estimates (when entering into the contract) will be completed within 2 years of the contract commencement date, provided the taxpayer satisfies the $10,000,000 gross receipts test described in paragraph (b)(3) of this section.

*(2)* * * *

(ii) Land improvements. For purposes of paragraph (b)(2)(i)(B) of this section, improvements to real property directly related to, and located on the site of, the dwelling units consist of improvements to land on which dwelling units (as described in paragraph (b)(2)(i)(A) of this section) are constructed, and common improvements as defined in paragraph (b)(2)(iv) of this section. A long-term construction contract is a home construction contract if a taxpayer (including a subcontractor working for a general contractor) meets the 80% test in paragraph (b)(2)(i) of this section as applied to either paragraph (b)(2)(i)(A) of this section or paragraph (b)(2)(i)(B) of this section, or both paragraphs (b)(2)(i)(A) and (b)(2)(i)(B) of this section, collectively.

(iii) Townhouses and rowhouses. For purposes of determining whether a long-term construction contract is a home construction contract under paragraph (b)(2) of this section, each townhouse or rowhouse is a separate building. For this purpose, the term townhouse and rowhouse includes an individual condominium unit.

(iv) Common improvements. (A) In general. A taxpayer includes in the cost of a dwelling unit or land its allocable share of the cost that the taxpayer incurs for any common improvements that benefit the dwelling unit or land.

(B) Definition. For purposes of this section, a common improvement is an improvement that the taxpayer is contractually obligated, or required by law, to construct within the tract or tracts of land containing the dwelling units (or the land on which dwelling units are to be constructed) and that benefits the dwelling units (or the land on which dwelling units are to be constructed). In general, a common improvement does not solely benefit any particular dwelling unit or any particular lot on which a dwelling unit is constructed. However, land clearing and grading are common improvements, even when performed on a particular lot. Other examples of common improvements are sidewalks, sewers, roads and clubhouses.

(v) Mixed use costs. If a contract involves the construction of both commercial units and dwelling units, a taxpayer must allocate the costs among the commercial units and dwelling units using a reasonable method or combination of reasonable methods. In general, the reasonableness of an allocation method will be based on facts and circumstances. Examples of methods that may be reasonable are specific identification, square footage, or fair market value.

* * * * *

### § 1.460-4 Methods of accounting for long-term contracts.

***Caution:*** The Treasury has not yet amended Reg § 1.460-4 to reflect changes made by P.L. 108-357.

**(a) Overview.** This section prescribes permissible methods of accounting for long-term contracts. Paragraph (b) of this section describes the percentage-of-completion method under section 460(b) (PCM) that a taxpayer generally must use to determine the income from a long-term contract. Paragraph (c) of this section lists permissible methods of accounting for exempt construction contracts described in § 1.460-3(b)(1) and describes the exempt-contract percentage-of-completion method (EPCM). Paragraph (d) of this section describes the completed-contract method (CCM), which is one of the permissible methods of accounting for exempt construction contracts. Paragraph (e) of this section describes the percentage-of-completion/capitalized-cost method (PCCM), which is a permissible method of accounting for qualified ship contracts described in § 1.460-2(d) and residential construction contracts described in § 1.460-3(c). Paragraph (f) of this section provides rules for determining the alternative minimum taxable income (AMTI) from long-term contracts that are not exempted under section 56. Paragraph (g) of this section provides rules concerning consistency in methods of accounting for long-term contracts. Paragraph (h) of this section provides examples illustrating the principles of this section. Paragraph (j) of this section provides rules for taxpayers that file consolidated tax returns. Finally, paragraph (k) of this section provides rules relating to a mid-contract change in taxpayer of a contract accounted for using a long-term contract method of accounting.

**(b) Percentage-of-completion method.** *(1) In general.* Under the PCM, a taxpayer generally must include in income the portion of the total contract price, as defined in paragraph (b)(4)(i) of this section, that corresponds to the percentage of the entire contract that the taxpayer has completed during the taxable year. The percentage of completion must be determined by comparing allocable contract costs incurred with estimated total allocable contract costs. Thus, the taxpayer includes a portion of the total contract price in gross income as the taxpayer incurs allocable contract costs.

*(2) Computations.* To determine the income from a long-term contract, a taxpayer—

(i) Computes the completion factor for the contract, which is the ratio of the cumulative allocable contract costs that the taxpayer has incurred through the end of the taxable year to the estimated total allocable contract costs that the taxpayer reasonably expects to incur under the contract;

(ii) Computes the amount of cumulative gross receipts from the contract by multiplying the completion factor by the total contract price;

(iii) Computes the amount of current-year gross receipts, which is the difference between the amount of cumulative gross receipts for the current taxable year and the amount of cumulative gross receipts for the immediately preceding taxable year (the difference can be a positive or negative number); and

(iv) Takes both the current-year gross receipts and the allocable contract costs incurred during the current year into account in computing taxable income.

*(3) Post-completion-year income.* If a taxpayer has not included the total contract price in gross income by the completion year, as defined in § 1.460-1(b)(6), the taxpayer must include the remaining portion of the total contract price in gross income for the taxable year following the completion year. For the treatment of post-completion-year costs, see paragraph (b)(5)(v) of this section. See § 1.460-6(c)(1)(ii) for application of the look-back method as a result of adjustments to total contract price.

*(4) Total contract price.* (i) In general— (A) Definition. Total contract price means the amount that a taxpayer reasonably expects to receive under a long-term contract, including holdbacks, retainages, and cost reimbursements. See § 1.460-6(c)(1)(ii) and (2)(vi) for application of the look-back method as a result of changes in total contract price.

(B) Contingent compensation. Any amount related to a contingent right under a contract, such as a bonus, award, incentive payment, and amount in dispute, is included in total contract price as soon as the taxpayer can reasonably predict that the amount will be earned, even if the all events test has not yet been met. For example, if a bonus is payable to a taxpayer for meeting an early completion date, the bonus is includible in total contract price at the time and to the extent that the taxpayer can reasonably predict the achievement of the corresponding objective. Similarly, a portion of the contract price that is in dispute is includible in total contract price at the time and to the extent that the taxpayer can reasonably predict that the dispute will be resolved in the taxpayer's favor (regardless of when the taxpayer actually receives payment or when the dispute is finally resolved). Total contract price does not include compensation that might be earned under any other agreement that the taxpayer expects to obtain from the same customer (e.g., exercised option or follow-on contract) if that other agreement is not aggregated under § 1.460-1(e). For the purposes of this paragraph (b)(4)(i)(B), a taxpayer can reasonably predict that an amount of contingent income will be earned not later than when the taxpayer includes that amount in income for financial reporting purposes under generally accepted accounting principles. If a taxpayer has not included an amount of contingent compensation in total contract price under this paragraph (b)(4)(i) by the taxable year following the completion year, the taxpayer must account for that amount of contingent compensation using a permissible method of accounting. If it is determined after the taxable year following the completion year that an amount included in total contract price will not be earned, the taxpayer should deduct that amount in the year of the determination.

(C) Non-long-term contract activities. Total contract price includes an allocable share of the gross receipts attributable to a non-long-term contract activity, as defined in § 1.460-1(d)(2), if the activity is incident to or necessary for the manufacture, building, installation, or construction of the subject matter of the long-term contract. Total contract price also includes amounts reimbursed for independent research and development expenses (as defined in § 1.460-1(b)(9)), or for bidding and proposal costs, under a federal or cost-plus long-term contract (as defined in section 460(d)), regardless of whether the research and development, or bidding and proposal, activities are incident to or necessary for the performance of that long-term contract.

(ii) Estimating total contract price. A taxpayer must estimate the total contract price based upon all the facts and circumstances known as of the last day of the taxable year. For this purpose, an event that occurs after the end of the taxable year must be taken into account if its occurrence was reasonably predictable and its income was subject to reasonable estimation as of the last day of that taxable year.

*(5) Completion factor.* (i) Allocable contract costs. A taxpayer must use a cost allocation method permitted under either § 1.460-5(b) or (c) to determine the amount of cumulative allocable contract costs and estimated total allocable contract costs that are used to determine a contract's completion factor. Allocable contract costs include a reimbursable cost that is allocable to the contract.

(ii) Cumulative allocable contract costs. To determine a contract's completion factor for a taxable year, a taxpayer must take into account the cumulative allocable contract costs that have been incurred, as defined in § 1.460-1(b)(8), through the end of the taxable year.

(iii) Estimating total allocable contract costs. A taxpayer must estimate total allocable contract costs for each long-term contract based upon all the facts and circumstances known as of the last day of the taxable year. For this purpose, an event that occurs after the end of the taxable year must be taken into account if its occurrence was reasonably predictable and its cost was subject to reasonable estimation as of the last day of that taxable year. To be considered reasonable, an estimate of total allocable contract costs must include costs attributable to delay, rework, change orders, technology or design problems, or other problems that reasonably can be predicted considering the nature of the contract and prior experience. However, estimated total allocable contract costs do not include any contingency allowance for costs that, as of the end of the taxable year, are not reasonably predicted to be incurred in the performance of the contract. For example, estimated total allocable contract costs do not include any costs attributable to factors not reasonably predictable at the end of the taxable year, such as third-party litigation, extreme weather conditions, strikes, and delays in securing required permits and licenses. In addition, the estimated costs of performing other agreements that are not aggregated with the contract under § 1.460-1(e) that the taxpayer expects to incur with the same customer (e.g., follow-on contracts) are not included in estimated total allocable contract costs for the initial contract.

(iv) Pre-contracting-year costs. If a taxpayer reasonably expects to enter into a long-term contract in a future taxable year, the taxpayer must capitalize all costs incurred prior to entering into the contract that will be allocable to that contract (e.g., bidding and proposal costs). A taxpayer is not required to compute a completion factor, or to include in gross income any amount, related to allocable contract costs for any taxable year ending before the contracting year or, if applicable, the 10-percent year defined in paragraph (b)(6)(i) of this section. In that year, the taxpayer is required to compute a completion factor that includes all allocable contract costs that have been incurred as of the end of that taxable year (whether previously capitalized or deducted) and to take into account in computing taxable income the related gross receipts and the previously capitalized allocable contract costs. If, however, a taxpayer determines in a subsequent year that it will not enter into the long-term contract, the taxpayer must account for these pre-contracting-year costs in that year (e.g., as a deduction or an inventoriable cost) using the appropriate rules contained in other sections of the Code or regulations.

(v) Post-completion-year costs. If a taxpayer incurs an allocable contract cost after the completion year, the taxpayer must account for that cost using a permissible method of accounting. See § 1.460-6(c)(1)(ii) for application of the look-back method as a result of adjustments to allocable contract costs.

*(6) 10-percent method.* (i) In general. Instead of determining the income from a long-term contract beginning with the contracting year, a taxpayer may elect to use the 10-percent method under section 460(b)(5). Under the 10-percent method, a taxpayer does not include in gross income any amount related to allocable contract costs until the taxable year in which the taxpayer has incurred at least 10 percent of the estimated total allocable contract costs (10-percent year). A taxpayer must treat costs incurred before the 10-percent year as pre-contracting-year costs described in paragraph (b)(5)(iv) of this section.

(ii) Election. A taxpayer makes an election under this paragraph (b)(6) by using the 10-percent method for all long-term contracts entered into during the taxable year of the election on its original federal income tax return for the election year. This election is a method of accounting and, thus, applies to all long-term contracts entered into during and after the taxable year of the election. An electing taxpayer must use the 10-percent method to apply the look-back method under § 1.460-6 and to determine alternative minimum taxable income under paragraph (f) of this section. This election is not available if a taxpayer uses the simplified cost-to-cost method described in § 1.460-5(c) to compute the completion factor of a long-term contract.

*(7) Terminated contract.* (i) Reversal of income. If a long-term contract is terminated before completion and, as a result, the taxpayer retains ownership of the property that is the subject matter of that contract, the taxpayer must reverse the transaction in the taxable year of termination. To reverse the transaction, the taxpayer reports a loss (or gain) equal to the cumulative allocable contract costs reported under the contract in all prior taxable years less the cumulative gross receipts reported under the contract in all prior taxable years.

(ii) Adjusted basis. As a result of reversing the transaction under paragraph (b)(7)(i) of this section, a taxpayer will have an adjusted basis in the retained property equal to the cumulative allocable contract costs reported under the contract in all prior taxable years. However, if the taxpayer received and retains any consideration or compensation from the customer, the taxpayer must reduce the adjusted basis in the retained property (but not below zero) by the fair market value of that consideration or compensation. To the extent that the amount of the consideration or compensation described in the preceding sentence exceeds the adjusted basis in the retained property, the taxpayer must include the excess in gross income for the taxable year of termination.

(iii) Look-back method. The look-back method does not apply to a terminated contract that is subject to this paragraph (b)(7).

**(c) Exempt contract methods.** *(1) In general.* An exempt contract method means the method of accounting that a taxpayer must use to account for all its long-term contracts (and any portion of a long-term contract) that are exempt from the requirements of section 460(a). Thus, an exempt contract method applies to exempt construction contracts, as defined in § 1.460-3(b); the non-PCM portion of a qualified ship contract, as defined in § 1.460-2(d); and the non-PCM portion of a residential construction contract, as defined in § 1.460-3(c). Permissible exempt contract methods include the PCM, the EPCM described in paragraph (c)(2) of this section, the CCM described in paragraph (d) of this section, or any other permissible method. See section 446.

*(2) Exempt-contract percentage-of-completion method.* (i) In general. Similar to the PCM described in paragraph (b) of this section, a taxpayer using the EPCM generally must include in income the portion of the total contract price, as described in paragraph (b)(4) of this section, that corresponds to the percentage of the entire contract that the taxpayer has completed during the taxable year. However, under the EPCM, the percentage of completion may be determined as of the end of the taxable year by using any method of cost comparison (such as comparing direct labor costs incurred to date to estimated total direct labor costs) or by comparing the work performed on the contract with the estimated total work to be performed, rather than by using the cost-to-cost comparison required by paragraphs (b)(2)(i) and (5) of this section, provided such method is used consistently and clearly reflects income. In addition, paragraph (b)(3) of this section (regarding post-completion-year income), paragraph (b)(6) of this section (regarding the 10-percent method) and § 1.460-6 (regarding the look-back method) do not apply to the EPCM.

(ii) Determination of work performed. For purposes of the EPCM, the criteria used to compare the work performed on a contract as of the end of the taxable year with the estimated total work to be performed must clearly reflect the earning of income with respect to the contract. For example, in the case of a roadbuilder, a standard of completion solely based on miles of roadway completed in a case where the terrain is substantially different may not clearly reflect the earning of income with respect to the contract.

**(d) Completed-contract method.** *(1) In general.* Except as otherwise provided in paragraph (d)(4) of this section, a taxpayer using the CCM to account for a long-term contract must take into account in the contract's completion year, as defined in § 1.460-1(b)(6), the gross contract price and all allocable contract costs incurred by the completion year. A taxpayer may not treat the cost of any materials and supplies that are allocated to a contract, but actually remain on hand when the contract is completed, as an allocable contract cost.

*(2) Post-completion-year income and costs.* If a taxpayer has not included an item of contingent compensation (i.e., amounts for which the all events test has not been satisfied) in gross contract price under paragraph (d)(3) of this section by the completion year, the taxpayer must account for this item of contingent compensation using a permissible method of accounting. If a taxpayer incurs an allocable contract cost after the completion year, the taxpayer must account for that cost using a permissible method of accounting.

*(3) Gross contract price.* Gross contract price includes all amounts (including holdbacks, retainages, and reimbursements) that a taxpayer is entitled by law or contract to receive, whether or not the amounts are due or have been paid. In addition, gross contract price includes all bonuses, awards, and incentive payments, such as a bonus for meeting an early completion date, to the extent the all events test is satisfied. If a taxpayer performs a non-long-term contract activity, as defined in § 1460-1(d)(2), that is incident to or necessary for the manufacture, building, installation, or construction of the subject matter of one or more of the taxpayer's long-term contracts, the taxpayer must include an allocable share of the gross receipts attributable to that activity in the gross contract price of the contract(s) benefitted by that activity. Gross contract price also includes amounts reimbursed for independent research and development expenses (as defined in § 1.460-1(b)(9)), or bidding and proposal costs, under a federal or cost-plus long-term contract (as defined in section 460(d)), regardless of whether the research and development, or bidding and proposal, activities are incident to or necessary for the performance of that long-term contract.

*(4) Contracts with disputed claims.* (i) In general. The special rules in this paragraph (d)(4) apply to a long-term contract accounted for using the CCM with a dispute caused by a customer's requesting a reduction of the gross contract price or the performance of additional work under the contract or by a taxpayer's requesting an increase in gross contract price, or both, on or after the date a taxpayer has tendered the subject matter of the contract to the customer.

(ii) Taxpayer assured of profit or loss. If the disputed amount relates to a customer's claim for either a reduction in price or additional work and the taxpayer is assured of either a profit or a loss on a long-term contract regardless of the outcome of the dispute, the gross contract price, reduced (but not below zero) by the amount reasonably in dispute, must be taken into account in the completion year. If the disputed amount relates to a taxpayer's claim for an increase in price and the taxpayer is assured of either a profit or a loss on a long-term contract regardless of the outcome of the dispute, the gross contract price must be taken into account in the completion year. If the taxpayer is assured a profit on the contract, all allocable contract costs incurred by the end of the completion year are taken into account in that year. If the taxpayer is assured a loss on the contract, all allocable contract costs incurred by the end of the completion year, reduced by the amount reasonably in dispute, are taken into account in the completion year.

(iii) Taxpayer unable to determine profit or loss. If the amount reasonably in dispute affects so much of the gross contract price or allocable contract costs that a taxpayer cannot determine whether a profit or loss ultimately will be realized from a long-term contract, the taxpayer may not take any of the gross contract price or allocable contract costs into account in the completion year.

(iv) Dispute resolved. Any part of the gross contract price and any allocable contract costs that have not been taken into account because of the principles described in paragraph (d)(4)(i), (ii), or (iii) of this section must be taken into account in the taxable year in which the dispute is resolved. If a taxpayer performs additional work under the contract because of the dispute, the term taxable year in which the dispute is resolved means the taxable year the additional work is completed, rather than the taxable year in which the outcome of the dispute is determined by agreement, decision, or otherwise.

**(e) Percentage-of-completion/capitalized-cost method.** Under the PCCM, a taxpayer must determine the income from a long-term contract using the PCM for the applicable percentage of the contract and its exempt contract method, as defined in paragraph (c) of this section, for the remaining percentage of the contract. For residential construction contracts described in § 1.460-3(c), the applicable percentage is 70 percent, and the remaining percentage is 30 percent. For qualified ship contracts described in § 1.460-2(d), the applicable percentage is 40 percent, and the remaining percentage is 60 percent.

**(f) Alternative minimum taxable income.** *(1) In general.* Under section 56(a)(3), a taxpayer (not exempt from the AMT under section 55(e)) must use the PCM to determine its AMTI from any long-term contract entered into on or after March 1, 1986, that is not a home construction contract, as defined in § 1.460-3(b)(2). For AMTI purposes, the PCM must include any election under paragraph (b)(6) of this section (concerning the 10-percent method) or under § 1.460-5(c) (concerning the simplified cost-to-cost method) that the taxpayer has made for regular tax purposes. For exempt construction contracts described in § 1.460-3(b)(1)(ii), a taxpayer must use the simplified cost-to-cost method to determine the completion factor for AMTI purposes. Except as provided in paragraph (f)(2) of this section, a taxpayer must use AMTI costs and AMTI methods, such as the depreciation method described in section 56(a)(1), to determine the completion factor of a long-term contract (except a home construction contract) for AMTI purposes.

*(2) Election to use regular completion factors.* Under this paragraph (f)(2), a taxpayer may elect for AMTI purposes to determine the completion factors of all of its long-term contracts using the methods of accounting and allocable contract costs used for regular federal income tax purposes. A taxpayer makes this election by using regular methods and regular costs to compute the completion factors of all long-term contracts entered into during the taxable year of the election for AMTI purposes on its original federal income tax return for the election year. This election is a method of accounting and, thus, applies to all long-term contracts entered into during and after the taxable year of the election. Although a taxpayer may elect to compute the completion factor of its long-term contracts using regular methods and regular costs, an election under this paragraph (f)(2) does not eliminate a taxpayer's obligation to comply with the requirements of section 55 when computing AMTI. For example, although a taxpayer may elect to use the depreciation methods used for regular tax purposes to compute the completion factor of its long-term contracts for AMTI purposes, the taxpayer must use the depreciation methods permitted by section 56 to compute AMTI.

**(g) Method of accounting.** A taxpayer that uses the PCM, EPCM, CCM, or PCCM, or elects the 10-percent method or special AMTI method (or changes to another method of accounting with the Commissioner's consent) must apply the method(s) consistently for all similarly classified long-term contracts, until the taxpayer obtains the Commissioner's consent under section 446(e) to change to another method of accounting. A taxpayer-initiated change in method of accounting will be permitted only on a cut-off basis (i.e., for contracts entered into on or after the year of change), and thus, a section 481(a) adjustment will not be permitted or required.

**(h) Examples.** The following examples illustrate the rules of this section:

*Example (1).* PCM—estimating total contract price. C, whose taxable year ends December 31, determines the income from long-term contracts using the PCM. On January 1, 2001, C enters into a contract to design and manufacture a satellite (a unique item). The contract provides that C will be paid $10,000,000 for delivering the completed satellite by December 1, 2002. The contract also provides that C will receive a $3,000,000 bonus for delivering the satellite by July 1, 2002, and an additional $4,000,000 bonus if the satellite successfully performs its mission for five years. C is unable to reasonably predict if the satellite will successfully perform its mission for five years. If on December 31, 2001, C should reasonably expect to deliver the satellite by July 1, 2002, the estimated total contract price is $13,000,000 ($10,000,000 unit price + $3,000,000 production-related bonus). Otherwise, the estimated total contract price is $10,000,000. In either event, the $4,000,000 bonus is not includible in the estimated total contract price as of December 31, 2001, because C is unable to reasonably predict that the satellite will successfully perform its mission for five years.

*Example (2).* PCM—computing income.

(i) C, whose taxable year ends December 31, determines the income from long-term contracts using the PCM. During 2001, C agrees to manufacture for the customer, B, a unique item for a total contract price of $1,000,000. Under C's contract, B is entitled to retain 10 percent of the total contract price until it accepts the item. By the end of 2001, C has incurred $200,000 of allocable contract costs and estimates that the total allocable contract costs will be $800,000. By the end of 2002, C has incurred $600,000 of allocable contract costs and estimates that the total allocable contract costs will be $900,000. In 2003, after completing the contract, C determines that the actual cost to manufacture the item was $750,000.

(ii) For each of the taxable years, C's income from the contract is computed as follows:

| | Taxable year | | |
|---|---|---|---|
| | 2001 | 2002 | 2003 |
| (A) Cumulative incurred costs | $ 200,000 | $ 600,000 | $ 750,000 |
| (B) Estimated total costs | 800,000 | 900,000 | 750,000 |
| (C) Completion factor: (A) (B) | 25.00% | 66.67% | 100.00% |
| (D) Total contract price | 1,000,000 | 1,000,000 | 1,000,000 |
| (E) Cumulative gross receipts: | 250,000 | 666,667 | 1,000,000 |
| (F) Cumulative gross receipts: (C)×(D) | (0) | (250,000) | (666,667) |
| (G) Current-year gross receipts | 250,000 | 416,667 | 333,333 |
| (H) Cumulative incurred costs | 200,000 | 600,000 | 750,000 |
| (I) Cumulative incurred costs (prior year) | (0) | (200,000) | (600,000) |
| (J) Current-year costs | 200,000 | 400,000 | 150,000 |
| (K) Gross income: (G) - (J) | $ 50,000 | $ 16,667 | $ 183,333 |

*Example (3).* PCM—computing income with cost sharing.

(i) C, whose taxable year ends December 31, determines the income from long-term contracts using the PCM. During 2001, C enters into a contract to manufacture a unique item. The contract specifies a target price of $1,000,000, a target cost of $600,000, and a target profit of $400,000. C and B will share the savings of any cost underrun (actual total incurred cost is less than target cost) and the additional cost of any cost overrun (actual total incurred cost is greater than target cost) as follows: 30 percent to C and 70 percent to B. By the end of 2001, C has incurred $200,000 of allocable contract costs and estimates that the total allocable contract costs will be $600,000. By the end of 2002, C has incurred $300,000 of allocable contract costs and estimates that the total allocable contract costs will be $400,000. In 2003, after completing the contract, C determines that the actual cost to manufacture the item was $700,000.

(ii) For each of the taxable years, C's income from the contract is computed as follows (note that the sharing of any cost underrun or cost overrun is reflected as an adjustment to C's target price under paragraph (b)(4)(i) of this section):

| | Taxable year | | |
|---|---|---|---|
| | 2001 | 2002 | 2003 |
| (A) Cumulative incurred costs | $ 200,000 | $ 300,000 | $ 700,000 |
| (B) Estimated total costs | 600,000 | 400,000 | 700,000 |
| (C) Completion factor: (A) (B) | 33.33% | 75.00% | 100.00% |
| (D) Target price | $1,000,000 | $1,000,000 | $1,000,000 |
| (E) Estimated total costs | 600,000 | 400,000 | 700,000 |
| (F) Target costs | 600,000 | 600,000 | 600,000 |
| (G) Cost (underrun)/overrun: (E)-(F) | 0 | (200,000) | 100,000 |
| (H) Adjustment rate | 70% | 70% | 70% |
| (I) Target price adjustment | (0) | (140,000) | 70,000 |
| (J) Total contract price: (D) + (I) | 1,000,000 | $ 860,000 | $1,070,000 |
| (K) Cumulative gross receipts: (C)×(J) | $ 333,333 | $ 645,000 | $1,070,000 |
| (L) Cumulative gross receipts: (prior year) | (0) | (333,333) | (645,000) |
| (M) Current-year gross receipts | 333,333 | 311,667 | 425,000 |
| (N) Cumulative incurred costs | 200,000 | 300,000 | 400,000 |
| (O) Cumulative incurred costs (prior year) | (0) | (200,000) | (300,000) |
| (P) Current-year costs | 200,000 | 100,000 | 400,000 |
| (Q) Gross income: (M) - (P) | $ 133,333 | $ 211,667 | $ 25,000 |

*Example (4).* PCM—10 percent method.

(i) C, whose taxable year ends December 31, determines the income from long-term contracts using the PCM. In November 2001, C agrees to manufacture a unique item for $1,000,000. C reasonably estimates that the total allocable contract costs will be $600,000. By December 31, 2001, C has received $50,000 in progress payments and incurred $40,000 of costs. C elects to use the 10 percent method effective for 2001 and all subsequent taxable years. During 2002, C receives $500,000 in progress payments and incurs $260,000 of costs. In 2003, C incurs an additional $300,000 of costs, C finishes manufacturing the item, and receives the final $450,000 payment.

(ii) For each of the taxable years, C's income from the contract is computed as follows:

| | Taxable year | | |
|---|---|---|---|
| | 2001 | 2002 | 2003 |
| (A) Cumulative incurred costs | $ 40,000 | $ 300,000 | $ 600,000 |
| (B) Estimated total costs | 600,000 | 600,000 | 600,000 |
| (C) Completion factor: (A) (B) | 6.67% | 50.00% | 100.00% |
| (D) Total contract price | 1,000,000 | 1,000,000 | 1,000,000 |
| (E) Cumulative gross receipts: (C)×(D)* | 0 | 500,000 | 1,000,000 |
| (F) Cumulative gross receipts: (prior year) | (0) | (0) | (500,000) |
| (G) Current-year gross receipts | 0 | 500,000 | 500,000 |
| (H) Cumulative incurred costs | 0 | 300,000 | 600,000 |
| (I) Cumulative incurred costs (prior year) | (0) | (0) | (300,000) |
| (J) Current-year costs | 0 | 300,000 | 300,000 |
| (K) Gross income: (G) - (J) | 0 | $ 200,000 | $ 200,000 |

* Unless (C) 10 percent

*Example (5).* PCM—contract terminated. C, whose taxable year ends December 31, determines the income from long-term contracts using the PCM. During 2001, C buys land and begins constructing a building that will contain 50 condominium units on that land. C enters into a contract to sell one unit in this condominium to B for $240,000. B gives C a $5,000 deposit toward the purchase price. By the end of 2001, C has incurred $50,000 of allocable contract costs on B's unit and estimates that the total allocable contract costs on B's unit will be $150,000. Thus, for 2001, C reports gross receipts of $80,000 ($50,000 $150,000 × $240,000), current-year costs of $50,000, and gross income of $30,000 ($80,000--$50,000). In 2002, after C has incurred an additional $25,000 of allocable contract costs on B's unit, B files for bankruptcy protection and defaults on the contract with C, who is permitted to keep B's $5,000 deposit as liquidated damages. In 2002, C reverses the transaction with B under paragraph (b)(7) of this section and reports a loss of $30,000 ($50,000-$80,000). In addition, C obtains an adjusted basis in the unit sold to B of $70,000 ($50,000 (current-year costs deducted in 2001)--$5,000 (B's forfeited deposit) + $25,000 (current-year costs incurred in 2002). C may not apply the look-back method to this contract in 2002.

*Example (6).* CCM—contracts with disputes from customer claims. In 2001, C, whose taxable year ends December 31, uses the CCM to account for exempt construction contracts. C enters into a contract to construct a bridge for B. The terms of the contract provide for a $1,000,000 gross contract price. C finishes the bridge in 2002 at a cost of $950,000. When B examines the bridge, B insists that C either repaint several girders or reduce the contract price. The amount reasonably in dispute is $10,000. In 2003, C and B resolve their dispute, C repaints the girders at a cost of $6,000, and C and B agree that the contract price is not to be reduced. Because C is assured a profit of $40,000 ($1,000,000--$10,000--$950,000) in 2002 even if the dispute is resolved in B's favor, C must take this $40,000 into account in 2002. In 2003, C will earn an additional $4,000 profit ($1,000,000--$956,000--$40,000) from the contract with B. Thus, C must take into account an additional $10,000 of gross contract price and $6,000 of additional contract costs in 2003.

*Example (7).* CCM—contracts with disputes from taxpayer claims. In 2003, C, whose taxable year ends December 31, uses the CCM to account for exempt construction contracts. C enters into a contract to construct a building for B. The terms of the contract provide for a $1,000,000 gross contract price. C finishes the building in 2004 at a cost of $1,005,000. B examines the building in 2004 and agrees that it meets the contract's specifications; however, at the end of 2004, C and B are unable to agree on the merits of C's claim for an additional $10,000 for items that C alleges are changes in contract specifications and B alleges are within the scope of the contract's original specifications. In 2005, B agrees to pay C an additional $2,000 to satisfy C's claims under the contract. Because the amount in dispute affects so much of the gross contract price that C cannot determine in 2004 whether a profit or loss will ultimately be realized, C may not taken any of the gross contract price or allocable contract costs into account in 2004. C must take into account $1,002,000 of gross contract price and $1,005,000 of allocable contract costs in 2005.

*Example (8).* CCM—contracts with disputes from taxpayer and customer claims. C, whose taxable year ends December 31, uses the CCM to account for exempt construction contracts. C constructs a factory for B pursuant to a long-term contract. Under the terms of the contract, B agrees to pay C a total of $1,000,000 for construction of the factory. C finishes construction of the factory in 2002 at a cost of $1,020,000. When B takes possession of the factory and begins operations in December 2002, B is dissatisfied with the location and workmanship of certain heating ducts. As of the end of 2002, C contends that the heating ducts are constructed in accordance with contract specifications. The amount of the gross contract price reasonably in dispute with respect to the heating ducts is $6,000. As of this time, C is claiming $14,000 in addition to the original contract price for certain changes in contract specifications which C alleges have increased his costs. B denies that these changes have increased C's costs. In 2003, the disputes between C and B are resolved by performance of additional work by C at a cost of $1,000 and by an agreement that the contract price would be revised downward to $996,000. Under these circumstances, C must include in his gross income for 2002, $994,000 (the gross contract price less the amount reasonably in dispute because of B's claim, or $1,000,000--$6,000). In 2002, C must also take into account $1,000,000 of allocable contract costs (costs incurred less the amounts in dispute attributable to both B's and C's claims, or $1,020,000--$6,000--$14,000). In 2003, C must take into account an additional $2,000 of gross contract price ($996,000--$994,000) and $21,000 of allocable contract costs ($1,021,000--$1,000,000).

**(i) [Reserved.]**

**(j) Consolidated groups and controlled groups.** *(1) Intercompany transactions.* (i) In general. Section 1.1502-13 does not apply to the income, gain, deduction, or loss from an intercompany transaction between members of a consolidated group, and section 267(f) does not apply to these items from an intercompany sale between members of a controlled group, to the extent—

(A) The transaction or sale directly or indirectly benefits, or is intended to benefit, another member's long-term contract with a nonmember;

(B) The selling member is required under section 460 to determine any part of its gross income from the transaction or sale under the percentage-of-completion method (PCM); and

(C) The member with the long-term contract is required under section 460 to determine any part of its gross income from the long-term contract under the PCM.

(ii) Definitions and nomenclature. The definitions and nomenclature under § 1.1502-13 and § 1.267(f)-1 apply for purposes of this paragraph (j).

*(2) Example.* The following example illustrates the principles of paragraph (j)(1) of this section.

*Example.* Corporations P, S, and B file consolidated returns on a calendar-year basis. In 1996, B enters into a long-term contract with X, a nonmember, to manufacture 5 airplanes for $500 million, with delivery scheduled for 1999. Section 460 requires B to determine the gross income from its contract with X under the PCM. S enters into a contract with B to manufacture for $50 million the engines that B will install on X's airplanes. Section 460 requires S to determine the gross income from its contract with B under the PCM. S estimates that it will incur $40 million of total contract costs during 1997 and 1998 to manufacture the engines. S incurs $10 million of contract costs in 1997 and $30 million in 1998. Under paragraph (j) of this section, S determines its gross income from the long-term contract under the PCM rather than taking its income or loss into account under section 267(f) or § 1.1502-13. Thus, S includes $12.5 million of gross receipts and $10 million of contract costs in gross income in 1997 and includes $37.5 million of gross receipts and $30 million of contract costs in gross income in 1998.

*(3) Effective dates.* (i) In general. This paragraph (j) applies with respect to transactions and sales occurring pursuant to contracts entered into in years beginning on or after July 12, 1995.

(ii) Prior law. For transactions and sales occurring pursuant to contracts entered into in years beginning before July 12, 1995, see the applicable regulations issued under sections 267(f) and 1502, including §§ 1.267(f)-1T, 1.267(f)-2T, and 1.1502-13(n) (as contained in the 26 CFR part 1 edition revised as of April 1, 1995).

*(4) Consent to change method of accounting.* For transactions and sales to which this paragraph (j) applies, the Commissioner's consent under section 446(e) is hereby granted to the extent any changes in method of accounting are necessary solely to comply with this section, provided the changes are made in the first taxable year of the taxpayer to which the rules of this paragraph (j) apply. Changes in method of accounting for these transactions are to be effected on a cut-off basis.

**(k) Mid-contract change in taxpayer.** *(1) In general.* The rules in this paragraph (k) apply if prior to the completion of a long-term contract accounted for using a long-term contract method by a taxpayer (old taxpayer), there is a transaction that makes another taxpayer (new taxpayer) responsible for accounting for income from the same contract. For purposes of this paragraph (k) and § 1.460-6(g), an old taxpayer also includes any old taxpayer(s) (e.g., predecessors) of the old taxpayer. In addition, a change in status from taxable to tax exempt or from domestic to foreign, or vice versa, will be considered a change in taxpayer. Finally, a contract will be treated as the same contract if the terms of the contract are not substantially changed in connection with the transaction, whether or not the customer agrees to release the old taxpayer from any or all of its obligations under the contract. The rules governing constructive completion transactions are provided in paragraph (k)(2) of this section, while the rules governing step-in-the-shoes transactions are provided in paragraph (k)(3) of this section. Special rules relating to the treatment of certain partnership transactions are provided in paragraphs (k)(2)(iv) and (k)(3)(v) of this section. For application of the look-back method to mid-contract changes in taxpayers for contracts accounted for using the PCM, see § 1.460-6(g).

*(2) Constructive completion transactions.* (i) Scope. The constructive completion rules in this paragraph (k)(2) apply to transactions (constructive completion transactions) that result in a change in the taxpayer responsible for reporting income from a contract and that are not described in paragraph (k)(3)(i) of this section. Constructive completion transactions generally include, for example, taxable sales under section 1001 and deemed asset sales under section 338.

(ii) Old taxpayer. The old taxpayer is treated as completing the contract on the date of the transaction. The total contract price (or, gross contract price in the case of a long-term contract accounted for under the CCM) for the old taxpayer is the sum of any amounts realized from the transaction that are allocable to the contract and any amounts the old taxpayer has received or reasonably expects to receive under the contract. Total contract price (or gross contract price) is reduced by any amount paid by the old taxpayer to the new taxpayer, and by any transaction costs, that are allocable to the contract. Thus, the old taxpayer's allocable contract costs determined under paragraph (b)(5) of this section do not include any consideration paid, or costs incurred, as a result of the transaction that are allocable to the contract. In the case of a transaction subject to section 338 or 1060, the amount realized from the transaction allocable to the contract is determined by using the residual method under §§ 1.338-6 and 1.338-7.

(iii) New taxpayer. The new taxpayer is treated as entering into a new contract on the date of the transaction. The new taxpayer must evaluate whether the new contract should be classified as a long-term contract within the meaning of § 1.460-1(b) and account for the contract under a permissible method of accounting. For a new taxpayer who accounts for a contract using the PCM, the total contract price is any amount the new taxpayer reasonably expects to receive under the contract consistent with paragraph (b)(4) of this section. Total contract price is reduced by the amount of any consideration paid by the new taxpayer as a result of the transaction, and by any transaction costs, that are allocable to the contract and is increased by the amount of any consideration received by the new taxpayer as a result of the transaction that is allocable to the contract. Similarly, the gross contract price for a contract accounted for using the CCM is all amounts the new taxpayer is entitled by law or contract to receive consistent with paragraph (d)(3) of this section, adjusted for any consideration paid (or received) by the new taxpayer as a result of the transaction, and for any transaction costs, that are allocable to the contract. Thus, the new taxpayer's allocable contract costs determined under paragraph (b)(5) of this section do not include any consideration paid, or costs incurred, as a result of the transaction that are allocable to the contract. In the case of a transaction subject to sections 338 or 1060, the amount of consideration paid that is allocable to the contract is determined by using the residual method under §§ 1.338-6 and 1.338-7.

(iv) Special rules relating to distributions of certain contracts by a partnership. (A) In general. The constructive completion rules of paragraph (k)(2) of this section apply both to the distribution of a contract accounted for under a long-term contract method of accounting by a partnership to a partner and to the distribution of an interest in a partnership (lower-tier partnership) holding (either directly or through other partnerships) one or more contracts accounted for under a long-term contract method of accounting by another partnership (upper-tier partnership). Notwithstanding the previous sentence, the constructive completion rules of paragraph (k)(2) of this section do not apply to a transfer by a partnership (transferor partnership) of all of its assets and liabilities to a second partnership (transferee partnership) in an exchange described in section 721, followed by a distribution of the interest in the transferee partnership in liquidation of the transferor partnership, under § 1.708-1(b)(4) (relating to terminations under section 708(b)(1)(B)) or § 1.708-1(c)(3)(i) (relating to certain partnership mergers). If a partnership that holds a contract accounted for under a long-term contract method of accounting terminates under section 708(b)(1)(A) because the number of its owners is reduced to one, the entire contract will be treated as being distributed from the partnership for purposes of the constructive completion rules, and the partnership must apply paragraph (k)(2) of this section immediately prior to the transaction or transactions resulting in the termination of the partnership.

(B) Old taxpayer. The partnership that distributes the contract is treated as the old taxpayer for purposes of paragraph (k)(2)(ii) of this section. For purposes of determining the total contract price (or gross contract price) under paragraph (k)(2)(ii) of this section, the fair market value of the contract is treated as the amount realized from the transaction. For purposes of determining each partner's distributive share of partnership items, any income or loss resulting from the constructive completion must be allocated among the partners of the old taxpayer as though the partnership closed its books on the date of the distribution.

(C) New taxpayer. The partner receiving the distributed contract is treated as the new taxpayer for purposes of paragraph (k)(2)(iii) of this section. For purposes of determining the total contract price (or gross contract price) under paragraph (k)(2)(iii) of this section, the new taxpayer's basis in the contract (including the uncompleted property, if applicable) after the distribution (as determined under section 732) is treated as consideration paid by the new taxpayer that is allocable to the contract. Thus, the total contract price (or gross contract price) of the new contract is reduced by the partner's basis in the contract (including the uncompleted property, if applicable) immediately after the distribution.

(D) Basis rules. For purposes of determining the new taxpayer's basis in the contract (including the uncompleted property, if applicable) under section 732, and the amount of any basis adjustment under section 734(b), the partnership's basis in the contract (including the uncompleted property, if applicable) immediately prior to the distribution is equal to—

(1) The partnership's allocable contract costs (including transaction costs);

(2) Increased (or decreased) by the amount of cumulative taxable income (or loss) recognized by the partnership on the contract through the date of the distribution (including amounts recognized as a result of the constructive completion); and

(3) Decreased by the amounts that the partnership has received or reasonably expects to receive under the contract.

(E) Section 751. (1) In general. Contracts accounted for under a long-term contract method of accounting are unrealized receivables within the meaning of section 751(c). For purposes of section 751, the amount of ordinary income or loss attributable to a contract accounted for under a long-term contract method of accounting is the amount of income or loss that the partnership would take into account under the constructive completion rules of paragraph (k)(2) of this section if the contract were disposed of for its fair market value in a constructive completion transaction, adjusted to account for any income or loss from the contract that is allocated under section 706 to that portion of the taxable year of the partnership ending on the date of the distribution, sale, or exchange.

(2) Ordering rules. Because the distribution of a contract accounted for under a long-term contract method of accounting is the distribution of an unrealized receivable, section 751(b) may apply to the distribution. A partnership that distributes a contract accounted for under a long-term contract method of accounting must apply paragraph (k)(2)(ii) of this section before applying the rules of section 751(b) to the distribution.

*(3) Step-in-the-shoes transactions.* (i) Scope. Except as otherwise provided in paragraph (k)(3)(v)(D) of this section, the step-in-the-shoes rules in this paragraph (k)(3) apply to the following transactions that result in a change in the taxpayer responsible for reporting income from a contract accounted for using a long-term contract method of accounting (step-in-the-shoes transactions)—

(A) Transfers to which section 361 applies if the transfer is in connection with a reorganization described in section 368(a)(1)(A), (C) or (F);

(B) Transfers to which section 361 applies if the transfer is in connection with a reorganization described in section 368(a)(1)(D) or (G), provided the requirements of section 354(b)(1)(A) and (B) are met;

(C) Distributions to which section 332 applies, provided the contract is transferred to an 80-percent distributee;

(D) Transfers described in section 351;

(E) Transfers to which section 361 applies if the transfer is in connection with a reorganization described in section 368(a)(1)(D) with respect to which the requirements of section 355 (or so much of section 356 as relates to section 355) are met;

(F) Transfers (e.g., sales) of S corporation stock;

(G) Conversion to or from an S corporation;

(H) Members joining or leaving a consolidated group;

(I) Contributions of contracts accounted for under a long-term contract method of accounting to which section 721(a) applies;

(J) Contributions of property (other than contracts accounted for under a long-term contract method of accounting) to a partnership that holds a contract accounted for under a long-term contract method of accounting;

(K) Transfers of partnership interests (other than transfers which cause the partnership to terminate under section 708(b)(1)(A));

(L) Distributions to which section 731 applies (other than the distribution of the contract); and

(M) Any other transaction designated in the Internal Revenue Bulletin by the Internal Revenue Service. See § 601.601(d)(2)(ii) of this chapter.

(ii) Old taxpayer. (A) In general. The new taxpayer will "step into the shoes" of the old taxpayer with respect to the contract. Thus, the old taxpayer's obligation to account for the contract terminates on the date of the transaction and is assumed by the new taxpayer, as set forth in paragraph (k)(3)(iii) of this section. As a result, an old taxpayer using the PCM is required to recognize income from the contract based on the cumulative allocable contract costs incurred as of the date of the transaction. Similarly, an old taxpayer using the CCM is not required to recognize any revenue and may not deduct allocable contract costs incurred with respect to the contract.

(B) Gain realized on the transaction. The amount of gain the old taxpayer realizes on the transfer of a contract in a step-in-the-shoes transaction must be determined after application of paragraph (k)(3)(ii)(A) of this section using the rules of paragraph (k)(2) of this section that apply to constructive completion transactions. (The amount of gain realized on a transfer of a contract is relevant, for example, in determining the amount of gain recognized with respect to the contract in a section 351 transaction in which the old taxpayer receives from the new taxpayer money or property other than stock of the transferee.)

(iii) New taxpayer. (A) Method of accounting. Beginning on the date of the transaction, the new taxpayer must account for the long-term contract by using the same method of accounting used by the old taxpayer prior to the transaction. The same method of accounting must be used for such contract regardless of whether the old taxpayer's method is the new taxpayer's principal method of accounting under § 1.381(c)(4)-1(b)(3) or whether the new taxpayer is otherwise eligible to use the old taxpayer's method. Thus, if the old taxpayer uses the PCM to account for the contract, the new taxpayer steps into the shoes of the old taxpayer with respect to its completion factor and percentage of completion methods (such as the 10-percent method), even if the new taxpayer has not elected such methods for similarly classified contracts. Similarly, if the old taxpayer uses the CCM, the new taxpayer steps into the shoes of the old taxpayer with respect to the CCM, even if the new taxpayer is not otherwise eligible to use the CCM. However, the new taxpayer is not necessarily bound by the old taxpayer's method for similarly classified contracts entered into by the new taxpayer subsequent to the transaction and must apply general tax principles, including section 381, to determine the appropriate method to account for these subsequent contracts. To the extent that general tax principles allow the taxpayer to account for similarly classified contracts using a method other than the old taxpayer's method, the taxpayer is not required to obtain the consent of the Commissioner to begin using such other method.

(B) Contract price. In the case of a long-term contract that has been accounted for under PCM, the total contract price for the new taxpayer is the sum of any amounts the old taxpayer or the new taxpayer has received or reasonably expects to receive under the contract consistent with paragraph (b)(4) of this section. Similarly, the gross contract price in the case of a long-term contract accounted for under the CCM includes all amounts the old taxpayer or the new taxpayer is entitled by law or by contract to receive consistent with paragraph (d)(3) of this section.

(C) Contract costs. Total allocable contract costs for the new taxpayer are the allocable contract costs as defined under paragraph (b)(5) of this section incurred by either the old taxpayer prior to, or the new taxpayer after, the transaction. Thus, any payments between the old taxpayer and the new taxpayer with respect to the contract in connection with the transaction are not treated as allocable contract costs.

(iv) Special rules related to certain corporate and partnership transactions. (A) Old taxpayer—basis adjustment. (1) In general. Except as provided in paragraph (k)(3)(iv)(A)(2) of this section, in the case of a transaction described in paragraph (k)(3)(i)(D), (E), or (I) of this section, the old taxpayer must adjust its basis in the stock or partnership interest of the new taxpayer by—

(i) Increasing such basis by the amount of gross receipts the old taxpayer has recognized under the contract; and

(ii) Reducing such basis by the amount of gross receipts the old taxpayer has received or reasonably expects to receive under the contract (except to the extent such gross receipts give rise to a liability other than a liability described in section 357(c)(3)).

(2) Basis adjustment in excess of stock or partnership interest basis. If the old and new taxpayer do not join in the filing of a consolidated Federal income tax return, the old taxpayer may not adjust its basis in the stock or partnership interest of the new taxpayer under paragraph (k)(3)(iv)(A)(1) of this section below zero and the old taxpayer must recognize ordinary income to the extent the basis in the stock or partnership interest of the new taxpayer otherwise would be adjusted below zero. If the old and new taxpayer join in the filing of a consolidated Federal income tax return, the old taxpayer must create an (or increase an existing) excess loss account to the extent the basis in the stock of the new taxpayer otherwise would be adjusted below zero under paragraph (k)(3)(iv)(A)(1) of this section. See § 1.1502-19 and 1.1502-32(a)(3)(ii).

(3) Subsequent dispositions of certain contracts. If the old taxpayer disposes of a contract in a transaction described in paragraph (k)(3)(i)(D), (E), or (I) of this section that the old taxpayer acquired in a transaction described in paragraph (k)(3)(i)(D), (E), or (I) of this section, the basis adjustment rule of this paragraph (k)(3)(iv)(A) is applied by treating the old taxpayer as having recognized the amount of gross receipts recognized by the previous old taxpayer under the contract and any amount recognized by the previous old taxpayer with respect to the contract in connection with the transaction in which the old taxpayer acquired the contract. In addition, the old taxpayer is treated as having received or as reasonably expecting to receive under the contract any amount the previous old taxpayer received or reasonably expects to receive under the contract. Similar principles will apply in the case of multiple successive transfers described in paragraph (k)(3)(i)(D), (E), or (I) of this section involving the contract.

(B) New taxpayer. (1) Contract price adjustment. Generally, payments between the old taxpayer and the new taxpayer with respect to the contract in connection with the transaction do not affect the contract price. Notwithstanding the preceding sentence and paragraph (k)(3)(iii)(B) of this section, however, in the case of transactions described in paragraph (k)(3)(i)(B), (D), (E), or (I) of this section, the total contract price (or gross contract price) must be reduced to the extent of any amount recognized by the old taxpayer with respect to the contract in connection with the transaction (e.g., any amount recognized under section 351(b) or section 357 that is attributable to the contract and any income recognized by the old taxpayer pursuant to the basis adjustment rule of paragraph (k)(3)(iv)(A) of this section).

(2) Basis in contract. The new taxpayer's basis in a contract (including the uncompleted property, if applicable) acquired in a transaction described in paragraphs (k)(3)(i)(A) through (E) or paragraph (k)(3)(i)(I) of this section will be computed under section 362, section 334, or section 723, as applicable. Upon a new taxpayer's completion (actual or constructive) of a CCM or a PCM contract acquired in a transaction described in paragraphs (k)(3)(i)(A) through (E) or paragraph (k)(3)(i)(I) of this section, the new taxpayer's basis in the contract (including the uncompleted property, if applicable) is reduced to zero. The new taxpayer is not entitled to a deduction or loss in connection with any basis reduction pursuant to this paragraph (k)(3)(iv)(B)(2).

(C) Definition of old taxpayer and new taxpayer for certain partnership transactions. For purposes of paragraphs (k)(3)(ii), (iii) and (iv) of this section, in the case of a transaction described in paragraph (k)(3)(i)(I) of this section, the partner contributing the contract to the partnership is treated as the old taxpayer, and the partnership receiving the contract from the partner is treated as the new taxpayer.

(D) Exceptions to step-in-the-shoes rules for S corporations. Upon a transfer described in paragraph (k)(3)(i)(F) of this section or a conversion described in paragraph (k)(3)(i)(G) of this section, paragraphs (k)(3)(ii) and (iii) of this section apply to a contract accounted for under a long-term contract method of accounting only if the S corporation's books are closed under section 1362(e)(3), section 1362(e)(6)(C), section 1362(e)(6)(D), section 1377(a)(2), or § 1.1502-76 on the date of the transfer or conversion. In these cases, the corporation is treated as both the old taxpayer and the new taxpayer for purposes of paragraphs (k)(3)(ii) and (iii) of this section. In all other cases involving these transfers, the corporation shall compute its income or loss from each contract accounted for under a long-term contract method of accounting for the period that includes the date of the transaction as though no change in taxpayer had occurred with respect to the contract, and must allocate the income or loss from the contract for that period in accordance with the rules generally applicable to transfers of S corporation stock and conversions to or from S corporation status. This paragraph (k)(3)(iv)(D) is applicable for transactions on or after July 16, 2004. In addition, this paragraph (k)(3)(iv)(D) may be relied upon for transactions on or after May 15, 2002.

(v) Special rules relating to certain partnership transactions. (A) Section 704(c). (1) Contributions of contracts. The principles of section 704(c)(1)(A), section 737, and the regulations thereunder apply to income or loss with respect to a contract accounted for under a long-term contract method of accounting that is contributed to a partnership. The amount of built-in income or built-in loss attributable to a contributed contract that is subject to section 704(c)(1)(A) is determined as follows. First, the contributing partner must take into account any income or loss required under paragraph (k)(3)(ii)(A) of this section for the period ending on the date of the contribution. Second, the partnership must determine the amount of income or loss that the contributing partner would take into account if the contract were disposed of for its fair market value in a constructive completion transaction. This calculation is treated as occurring immediately after the partner has applied paragraph (k)(3)(ii)(A) of this section, but before the contribution to the partnership. Finally, this amount is reduced by the amount of income, if any, that the contributing partner is required to recognize as a result of the contribution.

(2) Revaluations of partnership property. The principles of section 704(c) and § 1.704-3 apply to allocations of income or loss with respect to a long-term contract that is revalued by a partnership under § 1.704-1(b)(2)(iv)(f). The amount of built-in income or built-in loss attributable to such a contract is equal to the amount of income or loss that would be taken into account if, at the time of the revaluation, the contract were disposed of for its fair market value in a constructive completion transaction.

(3) Allocation methods. In the case of a contract accounted for under the CCM, any built-in income or loss under section 704(c) is taken into account in the year the contract is completed. In the case of a contract accounted for under a long-term contract method of accounting other than the CCM, any built-in income or loss under section 704(c) must be taken into account in a manner that reasonably accounts for the section 704(c) income or loss over the remaining term of the contract.

(B) Basis adjustments under sections 743(b) and 734(b). For purposes of §§ 1.743-1(d), 1.755-1(b), and 1.755-1(c), the amount of ordinary income or loss attributable to a contract accounted for under a long-term contract method of accounting is the amount of income or loss that the partnership would take into account under the constructive completion rules of paragraph (k)(2) of this section if, at the time of the sale of a partnership interest or the distribution to a partner, the partnership disposed of the contract for its fair market value in a constructive completion transaction. If all or part of the transferee's basis adjustment under section 743(b) or the partnership's basis adjustment under section 734(b) is allocated to a contract accounted for under a long-term contract method of accounting, the basis adjustment shall reduce or increase, as the case may be, the affected party's income or loss from the contract. In the case of a contract accounted for under the CCM, the basis adjustment is taken into account in the year in which the contract is completed. In the case of a contract accounted for under a long-term contract method of accounting other than the CCM, the portion of that basis adjustment that is recovered in each taxable year of the partnership must be determined by the partnership in a manner that reasonably accounts for the adjustment over the remaining term of the contract.

(C) Cross reference. See paragraph (k)(2)(iv)(E) of this section for rules relating to the application of section 751 to the transfer of an interest in a partnership holding a contract accounted for under a long-term contract method of accounting.

(D) Exceptions to step-in-the-shoes rules. Upon a contribution described in paragraph (k)(3)(i)(J) of this section, a transfer described in paragraph (k)(3)(i)(K) of this section, or a distribution described in paragraph (k)(3)(i)(L) of this section, paragraphs (k)(3)(ii) and (iii) of this section apply to a contract accounted for under a long-term contract method of accounting only if the partnership's books are properly closed with respect to that contract under section 706. In these cases, the partnership is treated as both the old taxpayer and the new taxpayer for purposes of paragraphs (k)(3)(ii) and (iii) of this section. In all other cases involving these transactions, the partnership shall compute its income or loss from each contract accounted for under a long-term contract method of accounting for the period that includes the date of the transaction as though no change in taxpayer had occurred with respect to the contract, and must allocate the income or loss from the contract for that period under a reasonable method complying with section 706.

*(4) Anti-abuse rule.* Notwithstanding this paragraph (k), in the case of a transaction entered into with a principal purpose of shifting the tax consequences associated with a long-term contract in a manner that substantially reduces the aggregate U.S. Federal income tax liability of the parties with respect to that contract, the Commissioner may allocate to the old (or new) taxpayer the income from that contract properly allocable to the old (or new) taxpayer. For example, the Commissioner may reallocate income from a long-term contract in a transaction in which a contract accounted for using the CCM, or using the PCM where the old taxpayer has received advance payments in excess of its contribution to the contract, is transferred to a tax indifferent party (e.g., a foreign person not subject to U.S. Federal income tax).

*(5) Examples.* The following examples illustrate the rules of this paragraph (k). For purposes of these examples, it is assumed that the contract is a long-term construction contract accounted for using the PCM prior to the transaction unless stated otherwise and the contract is not transferred with a principal purpose of shifting the tax consequences associated with a long-term contract in a manner that substantially reduces the aggregate U.S. Federal income tax liability of the parties with respect to that contract. The examples are as follows:

*Example (1).* Constructive completion—PCM. (i) Facts. In Year 1, X enters into a contract. The total contract price is $1,000,000 and the estimated total allocable contract costs are $800,000. In Year 1, X incurs costs of $200,000. In Year 2, X incurs additional costs of $400,000 before selling the contract as part of a taxable sale of its business in Year 2 to Y, an unrelated party. At the time of sale, X has received $650,000 in progress payments under the contract. The consideration allocable to the contract under section 1060 is $150,000. Pursuant to the sale, the new taxpayer Y immediately assumes X's contract obligations and rights. Y is required to account for the contract using the PCM. In Year 2, Y incurs additional allocable contract costs of $50,000. Y correctly estimates at the end of Year 2 that it will have to incur an additional $75,000 of allocable contract costs in Year 3 to complete the contract.

(ii) Old taxpayer. For Year 1, X reports receipts of $250,000 (the completion factor multiplied by total contract price ($200,000/$800,000 x $1,000,000)) and costs of $200,000, for a profit of $50,000. X is treated as completing the contract in Year 2 because it sold the contract. For purposes of applying the PCM in Year 2, the total contract price is $800,000 (the sum of the amounts received under the contract and the amount realized in the sale ($650,000 + $150,000)) and the total allocable contract costs are $600,000 (the sum of the costs incurred in Year 1 and Year 2 ($200,000 + $400,000)). Thus, in Year 2, X reports receipts of $550,000 (total contract price minus receipts already reported ($800,000 - $250,000)) and costs incurred in year 2 of $400,000, for a profit of $150,000.

(iii) New taxpayer. Y is treated as entering into a new contract in Year 2. The total contract price is $200,000 (the amount remaining to be paid under the terms of the contract less the consideration paid allocable to the contract ($1,000,000 - $650,000 - $150,000)). The estimated total allocable contract costs at the end of Year 2 are $125,000 (the allocable contract costs that Y reasonably expects to incur to complete the contract ($50,000 + $75,000)). In Year 2, Y reports receipts of $80,000 (the completion factor multiplied by the total contract price [($50,000/$125,000) x $200,000] and costs of $50,000 (the costs incurred after the purchase), for a profit of $30,000. For Year 3, Y reports receipts of $120,000 (total contract price minus receipts already reported ($200,000 - $80,000)) and costs of $75,000, for a profit of $45,000.

*Example (2).* Constructive completion—CCM. (i) Facts. The facts are the same as in Example 1, except that X and Y properly account for the contract under the CCM.

(ii) Old taxpayer. X does not report any income or costs from the contract in Year 1. In Year 2, the contract is deemed complete for X, and X reports its gross contract price of $800,000 (the sum of the amounts received under the contract and the amount realized in the sale ($650,000 + $150,000)) and its total allocable contract costs of $600,000 (the sum of the costs incurred in Year 1 and Year 2 ($200,000 + $400,000)) in that year, for a profit of $200,000.

(iii) New taxpayer. Y is treated as entering into a new contract in Year 2. Under the CCM, Y reports no gross receipts or costs in Year 2. Y reports its gross contract price of $200,000 (the amount remaining to be paid under the terms of the contract less the consideration paid allocable to the contract ($1,000,000 - $650,000 - $150,000)) and its total allocable contract costs of $125,000 (the allocable contract costs that Y incurred to complete the contract ($50,000 + $75,000)) in Year 3, the completion year, for a profit of $75,000.

*Example (3).* Step-in-the-shoes—PCM. (i) Facts. The facts are the same as in Example 1, except that X transfers the contract (including the uncompleted property) to Y in exchange for stock of Y in a transaction that qualifies as a statutory merger described in section 368(a)(1)(A) and does not result in gain or loss to X under section 361(a).

(ii) Old taxpayer. For Year 1, X reports receipts of $250,000 (the completion factor multiplied by total contract price ($200,000/$800,000 x $1,000,000)) and costs of $200,000, for a profit of $50,000. Because the mid-contract change in taxpayer results from a transaction described in paragraph (k)(3)(i) of this section, X is not treated as completing the contract in Year 2. In Year 2, X reports receipts of $500,000 (the completion factor multiplied by the total contract price and minus the Year 1 gross receipts [($600,000/$800,000 x $1,000,000) - $250,000]) and costs of $400,000, for a profit of $100,000.

(iii) New taxpayer. Because the mid-contract change in taxpayer results from a step-in-the-shoes transaction, Y must account for the contract using the same methods of accounting used by X prior to the transaction. Total contract price is the sum of any amounts that X and Y have received or reasonably expect to receive under the contract, and total allocable contract costs are the allocable contract costs of X and Y. Thus, the estimated total allocable contract costs at the end of Year 2 are $725,000 (the cumulative allocable contract costs of X and the estimated total allocable contract costs of Y ($200,000 + $400,000 + $50,000 + $75,000)). In Year 2, Y reports receipts of $146,552 (the completion factor multiplied by the total contract price minus receipts reported by the old taxpayer ([($650,000/$725,000) x $1,000,000] - $750,000) and costs of $50,000, for a profit of $96,552. For Year 3, Y reports receipts of $103,448 (the total contract price minus prior year receipts ($1,000,000 - $896,552)) and costs of $75,000, for a profit of $28,448.

*Example (4).* Step-in-the-shoes—CCM. (i) Facts. The facts are the same as in Example 3, except that X properly accounts for the contract under the CCM.

(ii) Old taxpayer. X reports no income or costs from the contract in Years 1, 2 or 3.

(iii) New taxpayer. Because the mid-contract change in taxpayer results from a step-in-the-shoes transaction, Y must account for the contract using the same method of accounting used by X prior to the transaction. Thus, in Year 3, the completion year, Y reports receipts of $1,000,000 and total contract costs of $725,000, for a profit of $275,000.

*Example (5).* Step in the shoes—PCM—basis adjustment. The facts are the same as in Example 3, except that X transfers the contract (including the uncompleted property) with a basis of $0 and $125,000 of cash to a new corporation, Z, in exchange for all of the stock of Z in a section 351 transaction. Thus, under section 358(a), X's basis in the Z stock is $125,000. Pursuant to paragraph (k)(3)(iv)(A)(1) of this section, X must increase its basis in the Z stock by the amount of gross receipts X recognized under the contract, $750,000 ($250,000 receipts in Year 1 + $500,000 receipts in Year 2), and reduce its basis by the amount of gross receipts X received under the contract, the $650,000 in progress payments. Accordingly, X's basis in the Z stock is $225,000. All other results are the same.

*Example (6).* Step in the shoes—CCM—basis adjustment. (i) Facts. The facts are the same as in Example 4, except that X receives progress payments of $800,000 (rather than $650,000) and transfers the contract (including the uncompleted property) with a basis of $600,000 and $125,000 of cash to a new corporation, Z, in exchange for all of the stock of Z in a section 351 transaction. X and Z do not join in filing a consolidated Federal income tax return.

(ii) Old taxpayer. X reports no income or costs under the contract in Years 1, 2, or 3. Under section 358(a), X's basis in Z is $725,000. Pursuant to paragraph (k)(3)(iv)(A)(1), X must reduce its basis in the stock of Z by $800,000, the progress payments received by X. However, X may not reduce its basis in the Z stock below zero pursuant paragraph (k)(3)(iv)(A)(2) of this section. Accordingly, X's basis in the Z stock is reduced by $725,000 to zero and X must recognize ordinary income of $75,000.

(iii) New taxpayer. Upon completion of the contract in Year 3, Z reports gross receipts of $925,000 ($1,000,000 original contract price - $75,000 income recognized by the old taxpayer pursuant to the basis adjustment rule of paragraph (k)(3)(iv)(A)) and total contract costs of $725,000, for a profit of $200,000.

*Example (7).* Step in the shoes—PCM—gain recognized in transaction. (i) Facts. The facts are the same as in Example 3, except that X transfers the contract (including the uncompleted property) with a basis of $0 and an unrelated capital asset with a value of $100,000 and a basis of $0 to a new corporation, Z, in exchange for stock of Z with a value of $200,000 and $50,000 of cash in a section 351 transaction.

(ii) Old taxpayer. For year 1, X reports receipts of $250,000 ($200,000/$800,000 x $1,000,000) and costs of $200,000, for a profit of $50,000. X is not treated as completing the contract in Year 2. In Year 2, X reports receipts of $500,000 (($600,000/$800,000 x $1,000,000 = $750,000 cumulative gross receipts) - $250,000 prior year cumulative gross receipts) and costs of $400,000, for a profit of $100,000. Under paragraph (k)(3)(ii)(B) of this section, X determines that the gain realized on the transfer of the contract to Z under the constructive completion rules of paragraph (k)(2)(ii) of this section is $50,000 (total contract price of $800,000 ($150,000 value allocable to the contract + $650,000 progress payments) - $750,000 previously recognized cumulative gross receipts - $0 costs incurred but not recognized). The gain realized on the transfer of the unrelated capital asset to Z is $100,000. The amount of gain X must recognize due to the receipt of $50,000 cash in the exchange is $50,000, of which $30,000 is allocated to the contract ($150,000 value of contract/$250,000 total value of property transferred to Z x $50,000) and is treated as ordinary income, and $20,000 is allocated to the unrelated capital asset ($100,000 value of capital asset/$250,000 total value of property transferred to Z x $50,000). Under section 358(a), X's basis in the Z stock is $0. However, pursuant to paragraph (k)(3)(iv)(A)(1) of this section, X must increase its basis in the Z stock by $750,000, the amount of gross receipts recognized under the contract, and must reduce its basis in the Z stock by $650,000, the amount of gross receipts X received under the contract. Therefore, X's basis in the Z stock is $100,000.

(iii) New taxpayer. Z must account for the contract using the same PCM method used by X prior to the transaction. Pursuant to paragraph (k)(3)(iv)(B)(1) of this section, the total contract price is $970,000 ($1,000,000 amount X and Z have received or reasonably expect to receive under the contract - $30,000 income recognized by X with respect to the contract as a result of the receipt of $50,000 cash in the transaction). In Year 2, Z reports gross receipts of $119,655 ($650,000/$725,000 x $970,000 = $869,655 current year cumulative gross receipts - $750,000 cumulative gross receipts reported by the old taxpayer) and costs of $50,000, for a profit of $69,655. In Year 3, Z reports gross receipts of $100,345 ($970,000-$869,655) and costs of $75,000, for a profit of $25,345.

*Example (8).* Step in the shoes—CCM—gain recognized in transaction. (i) Facts. The facts are the same as in Example 4, except that X transfers the contract (including the uncompleted property) with a basis of $600,000 and an unrelated capital asset with a value of $125,000 and a basis of $0 to a new corporation, Z, in exchange for all the stock of Z with a value of $175,000 and $100,000 of cash in a section 351 transaction. X and Z do not join in filing a consolidated Federal income tax return.

(ii) Old taxpayer. X reports no income or costs under the contract in Years 1, 2, or 3. Under paragraph (k)(3)(ii)(B), X determines that the gain realized on the transfer of the contract to Z under the constructive completion rules of paragraph (k)(2)(ii) of this section is $200,000 ($800,000 total contract price ($150,000 value allocable to the contract + $650,000 progress payments) - $600,000 costs incurred but not recognized). The gain realized on the transfer of the unrelated capital asset to Z is $125,000. The amount of gain X must recognize due to the receipt of $100,000 of cash in the exchange is $100,000, of which $54,545 is allocated to the contract ($150,000 value of the contract/$275,000 total value of property transferred to Z x $100,000) and is treated as ordinary income, and $45,455 is allocated to the unrelated capital asset ($125,000 value of capital asset/$275,000 total value of property transferred to Z x $100,000). Under section 358(a), X's basis in the Z stock is $600,000 ($600,000 basis in the contract and unrelated capital asset transferred - $100,000 cash received + $100,000 gain recognized). Pursuant to paragraph (k)(3)(iv)(A)(1) of this section, X must reduce its basis in the stock of Z by $650,000, the progress payments received under the contract. However, X may not reduce its basis in the Z stock below zero pursuant to paragraph (k)(3)(iv)(A)(2) of this section. Accordingly, X's basis in the Z stock is reduced by $600,000 to zero and X must recognize income of $50,000.

(iii) New taxpayer. Z must account for the contract using the same CCM used by X prior to the transaction. Pursuant to paragraph (k)(3)(iv)(B)(1) of this section, the total contract price is $895,455 ($1,000,000 original contract price - $54,545 income recognized by old taxpayer with respect to the contract as a result of the receipt of cash in the transaction - $50,000 income recognized by the old taxpayer pursuant to the basis adjustment rule of paragraph (k)(3)(iv)(A)). Accordingly, upon completion of the contract in Year 3, Z reports gross receipts of $895,455 and total contract costs of $725,000, for a profit of $170,455.

*Example (9).* Constructive completion—PCM—distribution of contract by partnership. (i) Facts. In Year 1, W, X, Y, and Z each contribute $100,000 to form equal partnership PRS. In Year 1, PRS enters into a contract. The total contract price is $1,000,000 and the estimated total allocable contract costs are $800,000. In Year 1, PRS incurs costs of $600,000 and receives $650,000 in progress payments under the contract. Under the contract, PRS performed all of the services required in order to be entitled to receive the progress payments, and there was no obligation to return the payments or perform any additional services in order to retain the payments. PRS properly accounts for the contract under the PCM. In Year 2, PRS distributes the contract to X in liquidation of X's interest. PRS incurs no costs and receives no progress payments in Year 2 prior to the distribution. At the time of the distribution, PRS's only asset other than the long-term contract and the partially constructed property is $450,000 cash ($400,000 initially contributed and $50,000 in excess progress payments). The fair market value of the contract is $150,000. Pursuant to the distribution, X assumes PRS's contract obligations and rights. In Year 2, X incurs additional allocable contract costs of $50,000. X correctly estimates at the end of Year 2 that X will have to incur an additional $75,000 of allocable contract costs in Year 3 to complete the contract (rather than $150,000 as originally estimated by PRS). Assume that X properly accounts for the contract under the PCM, that PRS has no income or loss other than income or loss from the contract, and that PRS has an election under section 754 in effect in Year 2.

(ii) Tax consequences to PRS. For Year 1, PRS reports receipts of $750,000 (the completion factor multiplied by total contract price ($600,000/$800,000 x $1,000,000)) and costs of $600,000, for a profit of $150,000, which is allocated equally among W, X, Y, and Z ($37,500 each). Immediately prior to the distribution of the contract to X in Year 2, the contract is deemed completed. Under paragraph (k)(2)(iv)(B) of this section, the fair market value of the contract ($150,000) is treated as the amount realized from the transaction. For purposes of applying the PCM in Year 2, the total contract price is $800,000 (the sum of the amounts received under the contract and the amount treated as realized from the transaction ($650,000 + $150,000)) and the total allocable contract costs are $600,000. Thus, in Year 2 PRS reports receipts of $50,000 (total contract price minus receipts already reported ($800,000 - $750,000)), and costs incurred in Year 2 of $0, for a profit of $50,000. Under paragraph (k)(2)(iv)(B) of this section, this profit must be allocated among W, X, Y, and Z as though the partnership closed its books on the date of the distribution. Accordingly, each partner's distributive share of this income is $12,500.

(iii) Tax consequences to X. X's basis in its interest in PRS immediately prior to the distribution is $150,000 (X's $100,000 initial contribution, increased by $37,500, X's distributive share of Year 1 income, and $12,500, X's distributive share of Year 2 income). Under paragraph (k)(2)(iv)(D) of this section, PRS's basis in the contract (including the uncompleted property, if applicable) immediately prior to the distribution is equal to $150,000 (the partnership's allocable contract costs, $600,000, increased by the amount of income recognized by PRS on the contract through the date of the distribution (including amounts recognized as a result of the constructive completion), $200,000, decreased by the amounts that the partnership has received or reasonably expects to receive under the contract, $650,000). Under section 732, X's basis in the contract (including the uncompleted property) after the distribution is $150,000. Under paragraph (k)(2)(iv)(C) of this section, X's basis in the contract (including the uncompleted property) is treated as consideration paid by X that is allocable to the contract. X's total contract price is $200,000 (the amount remaining to be paid under the terms of the contract less the consideration allocable to the contract ($350,000-$150,000)). For Year 2, X reports receipts of $80,000 (the completion factor multiplied by the total contract price [($50,000/$125,000) x $200,000]) and costs of $50,000 (the costs incurred after the distribution of the contract), for a profit of $30,000. For Year 3, X reports receipts of $120,000 (the total contract price minus receipts already reported ($200,000 - $80,000)) and costs of $75,000, for a profit of $45,000.

(iv) Section 734(b). Because X's basis in the contract (including the uncompleted property) immediately after the distribution, $150,000, is equal to PRS's basis in the contract (including the uncompleted property) immediately prior to the distribution, there is no basis adjustment under section 734(b).

*Example (10).* Constructive completion—CCM—distribution of contract by partnership. (i) Facts. The facts are the same as in Example 9, except that PRS and X properly account for the contract under the CCM.

(ii) Tax consequences to PRS. PRS reports no income or costs from the contract in Year 1. Immediately prior to the distribution of the contract to X in Year 2, the contract is deemed completed. Under paragraph (k)(2)(iv)(B) of this section, the fair market value of the contract ($150,000) is treated as the amount realized from the transaction. For purposes of applying the CCM in Year 2, the gross contract price is $800,000 (the sum of the amounts received under the contract and the amount treated as realized from the transaction ($650,000 + $150,000)) and the total allocable contract costs are $600,000. Thus, in Year 2 PRS reports profits of $200,000 ($800,000 - $600,000). This profit must be allocated among W, X, Y, and Z as though the partnership closed its books on the date of the distribution. Accordingly, each partner's distributive share of this income is $50,000.

(iii) Tax consequences to X. X's basis in its interest in PRS immediately prior to the distribution is $150,000 ($100,000 initial contribution, increased by $50,000, X's distributive share of Year 2 income). Under paragraph (k)(2)(iv)(D) of this section, PRS's basis in the contract (including the uncompleted property, if applicable) immediately prior to the distribution is equal to $150,000 (the partnership's allocable contract costs, $600,000, increased by the amount of cumulative taxable income recognized by PRS on the contract through the date of the distribution (including amounts recognized as a result of the constructive completion), $200,000, decreased by the amounts that the partnership has received or reasonably expects to receive under the contract, $650,000). Under section 732, X's basis in the contract (including the uncompleted property) after the distribution is $150,000. Under paragraph (k)(2)(iv)(C) of this section, X's basis in the contract is treated as consideration paid by X that is allocable to the contract. Under the CCM, X reports no gross receipts or costs in Year 2. For Year 3, the completion year, X reports its gross contract price of $200,000 (the amount remaining to be paid under the terms of the contract less the consideration allocable to the contract ($350,000 - $150,000)) and its total allocable contract costs of $125,000 (the allocable contract costs that X incurred to complete the contract ($50,000 + $75,000)), for a profit of $75,000.

(iv) Section 734(b). The results under section 734(b) are the same as in Example 9.

*Example (11).* Step-in-the-shoes—PCM—contribution of contract to partnership. (i) Facts. In Year 1, X enters into a contract that X properly accounts for under the PCM. The total contract price is $1,000,000 and the estimated total allocable contract costs are $800,000. In Year 1, X incurs costs of $600,000 and receives $650,000 in progress payments under the contract. Under the contract, X performed all of the services required in order to be entitled to receive the progress payments, and there was no obligation to return the payments or perform any additional services in order to retain the payments. In Year 2, X contributes the contract (including the uncompleted property) with a basis of $0 and $125,000 of cash to partnership PRS in exchange for a one-fourth partnership interest. X incurs costs of $10,000, and receives no progress payments in Year 2 prior to the contribution of the contract. X and the other three partners of PRS share equally in its capital, profits, and losses. The parties determine that, at the time of the contribution, the fair market value of the contract is $160,000. Following the contribution in Year 2, PRS incurs additional allocable contract costs of $40,000. PRS correctly estimates at the end of Year 2 that it will have to incur an additional $75,000 of allocable contract costs in Year 3 to complete the contract (rather than $150,000 as originally estimated by PRS).

(ii) Tax consequences to X. For Year 1, X reports receipts of $750,000 (the completion factor multiplied by the total contract price ($600,000/$800,000 x $1,000,000)) and costs of $600,000, for a profit of $150,000. Because the mid-contract change in taxpayer results from a transaction described in paragraph (k)(3)(i)(I) of this section, X is not treated as completing the contract in Year 2. Under paragraph (k)(3)(ii)(A) of this section, for Year 2, X reports receipts of $12,500 (the completion factor multiplied by the total contract price ($610,000/$800,000 x $1,000,000, or $762,500), decreased by receipts already reported, $750,000) and costs of $10,000, for a profit of $2,500. Under section 722, X's initial basis in its interest in PRS is $125,000. Pursuant to paragraph (k)(3)(iv)(A)(1) of this section, X must increase its basis in its interest in PRS by the amount of gross receipts X recognized under the contract, $762,500, and reduce its basis by the amount of gross receipts X received under the contract, the $650,000 in progress payments. Accordingly, X's basis in its interest in PRS is $237,500.

(iii) Tax consequences to PRS. Because the mid-contract change in taxpayer results from a step-in-the-shoes transaction, PRS must account for the contract using the same methods of accounting used by X prior to the transaction. The total contract price is the sum of any amounts that X and PRS have received or reasonably expect to receive under the contract, and total allocable contract costs are the allocable contract costs of X and PRS. For Year 2, PRS reports receipts of $134,052 (the completion factor multiplied by the total contract price [($650,000/$725,000) - $1,000,000], $896,552, decreased by receipts reported by X, $762,500) and costs of $40,000, for a profit of $94,052. For Year 3, PRS reports receipts of $103,448 (the total contract price minus prior year receipts ($1,000,000 x $896,552)) and costs of $75,000, for a profit of $28,448.

(iv) Section 704(c). The principles of section 704(c) and § 1.704-3 apply to allocations of income or loss with respect to the contract contributed by X. In this case, the amount of built-in income that is subject to section 704(c) is the amount of income or loss that the contributing partner would take into account if the contract were disposed of for its fair market value in a constructive completion transaction. This calculation is treated as occurring immediately after the partner has applied paragraph (k)(3)(ii)(A) of this section, but before the contribution to the partnership. In a constructive completion transaction, the total contract price would be $810,000 (the sum of the amounts received under the contract and the amount realized in the deemed sale ($650,000 + $160,000)). X would report receipts of $47,500 (total contract price minus receipts already reported ($810,000 - $762,500)) and costs of $0, for a profit of $47,500. Thus, the amount of built-in income that is subject to section 704(c) is $47,500. The partnership must apply section 704(c) to this income in a manner that reasonably accounts for the income over the remaining term of the contract. For example, in Year 2, PRS could allocate $26,810 to X under section 704(c) (the amount of built-in income, $47,500, multiplied by a fraction, the numerator of which is the completion factor for the year, $650,000/725,000, less the completion factor for the prior year, $610,000/$800,000, and the denominator of which is 100 percent reduced by the completion factor for the taxable year preceding the event creating the section 704(c) income or loss, $610,000/$800,000). The remaining $67,242 would be allocated equally among all of the partners. In Year 3, the completion year, PRS could allocate $20,690 to X under section 704(c) ($47,500 x [($725,000/$725,000 -$650,000/$725,000) / (100 percent - $610,000/$800,000)]). The remaining $7,758 would be allocated equally among all the partners.

*Example (12).* Step-in-the-shoes—CCM—contribution of contract to partnership. (i) Facts. The facts are the same as in Example 11, except that X and PRS properly account for the contract under the CCM, and X has a basis of $610,000 in the contract (including the uncompleted property).

(ii) Tax consequences to X. X reports no income or costs from the contract in Years 1 or 2. X is not treated as completing the contract in Year 2. Under section 722, X's initial basis in its interest in PRS is $735,000 (the sum of $125,000 cash and X's basis of $610,000 in the contract (including the uncompleted property)). Pursuant to paragraph (k)(3)(iv)(A)(1)(ii) of this section, X must reduce its basis in its interest in PRS by the amount of gross receipts X received under the contract, or $650,000. Accordingly, X's basis in its interest in PRS is $85,000.

(iii) Tax consequences to PRS. PRS must account for the contract using the same methods of accounting used by X prior to the transaction. Under the CCM, PRS reports no gross receipts or costs in Year 2. For Year 3, the completion year, PRS reports its gross contract price of $1,000,000 (the sum of any amounts that X and PRS have received or reasonably expect to receive under the contract), and total allocable contract costs of $725,000 (the allocable contract costs of X and PRS), for a profit of $275,000.

(iv) Section 704(c). In this case, the amount of built-in income that is subject to section 704(c) is the amount of income or loss that the contributing partner would take into account if the contract were disposed of for its fair market value in a constructive completion transaction. This calculation is treated as occurring immediately after the partner has applied paragraph (k)(3)(ii)(A) of this section, but before the contribution to the partnership. In a constructive completion transaction, X would report its gross contract price of $810,000 (the sum of the amounts received under the contract and the amount realized in the deemed sale ($650,000 + $160,000)) and its total allocable contract costs of $610,000, for a profit of $200,000. Thus, the amount of built-in income that is subject to section 704(c) is $200,000. Out of PRS's income of $275,000, in Year 3, $200,000 must be allocated to X under section 704(c), and the remaining $75,000 is allocated equally among all of the partners.

*Example (13).* Step-in-the-shoes—PCM—transfer of a partnership interest. (i) Facts. In Year 1, W, X, Y, and Z each contribute $100,000 to form equal partnership PRS. In Year 1, PRS enters into a contract. The total contract price is $1,000,000 and the estimated total allocable contract costs are $800,000. In Year 1, PRS incurs costs of $600,000 and receives $650,000 in progress payments under the contract. Under the contract, PRS performed all of the services required in order to be entitled to receive the progress payments, and there was no obligation to return the payment or perform any additional services in order to retain the payments. PRS properly accounts for the contract under the PCM. In Year 2, W transfers W's interest in PRS to T for $150,000. Assume that $10,000 of PRS's Year 2 costs are incurred prior to the transfer, $40,000 are incurred after the transfer; and that PRS receives no progress payments in Year 2. Also assume that the fair market value of the contract on the date of the transfer is $160,000, that PRS closes its books with respect to the contract under section 706 on the date of the transfer, and that PRS correctly estimates at the end of Year 2 that it will have to incur an additional $75,000 of allocable contract costs in Year 3 to complete the contract (rather than $150,000 as originally estimated by PRS).

(ii) Income reporting for period ending on date of transfer. For Year 1, PRS reports receipts of $750,000 (the completion factor multiplied by total contract price ($600,000/$800,000 x $1,000,000)) and costs of $600,000, for a profit of $150,000. This profit is allocated equally among W, X, Y, and Z ($37,500 each). Under paragraph (k)(3)(ii)(A) of this section, for the part of Year 2 ending on the date of the transfer of W's interest, PRS reports receipts of $12,500 (the completion factor multiplied by the total contract price ($610,000/$800,000 x $1,000,000) minus receipts already reported ($750,000)) and costs of $10,000 for a profit of $2,500. This profit is allocated equally among W, X, Y, and Z ($625 each).

(iii) Income reporting for period after transfer. PRS must continue to use the PCM. For the part of Year 2 beginning on the day after the transfer, PRS reports receipts of $134,052 (the completion factor multiplied by the total contract price decreased by receipts reported by PRS for the period ending on the date of the transfer [($650,000/$725,000 x $1,000,000)--$762,500]) and costs of $40,000, for a profit of $94,052. This profit is shared equally among T, X, Y, and Z ($23,513 each). For Year 3, PRS reports receipts of $103,448 (the total contract price minus prior year receipts ($1,000,000 - $896,552)) and costs of $75,000, for a profit of $28,448. The profit for Year 3 is shared equally among T, X, Y, and Z ($7,112 each).

(iv) Tax Consequences to W. W's amount realized is $150,000. W's adjusted basis in its interest in PRS is $138,125 ($100,000 originally contributed, plus $37,500, W's distributive share of PRS's Year 1 income, and $625, W's distributive share of PRS's Year 2 income prior to the transfer). Accordingly, W's income from the sale of W's interest in PRS is $11,875. Under paragraph (k)(2)(iv)(E) of this section, for purposes of section 751(a), the amount of ordinary income attributable to the contract is determined as follows. First, the partnership must determine the amount of income or loss from the contract that is allocated under section 706 to the period ending on the date of the sale ($625). Second, the partnership must determine the amount of income or loss that the partnership would take into account under the constructive completion rules of paragraph (k)(2) of this section if the contract were disposed of for its fair market value in a constructive completion transaction. Because PRS closed its books under section 706 with respect to the contract on the date of the sale, this calculation is treated as occurring immediately after the partnership has applied paragraph (k)(3)(ii)(A) of this section on the date of the sale. In a constructive completion transaction, the total contract price would be $810,000 (the sum of the amounts received under the contract and the amount realized in the deemed sale ($650,000 + $160,000)). PRS would report receipts of $47,500 (total contract price minus receipts already reported ($810,000 - $762,500)) and costs of $0, for a profit of $47,500. Thus, the amount of ordinary income attributable to the contract is $47,500, and W's share of that income is $11,875. Thus, under § 1.751-1(a), all of W's $11,875 of income from the sale of W's interest in PRS is ordinary income.

(v) Tax Consequences to T. T's adjusted basis for its interest in PRS is $150,000. Under § 1.743-1(d)(2), the amount of income that would be allocated to T if the contract were disposed of for its fair market value (adjusted to account for income from the contract for the portion of PRS's taxable year that ends on the date of the transfer) is $11,875. Under § 1.743-1(b), the amount of T's basis adjustment under section 743(b) is $11,875. Under paragraph (k)(3)(v)(B) of this section, the portion of T's basis adjustment that is recovered in Year 2 and Year 3 must be determined by PRS in a manner that reasonably accounts for the adjustment over the remaining term of the contract. For example, PRS could recover $6,703 of the adjustment in Year 2 (the amount of the basis adjustment, $11,875, multiplied by a fraction, the numerator of which is the excess of the completion factor for the year, $650,000/ $725,000, less the completion factor for the prior year, $610,000/ $800,000, and the denominator of which is 100 percent reduced by the completion factor for the taxable year preceding the transfer, $610,000/$800,000). T's distributive share of income in Year 2 from the contract would be adjusted from $23,513 to $16,810 as a result of the basis adjustment. In Year 3, the completion year, PRS could recover $5,172 of the adjustment ($11,875 x [($725,000/$725,000 -$650,000/$725,000) / (100 percent - $610,000/$800,000)]). T's distributive share of income in Year 3, the completion year, from the contract would be adjusted from $7,112 to $1,940 as a result of the basis adjustment.

*(6) Effective date.* Except as provided in paragraph (k)(3)(iv)(D) of this section, this paragraph (k) is applicable for transactions on or after May 15, 2002. Application of

the rules of this paragraph (k) to a transaction that occurs on or after May 15, 2002 is not a change in method of accounting.

---

T.D. 8597, 7/12/95, T.D. 8929, 1/10/2001, T.D. 8995, 5/14/2002, T.D. 9137, 7/15/2004.

---

PAR. 3. Section 1.460-4 is amended by:

1. Revising the third sentence in paragraph (c)(1).

2. Redesignating paragraph (g) as paragraph (g)(1) and revising newly redesignated paragraph (g)(1).

3. Adding a paragraph (g)(2).

4. Revising Example 5. of paragraph (h).

The revisions and additions read as follows:

**Proposed § 1.460-4 Methods of accounting for long-term contracts.** [*For Preamble, see ¶ 153,043*]

* * * * *

**(c)** * * *

*(1)* * * * Permissible exempt contract methods are the PCM, the EPCM described in paragraph (c)(2) of this section, the CCM described in paragraph (d) of this section, the accrual method, and any other permissible method. * * *

* * * * *

**(g) Method of accounting.** *(1) In general.* A taxpayer must apply its method(s) of accounting for long-term contracts consistently for all similarly classified long-term contracts until the taxpayer obtains the Commissioner's consent under section 446(e) to change to another method of accounting.

*(2) Taxpayer-initiated change in method of accounting.* (i) Change to PCM for long-term contracts for which PCM is required. A taxpayer-initiated change in method of accounting for long-term contracts (or portion thereof) for which income must be determined using the PCM described in paragraph (b) of this section and the costs allocation rules described in § 1.460-5(b) or (c) (required PCM contracts) from a method of accounting that does not comply with paragraph (b) of this section and § 1.460-5(b) or (c) to a method that complies with paragraph (b) of this section and § 1.460-5(b) or (c) must be applied to all required PCM contracts entered into before the year of change and not reported as completed as of the beginning of the year of change. Accordingly, a section 481(a) adjustment will be required.

(ii) Change from a permissible PCM method to another permissible PCM method for long-term contracts for which PCM is required. A taxpayer initiated change in method of accounting for required PCM contracts, as defined in paragraph (g)(2)(i) of this section (or a portion thereof), from a method of accounting that complies with paragraph (b) of this section and § 1.460-5(b) or (c) to another method of accounting that complies with paragraph (b) of this section and § 1.460-5(b) or (c) must be made on a cut-off basis and applied only to contracts entered into during and after the year of change. Accordingly, a section 481(a) adjustment will be neither permitted nor required.

(iii) Change to an exempt contract method for home construction contracts. A taxpayer-initiated change in method of accounting for home construction contracts, as defined in § 1.460-3(b)(2), to a permissible exempt contract method, as described in paragraph (c)(1) of this section, must be applied to all home construction contracts entered into before the year of change and not reported as completed as of the beginning of the year of change. Accordingly, a section 481(a) adjustment will be required.

(iv) Change to an exempt contract method for exempt contracts other than home construction contracts. A taxpayer-initiated change in method of accounting for long-term contracts (or portion thereof) not described in paragraphs (g)(2)(i), (ii) and (iii) of this section to a permissible exempt contract method as described in paragraph (c)(1) of this section must be applied to all contracts that are eligible to use the exempt contract method entered into before the year of change and not reported as completed as of the beginning of the year of change. Accordingly, a section 481(a) adjustment will be required.

**(h)** * * *

* * * * *

*Example (5).* PCM—contract terminated. C, whose taxable year ends December 31, determines the income from long-term contracts using the PCM. During 2001, C buys land and begins constructing a building that will contain 50 apartment units on that land. C enters into a contract to sell the building to B for $2,400,000. B gives C a $50,000 deposit toward the purchase price. By the end of 2001, C has incurred $500,000 of allocable contract costs on the building and estimates that the total allocable contract costs on the building will be $1,500,000. Thus, for 2001, C reports gross receipts of $800,000 ($500,000/$1,500,000 x $2,400,000), current-year costs of $500,000, and gross income of $300,000 ($800,000-$500,000). In 2002, after C has incurred an additional $250,000 of allocable contract costs on the building, B files for bankruptcy protection and defaults on the contract with C, who is permitted to keep B's $50,000 deposit as liquidated damages. In 2002, C reverses the transaction with B under paragraph (b)(7) of this section and reports a loss of $300,000 ($500,000-$800,000). In addition, C obtains an adjusted basis in the building sold to B of $700,000 ($500,000 (current-year costs deducted in 2001)-$50,000 (B's forfeited deposit) + $250,000 (current-year costs incurred in 2002). C may not apply the look-back method to this contract in 2002.

* * * * *

**§ 1.460-5 Cost allocation rules.**

***Caution:*** The Treasury has not yet amended Reg § 1.460-5 to reflect changes made by P.L. 108-357.

**(a) Overview.** This section prescribes methods of allocating costs to long-term contracts accounted for using the percentage-of-completion method described in § 1.460-4(b) (PCM), the completed-contract method described in § 1.460-4(d) (CCM), or the percentage-of-completion/capitalized-cost method described in § 1.460-4(e) (PCCM). Exempt construction contracts described in § 1.460-3(b) accounted for using a method other than the PCM or CCM are not subject to the cost allocation rules of this section (other than the requirement to allocate production-period interest under paragraph (b)(2)(v) of this section). Paragraph (b) of this section describes the regular cost allocation methods for contracts subject to the PCM. Paragraph (c) of this section describes an elective simplified cost allocation method for contracts subject to the PCM. Paragraph (d) of this section describes the cost allocation methods for exempt construction contracts reported using the CCM. Paragraph (e) of this section describes the cost allocation rules for contracts subject to the PCCM. Paragraph (f) of this section describes additional rules applicable to the cost allocation methods described in this section. Paragraph (g) of this section provides rules concerning consistency in method of allocating costs to long-term contracts.

**(b) Cost allocation method for contracts subject to PCM.** *(1) In general.* Except as otherwise provided in paragraph (b)(2) of this section, a taxpayer must allocate costs to each long-term contract subject to the PCM in the same manner that direct and indirect costs are capitalized to property produced by a taxpayer under § 1.263A-1(e) through (h). Thus, a taxpayer must allocate to each long-term contract subject to the PCM all direct costs and certain indirect costs properly allocable to the long-term contract (i.e., all costs that directly benefit or are incurred by reason of the performance of the long-term contract). However, see paragraph (c) of this section concerning an election to allocate contract costs using the simplified cost-to-cost method. As in section 263A, the use of the practical capacity concept is not permitted. See § 1.263A-2(a)(4).

*(2) Special rules.* (i) Direct material costs. The costs of direct materials must be allocated to a long-term contract when dedicated to the contract under principles similar to those in § 1.263A-11(b)(2). Thus, a taxpayer dedicates direct materials by associating them with a specific contract, including by purchase order, entry on books and records, or shipping instructions. A taxpayer maintaining inventories under § 1.471-1 must determine allocable contract costs attributable to direct materials using its method of accounting for those inventories (e.g., FIFO, LIFO, specific identification).

(ii) Components and subassemblies. The costs of a component or subassembly (component) produced by the taxpayer must be allocated to a long-term contract as the taxpayer incurs costs to produce the component if the taxpayer reasonably expects to incorporate the component into the subject matter of the contract. Similarly, the cost of a purchased component (including a component purchased from a related party) must be allocated to a long-term contract as the taxpayer incurs the cost to purchase the component if the taxpayer reasonably expects to incorporate the component into the subject matter of the contract. In all other cases, the cost of a component must be allocated to a long-term contract when the component is dedicated, under principles similar to those in § 1.263A-11(b)(2). A taxpayer maintaining inventories under § 1.471-1 must determine allocable contract costs attributable to components using its method of accounting for those inventories (e.g., FIFO, LIFO, specific identification).

(iii) Simplified production methods. A taxpayer may not determine allocable contract costs using the simplified production methods described in § 1.263A-2(b) and (c).

(iv) Costs identified under cost-plus long-term contracts and federal long-term contracts. To the extent not otherwise allocated to the contract under this paragraph (b), a taxpayer must allocate any identified costs to a cost-plus long-term contract or federal long-term contract (as defined in section 460(d)). Identified cost means any cost, including a charge representing the time-value of money, identified by the taxpayer or related person as being attributable to the taxpayer's cost-plus long-term contract or federal long-term contract under the terms of the contract itself or under federal, state, or local law or regulation.

(v) Interest. (A) In general. If property produced under a long-term contract is designated property, as defined in § 1.263A-8(b) (without regard to the exclusion for long-term contracts under § 1.263A-8(d)(2)(v)), a taxpayer must allocate interest incurred during the production period to the long-term contract in the same manner as interest is allocated to property produced by a taxpayer under section 263A(f). See §§ 1.263A-8 to 1.263A-12 generally.

(B) Production period. Notwithstanding § 1.263A-12(c) and (d), for purposes of this paragraph (b)(2)(v), the production period of a long-term contract—

(1) Begins on the later of—

(i) The contract commencement date, as defined in § 1.460-1(b)(7); or

(ii) For a taxpayer using the accrual method of accounting for long-term contracts, the date by which 5 percent or more of the total estimated costs, including design and planning costs, under the contract have been incurred; and

(2) Ends on the date that the contract is completed, as defined in § 1.460-1(c)(3).

(C) Application of section 263A(f). For purposes of this paragraph (b)(2)(v), section 263A(f)(1)(B)(iii) (regarding an estimated production period exceeding 1 year and a cost exceeding $1,000,000) must be applied on a contract-by-contract basis; except that, in the case of a taxpayer using an accrual method of accounting, that section must be applied on a property-by-property basis.

(vi) Research and experimental expenses. Notwithstanding § 1.263A-1(e)(3)(ii)(P) and (iii)(B), a taxpayer must allocate research and experimental expenses, other than independent research and development expenses (as defined in § 1.460-1(b)(9)), to its long-term contracts.

(vii) Service costs. (A) Simplified service cost method—(1) In general. To use the simplified service cost method under § 1.263A-1(h), a taxpayer must allocate the otherwise capitalizable mixed service costs among its long-term contracts using a reasonable method. For example, otherwise capitalizable mixed service costs may be allocated to each long-term contract based on labor hours or contract costs allocable to the contract. To be considered reasonable, an allocation method must be applied consistently and must not disproportionately allocate service costs to contracts expected to be completed in the near future.

*Example (2).* The following example illustrates the rule of this paragraph (b)(2)(vii)(A):

Example. Simplified service cost method. During 2001, C, whose taxable year ends December 31, produces electronic equipment for inventory and enters into long-term contracts to manufacture specialized electronic equipment. C's method of allocating mixed service costs to the property it produces is the labor-based, simplified service cost method described in § 1.263A-1(h)(4). For 2001, C's total mixed service costs are $100,000, C's section 263A labor costs are $500,000, C's section 460 labor costs (i.e., labor costs allocable to C's long-term contracts) are $250,000, and C's total labor costs are $1,000,000. To determine the amount of mixed service costs capitalizable under section 263A for 2001, C multiplies its total mixed service costs by its section 263A allocation ratio (section 263A labor costs  total labor costs). Thus, C's capitalizable mixed service costs for 2001 are $50,000 ($100,000 x $500,000  $1,000,000). Thereafter, C allocates its capitalizable mixed service costs to produced property remaining in ending inventory using its 263A allocation method (e.g., burden rate, simplified production). Similarly, to determine the amount of mixed service costs that are allocable to C's long-term contracts for 2001, C multiplies its total mixed service costs by its section 460 allocation ratio (section 460 labor  total labor costs). Thus, C's allocable mixed service contract costs for 2001 are $25,000 ($100,000 x $250,000 $1,000,000). Thereafter, C allocates its allocable mixed service costs to its long-term contracts proportionately based on its section 460 labor costs allocable to each long-term contract.

(B) Jobsite costs. If an administrative, service, or support function is performed solely at the jobsite for a specific long-term contract, the taxpayer may allocate all the direct and indirect costs of that administrative, service, or support function to that long-term contract. Similarly, if an administrative, service, or support function is performed at the jobsite solely for the taxpayer's long-term contract activities, the taxpayer may allocate all the direct and indirect costs of that administrative, service, or support function among all the long-term contracts performed at that jobsite. For this purpose, jobsite means a production plant or a construction site.

(C) Limitation on other reasonable cost allocation methods. A taxpayer may use any other reasonable method of allocating service costs, as provided in § 1.263A-1(f)(4), if, for the taxpayer's long-term contracts considered as a whole, the—

(1) Total amount of service costs allocated to the contracts does not differ significantly from the total amount of service costs that would have been allocated to the contracts under § 1.263A-1(f)(2) or (3);

(2) Service costs are not allocated disproportionately to contracts expected to be completed in the near future because of the taxpayer's cost allocation method; and

*(3) Taxpayer's cost allocation method is applied consistently.*

**(c) Simplified cost-to-cost method for contracts subject to the PCM.** *(1) In general.* Instead of using the cost allocation method prescribed in paragraph (b) of this section, a taxpayer may elect to use the simplified cost-to-cost method, which is authorized under section 460(b)(3)(A), to allocate costs to a long-term contract subject to the PCM. Under the simplified cost-to-cost method, a taxpayer determines a contract's completion factor based upon only direct material costs; direct labor costs; and depreciation, amortization, and cost recovery allowances on equipment and facilities directly used to manufacture or construct the subject matter of the contract. For this purpose, the costs associated with any manufacturing or construction activities performed by a subcontractor are considered either direct material or direct labor costs, as appropriate, and therefore must be allocated to the contract under the simplified cost-to-cost method. An electing taxpayer must use the simplified cost-to-cost method to apply the look-back method under § 1.460-6 and to determine alternative minimum taxable income under § 1.460-4(f).

*(2) Election.* A taxpayer makes an election under this paragraph (c) by using the simplified cost-to-cost method for all long-term contracts entered into during the taxable year of the election on its original federal income tax return for the election year. This election is a method of accounting and, thus, applies to all long-term contracts entered into during and after the taxable year of the election. This election is not available if a taxpayer does not use the PCM to account for all long-term contracts or if a taxpayer elects to use the 10-percent method described in § 1.460-4(b)(6).

**(d) Cost allocation rules for exempt construction contracts reported using the CCM.** *(1) In general.* For exempt construction contracts reported using the CCM, other than contracts described in paragraph (d)(3) of this section (concerning contracts of homebuilders that do not satisfy the $10,000,000 gross receipts test described in § 1.460-3(b)(3) or will not be completed within two years of the contract commencement date), a taxpayer must annually allocate the cost of any activity that is incident to or necessary for the taxpayer's performance under a long-term contract. A taxpayer must allocate to each exempt construction contract all direct costs as defined in § 1.263A-1(e)(2)(i) and all indirect costs either as provided in § 1.263A-1(e)(3) or as provided in paragraph (d)(2) of this section.

*(2) Indirect costs.* (i) Indirect costs allocable to exempt construction contracts. A taxpayer allocating costs under this paragraph (d)(2) must allocate the following costs to an exempt construction contract, other than a contract described in paragraph (d)(3) of this section, to the extent incurred in the performance of that contract—

(A) Repair of equipment or facilities;

(B) Maintenance of equipment or facilities;

(C) Utilities, such as heat, light, and power, allocable to equipment or facilities;

(D) Rent of equipment or facilities;

(E) Indirect labor and contract supervisory wages, including basic compensation, overtime pay, vacation and holiday pay, sick leave pay (other than payments pursuant to a wage continuation plan under section 105(d) as it existed prior to its repeal in 1983), shift differential, payroll taxes, and contributions to a supplemental unemployment benefits plan;

(F) Indirect materials and supplies;

(G) Noncapitalized tools and equipment;

(H) Quality control and inspection;

(I) Taxes otherwise allowable as a deduction under section 164, other than state, local, and foreign income taxes, to the extent attributable to labor, materials, supplies, equipment, or facilities;

(J) Depreciation, amortization, and cost-recovery allowances reported for the taxable year for financial purposes on equipment and facilities to the extent allowable as deductions under chapter 1 of the Internal Revenue Code;

(K) Cost depletion;

(L) Administrative costs other than the cost of selling or any return on capital;

(M) Compensation paid to officers other than for incidental or occasional services;

(N) Insurance, such as liability insurance on machinery and equipment; and

(O) Interest, as required under paragraph (b)(2)(v) of this section.

(ii) Indirect costs not allocable to exempt construction contracts. A taxpayer allocating costs under this paragraph (d)(2) is not required to allocate the following costs to an exempt construction contract reported using the CCM—

(A) Marketing and selling expenses, including bidding expenses;

(B) Advertising expenses;

(C) Other distribution expenses;

(D) General and administrative expenses attributable to the performance of services that benefit the taxpayer's activities as a whole (e.g., payroll expenses, legal and accounting expenses);

(E) Research and experimental expenses (described in section 174 and the regulations thereunder);

(F) Losses under section 165 and the regulations thereunder;

(G) Percentage of depletion in excess of cost depletion;

(H) Depreciation, amortization, and cost recovery allowances on equipment and facilities that have been placed in service but are temporarily idle (for this purpose, an asset is not considered to be temporarily idle on non-working days, and an asset used in construction is considered to be idle when it is neither en route to nor located at a job-site), and depreciation, amortization and cost recovery allowances under chapter 1 of the Internal Revenue Code in excess of depreciation, amortization, and cost recovery allowances reported by the taxpayer in the taxpayer's financial reports;

(I) Income taxes attributable to income received from long-term contracts;

(J) Contributions paid to or under a stock bonus, pension, profit-sharing, or annuity plan or other plan deferring the receipt of compensation whether or not the plan qualifies under section 401(a), and other employee benefit expenses paid or accrued on behalf of labor, to the extent the contributions or expenses are otherwise allowable as deductions under chapter 1 of the Internal Revenue Code. Other employee benefit expenses include (but are not limited to): Worker's compensation; amounts deductible or for whose payment reduction in earnings and profits is allowed under section 404A and the regulations thereunder; payments pursuant to a wage continuation plan under section 105(d) as it existed prior to its repeal in 1983; amounts includible in the gross income of employees under a method or arrangement of employer contributions or compensation which has the effect of a stock bonus, pension, profit-sharing, or annuity plan, or other plan deferring the receipt of compensation or providing deferred benefits; premiums on life and health insurance; and miscellaneous benefits provided for employees such as safety, medical treatment, recreational and eating facilities, membership dues, etc.;

(K) Cost attributable to strikes, rework labor, scrap and spoilage; and

(L) Compensation paid to officers attributable to the performance of services that benefit the taxpayer's activities as a whole.

*(3) Large homebuilders.* A taxpayer must capitalize the costs of home construction contracts under section 263A and the regulations thereunder, unless the contract will be completed within two years of the contract commencement date and the taxpayer satisfies the $10,000,000 gross receipts test described in § 1.460-3(b)(3).

**(e) Cost allocation rules for contracts subject to the PCCM.** A taxpayer must use the cost allocation rules described in paragraph (b) of this section to determine the costs allocable to the entire qualified ship contract or residential construction contract accounted for using the PCCM and may not use the simplified cost-to-cost method described in paragraph (c) of this section.

**(f) Special rules applicable to costs allocated under this section.** *(1) Nondeductible costs.* A taxpayer may not allocate any otherwise allocable contract cost to a long-term contract if any section of the Internal Revenue Code disallows a deduction for that type of payment or expenditure (e.g., an illegal bribe described in section 162(c)).

*(2) Costs incurred for non-long-term contract activities.* If a taxpayer performs a non-long-term contract activity, as defined in § 1.460-1(d)(2), that is incident to or necessary for the manufacture, building, installation, or construction of the subject matter of one or more of the taxpayer's long-term contracts, the taxpayer must allocate the costs attributable to that activity to such contract(s).

**(g) Method of accounting.** A taxpayer that adopts or elects a cost allocation method of accounting (or changes to another cost allocation method of accounting with the Commissioner's consent) must apply that method consistently for all similarly classified contracts, until the taxpayer obtains the Commissioner's consent under section 446(e) to change to another cost allocation method. A taxpayer-initiated change in cost allocation method will be permitted only on a cut-off basis (i.e., for contracts entered into on or after the year of change) and thus, a section 481(a) adjustment will not be permitted or required.

---

T.D. 8929, 1/10/2001.

---

PAR. 4. Section 1.460-5 is amended by:

1. Adding a new sentence to the end of paragraph (c)(2).

2. Revising paragraph (g).

The revision and addition read as follows:

**Proposed § 1.460-5 Cost allocation rules.** [*For Preamble, see ¶ 153,043*]

* * * * *

**(c)** * * *

*(2)* * * * Further, this election is not available if a taxpayer is changing from a cost allocation method other than as prescribed in paragraph (b) of this section, in which case the taxpayer must follow the procedures under § 1.446-1(e) for obtaining the Commissioner's consent for the change in method of accounting.

* * * * *

**(g) Method of accounting.** A taxpayer that adopts, elects, or otherwise changes to a cost allocation method of accounting (or changes to another cost allocation method of accounting with the Commissioner's consent) must apply that method consistently for all similarly classified contracts, until the taxpayer obtains the Commissioner's consent under section 446 to change to another cost allocation method. A taxpayer-initiated change in cost allocation method from a method that does not comply with the cost allocation rules of this section to a method that complies with the cost allocation rules of this section must be applied to all long-term contracts to which the rules of this section apply, including contracts entered into before the year of change and not reported as completed as of the beginning of the year of change. Accordingly, a section 481(a) adjustment is required. Any other taxpayer-initiated change in cost allocation method to a method permitted under the rules of this section must be made on a cut-off basis and applied only to contracts entered into during and after the year of change, in which case a section 481(a) adjustment will be neither permitted nor required.

**§ 1.460-6 Look-back method.**

***Caution:*** The Treasury has not yet amended Reg § 1.460-6 to reflect changes made by P.L. 105-34.

**(a) In general.** *(1) Introduction.* With respect to income from any long-term contract reported under the percentage of completion method, a taxpayer is required to pay or is entitled to receive interest under section 460(b) on the amount of tax liability that is deferred or accelerated as a result of overestimating or underestimating total contract price or contract costs. Under this look-back method, taxpayers are required to pay interest for any deferral of tax liability resulting from the underestimation of the total contract price or the overestimation of total contract costs. Conversely, if the total contract price is overestimated or the total contract costs are underestimated, taxpayers are entitled to receive interest for any resulting acceleration of tax liability. The computation of the amount of deferred or accelerated tax liability under the look-back method is hypothetical; application of the look-back method does not result in an adjustment to the taxpayer's tax liability as originally reported, as reported on an amended return, or as adjusted on examination. Thus, the look-back method does not correct for differences in tax liability that result from over- or under-estimation of contract price and costs and that are permanent because, for example, tax rates change during the term of the contract.

*(2) Overview.* Paragraph (b) explains which situations require application of the look-back method to income from a long-term contract. Paragraph (c) explains the operation of the three computational steps for applying the look-back method. Paragraph (d) provides guidance concerning the simplified marginal impact method. Paragraph (e) provides an elective method to minimize the number of times the look-back method must be reapplied to a single long-term contract. Paragraph (f) describes the reporting requirements for the look-back method and the tax treatment of look-back interest. Paragraph (g) provides rules for applying the look-back method when there is a transaction that changes the taxpayer that reports income from a long-term contract prior to the completion of a contract. Paragraph (h) provides examples illustrating the three computational steps for applying the look-back method. Paragraph (j) of this section provides guidance concerning the election not to apply the look-back method in de minimis cases.

**(b) Scope of look-back method.** *(1) In general.* The look-back method applies to any income from a long-term contract within the meaning of section 460(f) that is required to be reported under the percentage of completion method (as modified by section 460) for regular income tax purposes or for alternative minimum tax purposes. If a taxpayer uses the percentage of completion-capitalized cost method for long-term contracts, the look-back method applies for regular tax purposes only to the portion (40, 70, or 90 percent, whichever applies) of the income from the contract that is reported under the percentage of completion method. To the extent that the percentage of completion method is required to be used under § 1.460-1(g) with respect to income and expenses that are attributable to activities that benefit a related party's long-term contract, the look-back method also applies to these amounts, even if those activities are not performed under a contract entered into directly by the taxpayer.

*(2) Exceptions from section 460.* The look-back method generally does not apply to the regular taxable income from any long-term construction contract within the meaning of section 460(e)(4) that:

(i) Is a home construction contract within the meaning of section 460(e)(1)(A), or

(ii) Is not a home construction contract but is estimated to be completed within a 2-year period by a taxpayer whose average annual gross receipts for the 3 tax years preceding the tax year the contract is entered into do not exceed $10,000,000 (as provided in section 460(e)(1)(B)). These contracts are not subject to the look-back method for regular tax purposes, even if the taxpayer uses a version of the percentage of completion method permitted under § 1.451-3, unless the taxpayer has properly changed its method of accounting for these contracts to the percentage of completion method as modified by section 460(b). The look-back method, however, applies to the alternative minimum taxable income from a contract of this type, unless it is exempt from the required use of the percentage of completion method under section 56(a)(3).

*(3) De minimis exception.* Notwithstanding that the percentage of completion method is otherwise required to be used, the look-back method does not apply to any long-term contract that:

(i) Is completed within 2 years of the contract commencement date, and

(ii) Has a gross contract price (as of the completion of the contract) that does not exceed the lesser of $1,000,000 or 1 percent of the average annual gross receipts of the taxpayer for the 3 tax years preceding the tax year in which the contract is completed.

This de minimis exception is mandatory and, therefore, precludes application of the look-back method to any contract that meets the requirements of the exception. The de minimis exception applies for purposes of computing both regular taxable income and alternative minimum taxable income. Solely for this purpose, the determination of whether a long-term contract meets the gross receipts test for both alternative minimum tax and regular tax purposes is made based only on the taxpayer's regular taxable income.

*(4) Alternative minimum tax.* For purposes of computing alternative minimum taxable income, section 56(a)(3) generally requires long-term contracts within the meaning of section 460(f) (generally without regard to the exceptions in section 460(e)) to be accounted for using only the percentage of completion method as defined in section 460(b), including the look-back method of section 460(b), with respect to tax years beginning after December 31, 1986. However, section 56(a)(3) (and thus the look-back method) does not apply to any long-term contract entered into after June 20, 1988, and before the beginning of the first tax year that begins after September 30, 1990, that meets the conditions of both section 460(e)(1)(A) and clauses (i) and (ii) of section 460(e)(1)(B), and does not apply to any long-term contract entered into in a tax year that begins after September 30, 1990, that meets the conditions of section 460(e)(1)(A). A taxpayer that applies the percentage of completion method (and thus the look-back method) to income from a long-term contract only for purposes of determining alternative minimum taxable income, and not regular taxable income, must apply the look-back method to the alternative minimum taxable income in the year of contract completion and other filing years whether or not the taxpayer was liable for the alternative minimum tax for the filing year or for any prior year. Interest is computed under the look-back method to the extent that the taxpayer's total tax liability (including the alternative minimum tax liability) would have differed if the percentage of completion method had been applied using actual, rather than estimated, contract price and contract costs.

*(5) Effective date.* The look-back method, including the de minimis exception, applies to long-term contracts entered into after February 28, 1986. With respect to activities that are subject to section 460 solely because they benefit a long-term contract of a related party, the look-back method generally applies only if the related party's long-term contract was entered into after June 20, 1988, unless a principal purpose of the related-party arrangement is to avoid the requirements of section 460.

**(c) Operation of the look-back method.** *(1) Overview.* (i) In general. The amount of interest charged or credited to a taxpayer under the look-back method is computed in three steps. This paragraph (c) describes the three steps for applying the look-back method. These steps are illustrated by the examples in paragraph (h). The first step is to hypothetically reapply the percentage of completion method to all long-term contracts that are completed or adjusted in the current year (the "filing year"), using the actual, rather than estimated, total contract price and contract costs. Based on this reapplication, the taxpayer determines the amount of taxable income (and alternative minimum taxable income) that would have been reported for each year prior to the filing year that is affected by contracts completed or adjusted in the filing year if the actual, rather than estimated, total contract price and costs had been used in applying the percentage of completion method to these contracts, and to any other contracts completed or adjusted in a year preceding the filing year. If the percentage of completion method only applies to alternative minimum taxable income for contracts completed or adjusted in the filing year, only alternative minimum taxable income is recomputed in the first step. The second step is to compare what the tax liability would have been under the percentage of completion method (as reapplied in the first step) for each tax year for which the tax liability is affected by income from contracts completed or adjusted in the filing year (a "redetermination year") with the most recent determination of tax liability for that year to produce a hypothetical underpayments or overpayment of tax. The third step is to apply the rate of interest on overpayments designated under section 6621 of the Code, compounded daily, to the hypothetical underpayment or overpayment of tax for each redetermination year to compute interest that runs, generally, from the due date (determined without regard to extensions) of the return for the redetermination year to the due date (determined without regard to extensions) of the return for the filing year. The net amount of interest computed under the third step is paid by or credited to the taxpayer for the filing year. Paragraph (d) provides a simplified marginal impact method that simplifies the second step—the computation of hypothetical underpayments or overpayments of tax liability for redetermination years—and, in some cases, the third step—the determination of the time period for computing interest.

(ii) Post-completion revenue and expenses. (A) In general. Except as otherwise provided in section 460(b)(6) (see § 1.460-6(j) for method of electing) or § 1.460-6(e), a taxpayer must apply the look-back method to a long-term contract in the completion year and in any post-completion year for which the taxpayer must adjust total contract price or total allocable contract costs, or both, under the PCM. Any year in which the look-back method must be reapplied is treated as a filing year. See Example (3) of paragraph (h)(4) for an illustration of how the look-back method is applied to post-completion adjustments.

(B) Completion. A contract is considered to be completed for purposes of the look-back method in the year in which final completion and acceptance within the meaning of § 1.460-1(c)(3) have occurred.

(C) Discounting of contract price and contract cost adjustments subsequent to completion; election not to discount. (1) General rule. The amount of any post-completion adjustment to the total contract price or contract costs is discounted, solely for purposes of applying the look-back method, from its value at the time the amount is taken into account in computing taxable income to its value at the completion of the contract. The discount rate for this purpose is the Federal mid-term rate under section 1274(d) in effect at the time the amount is properly taken into account. For purposes of applying the look-back method for the completion year, no amounts are discounted, even if they are received after the completion year.

(2) Election not to discount. Notwithstanding the general requirement to discount post-completion adjustments, a taxpayer may elect not to discount contract price and contract cost adjustments with respect to any contract. The election not to discount is to be made on a contract-by-contract basis and is binding with respect to all post-completion adjustments that arise with respect to a contract for which an election has been made. An election not to discount with respect to any contract is made by stating that an election is being made on the taxpayer's timely filed Federal income tax return (determined with regard to extensions) for the first tax year after completion in which the taxpayer takes into account (i.e., includes in income or deducts) any adjustment to the contract price or contract costs. See § 301.9100-8 of this chapter.

(3) Year-end discounting convention. In the absence of an election not to discount, any revisions to the contract price and contract costs must be discounted to their value as of the completion of the contract in reapplying the look-back method. For this purpose, the period of discounting is the period between the completion date of the contract and the date that any adjustment is taken into account in computing taxable income. Although taxpayers may use the period between the months in which these two events actually occur, in many cases, these dates may not be readily identifiable. Therefore, for administrative convenience, taxpayers are permitted to use the period between the end of the tax years in which these events occur as the period of discounting provided that the convention is used consistently with respect to all post-completion adjustments for all contracts of the taxpayer the adjustments to which are discounted. In that case, the taxpayer must use as the discount rate the Federal mid-term rate under section 1274(d) as of the end of the tax year in which any revision is taken into account in computing taxable income.

(D) Revenue acceleration rule. Section 460(b)(1) imposes a special rule that requires a taxpayer to include in gross income, for the tax year immediately following the year of completion, any previously unreported portion of the total contract price (including amounts that the taxpayer expects to receive in the future) determined as of that year, even if the percentage of completion ratio is less than 100 percent because the taxpayer expects to incur additional allocable contract costs in a later year. At the time any remaining portion of the contract price is includible in income under this rule, no offset against this income is permitted for estimated future contract costs. To achieve the requirement to report all remaining contract revenue without regard to additional estimated costs, a taxpayer must include only costs actually incurred through the end of the tax year in the denominator of the percentage of completion ratio in applying the percentage of completion method for any tax years after the year of completion. The look-back method also must be reapplied for the year immediately following the year of completion if any portion of the contract price is includible in income in that year by reason of section 460(b)(1). For purposes of reapplying the look-back method as a result of this inclusion in income, the taxpayer must only include in the denominator of the percentage of completion ratio the actual contract costs incurred as of the end of the year, even if the taxpayer reasonably expects to incur additional allocable contract costs. To the extent that costs are incurred in a subsequent tax year, the look-back method is reapplied in that year (or a later year if the delayed reapplication method is used), and the taxpayer is entitled to receive interest for the post-completion adjustment to contract costs. Because this reapplication occurs subsequent to the completion year, only the cumulative costs incurred as of the end of the reapplication year are includible in the denominator of the percentage of completion ratio.

*(2) Look-back Step One.* (i) Hypothetical reallocation of income among prior tax years. For each filing year, a taxpayer must allocate total contract income among prior tax years, by hypothetically applying the percentage of completion method to all contracts that are completed or adjusted in the filing year using the rules of this paragraph (c)(2). The taxpayer must reallocate income from those contracts among all years preceding the filing year that are affected by those contracts using the total contract price and contract costs, as determined as of the end of the filing year ("actual contract price and costs"), rather than the estimated contract price and contract costs. The taxpayer then must determine the amount of taxable income and the amount of alternative minimum taxable income that would have been reported for each affected tax year preceding the filing year if the percentage of completion method had been applied on the basis of actual contract price and contract costs in reporting income from all contracts completed or adjusted in the filing year and in any preceding year. If the percentage of completion method only applies to alternative minimum taxable income from the contract, only alternative minimum taxable income is recomputed in the first step. For purposes of reallocating income (and costs if the 10-percent year changes for a taxpayer using the 10-percent method of section 460(b)(5)) under the look-back method, the method of computing the percentage of completion ratio is the same method used to report income from the contract on the taxpayer's return. (Thus, an election to use the 10-percent method or the simplified cost-to-cost method is taken into account). See Example (1) of paragraph (h)(2) for an illustration of Step One.

(ii) Treatment of estimated future costs in year of completion. If a taxpayer reasonably expects to incur additional allocable contract costs in a tax year subsequent to the year in which the contract is completed, the taxpayer includes the actual costs incurred as of the end of the completion year plus the additional allocable contract costs that are reasonably expected to be incurred (to the extent includible under the taxpayer's percentage of completion method) in the denominator of the percentage of completion ratio. The completion year is the only filing year for which the taxpayer may include additional estimated costs in the denominator of the percentage of completion ratio in applying the look-back method. If the look-back method is reapplied in any year after the completion year, only the cumulative costs incurred as of the end of the year of reapplication are includible in the denominator of the percentage of completion ratio in reapplying the look-back method.

(iii) Interim reestimates not considered. The look-back method cannot be applied to a contract before it is completed. Accordingly, for purposes of applying Step One, the actual total contract price and contract costs are substituted for the previous estimates of total contract price and contract costs only with respect to contracts that have been completed in the filing year and in a tax year preceding the filing year. No adjustments are made under Step One for contracts that have not been completed prior to the end of the current filing year, even if, as of the end of this year, the estimated total contract price or contract costs for these uncompleted contracts is different from the estimated amount that was used during any tax year for which taxable income is recomputed with respect to completed contracts under the look-back method for the current filing year.

(iv) Tax years in which income is affected. In general, because income under the percentage of completion method is generally reported as costs are incurred, the taxable income and alternative minimum taxable income are recomputed only for each year in which allocable contract costs were incurred. However, there will be exceptions to this general rule. For example, a taxpayer may be required to cumulatively adjust the income from a contract in a year in which no allocable contract costs are incurred if the estimated total contract price or contract costs was revised in that year. However, in applying the look-back method, no contract income is allocated to that year. Thus, there may be a difference between the amount of contract income originally reported for that year and the amount of contract income as reallocated. Similarly, because of the revenue acceleration rule of section 460(b)(1), income may be reported in the year immediately following the completion year even though no costs were incurred during that year and, in applying the look-back method in that year or another year, if additional costs are incurred or the contract price is adjusted in a later year, no income is allocated to the year immediately following the completion year.

(v) Costs incurred prior to contract execution; 10-percent method. (A) General rule. The look-back method does not require allocation of contract income to tax years before the contract was entered into. Costs incurred prior to the year a contract is entered into are first taken into account in the numerator of the percentage of completion ratio in the year the contract is entered into. A taxpayer using the 10-percent method must also use the 10-percent method in applying the look-back method, using actual total contract costs to determine the 10-percent year. Thus, contract income is never reallocated to a year before the 10-percent year as determined on the basis of actual contract costs. If the 10-percent year is earlier as a result of applying Step One of the look-back method, contract costs incurred up to and including the new 10-percent year (as determined based on actual contract costs), are reallocated from the original 10-percent year to the new 10-percent, and costs incurred in later years but before the old 10-percent year are reallocated to those years. If the 10-percent year is later as a result of applying Step One of the look-back method, contract costs incurred up to and including the new 10-percent year are reallocated from all prior years to the new 10-percent year. This is the only case in which costs are reallocated under the look-back method.

(B) Example. The application of the look-back method by a taxpayer using the 10-percent method is illustrated by the following example:

*Example.* Z elected to use the 10-percent method of section 460(b)(5) for reporting income under the percentage of completion method. Z entered into a contract in 1990 for a fixed price of $1,000x. During 1990, Z incurred allocable contract costs of $80x and estimated that it would incur a total of $900x for the entire contract. Since $80x is less than 10 percent of total estimated contract costs, Z reported no revenue from the contract in 1990 and deferred the $80x of costs incurred. In 1991, Z incurred an additional $620x of contract costs, and completed the contract. Accordingly, in its 1991 return, Z reported the entire contract price of $1,000x, and deducted the $620x of costs incurred in 1991 and the $80x of costs incurred in 1990.

Under section 460(b)(5), the 10-percent method applies both for reporting contract income and the look-back method. Under the look-back method, since the costs incurred in 1990 ($80x) exceed 10 percent of the actual total contract costs ($700x), Z is required to allocate $114x of contract revenue ($80x/$700x × $1,000x) and the $80x of costs incurred to 1990. Thus, application of the look-back method results in a net increase in taxable income for 1990 of $34x, solely for purposes of the look-back method.

(vi) Amount treated as contract price. (A) General rule. The amount that is treated as total contract price for purposes of applying the percentage of completion method and reapplying the percentage of completion method under the look-back method under Step One includes all amounts that the taxpayer expects to receive from the customer. Thus, amounts are treated as part of the contract price as soon as it is reasonably estimated that they will be received, even if the all-events test has not yet been met.

(B) Contingencies. Any amounts related to contingent rights or obligations, such as incentive fees or amounts in dispute, are not separated from the contract and accounted for under a non-long-term contract method of accounting, notwithstanding any provision in § 1.460-4(b)(4)(i), to the contrary. Instead, those amounts are treated as part of the total contract price in applying the percentage of completion method and the look-back method. For example, if an incentive fee under a contract to manufacture a satellite is payable to the taxpayer after a specified period of successful performance, the incentive fee is includible in the total contract price at the time and to the extent that it can reasonably be predicted that the performance objectives will be met. A portion of the contract price that is in dispute is included in the total contract price at the time and to the extent that the taxpayer can reasonably expect the dispute will be resolved in the taxpayer's favor (without regard to when the taxpayer receives payment for the amount in dispute or when the dispute is finally resolved).

(C) Change orders. In applying the look-back method, a change order with respect to a contract is not treated as a separate contract unless the change order would be treated as a separate contract under the rules for severing and aggregating contracts provided in § 1.460-1(e). Thus, if a change order is not treated as a separate contract, the contract price and contract costs attributable to the change order must be taken into account in allocating contract income to all tax years affected by the underlying contract.

*(3) Look-back Step Two: Computation of hypothetical overpayment or underpayment of tax.* (i) In general. Step Two involves the computation of a hypothetical overpayment or underpayment of tax for each year in which the tax liability is affected by income from contracts that are completed or adjusted in the filing year (a "redetermination year"). The application of Step Two depends on whether the taxpayer uses the simplified marginal impact method contained in paragraph (d) or the actual method described in this paragraph (c)(3). The remainder of this paragraph (c)(3) does not apply if a taxpayer uses the simplified marginal impact method.

(ii) Redetermination of tax liability. Under the method described in this paragraph (c)(3) (the "actual method"), a taxpayer, first, must determine what its regular and alternative minimum tax liability would have been for each redetermination year if the amounts of contract income allocated in Step One for all contracts completed or adjusted in the filing year and in any prior year were substituted for the amounts of contract income reported under the percentage of completion method on the taxpayer's original return (or as subsequently adjusted on examination, or by amended return). See Example (2) of paragraph (h)(3) for an illustration of Step Two.

(iii) Hypothetical underpayment or overpayment. After redetermining the income tax liability for each tax year affected by the reallocation of contract income, the taxpayer then determines the amount, if any, of the hypothetical underpayment or overpayment of tax for each of these redetermination years. The hypothetical underpayment or overpayment for each affected year is the difference between the tax liability as redetermined under the look-back method for that year and the amount of tax liability determined as of the latest of the following:

(A) The original return date;

(B) The date of a subsequently amended or adjusted return (if, however, the amended return is due to a carryback described in section 6611(f), see paragraph (c)(4)(iii)); or,

(C) The last previous application of the look-back method (in which case, the previous hypothetical tax liability is used).

(iv) Cumulative determination of tax liability. The redetermination of tax liability resulting from previous applications of the look-back method is cumulative. Thus, for example, in computing the amount of a hypothetical overpayment or underpayment of tax for a redetermination year, the current hypothetical tax liability is compared to the hypothetical tax liability for that year determined as of the last previous application of the look-back method.

(v) Years affected by look-back only. A redetermination of income tax liability under Step Two is required for every tax year for which the tax liability would have been affected by a change in the amount of income or loss for any other year for which a redetermination is required. For example, if the allocation of contract income under Step One changed the amount of a net operating loss that was carried back to a year preceding the year the taxpayer entered into the contract, the tax liability for the earlier year must be redetermined.

(vi) Definition of tax liability. For purposes of Step Two, the income tax liability must be redetermined by taking into account all applicable additions to tax, credits, and net operating loss carrybacks and carryovers. Thus, the tax, if any, imposed under section 55 (relating to alternative minimum tax) must be taken into account. For example, if the taxpayer did not pay alternative minimum tax, but would have paid alternative minimum tax for that year if actual rather than estimated contract price and costs had been used in determining contract income for the year, the amount of any hypothetical overpayment or underpayment of tax must be determined by comparing the hypothetical total tax liability (including hypothetical alternative minimum tax liability) with the actual tax liability for that year. The effect of taking these items into account in applying the look-back method is illustrated in Examples (4) through (7) of paragraphs (h)(5) through (h)(8) below.

*(4) Look-back Step Three: Calculation of interest on underpayment or overpayment.* (i) In general. After determining a hypothetical underpayment or overpayment of tax for each redetermination year, the taxpayer must determine the interest charged or credited on each of these amounts. Interest on the amount determined under Step Two is determined by applying the overpayment rate designated under section 6621, compounded daily. In general, the time period over which interest is charged on hypothetical underpayments or

credited on hypothetical overpayments begins at the due date (not including extensions) of the return for the redetermination year for which the hypothetical underpayment or overpayment determined in Step Two is computed. This time period generally ends on the earlier of:

(A) The due date (not including extensions) of the return for the filing year, and

(B) The date both

(1) The income tax return for the filing year is filed, and

(2) The tax for that year has been paid in full. If a taxpayer uses the simplified marginal impact method contained in paragraph (d), the remainder of this paragraph (c)(4) does not apply.

(ii) Changes in the amount of a loss or credit carryback or carryover. The time period for determining interest may be different in cases involving loss or credit carrybacks or carryovers in order to properly reflect the time period during which the taxpayer (in the case of an underpayment) or the Government (in the case of an overpayment) had the use of the amount determined to be a hypothetical underpayment or overpayment. Thus, if a reallocation of contract income under Step One results in an increase or decrease to a net operating loss carryback (but not a carryforward), the interest due or to be refunded must be computed on the increase or decrease in tax attributable to the change to the carryback only from the due date (not including extensions) of the return for the redetermination year that generated the carryback and not from the due date of the return for the redetermination year in which the carryback was absorbed. In the case of a change in the amount of a carryover as a result of applying the look-back method, interest is computed from the due date of the return for the year in which the carryover was absorbed. See Examples (8) and (9) of paragraph (h)(9) for an illustration of these rules.

(iii) Changes in the amount of tax liability that generated a subsequent refund. If the amount of tax liability for a redetermination year (as reported on the taxpayer's original return, as subsequently adjusted on examination, as adjusted by amended return, or as redetermined by the last previous application of the look-back method) is decreased by the application of the look-back method, and any portion of the redetermination year tax liability was absorbed by a loss or credit carryback arising in a year subsequent to the redetermination year, the look-back method applies as follows to properly reflect the time period of the use of the tax overpayment. To the extent the amount of tax absorbed because of the carryback exceeds the total hypothetical tax liability for the year (as redetermined under the look-back method) the taxpayer is entitled to receive interest only until the due date (not including extensions) of the return for the year in which the carryback arose.

*Example.* Upon the completion of a long-term contract in 1990, the taxpayer redetermines its tax liability for 1988 under the look-back method. This redetermination results in a hypothetical reduction of tax liability from $1,500x (actual liability originally reported) to $1,200x (hypothetical liability). In addition, the taxpayer had already received a refund of some or all of the actual 1988 tax by carrying back a net operating loss (NOL) that arose in 1989. The time period over which interest would be computed on the hypothetical overpayment of $300x for 1988 would depend on the amount of the refund generated by the carryback, as illustrated by the following three alternative situations:

(A) If the amount refunded because of the NOL is $1,500x: interest is credited to the taxpayer on the entire hypothetical overpayment of $300x from the due date of the 1988 return, when the hypothetical overpayment occurred, until the due date of the 1989 return, when the taxpayer received a refund for the entire amount of the 1988 tax, including the hypothetical overpayment.

(B) If the amount refunded because of the NOL is $1,000x: interest is credited to the taxpayer on the entire amount of the hypothetical overpayment of $300x from the due date of the 1988 return, when the hypothetical overpayment occurred, until the due date of the 1990 return. In this situation interest is credited until the due date of the return for the completion year of the contract, rather than the due date of the return for the year in which the carryback arose, because the amount refunded was less than the redetermined tax liability. Therefore, no portion of the hypothetical overpayment is treated as having been refunded to the taxpayer before the filing year.

(C) If the amount refunded because of the NOL is $1,300x-: interest is credited to the taxpayer on $100x ($1,300x − $1,200x) from the due date of the 1988 return until the due date of the 1989 return because only this portion of the total hypothetical overpayment is treated as having been refunded to the taxpayer before the filing year. However, the taxpayer did not receive a refund for the remaining $200x of the overpayment at that time and, therefore, is credited with interest on $200x through the due date of the tax return for 1990, the filing year. See Examples (10) and (11) of paragraph (h)(9) for a further illustration of this rule.

**(d) Simplified marginal impact method.** *(1) Introduction.* This paragraph (d) provides a simplified method for calculating look-back interest. Any taxpayer may elect this simplified marginal impact method, except that pass-through entities described in paragraph (d)(4) of this section are required to apply the simplified marginal impact method at the entity level with respect to domestic contracts and the owners of those entities do not apply the look-back method to those contracts. Under the simplified marginal impact method, a taxpayer calculates the hypothetical underpayments or overpayments of tax for a prior year based on an assumed marginal tax rate. A taxpayer electing to use the simplified marginal impact method must use the method for each long-term contract for which it reports income (except with respect to domestic contracts if the taxpayer is an owner in a widely held pass-through entity that is required to use the simplified marginal impact method at the entity level for those contracts).

*(2) Operation.* (i) In general. Under the simplified marginal impact method, income from those contracts that are completed or adjusted in the filing year is first reallocated in accordance with the procedures of Step One contained in paragraph (c)(2) of this section. Step Two is modified in the following manner. The hypothetical underpayment or overpayment of tax for each year of the contract (a "redetermination year") is determined by multiplying the applicable regular tax rate (as defined in paragraph (d)(2)(iii)) by the increase or decrease in regular taxable income (or, if it produces a greater amount, by multiplying the applicable alternative minimum tax rate by the increase or decrease in alternative minimum taxable income, whether or not the taxpayer would have been subject to the alternative minimum tax) that results from reallocating income to the tax year under Step One. Generally, the product of the alternative minimum tax rate and the increase or decrease in alternative minimum taxable income will be the greater of the two amounts described in the preceding sentence only with respect to con-

tracts for which a taxpayer uses the full percentage of completion method only for alternative minimum tax purposes and uses the completed contract method, or the percentage of completion-capitalized cost method, for regular tax purposes. Step Three is then applied. Interest is credited to the taxpayer on the net overpayment and is charged to the taxpayer on the net underpayment for each redetermination year from the due date (determined without regard to extensions) of the return for the redetermination year until the earlier of

(A) The due date (determined without regard to extensions) of the return for the filing year, and

(B) The first date by which both the return is filed and the tax is fully paid.

(ii) Applicable tax rate. For purposes of determining hypothetical underpayments or overpayments of tax under the simplified marginal impact method, the applicable regular tax rate is the highest rate of tax in effect for the redetermination year under section 1 in the case of an individual and under section 11 in the case of a corporation. The applicable alternative minimum tax rate is the rate of tax in effect for the taxpayer under section 55(b)(1). The highest rate is determined without regard to the taxpayer's actual rate bracket and without regard to any additional surtax imposed for the purpose of phasing out multiple tax brackets or exemptions.

(iii) Overpayment ceiling. The net hypothetical overpayment of tax for any redetermination year is limited to the taxpayer's total federal income tax liability for the redetermination year reduced by the cumulative amount of net hypothetical overpayments of tax for that redetermination year resulting from earlier applications of the look-back method. If the reallocation of contract income results in a net overpayment of tax and this amount exceeds the actual tax liability (as of the filing year) for the redetermination year, as adjusted for past applications of the look-back method and taking into account net operating loss, capital loss, or credit carryovers and carrybacks to that year, the actual tax so adjusted is treated as the overpayment for the redetermination year. This overpayment ceiling does not apply when the simplified marginal impact method is applied at the entity level by a widely held pass-through entity in accordance with paragraph (d)(4) of this section.

(iv) Example. The application of the simplified marginal impact method is illustrated by the following example:

*Example.* Corporation X, a calendar-year taxpayer, reports income from long-term contracts and elected the simplified marginal impact method when it filed its income tax return for 1989. X uses only the percentage of completion method for both regular taxable income and alternative minimum taxable income. X completed contracts A, B, and C in 1989 and, therefore, was required to apply the look-back method in 1989. Income was actually reported for these contracts in 1987, 1988, and 1989. X's applicable tax rate, as determined under section 11, for the redetermination years 1987 and 1988 was 40 percent and 34 percent, respectively. The amount of contract income originally reported and reallocated for contracts A, B, and C, and the net overpayments and under payments for the redetermination years are as follows:

| | 1987 | 1988 |
|---|---|---|
| Contract A: | | |
| Originally reported | $ 5,000x | $4,000x |
| Reallocated | 3,000x | 5,000x |
| Increase/(Decrease) | (2,000x) | 1,000x |
| Contract B: | | |
| Originally reported | 6,000x | 2,000x |
| Reallocated | 7,000x | 1,500x |
| Increase/(Decrease) | 1,000x | (500x) |
| Contract C: | | |
| Originally reported | 8,000x | 5,000x |
| Reallocated | 4,000x | 7,000x |
| Increase/(Decrease) | (4,000x) | 2,000x |
| Net Increase/(Decrease) | (5,000x) | 2,500x |
| Tentative (Underpayment)/Overpayment: | | |
| @.40 | 2,000x | |
| @.34 | | (850x) |
| Ceiling: | | |
| Actual Tax Liability (After Carryovers and Carrybacks) | 1,500x | 500x |
| Final (Underpayment)/Overpayment | 1,500x | (850x) |

Under the simplified marginal impact method, X determined a tentative hypothetical net overpayment for 1987 and a net underpayment for 1988. X determined these amounts by first aggregating the difference for contracts. A, B, and C between the amount of contract price originally reported and the amount of contract price as reallocated and, then, applying the highest regular tax rate to the aggregate decrease in income for 1987 and the aggregate increase in income for 1988.

However, X's overpayment for 1987 is subject to a ceiling based on X's total tax liability. Because the tentative net overpayment of tax for 1987 exceeds the actual tax liability for that year after taking into account carryovers and carrybacks to that year, the final overpayment under the simplified marginal impact method is the amount of tax liability paid instead of the tentative net overpayment. Since application of the look-back method for 1988 results in a tentative underpayment of tax, it is not subject to a ceiling. If the look-back method is applied in 1991, the ceiling amount for 1987 will be zero and the ceiling amount for 1988 will be $1,350.

X is entitled to receive interest on the hypothetical overpayment from March 15, 1988 to March 15, 1990, X is required to pay interest on the underpayment from March 15, 1989, to March 15, 1990.

*(3) Anti-abuse rule.* If the simplified marginal impact method is used with respect to any long-term contract (including a contract of a widely held pass-through entity), the district director may recompute interest for the contract (including domestic contracts of widely held pass-through entities) under the look-back method using the actual method (and without regard to the simplified marginal impact method). The district director may make such a recomputation only if the amount of income originally reported with respect to the contract for any redetermination year exceeds the amount of income reallocated under the look-back method with respect to that contract for that year (using actual contract price and contract costs) by the lesser of $1,000,000 or 20 percent of the amount of income as reallocated (i.e., based on actual contract price and contract costs) under the look-back method with respect to that contract for that year. In determining whether to exercise this authority upon examination of the Form 8697, the district director may take into account whether the taxpayer overreported income for a purpose of receiving interest under the look-back method on a hypothetical overpayment determined at the applicable tax rate. The district director also may take into account whether the taxpayer underreported income for the year in question with respect to other contracts. Notwithstanding the look-back method, the district director may require an adjustment to the tax liability for any open tax year

if the taxpayer did not apply the percentage of completion method properly on its original return.

*(4) Application.* (i) Required use by certain pass-through entities. (A) General rule. The simplified marginal impact method is required to be used with respect to income reported from domestic contracts by pass-through entity that is either a partnership, an S corporation, or a trust, and that is not closely held. With respect to contracts described in the preceding sentence, the simplified marginal impact method is applied by the pass-through entity at the entity level. For determining the amount of any hypothetical underpayment or overpayment, the applicable regular and alternative minimum tax rates, respectively, are generally the highest rates of tax in effect for corporations under section 11 and section 55(b)(1). However, the applicable regular and alternative minimum tax rates are the highest rates of tax imposed on individuals under section 1 and section 55(b)(1) if, at all times during the redetermination year involved (i.e., the year in which the hypothetical increase or decrease in income arises), more than 50 percent of the interests in the entity were held by individuals directly or through 1 or more pass-through entities.

(B) Closely held. A pass-through entity is closely held if, at any time during any redetermination year, 50 percent of more (by value) of the beneficial interests in that entity are held (directly or indirectly) by or for 5 or fewer persons. For this purpose, the term "person" has the same meaning as in section 7701(a)(1), except that a pass-through entity is not treated as a person. In addition, the constructive ownership rules of section 1563(e) apply by substituting the term "beneficial interest" for the term "stock" and by substituting the term "pass-through entity" for the term, "corporation" used in that section, as appropriate, for purposes of determining whether a beneficial interest in a pass-through entity is indirectly owned by any person.

(C) Examples. The following examples illustrate the application of the rules of paragraph (d)(4)(i):

*Example (1).* P, a partnership, began a long-term contract on March 1, 1986, and completed this contract in its tax year ending December 31, 1989. P used the percentage of completion method for all contract income. Substantially all of the income from the contract arose from U.S. sources. At all times during all of the years for which income was required to be reported under the contract, exactly 25 percent of the value of P's interests was owned by Corporation M. The remaining 75 percent of the value of P's interests was owned in equal shares by 15 unrelated individuals, who are also unrelated to Corporation M. M's ownership of P represents less than 50 percent of the value of the beneficial interests in P, and, therefore, viewed alone, is insufficient to make P a closely held partnership. In addition, because no 4 of the individual owners together own 25 percent or more of the remaining value of P's beneficial interests, there is no group of 5 owners that together own, directly or indirectly, 50 percent or more by value of the beneficial interests in P. Therefore, P is not closely held pass-through entity.

Because P is not a closely held pass-through entity, and because P completed the contract after the effective date of section 460(b)(4), P is required to use the simplified marginal impact method. Any interest computed under the look-back method will be paid to, or collected from, P, rather than its partners, and must be reported to each of the partners on Form 1065 as interest income or expense. Further, assume that, for the redetermination years, Corporation M is subject to alternative minimum tax at the rate of 20 percent and 3 of the individuals who own interests in P are subject to the highest marginal tax rate of 33 percent in 1988. Regardless of the actual marginal tax rates of its partners, P is required to determine the underpayment or overpayment of tax for each redetermination year at the entity level by applying a single rate to the increase or decrease in income resulting from the reallocation of contract income under the look-back method. Because more than 50 percent of the interests in P are held by individuals, P must use the highest rate specified in section 1 for each redetermination year. Thus, the rate applied by P is 50 percent for 1986, 38.5 percent for 1987, and 28 percent for 1988.

*Example (2).* Assume the same facts as in Example (1), except that one of the individuals, Individual I, who directly owns 5 percent of the value of the interests of P, also owns 100 percent of the stock of Corporation M. Section 1563(e)(4) of the Code provides that stock owned directly or indirectly by or for a corporation is considered to be owned by any person who owns 5 percent or more in value of its stock in that proportion which the value of the stock which that person so owns bears to the value of all the stock in that corporation. Because section 460(b)(4)(C)(iii) and this paragraph (d)(4) provide that rules similar to the constructive ownership rules of section 1563(e) apply in determining whether a pass-through entity is closely held, all of M's interest in P is attributed to I because I owns 100 percent of the value of the stock in M. Accordingly, because I's direct 5 percent and constructive 25 percent ownership of P, plus the interests owned by any 4 other individual partners, equals 50 percent or more of the value of the beneficial interests of P, P is a closely held pass-through entity within the meaning of section 460(b)(4)(C)(iii). Therefore, P cannot use the simplified marginal impact method at the entity level. Accordingly, each of the partners of P must separately apply the look-back method to their respective interests in the income and expenses attributable to the contract, but each partner may elect to use the simplified marginal impact method with respect to the partner's share of income from the contract.

(D) Domestic contracts. (1) General rule. A domestic contract is any contract substantially all of the income of which is from sources in the United States. For this purpose, "substantially all" of the income from a long-term contract is considered to be from United States sources if 95 percent or more of the gross income from the contract is from sources within the United States as determined under the rules in sections 861 through 865.

(2) Portion of contract income sourced. In determining whether substantially all of the gross income from a long-term contract is from United States sources, taxpayers must apply the allocation and apportionment principles of sections 861 through 865 only to the portion of the contract accounted for under the percentage of completion method. Under the percentage of completion method, gross income from a long-term contract includes all payments to be received under the contract (i.e., any amounts treated as contract price). Similarly, all costs taken into account in the computation of taxable income under the percentage of completion method are deducted from gross income rather than added to a cost of goods sold account that reduces gross income. Therefore, allocable contract costs are not considered in determining whether a long-term contract is a domestic contract or a foreign contract, even if, under the taxpayer's facts, the allocation of contract costs to any portion of a contract not accounted for under the percentage of completion method would affect the relative percentages of United States and foreign source gross income from the entire con-

tract if this portion of the contract were taken into account in applying the 95-percent test.

(E) Application to foreign contracts. If a widely held pass-through entity has some foreign contracts and some domestic contracts, the owners of the pass-through entity each apply the look-back method (using, if they elect, the simplified marginal impact method) to their respective share of the income and expense from foreign contracts. Moreover, in applying the look-back method to foreign contracts at the owner level, the owners do not take into account their share of increases or decreases in contract income resulting from the application of the simplified marginal impact method with respect to domestic contracts at the entity level.

(F) Effective date. The simplified marginal impact method must be applied to pass-through entities described in paragraph (d)(4)(i) of this section with respect to domestic contracts completed or adjusted in tax years for which the due date of the return (determined with regard to extensions) of the pass-through entity is after November 9, 1988.

(ii) Elective use. (A) General rule. As provided in paragraph (d)(4)(i) of this section, the simplified marginal impact method must be used by certain pass-through entities with respect to domestic contracts. C corporations, individuals, and owners of closely held pass-through entities may elect the simplified marginal impact method. Owners of other pass-through entities may also elect the simplified marginal impact method with respect to all contracts other than those for which the simplified marginal impact method is required to be applied at the entity level. This rule applies to foreign contracts of widely held pass-through entities. In the case of an electing owner in a pass-through entity, the simplified marginal impact method is applied at the owner level, instead of at the entity level, with respect to the owner's share of the long-term contract income and expense reported by the pass-through entity.

(B) Election requirements. A taxpayer elects the simplified marginal impact method by stating that the election is being made on a timely filed income tax return (determined with regard to extensions) for the first tax year the election is to apply. An election to use the simplified marginal impact method applies to all applications of the look-back method to all eligible long-term contracts for the tax year for which the election is made and for any subsequent tax year. The election may not be revoked without the consent of the Commissioner.

(C) Consolidated group consistency rule. In the case of a consolidated group of corporations, as defined in § 1.1502-1(h) an election to use the simplified marginal impact method is made by the common parent of the group. The election is binding on all other affected members of the group (including members that join the group after the election is made with respect to all applications of the look-back method after joining). If a member subsequently leaves the group, the election remains binding as to that member unless the Commissioner consents to a revocation of the election. If a corporation using the simplified marginal impact method joins a group that does not use the method, the election is automatically revoked with respect to all applications of the look-back method after it joins the group.

**(e) Delayed reapplication method.** *(1) In general.* For purposes of reapplying the look-back method after the year of contract completion, a taxpayer may elect the delayed reapplication method to minimize the number of required reapplications of the look-back method. Under this method, the look-back method is reapplied after the year of completion of a contract (or after a subsequent application of the look-back method) only when the first one of the following conditions is met with respect to the contract:

(i) The net undiscounted value of increases or decreases in the contract price occurring since the time of the last application of the look-back method exceeds the lesser of $1,000,000 or 10 percent of the total contract price as of that time,

(ii) The net undiscounted value of increases or decreases in the contract costs occurring since the time of the last application of the look-back method exceeds the lesser of $1,000,000 or 10 percent of the total contract price as of that time,

(iii) The taxpayer goes out of existence,

(iv) The taxpayer reasonably believes the contract is finally settled and closed, or

(v) Neither condition (e)(1)(i), (ii), (iii), nor (iv) above is met by the end of the fifth tax year that begins after the last previous application of the look-back method.

*(2) Time and manner of making election.* An election to use the delayed reapplication method may be made for any filing year for which the due date of the return (determined with regard to extensions) is after June 12, 1990. The election is made by a statement to that effect on the taxpayer's timely filed Federal income tax return (determined with regard to extensions) for the first tax year the election is to be effective. An election to use the delayed reapplication method is binding with respect to all long-term contracts for which the look-back method would be reapplied without regard to the election in the year of election and any subsequent year unless the Commissioner consents to a revocation of the election. In the case of a consolidated group of corporations, as defined in § 1.1502-1(h) an election to use the delayed reapplication method is made by the common parent of the group. The election is binding on all other affected members of the group (including members that join the group after the election is made with respect to contracts adjusted after joining). If a member subsequently leaves the group, the election remains binding as to that member unless the Commissioner consents to a revocation of the election. If a corporation that has made the election joins a consolidated group that has not made the election, the election is treated as revoked with respect to contracts adjusted after joining.

*(3) Examples.* The operation of this delayed reapplication method is illustrated by the following examples:

*Example (1).* X completes a contract in 1987, and applies the look-back method when its return for 1987 is filed. X properly uses $600,000 as the actual contract price in applying the look-back method. In 1990, as a result of the settlement of a dispute with its customer, X redetermines total contract price to be $640,000, and includes $40,000 in gross income. On its return for 1990, X states it is electing the delayed reapplication method. X is not required to reapply the look-back method at that time, because $40,000 does not exceed the lesser of $1,000,000 or 10 percent of the unadjusted contract price of $600,000, and 5 years have not passed since the last application of the look-back method.

*Example (2).* Assume the same facts as in Example (1), except that at the end of 1992, the fifth year after completion of the contract, no other adjustments to contract price or contract costs have occurred. X is required to reapply the look-back method in 1992 and, accordingly, redetermine its tax liability for each redetermination year. After redetermining the underpayment of tax for those years, X must compute the amount of interest charged on the underpayments. Although 1992 is the filing year, interest is due on the amount of each underpayment resulting from the adjustment only from the due date of the return for each redetermination year to the due date of the return for 1990 because the tax liability for the adjustment was fully paid in 1990. However, from the due of the 1990 return until the due date of the 1992 return, when the look-back method is reapplied for the adjustment, interest is due on the amount of interest attributable to the underpayments.

**(f) Look-back reporting.** *(1) Procedure.* The amount of any interest due from, or payable to, a taxpayer as a result of applying the look-back method is computed on Form 8697 for any filing year. In general, the look-back method is applied by the taxpayer that reports income from a long-term contract. See paragraph (g) of this section to determine who is responsible for applying the look-back method when, prior to the completion of a long-term contract, there is a transaction that changes the taxpayer that reports income from the contract.

*(2) Treatment of interest on return.* (i) General rule. The amount of interest required to be paid by a taxpayer is treated as an income tax under subtitle A, but only for purposes of subtitle F of the Code (other than sections 6654 and 6655), which addresses tax procedures and administration.

Thus, a taxpayer that fails to pay the amount of interest due is subject to any applicable penalties under subtitle F, including, for example, an underpayment penalty under section 6651, and the taxpayer also is liable for underpayment interest under section 6601. However, interest required to be paid under the look-back method is treated as interest expense for purposes of computing taxable income under subtitle A, even though it is treated as income tax liability for subtitle F purposes. Interest received under the look-back method is treated as taxable interest income for all purposes, and is not treated as a reduction in tax liability or a tax refund. The determination of whether or not interest computed under the look-back method is treated as tax is determined on a "net" basis for each filing year. Thus, if a taxpayer computes for the current filing year both hypothetical overpayments and hypothetical underpayments for prior years, the taxpayer has an increase in tax only if the interest computed on the underpayments for all those prior years exceeds the interest computed on the overpayments for all those prior years, for all contracts completed or adjusted for the year.

(ii) Timing of look-back interest. For purposes of determining taxable income under subtitle A of the Code, any amount of interest payable to the taxpayer under the look-back method is includible in gross income as interest income in the tax year it is properly taken into account under the taxpayer's method of accounting for interest income. Any amount of interest required to be paid is taken into account as interest expense arising from an underpayment of income tax in the tax year it is properly taken into account under the taxpayer's method of accounting for interest expense. Thus, look-back interest required to be paid by an individual, or by a pass-through entity on behalf of an individual owner (or beneficiary) under the simplified marginal impact method, is personal interest and, therefore, is disallowed in accordance with § 1.163-9T(b)(2). Interest determined at the entity level under the simplified marginal impact method is allocated among the owners (or beneficiaries) for reporting purposes in the same manner that interest income and interest expense are allocated to owners (or beneficiaries) and subject to the requirements of section 704 and any other applicable rules.

*(3) Statute of limitations and compounding of interest on look-back interest.* For guidance on the statute of limitations applicable to the assessment and collection of look-back interest owed by a taxpayer, see sections 6501 and 6502. A taxpayer's claim for credit or refund of look-back interest previously paid by or collected from a taxpayer is a claim for credit or refund of an overpayment of tax and is subject to the statute of limitations provided in section 6511. A taxpayer's claim for look-back interest (or interest payable on look-back interest) that is not attributable to an amount previously paid by or collected from a taxpayer is a general, non-tax claim against the federal government. For guidance on the statute of limitations that applies to general, non-tax claims against the federal government, see 28 U.S.C. sections 2401 and 2501. For guidance applicable to the compounding of interest when the look-back interest is not paid, see sections 6601 to 6622.

**(g) Mid-contract change in taxpayer.** *(1) In general.* The rules in this paragraph (g) apply if, as described in § 1.460-4(k), prior to the completion of a long-term contract accounted for using the PCM or the PCCM by a taxpayer (old taxpayer), there is a transaction that makes another taxpayer (new taxpayer) responsible for accounting for income from the same contract. The rules governing constructive completion transactions are provided in paragraph (g)(2) of this section, while the rules governing step-in-the-shoes transactions are provided in paragraph (g)(3) of this section. For purposes of this paragraph, pre-transaction years are all taxable years of the old taxpayer in which the old taxpayer accounted for (or should have accounted for) gross receipts from the contract, and post-transaction years are all taxable years of the new taxpayer in which the new taxpayer accounted for (or should have accounted for) gross receipts from the contract.

*(2) Constructive completion transactions.* In the case of a transaction described in § 1.460-4(k)(2)(i) (constructive completion transaction), the look-back method is applied by the old taxpayer with respect to pre-transaction years upon the date of the transaction and, if the new taxpayer uses the PCM or the PCCM to account for the contract, by the new taxpayer with respect to post-transaction years upon completion of the contract. The contract price and allocable contract costs to be taken into account by the old taxpayer or the new taxpayer in applying the look-back method are described in § 1.460-4(k)(2).

*(3) Step-in-the-shoes transactions.* (i) General rules. In the case of a transaction described in § 1.460-4(k)(3)(i) (step-in-the-shoes transaction), the look-back method is not applied at the time of the transaction, but is instead applied for the first time when the contract is completed by the new taxpayer. Upon completion of the contract, the look-back method is applied by the new taxpayer with respect to both pre-transaction years and post-transaction years, taking into account all amounts reasonably expected to be received by either the old or new taxpayer and all allocable contract costs incurred during both periods as described in § 1.460-4(k)(3). The new taxpayer is liable for filing the Form 8697 and for interest computed on hypothetical underpayments of tax, and is entitled to receive interest with respect to hypothetical overpayments of tax, for both pre- and post-transaction years. The old taxpayer will be secondarily liable for any interest required to be paid with respect to pre-transaction years reduced by any interest on pre-transaction overpayments.

(ii) Application of look-back method to pre-transaction period. (A) Contract price. The actual contract price for pre-transaction taxable years must be determined by the new taxpayer without regard to any contract price adjustment described in paragraph (k)(3)(iv)(B)(1) of this section.

(B) Method. The new taxpayer may apply the look-back method to each pre-transaction taxable year that is a redetermination year using the simplified marginal impact method described in paragraph (d) of this section (regardless of whether or not the old taxpayer would have actually used that method and without regard to the tax liability ceiling). But see paragraph (d)(4) of this section, which requires use of the simplified marginal impact method by certain pass-through entities.

(C) Interest accrual period. With respect to any hypothetical underpayment or overpayment of tax for a pre-transaction taxable year, interest accrues from the due date of the old taxpayer's tax return (not including extensions) for the taxable year of the underpayment or overpayment until the due date of the new taxpayer's return (not including extensions) for the completion year or the year of a post-completion adjustment, whichever is applicable.

(D) Information old taxpayer must provide. (1) In general. Except as provided in paragraph (g)(3)(ii)(D)(2) of this section, in order to help the new taxpayer to apply the look-back method with respect to pre-transaction taxable years, any old taxpayer that accounted for income from a long-term contract under the PCM or PCCM for either regular or alternative minimum tax purposes is required to provide the information described in this paragraph to the new taxpayer by the due date (not including extensions) of the old taxpayer's income tax return for the first taxable year ending on or after a step-in-the-shoes transaction described in § 1.460-4(k)(3)(i). The required information is as follows—

(i) The portion of the contract reported by the old taxpayer under PCM for regular and alternative minimum tax purposes (i.e., whether the old taxpayer used PCM, the 40/60 PCCM method, or the 70/30 PCCM method);

(ii) Any submethods used in the application of PCM (e.g., the simplified cost-to-cost method or the 10-percent method);

(iii) The amount of total contract price reported by year;

(iv) The numerator and the denominator of the completion factor by year;

(v) The due date (not including extensions) of the old taxpayer's income tax returns for each taxable year in which income was required to be reported;

(vi) Whether the old taxpayer was a corporate or a noncorporate taxpayer by year; and

(vii) Any other information required by the Commissioner by administrative pronouncement.

(2) Special rules for certain pass-through entity transactions. For purposes of paragraph (g)(3)(ii)(D)(1) of this section, in the case of a transaction described in § 1.460-4(k)(3)(i)(I), the contributing partner is treated as the old taxpayer, and the partnership is treated as the new taxpayer. In the case of transactions described in § 1.460-4(k)(3)(i)(F), (G), (J), (K), or (L), the old taxpayer is not required to provide the information described in paragraph (g)(3)(ii)(D)(1) of this section, because information necessary for the new taxpayer to apply the look-back method is provided by the pass-through entity. This paragraph (g)(3)(ii)(D) is applicable for transactions on or after August 6, 2003.

(iii) Application of look-back method to post-transaction years. With respect to post-transaction taxable years, the new taxpayer must use the same look-back method it uses for other contracts (i.e., the simplified marginal impact method or the actual method) to determine the amount of any hypothetical overpayment or underpayment of tax and the time period for computing interest on these amounts.

(iv) S corporation elections. Following the conversion of a C corporation into an S corporation, the look-back method is applied at the entity level with respect to contracts entered into prior to the conversion, notwithstanding section 460(b)(4)(B)(i).

*(4) Effective date.* Except as provided in paragraph (g)(3)(ii)(D) of this section, this paragraph (g) is applicable for transactions on or after May 15, 2002.

**(h) Examples.** *(1) Overview.* This paragraph provides computational examples of the rules of this section. Except as otherwise noted, the examples involve calendar-year taxpayers and involve long-term contracts subject to section 460 that are accounted for using the percentage of completion method, rather than the percentage of completion-capitalized cost method. If the percentage of completion-capitalized cost method were used by a taxpayer described in the examples, the amounts of contract income and expenses shown in the examples would be reduced, for purposes of determining regular taxable income, to the appropriate fraction (40, 70, or 90 percent) of contract items accounted for under the percentage of completion method. Tens of thousands of dollars ($00,000's) are omitted from the figures in the examples. The contracts described in the examples are assumed to be the taxpayers' only contracts that are subject to the look-back method of section 460. Except as otherwise stated, the examples assume that the taxpayer has no adjustments and preferences for purposes of section 55, so that alternative minimum taxable income is the same as taxable income, and no alternative minimum tax is imposed for the years involved. The examples assume that the taxpayer does not elect the 10-percent method, the simplified marginal impact method, or the delayed reapplication method.

*(2) Step One.* The following example illustrates the application of paragraph (c)(2);

*Example (1).* In 1989, W completes three long-term contracts, A, B, and C, entered into on January 1 of 1986, 1987, and 1988, respectively. For Contract A, W used the completed contract method of accounting. For Contract B, W used the percentage of completion-capitalized cost method of accounting, taking into account 60 percent of contract income under W's normal method of accounting, which was the completed contract method. For Contract C, W used the percentage of completion method of accounting. The total price for each contract was $1,000. In computing alternative minimum taxable income, W is required to use the percentage of completion method for Contracts B and C. W used regular tax costs for purposes of determining the degree of contract completion under the alternative minimum tax.

Contract A is not taken into account for purposes of applying the look-back method, because it is subject to neither section 460 nor section 56(a)(3). Thus, even if W had used the percentage of completion method as permitted under § 1.451-3, instead of the completed contract method, the look-back method would not be applicable because the Contract A was entered into before the effective date of section 460.

The actual costs allocated to Contracts B and C under section 460(c) and incurred in each year of the contract were as follows:

| Contract | 1987 | 1988 | 1989 | Total |
|---|---|---|---|---|
| B | $200 | $400 | $200 | $800 |
| C | 100 | 300 | 400 | 800 |

In applying the look-back method, the first step is to allocate the contract price among tax years preceding and including the completion year. That allocation would produce the following amounts of gross income for purposes of the regular tax. Note that no income from Contract C is allocated to 1987, the year before the contract was entered into, even though contract costs were incurred in 1987:

| Contract | 1987 | 1988 | 1989 |
|---|---|---|---|
| B | $100 (40% × $200/$800 × $1000) | $200 ((40% × $600/$800 × $1000) − $100) | $700 |
| C | 0 | 500 ($400/$800 × $1000) | 500 |

Because the percentage of completion-capitalized cost method may not be used for alternative minimum tax purposes, the allocation of contract income would produce the following amounts of gross income for purposes of computing alternative minimum taxable income:

| Contract | 1987 | 1988 | 1989 |
|---|---|---|---|
| B | $250 ($200/$800 × $1000) | $500 (($600/$800 × $1000) − $250) | $250 |
| C | 0 | 500 | 500 |

*(3) Step Two.* The following example illustrates the application of paragraph (c)(3):

*Example (2).* (i) X enters into two long-term contracts (D and E) in 1988. X determines its tax liability for 1988 as follows: e = estimate

a = amount originally reported (actual)
h = hypothetical

| | 1988 D | 1988 E | 1988 Total |
|---|---|---|---|
| 1988 contract costs | $ 3,000a | $ 2,000a | |
| Total contract costs | 8,000e | 8,000e | |
| Total contract price | 10,000e | 10,000e | |
| 1988 completion (%) | 37.5e | 25e | |
| 1988 gross income | 3,750a | 2,500e | |
| Less, 1988 costs | (3,000a) | (2,000a) | |
| 1988 net contract income | 750a | 500a | $1,250a |
| Other 1988 net income (loss) | | | (2,000a) |
| Taxable income (NOL) | | | (750a) |
| Tax | | | 0a |
| Refund from NOL carryback fully absorbed in 1985, at 46% | | | 345a |

(ii) X completes Contract D during 1989. X determines its taxable income for 1989 as follows:

| | 1989 D | 1989 E | 1989 Total |
|---|---|---|---|
| 1989 contract costs | $ 3,000a | 0a | |
| Total contract costs | 6,000a | $ 9,000e | |
| Total contract price | 10,000a | 10,000e | |
| 1989 completion (%) | 100a | 22.2e | |
| 1989 gross income/(loss) | 6,250a | (278a) | |
| Less, 1989 costs | (3,000a) | 0a | |
| 1989 net contract income | 3,250a | (278a) | $2,972a |
| Other 1989 net income (loss) | | | 0a |
| Taxable income (NOL) | | | 2,972a |
| Tax at 34% | | | 1,011a |

(iii) For purposes of the look-back method, X must reallocate the actual total contract D price between 1988 and 1989 based on the actual total contract D costs. This results in the following hypothetical underpayment of tax for 1988 for purposes of the look-back method. Note that X does not reallocate the contract E price in applying the look-back method in 1989 because contract E has not been completed, even though X's estimate of contract E costs has changed. The following computation is only for purposes of applying the look-back method, and does not result in the assessment of a tax deficiency.

| | 1988 | | |
|---|---|---|---|
| | D | E | Total |
| 1988 contract costs | $ 3,000a | $ 2,000a | |
| Total contract costs | 6,000a | 8,000e | |
| Total contract price | 10,000a | 10,000e | |
| 1988 completion (%) | 50a | 25e | |
| 1988 gross income | 5,000h | 2,500a | |
| Less, 1988 costs | (3,000a) | (2,000a) | |
| 1988 net contract income | 2,000h | 500a | $2,500h |
| Other 1988 net income (loss) | | | (2,000a) |
| Taxable income (NOL) | | | 500h |
| Tax at 34% | | | 170h |
| Less, previously computed tax | | | -0a |
| Underpayment of 1988 tax | | | 170h |
| Underpayment of 1985 tax from NOL carryback refund in 1988 | | | 345h |
| Total underpayment of tax | | | 515h |

For purposes of any subsequent application of the look-back method for which 1989 is a redetermination year, because the reallocation of contract income and redetermination of tax liability are cumulative, X will use for 1989 the amount of contract D income and the amount of tax liability that would have been reported in 1989 if X had used actual contract costs instead of the amounts that were originally reported using the estimate of $8,000. Assuming no subsequent revisions (due to, for example, adjustments to contract D price and costs determined after the end of 1989), this amount would be determined as follows:

| | 1989 | | |
|---|---|---|---|
| | D | E | Total |
| 1989 contract costs | $ 3,000a | 0a | |
| Total contract costs | 6,000a | $ 9,000e | |
| Total contract price | 10,000a | 10,000e | |
| 1989 completion (%) | 100a | 22.2e | |
| 1989 gross income | 5,000h | (278a) | |
| Less, 1989 costs | (3,000a) | 0a | |
| 1989 net contract income | 2,000h | (278a) | $1,722h |
| Other 1989 net income (loss) | | | 0a |
| Taxable income (NOL) | | | 1,722h |
| Tax at 34% | | | 585h |

(iv) X completes contract E during 1990. X determines its taxable income for 1990 as follows:

| | 1990 | | |
|---|---|---|---|
| | D | E | Total |
| 1990 contract costs | | $ 7,000a | |
| Total contract costs | | 9,000a | |
| Total contract price | | 10,000a | |
| 1990 completion (%) | | 100a | |
| 1990 gross income | | 7,778a | |
| Less, 1990 costs | | (7,000e) | |
| 1990 net contract income | | 778a | $778a |
| Other 1990 net income (loss) | | | 0a |
| Taxable income (NOL) | | | 778a |
| Tax at 34% | | | 265a |

(v) For purposes of the look-back method, X must reallocate the actual total contract E price between the 1988, 1989, and 1990, based on the actual total contract E costs. This results in the following hypothetical overpayment of tax for 1988. Note that X uses the amount of income for contract D determined in the last previous application of the look-back method, and not the amount of income actually reported:

| | 1988 | | |
|---|---|---|---|
| | D | E | Total |
| 1988 contract costs | $ 3,000a | $ 2,000a | |
| Total contract costs | $ 6,000a | $ 9,000a | |
| Total contract price | $10,000a | $10,000a | |
| 1988 completion (%) | 50a | 22.2a | |
| 1988 gross income | $ 5,000h | $ 2,222h | |
| Less, 1988 costs | ($ 3,000a) | ($ 2,000a) | |
| 1988 net contract income | $ 2,000h | $ 222h | $2,222h |
| Other 1988 net income (loss) | | | ($2,000a) |
| Taxable income (NOL) | | | $ 222h |
| Tax at 34% | | | $ 75h |
| Less, previously computed tax (based on most recent application of the look-back method) | | | $ 170h |
| Overpayment of 1988 tax | | | ($ 95h) |

In applying the look-back method to 1989, X again uses the amounts substituted as of the last previous application of the look-back method with respect to contract D. Thus, X computes its hypothetical underpayment for 1989 as follows:

| | 1989 | | |
|---|---|---|---|
| | D | E | Total |
| 1989 contract costs | $ 3,000a | 0a | |
| Total contract costs | $ 6,000a | $ 9,000a | |
| Total contract price | $10,000a | $10,000a | |
| 1989 completion (%) | 100a | 22.2a | |
| 1989 gross income | $ 5,000h | $ 0h | |
| Less, 1989 costs | ($ 3,000a) | ($ 0a) | |
| 1989 net contract income | $ 2,000h | 0a | $2,000h |
| Other 1989 net income (loss) | | | ($ 0a) |
| Taxable income (NOL) | | | $2,000h |
| Tax at 34% | | | $ 680h |
| Less, previously computed tax | | | $ 585h |
| Underpayment of 1989 tax | | | $ 95h |

For purposes of any subsequent application of the look-back method for which 1990 is a redetermination year, X will use for 1990 the amount of Contract E income, and the amount of tax liability, that was originally reported in 1990 because X's estimate of the total contract costs from $8,000 to $9,000 did not change after 1989. Without regard to any subsequent revisions, these amounts are the same as in the table in paragraph (h)(3)(iv) above.

*(4) Post-completion adjustments.* The following example illustrates the application of paragraph (c)(1)(ii):

*Example (3).* The facts are the same as in Example (2). In 1991, X settles a lawsuit against its customer in Contract E. The customer pays X an additional $3,000, without interest, in 1991. Applying the Federal mid-term rate then in effect, this $3,000 has a discounted value at the time of contract completion in 1990 of $2,700. X is required to apply the look-back method for 1991 even though no contract was completed in 1991. X must include the full $3,000 adjustment (which was not previously includible in total contract price) in gross income for 1991. X does not elect not to discount adjustments to the contract price or costs. Thus, X adjusts the contract price by the discounted amount of the adjustment and, therefore, uses $12,700 (not $13,000) for total Contract E price, rather than $10,000, which was used when the look-back method was first applied with respect to Contract E.

For purposes of the look-back method, X must allocate the revised total Contract E price of $12,700 between 1988, 1989 and 1990 based on the actual total Contract E costs, and compare the resulting revised tax liability with the tax liability determined for the last previous application of the look-back method involving those years. This results in the following hypothetical underpayments of tax for purposes of the look-back method:

r = revised

| | 1988 | | |
|---|---|---|---|
| | D | E | Total |
| 1988 contract costs | $ 3,000a | $ 2,000a | |
| Total contract costs | $ 6,000a | $ 9,000a | |
| Total contract price | $10,000a | $12,700r | |
| 1988 completion (%) | 50a | 22.2a | |
| 1988 gross income | $ 5,000h | $ 2,822rh | |
| Less, 1988 costs | ($ 3,000a) | ($ 2,000a) | |
| 1988 net contract income | $ 2,000h | 822rh | $2,222rh |
| Other 1988 net income (loss) | | | ($2,000a) |
| Taxable income | | | $ 822rh |
| Tax at 34% | | | $ 279rh |
| Less, previously computed tax | | | $ 75h |
| Underpayment of 1988 tax | | | $ 204rh |

No Contract E costs were incurred in 1989, and there is no hypothetical underpayment for 1989.

| | 1990 | | |
|---|---|---|---|
| | D | E | Total |
| 1990 contract costs | | $ 7,000a | |
| Total contract costs | | $ 9,000a | |
| Total contract price | | $12,700r | |
| 1990 completion (%) | | 100a | |
| 1990 gross income | | $ 9,878rh | |
| Less 1990 costs | | *($ 7,000a)* | |
| 1990 net contract income | | $ 2,878rh | $2,878rh |
| Other 1990 net income (loss) | | | 0a |
| Taxable income (NOL) | | | $2,878rh |
| Tax at 34% | | | $ 978rh |
| Less, previously computed tax | | | $ 265h |
| Underpayment of 1990 tax | | | $ 713rh |

In 1992, X incurs an additional cost of $1,000 allocable to the contract, which was not previously includible in total contract costs. Applying the Federal mid-term rate then in effect, the $1,000 has a discounted value at the time of contract completion of $800. X deducts this additional $1,000 in expenses in 1992. Based on this increase to contract costs, X reapplies the look-back method, and determines the following hypothetical underpayments for 1988, 1989 and 1990 for purposes of the look-back method:

| | 1988 | | |
|---|---|---|---|
| | D | E | Total |
| 1988 contract costs | $ 3,000a | $ 2,000a | |
| Total contract costs | $ 6,000a | $ 9,800r | |
| Total contract price | $10,000a | $12,700r | |
| 1988 completion (%) | 50a | 20.4r | |
| 1988 gross income | $ 5,000h | $ 2,592rh | |
| Less, 1988 costs | *($ 3,000a)* | *($ 2,000a)* | |
| 1988 net contract income | $ 2,000h | 592rh | $2,592rh |
| Other 1988 net income (loss) | | | *($2,000a)* |
| Taxable income (NOL) | | | $592rh |
| Tax at 34% | | | $201rh |
| Less, previously computed tax | | | $279rh |
| Overpayment of 1988 tax | | | ($78rh) |

No Contract E costs were incurred in 1989, and there is no hypothetical underpayment for 1989.

| | 1990 | | |
|---|---|---|---|
| | D | E | Total |
| 1990 contract costs | | | $7,000a |
| Total contract costs | | 9,800r | |
| Total contract price | | 12,700r | |
| 1990 completion (%) | | 92a | |
| 1990 gross income | | 9,071rh | |
| Less, 1990 costs | | (7,000a) | |
| 1990 Net contract income | | 2,071rh | $2,071rh |
| Other 1990 net income (loss) | | | 0a |
| Taxable income (NOL) | | | 2,071rh |
| Tax at 34% | | | 704rh |
| Less, previously computed tax | | | 978rh |
| Overpayment of 1990 tax | | | (274rh) |

*(5) Alternative minimum tax.* The operation of the look-back method in the case of a taxpayer liable for the alternative minimum tax as provided in paragraph (c)(3)(vi) is illustrated by the following examples:

*Example (4).* Y enters into a long-term contract in 1988 that is completed in 1989. Y used regular tax costs for purposes of determining the degree of contract completion under the alternative minimum tax.

| | |
|---|---|
| 1988 contract costs | $ 4,000a |
| Total contract costs | $ 8,000e |
| Total contract price | $20,000e |
| 1988 completion (%) | 50e |
| 1988 gross income | $10,000a |
| Less, 1988 contract costs | ($ 4,000a) |
| 1988 net contract income | $ 6,000a |
| Other 1988 net income/(loss) | ($ 3,400a) |
| Taxable income | $ 2,600a |
| Regular tax at 34% | 884a |
| Adjustments and preferences to produce alternative minimum taxable income | $ 600a |
| Alternative minimum taxable income | $ 3,200a |
| Tentative minimum tax at 20% | 640a |
| Tax liability | $ 884a |

In 1989, Y determines the following amounts:

| | |
|---|---|
| 1989 contract costs | $6,000a |
| Total contract costs | $10,000a |
| Total contract price | $20,000a |

(ii) For purposes of applying the look-back method, Y redetermines its tax liability for 1988, which results in a hypothetical overpayment of tax. This hypothetical overpayment is determined by comparing Y's original regular tax liability for 1988 with the hypothetical total tax liability (including alternative minimum tax liability) for that year because Y would have paid the alternative minimum tax if Y had used its actual contract costs to report income:

| | |
|---|---|
| 1988 contract costs | $ 4,000a |
| Total contract costs | $ 10,000a |
| Total contract price | $ 20,000a |
| 1988 completion (%) | 40a |
| 1988 gross income | $ 8,000h |
| less, 1988 contract costs | ($ 4,000a) |
| 1988 net contract income | $ 4,000h |
| Other 1988 net income/(loss) | ($ 3,400a) |
| Taxable income | $ 600h |
| Regular tax at 34% | $ 204h |
| Adjustments and preferences to produce alternative minimum taxable income | $ 600a |
| Alternative minimum taxable income | $ 1,200h |
| Tentative minimum tax at 20% | 240h |
| Alternative minimum tax | $ 36h |
| Total tax liability | $ 240h |
| less, previously computed tax | $ 884a |
| Underpayment/(overpayment) | ($ 644h) |

*(6) Credit carryovers.* The operation of the look-back method in the case of credit carryovers as provided in paragraph (c)(3)(v) is illustrated by the following example:

*Example (5).* Z enters into a contract in 1986 that is completed in 1987. Z determines its tax liability for 1986 as follows:

| | |
|---|---|
| 1986 contract costs | $ 400a |
| Total contract costs | $1,000e |
| Total contract price | $2,000e |
| 1986 completion (%) | 40e |
| 1986 gross income | $ 800a |
| Less, 1986 costs | ($ 400a) |
| 1986 net contract income | $ 400a |
| Other 1986 net income | $ 0a |
| Taxable income | $ 400a |
| Tax at 46% | $ 184a |
| Unused tax credits carried forward from 1985 allowable in 1986 | $ 350a |
| Net tax due | $ 0a |

Z determines the following amounts for 1987:

| | |
|---|---|
| 1987 contract costs | $ 400a |
| Total contract price | $2,000a |
| Total contract costs | $ 800a |

If Z had used actual rather than estimated contract costs in determining gross income for 1986, Z would have reported tax liability of $276 (46% × $600) rather than $184.

However, Z would have paid no additional tax for 1986 because its unused tax credits carried forward from 1985 would have been sufficient to offset this increased tax liability. Therefore, there is no hypothetical underpayment for 1986 for purposes of the look-back method. However, this hypothetical earlier use of the credit may increase the hypothetical tax liability for 1987 (or another subsequent year) for purposes of subsequent applications of the look-back method.

*(7) Net operating losses.* The operation of the look-back method in the case of net operating loss ("NOL") carryovers as provided in paragraph (c)(3)(v) is illustrated by the following example:

*Example (6).* A entered into a long-term contract in 1986, which was completed in 1987. A determined its tax liability for 1986 as follows:

| | |
|---|---|
| 1986 contract costs | $400a |
| Total contract costs | $1,000e |
| Total contract price | $2,000e |
| 1986 completion (%) | 40e |
| 1986 gross income | $800a |
| Less, 1986 costs | ($400a) |
| 1986 net contract income | $400a |
| Other 1986 net income/(loss) | ($1,000a) |
| Taxable income/(NOL) | ($600a) |
| Tax | $0a |

A elected to carry this loss forward to 1987 pursuant to section 172(b)(3)(C).

For 1987, A determined the following amounts:

| | |
|---|---|
| 1987 contract costs | $400a |
| Total contract costs | $800a |
| Total contract price | $2,000a |

If actual rather than estimated contract costs had been used in determining gross income for 1986, A would have reported $1,000 of gross income from the contract rather than $800, and thus would have reported a loss of $400 rather than $600. However, since A would have paid no tax for 1986 regardless of whether actual or estimated contract costs had been used, A does not have an underpayment for 1986 for purposes of the look-back method. If A had, instead, carried back the 1986 NOL, and this NOL had been absorbed in the tax years 1983 through 1985, it would have resulted in refunds of tax for those years in 1986. When A applies the look-back method, a hypothetical underpayment of tax would have resulted for those years due to a hypothetical reduction in the amount that would have been refunded if income had been reported on the basis of actual contract costs. See Example (2)(iii).

*(8) Alternative minimum tax credit.* The following example illustrates the application of the look-back method if affected by the alternative minimum tax credit as provided in paragraph (c)(3)(vi):

(i) Example (4), above illustrates that the reallocation of contract income under the look-back method can result in a hypothetical underpayment or overpayment determined using the alternative minimum tax rate, even though the taxpayer actually paid only the regular tax for that year. However, application of the look-back method had no effect on the difference between the amount of alternative minimum taxable income and the amount of regular taxable income taken into account in that year because the taxpayer was required to use the percentage of completion method for both regular and alternative minimum tax purposes and used the same version of the percentage of completion method for both regular and alternative minimum tax purposes (i.e., the taxpayer had made an election to use regular tax costs in determining the percentage of completion for purposes of computing alternative minimum taxable income).

(ii) The following example illustrates the application of the look-back method in the case of a taxpayer that does not use the percentage of completion method of accounting for long-term contracts in computing taxable income for regular tax purposes and thus must make an adjustment to taxable income to determine alternative minimum taxable income. The example also shows how interest is computed under the look-back method when the taxpayer is entitled to a credit under section 53 for minimum tax paid because of this adjustment.

*Example (7).* X is a taxpayer engaged in the construction of real property under contracts that are completed within a 24-month period and whose average annual gross receipts do not exceed $10,000,000. As permitted by section 460(e)(1)(B), X uses the completed contract method ("CCM") for regular tax purposes. However, X is engaged in the construction of commercial real property and, therefore, is required to use the percentage of completion method ("PCM") for alternative minimum tax ("AMT" ) purposes.

Assume that for 1988, 1989, and 1990, X has only one long-term contract, which is entered into in 1988 and completed in 1990. Assume further that X estimates gross income from the contract to be $2,000, total contract costs to be $1,000, and that the contract is 25 percent complete in 1988 and 75 percent complete in 1989. In 1990, the year of completion, the percentage of completion does not change but, upon completion, gross income from the contract is actually $3,000, instead of $2,000, and costs are actually $1,000.

For 1988, 1989, and 1990, X's income and tax liability using estimated contract price and costs are as follows:

| Estimates | 1988 | 1989 | 1990 |
|---|---|---|---|
| Regular tax: | | | |
| Long-term | | | |
| Contract-CCM | 0 | 0 | $2,000 |
| Other Income | 0 | $5,000 | 0 |
| Total Income | 0 | $5,000 | $2,000 |
| Tax @ 34% | 0 | $1,700 | $ 680 |
| AMT | | | |
| Gross Income | $500 | $1,000 | $1,500 |
| Deductions | $250) | $ (500) | $ (250) |
| Total long-term: | | | |
| Contract-PCM | $250 | $ 500 | $1,250 |
| Other Income | 0 | $5,000 | 0 |
| Total Income | $250 | $5,500 | $1,250 |
| Tax @ 20% | $ 50 | $1,100 | $ 250 |
| Tentative Minimum Tax | $ 50 | $1,100 | $ 250 |
| Regular Tax | 0 | $1,700 | $ 680 |
| Minimum Tax Credit | 0 | $ (50) | 0 |

| Net Tax Liability | $ 50 | $1,650 | $ 680 |
|---|---|---|---|

| Actual | 1988 | 1989 | 1990 |
|---|---|---|---|
| Regular tax: | | | |
| Long-term: | | | |
| Contract-CCM | 0 | 0 | $2,000 |
| Other Income | 0 | $5,000 | 0 |
| Total Income | 0 | $5,000 | $2,000 |
| Tax @ 34% | 0 | $1,700 | $ 680 |
| AMT | | | |
| Gross Income | $750 | $1,500 | $ 750 |
| Deductions | $250) | $ (500) | $ (250) |
| Total long-term: | | | |
| Contract-PCM | $500 | $1,000 | $ 500 |
| Other Income | 0 | $5,000 | 0 |
| Total Income | $500 | $6,000 | $ 500 |
| Tax @ 20% | $100 | $1,200 | $ 100 |
| Tentative Minimum Tax | $100 | $1,200 | $ 100 |
| Regular Tax | 0 | $1,700 | $ 680 |
| Minimum Tax Credit | 0 | $ (100) | 0 |
| Net Tax Liability | $100 | $1,600 | $ 680 |
| Underpayment | $ 50 | | |
| Overpayment | | $ 50 | |

As shown above, application of the look-back method results in a hypothetical underpayment of $50 for 1988 because X was subject to the alternative minimum tax for that year. Interest is charged to X on this $50 underpayment from the due date of X's 1988 return until the due date of X's 1990 return.

In 1989, although X was required to compute alternative minimum taxable income using the percentage of completion method, X was not required to pay alternative minimum tax. Nevertheless, the look-back method must be applied to 1989 because use of actual rather than estimated contract price in computing alternative minimum taxable income for 1988 would have changed the amount of the alternative minimum tax credit carried to 1989. Interest is paid to X on the resulting $50 overpayment from the due date of X's 1989 return until the due date of X's 1990 return.

*(9) Period for interest.* The following Examples (8) through (11) illustrate how to determine the period for computing interest as provided in paragraph (c)(4):

*Example (8).* The facts are the same as in Example (6), except that the contract is completed in 1988, and A determined the following amounts for 1987 and 1988:

For 1987:

| | |
|---|---|
| 1987 contract costs | 0 |
| Total contract costs | $1,000e |
| Total contract price | $2,000e |
| 1987 completion (%) | $ 40e |
| 1987 gross income | 0a |
| Less, 1987 costs | 0a |
| Other 1987 net income | $ 600a |
| Net operating loss carryforward from 1986 | $ (600a) |
| Taxable income | 0a |
| Tax | 0a |

For 1988:

| | |
|---|---|
| 1988 contract costs | $ 400a |
| Total contract costs | $ 800a |
| Total contract price | $2,000a |

If actual rather than estimated contract costs had been used in determining gross income for 1986, A would have reported $1,000 of gross income from the contract for 1986 rather than $800, and would have reported a net operating loss carryforward to 1987 of $400 rather than $600. Therefore, A would have reported taxable income of $200, and would have paid tax of $80 (i.e., $200 × 40%) for 1987. The due date for filing A's Federal income tax return for its 1988 taxable year is March 15. A obtains an extension and files its 1988 return on September 15, 1989. Under the look-back method, A is required to pay interest on the amount of this hypothetical underpayment ($80) computed from the due date (determined without regard to extensions) for A's return for 1987 (not 1986, even though 1986 was the year in which the net operating loss arose) until March 15 (not September 15), the due date (without regard to extensions) of A's return for 1988. A is required to pay additional interest from March 15 until September 15 on the amount of interest outstanding as of March 15 with respect to the hypothetical underpayment of $80.

*Example (9).* The facts are the same as in Example (6), except that A carries the net operating loss of $600 back to 1983 rather than forward to 1987, and receives a refund of $276 ($600 reduction in 1983 taxable income × 46% rate in effect in 1983). As in Example (6), if actual contract costs had been used, A would have reported a loss for 1986 of $400 rather than $600. Thus, A would have received a refund of 1983 tax of $184 ($400 × 46%) rather than $276. Under the look-back method A is required to pay interest on the difference in these two amounts ($92) computed from the due date (determined without regard to extensions) of A's return for 1986 (the year in which the carryback arose rather than 1983, the year in which it was used) until the due date of A's return for 1988..

*Example (10).* B enters into a long-term contract in 1986 that is completed in 1988. B determines its 1986 tax liability as follows:

| | |
|---|---|
| 1986 contract costs | $400a |
| Total contract costs | $1,000e |
| Total contract price | $2,000e |
| 1986 completion (%) | 40e |
| 1986 gross income | $800a |
| Less, 1986 costs | ($400a) |
| 1986 net contract income | $400a |
| Other 1986 net income | $2,000a |
| Taxable income | $2,400a |
| Tax at 46% | $1,104a |

B determines its tax liability for 1987 as follows:

| | |
|---|---|
| 1987 contract costs | $400a |
| Total contract costs | $1,600e |
| Total contract price | $2,000e |
| 1987 completion (%) | 50e |
| 1987 gross income | $200a |
| ( = (50% × $2,000) – $800 previously reported) less, 1987 costs | ($400a) |
| 1987 net contract income | ($200a) |
| Other 1987 net income/(loss) | ($2,200a) |
| Taxable income (NOL) | ($2,400a) |
| Tax | 0a |

Assume that B had no taxable income in either 1984 or 1985, so that the entire amount of the $2,400 net operating loss is carried back to 1986, and B receives a refund, with interest from the due date of B's 1987 return, of the entire $1,104 in tax that it paid for 1986.

In 1988, B determines the following amounts:

| | |
|---|---|
| 1988 contract costs | $ 800a |
| Total contract costs | $1,800a |
| Total contract price | $2,000a |

If B had used actual contract costs rather than estimated costs in determining its gross income for 1986, B would have had gross income from the contract of $500 rather than $800, and thus would have had taxable income of $2,100 rather than $2,400, and would have paid tax of $986 rather than $1,104. B is entitled to receive interest on the difference between these two amounts, the hypothetical overpayment of tax of $138. Interest is computed from the due date (without regard to extensions) of B's return for 1986 until the due date for B's return for 1987. Interest stops running at this date, because B's hypothetical overpayment of tax ended when B filed its original 1987 return and received a refund for the carryback to 1986, and interest on this refund began to run only from the due date of B's 1987 return. See section 6611(f).

*Example (11).* C enters into a long-term contract in 1986, its first year in business, which is completed in 1988. C determines its tax liability for 1986 as follows:

| | |
|---|---|
| 1986 contract costs | $ 400a |
| Total contract costs | $1,000e |
| Total contract price | $2,000e |
| 1986 completion (%) | 40e |
| 1986 gross income | $ 800a |
| less, 1986 costs | ($ 400a) |
| 1986 net contract income | $ 400a |
| Other 1986 net income | $2,000a |
| Taxable income (NOL) | $2,400a |
| Tax at 46% | $1,104a |

C determines its tax liability for 1987 as follows:

| | |
|---|---|
| 1987 contract costs | $400a |
| Total contract costs | $1,066e |
| Total contract price | $2,000e |
| 1987 completion (%) | 75e |
| 1987 gross income | $700a |
| Less, 1987 costs | ($400a) |
| 1987 net contract income | $300a |
| Other 1987 net income | ($2,450a) |
| Taxable income (NOL) | ($2,150a) |
| Tax | $10a |

C carries back the net operating loss to 1986, and files an amended return for 1986, showing taxable income of $250, and receives a refund of $989 (46% × $2,150). Interest on this refund begins to run only as of the due date of C's 1987 return. See section 6611(f).

In 1988, when the contract is completed, C determines the following amounts:

| | |
|---|---|
| 1988 contract costs | $ 800a |
| Total contract costs | $1,600a |
| Total contract price | $2,000a |

If C had used actual contract price and contract costs in determining gross income for 1986, it would have reported gross income from the contract of $500 rather than $800, taxable income of $2,100 rather than $2,400, and tax liability of $966 rather than $1,104.

If C had used actual contract price and contract costs in determining gross income for 1987, it would have reported gross income from the contract of $500 rather than $700, and would have reported a net operating loss of $2,350, rather than $2,150, which would have been carried back to 1986.

Under the look-back method, C receives interest with respect to a total 1986 hypothetical overpayment of $138 ($1,104 minus $966). C is credited with interest on $23 of this amount only from the due date of C's 1986 return until the due date of C's 1987 tax return, because this portion of C's total hypothetical overpayment for 1986 was refunded to C with interest computed from the due date of C's 1987 return and, therefore, was no longer held by the government. However, because the remainder of the total hypothetical overpayment of $115 was not refunded to C, C is credited with interest on this amount from the due date of C's 1986 return until the due date of C's 1988 tax return.

Under the look-back method, C receives no interest with respect to 1987, because C had no tax liability for 1987 using either estimated or actual contract price and costs.

**(i) [Reserved].**

**(j) Election not to apply look-back method in de minimis cases.** Section 460(b)(6) provides taxpayers with an election not to apply the look-back method to long-term contracts in de minimis cases, effective for contracts completed in taxable years ending after August 5, 1997. To make an election, a taxpayer must attach a statement to its timely filed original federal income tax return (including extensions) for the taxable year the election is to become effective or to an amended return for that year, provided the amended return is filed on or before March 31, 1998. This statement must have the legend "NOTIFICATION OF ELECTION UNDER SECTION 460(b)(6)"; provide the taxpayer's name and identifying number and the effective date of the election; and identify the trades or businesses that involve long-term contracts. An election applies to all long-term contracts completed during and after the taxable year for which the election is effective. An election may not be revoked without the Commissioner's consent. For taxpayers who elected to use the delayed reapplication method under paragraph (e) of this section, an election under this paragraph (j) automatically revokes the election to use the delayed reapplication method for contracts subject to section 460(b)(6). A consolidated group of corporations, as defined in § 1.1502-1(h), is subject to consistency rules analogous to those in paragraph (e)(2) of this section and in paragraph (d)(4)(ii)(C) of this section (concerning election to use simplified marginal impact method).

T.D. 8315, 10/12/90, amend T.D. 8775, 7/1/98, T.D. 8929, 1/10/2001, T.D. 8995, 5/14/2002, T.D. 9137, 7/15/2004.

PAR. 5. Section 1.460-6 is amended by:

1. Adding paragraph (c)(3)(vii).

2. Redesignating paragraph (d)(2)(iv) as paragraph (d)(2)(v).

3. Adding a new paragraph (d)(2)(iv).

The additions and revision read as follows:

**Proposed § 1.460-6 Look-back method.** [*For Preamble, see ¶ 153,043*]

* * * * *

**(c)** * * *

*(3)* * * *

(vii) Section 481(a) adjustments. For purposes of determining the hypothetical underpayment or overpayment of tax for any year, amounts reported as section 481(a) adjustments shall be taken into account in the tax year or years they are reported. However, any portion of a section 481(a) adjustment not yet reported as of the tax year in which the contract is completed shall be taken into account in the tax year the contract is completed for purposes of determining the hypothetical underpayment or overpayment of tax.

* * * * *

**(d)** * * *

*(2)* * * *

(iv) Section 481(a) adjustments. For purposes of determining the hypothetical underpayment or overpayment of tax for any year under the simplified marginal impact method, amounts reported as section 481(a) adjustments shall be taken into account in the tax year or years they are reported. However, any portion of a section 481(a) adjustment not yet reported as of the tax year in which the contract is completed shall be taken into account in the tax year the contract is completed for purposes of determining the hypothetical underpayment or overpayment of tax.

* * * * *

**§ 1.461-0 Table of contents.**

This section lists the captions that appear in the regulations under section 461 of the Internal Revenue Code.

T.D. 8408, 4/9/92, amend T.D. 8593, 4/7/95.

### § 1.461-1 General rules for taxable year of deduction.

***Caution:*** The Treasury has not yet amended Reg § 1.461-1 to reflect changes made by P.L. 94-455.

**(a) General rule.** *(1) Taxpayer using cash receipts and disbursements method.* Under the cash receipts and disbursements method of accounting, amounts representing allowable deductions shall, as a general rule, be taken into account for the taxable year in which paid. Further, a taxpayer using this method may also be entitled to certain deductions in the computation of taxable income which do not involve cash disbursements during the taxable year, such as the deductions for depreciation, depletion, and losses under sections 167, 611, and 165, respectively. If an expenditure results in the creation of an asset having a useful life which extends substantially beyond the close of the taxable year, such an expenditure may not be deductible, or may be deductible only in part, for the taxable year in which made. An example is an expenditure for the construction of improvements by the lessee on leased property where the estimated life of the improvements is in excess of the remaining period of the lease. In such a case, in lieu of the allowance for depreciation provided by section 167, the basis shall be amortized ratably over the remaining period of the lease. See section 178 and the regulations thereunder for rules governing the effect to be given renewal options in determining whether the useful life of the improvements exceeds the remaining term of the lease where a lessee begins improvements on leased property after July 28, 1958, other than improvements which on such date and at all times thereafter, the lessee was under a binding legal obligation to make. See section 263 and the regulations thereunder for rules relating to capital expenditures. See section 467 and the regulations thereunder for rules under which a liability arising out of the use of property pursuant to a section 467 rental agreement is taken into account.

*(2) Taxpayer using an accrual method.* (i) In general. Under an accrual method of accounting, a liability (as defined in § 1.446-1(c)(1)(ii)(B)) is incurred, and generally is taken into account for Federal income tax purposes, in the taxable year in which all the events have occurred that establish the fact of the liability, the amount of the liability can be determined with reasonable accuracy, and economic performance has occurred with respect to the liability. (See paragraph (a)(2)(iii)(A) of this section for examples of liabilities that may not be taken into account until a taxable year subsequent to the taxable year incurred, and see §§ 1.461-4 through 1.461-6 for rules relating to economic performance.) Applicable provisions of the Code, the Income Tax Regulations, and other guidance published by the Secretary prescribe the manner in which a liability that has been incurred is taken into account. For example, section 162 provides that the deductible liability generally is taken into account in the taxable year incurred through a deduction from gross income. As a further example, under section 263 or 263A, a liability that relates to the creation of an asset having a useful life extending substantially beyond the close of the taxable year is taken into account in the taxable year incurred through capitalization (within the meaning of § 1.263A-1(c)(3)), and may later affect the computation of taxable income through depreciation or otherwise over a period including subsequent taxable years, in accordance with applicable Internal Revenue Code sections and guidance published by the Secretary. The principles of this paragraph

(a)(2) also apply in the calculation of earnings and profits and accumulated earnings and profits.

(ii) Uncertainty as to the amount of a liability. While no liability shall be taken into account before economic performance and all of the events that fix the liability have occurred, the fact that the exact amount of the liability cannot be determined does not prevent a taxpayer from taking into account that portion of the amount of the liability which can be computed with reasonable accuracy within the taxable year. For example, A renders services to B during the taxable year for which A charges $10,000. B admits a liability to A for $6,000 but contests the remainder. B may take into account only $6,000 as an expense for the taxable year in which the services were rendered.

(iii) Alternative timing rules. (A) If any provision of the Code requires a liability to be taken into account in a taxable year later than the taxable year provided in paragraph (a)(2)(i) of this section, the liability is taken into account as prescribed in that Code provision. See, for example, section 267 (transactions between related parties) and section 464 (farming syndicates).

(B) If the liability of a taxpayer is subject to section 170 (charitable contributions), section 192 (black lung benefit trusts), section 194A (employer liability trusts), section 468 (mining and solid waste disposal reclamation and closing costs), or section 468A (certain nuclear decommissioning costs), the liability is taken into account as determined under that section and not under section 461 or the regulations thereunder. For special rules relating to certain loss deductions, see sections 165(e), 165(i), and 165(l), relating to theft losses, disaster losses, and losses from certain deposits in qualified financial institutions.

(C) Section 461 and the regulations thereunder do not apply to any amount allowable under a provision of the Code as a deduction for a reserve for estimated expenses.

(D) Except as otherwise provided in any Internal Revenue regulations, revenue procedure, or revenue ruling, the economic performance requirement of section 461(h) and the regulations thereunder is satisfied to the extent that any amount is otherwise deductible under section 404 (employer contributions to a plan of deferred compensation), section 404A (certain foreign deferred compensation plans), or section 419 (welfare benefit funds). See § 1.461-4(d)(2)(iii).

(E) Except as otherwise provided by regulations or other published guidance issued by the Commissioner (See § 601.601(b)(2) of this chapter), in the case of a liability arising out of the use of property pursuant to a section 467 rental agreement, the all events test (including economic performance) is considered met in the taxable year in which the liability is to be taken into account under section 467 and the regulations thereunder.

*(3) Effect in current taxable year of improperly accounting for a liability in a prior taxable year.* Each year's return should be complete in itself, and taxpayers shall ascertain the facts necessary to make a correct return. The expenses, liabilities, or loss of one year generally cannot be used to reduce the income of a subsequent year. A taxpayer may not take into account in a return for a subsequent taxable year liabilities that, under the taxpayer's method of accounting, should have been taken into account in a prior taxable year. If a taxpayer ascertains that a liability should have been taken into account in a prior taxable year, the taxpayer should, if within the period of limitation, file a claim for credit or refund of any overpayment of tax arising therefrom. Similarly, if a taxpayer ascertains that a liability was improperly taken into account in a prior taxable year, the taxpayer should, if within the period of limitation, file an amended return and pay any additional tax due. However, except as provided in section 905(c) and the regulations thereunder, if a liability is properly taken into account in an amount based on a computation made with reasonable accuracy and the exact amount of the liability is subsequently determined in a later taxable year, the difference, if any, between such amounts shall be taken into account for the later taxable year.

*(4) Deductions attributable to certain foreign income.* In any case in which, owing to monetary, exchange, or other restrictions imposed by a foreign country, an amount otherwise constituting gross income for the taxable year from sources without the United States is not includible in gross income of the taxpayer for that year, the deductions and credits properly chargeable against the amount so restricted shall not be deductible in such year but shall be deductible proportionately in any subsequent taxable year in which such amount or portion thereof is includible in gross income. See paragraph (b) of § 1.905-1 for rules relating to credit for foreign income taxes when foreign income is subject to exchange controls.

**(b) Special rule in case of death.** A taxpayer's taxable year ends on the date of his death. See section 443(a)(2) and paragraph (a)(2) of § 1.443-1. In computing taxable income for such year, there shall be deducted only amounts properly deductible under the method of accounting used by the taxpayer. However, if the taxpayer used an accrual method of accounting, no deduction shall be allowed for amounts accrued only by reason of his death. For rules relating to the inclusion of items of partnership deduction, loss, or credit in the return of a decedent partner, see subchapter K, chapter 1 of the Code, and the regulations thereunder.

**(c) Accrual of real property taxes.** *(1) In general.* If the accrual of real property taxes is proper in connection with one of the methods of accounting described in section 446(c), any taxpayer using such a method of accounting may elect to accrue any real property tax, which is related to a definite period of time, ratably over that period in the manner described in this paragraph. For example, assume that such an election is made by a calendar-year taxpayer whose real property taxes, applicable to the period from July 1, 1955, to June 30, 1956, amount to $1,200. Under section 461(c), $600 of such taxes accrue in the calendar year 1955, and the balance accrues in 1956. For special rule in the case of certain contested real property taxes in respect of which the taxpayer transfers money or other property to provide for the satisfaction of the contested tax, see § 1.461-2. For general rules relating to deductions for taxes, see section 164 and the regulations thereunder.

*(2) Special rules.* (i) Effective date. Section 461(c) and this paragraph do not apply to any real property tax allowable as a deduction under the Internal Revenue Code of 1939 for any taxable year beginning before January 1, 1954.

(ii) If real property taxes which relate to a period prior to the taxpayer's first taxable year beginning on or after January 1, 1954, would, but for section 461(c), be deductible in such first taxable year, the portion of such taxes which applies to the prior period is deductible in such first taxable year (in addition to the amount allowable under section 461(c)(1)).

*(3) When election may be made.* (i) Without consent. A taxpayer may elect to accrue real property taxes ratably in accordance with section 461(c) and this paragraph without the consent of the Commissioner for his first taxable year

beginning after December 31, 1953, and ending after August 16, 1954, in which the taxpayer incurs real property taxes. Such election must be made not later than the time prescribed by law for filing the return for such year (including extensions thereof). An election may be made by the taxpayer for each separate trade or business (and for nonbusiness activities, if accounted for separately). Such an election shall apply to all real property taxes of the trade business, or nonbusiness activity for which the election is made. The election shall be made in a statement submitted with the taxpayer's return for the first taxable year to which the election is applicable. The statement should set forth:

(a) The trades or businesses, or nonbusiness activity, to which the election is to apply, and the method of accounting used therein;

(b) The period of time to which the taxes are related; and

(c) The computation of the deduction for real property taxes for the first year of the election (or a summary of such computation)

(ii) With consent. A taxpayer may elect with the consent of the Commissioner to accrue real property taxes ratably in accordance with section 461(c) and this paragraph. A written request for permission to make such an election shall be submitted to the Commissioner of Internal Revenue, Washington 25, D. C., within 90 days after the beginning of the taxable year to which the election is first applicable, or before March 26, 1958, whichever date is later. The request for permission shall state:

(a) The name and address of the taxpayer;

(b) The trades or businesses, or nonbusiness activity, to which the election is to apply, and the method of accounting used therein;

(c) The taxable year to which the election first applies;

(d) The period to which the real property taxes relate;

(e) The computation of the deduction for real property taxes for the first year of election (or a summary of such computation); and

(f) An adequate description of the manner in which all real property taxes were deducted in the year prior to the year of election.

*(4) Binding effect of election.* An election to accrue real property taxes ratably under section 461(c) is binding upon the taxpayer unless the consent of the Commissioner is obtained under section 446(e) and paragraph (e) of § 1.446-1 to change such method of deducting real property taxes. If the last day prescribed by law for filing a return for any taxable year (including extensions thereof) to which section 461(c) is applicable falls before March 25, 1958, consent is hereby given for the taxpayer to revoke an election previously made to accrue real property taxes in the manner prescribed by section 461(c). If the taxpayer revokes his election under the preceding sentence, he must, on or before March 25, 1958, notify the district director for the district in which the return was filed of such revocation. For any taxable year for which such revocation is applicable, an amended return reflecting such revocation shall be filed on or before March 25, 1958.

*(5) Apportionment of taxes on real property between seller and purchaser.* For apportionment of taxes on real property between seller and purchaser, see section 164(d) and the regulations thereunder.

*(6) Examples.* The provisions of this paragraph are illustrated by the following examples:

*Example (1).* A taxpayer on an accrual method reports his taxable income for the taxable year ending June 30. He elects to accrue real property taxes ratably for the taxable year ending June 30, 1955 (which is his first taxable year beginning on or after January 1, 1954). In the absence of an election under section 461(c), such taxes would accrue on January 1 of the calendar year to which they are related. The real property taxes are $1,200 for 1954; $1,600 for 1955; and $1,800 for 1956. Deductions for such taxes for the fiscal years ending June 30, 1955, and June 30, 1956, are computed as follows:

**Fiscal year ending June 30, 1955**

| | |
|---|---|
| July through December 1954 | None[1] |
| January through June 1955 (6/12 of $1,600) | $ 800 |
| Deduction for fiscal year ending June 30, 1955 | 800 |

[1] The taxes for 1954 were deductible in the fiscal year ending June 30, 1954, since such taxes accrued on January 1, 1954.

**Fiscal year ending June 30, 1956**

| | |
|---|---|
| July through December 1955 (6/12 of $1,600) | $ 800 |
| January through June (6/12 of $1,800) | 900 |
| Deduction for fiscal year ending June 30, 1956 | 1,700 |

*Example (2).* A calendar-year taxpayer on an accrual method elects to accrue real property taxes ratably for 1954. In the absence of an election under section 461(c), such taxes would accrue on July 1 and are assessed for the 12-month period beginning on that date. The real property taxes assessed for the year ending June 30, 1954, are $1,200; $1,600 for the year ending June 30, 1955; and $1,800 for the year ending June 30, 1956. Deductions for such taxes for the calendar years 1954 and 1955 are computed as follows:

**Year ending December 31, 1954**

| | |
|---|---|
| January through June 1954 | None[1] |
| July through December 1954 (6/12 of $1,600) | $ 800 |
| Deduction for year ending December 31, 1954 | 800 |

[1] The entire tax of $1,200 for the year ended June 30, 1954, was deductible in the return for 1953, since such tax accrued on July 1, 1953.

**Year ending December 31, 1955**

| | |
|---|---|
| January through June 1955 6/12 of $1,600) | $ 800 |
| July through December 1955 6/12 of $1,800) | 900 |
| Deduction for year ending December 31, 1955 | 1,700 |

*Example (3).* A calendar-year taxpayer on an accrual method elects to accrue real property taxes ratably for 1954. In the absence of an election under section 461(c), such taxes, which relate to the calendar year 1954, are accruable on December 1 of the preceding calendar year. No deduction for real property taxes is allowable for the taxable year 1954 since such taxes accrued in the taxable year 1953 under section 23(c) of the Internal Revenue Code of 1939.

*Example (4).* A taxpayer on an accrual method reports his taxable income for the taxable year ending March 31. He elects to accrue real property taxes ratably for the taxable year ending March 31, 1955. In the absence of an election under section 461(c), such taxes are accruable on June 1 of the calendar year to which they relate. The real property taxes are $1,200 for 1954; $1,600 for 1955; and $1,800 for 1956. Deductions for such taxes for the taxable years ending March 31, 1955 and March 31, 1956, are computed as follows:

**Fiscal year ending March 31, 1955**

| | |
|---|---|
| April through December 1954 (9/12 of $1,200) | $ 900 |
| January through March 1955 (3/12 of $1,600) | 400 |
| Taxes accrued ratably in fiscal year ending March 31, 1955 | 1,300 |
| Tax relating to period January through March 1954, paid in June 1954, and not deductible in prior taxable years (3/12 of $1,200) | 300 |
| Deduction for fiscal year ending March 31, 1955 | 1,600 |

**Fiscal year ending March 31, 1956**

| | |
|---|---|
| April through December 1955 (9/12 of $1,600) | $1,200 |
| January through March 1956 (3/12 of $1,800) | 450 |
| Deduction for fiscal year ending March 31, 1956 | 1,650 |

*Example (5).* The facts are the same as in example (4) except that in June 1955, when the taxpayer pays his $1,600 real property taxes for 1955, he pays $400 of such amount under protest. Deductions for taxes for the taxable years ending March 31, 1955, and March 31, 1956, are computed as follows:

**Fiscal year ending March 31, 1955**

| | |
|---|---|
| April through December 1954 (9/12 of $1,200) | $ 900 |
| January through March 1955 (3/12 of $1,200, that is, $1,600 minus $400 (the contested portion which is not properly accruable)) | 300 |
| Taxes accrued ratably in fiscal year ending March 31, 1955 | 1,200 |
| Tax relating to period January through March 1954, paid in June 1954, and not deductible in prior taxable years (3/12 of $1,200) | 300 |
| Deduction for fiscal year ending March 31, 1955 | 1,500 |

**Fiscal year ending March 31, 1956**

| | |
|---|---|
| April through December 1955 (9/12 of $1,200) | $ 900 |
| January through March 1956 (3/12 of $1,800) | 450 |
| Taxes accrued ratably in fiscal year ending March 31, 1956 | 1,350 |
| Contested portion of tax relating to period January through December 1955, paid in June 1955, and deductible, under section 461(f), for taxpayer's fiscal year ending March 31, 1956 | 400 |
| Deduction for fiscal year ending March 31, 1956 | 1,750 |

**(d) Limitation on acceleration of accrual of taxes.** *(1)* Section 461(d)(1) provides that, in the case of a taxpayer whose taxable income is computed under an accrual method of accounting, to the extent that the time for accruing taxes is earlier than it would be but for any action of any taxing jurisdiction taken after December 31, 1960, such taxes are to be treated as accruing at the time they would have accrued but for such action. Any such action which, but for the provisions of section 461(d) and this paragraph, would accelerate the time for accruing a tax is to be disregarded in determining the time for accruing such tax for purposes of the deduction allowed for such tax. Such action is to be disregarded not only with respect to a taxpayer (whose taxable income is computed under an accrual method of accounting) upon whom the tax is imposed at the time of the action, but also with respect to such a taxpayer upon whom the tax is imposed at any time subsequent to such action. Thus, in the case of a tax imposed on property, the acceleration of the time for accruing taxes is to be disregarded not only with respect to the taxpayer who owned the property at the time of such acceleration, but also with respect to any subsequent owner of the property whose taxable income is computed under an accrual method of accounting. Similarly, such action is to be disregarded with respect to all property subject to such tax, even if such property is acquired after the action. Whenever the time for accruing taxes is to be disregarded in accordance with the provisions of this paragraph, the taxpayer shall accrue the tax at the time (original accrual date) the tax would have accrued but for such action, and shall, in the absence of any action of the taxing jurisdiction placing the time for accruing such tax at a time subsequent to the original accrual date, continue to accrue the tax as of the original accrual date for all future taxable years.

*(2)* For purposes of this paragraph—

(i) The term "a taxpayer whose taxable income is computed under an accrual method of accounting" means a taxpayer who, for Federal income tax purposes, accounts for any tax which is the subject of "any action" (as defined in subdivision (iii) of this subparagraph) under an accrual method of accounting. See section 446 and the regulations thereunder. If a taxpayer uses an accrual method as his overall method of accounting, it shall be presumed that he is "a taxpayer whose taxable income is computed under an accrual method of accounting." However, if the taxpayer establishes to the satisfaction of the district director that he has, for Federal income tax purposes, consistently accounted for such tax under the cash method of accounting, he shall be considered not to be "a taxpayer whose taxable income is computed under an accrual method of accounting."

(ii) The time for accruing taxes shall be determined under section 461 and the regulations in this section.

(iii) The term "any action" includes the enactment or reenactment of legislation, the adoption of an ordinance, the exercise of any taxing or administrative authority, or the taking of any other step, the result of which is an acceleration of the accrual event of any tax. The term also applies to the substitution of a substantially similar tax by either the original taxing jurisdiction or a substitute jurisdiction. However, the term does not include either a judicial interpretation, or an administrative determination by the Internal Revenue Service, as to the event which fixes the accrual date for the tax.

(iv) The term "any taxing jurisdiction" includes the District of Columbia, any State, possession of the United States, city, county, municipality, school district, or other political subdivision or authority, other than the United States, which imposes, assesses, or collects a tax.

*(3)* The provisions of this paragraph may be illustrated by the following examples:

*Example (1).* State X imposes a tax on intangible and tangible personal property used in a trade or business conducted in the State. The tax is assessed as of July 1, and becomes a lien as of that date. As a result of administrative and judicial decisions, July 1 is recognized as the proper date on which accrual method taxpayers may accrue their personal property tax for Federal income tax purposes. In 1961 State X, by legislative action, changes the assessment and lien dates from July 1, 1962, to December 31, 1961, for the property tax year 1962. The action taken by State X is considered to be "any action" of a taxing jurisdiction which results in the time for accruing taxes being earlier than it would have been but for that action. Therefore, for purposes of the deduction allowed for such tax, the personal property tax imposed by State X, for the property tax year 1962, shall be treated as though it accrued on July 1, 1962.

*Example (2).* Assume the same facts as in example (1) except that State X repeals the personal property tax and in lieu thereof enacts a franchise tax which is imposed on the privilege of conducting a trade or business within State X, and is based on the value of intangible and tangible personal property used in the trade or business. The franchise tax is to be assessed and will become a lien as of December 31, 1961, for the franchise tax year 1962, and on December 31 for all subsequent franchise tax years. Since the franchise tax is substantially similar to the former personal property tax and since the enactment of the franchise tax has the effect of accelerating the accrual date of the personal property tax from July 1, 1962, to December 31, 1961, the action taken by State X is considered to be "any action" of a taxing jurisdiction which results in the time for accruing taxes being earlier than it would have been but for that action. Therefore, for purposes of the deduction allowed for such tax, the franchise tax imposed by State X shall be treated as though it accrued on July 1, 1962, for the franchise tax year 1962, and on July 1 for all subsequent franchise tax years.

*Example (3).* Assume the same facts as in example (1) except that State X repealed the personal property tax and empowered the counties within the State to impose a personal property tax. Assuming the counties in State X subsequently imposed a personal property tax and chose December 31 of the preceding year as the assessment and lien date, the action of each of the counties would be considered to be "any action" of a taxing jurisdiction which results in the time for accruing taxes being earlier than it would have been but for that action since it is immaterial whether the original taxing jurisdiction or a substitute jurisdiction took the action.

*(4)* Section 461(d)(1) shall not be applicable to the extent that it would prevent the taxpayer and all other persons, including successors in interest, from ever taking into account, for Federal income tax purposes, any tax to which that section would otherwise apply. For example, assume that State Y imposes a personal property tax on tangible personal property used in a trade or business conducted in the State during a calendar year. The tax is assessed as of February 1 of the year following the personal property tax year, and becomes a lien as of that date. As a result of administrative and judicial decisions, February 1 of the following year is recognized as the proper date on which accrual method taxpayers may accrue the personal property tax for Federal income tax purposes. In 1962 State Y, by legislative action, changes the assessment and lien dates for the personal property tax year 1962 from February 1, 1963, to December 1, 1962, and to December 1 of the personal property tax year for all subsequent years. Corporation A, an accrual method taxpayer which uses the calendar year as its taxable year, pays the tax for 1962 on December 10, 1962. On December 15, 1962, the property which was taxed is completely destroyed and, on December 20, 1962, corporation A transfers all of its remaining assets to its shareholders, and is dissolved. Since corporation A is not in existence in 1963, and therefore could not take the personal property tax into account in computing its 1963 Federal income tax if February 1, 1963, is considered to be the time for accruing the tax, and no other person could ever take such tax into account in computing his Federal income tax, such tax shall be treated as accruing as of December 1, 1962. To the extent that any person other than the taxpayer may at any time take such tax into account in computing his taxable income, the provisions of section 461(d)(1) shall apply. Thus, upon the dissolution of a corporation or the termination of a partnership between the time which, but for the provisions of section 461(d)(1) and this paragraph, would be the time for accruing any tax which was the subject of "any action" (as defined in subdivision (iii) of subparagraph (2)), and the original accrual date, the corporation or the partnership would be entitled to a deduction for only that portion, if any, of such tax with respect to which it can establish, to the satisfaction of the district director, that no other taxpayer can properly take into account in computing his taxable income. However, to the extent that the corporation or partnership cannot establish, at the time of its dissolution or termination, as the case may be, that no other taxpayer would be entitled to take such tax into account in computing his taxable income, and it is subsequently determined that no other taxpayer is entitled to take such tax into account in computing his taxable income, the corporation or partnership may file a claim for refund for the year of its dissolution or termination (subject to the limitations prescribed in section 6511) and claim as a deduction therein the portion of such tax determined to be not deductible by any other taxpayer.

*(5)* Section 461(d) and this paragraph shall apply to taxable years ending after December 31, 1960.

**(e) Dividends or interest paid by certain savings institutions on certain deposits or withdrawable accounts.** *(1) Deduction not allowable.* (i) In general. Except as otherwise provided in this paragraph, pursuant to section 461(e) amounts paid to, or credited to the accounts of, depositors or holders of accounts as dividends or interest on their deposits or withdrawable accounts (if such amounts paid or credited are withdrawable on demand subject only to customary notice to withdraw) by a mutual savings bank not having capital stock represented by shares, a domestic building and loan association, or a cooperative bank shall not be allowed as a deduction for the taxable year to the extent such amounts are paid or credited for periods representing more than 12 months. The provisions of section 461(e) are applicable with respect to taxable years ending after December 31, 1962. Whether amounts are paid or credited for periods representing more than 12 months depends upon all the facts and circumstances in each case. For example, payments or credits which under all the facts and circumstances are in the nature of bona fide bonus interest or dividends paid or credited because a shareholder or depositor maintained a certain balance for more than 12 months, will not be considered made for more than 12 months, providing the regular payments or credits represent a period of 12 months or less. The nonallowance of a deduction to the taxpayer under section 461(e) and this subparagraph has no effect either on the proper time for reporting dividends or interest by a depositor or holder of a withdrawable account, or on the obligation of the taxpayer to make a return setting forth, among other (relating to returns regarding payments of interest) and the regulations thereunder. With respect to a short period (a taxable year consisting of a period of less than 12 months), amounts of dividends or interest paid or credited shall not be allowed as a deduction to the extent that such amounts are paid or credited for a period representing more than the number of months in such short period. In such a case, the rules contained in section 461(e) and this paragraph apply to the short period in a manner consistent with the application of such rules to a 12-month taxable year. Subparagraph (2) of this paragraph provides rules for computing amounts not allowed in the taxable year and subparagraph (3) provides rules for determining when such amounts are allowed. See section

7701(a)(19) and (32) and the regulations thereunder for the definitions of domestic building and loan association and cooperative bank.

(ii) Exceptions. The rule of nonallowance set forth in subdivision (i) of this subparagraph is not applicable to a taxpayer in the year in which it liquidates (other than following, or as part of, an acquisition of its assets in which the acquiring corporation, pursuant to section 381(a), takes into account certain items of the taxpayer, which for purposes of this paragraph shall be referred to as an acquisition described in section 381(a)). In addition, such rule of nonallowance is not applicable to a taxpayer which pays or credits grace interest or dividends to terminating depositors or shareholders, provided the total amount of the grace interest or dividends paid or credited during the payment or crediting period (for example, a quarterly or semiannual period) does not exceed 10 percent of the total amount of the interest or dividends paid or credited during such period, computed without regard to the grace interest or dividends. For example, providing the 10 percent limitation is met, the rule of nonallowance does not apply in a case in which a calendar year taxpayer, with regular interest payment dates of January 1, April 1, July 1, and October 1, pays grace interest for the period beginning October 1 to a depositor who terminates his account on December 10.

*(2) Computation of amounts not allowed as a deduction.* (i) Method of computation. The amount of the dividends or interest to which subparagraph (1) of this paragraph applies, which is not allowed as a deduction, shall be computed under the rules of this subparagraph. The amount which is not allowed as a deduction is the difference between the total amount of dividends or interest paid or credited to that class of accounts with respect to which a deduction is not allowed under subparagraph (1) of this paragraph during the taxable year (or short period, if applicable) and an amount which bears the same ratio to such total as the number 12 (or number of months in the short period) bears to the number of months with respect to which such amounts of dividends or interest are paid or credited.

(ii) Examples. The provisions of subdivision (i) of this subparagraph may be illustrated by the following examples:

*Example (1).* X Association, a domestic building and loan association filing its return on the basis of a calendar year, regularly credits dividends on its withdrawable accounts quarterly on the first day of the quarter following the quarter with respect to which they are earned. X changes the time of crediting dividends commencing with the credit for the fourth quarter of 1964. Such credit and all subsequent credits are made on the last day of the quarter with respect to which they are earned. As a result of this change X's credits for the year 1964 are as follows:

| Period With Respect To Which Earned | Date Credited In 1964 | Amount |
|---|---|---|
| 4th quarter, 1963 | Jan. 1 | $ 250,000 |
| 1st quarter, 1964 | Apr. 1 | 300,000 |
| 2d quarter, 1964 | July 1 | 300,000 |
| 3d quarter, 1964 | Oct. 1 | 300,000 |
| 4th quarter, 1964 | Dec. 31 | 350,000 |
| Total dividends credited | | 1,500,000 |

Since the change in the time of crediting dividends results in the crediting in 1964 of amounts of dividends representing periods totalling 15 months (October 1963 through December 1964), amounts shall not be allowed as a deduction in 1964 which are in excess of $1,200,000, which is the amount which bears the same ratio to the amounts of dividends credited during the year ($1,500,000) as the number 12 bears to the number of months (15) with respect to which such dividends are credited. Thus, $300,000 ($1,500,000 minus $1,200,000) is not allowed as a deduction in 1964.

*Example (2).* Y Association, a domestic building and loan association filing its return on the basis of a calendar year, regularly credits dividends on its withdrawable accounts on the basis of a semiannual period on March 31 and September 30 of each year. Y changes the period with respect to which credits are made from the semiannual period to the quarterly basis, commencing with the last quarter in 1964. The credit for this last quarter and all subsequent credits are made on the last day of the quarter with respect to which they are earned. As a result of this change, Y's credits for the year 1964 are as follows:

| Period With Respect To Which Earned | Date Credited In 1964 | Amount |
|---|---|---|
| 6-month period ending Mar. 31, 1964 | Mar. 31 | $300,000 |
| 6-month period ending Sept. 30, 1964 | Sept. 30 | 400,000 |
| 4th quarter, 1964 | Dec. 31 | 200,000 |
| Total dividends credited | | 900,000 |

Since the change in the basis of crediting dividends results in a crediting in 1964 of dividends representing periods totaling 15 months (October 1963 through December 1964), amounts shall not be allowed as a deduction in 1964 which are in excess of $720,000, which is the amount which bears the same ratio to the amounts of dividends credited during the year ($900,000) as the number 12 bears to the number of months (15) with respect to which such dividends are credited. Thus, $180,000 ($900,000 minus $720,000) is not allowed as a deduction in 1964.

*Example (3).* Z Association, a domestic building and loan association regularly files its return on the basis of a fiscal year ending on the last day of February and regularly credits dividends on its withdrawable accounts quarterly on the last day of the quarter with respect to which they are earned. Z receives approval from the Commissioner of Internal Revenue to change its accounting period to a calendar year and effects the change by filing a return for a short period ending on December 31, 1964. Dividend credits for the short period beginning on March 1 and ending on December 31, 1964, are as follows:

| Period With Respect To Which Earned | Date Credited In 1964 | Amount |
|---|---|---|
| January-March 1964 | Mar. 31 | $ 250,000 |
| April-June 1964 | June 30 | 300,000 |
| July-September 1964 | Sept. 30 | 300,000 |
| October-December 1964 | Dec. 31 | 350,000 |
| Total dividends credited | | 1,200,000 |

Since the change of accounting period results in amounts of dividends credited ($1,200,000) representing periods totaling 12 months (January through December 1964), and such periods represent more than the number of months (10) in the short period, an amount shall not be allowed as a deduction in such short period which is in excess of $1,000,000, which is the amount which bears the same ratio to the amount of dividends credited in the short period ($1,200,000) as the number of months (10) in the short period bears to the number of months (12) with respect to which such dividends are credited. Thus, $200,000 ($1,200,000 minus $1,000,000) is not allowed as a deduction in the short period.

*(3) When amounts allowable.* The amount of dividends or interest not allowed as a deduction under subparagraph (1) of this paragraph shall be allowed as follows (subject to the limitation that the total of the amounts so allowed shall not exceed the amount not allowed under subparagraph (1)):

(i) Such amount shall be allowed as a deduction in a later taxable year or years subject to the limitation that, when taken together with the deductions otherwise allowable in the later taxable year or years, it does not bring the deductions for any later taxable year to a total representing a period of more than 12 months (or number of months in the short period, if applicable). However, in any event, an amount otherwise allowable under subdivision (ii) of this subparagraph shall be allowed notwithstanding the fact that it may bring the deductions allowable to a total representing a period of more than 12 months (or number of months in the short period, if applicable).

(ii) In any case in which it is established to the satisfaction of the Commissioner that the taxpayer does not intend to avoid taxes, one-tenth of such amount shall be allowed as a deduction in each of the 10 succeeding taxable years—

(a) Commencing with the taxable year for which such amount is not allowed as a deduction under subparagraph (1), or

(b) In the case of such amount not allowed for a taxable year ending before July 1, 1964, commencing with either the first or second taxable year after the taxable year for which such amount is not allowed as a deduction under subparagraph (1) if the taxpayer has not taken a deduction on his return, or filed a claim for credit or refund, in respect of such amount under *(a)*. Normally, if the deduction not allowed under subparagraph (1) is a result of a change, not requested by the taxpayer, in the taxpayer's annual accounting period or dividend or interest payment or crediting dates solely as a consequence of a requirement of a Federal or State regulatory authority, or if the deduction is not allowed solely as a result of the taxpayer being a party to an acquisition to which section 381(a) applies, the Commissioner will permit the allowance of the amount not allowed in the manner provided in this subdivision. Nothing set forth in this subdivision shall be construed as permitting the allowance of a credit or refund for any year which is barred by the limitations on credit or refund provided by section 6511.

(iii) If the total of the amounts, if any, allowed under subdivisions (i) and (ii) of this subparagraph before the taxable year in which the taxpayer liquidates or otherwise ceases to engage in trade or business is less than the amount not allowed under subparagraph (1), there shall be allowed a deduction in such taxable year for the difference between the amount not allowed under subparagraph (1) and the amounts allowed, if any, as deductions under subdivisions (i) and (ii) unless the circumstances under which the taxpayer ceased to do business constitute an acquisition described in section 381(a) (relating to carryovers in certain corporate acquisitions). If the circumstances under which the taxpayer ceased to do business constitute an acquisition described in section 381(a), the acquiring corporation shall succeed to and take into account the balance of the amounts not allowed on the same basis as the taxpayer had it not ceased to engage in business.

T.D. 6282, 12/24/57, amend T.D. 6520, 12/23/60, T.D. 6710, 3/17/64, T.D. 6735, 5/18/64, T.D. 6772, 11/23/64, T.D. 6917, 5/1/67, T.D. 8408, 4/9/92, T.D. 8482, 8/6/93, T.D. 8554, 7/13/94, T.D. 8820, 5/17/99.

## § 1.461-2 Contested liabilities.

***Caution:*** The Treasury has not yet amended Reg § 1.461-2 to reflect changes made by P.L. 98-369.

**(a) General rule.** *(1) Taxable year of deduction.* If—

(i) The taxpayer contests an asserted liability,

(ii) The taxpayer transfers money or other property to provide for the satisfaction of the asserted liability,

(iii) The contest with respect to the asserted liability exists after the time of the transfer, and

(iv) But for the fact that the asserted liability is contested, a deduction would be allowed for the taxable year of the transfer (or, in the case of an accrual method taxpayer, for an earlier taxable year for which such amount would be accruable), then the deduction with respect to the contested amount shall be allowed for the taxable year of the transfer.

*(2) Exception.* Subparagraph (1) of this paragraph shall not apply in respect of the deduction for income, war profits, and excess profits taxes imposed by the authority of any foreign country or possession of the United States, including a tax paid in lieu of a tax on income, war profits, or excess profits otherwise generally imposed by any foreign country or by any possession of the United States.

*(3) Refunds includible in gross income.* If any portion of the contested amount which is deducted under subparagraph (1) of this paragraph for the taxable year of transfer is refunded when the contest is settled, such portion is includible in gross income except as provided in § 1.111-1, relating to recovery of certain items previously deducted or credited. Such refunded amount is includible in gross income for the taxable year of receipt, or for an earlier taxable year if properly accruable for such earlier year.

*(4) Examples.* The provisions of this paragraph are illustrated by the following examples:

*Example (1).* X Corporation, which uses an accrual method of accounting, in 1964 contests $20 of a $100 asserted real property tax liability but pays the entire $100 to the taxing authority. In 1968, the contest is settled and X receives a refund of $5. X deducts $100 for the taxable year 1964, and includes $5 in gross income for the taxable year 1968 (assuming § 1.111-1 does not apply to such amount). If in 1964 X pays only $80 to the taxing authority, X deducts only $80 for 1964. The result would be the same if X Corporation used the cash method of accounting.

*Example (2).* Y Corporation makes its return on the basis of a calendar year and uses an accrual method of accounting. Y's real property taxes are assessed and become a lien on December 1, but are not payable until March 1 of the following year. On December 10, 1964, Y contests $20 of the $100 asserted real property tax which was assessed and became a lien on December 1, 1964. On March 1, 1965, Y pays the entire $100 to the taxing authority. In 1968, the contest is settled and Y receives a refund of $5. Y deducts $80 for the taxable year 1964, deducts $20 for the taxable year 1965, and includes $5 in gross income for the taxable year 1968 (assuming § 1.111-1 does not apply to such amount).

**(b) Contest of asserted liability.** *(1) Asserted liability.* For purposes of paragraph (a)(1) of this section, the term "asserted liability" means an item with respect to which, but for the existence of any contest in respect of such item, a deduction would be allowable under an accrual method of accounting. For example, a notice of a local real estate tax assessment and a bill received for services may represent asserted liabilities.

*(2) Definition of the term "contest".* Any contest which would prevent accrual of a liability under section 461(a) shall be considered to be a contest in determining whether the taxpayer satisfies paragraph (a)(1)(i) of this section. A contest arises when there is a bona fide dispute as to the proper evaluation of the law or the facts necessary to determine the existence or correctness of the amount of an asserted liability. It is not necessary to institute suit in a court of law in order to contest an asserted liability. An affirmative act denying the validity or accuracy, or both, of an asserted liability to the person who is asserting such liability, such as including a written protest with payment of the asserted liability, is sufficient to commence a contest. Thus, lodging a protest in accordance with local law is sufficient to contest an asserted liability for taxes. It is not necessary that the affirmative act denying the validity or accuracy, or both, of an asserted liability be in writing if, upon examination of all the facts and circumstances, it can be established to the satisfaction of the Commissioner that a liability has been asserted and contested.

*(3) Example.* The provisions of this paragraph are illustrated by the following example:

*Example.* O Corporation makes its return on the basis of a calendar year and uses an accrual method of accounting. O receives a large shipment of typewriter ribbons from S Company on January 30, 1964, which O pays for in full on February 10, 1964. Subsequent to their receipt, several of the ribbons prove defective because of inferior materials used by the manufacturer. On August 9, 1964, O orally notifies S and demands refund of the full purchase price of the ribbons. After negotiations prove futile and a written demand is rejected by S, O institutes an action for the full purchase price. For purposes of paragraph (a)(1)(i) of this section, S has asserted a liability against O which O contests on August 9, 1964. O deducts the contested amount for 1964.

**(c) Transfer to provide for the satisfaction of an asserted liability.** *(1) In general.* (i) A taxpayer may provide for the satisfaction of an asserted liability by transferring money or other property beyond his control to—

(A) The person who is asserting the liability;

(B) An escrowee or trustee pursuant to a written agreement (among the escrowee or trustee, the taxpayer, and the person who is asserting the liability) that the money or other property be delivered in accordance with the settlement of the contest;

(C) An escrowee or trustee pursuant to an order of the United States or of any State or political subdivision thereof or any agency or instrumentality of the foregoing, or of a court, that the money or other property be delivered in accordance with the settlement of the contest; or

(D) A court with jurisdiction over the contest.

(ii) In order for money or other property to be beyond the control of a taxpayer, the taxpayer must relinquish all authority over the money or other property.

(iii) The following are not transfers to provide for the satisfaction of an asserted liability—

(A) Purchasing a bond to guarantee payment of the asserted liability;

(B) An entry on the taxpayer's books of account;

(C) A transfer to an account that is within the control of the taxpayer;

(D) A transfer of any indebtedness of the taxpayer or of any promise by the taxpayer to provide services or property in the future; and

(E) A transfer to a person (other than the person asserting the liability) of any stock of the taxpayer or of any stock or indebtedness of a person related to the taxpayer (as defined in section 267(b)).

*(2) Examples.* The provisions of this paragraph are illustrated by the following examples:

*Example (2).* M Corporation contests a $5,000 liability asserted against it by L Company for services rendered. To provide for the contingency that it might have to pay the liability, M establishes a separate bank account in its own name. M then transfers $5,000 from its general account to such separate account. Such transfer does not qualify as a transfer to provide for the satisfaction of an asserted liability because M has not transferred the money beyond its control.

*Example (3).* M Corporation contests a $5,000 liability asserted against it by L Company for services rendered. To provide for the contingency that it might have to pay the liability, M transfers $5,000 to an irrevocable trust pursuant to a written agreement among the trustee, M (the taxpayer), and L (the person who is asserting the liability) that the money shall be held until the contest is settled and then disbursed in accordance with the settlement. Such transfer qualifies as a transfer to provide for the satisfaction of an asserted liability.

**(d) Contest exists after transfer.** In order for a contest with respect to an asserted liability to exist after the time of transfer, such contest must be pursued subsequent to such time. Thus, the contest must have been neither settled nor abandoned at the time of the transfer. A contest may be settled by a decision, judgment, decree, or other order of any court of competent jurisdiction which has become final, or by written or oral agreement between the parties. For example, Z Corporation, which uses an accrual method of accounting, in 1964 contests a $100 asserted liability. In 1967 the contested liability is settled as being $80 which Z accrues and deducts for such year. In 1968 Z pays the $80. Section 461(f) does not apply to Z with respect to the transfer because a contest did not exist after the time of such transfer.

**(e) Deduction otherwise allowed.** *(1) In general.* The existence of the contest with respect to an asserted liability must prevent (without regard to section 461(f)) and be the only factor preventing a deduction for the taxable year of the transfer (or, in the case of an accrual method taxpayer, for an earlier taxable year for which such amount would be accruable) to provide for the satisfaction of such liability. Nothing in section 461(f) or this section shall be construed to give rise to a deduction since section 461(f) and this section relate only to the timing of deductions which are otherwise allowable under the Code.

*(2) Application of economic performance rules to transfers under section 461(f).* (i) A taxpayer using an accrual method of accounting is not allowed a deduction under section 461(f) in the taxable year of the transfer unless economic performance has occurred.

(ii) Economic performance occurs for liabilities requiring payment to another person arising out of any workers compensation act or any tort, or any other liability designated in § 1.461-4(g), as payments are made to the person to which the liability is owed. Except as provided in section 468B or the regulations thereunder, economic performance does not occur when a taxpayer transfers money or other property to a trust, an escrow account, or a court to provide for the satisfaction of an asserted workers compensation, tort, or other liability designated under § 1.461-4(g) that the taxpayer is contesting unless the trust, escrow account, or court is the person to which the liability is owed or the taxpayer's payment to the trust, escrow account, or court discharges the taxpayer's liability to the claimant. Rather, economic performance occurs in the taxable year the taxpayer transfers money or other property to the person that is asserting the workers compensation, tort, or other liability designated under § 1.461-4(g) that the taxpayer is contesting or in the taxable year that payment is made from a trust, an escrow account, or a court registry funded by the taxpayer to the person to which the liability is owed.

*(3) Examples.* The provisions of this paragraph are illustrated by the following examples:

*Example (1).* A, an individual, makes a gift of certain property to B, an individual. A pays the entire amount of gift tax assessed against him but contests his liability for the tax. Section 275(a)(3) provides that gift taxes are not deductible. A does not satisfy the requirement of paragraph (a)(1)(iv) of this section because a deduction would not be allowed for the taxable year of the transfer even if A did not contest his liability to the tax.

*Example (2).* Corporation X is a defendant in a class action suit for tort liabilities. In 2002, X establishes a trust for the purpose of satisfying the asserted liability and transfers $10,000,000 to the trust. The trust does not satisfy the requirements of section 468B or the regulations thereunder. In 2004, the trustee pays $10,000,000 to the plaintiffs in settlement of the litigation. Under paragraph (e)(2) of this section, economic performance with respect to X's liability to the plaintiffs occurs in 2004. X may deduct the $10,000,000 payment to the plaintiffs in 2004.

**(f) Treatment of money or property transferred to an escrowee, trustee, or court and treatment of any income attributable thereto. [Reserved]**

**(g) Effective dates.** *(1)* Except as otherwise provided, this section applies to transfers of money or other property in taxable years beginning after December 31, 1953, and ending after August 16, 1954.

*(2)* Paragraph (c)(1)(iii)(E) of this section applies to transfers of any stock of the taxpayer or any stock or indebtedness of a person related to the taxpayer on or after November 19, 2003.

*(3)* Paragraph (e)(2)(i) of this section applies to transfers of money or other property after July 18, 1984.

*(4)* Paragraph (e)(2)(ii) and paragraph (e)(3) Example 2 of this section apply to—

(i) Transfers after July 18, 1984, of money or other property to provide for the satisfaction of an asserted workers compensation or tort liability; and

(ii) Transfers in taxable years beginning after December 31, 1991, of money or other property to provide for the satisfaction of asserted liabilities designated in § 1.461-4(g) (other than liabilities for workers compensation or tort).

---

T.D. 6772, 11/23/64, amend T.D. 8408, 4/9/92, T.D. 9095, 11/19/2003, T.D. 9140, 7/19/2004.

---

**§ 1.461-3 Prepaid interest. [Reserved]**

**§ 1.461-4 Economic performance.**

**(a) Introduction.** *(1) In general.* For purposes of determining whether an accrual basis taxpayer can treat the amount of any liability (as defined in § 1.446-1(c)(1)(ii)(B)) as incurred, the all events test is not treated as met any earlier than the taxable year in which economic performance occurs with respect to the liability.

*(2) Overview.* Paragraph (b) of this section lists exceptions to the economic performance requirement. Paragraph (c) of this section provides cross-references to the definitions of certain terms for purposes of section 461(h) and the regulations thereunder. Paragraphs (d) through (m) of this section and § 1.461-6 provide rules for determining when economic performance occurs. Section 1.461-5 provides rules relating to an exception under which certain recurring items may be incurred for the taxable year before the year during which economic performance occurs.

**(b) Exceptions to the economic performance requirement.** Paragraph (a)(2)(iii)(B) of § 1.461-1 provides examples of liabilities that are taken into account under rules that operate without regard to the all events test (including economic performance).

**(c) Definitions.** The following cross-references identify certain terms defined for purposes of section 461(h) and the regulations thereunder:

*(1) Liability.* See paragraph (c)(1)(ii)(B) of § 1.446-1 for the definition of "liability."

*(2) Payment.* See paragraph (g)(1)(ii) of this section for the definition of "payment."

**(d) Liabilities arising out of the provision of services, property, or the use of property.** *(1) In general.* The principles of this paragraph (d) determine when economic performance occurs with respect to liabilities arising out of the performance of services, the transfer of property, or the use of property. This paragraph (d) does not apply to liabilities described in paragraph (e) (relating to interest expense) or paragraph (g) (relating to breach of contract, workers compensation, tort, etc.) of this section. In addition, except as otherwise provided in Internal Revenue regulations, revenue procedures, or revenue rulings this paragraph (d) does not apply to amounts paid pursuant to a notional principal contract. The Commissioner may provide additional rules in regulations, revenue procedures, or revenue rulings concerning the time at which economic performance occurs for items described in this paragraph (d).

*(2) Services or property provided to the taxpayer.* (i) In general. Except as otherwise provided in paragraph (d)(5) of this section, if the liability of a taxpayer arises out of the providing of services or property to the taxpayer by another person, economic performance occurs as the services or property is provided.

(ii) Long-term contracts. In the case of any liability of a taxpayer described in paragraph (d)(2)(i) of this section that is an expense attributable to a long-term contract with respect to which the taxpayer uses the percentage of completion method. economic performance occurs—

(A) As the services or property is provided; or, if earlier,

(B) As the taxpayer makes payment (as defined in paragraph (g)(1)(ii) of this section) in satisfaction of the liability to the person providing the services or property. See paragraph (k)(2) of this section for the effective date of this paragraph (d)(2)(ii).

(iii) Employee benefits. (A) In general. Except as otherwise provided in any Internal Revenue regulation, revenue procedure, or revenue ruling, the economic performance requirement is satisfied to the extent that any amount is otherwise deductible under section 404 (employer contributions to a plan of deferred compensation), section 404A (certain foreign deferred compensation plans), and section 419 (welfare benefit funds). See § 1.461-1(a)(2)(iii)(D).

(B) Property transferred in connection with performance of services. [Reserved]

(iv) Cross-references. See Examples 4 through 6 of paragraph (d)(7) of this section. See paragraph (d)(6) of this section for rules relating to when a taxpayer may treat services or property as provided to the taxpayer.

*(3) Use of property provided to the taxpayer.* (i) In general. Except as otherwise provided in this paragraph (d)(3) and paragraph (d)(5) of this section, if the liability of a taxpayer arises out of the use of property by the taxpayer, economic performance occurs ratably over the period of time the taxpayer is entitled to the use of the property (taking into account any reasonably expected renewal periods when necessary to carry out the purposes of section 461(h)). See Examples 6 through 9 of paragraph (d)(7) of this section.

(ii) Exceptions. (A) Volume, frequency of use, or income. If the liability of a taxpayer arises out of the use of property by the taxpayer and all or a portion of the liability is determined by reference to the frequency or volume of use of the property or the income from the property, economic performance occurs for the portion of the liability determined by reference to the frequency or volume of use of the property or the income from the property as the taxpayer uses the property or includes income from the property. See Examples 8 and 9 of paragraph (d)(7) of this section. This paragraph (d)(3)(ii) shall not apply if the District Director determines, that based on the substance of the transaction, the liability of the taxpayer for use of the property is more appropriately measured ratably over the period of time the taxpayer is entitled to the use of the property.

(B) Section 467 rental agreements. In the case of a liability arising out of the use of property pursuant to a section 467 rental agreement, economic performance occurs as provided in § 1.461-1(a)(2)(iii)(E).

*(4) Services or property provided by the taxpayer.* (i) In general. Except as otherwise provided in paragraph (d)(5) of this section, if the liability of a taxpayer requires the taxpayer to provide services or property to another person, economic performance occurs as the taxpayer incurs costs (within the meaning of § 1.446-1(c)(1)(ii)) in connection with the satisfaction of the liability. See Examples 1 through 3 of paragraph (d)(7) of this section.

(ii) Barter transactions. If the liability of a taxpayer requires the taxpayer to provide services, property, or the use of property, and arises out of the use of property by the taxpayer, or out of the provision of services or property to the taxpayer by another person. economic performance occurs to the extent of the lesser of—

(A) The cumulative extent to which the taxpayer incurs costs (within the meaning of § 1.446-1(c)(1)(ii)) in connection with its liability to provide the services of property; or

(B) The cumulative extent to which the services or property is provided to the taxpayer.

*(5) Liabilities that are assumed in connection with the sale of a trade or business.* (i) In general. If, in connection with the sale or exchange of a trade or business by a taxpayer, the purchaser expressly assumes a liability arising out of the trade or business that the taxpayer but for the economic performance requirement would have been entitled to incur as of the date of the sale, economic performance with respect to that liability occurs as the amount of the liability is properly included in the amount realized on the transaction by the taxpayer. See § 1.1001-2 for rules relating to the inclusion in amount realized from a discharge of liabilities resulting from a sale or exchange.

(ii) Trade or business. For purposes of this paragraph (d)(5), a trade or business is a specific group of activities carried on by the taxpayer for the purpose of earning income or profit if every operation that is necessary to the process of earning income or profit is included in the group. Thus, for example, the group of activities generally must include the collection of income and the payment of expenses.

(iii) Tax avoidance. This paragraph (d)(5) does not apply if the District Director determines that tax avoidance is one of the taxpayer's principal purposes for the sale or exchange.

*(6) Rules relating to the provision of services or property to a taxpayer.* The following rules apply for purposes of this paragraph (d):

(i) Services or property provided to a taxpayer include services or property provided to another person at the direction of the taxpayer.

(ii) A taxpayer is permitted to treat services or property as provided to the taxpayer as the taxpayer makes payment to the person providing the services or property (as defined in paragraph (g)(1)(ii) of this section), if the taxpayer can reasonably expect the person to provide the services or property within 3½ months after the date of payment.

(iii) A taxpayer is permitted to treat property as provided to the taxpayer when the property is delivered or accepted, or when title to the property passes. The method used by the taxpayer to determine when property is provided is a method of accounting that must comply with the rules of § 1.446-1(e). Thus, the method of determining when property is provided must be used consistently from year to year, and cannot be changed without the consent of the Commissioner.

(iv) If different services or items of property are required to be provided to a taxpayer under a single contract or agreement, economic performance generally occurs over the time each service is provided and as each item of property is provided. However, if a service or item of property to be provided to the taxpayer is incidental to other services or property to be provided under a contract or agreement, the taxpayer is not required to allocate any portion of the total contract price to the incidental service or property. For purposes of this paragraph (d)(6)(iv). Services or property is treated as incidental only if—

(A) The cost of the services or property is treated on the taxpayer's books and records as part of the cost of the other services or property provided under the contract; and

(B) The aggregate cost of the services or property does not exceed 10 percent of the total contract price.

*(7) Examples.* The following examples illustrate the principles of this paragraph (d). For purposes of these examples, it is assumed that the requirements of the all events test other than economic performance have been met, and that the recurring item exception is not used. Assume further that the examples do not involve section 467 rental agreements and, therefore, section 467 is not applicable. The examples are as follows:

*Example (1).* Services or property provided by the taxpayer.

(i) X corporation, a calendar year, accrual method taxpayer, is an oil company. During March 1990, X enters into an oil and gas lease with Y. In November 1990, X installs a platform and commences drilling. The lease obligates X to remove its offshore platform and well fixtures upon abandonment of the well or termination of the lease. During 1998, X removes the platform and well fixtures at a cost of $200,000.

(ii) Under paragraph (d)(4)(i) of this section, economic performance with respect to X's liability to remove the offshore platform and well fixtures occurs as X incurs costs in connection with that liability. X incurs these costs in 1998 as, for example, X's employees provide X with removal services (see paragraph (d)(2) of this section). Consequently, X incurs $200,000 for the 1998 taxable year. Alternatively, assume that during 1990 X pays Z $130,000 to remove the platform and fixtures, and that Z performs these removal services in 1998. Under paragraph (d)(2) of this section, X does not incur this cost until Z performs the services. Thus, economic performance with respect to the $130,000 X pays Z occurs in 1998.

*Example (2).* Services or property provided by the taxpayer.

(i) W corporation, a calendar year, accrual method taxpayer, sells tractors under a three-year warranty that obligates W to make any reasonable repairs to each tractor it sells. During 1990, W sells ten tractors. In 1992 W repairs, at a cost of $5,000, two tractors sold during 1990.

(ii) Under paragraph (d)(4)(i) of this section, economic performance with respect to W's liability to perform services under the warranty occurs as W incurs costs in connection with that liability. W incurs these costs in 1992 as, for example, replacement parts are provided to W (see paragraph (d)(2) of this section). Consequently, $5,000 is incurred by W for the 1992 taxable year.

*Example (3).* Services or property provided by the taxpayer; Long-term contracts.

(i) W corporation, a calendar year, accrual method taxpayer, manufactures machine tool equipment. In November 1992, W contracts to provide X corporation with certain equipment. The contract is not a long-term contract under section 460 or § 1.451-3. In 1992, W pays Z corporation $50,000 to lease from Z, for the one-year period beginning on January 1, 1993, testing equipment to perform quality control tests required by the agreement with X. In 1992, pursuant to the terms of a contract W pays Y corporation $100,000 for certain parts necessary to manufacture the equipment. The parts are provided to W in 1993. W's employees provide W with services necessary to manufacture the equipment during 1993, for which W pays $150,000 in 1993.

(ii) Under paragraph (d)(4) of this section, economic performance with respect to W's liability to provide the equipment to X occurs as W incurs costs in connection with that liability. W incurs these costs during 1993, as services, property, and the use of property necessary to manufacture the equipment are provided to W (see paragraphs (d)(2) and (d)(3) of this section). Thus, $300,000 is incurred by W for the 1993 taxable year. See section 263A and the regulations thereunder for rules relating to the capitalization and inclusion in inventory of these incurred costs.

(iii) Alternatively, assume that the agreement with X is a long-term contract as defined in section 460(f), and that W takes into account all items with respect to such contracts under the percentage of completion method as described in section 460(b)(1). Under paragraph (d)(2)(ii) of this section, the $100,000 W pays in 1992 for parts is incurred for the 1992 taxable year, for purposes of determining the percentage of completion under section 460(b)(1)(A). W's other costs under the agreement are incurred for the 1993 taxable year for this purpose.

*Example (4).* Services or property provided to the taxpayers.

(i) LP1, a calendar year, accrual method limited partnership, owns the working interest in a parcel of property containing oil and gas. During December 1990, LP1 enters into a turnkey contract with Z corporation pursuant to which LP1 pays Z $200,000 and Z is required to provide a completed well by the close of 1992. In May 1992, Z commences drilling the well, and, in December 1992, the well is completed.

(ii) Under paragraph (d)(2) of this section, economic performance with respect to LP1's liability for drilling and development services provided to LP1 by Z occurs as the services are provided. Consequently, $200,000 is incurred by LP1 for the 1992 taxable year.

*Example (5).* Services or property provided to the taxpayer.

(i) X corporation, a calendar year, accrual method taxpayer, is an automobile dealer. On January 15, 1990, X agrees to pay an additional $10 to Y, the manufacturer of the automobiles, for each automobile purchased by X from Y. Y agrees to provide advertising and promotional activities to X.

(ii) During 1990, X purchases from Y 1,000 new automobiles and pays to Y an additional $10,000 as provided in the agreement. Y, in turn, uses this $10,000 to provide advertising and promotional activities during 1992.

(iii) Under paragraph (d)(2) of this section, economic performance with respect to X's liability for advertising and promotional services provided to X by Y occurs as the services are provided. Consequently, $10,000 is incurred by X for the 1992 taxable year.

*Example (6).* Use of property provided to the taxpayer; services or property provided to the taxpayer.

(i) V corporation, a calendar year, accrual method taxpayer, charters aircrafts. On December 20, 1990, V leases a jet aircraft from L for the four-year period that begins on January 1, 1991. The lease obligates V to pay L a base rental of $500,000 per year. In addition, the lease requires V to pay $25 to an escrow account for each hour that the aircraft is flown. The escrow account funds are held by V and are to be used by L to make necessary repairs to the aircraft. Any amount remaining in the escrow account upon termination of the lease is payable to V. During 1991, the aircraft is flown 1,000 hours and V pays $25,000 to the escrow account. The aircraft is repaired by L in 1993. In 1994, $20,000 is released from the escrow account to pay L for the repairs.

(ii) Under paragraph (d)(3)(i) of this section, economic performance with respect to V's base rental liability occurs ratably over the period of time V is entitled to use the jet aircraft. Consequently, the $500,000 rent is incurred by V for the 1991 taxable year and for each of the next three taxable years. Under paragraph (d)(2) of this section, economic performance with respect to the liability to place amounts in escrow occurs as the aircraft is repaired. Consequently, V incurs $20,00 for the 1993 taxable year.

*Example (7).* Use of property provided to the taxpayer.

(i) X corporation, a calendar year, accrual method taxpayer, manufactures and sells electronic circuitry. On November 15, 1990, X enters into a contract with Y that entitles X to the exclusive use of a product owned by Y for the five-year period beginning on January 1, 1991. Pursuant to the contract, X pays Y $100,000 on December 30, 1990.

(ii) Under paragraph (d)(3)(i) of this section, economic performance with respect to X's liability for the use of property occurs ratably over the period of time X is entitled to use the product. Consequently, $20,000 is incurred by X for 1991 and for each of the succeeding four taxable years.

*Example (8).* Use of property provided to the taxpayer.

(i) Y corporation, a calendar year, accrual method taxpayer, enters into a five year lease with Z for the use of a copy machine on July 1, 1991. Y also receives delivery of the copy machine on July 1, 1991. The lease obligates Y to pay Z a base rental payment of $6,000 per year at the beginning of each lease year and an additional charge of 5 cents per copy 30 days after the end of each lease year. The machine is used to make 50,000 copies during the first lease year; 20,000 copies in 1991 and 30,000 copies from January 1, 1992, to July 1, 1992. Y pays the $6,000 base rental payment to Z on July 1, 1991, and the $2,500 variable use payment on July 30, 1992.

(ii) Under paragraph (d)(3)(i) of this section, economic performance with respect to Y's base rental liability occurs ratably over the period of time Y is entitled to use the copy machine. Consequently, $3,000 rent is incurred by Y for the 1991 taxable year. Under paragraph (d)(3)(ii) of this section, economic performance with respect to Y's variable use portion of the liability occurs as Y uses the machine. Thus, the $1,000 of the $2,500 variable-use liability that relates to the 20,000 copies made in 1991 is incurred by Y for the 1991 taxable year.

*Example (9).* Use of property provided to the taxpayer.

(i) X corporation, a calendar year, accrual method taxpayer, enters into a five-year product distribution agreement with Y, on January 1, 1992. The agreement provides for a payment of $100,000 on January 1, 1992, plus 10 percent of the gross profits earned by X from distribution of the product. The variable income portion of X's liability is payable on April 1 of each subsequent year. On January 1, 1992, X pays Y $100,000. On April 1, 1993, X pays Y $3 million representing 10 percent of X's gross profits from January 1 through December 31, 1992.

(ii) Under paragraph (d)(3)(i) of this section, economic performance with respect to X's $100,000 payment occurs ratably over the period of time X is entitled to use the product. Consequently, $20,000 is incurred by X for each year of the agreement beginning with 1992. Under paragraph (d)(3)(ii) of this section, economic performance with respect to X's variable income portion of the liability occurs as the income is earned by X. Thus, the $3 million variable-income liability is incurred by X for the 1992 taxable year.

**(e) Interest.** In the case of interest, economic performance occurs as the interest cost economically accrues, in accordance with the principles of relevant provisions of the Code.

**(f) Timing of deductions from notional principal contracts.** Economic performance on a notional principal contract occurs as provided under § 1.446-3.

**(g) Certain liabilities for which payment is economic performance.** *(1) In general.* (i) Person to which payment must be made. In the case of liabilities described in paragraphs (g)(2) through (7) of this section, economic performance occurs when, and to the extent that, payment is made to the person to which the liability is owed. Thus, except as otherwise provided in paragraph (g)(1)(iv) of this section and § 1.461-6, economic performance does not occur as a taxpayer makes payments in connection with such a liability to any other person, including a trust, escrow account, court-administered fund, or any similar arrangement, unless the payments constitute payment to the person to which the liability is owed under paragraph (g)(1)(ii)(B) of this section. Instead, economic performance occurs as payments are made from that other person or fund to the person to which the liability is owed. The amount of economic performance that occurs as payment is made from the other person or fund to the person to which the liability is owed may not exceed the amount the taxpayer transferred to the other person or fund. For special rules relating to the taxation of amounts transferred to "qualified settlement funds," see section 468B and the regulations thereunder. The Commissioner may provide additional rules in regulations, revenue procedures, and revenue rulings concerning the time at which economic performance occurs for items described in this paragraph (g).

(ii) Payment to person to which liability is owed. Paragraph (d)(6) of this section provides that for purposes of paragraph (d) of this section (relating to the provision of services or property to the taxpayer) in certain cases a taxpayer may treat services or property as provided to the taxpayer as the taxpayer makes payments to the person providing the services or property. In addition, this paragraph (g) provides that in the case of certain liabilities of a taxpayer, economic performance occurs as the taxpayer makes payment to persons specified therein. For these and all other purposes of section 461(h) and the regulations thereunder:

(A) Payment. The term payment has the same meaning as is used when determining whether a taxpayer using the cash receipts and disbursements method of accounting has made a payment. Thus, for example, payment includes the furnishing of cash or cash equivalents and the netting of offsetting accounts. Payment does not include the furnishing of a note or other evidence of indebtedness of the taxpayer, whether or not the evidence is guaranteed by any other instrument (including a standby letter of credit) or by any third party (including a government agency). As a further example, payment does not include a promise of the taxpayer to provide services or property in the future (whether or not the promise is evidenced by a contract or other written agreement). In addition, payment does not include an amount transferred as a loan, refundable deposit, or contingent payment.

(B) Person to which payment is made. Payment to a particular person is accomplished if paragraph (g)(1)(ii)(A) of this section is satisfied and a cash basis taxpayer in the position of that person would be treated as having actually or constructively received the amount of the payment as gross income under the principles of section 451 (without regard to section 104(a) or any other provision that specifically excludes the amount from gross income). Thus, for example, the purchase of an annuity contract or any other asset generally does not constitute payment to the person to which a liability is owed unless the ownership of the contract or other asset is transferred to that person.

(C) Liabilities that are assumed in connection with the sale of a trade or business. Paragraph (d)(5) of this section provides rules that determine when economic performance occurs in the case of liabilities that are assumed in connection with the sale of a trade or business. The provisions of paragraph (d)(5) of this section also apply to any liability described in paragraph (g)(2) through (7) of this section that the purchaser expressly assumes in connection with the sale or exchange of a trade or business by a taxpayer, provided the taxpayer (but for the economic performance requirement) would have been entitled to incur the liability as of the date of the sale.

(iii) Person. For purposes of this paragraph (g), "person" has the same meaning as in section 7701(a)(1), except that it also includes any foreign state, the United States, any State or political subdivision thereof, any possession of the United States, and any agency or instrumentality of any of the foregoing.

(iv) Assignments. If a person that has a right to receive payment in satisfaction of a liability described in paragraphs (g)(2) through (7) of this section makes a valid assignment of that right to a second person, or if the right is assigned to the second person through operation of law, then payment to the second person in satisfaction of that liability constitutes payment to the person to which the liability is owed.

*(2) Liabilities arising under a workers compensation act or out of any tort, breach of contract, or violation of law.* If the liability of a taxpayer requires a payment or series of payments to another person and arises under any workers compensation act or out of any tort, breach of contract, or violation of law, economic performance occurs as payment is made to the person to which the liability is owed. See Example 1 of paragraph (g)(8) of this section. For purposes of this paragraph (g)(2)—

(i) A liability to make payments for services, property, or other consideration provided under a contract is not a liability arising out of a breach of that contract unless the payments are in the nature of incidental, consequential, or liquidated damages; and

(ii) A liability arising out of a tort, breach of contract, or violation of law includes a liability arising out of the settlement of a dispute in which a tort, breach of contract, or violation of law, respectively, is alleged.

*(3) Rebates and refunds.* If the liability of a taxpayer is to pay a rebate, refund, or similar payment to another person (whether paid in property, money, or as a reduction in the price of goods or services to be provided in the future by the taxpayer), economic performance occurs as payment is made to the person to which the liability is owed. This paragraph (g)(3) applies to all rebates. refunds, and payments or transfers in the nature of a rebate or refund regardless of whether they are characterized as a deduction from gross income, an adjustment to gross receipts or total sales, or an adjustment or addition to cost of goods sold. In the case of a rebate or refund made as a reduction in the price of goods or services to be provided in the future by the taxpayer, "payment" is deemed to occur as the taxpayer would otherwise be required to recognize income resulting from a disposition at an unreduced price. See Example 2 of paragraph (g)(8) of this section. For purposes of determining whether the recurring item exception of § 1.461-5 applies, a liability that arises out of a tort, breach of contract, or violation of law is not considered a rebate or refund.

*(4) Awards, prizes, and jackpots.* If the liability of a taxpayer is to provide an award, prize, jackpot, or other similar payment to another person, economic performance occurs as payment is made to the person to which the liability is owed. See Examples 3 and 4 of paragraph (g)(8) of this section.

*(5) Insurance, warranty, and service contracts.* If the liability of a taxpayer arises out of the provision to the taxpayer of insurance, or a warranty or service contract, economic performance occurs as payment is made to the person to which the liability is owed, See Examples 5 through 7 of paragraph (g)(8) of this section. For purposes of this paragraph (g)(5)—

(i) A warranty or service contract is a contract that a taxpayer enters into in connection with property bought or leased by the taxpayer, pursuant to which the other party to the contract promises to replace or repair the property under specified circumstances.

(ii) The term "insurance" has the same meaning as is used when determining the deductibility of amounts paid or incurred for insurance under section 162.

*(6) Taxes.* (i) In general. Except as otherwise provided in this paragraph (g)(6), if the liability of a taxpayer is to pay a tax, economic performance occurs as the tax is paid to the governmental authority that imposed the tax. For purposes of this paragraph (g)(6), payment includes payments of estimated income tax and payments of tax where the taxpayer subsequently files a claim for credit or refund. In addition, for purposes of this paragraph (g)(6), a tax does not include a charge collected by a governmental authority for specific extraordinary services or property provided to a taxpayer by the governmental authority. Examples of such a charge include the purchase price of a parcel of land sold to a taxpayer by a governmental authority and a charge for labor engaged in by government employees to improve that parcel. In certain cases, a liability to pay a tax is permitted to be taken into account in the taxable year before the taxable year during which economic performance occurs under the recurring item exception of § 1.461-5. See Example 8 of paragraph (g)(8) of this section.

(ii) Licensing fees. If the liability of a taxpayer is to pay a licensing or permit fee required by a governmental authority, economic performance occurs as the fee is paid to the governmental authority, or as payment is made to any other person at the direction of the governmental authority.

(iii) Exceptions. (A) Real property taxes. If a taxpayer has made a valid election under section 461(c), the taxpayer's accrual for real property taxes is determined under section 461(c). Otherwise, economic performance with respect to a property tax liability occurs as the tax is paid, as specified in paragraph (g)(6)(i) of this section.

(B) Certain foreign taxes. If the liability of a taxpayer is to pay an income, war profits, or excess profits tax that is imposed by the authority of any foreign country or possession of the United States and is creditable under section 901 (including a creditable tax described in section 903 that is paid in lieu of such a tax), economic performance occurs when the requirements of the all events test (as described in § 1.446-1(c)(1)(ii)) other than economic performance are met, whether or not the taxpayer elects to credit such taxes under section 901(a).

*(7) Other liabilities.* In the case of a taxpayer's liability for which economic performance rules are not provided elsewhere in this section or in any other Internal Revenue regulation, revenue ruling or revenue procedure, economic performance occurs as the taxpayer makes payments in satisfaction of the liability to the person to which the liability is owed. This paragraph (g)(7) applies only if the liability cannot properly be characterized as a liability covered by rules provided elsewhere in this section. If a liability may properly be characterized as, for example, a liability arising from the provision of services or property to, or by, a taxpayer, the determination as to when economic performance

occurs with respect to that liability is made under paragraph (d) of this section and not under this paragraph (g)(7).

*(8) Examples.* The following examples illustrate the principles of this paragraph (g). For purposes of these examples, it is assumed that the requirements of the all events test other than economic performance have been met and, except as otherwise provided, that the recurring item exception is not used.

*Example (1).* Liabilities arising out of a tort.

(i) During the period 1970 through 1975, Z corporation, a calendar year, accrual method taxpayer, manufactured and distributed industrial products that contained carcinogenic substances. In 1992, a number of lawsuits are filed against Z alleging damages due to exposure to these products. In settlement of a lawsuit maintained by A, Z agrees to purchase an annuity contract that will provide annual payments to A of $50,000 for a period of 25 years. On December 15, 1992, Z pays W, an unrelated life insurance company, $491,129 for such an annuity contract. Z retains ownership of the annuity contract.

(ii) Under paragraph (g)(2) of this section, economic performance with respect to Z's liability to A occurs as each payment is made to A. Consequently, $50,000 is incurred by Z for each taxable year that a payment is made to A under the annuity contract. (Z must also include in income a portion of amounts paid under the annuity, pursuant to section 72.) The result is the same if in 1992 Z secures its obligation with a standby letter of credit.

(iii) If Z later transfers ownership of the annuity contract to A, an amount equal to the fair market value of the annuity on the date of transfer is incurred by Z in the taxable year of the transfer (see paragraph (g)(1)(ii)(B) of this section). In addition, the transfer constitutes a transaction to which section 1001 applies.

*Example (2).* Rebates and refunds.

(i) X corporation. a calendar year, accrual method taxpayer, manufactures and sells hardware products. X enters into agreements that entitle each of its distributors to a rebate (or discount on future purchases) from X based on the amount of purchases made by the distributor from X during any calendar year. During the 1992 calendar year, X becomes liable to pay a $2,000 rebate to distributor A. X pays A $1,200 of the rebate on January 15, 1993, and the remaining $800 on October 15, 1993. Assume the rebate is deductible (or allowable as an adjustment to gross receipts or cost of goods sold) when incurred.

(ii) If X does not adopt the recurring item exception described in § 1.461-5 with respect to rebates and refunds, then under paragraph (g)(3) of this section, economic performance with respect to the $2,000 rebate liability occurs in 1993. However, if X has made a proper election under § 1.461-5, and as of December 31, 1992, all events have occurred that determine the fact of the rebate liability, X incurs $1,200 for the 1992 taxable year. Because economic performance (payment) with respect to the remaining $800 does not occur until October 15, 1993 (more than 8½ months after the end of 1992), X cannot use the recurring item exception for this portion of the liability (see § 1.461-5). Thus, the $800 is not incurred by X until the 1993 taxable year. If, instead of making the cash payments to A during 1993, X adjusts the price of hardware purchased by A that is delivered to A during 1993, X's "payment" occurs as X would otherwise be required to recognize income resulting from a disposition at an unreduced price.

*Example (3).* Awards, prizes, and jackpots.

(i) W corporation, a calendar year, accrual method taxpayer, produces and sells breakfast cereal. W conducts a contest pursuant to which the winner is entitled to $10,000 per year for a period of 20 years. On December 1, 1992, A is declared the winner of the contest and is paid $10,000 by W. In addition, on December 1 of each of the next nineteen years, W pays $10,000 to A.

(ii) Under paragraph (g)(4) of this section, economic performance with respect to the $200,000 contest liability occurs as each of the $10,000 payments is made by W to A. Consequently, $10,000 is incurred by W for the 1992 taxable year and for each of the succeeding nineteen taxable years.

*Example (4).* Awards, prizes, and jackpots.

(i) Y corporation, a calendar year, accrual method taxpayer, owns a casino that contains progressive slot machines. A progressive slot machine provides a guaranteed jackpot amount that increases as money is gambled through the machine until the jackpot is won or until a maximum predetermined amount is reached. On July 1, 1993, the guaranteed jackpot amount on one of Y's slot machines reaches the maximum predetermined amount of $50,000. On October 1, 1994, the $50,000 jackpot is paid to B.

(ii) Under paragraph (g)(4) of this section economic performance with respect to the $50,000 jackpot liability occurs on the date the jackpot is paid to B. Consequently, $50,000 is incurred by Y for the 1994 taxable year.

*Example (5).* Insurance, warranty, and service contracts.

(i) V corporation, a calendar year, accrual method taxpayer, manufactures toys. V enters into a contract with W, an unrelated insurance company, on December 15, 1992. The contract obligates V to pay W a premium of $500,000 before the end of 1995. The contract obligates W to satisfy any liability of V resulting from claims made during 1993 or 1994 against V by any third party for damages attributable to defects in toys manufactured by V. Pursuant to the contract, V pays W a premium of $500,000 on October 1, 1995.

(ii) Assuming the arrangement constitutes insurance, under paragraph (g)(5) of this section economic performance occurs as the premium is paid. Thus, $500,000 is incurred by V for the 1995 taxable year.

*Example (6).* Insurance, warranty, and service contracts.

(i) Y corporation, a calendar year, accrual method taxpayer, is a common carrier. On December 15, 1992, Y enters into a contract with Z, an unrelated insurance company, under which Z must satisfy any liability of Y that arises during the succeeding 5 years for damages under a workers compensation act or out of any tort, provided the event that causes the damages occurs during 1993 or 1994. Under the contract, Y pays $360,000 to Z on December 31, 1993.

(ii) Assuming the arrangement constitutes insurance, under paragraph (g)(5) of this section economic performance occurs as the premium is paid. Consequently, $360,000 is incurred by Y for the 1993 taxable year. The period for which the $360,000 amount is permitted to be taken into account is determined under the capitalization rules because the insurance contract is an asset having a useful life extending substantially beyond the close of the taxable year.

*Example (7).* Insurance, warranty, and service contracts. Assume the seine facts as in Example 6, except that Y is obligated to pay the first $5,000 of any damages covered by the arrangement with Z. Y is, in effect, self-insured to the extent of this $5,000 "deductible." Thus, under paragraph (g)(2) of this section, economic performance with respect to the $5,000 liability does not occur until the amount is paid to the person to which the tort or workers compensation liability is owed.

*Example (8).* Taxes.

(i) The laws of State A provide that every person owning personal property located in State A on the first day of January shall be liable for tax thereon and that a lien for the tax shall attach as of that date. In addition, the laws of State A provide that 60% of the tax is due on the first day of December following the lien date and the remaining 40% is due on the first day of July of the succeeding year. On January 1, 1992, X corporation, a calendar year, accrual method taxpayer, owns personal property located in State A. State A imposes a $10,000 tax on S with respect to that property on January 1, 1992. X pays State A $6,000 of the tax on December 1, 1992, and the remaining $4,000 on July 1, 1993.

(ii) Under paragraph (g)(6) of this section, economic performance with respect to $6,000 of the tax liability occurs on December 1, 1992. Consequently, $6,000 is incurred by X for the 1992 taxable year. Economic performance with respect to the remaining $4,000 of the tax liability occurs on July 1, 1993. If X has adopted the recurring item exception described in § 1.461-5 as a method of accounting for taxes, and as of December 31, 1992, all events have occurred that determine the liability of X for the remaining $4,000, X also incurs $4,000 for the 1992 taxable year. If X does not adopt the recurring item exception method, the $4,000 is not incurred by X until the 1993 taxable year.

**(h) Liabilities arising under the Nuclear Waste Policy Act of 1982.** Notwithstanding the principles of paragraph (d) of this section, economic performance with respect to the liability of an owner or generator of nuclear waste to make payments to the Department of Energy ("DOE") pursuant to a contract required by the Nuclear Waste Policy Act of 1982 (Pub. L. 97-425, 42 U.S.C. 10101-10226 (1982)) occurs as each payment under the contract is made to DOE and not when DOE satisfies its obligations under the contract. This rule applies to the continuing fee required by 42 U.S.C. 10222(a)(2) (1982), as well as the one-time fee required by 42 U.S.C. 10222(a)(3) (1982). For rules relating to when economic performance occurs with respect to interest, see paragraph (e) of this section.

**(i) [Reserved]**

**(j) Contingent liabilities. [Reserved]**

**(k) Special effective dates.** *(1) In general.* Except as otherwise provided in this paragraph (k), section 461(h) and this section apply to liabilities that would, under the law in effect before the enactment of section 461(h), be allowable as a deduction or otherwise incurred after July 18, 1984. For example, the economic performance requirement applies to all liabilities arising under a workers compensation act or out of any tort that would, under the law in effect before the enactment of section 461(h), be incurred after July 18, 1984. For taxable years ending before April 7, 1995, see Q&A-2 of § 1.461-7T (as it appears in 26 CFR part 1 revised April 1, 1995), which provides an election to make this change in method of accounting applicable to either the portion of the first taxable year that occurs after July 18, 1984 (part-year change method), or the entire first taxable year ending after July 18, 1984 (full-year change method). With respect to the effective date rules for interest, section 461(h) applies to interest accruing under any obligation (whether or not evidenced by a debt instrument) if the obligation is incurred in any transaction occurring after June 8, 1984, and is not incurred under a written contract which was binding on March 1, 1984, and at all times thereafter until the obligation is incurred. Interest accruing under an obligation described in the preceding sentence is subject to section 461(h) even if the interest accrues before July 19, 1984. Similarly, interest accruing under any obligation incurred in a transaction occurring before June 9, 1984, (or under a written contract which was binding on March 1, 1984, and at all times thereafter until the obligation is incurred) is not subject to section 461(h) even to the extent the interest accrues after July 18, 1984.

*(2) Long-term contracts.* Except as otherwise provided in paragraph (M)(2) of this section, In the case of liabilities described in paragraph (d)(2)(ii) of this section (relating to long-term contracts), paragraph (d)(2)(ii) of this section applies to liabilities that would, but for the enactment of section 461(h), be allowable as a deduction or otherwise incurred for taxable years beginning after December 31, 1991.

*(3) Payment liabilities.* Except as otherwise provided in paragraph (m)(2) of this section, in the case of liabilities described in paragraph (g) of this section (other than liabilities arising under a workers compensation act or out of any tort described in paragraph (g)(2) of this section), paragraph (g) of this section applies to liabilities that would, but for the enactment of section 461(h), be allowable as a deduction or otherwise incurred for taxable years beginning after December 31, 1991.

**(l) [Reserved]**

**(m) Change in method of accounting required by this section.** *(1) In general.* For the first taxable year ending after July 18, 1984, a taxpayer is granted the consent of the Commissioner to change its method of accounting for liabilities to comply with the provisions of this section pursuant to any of the following procedures:

(i) For taxable years ending before April 7, 1995, the part-year change in method election described in Q&A-2 through Q&A-6 and Q&A-8 through Q&A-10 of § 1.461-7T (as it appears in 26 CFR part 1 revised April 1, 1995);

(ii) For taxable years ending before April 7, 1995, the full-year change in method election described in Q&A-2 through Q&A-6 and Q&A-8 through Q&A-10 of § 1.461-7T (as it appears in 26 CFR part 1 revised April 1, 1995); or

(iii) For taxable years ending before April 7, 1995, if no election is made, the cut-off method described in Q&A-1 and Q&A-11 of § 1.461-7T (as it appears in 26 CFR part 1 revised April 1, 1995).

*(2) Change in method of accounting for long-term contracts and payment liabilities.* (i) First taxable year beginning after December 31, 1991. For the first taxable year beginning after December 31, 1991, a taxpayer is granted the consent of the Commissioner to change its method of accounting for long-term contract liabilities described in paragraph (D)(2)(ii) of this section and payment liabilities described in paragraph (g) of this section (other than liabilities arising under a workers compensation act or out of any tort described in paragraph (g)(2) of this section) to comply with the provisions of this section. The change must be made in accordance with paragraph (m)(1)(ii) or (m)(1)(iii) of this section, except the effective date is the first day of the first taxable year beginning December 31, 1991.

(ii) Retroactive change in method of accounting for long-term contracts and payment liabilities. For the first taxable year beginning after December 31, 1989, or the first taxable year beginning after December 31, 1990, a taxpayer is granted the consent of the Commissioner to change its method of accounting for long-term contract liabilities described in paragraph (d)(2)(ii) of this section and payment liabilities described in paragraph (g) of this section (other than liabilities arising under a workers compensation act or out of any tort described in paragraph (g)(2) of this section) to comply with the provisions of this section. The change must be made in accordance with paragraph (m)(1)(ii) or (m)(1)(iii) of this section, except the effective date is the first day of the first taxable year beginning after December 31, 1989, or the first day of the first taxable year beginning after December 31, 1990. For taxable years ending before April 7, 1995, the taxpayer may make the change in method of accounting, including a full-year change in method election under paragraph (m)(1)(ii) of this section and Q&A-5 of § 1.461-7T (as it appears in 26 CFR part 1 revised April 1, 1995), by filing an amended return for such year, provided the amended return is filed on or before October 7, 1992.

---

T.D. 8408, 4/9/92, amend T.D. 8491, 10/8/93, T.D. 8593, 4/7/95, T.D. 8820, 5/17/99.

---

### § 1.461-5 Recurring item exception.

**(a) In general.** Except as otherwise provided in paragraph (c) of this section, a taxpayer using an accrual method of accounting may adopt the recurring item exception described in paragraph (b) of this section as method of accounting for one or more types of recurring items incurred by the taxpayer. In the case of the "other payment liabilities" described in § 1.461-4(g)(7), the Commissioner may provide for the application of the recurring item exception by regulation, revenue procedure or revenue ruling.

**(b) Requirements for use of the exception.** *(1) General rule.* Under the recurring item exception, a liability is treated as incurred for a taxable year if—

(i) As of the end of that taxable year, all events have occurred that establish the fact of the liability and the amount of the liability can be determined with reasonable accuracy;

(ii) Economic performance with respect to the liability occurs on or before the earlier of—

(A) The date the taxpayer files a timely (including extensions) return for that taxable year; or

(B) The 15th day of the 9th calendar month after the close of that taxable year;

(iii) The liability is recurring in nature; and

(iv) Either—

(A) The amount of the liability is not material; or

(B) The accrual of the liability for that taxable year results in a better matching of the liability with the income to which it relates than would result from accruing the liability for the taxable year in which economic performance occurs.

*(2) Amended returns.* A taxpayer may file an amended return treating a liability as incurred under the recurring item exception for a taxable year if economic performance with respect to the liability occurs after the taxpayer files a return for that year, but within 8 ½ months after the close of that year.

*(3) Liabilities that are recurring in nature.* A liability is recurring if it can generally be expected to be incurred from one taxable year to the next. However, a taxpayer may treat such a liability as recurring in nature even if it is not incurred by the taxpayer in each taxable year. In addition, a liability that has never previously been incurred by a taxpayer may be treated as recurring if it is reasonable to expect that the liability will be incurred on a recurring basis in the future.

*(4) Materiality requirement.* For purposes of this paragraph (b):

(i) In determining whether a liability is material, consideration shall be given to the amount of the liability in absolute terms and in relation to the amount of other items of income and expense attributable to the same activity.

(ii) A liability is material if it is material for financial statement purposes under generally accepted accounting principles.

(iii) A liability that is immaterial for financial statement purposes under generally accepted accounting principles may be material for purposes of this paragraph (b).

*(5) Matching requirement.* (i) In determining whether the matching requirement of paragraph (b)(1)(iv)(B) of this section is satisfied, generally accepted accounting principles are an important factor, but are not dispositive.

(ii) In the case of a liability described in paragraph (g)(3) (rebates and refunds), paragraph (g)(4) (awards, prizes, and jackpots), paragraph (g)(5) (insurance, warranty, and service contracts), paragraph (g)(6) (taxes), or paragraph (h) (continuing fees under the Nuclear Waste Policy Act of 1982) of § 1.461-4, the matching requirement of paragraph (b)(1)(iv)(B) of this section shall be deemed satisfied.

**(c) Types of liabilities not eligible for treatment under the recurring item exception.** The recurring item exception does not apply to any liability of a taxpayer described in paragraph (e) (interest), paragraph (g)(2) (workers compensation, tort, breach of contract, and violation of law), or paragraph (g)(7) (other liabilities) of § 1.461-4. Moreover, the recurring item exception does not apply to any liability incurred by a tax shelter, as defined in section 461(i) and § 1.448-1T(b).

**(d) Time and manner of adopting the recurring item exception.** *(1) In general.* The recurring item exception is a method of accounting that must be consistently applied with respect to a type of item, or for all items, from one taxable year to the next in order to clearly reflect income. A taxpayer is permitted to adopt the recurring item exception as part of its method of accounting for any type of item for the first taxable year in which that type of item is incurred. Except as otherwise provided, the rules of section 446(e) and § 1.446-1(e) apply to changes to or from the recurring item exception as a method of accounting. For taxable years ending before April 7, 1995, see Q&A-7 of § 1.461-7T (as it appears in 26 CFR part 1 revised April 1, 1995) for rules concerning the time and manner of adopting the recurring item exception for taxable years that include July 19, 1984. For purposes of this section, items are to be classified by type in a manner that results in classifications that are no less inclusive than the classifications of production costs provided in the full-absorption regulations of § 1.471-11(b) and (c), whether or not the taxpayer is required to maintain inventories.

*(2) Change to the recurring item exception method for the first taxable year beginning after December 31, 1991.* (i) In general. For the first taxable year beginning after December 31, 1991, a taxpayer is granted the consent of the Commissioner to change to the recurring item exception method of accounting. A taxpayer is also granted the consent of the Commissioner to expand or modify its use of the recurring item exception method for the first taxable year beginning after December 31, 1991. For each trade or business for which a taxpayer elects to use the recurring item exception method, the taxpayer must use the same method of change (cut-off or full-year change) it is using for that trade or busi-

ness under § 1.461-4(m). For taxable years ending before April 7, 1995, see Q&A-11 of § 1.461-7T (as it appears in 26 CFR part 1 revised April 1, 1995) for an explanation of how amounts are taken into account under the cut- off method (except that, for purposes of this paragraph (d)(2), the change applies to all amounts otherwise incurred on or after the first day of the first taxable year beginning after December 31, 1991). For taxable years ending before April 7, 1995, see Q&A-6 of § 1.461-7T (as it appears in 26 CFR part 1 revised April 1, 1995) for an explanation of how amounts are taken into account under the full-year change method (except that the change in method occurs on the first day of the first taxable year beginning after December 31, 1991). For taxable years ending before April 7, 1995, the full-year change in method may result in a section 481(a) adjustment that must be taken into account in the manner described in Q&A-8 and Q&A-9 of § 1.461-7T (as it appears in 26 CFR part 1 revised April 1, 1995) (except that the taxable year of change is the first taxable year beginning after December 31, 1991).

(ii) Manner of changing to the recurring item exception method. For the first taxable year beginning after December 31, 1991, a taxpayer may change to the recurring item exception method by accounting for the item on its timely filed original return for such taxable year (including extensions). For taxable years ending before April 7, 1995, the automatic consent of the Commissioner is limited to those items accounted for under the recurring item exception method on the timely filed return, unless the taxpayer indicates a wider scope of change by filing the statement provided in Q&A-7(b)(2) of § 1.461-7T (as it appears in 26 CFR part 1 revised April 1, 1995).

*(3) Retroactive change to the recurring item exception method.* For the first taxable year beginning after December 31, 1989, or December 31, 1990, a taxpayer is granted consent of the Commissioner to change to the recurring item exception method of accounting, provided the taxpayer complies with paragraph (d)(2) of this section on either the original return for such year or on an amended return for such year filed on or before October 7, 1991. For this purpose the effective date is the first day of the first taxable year beginning after December 31, 1989, or the first day of the first taxable year beginning after December 31, 1990. A taxpayer is also granted the consent of the Commissioner to expand or modify its use of the recurring item exception method for the first taxable year beginning after December 31, 1989, December 31, 1990, or December 31, 1991.

**(e) Examples.** The following examples illustrate the principles of this section:

*Example (1).* Requirements for the use of the recurring item exception.

(i) Y corporation, a calendar year, accrual method taxpayer, manufactures and distributes video cassette recorders. Y timely files its federal income tax return for each taxable year on the extended due date for the return (September 15, of the following taxable year). Y offers to refund the price of a recorder to a purchaser not satisfied with the recorder. During 1992, 100 purchasers request a refund of the $500 purchase price. Y refunds $30,000 on or before September 15, 1993, and the remaining $20,000 after such date but before the end of 1993.

(ii) Under paragraph (g)(3) of § 1.461-4, economic performance with respect to $30,000 of the refund liability occurs on September 15, 1993. Assume the refund is deductible (or allowable as an adjustment to gross receipts or cost of goods sold) when incurred. If Y does not adopt the recurring item exception with respect to rebates and refunds, the $30,000 refund is incurred by Y for the 1993 taxable year. However, if Y has properly adopted the recurring item exception method of accounting under this section, and as of December 31, 1992, all events have occurred that determine the fact of the liability for the $30,000 refund, Y incurs that amount for the 1992 taxable year. Because economic performance (payment) with respect to the remaining $20,000 occurs after September 15, 1993 (more than 8½ months after the end of 1992), that amount is not eligible for recurring item treatment under this section. Thus, the $20,000 amount is not incurred by Y until the 1993 taxable year.

*Example (2).* Requirements for use of the recurring item exception; amended returns. The facts are the same as in Example 2, except that Y files its income tax return for 1992 on March 15, 1993, and Y does not refund the price of any recorder before that date. Under paragraph (b)(1) of this section, the refund liability is not eligible for the recurring item exception because economic performance with respect to the refund does not occur before Y files a return for the taxable year for which the item would have been incurred under the exception. However, since economic performance occurs within 8½ months after 1992, Y may file an amended return claiming the $30,000 as incurred for its 1992 taxable year (see paragraph (b)(2) of this section).

T.D. 8408, 4/9/92, amend T.D. 8593, 4/7/95.

### § 1.461-6 Economic performance when certain liabilities are assigned or are extinguished by the establishment of a fund.

**(a) Qualified assignments of certain personal injury liabilities under section 130.** In the case of a qualified assignment (within the meaning of section 130(c)), economic performance occurs as a taxpayer-assignor makes payments that are excludible from the income of the assignee under section 130(a).

**(b) Section 468B.** Economic performance occurs as a taxpayer makes qualified payments to a designated settlement fund under section 468B, relating to special rules for designated settlement funds.

**(c) Payments to other funds or persons that constitute economic performance. [Reserved]**

**(d) Effective dates.** The rules in paragraph (a) of this section apply to payments after July 18, 1984.

T.D. 8408, 4/9/92.

### § 301.9100-16T Election to accrue vacation pay (temporary).

**(a) In general.** Section 463 provides that taxpayers whose taxable income is computed under an accrual method of accounting may elect without the consent of the Commissioner, to deduct certain amounts with respect to vacation pay which, because of contingencies, would not otherwise be deductible. Such election must apply to the liability for all vacation pay accounts maintained by the taxpayer within a single trade or business if the liability is contingent when vacation pay is earned.

**(b) Time for making election.** *(1)* In the case of a taxpayer who established or maintained a vacation pay account pursuant to I.T. 3956 and who continued to maintain such account pursuant to section 97 of the Technical Amendments Act of 1958, as amended, for its last taxable year ending before January 1, 1973, the election must be made for each trade or business for which such account was maintained on or before the later of (i) July 21, 1975, or (ii) the due date for filing the income tax return (determined with regard to any extensions of time granted the taxpayer for filing such return) for the first taxable year beginning after December 31, 1973. The election pursuant to this paragraph shall be effective with respect to an account described in this paragraph (b)(1) for taxable years ending after December 31, 1972. Failure to file such election shall constitute a change in the method of accounting for vacation pay for the first taxable year ending after December 31, 1972. Such change in accounting method will be considered a change initiated by the taxpayer.

*(2)* In the case of a trade or business of a taxpayer to which paragraph (b)(1) does not apply, the election provided for in this section may be made for any taxable year beginning after December 31, 1973, by making the election not later than (i) July 21, 1975, or (ii) the due date for filing the income tax return (determined with regard to any extensions of time granted the taxpayer for filing such return) for the first taxable year for which the election is made.

*(3)* A taxpayer who elects under section 463 to treat vacation pay as provided in this section and who wishes to revoke such election may only do so with the consent of the Commissioner. Such revocation shall constitute a change in the method of accounting.

**(c) Manner of making election.** *(1)* Except as otherwise provided in paragraph (c)(2) of this section, the election provided for in this section must be made by means of a statement attached to a timely filed income tax return. The statement shall indicate that the taxpayer is electing to apply the provisions of section 463, and shall contain the following information:

(i) The taxpayer's name and a description of each vacation pay plan to which the election is to apply.

(ii) A schedule with appropriate explanations showing—

(A) In the case of a vacation pay account established or maintained pursuant to I.T. 3956 and section 97 of the Technical Amendments Act of 1958, as amended,

(1) The balance of each such vacation pay account maintained by the taxpayer, and

(2) The amount, determined as if the taxpayer had maintained a vacation pay account for the last taxable year ending before January 1, 1973, representing the taxpayer's liability for vacation pay earned by employees, before the close of the taxable year and payable during such taxable year or within 12 months following the close of such taxable year.

(B) In the case of other vacation pay accounts, the amount of the closing balances the taxpayer would have had for the taxpayer's 3 taxable years immediately preceding the taxable year for which the election was made, had the taxpayer maintained an account representing the taxpayer's liability for vacation pay earned by the employees before the close of the taxable year and payable during the taxable year or within 12 months following the close of the taxable year throughout the 3 immediately preceding taxable years.

(iii) The amounts accrued and deducted for prior years for vacation pay but not paid at the close of the taxable year preceding the year for which the election is made.

*(2)* Where a taxpayer has filed its return for a taxable year beginning after December 31, 1973 prior to July 21, 1975, and has not made the election pursuant to this section, the election may be made by filing an amended return (showing adjustments, in any) for such year and attaching the statement required by paragraph (c)(1) of this section on or before July 21, 1975.

**(d)** The time for making the election may be illustrated by the following examples:

*Example (1).* X, whose taxable year begins on February 1, files its return based on the accrual method of accounting. X has continuously accrued and deducted for income tax purposes contingent amounts of vacation pay, pursuant to I.T. 3956. Pursuant to section 463 and these regulations, in order for X to continue accruing and deducting its vacation pay amounts, X must elect to account for vacation pay under section 463 by attaching the election to its timely filed return for its taxable year ending on January 31, 1975 or if X has already filed such return by July 21, 1975 without such election, by filing the election statement with an amended return by July 21, 1975. If X does not make the election under section 463, X will be treated as having initiated a change in its method of accounting for vacation pay in its taxable year ending on January 31, 1973.

*Example (2).* Y, a calendar year taxpayer, files its returns based on the accrual method of accounting. Y deducted its vacation pay amounts only when paid since such amounts were contingent when earned and Y was not entitled to the benefits of I.T. 3956. Y may elect for its taxable year ending on December 31, 1974, to deduct certain amounts with respect to contingent vacation pay which were not otherwise deductible, by filing an election pursuant to these regulations with its timely filed income tax return for such year or if such return was already filed by [insert date 90 days after publication of this document as a Treasury decision], without such election, by filing the election with an amended return filed by July 21, 1975. If Y does not make the election for its taxable year ending on December 31, 1974, Y may make the election with respect to any subsequent taxable year by filing an election with its return for such year.

T.D. 7353, 4/18/75, amend T.D. 8435, 9/18/92.

**Proposed § 1.465-1 General rules; limitation of deductions to amount at risk.** [*For Preamble, see ¶ 150,479*]

***Caution:*** The Treasury has not yet amended Reg § 1.465-1 to reflect changes made by P.L. 101-508, P.L. 99-514, P.L. 98-369, P.L. 96-222.

**(a) In general.** For taxable years beginning after December 31, 1975, section 465 generally limits the amount of any loss described in section 465(d) that is otherwise deductible in connection with an activity described in section 465(c)(1). Under section 465 the amount of the loss is allowed as a deduction only to the extent that the taxpayer is at risk with respect to the activity at the close of the taxable year. The determination of the amount the taxpayer is at risk in cases where the activity is engaged in by an entity separate from the taxpayer is made as of the close of the taxable year of the entity engaging in the activity (for example, a partnership). For the purposes of these regulations, in cases where the activity is engaged in by an entity separate from the taxpayer references to a taxable year shall apply to the taxable year of the entity unless otherwise stated. For rules determining the amount at risk and for more specific rules regarding the effective dates, see §§ 1.465-20 through 1.465-25 and 1.465-95.

**(b) Substance over form.** In applying section 465 and these regulations, substance will prevail over form. Regardless of the form a transaction may take, the taxpayer's amount at risk will not be increased if the transaction is inconsistent with normal commercial practices or is, in essence, a device to avoid section 465. See § 1.465-4 for rules regarding attempts to avoid the at risk provisions.

**(c) Activities.** See sections 465(c)(1)(A) through (D) and §§ 1.465-42 through 1.465-45 for the activities to which section 465 applies for taxable years beginning generally after December 31, 1975. These activities are holding, producing, or distributing movies and video tapes, farming, leasing of personal property, and exploring for or exploiting oil and gas resources. See section 465(c)(3) and section 465(c)(1)(E) for additional activities to which section 465 applies for taxable years beginning generally after December 31, 1978.

**(d) Taxpayers affected by at risk provisions.** *(1)* For taxable years beginning generally after December 31, 1975, section 465 applies to all noncorporate taxpayers, to electing small business corporations (as defined in section 1371(b)), and to personal holding companies (as defined in section 542). For special rules relating to electing small business corporations, see § 1.465-10.

*(2)* See section 465(a)(1)(C) for additional taxpayers to whom section 465 applies for taxable years beginning generally after December 31, 1978.

**(e) Basis.** The provisions of section 465 and the regulations thereunder are only intended to limit the extent to which certain losses in connection with covered activities may be deducted in a given year by a taxpayer. Section 465 does not apply for other purposes, such as determining adjusted basis. Thus, for example, the adjusted basis of a partner in a partnership interest is not affected by section 465.

**§ 1.465-1T Aggregation of certain activities.**

**(a) General rule.** A partner in a partnership or an S corporation shareholder may aggregate and treat as a single activity—

*(1)* The holding, production, or distribution of more than one motion picture film or video tape by the partnership or S corporation,

*(2)* The farming (as defined in section 464(e)) of more than one farm by the partnership or S corporation,

*(3)* The exploration for, or exploitation of, oil and gas resources with respect to more than one oil and gas property by the partnership or S corporation, or

*(4)* The exploration for, or exploitation of, geothermal deposits (within the meaning of section 613(e)(3)) with respect to more than one geothermal property by the partnership or S corporation.

Thus, for example, if a partnership or S corporation is engaged in the activity of exploring for, or exploiting, oil and gas resources with respect to 10 oil and gas properties, a partner or S corporation shareholder may aggregate those properties and treat the aggregated oil and gas activities as a single activity. If that partnership or S corporation also is engaged in the activity of farming with respect to two farms, the partner or shareholder may aggregate the farms and treat the aggregated farming activities as a single separate activity. Except as provided in section 465(c)(2)(B)(ii), the partner or shareholder cannot aggregate the farming activity with the oil and gas activity.

**(b) Effective date.** This section shall apply to taxable years beginning during 1984.

T.D. 8012, 3/7/85.

**§ 7.465-1 Amounts at risk with respect to activities begun prior to effective date; in general.**

***Caution:*** The Treasury has not yet amended Reg § 7.465-1 to reflect changes made by P.L. 98-369, P.L. 97-354, P.L. 96-222, P.L. 95-600.

Section 465 provides that a taxpayer (other than a corporation which is not a subchapter S corporation or a personal holding company) engaged in certain activities may not deduct losses from such activity to the extent the losses exceed the amount the taxpayer is at work with respect to the activity. For the types of activities to which section 465 applies and for determining what constitutes a separate activity, see section 465(c). Section 465 generally applies to losses attributable to amounts paid or incurred in taxable years beginning after December 31, 1975. For the purposes of applying the at risk limitation to activities begun before the effective date of the provision (and which were not excepted from application of the provision), it is necessary to determine the amount at risk as of the first day of the first taxable year beginning after December 31, 1975. The amount at risk in an activity as of the first day of the first taxable year of the taxpayer beginning after December 31, 1975, (for the purposes of § 7.465-1 through 7.465-5 such first day shall be referred to as the effective date) shall be determined according to the rules provided in sections 7.465-2 through 7.465-5.

T.D. 7504, 8/19/77.

PAR. 2. Sections 7.465-1 through 7.465-5 of this chapter (26 CFR Part 7), promulgated by Treasury Decision 7504, are hereby revoked.

**Proposed § 7.465-1 Through 7.465-5 [Revoked]** [*For Preamble, see ¶ 150,479*]

**Proposed § 1.465-2 General rules; allowance of deductions.** [*For Preamble, see ¶ 150,479*]

***Caution:*** The Treasury has not yet amended Reg § 1.465-2 to reflect changes made by P.L. 101-508, P.L. 99-514, P.L. 98-369, P.L. 96-222.

**(a) In general.** In any taxable year, there are two ways in which deductions allocable to an activity to which section 465 applies will be allowable under section 465. First, deductions allocable to an activity and otherwise allowable will be allowable in a taxable year to the extent of income received or accrued from the activity in that taxable year. See the example at § 1.465-11(c)(2). Thus, to the extent there is income from the activity in a taxable year, deductions allocable to that activity will be allowable without regard to the amount at risk. Second, losses from the activity (that is, the excess of deductions allocable to the activity over the income received or accrued from the activity) will be allowable to the extent the taxpayer is at risk with respect to that activity at the close of the taxable year. See the example at § 1.465-11(a)(2). Also see §§ 1.465-11 through 1.465-13 for the definition of loss.

**(b) Carryover of loss.** A loss which is disallowed by reason of section 465(a) shall be treated as a deduction for the succeeding taxable year with respect to the same activity to which it is allocable. In the succeeding taxable year there will again be two ways for the deduction to be allowable. There is no limit to the number of years to which a taxpayer may carry over a loss disallowed solely by reason of section 465(a).

### § 7.465-2 Determination of amount at risk.

***Caution:*** The Treasury has not yet amended Reg § 7.465-2 to reflect changes made by P.L. 98-369, P.L. 97-354, P.L. 96-222, P.L. 95-600.

**(a) Initial amount.** The amount a taxpayer is at risk on the effective date with respect to an activity to which section 465 applies shall be determined in accordance with this section. The initial amount the taxpayer is at risk in the activity shall be the taxpayer's initial basis in the activity as modified by disregarding amounts described in section 465(b)(3) or (4) (relating generally to amounts protected against loss or borrowed from related persons).

**(b) Succeeding adjustments.** For each taxable year ending before the effective date, the initial amount at risk shall be increased and decreased by the items which increased and decreased the taxpayer's basis in the activity in that year as modified by disregarding the amounts described in section 465(b)(3) or (4).

**(c) Application of losses and withdrawals.** *(1)* Losses described in section 465(d) which are incurred in taxable years beginning prior to January 1, 1976 and deducted in such taxable years, will be treated as reducing first that portion of the taxpayer's basis which is attributable to amounts not at risk. On the other hand, withdrawals made in taxable years beginning before January 1, 1976, will be treated as reducing the amount which the taxpayer is at risk.

*(2)* Therefore, if in a taxable year beginning prior to January 1, 1976 there is a loss described in section 465(d), it shall reduce the amount at risk only to the extent it exceeds the amount of the taxpayer's basis which is not at risk. For the purposes of this paragraph, the taxpayer's basis which is not at risk is that portion of the taxpayer's basis in the activity (as of the close of the taxable year and prior to reduction for the loss) which is attributable to amounts described in section 465(b)(3) or (4).

**(d) Amount at risk shall not be less than zero.** If, after determining the amount described in paragraph (a), (b), and (c) of this section, the amount at risk (but for this paragraph) would be less than zero, the amount at risk on the effective date shall be zero.

---

T.D. 7504, 8/19/77.

---

### Proposed § 1.465-3 General rules; amount at risk below zero. [*For Preamble, see ¶ 150,479*]

***Caution:*** The Treasury has not yet amended Reg § 1.465-3 to reflect changes made by P.L. 101-508, P.L. 99-514, P.L. 98-369, P.L. 96-222.

**(a) Loss deductions.** The amount of loss which is allowed for a taxable year cannot reduce a taxpayer's amount at risk below zero. Otherwise allowable losses for a taxable year which exceed a taxpayer's amount at risk shall be treated in accordance with § 1.465-2.

**(b) Negative at risk.** A taxpayer's amount at risk may be reduced below zero. For example, if a taxpayer's amount at risk in an activity is $100 and if $120 is distributed to the taxpayer from the activity, (or if a $120 recourse loan is converted to nonrecourse), the taxpayer's amount at risk is reduced to negative $20. In that event, for the taxpayer to restore the amount the taxpayer is at risk in the activity to zero, the amount at risk must be increased by $20. Thus, in such a case if in the succeeding taxable year the taxpayer incurs a loss described in section 465(d) of $40, the amount at risk must be increased by $60 ($40 + $20) in order for the full $40 to be allowed under section 465.

**(c) Recapture of certain loss deductions.** For taxable years beginning after December 31, 1978 see section 465(e) for rules relating to the recapture of certain loss deductions.

### § 7.465-3 Allocation of loss for different taxable years.

If the taxable year of the entity conducting the activity differs from that of the taxpayer, the loss attributable to the activity for the first taxable year of the entity ending after the beginning of the first taxable year of the taxpayer beginning after December 31, 1975, shall be allocated in the following manner. That portion of the loss from the activity for such taxable year of the entity which bears the same ratio as the number of days in such taxable year before January 1, 1976, divided by the total number of days in the taxable year, shall be attributable to taxable years of the taxpayer beginning before January 1, 1976. Consequently, that portion shall be treated in accordance with § 7.465-2.

---

T.D. 7504, 8/19/77.

---

### Proposed § 1.465-4 General rules; rules regarding attempts to avoid the at risk provisions. [*For Preamble, see ¶ 150,479*]

***Caution:*** The Treasury has not yet amended Reg § 1.465-4 to reflect changes made by P.L. 101-508, P.L. 99-514, P.L. 98-369, P.L. 96-222.

**(a) General rule.** If a taxpayer engages in a pattern of conduct which is not within normal commercial practice or has the effect of avoiding the provisions of section 465, the taxpayer's amount at risk may be adjusted to reflect more accurately the amount which is actually at risk. For example, increases in the amount at risk occurring toward the close of a taxable year which have the effect of increasing the amount of losses which will be allowed to the taxpayer under section 465 for the taxable year will be examined closely. If, considering all the facts and circumstances, it appears that the event which increases the amount at risk at the close of the taxable year will be accompanied by an event which decreases the amount at risk after the close of the taxable year, these amounts will be disregarded in determining the amount at risk unless the taxpayer can establish—

*(1)* The existence of a valid business purpose for increasing and then decreasing the amount at risk; and

*(2)* That the increases and decreases are not a device for avoiding section 465.

**(b) Facts and circumstances.** The facts and circumstances to be considered include—

*(1)* The length of time between the increase and decrease in the amount at risk;

*(2)* The nature of the activity and deviations from normal business practice in the conduct of that activity;

*(3)* The use of those amounts which increased the amount at risk toward the close of the taxable year;

*(4)* Contractual arrangements between parties to the activity; and

*(5)* The occurrence of unanticipated events which make the decrease in the amount at risk necessary.

### § 7.465-4 Insufficient records.

If sufficient records do not exist to accurately determine under § 7.465-2 the amount which a taxpayer is at risk on the effective date, the amount at risk shall be the taxpayer's basis in the activity reduced (but not below zero) by the taxpayer's share of amounts described in section 465(b)(3) or (4) with respect to the activity on the day before the effective date.

T.D. 7504, 8/19/77.

**Proposed § 1.465-5 General rules; recourse liabilities which become nonrecourse upon the occurrence of an event.** [*For Preamble, see ¶ 150,479*]

***Caution:*** The Treasury has not yet amended Reg § 1.465-5 to reflect changes made by P.L. 101-508, P.L. 99-514, P.L. 98-369, P.L. 96-222.

In the case of liabilities which are recourse for a period of time and then after the occurrence of an event or lapse of a period of time become nonrecourse, a taxpayer shall be considered at risk during the period of recourse liability if—

**(a)** On the basis of all the facts and circumstances, the reasons for entering into such a borrowing arrangement are primarily business motivated and not primarily related to Federal income tax consequences; and

**(b)** Such a borrowing arrangement is consistent with the normal commercial practice of financing the activity for which the money is being borrowed.

**§ 7.465-5 Examples.**

***Caution:*** The Treasury has not yet amended Reg § 7.465-5 to reflect changes made by P.L. 98-369, P.L. 97-354, P.L. 96-222, P.L. 95-600.

The provisions of § 7.465-1 and § 7.465-2 may be illustrated by the following examples:

*Example (1).* J and K, as equal partners, form partnership JK on January 1, 1975. Partnership JK is engaged solely in an activity described in section 465(c)(1). On January 1, 1975, each partner contributes $10,000 in cash from personal assets to JK. On July 1, 1975, JK borrows $40,000 (of which J's share is $20,000) from a bank under a nonrecourse financing arrangement secured only by the new equipment (for use in the activity) purchased with the $40,000. On September 1, 1975, JK reduces the amount due on the loan to $36,000 (of which J's share is $18,000). On October 1, 1975, JK distributes $3,000 to each partner. For taxable year 1975, JK has no income or loss. Although J's basis in the activity is $25,000 ($10,000 + $18,000 – $3,000) J's amount at risk on the effective date is $7,000 determined as follows:

| | |
|---|---|
| Initial amount at risk | $10,000 |
| Plus: Items which increased basis other than amounts described in sec. 465(b)(3) or (4) | 0 |
| Total | 10,000 |
| Less: Distribution | 3,000 |
| J's amount at risk on effective date | 7,000 |

*Example (2).* Assume the same facts as in Example (1) except that JK has a loss (as described in section 465(d)) for 1975 of which J's share is $12,000. Although J's basis in the activity is $13,000 ($10,000 + $18,000 – ($3,000 + $12,000)) J's amount at risk on the effective date is $7,000 determined as follows:

| | |
|---|---|
| Initial amount at risk | $10,000 |
| Plus: Items which increased basis other than amounts described in sec. 465(b)(3) or (4) | 0 |
| Total | 10,000 |
| Less: Distribution | 3,000 |
| Portion of loss ($12,000) in excess of portion of basis not at risk ($18,000) | 0 |
| | 3,000 |
| J's amount at risk on effective date | 7,000 |

*Example (3).* Assume the same facts as in Example (1) except that JK has a loss (as described in section 465(d)) for 1975, and J's share is $23,000. J's basis in the activity is $2,000 ($10,000 + $18,000 – ($3,000 + $23,000)). The amount at risk on the effective date is determined as follows:

| | |
|---|---|
| Initial amount at risk | $10,000 |
| Plus: Items which increased basis other than amounts described in sec. 465(b)(3) or (4) | 0 |
| | $10,000 |
| Less: Distribution | 3,000 |
| Portion of loss ($23,000) in excess of portion of basis not at risk ($18,000) | 5,000 |
| | 8,000 |
| J's amount at risk on the effective date | 2,000 |

T.D. 7504, 8/19/77.

**Proposed § 1.465-6 General rules; amounts protected against loss.** [*For Preamble, see ¶ 150,479*]

***Caution:*** The Treasury has not yet amended Reg § 1.465-6 to reflect changes made by P.L. 101-508, P.L. 99-514, P.L. 98-369, P.L. 96-222.

**(a) In general.** Notwithstanding any other provision in any regulation under section 465, assets of a taxpayer (including money) contributed to an activity shall not be treated as increasing the taxpayer's amount at risk to the extent the taxpayer is protected against loss of such assets. In addition, amounts borrowed by a taxpayer shall not be considered at risk to the extent the taxpayer is protected against loss of the borrowed amount. Similarly, such amounts shall not be considered at risk if the taxpayer is protected against loss of the property pledged as security and the taxpayer is not personally liable for repayment.

**(b) Contributions from other partners.** A partner shall not be at risk with respect to any partnership liability to the extent the partner would be entitled to contributions from other partners if the partner were called upon to pay the partnership's creditor, because to that extent the partner is protected against loss. See § 1.465-24(a)(2)(ii) for an example relating to the treatment of contributions by partners.

**(c) Contingent liabilities.** If a taxpayer is liable for repayment of an amount borrowed only upon the occurrence of a contingency, the taxpayer shall not be considered at risk with respect to such amount if the likelihood of the contingency occurring is such that the taxpayer is effectively protected against loss. Conversely, the taxpayer will be considered at risk if the likelihood of the contingency occurring is such that the taxpayer is not effectively protected against loss, or if the protection against loss does not cover all likely possibilities. For example, a taxpayer who obtains casualty insurance or insurance protection against tort liability will not ordinarily be considered "not at risk" solely because of such hazard insurance protection.

**(d) Guarantors.** If a taxpayer guarantees repayment of an amount borrowed by another person (primary obligor) for use in an activity, the guarantee shall not increase the taxpayer's amount at risk. If the taxpayer repays to the creditor the amount borrowed by the primary obligor, the taxpayer's amount at risk shall be increased at such time as the taxpayer has no remaining legal rights against the primary obligor.

**(e) Examples.** The provisions of this section may be illustrated by the following examples:

*Example (1).* A, an individual, borrows $6,000 from a bank for use in an activity described in section 465(c)(1). A is not personally liable for repayment of the loan but instead pledges as security assets not used in the activity with a net fair market value of $6,000. However B, a third party, guarantees A that A's entire loss from the activity will be repaid to A by B. Since A is protected against loss on the loan, A's amount at risk is not increased as a result of the entire transaction.

*Example (2).* Assume the same facts as in example (1) except that B, instead of guaranteeing A's entire loss from the activity, guarantees A against loss of A's security in excess of $2,000. Accordingly, A is considered as having pledged as security assets with a net fair market value of $2,000. Under § 1.465-25(a)(1), A's amount at risk is increased by $2,000.

*Example (3).* C, an individual, is engaged in the activity of farming. C borrows $10,000 for use on the farm from an unrelated third party. As security C pledges future crops. Under the general terms of the loan agreement C is not personally liable for repayment of the $10,000. There is, however, one exception to this general provision. C will be personally liable if the crops are destroyed as the result of flooding. While drought is a constant concern for farmers in the area, flooding is not. Accordingly, although C is personally liable in the event of flooding, C's amount at risk will not be increased unless flooding actually occurs and destroys the crops, because the likelihood of flooding is such that C is effectively protected against loss. If the contingency does occur, C's amount at risk is increased at the end of the year in which it occurs.

*Example (4).* D, an individual calendar year taxpayer, is engaged in the activity of producing motion picture films. In 1979 D borrows $100,000 for use in the activity from E, the promoter. D is personally liable for repayment of the loan. E has neither a capital interest in the activity nor an interest in the net profits of the activity. Therefore, E is not considered a person with an interest in the activity other than that of a creditor. See § 1.465-8(b). However, E agrees to protect D against loss of up to the first $40,000 of losses from the activity. Thus, under the agreement D will not bear the economic burden of any loss until the total losses exceed $40,000. All of the losses in excess of $40,000 will be borne by D. As a result of this protection against-loss agreement, the $100,000 borrowed for use in the activity will increase D's amount at risk by $60,000. At the close of 1979, D's losses from the activity amount to $70,000. However, because D's amount at risk is only $60,000, D will only be permitted to deduct $60,000. The remaining $10,000 of deductions shall be treated in accordance with § 1.465-2(b).

**Proposed § 1.465-7 General rules; amounts loaned to the activity by the taxpayer.** [*For Preamble, see ¶ 150,479*]

***Caution:*** The Treasury has not yet amended Reg § 1.465-7 to reflect changes made by P.L. 101-508, P.L. 99-514, P.L. 98-369, P.L. 96-222.

**(a) Partners.** The amount at risk in an activity of a partner who lends the partnership money for use in the activity shall be increased by the amount by which that partner's basis in the partnership is increased under § 1.752-1(e) due to the incurrence by the partnership of that liability. The amount at risk of any other partners shall not be increased as a result of the loan.

**(b) Shareholders of electing small business corporations.** For rules relating to amounts loaned by a shareholder to an electing small business corporation, see § 1.465-10(c).

**(c) Special rules.** For special rules relating to amounts borrowed from persons with an interest in the activity other than that of a creditor and amounts borrowed from persons with a special relationship to the taxpayer, see section 465(b)(3) and §§ 1.465-8 and 1.465-20.

**§ 1.465-8 General rules; interest other than that of a creditor.**

**(a) In general.** *(1) Amounts borrowed.* This section applies to amounts borrowed for use in an activity described in section 465(c)(1) or (c)(3)(A). Amounts borrowed with respect to an activity will not increase the borrower's amount at risk in the activity if the lender has an interest in the activity other than that of a creditor or is related to a person (other than the borrower) who has an interest in the activity other than that of a creditor. This rule applies even if the borrower is personally liable for the repayment of the loan or the loan is secured by property not used in the activity. For additional rules relating to the treatment of amounts borrowed from these persons, see § 1.465-20.

*(2) Certain borrowed amounts excepted.* (i) For purposes of determining a corporation's amount at risk, an interest in the corporation as a shareholder is not an interest in any activity of the corporation. Thus, amounts borrowed by a corporation from a shareholder may increase the corporation's amount at risk.

(ii) For purposes of determining a taxpayer's amount at risk in an activity of holding real property, paragraph (a)(1) of this section does not apply to financing that is secured by real property used in the activity and is either—

(A) Qualified nonrecourse financing described in section 465(b)(6)(B); or

(B) Financing that, if it were nonrecourse, would be financing described in section 465(b)(6)(B).

**(b) Loans for which the borrower is personally liable for repayment.** *(1) General rule.* If a borrower is personally liable for the repayment of a loan for use in an activity, a person shall be considered a person with an interest in the activity other than that of a creditor only if the person has either a capital interest in the activity or an interest in the net profits of the activity.

*(2) Capital interest.* For the purposes of this section a capital interest in an activity means an interest in the assets of the activity which is distributable to the owner of the capital interest upon the liquidation of the activity. The partners of a partnership and the shareholders of an S corporation are considered to have capital interests in the activities conducted by the partnership or S corporation.

*(3) Interest in net profits.* For the purposes of this section it is not necessary for a person to have any incidents of ownership in the activity in order to have an interest in the net profits of the activity. For example, an employee or independent contractor any part of whose compensation is determined with reference to the net profits of the activity will be considered to have an interest in the net profits of the activity.

(4) *Examples.* The provisions of this paragraph may be illustrated by the following examples:

*Example (1).* A, the owner of a herd of cattle sells the herd to partnership BCD. BCD pays A $10,000 in cash and executes a note for $30,000 payable to A. Each of the three partners, B, C, and D, assumes personal liability for repayment of the amount owed A. In addition, BCD enters into an agreement with A under which A is to take care of the cattle for BCD in return for compensation equal to 6 percent of BCD's net profits from the activity. Because A has an interest in the net profits of BCD's farming activity, A is considered to have an interest in the activity other than that of a creditor. Accordingly, amounts payable to A for use in that activity do not increase the partners' amount at risk even though the partners assume personal liability for repayment.

*Example (2).* Assume the same facts as in Example 1 except that instead of receiving compensation equal to 6 percent of BCD's net profits from the activity, A instead receives compensation equal to 1 percent of the gross receipts from the activity. A does not have a capital interest in BCD. A's interest in the gross receipts is not considered an interest in the net profits. Because B, C, and D assumed personal liability for the amounts payable to A, and A has neither a capital interest nor an interest in the net profits of the activity, A is not considered to have an interest in the activity other than that of a creditor with respect to the $30,000 loan. Accordingly, B, C, and D are at risk for their share of the loan if the other provisions of section 465 are met.

*Example (3).* Assume the same facts as in Example 1 except that instead of receiving compensation equal to 6 percent of BCD's net profits from the activity, A instead receives compensation equal to 6 percent of the net profits from the activity or $15,000, whichever is greater. A is considered to have an interest in the net profits from the activity and accordingly will be treated as a person with an interest in the activity other than that of a creditor.

**(c) Nonrecourse loans secured by assets with a readily ascertainable fair market value.** *(1) General rule.* This paragraph shall apply in the case of a nonrecourse loan for use in an activity where the loan is secured by property which has a readily ascertainable fair market value. In the case of such a loan a person shall be considered a person with an interest in the activity other than that of a creditor only if the person has either a capital interest in the activity or an interest in the net profits of the activity.

*(2) Example.* The provisions of this paragraph (c) may be illustrated by the following example:

*Example.* X is an investor in an activity described in section 465(c)(1). In order to raise money for the investment, X borrows money from A, the promoter (the person who brought X together with other taxpayers for the purpose of investing in the activity). The loan is secured by stock unrelated to the activity which is listed on a national securities exchange. X's stock has a readily ascertainable fair market value. A does not have a capital interest in the activity or an interest in its net profits. Accordingly, with respect to the loan secured by X's stock, A does not have an interest in the activity other than that of a creditor.

**(d) Nonrecourse loans secured by assets without a readily ascertainable fair market value.** *(1) General rule.* This paragraph shall apply in the case of a nonrecourse loan for use in an activity where the loan is secured by property which does not have a readily ascertainable fair market value. In the case of such a loan a person shall be considered a person with an interest in the activity other than that of a creditor if the person stands to receive financial gain (other than interest) from the activity or from the sale of interests in the activity. For the purposes of this section persons who stand to receive financial gain from the activity include persons who receive compensation for services rendered in connection with the organization or operation of the activity or for the sale of interests in the activity. Such a person will generally include the promoter of the activity who organizes the activity or solicits potential investors in the activity.

*(2) Example.* The provisions of this paragraph (d) may be illustrated by the following example:

*Example.* A is the promoter of an activity described in section 465(c)(1). As the promoter, A organizes the activity and solicits potential investors. For these services A is paid a flat fee of $130x. This fee is paid out of the amounts contributed by the investors to the activity. X, one of the investors in the activity, borrows money from A for use in the activity. X is not personally liable for repayment to A of the amount borrowed. As security for the loan, X pledges an asset which does not have a readily ascertainable fair market value. A is considered a person with an interest in the activity other than that of a creditor with respect to this loan because the asset pledged as security does not have a readily ascertainable fair market value, X is not personally liable for repayment of the loan, and A received financial gain from the activity. Accordingly, X's amount at risk in the activity is not increased despite the fact that property was pledged as security.

**(e) Effective date.** This section applies to amounts borrowed after May 3, 2004.

---

T.D. 9124, 4/30/2004.

---

**Proposed § 1.465-9 General rules; rules of construction.**

[*For Preamble, see ¶ 150,479*]

***Caution:*** The Treasury has not yet amended Reg § 1.465-9 to reflect changes made by P.L. 101-508, P.L. 99-514, P.L. 98-369, P.L. 96-222.

**(a) Amounts protected against loss.** Section 465(b)(4) and § 1.465-6 provide special rules relating to amounts protected against loss which override the other rules contained in section 465. Where the regulations under section 465 refer to cash or property contributed to an activity and amounts borrowed for use in an activity, it may be assumed that such cash, property, or amounts are not protected against loss under section 465(b)(4) unless expressly provided otherwise.

**(b) Amounts borrowed for use in an activity.** Section 465(b)(3) and § 1.465-20 contain special rules relating to treatment of amounts borrowed from certain persons. Where the regulations under section 465 refer to amounts borrowed for use in an activity, it may be assumed that such amounts are borrowed neither from a person with an interest (other than an interest as a creditor) in the activity nor from a person who has a special relationship to the taxpayer specified within any one of the paragraphs of section 267(b), unless expressly provided otherwise.

**(c) Use of the term "activity".** For the purposes of the regulations under section 465, unless expressly provided otherwise, use of the term "activity" shall refer to an activity which is described in section 465(c)(1).

**(d) Single activity.** For the purposes of the regulations under section 465, unless otherwise stated, it is assumed that an entity conducting an activity is engaged only in that one activity.

**(e) Double counting of additions and reductions to amount at risk.** An amount, or portion of an amount (which is contributed, borrowed, etc.), can only increase or decrease a taxpayer's amount at risk one time. Thus, if a portion of an amount increases a taxpayer's amount at risk under more than one section of the regulations, that portion can increase the taxpayer's amount at risk in the activity only once.

**(f) Personal funds or personal assets.** For the purposes of the regulations under section 465, unless otherwise stated, the terms "personal funds" and "personal assets" of a taxpayer refer to funds and assets which—

*(1)* Are owned by the taxpayer;

*(2)* Are not acquired through borrowing; and

*(3)* Have a basis equal to their fair market value.

**(g) Foreclosure.** If a foreclosure occurs within an activity, it will be treated as a disposition of the asset which is the subject of the foreclosure. For rules relating to dispositions, see § 1.465-66.

**Proposed § 1.465-10 General rules; rules relating to subchapter S corporations and their shareholders.** [*For Preamble, see ¶ 150,479*]

***Caution:*** The Treasury has not yet amended Reg § 1.465-10 to reflect changes made by P.L. 101-508, P.L. 99-514, P.L. 98-369, P.L. 96-222.

**(a) In general.** In the case of electing small business corporations (as defined in section 1371(b)) the at risk rules of section 465 apply at both the corporate level and the shareholder level. Therefore, losses from an activity can be deducted by the corporation only to the extent that the corporation is at risk in the activity. In addition, each shareholder will be allowed a loss in the activity only to the extent that the shareholder is at risk in the activity.

**(b) Determination of corporation's amount at risk.** *(1) General rule.* Except as provided in paragraph (b)(2) of this section, an electing small business corporation's amount at risk in an activity is determined in the same manner as that of any other taxpayer.

*(2) Special rule for certain borrowed amounts.* Amounts borrowed by an electing small business corporation from one or more of its shareholders may increase the corporation's amount at risk, notwithstanding the fact that the shareholders have an interest in the activity other than that of a creditor.

**(c) Determination of shareholder's amount at risk.** The amount at risk of a shareholder of an electing small business corporation (as described in section 1371(b)) shall be adjusted to reflect any increase or decrease in the adjusted basis of any indebtedness of the corporation to the shareholder described in section 1374(c)(2)(B).

**(d) Example.** The provisions of this section may be illustrated by the following example:

*Example.* A is the single shareholder in X, an electing small business corporation engaged in an activity described in section 465(c)(1). A contributed $50,000 to X in exchange for its stock under section 351. In addition, A borrowed $40,000 for which A assumed personal liability. A then loaned the entire amount to X for use in the activity. During its taxable year, X had a net operating loss of $75,000. At the close of the taxable year (without reduction for any losses of X) A's amount at risk is $90,000 ($50,000 + $40,000). However, it is also necessary to determine X's amount at risk in the activity. X is also at risk for the $40,000 borrowed from A and expended in the activity. Therefore, X's amount at risk in the activity is $90,000 ($50,000 + $40,000). Because X's amount at risk in the activity ($90,000) exceeds the net operating loss ($75,000), the entire loss is allowed to the corporation and allocated to A. Since A's amount at risk ($90,000) also exceeds the loss ($75,000) A will be allowed the entire loss deduction.

**Proposed § 1.465-11 Definition of loss; in general.** [*For Preamble, see ¶ 150,479*]

**(a) In general.** *(1) Loss.* A taxpayer has a loss described in section 465(d) in a taxable year in an amount equal to the excess of allowable deductions allocable to an activity over the income received or accrued from the activity by the taxpayer for the taxable year. Such loss is referred to as a section 465(d) loss in the regulations under section 465. See § 1.465-13 for the definition of allowable deductions allocable to an activity and § 1.465-12 for a definition of income from the activity.

*(2) Example.* The application of this paragraph may be illustrated by the following example:

*Example.* In 1977 B, a calendar year individual, contributes $15,000 to an activity described in section 465(c)(1). During 1977 B has income of $20,000 from the activity and has allowable deductions of $45,000 from the activity. From this $45,000 of allowable deductions, B must first take a deduction of $20,000 to reflect the income received by B from the activity in 1977. The remaining $25,000 ($45,000G1T1 – $20,000) is B's section 465(d) loss. Assuming B's amount at risk in the activity is $15,000 at the close of 1977, B is also allowed to deduct $15,000 of the $25,000 section 465(d) loss for 1977. The remaining $10,000 ($25,000G1T1 – $15,000) of the section 465(d) loss which is not allowed as a deduction for 1977 will be treated as a deduction allocable to the activity for 1978.

**(b) Carryover loss.** For the carryover of losses disallowed by section 465, see § 1.465-2(b)

**(c) Loss with no amount at risk.** *(1) In general.* A section 465(d) loss is determined without regard to the amount at risk. Thus, even if the taxpayer has no amount at risk in the activity, deductions are allowable under section 465 for a taxable year to the extent there is income from the activity in that taxable year.

*(2) Example.* The provisions of this paragraph may be illustrated by the following example:

*Example.* Before taking into account any gain or loss during 1978, the amount that C, a calendar year taxpayer, is at risk in an activity described in section 465(c)(1) is equal to minus $20,000. During 1978 C has deductions of $10,000 allocable to the activity and income of $15,000 from the activity. Because the income from the activity exceeds the amount of allocable deductions from the activity, there is no section 465(d) loss in 1978 to be disallowed under section 465(a). Thus, although C has a negative amount at risk, C is permitted to take deductions in the amount of $10,000 for 1978.

**Proposed § 1.465-12 Definition of loss; income from the activity.** [*For Preamble, see ¶ 150,479*]

***Caution:*** The Treasury has not yet amended Reg § 1.465-12 to reflect changes made by P.L. 101-508, P.L. 99-514, P.L. 98-369, P.L. 96-222.

**(a) In general.** Income received or accrued from an activity includes gain recognized upon the disposition of the activity or an interest in the activity in accordance with

§ 1.465-66. For the purposes of this section and the determinations made under section 465(d), the character of any gain is irrelevant. Thus, all short-term capital gains and long-term capital gains attributable to the activity shall be included as income from the activity. For more rules relating to income from an activity see §§ 1.465-42 through 1.465-45.

**(b) Example.** The provisions of this section may be illustrated by the following example:

*Example.* On February 1, 1977, A, an individual on a calendar year, purchases a piece of equipment to be used in an activity described in section 465(c)(1)(C). A bought the equipment for $50,000, paying $5,000 from personal assets and borrowing $45,000 from a bank on a nonrecourse basis secured only by the newly purchased equipment. On February 1, 1977, A has a basis in the activity of $50,000 and an initial amount at risk of $5,000, at the close of 1977 after the application of section 465, A's basis has been reduced to $35,000, A's amount at risk has been reduced to zero, and A has a loss of $10,000 disallowed by reason of section 465(a). In 1978, the bank forecloses on the equipment when it is still encumbered by the $45,000 loan. Assuming there were no other transactions relating to this activity, A recognizes a $10,000 gain ($45,000 – $35,000) on this disposition. For purposes of section 465(d), this $10,000 of gain is income from the activity, and the $10,000 of disallowed loss in 1977 is treated as a deduction for 1978. Since the income from the activity for 1978 ($10,000) is equal to the deductions attributable to the activity for 1978 ($10,000), there is no section 465(d) loss for 1978. Therefore, the $10,000 of gain is included in gross income in 1978 and the $10,000 of disallowed loss is allowed as a deduction for 1978.

**Proposed § 1.465-13 Definition of loss; deductions from the activity.** [*For Preamble, see ¶ 150,479*]

***Caution:*** The Treasury has not yet amended Reg § 1.465-13 to reflect changes made by P.L. 101-508, P.L. 99-514, P.L. 98-369, P.L. 96-222.

**(a) General rule.** For the purposes of section 465 allowable deductions allocable to an activity are those otherwise allowable deductions incurred in a trade or business or for the production of income from the activity. For the purposes of this section—capital losses shall be treated as deductions without regard to section 1211. See § 1.465-38 for rules relating to the order in which deductions are to be allowed and § 1.465-2(b) for the treatment of loss deductions which are disallowed by section 465.

**(b) Capital gain.** *(1) In general.* For the purposes of section 465 the deduction for capital gains provided for in section 1202 shall not be treated as a deduction allocable to an activity. Therefore, the capital gain deduction described in section 1202 will not be subject to the limitations of section 465(a) and has no effect on the amount at risk.

*(2) Example.* The provision of paragraph (b)(1) of this section may be illustrated by the following example:

*Example.* At the close of 1976 A, an individual and a calendar year taxpayer, has $1,000 of section 465(d) losses disallowed under section 465(a) for an activity described in section 465(c)(1). Before A has any other deductions allocable to the activity, A sells the entire activity, realizing $1,900 of long term capital gain. For 1977 A is allowed a deduction of $950 under section 1202. Other than the disallowed loss of $1,000 and the section 1202 deduction, A has no other deductions. In accordance with § 1.465-66 A has received $1,900 income from the activity. Since the $950 deduction under section 1202 is not allocable to the activity, the only deduction allocable to the activity for 1977 is the $1,000 disallowed in 1976. Therefore, for 1977 $1,900 will be included in gross income, $950 is allowed as a deduction, and in addition the full disallowed loss of $1,000 is allowed as a deduction since it is not in excess of the income from the activity ($1,900).

**(c) Dual use of assets or personnel.** Proper allocation rules are necessary if assets or personnel are used either in two or more separate activities referred to in section 465(c)(2), or in one or more activities referred to in section 465(c)(2) and an activity to which section 465 does not apply. In such a case the deductions attributable to the use of these assets or personnel must be allocated between the activities on a reasonable basis.

**§ 1.465-20 Treatment of amounts borrowed from certain persons and amounts protected against loss.**

**(a) General rule.** The following amounts are treated in the same manner as borrowed amounts for which the taxpayer has no personal liability and for which no security is pledged—

*(1)* Amounts that do not increase the taxpayer's amount at risk because they are borrowed from a person who has an interest in the activity other than that of a creditor or from a person who is related to a person (other than the taxpayer) who has an interest in the activity other than that of a creditor; and

*(2)* Amounts (whether or not borrowed) that are protected against loss.

**(b) Interest other than that of a creditor; cross reference.** See § 1.465-8 for additional rules relating to amounts borrowed from a person who has an interest in the activity other than that of a creditor or is related to a person (other than the taxpayer) who has an interest in the activity other than that of a creditor.

**(c) Amounts protected against loss; cross reference.** See § 1.465-6 for rules relating to amounts protected against loss.

**(d) Effective date.** This section applies to amounts borrowed after May 3, 2004.

---

T.D. 9124, 4/30/2004.

---

**Proposed § 1.465-22 Effect on amount at risk of money transactions.** [*For Preamble, see ¶ 150,479*]

***Caution:*** The Treasury has not yet amended Reg § 1.465-22 to reflect changes made by P.L. 98-369.

**(a) Money contributed to activity.** A taxpayer's amount at risk in an activity shall be increased by the amount of personal funds the taxpayer contributes to the activity. For this purpose a contribution by a partner to a partnership conducting only one activity is a contribution to the activity. However, a partner's amount at risk shall not be increased by the amount which the partner is required under the partnership agreement to contribute until such time as the contribution is actually made. Neither shall a partner's amount at risk be increased in the case of a note payable to the partnership for which a partner is personally liable until such time as the proceeds of the note are actually devoted to the activity. See § 1.465-10 for rules relating to amounts loaned by a shareholder to an electing small business corporation. See § 1.465-7(a) for the treatment of a loan by a partner to the partnership.

**(b) Withdrawal of money from the activity.** A taxpayer's amount at risk in an activity shall be decreased by the amount of money withdrawn from the activity by or on behalf of the taxpayer. Amounts withdrawn from an activity include distributions from a partnership or an electing small business corporation (as defined in section 1371(b)). In the case of a taxpayer who is a shareholder of an electing small business corporation (as defined in section 1371(b)), withdrawals shall include repayments of any indebtedness of the corporation to the shareholder described in section 1374(c)(2)(B) to the extent of any decrease in the shareholder's adjusted basis of such indebtedness. For the treatment of amounts already used in an activity which are used to repay a loan, see §§ 1.465-24(b)(2)(i) and 1.465-25(b)(2).

**(c) Effect of income and loss from activity on amount at risk.** *(1) Income.* A taxpayer's amount at risk in an activity shall be increased by an amount equal to the excess of the taxpayer's share of all items of income received or accrued from the activity during the taxable year over the taxpayer's share of allowable deductions which are allocable to the activity for the taxable year. A taxpayer's amount at risk in an activity shall also be increased by the taxpayer's share of tax-exempt receipts of the activity.

*(2) Loss.* A taxpayer's amount at risk in an activity shall be decreased by the amount of loss from the activity allowed as a deduction to the taxpayer under section 465(a). A loss shall reduce a taxpayer's amount at risk in the activity at the close of the taxable year after the taxable year for which the loss is allowable. A taxpayer's amount at risk in an activity shall be decreased by the taxpayer's share of expenses relating to the production of tax-exempt receipts of the activity which are not deductible in determining taxable income from the activity.

*(3) Cross references.* For the definition of income from the activity, see § 1.465-12. For definition of loss from the activity, see section 465(d) and § 1.465-11. For the timing of increases and decreases to the amount at risk, see § 1.465-39.

**(d) Payment to seller.** Payment by a purchaser to the seller for an interest in an activity shall be treated by the purchaser as if the payment to the seller were a contribution to the activity. For rules relating to the contribution of borrowed amounts see §§ 1.465-20, 1.465-24, and 1.465-25.

**Proposed § 1.465-23 Effect on amount at risk of property transactions.** [*For Preamble, see ¶ 150,479*]

***Caution:*** The Treasury has not yet amended Reg § 1.465-23 to reflect changes made by P.L. 101-508, P.L. 98-369.

**(a) Contributions of property.** *(1) Contribution of unencumbered property.* When a taxpayer contributes unencumbered property to an activity, the taxpayer's amount at risk in the activity shall be increased by the adjusted basis of the contributed property. However, see §§ 1.465-20, 1.465-24, and 1.465-25 for rules relating to the contribution to the activity of property that has been purchased with borrowed funds.

*(2) Contribution of encumbered property.* (i) Except as may otherwise result due to the application of § 1.465-20, when a taxpayer contributes to an activity property that is subject only to liabilities for which the taxpayer is personally liable for repayment, the taxpayer's amount at risk in the activity shall be increased by the adjusted basis of the contributed property.

(ii) Except as may otherwise result due to the application of § 1.465-20, when a taxpayer contributes to an activity property that is subject to a liability for which the taxpayer is not personally liable for repayment, the taxpayer's amount at risk is increased by the adjusted basis in the property and is decreased by the amount of encumbrances to which the property is subject which would not have increased the taxpayer's amount at risk if incurred for use in the activity. If after contribution of the property to the activity such an encumbrance is reduced, it shall be treated as the repayment of a loan used in the activity for which the taxpayer is not personally liable and for which there is no property used outside the activity pledged as security. See § 1.465-25(b)(2)(i).

If the basis of such property is decreased (for example due to depreciation) prior to contribution to the activity, the portion of the basis consisting of amounts which would have increased the taxpayer's amount at risk if contributed directly to the activity will be decreased first.

(iii) The provisions of this paragraph may be illustrated by the following examples.

*Example (1).* In 1976 A, a calendar year individual taxpayer, purchases an asset for $5,000 financed in part by a $3,000 nonrecourse loan secured only by the asset and in part by $2,000 of cash from personal funds. Thereafter, in 1976 A contributes the asset to an activity before any of the nonrecourse debt has been repaid. Under § 1.465-23(a)(2)(ii), A's amount at risk in the activity will be increased to the extent the taxpayer's adjusted basis in the asset consists of amounts which would have increased the taxpayer's amount at risk if contributed directly to the activity. In this instance the $3,000 nonrecourse loan is secured by an asset used in the activity. Because these loan proceeds would not increase the amount at risk if contributed directly to the activity, they will not increase the amount at risk in this case. However, the $2,000 of personal funds used for part payment of the asset would have increased A's amount at risk in the activity by $2,000 if contributed directly to the activity. Consequently, A's amount at risk in the activity is increased by $2,000 as a result of the contribution of the asset to the activity.

*Example (2).* In 1976 B, a calendar year individual taxpayer, purchases an asset for $5,000 financed in part by a $3,000 nonrecourse loan secured only by the asset and in part by $2,000 of cash from personal funds. B uses the asset in an activity to which section 465 does not apply and takes $1,000 of depreciation. Thereafter, B contributes the asset to an activity described in section 465(c)(1). None of the nonrecourse debt had been repaid at the time of the contribution. Under § 1.465-23(a)(2)(ii) the $1,000 of depreciation will be deducted first from the portion of the basis that consists of amounts which would have increased the taxpayer's amount at risk in the activity if contributed directly to the activity. This means that at the time of contribution to the activity the asset has an adjusted basis of $4,000, consisting in part of a $3,000 nonrecourse loan and in part of $1,000 of personal funds which would have increased B's amount at risk in the activity if contributed directly to the activity. Consequently, B's amount at risk in the activity is increased by $1,000 as a result of the contribution of the asset to the activity.

**(b) Adjusted basis.** *(1)* For the purpose of this section the adjusted basis is that adjusted basis which would have been used in determining the amount of loss if the property were sold immediately after being contributed to the activity.

*(2)* The provisions of this paragraph may be illustrated by the following examples:

*Example (1).* In 1972 A, an individual calendar year taxpayer, purchases a car for $5,000 using person assets to pay the seller. From 1972 through 1975 the car is used solely for A's personal nonbusiness needs. On January 1, 1976, A converts the use of the car and begins using the car solely for business purposes. On January 1, 1976, the fair market value of the car is $2,400. For 1976 A is allowed a deduction of $600 for depreciation of the car. On January 1, 1977, A contributes the car to an activity described in section 465(c)(1). If on January 1, 1977, the car had been sold the allowable loss would have been the excess (if any) of $1,800 ($2,400−$600) over the amount realized on the sale (see § 1.165-7(a)(5)). As a result of contributing the car, A's amount at risk in the activity is increased by $1,800.

*Example (2).* Assume the same facts as in example (1) except that A contributes the car to the activity described in section 465(c)(1) on January 1, 1976. On that date the car is converted from personal use to use in a trade or business or for the production of income. If the car were to be sold thereafter, the loss would be determined with reference to an adjusted basis of $2,400. Accordingly, A's amount at risk is increased by $2,400.

**(c) Distribution of property.** A taxpayer's amount at risk in an activity shall be decreased by—

*(1)* The adjusted basis in the hands of the taxpayer of property (other than money) which is withdrawn by or on behalf of the taxpayer from the activity; less

*(2)* The amount of liabilities to which the property is subject to for which the taxpayer is not personally liable.

If a taxpayer is distributed property described in this paragraph, repayment of the liability by the taxpayer after the distribution shall not increase the taxpayer's amount at risk.

**(d) Use of property as security for a nonrecourse loan.** For rules relating to the treatment of a taxpayer's amount at risk when the taxpayer pledges property as security for a nonrecourse loan, see § 1.465-25.

**(e) Contribution of property previously serving as security for a nonrecourse loan.** For rules relating to the treatment of a taxpayer's amount at risk when the taxpayer contributes to an activity property that had served as security for a nonrecourse loan used in the activity, see § 1.465-25(a)(3).

**Proposed § 1.465-24 Effect on amount at risk of loans for which borrower is personally liable for repayment.** [*For Preamble, see ¶ 150,479*]

***Caution:*** The Treasury has not yet amended Reg § 1.465-24 to reflect changes made by P.L. 101-508, P.L. 98-369, P.L. 96-222.

**(a) Creation of loan.** *(1) General rule.* A taxpayer's amount at risk in an activity is increased by the amount of any liability incurred in the conduct of an activity for use in the activity to the extent the taxpayer is personally liable for repayment of the liability.

*(2) Partnerships.* (i) When a partnership incurs a liability in the conduct of an activity and under state law members of the partnership may be held personally liable for repayment of the liability, each partner's amount at risk is increased to the extent the partner is not protected against loss. To the extent the partner is protected against loss (such as through a right of contribution), the liability shall be treated in the same manner as amounts borrowed for which the taxpayer has no personal liability and for which no security is pledged. See § 1.465-25.

(ii) The application of this paragraph may be illustrated by the following example:

*Example.* A and B are equal general partners in partnership AB, which is engaged solely in an activity described in section 465(c)(1). AB borrows $25,000 from a bank to purchase equipment to be used in the activity. In addition to giving the bank a security interest in the newly purchased equipment, A and B each assumes personal liability for the loan. Although either A or B could be called upon by the bank to repay the entire $25,000, in such instance the partner who paid would be entitled to $12,500 from the other partner. Thus, although each is personally liable for $25,000, each is protected against loss in excess of $12,500. Accordingly, the loan increases the amount each is at risk with respect to the activity by $12,500.

*(3) Small business corporations.* The amount at risk of a shareholder of an electing small business corporation (as defined in section 1371(b)) shall not be increased by indebtedness incurred by the corporation from persons other than that shareholder. For treatment of indebtedness described in section 1374(c)(2)(B) (relating to loans by shareholders to electing small business corporations), see § 1.465-10(c).

**(b) Repayment of loan.** *(1) General rule.* (i) Except as otherwise provided in this paragraph, the repayment by the taxpayer of a liability for which the taxpayer is personally liable does not affect the taxpayer's amount at risk. For this purpose, whether a taxpayer is considered personally liable for repayment of a liability is determined at the time of repayment.

(ii) The provisions of paragraph (b)(1) of this section, may be illustrated by the following examples:

*Example (1).* In 1977 A, an individual calendar year taxpayer, borrows $10,000 from a bank, assuming personal liability for repayment, for use in partnership AB, which is engaged solely in an activity. At the close of 1977 A's amount at risk is $10,000. In December of 1978 A takes $3,000 of personal funds and uses these funds to repay the bank. If no other factors occur during the year to affect A's amount at risk in the activity, A's amount at risk will be $10,000 at the close of 1978 because the repayment with personal assets of a liability for which A was personally liable does not affect A's amount at risk in the activity.

*Example (2).* In 1977 B, a calendar year taxpayer, borrows $5,000 for use in an activity. B is personally liable for the repayment of the loan. At the end of 1977 B's amount at risk in the activity is $5,000. In 1978 when the amount of the loan is still $5,000, the loan obligation is purchased by C, a person who has an interest (other than interest as a creditor) in the activity. As a result of C's interest in the activity the loan is not treated in the same manner as a loan for which B is personally liable for repayment as long as C is the holder of the note. See § 1.465-20. Accordingly, B's amount at risk in the activity is decreased by $5,000, and repayments on the note made by B to C are not governed by this section. See § 1.465-5 for the effect on the amount at risk of loans which convert from recourse to nonrecourse. See § 1.465-25 for the effect on the amount at risk of repayments of a loan for which the borrower is not personally liable for repayment.

*(2) Repayments using amounts which would not increase the taxpayer's amount at risk if contributed to the activity.* (i) If a taxpayer repays a loan for which the taxpayer is personally liable with assets already in the activity, the taxpayer's amount at risk in the activity will be decreased by the adjusted basis (as defined in § 1.465-23(b)(1)) of such assets. If the taxpayer repays a loan for which the taxpayer is personally liable with funds which, if contributed to the activity, would not increase the taxpayer's amount at risk,

the taxpayer's amount at risk shall be decreased to the extent of the repayment. Thus, for example, if a taxpayer repays a loan for which the taxpayer is personally liable with funds received from a nonrecourse loan secured by property used in the activity, the taxpayer's amount at risk shall be decreased to the extent of the repayment. The payment by a partnership of a liability which, pursuant to paragraph (a)(2) of this section, is deemed to be incurred by a partner in the conduct of the activity shall decrease the partner's amount at risk in the activity to the extent such partner's basis in the partnership is decreased due to the payment of the liability by the partnership.

(ii) The provisions of paragraph (b)(2) of this section may be illustrated by the following example:

*Example.* In 1977 A, an individual calendar year taxpayer, borrows $10,000 from a bank, assuming personal liability for repayment, for use in partnership AB, which is engaged solely in an activity described in section 465(c)(1). At the close of 1977 A's amount at risk in the activity is $10,000. In December of 1978 A borrows $3,000 for which A is not personally liable and which is secured by property used in the activity, and uses the funds to pay the bank. If no other factors occur during the year to affect A's amount at risk in the activity, A's amount at risk will be decreased by the amount of the repayment because A used funds for the repayment which would not have increased A's amount at risk had they been contributed to the activity. Therefore, at the close of 1978 A's amount at risk is $7,000. The result would be the same if the $3,000 used for the repayment of the loan were withdrawn from AB. See § 1.465-22.

*(3) Repayment of a loan for which others are personally liable.* Where more than one person is personally liable for repayment of a loan, repayment of that portion of the loan for which the taxpayer is personally liable and not protected against loss shall be treated in accordance with § 1.465-24(b). Repayment of that portion of the loan for which the taxpayer is protected against loss (such as through a right of contribution) shall be treated as a repayment of a loan for which the taxpayer has no personal liability and for which no security is pledged. See § 1.465-25. Also, see the example at paragraph (a)(2) of this section.

**Proposed § 1.465-25 Effect on amount at risk of loan for which borrower is not personally liable for repayment.** [*For Preamble, see ¶ 150,479*]

***Caution:*** The Treasury has not yet amended Reg § 1.465-25 to reflect changes made by P.L. 98-369.

**(a) Nonrecourse loan for which taxpayer pledges property not used in the activity.** *(1) In general.* A taxpayer's amount at risk in an activity is increased by amounts borrowed for use in the activity when the taxpayer is not personally liable for repayment of the loan if the taxpayer pledges as security property not used in the activity. However, the amount of the increase shall not exceed the net fair market value (as defined in paragraph (a)(4) of this section) of the pledged property. If the net fair market value of the security changes (in accordance with paragraph (a)(4) of this section) after the loan is made, a redetermination shall be made of the taxpayer's amount at risk in the activity using the new net fair market value.

*(2) Repayment of loan.* To the extent a taxpayer's amount at risk is increased by a portion of a liability described in paragraph (a)(1) of this section, the taxpayer's repayment of that portion of the liability will be treated in the same manner as the repayment of a loan for which the taxpayer is personally liable in accordance with § 1.465-24(b). However, to the extent the amount of the liability exceeds the net fair market value of property not used in the activity which secures the loan, repayment of that portion of the liability is considered as the repayment of a loan for which the taxpayer is not personally liable and has not pledged property used outside the activity in accordance with paragraph (b)(2)(i) of this section. Repayments of the loan are considered to be made first in respect of that portion of the loan which exceeds the net fair market value of property not used in the activity which secures the loan. If a portion of an amount borrowed is used in the activity and a portion is used outside the activity, repayment will be considered made first in respect of the portion used outside the activity.

*(3) Contribution of security to activity.* If property which is pledged as security for an amount borrowed for use in an activity is subsequently contributed to the activity, the amount at risk shall be redetermined in accordance with this section as though the net fair market value of the security had been reduced to zero. This will reduce the amount at risk in accordance with § 1.465-25(a)(1). Furthermore, the contribution of the property to the activity will be treated as a contribution of unencumbered property and will increase the amount at risk in accordance with § 1.465-23(a)(1).

*(4) Net fair market value; changes in net fair market value.* The net fair market value of property is the amount by which the property's fair market value at the date it is pledged as security exceeds the total amount of superior liens to which it is subject. Subsequent changes in the fair market value of the property are not taken into account for purposes of determining net fair market value. However, to the extent the amount of superior liens changes during a taxable year the net fair market value shall be adjusted at the close of the taxable year. Thus, the net fair market value of property will be reduced to the extent of increases in superior liens to which the property is subject and will be increased to the extent of decreases in superior liens of which the property is relieved. For purposes of determining the effect of superior liens on the calculations described in this paragraph, it is not relevant that other property is also subject to any such superior lien. If a portion of an amount borrowed which is secured by property described in this section is not contributed to an activity, that portion shall be treated as a superior lien on such property, thus reducing its net fair market value in accordance with § 1.465-25(a)(4).

**(b) Nonrecourse loan for which a taxpayer pledges assets used in the activity.** *(1) In general.* (i) Borrowed funds used in the activity. A taxpayer's amount at risk is unaffected by amounts borrowed for use in an activity where the taxpayer is not personally liable for repayment of the loan and has not pledged as security property used outside the activity. Thus, a taxpayer's amount at risk in a partnership activity is unaffected to the extent the taxpayer borrows for use in the partnership money secured only by the partnership interest. Where a partnership borrows amounts for use in the activity pledging only property used in the activity for repayment of the loan, and neither the partnership nor any partner is personally liable for repayment of the loan, the loan shall be treated by each partner as a loan which is described in this paragraph.

(ii) Borrowed funds used outside the activity. A taxpayer's amount at risk is affected by amounts borrowed for use outside the activity where the taxpayer is not personally liable for repayment of the loan and has pledged as security only property used in the activity. In such a case, the taxpayer's amount at risk in the activity is decreased by an amount equal to the amount borrowed for use outside the activity. This result is unchanged if the only security for the loan is the taxpayer's interest in the activity. If the taxpayer has pledged as security property, some of which is used in the activity (including for this purpose the taxpayer's interest in the activity) and some of which is not, the taxpayer's amount at risk in the activity shall be reduced by the excess, if any, of amounts borrowed for use outside the activity over the net fair market value of the security not used in the activity.

*(2) Repayment of loan.* (i) Borrowed funds used in the activity. Where a taxpayer's amount at risk was not increased as a result of the rule contained in paragraph (b)(1)(i) of this section, a subsequent repayment of the loan by the taxpayer will increase the taxpayer's amount at risk to the extent of the repayment. However, if the amount used to repay the loan would not have increased the taxpayer's amount at risk in the activity if the amount had been contributed to the activity, the repayment will not increase the taxpayer's amount at risk. Thus, for example, if a nonrecourse loan (the proceeds of which were used in the activity) which did not increase the taxpayer's amount at risk is repaid with money borrowed by the taxpayer with a second nonrecourse loan secured only by property used in the activity, the taxpayer's amount at risk will not be increased by the repayment. When a liability described in paragraph (b)(1)(i) of this section is repaid with assets already used in the activity, the taxpayer's amount at risk will not be affected as a result of the repayment. Therefore, when a partnership incurs such a liability and thereafter repays it with assets used in the activity, no partner's amount at risk is affected upon the incurrence of the liability or upon repayment.

(ii) Borrowed funds not used in the activity. A taxpayer's amount at risk is affected by the repayment by the taxpayer of amounts borrowed for use outside the activity where the taxpayer is not personally liable for repayment of the loan and has pledged as security only property used in the activity (including for this purpose the taxpayer's interest in the activity). In such a case the taxpayer's amount at risk in the activity is increased by the amount of the repayment. If the taxpayer has pledged as security property, some of which is used in the activity and some of which is not, upon repayment the taxpayer's amount at risk in the activity will be increased by the lesser of the amount of the repayment made by the taxpayer or the amount (if any) by which the outstanding liability (immediately before repayment) exceeds the net fair market value of the property not used in the activity which is pledged as security. However, if the amount used to repay the loan would not have increased the taxpayer's amount at risk in the activity if the amount had been contributed to the activity, the repayment will not increase the amount at risk. Thus, if the repayment is made using assets already in the activity, the repayment will not increase the taxpayer's amount at risk.

*(3) Examples.* The provisions of this section may be illustrated by the following examples:

*Example (1).* (i) In 1977 A, a calendar year individual, pledges A's house (which is not used in the activity) as well as an asset used in the activity as security to borrow $8,000 on a nonrecourse basis to be used in an activity. On the day the house is pledged as security, its fair market value is $60,000, and it is subject to a superior lien of $54,000. If the amount of the superior lien is not reduced during the balance of the year, at the close of 1977 the net fair market value of the house is $6,000 ($60,000 – $54,000), since the net fair market value of the security ($6,000) is less than the amount borrowed ($8,000), the increase in A's amount at risk is limited to $6,000.

(ii) In 1978 A reduces the amount of the superior lien on the house to $53,000. Accordingly, the house's net fair market value at the close of 1978 is $7,000 ($60,000 – $53,000). In accordance with paragraph (a)(4) of this section, a redetermination of the amount at risk is made using the new net fair market value. Using the new value, the amount borrowed ($8,000) is still more than the net fair market value ($7,000). Therefore, the new net fair market value would be used to measure the increase in A's amount at risk in the activity. The new amount determined under paragraph (a)(4) of this section ($7,000) exceeds the earlier amount determined under this section ($6,000) by $1,000. Thus, A's amount at risk is increased by $1,000.

(iii) In 1979 the fair market value of A's house increases to $75,000. On December 31, 1979, A obtains a $10,000 second mortgage on the house. The second mortgage is made superior to the lien for the $8,000 loan made in 1977. At the close of 1979 the original lien on the house has been reduced to $52,000 and the second mortgage is $10,000. Since changes in the fair market value of security are ignored for purposes of determining net fair market value, the net fair market value of the house at the end of 1979 is determined by comparing its fair market value at the time the $8,000 was borrowed in 1977, $60,000, with the amount of superior liens outstanding at the end of 1979, $62,000 ($52,000 + $10,000). Since the fair market value of the house as so determined is less than the total of the superior liens to which the house is subject at the end of 1979, the net fair market value of the house at that time is 0. In accordance with paragraph (a)(4) of this section a redetermination of the amount at risk is made using the new net fair market value. Using the new value the amount borrowed ($8,000) is still more than the net fair market value (0). Therefore, the new net fair market value would be used to measure the increase in A's amount at risk in the activity. The new amount determined under paragraph (a)(4) of this section (0) is less than the earlier amount determined under this section ($7,000) by $7,000. Thus, A's amount at risk is decreased by $7,000.

*Example (2).* (i) In 1977 B, a calendar year individual, pledges shares of stock that are not used in the activity as security to borrow $20,000 on a nonrecourse basis to be used in an activity. On the day the shares are pledged, they are worth $40,000 and are not subject to any superior liens. At the close of 1977 the fair market value of the shares is $30,000. Nevertheless, at the close of 1977 the net fair market value of the shares is $40,000, because changes in the fair market value of security are ignored for purposes of determining net fair market value. Since the net fair market value of the shares ($40,000) is greater than the amount borrowed ($20,000), B's amount at risk in the activity is increased by $20,000.

(ii) In 1978, B, using personal assets, repays $4,000 of the loan secured by the shares of stock. In accordance with paragraph (a)(2) of this section, repayments of such a loan are treated like repayments of a loan for which the taxpayer is personally liable. Thus, B's amount at risk is not affected by the repayment.

(iii) In 1979 the shares of stock are made subject to a $30,000 lien superior to the previous lien. At the close of 1979 the net fair market value of the shares of stock is $10,000 ($40,000 fair market value minus $30,000 superior lien). Accordingly, a redetermination must be made of B's amount at risk. Since the new net fair market value of the shares of stock ($10,000) is less than the amount of the loan outstanding ($16,000), the net fair market value is used to measure any change in A's amount at risk. The new amount determined under this section ($10,000) is less than the earlier amount determined under this section ($16,000) by $6,000. Thus, in accordance with paragraph (a) of this section B's amount at risk is decreased under this section by $6,000.

(iv) In 1980 B repays $7,000 of the loan secured by the shares of stock. In accordance with paragraph (a)(2) of this section the repayment is first deemed to be made in respect of that portion of the loan, $6,000, which exceeds the net fair market value of property not used in the activity which secures the loan. Pursuant to paragraph (b)(2)(i) of this section the repayment will result in a corresponding increase of $6,000 in the amount at risk. The remaining $1,000 repayment is treated under paragraph (a)(2) of this section in the same manner as the repayment of a loan for which the taxpayer is personally liable. Repayment of such a loan results in no change in the amount at risk. Accordingly, as a result of the $7,000 repayment, B's amount at risk is increased by $6,000.

*Example (3).* (i) In 1977 C, a calendar year individual, purchases an asset for $10,000 for use in an activity. C pays for the asset with $2,000 of personal funds and a purchase money mortgage of $8,000 on which C is not personally liable. At the end of 1977 C still owes $8,000 on the purchase money mortgage. As a result of this transaction C's amount at risk in the activity is increased by $2,000.

(ii) In 1978 C repays $3,000 of the purchase money mortgage, $2,000 with personal funds from outside the activity and $1,000 with funds from within the activity. Since the $2,000 of funds from outside the activity can increase C's amount at risk if contributed to the activity, their use to repay the loan will increase C's amount at risk by $2,000. The additional $1,000 of repayment is from funds already within the activity. Accordingly, the use of those funds to repay the loan does not increase C's amount at risk in the activity.

*Example (4).* (i) In 1977 D, a calendar year individual, borrows $5,000 for use in a farming activity described in section 465(c)(1)(B). D is personally liable on the loan. At the end of 1977 the $5,000 loan remains outstanding. Accordingly, D's amount at risk in the activity is increased by $5,000.

(ii) In 1979 D requests the lender to convert the $5,000 loan into a nonrecourse loan secured by assets in the farming activity. The lender agrees to the request. Assuming that § 1.465-5 applies and the recourse loan increases D's amount at risk prior to conversion, the conversion of the loan from recourse to nonrecourse reduces D's amount at risk by $5,000 at the close of 1979.

(iii) In 1980 D repays $1,000 of the $5,000 loan with personal funds from outside the activity and $2,000 with money from the activity. The repayment of $3,000 of the loan increases D's amount at risk to the extent a contribution of amounts used to repay the loan would have increased the taxpayer's amount at risk in the activity. Since $2,000 from the activity was used to repay the loan, D's amount at risk in the activity is not increased to the extent of that $2,000. However, the $1,000 from outside the activity would have increased the amount at risk if it were contributed to the activity. Therefore, at the end of 1980 D's amount at risk will be increased by $1,000.

*Example (5).* E and F form partnership EF to engage in an activity described in section 465(c)(1). Partnership EF borrows $20,000 secured by a purchase money mortgage for which neither of the partners is personally liable and uses the funds to purchase an asset for use in the activity. This transaction does not increase the amount E and F are at risk in the activity. Thereafter, EF repays $5,000 of the purchase money mortgage with funds from the activity. Pursuant to paragraph (c) of this section the repayment by EF has no effect on the amount E and F are at risk in the activity.

*Example (6).* A, an individual calendar year taxpayer, is engaged in a farming activity described in section 465(c)(1)(B). On January 6, 1978, A borrows $8,000 using machinery from the activity as security. A is not personally liable for repayment of the loan. A uses the $8,000 (along with $2,000 from personal funds) to purchase an automobile for use outside the activity. Subsequently, A pledges the automobile as security to borrow $8,000. A uses this $8,000 to purchase a truck which is contributed to the farming activity in August of 1978. Section 465(b)(2) provides that no property shall be taken into account as security if it is directly or indirectly financed by indebtedness which is secured by property used in the activity. Accordingly, if no other events affecting A's amount at risk occur in 1978, A's amount at risk in the farming activity at the close of 1978 will be the same as it was at the close of 1977.

**(c) Repayment of nonrecourse liability by a partnership.** The repayment by a partnership of a liability for which a taxpayer is not personally liable and for which that taxpayer has not pledged as security assets used outside the activity shall not affect the taxpayer's amount at risk.

**Proposed § 1.465-26 Effect of transfers by gift or at death on amount at risk; cross reference.** [*For Preamble, see ¶ 150,479*]

For rules relating to the effect on the amount at risk of transfers by gift or at death, see §§ 1.465-57 through 1.465-59.

**§ 1.465-27 Qualified nonrecourse financing.**

**(a) In general.** Notwithstanding any provision of section 465(b) or the regulations under section 465(b), for an activity of holding real property, a taxpayer is considered at risk for the taxpayer's share of any qualified nonrecourse financing which is secured by real property used in such activity.

**(b) Qualified nonrecourse financing secured by real property.** *(1) In general.* For purposes of section 465(b)(6) and this section, the term qualified nonrecourse financing means any financing—

(i) Which is borrowed by the taxpayer with respect to the activity of holding real property;

(ii) Which is borrowed by the taxpayer from a qualified person or represents a loan from any federal, state, or local government or instrumentality thereof, or is guaranteed by any federal, state, or local government;

(iii) For which no person is personally liable for repayment, taking into account paragraphs (b)(3), (4), and (5) of this section; and

(iv) Which is not convertible debt.

*(2) Security for qualified nonrecourse financing.* (i) Types of property. For a taxpayer to be considered at risk under section 465(b)(6), qualified nonrecourse financing must be secured only by real property used in the activity of holding real property. For this purpose, however, property that is incidental to the activity of holding real property will be disregarded. In addition, for this purpose, property that is neither real property used in the activity of holding real property nor incidental property will be disregarded if the aggregate gross

fair market value of such property is less than 10 percent of the aggregate gross fair market value of all the property securing the financing.

(ii) Look-through rule for partnerships. For purposes of paragraph (b)(2)(i) of this section, a borrower shall be treated as owning directly its proportional share of the assets in a partnership in which the borrower owns (directly or indirectly through a chain of partnerships) an equity interest.

*(3) Personal liability; partial liability.* If one or more persons are personally liable for repayment of a portion of a financing, the portion of the financing for which no person is personally liable may qualify as qualified nonrecourse financing.

*(4) Partnership liability.* For purposes of section 465(b)(6) and this paragraph (b), the personal liability of any partnership for repayment of a financing is disregarded and, provided the requirements contained in paragraphs (b)(1)(i), (ii), and (iv) of this section are satisfied, the financing will be treated as qualified nonrecourse financing secured by real property if—

(i) The only persons personally liable to repay the financing are partnerships;

(ii) Each partnership with personal liability holds only property described in paragraph (b)(2)(i) of this section (applying the principles of paragraph (b)(2)(ii) of this section in determining the property held by each partnership); and

(iii) In exercising its remedies to collect on the financing in a default or default-like situation, the lender may proceed only against property that is described in paragraph (b)(2)(i) of this section and that is held by the partnership or partnerships (applying the principles of paragraph (b)(2)(ii) of this section in determining the property held by the partnership or partnerships).

*(5) Disregarded entities.* Principles similar to those described in paragraph (b)(4) of this section shall apply in determining whether a financing of an entity that is disregarded for federal tax purposes under § 301.7701-3 of this chapter is treated as qualified nonrecourse financing secured by real property.

*(6) Examples.* The following examples illustrate the rules of this section:

*Example (1).* Personal liability of a partnership; incidental property.

(i) X is a limited liability company that is classified as a partnership for federal tax purposes. X engages only in the activity of holding real property. In addition to real property used in the activity of holding real property, X owns office equipment, a truck, and maintenance equipment that it uses to support the activity of holding real property. X borrows $500 to use in the activity. X is personally liable on the financing, but no member of X and no other person is liable for repayment of the financing under local law. The lender may proceed against all of X's assets if X defaults on the financing.

(ii) Under paragraph (b)(2)(i) of this section, the personal property is disregarded as incidental property used in the activity of holding real property. Under paragraph (b)(4) of this section, the personal liability of X for repayment of the financing is disregarded and, provided the requirements contained in paragraphs (b)(1)(i), (ii), and (iv) of this section are satisfied, the financing will be treated as qualified nonrecourse financing secured by real property.

*Example (2).* Bifurcation of a financing. The facts are the same as in Example 1, except that A, a member of X, is personally liable for repayment of $100 of the financing. If the requirements contained in paragraphs (b)(1)(i), (ii), and (iv) of this section are satisfied, then under paragraph (b)(3) of this section, the portion of the financing for which A is not personally liable for repayment ($400) will be treated as qualified nonrecourse financing secured by real property.

*Example (3).* Personal liability; tiered partnerships.

(i) UTP1 and UTP2, both limited liability companies classified as partnerships, are the only general partners in Y, a limited partnership. Y borrows $500 with respect to the activity of holding real property. The financing is a general obligation of Y. UTP1 and UTP2, therefore, are personally liable to repay the financing. Under section 752, UTP1's share of the financing is $300, and UTP2's share is $200. No person other than Y, UTP1, and UTP2 is personally liable to repay the financing. Y, UTP1, and UTP2 each hold only real property.

(ii) Under paragraph (b)(4) of this section, the personal liability of Y, UTP1, and UTP2 to repay the financing is disregarded and, provided the requirements of paragraphs (b)(1)(i), (ii), and (iv) of this section are satisfied, UTP1's $300 share of the financing and UTP2's $200 share of the financing will be treated as qualified nonrecourse financing secured by real property.

*Example (4).* Personal liability; tiered partnerships. The facts are the same as in Example 3, except that Y's general partners are UTP1 and B, an individual. Because B, an individual, is also personally liable to repay the $500 financing, the entire financing fails to satisfy the requirement in paragraph (b)(1)(iii) of this section. Accordingly, UTP1's $300 share of the financing will not be treated as qualified nonrecourse financing secured by real property.

*Example (5).* Personal liability; tiered partnerships. The facts are the same as in Example 3, except that Y is a limited liability company and UTP1 and UTP2 are not personally liable for the debt. However, UTP1 and UTP2 each pledge property as security for the loan that is other than real property used in the activity of holding real property and other than property that is incidental to the activity of holding real property. The fair market value of the property pledged by UTP1 and UTP2 is greater than 10 percent of the sum of the aggregate gross fair market value of the property held by Y and the aggregate gross fair market value of the property pledged by UTP1 and UTP2. Accordingly, the financing fails to satisfy the requirement in paragraph (b)(1)(iii) of this section by virtue of its failure to satisfy paragraph (b)(4)(iii) of this section. Therefore, the financing is not qualified nonrecourse financing secured by real property.

*Example (6).* Personal liability; Disregarded entity.

(i) X is a single member limited liability company that is disregarded as an entity separate from its owner for federal tax purposes under § 301.7701-3 of this chapter. X owns certain real property and property that is incidental to the activity of holding the real property. X does not own any other property. For federal tax purposes, A, the sole member of X, is considered to own all of the property held by X and is engaged in the activity of holding real property through X. X borrows $500 and uses the proceeds to purchase additional real property that is used in the activity of holding real property. X is personally liable to repay the financing, but A is not personally liable for repayment of the financing under local law. The lender may proceed against all of X's assets if X defaults on the financing.

(ii) X is disregarded so that the assets and liabilities of X are treated as the assets and liabilities of A. However, A is not personally liable for the $500 liability. Provided that the requirements contained in paragraphs (b)(1)(i), (ii), and (iv) of this section are satisfied, the financing will be treated as qualified nonrecourse financing secured by real property with respect to A.

**(c) Effective date.** This section is effective for any financing incurred on or after August 4, 1998. Taxpayers, however, may apply this section retroactively for financing incurred before August 4, 1998.

T.D. 8777, 8/3/98.

**Proposed § 1.465-38 Ordering rules.** [*For Preamble, see ¶ 150,479*]

***Caution:*** The Treasury has not yet amended Reg § 1.465-38 to reflect changes made by P.L. 98-369.

**(a) In general.** In determining which items of deductions otherwise allowable are to be allowed under section 465(a), the following ordering system shall be used:

*(1)* First, all capital losses shall be allowed.

*(2)* Second, all items of deduction entering into the computation under section 1231 shall be allowed.

*(3)* Third, all items of deduction to the extent they do not constitute items of tax preference under section 57 and are not described in paragraph (a)(1) or (2) of this section shall be allowed.

*(4)* Fourth, all items of tax preference under section 57 not described in paragraph (a)(1) or (2) of this section shall be allowed.

**(b) Retention of identity.** When treated as deductions in succeeding taxable years, deductions which are disallowed under section 465(a) shall retain their identity according to the classifications enumerated in paragraph (a) of this section.

**(c) Special rule.** Deductions described in paragraph (a)(4) of this section (relating to tax preference items) which are disallowed by section 465(a) shall be further subdivided according to the taxable year in which they were originally paid or accrued. When such deductions are allowed, those deductions paid or accrued in the earliest taxable years shall be allowed first.

**(d) Examples.** The provisions of this section may be illustrated by the following examples:

*Example (1).* A, an individual calendar year taxpayer, is engaged in an activity described in section 465(c)(1). At the close of 1977 A is at risk $1,000 in the activity. During 1978 A had $3,000 of income from the activity and $7,500 of deductions allocated to the activity. Of the $7,500 of deductions $2,500 are of the type described in § 1.465-38(a)(3) and $5,000 are of the type described in § 1.465-38(a)(4). Assuming nothing else has occurred during 1978 to affect A's amount at risk, A will be allowed $4,000 of deductions and $3,500 of deductions will be disallowed. Since A has no deductions described in § 1.465-38(a)(1) or § 1.465-38(a)(2), the $4,000 of allowed deductions will consist of the entire $2,500 described in § 1.465-38(a)(3) and $1,500 of the $5,000 deductions described in § 1.465-38(a)(4). The $3,500 deductions disallowed will consist of deductions in § 1.465-38(a)(4).

*Example (2).* Assume the same facts as in example (1), and in addition during 1979 A has income from the activity of $10,000. During 1979 A incurred $14,000 of deductions of which $4,000 are described in § 1.465-38(a)(3) and $10,000 are described in § 1.465-38(a)(4). When A's current deductions are added to the deductions which were not allowed and therefore carried over from 1978, A's total deductions from the activity for 1979 are $17,500 ($14,000 + $3,500), of which $4,000 are described in § 1.465-38(a)(3) and $13,500 are described in § 1.465-38(a)(4) ($10,000 + $3,500). Of the $13,500 of deductions described in § 1.465-38(a)(4), $3,500 are from 1978 and $10,000 are from 1979. Assuming nothing occurs during 1979 to affect A's amount at risk, A will be allowed deductions from the activity in the amount of $10,000 (see § 1.465-2(a)). Since A has no deductions described in § 1.465-38(a)(1) or § 1.465-38(a)(2), the entire $10,000 of deductions will come from those deductions described in § 1.465-38(a)(3) and § 1.465-38(a)(4). Of A's $17,500 of deductions from the activity the entire $4,000 described in § 1.465-38(a)(3) will be allowed. Of the $13,500 deductions described in § 1.465-38(a)(4), $6,000 will be allowed. Pursuant to § 1.465-38(c) deductions described in § 1.465-38(a)(4) and occurring in the earliest years shall be allowed first. Accordingly, the $6,000 deductions described in § 1.465-38(a)(4) which are to be allowed shall consist of the entire $3,500 attributable to 1978 and $2,500 of the $10,000 deductions described in § 1.465-38(a)(4) attributable to 1979. The remaining $7,500 of deductions described in § 1.465-38(a)(4) and attributable to 1979 will be carried over and treated as deductions from the activity for 1980.

**Proposed § 1.465-39 Timing of increases and decreases to the amount at risk.** [*For Preamble, see ¶ 150,479*]

***Caution:*** The Treasury has not yet amended Reg § 1.465-39 to reflect changes made by P.L. 98-369, P.L. 96-222.

**(a) General rule.** Except as provided in paragraph (b) of this section, factors which increase or decrease the amount a taxpayer is at risk in a taxable year shall so increase or decrease the amount at risk before determining the amount of section 465(d) loss which is allowed for the year.

**(b) Exception.** Section 465(d) losses which are allowed as deductions for a taxable year under section 465 reduce the amount a taxpayer is at risk with respect to that activity at the close of the immediately succeeding taxable year of the taxpayer.

**(c) Procedure.** The amount a taxpayer is at risk in an activity at the close of a taxable year of the taxpayer is determined by—

*(1)* Reducing the amount at risk in the activity at the close of the preceding taxable year by the amount of the section 465(d) loss which was allowed as a deduction in the preceding taxable year;

*(2)* Increasing the amount at risk in the activity (determined after the application of paragraph (c)(1) of this section) by all factors occurring during the taxable year which increase the amount at risk; and

*(3)* Decreasing the amount at risk in the activity (determined after the application of paragraph (c)(2) of this section) by all factors occurring during the taxable year which decrease the amount at risk.

See § 1.465-41 for illustrations of the operation of this section.

**Proposed § 1.465-41 Examples.** [*For Preamble, see ¶ 150,479*]

***Caution:*** The Treasury has not yet amended Reg § 1.465-41 to reflect changes made by P.L. 98-369, P.L. 96-222.

The provisions of § 1.465-1 through 1.465-40 may be illustrated by the following examples:

*Example (1).* On January 1, 1976, A and B as equal partners form partnership AB. Both A and B, as well as partnership AB, are calendar year taxpayers. On January 1, 1976, A and B each contributes $5,000 from personal assets to AB. On August 1, 1976, AB borrows $6,000 from a bank with A and B each assuming personal liability. On December 31, 1976, AB reduces the amount outstanding on the loan to $4,500. AB has neither loss nor income for 1976. As of December 31, 1976, A's amount at risk in the activity engaged in by AB is determined as follows:

| | |
|---|---|
| Amount at risk in activity as of Jan. 1, 1976 | $ 0 |
| Plus: | |
| Contributions | 5,000 |
| Allocable share of loan for which personal liability was assumed ($6,000 divided by 2) | 3,000 |
| | $8,000 |
| Less: | |
| Allocable share of net reduction in personal liability (See § 1.465-24(b)(2)(i)) ($6,000 minus $4,500 divided by 2) | 750 |
| Amount at risk in activity as of Dec 31, 1976 | $7,250 |

*Example (2).* Assume the same facts as in example (1) and in addition on February 1, 1977, AB borrows $20,000 under a nonrecourse financing arrangement with the lender taking as security equipment purchased with the newly acquired funds. On May 1, 1977 AB reduces the amount outstanding on the loan on which A and B have assumed personal liability to $4,000 ($4,500G_IT_I +22 $500). On August 1, 1977 AB reduces the principal amount due on the nonrecourse loan to $19,000. On October 1, 1977 AB distributes $2,000 each to both A and B. On December 1, 1977 AB reduces the amount outstanding on the loan on which A and B have assumed personal liability to $2,500 ($4,000G1T1 × $1,500). A and B are each allocated $3,000 as their distributive share of partnership income for its taxable year ending December 31, 1977. As of December 31, 1977, A's amount at risk in the activity engaged in by AB is determined as follows:

| | | |
|---|---|---|
| Amount at risk in activity as of 1/1/77 | | $ 7,250 |
| Plus: | | |
| Income from the activity | | 3,000 |
| | | $10,250 |
| Less: | | |
| Allocable share of net reduction in personal liability—5/1/77 ($500 ÷ 2) | $ 250 | |
| Allocable share of net reduction in personal liability—12/1/77 ($1,500 ÷ 2) | 750 | |
| Distribution | 2,000 | 3,000 |
| Amount at risk in activity as of 12/31/77 | | $ 7,250 |

The $20,000 nonrecourse loan does not affect the amount at risk of either A or B because neither of them assumed personal liability and neither of them pledged property not used in the activity as security. Under § 1.465-25(b)(2) the reduction in the nonrecourse liability did not reduce either partner's amount at risk, because the loan was repaid with amounts already in the activity. Under § 1.465-24(b)(2) the reduction in personal liability did reduce the amount at risk, because the repayment was made with amounts already in the activity.

*Example (3).* Assume the same facts as in example (2) and in addition on March 1, 1978, A and B each contributes $1,000 to AB. On September 1, 1978 A and B each contributes $1,500 to AB and on the same date AB reduces the outstanding amount due on the loan for which A and B are personally liable to zero and also repays $500 on the loan for which A and B had not assumed personal liability. For AB's taxable year ending December 1978 A and B each has $10,500 of section 465(d) losses. As of December 31, 1978, A's amount at risk for the activity engaged in by AB is determined as follows:

| | |
|---|---|
| Amount at risk in activity as of 1/1/78 | $7,250 |
| Plus: | |
| Contribution—3/1/78 | 1,000 |
| Contribution—9/1/78 | 1,500 |
| | $9,750 |
| Less: | |
| Allocable share of net reduction in personal liability ($2,500 ÷ 2) | 1,250 |
| Amount at risk in activity as of 12/31/78 | $8,500 |

A was allocated $10,500 in partnership losses. Since A's amount at risk as of December 31, 1978 is only $8,500, A's loss deduction for the activity will also be so limited. Thus, A may take a loss deduction of $8,500 for 1978. This deduction will decrease A's amount at risk at the close of 1979. The $2,000 not allowed as a loss deduction for 1978 will be treated as a deduction in 1979. Under § 1.465-25(b)(2)(i) the reduction in nonrecourse liability did not reduce either partner's amount at risk, because the loan was repaid with amounts already in the activity.

*Example (4).* Assume the same facts as in example (3) and in addition on March 1, 1979, A and B each contributes $1,000 to AB. For AB's taxable year ending December 31, 1979, A and B are each allocated $500 as their share of partnership income (which is calculated without regard to the $2,000 loss deduction disallowed in 1978). As of December 31, 1979, A's amount at risk in the activity engaged in by AB is determined as follows:

| | |
|---|---|
| Amount at risk in activity as of 1/1/79 | $8,500 |
| Less: | |
| Loss allowed in 1978 | 8,500 |
| | $ 0 |
| Plus: | |
| Contribution | 1,000 |
| Amount at risk in activity as of 12/31/79 | $1,000 |

A had a $2,000 loss deduction which was not allowed in 1978 and is treated as a deduction for 1979. Since $500 is A's distributive share of partnership income (which is calculated without regard to such deduction), A's section 465(d) loss for 1979 is $1,500 ($2,000−$500). Since A is at risk $1,000 as of December 31, 1979, only $1,000 is allowable as loss deduction for 1979. The remaining $500 is treated as a deduction for 1980. Therefore, of the $2,000 disallowed loss deduction for 1978 treated as a deduction for 1979, $500 is deductible by reason of A's share of partnership income, $1,000 is deductible because A was at risk $1,000, and the remaining $500 is not deductible for 1979 but is treated as a deduction allocable to the activity for 1980.

*Example (5).* On July 1, 1976, C, along with many other persons, forms partnership W.C. is a calendar year taxpayer and partnership W is on a taxable year ending June 30. On July 1, 1976, C contributes $3,000 to W. On August 1, 1976, W borrows a sum of money for which C's allocable share of personal liability is $7,500. On October 1, 1976, W borrows a sum of money under a nonrecourse financing arrangement with respect to which C's allocable share is $10,000. On March 1, 1977, W repays a portion of the loan for which C is personally liable, thereby reducing C's personal liability to $6,000. C's allocable share of W's losses for the taxable year ending June 30, 1977, is $13,000. On September 1, 1977, C contributes unencumbered personal assets with an adjusted basis of $6,000 to W. On November 1, 1977, W repays another portion of the loan for which C is personally liable, reducing C's personal liability to $5,000. On December 1, 1977, W repays part of the nonrecourse loan thereby reducing C's allocable portion of the amount outstanding to $8,000. The amount of loss deduction which C is allowed for 1977 is determined as follows:

| | |
|---|---|
| Amount at risk in activity as of 7/1/76 (prior to contribution) | $ 0 |
| Plus: | |
| Contribution—7/1/76 | 3,000 |
| Allocable share of loan for which personal liability was assumed | 7,500 |
| | $10,500 |
| Less: | |
| Allocable share of net reduction in personal liability | 1,500 |
| Amount at risk in activity as of 6/30/77 | $ 9,000 |

Although C's allocable share of W's losses for the taxable year ending June 30, 1977, is $13,000, C's allowable loss deduction is limited to the amount at risk as of the close of the partnership's taxable year. Thus, C's loss deduction for the taxable year ending December 31, 1977, is $9,000. The $4,000 not allowed as a loss deduction in 1977 will be treated as a deduction in 1978. The fact that prior to December 31, 1977, but after the close of W's taxable year on June 30, 1977, C made a contribution to W does not increase the amount of loss which C may deduct for 1977. That amount is limited to the amount C was at risk in the activity as of the close of W's taxable year.

*Example (6).* Assume the same facts as in example (5), and in addition for the taxable year ending June 30, 1978, C's allocable share of W's losses is $250 (which is calculated without regard to the $4,000 loss deduction carryover from 1977). On October 1, 1978, W distributes $2,000 to C. The amount of loss deduction which C is allowed for 1978 is determined as follows:

| | |
|---|---|
| Amount at risk in activity as of 7/1/77 | $9,000 |
| Less: | |
| Loss allowed in 1977 | 9,000 |
| | $ 0 |
| Plus: | |
| Contribution—9/1/77 | 6,000 |
| Less: | |
| Net reduction in personal liability 11/1/77 | 1,000 |
| Amount at risk in activity as of 6/30/78 | $5,000 |

C has $4,000 of deductions which were not allowed in 1977 as well as $250 of current loss for W's taxable year ending June 30, 1978. Since $4,250, the entire amount of section 465(d) loss ($4,000 + $250), is less than the amount at risk as of the close of W's taxable year, the entire amount is allowable as a deduction for C's taxable year ending December 31, 1978. The fact that prior to December 31, 1978, but after the close of W's taxable year on June 30, 1978, W made a distribution to C does not decrease the amount of allowable loss which C may deduct in 1978 unless § 1.465-4 is found to apply.

*Example (7).* Assume the facts as in example (6), and in addition for W's taxable year ending June 30, 1979, C's allocable share of income is $1,000. No other events occur which affect C's amount at risk. C's amount at risk as of June 30, 1979, is determined as follows:

| | |
|---|---|
| Amount at risk in activity as of 7/1/78 | $5,000 |
| Less: | |
| Loss allowed in 1978 | 4,250 |
| | $ 750 |
| Plus: | |
| Income from the activity | 1,000 |
| | $1,750 |
| Less: | |
| Distribution—10/1/78 | 2,000 |
| Amount at risk in activity as of 6/30/79 | $ (250) |

For the recapture of certain losses where the amount at risk is less than zero, see section 465(e).

**Proposed § 1.465-42 Activities to which section 465 applies; holding, producing, or distributing motion picture films or video tapes.** [*For Preamble, see ¶ 150,479*]

***Caution:*** The Treasury has not yet amended Reg § 1.465-42 to reflect changes made by P.L. 98-369.

**(a) In general.** Section 465 applies to any taxpayer described in § 1.465-1(d) who is engaged in the activity of holding, producing, or distributing motion picture films or video tapes either as a trade or business or for the production of income.

**(b) Loss.** All receipts related to holding, producing, or distributing motion picture films or video tapes and all items of deduction incurred with respect to such receipts are to be taken into account in determining whether there is a section 465(d) loss.

**(c) Separate activities.** *(1) General rule.* Except in the case of a partner's interest in a partnership or a shareholder's interest in an electing small business corporation, a taxpayer's interest in each different film or video tape shall be considered a separate activity. Thus, if an individual has an interest in four different films, each film represents a separate activity to that individual and that individual has a separate section 465(d) loss and a separate amount at risk with respect to each film.

*(2) Partners and shareholders.* In the case of a partner's interest in a partnership or a shareholder's interest in an electing small business corporation, all films and video tapes in which the partnership or corporation has an interest shall be treated as one activity of the partner or shareholder. Thus, if a partnership has an interest in three different films and two different video tapes, the five films and video tapes will constitute one activity for each partner. This means that all items of income allocated to a partner from the films and video tapes shall be aggregated with all items of deductions allocated to that partner from the films and video tapes so as to result in one amount at risk and one section 465(d) loss (if any) for each partner.

**(d) Different film or video tape.** *(1) General rule.* For the purposes of paragraph (c) of this section, a different film or video tape is one—

(i) In which the finished product is viewed as a single work; and

(ii) Which is of a length such that individuals could normally be expected to view it in one sitting.

For the purposes of paragraph (c) of this section, a movie or video tape can consist of more than one reel.

*(2) Special rule.* In cases where more than one film or video tape exists as a result of applying paragraph (d)(1)(ii) of this section, each portion of the film or video tape which is intended to be viewed in a separate sitting shall be a different film or video tape.

**Proposed § 1.465-43 Activities to which section 465 applies; farming.** [*For Preamble, see ¶ 150,479*]

***Caution:*** The Treasury has not yet amended Reg § 1.465-43 to reflect changes made by P.L. 98-369.

**(a) In general.** Section 465 applies to any taxpayer described in § 1.465-1(d) who is engaged in farming (as defined in section 464(e)) as a trade or business or for the production of income.

**(b) Loss.** All receipts related to the farming activity and all items of deduction incurred with respect to such receipts are to be taken into account in determining whether there is a section 465(d) loss.

**(c) Separate activities.** For each farm rules similar to those found in § 1.465-42(c) shall apply for purposes of determining what constitutes a separate activity.

**(d) Farm.** As used in this section, the term "farm" includes all property where the cultivation of land or the raising or harvesting of any agricultural or horticultural commodity occurs, including the raising, shearing, feeding, caring for, training, and management of animals. For purposes of the preceding sentence, trees (other than trees bearing fruit or nuts) shall not be treated as an agricultural or horticultural commodity.

**(e) Farm activity.** When a procedure for the processing of products grown or animals raised on a farm is carried on within the physical boundaries of a farm, it is necessary to determine whether such activity constitutes a farm activity. In such event, the facts and circumstances of each case must be evaluated. Generally, the most significant facts and circumstances in making this determination include—

*(1)* The similarity of the product as processed to the product as it is being grown or raised;

*(2)* The consistency with normal commercial practice of conducting the procedure within the physical boundaries of a farm; and

*(3)* The necessity of the procedure to obtain a marketable product.

If is determined that the processing procedure is a nonfarm activity, receipts and expenditures from the farm activity and the nonfarm activity cannot be aggregated, and section 465 shall apply only to the receipts and expenditures from the farm activity.

**(f) Examples.** The provisions of paragraph (e) of this section may be illustrated by the following examples.

*Example (1).* A operates a farm where A plants and harvests potatoes. On one portion of the farm A also operates a plant in which the potatoes are processed into potato chips. These potato chips are then shipped to various distributors who bag and sell the potato chips to retailers. The processing of potato chips by A shall not be considered a farm activity. The processing neither results in a final product (potato chip) similar to the product as grown (potato) nor is it necessary to obtain a marketable product.

*Example (2).* B is engaged in the farm activity of growing tobacco. Among the steps B takes to produce a product that is marketable is to maintain a warehouse within the physical boundaries of the farm for the purpose of curing and packing the tobacco that B has grown on the farm. There is no market for the tobacco in the form it takes when harvested. The curing and packing aspect of B's operations is a farm activity, because the final product as processed is similar to the product as grown, and the procedure is necessary to obtain a marketable product.

*Example (3).* C is engaged in growing wine grapes. In addition, C operates a winery within the boundaries of the farm. The capacity of C's winery is such that C purchases grapes from neighboring farms for use in making the wine in addition to using grapes grown in C's own vineyard. Most of the grape growers in the region of C's vineyard do not operate their own wineries but, instead, sell their grapes to a winery. Therefore the operation of the winery on the farm is not consistent with normal commercial practice. Thus, the operation of the winery is not a farm activity. The end product of the winery (wine) is not similar to the product as grown (grapes). In addition, harvested grapes are a marketable commodity without further processing. The result is the same even if the size of C's winery is such that it can only accommodate the grapes grown by C.

*Example (4).* D operates a farm on which D raises Black Angus steers. In addition, D maintains facilities on the farm to slaughter the steers. D has a contract with several grocery stores and restaurants in the area to provide them with this meat. Under these circumstances the slaughtering facilities will not be considered a farm activity.

**Proposed § 1.465-44 Activities to which section 465 applies; leasing section 1245 property.** [*For Preamble, see ¶ 150,479*]

***Caution:*** The Treasury has not yet amended Reg § 1.465-44 to reflect changes made by P.L. 98-369.

**(a) In general.** Section 465 applies to any taxpayer described in § 1.465-1(d)(1) who is engaged in the leasing of any section 1245 property (as defined in section 1245(a)(3)) as a trade or business or for the production of income. However, see section 465(c)(3)(D)(ii) for special exceptions relating to certain corporations engaged in equipment leasing.

**(b) Loss.** All receipts related to the leasing of section 1245 property and all items of deduction incurred with respect to such receipts are to be taken into account in determining whether there is a section 465(d) loss.

**(c) Separate activities.** *(1) General rule.* For each section 1245 property which is leased or held for leasing, rules similar to those found in § 1.465-42(c) shall apply for purposes of determining what constitutes a separate activity.

*(2) Section 1245 property.* For the purposes of section 465 where several section 1245 properties, such as parts of a computer system, comprise one unit under the same lease agreement and are neither separately financed nor subject to different lease terms, the properties will be considered one section 1245 property.

**(d) Lease.** For the purposes of section 465, a lease is any arrangement or agreement, formal or informal, written or oral, whereby the owner of property receives consideration in any form for the use of the property by another party. Whether a specific transaction constitutes a lease or sale shall be determined on the basis of the particular facts and circumstances.

**(e) Ancillary leasing of section 1245 property.** Section 465 shall not apply to amounts received or accrued where the leasing of section 1245 property is incidental to making real property available as living accommodations (such as where an unfurnished rental apartment is equipped with a stove or refrigerator). Section 465 shall also not apply to amounts received or accrued where the leasing of section 1245 property is incidental to the furnishing of services.

**Proposed § 1.465-45 Activities to which section 465 applies; exploring for, or exploiting, oil and gas resources.** [*For Preamble, see ¶ 150,479*]

***Caution:*** The Treasury has not yet amended Reg § 1.465-45 to reflect changes made by P.L. 98-369.

**(a) In general.** Section 465 applies to any taxpayer described in § 1.465-1(d) who is engaged in exploring for, or exploiting, oil and gas resources as a trade or business or for the production of income.

**(b) Loss.** All receipts related to exploring for, or exploiting, oil and gas resources and which constitute gross income from the property within the meaning of section 613, and all items of deduction incurred with respect to such receipts, are to be taken into account in determining whether there is a section 465(d) loss.

**(c) Separate activities.** For each separate oil and gas property (as defined under section 614) rules similar to those found in § 1.465-42(c) shall apply for purposes of determining what constitutes a separate activity.

**(d) Depletion.** In the case of exploring for, or exploiting, oil and gas resources a taxpayer's allowable deduction under section 611 (relating to an allowance for depletion) shall be considered a deduction incurred in the production of income from the activity. Therefore, it must be taken into account in determining the taxpayer's section 465(d) loss. A taxpayer's amount at risk in an activity shall be increased by the excess of the deductions for depletion over the basis of the property (used within the activity) subject to depletion.

**Proposed § 1.465-66 Transfers and dispositions; general rule.** [*For Preamble, see ¶ 150,479*]

***Caution:*** The Treasury has not yet amended Reg § 1.465-66 to reflect changes made by P.L. 98-369.

**(a) General rule.** In the case of a transfer or other disposition of all or part of either an activity or an interest in an activity during a taxable year, any gain recognized on the transfer or disposition shall be treated as income from the activity in accordance with § 1.465-12. In the case of a liquidation by a partnership of a partner's interest in that partnership, or complete redemption by an electing small business corporation of a shareholder's stock in that corporation, the provisions of this section shall apply. In general, this section will cause amounts disallowed by section 465 in previous taxable years to be allowed for the taxable year of transfer or disposition. In addition, any gain recognized as the result of a transfer or disposition of an asset which was at one time used in an activity shall be treated as income from the activity, notwithstanding the fact that the taxpayer's participation in the activity ended prior to the transfer or disposition.

**(b) Examples.** The provisions of this section may be illustrated by the following examples:

*Example (1).* On January 1, 1976, A and B as equal partners form partnership AB. A and B, as well as AB, are calendar year taxpayers. After the close of taxable year 1978 A's basis in AB is $3,000, A's amount at risk is zero, and A has $7,000 of losses from the activity which would have been allowed but for section 465(a). AB's assets are subject to a nonrecourse loan of $20,000, of which A's share is $10,000. On January 1, 1979, C purchases A's interest in AB for $11,000. C pays A $1,000 in cash and takes a 50 percent interest in the partnership, which is renamed BC. BC's assets are still encumbered to the extent of $20,000. A's amount realized is $11,000, which includes $1,000 cash as well as the amount of the encumbrance on A's share of AB's asset ($10,000). Therefore, A's gain is $8,000 ($11,000 – $3,000). This $8,000 is income from the activity. Assuming A is entitled to no deductions allocable to the activity for 1979 other than those disallowed in 1978 under section 465(a), income allocable to the activity for 1979 ($8,000) will exceed the deductions ($7,000). Consequently, A will not have a section 465(d) loss from the activity in 1979 because $7,000 is less than the amount of income from the activity for 1979 ($8,000). The $7,000 of deductions will be allowed for 1979.

*Example (2).* On January 1, 1978, D, an individual, purchases a piece of equipment to be used in an activity described in section 465(c)(1)(C). D purchases the equipment for $10,000, paying $1,000 from personal assets and borrowing $9,000 from a bank. The loan from the bank is a nonrecourse loan secured by the equipment. After the close of 1980 D's basis in the equipment is $2,000 and the amount at risk in the activity is zero. As of the beginning of 1981 D has $7,000 of losses which would be allowed but for section 465(a). The equipment is still encumbered by the $9,000 loan. On January 1, 1981, D gives the piece of equipment to a relative, E. The fair market value of the equipment at the time of the transfer is $9,500. E pays no cash to D but takes the equipment still subject to the nonrecourse loan. D's amount realized on the transfer is $9,000, attributable to the liabilities to which the equipment is subject. D must recognize $7,000 ($9,000 – $2,000) of income on the disposition. This $7,000 is income from the activity. Assuming D is entitled to no deductions allocable to the activity for 1981 other than those disallowed in 1980 under section 465(a) the income allocable from the activity for 1981 ($7,000) will equal the deductions allocable to the activity for 1981 ($7,000). Consequently, D will not have a section 465(d) loss from the activity in 1981 and the $7,000 of deductions will be allowed for 1981, because there is an equal amount of income from the activity in that year.

*Example (3).* E, an individual calendar year taxpayer, is a partner in partnership EFGH, which is also a calendar year taxpayer. At the close of 1978 E's amount at risk is zero, E's adjusted basis is $350, and E has deductions disallowed by section 465 in the amount of $50. E's share of nonrecourse liabilities of the partnership is $400. At the close of 1979 none of the figures has changed and EFGH distributes property (which is not described in section 751) to E in complete liquidation of E's interest in EFGH. Under section 752(b) E is treated as receiving $400. Under section 732(b), E's basis of $350 is reduced to zero. E must recognize $50 of gain ($400 – $350). Under this section, E has income from the activity in the amount of the gain recognized ($50). This will allow E to deduct the $50 of deductions previously suspended. In 1979 E will not have a section 465(d) loss from the activity.

**Proposed § 1.465-67 Transfers and dispositions; pass through of losses suspended under section 465(a).** [*For Preamble, see ¶ 150,479*]

***Caution:*** The Treasury has not yet amended Reg § 1.465-67 to reflect changes made by P.L. 98-369, P.L. 96-222.

**(a) Applicability.** This section shall apply to any transfer or disposition in which—

*(1)* The taxpayer transfers or disposes of such taxpayer's entire interest in the activity or the entity conducting the activity,

*(2)* The basis of the transferee is determined in whole or in part by reference to the basis of the transferor; and

*(3)* The transferor has suspended losses under section 465(a) at the time of the transfer or disposition.

For the treatment of any gain recognized by the transferor, see § 1.465-66.

**(b) Pass through of suspended losses.** If at the close of the taxable year in which the transfer or disposition occurs, the amount of the transferor's section 465(d) loss from the activity is in excess of the transferor's amount at risk in the activity, such excess shall be added to the transferor's basis in the activity. The preceding sentence is to be applied after the determination of any gain to the transferor and is to be used solely for the purpose of determining the basis of the property in the hands of the transferee.

**Proposed § 1.465-68 Transfers and dispositions; amounts at risk in excess of losses disallowed.** [*For Preamble, see ¶ 150,479*]

***Caution:*** The Treasury has not yet amended Reg § 1.465-68 to reflect changes made by P.L. 98-369, P.L. 96-222.

**(a) Applicability.** This section shall apply to any transfer or disposition (except a transfer at death) in which—

*(1)* The taxpayer transfers or disposes of such taxpayer's entire interest in the activity or the entity conducting the activity;

*(2)* The basis of the transferee is determined in whole or in part by reference to the basis of the transferor; and

*(3)* The transferor has an amount at risk which is in excess of losses from the activity.

**(b) General rule.** At the close of the transferor's taxable year in which the transfer or disposition occurs, the transferor's amount at risk in the activity (after being reduced by the transferor's losses from that activity for that taxable year) shall be added to the transferee's amount at risk. In addition, the transferee's amount at risk shall be increased by the amount that the transferee's basis is increased under section 1015(d) (relating to gift tax paid by the transferor).

**(c) Limitation.** The amount by which the transferee's amount at risk is increased under paragraph (b) of this section shall be limited to the amount of the transferee's basis which exceeds the amount considered paid by the transferee at the time of the transfer. For the purposes of this section the amount considered paid by the transferee includes the amount of liabilities to which the transferred property is subject.

**(d) Examples.** The provisions of this section may be illustrated by the following examples:

*Example (1).* On December 31, 1978, F, an individual, makes a gift to G of F's entire interest in an activity described in section 465(c)(1). F had engaged in the activity as an individual. As of the close of 1978 F's amount at risk in the activity is $500, F's adjusted basis in the activity is $9,500, the fair market value of the activity is $20,000, and the activity is subject to a nonrecourse liability of $9,000. G does not pay any cash to F but takes the gift subject to the $9,000 liability. Since F's amount at risk in the activity is $500 at the close of the year, this amount shall be added to G's amount at risk. This amount is not limited by paragraph (c) of this section, because the amount of G's adjusted basis which exceeds the amount G is considered to have paid at the time of the transfer is also $500 ($9,500 – $9,000). Therefore, G is at risk in the amount of $500.

*Example (2).* Assume the same facts as in example (1), except that in addition to G taking the gift subject to the $9,000 liability, G also pays F $1,500 in cash. Regardless of how much F is at risk, G's amount at risk will not be increased as the result of this section. This is because the amount of increase is limited to the excess of G's basis ($10,500, consisting of the $9,000 liability, plus the $1,500 cash paid to F) over the amount G is considered to have paid F ($9,000 + $1,500 = $10,500). Since the excess is zero (10,500 – $10,500), the amount of increase under § 1.465-68 (b) is also zero. G's amount at risk will be increased, however, under § 1.465-22(d) by the $1,500 cash paid to F, and therefore, G's amount at risk is $1,500.

**Proposed § 1.465-69 Transfers and dispositions; amounts at risk in excess of losses disallowed with respect to transfers at death.** [*For Preamble, see ¶ 150,479*]

**(a) Applicability.** If after the close of the taxable year in which a decedent dies, the decedent's amount at risk in the activity (after being reduced by losses previously suspended under section 465(a)) is greater than zero, such amount shall be added to the successor's amount at risk. However, this amount must be adjusted to reflect changes, if any, in the amount at risk occurring as the result of the decedent's death. The successor's amount at risk shall also be increased by the amount which the successor's basis in the activity is increased under section 1014 or 1023(h), (c), (d), and (e).

**(b) Example.** The provisions of this section may be illustrated by the following example:

*Example.* H, an individual, is engaged in an activity described in section 465(c)(1) for a taxable year in which section 1023 applies. On December 31 of such year, H dies. On that date H's basis in the activity is $6,000, H's amount at risk in the activity is $2,500, and the fair market value of the activity is $12,500. Under H's will, J is the sole beneficiary of H's interest in the activity. During the period between H's death and the time J succeeded to the activity nothing occurred which affected the amount at risk. Under sections 1023(h), (c), (d), and (e), the basis of the activity in the hands of J is increased by $5,000, which when added to H's basis of $6,000, gives J a basis in the activity of $11,000. To determine J's amount at risk in the activity, H's amount at risk in the activity ($42,500) is added to the amount by which J's basis in the activity is increased under sections 1023(h), (c), (d), and (e) ($5,000). Therefore, J's amount at risk in the activity is $7,500 ($2,500 + $5,000).

**Proposed § 1.465-75 Amounts at risk with respect to activities begun prior to effective date; in general.** [*For Preamble, see ¶ 150,479*]

Section 465 generally applies to losses attributable to amounts paid or incurred in taxable years beginning after December 31, 1975. For the purposes of applying the at risk limitation to activities begun before the effective date of the provision (and which were not excepted from application of the provision), it is necessary to determine the amount at risk as of the first day of the first taxable year beginning after December 31, 1975. The amount at risk in an activity as of the first day of the first taxable year of the taxpayer beginning after December 31, 1975 (for the purposes of §§ 1.465-75 through 1.465-79, such first day shall be referred to as the effective date) shall be determined according to the rules provided in §§ 1.465-76 through 1.465-79.

**Proposed § 1.465-76 Amounts at risk with respect to activities begun prior to effective date; determination of amount at risk.** [*For Preamble, see ¶ 150,479*]

**(a) Initial amount.** The amount a taxpayer is at risk on the effective date with respect to an activity to which section 465 applies shall be determined in accordance with this section. The initial amount the taxpayer is at risk in the activity shall be the taxpayer's initial basis in the activity as modified by disregarding amounts described in section 465(b)(3) or (4) (relating generally to amounts protected against loss or borrowed from related persons).

**(b) Succeeding adjustments.** For each taxable year ending before the effective date, the initial amount at risk shall be increased and decreased by the items which increased and decreased the taxpayer's basis in the activity in that year as modified by disregarding the amounts described in section 465(b)(3) or (4).

**(c) Application of losses and withdrawals.** *(1)* Losses described in section 465(d) which are incurred in taxable years beginning prior to January 1, 1976 and deducted in such taxable years will be treated as reducing first that portion of the taxpayer's basis which is attributable to amounts not at risk. On the other hand, withdrawals made in taxable years beginning before January 1, 1976 will be treated as reducing the amount which the taxpayer is at risk.

*(2)* Therefore, if in a taxable year beginning prior to January 1, 1976 there is a loss described in section 465(d), it shall reduce the amount at risk only to the extent it exceeds the amount of the taxpayer's basis which is not at risk. For the purposes of this paragraph the taxpayer's basis which is not at risk is that portion of the taxpayer's basis in the activity (as of the close of the taxable year and prior to reduction for the loss) which is attributable to amounts described in section 465(b)(3) or (4).

**(d) Amount at risk shall not be less than zero.** If, after determining the amount described in paragraph (a), (b), and (c) of this section, the amount at risk (but for this paragraph) would be less than zero, the amount at risk on the effective date shall be zero.

**Proposed § 1.465-77 Amounts at risk with respect to activities begun prior to effective date; allocation of loss for different taxable years.** [*For Preamble, see ¶ 150,479*]

If the taxable year of the entity conducting the activity differs from that of the taxpayer, the loss attributable to the activity for the first taxable year of the entity ending after the beginning of the first taxable year of the taxpayer beginning after December 31, 1975, shall be allocated in the following manner: That portion of the loss from the activity for such taxable year of the entity which is attributable to taxable years of the taxpayer beginning before January 1, 1976, is that portion which bears the same ratio to the total loss as the number of days in such taxable year before January 1, 1976, bears to the total number of days in the entire taxable year. Consequently, that portion shall be treated in accordance with § 1.465-76.

**Proposed § 1.465-78 Amounts at risk with respect to activities begun prior to effective date; insufficient records.** [*For Preamble, see ¶ 150,479*]

If sufficient records do not exist to accurately determine under § 1.465-76 the amount which a taxpayer is at risk on the effective date, the amount at risk shall be the taxpayer's basis in the activity reduced (but not below zero) by the taxpayer's share of amounts described in section 465(b)(3) or (4) with respect to the activity on the day before the effective date.

**Proposed § 1.465-79 Amounts at risk with respect to activities begun prior to effective date; examples.** [*For Preamble, see ¶ 150,479*]

The provisions of § 1.465-75 and § 1.465-76 may be illustrated by the following examples:

*Example (1).* J and K, as equal partners, form partnership JK on January 1, 1975 to engage in an activity described in section 465(c)(1). Both J and K, as well as JK, are calendar year taxpayers. On January 1, 1975, each partner contributes $10,000 in cash from personal assets to JK. On July 1, 1975, JK borrows $40,000 (of which J's share is $20,000) from a bank under a nonrecourse financing arrangement secured only by the new equipment purchased with the $40,000 for use in the activity. On September 1, 1975, JK reduces the amount due on the loan to $36,000 (of which J's share is $18,000). On October 1, 1975, JK distributes $3,000 to each partner. For taxable year 1975, JK has no income or loss. Although J's basis in the activity is $25,000 ($10,000 + $18,000 − $3,000). J's amount at risk on the effective date is $7,000, determined as follows:

| | |
|---|---|
| *Initial amount at risk* | $10,000 |
| Plus: | |
| Items which increased basis other than amounts described in section 465(b)(3) or (4) | 0 |
| | $10,000 |
| Less: | |
| Distribution | 3,000 |
| J's amount at risk on effective date | $ 7,000 |

*Example (2).* Assume the same facts as in example (1) except that JK has a section 465(d) loss for 1975, of which J's share is $12,000. Although J's basis in the activity is $13,000 ($10,000 + $18,000 − ($3,000 + $12,000)), J's amount at risk on the effective date is $7,000. determined as follows:

| | |
|---|---|
| *Initial amount at risk* | $10,000 |
| Plus: | |
| Items which increased basis other than amounts described in section 465(b)(3) or (4) | 0 |
| | $10,000 |
| Less: | |
| Distribution plus portion of loss ($12,000) in excess of portion of basis not at risk ($18,000) ($3,000 + 0) | 3,000 |
| J's amount at risk on effective date | $ 7,000 |

*Example (3).* Assume the same facts as in example (1) except that JK has a section 465(d) loss for 1975, and J's share is $23,000. J's basis in the activity is $2,000 ($10,000 + $18,000 − ($3,000 + $23,000)). The amount at risk on the effective date is determined as follows:

| | | |
|---|---|---|
| *Initial amount at risk* | | $10,000 |
| Plus: | | |
| Items which increased basis other than amounts described in section 465(b)(3) or (4) | | 0 |
| | | $10,000 |
| Less: | | |
| Distribution | $3,000 | |
| Portion of loss ($23,000) in excess of portion of basis not at risk ($18,000) | 5,000 | 8,000 |
| J's amount at risk on the effective date | | $ 2,000 |

**Proposed § 1.465-95 Effective date.** [*For Preamble, see ¶ 150,479*]

**(a) In general.** Except as otherwise provided, the regulations under section 465 shall apply to losses attributable to amounts paid or incurred in taxable years beginning after December 31, 1975. For purposes of this paragraph, any amount allowed or allowable for depreciation, amortization, or depletion for any period shall be treated as an amount paid or incurred in such period.

**(b) Special rules.** For special rules relating to the effective date of section 465 with respect to certain leasing activities and certain movie and video tape activities, see section 204(c)(2) and (3) of the Tax Reform Act of 1976 (90 Stat. 1532).

**§ 1.466-1 Method of accounting for the redemption cost of qualified discount coupons.**

***Caution:*** The Treasury has not yet amended Reg § 1.466-1 to reflect changes made by 99-514.

**(a) Introduction.** Section 466 permits taxpayers who elect to use the method of accounting described in section 466 to deduct the redemption cost (as defined in paragraph (b) of this section) of qualified discount coupons (as defined in paragraph (c) of this section) outstanding at the end of the taxable year and redeemed during the redemption period (within the meaning of paragraph (d)(2) of this section) in addition to the redemption cost of qualified discount coupons redeemed during the taxable year which were not deducted for a prior taxable year. For the taxable year in which the taxpayer first uses this method of accounting, the taxpayer is not allowed to deduct the redemption costs of qualified discount coupons redeemed during the taxable year that would have been deductible for the prior taxable year had the taxpayer used this method of accounting for such prior year. (See paragraph (e) of this section for rules describing how this amount should be taken into account.) A taxpayer must use the accrual method of accounting for any trade or business for which and election is made under section 466. Furthermore, the taxpayer must make an election in accordance with the rules in section 466(d) and § 1.466-3 for that trade or business. The method of accounting in section 466 is applicable only to the taxpayer's redemption of qualified discount coupons. Section 466 does not apply to trading stamps or premium coupons, which are subject to the method of accounting in § 1.451-4, or to discount coupons that are not qualified discount coupons.

**(b) Redemption costs.** *(1) Costs deductible under section 466.* The deduction allowed by section 466 applies only to the redemption cost of qualified discount coupons. The term "redemption cost" means an amount equal to:

(i) The lesser of:

(A) The amount of the discount stated on the coupon, or

(B) The cost incurred by the taxpayer for paying the discount; plus

(ii) The amount payable to the retailer (or other person redeeming the coupon from the person receiving the price discount) for services in redeeming the coupon.

The amount payable to the retailer or other person for services in redeeming the coupon is allowed only if the amount payable is stated on the coupon.

*(2) Costs not deductible under section 466.* The term "redemption cost" includes only the amounts stated in paragraph (b)(1) of this section. Amounts other than those mentioned in paragraph (b)(1) of this section cannot be deducted under the method of accounting described in section 466 even though such amounts are incurred in relation to the redemption of qualified discount coupons. Therefore, those amounts must be taken into account as if section 466 did not apply. Examples of such amounts are fees paid to the redemption center or clearinghouse and amounts payable to the retailer in excess of the amount stated on the coupon.

**(c) Qualified discount coupons.** *(1) General rule.* In order for a discount coupon (as defined in paragraph (c)(2)(i) of this section) to be considered a qualified discount coupon, all of the following requirements must be met:

(i) The coupon must have been issued by and must be redeemable by the taxpayer;

(ii) The coupon must allow a discount on the purchase price of merchandise or other tangible personal property;

(iii) The face amount of the coupon must not exceed five dollars;

(iv) The coupon, by its terms, may not be used with other coupons to bring about a price discount reimbursable by the issuer of more than five dollars with respect to any item; and

(v) There must exist a redemption chain (as defined in paragraph (c)(2)(ii) of this section) with respect to the coupon.

*(2) Definitions.* (i) Discount coupon. A discount coupon is a sales promotion device used to encourage the purchase of a specific product by allowing a purchaser of that product to receive a discount on its purchase price. The term "discount coupon" does not include trading stamps or premium coupons, which are subject to the method of accounting in § 1.451-4. A discount coupon may or may not be issued as part of a prior purchase. A discount coupon normally entitles its holders to receive nothing more than a reduction in the sales price of one of the issuer's products. The discount may be stated in terms of a cash amount, a percentage or fraction of the purchase price, a "two for the price of one" deal, or any other similar provision. A discount coupon need not be printed on paper in the form usually associated with coupons; it may be a token or other object so long as it functions as a coupon.

(ii) Redemption chain. A redemption chain exists when the issuer redeems the coupon from some person other than the customer who used the coupon to receive the price discount. Thus, in order to be treated as a qualified discount coupon, the coupon must be issued by the person that initially redeems the coupon from the customer. For purposes of determining whether a redemption chain exists, corporations that are members of the same controlled group of corporations (as defined in section 1563(a)) as the issuer of the coupon shall be treated as the issuer. Thus, if the issuer of the coupon and the retailer that initially redeems the coupon from the customer are members of the same controlled group of corporations, the coupon shall not be treated as a qualified discount coupon.

**(d) Deduction for coupons redeemed during the redemption period.** *(1) General rule.* Two special conditions must be met before the cost of redeeming qualified discount coupons during the redemption period can be deducted from the taxpayer's gross income for the taxable year preceding the redemption period. First, the qualified discount coupons must have been outstanding at the close of such taxable year. Second, the qualified discount coupons must have been received by the taxpayer before the close of the redemption period for that taxable year.

*(2) Redemption period.* The taxpayer can select any redemption period so long as the period does not extend longer than 6 months after the close of the taxpayer's taxable year. A change in the redemption period so selected shall be treated as a change in method of accounting.

*(3) Coupons received.* The deduction provided for in section 466(a)(1) is limited to the redemption costs associated with coupons that are actually received by the taxpayer within the redemption period. For purposes of this paragraph, if the issuer uses a redemption agent or clearinghouse to group, count, and verify coupons after they have been redeemed by a retailer, the coupons received by the redemption agent or clearinghouse will be considered to have been received by the issuer. Nothing in section 466, however, allows deductions to be made on the basis of estimated redemptions, whether such estimates are made by either the issuer or some other party.

**(e) Transitional adjustment.** *(1) In general.* An election to change from some other method of accounting for the redemption of discount coupons to the method of accounting described in section 466 is a change in method of accounting that requires a transitional adjustment. Unless the taxpayer can qualify for a waiver of the suspense account requirement as provided for in section 373(c) of the Revenue Act of 1978 (92 Stat. 2865), the taxpayer should compute the transitional adjustment described in section 481(a)(2) according to the rules contained in this section. This adjustment should be taken into account according to the special rules in subsections (e) and (f) of section 466.

*(2) Net increase in taxable income.* In the case of a transitional adjustment that would result in a net increase in taxable income under section 481(a)(2) for the year of change, that increase should be taken into income over a ten-year period consisting of the year of change and the immediately succeeding nine taxable years. For example, assume that A, a calendar year taxpayer, makes an election to use the method of accounting described in section 466 for the year 1980 and for subsequent years. Assume further that the amount of the transitional adjustment computed under section 481(a)(2) would result in a net increase taxable income of $100 for 1980. Under these facts, A should increase taxable income for 1980 and each of the next nine taxable years by $10.

*(3) Suspense account.* (i) In general. In the case of a transitional adjustment that would result in a net decrease in taxable income under section 481(a)(2) for the year of change, in lieu of applying section 481, the taxpayer must establish a separate suspense account for each trade or business for which the taxpayer has made an election to use section 466. The computation of the initial opening balance in the suspense account is described in paragraph (e)(3)(ii)(A) of this section. An initial adjustment to gross income for the year of election is described in paragraph (e)(3)(ii)(B) of this section. Annual adjustments to the suspense account are described in paragraph (e)(3)(iii)(A) of this section, and gross income adjustments are described in paragraph (e)(3)(iii)(B) of this section. Examples are provided in paragraph (e)(4) of this section. The effect of the suspense account is to defer some part of, or all of, the deduction of the transitional adjustment until the taxpayer no longer redeems discount coupons in connection with the trade or business to which the suspense account relates.

(ii) Establishing a suspense account. (A) Initial opening balance. To compute the initial opening balance of the suspense account for the first taxable year for which the election to use section 466 is effective, the taxpayer must determine the dollar amount of the deduction that would have been allowed for qualified discount coupon redemption costs during the redemption period for each of the three immediately preceding taxable years had the election to use section 466 been in effect for those years. The initial opening balance of the suspense account is the largest such dollar amount reduced by the sum of the adjustments attributable to the change in method of accounting that increase income for the year of change.

(B) Initial year adjustment. If, in computing the initial opening balance, the largest dollar amount of deduction that would have been allowed in any of the three prior years exceeds the actual cost of redeeming qualified discount coupons received during the redemption period following the close of the year immediately preceding the year of election, the excess is included in income in the year of election. Section 481(b) does not apply to this increase in gross income.

(iii) Annual adjustments. (A) Adjustment to the suspense account. Adjustments are made to the suspense account each year to account for fluctuations in coupon redemptions. To compute the annual adjustment, the taxpayer must determine the amount to be deducted under section 466(a)(1) for the taxable year. If the amount is less than the opening balance in the suspense account for the taxable year, the balance in the suspense account is reduced by the difference. Conversely, if such amount is greater than the opening balance in the suspense account for the taxable year, the account is increased by the difference (but not to an amount in excess of the initial opening balance described in paragraph (e)(3)(ii) of this section). Therefore, the balance in the suspense account will never be greater than the initial opening balance in the suspense account determined in paragraph (e)(3)(ii) of this section. However, the balance in the suspense account after adjustments may be less than this initial opening balance in the suspense account.

(B) Gross income adjustments. Adjustments to the suspense account for years subsequent to the year of the election also produce adjustments in the taxpayer's gross income. Adjustments which reduce the balance in the suspense account reduce gross income for the year in which the adjustment to the suspense account is made. Adjustments which increase the balance in the suspense account increase gross income for the year in which the adjustment to the suspense account is made.

*(4) Examples.* (i) The provisions of paragraph (e)(3) of this section may be illustrated by the following examples:

*Example (1).* Assume that the issuer of qualified discount coupons makes a timely election under section 466 for its taxable year ending December 31, 1979, and does not select a coupon redemption period shorter than the statutory period of 6 months. Assume further that the taxpayer's qualified discount coupon redemption costs in the first 6 months of 1977, 1978, and 1979 were $7, $13, and $8 respectively, and that the accounting change adjustments that increase income for 1979 are $10. Since the accounting change adjustment that increases income for 1979, ($10), is greater than the taxpayer's discount coupon redemptions during the first 6 months of 1979 ($8), the net section 481(a)(2) adjustment for the year of change results in a positive adjustment. Because of this, a suspense account is not required. The taxpayer should instead follow the rules in section 466(f) and in paragraph (e)(2) of this section in order to take this positive transitional adjustment into account.

*Example (2).* Assume the same facts as in example (1), except that the sum of the accounting change adjustments that increase income for 1979 is equal to $2. Under these facts the initial opening balance in the suspense account on January 1, 1979 would be $11 (that is, the largest dollar amount of qualified coupon redemption costs in the pertinent years ($13), reduced by the sum of the accounting change adjustments that increase income in the year of change ($2)). Since the coupon redemption costs taken into account in determining the initial opening balance ($13 in 1978) exceed the actual redemption costs in the first 6 months of the taxable year for which the election is first effective ($8 in 1979), the excess of $5 is added to gross income for the year of election (1979).

*Example (3).* Assume, in addition to the facts of example (2), that coupon redemption costs during the redemption period for the 1979 taxable year are $7. Since the qualifying redemption costs ($7) during the redemption period for the taxable year are less than the opening balance in the suspense account ($11) the taxpayer must reduce the suspense account balance by the difference ($4). The taxpayer is also allowed to take a deduction equal to the amount of this adjustment to the suspense account. Thus, the net amount deductible for the 1979 taxable year after taking into account the coupon redemptions during the redemption period, the amount deductible because of the decrease in the suspense account, and the initial year adjustment determined in example (2) is $6 ($7 + $4 – $5).

*Example (4).* Assume, in addition to the facts of example (3), that coupon redemption costs during the redemption period for the 1980 taxable year are $10. Since the qualifying redemption costs during the redemption period for the taxable year ($10) exceed the opening balance of the suspense account at the beginning of the taxable year ($7), the suspense account must be increased by the difference ($3). The taxpayer must also include $3 in gross income for the taxable year. Thus, the net amount deductible for the 1980 taxable year is $7 ($10 – $3).

*Example (5).* Assume, in addition to the facts of example (4), that coupon redemption costs during the redemption period for the 1981 taxable year are $12. Since the qualifying redemption costs for the 1981 taxable year ($12) exceed the opening balance of the suspense account at the beginning of the taxable year ($10), the suspense account must be increased by the difference ($2) but not above the initial opening balance ($11). Thus, the taxpayer will increase the balance by $1. The taxpayer must also include $1 in gross income for the taxable year. Thus, the net amount deductible for the 1981 taxable year is $11 ($12 – $1).

(ii) The following table summarizes examples (2) through (5):

| | Years ending Dec. 31— | | | | | |
|---|---|---|---|---|---|---|
| | 1977 | 1978 | 1979 | 1980 | 1981 | 1982 |
| Facts: | | | | | | |
| Actual coupon redemption costs in first six months | $7 | $13 | $8 | $7 | $10 | $12 |
| Accounting change adjustments that increase income in year of change | — | — | 2 | — | — | — |
| Net adjustment decreasing income in year of change under sec. 481(a)(2) | — | — | 6 | — | — | — |
| Adjustment to suspense account: | | | | | | |
| Opening balance | | | 11 | 7 | 10 | 11 |
| Addition to account | | | | 3 | 1 | |
| Reduction to account | — | — | (4) | — | — | — |
| Opening balance for next year | — | — | 7 | 10 | 11 | — |
| Amount deductible: | | | | | | |
| Initial year adjustment | | | (5) | | | |
| Amount of deductible as actual coupon redemptions during redemption period | | | 7 | 10 | 12 | |
| Adjustment for increase in suspense account | | | | (3) | (1) | |
| Adjustment for decrease in suspense account | — | — | 4 | — | — | — |
| Net amount deductible for the year for coupons redeemed during the redemption period | | | 6 | 7 | 11 | |

**(f) Subchapter C transactions.** *(1) General rule.* If a transfer of substantially all the assets of a trade or business in which discount coupons are redeemed is made to an acquiring corporation, and if the acquiring corporation determines its basis in these assets, in whole or part, with reference to the basis of these assets in the hands of the transferor, then for the purposes of section 466(e) the principles of section 381 and § 1.381(c)(4)-1 will apply. The application of this rule is not limited to the transactions described in section 381(a). Thus, the rule also applies, for example, to transactions described in section 351.

*(2) Special rules.* If, in the case of a transaction described in paragraph (f)(1) of this section, an acquiring corporation acquires assets that were used in a trade or business that was not subject to a section 466 election from a transferor that is owned or controlled directly (or indirectly through a chain or corporations) by the same interests, and if the acquiring corporation uses the acquired assets in a trade or business for which the acquiring corporation later makes an election to

use section 466, then the acquiring corporation must establish a suspense account by taking into account not only its own experience but also the transferor's experience when the transferor held the assets in its trade or business. Furthermore, the transferor is not allowed a deduction for qualified discount coupons redeemed after the date of the transfer attributable to discount coupons issued by the transferor before the date of the transfer. Such redemptions shall be considered to be made by the acquiring corporation.

*(3) Example.* The provisions of paragraph (f)(2) of this section may be illustrated by the following example:

*Example.* Corporation S, a calendar year taxpayer, is a wholly owned subsidiary of Corporation P, a calendar year taxpayer. On December 31, 1982, S acquires from P substantially all of the assets used in a trade or business in which qualified discount coupons are redeemed. P has not made an election under section 466 with respect to the redemption costs of the qualified discount coupons issued in connection with that trade or business. S makes an election to use section 466 for its taxable year ending December 31, 1983, for the trade or business in which the acquired assets are used, and selects a redemption period of 6 months. Assume that P's qualified discount coupon redemption costs in the first 6 months of 1981 and 1982 were $120 and $140 respectively. Assume further that S's qualified discount coupon redemption costs in the first 6 months of 1983 were $130, and that there are no accounting change adjustments that increase income with respect to the election. S must establish a suspense account by taking into account the largest dollar amount of deductions that would have been allowed under section 466(a)(1) for the 3 immediately preceding taxable years of P, including both P's and S's experience with respect to costs actually incurred during the redemption periods relating to those years. Thus, the initial opening balance of S's suspense account is $140. S must also make an initial year adjustment of $10 ($140 – $130), which S must include in income for S's taxable year ending December 31, 1983. P may not take a deduction for the qualified coupon redemptions made after December 31, 1982, that are attributable to coupons issued by P before December 31, 1982. Thus, none of the $130 qualified discount coupon redemption costs incurred by S during the first six months of 1983 may be deducted by P.

---

T.D. 8022, 4/30/85.

---

### § 1.466-2 Special protective election for certain taxpayers.

**(a) General rule.** Section 373(c) of the Revenue Act of 1978 (92 Stat. 2865) allows certain taxpayers, who in prior years have accounted for discount coupons under a method of accounting reasonably similar to the method described in § 1.451-4, to elect to treat that method of accounting as a proper one for those prior years. There are several differences between this protective election and the section 466(d) election. First, the protective election applies only to a single continuous period of taxable years the last year of which ends before January 1, 1979. Second, an otherwise qualifying protective election may apply to coupons which are discount coupons but which would not be treated as qualified discount coupons under Code section 466. Third, certain expenses such as the cost of redemption center service fees, and amounts that are payable to the retailer (or other person redeeming the coupons from the person receiving the price discount) for services in redeeming the coupons but that are not stated on the coupon, can be subtracted from gross receipts for prior years covered by a protective election (if treated as deductible under the accounting method for such years), even though such expenses would not be deductible under Code section 466.

**(b) Requirements.** In order to qualify for this special protective election, the following conditions must be met:

*(1)* For a continuous period of one or more prior taxable years, (the last year of which ends before Jan. 1, 1979), the taxpayer must have used a method of accounting for discount coupons that is reasonably similar to the method provided in § 1.451-4 or its predecessors under the Internal Revenue Code of 1954;

*(2)* The taxpayer must make an election under section 466 of the Internal Revenue Code of 1954 according to the rules contained in § 1.466-3 for its first taxable year ending after December 31, 1978; and

*(3)* The taxpayer must make an election under section 373(c) of the Revenue Act of 1978 according to the rules contained in § 1.466-4 for its first taxable year ending after December 31, 1978.

**(c) Amount to be subtracted from gross receipts.** The amount the taxpayer may subtract under this section for the redemption costs of coupons shall include only:

*(1)* Costs of the type permitted by § 1.451-4 to be included in the estimated average cost of redeeming coupons, plus

*(2)* Any amount designated or referred to on the coupon payable by the taxpayer to the person who allowed the discount on a sale by such person to the user of the coupon.

Nothing in this paragraph shall allow an item to be deducted more than once.

**(d) Right to amend prior tax returns.** This paragraph applies only to those taxpayers who have agreed in a prior year to discontinue the use of the method of accounting described in § 1.451-4 for discount coupon redemptions. If the taxpayer used such method of accounting on the original return filed for the prior taxable year, and if any such year is not closed under the statute of limitations or by reason of a closing agreement with the Internal Revenue Service, a taxpayer who has made a protective election may file an amended return and a claim for refund for such years. In this amended return, the taxpayer should account for its discount coupon redemptions, according to the method of accounting described in § 1.451-4. This is not to be construed, however, to abrogate in any way the rules regarding the close of taxable years due to the statute of limitations or a binding closing agreement between the Internal Revenue Service and the taxpayer.

**(e) Suspense account not required.** If the following three conditions are satisfied, the taxpayer need not establish the suspense account otherwise required by section 466(e). First, the taxpayer must make a timely election under these rules to protect prior years. Second, the method of accounting used in those years must have been used for all discount coupons issued by the taxpayer in those years in all the taxpayer's separate trades or

businesses in which coupons were issued. Third, either before or after an amendment to the taxpayer's tax returns as described in paragraph (d) of this section, a method of accounting reasonably similar to the method of accounting described in § 1.451-4 must have been used for the taxable year ending on or before December 31, 1978. If these conditions are met, the taxpayer will treat the election of the method under section 466 as a change in method of accounting to which the rules in section 481 and the regulations thereunder apply.

**(f) Definition: reasonably similar.** For purposes of paragraphs (b)(1) and (e) of this section, a taxpayer will be considered to have used a method of accounting for discount coupons that is "reasonably similar" to the method of accounting provided in § 1.451-4 if the taxpayer followed the method of accounting described in § 1.451-4 as if that method were a valid method of accounting for discount coupon redemptions.

T.D. 8022, 5/1/85.

## § 1.466-3 Manner of and time for making election under section 466.

**(a) In general.** Section 466 provides a special method of accounting for accrual basis taxpayers who issue qualified discount coupons (as defined in section 466(b)). In order to use the special method under section 466, a taxpayer must make an election with respect to the trade or business in connection with which the qualified discount coupons are issued. If a taxpayer issues qualified discount coupons in connection with more than one trade or business, the taxpayer may use the special method of accounting under section 466 only with respect to the qualified discount coupons issued in connection with a trade or business for which an election is made. The election must be made in the manner prescribed in this section. The election does not require the prior consent of the Internal Revenue Service. An election under section 466 is effective for the taxable year for which it is made and for all subsequent taxable years, unless the taxpayer secures the prior consent of the Internal Revenue Service to revoke such election.

**(b) Manner of and time for making election.** *(1) General rule.* Except as provided in paragraph (b)(2) of this section, an election is made under section 466 and this section by filing a statement of election containing the information described in paragraph (c) of this section with the taxpayer's income tax return for the taxpayer's first taxable year for which the election is made. The election must be made not later than the time prescribed by law (including extensions thereof) for filing the income tax return for the first taxable year for which the election is made. Thus, the election may not be made for a taxable year by filing an amended income tax return after the time prescribed (including extensions) for filing the original return for such year.

*(2) Transitional rule.* If the last day of the time prescribed by law (including extensions thereof) for filing a taxpayer's income tax return for the taxpayer's first taxable year ending after December 31, 1978, falls before December 3, 1979, and the taxpayer does not make an election under section 466 with respect to such taxable year in the manner prescribed by paragraph (b)(1) of this section, an election is made under section 466 and this section with respect to such taxable year if—

(i) Within the time prescribed by law (including extensions thereof) for filing the taxpayer's income tax return for such taxable year, the taxpayer has made a reasonable effort to notify the Commissioner of the taxpayer's intent to make an election under section 466 with respect to such taxable year, and

(ii) Before January 2, 1980, the taxpayer files a statement of election containing the information described in paragraph (c) of this section to be associated with the taxpayer's income tax return for such taxable year.

For purposes of paragraph (b)(2)(i) of this section, a reasonable effort to notify the Commissioner of an intent to make an election under section 466 with respect to a taxable year includes the timely filing of an income tax return for such taxable year if the taxable income reported on the return reflects a deduction for the redemption costs of qualified discount coupons as determined under section 466(a).

**(c) Required information.** The statement of election required by paragraph (b) of this section must indicate that the taxpayer (identified by name, address, and taxpayer identification number) is making an election under section 466 and must set forth the following information:

*(1)* A description of each trade or business for which the election is made;

*(2)* The first taxable year for which the election is made;

*(3)* The redemption period (as defined in section 466(c)(2)) for each trade or business for which the election is made;

*(4)* If the taxpayer is required to establish a suspense account under section 466(e) for a trade or business for which the election is made, the initial opening balance of such account (as defined in section 466(e)(2)) for each such trade or business; and

*(5)* In the case of an election under section 466 that results in a net increase in taxable income under section 481(a)(2), the amount of such net increase.

The statement of election should be made on a Form 3115, which need contain no information other than that required by this paragraph or paragraph (c) of § 1.466-4.

T.D. 8022, 5/1/85

## § 1.466-4 Manner of and time for making election under section 373(c) of the Revenue Act of 1978.

**(a) In general.** Section 373(c)(2) of the Revenue Act of 1978 (92 Stat. 2865) provides an election for taxpayers who satisfy the requirements of section 373(c)(2)(A) (i) and (ii) of the Act. The election is made with respect to a method of accounting for the redemption costs of discount coupons used by the electing taxpayer in a continuous period of one or more taxable years ending before January 1, 1979. The election must be made in the manner prescribed by this section. The election does not require the prior consent of the Internal Revenue Service.

**(b) Manner of and time for making election.**

*(1) General rule.* Except as provided in paragraph (b)(2) of this section, the election under section 373(c) of the Revenue Act of 1978 is made by filing a statement of election containing the information described in paragraph (c) of this section with the taxpayer's income tax return for the taxpayer's first taxable year ending after December 31, 1978. The election must be made not later than the time prescribed by law (including extensions thereof) for filing the income tax return for the taxpayer's first taxable year ending after December 31, 1978. Thus, the election may not be made with an amended income tax return for such year filed after the time prescribed (including extensions) for filing the original return.

*(2) Transitional rule.* If the last day of the time prescribed by law (including extensions thereof) for filing a taxpayer's income tax return for the taxpayer's first taxable year ending

after December 31, 1978, falls before December 3, 1979, and the taxpayer does not make an election in the manner prescribed by paragraph (b)(1) of this section, an election is made under section 373(c) of the Act and this section with respect to a continuous period if—

(i) Within the time prescribed by law (including extensions thereof) for filing the taxpayer's income tax return for the taxpayer's first taxable year ending after December 31, 1978, the taxpayer has made a reasonable effort to notify the Commissioner of the taxpayer's intent to make election under section 373(c) of the Act with respect to the continuous period, and

(ii) Before January 2, 1980, the taxpayer files a statement of election containing the information described in paragraph (c) of this section to be associated with the taxpayer's income tax return for the taxpayer's first taxable year ending after December 31, 1978.

**(c) Required information.** The statement of election required by paragraph (b) of this section must indicate that the taxpayer (identified by name, address, and taxpayer identification number) is making an election under section 373(c) of the Revenue Act of 1978 and must set forth the taxable years in the continuous period for which the election is made. The statement of election should be made on the same form 3115 on which the taxpayer has made a statement of election under section 466. The Form 3115 need contain no information other than that required by this paragraph or paragraph (c) of § 1466-3.

---

T.D. 8022, 5/1/85

---

**§ 1.467-0 Table of contents.**

This section lists the captions that appear in §§ 1.467-1 through 1.467-9.

(4) Allocation of fixed rent within a period.

(5) Rental period length.

*§ 1.467-2 Rent accrual for section 467 rental agreements without adequate interest.*

(a) Section 467 rental agreements for which proportional rental accrual is required.

(b) Adequate interest on fixed rent.

(1) In general.

(2) Section 467 rental agreements that provide for a variable rate of interest.

(3) Agreements with both deferred and prepaid rent.

(c) Computation of proportional rental amount.

(1) In general.

(2) Section 467 rental agreements that provide for a variable rate of interest.

(d) Present value.

(e) Applicable Federal rate.

(1) In general.

(2) Source of applicable Federal rates.

(3) 110 percent of applicable Federal rate.

(4) Term of the section 467 rental agreement.

(i) In general.

(ii) Section 467 rental agreements with variable interest.

(f) Examples.

*§ 1.467-3 Disqualified leasebacks and long-term agreements.*

(a) General rule.

(b) Disqualified leaseback or long-term agreement.

(1) In general.

(2) Leaseback.

(3) Long-term agreement.

(i) In general.

(ii) Statutory recovery period.

(A) In general.

(B) Special rule for rental agreements relating to properties having different statutory recovery periods.

(c) Tax avoidance as principal purpose for increasing or decreasing rent.

(1) In general.

(2) Tax avoidance.

(i) In general.

(ii) Significant difference in tax rates.

(iii) Special circumstances.

(3) Safe harbors.

(4) Uneven rent test.

(i) In general.

(ii) Special rule for real estate.

(iii) Operating rules.

(d) Calculating constant rental amount.

(1) In general.

(2) Initial or final short periods.

(3) Method to determine constant rental amount; no short periods.

(i) Step 1.

(ii) Step 2.

(iii) Step 3.

(e) Examples.

*§ 1.467-4 Section 467 loan.*

(a) In general.

(1) Overview.

(2) No section 467 loan in the case of certain section 467 rental agreements.

(3) Rental agreements subject to constant rental accrual.

(4) Special rule in applying the provisions of § 1.467-7(e), (f), or (g).

(b) Principal balance.

(1) In general.

(2) Section 467 rental agreements that provide for prepaid fixed rent and adequate interest.

(3) Timing of payments.

(c) Yield.

(1) In general.

(i) Method of determining yield.

(ii) Method of stating yield.

(iii) Rounding adjustments.

(2) Yield of section 467 rental agreements for which constant rental amount or proportional rental amount is computed.

(3) Yield for purposes of applying paragraph (a)(4) of this section.

(4) Determination of present values.

(d) Contingent payments.

(e) Section 467 rental agreements that call for payments before or after the lease term.

(f) Examples.

*§ 1.467-5 Section 467 rental agreements with variable interest.*

(a) Variable interest on deferred or prepaid rent.

(1) In general.

(2) Exceptions.

(b) Variable rate treated as fixed.

(1) In general.

(2) Variable interest adjustment amount.

(i) In general.

(ii) Positive or negative adjustment.

(3) Section 467 loan balance.

(c) Examples.

*§ 1.467-6 Section 467 rental agreements with contingent payments. [Reserved]*

*§ 1.467-7 Section 467 recapture and other rules relating to dispositions and modifications.*

(a) Section 467 recapture.

(b) Recapture amount.

(1) In general.

(2) Prior understated inclusion.

(3) Section 467 gain.

(i) In general.

(ii) Certain dispositions.

(c) Special rules.

(1) Gifts.

(2) Dispositions at death.
(3) Certain tax-free exchanges.
(i) In general.
(ii) Dispositions covered.
(A) In general.
(B) Transfers to certain tax-exempt organizations.
(4) Dispositions by transferee.
(5) Like-kind exchanges and involuntary conversions.
(6) Installment sales.
(7) Dispositions covered by section 170(e), 341(e)(12), or 751(c).
(d) Examples.
(e) Other rules relating to dispositions.
(1) In general.
(2) Treatment of section 467 loan.
(3) [Reserved]
(4) Examples.
(f) Treatment of assignments by lessee and lessee-financed renewals.
(1) Substitute lessee use.
(2) Treatment of section 467 loan.
(3) Lessor use.
(4) Examples.
(g) Application of section 467 following a rental agreement modification.
(1) Substantial modifications.
(i) Treatment of pre-modification items.
(ii) Computations with respect to post-modification items.
(iii) Adjustments.
(A) Adjustment relating to certain prepayments.
(B) Adjustment relating to retroactive beginning of lease term.
(iv) Coordination with rules relating to dispositions and assignments.
(A) Dispositions.
(B) Assignments.
(2) Other modifications.
(i) Computation of section 467 loan for modified agreement.
(ii) Change in balance of section 467 loan.
(iii) Section 467 rent and interest after the modification.
(iv) Applicable Federal rate.
(v) Modification effective within a rental period.
(vi) Other adjustments.
(vii) Coordination with rules relating to dispositions and assignments.
(viii) Exception for agreements entered into prior to effective date of section 467.
(3) Adjustment by Commissioner.
(4) Effective date of modification.
(5) Examples.
(h) Omissions or duplications.
(1) In general.
(2) Example.

*§ 1.467-8 Automatic consent to change to constant rental accrual for certain rental agreements.*
(a) General rule.
(b) Agreements to which automatic consent applies.

*§ 1.467-9 Effective dates and automatic method changes for certain agreements.*
(a) In general.
(b) Automatic consent for certain rental agreements.
(c) Application of regulation project IA-292-84 to certain leasebacks and long-term agreements.
(d) Entered into.
(e) Change in method of accounting.
(1) In general.
(2) Application of regulation project IA-292-84.
(3) Automatic change procedures.

T.D. 8820, 5/17/99, T.D. 8917, 1/4/2001.

**§ 1.467-1 Treatment of lessors and lessees generally.**

**(a) Overview.** *(1) In general.* When applicable, section 467 requires a lessor and lessee of tangible property to treat rents consistently and to use the accrual method of accounting (and time value of money principles) regardless of their overall method of accounting. In addition, in certain cases involving tax avoidance, the lessor and lessee must take rent and stated or imputed interest into account under a constant rental accrual method, pursuant to which the rent is treated as accruing ratably over the entire lease term.

*(2) Cases in which rules are inapplicable.* Section 467 applies only to leases (or other similar arrangements) that constitute section 467 rental agreements as defined in paragraph (c) of this section. For example, a rental agreement is not a section 467 rental agreement, and, therefore, is not subject to the provisions of this section and §§ 1.467-2 through 1.467-9 (the section 467 regulations), if it specifies equal amounts of rent for each month throughout the lease term and all payments of rent are due in the calendar year to which the rent relates (or in the preceding or succeeding calendar year). In addition, the section 467 regulations do not apply to a rental agreement that requires total rents of $250,000 or less. For purposes of determining whether the agreement has total rents of $250,000 or less, certain specified contingent rent is disregarded.

*(3) Summary of rules.* (i) Basic rules. Paragraph (c) of this section provides rules for determining whether a rental agreement is a section 467 rental agreement. Paragraphs (d) and (e) of this section provide rules for determining the amount of rent and interest, respectively, required to be taken into account by a lessor and lessee under a section 467 rental agreement. Paragraphs (f) through (h) and (j) of this section provide various definitions and special rules relating to the application of the section 467 regulations. Paragraph (i) of this section is reserved.

(ii) Special rules. Section 1.467-2 provides rules for section 467 rental agreements that have deferred or prepaid rents without providing for adequate interest. Section 1.467-3 provides rules for application of the constant rental accrual method, including criteria for determining whether an agreement is subject to this method. Section 1.467-4 provides rules for establishing and adjusting a section 467 loan (the amount that a lessor is deemed to have loaned to the lessee, or vice versa, pursuant to the application of the section 467 regulations). Section 1.467-5 provides rules for applying the section 467 regulations where a rental agreement requires payments of interest at a variable rate. Section 1.467-6, relating to the treatment of certain section 467 rental agreements with contingent payments, is reserved. Section 1.467-7 provides rules for the treatment of dispositions by a lessor of property subject to a section 467 rental agreement and the treatment of assignments by lessees and certain lessee-financed renewals of a section 467 rental agreement. Section 1.467-7 also provides rules for the treatment of modified rental agreements. Section 1.467-8 provides special transitional rules relating to the method of accounting for certain rental agreements entered into on or before May 18, 1999. Finally, § 1.467-9 provides the effective date rules for the section 467 regulations.

*(4) Scope of rules.* No inference should be drawn from any provision of this section or §§ 1.467-2 through 1.467-9 concerning whether—

(i) For Federal tax purposes, an arrangement constitutes a lease; or

(ii) For Federal tax purposes, any obligation of the lessee under a rental agreement is treated as rent.

*(5) Application of other authorities.* Notwithstanding section 467 and the regulations thereunder, other authorities such as section 446(b) clear-reflection-of-income principles, section 482, and the substance-over-form doctrine, may be applied by the Commissioner to determine the income and expense from a rental agreement (including the proper allocation of fixed rent under a rental agreement).

**(b) Method of accounting for section 467 rental agreements.** If a rental agreement is a section 467 rental agreement, as described in paragraph (c) of this section, the lessor and lessee must each take into account for any taxable year the sum of—

*(1)* The section 467 rent for the taxable year (as defined in paragraph (d) of this section); and

*(2)* The section 467 interest for the taxable year (as defined in paragraph (e) of this section).

**(c) Section 467 rental agreements.** *(1) In general.* Except as otherwise provided in paragraph (c)(4) of this section, the term section 467 rental agreement means a rental agreement, as defined in paragraph (h)(12) of this section, that has increasing or decreasing rents (as described in paragraph (c)(2) of this section), or deferred or prepaid rents (as described in paragraph (c)(3) of this section).

*(2) Increasing or decreasing rent.* (i) Fixed rent. (A) In general. A rental agreement has increasing or decreasing rent if the annualized fixed rent, as described in paragraph (j)(3) of this section, allocated to any rental period exceeds the annualized fixed rent allocated to any other rental period in the lease term.

(B) Certain rent holidays disregarded. Notwithstanding the provisions of paragraph (c)(2)(i)(A) of this section, a rental agreement does not have increasing or decreasing rent if the increasing or decreasing rent is solely attributable to a rent holiday provision allowing reduced rent (or no rent) for a period of three months or less at the beginning of the lease term.

(ii) Fixed rent allocated to a rental period. (A) Specific allocation. (1) In general. If a rental agreement provides a specific allocation of fixed rent, as described in paragraph (c)(2)(ii)(A)(2) of this section, the amount of fixed rent allocated to each rental period during the lease term is the amount of fixed rent allocated to that period by the rental agreement.

(2) Rental agreements specifically allocating fixed rent. A rental agreement specifically allocates fixed rent if the rental agreement unambiguously specifies, for periods no longer than a year, a fixed amount of rent for which the lessee becomes liable on account of the use of the property during that period, and the total amount of fixed rent specified is equal to the total amount of fixed rent payable under the lease. For example, a rental agreement providing that rent is $100,000 per calendar year, and providing for total payments of fixed rent equal to the total amount specified, specifically allocates rent. A rental agreement stating only when rent is payable does not specifically allocate rent.

(B) No specific allocation. If a rental agreement does not provide a specific allocation of fixed rent (for example, because the total amount of fixed rent specified is not equal to the total amount of fixed rent payable under the lease), the amount of fixed rent allocated to a rental period is the amount of fixed rent payable during that rental period. If an amount of fixed rent is payable before the beginning of the lease term, it is allocated to the first rental period in the lease term. If an amount of fixed rent is payable after the end of the lease term, it is allocated to the last rental period in the lease term.

(iii) Contingent rent. (A) In general. A rental agreement has increasing or decreasing rent if it requires (or may require) the payment of contingent rent (as defined in paragraph (h)(2) of this section), other than contingent rent described in paragraph (c)(2)(iii)(B) of this section.

(B) Certain contingent rent disregarded. For purposes of this paragraph (c)(2)(iii), rent is disregarded to the extent it is contingent as the result of one or more of the following provisions—

(1) A qualified percentage rents provision, as defined in paragraph (h)(8) of this section;

(2) An adjustment based on a reasonable price index, as defined in paragraph (h)(10) of this section;

(3) A provision requiring the lessee to pay third-party costs, as defined in paragraph (h)(15) of this section;

(4) A provision requiring the payment of late payment charges, as defined in paragraph (h)(4) of this section;

(5) A loss payment provision, as defined in paragraph (h)(7) of this section;

(6) A qualified TRAC provision, as defined in paragraph (h)(9) of this section;

(7) A residual condition provision, as defined in paragraph (h)(13) of this section;

(8) A tax indemnity provision, as defined in paragraph (h)(14) of this section;

(9) A variable interest rate provision, as defined in paragraph (h)(16) of this section; or

(10) Any other provision provided in regulations or other published guidance issued by the Commissioner, but only if the provision is designated as contingent rent to be disregarded for purposes of this paragraph (c)(2)(iii).

*(3) Deferred or prepaid rent.* (i) Deferred rent. A rental agreement has deferred rent under this paragraph (c)(3) if the cumulative amount of rent allocated as of the close of a calendar year (determined under paragraph (c)(3)(iii) of this section) exceeds the cumulative amount of rent payable as of the close of the succeeding calendar year.

(ii) Prepaid rent. A rental agreement has prepaid rent under this paragraph (c)(3) if the cumulative amount of rent payable as of the close of a calendar year exceeds the cumulative amount of rent allocated as of the close of the succeeding calendar year (determined under paragraph (c)(3)(iii) of this section).

(iii) Rent allocated to a calendar year. For purposes of this paragraph (c)(3), the rent allocated to a calendar year is the sum of—

(A) The fixed rent allocated to any rental period (determined under paragraph (c)(2)(ii) of this section) that begins and ends in the calendar year;

(B) A ratable portion of the fixed rent allocated to any other rental period that begins or ends in the calendar year; and (C) Any contingent rent that accrues during the calendar year.

(iv) Examples. The following examples illustrate the application of this paragraph (c)(3):

*Example (1).* (i) A and B enter into a rental agreement that provides for the lease of property to begin on January 1, 2000, and end on December 31, 2003. The rental agreement provides that rent of $100,000 accrues during each year of the lease term. Under the rental agreement, no rent is payable during calendar year 2000, a payment of $100,000 is to be made on December 31, 2001, and December 31, 2002, and a payment of $200,000 is to be made on December 31, 2003. A and B both select the calendar year as their rental period. Thus, the amount of rent allocated to each rental period under paragraph (c)(2)(ii) of this section is $100,000. Therefore, the rental agreement does not have increasing or decreasing rent as described in paragraph (c)(2)(i) of this section.

(ii) Under paragraph (c)(3)(i) of this section, a rental agreement has deferred rent if, at the close of a calendar year, the cumulative amount of rent allocated under paragraph (c)(3)(iii) of this section exceeds the cumulative amount of rent payable as of the close of the succeeding year. In this example, there is no deferred rent: the rent allocated to 2000 ($100,000) does not exceed the cumulative rent payable as of December 31, 2001 ($100,000); the rent allocated to 2001 and preceding years ($200,000) does not exceed the cumulative rent payable as of December 31, 2002 ($200,000); the rent allocated to 2002 and preceding years ($300,000) does not exceed the cumulative rent payable as of December 31, 2003 ($400,000); and the rent allocated to 2003 and preceding years ($400,000) does not exceed the cumulative rent payable as of December 31, 2004 ($400,000). Therefore, because the rental agreement does not have increasing or decreasing rent and does not have deferred or prepaid rent, the rental agreement is not a section 467 rental agreement.

*Example (2).* (i) A and B enter into a rental agreement that provides for a 10-year lease of personal property, beginning on January 1, 2000, and ending on December 31, 2009. The rental agreement provides for accruals of rent of $10,000 during each month of the lease term. Under paragraph (c)(3)(iii) of this section, $120,000 is allocated to each calendar year. The rental agreement provides for a $1,200,000 payment on December 31, 2000.

(ii) The rental agreement does not have increasing or decreasing rent as described in paragraph (c)(2)(i) of this section. The rental agreement, however, provides prepaid rent under paragraph (c)(3)(ii) of this section because the cumulative amount of rent payable as of the close of a calendar year exceeds the cumulative amount of rent allocated as of the close of the succeeding calendar year. For example, the cumulative amount of rent payable as of the close of 2000 ($1,200,000 is payable on December 31, 2000) exceeds the cumulative amount of rent allocated as of the close of 2001, the succeeding calendar year ($240,000). Accordingly, the rental agreement is a section 467 rental agreement.

*(4) Rental agreements involving total payments of $250,000 or less.* (i) In general. A rental agreement is not a section 467 rental agreement if, as of the agreement date (as defined in paragraph (h)(1) of this section), it is not reasonably expected that the sum of the aggregate amount of rental payments under the rental agreement and the aggregate value of all other consideration to be received for the use of property (taking into account any payments of contingent rent, and any other contingent consideration) will exceed $250,000.

(ii) Special rules in computing amount described in paragraph (c)(4)(i) of this section of this section. The following rules apply in determining the amount described in paragraph (c)(4)(i) of this section:

(A) Stated interest on deferred rent is not taken into account. However, the Commissioner may recharacterize a portion of stated interest as additional rent if a rental agreement provides for interest on deferred rent at a rate that, in light of all of the facts and circumstances, is clearly greater than the arm's-length rate of interest that would have been charged in a lending transaction between the lessor and lessee.

(B) Consideration that does not involve a cash payment is taken into account at its fair market value. A liability that is either assumed or secured by property acquired subject to the liability is taken into account at the sum of its remaining principal amount and accrued interest (if any) thereon or, in the case of an obligation originally issued at a discount, at the sum of its adjusted issue price and accrued qualified stated interest (if any), within the meaning of § 1.1273-1(c)(1).

(C) All rental agreements that are part of the same transaction or a series of related transactions involving the same lessee (or any related person) and the same lessor (or any related person) are treated as a single rental agreement. Whether two or more rental agreements are part of the same transaction or a series of related transactions depends on all the facts and circumstances.

(D) If an agreement includes a provision increasing or decreasing rent payable solely as a result of an adjustment based on a reasonable price index, the amount described in paragraph (c)(4)(i) of this section must be determined as if the applicable price index did not change during the lease term.

(E) If an agreement includes a variable interest rate provision (as defined in paragraph (h)(16) of this section), the amount described in paragraph (c)(4)(i) of this section must be determined by using fixed rate substitutes (determined in the same manner as under § 1.1275-5(e), treating the agreement date as the issue date) for the variable rates of interest applicable to the lessor's indebtedness.

(F) Contingent rent described in paragraphs (c)(2)(iii)(B)(3) through (8) of this section is not taken into account.

**(d) Section 467 rent.** *(1) In general.* The section 467 rent for a taxable year is the sum of—

(i) The fixed rent for any rental period (determined under paragraph (d)(2) of this section) that begins and ends in the taxable year;

(ii) A ratable portion of the fixed rent for any other rental period beginning or ending in the taxable year; and

(iii) In the case of a section 467 rental agreement that provides for contingent rent, the contingent rent that accrues during the taxable year.

*(2) Fixed rent for a rental period.* (i) Constant rental accrual. In the case of a section 467 rental agreement that is a disqualified leaseback or long-term ageement (as described in § 1.467-3(b)), the fixed rent for a rental period is the constant rental amount (as determined under § 1.467-3(d)).

(ii) Proportional rental accrual. In the case of a section 467 rental agreement that is not described in paragraph (d)(2)(i) of this section, and does not provide adequate interest on fixed rent (as determined under § 1.467-2(b)), the fixed rent for a rental period is the proportional rental amount (as determined under § 1.467-2(c)).

(iii) Section 467 rental agreement accrual. In the case of a section 467 rental agreement that is not described in either paragraph (d)(2)(i) or (ii) of this section, the fixed rent for a rental period is the amount of fixed rent allocated to the rental period under the rental agreement, as determined under paragraph (c)(2)(ii) of this section.

**(e) Section 467 interest.** *(1) In general.* The section 467 interest for a taxable year is the sum of—

(i) The interest on fixed rent for any rental period that begins and ends in the taxable year;

(ii) A ratable portion of the interest on fixed rent for any other rental period beginning or ending in the taxable year; and

(iii) In the case of a section 467 rental agreement that provides for contingent rent, any interest that accrues on the contingent rent during the taxable year.

*(2) Interest on fixed rent for a rental period.* (i) In general. Except as provided in paragraph (e)(2)(ii) of this section and § 1.467-5(b)(1)(ii), the interest on fixed rent for a rental period is equal to the product of—

(A) The principal balance of the section 467 loan (as described in § 1.467-4(b)) at the beginning of the rental period; and

(B) The yield of the section 467 loan (as described in § 1.467-4(c)).

(ii) Section 467 rental agreements with adequate interest. Except in the case of a section 467 rental agreement that is a disqualified leaseback or long-term agreement, if a section 467 rental agreement provides adequate interest under § 1.467-2(b)(1)(i) (agreements with no deferred or prepaid rent) or § 1.467-2(b)(1)(ii) (agreements with adequate interest stated at a single fixed rate), the interest on fixed rent for a rental period is the amount of interest provided in the rental agreement for the period.

*(3) Treatment of interest.* If the section 467 interest for a rental period is a positive amount, the lessor has interest income and the lessee has an interest expense. If the section 467 interest for a rental period is a negative amount, the lessee has interest income and the lessor has an interest expense. Section 467 interest is treated as interest for all purposes of the Internal Revenue Code.

**(f) Substantial modification of a rental agreement.** *(1) Treatment as new agreement.* (i) In general. If a substantial modification of a rental agreement occurs after June 3, 1996, the post-modification agreement is treated as a new agreement and the date on which the modification occurs is treated as the agreement date in applying section 467 and the regulations thereunder to the post-modification agreement. Thus, for example, the post-modification agreement is treated as a new agreement entered into on the date the modification occurs for purposes of determining whether it is a section 467 rental agreement under this section, whether it is a disqualified leaseback or long-term agreement under § 1.467-3, and whether it is entered into after the applicable effective date in § 1.467-9.

(ii) Limitation. In the case of a substantial modification of a rental agreement occurring on or before May 18, 1999, this paragraph (f) applies only if—

(A) The rental agreement was a disqualified leaseback or long-term agreement before the modification and the agreement date, determined without regard to the modification, is after June 3, 1996; or

(B) The post-modification agreement would, after application of the rules in this paragraph (f) (other than the special rule for disqualified agreements in paragraph (f)(4)(iii) of this section), be a disqualified leaseback or long-term agreement.

*(2) Post-modification agreement; in general.* For purposes of determining whether a post-modification agreement is a section 467 rental agreement or a disqualified leaseback or long-term agreement under paragraph (f)(1) of this section, the terms of the post-modification agreement are, except as provided in paragraph (f)(4) of this section, only those terms that provide for rights and obligations relating to post-modification items (within the meaning of paragraph (f)(5)(iv) of this section).

*(3) Other effects of a modification.* For rules relating to amounts that must be taken into account following certain modifications, see § 1.467-7(g).

*(4) Special rules.* (i) Carryover of character; leasebacks. If an agreement is a leaseback prior to its modification and the lessee prior to the modification (or a related person) is the lessee after the modification, the post-modification agreement is a leaseback even if the post-modification lessee did not have an interest in the property at any time during the two-year period ending on the date on which the modification occurs.

(ii) Carryover of character; long-term agreements. If an agreement is a long-term agreement prior to its modification and the entire agreement (as modified) would be a long-term agreement, the post-modification agreement is a long-term agreement.

(iii) Carryover of character; disqualified agreements. If an agreement (as in effect before its modification) is a disqualified leaseback or long-term agreement as the result of a determination (whether occurring before or after the modification) under § 1.467-3(b)(1)(ii) and the post-modification agreement is a section 467 rental agreement (or the entire agreement (as modified) would be a section 467 rental agreement), the post-modification agreement will, notwithstanding its treatment as a new agreement under paragraph (f)(1)(i) of this section, be subject to constant rental accrual unless the Commissioner determines that, because of the absence of tax avoidance potential, the post-modification agreement should not be treated as a disqualified leaseback or long-term agreement.

(iv) Allocation of rent. If the entire agreement (as modified) provides a specific allocation of fixed rent, as described in paragraph (c)(2)(ii)(A)(2) of this section, the post-modification agreement is treated as an agreement that provides a specific allocation of fixed rent. If the entire agreement (as modified) does not provide a specific allocation of fixed rent, the fixed rent allocated to rental periods during the lease term of the post-modification agreement is determined by applying the rules of paragraph (c)(2)(ii)(B) of this section to the entire agreement (as modified).

(v) Difference between aggregate rent and interest and aggregate payments. (A) In general. Except as provided in paragraph (f)(4)(v)(B) of this section, a post-modification agreement described in paragraph (f)(4)(v)(C) of this section is treated as a section 467 rental agreement subject to proportional rental accrual (determined under § 1.467-2(c)).

(B) Constant rental accrual prior to the modification. A post-modification agreement described in paragraph (f)(4)(v)(C) of this section is treated as a section 467 rental agreement subject to constant rental accrual if—

(1) Constant rental accrual is required under paragraph (f)(4)(iii) of this section; or

(2) The post-modification agreement involves total payments of more than $250,000 (as described in paragraph (c)(4) of this section), and the Commissioner determines that the post-modification agreement is a disqualified leaseback or long-term agreement.

(C) Agreements described in this paragraph (f)(4)(v)(C). A post-modification agreement is described in this paragraph (f)(4)(v)(C) if the aggregate amount of fixed rent and stated interest treated as post-modification items does not equal the aggregate amount of payments treated as post-modification items.

(vi) Principal purpose of tax avoidance. If a principal purpose of a substantial modification is to avoid the purpose or intent of section 467 or the regulations thereunder, the Commissioner may treat the entire agreement (as modified) as a single agreement for purposes of section 467 and the regulations thereunder.

*(5) Definitions.* The following definitions apply for purposes of this paragraph (f) and § 1.467-7(g):

(i) A modification of a rental agreement is any alteration, including any deletion or addition, in whole or in part, of a legal right or obligation of the lessor or lessee thereunder, whether the alteration is evidenced by an express agreement (oral or written), conduct of the parties, or otherwise.

(ii) A modification is substantial only if, based on all of the facts and circumstances, the legal rights or obligations that are altered and the degree to which they are altered are economically substantial. A modification of a rental agreement will not be treated as substantial solely because it is not described in paragraph (f)(6) of this section.

(iii) A modification occurs on the earlier of the first date on which there is a binding contract that substantially sets forth the terms of the modification or the date on which agreement to such terms is otherwise evidenced.

(iv) Post-modification items with respect to any modification of a rental agreement are all items (other than pre-modification items) provided under the terms of the entire agreement (as modified).

(v) Pre-modification items with respect to any modification of a rental agreement are pre-modification rent, interest thereon, and payments allocable thereto (whether payable before or after the modification.) For this purpose—

(A) Pre-modification rent is rent allocable to periods before the effective date of the modification, but only to the extent such rent is payable under the entire agreement (as modified) at the time such rent was due under the agreement in effect before the modification; and

(B) Pre-modification items are identified by applying payments, in the order payable under the entire agreement (as modified) unless the agreement specifies otherwise, to rent and interest thereon in the order in which amounts accrue.

(vi) The entire agreement (as modified) with respect to any modification is the agreement consisting of pre-modification terms providing for rights and obligations that are not affected by the modification and post-modification terms providing for rights and obligations that differ from the rights and obligations under the agreement in effect before the modification. For example, if a 10-year rental agreement that provides for rent of $25,000 per year is modified at the end of the 5th year to provide for rent of $30,000 per year in subsequent years, the entire agreement (as modified) provides for a 10-year lease term and provides for rent of $25,000 per year in years 1 through 5 and rent of $30,000 per year in years 6 through 10. The result would be the same if the modification provided for both the increase in rent and the substitution of a new lessee.

*(6) Safe harbors.* Notwithstanding the provisions of paragraph (f)(5) of this section, a modification of a rental agreement is not a substantial modification if the modification occurs solely as the result of one or more of the following--

(i) The refinancing of any indebtedness incurred by the lessor to acquire the property subject to the rental agreement and secured by such property (or any refinancing thereof) but only if all of the following conditions are met—

(A) Neither the amount, nor the time for payment, of the principal amount of the new indebtedness differs from the amount and time for payment of the remaining principal amount of the refinanced indebtedness, except for de minimis changes;

(B) For each of the remaining rental periods, the rent allocation schedule, the payments of rent and interest, and the amount accrued under section 467 are changed only to the extent necessary to take into account the change in financing costs, and such changes are made pursuant to the terms of the rental agreement in effect before the modification;

(C) The lessor and the lessee are not related persons to each other or to any lender to the lessor with respect to the property (whether under the refinanced indebtedness or the new indebtedness); and

(D) With respect to the indebtedness being refinanced, the lessor was granted a unilateral option (within the meaning of § 1.1001-3(c)(3)) by the creditor to repay the refinanced indebtedness, exercisable with or without the lessee's consent;

(ii) A change in the obligation of the lessee to make any of the contingent payments described in paragraphs (c)(2)(iii)(B)(3) through (8) of this section; or

(iii) A change in the amount of fixed rent allocated to a rental period that, when combined with all previous changes in the amount of fixed rent allocated to the rental period, does not exceed one percent of the fixed rent allocated to that rental period prior to the modification.

*(7) Special rules for certain transfers.* (i) In general. For purposes of this paragraph (f), a substitution of a new lessee or a sale, exchange, or other disposition by a lessor of property subject to a rental agreement will not, by itself, be treated as a substantial modification unless a principal purpose of the transaction giving rise to the modification is the avoidance of Federal income tax. In determining whether a principal purpose of the transaction giving rise to the modification is the avoidance of Federal income tax--

(A) The safe harbors and other principles of § 1.467-3(c) are taken into account; and

(B) The Commissioner may treat the post-modification agreement as a new agreement or treat the entire agreement (as modified) as a single agreement.

(ii) Exception. Notwithstanding the provisions of paragraph (f)(7)(i) of this section, the continuing lessor and the new lessee (in the case of a substitution of a new lessee) or the new lessor and the continuing lessee (in the case of a sale, exchange, or other disposition by a lessor of property subject to a rental agreement) may, in appropriate cases, request the Commissioner to treat the transaction as if it were a substantial modification in order to have the provisions of paragraph (f)(4)(iii) of this section and § 1.467-7(g)(1) apply to the transaction.

**(g) Treatment of amounts payable by lessor to lessee.** *(1) Interest.* For purposes of determining present value, any amounts payable by the lessor to the lessee as interest on prepaid rent are treated as negative amounts.

*(2) Other amounts. [Reserved]*

**(h) Meaning of terms.** The following meanings apply for purposes of this section and §§ 1.467-2 through 1.467-9:

*(1)* Agreement date means the earlier of the lease date or the first date on which there is a binding written contract that substantially sets forth the terms under which the property will be leased.

*(2)* Contingent rent means any rent that is not fixed rent, including any amount reflecting an adjustment based on a reasonable price index (as defined in paragraph (h)(10) of this section) or a variable interest rate provision (as defined in paragraph (h)(16) of this section).

*(3)* Fixed rent means any rent to the extent its amount and the time at which it is required to be paid are fixed and determinable under the terms of the rental agreement as of the lease date. The following rules apply for the purpose of determining the extent to which rent is fixed rent:

(i) The possibility of a breach, default, or other early termination of the rental agreement and any adjustments based on a reasonable price index or a variable interest rate provision are disregarded.

(ii) Rent will not fail to be treated as fixed rent merely because of the possibility of impairment by insolvency, bankruptcy, or other similar circumstances.

(iii) If the lease term (as defined in paragraph (h)(6) of this section) includes one or more periods as to which either the lessor or the lessee has an option to renew or extend the term of the agreement, rent will not fail to be treated as fixed rent merely because the option has not been exercised.

(iv) If the lease term includes one or more periods during which a substitute lessee or lessor may have use of the property, rent will not fail to be treated as fixed rent merely because the contingencies relating to the obligation of the lessee (or a related person) to make payments in the nature of rent have not occurred.

(v) If either the lessor or the lessee has an unconditional option or options, exercisable on one or more dates during the lease term, that, if exercised, require payments of rent to be made under an alternative payment schedule or schedules, the amount of fixed rent and the dates on which such rent is required to be paid are determined on the basis of the payment schedule that, as of the agreement date, is most likely to occur. If payments of rent are made under an alternative payment schedule that differs from the payment schedule assumed in applying the preceding sentence, then, for purposes of paragraph (f) of this section, the rental agreement is treated as having been modified at the time the option to make payments on such alternative schedule is exercised.

*(4)* Late payment charge means any amount required to be paid by the lessee to the lessor as additional compensation for the lessee's failure to make any payment of rent under a rental agreement when due.

*(5)* Lease date means the date on which the lessee first has the right to use of the property that is the subject of the rental agreement.

*(6)* Lease term means the period during which the lessee has use of the property subject to the rental agreement, including any option of the lessor to renew or extend the term of the agreement. An option of the lessee to renew or extend the term of the agreement is included in the lease term only if it is expected, as of the agreement date, that the option will be exercised. For this purpose, a lessee is generally expected to exercise an option if, for example, as of the agreement date the rent for the option period is less than the expected fair market value rental for such period. The lessor's or lessee's determination that an option period is either included in or excluded from the lease term is not binding on the Commissioner. If the lessee (or a related person) agrees that one or both of them will or could be obligated to make payments in the nature of rent (within the meaning of § 1.168(i)-2(b)(2)) for a period when another lessee (the substitute lessee) or the lessor will have use of the property subject to the rental agreement, the Commissioner may, in appropriate cases, treat the period when the substitute lessee or lessor will have use of the property as part of the lease term. See § 1.467-7(f) for special rules applicable to the lessee, substitute lessee, and lessor. This paragraph (h)(6) applies to section 467 rental agreements entered into after March 6, 2001. However, taxpayers may choose to apply this paragraph (h)(6) to any rental agreement that is described in § 1.467-9(a) and is entered into on or before March 6, 2001.

*(7)* A loss payment provision means a provision that requires the lessee to pay the lessor a sum of money (which may be either a stipulated amount or an amount determined by reference to a formula or other objective measure) if the property subject to the rental agreement is lost, stolen, damaged or destroyed, or otherwise rendered unsuitable for any use (other than for scrap purposes).

*(8)* A qualified percentage rents provision means a provision pursuant to which the rent is equal to a fixed percentage of the lessee's receipts or sales (whether or not receipts or sales are adjusted for returned merchandise or Federal, state, or local sales taxes), but only if the percentage does not vary throughout the lease term. A provision will not fail to be treated as a qualified percentage rents provision solely by reason of one or more of the following additional terms:

(i) Differing percentages of receipts or sales apply to different departments or separate floors of a retail store, but only if the percentage applicable to a particular department or floor does not vary throughout the lease term.

(ii) The percentage is applied to receipts or sales in excess of determinable dollar amounts, but only if the determinable dollar amounts are fixed and do not vary throughout the lease term.

*(9)* A qualified TRAC provision means a terminal rental adjustment clause (as defined in section 7701(h)(3)) contained in a qualified motor vehicle operating agreement (as defined in section 7701(h)(2)), but only if the adjustment to the rental price is based on a reasonable estimate, determined as of any date between the agreement date and the lease date (or, in the event the agreement date is the same as

or later than the lease date, determined as of the agreement date), of the fair market value of the motor vehicle (including any trailer) at the end of the lease term.

*(10)* An adjustment is based on a reasonable price index if the adjustment reflects inflation or deflation occurring over a period during the lease term and is determined consistently under a generally recognized index for measuring inflation or deflation (for example, the non-seasonally adjusted U.S. City Average All Items Consumer Price Index for All Urban Consumers (CPI-U), which is published by the Bureau of Labor Statistics of the Department of Labor). An adjustment will not fail to be treated as one that is based on a reasonable price index merely because the adjustment may be limited to a fixed percentage, but only if the parties reasonably expect, as of any date between the agreement date and the lease date (or, in the event the agreement date is the same as the lease date, as of such date), that the fixed percentage will actually limit the amount of the rent payable during less than 50 percent of the lease term.

*(11)* For purposes of determining whether a section 467 rental agreement is a leaseback within the meaning of § 1.467-3(b)(2), two persons are related persons if they are related persons within the meaning of section 465(b)(3)(C). In all other cases, two persons are related persons if they either have a relationship to each other that is specified in section 267(b) or section 707(b)(1) or are related entities within the meaning of sections 168(h)(4)(A), (B), or (C).

*(12)* Rental agreement includes any agreement, whether written or oral, that provides for the use of tangible property and is treated as a lease for Federal income tax purposes.

*(13)* A residual condition provision means a provision in a rental agreement that requires a payment to be made by either the lessor or the lessee to the other party based on the difference between the actual condition of the property subject to the agreement, determined as of the expiration of the lease term, and the expected condition of the property at the expiration of the lease term, as set forth in the rental agreement. The amount of any such payment may be determined by reference to any objective measure relating to the use or condition of the property, such as miles, hours or other duration of use, units of production, or similar measure. A provision will be treated as a residual condition provision only if the payment represents compensation for the use of, or wear and tear on, the property in excess of, or below, a standard set forth in the rental agreement, and the standard is reasonably expected, as of any date between the agreement date and the lease date (or, in the event the agreement date is the same as or later than the lease date, as of the agreement date), to be met at the expiration of the lease term.

*(14)* A tax indemnity provision means a provision in a rental agreement that may require the lessee to make one or more payments to the lessor in the event that the Federal, foreign, state, or local income tax consequences actually realized by a lessor from owning the property subject to the rental agreement and leasing it to the lessee differ from the consequences reasonably expected by the lessor, but only if the differences in such consequences result from a misrepresentation, act, or failure to act on the part of the lessee, or any other factor not within the control of the lessor or any related person.

*(15)* Third-party costs include any real estate taxes, insurance premiums, maintenance costs, and any other costs (excluding a debt service cost) that relate to the leased property and are not within the control of the lessor or lessee or any person related to the lessor or lessee.

*(16)* A variable interest rate provision means a provision in a rental agreement that requires the rent payable by the lessee to the lessor to be adjusted by the dollar amount of changes in the amount of interest payable by the lessor on any indebtedness that was incurred to acquire the property subject to the rental agreement (or any refinancing thereof), but—

(i) Only to the extent the changes are attributable to changes in the interest rate; and

(ii) Only if the indebtedness provides for interest at one or more qualified floating rates (within the meaning of § 1.1275-5(b)), or the changes are attributable to a refinancing at a fixed rate or one or more qualified floating rates.

**(i) [Reserved].**

**(j) Computational rules.** For purposes of this section and §§ 1.467-2 through 1.467-9, the following rules apply--

*(1) Counting conventions.* Any reasonable counting convention may be used (for example, 30 days per month/360 days per year) to determine the length of a rental period or to perform any computation. Rental periods of the same descriptive length, for example annual, semiannual, quarterly, or monthly, may be treated as being of equal length.

*(2) Conventions regarding timing of rent and payments.* (i) In general. For purposes of determining present values and yield only, except as otherwise provided in this section and §§ 1.467-2 through 1.467-8—

(A) The rent allocated to a rental period is taken into account on the last day of the rental period;

(B) Any amount payable during the first half of the first rental period is treated as payable on the first day of that rental period;

(C) Any amount payable during the first half of any other rental period is treated as payable on the last day of the preceding rental period;

(D) Any amount payable during the second half of a rental period is treated as payable on the last day of the rental period; and

(E) Any amount payable at the midpoint of a rental period is treated, in applying this paragraph (j)(2), as an amount payable during the first half of the rental period.

(ii) Time amount is payable. For purposes of this section and §§ 1.467-2 through 1.467-9, an amount is payable on the last day for timely payment (that is, the last day such amount may be paid without incurring interest, computed at an arm's-length rate, a substantial penalty, or other substantial detriment (such as giving the lessor the right to terminate the agreement, bring an action to enforce payment, or exercise other similar remedies under the terms of the agreement or applicable law)). This paragraph (j)(2)(ii) applies to section 467 rental agreements entered into after March 6, 2001. However, taxpayers may choose to apply this paragraph (j)(2)(ii) to any rental agreement that is described in § 1.467-9(a) and is entered into on or before March 6, 2001.

*(3) Annualized fixed rent.* Annualized fixed rent is determined by multiplying the fixed rent allocated to the rental period under paragraph (c)(2)(ii) of this section by the number of periods of the rental period's length in a calendar year. Thus, if the fixed rent allocated to a rental period is $10,000 and the rental period is one month, the annualized fixed rent for that rental period is $120,000 ($10,000 times 12).

*(4) Allocation of fixed rent within a period.* A rental agreement that allocates fixed rent to any period is treated as

allocating fixed rent ratably within that period. Thus, if a rental agreement provides that $120,000 is allocated to each calendar year in the lease term, $10,000 of rent is allocated to each calendar month.

*(5) Rental period length.* Except as provided in § 1.467-3(d)(1) (relating to agreements for which constant rental accrual is required), rental periods may be of any length, may vary in length, and may be different as between the lessor and the lessee as long as—

(i) The rental periods are one year or less, cover the entire lease term, and do not overlap;

(ii) Each scheduled payment under the rental agreement (other than a payment scheduled to occur before or after the lease term) occurs within 30 days of the beginning or end of a rental period; and

(iii) In the case of a rental agreement that does not provide a specific allocation of fixed rent, the rental periods selected do not cause the agreement to be treated as a section 467 rental agreement unless all alternative rental period schedules would result in such treatment.

T.D. 8820, 5/17/99, T.D. 8917, 1/4/2001.

**§ 1.467-2 Rent accrual for section 467 rental agreements without adequate interest.**

**(a) Section 467 rental agreements for which proportional rental accrual is required.** Under § 1.467-1(d)(2)(ii), the fixed rent for each rental period is the proportional rental amount, computed under paragraph (c) of this section, if—

*(1)* The section 467 rental agreement is not a disqualified leaseback or long-term agreement under § 1.467-3(b); and

*(2)* The section 467 rental agreement does not provide adequate interest on fixed rent under paragraph (b) of this section.

**(b) Adequate interest on fixed rent.** *(1) In general.* A section 467 rental agreement provides adequate interest on fixed rent if, disregarding any contingent rent—

(i) The rental agreement has no deferred or prepaid rent as described in § 1.467-1(c)(3);

(ii) The rental agreement has deferred or prepaid rent, and—

(A) The rental agreement provides interest (the stated rate of interest) on deferred or prepaid fixed rent at a single fixed rate (as defined in § 1.1273-1(c)(1)(iii));

(B) The stated rate of interest on fixed rent is no lower than 110 percent of the applicable Federal rate (as defined in paragraph (e)(3) of this section);

(C) The amount of deferred or prepaid fixed rent on which interest is charged is adjusted at least annually to reflect the amount of deferred or prepaid fixed rent as of a date no earlier than the date of the preceding adjustment and no later than the date of the succeeding adjustment; and

(D) The rental agreement requires interest to be paid or compounded at least annually;

(iii) The rental agreement provides for deferred rent but no prepaid rent, and the sum of the present values (within the meaning of paragraph (d) of this section) of all amounts payable by the lessee as fixed rent (and interest, if any, thereon) is equal to or greater than the sum of the present values of the fixed rent allocated to each rental period; or

(iv) The rental agreement provides for prepaid rent but no deferred rent, and the sum of the present values of all amounts payable by the lessee as fixed rent, plus the sum of the negative present values of all amounts payable by the lessor as interest, if any, on prepaid fixed rent, is equal to or less than the sum of the present values of the fixed rent allocated to each rental period.

*(2) Section 467 rental agreements that provide for a variable rate of interest.* For purposes of the adequate interest test under paragraph (b)(1) of this section, if a section 467 rental agreement provides for variable interest, the rental agreement is treated as providing for fixed rates of interest on deferred or prepaid fixed rent equal to the fixed rate substitutes (determined in the same manner as under § 1.1275-5(e), treating the agreement date as the issue date) for the variable rates called for by the rental agreement. For purposes of this section, a rental agreement provides for variable interest if all stated interest provided by the agreement is paid or compounded at least annually at a rate or rates that meet the requirements of § 1.1275-5(a)(3)(i)(A) or (B) and (a)(4).

*(3) Agreements with both deferred and prepaid rent.* If an agreement has both deferred and prepaid rent, the agreement provides adequate interest under paragraph (b)(1) of this section if the conditions set forth in paragraph (b)(1)(ii)(A) through (D) of this section are met for both the prepaid and the deferred rent. For purposes of this paragraph (b)(3), an agreement will be considered to meet the condition set forth in paragraph (b)(1)(ii)(A) of this section if the agreement provides a single fixed rate of interest on the deferred rent and a single fixed rate of interest on the prepaid rent, even if those rates are not the same. This paragraph (b)(3) applies to section 467 rental agreements entered into after March 6, 2001. However, taxpayers may choose to apply this paragraph (b)(3) to any rental agreement that is described in § 1.467-9(a) and is entered into on or before March 6, 2001.

**(c) Computation of proportional rental amount.** *(1) In general.* The proportional rental amount for a rental period is the amount of fixed rent allocated to the rental period under § 1.467-1(c)(2)(ii), multiplied by a fraction. The numerator of the fraction is the sum of the present values of the amounts payable under the terms of the section 467 rental agreement as fixed rent and interest thereon. The denominator of the fraction is the sum of the present values of the fixed rent allocated to each rental period under the rental agreement.

*(2) Section 467 rental agreements that provide for a variable rate of interest.* To calculate the proportional rental amount for a section 467 rental agreement that provides for a variable rate of interest, see § 1.467-5.

**(d) Present value.** For purposes of determining adequate interest under paragraph (b) of this section or the proportional rental amount under paragraph (c) of this section, the present value of any amount is determined using a discount rate equal to 110 percent of the applicable Federal rate. In general, present values are determined as of the first day of the first rental period in the lease term. However, if a section 467 rental agreement calls for payments of fixed rent prior to the lease term, present values are determined as of the first day a fixed rent payment is called for by the agreement. For purposes of the present value determination under paragraph (b)(1)(iv) of this section, the fixed rent allocated to a rental period must be discounted from the first day of the rental period. For other conventions and rules relating to the determination of present value, see § 1.467-1(g) and (j).

**(e) Applicable Federal rate.** *(1) In general.* The applicable Federal rate for a section 467 rental agreement is the applicable Federal rate in effect on the agreement date. The applicable Federal rate for a rental agreement means—

(i) The Federal short-term rate if the term of the rental agreement is not over 3 years;

(ii) The Federal mid-term rate if the term of the rental agreement is over 3 years but not over 9 years; and

(iii) The Federal long-term rate if the term of the rental agreement is over 9 years.

*(2) Source of applicable Federal rates.* The Internal Revenue Service publishes the applicable Federal rates, based on annual, semiannual, quarterly, and monthly compounding, each month in the Internal Revenue Bulletin (see § 601.601(d) of this chapter). However, the applicable Federal rates may be based on any compounding assumption. To convert a rate based on one compounding assumption to an equivalent rate based on a different compounding assumption, see § 1.1272-1(j), Example 1.

*(3) 110 percent of applicable Federal rate.* For purposes of § 1.467-1, this section and §§ 1.467-3 through 1.467-9, 110 percent of the applicable Federal rate means 110 percent of the applicable Federal rate based on semiannual compounding or any rate based on a different compounding assumption that is equivalent to 110 percent of the applicable Federal rate based on semiannual compounding. The Internal Revenue Service publishes 110 percent of the applicable Federal rates, based on annual, semiannual, quarterly, and monthly compounding, each month in the Internal Revenue Bulletin (see § 601.601(d)(2) of this chapter).

*(4) Term of the section 467 rental agreement.* (i) In general. For purposes of determining the applicable Federal rate under this paragraph (e), the term of the section 467 rental agreement includes the lease term, any period before the lease term beginning with the first day an amount of fixed rent is payable under the terms of the rental agreement, and any period after the lease term ending with the last day an amount of fixed rent or interest thereon is payable under the rental agreement.

(ii) Section 467 rental agreements with variable interest. If a section 467 rental agreement provides variable interest on deferred or prepaid fixed rent, the term of the rental agreement for purposes of calculating the applicable Federal rate is the longest period between interest rate adjustment dates, or, if the rental agreement provides an initial fixed rate of interest on deferred or prepaid fixed rent, the period between the agreement date and the last day the fixed rate applies, if this period is longer. If, as described in § 1.1274-4(c)(2)(ii), the rental agreement provides for a qualified floating rate (as defined in § 1.1275-5(b)) that in substance resembles a fixed rate, the applicable Federal rate is determined by reference to the lease term.

**(f) Examples.** The following examples illustrate the application of this section. In each of these examples it is assumed that the rental agreement is not a disqualified leaseback or long-term agreement subject to constant rental accrual. The examples are as follows:

*Example (1).* (i) C agrees to lease property from D for five years beginning on January 1, 2000, and ending on December 31, 2004. The section 467 rental agreement provides that rent of $100,000 accrues in each calendar year in the lease term and that rent of $500,000 plus $120,000 of interest is payable on December 31, 2004. Assume that the parties select the calendar year as the rental period and that 110 percent of the applicable Federal rate is 10 percent, compounded annually.

(ii) The rental agreement has deferred rent under § 1.467-1(c)(3)(i) because the fixed rent allocated to calendar years 2000, 2001, and 2002 is not paid until 2004. In addition, because the rental agreement does not state an interest rate, the rental agreement does not satisfy the requirements of paragraph (b)(1)(ii) of this section.

(iii)

(A) Because the rental agreement has deferred fixed rent and no prepaid rent, the agreement has adequate interest only if the present value test provided in paragraph (b)(1)(iii) of this section is met. The present value of all fixed rent and interest payable under the rental agreement is $384,971.22, determined as follows: $\$620{,}000/(1.10)^5 = \$384{,}971.22$. The present value of all fixed rent allocated under the rental agreement (discounting the amount of fixed rent allocated to a rental period from the last day of the rental period) is $379,078.68, determined as follows:

$$\$379{,}078.68 = \$100{,}000 \times \frac{1 - (1.10)^{-5}}{.10}$$

(B) The rental agreement provides adequate interest on fixed rent because the present value of the single amount payable under the section 467 rental agreement exceeds the sum of the present values of fixed rent allocated.

(iv) For an example illustrating the computation of the yield on the rental agreement and the allocation of the interest and rent provided for under the rental agreement, see § 1.467-4(f), Example 2.

*Example (2).* (i) E and F enter into a section 467 rental agreement for the lease of equipment beginning on January 1, 2000, and ending on December 31, 2004. The rental agreement provides that rent of $100,000 accrues for each calendar month during the lease term. All rent is payable on December 31, 2004, together with interest on accrued rent at a qualified floating rate set at a current value (as defined in § 1.1275-5(a)(4)) that is compounded at the end of each calendar month and adjusted at the beginning of each calendar month throughout the lease term. Therefore, the rental agreement provides for variable interest within the meaning of paragraph (b)(2) of this section.

(ii) On the agreement date the qualified floating rate is 7.5 percent, and 110 percent of the applicable Federal rate, as defined in paragraph (e)(3) of this section, based on monthly compounding, is 7 percent. Under paragraph (b)(2) of this section, the fixed rate substitute for the qualified floating rate is 7.5 percent and the agreement is treated as providing for interest at this fixed rate for purposes of determining whether adequate interest is provided under paragraph (b) of this section. Accordingly, the requirements of paragraph (b)(1)(ii) of this section are satisfied, and the rental agreement has adequate interest.

*Example (3).* (i) X and Y enter into a section 467 rental agreement for the lease of real property beginning on January 1, 2000, and ending on December 31, 2002. The rental agreement provides that rent of $800,000 is allocable to 2000, $1,000,000 is allocable to 2001, and $1,200,000 is allocable to 2002. Under the rental agreement, Y must make a $3,000,000 payment on December 31, 2002. Assume that both X and Y choose the calendar year as the rental period, X and Y are calendar year taxpayers, and 110 percent of the applicable Federal rate is 8.5 percent compounded annually.

(ii) The rental agreement fails to provide adequate interest under paragraph (b)(1) of this section. Therefore, under § 1.467-1(d)(2)(ii), the fixed rent for each rental period is the proportional rental amount.

(iii)

(A) The proportional rental amount is computed under paragraph (c) of this section. Because the rental agreement does not call for any fixed rent payments prior to the lease term, under paragraph (d) of this section, the present value is determined as of the first day of the first rental period in the lease term. The present value of the single amount payable by the lessee under the rental agreement is computed as follows:

$$\$2{,}348{,}724.30 = \frac{\$3{,}000{,}000}{(1 + .085)^3}$$

(B) The sum of the present values of the fixed rent allocated to each rental period (discounting the fixed rent allocated to a rental period from the last day of such rental period) is computed as follows:

$$\$2{,}526{,}272.20 = \frac{\$800{,}000}{(1 + .085)} + \frac{\$1{,}000{,}000}{(1 + .085)^2} + \frac{\$1{,}200{,}000}{(1 + .085)^3}$$

(C) Thus, the fraction for determining the proportional rental amount is .9297194 ($2,348,724.30/$2,526,272.20). The section 467 interest for each of the taxable years within the lease term is computed and taken into account as provided in § 1.467-4. The section 467 rent for each of the taxable years within the lease term is as follows:

| Taxable year | Section 467 rent |
|---|---|
| 2000 | $ 743,775.52 ($ 800,000 × .9297194). |
| 2001 | $ 929,719.40 ($1,000,000 × .9297194). |
| 2002 | $ 1,115,663.28 ($1,200,000 × .9297194). |

T.D. 8820, 5/17/99, T.D. 8917, 1/4/2001.

### § 1.467-3 Disqualified leasebacks and long-term agreements.

**(a) General rule.** Under § 1.467-1(d)(2)(i), constant rental accrual (as described under paragraph (d) of this section) must be used to determine the fixed rent for each rental period in the lease term if the section 467 rental agreement is a disqualified leaseback or long-term agreement within the meaning of paragraph (b) of this section. Constant rental accrual may not be used in the absence of a determination by the Commissioner, pursuant to paragraph (b)(1)(ii) of this section, that the rental agreement is disqualified. Such determination may be made either on a case-by-case basis or in regulations or other guidance published by the Commissioner (see § 601.601(d)(2) of this chapter) providing that a certain type or class of leaseback or long-term agreement will be treated as disqualified and subject to constant rental accrual.

**(b) Disqualified leaseback or long-term agreement.** *(1) In general.* A leaseback (as defined in paragraph (b)(2) of this section) or a long-term agreement (as defined in paragraph (b)(3) of this section) is disqualified only if—

(i) A principal purpose for providing increasing or decreasing rent is the avoidance of Federal income tax (as described in paragraph (c) of this section);

(ii) The Commissioner determines that, because of the tax avoidance purpose, the agreement should be treated as a disqualified leaseback or long-term agreement; and

(iii) For section 467 rental agreements entered into before July 19, 1999, the amount determined with respect to the rental agreement under § 1.467-1(c)(4) (relating to the exception for rental agreements involving total payments of $250,000 or less) exceeds $2,000,000.

*(2) Leaseback.* A section 467 rental agreement is a leaseback if the lessee (or a related person) had any interest (other than a de minimis interest) in the property at any time during the two-year period ending on the agreement date. For this purpose, interests in property include options and agreements to purchase the property (whether or not the lessee or related person was considered the owner of the property for Federal income tax purposes) and, in the case of subleased property, any interest as a sublessor.

*(3) Long-term agreement.* (i) In general. A section 467 rental agreement is a long-term agreement if the lease term exceeds 75 percent of the property's statutory recovery period. (ii) Statutory recovery period. (A) In general. The term statutory recovery period means—

(1) In the case of property depreciable under section 168, the applicable period determined under section 467(e)(3)(A);

(2) In the case of land, 19 years; and

(3) In the case of any other tangible property, the period that would apply under section 467(e)(3)(A) if the property were property to which section 168 applied. (B) Special rule for rental agreements relating to properties having different statutory recovery periods. In the case of a rental agreement relating to two or more related properties that have different statutory recovery periods, the statutory recovery period for purposes of paragraph (b)(3)(ii)(A) of this section is the weighted average, based on the fair market values of the properties on the agreement date, of the statutory recovery periods of each of the properties.

**(c) Tax avoidance as principal purpose for increasing or decreasing rent.** *(1) In general.* In determining whether a principal purpose for providing increasing or decreasing rent is the avoidance of Federal income tax, all relevant facts and circumstances are taken into account. However, an agreement will not be treated as a disqualified leaseback or long-term agreement if either of the safe harbors set forth in paragraph (c)(3) of this section is met. The mere failure of a leaseback or long-term agreement to meet one of these safe harbors will not, by itself, cause the agreement to be treated as one in which tax avoidance was a principal purpose for providing increasing or decreasing rent.

*(2) Tax avoidance.* (i) In general. If, as of the agreement date, a significant difference between the marginal tax rates of the lessor and lessee can reasonably be expected at some time during the lease term, the agreement will be closely scrutinized and clear and convincing evidence will be required to establish that tax avoidance is not a principal purpose for providing increasing or decreasing rent. The term "marginal tax rate" means the percentage determined by dividing one dollar into the amount of the increase or decrease in the Federal income tax liability of the taxpayer that would result from an additional dollar of rental income or deduction.

(ii) Significant difference in tax rates. A significant difference between the marginal tax rates of the lessor and lessee is reasonably expected if—

(A) The rental agreement has increasing rents and the lessor's marginal tax rate is reasonably expected to exceed the lessee's marginal tax rate by more than 10 percentage points during any rental period to which the rental agreement allocates annualized fixed rent that is less than the average rent allocated to all calendar years (determined by taking into account the rules set forth in paragraph (c)(4)(iii) of this section); or

(B) The rental agreement has decreasing rents and the lessee's marginal tax rate is reasonably expected to exceed the lessor's marginal tax rate by more than 10 percentage points during any rental period to which the rental agreement allocates annualized fixed rent that is greater than the average rent allocated to all calendar years (determined by taking into account the rules set forth in paragraph (c)(4)(iii) of this section).

(iii) Special circumstances. In determining the expected marginal tax rates of the lessor and lessee, net operating loss and credit carryovers and any other attributes or special circumstances reasonably expected to affect the Federal income tax liability of the taxpayer (including the alternative minimum tax) are taken into account. For example, in the case of a partnership or S corporation, the amount of rental income or deduction that would be allocable to the partners or shareholders, respectively, is taken into account.

*(3) Safe harbors.* Tax avoidance will not be considered a principal purpose for providing increasing or decreasing rent if—

(i) The uneven rent test (as defined in paragraph (c)(4) of this section) is met; or

(ii) The increase or decrease in rent is wholly attributable to one or more of the following provisions—

(A) A contingent rent provision set forth in § 1.467-1(c)(2)(iii)(B); or

(B) A single rent holiday provision allowing reduced rent (or no rent) for one consecutive period during the lease term, but only if—

(1) The rent holiday is for a period of three months or less at the beginning of the lease term and for no other period; or

(2) The duration of the rent holiday is reasonable, determined by reference to commercial practice (as of the agreement date) in the locality where the use of the property occurs, and does not exceed the lesser of 24 months or 10 percent of the lease term.

*(4) Uneven rent test.* (i) In general. The uneven rent test is met if the rent allocated to each calendar year does not vary from the average rent allocated to all calendar years (determined in accordance with the rules set forth in paragraph (c)(4)(iii) of this section) by more than 10 percent.

(ii) Special rule for real estate. Paragraph (c)(4)(i) of this section is applied by substituting "15 percent" for "10 percent" if the rental agreement is a long-term agreement and at least 90 percent of the property subject to the agreement (determined on the basis of fair market value as of the agreement date) consists of real property (as defined in § 1.856-3(d)).

(iii) Operating rules. In determining whether the uneven rent test has been met, the following rules apply:

(A) Any contingent rent attributable to a provision set forth in § 1.467-1(c)(2)(iii)(B)(3) through (9) is disregarded.

(B) If the lease term includes one or more partial calendar years (a period less than a complete calendar year), the average rent allocated to each calendar year is the total rent allocated under the rental agreement, divided by the actual length (in years) of the lease term. The rent allocated to a partial calendar year is annualized by multiplying the allocated rent by the number of periods of the partial calendar year's length in a full calendar year and the annualized rent is treated as the amount of rent allocated to that year in determining whether the uneven rent test is met.

(C) In the case of a rental agreement not described in paragraph (c)(4)(ii) of this section, an initial rent holiday period and any rent allocated to such period are disregarded for purposes of this paragraph (c)(4) if taking such period and rent into account would cause the agreement to fail to meet the uneven rent test. For purposes of this paragraph (c)(4), an initial rent holiday period is any period of three months or less at the beginning of the lease term during which annualized fixed rent (determined by treating such period as a rental period for purposes of § 1.467-1(j)(3)) is less than the average rent allocated to all calendar years (determined before the application of this paragraph (c)(4)(iii)(C)).

(D) In the case of a rental agreement described in paragraph (c)(4)(ii) of this section, one qualified rent holiday period and any rent allocated to such period are disregarded for purposes of this paragraph (c)(4) if taking such period and rent into account would cause the agreement to fail the uneven rent test. For this purpose, a qualified rent holiday period is a consecutive period that is an initial rent holiday period or that meets the following conditions:

(1) The period does not exceed the lesser of 24 months or 10 percent of the lease term (determined before the application of this paragraph (c)(4)(iii)(D)).

(2) Annualized fixed rent during the period (determined by treating the period as a rental period for purposes of § 1.467-1(j)(3)) is less than the average rent allocated to all calendar years (determined before the application of this paragraph (c)(4)(iii)(D)).

(3) Providing less than average rent for the period is reasonable, determined by reference to commercial practice (as of the agreement date) in the locality where the use of the property occurs.

(E) If the rental agreement contains a variable interest rate provision, the uneven rent test is applied by treating the rent as having been fixed under the terms of the rental agreement for the entire lease term using fixed rate substitutes (determined in the same manner as § 1.1275-5(e), treating the agreement date as the issue date) for the variable rates of interest provided under the terms of the lessor's indebtedness.

**(d) Calculating constant rental amount.** *(1) In general.* Except as provided in paragraph (d)(2) of this section, the constant rental amount is the amount that, if paid at the end of each rental period, would result in a present value equal to the present value of all amounts payable under the disqualified leaseback or long-term agreement as rent and interest. In computing the constant rental amount, the rules for determining present value are the same as those provided in § 1.467-2(d) for computing the proportional rental amount. If constant rental accrual is required, all rental periods (other than an initial or final short period of not more than one month) must be equal in length and satisfy the requirements of § 1.467-1(j)(5).

*(2) Initial or final short periods.* If a disqualified leaseback or long-term agreement has an initial or final short rental period, the constant rental amount for the initial or final short period may be determined under any reasonable method. However, the sum of the present values of all the constant rental amounts must equal the present values of all amounts payable under the disqualified leaseback or long-term agreement as rent and interest. Any adjustment necessary to eliminate the section 467 loan balance because of the method used to determine the constant rental amount for short periods must be taken into account as section 467 rent for the final rental period.

(3) Method to determine constant rental amount; no short periods—

(i) Step 1. Determine the present value of amounts payable under the disqualified leaseback or long-term agreement as rent or interest.

(ii) Step 2. Determine the present value of $1 to be received at the end of each rental period during the lease term as of the first day of the first rental period during the lease term (or, if earlier, the first day a rent payment is required under the rental agreement).

(iii) Step 3. Divide the amount determined in paragraph (d)(3)(i) of this section (Step 1) by the number of dollars determined in paragraph (d)(3)(ii) of this section (Step 2).

**(e) Examples.** The following examples illustrate the application of this section:

*Example (1).* (i) K, lessor, and L, lessee, enter into a long-term agreement for a 10-year lease of personal property beginning on January 1, 2000. K and L are C corporations that use the calendar year as their taxable year. K does not have any unused losses or credits from taxable years preceding 2000. In addition, as of the agreement date, K expects that it will be subject to the maximum rate of tax imposed by section 11 in 2000 and that it will not be limited in its ability to use any losses or credits. As of the agreement date, L expects that it will be subject to the alternative minimum tax imposed by section 55 in 2000. The rental agreement provides for rent allocations in each year of the lease term, as follows:

| Year | Allocation |
|---|---|
| 2000 | $427,500 |
| 2001 | 442,500 |
| 2002 | 457,500 |
| 2003 | 472,500 |
| 2004 | 487,500 |
| 2005 | 502,500 |
| 2006 | 517,500 |
| 2007 | 532,500 |
| 2008 | 547,500 |
| 2009 | 562,500 |

As described in paragraph (c)(2) of this section, as of the agreement date, a significant difference between the marginal tax rates of the lessor and lessee can reasonably be expected at some time during the lease term. First, the rental agreement has increasing rents. Second, the lessor's marginal tax rate exceeds the lessee's marginal tax rate by more than 10 percentage points during a rental period to which the rental agreement allocates less than a ratable portion of the aggregate amount of rent payable under the agreement. For example, for the year 2000, the lessor's expected marginal tax rate is 35 percent, the percentage determined by dividing the increase in the Federal income tax liability of K that would result from an additional dollar of rental income ($.35) by $1. Because the lessee is subject to the alternative minimum tax, the lessee's expected marginal tax rate for 2000 is 20 percent, the percentage determined by dividing the decrease in the Federal income tax liability (taking into account both the decrease in the lessee's regular tax and the increase in the lessee's alternative minimum tax) that would result from an additional dollar of rental deduction ($.20) by $1. Further, for the year 2000, the rent allocated in accordance with the rental agreement is $427,500, which is less than a ratable portion of the aggregate amount of rental payments, $495,000, determined by dividing the total rents payable under the agreement ($4,950,000) by the number of years in the lease term (10). Thus, because a significant difference between the marginal tax rates of the lessor and lessee can reasonably be expected during the lease term, the agreement will be closely scrutinized and clear and convincing evidence will be required to establish that tax avoidance is not a principal purpose for providing increasing rent.

*Example (2).* (i) A and B enter into a long-term agreement for a 5-year lease of personal property beginning on July 1, 2000, and ending on June 30, 2005. The rental agreement provides that the rent is allocated to the calendar years in the lease term in accordance with the following schedule and is paid at successive six-month intervals (on December 31 and June 30) during the lease term:

| Year | Amount |
|---|---|
| 2000 | $ 450,000 |
| 2001 | 900,000 |
| 2002 | 900,000 |
| 2003 | 1,100,000 |
| 2004 | 1,100,000 |
| 2005 | 550,000 |

(ii) In determining whether the uneven rent test described in paragraph (c)(4)(i) of this section is met, the total amount of rent allocated under the rental agreement is $5,000,000, and the lease term is five years. The average rent for each year is $1,000,000 (see paragraph (c)(4)(iii)(B) of this section), and the uneven rent test is met if the rent for each year is not less than $900,000 and not more than $1,100,000. The test is met for 2000 because the annualized rent for that year is $900,000. The test is met for 2005 because the annualized rent for that year is $1,100,000. The test is met for each of the years 2001 through 2004 because the rent for each of these years is not less than $900,000 and not more than $1,100,000. Accordingly, because the uneven rent test of paragraph (c)(4)(i) of this section is met, the long-term agreement will not be treated as disqualified.

*Example (3).* (i) C and D enter into a long-term agreement for a lease of personal property beginning on October 1, 1999, and ending on December 31, 2005. The rental agreement provides that the rent is allocated to the calendar years in the lease term in accordance with the following schedule and is paid at successive six-month intervals (on December 31 and June 30) during the lease term:

| Year | Amount |
|---|---|
| 1999 | $ 0 |
| 2000 | 900,000 |
| 2001 | 900,000 |
| 2002 | 900,000 |
| 2003 | 1,100,000 |
| 2004 | 1,100,000 |
| 2005 | 1,100,000 |

(ii) The three-month rent holiday period at the beginning of the lease term is an initial rent holiday within the meaning of paragraph (c)(4)(iii)(C) of this section. Moreover, the agreement would fail the uneven rent test if the rent holiday period and the rent allocated to the period were taken into account. Thus, under paragraph (c)(4)(iii)(C) of this section, the period and the rent allocated to the period are disregarded for purposes of applying the uneven rent test. In that case, the lease term is six years, and the uneven rent test is met because the average rent for each year in the lease term is $1,000,000 and the rent for each calendar year in the lease term is not less than $900,000 nor more than $1,100,000.

Accordingly, the long-term agreement will not be treated as disqualified.

*Example (4).* (i) E and F enter into a long-term agreement for a 6-year lease of personal property beginning on January 1, 2000, and ending on December 31, 2005. The rental agreement provides that the rent allocated to the calendar years in the lease term and paid at successive six-month intervals (on June 30 and December 31) during the lease term is the sum of the interest on the lessor's indebtedness, in the amount of $4,637,577, and an amount determined in accordance with the following schedule:

| Year | Amount |
|---|---|
| 2000 | $ 539,574 |
| 2001 | 583,603 |
| 2002 | 631,225 |
| 2003 | 886,773 |
| 2004 | 959,090 |
| 2005 | 1,037,352 |

(ii) Assume further that the lessor's indebtedness bears interest at the rate of 2 percent in excess of the 6-month London Interbank Offered Rate (LIBOR) in effect on the first day of the 6-month period for each rental period and that, on the agreement date, the interest rate under this formula would be 8 percent. If the interest rate remained fixed during the entire lease term, the formula for determining the rent payable by the lessee would result in payments of rent in the amount of $450,000 for each six-month period in 2000, 2001, and 2002, and $550,000 for each six-month period in 2003, 2004, and 2005.

(iii) Under paragraph (c)(4)(iii)(E) of this section, the fixed rate substitute for the variable interest rate provision produces a schedule of fixed rents that meets the uneven rent test of paragraph (c)(4)(i) of this section. Thus, even if the actual rents payable under the rental agreement do not meet the uneven rent test because of fluctuations in the 6-month LIBOR, the uneven rent test will be treated as having been met, and the long-term agreement will not be treated as disqualified.

*Example (5).* (i) G and H enter into a long-term agreement for a 5-year lease of personal property beginning on January 1, 2000, and ending on December 31, 2004. The rental agreement provides that the rent is payable to G at the rate of $40,000 per month in arrears, subject to an adjustment based on changes in prevailing interest rates during the lease term. Under this adjustment, the lessor is entitled to receive an amount equal to the sum of a specified dollar amount, which increases each month as payments of rent are made, and interest on a notional principal amount (as defined in § 1.446-3(c)(3)) at a qualified floating rate (as defined in § 1.1275-5(b)). The notional principal amount is initially established at 80 percent of the cost of the property. As each payment of rent is made, the notional principal amount is reduced (but not below zero) to an amount that would represent the outstanding principal balance of a loan the payments on which are equal to the monthly payments of rent. As of the agreement date, the value of the qualified floating rate is 9 percent. Although G did not incur indebtedness specifically for the purpose of acquiring the property, the parties agreed to the adjustment provisions in order to compensate G for its general costs of borrowing.

(ii) The adjustment provision produces a schedule of rent payments that is virtually identical to the schedule that would have resulted if G had actually borrowed money in an amount and on terms identical to the terms used in determining interest on the notional principal amount and the adjustment were based on that indebtedness. An adjustment based on actual indebtedness of the lessor would have been a variable interest rate provision eligible for a safe harbor under paragraph (c)(3)(ii)(A) of this section. Accordingly, based on all the facts and circumstances, the adjustment provision did not have as one of its principal purposes the avoidance of Federal income tax, and thus the long-term agreement will not be treated as disqualified.

*Example (6).* (i) X and Y enter into a leaseback for a 5-year lease of personal property beginning on January 1, 1998, and ending on December 31, 2002. The rental agreement provides that $0 of rent is allocated to years 1998, 1999, and 2000, and that rent of $17,500,000 is allocated to years 2001 and 2002. The rental agreement provides that the rent allocated to each year is payable on December 31 of that year. Assume all rental periods are the calendar year. Assume also that 110 percent of the applicable Federal rate based on annual compounding is 12 percent.

(ii)

(A) If the Commissioner determines that the leaseback is disqualified, the constant rental amount is computed as follows:

(B) Step 1 in calculating the constant rental amount is to determine the present value of the two payments due under the rental agreement as follows:

$$\$21{,}051{,}536 = \frac{\$17{,}500{,}000}{(1.12)^4} + \frac{\$17{,}500{,}000}{(1.12)^5}$$

(iii) Because no amounts of rent are payable before the lease term, Step 2 in calculating the constant rental amount is to determine the present value as of the first day of the lease term of $1 to be received at the end of each rental period during the lease term. This results in a present value of $3.6047762. In Step 3 the amount determined in Step 1 is divided by the number of dollars determined in Step 2. Thus, the constant rental amount is $5,839,901 for each calendar year during the lease term computed as follows:

$$\$5{,}839{,}901 = \frac{\$21{,}051{,}536}{3.6047762}$$

T.D. 8820, 5/17/99, T.D. 8917, 1/4/2001.

## § 1.467-4 Section 467 loan.

**(a) In general.** *(1) Overview.* Except as provided in paragraph (a)(2) of this section, the section 467 loan rules of this section apply to a section 467 rental agreement if, as of the first day of a rental period, there is a difference between the amount of fixed rent payable under the rental agreement on or before the first day and the amount of fixed rent required to be accrued in accordance with § 1.467-1(d)(2) before the first day. Paragraph (b) of this section provides rules for computing the principal balance of a section 467 loan at the beginning of any rental period. The principal balance of a section 467 loan may be positive or negative. For Federal tax purposes, if the principal balance is positive, the amount represents a loan from the lessor to the lessee, and if the principal balance is negative, the amount represents a loan from the lessee to the lessor.

*(2) No section 467 loan in the case of certain section 467 rental agreements.* Except as provided in paragraphs (a)(3) and (4) of this section, this section does not apply to section 467 rental agreements that provide adequate interest under § 1.467-2(b)(1)(i) (agreements with no deferred or prepaid rent) or § 1.467-2(b)(1)(ii) (agreements with deferred or pre-

paid rent that provide adequate stated interest at a single fixed rate).

*(3) Rental agreements subject to constant rental accrual.* Notwithstanding the provisions of paragraph (a)(2) of this section, this section applies to rental agreements subject to constant rental accrual under § 1.467-3 (relating to disqualified leasebacks or long-term agreements).

*(4) Special rule in applying the provisions of § 1.467-7(e), (f), or (g).* Notwithstanding the provisions of paragraph (a)(2) of this section, section 467 loan balances must be computed for section 467 rental agreements that are not subject to constant rental accrual under § 1.467-3 and that provide adequate interest under § 1.467-2(b)(1)(i) or (ii), but only for purposes of applying the provisions of § 1.467-7(e) (relating to dispositions of property subject to a section 467 rental agreement), § 1.467-7(f) (relating to assignments by lessees and lessee-financed renewals), and § 1.467-7(g) (relating to modifications of rental agreements).

**(b) Principal balance.** *(1) In general.* Except as provided in paragraph (b)(2) of this section or in § 1.467-7(e), (f), or (g), the principal balance of the section 467 loan at the beginning of a rental period equals—

(i) The fixed rent accrued in preceding rental periods;

(ii) Increased by the sum of--

(A) The interest on fixed rent includible in the gross income of the lessor for preceding rental periods; and

(B) Any amount payable by the lessor on or before the first day of the rental period as interest on prepaid fixed rent; and

(iii) Decreased by the sum of—

(A) The interest on prepaid fixed rent includible in the gross income of the lessee for preceding rental periods; and

(B) Any amount payable by the lessee on or before the first day of the rental period as fixed rent or interest thereon.

*(2) Section 467 rental agreements that provide for prepaid fixed rent and adequate interest.* If a section 467 rental agreement calls for prepaid fixed rent and provides adequate interest under § 1.467-2(b)(1)(iv), the principal balance of the section 467 loan at the beginning of a rental period equals the principal balance determined under paragraph (b)(1) of this section, plus the fixed rent accrued for that rental period.

*(3) Timing of payments.* For purposes of this paragraph (b), the day on which an amount is payable is determined under the rules of § 1.467-1(j)(2)(i)(B) through (E) and § 1.467-1(j)(2)(ii).

**(c) Yield.** *(1) In general.* (i) Method of determining yield. Except as provided in paragraphs (c)(2) and (3) of this section, the yield of a section 467 loan is the discount rate at which the sum of the present values of all amounts payable by the lessee as fixed rent and interest on fixed rent, plus the sum of the present values of all amounts payable by the lessor as interest on prepaid fixed rent, equals the sum of the present values of the fixed rent that accrues in accordance with § 1.467-1(d)(2). The yield must be constant over the term of the section 467 rental agreement and, when expressed as a percentage, must be calculated to at least two decimal places.

(ii) Method of stating yield. In determining the section 467 interest for a rental period, the yield of the section 467 loan must be stated appropriately by taking into account the length of the rental period. Section 1.1272-1(j), Example 1, provides a formula for converting a yield based on a period of one length to an equivalent yield based on a period of a different length.

(iii) Rounding adjustments. Any adjustment necessary to eliminate the section 467 loan because of rounding the yield to two or more decimal places must be taken into account as an adjustment to the section 467 interest for the final rental period determined as provided in paragraph (e) of this section.

*(2) Yield of section 467 rental agreements for which constant rental amount or proportional rental amount is computed.* In the case of a section 467 rental agreement to which § 1.467-1(d)(2)(i) or (ii) applies, the yield of the section 467 loan equals 110 percent of the applicable Federal rate (based on a compounding period equal to the length of the rental period).

*(3) Yield for purposes of applying paragraph (a)(4) of this section.* For purposes of applying paragraph (a)(4) of this section, the yield of the section 467 loan balance of any party, or prior party, to a section 467 rental agreement for a period is the same for all parties and is the yield that results in the net accrual of positive or negative interest for that period equal to the amount of such interest that accrues under the terms of the rental agreement for that period. For example, if property subject to a section 467 rental agreement is sold (transferred) and the beginning section 467 loan balance of the transferor (as described in § 1.467-7(e)(2)(i)) is positive and the beginning section 467 loan balance of the transferee (as described in § 1.467-7(e)(2)(ii)) is negative, the yield on each of these loan balances for any period is the same for all parties and is the yield that results in the net accrual of positive or negative interest, taking into account the aggregate positive or negative interest on the section 467 loan balances of both the transferor and transferee, equal to the amount of such interest that accrues under the terms of the rental agreement for that period.

*(4) Determination of present values.* The rules for determining present value in computing the yield of a section 467 loan are the same as those provided in § 1.467-2(d) for computing the proportional rental amount.

**(d) Contingent payments.** Except as otherwise required, contingent payments are not taken into account in calculating either the yield or the principal balance of a section 467 loan.

**(e) Section 467 rental agreements that call for payments before or after the lease term.** If a section 467 rental agreement calls for the payment of fixed rent or interest thereon before the beginning of the lease term, this section is applied by treating the period beginning on the first day an amount is payable and ending on the day before the beginning of the first rental period of the lease term as one or more rental periods. If a rental agreement calls for the payment of fixed rent or interest thereon after the end of the lease term, this section is applied by treating the period beginning on the day after the end of the last rental period of the lease term and ending on the last day an amount of fixed rent or interest thereon is payable as one or more rental periods. Rental period length for the period before the lease term or after the lease term is determined in accordance with the rules of § 1.467-1(j)(5).

**(f) Examples.** The following examples illustrate the application of this section:

*Example (1).* (i)

(A) A leases property to B for a three-year period beginning on January 1, 2000, and ending on December 31, 2002.

The section 467 rental agreement has the following rent allocation schedule and payment schedule:

| | Rent Allocation | Payment |
|---|---|---|
| 2000 | $400,000 | |
| 2001 | 600,000 | |
| 2002 | 800,000 | $1,800,000 |

(B) The rental agreement requires a $1.8 million payment to be made on December 31, 2002, but does not provide for interest on deferred rent. Assume A and B choose the calendar year as the rental period length and that 110 percent of the applicable Federal rate based on annual compounding is 10 percent. Assume also that the agreement is not a leaseback or long-term agreement and, therefore, is not subject to constant rental accrual.

(ii) Because the section 467 rental agreement does not provide adequate interest under § 1.467-2(b) and is not subject to constant rental accrual, the fixed rent that accrues during each rental period is the proportional rental amount as described in § 1.467-2(c). The proportional rental amounts for each rental period are as follows:

| | |
|---|---|
| 2000 | $370,370.37 |
| 2001 | 555,555.56 |
| 2002 | 740,740.73 |

(iii) A section 467 loan arises at the beginning of the second rental period because the rent payable on or before that day (zero) is less than the fixed rent accrued under § 1.467-1(d)(2) in all preceding rental periods ($370,370.37). Under paragraph (c)(2) of this section, the yield of the loan is equal to 110 percent of the applicable Federal rate (10 percent compounded annually). Because no payments are treated as made on or before the first day of the second rental period, the principal balance of the loan at the beginning of the second rental period is $370,370.37. The interest for the second rental period on fixed rent is $37,037.04 (.10 x $370,370.37) and, under § 1.467-1(e)(3), is treated as interest income of the lessor and as an interest expense of the lessee.

(iv) Because no payments are made on or before the first day of the third rental period, the principal balance of the loan at the beginning of the third rental period is equal to the fixed rent accrued during the first and second rental periods plus the lessor's interest income on fixed rent for the second rental period ($962,962.97 = $370,370.37 + $555,555.56 + $37,037.04). The interest for the third rental period on fixed rent is $96,296.30 (.10 × $962,962.97). Thus, the sum of the fixed rent and interest on fixed rent for the three rental periods is equal to the total amount paid over the lease term (first year fixed rent accrual, $370,370.37, plus second year fixed rent and interest accrual, $555,555.56 + $37,037.04, plus third year fixed rent and interest accrual, $740,740.73 + $96,296.30, equals $1,800,000). B takes the amounts of interest and rent into account as interest and rent expense, respectively, and A takes such amounts into account as interest and rent income, respectively, for the calendar years identified above, regardless of their respective overall methods of accounting.

*Example (2).* (i) The facts are the same as in Example 1, § 1.467-2(f). C agrees to lease property from D for five years beginning on January 1, 2000, and ending on December 31, 2004. The section 467 rental agreement provides that rent of $100,000 accrues in each calendar year in the lease term and that rent of $500,000 plus $120,000 of interest is payable on December 31, 2004. The parties select the calendar year as the rental period, and 110 percent of the applicable Federal rate is 10 percent, compounded annually. The rental agreement has deferred rent but provides adequate interest on fixed rent.

(ii)

(A) Pursuant to paragraph (c)(1) of this section, the yield of the section 467 loan is 10.775078%, compounded annually. The following is a schedule of the rent allocable to each rental period during the lease term, the balance of the section 467 loan as of the end of each rental period (determined, in the case of the calendar year 2004, without regard to the single payment of rent and interest in the amount of $620,000 payable on the last day of the lease term), and the interest on the section 467 loan allocable to each rental period:

| Calendar year | Section 467 interest | Section 467 rent | Section 467 Loan balance |
|---|---|---|---|
| 2000 | $ 0 | $100,000.00 | $100,000.00 |
| 2001 | 10,775.08 | 100,000.00 | 210,775.08 |
| 2002 | 22,711.18 | 100,000.00 | 333,486.26 |
| 2003 | 35,933.41 | 100,000.00 | 469,419.67 |
| 2004 | 50,580.33 | 100,000.00 | 620,000.00 |

(B) C takes the amounts of interest and rent into account as expense and D takes such amounts into account as income for the calendar years identified above, regardless of their respective overall methods of accounting.

T.D. 8820, 5/17/99.

## § 1.467-5 Section 467 rental agreements with variable interest.

**(a) Variable interest on deferred or prepaid rent.** *(1) In general.* This section provides rules for computing section 467 rent and interest in the case of section 467 rental agreements providing variable interest. For purposes of this section, a rental agreement provides for variable interest if the rental agreement provides for stated interest that is paid or compounded at least annually at a rate or rates that meet the requirements of § 1.1275-5(a)(3)(i)(A) or (B) and (a)(4). If a section 467 rental agreement provides for interest that is neither variable interest nor fixed interest, the agreement provides for contingent payments.

*(2) Exceptions.* This section is not applicable to section 467 rental agreements that provide adequate interest under § 1.467-2(b)(1)(i) (agreements with no deferred or prepaid rent) or (b)(1)(ii) (rental agreements with stated interest at a single fixed rate). The exceptions in this paragraph (a)(2) do not apply to rental agreements subject to constant rental accrual under § 1.467-3.

**(b) Variable rate treated as fixed.** *(1) In general.* If a section 467 rental agreement provides variable interest—

(i) The fixed rate substitutes (determined in the same manner as under § 1.1275-5(e), treating the agreement date as the issue date) for the variable rates of interest on deferred or prepaid fixed rent provided by the rental agreement must be used in computing the proportional rental amount under § 1.467-2(c), the constant rental amount under § 1.467-3(d), the principal balance of a section 467 loan under § 1.467-4(b), and the yield of a section 467 loan under § 1.467-4(c); and

(ii) The interest on fixed rent for any rental period is equal to the amount that would be determined under § 1.467-1(e)(2) if the section 467 rental agreement did not provide variable interest, using the fixed rate substitutes determined under paragraph (b)(1)(i) of this section in place of the variable rates called for by the rental agreement, plus the variable interest adjustment amount provided in paragraph (b)(2) of this section.

*(2) Variable interest adjustment amount.*

(i) In general. The variable interest adjustment amount for a rental period equals the difference between—

(A) The amount of interest that, without regard to section 467, would have accrued during the rental period under the terms of the section 467 rental agreement; and

(B) The amount of interest that, without regard to section 467, would have accrued during the rental period under the terms of the section 467 rental agreement using the fixed rate substitutes determined under paragraph (b)(1)(i) of this section in place of the variable interest rates called for by the rental agreement.

(ii) Positive or negative adjustment. If the amount determined under paragraph (b)(2)(i)(A) of this section is greater than the amount determined under paragraph (b)(2)(i)(B) of this section, the variable interest adjustment amount is positive. If the amount determined under paragraph (b)(2)(i)(A) of this section is less than the amount determined under paragraph (b)(2)(i)(B) of this section, the variable interest adjustment amount is negative.

*(3) Section 467 loan balance.* The variable interest adjustment amount is not taken into account in determining the principal balance of a section 467 loan under § 1.467-4(b). Instead, the section 467 loan balance is computed as if all amounts payable under the section 467 rental agreement were based on the fixed rate substitutes determined under paragraph (b)(1)(i) of this section.

**(c) Examples.** The following examples illustrate the application of this section:

*Example (1).* (i) X and Y enter into a section 467 rental agreement for the lease of personal property beginning on January 1, 2000, and ending on December 31, 2002. The rental agreement allocates $100,000 of rent to 2000, $200,000 to 2001, and $100,000 to 2002, and requires the lessee to pay all $400,000 of rent on December 31, 2002. The rental agreement requires the accrual of interest on unpaid accrued rent at two different qualified floating rates (as defined in § 1.1275-5(b)), one for 2001 and the other for 2002, such interest to be paid on December 31 of the year it accrues. The rental agreement provides that the qualified floating rate is set at a current value within the meaning of § 1.1275-5(a)(4). Assume that on the agreement date, 110 percent of the applicable Federal rate is 10 percent, compounded annually. Assume also that the agreement is not a leaseback or long-term agreement and, therefore, is not subject to constant rental accrual.

(ii) To determine if the section 467 rental agreement provides for adequate interest under § 1.467-2(b), § 1.467-2(b)(2) requires the use of fixed rate substitutes (in this example determined in the same manner as under § 1.1275-5(e)(3)(i) treating the agreement date as the issue date) in place of the variable rates called for by the rental agreement. Assume that on the agreement date the qualified floating rates, and therefore the fixed rate substitutes, relating to 2001 and 2002 are 10 and 15 percent compounded annually. Taking into account the fixed rate substitutes, the sum of the present values of all amounts payable by the lessee as fixed rent and interest thereon is greater than the sum of the present values of the fixed rent allocated to each rental period. Accordingly, the rental agreement provides adequate interest under § 1.467-2(b)(1)(iii) and the fixed rent accruing in each calendar year during the rental agreement is the fixed rent allocated under the rental agreement.

(iii) Because the section 467 rental agreement provides for variable interest on unpaid accrued fixed rent at qualified floating rates and the qualified floating rates are set at a current value, the requirements of § 1.1275-5(a)(3)(i)(A) and (4) are met and the rental agreement provides for variable interest within the meaning of paragraph (a)(1) of this section. Therefore, under paragraph (b)(1)(i) of this section, the yield of the section 467 loan is computed based on the fixed rate substitutes. Under § 1.467-4(c), the constant yield (rounded to two decimal places) equals 13.63 percent compounded annually. Based on the fixed rate substitutes, the fixed rent, interest on fixed rent, and the principal balance of the section 467 loan, for each calendar year during the lease term, are as follows:

| | Accrued rent | Accrued interest | Projected payment | Cumulative loan |
|---|---|---|---|---|
| 2000 | $100,000 | $0 | $0 | $100,000 |
| 2001 | 200,000 | 13,630 | (10,000) | 303,630 |
| 2002 | 100,000 | 41,370 | (445,000) | 0 |

(iv) To compute the actual reported interest on fixed rent for each calendar year, the variable interest adjustment amount, as described in paragraph (b)(2) of this section, must be added to the accrued interest determined in paragraph (iii) of this Example 1. Assume that the variable rates for 2001 and 2002 are actually 11 and 14 percent, respectively. Without regard to section 467, the interest that would have accrued during each calendar year under the terms of the section 467 rental agreement, and the interest that would have accrued under the terms of the rental agreement using the fixed rate substitutes determined under paragraph (b)(1)(i) of this section are as follows:

| | Accrued interest under rental agreement | Accrued interest using fixed rate substitutes |
|---|---|---|
| 2000 | $ 0 | $ 0 |
| 2001 | 11,000 | 10,000 |
| 2002 | 42,000 | 45,000 |

(v) Under paragraph (b)(2) of this section, the variable interest adjustment amount is $1,000 ($11,000 – $10,000) for 2001 and is – $3,000 ($42,000 – $45,000) for 2002. Thus, under paragraph (b)(1)(ii) of this section, the actual interest on fixed rent for 2001 is $14,630 ($13,630 + $1,000) and for 2002 is $38,370 ($41,370 – $3,000).

*Example (2).* (i) The facts are the same as in Example 1 except that 110 percent of the applicable Federal rate is 15 percent compounded annually and the section 467 rental agreement does not provide adequate interest under § 1.467-2(b). Consequently, the fixed rent for each calendar year during the lease is the proportional rental amount.

(ii) The sum of the present values of the fixed rent provided for each calendar year during the lease term, discounted at 15 percent compounded annually, equals $303,936.87.

(iii)

(A) Paragraph (b)(1)(i) of this section requires the proportional rental amount to be computed based on the assumption that interest will accrue and be paid based on the fixed rate substitutes. Thus, the sum of the present values of the projected payments under the section 467 rental agreement equals $300,156.16, computed as follows:

| | | |
|---|---|---|
| $ | $10{,}000/(1.15)^2$ = | $ 7,561.44 |
| | $445{,}000/(1.15)^3$ = | 292,594.72 |
| | | $300,156.16 |

(B) The fraction for computing the proportional rental amount equals .9875609 ($300,156.16/$303,936.87).

(iv) Based on the fixed rate substitutes, the fixed rent, interest on fixed rent, and the balance of the section 467 loan for each calendar year during the lease term are as follows:

| | Proportional rent | Accrued interest | Projected payment | Cumulative loan |
|---|---|---|---|---|
| 2000 | $98,756.09 | $0.00 | $0 | $ 98,756.09 |
| 2001 | 197,512.18 | 14,813.41 | (10,000) | 301,081.68 |
| 2002 | 98,756.09 | 45,162.23 | (445,000) | 0.00 |

(v) The variable interest adjustment amount in this example is the same as in Example 1. Under paragraph (b)(1)(ii) of this section, the actual interest on fixed rent for 2001 is $15,813.41 ($14,813.41 + $1,000) and for 2002 is $42,162.23 ($45,162.23 – $3,000).

T.D. 8820, 5/17/99.

### § 1.467-6 Section 467 rental agreements with contingent payments. [Reserved].

T.D. 8820, 5/17/99.

### § 1.467-7 Section 467 recapture and other rules relating to dispositions and modifications.

***Caution:*** The Treasury has not yet amended Reg § 1.467-7 to reflect changes made by P.L. 108-27.

**(a) Section 467 recapture.** Notwithstanding any other provision of the Internal Revenue Code, except as provided in paragraph (c) of this section, a lessor disposing of property in a transaction to which this paragraph (a) applies must recognize the recapture amount (determined under paragraph (b) of this section) and treat that amount as ordinary income. This paragraph (a) applies to any disposition of property subject to a section 467 rental agreement that--

*(1)* Is a leaseback (as defined in § 1.467-3(b)(2)) or a long-term agreement (as defined in § 1.467-3(b)(3));

*(2)* Is not disqualified under § 1.467-3(b)(1); and

*(3)* Allocates to any rental period fixed rent that, when annualized, exceeds the annualized fixed rent allocated to any preceding rental period.

**(b) Recapture amount.** *(1) In general.* The recapture amount for a disposition is the lesser of—

(i) The prior understated inclusion (determined under paragraph (b)(2) of this section); or

(ii) The section 467 gain (determined under paragraph (b)(3) of this section).

*(2) Prior understated inclusion.* The prior understated inclusion is the excess (if any) of—

(i) The aggregate amount of section 467 rent and section 467 interest for the period during which the lessor held the property, determined as if the section 467 rental agreement were a disqualified leaseback or long-term agreement subject to constant rental accrual under § 1.467-3; over

(ii) The aggregate amount of section 467 rent and section 467 interest accrued by the lessor during that period.

*(3) Section 467 gain.*

(i) In general. Except as otherwise provided in paragraph (b)(3)(ii) of this section, the section 467 gain is the excess (if any) of—

(A) The amount realized from the disposition; over

(B) The sum of the adjusted basis of the property and the amount of any gain from the disposition that is treated as ordinary income under any provision of subtitle A of the Internal Revenue Code other than section 467(c) (for example, section 1245 or 1250).

(ii) Certain dispositions. In the case of a disposition that is not a sale or exchange, the section 467 gain is the excess (if any) of the fair market value of the property on the date of disposition over the amount determined under paragraph (b)(3)(i)(B) of this section.

**(c) Special rules.** *(1) Gifts.* Paragraph (a) of this section does not apply to a disposition by gift. However, see paragraph (c)(4) of this section for dispositions by transferees. If a disposition is in part a sale or exchange and in part a gift, paragraph (a) of this section applies to the disposition but the prior understated inclusion is determined by taking into account only section 467 rent and section 467 interest properly allocable to the portion of the property not disposed of by gift.

*(2) Dispositions at death.* Paragraph (a) of this section does not apply to a disposition if the basis of the property in the hands of the transferee is determined under section 1014(a). This paragraph (c)(2) does not apply to property which constitutes a right to receive an item of income in respect of a decedent. See sections 691 and 1014(c).

*(3) Certain tax-free exchanges.* (i) In general. The recapture amount in the case of a disposition to which this paragraph (c)(3) applies is limited to the amount of gain recognized to the transferor (determined without regard to paragraph (a) of this section), reduced by the amount of any gain from the disposition that is treated as ordinary income under any provision of subtitle A of the Internal Revenue Code other than section 467(c). However, see paragraph (c)(4) of this section for dispositions by transferees.

(ii) Dispositions covered. (A) In general. Except as provided in paragraph (c)(3)(ii)(B) of this section, this paragraph (c)(3) applies to a disposition of property if the basis of the property in the hands of the transferee is determined by reference to its basis in the hands of the transferor by reason of the application of section 332, 351, 361, 721, or 731. (B) Transfers to certain tax-exempt organizations. This paragraph (c)(3) does not apply to a disposition to an organization (other than a cooperative described in section 521) which is exempt from tax imposed by chapter 1, subtitle A of the Internal Revenue Code (a tax-exempt entity) except to the extent the property is used in an activity the income from which is subject to tax under section 511(a) (a section 511(a) activity). However, if assets used to any extent in a section 511(a) activity are disposed of by the tax-exempt entity, then, notwithstanding any other provision of law (except section 1031 or section 1033) the recapture amount with respect to such disposition, to the extent attributable under paragraph (c)(4) of this section to the period of the transferor's ownership of the property prior to the first disposition, shall be included in the tax-exempt entity's unrelated business taxable income. To the extent that the tax-exempt entity ceases to use the property in a section 511(a) activity, the entity will be treated for purposes of this paragraph (c)(3) and paragraph (c)(4) of this section as having disposed of the property to such extent on the date of the cessation.

*(4) Dispositions by transferee.* If the recapture amount with respect to a disposition of property (the first disposition) is limited under paragraph (c)(1) or (3) of this section and the transferee subsequently disposes of the property in a transaction to which paragraph (a) of this section applies, the prior understated inclusion determined under paragraph (b)(2) of this section is computed by taking into account the amounts attributable to the period of the transferor's ownership of the property prior to the first disposition. Thus, for example, the section 467 rent and section 467 interest that would have been taken into account by the transferee if the section 467 rental agreement were a disqualified leaseback or long-term agreement subject to constant rental accrual include the amounts that would have been taken into account by the transferor, and the aggregate amount of section 467 rent and section 467 interest accrued by the transferee includes the aggregate amount of section 467 rent and section 467 interest that was taken into account by the transferor. The prior understated inclusion determined under this paragraph (c)(4) must be reduced by any recapture amount taken into account under paragraph (a) of this section by the transferor.

*(5) Like-kind exchanges and involuntary conversions.* If property is disposed of or converted and, before the application of paragraph (a) of this section, gain is not recognized in whole or in part under section 1031 or 1033, then the amount of section 467 gain taken into account by the lessor is limited to the sum of—

(i) The amount of gain recognized on the disposition or conversion of the property (determined without regard to paragraph (a) of this section); and

(ii) The fair market value of property acquired that is not subject to the same section 467 rental agreement and that is not taken into account under paragraph (c)(5)(i) of this section.

*(6) Installment sales.* In the case of an installment sale of property to which paragraph (a) of this section applies—

(i) The recapture amount is recognized and treated as ordinary income in the year of the disposition; and

(ii) Any gain in excess of the recapture amount is reported under the installment method of accounting if and to the extent that method is otherwise available under section 453.

*(7) Dispositions covered by section 170(e), 341(e)(12), or 751(c).* For purposes of sections 170(e), 341(e)(12), and 751(c), amounts treated as ordinary income under paragraph (a) of this section must be treated in the same manner as amounts treated as ordinary income under section 1245 or 1250.

**(d) Examples.** The following examples illustrate the application of paragraphs (a), (b), and (c) of this section. In each of these examples the transferor of property subject to a section 467 rental agreement is entitled to the rent for the day of the disposition. The examples are as follows:

*Example (1).* (i) (A) X and Y enter into a section 467 rental agreement for a 5-year lease of personal property beginning on January 1, 2000, and ending on December 31, 2004. The rental agreement provides that the calendar year will be the rental period and that rents accrue and are paid in the following pattern:

| | Allocation | Payment |
|---|---|---|
| 2000 | $ 0 | $ 0 |
| 2001 | 87,500 | 0 |
| 2002 | 87,500 | 175,000 |
| 2003 | 87,500 | 175,000 |
| 2004 | 87,500 | 0 |

(B) Assume that both X and Y are calendar year taxpayers and that 110 percent of the applicable Federal rate is 11 percent, compounded annually. Assume also that the rental agreement is a long-term agreement (as defined in § 1.467-3(b)(3)), but it is not a disqualified leaseback or long-term agreement. Further, because the agreement does not provide prepaid or deferred rent, proportional rental accrual is not applicable. (See § 1.467-2(b)(1)(i)). Therefore, the rent taken into account under § 1.467-1(d)(2) is the fixed rent allocated to the rental periods under § 1.467-1(c)(2)(ii).

(ii) On December 31, 2000, X sells the property subject to the section 467 rental agreement to an unrelated person for $575,000. At the time of the sale, X's adjusted basis in the property is $175,000. Thus, X's gain on the sale of the property is $400,000. Assume that $175,000 of this gain would be treated as ordinary income under provisions of the Internal Revenue Code other than section 467(c). Under paragraph (a) of this section, X is required to take the recapture amount into account as ordinary income. Under paragraph

(b) of this section, the recapture amount is the lesser of the prior understated inclusion or the section 467 gain.

(iii) (A) In computing the prior understated inclusion under paragraph (b)(2) of this section, assume that the section 467 rent and section 467 interest (based on constant rental accrual) would be taken into account as follows if the section 467 rental agreement were a disqualified long-term agreement:

| | Section 467 rent | Section 467 interest |
|---|---|---|
| 2000 | $65,812.55 | $0 |
| 2001 | $65,812.55 | 7,239.38 |
| 2002 | $65,812.55 | 15,275.09 |
| 2003 | $65,812.55 | 4,944.73 |
| 2004 | $65,812.55 | (6,521.95) |

(B) The total amount of section 467 rent and section 467 interest for 2000, based on constant rental accrual, is $65,812.55. Since X did not take any section 467 rent or section 467 interest into account in 2000, the prior understated inclusion is also $65,812.55. X's section 467 gain is $225,000, which is the excess of the gain realized ($400,000) over the amount of that gain treated as ordinary income under non-section 467 provisions ($175,000). Accordingly, the recapture amount (the lesser of the prior understated inclusion or the section 467 gain) treated as ordinary income is $65,812.55.

*Example (2).* (i) The facts are the same as in Example 1, except that the section 467 rental agreement specifies that rents accrue and are paid in the following pattern:

| | Allocation | Payment |
|---|---|---|
| 2000 | $60,000 | $ 0 |
| 2001 | 65,000 | 0 |
| 2002 | 70,000 | 175,000 |
| 2003 | 75,000 | 175,000 |
| 2004 | 80,000 | 0 |

(ii)

(A) Assume the section 467 rental agreement does not provide for adequate interest under § 1.467-2(b), and, therefore, the fixed rent for a rental period is the proportional rental amount. See § 1.467-1(d)(2)(ii). Under § 1.467-2(c), the following amounts would be required to be taken into account:

| | Section 467 rent | Section 467 interest |
|---|---|---|
| 2000 | $57,260.43 | $0 |
| 2001 | $62,032.13 | 6,298.65 |
| 2002 | $66,803.83 | 13,815.03 |
| 2003 | $71,575.53 | 3,433.11 |
| 2004 | $76,347.23 | (7,565.94) |

(B) The amount of section 467 rent and section 467 interest taken into account by X for 2000 is $57,260.43. Thus, the prior understated inclusion is $8,552.12 (the excess of the amount of section 467 rent and section 467 interest based on constant rental accrual for 2000, $65,812.55, over the amount of section 467 rent and section 467 interest actually taken into account, $57,260.43). Since the prior understated inclusion is less than the section 467 gain ($225,000, as determined in Example 1(iii)(B)), the recapture amount treated as ordinary income is also $8,552.12.

*Example (3).* (i) The facts are the same as in Example 1, except that, instead of selling the property, X transfers the property to S on December 31, 2002, in exchange for stock of S in a transaction that meets the requirements of section 351(a). Under paragraph (c)(3) of this section, because of the application of section 351, X is not required to take into account any section 467 recapture.

(ii) On December 31, 2003, S sells the property subject to the section 467 rental agreement to an unrelated person for $450,000. At the time of the sale, S's adjusted basis in the property is $105,000. Thus, S's gain on the sale of the property is $345,000. Assume that $245,000 of this gain would be treated as ordinary income under provisions of the Internal Revenue Code other than section 467(c). Under paragraph (a) of this section, S is required to take the recapture amount into account as ordinary income which, under paragraph (b) of this section, is the lesser of the prior understated inclusion or the section 467 gain.

(iii) S owned the property in 2003 and, under paragraph (c)(4) of this section, for purposes of determining S's prior understated inclusion, S is treated as if it had owned the property during the years 2000 through 2002. In computing S's prior understated inclusion under paragraph (b)(2) of this section, the section 467 rent and section 467 interest based on constant rental accrual are the same as the amounts set forth in the schedule in Example 1(iii)(A). Thus, the constant rental amount for 2000, 2001, 2002, and 2003 is $290,709.40 ((4 × $65,812.55) + $7,239.38 + $15,275.09 + $4,944.73). The section 467 rent and section 467 interest actually taken into account prior to the disposition is $262,500. Thus, S's prior understated inclusion is $28,209.40 ($290,709.40 minus $262,500 (3 × $87,500)). S's section 467 gain is $100,000, the difference between the gain realized on the disposition ($345,000) and the amount of gain that is treated as ordinary income under non-section 467 Code provisions ($245,000). Accordingly, S's recapture amount, the lesser of the prior understated inclusion or the section 467 gain, is $28,209.40.

**(e) Other rules relating to dispositions.** *(1) In general.* If there is a sale, exchange, or other disposition of property subject to a section 467 rental agreement (the transfer), the section 467 rent and, if applicable, section 467 interest for a period are taken into account by the owner of the property during the period. The following rules apply in determining the section 467 rent and section 467 interest for the portion of the rental period ending immediately prior to the transfer:

(i) The section 467 rent and section 467 interest for the portion of the rental period ending immediately prior to the transfer are a pro rata portion of the section 467 rent and the section 467 interest, respectively, for the rental period. Such amounts are also taken into account in determining the transferor's section 467 loan balance, prior to any adjustment thereof that may be required under paragraph (h) of this section, immediately before the transfer.

(ii) If the transferor of the property is entitled to the rent for the day of transfer, the transfer is treated as occurring at the end of the day of the transfer.

(iii) If the transferee of the property is entitled to the rent for the day of transfer, the transfer is treated as occurring at the beginning of the day of the transfer.

*(2) Treatment of section 467 loan.* If there is a transfer described in paragraph (e)(1) of this section, the following rules apply in determining the transferor's and the transferee's section 467 loans for the period after the transfer, the

amount realized by the transferor, and the transferee's basis in the property:

(i) The beginning balance of the transferor's section 467 loan is equal to the net present value at the time of the transfer (but after giving effect to the transfer) of all subsequent amounts payable as fixed rent and interest on fixed rent to the transferor and all subsequent amounts payable as interest on prepaid fixed rent by the transferor. The transferor must continue to take into account interest on the transferor's section 467 loan balance after the date of the transfer.

(ii) The beginning balance of the transferee's section 467 loan is equal to the principal balance of the transferor's section 467 loan immediately before the transfer reduced (below zero, if appropriate) by the beginning balance of the transferor's section 467 loan. Amounts payable to the transferor are not taken into account in adjusting the transferee's section 467 loan balance.

(iii) If the beginning balance of the transferee's section 467 loan is negative, the transferor and transferee must treat the balance as a liability that is either assumed in connection with the transfer of the property or secured by the property acquired subject to the liability. If the beginning balance of the transferee's section 467 loan is positive, the transferor and transferee must treat the balance as an additional asset acquired in connection with the transfer of the property. In the case of a positive beginning balance of the transferee's section 467 loan, the transferee will have an initial cost basis in the section 467 loan equal to the lesser of the beginning balance of the loan or the aggregate consideration for the transfer of the property subject to the section 467 rental agreement and the transfer of the transferor's interest in the section 467 loan.

*(3) [Reserved].*

*(4) Examples.* The following examples illustrate the application of this paragraph (e). In each of these examples the transferor of property subject to a section 467 rental agreement is entitled to the rent for the day of the transfer. The examples are as follows:

*Example (1).* (i) Q and R enter into a section 467 rental agreement for a 5-year lease of personal property beginning on January 1, 2000, and ending on December 31, 2004. The rental agreement provides that $0 of rent is allocated to 2000, 2001, and 2002, and $1,750,000 is allocated to each of the years 2003 and 2004. The rental agreement provides that the calendar year will be the rental period and that the rent allocated to each calendar year is payable on the last day of that calendar year. Assume that both Q and R are calendar year taxpayers and that 110 percent of the applicable Federal rate is 11 percent, compounded annually. Assume further that the rental agreement is a disqualified long-term agreement (as defined in § 1.467-3(b)(3)) and that the section 467 rent, the section 467 interest, and the section 467 loan balance would be the following amounts:

| Calendar year | Payment | Section 467 interest | Section 467 rent | Section 467 loan balance |
|---|---|---|---|---|
| 2000 | $0 | $0 | $592,905.87 | $592,905.87 |
| 2001 | 0 | 65,219.65 | 592,905.87 | 1,251,031.39 |
| 2002 | 0 | 137,613.45 | 592,905.87 | 1,981,550.71 |
| 2003 | 1,750,000.00 | 217,970.58 | 592,905.87 | 1,042,427.16 |
| 2004 | 1,750,000.00 | 114,666.97 | 592,905.87 | 0 |

(ii) On December 31, 2002, Q sells the property subject to the section 467 rental agreement to P, an unrelated person, for $3,000,000. Q does not retain the right to receive any amounts payable by R under the rental agreement after the date of sale, but the agreement is not otherwise modified. At the time of the sale, Q's adjusted basis in the property is $975,000. Assume that, under § 1.467-1(f)(7), the disposition is not a substantial modification. Further, the Commissioner does not determine that the treatment of the agreement as a disqualified long-term agreement should be changed and, under § 1.467-1(f)(4)(iii), the agreement remains subject to constant rental accrual. Thus, under paragraph (g)(2)(iii) of this section, section 467 rent and section 467 interest for periods after the disposition will be taken into account on the basis of constant rental accrual applied to the terms of the entire agreement (as modified).

(iii) Under paragraph (e)(2)(ii) of this section, the beginning balance of P's section 467 loan is $1,981,550.71. P's section 467 loan balance is computed by reducing the balance of the section 467 loan immediately before the transfer ($1,981,550.71) by the beginning balance of the transferor's section 467 loan ($0 because Q does not retain the right to receive any amounts payable under the rental agreement subsequent to the transfer).

(iv) Q will be treated as if it had received $1,981,550.71 from the disposition of the section 467 loan and $1,018,449.29 from the sale of the property subject to the rental agreement. Thus, Q's gain on the sale of the property is $43,449.29 ($1,018,449.29 amount realized less $975,000 adjusted basis). Q's gain is not subject to the recapture provisions of section 467(c) and paragraph (a) of this section because the rental agreement was disqualified under § 1.467-3(b)(1) and, thus, the requirement of paragraph (a)(2) of this section is not met. Q recognizes no gain on the disposition of the section 467 loan because Q's basis in the loan equals the amount considered received for the loan. Further, Q does not take into account any of the section 467 rent or section 467 interest attributable to periods after the transfer of the property.

(v) P is treated as if it had acquired the property and the positive balance in the transferee's section 467 loan. P's cost basis in the property is $1,018,449.29, and its cost basis in the section 467 loan immediately following the transfer is $1,981,550.71. P takes section 467 rent and section 467 interest into account for the calendar years 2002 and 2003 under the constant rental accrual method and, accordingly, treats payments received under the rental agreement as recoveries of the principal balance of the section 467 loan (as adjusted from time to time).

*Example (2).* (i) The facts are the same as Example 1, except that on December 31, 2002, Q transfers the property to P in exchange for stock of P having a fair market value of $3,000,000 and the transaction meets the requirements of section 351(a).

(ii) Q is treated as having transferred two assets to P, the property subject to the rental agreement and the positive balance of the section 467 loan. Under section 351(a), because only stock of P is received by Q, Q does not recognize any of the gain realized on the transaction. Pursuant to section 358(a), the basis of Q in the P stock received in the exchange is the same as the aggregate basis of the property exchanged, or $2,956,550.71 (the sum of the balance of the section 467 loan, $1,981,550.71, and the adjusted basis of the property, $975,000). Q does not take into account any of the section 467 rent or section 467 interest attributable to periods after the transfer of the property.

(iii) P is treated as if it had acquired the property and the positive balance in the transferee's section 467 loan in the transaction. Pursuant to section 362(a), P's basis in each asset is the same as the basis of Q immediately preceding the transfer. Thus, the basis of P in the property subject to the rental agreement is $975,000, and the basis of P in the section 467 loan immediately following the transfer is $1,981,550.71. P takes section 467 rent and section 467 interest into account for the calendar years 2003 and 2004 under the constant rental accrual method and, accordingly, treats payments received under the rental agreement as recoveries of the principal balance of the section 467 loan (as adjusted from time to time).

**(f) Treatment of assignments by lessee and lessee-financed renewals.** *(1) Substitute lessee use.* If a lessee assigns its interest in a section 467 rental agreement to a substitute lessee, or if a period when a substitute lessee has the use of property subject to a section 467 rental agreement is otherwise included in the lease term under § 1.467-1(h)(6), the section 467 rent for a period is taken into account by the person having the use of the property during the period. The following rules apply in determining the section 467 rent and section 467 interest for the portion of the rental period ending immediately prior to the assignment:

(i) The section 467 rent and section 467 interest for the portion of the rental period ending immediately prior to the assignment are a pro rata portion of the section 467 rent and the section 467 interest, respectively, for the rental period. Such amounts are also taken into account in determining the lessee's section 467 loan balance, prior to any adjustment thereof that may be required under paragraph (h) of this section, immediately before the substitute lessee first has use of the property.

(ii) If the lessee is liable for the rent for the day that the substitute lessee first has use of the property, the substitute lessee's use shall be treated as beginning at the end of that day.

(iii) If the substitute lessee is liable for the rent for the day that the substitute lessee first has use of the property, the substitute lessee's use shall be treated as beginning at the beginning of that day.

*(2) Treatment of section 467 loan.* If, as described in paragraph (f)(1) of this section, a lessee assigns its interest in a section 467 rental agreement to a substitute lessee or a period when a substitute lessee has the use of property subject to a section 467 rental agreement is otherwise included in the lease term under § 1.467-1(h)(6), the following rules apply in determining the amount of the lessee's and the substitute lessee's section 467 loans for the period when the substitute lessee has use of the property and in computing the taxable income of the lessee and substitute lessee:

(i) The beginning balance of the lessee's section 467 loan is equal to the net present value, as of the time the substitute lessee first has use of the property (but after giving effect to the transfer of the right to use the property), of all amounts subsequently payable by the lessee as fixed rent and interest on fixed rent and all amounts subsequently payable as interest on prepaid fixed rent to the lessee. For purposes of this paragraph (f), any amount otherwise payable by the lessee is not treated as an amount subsequently payable by the lessee to the extent that such payment, if made by the lessee, would give rise to a right of contribution or other similar claim against the substitute lessee or any other person. The lessee must continue to take into account interest on the lessee's section 467 loan balance after the substitute lessee first has use of the property.

(ii) The beginning balance of the substitute lessee's section 467 loan is equal to the principal balance of the lessee's section 467 loan immediately before the substitute lessee first has use of the property reduced (below zero, if appropriate) by the beginning balance of the lessee's section 467 loan. Amounts payable by the lessee to any person other than the substitute lessee (or a related person) or payable to the lessee by any person other than the substitute lessee (or a related person) are not taken into account in adjusting the substitute lessee's section 467 loan balance.

(iii) If the beginning balance of the substitute lessee's section 467 loan is positive, the beginning balance is treated as—

(A) Gross receipts of the lessee for the taxable year in which the substitute lessee first has use of the property; and

(B) A liability that is either assumed in connection with the transfer of the leasehold interest to the substitute lessee or secured by property acquired subject to the liability.

(iv) If the beginning balance of the substitute lessee's section 467 loan is negative, the following rules apply:

(A) If the principal balance of the lessee's section 467 loan immediately before the substitute lessee first has use of the property was negative, any consideration paid by the substitute lessee to the lessee in conjunction with the transfer of the use of the property shall be treated as a nontaxable return of capital to the lessee to the extent that—

(1) The consideration does not exceed the amount owed to the lessee under the lessee's section 467 loan balance immediately before the substitute lessee first has use of the property; and

(2) The lessee has basis in the principal balance of the lessee's section 467 loan immediately before the substitute lessee first has use of the property.

(B) Except as provided in paragraph (f)(2)(iv)(D) of this section, the excess, if any, of the beginning balance of the amount owed to the substitute lessee under the section 467 loan, over any consideration paid by the substitute lessee to the lessee in conjunction with the transfer of the use of the property, is treated as an amount incurred by the lessee for the taxable year in which the substitute lessee first has use of the property.

(C) To the extent the beginning balance of the amount owed to the substitute lessee under the section 467 loan exceeds any consideration paid by the substitute lessee to the lessee in conjunction with the transfer of the use of the property, repayments of the beginning balance are items of gross income of the substitute lessee in the taxable year in which repayment occurs (determined by applying any repayment first to the beginning balance of the substitute lessee's section 467 loan).

(D) Any amount incurred by the lessee under paragraph (f)(2)(iv)(B) of this section with respect to a transfer of the use of property (the current transfer) shall be reduced (but not below zero) to the extent that the lessee, in its capacity, if any, as a substitute lessee with respect to an earlier transfer of the use of the property would have recognized additional gross income under paragraph (f)(2)(iv)(C) of this section if the current transfer had not occurred.

(v) For purposes of paragraph (f)(2)(iv)(C) of this section, repayments occur as the negative balance is amortized through the net accrual of rent and negative interest.

*(3) Lessor use.* If a period when the lessor has the use of property subject to a section 467 rental agreement is included in the lease term under § 1.467-1(h)(6), the section 467 rent for the period is not taken into account and the lessor is treated as a substitute lessee for purposes of this paragraph (f).

*(4) Examples.* The following examples illustrate the application of this paragraph (f). In each of these examples, the substitute lessee is liable for the rent for the day on which the substitute lessee first has use of the property subject to the section 467 rental agreement. Further, assume that in each example the lessee assignment is not a substantial modification under § 1.467-1(f). The examples are as follows:

*Example (1).* (i) The facts are the same as in Example 1 of paragraph (e)(4) of this section, except that on December 31, 2001, R, the lessee, contracts to assign its entire remaining interest in the leasehold to S, a calendar year taxpayer. The assignment becomes effective at the beginning of January 1, 2002. Pursuant to the terms of the assignment, R agrees with S that R will make $1,400,000 of the $1,750,000 rental payment required on December 31, 2003.

(ii) Under paragraph (f)(2)(i) of this section, R's section 467 loan balance as of the beginning of January 1, 2002, the time S first has use of the property, is $1,136,271.41 ($1,400,000/ (1.11)2). Under paragraph (f)(2)(ii) of this section, S's section 467 loan balance as of the beginning of January 1, 2002, is $114,759.98 (the principal balance of R's section 467 loan immediately before S has use of the property ($1,251,031.39), less R's section 467 loan balance at the beginning of January 1, 2002 ($1,136,271.41)).

(iii) Because S's $114,759.98 section 467 loan balance is positive, under paragraph (f)(2)(iii)(A) of this section, such amount is treated as gross receipts of R for 2002, R's taxable year in which S first has use of the property. R will treat the $114,759.98 as an amount received in exchange for the transfer of the leasehold interest. Under paragraph (f)(2)(iii)(B) of this section, S will treat that amount as a liability assumed in acquiring the leasehold interest. Thus, S's cost basis in the leasehold interest is $114,759.98.

(iv) Under paragraph (f)(1) of this section, S takes the section 467 rent attributable to the property into account for the period beginning on January 1, 2002. For 2002, S takes section 467 interest into account based on S's section 467 loan balance at the beginning of 2002. S's amounts payable, section 467 rent, section 467 interest, and end-of-year section 467 loan balances for calendar years 2002 through 2004 are as follows:

| Calendar year | Payment | Section 467 interest | Section 467 rent | Section 467 loan balance |
|---|---|---|---|---|
| Beginning | | | | $114,759.98 |
| 2002 | $0 | $ 12,623.60 | $592,905.87 | 720,289.45 |
| 2003 | 350,000.00 | 79,231.83 | 592,905.87 | 1,042,427.15 |
| 2004 | 1,750,000.00 | 114,666.98 | 592,905.87 | 0 |

(v) Under paragraph (f)(2)(i) of this section, R must continue to take into account section 467 interest on R's section 467 loan balance after S first has use of the property. R's section 467 loan balance beginning when S first has use of the property is $1,136,271.41. R's section 467 interest and end-of-year section 467 loan balances for calendar years 2002 through 2003 are as follows:

| Calendar year | Payment | Section 467 interest | Section 467 loan balance |
|---|---|---|---|
| Beginning | | | $1,136,271.41 |
| 2002 | $0 | $124,989.85 | 1,261,261.26 |
| 2003 | 1,400,000.00 | 138,738.74 | 0 |

*Example (2).* (i) On January 1, 2000, B leases tangible personal property from C for a period of five years. The rental agreement provides that the rental period is the calendar year and that rent payments are due at the end of the calendar year. The rental agreement does not provide for interest on prepaid rent. Assume that B and C are both calendar year taxpayers and that 110 percent of the applicable Federal rate is 10 percent, compounded annually. The rental agreement allocates rents and provides for payments of rent as follows:

| Calendar year | Rent | Payments |
|---|---|---|
| 2000 | $200,000 | $400,000 |
| 2001 | 200,000 | 300,000 |
| 2002 | 200,000 | 200,000 |
| 2003 | 200,000 | 100,000 |
| 2004 | 200,000 | 0 |

(ii) The rental agreement has prepaid rent within the meaning of § 1.467-1(c)(3)(ii) because the cumulative amount of rent payable through the end of 2001 ($700,000) exceeds the cumulative amount of rent allocated to calendar years 2000 through 2002 ($600,000). Because the rental agreement does not provide for adequate interest on prepaid fixed rent, the rent for each calendar year during the lease term is the proportional rental amount, as described in § 1.467-2(c). The amounts payable, section 467 rent, section 467 interest, and end-of-year section 467 loan balances for each calendar year are as follows:

| Calendar year | Payment | Section 467 interest | Section 467 rent | Section 467 loan balance |
|---|---|---|---|---|
| 2000 | $400,000 | $0 | $218,987.40 | ($ 181,012.60) |
| 2001 | 300,000 | (18,101.26) | 218,987.40 | ( 280,126.46) |
| 2002 | 200,000 | (28,012.64) | 218,987.40 | ( 289,151.70) |
| 2003 | 100,000 | (28,915.17) | 218,987.40 | ( 199,079.47) |
| 2004 | 0 | (19,907.93) | 218,987.40 | 0 |

(iii) On December 31, 2001, B contracts to assign its entire remaining interest in the leasehold to D, a calendar year taxpayer. The assignment becomes effective at the beginning of January 1, 2002. D pays B $278,000 on January 1, 2002, in conjunction with the assignment of the leasehold interest. Under the terms of the assignment, B is not obligated to make any rental payments due after the assignment.

(iv) Under paragraph (f)(2)(i) of this section, B's section 467 loan balance as of the beginning of January 1, 2002, the time D first has use of the property, is zero because D is obligated to make all rent payments due after the assignment of the leasehold interest. Under paragraph (f)(2)(ii) of this section, D's section 467 loan balance as of the beginning of January 1, 2002, is negative $280,126.46 (the principal balance of B's section 467 loan immediately before D has use of the property (negative $280,126.46), less B's section 467 loan balance when D first has use of the property (zero)). Because D's beginning section 467 loan balance is negative, paragraph (f)(2)(iv) of this section applies.

(v) Because B's $280,126.46 section 467 loan balance at the end of 2001 (that is, immediately before D has use of the property) is negative, paragraph (f)(2)(iv)(A) of this section applies. B's loan balance is the amount owed to B under the section 467 loan and consists of the excess of B's payments to C over the net amount of rent and negative interest B has taken into account through the end of 2001. Thus, B's basis in the negative section 467 loan balance at the end of 2001 is $280,126.46. Because the $278,000 paid by D to B in conjunction with the transfer of the leasehold interest does not exceed the amount owed to B under the section 467 loan at the end of 2001, and does not exceed B's basis in that loan balance, under paragraph (f)(2)(iv)(A) of this section B treats the $278,000 payment from D as a nontaxable return of capital.

(vi) The beginning balance of the amount owed to D under the section 467 loan ($280,126.46) exceeds by $2,126.46 the $278,000 paid by D to B in conjunction with the transfer of the leasehold interest. Paragraph (f)(2)(iv)(B) of this section treats the $2,126.46 as an amount incurred by B in 2002, B's taxable year in which D first has use of the property. Paragraph (f)(2)(iv)(D) of this section does not apply to reduce the amount incurred by B because B is the original lessee under the section 467 rental agreement.

(vii) Under paragraph (f)(1) of this section, D takes the section 467 rent into account for the period beginning when D first has use of the property. D takes section 467 interest into account based on a beginning section 467 loan balance of negative $280,126.46.

(viii) The beginning balance of the amount owed to D under the section 467 loan ($280,126.46) exceeds by $2,126.46 the $278,000 paid by D to B in conjunction with the transfer of the leasehold interest. Under paragraph (f)(2)(iv)(C) of this section, D must include this amount in gross income in 2002, the year in which this amount of D's beginning section 467 loan balance is paid through the net accrual of rent and negative interest. This inclusion in gross income ensures that the reductions in D's taxable income attributable to the section 467 rental agreement will not exceed the actual amount of D's expenditures.

**(g) Application of section 467 following a rental agreement modification.** *(1) Substantial modifications.* The following rules apply to any substantial modification of a rental agreement occurring after May 18, 1999 unless the entire agreement (as modified) is treated as a single agreement under § 1.467-1(f)(4)(vi):

(i) Treatment of pre-modification items. The lessor and lessee must take pre-modification items (within the meaning of § 1.467-1(f)(5)(v)) into account under their method of accounting used before the modification to report income and expense attributable to the rental agreement.

(ii) Computations with respect to post-modification items. In computing section 467 rent, section 467 interest, and the amount of the section 467 loan with respect to post-modification items--

(A) Post-modification items are treated as provided under a rental agreement (the post-modification agreement) separate from the agreement under which pre-modification items are provided;

(B) The lease term of the post-modification agreement begins at the beginning of the first period for which rent other than pre-modification rent is provided; and

(C) The applicable Federal rate for the post-modification agreement is the applicable Federal rate in effect on the day on which the modification occurs.

(iii) Adjustments.

(A) Adjustment relating to certain prepayments. If any payments before the beginning of the lease term of the post-modification agreement are post-modification items, the lessor and lessee must take into account, in the taxable year in which the modification occurs, any adjustment necessary to prevent duplication with respect to such payments or the omission of interest thereon for periods before the beginning of the lease term.

(B) Adjustment relating to retroactive beginning of lease term. If the lease term of a post-modification agreement begins before the date on which the modification occurs, the lessor and lessee must take into account in the taxable year in which the modification occurs any amount necessary to prevent the duplication or omission of rent or interest for the period after the beginning of the lease term of the post-modification agreement and before the beginning of the taxable year in which the modification occurs. For this purpose, the amount necessary to prevent duplication or omission is determined after taking into account any adjustments required by the Commissioner for taxable years ending prior to the beginning of the taxable year in which the modification occurs. In determining any adjustments required by the Commissioner for taxable years ending prior to the beginning of the taxable year in which the modification occurs, the Commissioner will disregard the modification.

(iv) Coordination with rules relating to dispositions and assignments. (A) Dispositions. If the modification involves a sale, exchange, or other disposition of the property subject to the rental agreement—

(1) Adjustments required under this paragraph (g) are taken into account before applying paragraphs (a), (b), (c), and (e) of this section;

(2) The prior understated inclusion for purposes of paragraph (b) of this section is the sum of the prior understated inclusion with respect to pre-modification items and the prior understated inclusion with respect to post-modification items; and

(3) Paragraph (e) of this section applies separately with respect to pre-modification items and post-modification items.

(B) Assignments. If the modification involves an assignment of the lessee's interest in the rental agreement to a substitute lessee or a substitute lessee having use of the property during a period otherwise included in the lease term—

(1) Adjustments required under this paragraph (g) are taken into account before applying paragraph (f) of this section; and

(2) Paragraph (f) of this section applies separately with respect to pre-modification items and post-modification items.

*(2) Other modifications.* The following rules apply to a modification (other than a substantial modification) of a rental agreement occurring after May 18, 1999:

(i) Computation of section 467 loan for modified agreement. The amount of the section 467 loan relating to the agreement is computed as of the effective date of the modification. The section 467 rent and section 467 interest for periods before the effective date of the modification are determined, solely for purposes of computing the amount of the section 467 loan, under the terms of the entire agreement (as modified).

(ii) Change in balance of section 467 loan. (A) If the balance of the section 467 loan determined under paragraph (g)(2)(i) of this section is greater than the balance of the section 467 loan immediately before the effective date of the modification, the difference is taken into account, in the taxable year in which the modification occurs, as additional rent.

(B) If the balance of the section 467 loan determined under paragraph (g)(2)(i) of this section is less than the balance of the section 467 loan immediately before the effective date of the modification, the difference is taken into account, in the taxable year in which the modification occurs, as a reduction of the rent previously taken into account by the lessor and lessee.

(C) For purposes of this paragraph (g)(2)(ii), a negative balance is less than a positive balance, a zero balance, or any other negative balance that is closer to a zero balance.

(iii) Section 467 rent and interest after the modification. The section 467 rent and section 467 interest for periods after the effective date of the modification are determined under the terms of the entire agreement (as modified).

(iv) Applicable Federal rate. The applicable Federal rate for the agreement does not change as a result of the modification.

(v) Modification effective within a rental period. If the effective date of a modification does not coincide with the beginning or end of a rental period under the agreement in effect before the modification, the section 467 rent and section 467 interest for the portion of the rental period ending immediately prior to the effective date of the modification are a pro rata portion of the section 467 rent and the section 467 interest, respectively, for the rental period. Such amounts are also taken into account in determining the section 467 loan balance, prior to any adjustment thereof that may be required under paragraph (h) of this section, immediately before the effective date of the modification. Similar rules apply with respect to the section 467 rent and section 467 interest determined under the terms of the entire agreement (as modified) for purposes of computing the amount of the section 467 loan under paragraph (g)(2)(i) of this section and the section 467 rent and section 467 interest for a partial rental period beginning on the effective date of the modification.

(vi) Other adjustments. The lessor and lessee must take into account, in the taxable year in which a retroactive modification occurs, any amount necessary to prevent the duplication or omission of rent or interest for the period before the beginning of the taxable year in which the modification occurs.

(vii) Coordination with rules relating to dispositions and assignments. If the modification involves a sale, exchange, or other disposition of the property subject to the rental agreement, an assignment of the lessee's interest in the rental agreement to a substitute lessee or a substitute lessee having use of the property during a period otherwise included in the lease term, adjustments required under this paragraph (g) are taken into account before applying paragraphs (a), (b), (c), (e), and (f) of this section.

(viii) Exception for agreements entered into prior to effective date of section 467. This paragraph (g)(2) does not apply to a modification of a rental agreement that is not subject to section 467 because of the effective date provisions of section 92(c) of the Tax Reform Act of 1984 (Public Law 98-369 (98 Stat. 612)).

*(3) Adjustment by Commissioner.* If the entire agreement (as modified) is treated as a single agreement under § 1.467-1(f)(4)(vi), the Commissioner may require adjustments to taxable income to reflect the effect of the modification, including adjustments that are similar to those required under paragraph (g)(2) of this section.

*(4) Effective date of modification.* The effective date of a modification of a rental agreement occurs at the earliest of--

(i) The date on which the modification occurs;

(ii) The beginning of the first period for which the amount of rent or interest provided under the entire agreement (as modified) differs from the amount of rent or interest provided under the agreement in effect before the modification;

(iii) The due date of the first payment, under either the entire agreement (as modified) or the agreement in effect before the modification, that is not identical, in due date and amount, under both such agreements;

(iv) The date, in the case of a modification involving the substitution of a new lessor, on which the property subject to the rental agreement is transferred; or

(v) The date, in the case of a modification involving the substitution of a new lessee, on which the substitute lessee first has use of the property subject to the rental agreement.

*(5) Examples.* The following examples illustrate the application of this paragraph (g):

*Example (1).* (i) F, a cash method lessor, and G, an accrual method lessee, agree to a 7-year lease of tangible personal property for the period beginning on January 1, 1998, and ending on December 31, 2004. The rental agreement allocates $100,000 of rent to each calendar year during the lease term, such rent to be paid December 31 following the close of the calendar year to which it is allocated. Because the rental agreement does not provide for increasing rent, or deferred rent within the meaning of section 467(d)(1)(A), section 467 does not apply to the rental agreement.

(ii) Prior to January 1, 2001, G timely makes the $100,000 rental payments required as of December 31, 1999, and December 31, 2000. On January 1, 2001, F and G modify the rental agreement payment schedule to provide for a single final payment of $500,000 on December 31, 2004. Assume that the change is a substantial modification within the meaning of § 1.467-1(f)(5)(ii). Because the modification occurs after May 18, 1999, the post-modification agreement is treated, under § 1.467-1(f)(1), as a new agreement for purposes of determining whether it is a section 467 rental agreement.

(iii) Under § 1.467-1(f)(5)(v), the $200,000 of rent allocated to calendar years 1998 and 1999 (periods prior to the modification) constitutes pre-modification rent, and the $100,000 rent payments made on December 31, 1999, and December 31, 2000, constitute pre-modification payments. Although calendar year 2000 is also prior to the modification, the rent allocated to calendar year 2000 is not pre-modification rent and the related payment is not a pre-modification payment because the modification changed the time at which that rent is payable. See § 1.467-1(f)(5)(v)(A).

(iv) Under paragraph (g)(1)(i) of this section, F and G take pre-modification rent and pre-modification payments into account under the method of accounting they used to report income and deductions attributable to the pre-modification agreement.

(v) Under § 1.467-1(f)(1)(i), the post-modification agreement providing rent for the period beginning on January 1, 2000, and ending on December 31, 2004, is treated as a new rental agreement. This rental agreement allocates $100,000 of rent to each of the calendar years 2000 through 2004 and provides for a single rental payment of $500,000 on December 31, 2004. Because the post-modification agreement provides for deferred rent under § 1.467-1(c)(3)(i), section 467 applies. Further, the post-modification agreement does not provide for adequate interest on fixed rent, and therefore F and G must account for fixed rent and interest on fixed rent using proportional rental accrual. Under paragraph (g)(1)(iii) of this section, for their taxable years which include January 1, 2001, F and G must adjust reported rent for the difference between the rent taken into account for the calendar year 2000 under the unmodified agreement and the proportional rental amount for that year under the post-modification agreement.

*Example (2).* (i) On January 1, 2000, X, lessee, and Y, lessor, enter into a rental agreement for a 6-year lease of tangible personal property beginning January 1, 2000, and ending December 31, 2005. The agreement provides that the calendar year is the rental period and all rent payments are due on July 15 of all years in which a payment is required. Assume the agreement is not a disqualified leaseback or long-term agreement within the meaning of § 1.467-3(b), and has the following allocation schedule and payment schedule:

| Year | Allocation | Payment |
|---|---|---|
| 2000 | $800,000 | $0 |
| 2001 | 900,000 | 0 |
| 2002 | 1,000,000 | 1,500,000 |
| 2003 | 1,000,000 | 1,500,000 |
| 2004 | 1,100,000 | 1,500,000 |
| 2005 | 1,200,000 | 1,500,000 |

(ii) The rental agreement has deferred rent within the meaning of § 1.467-1(c)(3)(i) because the rent allocated to 2000 is not payable until 2002 and some of the rent allocable to 2001 is not payable until 2003. Further, the rental agreement does not provide adequate interest on fixed rent within the meaning of § 1.467-2(b). Therefore, the rent amount to be accrued by X and Y for each rental period is the proportional rental amount, as described in § 1.467-2(c). Assuming 110 percent of the applicableFederal rate is 10 percent compounded annually, the section 467 rent, interest, and loan balances are as follows:

| Year | Rent | Interest | Loan balance |
|---|---|---|---|
| 2000 | $736,949.55 | $0 | $736,949.55 |
| 2001 | 829,068.24 | 73,694.96 | 1,639,712.75 |
| 2002 | 921,186.94 | 163,971.28 | 1,224,870.97 |
| 2003 | 921,186.94 | 122,487.10 | 768,545.01 |
| 2004 | 1,013,305.63 | 76,854.50 | 358,705.14 |
| 2005 | 1,105,424.33 | 35,870.53 | 0 |

(iii)

(A) On January 1, 2004, X and Y agree that the $1,500,000 payment scheduled for July 15, 2005, will be made in three equal installments on June 15, 2005, July 15, 2005, and August 15, 2005. Under § 1.467-1(j)(2)(i)(C) (relating to timing conventions), the payment to be made on June 15, 2005, is treated as if it were payable on December 31, 2004, for purposes of determining present values and yield of the section 467 loan. Assume that this change, which results in the following allocation schedule and payment schedule, is not a substantial modification within the meaning of § 1.467-1(f)(5)(ii):

| Year | Allocation | Payment |
|---|---|---|
| 2000 | $800,000 | $0 |
| 2001 | 900,000 | 0 |
| 2002 | 1,000,000 | 1,500,000 |
| 2003 | 1,000,000 | 1,500,000 |
| 2004 | 1,100,000 | 2,000,000 |
| 2005 | 1,200,000 | 1,000,000 |

(B) The agreement remains subject to proportional rental accrual after the modification because it has deferred rent and does not provide adequate interest on fixed rent within the meaning of § 1.467-2(b).

(iv) Because the modification occurs after May 18, 1999, and is not substantial within the meaning of § 1.467-1(f)(5)(ii), paragraph (g)(2) of this section applies. Under paragraph (g)(2)(i) of this section, the amount of the section 467 loan relating to the modified agreement is computed as of the effective date of the modification, and, solely for purposes of recomputing the amount of the section 467 loan, the section 467 rent and section 467 interest for periods before the modification are determined under the terms of the entire agreement (as modified). In addition, the applicable Federal rate does not change as a result of the modification. Thus, the recomputed section 467 rent, interest, and loan balances are as follows:

| Year | Rent | Interest | Loan balance |
|---|---|---|---|
| 2000 | $742,242.59 | $0 | $742,242.59 |
| 2001 | 835,022.91 | 74,224.26 | 1,651,489.76 |
| 2002 | 927,803.24 | 165,148.98 | 1,244,441.98 |
| 2003 | 927,803.24 | 124,444.20 | 796,689.42 |
| 2004 | 1,020,583.56 | 79,668.94 | (103,058.08) |
| 2005 | 1,113,363.88 | (10,305.80) | 0 |

(v) Under paragraph (g)(2)(ii) of this section, the difference between the section 467 loan balance immediately before the effective date of the modification and the recomputed section 467 loan balance as of the effective date of the modification is taken into account. In this example, the loan balance immediately before the effective date of the modification is $768,545.01 and the recomputed loan balance as of the effective date of the modification is $796,689.42. Thus, because the recomputed loan balance exceeds the original loan balance, the difference ($28,144.41) is taken into account, in the taxable year in which the modification occurs, as additional rent. Beginning on January 1, 2004, section 467 rent and interest are taken into account by X and Y in accordance with the recomputed rent schedule set forth in paragraph (iv) of this example.

**(h) Omissions or duplications.** *(1) In general.* In applying the rules of this section in conjunction with the rules of §§ 1.467-1 through 1.467-5, adjustments must be made to the extent necessary to prevent the omission or duplication of items of income, deduction, gain, or loss. For example, if a transferee lessor acquires property subject to a section 467 rental agreement at other than the beginning or end of a rental period, and the transferee lessor's beginning section 467 loan balance differs from the transferor lessor's section 467 loan balance immediately prior to the transfer, it will be necessary to treat the rental period that includes the day of transfer as consisting of two rental periods, one beginning at the beginning of the rental period that includes the day of transfer and ending with or immediately prior to the transfer and one beginning with or immediately after the transfer and ending immediately prior to the beginning of the succeeding rental period. Because the substitution of two rental periods for one rental period may change the proportional rental amount or constant rental amount, the change in rental periods should be treated as a modification of the rental agreement that occurs immediately prior to the transfer. The change in rental periods, by itself, is not treated as a substantial modification of the rental agreement although the substitution of a new lessor may constitute a substantial modification of the rental agreement. Likewise, § 1.467-1(j)(2), which provides rules regarding when amounts are treated as payable, is designed to simplify calculations of present values, section 467 loan balances, and proportional and constant rental amounts. These simplifying conventions assume that there will be no change in the lessor or lessee under a section 467 rental agreement and that the terms of the section 467 rental agreement will not be modified. Therefore, as illustrated in the example in paragraph (h)(2) of this section, when actual events do not reflect these assumptions, it may be necessary to alter the application of these rules to properly reflect taxable income.

*(2) Example.* The following example illustrates an application of this paragraph (h):

*Example.* (i) J leases tangible personal property from K for five years beginning on January 1, 2000, and ending on December 31, 2004. Under the rental agreement, rent is payable on July 15 of the calendar year to which it is allocated. Both J and K treat the calendar year as the rental period. The allocation of rent and payments of rent required under the rental agreement are as follows:

| Calendar year | Rent | Payments |
|---|---|---|
| 2000 | $200,000 | $450,000 |
| 2001 | 200,000 | 250,000 |
| 2002 | 200,000 | 200,000 |
| 2003 | 200,000 | 100,000 |
| 2004 | 200,000 | 0 |

(ii) The rental agreement does not provide for interest on prepaid rent. The rental agreement has prepaid rent under § 1.467-1(c)(3)(ii) because the rent payable at the end of 2000 exceeds the cumulative amount of rent allocated to 2000 and 2001. Therefore, J and K must take section 467 rent into account under the proportional rental method of § 1.467-2(c). Assume that 110 percent of the applicable Federal rate is 10 percent, compounded annually. The section 467 rent, section 467 interest, amounts payable, and section 467 loan balances for each of the calendar years under the terms of the rental agreement are as follows:

| Calendar Year | Section 467 rent | Section 467 interest | Payments | Section 467 loan balance |
|---|---|---|---|---|
| 2000 | $220,077.48 | $0 | $450,000 | $(229,922.52) |
| 2001 | 220,077.48 | (22,992.25) | 250,000 | (282,837.29) |
| 2002 | 220,077.48 | (28,283.73) | 200,000 | (291,043.54) |
| 2003 | 220,077.48 | (29,104.35) | 100,000 | (200,070.41) |
| 2004 | 220,077.48 | (20,007.07) | 0 | 0 |

(iii) On January 1, 2002, J and K amend the terms of the rental agreement to advance the due date of the $200,000 payment originally due on July 15, 2002, to June 15, 2002. This change in the payment schedule constitutes a modification of the terms of the rental agreement within the meaning of § 1.467-1(f)(5)(i). Assume, however, that the change is not a substantial modification within the meaning of § 1.467-1(f)(5)(ii). Because the modification occurs after May 18, 1999, and is not substantial, paragraph (g)(2) of this section applies. Thus, the section 467 loan balance at the beginning of 2002 must be recomputed as if the June 15, 2002, payment date had been included in the terms of the pre-modification rental agreement. If this had been the case, the section 467 rent, section 467 interest, amounts payable, and section 467 loan balances for each of the calendar years under the terms of the rental agreement would have been as follows:

| Calendar | Section 467 rent | Section 467 interest | Payments | Section 467 loan balance |
|---|---|---|---|---|
| 2000 | $224,041.38 | $0 | $450,000 | $(225,958.62) |
| 2001 | 224,041.38 | (22,595.86) | 450,000 | (474,513.10) |
| 2002 | 224,041.38 | (47,451.31) | 0 | (297,923.03) |
| 2003 | 224,041.38 | (29,792.30) | 100,000 | (203,673.95) |
| 2004 | 224,041.38 | (20,367.43) | 0 | 0 |

(iv) Section 1.467-4(b)(3) incorporates the conventions of § 1.467-1(j)(2) in determining when amounts are treated as payable for purposes of determining the section 467 loan balance. Section 1.467-1(j)(2)(i)(C) treats amounts payable during the first half of any rental period except the first rental period as payable on the last day of the preceding rental period. Therefore, because June 15, 2002, occurs in the first half of 2002, in determining the section 467 loan balance at the beginning of 2002 under the amended terms of the rental agreement, the $200,000 payment due on June 15, 2002, is treated as payable on December 31, 2001.

(v) Under paragraph (g)(2)(ii)(B) of this section, if the recomputed section 467 loan balance is less than the section 467 loan balance immediately before the modification, the difference is taken into account as a reduction of the rent previously taken into account by the lessor and the lessee. In this example, the recomputed section 467 loan balance immediately after the modification is negative $474,513.10 and the section 467 loan balance immediately before the modification is negative $282,837.29. However, the section 467 loan balance immediately before the modification does not take into account the $200,000 payment originally payable on July 15, 2002, whereas, under the conventions of § 1.467-1(j)(2)(i)(C), the recomputed section 467 loan balance immediately after the modification takes into account that $200,000 payment because it is now payable in the first half of the rental period (June 15). Under these circumstances, if the recomputed section 467 loan balance immediately after the modification is treated as negative $474,513.10 for purposes of applying paragraph (g)(2)(ii)(B) of this section, K's gross income and J's deductions attributable to the section 467 rental agreement will be understated by $200,000. Therefore, under paragraph (h)(1) of this section, only for purposes of applying paragraph (g)(2)(ii)(B) of this section, the $200,000 payment due on June 15, 2002, should not be taken into account in determining the recomputed section 467 loan balance immediately after the modification.

T.D. 8820, 5/17/99.

### § 1.467-8 Automatic consent to change to constant rental accrual for certain rental agreements.

**(a) General rule.** For the first taxable year ending after May 18, 1999, a taxpayer may change to the constant rental accrual method, as described in § 1.467-3, for all of its section 467 rental agreements described in paragraph (b) of this section. A change to the constant rental accrual method is a change in method of accounting to which the provisions of sections 446 and 481 and the regulations thereunder apply. A taxpayer changing its method of accounting in accordance with this section must follow the automatic change in accounting method provisions of Rev. Proc. 98-60 (see § 601.601(d)(2) of this chapter) except, for purposes of this paragraph (a), the scope limitations in section 4.02 of Rev. Proc. 98-60 are not applicable. Taxpayers changing their method of accounting in accordance with this section must do so for all of their section 467 rental agreements described in paragraph (b) of this section.

**(b) Agreements to which automatic consent applies.** A section 467 rental agreement is described in this paragraph (b) if—

*(1)* The property subject to the section 467 rental agreement is financed with an "exempt facility bond" within the meaning of section 142;

*(2)* The facility subject to the section 467 rental agreement is described in section 142(a)(1), (2), (3), or (12);

*(3)* The section 467 rental agreement does not include a specific allocation of fixed rent within the meaning of § 1.467-1(c)(2)(ii)(A)(2); and

*(4)* The section 467 rental agreement was entered into on or before May 18, 1999.

T.D. 8820, 5/17/99.

### § 1.467-9 Effective dates and automatic method changes for certain agreements.

**(a) In general.** Sections 1.467-1 through 1.467-7 are applicable for—

*(1)* Disqualified leasebacks and long-term agreements entered into after June 3, 1996; and

*(2)* Rental agreements not described in paragraph (a)(1) of this section that are entered into after May 18, 1999.

**(b) Automatic consent for certain rental agreements.** Section 1.467-8 applies only to rental agreements described in § 1.467-8.

**(c) Application of regulation project IA-292-84 to certain leasebacks and long-term agreements.** In the case of any leaseback or long-term agreement (other than a disqualified leaseback or long-term agreement) entered into after June 3, 1996, and on or before May 18, 1999, a taxpayer may choose to apply the provisions of regulation project IA-

292-84 (1996-2 C.B. 462)(see § 601.601(d)(2) of this chapter).

**(d) Entered into.** For purposes of this section and § 1.467-8, a rental agreement is entered into on its agreement date (within the meaning of § 1.467-1(h)(1) and, if applicable, § 1.467-1(f)(1)(i)).

**(e) Change in method of accounting.** *(1) In general.* For the first taxable year ending after May 18, 1999, a taxpayer is granted consent of the Commissioner to change its method of accounting for rental agreements described in paragraph (a)(2) of this section to comply with the provisions of §§ 1.467-1 through 1.467-7.

*(2) Application of regulation project IA-292-84.* For the first taxable year ending after May 18, 1999, a taxpayer is granted consent of the Commissioner to change its method of accounting for any rental agreement described in paragraph (c) of this section to comply with the provisions of regulation project IA-292-84 (1996-2 C.B. 462) (see § 601.601(d)(2) of this chapter).

*(3) Automatic change procedures.* A taxpayer changing its method of accounting in accordance with this paragraph (e) must follow the automatic change in accounting method provisions of Rev. Proc. 98-60 (see § 601.601(d)(2) of this chapter) except, for purposes of this paragraph (e), the scope limitations in section 4.02 of Rev. Proc. 98-60 are not applicable. A method change in accordance with paragraph (e)(1) of this section is made on a cut-off basis so no adjustment under section 481(a) is required.

---

T.D. 8820, 5/17/99.

---

**§ 1.468A-0 Nuclear decommissioning costs; table of contents.**

This section lists the paragraphs contained in §§ 1.468A-1 through 1.468A-9.

---

T.D. 9512, 12/22/2010

---

**§ 1.468A-1 Nuclear decommissioning costs; general rules.**

**(a) Introduction.** Section 468A provides an elective method for taking into account nuclear decommissioning costs for Federal income tax purposes. In general, an eligible taxpayer that elects the application of section 468A pursuant to the rules contained in § 1.468A-7 is allowed a deduction (as determined under § 1.468A-2) for the taxable year in which the taxpayer makes a cash payment to a nuclear decommissioning fund. Taxpayers using an accrual method of accounting that do not elect the application of section 468A are not allowed a deduction for nuclear decommissioning costs prior to the taxable year in which economic performance occurs with respect to such costs (see section 461(h)).

**(b) Definitions.** The following terms are defined for purposes of section 468A and § 1.468A-1 through 1.468A-9:

*(1)* The term eligible taxpayer means any taxpayer that possesses a qualifying interest in a nuclear power plant (including a nuclear power plant that is under construction).

*(2)* The term qualifying interest means—

(i) A direct ownership interest; and

(ii) A leasehold interest in any portion of a nuclear power plant if—

(A) The holder of the leasehold interest is primarily liable under Federal or State law for decommissioning such portion of the nuclear power plant; and

(B) No other person establishes a nuclear decommissioning fund with respect to such portion of the nuclear power plant.

*(3)* The term direct ownership interest includes an interest held as a tenant in common or joint tenant, but does not include stock in a corporation that owns a nuclear power plant or an interest in a partnership that owns a nuclear power plant. Thus, in the case of a partnership that owns a nuclear power plant, the election under section 468A must be made by the partnership and not by the partners. In the case of an unincorporated organization described in § 1.761-2(a)(3) that elects under section 761(a) to be excluded from the application of subchapter K, each taxpayer that is a co-owner of the nuclear power plant is eligible to make a separate election under section 468A.

*(4)* The terms nuclear decommissioning fund and qualified nuclear decommissioning fund mean a fund that satisfies the requirements of § 1.468A-5. The term nonqualified fund means a fund that does not satisfy those requirements.

*(5)* The term nuclear power plant means any nuclear power reactor that is used predominantly in the trade or business of the furnishing or sale of electric energy. Each unit (that is, nuclear reactor) located on a multi-unit site is a separate nuclear power plant. The term nuclear power plant also

includes the portion of the common facilities of a multi-unit site allocable to a unit on that site.

*(6)* The term nuclear decommissioning costs or decommissioning costs includes all otherwise deductible expenses to be incurred in connection with the entombment, decontamination, dismantlement, removal and disposal of the structures, systems and components of a nuclear power plant, whether that nuclear power plant will continue to produce electric energy or has permanently ceased to produce electric energy. Such term includes all otherwise deductible expenses to be incurred in connection with the preparation for decommissioning, such as engineering and other planning expenses, and all otherwise deductible expenses to be incurred with respect to the plant after the actual decommissioning occurs, such as physical security and radiation monitoring expenses. Such term also includes costs incurred in connection with the construction, operation, and ultimate decommissioning of a facility used solely to store, pending acceptance by the government for permanent storage or disposal, spent nuclear fuel generated by the nuclear power plant or plants located on the same site as the storage facility. Such term does not include otherwise deductible expenses to be incurred in connection with the disposal of spent nuclear fuel under the Nuclear Waste Policy Act of 1982 (Pub. L. 97-425). An expense is otherwise deductible for purposes of this paragraph (b)(6) if it would be deductible under chapter 1 of the Internal Revenue Code without regard to section 280B.

*(7)* The term public utility commission means any State or political subdivision thereof, any agency, instrumentality or judicial body of the United States, or any judicial body, commission or other similar body of the District of Columbia or of any State or any political subdivision thereof that establishes or approves rates for the furnishing or sale of electric energy.

*(8)* The term ratemaking proceeding means any proceeding before a public utility commission in which rates for the furnishing or sale of electric energy are established or approved. Such term includes a generic proceeding that applies to two or more taxpayers that are subject to the jurisdiction of a single public utility commission.

*(9)* The term special transfer means any transfer of funds to a qualified nuclear decommissioning fund pursuant to § 1.468A-8.

**(c) Special rules applicable to certain experimental nuclear facilities.** *(1)* The owner of a qualifying interest in an experimental nuclear facility possesses a qualifying interest in a nuclear power plant for purposes of paragraph (b) of this section if such person is engaged in the trade or business of the furnishing or sale of electric energy.

*(2)* An owner of stock in a corporation that owns an experimental nuclear facility possesses a qualifying interest in a nuclear power plant for purposes of paragraph (b)(1) of this section if—

(i) Such stockholder satisfies the conditions of paragraph (c)(1) of this section; and

(ii) The corporation that directly owns the facility is not engaged in the trade or business of the furnishing or sale of electric energy.

*(3)* For purposes of this paragraph (c), an experimental nuclear facility is a nuclear power reactor that is used predominantly for the purpose of conducting experimentation and research.

T.D. 9512, 12/22/2010

**§ 1.468A-2 Treatment of electing taxpayer.**

**(a) In general.** An eligible taxpayer that elects the application of section 468A pursuant to the rules contained in § 1.468A-7 (an electing taxpayer) is allowed a deduction for the taxable year in which the taxpayer makes a cash payment (or is deemed to make a cash payment as provided in paragraph (c) of this section) to a nuclear decommissioning fund and for any taxable year in which a deduction is allowed for a special transfer described in § 1.468A-8. The amount of the deduction for any taxable year equals the total amount of cash payments made (or deemed made) by the electing taxpayer to a nuclear decommissioning fund (or nuclear decommissioning funds) during such taxable year under this section, plus any amount allowable as a deduction in that taxable year for a special transfer described in § 1.468A-8. The amount of a special transfer permitted under § 1.468A-8 is not treated as a cash payment for purposes of this paragraph (a), and a taxpayer making a special transfer is allowed a ratable deduction in each taxable year during the remaining useful life of the nuclear power plant for the special transfer. A payment may not be made (or deemed made) to a nuclear decommissioning fund before the first taxable year in which all of the following conditions are satisfied:

*(1)* The construction of the nuclear power plant to which the nuclear decommissioning fund relates has commenced.

*(2)* A ruling amount is applicable to the nuclear decommissioning fund (see § 1.468A-3).

**(b) Limitation on payments to a nuclear decommissioning fund.** *(1) In general.* For purposes of paragraph (a) of this section, the maximum amount of cash payments made (or deemed made) to a nuclear decommissioning fund under paragraph (a) of this section during any taxable year shall not exceed the ruling amount applicable to the nuclear decommissioning fund for such taxable year (as determined under § 1.468A-3).

*(2) Excess contributions not deductible.* If the amount of cash payments made (or deemed made) to a nuclear decommissioning fund during any taxable year exceeds the limitation of paragraph (b)(1) of this section, the excess is not deductible by the electing taxpayer. In addition, see paragraph (c) of § 1.468A-5 for rules which provide that the Internal Revenue Service may disqualify a nuclear decommissioning fund if the amount of cash payments made (or deemed made) to a nuclear decommissioning fund during any taxable year exceeds the limitation of paragraph (b)(1) of this section.

*(3) Special transfer disregarded.* The amount of a special transfer permitted under § 1.468A-8 is not treated as a cash payment for purposes of this paragraph (b).

**(c) Deemed payment rules.** *(1) In general.* The amount of any cash payment made by an electing taxpayer to a nuclear decommissioning fund on or before the 15th day of the third calendar month after the close of any taxable year (the deemed payment deadline date) shall be deemed made during such taxable year if the electing taxpayer irrevocably designates the amount as relating to such taxable year on its timely filed Federal income tax return for such taxable year (see § 1.468A-7(b)(4)(iii) and (iv) for rules relating to such designation).

*(2) Cash payment by customer.* The amount of any cash payment made by a customer of an electing taxpayer to a

nuclear decommissioning fund of such electing taxpayer shall be deemed made by the electing taxpayer if the amount is included in the gross income of the electing taxpayer in the manner prescribed by section 88 and § 1.88-1.

**(d) Treatment of distributions.** *(1) In general.* Except as otherwise provided in paragraph (d)(2) of this section, the amount of any actual or deemed distribution from a nuclear decommissioning fund shall be included in the gross income of the electing taxpayer for the taxable year in which the distribution occurs. The amount of any distribution of property equals the fair market value of the property on the date of the distribution. See § 1.468A-5(c) and (d) for rules relating to the deemed distribution of the assets of a nuclear decommissioning fund in the case of a disqualification or termination of the fund. A distribution from a nuclear decommissioning fund shall include an expenditure from the fund or the use of the fund's assets--

(i) To satisfy, in whole or in part, the liability of the electing taxpayer for decommissioning costs of the nuclear power plant to which the fund relates; and

(ii) To pay administrative costs and other incidental expenses of the fund.

*(2) Exceptions to inclusion in gross income.* (i) Payment of administrative costs and incidental expenses. The amount of any payment by a nuclear decommissioning fund for administrative costs or other incidental expenses of such fund (as defined in § 1.468A-5(a)(3)(ii)) shall not be included in the gross income of the electing taxpayer unless such amount is paid to the electing taxpayer (in which case the amount of the payment is included in the gross income of the electing taxpayer under section 61).

(ii) Withdrawals of excess contributions. The amount of a withdrawal of an excess contribution (as defined in § 1.468A-5(c)(2)(ii)) by an electing taxpayer pursuant to the rules of § 1.468A-5(c)(2) shall not be included in the gross income of the electing taxpayer. See paragraph (b)(2) of this section, which provides that the payment of such amount to the nuclear decommissioning fund is not deductible by the electing taxpayer.

(iii) Actual distributions of amounts included in gross income as deemed distributions. If the amount of a deemed distribution is included in the gross income of the electing taxpayer for the taxable year in which the deemed distribution occurs, no further amount is required to be included in gross income when the amount of the deemed distribution is actually distributed by the nuclear decommissioning fund. The amount of a deemed distribution is actually distributed by a nuclear decommissioning fund as the first actual distributions are made by the nuclear decommissioning fund on or after the date of the deemed distribution.

**(e) Deduction when economic performance occurs.** An electing taxpayer using an accrual method of accounting is allowed a deduction for nuclear decommissioning costs no earlier than the taxable year in which economic performance occurs with respect to such costs (see section 461(h)(2)). The amount of nuclear decommissioning costs that is deductible under this paragraph (e) is determined without regard to section 280B (see § 1.468A-1(b)(6)). A deduction is allowed under this paragraph (e) whether or not a deduction was allowed with respect to such costs under section 468A(a) and paragraph (a) of this section for an earlier taxable year.

T.D. 9512, 12/22/2010

**§ 1.468A-3 Ruling amount.**

**(a) In general.** *(1)* Except as otherwise provided in paragraph (g) of this section or in § 1.468A-8 (relating to deductions for special transfers into a nuclear decommissioning fund), an electing taxpayer is allowed a deduction under section 468A(a) for the taxable year in which the taxpayer makes a cash payment (or is deemed to make a cash payment) to a nuclear decommissioning fund only if the taxpayer has received a schedule of ruling amounts for the nuclear decommissioning fund that includes a ruling amount for such taxable year. Except as provided in paragraph (a)(4) or (5) of this section, a schedule of ruling amounts for a nuclear decommissioning fund (schedule of ruling amounts) is a ruling (within the meaning of § 601.201(a)(2) of this chapter) specifying the annual payments (ruling amounts) that, over the taxable years remaining in the funding period as of the date the schedule first applies, will result in a projected balance of the nuclear decommissioning fund as of the last day of the funding period equal to (and in no event greater than) the amount of decommissioning costs allocable to the fund. The projected balance of a nuclear decommissioning fund as of the last day of the funding period shall be calculated by taking into account the fair market value of the assets of the fund as of the first day of the first taxable year to which the schedule of ruling amounts applies and the estimated rate of return to be earned by the assets of the fund after payment of the estimated administrative costs and incidental expenses to be incurred by the fund (as defined in § 1.468A-5(a)(3)(ii)), including all Federal, State and local income taxes to be incurred by the fund (the after-tax rate of return). See paragraph (c) of this section for a definition of funding period and paragraph (d) of this section for guidance with respect to the amount of decommissioning costs allocable to a fund.

*(2)* Each schedule of ruling amounts must be consistent with the principles and provisions of this section and must be based on reasonable assumptions concerning--

(i) The after-tax rate of return to be earned by the assets of the qualified nuclear decommissioning fund;

(ii) The total estimated cost of decommissioning the nuclear power plant (see paragraph (d)(2) of this section); and

(iii) The frequency of contributions to a nuclear decommissioning fund for a taxable year (for example, monthly, quarterly, semi-annual or annual contributions).

*(3)* The Internal Revenue Service (IRS) shall provide a schedule of ruling amounts that is identical to the schedule of ruling amounts proposed by the taxpayer in connection with the taxpayer's request for a schedule of ruling amounts (see paragraph (e)(2)(viii) of this section), but no schedule of ruling amounts shall be provided unless the taxpayer's proposed schedule of ruling amounts is consistent with the principles and provisions of this section and is based on reasonable assumptions. If a proposed schedule of ruling amounts is not consistent with the principles and provisions of this section or is not based on reasonable assumptions, the taxpayer may propose an amended schedule of ruling amounts that is consistent with such principles and provisions and is based on reasonable assumptions.

*(4)* The taxpayer bears the burden of demonstrating that the proposed schedule of ruling amounts is consistent with the principles and provisions of this section and is based on reasonable assumptions. If a public utility commission established or approved the currently applicable rates for the furnishing or sale by the taxpayer of electricity from the plant, the taxpayer can generally satisfy this burden of proof by

demonstrating that the schedule of ruling amounts is calculated using the assumptions used by the public utility commission in its most recent order. In addition, a taxpayer that owns an interest in a deregulated nuclear plant may submit assumptions used by a public utility commission that formerly had regulatory jurisdiction over the plant as support for the assumptions used in calculating the taxpayer's proposed schedule of ruling amounts, with the understanding that the assumptions used by the public utility commission may be given less weight if they are out of date or were developed in a proceeding for a different taxpayer. The use of other industry standards, such as the assumptions underlying the taxpayer's most recent financial assurance filing with the NRC, are an alternative means of demonstrating that the taxpayer has calculated its proposed schedule of ruling amounts on a reasonable basis. Consistency with financial accounting statements is not sufficient, in the absence of other supporting evidence, to meet the taxpayer's burden of proof under this paragraph (a)(4).

*(5)* The IRS will approve, at the request of the taxpayer, a formula or method for determining a schedule of ruling amounts (rather than providing a schedule specifying a dollar amount for each taxable year) if the formula or method is consistent with the principles and provisions of this section and is based on reasonable assumptions. See paragraph (f)(1)(ii) of this section for a special rule relating to the mandatory review of ruling amounts that are determined pursuant to a formula or method.

*(6)* The IRS may, in its discretion, provide a schedule of ruling amounts that is determined on a basis other than the rules of paragraphs (a) through (d) of this section if—

(i) In connection with its request for a schedule of ruling amounts, the taxpayer explains the need for special treatment and sets forth an alternative basis for determining the schedule of ruling amounts; and

(ii) The IRS determines that special treatment is consistent with the purpose of section 468A.

**(b) Level funding limitation.** *(1)* Except as otherwise provided in paragraph (b)(3) of this section, the ruling amount specified in a schedule of ruling amounts for any taxable year in the funding period (as defined in paragraph (c) of this section) shall not be less than the ruling amount specified in such schedule for any earlier taxable year.

*(2)* The ruling amount specified in a schedule of ruling amounts for a taxable year after the end of the funding period may be less than the ruling amount specified in such schedule for an earlier taxable year.

*(3)* The ruling amount specified in a schedule of ruling amounts for the last taxable year in the funding period may be less than the ruling amount specified in such schedule for an earlier taxable year if, when annualized, the amount specified for the last taxable year is not less than the amount specified for such earlier taxable year. The amount specified for the last taxable year is annualized by—

(i) Determining the number of days between the beginning of the taxable year and the end of the plant's estimated useful life;

(ii) Dividing the amount specified for the last taxable year by such number of days; and

(iii) Multiplying the result by the number of days in the last taxable year (generally 365).

**(c) Funding period.** *(1) In general.* For purposes of this section, the funding period for a nuclear decommissioning fund is the period that—

(i) Begins on the first day of the first taxable year for which a deductible payment is made (or deemed made) to such nuclear decommissioning fund (see § 1.468A-2(a) for rules relating to the first taxable year for which a payment may be made (or deemed made) to a nuclear decommissioning fund); and

(ii) Ends on the last day of the taxable year that includes the last day of the estimated useful life of the nuclear power plant to which the nuclear decommissioning fund relates.

*(2) Estimated useful life.* The last day of the estimated useful life of a nuclear power plant is determined under the following rules:

(i) Except as provided in paragraph (c)(2)(ii) of this section—

(A) The last day of the estimated useful life of a nuclear power plant that has been included in rate base for ratemaking purposes in any ratemaking proceeding that established rates for a period before January 1, 2006, is the date used in the first such ratemaking proceeding as the estimated date on which the nuclear power plant will no longer be included in the taxpayer's rate base for ratemaking purposes;

(B) The last day of the estimated useful life of a nuclear power plant that is not described in paragraph (c)(2)(i)(A) of this section is the last day of the estimated useful life of the plant determined as of the date it is placed in service;

(C) A taxpayer with an interest in a plant that is not described in paragraph (c)(2)(i)(A) of this section may use any reasonable method for determining the last day of such estimated useful life; and

(D) A reasonable method for purposes of paragraph (c)(2)(i)(C) of this section may include use of the period for which a public utility commission has included a comparable nuclear power plant in rate base for ratemaking purposes.

(ii) If it can be established that the estimated useful life of the nuclear power plant will end on a date other than the date determined under paragraph (c)(2)(i) of this section, the taxpayer may use such other date as the last day of the estimated useful life but is not required to do so. If the last day of the estimated useful life was determined under paragraph (c)(2)(i)(A) of this section and the most recent ratemaking proceeding used an alternative date as the estimated date on which the nuclear power plant will no longer be included rate base, the most recent ratemaking proceeding will generally be treated as establishing such alternative date as the last day of the estimated useful life.

**(d) Decommissioning costs allocable to a fund.** The amount of decommissioning costs allocable to a nuclear decommissioning fund is determined for purposes of this section by applying the following rules and definitions:

*(1) General rule.* The amount of decommissioning costs allocable to a nuclear decommissioning fund is the taxpayer's share of the total estimated cost of decommissioning the nuclear power plant to which the fund relates.

*(2) Total estimated cost of decommissioning.* Under paragraph (a)(2) of this section, the taxpayer must demonstrate the reasonableness of the assumptions concerning the total estimated cost of decommissioning the nuclear power plant.

*(3) Taxpayer's share.* The taxpayer's share of the total estimated cost of decommissioning a nuclear power plant equals the total estimated cost of decommissioning such nuclear power plant multiplied by the percentage of such nuclear power plant that the qualifying interest of the taxpayer represents. (See § 1.468A-1(b)(2) for circumstances in

which a taxpayer possesses a qualifying interest in a nuclear power plant).

**(e) Manner of requesting schedule of ruling amounts.** *(1) In general.* (i) In order to receive a ruling amount for any taxable year, a taxpayer must file a request for a schedule of ruling amounts that complies with the requirements of this paragraph (e), the applicable procedural rules set forth in § 601.201(e) of this chapter (Statement of Procedural Rules), and the requirements of any applicable revenue procedure that is in effect on the date the request is filed.

(ii) A separate request for a schedule of ruling amounts is required for each nuclear decommissioning fund established by a taxpayer. (See paragraph (a) of § 1.468A-5 for rules relating to the number of nuclear decommissioning funds that a taxpayer can establish.)

(iii) Except as provided by §§ 1.468A-5(a)(1)(iv) (relating to certain unincorporated organizations that may be taxable as corporations) and 1.468A-8 (relating to a special transfer under section 468A(f)(1)), a request for a schedule of ruling amounts must not contain a request for a ruling on any other issue, whether the issue involves section 468A or another section of the Internal Revenue Code.

(iv) In the case of an affiliated group of corporations that join in the filing of a consolidated return, the common parent of the group may request a schedule of ruling amounts for each member of the group that possesses a qualifying interest in the same nuclear power plant by filing a single submission with the IRS.

(v) The IRS will not provide or revise a ruling amount applicable to a taxable year in response to a request for a schedule of ruling amounts that is filed after the deemed payment deadline date (as defined in § 1.468A-2(c)(1)) for such taxable year. In determining the date when a request is filed, the principles of sections 7502 and 7503 shall apply.

(vi) Except as provided in paragraph (e)(1)(vii) of this section, a request for a schedule of ruling amounts shall be considered filed only if such request complies substantially with the requirements of this paragraph (e).

(vii) If a request does not comply substantially with the requirements of this paragraph (e), the IRS will notify the taxpayer of that fact. If the information or materials necessary to comply substantially with the requirements of this paragraph (e) are provided to the IRS within 30 days after this notification, the request will be considered filed on the date of the original submission. In addition, the request will be considered filed on the date of the original submission in a case in which the information and materials are provided more than 30 days after the notification if the IRS determines that the electing taxpayer made a good faith effort to provide the applicable information or materials within 30 days after notification and also determines that treating the request as filed on the date of the original submission is consistent with the purposes of section 468A. In any other case in which the information or materials necessary to comply substantially with the requirements of this paragraph (e) are not provided within 30 days after the notification, the request will be considered filed on the date that all information or materials necessary to comply with the requirements of this paragraph (e) are provided.

*(2) Information required.* A request for a schedule of ruling amounts must contain the following information:

(i) The taxpayer's name, address, and taxpayer identification number.

(ii) Whether the request is for an initial schedule of ruling amounts, a mandatory review of the schedule of ruling amounts (see paragraph (f)(1) of this section), or an elective review of the schedule of ruling amounts (see paragraph (f)(2) of this section).

(iii) The name and location of the nuclear power plant with respect to which a schedule of ruling amounts is requested.

(iv) A description of the taxpayer's qualifying interest in the nuclear power plant and the percentage of such nuclear power plant that the qualifying interest of the taxpayer represents.

(v) Where applicable, an identification of each public utility commission that establishes or approves rates for the furnishing or sale by the taxpayer of electric energy generated by the nuclear power plant, and, for each public utility commission identified—

(A) Whether the public utility commission has determined the amount of decommissioning costs to be included in the taxpayer's cost of service for ratemaking purposes;

(B) The amount of decommissioning costs that are to be included in the taxpayer's cost of service for each taxable year under the current determination and amounts that otherwise are required to be included in the taxpayer's income under section 88 and the regulations thereunder;

(C) A description of the assumptions, estimates and other factors used by the public utility commission to determine the amount of decommissioning costs;

(D) A copy of such portions of any order or opinion of the public utility commission as pertain to the public utility commission's most recent determination of the amount of decommissioning costs to be included in cost of service; and

(E) A copy of each engineering or cost study that was relied on or used by the public utility commission in determining the amount of decommissioning costs to be included in the taxpayer's cost of service under the current determination.

(vi) A description of the assumptions, estimates and other factors that were used by the taxpayer to determine the amount of decommissioning costs, including each of the following if applicable:

(A) A description of the proposed method of decommissioning the nuclear power plant (for example, prompt removal/dismantlement, safe storage entombment with delayed dismantlement, or safe storage mothballing with delayed dismantlement).

(B) The estimated year in which substantial decommissioning costs will first be incurred.

(C) The estimated year in which the decommissioning of the nuclear power plant will be substantially complete (see § 1.468A-5(d)(3) for a definition of substantial completion of decommissioning).

(D) The total estimated cost of decommissioning expressed in current dollars (that is, based on price levels in effect at the time of the current determination).

(E) The total estimated cost of decommissioning expressed in future dollars (that is, based on anticipated price levels when expenses are expected to be paid).

(F) For each taxable year in the period that begins with the year specified in paragraph (e)(2)(vi)(B) of this section (the estimated year in which substantial decommissioning costs will first be incurred) and ends with the year specified in paragraph (e)(2)(vi)(C) of this section (the estimated year in which the decommissioning of the nuclear power plant will be substantially complete), the estimated cost of decommissioning expressed in future dollars.

(G) A description of the methodology used in converting the estimated cost of decommissioning expressed in current dollars to the estimated cost of decommissioning expressed in future dollars.

(H) The assumed after-tax rate of return to be earned by the assets of the qualified nuclear decommissioning fund.

(I) A copy of each engineering or cost study that was relied on or used by the taxpayer in determining the amount of decommissioning costs.

(vii) A proposed schedule of ruling amounts for each taxable year remaining in the funding period as of the date the schedule of ruling amounts will first apply.

(viii) A description of the assumptions, estimates and other factors that were used in determining the proposed schedule of ruling amounts, including, if applicable—

(A) The funding period (as such term is defined in paragraph (c) of this section);

(B) The assumed after-tax rate of return to be earned by the assets of the nuclear decommissioning fund;

(C) The fair market value of the assets (if any) of the nuclear decommissioning fund as of the first day of the first taxable year to which the schedule of ruling amounts will apply;

(D) The amount expected to be earned by the assets of the nuclear decommissioning fund (based on the after-tax rate of return applicable to the fund) over the period that begins on the first day of the first taxable year to which the schedule of ruling amounts will apply and ends on the last day of the funding period;

(E) The amount of decommissioning costs allocable to the nuclear decommissioning fund (as determined under paragraph (d) of this section);

(F) The total estimated cost of decommissioning (as determined under paragraph (d)(2) of this section); and

(G) The taxpayer's share of the total estimated cost of decommissioning (as such term is defined in paragraph (d)(3) of this section).

(ix) If the request is for a revised schedule of ruling amounts, the after-tax rate of return earned by the assets of the nuclear decommissioning fund for each taxable year in the period that begins with the date of the initial contribution to the fund and ends with the first day of the first taxable year to which the revised schedule of ruling amounts applies.

(x) If applicable, an explanation of the need for a schedule of ruling amounts determined on a basis other than the rules of paragraphs (a) through (d) of this section and a description of an alternative basis for determining a schedule of ruling amounts (see paragraph (a)(5) of this section).

(xi) A chart or table, based upon the assumed after-tax rate of return to be earned by the assets of the nuclear decommissioning fund, setting forth the years the fund will be in existence, the annual contribution to the fund, the estimated annual earnings of the fund and the cumulative total balance in the fund.

(xii) If the request is for a revised schedule of ruling amounts, a copy of the schedule of ruling amounts that the revised schedule would replace.

(xiii) If the request for a schedule of ruling amounts contains a request, pursuant to § 1.468A-5(a)(1)(iv), that the IRS rule whether an unincorporated organization through which the assets of the fund are invested is an association taxable as a corporation for Federal tax purposes, a copy of the legal documents establishing or otherwise governing the organization.

(xiv) Any other information required by the IRS that may be necessary or useful in determining the schedule of ruling amounts.

*(3) Administrative procedures.* The IRS may prescribe administrative procedures that supplement the provisions of paragraph (e)(1) and (2) of this section. In addition, the IRS may, in its discretion, waive the requirements of paragraph (e)(1) and (2) of this section under appropriate circumstances.

**(f) Review and revision of schedule of ruling amounts.** *(1) Mandatory review.* (i) Any taxpayer that has obtained a schedule of ruling amounts pursuant to paragraph (e) of this section must file a request for a revised schedule of ruling amounts on or before the deemed payment deadline date for the 10th taxable year that begins after the taxable year in which the most recent schedule of ruling amounts was received. If the taxpayer calculated its most recent schedule of ruling amounts on any basis other than an order issued by a public utility commission, the taxpayer must file a request for a revised schedule of ruling amounts on or before the deemed payment deadline date for the 5th taxable year that begins after the taxable year in which the most recent schedule of ruling amounts was received.

(ii) (A) Any taxpayer that has obtained a formula or method for determining a schedule of ruling amounts for any taxable year under paragraph (a)(5) of this section must file a request for a revised schedule on or before the earlier of the deemed payment deadline for the 5th taxable year that begins after its taxable year in which the most recent formula or method was approved or the deemed payment deadline for the first taxable year that begins after a taxable year in which there is a substantial variation in the ruling amount determined under the most recent formula or method. There is a substantial variation in the ruling amount determined under the formula or method in effect for a taxable year if the ruling amount for the year and the ruling amount for any earlier year since the most recent formula or method was approved differ by more than 50 percent of the smaller amount.

(B) Any taxpayer that has determined its ruling amount for any taxable year under a formula prescribed by § 1.468A-6 (which prescribes ruling amounts for the taxable year in which there is a disposition of a qualifying interest in a nuclear power plant) must file a request for a revised schedule of ruling amounts on or before the deemed payment deadline for its first taxable year that begins after the disposition.

(iii) A taxpayer requesting a schedule of deduction amounts for a nuclear decommissioning fund under § 1.468A-8 must also request a revised schedule of ruling amounts for the fund. The revised schedule of ruling amounts must apply beginning with the first taxable year following the first year in which a deduction is allowed under the schedule of deduction amounts.

(iv) If the operating license of the nuclear power plant to which a nuclear decommissioning fund relates is renewed, the taxpayer maintaining the fund must request a revised schedule of ruling amounts. The request for the revised schedule must be submitted on or before the deemed payment deadline for the taxable year that includes the date on which the operating license is renewed.

(v) A request for a schedule of ruling amounts required by this paragraph (f)(1) must be made in accordance with the rules of paragraph (e) of this section. If a taxpayer does not properly file a request for a revised schedule of ruling amounts by the date provided in paragraph (f)(1)(i), (ii) or (iv) of this section (whichever is applicable), the taxpayer's ruling amount for the first taxable year to which the revised schedule of ruling amounts would have applied and for all succeeding taxable years until a new schedule is obtained shall be zero dollars, unless, in its discretion, the IRS provides otherwise in such new schedule of ruling amounts. Thus, if a taxpayer is required to request a revised schedule of ruling amounts under any provision of this section, and each ruling amount in the revised schedule would equal zero dollars, the taxpayer may, instead of requesting a new schedule of ruling amounts, begin treating the ruling amounts under its most recent schedule as equal to zero dollars.

*(2) Elective review.* Any taxpayer that has obtained a schedule of ruling amounts pursuant to paragraph (e) of this section can request a revised schedule of ruling amounts. Such a request must be made in accordance with the rules of paragraph (e) of this section; thus, the IRS will not provide a revised ruling amount applicable to a taxable year in response to a request for a schedule of ruling amounts that is filed after the deemed payment deadline date for such taxable year (see paragraph (e)(1)(vi) of this section).

*(3) Determination of revised schedule of ruling amounts.* A revised schedule of ruling amounts for a nuclear decommissioning fund shall be determined under this section without regard to any schedule of ruling amounts for such nuclear decommissioning fund that was issued prior to such revised schedule. Thus, a ruling amount specified in a revised schedule of ruling amounts for any taxable year in the funding period can be less than one or more ruling amounts specified in a prior schedule of ruling amounts for a prior taxable year.

**(g) Special rule permitting payments to a nuclear decommissioning fund before receipt of an initial or revised ruling amount applicable to a taxable year.** *(1)* If an electing taxpayer has filed a timely request for an initial or revised ruling amount for a taxable year beginning on or after January 1, 2006, and does not receive the ruling amount on or before the deemed payment deadline date for such taxable year, the taxpayer may make a payment to a nuclear decommissioning fund on the basis of the ruling amount proposed in the taxpayer's request. Thus, under the preceding sentence, an electing taxpayer may make a payment to a nuclear decommissioning fund for such taxable year that does not exceed the ruling amount proposed by the taxpayer for such taxable year in a timely filed request for a schedule of ruling amounts.

*(2)* If an electing taxpayer makes a payment to a nuclear decommissioning fund for any taxable year pursuant to paragraph (g)(1) of this section and the ruling amount that is provided by the IRS is greater than the ruling amount proposed by the taxpayer for such taxable year, the taxpayer is not allowed to make an additional payment to the fund for such taxable year after the deemed payment deadline date for such taxable year.

*(3)* If the payment or transfer that an electing taxpayer makes to a nuclear decommissioning fund for any taxable year pursuant to paragraph (g)(1) of this section exceeds the ruling amount that is provided by the IRS for such taxable year, the following rules apply:

(i) The amount of the excess is an excess contribution (as defined in § 1.468A-5(c)(2)(ii)) for such taxable year.

(ii) The amount of the excess contribution is not deductible (see § 1.468A-2(b)(2)) and must be withdrawn by the taxpayer pursuant to the rules of § 1.468A-5(c)(2)(i).

(iii) The taxpayer must withdraw the after-tax earnings on the excess contribution.

(iv) If the taxpayer claimed a deduction for the excess contribution, the taxpayer should file an amended return for the taxable year.

T.D. 9512, 12/22/2010

## § 1.468A-4 Treatment of nuclear decommissioning fund.

**(a) In general.** A nuclear decommissioning fund is subject to tax on all of its modified gross income (as defined in paragraph (b) of this section). The rate of tax is 20 percent for taxable years beginning after December 31, 1995. This tax is in lieu of any other tax that may be imposed under subtitle A of the Internal Revenue Code (Code) on the income earned by the assets of the nuclear decommissioning fund.

**(b) Modified gross income.** For purposes of this section, the term modified gross income means gross income as defined under section 61 computed with the following modifications:

*(1)* The amount of any payment or special transfer to the nuclear decommissioning fund with respect to which a deduction is allowed under section 468A(a) or section 468A(f) is excluded from gross income.

*(2)* A deduction is allowed for the amount of administrative costs and other incidental expenses of the nuclear decommissioning fund (including taxes, legal expenses, accounting expenses, actuarial expenses and trustee expenses, but not including decommissioning costs) that are otherwise deductible and that are paid by the nuclear decommissioning fund to any person other than the electing taxpayer. An expense is otherwise deductible for purposes of this paragraph (b)(2) if it would be deductible under chapter 1 of the Code in determining the taxable income of a corporation. For example, because Federal income taxes are not deductible under chapter 1 of the Code in determining the taxable income of a corporation, the tax imposed by section 468A(e)(2) and paragraph (a) of this section is not deductible in determining the modified gross income of a nuclear decommissioning fund. Similarly, because certain expenses allocable to tax-exempt interest income are not deductible under section 265 in determining the taxable income of a corporation, such expenses are not deductible in determining the modified gross income of a nuclear decommissioning fund.

*(3)* A deduction is allowed for the amount of an otherwise deductible loss that is sustained by the nuclear decommissioning fund in connection with the sale, exchange or worthlessness of any investment. A loss is otherwise deductible for purposes of this paragraph (b)(3) if such loss would be deductible by a corporation under section 165(f) or (g) and sections 1211(a) and 1212(a).

*(4)* A deduction is allowed for the amount of an otherwise deductible net operating loss of the nuclear decommissioning fund. For purposes of this paragraph (b), the net operating loss of a nuclear decommissioning fund for a taxable year is

the amount by which the deductions allowable under paragraphs (b)(2) and (3) of this section exceed the gross income of the nuclear decommissioning fund computed with the modification described in paragraph (b)(1) of this section. A net operating loss is otherwise deductible for purposes of this paragraph (b)(4) if such a net operating loss would be deductible by a corporation under section 172(a).

**(c) Special rules.** *(1) Period for computation of modified gross income.* The modified gross income of a nuclear decommissioning fund must be computed on the basis of the taxable year of the electing taxpayer. If an electing taxpayer changes its taxable year, each nuclear decommissioning fund of the electing taxpayer must change to the new taxable year. See section 442 and § 1.442-1 for rules relating to the change to a new taxable year.

*(2) Gain or loss upon distribution of property by a fund.* A distribution of property by a nuclear decommissioning fund (whether an actual distribution or a deemed distribution) shall be considered a disposition of property by the nuclear decommissioning fund for purposes of section 1001. In determining the amount of gain or loss from such disposition, the amount realized by the nuclear decommissioning fund shall be the fair market value of the property on the date of disposition.

*(3) Denial of credits against tax.* The tax imposed on the modified gross income of a nuclear decommissioning fund under paragraph (a) of this section is not to be reduced or offset by any credits against tax provided by part IV of subchapter A of chapter 1 of the Code other than the credit provided by section 31(c) for amounts withheld under section 3406 (back-up withholding).

*(4) Other corporate taxes inapplicable.* Although the modified gross income of a nuclear decommissioning fund is subject to tax at the rate specified by section 468A(e)(2) and paragraph (a) of this section, a nuclear decommissioning fund is not subject to the other taxes imposed on corporations under subtitle A of the Code. For example, a nuclear decommissioning fund is not subject to the alternative minimum tax imposed by section 55, the accumulated earnings tax imposed by section 531, the personal holding company tax imposed by section 541, and the alternative tax imposed on a corporation under section 1201(a).

**(d) Treatment as corporation for purposes of subtitle F.** For purposes of subtitle F of the Code and §§ 1.468A-1 through 1.468A-9, a nuclear decommissioning fund is to be treated as if it were a corporation and the tax imposed by section 468A(e)(2) and paragraph (a) of this section is to be treated as a tax imposed by section 11. Thus, for example, the following rules apply:

*(1)* A nuclear decommissioning fund must file a return with respect to the tax imposed by section 468A(e)(2) and paragraph (a) of this section for each taxable year (or portion thereof) that the fund is in existence even though no amount is included in the gross income of the fund for such taxable year. The return is to be made on Form 1120-ND in accordance with the instructions relating to such form. For purposes of this paragraph (d)(1), a nuclear decommissioning fund is in existence for the period that—

(i) Begins on the date that the first deductible payment is actually made to such nuclear decommissioning fund; and

(ii) Ends on the date of termination (see § 1.468A-5(d)), the date that the entire fund is disqualified (see § 1.468A-5(c)), or the date that the electing taxpayer disposes of its entire qualifying interest in the nuclear power plant to which the nuclear decommissioning fund relates (other than in connection with the transfer of the entire fund to the person acquiring such interest), whichever is applicable.

*(2)* For each taxable year of the nuclear decommissioning fund, the return described in paragraph (d)(1) of this section must be filed on or before the 15th day of the third month following the close of such taxable year unless the nuclear decommissioning fund is granted an extension of time for filing under section 6081. If such an extension is granted for any taxable year, the return for such taxable year must be filed on or before the extended due date for such taxable year.

*(3)* A nuclear decommissioning fund must provide its employer identification number on returns, statements and other documents as required by the forms and instructions relating thereto. The employer identification number is obtained by filing a Form SS-4, Application for Employer Identification Number, in accordance with the instructions relating thereto.

*(4)* A nuclear decommissioning fund must deposit all payments of tax imposed by section 468A(e)(2) and paragraph (a) of this section (including any payments of estimated tax) with an authorized government depositary in accordance with § 1.6302-1.

*(5)* A nuclear decommissioning fund is subject to the addition to tax imposed by section 6655 in case of a failure to pay estimated income tax. For purposes of section 6655 and this section—

(i) The tax with respect to which the amount of the underpayment is computed in the case of a nuclear decommissioning fund is the tax imposed by section 468A(e)(2) and paragraph (a) of this section; and

(ii) The taxable income with respect to which the nuclear decommissioning fund's status as a large corporation is measured is modified gross income (as defined by paragraph (b) of this section).

---

T.D. 9512, 12/22/2010

---

### § 1.468A-5 Nuclear decommissioning fund qualification requirements; prohibitions against self-dealing; disqualification of nuclear decommissioning fund; termination of fund upon substantial completion of decommissioning.

**(a) Qualification requirements.** *(1) In general.* (i) A nuclear decommissioning fund must be established and maintained at all times in the United States pursuant to an arrangement that qualifies as a trust under State law. Such trust must be established for the exclusive purpose of providing funds for the decommissioning of one or more nuclear power plants, but a single trust agreement may establish multiple funds for such purpose. Thus, for example—

(A) Two or more nuclear decommissioning funds can be established and maintained pursuant to a single trust agreement; and

(B) One or more funds that are to be used for the decommissioning of a nuclear power plant and that do not qualify as nuclear decommissioning funds under this paragraph (a) can be established and maintained pursuant to a trust agreement that governs one or more nuclear decommissioning funds.

(ii) A separate nuclear decommissioning fund is required for each electing taxpayer and for each nuclear power plant with respect to which an electing taxpayer possesses a qualifying interest. The Internal Revenue Service (IRS) will issue a separate schedule of ruling amounts with respect to each nuclear decommissioning fund, and each nuclear decommissioning fund must file a separate income tax return even if other nuclear decommissioning funds or nonqualified funds are established and maintained pursuant to the trust agreement governing such fund or the assets of other nuclear decommissioning funds or nonqualified funds are pooled with the assets of such fund.

(iii) An electing taxpayer can maintain only one nuclear decommissioning fund for each nuclear power plant with respect to which the taxpayer elects the application of section 468A. If a nuclear power plant is subject to the ratemaking jurisdiction of two or more public utility commissions and any such public utility commission requires a separate fund to be maintained for the benefit of ratepayers whose rates are established or approved by the public utility commission, the separate funds maintained for such plant (whether or not established and maintained pursuant to a single trust agreement) shall be considered a single nuclear decommissioning fund for purposes of section 468A and §§ 1.468A-1 through 1.468A-4, this section and §§ 1.468A-7 through 1.468A-9. Thus, for example, the IRS will issue one schedule of ruling amounts with respect to such nuclear power plant, the nuclear decommissioning fund must file a single income tax return (see § 1.468A-4(d)(1)), and, if the IRS disqualifies the nuclear decommissioning fund, the assets of each separate fund are treated as distributed on the date of disqualification (see paragraph (c)(3) of this section).

(iv) If assets of a nuclear decommissioning fund are (or will be) invested through an unincorporated organization, within the meaning of § 301.7701-2 of this chapter, the IRS will rule, if requested, whether the organization is an association taxable as a corporation for Federal tax purposes. A request for this ruling may be made by the electing taxpayer as part of its request for a schedule of ruling amounts or as part of a request under § 1.468A-8 for a schedule of deduction amounts.

*(2) Limitation on contributions.* Except as otherwise provided in § 1.468A-8 (relating to special transfers under section 468A(f)), a nuclear decommissioning fund is not permitted to accept any contributions in cash or property other than cash payments with respect to which a deduction is allowed under section 468A(a) and § 1.468A-2(a). Thus, for example, except in the case of a special transfer pursuant to § 1.468A-8, securities may not be contributed to a nuclear decommissioning fund even if the taxpayer or a fund established by the taxpayer previously held such securities for the purpose of providing funds for the decommissioning of a nuclear power plant.

*(3) Limitation on use of fund.* (i) In general. The assets of a nuclear decommissioning fund are to be used exclusively—

(A) To satisfy, in whole or in part, the liability of the electing taxpayer for decommissioning costs of the nuclear power plant to which the nuclear decommissioning fund relates;

(B) To pay administrative costs and other incidental expenses of the nuclear decommissioning fund; and

(C) To the extent that the assets of the nuclear decommissioning fund are not currently required for the purposes described in paragraph (a)(3)(i)(A) or (B) of this section, to make investments.

(ii) Definition of administrative costs and expenses. For purposes of paragraph (a)(3)(i) of this section, the term administrative costs and other incidental expenses of a nuclear decommissioning fund means all ordinary and necessary expenses incurred in connection with the operation of the nuclear decommissioning fund. Such term includes the tax imposed by section 468A(e)(2) and § 1.468A-4(a), any State or local tax imposed on the income or the assets of the fund, legal expenses, accounting expenses, actuarial expenses and trustee expenses. Such term does not include decommissioning costs or the payment of insurance premiums on a policy to pay for the nuclear decommissioning costs of a nuclear power plant. Such term also does not include the excise tax imposed on the trustee or other disqualified person under section 4951 or the reimbursement of any expenses incurred in connection with the assertion of such tax unless such expenses are considered reasonable and necessary under section 4951(d)(2)(C) and it is determined that the trustee or other disqualified person is not liable for the excise tax.

*(4) Trust provisions.* Each qualified nuclear decommissioning fund trust agreement must provide that assets in the fund must be used as authorized by section 468A and §§ 1.468A-1 through 1.468A-9 and that the agreement may not be amended so as to violate section 468A or §§ 1.468A-1 through 1.468A-9.

**(b) Prohibitions against self-dealing.**

*(1) In general.* Except as otherwise provided in this paragraph (b), the excise taxes imposed by section 4951 shall apply to each act of self-dealing between a disqualified person and a nuclear decommissioning fund.

*(2) Self-dealing defined.* For purposes of this paragraph (b), the term self-dealing means any act described in section 4951(d), except--

(i) A payment by a nuclear decommissioning fund for the purpose of satisfying, in whole or in part, the liability of the electing taxpayer for decommissioning costs of the nuclear power plant to which the nuclear decommissioning fund relates;

(ii) A withdrawal of an excess contribution by the electing taxpayer pursuant to the rules of paragraph (c)(2) of this section;

(iii) A withdrawal by the electing taxpayer of amounts that have been treated as distributed under paragraph (c)(3) of this section;

(iv) A payment of amounts remaining in a nuclear decommissioning fund to the electing taxpayer after the termination of such fund (as determined under paragraph (d) of this section);

(v) Any act described in section 4951(d)(2)(B) or (C);

(vi) Any act that is described in § 53.4951-1(c) of this chapter and is undertaken to facilitate the temporary investment of assets or the payment of reasonable administrative expenses of the nuclear decommissioning fund; or

(vii) A payment by a nuclear decommissioning fund for the performance of trust functions and certain general banking services by a bank or trust company that is a disqualified person if the banking services are reasonable and necessary to carry out the purposes of the fund and the compensation paid to the bank or trust company for such services, taking into account the fair interest rate for the use of the funds by the bank or trust company, is not excessive.

*(3) Disqualified person defined.* For purposes of this paragraph (b), the term disqualified person includes each person described in section 4951(e)(4) and § 53.4951-1(d).

*(4) General banking services.* The general banking services allowed by paragraph (b)(2)(vii) of this section are—

(i) Checking accounts, as long as the bank does not charge interest on any overwithdrawals;

(ii) Savings accounts, as long as the fund may withdraw its funds on no more than 30 days' notice without subjecting itself to a loss of interest on its money for the time during which the money was on deposit; and

(iii) Safekeeping activities (see § 53.4941(d)-3(c)(2), Example 3, of this chapter).

**(c) Disqualification of nuclear decommissioning fund.** *(1) In general.* (i) Disqualification events. Except as otherwise provided in paragraph (c)(2) of this section, the IRS may, in its discretion, disqualify all or any portion of a nuclear decommissioning fund if at any time during a taxable year of the fund—

(A) The fund does not satisfy the requirements of paragraph (a) of this section; or

(B) The fund and a disqualified person engage in an act of self-dealing (as defined in paragraph (b)(2) of this section).

(ii) Date of disqualification. (A) Except as otherwise provided in this paragraph (c)(1)(ii), the date on which a disqualification under this paragraph (c) will take effect (date of disqualification) is the date that the fund does not satisfy the requirements of paragraph (a) of this section or the date on which the act of self-dealing occurs, whichever is applicable.

(B) If the IRS determines, in its discretion, that the disqualification should take effect on a date subsequent to the date specified in paragraph (c)(1)(ii)(A) of this section, the date of disqualification is such subsequent date.

(iii) Notice of disqualification. The IRS will notify the electing taxpayer of the disqualification of a nuclear decommissioning fund and the date of disqualification by registered or certified mail to the last known address of the electing taxpayer (the notice of disqualification). For further guidance regarding the definition of last known address, see § 301.6212-2 of this chapter.

*(2) Exception to disqualification.* (i) In general. A nuclear decommissioning fund will not be disqualified under paragraph (c)(1) of this section by reason of an excess contribution or the withdrawal of such excess contribution by an electing taxpayer if the amount of the excess contribution is withdrawn by the electing taxpayer on or before the date prescribed by law (including extensions) for filing the return of the nuclear decommissioning fund for the taxable year to which the excess contribution relates. In the case of an excess contribution that is the result of a payment made pursuant to § 1.468A-3(g)(1), a nuclear decommissioning fund will not be disqualified under paragraph (c)(1) of this section if the amount of the excess contribution is withdrawn by the electing taxpayer on or before the later of—

(A) The date prescribed by law (including extensions) for filing the return of the nuclear decommissioning fund for the taxable year to which the excess contribution relates; or

(B) The date that is 30 days after the date that the taxpayer receives the ruling amount for such taxable year.

(ii) Excess contribution defined. For purposes of this section, an excess contribution is the amount by which cash payments made (or deemed made) to a nuclear decommissioning fund during any taxable year exceed the payment limitation contained in section 468A(b) and § 1.468A-2(b). The amount of a special transfer permitted under § 1.468A-8 is not treated as a cash payment for this purpose.

(iii) Taxation of income attributable to an excess contribution. The income of a nuclear decommissioning fund attributable to an excess contribution is required to be included in the gross income of the nuclear decommissioning fund under § 1.468A-4(b).

*(3) Disqualification treated as distribution.* If all or any portion of a nuclear decommissioning fund is disqualified under paragraph (c)(1) of this section, the portion of the nuclear decommissioning fund that is disqualified is treated as distributed to the electing taxpayer on the date of disqualification. Such a distribution shall be treated for purposes of section 1001 as a disposition of property held by the nuclear decommissioning fund (see § 1.468A-4(c)(2)). In addition, the electing taxpayer must include in gross income for the taxable year that includes the date of disqualification an amount equal to the fair market value of the distributable assets of the nuclear decommissioning fund multiplied by the fraction of the nuclear decommissioning fund that was disqualified under paragraph (c)(1) of this section. For this purpose, the fair market value of the distributable assets of the nuclear decommissioning fund is equal to the fair market value of the assets of the fund determined as of the date of disqualification, reduced by—

(i) The amount of any excess contribution that was not withdrawn before the date of disqualification if no deduction was allowed with respect to such excess contribution;

(ii) The amount of any deemed distribution that was not actually distributed before the date of disqualification (as determined under § 1.468A-2(d)(2)(iii)) if the amount of the deemed distribution was included in the gross income of the electing taxpayer for the taxable year in which the deemed distribution occurred; and

(iii) The amount of any tax that—

(A) Is imposed on the income of the fund;

(B) Is attributable to income taken into account before the date of disqualification or as a result of the disqualification; and

(C) Has not been paid as of the date of disqualification.

*(4) Further effects of disqualification.* Contributions made to a disqualified fund after the date of disqualification are not deductible under section 468A(a) and § 1.468A-2(a), or, if the fund is disqualified only in part, are deductible only to the extent provided in the notice of disqualification. In addition, if any assets of the fund that are deemed distributed under paragraph (c)(3) of this section are held by the fund after the date of disqualification (or if additional assets are acquired with nondeductible contributions made to the fund after the date of disqualification), the income earned by such assets after the date of disqualification must be included in the gross income of the electing taxpayer (see section 671) to the extent that such income is otherwise includible under chapter 1 of the Internal Revenue Code (Code). An electing taxpayer can establish a nuclear decommissioning fund to replace a fund that has been disqualified in its entirety only if the IRS specifically consents to the establishment of a replacement fund in connection with the issuance of an initial schedule of ruling amounts for such replacement fund.

**(d) Termination of nuclear decommissioning fund upon substantial completion of decommissioning.** *(1) In general.* Upon substantial completion of the decommissioning of a nuclear power plant to which a nuclear decommissioning fund relates, such nuclear decommissioning fund shall be considered terminated and treated as having distributed all of its assets on the date the termination occurs (the termination date). Such a distribution shall be treated for purposes of section 1001 as a disposition of property held by the nuclear decommissioning fund (see § 1.468A-4(c)(2)). In addition, the electing taxpayer shall include in gross income for the taxable year in which the termination occurs an amount equal to the fair market value of the assets of the fund determined as of the termination date, reduced by—

(i) The amount of any deemed distribution that was not actually distributed before the termination date if the amount of the deemed distribution was included in the gross income of the electing taxpayer for the taxable year in which the deemed distribution occurred; and

(ii) The amount of any tax that—

(A) Is imposed on the income of the fund;

(B) Is attributable to income taken into account before the termination date or as a result of the termination; and

(C) Has not been paid as of the termination date.

*(2) Additional rules.* Contributions made to a nuclear decommissioning fund after the termination date are not deductible under section 468A(a) and § 1.468A-2(a). In addition, if any assets are held by the fund after the termination date, the income earned by such assets after the termination date must be included in the gross income of the electing taxpayer (see section 671) to the extent that such income is otherwise includible under chapter 1 of the Code. Finally, under § 1.468A-2(e), an electing taxpayer using an accrual method of accounting is allowed a deduction for nuclear decommissioning costs that are incurred during any taxable year even if such costs are incurred after substantial completion of decommissioning (for example, expenses incurred to monitor or safeguard the plant site).

*(3) Substantial completion of decommissioning and termination date.* (i) The substantial completion of the decommissioning of a nuclear power plant occurs on the date that the maximum acceptable radioactivity levels mandated by the Nuclear Regulatory Commission with respect to a decommissioned nuclear power plant are satisfied (the substantial completion date). Except as otherwise provided in paragraph (d)(3)(ii) of this section, the substantial completion date is also the termination date.

(ii) If a significant portion of the total estimated decommissioning costs with respect to a nuclear power plant are not incurred on or before the substantial completion date, an electing taxpayer may request, and the IRS will issue, a ruling that designates a date subsequent to the substantial completion date as the termination date. The termination date designated in the ruling will not be later than the last day of the third taxable year after the taxable year that includes the substantial completion date. The request for a ruling under this paragraph (d)(3)(ii) must be filed during the taxable year that includes the substantial completion date and must comply with the procedural rules in effect at the time of the request.

---

T.D. 9512, 12/22/2010

---

## § 1.468A-6 Disposition of an interest in a nuclear power plant.

**(a) In general.** This section describes the Federal income tax consequences of a transfer of the assets of a nuclear decommissioning fund (Fund) within the meaning of § 1.468A-1(b)(4) in connection with a sale, exchange, or other disposition by a taxpayer (transferor) of all or a portion of its qualifying interest in a nuclear power plant to another taxpayer (transferee). This section also explains how a schedule of ruling amounts will be determined for the transferor and transferee. For purposes of this section, a nuclear power plant includes a plant that previously qualified as a nuclear power plant and that has permanently ceased to produce electricity.

**(b) Requirements.** This section applies if—

*(1)* Immediately before the disposition, the transferor maintained a Fund with respect to the interest disposed of; and

*(2)* Immediately after the disposition—

(i) The transferee maintains a Fund with respect to the interest acquired;

(ii) The interest acquired is a qualifying interest of the transferee in the nuclear power plant;

*(3)* In connection with the disposition, either—

(i) The transferee acquires part or all of the transferor's qualifying interest in the plant and a proportionate amount of the assets of the transferor's Fund (all such assets if the transferee acquires the transferor's entire qualifying interest in the plant) is transferred to a Fund of the transferee; or

(ii) The transferee acquires the transferor's entire qualifying interest in the plant and the transferor's entire Fund is transferred to the transferee; and

*(4)* The transferee continues to satisfy the requirements of § 1.468A-5(a)(1)(iii), which permits an electing taxpayer to maintain only one Fund for each plant.

**(c) Tax consequences.** A disposition that satisfies the requirements of paragraph (b) of this section will have the following tax consequences at the time it occurs:

*(1) The transferor and its Fund.* (i) Except as provided in paragraph (c)(1)(ii) of this section, neither the transferor nor the transferor's Fund will recognize gain or loss or otherwise take any income or deduction into account by reason of the transfer of a proportionate amount of the assets of the transferor's Fund to the transferee's Fund (or by reason of the transfer of the transferor's entire Fund to the transferee). For purposes of §§ 1.468A-1 through 1.468A-9, this transfer (or the transfer of the transferor's Fund) will not be considered a distribution of assets by the transferor's Fund.

(ii) Notwithstanding paragraph (c)(1)(i) of this section, if the transferor has made a special transfer under § 1.468A-8 prior to the transfer of the Fund or Fund assets, any deduction with respect to that special transfer allowable under section 468A(f)(2) for a taxable year ending after the date of the transfer of the Fund or Fund assets (the unamortized special transfer deduction) is allowed under section 468A(f)(2)(C) for the taxable year that includes the date of the transfer of the Fund or Fund assets. If the taxpayer transfers only a portion of its interest in a nuclear power plant, only the corresponding portion of the unamortized special transfer deduction qualifies for the acceleration under section 468A(f)(2)(C).

*(2) The transferee and its Fund.* Neither the transferee nor the transferee's Fund will recognize gain or loss or otherwise take any income or deduction into account by reason of the transfer of a proportionate amount of the assets of the transferor's Fund to the transferee's Fund (or by reason of the transfer of the transferor's Fund to the transferee). For purposes of §§ 1.468A-1 through 1.468A-9, this transfer (or the transfer of the transferor's Fund) will not constitute a payment or a contribution of assets by the transferee to its Fund.

*(3) Basis.* Transfers of assets of a Fund to which this section applies do not affect basis. Thus, the transferee's Fund will have a basis in the assets received from the transferor's Fund that is the same as the basis of those assets in the transferor's Fund immediately before the disposition.

**(d) Determination of proportionate amount.** For purposes of this section, a transferor of a qualifying interest in a nuclear power plant is considered to transfer a proportionate amount of the assets of its Fund to a Fund of a transferee of the interest if, on the date of the transfer of the interest, the percentage of the fair market value of the Fund's assets attributable to the assets transferred equals the percentage of the transferor's qualifying interest that is transferred.

**(e) Calculation of schedule of ruling amounts and schedule of deduction amounts for dispositions described in this section.** *(1) Transferor.* If a transferor disposes of all or a portion of its qualifying interest in a nuclear power plant in a transaction to which this section applies, the transferor's schedule of ruling amounts with respect to the interests disposed of and retained (if any) and, if applicable, the amount allowable as a deduction for a special transfer under § 1.468A-8 will be determined under the following rules:

(i) Taxable year of disposition; ruling amount. If the transferor does not file a request for a revised schedule of ruling amounts on or before the deemed payment deadline for the taxable year of the transferor in which the disposition of its interest in the nuclear power plant occurs (that is, the date that is two and one-half months after the close of that year), the transferor's ruling amount with respect to that plant for that year will equal the sum of

(A) The ruling amount contained in the transferor's current schedule of ruling amounts with respect to that plant for that taxable year multiplied by the portion of the qualifying interest that is retained (if any); and

(B) The ruling amount contained in the transferor's current schedule of ruling amounts with respect to that plant for that taxable year multiplied by the product of—

(1) The portion of the transferor's qualifying interest that is disposed of; and

(2) A fraction, the numerator of which is the number of days in that taxable year that precede the date of disposition, and the denominator of which is the number of days in that taxable year.

(ii) Taxable year of disposition; deduction under § 1.468A-8. If the transferor has elected to make a special transfer under section 468A(f), the amount allowable as a deduction under § 1.468A-8 for the taxable year in which it transfers a portion of its interest in the nuclear plant is equal to the deduction amount for that taxable year from its existing schedule of deduction amounts multiplied by the percentage of its interest that it retains. This deduction is in addition to the deduction described in paragraph (c)(1)(ii) of this section.

(iii) Taxable years after the year of disposition. A transferor that retains a qualifying interest in a nuclear power plant must file a request for a revised schedule of ruling amounts (and, if applicable, a revised schedule of deduction amounts) with respect to that interest on or before the deemed payment deadline for the first taxable year of the transferor beginning after the disposition. See §§ 1.468A-3(f)(1)(ii)(B) and 1.468A-8(c)(3). If the transferor does not timely file such a request, the transferor's ruling amount and the transferor's deduction amount under § 1.468A-8 with respect to that interest for the affected year or years will be zero, unless the Internal Revenue Service (IRS) waives the application of this paragraph (e)(1)(iii) upon a showing of good cause for the delay.

*(2) Transferee.* If a transferee acquires all or a portion of a transferor's qualifying interest in a nuclear power plant in a transaction to which this section applies, the transferee's schedule of ruling amounts with respect to the interest acquired will be determined under the following rules:

(i) Taxable year of disposition. If the transferee does not file a request for a schedule of ruling amounts on or before the deemed payment deadline for the taxable year of the transferee in which the disposition occurs (that is, the date that is two and one-half months after the close of that year), the transferee's ruling amount with respect to the interest acquired in the nuclear power plant for that year is equal to the amount contained in the transferor's current schedule of ruling amounts for that plant for the taxable year of the transferor in which the disposition occurred, multiplied by the product of—

(A) The portion of the transferor's qualifying interest that is transferred; and

(B) A fraction, the numerator of which is the number of days in the taxable year of the transferor including and following the date of disposition, and the denominator of which is the number of days in that taxable year.

(ii) Taxable years after the year of disposition. A transferee of a qualifying interest in a nuclear power plant must file a request for a revised schedule of ruling amounts with respect to that interest on or before the deemed payment deadline for the first taxable year of the transferee beginning after the disposition. See § 1.468A-3(f)(1)(ii)(B). If the transferee does not timely file such a request, the transferee's ruling amount with respect to that interest for the affected year or years will be zero, unless the IRS waives the application of this paragraph (e)(2)(ii) upon a showing of good cause for the delay.

*(3) Examples.* The following examples illustrate the provisions of this paragraph (e):

*Example (1).* (i) X Corporation is a calendar year taxpayer engaged in the sale of electric energy generated by a nuclear power plant. The plant is owned entirely by X. On May 27, 2010, X transfers a 60-percent qualifying interest in the plant to Y Corporation, a calendar year taxpayer. Before the transfer, X had received a schedule of ruling amounts containing an annual ruling amount of $10 million for the taxable years 2005 through 2025. For 2010, neither X nor Y files a request for a revised schedule of ruling amounts.

(ii) Under paragraph (e)(1)(i) of this section, X's ruling amount for 2010 is calculated as follows: ($10,000,000 x .40) + ($10,000,000 x .60 x 146/365)=$6,400,000. Under paragraph (e)(2)(i) of this section, Y's ruling amount for 2010 is calculated as follows: $10,000,000 x .60 x 219/365=$3,600,000. Under paragraphs (e)(1)(iii) and (e)(2)(ii) of this section, X and Y must file requests for revised schedules of ruling amounts by March 15, 2012.

*Example (2).* Y Corporation, the sole owner of a nuclear power plant, is a calendar year taxpayer. In year 1, Y elects to make a special transfer under section 468A(f)(1) to the nuclear decommissioning fund Y maintains with respect to the plant. The amount of the special transfer is $100x, and the remaining useful life of the plant is 20 years. Y obtains a schedule of deduction amounts under § 1.468A-8T(c) permitting a $5x deduction each year over the 20-year remaining useful life, and deducts $5x of the special transfer amount in year 1, year 2, year 3, and year 4. On the first day of year 5, Y transfers a 25% interest in the plant to an unrelated party. Under paragraph (c)(1)(ii) of this section, Y may deduct in Year 5 the unamortized special transfer deduction corresponding to the portion of the plant transferred (25 percent of $80x or $20x). In addition, under paragraph (e)(1)(ii) of this section, Y may deduct the portion of the deduction amount for year 5 from the schedule of deduction amounts corresponding to its retained interest in the plant (75 percent of $5x or $3.75x). Pursuant to paragraph (e)(1)(iii) of this section, Y must file a request for a revised schedule of ruling amounts by March 15 of year 6.

**(f) Anti-abuse provision.** The IRS may treat a disposition as satisfying the requirements of this section if the IRS determines that this treatment is necessary or appropriate to carry out the purposes of section 468A and §§ 1.468A-1 through 1.468A-9.

T.D. 9512, 12/22/2010

**§ 1.468A-7 Manner of and time for making election.**

**(a) In general.** An eligible taxpayer is allowed a deduction for the taxable year in which the taxpayer makes a cash payment (or is deemed to make a cash payment) to a nuclear decommissioning fund or for a special transfer under § 1.468A-8 only if the taxpayer elects the application of section 468A. A separate election is required for each nuclear decommissioning fund and for each taxable year with respect to which payments are to be deducted under section 468A or a special transfer is made under § 1.468A-8. In the case of an affiliated group of corporations that join in the filing of a consolidated return for a taxable year, the common parent must make a separate election on behalf of each member whose payments to a nuclear decommissioning fund during such taxable year are to be deducted under section 468A and each member that makes a special transfer under § 1.468A-8 with respect to such year. The election under section 468A for any taxable year is irrevocable and must be made by attaching a statement (Election Statement) and a copy of the schedule of ruling amounts provided pursuant to the rules of § 1.468A-3 to the taxpayer's Federal income tax return (or, in the case of an affiliated group of corporations that join in the filing of a consolidated return, the consolidated return) for such taxable year. The return to which the Election Statement and a copy of the schedule of ruling amounts is attached must be filed on or before the time prescribed by law (including extensions) for filing the return for the taxable year with respect to which payments are to be deducted under section 468A.

**(b) Required information.** The Election Statement must include the following information:

*(1)* The legend "Election Under Section 468A" typed or legibly printed at the top of the first page.

*(2)* The electing taxpayer's name, address and taxpayer identification number (or, in the case of an affiliated group of corporations that join in the filing of a consolidated return, the name, address and taxpayer identification number of each electing taxpayer).

*(3)* The taxable year for which the election is made.

*(4)* For each nuclear decommissioning fund for which an election is made—

(i) The name and location of the nuclear power plant to which the fund relates;

(ii) The name and employer identification number of the nuclear decommissioning fund;

(iii) The total amount of actual cash payments made to the nuclear decommissioning fund during the taxable year that were not treated as deemed cash payments under § 1.468A-2(c)(1) for a prior taxable year;

(iv) The total amount of cash payments deemed made to the nuclear decommissioning fund under § 1.468A-2(c)(1) for the taxable year;

(v) The total amount of any special transfers (whether in cash or property) made to the nuclear decommissioning fund under § 1.468A-8 during the taxable year that were not treated as deemed transfers under § 1.468A-8(a)(4) for a prior taxable year;

(vi) The total amount of any special transfers (whether in cash or property) deemed made to the nuclear decommissioning fund under § 1.468A-8(a)(4) for the taxable year; and

(vii) For each item of property included in the amounts described in paragraph (b)(4)((v) or (vi) of this section, the amount of the item of property and whether the basis of the item of property is determined under § 1.468A-8(b)(5)(iii)(A) or § 1.468A-8(b)(5)(iii)(B).

T.D. 9512, 12/22/2010

**§ 1.468A-8 Special transfers to qualified funds pursuant to section 468A(f) (temporary).**

**(a) General rule.** *(1) In general.* In general. Under section 468A(f), a taxpayer maintaining a qualified nuclear decommissioning fund with respect to a nuclear power plant may transfer cash or property into the fund (a special transfer). The special transfer is not subject to the ruling amount limitation in section 468A(b) and is not treated as a cash payment for purposes of that limitation. Thus, a taxpayer may, in the same taxable year, pay the ruling amount and make a special transfer into the fund. A special transfer may be made in cash, property, or both cash and property. The amount of a special transfer (that is, the amount of cash and the fair market value of property transferred) may not exceed the present value of the pre-2005 nonqualifying amount of nuclear decommissioning costs with respect to the nuclear power plant. The taxpayer is entitled to a deduction against income for a special transfer, as described in paragraph (b) of this section. A special transfer may not be made to a nuclear decommissioning fund before the first taxable year in which a deduction amount is applicable to the nuclear decommissioning fund (see paragraph (c) of this section).

*(2) Pre-2005 nonqualifying amount.*

(i) In general. The present value of the pre-2005 nonqualifying amount of nuclear decommissioning costs with respect to a nuclear power plant is the amount equal to the pre-2005 nonqualifying percentage of the present value of the estimated future decommissioning costs (as defined in § 1.468A-1(b)(6)) with respect to the nuclear power plant as of the first day of the taxable year of the taxpayer in which the special transfer is made or deemed made (or a later date that is on or before the date on which the special transfer is expected to be made if the taxpayer establishes to the satisfaction of the IRS that the determination of present value as of such date is reasonable and consistent with the principles and provisions of this section). For this purpose, the pre-2005 nonqualifying percentage for the plant is 100 percent reduced by the sum of—

(A) The qualifying percentage (within the meaning of § 1.468A-3(d)(4) as in effect on December 31, 2005) used in determining the taxpayer's last schedule of ruling amounts for the nuclear decommissioning fund under the law in effect before the enactment of the Energy Policy Act of 2005 (that is, the percentage of the plant's total nuclear decommissioning costs that were permitted to be funded through the fund under the law in effect before the enactment of the Energy Policy Act of 2005); and

(B) The percentage of decommissioning costs transferred in any previous special transfer (that is, the amount transferred as a percentage of the present value of the estimated future costs of decommissioning as of the first day of the taxable year in which such previous transfer was made).

(ii) Pre-2005 nonqualifying amount of transferee. If there is a transfer of a nuclear decommissioning fund or part or all of its assets and § 1.468A-6 applies to the transfer, the pre-2005 nonqualifying amount determined with respect to the transferee is equal to the pre-2005 nonqualifying amount (or a proportionate part of the pre-2005 nonqualifying amount) that would have been determined with respect to the transferor but for such transfer.

*(3) Transfers in multiple years.* A taxpayer making a special transfer is not required to transfer the entire eligible amount in a single year. The requirements of paragraph (c) of this section apply separately to each year in which a special transfer is made. In calculating the amount of any subsequent transfer, the taxpayer must reduce the pre-2005 nonqualifying percentage under paragraph (a)(2) of this section to take into account all previous transfers. For example, if a taxpayer has a pre-2005 nonqualifying percentage of 40 percent, and transfers half of the eligible amount in a special transfer, any subsequent transfer must be calculated on the basis of a pre-2005 nonqualifying percentage of 20 percent.

*(4) Deemed payment rules.* (i) In general. The amount of any special transfer (whether in cash or property) described in § 1.468A-8 and made by an electing taxpayer to a nuclear decommissioning fund on or before the 15th day of the third calendar month after the close of any taxable year (the deemed payment deadline date) shall be deemed made during such taxable year if the electing taxpayer irrevocably designates the amount as relating to such taxable year on its timely filed Federal income tax return for such taxable year or, in the case of special transfers described in paragraph (a)(4)(ii) of this section, on an amended return for such taxable year (see § 1.468A-7(b)(4)(v) and (vi) for rules relating to such designation).

(ii) Special rule for certain special transfers. Special transfers that the electing taxpayer designates as relating to a taxable year beginning after December 31, 2005, and ending before January 1, 2010, which are actually made within 90 days after the electing taxpayer receives a ruling from the Secretary relating to the special transfer are deemed made during the taxable year designated as the year to which the special transfer relates.

**(b) Deduction for amounts transferred.** *(1) In general.* (i) Except as provided in this paragraph (b), the deduction for any special transfer is allowed ratably over the remaining useful life of the nuclear power plant. The amount of the deduction for any taxable year is the deduction amount for such year specified in the schedule of deduction amounts required under paragraph (c) of this section.

(ii) For purposes of this paragraph (b), the remaining useful life of the nuclear power plant is the period beginning on the first day of the taxable year during which the transfer is made and ending on the last day of the taxable year that includes the last day of the estimated useful life of the nuclear power plant. The last day of the estimated useful life of the nuclear power plant is determined for this purpose under the rules of § 1.468A-3(c)(2).

*(2) Amount of deduction.* (i) General rule. Except as provided in this paragraph (b)(2), the deduction for property contributed in a special transfer is limited to the lesser of the fair market value of the property contributed or the taxpayer's basis in that property.

(ii) Election. (A) In general. If the fair market value of the property contributed is less than the taxpayer's adjusted basis in such property as of the date the property is contributed and the fund elects to treat the fair market value of the property as its adjusted basis in the property, the taxpayer may deduct an amount equal to the adjusted basis of the contributed property.

(B) Manner of making election. The election described in paragraph (b)(2)(ii)(A) of this section is made for property contributed in a special transfer by attaching a description of the property and a statement that the fund is making an election under § 1.468A-8(b)(2)(ii) with respect to the property to the return of the fund for the taxable year in which the property is contributed to the fund.

(C) Election allowed for property transferred prior to December 23, 2010. The election described in paragraph (b)(2)(ii)(A) of this section may be made and a deduction equal to adjusted basis will be allowed for property contributed in a special transfer prior to December 23, 2010. The election in such a case may be made on an amended return of the fund for the taxable year in which the property is contributed to the fund and the transferor may amend previously filed returns to claim a deduction calculated by reference to the adjusted basis of the property.

*(3) Denial of deduction for previously deducted amounts.* If a deduction (other than a deduction under section 468A) has been allowed to the taxpayer (or a predecessor) on account of expected decommissioning costs for a nuclear power plant (a nonconforming deduction) or an amount otherwise includible in income has been excluded from the gross income of the taxpayer (or a predecessor) on account of such expected decommissioning costs (a nonconforming exclusion), the deduction allowed for a special transfer to the nuclear decommissioning fund maintained with respect to the plant is reduced. In the case of a single special transfer of the full eligible amount, the reduction is equal to the aggregate amount of all nonconforming deductions and nonconforming exclusions. In the case of a transfer of less than the full eligible amount, the reduction is a ratable portion of such aggregate amount.

*(4) Transfers of qualified nuclear decommissioning funds.* (i) If a special transfer is made to any qualified nuclear decommissioning fund, there is a subsequent transfer of the fund or the assets of the fund (a fund transfer), and § 1.468-6 applies to the fund transfer, any amount of the deduction under paragraph (b) of this section allocable to taxable years ending after the date of the fund transfer will be allowed as a current deduction to the transferor for the taxable year that includes the date of the fund transfer. See § 468A-6(c) for additional rules concerning transfers of decommissioning funds, including the transfer of a portion of the taxpayer's interest in a nuclear power plant. If a taxpayer transfers only part of the fund or the fund's assets, the rules in this paragraph (b)(4) apply only to the corresponding portion of the deduction under paragraph (b) of this section.

(ii) If a deduction is allowed to the transferor under paragraph (b)(4)(i) of this section and the transferee is related to the transferor, the Internal Revenue Service (IRS) will not approve the transferee's schedule of ruling amounts for taxable years beginning after the date of the transfer unless the ruling amounts are deferred in a manner that results in recapture of the acceleration amount. For this purpose— (A)

The acceleration amount is the difference between the deduction allowed under this paragraph (b)(4) and the present value as of the beginning of the acceleration period of the deductions that, but for the transfer, would have been allowed under this paragraph (b) for taxable years during the acceleration period;

(B) The acceleration amount is recaptured if the aggregate present value of the ruling amounts at the beginning of the acceleration period is equal to the amount by which the aggregate present value of the ruling amounts that would have been approved but for this paragraph (b)(4)(ii) exceeds the acceleration amount; (C) The acceleration period is the period from the first day of the transferor's first taxable year beginning after the date of the transfer until the end of the plant's remaining useful life;

(D) Present values will be determined using the assumptions that are used in determining the transferee's first schedule of ruling amounts; and

(E) A transferor and a transferee are related if their relationship is specified in section 267(b) or section 707(b)(1) or they are treated as a single taxpayer under section 41(f)(1)(A) or (B).

*(5) Special rules.* (i) Gain or loss not recognized on transfers to fund. No gain or loss will be recognized on any special transfer.

(ii) Taxpayer basis in fund. Notwithstanding any other provision of the Internal Revenue Code (Code) and regulations, the taxpayer's basis in the fund is not increased by reason of the special transfer.

(iii) Fund basis in transferred property. (A) In general. Except as provided in paragraph (b)(5)(iii)(B) of this section, the fund's basis in any property transferred in a special transfer is the same as the transferor's basis in the property immediately before the transfer.

(B) Basis in case of election. If a fund makes the election described in paragraph (b)(2)(ii) of this section, the fund's basis in the property transferred is the fair market value of the property on the date of transfer.

**(c) Schedule of deductions required.** *(1) In general.* A taxpayer may not make a special transfer to a qualified nuclear decommissioning fund unless the taxpayer requests from the IRS a schedule of deduction amounts in connection with such transfer. A schedule of deduction amounts for a nuclear decommissioning fund (schedule of deduction amounts) is a ruling (within the meaning of § 601.201(a)(2) of this chapter) specifying the annual deductions (deduction amounts) that, over the taxable years in the remaining useful life of the nuclear power plant, will result in the deduction of the entire amount of the special transfer. Such a request may be combined with a request for a schedule of ruling amounts under § 1.468A-3(a). In the case of a combined request, the schedule of deduction amounts requested under this paragraph (c)(1) must be stated separately from the schedule of ruling amounts requested under § 1.468A-3(a) and approval of the schedule of deduction amounts under this section will constitute a separate ruling. A request for a schedule of deduction amounts must comply with all provisions of paragraph (d) of this section.

*(2) Transfers in multiple taxable years.* A taxpayer making a special transfer in more than one taxable year pursuant to paragraph (a)(3) of this section must request a separate schedule of deduction amounts in connection with each special transfer. More than one schedule of deduction amounts can be requested in a single ruling request to the Secretary and the Secretary will provide, in a single ruling, separate schedules of deduction amounts for each of a series of special transfers provided that each request for a separate schedule of deduction amounts complies with all requirements of this paragraph.

*(3) Transfer of partial interest in fund.* If a taxpayer transfers part of a fund or a fund's assets and is allowed a deduction under paragraph (b)(3) of this section, the taxpayer must request a new schedule of deduction amounts in connection with the transfer.

*(4) Special transfer permitted before receipt of schedule.* If an electing taxpayer has filed a timely request for a schedule of deduction amounts in connection with a special transfer for a taxable year and does not receive the schedule of deduction amounts before the deemed payment deadline for such taxable year, the taxpayer may make a special transfer to the nuclear decommissioning fund on the basis of the special transfer amount proposed in the taxpayer's request. If the schedule of deduction amounts provided by the Secretary is based on a special transfer amount that differs from the special transfer amount proposed in the taxpayer's request, rules similar to the rules of § 1.468A-3(g)(2) and (3) shall apply.

**(d) Manner of requesting schedule of deduction amounts.** *(1) In general.* (i) In order to receive a deduction amount for any taxable year, a taxpayer must file a request for a schedule of deduction amounts that complies with the requirements of this paragraph (d), the applicable procedural rules set forth in § 601.201(e) of this chapter (Statement of Procedural Rules) and the requirements of any applicable revenue procedure that is in effect on the date the request is filed.

(ii) A separate request for a schedule of deduction amounts is required for each nuclear decommissioning fund established by a taxpayer (see § 1.468A-5(a) for rules relating to the number of nuclear decommissioning funds that a taxpayer can establish).

(iii) Except as provided by § 1.468A-5(a)(1)(iv) (relating to certain unincorporated organizations that may be taxable as corporations) and § 1.468A-3 (relating to a request for a schedule of ruling amounts), a request for a schedule of deduction amounts must not contain a request for a ruling on any other issue, whether the issue involves section 468A or another section of the Code.

(iv) In the case of an affiliated group of corporations that join in the filing of a consolidated return, the common parent of the group may request a schedule of deduction amounts for each member of the group that possesses a qualifying interest in the same nuclear power plant by filing a single submission with the IRS.

(v) Except as provided in paragraph (d)(1)(vi) of this section, the IRS will not provide or revise a deduction amount applicable to a taxable year in response to a request for a schedule of deduction amounts that is filed after the deemed payment deadline date (as defined in paragraph (a)(4) of this section) for such taxable year.

(vi) For special transfers relating to taxable years beginning after December 31, 2005, and before January 1, 2010, the IRS will not provide a deduction amount in response to a request for a schedule of deduction amounts that is filed after February 22, 2011.

(vii) Except as provided in paragraph (d)(1)(viii) of this section, a request for a schedule of deduction amounts shall be considered filed only if such request complies substantially with the requirements of this paragraph (d). In determining the date when a request is filed, the principles of sections 7502 and 7503 shall apply.

(viii) If a request does not comply substantially with the requirements of this paragraph (d), the IRS will notify the taxpayer of that fact. If the information or materials necessary to comply substantially with the requirements of this paragraph (d) are provided to the IRS within 30 days after this notification, the request will be considered filed on the date of the original submission. In addition, the request will be considered filed on the date of the original submission in a case in which the information and materials are provided more than 30 days after the notification if the IRS determines that the electing taxpayer made a good faith effort to provide the applicable information or materials within 30 days after notification and also determines that treating the request as filed on the date of the original submission is consistent with the purposes of section 468A. In any other case in which the information or materials necessary to comply substantially with the requirements of this paragraph (d) are not provided within 30 days after the notification, the request will be considered filed on the date that all information or materials necessary to comply with the requirements of this paragraph (d) are provided.

*(2) Information required.* A request for a schedule of deduction amounts must contain the following information:

(i) The taxpayer's name, address and taxpayer identification number.

(ii) Whether the request is for an initial schedule of deduction amounts or a schedule of deduction amounts for a subsequent special transfer.

(iii) The name and location of the nuclear power plant with respect to which a schedule of deduction amounts is requested.

(iv) A description of the taxpayer's qualifying interest in the nuclear power plant and the percentage of such nuclear power plant that the qualifying interest of the taxpayer represents.

(v) The present value of the estimated future decommissioning costs (as defined in § 1.468A-1(b)(6)) with respect to the taxpayer's qualifying interest in the nuclear power plant as of the first day of the taxable year of the taxpayer in which a transfer is made under this section.

(vi) A description of the assumptions, estimates and other factors that were used by the taxpayer to determine the amount of decommissioning costs, including each of the following if applicable:

(A) A description of the proposed method of decommissioning the nuclear power plant (for example, prompt removal/dismantlement, safe storage entombment with delayed dismantlement, or safe storage mothballing with delayed dismantlement).

(B) The estimated year in which substantial decommissioning costs will first be incurred.

(C) The estimated year in which the decommissioning of the nuclear power plant will be substantially complete (see § 1.468A-5(d)(3) for a definition of substantial completion of decommissioning).

(D) The total estimated cost of decommissioning expressed in current dollars (that is, based on price levels in effect at the time of the current determination).

(E) The total estimated cost of decommissioning expressed in future dollars (that is, based on anticipated price levels when expenses are expected to be paid).

(F) For each taxable year in the period that begins with the year specified in paragraph (d)(2)(vi)(B) of this section (the estimated year in which substantial decommissioning costs will first be incurred) and ends with the year specified in paragraph (d)(2)(vi)(C) of this section (the estimated year in which the decommissioning of the nuclear power plant will be substantially complete), the estimated cost of decommissioning expressed in future dollars.

(G) A description of the methodology used in converting the estimated cost of decommissioning expressed in current dollars to the estimated cost of decommissioning expressed in future dollars.

(H) The assumed after-tax rate of return to be earned by the amounts collected for decommissioning.

(I) A copy of each engineering or cost study that was relied on or used by the taxpayer in determining the amount of decommissioning costs.

(vii) The taxpayer's pre-2005 nonqualifying percentage (as defined in paragraph (a)(2) of this section).

(viii) The estimated useful life of the nuclear power plant (as such term is defined in paragraph (b)(1)(ii) or (iii) of this section).

(ix) If the request is for a subsequent schedule of deduction amounts, the amount of the previous special transfer and the present value of the estimated future decommissioning costs (as defined in § 1.468A-1(b)(6)) with respect to the taxpayer's qualifying interest in the nuclear power plant as of the first day of the taxable year of the taxpayer in which the previous special transfer was made.

(x) If the request is for a subsequent schedule of deduction amounts, a copy of all schedules of deduction amounts that relate to the nuclear power plant to which the request relates and that were previously issued to the taxpayer making the request.

(xi) If the request for a schedule of deduction amounts contains a request, pursuant to § 1.468A-5(a)(1)(iv), that the IRS rule whether an unincorporated organization through which the assets of the fund are invested is an association taxable as a corporation for Federal tax purposes, a copy of the legal documents establishing or otherwise governing the organization.

(xii) Any other information required by the IRS that may be necessary or useful in determining the schedule of deduction amounts.

*(3) Statement required.* A taxpayer requesting a schedule of deduction amounts under this paragraph (d) must submit a statement that any nonconforming deductions and nonconforming exclusions have reduced the deduction allowed for the special transfer in accordance with paragraph (b)(2) of this section.

*(4) Administrative procedures.* The IRS may prescribe administrative procedures that supplement the provisions of paragraphs (d)(1) and (2) of this section. In addition, the IRS may, in its discretion, waive the requirements of paragraphs (d)(1) and (2) of this section under appropriate circumstances.

T.D. 9512, 12/22/2010

**§ 1.468A-9 Effective/applicability date.**

Sections 1.468A-1 through 1.468A-8 are effective on December 23, 2010 and apply with respect to taxable years ending after such date. Special rules that are provided for taxable years ending on or before such date, such as the special rule for certain special transfers contained in § 1.468A-8(a)(4)(ii), apply with respect to such taxable years. In addition, a taxpayer may apply the provisions of §§ 1.468A-1 through 1.468A-8 with respect to a taxable year ending on or before December 23, 2010 if all such provisions are consistently applied.

T.D. 9512, 12/22/2010

### § 1.468B Designated settlement funds.

A designated settlement fund, as defined in section 468B(d)(2), is taxed in the manner described in § 1.468B-2. The rules for transferors to a qualified settlement fund described in § 1.468B-3 apply to transferors to a designated settlement fund. Similarly, the rules for claimants of a qualified settlement fund described in § 1.468B-4 apply to claimants of a designated settlement fund. A fund, account, or trust that does not qualify as a designated settlement fund is, however, a qualified settlement fund if it meets the requirements of a qualified settlement fund described in § 1.468B-1.

T.D. 8459, 12/18/92.

### § 1.468B-0 Table of contents.

This section lists the table of contents for §§ 1.468B-1 through 1.468B-9.

T.D. 8459, 12/18/92, amend T.D. 9249, 2/3/2006, T.D. 9413, 7/7/2008.

### § 1.468B-1 Qualified settlement funds.

**(a) In general.** A qualified settlement fund is a fund, account, or trust that satisfies the requirements of paragraph (c) of this section.

**(b) Coordination with other entity classifications.** If a fund, account, or trust that is a qualified settlement fund could be classified as a trust within the meaning of § 301.7701-4 of this chapter, it is classified as a qualified settlement fund for all purposes of the Internal Revenue Code (Code). If a fund, account, or trust, organized as a trust under applicable state law, is a qualified settlement fund, and could be classified as either an association (within the meaning of § 301.7701-2 of this chapter) or a partnership (within the meaning of § 301.7701-3 of this chapter), it is classified as a qualified settlement fund for all purposes of the Code. If a fund, account, or trust, established for contested liabilities pursuant to § 1.461-2(c)(1) is a qualified settlement fund, it is classified as a qualified settlement fund for all purposes of the Code.

**(c) Requirements.** A fund, account, or trust satisfies the requirements of this paragraph (c) if—

*(1)* It is established pursuant to an order of, or is approved by, the United States, any state (including the District of Columbia), territory, possession, or political subdivision thereof, or any agency or instrumentality (including a court of law) of any of the foregoing and is subject to the continuing jurisdiction of that governmental authority;

*(2)* It is established to resolve or satisfy one or more contested or uncontested claims that have resulted or may result from an event (or related series of events) that has occurred and that has given rise to at least one claim asserting liability—

(i) Under the Comprehensive Environmental Response, Compensation and Liability Act of 1980 (hereinafter referred to as CERCLA), as amended, 42 U.S.C. 9601 *et seq.*; or

(ii) Arising out of a tort, breach of contract, or violation of law; or

(iii) Designated by the Commissioner in a revenue ruling or revenue procedure; and

*(3)* The fund, account, or trust is a trust under applicable state law, or its assets and otherwise segregated from other assets of the transferor (and related persons).

**(d) Definitions.** For purposes of this section—

*(1) Transferor.* A "transferor" is a person that transfers (or on behalf of whom an insurer or other person transfers) money or property to a qualified settlement fund to resolve or satisfy claims described in paragraph (c)(2) of this section against that person.

*(2) Related person.* A "related person" is any person who is related to the transferor within the meaning of sections 267(b) or 707(b)(1).

**(e) Governmental order or approval requirement.** *(1) In general.* A fund, account, or trust is "ordered by" or "approved by" a governmental authority described in paragraph (c)(1) of this section when the authority issues its initial or preliminary order to establish, or grants its initial or preliminary approval of, the fund, account, or trust, even if that order or approval may be subject to review or revision. Except as otherwise provided in paragraph (j)(2) of this section, the governmental authority's order or approval has no retroactive effect and does not permit a fund, account, or trust to be a qualified settlement fund prior to the date the order is issued or the approval is granted.

*(2) Arbitration panels.* An arbitration award that orders the establishment of, or approves, a fund, account, or trust is an order or approval of a governmental authority described in paragraph (c)(1) of this section if—

(i) The arbitration award is judicially enforceable;

(ii) The arbitration award is issued pursuant to a bona fide arbitration proceeding in accordance with rules that are approved by a governmental authority described in paragraph (c)(1) of this section (such as self-regulatory organization-administered arbitration proceedings in the securities industry); and

(iii) The fund, account, or trust is subject to the continuing jurisdiction of the arbitration panel, the court of law that has jurisdiction to enforce the arbitration award, or the governmental authority that approved the rules of the arbitration proceeding.

**(f) Resolve or satisfy requirement.** *(1) Liabilities to provide services or property.* Except as otherwise provided in paragraph (f)(2) of this section, a liability is not described in paragraph (c)(2) of this section if it is a liability for the provision of services or property, unless the transferor's obligation to provide services or property is extinguished by a transfer or transfers to the fund, account, or trust.

*(2) CERCLA liabilities.* A transferor's liability under CERCLA to provide services or property is described in paragraph (c)(2) of this section if following its transfer to a fund, account, or trust the transferor's only remaining liability to the Environmental Protection Agency (if any) is a remote, future obligation to provide services or property.

**(g) Excluded liabilities.** A liability is not described in paragraph (c)(2) of this section if it—

*(1)* Arises under a workers compensation act or a self-insured health plan;

*(2)* Is an obligation to refund the purchase price of, or to repair or replace, products regularly sold in the ordinary course of the transferor's trade or business;

*(3)* Is an obligation of the transferor to make payments to its general trade creditors or debtholders that relates to a title 11 or similar case (as defined in section 368(a)(3)(A)), or a workout; or

*(4)* Is designated by the Commissioner in a revenue ruling or a revenue procedure (see § 601.601(d)(2)(ii) *(b)* of this chapter).

**(h) Segregation requirement.** *(1) In general.* If it is not a trust under applicable state law, a fund, account, or trust satisfies the requirements of paragraph (c)(3) of this section if its assets are physically segregated from other assets of the transferor (and related persons). For example, cash held by a transferor in a separate bank account satisfies the segregation requirement of paragraph (c)(3) of this section.

*(2) Classification of fund established to resolve or satisfy allowable and non-allowable claims.* If a fund, account, or trust is established to resolve or satisfy claims described in paragraph (c)(2) of this section as well as other types of claims *(i.e.,* non-allowable claims) arising from the same event or related series of events, the fund is a qualified settlement fund. However, under § 1.468B-3(c), economic performance does not occur with respect to transfers to the qualified settlement fund for non-allowable claims.

**(i) [Reserved]**

**(j) Classification of fund prior to satisfaction of requirements in paragraph (c) of this section.** *(1) In general.* If a fund, account, or trust is established to resolve or satisfy claims described in paragraph (c)(2) of this section, the assets of the fund, account, or trust are treated as owned by the transferor of those assets until the fund, account, or trust also meets the requirements of paragraphs (c)(1) and (3) of this section. On the date the fund, account, or trust satisfies all the requirements of paragraph (c) of this section, the transferor is treated as transferring the assets to a qualified settlement fund.

*(2) Relation-back rule.* (i) In general. If a fund, account, or trust meets the requirements of paragraphs (c)(2) and (c)(3) of this section prior to the time it meets the requirements of paragraph (c)(1) of this section, the transferor and administrator (as defined in § 1.468B-2(k)(3)) may jointly elect (a relation-back election) to treat the fund, account, or trust as coming into existence as a qualified settlement fund on the later of the date the fund, account, or trust meets the requirements of paragraphs (c)(2) and (c)(3) of this section or January 1 of the calendar year in which all the requirements of paragraph (c) of this section are met. If a relation-back election is made, the assets held by the fund, account, or trust on the date the qualified settlement fund is treated as coming into existence are treated as transferred to the qualified settlement fund on that date.

(ii) Relation-back election. A relation-back election is made by attaching a copy of the election statement, signed by each transferor and the administrator, to (and as part of) the timely filed income tax return (including extensions) of the qualified settlement fund for the taxable year in which the fund is treated as coming into existence. A copy of the election statement must also be attached to (and as part of) the timely filed income tax return (including extensions), or an amended return that is consistent with the requirements of §§ 1.468B-1 through 1.468B-4, of each transferor for the taxable year of the transferor that includes the date on which the qualified settlement fund is treated as coming into existence. The election statement must contain—

(A) A legend, "§ 1.468B-1 Relation-Back Election", at the top of the first page;

(B) Each transferor's name, address, and taxpayer identification number;

(C) The qualified settlement fund's name, address, and employer identification number;

(D) The date as of which the qualified settlement fund is treated as coming into existence; and

(E) A schedule describing each asset treated as transferred to the qualified settlement fund on the date the fund is treated as coming into existence. The schedule of assets does not have to identify the amount of cash or the property treated as transferred by a particular transferor. If the schedule does not identify the transferor of each asset, however, each transferor must include with the copy of the election statement that is attached to its income tax return (or amended return) a schedule describing each asset the transferor is treated as transferring to the qualified settlement fund.

**(k) Election to treat a qualified settlement fund as a subpart E trust.** *(1) In general.* If a qualified settlement fund has only one transferor (as defined in paragraph (d)(1) of this section), the transferor may make an election (grantor trust election) to treat the qualified settlement fund as a trust all of which is owned by the transferor under section 671 and the regulations thereunder. A grantor trust election may be made whether or not the qualified settlement fund would be classified, in the absence of paragraph (b) of this section, as a trust all of which is treated as owned by the transferor under section 671 and the regulations thereunder. A grantor trust election may be revoked only for compelling circumstances upon consent of the Commissioner by private letter ruling.

*(2) Manner of making grantor trust election.*

(i) In general. To make a grantor trust election, a transferor must attach an election statement satisfying the requirements of paragraph (k)(2)(ii) of this section to a timely filed (including extensions) Form 1041, "U.S. Income Tax Return for Estates and Trusts," that the administrator files on behalf of the qualified settlement fund for the taxable year in which the qualified settlement fund is established. However, if a Form 1041 is not otherwise required to be filed (for example, because the provisions of § 1.671-4(b) apply), then the transferor makes a grantor trust election by attaching an election statement satisfying the requirements of paragraph (k)(2)(ii) of this section to a timely filed (including extensions) income tax return of the transferor for the taxable year in which the qualified settlement fund is established. See § 1.468B-5(c)(2) for transition rules.

(ii) Requirements for election statement. The election statement must include a statement by the transferor that the transferor will treat the qualified settlement fund as a grantor trust. The election statement must include the transferor's name, address, taxpayer identification number, and the legend, "§ 1.468B-1(k) Election." The election statement and the statement described in § 1.671-4(a) may be combined into a single statement.

*(3) Effect of making the election.* If a grantor trust election is made--

(i) Paragraph (b) of this section, and §§ 1.468B-2, 1.468B-3, and 1.468B-5(a) and (b) do not apply to the qualified settlement fund. However, this section (except for paragraph (b) of this section) and § 1.468B-4 apply to the qualified settlement fund;

(ii) The qualified settlement fund is treated, for Federal income tax purposes, as a trust all of which is treated as owned by the transferor under section 671 and the regulations thereunder;

(iii) The transferor must take into account in computing the transferor's income tax liability all items of income, deduction, and credit (including capital gains and losses) of the qualified settlement fund in accordance with § 1.671-3(a)(1); and

(iv) The reporting obligations imposed by § 1.671-4 on the trustee of a trust apply to the administrator.

**(l) Examples.** The following examples illustrate the rules of this section:

*Example (1).* In a class action brought in a United States federal district court, the court holds that the defendant, Corporation X, violated certain securities laws and must pay damages in the amount of $150 million. Pursuant to an order of the court, Corporation X transfers $50 million in cash and transfers property with a fair market value of $75 million to a state law trust. The trust will liquidate the property and distribute the cash proceeds to the plaintiffs in the class action. The trust is a qualified settlement fund because it was established pursuant to the order of a federal district court to resolve or satisfy claims against Corporation X for securities law violations that have occurred.

*Example (2).* (i) Assume the same facts as in *Example 1,* except that Corporation X and the class of plaintiffs reach an out-of-court settlement that requires Corporation X to establish and fund a state law trust before the settlement agreement is submitted to the court for approval. The trust is not a qualified settlement fund because it neither is established pursuant to an order of, nor has it been approved by, a governmental authority described in paragraph (c)(1) of this section.

*Example (3).* On June 1, 1994, Corporation Y establishes a fund to resolve or satisfy claims against it arising from the violation of certain securities laws. On that date, Corporation Y transfers $10 million to a segregated account. On December 1, 1994, a federal district court approves the fund. Assuming Corporation Y and the administrator of the qualified settlement fund do not make a relation-back election, Corporation Y is treated as the owner of the $10 million, and is taxable on any income earned on that money, from June 1 through November 30, 1994. The fund is a qualified settlement fund beginning on December 1, 1994.

*Example (4).* (i) On September 1, 1993, Corporation X, which has a taxable year ending on October 31, enters into a settlement agreement with a plaintiff class for asserted tort liabilities. Under the settlement agreement, Corporation X makes two $50 million payments into a segregated fund, one on September 1, 1993, and one on October 1, 1993, to resolve or satisfy the tort liabilities. A federal district court approves the settlement agreement on November 1, 1993.

(ii) The administrator of the fund and Corporation X elect to treat the fund as a qualified settlement fund prior to governmental approval under the relation-back rule of paragraph (j)(2) of this section. The administrator must attach the relation-back election statement to the fund's income tax return for calendar year 1993, and Corporation X must attach the election to its original or amended income tax return for its taxable year ending October 31, 1993.

(iii) Pursuant to the relation-back election, the fund begins its existence as a qualified settlement fund on September 1, 1993, and Corporation X is treated as transferring $50 million to the qualified settlement fund on September 1, 1993, and $50 million on October 1, 1993.

(iv) With respect to these transfers, Corporation X must provide the statement described in § 1.468B-3(e) to the administrator of the qualified settlement fund by February 15, 1994, and must attach a copy of this statement to its original or amended income tax return for its taxable year ending October 31, 1993.

*Example (5).* Assume the same facts as in *Example 4,* except that the court approves the settlement on May 1, 1994. The administrator must attach the relation-back election statement to the fund's income tax return for calendar year 1994, and Corporation X must attach the election statement to its original or amended income tax return for its taxable year ending October 31, 1994. Pursuant to this election, the fund begins its existence as a qualified settlement fund on January 1, 1994. In addition, Corporation X is treated as transferring to the qualified settlement fund all amounts held in the fund on January 1, 1994. With respect to the transfer, Corporation X must provide the statement described in § 1.468B-3(e) to the administrator of the qualified settlement fund by February 15, 1995, and must attach a copy of this statement to its income tax return for its taxable year ending October 31, 1994.

*Example (6).* Corporation Z establishes a fund that meets all the requirements of section 468B(d)(2) for a designated settlement fund, except that Corporation Z does not make the election under section 468B(d)(2)(F). Although the fund does not qualify as a designated settlement fund, it is a qualified settlement fund because the fund meets the requirements of paragraph (c) of this section.

*Example (7).* Corporation X owns and operates a landfill in State A. State A requires Corporation X to transfer money to a trust annually based on the total tonnage of material placed in the landfill during the year. Under the laws of State A, Corporation X will be required to perform (either itself or through contractors) specified closure activities when the landfill is full, and the trust assets will be used to reimburse Corporation X for those closure costs. The trust is not a qualified settlement fund because it is established to secure the liability of Corporation X to perform the closure activities.

T.D. 8459, 12/18/92, amend T.D. 9249, 2/3/2006.

### § 1.468B-2 Taxation of qualified settlement funds and related administrative requirements.

**(a) In general.** A qualified settlement fund is a United States person and is subject to tax on its modified gross income for any taxable year at a rate equal to the maximum rate in effect for that taxable year under section 1(e).

**(b) Modified gross income.** The "modified gross income" of a qualified settlement fund is its gross income, as defined in section 61, computed with the following modifications—

*(1)* In general, amounts transferred to the qualified settlement fund by, or on behalf of, a transferor to resolve or satisfy a liability for which the fund is established are excluded from gross income. However, dividends on stock of a transferor (or a related person), interest on debt of a transferor (or a related person), and payments in compensation for late or delayed transfers, are not excluded from gross income.

*(2)* A deduction is allowed for administrative costs and other incidental expenses incurred in connection with the operation of the qualified settlement fund that would be deductible under chapter 1 of the Internal Revenue Code in determining the taxable income of a corporation. Administrative costs and other incidental expenses include state and local taxes, legal, accounting, and actuarial fees relating to the operation of the qualified settlement fund, and expenses arising from the notification of claimants and the processing of their claims. Administrative costs and other incidental expenses do not include legal fees incurred by, or on behalf of, claimants.

*(3)* A deduction is allowed for losses sustained by the qualified settlement fund in connection with the sale, exchange, or worthlessness of property held by the fund to the extent the losses would be deductible in determining the taxable income of a corporation under section 165(f) or (g), and sections 1211(a) and 1212(a).

*(4)* A deduction is allowed for the amount of a net operating loss of the qualified settlement fund to the extent the loss would be deductible in determining the taxable income of a corporation under section 172(a). For purposes of this paragraph (b)(4), the net operating loss of a qualified settlement fund for a taxable year is the amount by which the deductions allowed under paragraphs (b)(2) and (b)(3) of this section exceed the gross income of the fund computed with the modification described in paragraph (b)(1) of this section.

**(c) Partnership interests held by a qualified settlement fund on February 14, 1992.** *(1) In general.* For taxable years ending prior to January 1, 2003, a qualified settlement fund that holds a partnership interest it acquired prior to February 15, 1992, is allowed a deduction for its distributive share of that partnership's items of loss, deduction, or credit described in section 702(a) that would be deductible in determining the taxable income (or in the case of a credit, the income tax liability) of a corporation to the extent of the fund's distributive share of that partnership's items of income and gain described in section 702(a) for the same taxable year. For purposes of this paragraph (c)(1), a distributive share of a partnership credit is treated as a deduction in an amount equal to the amount of the credit divided by the rate described in paragraph (a) of this section.

*(2) Limitation on changes in partnership agreements and capital contributions.* For purposes of paragraph (c)(1) of this section, changes in a qualified settlement fund's distributive share of items of income, gain, loss, deduction, or credit are disregarded if—

(i) They result from a change in the terms of the partnership agreement on or after December 18, 1992 or a capital contribution to the partnership on or after December 18, 1992 unless the partnership agreement as in effect prior to December 18, 1992 requires the contribution; and

(ii) A principal purpose of the change in the terms of the partnership agreement or the capital contribution is to circumvent the limitation described in paragraph (c)(1) of this section.

**(d) Distributions to transferors and claimants.** Amounts that are distributed by a qualified settlement fund to, or on behalf of, a transferor or a claimant are not deductible by the fund.

**(e) Basis of property transferred to a qualified settlement fund.** A qualified settlement fund's initial basis in property it receives from a transferor (or from an insurer or other person on behalf of a transferor) is the fair market value of that property on the date of transfer to the fund.

**(f) Distribution of property.** A qualified settlement fund must treat a distribution of property as a sale or exchange of that property for purposes of section 1001(a). In computing gain or loss, the amount realized by the qualified settlement fund is the fair market value of the property on the date of distribution.

**(g) Other taxes.** The tax imposed under paragraph (a) of this section is in lieu of any other taxation of the income of a qualified settlement fund under subtitle A of the Internal Revenue Code. Thus, a qualified settlement fund is not subject to the alternative minimum tax of section 55, the accumulated earnings tax of section 531, the personal holding company tax of section 541, or the maximum capital gains rate of section 1(h). A qualified settlement fund is, however, subject to taxes that are not imposed on the income of a taxpayer, such as the tax on transfers of property to foreign entities under section 1491.

**(h) Denial of credits against tax.** The tax imposed on the modified gross income of a qualified settlement fund under paragraph (a) of this section may not be reduced or offset by any credits against tax provided by part IV of subchapter A of chapter 1 of the Internal Revenue Code.

**(i) [Reserved]**

**(j) Taxable year and accounting method.** The taxable year of a qualified settlement fund is the calendar year. A qualified settlement fund must use an accrual method of accounting within the meaning of section 446(c).

**(k) Treatment as corporation for purposes of subtitle F.** Except as otherwise provided in § 1.468B-5(b), for purposes of subtitle F of the Internal Revenue Code, a qualified settlement fund is treated as a corporation and any tax imposed under paragraph (a) of this section is treated as a tax imposed by section 11. Subtitle F rules that apply to qualified settlement funds include, but are not limited to—

*(1)* A qualified settlement fund must file an income tax return with respect to the tax imposed under paragraph (a) of this section for each taxable year that the fund is in existence, whether or not the fund has gross income for that taxable year.

*(2)* A qualified settlement fund is in existence for the period that—

(i) Begins on the first date on which the fund is treated as a qualified settlement fund under § 1.468B-1; and

(ii) Ends on the earlier of the date the fund—

(A) No longer satisfies the requirements of § 1.468B-1; or

(B) No longer has any assets and will not receive any more transfers. (See paragraph (m) of this section for procedures for the prompt assessment of tax).

*(3)* The income tax return of the qualified settlement fund must be filed on or before March 15 of the year following the close of the taxable year of the qualified settlement fund unless the fund is granted an extension of time for filing under section 6081. The return must be made by the administrator of the qualified settlement fund. The "administrator" (which may include a trustee if the qualified settlement fund is a trust) of a qualified settlement fund is, in order of priority—

(i) The person designated, or approved, by the governmental authority that ordered or approved the fund for purposes of § 1.468B-1(c)(1);

(ii) The person designated in the escrow agreement, settlement agreement, or other similar agreement governing the fund;

(iii) The escrow agent, custodian, or other person in possession or control of the fund's assets; or

(iv) The transferor or, if there are multiple transferors, all the transferors, unless an agreement signed by all the transferors designates a single transferor as the administrator.

*(4)* The administrator of a qualified settlement fund must obtain an employer identification number for the fund.

*(5)* A qualified settlement fund must deposit all payments of tax imposed under paragraph (a) of this section (including any payments of estimated tax) with an authorized government depositary in accordance with § 1.6302-1.

*(6)* A qualified settlement fund is subject to the addition to tax imposed by section 6655 in the case of an underpayment of estimated tax computed with respect to the tax imposed under paragraph (a) of this section. For purposes of section 6655(g)(2), a qualified settlement fund's taxable income is its modified gross income and a transferor is not considered a predecessor of a qualified settlement fund.

**(l) Information reporting and withholding requirements.** *(1) Payments to a qualified settlement fund.* Payments to a qualified settlement fund are treated as payments to a corporation for purposes of the information reporting requirements of part III of subchapter A of chapter 61 of the Internal Revenue Code.

*(2) Payments and distributions by a qualified settlement fund.* (i) In general. Payments and distributions by a qualified settlement fund are subject to the information reporting requirements of part III of subchapter A of chapter 61 of the Internal Revenue Code (Code), and the withholding requirements of subchapter A of chapter 3 of subtitle A and subtitle C of the Code.

(ii) Special rules. The following rules apply with respect to payments and distributions by a qualified settlement fund—

(A) A qualified settlement fund must make a return for, or must withhold tax on, a distribution to a Claimant if one or more transferors would have been required to make a return or withhold tax had that transferor made the distribution directly to the claimant;

(B) For purposes of sections 6041(a) and 6041A, if a qualified settlement fund makes a payment or distribution to a transferor, the fund is deemed to make the payment or distribution to the transferor in the course of a trade or business;

(C) For purposes of sections 6041(a) and 6041A, if a qualified settlement fund makes a payment or distribution on behalf of a transferor or a claimant, the fund is deemed to make the payment or distribution to the recipient of that payment or distribution in the course of a trade or business;

(D) With respect to a distribution or payment described in paragraph (l)(2)(ii)(C) of this section and the information reporting requirements of part III of subchapter A of chapter 61 of the Internal Revenue Code, the qualified settlement fund is also deemed to have made the distribution or payment to the transferor or claimant.

**(m) Request for prompt assessment.** A qualified settlement fund is eligible to request the prompt assessment of tax under section 6501(d). For purposes of section 6501(d), a qualified settlement fund is treated as dissolving on the date the fund no longer has any assets (other than a reasonable reserve for potential tax liabilities and related professional fees) and will not receive any more transfers.

**(n) Examples.** The following examples illustrate the rules of this section:

*Example (1).* On June 30, 1993, a United States federal district court approves the settlement of a lawsuit under which Corporation X must transfer $10,833,000 to a qualified settlement fund on August 1, 1993. The $10,833,000 includes $10 million of damages incurred by plaintiffs on October 1, 1992, and $833,000 of interest calculated at 10 percent annually from October 1, 1992, to August 1, 1993. The $833,000 of interest is not a payment to the qualified settlement fund in compensation for a late or delayed transfer to the fund within the meaning of paragraph (b)(1) of this section because the payment of $10,833,000 to the fund is not due until August 1, 1993.

*Example (2).* Assume the same facts as in Example 1 except that the settlement agreement also provides for interest to accrue at a rate of 12 percent annually on any amount not transferred to the qualified settlement fund on August 1, 1993, and the only transfer Corporation X makes to the fund is $11,374,650 on January 1, 1994. The additional payment of $541,650 ($11,374,650 paid on January 1, 1994, less $10,833,000 due on August 1, 1993) is a payment to the qualified settlement fund in compensation for a late or delayed transfer to the fund within the meaning of paragraph (b)(1) of this section.

---

T.D. 8459, 12/18/92.

---

**§ 1.468B-3 Rules applicable to the transferor.**

**(a) Transfer of property.** *(1) In general.* A transferor must treat a transfer of property to a qualified settlement fund as a sale or exchange of that property for purposes of section 1001(a). In computing the gain or loss, the amount realized by the transferor is the fair market value of the property on the date the transfer is made (or is treated as made under § 1.468B-1(g)) to the qualified settlement fund. Because the issuance of a transferor's debt, obligation to provide services or property in the future, or obligation to make a payment described in § 1.461-4(g), is generally not a transfer of property by the transferor, it generally does not result in gain or loss to the transferor under this paragraph (a)(1). If a person other than the transferor transfers property to a qualified settlement fund, there may be other tax consequences as determined under general federal income tax principles.

*(2) Anti-abuse rule.* The Commissioner may disallow a loss resulting from the transfer of property to a qualified settlement fund if the Commissioner determines that a principal purpose for the transfer was to claim the loss and—

(i) The transferor places significant restrictions on the fund's ability to use or dispose of the property; or

(ii) The property (or substantially similar property) is distributed to the transferor (or a related person).

**(b) Qualified appraisal requirement for transfers of certain property.** *(1) In general.* A transferor must obtain a qualified appraisal to support a loss or deduction it claims with respect to a transfer to a qualified settlement fund of the following types of property—

(i) Nonpublicly traded securities (as defined in § 1.170A-13(c)(7)(ix)) issued by the transferor (or a related person); and

(ii) Interests in the transferor (if the transferor is a partnership) and in a partnership in which the transferor (or a related person) is a direct or indirect partner.

*(2) Provision of copies.* The transferor must provide a copy of the qualified appraisal to the administrator of the qualified settlement fund no later than February 15 of the year following the calendar year in which the property is transferred. The transferor also must attach a copy of the qualified appraisal to (and as part of) its timely filed income tax return (including extensions) for the taxable year of the transferor in which the transfer is made.

*(3) Qualified appraisal.* A "qualified appraisal" is a written appraisal that—

(i) Is made within 60 days before or after the date the property is transferred to the qualified settlement fund;

(ii) Is prepared, signed, and dated by an individual who is a qualified appraiser within the meaning of § 1.170A-13(c)(5);

(iii) Includes the information required by paragraph (b)(4) of this section; and

(iv) Does not involve an appraisal fee of the type prohibited by § 1.170A-13(c)(6).

*(4) Information included in a qualified appraisal.* A qualified appraisal must include the following information—

(i) A description of the appraised property;

(ii) The date (or expected date) of the property's transfer to the qualified settlement fund;

(iii) The appraised fair market value of the property on the date (or expected date) of transfer;

(iv) The method of valuing the property, such as the comparable sales approach;

(v) The specific basis for the valuation, such as specific comparable sales or statistical sampling, including a justification for using comparable sales or statistical sampling a and an explanation of the procedure employed;

(vi) The terms of any agreement or understanding entered into (or expected to be entered into) by or on behalf of the transferor (or a related person) or the qualified settlement fund that relates to the use, sale, or other disposition of the transferred property, including, for example, the terms of any agreement or understanding that temporarily or permanently—

(A) Restricts the qualified settlement fund's right to use or dispose of the property; or

(B) Reserves to, or confers upon, any person other than the qualified settlement fund any right (including designating another person as having the right) to income from the property, to possess the property (including the right to purchase or otherwise acquire the property), or to exercise any voting rights with respect to the property;

(vii) The name, address, and taxpayer identification number of the qualified appraiser; and if the qualified appraiser is acting in his or her capacity as a partner in a partnership, an employee of any person, or an independent contractor engaged by a person other than the transferor, the name, address, and taxpayer identification number of the partnership or the person who employs or engages the qualified appraiser;

(viii) The qualifications of the qualified appraiser, including the appraiser's background, experience, education, and membership, if any, in professional appraisal associations; and

(ix) A statement that the appraisal was prepared for income tax purposes.

*(5) Effect of signature of the qualified appraiser.* Any appraiser who falsely or fraudulently overstates the value of the transferred property referred to in a qualified appraisal may be subject to a civil penalty under section 6701 for aiding and abetting an understatement of tax liability and may have appraisals disregarded pursuant to 31 U.S.C. 330(c).

**(c) Economic performance.** *(1) In general.* Except as otherwise provided in this paragraph (c), for purposes of section 461(h), economic performance occurs with respect to a liability described in § 1.468B-1(c)(2) (determined with regard to § 1.468B-1(f) and (g)) to the extent the transferor makes a transfer to a qualified settlement fund to resolve or satisfy the liability.

*(2) Right to a refund or reversion.* (i) In general. Economic performance does not occur to the extent—

(A) The transferor (or a related person) has a right to a refund or reversion of a transfer if that right is exercisable currently and without the agreement of an unrelated person that is independent or has an adverse interest (e.g., the court or agency that approved the fund, or the fund claimants); or

(B) Money or property is transferred under conditions that allow its refund or reversion by reason of the occurrence of an event that is certain to occur, such as the passage of time, or if restrictions on its refund or reversion are illusory.

(ii) Right extinguished. With respect to a transfer described in paragraph (c)(2)(i) of this section, economic performance is deemed to occur on the date, and to the extent, the transferor's right to a refund or reversion is extinguished.

*(3) Obligations of a transferor.* Economic performance does not occur when a transferor transfers to a qualified settlement fund its debt (or the debt of a related person). Instead, economic performance occurs as the transferor (or related person) makes principal payments on the debt. Similarly, economic performance does not occur when a transferor transfers to a qualified settlement fund its obligation (or the obligation of a related person) to provide services or property in the future, or to make a payment described in § 1.461-4(g). Instead, economic performance with respect to such an obligation occurs as services, property or payments are provided or made to the qualified settlement fund or a claimant.

**(d) Payment of insurance amounts.** No deduction is allowed to a transferor for a transfer to a qualified settlement fund to the extent the transferred amounts represent amounts received from the settlement of an insurance claim and are excludable from gross income. If the settlement of an insurance claim occurs after a transferor makes a transfer to a qualified settlement fund for which a deduction has been taken, the transferor must include in income the amounts received from the settlement of the insurance claim to the extent of the deduction.

**(e) Statement to the qualified settlement fund and the Internal Revenue Service.** *(1) In general.* A transferor must provide the statement described in paragraph (e)(2) of this section to the administrator of a qualified settlement fund no later than February 15 of the year following each calendar year in which the transferor (or an insurer or other person on behalf of the transferor) makes a transfer to the fund. The transferor must attach a copy of the statement to (and as part of) its timely filed income tax return (including extensions) for the taxable year of the transferor in which the transfer is made.

*(2) Required statement.* (i) In general. The statement required by this paragraph (e) must provide the following information—

(A) A legend, "§ 1.468B-3 Statement", at the top of the first page;

(B) The transferor's name, address, and taxpayer identification number;

(C) The qualified settlement fund's name, address, and employer identification number;

(D) The date of each transfer;

(E) The amount of cash transferred; and

(F) A description of property transferred and its fair market value on the date of transfer.

(ii) Combined statements. If a qualified settlement fund has more than one transferor, any two or more of the transferors may provide a combined statement to the administrator that does not identify the amount of cash or the property transferred by a particular transferor. If a combined statement is used, however, each transferor must include with its copy of the statement that is attached to its income tax return a schedule describing each asset that the transferor transferred to the qualified settlement fund.

**(f) Distributions to transferors.** *(1) In general.* A transferor must include in gross income any distribution (including a deemed distribution described in paragraph (f)(2) of this section) it receives from a qualified settlement fund. If property is distributed, the amount includible in gross income and the basis in that property, is the fair market value of the property on the date of the distribution.

*(2) Deemed distributions.* (i) Other liabilities. If a qualified settlement fund makes a distribution on behalf of a transferor to a person that is not a claimant, or to a claimant to resolve or satisfy a liability of the transferor (or a related person) other than a liability described in § 1.468B-1(c)(2) for which the fund was established, the distribution is deemed made by the fund to the transferor. The transferor, in turn, is deemed to have made a payment to the actual recipient.

(ii) Constructive receipt. To the extent a transferor acquires a right to a refund or reversion described in paragraph (c)(2) of this section of all or a portion of the assets of a qualified settlement fund subsequent to the transfer of those assets to the fund, the fund is deemed to distribute those assets to the transferor on the date the right is acquired.

*(3) Tax benefit rule.* A distribution described in paragraph (f)(1) or (f)(2) of this section is excluded from the gross income of a transferor to the extent provided by section 111(a).

**(g) Example.** The following example illustrates the rules of this section:

*Example.* On March 1, 1993, Individual A transfers $1 million to a qualified settlement fund to resolve or satisfy claims against him resulting from certain violations of securities laws. Individual A uses the cash receipts and disbursements method of accounting. Since Individual A does not use the accrual method of accounting, the economic performance rules of paragraph (c) of this section are not applicable. Therefore, whether, when, and to what extent Individual A can deduct the transfer is determined under applicable provisions of the Internal Revenue Code, such as sections 162 and 461.

T.D. 8459, 12/18/92.

## § 1.468B-4 Taxability of distributions to claimants.

Whether a distribution to a claimant is includible in the claimant's gross income is generally determined by reference to the claim in respect of which the distribution is made and as if the distribution were made directly by the transferor. For example, to the extent a distribution is in satisfaction of damages on account of personal injury or sickness, the distribution may be excludable from gross income under section 104(a)(2). Similarly, to the extent a distribution is in satisfaction of a claim for foregone taxable interest, the distribution is includible in the claimant's gross income under section 61(a)(4).

T.D. 8459, 12/18/92.

## § 1.468B-5 Effective dates and transition rules applicable to qualified settlement funds.

**(a) In general.** Section 468B, including section 468B(g), is effective as provided in the Tax Reform Act of 1986 and the Technical and Miscellaneous Revenue Act of 1988. Except as otherwise provided in this section, §§ 1.468B-1 through 1.468B-4 are effective on January 1, 1993. Thus, the regulations apply to income of a qualified settlement fund earned after December 31, 1992, transfers to a fund after December 31, 1992, and distributions from a fund after December 31, 1992. For purposes of § 1.468B-3(c) (relating to economic performance), previously transferred assets held by a qualified settlement fund on the date these regulations first apply to the fund (i.e., January 1, 1993, or the earlier date provided under paragraph (b)(2) of this section) are treated as transferred to the fund on that date, to the extent no taxpayer has previously claimed a deduction for the transfer.

**(b) Taxation of certain pre-1996 fund income.** *(1) Reasonable method.* (i) In general. With-respect to a fund, account, or trust established after August 16, 1986, but prior to February 15, 1992, that satisfies (or, if it no longer exists, would have satisfied) the requirements of § 1.468B-1(c), the Internal Revenue Service will not challenge a reasonable, consistently applied method of taxation for transfers to the fund, income earned by the fund, and distributions made by the fund after August 16, 1986, but prior to January 1, 1996. A method is generally considered reasonable if, depending on the facts and circumstances, all transferors and the administrator of the fund have consistently treated transfers to the fund, income earned by the fund, and distributions made by the fund after August 16, 1986, as if the fund were—

(A) A grantor trust and the transferors are the grantors;

(B) A complex trust and the transferors are the grantors; or

(C) A designated settlement fund.

(ii) Qualified settlement funds established after February 14, 1992, but before January 1, 1993. With respect to a fund, account, or trust established after February 14, 1992, but prior to January 1, 1993, that satisfies the requirements of § 1.468B-1(c), the Internal Revenue Service will not challenge a reasonable, consistently applied method of taxation as described in paragraph (b)(1)(i) of this section for transfers to, income earned by, and distributions made by the fund prior to January 1, 1993. However, pursuant to paragraph (a) of this section, sections 1.468B-1 through 1.468B-4 apply to transfers to, income earned by, and distributions made by the qualified settlement fund after 1992.

(iii) Use of cash method of accounting. For purposes of paragraphs (b)(i) and (b)(ii) of this section, for taxable years beginning prior to January 1, 1996, the Internal Revenue Service will not challenge the use of the cash receipts and disbursement method of accounting by a fund, account, or trust.

(iv) Unreasonable position. In no event is it a reasonable position to assert, pursuant to Rev. Rul. 71-119 (see § 601.601(d)(2)(ii)(b) of this chapter), that there is no current taxation of the income of a fund established after August 16, 1986.

(v) Waiver of penalties. For taxable years beginning prior to January 1, 1993, if a fund, account or trust is subject to section 468B(g) and the Internal Revenue Service does not challenge the method of taxation for transfers to, income earned by, and distributions made by, the fund pursuant to paragraph (b)(1)(i) or (b)(1)(ii) of this section, penalties will not be imposed in connection with the use of such method. For example, the penalties under section 6655 for failure to pay estimated tax, section 6651(a)(1) for failure to file a return, section 6651(a)(2) for failure to pay tax, section 6656 for failure to make deposit of taxes, and section 6662 for accuracy-related underpayments will generally not be imposed.

*(2) Election to apply qualified settlement fund rules.* (i) In general. The person that will be the administrator of a qualified settlement fund may elect to apply §§ 1.468B-1 through 1.468B-4 to transfers to, income earned by, and distributions made by, the fund in taxable years ending after August 16, 1986. The election is effective beginning on the first day of the earliest open taxable year of the qualified settlement fund. For purposes of this paragraph (b)(2), a taxable year is

considered open if the period for assessment and collection of tax has not expired pursuant to the rules of section 6501. The election statement must provide the information described in paragraph (b)(2)(ii) of this section and must be signed by the person that will be the administrator. Such person must also provide each transferor of the qualified settlement fund with a copy of the election statement on or before March 15, 1993.

(ii) Election statement. The election statement must provide the following information—

(A) A legend, "§ 1.468B-5(b)(2) Election", at the top of the first page;

(B) Each transferor's name, address, and taxpayer identification number;

(C) The qualified settlement fund's name, address, and employer identification number; and

(D) The date the qualified settlement fund was established within the meaning of § 1.468B-1(j).

(iii) Due date of returns and amended returns. The election statement described in paragraph (b)(2)(ii) of this section must be filed with, and as part of, the qualified settlement fund's timely filed tax return for the taxable year ended December 31, 1992. In addition, the qualified settlement fund must file an amended return that is consistent with the requirements of §§ 1.468B-1 through 1.468B-4 for any taxable year to which the election applies in which the fund took a position inconsistent with those requirements. Any such amended return must be filed no later than March 15, 1993, and must include a copy of the election statement described in paragraph (b)(2)(ii) of this section.

(iv) Computation of interest and waiver of penalties. For purposes of section 6601 and section 6611, the income tax return for each taxable year of the qualified settlement fund to which the election applies is due on March 15 of the year following the taxable year of the fund. For taxable years of a qualified settlement fund ending prior to January 1, 1993, the income earned by the fund is deemed to have been earned on December 31 of each taxable year for purposes of section 6655. Thus, the addition to tax for failure to pay estimated tax under section 6655 will not be imposed. The penalty for failure to file a return under section 6651(a)(1), the penalty for failure to pay tax under section 6651(a)(2), the penalty for failure to make deposit of taxes under section 6656, and the accuracy-related penalty under section 6662 will not be imposed on a qualified settlement fund if the fund files its tax returns for taxable years ending prior to January 1, 1993, and pays any tax due for those taxable years, on or before March 15, 1993.

**(c) Grantor trust elections under § 1.468B-1(k).** *(1) In general.* A transferor may make a grantor trust election under § 1.468B-1(k) if the qualified settlement fund is established after February 3, 2006.

*(2) Transition rules.* A transferor may make a grantor trust election under § 1.468B-1(k) for a qualified settlement fund that was established on or before February 3, 2006, if the applicable period of limitation on filing an amended return has not expired for both the qualified settlement fund's first taxable year and all subsequent taxable years and the transferor's corresponding taxable year or years. A grantor trust election under this paragraph (c)(2) requires that the returns of the qualified settlement fund and the transferor for all affected taxable years are consistent with the grantor trust election. This requirement may be satisfied by timely filed original returns or amended returns filed before the applicable period of limitation expires.

*(3) Qualified settlement funds established by the U.S. government on or before February 3, 2006.* If the U.S. government, or any agency or instrumentality thereof, established a qualified settlement fund on or before February 3, 2006, and the fund would have been classified as a trust all of which is treated as owned by the U.S. government under section 671 and the regulations thereunder without regard to the regulations under section 468B, then the U.S. government is deemed to have made a grantor trust election under § 1.468B-1(k), and the election is applicable for all taxable years of the fund.

T.D. 8459, 12/18/92, amend T.D. 9249, 2/3/2006.

### § 1.468B-6 Escrow accounts, trusts, and other funds used during deferred exchanges of like-kind property under section 1031(a)(3).

**(a) Scope.** This section provides rules under section 468B(g) relating to the current taxation of escrow accounts, trusts, and other funds used during deferred exchanges.

**(b) Definitions.** The definitions in this paragraph (b) apply for purposes of this section.

*(1) In general.* Deferred exchange, escrow agreement, escrow holder, exchange agreement, qualified escrow account, qualified intermediary, qualified trust, relinquished property, replacement property, taxpayer, trust agreement, and trustee have the same meanings as in § 1.1031(k)-1; deferred exchange also includes any exchange intended to qualify as a deferred exchange, and qualified intermediary also includes any person or entity intended by a taxpayer to be a qualified intermediary within the meaning of § 1.1031(k)-1(g)(4).

*(2) Exchange funds.* Exchange funds means relinquished property, cash, or cash equivalent that secures an obligation of a transferee to transfer replacement property, or proceeds from a transfer of relinquished property, held in a qualified escrow account, qualified trust, or other escrow account, trust, or fund in a deferred exchange.

*(3) Exchange facilitator.* Exchange facilitator means a qualified intermediary, transferee, escrow holder, trustee, or other party that holds exchange funds for a taxpayer in a deferred exchange pursuant to an escrow agreement, trust agreement, or exchange agreement.

*(4) Transactional expenses.* (i) In general. Except as provided in paragraph (b)(4)(ii) of this section, transactional expenses means transactional items within the meaning of § 1.1031(k)-1(g)(7)(ii).

(ii) Special rule for certain fees for exchange facilitator services. The fee for the services of an exchange facilitator is not a transactional expense unless the escrow agreement, trust agreement, or exchange agreement, as applicable, provides that—

(A) The amount of the fee payable to the exchange facilitator is fixed on or before the date of the transfer of the relinquished property by the taxpayer (either by stating the fee as a fixed dollar amount in the agreement or determining the fee by a formula, the result of which is known on or before the transfer of the relinquished property by the taxpayer); and

(B) The amount of the fee is payable by the taxpayer regardless of whether the earnings attributable to the exchange funds are sufficient to pay the fee.

**(c) Taxation of exchange funds.** *(1) Exchange funds generally treated as loaned to an exchange facilitator.* Except as provided in paragraph (c)(2) of this section, exchange funds are treated as loaned from a taxpayer to an exchange facilitator (exchange facilitator loan). If a transaction is treated as an exchange facilitator loan under this paragraph (c)(1), the exchange facilitator must take into account all items of income, deduction, and credit (including capital gains and losses) attributable to the exchange funds. See § 1.7872-16 to determine if an exchange facilitator loan is a below-market loan for purposes of section 7872 and § 1.7872-5(b)(16) to determine if an exchange facilitator loan is exempt from section 7872.

*(2) Exchange funds not treated as loaned to an exchange facilitator.* (i) Scope. This paragraph (c)(2) applies if, in accordance with an escrow agreement, trust agreement, or exchange agreement, as applicable, all the earnings attributable to a taxpayer's exchange funds are paid to the taxpayer.

(ii) Earnings attributable to the taxpayer's exchange funds. (A) Separately identified account. If an exchange facilitator holds all of the taxpayer's exchange funds in a separately identified account, the earnings credited to that account are deemed to be all the earnings attributable to the taxpayer's exchange funds for purposes of paragraph (c)(2)(i) of this section. In general, a separately identified account is an account established under the taxpayer's name and taxpayer identification number with a depository institution. For purposes of paragraph (c)(2)(i) of this section, a sub-account will be treated as a separately identified account if the master account under which the sub-account is created is established with a depository institution, the depository institution identifies the sub-account by the taxpayer's name and taxpayer identification number, and the depository institution specifically credits earnings to the sub-account.

(B) Allocation of earnings in commingled accounts. If an exchange facilitator commingles (for investment or otherwise) the taxpayer's exchange funds with other funds or assets, all the earnings attributable to the taxpayer's exchange funds are paid to the taxpayer if all of the earnings attributable to the commingled funds or assets that are allocable on a pro-rata basis (using a reasonable method that takes into account the time that the exchange funds are in the commingled account, actual rate or rates of return, and the respective account balances) to the taxpayer's exchange funds either are paid to the taxpayer or are treated as paid to the taxpayer under paragraph (c)(2)(ii)(C) of this section.

(C) Transactional expenses. Any payment from the taxpayer's exchange funds, or from the earnings attributable to the taxpayer's exchange funds, for a transactional expense of the taxpayer (as defined in paragraph (b)(4) of this section) is treated as first paid to the taxpayer and then paid by the taxpayer to the recipient.

(iii) Treatment of the taxpayer. If this paragraph (c)(2) applies, exchange funds are not treated as loaned from a taxpayer to an exchange facilitator. The taxpayer must take into account all items of income, deduction, and credit (including capital gains and losses) attributable to the exchange funds.

**(d) Information reporting requirements.** A payor (as defined in § 1.6041-1) must report the income attributable to exchange funds to the extent required by the information reporting provisions of subpart B, Part III, subchapter A, chapter 61, Subtitle F of the Internal Revenue Code, and the regulations under those provisions. See § 1.6041-1(f) for rules relating to the amount to be reported when fees, expenses or commissions owed by a payee to a third party are deducted from a payment.

**(e) Examples.** The provisions of this section are illustrated by the following examples in which T is a taxpayer that uses a calendar taxable year and the cash receipts and disbursements method of accounting. The examples are as follows:

*Example (1).* All earnings attributable to exchange funds paid to taxpayer. (i) T enters into a deferred exchange with R. The sales agreement provides that T will transfer property (the relinquished property) to R and R will transfer replacement property to T. R's obligation to transfer replacement property to T is secured by cash equal to the fair market value of the relinquished property, which R will deposit into a qualified escrow account that T establishes with B, a depository institution. T enters into an escrow agreement with B that provides that all the earnings attributable to the exchange funds will be paid to T.

(ii) On November 1, 2008, T transfers property to R and R deposits $2,100,000 in T's qualified escrow account with B. Between November 1 and December 31, 2008, B credits T's account with $14,000 of interest. During January 2009, B credits T's account with $7000 of interest. On February 1, 2009, R transfers replacement property worth $2,100,000 to T and B pays $2,100,000 from the qualified escrow account to R. Additionally, on February 1, 2009, B pays the $21,000 of interest to T.

(iii) Under paragraph (b) of this section, the $2,100,000 deposited with B constitutes exchange funds and B is an exchange facilitator. Because all the earnings attributable to the exchange funds are paid to T in accordance with the escrow agreement, paragraph (c)(2) of this section applies. The exchange funds are not treated as loaned from T to B. T must take into account in computing T's income tax liability for 2008 the $14,000 of earnings credited to the qualified escrow account in 2008 and for 2009 the $7,000 of earnings credited to the qualified escrow account in 2009.

*Example (2).* Payment of transactional expenses from earnings. (i) The facts are the same as in Example 1, except that the escrow agreement provides that, prior to paying the earnings to T, B may deduct any amounts B has paid to third parties for T's transactional expenses. B pays a third party $350 on behalf of T for a survey of the replacement property. After deducting $350 from the earnings attributable to T's qualified escrow account, B pays T the remainder ($20,650) of the earnings.

(ii) Under paragraph (b)(4) of this section, the cost of the survey is a transactional expense. Under paragraph (c)(2)(ii)(C) of this section, the $350 that B pays for the survey is treated as first paid to T and then from T to the third party. Therefore, all the earnings attributable to T's exchange funds are paid or treated as paid to T in accordance with the escrow agreement, and paragraph (c)(2) of this section applies. The exchange funds are not treated as loaned from T to B, and T must take into account in computing T's income tax liability the $21,000 of earnings credited to the qualified escrow account.

*Example (3).* Earnings retained by exchange facilitator as compensation for services. (i) The facts are the same as in Example 1, except that the escrow agreement provides that B also may deduct any outstanding fees owed by T for B's services in facilitating the deferred exchange. In accordance with paragraph (b)(4)(ii) of this section, the escrow agreement provides for a fixed fee of $1,200 for B's services, which is payable by T regardless of the amount of earnings attributable to the exchange funds. Because the earnings on the exchange funds in this case exceed $1,200, B retains $1,200 as the unpaid portion of its fee and pays T the remainder ($19,800) of the earnings.

(ii) Under paragraph (b)(4) of this section, B's fee is treated as a transactional expense. Under paragraph (c)(2)(ii)(C) of this section, the $1200 that B retains for its fee is treated as first paid to T and then from T to B. Therefore, all the earnings attributable to T's exchange funds are paid or treated as paid to T in accordance with the escrow agreement, and paragraph (c)(2) of this section applies. The exchange funds are not treated as loaned from T to B, and T must take into account in computing T's income tax liability the $21,000 of earnings credited to the qualified escrow account.

*Example (4)*. Exchange funds deposited by exchange facilitator with related depository institution in account in taxpayer's name. (i) The facts are the same as in Example 1 except that, instead of entering into an escrow agreement, T enters into an exchange agreement with QI, a qualified intermediary. The exchange agreement provides that R will pay $2,100,000 to QI, QI will deposit $2,100,000 into an account with a depository institution under T's name and taxpayer identification number (TIN), and all the earnings attributable to the account will be paid to T.

(ii) On May 1, 2008, T transfers property to QI, QI transfers the property to R, R delivers $2,100,000 to QI, and QI deposits $2,100,000 into a money market account with depository institution B under T's name and TIN. B and QI are members of the same consolidated group of corporations within the meaning of section 1501. Between May 1 and September 1, 2008, the account earns $28,000 of interest at the stated rate established by B. During the period May 1 to September 1, 2008, B invests T's exchange funds and earns $40,000. On September 1, 2008, QI uses $2,100,000 of the funds in the account to purchase replacement property identified by T and transfers the replacement property to T. B pays to T the $28,000 of interest earned on the money market account at the stated rate.

(iii) Under paragraph (b) of this section, the $2,100,000 QI receives from R for the relinquished property is exchange funds and QI is an exchange facilitator. B is not an exchange facilitator. T has not entered into an escrow agreement, trust agreement, or exchange agreement with B, and QI, not B, holds the exchange funds on behalf of T. Under paragraph (c)(2)(ii)(A) of this section, the $40,000 B earns from investing T's exchange funds are not treated as earnings attributable to T's exchange funds. Because all the earnings attributable to T's exchange funds are paid to T in accordance with the exchange agreement, paragraph (c)(2) of this section applies. The exchange funds are not treated as loaned from T to QI, and T must take into account in computing T's income tax liability for 2008 the $28,000 of interest earned on the money market account.

*Example (5)*. Earnings of related depository institution credited to exchange facilitator. (i) The facts are the same as in Example 4, except that at the end of each taxable year, B credits a portion of its earnings on deposits to QI. The amount credited is based on the total amount of exchange funds QI has deposited with B during the year. At the end of the 2008 taxable year, B credits $152,500 of B's earnings to QI.

(ii) Under paragraph (c)(2)(ii)(A) of this section, no part of the $152,500 credited by B to QI is earnings attributable to T's exchange funds. Therefore, all of the earnings attributable to the exchange funds are paid to T in accordance with the exchange agreement, and paragraph (c)(2) of this section applies. The exchange funds are not treated as loaned from T to QI, and T must take into account in computing T's income tax liability for 2008 the $28,000 of interest earned on T's account.

*Example (6)*. Exchange funds deposited by exchange facilitator with unrelated depository institution in sub-account in taxpayer's name. (i) The facts are the same as in Example 4, except that QI and B are unrelated and the money market account in which QI deposits the $2,100,000 received from T is a sub-account within a master account QI maintains with B in QI's name and TIN. The master account includes other sub-accounts, each in the name and TIN of a taxpayer that has entered into an exchange agreement with QI, into which QI deposits each taxpayer's exchange funds. Each month, B transfers to QI's master account an additional amount of interest based upon the average daily balance of all exchange funds within the master account during the month. At the end of the 2008 taxable year, B has credited $152,500 of additional interest to QI.

(ii) Under paragraph (c)(2)(ii)(A) of this section, no part of the $152,500 credited by B to QI is earnings attributable to T's exchange funds. Therefore, all of the earnings attributable to the exchange funds are paid to T in accordance with the exchange agreement, and paragraph (c)(2) of this section applies. The exchange funds are not treated as loaned from T to QI, and T must take into account in computing T's income tax liability for 2008 the $28,000 of interest earned on T's account.

*Example (7)*. Marketing fee paid to exchange facilitator. (i) The facts are the same as in Example 4, except that at the end of each taxable year, B pays a marketing fee to QI for using B as its depository institution for exchange funds. The amount of the fee is based on the total amount of exchange funds QI has deposited with B during the year.

(ii) Under paragraph (c)(2)(ii)(A) of this section, no part of the marketing fee that B pays to QI is earnings attributable to T's exchange funds. Therefore, all of the earnings attributable to the exchange funds are paid to T in accordance with the exchange agreement, and paragraph (c)(2) of this section applies. The exchange funds are not treated as loaned from T to QI, and T must take into account in computing T's income tax liability for 2008 the $28,000 of interest earned on T's account.

*Example (8)*. Stated rate of interest on account less than earnings attributable to exchange funds. (i) The facts are the same as in Example 4, except that the exchange agreement provides only that QI will pay T a stated rate of interest. QI invests the exchange funds and earns $40,000. The exchange funds earn $28,000 at the stated rate of interest, and QI pays the $28,000 to T.

(ii) Paragraph (c)(1) of this section applies and the exchange funds are treated as loaned from T to QI. QI must take into account in computing QI's income tax liability all items of income, deduction, and credit (including capital gains and losses) attributable to the exchange funds. Paragraph (c)(2) of this section does not apply because QI does not pay all the earnings attributable to the exchange funds to T. See §§ 1.7872-5 and 1.7872-16 for rules relating to exchange facilitator loans.

*Example (9)*. All earnings attributable to commingled exchange funds paid to taxpayer. (i) The facts are the same as in Example 4, except that the exchange agreement does not specify how the $2,100,000 QI receives from R must be invested.

(ii) On May 1, 2008, QI deposits the $2,100,000 with B in a pre-existing interest-bearing account under QI's name and TIN. The account has a total balance of $5,275,000 immediately thereafter. On the last day of each month between May and September, 2008, the account earns interest as follows: $17,583 in May, $17,642 in June, $18,756 in July, and $17,472 in August. On July 11, 2008, QI deposits $500,000 in the account. On August 15, 2008, QI withdraws $1,175,000 from the account.

(iii) QI calculates T's pro-rata share of the earnings allocable to the $2,100,000 based on the actual return, the average daily principal balances, and a 30-day month convention, as follows:

| Month | Account's avg. daily bal. | T's avg. daily bal. | T's share* (percent) | Monthly interest | T's end. bal.** |
|---|---|---|---|---|---|
| May | $5,275,000 | $2,100,000 | 39.8 | $17,583 | $2,106,998 |
| June | 5,292,583 | 2,106,998 | 39.8 | 17,642 | 2,114,020 |
| July | 5,643,558 | 2,114,020 | 37.5 | 18,756 | 2,121,054 |
| August | 5,035,647 | 2,121,054 | 42.1 | 17,472 | 2,128,410 |

(iv) On September 1, 2008, QI uses $2,100,000 of the funds to purchase replacement property identified by T and transfers the property to T. QI pays $28,410, the earnings of the account allocated to T's exchange funds, to T.

(v) Because QI uses a reasonable method to calculate the pro-rata share of account earnings allocable to T's exchange funds in accordance with paragraph (c)(2)(ii)(B) of this section, and pays all those earnings to T, paragraph (c)(2) of this section applies. The exchange funds are not treated as loaned from T to QI. T must take into account in computing T's income tax liability for 2008 the $28,410 of earnings attributable to T's exchange funds.

**(f) Effective/applicability dates.** *(1) In general.* This section applies to transfers of relinquished property made by taxpayers on or after October 8, 2008.

*(2) Transition rule.* With respect to transfers of relinquished property made by taxpayers after August 16, 1986, but before October 8, 2008, the Internal Revenue Service will not challenge a reasonable, consistently applied method of taxation for income attributable to exchange funds.

T.D. 9249, 2/3/2006, amend T.D. 9413, 7/7/2008.

### § 1.468B-7 Pre-closing escrows.

**(a) Scope.** This section provides rules under section 468B(g) for the current taxation of income of a pre-closing escrow.

**(b) Definitions.** For purposes of this section—

*(1)* A pre-closing escrow is an escrow account, trust, or fund—

(i) Established in connection with the sale or exchange of real or personal property;

(ii) Funded with a down payment, earnest money, or similar payment that is deposited into the escrow prior to the sale or exchange of the property;

(iii) Used to secure the obligation of the purchaser to pay the purchase price for the property;

(iv) The assets of which, including any income earned thereon, will be paid to the purchaser or otherwise distributed for the purchaser's benefit when the property is sold or exchanged (for example, by being distributed to the seller as a credit against the purchase price); and

(v) Which is not an escrow account or trust established in connection with a deferred exchange under section 1031(a)(3).

*(2)* Purchaser means, in the case of an exchange, the intended transferee of the property whose obligation to pay the purchase price is secured by the pre-closing escrow;

*(3)* Purchase price means, in the case of an exchange, the required consideration for the property; and

*(4)* Administrator means the escrow agent, escrow holder, trustee, or other person responsible for administering the pre-closing escrow.

**(c) Taxation of pre-closing escrows.** The purchaser must take into account in computing the purchaser's income tax liability all items of income, deduction, and credit (including capital gains and losses) of the pre-closing escrow. In the case of an exchange with a single pre-closing escrow funded by two or more purchasers, each purchaser must take into account in computing the purchaser's income tax liability all items of income, deduction, and credit (including capital gains and losses) earned by the pre-closing escrow with respect to the money or property deposited in the pre-closing escrow by or on behalf of that purchaser.

**(d) Reporting obligations of the administrator.** For each calendar year (or portion thereof) that a pre-closing escrow is in existence, the administrator must report the income of the pre-closing escrow on Form 1099 to the extent required by the information reporting provisions of subpart B, Part III, subchapter A, chapter 61, Subtitle F of the Internal Revenue Code and the regulations thereunder. See § 1.6041-1(f) for rules relating to the amount to be reported when fees, expenses, or commissions owed by a payee to a third party are deducted from a payment.

**(e) Examples.** The provisions of this section may be illustrated by the following examples:

*Example (1).* P enters into a contract with S for the purchase of residential property owned by S for the price of $200,000. P is required to deposit $10,000 of earnest money into an escrow. At closing, the $10,000 and the interest earned thereon will be credited against the purchase price of the property. The escrow is a pre-closing escrow. P is taxable on the interest earned on the pre-closing escrow prior to closing.

*Example (2).* X and Y enter into a contract in which X agrees to exchange certain construction equipment for residential property owned by Y. The contract requires X and Y to each deposit $10,000 of earnest money into an escrow. At closing, $10,000 and the interest earned thereon will be paid to X and $10,000 and the interest earned thereon will be paid to Y. The escrow is a pre-closing escrow. X is taxable on the interest earned prior to closing on the $10,000 of

*. T's Average Daily Balance / Account's Average Daily Balance.
**. T's beginning balance + [(T's share) (Monthly Interest)].

funds X deposited in the pre-closing escrow. Similarly, Y is taxable on the interest earned prior to closing on the $10,000 of funds Y deposited in the pre-closing escrow.

**(f) Effective dates.** *(1) In general.* This section applies to pre-closing escrows established after February 3, 2006.

*(2) Transition rule.* With respect to a pre-closing escrow established after August 16, 1986, but on or before February 3, 2006, the Internal Revenue Service will not challenge a reasonable, consistently applied method of taxation for income earned by the escrow or a reasonable, consistently applied method for reporting the income.

T.D. 9249, 2/3/2006.

**§ 1.468B-8 Contingent-at-closing escrows. [Reserved]**

T.D. 9249, 2/3/2006.

**Proposed § 1.468B-8 Contingent at-closing escrows.** [*For Preamble, see ¶ 151,955*]

• ***Caution:*** This Notice of Proposed Rulemaking was partially finalized by TD 9249, 2/3/2006. Reg. § 1.468B-6 was withdrawn by Prop Rule 71-25, 2/7/2006. Reg. § 1.468B-8 remains proposed.

**(a) Scope.** This section provides rules under section 468B(g) for the taxation of income earned on a contingent at-closing escrow, which is defined in paragraph (b) of this section. No inference should be drawn from this section concerning the tax treatment of a contingent at-closing escrow, or of parties to the escrow, under sections of the Internal Revenue Code other than section 468B. See also paragraph (d) of this section.

**(b) Definitions.** For purposes of this section, the following definitions apply—

*Administrator* means an escrow agent, escrow holder, trustee, or other person responsible for administering an escrow account, trust, or fund (the purchaser or the seller may be the administrator);

*Contingent at-closing escrow* means an escrow account, trust, or fund that satisfies the following requirements—

*(1)* The escrow is established in connection with the sale or exchange (other than an exchange to which section 354, 355, or 356 applies) of real or personal property used in a trade or business or held for investment (including stock in a corporation or an interest in a partnership);

*(2)* Depending on whether events specified in the agreement between the purchaser and the seller that are subject to bona fide contingencies (not including events that are certain, or reasonably certain, to occur, such as the passage of time, or that are certain, or reasonably certain, not to occur) either occur or fail to occur, the escrow's assets (except for assets set aside for taxes or expenses) will be distributable—

(i) Entirely to the purchaser;

(ii) Entirely to the seller; or

(iii) In part, to the purchaser with the remainder to the seller; and

*(3)* The escrow is not a qualified escrow account or qualified trust established in connection with a deferred exchange under section 1031(a)(3);

*Determination date* means the date on which (or by which) the last of the events subject to a bona fide contingency specified in the agreement between the purchaser and the seller (referred to in the definition of contingent at-closing escrow) has either occurred or failed to occur;

*Purchaser* means, in the case of an exchange of property, the transferee of the property; and

*Seller* means, in the case of an exchange of property, the transferor of the property.

**(c) Tax liability of purchaser and seller for the period prior to the determination date.** For the period prior to the determination date, the purchaser is treated as owning the assets of the contingent at-closing escrow for federal income tax purposes. Thus, in computing the purchaser's income tax liability, the purchaser must take into account all items of income, deduction, and credit (including capital gains and losses) of the escrow until the determination date.

**(d) Transfer of interest in the assets of the escrow on the determination date.** No inference should be drawn from this section whether, for purposes of Internal Revenue Code sections other than 468B, there is a transfer of ownership of the assets of a contingent at-closing escrow on the determination date from the purchaser to the seller or from the seller to the purchaser, or the tax consequences of such a transfer. Thus, for example, if there is a transfer of ownership of the assets of the escrow from the purchaser to the seller on the determination date for purposes of other Code sections, no inference should be drawn from this section whether any portion of the amount transferred is unstated interest. See § 1.483-4.

**(e) Tax liability of purchaser and seller for the period beginning on the determination date.** For the period beginning on the determination date, the purchaser and the seller must each take into account in determining their income tax liabilities the income, deductions, and credits (including capital gains and losses) corresponding to their ownership interests in the assets of the escrow.

**(f) Statement required to be provided to administrator within 30 days after the determination date.** Within 30 days after the determination date, the purchaser and the seller must provide the administrator with a written statement that—

*(1)* Is signed by the purchaser and the seller;

*(2)* Specifies the determination date; and

*(3)* Specifies the purchaser's and seller's ownership interests in each asset of the escrow.

**(g) Reporting obligations of the administrator.** *(1) In general.* The administrator of a contingent at-closing escrow must, for each calendar year (or portion thereof) that the escrow is in existence, report the income of the escrow on Forms 1099 in accordance with the information reporting requirements of subpart B, Part III, subchapter A, chapter 61, Subtitle F of the Internal Revenue Code. The Forms 1099 must show as payor the administrator of the escrow and as payee the person (or persons) treated as the payee (or payees) under paragraph (g)(2) of this section.

*(2) Person treated as payee.* In satisfying the reporting obligations of paragraph (g)(1) of this section, the following rules apply to the administrator—

(i) For the period prior to the determination date, the administrator must treat the purchaser as the payee of the income of the escrow;

(ii) For the period beginning on the determination date, if the written statement described in paragraph (f) of this section is timely provided to the administrator, the administrator must treat as the payee (or payees) of the income of the escrow the purchaser or seller (or both) in accordance with their respective ownership interests as shown on the statement; and

(iii) If the written statement described in paragraph (f) of this section is not provided to the administrator, the administrator must continue to treat the purchaser as the payee of the income of the escrow.

*(3) Relief from penalties for filing incorrect information return or payee statement.* For purposes of sections 6721 and 6722, the administrator will not be treated as failing to file or furnish a correct information return or payee statement solely because, in preparing a Form 1099, the administrator relies on a statement described in paragraph (f) of this section and therefore treats the purchaser or seller (or both) as the payee (or payees) of the income of the escrow in accordance with their respective ownership interests in the assets of the escrow as shown on the statement. If a statement described in paragraph (f) of this section is not provided to the administrator, the administrator will not be treated as failing to file or furnish a correct information return or payee statement solely because, in preparing a Form 1099, the administrator relies on the absence of the statement and therefore treats the purchaser as the payee.

**(h) Effective date.** *(1) In general.* The provisions of this section apply to contingent at-closing escrows that are established after the date of publication of final regulations in the Federal Register.

*(2) Transition rule.* With respect to a contingent at-closing escrow established after August 16, 1986, but on or before the date of publication of final regulations in the Federal Register, the Internal Revenue Service will not challenge a reasonable, consistently applied method of taxation for income earned by the escrow. The Internal Revenue Service will also not challenge a reasonable, consistently applied method for reporting such income.

**(i) [Reserved]**

**(j) Example.** The provisions of this section may be illustrated by the following example:

*Example.* (i) P and S are corporations. In 1999, P enters into a contract with S for the purchase of rental real estate. On October 1, 1999, the date of sale, S transfers the real estate to P, and P pays S a portion of the purchase price, $9,000,000. P deposits the remaining portion of the purchase price, $850,000, into an escrow account as required by the contract. H is the escrow holder.

(ii) The contract provides that the escrow balance as of November 1, 2000, is payable entirely to P, entirely to S, or partially to P and partially to S depending on the amount, if any, by which the average rental income from the real estate during a specified testing period ending on September 30, 2000, exceeds one or more specified earnings targets.

(iii) According to the terms of the contract, the income earned on the escrow must be accumulated and is not currently distributable to P or S during the period prior to November 1, 2000.

(iv) During the testing period specified in the contract between P and S, the average rental income earned on the property exceeds one (but not all) of the specified earnings targets. As a result, on September 30, 2000, the end of the testing period, P became entitled to 40% of the escrow assets and S became entitled to 60% of the escrow assets.

(v) On October 30, 2000, P and S provide H with the written statement described in paragraph (f) of this section. The written statement is thus provided within 30 days of September 30, 2000. The statement indicates that P's ownership interest in each asset of the escrow is 40 percent and S's ownership interest in each asset is 60 percent.

(vi) The escrow is a contingent at-closing escrow. September 30, 2000, is the determination date because this is the date on which the testing period ends. As of this date, all contingencies specified in the contract are resolved.

(vii) P must take into account all of the income, deductions, and credits (including capital gains and losses) of the escrow in computing P's income tax liability for the period prior to September 30, 2000. See paragraph (c) of this section.

(viii) For the period beginning on September 30, 2000, P must take into account in computing P's income tax liability 40 percent of each item of income, deduction, and credit of the escrow (including capital gains and losses), and S must take into account in computing S's income tax liability 60 percent of these items. See paragraph (e) of this section.

(ix) H is subject to the information reporting requirements of paragraph (g)(1) of this section. H must file Forms 1099 and furnish payee statements to reflect the fact that prior to September 30, 2000, P is the payee of all the income of the escrow, and for the period beginning on September 30, 2000, P is the payee of 40 percent of the income, and S is the payee of 60 percent of the income.

**§ 1.468B-9 Disputed ownership funds.**

**(a) Scope.** This section provides rules under section 468B(g) relating to the current taxation of income of a disputed ownership fund.

**(b) Definitions.** For purposes of this section—

*(1)* Disputed ownership fund means an escrow account, trust, or fund that—

(i) Is established to hold money or property subject to conflicting claims of ownership;

(ii) Is subject to the continuing jurisdiction of a court;

(iii) Requires the approval of the court to pay or distribute money or property to, or on behalf of, a claimant, transferor, or transferor-claimant; and

(iv) Is not a qualified settlement fund under § 1.468B-1, a bankruptcy estate (or part thereof) resulting from the commencement of a case under title 11 of the United States Code, or a liquidating trust under § 301.7701-4(d) of this chapter (except as provided in paragraph (c)(2)(ii) of this section);

*(2)* Administrator means a person designated as such by a court having jurisdiction over a disputed ownership fund, however, if no person is designated, the administrator is the escrow agent, escrow holder, trustee, receiver, or other person responsible for administering the fund;

*(3)* Claimant means a person who claims ownership of, in whole or in part, or a legal or equitable interest in, money or property immediately before and immediately after that property is transferred to a disputed ownership fund;

*(4)* Court means a court of law or equity of the United States or of any state (including the District of Columbia), territory, possession, or political subdivision thereof;

*(5)* Disputed property means money or property held in a disputed ownership fund subject to the claimants' conflicting claims of ownership;

*(6)* Related person means any person that is related to a transferor within the meaning of section 267(b) or 707(b)(1);

*(7)* Transferor means, in general, a person that transfers disputed property to a disputed ownership fund, except that—

(i) If disputed property is transferred by an agent, fiduciary, or other person acting in a similar capacity, the transferor is the person on whose behalf the agent, fiduciary, or other person acts; and

(ii) A payor of interest or other income earned by a disputed ownership fund is not a transferor within the meaning of this section (unless the payor is also a claimant);

*(8)* Transferor-claimant means a transferor that claims ownership of, in whole or in part, or a legal or equitable interest in, the disputed property immediately before and immediately after that property is transferred to the disputed ownership fund. Because a transferor-claimant is both a transferor and a claimant, generally the terms transferor and claimant also include a transferor-claimant. See paragraph (d) of this section for rules applicable only to transferors that are not transferor-claimants and paragraph (e) of this section for rules applicable only to transferors that are also transferor-claimants.

**(c) Taxation of a disputed ownership fund.** *(1) In general.* For Federal income tax purposes, a disputed ownership fund is treated as the owner of all assets that it holds. A disputed ownership fund is treated as a C corporation for purposes of subtitle F of the Internal Revenue Code, and the administrator of the fund must obtain an employer identification number for the fund, make all required income tax and information returns, and deposit all tax payments. Except as otherwise provided in this section, a disputed ownership fund is taxable as—

(i) A C corporation, unless all the assets transferred to the fund by or on behalf of transferors are passive investment assets. For purposes of this section, passive investment assets are assets of the type that generate portfolio income within the meaning of § 1.469-2T(c)(3)(i); or

(ii) A qualified settlement fund, if all the assets transferred to the fund by or on behalf of transferors are passive investment assets. A disputed ownership fund taxable as a qualified settlement fund under this section is subject to all the provisions contained in § 1.468B-2, except that the rules contained in paragraphs (c)(3), (4), and (c)(5)(i) of this section apply in lieu of the rules in § 1.468B-2(b)(1), (d), (e), (f) and (j).

*(2) Exceptions.* (i) The claimants to a disputed ownership fund may submit a private letter ruling request proposing a method of taxation different than the method provided in paragraph (c)(1) of this section.

(ii) The trustee of a liquidating trust established pursuant to a plan confirmed by the court in a case under title 11 of the United States Code may, in the liquidating trust's first taxable year, elect to treat an escrow account, trust, or fund that holds assets of the liquidating trust that are subject to disputed claims as a disputed ownership fund. Pursuant to this election, creditors holding disputed claims are not treated as transferors of the money or property transferred to the disputed ownership fund. A trustee makes the election by attaching a statement to the timely filed Federal income tax return of the disputed ownership fund for the taxable year for which the election becomes effective. The election statement must include a statement that the trustee will treat the escrow account, trust, or fund as a disputed ownership fund and must include a legend, "§ 1.468B-9(c) Election," at the top of the page. The election may be revoked only upon consent of the Commissioner by private letter ruling.

*(3) Property received by the disputed ownership fund.* (i) Generally excluded from income. In general, a disputed ownership fund does not include an amount in income on account of a transfer of disputed property to the disputed ownership fund. However, the accrual or receipt of income from the disputed property in a disputed ownership fund is not a transfer of disputed property to the fund. Therefore, a disputed ownership fund must include in income all income received or accrued from the disputed property, including items such as—

(A) Payments to a disputed ownership fund made in compensation for late or delayed transfers of money or property;

(B) Dividends on stock of a transferor (or a related person) held by the fund; and

(C) Interest on debt of a transferor (or a related person) held by the fund.

(ii) Basis and holding period. In general, the initial basis of property transferred by, or on behalf of, a transferor to a disputed ownership fund is the fair market value of the property on the date of transfer to the fund, and the fund's holding period begins on the date of the transfer. However, if the transferor is a transferor-claimant, the fund's initial basis in the property is the same as the basis of the transferor-claimant immediately before the transfer to the fund, and the fund=s holding period for the property is determined under section 1223(2).

*(4) Property distributed by the disputed ownership fund.* (i) Computing gain or loss. Except in the case of a distribution or deemed distribution described in paragraph (e)(3) of this section, a disputed ownership fund must treat a distribution of disputed property as a sale or exchange of that property for purposes of section 1001(a). In computing gain or loss, the amount realized by the disputed ownership fund is the fair market value of that property on the date of distribution.

(ii) Denial of deduction. A disputed ownership fund is not allowed a deduction for a distribution of disputed property or of the net after-tax income earned by the disputed ownership fund made to or on behalf of a transferor or claimant.

*(5) Taxable year and accounting method.* (i) A disputed ownership fund taxable as a C corporation under paragraph (c)(1)(i) of this section may compute taxable income under any accounting method allowable under section 446 and is not subject to the limitations contained in section 448. A disputed ownership fund taxable as a C corporation may use any taxable year allowable under section 441.

(ii) A disputed ownership fund taxable as a qualified settlement fund under paragraph (c)(1)(ii) of this section may compute taxable income under any accounting method allowable under section 446 and may use any taxable year allowable under section 441.

(iii) Appropriate adjustments must be made by a disputed ownership fund or transferors to the fund to prevent the fund and the transferors from taking into account the same item of income, deduction, gain, loss, or credit (including capital gains and losses) more than once or from omitting such items. For example, if a transferor that is not a transferor-claimant uses the cash receipts and disbursements method of accounting and transfers an account receivable to a disputed ownership fund that uses an accrual method of accounting, at the time of the transfer of the account receivable to the disputed ownership fund, the transferor must include in its gross income the value of the account receivable because, under paragraph (c)(3)(ii) of this section, the disputed ownership fund will take a fair market value basis in the receivable and will not include the fair market value in its income when received from the transferor or when paid by the customer. If the account receivable were transferred to the disputed ownership fund by a transferor-claimant using the cash receipts and disbursements method, however, the disputed ownership fund would take a basis in the receivable equal to the transferor's basis, or $0, and would be required to report the income upon collection of the account.

*(6) Unused carryovers.* Upon the termination of a disputed ownership fund, if the fund has an unused net operating loss carryover under section 172, an unused capital loss carryover under section 1212, or an unused tax credit carryover, or if the fund has, for its last taxable year, deductions in excess of gross income, the claimant to which the fund's net assets are distributable will succeed to and take into account the fund's unused net operating loss carryover, unused capital loss carryover, unused tax credit carryover, or excess of deductions over gross income for the last taxable year of the fund. If the fund's net assets are distributable to more than one claimant, the unused net operating loss carryover, unused capital loss carryover, unused tax credit carryover, or excess of deductions over gross income for the last taxable year must be allocated among the claimants in proportion to the value of the assets distributable to each claimant from the fund. Unused carryovers described in this paragraph (c)(6) are not money or other property for purposes of paragraph (e)(3)(ii) of this section and thus are not deemed transferred to a transferor-claimant before being transferred to the claimants described in this paragraph (c)(6).

**(d) Rules applicable to transferors that are not transferor-claimants.** The rules in this paragraph (d) apply to transferors (as defined in paragraph (b)(7) of this section) that are not transferor-claimants (as defined in paragraph (b)(8) of this section).

*(1) Transfer of property.* A transferor must treat a transfer of property to a disputed ownership fund as a sale or other disposition of that property for purposes of section 1001(a). In computing the gain or loss on the disposition, the amount realized by the transferor is the fair market value of the property on the date the transfer is made to the disputed ownership fund.

*(2) Economic performance.* (i) In general. For purposes of section 461(h), if a transferor using an accrual method of accounting has a liability for which economic performance would otherwise occur under § 1.461-4(g) when the transferor makes payment to the claimant or claimants, economic performance occurs with respect to the liability when and to the extent that the transferor makes a transfer to a disputed ownership fund to resolve or satisfy that liability.

(ii) Obligations of the transferor. Economic performance does not occur when a transferor using an accrual method of accounting issues to a disputed ownership fund its debt (or provides the debt of a related person). Instead, economic performance occurs as the transferor (or related person) makes principal payments on the debt. Economic performance does not occur when the transferor provides to a disputed ownership fund its obligation (or the obligation of a related person) to provide property or services in the future or to make a payment described in § 1.461-4(g)(1)(ii)(A). Instead, economic performance occurs with respect to such an obligation as property or services are provided or payments are made to the disputed ownership fund or a claimant. With regard to interest on a debt issued or provided to a disputed ownership fund, economic performance occurs as determined under § 1.461-4(e).

*(3) Distributions to transferors.* (i) In general. Except as provided in section 111(a) and paragraph (d)(3)(ii) of this section, the transferor must include in gross income any distribution to the transferor (including a deemed distribution described in paragraph (d)(3)(iii) of this section) from the disputed ownership fund. If property is distributed, the amount includible in gross income and the basis in that property are generally the fair market value of the property on the date of distribution.

(ii) Exception. A transferor is not required to include in gross income a distribution of money or property that it previously transferred to the disputed ownership fund if the transferor did not take into account, for example, by deduction or capitalization, an amount with respect to the transfer either at the time of the transfer to, or while the money or property was held by, the disputed ownership fund. The transferor's gross income does not include a distribution of money from the disputed ownership fund equal to the net after-tax income earned on money or property transferred to the disputed ownership fund by the transferor while that money or property was held by the fund. Money distributed to a transferor by a disputed ownership fund will be deemed to be distributed first from the money or property transferred to the disputed ownership fund by that transferor, then from the net after-tax income of any money or property transferred to the disputed ownership fund by that transferor, and then from other sources.

(iii) Deemed distributions. If a disputed ownership fund makes a distribution of money or property on behalf of a transferor to a person that is not a claimant, the distribution is deemed made by the fund to the transferor. The transferor, in turn, is deemed to make a payment to the actual recipient.

**(e) Rules applicable to transferor-claimants.** The rules in this paragraph (e) apply to transferor-claimants (as defined in paragraph (b)(8) of this section).

*(1) Transfer of property.* A transfer of property by a transferor-claimant to a disputed ownership fund is not a sale or other disposition of the property for purposes of section 1001(a).

*(2) Economic performance.* (i) In general. For purposes of section 461(h), if a transferor-claimant using an accrual method of accounting has a liability for which economic performance would otherwise occur under § 1.461-4(g) when the transferor-claimant makes payment to another claimant, economic performance occurs with respect to the liability when and to the extent that the disputed ownership fund transfers money or property to the other claimant to resolve or satisfy that liability.

(ii) Obligations of the transferor-claimant. Economic performance does not occur when a disputed ownership fund transfers the debt of a transferor-claimant (or of a person related to the transferor-claimant) to another claimant. Instead, economic performance occurs as principal payments on the debt are made to the other claimant. Economic performance does not occur when a disputed ownership fund transfers to another claimant the obligation of a transferor-claimant (or of a person related to the transferor-claimant) to provide property or services in the future or to make a payment described in § 1.461-4(g)(1)(ii)(A). Instead, economic performance occurs with respect to such an obligation as property or services are provided or payments are made to the other claimant. With regard to interest on a debt issued or provided to a disputed ownership fund, economic performance occurs as determined under § 1.461-4(e).

*(3) Distributions to transferor-claimants.* (i) In general. The gross income of a transferor-claimant does not include a distribution to the transferor-claimant (including a deemed distribution described in paragraph (e)(3)(ii) of this section) of money or property from a disputed ownership fund that the transferor-claimant previously transferred to the fund, or the net after-tax income earned on that money or property while it was held by the fund. If such property is distributed to the transferor-claimant by the disputed ownership fund, then the transferor-claimant's basis in the property is the same as the disputed ownership fund's basis in the property immediately before the distribution.

(ii) Deemed distributions. If a disputed ownership fund makes a distribution of money or property to a claimant or makes a distribution of money or property on behalf of a transferor-claimant to a person that is not a claimant, the distribution is deemed made by the fund to the transferor-claimant. The transferor-claimant, in turn, is deemed to make a payment to the actual recipient.

**(f) Distributions to claimants other than transferor-claimants.** Whether a claimant other than a transferor-claimant must include in gross income a distribution of money or property from a disputed ownership fund generally is determined by reference to the claim in respect of which the distribution is made.

**(g) Statement to the disputed ownership fund and the Internal Revenue Service with respect to transfers of property other than cash.** *(1) In general.* By February 15 of the year following each calendar year in which a transferor (or other person acting on behalf of a transferor) makes a transfer of property other than cash to a disputed ownership fund, the transferor must provide a statement to the administrator of the fund setting forth the information described in paragraph (g)(3) of this section. The transferor must attach a copy of this statement to its return for the taxable year of transfer.

*(2) Combined statements.* If a disputed ownership fund has more than one transferor, any two or more transferors may provide a combined statement to the administrator. If a combined statement is used, each transferor must attach a copy of the combined statement to its return and maintain with its books and records a schedule describing each asset that the transferor transferred to the disputed ownership fund.

*(3) Information required on the statement.* The statement required by paragraph (g)(1) of this section must include the following information—

(i) A legend, "§ 1.468B-9 Statement," at the top of the first page;

(ii) The transferor's name, address, and taxpayer identification number;

(iii) The disputed ownership fund's name, address, and employer identification number;

(iv) A statement declaring whether the transferor is a transferor-claimant;

(v) The date of each transfer;

(vi) A description of the property (other than cash) transferred; and

(vii) The disputed ownership fund's basis in the property and holding period on the date of transfer as determined under paragraph (c)(3)(ii) of this section.

**(h) Examples.** The following examples illustrate the rules of this section:

*Example (1).* (i) X Corporation petitions the United States Tax Court in 2006 for a redetermination of its tax liability for the 2003 taxable year. In 2006, the Tax Court determines that X Corporation is liable for an income tax deficiency for the 2003 taxable year. X Corporation files an appellate bond in accordance with section 7485(a) and files a notice of appeal with the appropriate United States Court of Appeals. In 2006, the Court of Appeals affirms the decision of the Tax Court and the United States Supreme Court denies X Corporation's petition for a writ of certiorari.

(ii) The appellate bond that X Corporation files with the court for the purpose of staying assessment and collection of deficiencies pending appeal is not an escrow account, trust or fund established to hold property subject to conflicting claims of ownership. Although X Corporation was found liable for an income tax deficiency, ownership of the appellate bond is not disputed. Rather, the bond serves as security for a disputed liability. Therefore, the bond is not a disputed ownership fund.

*Example (2).* (i) The facts are the same as Example 1, except that X Corporation deposits United States Treasury bonds with the Tax Court in accordance with section 7845(c)(2) and 31 U.S.C. 9303.

(ii) The deposit of United States Treasury bonds with the court for the purpose of staying assessment and collection of deficiencies while X Corporation prosecutes an appeal does not create a disputed ownership fund because ownership of the bonds is not disputed.

*Example (3).* (i) Prior to A's death, A was the insured under a life insurance policy issued by X, an insurance company. X uses an accrual method of accounting. Both A's current spouse and A's former spouse claim to be the beneficiary under the policy and entitled to the policy proceeds ($1 million). In 2005, X files an interpleader action and deposits $1 million into the registry of the court. On June 1, 2006, a final determination is made that A's current spouse is the beneficiary under the policy and entitled to the money held in the registry of the court. The interest earned on the registry account is $12,000. The money in the registry account is distributed to A's current spouse.

(ii) The money held in the registry of the court consisting of the policy proceeds and the earnings thereon are a disputed ownership fund taxable as if it were a qualified settlement fund. See paragraphs (b)(1) and (c)(1)(ii) of this section. The fund's gross income does not include the $1 million transferred to the fund by X, however, the $12,000 interest is included in the fund's gross income in accordance with its method of accounting. See paragraph (c)(3)(i) of this section. Under paragraph (c)(4)(ii) of this section, the fund is not allowed a deduction for a distribution to A's current spouse of the $1 million or the interest income earned by the fund.

(iii) X is a transferor that is not a transferor-claimant. See paragraphs (b)(7) and (b)(8) of this section.

(iv) Whether A's current spouse must include in income the $1 million insurance proceeds and the interest received from the fund is determined under other provisions of the Internal Revenue Code. See paragraph (f) of this section.

*Example (4).* (i) Corporation B and unrelated individual C claim ownership of certain rental property. B uses an accrual method of accounting. The rental property is property used in a trade or business. B claims to have purchased the property from C's father. However, C asserts that the purported sale to B was ineffective and that C acquired ownership of the property through intestate succession upon the death of C's father. For several years, B has maintained and received the rent from the property.

(ii) Pending the resolution of the title dispute between B and C, the title to the rental property is transferred to a court-supervised registry account on February 1, 2005. On that date the court appoints R as receiver for the property. R collects the rent earned on the property and hires employees necessary for the maintenance of the property. The rents paid to R cannot be distributed to B or C without the court's approval.

(iii) On June 1, 2006, the court makes a final determination that the rental property is owned by C. The court orders C to refund to B the purchase price paid by B to C's father plus interest on that amount from February 1, 2005. The court also orders that a distribution be made to C of all funds held in the court registry consisting of the rent collected by R and the income earned thereon. C takes title to the rental property.

(iv) The rental property and the funds held by the court registry are a disputed ownership fund under paragraph (b)(1) of this section. The fund is taxable as if it were a C corporation because the rental property is not a passive investment asset within the meaning of paragraph (c)(1)(i) of this section.

(v) The fund's gross income does not include the value of the rental property transferred to the fund by B. See paragraph (c)(3)(i) of this section. Under paragraph (c)(3)(ii) of this section, the fund's initial basis in the property is the same as B's adjusted basis immediately before the transfer to the fund and the fund's holding period is determined under section 1223(2). The fund's gross income includes the rents collected by R and any income earned thereon. For the period between February 1, 2005, and June 1, 2006, the fund may be allowed deductions for depreciation and for the costs of maintenance of the property because the fund is treated as owning the property during this period. See sections 162, 167, and 168. Under paragraph (c)(4)(ii) of this section, the fund may not deduct the distribution to C of the property, or the rents (or any income earned thereon) collected from the property while the fund holds the property. No gain or loss is recognized by the fund from this distribution or from the fund's transfer of the rental property to C pursuant to the court's determination that C owns the property. See paragraphs (c)(4)(i) and (e)(3) of this section.

(vi) B is the transferor to the fund. Under paragraphs (b)(8) and (e)(1) of this section, B is a transferor-claimant and does not recognize gain or loss under section 1001(a) on transfer of the property to the disputed ownership fund. The money and property distributed from the fund to C is deemed to be distributed first to B and then transferred from B to C. See paragraph (e)(3)(ii) of this section. Under paragraph (e)(2)(i) of this section, economic performance occurs when the disputed ownership fund transfers the property and any earnings thereon to C. The income tax consequences of the deemed transfer from B to C as well as the income tax consequences of C's refund to B of the purchase price paid to C's father and interest thereon are determined under other provisions of the Internal Revenue Code.

**(i)** [Reserved]

**(j) Effective dates.** *(1) In general.* This section applies to disputed ownership funds established after February 3, 2006.

*(2) Transition rule.* With respect to a disputed ownership fund established after August 16, 1986, but on or before February 3, 2006, the Internal Revenue Service will not challenge a reasonable, consistently applied method of taxation for income earned by the fund, transfers to the fund, and distributions made by the fund.

T.D. 9249, 2/3/2006.

### § 1.469-0 Table of contents.

This section lists the captions that appear in the regulations under section 469.

(1) In general.
(2) Exceptions.
(b) Taxpayers to whom these rules apply.
(c) Cross references.
(1) Definition of passive activity.
(2) Passive activity loss.
(3) Passive activity credit.
(4) Effect of rules for other purposes.
(5) Special rule for oil and gas working interests.
(6) Treatment of disallowed losses and credits.
(7) Corporations subject to section 469.
(8) [Reserved]
(9) Joint returns.
(10) Material participation.
(11) Effective date and transition rules.
(12) Future regulations.
(d) Effect of section 469 and the regulations thereunder for other purposes.
(1) Treatment of items of passive activity income and gain.
(2) Coordination with sections 613A(d) and 1211 [Reserved].
(3) Treatment of passive activity losses.
(e) Definition of "passive activity".
(1) In general.
(2) Trade or business activity [Reserved].
(3) Rental Activity.
(i) In general.
(ii) Exceptions.
(iii) Average period of customer use [Reserved].
(A) In general [Reserved].
(B) Average use factor [Reserved].
(C) Average period of customer use for class of property [Reserved].
(D) Period of Customer use [Reserved].
(E) Class of property [Reserved].
(F) Gross rental income and daily rent [Reserved].
(iv) Significant personal services.
(A) In general.
(B) Excluded services
(v) Extraordinary personal services.
(vi) Rental of property incidental to a nonrental activity of the taxpayer.
(A) In general.
(B) Property held for investment.
(C) Property used in a trade or business.
(D) Lodging rented for convenience of employer [Reserved].
(E) Unadjusted basis [Reserved].
(vii) Property made available for use in a nonrental activity conducted by a partnership, S corporation or joint venture in which the taxpayer owns an interest.
(viii) Examples.
(4) Special rules for oil and gas working interests.
(i) In general.
(ii) Exception for deductions attributable to a period during which liability is limited.
(A) In general.
(B) Coordination with rules governing the identification of disallowed passive activity deductions.
(C) Meaning of certain terms.
(1) Allocable deductions
(2) Disqualified deductions.
(3) Net loss.
(4) Ratable portion.
(iii) Examples.
(iv) Definition of "working interest" [Reserved].
(v) Entities that limit liability.
(A) General rule.
(B) Other limitations disregarded.
(C) Examples.
(vi) Cross reference to special rule for income from certain oil or gas properties.
(5) Rental of dwelling unit [Reserved].
(6) Activity of trading personal property.
(i) In general.
(ii) Personal property.
(iii) Example.
(f) Treatment of disallowed passive activity losses and credits.
(1) Scope of this paragraph.
(2) Identification of disallowed passive activity deductions.
(i) Allocation of disallowed passive activity deductions.
(A) General rule.
(B) Loss from an activity.
(C) Significant participation passive activities.
(D) Examples.
(ii) Allocation with loss activities.
(A) In general.
(B) Excluded deductions.
(iii) Separately identified deductions.
(3) Identification of disallowed credits from passive activities.
(i) General rule.
(ii) Coordination rule.
(iii) Separately identified credits.
(4) Carryover of disallowed deductions and credits [Reserved].
(i) In general.
(ii) Operations continued through C corporations or similar entities.
(iii) Examples.
(g) Application of these rules to C corporations.
(1) In general.
(2) Definitions.
(3) Participation of corporations.
(i) Material participation.
(ii) Significant participation.
(iii) Participation of individual.

(4) Modified computation of passive activity loss in the case of closely held corporations.

(i) In general.

(ii) Net active income.

(iii) Examples.

(5) Allowance of passive activity credit of closely held corporations to extent of net active income tax liability.

(i) In general.

(ii) Net active income tax liability.

(h) Special rules for affiliated group filing consolidated return.

(1) [Reserved]

(2) [Reserved]

(3) Disallowance of consolidated group's passive activity loss or credit.

(4) Status and participation of members [Reserved].

(i) Determination by reference to status and participation of group [Reserved].

(ii) Determination of status and participation of consolidated group [Reserved].

(5) Modification of rules for identifying disallowed passive activity deductions and credits.

(i) Identification of disallowed deductions.

(ii) Ratable portion of disallowed passive activity losses.

(iii) Identification of disallowed credits.

(6) [Reserved]

(7) Disposition of stock of a member of an affiliated group.

(8) Dispositions of property used in multiple activities.

(i) [Reserved]

(j) Spouses filing joint returns.

(1) In general.

(2) Exceptions of treatment as one taxpayer.

(i) Identification of disallowed deductions and credits.

(ii) Treatment of deductions disallowed under sections 704(d), 1366(d) and 465.

(iii) Treatment of losses from working interests.

(3) Joint return no longer filed.

(4) Participation of spouses.

(k) Former passive activities and changes in status of corporations [Reserved].

*§ 1.469-2 Passive activity loss.*

(a) through (c)(2) (ii) [Reserved].

(iii) Disposition of substantially appreciated property formerly used in a nonpassive activity.

(A) In general.

(B) Date of disposition.

(C) Substantially appreciated property.

(D) Investment property.

(E) Coordination with § 1.469-2T(c)(2)(ii).

(F) Coordination with section 163(d).

(G) Examples.

(iv) Taxable acquisitions.

(v) Property held for sale to customers.

(A) Sale incidental to another activity.

(1) Applicability.

(i) In general.

(ii) Principal purpose.

(2) Dealing activity not taken into account.

(B) Use in a nondealing activity incidental to sale.

(C) Examples.

(c) (3) through (c)(5) [Reserved].

(6) Gross income from certain oil or gas properties.

(i) In general.

(ii) Gross and net passive income from the property.

(iii) Property.

(iv) Examples 1 and 2.

(c) (6)(iv) Example 3 through (c)(7)(iii) [Reserved].

(c) (7)(iv) through (vi) (no paragraph heading).

(d) (1) through (d)(2)(viii) [Reserved].

(d) (2)(ix) through (d)(2)(xii) (no paragraph heading).

(d) (2)(x) through (d)(2)(xi) [Reserved].

(d) (2)(xii) (no paragraph heading).

(d) (3) through (d)(5)(ii) [Reserved].

(d) (5)(iii)(A) Applicability of rules in § 1.469-2T(c)(2).

(d) (5)(iii)(B) through (d)(6)(v)(D) [Reserved].

(d) (6)(v)(E) (no paragraph heading).

(d) (6)(v)(F) through (d)(7) [Reserved].

(8) Taxable year in which item arises.

(e) (1) through (e)(2) (i) [Reserved].

(ii) Section 707(c).

(iii) Payments in liquidation of a partner's interest in partnership property.

(A) In general.

(B) Payments in liquidation of a partner's interest in unrealized receivables and goodwill under section 736(a).

(e) (3)(i) through (iii)(A) [Reserved].

(e) (3)(iii)(B) (no paragraph heading).

(e) (3)(iii)(C) through (f)(4) [Reserved].

(5) Net income from certain property rented incidental to development activity.

(i) In general.

(ii) Commencement of use.

(iii) Services performed for the purpose of enhancing the value of property.

(iv) Examples.

(6) Property rented to a nonpassive activity.

(f) (7) through (f)(9)(ii) [Reserved].

(f) (9)(iii) through (f)(9)(iv) (no paragraph heading).

(10) Coordination with section 163(d).

(f) (11) [Reserved].

*§ 1.469-2T Passive activity loss (temporary).*

(a) Scope of this section.

(b) Definition of passive activity loss.

(1) In general.

(2) Cross reference.

(c) Passive activity group income.

(1) In general.

(2) Treatment of gain from disposition of an interest in an activity or an interest in property used in an activity.

(i) In general.

(A) Treatment of gain.

(B) Dispositions of partnership interest and S corporation stock.

(C) Interest in property.

(D) Examples.

(ii) Disposition of property used in more than one activity in 12-month period preceding disposition.

(iii) Disposition of substantially appreciated property used in nonpassive activity [Reserved].

(A) In general [Reserved].

(B) Date of disposition [Reserved].

(C) Substantially appreciated property [Reserved].

(D) Investment property [Reserved].

(E) Coordination with paragraph (c)(2)(ii) of this section [Reserved].

(F) Coordination with section 163(d) [Reserved].

(G) Examples [Reserved].

(iv) Taxable acquisitions [Reserved].

(v) Property held for sale to customers [Reserved].

(A) Sale incidental to another activity [Reserved].

(1) Applicability [Reserved].

(i) In general [Reserved].

(ii) Principal purpose [Reserved].

(2) Dealing activity not taken into account [Reserved].

(B) Use in a nondealing activity incidental to sale [Reserved].

(C) Examples [Reserved].

(3) Items of portfolio income specifically excluded.

(i) In general.

(ii) Gross income derived in the ordinary course of a trade or business.

(iii) Special rules.

(A) Income from property held for investment by dealer.

(B) Royalties derived in the ordinary course of the trade or business of licensing intangible property.

(1) In general.

(2) Substantial services or costs.

(i) In general.

(ii) Exception.

(iii) Expenditures taken into account.

(3) Passthrough entities.

(4) Cross reference.

(C) Mineral production payments.

(iv) Examples.

(4) Items of personal service income specifically excluded.

(i) In general.

(ii) Example.

(5) Income from section 481 adjustments.

(i) In general.

(ii) Positive section 481 adjustments.

(iii) Ratable portion.

(6) Gross income from certain oil or gas properties [Reserved].

(i) In general [Reserved].

(ii) Gross and net passive income from the properties [Reserved].

(iii) Property [Reserved].

(iv) Examples.

(7) Other items specifically excluded.

(d) Passive activity deductions.

(1) In general.

(2) Exceptions.

(3) Interest expense.

(4) Clearly and directly allocable expenses.

(5) Treatment of loss from disposition.

(i) In general.

(ii) Disposition of property used in more than one activity in 12-month period preceding disposition.

(iii) Other applicable rules.

(A) Applicability or rules in paragraph (c)(2).

(B) Dispositions of partnership interest and S corporation stock.

(6) Coordination with other limitations on deductions that apply before section 469.

(i) In general.

(ii) Proration of deductions disallowed under basis limitations.

(A) Deductions disallowed under section 704(d).

(B) Deductions disallowed under section 1366(d).

(iii) Proration of deductions disallowed under at-risk limitations.

(iv) Coordination of basis and at-risk limitations.

(v) Separately identified items of deduction and loss.

(7) Deductions from section 481 adjustment.

(i) In general.

(ii) Negative section 481 adjustment.

(iii) Ratable portion.

(8) Taxable year in which item arises.

(e) Special rules for partners and S corporation shareholders.

(1) In general.

(2) Payments under sections 707(a), 707(c), and 736(b).

(i) Section 707(a).

(ii) Section 707(c).

(iii) Payments in liquidation of a partner's interest in partnership property.

(A) In general.

(B) Payments in liquidation of a partner's interest of a partnership property.

(3) Sale or exchange of interest in passthrough entity.

(i) Application of this paragraph (e)(3).

(ii) General rule.

(A) Allocation among activities.

(B) Ratable portions.

(1) Disposition on which gain is recognized.

(2) Disposition on which loss is recognized.

(C) Default rule.

(D) Special rules.

(1) Applicable valuation date.

(i) In general.

(ii) Exception.

(2) Basis adjustment.

(3) Tiered passthrough entities.

(E) Meaning of certain terms.

(iii) Treatment of gain allocated to certain passive activities as not from a passive activity.

(iv) Dispositions occurring in taxable years beginning before February 19, 1988.

(A) In general.

(B) Exceptions.

(v) Treatment of portfolio assets.

(vi) Definitions.

(vii) Examples.

(f) Recharacterization of passive income in certain situations.

(1) In general.

(2) Special rule for significant participation.

(i) In general.

(ii) Significant participation passive activity.

(iii) Example.

(3) Rental of nondepreciable property.

(4) Net interest income from passive equity-financed lending activity.

(i) In general.

(ii) Equity-financed lending activity.

(A) In general.

(B) Certain liabilities not taken into account.

(iii) Equity-financed interest income.

(iv) Net interest income.

(v) Interest-bearing assets.

(vi) Liabilities incurred in the activity.

(vii) Average outstanding balance.

(viii) Example.

(5) Net income from certain property rented incidental to development activity.

(i) In general [Reserved].

(ii) Commencement of use [Reserved].

(iii) Services performed for the purpose of enhancing the value of property [Reserved].

(iv) Examples [Reserved].

(6) Property rented to a nonpassive activity.

(7) Special rules applicable to the acquisition of an interest of a passthrough entity engaged in the trade or business of licensing intangible property.

(i) In general.

(ii) Royalty income from property.

(iii) Exceptions.

(iv) Capital expenditures.

(v) Example.

(8) Limitation on recharacterized income.

(9) Meaning of certain terms.

(10) Coordination with section 163(d).

(11) Effective date.

*§ 1.469-3 Passive activity credit.*

(a) through (d) [Reserved).

(e) Coordination with section 38(b).

(f) Coordination with section 50.

(g) [Reserved].

*§ 1.469-3T Passive activity credit (temporary).*

(a) Computation of passive activity credit.

(b) Credits subject to section 469.

(1) In general.

(2) Treatment of credits attributed to qualified progress expenditures.

(3) Special rule for partners and S corporations shareholders.

(4) Exception for pre-1987 credits.

(c) Taxable year to which credit is attributable.

(d) Regular tax liability allocable to passive activities.

(1) In general.

(2) Regular tax liability.

(e) Coordination with section 38(b) [Reserved].

(f) Coordination with section 47 [Reserved].

(g) Examples.

*§ 1.469-4 Definition of activity.*

(a) Scope and purpose.

(b) Definitions.

(1) Trade or business activities.

(2) Rental activities.

(c) General rules for grouping activities.

(1) Appropriate economic unit.

(2) Facts and circumstances test.

(3) Examples.

(d) Limitation on grouping certain activities.

(1) Grouping rental activities with other trade or business activities.

(i) Rule.

(ii) Examples.

(2) Grouping real property rentals and personal property rentals prohibited.

(3) Certain activities of limited partners and limited entrepreneurs.

(i) In general.

(ii) Example.

(4) Other activities identified by the Commissioner.

(5) Activities conducted through section 469 entities.

(i) In general.

(ii) Cross reference.

(e) Disclosure and consistency requirements.

(1) Original groupings.

(2) Regroupings.

(f) Grouping by Commissioner to prevent tax avoidance.

(1) Rule.

(2) Example.

(g) Treatment of partial dispositions.

(h) Rules for grouping rental real estate activities for taxpayers qualifying under section 469(c)(7).

*§ 1.469-5 Material participation.*

(a) through (e) [Reserved].

(f) Participation.

(1) In general.

(f) (2) through (h)(2) [Reserved].

(3) Coordination with rules governing the treatment of passthroughs entities.

(i) [Reserved].

(j) Material participation for preceding taxable years.

(1) In general.

(2) Material participation test for taxable years beginning before January 1, 1987

(k) Examples (1) through (4) [Reserved].

(k) Example (5).

(k) Examples (6) through (8) [Reserved].

*§ 1.469-5T Material participation (temporary).*

(a) In general.

(b) Facts and circumstances.

(1) In general [Reserved].

(2) Certain participation insufficient to constitute material participation under this paragraph (b).

(i) Participation satisfying standards not contained in section 469.

(ii) Certain management activities.

(iii) Participation less than 100 hours.

(c) Significant participation activity.

(1) In general.

(2) Significant participation.

(d) Personal service activity.

(e) Treatment of limited partners.

(1) General rule.

(2) Exceptions.

(3) Limited partnership interest.

(i) In general.

(ii) Limited partner holding general partner interest.

(f) Participation [Reserved].

(1) In general [Reserved].

(2) Exceptions.

(i) Certain work not customarily done by owners.

(ii) participation as an investor.

(A) In general.

(B) Work done in individual's capacity as an investor.

(3) Participation of spouses.

(4) Methods of proof.

(g) Material participation of trust and estates [Reserved].

(h) Miscellaneous rules.

(1) Participation of corporations.

(2) Treatment of certain retired farmers and surviving spouses of retired or disabled farmers.

(3) Coordination with rules governing the treatment of passthroughs entities [Reserved].

(i) [Reserved].

(j) Material participation for preceding taxable years [Reserved].

(1) In general [Reserved].

(2) Material participation for taxable years beginning before January 1, 1987 [Reserved].

(k) Examples.

*§ 1.469-6 Treatment of losses upon certain dispositions. [Reserved]*

*§ 1.469-7 Treatment of self-charged items of interest income and deduction.*

(a) In general.

(1) Applicability and effect of rules.

(2) Priority of rules in this section.

(b) Definitions.

(1) Passthrough entity.

(2) Taxpayer's share.

(3) Taxpayer's indirect interest.

(4) Entity taxable year.

(5) Deductions for a taxable year.

(c) Taxpayer loans to passthrough entity.

(1) Applicability.

(2) General rule.

(3) Applicable percentage.

(d) Passthrough entity loans to taxpayer.

(1) Applicability.

(2) General rule.

(3) Applicable percentage.

(e) Identically-owned passthrough entities.

(1) Applicability.

(2) General rule.

(3) Example.

(f) Identification of properly allocable deductions.

(g) Election to avoid application of the rules of this section.

(1) In general.

(2) Form of election.

(3) Period for which election applies.

(4) Revocation.

(h) Examples.

*§ 1.469-8 Application of section 469 to trust, estates, and their beneficiaries. [Reserved]*

*§ 1.469-9 Rules for certain rental real estate activities.*

(a) Scope and purpose.

(b) Definitions.

(1) Trade or business.

(2) Real property trade or business.

(3) Rental real estate.

(4) Personal services.

(5) Material participation.

(6) Qualifying taxpayer.

(c) Requirements for qualifying taxpayers.

(1) In general.

(2) Closely held C corporations.

(3) Requirement of material participation in the real property trades or businesses.

(4) Treatment of spouses.

(5) Employees in real property trades or businesses.

(d) General rule for determining real property trades or businesses.

(1) Facts and circumstances.

(2) Consistency requirement.

(e) Treatment of rental real estate activities of a qualifying taxpayer.

(1) In general.

(2) Treatment as a former passive activity.

(3) Grouping rental real estate activities with other activities.

(i) In general.

(ii) Special rule for certain management activities.

(4) Example.

(f) Limited partnership interests in rental real estate activities.

(1) In general.

(2) De minimis exception.

(g) Election to treat all interests in rental real estate as a single rental real estate activity.

(1) In general.

(2) Certain changes not material.

(3) Filing a statement to make or revoke the election.

(h) Interests in rental real estate held by certain passthrough entitites.

(1) General rule.

(2) Special rule if a qualifying taxpayer holds a fifty-percent or greater interest in a passthrough entity.

(3) Special rule for interests held in tiered passthrough entities.

(i) [Reserved].

(j) $25,000 offset for rental real estate activities of qualifying taxpayers.

(1) In general.

(2) Example.

*§ 1.469-10 Application of section 469 to publicly traded partnerships. [Reserved]*

*§ 1.469-11 Effective date and transition rules.*

(a) Generally applicable effective dates.

(b) Additional effective dates.

(1) Application of 1992 amendments for taxable years beginning before October 4, 1994.

(2) Additional transition rule for 1992 amendments.

(3) Fresh starts under consistency rules.

(i) Regrouping when tax liability is first determined under Project PS-1-89.

(ii) Regrouping when tax liability is first determined under § 1.469-4.

(iii) Regrouping when taxpayer is first subject to section 469(c)(7).

(4) Certain investment credit property.

(c) Special rules.

(1) Application of certain income recharacterization rules and self-charged rules.

(i) Certain recharacterization rules inapplicable in 1987.

(ii) Property rented to a nonpassive activity.

(iii) Self-charged rules.

(2) Qualified low-income housing projects.

(3) Effect of events occurring in years prior to 1987.

(d) Examples.

T.D. 8417, 5/11/92, amend T.D. 8477, 2/22/93, T.D. 8495, 11/3/93, T.D. 8565, 10/3/94, T.D. 8597, 7/12/95, T.D. 8645, 12/21/95, T.D. 9013, 8/20/2002.

**§ 1.469-1 General rules.**

***Caution:*** The Treasury has not yet amended Reg § 1.469-1 to reflect changes made by P.L. 103-66.

**(a) through (c)(7) [Reserved]**

**(c)** *(8) Consolidated groups.* Rules relating to the application of section 469 to consolidated groups are contained in paragraph (h) of this section.

*(9) through (d)(1) [Reserved]*

**(d)** *(2)* Coordination with sections 613A(d) and 1211. A passive activity deduction that is not disallowed for the taxable year under section 469 and the regulations thereunder may nonetheless be disallowed for the taxable year under section 613A(d) or 1211. The following example illustrates the application of this paragraph (d)(2):

*Example.* In 1993, an individual derives $10,000 of ordinary income from passive activity X, no gains from the sale or exchange of capital assets or assets used in a trade or business, $12,000 of capital loss from passive activity Y, and no income, gain, deductions, or losses from any other passive activity. The capital loss from activity Y is a passive activity deduction (within the meaning of § 1.469-2T(d)). Under section 469 and the regulations thereunder, the taxpayer is allowed $10,000 of the $12,000 passive activity deduction and has a $2,000 passive activity loss for the taxable year. Since the $10,000 passive activity deduction allowed under section 469 is a capital loss, such deduction is allowable for the taxable year only to the extent provided under section 1211. Therefore, the taxpayer is allowed $3,000 of the $10,000 capital loss under section 1211 and has a $7,000 capital loss carryover (within the meaning of section 1212(b)) to the succeeding taxable year. *(3)* **through (e)***(1)* **[Reserved]**

**(e)** *(2)* Trade or business activities. Trade or business activities are activities that constitute trade or business activities within the meaning of § 1.469-4(b)(1). *(3)* (i) through **(e)***(3)*(ii) [Reserved] (iii) Average period of customer use.

(A) In general. For purposes of this paragraph (e)(3), the average period of customer use for property held in connection with an activity (the activity's average period of customer use) is the sum of the average use factors for each class of property held in connection with the activity.

(B) Average use factor. The average use factor for a class of property held in connection with an activity is the average period of customer use for that class of property multiplied by the fraction obtained by dividing—

(1) The activity's gross rental income attributable to that class of property; by

(2) The activity's gross rental income.

(C) Average period of customer use for class of property. In determining an activity's average period of customer use for a taxable year, the average period of customer use for a class of property held in connection with an activity is determined by dividing—

(1) The aggregate number of days in all periods of customer use for property in the class (taking into account only periods that end during the taxable year or that include the last day of the taxable year); by

(2) The number of those periods of customer use.

(D) Period of customer use. Each period during which a customer has a continuous or recurring right to use an item of property held in connection with the activity (without regard to whether the customer uses the property for the entire period or whether the right to use the property is pursuant to a single agreement or to renewals thereof) is treated for purposes of this paragraph (e)(3)(iii) as a separate period of customer use. The duration of a period of customer use that includes the last day of a taxable year may be determined on the basis of reasonable estimates.

(E) Class of property. Taxpayers may organize property into classes for purposes of this paragraph (e)(3)(iii) using any method under which items of property for which the amount of the daily rent differs significantly are not included in the same class.

(F) Gross rental income and daily rent. In determining an activity's average period of customer use for a taxable year—

(1) The activity's gross rental income is the gross income from the activity for the taxable year taking into account only income that is attributable to amounts paid for the use of property;

(2) The activity's gross rental income attributable to a class of property is the gross income from the activity for the taxable year taking into account only income that is attributable to amounts paid for the use of property in that class; and

(3) The daily rent for items of property may be determined on any basis that reasonably reflects differences during the taxable year in the amounts ordinarily paid for one day's use of those items of property.

(iv) through **(e)***(3)*(vi)(C) [Reserved]

(vi) (D) Lodging rented for convenience of employer. The provision of lodging to an employee or to an employee's spouse or dependents is treated as incidental to the activity (or activities) of the taxpayer in which the employee performs services if the lodging is furnished for the taxpayer's convenience (within the meaning of section 119).

(E) Unadjusted basis. For purposes of this paragraph (e)(3)(vi), the term unadjusted basis means adjusted basis determined without regard to any adjustment described in section 1016 that decreases basis. (vii) through **(e)***(4)*(iii) [Reserved] *(4)* (iv) Definition of "working interest." For purposes of section 469 and the regulations thereunder, the term working interest means a working or operating mineral interest in any tract or parcel of land (within the meaning of § 1.612-4(a)). (v) through **(f)***(3)* [Reserved]

**(f)** *(4)* Carryover of disallowed deductions and credits—

(i) In general. In the case of an activity of a taxpayer with respect to which any deductions or credits are disallowed for a taxable year under § 1.469-1T(f)(2) or (f)(3) (the loss activity)—

(A) The disallowed deductions or credits is allocated among the taxpayer's activities for the succeeding taxable year in a manner that reasonably reflects the extent to which each activity continues the loss activity; and

(B) The disallowed deductions or credits allocated to an activity under paragraph (f)(4)(i)(A) of this section shall be treated as deductions or credits from the activity for the succeeding taxable year.

(ii) Business continued through C corporations or similar entities. If a taxpayer continues part or all of a loss activity through a C corporation or similar entity (C corporation entity), the taxpayer's interest in the C corporation entity shall be treated for purposes of this paragraph (f)(4) as an interest in a passive activity that continues that loss activity in whole or part. An entity is similar to a C corporation for this purpose if the owners of interests in the entity derive only portfolio income (within the meaning of § 1.469-2T(c)(3)(i)) from the interests.

(iii) Examples. The following examples illustrate the application of this paragraph (f)(4). In each example, the taxpayer is an individual whose taxable year is the calendar year.

*Example (1).* (i) The taxpayer owns interests in a convenience store and an apartment building. In each taxable year, the taxpayer's interests in the convenience store and the apartment building are treated under § 1.469-4 as interests in two separate passive activities of the taxpayer. A $5,000 loss from the convenience-store activity and a $3,000 loss from the apartment-building activity are disallowed under § 1.469-1T(f)(2) for 1993. Under § 1.469-1T(f)(2), the $5,000 loss from the convenience-store activity is allocated among the passive activity deductions from that activity for 1993, and the $3,000 loss from the apartment-building activity is treated similarly.

(ii) In 1994, the convenience store is continued in a single activity, and the section 469 activities that constituted the apartment building is similarly continued in a separate activity. Thus, the disallowed deductions from the convenience-store activity for 1993 must be allocated under paragraph (f)(4)(i)(A) of this section to the taxpayer's convenience-store activity in 1994. Similarly, the disallowed deductions from the apartment-building activity for 1993 must be allocated to the taxpayer's apartment-building activity in 1994. Under paragraph (f)(4)(i)(B) of this section, the disallowed deductions allocated to the convenience-store activity in 1994 are treated as deductions from that activity for 1994, and the disallowed deductions allocated to the apartment-building activity for 1994 are treated as deductions from the apartment-building activity for 1994.

*Example (2).* (i) In 1993, the taxpayer acquires a restaurant and a catering business. Assume that in 1993 and 1994 the restaurant and the catering business are treated under § 1.469-4 as an interest in a single passive activity of the taxpayer (the restaurant and catering activity). A $10,000 loss from the activity is disallowed under § 1.469-1T(f)(2) for 1994. Assume that in 1995, the taxpayer's interests in the restaurant and the catering business are treated under § 1.469-4 as interests in two separate passive activities of the taxpayer.

(ii) Under § 1.469-1T(f)(2), the $10,000 loss from the restaurant and catering activity is allocated among the passive activity deductions from that activity for 1994. In 1995, the businesses that constituted the restaurant and catering activity are continued, but are treated as two separate activities under § 1.469-4. Thus, the disallowed deductions from the restaurant and catering activity for 1994 must be allocated under paragraph (f)(4)(i)(A) of this section between the restaurant activity and the catering activity in 1995 in a manner that reasonably reflects the extent to which each of the activities continues the single restaurant and catering activity. Under paragraph (f)(4)(i)(B) of this section, the disallowed deductions allocated to the restaurant activity in 1995 are treated as deductions from the restaurant activity for 1995, and the disallowed deductions allocated to the catering activity in 1995 are treated as deductions from the catering activity for 1995.

*Example (3).* (i) In 1993, the taxpayer acquires a restaurant and a catering business. Assume that in 1993 and 1994 the restaurant and the catering business are treated under

§ 1.469-4 as an interest in a single passive activity of the taxpayer (the restaurant and catering activity). A $10,000 loss from the activity is disallowed under § 1.469-1T(f)(2) for 1994. Assume that in 1995, the taxpayer's interests in the restaurant and the catering business are treated under § 1.469-4 as interests in two separate passive activities of the taxpayer. In addition, a $20,000 loss from the activity was disallowed under § 1.469-1T(f)(2) for 1993, and the gross income and deductions (including deductions that were disallowed for 1993 under § 1.469-1T(f)(2)) from the restaurant and catering business for 1993 and 1994 are as follows:

| | Restaurant | Catering Business |
|---|---|---|
| 1993: | | |
| Gross income | $20,000 | $60,000 |
| Deductions | 40,000 | 60,000 |
| Net income (loss) | (20,000) | |
| 1994: | | |
| Gross income | 40,000 | 50,000 |
| Deductions | 30,000[1] | 70,000[2] |
| Net income (loss) | 10,000 | (20,000) |

[1] Includes $8,000 of deductions that were disallowed for 1993 ($20,000 × $40,000/$100,000).

[2] Includes $12,000 of deductions that were disallowed for 1993 ($20,000 × $60,000/$100,000).

(ii) Under paragraph (f)(4)(i)(A) of this section, the disallowed deductions from the restaurant and catering activity must be allocated among the taxpayer's activities for the succeeding year in a manner that reasonably reflects the extent to which those activities continue the restaurant and catering activity. The remainder of this example describes a number of allocation methods that will ordinarily satisfy the requirement of paragraph (f)(4)(i)(A) of this section. The description of specific allocation methods in this example does not preclude the use of other reasonable allocation methods for purposes of paragraph (f)(4)(i)(A) of this section.

(iii) Ordinarily, an allocation of disallowed deductions from the restaurant to the restaurant activity and disallowed deductions from the catering business to the catering activity would satisfy the requirement of paragraph (f)(4)(i)(A) of this section. Under § 1.469-1T(f)(2)(ii), a ratable portion of each deduction from the restaurant and catering activity is disallowed for 1994. Thus, $3,000 of the 1994 deductions from the restaurant are disallowed ($10,000 × $30,000/$100,000), and $7,000 of the 1994 deductions from the catering business are disallowed ($10,000 × $70,000/$100,000). Thus, the taxpayer can ordinarily treat $3,000 of the disallowed deductions as deductions from the restaurant activity for 1995, and $7,000 of the disallowed deductions as deductions from the catering activity for 1995.

(iv) Ordinarily, an allocation of disallowed deductions between the restaurant activity and catering activity in proportion to the losses from the restaurant and from the catering business for 1994 would also satisfy the requirement of paragraph (f)(4)(i)(A) of this section. If the restaurant and the catering business had been treated as separate activities in 1994, the restaurant activity would have had net income of $10,000 and the catering activity would have had a $20,000 loss. Thus, the taxpayer can ordinarily treat all $10,000 of disallowed deductions as deductions from the catering activity for 1995.

(v) Ordinarily, an allocation of disallowed deductions between the restaurant activity and catering activity in proportion to the losses from the restaurant and from the catering business for 1994 (determined as if the restaurant and the catering business had been separate activities for all taxable years) would also satisfy the requirement of paragraph (f)(4)(i)(A) of this section. If the restaurant and the catering business had been treated as separate activities for all taxable years, the entire $20,000 loss from the restaurant in 1993 would have been allocated to the restaurant activity in 1994, and the gross income and deductions from the separate activities for 1994 would be as follows:

| | Restaurant | Catering Business |
|---|---|---|
| Gross income | $40,000 | $50,000 |
| Deductions | 42,000 | 58,000 |
| Net income (loss) | (2,000) | (8,000) |

Thus, the taxpayer can ordinarily treat $2,000 of the disallowed deductions as deductions from the restaurant activity for 1995, and $8,000 of the disallowed deductions as deductions from the catering activity for 1995.

*Example (4).* (i) The taxpayer is a partner in a law partnership that acquires a building in December 1993 for use in the partnership's law practice. In taxable year 1993, four floors that are not needed in the law practice are leased to tenants; in taxable year 1994, two floors are leased to tenants; in taxable years after 1994, only one floor is leased to tenants and the rental operations are insubstantial. Assume that under § 1.469-4, the law practice and the rental property are treated as a trade or business activity and a separate rental activity for taxable years 1993 and 1994. Assume further that the law practice and the rental operations are a single trade or business activity for taxable years after 1994 under § 1.469-4. The trade or business activity is not a passive activity of the taxpayer. The rental activity, however, is a passive activity. Under § 1.469-1T(f)(2), a $12,000 loss from the rental activity is disallowed for 1993 and a $9,000 loss from the rental activity is disallowed for 1994.

(ii) Under § 1.469-1T(f)(2), the $12,000 loss from the rental activity for 1993 is allocated among the passive activity deductions from that activity for 1993. In 1994, the business of the rental activity is continued in two separate activities. Only two floors of the building remain in the rental activity, and the other two floors (i.e., the floors that were leased to tenants in 1993, but not in 1994) are used in the taxpayer's law-practice activity. Thus, the disallowed deductions from the rental activity for 1993 must be allocated under paragraph (f)(4)(i)(A) of this section between the rental activity and the law-practice activity in a manner that reasonably reflects the extent to which each of the activities continues business on the four floors that were leased to tenants in 1993. In these circumstances, the requirement of paragraph (f)(4)(i)(A) of this section would ordinarily be satisfied by any of the allocation methods illustrated in Example 3 or by an allocation of 50 percent of the disallowed deductions to each activity. Under paragraph (f)(4)(i)(B) of this section, the disallowed deductions allocated to the rental activity in 1994 are treated as deductions from the rental activity for 1994, and the disallowed deductions ($6,000) allocated to the law-practice activity in 1994 are treated as deductions from the law-practice activity for 1994.

(iii) Under § 1.469-1T(f)(2), the $9,000 loss from the rental activity for 1994 is allocated among the passive activity deductions from that activity for 1994. In 1995, the rental activity is continued in the taxpayer's law-practice activity. Thus, the disallowed deductions from the rental activity for

1994 must be allocated under paragraph (f)(4)(ii) of this section to the taxpayer's law-practice activity in 1995. Under paragraph (f)(4)(i)(B) of this section, the disallowed deductions allocated to the law-practice activity are treated as deductions from the law-practice activity for 1995.

(iv) Rules relating to former passive activities will be contained in paragraph (k) of this section. Under those rules, any disallowed deductions from the rental activity that are treated as deductions from the law-practice activity will be treated as unused deductions that are allocable to a former passive activity.

*Example (5).* (i) The taxpayer owns stock in a corporation that is an S corporation for the taxpayer's 1993 taxable year and a C corporation thereafter. The only activity of the corporation is a rental activity. For 1993, the taxpayer's pro rata share of the corporation's loss from the rental activity is $5,000, and the entire loss is disallowed under § 1.469-1T(f)(2) of this section.

(ii) Under § 1.469-1T(f)(2), the taxpayer's $5,000 loss from the rental activity is allocated among the taxpayer's deductions from that activity for 1993. In 1994, the rental activity is continued through a C corporation, and the taxpayer's interest in the C corporation is treated under paragraph (f)(4)(ii) of this section as a passive activity that continues the rental activity (the C corporation activity) for purposes of allocating the previously disallowed loss. Thus, the disallowed deductions from the rental activity for 1993 must be allocated under paragraph (f)(4)(i)(A) of this section to the taxpayer's C corporation activity in 1994, and are treated under paragraph (f)(4)(i)(B) of this section as deductions from the C corporation activity for 1994.

(iii) Treating the taxpayer's interest in the C corporation as an interest in a passive activity that continues the business of the rental activity does not change the character of the taxpayer's dividend income from the C corporation. Thus, the taxpayer's dividend income is portfolio income (within the meaning of § 1.469-2T(c)(3)(i)) and is not included in passive activity gross income. Accordingly, the taxpayer's loss from the C corporation activity for 1994 is $5,000.

*Example (6).* (i) The taxpayer owns stock in a corporation that is an S corporation for the taxpayer's 1993 taxable year and a C corporation thereafter. The only activity of the corporation is a rental activity. For 1993, the taxpayer's pro rata share of the corporation's loss from the rental activity is $5,000, and the entire loss is disallowed under § 1.469-1T(f)(2). The taxpayer has $2,000 in income from other passive activities for 1994, and as a result, only 60% of the taxpayer's loss from the C corporation activity ($3,000) is disallowed for 1994 under § 1.469-1T(f)(2).

(ii) Under § 1.469-1T(f)(2), the $3,000 disallowed loss from the C corporation activity is allocated among the passive activity deductions from that activity for 1994. In effect therefore, 60 percent of each disallowed deduction from the rental activity for 1993 is again disallowed for 1994.

(iii) Under paragraph (f)(4) of this section, the taxpayer's interest in the C corporation is treated as a loss activity and as an interest in a passive activity that continues the business of that loss activity for 1995. Thus, the disallowed deductions from the C corporation activity for 1994 must be allocated under paragraph (f)(4)(i)(A) of this section to the taxpayer's C corporation activity in 1995, and are treated under paragraph (f)(4)(i)(B) of this section as deductions from that activity for 1995.

**(g)** *(1)* **through (g)***(4)*(ii)(B) **[Reserved]**

*(4)* (ii) (C) Portfolio income (within the meaning of § 1.469-2T(c)(3)(i)), including any gross income that is treated as portfolio income under any other provision of the regulations (See, e.g., § 1.469-2(c)(2)(iii)(F) (relating to gain from the disposition of substantially appreciated property formerly held for investment) and § 1.469-2(f)(10) (relating to certain recharacterized passive activity gross income))

*(5) [Reserved]*

**(h)** *(1) In general.* This paragraph (h) provides rules for applying section 469 in computing a consolidated group's consolidated taxable income and consolidated tax liability (and the separate taxable income and tax liability of each member).

*(2) Definitions.* The definitions and nomenclature in the regulations under section 1502 apply for purposes of this paragraph (h). See, e.g., §§ 1.1502-1 (definitions of group, consolidated group, member, subsidiary, and consolidated return year), 1.1502-2 (consolidated tax liability), 1.1502-11 (consolidated taxable income), 1.1502-12 (separate taxable income), 1.1502-13 (intercompany transactions), 1.1502-21 (net operating losses), and 1.1502-22 (consolidated net capital gain and loss).

*(3) [Reserved]*

*(4)* Status and participation of members. (i) Determination by reference to status and participation of group. For purposes of section 469 and the regulations thereunder—

(A) Each member of a consolidated group shall be treated as a closely held corporation or personal service corporation, respectively, for the taxable year, if and only if the consolidated group is treated (under the rules of paragraph (h)(4)(ii) of this section) as a closely held corporation or personal service corporation for that year; and

(B) The determination of whether a trade or business activity (within the meaning of paragraph (e)(2) of this section) conducted by one or more members of a consolidated group is a passive activity of the members is made by reference to the consolidated group's participation in the activity.

(ii) Determination of status and participation of consolidated group. For purposes of determining under § 1.469-1T(g)(2) whether a consolidated group is treated as a closely held corporation or a personal service corporation, and determining under § 1.469-1T(g)(3) whether the consolidated group materially or significantly participates in any activity conducted by one or more members of the group—

(A) The members of the consolidated group shall be treated as one corporation;

(B) Only the outstanding stock of the common parent shall be treated as outstanding stock of the corporation;

(C) An employee of any member of the group shall be treated as an employee of the corporation; and

(D) An activity is treated as the principal activity of the corporation if and only if it is the principal activity (within the meaning of § 1.441-3(e)) of the consolidated group.

*(5) [Reserved]*

*(6) Intercompany transactions.* (i) In general. Section 1.1502-13 applies to determine the treatment under section 469 of intercompany items and corresponding items from intercompany transactions between members of a consolidated group. For example, the matching rule of § 1.1502-13(c) treats the selling member (S) and the buying member (B) as divisions of a single corporation for purposes of determining whether S's intercompany items and B's corresponding items are from a passive activity. Thus, for purposes of ap-

plying § 1.469-2(c)(2)(iii) and § 1.469-2T(d)(5)(ii) to property sold by S to B in an intercompany transaction—

(A) S and B are treated as divisions of a single corporation for determining the uses of the property during the 12-month period preceding its disposition to a nonmember, and generally have an aggregate holding period for the property; and

(B) § 1.469-2(c)(2)(iv) does not apply.

(ii) Example. The following example illustrates the application of this paragraph (h)(6).

*Example.* (i) P, a closely held corporation, is the common parent of the P consolidated group. P owns all of the stock of S and B. X is a person unrelated to any member of the P group. S owns and operates equipment that is not used in a passive activity. On January 1 of Year 1, S sells the equipment to B at a gain. B uses the equipment in a passive activity and does not dispose of the equipment before it has been fully depreciated.

(ii) Under the matching rule of § 1.1502-13(c), S's gain taken into account as a result of B's depreciation is treated as gain from a passive activity even though S used the equipment in a nonpassive activity.

(iii) The facts are the same as in paragraph (a) of this Example, except that B sells the equipment to X on December 1 of Year 3 at a further gain. Assume that if S and B were divisions of a single corporation, gain from the sale to X would be passive income attributable to a passive activity. To the extent of B's depreciation before the sale, the results are the same as in paragraph (ii) of this Example. B's gain and S's remaining gain taken into account as a result of B's sale are treated as attributable to a passive activity.

(iv) The facts are the same as in paragraph (iii) of this Example, except that B recognizes a loss on the sale to X. B's loss and S's gain taken into account as a result of B's sale are treated as attributable to a passive activity.

(iii) Effective dates. This paragraph (h)(6) applies with respect to transactions occurring in years beginning on or after July 12, 1995. For transactions occurring in years beginning before July 12, 1995, see § 1.469-1T(h)(6) (as contained in the 26 CFR part 1 edition revised as of April 1, 1995). *(7)* through (k) [Reserved]

T.D. 8417, 5/11/92, amend T.D. 8597, 7/12/95, T.D. 8677, 6/26/96, T.D. 8823, 6/25/99, T.D. 8996, 5/16/2002.

PAR. 2. In the list below, for each section indicated in the left column, remove the old language in the middle column and add the new language in the right column.

| Affected Section | Remove | Add |
|---|---|---|
| 1.46-1(p)(2)(iv) | paragraph (b)(1) of § 1.441-2 | § 1.441-2 |
| 1.48-3(d)(1)(iii) | paragraph (b)(1) of § 1.441-2 | § 1.441-2 |
| 1.280H-1T(a), last sentence | | |
| 1.443-1(b)(1)(ii) | § 1.441-4T(d) and paragraph (c)(5) of § 1.441-2 | § 1.441-3(c) and § 1.441-1(b)(2)(ii). |
| 1.444-1T(a)(1), first sentence | § 1.444-4T(d) | § 1.441-3(c) |
| 1.444-2T(a), last sentence | | |
| 1.448-1(h)(2)(ii)(B)(1) | § 1.441-4T(d) | § 1.441-3(c) |
| 1.469-1(h)(4)(ii)(D) | § 1.441-2T(b)(1) | § 1.441-2(c) |
| 1.469-1T(g)(2)(i) | § 1.441-4T(f) | § 1.441-3(e) |
| 1.1561-1(c)(2) | § 1.441-4T(d) | § 1.441-2 |
| | See paragraph (b)(1) of § 1.441-2 | See § 1.441-2 |
| 1.6654-2(a), concluding text | paragraph (b) of § 1.441-2 | § 1.441-2(c) |
| 1.6655-2(a)(4), first sentence | paragraph (b) of § 1.441-2 | § 1.441-1(b) |

**Proposed § 1.469-1** [*For Preamble, see ¶ 152,177*]

• ***Caution:*** This Notice of Proposed Rulemaking was partially finalized by T.D. 8996, issued on 5/16/2002. Proposed regulation §§ 1.46-1, 1.48-3, 1.280H-1T, 1.443-1, 1.444-1T, 1.444-2T, 1.448-1, 1.469-1, 1.469-1T, 1.898-4, 1.1561-1, 1.6654-2, 1.6655-2 and 301.7701(b)-6 remains in effect.

**§ 1.469-1T General rules (temporary).**

***Caution:*** The Treasury has not yet amended Reg § 1.469-1T to reflect changes made by P.L. 104-188.

**(a) Passive activity loss and credit disallowed.** *(1) In general.* Except as otherwise provided in paragraph (a)(2) of this section—

(i) The passive activity loss for the taxable year shall not be allowed as a deduction; and

(ii) The passive activity credit for the taxable year shall not be allowed.

*(2) Exceptions.* Paragraph (a)(1) of this section shall not apply to the passive activity loss or the passive activity credit for the taxable year to the extent provided in—

(i) Section 469(i) and the rules to be contained in § 1.469-9T (relating to losses and credits attributable to certain rental real estate activities); and

(ii) Section 1.469-11T (relating to losses and credits attributable to certain pre-enactment interests in activities).

**(b) Taxpayers to whom these rules apply.** The rules of section 469 and the regulations thereunder generally apply to—

*(1)* Individuals;

*(2)* Trusts (other than trusts (or portions of trusts) described in section 671);

*(3)* Estates;

*(4)* Personal service corporations (within the meaning of paragraph (g)(2)(i) of this section); and

*(5)* Closely held corporations (within the meaning of paragraph (g)(2)(ii) of this section).

**(c) Cross references.** *(1) Definition of "passive activity."* Rules relating to the definition of the term "passive activity" are contained in paragraph (e) of this section.

*(2) Passive activity loss.* Rules relating to the computation of the passive activity loss for the taxable year are contained in § 1.469-2T.

*(3) Passive activity credit.* Rules relating to the computation of the passive activity credit for the taxable year are contained in § 1.469-3T.

*(4) Effect of rules for other purposes.* Rules relating to the effect of section 469 and the regulations thereunder for other purposes under the Code are contained in paragraph (d) of this section.

*(5) Special rule for oil and gas working interests.* Rules relating to the treatment of losses and credits from certain interests in oil and gas wells are contained in paragraph (e)(4) of this section.

*(6) Treatment of disallowed losses and credits.* Paragraph (f) of this section contains rules relating to—

(i) The treatment of deductions from passive activities in taxable years in which the passive activity loss is disallowed in whole or in part under paragraph (a)(1)(i) of this section; and

(ii) The treatment of credits from passive activities in taxable years in which the passive activity credit is disallowed in whole or in part under paragraph (a)(1)(ii) of this section.

*(7) Corporations subject to section 469.* Rules relating to the application of section 469 and regulations thereunder to C corporations are contained in paragraph (g) of this section.

*(8) [Reserved]*

*(9) Joint returns.* Rules relating to the application of section 469 and the regulations thereunder to spouses filing a joint return for the taxable year are contained in paragraph (j) of this section.

*(10) Material participation.* Rules defining the term "material participation" are contained in § 1.469-5T.

*(11) Effective date and transition rules.* Rules relating to the effective date of section 469 and the regulations thereunder and transition rules applicable to pre-enactment interests in activities are contained in § 1.469-11T.

*(12) Future regulations.* (i) Rules relating to former passive activities and changes in corporate status will be contained in paragraph (k) of this section.

(ii) Rules relating to the definition of "activity" will be contained in § 1.469-4T.

(iii) Rules relating to the treatment of deductions from activities that are disposed of in certain transactions will be contained in § 1.469-6T.

(iv) Rules relating to the treatment of self-charged items of income and expense will be contained in § 1.469-7T.

(v) Rules relating to the application of section 469 and the regulations thereunder to trusts, estates, and their beneficiaries will be contained in § 1.469-8T.

(vi) Rules relating to the treatment of income, deductions, and credits from certain rental real estate activities of individuals and certain estates will be contained in § 1.469-9T.

(vii) Rules relating to the application of section 469 to publicly traded partnerships will be contained in § 1.469-10T.

**(d) Effect of section 469 and the regulations thereunder for other purposes.** *(1) Treatment of items of passive activity income and gain.* Neither the provisions of section 469(a)(1) and paragraph (a)(1) of this section nor the characterization of items of income or deduction as passive activity gross income (within the meaning of § 1.469-2T(c)) or passive activity deductions (within the meaning of § 1.469-2T(d)) affects the treatment of any item of income or gain under any provision of the Internal Revenue Code other than section 469. The following example illustrates the application of this paragraph (d)(1):

*Example.* (i) In 1991, an individual's only income and loss from passive activities are a $10,000 capital gain from passive activity X and a $12,000 ordinary loss from passive activity Y. The taxpayer also has a $10,000 capital loss that is not derived from a passive activity.

(ii) Under § 1.469-2T(b), the taxpayer has a $2,000 passive activity loss for the taxable year. The only effect of section 469 and the regulations thereunder is to disallow a deduction for the taxpayer's $2,000 passive activity loss for the taxable year. Thus, the taxpayer's capital loss for the taxable year is allowed because the $10,000 capital gain from passive activity X is taken into account under section 1211(b) in computing the taxpayer's allowable capital loss for the year.

*(2) Coordination with sections 613A(d) and 1211. [Reserved]* See § 1.469-1(d)(2) for rules relating to this paragraph.

*(3) Treatment of passive activity losses.* Except as otherwise provided by regulations, a deduction that is disallowed for a taxable year under section 469 and the regulations thereunder is not taken into account as a deduction that is allowed for the taxable year in computing the amount subject to any tax imposed by subtitle A of the Internal Revenue Code. The following example illustrates the application of this paragraph (d)(3):

*Example.* An individual has a $5,000 passive activity loss for a taxable year, all of which is disallowed under paragraph (a)(1) of this section. All of the disallowed loss is allocated under paragraph (f) of this section to activities that are trades or businesses (within the meaning of section 1402(c)). Such loss is not taken into account for the taxable year in computing the taxpayer's taxable income subject to tax under section 1. In addition, under this paragraph (d)(3), such loss is not taken into account for the taxable year in computing the taxpayer's net earnings from self-employment subject to tax under section 1401.

**(e) Definition of "passive activity".** *(1) In general.* Except as otherwise provided in this paragraph (e), an activity is a passive activity of the taxpayer for a taxable year if and only if the activity—

(i) Is a trade or business activity (within the meaning of paragraph (e)(2) of this section) in which the taxpayer does not materially participate for such taxable year; or

(ii) Is a rental activity (within the meaning of paragraph (e)(3) of this section), without regard to whether or to what extent the taxpayer participates in such activity.

*(2) Trade or business activity. [Reserved]* See § 1.469-1(e)(2) for rules relating to this paragraph.

*(3) Rental activity.* (i) In general. Except as otherwise provided in this paragraph (e)(3), an activity is a rental activity for a taxable year if—

(A) During such taxable year, tangible property held in connection with the activity is used by customers or held for use by customers; and

(B) The gross income attributable to the conduct of the activity during such taxable year represents (or, in the case of an activity in which property is held for use by customers, the expected gross income from the conduct of the activity will represent) amounts paid or to be paid principally for the use of such tangible property (without regard to whether the use of the property by customers is pursuant to a lease or pursuant to a service contract or other arrangement that is not denominated a lease).

(ii) Exceptions. For purposes of this paragraph (e)(3), an activity involving the use of tangible property is not a rental activity for a taxable year if for such taxable year—

(A) The average period of customer use for such property is seven days or less;

(B) The average period of customer use for such property is 30 days or less, and significant personal services (within the meaning of paragraph (e)(3)(iv) of this section) are provided by or on behalf of the owner of the property in connection with making the property available for use by customers;

(C) Extraordinary personal services (within the meaning of paragraph (e)(3)(v) of this section) are provided by or on behalf of the owner of the property in connection with making such property available for use by customers (without regard to the average period of customer use);

(D) The rental of such property is treated as incidental to a nonrental activity of the taxpayer under paragraph (e)(3)(vi) of this section;

(E) The taxpayer customarily makes the property available during defined business hours for nonexclusive use by various customers; or

(F) The provision of the property for use in an activity conducted by a partnership, S corporation, or joint venture in which the taxpayer owns an interest is not a rental activity under paragraph (e)(3)(vii) of this section.

(iii) Average period of customer use. [Reserved] See § 1.469-1(e)(3)(iii) for rules relating to this paragraph.

(iv) Significant personal services. (A) In general. For purposes of paragraph (e)(3)(ii)(B) of this section, personal services include only services performed by individuals, and do not include excluded services (within the meaning of paragraph (e)(3)(iv)(B) of this section). In determining whether personal services provided in connection with making property available for use by customers are significant, all of the relevant facts and circumstances shall be taken into account. Relevant facts and circumstances include the frequency with which such services are provided, the type and amount of labor required to perform such services, and the value of such services relative to the amount charged for the use of the property.

(B) Excluded services. For purposes of paragraph (e)(3)(iv)(A) of this section, the term "excluded services" means, with respect to any property made available for use by customers—

(1) Services necessary to permit the lawful use of the property;

(2) Services performed in connection with the construction of improvements to the property, or in connection with the performance of repairs that extend the property's useful life for a period substantially longer than the average period for which such property is used by customers; and

(3) Services, provided in connection with the use of any improved real property, that are similar to those commonly provided in connection with long-term rentals of high-grade commercial or residential real property (e.g., cleaning and maintenance of common areas, routine repairs, trash collection, elevator service, and security at entrances or perimeters).

(v) Extraordinary personal services. For purposes of paragraph (e)(3)(ii)(C) of this section, extraordinary personal services are provided in connection with making property available for use by customers only if the services provided in connection with the use of the property are performed by individuals, and the use by customers of the property is incidental to their receipt of such services. For example, the use by patients of a hospital's boarding facilities generally is incidental to their receipt of the personal services provided by the hospital's medical and nursing staff. Similarly, the use by students of a boarding school's dormitories generally is incidental to their receipt of the personal services provided by the school's teaching staff.

(vi) Rental of property incidental to a nonrental activity of the taxpayer. (A) In general. For purposes of paragraph (e)(3)(ii)(D) of this section, the rental of property shall be treated as incidental to a nonrental activity of the taxpayer only to the extent provided in this paragraph (e)(3)(vi).

(B) Property held for investment. The rental of property during a taxable year shall be treated as incidental to an activity of holding such property for investment if and only if—

(1) The principal purpose for holding the property during such taxable year is to realize gain from the appreciation of the property (without regard to whether it is expected that such gain will be realized from the sale or exchange of the property in its current state of development); and

(2) The gross rental income from the property for such taxable year is less than two percent of the lesser of—

(i) The unadjusted basis of such property; and

(ii) The fair market value of such property.

(C) Property used in a trade or business. The rental of property during a taxable year shall be treated as incidental to a trade or business activity (within the meaning of paragraph (e)(2) of this section) if and only if—

(1) The taxpayer owns an interest in such trade or business activity during the taxable year;

(2) The property was predominantly used in such trade or business activity during the taxable year or during at least two of the five taxable years that immediately precede the taxable year; and

(3) The gross rental income from such property for the taxable year is less than two percent of the lesser of—

(i) The unadjusted basis of such property; and

(ii) The fair market value of such property.

(D) Lodging for convenience of employer. [Reserved] See § 1.469-1(e)(3)(vi)(D) for rules relating to this paragraph.

(E) Unadjusted basis. [Reserved] See § 1.469-1(e)(3)(vi)(E) for rules relating to this paragraph.

(vii) Property made available for use in a nonrental activity conducted by a partnership, S corporation, or joint venture in which the taxpayer owns an interest. If the taxpayer owns an interest in a partnership, S corporation, or joint venture conducting an activity other than a rental activity, and the taxpayer provides property for use in the activity in the taxpayer's capacity as an owner of an interest in such partnership, S corporation, or joint venture, the provision of such property is not a rental activity. Thus, if a partner contributes the use of property to a partnership, none of the partner's distributive share of partnership income is income from a rental activity unless the partnership is engaged in a rental activity. In addition, a partner's gross income attributable to a payment described in section 707(c) is not income from a rental activity under any circumstances (see § 1.469-2T(e)(2)). The determination of whether property used in an activity is provided by the taxpayer in the taxpayer's capacity as an owner of an interest in a partnership, S corporation, or joint venture shall be made on the basis of all of the facts and circumstances.

(viii) Examples. The following examples illustrate the application of this paragraph (e)(3):

*Example (1).* The taxpayer is engaged in an activity of leasing photocopying equipment. The average period of customer use for the equipment exceeds 30 days. Pursuant to the lease agreements, skilled technicians employed by the taxpayer maintain the equipment and service malfunctioning equipment for no additional charge. Service calls occur frequently (three times per week on average) and require substantial labor. The value of the maintenance and repair services (measured by the cost to the taxpayer of employees performing these services) exceeds 50 percent of the amount charged for the use of the equipment. Under these facts, services performed by individuals are provided in connection with the use of the photocopying equipment, but the customers' use of the photocopying equipment is not incidental to their receipt of the services. Therefore, extraordinary personal services (within the meaning of paragraph (e)(3)(v) of this section) are not provided in connection with making the photocopying equipment available for use by customers, and the activity is a rental activity.

*Example (2).* The facts are the same as in example (1), except that the average period of customer use for the photocopying equipment exceeds seven days but does not exceed 30 days. Under these facts, significant personal services (within the meaning of paragraph (e)(3)(iv) of this section) are provided in connection with making the photocopying equipment available for use by customers and, under paragraph (e)(3)(ii)(B) of this section, the activity is not a rental activity.

*Example (3).* The taxpayer is engaged in an activity of transporting goods for customers. In conducting the activity, the taxpayer provides tractor-trailers to transport goods for customers pursuant to arrangements under which the tractor-trailers are selected by the taxpayer, may be replaced at the sole option of the taxpayer, and are operated and maintained by drivers and mechanics employed by the taxpayer. The average period of customer use for the tractor-trailers exceeds 30 days. Under these facts, the use of tractor-trailers by the taxpayer's customers is incidental to their receipt of personal services provided by the taxpayer. Accordingly, the services performed in the activity are extraordinary personal services (within the meaning of paragraph (e)(3)(v) of this section) and, under paragraph (e)(3)(ii)(C) of this section, the activity is not a rental activity.

*Example (4).* The taxpayer is engaged in an activity of owning and operating a residential apartment hotel. For the taxable year, the average period of customer use for apartments exceeds seven days but does not exceed 30 days. In addition to cleaning public entrances, exits, stairways, and lobbies, and collecting and removing trash, the taxpayer provides a daily maid and linen service at no additional charge. All of the services other than maid and linen service are excluded services (within the meaning of paragraph (e)(3)(iv)(B) of this section), because such services are similar to those commonly provided in connection with long-term rentals of high-grade residential real property. The value of the maid and linen services (measured by the cost to the taxpayer of employees performing such services) is less than 10 percent of the amount charged to tenants for occupancy of apartments. Under these facts, neither significant personal services (within the meaning of paragraph (e)(3)(iv) of this section) nor extraordinary personal services (within the meaning of paragraph (e)(3)(v) of this section) are provided in connection with making apartments available for use by customers. Accordingly, the activity is a rental activity.

*Example (5).* The taxpayer owns 1,000 acres of unimproved land with a fair market value of $350,000 and an unadjusted basis of $210,000. The taxpayer holds the land for the principal purpose of realizing gain from appreciation. In order to defray the cost of carrying the land, the taxpayer leases the land to a rancher, who uses the land to graze cattle and pays rent of $4,000 per year. Thus, the gross rental income from the land is less than two percent of the lesser of the fair market value and the unadjusted basis of the land (.02 × $210,000 = $4,200). Accordingly, under paragraph (e)(3)(ii)(D) of this section, the rental of the land is not a rental activity because the rental is treated under paragraph (e)(3)(vi)(B) of this section as incidental to an activity of holding the property for investment.

*Example (6).* (i) A calendar year taxpayer owns an interest in a farming activity which is a trade or business activity (within the meaning of paragraph (e)(2) of this section) and owns farmland which was used in the farming activity in 1985 and 1986. The fair market value of the farmland is $350,000 and its unadjusted basis is $210,000. In 1987, 1988, and 1989, the taxpayer continues to own an interest in the farming activity but does not use the land in the activity. In 1987, the taxpayer leases the land for $4,000 to a rancher, who uses the land to graze cattle. In 1988, the taxpayer leases the land for $10,000 to a film production company, which uses the land to film scenes for a movie. In 1989, the taxpayer again leases the land for $4,000 to the rancher.

(ii) For 1987 and 1989, the taxpayer owns an interest in a trade or business activity, and the farmland which the taxpayer leases to the rancher was used in such activity for two out of five immediately preceding taxable years. In addition, the gross rental income from the land ($4,000) is less than two percent of the lesser of the fair market value and the unadjusted basis of the land (.02 × $210,000 treated under paragraph (e)(3)(vi)(C) of this section as incidental to the taxpayer's farming activity, and is not a rental activity.

(iii) Because the taxpayer's gross rental income from the land for 1988 ($10,000) is not less than two percent of the lesser of the fair market value and the unadjusted basis of the land, the requirement of paragraph (e)(3)(vi)(C)(3) of this section is not met. Therefore, the taxpayer's rental of the land in 1988 is not treated as incidental to the taxpayer's farming activity and is a rental activity.

*Example (7).* (i) In 1988, the taxpayer acquires vacant land for the purpose of constructing a shopping mall. Before commencing construction, the taxpayer leases the land under a one-year lease to an automobile dealer, who uses the land to park cars held in its inventory. The taxpayer commences construction of the shopping mall in 1989.

(ii) The taxpayer acquired the land for the principal purpose of constructing the shopping mall, not for the principal purpose of realizing gain from the appreciation of the property. Therefore, the rental of the property in 1988 is not treated under paragraph (e)(3)(vi)(B) of this section as incidental to an activity of holding the property for investment.

(iii) The land has not been used in any taxable year in any trade or business of the taxpayer. Therefore, the rental of the property in 1988 is not treated under paragraph (e)(3)(vi)(C) of this section as incidental to a trade or business activity.

(iv) Since the rental of the land in 1988 is not treated under paragraph (e)(3)(vi) of this section as incidental to a nonrental activity of the taxpayer, the rental of the land in 1988 is a rental activity. See § 1.469-2T(f)(3) for a special rule relating to the treatment of gross income from the rental of nondepreciable property.

*Example (8).* The taxpayer makes farmland available to a tenant farmer pursuant to an arrangement designated a "crop-share lease." Under the arrangement, the tenant is required to use the tenant's best efforts to farm the land and produce marketable crops. The taxpayer is obligated to pay 50 percent of the costs incurred in the activity (without regard to whether any crops are successfully produced or marketed), and is entitled to 50 percent of the crops produced (or 50 percent of the proceeds from marketing the crops). For purposes of paragraph (e)(3)(vii) of this section, the taxpayer is treated as providing the farmland for use in a farming activity conducted by a joint venture in the taxpayer's capacity as an owner of an interest in the joint venture. Accordingly, under paragraph (e)(3)(ii)(F) of this section, the taxpayer is not engaged in a rental activity, without regard to whether the taxpayer performs any services in the farming activity.

*Example (9).* The taxpayer owns a taxicab which the taxpayer operates during the day and leases to another driver for use at night under a one-year lease. Under the terms of the lease, the other driver is charged a fixed rental for use of the taxicab. Assume that, under the rules to be contained in § 1.469-4T, the taxpayer is engaged in two separate activities, an activity of operating the taxicab and an activity of making the taxicab available for use by the other driver. Under these facts, the period for which the other driver uses the taxicab exceeds 30 days, and the taxpayer does not provide extraordinary personal services in connection with making the taxicab available to the other driver. Accordingly, the lease of the taxicab is a rental activity.

*Example (10).* The taxpayer operates a golf course. Some customers of the golf course pay greens fees upon each use of the golf course, while other customers purchase weekly, monthly, or annual passes. The golf course is open to all customers from sunrise to sunset every day of the year except certain holidays and days on which the taxpayer determines that the course is too wet for play. The taxpayer thus makes the golf course available during prescribed hours for nonexclusive use by various customers. Accordingly, under paragraph (e)(3)(ii)(E) of this section, the taxpayer is not engaged in a rental activity, without regard to the average period of customer use for the golf course.

*(4) Special rule for oil and gas working interests.* (i) In general. Except as otherwise provided in paragraph (e)(4)(ii) of this section, an interest in an oil or gas well drilled or operated pursuant to a working interest (within the meaning of paragraph (e)(4)(iv) of this section) of a taxpayer is not an interest in a passive activity for the taxpayer's taxable year (without regard to whether the taxpayer materially participates in such activity) if at any time during such taxable year the taxpayer holds such working interest either—

(A) Directly; or

(B) Through an entity that does not limit the liability of the taxpayer with respect to the drilling or operation of such well pursuant to such working interest.

(ii) Exception for deductions attributable to a period during which liability is limited. (A) In general. If paragraph (e)(4)(i) of this section applies for a taxable year to the taxpayer's interest in an oil or gas well that would, but for the application of paragraph (e)(4)(i) of this section, be an interest in a passive activity for the taxable year, and the taxpayer has a net loss (within the meaning of paragraph (e)(4)(ii)(C)(3) of this section) from the well for the taxable year—

(1) The taxpayer's disqualified deductions (within the meaning of paragraph (e)(4)(ii)(C)(2) of this section) from such oil or gas well for such year shall be treated as passive activity deductions for such year (within the meaning of § 1.469-2T(d)); and

(2) A ratable portion (within the meaning of paragraph (e)(4)(ii)(C)(4) of this section) of the taxpayer's gross income from such oil or gas well for such year shall be treated as passive activity gross income for such year (within the meaning of § 1.469-2T(c)).

(B) Coordination with rules governing the identification of disallowed passive activity deductions. If gross income and deductions from an activity for a taxable year are treated as passive activity gross income and passive activity deductions under paragraph (e)(4)(ii)(A) of this section, such activity shall be treated as a passive activity for such year for purposes of applying paragraph (f)(2) and (4) of this section.

(C) Meaning of certain terms. For purposes of this paragraph (e)(4)(ii), the following terms shall have the meanings set forth below:

(1) Allocable deductions. The deductions allocable to a taxable year are any deductions that arise in such year (within the meaning of § 1.469-2T(d)(8)) and any deductions that are treated as deductions for such year under paragraph (f)(4) of this section.

(2) Disqualified deductions. The taxpayer's "disqualified deductions" from an oil or gas well for a taxable year are the taxpayer's deductions—

(i) That are attributable to such well and allocable to the taxable year; and

(ii) With respect to which economic performance (within the meaning of section 461(h), without regard to section 461(h)(3) or (i)(2)) occurs at a time during which the taxpayer's only interest in the working interest is held through an entity that limits the taxpayer's liability with respect to the drilling or operation of such well.

(3) Net loss. The "net loss" of a taxpayer from an oil or gas well for a taxable year equals the amount by which the taxpayer's deductions that are attributable to such oil or gas

well and allocable to such year exceeds the gross income of the taxpayer from such well for such year.

(4) Ratable portion. The "ratable portion" of the taxpayer's gross income from an oil or gas well for a taxable year equals the total amount of such gross income multiplied by the fraction obtained by dividing—

(i) The disqualified deductions from such oil or gas well for the taxable year; by

(ii) The total amount of the deductions that are attributable to such oil or gas well and allocable to the taxable year.

(iii) Examples. The following examples illustrate the application of paragraph (e)(4)(i) and (ii) of this section:

*Example (1).* (i) A, a calendar year individual, acquires on January 1, 1987, a general partnership interest in P, a calendar year partnership that holds a working interest in an oil or gas property. Pursuant to the partnership agreement, A is entitled to convert the general partnership interest into a limited partnership interest at any time. On December 1, 1987, pursuant to a contract with D, an independent drilling contractor, P commences drilling a single well pursuant to the working interest. Under the drilling contract, P pays D for the drilling only as the work is performed. All drilling costs are deducted by P in the year in which they are paid. At the end of 1987, A converts the general partnership interest into a limited partnership interest, effective immediately. The drilling of the well is completed on February 28, 1988. A's interest in the well would but for this paragraph (e)(4) be an interest in a passive activity.

(ii) Throughout 1987, A holds the working interest through an entity that does not limit A's liability with respect to the drilling of the well pursuant to the working interest. In 1988, however, A holds the working interest through an entity that limits A's liability with respect to the drilling and operation of the well throughout such year. Accordingly, under paragraph (e)(4)(i) of this section, A's interest in P's well is not an interest in a passive activity for 1987 but is an interest in a passive activity for 1988. Moreover, since economic performance occurs in 1987 with respect to all items of deduction for drilling costs that are allocable to 1987, A has no disqualified deductions for 1987.

*Example (2).* The facts are the same as in example (1), except that all costs of drilling under the contract with D (including costs of drilling performed after 1987) are paid before the end of 1987 and A has a net loss for 1987. In addition, A has $15,000 of total deductions that are attributable to the well and allocable to 1987, but economic performance (as that term is used in paragraph (e)(4)(ii)(C)(2)(ii) of this section) does not occur with respect to $5,000 of those deductions until 1988. Under paragraph (e)(4)(ii) of this section, the $5,000 of deductions with respect to which economic performance occurs in 1988 are disqualified deductions and are treated as passive activity deductions for 1987. In addition, one-third ($5,000/$15,000) of A's gross income from the well for 1987 is treated as passive activity gross income.

(iv) Definition of "working interest." [Reserved] See § 1.469-1(e)(4)(iv) for rules relating to this paragraph.

(v) Entities that limit liability. (A) General rule. For purposes of paragraph (e)(4)(i)(B) of this section, an entity limits the liability of the taxpayer with respect to the drilling or operation of a well pursuant to a working interest held through such entity if the taxpayer's interest in the entity is in the form of—

(1) A limited partnership interest in a partnership in which the taxpayer is not a general partner;

(2) Stock in a corporation; or

(3) An interest in any entity (other than a limited partnership or corporation) that, under applicable State law, limits the potential liability of a holder of such an interest for all obligations of the entity to a determinable fixed amount (for example, the sum of the taxpayer's capital contributions).

(B) Other limitations disregarded. For purposes of this paragraph (e) (4), protection against loss through any of the following is not taken into account in determining whether a taxpayer holds a working interest through an entity that limits the taxpayer's liability:

(1) An indemnification agreement;

(2) A stop loss arrangement;

(3) Insurance;

(4) Any similar arrangement; or

(5) Any combination of the foregoing.

(C) Examples. The following examples illustrate the application of this paragraph (e)(4)(v):

*Example (1).* A owns a 20 percent interest as a general partner in the capital and profits of P, a partnership which owns oil or gas working interests. The other partners of P agree to indemnify A against liability in excess of A's capital contribution for any of P's costs and expenses with respect to P's working interests. As a general partner, however, A is jointly and severally liable for all of P's liabilities and, under paragraph (e)(4)(v)(B)(1) of this section, the indemnification agreement is not taken into account in determining whether A holds the working interests through an entity that limits A's liability. Accordingly, the partnership does not limit A's liability with respect to the drilling or operation of wells pursuant to the working interests.

*Example (2).* B owns a 10 percent interest in X, an entity (other than a limited partnership or corporation) created under applicable State law to hold working interests in oil or gas properties. Under applicable State law, B is liable without limitation for 10 percent of X's costs and expenses with respect to X's working interests but is not liable for the remaining 90 percent of such costs and expenses. Since B's liability for the obligations of X is not limited to a determinable fixed amount (within the meaning of paragraph (e)(4)(v)(A)(3) of this section), the entity does not limit B's liability with respect to the drilling or operation of wells pursuant to the working interests.

*Example (3).* C is both a general partner and a limited partner in a partnership that owns a working interest in oil or gas property. Because C owns an interest as a general partner in each well drilled pursuant to the working interest, C's entire interest in each well drilled pursuant to the working interest is treated under paragraph (e)(4)(i) of this section as an interest in an activity that is not a passive activity (without regard to whether C materially participates in such activity).

(vi) Cross reference to special rule for income from certain oil or gas properties. A special rule relating to the treatment of income from certain interests in oil or gas properties is contained in § 1.469-2T(c)(6).

*(5) Rental of dwelling unit. [Reserved]* See § 1.469-2(d)(2)(xii) for rules relating to this paragraph.

*(6) Activity of trading personal property.* (i) In general. An activity of trading personal property for the account of owners of interests in the activity is not a passive activity

(without regard to whether such activity is a trade or business activity (within the meaning of paragraph (e)(2) of this section)).

(ii) Personal property. For purposes of this paragraph (e)(6), the term "personal property" means personal property (within the meaning of section 1092(d), without regard to paragraph (3) thereof).

(iii) Example. The following example illustrates the application of this paragraph (e)(6):

*Example.* A partnership is a trader of stocks, bonds, and other securities (within the meaning of section 1236(c)). The capital employed by the partnership in the trading activity consists of amounts contributed by the partners in exchange for their partnership interests, and funds borrowed by the partnership. The partnership derives gross income from the activity in the form of interest, dividends, and capital gains. Under these facts, the partnership is treated as conducting an activity of trading personal property for the account of its partners. Accordingly, under this paragraph (e)(6), the activity is not a passive activity.

**(f) Treatment of disallowed passive activity losses and credits.** *(1) Scope of this paragraph.* The rules in this paragraph (f)—

(i) Identify the passive activity deductions that are disallowed for any taxable year in which all or a portion of the taxpayer's passive activity loss is disallowed under paragraph (a)(1)(i) of this section;

(ii) Identify the credits from passive activities that are disallowed for any taxable year in which all or a portion of the taxpayer's passive activity credit is disallowed under paragraph (a)(1)(ii) of this section; and

(iii) Provide for the carryover of disallowed deductions and credits.

*(2) Identification of disallowed passive activity deductions.* (i) Allocation of disallowed passive activity loss among activities. (A) General rule. If all or any portion of the taxpayer's passive activity loss is disallowed for the taxable year under paragraph (a)(1)(i) of this section, a ratable portion of the loss (if any) from each passive activity of the taxpayer is disallowed. For purposes of the preceding sentence, the ratable portion of a loss from an activity is computed by multiplying the passive activity loss that is disallowed for the taxable year by the fraction obtained by dividing—

(1) The loss from the activity for the taxable year; by

(2) The sum of the losses for the taxable year from all activities having losses for such year.

(B) Loss from an activity. For purposes of this paragraph (f)(2)(i), the term "loss from an activity" means—

(1) The amount by which the passive activity deductions from the activity for the taxable year (within the meaning of § 1.469-2T(d)) exceed the passive activity gross income from the activity for the taxable year (within the meaning of § 1.469-2T(c)); reduced by

(2) Any part of such amount that is allowed under section 469(i) and the rules to be contained in § 1.469-9T (relating to the $25,000 allowance for certain rental real estate activities).

(C) Significant participation passive activities. If the taxpayer's passive activity gross income from significant participation passive activities (within the meaning of § 1.469-2T(f)(2)(ii)) for the taxable year (determined without regard to § 1.469-2T(f)(2) through (4)) exceeds the taxpayer's passive activity deductions from such activities for the taxable year, such activities shall be treated, solely for purposes of applying this paragraph (f)(2)(i) for the taxable year, as a single activity that does not have a loss for such taxable year.

(D) Examples. The following examples illustrate the application of this paragraph (f)(2)(i):

*Example (1).* An individual holds interests in three passive activities, A, B, and C. The gross income and deductions from these activities for the taxable year are as follows:

| | A | B | C | Total |
|---|---|---|---|---|
| Gross income | $ 7,000 | $4,000 | $12,000 | $23,000 |
| Deductions | (16,000) | (20,000) | (8,000) | (44,000) |
| Net income (loss) | ($ 9,000) | ($16,000) | $ 4,000 | ($21,000) |

The taxpayer's $21,000 passive activity loss for the taxable year is disallowed under paragraph (a)(1)(i) of this section. Therefore, a ratable portion of the losses from activities A and B is disallowed. The disallowed portion of each loss is determined as follows:

| | | | | | |
|---|---|---|---|---|---|
| A: | $21,000 | × | $ 9,000/$25,000 | = | $ 7,560 |
| B: | $21,000 | × | $16,000/$25,000 | = | $13,440 |
| | | | Total | | $21,000 |

*Example (2).* An individual holds interests in four passive activities, A, B, C, and D. The results of operations of these activities for the taxable year are as follows:

| | A | B | C | D | Total |
|---|---|---|---|---|---|
| Gross income | 15,000 | 5,000 | 10,000 | 10,000 | 40,000 |
| Deductions | (5,000) | (10,000) | (20,000) | (8,000) | (43,000) |
| Net income (loss) | 10,000 | (5,000) | (10,000) | 2,000 | (3,000) |

Activities A and B are significant participation passive activities (within the meaning of § 1.469-2T(f)(2)(ii)). The gross income from those activities for the taxable year ($20,000) exceeds the passive activity deductions from those activities for the taxable year ($15,000) by $5,000 and, under § 1.469-2T(f)(2), $5,000 of gross income from those activities is treated as not from a passive activity. Therefore, solely for purposes of applying this paragraph (f)(2)(i) for the taxable year, activities A and B are treated as a single activity that does not have a loss for the taxable year. Under § 1.469-2T(b), the taxpayer's passive activity loss for the taxable year is $8,000 ($43,000 of passive activity deductions minus $35,000 of passive activity gross income). The result of treating activities A and B as a single activity that does not have a loss for the taxable year is that none of the $8,000 passive activity loss is allocated under this paragraph (f)(2)(i) to activity B for the taxable year, even though the taxpayer incurred a loss in that activity for the taxable year.

(ii) Allocation within loss activities. (A) In general. If all or any portion of a taxpayer's loss from an activity is disallowed under paragraph (f)(2)(i) of this section for the taxable year, a ratable portion of each passive activity deduction (other than an excluded deduction (within the meaning of paragraph (f)(2)(ii)(B) of this section)) of the taxpayer from such activity is disallowed. For purposes of the preceding sentence, the ratable portion of a passive activity deduction of a taxpayer is the amount of the disallowed portion of the taxpayer's loss from the activity (within the meaning of paragraph (f)(2)(i)(B) of this section) for the taxable year multiplied by the fraction obtained by dividing—

(1) The amount of such deduction; by

(2) The sum of all passive activity deductions (other than excluded deductions (within the meaning of paragraph (f)(2)(ii)(B) of this section)) of the taxpayer from such activity for the taxable year.

(B) Excluded deductions. The term "excluded deduction" means any passive activity deduction of a taxpayer that is taken into account in computing the taxpayer's net income from an item of property for a taxable year in which an amount of the taxpayer's gross income from such item of property is treated as not from a passive activity under § 1.469-2T(c)(6) or § 1.469-2T(f)(5), (6), or (7).

(iii) Separately identified deductions. In identifying the deductions from an activity that are disallowed under this paragraph (f)(2), the taxpayer need not account separately for a deduction unless such deduction may, if separately taken into account, result in an income tax liability for any taxable year different from that which would result were such deduction not taken into account separately. For related rules applicable to partnerships and S corporations, see § 1.702-1(a)(8)(ii) and section 1366(a)(1)(A), respectively. Deductions that must be accounted for separately include (but are not limited to) deductions that—

(A) Arise in a rental real estate activity (within the meaning of section 469(i) and the rules to be contained § 1.469-9T) in taxable years in which the taxpayer actively participates (within the meaning of section 469(i) and the rules to be contained in § 1.469-9T) in such activity;

(B) Arise in a rental real estate activity (within the meaning of section 469(i) and the rules to be contained in § 1.469-9T) in taxable years in which the taxpayer does not actively participate (within the meaning of section 469(i) and the rules to be contained in § 1.469-9T) in such activity; or

(C) Are taken into account under section 1211 (relating to the limitation on capital losses) or section 1231 (relating to property used in a trade or business and involuntary conversions).

*(3) Identification of disallowed credits from passive activities.* (i) General rule. If all or any portion of the taxpayer's passive activity credit is disallowed for the taxable year under paragraph (a)(1)(ii) of this section, a ratable portion of each credit from each passive activity of the taxpayer is disallowed. For purposes of the preceding sentence, the ratable portion of a credit of a taxpayer is computed by multiplying the portion of the taxpayer's passive activity credit that is disallowed for the taxable year by the fraction obtained by dividing—

(A) The amount of the credit; by

(B) The sum of all of the taxpayer's credits from passive activities for the taxable year.

(ii) Coordination rule. For purposes of paragraph (f)(3)(i) of this section, the credits from a passive activity do not include any credit or portion of a credit that—

(A) Is allowed for the taxable year under section 469(i) and the rules to be contained in § 1.469-9T (relating to the $25,000 allowance for certain rental real estate activities); or

(B) Increases the basis of property during the taxable year under section 469(j)(a) and the rules to be contained in § 1.469-6T (relating to the election to increase the basis of certain property by disallowed credits).

(iii) Separately identified credits. In identifying the credits from an activity that are disallowed under this paragraph (f)(3), the taxpayer need not account separately for any credit unless such credit may, if separately taken into account, result in an income tax liability for any taxable year different from that which would result were such credit not taken into account separately. For related rules applicable to partnerships and S corporations, see § 1.702-1(a)(8)(ii) and section 1366 (a)(1)(A), respectively. Credits that must be accounted for separately include (but are not limited to)—

(A) Credits (other than the low-income housing and rehabilitation investment credits) from a rental real estate activity (within the meaning of section 469(i) and the rules to be contained in § 1.469-9T) that arise in a taxable year in which the taxpayer actively participates (within the meaning of section 469(i) and the rules to be contained in § 1.469-9T) in such activity;

(B) Credits (other than the low-income housing and rehabilitation investment credits) from a rental real estate activity (within the meaning of section 469(i) and the rules to be contained in § 1.469-9T) that arise in a taxable year in which the taxpayer does not actively participate (within the meaning of section 469(i) and the rules to be contained in § 1.469-9T) in such activity;

(C) Low-income housing and rehabilitation investment credits from a rental real estate activity (within the meaning of section 469(i) and the rules to be contained in § 1.469-9T); and

(D) Any credit that is subject to the limitations of sections 26(a), 28(d)(2), 29(b)(5), or 38(c) in a manner that differs from the manner in which any other credit is subject to such limitations.

*(4) Carryover of disallowed deductions and credits. [Reserved]* See § 1.469-1(f)(4) for rules relating to this paragraph.

**(g) Application of these rules to C corporations.** *(1) In general.* Except as otherwise provided in the rules to be contained in paragraph (k) of this section, section 469 and the regulations thereunder do not apply to any corporation that is not a personal service corporation or a closely held corporation for the taxable year. See paragraph (g)(4) and (5) of this section for special rules for computing the passive activity loss and passive activity credit, respectively, of a closely held corporation.

*(2) Definitions.* For purposes of section 469 and the regulations thereunder—

(i) The term "personal service corporation" means a C corporation that is a personal service corporation for the taxable year (within the meaning of § 1.441-3(c)); and

(ii) The term "closely held corporation" means a C corporation that meets the stock ownership requirements of section 542(a)(2) (taking into account the modifications in section 465(a)(3)) for the taxable year and is not a personal service corporation for such year.

*(3) Participation of corporations.* (i) Material participation. For purposes of section 469 and the regulations thereunder, a corporation described in paragraph (g)(2) of this section shall be treated as materially participating in an activity for a taxable year if and only if—

(A) One or more individuals, each of whom is treated under paragraph (g)(3)(iii) of this section as materially participating in such activity for the taxable year, directly or indirectly hold (in the aggregate) more than 50 percent (by value) of the outstanding stock of such corporation; or

(B) In the case of a closely held corporation (within the meaning of paragraph (g)(2)(ii) of this section), the requirements of section 465(c)(7)(C) (without regard to clause (iv) thereof and taking into account section 465(c)(7)(D)) are met with respect to such activity.

(ii) Significant participation. For purposes of § 1.469-2T(f)(2), an activity of a corporation described in paragraph (g)(2) of this section shall be treated as a significant participation passive activity for a taxable year if and only if—

(A) The corporation is not treated as materially participating in such activity for the taxable year; and

(B) One or more individuals, each of whom is treated under paragraph (g)(3)(iii) of this section as significantly participating in such activity, directly or indirectly hold (in the aggregate) more than 50 percent (by value) of the outstanding stock of such corporation.

(iii) Participation of individual. Whether an individual is treated for purposes of this paragraph (g)(3) as materially participating or significantly participating in an activity of a corporation shall be determined under the rules of § 1.469-5T, except that in applying such rules—

(A) All activities of the corporation shall be treated as activities in which the individual holds an interest in determining whether the individual participates (within the meaning of § 1.469-5T(f)) in an activity of the corporation; and

(B) The individual's participation in all activities other than activities of the corporation shall be disregarded in determining whether the individual's participation in an activity of the corporation is treated as material participation under § 1.469-5T(a)(4) (relating to material participation in significant participation activities).

*(4) Modified computation of passive activity loss in the case of closely held corporations.* (i) In general. A closely held corporation's passive activity loss for the taxable year is the amount, if any, by which the corporation's passive activity deductions for the taxable year (within the meaning of § 1.469-2T(d)) exceed the sum of—

(A) The corporation's passive activity gross income for the taxable year (within the meaning of § 1.469-2T(c)); and

(B) The corporation's net active income for the taxable year.

(ii) Net active income. For purposes of this paragraph (g)(4), a corporation's net active income for the taxable year is such corporation's taxable income for the taxable year, determined without regard to the following items for the year:

(A) Passive activity gross income;

(B) Passive activity deductions;

(C) [Reserved] See § 1.469-1(g)(4)(ii)(C) for rules relating to this paragraph.

(D) Gross income that is treated under § 1.469-2T(c)(6) (relating to gross income from certain oil or gas properties) as not from a passive activity;

(E) Gross income and deductions from any trade or business activity (within the meaning of paragraph (e)(2) of this section) that is described in paragraph (e)(6) of this section (relating to certain activities of trading personal property) but only if the corporation did not materially participate in such activity for the taxable year;

(F) Deductions described in § 1.469-2T(d)(2)(i), (ii), and (iv) (relating to certain deductions attributable to portfolio income); and

(G) Interest expense allocated under § 1.163-8T to a portfolio expenditure (within the meaning of § 1.163-8T(b)(6)).

(iii) Examples. The following examples illustrate the application of this paragraph (g)(4):

*Example (1).* (i) For 1987, X, a closely held corporation, is engaged in two activities, a trade or business activity in which X materially participates for 1987 and a rental activity. X also holds portfolio investments. For 1987, X has the following gross income and deductions:

| | |
|---|---|
| Gross Income: | |
| Rents | $ 60,000 |
| Gross income from business | 100,000 |
| Portfolio income | 35,000 |
| Total | $195,000 |
| Deductions: | |
| Rental deductions | ($100,000) |
| Business deductions | (80,000) |
| Interest expense allocable to portfolio expenditures under Sec. 1.163-8T | (10,000) |
| Deductions (other than interest expense) clearly and directly allocable to portfolio income | (5,000) |
| Total | ($195,000) |

(ii) The corporation's net active income for 1987 is $20,000, computed as follows:

| | | | |
|---|---|---|---|
| Gross income | | $ 195,000 | |
| Amounts not taken into account in computing net active income: | | | |
| Rents (see paragraph (g)(4)(ii)(A) of this section) | $ 60,000 | | |
| Portfolio income (see paragraph (g)(4)(ii)(C) of this section) | $ 35,000 | | |
| | $ 95,000 | ($ 95,000) | |
| Gross income taken into account in computing net active income | | $ 100,000 | $ 100,000 |
| Deductions | | ($ 195,000) | |
| Amounts not taken into account in computing net active income: | | | |
| Rental deductions (see paragraph (g)(4)(ii)(B) of this section) | ($ 100,000) | | |
| Interest expense allocated to portfolio expenditures (see paragraph (g)(4)(ii)(G) of this section) | ($ 10,000) | | |

| | | |
|---|---|---|
| Other deductions clearly and directly allocable to portfolio income (see paragraph (g)(4)(ii)(F) of this section) | ($ 5,000) | |
| | ($ 115,000) | $ 115,000 |
| Deductions taken into account in computing net active income | ($ 80,000) | ($ 80,000) |
| Net active income | | $ 20,000 |

(iii) Under paragraph (g)(4)(i) of this section, X's passive activity loss for 1987 is $20,000, the amount by which the passive activity deductions for the taxable year ($100,000) exceed the sum of (a) the passive activity gross income for the taxable year ($60,000) and (b) the net active income for the taxable year ($20,000). Under paragraph (f)(4) of this section, the $20,000 of deductions from X's rental activity that are disallowed for 1987 are treated as deductions from the rental activity for 1988. If computed without regard to the net active income for the taxable year, X's passive activity loss would be $40,000 ($100,000 of rental deductions minus $60,000 of rental income). Thus, the effect of the rule in paragraph (g)(4)(i) of this section is to reduce the corporation's passive activity loss for the taxable year by the amount of the corporation's net active income for such year.

(iv) Under these facts, X's taxable income for 1987 is $20,000, computed as follows:

| | | |
|---|---|---|
| Gross income | | $195,000 |
| Deductions | | |
| Total Deductions | ($195,000) | |
| Passive activity loss | $20,000 | |
| Allowable deductions | ($175,000) | ($175,000) |
| Taxable income | | $20,000 |

*Example (2).* (i) The facts are the same as in example (1), except that, in 1988, X has a loss from the trade or business activity, and a net operating loss ("NOL") of $15,000 that is carried back under section 172 (b) to 1987. Since NOL carrybacks are taken into account in computing net active income, X's net active income for 1987 must be recomputed as follows:

| | |
|---|---|
| Net active income before NOL carryback | $20,000 |
| NOL carryback | ($15,000) |
| Net active income | $5,000 |

(ii) Under these facts, X's disallowed passive activity loss for 1987 is $35,000, the amount by which the passive activity deductions for the taxable year ($100,000) exceed the sum of (a) the passive activity gross income for the taxable year ($60,000) and (b) the net active income for the taxable year ($5,000).

(iii) Under paragraph (f) (4) of this section, the $35,000 of deductions from X's rental activity that are disallowed for 1987 are treated as deductions from the rental activity for 1988. X's taxable income for 1987 is $20,000, computed as follows:

| | | |
|---|---|---|
| Gross income | | $195,000 |
| Deductions | | |
| Total deductions | ($210,000) | |
| Passive activity loss | $35,000 | |
| Allowable deductions | ($175,000) | ($175,000) |
| Taxable income | | $20,000 |

Thus, taking the NOL carryback into account in computing net active income for 1987 does not affect X's taxable income for 1987, but increases the deductions treated under paragraph (f)(4) as deductions from X's rental activity for 1988 and decreases X's NOL carryover to years other than 1987.

*(5) Allowance of passive activity credit of closely held corporations to extent of net active income tax liability.* (i) In general. Solely for purposes of determining the amount disallowed under paragraph (a)(1)(ii) of this section, a closely held corporation's passive activity credit for the taxable year shall be reduced by such corporation's net active income tax liability for such year.

(ii) Net active income tax liability. For purposes of paragraph (g)(5)(i) of this section, a corporation's net active income tax liability for a taxable year is the amount (if any) by which—

(A) The corporation's regular tax liability (within the meaning of section 26(b)) for the taxable year, determined by reducing the corporation's taxable income for such year by an amount equal to the excess (if any) of the corporation's passive activity gross income for such year over the corporation's passive activity deductions for such year; exceeds

(B) The sum of—

(1) The corporation's regular tax liability for the taxable year, determined by reducing the corporation's taxable income for such year by an amount equal to the excess (if any) of the sum of the corporation's net active income (within the meaning of paragraph (g)(4)(ii) of this section) and passive activity gross income for such year over the corporation's passive activity deductions for such year; and

(2) The corporation's credits (other than credits from passive activities) that are allowable for the taxable year (without regard to the limitations contained in sections 26(a), 28(d)(2), 29(b)(5), 38(c), and 469).

**(h) Special rules for affiliated group filing consolidated return.** *(1) [Reserved]*

*(2) [Reserved]*

*(3) Disallowance of consolidated group's passive activity loss or credit.* A consolidated group's passive activity loss or passive activity credit for the taxable year shall be disallowed to the extent provided in paragraph (a) of this section. For purposes of the preceding sentence, a consolidated group's passive activity loss and passive activity credit shall be determined by taking into account the following items of each member of such group:

(i) Passive activity gross income;

(ii) Passive activity deductions;

(iii) Net active income (in the case of a consolidated group treated as a closely held corporation under paragraph (h)(4)(ii) of this section); and

(iv) Credits from passive activities.

*(4) [Reserved]* See § 1.469-1(h)(4) for rules relating to this paragraph.

*(5) Modification of rules for identifying disallowed passive activity deductions and credits.* (i) Identification of dis-

allowed deductions. In applying paragraph (f)(2) and (4) of this section to a consolidated group for purposes of identifying the passive activity deductions of such consolidated group and of each member of such consolidated group that are disallowed for the taxable year and treated as deductions from activities for the succeeding taxable year, the following rules shall apply:

(A) A ratable portion (within the meaning of paragraph (h)(5)(ii) of this section) of the passive activity loss of the consolidated group that is disallowed for the taxable year shall be allocated to each member of the group;

(B) Paragraph (f)(2) of this section shall then be applied to each member of the group as if—

(1) Such member were a separate taxpayer; and

(2) The amount allocated to such member under paragraph (h)(5)(i)(A) of this section were the amount of such member's passive activity loss that is disallowed for the taxable year; and

(C) Paragraph (f)(4) of this section shall be applied to each member of the group as if it were a separate taxpayer.

(ii) Ratable portion of disallowed passive activity loss. For purposes of paragraph (h)(5)(i)(A) of this section, a member's ratable portion of the disallowed passive activity loss of the consolidated group is the amount of such disallowed loss multiplied by the fraction obtained by dividing—

(A) The amount of the passive activity loss of such member of the consolidated group that would be disallowed for the taxable year if the items of gross income and deduction of such member were the only items of the group for such year; by

(B) The sum of the amounts described in paragraph (h)(5)(ii)(A) of this section for all members of the group.

(iii) Identification of disallowed credits. In applying paragraph (f)(3) of this section to a consolidated group for purposes of identifying the credits from passive activities of members of such consolidated group that are disallowed for the taxable year, the consolidated group shall be treated as one taxpayer. Thus, a ratable portion of each of the group's credits from passive activities is disallowed.

*(6) [Reserved]*

*(7) Disposition of stock of a member of an affiliated group.* Any gain recognized by a member on the disposition of stock of a subsidiary (including income resulting from the recognition of an excess loss account under § 1.1502-19) shall be treated as portfolio income (within the meaning of § 1.469-2T(c)(3)(i)).

*(8) Dispositions of property used in multiple activities.* The determination of whether § 1.469-2T(c)(2)(ii) or (iii) or (d)(5)(ii) applies to a disposition (including a deemed disposition described in paragraph (h)(6)(iii)(C)(1) of this section) of property by a member of a consolidated group shall be made by treating such member as having held the property for the entire period that the group has owned such property and as having used the property in all of the activities in which the group has used such property.

**(i) [Reserved]**

**(j) Spouses filing joint return.** *(1) In general.* Except as otherwise provided in the regulations under section 469, spouses filing a joint return for a taxable year shall be treated for such year as one taxpayer for purposes of section 469 and the regulations thereunder. Thus, for example, spouses filing a joint return are treated as one taxpayer for purposes of—

(i) Section 1.469-2T (relating generally to the computation of such taxpayer's passive activity loss); and

(ii) Paragraph (f) of this section (relating to the allocation of such taxpayer's disallowed passive activity loss and passive activity credit among activities and the identification of disallowed passive activity deductions and credits from passive activities).

*(2) Exceptions to treatment as one taxpayer.* (i) Identification of disallowed deductions and credits. For purposes of paragraph (f)(2)(iii) and (3)(iii) of this section, spouses filing a joint return for the taxable year must account separately for the deductions and credits attributable to the interests of each spouse in any activity.

(ii) Treatment of deductions disallowed under sections 704(d), 1366(d), and 465. Notwithstanding any other provision of this section or § 1.469-2T, this paragraph (j) shall not affect the application of section 704(d), section 1366 (d), or section 465 to taxpayers filing a joint return for the taxable year.

(iii) Treatment of losses from working interests. Paragraph (e)(4) of this section (relating to losses and credits from certain interests in oil and gas wells) shall be applied by treating a husband and wife (whether or not filing a joint return) as separate taxpayers.

*(3) Joint return no longer filed.* If an individual—

(A) Does not file a joint return for the taxable year; and

(B) Filed a joint return for the immediately preceding taxable year;

then the passive activity deductions and credits allocable to such individual's activities for the taxable year under paragraph (f)(4) of this section shall be determined by taking into account the items of deduction and credit attributable to such individual's interests in passive activities for the immediately preceding taxable year. See paragraph (j)(2)(i) of this section.

*(4) Participation of spouses.* Rules treating an individual's participation in an activity as participation of such individual's spouse in such activity (without regard to whether the spouses file a joint return) are contained in § 1.469-5T(f)(3).

**(k) Former passive activities and changes in status of corporations. [Reserved]**

---

T.D. 8175, 2/19/88, amend T.D. 8253, 5/11/89, T.D. 8319, 11/19/90, T.D. 8417, 5/11/92, T.D. 8560, 8/12/94, T.D. 8597, 7/12/95, T.D. 8996, 5/16/2002.

---

PAR. 2. In the list below, for each section indicated in the left column, remove the old language in the middle column and add the new language in the right column.

| Affected Section | Remove | Add |
|---|---|---|
| 1.46-1(p)(2)(iv) | paragraph (b)(1) of § 1.441-2 | § 1.441-2 |
| 1.48-3(d)(1)(iii) | paragraph (b)(1) of § 1.441-2 | § 1.441-2 |
| 1.280H-1T(a), last sentence | § 1.441-4T(d) | § 1.441-3(c) |
| 1.443-1(b)(1)(ii) | and paragraph (c)(5) of § 1.441-2 | and § 1.441-1(b)(2)(ii). |
| 1.444-1T(a)(1), first sentence | § 1.444-4T(d) | § 1.441-3(c) |
| 1.444-2T(a), last sentence | § 1.441-4T(d) | § 1.441-3(c) |
| 1.448-1(h)(2)(ii)(B)(1) | § 1.441-2T(b)(1) | § 1.441-2(c) |
| 1.469-1(h)(4)(ii)(D) | § 1.441-4T(f) | § 1.441-3(e) |
| 1.469-1T(g)(2)(i) | § 1.441-4T(d) | § 1.441-2 |
| 1.1561-1(c)(2) | See paragraph (b)(1) of § 1.441-2 | See § 1.441-2 |
| 1.6654-2(a), concluding text | paragraph (b) of § 1.441-2 | § 1.441-2(c) |
| 1.6655-2(a)(4), first sentence | paragraph (b) of § 1.441-2 | § 1.441-1(b) |

**Proposed § 1.469-1T** *[For Preamble, see ¶ 152,177]*

• ***Caution:*** This Notice of Proposed Rulemaking was partially finalized by T.D. 8996, issued on 5/16/2002. Proposed regulation §§ 1.46-1, 1.48-3, 1.280H-1T, 1.443-1, 1.444-1T, 1.444-2T, 1.448-1, 1.469-1, 1.469-1T, 1.898-4, 1.1561-1, 1.6654-2, 1.6655-2 and 301.7701(b)-6 remains in effect.

**§ 1.469-2 Passive activity loss.**

***Caution:*** The Treasury has not yet amended Reg § 1.469-2 to reflect changes made by P.L. 104-188, P.L. 103-66.

**(a)** through (c)(2)(ii) (Reserved)

**(c)** *(2)* (iii) Disposition of substantially appreciated property formerly used in nonpassive activity. (A) In general. If an interest in property used in an activity is substantially appreciated at the time of its disposition, any gain from the disposition shall be treated as not from a passive activity unless the interest in property was used in a passive activity for either—

(1) 20 percent of the period during which the taxpayer held the interest in property; or

(2) The entire 24-month period ending on the date of the disposition.

(B) Date of disposition. For purposes of this paragraph (c)(2)(iii), a disposition of an interest in property is deemed to occur on the date that the interest in property becomes subject to an oral or written agreement that either requires the owner or gives the owner an option to transfer the interest in property for consideration that is fixed or otherwise determinable on that date.

(C) Substantially appreciated property. For purposes of this paragraph (c)(2)(iii), an interest in property is substantially appreciated if the fair market value of the interest in property exceeds 120 percent of the adjusted basis of the interest.

(D) Investment property. For purposes of this paragraph (c)(2)(iii), an interest in property is treated as an interest in property used in an activity other than a passive activity and as an interest in property held for investment for any period during which the interest is held through a C corporation or similar entity. An entity is similar to a C corporation for this purpose if the owners of interests in the entity derive only portfolio income (within the meaning of § 1.469-2T) from the interests.

(E) Coordination with § 1.469-2T(c)(2)(ii). If § 1.469-2T(c)(2)(ii) applies to the disposition of an interest in property, this paragraph (6)(2)(iii) applies only to that portion of the gain from the disposition of the interest in property that is characterized as gain from a passive activity after the application of § 1.469-2T(c)(2)(ii).

(F) Coordination with section 163(d). Gain that is treated as not from a passive activity under this paragraph (c)(2)(iii) is treated as income described in section 469(e)(1)(A) and § 1.469-2T(c)(3)(i) if and only if the gain is from the disposition of an interest in property that was held for investment for more than 50 percent of the period during which the taxpayer held that interest in property in activities other than passive activities.

(G) Examples. The following examples illustrate the application of this paragraph (c)(2)(iii):

*Example (1).* A acquires a building on January 1, 1993, and uses the building in a trade or business activity in which A materially participates until March 31, 2004. On April 1, 2004, A leases the building to B. On Decemner 31, 2005, A sells the building. At the time of the sale, A's interest in the building is substantially appreciated (within the meaning of paragraph (c)(2)(iii)(C) of this section). Assuming A's lease of the building to B constitutes a rental activity (within the meaning of § 1.469-1T(e)(3)), the building is used in a passive activity for 21 months (April 1, 2004, through December 31, 2005). Thus, the building was not used in a passive activity for the entire 24-month period ending on the date of the sale. In addition, the 21-month period during which the building was used in a passive activity is less than 20 percent of A's holding period for the building (13 years). Therefore, the gain from the sale is treated under this paragraph (c)(2)(iii) as not from a passive activity.

*Example (2).* (i) A, an individual, is a stockholder of corporation X. X is a C corporation until December 31, 1993, and is an S corporation thereafter. X acquires a building on January 1, 1993, and sells the building on March 1, 1994. At the time of the sale, A's interest in the building held through X is substantially appreciated (within the meaning of paragraph (c)(2)(iii)(C) of this section). The building is leased to various tenants at all times during the period in which it is held by X. Assume that the lease of the building would constitute a rental activity (within the meaning of § 1.469-1T(e)(3)) with respect to a person that holds the building directly or through an S corporation.

(ii) Paragraph (c)(2)(iii)(D) of this section provides that an interest in property is treated for purposes of this paragraph (c)(2)(iii) as used in an activity other than a passive activity and as held for investment for any period during which the interest is held through a C corporation. Thus, for purposes of determining the character of A's gain from the sale of the building, A's interest in the building is treated as an interest in property held for investment for the period from January 1, 1993, to December 31, 1993, and as an interest in property used in a passive activity for the period from January 1, 1994, to February 28, 1994.

(iii) A's interest in the building was not used in a passive activity for the entire 24-month period ending on the date of the sale. In addition, the 2- month period during which A's interest in the building was used in a passive activity is less than 20 percent of the period during which A held an interest in the building (14 months). Therefore, the gain from the sale is treated under this paragraph (c)(2)(iii) as not from a passive activity.

(iv) Under paragraph (c)(2)(iii)(F) of this section, gain that is treated as nonpassive under this paragraph (c)(2)(iii) is treated as portfolio income (within the meaning of § 1.469-2T(c)(3)(i)) if the gain is from the disposition of an interest in property that was held for investment for more than 50 percent of the period during which the taxpayer held the interest in activities other than passive activities. In this case, A's interest in the building was treated as held for investment for the entire period during which it was used in activities other than passive activities (i.e., the 12-month period from January 1, 1993, to December 31, 1993). Accordingly, A's gain from the sale is treated under this paragraph (c)(2)(iii) as portfolio income.

(iv) Taxable acquisitions. If a taxpayer acquires an interest in property in a transaction other than a nonrecognition transaction (within the meaning of section 7701(a)(45)), the ownership and use of the interest in property before the transaction is not taken into account for purposes of applying this paragraph (c)(2) to any subsequent disposition of the interest in property by the taxpayer.

(v) Property held for sale to customers. (A) Sale incidental to another activity. (1) Applicability. (i) In general. This paragraph (c)(2)(v)(A) applies to the disposition of a taxpayer's interest in property if and only if—

(A) At the time of the disposition, the taxpayer holds the interest in property in an activity that, for purposes of section 1221(1), involves holding the property or similar property primarily for sale to customers in the ordinary course of a trade or business (a dealing activity);

(B) One or more other activities of the taxpayer do not involve holding similar property for sale to customers in the ordinary course of a trade or business (nondealing activities) and the interest in property was used in the nondealing activity or activities for more than 80 percent of the period during which the taxpayer held the interest in property; and

(C) The interest in property was not acquired and held by the taxpayer for the principal purpose of selling the interest to customers in the ordinary course of a trade or business.

(ii) Principal purpose. For purposes of this paragraph (c)(2)(v)(A), a taxpayer is rebuttably presumed to have acquired and held an interest in property for the principal purpose of selling the interest to customers in the ordinary course of a trade or business if—

(A) The period during which the interest in property was used in nondealing activities of the taxpayer does not exceed the lesser of 24 months or 20 percent of the recovery period (within the meaning of section 168) applicable to the property; or

(B) The interest in property was simultaneously offered for sale to customers and used in a nondealing activity of the taxpayer for more than 25 percent of the period during which the interest in property was used in nondealing activities of the taxpayer.

For purposes of the preceding sentence, an interest in property is not considered to be offered for sale to customers solely because a lessee of the property has been granted an option to purchase the property.

(2) Dealing activity not taken into account. If paragraph (c)(2)(v)(A) applies to the disposition of a taxpayer's interest in property, holding the interest in the dealing activity is treated, for purposes of § 1.469- 2T(c)(2), as the use of the interest in the last nondealing activity of the taxpayer in which the interest in property was used prior to its disposition.

(B) Use in a nondealing activity incidental to sale. If paragraph (c)(2)(v)(A) of this section does not apply to the disposition of a taxpayer's interest in property that is held in a dealing activity of the taxpayer at the time of disposition, the use of the interest in property in a nondealing activity of the taxpayer for any period during which the interest in property is also offered for sale to customers is treated, for purposes of § 1.469- 2T(c)(2), as the use of the interest in property in the dealing activity of the taxpayer.

(C) Examples. The following examples illustrate the application of this paragraph (c)(2)(v):

*Example (1).* (i) The taxpayer acquires a residential apartment building on January 1, 1993, and uses the building in a rental activity. In January 1996, the taxpayer converts the apartments into condominium units. After the conversion, the taxpayer holds the condominium units for sale to customers in the ordinary course of a trade or business of dealing in condominium units. (Assume that these are dealing operations treated as separate activities under § 1.469-4, and that the taxpayer materially participates in the activity.) In addition, the taxpayer continues to use the units in the rental activity until they are sold. The units are first held for sale on January 1, 1996, and the last unit is sold on December 31, 1996.

(ii) This paragraph (c)(2)(v) provides that holding an interest in property in a dealing activity (the marketing of the property) is treated for purposes of § 1.469-2t(c)(2) as the use of the interest in a nondealing activity if the marketing of the property is incidental to the nondealing use. Under paragraph (c)(2)(v)(A)(2) of this section, the interests in property are treated as used in the last nondealing activity in which they were used prior to their disposition. In addition, paragraph (c)(2)(v)(A)(1) of this section provides rules for determining whether the marketing of the property is incidental to the use of an interest in property in a nondealing activity. Under these rules, the marketing of the property is treated as incidental to the use in a nondealing activity if the interest in property was used in nondealing activities for more than 80 percent of the taxpayer's holding period in the property (the holding period requirement) and the taxpayer did not acquire and hold the interest in property for the principal purpose of selling it to customers in the ordinary course of a trade or business (a dealing purpose).

(iii) In this case, the apartments were used in a rental activity for the entire period during which they were held by the taxpayer. Thus, the apartments were used in a nondealing activity for more than 80 percent of the taxpayer's holding period in the property, and the marketing of the property satisfies the holding period requirement.

(iv) Paragraph (c)(2)(v)(A)(1)(ii) of this section provides that a taxpayer is rebuttably presumed to have a dealing purpose unless the interest in property was used in nondealing activities for more than 24 months or 20 percent of the property's recovery period (whichever is less). The same presumption applies if the interest in property was offered for sale to customers during more than 25 percent of the period in which the interest was held in nondealing activities. In this case, the taxpayer used each apartment in a nondealing activity (the rental activity) for a period of 36 to 48 months (i.e., from January 1, 1993, to the date of sale in the period from January through December 1996). Thus, the apartments were used in nondealing activities for more than 24 months, and the first of the rebuttable presumptions described above does not apply. In addition, the apartments were offered for sale to customers for up to 12 months (depending on the month in which the apartment was sold) during the period in which the apartments were used in a nondealing activity. The percentage obtained by dividing the period during which an apartment was held for sale to customers by the period during which the apartment was used in nondealing activities ranges from zero in the case of apartments sold on January 1, 1996, to 25 percent (i.e., 12 months/48 months) in the case of apartments sold on December 31, 1996. Thus, no apartment was offered for sale to customers during more than 25 percent of the period in which it was used in nondealing activities, and the second rebuttable presumption does not apply.

(v) Because neither of the rebuttable presumptions in paragraph (c)(2)(v)(A)(1)((ii) of this section applies in this case, the taxpayer will not be treated as having a dealing purpose unless other facts and circumstances establish that the taxpayer acquired and held the apartments for the principal purpose of selling the apartments to customers in the ordinary course of a trade or business. Assume that none of the facts and circumstances suggest that the taxpayer had such a purpose. If that is the case, the taxpayer does not have a dealing purpose.

(vi) The marketing of the property satisfies the holding period requirement, and the taxpayer does not have a dealing purpose. Thus, holding the apartments in the taxpayer's dealing activity is treated for purposes of this paragraph (c)(2) as the use of the apartments in a nondealing activity. In this case, the rental activity is the only nondealing activity in which the apartments were used prior to their disposition. Thus, the apartments are treated under paragraph (c)(2)(v)(A)(2) of this section as interests in property that were used only in the rental activity for the entire period during which the taxpayer held the interests. Accordingly, the rules in § 1.469-2T(c)(2)(ii) and paragraph (c)(2)(iii) of this section do not apply, and all gain from the sale of the apartments is treated as passive activity gross income.

*Example (2).* (i) The taxpayer acquires a residential apartment building on January 1, 1993, and uses the building in a rental activity. The taxpayer converts the apartments into condominium units on July 1, 1993. After the conversion, the taxpayer holds the condominium units for sale to customers in the ordinary course of a trade or business of dealing in condominium units. (Assume that these are dealing operations treated as separate activities under § 1.469-4, and that the taxpayer materially participates in the activities.) In addition, the taxpayer continues to use the units in the rental activity until they are sold. The first unit is sold on January 1, 1994, and the last unit is sold on December 31, 1996.

(ii) In this case, all of the apartments were simultaneously offered for sale to customers and used in a nondealing activity of the taxpayer for more than 25 percent of the period during which the apartments were used in nondealing activities. Thus, the taxpayer is rebuttably presumed to have acquired the apartments (including apartments that are used in the rental activity for at least 24 months) for the principal purpose of selling them to customers in the ordinary course of a trade or business. Assume that the facts and circumstances do not rebut this presumption. If that is the case, the taxpayer has a dealing purpose, and paragraph (c)(2)(v)(A) of this section does not apply to the disposition of the apartments.

(iii) Paragraph (c)(2)(v)(B) of this section provides that if paragraph (c)(2)(v)(A) of this section does not apply to the disposition of a taxpayer's interest in property that is held in a dealing activity of the taxpayer at the time of the disposition, the use of the interest in property in any nondealing activity of the taxpayer for any period during which the interest is also offered for sale to customers is treated as incidental to the use of the interest in the dealing activity. Accordingly, for purposes of applying the rules of § 1.469-2T(c)(2) to the disposition of the apartments, the rental of the apartments after July 1, 1993, is treated as the use of the apartments in the taxpayer's dealing activity.

*Example (3).* (i) The taxpayer acquires a residential apartment building on January 1, 1993, and uses the building in a rental activity. In January 1996, the taxpayer converts the apartments into condominium units. After the conversion, the taxpayer holds the condominium units for sale to customers in the ordinary course of a trade or business of dealing in condominium units. (Assume that these are dealing operations treated as separate activities under § 1.469-4, and that the taxpayer materially participates in the activities.) In addition, the taxpayer continues to use the units in the rental activity until they are sold. The units are first held for sale on January 1, 1996, and the last unit is sold in 1997.

(ii) The treatment of apartments sold in 1996 is the same as in Example 1. The apartments sold in 1997, however, were simultaneously offered for sale to customers and used in a nondealing activity for more than 25 percent of the period during which the apartments were used in nondealing activities. (For example, an apartment that is sold on January 31, 1997, has been offered for sale for 13 months or 26.1 percent of the 49-month period during which it was used in nondealing activities.) Thus, the taxpayer is rebuttably presumed to have acquired the apartments sold in 1997 for the principal purpose of selling them to customers in the ordinary course of a trade of business. Assume that the facts and circumstances do not rebut this presumption. In that case, the marketing of the apartments sold in 1997 does not satisfy the principal purpose requirement, and paragraph (c)(2)(v)(A) of this section does not apply to the disposition of those apartments. Accordingly, for purposes of applying the rules of § 1.469-2T(c)(2) to the disposition of the apartments sold in 1977, the rental of the apartments after January 1, 1996, is treated, under paragraph (c)(2)(v)(B) of this section, as the use of the apartments in the taxpayer's dealing activity.

*(3)* through (c)(5) (Reserved)

*(6) Gross income from certain oil or gas properties.* (i) In general. Notwithstanding any other provision of the regulations under section 469, passive activity gross income for any taxable year does not include an amount of the taxpayer's gross passive income for the year from a property described in this paragraph (c)(6)(i) equal to the taxpayer's net passive income from the property for the year. Property is described in this paragraph (c)(6)(i) if the property is—

(A) An oil or gas property that includes an oil or gas well if, for any prior taxable year beginning after December 31, 1996, any of the taxpayer's loss from the well was treated, solely by reason of § 1.469-1T(e)(4) (relating to a special rule for losses from oil and gas working interests), and not by reason of the taxpayer's material participation in the activity, as a loss that is not from a passive activity; or

(B) Any property the basis of which is determined in whole or in part by reference to the basis of property described in paragraph (c)(6)(i)(A) of this section.

(ii) Gross and net passive income from the property. For purposes of this paragraph (c)(6)—

(A) The taxpayer's gross passive income for any taxable year from any property described in paragraph (c)(6)(i) of this section is any passive activity gross income for the year (determined without regard to this paragraph (c)(6) and § 1.469-2T(f)) from the property;

(B) The taxpayer's net passive income for any taxable year from any property described in paragraph (c)(6)(i) of this section is the excess, if any, of—

(1) The taxpayer's gross passive income for the taxable year from the property; over

(2) Any passive activity deductions for the taxable year (including any deduction treated as a deduction for the year under § 1.469-1T(f)(4)) that are reasonably allocable to the income; and

(C) if any oil or gas well or other item of property (the item) is included in two or more properties described in paragraph (c)(6)(i) of this section (the properties), the taxpayer must allocate the passive activity gross income (determined without regard to this paragraph (c)(6) and § 1.469-2T(f) from the item and the passive activity deductions reasonably allocable to the item among the properties.

(iii) Property. For purposes of paragraph (c)(6)(i)(A) of this section, the term "property" does not have the meaning given the term by section 614(a) or the regulations thereunder, and an oil or gas property that includes an oil or gas well is—

(A) The well; and

(B) Any other item of property (including any oil or gas well) the value of which is directly enhanced by any drilling, logging, seismic testing, or other activities the costs of which were taken into account in determining the amount of the taxpayer's income or loss from the well.

(iv) Examples. The following examples illustrate the application of this paragraph (c)(6):

*Example (1).* A is a general partner in partnership P and a limited partner in partnership R. P and R own oil and gas working interests in two separate tracts of land acquired from two separate landowners. In 1993, P drills a well on its tract, and A's distributive share of P's losses from drilling the well are treated under § 1.469-1T(e)(4) as not from a passive activity. In the course of selecting the drilling site and drilling the well, P develops information indicating that the reservior in which the well was drilled underlies R's tract as well as P's. Under these facts, P's and R's tracts are treated as one property for purposes of this paragraph (c)(6), even if A's interests in the mineral deposits in the tracts are treated as separate properties under section 614(a). Accordingly, in 1994 and subsequent years, A's distributive share of both P's and R's income and expenses from their respective tracts is taken into account in computing A's net passive income from the property for purposes of this paragraph (c)(6).

*Example (2).* B is a general partner in partnership S. S owns an oil and gas working interest in a single tract of land. In 1993, S drills a well, and B's distributive share of S's losses from drilling the well is treated under § 1.469-1T(e)(4) as not from a passive activity. In the course of drilling the well, S discovers two oil-bearing formations, one underlying the other. On December 1, 1993, S completes the well in the underlying formation. On January 1, 1994, B converts B's entire general partnership interest in S into a limited partnership interest. In 1994, S completes in, and commences production from, the shallow formation. Under these facts, the two mineral deposits in S's tract are treated as one property for purposes of this paragraph (c)(6), even if they are treated as separate properties under section 614(a). Accordingly, B's distributive share of S's income and expenses from both the underlying formation and from recompletion in and production from the shallow formation is taken into account in computing B's net passive income from the property for purposes of this paragraph (c)(6).

*Example (3).* through (c)(7)(iii) (Reserved)

*(7)* (iv) Gross income of an individual from a covenant by such individual not to compete;

(v) Gross income that is treated as not from a passive activity under any provision of the regulations under section 469, including but not limited to § 1.469-1T(h)(6) (relating to income from intercompany transactions of members of an affiliated group of corporations filing a consolidated return) and § 1.469-2T(f) and paragraph (f) of this section (relating to recharacterized passive income);

(vi) Gross income attributable to the reimbursement of a loss from fire, storm, shipwreck, or other casualty, or from theft (as such terms are used in section 165(c)(3)) if—

(A) The reimbursement is included in gross income under § 1.165- 1(d)(2)(iii) (relating to reimbursements of losses that the taxpayer deducted in a prior taxable year); and

(B) The deduction for the loss was not a passive activity deduction; and

(vii) Gross income or gain allocable to business or rental use of a dwelling unit for any taxable year in which section 280A(c)(5) applies to such business or rental use.

**(d)** *(1)* through (d)(2)(viii) (Reserved).

*(2)* (ix) An item of loss or deduction that is carried to the taxable year under section 172(a), section 613A(d), section 1212(a)(1) (in the case of corporations), or section 1212(b) (in the case of taxpayers other than corporations);

(x) An item of loss or deduction that would have been allowed for a taxable year beginning before January 1, 1987, but for section 704(d), 1366, or 465;

(xi) A deduction for a loss from fire, storm, shipwreck, or other casualty, or from theft (as such terms are used in section 165(c)(3)) if losses that are similar in cause and severity do not recur regularly in the conduct of the activity; and

(xii) A deduction or loss allocable to business or rental use of a dwelling unit for any taxable year in which section 280(c)(5) applies to such business or rental use.

*(3)* through (d)(5)(ii) (Reserved)

*(5)* (iii) Other applicable rules. (A) Applicability of rules in § 1.469- 2T(c)(2). For purposes of this paragraph (d)(5), a taxpayer's interests in property used in an activity and the amounts allocated to the interests shall be determined under § 1.469-2T(2)(i)(C). In addition, the rules contained in paragraph (c)(2) (iv) and (v) of this section apply in determining for purposes of this paragraph (d)(5) the activity (or activities) in which an interest in property is used at the time of its disposition and during the 12- month period ending on the date of its disposition.

(B) through (d)(6)(v)(D) (Reserved)

*(6)* (v) (E) Are taken into account under section 613A(d) (relating to limitations on certain depletion deductions), section 1211 (relating to the limitation on capital losses), or section 1231 (relating to property used in a trade or business and involuntary conversions); or

(F) through (d)(7) (Reserved)

*(8) Taxable year in which item arises.* For purposes of § 1.469-2T(d), an item of deduction arises in the taxable year in which the item would be allowable as a deduction under the taxpayer's method of accounting if taxable income for all taxable years were determined without regard to sections 469, 613A(d) and 1211.

**(e)** *(1)* through (e)(2)(i) (Reserved)

*(2)* (ii) Section 707(c). Except as provided in paragraph (e)(2)(iii)(B) of this section, any payment to a partner for services or the use of capital that is described in section 707(c), including any payment described in section 736(a)(2) (relating to guaranteed payments made in liquidation of the interest of a retiring or deceased partner), is characterized as a payment for services or as the payment of interest, respectively, and not as a distributive share of partnership income.

(iii) Payments in liquidation of a partner's interest in partnership property. (A) In general. If any gain or loss is taken into account by a retiring partner (or any other person that owns (directly or indirectly) an interest in the partner if the partner is a passthrough entity) or a deceased partner's successor in interest as a result of a payment to which section 736(b) (relating to payments made in exchange for a retired or deceased partner's interest in partnership property) applies, the gain or loss is treated as passive activity gross income or a passive activity deduction only to the extent that the gain or loss would have been passive activity gross income or a passive activity deduction of the retiring or deceased partner (or the other person) if it had been recognized at the time the liquidation of the partner's interest commenced.

(B) Payments in liquidation of a partner's interest in unrealized receivables and goodwill under section 736(a). (1) If a payment is made in liquidation of a retiring or deceased partner's interest, the payment is described in section 736(a), and any income—

(i) Is taken into account by the retiring partner (or any other person that owns (directly or indirectly) an interest in the partner if the partner is a passthrough entity) or the deceased partner's successor in interest as a result of the payment; and

(ii) s attributable to the portion (if any) of the payment that is allocable to the unrealized receivables (within the meaning of section 751(c)) and goodwill of the partnership; the percentage of the income that is treated as passive activity gross income shall not exceed the percentage of passive activity gross income that would be included in the gross income that the retiring or deceased partner (or the other person) would have recognized if the unrealized receivables and goodwill had been sold at the time that the liquidation of the partner's interest commenced.

(2) For purposes of this paragarph (e)(2)(iii)(B), the portion (if any) of a payment under section 736(a) that is allocable to unrealized receivables and goodwill of a partnership shall be determined in accordance with the principles employed under § 1.736-1(b) for determining the portion of a payment made under section 736 that is treated as a distribution under section 736(b).

*(3)* (i) through (iii)(A) (Reserved)

(iii)

(B) An amount of gain that would have been treated as gain that is not from a passive activity under paragraph (c)(2)(iii) of this section (relating to substantially appreciated property formerly used in a nonpassive activity), paragraph (c)(6) of this section (relating to certain oil or gas properties), § 1.469-2T(f)(5) (relating to certain property rented incidental to development), paragraph (f)(6) of this section (relating to property rented to a nonpassive activity), or § 1.469-2T(f)(7) (relating to certain interests in a passthrough entity engaged in the trade or business of licensing intangible property) would have been allocated to the holder (or such other person) with respect to the interest if all of the property used in passive activity had been sold immediately prior to the disposition for its fair market value on the applicable valuation date (within the meaning of § 1.469-2T(e)(3)(ii)(D)(1)); and

(C) through (f)(4) (Reserved)

**(f)** *(5) Net income from certain property rented incidental to development activity.* (i) In general. An amount of the taxpayer's gross rental activity income for the taxable year from an item of property equal to the net rental activity income for the year from the item of property shall be treated as not from a passive activity if—

(A) Any gain from the sale, exchange, or other disposition of the item of property is included in the taxpayer's income for the taxable year;

(B) The taxpayer's use of the item of property in an activity involving the rental of the property commenced less than 12 months before the date of the disposition (within the meaning of paragraph (c)(2)(iii)(B) of this section) of such property; and

(C) The taxpayer materially participated (within the meaning of § 1.469-5T) or significantly participated (within the meaning of § 1.469- 5T(c)(2)) for any taxable year in an activity that involved for such year the performance of services for the purpose of enhancing the value of such item of property (or any other item of property if the basis of the item of property that is sold, exchanged, or otherwise disposed of is determined in whole or in part by reference to the basis of such other item of property).

(ii) Commencement of use. (A) In general. For purposes of paragraph (f)(5)(i)(B) of this section, a taxpayer's use of an item of property in an activity involving the rental of the property commences on the first date on which—

(1) The taxpayer owns an interest in the property;

(2) Substantially all of the property is rented (or is held out for rent and is in a state of readiness for rental); and

(3) No significant value-enhancing services (within the meaning of paragraph (f)(5)(ii)(B) of this section) remain to be performed.

(B) Value-enhancing services. For purposes of this paragraph (f)(5)(ii), the term value-enhancing services means the services described in paragraphs (f)(5) (i)(C) and (iii) of this section, except that the term does not include lease-up. Thus, in cases in which this paragraph (f)(5) applies solely because substantial lease-up remains to be performed (see paragraph (f)(5)(iii)(C) of this section), the twelve month period described in paragraph (f)(5)(i)(B) of this section will begin when the taxpayer acquires an interest in the property if substantially all of the property is held out for rent and is in a state of readiness for rental on that date.

(iii) Services performed for the purpose of enhancing the value of property. For purposes of paragraph (f)(5)(i)(C) of this section, services that are treated as performed for the purpose of enhancing the value of an item of property include but are not limited to—

(A) Construction;

(B) Renovation; and

(C) Lease-up (unless more than 50 percent of the property is leased on the date that the taxpayer acquires an interest in the property).

(iv) Examples. The following examples illustrate the application of this paragraph (f)(5):

*Example (1).* (i) A, a calendar year individual, is a partner in P, a calendar year partnership, which develops real estate. In 1993, P acquires an interest in undeveloped land and arranges for the financing and construction of an office building on the land. Construction is completed in February *58788 1995, and substantially all of the building is either rented or held out for rent and in a state of readiness for rental beginning on March 1, 1995. Twenty percent of the building is leased as of March 1, 1995.

(ii) P rents the building (or holds it out for rent) for the remainder of 1995 and all of 1996, and sells the building on February 1, 1997, pursuant to a contract entered into on January 15, 1996. P did not hold the building (or any other buildings) for sale to customers in the ordinary course of P's trade or business (see paragraph (c)(2)(v) of this section). A's distributive share of P's taxable losses from the rental of the building is $50,000 for 1995 and $30,000 for 1996. All of A's losses from the rental of the building are disallowed under 1.469-1(a)(1)(i) (relating to the disallowance of the passive activity loss for the taxable year). A's distributive share of P's gain from the sale of the building is $150,000. A has no other gross income or deductions from the activity of renting the building.

(iii) The real estate development activity that A holds through P in 1993, 1994, and 1995 involves the performance of services (e.g., construction) for the purpose of enhancing the value of the building. Accordingly, an amount equal to A's net rental activity income from the building may be treated as gross income that is not from a passive activity if A's use of the building in an activity involving the rental of the building commenced less that 12 months before the date of the disposition of the building. In this case, the date of the disposition of the building is January 15, 1996, the date of the binding contract for its sale.

(iv) (A) A taxpayer's use of an item of property in an activity involving the rental of the property commences on the first date on which— (1) The taxpayer owns an interest in the item of property;

(2) Substantially all of the property is rented (or is held out for rent and is in a state of readiness for rental); and

(3) No significant value-enhancing services (within the meaning of paragraph (f)(5)(ii)(B) of this section) remain to be performed.

(B) In this case, A's use of the building in an activity involving the rental of the building commenced on March 1, 1995, less than 12 months before January 15, 1996, the date of disposition. Accordingly, if A materially (or significantly) participated in the real estate development activity in 1993, 1994, or 1995 (without regard to whether A materially participated in the activity in more than one of those years), an amount of A's gross rental activity income from the building for 1997 equal to A's net rental activity income from the building for 1997 is treated under this paragraph (f)(5) as gross income that is not from a passive activity. Under paragraph (f)(9)(iv) of this section, A's net rental activity income from the building for 1997 is $70,000 ($150,000 distributive share of gain from the disposition of the building minus $80,000 of reasonably allocable passive activity deductions).

*Example (2).* (i) X, a calendar year taxpayer subject to section 469, acquires a building on February 1, 1994, when the building is 25 percent leased. During 1994, X rents the building (or holds it out for rent) and materially participates in an activity that involves the lease-up of the building. X's activities do not otherwise involve the performance of construction or other services for the purpose of enhancing the value of the building, and X does not hold the building (or any other building) for sale to customers in the ordinary course of X's trade or business. X sells the building on December 1, 1994.

(ii) (A) Under paragraph (f)(5)(iii)(C) of this section, lease-up is considered a service performed for the purpose of enhancing the value of property unless more than 50 percent of the property is leased on the date the taxpayer acquires an interest in the property. Under paragraph (f)(5)(ii)(B) of this section, however, lease-up is not considered a value-enhancing service for purposes of determining when the taxpayer commences using an item of property in an activity involving the rental of the property. Accordingly, X's acquisition of the building constitutes a commencement of X's use of the building in a rental activity, because February 1, 1994, is the first date on which—

(1) The taxpayer owns an interest in the item of property;

(2) Substantially all of the property is held out for rent; and

(3) No significant value-enhancing services (within the meaning of paragraph (f)(5)(ii)(B) of this section) remain to be performed.

(B) In this case, X disposes of the property within 12 months of the date X commenced using the building in a rental activity. Accordingly, an amount of X's gross rental activity income for 1994 equal to X's net rental activity income from the building for 1994 is treated under this paragraph (f)(5) as gain that is not from a passive activity.

*Example (2).* The facts are the same as in Example 2, except that at the time X acquires the building it is 60 percent leased. Under paragraph (f)(5)(iii)(C) of this section, lease-up is not considered a service performed for the purpose of enhancing the value of property if more than 50 percent of the property is leased on the date the taxpayer acquires an interest in the property. Therefore, additional lease-up performed by X is not taken into account under this paragraph (f)(5). Since X's activities do not otherwise involve the performance of services for the purpose of enhancing the value of the building, none of X's gross rental activity income from the building will be treated as income that is not from a passive activity under this paragraph (f)(5).

*(6) Property rented to a nonpassive activity.* An amount of the taxpayer's gross rental activity income for the taxable year from an item of property equal to the net rental activity income for the year from that item of property is treated as not from a passive activity if the property—

(i) Is rented for use in a trade or business activity (within the meaning of paragraph (e)(2) of this section) in which the taxpayer materially participates (within the meaning of § 1.469-5T) for the taxable year; and

(ii) Is not described in § 1.469-2T(f)(5).

*(7)* through (f)(9)(ii) (Reserved)

*(9)* (iii) The gross rental activity income for a taxable year from an item of property is any passive activity gross income (determined without regard to § 1.469-2T(f)(2) through (f)(6)) that—

(A) Is income for the year from the rental or disposition of such item of property; and

(B) In the case of income from the disposition of such item of property, is income from an activity that involved the rental of such item of property during the 12-month period ending on the date of the disposition (see § 1.469-2T(c)(2)(ii)); and

(iv) The net rental activity income from an item of property for the taxable year is the excess, if any, of—

(A) The gross rental activity income from the item of property for the taxable year; over

(B) Any passive activity deductions for the taxable year (including any deduction treated as a deduction for the year under § 1.469-1(f)(4)) that are reasonably allocable to the income.

*(10) Coordination with section 163(d).* Gross income that is treated as not from a passive activity under § 1.469-2T(f)(3), (4), or (7) is treated as income described in section 469(e)(1)(A) and § 1.469-2T(c)(3)(i) except in determining whether—

(i) Any property is treated for purposes of section 469(e)(1)(A)(ii)(I) and § 1.469-2T(c)(3)(i)(C) as property that produces income of a type described in § 1.469-2T(c)(3)(i)(A);

(ii) Any property is treated for purposes of section 469(e)(1)(A) (ii)(II) and § 1.469-2T(c)(3)(i)(D) as property held for investment;

(iii) An expense (other than interest expense) is treated for purposes of section 469(e)(1)(A)(i)(II) and § 1.469-2T(d)(4) as clearly and directly allocable to portfolio income (within the meaning of § 1.469-2T(c)(3)(i); and

(iv) Interest expense is allocated under § 1.163-8T to an investment expenditure (within the meaning of § 1.163-8T(b)(3)) or to a passive activity expenditure (within the meaning of § 1.163-8T(b)(4)).

*(11)* [Reserved]

---

T.D. 8417, 5/11/92, amend T.D. 8477, 2/22/93, T.D. 8495, 11/3/93.

---

### § 1.469-2T Passive activity loss (temporary).

***Caution:*** The Treasury has not yet amended Reg § 1.469-2T to reflect changes made by P.L. 103-66.

**(a) Scope of this section.** This section contains rules for determining the amount of the taxpayer's passive activity loss for the taxable year for purposes of section 469 and the regulations thereunder. The rules contained in this section—

*(1)* Provide general guidance for identifying items of income and deduction that are taken into account in determining the amount of the passive activity loss for the taxable year;

*(2)* Specify particular items of income and deduction that are not taken into account in determining the amount of the passive activity loss for the taxable year; and

*(3)* Specify the manner in which provisions of the Internal Revenue Code and the regulations, other than section 469 and the regulations thereunder, are applied for purposes of determining the extent to which items of deduction are taken into account for a taxable year in computing the amount of the passive activity loss for such year.

**(b) Definition of passive activity loss.** *(1) In general.* In the case of a taxpayer other than a closely held corporation (within the meaning of § 1.469-1T(g)(2)(ii)), the passive activity loss for the taxable year is the amount, if any, by which the passive activity deductions for the taxable year exceed the passive activity gross income for the taxable year.

*(2) Cross references.* See paragraph (c) of this section for the definition of "passive activity gross income," paragraph (d) of this section for the definition of "passive activity deduction," and § 1.469-1T(g)(4) for the computation of the passive activity loss of a closely held corporation.

**(c) Passive activity gross income.** *(1) In general.* Except as otherwise provided in the regulations under section 469, passive activity gross income for a taxable year includes an item of gross income if and only if such income is from a passive activity.

*(2) Treatment of gain from disposition of an interest in an activity or an interest in property used in an activity.* (i) In general. (A) Treatment of gain. Except as otherwise provided in the regulations under section 469, any gain recognized upon the sale, exchange, or other disposition (a "disposition") of an interest in property used in an activity at the time of the disposition or of an interest in an activity held through a partnership or S corporation is treated in the following manner:

(1) The gain is treated as gross income from such activity for the taxable year or years in which it is recognized;

(2) If the activity is a passive activity of the taxpayer for the taxable year of the disposition, the gain is treated as passive activity gross income for the taxable year or years in which it is recognized; and

(3) If the activity is not a passive activity of the taxpayer for the taxable year of the disposition, the gain is treated as not from a passive activity.

(B) Dispositions of partnership interests and S corporation stock. A partnership interest or S corporation stock is not property used in an activity for purposes of this paragraph (c)(2). See paragraph (e)(3) of this section for rules treating the gain recognized upon the disposition of a partnership interest or S corporation stock as gain from the disposition of interests in the activities in which the partnership or S corporation has an interest.

(C) Interest in property. For purposes of applying this paragraph (c)(2) to a disposition of property—

(1) Any material portion of the property that was used, at any time before the disposition, in any activity at a time when the remainder of the property was not used in such activity shall be treated as a separate interest in property; and

(2) The amount realized from the disposition and the adjusted basis of the property must be allocated among the separate interests in a reasonable manner.

(D) Examples. The following examples illustrate the application of this paragraph (c)(2)(i):

*Example (1).* A owns an interest in a trade or business activity in which A has never materially participated. In 1987, A sells equipment that was used exclusively in the activity and realizes a gain on the sale. Under paragraph (c)(2)(i)(A)(2) of this section, the gain is passive activity gross income.

*Example (2).* B owns an interest in a trade or business activity in which B materially participates for 1987. In 1987, B sells a building used in the activity in an installment sale and realizes a gain on the sale. B does not materially participate in the activity for 1988 or any subsequent year. Under paragraph (c)(2)(i)(A)(3) of this section, none of B's gain from the sale (including gain taken into account after 1987) is passive activity gross income.

*Example (3).* C enters into a contract to acquire property used by the seller in a rental activity. Before acquiring the property pursuant to the contract, C sells all rights under the contract and realizes a gain on the sale. Since C's rights under the contract are not property used in a rental activity, the gain is not income from a rental activity. The result would be the same if C owned an option to acquire the property and sold the option.

*Example (4).* D sells a ten-floor office building. D owned the building for three years preceding the sale and at all times during that period used seven floors of the building in a trade or business activity and three floors in a rental activity. The fair market value per square foot is substantially the same throughout the building, and D did not maintain a separate adjusted basis for any part of the building. Under paragraph (c)(2)(i)(C)(1) of this section, the seven floors used in the trade or business activity and the three floors used in the rental activity are treated as separate interests in property. Under paragraph (c)(2)(i)(C)(2) of this section, the amount realized and the adjusted basis of the building must be allocated between the separate interests in a reasonable manner. Under these facts, an allocation based on the square footage of the parts of the building used in each activity would be reasonable.

*Example (5).* The facts are the same as in example (4), except that two of the seven floors used in the trade or business activity were used in the rental activity until five months before the sale. Under paragraph (c)(2)(i)(C)(1) of this section, the five floors used exclusively in the trade or business activity and the two floors used first in the rental activity and then in the trade or business activity are treated as separate interests in property. See paragraph (c)(2)(ii) of this section for rules for allocating amount realized and adjusted basis upon a disposition of an interest in property used in more than one activity during the 12-month period ending on the date of the disposition.

(ii) Disposition of property used in more than one activity in 12-month period preceding disposition. In the case of a disposition of an interest in property that is used in more than one activity during the 12-month period ending on the date of the disposition, the amount realized from the disposition and the adjusted basis of such interest must be allocated among such activities on a basis that reasonably reflects the use of such interest in property during such 12-month period. For purposes of this paragraph (c)(2)(ii), an allocation of the amount realized and adjusted basis solely to the activity in which an interest in property is predominantly used during the 12-month period ending on the date of the disposition reasonably reflects the use of such interest in property if the fair market value of such interest does not exceed the lesser of—

(A) $10,000; and

(B) 10 percent of the sum of the fair market value of such interest and the fair market value of all other property used in such activity immediately before the disposition.

The following examples illustrate the application of this paragraph (c)(2)(ii):

*Example (1).* The facts are the same as in example (5) of paragraph (c)(2)(i)(D) of this section. Under paragraph (c)(2)(i)(C)(2) of this section, D allocates the amount realized and adjusted basis of the building 30 percent to the three floors used exclusively in the rental activity, 50 percent to the five floors used exclusively in the trade or business activity, and 20 percent to the two floors used first in the rental activity and then in the trade or business activity. Under this paragraph (c)(2)(ii), the amount realized and adjusted basis allocated to the two floors that were used in both activities during the 12-month period ending on the date of the disposition must also be allocated between such activities. Under these facts, an allocation of 7/12 of such amounts to the rental activity and 5/12 of such amounts to the trade or business activity would reasonably reflect the use of the two floors during the 12-month period ending on the date of the disposition.

*Example (2).* B is a limited partner in a partnership that sells a tractor-trailer. During the 12-month period ending on the date of the sale, the tractor-trailer was used in several activities, and the partnership allocates the amount realized from the disposition and the adjusted basis of the tractor-trailer among the activities based on the number of days during the 12-month period that the partnership used the tractor-trailer in each activity. Under these facts, the partnership's allocation reasonably reflects the use of the tractor-trailer during the 12-month period ending on the date of the sale.

*Example (3).* C sells a personal computer for $8,000. During the 12-month period ending on the date of the sale, 70 percent of C's use of the computer was in a passive activity. Immediately before the sale, the fair market value of all property used in the passive activity (including the personal computer) was $200,000. Under these facts, the computer was predominantly used in the passive activity during the 12-month period ending on the date of the sale, and the value of the computer, as measured by its sale price ($8,000), does not exceed the lesser of (a) $10,000, and (b) 10 percent of the value of all property used in the activity immediately before the sale ($20,000). C allocates the amount realized and the adjusted basis solely to the passive activity. Under this paragraph (c)(2)(ii), C's allocation reasonably reflects the use of the computer during the 12-month period ending on the date of the sale.

(iii) Disposition of substantially appreciated property formerly used in nonpassive activity. [Reserved] See § 1.469-4(c)(2)(iii) for rules relating to this paragraph.

(iv) Taxable acquisitions. [Reserved} See § 1.469-2(c)(iv) for rules relating to this paragraph.

(v) Property held for sale to customers. [Reserved] See § 1.469-2(c)(v) for rules relating to this paragraph.

*(3) Items of portfolio income specifically excluded.* (i) In general. Passive activity gross income does not include portfolio income. For purposes of the preceding sentence, portfolio income includes all gross income, other than income derived in the ordinary course of a trade or business (within the meaning of paragraph (c)(3)(ii) of this section), that is attributable to—

(A) Interest (including amounts treated as interest under paragraph (e)(2)(ii) of this section, relating to certain payments to partners for the use of capital); annuities; royalties (including fees and other payments for the use of intangible property); dividends on C corporation stock; and income (including dividends) from a real estate investment trust (within the meaning of section 856), regulated investment company (within the meaning of section 851), real estate mortgage investment conduit (within the meaning of section 860D), common trust fund (within the meaning of section 584), controlled foreign corporation (within the meaning of section 957), qualified electing fund (within the meaning of section 1295(a)), or cooperative (within the meaning of section 1381(a));

(B) Dividends on S corporation stock (within the meaning of section 1368(c)(2));

(C) The disposition of property that produces income of a type described in paragraph (c)(3)(i)(A) of this section; and

(D) The disposition of property held for investment (within the meaning of section 163(d)).

(ii) Gross income derived in the ordinary course of a trade or business. Solely for purposes of paragraph (c)(3)(i) of this section, gross income derived in the ordinary course of a trade or business includes only—

(A) Interest income on loans and investments made in the ordinary course of a trade or business of lending money;

(B) Interest on accounts receivable arising from the performance of services or the sale of property in the ordinary course of a trade or business of performing such services or selling such property, but only if credit is customarily offered to customers of the business;

(C) Income from investments made in the ordinary course of a trade or business of furnishing insurance or annuity contracts or reinsuring risks underwritten by insurance companies;

(D) Income or gain derived in the ordinary course of an activity of trading or dealing in any property if such activity constitutes a trade or business (but see paragraph (c)(3)(iii)(A) of this section);

(E) Royalties derived by the taxpayer in the ordinary course of a trade or business of licensing intangible property (within the meaning of paragraph (c)(3)(iii)(B) of this section);

(F) Amounts included in the gross income of a patron of a cooperative (within the meaning of section 1381(a), without regard to paragraph (2)(A) or (C) thereof) by reason of any payment or allocation to the patron based on patronage occurring with respect to a trade or business of the patron; and

(G) Other income identified by the Commissioner as income derived by the taxpayer in the ordinary course of a trade or business.

(iii) Special rules (A) Income from property held for investment by dealer. For purposes of paragraph (c)(3)(i) of this section, a dealer's income or gain from an item of property is not derived by the dealer in the ordinary course of a trade or business of dealing in such property if the dealer held the property for investment at any time before such income or gain is recognized.

(B) Royalties derived in the ordinary course of the trade or business of licensing intangible property. (1) In general. Royalties received by any person with respect to a license or other transfer of any rights in intangible property shall be considered to be derived in the ordinary course of the trade or business of licensing such property only if such person—

(i) Created such property; or

(ii) Performed substantial services or incurred substantial costs with respect to the development or marketing of such property.

(2) Substantial services or costs. (i) In general. Except as provided in paragraph (c)(3)(iii)(B)(2)(ii) of this section, the determination of whether a person has performed substantial services or incurred substantial costs with respect to the development or marketing of an item of intangible property shall be made on the basis of all the facts and circumstances.

(ii) Exception. A person has performed substantial services or incurred substantial costs for a taxable year with respect to the development or marketing of an item of intangible property if—

(a) The expenditures reasonably incurred by such person in such taxable year with respect to the development or marketing of the property exceed 50 percent of the gross royalties from licensing such property that are includible in such person's gross income for the taxable year; or

(b) The expenditures reasonably incurred by such person in such taxable year and all prior taxable years with respect to the development or marketing of the property exceed 25 percent of the aggregate capital expenditures (without any adjustment for amortization) made by such person with respect to the property in all such taxable years.

(iii) Expenditures taken into account. For purposes of paragraph (c)(3)(iii)(B)(2)(ii) of this section, expenditures in a taxable year include amounts chargeable to capital account for such year without regard to the year or years (if any) in which any deduction for such expenditure is allowed.

(3) Passthrough entities. For purposes of this paragraph (c)(3)(iii)(B), in the case of any intangible property held by a partnership, S corporation, estate, or trust, the determination of whether royalties from such property are derived in the ordinary course of a trade or business shall be made by applying the rules of this paragraph (c)(3)(iii)(B) to such entity and not to any holder of an interest in such entity.

(4) Cross reference. For special rules applicable to certain gross income from a trade or business of licensing intangible property, see paragraph (f)(7) of this section.

(C) Mineral production payments. For purposes of section 469 and the regulations thereunder—

(1) If a mineral production payment is treated as a loan under section 636, the portion of any payment in discharge of the production payment that is the equivalent of interest shall be treated as interest; and

(2) If a mineral production payment is not treated as a loan under section 636, payments in discharge of the production payment shall be treated as royalties.

(iv) Examples. The following examples illustrate the application of this paragraph (c)(3):

*Example (1).* A, an individual engaged in the trade or business of farming, disposes of farmland in an installment sale. A is not engaged in a trade or business of selling farmland. Therefore, A's interest income from the installment note is not gross income derived in the ordinary course of a trade or business.

*Example (2).* P, a partnership, operates a rental apartment building for low-income tenants in City Y. Under Y's laws relating to the operation of low-income housing, P is required to maintain a reserve fund to pay for the maintenance and repair of the building. P invests the reserve fund in short-term interest-bearing deposits. Because P's interest income from the investment of the reserve fund is not interest income described in paragraph (c)(3)(ii) of this section, such income is not treated as derived in the ordinary course of a trade or business. Accordingly, P's interest income from the deposits is portfolio income (within the meaning of paragraph (c)(3)(i) of this section).

*Example (3).* (i) B is a partner in a partnership that is engaged in an activity involving the conduct of a trade or business of dealing in securities. On February 1, the partnership acquires certain securities for investment (within the meaning of section 163(d)). On February 2, before recognizing any income with respect to the securities, the partnership determines that it would be advisable to hold the securities primarily for sale to customers and subsequently sells them to customers in the ordinary course of its business.

(ii) Under paragraph (c)(3)(iii)(A) of this section, income or gain from any security (including any security acquired pursuant to an investment of working capital) held by a dealer for investment at any time before such income or gain is recognized is not treated for purposes of paragraph (c)(3)(i) of this section as derived by the dealer in the ordinary course of its trade or business of dealing in securities. Accordingly, B's distributive share of the partnership's interest, dividends, or gains from the securities acquired by the partnership for investment on February 1 is portfolio income of B, notwithstanding that such securities were held by the partnership, subsequent to February 1, primarily for sale to customers in the ordinary course of the partnership's trade or business of dealing in securities.

*Example (4).* C is a partner in a partnership that is engaged in an activity of trading or dealing in royalty interests in mineral properties. The partnership derives royalty income from royalty interests held in the activity. If the activity is a trade or business activity, C's distributive share of the partnership's royalty income from such royalty interests is treated under paragraph (c)(3)(ii)(D) of this section as derived in the ordinary course of the partnership's trade or business.

*Example (5).* (i) D, a calendar year individual, is a partner in a calendar year partnership that is engaged in an activity of developing and marketing a design for a system that reduces air pollution in office buildings. D has a 10 percent distributive share of all items of partnership income, gain, loss, deduction, and credit. In 1987, the partnership acquired the rights to the design for $100,000. In 1987, 1988, and 1989, the partnership incurs expenditures with respect to the development and marketing of the design, and derives gross royalties from licensing the design, in the amounts set forth in the table below. The expenditures incurred in 1987 and 1988 are currently deductible expenses. The expenditures incurred in 1989 are capitalized and may be deducted only in subsequent taxable years.

| Year | Gross Royalties | Expenditures | Cumulative Capital Expenditures |
|---|---|---|---|
| 1987 | $20,000 | $8,000 | $100,000 |
| 1988 | 20,000 | 12,000 | 100,000 |
| 1989 | 60,000 | 15,000 | 115,000 |
| 1990 | 120,000 | -0- | 115,000 |

(ii) Under paragraph (c)(3)(iii)(B)(3) of this section, the determination of whether royalties from intangible property are derived in the ordinary course of a trade or business of a partnership is made by applying the rules of paragraph (c)(3)(iii)(B) of this section to the partnership rather than the partners. The expenditures reasonably incurred by the partnership in 1987 with respect to the development or marketing of the design ($8,000) do not exceed 50 percent of the partnership's gross royalties for such year from licensing the design ($20,000). In addition, the sum of such expenditures incurred in 1987 and all prior taxable years ($8,000) does not exceed 25 percent of the aggregate capital expenditures made by the partnership in all such taxable years with respect to the design ($100,000). Accordingly, for 1987, the partnership is not treated under paragraph (c)(3)(iii)(B)(2)(ii) of this section as performing substantial services or incurring substantial costs with respect to the development or marketing of the design. Therefore, unless all of the facts and circumstances indicate that the partnership performed substantial services or incurred substantial costs with respect to the development or marketing of the design, D's distributive share of the partnership's royalty income for 1987 is portfolio income.

(iii) As of the end of 1988, the sum of the expenditures reasonably incurred by the partnership during such taxable year and all prior taxable years with respect to the development or marketing of the design ($20,000) does not exceed 25 percent of the aggregate capital expenditures made by the partnership in all such years with respect to the design ($100,000). However, the amount of such expenditures incurred by the partnership in 1988 ($12,000) exceeds 50 percent of the partnership's gross royalties for such year from licensing the design ($20,000). Accordingly, for 1988, under paragraph (c)(3)(iii)(B)(2)(ii)(a) of this section, the partnership is treated as performing substantial services or incurring substantial costs with respect to the development or marketing of the design, and D's distributive share of the partnership's royalty income for 1988 is considered for purposes of paragraph (c)(3)(i) of this section to be derived in the ordinary course of a trade or business and therefore is not portfolio income.

(iv) The expenditures reasonably incurred by the partnership in 1989 with respect to the development or marketing of the design ($15,000) do not exceed 50 percent of the partnership's gross royalties for such year from licensing the design ($60,000). However, the sum of such expenditures incurred by the partnership in 1989 and all prior taxable years ($35,000) exceeds 25 percent of the partnership's aggregate capital expenditures made in all such years with respect to the design ($115,000). Accordingly, for 1989, under paragraph (c)(3)(iii)(B)(2)(ii)(b) of this section, the partnership is treated as performing substantial services or incurring substantial costs with respect to the development or marketing of the design, and D's distributive share of the partnership's royalty income in 1989 is considered for purposes of paragraph (c)(3)(i) of this section to be derived in the ordinary course of a trade or business and therefore is not portfolio income.

(v) The result for 1990 is the same as for 1989, notwithstanding that the partnership incurs no expenditures in 1990 with respect to the development or marketing of the design.

*Example (6).* The facts are the same as in example (5), except that, for 1987, D's distributive share of the partnership's development and marketing costs is 15 percent, while D's distributive share of the partnership's gross royalties is 10 percent. Although D's distributive share of the expenditures reasonably incurred by the partnership during 1987 with respect to the development and marketing of the design ($1,200) is more than 50 percent of D's distributive share of the partnership's gross royalties from licensing the design ($2,000), D is not treated as performing substantial services or incurring substantial costs with respect to the development or marketing of the design for 1987 under paragraph (c)(3)(iii)(B)(2)(ii)(a) of this section. This is because, under paragraph (c)(3)(iii)(B)(3) of this section, the determination of whether the royalties are derived in the ordinary course of a trade or business is made by applying paragraph (c)(3)(iii)(B) of this section to the partnership, and not to D.

*(4) Items of personal service income specifically excluded.* (i) In general. Passive activity gross income does not include compensation paid to or on behalf of an individual for personal services performed or to be performed by such individual at any time. For purposes of this paragraph (c)(4), compensation for personal services includes only—

(A) Earned income (within the meaning of section 911(d)(2)(A)), including gross income from a payment described in paragraph (e)(2) of this section that represents compensation for the performance of services by a partner;

(B) Amounts includible in gross income under section 83;

(C) Amounts includible in gross income under sections 402 and 403;

(D) Amounts (other than amounts described in paragraph (c)(4)(i)(C) of this section) paid pursuant to retirement, pension, and other arrangements for deferred compensation for services;

(E) Social security benefits (within the meaning of section 86(d)) includible in gross income under section 86; and

(F) Other income identified by the Commissioner as income derived by the taxpayer from personal services;

provided, however, that no portion of a partner's distributive share of partnership income (within the meaning of section 704(b)) or a shareholder's pro rata share of income from an S corporation (within the meaning of section 1377(a)) shall be treated as compensation for personal services.

(ii) Example. The following example illustrates the application of this paragraph (c)(4):

*Example.* C owns 50 percent of the stock of X, an S corporation. X owns rental real estate, which it manages. X pays C a salary for services performed by C on behalf of X in connection with the management of X's rental properties. Under this paragraph (c)(4), although C's pro rata share of X's gross rental income is passive activity gross income (even if the salary paid to C is less than the fair market value of C's services), the salary paid to C does not constitute passive activity gross income.

*(5) Income from section 481 adjustment.* (i) In general. If a change in accounting method results in a positive section 481 adjustment with respect to an activity, a ratable portion (within the meaning of paragraph (c)(5)(iii) of this section) of the amount taken into account for a taxable year as a net positive section 481 adjustment by reason of such change shall be treated as gross income from the activity for such taxable year, and such gross income shall be treated as passive activity gross income if and only if such activity is a passive activity for the year of the change (within the meaning of section 481(a)).

(ii) Positive section 481 adjustments. For purposes of applying this paragraph (c)(5)—

(A) The term "net positive section 481 adjustment" means the increase (if any) in taxable income taken into account under section 481(a) to prevent amounts from being duplicated or omitted by reason of a change in accounting method; and

(B) The term "positive section 481 adjustment with respect to an activity" means the increase (if any) in taxable income that would be taken into account under section 481(a) to prevent only the duplication or omission of amounts from such activity by reason of the change in accounting method.

(iii) Ratable portion. The ratable portion of the amount taken into account as a net positive section 481 adjustment for a taxable year by reason of a change in accounting method is determined with respect to an activity by multiplying such amount by the fraction obtained by dividing—

(A) The positive section 481 adjustment with respect to the activity; by

(B) The sum of the positive section 481 adjustments with respect to all of the activities of the taxpayer.

*(6) Gross income from certain oil or gas properties.* (i) In general. [Reserved] See § 1.469-2(c)(6)(i) for rules relating to this paragraph.

(ii) Gross and net passive income from the property. [Reserved] See § 1.469-2(c)(6)(ii) for rules relating to this paragraph.

(iii) Property. [Reserved] See § 1.469-2(c)(6)(iii) for rules relating to this paragraph.

(iv) Examples. The following examples illustrate the application of this paragraph (c)(6):

*Example (1).* [Reserved] See § 1.469-2(c)(6)(iv) Example 1.

*Example (2).* [Reserved] See § 1.469-2(c)(6)(iv) Example 2.

*Example (3).* C is a general partner in partnership T and a limited partner in partnership U. T and U both own oil and gas working interests in tracts of land in County X. In 1987, T drills a well, and C's distributive share of T's losses from drilling the well is treated under § 1.469-1T(e)(4) as not from a passive activity. In the course of selecting the drilling site and drilling the well, T develops information indicating a significant probability that substantial oil and gas reserves underlie most portions of County X. As a result, the value of all oil and gas properties in County X is enhanced. The information developed by T does not, however, indicate that the reservoir in which T's well is drilled underlies U's tract. Under these facts, T's and U's tracts are not treated as one property for purposes of this paragraph (c)(6), because the value of U's tract is not directly enhanced by T's activities.

*(7) Other items specifically excluded.* Notwithstanding any other provision of the regulations under section 469, passive activity gross income does not include the following:

(i) Gross income of an individual from intangible property, such as a patent, copyright, or literary, musical, or artistic composition, if the taxpayer's personal efforts significantly contributed to the creation of such property;

(ii) Gross income from a qualified low-income housing project (within the meaning of section 502 of the Tax Reform Act of 1986) for any taxable year in the relief period (within the meaning of section 502(b) of such Act);

(iii) Gross income attributable to a refund of any state, local, or foreign income, war profits, or excess profits tax;

(iv) [Reserved] See § 1.469-2(c)(7)(iv) for rates relating to this paragraph (c)(7)(iv).

(v) [Reserved] See § 1.469-2(c)(7)(v) for rules relating to this paragraph (c)(7)(v).

(vi) [Reserved] See § 1.469-2(c)(7)(vi) for rules relating to this paragraph (c)(7)(vi).

**(d) Passive activity deductions.** *(1) In general.* Except as otherwise provided in section 469 and the regulations thereunder, a deduction is a passive activity deduction for a taxable year if and only if such deduction—

(i) Arises (within the meaning of paragraph (d)(8) of this section) in connection with the conduct of an activity that is a passive activity for the taxable year; or

(ii) Is treated as a deduction from an activity under § 1.469-1T(f)(4) for the taxable year. The following example illustrates the application of this paragraph (d)(1):

*Example.* (i) In 1987, A, a calendar year individual, acquires a partnership interest in R, a calendar year partnership. R's only activity is a trade or business activity in which A materially participates for 1987. R incurs a loss in 1987. A's distributive share of R's 1987 loss is $1,000. However, A's basis in the partnership interest at the end of 1987 (without regard to A's distributive share of partnership loss) is $600; accordingly, section 704(d) disallows any deduction in 1987 for $400 of A's distributive share of R's loss. The remainder of A's distributive share of R's loss would be allowed as a deduction for 1987 if taxable income for all taxable years were determined without regard to sections 469, 613A(d), and 1211. See paragraph (d)(8) of this section.

(ii) A does not materially participate in R's activity for 1988. In 1988, R again incurs a loss, and A's distributive share of the loss is again $1,000. At the end of 1988, A's basis in the partnership interest (without regard to A's distributive share of partnership loss) is $2,000; accordingly, in 1988 section 704(d) does not limit A's deduction for either A's $1,000 distributive share of R's 1988 loss or the $400 loss carried over from 1987 under the second sentence of section 704(d). These losses would be allowed as a deduction for 1988 if taxable income for all taxable years were determined without regard to sections 469, 613A(d), and 1211. See paragraph (d)(8) of this section.

(iii) Under these facts, only $400 of A's distributive share of R's deductions from the activity are disallowed under section 704(d) in 1987. A's remaining deductions from the activity are treated as deductions that arise in connection with the activity for 1987 under paragraph (d)(8) of this section. Because A materially participates in the activity for 1987, the activity is not a passive activity (within the meaning of § 1.469-1T(e)(1)) of A for such year. Accordingly, the deductions that are not disallowed in 1987 are not passive activity deductions.

(iv) A does not materially participate in R's activity for 1988. Accordingly, the activity is a passive activity of A for such year. No portion of A's distributive share of R's deductions from the activity is disallowed under section 704(d) in 1988. Accordingly, A's distributive share of R's deductions for 1988 and the $400 of deductions carried over from 1987 are both treated under paragraph (d)(8) of this section as deductions that arise in 1988. Since the activity is a passive activity for 1988, such deductions are passive activity deductions.

*(2) Exceptions.* Passive activity deductions do not include—

(i) A deduction for an item of expense (other than interest) that is clearly and directly allocable (within the meaning of paragraph (d)(4) of this section) to portfolio income (within the meaning of paragraph (c)(3)(i) of this section);

(ii) A deduction allowed under section 243, 244, or 245 with respect to any dividend that is not included in passive activity gross income;

(iii) Interest expense (other than interest expense described in paragraph (d)(3) of this section);

(iv) A deduction for a loss from the disposition of property of a type that produces portfolio income (within the meaning of paragraph (c)(3)(i) of this section);

(v) A deduction that, under section 469(g) and § 1.469-6T (relating to the allowance of passive activity losses upon certain dispositions of interests in passive activities), is treated as a deduction that is not a passive activity deduction;

(vi) A deduction for any state, local, or foreign income, war profits, or excess profits tax;

(vii) A miscellaneous itemized deduction (within the meaning of section 67(b)) that is subject to disallowance in whole or in part under section 67(a) (without regard to whether any amount of such deduction is disallowed under section 67);

(viii) A deduction allowed under section 170 for a charitable contribution;

(ix) [Reserved] See § 1.469-2(d)(2)(ix) for rules relating to this paragraph.

(x) [Reserved] See § 1.469-2(d)(2)(x) for rules relating to this paragraph (d)(2)(x).

(xi) [Reserved] See § 1.469-2(d)(2)(xi) for rules relating to this paragraph (d)(2)(xi).

*(3) Interest expense.* Except as otherwise provided in the regulations under section 469, interest expense is taken into account as a passive activity deduction if and only if such interest expense—

(i) Is allocated under § 1.163-8T to a passive activity expenditure (within the meaning of § 1.163-8T(b)(4)); and

(ii) Is not—

(A) Qualified residence interest (within the meaning of § 1.163-10T); or

(B) Capitalized pursuant to a capitalization provision (within the meaning of § 1.163-8T(m)(7)(i)).

*(4) Clearly and directly allocable expenses.* For purposes of section 469 and the regulations thereunder, an expense (other than interest expense) is clearly and directly allocable to portfolio income (within the meaning of paragraph (c)(3)(i) of this section) if and only if such expense is incurred as a result of, or incident to, an activity in which such gross income is derived or in connection with property from which such gross income is derived. For example, general and administrative expenses and compensation paid to officers attributable to the performance of services that do not

directly benefit or are not incurred by reason of a particular activity or particular property are not clearly and directly allocable to portfolio income (within the meaning of paragraph (c)(3)(i) of this section).

*(5) Treatment of loss from disposition.* (i) In general. Except as otherwise provided in the regulations under section 469—

(A) Any loss recognized in any year upon the sale, exchange, or other disposition (a "disposition") of an interest in property used in an activity at the time of the disposition or of an interest in an activity held through a partnership or S corporation and any deduction allowed on account of the abandonment or worthlessness of such an interest is treated as a deduction from such activity; and

(B) Any such deduction is a passive activity deduction if and only if the activity is a passive activity of the taxpayer for the taxable year of the disposition (or other event giving rise to the deduction).

(ii) Disposition of property used in more than one activity in 12-month period preceding disposition. In the case of a disposition of an interest in property that is used in more than one activity during the 12-month period ending on the date of the disposition, the amount realized from the disposition and the adjusted basis of such interest must be allocated among such activities in the manner described in paragraph (c)(2)(ii) of this section.

(iii) Other applicable rules. (A) Applicability of rules in paragraph (c)(2). [Reserved] See § 1.469-2(d)(5)(iii)(A) for rules relating to this paragraph.

(B) Dispositions of partnership interests and S corporation stock. A partnership interest or S corporation stock is not property used in an activity for purposes of this paragraph (d)(5). See paragraph (e)(3) of this section for rules treating the loss recognized upon the disposition of a partnership interest or S corporation stock as loss from the disposition of interests in the activities in which the partnership or S corporation has an interest.

*(6) Coordination with other limitations on deductions that apply before section 469.* (i) In general. An item of deduction from a passive activity that is disallowed for a taxable year under section 704(d), 1366(d), or 465 is not a passive activity deduction for the taxable year. Paragraphs (d)(6)(ii) and (iii) of this section provide rules for determining the extent to which items of deduction from a passive activity are disallowed for a taxable year under sections 704(d), 1366(d), and 465.

(ii) Proration of deductions disallowed under basis limitations. (A) Deductions disallowed under section 704(d). If any amount of a partner's distributive share of a partnership's loss for the taxable year is disallowed under section 704(d), a ratable portion of the partner's distributive share of each item of deduction or loss of the partnership is disallowed for the taxable year. For purposes of the preceding sentence, the ratable portion of an item of deduction or loss is the amount of such item multiplied by the fraction obtained by dividing—

(1) The amount of the partner's distributive share of partnership loss that is disallowed for the taxable year; by

(2) The sum of the partner's distributive shares of all items of deduction and loss of the partnership for the taxable year.

(B) Deductions disallowed under section 1366(d). If any amount of an S corporation shareholder's pro rata share of an S corporation's loss for the taxable year is disallowed under section 1366(d), a ratable portion of the taxpayer's pro rata share of each item of deduction or loss of the S corporation is disallowed for the taxable year. For purposes of the preceding sentence, the ratable portion of an item of deduction or loss is the amount of such item multiplied by the fraction obtained by dividing—

(1) The amount of the shareholder's pro rata share of S corporation loss that is disallowed for the taxable year; by

(2) The sum of the shareholder's pro rata shares of all items of deduction and loss of the corporation for the taxable year.

(iii) Proration of deductions disallowed under at-risk limitation. If any amount of the taxpayer's loss from an activity (within the meaning of section 465(c)) is disallowed under section 465 for the taxable year, a ratable portion of each item of deduction or loss from the activity is disallowed for the taxable year. For purposes of the preceding sentence, the ratable portion of an item of deduction or loss is the amount of such item multiplied by the fraction obtained by dividing—

(1) The amount of the loss from the activity that is disallowed for the taxable year; by

(2) The sum of all deductions from the activity for the taxable year.

(iv) Coordination of basis and at-risk limitations. The portion of any item of deduction or loss that is disallowed for the taxable year under section 704(d) or 1366(d) is not taken into account for the taxable year in determining the loss from an activity (within the meaning of section 465(c)) for purposes of applying section 465.

(v) Separately identified items of deduction and loss. In identifying the items of deduction and loss from an activity that are not disallowed under sections 704(d), 1366(d), and 465 (and that therefore may be treated as passive activity deductions), the taxpayer need not account separately for any item of deduction or loss unless such item may, if separately taken into account, result in an income tax liability different from that which would result were such item of deduction or loss not taken into account separately. For related rules applicable to partnerships and S corporations, see § 1.702-1(a)(8)(ii) and section 1366(a)(1)(A), respectively. Items of deduction or loss that must be accounted for separately include (but are not limited to) items of deduction or loss that—

(A) Are attributable to separate activities (within the meaning of the rules to be contained in § 1.469-4T);

(B) Arise in a rental real estate activity (within the meaning of section 469(i) and the rules to be contained in § 1.469-9T) in taxable years in which the taxpayer actively participates (within the meaning of section 469(i) and the rules to be contained in § 1.469-9T) in such activity;

(C) Arise in a rental real estate activity (within the meaning of section 469(i) and the rules to be contained in § 1.469-9T) in taxable years in which the taxpayer does not actively participate (within the meaning of section 469(i) and the rules to be contained in § 1.469-9T) in such activity;

(D) Arose in a taxable year beginning before 1987 and were not allowed for such taxable year under section 704(d), 1366(d), or 465(a)(2);

(E) [Reserved] See § 1.469-2(d)(6)(v)(E) for rules relating to this paragraph.

(F) Are attributable to pre-enactment interests in activities (within the meaning of § 1.469-11T(c)).

*(7) Deductions from section 481 adjustment.* (i) In general. If a change in accounting method results in a negative section 481 adjustment with respect to an activity, a ratable portion (within the meaning of paragraph (d)(7)(iii) of this section) of the amount taken into account for a taxable year as a net negative section 481 adjustment by reason of such change shall be treated as a deduction from the activity for such taxable year, and such deduction shall be treated as a passive activity deduction if and only if such activity is a passive activity for the year of the change (within the meaning of section 481(a)). See the rules to be contained in § 1.469-1T(k) for the treatment of passive activity deductions from an activity in taxable years in which the activity is a former passive activity.

(ii) Negative section 481 adjustments. For purposes of applying this paragraph (d)(7)—

(A) The term "net negative section 481 adjustment" means the decrease (if any) in taxable income taken into account under section 481(a) to prevent amounts from being duplicated or omitted by reason of a change in accounting method; and

(B) The term "negative section 481 adjustment with respect to an activity" means the decrease (if any) in taxable income that would be taken into account under section 481(a) to prevent only the duplication or omission of amounts from such activity by reason of the change in accounting method.

(iii) Ratable portion. The ratable portion of the amount taken into account as a net negative section 481 adjustment for a taxable year by reason of a change in accounting method is determined with respect to an activity by multiplying such amount by the fraction obtained by dividing—

(A) The negative section 481 adjustment with respect to the activity; by

(B) The sum of the negative section 481 adjustments with respect to all of the activities of the taxpayer.

*(8) Taxable year in which item arises. [Reserved]* See § 1.469-2(d)(8) for rules relating to this paragraph.

**(e) Special rules for partners and S corporation shareholders.** *(1) In general.* For purposes of section 469 and the regulations thereunder, the character (as an item of passive activity gross income or passive activity deduction) of each item of gross income and deduction allocated to a taxpayer from a partnership or S corporation (a "passthrough entity") shall be determined, in any case in which participation is relevant, by reference to the participation of the taxpayer in the activity (or activities) that generated such item. Such participation is determined for the taxable year of the passthrough entity (and not the taxable year of the taxpayer). The following example illustrates the application of this paragraph (e)(1):

*Example.* A, a calendar year individual, is a partner in a partnership that has a taxable year ending January 31. During its taxable year ending on January 31, 1988, the partnership engages in a single trade or business activity. For the period from February 1, 1987, through January 31, 1988, A does not materially participate in this activity. In A's calendar year 1988 return, A's distributive share of the partnership's gross income and deductions from the activity must be treated as passive activity gross income and passive activity deductions, without regard to A's participation in the activity from February 1, 1988, through December 31, 1988. See also § 1.469-11T(a)(4) (relating to the effective date of, and transition rules under, section 469 and the regulations thereunder).

*(2) Payments under sections 707(a), 707(c), and 736(b).* Items of gross income and deduction attributable to a transaction described in section 707(a), 707(c), or 736(b) shall be characterized for purposes of section 469 and the regulations thereunder in accordance with the following rules:

(i) Section 707(a). Any item of gross income or deduction attributable to a transaction that is treated under section 707(a) as a transaction between a partnership and a partner acting in a capacity other than as a member of such partnership shall be characterized for purposes of section 469 and the regulations thereunder in a manner that is consistent with the treatment of such transaction under section 707(a).

(ii) Section 707(c). [Reserved] See § 1.469-2(e)(ii) for rules relating to this paragraph.

(iii) Payments in liquidation of a partner's interest in partnership property. [Reserved] See § 1.469-2(e)(iii) for rules relating to this paragraph.

*(3) Sale or exchange of interest in passthrough entity.* (i) Application of this paragraph (e)(3). In the case of the sale, exchange, or other disposition (a "disposition") of an interest in a passthrough entity, the amount of the seller's gain or loss from each activity in which such entity has an interest is determined, for purposes of section 469 and the regulations thereunder, under this paragraph (e)(3). In the case of any such disposition, except as otherwise provided in paragraph (e)(3)(iii) or (iv) of this section, paragraph (e)(3)(ii) of this section shall apply. See paragraphs (c)(2) and (d)(5) of this section for rules for determining the character of gain or loss, respectively, recognized upon a disposition of an interest in an activity held through a passthrough entity.

(ii) General rule. (A) Allocation among activities. Except as otherwise provided in this paragraph (e)(3)(ii) or in paragraph (e)(3)(iii) or (iv) of this section, if a holder of an interest in a passthrough entity disposes of such interest, a ratable portion (within the meaning of paragraph (e)(3)(ii)(B) of this section) of any gain or loss from such disposition shall be treated as gain or loss from the disposition of an interest in each trade or business, rental, or investment activity in which such passthrough entity owns an interest on the applicable valuation date.

(B) Ratable portion. (1) Dispositions on which gain is recognized. The ratable portion of any gain from the disposition of an interest in a passthrough entity that is allocable to an activity described in paragraph (e)(3)(ii)(A) of this section is determined by multiplying the amount of such gain by the fraction obtained by dividing—

(i) The amount of net gain (within the meaning of paragraph (e)(3)(ii)(E) (3) of this section) that would have been allocated to the holder of such interest with respect thereto if the passthrough entity had sold its entire interest in such activity for its fair market value on the applicable valuation date; by

(ii) The sum of the amounts of net gain that would have been allocated to the holder of such interest with respect thereto if the passthrough entity had sold its entire interest in each appreciated activity (within the meaning of paragraph (e)(3)(ii)(E)(1) of this section) described in paragraph (e)(3)(ii)(A) of this section for the fair market value of each such activity on the applicable valuation date.

(2) Dispositions on which loss is recognized. The ratable portion of any loss from the disposition of an interest in a passthrough entity that is allocable to an activity described in paragraph (e)(3)(ii)(A) of this section is determined by multiplying the amount of such loss by the fraction obtained by dividing—

(i) The amount of net loss (within the meaning of paragraph (e)(3)(ii)(E) (4) of this section) that would have been allocated to the holder of such interest with respect thereto if the passthrough entity had sold its entire interest in such activity for its fair market value on the applicable valuation date; by

(ii) The sum of the amounts of net loss that would have been allocated to the holder of such interest with respect thereto if the passthrough entity had sold its entire interest in each depreciated activity (within the meaning of paragraph (e)(3)(ii)(E)(2) of this section) described in paragraph (e)(3)(ii)(A) of this section for the fair market value of each such activity on the applicable valuation date.

(C) Default rule. If the gain or loss recognized upon the disposition of an interest in a passthrough entity cannot be allocated under paragraph (e)(3)(ii)(A) of this section, such gain or loss shall be allocated among the activities described in paragraph (e)(3)(ii)(A) of this section in proportion to the respective fair market values of the passthrough entity's interests in such activities at the applicable valuation date, and the gain or loss allocated to each activity of the passthrough entity shall be treated as gain or loss from the disposition of an interest in such activity.

(D) Special rules. For purposes of this paragraph (e)(3)(ii), the following rules shall apply:

(1) Applicable valuation date. (i) In general. Except as otherwise provided in paragraph (e)(3)(ii)(D)(1)(ii) of this section, the applicable valuation date with respect to any disposition of an interest in a passthrough entity is whichever one of the following dates is selected by the passthrough entity:

(a) The beginning of the taxable year of the passthrough entity in which such disposition occurs; or

(b) The date on which such disposition occurs.

(ii) Exception. If, after the beginning of a passthrough entity's taxable year in which a holder's disposition of an interest in such passthrough entity occurs and before the time of such disposition—

(a) The passthrough entity disposes of more than 10 percent of its interest (by value as of the beginning of such taxable year) in any activity;

(b) More than 10 percent of the property (by value as of the beginning of such taxable year) used in any activity of the passthrough entity is disposed of; or

(c) The holder of such interest contributes to the passthrough entity substantially appreciated property or substantially depreciated property with a total fair market value or adjusted basis, respectively, which exceeds 10 percent of the total fair market value of the holder's interest in the passthrough entity as of the beginning of such taxable year;

then the applicable valuation date shall be the date immediately preceding the date on which such disposition occurs.

(2) Basis adjustments. Any adjustment to the basis of partnership property under section 743(b) made with respect to the holder of an interest in a partnership shall be taken into account in computing the net gain or net loss that would have been allocated to the holder with respect to such interest if the partnership had sold its entire interest in an activity.

(3) Tiered passthrough entities. In the case of a disposition of an interest in a passthrough entity (the "subsidiary passthrough entity") by a holder that is also a passthrough entity, any gain or loss from such disposition that is taken into account by any person that owns (directly or indirectly) an interest in such holder shall be allocated among the activities of the subsidiary passthrough entity by applying the rules of this paragraph (e)(3)(ii) to the person taking such gain or loss into account as if such person had been the holder of an interest in such subsidiary passthrough entity and had recognized such gain or loss as a result of a disposition of such interest.

(E) Meaning of certain terms. For purposes of this paragraph (e)(3)(ii)—

(1) An activity is an appreciated activity with respect to a holder that has disposed of an interest in a passthrough entity if a net gain would have been allocated to the holder with respect to such interest if the passthrough entity had sold its entire interest in such activity for its fair market value on the applicable valuation date;

(2) An activity is a depreciated activity with respect to a holder that has disposed of an interest in a passthrough entity if a net loss would have been allocated to the holder with respect to such interest if the passthrough entity had sold its entire interest in such activity for its fair market value on the applicable valuation date;

(3) The term "net gain" means, with respect to the sale of a passthrough entity's entire interest in an activity, the amount by which the gains from the sale of all of the property used by (or representing the interest of) the passthrough entity in such activity exceed the losses (if any) from such sale;

(4) The term "net loss" means, with respect to the sale of a passthrough entity's entire interest in an activity, the amount by which the losses from the sale of all of the property used by (or representing the interest of) the passthrough entity in such activity exceed the gains (if any) from such sale.

(iii) Treatment of gain allocated to certain passive activities as not from a passive activity. If, in the case of a disposition of an interest in a passthrough entity—

(A) An amount of gain recognized on account of such disposition by the holder of such interest (or any other person that owns (directly or indirectly) an interest in such holder if such holder is a passthrough entity) is allocated to a passive activity of such holder (or such other person) under paragraph (e)(3)(ii) of this section;

(B) [Reserved] See § 1.469-2(e)(3)(iii)(B) for rules relating to this paragraph.

(C) The amount of the gain of the holder (or such other person) described in paragraph (e)(3)(iii)(B) of this section exceeds 10 percent of the amount of the gain of the holder (or such other person) described in paragraph (e)(3)(iii)(A) of this section;

then the gain of the holder (or such other person) that is described in paragraph (e)(3)(iii)(A) of this section shall be treated as gain that is not from a passive activity to the extent that such gain does not exceed the amount of the gain of the holder (or such other person) described in paragraph (e)(3)(iii)(B) of this section. For purposes of applying the preceding sentence to the disposition of an interest in a partnership, the amount of gain that would have been allocated to the holder (or such other person) if all of the property used in an activity had been sold shall be determined by taking into account any adjustment to the basis of partnership property made with respect to such holder (or such other person) under section 743(b).

(iv) Dispositions occurring in taxable years beginning before February 19, 1988. (A) In general. Except as otherwise provided in this paragraph (e)(3)(iv), if the holder of an interest in a passthrough entity sells, exchanges, or otherwise disposes of all or part of such interest during a taxable year of such entity beginning prior to February 19, 1988, any gain or loss recognized from such disposition shall be allocated among the activities of the passthrough entity under any reasonable method selected by the passthrough entity, and the gain or loss allocated to each activity of the passthrough entity shall be treated as gain or loss from the disposition of an interest in such activity. For purposes of the preceding sentence, a reasonable method shall include the method prescribed by paragraph (e)(3)(ii) of this section. In addition, a method that allocates gain or loss among the passthrough entity's activities on the basis of the fair market value, cost, or adjusted basis of the property used in such activities shall generally be considered a reasonable method for purposes of this paragraph (e)(3)(iv).

(B) Exceptions. This paragraph (e)(3)(iv) shall not apply to any disposition of an interest in a passthrough entity occurring after February 19, 1988 if after such date, but before the holder's disposition of such interest, the holder (or any other person that owns (directly or indirectly) an interest in such holder if such holder is a passthrough entity) contributes to the passthrough entity substantially appreciated portfolio assets or any other substantially appreciated property that was used in any trade or business activity (within the meaning of § 1.469-1T(e)) of the holder (or such other person) during—

(1) The taxable year of such person in which such contribution occurs; or

(2) The immediately preceding taxable year of such person; but only if such person materially participated (within the meaning of § 1.469-5T) in the activity for such year.

(v) Treatment of portfolio assets. For purposes of this paragraph (e)(3), all portfolio assets owned by a passthrough entity shall be treated as held in a single investment activity.

(vi) Definitions. For purposes of this paragraph (e)(3)—

(A) The term "portfolio asset" means any property of a type that produces portfolio income (within the meaning of paragraph (c)(3)(i) of this section);

(B) The term "substantially appreciated property" means property with a fair market value that exceeds 120 percent of its adjusted basis; and

(C) The term "substantially depreciated property" means property with an adjusted basis that exceeds 120 percent of its fair market value.

(vii) Examples. The following examples illustrate the application of this paragraph (e)(3):

*Example (1).* (i) A owns a one-half interest in P, a calendar year partnership. In 1993, A sells 50 percent of such interest for $50,000. A's adjusted basis for the interest sold is $30,000. Thus, A recognizes $20,000 of gain from the sale. P is engaged in three trade or business activities, X, Y, and Z, and owns marketable securities that are portfolio assets. For 1993, A materially participates in activity Z, but does not participate in activities X and Y. Paragraph (c)(2)(iii) of this section would not have applied to any of the gain that A would have been allocated if, immediately before A's sale, P had disposed of all of the property used in its trade or business activities. During the portion of 1993 preceding A's sale, P did not sell any of the property used in its activities, and A did not contribute any property to P.

(ii) Under paragraph (e)(3)(ii) of this section, a ratable portion of A's $20,000 gain is allocated to each appreciated activity in which P owned an interest on the applicable valuation date (within the meaning of paragraph (e)(3)(ii)(D)(1) of this section). For this purpose, paragraph (e)(3)(v) of this section treats the marketable securities owned by P as a single investment activity.

(iii) P selects the beginning of 1993 as the applicable valuation date pursuant to paragraph (e)(3)(ii)(D)(1)(i) of this section. P is not required to use the date of A's sale as the applicable valuation date under paragraph (e)(3)(ii)(D)(1)(ii) of this section because during the portion of 1993 preceding A's sale, P did not sell any of its property and A did not contribute any property to P. At the beginning of 1993, the fair market value and adjusted basis of the property used in P's activities are as follows:

| | Adjusted Basis | Fair Market Value |
|---|---|---|
| X | $ 68,000 | $ 48,000 |
| Y | 30,000 | 62,000 |
| Z | 20,000 | 80,000 |
| Marketable securities | 2,000 | 10,000 |
| Total | $120,000 | $200,000 |

(iv) Under paragraph (e)(3)(ii)(B) of this section, the portion of A's $20,000 gain that is allocated to an appreciated activity of P (i.e., activities Y and Z and the marketable securities) is the amount of such gain multiplied by the fraction obtained by dividing (a) the net gain that would have been allocated to A with respect to the interest sold by A if P had sold its entire interest in such activity at the beginning of 1993 by (b) the sum of the amounts of net gain that would have been allocated to A with respect to the interest sold by A if P had sold its entire interest in each appreciated activity at the beginning of 1993.

(v) If P had sold its entire interest in activities Y and Z and the marketable securities at the beginning of 1993, A would have been allocated the following amounts of net gain with respect to the interest in P that A sold in 1993:

| Activity | Net Gain |
|---|---|
| Y | $ 8,000 |
| Z | 15,000 |
| Marketable securities | 2,000 |
| Total | $25,000 |

(vi) Accordingly, under paragraph (e)(3)(ii) of this section, $6,400 of A's $20,000 gain ($20,000 × $8,000/$25,000) is allocated to activity Y, $12,000 of A's $20,000 gain ($20,000 × $15,000/$25,000) is allocated to activity Z, and $1,600 of A's $20,000 gain ($20,000 × $2,000/$25,000) is allocated to the marketable securities. The gain allocated to activity Y is passive activity gross income. None of that gain is treated as gain that is not from a passive activity under paragraph (e)(3)(iii) of this section because paragraph (c)(2)(iii) of this section would not have applied to any of the gain that A would have been allocated if P had sold all of the property used in activity Y immediately prior to A's sale.

*Example (2).* (i) B and C, calendar year individuals, are equal partners in calendar year partnership R, which they formed on January 1, 2005, with contributions of property and money. The only item of property (other than money) contributed by B was a building that B had used for 12 years preceding the contribution in an activity that was not a passive activity during such period. At the time of its contribution, the building had an adjusted basis of $40,000 and a fair market value of $66,000. R is engaged in a single activity: the sale of equipment to customers in the ordinary course of the business of dealing in such property. R uses the building contributed by B in the dealership activity. B did not materially participate in the dealership activity during 2005. On July 1, 2005, D purchases one-half of B's interest in R for $37,500 in cash. At the time of the sale, the balance sheet of R, which uses the accrual method of accounting, is as follows:

**Assets**

| | Adjusted Basis Per Books | Fair Market Value |
|---|---|---|
| Cash | $ 30,000 | $ 30,000 |
| Accounts receivable —Dealership | 20,000 | 18,000 |
| Inventory —Dealership | 52,000 | 66,000 |
| Building | 40,000 | 66,000 |
| Total | $142,000 | $180,000 |

**Liabilities And Capital**

| | | Adjusted Basis Per Books | Fair Market Value |
|---|---|---|---|
| Liabilities | | $ 30,000 | $ 30,000 |
| Capital | B | 47,000 | 75,000 |
| | C | 65,000 | 75,000 |
| Total | | $142,000 | $180,000 |

Thus, B's gain from the sale is $14,000 ($45,000 amount realized from the sale (consisting of $37,500 of cash and $7,500 of liabilities assumed by the purchaser) minus B's $31,000 adjusted basis for the interest sold (one-half of B's total adjusted basis of $62,000)).

(ii) Under paragraph (e)(3)(ii) of this section, all $14,000 of B's gain from the sale is allocated to R's dealership activity, which is a passive activity of B for 2005. If, however, R had sold its interest in the building immediately prior to B's sale for its fair market value on the applicable valuation date (the valuation date selected by R is irrelevant since the building had a fair market value of $66,000 at the beginning of 2005 and at the time of the sale), B would have been allocated $13,000 of gain under section 704(c) with respect to the interest in R that B sold to D. This gain would have been treated as gain that is not from a passive activity under paragraph (c)(2)(iii) of this section and would have exceeded 10 percent of the total amount of B's gain that is allocated to the dealership activity under paragraph (e)(3)(ii) of this section. Accordingly, under paragraph (e)(3)(iii) of this section, B's gain from the sale ($14,000) is treated as gain that is not from a passive activity to the extent that such gain does not exceed the amount of gain subject to paragraph (c)(2)(iii) of this section that B would have been allocated with respect to the interest sold to D if R had sold all of the property used in the dealership activity immediately prior to B's sale ($13,000). Thus, $13,000 of B's gain from the sale is treated as gain that is not from a passive activity.

**(f) Recharacterization of passive income in certain situations.** *(1) In general.* This paragraph (f) sets forth rules that require income from certain passive activities to be treated as income that is not from a passive activity (regardless of whether such income is treated as passive activity gross income under section 469 or any other provision of the regulations thereunder). For definitions of certain terms used in this paragraph (f), see paragraph (f)(9) of this section.

*(2) Special rule for significant participation.* (i) In general. An amount of the taxpayer's gross income from each significant participation passive activity for the taxable year equal to a ratable portion of the taxpayer's net passive income from such activity for the taxable year shall be treated as not from a passive activity if the taxpayer's passive activity gross income from all significant participation passive activities for the taxable year (determined without regard to paragraph (f)(2) through (4) of this section) exceeds the taxpayer's passive activity deductions from all such activities for such year. For purposes of this paragraph (f)(2), the ratable portion of the net passive income from an activity is determined by multiplying the amount of such income by the fraction obtained by dividing—

(A) The amount of the excess described in the preceding sentence; by

(B) The amount of the excess described in the preceding sentence taking into account only significant participation passive activities from which the taxpayer has net passive income for the taxable year.

(ii) Significant participation passive activity. For purposes of this paragraph (f)(2), the term "significant participation passive activity" means any trade or business activity (within the meaning of § 1.469-1T (e)(2)) in which the taxpayer significantly participates (within the meaning of § 1.469-5T(c)(2)) for the taxable year but in which the taxpayer does not materially participate (within the meaning of § 1.469-5T) for such year.

(iii) Example. The following example illustrates the application of this paragraph (f)(2):

*Example.* (i) A owns interests in three trade or business activities, X, Y, and Z. A does not materially participate in any of these activities for the taxable year, but participates in activity X for 110 hours, in activity Y for 160 hours, and in activity Z for 125 hours. A owns no interest in any other trade or business activity in which A does not materially participate for the taxable year but in which A participates for more than 100 hours during the taxable year. A's net passive income (or loss) for the taxable year from activities X, Y, and Z is as follows:

| | X | Y | Z |
|---|---|---|---|
| Passive activity gross income | $600 | $700 | $900 |
| Passive activity deductions | (200) | (1,000) | (300) |
| Net passive income | $400 | ($300) | $600 |

(ii) Under paragraph (f)(2)(ii) of this section, activities X, Y, and Z are A's only significant participation passive activities for the taxable year. A's passive activity gross income from significant participation passive activities ($2,200) exceeds A's passive activity deductions from significant participation passive activities ($1,500) by $700 for such year. Therefore, under paragraph (f)(2)(i) of this section, a ratable portion of A's gross income from activities X and Z (A's significant participation passive activities with net passive income for the taxable year) is treated as gross income that is not from a passive activity. The ratable portion is determined by dividing (a) the amount by which A's passive activity gross income from significant participation passive activities exceeds A's passive activity deductions from significant participation passive activities for the taxable year ($700) by (b) such excess taking into account only A's significant participation passive activities having net passive income for the taxable year ($1,000). Accordingly, $280 of gross income from activity X ($400 × 700/1000) and $420 of gross income from activity Z ($600 × 700/1000) is treated as gross income that is not from a passive activity.

*(3) Rental of nondepreciable property.* If less than 30 percent of the unadjusted basis of the property used or held for use by customers in a rental activity (within the meaning of § 1.469-1T(e)(3)) during the taxable year is subject to the allowance for depreciation under section 167, an amount of the taxpayer's gross income from the activity equal to the taxpayer's net passive income from the activity shall be treated as not from a passive activity. For purposes of this paragraph (f)(3), the term "unadjusted basis" means adjusted basis determined without regard to any adjustment described in section 1016 that decreases basis. The following example illustrates the application of this paragraph (f)(3):

*Example.* C is a limited partner in a partnership. The partnership acquires vacant land for $300,000, constructs improvements on the land at a cost of $100,000, and leases the land and improvements to a tenant. The partnership then sells the land and improvements for $600,000, thereby realizing a gain on the disposition. The unadjusted basis of the improvements ($100,000) equals 25 percent of the unadjusted basis of all property ($400,000) used in the rental activity. Therefore, under this paragraph (f)(3), an amount of C's gross income from the activity equal to the net passive income from the activity (which is computed by taking into account the gain from the disposition, including gain allocable to the improvements) is treated as not from a passive activity.

*(4) Net interest income from passive equity-financed lending activity.* (i) In general. An amount of the taxpayer's gross income for the taxable year from any equity-financed lending activity equal to the lesser of—

(A) The taxpayer's equity-financed interest income from the activity for such year; and

(B) The taxpayer's net passive income from the activity for such year shall be treated as not from a passive activity.

(ii) Equity-financed lending activity. (A) In general. For purposes of this paragraph (f)(4), an activity is an equity-financed lending activity for a taxable year if—

(1) The activity involves a trade or business of lending money; and

(2) The average outstanding balance of the liabilities incurred in the activity for the taxable year does not exceed 80 percent of the average outstanding balance of the interest-bearing assets held in the activity for such year.

(B) Certain liabilities not taken into account. For purposes of paragraph (f)(4)(ii)(A)(2) of this section, liabilities incurred principally for the purpose of increasing the percentage described in paragraph (f)(4)(ii)(A)(2) of this section shall not be taken into account in computing such percentage.

(iii) Equity-financed interest income. For purposes of this paragraph (f)(4), the taxpayer's equity-financed interest income from an activity for a taxable year is the amount of the taxpayer's net interest income from the activity for such year multiplied by the fraction obtained by dividing—

(A) The excess of the average outstanding balance for such year of the interest-bearing assets held in the activity over the average outstanding balance for such year of the liabilities incurred in the activity; by

(B) The average outstanding balance for such year of the interest-bearing assets held in the activity.

(iv) Net interest income. For purposes of this paragraph (f)(4), the net interest income from an activity for a taxable year is—

(A) The gross interest income from the activity for such year; reduced by

(B) Expenses from the activity (other than interest on liabilities described in paragraph (f)(4)(vi) of this section) for such year that are reasonably allocable to such gross interest income.

(v) Interest-bearing assets. For purposes of this paragraph (f)(4), the interest-bearing assets held in an activity include all assets that produce interest income, including loans to customers.

(vi) Liabilities incurred in the activity. For purposes of this paragraph (f)(4), liabilities incurred in an activity include all fixed and determinable liabilities incurred in the activity that bear interest or are issued with original issue discount other than debts secured by tangible property used in the activity. In the case of an activity conducted by an entity in which the taxpayer owns a interest, liabilities incurred in an activity include only liabilities with respect to which the entity is the borrower.

(vii) Average outstanding balance. For purposes of this paragraph (f)(4), the average outstanding balance of liabilities incurred in an activity or of the interest-bearing assets held in an activity may be computed on a daily, monthly, or quarterly basis at the option of the taxpayer.

(viii) Example. The following example illustrates the application of this paragraph (f)(4):

*Example.* (i) A, a calendar year individual, acquires on January 1, 1988, a limited partnership interest in P, a calendar year partnership. Under the partnership agreement, A has a one percent share of each item of income, gain, loss, deduction, and credit of P. A acquires the partnership interest for $90,000, using $50,000 of unborrowed funds and $40,000 of proceeds of a loan bearing interest at an annual rate of 10 percent. A pays $4,000 of interest on the loan in 1988.

(ii) P's sole activity is a trade or business of lending money. A does not materially participate in the activity for 1988. During 1988, the average outstanding balance of P's interest-bearing assets (including loans to customers, temporary deposits with other lending institutions, and government and corporate securities) is $20 million. P incurs numerous interest-bearing liabilities in connection with its lending activity, including liabilities for deposits taken from customers, unsecured short-term and long-term loans from other lending institutions, and a mortgage loan secured by the building, owned by P, in which P conducts its business. For 1988, the average outstanding balance of all of these liabilities (other than the mortgage loan) is $11 million. None of these liabilities was incurred by P principally for the purpose of increasing the percentage described in paragraph (f)(4)(ii)(A)(2) of this section.

(iii) The interest income derived by P for 1988 from its interest-bearing assets is $2.2 million. The interest expense paid by P for 1988 with respect to the liabilities incurred in connection with its lending activity (other than the mortgage loan) is $990,000. P's other expenses for 1988 that are reasonably allocable to P's gross interest income (including expenses for advertising, loan processing and servicing, and insurance and depreciation on P's building) total $250,000. P's interest expense for 1988 on the mortgage loan secured by the building used in P's lending activity is $50,000. All of the interest expense paid or incurred by P for 1988 is allocated under § 1.163-8T to expenditures in connection with P's lending activity.

(iv) Under paragraph (f)(4)(ii) of this section, P's activity is an equity-financed lending activity for 1988, since, for 1988, the activity involves a trade or business of lending money and the average outstanding balance of the liabilities incurred in the activity ($11 million) does not exceed 80 percent of the average outstanding balance of the interest-bearing assets held in the activity ($20 million). Accordingly, under paragraph (f)(4)(i) of this section, an amount of A's gross income from the activity equal to the lesser of (a) A's equity-financed interest income from the activity for 1988, or (b) A's net passive income from the activity for 1988, is treated as income that is not from a passive activity.

(v) Under paragraph (f)(4)(iii) of this section, A's equity-financed interest income from the activity for 1988 is determined by multiplying A's net interest income from the activity for 1988 by the fraction obtained by dividing $9 million (the excess of the average interest-bearing assets for 1988 over the average interest-bearing liabilities for 1988) by $20 million (the average interest-bearing assets for 1988). Under paragraph (f)(4)(iv) of this section, A's net interest income from the activity for 1988 is $19,000 (A's distributive share of $2.2 million of gross interest income less A's distributive share of $300,000 of expenses described in paragraph (f)(4)(iv)(B) of this section, including interest expense on the mortgage loan). A's distributive share of P's other interest expense ($990,000) is not taken into account in computing A's net interest income for 1988. Accordingly, A's equity-financed interest income from the activity for 1988 is $8,550 ($19,000 × $9 million/$20 million).

(vi) Under paragraph (f)(9)(i) of this section, A's net passive income from the activity for 1988 is determined by taking into account A's distributive share of P's gross income and deductions from the activity for 1988, as well as any interest expense incurred by A individually that is taken into account under § 1.163-8T in determining A's income or loss from the activity for 1988. Assuming that for 1988 all $4,000 of interest expense on the loan that A used to finance the acquisition of A's interest in P is allocated under § 1.163-8T to expenditures of A in connection with the lending activity for 1988, A's net passive income from the activity for 1988 is $5,100, computed as set forth in the following table:

| | |
|---|---|
| *Gross income* | |
| Interest income | $22,000 |
| *Deductions* | |
| Distributive share of P's expenses from the activity | (12,900) |
| Interest expense on A's acquisition debt | (4,000) |
| Net passive income | $5,100 |

(vii) A's net passive income from the activity for 1988 ($5,100) is less than A's equity-financed income from the activity for 1988 ($8,550). Accordingly, under this paragraph (f)(4), $5,100 of A's gross income from the activity for 1988 is treated as not from a passive activity.

*(5) Net income from certain property rented incidental to development activity.* (i) In general. [Reserved] See § 1.469-2(f)(5)(i) for rules relating to this paragraph.

(ii) Commencement. [Reserved] See § 1.469-2(f)(5)(ii) for rules relating to this paragraph (f)(5)(ii).

(iii) Services performed for the purpose of enhancing the value of property. [Reserved] See § 1.469-2(f)(5)(iii) for rules relating to this paragraph (f)(5)(iii).

(iv) Examples. [Reserved] See § 1.469-2(f)(5)(iv) for examples relating to this paragraph (f)(5)(iv).

*(6) Property rented to a nonpassive activity.* [Reserved] See § 1.469-2(f)(6) for rules relating to this paragraph.

*(7) Special rules applicable to the acquisition of an interest in a passthrough entity engaged in the trade or business of licensing intangible property.* (i) In general. If a taxpayer acquires an interest in an entity described in paragraph (c)(3)(iii)(B)(3) of this section (the "development entity") after the development entity has created an item of intangible property or performed substantial services or incurred substantial costs with respect to the development or marketing of an item of intangible property, an amount of the taxpayer's gross royalty income for the taxable year from such item of property equal to the taxpayer's net royalty income for the year from such item of property shall be treated as not from a passive activity.

(ii) Royalty income from property. For purposes of this paragraph (f)(7)—

(A) A taxpayer's gross royalty income for a taxable year from an item of property is the taxpayer's share of passive activity gross income for such year (determined without regard to paragraph (f)(2) through (7) of this section) from the licensing or transfer of any right in such property; and

(B) A taxpayer's net royalty income for a taxable year from an item of property is the excess, if any, of—

(1) The taxpayer's gross royalty income for the taxable year from such item of property; over

(2) Any passive activity deductions for such taxable year (including any deduction treated as a deduction for such year under § 1.469-1T(f)(4)) that are reasonably allocable to such item of property.

(iii) Exceptions. Paragraph (f)(7)(i) of this section shall not apply to a taxpayer's gross royalty income for a taxable year from the licensing of an item of intangible property if—

(A) The expenditures reasonably incurred by the development entity for the taxable year of the entity ending with or within the taxpayer's taxable year with respect to the development or marketing of such property satisfy paragraph (c)(3)(iii)(B)(2)(ii)(a) of this section; or

(B) The taxpayer's share of the expenditures reasonably incurred by the development entity with respect to the development or marketing of such property for all taxable years of the entity beginning with the taxable year of the entity in which the taxpayer acquired the interest in the entity and ending with the taxable year of the entity ending with or within the taxpayer's current taxable year exceeds 25 percent of the fair market value of the taxpayer's interest in such property at the time the taxpayer acquired the interest in the entity.

(iv) Capital expenditures. For purposes of paragraph (f)(7)(iii)(B) of this section, a capital expenditure shall be taken into account for the taxable year of the entity in which such expenditure is chargeable to capital account, and the taxpayer's share of such expenditure shall be determined as though such expenditure were allowed as a deduction for such year.

(v) Example. The following example illustrates the application of this paragraph (f)(7):

*Example.* (i) The facts are the same as in example (5) in paragraph (c)(3)(iv) of this section, except that, in 1988, D's 10 percent partnership interest is sold to F for $13,000, all of which is attributable to the design licensed by the partnership.

(ii) For 1988, the expenditures reasonably incurred by the partnership with respect to the development or marketing of the design satisfy paragraph (c)(3)(iii)(B)(2)(ii)(a) of this section. Accordingly, under paragraph (f)(7)(iii)(A) of this section, paragraph (f)(7)(i) of this section does not apply to F's distributive share of the partnership's gross income from licensing the design.

(iii) For 1989, the expenditures reasonably incurred by the partnership with respect to the development or marketing of the design do not satisfy paragraph (c)(3)(iii)(B)(2)(ii)(a) of this section. Moreover, F's distributive share of such expenditures reasonably incurred by the partnership for 1988 and 1989 ($27,000 × .10 = $2,700) does not exceed 25 percent of the fair market value of F's interest in the design at the time F acquired the partnership interest ($13,000). Accordingly, neither of the exceptions provided in paragraph (f)(7)(iii) of this section applies for 1989 and, under paragraph (f)(7)(i) of this section, an amount of F's gross royalty income from the design equal to F's net royalty income from the design is treated as not from a passive activity.

*(8) Limitation on recharacterized income.* The amount of gross income from an activity that is treated as not from a passive activity for the taxable year under subparagraphs (f)(2) through (4) of this paragraph (f) shall not exceed the greatest amount of gross income treated as not from a passive activity under any one of such subparagraphs.

*(9) Meaning of certain terms.* For purposes of this paragraph (f), the terms set forth below shall have the following meanings:

(i) The net passive income from an activity for a taxable year is the amount by which the taxpayer's passive activity gross income from the activity for the taxable year (determined without regard to paragraph (f)(2) through (4) of this section) exceeds the taxpayer's passive activity deductions from the activity for such year;

(ii) The net passive loss from an activity for a taxable year is the amount by which the taxpayer's passive activity deductions from the activity for the taxable year exceeds the taxpayer's passive activity gross income from the activity for such year (determined without regard to paragraph (f) (2) through (4) of this section).

(iii) [Reserved] See § 1.469-2(f)(9)(iii) for rules relating to this paragraph.

(iv) [Reserved] See § 1.469-2(f)(9)(iv) for rules relating to this paragraph.

*(10) Coordination with section 163(d).* [Reserved] See paragraph 1.469-2(f)(10) for rules relating to this paragraph.

*(11) Effective date.* For the effective date of the rules in this paragraph (f), see § 1.469-11T (relating to effective date and transition rules).

---

T.D. 8175, 2/19/88, amend T.D. 8253, 5/11/89, T.D. 8290, 2/23/90, T.D. 8318, 11/16/90, T.D. 8417, 5/11/92, T.D. 8477, 2/22/93, T.D. 8495, 11/3/93.

---

## § 1.469-3 Passive activity credit.

**(a) through (d) [Reserved]**

**(e) Coordination with section 38(b).** Any credit described in section 38(b)(1) through (5) is taken into account in computing the current year business credit for the first taxable year in which the credit is subject to section 469 and is not disallowed by section 469 and the regulations thereunder.

**(f) Coordination with section 50.** In the case of any cessation described in section 50(a)(1) or (2), the credits allocable to the taxpayer's activities under § 1.469-1(f)(4) shall be adjusted by reason of the cessation.

**(g) [Reserved]**

---

T.D. 8417, 5/11/92.

---

## § 1.469-3T Passive activity credit (temporary).

***Caution:*** The Treasury has not yet amended Reg § 1.469-3T to reflect changes made by P.L. 103-66.

**(a) Computation of passive activity credit.** The taxpayer's passive activity credit for the taxable year is the amount (if any) by which—

*(1)* The sum of all of the taxpayer's credits that are subject to section 469 for such year; exceeds

*(2)* The taxpayer's regular tax liability allocable to all passive activities for such year.

**(b) Credits subject to section 469.** *(1) In general.* Except as otherwise provided in this paragraph (b), a credit is subject to section 469 for a taxable year if and only if—

(i) Such credit—

(A) Is attributable to such taxable year and arises in connection with the conduct of an activity that is a passive activity for such taxable year; and

(B) Is described in—

(1) Section 38(b)(1) through (5) (relating to general business credits);

(2) Section 27(b) (relating to corporations described in section 936);

(3) Section 28 (relating to clinical testing of certain drugs); or

(4) Section 29 (relating to fuel from nonconventional sources); or

(ii) Such credit is allocable to an activity for such taxable year under § 1.469-1T(f)(4).

*(2) Treatment of credits attributable to qualified progress expenditures.* Any credit attributable to an increase in qualified investment under section 46(d)(1)(A) (relating to qualified progress expenditures) with respect to progress expenditure property (as defined in section 46(d)(2)) is subject to section 469 for a taxable year if—

(i) Such credit is attributable to such taxable year;

(ii) Such credit is described in paragraph (b)(1)(i)(B) of this section; and

(iii) It is reasonable to believe that such progress expenditure property will be used in a passive activity of the taxpayer when it is placed in service.

*(3) Special rule for partners and S corporation shareholders.* The character of a credit of a taxpayer arising in connection with an activity conducted by a partnership or S corporation (as a credit subject to section 469) shall be determined, in any case in which participation is relevant, by

reference to the participation of the taxpayer in such activity. Such participation is determined for the taxable year of the partnership or S corporation (and not the taxable year of the taxpayer). See § 1.469-2T(e)(1).

*(4) Exception for pre-1987 credits.* A credit is not subject to section 469 if it is attributable to a taxable year of the taxpayer beginning prior to January 1, 1987.

**(c) Taxable year to which credit is attributable.** A credit is attributable to the taxable year in which such credit would be (or would have been) allowed if the credits allowed for all taxable years were determined without regard to the limitations contained in sections 26(a), 28(d)(2), 29(b)(5), 38(c), and 469.

**(d) Regular tax liability allocable to passive activities.** *(1) In general.* For purposes of paragraph (a) (2) of this section, the taxpayer's regular tax liability allocable to all passive activities for the taxable year is the excess (if any) of—

(i) The taxpayer's regular tax liability for such taxable year; over

(ii) The amount of such regular tax liability determined by reducing the taxpayer's taxable income for such year by the excess (if any) of the taxpayer's passive activity gross income for such year over the taxpayer's passive activity deductions for such year.

*(2) Regular tax liability.* For purposes of this section, the term "regular tax liability" has the meaning given such term in section 26 (b).

**(e) Coordination with section 38(b). [Reserved]** See § 1.469-3(e) for rules relating to this paragraph.

**(f) Coordination with section 50. [Reserved]** See § 1.469-3(f) for rules relating to this paragraph.

**(g) Examples.** The following examples illustrate the application of this section:

*Example (1).* (i) A, a calendar year individual, is a general partner in calendar year partnership P. P purchases a building in 1987 and, in 1987, 1988, and 1989, incurs rehabilitation costs with respect to the building. The building is placed in service in the rental activity in 1989. P's rehabilitation costs are qualified rehabilitation expenditures (within the meaning of section 48(g)(2)) and are taken into account in determining the amount of the investment credit for rehabilitation expenditures. P's qualified rehabilitation expenditures are not qualified progress expenditures (within the meaning of section 46(d)).

(ii) Because, under section 46(c)(1), the credit is allowable for the taxable year in which the rehabilitated property is placed in service, the credit allowable for P's qualified rehabilitation expenditures arises in connection with the activity in which the property is placed in service. In addition, the credit is attributable to 1989, the year in which the property is placed in service, because it would be allowed for such year if A's credits allowed for all taxable years were determined without regard to the limitations contained in sections 26(a), 28(d)(2), 29(b)(5), 38(c), and 469. Accordingly, under paragraph (b) (1) of this section, A's distributive share of the credit is subject to section 469 for 1989 because the credit arises in connection with a rental activity for such year.

*Example (2).* The facts are the same as in example (1), except that the rehabilitation costs are incurred in anticipation of placing the building in service in a rental activity, the qualified rehabilitation expenditures in 1987 and 1988 are qualified progress expenditures ("QPEs") (within the meaning of section 46(d)(3)), the improvements resulting from the expenditures are progress expenditure property (within the meaning of paragraph (d)(2) of this section), and it is reasonable to expect that such property will be transition property (within the meaning of section 49(e)) when the property is placed in service. Therefore, under section 46(d)(1)(A), the qualified investment for 1987 and 1988 is increased by an amount equal to the aggregate of the applicable percentage of the qualified rehabilitation expenditures incurred in such years. The credits that are based on these expenditures are attributable (under paragraph (c) of this section) to 1987 and 1988, respectively. It is reasonable to believe in 1987 and 1988 that the progress expenditure property will be used in a rental activity when it is placed in service. Accordingly, under paragraph (b)(2) of this section, A's distributive share of the credit for 1987 and 1988 is subject to section 469. Under paragraph (b)(1) of this section (as in example (1)), A's distributive share of the credit for 1989 is also subject to section 469.

*Example (3).* (i) B, a single individual, acquires an interest in a partnership that, in 1988, rehabilitates a building and places it in service in a trade or business activity in which B does not materially participate. For 1988, B has the following items of gross income, deduction, and credit:

| | | |
|---|---|---|
| *Gross income* | | |
| Income other than passive activity gross income | $110,000 | |
| Passive activity gross income | 20,000 | $ 130,000 |
| *Deductions* | | |
| Deductions other than passive activity deductions | $ 23,950 | |
| Passive activity deductions | 18,000 | (41,950) |
| Taxable income | | 88,050 |
| *Credits* | | |
| Rehabilitation credit from the passive activity | | $ 8,000 |

(ii) For 1988, the amount by which B's passive activity gross income exceeds B's passive activity deductions (B's net passive income) is $2,000. Under paragraph (d) of this section, B's regular tax liability allocable to passive activities for 1988 is determined as follows:

| | | |
|---|---|---|
| (A) Taxable income | $88,050.00 | |
| (B) Regular tax liability | | $24,578.50 |
| (C) Taxable income minus net passive income | 86,050.00 | |
| (D) Regular tax liability for taxable income of $86,050.00 | | 23,918.50 |
| (E) Regular tax liability allocable to passive activities ((B) minus (D)) | | $ 660.00 |

(iii) Under paragraph (a) of this section, B's passive activity credit for 1988 is the amount by which B's credits that are subject to section 469 for 1988 ($8,000) exceed B's regular tax liability allocable to passive activities for 1988 ($660.00). Accordingly, B's passive activity credit for 1988 is $7,340.

*Example (4).* (i) The facts are the same as in example (3) except that, in 1988, B also has additional deductions of $100,000 from a trade or business activity in which B materially participates for 1988. Thus, B has a taxable loss for 1988 of $11,950, determined as follows:

| | | |
|---|---|---|
| *Gross income* | | |
| Income other than passive activity gross income | $110,000 | |
| Passive activity gross income | 20,000 | $ 130,000 |
| *Deductions* | | |
| Deductions other than passive activity deductions | $123,950 | |
| Passive activity deductions | 18,000 | (141,950) |
| Taxable income | | ($ 11,950) |

(ii) Under section 26(b) and paragraph (d)(2) of this section, the regular tax liability for a taxable year cannot exceed the tax imposed by chapter 1 of subtitle A of the Internal Revenue Code for the taxable year. Therefore, under paragraph (d)(1) of this section, B's regular tax liability allocable to passive activities for 1988 is zero. Although B's net operating loss for the taxable year is reduced by B's net passive income, and B's regular tax liability for other taxable years may increase as a result of the reduction, such an increase does not change B's regular tax liability allocable to passive activities for 1988. Accordingly, B's passive activity credit for 1988 is $8,000.

T.D. 8175, 2/19/88, amend T.D. 8253, 5/11/89, T.D. 8417, 5/11/92.

## § 1.469-4 Definition of activity.

**(a) Scope and purpose.** This section sets forth the rules for grouping a taxpayer's trade or business activities and rental activities for purposes of applying the passive activity loss and credit limitation rules of section 469. A taxpayer's activities include those conducted through C corporations that are subject to section 469, S corporations, and partnerships.

**(b) Definitions.** The following definitions apply for purposes of this section—

*(1) Trade or business activities.* Trade or business activities are activities, other than rental activities or activities that are treated under § 1.469-1T(e)(3)(vi)(B) as incidental to an activity of holding property for investment, that—

(i) Involve the conduct of a trade or business (within the meaning of section 162);

(ii) Are conducted in anticipation of the commencement of a trade or business; or

(iii) Involve research or experimental expenditures that are deductible under section 174 (or would be deductible if the taxpayer adopted the method described in section 174(a)).

*(2) Rental activities.* Rental activities are activities that constitute rental activities within the meaning of § 1.469-1T(e)(3).

**(c) General rules for grouping activities.** *(1) Appropriate economic unit.* One or more trade or business activities or rental activities may be treated as a single activity if the activities constitute an appropriate economic unit for the measurement of gain or loss for purposes of section 469.

*(2) Facts and circumstances test.* Except as otherwise provided in this section, whether activities constitute an appropriate economic unit and, therefore, may be treated as a single activity depends upon all the relevant facts and circumstances. A taxpayer may use any reasonable method of applying the relevant facts and circumstances in grouping activities. The factors listed below, not all of which are necessary for a taxpayer to treat more than one activity as a single activity, are given the greatest weight in determining whether activities constitute an appropriate economic unit for the measurement of gain or loss for purposes of section 469—

(i) Similarities and differences in types of trades or businesses;

(ii) The extent of common control;

(iii) The extent of common ownership;

(iv) Geographical location; and

(v) Interdependencies between or among the activities (for example, the extent to which the activities purchase or sell goods between or among themselves, involve products or services that are normally provided together, have the same customers, have the same employees, or are accounted for with a single set of books and records).

*(3) Examples.* The following examples illustrate the application of this paragraph (c).

*Example (1).* Taxpayer C has a significant ownership interest in a bakery and a movie theater at a shopping mall in Baltimore and in a bakery and a movie theater in Philadelphia. In this case, after taking into account all the relevant facts and circumstances, there may be more than one reasonable method for grouping C's activities. For instance, depending on the relevant facts and circumstances, the following groupings may or may not be permissible: a single activity; a movie theater activity and a bakery activity; a Baltimore activity and a Philadelphia activity; or four separate activities. Moreover, once C groups these activities into appropriate economic units, paragraph (e) of this section requires C to continue using that grouping in subsequent taxable years unless a material change in the facts and circumstances makes it clearly inappropriate.

*Example (2).* Taxpayer B, an individual, is a partner in a business that sells non-food items to grocery stores (partnership L). B also is a partner in a partnership that owns and operates a trucking business (partnership Q). The two partnerships are under common control. The predominant portion of Q's business is transporting goods for L, and Q is the only trucking business in which B is involved. Under this section, B appropriately treats L's wholesale activity and Q's trucking activity as a single activity.

**(d) Limitation on grouping certain activities.** The grouping of activities under this section is subject to the following limitations:

*(1) Grouping rental activities with other trade or business activities.* (i) Rule. A rental activity may not be grouped with a trade or business activity unless the activities being grouped together constitute an appropriate economic unit under paragraph (c) of this section and—

(A) The rental activity is insubstantial in relation to the trade or business activity;

(B) The trade or business activity is insubstantial in relation to the rental activity; or

(C) Each owner of the trade or business activity has the same proportionate ownership interest in the rental activity, in which case the portion of the rental activity that involves the rental of items of property for use in the trade or business activity may be grouped with the trade or business activity.

(ii) Examples. The following examples illustrate the application of paragraph (d)(1)(i) of this section:

*Example (1).* (i) H and W are married and file a joint return. H is the sole shareholder of an S corporation that conducts a grocery store trade or business activity. W is the sole shareholder of an S corporation that owns and rents out a building. Part of the building is rented to H's grocery store trade or business activity (the grocery store rental). The grocery store rental and the grocery store trade or business are not insubstantial in relation to each other.

(ii) Because they file a joint return, H and W are treated as one taxpayer for purposes of section 469. See § 1.469-1T(j). Therefore, the sole owner of the trade or business activity (taxpayer H-W) is also the sole owner of the rental activity. Consequently, each owner of the trade or business activity has the same proportionate ownership interest in the rental activity. Accordingly, the grocery store rental and the grocery store trade or business activity may be grouped together (under paragraph (d)(1)(i) of this section) into a single trade or business activity, if the grouping is appropriate under paragraph (c) of this section.

*Example (2).* Attorney D is a sole practitioner in town X. D also wholly owns residential real estate in town X that D rents to third parties. D's law practice is a trade or business activity within the meaning of paragraph (b)(1) of this section. The residential real estate is a rental activity within the meaning of § 1.469-1T(e)(3) and is insubstantial in relation to D's law practice. Under the facts and circumstances, the law practice and the residential real estate do not constitute an appropriate economic unit under paragraph (c) of this section. Therefore, D may not treat the law practice and the residential real estate as a single activity.

*(2) Grouping real property rentals and personal property rentals prohibited.* An activity involving the rental of real property and an activity involving the rental of personal property (other than personal property provided in connection with the real property or real property provided in connection with the personal property) may not be treated as a single activity.

*(3) Certain activities of limited partners and limited entrepreneurs.* (i) In general. Except as provided in this paragraph, a taxpayer that owns an interest as a limited partner or a limited entrepreneur (as defined in section 464(e)(2)), in an activity described in section 465(c)(2), may not group that activity with any other activity. A taxpayer that owns an interest as a limited partner or a limited entrepreneur in an activity described in the preceding sentence may group that activity with another activity in the same type of business if the grouping is appropriate under the provisions of paragraph (c) of this section.

(ii) Example. The following example illustrates the application of this paragraph (d)(3):

*Example.* (i) Taxpayer A, an individual, owns and operates a farm. A is also a member of M, a limited liability company that conducts a cattle-feeding business. A does not actively participate in the management of M (within the meaning of section 464(e)(2)(B)). IN addition, A is a limited partner in N, a limited partnership engaged in oil and gas production.

(ii) Because A does not actively participate in the management of M, A is a limited entrepreneur in M's activity. M's cattle-feeding business is described in section 465(c)(1)(B) (relating to farming) and may not be grouped with any other activity that does not involve farming. Moreover, A's farm may not be grouped with the cattle-feeding activity unless the grouping constitutes an appropriate economic unit for the measurement of gain or loss for purposes of section 469.

(iii) Because A is a limited partner in N and N's activity is described in section 465(c)(1)(D) (relating to exploring for, or exploiting, oil and gas resources), A may not group N's oil and gas activity with any other activity that does not involve exploring for, or exploiting, oil and gas resources. Thus, N's activity may not be grouped with A's farm or with M's cattle-feeding business.

*(4) Other activities identified by the Commissioner.* A taxpayer that owns an interest in an activity identified in guidance issued by the Commissioner as an activity covered by this paragraph (d)(4) may not group that activity with any other activity, except as provided in the guidance issued by the Commissioner.

*(5) Activities conducted through section 469 entries.* (i) In general. A C corporation subject to section 469, an S corporation, or a partnership (a section 469 entry) must group its activities under the rules of this section. Once the section 469 entity groups its activities, a shareholder or partner may group those activities with each other, with activities conducted directly by the shareholder or partner, and with activities conducted through other section 469 entities, in accordance with the rules of this section. A shareholder or partner may not treat activities group together by a section 469 entity as separate activities.

(ii) Cross reference. An activity that a taxpayer conducts through a C corporation subject to section 469 may be grouped with another activity of the taxpayer, but only for purposes of determining whether the taxpayer materially or significantly participates in the other activity. See § 1.469-2T(c)(3)(i)(A) and (c)(4)(i) for the rules regarding dividends on C corporation stock and compensation paid for personal services.

**(e) Disclosure and consistency requirements.** *(1) Original groupings.* Except as provided in paragraph (e)(2) of this section and § 1.469-11, once a taxpayer has grouped activities under this section, the taxpayer may not regroup those activities in subsequent taxable years. Taxpayers must comply with disclosure requirements that the Commissioner may prescribe with respect to both their original groupings and the addition and disposition of specific activities within those chosen groupings in subsequent taxable years.

*(2) Regroupings.* If it is determined that a taxpayer's original grouping was clearly inappropriate or a material change in the facts and circumstances has occurred that makes the original grouping clearly inappropriate, the taxpayer must regroup the activities and must comply with disclosure requirements that the Commissioner may prescribe.

**(f) Grouping by Commissioner to prevent tax avoidance.** *(1) Rule.* The Commissioner may regroup a taxpayer's activities if any of the activities resulting from the taxpayer's grouping is not an appropriate economic unit and a principal purpose of the taxpayer's grouping (or failure to regroup under paragraph (e) of this section) is to circumvent the underlying purposes of section 469.

*(2) Example.* The following example illustrates the application of this paragraph (f):

*Example.* (i) Taxpayers D, E, F, G, and H are doctors who operate separate medical practices. D invested in a tax shelter several years ago that generates passive losses and the other doctors intend to invest in real estate that will generate passive losses. The taxpayers form a partnership to engage in the trade or business of acquiring and operating X-ray equipment. In exchange for equipment contributed to the partnership, the taxpayers receive limited partnership interests. The partnership is managed by a general partner selected by the taxpayers; the taxpayers do not materially participate in its operations. Substantially all of the partnership's services are provided to the taxpayers or their patients, roughly in proportion to the doctors' interests in the partnership. Fees for the partnership's services are set at a level equal to the amounts that would be charged if the partnership were dealing with the taxpayers at arm's length and are expected to assure the partnership a profit. The taxpayers treat the partnership's services as a separate activity from their medical practices and offset the income generated by the partnership against their passive losses.

(ii) For each of the taxpayers, the taxpayer's own medical practice and the services provided by the partnership constitute an appropriate economic unit, but the services provided by the partnership do not separately constitute an appropriate economic unit. Moreover, a principal purpose of treating the medical practices and the partnership's services as separate activities is to circumvent the underlying purposes of section 469. Accordingly, the Commissioner may require the taxpayers to treat their medical practices and their interests in the partnership as a single activity, regardless of whether the separate medical practices are conducted through C corporations subject to section 469, S corporations, partnerships, or sole proprietorships. The Commissioner may assert penalties under section 6662 against the taxpayers in appropriate circumstances.

**(g) Treatment of partial dispositions.** A taxpayer may, for the taxable year in which there is a disposition of substantially all of an activity, treat the part disposed of as a separate activity, but only if the taxpayer can establish with reasonable certainty—

*(1)* The amount of deductions and credits allocable to that part of the activity for the taxable year under § 1.469-1(f)(4) (relating to carryover of disallowed deductions and credits); and

*(2)* The amount of gross income and of any other deductions and credits allocable to that part of the activity for the taxable year.

**(h) Rules for grouping rental real estate activities for taxpayers qualifying under section 469(c)(7).** See § 1.469-9 for rules for certain rental real estate activities.

T.D. 8565, 10/3/94, amend T.D. 8645, 12/21/95.

### § 1.469-4T Definition of activity (temporary).

• ***Caution:*** Under Code Sec. 7805, temporary regulations expire within three years of the date of issuance. This temporary regulation was issued on 5/11/89.

**(a) Overview.** *(1) Purpose and effect of overview.* This paragraph (a) contains a general description of the rules contained in this section and is intended solely as an aid to readers. The provisions of this paragraph (a) are not a substitute for the more detailed rules contained in the remainder of this section and cannot be relied upon in cases in which those rules qualify the general description contained in this paragraph (a).

*(2) Scope and structure of § 1.469-4T.* This section provides rules under which a taxpayer's business and rental operations are treated as one or more activities for purposes of section 469 and the regulations thereunder. (See paragraph (b)(2)(ii) of this section for the definition of business and rental operations.) In general, these rules are divided into three groups:

(i) Rules that identify the business and rental operations that constitute an undertaking (the undertaking rules).

(ii) Rules that identify the undertaking or undertakings that constitute an activity (the activity rules).

(iii) Rules that apply only under certain special circumstances (the special rules).

*(3) Undertaking rules.* (i) In general. The undertaking is generally the smallest unit that can constitute an activity. (See paragraph (b)(1) of this section for the general rule and paragraph (k)(2)(iii) of this section for a special rule that permits taxpayers to treat a single rental real estate undertaking as multiple activities.) An undertaking may include diverse business and rental operations.

(ii) Basic undertaking rule. The basic undertaking rule identifies the business and rental operations that constitute an undertaking by reference to their location and ownership. Under this rule, business and rental operations that are conducted at the same location and are owned by the same person are generally treated as part of the same undertaking. Conversely, business and rental operations generally constitute separate undertakings to the extent that they are conducted at different locations or are not owned by the same person. (See paragraph (c)(2)(i) of this section.).

(iii) Circumstances in which location is disregarded. In some circumstances, the undertaking in which business and rental operations are included does not depend on the location at which the operations are conducted. Operations that are not conducted at any fixed place of business or that are conducted at the customer's place of business are treated as part of the undertaking with which the operations are most closely associated (see paragraph (c)(2)(iii)(C) of this section). In addition, operations that are conducted at a location but do not relate to the production of property at that location or to the transaction of business with customers at that location are treated, in effect, as part of the undertaking or undertakings that the operations support (see paragraph (c)(2)(ii) of this section).

(iv) Rental undertakings. The basic undertaking rule is also modified if the undertaking determined under that rule includes both rental and nonrental operations. In such cases, the rental operations and the nonrental operations generally must be treated as separate undertakings (see paragraph (d)(1) of this section). This rule does not apply if more than 80 percent of the income of the undertaking determined under the basic rule is attributable to one class of operations (i.e., rental or nonrental) or if the rental operations would not be treated as part of a rental activity because of the exceptions contained in § 1.469-1T(e)(3)(ii) (see paragraph (d)(2) of this section). In applying the rental undertaking rules, short-term rentals of real property (e.g., hotel-room rentals) are generally treated as nonrental operations (see paragraph (d)(3)(ii) of this section).

(v) Oil and gas wells. Another exception to the basic undertaking rule treats oil and gas wells that are subject to the working-interest exception in § 1.469-1T(e)(4) as separate undertakings (see paragraph (e) of this section).

*(4) Activity rules.* (i) In general. The basic activity rule treats each undertaking in which a taxpayer owns an interest as a separate activity of the taxpayer (see paragraph (b)(1) of this section). In the case of trade or business undertakings, professional service undertakings, and rental real estate undertakings, additional rules may either require or permit the aggregation of two or more undertakings into a single activity.

(ii) Aggregation of trade or business undertakings. (A) Trade or business undertakings. Trade or business undertakings include all nonrental undertakings other than oil and gas undertakings described in paragraph (a)(3)(v) of this section and professional service undertakings described in paragraph (a)(4)(iii) of this section (see paragraph (f)(1)(ii) of this section).

(B) Similar, commonly-controlled undertakings treated as a single activity. An aggregation rule treats trade or business undertakings that are both similar and controlled by the same interests as part of the same activity. This rule is, however, generally inapplicable to small interests held by passive investors in such undertakings, except to the extent such interests are held through the same passthrough entity. (See paragraph (f)(2) of this section.) Undertakings are similar for purposes of this rule if more than half (by value) of their operations are in the same line of business (as defined in a revenue procedure issued pursuant to paragraph (f)(4)(iv) of this section) or if the undertakings are vertically integrated (see paragraph (f)(4)(iii) of this section). All the facts and circumstances are taken into account in determining whether undertakings are controlled by the same interests for purposes of the aggregation rule (see paragraph (j)(1) of this section). If, however, each member of a group of five or fewer persons owns a substantial interest in each of the undertakings, the undertakings may be rebuttably presumed to be controlled by the same interests (see paragraph (j)(2) and (3) of this section).

(C) Integrated businesses treated as a single activity. Trade or business undertakings (including undertakings that have been aggregated because of their similarity and common control) are subject to a second aggregation rule. Under this rule undertakings that constitute an integrated business and are controlled by the same interests must be treated as part of the same activity. (See paragraph (g) of this section.)

(iii) Aggregation of professional service undertakings. Professional service undertakings are nonrental undertakings that predominantly involve the provision of services in the fields of health, law, engineering, architecture, accounting, actuarial science, performing arts, or consulting (see paragraph (h)(1)(ii) of this section). In general, professional service undertakings that are either similar, related, or controlled by the same interests must be treated as part of the same activity (see paragraph (h)(2) of this section). The rules for determining whether trade or business undertakings are controlled by the same interests also apply with respect to professional service undertakings. Professional service undertakings are similar, however, if more than 20 percent (by value) of their operations are in the same field, and two professional service undertakings are related if one of the undertakings derives more than 20 percent of its gross income from persons who are customers of the other undertaking (see paragraph (h)(3) of this section).

(iv) Rules for rental real estate. (A) Taxpayers permitted to determine rental real estate activities. The rules for aggregating rental real estate undertakings are generally elective. They permit taxpayers to treat any combination of rental real estate undertakings as a single activity. Taxpayers may also divide their rental real estate undertakings and then treat portions of the undertakings as separate activities or recombine the portions into activities that include parts of different undertakings. (See paragraph (k)(2)(i) and (iii) of this section.)

(B) Limitations on fragmentation and aggregation of rental real estate. Taxpayers may not fragment their rental real estate in a manner that is inconsistent with their treatment of such property in prior taxable years or with the treatment of such property by the passthrough entity through which it is held (see paragraph (k)(2)(ii) and (3) of this section). There are no comparable limitations on the aggregation of rental real estate into a single activity. If however, the income or gain from a rental real estate undertaking is subject to recharacterization under § 1.469-2T(f)(3) (relating to the rental of nondepreciable property), a coordination rule provides that the undertaking must be treated as a separate activity (see paragraph (k)(6) of this section.)

(v) Election to treat nonrental undertakings as separate activities. Another elective rule permits taxpayers to treat a nonrental undertaking as a separate activity even if the undertaking would be treated as part of a larger activity under the aggregation rules applicable to the undertaking (see paragraph (o)(2) of this section). This elective rule is limited by consistency requirements similar to those that apply to rental real estate operations (see paragraph (o)(3) and (4) of this section). Moreover, in cases in which a taxpayer elects to treat a nonrental undertaking as a separate activity, the taxpayer's level of participation (i.e., material, significant, or otherwise) in the separate activity is the same as the taxpayer's level of participation in the larger activity in which the undertaking would be included but for the election (see paragraph (o)(6) of this section).

*(5) Special rules.* (i) Consolidated groups and publicly traded partnerships. Special rules apply to the business and rental operations of consolidated groups of corporations and publicly traded partnerships. Under these rules, a consolidated group is treated as one taxpayer in determining its activities and those of its members (see paragraph (m) of this section), and business and rental operations owned through a publicly traded partnership cannot be aggregated with operations that are not owned through the partnership (see paragraph (n) of this section).

(ii) Transitional rule. A special rule applies for taxable years ending before August 10, 1989. In those years, taxpayers may organize business and rental operations into activities under any reasonable method (see paragraph (p)(1) of this section). A taxpayer will also be permitted to use any reasonable method to allocate disallowed deductions and credits among activities for the first taxable year in which the taxpayer's activities are determined under the general rules of § 1.469-4T (see paragraph (p)(3) of this section).

**(b) General rule and definitions of general application.** *(1) General rule.* Except as otherwise provided in this section, each undertaking in which a taxpayer owns an interest shall be treated as a separate activity of the taxpayer. See paragraphs (f), (g), and (h) of this section for rules requiring certain nonrental undertakings to be treated as part of the same activity and paragraph (k) of this section for rules identifying the rental real estate undertakings (or portions thereof) that are included in an activity.

*(2) Definitions of general application.* The following definitions set forth the meaning of certain terms for purposes of this section:

(i) Passthrough entity. The term "passthrough entity" means a partnership, S corporation, estate, or trust.

(ii) Business and rental operations. (A) In general. Except as provided in paragraph (b)(2)(ii)(B) of this section, the term "business and rental operations" means all endeavors that are engaged in for profit or the production of income and satisfy one or more of the following conditions for the taxable year:

(1) Such endeavors involve the conduct of a trade or business (within the meaning of section 162) or are conducted in anticipation of such endeavors becoming a trade or business;

(2) Such endeavors involve making tangible property available for use by customers; or

(3) Research or experimental expenditures paid or incurred with respect to such endeavors are deductible under section 174 (or would be deductible if the taxpayer adopted the method described in section 174(a)).

(B) Operations conducted through nonpassthrough entities. For purposes of applying section 469 and the regulations thereunder, a taxpayer's activities do not include operations that a taxpayer conducts through one or more entities (other than passthrough entities). The following example illustrates the operation of this paragraph (b)(2)(ii)(B):

*Example.* (i) A, an individual, owns stock of X, a closely held corporation (within the meaning of § 1.469-1T(g)(2)(ii) that is directly engaged in the conduct of a real estate development business. A participates in X's real estate development business, but does not own any interest in the business other than through ownership of the stock of X.

(ii) X is subject to section 469 (see § 1.469-1T(b)(5)) and does not hold the real estate development business through another entity. Accordingly, for purposes of section 469 and the regulations thereunder, the operations of X's real estate development business are treated as part of X's activities.

(iii) A is also subject to section 469 (see § 1.469-1T(b)(1)), but A's only interest in the real estate development business is held through X. X is a C corporation and therefore is not a passthrough entity. Thus, for purposes of section 469 and the regulations thereunder, A's activities do not include the operations of X's real estate development business. Accordingly, A's participation in X's business is not participation in an activity of A, and is not taken into account in determining whether A materially participates (within the meaning of § 1.469-5T) or significantly participates (within the meaning of § 1.469-1T(c)(2)) in any activity. (See, however, § 1.469-1T(g)(3) for rules under which a shareholder's participation is taken into account for purposes of determining whether a corporation materially or significantly participates in an activity.

**(c) Undertaking.** *(1) In general.* Except as otherwise provided in paragraphs (d), (e), and (k)(2)(iii) of this section, business and rental operations that constitute a separate source of income production shall be treated as a single undertaking that is separate from other undertakings.

*(2) Operations treated as a separate source of income production.* (i) In general. Except as otherwise provided in this paragraph (c)(2), business and rental operations shall be treated for purposes of this paragraph (c) as a separate source of income production if and only if—

(A) Such operations are conducted at the same location (within the meaning of paragraph (c)(2)(iii) of this section) and are owned by the same person (within the meaning of paragraph (c)(2)(v) of this section); and

(B) Income-producing operations (within the meaning of paragraph (c)(2)(iv) of this section) owned by such person are conducted at such location.

(ii) Treatment of support operations. (A) In general. For purposes of section 469 and the regulations thereunder—

(1) The support operations conducted at a location shall not be treated as part of an undertaking under paragraph (c)(2)(i) of this section; and

(2) The income and expenses that are attributable to such operations and are reasonably allocable to an undertaking conducted at a different location shall be taken into account in determining the income or loss from the activity or activities that include such undertaking.

(B) Support operations. For purposes of this paragraph (c)(2), the business and rental operations conducted at a location are treated as support operations to the extent that—

(1) Such operations and an undertaking that is conducted at a different location are owned by the same person (within the meaning of paragraph (c)(2)(v) of this section);

(2) Such operations involve the provision of property or services to such undertaking; and

(3) Such operations are not income-producing operations (within the meaning of paragraph (c)(2)(iv) of this section).

(iii) Location. For purposes of this paragraph (c)(2)—

(A) The term "location" means, with respect to any business and rental operations, a fixed place of business at which such operations are regularly conducted;

(B) Business and rental operations are conducted at the same location if they are conducted in the same physical structure or within close proximity of one another;

(C) Business and rental operations that are not conducted at a fixed place of business or that are conducted on the customer's premises shall be treated as operations that are conducted at the location (other than the customer's premises) with which they are most closely associated;

(D) All the facts and circumstances (including, in particular, the factors listed in paragraph (c)(3) of this section) are taken into account in determining the location with which business and rental operations are most closely associated; and

(E) Oil and gas operations that are conducted for the development of a common reservoir are conducted within close proximity of one another.

(iv) Income-producing operations. For purposes of this paragraph (c)(2), the term "income-producing operations" means business and rental operations that are conducted at a location and relate to (or are conducted in reasonable anticipation of)—

(A) The production of property at such location;

(B) The sale of property to customers at such location;

(C) The performance of services for customers at such location;

(D) Transactions in which customers take physical possession at such location of property that is made available for their use; or

(E) Any other transactions that involve the presence of customers at such location.

(v) Ownership by the same person. For purposes of this paragraph (c)(2), business and rental operations are owned by the same person if and only if one person (within the meaning of section 7701(a)(1)) is the direct owner of such operations.

*(3) Facts and circumstances determinations.* In determining whether a location is the location with which business and rental operations are most closely associated for purposes of paragraph (c)(2)(iii)(D) of this section, the following relationships between operations that are conducted at such location and other operations are generally the most significant:

(i) The extent to which other persons conduct similar operations at one location;

(ii) Whether such operations are treated as a unit in the primary accounting records reflecting the results of such operations;

(iii) The extent to which other persons treat similar operations as a unit in the primary accounting records reflecting the results of such similar operations;

(iv) The extent to which such operations involve products or services that are commonly provided together;

(v) The extent to which such operations serve the same customers;

(vi) The extent to which the same personnel, facilities, or equipment are used to conduct such operations;

(vii) The extent to which such operations are conducted in coordination with or reliance upon each other;

(viii) The extent to which the conduct of any such operations is incidental to the conduct of the remainder of such operations;

(ix) The extent to which such operations depend on each other for their economic success; and

(x) Whether such operations are conducted under the same trade name.

*(4) Examples.* The following examples illustrate the application of this paragraph (c). In each example that does not state otherwise, the taxpayer is an individual and the facts, analysis, and conclusion relate to a single taxable year.

*Example (1).* The taxpayer is the sole owner of a department store and a restaurant and conducts both businesses in the same building. Thus, the department store and restaurant operations are conducted at the same location (within the meaning of paragraph (c)(2)(iii) of this section) and are owned by the same person (i.e., the taxpayer is the direct owner of the operations). In addition, the taxpayer conducts income-producing operations (within the meaning of paragraph (c)(2)(iv) of this section) at the location (i.e., property is sold to customers and services are performed for customers on the premises of the department store). Accordingly, the department store and restaurant operations are treated as a separate source of income production (see paragraph (c)(2) of this section) and as a single undertaking that is separate from other undertakings (see paragraph (c)(1) of this section).

*Example (2).* (i) The facts are the same as in example (1), except that the taxpayer is also the sole owner of an automotive center that services automobiles and sells tires, batteries, motor oil, and accessories. The taxpayer operates the automotive center in a separate structure in the shopping mall in which the department store is located. Although the automotive center operations and the department store and restaurant operations are not conducted in the same physical structure, they are conducted within close proximity (within the meaning of paragraph (c)(2)(iii)(B) of this section) of one another. Thus, the department store, restaurant, and automotive center operations are conducted at the same location (within the meaning of paragraph (c)(2)(iii) of this section).

(ii) As in example (1), the operations conducted at the same location are owned by the same person, and the taxpayer conducts income-producing operations (within the meaning of paragraph (c)(2)(iv) of this section) at the location. Accordingly, the department store, restaurant, and automotive center operations are treated as a separate source of income production (see paragraph (c)(2) of this section) and as a single undertaking that is separate from other undertakings (see paragraph (c)(1) of this section).

*Example (3).* (i) The facts are the same as in example (2), except that the automotive center is located several blocks from the shopping mall. As in example (1), the department store and restaurant operations are treating as a single undertaking that is separate from other undertakings. Because, however, the automotive center operations are not conducted within close proximity (within the meaning of paragraph (c)(2)(iii)(B) of this section) of the department store and restaurant operations, all of the taxpayer's operations are not conducted at the same location (within the meaning of paragraph (c)(2)(iii) of this section).

(ii) All of the automotive center operations are conducted at the same location (within the meaning of paragraph (c)(2)(iii) of this section) and are owned by the same person (i.e., the taxpayer is the direct owner of the operations). In addition, the taxpayer conducts income producing operations (within the meaning of paragraph (c)(2)(iv) of this section) at the location (i.e., property is sold to customers and services are performed for customers on the premises of the automotive center). Accordingly, the automotive center operations are also treated as a separate source of income production (see paragraph (c)(2) of this section) and as a single undertaking that is separate from other undertakings (see paragraph (c)(1) of this section). See, however, paragraph (g) of this section for rules under which certain trade or business activities are treated as a single activity.

*Example (4).* The taxpayer is the sole owner of a building and rents residential, office, and retail space in the building to various tenants. The taxpayer manages these rental operations from an office located in the building. The rental operations are conducted at the same location (within the meaning of paragraph (c)(2)(iii) of this section) and are owned by the same person (i.e., the taxpayer is the direct owner of the operations). In addition, the taxpayer conducts income-producing operations (within the meaning of paragraph (c)(2)(iv) of this section) at the location (i.e., customers take physical possession in the building of property made available for their use). Accordingly, the rental operations are treated as a separate source of income production (see paragraph (c)(2) of this section) and as a single undertaking that is separate from other undertakings (see paragraph (c)(1) of this section). See paragraph (d) of this section for rules for determining whether this undertaking is a rental undertaking and paragraph (k) of this section for rules for identifying rental real estate activities.

*Example (5).* (i) The facts are the same as in example (4), except that the taxpayer also uses the rental office in the building ("Building #1") to manage rental operations in another building (" Building #2") that the taxpayer owns. The rental operations conducted in Building #2 are treated as a separate source of income production under paragraph (c)(2) of this section and as a single undertaking that is separate from other undertakings (the "Building #2 undertaking") under paragraph (c)(1) of this section.

(ii) The operations conducted at the rental office in Building #1 and the Building #2 undertaking are owned by the same person (i.e., the taxpayer is the direct owner of the operations). In addition, the operations conducted at the rental office with respect to the Building #2 undertaking relate to transactions in which customers take physical possession at another location of property that is made available for their use (i.e., the operations are not income-producing operations (within the meaning of paragraph (c)(2)(iv) of this section)). Thus, to the extent the operations conducted at the rental office involve the management of the Building #2 undertaking, they are support operations (within the meaning of paragraph (c)(2)(ii)(B) of this section) with respect to the Building #2 undertaking.

(iii) Paragraph (c)(2)(ii)(A)(1) of this section provides that support operations are not treated as part of an undertaking under paragraph (c)(2)(i) of this section. Therefore, the support operations conducted at the rental office are not treated as part of the undertaking that consists of the rental operations conducted in Building #1 (the "Building #1 undertaking"). Paragraph (c)(2)(ii)(A)(2) of this section provides that the income and expenses that are attributable to support operations and are reasonably allocable to an undertaking conducted at a different location shall be taken into account in determining the income or loss from the activity that includes such undertaking. Accordingly, the income and expenses of the rental office that are reasonably allocable to the Building #2 undertaking are taken into account in determining the income or loss from the activity or activities that include the Building #2 undertaking. See paragraph (k) of this section for rules for identifying rental real estate activities.

(iv) Rental office operations that involve the management of rental operations conducted in Building #1 are not support operations (within the meaning of paragraph (c)(2)(ii)(B) of this section) because they relate to an undertaking that is conducted at the same location (the "Building #1 undertaking"). Thus, the rules for support operations in paragraph (c)(2)(ii)(A) of this section do not apply to such operations, and they are treated as part of the Building #1 undertaking.

*Example (6).* (i) The taxpayer conducts business and rental operations at eleven different locations (within the meaning of paragraph (c)(2)(iii) of this section). At ten of the locations the taxpayer owns grocery stores, and at the eleventh location the taxpayer owns a warehouse that receives goods and supplies them to the taxpayer's stores. The operations of each store are conducted at the same location (within the meaning of paragraph (c)(2)(iii) of this section) and are owned by the same person (i.e., the taxpayer is the direct owner of the operations). In addition, the taxpayer conducts income-producing operations (within the meaning of paragraph (c)(2)(iv) of this section) at each location (i.e., property is sold to customers on the store premises, and customers take physical possession on the store premises of property made available for their use). Accordingly, the operations of each of the ten grocery stores are treated as a separate source of income production (see paragraph (c)(2) of this section), and each store is treated as a single undertaking (a "grocery store undertaking") that is separate from other undertakings (see paragraph (c)(1) of this section). The operations conducted at the warehouse, however, do not include any income-producing operations (within the meaning of paragraph (c)(2)(iv) of this section). Accordingly, the warehouse operations do not satisfy the requirements of paragraph (c)(2)(i) of this section and are not treated as a separate undertaking under paragraph (c)(1) of this section.

(ii) The warehouse operations and the grocery store undertakings are owned by the same person (i.e., the taxpayer is the direct owner of the operations), the operations conducted at the warehouse involve the provision of property to the grocery store undertakings, and the warehouse operations are not income-producing operations (within the meaning of paragraph (c)(2)(iv) of this section). Thus, the warehouse operations are support operations (within the meaning of paragraph (c)(2)(ii)(B) of this section) with respect to the grocery store undertakings. Paragraph (c)(2)(ii)(A)(2) of this section provides that the income and expenses that are attributable to support operations and are reasonably allocable to an undertaking conducted at a different location shall be taken into account in determining the income or loss from the activity or activities that include such undertaking. Accordingly, the income and expenses of the warehouse operations that are reasonably allocable to a grocery store undertaking are taken into account in determining the income or loss from the activity or activities that include such undertaking. See paragraph (f) of this section for rules under which certain similar, commonly-controlled undertakings are treated as a single activity.

*Example (7).* (i) The facts are the same as in example (6), except that the warehouse operations also include the sale of goods to grocery stores that the taxpayer does not own ("other grocery stores"). Because of these sales, the taxpayer conducts income-producing operations (within the meaning of paragraph (c)(2)(iv) of this section) at the warehouse. The warehouse operations are conducted at the same location (within the meaning of paragraph (c)(2)(iii) of this section) and are owned by the same person (i.e., the taxpayer is the direct owner of the operations). Accordingly, prior to the application of the rules for support operations in paragraph (c)(2)(ii) of this section, the warehouse operations are treated as a separate source of income production (see paragraph (c)(2) of this section) and as a single undertaking (the "separate warehouse undertaking") that is separate from other undertakings (see paragraph (c)(1) of this section).

(ii) As in example (6), the warehouse operations that involve supplying goods to the taxpayer's grocery store undertakings are support operations with respect to those undertakings. Therefore, those operations are not treated as part of the separate warehouse undertaking (see paragraph (c)(2)(ii)(A)(1) of this section), and the income and expenses of such operations are taken into account, as in example (6), in determining the income or loss from the activity or activities that include the taxpayer's grocery store undertakings.

*Example (8).* (i) A partnership is formed to acquire real property and construct a building on the property. The partnership hires brokers to locate a suitable parcel of land, lawyers to negotiate zoning variances, easements, and building permits, and architects and engineers to design the improvements. After the architects and engineers have designed the improvements and other preliminaries have been completed, the partnership hires a general contractor who hires subcontractors and oversees construction. During the construction process and after construction has been completed, the partnership leases out space in the building. The partnership then operates the building as a rental property. The operations of acquiring the real property, negotiating contracts, overseeing the designing and construction of the improvements, leasing up the building, and operating the building are conducted at an office (the "management office") that is not at the same location (within the meaning of paragraph (c)(2)(iii) of this section) as the building.

(ii) The operations conducted at the building site (e.g., excavating the land, pouring the concrete for the foundation, erecting the frame of the building, completing the exterior of the building, and building out the interior of the building) are conducted at the same location (within the meaning of paragraph (c)(2)(iii) of this section) and are owned by the same person (i.e., the partnership is the direct owner of the operations). In addition, the partnership conducts income-producing operations (within the meaning of paragraph (c)(2)(iv) of this section) at the location (i.e., during the construction period property (the building) is produced at the building site, and during the rental period customers take physical possession in the building of property made available for their use). Accordingly, the operations conducted at the building site are treated as a separate source of income production (see paragraph (c)(2) of this section) and as a single undertaking that is separate from other undertakings (see paragraph (c)(1) of this section).

(iii) The operations conducted at the management office and the undertaking conducted at the building site are owned by the same person (i.e., the partnership is the direct owner of the operations). In addition, the operations conducted at the management office relate to transactions in which customers take physical possession at another location of property that is made available for their use (i.e., the operations are not income-producing operations (within the meaning of paragraph (c)(2)(iv) of this section)). Thus, to the extent the operations conducted at the management office involve the provision of services to the undertaking conducted at the building site, they are support operations (within the meaning of paragraph (c)(2)(ii)(B) of this section) with respect to such undertaking.

(iv) Paragraph (c)(2)(ii)(A)(2) of this section provides that the income and expenses of support operations that are reasonably allocable to an undertaking conducted at a different location shall be taken into account in determining the income or loss from the activity that includes such undertaking. Accordingly, the income and expenses of the management office that are reasonably allocable to the undertaking conducted at the building site are taken into account in determining the income or loss from the activity or activities that include such undertaking.

(v) Until the building is first held out for rent and is in a state of readiness for rental, the undertaking conducted at the building site is a trade or business undertaking (within the meaning of paragraph (f)(1)(ii) of this section). See paragraph (d) of this section for rules for determining whether the undertaking is a rental undertaking for periods after the building is first held out for rent and is in a state or readiness for rental and paragraph (k) of this section for rules for identifying rental real estate activities.

*Example (9).* The taxpayer owns 15 oil wells pursuant to a single working interest (within the meaning of § 1.469-1T(e)(4)(iv). All of the wells are drilled and operated for the development of a common reservoir. Thus, all of the wells are at the same location (see paragraph (c)(2)(iii)(E) of this section). All of the wells are owned by the same person (i.e., the taxpayer is the direct owner of the operations), and the taxpayer conducts income-producing operations (within the meaning of paragraph (c)(2)(iv) of this section) at the location (i.e., oil wells are drilled in reasonable anticipation of producing oil at the location). Accordingly, the operations of the wells are treated as a separate source of income production (see paragraph (c)(2) of this section) and as a single undertaking that is separate from other undertakings (see paragraph (c)(1) of this section). See paragraph (e) of this section for rules under which certain oil and gas operations are treated as multiple undertakings even if they would be part of the same undertaking under the rules of this paragraph (c).

*Example (10).* (i) Partnership X owns an automobile dealership and partnership Y owns an automobile repair shop. The dealership and repair shop operations are conducted in the same physical structure. Individuals A, B, and C are the only partners in partnerships X and Y, and each of the partners owns a one-third interest in both partnerships.

(ii) The dealership operations and the repair-shop operations are conducted at the same location (within the meaning of paragraph (c)(2)(iii) of this section), but are owned by different persons (i.e., X is the direct owner of the dealership operations, and Y is the direct owner of the repair-shop operations). Moreover, indirect ownership of the operations is not taken into account under paragraph (c)(2)(v) of this section. Thus, it is irrelevant that the two partnerships are owned by the same persons in identical proportions. Accordingly, the dealership and repair-shop operations are not treated as part of the same source of income production (see paragraph (c)(2) of this section) or as a single undertaking that is separate from other undertakings (see paragraph (c)(1) of this section). See, however, paragraph (g) of this section for rules under which certain trade or business activities are treated as a single activity.

*Example (11).* (i) The taxpayer owns and operates a delivery service. The business consists of a central office, retail establishments, and messengers who transport packages from one place to another. Customers may bring their packages to a retail establishment for delivery elsewhere or, by calling the central office, may have packages picked up at their homes or offices. The central office dispatches messengers and coordinates all pickups and deliveries. Customers may pay for deliveries when they drop off or pick up packages at a retail establishment, or the central office will bill the customer for services rendered. In addition, many packages are routed through the central office.

(ii) The operations conducted at the central office are conducted at the same location (within the meaning of paragraph (c)(2)(iii) of this section) and are owned by the same person (i.e., the taxpayer is the direct owner of the operations). The operations actually conducted at the central office, however, do not include any income-producing operations (within the meaning of paragraph (c)(2)(iv) of this section).

(iii) Under paragraph (c)(2)(iii)(C) and (D) of this section, business and rental operations that are not conducted at a fixed place of business or that are conducted on the customer's premises are treated as operations that are conducted at the location (other than the customer's premises) with which they are most closely associated, and all the facts and circumstances are taken into account in determining the location with which business and rental operations are most closely associated. The facts and circumstances in this case (including the facts that the central office dispatches messengers, coordinates all pickups and deliveries, and is the transshipment point for many packages) establish that the operations of delivering packages from one location to another are most closely associated with the central office. Thus, the delivery operations are treated as operations that are conducted at the central office, and the deliveries are treated as income-producing operations (i.e., the performance of services for customers) that the taxpayer conducts at the central office. Accordingly, the operations conducted at the central office are treated as a separate source of income production (see paragraph (c)(2) of this section) and as a single undertaking that is separate from other undertakings (see paragraph (c)(1) of this section).

(iv) The operations conducted at each retail establishment are conducted at the same location (within the meaning of paragraph (c)(2)(iii) of this section) and are owned by the same person (i.e., the taxpayer is the direct owner of the operations). At each retail establishment, the taxpayer's operations include transactions that involve the presence of customers at the establishment. Thus, the taxpayer conducts income-producing operations (within the meaning of paragraph (c)(2)(iv)(E) of this section) at the retail establishments. Accordingly, the operations of each retail establishment are treated as a separate source of income production (see paragraph (c)(2) of this section) and as a single undertaking that is separate from other undertakings (see paragraph (c)(1) of this section). See, however, paragraph (f) of this section for rules under which certain similar, commonly-controlled undertakings are treated as a single activity.

*Example (12).* (i) The taxpayer is the sole owner of a saw mill and a lumber yard. The taxpayer's business operations consist of converting timber into lumber and other wood products and selling the resulting products. The timber is processed at the saw mill, and the resulting products are transported to the lumber yard where they are sold. The saw mill and the lumber yard are at different locations (within the meaning of paragraph (c)(2)(iii) of this section). The transportation operations are managed at the saw mill.

(ii) The operations conducted at the saw mill are conducted at the same location (within the meaning of paragraph (c)(2)(iii) of this section) and are owned by the same person (i.e., the taxpayer is the direct owner of the operations). In addition, the taxpayer conducts income-producing operations (within the meaning of paragraph (c)(2)(iv) of this section) at the location (i.e., lumber is produced at the mill). Similarly, the selling operations at the lumber yard are conducted at the same location (within the meaning of paragraph (c)(2)(iii) of this section) and are owned by the same person (i.e., the taxpayer is the direct owner of the operations). In addition, the taxpayer conducts income-producing operations (within the meaning of paragraph (c)(2)(iv) of this section) at the location (i.e., lumber is sold to customers at the lumber yard). Thus, the milling operations and the selling operations are treated as separate sources of income production (see paragraph (c)(2) of this section) and as separate undertakings (see paragraph (c)(1) of this section).

(iii) The operations conducted at the mill involve the provision of property to the lumber-yard undertaking. Nonetheless, the milling operations are income-producing operations because they relate to the production of property at the mill, and an undertaking's income-producing operations are not treated as support operations (see paragraph (c)(2)(ii)(B)(3) of this section). Accordingly, the milling operations are not support operations with respect to the lumber-yard undertaking. See, however, paragraph (f) of this section for rules under which certain vertically-integrated undertakings are treated as part of the same activity.

(iv) The operations of transporting finished products from the saw mill to the lumber yard are not conducted at a fixed location. Under paragraphs (c)(2)(iii)(C) and (D) of this section, business and rental operations that are not conducted at a fixed place of business or that are conducted on the customer's premises are treated as operations that are conducted at the location (other than the customer's premises) with which they are most closely associated, and all the facts and circumstances are taken into account in determining the location with which business and rental operations are most closely associated. The facts and circumstances in this case (including the fact that the transportation operations are managed at the saw mill) establish that the transportation operations are most closely associated with the saw mill. Thus, the transportation operations are treated as operations that are conducted at the mill and as part of the undertaking that consists of the milling operations.

**(d) Rental undertaking.** *(1) In general.* This paragraph (d) applies to operations that are treated, under paragraph (c) of this section and before the application of paragraph (d)(1)(i) of this section, as a single undertaking that is separate from other undertakings (a "paragraph (c) undertaking"). For purposes of this section—

(i) A paragraph (c) undertaking's rental operations and its operations other than rental operations shall be treated, except as otherwise provided in paragraph (d)(2) of this section, as two separate undertakings;

(ii) The income and expenses that are reasonably allocable to an undertaking (determined after the application of paragraph (d)(1)(i) of this section) shall be taken into account in determining the income or loss from the activity or activities that include such undertaking; and

(iii) An undertaking (determined after the application of paragraph (d)(1)(i) of this section) shall be treated as a rental undertaking if and only if such undertaking, considered as a separate activity, would constitute a rental activity (within the meaning of § 1.469-1T(e)(3)).

*(2) Exceptions.* Paragraph (d)(1)(i) of this section shall not apply to a paragraph (c) undertaking for any taxable year in which—

(i) The rental operations of the paragraph (c) undertaking, considered as a separate activity, would not constitute a rental activity (within the meaning of § 1.469-1T(e)(3));

(ii) Less than 20 percent of the gross income of the paragraph (c) undertaking is attributable to rental operations; or

(iii) Less than 20 percent of the gross income of the paragraph (c) undertaking is attributable to operations other than rental operations.

*(3) Rental operations.* For purposes of this paragraph (d), a paragraph (c) undertaking's rental operations are determined under the following rules:

(i) General rule. Except as otherwise provided in paragraph (d)(3)(ii) or (iii) of this section, a paragraph (c) undertaking's rental operations are all of the undertaking's business and rental operations that involve making tangible property available for use by customers and the provision of property and services in connection therewith.

(ii) Real property provided for short-term use. A paragraph (c) undertaking's operations that involve making short-term real property available for use by customers and the provision of property and services in connection therewith shall not be treated as rental operations if such operations, considered as a separate activity, would not constitute a rental activity. An item of property is treated as short-term real property for this purpose if and only if such item is real property that the paragraph (c) undertaking makes available for use by customers and the average period of customer use (within the meaning of § 1.469-1T(e)(3)(iii)) for all of the paragraph (c) undertaking's real property of the same type as such item is 30 days or less.

(iii) Property made available to licensees. A paragraph (c) undertaking's operations that involve making tangible property available during defined business hours for nonexclusive use by various customers shall not be treated as rental operations. (See § 1.469-1T(e)(3)(ii)(E).)

*(4) Examples.* The following examples illustrate the application of this paragraph (d). In each example that does not state otherwise, the taxpayer is an individual and the facts, analysis, and conclusions relate to a single taxable year.

*Example (1).* The taxpayer owns a building in which the taxpayer rents office space to tenants and operates a parking garage that is used by tenants and other persons. (Assume that, under paragraph (c)(1) of this section, the operations conducted in the building are treated as a single paragraph (c) undertaking.) The taxpayer's tenants typically occupy an office for at least one year, and the services provided to tenants are those customarily provided in office buildings. Some persons (including tenants) rent spaces in the parking garage on a monthly or annual basis. In general, however, spaces are rented on an hourly or daily basis, and the average period for which all customers (including tenants) use the parking garage is less than 24 hours. The paragraph (c) undertaking derives 75 percent of its gross income from office-space rentals and 25 percent of its gross income from the parking garage. The operations conducted in the building are not incidental to any other activity of the taxpayer (within the meaning of § 1.469-1T(e)(3)(vi)).

(ii) The parking spaces are real property and the average period of customer use (within the meaning of § 1.469-1T(e)(3)(iii)) for the parking spaces is 30 days or less. Thus, the parking spaces are short-term real properties (within the meaning of paragraph (d)(3)(ii) of this section). (For this purpose, individual parking spaces that are rented on a monthly or annual basis are, nevertheless, short-term real properties because all the parking spaces are property of the same type, and the average rental period taking all parking spaces into account is 30 days or less.) In addition, the parking-garage operations involve making short-term real properties available for use by customers and the provision of property and services in connection therewith.

(iii) Paragraph (d)(3)(i) and (ii) of this section provides, in effect, that a paragraph (c) undertaking's operations that involve making short-term real properties available for use by customers and the provision of property and services in connection therewith are treated as rental operations if and only if the operations, considered as a separate activity, would constitute a rental activity (within the meaning of § 1.469-1T(e)(3)). In this case, the parking-garage operations, if considered as a separate activity, would not constitute a rental activity because the average period of customer use for the parking spaces is seven days or less (see § 1.469-1T(e)(3)(ii)(A)). Accordingly, the parking-garage operations are not treated as rental operations.

(iv) The paragraph (c) undertaking's remaining operations involve the provision of tangible property (the office spaces) for use by customers and the provision of property and services in connection therewith. The average period of customer use for the office spaces exceeds 30 days. Thus, the office spaces are not short-term real properties, and the undertaking's operations involving the rental of office spaces are rental operations.

(v) Paragraph (d)(1)(i) of this section provides, with certain exceptions, that a paragraph (c) undertaking's rental operations and its operations other than rental operations are treated as two separate undertakings. In this case, at least 20 percent of the paragraph (c) undertaking's gross income is attributable to rental operations (the office-space operations) and at least 20 percent is attributable to operations other than rental operations (the parking-garage operations). Thus, the exceptions in paragraph (d)(2)(ii) and (iii) of this section do not apply. In addition, the average period of customer use for the office spaces exceeds 30 days, extraordinary personal services (within the meaning of § 1.469-1T(e)(3)(v)) are not provided, and the rental of the office spaces is not treated as incidental to a nonrental activity under § 1.469-1T(e)(3)(vi) (relating to incidental rentals that are not treated as a rental activity). Thus, the rental operations, if considered as a separate activity, would constitute a rental activity, and the exception in paragraph (d)(2)(i) of this section does not apply. Accordingly, the rental operations and the parking-garage operations are treated as two separate undertakings (the "office-space undertaking" and the "parking-garage undertaking").

(vi) Paragraph (d)(1)(iii) of this section provides that an undertaking (determined after the application of paragraph (d)(1)(i) of this section) is treated as a rental undertaking if and only if the undertaking, considered as a separate activity, would constitute a rental activity. In this case, the office-space undertaking, if considered as a separate activity, would constitute a rental activity (see (v) above), and the parking-garage undertaking, if considered as a separate activity, would not constitute a rental activity (see (iii) above). Accordingly, the office-space undertaking is treated as a rental undertaking, and the parking-garage undertaking is not.

*Example (2).* (i) The taxpayer owns a building in which the taxpayer rents apartments to tenants and operates a restaurant. (Assume that, under paragraph (c)(1) of this section, the operations conducted in the building are treated as a single paragraph (c) undertaking.) The taxpayer's tenants typically occupy an apartment for at least one year, and the services provided to tenants are those customarily provided in residential apartment buildings. The paragraph (c) undertaking derives 85 percent of its gross income from apartment rentals and 15 percent of its gross income from the restaurant. The operations conducted in the building are not incidental to any other activity of the taxpayer (within the meaning of § 1.469-1T(e)(3)(vi)).

(ii) The operations with respect to apartments (the "apartment operations") involve the provision of tangible property (the apartments) for use by customers and the provision of property and services in connection therewith. In addition, the apartments are not short-term real properties (within the meaning of paragraph (d)(3)(ii) of this section) because the average period of customer use (within the meaning of § 1.469-1T(e)(3)(iii)) for the apartments exceeds 30 days. Accordingly, the apartment operations are rental operations (within the meaning of paragraph (d)(3) of this section). The restaurant operations do not involve the provision of tangible property for use by customers or the provision of property or services in connection therewith. Thus, the restaurant operations are not rental operations.

(iii) Paragraph (d)(1)(i) of this section provides, with certain exceptions, that a paragraph (c) undertaking's rental operations and its operations other than rental operations are treated as two separate undertakings. In this case, however, the exception in paragraph (d)(2)(iii) of this section applies because less than 20 percent of the paragraph (c) undertaking's gross income is attributable to operations other than rental operations (the restaurant operations). Accordingly, the rental operations and the restaurant operations are not treated as two separate undertakings under paragraph (d)(1)(i) of this section.

(iv) Paragraph (d)(1)(iii) of this section provides that an undertaking (determined after the application of paragraph (d)(1)(i) of this section) is treated as a rental undertaking if and only if the undertaking, considered as a separate activity, would constitute a rental activity. In this case, the undertaking (determined after the application of paragraph (d)(1)(i) of this section) includes both the apartment operations and the restaurant operations, and the gross income of this undertaking represents amounts paid principally for the use of tangible property (the apartments). Moreover, the average period of customer use for the apartments exceeds 30 days, extraordinary personal services (within the meaning of § 1.469-1T(e)(3)(v)) are not provided, and the rental of the apartments is not treated as incidental to a nonrental activity under § 1.469-1T(e)(3)(vi) (relating to incidental rentals that are not treated as a rental activity). Thus, the undertaking, if considered as a separate activity, would constitute a rental activity. Accordingly, the undertaking is treated as a rental undertaking.

*Example (3).* (i) The taxpayer owns a building in which the taxpayer rents hotel rooms, meeting rooms, and parking spaces to customers, rents space to various retailers, and operates a restaurant and health club. (Assume that, under paragraph (c)(1) of this section, the operations conducted in the building are treated as a single paragraph (c) undertaking.) Although some customers occupy hotel rooms for extended periods (including some customers who reside in the hotel), customers use hotel rooms for an average period of two days and meeting rooms for an average period of one day. The services provided to persons using the hotel rooms and meeting rooms are those customarily provided in hotels (including wake-up calls, valet services, and delivery of food and beverages to rooms). Some customers rent spaces in the parking garage on a monthly or annual basis. In general, however, parking spaces are rented on an hourly or daily basis, and the average period for which customers use the parking garage is less than 24 hours. Retail tenants typically occupy their space for at least one year, and the services provided to retail tenants are those customarily provided in commercial buildings. The paragraph (c) undertaking derives 45 percent of its gross income from renting hotel rooms, meeting rooms, and parking spaces, 35 percent of its gross income from renting retail space, and 20 percent of its gross income from the restaurant and health club. The operations conducted in the building are not incidental to any other activity of the taxpayer (within the meaning of § 1.469-1T(e)(3)(vi)).

(ii) The parking spaces, hotel rooms, and meeting rooms are real property of three different types, but the average period of customer use (within the meaning of § 1.469-1T(e)(3)(iii)) for property of each type is 30 days or less. Thus, the parking spaces, hotel rooms, and meeting rooms are short-term real properties. (For this purpose, individual parking spaces or hotel rooms that are rented for extended periods are, nevertheless, short-term real properties if the average rental period for all parking spaces is 30 days or less and the average rental period for all hotel rooms is 30 days or less.) In addition, the parking garage operations, the operations with respect to hotel rooms (the "hotel-room operations"), and the operations with respect to meeting rooms (the "meeting-room operations") involve making short-term real properties available for use by customers and the provision of property and services in connection therewith.

(iii) Paragraph (d)(3)(i) and (ii) of this section provides, in effect, that a paragraph (c) undertaking's operations that involve making short-term real properties available for use by customers and the provision of property and services in connection therewith are treated as rental operations if and only if the operations, considered as a separate activity, would constitute a rental activity (within the meaning of § 1.469-1T(e)(3)). In this case the parking-garage, hotel-room and meeting-room operations, if considered as separate activities, would not constitute rental activities because the average period of customer use for parking spaces, hotel rooms, and meeting rooms does not exceed seven days (see § 1.469-1T(e)(3)(ii)(A)). Accordingly, the parking-garage, hotel-room, and meeting-room operations are not treated as rental operations.

(iv) The operations with respect to retail space in the building (the "retail-space operations") involve the provision of tangible property (the retail spaces) for use by customers and the provision of property and services in connection therewith. In addition, the retail spaces are not short-term real properties (within the meaning of paragraph (d)(3)(ii) of this section) because the average period of customer use (within the meaning of § 1.469-1T(e)(3)(iii)) for the retail spaces exceeds 30 days. Accordingly, the retail-space operations are rental operations.

(v) The health-club operations involve making tangible property available for use by customers, but the property is customarily made available during defined business hours for nonexclusive use by various customers. Accordingly, the health-club operations are not rental operations (see paragraph (d)(3)(iii) of this section). The restaurant operations do not involve the provision of tangible property for use by customers or the provision of property or services in connection therewith. Accordingly, the restaurant operations also are not rental operations.

(vi) Paragraph (d)(1)(i) of this section provides, with certain exceptions, that a paragraph (c) undertaking's rental operations and its operations other than rental operations are treated as two separate undertakings. In this case, at least 20 percent of the paragraph (c) undertaking's gross income is attributable to rental operations (35 percent of the paragraph (c) undertaking's gross income is from the retail-space operations) and at least 20 percent is attributable to operations other than rental operations (45 percent from the hotel-room, meeting-room and parking-garage operations and 20 percent from the restaurant and health-club operations). Thus, the exceptions in paragraph (d)(2)(ii) and (iii) of this section do not apply. In addition, the average period of customer use for the retail space exceeds 30 days, extraordinary personal services (within the meaning of § 1.469-1T(e)(3)(v)) are not provided, and the rental of the retail space is not treated as incidental to a nonrental activity under § 1.469-1T(e)(3)(vi) (relating to incidental rentals that are not treated as a rental activity). Thus, the retail-space operations, if considered as a separate activity, would constitute a rental activity, and the exception in paragraph (d)(2)(i) of this section does not apply. Accordingly, the retail-space operations are treated as an undertaking (the "retail-space undertaking") and all the other operations conducted in the building (i.e., renting hotel and meeting rooms and parking spaces and operating the restaurant and health club) are treated as a separate undertaking (the "hotel undertaking").

(vii) Paragraph (d)(1)(iii) of this section provides that an undertaking (determined after the application of paragraph (d)(1)(i) of this section) is treated as a rental undertaking if and only if the undertaking, considered as a separate activity, would constitute a rental activity. In this case, the retail-space undertaking, if considered as a separate activity, would constitute a rental activity (see (iv) above). Accordingly, the retail-space undertaking is treated as a rental undertaking. The hotel undertaking, if considered as a separate activity, would not constitute a rental activity because all tangible property provided for the use of customers in the hotel undertaking is either property for which the average period of customer use is seven days or less (see § 1.469-1T(e)(3)(ii)(A)) or property customarily made available during defined business hours for nonexclusive use by various customers (see § 1.469-1T(e)(3)(ii)(E)). Accordingly, the hotel undertaking is not treated as a rental undertaking.

*Example (4).* (i) A law partnership owns a ten-story building. The partnership uses eight floors of the building in its law practice and leases two floors to one or more tenants. (Assume that, under paragraph (c)(1) of this section, the operations conducted in the building are treated as a single paragraph (c) undertaking.) Tenants typically occupy space on the two rented floors for at least one year, and the services provided to tenants are those customarily provided in office buildings. The paragraph (c) undertaking derives 90 percent of its gross income from rendering legal services and 10 percent of its gross income from renting space. The operations conducted in the building are not incidental to any other activity of the taxpayer (within the meaning of § 1.469-1T(e)(3)(vi)).

(ii) The operations with respect to the office space leased to tenants (the "office-space operations") involve the provision of tangible property (the office space) for use by customers and the provision of property and services in connection therewith. In addition, the office spaces are not short-term real properties (within the meaning of paragraph (d)(3)(ii) of this section) because the average period of customer use (within the meaning of § 1.469-1T(e)(3)(iii)) for the office space exceeds 30 days. Accordingly, the office-space operations are rental operations (within the meaning of paragraph (d)(3) of this section).

(iii) The operations that involve the performance of legal services (the "law-practice operations") do not involve the provision of tangible property for use by customers or the provision of property or services in connection therewith. Accordingly, the law-practice operations are not rental operations.

(iv) Paragraph (d)(1)(i) of this section provides, with certain exceptions, that a paragraph (c) undertaking's rental operations and its operations other than rental operations are treated as two separate undertakings. In this case, however, the exception in paragraph (d)(2)(ii) of this section applies because less than 20 percent of the paragraph (c) undertaking's gross income is attributable to rental operations (the office-space operations). Accordingly, the law-practice operations and the office-space operations are not treated as two separate undertakings under paragraph (d)(1)(i) of this section.

(v) Paragraph (d)(1)(iii) of this section provides that an undertaking (determined after the application of paragraph (d)(1)(i) of this section) is treated as a rental undertaking only if the undertaking, considered as a separate activity, would constitute a rental activity. In this case, the undertaking (determined after the application of paragraph (d)(1)(i) of this section) includes both the law-practice operations and the office-space operations, and the gross income of this undertaking does not represent amounts paid principally for the use of tangible property. Thus, the undertaking, if considered as a separate activity, would not constitute a rental activity. Accordingly, the undertaking is not treated as a rental undertaking.

*Example (5).* (i) The facts are the same as in example (4), except that the building is owned by a separate partnership (the "real estate partnership"), which leases eight floors of the building to the law partnership for use in its law practice and two floors to one or more other tenants. The law partnership and real estate partnership are owned by the same individuals in identical proportions.

(ii) The operations conducted in the building are owned by two different persons (i.e., the law partnership and the real estate partnership). (See paragraph (c)(2)(v) of this section.) Thus, the operations conducted in the building are not treated as a single undertaking under paragraph (c)(1) of this section. Instead, each partnership's share of such operations is treated as a separate paragraph (c) undertaking (the "law-practice undertaking" and the "office-space undertaking").

(iii) Paragraph (d)(1)(iii) of this section provides that an undertaking (determined after the application of paragraph (d)(1)(i) of this section) is treated as a rental undertaking if and only if the undertaking, considered as a separate activity, would constitute a rental activity. In this case, the office-space undertaking, if considered as a separate activity, would constitute a rental activity because all of the undertaking's gross income (including rents paid by the law partnership) represents amounts paid principally for the use of tangible property (the office space), the average period of customer use for the office space exceeds 30 days, extraordinary personal services (within the meaning of § 1.469-1T(e)(3)(v)) are not provided, and the rental of the office space is not treated as incidental to a nonrental activity under § 1.469-1T(e)(3)(vi) (relating to incidental rentals that are not treated as a rental activity). Accordingly, the office-space undertaking is treated as a rental undertaking. See, however, § 1.469-2T(f)(6) (relating to certain rentals of property to a trade or business activity in which the taxpayer materially participates).

(iv) The law-practice undertaking, if considered as a separate activity, would not constitute a rental activity because none of the undertaking's gross income represents amounts paid principally for the use of tangible property. Accordingly, the law-practice undertaking is not treated as a rental undertaking.

*Example (6).* (i) The taxpayer owns a building in which the taxpayer operates a nursing home and a medical clinic. (Assume that, under paragraph (c)(1) of this section, the operations conducted in the building are treated as a single paragraph (c) undertaking.) The nursing-home operations consist of renting apartments in the nursing home to elderly and handicapped persons and providing medical care, meals, and social activities. (Assume that these services are extraordinary personal services (within the meaning of § 1.469-1T(e)(3)(v)). The medical clinic provides medical care to nursing-home residents and other individuals. Nursing-home residents typically occupy an apartment for at least one year. The paragraph (c) undertaking derives 55 percent of its gross income from nursing-home operations (including the provision of medical services to nursing-home residents) and 45 percent of its gross income from medical-clinic operations. The operations conducted in the building are not incidental to any other activity of the taxpayer (within the meaning of § 1.469-1T(e)(3)(vi)).

(ii) The paragraph (c) undertaking's nursing-home operations involve the provision of tangible property (the apartments) for use by customers and the provision of property and services in connection therewith. In addition, the apartments are not short-term real properties (within the meaning of paragraph (d)(3)(ii) of this section) because the average period of customer use (within the meaning of § 1.469-1T(e)(3)(iii)) for the apartments exceeds 30 days. Accordingly, the nursing-home operations are rental operations (within the meaning of paragraph (d)(3) of this section). The medical-clinic operations do not involve the provision of tangible property for use by customers or the provision of property or services in connection therewith. Thus, the medical-clinic operations are not rental operations.

(iii) Paragraph (d)(1)(i) of this section provides, with certain exceptions, that a paragraph (c) undertaking's rental operations and its operations other than rental operations are treated as two separate undertakings. In this case, however, the nursing-home operations, if considered as a separate activity, would not constitute a rental activity because extraordinary personal services are provided in connection with making nursing-home apartments available for use by customers (see § 1.469-T(e)(3)(ii)(C)). Thus, the exception in paragraph (d)(2)(i) of this section applies, and the nursing-home operations and the medical-clinic operations are not treated as two separate undertakings under paragraph (d)(1)(i) of this section.

(iv) Paragraph (d)(1)(iii) of this section provides that an undertaking (determined after the application of paragraph (d)(1)(i) of this section) is treated as a rental undertaking only if the undertaking, considered as a separate activity, would constitute a rental activity. In this case, the nursing-home operations, if considered as a separate activity, would not constitute a rental activity (see (iii) above). Thus, an undertaking that includes no rental operations other than the nursing-home operations would not, if considered as a separate activity, constitute a rental activity. Accordingly, the undertaking is not treated as a rental undertaking.

*Example (7).* (i) The taxpayer rents and sells videocassettes. (Assumes that, under paragraph (c)(1) of this section, the videocassette operations are treated as a single paragraph (c) undertaking.) Renters of videocassettes typically keep the videocassettes for one or two days, and do not receive any other property or services in connection with videocassette rentals. The paragraph (c) undertaking derives 70 percent of its gross income from renting videocassettes and 30 percent of its gross income from selling videocassettes. The videocassette operations are not incidental to any other activity of the taxpayer (within the meaning of § 1.469-1T(e)(3)(vi)).

(ii) The rental of videocassettes involves the provision of tangible property (the videocassettes) for use by customers. In addition, the special rules for short-term real properties contained in paragraph (d)(3)(ii) of this section do not apply in this case because the videocassettes are not real property. Thus, the operations that involve videocassette rentals are rental operations (within the meaning of paragraph (d)(3) of this section). The sale of videocassettes does not involve the provision of tangible property for use by customers or the provision of property or services in connection therewith. Thus, the operations that involve videocassette sales are not rental operations.

(iii) Paragraph (d)(1)(i) of this section provides, with certain exceptions, that a paragraph (c) undertaking's rental operations and its operations other than rental operations are treated as two separate undertakings. In this case, however, the rental operations, if considered as a separate activity, would not constitute a rental activity because the average period of customer use for rented videocassettes does not exceed seven days (see § 1.469-1T(e)(3)(ii)(A)). Accordingly, the exception in paragraph (d)(2)(i) of this section applies, and the videocassette-rental operations and videocassette-sales operations are not treated as two separate undertakings under paragraph (d)(1)(i) of this section.

(iv) Paragraph (d)(1)(iii) of this section provides that an undertaking (determined after the application of paragraph (d)(1)(i) of this section) is treated as a rental undertaking only if the undertaking, considered as a separate activity, would constitute a rental activity. In this case, the videocassette-rental operations, if considered as a separate activity, would not constitute a rental activity (see (iii) above). Thus, an undertaking that includes no rental operations other than the videocassette-rental operations would not, if considered as a separate activity, constitute a rental activity. Accordingly, the undertaking is not treated as a rental undertaking.

*Example (8).* (i) The taxpayer owns a building in which the taxpayer sells, leases, and services automobiles. (Assume that, under paragraph (c)(1) of this section, the operations conducted in the building are treated as a single paragraph (c) undertaking.) The minimum lease term for any leased automobile is 31 days, and the services provided to lessees (including periodic oil changes, lubrication, and routine services and repairs) are those customarily provided in long-term automobile leases. The paragraph (c) undertaking derives 75 percent of its gross income from selling automobiles, 15 percent of its gross income from servicing automobiles other than leased automobiles, and 10 percent of its gross income from leasing automobiles. The taxpayer's automobile operations are not incidental to any other activity of the taxpayer (within the meaning of § 1.469-1T(e)(3)(vi)).

(ii) The paragraph (c) undertaking's automobile-leasing operations involve the provision of tangible property (the automobiles) for use by customers and the provision of services in connection therewith. In addition, the special rules for short-term real properties contained in paragraph (d)(3)(ii) of this section do not apply in this case because the automobiles are not real property. Accordingly, the automobile-leasing operations are rental operations (within the meaning of paragraph (d)(3) of this section). The paragraph (c) undertaking's automobile-sales operations and servicing operations for automobiles other than leased automobiles (the "selling-and-servicing operations") do not involve the provision of tangible property for use by customers or the provision of property or services in connection therewith. Thus, the selling-and-servicing operations are not rental operations.

(iii) Paragraph (d)(1)(i) of this section provides, with certain exceptions, that a paragraph (c) undertaking's rental operations and its operations other than rental operations are treated as two separate undertakings. In this case, however, the exception in paragraph (d)(2)(ii) of this section applies because less than 20 percent of the paragraph (c) undertaking's gross income is attributable to rental operations (the "automobile-leasing operations" ). Accordingly, the rental operations and the selling-and-servicing operations are not treated as two separate undertakings under paragraph (d)(1)(i) of this section.

(iv) Paragraph (d)(1)(iii) of this section provides that an undertaking (determined after the application of paragraph (d)(1)(i) of this section) is treated as a rental undertaking only if the undertaking, considered as a separate activity, would constitute a rental activity. In this case, the undertaking (determined after the application of paragraph (d)(1)(i) of this section) includes both the selling-and-servicing operations and the automobile-leasing operations, and the gross income of the undertaking does not represent amounts paid principally for the use of tangible property. Thus, the undertaking, if considered as a separate activity, would not constitute a rental activity. Accordingly, the undertaking is not treated as a rental undertaking.

*Example (9).* (i) The facts are the same as in example (8), except that the paragraph (c) undertaking derives 60 percent of its gross income from selling automobiles, 15 percent of its gross income from servicing automobiles other than leased automobiles, and 25 percent of its gross income from leasing automobiles.

(ii) Paragraph (d)(1)(i) of this section provides, with certain exceptions, that a paragraph (c) undertaking's rental operations and its operations other than rental operations are treated as two separate undertakings. In this case, more than 20 percent of the paragraph (c) undertaking's gross income is attributable to rental operations (the automobile-leasing operations), and more than 20 percent is attributable to operations other than rental operations (the selling-and-servicing operations). Thus, the exceptions in paragraph (d)(2)(ii) and (iii) of this section do not apply. In addition, the average period of customer use for leased automobiles exceeds 30 days, extraordinary personal services (within the meaning of § 1.469-1T(e)(3)(v)) are not provided, and the leasing of the automobiles is not treated as incidental to a nonrental activity under § 1.469-1T(e)(3)(vi) (relating to incidental rentals that are not treated as a rental activity). Thus, the leasing operations, if considered as a separate activity, would constitute a rental activity, and the exception in paragraph (d)(2)(i) of this section does not apply. Accordingly, the rental operations and the selling-and-servicing operations are treated as two separate undertakings (the "automobile-leasing undertaking" and the "automobile selling-and-servicing undertaking").

(iii) Paragraph (d)(1)(iii) of this section provides that an undertaking (determined after the application of paragraph (d)(1)(i) of this section) is treated as a rental undertaking if and only if the undertaking, considered as a separate activity, would constitute a rental activity. In this case, the automobile-leasing undertaking would, if considered as a separate activity, constitute a rental activity, and the automobile selling-and-servicing undertaking would not, if considered as a separate activity, constitute a rental activity (see example (8) and (ii) above). Accordingly, the automobile-leasing undertaking is treated as a rental undertaking, and the automobile selling-and-servicing undertaking is not.

**(e) Special rules for certain oil and gas operations.** *(1) Wells treated as nonpassive under § 1.469-1T(e)(4)(i).* An oil or gas well shall be treated as an undertaking that is separate from other undertakings in determining the activities of a taxpayer for a taxable year if the following conditions are satisfied:

(i) The well is drilled or operated pursuant to a working interest (within the meaning of § 1.469-1T(e)(4)(iv)) and at any time during such taxable year the taxpayer holds such working interest either—

(A) Directly; or

(B) Through an entity that does not limit the liability of the taxpayer with respect to the drilling or operation of such well pursuant to such working interest; and

(ii) The taxpayer would not be treated as materially participating (within the meaning of § 1.469-5T) for the taxable year in the activity in which such well would be included if the taxpayer's activities were determined without regard to this paragraph (e).

*(2) Business and rental operations that constitute an undertaking.* In any case in which an oil or gas well is treated under this paragraph (e) as an undertaking that is separate from other undertakings, the business and rental operations that constitute such undertaking are the business and rental operations that are attributable to such well.

*(3) Examples.* The following examples illustrate the application of this paragraph (e). In each example, the taxpayer is an individual whose taxable year is the calendar year.

*Example (1).* During 1989, A directly owns an undivided interest in a working interest (within the meaning of § 1.469-1T(e)(4)(iv)) in two oil wells. A does not participate in the activity in which the wells would be included if A's activities were determined without regard to this paragraph (e). Under paragraph (e)(1) of this section, each well is treated as a separate undertaking in determining A's activities for 1989 because A holds the working interest directly and would not be treated as materially participating for 1989 in the activity in which the wells would be included if A's activities were determined without regard to this paragraph (e). The aggregation rules in paragraph (f) of this section do not apply to these undertakings (see paragraph (f)(1)(ii)(B) of this section). Thus, each of the undertakings is treated as a separate activity under paragraph (b)(1) of this section. The result is the same even if A has net income from one or both wells for 1989 and even if the wells would otherwise be treated as part of the same undertaking under paragraph (c) of this section. The result would also be the same if A held the working interest through an entity, such as a general partnership, that does not limit A's liability with respect to the drilling or operation of the wells pursuant to the working interest.

*Example (2).* (i) During 1989, B is a general partner in a partnership that owns a working interest (within the meaning of § 1.469-1T(e)(4)(iv)) in an oil well. B does not own any interest in the well other than through the partnership. At the end of 1989, however, B's partnership interest is converted into a limited partnership interest, and during 1990 B holds the working interest only as a limited partner. B does not participate in the activity in which the well would be included if B's activities were determined without regard to this paragraph (e).

(ii) Under paragraph (e)(1) of this section, the well is treated as a separate undertaking in determining B's activities for 1989 because B holds the working interest during 1989 through an entity that does not limit B's liability with respect to the drilling or operation of the well pursuant to the working interest, and B would not be treated as materially participating for 1989 in the activity in which the well would be included if B's activities were determined without regard to this paragraph (e). Throughout 1990, however, B's liability with respect to the drilling and operation of the well is limited by the entity through which B holds the working interest (i.e., the limited partnership). Accordingly, paragraph (e)(1) of this section does not apply to the well in 1990, and the well may be included under paragraph (c) of this section in an undertaking that includes other operations.

*Example (3).* The facts are the same as in example (2), except that B's partnership interest is converted into a limited partnership interest at the end of November 1989. An oil or gas well may be treated as a separate undertaking under paragraph (e)(1) of this section if at any time during the taxable year the taxpayer holds a working interest in the well directly or through an entity that does not limit the taxpayer's liability with respect to the drilling or operation of the well pursuant to the working interest (see § 1.469-1T(e)(4)(i)). Thus, although B's liability with respect to the drilling and operation of the well is limited during December 1989, the result in both 1989 and 1990 is the same as in example (2). In 1989, however, disqualified deductions and a ratable portion of the gross income from the well may be treated under § 1.469-1T(e)(4)(ii) as passive activity deductions and passive activity gross income, respectively.

**(f) Certain trade or business undertakings treated as part of the same activity.** *(1) Applicability.* (i) In general. This paragraph (f) applies to a taxpayer's interests in trade or business undertakings (within the meaning of paragraph (f)(1)(ii) of this section).

(ii) Trade or business undertaking. For purposes of this paragraph (f), the term "trade or business undertaking" means any undertaking in which a taxpayer has an interest, other than—

(A) A rental undertaking (within the meaning of paragraph (d) of this section);

(B) An oil or gas well treated as an undertaking that is separate from other undertakings under paragraph (e) of this section; or

(C) A professional service undertaking (within the meaning of paragraph (h) of this section).

*(2) Treatment as part of the same activity.* A taxpayer's interests in two or more trade or business undertakings that are similar (within the meaning of paragraph (f)(4) of this section) and controlled by the same interests (within the meaning of paragraph (j) of this section) shall be treated as part of the same activity of the taxpayer for any taxable year in which the taxpayer—

(i) Owns interests in each such undertaking through the same passthrough entity;

(ii) Owns a direct or substantial indirect interest (within the meaning of paragraph (f)(3) of this section) in each such undertaking; or

(iii) Materially or significantly participates (within the meaning of § 1.469-5T) in the activity that would result if such undertakings were treated as part of the same activity.

*(3) Substantial indirect interest.* (i) In general. For purposes of this paragraph (f), a taxpayer owns a substantial indirect interest in an undertaking for a taxable year if at any time during such taxable year the taxpayer's ownership percentage (determined in accordance with paragraph (j)(3) of this section) in a passthrough entity that directly owns such undertaking exceeds ten percent.

(ii) Coordination rule. A taxpayer shall be treated for purposes of this paragraph (f) as owning a substantial indirect interest in each of two or more undertakings for any taxable year in which—

(A) Such undertakings are treated as part of the same activity of the taxpayer under paragraph (f)(2)(i) of this section; and

(B) The taxpayer owns a substantial indirect interest (within the meaning of paragraph (f)(3)(i) of this section) in any such undertaking.

*(4) Similar undertakings.* (i) In general. Except as provided in paragraph (f)(4)(iii) of this section, two undertakings are similar for purposes of this paragraph (f) if and only if—

(A) There are predominant operations in each such undertaking; and

(B) The predominant operations of both undertakings are in the same line of business.

(ii) Predominant operations. For purposes of paragraph (f)(4)(i)(A) of this section, there are predominant operations in an undertaking if more than 50 percent of the undertaking's gross income is attributable to operations in a single line of business.

(iii) Vertically-integrated undertakings. If an undertaking (the "supplier undertaking") provides property or services to other undertakings (the "recipient undertakings"), the following rules apply for purposes of this paragraph (f):

(A) Supplier undertaking similar to recipient undertaking. If the supplier undertaking predominantly involves the provision of property and services to a recipient undertaking that is controlled by the same interests (within the meaning of paragraph (j) of this section), the supplier undertaking shall be treated as similar to the recipient undertaking. For purposes of applying the preceding sentence—

(1) If a supplier undertaking and two or more recipient undertakings that are similar (within the meaning of paragraph (f)(4)(i) of this section) are controlled by the same interests, such recipient undertakings shall be treated as a single undertaking; and

(2) A supplier undertaking predominantly involves the provision of property and services to a recipient undertaking for any taxable year in which such recipient undertaking obtains more than 50 percent (by value) of all property and services provided by the supplier undertaking.

(B) Recipient undertaking similar to supplier undertaking. If the supplier undertaking is the predominant provider of property and services to a recipient undertaking that is controlled by the same interests (within the meaning of paragraph (j) of this section), the recipient undertaking shall be treated, except as otherwise provided in paragraph (f)(4)(iii)(C) of this section, as similar to the supplier undertaking. For purposes of the preceding sentence, a supplier undertaking is the predominant provider of property and services to a recipient undertaking for any taxable year in which the supplier undertaking provides more than 50 percent (by value) of all property and services obtained by the recipient undertaking.

(C) Coordination rules. (1) Paragraph (f)(4)(iii)(B) of this section does not apply if, under paragraph (f)(4)(iii)(A) of this section—

(i) The supplier undertaking is treated as an undertaking that is similar to any recipient undertaking;

(ii) The recipient undertaking is treated as a supplier undertaking that is similar to another recipient undertaking; or

(iii) Another supplier undertaking is treated as an undertaking that is similar to the recipient undertaking.

(2) If paragraph (f)(4)(iii)(A) of this section applies to a supplier undertaking, the supplier undertaking shall be treated as similar to undertakings that are similar to the recipient undertaking and shall not otherwise be treated as similar to undertakings to which the supplier undertaking would be similar without regard to paragraph (f)(4)(iii) of this section.

(3) If paragraph (f)(4)(iii)(B) of this section applies to a recipient undertaking, the recipient undertaking shall be treated as similar to undertakings that are similar to the supplier undertaking and shall not otherwise be treated as similar to undertakings to which the recipient undertaking would be similar without regard to paragraph (f)(4)(iii) of this section.

(iv) Lines of business. The Commissioner shall establish, by revenue procedure, lines of business for purposes of this paragraph (f)(4). Business and rental operations that are not included in the lines of business established by the Commissioner shall nonetheless be included in a line of business for purposes of this paragraph (f)(4). Such operations shall be included in a single line of business or in multiple lines of business on a basis that reasonably reflects—

(A) Similarities and differences in the property or services provided pursuant to such operations and in the markets to which such property or services are offered; and

(B) The treatment within the lines of business established by the Commissioner of operations that are comparable in their similarities and differences.

*(5) Examples.* The following examples illustrate the application of this paragraph (f). In each example that does not state otherwise, the taxpayer is an individual and the facts, analysis, and conclusions relate to a single taxable year.

*Example (1).* (i) The taxpayer is a partner in partnerships A, B, C, and D and owns a five-percent interest in each partnership. Each partnership owns a single undertaking (undertakings A, B, C, and D), and the undertakings are trade or business undertakings (within the meaning of paragraph (f)(1)(ii) of this section) that are controlled by the same interests (within the meaning of paragraph (j) of this section). In addition, undertakings A, B, and D are similar (within the meaning of paragraph (f)(4) of this section). The taxpayer is not related to any of the other partners, and does not participate in any of the undertakings.

(ii) In general, each undertaking in which a taxpayer owns an interest is treated as a single activity that is separate from other activities of the taxpayer (see paragraph (b)(1) of this section). This paragraph (f) provides aggregation rules for trade or business undertakings that are similar and controlled by the same interests. These aggregation rules do not apply, however, unless the taxpayer owns interests in the undertakings through the same passthrough entity, owns direct or substantial indirect interests in the undertakings, or materially or significantly participates in the undertakings. In this case, the taxpayer does not satisfy any of these conditions, and the aggregation rules in this paragraph (f) do not apply. Accordingly, except as otherwise provided in paragraph (g) of this section (relating to an aggregation rule for integrated businesses), undertakings A, B, C, and D are treated as separate activities of the taxpayer under paragraph (b)(1) of this section.

*Example (2).* (i) The facts are the same as in example (1), except that the taxpayer owns a 25-percent interest in partnership A, a 15-percent interest in partnership B, and a 40-percent interest in partnership C.

(ii) Paragraph (f)(2)(ii) of this section provides that trade or business undertakings that are similar and controlled by the same interests are treated as part of the same activity of the taxpayer if the taxpayer owns a direct or substantial indirect interest in each such undertaking. In this case, the taxpayer owns more than ten percent of partnerships A, B, and C, and these partnerships directly own undertakings A, B, and C. Thus, the taxpayer owns a substantial indirect interest in undertakings A, B, and C (see paragraph (f)(3)(i) of this section). Of these undertakings, only undertakings A and B are both similar and controlled by the same interests. Accordingly, the taxpayer's interests in undertakings A and B are treated as part of the same activity. As in example (1), the aggregation rules in this paragraph (f) do not apply to undertakings C and D, and except as otherwise provided in paragraph (g) of this section, undertakings C and D are treated as separate activities.

*Example (3).* (i) The facts are the same as in example (1), except that the taxpayer participates (within the meaning of § 1.469-5T(f)) for 60 hours in undertaking A and for 60 hours in undertaking B.

(ii) Paragraph (f)(2)(iii) of this section provides that trade or business undertakings that are similar and controlled by the same interests are treated as part of the same activity of the taxpayer if the taxpayer materially or significantly participates (within the meaning of § 1.469-5T) in the activity that would result from the treatment of similar, commonly-controlled undertakings as part of the same activity. In this case, the activity that would result from treating the similar, commonly-controlled undertakings as part of the same activity consists of undertakings A, B, and D, and the taxpayer participates for 120 hours in the activity that results from this treatment. Accordingly, undertakings A, B, and D are treated as part of the same activity because the taxpayer significantly participates (within the meaning of § 1.469-5T(c)(2)) in the activity that results from this treatment. The result is the same whether the taxpayer participates in one, two, or all three of the similar, commonly-controlled undertakings, so long as the taxpayer's aggregate participation in undertakings A, B, and D exceeds 100 hours. As in example (1), the aggregation rules in this paragraph (f) do not apply to undertaking C, and except as otherwise provided in paragraph (g) of this section, undertaking C is treated as a separate activity.

*Example (4).* (i) The taxpayer owns a 5-percent interest in partnership A. Partnership A owns interests in partnerships B and C, each of which owns a single undertaking (undertakings B and C). In addition, the taxpayer is a partner in partnerships C and D and directly owns a 15-percent interest in each partnership. Partnership D also owns a single undertaking (undertaking D). Undertakings B, C, and D are trade or business undertakings (within the meaning of paragraph (f)(1)(ii) of this section) that are similar (within the meaning of paragraph (f)(4) of this section) and controlled by the same interests (within the meaning of paragraph (j) of this section). The taxpayer does not participate in undertaking B, C, or D.

(ii) Paragraph (f)(2)(i) of this section provides that trade or business undertakings that are similar and controlled by the same interests are treated as part of the same activity of the taxpayer if the taxpayer owns interests in the undertakings through the same passthrough entity. In this case, the taxpayer owns interests in undertakings B and C through partnership A. Thus, the taxpayer's interests in undertakings B and C are treated as part of the same activity.

(iii) Paragraph (f)(2)(ii) of this section provides that trade or business undertakings that are similar and controlled by the same interests are treated as part of the same activity of the taxpayer if the taxpayer owns a direct or substantial indirect interest in each such undertaking. In this case, the taxpayer owns more than ten percent of partnerships C and D, and these partnerships directly own undertakings C and D. Thus, the taxpayer owns a substantial indirect interest in undertakings C and D (see paragraph (f)(3)(i) of this section).

(iv) The coordination rule in paragraph (f)(3)(ii) of this section applies to undertakings B and C because they are treated as part of the same activity under paragraph (f)(2)(i) of this section, and the taxpayer owns a substantial indirect interest in undertaking C. Under the coordination rule, the taxpayer is treated as owning a substantial indirect interest in undertaking B as well as undertaking C. Accordingly, the taxpayer's interests in undertakings B, C, and D are treated as part of the same activity.

*Example (5).* (i) Undertakings A, B, C, and D are trade or business undertakings (within the meaning of paragraph (f)(1)(ii) of this section), each of which involves the operation of a department store, restaurants, and movie theaters. The following table shows, for each undertaking, the percentages of gross income attributable to the various operations of the undertaking.

| | Department Store | Restaurants | Movie Theaters |
|---|---|---|---|
| Undertaking A | 70% | 20% | 10% |
| Undertaking B | 60% | 20% | 20% |
| Undertaking C | 35% | 35% | 30% |
| Undertaking D | 35% | 10% | 55% |

(ii) Paragraph (f)(4)(i) of this section provides that two undertakings are similar for purposes of this paragraph (f) if and only if there are predominant operations in each undertaking and the predominant operations of the two undertakings are in the same line of business. (Assume that the applicable revenue procedure provides that "general merchandise stores," "eating and drinking places," and "motion picture services" are three separate lines of business.)

(iii) Undertaking A and undertaking B each derives more than 50 percent of its gross income from department-store operations, which are in the general-merchandise-store line of business. Thus, there are predominant operations in undertaking A and undertaking B, and the predominant operations of the two undertakings are in the same line of business. Accordingly, undertakings A and B are similar.

(iv) Undertaking C does not derive more than 50 percent of its gross income from operations in any single line of business. Thus, there are no predominant operations in undertaking C, and undertaking C is not similar to any of the other undertakings.

(v) Undertaking D derives more than 50 percent of its gross income from movie-theater operations, which are in the motion-picture-services line of business. Thus, there are predominant operations in undertaking D. The predominant operations of undertaking D, however, are not in the same line of business as those of undertakings A and B. Accordingly, undertaking D is not similar to undertakings A and B.

*Example (6).* (i) Undertakings A and B are trade or business undertakings (within the meaning of paragraph (f)(1)(ii) of this section) that derive all of their gross income from the sale of automobiles. Undertakings C and D derive all of their gross income from the rental of automobiles. Undertaking C is not a rental undertaking (within the meaning of paragraph (d)(1)(iii) of this section) because the average period of customer use (within the meaning of § 1.469-1T(e)(3)(iii)) for its automobiles does not exceed seven days (see § 1.469-1T(e)(3)(ii)(A)). Undertaking D, on the other hand, leases automobiles for periods of one year or more and is a rental undertaking.

(ii) Paragraph (f)(4)(i) of this section provides that two undertakings are similar for purposes of this paragraph (f) if and only if there are predominant operations in each undertaking and the predominant operations of the two undertakings are in the same line of business. (Assume that the applicable revenue procedure provides that (a) "automotive dealers and service stations" (automotive retail) and (b) "auto repair, services (including rentals), and parking" (automotive services) are two separate lines of business.)

(iii) Undertakings A and B both derive more than 50 percent of their gross income from operations in the automotive-retail line of business (the automobile-sales operations). Similarly, undertakings C and D both derive more than 50 percent of their gross income from operations in the automotive-services line of business (the automobile-rental operations). Thus, there are predominant operations in each undertaking, the predominant operations of undertakings A and B are in the same line of business, and the predominant operations of undertakings C and D are in the same line of business. Accordingly, undertakings A and B are similar, undertakings C and D are similar, and undertakings A and B are not similar to undertakings C and D.

(iv) Paragraph (f)(1) of this section provides that this paragraph (f) applies only to trade or business undertakings and that a rental undertaking is not a trade or business undertaking. Accordingly, this paragraph (f) does not apply to undertaking D, and undertakings C and D, although similar, are not treated, under this paragraph (f), as part of the same activity.

*Example (7).* (i) Undertakings A, B, and C are trade or business undertakings (within the meaning of paragraph (f)(1)(ii) of this section) that involve real estate operations. Undertaking A derives all of its gross income from the development of real property, undertaking B derives all of its gross income from the management of real property and the performance of services as a leasing agent with respect to real property, and undertaking C derives all of its gross income from buying, selling, or arranging purchases and sales of real property. Undertaking D derives all of its gross income from the rental of residential apartments and is a rental undertaking (within the meaning of paragraph (d)(1)(iii) of this section).

(ii) Paragraph (f)(4)(i) of this section provides that two undertakings are similar for purposes of this paragraph (f) if there are predominant operations in each undertaking and the predominant operations of the two undertakings are in the same line of business. (Assume that the applicable revenue procedure provides that real estate development and services (including the development and management of real property, dealing in real property, and the performance of services as a leasing agent with respect to real property) is a single line of business (the "real-estate" line of business).)

(iii) Undertakings A, B, and C all derive more than 50 percent of their gross income from operations in the real-estate line of business. Thus, there are predominant operations in undertakings A, B, and C, and the predominant operations of the three undertakings are in the same line of business. Accordingly, undertakings A, B, and C are similar.

(iv) Undertaking D also derives more than 50 percent of its gross income from operations in the real-estate line of business. Thus, there are predominant operations in undertaking D, and the predominant operations of undertaking D are in the same line of business as those of undertakings A, B, and C. Paragraph (f)(1) of this section provides, however, that this paragraph (f) applies only to trade or business undertakings and that a rental undertaking is not a trade or business undertaking. Accordingly, this paragraph (f) does not apply to undertaking D, and undertaking D, although similar to undertakings A, B, and C, is not treated, under this paragraph (f), as part an activity that includes undertaking A, B, or C.

*Example (8).* (i) Undertakings A and B are trade or business undertakings (within the meaning of paragraph (f)(1)(ii) of this section), both of which involve the provision of moving services. Undertaking A derives its gross income principally from local moves, and undertaking B derives its gross income principally from long-distance moves.

(ii) Paragraph (f)(4)(i) of this section provides that two undertakings are similar for purposes of this paragraph (f) if there are predominant operations in each undertaking and the predominant operations of the two undertakings are in the same line of business. Under paragraph (f)(4)(iv) of this section, operations that are not in the lines of business established by the applicable revenue procedure are nonetheless included in a line of business. In addition, such operations are included in a single line of business or in multiple lines of business on a basis that reasonably reflects (a) similarities and differences in the property or services provided pursuant to such operations and in the markets to which such property or services are offered, and (b) the treatment within the lines of business established by the Commissioner of operations that are comparable in their similarities and differences. (Assume that the provision of moving services is not in any line of business established by the Commissioner and that within the lines of business established by the Commissioner services that differ only in the distance over which they are performed (e.g., local and long-distance telephone services) are generally treated as part of the same line of business.)

(iii) Undertakings A and B provide the same types of services to similar customers, and the only significant difference in the services provided is the distance over which they are performed. Thus, treating local and long-distance moving services as a single line of business (the "moving-services" line of business) reasonably reflects the treatment within the lines of business established by the Commissioner of operations that are comparable in their similarities and differences.

(iv) Each undertaking derives more than 50 percent of its gross income from operations in the moving-services line of business. Thus, there are predominant operations in each undertaking, and the predominant operations of the two undertakings are in the same line of business. Accordingly, undertakings A and B are similar.

*Example (9).* (i) Undertakings A, B, C, D, and E are trade or business undertakings (within the meaning of paragraph (f)(1)(ii) of this section) and are controlled by the same interests (within the meaning of paragraph (j) of this section). Undertakings A, B, and C derive all of their gross income from retail sales of dairy products, and undertakings D and E derive all of their gross income from the processing of dairy products. Undertakings D and E sell less than ten percent of their dairy products to undertakings A, B, and C, and sell the remainder to unrelated undertakings. Undertakings A, B, and C purchase less than ten percent of their inventory from undertakings D and E and purchase the remainder from unrelated undertakings.

(ii) Paragraph (f)(4)(i) of this section provides that, except as provided in paragraph (f)(4)(iii) of this section, undertakings are similar for purposes of this paragraph (f) if and only if there are predominant operations in each undertaking and the predominant operations of the undertakings are in the same line of business. (Assume that the applicable revenue procedure provides that (a) "food stores" and (b) "manufacturing—food and kindred products" are two separate lines of business.)

(iii) Undertakings A, B, and C all derive more than 50 percent of their gross income from operations in the food-store line of business (the dairy-sales operations). Thus, there are predominant operations in undertakings A, B, and C, and the predominant operations of the three undertakings are in the same line of business. Accordingly, undertakings A, B, and C are similar.

(iv) Undertakings D and E both derive more than 50 percent of their gross income from operations in the food-manufacturing line of business (the dairy-processing operations). Thus, there are predominant operations in undertakings D and E, and the predominant operations of the two undertakings are in the same line of business. Accordingly, undertakings D and E are similar. The predominant operations of undertakings D and E are not in the same line of business as those of undertakings A, B, and C. Accordingly, undertakings D and E are not similar to undertakings A, B, and C.

(v) Paragraph (f)(4)(iii) of this section provides rules under which certain undertakings whose operations are not in the same line of business nevertheless are similar to one another if one of the undertakings (the "supplier undertaking") provides property or services to the other undertaking (the "recipient undertaking"), and the undertakings are controlled by the same interests. These rules apply, however, only if the supplier undertaking predominantly involves the provision of property and services to the recipient undertaking (see paragraph (f)(4)(iii)(A) of this section), or the supplier undertaking is the predominant provider of property and services to the recipient undertaking (see paragraph (f)(4)(iii)(B) of this section). In this case, undertakings D and E are supplier undertakings, and undertakings A, B, and C are recipient undertakings. Undertakings D and E, however, sell less than ten percent of their dairy products to undertakings A, B, and C and thus do not predominantly involve the provision of property and services to recipient undertakings. Similarly, undertakings D and E are not the predominant providers of property and services to undertakings A, B, and C. Thus, the rules for vertically-integrated undertakings in paragraph (f)(4)(iii) of this section do not apply in this case.

*Example (10).* (i) The facts are the same as in example (9), except that undertaking D sells 75 percent of its dairy products to undertakings A, B, and C.

(ii) Paragraph (f)(4)(iii)(A) of this section applies if a supplier undertaking predominantly involves the provision of property to a recipient undertaking that is controlled by the same interests. Paragraph (f)(4)(iii)(A)(2) of this section provides that a supplier undertaking predominantly involves the provision of property to a recipient undertaking if the supplier undertaking provides more than 50 percent of its property to such recipient undertaking. In addition, paragraph (f)(4)(iii)(A)(1) of this section provides that if a supplier undertaking and two or more similar recipient undertakings are controlled by the same interests, the recipient undertakings are treated as a single undertaking for purposes of applying paragraph (f)(4)(iii)(A) of this section. Undertakings D and E both provide dairy products to undertakings A, B, and C. Thus, for purposes of paragraph (f)(4)(iii) of this section, undertakings D and E are supplier undertakings and undertakings A, B, and C are recipient undertakings. Undertaking D predominantly involves the provision of property to undertakings A, B, and C. Moreover, undertakings A, B, and C are treated as a single undertaking under paragraph (f)(4)(iii)(A)(1) of this section because undertakings A, B, and C are similar to one another under paragraph (f)(4)(i) of this section, and undertakings A, B, C, and D are controlled by the same interests. Accordingly, paragraph (f)(4)(iii)(A) of this section applies to undertakings A, B, C, and D.

(iii) If paragraph (f)(4)(iii)(A) of this section applies to supplier and recipient undertakings, the supplier undertaking is treated under paragraph (f)(4)(iii)(A) and (C)(2) of this section as an undertaking that is similar to the recipient undertakings and to undertakings to which the recipient undertakings are similar. Accordingly, undertaking D is similar, for purposes of this paragraph (f), to undertakings A, B, and C.

(iv) Undertaking E does not predominantly involve the provision of property to undertakings A, B, and C, or to any other related undertakings. Thus, paragraph (f)(4)(iii)(A) of this section does not apply to undertaking E, and undertaking E is not similar to undertakings A, B, and C.

Moreover, undertakings D and E are not similar because, under paragraph (f)(4)(iii)(C)(2) of this section, undertaking D is not similar to any undertaking that is not similar to undertakings A, B, and C.

*Example (11).* (i) The facts are the same as in example (10), except that 75 percent of undertaking D's dairy products are sold to undertakings A and B, and none are sold to undertaking C.

(ii) In this case, undertaking D is a supplier undertaking only with respect to undertakings A and B. Accordingly, paragraph (f)(4)(iii)(A) applies only to undertakings A, B, and D. As in example (10), undertaking D is similar to undertakings A and B, and is not similar to undertaking E. In addition, if paragraph (f)(4)(iii)(A) of this section applies to supplier and recipient undertakings, the supplier undertaking is treated under paragraph (f)(4)(iii)(C)(2) of this section as an undertaking that is similar to the recipient undertakings and undertakings to which the recipient undertakings are similar. Accordingly, even though undertaking D does not provide any property or services to undertaking C, undertaking D is similar to undertaking C because undertaking C is similar to undertakings A and B.

*Example (12).* (i) The facts are the same as in example (9), except that undertakings A and B purchase 80 percent of their inventory from undertaking D.

(ii) Paragraph (f)(4)(iii)(B) of this section applies, except as provided in paragraph (f)(4)(iii)(C) of this section, if a supplier undertaking is the predominant provider of property to a recipient undertaking that is controlled by the same interests. Undertakings D and E both provide dairy products to undertakings A, B, and C. Thus, for purposes of paragraph (f)(4)(iii) of this section, undertakings D and E are supplier undertakings, and undertakings A, B, and C are recipient undertakings. In addition, undertaking D is the predominant provider of property and services to undertakings A and B, and undertakings A, B and D are controlled by the same interests. Thus, except as provided in paragraph (f)(4)(iii)(C) of this section, paragraph (f)(4)(iii)(B) of this section applies to undertakings A, B, and D.

(iii) The coordination rules in paragraph (f)(4)(iii)(C)(1) of this section provide that paragraph (f)(4)(iii)(B) of this section does not apply in certain cases to which paragraph (f)(4)(iii)(A) of this section applies. These coordination rules would apply if undertaking D or E (or any other undertaking that is controlled by the interests that control undertakings A, B, and C) predominantly involved the provision of property and services to undertakings A, B, and C. The coordination rules in paragraph (f)(4)(iii)(C)(1) of this section would also apply if undertaking A, B, or D predominantly involved the provision of property or services to a recipient undertaking that is controlled by the same interests. Assume that these coordination rules do not apply in this case.

(iv) If paragraph (f)(4)(iii)(B) of this section applies to supplier and recipient undertakings, the recipient undertakings are treated under paragraph (f)(4)(iii)(B) and (C)(3) of this section as undertakings that are similar to the supplier undertaking and to undertakings to which the supplier undertaking is similar. Accordingly, undertakings A and B are similar, for purposes of this paragraph (f), to undertaking D and, because undertakings D and E are similar, to undertaking E.

(v) The principal providers of property and services to undertaking C are unrelated undertakings. Thus, paragraph (f)(4)(iii)(B) of this section does not apply to undertaking C, and undertaking C is not similar to undertakings D and E. Moreover, undertaking C is not similar to undertakings A and B because, under paragraph (f)(4)(iii)(C)(3) of this section, undertakings A and B are not similar to any undertaking that is not similar to undertaking D.

*Example (13).* (i) Undertakings A through Z are trade or business undertakings (within the meaning of paragraph (f)(1)(ii) of this section) and are controlled by the same interests (within the meaning of paragraph (j) of this section). Undertaking A derives all of its gross income from the manufacture and sale of men's and women's clothing, undertaking B derives all of its gross income from sales of men's and women's clothing to retail stores, and undertakings C through Z derive all of their gross income from retail sales of men's and women's clothing. Undertaking A sells clothing exclusively to undertaking B. Undertaking B sells 75 percent of its clothing to undertakings C through Z, and sells the remainder to unrelated retail stores. Undertaking B purchases 80 percent of its inventory from undertaking A, and undertakings C through Z purchase 60 to 90 percent of their inventory from undertaking B.

(ii) Paragraph (f)(4)(iii)(A) of this section applies if a supplier undertaking predominantly involves the provision of property to a recipient undertaking that is controlled by the same interests. In addition, paragraph (f)(4)(iii)(A)(1) of this section provides that if a supplier undertaking and two or more similar recipient undertakings are controlled by the same interests, the recipient undertaking are treated as a single undertaking for this purpose. Undertaking B provides men's and women's clothing to undertaking C through Z. Thus, for purposes of paragraph (f)(4)(iii) of this section, undertaking B is a supplier undertaking and undertakings C through Z are recipient undertakings. In addition, undertaking B predominantly involves the provision of property to undertakings C through Z, and undertakings C through Z are treated as a single undertaking for purposes of paragraph (f)(4)(iii)(A) of this section. Accordingly, paragraph (f)(4)(iii)(A) of this section applies to undertakings B and C through Z.

(iii) If paragraph (f)(4)(iii)(A) of this section applies to supplier and recipient undertakings, the supplier undertaking is treated under paragraph (f)(4)(iii)(A) of this section as an undertaking that is similar to the recipient undertakings. Accordingly, undertaking B is similar, for purposes of this paragraph (f), to undertakings C through Z.

(iv) Undertaking A provides men's and women's clothing to undertaking B. Thus, for purposes of paragraph (f)(4)(iii) of this section, undertaking A is a supplier undertaking and undertaking B is a recipient undertaking. In addition, undertaking A predominantly involves the provision of property to undertaking B, and undertakings A and B are controlled by the same interests. Accordingly, paragraph (f)(4)(iii)(A) of this section applies to undertakings A and B, and undertaking A is similar to undertaking B.

(v) If paragraph (f)(4)(iii)(A) of this section applies to supplier and recipient undertakings, the supplier undertaking is treated under paragraph (f)(4)(iii)(C)(2) of this section as an undertaking that is similar to undertakings to which the recipient undertakings are similar. Accordingly, undertaking A is also similar, for purposes of this paragraph (f), to undertakings C through Z.

(vi) The coordination rule in paragraph (f)(4)(iii)(C)(1)(i) of this section provides that paragraph (f)(4)(iii)(B) of this section does not apply if, as described above, the supplier undertaking predominantly involves the provision of property to recipient undertakings and is treated under paragraph (f)(4)(iii)(A) of this section as an undertaking that is similar to such recipient undertakings. Accordingly, paragraph (f)(4)(iii)(B) of this section does not apply to undertakings B through Z, even though undertaking B is the predominant provider of property and services to undertakings C through Z, and undertakings B through Z are controlled by the same interests. For the same reason, paragraph (f)(4)(iii)(B) of this section does not apply to undertaking A and B. (Paragraph (f)(4)(iii)(B) of this section is also inapplicable to undertakings A and B because the coordination rule in paragraph (f)(4)(iii)(C)(1)(ii) of this section applies if the recipient undertaking (undertaking B) is itself a supplier undertaking that is treated under paragraph (f)(4)(iii)(A) of this section as an undertaking that is similar to its recipient undertakings (undertakings C through Z).)

**(g) Integrated businesses.** *(1) Applicability.* (i) In general. This paragraph (g) applies to a taxpayer's interests in trade or business activities (within the meaning of paragraph (g)(1)(ii) of this section).

(ii) Trade or business activity. For purposes of this paragraph (g), the term "trade or business activity" means any activity (determined without regard to this paragraph (g)) that consists of interests in one or more trade or business undertakings (within the meaning of paragraph (f)(1)(ii) of this section).

*(2) Treatment as a single activity.* A taxpayer's interests in two or more trade or business activities shall be treated as a single activity if and only if—

(i) The operations of such trade or business activities constitute a single integrated business, activities constitute a single integrated business; and

(ii) Such activities are controlled by the same interests (within the meaning of paragraph (j) of this section).

*(3) Facts and circumstances test.* In determining whether the operations of two or more trade or business activities constitute a single integrated business for purposes of this paragraph (g), all the facts and circumstances are taken into account, and the following factors are generally the most significant:

(i) Whether such operations are conducted at the same location;

(ii) The extent to which other persons conduct similar operations at one location;

(iii) Whether such operations are treated as a unit in the primary accounting records reflecting the results of such operations;

(iv) The extent to which other persons treat similar operations as a unit in the primary accounting records reflecting the results of such similar operations;

(v) Whether such operations are owned by the same person (within the meaning of paragraph (c)(2)(v) of this section);

(vi) The extent to which such operations involve products or services that are commonly provided together;

(vii) The extent to which such operations serve the same customers;

(viii) The extent to which the same personnel, facilities, or equipment are used to conduct such operations;

(ix) The extent to which such operations are conducted in coordination with or reliance upon each other;

(x) The extent to which the conduct of any such operations is incidental to the conduct of the remainder of such operations;

(xi) The extent to which such operations depend on each other for their economic success; and

(xii) Whether such operations are conducted under the same trade name.

*(4) Examples.* The following examples illustrate the application of this paragraph (g). The facts, analysis, and conclusion in each example relate to a single taxable year, and the trade or business activities described in each example are controlled by the same interests (within the meaning of paragraph (j) of this section).

*Example (1).* (i) The taxpayer owns a number of department stores and auto-supply stores. Some of the taxpayer's department stores include auto-supply departments. In other cases, the taxpayer operates a department store and an auto-supply store at the same location (within the meaning of paragraph (c)(2)(iii) of this section), or at different locations from which the same group of customers can be served. In cases in which a department store and an auto-supply store are operated at the same location, the department-store operations are the predominant operations (within the meaning of paragraph (f)(4)(ii) of this section), and the undertaking that includes the stores is treated as a department-store undertaking for purposes of paragraph (f) of this section. Under paragraph (f) of this section, the department-store undertakings are all treated as part of the same activity of the taxpayer (the "department-store activity"). Similarly, the auto-supply undertakings (i.e., the auto-supply stores that are not operated at a department-store location) are all treated as part of the same activity (the "auto-supply activity"). (Assume that department-store undertakings and auto-supply undertakings are not similar and are not treated as part of the same activity under paragraph (f) of this section.)

(ii) The department stores and auto-supply stores use a common trade name and coordinate their marketing activities (e.g., the stores advertise in the same catalog and the same newspaper supplements, honor the same credit cards (including credit cards issued by the department stores), and jointly conduct sales and other promotional activities). Although sales personnel generally work only in a particular store or in a particular department within a store, other employees (e.g., cashiers, janitorial and maintenance workers, and clerical staff) may work in or perform services for various stores, including both department and auto-supply stores. In addition, the management of store operations is organized on a geographical basis, and managers above the level of the individual store generally supervise operations in both types of store. A central office provides payroll, financial, and other support services to all stores and establishes pricing and other business policies. Most inventory for both types of stores is acquired through a central purchasing department and inventory for all stores in an area is stored in a common warehouse.

(iii) Based on the foregoing facts and circumstances, the operations of the department-store activity and the auto-supply activity constitute an integrated business. Paragraph (g)(3) of this section provides that the factors relevant to this determination include the conduct of department-store and auto-supply operations at the same location, the location of department and auto-supply stores at sites where the same group of customers can be served, the treatment of all such operations as a unit in the taxpayer's financial statements, the taxpayer's ownership and the common management of all such operations, the use of the same personnel, facilities, and equipment to conduct and support the operations, the use of a common trade name, and the coordination (as evidenced by the coordinated marketing activities) of department-store and auto-supply operations.

(iv) Paragraph (g)(2) of this section provides that a taxpayer's interests in two or more trade or business activities (within the meaning of paragraph (g)(1)(ii) of this section) are treated as a single activity of the taxpayer if the operations of such activities constitute an integrated business and the activities are controlled by the same interests. The department-store activity and the auto-supply activity consist of trade or business undertakings and, thus, are trade or business activities. In addition, the activities are controlled by the same interests (the taxpayer), and the operations of the activities constitute an integrated business. Accordingly, the department-store activity and the auto-supply activity are treated as a single activity of the taxpayer.

*Example (2).* (i) The taxpayer owns a number of stores that sell stereo equipment and a repair shop that services stereo equipment. Under paragraph (f) of this section, the stores are all treated as part of the same activity of the taxpayer (the "store activity" ). The repair shop does not sell stereo equipment, does not predominantly involve the provision of services to the taxpayer's stores, and is treated as a separate activity (the "repair-shop activity"). (Assume that stereo-sales undertakings and stereo-repair undertakings are not similar and are not treated as part of the same activity under paragraph (f) of this section.)

(ii) The stores sell stereo equipment produced by manufacturers for which the stores are an authorized distributor. The repair shop's operations principally involve the servicing of stereo equipment produced by the same manufacturers. These operations include repairs on equipment under warranty for which reimbursement is received from the manufacturer and reconditioning of equipment taken as trade-ins by the taxpayer's stores. The majority of the operations, however, involve repairs that are performed for customers and are not covered by a warranty. The taxpayer's distribution agreements with manufacturers generally require the taxpayer to repair and service equipment produced by the manufacturer both during and after the warranty period. In some cases, the distribution agreements require that the taxpayer's repair facility meet the manufacturer's standards and provide for periodic inspections to ensure that these standards are met.

(iii) The stores and the repair shop use a common trade name. Sales personnel generally work only in a particular store and stereo technicians work only in the repair shop. The stores and the repair shop are, however, managed from a central office, which supervises both store and repair-shop operations, provides payroll, financial, and other support services to the stores and the repair shop, and establishes pricing and other business policies. In addition, inventory for the stores and supplies for the repair shop are acquired through a central purchasing department and are stored in a single warehouse.

(iv) Based on the foregoing facts and circumstances, the operations of the store activity and the repair-shop activity constitute an integrated business. Paragraph (g)(3) of this section provides that the factors relevant to this determination include the treatment of all such operations as a unit in the taxpayer's financial statements, the taxpayer's ownership and the common management of all such operations, the use of the same personnel and facilities to support the operations, the use of a common trade name, the extent to which the same customers patronize both the stores and the repair shop, the similarity of the products (i.e., stereo equipment) involved in both store and repair-shop operations, and the extent to which the provision of repair services contributes to the taxpayer's ability to obtain the stereo equipment sold in store operations.

(v) Paragraph (g)(2) of this section provides that a taxpayer's interests in two or more trade or business activities (within the meaning of paragraph (g)(1)(ii) of this section) are treated as a single activity of the taxpayer if the operations of such activities constitute an integrated business and the activities are controlled by the same interests. The store activity and repair-shop activity consist of trade or business undertakings and thus are trade or business activities. In addition, the activities are controlled by the same interests (the taxpayer), and the operations of the activities constitute an integrated business. Accordingly, the store activity and the repair-shop activity are treated as a single activity of the taxpayer.

*Example (3).* (i) The taxpayer owns interests in three partnerships. One partnership owns a television station, the second owns a professional sports franchise, and the third owns a motion-picture production company. The operations of the partnerships are treated as three separate undertakings. Although other persons own interests in the partnerships, all three undertakings are controlled (within the meaning of paragraph (j) of this section) by the taxpayer. The operations of the partnerships are treated as three separate activities (the "television activity," the "sports activity," and the "motion-picture activity"). (Assume that the undertakings are not similar and are not treated as part of the same activity under paragraph (f) of this section.)

(ii) Each partnership prepares financial statements that reflect only the results of that partnership's operations, and each of the activities is conducted under its own trade name. The taxpayer participates extensively in the management of each partnership and makes the major business decisions for all three partnerships. Each partnership, however, employs separate management and other personnel who conduct its operations on a day-to-day basis. The taxpayer generally arranges the partnerships' financing and often obtains loans for two, or all three, partnerships from the same source. Although the assets of one partnership are not used as security for loans to another partnership, the taxpayer's interest in a partnership may secure loans to the other partnerships. The television station broadcasts the sports franchise's games, and the motion-picture production company occasionally prepares programming for the television station. In addition, support staff of one partnership may, during periods of peak activity or in the case of emergency, be made available to another partnership on a temporary basis. There are no other significant transactions between the partnerships. Moreover, all transactions between the partnerships involve essentially the same terms as would be provided in transactions between unrelated persons.

(iii) Based on the foregoing facts and circumstances, the television activity, the sports activity, and the motion-picture activity constitute three separate businesses. Paragraph (g)(3) of this section provides that the factors relevant to this determination include the treatment of the activities as separate units in the partnerships' financial statements, the use of a different trade name for each activity, the separate day-to-day management of the activities, and the limited extent to which the activities contribute to or depend on each other (as evidenced by the small number of significant transactions between the partnerships and the arm's length nature of those transactions). The taxpayer's participation in management and financing are taken into account in this determination, as are the transactions between the partnerships, but these factors do not of themselves support a determination that the activities constitute an integrated business.

(iv) Paragraph (g)(2) of this section provides that a taxpayer's interests in two or more trade or business activities (within the meaning of paragraph (g)(1)(ii) of this section) are treated as a single activity of the taxpayer only if the operations of such activities constitute an integrated business and the activities are controlled by the same interests. In this case, the taxpayer's activities do not constitute an integrated business, and the aggregation rule in paragraph (g)(2) of this section does not apply. Accordingly, the television activity, the sports activity, and the motion-picture activity are treated as three separate activities of the taxpayer.

**(h) Certain professional service undertakings treated as a single activity.** *(1) Applicability.* (i) In general. This paragraph (h) applies to a taxpayer's interests in professional service undertakings (within the meaning of paragraph (h)(1)(ii) of this section).

(ii) Professional service undertaking. For purposes of this paragraph (h), an undertaking is treated as a professional service undertaking for any taxable year in which the undertaking derives more than 50 percent of its gross income from the provision of services that are treated, for purposes of section 448(d)(2)(A) and the regulations thereunder, as services performed in the fields of health, law, engineering, architecture, accounting, actuarial science, performing arts, or consulting.

*(2) Treatment as a single activity.* (i) Undertakings controlled by the same interest. A taxpayer's interests in two or more professional service undertakings that are controlled by the same interests (within the meaning of paragraph (j) of this section) shall be treated as part of the same activity of the taxpayer.

(ii) Undertakings involving significant similar or significant related services. A taxpayer's interests in two or more professional service undertakings that involve the provision of significant similar services or significant related services shall be treated as part of the same activity of the taxpayer.

(iii) Coordination rule. (A) Except as provided in paragraph (h)(2)(iii)(B) of this section, a taxpayer's interests in two or more undertakings (the "original undertakings") that are treated as part of the same activity of the taxpayer under the provisions of paragraph (h)(2)(i) or (ii) of this section shall be treated as interests in a single professional service undertaking (the "aggregated undertaking") for purposes of reapplying such provisions.

(B) If any original undertaking included in an aggregated undertaking and any other undertaking that is not included in such aggregated undertaking involve the provision of significant similar or related services, the aggregated undertaking and such other undertaking shall be treated as undertakings that involve the provision of significant similar or related services for purposes of reapplying the provisions of paragraph (h)(2)(ii) of this section.

*(3) Significant similar or significant related services.* For purposes of this paragraph (h)—

(i) Services (other than consulting services) in any field described in paragraph (h)(1)(ii) of this section are similar to all other services in the same field;

(ii) All the facts and circumstances are taken into account in determining whether consulting services are similar;

(iii) Two professional service undertakings involve the provision of significant similar services if and only if—

(A) Each such undertaking provides significant professional services; and

(B) Significant professional services provided by one such undertaking are similar to significant professional services provided by the other such undertaking;

(iv) Services are significant professional services if and only if such services are in a field described in paragraph (h)(1)(ii) of this section and more than 20 percent of the undertaking's gross income is attributable to services in such field (or, in the case of consulting services, to similar services in such field); and

(v) Two professional service undertakings involve the provision of significant related services if and only if more than 20 percent of the gross income of one such undertaking is derived from customers that are also customers of the other such undertaking.

*(4) Examples.* The following examples illustrate the application of this paragraph (h). In each example that does not state otherwise, the taxpayer is an individual, and the facts, analysis, and conclusions relate to a single taxable year.

*Example (1).* (i) The taxpayer is a partner in a law partnership that has offices in various cities. Some of the partnership's offices provide a full range of legal services. Other offices, however, specialize in a particular area or areas of the law (e.g., litigation, tax law, corporate law, etc.). In either case, substantially all of the office's gross income is derived from the provision of legal services. Under paragraph (c)(1) of this section, each of the law partnership's offices is treated as a single undertaking that is separate from other undertakings (a "law-office undertaking").

(ii) Each law-office undertaking derives more than 50 percent of its gross income from the provision of services in the field law. Thus, each such undertaking is treated as a professional service undertaking (within the meaning of paragraph (h)(1)(ii) of this section).

(iii) Each law-office undertaking derives more than 20 percent of its gross income from services in the field of law. Thus, each such undertaking involves significant professional services (within the meaning of paragraph (h)(3)(iv) of this section) in the field of law. In addition, all services in the field of law are treated as similar services under paragraph (h)(3)(i) of this section. Thus, the law-office undertakings involve the provision of significant similar services (within the meaning of paragraph (h)(3)(iii) of this section).

(iv) Paragraph (h)(2)(ii) of this section provides that a taxpayer's interest in professional service undertakings that involve the provision of significant similar services are treated as part of the same activity of the taxpayer. Accordingly, the taxpayer's interests in the law-office undertakings are treated as part of the same activity of the taxpayer under paragraph (h)(2)(ii) of this section even if the undertakings are not controlled by the same interests (within the meaning of paragraph (j) of this section).

*Example (2).* (i) The taxpayer is a partner in medical partnerships A and B. Both partnerships derive all of their gross income from the provision of medical services, but partnership A specializes in internal medicine and partnership B operates a radiology laboratory. Under paragraph (c)(1) of this section, the medical-service business of each partnership is treated as a single undertaking that is separate from other undertakings (a "medical-service undertaking"). Partnerships A and B are not controlled by the same interests (within the meaning of paragraph (j) of this section).

(ii) Each partnership's medical-service undertaking derives more than 50 percent of its gross income from the provision of services in the field of health. Thus, each partnership's medical-service undertaking is treated as a professional service undertaking (within the meaning of paragraph (h)(1)(ii) of this section).

(iii) Each partnership's medical-service undertaking derives more than 20 percent of its gross income from services in the field of health. Thus, each such undertaking involves significant professional services (within the meaning of paragraph (h)(3)(iv) of this section) in the field of health. In addition, all services in the field of health are treated as similar services under paragraph (h)(3)(i) of this section. Thus, the medical-services undertakings of partnerships A and B involve the provision of significant similar services (within the meaning of paragraph (h)(3)(iii) of this section).

(iv) Paragraph (h)(2)(ii) of this section provides that a taxpayer's interests in professional service undertakings that involve the provision of significant similar services are treated as part of the same activity of the taxpayer. Accordingly, the taxpayer's interests in the medical-service undertakings of partnerships A and B are treated as part of the same activity of the taxpayer under paragraph (h)(2)(ii) of this section even though the undertakings are not controlled by the same interests.

*Example (3).* (i) The facts are the same as in example (2), except that the taxpayer withdraws from partnership A in 1989 and becomes a partner in partnership B in 1990. In addition, the taxpayer was a full-time participant in the operations of partnership A from 1970 through 1989, but does not participate in the operations of partnership B.

(ii) Paragraph (h)(2)(ii) of this section provides that a taxpayer's interests in professional service undertakings that involve the provision of significant similar services are treated as part of the same activity of the taxpayer. This rule is not limited to cases in which the taxpayer holds such interests simultaneously. Thus, as in example (2), the taxpayer's interests in the medical-service undertakings of partnerships A and B are treated as part of the same activity of the taxpayer.

(iii) The activity that includes the taxpayer's interests in the medical-service undertakings of partnerships A and B is a personal service activity (within the meaning of § 1.469-5T(d)) because it involves the performance of personal services in the field of health. In addition, the taxpayer materially participated in the activity for three or more taxable years preceding 1990 (see § 1.469-5T(j)(1)). Thus, even if the taxpayer does not work in the activity after 1989, the taxpayer is treated, under § 1.469-5T(a)(6), as materially participating in the activity for 1990 and subsequent taxable years.

*Example (4).* (i) The taxpayer is a partner in an accounting partnership that has offices in various cities (partnership A) and in a management-consulting partnership that has a single office (partnership B). Each of partnership A's offices derives substantially all of its gross income from services in the field of accounting, and partnership B derives substantially all of its gross income from services in the field of consulting. Under paragraph (c)(1) of this section, partnership B's consulting business is treated as a single undertaking that is separate from other undertakings (the "consulting undertaking") and each of partnership A's offices is similarly treated (the "accounting undertakings"). The accounting undertakings are controlled by the same interests, but partnerships A and B are not controlled by the same interests (within the meaning of paragraph (j) of this section). Partnership B's consulting business derives 50 percent of its gross income from customers of partnership A's accounting undertakings, but does not derive more than 20 percent of its gross income from the customers of any single accounting undertaking.

(ii) Each accounting undertaking derives more than 50 percent of its gross income from the provision of services in the field of accounting, and the consulting undertaking derives more than 50 percent of its gross income from the provision of services in the field of consulting. Thus, each accounting undertaking is treated as a professional service undertaking (within the meaning of paragraph (h)(1)(ii) of this section), and the consulting undertaking is also treated as a professional service undertaking.

(iii) Each accounting undertaking derives more than 20 percent of its gross income from services in the field of accounting. Thus, each such undertaking involves significant professional services (within the meaning of paragraph (h)(3)(iv) of this section) in the field of accounting. In addition, all services in the field of accounting are treated as similar services under paragraph (h)(3)(i) of this section. Thus, the accounting undertakings involve the provision of significant similar services (within the meaning of paragraph (h)(3)(iii) of this section).

(iv) Paragraph (h)(2)(i) and (ii) of this section provides that a taxpayer's interests in professional service undertakings that are controlled by the same interests or that involve the provision of significant similar services are treated as part of the same activity of the taxpayer. The accounting undertakings are controlled by the same interests (see (i) above) and involve the provision of significant similar services (see (iii) above). Accordingly, the taxpayer's interests in the accounting undertakings are treated as part of the same activity under paragraph (h)(2)(i) and (ii) of this section.

(v) The consulting undertaking derives more than 20 percent of its gross income from services in the field of consulting. If, based on all the facts and circumstances, these services are determined to be similar consulting services under paragraph (h)(3)(ii) of this section, the consulting undertaking involves significant professional services (within the meaning of paragraph (h)(3)(iv) of this section). In this case, however, the consulting undertaking and the accounting undertakings do not involve the provision of significant similar services (within the meaning of paragraph (h)(3)(iii) of this section) because consulting services and accounting services are not treated as similar services under paragraph (h)(3)(i) of this section.

(vi) The consulting undertaking does not derive more than 20 percent of its gross income from the customers of any single accounting undertaking of partnership A. If, however, partnership A's accounting undertakings are aggregated, the consulting undertaking derives more than 20 percent of its gross income from customers of the aggregated undertakings. Paragraph (h)(3)(v) of this section provides that two professional service undertakings involve the provision of significant related services if more than 20 percent of the gross income of one undertaking is derived from customers of the other undertaking. For purposes of applying this rule, partnership A's accounting undertakings are treated as a single undertaking under paragraph (h)(2)(iii) of this section because the accounting undertakings are treated as part of the same activity under paragraph (h)(2)(i) and (ii) of this section. Thus, the consulting undertaking and the accounting undertakings involve the provision of significant related services.

(vii) Paragraph (h)(2)(ii) of this section provides that a taxpayer's interests in professional service undertakings that involve the provision of significant related services are treated as part of the same activity of the taxpayer. Accordingly, the taxpayer's interests in the consulting undertaking and the accounting undertakings are treated as part of the same activity of the taxpayer under paragraph (h)(2)(ii) of this section.

*Example (5).* (i) The facts are the same as in example (4), except that partnership B's consulting business derives only 15 percent of its gross income from customers of partnership A's accounting undertakings.

(ii) As in example (4), the taxpayer's interests in the accounting undertakings are treated as part of the same activity under paragraph (h)(2)(i) and (ii) of this section and are treated under paragraph (h)(2)(iii) of this section as a single undertaking for purposes of reapplying those provisions. In this case, however, the consulting undertaking does not derive more than 20 percent of its gross income from the customers of partnership A's accounting undertakings. Thus, the consulting undertaking and the accounting undertakings do not involve the provision of significant related services. Accordingly, the accounting undertakings and the consulting undertaking are not treated as part of the same activity under paragraph (h)(2)(i) or (ii) of this section because they are not controlled by the same interests and do not involve the provision of significant similar or related services.

*Example (6).* (i) The taxpayer is a partner in partnerships A, B, and C. Partnership A derives substantially all of its gross income from the provision of engineering services, partnership B derives substantially all of its gross income from the provision of architectural services, and partnership C derives 40 percent of its gross income from the provision of engineering services and the remainder from the provision of architectural services. Under paragraph (c)(1) of this section, each partnership's service business is treated as a single undertaking that is separate from other undertakings. Partnerships A, B, and C are not controlled by the same interests (within the meaning of paragraph (j) of this section).

(ii) Each partnership's undertaking derives more than 50 percent of its gross income from the provision of services in the fields of architecture and engineering. Thus, each such undertaking is treated as a professional service undertaking (within the meaning of paragraph (h)(1)(ii) of this section).

(iii) Partnership A's undertaking ("undertaking A") derives more than 20 percent of its gross income from services in the field of engineering, partnership B's undertaking ("undertaking B") derives more than 20 percent of its gross income from services in the field of architecture, and partnership C's undertaking ("undertaking C") derives more than 20 percent of its gross income from services in the field of engineering and more than 20 percent of its gross income from services in the field of architecture. Thus, undertaking A involves significant services in the field of engineering, undertaking B involves significant services in the field of architecture, and undertaking C involves significant services in both fields. Under paragraph (h)(3)(i) of this section, all services within each field are treated as similar services, but engineering services and architectural services are not treated as similar services. Thus, undertakings A and C, and undertakings B and C, involve the provision of significant similar services (within the meaning of paragraph (h)(3)(iii) of this section).

(iv) Paragraph (h)(2)(ii) of this section provides that a taxpayer's interests in professional service undertakings that involve the provision of significant similar services are treated as part of the same activity of the taxpayer. Accordingly, the taxpayer's interests in undertakings A and C are treated as part of the same activity of the taxpayer.

(v) Under paragraph (h)(2)(iii)(A) of this section, undertakings A and C are also treated as a single undertaking for purposes of determining whether undertaking B involves the provision of significant similar services. Paragraph (h)(2)(iii)(B) of this section in effect provides that treating undertakings A and C as a single undertaking does not affect the conclusion that the architectural services provided by undertakings B and C are significant similar services. Thus, undertaking B and the single undertaking in which undertakings A and C are included under paragraph (h)(3)(iii) of this section involve the provision of significant similar services, and the taxpayer's interests in undertakings A, B, and C are treated as part of the same activity of the taxpayer under paragraph (h)(2)(ii) of this section.

**(i) [Reserved]**

**(j) Control by the same interests and ownership percentage.** *(1) In general.* Except as otherwise provided in paragraph (j)(2) of this section, all the facts and circumstances are taken into account in determining, for purposes of this section, whether undertakings are controlled by the same interests. For this purpose, control includes any kind of control, direct or indirect, whether legally enforceable, and however exercisable or exercised. It is the reality of control that is determinative, and not its form or mode of exercise.

*(2) Presumption.* (i) In general. Undertakings are rebuttably presumed to be controlled by the same interests if such undertakings are part of the same common-ownership group.

(ii) Common-ownership group. Except as provided in paragraph (j)(2)(iii) of this section, two or more undertakings of a taxpayer are part of the same common-ownership group for purposes of this paragraph (j)(2) if and only if the sum of the common-ownership percentages of any five or fewer persons (within the meaning of section 7701(a)(1), but not including passthrough entities) with respect to such undertakings exceeds 50 percent. For this purpose, the common-ownership percentage of a person with respect to such undertakings is the person's smallest ownership percentage (determined in accordance with paragraph (j)(3) of this section) in any such undertaking.

(iii) Special aggregation rule. If, without regard to this paragraph (j)(2)(iii), an undertaking of a taxpayer is part of two or more common-ownership groups, any undertakings of the taxpayer that are part of any such common-ownership group shall be treated for purposes of this paragraph (j)(2) as part of a single common-ownership group in determining the activities of such taxpayer.

*(3) Ownership percentage.* (i) In general. For purposes of this section, a person's ownership percentage in an undertaking or in a passthrough entity shall include any interest in such undertaking or passthrough entity that the person holds directly and the person's share of any interest in such undertaking or passthrough entity that is held through one or more passthrough entities.

(ii) Passthrough entities. The following rules apply for purposes of applying paragraph (j)(3)(i) of this section:

(A) A partner's interest in a partnership and share of any interest in a passthrough entity or undertaking held through a partnership shall be determined on the basis of the greater of such partner's percentage interest in the capital (by value) of such partnership or such partner's largest distributive share of any item of income or gain (disregarding guaranteed payments under section 707(c)) of such partnership.

(B) A shareholder's interest in an S corporation and share of any interest in a passthrough entity or undertaking held through an S corporation shall be determined on the basis of such shareholder's stock ownership.

(C) A beneficiary's interest in a trust or estate and share of any interest in a passthrough entity or undertaking held through a trust or estate shall not be taken into account.

(iii) Attribution rules. (A) In general. Except as otherwise provided in paragraph (j)(3)(iii)(B) of this section, a person's ownership percentage in a passthrough entity or in an undertaking shall be determined by treating such person as the owner of any interest that a person related to such person owns (determined without regard to this paragraph (j)(3)(iii)) in such passthrough entity or in such undertaking.

(B) Determination of common-ownership percentage. The common-ownership percentage of five or fewer persons with respect to two or more undertakings shall be determined, in any case in which, after the application of paragraph (j)(3)(iii)(A) of this section, two or more such persons own the same interest in any such undertaking (the "related-party owners") by treating as the only owner of such interest (or portion thereof) the related-party owner whose ownership of such interest (or a portion thereof) would result in the highest common-ownership percentage.

(C) Related person. A person is related to another person for purposes of this paragraph (j)(3)(iii) if the relationship of such persons is described in section 267(b) or 707(b)(1).

*(4) Special rule for trade or business activities.* In determining whether two or more trade or business activities are controlled by the same interests for purposes of paragraph (g) of this section, each such activity shall be treated as a separate undertaking in applying this paragraph (j).

*(5) Examples.* The following examples illustrate the application of this paragraph (j):

*Example (1).* (i) Partnership X is the sole owner of an undertaking (undertaking X), and partnership Y is the sole owner of another undertaking (undertaking Y). Individuals A, B, C, D, and E are the only partners in partnerships X and Y, and the partnership agreements of both X and Y provide that no action may be taken or decision made on behalf of the partnership without the unanimous consent of the partners. Moreover, each partner actually participates in, and agrees to, all major decisions that affect the operations of either partnership. The ownership percentages (within the meaning of paragraph (j)(3) of this section) of A, B, C, D, and E in each partnership (and in the undertaking owned by the partnership) are as follows:

| Partner | Partnership/Undertaking | |
|---|---|---|
| | X (percent) | Y (percent) |
| A | 15 | 5 |
| B | 10 | 60 |
| C | 10 | 20 |
| D | 77 | 12 |
| E | 8 | 20 |
| | 120 | 117 |

The sum of the ownership percentages exceeds 100 percent for both X and Y because, under paragraph (j)(3)(ii)(A) of this section, each partner's ownership percentage is determined on the basis of the greater of the partner's percentage interest in the capital of the partnership or the partner's largest distributive share of any item of income or gain of the partnership.)

(ii) Paragraph (j)(2)(ii) of this section provides that a person's common-ownership percentage with respect to any two or more undertakings is the person's smallest ownership percentage in any such undertaking. Thus, the common-ownership percentages of A, B, C, D, and E with respect to undertakings X and Y are as follows:

| Partner | Common-ownership percentage |
|---|---|
| A | 5 |
| B | 10 |
| C | 10 |
| D | 12 |
| E | 8 |
| | 45 |

(iii) Paragraph (j)(2)(i) of this section provides that undertakings are rebuttably presumed to be controlled by the same interests if the undertakings are part of the same common-ownership group. In general, undertakings are part of a common-ownership group only if the sum of the common-ownership percentages of any five or fewer persons with respect to such undertakings exceeds 50 percent. In this case, the sum of the partners' common-ownership percentages with respect to undertakings X and Y is only 45 percent. Thus, undertakings X and Y are not part of the same common-ownership group.

(iv) If the presumption in paragraph (j)(2)(i) of this section does not apply, all the facts and circumstances are taken into account in determining whether undertakings are controlled by the same interests (see paragraph (j)(1) of this section). In this case, all actions and decisions in both undertakings require the unanimous consent of the same persons and each of those persons actually participates in, and agrees to, all major decisions. Accordingly, undertakings X and Y are controlled by the same interests (i.e., A, B, C, D, and E).

*Example (2).* (i) Partnerships W, X, Y, and Z are each the sole owner of an undertaking (undertakings W, X, Y, and Z). Individuals A, B, and C are partners in each of the four partnerships, and the remaining interests in each partnership are owned by a number of unrelated individuals, none of whom owns more than a one-percent interest in any of the partnerships. The ownership percentages (within the meaning of paragraph (j)(3) of this section) of A, B, and C in each partnership (and in the undertaking owned by the partnership) are as follows:

| Partnership/Undertaking | Partner | | |
|---|---|---|---|
| | A | B | C |
| W | 23% | 21% | 40% |
| X | 19% | 30% | 22% |
| Y | 25% | 25% | 20% |
| Z | 8% | 4% | 2% |

(ii) Paragraph (j)(2)(ii) of this section provides that a person's common-ownership percentage with respect to any two or more undertakings is the person's smallest ownership percentage in any such undertaking. Thus, the common-ownership percentages of A, B, and C in undertakings W, X, Y, and Z are as follows:

| Partner | Common-ownership percentage |
|---|---|
| A | 8 |
| B | 4 |
| C | 2 |
| | 14 |

(iii) The sum of the common-ownership percentages of A, B, and C with respect to undertakings W, X, Y, and Z is 14 percent, and no other person owns more than a one-percent interest in any of the undertakings. Thus, the sum of the common-ownership percentages of any five or fewer persons with respect to all four undertakings cannot exceed 50 percent. Accordingly, undertakings W, X, Y, and Z are not part of the same common-ownership group (see paragraph (j)(2)(ii) of this section) and are not rebuttably presumed to be controlled by the same interests (see paragraph (j)(2)(i) of this section).

(iv) The common-ownership percentages of A, B, and C in undertakings W, X, and Y are as follows:

| Partner | Common-ownership percentage |
|---|---|
| A | 19 |
| B | 21 |
| C | 20 |
| | 60 |

(v) The sum of the common-ownership percentages of A, B, and C, taking into account only undertakings W, X, and Y, is 60 percent. Because the sum of the common-ownership percentages exceeds 50 percent, undertakings W, X, and Y are part of the same common-ownership group (see paragraph (j)(2)(ii) of this section and are rebuttably presumed to be controlled by the same interests (see paragraph (j)(2)(i) of this section).

*Example (3).* (i) Corporation X, an S corporation, is the sole owner of an undertaking (undertaking X), and corporation Y, another S corporation, is the sole owner of another undertaking (undertaking Y). Individuals A, B, and C are shareholders in corporations X and Y. Both A and B are related (within the meaning of paragraph (j)(3)(iii)(C) of this section) to C, but not to each other. A, B, and C are not related to any other person that owns an interest in either corporation X or corporation Y. The ownership percentages (determined without regard to the attribution rules of paragraph (j)(3)(iii) of this section) of A, B, and C in each corporation (and in the undertaking owned by the corporation) are as follows:

**Corporation/Undertaking**

| Shareholder | X (percent) | Y (percent) |
|---|---|---|
| A | 20 | |
| B | | 20 |
| C | 5 | 5 |

(ii) In general, a person's ownership percentage is determined by treating the person as the owner of interests that are actually owned by related persons (see paragraph (j)(3)(iii)(A) of this section). If A, B, and C are treated as owning interests that are actually owned by related persons, their ownership percentages are as follows:

**Corporation/Undertaking**

| Shareholder | X (percent) | Y (percent) |
|---|---|---|
| A | 25 | 5 |
| B | 5 | 25 |
| C | 25 | 25 |

(iii) Paragraph (j)(3)(iii)(B) of this section provides that, in determining the sum of the common-ownership percentages of any five or fewer persons with respect to any undertakings, each interest in such undertakings is counted only once. If two or more persons are treated as owners of the same interest under paragraph (j)(3)(iii)(A) of this section, the person whose ownership would result in the highest sum is treated as the only owner of the interest. In this case, C's common-ownership percentage with respect to undertakings X and Y, determined by treating C as the owner of the interests actually owned by A and B, is 25 percent. If, however, A and B are treated as the owners of the interests actually owned by C, each has a common-ownership percentage of only five percent. Thus, in determining the sum of common-ownership percentages with respect to undertakings X and Y, C is treated as the owner of the interests actually owned by A and B because this treatment results in the highest sum of common-ownership percentages with respect to such undertakings.

*Example (4).* (i) The ownership percentages of individuals A, B, and C in undertakings X, Y, and Z are as follows:

**Undertaking**

| Individual | X | Y | Z |
|---|---|---|---|
| A | 30% | 30% | 30% |
| B | 30% | 30% | 30% |
| C | | 30% | 30% |

No other person owns an interest in more than one of the undertakings.

(ii) Paragraph (j)(2)(ii) of this section provides that a person's common ownership percentage with respect to any two or more undertakings is the person's smallest ownership percentage in any such undertaking. Thus, A's common-ownership percentage with respect to undertakings X, Y, and Z is 30 percent, and the common-ownership percentages of B and C (and all other persons owning interests in such undertakings) with respect to such undertakings is zero. Accordingly, the sum of the common ownership percentages with respect to undertakings X, Y, and Z is only 30 percent, and undertakings X, Y, and Z are not treated as part of the same common-ownership group under paragraph (j)(2)(ii) of this section.

(iii) B's common-ownership percentage with respect to undertakings X and Y is 30 percent, and the sum of A's and B's common-ownership percentages with respect to such undertakings is 60 percent. Thus, undertakings X and Y are treated as part of the same common-ownership group under paragraph (j)(2)(ii) of this section. Similarly, C's common-ownership percentage with respect to undertakings Y and Z is 30 percent, and the sum of A's and C's common-ownership percentages with respect to such undertakings is 60 percent. Thus, undertakings Y and Z are also treated as part of the same common-ownership group under paragraph (j)(2)(ii) of this section.

(iv) Paragraph (j)(2)(iii) of this section requires the aggregation of common-ownership groups that include the same undertaking. In this case, undertaking Y is treated as part of the common-ownership group XY and as part of the common-ownership group YZ. Accordingly, undertakings X, Y, and Z are treated as part of a single common-ownership group and are rebuttably presumed to be controlled by the same interests (see paragraph (j)(2)(i) of this section) even though B does not own an interest in undertaking Z and C does not own an interest in undertaking X. The fact that B and C are not common owners with respect to undertakings X and Z is taken into account, however, in determining whether this presumption is rebutted.

**(k) Identification of rental real estate activities.** *(1) Applicability.* (i) In general. Except as otherwise provided in paragraph (k)(6) of this section, this paragraph (k) applies to a taxpayer's interests in rental real estate undertakings (within the meaning of paragraph (k)(1)(ii) of this section).

(ii) Rental real estate undertaking. For purposes of this paragraph (k), a rental real estate undertaking is a rental undertaking (within the meaning of paragraph (d) of this section) in which at least 85 percent of the unadjusted basis (within the meaning of § 1.469-2T(f)(3)) of the property made available for use by customers is real property. For this purpose the term "real property" means any tangible property other than tangible personal property (within the meaning of § 1.48-1(c)).

*(2) Identification of activities.* (i) Multiple undertakings treated as a single activity or multiple activities by taxpayer. Except as otherwise provided in this paragraph (k), a taxpayer may treat two or more rental real estate undertakings (determined after the application of paragraph (k)(2)(ii) and (iii) of this section) as a single activity or may treat such undertakings as separate activities.

(ii) Multiple undertakings treated as a single activity by passthrough entity. A taxpayer must treat two or more rental real estate undertakings as a single rental real estate undertaking for a taxable year if any passthrough entity through which the taxpayer holds such undertakings treats such undertakings as a single activity on the applicable return of the passthrough entity for the taxable year of the taxpayer.

(iii) Single undertaking treated as multiple undertakings. Notwithstanding that a taxpayer's interest in leased property would, but for the application of this paragraph (k)(2)(iii), be treated as used in a single rental real estate undertaking, the taxpayer may, except as otherwise provided in paragraph (k)(3) of this section, treat a portion of the leased property (including a ratable portion of any common areas or facilities) as a rental real estate undertaking that is separate from the undertaking or undertakings in which the remaining portion of the property is treated as used. This paragraph (k)(2)(iii) shall apply for a taxable year if and only if—

(A) Such portion of the leased property can be separately conveyed under applicable State and local law (taking into account the limitations, if any, imposed by any special rules or procedures, such as condominium conversion laws, restricting the separate conveyance of parts of the same structure); and

(B) The taxpayer holds such leased property directly or through one or more passthrough entities, each of which treats such portion of the leased property as a separate activity on the applicable return of the passthrough entity for the taxable year of the taxpayer.

*(3) Treatment in succeeding taxable years.* All rental real estate undertakings or portions of such undertakings that are treated, under this paragraph (k), as part of the same activity for a taxable year ending after August 9, 1989 must be treated as part of the same activity in each succeeding taxable year.

*(4) Applicable return of passthrough entity.* For purposes of this paragraph (k), the applicable return of a passthrough entity for a taxable year of a taxpayer is the return reporting the passthrough entity's income, gain, loss, deductions, and credits taken into account by the taxpayer for such taxable year.

*(5) Evidence of treatment required.* For purposes of this paragraph (k), a person (including a passthrough entity) does not treat a rental real estate undertaking as multiple undertakings for a taxable year or, except as otherwise provided in paragraph (k)(2)(ii) or (3) of this section, treat multiple rental real estate undertakings as a single undertaking for a taxable year unless such treatment is reflected on a schedule attached to the person's return for the taxable year.

*(6) Coordination rule for rental of nondepreciable property.* This paragraph (k) shall not apply to a rental real estate undertaking if less than 30 percent of the unadjusted basis (within the meaning of § 1.469-2T(f)(3)) of property used or held for use by customers in such undertaking during the taxable year is subject to the allowance for depreciation under section 167.

*(7) Coordination rule for rental of dwelling unit.* For any taxable year in which section 280A(c)(5) applies to a taxpayer's use of a dwelling unit—

(i) Paragraph (k)(2) and (3) of this section shall not apply to the taxpayer's interest in such dwelling unit; and

(ii) The taxpayer's interest in such dwelling unit shall be treated as a separate activity of the taxpayer.

*(8) Examples.* The following examples illustrate the application of this paragraph (k). In each example, the taxpayer is an individual whose taxable year is the calendar year.

*Example (1).* (i) In 1989, the taxpayer directly owns five condominium units (units A, B, C, D, and E) in three different buildings. Units A, B, and C are in one of the buildings and constitute a single rental real estate undertaking (within the meaning of paragraph (k)(1)(ii) of this section). Units D and E are in the other two buildings, and each of these units constitutes a separate rental real estate undertaking. Each of the units can be separately conveyed under applicable State and local law.

(ii) Paragraph (k)(2)(iii) of this section permits a taxpayer to treat a portion of the property included in a rental real estate undertaking as a separate rental real estate undertaking if the property can be separately conveyed under applicable State and local law and the taxpayer owns the property directly. Thus, the taxpayer can treat units A, B, and C as three separate undertakings. Alternatively, the taxpayer could treat two of those units (e.g., units A and C) as an undertaking and the remaining unit as a separate undertaking, or could treat units A, B, and C as a single undertaking.

(iii) Paragraph (k)(2)(i) of this section permits a taxpayer to treat two or more rental real estate undertakings as a single activity, or to treat such undertakings as separate activities. Thus, the taxpayer, by combining undertakings, can treat all five units as a single activity. Alternatively, the taxpayer could treat each undertaking as a separate activity, or could combine some, but not all, undertakings. Thus, for example, the taxpayer could treat units A, B, C, and D as an activity and unit E as a separate activity.

(iv) For purposes of paragraph (k)(2)(i) of this section, a taxpayer's rental real estate undertakings are determined after the application of paragraph (k)(2)(iii) of this section. Thus, the taxpayer, by treating units as separate undertakings under paragraph (k)(2)(iii) of this section and combining them with other units under paragraph (k)(2)(i) of this section, can treat any combination of units as a single activity. For example, the taxpayer could treat units A and B as a separate rental real estate undertaking, and then treat units A, B, and D as a single activity. In that case, the taxpayer could treat units C and E either as a single activity or as two separate activities.

*Example (2).* (i) The facts are the same as in example (1). In addition, the taxpayer treats all five units as a single activity for 1989 and sells unit E in 1990. (See paragraph (k)(5) of this section for a rule providing that the units are treated as a single activity only if such treatment is reflected on a schedule attached to the taxpayer's return.)

(ii) Under paragraph (k)(3) of this section, rental real estate undertakings that are treated as part of the same activity for a taxable year must be treated as part of the same activity in each succeeding year. In this case, all five units were treated as part of the same activity for 1989 and must therefore be treated as part of the same activity for 1990. Accordingly, the taxpayer's sale of unit E in 1990 cannot be treated as a disposition of the taxpayer's entire interest in an activity for purposes of section 469(g) and the rules to be contained in § 1.469-6T (relating to the treatment of losses upon certain dispositions of passive and former passive activities).

*Example (3).* (i) The facts are the same as in example (1), except that the taxpayer is a partner in a partnership that is the direct owner of the five condominium units. In its return for its taxable year ending on November 30, 1989, the partnership treats the five units as a single activity. (See paragraph (k)(5) of this section for a rule providing that the units are treated as a single activity only if such treatment is reflected on a schedule attached to the partnership's return.) The partnership sells unit E on November 1, 1990.

(ii) Paragraph (k)(2)(ii) of this section provides that a taxpayer who holds rental real estate undertakings through a passthrough entity must treat those undertakings as a single rental real estate undertaking if they are treated as a single activity on the applicable return of the passthrough entity. Under paragraph (k)(4) of this section, the applicable return of the partnership for the taxpayer's 1989 taxable year is the partnership's return for its taxable year ending on November 30, 1989. Accordingly, the taxpayer must treat the five condominium units as a single rental real estate undertaking (and thus as part of the same activity) for 1989 because they are treated as a single activity on the partnership's return for its taxable year ending in 1989.

(iii) Under paragraph (k)(3) of this section, the taxpayer must continue treating the condominium units as part of the same activity for taxable years after 1989. Accordingly, as in example (2), the five condominium units are treated as part of the same activity for 1990, and the sale of unit E in 1990 cannot be treated as a disposition of the taxpayer's interest in an activity for purposes of section 469(g) and the rules to be contained in § 1.469-6T.

*Example (4).* (i) The taxpayer owns a shopping center and a vacant lot that are separate rental real estate undertakings (within the meaning of paragraph (k)(1)(ii) of this section). The taxpayer rents space in the shopping center to various tenants and rents the vacant lot to a parking lot operator. Most of the unadjusted basis of the property used in the shopping-center undertaking (taking into account the land on which the shopping center is built) is subject to the allowance for depreciation, but no depreciable property is used in the parking-lot undertaking.

(ii) This paragraph (k) provides rules for identifying rental real estate activities (including the rule in paragraph (k)(2)(i) of this section that permits a taxpayer to treat two or more rental real estate undertakings as a single activity). Paragraph (k)(6) of this section provides, however, that these rules do not apply to a rental real estate undertaking if less than 30 percent of the unadjusted basis of the property used in the undertaking is subject to the allowance for depreciation. Thus, the taxpayer may not combine the parking-lot undertaking, which includes no depreciable property, with the shopping-center undertaking or any other rental real estate undertaking under paragraph (k)(2)(i) of this section. Accordingly, the parking lot undertaking is treated as a separate activity under paragraph (b)(1) of this section.

*Example (5).* (i) The facts are the same as in example (4), except that the shopping center and the vacant lot are at the same location (within the meaning of paragraph (c)(2)(iii) of this section) and are part of the same rental real estate undertaking (within the meaning of paragraph (k)(1)(ii) of this section). Taking into account the property used in the shopping center operations (including the land on which the shopping center is built) and the vacant lot, 50 percent of the unadjusted basis of the property used in the undertaking is subject to the allowance for depreciation.

(ii) In this case, the vacant lot is used in a rental real estate undertaking in which depreciable property is also used. Moreover, the exception in paragraph (k)(6) of this section does not apply to the undertaking consisting of the shopping center and the parking lot because at least 30 percent of unadjusted basis of the property used in the undertaking is subject to the allowance for depreciation. Accordingly, the taxpayer may combine the undertaking with other rental real estate undertakings and treat the combined undertakings as a single activity under paragraph (k)(2)(i) of this section.

**(l) [Reserved]**

**(m) Consolidated groups.** *(1) In general.* The activities of a consolidated group (within the meaning of § 1.469-1T(h)(2)(ii)) and of each member of such group shall be determined under this section as if the consolidated group were one taxpayer.

*(2) Examples.* The following examples illustrate the application of this paragraph (m). In each example, the facts, analysis, and conclusions relate to a single taxable year.

*Example (1).* (i) Corporations M, N, and O are the members of a consolidated group (within the meaning of § 1.469-1T(h)(2)(ii)). Under § 1.469-1T(h)(4)(i)(A) and (ii), the consolidated group and its members are treated as closely held corporations (within the meaning of § 1.469-1T(g)(2)(ii)). Each member of the consolidated group owns a two-percent interest in partnership X and a two-percent interest in partnership Y, and owns interests in a number of trade or business undertakings (within the meaning of paragraph (f)(1)(ii) of this section) through the partnerships. Each of these undertakings is directly owned by partnership X or Y, and all the undertakings of partnerships X and Y are controlled by the same interests (within the meaning of paragraph (j) of this section) and are similar (within the meaning of paragraph (f)(4) of this section). The employees of the consolidated group and the shareholders of its common parent do not participate in the undertakings that the member corporations own through the partnerships.

(ii) Paragraph (f)(2)(i) of this section provides that trade or business undertakings that are similar and controlled by the same interests are treated as part of the same activity of the taxpayer if the taxpayer owns interests in the undertakings through the same passthrough entity. In this case, the member corporations own interests in similar, commonly-controlled undertakings through both partnerships, and such interests are treated under this paragraph (m) as interests owned by one taxpayer (the consolidated group). Accordingly, the member corporations' interests in the undertakings owned through partnership X are treated as part of the same activity of the consolidated group, and their interests in the undertakings owned through partnership Y are treated similarly.

*Example (2).* (i) The facts are the same as in example (1), except that each member of the consolidated group owns a five-percent interest in partnership X and a five-percent interest in partnership Y.

(ii) Paragraph (f)(2)(ii) of this section provides that trade or business undertakings that are similar and controlled by the same interests are treated as part of the same activity of the taxpayer if the taxpayer owns a direct or substantial indirect interest in each such undertaking. In this case, the member corporations own, in the aggregate, a 15-percent interest in partnership X and a 15-percent interest in partnership Y, and such interests are treated under this paragraph (m) as interests owned by one taxpayer (the consolidated group). Thus, the consolidated group owns a substantial indirect interest in the similar, commonly-controlled undertakings owned by partnerships X and Y (see paragraph (f)(3)(i) of this section). Accordingly, the member corporations' interests in the undertakings owned through partnerships X and Y are treated as part of the same activity of the consolidated group.

**(n) Publicly traded partnerships.** The rules of this section shall apply to a taxpayer's interest in business and rental operations held through a publicly traded partnership (within the meaning of section 469(k)(2)) as if the taxpayer had no interest in any other business and rental operations. The following example illustrates the application of this paragraph (n):

*Example.* (i) The taxpayer, an individual, owns a 20-percent interest in partnership X and a 15-percent interest in partnership Y. Partnership X directly owns a hotel ("hotel 1") and a commercial office building ("building 1"). Partnership Y directly owns two hotels ("hotels 2 and 3") and two commercial office buildings ("buildings 2 and 3"). Each of the three hotels is a separate trade or business undertaking (within the meaning of paragraph (f)(1)(ii) of this section), and each of the three office buildings is a separate rental real estate undertaking (within the meaning of paragraph (k)(1)(ii) of this section). The three hotel undertakings are similar (within the meaning of paragraph (f)(4) of this section) and are controlled by the same interests (within the meaning of paragraph (j) of this section). Partnership X is not a publicly traded partnership (within the meaning of section 469(k)(2)). Partnership Y, however, is a publicly traded partnership and is not treated as a corporation under section 7704.

(ii) This paragraph (n) provides that the rules of this section apply to a taxpayer's interest in business and rental operations held through a publicly traded partnership as if the taxpayer had no interest in any other business and rental operations. Thus, undertakings owned through partnership Y may be treated as part of the same activity under the rules of this section, but an undertaking owned through partnership Y and an undertaking that is not owned through partnership Y may not be treated as part of the same activity.

(iii) Paragraph (f)(2)(i) of this section provides that a taxpayer's interests in two or more trade or business undertakings that are similar and controlled by the same interests are treated as part of the same activity if the taxpayer owns interests in each undertaking through the same passthrough entity. Partnership Y's hotel undertakings (i.e., hotels 2 and 3) are similar and are controlled by the same interests. In addition, the taxpayer owns interests in both undertakings through the same partnership. Accordingly, the taxpayer's interests in partnership Y's hotel undertakings are treated as part of the same activity.

(iv) The hotel undertaking owned through partnership X (i.e., hotel 1) and the hotel undertakings owned through partnership Y are similar and controlled by the same interests, and the taxpayer owns a substantial indirect interest in each of the undertakings (see paragraph (f)(3)(i) of this section). Thus, the three undertakings would ordinarily be treated as part of the same activity under paragraph (f)(2)(ii) of this section. Under this paragraph (n), however, undertakings that are owned through a publicly traded partnership cannot be treated as part of the same activity as any undertaking not owned through that partnership. Accordingly, the hotel undertaking that the taxpayer owns through partnership X and the hotel undertakings that the taxpayer owns through partnership Y are treated as two separate activities.

(v) Paragraph (k)(2)(i) of this section provides that, with certain exceptions, a taxpayer may treat two or more rental real estate undertakings as a single activity or as separate activities. Thus, the taxpayer's interests in the rental real estate undertakings owned through partnership Y (i.e., buildings 2 and 3) may be treated as a single activity or as separate activities. Under this paragraph (n), however, undertakings that are owned through a publicly traded partnership cannot be treated as part of the same activity as any undertaking not owned through that partnership. Accordingly, the taxpayer's interest in the rental real estate undertaking owned through partnership X (building 1) cannot be treated as part of an activity that includes any rental real estate undertaking owned through partnership Y.

**(o) Elective treatment of undertakings as separate activities.** *(1) Applicability.* This paragraph applies to a taxpayer's interest in any undertaking (other than a rental real estate undertaking (within the meaning of paragraph (k)(1)(ii) of this section)) that would otherwise be treated under this section as part of an activity that includes the taxpayer's interest in any other undertaking.

*(2) Undertakings treated as separate activities.* Except as otherwise provided in this paragraph (o), a person (including a passthrough entity) shall treat an undertaking to which this paragraph (o) applies as an activity separate from the remainder of the activity in which such undertaking would otherwise be included for a taxable year if and only if, for such taxable year or any preceding taxable year, such person made an election with respect to such undertaking under this paragraph (o).

*(3) Multiple undertakings treated as a single activity by passthrough entity.* A person (including a passthrough entity) must treat interests in two or more undertakings as part of the same activity for a taxable year if any passthrough entity through which the person holds such undertakings treats such undertakings as part of the same activity on the applicable return of the passthrough entity for the taxable year of such person.

*(4) Multiple undertakings treated as a single activity for a preceding taxable year.* If a person (including a passthrough entity) treats undertakings as part of the same activity on such person's return for a taxable year ending after August 9, 1989, such person may not treat such undertakings as part of different activities under this paragraph (o) for any subsequent taxable year.

*(5) Applicable return of passthrough entity.* For purposes of this paragraph (o), the applicable return of a passthrough entity for a taxable year of a taxpayer is the return reporting the passthrough entity's income, gain, loss, deductions, and credits taken into account by the taxpayer for such taxable year.

*(6) Participation.* The following rules apply to multiple activities (the "separate activities") that would be treated as a single activity (the "original activity") if the taxpayer's activities were determined without regard to this paragraph (o):

(i) The taxpayer shall be treated as materially participating (within the meaning of § 1.469-5T) for the taxable year in the separate activities if and only if the taxpayer would, but for the application of this paragraph (o), be treated as materially participating for the taxable year in the original activity.

(ii) The taxpayer shall be treated as significantly participating (within the meaning of § 1.469-5T(c)(2)) for the taxable year in the separate activities if and only if the taxpayer would, but for the application of this paragraph (o), be treated as significantly participating for the taxable year in the original activity.

*(7) Election.* (i) In general. A person makes an election with respect to an undertaking under this paragraph (o) by attaching the written statement described in paragraph (o)(7)(ii) of this section to such person's return for the taxable year for which the election is made (see paragraph (o)(2) of this section).

(ii) Written statement. The written statement required by paragraph (o)(7)(i) of this section must—

(A) State the name, address, and taxpayer identification number of the person making the election;

(B) Contain a declaration that an election is being made under § 1.469-4T(o);

(C) Identify the undertaking with respect to which such election is being made; and

(D) Identify the remainder of the activity in which such undertaking would otherwise be included.

*(8) Examples.* The following examples illustrate the application of this paragraph (o):

*Example (1).* (i) During 1989, the taxpayer, an individual whose taxable year is the calendar year, acquires and is the direct owner of ten grocery stores. The operations of each grocery store are treated under paragraph (c)(1) of this section as a single undertaking that is separate from other undertakings (a "grocery-store undertaking"), and the taxpayer's interests in the grocery-store undertakings would be treated as part of the same activity of the taxpayer under paragraph (f)(2) of this section.

(ii) Paragraph (o)(2) of this section provides that, with certain exceptions, undertakings that would be treated as part of the same activity under other rules in this section may, at the election of the taxpayer, be treated as separate activities. Thus, the taxpayer may elect to treat each grocery-store undertaking as a separate activity for 1989. Alternatively, the taxpayer may combine grocery-store undertakings in any manner and treat each combination of undertakings (and each uncombined undertaking) as a separate activity for 1989. In either case, the election must be made by attaching the written statement described in paragraph (o)(7)(ii) of this section to the taxpayer's 1989 return.

*Example (2).* (i) The facts are the same as in example (1). In addition, the taxpayer, in 1989, elects to treat each grocery-store undertaking as a separate activity and participates for 15 hours in each of the grocery-store undertakings.

(ii) The taxpayer's interest in each grocery-store undertaking is treated, under paragraph (o)(2) of this section, as a separate activity of the taxpayer for 1989 (a "grocery-store activity"). In 1989, however, the taxpayer participates for more than 100 hours in the activity in which the undertakings would be included (but for the election to treat the grocery-store undertakings as separate activities) and would be treated under § 1.469-5T(c)(2) as significantly participating in such activity. Accordingly, the taxpayer is treated under paragraph (o)(6)(ii) of this section as significantly participating in each of the grocery-store activities for 1989.

*Example (3).* (i) The facts are the same as in example (1). In addition, the taxpayer, in 1989, elects to treat each grocery-store undertaking as a separate activity. The taxpayer does not participate in any of the grocery-store undertakings in 1989 or 1990, and sells one of the grocery stores in 1990.

(ii) As in example (2), the taxpayer's interests in each grocery-store undertaking is treated, under paragraph (o)(2) of this section, as a separate activity of the taxpayer for 1989. Because the taxpayer elected to treat the undertakings as separate activities for a preceding taxable year (1989), each grocery-store undertaking is also treated, under paragraph (o)(2) of this section, as a separate activity of the taxpayer for 1990. In addition, each of the taxpayer's grocery-store activities is a passive activity for 1989 and 1990 because the taxpayer does not participate in any of the grocery store undertakings for 1989 and 1990. Accordingly, the taxpayer's sale of the grocery store will generally be treated as a disposition of the taxpayer's entire interest in a passive activity for purposes of section 469(g) and the rules to be contained in § 1.469-6T (relating to the treatment of losses upon certain dispositions of passive and former passive activities).

*Example (4).* (i) The facts are the same as in example (3), except that the taxpayer elects to treat the grocery-store undertakings as two separate activities. One of the activities includes three grocery-store undertakings, and the store sold in 1990 is part of this activity. The other activity includes the seven remaining grocery-store undertakings.

(ii) Paragraph (o)(4) of this section provides that a person who treats undertakings as part of the same activity for a taxable year ending after August 9, 1989, may not elect to treat those undertakings as separate activities for a subsequent taxable year. The grocery store sold in 1990 was treated for 1989 as part of an activity that includes two other grocery stores. Thus, those three stores must be treated as part of the same activity for 1990. Accordingly, the taxpayer's sale of the grocery store cannot be treated as a disposition of the taxpayer's entire interest in a passive activity for purposes of section 469(g) and the rules to be contained in § 1.469-6T.

*Example (5).* (i) The facts are the same as in example (1), except that the taxpayer is a partner in a partnership that acquires and is the direct owner of the ten grocery stores. The taxable year of the partnership ends on November 30, and the partnership acquires the grocery stores in its taxable year ending on November 30, 1989. In its return for that taxable year, the partnership treats the grocery-store undertakings as a single activity.

(ii) Paragraph (o)(3) of this section provides that a person who holds undertakings through a passthrough entity may not elect to treat those undertakings as separate activities if they are treated as part of the same activity on the applicable return of the passthrough entity. Under paragraph (o)(5) of this section, the applicable return of the partnership for the taxpayer's 1989 taxable year is the partnership's return for its taxable year ending on November 30, 1989. Accordingly, the taxpayer must treat the grocery-store undertakings as a single activity for 1989 because those undertakings are treated as a single activity on the partnership's return for its taxable year ending in 1989.

(iii) Under paragraph (o)(4) of this section, the taxpayer must continue treating the grocery-store undertakings as part of the same activity for taxable years after 1989. This rule applies even if the partnership subsequently distributes its interest in the grocery stores to the taxpayer, and the taxpayer becomes the direct owner of the grocery-store undertakings.

**(p) Special rule for taxable years ending before August 10, 1989.** *(1) In general.* For purposes of applying section 469 and the regulations thereunder for a taxable year ending before August 10, 1989, a taxpayer's business and rental operations may be organized into activities under the rules or paragraphs (b) through (n) of this section or under any other reasonable method. For example, for such taxable years a taxpayer may treat each of the taxpayer's undertakings as a separate activity, or a taxpayer may treat undertakings that involve the provision of similar goods or services as a single activity.

*(2) Unreasonable methods.* A method of organizing business and rental operations into activities is not reasonable if such method—

(i) Treats rental operations (within the meaning of paragraph (d)(3) of this section) that are not ancillary to a trade or business activity (within the meaning of § 1.469-1T(e)(2)) as part of a trade or business activity;

(ii) Treats operations that are not rental operations and are not ancillary to a rental activity (within the meaning of § 1.469-1T(e)(3)) as part of a rental activity;

(iii) Includes in a passive activity of a taxpayer any oil or gas well that would be treated, under paragraph (e)(1) of this section, as a separate undertaking in determining the taxpayer's activities;

(iv) Includes in a passive activity of a taxpayer any interest in a dwelling unit that would be treated, under paragraph (K)(7) of this section, as a separate activity of the taxpayer; or

(v) Is inconsistent with the taxpayer's method of organizing business and rental operations into activities for the taxpayer's first taxable year beginning after December 31, 1986.

*(3) Allocation of disallowed deductions in succeeding taxable year.* If any of the taxpayer's passive activity deductions or the taxpayer's credits from passive activities are disallowed under § 1.469-1T for the last taxable year of the taxpayer ending before August 10, 1989, such disallowed deductions or credits shall be allocated among the taxpayer's activities for the first taxable year of the taxpayer ending after August 9, 1989, using any reasonable method. See § 1.469-1T(f)(4).

T.D. 8253, 5/11/89.

## § 1.469-5 Material participation.

**(a) through (e) [Reserved]**

**(f) Participation.** *(1) In general.* Except as otherwise provided in this paragraph (f), any work done by an individual (without regard to the capacity in which the individual does the work) in connection with an activity in which the individual owns an interest at the time the work is done shall be treated for purposes of this section as participation of the individual in the activity.

*(2)* through (h)(2) [Reserved]

**(h)** *(3) Coordination with rules governing the treatment of passthrough entities.* If a taxpayer takes into account for a taxable year of the taxpayer any item of gross income or deduction from a partnership or S corporation that is characterized as an item of gross income or deduction from an activity in which the taxpayer materially participated under § 1.469-2T(e)(1), the taxpayer is treated as materially participating in the activity for the taxable year for purposes of applying § 1.469-5T(a)(5) and (6) to any succeeding taxable year of the taxpayer.

**(i) [Reserved]**

**(j) Material participation for preceding taxable years.** *(1) In general.* For purposes of § 1.469-5T(a)(5) and (6), a taxpayer has materially participated in an activity for a preceding taxable year if the activity includes significant section 469 activities that are substantially the same as significant section 469 activities that were included in an activity in which the taxpayer materially participated (determined without regard to § 1.469-5T(a)(5)) for the preceding taxable year.

*(2) Material participation for taxable years beginning before January 1, 1987.* In any case in which it is necessary to determine whether an individual materially participated in any activity for a taxable year beginning before January 1, 1987 (other than a taxable year of a partnership, S corporation, estate, or trust ending after December 31, 1986), the determination shall be made without regard to paragraphs (a)(2) through (7) of this section.

**(k) Examples.** Example (1) through Example (4) [Reserved]

*Example (5).* In 1993, D, an individual, acquires stock in an S corporation engaged in a trade or business activity (within the meaning of § 1.469-1(e)(2)). For every taxable year from 1993 through 1997, D is treated as materially participating (without regard to § 1.469-5T(a)(5)) in the activity. D retires from the activity at the beginning of 1998, and would not be treated as materially participating in the activity for 1998 and subsequent taxable years if material participation of those years were determined without regard to § 1.469-5T(a)(5). Under § 1.469-5T(a)(5) of this section, however, D is treated as materially participating in the activity for taxable years 1998 through 2003 because D materially participated in the activity (determined without regard to § 1.469-5T(a)(5) for five taxable years during the ten taxable years that immediately precede each of those years. D is not treated under § 1.469-5T(a)(5) as materially participating in the activity for taxable years beginning after 2003 because for those years D has not materially participated in the activity (determined without regard to § 1.469-5T(a)(5) for five of the last ten immediately preceding taxable years.

T.D. 8417, 5/11/92.

## § 1.469-5T Material participation (temporary).

**(a) In general.** Except as provided in paragraphs (e) and (h)(2) of this section, an individual shall be treated, for purposes of section 469 and the regulations thereunder, as materially participating in an activity for the taxable year if and only if—

*(1)* The individual participates in the activity for more than 500 hours during such year.

*(2)* The individual's participation in the activity for the taxable year constitutes substantially all of the participation in such activity of all individuals (including individuals who are not owners of interests in the activity) for such year;

*(3)* The individual participates in the activity for more than 100 hours during the taxable year, and such individual's participation in the activity for the taxable year is not less

than the participation in the activity of any other individual (including individuals who are not owners of interests in the activity) for such year;

*(4)* The activity is a significant participation activity (within the meaning of paragraph (c) of this section) for the taxable year, and the individual's aggregate participation in all significant participation activities during such year exceeds 500 hours;

*(5)* The individual materially participated in the activity (determined without regard to this paragraph (a)(5)) for any five taxable years (whether or not consecutive) during the ten taxable years that immediately precede the taxable year;

*(6)* The activity is a personal service activity (within the meaning of paragraph (d) of this section), and the individual materially participated in the activity for any three taxable years (whether or not consecutive) preceding the taxable year; or

*(7)* Based on all of the facts and circumstances (taking into account the rules in paragraph (b) of this section), the individual participates in the activity on a regular, continuous, and substantial basis during such year.

**(b) Facts and circumstances.** *(1) In general. [Reserved]*

*(2) Certain participation insufficient to constitute material participation under this paragraph (b).* (i) Participation satisfying standards not contained in section 469. Except as provided in section 469(h)(3) and paragraph (h)(2) of this section (relating to certain retired individuals and surviving spouses in the case of farming activities), the fact that an individual satisfies the requirements of any participation standard (whether or not referred to as "material participation") under any provision (including sections 1402 and 2032A and the regulations thereunder) other than section 469 and the regulations thereunder shall not be taken into account in determining whether such individual materially participates in any activity for any taxable year for purposes of section 469 and the regulations thereunder.

(ii) Certain management activities. An individual's services performed in the management of an activity shall not be taken into account in determining whether such individual is treated as materially participating in such activity for the taxable year under paragraph (a)(7) of this section unless, for such taxable year—

(A) No person (other than such individual) who performs services in connection with the management of the activity receives compensation described in section 911(d)(2)(A) in consideration for such services; and

(B) No individual performs services in connection with the management of the activity that exceed (by hours) the amount of such services performed by such individual.

(iii) Participation less than 100 hours. If an individual participates in an activity for 100 hours or less during the taxable year, such individual shall not be treated as materially participating in such activity for the taxable year under paragraph (a)(7) of this section.

**(c) Significant participation activity.** *(1) In general.* For purposes of paragraph (a)(4) of this section, an activity is a significant participation activity of an individual if and only if such activity—

(i) Is a trade or business activity (within the meaning of § 1.469-1T(e)(2)) in which the individual significantly participates for the taxable year; and

(ii) Would be an activity in which the individual does not materially participate for the taxable year if material participation for such year were determined without regard to paragraph (a)(4) of this section.

*(2) Significant participation.* An individual is treated as significantly participating in an activity for a taxable year if and only if the individual participates in the activity for more than 100 hours during such year.

**(d) Personal service activity.** An activity constitutes a personal service activity for purposes of paragraph (a)(6) of this section if such activity involves the performance of personal services in—

*(1)* The fields of health, law, engineering, architecture, accounting, actuarial science, performing arts, or consulting; or

*(2)* Any other trade or business in which capital is not a material income-producing factor.

**(e) Treatment of limited partners.** *(1) General rule.* Except as otherwise provided in this paragraph (e), an individual shall not be treated as materially participating in any activity of a limited partnership for purposes of applying section 469 and the regulations thereunder to—

(i) The individual's share of any income, gain, loss, deduction, or credit from such activity that is attributable to a limited partnership interest in the partnership; and

(ii) Any gain or loss from such activity recognized upon a sale or exchange of such an interest.

*(2) Exceptions.* Paragraph (e)(1) of this section shall not apply to an individual's share of income, gain, loss, deduction, and credit for a taxable year from any activity in which the individual would be treated as materially participating for the taxable year under paragraph (a)(1), (5), or (6) of this section if the individual were not a limited partner for such taxable year.

*(3) Limited partnership interest.* (i) In general. Except as provided in paragraph (e)(3)(ii) of this section, for purposes of section 469(h)(2) and this paragraph (e), a partnership interest shall be treated as a limited partnership interest if—

(A) Such interest is designated a limited partnership interest in the limited partnership agreement or the certificate of limited partnership, without regard to whether the liability of the holder of such interest for obligations of the partnership is limited under the applicable State law; or

(B) The liability of the holder of such interest for obligations of the partnership is limited, under the law of the State in which the partnership is organized, to a determinable fixed amount (for example, the sum of the holder's capital contributions to the partnership and contractual obligations to make additional capital contributions to the partnership).

(ii) Limited partner holding general partner interest. A partnership interest of an individual shall not be treated as a limited partnership interest for the individual's taxable year if the individual is a general partner in the partnership at all times during the partnership's taxable year ending with or within the individual's taxable year (or the portion of the partnership's taxable year during which the individual (directly or indirectly) owns such limited partnership interest).

**(f) Participation.** *(1) [Reserved]* See § 1.469-5(f)(1) for rules relating to this paragraph.

*(2) Exceptions.* (i) Certain work not customarily done by owners. Work done in connection with an activity shall not be treated as participation in the activity for purposes of this section if—

(A) Such work is not of a type that is customarily done by an owner of such an activity; and

(B) One of the principal purposes for the performance of such work is to avoid the disallowance, under section 469 and the regulations thereunder, of any loss or credit from such activity.

(ii) Participation as an investor. (A) In general. Work done by an individual in the individual's capacity as an investor in an activity shall not be treated as participation in the activity for purposes of this section unless the individual is directly involved in the day-to-day management or operations of the activity.

(B) Work done in individual's capacity as an investor. For purposes of this paragraph (f)(2)(ii), work done by an individual in the individual's capacity as an investor in an activity includes—

(1) Studying and reviewing financial statements or reports on operations of the activity;

(2) Preparing or compiling summaries or analyses of the finances or operations of the activity for the individual's own use; and

(3) Monitoring the finances or operations of the activity in a non-managerial capacity.

*(3) Participation of spouse.* In the case of any person who is a married individual (within the meaning of section 7703) for the taxable year, any participation by such person's spouse in the activity during the taxable year (without regard to whether the spouse owns an interest in the activity and without regard to whether the spouses file a joint return for the taxable year) shall be treated, for purposes of applying section 469 and the regulations thereunder to such person, as participation by such person in the activity during the taxable year.

*(4) Methods of proof.* The extent of an individual's participation in an activity may be established by any reasonable means. Contemporaneous daily time reports, logs, or similar documents are not required if the extent of such participation may be established by other reasonable means. Reasonable means for purposes of this paragraph may include but are not limited to the identification of services performed over a period of time and the approximate number of hours spent performing such services during such period, based on appointment books, calendars, or narrative summaries.

**(g) Material participation of trusts and estates. [Reserved]**

**(h) Miscellaneous rules.** *(1) Participation of corporations.* For rules relating to the participation in an activity of a personal service corporation (within the meaning of § 1.469-1T(g)(2)(i)) or a closely held corporation (within the meaning of § 1.469-1T(g)(2)(ii)), see § 1.469-1T(g)(3).

*(2) Treatment of certain retired farmers and surviving spouses of retired or disabled farmers.* An individual shall be treated as materially participating for a taxable year in any trade or business activity of farming if paragraph (4) or (5) of section 2032A(b) would cause the requirements of section 2032A(b)(1)(C)(ii) to be met with respect to real property used in such activity had the individual died during such taxable year.

*(3) Coordination with rules governing the treatment of passthrough entities. [Reserved]* See § 1.469-5(h)(3) for rules relating to this paragraph.

**(i) [Reserved]**

**(j) Material participation for preceding taxable years. [Reserved]** See § 1.469-5(j) for rules relating to this paragraph.

**(k) Examples.** The following examples illustrate the application of this section:

*Example (1).* A, a calendar year individual, owns all of the stock of X, a C corporation. X is the general partner, and A is the limited partner, in P, a calendar year partnership. P has a single activity, a restaurant, which is a trade or business activity (within the meaning of § 1.469-1T(e)(2)). During the taxable year, A works for an average of 30 hours per week in connection with P's restaurant activity. Under paragraphs (a)(1) and (e)(2) of this section, A is treated as materially participating in the activity for the taxable year because A participates in the restaurant activity during such year for more than 500 hours. In addition, under § 1.469-1T(g)(3)(i), A's participation will cause X to be treated as materially participating in the restaurant activity.

*Example (2).* The facts are the same as in example (1), except that the partnership agreement provides that P's restaurant activity is to be managed by X, and A's work in the activity is performed pursuant to an employment contract between A and X. Under paragraph (f)(1) of this section, work done by A in connection with the activity in any capacity is treated as participation in the activity by A. Accordingly, the conclusion is the same as in example (1). The conclusion would be the same if A owned no stock in X at any time, although in that case A's participation would not be taken into account in determining whether X materially participates in the restaurant activity.

*Example (3).* B, an individual, is employed full-time as a carpenter. B also owns an interest in a partnership which is engaged in a van conversion activity, which is a trade or business activity (within the meaning of § 1.469-1T(e)(2)). B and C, the other partner, are the only participants in the activity for the taxable year. The activity is conducted entirely on Saturdays. Each Saturday throughout the taxable year, B and C work for eight hours in the activity. Although B does not participate in the activity for more than 500 hours during the taxable year, under paragraph (a)(3) of this section, B is treated for such year as materially participating in the activity because B participates in the activity for more than 100 hours during the taxable year, and B's participation in the activity for such year is not less than the participation of any other person in the activity for such year.

*Example (4).* C, an individual, is employed full-time as an accountant. C also owns interests in a restaurant and a shoe store. The restaurant and shoe store are trade or business activities (within the meaning of § 1.469-1T(e)(2)) that are treated as separate activities under the rules to be contained in § 1.469-4T. Each activity has several full-time employees. During the taxable year, C works in the restaurant activity for 400 hours and in the shoe store activity for 150 hours. Under paragraph (c) of this section, both the restaurant and shoe store activities are significant participation activities of C for the taxable year. Accordingly, since C's aggregate participation in the restaurant and shoe store activities during the taxable year exceeds 500 hours, C is treated under paragraph (a)(4) of this section as materially participating in both activities.

*Example (5).* [Reserved] See § 1.469-5(k) Example 5 for this example.

*Example (6).* The facts are the same as in example (5), except that D does not acquire any stock in the S corporation until 1994. Under paragraph (f)(1) of this section, D is not treated as participating in the activity for any taxable year prior to 1994 because D does not own an interest in the activity for any such taxable year. Accordingly, D materially participates in the activity for only one taxable year prior to 1995, and D is not treated under paragraph (a)(5) of this section as materially participating in the activity for 1995 or subsequent taxable years.

*Example (7).* (i) E, a married individual filing a separate return for the taxable year, is employed full-time as an attorney. E also owns an interest in a professional football team that is a trade or business activity (within the meaning of § 1.469-1T(e)(2)). E does no work in connection with this activity. E anticipates that, for the taxable year, E's deductions from the activity will exceed E's gross income from the activity and that, if E does not materially participate in the activity for the taxable year, part or all of F's passive activity loss for the taxable year will be disallowed under § 1.469-1T(a)(1)(i). Accordingly, E pays E's spouse to work as an office receptionist in connection with the activity for an average of 15 hours per week during the taxable year.

(ii) Under paragraph (f)(3) of this section, any participation in the activity by E's spouse is treated as participation in the activity by E. However, under paragraph (f)(2)(i) of this section, the work done by E's spouse is not treated as participation in the activity because work as an office receptionist is not work of a type customarily done by an owner of a football team, and one of E's principal purposes for paying E's spouse to do this work is to avoid the disallowance under § 1.469-1T(a)(1)(i) of E's passive activity loss. Accordingly, E is not treated as participating in the activity for the taxable year.

*Example (8).* (i) F, an individual, owns an interest in a partnership that feeds and sells cattle. The general partner of the partnership periodically mails F a letter setting forth certain proposed actions and decisions with respect to the cattle-feeding operation. Such actions and decisions include, for example, what kind of feed to purchase, how much to purchase, and when to purchase it, how often to feed cattle, and when to sell cattle. The letters explain the proposed actions and decisions, emphasize that taking or not taking a particular action or decision is solely within the discretion of F and other partners, and ask F to indicate a decision with respect to each proposed action by answering certain questions. The general partner receives a fee that constitutes earned income (within the meaning of section 911(d)(2)(A)) for managing the cattle-feeding operation. F is not treated as materially participating in the cattle-feeding operation under paragraph (a)(1) through (6) of this section.

(ii) F's only participation in the cattle-feeding operation is to make certain managerial decisions. Under paragraph (b)(2)(ii) of this section, such management services are not taken into account in determining whether the taxpayer is treated as materially participating in the activity for a taxable year under paragraph (a)(7) of this section if any other person performs services in connection with the management of the activity and receives compensation described in section 911(d)(2)(A) for such services. Therefore, F is not treated as materially participating for the taxable year in the cattle-feeding operation.

T.D. 8175, 2/19/88, amend T.D. 8253, 5/11/89, T.D. 8417, 5/11/92.

### § 1.469-6 Treatment of losses upon certain dispositions. [Reserved]

### § 1.469-7 Treatment of self-charged items of interest income and deduction.

**(a) In general.** *(1) Applicability and effect of rules.* This section sets forth rules that apply, for purposes of section 469 and the regulations thereunder, in the case of a lending transaction (including guaranteed payments for the use of capital under section 707(c)) between a taxpayer and a passthrough entity in which the taxpayer owns a direct or indirect interest, or between certain passthrough entities. The rules apply only to items of interest income and interest expense that are recognized in the same taxable year. The rules—

(i) Treat certain interest income resulting from these lending transactions as passive activity gross income;

(ii) Treat certain deductions for interest expense that is properly allocable to the interest income as passive activity deductions; and

(iii) Allocate the passive activity gross income and passive activity deductions resulting from this treatment among the taxpayer's activities.

*(2) Priority of rules in this section.* The character of amounts treated under the rules of this section as passive activity gross income and passive activity deductions and the activities to which these amounts are allocated are determined under the rules of this section and not under the rules of § § 1.163-8T, 1.469-2(c) and (d), and 1.469-2T(c) and (d).

**(b) Definitions.** The following definitions set forth the meaning of certain terms for purposes of this section:

*(1) Passthrough entity.* The term passthrough entity means a partnership or an S corporation.

*(2) Taxpayer's share.* A taxpayer's share of an item of income or deduction of a passthrough entity is the amount treated as an item of income or deduction of the taxpayer for the taxable year under section 702 (relating to the treatment of distributive shares of partnership items as items of partners) or section 1366 (relating to the treatment of pro rata shares of S corporation items as items of shareholders).

*(3) Taxpayer's indirect interest.* The taxpayer has an indirect interest in an entity if the interest is held through one or more passthrough entities.

*(4) Entity taxable year.* In applying this section for a taxable year of a taxpayer, the term entity taxable year means the taxable year of the passthrough entity for which the entity reports items that are taken into account under section 702 or section 1366 for the taxpayer's taxable year.

*(5) Deductions for a taxable year.* The term deductions for a taxable year means deductions that would be allowable for the taxable year if the taxpayer's taxable income for all taxable years were determined without regard to sections 163(d), 170(b), 469, 613A(d), and 1211.

**(c) Taxpayer loans to passthrough entity.** *(1) Applicability.* Except as provided in paragraph (g) of this section, this paragraph (c) applies with respect to a taxpayer's interest in a passthrough entity (borrowing entity) for a taxable year if—

(i) The borrowing entity has deductions for the entity taxable year for interest charged to the borrowing entity by persons that own direct or indirect interests in the borrowing entity at any time during the entity taxable year (the borrowing entity's self-charged interest deductions);

(ii) The taxpayer owns a direct or an indirect interest in the borrowing entity at any time during the entity taxable year and has gross income for the taxable year from interest charged to the borrowing entity by the taxpayer or a passthrough entity through which the taxpayer holds an interest in the borrowing entity (the taxpayer's income from interest charged to the borrowing entity); and

(iii) The taxpayer's share of the borrowing entity's self-charged interest deductions includes passive activity deductions.

*(2) General rule.* If any of the borrowing entity's self-charged interest deductions are allocable to an activity for a taxable year in which this paragraph (c) applies, the passive activity gross income and passive activity deductions from that activity are determined under the following rules—

(i) The applicable percentage of each item of the taxpayer's income for the taxable year from interest charged to the borrowing entity is treated as passive activity gross income from the activity; and

(ii) The applicable percentage of each deduction for the taxable year for interest expense that is properly allocable (within the meaning of paragraph (f) of this section) to the taxpayer's income from the interest charged to the borrowing entity is treated as a passive activity deduction from the activity.

*(3) Applicable percentage.* In applying this paragraph (c) with respect to a taxpayer's interest in a borrowing entity, the applicable percentage is separately determined for each of the taxpayer's activities. The percentage applicable to an activity for a taxable year is obtained by dividing—

(i) The taxpayer's share for the taxable year of the borrowing entity's self-charged interest deductions that are treated as passive activity deductions from the activity by

(ii) The greater of—

(A) The taxpayer's share for the taxable year of the borrowing entity's aggregate self-charged interest deductions for all activities (regardless of whether these deductions are treated as passive activity deductions); or

(B) The taxpayer's aggregate income for the taxable year from interest charged to the borrowing entity for all activities of the borrowing entity.

**(d) Passthrough entity loans to taxpayer.** *(1) Applicability.* Except as provided in paragraph (g) of this section, this paragraph (d) applies with respect to a taxpayer's interest in a passthrough entity (lending entity) for a taxable year if—

(i) The lending entity has gross income for the entity taxable year from interest charged by the lending entity to persons that own direct or indirect interests in the lending entity at any time during the entity taxable year (the lending entity's self-charged interest income);

(ii) The taxpayer owns a direct or an indirect interest in the lending entity at any time during the entity taxable year and has deductions for the taxable year for interest charged by the lending entity to the taxpayer or a passthrough entity through which the taxpayer holds an interest in the lending entity (the taxpayer's deductions for interest charged by the lending entity); and

(iii) The taxpayer's deductions for interest charged by the lending entity include passive activity deductions.

*(2) General rule.* If any of the taxpayer's deductions for interest charged by the lending entity are allocable to an activity for a taxable year in which this paragraph (d) applies, the passive activity gross income and passive activity deductions from that activity are determined under the following rules—

(i) The applicable percentage of the taxpayer's share for the taxable year of each item of the lending entity's self-charged interest income is treated as passive activity gross income from the activity.

(ii) The applicable percentage of the taxpayer's share for the taxable year of each deduction for interest expense that is properly allocable (within the meaning of paragraph (f) of this section) to the lending entity's self-charged interest income is treated as a passive activity deduction from the activity.

*(3) Applicable percentage.* In applying this paragraph (d) with respect to a taxpayer's interest in a lending entity, the applicable percentage is separately determined for each of the taxpayer's activities. The percentage applicable to an activity for a taxable year is obtained by dividing—

(i) The taxpayer's deductions for the taxable year for interest charged by the lending entity, to the extent treated as passive activity deductions from the activity; by

(ii) The greater of—

(A) The taxpayer's aggregate deductions for all activities for the taxable year for interest charged by the lending entity (regardless of whether these deductions are treated as passive activity deductions); or

(B) The taxpayer's aggregate share for the taxable year of the lending entity's self-charged interest income for all activities of the lending entity.

**(e) Identically-owned passthrough entities.** *(1) Applicability.* Except as provided in paragraph (g) of this section, this paragraph (e) applies with respect to lending transactions between passthrough entities if each owner of the borrowing entity has the same proportionate ownership interest in the lending entity.

*(2) General rule.* To the extent an owner shares in interest income from a loan between passthrough entities described in paragraph (e)(1) of this section, the owner is treated as having made the loan to the borrowing passthrough entity and paragraph (c) of this section applies to determine the applicable percentage of portfolio income or properly allocable interest expense that is recharacterized as passive.

*(3) Example.* The following example illustrates the application of this paragraph (e):

*Example.* (i) A and B, both calendar year taxpayers, each own a 50-percent interest in the capital and profits of partnerships RS and XY, both calendar year partnerships. Under the partnership agreements of RS and XY, A and B are each entitled to a 50-percent distributive share of each partnership's income, gain, loss, deduction, or credit. RS makes a $20,000 loan to XY and XY pays RS $2,000 of interest for the taxable year. A's distributive share of interest income attributable to this loan is $1,000 (50 percent x $2,000). XY uses all of the proceeds received from RS in a passive activity. A's distributive share of interest expense attributable to the loan is $1,000 (50 percent x $2,000).

(ii) This paragraph (e) applies in determining A's passive activity gross income because RS and XY are identically-owned passthrough entities as described in paragraph (e)(1) of this section. Under paragraph (e)(2) of this section, the RS-to-XY loan is treated as if A made the loan to XY. Therefore, A must apply paragraph (c) of this section to determine the applicable percentage of portfolio income that is recharacterized as passive income.

(iii) Paragraph (c) of this section applies in determining A's passive activity gross income because: XY has deductions for interest charged to XY by RS for the taxable year (XY's self-charged interest deductions); A owns an interest in XY during XY's taxable year and has gross income for the taxable year from interest charged to XY by RS; and A's share of XY's self-charged interest deductions includes passive activity deductions. See paragraph (c)(1) of this section.

(iv) Under paragraph (c)(2)(i) of this section, the applicable percentage of A's interest income is recharacterized as passive activity gross income from the activity. Paragraph (c)(3) of this section provides that the applicable percentage is obtained by dividing A's share for the taxable year of XY's self-charged interest deductions that are treated as passive activity deductions from the activity ($1,000) by the greater of A's share for the taxable year of XY's self-charged interest deductions ($1,000), or A's income for the year from interest charged to XY ($1,000). Thus, A's applicable percentage is 100 percent ($1,000/$1,000), and $1,000 (100 percent x $1,000) of A's income from interest charged to XY is treated as passive activity gross income from the passive activity.

**(f) Identification of properly allocable deductions.** For purposes of this section, interest expense is properly allocable to an item of interest income if the interest expense is allocated under § 1.163-8T to an expenditure that—

*(1)* Is properly chargeable to capital account with respect to the investment producing the item of interest income; or

*(2)* May reasonably be taken into account as a cost of producing the item of interest income.

**(g) Election to avoid application of the rules of this section.** *(1) In general.* Paragraphs (c), (d) and (e) of this section shall not apply with respect to any taxpayer's interest in a passthrough entity for a taxable year if the passthrough entity has made, under this paragraph (g), an election that applies to the entity's taxable year.

*(2) Form of election.* A passthrough entity makes an election under this paragraph (g) by attaching to its return (or amended return) a written statement that includes the name, address, and taxpayer identification number of the passthrough entity and a declaration that an election is being made under this paragraph (g).

*(3) Period for which election applies.* An election under this paragraph (g) made with a return (or amended return) for a taxable year applies to that taxable year and all subsequent taxable years that end before the date on which the election is revoked.

*(4) Revocation.* An election under this paragraph (g) may be revoked only with the consent of the Commissioner.

**(h) Examples.** The following examples illustrate the principles of this section. The examples assume for purposes of simplifying the presentation, that the lending transactions described do not result in foregone interest (within the meaning of section 7872(e)(2)), original issue discount (within the meaning of section 1273), or total unstated interest (within the meaning of section 483(b)).

*Example (1).* (i) A and B, two calendar year individuals, each own 50-percent interests in the capital, profits and losses of AB, a calendar year partnership. AB is engaged in a single rental activity within the meaning of § 1.469-1T(e)(3). AB borrows $50,000 from A and uses the loan proceeds in the rental activity. AB pays $5,000 of interest to A for the taxable year. A and B each incur $2,500 of interest expense as their distributive share of AB's interest expense.

(ii) AB has self-charged interest deductions for the taxable year (i.e., the deductions for interest charged to AB by A); A owns a direct interest in AB during AB's taxable year and has income for A's taxable year from interest charged to AB; and A's share of AB's self-charged interest deductions includes passive activity deductions. Accordingly, paragraph (c) of this section applies in determining A's passive activity gross income. See paragraph (c)(1) of this section.

(iii) Under paragraph (c)(2)(i) of this section, the applicable percentage of A's interest income is recharacterized as passive activity gross income from AB's rental activity. Paragraph (c)(3) of this section provides that the applicable percentage is obtained by dividing A's share for the taxable year of AB's self-charged interest deductions that are treated as passive activity deductions from the activity ($2,500) by the greater of A's share for the taxable year of AB's self-charged interest deductions ($2,500), or A's income for the taxable year from interest charged to AB ($5,000). Thus, A's applicable percentage is 50 percent ($2,500/$5,000), and $2,500 (50 percent x $5,000) of A's income from interest charged to AB is treated as passive activity gross income from the passive activity A conducts through AB.

(iv) Because B does not have any gross income for the year from interest charged to AB, this section does not apply to B. See paragraph (c)(1)(ii) of this section.

*Example (2).* (i) C and D, two calendar year taxpayers, each own 50-percent interests in the capital and profits of CD, a calendar year partnership. CD is engaged in a single rental activity, within the meaning of § 1.469-1T(e)(3). C obtains a $10,000 loan from a third-party lender, and pays the lender $900 in interest for the taxable year. C lends the $10,000 to CD, and receives $1,000 of interest income from CD for the taxable year. D lends $20,000 to CD and receives $2,000 of interest income from CD for the taxable year. CD uses all of the proceeds in the rental activity. C and D are each allocated $1,500 (50 percent x $3,000) of interest expense as their distributive share of CD's interest expense for the taxable year.

(ii) CD has self-charged interest deductions for the taxable year (i.e., deductions for interest charged to CD by C and D); C and D each own direct interests in CD during CD's taxable year and have gross income for the taxable year from interest charged to CD; and both C's and D's shares of CD's self-charged interest deductions include passive activity deductions. Accordingly, paragraph (c) of this section applies in determining C's and D's passive activity gross income. See paragraph (c)(1) of this section.

(iii) Under paragraph (c)(2)(i) of this section, the applicable percentage of each partner's interest income is recharacterized as passive activity gross income from CD's rental activity. Paragraph (c)(3) of this section provides that C's applicable percentage is obtained by dividing C's share for the taxable year of CD's self-charged interest deductions that are treated as passive activity deductions from the activity ($1,500) by the greater of C's share for the taxable year of CD's self-charged interest deductions ($1,500), or C's income for the taxable year from interest charged to CD ($1,000). Thus, C's applicable percentage is 100 percent ($1,500/$1,500), and all of C's income from interest charged to CD ($1,000) is treated as passive activity gross income from the passive activity C conducts through CD. Similarly, D's applicable percentage is obtained by dividing D's share for the taxable year of CD's self-charged interest deductions that are treated as passive activity deductions from the activity ($1,500) by the greater of D's share for the taxable year of CD's self-charged interest deductions ($1,500), or D's income for the taxable year from interest charged to CD ($2,000). Thus, D's applicable percentage is 75 percent ($1,500/$2,000), and $1,500 (75 percent x $2,000) of D's income from interest charged to CD is treated as passive activity gross income from the rental activity.

(iv) The $900 of interest expense that C pays to the third-party lender is allocated under § 1.163-8T(c)(1) to an expenditure that is properly chargeable to capital account with respect to the loan to CD. Thus, the expense is properly allocable to the interest income C receives from CD (see paragraph (f) of this section). Under paragraph (c)(2)(ii) of this section, the applicable percentage of C's deductions for the taxable year for interest expense that is properly allocable to C's income from interest charged to CD is recharacterized as a passive activity deduction from CD's rental activity. Accordingly, all of C's $900 interest deduction is treated as a passive activity deduction from the rental activity.

*Example (3).* (i) E and F, calendar year taxpayers, each own 50 percent of the stock of X, a calendar year S corporation. E borrows $30,000 from X, and pays X $3,000 of interest for the taxable year. E uses $15,000 of the loan proceeds to make a personal expenditure (as defined in § 1.163-8T(b)(5)), and uses $15,000 of loan proceeds to purchase a trade or business activity in which E does not materially participate (within the meaning of § 1.469-5T) for the taxable year. E and F each receive $1,500 as their pro rata share of X's interest income from the loan for the taxable year.

(ii) X has gross income for X's taxable year from interest charged to E (X's self-charged interest income); E owns a direct interest in X during X's taxable year and has deductions for the taxable year for interest charged by X; and E's deductions for interest charged by X include passive activity deductions. Accordingly, paragraph (d) of this section applies in determining E's passive activity gross income. See paragraph (d)(1) of this section.

(iii) Under the rules in paragraph (d)(2)(i) of this section, the applicable percentage of E's share of X's self-charged interest income is recharacterized as passive activity gross income from the activity. Paragraph (d)(3) of this section provides that the applicable percentage is obtained by dividing E's deductions for the taxable year for interest charged by X, to the extent treated as passive activity deductions from the activity ($1,500), by the greater of E's deductions for the taxable year for interest charged by X, regardless of whether those deductions are treated as passive activity deductions ($3,000), or E's share for the taxable year of X's self-charged interest income ($1,500). Thus, E's applicable percentage is 50 percent ($1,500/$3,000), and $750 (50 percent x $1,500) of E's share of X's self-charged interest income is treated as passive activity gross income.

(iv) Because F does not have any deductions for the taxable year for interest charged by X, this section does not apply to F. See paragraph (d)(1)(ii) of this section.

*Example (4).* (i) This Example 4 illustrates the application of this section to a partner that has a different taxable year from the partnership. The facts are the same as in Example 1 except as follows: Partnership AB has properly adopted a fiscal year ending June 30 for federal tax purposes; AB borrows the $50,000 from A on October 1, 1990; and under the terms of the loan, AB must pay A $5,000 in interest annually, in quarterly installments, for a term of 2 years.

(ii) For A's taxable years from 1990 through 1993 and AB's corresponding entity taxable years (as defined in paragraph (b)(4) of this section) A's interest income and AB's interest deductions from the loan are as follows:

| | A's Interest Income | AB's Interest Deductions |
|---|---|---|
| 1990 | $1,250 | 0 |
| 1991 | $5,000 | $3,750 |
| 1992 | $3,750 | $5,000 |
| 1993 | 0 | $1,250 |

(iii) For A's taxable year ending December 31, 1990, the corresponding entity taxable year is AB's taxable year ending June 30, 1990. Because AB does not have any deductions for the entity taxable year for interest charged to AB by A, paragraph (c) of this section does not apply in determining A's passive activity gross income for 1990 (see paragraph (c)(1)(i) of this section). Accordingly, A reports $1,250 of portfolio income on A's 1990 income tax return.

(iv) For A's taxable year ending December 31, 1991, the corresponding entity taxable year ends on June 30, 1991. AB has $3,750 of deductions for the entity taxable year for interest charged to AB by A (AB's self-charged interest deductions); A owns a direct interest in AB during the entity taxable year and has $5,000 of interest income for A's taxable year from interest charged to AB; and A's share of AB's self-charged interest deductions includes passive activity deductions. Accordingly, paragraph (c) of this section applies in determining A's passive activity gross income.

(v) Under paragraph (c)(2)(i) of this section, the applicable percentage of A's 1991 interest income is recharacterized as passive activity gross income from the activity. Paragraph (c)(3) of this section provides that the applicable percentage is obtained by dividing A's share for A's 1991 taxable year of AB's self-charged interest deductions that are treated as passive activity deductions from the activity (50 percent x $3,750 = $1,875) by the greater of A's share for A's taxable year of AB's self-charged interest deductions ($1,875), or A's income for A's taxable year from interest charged to AB ($5,000). Thus, A's applicable percentage is 37.5 percent ($1,875/$5,000), and $1,875 (37.5 percent x $5,000) of A's income from interest charged to AB is treated as passive activity gross income from the passive activity A conducts through AB.

(vi) For A's taxable year ending December 31, 1992, the corresponding entity taxable year ends on June 30, 1992. AB has $5,000 of deductions for the entity taxable year for interest charged to AB by A (AB's self-charged interest deductions); A owns a direct interest in AB during the entity taxable year and has $3,750 of gross income for A's taxable year from interest charged to AB; and A's share of AB's self-charged interest deductions includes passive activity deductions. Accordingly, paragraph (c) of this section applies in determining A's passive activity gross income.

(vii) The applicable percentage for 1992 is obtained by dividing A's share for A's 1992 taxable year of AB's self-charged interest deductions that are treated as passive activity deductions from the activity ($2,500) by the greater of A's share for A's taxable year of AB's self-charged interest deductions ($2,500), or A's income for A's taxable year from interest charged to AB ($3,750). Thus, A's applicable percentage is 66 2/3 percent ($2,500/$3,750), and $2,500 (66 2/3 percent x $3,750) of A's income from interest charged to AB is treated as passive activity gross income from the passive activity A conducts through AB.

(viii) Paragraph (c) of this section does not apply in determining A's passive activity gross income for the taxable year ending December 31, 1993, because A has no gross income for the taxable year from interest charged to AB (see paragraph (c)(1)(ii) of this section). A's share of AB's self-charged interest deductions for the entity taxable year ending June 30, 1993 ($625) is taken into account as a passive activity deduction on A's 1993 income tax return.

(ix) Because B does not have any gross income from interest charged to AB for any of the taxable years, this section does not apply to B. See paragraph (c)(1)(ii) of this section.

*Example (5).* (i) This Example 5 illustrates the application of the rules of this section in the case of a taxpayer who has an indirect interest in a partnership. G, a calendar year taxpayer, is an 80-percent partner in partnership UTP. UTP owns a 25-percent interest in the capital and profits of partnership LTP. UTP and LTP are both calendar year partnerships. The partners of LTP conduct a single passive activity through LTP. UTP obtains a $10,000 loan from a bank, and pays the bank $1,000 of interest per year. G's distributive share of the interest paid to the bank is $800 (80 percent x $1,000). UTP uses the $10,000 debt proceeds and another $10,000 of cash to make a loan to LTP, and LTP pays UTP $2,000 of interest for the taxable year. G's distributive share of interest income attributable to the UTP-to-LTP loan is $1,600 (80 percent x $2,000). LTP uses all of the proceeds received from UTP in the passive activity. UTP's distributive share of interest expense attributable to the UTP-to-LTP loan is $500 (25 percent x $2,000). G's distributive share of interest expense attributable to the UTP-to-LTP loan is $400 (80 percent x $500).

(ii) LTP has deductions for interest charged to LTP by UTP for the taxable year (LTP's self-charged interest deductions); G owns an indirect interest in LTP during LTP's taxable year and has gross income for the taxable year from interest charged to LTP by a passthrough entity (UTP) through which G owns an interest in LTP; and G's share of LTP's self-charged interest deductions includes passive activity deductions. Accordingly, paragraph (c) of this section applies in determining G's passive activity gross income. See paragraph (c)(1) of this section.

(iii) Under paragraph (c)(2)(i) of this section, the applicable percentage of G's interest income is recharacterized as passive activity gross income from the activity. Paragraph (c)(3) of this section provides that the applicable percentage is obtained by dividing G's share for the taxable year of LTP's self-charged interest deductions that are treated as passive activity deductions from the activity ($400) by the greater of G's share for the taxable year of LTP's self-charged interest deductions ($400), or G's income for the year from interest charged to LTP ($1,600). Thus, G's applicable percentage is 25 percent ($400/$1,600), and $400 (25 percent x $1,600) of G's income from interest charged to LTP is treated as passive activity gross income from the passive activity that G conducts through UTP and LTP.

(iv) G's $800 distributive share of the interest expense that UTP pays to the third-party lender is allocated under § 1.163-8T(c)(1) to an expenditure that is properly chargeable to capital account with respect to the loan to LTP. Thus, the expense is a deduction properly allocable to the interest income that G receives as a result of the UTP-to-LTP loan (see paragraph (f) of this section). Under paragraph (c)(2)(ii) of this section, the applicable percentage of G's deductions for the taxable year for interest expense that is properly allocable to G's income from interest charged by UTP to LTP is recharacterized as a passive activity deduction from LTP's passive activity. Accordingly, $200 (25 percent x $800) of G's interest deduction is treated as a passive activity deduction from LTP's activity.

*Example (6).* (i) This Example 6 illustrates the application of the rules of this section in the case of a taxpayer who conducts two passive activities through a passthrough entity. J, a calendar year taxpayer, is the 100-percent shareholder of Y, a calendar year S corporation. J conducts two passive activities through Y: a rental activity and a trade or business activity in which J does not materially participate. Y borrows $80,000 from J, and uses $60,000 of the loan proceeds in the rental activity and $20,000 of the loan proceeds in the passive trade or business activity. Y pays $8,000 of interest to J for the taxable year, and J incurs $8,000 of interest expense as J's distributive share of Y's interest expense.

(ii) Y has self-charged interest deductions for the taxable year (i.e., the deductions for interest charged to Y by J); J owns a direct interest in Y during Y's taxable year and has gross income for J's taxable year from interest charged to Y; and J's share of Y's self-charged interest deductions includes passive activity deductions. Accordingly, paragraph (c) of this section applies in determining J's passive activity gross income. See paragraph (c)(1) of this section.

(iii) Under paragraph (c)(2)(i) of this section, the applicable percentage of J's interest income is recharacterized as passive activity gross income attributable to the rental activity. Paragraph (c)(3) of this section provides that the applicable percentage is obtained by dividing J's share for the taxable year of Y's self-charged interest deductions that are treated as passive activity deductions from the rental activity ($6,000) by the greater of J's share for the taxable year of Y's self-charged interest deductions ($8,000), or J's income for the taxable year from interest charged to Y ($8,000). Thus, J's applicable percentage is 75 percent ($6,000/$8,000), and $6,000 (75 percent x $8,000) of J's income from interest charged to Y is treated as passive activity gross income from the rental activity J conducts through Y.

(iv) Under paragraph (c)(2)(i) of this section, the applicable percentage of J's interest income is recharacterized as passive activity gross income attributable to the passive trade or business activity. Paragraph (c)(3) of this section provides that the applicable percentage is obtained by dividing J's share for the taxable year of Y's self-charged interest deductions that are treated as passive activity deductions from the passive trade or business activity ($2,000) by the greater of J's share for the taxable year of Y's self-charged interest deductions ($8,000), or J's income for the taxable year from interest charged to Y ($8,000). Thus, J's applicable percentage is 25 percent ($2,000/$8,000), and $2,000 of J's income from interest charged to Y is treated as passive activity gross income from the passive trade or business activity J conducts through Y.

T.D. 9013, 8/20/2002.

### § 1.469-8 Application of section 469 to trust, estates, and their beneficiaries. [Reserved]

### § 1.469-9 Rules for certain rental real estate activities.

***Caution:*** The Treasury has not yet amended Reg § 1.469-9 to reflect changes made by P.L. 108-357.

**(a) Scope and purpose.** This section provides guidance to taxpayers engaged in certain real property trades or businesses on applying section 469(c)(7) to their rental real estate activities.

**(b) Definitions.** The following definitions apply for purposes of this section:

*(1) Trade or business.* A trade or business is any trade or business determined by treating the types of activities in § 1.469-4(b)(1) as if they involved the conduct of a trade or business, and any interest in rental real estate, including any interest in rental real estate that gives rise to deductions under section 212.

*(2) Real property trade or business.* Real property trade or business is defined in section 469(c)(7)(C).

*(3) Rental real estate.* Rental real estate is any real property used by customers or held for use by customers in a rental activity within the meaning of § 1.469-1T(e)(3). However, any rental real estate that the taxpayer grouped with a trade or business activity under § 1.469-4(d)(1)(i)(A) or (C) is not an interest in rental real estate for purposes of this section.

*(4) Personal services.* Personal services means any work performed by an individual in connection with a trade or business. However, personal services do not include any work performed by an individual in the individual's capacity as an investor as described in § 1.469-5T(f)(2)(ii).

*(5) Material participation.* Material participation has the same meaning as under § 1.469-5T. Paragraph (f) of this section contains rules applicable to limited partnership interests in rental real estate that a qualifying taxpayer elects to aggregate with other interests in rental real estate of that taxpayer.

*(6) Qualifying taxpayer.* A qualifying taxpayer is a taxpayer that owns at least one interest in rental real estate and meets the requirements of paragraph (c) of this section.

**(c) Requirements for qualifying taxpayers.** *(1) In general.* A qualifying taxpayer must meet the requirements of section 469(c)(7)(B).

*(2) Closely held C corporations.* A closely held C corporation meets the requirements of paragraph (c)(1) of this section by satisfying the requirements of section 469(c)(7)(D)(i). For purposes of section 469(c)(7)(D)(i), gross receipts do not include items of portfolio income within the meaning of § 1.469-2T(c)(3).

*(3) Requirement of material participation in the real property trades or businesses.* A taxpayer must materially participate in a real property trade or business in order for the personal services provided by the taxpayer in that real property trade or business to count towards meeting the requirements of paragraph (c)(1) of this section.

*(4) Treatment of spouses.* Spouses filing a joint return are qualifying taxpayers only if one spouse separately satisfies both requirements of section 469(c)(7)(B). In determining the real property trades or businesses in which a married taxpayer materially participates (but not for any other purpose under this paragraph (c)), work performed by the taxpayer's spouse in a trade or business is treated as work performed by the taxpayer under § 1.469-5T(f)(3), regardless of whether the spouses file a joint return for the year.

*(5) Employees in real property trades or businesses.* For purposes of paragraph (c)(1) of this section, personal services performed during a taxable year as an employee generally will be treated as performed in a trade or business but will not be treated as performed in a real property trade or business, unless the taxpayer is a five-percent owner (within the meaning of section 416(i)(1)(B)) in the employer. If an employee is not a five-percent owner in the employer at all times during the taxable year, only the personal services performed by the employee during the period the employee is a five-percent owner in the employer will be treated as performed in a real property trade or business.

**(d) General rule for determining real property trades or businesses.** *(1) Facts and circumstances.* The determination of a taxpayer's real property trades or businesses for purposes of paragraph (c) of this section is based on all of the relevant facts and circumstances. A taxpayer may use any reasonable method of applying the facts and circumstances in determining the real property trades or businesses in which the taxpayer provides personal services. Depending on the facts and circumstances, a real property trade or business consists either of one or more than one trade or business specifically described in section 469(c)(7)(C). A taxpayer's grouping of activities under § 1.469-4 does not control the determination of the taxpayer's real property trades or businesses under this paragraph (d).

*(2) Consistency requirement.* Once a taxpayer determines the real property trades or businesses in which personal services are provided for purposes of paragraph (c) of this section, the taxpayer may not redetermine those real property trades or businesses in subsequent taxable years unless the original determination was clearly inappropriate or there has been a material change in the facts and circumstances that makes the original determination clearly inappropriate.

**(e) Treatment of rental real estate activities of a qualifying taxpayer.** *(1) In general.* Section 469(c)(2) does not apply to any rental real estate activity of a taxpayer for a taxable year in which the taxpayer is a qualifying taxpayer under paragraph (c) of this section. Instead, a rental real estate activity of a qualifying taxpayer is a passive activity under section 469 for the taxable year unless the taxpayer materially participates in the activity. Each interest in rental real estate of a qualifying taxpayer will be treated as a separate rental real estate activity, unless the taxpayer makes an election under paragraph (g) of this section to treat all interests in rental real estate as a single rental real estate activity. Each separate rental real estate activity, or the single combined rental real estate activity if the taxpayer makes an election under paragraph (g), will be an activity of the taxpayer for all purposes of section 469, including the former passive activity rules under section 469(f) and the disposition rules under section 469(g). However, section 469 will continue to be applied separately with respect to each publicly traded partnership, as required under section 469(k), notwithstanding the rules of this section.

*(2) Treatment as a former passive activity.* For any taxable year in which a qualifying taxpayer materially participates in a rental real estate activity, that rental real estate activity will be treated as a former passive activity under section 469(f) if disallowed deductions or credits are allocated to the activity under § 1.469-1(f)(4).

*(3) Grouping rental real estate activities with other activities.* (i) In general. For purposes of this section, a qualifying taxpayer may not group a rental real estate activity with any other activity of the taxpayer. For example, if a qualifying taxpayer develops real property, constructs buildings, and owns an interest in rental real estate, the taxpayer's interest in rental real estate may not be grouped with the taxpayer's development activity or construction activity. Thus, only the participation of the taxpayer with respect to the rental real estate may be used to determine if the taxpayer materially participates in the rental real estate activity under § 1.469-5T.

(ii) Special rule for certain management activities. A qualifying taxpayer may participate in a rental real estate activity through participation, within the meaning of §§ 1.469-5(f) and 5T(f), in an activity involving the management of rental real estate (even if this management activity is conducted through a separate entity). In determining whether the taxpayer materially participates in the rental real estate activity, however, work the taxpayer performs in the management activity is taken into account only to the extent it is performed in managing the taxpayer's own rental real estate interests.

*(4) Example.* The following example illustrates the application of this paragraph (e).

*Example.* (i) Taxpayer B owns interests in three rental buildings, U, V and W. In 1995, B has $30,000 of disallowed passive losses allocable to Building U and $10,000 of disallowed passive losses allocable to Building V under § 1.469-1(f)(4). In 1996, B has $5,000 of net income from building U, $5,000 of net losses from building V, and $10,000 of net income from building W. Also in 1996, B is a qualifying taxpayer within the meaning of paragraph (c) of this section. Each building is treated as a separate activity of B under paragraph (e)(1) of this section, unless B makes the election under paragraph (g) to treat the three buildings as a single rental real estate activity. If the buildings are treated as separate activities, material participation is determined separately with respect to each building. If B makes the election under paragraph (g) to treat the buildings as a single activity, all participation relating to the buildings is aggregated in determining whether B materially participates in the combined activity.

(ii) Effective beginning in 1996, B makes the election under paragraph (g) to treat the three buildings as a single rental real estate activity. B works full-time managing the three buildings and thus materially participates in the combined activity in 1996 (even if B conducts this management function through a separate entity, including a closely held C corporation). Accordingly, the combined activity is not a passive activity of B in 1996. Moreover, as a result of the election under paragraph (g), disallowed passive losses of $40,000 ($30,000 + $10,000) are allocated to the combined activity. B's net income from the activity for 1996 is $10,000 ($5,000 − $5,000 + $10,000). This net income is nonpassive income for purposes of section 469. However, under section 469(f), the net income from a former passive activity may be offset with the disallowed passive losses from the same activity. Because Buildings U, V and W are treated as one activity for all purposes of section 469 due to the election under paragraph (g), and this activity is a former passive activity under section 469(f), B may offset the $10,000 of net income from the buildings with an equal amount of disallowed passive losses allocable to the buildings, regardless of which buildings produced the income or losses. As a result, B has $30,000 ($40,000 − $10,000) of disallowed passive losses remaining from the buildings after 1996.

**(f) Limited partnership interests in rental real estate activities.** *(1) In general.* If a taxpayer elects under paragraph (g) of this section to treat all interests in rental real estate as a single rental real estate activity, and at least one interest in rental real estate is held by the taxpayer as a limited partnership interest (within the meaning of § 1.469-5T(e)(3)), the combined rental real estate activity will be treated as a limited partnership interest of the taxpayer for purposes of determining material participation. Accordingly, the taxpayer will not be treated under this section as materially participating in the combined rental real estate activity unless the taxpayer materially participates in the activity under the tests listed in § 1.469-5T(e)(2) (dealing with the tests for determining the material participation of a limited partner).

*(2) De minimis exception.* If a qualifying taxpayer elects under paragraph (g) of this section to treat all interests in rental real estate as a single rental real estate activity, and the taxpayer's share of gross rental income from all of the taxpayer's limited partnership interests in rental real estate is less than ten percent of the taxpayer's share of gross rental income from all of the taxpayer's interests in rental real estate for the taxable year, paragraph (f)(1) of this section does not apply. Thus the taxpayer may determine material participation under any of the tests listed in § 1.469-5T(a) that apply to rental real estate activities.

**(g) Election to treat all interests in rental real estate as a single rental real estate activity.** *(1) In general.* A qualifying taxpayer may make an election to treat all of the taxpayer's interests in rental real estate as a single rental real estate activity. This election is binding for the taxable year in which it is made and for all future years in which the taxpayer is a qualifying taxpayer under paragraph (c) of this section, even if there are intervening years in which the taxpayer is not a qualifying taxpayer. The election may be made in any year in which the taxpayer is a qualifying taxpayer, and the failure to make the election in one year does not preclude the taxpayer from making the election in a subsequent year. In years in which the taxpayer is not a qualifying taxpayer, the election will not have effect and the taxpayer's activities will be those determined under § 1.469-4. If there is a material change in the taxpayer's facts and circumstances, the taxpayer may revoke the election using the procedure described in paragraph (g)(3) of this section.

*(2) Certain changes not material.* The fact that an election is less advantageous to the taxpayer in a particular taxable year is not, of itself, a material change in the taxpayer's facts and circumstances. Similarly, a break in the taxpayer's status as a qualifying taxpayer is not, of itself, a material change in the taxpayer's facts and circumstances.

*(3) Filing a statement to make or revoke the election.* A qualifying taxpayer makes the election to treat all interests in rental real estate as a single rental real estate activity by filing a statement with the taxpayer's original income tax return for the taxable year. This statement must contain a declaration that the taxpayer is a qualifying taxpayer for the taxable year and is making the election pursuant to section 469(c)(7)(A). The taxpayer may make this election for any taxable year in which section 469(c)(7) is applicable. A taxpayer may revoke the election only in the taxable year in which a material change in the taxpayer's facts and circumstances occurs or in a subsequent year in which the facts and circumstances remain materially changed from those in the taxable year for which the election was made. To revoke the election, the taxpayer must file a statement with the taxpayer's original income tax return for the year of revocation. This statement must contain a declaration that the taxpayer is revoking the election under section 469(c)(7)(A) and an explanation of the nature of the material change.

**(h) Interests in rental real estate held by certain passthrough entities.** *(1) General rule.* Except as provided in paragraph (h)(2) of this section, a qualifying taxpayer's interest in rental real estate held by a partnership or an S corporation (passthrough entity) is treated as a single interest in rental real estate if the passthrough entity grouped its rental real estate as one rental activity under § 1.469-4(d)(5). If the passthrough entity grouped its rental real estate into separate rental activities under § 1.469-4(d)(5), each rental real estate activity of the passthrough entity will be treated as a separate interest in rental real estate of the qualifying taxpayer. However, the qualifying taxpayer may elect under paragraph (g) of this section to treat all interests in rental real estate, including the rental real estate interests held through passthrough entities, as a single rental real estate activity.

*(2) Special rule if a qualifying taxpayer holds a fifty-percent or greater interest in a passthrough entity.* If a qualifying taxpayer owns, directly or indirectly, a fifty-percent or greater interest in the capital, profits, or losses of a passthrough entity for a taxable year, each interest in rental real estate held by the passthrough entity will be treated as a separate interest in rental real estate of the qualifying taxpayer, regardless of the passthrough entity's grouping of activities under § 1.469-4(d)(5). However, the qualifying taxpayer may elect under paragraph (g) of this section to treat all interests in rental real estate, including the rental real estate interests held through passthrough entities, as a single rental real estate activity.

*(3) Special rule for interests held in tiered passthrough entities.* If a passthrough entity owns a fifty-percent or greater interest in the capital, profits, or losses of another passthrough entity for a taxable year, each interest in rental real estate held by the lower-tier entity will be treated as a separate interest in rental real estate of the upper-tier entity, regardless of the lower-tier entity's grouping of activities under § 1.469-4(d)(5).

**(i) [Reserved]**

**(j) $25,000 offset for rental real estate activities of qualifying taxpayers.** *(1) In general.* A qualifying taxpayer's passive losses and credits from rental real estate activities (including prior-year disallowed passive activity losses and credits from rental real estate activities in which the taxpayer materially participates) are allowed to the extent permitted under section 469(i). The amount of losses or credits allowable under section 469(i) is determined after the rules of this section are applied. However, losses allowable by reason of this section are not taken into account in determining adjusted gross income for purposes of section 469(i)(3).

*(2) Example.* The following example illustrates the application of this paragraph (j).

*Example.* (i) Taxpayer A owns building X and building Y, both interests in rental real estate. In 1995, A is a qualifying taxpayer within the meaning of paragraph (c) of this section. A does not elect to treat X and Y as one activity under section 469(c)(7)(A) and paragraph (g) of this section. As a result, X and Y are treated as separate activities pursuant to section 469(c)(7)(A)(ii). A materially participates in X which has $100,000 of passive losses disallowed from prior years and produces $20,000 of losses in 1995. A does not materially participate in Y which produces $40,000 of income in 1995. A also has $50,000 of income from other nonpassive sources in 1995. A otherwise meets the requirements of section 469(i).

(ii) Because X is not a passive activity in 1995, the $20,000 of losses produced by X in 1995 are nonpassive losses that may be used by A to offset part of the $50,000 of nonpassive income. Accordingly, A is left with $30,000 ($50,000 – $20,000) of nonpassive income. In addition, A may use the prior year disallowed passive losses of X to offset any income from X and passive income from other sources. Therefore, A may offset the $40,000 of passive income from Y with $40,000 of passive losses from X.

(iii) Because A has $60,000 ($100,000 – $40,000) of passive losses remaining from X and meets all of the requirements of section 469(i), A may offset up to $25,000 of nonpassive income with passive losses from X pursuant to section 469(i). As a result, A has $5,000 ($30,000 – $25,000) of nonpassive income remaining and disallowed passive losses from X of $35,000 ($60,000 – $25,000) in 1995.

T.D. 8645, 12/21/95.

### § 1.469-10 Application of section 469 to publicly traded partnerships.

**(a) [Reserved].**

**(b) Publicly traded partnership.** *(1) In general.* For purposes of section 469(k), a partnership is a publicly traded partnership only if the partnership is a publicly traded partnership as defined by in § 1.7704-1.

*(2) Effective date.* This section applies for taxable years of a partnership beginning on or after December 17, 1998.

T.D. 8799, 12/16/98.

### § 1.469-11 Effective date and transition rules.

**(a) Effective date and transition rules.** Except as otherwise provided in this section—

*(1)* The rules contained in §§ 1.469-1, 1.469-1T, 1.469-2, 1.469-2T, 1.469-3, 1.469-3T, 1.469-4, 1.469-5, and 1.469-5T apply for taxable years ending after May 10, 1992.

*(2)* The rules contained in 26 CFR 1.469-1T, 1.469-2T, 1.469-3T, 1.469-4T, 1.469-5T, 1.469-11T(b) and (c) (as contained in the CFR edition revised as of April 1, 1992) apply for taxable years beginning after December 31, 1986, and ending on or before May 10, 1992;

*(3)* The rules contained in § 1.469-9 apply for taxable years beginning on or after January 1, 1995, and to elections made under § 1.469-9(g) with returns filed on or after January 1, 1995;

*(4)* The rules contained in § 1.469-7 apply for taxable years ending after December 31, 1986; and

*(5)* This section applies for taxable years beginning after December 31, 1986.

**(b) Additional effective dates.** *(1) Application of 1992 amendments for taxable years beginning before October 4, 1994.* Except as provided in paragraph (b)(2) of this section, for taxable years that end after May 10, 1992, and begin before October 4, 1994, a taxpayer may determine tax liability in accordance with Project PS-1-89 published at 1992-1 C.B. 1219 (see § 601.601(d)(2)(ii)(b) of this chapter).

*(2) Additional transition rule for 1992 amendments.* If a taxpayer's first taxable year ending after May 10, 1992, begins on or before that date, the taxpayer may treat the taxable year, for purposes of paragraph (a) of this section, as a taxable year ending on or before May 10, 1992.

*(3) Fresh starts under consistency rules.* (i) Regrouping when tax liability is first determined under Project PS-1-89. For the first taxable year in which a taxpayer determines its tax liability under Project PS-1-89, the taxpayer may regroup its activities without regard to the manner in which the activities were grouped in the preceding taxable year and must regroup its activities if the grouping in the preceding taxable year is inconsistent with the rules of Project PS-1-89.

(ii) Regrouping when tax liability is first determined under § 1.469-4. For the first taxable year in which a taxpayer determines its tax liability under § 1.469-4, rather than under the rules of Project PS-1-89, the taxpayer may regroup its activities without regard to the manner in which the activities were grouped in the preceding taxable year and must regroup its activities if the grouping in the preceding taxable year is inconsistent with the rules of § 1.469-4.

(iii) Regrouping when taxpayer is first subject to section 469(c)(7). For the first taxable year beginning after December 31, 1993, a taxpayer may regroup its activities to the extent necessary or appropriate to avail itself of the provisions of section 469(c)(7) and without regard to the manner in which the activities were grouped in the preceding taxable year.

*(4) Certain investment credit property.* (i) The rules contained in § 1.469-3(f) apply with respect to property placed in service after December 31, 1990 (other than property described in section 11813(c)(2) of the Omnibus Reconciliation Act of 1990 (P.L. 101-508)).

(ii) The rules contained in 26 CFR 1.469-3T(f) (as contained in the CFR edition revised as of April 1, 1992) apply with respect to property placed in service on or before December 31, 1990, and property described in section 11813(c)(2) of the Omnibus Reconciliation Act of 1990.

**(c) Special rules.** *(1) Application of certain income recharacterization rules and self-charged rules.* (i) Certain recharacterization rules inapplicable in 1987. No amount of gross income shall be treated under § 1.469-2T(f)(3) through (7) as income that is not from a passive activity for any taxable year of the taxpayer beginning before January 1, 1988.

(ii) Property rented to a nonpassive activity. In applying § 1.469-2(f)(6) or § 1.469-2T(f)(6) to a taxpayer's rental of an item of property, the taxpayer's net rental activity income (within the meaning of § 1.469-2(f)(9)(iv) or § 1.469-2T(f)(9)(iv)) from the property for any taxable year beginning after December 31, 1987, does not include the portion of the income (if any) that is attributable to the rental of that item of property pursuant to a written binding contract entered into before February 19, 1988.

(iii) Self-charged rules. For taxable years beginning before June 4, 1991—

(1) A taxpayer is not required to apply the rules in § 1.469-7 in computing the taxpayer's passive activity loss and passive activity credit; and

(2) A taxpayer that owns an interest in a passthrough entity may use any reasonable method of offsetting items of interest income and interest expense from lending transactions between the passthrough entity and its owners or between identically-owned passthrough entities (as defined in § 1.469-7(e)) to compute the taxpayer's passive activity loss and passive activity credit. Items from nonlending transactions cannot be offset under the self-charged rules.

*(2) Qualified low-income housing projects.* For a transitional rule concerning the application of section 469 to losses from qualified low-income housing projects, see section 502 of the Tax Reform Act of 1986.

*(3) Effect of events occurring in years prior to 1987.* The treatment for a taxable year beginning after December 31, 1986, of any item of income, gain, loss, deduction, or credit as an item of passive activity gross income, passive activity deduction, or credit from a passive activity, is determined as if section 469 and the regulations thereunder had been in effect for taxable years beginning before January 1, 1987, but without regard to any passive activity loss or passive activity credit that would have been disallowed for any taxable year beginning before January 1, 1987, if section 469 and the regulations thereunder had been in effect for that year. For example, in determining whether a taxpayer materially participates in an activity under § 1.469-5T(a)(5) (relating to taxpayers who have materially participated in an activity for five of the ten immediately preceding taxable years) for any taxable year beginning after December 31, 1986, the taxpayer's participation in the activity for all prior taxable years (including taxable years beginning before 1987) is taken into account. See § 1.469-5(j) (relating to the determination of material participation for taxable years beginning before January 1, 1987).

**(d) Examples.** The following examples illustrate the application of paragraph (c) of this section:

*Example (1).* A, a calendar year individual, is a partner in a partnership with a taxable year ending on January 31. During its taxable year ending January 31, 1987, the partnership was engaged in a single activity involving the conduct of a trade or business. In applying section 469 and the regulations thereunder to A for calendar year 1987, A's distributive share of partnership items for the partnership's taxable year ending January 31, 1987, is taken into account. Therefore, under § 1.469-2T(e)(1) and paragraph (c)(3) of this section, A's participation in the activity throughout the partnership's taxable year beginning February 1, 1986, and ending January 31, 1987, is taken into account for purposes of determining the character under section 469 of the items of gross income, deduction, and credit allocated to A for the partnership's taxable year ending January 31, 1987.

*Example (2).* B, a calendar year individual, is a beneficiary of a trust described in section 651 that has a taxable year ending January 31. The trust conducts a rental activity (within the meaning of § 1.469-1T(e)(3)). Because the trust's taxable year ending January 31, 1987, began before January 1, 1987, section 469 and the regulations thereunder do not applying to the trust for that year. Section 469 and the regulations thereunder do apply, however, to B for B's calendar year 1987. Therefore, income of the trust from the rental activity for the trust's taxable year ending January 31, 1987, that is included in B's gross income for 1987 is taken into account in apply section 469 to B for 1987.

T.D. 8417, 5/11/92, amend T.D. 8565, 10/3/94, T.D. 8645, 12/21/95, T.D. 9013, 8/20/2002.

## § 1.471-1 Need for inventories.

In order to reflect taxable income correctly, inventories at the beginning and end of each taxable year are necessary in every case in which the production, purchase, or sale of merchandise is an income-producing factor. The inventory should include all finished or partly finished goods and, in the case of raw materials and supplies, only those which have been acquired for sale or which will physically become a part of merchandise intended for sale, in which class fall containers, such as kegs, bottles, and cases, whether returnable or not, if title thereto will pass to the purchaser of the product to be sold therein. Merchandise should be included in the inventory only if title thereto is vested in the taxpayer. Accordingly, the seller should include in his inventory goods under contract for sale but not yet segregated and applied to the contract and goods out upon consignment, but should exclude from inventory goods sold (including containers), title to which has passed to the purchaser. A purchaser should include in inventory merchandise purchased (including containers), title to which has passed to him, although such merchandise is in transit or for other reasons has not been reduced to physical possession, but should not include goods ordered for future delivery, transfer of title to which has not yet been effected. (But see § 1.472-1.)

T.D. 6336, 12/1/58.

### § 1.471-2 Valuation of inventories.

**(a)** Section 471 provides two tests to which each inventory must conform:

*(1)* It must conform as nearly as may be to the best accounting practice in the trade or business, and

*(2)* It must clearly reflect the income.

**(b)** It follows, therefore, that inventory rules cannot be uniform but must give effect to trade customs which come within the scope of the best accounting practice in the particular trade or business. In order to clearly reflect income, the inventory practice of a taxpayer should be consistent from year to year, and greater weight is to be given to consistency than to any particular method of inventorying or basis of valuation so long as the method or basis used is in accord with §§ 1.471-1 through 1.471-11.

**(c)** The bases of valuation most commonly used by business concerns and which meet the requirements of section 471 are (1) cost and (2) cost or market, whichever is lower. (For inventories by dealers in securities, see § 1.471-5.) Any goods in an inventory which are unsalable at normal prices or unusable in the normal way because of damage, imperfections, shop wear, changes of style, odd or broken lots, or other similar causes, including second-hand goods taken in exchange, should be valued at bona fide selling prices less direct cost of disposition, whether subparagraph (1) or (2) of this paragraph is used, or if such goods consist of raw materials or partly finished goods held for use or consumption, they shall be valued upon a reasonable basis, taking into consideration the usability and the condition of the goods, but in no case shall such value be less than the scrap value. Bona fide selling price means actual offering of goods during a period ending not later than 30 days after inventory date. The burden of proof will rest upon the taxpayer to show that such exceptional goods as are valued upon such selling basis come within the classifications indicated above, and he shall maintain such records of the disposition of the goods as will enable a verification of the inventory to be made.

**(d)** In respect of normal goods, whichever method is adopted must be applied with reasonable consistency to the entire inventory of the taxpayer's trade or business except as to those goods inventoried under the last-in, first-out method authorized by section 472 or to animals inventoried under the elective unit-livestock-price-method authorized by § 1.471-6. See paragraph (d) of § 1.446-1 for rules permitting the use of different methods of accounting if the taxpayer has more than one trade or business. Where the taxpayer is engaged in more than one trade or business the Commissioner may require that the method of valuing inventories with respect to goods in one trade or business also be used with respect to similar goods in other trades or businesses if, in the opinion of the Commissioner, the use of such method with respect to such other goods is essential to a clear reflection of income. Taxpayers were given an option to adopt the basis of either (1) cost or (2) cost or market, whichever is lower, for their 1920 inventories. The basis properly adopted for that year or any subsequent year is controlling, and a change can now be made only after permission is secured from the Commissioner. Application for permission to change the basis of valuing inventories shall be made in writing and filed with the Commissioner as provided in paragraph (e) of § 1.446-1. Goods taken in the inventory which have been so intermingled that they cannot be identified with specific invoices will be deemed to be the goods most recently purchased or produced, and the cost thereof will be the actual cost of the goods purchased or produced during the period in which the quantity of goods in the inventory has been acquired. But see section 472 as to last-in, first-out inventories. Where the taxpayer maintains book inventories in accordance with a sound accounting system in which the respective inventory accounts are charged with the actual cost of the goods purchased or produced and credited with the value of goods used, transferred, or sold, calculated upon the basis of the actual cost of the goods acquired during the taxable year (including the inventory at the beginning of the year), the net value as shown by such inventory accounts will be deemed to be the cost of the goods on hand. The balances shown by such book inventories should be verified by physical inventories at reasonable intervals and adjusted to conform therewith.

**(e)** Inventories should be recorded in a legible manner, properly computed and summarized, and should be preserved as a part of the accounting records of the taxpayer. The inventories of taxpayers on whatever basis taken will be subject to investigation by the district director, and the taxpayer must satisfy the district director of the correctness of the prices adopted.

**(f)** The following methods, among others, are sometimes used in taking or valuing inventories, but are not in accord with the regulations in this part:

*(1)* Deducting from the inventory a reserve for price changes, or an estimated depreciation in the value thereof.

*(2)* Taking work in process, or other parts of the inventory, at a nominal price or at less than its proper value.

*(3)* Omitting portions of the stock on hand.

*(4)* Using a constant price or nominal value for so-called normal quantity of materials or goods in stock.

*(5)* Including stock in transit, shipped either to or from the taxpayer, the title to which is not vested in the taxpayer.

*(6)* Segregating indirect production costs into fixed and variable production cost classifications (as defined in § 1.471-11(b)(3)(ii) and allocating only the variable costs to the cost of goods produced while treating fixed costs as period costs which are currently deductible. This method is commonly referred to as the "direct cost" method.

*(7)* Treating all or substantially all indirect production costs (whether classified as fixed or variable) as period costs which are currently deductible. This method is generally referred to as the "prime cost" method.

T.D. 6336, 12/1/58, amend T.D. 7285, 9/14/73.

### § 1.471-3 Inventories at cost.

Cost means:

**(a)** In the case of merchandise on hand at the beginning of the taxable year, the inventory price of such goods.

**(b)** In the case of merchandise purchased since the beginning of the taxable year, the invoice price less trade or other discounts, except strictly cash discounts approximating a fair interest rate, which may be deducted or not at the option of the taxpayer, provided a consistent course is followed. To this net invoice price should be added transportation or other necessary charges incurred in acquiring possession of the goods. For taxpayers acquiring merchandise for resale that are subject to the provisions of section 263A, see §§ 1.263A-1 and 1.263A-3 for additional amounts that must be included in inventory costs.

**(c)** In the case of merchandise produced by the taxpayer since the beginning of the taxable year, (1) the cost of raw materials and supplies entering into or consumed in connection with the product, (2) expenditures for direct labor, and (3) indirect production costs incident to and necessary for the production of the particular article, including in such indirect production costs an appropriate portion of management expenses, but not including any cost of selling or return on capital, whether by way of interest or profit. See §§ 1.263A-1 and 1.263A-2 for more specific rules regarding the treatment of production costs.

**(d)** In any industry in which the usual rules for computation of cost of production are inapplicable, costs may be approximated upon such basis as may be reasonable and in conformity with established trade practice in the particular industry. Among such cases are: (1) Farmers and raisers of livestock (see § 1.471-6); (2) miners and manufacturers who by a single process or uniform series of processes derive a product of two or more kinds, sizes, or grades, the unit cost of which is substantially alike (see § 1.471-7); and (3) retail merchants who use what is known as the "retail method" in ascertaining approximate cost (see § 1.471-8).

Notwithstanding the other rules of this section, cost shall not include an amount which is of a type for which a deduction would be disallowed under section 162(c), (f), or (g) and the regulations thereunder in the case of a business expense.

T.D. 6336, 12/1/58, amend T.D. 7285, 9/14/73, T.D. 7345, 2/9/75, T.D. 8131, 3/24/87, T.D. 8482, 8/6/93.

PAR. 6. Section 1.471-3 is amended by:

1. Adding paragraphs (e) and (g).

2. Designating the undesignated text following paragraph (d) as paragraph (f).

The additions read as follows:

**Proposed § 1.471-3 Inventories at cost.** [*For Preamble, see ¶ 153,199*]

* * * * *

**(e)** The amount of an allowance, discount, or price rebate a taxpayer earns by selling specific merchandise is a reduction in the cost (as determined under paragraph (a), (b), or (d) of this section) of the merchandise sold or deemed to be sold under the inventory cost flow assumption (such as first-in, first-out; last-in, first-out; or a specific-goods method) the taxpayer uses to identify the costs in ending inventory. This amount decreases cost of goods sold and does not reduce the inventory cost or value of goods on hand at the end of the taxable year.

* * * * *

**(e) Effective/applicability date.** Paragraph (f) of this section applies to taxable years ending on or after the date these regulations are published as final regulations in the Federal Register.

**§ 1.471-4 Inventories at cost or market, whichever is lower.**

**(a) In general.** *(1) Market definition.* Under ordinary circumstances and for normal goods in an inventory, market means the aggregate of the current bid prices prevailing at the date of the inventory of the basic elements of cost reflected in inventories of goods purchased and on hand, goods in process of manufacture, and finished manufactured goods on hand. The basic elements of cost include direct materials, direct labor, and indirect costs required to be included in inventories by the taxpayer (e.g., under section 263A and its underlying regulations for taxpayers subject to that section). For taxpayers to which section 263A applies, for example, the basic elements of cost must reflect all direct costs and all indirect costs properly allocable to goods on hand at the inventory date at the current bid price of those costs, including but not limited to the cost of purchasing, handling, and storage activities conducted by the taxpayer, both prior to and subsequent to acquisition or production of the goods. The determination of the current bid price of the basic elements of costs reflected in goods on hand at the inventory date must be based on the usual volume of particular cost elements purchased (or incurred) by the taxpayer.

*(2) Fixed price contracts.* Paragraph (a)(1) of this section does not apply to any goods on hand or in process of manufacture for delivery upon firm sales contracts (i.e., those not legally subject to cancellation by either party) at fixed prices entered into before the date of the inventory, under which the taxpayer is protected against actual loss. Any such goods must be inventoried at cost.

*(3) Examples.* The valuation principles in paragraph (a)(1) of this section are illustrated by the following examples:

*Example (1).* (i) Taxpayer A manufactures tractors. A values its inventory using cost or market, whichever is lower, under paragraph (a)(1) of this section. At the end of 1994, the cost of one of A's tractors on hand is determined as follows:

| | |
|---|---|
| Direct materials | $ 3,000 |
| Direct labor | 4,000 |
| Indirect costs under section 263A | 3,000 |
| Total section 263A costs (cost) | $ 10,000 |

(ii) A determines that the aggregate of the current bid prices of the materials, labor, and overhead required to reproduce the tractor at the end of 1994 are as follows:

| | |
|---|---|
| Direct materials | $ 3,100 |
| Direct labor | 4,100 |
| Indirect costs under section 263A | 3,100 |
| Total section 263A costs (market) | $ 10,300 |

(iii) In determining the lower of cost or market value of the tractor, A compares the cost of the tractor, $10,000, with the market value of the tractor, $10,300, in accordance with paragraph (c) of this section. Thus, under this section, A values the tractor at $10,000.

*Example (2).* (i) Taxpayer B purchases and resells several lines of shoes and is subject to section 263A. B values its inventory using cost or market, whichever is lower, under paragraph (a)(1) of this section. At the end of 1994, the cost of one pair of shoes on hand is determined as follows:

| | |
|---|---|
| Acquisition cost | $ 200 |
| Indirect costs under section 263A | 10 |
| Total section 263A costs (cost) | $ 210 |

(ii) B determines the aggregate current bid prices prevailing at the end of 1994 for the elements of cost (both direct costs and indirect costs incurred prior and subsequent to acquisition of the shoes) based on the volume of the elements usually purchased (or incurred) by B as follows:

| | | |
|---|---|---|
| Acquisition cost | $ | 178 |
| Indirect costs under section 263A | | 12 |
| Total § 263A costs (market) | $ | 190 |

(iii) In determining the lower of cost or market value of the shoes, B compares the cost of the pair of shoes, $210, with the market value of the shoes, $190, in accordance with paragraph (c) of this section. Thus, under this section, B values the shoes at $190.

**(b) Inactive markets.** Where no open market exists or where quotations are nominal, due to inactive market conditions, the taxpayer must use such evidence of a fair market price at the date or dates nearest the inventory as may be available, such as specific purchases or sales by the taxpayer or others in reasonable volume and made in good faith, or compensation paid for cancellation of contracts for purchase commitments. Where the taxpayer in the regular course of business has offered for sale such merchandise at prices lower than the current price as above defined, the inventory may be valued at such prices less direct cost of disposition, and the correctness of such prices will be determined by reference to the actual sales of the taxpayer for a reasonable period before and after the date of the inventory. Prices which vary materially from the actual prices so ascertained will not be accepted as reflecting the market.

**(c) Comparison of cost and market.** Where the inventory is valued upon the basis of cost or market, whichever is lower, the market value of each article on hand at the inventory date shall be compared with the cost of the article, and the lower of such values shall be taken as the inventory value of the article.

**(d) Effective date.** This section applies to inventory valuations for taxable years beginning after December 31, 1993. For taxable years beginning before January 1, 1994, taxpayers must take reasonable positions on their federal income tax returns with respect to the application of section 263A, and must have otherwise complied with § 1.471-4 (as contained in the 26 CFR part 1 edition revised April 1, 1993). For purposes of this paragraph (d), a reasonable position as to the application of section 263A is a position consistent with the temporary regulations, revenue rulings, revenue procedures, notices, and announcements concerning section 263A applicable in taxable years beginning before January 1, 1994. (See § 601.601(d)(2)(ii)(b) of this chapter.)

T.D. 6336, 12/1/58, amend T.D. 8482, 8/6/93.

## § 1.471-5 Inventories by dealers in securities.

A dealer in securities who in his books of account regularly inventories unsold securities on hand either—

**(a)** At cost,

**(b)** At cost or market, whichever is lower, or

**(c)** At market value,

may make his return upon the basis upon which his accounts are kept, provided that a description of the method employed is included in or attached to the return, that all the securities are inventoried by the same method, and that such method is adhered to in subsequent years, unless another method is authorized by the Commissioner pursuant to a written application therefor filed as provided in paragraph (e) of § 1.446-1. A dealer in securities in whose books of account separate computations of the gain or loss from the sale of the various lots of securities sold are made on the basis of the cost of each lot shall be regarded, for the purposes of this section, as regularly inventorying his securities at cost. For the purposes of this section, a dealer in securities is a merchant of securities, whether an individual, partnership, or corporation, with an established place of business, regularly engaged in the purchase of securities and their resale to customers; that is, one who as a merchant buys securities and sells them to customers with a view to the gains and profits that may be derived therefrom. If such business is simply a branch of the activities carried on by such person, the securities inventoried as provided in this section may include only those held for purposes of resale and not for investment. Taxpayers who buy and sell or hold securities for investment or speculation, irrespective of whether such buying or selling constitutes the carrying on of a trade or business, and officers of corporations and members of partnerships who in their individual capacities buy and sell securities, are not dealers in securities within the meaning of this section. See §§ 1.263A-1 and 1.263A-3 for rules regarding the treatment of costs with respect to property acquired for resale.

T.D. 6336, 12/1/58, amend T.D. 8131, 3/24/87, T.D. 8482, 8/6/93.

## § 1.471-6 Inventories of livestock raisers and other farmers.

**(a)** A farmer may make his return upon an inventory method instead of the cash receipts and disbursements method. It is optional with the taxpayer which of these methods of accounting is used but, having elected one method, the option so exercised will be binding upon the taxpayer for the year for which the option is exercised and for subsequent years unless another method is authorized by the Commissioner as provided in paragraph (e) of § 1.446-1.

**(b)** In any change of accounting method from the cash receipts and disbursements method to an inventory method, adjustments shall be made as provided in section 481 (relating to adjustments required by change in method of accounting) and the regulations thereunder.

**(c)** Because of the difficulty of ascertaining actual cost of livestock and other farm products, farmers who render their returns upon an inventory method may value their inventories according to the "farm-price method", and farmers raising livestock may value their inventories of animals according to either the "farm-price method" or the "unit-livestock-price method". In addition, these inventory methods may be used to account for the costs of property produced in a farming business that are required to be capitalized under section 263A regardless of whether the property being produced is otherwise treated as inventory by the taxpayer, and regardless of whether the taxpayer is otherwise using the cash or an accrual method of accounting.

**(d)** The "farm-price method" provides for the valuation of inventories at market price less direct cost of disposition. If this method of valuation is used, it generally must be applied to all property produced by the taxpayer in the trade or business of farming, except as to livestock accounted for, at the taxpayer's election, under the unit livestock method of accounting. However, see § 1.263A-4(c)(3) for an exception to this rule. If the use of the "farm-price method" of valuing inventories for any taxable year involves a change in method of valuing inventories from that employed in prior years, permission for such change shall first be secured from the Commissioner as provided in paragraph (e) of § 1.446-1.

**(e)** The "unit-livestock-price method" provides for the valuation of the different classes of animals in the inventory at a standard unit price for each animal within a class. A livestock raiser electing this method of valuing his animals must adopt a reasonable classification of the animals in his inventory with respect to the age and kind included so that the unit prices assigned to the several classes will reasonably account for the normal costs incurred in producing the animals within such classes. Thus, if a cattle raiser determines that it costs approximately $15 to produce a calf, and $7.50 each year to raise the calf to maturity, his classifications and unit prices would be as follows: Calves, $15; yearlings, $22.50; 2-year olds, $30; mature animals, $37.50. The classification selected by the livestock raiser, and the unit prices assigned to the several classes, are subject to approval by the district director upon examination of the taxpayer's return.

**(f)** A taxpayer that elects to use the "unit-livestock-price method" must apply it to all livestock raised, whether for sale or for draft, breeding, or dairy purposes. The inventoriable costs of animals raised for draft, breeding, or dairy purposes can, at the election of the livestock raiser, be included in inventory or treated as property used in a trade or business subject to depreciation after maturity. See § 1.263A-4 for rules regarding the computation of inventoriable costs for purposes of the unit-livestock-price method. Once established, the methods of accounting used by the taxpayer to determine unit prices and to classify animals must be consistently applied in all subsequent taxable years. A taxpayer that uses the unit-livestock-price method must annually reevaluate its unit prices and adjust the prices either upward to reflect increases, or downward to reflect decreases, in the costs of raising livestock. The consent of the Commissioner is not required to make such upward or downward adjustments. No other changes in the classification of animals or unit prices may be made without the consent of the Commissioner. See § 1.446-1(e) for procedures for obtaining the consent of the Commissioner. The provisions of this paragraph (f) apply to taxable years ending after October 28, 2002.

**(g)** A livestock raiser who uses the "unit-livestock-price method" must include in his inventory at cost any livestock purchased, except that animals purchased for draft, breeding, or dairy purposes can, at the election of the livestock raiser, be included in inventory or be treated as property used in a trade or business subject to depreciation after maturity. If the animals purchased are not mature at the time of purchase, the cost should be increased at the end of each taxable year in accordance with the established unit prices, except that no increase is to be made in the taxable year of purchase if the animal is acquired during the last six months of that year. If the records maintained permit identification of a purchased animal, the cost of such animal will be eliminated from the closing inventory in the event of its sale or loss. Otherwise, the first-in, first-out method of valuing inventories must be applied.

**(h)** If a taxpayer using the "farm-price method" desires to adopt the "unit-livestock-price method" in valuing his inventories of livestock, permission for the change shall first be secured from the Commissioner as provided in paragraph (e) of § 1.446-1. However, a taxpayer who has filed returns on the basis of inventories at cost, or cost or market whichever is lower, may adopt the "unit-livestock-price method" for valuing his inventories of livestock without formal application for permission, but the classifications and unit prices selected are subject to approval by the district director upon examination of the taxpayer's return. A livestock raiser who has adopted a constant unit-price method of valuing livestock inventories and filed returns on that basis will be considered as having elected the "unit-livestock-price method".

**(i)** If returns have been made in which the taxable income has been computed upon incomplete inventories, the abnormality should be corrected by submitting with the return for the current taxable year a statement for the preceding taxable year. In this statement such adjustments shall be made as are necessary to bring the closing inventory for the preceding taxable year into agreement with the opening complete inventory for the current taxable year. If necessary clearly to reflect income, similar adjustments may be made as at the beginning of the preceding year or years, and the tax, if any be due, shall be assessed and paid at the rate of tax in effect for such year or years.

---

T.D. 6336, 12/1/58, amend T.D. 8131, 3/24/87, T.D. 8729, 8/21/97, T.D. 8897, 8/18/2000, T.D. 9019, 10/25/2002.

---

### § 1.471-7 Inventories of miners and manufacturers.

A taxpayer engaged in mining or manufacturing who by a single process or uniform series of processes derives a product of two or more kinds, sizes, or grades, the unit cost of which is substantially alike, and who in conformity to a recognized trade practice allocates an amount of cost to each kind, size, or grade of product, which in the aggregate will absorb the total cost of production, may, with the consent of the Commissioner, use such allocated cost as a basis for pricing inventories, provided such allocation bears a reasonable relation to the respective selling values of the different kinds, sizes, or grades of product. See section 472 as to last-in, first-out inventories.

---

T.D. 6336, 12/1/58.

---

### § 1.471-8 Inventories of retail merchants.

**(a)** Retail merchants who employ what is known as the "retail method" of pricing inventories may make their returns upon that method, provided that the use of such method is designated upon the return, that accurate accounts are kept, and that such method is consistently adhered to unless a change is authorized by the Commissioner as provided in paragraph (e) of § 1.446-1. Under the retail method the total of the retail selling prices of the goods on hand at the end of the year in each department or of each class of goods is reduced to approximate cost by deducting therefrom an amount which bears the same ratio to such total as—

*(1)* The total of the retail selling prices of the goods included in the opening inventory plus the retail selling prices of the goods purchased during the year, with proper adjustment to such selling prices for all mark-ups and mark-downs, less

*(2)* The cost of the goods included in the opening inventory plus the cost of the goods purchased during the year, bears to (1).

The result should represent as accurately as may be the amounts added to the cost price of the goods to cover selling and other expenses of doing business and for the margin of profit. See §§ 1.263A-1 and 1.263A-3 for rules regarding the computation of costs with respect to property acquired for resale.

**(b)** For further adjustments to be made in the case of a retail merchant using the last-in, first-out inventory method authorized by section 472, see paragraph (k) of § 1.472-1.

**(c)** A taxpayer maintaining more than one department in his store or dealing in classes of goods carrying different percentages of gross profit should not use a percentage of profit based upon an average of his entire business. But should compute and use in valuing his inventory the proper percentages for the respective departments or classes of goods.

**(d)** A taxpayer (other than one using the last-in, first-out inventory method) who previously has determined inventories in accordance with the retail method, except that, to obtain a basis of approximate cost or market, whichever is lower, has consistently and uniformly followed the practice of adjusting the retail selling prices of the goods included in the opening inventory and purchased during the taxable year for mark-ups but not for mark-downs, may continue such practice subject to the conditions prescribed in this section. The adjustments must be bona fide and consistent and uniform. Where mark-downs are not included in the adjustments, mark-ups made to cancel or correct mark-downs shall not be included; and the mark-ups included must be reduced by the mark-downs made to cancel or correct such mark-ups.

**(e)** In no event shall mark-downs not based on actual reduction of retail sale prices, such as mark-downs based on depreciation and obsolescence, be recognized in determining the retail selling prices of the goods on hand at the end of the taxable year.

**(f)** A taxpayer (other than one using the last-in, first-out inventory method) who previously has determined inventories without following the practice of eliminating mark-downs in making adjustments to retail selling prices may adopt such practice, provided permission to do so is obtained in accordance with, and subject to the terms provided by, paragraph (e) of § 1.446-1. A taxpayer filing a first return of income may adopt such practice subject to approval by the district director upon examination of the return.

**(g)** A taxpayer using the last-in, first-out inventory method in conjunction with retail computations must adjust retail selling prices for mark-downs as well as mark-ups, in order that there may be reflected the approximate cost of the goods on hand at the end of the taxable year regardless of market values.

T.D. 6336, 12/1/58, amend T.D. 8131, 3/24/87, T.D. 8482, 8/6/93.

### § 1.471-9 Inventories of acquiring corporations.

For additional rules in the case of certain corporate acquisitions specified in section 381(a), see section 381(c)(5) and the regulations thereunder.

T.D. 6336, 12/1/58.

### § 1.471-10 Applicability of long-term contract methods.

See § 1.460-2 for rules providing for the application of the long-term contract methods to certain manufacturing contracts.

T.D. 7397, 11/14/76, T.D. 8067, 12/30/85, T.D. 8929, 1/10/2001.

### § 1.471-11 Inventories of manufacturers.

**(a) Use of full absorption method of inventory costing.** In order to conform as nearly as may be possible to the best accounting practices and to clearly reflect income (as required by section 471 of the Code), both direct and indirect production costs must be taken into account in the computation of inventoriable costs in accordance with the "full absorption" method of inventory costing. Under the full absorption method of inventory costing production costs must be allocated to goods produced during the taxable year, whether sold during the taxable year or in inventory at the close of the taxable year determined in accordance with the taxpayer's method of identifying goods in inventory. Thus, the taxpayer must include as inventoriable costs all direct production costs and, to the extent provided by paragraphs (c) and (d) of this section, all indirect production costs. For purposes of this section, the term "financial reports" means financial reports (including consolidated financial statements) to shareholders, partners, beneficiaries or other proprietors and for credit purposes. See also § 1.263A-1T with respect to the treatment of production costs incurred in taxable years beginning after December 31, 1986, and before January 1, 1994. See also §§ 1.263A-1 and 1.263A-2 with respect to the treatment of production costs incurred in taxable years beginning after December 31, 1993.

**(b) Production costs.** *(1) In general.* Costs are considered to be production costs to the extent that they are incident to and necessary for production or manufacturing operations or processes. Production costs include direct production costs and fixed and variable indirect production costs.

*(2) Direct production costs.* (i) Costs classified as "direct production costs" are generally those costs which are incident to and necessary for production or manufacturing operations or processes and are components of the cost of either direct material or direct labor. Direct material costs include the cost of those materials which become an integral part of the specific product and those materials that are consumed in the ordinary course of manufacturing and can be identified or associated with particular units or groups of units of that product. See § 1.471-3 for the elements of direct material costs. Direct labor costs include the cost of labor which can be identified or associated with particular units or groups of units of a specific product. The elements of direct labor costs include such items as basic compensation, overtime pay, vacation and holiday pay, sick leave pay (other than payments pursuant to a wage continuation plan under section 105(d)), shift differential, payroll taxes and payments to a supplemental unemployment benefit plan paid or incurred on behalf of employees engaged in direct labor. For the treatment of rework labor, scrap, spoilage costs, and any other costs not specifically described as direct production costs see § 1.471-11(c)(2).

(ii) Under the full absorption method, a taxpayer must take into account all items of direct production cost in his inventoriable costs. Nevertheless, a taxpayer will not be treated as using an incorrect method of inventory costing if he treats any direct production costs as indirect production costs, provided such costs are allocated to the taxpayer's ending inventory to the extent provided by paragraph (d) of this section. Thus, for example, a taxpayer may treat direct labor costs as part of indirect production costs (for example (by use of the conversion cost method), provided all such costs are allocated to ending inventory to the extent provided by paragraph (d) of this section.

*(3) Indirect production costs.* (i) In general. The term "indirect production costs" includes all costs which are incident to and necessary for production or manufacturing operations or processes other than direct production costs (as defined in subparagraph (2) of this paragraph). Indirect production costs may be classified as to kind or type in accordance with acceptable accounting principles so as to enable convenient identification with various production or manufacturing activities or functions and to facilitate reasonable groupings of such costs for purposes of determining unit product costs.

(ii) Fixed and variable classifications. For purposes of this section, fixed indirect production costs are generally those costs which do not vary significantly with changes in the amount of goods produced at any given level of production capacity. These fixed costs may include, among other costs, rent and property taxes on buildings and machinery incident to and necessary for manufacturing operations or processes. On the other hand, variable indirect production costs are generally those costs which do vary significantly with changes in the amount of goods produced at any given level of production capacity. These variable costs may include, among other costs, indirect materials, factory janitorial supplies, and utilities. Where a particular cost contains both fixed and variable elements, these elements should be segregated into fixed and variable classifications to the extent necessary under the taxpayer's method of allocation, such as for the application of the practical capacity concept (as described in paragraph (d)(4) of this section).

**(c) Certain indirect and production costs.** *(1) General rule.* Except as provided in paragraph (c)(3) of this section and in paragraph (d)(6)(v) of § 1.451-3, in order to determine whether indirect production costs referred to in paragraph (b) of this section must be included in a taxpayer's computation of the amount of inventoriable costs, three categories of costs have been provided in subparagraph (2) of this paragraph. Costs described in subparagraph (2)(i) of this paragraph must be included in the taxpayer's computation of the amount of inventoriable costs, regardless of their treatment by the taxpayer in his financial reports. Costs described in subparagraph (2)(ii) of this paragraph need not enter into the taxpayer's computation of the amount of inventoriable costs, regardless of their treatment by the taxpayer in his financial reports. Costs described in subparagraph (2)(iii) of this paragraph must be included in or excluded from the taxpayer's computation of the amount inventoriable costs in accordance with the treatment of such costs by the taxpayer in his financial reports and generally accepted accounting principles. For the treatment of indirect production costs described in subparagraph (2) of this paragraph in the case of a taxpayer who is not using comparable methods of accounting for such costs for tax and financial reporting see paragraph (c)(3) of this section. For contracts entered into after December 31, 1982, notwithstanding this section, taxpayers who use an inventory method of accounting for extended period long-term contracts (as defined in paragraph (b)(3) of § 1.451-3) for tax purposes may be required to use the cost allocation rules provided in paragraph (d)(6) of § 1.451-3 rather than the cost allocation rules provided in this section. See paragraph (d)(6)(v) of § 1.451-3. After a taxpayer has determined which costs must be treated as indirect production costs includible in the computation of the amount of inventoriable costs, such costs must be allocated to a taxpayer's ending inventory in a manner prescribed by paragraph (d) of this section.

*(2) Includibility of certain indirect production costs.* (i) Indirect production costs included in inventoriable costs. Indirect production costs which must enter into the computation of the amount of inventoriable costs (regardless of their treatment by a taxpayer in his financial reports) include:

(a) Repair expenses,

(b) Maintenance,

(c) Utilities, such as heat, power and light,

(d) Rent,

(e) Indirect labor and production supervisory wages, including basic compensation, overtime pay, vacation and holiday pay, sick leave pay (other than payments pursuant to a wage continuation plan under section 105(d), shift differential, payroll taxes and contributions to a supplemental unemployment benefit plan,

(f) Indirect materials and supplies,

(g) Tools and equipment not capitalized, and

(h) Costs of quality control and inspection,

to the extent, and only to the extent, such costs are incident to and necessary for production or manufacturing operations or processes.

(ii) Costs not included in inventoriable costs. Costs which are not required to be included for tax purposes in the computation of the amount of inventoriable costs (regardless of their treatment by a taxpayer in his financial reports) include:

(a) Marketing expenses,

(b) Advertising expenses,

(c) Selling expenses,

(d) Other distribution expenses,

(e) Interest,

(f) Research and experimental expenses including engineering and product development expenses,

(g) Losses under section 165 and the regulations thereunder,

(h) Percentage depletion in excess of cost depletion,

(i) Depreciation and amortization reported for Federal income tax purposes in excess of depreciation reported by the taxpayer in his financial reports,

(j) Income taxes attributable to income received on the sale of inventory,

(k) Pension contributions to the extent that they represent past services costs,

(l) General and administrative expenses incident to and necessary for the taxpayer's activities as a whole rather than to production or manufacturing operations or processes, and

(m) Salaries paid to officers attributable to the performance of services which are incident to and necessary for the taxpayer's activities taken as a whole rather than to production or manufacturing operations or processes.

Notwithstanding the preceding sentence, if a taxpayer consistently includes in his computation of the amount of inventoriable costs any of the costs described in the preceding sentence, a change in such method of inclusion shall be considered a change in method of accounting within the meaning of sections 446, 481, and paragraph (e)(4) of this section.

(iii) Indirect production: costs includible in inventoriable costs depending upon treatment in taxpayer's financial reports. In the case of costs listed in this subdivision, the inclusion or exclusion of such costs from the amount of inventoriable costs for purposes of a taxpayer's financial reports shall determine whether such costs must be included in or excluded from the computation of inventoriable costs for tax purposes, but only if such treatment is not inconsistent with generally accepted accounting principles. In the case of costs which are not included in subdivision (i) or (ii) of this subparagraph, nor listed in this subdivision, whether such costs must be included in or excluded from the computation of inventoriable costs for tax purposes depends upon the extent to which such costs are similar to costs included in subdivision (i) or (ii), and if such costs are dissimilar to costs in subdivision (i) or (ii), such costs shall be treated as included in or excludable from the amount of inventoriable costs in accordance with this subdivision.

The costs listed in this subdivision are:

(a) Taxes. Taxes otherwise allowable as a deduction under section 164 (other than State and local and foreign income taxes) attributable to assets incident to and necessary for production or manufacturing operations or processes. Thus, for example, the cost of State and local property taxes imposed on a factory or other production facility and any State and local taxes imposed on inventory must be included in or excluded from the computation of the amount of inventoriable costs for tax purposes depending upon their treatment by a taxpayer in his financial reports.

(b) Depreciation and depletion. Depreciation reported in financial reports and cost depletion on assets incident to and necessary for production or manufacturing operations or processes. In computing cost depletion under this section, the adjusted basis of such assets shall be reduced by cost depletion and not by percentage depletion taken thereon.

(c) Employee benefits. Pension and profit-sharing contributions representing current service costs otherwise allowable as a deduction under section 404, and other employee benefits incurred on behalf of labor incident to and necessary for production or manufacturing operations or processes. These other benefits include workmen's compensation expenses, payments under a wage continuation plan described in section 105(d), amounts of a type which would be includible in the gross income of employees under nonqualified pension, profit-sharing and stock bonus plans, premiums on life and health insurance and miscellaneous benefits provided for employees such as safety, medical treatment, cafeteria, recreational facilities, membership dues, etc., which are otherwise allowable as deductions under chapter 1 of the Code.

(d) Costs attributable to strikes, rework labor, scrap and spoilage. Costs attributable to rework labor, scrap and spoilage which are incident to and necessary for production or manufacturing operations or processes and costs attributable to strikes incident to production or manufacturing operation or processes.

(e) Factory administrative expenses. Administrative costs of production (but not including any cost of selling or any return on capital) incident to and necessary for production or manufacturing operations or processes.

(f) Officers' salaries. Salaries paid to officers attributable to services performed incident to and necessary for production or manufacturing operations or processes.

(g) Insurance costs. Insurance costs incident to and necessary for production or manufacturing operations or processes such as insurance on production machinery and equipment.

A change in the taxpayer's treatment in his financial reports of costs described in this subdivision which results in a change in treatment of such costs for tax purposes shall constitute a change in method of accounting within the meaning of sections 446 and 481 to which paragraph (e) applies.

*(3) Exception.* Except as provided in paragraph (d)(6) of § 1.451-3, in the case of a taxpayer whose method of accounting for production costs in his financial reports is not comparable to his method of accounting for such costs for tax purposes (such as a taxpayer using the prime cost method for purposes of financial reports), the following rules apply:

(i) Indirect production costs included in inventoriable costs. Indirect production costs which must enter into the computation of the amount of inventoriable costs (to the extent, and only to the extent, such costs are incident to and necessary for production or manufacturing operations or processes) include:

(a) Repair expenses,

(b) Maintenance,

(c) Utilities, such as heat, power and light,

(d) Rent,

(e) Indirect labor and production supervisory wages, including basic compensation, overtime pay, vacation and holiday pay, sick leave pay (other than payments pursuant to a wage continuation plan under section 105(d)), shift differential, payroll taxes and contributions to a supplemental unemployment benefit plan,

(f) Indirect materials and supplies,

(g) Tools and equipment not capitalized,

(h) Costs of quality control and inspection,

(i) Taxes otherwise allowable as a deduction under section 164 (other than State and local and foreign income taxes.),

(j) Depreciation and amortization reported for financial purposes and cost depletion,

(k) Administrative costs of production (but not including any cost of selling or any return on capital) incident to and necessary for production or manufacturing operations or processes,

(l) Salaries paid to officers attributable to services performed incident to and necessary for production or manufacturing operations or processes, and

(m) Insurance costs incident to and necessary for production or manufacturing operations or processes such as insurance on production machinery and equipment.

(ii) Costs not included in inventoriable costs. Costs which are not required to be included in the computation of the amount of inventoriable costs include:

(a) Marketing expenses,

(b) Advertising expenses,

(c) Selling expenses,

(d) Other distribution expenses,

(e) Interest,

(f) Research and experimental expenses including engineering and product development expenses,

(g) Losses under section 165 and the regulations thereunder,

(h) Percentage depletion in excess of cost depletion,

(i) Depreciation reported for Federal income tax purposes in excess of depreciation reported by the taxpayer in his financial reports,

(j) Income taxes attributable to income received on the sale of inventory,

(k) Pension and profit-sharing contributions representing either past service costs or representing current service costs otherwise allowable as a deduction under section 404, and other employee benefits incurred on behalf of labor. These other benefits include workmen's compensation expenses, payments under a wage continuation plan described in section 105(d), amounts of a type which would be includible in the gross income of employees under nonqualified pension, profit-sharing and stock bonus plans, premiums on life and health insurance and miscellaneous benefits provided for employees such as safety, medical treatment, cafeteria, recreational facilities, membership dues, etc., which are otherwise allowable as deductions under chapter 1 of the Code,

(l) Cost attributable to strikes, rework labor, scrap and spoilage,

(m) General and administrative expenses incident to and necessary for the taxpayer's activities as a whole rather than to production or manufacturing operations or processes, and

(n) Salaries paid to officers attributable to the performance of services which are incident to and necessary for the taxpayer's activities as a whole rather than to production or manufacturing operations or processes.

**(d) Allocation methods.** *(1) In general.* Indirect production costs required to be included in the computation of the amount of inventoriable costs pursuant to paragraphs (b) and (c) of this paragraph must be allocated to goods in a taxpayer's ending inventory (determined in accordance with the taxpayer's method of identification) by the use of a method of allocation which fairly apportions such costs among the various items produced. Acceptable methods for allocating indirect production costs to the cost of goods in the ending inventory include the manufacturing burden rate method and the standard cost method. In addition, the practical capacity concept can be used in conjunction with either the manufacturing burden rate or standard cost method.

*(2) Manufacturing burden rate method.* (i) In general. Manufacturing burden rates may be developed in accordance with acceptable accounting principles and applied in a reasonable manner. In developing a manufacturing burden rate, the factors described in paragraph (d)(2)(ii) of this section may be taken into account. Furthermore, if the taxpayer chooses, he may allocate different indirect production costs on the basis of different manufacturing burden rates. Thus, for example, the taxpayer may use one burden rate for allocating rent and another burden rate for allocating utilities. The method used by the taxpayer in allocating such costs in his financial reports shall be given great weight in determining whether the taxpayer's method employed for tax purposes fairly allocates indirect production costs to the ending inventory. Any change in a manufacturing burden rate which is merely a periodic adjustment to reflect current operating conditions, such as increases in automation or changes in operation, does not constitute a change in method of accounting under section 446. However, a change in the concept upon which such rates are developed does constitute a change in method of accounting requiring the consent of the Commissioner. The taxpayer shall maintain adequate records and working papers to support all manufacturing burden rate calculations.

(ii) Development of manufacturing burden rate. The following factors, among others, may be taken into account in developing manufacturing burden rates:

(a) The selection of an appropriate level of activity and period of time upon which to base the calculation of rates which will reflect operating conditions for purposes of the unit costs being determined;

(b) The selection of an appropriate statistical base such as direct labor hours, direct labor dollars, or machine hours, or a combination thereof, upon which to apply the overhead rate to determine production costs; and

(c) The appropriate budgeting, classification and analysis of expenses (for example, the analysis of fixed and variable costs).

(iii) Operation of the manufacturing burden rate method (a) The purpose of the manufacturing burden rate method used in conjunction with the full absorption method of inventory costing is to allocate an appropriate amount of indirect production costs to a taxpayer's goods in ending inventory by the use of predetermined rates intended to approximate the actual amount of indirect production costs incurred. Accordingly, the proper use of the manufacturing burden rate method under this section requires that any net negative or net positive difference between the total predetermined amount of indirect production costs allocated to the goods in ending inventory and the total amount of indirect production costs actually incurred and required to be allocated to such goods (i.e., the under or over-applied burden) must be treated as an adjustment to the taxpayer's ending inventory in the taxable year in which such difference arises. However, if such adjustment is not significant in amount in relation to the taxpayer's total actual indirect production costs for the year then such adjustment need not be allocated to the taxpayer's goods in ending inventory unless such allocation is made in the taxpayer's financial reports. The taxpayer must treat both positive and negative adjustments consistently.

(b) Notwithstanding subdivision (a), the practical capacity concept may be used to determine the total amount of fixed indirect production costs which must be allocated to goods in ending inventory. See subparagraph (4) of this paragraph.

*(3) Standard cost method.* (i) In general. A taxpayer may use the so-called "standard cost" method of allocating inventoriable costs to the goods in ending inventory, provided he treats variances in accordance with the procedures prescribed in paragraph (d)(3)(ii) of this section. The method used by the taxpayer in allocating such costs in his financial reports shall be given great weight in determining whether the taxpayer's method employed for tax purposes fairly allocates indirect production costs to the ending inventory. For purposes of this subparagraph, a "net positive overhead variance" shall mean the excess of total standard (or estimated) indirect production costs over total actual indirect production costs and a "net negative overhead variance" shall mean the excess of total actual indirect production costs over total standard (or estimated) indirect production costs.

(ii) Treatment of variances. (a) The proper use of the standard cost method pursuant to this subparagraph requires that a taxpayer must reallocate to the goods in ending inventory a pro rata portion of any net negative or net positive overhead variances and any net negative or net positive direct production cost variances. The taxpayer must apportion such variances among his various items in ending inventory. However, if such variances are not significant in amount in relation to the taxpayer's total actual indirect production costs for the year then such variances need not be allocated to the taxpayer's goods in ending inventory unless such allocation is made in the taxpayer's financial reports. The taxpayer must treat both positive and negative variances consistently.

(b) Notwithstanding subdivision (a), the practical capacity concept may be used to determine the total amount of fixed indirect production costs which must be allocated to goods in ending inventory. See subparagraph (4) of this paragraph.

*(4) Practical capacity concept.* (i) In general. Under the practical capacity concept, the percentage of practical capacity represented by actual production (not greater than 100 percent), as calculated under subdivision (ii) of this subparagraph, is used to determine the total amount of fixed indirect production costs which must be included in the taxpayer's computation of the amount of inventoriable costs. The portion of such costs to be included in the taxpayer's computation of the amount of inventoriable costs is then combined with variable indirect production costs and both are allocated to the goods in ending inventory in accordance with this par-

agraph. See the example in subdivision (ii)(d) of this subparagraph. The difference (if any) between the amount of all fixed indirect production costs and the fixed indirect production costs which are included in the computation of the amount of inventoriable costs under the practical capacity concept is allowable as a deduction for the taxable year in which such difference occurs.

(ii) Calculation of practical capacity. (a) In general. Practical capacity and theoretical capacity (as described in (c) of this subdivision) may be computed in terms of tons, pounds, yards, labor hours, machine hours, or any other unit of production appropriate to the cost accounting system used by a particular taxpayer. The determination of practical capacity and theoretical capacity should be modified from time to time to reflect a change in underlying facts and conditions such as increased output due to automation or other changes in plant operation. Such a change does not constitute a change in method of accounting under sections 446 and 481.

(b) Based upon taxpayer's experience. In selecting an appropriate level of production activity upon which to base the calculation of practical capacity, the taxpayer shall establish the production operating conditions expected during the period for which the costs are being determined, assuming that the utilization of production facilities during operations will be approximately at capacity. This level of production activity is frequently described as practical capacity for the period and is ordinarily based upon the historical experience of the taxpayer. For example, a taxpayer operating on a 5-day, 8-hour basis may have a "normal" production of 100,000 units a year based upon three years of experience.

(c) Based upon theoretical capacity. Practical capacity may also be established by the use of "theoretical" capacity, adjusted for allowances for estimated inability to achieve maximum production, such as machine breakdown, idle time, and other normal work stoppages. Theoretical capacity is the level of production the manufacturer could reach if all machines and departments were operated continuously at peak efficiency.

(d) Example. The provisions of (c) of this subdivision may be illustrated by the following example:

Corporation X operates a stamping plant with a theoretical capacity of 50 units per hour. The plant actually operates 1960 hours per year based on an 8-hour day, 5 day week basis and 15 shut-down days for vacations and holidays. A reasonable allowance for down time (the time allowed for ordinary and necessary repairs and maintenance) is 5 percent of practical capacity before reduction for down time. Assuming no loss of production during starting up, closing down, or employee work breaks, under these facts and circumstances X may properly make a practical capacity computation as follows:

| | |
|---|---|
| Practical capacity without allowance for down time based on theoretical capacity per hour is (1900 × 50) | 98,000 |
| Reduction for down time (98,000 × 5 percent) | 4,900 |
| Practical capacity | 93,100 |

The 93,100 unit level of activity (i.e., practical capacity) would, therefore, constitute an appropriate base for calculating the amount of fixed indirect production costs to be included in the computation of the amount of inventoriable costs for the period under review. On this basis if only 76,000 units were produced for the period, the effect would be that approximately 81.6 percent (76,000, the actual number of units produced, divided by 93,100, the maximum number of units producible at practical capacity) of the fixed indirect production costs would be included in the computation of the amount of inventoriable costs during the year. The portion of the fixed indirect production costs not so included in the computation of the amount of inventoriable costs would be deductible in the year in which paid or incurred. Assume further that 7,600 units were on hand at the end of the taxable year and the 7,600 units were in the same proportion to the total units produced. Thus, 10 percent (7,600 units in inventory at the end of the taxable year, divided by 76,000, the actual number of units produced) of the fixed indirect production costs included in the computation of the amount of inventoriable costs (the above-mentioned 81.6 percent) and 10 percent of the variable indirect production costs would be included in the cost of the goods in the ending inventory, in accordance with a method of allocation provided by this paragraph.

**(e) Transition to full absorption method of inventory costing.** *(1) In general.* (i) Mandatory requirement. A taxpayer not using the full absorption method of inventory costing, as prescribed by paragraph (a) of this section, must change to that method. Any change to the full absorption method must be made by the taxpayer with respect to all trades or businesses of the taxpayer to which this section applies. A taxpayer not using the full absorption method of inventory costing, as prescribed by paragraph (a) of this section, who makes the special election provided in subdivision (ii) of this subparagraph during the transition period described in subdivision (ii) of this subparagraph need not change to the full absorption method of inventory costing for taxable years prior to the year for which such election is made. In determining whether the taxpayer is changing to a more or less inclusive method of inventory costing, all positive and negative adjustments for all items and all trades or businesses of the taxpayer shall be aggregated. If the net adjustment is positive, paragraph (e)(3) shall apply, and if the net adjustment is negative, paragraph (e)(4) shall apply to the change. The rules otherwise prescribed in sections 446 and 481 and the regulations thereunder shall apply to any taxpayer who fails to make the special election in subdivision (ii) of this subparagraph. The transition rules of this paragraph are available only to those taxpayers who change their method of inventory costing.

(ii) Special election during two-year-transition period. If a taxpayer elects to change to the full absorption method of inventory costing during the transition period provided herein, he may elect on Form 3115 to change to such full absorption method of inventory costing and, in so doing, employ the transition procedures and adopt any of the transition methods prescribed in subparagraph (3) of this paragraph. Such election shall be made during the first 180 days of any taxable year beginning on or after September 19, 1973 and before September 19, 1975 (i.e., the "transition period") and the change in inventory costing method shall be made for the taxable year in which the election is made. Notwithstanding the preceding sentence if the taxpayer's prior returns have been examined by the Service prior to September 19, 1973, and there is a pending issue involving the taxpayer's method of inventory costing, the taxpayer may request the application of this regulation by agreeing and filing a letter to that effect with the district director, within 90 days after September 19, 1973 to change to the full absorption method for the first taxable year of the taxpayer beginning after September 19, 1973 and subsequently filing Form 3115 within the first 180 days of such taxable year of change.

(iii) Change initiated by the Commissioner. A taxpayer who properly makes an election under subdivision (ii) of this subparagraph shall be considered to have made a change in method of accounting not initiated by the taxpayer, notwithstanding the provisions of § 1.481-1(c)(5). Thus, any of the taxpayer's "pre-1954 inventory balances" with respect to such inventory shall not be taken into account as an adjustment under section 481. For purposes of this paragraph, a "pre-1954 inventory balance" is the net amount of the adjustments which would have been required if the taxpayer had made such change in his method of accounting with respect to his inventory in his first taxable year which began after December 31, 1953, and ended after August 16, 1954. See section 481(a)(2) and § 1.481-3.

*(2) Procedural rules for change.* If a taxpayer makes an election pursuant to subparagraph (1)(ii) of this paragraph, the Commissioner's consent will be evidenced by a letter of consent to the taxpayer, setting forth the values of inventory, as provided by the taxpayer, determined under the full absorption method of inventory costing, except to the extent that no determination of such values is necessary under subparagraph (3)(ii)(B) of this paragraph (the cut off method), the amount of the adjustments (if any) required to be taken into account by section 481, and the treatment to be accorded to any such adjustments. Such full absorption values shall be subject to verification on examination by the district director. The taxpayer shall preserve at his principal place of business all records, data, and other evidence relating to the full absorption values of inventory.

(3) Transition methods. In the case of a taxpayer who properly makes an election under subparagraph (1)(ii) of this paragraph during the transition period—

(i) 10-year adjustment period. Such taxpayer may elect to take any adjustment required by section 481 with respect to any inventory being revalued under the full absorption method into account ratably over a period designated by the taxpayer at the time of such election, not to exceed the lesser of 10 taxable years commencing with the year of transition or the number of years the taxpayer has been on the inventory method from which he is changing. If the taxpayer dies or ceases to exist in a transaction other than one to which section 381(a) of the Code applies or if the taxpayer's inventory (determined under the full absorption method) on the last day of any taxable year is reduced (by other than a strike or involuntary conversion) by more than an amount equal to 33⅓ percent of the taxpayer's inventory (determined under the full absorption method) as of the beginning of the year of change, the entire amount of the section 481 adjustment not previously taken into account in computing income shall be taken into account in computing income for the taxable year in which such taxpayer so ceases to exist or such taxpayer's inventory is so reduced.

(ii) Additional rules for LIFO taxpayers. A taxpayer who uses the LIFO method of inventory identification may either—

(a) Employ the special transition rules described in subdivision (i) of this subparagraph. Accordingly, all LIFO layers must be revalued under the full absorption method and the section 481 adjustment must be computed for all items in all layers in inventory, but no pre-1954 inventory balances shall be taken into account as adjustments under section 481; or

(b) (1) Employ a cut-off method whereby the full absorption method is only applied in costing layers of inventory acquired during all taxable years beginning with the year for which an election is made under subparagraph (e)(1)(ii).

(2) In the case of a taxpayer using dollar value LIFO, employ a cut-off method whereby the taxpayer must use, for the year of change, the full absorption method in computing the base year cost and current cost of a dollar value inventory pool for the beginning of such year. The taxpayer shall not be required to recompute his LIFO inventories based on the full absorption method for a taxable year beginning prior to the year of change to the full absorption method. The base cost and layers of increment previously computed shall be retained and treated as if such base cost and layers of increment had been computed under the method authorized by this section. The taxpayer shall use the year of change as the base year in applying the double extension method or other method approved by the Commissioner, instead of the earliest year for which he adopted the LIFO method for any items in the pool.

*(4) Transition to full absorption method of inventory costing from a method more inclusive of indirect production costs.* (i) Taxpayer has not previously changed to his present method pursuant to subparagraphs (1), (2), and (3) of this paragraph. If a taxpayer wishes to change to the full absorption method of inventory costing (as prescribed by paragraph (a) of this section) from a method of inventory costing which is more inclusive of indirect production costs and he has not previously changed to his present method by use of the special transition rules provided by subparagraphs (1), (2) and (3) of this paragraph, he may elect on Form 3115 to change to the full absorption method of inventory costing and, in so doing, take into account any resulting section 481 adjustment generally over 10 taxable years commencing with the year of transition. The Commissioner's consent to such election will be evidenced by a letter of consent to the taxpayer setting forth the values of inventory, as provided by the taxpayer determined under the full absorption method of inventory costing, except to the extent that no determination of such values is necessary under subparagraph (3)(ii)(b) of this paragraph, the amount of the adjustments (if any) required to be taken into account by section 481, and the treatment to be accorded such adjustments, subject to terms and conditions specified by the Commissioner to prevent distortions of income. Such election must be made within the transition period described in subparagraph (1)(ii) of this paragraph. A change pursuant to this subparagraph shall be a change initiated by the taxpayer as provided by § 1.481-1(c)(5). Thus, any of the taxpayers "pre-1954 inventory balances" will be taken into account as an adjustment under section 481.

(ii) Taxpayer has previously changed to his present method pursuant to subparagraphs (1), (2), and (3) of this paragraph or would satisfy all the requirements of subdivision (i) of this subparagraph but fails to elect within the transition period. If a taxpayer wishes to change to the full absorption method of inventory costing (as prescribed by paragraph (a) of this section) from a method of inventory costing which is more inclusive of indirect production costs and he has previously changed to his present method pursuant to subparagraphs (1), (2), and (3) of this paragraph or he would satisfy the requirements of subdivision (i) of this subparagraph but he fails to elect within the transition period, he must secure the consent of the Commissioner prior to making such change.

---

T.D. 7285, 9/14/73, amend T.D. 8067, 12/30/85, T.D. 8131, 3/24/87, T.D. 8482, 8/6/93.

---

**Proposed § 1.471-12 Nonfinancial customer paper.** [*For Preamble, see ¶ 151,953*]

Nonfinancial customer paper, as defined in section 475(c)(4)(B), may not be treated as inventory except as provided in § 1.475(c)-2(d). This section applies to taxable years ending on or after January 28, 1999.

**§ 1.472-1 Last-in, first-out inventories.**

**(a)** Any taxpayer permitted or required to take inventories pursuant to the provisions of section 471, and pursuant to the provisions of §§ 1.471-1 to 1.471-9, inclusive, may elect with respect to those goods specified in his application and properly subject to inventory to compute his opening and closing inventories in accordance with the method provided by section 472, this section, and § 1.472-2. Under this last-in, first-out (LIFO) inventory method, the taxpayer is permitted to treat those goods remaining on hand at the close of the taxable year as being:

*(1)* Those included in the opening inventory of the taxable year, in the order of acquisition and to the extent thereof, and

*(2)* Those acquired during the taxable year.

The LIFO inventory method is not dependent upon the character of the business in which the taxpayer is engaged, or upon the identity or want of identity through commingling of any of the goods on hand, and may be adopted by the taxpayer as of the close of any taxable year.

**(b)** If the LIFO inventory method is used by a taxpayer who regularly and consistently, in a manner similar to hedging on a futures market, matches purchases with sales, then firm purchases and sales contracts (i.e., those not legally subject to cancellation by either party) entered into at fixed prices on or before the date of the inventory may be included in purchases or sales, as the case may be, for the purpose of determining the cost of goods sold and the resulting profit or loss, provided that this practice is regularly and consistently adhered to by the taxpayer and provided that, in the opinion of the Commissioner, income is clearly reflected thereby.

**(c)** A manufacturer or processor who has adopted the LIFO inventory method as to a class of goods may elect to have such method apply to the raw materials only (including those included in goods in process and in finished goods) expressed in terms of appropriate units. If such method is adopted, the adjustments are confined to costs of the raw material in the inventory and the cost of the raw material in goods in process and in finished goods produced by such manufacturer or processor and reflected in the inventory. The provisions of this paragraph may be illustrated by the following examples:

*Example (1).* Assume that the opening inventory had 10 units of raw material, 10 units of goods in process, and 10 units of finished goods, and that the raw material cost was 6 cents a unit, the processing cost 2 cents a unit, and overhead cost 1 cent a unit. For the purposes of this example, it is assumed that the entire amount of goods in process was 50 percent processed.

**Opening Inventory**

| | Raw material | Goods in process | Finished goods |
|---|---|---|---|
| Raw material | $0.60 | $0.60 | $0.60 |
| Processing cost | | .10 | .20 |
| Overhead | | .05 | .10 |

In the closing inventory there are 20 units of raw material, 6 units of goods in process, and 8 units of finished goods and the costs were: Raw material 10 cents, processing cost 4 cents, and overhead 1 cent.

**Closing Inventory (Based On Cost And Prior To Adjustment)**

| | Raw material | Goods in process | Finished goods |
|---|---|---|---|
| Raw material | $2.00 | $0.60 | $0.80 |
| Processing costs | | .12 | .32 |
| Overhead | | .03 | .08 |
| Total | 2.00 | .75 | 1.20 |

There were 30 units of raw material in the opening inventory and 34 units in the closing inventory. The adjustment to the closing inventory would be as follows:

**Closing Inventory As Adjusted**

| | Raw material | Goods in process | Finished goods |
|---|---|---|---|
| Raw materials: | | | |
| 20 at 6 cents | $1.20 | | |
| 6 at 6 cents | | $0.36 | |
| 4 at 6 cents | | | $0.24 |
| 4 at 10 cents[1] | | | .40 |
| Processing costs | | .12 | .32 |
| Overhead | | .03 | .08 |
| Total | 1.20 | .51 | 1.04 |

[1] This excess is subject to determination of price under section 472(b)(1) and § 1.472-2. If the excess falls in goods in process, the same adjustment is applicable.

The only adjustment to the closing inventory is the cost of the raw material; the processing costs and overhead cost are not changed.

*Example (2).* Assume that the opening inventory had 5 units of raw material, 10 units of goods in process, and 20 units of finished goods, with the same prices as in example (1), and that the closing inventory had 20 units of raw material, 20 units of goods in process, and 10 units of finished goods, with raw material costs as in the closing inventory in example (1). The adjusted closing inventory would be as follows in so far as the raw material is concerned:

| | |
|---|---|
| Raw material, 20 at 6 cents | $1.20 |
| Goods in process: | |
| 15 at 6 cents | .90 |
| 5 at 10 cents[1] | .50 |
| Finished goods: | |
| None at 6 cents | .00 |
| 10 at 10 cents[1] | 1.00 |

[1] This excess is subject to determination of price under section 472(b)(1) and § 1.472-2.

The 20 units of raw material in the raw state plus 15 units of raw material in goods in process make up the 35 units of raw material that were contained in the opening inventory.

**(d)** For the purposes of this section, raw material in the opening inventory must be compared with similar raw material in the closing inventory. There may be several types of raw materials, depending upon the character, quality, or price, and each type of raw material in the opening inventory must be compared with a similar type in the closing inventory.

**(e)** In the cotton textile industry there may be different raw materials depending upon marked differences in length of staple, in color or grade of the cotton. But where different staple lengths or grades of cotton are being used at different times in the same mill to produce the same class of goods, such differences would not necessarily require the classification into different raw materials.

**(f)** As to the pork packing industry a live hog is considered as being composed of various raw materials, different cuts of a hog varying markedly in price and use. Generally a hog is processed into approximately 10 primal cuts and several miscellaneous articles. However, due to similarity in price and use, these may be grouped into fewer classifications, each group being classed as one raw material.

**(g)** When the finished product contains two or more different raw materials as in the case of cotton and rayon mixtures, each raw material is treated separately and adjustments made accordingly.

**(h)** Upon written notice addressed to the Commissioner of Internal Revenue, Attention T:R, Washington 25, D. C., by the taxpayer, a taxpayer who has heretofore adopted the LIFO inventory method in respect of any goods may adopt the method authorized in this section and limit the election to the raw material including raw materials entering into goods in process and in finished goods. If this method is adopted as to any specific goods, it must be used exclusively for such goods for any prior taxable year (not closed by agreement) to which the prior election applies and for all subsequent taxable years, unless permission to change is granted by the Commissioner.

**(i)** The election may also be limited to that phase in the manufacturing process where a product is produced that is recognized generally as a salable product as, for example, in the textile industry where one phase of the process is the production of yarn. Since yarn is generally recognized as a salable product, the election may be limited to that portion of the process when yarn is produced. In the case of copper and brass processors, the election may be limited to the production of bars, plates, sheets, etc., although these may be further processed into other products.

**(j)** The election may also apply to any one raw material, when two or more raw materials enter into the composition of the finished product; for example, in the case of cotton and rayon yarn, the taxpayer may elect to inventory the cotton only. However, a taxpayer who has previously made an election to use the LIFO inventory method may not later elect to exclude any raw materials that were covered by such previous election.

**(k)** If a taxpayer using the retail method of pricing inventories, authorized by § 1.471-8, elects to use in connection therewith the LIFO inventory method authorized by section 472 and this section, the apparent cost of the goods on hand at the end of the year, determined pursuant to § 1.471-8, shall be adjusted to the extent of price changes therein taking place after the close of the preceding taxable year. The amount of any apparent inventory increase or decrease to be eliminated in this adjustment shall be determined by reference to acceptable price indexes establishes to the satisfaction of the Commissioner. Price indexes prepared by the United States Bureau of Labor Statistics which are applicable to the goods in question will be considered acceptable to the Commissioner. Price indexes which are based upon inadequate records, or which are not subject to complete and detailed audit within the Internal Revenue Service, will not be approved.

**(l)** If a taxpayer uses consistently the so-called "dollar-value" method of pricing inventories, or any other method of computation established to the satisfaction of the Commissioner as reasonably adaptable to the purpose and intent of section 472 and this section, and if such taxpayer elects under section 472 to use the LIFO inventory method authorized by such section, the taxpayer's opening and closing inventories shall be determined under section 472 by the use of the appropriate adaptation. See § 1.472-8 for rules relating to the use of the dollar-value method.

T.D. 6336, 12/1/58, amend T.D. 6539, 1/19/61.

### § 1.472-2 Requirements incident to adoption and use of LIFO inventory method.

Except as otherwise provided in § 1.472-1 with respect to raw material computations, with respect to retail inventory computations, and with respect to other methods of computation established to the satisfaction of the Commissioner as reasonably adapted to the purpose and intent of section 472, and in § 1.472-8 with respect to the "dollar-value" method, the adoption and use of the LIFO inventory method is subject to the following requirements:

**(a)** The taxpayer shall file an application to use such method specifying with particularity the goods to which it is to be applied.

**(b)** The inventory shall be taken at cost regardless of market value.

**(c)** Goods of the specified type included in the opening inventory of the taxable year for which the method is first used shall be considered as having been acquired at the same time and at a unit cost equal to the actual cost of the aggregate divided by the number of units on hand. The actual cost of the aggregate shall be determined pursuant to the inventory method employed by the taxpayer under the regulations applicable to the prior taxable year with the exception that restoration shall be made with respect to any writedown to market values resulting from the pricing of former inventories.

**(d)** Goods of the specified type on hand as of the close of the taxable year in excess of what were on hand as of the beginning of the taxable year shall be included in the closing inventory, regardless of identification with specific invoices and regardless of specific cost accounting records, at costs determined pursuant to the provisions of subparagraph (1) or (2) of this paragraph, dependent upon the character of the transactions in which the taxpayer is engaged:

*(1)* (i) In the case of a taxpayer engaged in the purchase and sale of merchandise, such as a retail grocer or druggist, or engaged in the initial production of merchandise and its sale without processing, such as a miner selling his ore output without smelting or refining, such costs shall be determined—

(a) By reference to the actual cost of the goods most recently purchased or produced;

(b) By reference to the actual cost of the goods purchased or produced during the taxable year in the order of acquisition;

(c) By application of an average unit cost equal to the aggregate cost of all of the goods purchased or produced throughout the taxable year divided by the total number of units so purchased or produced, the goods reflected in such inventory increase being considered for the purposes of section 472 as having been acquired all at the same time; or

(d) Pursuant to any other proper method which, in the opinion of the Commissioner, clearly reflects income.

(ii) Whichever of the several methods of valuing the inventory increase is adopted by the taxpayer and approved by the Commissioner shall be consistently adhered to in all subsequent taxable years so long as the LIFO inventory method is used by the taxpayer.

(iii) The application of subdivisions (i) and (ii) of this subparagraph may be illustrated by the following examples:

*Example (1).* Suppose that the taxpayer adopts the LIFO inventory method for the taxable year 1957 with an opening inventory of 10 units at 10 cents per unit, that it makes 1957 purchases of 10 units as follows:

| | | | |
|---|---|---|---|
| January | 1 at | $0.11 = | $0.11 |
| April | 2 at | .12 = | .24 |
| July | 3 at | .13 = | .39 |
| October | 4 at | .14 = | .56 |
| Totals | 10 | | 1.30 |

and that it has a 1957 closing inventory of 15 units. This closing inventory, depending upon the taxpayer's method of valuing inventory increases, will be computed as follows:

(a) Most recent purchases—

| | | | |
|---|---|---|---|
| 10 at | $0.10 | | $1.00 |
| 4 at | .14 | (October) | .56 |
| 1 at | .13 | (July) | .13 |
| Totals 15 | | | 1.69 |

or

(b) In order of acquisition—

| | | | |
|---|---|---|---|
| 10 at | $0.10 | | $1.00 |
| 1 at | .11 | (January) | .11 |
| 2 at | .12 | (April) | .24 |
| 2 at | .13 | (July) | .26 |
| Totals 15 | | | 1.61 |

or

(c) At an annual average—

| | | | |
|---|---|---|---|
| 10 at | $0.10 | | $1.00 |
| 5 at | .13 | (130/10) | .65 |
| Totals 15 | | | 1.65 |

*Example (2).* Suppose that the taxpayer's closing inventory for 1958, the year following that involved in example (1) of this subdivision, reflects an inventory decrease for the year, and not an increase; suppose that there is, accordingly, a 1958 closing inventory of 13 units. Inasmuch as the decreased closing inventory will be determined wholly by reference to the 15 units reflected in the opening inventory for the year, and will be taken "in the order of acquisition" pursuant to section 472(b)(1), and inasmuch as the character of the taxpayer's opening inventory for 1958 will be dependent upon its method of valuing its 5-unit inventory increase for 1957, the closing inventory for 1958 will be computed as follows:

(a) In case the increase for 1957 was taken by reference to the most recent purchases—

| | | | |
|---|---|---|---|
| 10 at | $0.10 | (from 1956) | $1.00 |
| 1 at | .13 | (July 1957) | .13 |
| 2 at | .14 | (October 1957) | .28 |
| Totals 13 | | | 1.41 |

or

(b) In case the increase for 1957 was taken in the order of acquisition—

| | | | |
|---|---|---|---|
| 10 at | $0.10 | (from 1956) | $1.00 |
| 1 at | .11 | (January 1957) | .11 |
| 2 at | .12 | (April 1957) | .24 |
| Totals 13 | | | 1.35 |

or

(c) In case the increase for 1957 was taken on the basis of an average—

| | | | |
|---|---|---|---|
| 10 at | $0.10 | (from 1956) | $1.00 |
| 3 at | .13 | (from 1957) | .39 |
| Totals 13 | | | 1.39 |

*(2)* In the case of a taxpayer engaged in manufacturing, fabricating, processing, or otherwise producing merchandise, such costs shall be determined:

(i) In the case of raw materials purchased or initially produced by the taxpayer, in the manner elected by the taxpayer under subparagraph (1) of this paragraph to the same extent as if the taxpayer were engaged in purchase and sale transactions; and

(ii) In the case of good in process, regardless of the stage to which the manufacture, fabricating, or processing may have advanced, and in the case of finished goods, pursuant to any proper method which, in the opinion of the Commissioner, clearly reflects income.

**(e) LIFO conformity requirement.** *(1) In general.* The taxpayer must establish to the satisfaction of the Commissioner that the taxpayer, in ascertaining the income, profit, or loss for the taxable year for which the LIFO inventory method is first used, or for any subsequent taxable year, for credit purposes or for purposes of reports to shareholders, partners, or other proprietors, or to beneficiaries, has not used any inventory method other than that referred to in § 1.472-1 or at variance with the requirement referred to in § 1.472-2(c). See paragraph (e)(2) of this section for rules relating to the meaning of the term "taxable year" as used in this paragraph. The following are not considered at variance with the requirement of this paragraph:

(i) The taxpayer's use of an inventory method other than LIFO for purposes of ascertaining information reported as a supplement to or explanation of the taxpayer's primary presentation of the taxpayer's income, profit, or loss for a taxable year in credit statements or financial reports (including preliminary and unaudited financial reports). See paragraph (e)(3) of this section for rules relating to the reporting of supplemental and explanatory information ascertained by the use of an inventory method other than LIFO.

(ii) The taxpayer's use of an inventory method other than LIFO to ascertain the value of the taxpayer's inventory of goods on hand for purposes of reporting the value of such inventories as assets. See paragraph (e)(4) of this section for rules relating to such disclosures.

(iii) The taxpayer's use of an inventory method other than LIFO for purposes of ascertaining information reported in internal management reports. See paragraph (e)(5) of this section for rules relating to such reports.

(iv) The taxpayer's use of an inventory method other than LIFO for purposes of issuing reports or credit statements covering a period of operations that is less than the whole of a taxable year for which the LIFO method is used for Federal income tax purposes. See paragraph (e)(6) of this section for rules relating to series of interim reports.

(v) The taxpayer's use of the lower of LIFO cost or market method to value LIFO inventories for purposes of financial reports and credit statements. However, except as provided in paragraph (e)(7) of this section, a taxpayer may not use market value in lieu of cost to value inventories for purposes of financial reports or credit statements.

(vi) The taxpayer's use of a costing method or accounting method to ascertain income, profit, or loss for credit purposes or for purposes of financial reports if such costing method or accounting method is neither inconsistent with the inventory method referred to in § 1.472-1 nor at variance with the requirement referred to in § 1.472-2(c), regardless of whether such costing method or accounting method is used by the taxpayer for Federal income tax purposes. See paragraph (e)(8) of this section for examples of such costing methods and accounting methods.

(vii) For credit purposes or for purposes of financial reports, the taxpayer's treatment of inventories, after such inventories have been acquired in a transaction to which section 351 applies from a transferor that used the LIFO method with respect to such inventories, as if such inventories had the same acquisition dates and costs as in the hands of the transferor.

(viii) For credit purposes or for purposes of financial reports relating to a taxable year, the taxpayer's determination of income, profit, or loss for the taxable year by valuing inventories in accordance with the procedures described in section 472(b)(1) and (3), notwithstanding that such valuation differs from the valuation of inventories for Federal income tax purposes because the taxpayer either—

(A) Adopted such procedures for credit or financial reporting purposes beginning with an accounting period other than the taxable year for which the LIFO method was first used by the taxpayer for Federal income tax purposes, or

(B) With respect to such inventories treated a business combination for credit or financial reporting purposes in a manner different from the treatment of the business combination for Federal income tax purposes.

*(2) One-year periods of other than a taxable year.* The rules of this paragraph relating to the determination of income, profit, or loss for a taxable year and credit statements or financial reports that cover a taxable year also apply to the determination of income, profit, or loss for a one-year period other than a taxable year and credit statements or financial reports that cover a one-year period other than a taxable year, but only if the one-year period both begins and ends in a taxable year or years for which the taxpayer uses the LIFO method for Federal income tax purposes. For example, the requirements of paragraph (e)(1) of this section apply to a taxpayer's determination of income for purposes of a credit statement that covers a 52-week fiscal year beginning and ending in a taxable year for which the taxpayer uses the LIFO method for Federal income tax purposes. Similarly, in the case of a calendar year taxpayer, the requirements of paragraph (e)(1) of this section apply to the taxpayer's determination of income for purposes of a credit statement that covers the period October 1, 1981, through September 30, 1982, if the taxpayer uses the LIFO method for Federal income tax purposes in taxable years 1981 and 1982. However, the Commissioner will waive any violation of the requirements of this paragraph in the case of a credit statement or financial report that covers a one-year period other than a taxable year if the report was issued before January 22, 1981.

*(3) Supplemental and explanatory information.* (i) Face of the income statement. Information reported on the face of a taxpayer's financial income statement for a taxable year is not considered a supplement to or explanation of the taxpayer's primary presentation of the taxpayer's income, profit, or loss for the taxable year in credit statements or financial reports. For purposes of paragraph (e)(3) of this section, the face of an income statement does not include notes to the income statement presented on the same page as the income statement, but only if all notes to the financial income statement are presented together.

(ii) Notes to the income statement. Information reported in notes to a taxpayer's financial income statement is considered a supplement to or explanation of the taxpayer's primary presentation of income, profit, or loss for the period covered by the income statement if all notes to the financial income statement are presented together and if they accompany the income statement in a single report. If notes to an income statement are issued in a report that does not include the income statement, the question of whether the information reported therein is supplemental or explanatory is determined under the rules in paragraph (e)(3)(iv) of this section.

(iii) Appendices and supplements to the income statement. Information reported in an appendix or supplement to a taxpayer's financial income statement is considered a supplement to or explanation of the taxpayer's primary presentation of income, profit, or loss for the period covered by the income statement if the appendix or supplement accompanies the income statement in a single report and the information reported in the appendix or supplement is clearly identified as a supplement to or explanation of the taxpayer's primary presentation of income, profit, or loss as reported on the face of the taxpayer's income statement. If an appendix or supplement to an income statement is issued in a report that does not include the income statement, the question of whether the information reported therein is supplemental or explanatory is determined under the rules in paragraph (e)(3)(iv) of this section. For purposes of paragraph (e)(3)(iii) of this section, an appendix or supplement to an income statement includes written statements, schedules, and reports that are labelled supplements or appendices to the income statement. However, sections of an annual report such as those labelled "President's Letter", "Management's Analysis", "Statement of Changes in Financial Position", "Summary of Key Figures", and similar sections are reports described in paragraph (e)(3)(iv) of this section and are not considered "supplements or appendices to an income statement within the meaning of paragraph (e)(3)(iii) of this section, regardless of whether such sections are also labelled as supplements or appendices. For purposes of paragraph (e)(3)(iii) of this section, information is considered to be clearly identified as a supplement to or explanation of the taxpayer's primary presentation of income, profit, or loss as reported on the face of the taxpayer's income statement if the information either—

(A) Is reported in an appendix or supplement that contains a general statement identifying all such supplemental or explanatory information;

(B) Is identified specifically as supplemental or explanatory by a statement immediately preceding or following the disclosure of the information;

(C) Is disclosed in the context of making a comparison to corresponding information disclosed both on the face of the taxpayer's income statement and in the supplement or appendix; or

(D) Is a disclosure of the effect on an item reported on the face of the taxpayer's income statement of having used the LIFO method.

For example, a restatement of cost of goods sold based on an inventory method other than LIFO is considered to be clearly identified as supplemental or explanatory information if the supplement or appendix containing the restatement contains a general statement that all information based on such inventory method is reported in the appendix or supplement as a supplement to or explanation of the taxpayer's primary presentation of income, profit, or loss as reported on the face of the taxpayer's income statement.

(iv) Other reports; in general. The rules of paragraph (e)(3)(iv), (v), and (vi) of this section apply to the following types of reports: news releases; letters to shareholders, partners, or other proprietors or beneficiaries; oral statements at press conferences, shareholders' meetings or securities analysts' meetings; sections of an annual report such as those labelled "President's Letter", "Management's Analysis", "Statement of Changes in Financial Position", "Summary of Key Figures", and similar sections; and reports other than a taxpayer's income statement or accompanying notes, appendices, or supplements. Information disclosed in such a report is considered a supplement to or explanation of the taxpayer's primary presentation of income, profit, or loss for the period covered by an income statement if the supplemental or explanatory information is clearly identified as a supplement to or explanation of the taxpayer's primary presentation of income, profit, or loss as reported on the face of the taxpayer's income statement and the specific item of information being explained or supplemented, such as the cost of goods sold, net income, or earnings per share ascertained using the LIFO method, is also reported in the other report.

(v) Other reports; disclosure of non-LIFO income. For purposes of paragraph (e)(3)(iv) of this section, supplemental or explanatory information is considered to have been clearly identified as such if it would be considered to have been clearly identified as such under the rules of paragraph (e)(3)(iii) of this section, relating to information reported in supplements or appendices to an income statement. For example, if at a securities analysts' meeting the following question is asked, "What would the reported earnings per share for the year have been if the FIFO method had been used to value inventories?", it would be permissible to respond "Reported earnings per share for the year were $6.00. If the company had used the FIFO method to value inventories this year and had computed earnings based upon the following assumptions, earnings per share would have been $8.20. FIFO earnings are based on the following assumptions:

"(A) The use of the same effective tax rate as used in computing LIFO earnings, and

"(B) All other conditions and assumptions remain the same, including—

"(1) The use of the LIFO method for Federal income tax purposes and

"(2) The investment of the tax savings resulting from such use of the LIFO method, the income from which is included in both LIFO and FIFO earnings."

(vi) Other reports; disclosure of effect on income. For purposes of paragraph (e)(3)(iv) of this section, if the only supplement to or explanation of a specific item is the effect on the item of having used LIFO instead of a method other than LIFO to value inventories, it is not necessary to also report the specific item. For example, if at a shareholders' meeting the question is asked, "What was the effect on reported earnings per share of not having used FIFO to value inventories?", it would be permissible to respond "If earnings would have been computed on the basis of the following assumptions, the use of LIFO instead of FIFO to value inventories would have decreased reported earnings per share by $2.20. FIFO earnings are based on the following assumptions:

(A) The use of the same effective tax rate as used in computing LIFO earnings, and

(B) All other conditions and assumptions remain the same, including—

(1) The use of the LIFO method for Federal income tax purposes and

(2) The investment of the tax savings resulting from such use of the LIFO method, the income from which is included in both LIFO and FIFO earnings.

*(4) Inventory asset value disclosures.* Under paragraph (e)(1)(ii) of this section, the use of an inventory method other than LIFO to ascertain the value of the taxpayer's inventories for purposes of reporting the value of the inventories as assets is not considered the ascertainment of income, profit, or loss and therefore is not considered at variance with the requirement of paragraph (e)(1) of this section. Therefore, a taxpayer may disclose the value of inventories on a balance sheet using a method other than LIFO to identify the inventories, and such a disclosure will not be considered at variance with the requirement of paragraph (e)(1) of this section. However, the disclosure of income, profit, or loss for a taxable year on a balance sheet issued to creditors, shareholders, partners, other proprietors, or beneficiaries is considered at variance with the requirement of paragraph (e)(1) of this section if such income information is ascertained using an inventory method other than LIFO and such income information is for a taxable year for which the LIFO method is used for Federal income tax purposes. Therefore, a balance sheet that discloses the net worth of a taxpayer, determined as if income had been ascertained using an inventory method other than LIFO, may be at variance with the requirement of paragraph (e)(1) of this section if the disclosure of net worth is made in a manner that also discloses income, profit, or loss for a taxable year.

However, a disclosure of income, profit, or loss using an inventory method other than LIFO is not considered at variance with the requirement of paragraph (e)(1) of this section if the disclosure is made in the form of either a footnote to the balance sheet or a parenthetical disclosure on the face of the balance sheet. In addition, an income disclosure is not considered at variance with the requirement of paragraph (e)(1) of this section if the disclosure is made on the face of a supplemental balance sheet labelled as a supplement to the taxpayer's primary presentation of financial position, but only if, consistent with the rules of paragraph (e)(3) of this section, such a disclosure is clearly identified as a supplement to or explanation of the taxpayer's primary presentation of financial income as reported on the face of the taxpayer's income statement.

*(5) Internal management reports. [Reserved]*

*(6) Series of interim reports.* For purposes of paragraph (e)(1)(iv) of this section, a series of credit statements or financial reports is considered a single statement or report covering a period of operations if the statements or reports in the series are prepared using a single inventory method and can be combined to disclose the income, profit, or loss for the period. However, the Commissioner will waive any violation of the requirement of this paragraph in the case of a series of interim reports issued before February 6, 1978, that cover a taxable year, or a series of interim reports is-

sued before January 22, 1981 that cover a one-year period other than a taxable year.

*(7) Market value.* The Commissioner will waive any violation of the requirement of this paragraph in the case of a taxpayer's use of market value in lieu of cost for a credit statement or financial report issued before January 22, 1981. However, the special rule of this (7) applies only to a taxpayer's use of market value in lieu of cost and does not apply to the use of a method of valuation such as market value in lieu of cost but not more than FIFO cost.

*(8) Use of different methods.* The following are examples of costing methods and accounting methods that are neither inconsistent with the inventory method referred to in § 1.472-1 nor at variance with the requirement of § 1.472-2(c) and which, under paragraph (e)(1)(vi) of this section, may be used to ascertain income, profit, or loss for credit purposes or for purposes of financial reports regardless of whether such method is also used by the taxpayer for Federal income tax purposes:

(i) Any method relating to the determination of which costs are includible in the computation of the cost of inventory under the full absorption inventory method.

(ii) Any method of establishing pools for inventory under the dollar-value LIFO inventory method.

(iii) Any method of determining the LIFO value of a dollar-value inventory pool, such as the double-extension method, the index method, and the link chain method.

(iv) Any method of determining or selecting a price index to be used with the index or link chain method of valuing inventory pools under the dollar-value LIFO inventory method.

(v) Any method permitted under § 1.472-8 for determining the current-year cost of closing inventory for purposes of using the dollar-value LIFO inventory method.

(vi) Any method permitted under § 1.472-2(d) for determining the cost of goods in excess of goods on hand at the beginning of the year for purposes of using a LIFO method other than the dollar-value LIFO method.

(vii) Any method relating to the classification of an item as inventory or a capital asset.

(viii) The use of an accounting period other than the period used for Federal income tax purposes.

(ix) The use of cost estimates.

(x) The use of actual cost of cut timber or the cost determined under section 631(a).

(xi) The use of inventory costs unreduced by any adjustment required by the application of section 108 and section 1017, relating to discharge of indebtedness.

(xii) The determination of the time when sales or purchases are accrued.

(xiii) The use of a method to allocate basis in the case of a business combination other than the method used for Federal income tax purposes.

(xiv) The treatment of transfers of inventory between affiliated corporations in a manner different from that required by § 1.1502-13.

*(9) Reconciliation of LIFO inventory values.* A taxpayer may be required to reconcile differences between the value of inventories maintained for credit or financial reporting purposes and for Federal income tax purposes in order to show that the taxpayer has satisfied the requirements of this paragraph.

**(f)** Goods of the specified type on hand as of the close of the taxable year preceding the taxable year for which this inventory method is first used shall be included in the taxpayer's closing inventory for such preceding taxable year at cost determined in the manner prescribed in paragraph (c) of this section.

**(g)** The LIFO inventory method, once adopted by the taxpayer with the approval of the Commissioner, shall be adhered to in all subsequent taxable years unless—

*(1)* A change to a different method is approved by the Commissioner; or

*(2)* The Commissioner determines that the taxpayer, in ascertaining income, profit, or loss for the whole of any taxable year subsequent to his adoption of the LIFO inventory method, for credit purposes or for the purpose of reports to shareholders, partners, or other proprietors, or to beneficiaries, has used any inventory method at variance with that referred to in § 1.472-1 and requires of the taxpayer a change to a different method for such subsequent taxable year or any taxable year thereafter.

**(h)** The records and accounts employed by the taxpayer in keeping his books shall be maintained in conformity with the inventory method referred to in § 1.472-1; and such supplemental and detailed inventory records shall be maintained as will enable the district director readily to verify the taxpayer's inventory computations as well as his compliance with the requirements of section 472 and §§ 1.472-1 through 1.472-7.

**(i)** Where the taxpayer is engaged in more than one trade or business, the Commissioner may require that if the LIFO method of valuing inventories is used with respect to goods in one trade or business the same method shall also be used with respect to similar goods in the other trades or businesses if, in the opinion of the Commissioner, the use of such method with respect to such other goods is essential to a clear reflection of income.

---

T.D. 6336, 12/1/58, amend T.D. 6539, 1/19/61, T.D. 7756, 1/16/81.

---

Section 1.472-2 is amended as follows:

1. Paragraph (c) is revised to read as set forth below.

2. Paragraph (f) is removed.

**Proposed § 1.472-2 Requirements incident to the adoption and use of LIFO Inventory method.** [*For Preamble, see ¶ 150,819*]

* * * * *

**(c)** *(1)* Goods of the specified type included in the opening inventory of the taxable year for which the method is first used shall be considered as having been acquired at the same time and at a unit cost equal to the actual cost of the aggregate divided by the number of units on hand. The actual cost of the aggregate shall be determined pursuant to the inventory method employed by the taxpayer under the regulations applicable to the prior taxable year with the exception that restoration to the opening inventory of the taxable year for which the LIFO method is first used shall be made with respect to any writedown to market values resulting from the pricing of former inventories.

*(2)* In the case of a taxpayer first using the LIFO method before January 1, 1982, goods of the specified type on hand as of the close of the taxable year preceding the taxable year for which this inventory method is first used shall be included in the taxpayer's closing inventory for such preceding

taxable year at a cost determined in the manner prescribed in paragraph (c)(1) of this section.

*(3) In the case of a taxpayer first using the LIFO method after December 31, 1981—*

(i) The amount arising from the restoration referred to in paragraph (c)(1) of this section shall be included in the taxpayer's gross income ratably in each of the three taxable years beginning with the taxable year for which the LIFO method is first used.

(ii) Neither an adjustment to the closing inventory nor an amended return shall be required for the taxable year preceding the taxable year for which the LIFO method is first used.

(iii) The provisions of paragraph (c)(3) of this section may be illustrated by the following example:

*Example.* X, a calendar year taxpayer, first adopts the LIFO method for 1982 and the closing inventory for 1981 included a writedown to market values of $9,000. Such writedown amount shall be restored to the 1982 opening inventory and $3,000 shall be included in X's gross income in each of the taxable years 1982, 1983, and 1984.

* * * * *

### § 1.472-3 Time and manner of making election.

**(a)** The LIFO inventory method may be adopted and used only if the taxpayer files with his income tax return for the taxable year as of the close of which the method is first to be used a statement of his election to use such inventory method. The statement shall be made on Form 970 pursuant to the instructions printed with respect thereto and to the requirements of this section, or in such other manner as may be acceptable to the Commissioner. Such statement shall be accompanied by an analysis of all inventories of the taxpayer as of the beginning and as of the end of the taxable year for which the LIFO inventory method is proposed first to be used, and also as of the beginning of the prior taxable year. In the case of a manufacturer, this analysis shall show in detail the manner in which costs are computed with respect to raw materials, goods in process, and finished goods, segregating the products (whether in process or finished goods) into natural groups on the basis of either (1) similarity in factory processes through which they pass, or (2) similarity of raw materials used, or (3) similarity in style, shape, or use of finished products. Each group of products shall be clearly described.

**(b)** The taxpayer shall submit for the consideration of the Commissioner in connection with the taxpayer's adoption or use of the LIFO inventory method such other detailed information with respect to his business or accounting system as may be at any time requested by the Commissioner.

**(c)** As a condition to the taxpayer's use of the LIFO inventory method, the Commissioner may require that the method be used with respect to goods other than those specified in the taxpayer's statement of election if, in the opinion of the Commissioner, the use of such method with respect to such other goods is essential to a clear reflection of income.

**(d)** Whether or not the taxpayer's application for the adoption and use of the LIFO inventory method should be approved, and whether or not such method, once adopted, may be continued, and the propriety of all computations incidental to the use of such method, will be determined by the Commissioner in connection with the examination of the taxpayer's income tax returns.

T.D. 6336, 12/1/58, amend T.D. 7295, 12/11/73.

### § 1.472-4 Adjustments to be made by taxpayer.

A taxpayer may not change to the LIFO method of taking inventories unless, at the time he files his application for the adoption of such method, he agrees to such adjustments incident to the change to or from such method, or incident to the use of such method, in the inventories of prior taxable years or otherwise, as the district director upon the examination of the taxpayer's returns may deem necessary in order that the true income of the taxpayer will be clearly reflected for the years involved.

T.D. 6336, 12/1/58.

### § 1.472-5 Revocation of election.

An election made to adopt and use the LIFO inventory method is irrevocable, and the method once adopted shall be used in all subsequent taxable years, unless the use of another method is required by the Commissioner, or authorized by him pursuant to a written application therefor filed as provided in paragraph (e) of § 1.446-1.

T.D. 6336, 12/1/58.

### § 1.472-6 Change from LIFO inventory method.

If the taxpayer is granted permission by the Commissioner to discontinue the use of LIFO method of taking inventories, and thereafter to use some other method, or if the taxpayer is required by the Commissioner to discontinue the use of the LIFO method by reason of the taxpayer's failure to conform to the requirements detailed in § 1.472-2, the inventory of the specified goods for the first taxable year affected by the change and for each taxable year thereafter shall be taken—

**(a)** In conformity with the method used by the taxpayer under section 471 in inventorying goods not included in his LIFO inventory computations; or

**(b)** If the LIFO inventory method was used by the taxpayer with respect to all of his goods subject to inventory, then in conformity with the inventory method used by the taxpayer prior to his adoption of the LIFO inventory method; or

**(c)** If the taxpayer had not used inventories prior to his adoption of the LIFO inventory method and had no goods currently subject to inventory by a method of than the LIFO inventory method, then in conformity with such inventory method as may be selected by the taxpayer and approved by the Commissioner as resulting in a clear reflection of income; or

**(d)** In any event, in conformity with any inventory method to which the taxpayer may change pursuant to application approved by the Commissioner.

T.D. 6336, 12/1/58.

### § 1.472-7 Inventories of acquiring corporations.

For additional rules in the case of certain corporate acquisitions specified in section 381(a), see section 381(c)(5) and the regulations thereunder.

T.D. 6336, 12/1/58.

### § 1.472-8 Dollar-value method of pricing LIFO inventories.

**(a) Election to use dollar-value method.** Any taxpayer may elect to determine the cost of his LIFO inventories under the so-called "dollar-value" LIFO method, provided such method is used consistently and clearly reflects the income of the taxpayer in accordance with the rules of this section. The dollar-value method of valuing LIFO inventories is a method of determining cost by using a "base-year" cost expressed in terms of total dollars rather than the quantity and price of specific goods as the unit of measurement. Under such method the goods contained in the inventory are grouped into a pool or pools as described in paragraphs (b) and (c) of this section. The term "base-year cost" is the aggregate of the cost (determined as of the beginning of the taxable year for which the LIFO method is first adopted, i.e., the base date) of all items in a pool. The taxable year for which the LIFO method is first adopted with respect to any item in the pool is the "base year" for that pool, except as provided in paragraph (g)(3) of this section. Liquidations and increments of items contained in the pool shall be reflected only in terms of a net liquidation or increment for the pool as a whole. Fluctuations may occur in quantities of various items within the pool, new items which properly fall within the pool may be added, and old items may disappear from the pool, all without necessarily effecting a change in the dollar value of the pool as a whole. An increment in the LIFO inventory occurs when the end of the year inventory for any pool expressed in terms of base-year cost is in excess of the beginning of the year inventory for that pool expressed in terms of base-year cost. In determining the inventory value for a pool, the increment, if any, is adjusted for changing unit costs or values by reference to a percentage, relative to base-year-cost, determined for the pool as a whole. See paragraph (e) of this section. See also paragraph (f) of this section for rules relating to the change to the dollar-value LIFO method from another LIFO method.

**(b) Principles for establishing pools of manufacturers and processors.** *(1) Natural business unit pools.* A pool shall consist of all items entering into the entire inventory investment for a natural business unit of a business enterprise, unless the taxpayer elects to use the multiple pooling method provided in subparagraph (3) of this paragraph. Thus, if a business enterprise is composed of only one natural business unit, one pool shall be used for all of its inventories, including raw materials, goods in process, and finished goods. If, however, a business enterprise is actually composed of more than one natural business unit, more than one pool is required. Where similar types of goods are inventoried in two or more natural business units of the taxpayer, the Commissioner may apportion or allocate such goods among the various natural business units, if he determines that such apportionment or allocation is necessary in order to clearly reflect the income of such taxpayer. Where a manufacturer or processor is also engaged in the wholesaling or retailing of goods purchased from others, any pooling of the LIFO inventory of such purchased goods for the wholesaling or retailing operations shall be determined in accordance with the rules of paragraph (c) of this section.

*(2) Definition of natural business unit.* (i) Whether an enterprise is composed of more than one natural business unit is a matter of fact to be determined from all the circumstances. The natural business divisions adopted by the taxpayer for internal management purposes, the existence of separate and distinct production facilities and processes, and the maintenance of separate profit and loss records with respect to separate operations are important considerations in determining what is a business unit, unless such divisions, facilities, or accounting records are set up merely because of differences in geographical location. In the case of a manufacturer or processor, a natural business unit ordinarily consists of the entire productive activity of the enterprise within one product line or within two or more related product lines including (to the extent engaged in by the enterprise) the obtaining of materials, the processing of materials, and the selling of manufactured or processed goods. Thus, in the case of a manufacturer or processor, the maintenance and operation of a raw material warehouse does not generally constitute, of itself, a natural business unit. If the taxpayer maintains and operates a supplier unit the production of which is both sold to others and transferred to a different unit of the taxpayer to be used as a component part of another product, the supplier unit will ordinarily constitute a separate and distinct natural business unit. Ordinarily, a processing plant would not in itself be considered a natural business unit if the production of the plant, although saleable at this stage, is not sold to others, but is transferred to another plant of the enterprise, not operated as a separate division, for further processing or incorporation into another product. On the other hand, if the production of a manufacturing or processing plant is transferred to a separate and distinct division of the taxpayer, which constitutes a natural business unit, the supplier unit itself will ordinarily be considered a natural business unit. However, the mere fact that a portion of the production of a manufacturing or processing plant may be sold to others at a certain stage of processing with the remainder of the production being further processed or incorporated into another product will not of itself be determinative that the activities devoted to the production of the portion sold constitute a separate business unit. Where a manufacturer or processor is also engaged in the wholesaling or retailing of goods purchased from others, the wholesaling or retailing operations with respect to such purchased goods shall not be considered a part of any manufacturing or processing unit.

(ii) The rules of this subparagraph may be illustrated by the following examples:

*Example (1).* A corporation manufacturers, in one division, automatic clothes washers and driers of both commercial and domestic grade as well as electric ranges, mangles, and dishwashers. The corporation manufactures, in another division, radios and television sets. The manufacturing facilities and processes used in manufacturing the radios and television sets are distinct from those used in manufacturing the automatic clothes washers, etc. Under these circumstances, the enterprise would consist of two business units and two pools would be appropriate, one consisting of all of the LIFO inventories entering into the manufacture of clothes washers and dries, electric ranges mangles, and dishwashers and the other consisting of all of the LIFO inventories entering into the production of radio and television sets.

*Example (2).* A taxpayer produces plastics in one of the its plants. Substantial amounts of the production are sold as plastics. The remainder of the production is shipped to a second plant of the taxpayer for the production of plastic toys which are sold to customers. The taxpayer operates his plastics plant and toy plant as separate divisions. Because of the different product lines and the separate divisions the taxpayer has two natural business units.

*Example (3).* A taxpayer is engaged in the manufacture of paper. At one stage of processing, uncoated paper is produced. Substantial amounts of uncoated paper are sold at this stage of processing. The remainder of the uncoated paper is transferred to the taxpayer's finishing mill where coated paper is produced and sold. This taxpayer has only one natural business unit since coated and uncoated paper are within the same product line.

*(3) Multiple pools.* (i) Principles for establishing multiple pools. (a) A taxpayer may elect to establish multiple pools for inventory items which are not within a natural business unit as to which the taxpayer has adopted the natural business unit method of pooling as provided in subparagraph (1) of this paragraph. Each such pool shall ordinarily consist of a group of inventory items which are substantially similar. In determining whether such similarity exists, consideration shall be given to all the facts and circumstances. The formulation of detailed rules for selection of pools applicable to all taxpayers is not feasible. Important considerations to be taken into account include, for example, whether there is substantial similarity in the types of raw materials used or in the processing operations applied; whether the raw materials used are readily interchangeable; whether there is similarity in the use of the products; whether the groupings are consistently followed for purposes of internal accounting and management; and whether the groupings follow customary business practice in the taxpayer's industry. The selection of pools in each case must also take into consideration such factors as the nature of the inventory items subject to the dollar-value LIFO method and the significance of such items to the taxpayer's business operations. Where similar types of goods are inventoried in natural business units and multiple pools of the taxpayer, the Commissioner may apportion or allocate such goods among the natural business units and the multiple pools, if he determines that such apportionment or allocation is necessary in order to clearly reflect the income of the taxpayer.

(b) Raw materials which are substantially similar shall be pooled together in accordance with the principles of this subparagraph. However, inventories of raw or unprocessed materials of an unlike nature may not be placed into one pool, even though such materials become part of otherwise identical finished products.

(c) Finished goods and goods-in-process in the inventory shall be placed into pools classified by major classes or types of goods. The same class or type of finished goods and goods-in-process shall ordinarily be included in the same pool. Where the material content of a class of finished goods and goods-in-process included in a pool has been changed, for example, to conform with current trends in an industry, a separate pool of finished goods and goods-in-process will not ordinarily be required unless the change in material content results in a substantial change in the finished goods.

(d) The requirement that pools be established by major types of materials or major classes of goods is not to be construed so as to preclude the establishment of a miscellaneous pool. Since a taxpayer may elect the dollar-value LIFO method with respect to all or any designated goods in his inventory, there may be a number of such inventory items covered in the election. A miscellaneous pool shall consist only of items which are relatively insignificant in dollar value by comparison with other inventory items in the particular trade or business and which are not properly includible as part of another pool.

Raw materials content pools. The dollar-value method of pricing LIFO inventories may be used in conjunction with the raw materials content method authorized in § 1.472-1. Raw materials (including the raw material content of finished goods and goods-in-process) which are substantially similar shall be pooled together in accordance with the principles of subdivision (i) of this subparagraph. However, inventories of materials of an unlike nature may not be placed into one pool, even though such materials become part of otherwise identical finished products.

*(4) IPIC method pools.* A manufacturer or processor that elects to use the inventory price index computation method described in paragraph (e)(3) of this section (IPIC method) for a trade or business may elect to establish dollar-value pools for those items accounted for using the IPIC method based on the 2-digit commodity codes (i.e., major commodity groups) in Table 6 (Producer price indexes and percent changes for commodity groupings and individual items, not seasonally adjusted) of the "PPI Detailed Report" published monthly by the United States Bureau of Labor Statistics (available from New Orders, Superintendent of Documents, PO Box 371954, Pittsburgh, PA 15250-7954). A taxpayer electing to establish dollar-value pools under this paragraph (b)(4) may combine IPIC pools that comprise less than 5 percent of the total current-year cost of all dollar-value pools to form a single miscellaneous IPIC pool. A taxpayer electing to establish dollar-value pools under this paragraph (b)(4) may combine a miscellaneous IPIC pool that comprises less than 5 percent of the total current-year cost of all dollar-value pools with the largest IPIC pool. Each of these 5 percent rules is a method of accounting. A taxpayer may not change to, or cease using, either 5 percent rule without obtaining the Commissioner's prior consent. Whether a specific IPIC pool or the miscellaneous IPIC pool satisfies the applicable 5 percent rule must be determined in the year of adoption or year of change (whichever is applicable) and redetermined every third taxable year. Any change in pooling required or permitted as a result of a 5 percent rule is a change in method of accounting. A taxpayer must secure the consent of the Commissioner pursuant to § 1.446-1(e) before combining or separating pools and must combine or separate its IPIC pools in accordance with paragraph (g)(2) of this section.

**(c) Principles for establishing pools for wholesalers, retailers, etc.** *(1) In general.* Items of inventory in the hands of wholesalers, retailers, jobbers, and distributors shall be placed into pools by major lines, types, or classes of goods. In determining such groupings, customary business classifications of the particular trade in which the taxpayer is engaged is an important consideration. An example of such customary business classification is the department in the department store. In such case practices are relatively uniform throughout the trade, and departmental grouping is peculiarly adapted to the customs and needs of the business. However, in appropriate cases, the principles set forth in paragraphs (b)(1) and (2) of this section, relating to pooling by natural business units, may be used, with permission of the Commissioner, by wholesalers, retailers, jobbers, or distributors. Where a wholesaler or retailer is also engaged in the manufacturing or processing of goods, the pooling of the LIFO inventory for the manufacturing or processing operations shall be determined in accordance with the rules of paragraph (b) of this section.

*(2) IPIC method pools.* A retailer that elects to use the inventory price index computation method described in paragraph (e)(3) of this section (IPIC method) for a trade or business may elect to establish dollar-value pools for those items accounted for using the IPIC method based on either the general expenditure categories (i.e., major groups) in Table 3 (Consumer Price Index for all Urban Consumers (CPI-U): U.S. city average, detailed expenditure categories) of the "CPI Detailed Report" or the 2-digit commodity codes (i.e., major commodity groups) in Table 6 (Producer price indexes and percent changes for commodity groupings and individual

items, not seasonally adjusted) of the "PPI Detailed Report." A wholesaler, jobber, or distributor that elects to use the IPIC method for a trade or business may elect to establish dollar-value pools for any group of goods accounted for using the IPIC method and included within one of the 2-digit commodity codes (i.e., major commodity groups) in Table 6 (Producer price indexes and percent changes for commodity groupings and individual items, not seasonally adjusted) of the "PPI Detailed Report." The "CPI Detailed Report" and the "PPI Detailed Report" are published monthly by the United States Bureau of Labor Statistics (BLS) (available from New Orders, Superintendent of Documents, P.O. Box 371954, Pittsburgh, PA 15250-7954). A taxpayer electing to establish dollar-value pools under this paragraph (c)(2) may combine IPIC pools that comprise less than 5 percent of the total current-year cost of all dollar-value pools to form a single miscellaneous IPIC pool. A taxpayer electing to establish pools under this paragraph (c)(2) may combine a miscellaneous IPIC pool that comprises less than 5 percent of the total current-year cost of all dollar-value pools with the largest IPIC pool. Each of these 5 percent rules is a method of accounting. Thus, a taxpayer may not change to, or cease using, either 5 percent rule without obtaining the Commissioner's prior consent. Whether a specific IPIC pool or the miscellaneous IPIC pool satisfies the applicable 5 percent rule must be determined in the year of adoption or year of change (whichever is applicable) and redetermined every third taxable year. Any change in pooling required or permitted under a 5 percent rule is a change in method of accounting. A taxpayer must secure the consent of the Commissioner pursuant to section 1.446-1(e) before combining or separating pools and must combine or separate its IPIC pools in accordance with paragraph (g)(2) of this section.

**(d) Determination of appropriateness of pools.** Whether the number and the composition of the pools used by the taxpayer is appropriate, as well as the propriety of all computations incidental to the use of such pools, will be determined in connection with the examination of the taxpayer's income tax returns. Adequate records must be maintained to support the base-year unit cost as well as the current-year unit cost for all items priced on the dollar-value LIFO inventory method, regardless of the method authorized by paragraph (e) of this section which is used in computing the LIFO value of the dollar-value pool. The pool or pools selected must be used for the year of adoption and for all subsequent taxable years unless a change is required by the Commissioner in order to clearly reflect income, or unless permission to change is granted by the Commissioner as provided in paragraph (e) of § 1.446-1. However, see paragraph (h) of this section for authorization to change the method of pooling in certain specified cases.

**(e) Methods of computation of the LIFO value of a dollar-value pool.** *(1) Methods authorized.* A taxpayer may ordinarily use only the so-called "double-extension" method for computing the base-year and current-year cost of a dollar-value inventory pool. Where the use of the double-extension method is impractical, because of technological changes, the extensive variety of items, or extreme fluctuations in the variety of the items, in a dollar-value pool, the taxpayer may use an index method for computing all or part of the LIFO value of the pool. An index may be computed by double-extending a representative portion of the inventory in a pool or by the use of other sound and consistent statistical methods. The index used must be appropriate to the inventory pool to which it is to be applied. The appropriateness of the method of computing the index and the accuracy, reliability, and suitability of the use of such index must be demonstrated to the satisfaction of the district director in connection with the examination of the taxpayer's income tax returns. The use of any so-called "link-chain" method will be approved for taxable years beginning after December 31, 1960, only in those cases where the taxpayer can demonstrate to the satisfaction of the district director that the use of either an index method or the double-extension method would be impractical or unsuitable in view of the nature of the pool. A taxpayer using either an index or link-chain method shall attach to his income tax return for the first taxable year beginning after December 31, 1960, for which the index or link-chain method is used, a statement describing the particular link-chain method or the method used in computing the index. The statement shall be in sufficient detail to facilitate the determination as to whether the method used meets the standards set forth in this subparagraph. In addition, a copy of the statement shall be filed with the Commissioner of Internal Revenue, Attention: T:R, Washington 25, D.C. The taxpayer shall submit such other information as may be requested with respect to such index or link-chain method. Adequate records must be maintained by the taxpayer to support the appropriateness, accuracy, and reliability of an index or link-chain method. A taxpayer may request the Commissioner to approve the appropriateness of an index or link-chain method for the first taxable year beginning after December 31, 1960, for which it is used. Such request must be submitted within 90 days after the beginning of the first taxable year beginning after December 31, 1960, in which the taxpayer desires to use the index or link-chain method, or on or before May 1, 1961, whichever is later. A taxpayer entitled to use the retail method of pricing LIFO inventories authorized by paragraph (k) of § 1.472-1 may use retail price indexes prepared by the United States Bureau of Labor Statistics. Any method of computing the LIFO value of a dollar-value pool must be used for the year of adoption and all subsequent taxable years, unless the taxpayer obtains the consent of the Commissioner in accordance with paragraph (e) of § 1.446-1 to use a different method.

*(2) Double-extension method.* (i) Under the double-extension method the quantity of each item in the inventory pool at the close of the taxable year is extended at both base-year unit cost and current-year unit cost. The respective extensions at the two costs are then each totaled. The first total gives the amount of the current inventory in terms of base-year cost and the second total gives the amount of such inventory in terms of current-year cost.

(ii) The total current-year cost of items making up a pool may be determined—

(a) By reference to the actual cost of the goods most recently purchased or produced;

(b) By reference to the actual cost of the goods purchased or produced during the taxable year in the order of acquisition;

(c) By application of an average unit cost equal to the aggregate cost of all of the goods purchased or produced throughout the taxable year divided by the total number of units so purchased or produced; or

(d) Pursuant to any other proper method which, in the opinion of the Commissioner, clearly reflects income.

(iii) Under the double-extension method a base-year unit cost must be ascertained for each item entering a pool for the first time subsequent to the beginning of the base-year. In such a case, the base-year unit cost of the entering item shall be the current-year cost of that item unless the taxpayer is able to reconstruct or otherwise establish a different cost. If the entering item is a product or raw material not in existence on the base date, its cost may be reconstructed, that is, the taxpayer using reasonable means may determine what the cost of the item would have been had it been in existence in the base year. If the item was in existence on the base date but not stocked by the taxpayer, he may establish, by using available data or records, what the cost of the item would have been to the taxpayer had he stocked the item. If the base-year unit cost of the entering item is either reconstructed or otherwise established to the satisfaction of the Commissioner, such cost may be used as the base-year unit cost in applying the double-extension method. If the taxpayer does not reconstruct or establish to the satisfaction of the Commissioner a base-year unit cost, but does reconstruct or establish to the satisfaction of the Commissioner the cost of the item at some year subsequent to the base year, he may use the earliest cost which he does reconstruct or establish as the base-year unit cost.

(iv) To determine whether there is an increment or liquidation in a pool for a particular taxable year, the end of the year inventory of the pool expressed in terms of the base-year cost is compared with the beginning of the year inventory of the pool expressed in terms of base-year cost. When the end of the year inventory of the pool is in excess of the beginning of the year inventory of the pool, an increment occurs in the pool for that year. If there is an increment for the taxable year, the ratio of the total current-year cost of the pool to the total base-year cost of the pool must be computed. This ratio when multiplied by the amount of the increment measured in terms of base-year cost gives the LIFO value of such increment. The LIFO value of each such increment is hereinafter referred to in this section as the "layer of increment" and must be separately accounted for and a record thereof maintained as a separate layer of the pool, and may not be combined with a layer of increment occurring in a different year. On the other hand, when the end of the year inventory of the pool is less than the beginning of the year inventory of the pool, a liquidation occurs in the pool for that year. Such liquidation is to be reflected by reducing the most recent layer of increment by the excess of the beginning of the year inventory over the end of the year inventory of the pool. However, if the amount of the liquidation exceeds the amount of the most recent layer of increment, the preceding layers of increment in reverse chronological order are to be successively reduced by the amount of such excess until all the excess is absorbed. The base-year inventory is to be reduced by liquidation only to the extent that the aggregate of all liquidation exceeds the aggregate of all layers of increment.

(v) The following examples illustrate the computation of the LIFO value of inventories under the double-extension method.

*Example (1).* (a) A taxpayer elects, beginning with the calendar year 1961, to compute his inventories by use of the LIFO inventory method under section 472 and further elects to use the dollar-value method in pricing such inventories as provided in paragraph (a) of this section. He creates Pool No. 1 for items A, B, and C. The composition of the inventory for Pool No. 1 at the base date, January 1, 1961, is as follows.

| Items | Units | Unit Cost | Total Cost |
|---|---|---|---|
| A | 1,000 | $5 | $5,000 |
| B | 2,000 | 4 | 8,000 |
| C | 500 | 2 | 1,000 |
| Total base-year cost at Jan. 1, 1961 | | | 14,000 |

(b) The closing inventory of Pool No. 1 at December 31, 1961, contains 3,000 units of A, 1,000 units of B, and 500 units of C. The taxpayer computes the current-year cost of the items making up the pool by reference to the actual cost of goods most recently purchased. The most recent purchases of items A, B, and C are as follows:

| Item | Purchase Date | Quantity Purchased | Unit Cost |
|---|---|---|---|
| A | Dec. 15, 1961 | 3,500 | $6.00 |
| B | Dec. 10, 1961 | 2,000 | 5.00 |
| C | Nov. 1, 1961 | 500 | 2.50 |

(c) The inventory of Pool No. 1 at December 31, 1961, shown at base-year and current year cost is as follows:

| Item | Quantity | Dec. 31, 1961, Inventory At Jan. 1, 1961, Base-Year Cost | | Dec. 31, 1961, Inventory At Current-Year Cost | |
|---|---|---|---|---|---|
| | | Unit Cost | Amount | Unit Cost | Amount |
| A | 3,000 | $5.00 | $15,000 | $6.00 | $18,000 |
| B | 1,000 | 4.00 | 4,000 | 5.00 | 5,000 |
| C | 500 | 2.00 | 1,000 | 2.50 | 1,250 |
| Total | | | $20,000 | | $24,250 |

(d) If the amount of the December 31, 1961, inventory at base-year cost were equal to, or less than, the base-year cost of $14,000 at January 1, 1961, such amount would be the closing LIFO inventory at December 31, 1961. However, since the base-year cost of the closing LIFO inventory at December 31, 1961, amounts to $20,000, and is in excess of the $14,000 base-year cost of the opening inventory for that year, there is a $6,000 increment in Pool No. 1 during the year. This increment must be valued at current-year cost, i.e., the ratio of 24,250/20,000, or 121.25 percent. The LIFO value of the inventory at December 31, 1961, is $21,275, computed as follows:

**Pool No. 1**

| | Dec. 31, 1961, Inventory At Jan. 1, 1961, Base-Year Cost | Ratio Of Total Current-Year Cost To Total Base-Year Cost | Dec. 31, 1961, Inventory At LIFO Value |
|---|---|---|---|
| | | Percent | |
| Jan. 1, 1961, base cost | 14,000 | 100.00 | $14,000 |
| Dec. 31, 1961, increment | 6,000 | 121.25 | 7,275 |
| Total | 20,000 | | 21,275 |

*Example (2).* (a) Assume the taxpayer in example (1) during the year 1962 completely disposes of item C and purchases item D. Assume further that item D is properly includible in Pool No. 1 under the provisions of this section.

The closing inventory on December 31, 1962, consists of quantities at current-year unit cost, as follows:

| Items | Units | Current-year Unit Cost Dec. 31, 1962 |
|---|---|---|
| A | 2,000 | $6.50 |
| B | 1,500 | 6.00 |
| D | 1,000 | 5.00 |

(b) The taxpayer establishes that the cost of item D, had he acquired it an January 1, 1961, would have been $2.00 per unit. Such cost shall be used as the base-year unit cost for item D, and the LIFO computations at December 31, 1962, are made as follows:

| Item | Quantity | Dec. 31, 1962, Inventory At Jan. 1, 1961, Base-Year Cost | | Dec. 31, 1962, Inventory At Current-Year Cost | |
|---|---|---|---|---|---|
| | | Unit Cost | Amount | Unit Cost | Amount |
| A | 2,000 | $5.00 | $10,000 | $6.50 | $13,000 |
| B | 1,500 | 4.00 | 6,000 | 6.00 | 9,000 |
| D | 1,000 | 2.00 | 2,000 | 5.00 | 5,000 |
| Total | | | 18,000 | | 27,000 |

(c) Since the closing inventory at base-year cost, $18,000, is less than the 1962 opening inventory at base-year cost, $20,000, a liquidation of $2,000 has occurred during 1962. This liquidation is to be reflected by reducing the most recent layer of increment. The LIFO value of the inventory at December 31, 1962, is $18,850, and is summarized as follows:

**Pool No. 1**

| | Dec. 31, 1962, Inventory At Jan. 1, 1961, Base-Year Cost | Ratio Of Total Current-Year Cost To Total Base-Year Cost | Dec. 31, 1962, Inventory At LIFO Value |
|---|---|---|---|
| | | Percent | |
| Jan. 1, 1961, base cost | 14,000 | 100.00 | $14,000 |
| Dec. 31, 1961, increment | 4,000 | 121.25 | 4,850 |
| Total | 18,000 | | 18,850 |

*(3) Inventory price index computation (IPIC) method.* (i) In general. The inventory price index computation method provided by this paragraph (e)(3) (IPIC method) is an elective method of determining the LIFO value of a dollar-value pool using consumer or producer price indexes published by the United States Bureau of Labor Statistics (BLS). A taxpayer using the IPIC method must compute a separate inventory price index (IPI) for each dollar-value pool. This IPI is used to convert the total current-year cost of the items in a dollar-value pool to base-year cost in order to determine whether there is an increment or liquidation in terms of base-year cost and, if there is an increment, to determine the LIFO inventory value of the current year's layer of increment (layer). Using one IPI to compute the base-year cost of a dollar-value pool for the current taxable year and using a different IPI to compute the LIFO inventory value of the current taxable year's layer is not permitted under the IPIC method. The IPIC method will be accepted by the Commissioner as an appropriate method of computing an index, and the use of that index to compute the LIFO value of a dollar-value pool will be accepted as accurate, reliable, and suitable. The appropriateness of a taxpayer's computation of an IPI, which includes all the steps described in paragraph (e)(3)(iii) of this section, will be determined in connection with an examination of the taxpayer's federal income tax return. A taxpayer using the IPIC method may elect to establish dollar-value pools according to the special rules in paragraphs (b)(4) and (c)(2) of this section or the general rules in paragraphs (b) and (c) of this section. Taxpayers eligible to use the IPIC method are described in paragraph (e)(3)(ii) of this section. The manner in which an IPI is computed is described in paragraph (e)(3)(iii) of this section. Rules relating to the adoption of, or change to, the IPIC method are in paragraph (e)(3)(iv) of this section.

(ii) Eligibility. Any taxpayer electing to use the dollar-value LIFO method may elect to use the IPIC method. Except as provided in this paragraph (e)(3)(ii) or in other published guidance, a taxpayer that elects to use the IPIC method for a specific trade or business must use that method to account for all items of dollar-value LIFO inventory. A taxpayer that uses the retail price indexes computed by the BLS and published in "Department Store Inventory Price Indexes" (available from the BLS by calling (202) 606-6325 and entering document code 2415) may elect to use the IPIC method for items that do not fall within any of the major groups listed in "Department Store Inventory Price Indexes."

(iii) Computation of an inventory price index. (A) In general. The computation of an IPI for a dollar-value pool requires the following four steps, which are described in more detail in this paragraph (e)(3)(iii): First, selection of a BLS table and an appropriate month; second, assignment of items in a dollar-value pool to BLS categories (selected BLS categories); third, computation of category inflation indexes for selected BLS categories; and fourth, computation of the IPI. A taxpayer may compute the IPI for each dollar-value pool using either the double-extension method (double-extension IPIC method) or the link-chain method (link-chain IPIC method), without regard to whether the use of a double-extension method is impractical or unsuitable. The use of either the double-extension IPIC method or the link-chain IPIC method is a method of accounting, and the adopted method must be applied consistently to all dollar-value pools within a trade or business accounted for under the IPIC method. A taxpayer that wants to change from the double-extension IPIC method to the link-chain IPIC method, or vice versa, must secure the consent of the Commissioner under § 1.446-1(e). This change must be made with a new base year as described in paragraph (e)(3)(iv)(B)(1).

(B) Selection of BLS table and appropriate month. (1) In general. Under the IPIC method, an IPI is computed using the consumer or producer price indexes for certain categories (BLS price indexes and BLS categories, respectively) listed in the selected BLS table of the "CPI Detailed Report" or the "PPI Detailed Report" for the appropriate month.

(2) BLS table selection. Manufacturers, processors, wholesalers, jobbers, and distributors must select BLS price in-

dexes from Table 6 (Producer price indexes and percent changes for commodity groupings and individual items, not seasonally adjusted) of the "PPI Detailed Report", unless the taxpayer can demonstrate that selecting BLS price indexes from another table of the "PPI Detailed Report" is more appropriate. Retailers may select BLS price indexes from either Table 3 (Consumer Price Index for all Urban Consumers (CPI-U): U.S. city average, detailed expenditure categories) of the "CPI Detailed Report" or from Table 6 (or another more appropriate table) of the "PPI Detailed Report." The selection of a BLS table is a method of accounting and must be used for the taxable year of adoption and all subsequent years, unless the taxpayer obtains the Commissioner's consent under § 1.446-1(e) to change its table selection. A taxpayer that changes its BLS table must establish a new base year in the year of change as described in paragraph (e)(3)(iv)(B) of this section.

(3) Appropriate month. In the case of a retailer using the retail method, the appropriate month is the last month of the retailer's taxable year. In the case of all other taxpayers, the appropriate month is the month most consistent with the method used to determine the current-year cost of the dollar-value pool under paragraph (e)(2)(ii) of this section and the taxpayer's history of inventory production or purchases during the taxable year. A taxpayer not using the retail method may annually select an appropriate month for each dollar-value pool or make an election on Form 970, "Application to Use LIFO Inventory Method," to use a representative appropriate month (representative month). An election to use a representative month is a method of accounting and the month elected must be used for the taxable year of the election and all subsequent taxable years, unless the taxpayer obtains the Commissioner's consent under § 1.446-1(e) to change or revoke its election.

(4) Examples. The following examples illustrate the rules of this paragraph (e)(3)(iii)(B)(3):

*Example (1).* Determining an appropriate month. A wholesaler of seasonal goods timely files a Form 970, "Application to Use LIFO Inventory Method," for the taxable year ending December 31, 2001. The taxpayer indicates elections to use the dollar-value LIFO method, to determine the current-year cost using the earliest acquisitions method in accordance with paragraph (e)(2)(ii)(b) of this section, and to use the IPIC method under paragraph (e)(3) of this section. Although the taxpayer purchases inventory items regularly throughout the year, the items purchased vary according to the seasons. The seasonal items on hand at December 31, 2001, are purchased between October and December. Thus, based on the taxpayer's use of the earliest acquisitions method of determining current-year cost and its experience with inventory purchases, the appropriate month for the items represented in the ending inventory at December 31, 2001, is October.

*Example (2).* Electing a representative month. A retailer not using the retail method timely files a Form 970, "Application to Use LIFO Inventory Method," for the taxable year ending December 31, 2001. The taxpayer indicates elections to use the dollar-value LIFO method, the most recent purchases method of determining current-year cost under paragraph (e)(2)(ii)(a) of this section, the IPIC method under paragraph (e)(3) of this section, and December as its representative month under paragraph (e)(3)(iii)(B)(3) of this section. The items in the taxpayer's ending inventory are purchased fairly uniformly throughout the year, with the first purchases normally occurring in January and the last purchases normally occurring in December. The taxpayer's election to use December as its representative month is permissible because the taxpayer elected to use the most recent purchases method and the taxpayer's last purchases of the taxable year normally occur during December, the last month of the taxpayer's taxable year.

*Example (3).* Changing representative month. The facts are the same as in Example 2, except the taxpayer files a Form 3115, "Application for Change in Accounting Method," requesting permission to change to the earliest acquisitions method of determining current-year cost in accordance with paragraph (e)(2)(ii)(b) of this section and to change its representative month from December to January beginning with the taxable year ending December 31, 2003. If the Commissioner consents to the taxpayer's request to change to the earliest acquisitions method, December will no longer be a permissible representative month for this taxpayer because of the absence of a nexus between the earliest acquisitions method, the month of December (the last month of the taxpayer's taxable year), and the taxpayer's experience with inventory purchases during the year. Thus, the Commissioner will permit the taxpayer to change its representative month to January, the first month of the taxpayer's taxable year.

*Example (4).* Changing representative month. The facts are the same as in Example 2. In 2002, the taxpayer changes its annual accounting period to a taxable year ending June 30, which requires the taxpayer to file a return for the short taxable year beginning January 1, 2002, and ending June 30, 2002. As a result, December is no longer a permissible representative month because of the absence of a nexus between the most recent purchases method, the month of December, and the taxpayer's experience with inventory purchases during the year. The taxpayer should file a Form 3115 requesting permission to change its representative month from December to June beginning with the short taxable year ending June 30, 2002. Because the taxpayer's last purchases of the taxable year now will occur in June, the Commissioner will consent to the taxpayer's request to change its representative month to June.

*Example (5).* Changing representative month. The facts are the same as in Example 2, except that the taxpayer elects to use January as its representative month. The taxpayer timely files a Form 3115 requesting permission to change its representative month from January to December beginning with the taxable year ending December 31, 2003. January is not a permissible representative month because of the absence of a nexus between the most recent purchases method, the taxpayer's history of inventory purchases, and the month of January, the first month in the taxpayer's taxable year. Because December is a permissible representative month, the Commissioner will permit the taxpayer to change its representative month to December.

(C) Assignment of inventory items to BLS categories. (1) In general. Except as provided in paragraph (e)(3)(iii)(C)(2) of this section, a taxpayer must assign each item in a dollar-value pool to the most-detailed BLS category of the selected BLS table that contains that item. For example, in Table 6 of the "PPI Detailed Report" for a given month, the commodity codes for the various BLS categories run from 2 to 8 digits, with the least-detailed BLS categories having a 2-digit code and the most-detailed BLS categories usually (but not always) having an 8-digit code. For purposes of assigning items to the most-detailed BLS category, manufacturers and processors must assign each raw material item to the most-detailed PPI category that includes that raw material and must assign each finished good item to the most-detailed PPI category that includes that finished good. In addition, manufacturers and processors must assign each work-in-process (WIP) item to the most-detailed PPI category that includes the finished good into which the item will be manufactured or processed. For this purpose, finished good means a salable item that the taxpayer regularly sells. For example, a gasoline-engine manufacturer that also manufactures the pistons used in those engines and regularly sells some of the pistons (e.g., to retailers of replacement parts) must assign both finished pistons that have not been affixed to an engine block and piston WIP items to the most-detailed PPI category that includes pistons. Finished pistons that have been affixed to an engine block must be assigned to the most-detailed PPI category that includes gasoline engines. In contrast, if sales of these pistons occur infrequently, the taxpayer must assign both finished pistons and piston WIP items to the most-detailed PPI category that includes gasoline engines.

(2) 10 percent method. Instead of assigning each item in a dollar-value pool to the most-detailed BLS categories, as described in paragraph (e)(3)(iii)(C)(1) of this section, a taxpayer may elect to use the 10 percent method described in this paragraph (e)(3)(iii)(C)(2). Under the 10 percent method, items are assigned to BLS categories using a three-step procedure. First, when the current-year cost of a specific item is 10 percent or more of the total current-year cost of the dollar-value pool, the taxpayer must assign that item to the most-detailed BLS category that includes that item (10 percent BLS category). Any other item that is includible in that 10 percent BLS category (other than an item that qualifies for its own 10 percent BLS category under the preceding sentence) must be assigned to that 10 percent BLS category. Second, if one or more items have not been assigned to BLS categories in the first step, the taxpayer must investigate successively less-detailed BLS categories and assign the unassigned item(s) to the first BLS category that contains unassigned items whose current-year cost, in the aggregate, is 10 percent or more of the total current-year cost of the dollar-value pool (also, 10 percent BLS categories). This step must be repeated until all the items in the dollar-value pool have been included in an appropriate 10 percent BLS category, the current-year cost of the unassigned items, in the aggregate, is less than 10 percent of the total current-year cost of the dollar-value pool, or the taxpayer determines that a single BLS category is not appropriate for the aggregate of the unassigned items. Third, if items in a dollar-value pool have not been assigned to a 10 percent BLS category because the current-year cost of those items, in the aggregate, is less than 10 percent of the total current-year cost of the dollar-value pool, the taxpayer must assign those items to the most-detailed BLS category that includes all those items (also, a 10 percent category). On the other hand, if items in a dollar-value pool have not been assigned to a 10 percent BLS category because the taxpayer determines that a single BLS category is not appropriate for the aggregate of those items, the taxpayer must assign each of those items to a single miscellaneous BLS category created by the taxpayer (also, a 10 percent category). In no event may a taxpayer assign items in a dollar-value pool to a BLS category that is less detailed than either the major groups of consumer goods described in Table 3 of the monthly "CPI Detailed Report" or the major commodity groups of producer goods described in Table 6 of the monthly "PPI Detailed Report." Principles similar to those described in paragraph (e)(3)(iii)(C)(1) apply for purposes of assigning raw material, work-in-process, and finished good items to the most-detailed BLS category under the 10 percent method.

(3) Change in method of accounting. The 10 percent method of assigning items in a dollar-value pool to BLS categories is a method of accounting. In addition, a taxpayer's selection of a BLS category for a specific item is a method of accounting. However, the assignment of items to different BLS categories solely as a result of the application of the 10 percent method is a change in underlying facts and not a change in method of accounting. Likewise, the selection of a new BLS category for a specific item as a result of a revision to a BLS table is a change in underlying facts and not a change in method of accounting. A taxpayer that wants to change its method of selecting BLS categories (i.e., to or from the 10-percent method) or of selecting a BLS category for a specific item must secure the Commissioner's consent in accordance with § 1.446-1(e). A taxpayer that voluntarily changes its method of selecting BLS categories or of selecting a BLS category for a specific item must establish a new base year in the year of change as described in paragraph (e)(3)(iv)(B) of this section.

(D) Computation of a category inflation index. (1) In general. As described in more detail in this paragraph (e)(3)(iii)(D), a category inflation index reflects the inflation that occurs in the BLS price indexes for a selected BLS category (or, if applicable,10 percent BLS category) during the relevant measurement period.

(2) BLS price indexes. The BLS price indexes are the cumulative indexes published in the selected BLS table for the appropriate month. A taxpayer may elect to use either preliminary or final BLS price indexes for the appropriate month, provided that the selected BLS price indexes are used consistently. However, a taxpayer that elects to use final BLS price indexes for the appropriate month must use preliminary BLS price indexes for any taxable year for which the taxpayer files its original federal income tax return before the BLS publishes final BLS price indexes for the appropriate month. If a BLS price index for a most-detailed or 10 percent BLS category is not otherwise available for the appropriate or representative month (but not because the BLS categories in the BLS table have been revised), the taxpayer must use the BLS price index for the next most-detailed BLS category that includes the specific item(s) in the most-detailed or 10 percent BLS category. If a BLS price index is not otherwise available for the appropriate or representative month because the BLS categories in the BLS table have been revised, the rules of paragraph (e)(3)(iii)(D)(4) of this section apply.

(3) Category inflation index. (i) In general. Except as provided in paragraph (e)(3)(iii)(D)(4) of this section (concerning compound category inflation indexes) or (e)(3)(iii)(D)(5) of this section (concerning category inflation indexes for certain 10 percent BLS categories), a category inflation index for a selected BLS category (or, if applicable, 10 percent BLS category) is computed under the rules of this paragraph (e)(3)(iii)(D)(3).

(ii) Double-extension IPIC method. In the case of a taxpayer using the double-extension IPIC method, the category inflation index for a BLS category is the quotient of the BLS price index for the appropriate or representative month of the current year divided by the BLS price index for the appropriate month of the taxable year preceding the base year (base month). However, if the taxpayer did not have an opening inventory in the year that its election to use the dollar-value LIFO method and double-extension IPIC method became effective, the category inflation index for a BLS category is the quotient of the BLS price index for the appropriate or representative month of the current year divided by the BLS price index for the month immediately preceding the month of the taxpayer's first inventory production or purchase.

(iii) Link-chain IPIC method. In the case of a taxpayer using the link-chain IPIC method, the category inflation index for a BLS category is the quotient of the BLS price index for the appropriate or representative month of the current year divided by the BLS price index for the appropriate month used for the immediately preceding taxable year. However, if the taxpayer did not have an opening inventory in the year that its election to use the dollar-value LIFO method and link-chain IPIC method became effective, the category inflation index for a BLS category for the year of election is the quotient of the BLS price index for the appropriate or representative month of the current year divided by the BLS price index for the month immediately preceding the month of the taxpayer's first inventory production or purchase.

(iv) Special rules concerning representative months. A taxpayer electing to use a representative month under paragraph (e)(3)(iii)(B)(3) of this section must use an appropriate month, rather than the representative month, to determine category inflation indexes in the circumstances described in this paragraph (e)(3)(iii)(D)(3)(iv) and in other similar circumstances. For example, in the case of a short taxable year, the category inflation index should reflect the inflation that occurs from the base month (in the case of the double-extension IPIC method), or the appropriate or representative month used for the preceding taxable year (in the case of the link-chain IPIC method), and the appropriate month for the short taxable year. Similarly, if a taxpayer using the link-chain IPIC method is granted consent to change both its method of determining the current-year cost of a dollar-value pool and its representative month, the category inflation index for the year of change should reflect the inflation that occurs between the old representative month used for the preceding taxable year and the new representative month used for the year of change.

(4) Compound category inflation index for revised BLS categories or price indexes. (i) In general. Periodically, the BLS revises a BLS table to add one or more new BLS categories, eliminate one or more previously reported BLS categories, or reset the base-year BLS price index of one or more BLS categories. If the BLS has revised the applicable BLS table for a taxable year, a taxpayer must compute the category inflation index for each BLS category for which the taxpayer cannot compute a category inflation index in accordance with paragraph (e)(3)(iii)(D)(3) of this section (affected BLS category) using a reasonable method, provided the method is used consistently for all affected BLS categories within a particular taxable year. For example, if the BLS revised the CPI by adding new BLS categories as of January 2001 and eliminating some previously reported BLS categories as of December 2000, January 2002 would be the first month for which it would be possible to compute a category inflation index for a 12-month period using the BLS price indexes for any affected category. The compound category inflation index described in paragraph (e)(3)(iii)(D)(4)(ii) of this section is a reasonable method of computing the category inflation index for an affected BLS category.

(ii) Computation of compound category inflation index. When the applicable BLS table is revised as described in paragraph (e)(3)(iii)(D)(4)(i) of this section, a taxpayer may use the procedure described in this paragraph (e)(3)(iii)(D)(4)(ii) to compute a compound category inflation index for each affected BLS category represented in the taxpayer's ending inventory. For this purpose, a compound category inflation index is the product of the category inflation index for the "first portion" multiplied by the corresponding category inflation index for the "second portion." The category inflation index for the first portion must reflect the inflation that occurs between the end of the base month (in the case of the double-extension IPIC method), or the preceding year's appropriate or representative month (in the case of the link-chain IPIC method), and the end of the last month covered by the unrevised BLS table based on the old BLS category. The corresponding category inflation index for the second portion must reflect the inflation that occurs between the beginning of the first month covered by the revised BLS table based on the new BLS category and the end of the current year's appropriate or representative month. First, using the revised BLS table for the current-year's appropriate or representative month, the taxpayer assigns items in the dollar-value pool using its method of assigning items to BLS categories as described in paragraph (e)(3)(iii)(C) of this section. Second, for each affected BLS category represented in the ending inventory, the taxpayer computes the category inflation index for the second portion using this formula: [A/B], where A equals the BLS price index for the current year's appropriate or representative month and B equals the BLS price index for the last month covered by the unrevised BLS table (as published for the first month of the revised BLS table). Third, using the unrevised BLS table for the base month (in the case of the double extension IPIC method) or the preceding year's appropriate or representative month (in the case of the link-chain IPIC method), the taxpayer assigns each of the items in the dollar-value pool using its method of assigning items to BLS categories. Fourth, for each affected BLS category represented in the ending inventory, the taxpayer computes the category inflation index for the first portion using this formula: [C/D], where C equals the BLS price index for the last month covered by the unrevised BLS table (as published for the last month of the unrevised BLS table) and D equals the BLS price index for the base month (in the case of the double-extension IPIC method) or the preceding year's appropriate or representative month (in the case of the link-chain IPIC method). Fifth, for each affected BLS category represented in the ending inventory, the taxpayer computes the compound category inflation index using this formula: [X*Y], where X equals the category inflation index for the second portion, and Y equals the corresponding category inflation index for the first portion. For the purpose of computing the compound category inflation index for each affected BLS category, the corresponding category inflation index for the first portion is the category inflation index for the unrevised BLS category that includes the specific inventory item(s) included in the revised BLS category. If items included in a single revised BLS category had been included in separate BLS categories before the revision of the BLS table, the corresponding category inflation index for the first portion is the weighted harmonic mean of the category inflation indexes for these unrevised BLS categories. See paragraph (e)(3)(iii)(E)(1) of this section for a formula of the weighted harmonic mean. When computing this weighted-average category inflation index, a taxpayer must use the current-year costs (or in the case of a retailer using the retail method, the retail selling prices) in ending inventory as the weights.

(iii) New base year. A taxpayer may establish a new base year in the year following the taxable year for which the taxpayer computed a compound category inflation index under this paragraph (e)(3)(iii)(D)(4) for one or more affected BLS categories in a dollar-value pool. See paragraph (e)(3)(iv)(B) of this section for the procedures and computations incident to establishing a new base year.

(iv) Examples. The following examples illustrate the rules of this paragraph (e)(3)(iii)(D)(4):

*Example (1).* BLS categories eliminated.

(i) A retailer, whose taxable year ends January 31, elected to account for its inventories using the dollar-value LIFO method and double-extension IPIC method (based on the CPI), beginning with the taxable year ending January 31, 1997. The taxpayer does not use the retail method, but elected to use January as its representative month. On January 31, 1999, the taxpayer's only dollar-value pool contains only two items--lemons and peaches. The total current-year cost of these items is as follows: lemons, $40, and peaches, $30.

(ii) The CPI was revised in October of 1998 to eliminate the "Citrus fruits" subcategory of "Other fresh fruits." In addition, the base-year BLS price index for "Other fresh fruits" was reset to 100.00 as of October 1, 1998. In relevant part, the January 1999 CPI permits the assignment of both lemons and peaches to "Other fresh fruits." The January 1999 BLS price indexes for "Citrus fruits" and "Other fresh fruits" are 96.6 and 105.6, respectively. In relevant part, the September 1998 CPI permits the assignment of lemons to "Citrus fruits" and peaches to "Other fresh fruits." The September 1998 BLS price indexes for "Citrus fruits" and "Other fresh fruits" are 194.9 and 294.9, respectively, and the January 1997 BLS price indexes for "Citrus fruits" and "Other fresh fruits" are 190.2 and 290.2, respectively.

(iii) Because the BLS eliminated the category, "Citrus fruits," as of October 1998, it did not publish a BLS price index for that category in the January 1999 CPI. Thus, the taxpayer cannot compute a category inflation index for "Citrus fruits" under the normal procedures, but may compute a compound category inflation index for that affected BLS category using the procedures described in paragraph (e)(3)(iii)(D)(4)(ii) of this section.

(iv) The taxpayer computes a compound category inflation index for the two BLS categories that formerly included lemons and peaches. The taxpayer first assigns lemons and peaches to "Other fresh fruits," the most-detailed index in the January 1999 CPI, and then computes the category inflation index for the second portion as follows:

| Item | 1999 category | Jan 1999 index/Sept 1998 index (as published in Oct. 1998) | Category inflation index |
|---|---|---|---|
| Lemons and Peaches | Other fresh fruits | 105.6/100.0 | 1.0560 |

(v) The taxpayer assigns the lemons and peaches to the most-detailed BLS categories in the January 1998 CPI as follows: lemons to "Citrus fruits" and peaches to "Other fresh fruits." Then, the taxpayer computes the category inflation index for the first portion as follows:

| Item | 1998 category | Sept 1998 index (as published in Sept.1998)/Jan 1997 | Category inflation index |
|---|---|---|---|
| Lemons | Citrus fruits | 194.9/190.2 | 1.0247 |
| Peaches | Other fresh Fruits | 294.9/290.2 | 1.0162 |

(vi) Because lemons and peaches, which are included together in the revised "Other fresh fruits" category, had been included in separate BLS categories before the BLS table was revised, the taxpayer must compute a single corresponding category inflation index for the affected BLS categories for the first portion. This corresponding category inflation index is the weighted harmonic mean of the separate corresponding category inflation indexes for the first portion using the cost of the items in ending inventory as the weights. The taxpayer computes the corresponding category inflation index for "Other fresh fruits" for the first portion as follows:

| Item | (I) Weight (cost of item) | (II) Category inflation index | (III) Quotient:(I)/(II) |
|---|---|---|---|
| Lemons | $40.00 | 1.0247 | $39.04 |
| Peaches | 30.00 | 1.0162 | 29.52 |
| Total | 70.00 | | 68.56 |

| (IV) Sum of weights | (V) Sum of (weight/category inflation index) | (VI) Weighted harmonic mean of other fresh fruits: (IV)/(V) |
|---|---|---|
| $70.00 | $68.56 | 1.0210 |

(vii) Finally, the taxpayer computes the compound category inflation index for Other fresh fruits as follows:

| Item | (I) Category inflation index (second portion) | (II) Category inflation index (first portion) | (III) Compound category inflation index (I)*(II) |
|---|---|---|---|
| Other fresh fruits | 1.0560 | 1.0210 | 1.0782 |

(viii) The taxpayer may establish a new base year for the taxable year ending January 31, 2000.

*Example (2).* BLS categories separated.

(i) The facts are the same as in Example 1, except prior to October 1998, both lemons and peaches were assigned to "Other fresh fruits" and in the October 1998 CPI, the BLS created a new category, "Citrus fruits," for citrus fruits, such as lemons. Moreover, the BLS reset the base-year BLS price index for "Other fresh fruits" to 100.0 as of October 1, 1998. As a result of these changes, the taxpayer may no longer assign lemons to "Other fresh fruits."

(ii) Because "Citrus fruits" is new as of October 1998, the BLS did not publish a BLS price index for this BLS category in the January 1999 CPI. Thus, because the taxpayer cannot compute a category inflation index for "Citrus fruits" under the normal procedures, the taxpayer may compute a compound category inflation index for the affected BLS category using the procedures described in paragraph (e)(3)(iii)(D)(4)(ii) of this section.

(iii) Based on the January 1999 CPI, the taxpayer assigns lemons to "Citrus fruits" and peaches to "Other fresh fruits." Then, the taxpayer computes a compound category inflation index for each of the two BLS categories. The computation of the category inflation index for the second portion is as follows:

| Item | 1999 category | Jan 1999 index/Sept.1998 index (as published in Oct 1998) | Category inflation index |
|---|---|---|---|
| Lemons | Citrus fruits | 96.6/100 | 0.9660 |
| Peaches | Other fresh fruits | 105.6/100 | 1.0560 |

(iv) Then, the taxpayer computes the category inflation index for the first portion as follows:

| Item | 1998 category | Sept 1998 index (as published in Sept 1998)/Jan 1997 | Category inflation index |
|---|---|---|---|
| Lemons & Peaches | Other fresh fruits | 294.9/290.2 | 1.0162 |

(v) Finally, the taxpayer computes the compound category inflation index for "Citrus fruits" and "Other fresh fruits":

| Item | (I) Category inflation index (second portion) | (II) Category inflation index (first portion) | (III) Compound category inflation index: (I)*(II) |
|---|---|---|---|
| Citrus fruits | 0.9660 | 1.0162 | 0.9816 |
| Other fresh fruits | 1.0560 | 1.0162 | 1.0731 |

(vi) The taxpayer may establish a new base year for the taxable year ending January 31, 2000.

(5) 10 percent method. (i) Applicability. A taxpayer that elects to use the 10 percent method described in paragraph (e)(3)(iii)(C)(2) of this section must compute a category inflation index for a less-detailed 10 percent BLS category as provided in this paragraph (e)(3)(iii)(D)(5). A less-detailed 10 percent category is a BLS category that—

(A) subsumes two or more BLS categories;

(B) Does not have a single assigned item whose current-year cost is 10 percent or more of the current-year cost of all the items in the dollar-value pool;

(C) Has at least one item in at least one of the subsumed BLS categories; and

(D) Has at least one subsumed BLS category that either does not have any assigned items or is a separate 10 percent BLS category.

(ii) Determination of category inflation index. If the rules of this paragraph (e)(3)(iii)(D)(5) apply, the category inflation index for the less-detailed 10 percent BLS category is equal to the weighted arithmetic mean of the category inflation index (or, compound category inflation index, if applicable) for each of the subsumed BLS categories that have been assigned at least one item from the taxpayer's dollar-value pool (excluding any item that is properly assigned to a separate 10 percent BLS category). [Weighted Arithmetic Mean = Sum of (Weight x Category Inflation Index)]/Sum of Weights]. The appropriate weight for each of the most-detailed BLS categories referenced in the preceding sentence is the corresponding BLS weight. Currently, in January of each year, the BLS publishes the BLS weights determined for December of the preceding year. In the case of a taxpayer using the double-extension IPIC method, the BLS weights for December of the taxable year preceding the base year are to be used for all taxable years. In the case of a taxpayer using the link-chain IPIC method, the BLS weights for December of a given calendar year are to be used for taxable years that end during the 12-month period that begins on July 1 of the following calendar year. However, if the BLS weights are not published for all of the most-detailed BLS categories referenced above, the taxpayer may use the current-year cost (or in the case of a retailer using the retail method, the retail selling prices) of all items assigned to a specific most-detailed BLS category as the appropriate weight for that category, but must compute a weighted harmonic mean. See paragraph (e)(3)(iii)(E)(1) of this section for a formula of the weighted harmonic mean.

(E) Computation of Inventory Price Index (IPI), (1) Double-extension IPIC method. Under the double-extension IPIC method, the IPI for a dollar-value pool is the weighted harmonic mean of the category inflation indexes (or, if applicable, compound category inflation indexes) determined under paragraph (e)(3)(iii)(D) of this section for each selected BLS category (or, if applicable 10 percent BLS category) represented in the taxpayer's dollar-value pool at the end of the taxable year. The formula for computing the weighted harmonic mean of the category inflation indexes is: [Sum of Weights/Sum of (Weight/ Category Inflation Index)]. The weights to be used when computing this weighted harmonic mean are the current-year costs (or, in the case of a retailer using the retail method, the retail selling prices) in each selected BLS category represented in the dollar-value pool at the end of the taxable year.

(2) Link-chain IPIC method. Under the link-chain IPIC method, the IPI for a dollar-value pool is the product of the weighted harmonic mean of the category inflation indexes (or, if applicable, the compound category inflation indexes) determined under paragraph (e)(3)(iii)(D) of this section for each selected BLS category (or, if applicable, 10 percent BLS category) represented in the taxpayer's dollar-value pool at the end of the taxable year multiplied by the IPI for the immediately preceding taxable year. The formula for computing the weighted harmonic mean of the category inflation indexes is: [Sum of Weights/Sum of (Weight/Category Inflation Index)]. The weights to be used when computing this weighted harmonic mean are the current-year costs (or, in the case of a retailer using the retail method, the retail selling prices) in each selected BLS category represented in the dollar-value pool at the end of the taxable year.

(3) Examples. The following examples illustrate the rules of this paragraph (e)(3)(iii)(E):

*Example (1).* Double-extension method.

(i) Introduction. R is a retail furniture merchant that does not use the retail method. For the taxable year ending December 31, 2000, R used the first-in, first-out method of identifying inventory and valued its inventory at cost. The total cost of R's inventory on December 31, 2000, was $850,000. R elected to use the dollar-value LIFO and double-extension IPIC methods for its taxable year ending December 31, 2001. R does not elect to use the 10 percent method described in paragraph (e)(3)(iii)(C)(2) of this section. R determines the current-year cost of the items using the actual cost of the most recently purchased goods. R elected to pool its inventory based on the major groups in Table 6 of the monthly "PPI Detailed Report" in accordance with the special IPIC pooling rules of paragraph (b)(4) of this section. All items in R's inventory fall within the 2-digit commodity code in Table 6 of the monthly "PPI Detailed Report" for "furniture and household durables." Therefore, R will maintain a single dollar-value pool.

(ii) Select a BLS table and appropriate month for 2001. R determines that the appropriate month for 2001 is October. R also determines that the appropriate month for 2000 would have been December if R had used the IPIC method for that year.

(iii) Assign inventory items to BLS categories for 2001. For 2001, R assigns all items in the dollar-value pool to the most-detailed BLS categories listed in Table 6 of the October 2001 "PPI Detailed Report" that contain those items. The BLS categories and the current-year cost of the items assigned to them are summarized as follows:

| Commodity code | Category | Current-year cost |
|---|---|---|
| 12120101 | Living Room Table | $111,924.00 |
| 12120211 | Dining Room Table | 159,578.00 |
| 12120216 | Dining Room Chairs | 98,639.00 |
| 12130101 | Upholstered Sofas | 332,488.00 |
| 12130111 | Upholstered Chairs | 218,751.00 |
| Total | | 921,380.00 |

(iv) Compute category inflation indexes for 2001. Because R elected to use the double-extension IPIC method and did not elect the 10 percent method, the category inflation indexes are computed in accordance with paragraph (e)(3)(iii)(D)(3)(ii) of this section (BLS price indexes for October 2001 divided by BLS price indexes for December 2000). R computes the category inflation indexes for 2001 as follows:

| Category | (I) Oct 2001 index | (II) Dec 2000 index | (III) Category inflation index: (I)/(II) |
|---|---|---|---|
| Living Room Table | 172.4 | 169.2 | 1.018913 |
| Dining Room Table | 171.9 | 168.1 | 1.022606 |
| Dining Room Chairs | 172.8 | 169.7 | 1.018268 |
| Upholstered Sofas | 142.2 | 140.9 | 1.009226 |
| Upholstered Chairs | 134.1 | 132.5 | 1.012075 |

(v) Compute IPI for 2001. R must compute the IPI for 2001, which is the weighted harmonic mean of the category inflation indexes for 2001. The formula for the weighted harmonic mean provided in paragraph (e)(3)(iii)(E)(1) of this section is [Sum of Weights/Sum of (Weight/Category Inflation Index)]. The IPI for 2001 is computed as follows:

| Category | (I) Weight | (II) Category inflation index | (III) Quotient:(I)/(II) |
|---|---|---|---|
| Living Room Table | $111,924.00 | 1.018913 | $109,846.47 |
| Dining Room Table | 159,578.00 | 1.022606 | 156,050.33 |
| Dining Room Chairs | 98,639.00 | 1.018268 | 96,869.39 |
| Upholstered Sofas | 332,488.00 | 1.009226 | 329,448.51 |
| Upholstered Chairs | 218,751.00 | 1.012075 | 216,141.10 |
| Total | $921,380.00 | | $908,355.80 |

| (IV) Sum of weights | (V) Sum of (weight/category inflation index) | (VI) Inventory price index: (IV)/(V) |
|---|---|---|
| $921,380.00 | $908,355.80 | 1.01433821 |

(vi) Determine the LIFO value of the dollar-value pool for 2001. For 2001, R determines the total base-year cost of its ending inventory by dividing the total current-year cost of the items in the dollar-value pool by the IPI for 2001. The total base-year cost of R's ending inventory is $908,355.80 ($921,380/1.01433821). Comparing the base-year cost of the ending inventory to the base-year cost of the beginning inventory, R determines that the base-year cost of the 2001 increment is $58,355.80 ($908,355.80--$850,000.00). R multiplies the base-year cost of the 2001 increment by the IPI for 2001 and determines that the LIFO value of the 2001 layer is $59,192.52 ($58,355.80 * 1.01433821). Thus, the LIFO value of R's total inventory at the end of 2001 is $909,192.52 ($850,000.00 (opening inventory) + $59,192.52 (2001 layer)).

(vii) Select a BLS table and appropriate month for 2002. For 2002.0, R must compute a new IPI under the double-extension IPIC method to determine the LIFO value of its dollar-value pool. R determines that the appropriate month for 2002 is November.

(viii) Assign inventory items to BLS categories for 2002. For 2002, R assigns all items in the dollar-value pool to the most-detailed BLS categories listed in Table 6 of the November 2002 "PPI Detailed Report" that contain those items. The BLS categories and the current-year cost of the items assigned to them are summarized as follows:

| Commodity code | Category | Current-year cost |
|---|---|---|
| 12120103 | Living Room Desks | $125,008.00 |
| 12120211 | Dining Room Table | 136,216.00 |
| 12120216 | Dining Room Chairs | 113,569.00 |
| 12130101 | Upholstered Sofas | 343,900.00 |
| 12130111 | Upholstered Chairs | 233,050.00 |
| Total | | $951,743.00 |

(ix) Compute category inflation indexes for 2002. Because R uses the double-extension IPIC method and did not elect the 10 percent method, the category inflation indexes are computed in accordance with paragraph (e)(3)(iii)(D)(3)(ii) of this section (BLS price indexes for November 2002 divided by BLS price indexes for December 2000). R computes the category inflation indexes for 2002 as follows:

| Category | Nov (I) 2002 index | Dec (II) 2000 index | (III) Category inflation index (I)/(II) |
|---|---|---|---|
| Living Room Desks | 172.6 | 160.3 | 1.076731 |
| Dining Room Table | 174.8 | 168.1 | 1.039857 |
| Dining Room Chairs | 177.0 | 169.7 | 1.043017 |
| Upholstered Sofas | 144.9 | 140.9 | 1.028389 |
| Upholstered Chairs | 136.6 | 132.5 | 1.030943 |

(x) Compute IPI for 2002. R must compute the IPI for 2002, which is the weighted harmonic mean [Sum of Weights/Sum of (Weight/ Category Inflation Index)] of the category inflation indexes for 2002. The IPI for 2002 is computed as follows:

| Category | (I) Weight | (II) Category inflation index | (III) Quotient: (I)/(II) |
|---|---|---|---|
| Living Room Desks | $125,008.00 | 1.076731 | $116,099.56 |
| Dining Room Table | 136,216.00 | 1.039857 | 130,994.93 |
| Dining Room Chairs | 113,569.00 | 1.043017 | 108,885.09 |
| Upholstered Sofas | 343,900.00 | 1.028389 | 334,406.53 |
| Upholstered Chairs | 233,050.00 | 1.030943 | 226,055.17 |
| Total | 951,743.00 | | 916,441.28 |

| (IV) Sum of weights | (V) Category inflation index | (VI) Inventory price index: (IV)/(V) |
|---|---|---|
| $951,743.00 | $916,441.28 | 1.03852044 |

(xi) Determine the LIFO value of the pool for 2002. For 2002, R determines the total base-year cost of its ending inventory by dividing the total current-year cost of the items in the dollar-value pool by the IPI for 2002. The total base-year cost of the ending inventory is $916,441.28 ($951,743.00/1.03852044). Comparing the base-year cost of the ending inventory to the base-year cost of the beginning inventory, R determines that the base-year cost of the 2002 increment is $8,085.48 ($916,441.28-$908,355.80). R multiplies the base-year cost of the 2002 increment by the IPI for 2002 and determines that the LIFO value of the 2002 layer is $8,396.94 ($8,085.48 * 1.03852044). Thus, the LIFO value of R's total inventory at the end of 2002 is $917,589.46 ($850,000.00 (opening inventory) + $59,192.52 (2001 layer) + $8,396.94 (2002 layer)).

*Example (2).* Link-chain method.

(i) Introduction. The facts are the same as Example 1, except that R uses the link-chain IPIC method. The double-extension IPIC method and the link-chain IPIC method yield the same results for the first taxable year in which the dollar-value LIFO and IPIC methods are used. Therefore, this example illustrates only how R will compute the IPI for, and determine the LIFO value of, its dollar-value pool for 2002.

(ii) Select a BLS table and appropriate month for 2002. R determines that the appropriate month for 2002 is November.

(iii) Assign inventory items to BLS categories for 2002. For 2002, R assigns all items in the dollar-value pool to the most-detailed BLS categories listed in Table 6 of the November 2002 "PPI Detailed Report" that contain those items. The BLS categories and the current-year cost of the items assigned to them are summarized as follows:

| Commodity code | Category | Current-year cost |
|---|---|---|
| 12120103 | Living Room Desks | $125,008.00 |
| 12120211 | Dining Room Table | 136,216.00 |
| 12120216 | Dining Room Chairs | 113,569.00 |
| 12130101 | Upholstered Sofas | 343,900.00 |
| 12130111 | Upholstered Chairs | 233,050.00 |
| Total | | 951,743.00 |

(iv) Compute category inflation indexes for 2002. Because R uses the link-chain IPIC method and did not elect the 10 percent method, the category inflation indexes are computed in accordance with paragraph (e)(3)(iii)(D)(3)(iii) of this section (BLS price indexes for November 2002 divided by BLS price indexes for October 2001). R computes the category inflation indexes for 2002 as follows:

| Category | Nov (I) 2002 index | Oct (II) 2001 index | (III) Category inflation index: (I)/(II) |
|---|---|---|---|
| Living Room Desks | 172.6 | 162.0 | 1.065432 |
| Dining Room Table | 174.8 | 171.9 | 1.016870 |
| Dining Room Chairs | 177.0 | 172.8 | 1.024306 |
| Upholstered Sofas | 144.9 | 142.2 | 1.018987 |
| Upholstered Chairs | 136.6 | 134.1 | 1.018643 |

(v) Compute IPI for 2002. As provided in paragraph (e)(3)(iii)(E)(2) of this section, R must compute the IPI for 2002 by multiplying the weighted harmonic mean of the category inflation indexes for 2002 by the IPI for 2001. The IPI for 2002 is computed as follows:

| Category | (I) Weight | (II) Category inflation index | (III) Quotient: (I)/(II) |
|---|---|---|---|
| Living Room Desks | $125,008.00 | 1.065432 | $117,330.81 |
| Dining Room Table | 136,216.00 | 1.016870 | 133,956.16 |
| Dining Room Chairs | 113,569.00 | 1.024306 | 110,874.09 |
| Upholstered Sofas | 343,900.00 | 1.018987 | 337,492.04 |
| Upholstered Chairs | 233,050.00 | 1.018643 | 228,784.77 |
| Total | 951,743.00 | | 928,437.87 |

| (IV) Sum of weights | (V) Sum of (weight/ category inflation index) | (VI) Weighted harmonic mean of category inflation indexes for 2002: (IV)/(V) | (VII) Inventory price index for 2001 | (VIII) Inventory price index for 2002: (VI)*(VII) |
|---|---|---|---|---|
| $951,743.00 | $928,437.87 | 1.02510144 | 1.01433821 | 1.03979956 |

(vi) Determine the LIFO value of the pool for 2002. R determines the total base-year cost of its ending inventory by dividing the total current-year cost of the items in the dollar-value pool by the IPI for 2002. The total base-year cost of the ending inventory is $915,313.91 ($951,743.00 / 1.03979956). Comparing the base-year cost of the ending inventory to the base-year cost of the beginning inventory, R determines that the base-year cost of the 2002 layer is $6,958.11 ($915,313.91-$908,355.80). R multiplies the base-year cost of the 2002 layer by the IPI for 2002 and determines that the LIFO value of the 2002 layer is $7,235.04 ($6,958.11 * 1.03979956). Thus, the LIFO value of R's total inventory at the end of 2002 is $916,427.56 ($850,000.00 (opening inventory) + $59,192.52 (2001 layer) + $7,235.04 (2002 layer)).

(iv) Adoption or change of method. (A) Adoption or change to IPIC method. The use of an inventory price index computed under the IPIC method is a method of accounting. A taxpayer permitted to adopt the dollar-value LIFO method without first securing the Commissioner's consent also may adopt the IPIC method without first securing the Commissioner's consent. The IPIC method may be adopted and used, however, only if the taxpayer provides the following information on a Form 970, "Application to Use LIFO Inventory Method," or in another manner as may be acceptable to the Commissioner: A complete list of dollar-value pools (including a description of the items in each dollar-value pool); the BLS table (i.e., CPI or PPI) selected for each dollar-value pool; the representative month, if applicable, elected for each dollar-value pool; the BLS categories to which the items in each dollar-value pool will be assigned; the method of assigning items to BLS categories (e.g., the 10 percent method) for each dollar-value pool; and the method of computing the IPI (i.e., double-extension IPIC method or link-chain IPIC method) for each dollar-value pool. In the case of a taxpayer permitted to adopt the IPIC method without requesting the Commissioner's consent, the Form 970 must be attached to the taxpayer's income tax return for the taxable year of adoption. In all other cases, a taxpayer may change to the IPIC method only after securing the Commissioner's consent as provided in § 1.446-1(e). In these latter cases, the Form 970 containing the information described in this paragraph (e)(3)(iv)(A) must be attached to a Form 3115, "Application for Change in Accounting Method," filed as required by § 1.446-1(e). A taxpayer that simultaneously changes to the dollar-value LIFO and IPIC methods from another LIFO method must apply the rules of paragraph (f)(2) of this section before applying the rules of paragraph (e)(3)(iv)(B)(1) of this section. To satisfy the requirements of § 1.472-2(h), taxpayers must maintain adequate books and records, including those concerning the use of the IPIC method and necessary computations. Notwithstanding the rules in paragraph (e)(1) of this section, a taxpayer that adopts, or changes to, the link-chain IPIC method is not required to demonstrate that the use of any other method of determining the LIFO value of a dollar-value pool is impractical.

(B) New base year. (1) Voluntary change. (i) In general. In the case of a taxpayer using a non-IPIC method to determine the LIFO value of inventory, the layers previously determined under that method, if any, and the LIFO values of those layers are retained if the taxpayer voluntarily changes to the IPIC method. Instead of using the earliest taxable year for which the taxpayer adopted the LIFO method for any items in the dollar-value pool, the year of change is used as the new base year for the purpose of determining the amount of increments and liquidations, if any, for the year of change and subsequent taxable years. The base-year cost of the layers in a dollar-value pool at the beginning of the year of change must be restated in terms of new base-year cost using the year of change as the new base year and, if applicable, the indexes for the previously determined layers must be recomputed accordingly. The recomputed indexes will be used to determine the LIFO value of subsequent liquidations. For purposes of computing an IPI under paragraph (e)(3)(iii)(E) of this section, the IPI for the immediately preceding year is 1.00. The new total base-year cost of the items in a dollar-value pool for the purpose of determining future increments and liquidations is equal to the total current-year cost of the items in the dollar-value pool (determined using the taxpayer's method of determining the total current-year cost of the items in the dollar-value pool under paragraph (e)(2)(ii) of this section). A taxpayer must allocate this new total base-year cost to each layer based on the ratio of the old base-year cost of the layer to the old total base-year cost of the dollar-value pool.

(ii) Example. The following example illustrates the rules of this paragraph (e)(3)(iv)(B)(1):

*Example.* (i) In 1990, X elected to use a dollar-value LIFO method (other than the IPIC method) for its single dollar-value pool. X is granted permission to change to the link-chain IPIC method, beginning with the taxable year ending December 31, 2001. X will continue using a single dollar-value pool. X's beginning inventory as of January 1, 2001, computed using its former inventory method, is as follows:

| Layer | (I) Base-year cost | (II) Inflation index | (III) LIFO value: (I) * (II) |
|---|---|---|---|
| Base layer | $135,000 | 1.00 | $135,000 |
| 1991 layer | 20,000 | 1.43 | 28,600 |
| 1994 layer | 60,000 | 1.55 | 93,000 |
| 1995 layer | 13,000 | 1.59 | 20,670 |
| 1997 layer | 2,000 | 1.61 | 3,220 |
| Total | 230,000 | | 280,490 |

(ii) Under X's method of determining the current-year cost of items in a dollar-value pool, the current-year cost of the beginning inventory is $391,000. Thus, X's new base-year cost as of January 1, 2001, is $391,000. X allocates this new base-year cost to each layer based on the ratio of old base-year cost of the layer to the total old base-year cost of the dollar-value pool. To recompute the inflation indexes for each of its layers, X divides the LIFO value of each layer by the new base-year cost attributable to the layer. The new base-year cost, recomputed inflation indexes, and LIFO value of X's layers as of January 1, 2001, are as follows:

| Layer | (I) Base-year cost | (II) Inflation index | (III) LIFO value: (I) * (II) |
|---|---|---|---|
| Base layer | $229,500 | 0.588235 | $135,000 |
| 1991 layer | 34,000 | 0.841176 | 28,600 |
| 1994 layer | 102,000 | 0.911765 | 93,000 |
| 1995 layer | 22,100 | 0.935294 | 20,670 |
| 1997 layer | 3,400 | 0.947059 | 3,220 |
| Total | 391,000 | | 280,490 |

(iii) In 2001, the current-year cost of X's ending inventory is $430,139. The weighted harmonic mean of the category inflation indexes applicable to X's ending inventory is 1.075347, and in accordance with paragraph (e)(3)(iv)(B)(1)(i) of this section, the inflation index for the immediately preceding taxable year is 1.00. Thus, X's IPI for 2001 is 1.075347 (1.00 * 1.075347). The total base-year cost of X's ending inventory is $400,000 ($430,139/1.075347). The base-year cost, IPI, and LIFO value of X's layers as of December 31, 2001, are as follows:

| Layer | (I) Base-year cost | (II) Inventory price index | (III) LIFO value: (I) * (II) |
|---|---|---|---|
| Base layer | $229,500 | 0.588235 | $135,000 |
| 1991 layer | 34,000 | 0.841176 | 28,600 |
| 1994 layer | 102,000 | 0.911765 | 93,000 |
| 1995 layer | 22,100 | 0.935294 | 20,670 |
| 1997 layer | 3,400 | 0.947059 | 3,220 |
| 2001 layer | 9,000 | 1.075347 | 9,678 |
| Total | 400,000 | | 290,168 |

(iv) In 2002, the current-year cost of X's ending inventory is $418,000. The weighted harmonic mean of the category inflation indexes applicable to X's ending inventory is 1.02292562, and the IPI for the immediately preceding year is 1.075347. Thus, X's IPI for 2001 is 1.10 (1.075347 * 1.02292562). The total base-year cost of X's ending inventory is $380,000 ($418,000/1.10), which results in a liquidation of $20,000 ($400,000-$380,000) in terms of base-year cost. This liquidation eliminates the 2001 layer ($9,000 base-year cost), the 1997 layer ($3,400 base-year cost), and part of the 1995 layer ($7,600 base-year cost). The base-year cost, indexes, and LIFO value of X's layers as of December 31, 2002, are as follows:

| Layer | (I) Base-year cost | (II) Inventory price index | (III) LIFO value: (I) * (II) |
|---|---|---|---|
| Base layer | $229,500 | 0.588235 | $135,000 |
| 1991 layer | 34,000 | 0.841176 | 28,600 |
| 1994 layer | 102,000 | 0.911765 | 93,000 |
| 1995 layer | 14,500 | 0.935294 | 13,562 |
| Total | 380,000 | | 270,162 |

(2) Involuntary change. (i) In general. If a taxpayer uses a non-IPIC method to compute the LIFO value of a dollar-value pool, and if the Commissioner determines that the taxpayer's method does not clearly reflect income, the Commissioner may require the taxpayer to change to the IPIC method. If the Commissioner requires a taxpayer to change to the IPIC method, and the taxpayer does not provide sufficient information from its books and records to compute an adjustment under section 481, the Commissioner may implement the change using the simplified transition method described in paragraph (e)(3)(iv)(B)(2)(ii) of this section.

(ii) Simplified Transition Method. Under the simplified transition method, the Commissioner will recompute the LIFO value of each dollar-value pool as of the beginning of the year of change using the double-extension IPIC method or the link-chain IPIC method. The adjustment under section 481 is equal to the difference between the recomputed LIFO value and the LIFO value of the pool determined under the taxpayer's former method. The Commissioner will compute an IPI using the double-extension IPIC method or link-chain IPIC method for each taxable year in which the LIFO method was used by the taxpayer based on the assumptions that the ending inventory of the pool in each taxable year was comprised of items that fall into the same BLS categories as the items in the ending inventory of the year of change and that the relative weights of those BLS categories in all prior years were the same as the relative weights of those BLS categories in the ending inventory of the year of change. The base-year cost of the items in a dollar-value pool at the end of a taxable year will be determined by dividing the IPI computed for the taxable year into the current-year cost of the items in that pool determined in accordance with paragraph (e)(2)(ii) of this section. If the comparison of the base-year cost of the beginning and ending inventory produces a current-year increment, the base-year cost of that increment will be multiplied by the IPI computed for that taxable year to determine the LIFO value of that layer.

(iii) Example. The following example illustrates the rules of this paragraph (e)(3)(iv)(B)(2)(ii).

*Example.* (i) Z began using a dollar-value LIFO method other than the IPIC method in the taxable year ending December 31, 1998, and maintains a single dollar-value pool. Z's beginning inventory as of January 1, 2000, computed using its method of accounting, was as follows:

| Layer | (I) Base-year cost | (II) Inflation index | (III) LIFO value: (I) * (II) |
|---|---|---|---|
| Base layer | $105,000 | 1.00 | $105,000 |
| 1998 layer | 3,000 | 1.40 | 4,200 |
| Total | 108,000 | | 109,200 |

(ii) Upon examining Z's federal income tax return for the taxable year ending December 31, 2000, the examining agent determines that Z's dollar-value LIFO method does not clearly reflect income. The examining agent chooses to change Z to the double-extension IPIC method for 2000 and implements the change using the simplified transition method as follows. First, the inventory in Z's dollar-value pool at the end of 2000 is assigned to the most-detailed categories in the CPI or PPI, whichever is appropriate. Assume that 80 percent of the current-year cost of Z's inventory as of December 31, 2000, is assigned to Category 1, 10 percent is assigned to Category 2, and 10 percent is assigned to Category 3. Assume further that the current-year cost of the inventory in Z's dollar-value pool at the end of 1998 and 1999 was $133,000 and $145,000, respectively.

(iii) The category inflation indexes for 1998 computed under the double-extension IPIC method are 1.17 for Category 1, 1.26 for Category 2, and 1.19 for Category 3. The weights to be used in computing the IPI for 1998 are $106,400 ($133,000 * 80 percent) for Category 1, $13,300 ($133,000 * 10 percent) for Category 2, and $13,300 ($133,000 * 10 percent) for Category 3. The IPI for 1998 is computed as follows:

| Category | (I) Weight | (II) Category inflation index | (III) Quotient: (I)/(II) |
|---|---|---|---|
| 1 | $106,400 | 1.17 | 90,940 |
| 2 | 13,300 | 1.26 | 10,556 |
| 3 | 13,300 | 1.19 | 11,176 |
| Total | 133,000 | | 112,672 |

| (IV) Sum of weights | (V) Sum of (weight/category inflation index) | (VI) Inventory price index: (IV)/(V) |
|---|---|---|
| $133,000 | $112,672 | 1.180417 |

(iv) The base-year cost of the inventory in Z's pool at the end of 1998 is $112,672 ($133,000/1.180417), and the base-year cost of the 1998 increment is $7,672 ($112,672-$105,000). The LIFO value of the 1998 layer is $9,056 ($7,672 x 1.180417).

(v) The category inflation indexes for 1999 computed under the double-extension IPIC method were 1.21 for Category 1, 1.29 for Category 2 and 1.23 for Category 3. The weights to be used in computing the IPI for 1999 are $116,000 ($145,000 x 80 percent) for Category 1, $14,500 ($145,000 x 10 percent) for Category 2, and $14,500 ($145,000 x 10 percent) for Category 3. The IPI for 1999 is computed as follows:

| Category | (I) Weight | (II) Category inflation index | (III) Quotient: (I)/(II) |
|---|---|---|---|
| 1 | $116,000 | 1.21 | $ 95,868 |
| 2 | 14,500 | 1.29 | 11,240 |
| 3 | 14,500 | 1.23 | 11,789 |
| Total | 145,000 | | 118,897 |

| (IV) Sum of weights | (V) Sum of (weight/category inflation index) | (VI) Inventory price index: (IV)/(V) |
|---|---|---|
| $145,000 | $118,897 | 1.219543 |

(vi) The base-year cost of the inventory in Z's pool at the end of 1999 is $118,897 ($145,000/1.219543), and the base-year cost of the 1999 layer is $6,225 ($118,897-$112,672). The LIFO value of the 1999 layer is $7,592 ($6,225 x 1.219543).

(vii) The LIFO value of Z's dollar-value pool at the end of 1999 computed under the double-extension IPIC method is as follows:

| Layer | (I) Base-year cost | (II) Inventory price index | (III) LIFO value: (I) * (II) |
|---|---|---|---|
| Base layer | $105,000 | 1.000000 | $105,000 |
| 1998 layer | 7,672 | 1.180417 | 9,056 |
| 1999 layer | 6,225 | 1.219542 | 7,592 |
| Total | 118,897 | | 121,648 |

(viii) The section 481(a) adjustment is equal to the difference between the LIFO value of the inventory at the beginning of 2000 computed under Z's former method of accounting and recomputed by the examining agent under the double-extension IPIC method, or $12,448 ($121,648--$109,200).

(ix) Finally, the examining agent will recompute Z's taxable income for 2000 and succeeding taxable years using the double-extension IPIC method.

(v) Effective date. (A) In general. The rules of this paragraph (e)(3) and paragraphs (b)(4) and (c)(2) of this section are applicable for taxable years ending on or after December 31, 2001.

(B) Change in method of accounting. Any change in a taxpayer's method of accounting necessary to comply with this paragraph (e)(3) or with paragraphs (b)(4) or (c)(2) of this section is a change in method of accounting to which the provisions of section 446 and the regulations thereunder apply. For the first or second taxable year ending on or after

December 31, 2001, a taxpayer is granted the consent of the Commissioner to change its method of accounting to a method required or permitted by this paragraph (e)(3) and paragraphs (b)(4) and (c)(2) of this section. A taxpayer that wants to change its method of accounting under this paragraph (e)(3)(v) must follow the automatic consent procedures in Rev. Proc. 2002-9 (2002-3 I.R.B. xxx) (see § 601.601(d)(2) of this chapter). However, the scope limitations in section 4.02 of Rev. Proc. 2002-9 do not apply, and the five-year limitation on the readoption of the LIFO method under section 10.01(2) of the Appendix is waived. In addition, if the taxpayer's method of accounting for its LIFO inventories is an issue under consideration at the time the application is filed with the national office, the audit protection of section 7 of Rev. Proc. 2002-9 does not apply. If a taxpayer changing its method of accounting under this paragraph (e)(3)(v)(B) is under examination, before an appeals office, or before a federal court with respect to any income tax issue, the taxpayer must provide a copy of the application to the examining agent(s), appeals officer or counsel for the government, as appropriate, at the same time it files the application with the national office. Any change under this paragraph (e)(3)(v)(B) must be made using a cut-off method and new base year. See paragraph (e)(3)(iv)(B)(1) of this section for an example of this computation. Because a change under this paragraph (e)(3)(v)(B) is made using a cut-off method, a section 481(a) adjustment is not permitted. However, a taxpayer changing its method of accounting under this paragraph (e)(3)(v)(B) must comply with the requirements of section 10.06(3) of the APPENDIX of Rev. Proc. 2002-9 (concerning bargain purchases).

**(f) Change to dollar-value method from another method of pricing LIFO inventories.** *(1) Consent required.* Except as provided in § 1.472-3 in the case of a taxpayer electing to use a LIFO inventory method for the first time, or in the case of a taxpayer changing to the dollar-value method and continuing to use the same pools as were used under another LIFO method, a taxpayer using another LIFO method of pricing inventories may not change to the dollar-value method of pricing such inventories unless he first secures the consent of the Commissioner in accordance with paragraph (e) of § 1.446-1.

*(2) Method of converting inventory.* Where the taxpayer changes from one method of pricing LIFO inventories to the dollar-value method, the ending LIFO inventory for the taxable year immediately preceding the year of change shall be converted to the dollar-value LIFO method. This is done to establish the base-year cost for subsequent calculations. Thus, if the taxpayer was previously valuing LIFO inventories on the specific goods method, these separate values shall be combined into appropriate pools. For this purpose, the base year for the pool shall be the earliest taxable year for which the LIFO inventory method had been adopted for any item in that pool. No change will be made in the overall LIFO value of the opening inventory for the year of change as a result of the conversion, and that inventory will merely be restated in the manner used under the dollar-value method. All layers of increment for such inventory must be retained, except that all layers of increment which occurred in the same taxable year must be combined. The following examples illustrate the provisions of this subparagraph:

*Example (1).* (i) Assume that the taxpayer has used another LIFO method for finished goods since 1954 and has complied with all the requirements prerequisite for a change to the dollar-value method. Items A, B, and C, which have previously been inventoried under the specific goods LIFO method, may properly be included in a single dollar-value LIFO pool. The LIFO inventory value of items A, B, and C at December 31, 1960, is $12,200, computed as follows:

| Year | Base Quantity And Yearly Increments | Unit Cost Value | Dec. 31, 1960, Inventory At LIFO |
|---|---|---|---|
| Item A | | | |
| 1954 (base year) | 100 | $1 | $100 |
| 1955 | 200 | 2 | 400 |
| 1956 | 100 | 4 | 400 |
| 1960 | 100 | 6 | 600 |
| Total | 500 | | 1,500 |
| Item B | | | |
| 1954 (base year) | 300 | 6 | 1,800 |
| 1955 | 100 | 8 | 800 |
| 1960 | 50 | 10 | 500 |
| Total | 450 | | 3,100 |
| Item C | | | |
| 1954 (base year) | 1,000 | 4 | 4,000 |
| 1955 | 200 | 6 | 1,200 |
| 1956 | 300 | 8 | 2,400 |
| Total | 1,500 | | 7,600 |
| LIFO value of items A, B, and C at Dec. 31, 1960 | | | 12,200 |

There were no increments in the years 1957, 1958, or 1959.

(ii) The computation of the ratio of the total current-year cost to the total base-year cost for the base year and each layer of increment in Pool No. 1 as shown as follows:

| Item | 1954 Base-Year Unit Cost | Year 1954 | Increments 1955 | 1956 | 1960 |
|---|---|---|---|---|---|
| A | | | | | |
| Base-year cost | $1.00 | $100 | $200 | $100 | $100 |
| Total—LIFO | | 100 | 400 | 400 | 600 |
| B | | | | | |
| Base-year cost | 6.00 | 1,800 | 600 | | 300 |
| LIFO value | | 1,800 | 800 | | 500 |
| C | | | | | |
| Base-year cost | 4.00 | 4,000 | 800 | 1,200 | |
| LIFO value | | 4,000 | 1,200 | 2,400 | |
| Total—Base-year cost | | 5,900 | 1,600 | 1,300 | 400 |
| Total—LIFO value | | 5,900 | 2,400 | 2,800 | 1,100 |
| Ratio of total current-year cost to total base-year cost (percent) | | 100.00 | 150.00 | 215.38 | 275.00 |

(iii) On the basis of the foregoing computations, the LIFO inventory of Pool No. 1, at December 31, 1960, is restated as follows:

| | Dec. 31, 1960, Inventory At Base-Year Cost | Ratio Of Total Current-Year Cost To Total Base-Year Cost | Dec. 31, 1960, Inventory At LIFO Value |
|---|---|---|---|
| | | Percent | |
| 1954 base cost | 5,900 | 100.00 | $5,900 |
| 1955 increment | 1,600 | 150.00 | 2,400 |
| 1956 increment | 1,300 | 215.38 | 2,800 |
| 1960 increment | 400 | 275.00 | 1,100 |
| Total | 9,200 | | 12,200 |

*Example (2).* Assume the same facts as in example (1) and assume further that the base-year cost of Pool No. 1 at December 31, 1961, is $8,350. Since the closing inventory for the taxable year 1961 at base-year cost is less than the opening inventory for that year at base-year cost, a liquidation has occurred during 1961. This liquidation absorbs all of the 1960 layer of increment and part of the 1956 layer of increment. The December 31, 1961, inventory is $10,131, computed as follows:

| | Dec. 31, 1961, Inventory At Base-Year Cost | Ratio Of Total Current-Year Cost To Total Base-Year Cost | Dec. 31, 1961, Inventory At LIFO Value |
|---|---|---|---|
| | | Percent | |
| 1954 base cost | 5,900 | 100.00 | $5,900 |
| 1955 increment | 1,600 | 150.00 | 2,400 |
| 1956 increment | 850 | 215.38 | 1,831 |
| Total | 8,350 | | 10,131 |

**(g) Transitional rules.** *(1) Change in method of pooling.* Any method of pooling authorized by this section and used by the taxpayer in computing his LIFO inventories under the dollar-value method shall be treated as a method of accounting. Any method of pooling which is authorized by this section shall be used for the year of adoption and for all subsequent taxable years unless a change is required by the Commissioner in order to clearly reflect income, or unless permission to change is granted by the Commissioner as provided in paragraph (e) of § 1.446-1. Where the taxpayer changes from one method of pooling to another method of pooling permitted by this section, the ending LIFO inventory for the taxable year preceding the year of change shall be restated under the new method of pooling.

*(2) Manner of combining or separating dollar-value pools.* (i) A taxpayer who has been using the dollar-value LIFO method and who is permitted or required to change his method of pooling, shall combine or separate the LIFO value of his inventory for the base year and each yearly layer of increment in order to conform to the new pool or pools. Each yearly layer of increment in the new pool or pools must be separately accounted for and a record thereof maintained, and any liquidation occurring in the new pool or pools subsequent to the formation thereof shall be treated in the same manner as if the new pool or pools had existed from the date the taxpayer first adopted the LIFO inventory method. The combination or separation of the LIFO value of his inventory for the base year and each yearly layer of increment shall be made in accordance with the appropriate method set forth in this subparagraph, unless the use of a different method is approved by the Commissioner.

(ii) Where the taxpayer is permitted or required to separate a pool into more than one pool, the separation shall be made in the following manner: First, each item in the former pool shall be placed in an appropriate new pool. Every item in each new pool is then extended at its base-year unit cost and the extensions are totaled. Each total is the amount of inventory for each new pool expressed in terms of base-year cost. Then a ratio of the total base-year cost of each new pool to the base-year cost of the former pool is computed. The resulting ratio is applied to the amount of inventory for the base year and each yearly layer of increment of the former pool to obtain an allocation to each new pool of the base-year inventory of the former pool and subsequent layers of increment thereof. The foregoing may be illustrated by the following example of a change for the taxable year 1961:

*Example.* (a) Assume that items A, B, C, and D are all grouped together in one pool prior to December 31, 1960. The LIFO inventory value at December 21, 1960, is computed as follows:

| | Pool ABCD | | |
|---|---|---|---|
| | Dec. 31, 1960, Inventory At Jan. 1, 1956, Base-Year Cost | Ratio Of Total Current-Year Cost To Total Base-Year Cost | Dec. 31, 1960, Inventory At LIFO Value |
| | | Percent | |
| Jan. 1, 1956, base cost | 10,000 | 100 | $10,000 |
| Dec. 31, 1956, increment | 1,000 | 110 | 1,100 |
| Dec. 31, 1958, increment | 5,000 | 120 | 6,000 |
| Dec. 31, 1960, increment | 4,000 | 125 | 5,000 |
| Total | 20,000 | | 22,100 |

(b) The extension of the quantity of items A, B, C, and D at respective base-year unit costs is as follows:

| Item | Quantity | Base-Year Unit Cost | Amount |
|---|---|---|---|
| A | 2,000 | $2 | $4,000 |
| B | 1,000 | 3 | 3,000 |
| C | 1,000 | 5 | 5,000 |
| D | 4,000 | 2 | 8,000 |
| Total | | | 20,000 |

(c) Under the provisions of this section the taxpayer separates former Pool ABCD into two pools, Pool AB and Pool CD. The computation of the ratio of total base-year cost for each of the new pools to the base-year cost of the former pool is as follows:

| Item | Total Base-Year Cost | Ratio |
|---|---|---|
| Pool AB: | | |
| A | $4,000 | |

| | | |
|---|---|---|
| B | 3,000 | |
| | 7,000 | 7,000/20,000 |
| Pool CD: | | |
| C | 5,000 | |
| D | 8,000 | |
| | 13,000 | 13,000/20,000 |
| Total for pool ABCD | 20,000 | |

(d) The ratio of the base-year cost of new Pools AB and CD to the base-year cost of former Pool ABCD is 7,000/20,000 and 13,000/20,000, respectively. The allocation of the January 1, 1956 base cost and subsequent yearly layers of increment of former Pool ABCD to new Pools AB and CD is as follows:

| | Base-Year Cost To Be Allocated | Pool AB | Pool CD |
|---|---|---|---|
| Jan. 1, 1956, base cost | $10,000 | $3,500 | $6,500 |
| Dec. 31, 1956, increment | 1,000 | 350 | 650 |
| Dec. 31, 1958, increment | 5,000 | 1,750 | 3,250 |
| Dec. 31, 1960, increment | 4,000 | 1,400 | 2,600 |
| Total | 20,000 | 7,000 | 13,000 |

(e) The LIFO value of new Pools AB and CD at December 31, 1960, as allocated, is as follows:

| | Dec. 31, 1960, Inventory At Jan. 1, 1956, Base-Year Cost | Ratio Of Total Current-Year Cost To Total Base-Year Cost | Dec. 31, 1960, Inventory At LIFO Value |
|---|---|---|---|
| | | Percent | |
| Pool AB | | | |
| Jan. 1, 1956, base cost | 3,500 | 100 | $3,500 |
| Dec. 31, 1956, increment | 350 | 110 | 385 |
| Dec. 31, 1958, increment | 1,750 | 120 | 2,100 |
| Dec. 31, 1960, increment | 1,400 | 125 | 1,750 |
| Total | 7,000 | | 7,735 |
| Pool CD | | | |
| Jan. 1, 1956, base cost | 6,500 | 100 | 6,500 |
| Dec. 31, 1956, increment | 650 | 110 | 715 |
| Dec. 31, 1958, increment | 3,250 | 120 | 3,900 |
| Dec. 31, 1960, increment | 2,600 | 125 | 3,250 |
| Total | 13,000 | | 14,365 |

(iii) Where the taxpayer is permitted or required to combine two or more pools having the same base year, they shall be combined into one pool in the following manner: The LIFO value of the base-year inventory of each of the former pools is combined to obtain a LIFO value of the base-year inventory for the new pool. Then, any layers of increment in the various pools which occurred in the same taxable year are combined into one total layer of increment for that taxable year. However, layers of increment which occurred in different taxable years may not be combined. In combining the layers of increment a new ratio of current-year cost to base-year cost is computed for each of the combined layers of increment. The foregoing may be illustrated by the following example:

*Example.* (a) Assume the taxpayer has two pools at December 31, 1960. Under the provisions of this section the taxpayer combines these pools into a single pool as of January 1, 1961. The LIFO inventory value of each pool at December 31, 1960, is shown as follows:

| | Dec. 31, 1960, Inventory At Jan. 1, 1957, Base-Year Cost | Ratio Of Total Current-Year Cost To Total Base-Year Cost | Dec. 31, 1960, Inventory At LIFO Value |
|---|---|---|---|
| Pool No. 1 | | Percent | |
| Jan. 1, 1957, base cost | 10,000 | 100 | $10,000 |
| Dec. 31, 1957, increment | 2,000 | 110 | 2,200 |
| Dec. 31, 1960, increment | 1,000 | 120 | 1,200 |
| Total | 13,000 | | 13,400 |
| Pool No. 2 | | | |
| Jan. 1, 1957, base cost | 5,000 | 100 | 5,000 |
| Dec. 31, 1960, increment | 3,000 | 140 | 4,200 |
| Total | 8,000 | | 9,200 |

(b) The computation of the ratio of the total current-year cost to the total base-year cost for the base year and each yearly layer of increment in the new pool is as follows:

| Pool | Base Year 1957 | Increments Dec. 31, 1957 | Increments Dec. 31, 1960 |
|---|---|---|---|
| No. 1: | | | |
| Base-year cost | $10,000 | $2,000 | $1,000 |
| LIFO value | 10,000 | 2,200 | 1,200 |
| No. 2: | | | |
| Base-year cost | 5,000 | | 3,000 |
| LIFO value | 5,000 | | 4,200 |
| Total, base-year cost | 15,000 | 2,000 | 4,000 |
| Total, LIFO value | 15,000 | 2,200 | 5,400 |
| Ratio of total current-year cost to total base-year cost (per-cent) | 100 | 110 | 135 |

(c) On the basis of the foregoing computations, the LIFO inventory of the new pool at December 31, 1960, is restated as follows:

| | Dec. 31, 1960, Inventory At Jan. 1, 1957, Base-Year Cost | Ratio Of Total Current-Year Cost To Total Base-Year Cost | Dec. 31, 1960, Inventory At LIFO Value |
|---|---|---|---|
| | | Percent | |
| Jan. 1, 1957, base cost | 15,000 | 100 | $15,000 |
| Dec. 31, 1957, increment | 2,000 | 110 | 2,200 |
| Dec. 31, 1960, increment | 4,000 | 135 | 5,400 |
| Total | 21,000 | | 22,600 |

(iv) In combining pools having different base years, the principles set forth in subdivision (iii) of this subparagraph are to be applied, except that all base years subsequent to the earliest base year shall be treated as increments, and the base-year costs for all pools having a base year subsequent to the earliest base year of any pool shall be redetermined in terms of the base cost for the earliest base year. The foregoing may be illustrated by the following example:

*Example.* (a) Assume that the taxpayer has two pools at December 31, 1960. Under the provisions of this section the taxpayer combines these pools into a single pool as of January 1, 1961. The LIFO inventory value of each pool at December 31, 1960, is shown as follows:

| | Dec. 31, 1960, Inventory At Jan. 1, 1956, Base-Year Cost | Ratio Of Total Current-Year Cost To Total Base-Year Cost | Dec. 31, 1960, Inventory At LIFO Value |
|---|---|---|---|
| Pool No. 1 | | Percent | |
| Jan. 1, 1956, base cost | 7,000 | 100 | $7,000 |
| Dec. 31, 1956, increment | 1,000 | 105 | 1,050 |
| Dec. 31, 1957, increment | 500 | 110 | 550 |
| Dec. 31, 1958, increment | 500 | 110 | 550 |
| Dec. 31, 1960, increment | 1,000 | 120 | 1,200 |
| Total | 10,000 | | 10,350 |

| | Dec. 31, 1960, Inventory At Jan. 1, 1958, Base-Year Cost | Ratio Of Total Current-Year Cost To Total Base-Year Cost | Dec. 31, 1960, Inventory At LIFO Value |
|---|---|---|---|
| Pool No. 2 | | | |
| Jan. 1, 1958, base cost | 3,500 | 100 | $3,500 |
| Dec. 31, 1958, increment | 1,000 | 110 | 1,100 |
| Dec. 31, 1959, increment | 500 | 115 | 575 |
| Total | 5,000 | | 5,175 |

(b) The next step is to redetermine the 1958 base-year cost for Pool No. 2 in terms of 1956 base-year cost. January 1, 1956 base-year unit cost must be reconstructed or established in accordance with paragraph (e)(2) of this section for each item in Pool No. 2. Such costs are assumed to be $9.00 for item A, $20.00 for item B, and $1.80 for item C. A ratio of the 1958 total base year cost to the 1956 total base-year cost for Pool No. 2 is computed as follows:

| Item | Quantity | Jan. 1, 1956, Base-Year Unit Cost | Jan. 1, 1956 Base-Year Cost |
|---|---|---|---|
| A | 250 | $9.00 | $2,250 |
| B | 75 | 20.00 | 1,500 |
| C | 500 | 1.80 | 900 |
| Total | | | 4,650 |

| Item | Quantity | Jan. 1, 1958, Base-Year Unit Cost | Jan. 1, 1958 Base-Year Cost |
|---|---|---|---|
| A | 250 | $10.00 | $2,500 |
| B | 75 | 20.00 | 1,500 |
| C | 500 | 2.00 | 1,000 |
| Total | | | 5,000 |

(c) The ratio of the 1956 total base-year cost to the 1958 total base-year cost for Pool No. 2 is 4,650/5,000 or 93 percent. The January 1, 1958 base cost and each yearly layer of increment at 1958 base-year cost is multiplied by this ratio. Such computation is as follows:

| | Dec. 31, 1960, Inventory At Jan. 1, 1958, Base-Year Cost | Ratio | Dec. 31, 1960, Inventory Restated At Jan. 1, 1956, Base-Year Cost |
|---|---|---|---|
| | | Percent | |
| Jan. 1, 1958, base cost | 3,500 | 93 | $3,255 |
| Dec. 31, 1958, increment | 1,000 | 93 | 930 |
| Dec. 31, 1959, increment | 500 | 93 | 465 |
| Total | | | 4,650 |

(d) The computation of the ratio of the total current-year cost to the total base-year cost for the base year (1956) and each yearly layer of increment in the new pool is as follows:

| Pool | Base Year 1956 | Increments Dec. 31, 1956 | Dec. 31, 1957 | Dec. 31, 1958 | Dec. 31, 1959 | Dec. 31, 1960 |
|---|---|---|---|---|---|---|
| No. 1: | | | | | | |
| Base-year cost | $7,000 | $1,000 | $500 | $500 | | $1,000 |
| LIFO value | 7,000 | 1,050 | 550 | 550 | | 1,200 |
| No. 2: | | | | | | |
| Base-year cost as restated | | | 3,255 | 930 | $465 | |
| LIFO value | | | 3,500 | 1,100 | 575 | |
| Total, base-year cost | 7,000 | 1,000 | 3,755 | 1,430 | 465 | 1,000 |
| Total, LIFO value | 7,000 | 1,050 | 4,050 | 1,650 | 575 | 1,200 |
| Ratio of total current-year cost to total base-year cost (percent) | 100.00 | 105.00 | 107.86 | 115.38 | 123.66 | 120.00 |

(e) On the basis of the foregoing computation, the LIFO inventory of the new pool at December 31, 1960, is restated as follows:

| | Dec. 31, 1960, Inventory At Jan. 1, 1956, Base-Year Cost | Ratio Of Total Current-Year Cost To Total Base-Year Cost | Dec. 31, 1960, Inventory At LIFO Value |
|---|---|---|---|
| | | Percent | |
| Jan. 1, 1956, base cost | 7,000 | 100.00 | $7,000 |
| Dec. 31, 1956, increment | 1,000 | 105.00 | 1,050 |
| Dec. 31, 1957, increment | 3,755 | 107.86 | 4,050 |
| Dec. 31, 1958, increment | 1,430 | 115.38 | 1,650 |
| Dec. 31, 1959, increment | 465 | 123.66 | 575 |
| Dec. 31, 1960, increment | 1,000 | 120.00 | 1,200 |
| Total | 14,650 | | 15,525 |

*(3) Change in methods of computation of the LIFO value of a dollar-value pool.* For the first taxable year beginning after December 31, 1960, the taxpayer must use a method authorized by paragraph (e)(1) of this section in computing the base-year cost and current-year cost of a dollar-value inventory pool for the end of such year. If the taxpayer had previously used any methods other than one authorized by paragraph (e)(1) of this section, he shall not be required to recompute his LIFO inventories for taxable years beginning on or before December 31, 1960, under a method authorized by such paragraph. The base cost and layers of increment previously computed by such other method shall be retained and treated as if such base cost and layers of increment had been computed under a method authorized by paragraph (e)(1) of this section. The taxpayer shall use the year of change as the base year in applying the double-extension method or other method approved by the Commissioner, instead of the earliest year for which he adopted the LIFO method for any items in the pool.

**(h) LIFO inventories received in certain nonrecognition transactions.** *(1) In general.* Except as provided in paragraph (h)(3) of this section, if inventory items accounted for under the LIFO method are received in a transaction described in paragraph (h)(2) of this section, then, for the purpose of determining future increments and liquidations, the transferee must use the year of transfer as the base year and must use its current-year cost (computed under the transferee's method of accounting) of those items as their new base-year cost. If the transferee had opening inventories in the year of transfer, then, for the purpose of determining future increments and liquidations, the transferee must use its current-year cost (computed under the transferee's method of accounting) of those inventories as their new base-year cost. For this purpose, "opening inventory" refers to all items owned by the transferee before the transfer for which the transferee uses, or elects to use, the LIFO method. The total new base-year cost of the transferee's inventory as of the beginning of the year of transfer is equal to the new base-year cost of the inventory received from the transferor and the new base-year cost of the transferee's opening inventory. The index (or, the cumulative index in the case of the link-chain method) for the year immediately preceding the year of transfer is 1.00. The base-year cost of any layers in the dollar-value pool, as determined after the transfer, must be recomputed accordingly. See paragraph (e)(3)(iv)(B)(1) of this section for an example of this computation.

*(2) Transactions to which this paragraph (h) applies.* The rules in this paragraph (h) apply to a transaction in which—

(i) The transferee determines its basis in the inventories, in whole or in part, by reference to the basis of the inventories in the hands of the transferor;

(ii) The transferor used the dollar-value LIFO method to account for the transferred inventories;

(iii) The transferee uses the dollar-value LIFO method to account for the inventories in the year of the transfer; and

(iv) The transaction is not described in section 381(a).

*(3) Anti-avoidance rule.* The rules in this paragraph (h) do not apply to a transaction entered into with the principal purpose to avail the transferee of a method of accounting that would be unavailable to the transferor (or would be unavailable to the transferor without securing consent from the Commissioner). In determining the principal purpose of a transfer, consideration will be given to all of the facts and circumstances. However, a transfer is deemed made with the principal purpose to avail the transferee of a method of accounting that would be unavailable to the transferor without securing consent from the Commissioner if the transferor acquired inventory in a bargain purchase within the five taxable years preceding the year of the transfer and used a dollar-value LIFO method to account for that inventory that did

not treat the bargain purchase inventory and physically identical inventory acquired at market prices as separate items. Inventory is deemed acquired in a bargain purchase if the actual cost of the inventory (or, if appropriate, the allocated cost of the inventory) was less than or equal to 50 percent of the replacement cost of physically identical inventory. Inventory is not considered acquired in a bargain purchase if the actual cost of the inventory (or, if appropriate, the allocated cost of the inventory) was greater than or equal to 75 percent of the replacement cost of physically identical inventory.

*(4) Effective date.* The rules of this paragraph (h) are applicable for transfers that occur during a taxable year ending on or after December 31, 2001.

---

T.D. 6539, 1/19/61, amend T.D. 7814, 3/15/82, T.D. 8976, 1/8/2002.

---

**§ 1.475-0 Table of contents.**

This section lists the major captions in §§ 1.475(a)-3, 1.475(a)-4, 1.475(b)-1, 1.475(b)-2, 1.475(b)-4, 1.475(c)-1, 1.475(c)-2, 1.475(d)-1 and 1.475(g)-1.

(d) Special rule for hedges of another member's risk.

(e) Transitional rules.

(1) Stock, partnership, and beneficial ownership interests in certain controlled corporations, partnerships, and trusts before January 23, 1997.

(i) In general.

(ii) Control defined.

(iii) Applicability.

(2) Dealers in notional principal contracts and derivatives acquired before January 23, 1997.

(i) General rule.

(ii) Exception for securities not acquired in dealer capacity.

(iii) Applicability.

*§ 1.475(b)-2 Exemptions—identification requirements.*

(a) Identification of the basis for exemption.

(b) Time for identifying a security with a substituted basis.

(c) Integrated transactions under § 1.1275-6.

(1) Definitions.

(2) Synthetic debt held by a taxpayer as a result of legging in.

(3) Securities held after legging out.

*§ 1.475(b)-3 [Reserved]*

*§ 1.475(b)-4 Exemptions—transitional issues.*

(a) Transitional identification.

(1) Certain securities previously identified under section 1236.

(2) Consistency requirement for other securities.

(b) Corrections on or before January 31, 1994.

(1) Purpose.

(2) To conform to § 1.475(b)-1(a).

(i) Added identifications.

(i) Limitations.

(3) To conform to § 1.475(b)-1(c).

(c) Effect of corrections.

*§ 1.475(c)-1 Definitions—dealer in securities.*

(a) Dealer-customer relationship.

(1) [Reserved].

(2) Transactions described in section 475(c)(1)(B).

(i) In general.

(ii) Examples.

(3) Related parties.

(i) General rule.

(ii) Special rule for members of a consolidated group.

(iii) The intragroup-customer election.

(A) Effect of election.

(B) Making and revoking the election.

(iv) Examples.

(b) Sellers of nonfinancial goods and services.

(1) Purchases and sales of customer paper.

(2) Definition of customer paper.

(3) Exceptions.

(4) Election not to be governed by the exception for sellers of nonfinancial goods or services.

(i) Method of making the election.

(A) Taxable years ending after December 24, 1996.

(B) Taxable years ending on or before December 24, 1996.

(ii) Continued applicability of an election.

(c) Taxpayers that purchase securities from customers but engage in no more than negligible sales of the securities.

(1) Exemption from dealer status.

(i) General rule.

(ii) Election to be treated as a dealer.

(2) Negligible sales.

(3) Special rules for members of a consolidated group.

(i) Intragroup-customer election in effect.

(ii) Intragroup-customer election not in effect.

(4) Special rules.

(5) Example.

(d) Issuance of life insurance products.

*§ 1.475(c)-2 Definitions—security.*

(a) Items that are not securities.

(b) Synthetic debt that § 1.1275-6(b) treats the taxpayer as holding.

(c) Negative value REMIC residuals acquired before January 4, 1995.

(1) Description.

(2) Special rules applicable to negative value REMIC residuals acquired before January 4, 1995.

*§ 1.475(d)-1 Character of gain or loss.*

(a) Securities never held in connection with the taxpayer's activities as a dealer in securities.

(b) Ordinary treatment for notional principal contracts and derivatives held by dealers in notional principal contracts and derivatives.

*§ 1.475(g)-1 Effective dates.*

T.D. 8700, 12/23/96, amend T.D. 9328, 6/11/2007.

**Proposed § 1.475(a)-1 Mark to market of debt instruments.** [*For Preamble, see ¶ 151,647*]

• ***Caution:*** Proposed regulations 1.475-0, 1.475(a)-3, 1.475(b)-4, 1.475(c)-1, 1.475(c)-2, and 1.475(e)-1 were finalized by T.D. 8700, 12/23/96. Prop. reg. §§ 1.475(a)-1, 1.475(a)-2 and 1.475(b)-3 remain proposed.

***Caution:*** The Treasury has not yet amended Reg § 1.475(a)-1 to reflect changes made by P.L. 104-188.

**(a) Overview.** This section provides rules for taking into account interest accruals and gain and loss on a debt instrument to which section 475(a) applies. Paragraph (b) of this section clarifies that the mark-to-market computation affects neither the amount treated as interest earned from a debt instrument nor the taxable year in which that interest is taken into account. Paragraph (c) of this section prescribes general rules. Paragraph (d) of this section prescribes additional rules for instruments acquired with market discount. Paragraph (e) of this section provides rules for taking into account market discount that accrued on a bond before the bond became subject to the mark-to-market requirements. Paragraph (f) of this section prescribes rules for computing the mark-to-market gain or loss on partially or wholly worthless debts, and paragraph (g) provides rules for dealers accounting for bad debts using a reserve method of accounting.

**(b) No effect on amount of market discount, acquisition premium, or bond premium.** Marking a debt instrument to market does not create, increase, or reduce market discount, acquisition premium, or bond premium, nor does it affect the adjusted issue price of, or accruals of original issue discount (OID) on, a bond issued with OID.

**(c) Accrual of interest, discount, and premium.** In general, the amount of gain or loss from marking a debt instrument to market is computed after adjustments to basis for accruals of stated interest, discount, and premium.

*(1) Qualified stated interest.* Immediately before a debt instrument is marked to market under section 475(a), the holder of the instrument must take any unpaid accrued qualified stated interest into account and must correspondingly increase the basis of the instrument. The holder must later decrease the basis of the instrument when accrued qualified stated interest is actually received. (See § 1.1273-1(c) for the definition of qualified stated interest and § 1.446-2(b) for the rule governing its accrual.)

*(2) General rule regarding accrual of discount.* If a bond that was acquired with OID or market discount is marked to market under section 475(a), then, immediately before the bond is marked to market, the discount accrued through that date (determined under section 1272, 1275(d), or 1276, as applicable) is included in gross income, to the extent not previously included, and the bond's basis is correspondingly increased for amounts so included. (Because accrued OID is determined under all of the rules of section 1272 and the regulations thereunder, it is computed taking into account the reduction for acquisition premium that is required by section 1272(a)(7).) See paragraph (d) of this section, which requires the current inclusion in income of market discount on bonds marked to market. See paragraph (e) of this section for exceptions, and additional rules, for market discount bonds that become subject to section 475(a) after acquisition.

*(3) Bond premium.* If a debt instrument that is subject to the basis adjustment required by section 1016(a)(5) or (6) is marked to market under section 475(a), then, immediately before the debt instrument is marked to market, the required basis adjustment must be made. Accordingly, the mark-to-market adjustment is computed after the basis of the debt instrument has been adjusted under section 1016(a)(5) or (6) for disallowed amortizable bond premium (in the case of tax-exempt bonds) or deductible bond premium (in the case of taxable bonds). If an election under section 171(c) is made after the first taxable year in which section 475(a) applies to the bond, the amount of bond premium is determined under section 171(b)(1) without regard to any basis adjustments that may have been required as a result of the bond being marked to market in prior taxable years. See paragraph (b) of this section for the rule that marking a debt instrument to market does not affect bond premium.

**(d) Mandatory current inclusion of market discount.** *(1) General rule.* If section 475(a) applies to a bond during any portion of a taxable year, gross income for that taxable year includes the market discount attributable to the portion of the year to which section 475(a) applies (as determined under section 1276(b)). Section 1276 does not apply to the bond except with respect to market discount, if any, that accrued before the bond became subject to section 475(a). Similarly, section 1277 does not apply to the bond except with respect to any net direct interest expense (as defined in section 1277(c)) that accrued before the bond became subject to section 475(a). See paragraph (e) of this section for additional rules governing this situation. For purposes of the Code other than the purposes described in the last sentence of section 1278(b)(1), any amount included in gross income under this paragraph (d)(1) is treated as interest. The bond's basis is correspondingly increased for any amount so included in gross income.

*(2) Interaction with section 1278(b).* Paragraph (d)(1) of this section applies to a dealer, even if the dealer has not elected under section 1278(b) to include market discount currently. If the dealer has not made that election, however, this paragraph (d) does not require current inclusion of market discount on any bond to which section 475(a) does not apply.

**(e) Recognition of market discount that accrued before section 475(a) applies to a market discount bond.** *(1) General rule.* In the case of a debt instrument that is acquired with market discount, that is not subject to an election under section 1278(b), and that first becomes subject to section 475(a) in the taxpayer's hands on a date after its acquisition, this paragraph (e) governs the recognition of market discount that is attributable (as determined under section 1276(b)) to any period before section 475(a) applies to the debt instrument. To the extent that the market discount described in the preceding sentence is greater than the excess, if any, of the fair market value of the debt instrument at the time it became subject to section 475(a) over its adjusted basis at that time, section 1276(a)(1) applies to any gain recognized under section 475(a). To the extent of any remaining market discount that had accrued before section 475(a) became applicable, section 1276(a) applies no later than it would have applied if section 475(a) did not apply to the bond. For example, section 1276(a) applies to the previously accrued market discount as partial principal payments are made. Except as provided in the preceding sentences, gain recognized under section 475(a) is not recharacterized as interest by section 1276(a).

*(2) Examples.* The rules of paragraphs (d) and (e) of this section are illustrated by the following examples:

*Example (1).* (i) Facts. Bond X was issued on January 1, 1996, for $1,000. Bond X matures on December 31, 2005, provides for a principal payment of $1,000 on the maturity date, and provides for interest payments at a rate of 8%, compounded annually, on December 31 of each year. D is a dealer in securities within the meaning of section 475(c)(1). On January 1, 1997, D purchased bond X for $955. D had not elected under section 1278(b) to include market discount in gross income currently. Under section 475(b), section 475(a) did not apply to bond X until January 1, 1999, at which time bond X had a fair market value of $961. On December 31, 1999, bond X had a fair market value of $980.

(ii) Holdings. In the absence of an election under section 1276(b)(2), market discount on bond X accrues under section 1276(b)(1) at the rate of $5 per year. On January 1, 1999, when bond X became subject to section 475(a), $10 of market discount had accrued, but the excess of the bond's fair market value on January 1, 1999, over its adjusted basis on that date (the built-in gain) was only $6 ($961 – $955). During 1999, D is required to include as interest income the

$5 of market discount that accrues during that year, and D increases by that amount its basis in the bond and the amount to be used in computing mark-to-market gain or loss. On December 31, 1999, B must mark bond X to market and recognize a gain of $14 ($980 − [$961 + $5]). Under section 1276(a)(1) and (4) and paragraph (e)(1) of this section, $4 of that $14 gain is treated as interest income. The $4 is the amount by which the market discount of $10 that had accrued on January 1, 1999, exceeded the $6 built-in gain on that date.

*Example (2).* (i) Facts. The facts are the same as in Example 1, except that, in addition, D sells bond X for its fair market value of $1,000 on June 30, 2000.

(ii) Holdings. Immediately before the sale, D is required to include as interest income the $2.50 of market discount that accrued during the portion of the year through June 30, and D increases by that amount its basis in the bond and the amount to be used in computing mark-to-market gain or loss. Also, under § 1.475(a)-2, immediately before the sale, D recognizes $17.50 of mark-to-market gain (the increase in value since the preceding mark to market, less the basis increase of $2.50 from the market discount accrual. See § 1.475(a)-2). On the sale, D also recognizes the $6 of built-in gain, all of which is recharacterized as ordinary interest income under section 1276(a)(4).

*Example (3).* (i) Facts. The facts are the same as in Example 1, except that, during 2001, the issuer of bond X made a partial principal payment in the amount of $20.

(ii) Holdings. Under paragraph (e)(1) of this section and section 1276(a)(4), $6 of the partial principal payment is included in D's 2001 income as interest income. The $6 is the portion of the $10 of market discount that had accrued at the time bond X became subject to section 475(a) and that had not previously caused gain or a partial principal payment to be treated as interest income.

**(f) Worthless debts.** *(1) Computation of mark-to-market gain or loss.* This paragraph (f) applies to any dealer that, under section 475(a)(2), marks to market either a debt that was charged off during the year because it became partially worthless or a debt that became wholly worthless during the taxable year (without regard to whether the debt was charged off). Any gain or loss attributable to marking a debt to market is determined by deeming the debt's adjusted basis to be the debt's adjusted basis under § 1.1011-1, less the amount charged off during the taxable year or during any prior taxable year, to the extent that amount has not previously reduced tax basis. A debt that becomes wholly worthless is deemed to have an adjusted basis of zero. The deemed adjusted basis, however, is used solely for this paragraph (f). Thus, any portion of a loss attributable to a bad debt continues to be accounted for under the bad debt provisions of the Code, and the basis of the debt continues to be adjusted as otherwise required under the Code.

*(2) Treatment of mark-to-market gain or loss.* To the extent that a debt has been previously charged off, mark-to-market gain is treated as a recovery. Thus, for example, a dealer using the section 585 reserve method of accounting for bad debts must credit to the reserve any portion of mark-to-market gain that is treated as a recovery of a bad debt previously charged to the reserve account, and the dealer must include any excess in gross income as required by § 1.585-3(a). Similarly, if a dealer is a large bank that changed to the specific charge-off method of accounting for bad debts using the elective cut-off procedures described in § 1.585-7, the dealer must charge to the reserve for pre-disqualification loans all losses recognized as a result of marking to market a debt that is a pre-disqualification loan within the meaning of § 1.585-7(b)(2). Marking a pre-disqualification loan to market, however, is not a disposition of that loan under § 1.585-7(d).

**(g) Additional rules applicable to reserve-method taxpayers.** If a dealer accounts for bad debts using the reserve method of accounting under section 585 or 593, the following additional rules apply in computing a reasonable addition to a reserve—

*(1)* To determine the amount of total loans outstanding, the outstanding balance on a debt that is marked to market is increased or decreased by the amount of any mark-to-market gain or loss recognized, except that the outstanding balance of the debt may never exceed the actual balance currently due; and

*(2)* If the reasonable addition to the reserve is computed based on a percentage of taxable income, any gain or loss attributable to marking a debt to market must be taken into account in computing taxable income.

**(h) Example.** This example illustrates paragraphs (f) and (g) of this section.

*Example.* (i) B, a calendar year taxpayer, is a dealer that marks some of its debts to market under section 475(a)(2). Additionally, B is a bank that accounts for bad debts using the section 585 reserve method of accounting. B has not made an election to use the conformity method of accounting described in § 1.166-2(d)(3).

(ii) On December 31, 1995, B has total loans outstanding of $1,000,000 and a bad debt reserve balance of $1000. Among the loans that B marks to market is loan X. On January 1, 1995, loan X had a book and tax basis of $100. During the taxable year, loan X became partially worthless, and B charged off the loan by $5. Thus, loan X had a book basis of $95 and a tax basis of $100. The fair market value of loan X was $94 on December 31, 1995.

(iii) B computes the amount of gain or loss to be taken into account under section 475(a)(2) with respect to loan X using the rules of paragraph (f) of this section. Under paragraph (f)(1) of this section, B treats the adjusted tax basis of loan X as having been reduced by the $5 charge-off. Thus, B determines that it is required to take into account a $1 mark-to-market loss based on the difference between B's adjusted basis in loan X of $95, as determined under paragraph (f)(1) of this section, and loan X's fair market value of $94.

(iv) Further, B decides to claim a bad debt deduction with respect to loan X in 1995, rather than waiting until loan X becomes totally worthless. Thus, B charges the $5 of partial worthlessness to its reserve for bad debts. In computing a reasonable addition to the reserve under section 585(b), B reduces the amount of its total loans outstanding by $6 ($5 charged to the reserve for bad debts, plus $1 mark-to-market loss).

(v) On December 31, 1997, loan X has a fair market value of $93 and an adjusted basis (and outstanding principal balance) of $90. No additional worthlessness occurred with respect to loan X in 1996 or 1997. B determines that it is required to recognize a $3 mark-to-market gain with respect to loan X. Because B previously charged $5 to the bad debt reserve with respect to loan X, the entire $3 is a recovery item and must be credited to the bad debt reserve. See paragraph (f)(2) of this section. In computing a reasonable addition to the reserve for 1997, B does not increase the balance of its total loans outstanding by the $3 mark-to-market gain, because that adjustment would increase the balance to an amount in excess of the actual outstanding principal balance of $90. See paragraph (g)(1) of this section.

**Proposed § 1.475(a)-2 Mark to market upon disposition of security by a dealer.** [*For Preamble, see ¶ 151,647*]

• ***Caution:*** Proposed regulations 1.475-0, 1.475(a)-3, 1.475(b)-4, 1.475(c)-1, 1.475(c)-2, and 1.475(e)-1 were finalized by T.D. 8700, 12/23/96. Prop. reg. §§ 1.475(a)-1, 1.475(a)-2 and 1.475(b)-3 remain proposed.

**(a) General rule.** If a dealer in securities ceases to be the owner of a security for federal income tax purposes and if the security would have been marked to market under section 475(a) if the dealer's taxable year had ended immediately before the dealer ceases to own it, then (whether or not the security is inventory in the hands of the dealer) the dealer must recognize gain or loss on the security as if it were sold for its fair market value immediately before the dealer ceases to own it, and gain or loss is taken into account at that time. The amount of any gain or loss subsequently realized must be properly adjusted, in the form of a basis adjustment or otherwise, for gain or loss taken into account under this paragraph (a). See § 1.475(b)-4(b) for the rule governing when a security with substituted basis must be identified if it is to be exempted from the application of section 475(a).

**(b) Example.** The rule of paragraph (a) of this section is illustrated by the following example.

*Example.* (i) Facts. D is a dealer in securities within the meaning of section 475(c)(1) and is a member of a consolidated group that uses the calendar year as its taxable year. On February 1, 1995, D acquired for $100 a debt instrument issued by an unrelated party. On June 1, 1995, D sold the debt instrument to another member of the group, M1, for $110, which was the fair market value of the security on that date. D would have been required to mark the debt instrument to market under section 475(a) if its taxable year had ended immediately before it sold the debt instrument to M1.

(ii) Holding. Under paragraph (a) of this section, D marks the debt instrument to market immediately before the sale to M1 and takes into account $10 of gain. The gain is not deferred intercompany gain. As a result, D's basis in the debt instrument increases to $110 immediately before the sale. Accordingly, there is no gain or loss on the sale, and M1's basis in the debt instrument is $110.

**§ 1.475(a)-3 Acquisition by a dealer of a security with a substituted basis.**

**(a) Scope.** This section applies if—

*(1)* A dealer in securities acquires a security that is subject to section 475(a) and the dealer's basis in the security is determined, in whole or in part, by reference to the basis of that security in the hands of the person from whom the security was acquired; or

*(2)* A dealer in securities acquires a security that is subject to section 475(a) and the dealer's basis in the security is determined, in whole or in part, by reference to other property held at any time by the dealer.

**(b) Rules.** If this section applies to a security—

*(1)* Section 475(a) applies only to changes in value of the security occurring after the acquisition; and

*(2)* Any built-in gain or loss with respect to the security (based on the difference between the fair market value of the security on the date the dealer acquired it and its basis to the dealer on that date) is taken into account at the time, and has the character, provided by the sections of the Internal Revenue Code that would apply to the built-in gain or loss if section 475(a) did not apply to the security.

T.D. 8700, 12/23/96.

**§ 1.475(a)-4 Valuation safe harbor.**

**(a) Overview.** *(1) Purpose.* This section sets forth a safe harbor that, under certain circumstances, permits taxpayers to elect to use the values of positions reported on certain financial statements as the fair market values of those positions for purposes of section 475. This safe harbor is based on the principle that, if a mark-to-market method used for financial reporting is sufficiently consistent with the requirements of section 475 and if the financial statement employing that method has certain indicia of reliability, then the values used on that financial statement may be used for purposes of section 475. If other provisions of the Internal Revenue Code or regulations require adjustments to fair market value, use of the safe harbor does not eliminate the need for those adjustments. See paragraph (e) of this section.

*(2) Dealer business model.* The safe harbor is based on the business model for a derivatives dealer. Under this model, the dealer seeks to capture and profit from bid-ask spreads in the marketplace by entering into substantially offsetting positions with customers that will remain on the derivatives dealer's books over their terms. Because the positions in the aggregate tend to offset each other, the dealer has achieved a predictable net cash flow (for example, a synthetic annuity) that reflects the captured bid-ask spread. This net cash flow is generally impervious to market fluctuations in the values on which the component derivatives are based. Section 475 requires current recognition of the present value of the net cash flow attributable to the capture of these spreads.

*(3) Summary of paragraphs.* Paragraph (b) of this section sets forth the safe harbor. To determine who may use the safe harbor, paragraph (c) of this section defines the term "eligible taxpayer." Paragraph (d) of this section sets forth the basic requirements for determining whether the method used for financial reporting is sufficiently consistent with the requirements of section 475. Paragraph (e) of this section describes adjustments to the financial statement values that may be required for purposes of applying this safe harbor. Paragraph (f) of this section describes the procedure for making the safe harbor election and the conditions under which the election may be revoked. Paragraph (g) of this section provides that the Commissioner will issue a revenue procedure that lists the types of securities and commodities that are eligible positions for purposes of the safe harbor. Using rules for determining priorities among financial statements, paragraph (h) of this section defines the term "applicable financial statement" and so describes the financial statement, if any, whose values may be used in the safe harbor. In some cases, as required by paragraph (j) of this section, the safe harbor is available only if the taxpayer's operations make significant business use of financial statement values. Paragraph (k) of this section sets forth requirements for record retention and record production. Paragraph (m) of this section provides that the Commissioner may use fair market values that clearly reflect income, but which differ from values used on the applicable financial statement, if an

electing taxpayer fails to comply with the recordkeeping and record production requirements of paragraph (k) of this section.

**(b) Safe harbor.** *(1) General rule.* Subject to any adjustment required by paragraph (e) of this section, if an eligible taxpayer uses an eligible method for the valuation of an eligible position on its applicable financial statement and the eligible taxpayer is subject to the election described in paragraph (f) of this section, the value that the eligible taxpayer assigns to that eligible position on its applicable financial statement is the fair market value of the eligible position for purposes of section 475 and must be used for purposes of section 475, even if that value is not the fair market value of the position for any other purpose of the internal revenue laws. Notwithstanding the rule set forth in this paragraph, the Commissioner may, in certain circumstances, use fair market values that clearly reflect income but differ from the values used on the applicable financial statement. See paragraph (m) of this section.

*(2) Example.* Use of eligible and non-eligible methods. X uses eligible methods on its applicable financial statement for some, but not all, securities and commodities that are eligible positions. When X elects into the safe harbor, the election applies to all eligible positions for which X has an eligible method. Therefore, once the election is in effect, the financial statement values for eligible positions for which X has an eligible method are the fair market values of those eligible positions for purposes of section 475. Since X, however, does not have an eligible method for all eligible positions, those eligible positions for which X does not have an eligible method remain subject to the fair market value requirements of section 475 as set out in case law and otherwise.

*(3) Scope of the safe harbor.* The safe harbor may be used only to determine values for eligible positions that are properly marked to market under section 475. It does not determine whether any positions may or may not be subject to mark-to-market accounting under section 475.

**(c) Eligible taxpayer.** An eligible taxpayer is—

*(1)* A dealer in securities, as defined in section 475(c)(1); or

*(2)* A dealer in commodities, as defined in section 475(e), that is subject to an election under section 475(e).

**(d) Eligible method.** *(1) Sufficient consistency.* An eligible method is a mark-to-market method that is sufficiently consistent with the requirements of a mark-to-market method under section 475. To be sufficiently consistent with the requirements of a mark-to-market method under section 475, the eligible method must satisfy all of the requirements of paragraph (d)(2) and paragraph (d)(3) of this section.

*(2) General requirements.* The method—

(i) Frequency. Must require a valuation of the eligible position no less frequently than annually, including a valuation as of the last business day of the taxable year;

(ii) Recognition at the mark. Must recognize into income on the income statement for each taxable year mark-to-market gain or loss based upon the valuation or valuations described in paragraph (d)(2)(i) of this section;

(iii) Recognition on disposition. Must require, on disposition of the eligible position, recognition into income (on the income statement for the taxable year of disposition) as if a year-end mark occurred immediately before such disposition; and

(iv) Fair value standard. Must require use of a valuation standard that arrives at fair value in accordance with U.S. Generally Accepted Accounting Principles (U.S. GAAP).

*(3) Limitations.* (i) Bid-ask method. (A) General rule. Except for eligible positions that are traded on a qualified board or exchange, as defined in section 1256(g)(7), or eligible positions that the Commissioner designates in a revenue procedure or other published guidance, the valuation standard used must not, other than on a de minimis portion of a taxpayer's positions, permit values at or near the bid or ask value. Consequently, the valuation method described in § 1.471-4(a)(1) fails to satisfy this paragraph (d)(3)(i)(A).

(B) Safe harbor. The restriction in paragraph (d)(3)(i)(A) of this section is satisfied if the method consistently produces values that are closer to the mid-market values than they are to the bid or ask values.

(ii) Valuations based on present values of projected cash flows. If the method of valuation consists of projecting cash flows from an eligible position or positions and determining the present value of those cash flows, the method must not take into account any cash flows attributable to a period or time on or before the valuation date. In addition, adjustment of the gain or loss recognized on the mark may be required with respect to payments that will be made after the valuation date to the extent that portions of the payments have been recognized for tax purposes before the valuation and appropriate adjustment has not been made for purposes of determining financial statement value.

(iii) Accounting for costs and risks. Valuations may account for appropriate costs and risks, but no cost or risk may be accounted for more than once, either directly or indirectly. Further, no valuation adjustment for any cost or risk may be made for purposes of this safe harbor if that valuation adjustment is not also permitted by, and taken for, U.S. GAAP purposes on the taxpayer's applicable financial statement. If appropriate, the costs and risks that may be accounted for include, but are not limited to, credit risk (appropriately adjusted for any credit enhancement), future administrative costs, and model risk. An adjustment for credit risk is implicit in computing the present value of cash flows using a discount rate greater than a risk-free rate. Accordingly, a determination of whether any further downward adjustment to value for credit risk is warranted, or whether an upward adjustment is required, must take that implicit adjustment into consideration.

*(4) Examples.* The following examples illustrate this paragraph (d):

*Example (1).* (i) X, a calendar year taxpayer, is a dealer in securities within the meaning of section 475(c)(1). X generally maintains a balanced portfolio of interest rate swaps and other interest rate derivatives, capturing bid-ask spreads and keeping its market exposure within desired limits (using, if necessary, additional derivatives for this purpose). X uses a mark-to-market method on a statement that it is required to file with the United States Securities and Exchange Commission (SEC) and that satisfies paragraph (d)(2) of this section with respect to both the contracts with customers and the additional derivatives. When determining the amount of any gain or loss realized on a sale, exchange, or termination of a position, X makes a proper adjustment for amounts taken into account respecting payments or receipts. All of X's counterparties on the derivatives have credit ratings of AA/aa, according to standard credit ratings obtained from private credit rating agencies.

(ii) Under X's valuation method, as of each valuation date, X determines a mid-market probability distribution of future cash flows under the derivatives and computes the present values of these cash flows. In computing these present values, X uses an industry standard yield curve that is appropriate for obligations by persons with credit ratings of AA/aa. In addition, based on information that includes its own knowledge about the counterparties, X adjusts some of these present values either upward or downward to reflect X's reasonable judgment about the extent to which the true credit status of each counterparty's obligation, taking credit enhancements into account, differs from AA/aa.

(iii) X's methodology does not violate the requirement in paragraph (d)(3)(iii) of this section that the same cost or risk not be taken into account, directly or indirectly, more than once.

*Example (2).* (i) The facts are the same as in Example 1, except that X uses a AAA/aaa rate to discount the payments to be received under the derivatives. Based on information that includes its own knowledge about the counterparties, X adjusts these present values to reflect X's reasonable judgment about the extent to which the true credit status of each counterparty's obligation, taking credit enhancements into account, differs from a AAA/aaa obligation.

(i) X's methodology does not violate the requirement in paragraph (d)(3)(iii) of this section that the same cost or risk not be taken into account, directly or indirectly, more than once.

*Example (3).* (i) The facts are the same as in Example 1, except that, after computing present values using the discount rates that are appropriate for obligors with credit ratings of AA/aa, and based on information that includes X's own knowledge about the counterparties, X adjusts some of these present values either upward or downward to reflect X's reasonable judgment about the extent to which the true credit status of each counterparty's obligation, taking credit enhancements into account, differs from AAA/aaa.

(ii) X's methodology violates the requirement in paragraph (d)(3)(iii) of this section that the same cost or risk not be taken into account, directly or indirectly, more than once. By using a AA/ aa discount rate, X's method takes into account the difference between risk-free obligations and AA/aa obligations. This difference includes the difference between a rating of AAA/aaa and one of AA/ aa. By adjusting values for the difference between a rating of AAA/ aaa and one of AA/aa, X takes into account risks that it had already accounted for through the discount rates that it used. The same result would occur if X judged some of its counterparties' obligations to be of AAA/aaa quality but X failed to adjust the values of those obligations to reflect the difference between a rating of AAA/aaa and one of AA/aa.

*Example (4).* (i) The facts are the same as in Example 1, except that X determines the mid-market value for each derivative and then subtracts the corresponding part of the bid-ask spread.

(ii) X's methodology violates the rule in paragraph (d)(3)(i) of this section that forbids valuing positions at or near the bid or ask value.

*Example (5).* (i) The facts are the same as in Example 1, and, in addition, X's adjustments for all risks and costs, including credit risk, future administrative costs and model risk, may occasionally cause the adjusted value of an eligible position to be at or near the bid value or ask value.

(ii) X's methodology does not violate the rule in paragraph (d)(3)(i)(A) of this section that forbids valuing eligible positions at or near the bid or ask value.

**(e) Compliance with other rules.** Notwithstanding any other provisions of this section, the fair market values for purposes of the safe harbor must be consistent with section 482, or rules that adopt section 482 principles, when applicable. For example, if a notional principal contract is subject to section 482 or section 482 principles, the values of future cash flows taken into account in determining the value of the contract for purposes of section 475 must be consistent with section 482.

**(f) Election.** *(1) Making the election.* Unless the Commissioner prescribes otherwise, an eligible taxpayer elects under this section by filing with the Commissioner a statement declaring that the taxpayer makes the safe harbor election in this section for all eligible positions for which it has an eligible method. In addition to any other information that the Commissioner may require, the statement must describe the taxpayer's applicable financial statement for the first taxable year for which the election is effective and must state that the taxpayer agrees to provide upon the request of the Commissioner all information, records, and schedules in the manner required by paragraph (k) of this section. The statement must be attached to a timely filed Federal income tax return (including extensions) for the taxable year for which the election is first effective.

*(2) Duration of the election.* Once made, the election continues in effect for all subsequent taxable years unless revoked.

*(3) Revocation.* (i) By the taxpayer. An eligible taxpayer that is subject to an election under this section may revoke the election only with the consent of the Commissioner.

(ii) By the Commissioner. The Commissioner, after consideration of the relevant facts and circumstances, may revoke an election under this section, effective beginning with the first open year for which the election is effective or with any subsequent year, if—

(A) The taxpayer fails to comply with paragraph (k) of this section (concerning record retention and production) and the taxpayer does not show reasonable cause for this failure;

(B) The taxpayer ceases to have an applicable financial statement or ceases to use an eligible method; or

(C) For any other reason, no more than a de minimis number of eligible positions, or no more than a de minimis fraction of the taxpayer's eligible positions, are covered by the safe harbor in paragraph (b) of this section.

*(4) Re-election.* If an election is revoked, either by the Commissioner or by the taxpayer, the taxpayer (or any successor in interest of the taxpayer) may not make the election without the consent of the Commissioner for any taxable year that begins before the date that is six years after the first day of the earliest taxable year affected by the revocation.

**(g) Eligible positions.** For any taxpayer, an eligible position is any security or commodity that the Commissioner in a revenue procedure or other published guidance designates as an eligible position with respect to that taxpayer for purposes of this safe harbor.

**(h) Applicable financial statement.** *(1) Definition.* An eligible taxpayer's applicable financial statement for a taxable year is the taxpayer's primary financial statement for that year if that primary financial statement is described in paragraph (h)(2)(i) of this section (concerning statements required to be filed with the SEC) or if that primary financial statement both meets the requirements of paragraph (j) of this section (concerning significant business use) and is described in either paragraph (h)(2)(ii) or (iii) of this section. Otherwise, or if the taxpayer does not have a primary financial statement for the taxable year, the taxpayer does not have an applicable financial statement for the taxable year.

*(2) Primary financial statement.* For any taxable year, an eligible taxpayer's primary financial statement is the financial statement, if any, described in one or more of paragraphs (h)(2)(i), (ii), and (iii) of this section. If more than one financial statement of the taxpayer for the year is so described, the primary financial statement is the one first described in paragraphs (h)(2)(i), (ii), and (iii) of this section. A taxpayer has only one primary financial statement for any taxable year.

(i) Statement required to be filed with the Securities and Exchange Commission (SEC). A financial statement that is prepared in accordance with U.S. GAAP and that is required to be filed with the SEC, such as the 10—K or the Annual Statement to Shareholders.

(ii) Statement filed with a Federal agency other than the Internal Revenue Service. A financial statement that is prepared in accordance with U.S. GAAP and that is required to be provided to the Federal government or any of its agencies other than the Internal Revenue Service (IRS).

(iii) Certified audited financial statement. A certified audited financial statement that is prepared in accordance with U.S. GAAP; that is given to creditors for purposes of making lending decisions, given to equity holders for purposes of evaluating their investment in the eligible taxpayer, or provided for other substantial non-tax purposes; and that the taxpayer reasonably anticipates will be directly relied on for the purposes for which it was given or provided.

*(3) Example.* Primary financial statement. X prepares financial statement FS1, which is required to be filed with a Federal government agency other than the SEC or the IRS. FS1 is thus described in paragraph (h)(2)(ii) of this section. X also prepares financial statement FS2, which is a certified audited financial statement that is given to creditors and that X reasonably anticipates will be relied on for purposes of making lending decisions. FS2 is thus described in paragraph (h)(2)(iii) of this section. Because FS1, which is described in paragraph (h)(2)(ii) of this section, is described before FS2, which is described in paragraph (h)(2)(iii) of this section, FS1 is X's primary financial statement.

*(4) Financial statements of equal priority.* If the rules of paragraph (h)(2) of this section cause two or more financial statements to be of equal priority, then the statement that results in the highest aggregate valuation of eligible positions being marked to market under section 475 is the primary financial statement.

*(5) Consolidated groups.* If the taxpayer is a member of an affiliated group that files a consolidated return, the primary financial statement of the taxpayer is the primary financial statement, if any, of the common parent (within the meaning of section 1504(a)(1)) of the consolidated group.

*(6) Supplement or amendment to a financial statement.* A financial statement includes any supplement or amendment to the financial statement.

*(7) Certified audited financial statement.* For purposes of this paragraph (h), a financial statement is a certified audited financial statement if it is certified by an independent certified public accountant from a Registered Public Accounting firm, as defined in section 2(a)(12) of the Sarbanes-Oxley Act of 2002, Public Law 107-204, 116 Stat. 746 (July 30, 2002), 15 U.S.C. § 7201(a)(12), and rules promulgated under that Act, and is—

(i) Certified to be fairly presented (a "clean" opinion);

(ii) Certified to be fairly presented subject to a concern about a contingency, other than a contingency relating to the value of eligible positions (a qualified "subject to" opinion); or

(iii) Certified to be fairly presented except for a method of accounting with which the Certified Public Accountant disagrees and which is not a method used to determine the value of an eligible position held by the eligible taxpayer (a qualified "except for" opinion).

**(i)** [Reserved].

**(j) Significant business use.** *(1) In general.* A financial statement is described in this paragraph (j) if—

(i) The financial statement contains values for eligible positions;

(ii) The eligible taxpayer makes significant use of financial statement values in most of the significant management functions of its business; and

(iii) That use is related to the management of all or substantially all of the eligible taxpayer's business.

*(2) Financial statement value.* For purposes of this paragraph (j), the term financial statement value means—

(i) A value that is taken from the financial statement; or

(ii) A value that is produced by a process that is in all respects identical to the process that produces the values that appear on the financial statement but that is not taken from the statement because either—

(A) The value was determined as of a date for which the financial statement does not value eligible positions; or

(B) The value is used in the management of the business before the financial statement has been prepared.

*(3) Management functions of a business.* For purposes of this paragraph (j), the term management functions of a business refers to the financial and commercial oversight of the business. Oversight includes, but is not limited to, senior management review of business-unit profitability, market risk measurement or management, credit risk measurement or management, internal allocation of capital, and compensation of personnel. Management functions of a business do not include either tax accounting or reporting the results of operations to persons other than directors or employees.

*(4) Significant use.* If an eligible taxpayer uses financial statement values for some significant management functions and uses values that are not financial statement values for other significant management functions, then the determination of whether the taxpayer has made significant use of the financial statement values is made on the basis of all the facts and circumstances. This determination must particularly take into account whether the taxpayer's reliance on the financial statement values exposes the taxpayer to material adverse economic consequences if the values are incorrect.

**(k) Retention and production of records.** *(1) In general.* In addition to all records that section 6001 otherwise requires to be retained, an eligible taxpayer subject to the election provided by this section must keep, and timely provide to the Commissioner upon request, records and books of account that are sufficient to establish that the financial statement to which the income tax return conforms is the taxpayer's applicable financial statement, that the method used on that statement is an eligible method, and that the values used for eligible positions for purposes of section 475 are the values used in the applicable financial statement. This obligation extends to all records and books that are required to be maintained for any period for financial or regulatory reporting purposes, even if these records or books may not otherwise be specifically covered by section 6001. All records and books described in this paragraph (k) must be maintained for the period described in paragraph (k)(4) of this section, even if a lesser period of retention applies for financial statement or regulatory purposes.

*(2) Specific requirements.* (i) Verification and reconciliation. Unless the Commissioner otherwise provides—

(A) In general. An eligible taxpayer must provide books and records to verify the appropriate use of the safe harbor and reconciliation schedules between the applicable financial statement for the taxable year and the Federal income tax return for that year. The required verification materials and reconciliation schedules include all supporting schedules, exhibits, computer programs, and any other information used in producing the values and schedules, including the documentation of rules and procedures governing determination of the values. The required reconciliation schedules must also include a detailed explanation of any adjustments necessitated by the imperfect overlap between the eligible positions that the taxpayer marks to market under section 475 and the eligible positions for which the applicable financial statement uses an eligible method. In the time and manner provided by the Commissioner, a corporate taxpayer subject to this paragraph (k) must reconcile the net income amount reported on its applicable financial statement to the amount reported on the applicable forms and schedules on its Federal income tax return (such as the Schedule M-1, "Net Income(Loss) Reconciliation for Corporations With Total Assets of $10 Million or More"; Schedule M-3, "Net Income(Loss) Reconciliation for Corporations With Total Assets of $10 Million or More"; and Form 1120F, "U.S. Income Tax Return of a Foreign Corporation"). Eligible taxpayers that are not otherwise required to file a Schedule M-1 or Schedule M-3 must reconcile net income using substitute schedules similar to Schedule M-1 and Schedule M-3, and these substitute schedules must be attached to the return.

(B) Values on books and records with supporting schedules. The books and records must state the value used for each eligible position separately from the value used for any other eligible position. However, an eligible taxpayer may make adjustments to values on a pooled basis, if the taxpayer demonstrates that it can compute gain or loss attributable to the sale or other disposition of an individual eligible position.

(C) Consolidation schedules. An eligible taxpayer must provide a schedule showing the consolidation and de-consolidation that is used in preparing the applicable financial statement, along with exhibits and subordinate schedules. This schedule must provide information that addresses the differences for consolidation and de-consolidation between the applicable financial statement and the Federal income tax return.

(ii) Instructions provided by the Commissioner. The Commissioner may provide an alternative time or manner in which an eligible taxpayer subject to this paragraph (k) must establish that the same values used for eligible positions on the applicable financial statement are also the values used for purposes of section 475 on the Federal income tax return.

*(3) Time for producing records.* All documents described in this paragraph (k) must be produced within 30 days of a request by the Commissioner, unless the Commissioner grants a written extension. Generally, the Commissioner will exercise his discretion to excuse a minor or inadvertent failure to provide requested documents if the taxpayer shows reasonable cause for the failure, has made a good faith effort to comply with the requirement to produce records, and promptly remedies the failure. For failures to maintain, or timely produce, records, see paragraph (f)(3)(ii) of this section (allowing the Commissioner to revoke the election), and see paragraph (m) of this section (allowing the Commissioner, but not the taxpayer, to use for eligible positions that otherwise might be subject to the safe harbor fair market values that clearly reflect income but that are different from the values used on the applicable financial statement).

*(4) Retention period for records.* All materials required by this paragraph (k) and section 6001 must be retained as long as their contents may become material in the administration of any internal revenue law.

*(5) Agreements with the Commissioner.* The Commissioner and an eligible taxpayer may enter into a written agreement that establishes, for purposes of this paragraph (k), which records must be maintained, how they must be maintained, and for how long they must be maintained.

**(l)** [Reserved].

**(m) Use of different values.** If, with respect to the records that relate to certain eligible positions for a taxable year, the taxpayer fails to satisfy paragraph (k) of this section (concerning record retention and record production), then, for those eligible positions for that year, the Commissioner may use values that the Commissioner determines to be fair market values that are appropriate to clearly reflect income, even if the values so determined are different from the values reported for those positions on the applicable financial statement. See also paragraph (f)(3)(ii) of this section (concerning revocation of the election by the Commissioner when a taxpayer does not produce required records and fails to demonstrate reasonable cause for the failure).

T.D. 9328, 6/11/2007.

### § 1.475(b)-1 Scope of exemptions from mark-to-market requirement.

**(a) Securities held for investment or not held for sale.** Except as otherwise provided by this section and subject to the identification requirements of section 475(b)(2), a security is held for investment (within the meaning of section 475(b)(1)(A)) or not held for sale (within the meaning of section 475(b)(1)(B)) if it is not held by the taxpayer primarily for sale to customers in the ordinary course of the taxpayer's trade or business.

**(b) Securities deemed identified as held for investment.** *(1) In general.* The following items held by a dealer in securities are per se held for investment within the meaning of section 475(b)(1)(A) and are deemed to be properly identified as such for purposes of section 475(b)(2)—

(i) Except as provided in paragraph (b)(3) of this section, stock in a corporation, or a partnership or beneficial ownership interest in a widely held or publicly traded partnership or trust, to which the taxpayer has a relationship specified in paragraph (b)(2) of this section; or

(ii) A contract that is treated for federal income tax purposes as an annuity, endowment, or life insurance contract (see sections 72, 817, and 7702).

*(2) Relationships.* (i) General rule. The relationships specified in this paragraph (b)(2) are—

(A) Those described in section 267(b)(2), (3), (10), (11), or (12); or

(B) Those described in section 707(b)(1)(A) or (B).

(ii) Attribution. The relationships described in paragraph (b)(2)(i) of this section are determined taking into account sections 267(c) and 707(b)(3), as appropriate.

(iii) Trusts treated as partnerships. For purposes of this paragraph (b)(2), the phrase partnership or trust is substituted for the word partnership in sections 707(b)(1) and (3), and a reference to beneficial ownership interest is added to each reference to capital interest or profits interest in those sections.

*(3) Securities traded on certain established financial markets.* Paragraph (b)(1)(i) of this section does not apply to a security if—

(i) The security is actively traded within the meaning of § 1.1092(d)-1(a) taking into account only established financial markets identified in § 1.1092(d)-1(b)(1)(i) or (ii) (describing national securities exchanges and interdealer quotation systems);

(ii) Less than 15 percent of all of the outstanding shares or interests in the same class are held by the taxpayer and all persons having a relationship to the taxpayer that is specified in paragraph (b)(2) of this section; and

(iii) If the security was acquired (e.g., on original issue) from a person having a relationship to the taxpayer that is specified in paragraph (b)(2) of this section, then, after the time the security was acquired—

(A) At least one full business day has passed, and

(B) There has been significant trading involving persons not having a relationship to the taxpayer that is specified in paragraph (b)(2) of this section.

*(4) Changes in status.* (i) Onset of prohibition against marking. (A) Once paragraph (b)(1) of this section begins to apply to the security and for so long as it continues to apply, section 475(a) does not apply to the security in the hands of the taxpayer.

(B) If a security has not been timely identified under section 475(b)(2) and, after the last day on which such an identification would have been timely, paragraph (b)(1) of this section begins to apply to the security, then the dealer must recognize gain or loss on the security as if it were sold for its fair market value as of the close of business of the last day before paragraph (b)(1) of this section begins to apply to the security, and gain or loss is taken into account at that time.

(ii) Termination of prohibition against marking. If a taxpayer did not timely identify a security under section 475(b)(2), and paragraph (b)(1) of this section applies to the security on the last day on which such an identification would have been timely but thereafter ceases to apply—

(A) An identification of the security under section 475(b)(2) is timely if made on or before the close of the day paragraph (b)(1) of this section ceases to apply; and

(B) Unless the taxpayer timely identifies the security under section 475(b)(2) (taking into account the additional time for identification that is provided by paragraph (b)(4)(ii)(A) of this section), section 475(a) applies to changes in value of the security after the cessation in the same manner as under section 475(b)(3).

(iii) Examples. These examples illustrate this paragraph (b)(4):

*Example (1).* Onset of prohibition against marking. (A) Facts. Corporation H owns 75 percent of the stock of corporation D, a dealer in securities within the meaning of section 475(c)(1). On December 1, 1995, D acquired less than half of the stock in corporation X. D did not identify the stock for purposes of section 475(b)(2). On July 17, 1996, H acquired from other persons 70 percent of the stock of X. As a result, D and X became related within the meaning of paragraph (b)(2)(i) of this section. The stock of X is not described in paragraph (b)(3) of this section (concerning some securities traded on certain established financial markets).

Holding. Under paragraph (b)(4)(i) of this section, D recognizes gain or loss on its X stock as if the stock were sold for its fair market value at the close of business on July 16, 1996, and the gain or loss is taken into account at that time. As with any application of section 475(a), proper adjustment is made in the amount of any gain or loss subsequently realized. After July 16, 1996, section 475(a) does not apply to D's X stock while paragraph (b)(1)(i) of this section (concerning the relationship between X and D) continues to apply.

*Example (2).* Termination of prohibition against marking; retained securities identified as held for investment.

(A) Facts. On July 1, 1996, corporation H owned 60 percent of the stock of corporation Y and all of the stock of corporation D, a dealer in securities within the meaning of section 475(c)(1). Thus, D and Y are related within the meaning of paragraph (b)(2)(i) of this section. Also on July 1, 1996, D acquired, as an investment, 10 percent of the stock of Y. The stock of Y is not described in paragraph (b)(3) of this section (concerning some securities traded on certain established financial markets). When D acquired its shares of Y stock, it did not identify them for purposes of section 475(b)(2). On December 24, 1996, D identified its shares of Y stock as held for investment under section 475(b)(2). On December 30, 1996, H sold all of its shares of stock in Y to an unrelated party. As a result, D and Y ceased to be related within the meaning of paragraph (b)(2)(i) of this section.

(B) Holding. Under paragraph (b)(4)(ii)(A) of this section, identification of the Y shares is timely if done on or before the close of December 30, 1996. Because D timely identified its Y shares under section 475(b)(2), it continues after December 30, 1996, to refrain from marking to market its Y stock.

*Example (3).* Termination of prohibition against marking; retained securities not identified as held for investment.

(A) Facts. The facts are the same as in Example 2 above, except that D did not identify its stock in Y for purposes of section 475(b)(2) on or before December 30, 1996. Thus, D did not timely identify these securities under section 475(b)(2) (taking into account the additional time for identification provided in paragraph (b)(4)(ii)(A) of this section).

(B) Holding. Under paragraph (b)(4)(ii)(B) of this section, section 475(a) applies to changes in value of D's Y stock after December 30, 1996, in the same manner as under section 475(b)(3). Thus, any appreciation or depreciation that occurred while the securities were prohibited from being marked to market is suspended. Further, section 475(a) applies only to those changes occurring after December 30, 1996.

*Example (4).* Acquisition of actively traded stock from related party.

(A) Facts. Corporation P is the parent of a consolidated group whose taxable year is the calendar year, and corporation M, a member of that group, is a dealer in securities within the meaning of section 475(c)(1). Corporation M regularly acts as a market maker with respect to common and preferred stock of corporation P. Corporation P has outstanding 2,000,000 shares of series X preferred stock, which are traded on a national securities exchange. During the business day on December 29, 1997, corporation P sold 100,000 shares of series X preferred stock to corporation M for $100 per share. Subsequently, also on December 29, 1997, persons not related to corporation M engaged in significant trading of the series X preferred stock. At the close of business on December 30, 1997, the fair market value of series X stock was $99 per share. At the close of business on December 31, 1997, the fair market value of series X stock was $98.50 per share. Corporation M sold the series X stock on the exchange on January 2, 1998. At all relevant times, corporation M and all persons related to M owned less than 15% of the outstanding series X preferred stock.

(B) Holding. The 100,000 shares of series X preferred stock held by corporation M are not subject to mark-to-market treatment under section 475(a) on December 29, 1997, because at that time the stock was held for less than one full business day and is therefore treated as properly identified as held for investment. At the close of business on December 30, 1997, that prohibition on marking ceases to apply, and section 475(b)(3) begins to apply. The built-in loss is suspended, and subsequent appreciation and depreciation are subject to section 475(a). Accordingly, when corporation M marks the series X stock to market at the close of business on December 31, 1997, under section 475(a) it recognizes and takes into account a loss of $.50 per share. Under section 475(b)(3), when corporation M sells the series X stock on January 2, 1998, it takes into account the suspended loss, that is, the difference between the $100 per share it paid corporation P for that stock and the $99-per-share fair market value when section 475(b)(1) ceased to be apply to the stock. No deduction, however, is allowed for that loss. (See section 1.1502-13(f)(6), under which no deduction is allowed to a member of a consolidated group for a loss with respect to a share of stock of the parent of that consolidated group, if the member does not take the gain or loss into account pursuant to section 475(a).)

**(c) Securities deemed not held for investment; dealers in notional principal contracts and derivatives.** *(1)* Except as otherwise determined by the Commissioner in a revenue ruling, revenue procedure, or letter ruling, section 475(b)(1)(A) (exempting from mark-to-market accounting certain securities that are held for investment) does not apply to a security if—

(i) The security is described in section 475(c)(2)(D) or (E) (describing certain notional principal contracts and derivative securities); and

(ii) The taxpayer is a dealer in such securities.

*(2)* See § 1.475(d)-1(b) for a rule concerning the character of gain or loss on securities described in this paragraph (c).

**(d) Special rule for hedges of another member's risk.** A taxpayer may identify under section 475(b)(1)(C) (exempting certain hedges from mark-to-market accounting) a security that hedges a position of another member of the taxpayer's consolidated group if the security meets the following requirements—

*(1)* The security is a hedging transaction within the meaning of § 1.1221-2(b);

*(2)* The security is timely identified as a hedging transaction under § 1.1221-2(f) (including identification of the hedged item); and

*(3)* The security hedges a position that is not marked to market under section 475(a).

**(e) Transitional rules.** *(1) Stock, partnership, and beneficial ownership interests in certain controlled corporations, partnerships, and trusts before January 23, 1997.* (i) In general. The following items held by a dealer in securities are per se held for investment within the meaning of section 475(b)(1)(A) and are deemed to be properly identified as such for purposes of section 475(b)(2)—

(A) Stock in a corporation that the taxpayer controls (within the meaning of paragraph (e)(1)(ii) of this section); or

(B) A partnership or beneficial ownership interest in a widely held or publicly traded partnership or trust that the taxpayer controls (within the meaning of paragraph (e)(1)(ii) of this section).

(ii) Control defined. Control means the ownership, directly or indirectly through persons described in section 267(b) (taking into account section 267(c)), of—

(A) 50 percent or more of the total combined voting power of all classes of stock entitled to vote; or

(B) 50 percent or more of the capital interest, the profits interest, or the beneficial ownership interest in the widely held or publicly traded partnership or trust.

(iii) Applicability. The rules of this paragraph (e)(1) apply only before January 23, 1997.

*(2) Dealers in notional principal contracts and derivatives acquired before January 23, 1997.* (i) General rule. Section 475(b)(1)(A) (exempting certain securities from mark-to-market accounting) does not apply to a security if—

(A) The security is described in section 475(c)(2)(D) or (E) (describing certain notional principal contracts and derivative securities); and

(B) The taxpayer is a dealer in such securities.

(ii) Exception for securities not acquired in dealer capacity. This paragraph (e)(2) does not apply if the taxpayer establishes unambiguously that the security was not acquired in the taxpayer's capacity as a dealer in such securities.

(iii) Applicability. The rules of paragraph (e)(2) apply only to securities acquired before January 23, 1997.

T.D. 8700, 12/23/96, amend T.D. 8985, 3/15/2002.

**§ 1.475(b)-2 Exemptions—identification requirements.**

**(a) Identification of the basis for exemption.** An identification of a security as exempt from mark to market does not satisfy section 475(b)(2) if it fails to state whether the security is described in—

*(1)* Either of the first two subparagraphs of section 475(b)(1) (identifying a security as held for investment or not held for sale); or

*(2)* The third subparagraph thereof (identifying a security as a hedge).

**(b) Time for identifying a security with a substituted basis.** For purposes of determining the timeliness of an identification under section 475(b)(2), the date that a dealer acquires a security is not affected by whether the dealer's basis in the security is determined, in whole or in part, either by reference to the basis of the security in the hands of the person from whom the security was acquired or by reference to other property held at any time by the dealer. See § 1.475(a)-3 for rules governing how the dealer accounts for such a security if this identification is not made.

**(c) Integrated transactions under § 1.1275-6.** *(1) Definitions.* The following terms are used in this paragraph (c) with the meanings that are given to them by § 1.1275-6: integrated transaction, legging into, legging out, qualifying debt instrument, § 1.1275-6 hedge, and synthetic debt instrument.

*(2) Synthetic debt held by a taxpayer as a result of legging in.* If a taxpayer is treated as the holder of a synthetic debt instrument as the result of legging into an integrated transaction, then, for purposes of the timeliness of an identification under section 475(b)(2), the synthetic debt instrument is treated as having the same acquisition date as the qualifying debt instrument. A pre-leg-in identification of the qualifying debt instrument under section 475(b)(2) applies to the integrated transaction as well.

*(3) Securities held after legging out.* If a taxpayer legs out of an integrated transaction, then, for purposes of the timeliness of an identification under section 475(b)(2), the qualifying debt instrument, or the § 1.1275-6 hedge, that remains in the taxpayer's hands is generally treated as having been acquired, originated, or entered into, as the case may be, immediately after the leg-out. If any loss or deduction determined under § 1.1275-6(d)(2)(ii)(B) is disallowed by § 1.1275-6(d)(2)(ii)(D) (which disallows deductions when a taxpayer legs out of an integrated transaction within 30 days of legging in), then, for purposes of this section and section 475(b)(2), the qualifying debt instrument that remains in the taxpayer's hands is treated as having been acquired on the same date that the synthetic debt instrument was treated as having been acquired.

---

T.D. 8700, 12/23/96.

---

**Proposed § 1.475(b)-3 Exemption of securities in certain securitization transactions.** [*For Preamble, see ¶ 151,647*]

• ***Caution:*** Proposed regulations 1.475-0, 1.475(a)-3, 1.475(b)-4, 1.475(c)-1, 1.475(c)-2, and 1.475(e)-1 were finalized by T.D. 8700, 12/23/96. Prop. reg. §§ 1.475(a)-1, 1.475(a)-2 and 1.475(b)-3 remain proposed.

**(a) Exemption of contributed assets.** If a taxpayer expects to contribute securities (for example, mortgages) to a trust or other entity, including a REMIC, in exchange for interests therein (including ownership interests or debt issued by the trust or other entity), the contributed securities qualify as held for investment (within the meaning of section 475(b)(1)(A)) or not held for sale (within the meaning of section 475(b)(1)(B)) only if the taxpayer expects each of the interests received (whether or not a security within the meaning of section 475(c)(2)) to be either held for investment or not held for sale to customers in the ordinary course of the taxpayer's trade or business.

**(b) Exemption of resulting interests.** *(1) General rule.* If a taxpayer contributes securities to a trust or other entity in exchange for interests therein (including ownership interests or debt issued by the trust or other entity) and if, for federal income tax purposes, the ownership of the interests received is not treated as ownership of the securities contributed, the interests received may be identified as being described in section 475(b)(1), even if some or all of the contributed securities were not so described and could not have been so identified. For purposes of determining the timeliness of an identification of an interest received, the interest is treated as acquired on the day of its receipt.

*(2) Examples.* The following examples illustrate the principles of paragraph (b)(1) of this section.

*Example (1).* Identification of REMIC regular interests. If a taxpayer holds mortgages that are marked to market under section 475 and the taxpayer contributes the mortgages to a REMIC in exchange for REMIC regular interests that are described in section 475(b)(1), the taxpayer may identify the regular interests as exempt from mark-to-market treatment. This is permissible because REMIC regular interests are debt securities issued by the REMIC and do not represent continued ownership of the contributed mortgages.

*Example (2).* Identification of interests in a grantor trust. If a taxpayer contributes securities to a grantor trust and receives beneficial interests therein and if the taxpayer marked the contributed securities to market under section 475, the taxpayer cannot identify the beneficial interests in the grantor trust as exempt from mark-to-market treatment. Because ownership of a beneficial interest in a grantor trust represents continued ownership of an undivided interest in the contributed assets, no new security has been acquired.

**§ 1.475(b)-4 Exemptions—transitional issues.**

**(a) Transitional identification.** *(1) Certain securities previously identified under section 1236.* If, as of the close of the last taxable year ending before December 31, 1993, a security was identified under section 1236 as a security held for investment, the security is treated as being identified as held for investment for purposes of section 475(b).

*(2) Consistency requirement for other securities.* In the case of a security (including a security described in section 475(c)(2)(F)) that is not described in paragraph (a)(1) of this section and that was held by the taxpayer as of the close of the last taxable year ending before December 31, 1993, the security is treated as having been properly identified under section 475(b)(2) or 475(c)(2)(F)(iii) if the information contained in the dealer's books and records as of the close of that year supports the identification. If there is any ambiguity in those records, the taxpayer must, no later than January 31, 1994, place in its records a statement resolving this ambiguity and indicating unambiguously which securities are to be treated as properly identified. Any information that supports treating a security as having been properly identified under section 475(b)(2) or (c)(2)(F)(iii) must be applied consistently from one security to another.

**(b) Corrections on or before January 31, 1994.** *(1) Purpose.* This paragraph (b) allows a taxpayer to add or remove certain identifications covered by § 1.475(b)-1.

*(2) To conform to § 1.475(b)-1(a).* (i) Added identifications. To the extent permitted by paragraph (b)(2)(ii) of this section, a taxpayer may identify as being described in section 475(b)(1)(A) or (B)—

(A) A security that was held for immediate sale but was not held primarily for sale to customers in the ordinary course of the taxpayer's trade or business (for example, a trading security); or

(B) An evidence of indebtedness that was not held for sale to customers in the ordinary course of the taxpayer's trade or business and that the taxpayer intended to hold for less than one year.

(ii) Limitations. An identification described in paragraph (b)(2)(i) of this section is permitted only if—

(A) Prior to December 28, 1993, the taxpayer did not identify as being described in section 475(b)(1)(A) or (B) any of the securities described in paragraph (b)(2)(i) of this section;

(B) The taxpayer identifies every security described in paragraph (b)(2)(i) of this section for which a timely identification of the security under section 475(b)(2) cannot be made after the date on which the taxpayer makes these added identifications; and

(C) The identification is made on or before January 31, 1994.

*(3) To conform to § 1.475(b)-1(c).* On or before January 31, 1994, a taxpayer described in § 1.475(b)-1(e)(2)(i)(B) may remove an identification under section 475(b)(1)(A) of a security described in § 1.475(b)-1(e)(2)(i)(A).

**(c) Effect of corrections.** An identification added under paragraph (a)(2) or (b)(2) of this section is timely for purposes of section 475(b)(2) or (c)(2)(F)(iii). An identification removed under paragraph (a)(2) or (b)(3) of this section does not subject the taxpayer to the provisions of section 475(d)(2).

T.D. 8700, 12/23/96.

### § 1.475(c)-1 Definitions—dealer in securities.

***Caution:*** The Treasury has not yet amended Reg § 1.475(c)-1 to reflect changes made by P.L. 105-206.

**(a) Dealer-customer relationship.** Whether a taxpayer is transacting business with customers is determined on the basis of all of the facts and circumstances.

*(1) [Reserved].*

*(2) Transactions described in section 475(c)(1)(B).* (i) In general. For purposes of section 475(c)(1)(B), the term dealer in securities includes, but is not limited to, a taxpayer that, in the ordinary course of the taxpayer's trade or business, regularly holds itself out as being willing and able to enter into either side of a transaction enumerated in section 475(c)(1)(B).

(ii) Examples. The following examples illustrate the rules of this paragraph (a)(2). In the following examples, B is a bank and is not a member of a consolidated group:

*Example (1).* B regularly offers to enter into interest rate swaps with other persons in the ordinary course of its trade or business. B is willing to enter into interest rate swaps under which it either pays a fixed interest rate and receives a floating rate or pays a floating rate and receives a fixed rate. B is a dealer in securities under section 475(c)(1)(B), and the counterparties are its customers.

*Example (2).* B, in the ordinary course of its trade or business, regularly holds itself out as being willing and able to enter into either side of positions in a foreign currency with other banks in the interbank market. B's activities in the foreign currency make it a dealer in securities under section 475(c)(1)(B), and the other banks in the interbank market are its customers.

*Example (3).* B engages in frequent transactions in a foreign currency in the interbank market. Unlike the facts in Example 2, however, B does not regularly hold itself out as being willing and able to enter into either side of positions in the foreign currency, and all of B's transactions are driven by its internal need to adjust its position in the currency. No other circumstances are present to suggest that B is a dealer in securities for purposes of section 475(c)(1)(B). B's activity in the foreign currency does not qualify it as a dealer in securities for purposes of section 475(c)(1)(B), and its transactions in the interbank market are not transactions with customers.

*(3) Related parties.* (i) General rule. Except as provided in paragraph (a)(3)(ii) of this section (concerning transactions between members of a consolidated group, as defined in § 1.1502-1(h)), a taxpayer's transactions with related persons may be transactions with customers for purposes of section 475. For example, if a taxpayer, in the ordinary course of the taxpayer's trade or business, regularly holds itself out to its foreign subsidiaries or other related persons as being willing and able to enter into either side of transactions enumerated in section 475(c)(1)(B), the taxpayer is a dealer in securities within the meaning of section 475(c)(1), even if it engages in no other transactions with customers.

(ii) Special rule for members of a consolidated group. Solely for purposes of paragraph (c)(1) of section 475 (concerning the definition of dealer in securities) and except as provided in paragraph (a)(3)(iii) of this section, a taxpayer's transactions with other members of its consolidated group are not with customers. Accordingly, notwithstanding paragraph (a)(2) of this section, the fact that a taxpayer regularly holds itself out to other members of its consolidated group as being willing and able to enter into either side of a transaction enumerated in section 475(c)(1)(B) does not cause the taxpayer to be a dealer in securities within the meaning of section 475(c)(1)(B).

(iii) The intragroup-customer election. (A) Effect of election. If a consolidated group makes the intragroup-customer election, paragraph (a)(3)(ii) of this section (special rule for members of a consolidated group) does not apply to the members of the group. Thus, a member of a group that has made this election may be a dealer in securities within the meaning of section 475(c)(1) even if its only customer transactions are with other members of its consolidated group.

(B) Making and revoking the election. Unless the Commissioner otherwise prescribes, the intragroup-customer election is made by filing a statement that says, "[Insert name and employer identification number of common parent] hereby makes the Intragroup-Customer Election (as described in § 1.475(c)-1(a)(3)(iii) of the income tax regulations) for the taxable year ending [describe the last day of the year] and for subsequent taxable years." The statement must be signed by the common parent and attached to the timely filed federal income tax return for the consolidated group for that taxable year. The election applies for that year and continues in effect for subsequent years until revoked. The election may be revoked only with the consent of the Commissioner.

(iv) Examples. The following examples illustrate this paragraph (a)(3):

General Facts. HC, a hedging center, provides interest rate hedges to all of the members of its affiliated group (as defined in section 1504(a)(1)). Because of the efficiencies created by having a centralized risk manager, group policy prohibits members other than HC from entering into derivative interest rate positions with outside parties. HC regularly holds itself out as being willing and able to, and in fact does, enter into either side of interest rate swaps with its fellow members. HC periodically computes its aggregate position and hedges the net risk with an unrelated party. HC does not otherwise enter into interest rate positions with persons that are not members of the affiliated group. HC attempts to operate at cost, and the terms of its swaps do not factor in any risk of default by the affiliate. Thus, HC's affiliates receive somewhat more favorable terms then they would receive from an unrelated swaps dealer (a fact that may subject HC and its fellow members to reallocation of income under section 482). No other circumstances are present to suggest that HC is a dealer in securities for purposes of section 475(c)(1)(B).

*Example (1).* General rule for related persons. In addition to the General Facts stated above, assume that HC's affiliated group has not elected under section 1501 to file a consolidated return. Under paragraph (a)(3)(i) of this section, HC's transactions with its affiliates can be transactions with customers for purposes of section 475(c)(1). Thus, under paragraph (a)(2)(i) of this section, HC is a dealer in securities within the meaning of section 475(c)(1)(B), and the members of the group with which it does business are its customers.

*Example (2).* Special rule for members of a consolidated group. In addition to the General Facts stated above, assume that HC's affiliated group has elected to file consolidated returns and has not made the intragroup-customer election. Under paragraph (a)(3)(ii) of this section, HC's interest rate swap transactions with the members of its consolidated group are not transactions with customers for purposes of determining whether HC is a dealer in securities within the meaning of section 475(c)(1). Further, the fact that HC regularly holds itself out to members of its consolidated group as being willing and able to enter into either side of a transaction enumerated in section 475(c)(1)(B) does not cause HC to be a dealer in securities within the meaning of section 475(c)(1)(B). Because no other circumstances are present to suggest that HC is a dealer in securities for purposes of section 475(c)(1)(B), HC is not a dealer in securities.

*Example (3).* Intragroup-customer election. In addition to the General Facts stated above, assume that HC's affiliated group has elected to file a consolidated return but has also made the intragroup-customer election under paragraph (a)(3)(iii) of this section. Thus, the analysis and result are the same as in Example 1.

**(b) Sellers of nonfinancial goods and services.** *(1) Purchases and sales of customer paper.* Except as provided in paragraph (b)(3) of this section, if a taxpayer would not be a dealer in securities within the meaning of section 475(c)(1) but for its purchases and sales of debt instruments that, at the time of purchase or sale, are customer paper with respect to either the taxpayer or a corporation that is a member of the same consolidated group (as defined in § 1.1502-1(h)) as the taxpayer, then for purposes of section 475 the taxpayer is not a dealer in securities.

*(2) Definition of customer paper.* A debt instrument is customer paper with respect to a person at a point in time if—

(i) The person's principal activity is selling nonfinancial goods or providing nonfinancial services;

(ii) The debt instrument was issued by a purchaser of the goods or services at the time of the purchase of those goods or services in order to finance the purchase; and

(iii) At all times since the debt instrument was issued, it has been held either by the person selling those goods or services or by a corporation that is a member of the same consolidated group as that person.

*(3) Exceptions.* Paragraph (b)(1) of this section does not apply if—

(i) For purposes of section 471, the taxpayer accounts for any security (as defined in section 475(c)(2)) as inventory;

(ii) The taxpayer is subject to an election under paragraph (b)(4) of this section; or

(iii) The taxpayer is not described in paragraph (b)(2)(i) of this section and one or more debt instruments that are customer paper with respect to a corporation that is a member of the same consolidated group as the taxpayer are accounted for by the taxpayer, or by a corporation that is a member of the same consolidated group as the taxpayer, in a manner that allows recognition of unrealized gains or losses or deductions for additions to a reserve for bad debts.

*(4) Election not to be governed by the exception for sellers of nonfinancial goods or services.* (i) Method of making the election. Unless the Commissioner otherwise prescribes, an election under this paragraph (b)(4) must be made in the manner, and at the time, prescribed in this paragraph (b)(4)(i). The taxpayer must file with the Internal Revenue Service a statement that says, "[Insert name and taxpayer identification number of the taxpayer] hereby elects not to be governed by § 1.475(c)-1(b)(1) of the income tax regulations for the taxable year ending [describe the last day of the year] and for subsequent taxable years."

(A) Taxable years ending after December 24, 1996. If the first taxable year subject to an election under this paragraph (b)(4) ends after December 24, 1996, the statement must be attached to a timely filed federal income tax return for that taxable year.

(B) Taxable years ending on or before December 24, 1996. If the first taxable year subject to an election under this paragraph (b)(4) ends on or before December 24, 1996, and the election changes the taxpayer's taxable income for any taxable year the federal income tax return for which was filed before February 24, 1997, the statement must be attached to an amended return for the earliest such year that is so affected, and that amended return (and an amended return for any other such year that is so affected) must be filed not later than June 23, 1997. If the first taxable year subject to an election under this paragraph (b)(4) ends on or before December 24, 1996, but the taxpayer is not described in the preceding sentence, the statement must be attached to the first federal income tax return that is for a taxable year subject to the election and that is filed on or after February 24, 1997.

(ii) Continued applicability of an election. An election under this paragraph (b)(4) continues in effect for subsequent taxable years until revoked. The election may be revoked only with the consent of the Commissioner.

**(c) Taxpayers that purchase securities from customers but engage in no more than negligible sales of the securities.** *(1) Exemption from dealer status.* (i) General rule. A taxpayer that regularly purchases securities from customers in the ordinary course of a trade or business (including regularly making loans to customers in the ordinary course of a trade or business of making loans) but engages in no more than negligible sales of the securities so acquired is not a dealer in securities within the meaning of section 475(c)(1) unless the taxpayer elects to be so treated or, for purposes of section 471, the taxpayer accounts for any security (as defined in section 475(c)(2)) as inventory.

(ii) Election to be treated as a dealer. A taxpayer described in paragraph (c)(1)(i) of this section elects to be treated as a dealer in securities by filing a federal income tax return reflecting the application of section 475(a) in computing its taxable income.

*(2) Negligible sales.* Solely for purposes of paragraph (c)(1) of this section, a taxpayer engages in negligible sales of debt instruments that it regularly purchases from customers in the ordinary course of its business if, and only if, during the taxable year, either—

(i) The taxpayer sells all or part of fewer than 60 debt instruments, regardless how acquired; or

(ii) The total adjusted basis of the debt instruments (or parts of debt instruments), regardless how acquired, that the taxpayer sells is less than 5 percent of the total basis, immediately after acquisition, of the debt instruments that it acquires in that year.

*(3) Special rules for members of a consolidated group.* (i) Intragroup-customer election in effect. If a taxpayer is a member of a consolidated group that has made the intragroup-customer election (described in paragraph (a)(3)(iii) of this section), the negligible sales test in paragraph (c)(2) of this section takes into account all of the taxpayer's sales of debt instruments to other group members.

(ii) Intragroup-customer election not in effect. If a taxpayer is a member of a consolidated group that has not made the intragroup-customer election (described in paragraph (a)(3)(iii) of this section), the taxpayer satisfies the negligible sales test in paragraph (c)(2) of this section if either—

(A) The test is satisfied by the taxpayer, taking into account sales of debt instruments to other group members (as in paragraph (c)(3)(i) of this section); or

(B) The test is satisfied by the group, treating the members of the group as if they were divisions of a single corporation.

*(4) Special rules.* Whether sales of securities are negligible is determined without regard to—

(i) Sales of securities that are necessitated by exceptional circumstances and that are not undertaken as recurring business activities;

(ii) Sales of debt instruments that decline in quality while in the taxpayer's hands and that are sold pursuant to an established policy of the taxpayer to dispose of debt instruments below a certain quality; or

(iii) Acquisitions and sales of debt instruments that are qualitatively different from all debt instruments that the taxpayer purchases from customers in the ordinary course of its business.

*(5) Example.* The following example illustrates paragraph (c)(4)(iii) of this section:

*Example.* I, an insurance company, regularly makes policy loans to its customers but does not sell them. I, however, actively trades Treasury securities. No other circumstances are present to suggest that I is a dealer in securities for purposes of section 475(c)(1). Since the Treasuries are qualitatively different from the policy loans that I originates, under paragraph (c)(4)(iii) of this section, I disregards the purchases and sales of Treasuries in applying the negligible sales test in paragraph (c)(2) of this section.

**(d) Issuance of life insurance products.** A life insurance company that is not otherwise a dealer in securities within the meaning of section 475(c)(1) does not become a dealer in securities solely because it regularly issues life insurance products to its customers in the ordinary course of a trade or business. For purposes of the preceding sentence, the term life insurance product means a contract that is treated for federal income tax purposes as an annuity, endowment, or life insurance contract. See sections 72, 817, and 7702.

---

T.D. 8700, 12/23/96.

---

PAR. 4. In § 1.475(c)-1, paragraphs (b)(3)(i) and (b)(4)(ii) are revised to read as follows:

**Proposed § 1.475(c)-1 Definitions—dealer in securities.**
*[For Preamble, see ¶ 151,953]*

* * * * *

**(b)** * * *

*(3)* * * *

(i) For purposes of section 471, the taxpayer accounts for any security (as defined in section 475(c)) as inventory;

* * * * *

*(4)* * * *

(ii) Continued applicability of an election. (A) In general. Except as provided in paragraph (b)(4)(ii)(B) of this section, an election under this paragraph (b)(4) continues in effect for subsequent taxable years until revoked. The election may be revoked only with the consent of the Commissioner.

(B) Taxable years ending after July 22, 1998. An election under this paragraph (b)(4) is ineffective for taxable years ending after July 22, 1998.

* * * * *

**§ 1.475(c)-2 Definitions—security.**

***Caution:*** The Treasury has not yet amended Reg § 1.475(c)-2 to reflect changes made by P.L. 105-206.

**(a) Items that are not securities.** The following items are not securities within the meaning of section 475(c)(2) with respect to a taxpayer and, therefore, are not subject to section 475—

*(1)* A security (determined without regard to this paragraph (a)) if section 1032 prevents the taxpayer from recognizing gain or loss with respect to that security;

*(2)* A debt instrument issued by the taxpayer (including a synthetic debt instrument, within the meaning of § 1.1275-6(b)(4), that § 1.1275-6(b) treats the taxpayer as having issued); or

*(3)* A REMIC residual interest, or an interest or arrangement that is determined by the Commissioner to have substantially the same economic effect, if the residual interest or the interest or arrangement is acquired on or after January 4, 1995.

**(b) Synthetic debt that § 1.1275-6(b) treats the taxpayer as holding.** If § 1.1275-6 treats a taxpayer as the holder of a synthetic debt instrument (within the meaning of section 1.1275-6(b)(4)), the synthetic debt instrument is a security held by the taxpayer within the meaning of section 475(c)(2)(C).

**(c) Negative value REMIC residuals acquired before January 4, 1995.** A REMIC residual interest that is described in paragraph (c)(1) of this section or an interest or arrangement that is determined by the Commissioner to have substantially the same economic effect is not a security within the meaning of section 475(c)(2).

*(1) Description.* A residual interest in a REMIC is described in this paragraph (c)(1) if, on the date the taxpayer acquires the residual interest, the present value of the anticipated tax liabilities associated with holding the interest exceeds the sum of—

(i) The present value of the expected future distributions on the interest; and

(ii) The present value of the anticipated tax savings associated with holding the interest as the REMIC generates losses.

*(2) Special rules applicable to negative value REMIC residuals acquired before January 4, 1995.* Solely for purposes of this paragraph (c)—

(i) If a transferee taxpayer acquires a residual interest with a basis determined by reference to the transferor's basis, then the transferee is deemed to acquire the interest on the date the transferor acquired it (or is deemed to acquire it under this paragraph (c)(2)(i)).

(ii) Anticipated tax liabilities, expected future distributions, and anticipated tax savings are determined under the rules in § 1.860E-2(a)(3) and without regard to the operation of section 475.

(iii) Present values are determined under the rules in § 1.860E-2(a)(4).

---

T.D. 8700, 12/23/96.

---

PAR. 5. In § 1.475(c)-2, paragraph (d) is added to read as follows:

**Proposed § 1.475(c)-2 Definitions—security.** [*For Preamble, see ¶ 151,953*]

* * * * *

**(d) Inventory.** *(1) Nonfinancial customer paper is generally not marked to market under section 475.* Except as provided in paragraph (d)(3) of this section, nonfinancial customer paper (as defined in section 475(c)(4)(B)) is not a security even if it is inventory.

*(2) Treatment of nonfinancial customer paper under other sections of the Internal Revenue Code.* For nonfinancial customer paper that is not a security, the mark-to-market method of accounting and the lower-of-cost-or-market method of accounting are not permissible methods of accounting. See §§ 1.446-1(c)(2)(iii) and 1.471-12.

*(3) Nonfinancial customer paper treated as inventory.* [Reserved]

**§ 1.475(d)-1 Character of gain or loss.**

**(a) Securities never held in connection with the taxpayer's activities as a dealer in securities.** If a security is never held in connection with the taxpayer's activities as a dealer in securities, section 475(d)(3)(A) does not affect the character of gain or loss from the security, even if the taxpayer fails to identify the security under section 475(b)(2).

**(b) Ordinary treatment for notional principal contracts and derivatives held by dealers in notional principal contracts and derivatives.** Section 475(d)(3)(B)(ii) (concerning the character of gain or loss with respect to a security held by a person other than in connection with its activities as a dealer in securities) does not apply to a security if § 1.475(b)-1(c) and the absence of a determination by the Commissioner prevent section 475(b)(1)(A) from applying to the security.

---

T.D. 8700, 12/23/96.

---

PAR. 6. Section 1.475(e)-1 is redesignated as § 1.475(g)-1.

**Proposed § 1.475(e)-1 [Redesignated as § 1.475(g)-1]**

**Proposed § 1.475(e)-1 Election of mark-to-market accounting for dealers in commodities.** [*For Preamble, see ¶ 151,953*]

**(a) Time and manner of making election.** An election under section 475(e)(1) must be made in the time and manner prescribed by the Commissioner.

**(b) Application of securities dealer rules to electing commodities dealers.** Except as otherwise provided in this section or in other guidance prescribed by the Commissioner, the rules and administrative interpretations under section 475 for dealers in securities apply to dealers in commodities that make an election under section 475(e)(1).

**(c) Commodity derivatives deemed not held for investment.** *(1) In general.* Except as otherwise determined by the Commissioner in a revenue ruling, revenue procedure, or letter ruling, if a dealer in commodities that made an election under section 475(e)(1) holds a commodity described in section 475(e)(2)(B) or (C) (describing certain notional principal contracts and commodity derivatives), section 475(b)(1)(A) (exempting from mark-to-market accounting certain positions that are held for investment) does not apply to that commodity.

*(2) Character of commodity derivatives required to be marked to market.* If a commodity is required to be marked to market because of the application of paragraph (c)(1) of this section, the gain or loss with respect to that commodity is ordinary.

**(d) Same day identification.** An identification of a commodity as exempt from mark-to-market accounting under section 475(b)(2) is not effective unless it is made before the close of the day on which the commodity was acquired, originated, or entered into.

**Proposed § 1.475(f)-1 Procedures for electing mark-to-market accounting for traders.** [*For Preamble, see ¶ 151,953*]

**(a) Time and manner of making election.** An election under section 475(f)(1) or (2) must be made in the time and manner prescribed by the Commissioner.

**(b) Coordination with section 475(a).** If a dealer in securities also has a securities or commodities trading business or a commodities dealing business, the dealer may make an election under section 475(e)(1), (f)(1), or (f)(2) for that business.

**Proposed § 1.475(f)-2 Election of mark-to-market accounting for traders in securities or commodities.** [*For Preamble, see ¶ 151,953*]

**(a) Securities not held in connection with trading activities.** *(1) Taxpayer identification of investment securities.* If a trader in securities makes an election under section 475(f)(1)(A) (electing trader) and holds a security other than in connection with that trading business, the electing trader must identify that security in accordance with section 475(f)(1)(B)(ii). If the electing trader is also a dealer in securities, however, the preceding sentence applies only to securities described in section 475(b)(1) (without regard to section 475(b)(2)).

*(2) Satisfaction of Commissioner.* In no event is the requirement of section 475(f)(1)(B)(i) satisfied unless the electing trader demonstrates by clear and convincing evidence that a security has no connection to its trading activities.

*(3) Substantially similar securities held for trading and investment.* An electing trader that holds a security other than in connection with its trading business and also trades the same or substantially similar securities in no event satisfies the requirement of section 475(f)(1)(B)(i) unless the security is held in a separate, nontrading account maintained with a third party.

*(4) Consequences of failure to identify investment securities.* If an electing trader holds a security that is not held in connection with its trading business and fails to identify the security in a manner that satisfies the requirements of section 475(f)(1)(B)(ii)—

(i) The consequences described in section 475(d)(2) apply to the security; and

(ii) The character of the gain or loss with respect to the security is ordinary.

*(5) Commissioner identification of investment securities.* Notwithstanding paragraph (a)(4) of this section, the Commissioner may treat a security described in that paragraph as meeting the requirements of section 475(f)(1)(B)(i) and (ii).

**(b) Character of securities marked to market.** The gain or loss with respect to a security that is marked to market under section 475(f)(1)(A) is ordinary.

**(c) Application of securities dealer rules to electing traders.** Except as otherwise provided in this section or in other guidance prescribed by the Commissioner, the principles of the rules and administrative interpretations under section 475 for dealers in securities apply to traders in securities that make an election under section 475(f)(1).

**(d) Same day identification.** An identification of a security as exempt from mark-to-market accounting under section 475(f)(1)(B) is not effective unless it is made before the close of the day on which the security was acquired, originated, or entered into.

**(e) Application to traders in commodities.** *(1) General rule.* If a trader in commodities makes an election under section 475(f)(2), paragraphs (a), (b), (c), and (d) of this section apply to the trader in the same manner that they apply to a trader in securities who makes an election under section 475(f)(1).

*(2) Coordination with section 1256.* If a trader in commodities makes an election under section 475(f)(2) and trades section 1256 contracts that are commodities as defined in section 475(e)(2), then the rules of section 475(f) and paragraph (e)(1) of this section apply to those contracts, and not the capital character rules of section 1256.

### § 1.475(g)-1 Effective dates.

**(a) and (b) [Reserved].**

**(c)** Section 1.475(a)-3 (concerning acquisition by a dealer of a security with a substituted basis) applies to securities acquired, originated, or entered into on or after January 4, 1995.

**(d)** Section 1.475(a)-4 (concerning a safe harbor to use applicable financial statement values for purposes of section 475) applies to taxable years ending on or after June 12, 2007.

**(e)** Except as provided elsewhere in this paragraph (d), § 1.475(b)-1 (concerning the scope of exemptions from the mark-to-market requirement) applies to taxable years ending on or after December 31, 1993.

*(1)* Section 1.475(b)-1(b) applies as follows:

(i) Section 1.475(b)-1(b)(1)(i) (concerning equity interests issued by a related person) applies beginning June 19, 1996. If, on June 18, 1996, a security is subject to mark-to-market accounting and, on June 19, 1996, § 1.475(b)-1(b)(1) begins to apply to the security solely because of the effective dates in this paragraph (d) (rather than because of a change in facts), then the rules of section 1.475(b)-1(b)(4)(i)(A) (concerning the prohibition against marking) apply, but § 1.475(b)-1(b)(4)(i)(B) (imposing a mark to market on the day before the onset of the prohibition) does not apply.

(ii) Section 1.475(b)-1(b)(2) (concerning relevant relationships for purposes of determining whether equity interests in related persons are prohibited from being marked to market) applies beginning June 19, 1996.

(iii) Section 1.475(b)-1(b)(3) (concerning certain actively traded securities) applies beginning June 19, 1996, to securities held on or after that date, except for securities described in § 1.475(b)-1(e)(1)(i) (concerning equity interests issued by controlled entities). If a security is described in § 1.475(b)-1(e)(1)(i), § 1.475(b)-1(b)(3) applies only on or after January 23, 1997, if the security is held on or after that date. If § 1.475(b)-1(b)(1) ceases to apply to a security by virtue of the operation of this paragraph (d)(1)(iii), the rules of § 1.475(b)-1(b)(4)(ii) apply to the cessation.

(iv) Except to the extent provided in paragraph (d)(1) of this section, § 1.475(b)-1(b)(4) (concerning changes in status) applies beginning June 19, 1996.

*(2)* Section 1.475(b)-1(c) (concerning securities deemed not held for investment by dealers in notional principal contracts and derivatives) applies to securities acquired on or after January 23, 1997.

*(3)* Section 1.475(b)-1(d) (concerning the special rule for hedges of another member's risk) is effective for securities acquired, originated, or entered into on or after January 23, 1997.

**(f)** Section 1.475(b)-2 (concerning identification of securities that are exempt from mark to market treatment) applies as follows:

*(1)* Section 1.475(b)-2(a) (concerning the general rules for identification of basis for exemption from mark to market treatment) applies to identifications made on or after July 1, 1997.

*(2)* Section 1.475(b)-2(b) (concerning time for identifying a security with a substituted basis) applies to securities acquired, originated, or entered into on or after January 4, 1995.

*(3)* Section 1.475(b)-2(c) (concerning identification in the context of integrated transactions under § 1.1275-6) applies on and after August 13, 1996 (the effective date of § .1275-6).

**(g) [Reserved].**

**(h)** Section 1.475(b)-4 (concerning transitional issues relating to exemptions) applies to taxable years ending on or after December 31, 1993.

**(i)** Section 1.475(c)-1 applies as follows:

*(1)* Except as otherwise provided in this paragraph (h)(1), § 1.475(c)-1(a) (concerning the dealer-customer relationship) applies to taxable years beginning on or after January 1, 1995.

(i) [Reserved].

(ii) Section 1.475(c)-1(a)(2)(ii) (illustrating rules concerning the dealer-customer relationship) applies to taxable years beginning on or after June 20, 1996.

(iii) (A) Section 1.475(c)-1(a)(3) applies to taxable years beginning on or after June 20, 1996, except for transactions between members of the same consolidated group.

(B) For transactions between members of the same consolidated group, paragraph § 1.475(c)-1(a)(3) applies to taxable years beginning on or after December 24, 1996.

*(2)* Section 1.475(c)-1(b) (concerning sellers of nonfinancial goods and services) applies to taxable years ending on or after December 31, 1993.

*(3)* Except as otherwise provided in this paragraph (h)(3), § 1.475(c)-1(c) (concerning taxpayers that purchase securities but engage in no more than negligible sales of the securities) applies to taxable years ending on or after December 31, 1993.

(i) Section 1.475(c)-1(c)(3) (special rules for members of a consolidated group) is effective for taxable years beginning on or after December 24, 1996.

(ii) A taxpayer may rely on the rules set out in § 1.475(c)-1T(b) (as contained in 26 CFR part 1 revised April 1, 1996) for taxable years beginning before January 23, 1997, provided the taxpayer applies that paragraph reasonably and consistently.

*(4)* Section 1.475(c)-1(d) (concerning the issuance of life insurance products) applies to taxable years beginning on or after January 1, 1995.

**(j)** Section 1.475(c)-2 (concerning the definition of security) applies to taxable years ending on or after December 31, 1993. By its terms, however, § 1.475(c)-2(a)(3) applies only to residual interests or to interests or arrangements that are acquired on or after January 4, 1995; and the integrated transactions that are referred to in §§ 1.475(c)-2(a)(2) and 1.475(c)-2(b) exist only after August 13, 1996 (the effective date of § 1.1275-6).

**(k)** Section 1.475(d)-1 (concerning the character of gain or loss) applies to taxable years ending on or after December 31, 1993.

T.D. 8700, 12/23/96, amend T.D. 9328, 6/11/2007.

PAR. 8. Newly designated § 1.475(g)-1 is amended by revising paragraphs (h)(2) and (i) and adding paragraphs (k), (l), and (m) to read as follows:

**Proposed § 1.475(g)-1 Effective dates.** [*For Preamble, see ¶ 151,953*]

**(h)** * * *

*(2)* Section 1.475(c)-1(b) (concerning sellers of nonfinancial goods and services) applies as follows:

(i) Except as otherwise provided in this paragraph (h)(2), § 1.475(c)-1(b) applies to taxable years ending on or after December 31, 1993.

(ii) Section 1.475(c)-1(b)(4)(ii)(B) applies to taxable years ending after July 22, 1998.

* * * * *

**(i)** Section 1.475(c)-2 (concerning the definition of security) applies as follows:

*(1)* Section 1.475(c)-2(a), (b), and (c) (concerning the definition of security) applies to taxable years ending on or after December 31, 1993. By its terms, however, § 1.475(c)-2(a)(3) applies only to residual interests or to interests or arrangements acquired on or after January 4, 1995; and the integrated transactions that are referred to in § 1.475(c)-2(a)(2) and (b) exist only after August 13, 1996 (the effective date of § 1.1275-6).

*(2)* Section 1.475(c)-2(d) applies as follows:

(i) Section 1.475(c)-2(d)(1) applies to taxable years ending after July 22, 1998.

(ii) Section 1.475(c)-2(d)(2) applies to taxable years ending on or after January 28, 1999.

* * * * *

**(k)** Section 1.475(e)-1(a) (concerning the time and manner for making the mark-to-market election for dealers in commodities) applies to taxable years ending on or after January 28, 1999. Section 1.475(e)-1(b), (c) and (d) applies to commodities acquired on or after March 1, 1999.

**(l)** Section 1.475(f)-1 (procedures for electing mark-to-market accounting for traders in securities or commodities) applies to taxable years ending on or after January 28, 1999.

**(m)** Section 1.475(f)-2 (concerning the mark-to-market rules for traders in securities or commodities) applies to securities or commodities acquired on or after March 1, 1999.

**Proposed § 1.475(g)-2 Risk transfer agreements in a global dealing operation.** [*For Preamble, see ¶ 151,855*]

**(a) In general.** This section provides computational rules to coordinate the application of section 475 and § 1.446-4 with rules for allocation and sourcing under the global dealing regulations. If the requirements in paragraph (c) of this section are met, a risk transfer agreement (RTA) (as defined in paragraph (b) of this section) is accounted for under the rules of paragraph (d) of this section.

**(b) Definition of risk transfer agreement.** For purposes of this section, a risk transfer agreement (RTA) is a transfer of risk between two qualified business units (QBUs) (as defined in § 1.989(a)-1(b)) of the same taxpayer such that—

*(1)* The transfer is consistent with the business practices and risk management policies of each QBU;

*(2)* The transfer is evidenced in each QBU's books and records;

*(3)* Each QBU records the RTA on its books and records at a time no later than the time the RTA is effective; and

*(4)* Except to the extent required by paragraph (b)(3) of this section, the entry in the books and records of each QBU is consistent with that QBU's normal accounting practices.

**(c) Requirements for application of operational rule.** *(1)* The position in the RTA of one QBU (the hedging QBU) would qualify as a hedging transaction (within the meaning of § 1.1221-2(b)) with respect to that QBU if—

(i) The RTA were a transaction entered into with an unrelated party; and

(ii) For purposes of determining whether the hedging QBU's position satisfies the risk reduction requirement in § 1.1221-2(b), the only risks taken into account are the risks of the hedging QBU (that is, the risks that would be taken into account if the hedging QBU were a separate corporation that had made a separate-entity election under § 1.1221-2(d)(2));

*(2)* The other QBU (the marking QBU) is a regular dealer in securities (within the meaning of § 1.482-8(a)(2)(iii));

*(3)* The marking QBU would mark to market its position in the RTA under section 475 if the RTA were a transaction entered into with an unrelated party; and

*(4)* Income of the marking QBU is subject to allocation under § 1.482-8 to two or more jurisdictions or is sourced under § 1.863-3(h) to two or more jurisdictions.

**(d) Operational rule.** If the requirements in paragraph (c) of this section are met, each QBU that is a party to a RTA (as defined in paragraph (b) of this section) takes its position in the RTA into account as if that QBU had entered into the RTA with an unrelated party. Thus, the marking QBU marks its position to market, and the hedging QBU accounts for its position under § 1.446-4. Because this section only effects coordination with the allocation and sourcing rules, it does not affect factors such as the determination of the amount of interest expense that is incurred by either QBU and that is subject to allocation and apportionment under section 864(e) or 882(c).

### § 1.481-1 Adjustments in general.

**(a)** *(1)* Section 481 prescribes the rules to be followed in computing taxable income in cases where the taxable income of the taxpayer is computed under a method of accounting different from that under which the taxable income was previously computed. A change in method of accounting to which section 481 applies includes a change in the over-all method of accounting for gross income or deductions, or a change in the treatment of a material item. For rules relating to changes in methods of accounting, see section 446(e) and paragraph (e) of § 1.446-1. In computing taxable income for the taxable year of the change, there shall be taken into account those adjustments which are determined to be necessary solely by reason of such change in order to prevent amounts from being duplicated or omitted. The "year of the change" is the taxable year for which the taxable income of the taxpayer is computed under a method of accounting different from that used for the preceding taxable year.

*(2)* Unless the adjustments are attributable to a change in method of accounting initiated by the taxpayer, no part of the adjustments required by subparagraph (1) of this paragraph shall be based on amounts which were taken into account in computing income (or which should have been taken into account had the new method of accounting been used) for taxable years beginning before January 1, 1954, or ending before August 17, 1954 (hereinafter referred to as pre-1954 years).

**(b)** The adjustments specified in section 481(a) and this section shall take into account inventories, accounts receivable, accounts payable, and any other item determined to be necessary in order to prevent amounts from being duplicated or omitted.

**(c)** *(1)* The term "adjustments", as used in section 481, has reference to the net amount of the adjustments required by section 481(a) and paragraph (b) of this section. In the case of a change in the over-all method of accounting, such as from the cash receipts and disbursements method to an accrual method, the term "net amount of the adjustments" means the consolidation of adjustments (whether the amounts thereof represent increases or decreases in items of income or deductions) arising with respect to balances in various accounts, such as inventory, accounts receivable, and accounts payable, at the beginning of the taxable year of the change in method of accounting. With respect to the portion of the adjustments attributable to pre-1954 years, it is immaterial that the same items or class of items with respect to which adjustments would have to be made (for the first taxable year to which section 481 applies) do not exist at the time the actual change in method of accounting occurs. For purposes of section 481, only the net dollar balance is to be taken into account. In the case of a change in the treatment of a single material item, the amount of the adjustment shall be determined with reference only to the net dollar balances in that particular account.

*(2)* If a change in method of accounting is voluntary (i.e., initiated by the taxpayer), the entire amount of the adjustments required by section 481(a) is generally taken into account in computing taxable income in the taxable year of the change, regardless of whether the adjustments increase or decrease taxable income. See, however, §§ 1.446-1(e)(3) and 1.481-4 which provide that the Commissioner may prescribe the taxable year or years in which the adjustments are taken into account.

*(3)* If the change in method of accounting is involuntary (i.e., not initiated by the taxpayer), then only the amount of the adjustments required by section 481(a) that is attributable to taxable years beginning after December 31, 1953, and ending after August 16, 1954, (hereinafter referred to as post-1953 years) is taken into account. This amount is generally taken into account in computing taxable income in the taxable year of the change, regardless of whether the adjustments increase or decrease taxable income. See, however, §§ 1.446-1(e)(3) and 1.481-4 which provide that the Commissioner may prescribe the taxable year or years in which the adjustments are taken into account. See also § 1.481-3 for rules relating to adjustments attributable to pre-1954 years.

*(4)* For any adjustments attributable to post-1953 years that are taken into account entirely in the year of change and that increase taxable income by more than $3,000, the limitations on tax provided in section 481(b)(1) or (2) apply. See § 1.481-2 for rules relating to the limitations on tax provided by sections 481(b)(1) and (2).

*(5)* A change in the method of accounting initiated by the taxpayer includes not only a change which he originates by securing the consent of the Commissioner, but also a change from one method of accounting to another made without the advance approval of the Commissioner. A change in the taxpayer's method of accounting required as a result of an examination of the taxpayer's income tax return will not be considered as initiated by the taxpayer.

On the other hand, a taxpayer who, on his own initiative, changes his method of accounting in order to conform to the requirements of any Federal income tax regulation or ruling shall not, merely because of such fact, be considered to have made an involuntary change.

**(d)** Any adjustments required under section 481(a) that are taken into account during a taxable year must be properly taken into account for purposes of computing gross income, adjusted gross income, or taxable income in determining the amount of any item of gain, loss, deduction, or credit that depends on gross income, adjusted gross income, or taxable income.

T.D. 6366, 2/19/59, amend T.D. 8608, 8/4/95.

### § 1.481-2 Limitation on tax.

**(a) Three-year allocation.** Section 481(b)(1) provides a limitation on the tax under chapter 1 of the Internal Revenue Code for the taxable year of change that is attributable to the adjustments required under section 481(a) and § 1.481-1 if the entire amount of the adjustments is taken into account in the year of change. If such adjustments increase the taxpayer's taxable income for the taxable year of the change by more than $3,000, then the tax for such taxable year that is attributable to the adjustments shall not exceed the lesser of the tax attributable to taking such adjustments into account in computing taxable income for the taxable year of the change under section 481(a) and § 1.481-1, or the aggregate of the increases in tax that would result if the adjustments were included ratably in the taxable year of the change and the two preceding taxable years. For the purpose of computing the limitation on tax under section 481(b)(1), the adjustments shall be allocated ratably to the taxable year of the change and the two preceding taxable years, whether or not the adjustments are in fact attributable in whole or in part to such years. The limitation on the tax provided in this paragraph shall be applicable only if the taxpayer used the method of accounting from which the change was made in computing taxable income for the two taxable years preceding the taxable year of the change.

**(b) Allocation under new method of accounting.** Section 481(b)(2) provides a second alternative limitation on the tax for the taxable year of change under chapter 1 of the Internal Revenue Code that is attributable to the adjustments required under section 481(a) and § 1.481-1 where such adjustments increase taxable income for the taxable year of change by more than $3,000. If the taxpayer establishes from his books of account and other records what his taxable income would have been under the new method of accounting for one or more consecutive taxable years immediately preceding the taxable year of the change, and if the taxpayer in computing taxable income for such years used the method of accounting from which the change was made, then the tax attributable to the adjustments shall not exceed the smallest of the following amounts:

*(1)* The tax attributable to taking the adjustments into account in computing taxable income for the taxable year of the change under section 481(a) and § 1.481-1;

*(2)* The tax attributable to such adjustments computed under the 3-year allocation provided in section 481(b)(1), if applicable; or

*(3)* The net increase in the taxes under chapter 1 (or under corresponding provisions of prior revenue laws) which would result from allocating that portion of the adjustments to the one or more consecutive preceding taxable years to which properly allocable under the new method of accounting and from allocating the balance thereof to the taxable year of the change.

**(c) Rules for computation of tax.** *(1)* The first step in determining whether either of the limitations described in section 481(b)(1) or (2) applies is to compute the increase in tax for the taxable year of the change that is attributable to the increase in taxable income for such year resulting solely from the adjustments required under section 481(a) and § 1.481-1. This increase in tax is the excess of the tax for the taxable year computed by taking into account such adjustments under section 481(a) over the tax computed for such year without taking the adjustments into account.

*(2)* The next step is to compute under section 481(b)(1) the tax attributable to the adjustments referred to in paragraph (c)(1) of this section for the taxable year of the change and the two preceding taxable years as if an amount equal to one-third of the net amount of such adjustments had been received or accrued in each of such taxable years. The increase in tax attributable to the adjustments for each such taxable year is the excess of the tax for such year computed with the allocation of one-third of the net adjustments to such taxable year over the tax computed without the allocation of any part of the adjustments to such year. For the purpose of computing the aggregate increase in taxes for such taxable years, there shall be taken into account the increase or decrease in tax for any taxable year preceding the taxable year of the change to which no adjustment is allocated under section 481(b)(1) but which is affected by a net operating loss under section 162 or by a capital loss carryback or carryover under section 1212, determined with reference to taxable years with respect to which adjustments under section 481(b)(1) are allocated.

*(3)* In the event that the taxpayer satisfies the conditions set forth in section 481(b)(2), the next step is to determine the amount of the net increase in tax attributable to the adjustments referred to in paragraph (c)(1) of this section for:

(i) The taxable year of the change,

(ii) The consecutive taxable year or years immediately preceding the taxable year of the change for which the taxpayer can establish his taxable income under the new method of accounting, and

(iii) Any taxable year preceding the taxable year of the change to which no adjustment is allocated under section 481(b)(2), but which is affected by a net operating loss or by a capital loss carryover determined with reference to taxable years with respect to which such adjustments are allocated.

*(4)* The tax for the taxable year of the change shall be the tax for such year, computed without taking any of the adjustments referred to in paragraph (c)(1) of this section into account, increased by the smallest of the following amounts—

(i) The amount of tax for the taxable year of the change attributable solely to taking into account the entire amount of the adjustments required by section 481(a) and § 1.481-1;

(ii) The sum of the increases in tax liability for the taxable year of the change and the two immediately preceding taxable years that would have resulted solely from taking into account one-third of the amount of such adjustments required for each of such years as though such amounts had been properly attributable to such years (computed in accordance with paragraph (c)(2) of this section); or

(iii) The net increase in tax attributable to allocating such adjustments under the new method of accounting (computed in accordance with paragraph (c)(3) of this section).

*(5)* (i) In the case of a change in method of accounting by a partnership, the adjustments required by section 481 shall be made with respect to the taxable income of the partnership but the limitations on tax under section 481(b) shall apply to the individual partners. Each partner shall take into account his distributive share of the partnership items, as so adjusted, for the taxable year of the change. Section 481(b) applies to a partner whose taxable income is so increased by more than $3,000 as a result of such adjustments to the partnership taxable income. It is not necessary for the partner to have been a member of the partnership for the two taxable years immediately preceding the taxable year of the change of the partnership's accounting method in order to have the limitation provided by section 481(b)(1) apply. Further, a partner may apply section 481(b)(2) even though he was not a member of the partnership for all the taxable years affected by the computation thereunder.

(ii) In the case of a change in method of accounting by an electing small business corporation under subchapter S, chapter 1 of the Code, the adjustments required by section 481 shall be made with respect to the taxable income of such electing corporation in the year of the change, but the limitations on tax under section 481(b) shall apply to the individual shareholders. Section 481(b) applies to a shareholder of an electing small business corporation whose taxable income is so increased by more than $3,000 as a result of such adjustments to such corporation's taxable income. It is not necessary for the shareholder to have been a member of the electing small business corporation, or for such corporation to have been an electing small business corporation, for the two taxable years immediately preceding the taxable year of the change of the corporation's accounting method in order to have the limitation provided by section 481(b)(1) apply. Further, a shareholder may apply section 481(b)(2), even though he was not a shareholder, or the corporation was not an electing small business corporation, for all the taxable years affected by the computation thereunder.

*(6)* For the purpose of the successive computations of the limitations on tax under section 481(b)(1) or (2), if the treatment of any item under the provisions of the Internal Revenue Code of 1986 (or corresponding provisions of prior internal revenue laws) depends upon the amount of gross income, adjusted gross income, or taxable income (for example, medical expenses, charitable contributions, or credits against the tax), such item shall be determined for the purpose of each such computation by taking into account the proper portion of the amount of any adjustments required to be taken into account under section 481 in each such computation.

*(7)* The increase or decrease in the tax for any taxable year for which an assessment of any deficiency, or a credit or refund of any overpayment, is prevented by any law or rule of law, shall be determined by reference to the tax previously determined (within the meaning of section 1314(a)) for such year.

*(8)* In applying section 7807(b)(1), the provisions of chapter 1 (other than subchapter E, relating to tax on self-employment income) and chapter 2 of the Internal Revenue Code of 1939 shall be treated as the corresponding provisions of the Internal Revenue Code of 1939.

**(d) Examples.** The application of section 481(b)(1) and (2) may be illustrated by the following examples. Although the examples in this paragraph are based upon adjustments required in the case of a change in the over-all method of accounting, the principles illustrated would be equally applicable to adjustments required in the case of a change in method of accounting for a particular material item, provided the treatment of such adjustments is not specifically subject to some other provision of the Internal Revenue Code of 1986.

*Example (1).* An unmarried individual taxpayer using the cash receipts and disbursements method of accounting for the calendar year is required by the Commissioner to change to an accrual method effective with the year 1958. As of January 1, 1958, he had an opening inventory of $11,000. On December 31, 1958, he had a closing inventory of $12,500. Merchandise purchases during the year amounted to $22,500, and net sales were $32,000. Total deductible business expenses were $5,000. There were no receivables or payables at January 1, 1958. The computation of taxable income for 1958, assuming no other adjustments, using the new method of accounting follows:

| | | |
|---|---|---|
| Net sales | | $32,000 |
| Opening inventory | $11,000 | |
| Purchases | 22,500 | |
| Total | 33,500 | |
| Less closing inventory | 12,500 | |
| Cost of goods sold | | 21,000 |
| Gross profit | | 11,000 |
| Business expenses | | 5,000 |
| Business income | | 6,000 |
| Personal exemption and itemized deductions | | 1,600 |
| Taxable income | | 4,400 |

Under the cash receipts and disbursements method of accounting, only $9,000 of the $11,000 opening inventory had been included in the cost of goods sold and claimed as a deduction for the taxable years 1954 through 1957; the remaining $2,000 had been so accounted for in pre-1954 years. In order to prevent the same item from reducing taxable income twice, an adjustment of $9,000 must be made to the taxable income of 1958 under the provisions of section 481(a) and § 1.481-1. Since the change in method of accounting was not initiated by the taxpayer, the $2,000 of opening inventory which had been included in cost of goods sold in pre-1954 years is not taken into account. Taxable income for 1958 is accordingly increased by $9,000 under section 481(a) to $13,400. Assuming that the tax on $13,400 is $4,002 and that the tax on $4,400 (income without the adjustment) is $944, the increase in tax attributable to the adjustment, if taken into account for the taxable year of the change, would be the difference between the two, or $3,058. Since the adjustment required by section 481(a) and § 1.481-1 ($9,000) increases taxable income by more than $3,000, the increase in tax for the taxable year 1958 attributable to the adjustment of $9,000 (i.e., $3,058) may be limited under the provisions of section 481(b)(1) or (2). See examples (2) and (3).

*Example (2).* Assume that the taxpayer in example (1) used the cash receipts and disbursements method of accounting in computing taxable income for the years 1956 and 1957 and that the taxable income for these years determined under such method was $4,000 and $6,000, respectively. The section 481(b)(1) limitation on tax with a pro rata three-year allocation of the $9,000 adjustment is computed as follows:

| Taxable Year | Taxable Income Before Adjustment | Taxable Income With Adjustment | Assumed Total Tax | Assumed Tax Before Adjustment | Increase In Tax Attributable To Adjustment |
|---|---|---|---|---|---|
| 1956 | $4,000 | $7,000 | $1,660 | $840 | $820 |
| 1957 | 6,000 | 9,000 | 2,300 | 1,360 | 940 |
| 1958 | 4,400 | 7,400 | 1,780 | 944 | 836 |
| Total | | | | | 2,596 |

Since this increase in tax of $2,596 is less than the increase in tax attributable to the inclusion of the entire adjustment in the income for the taxable year of the change ($3,058), the limitation provided by section 481(b)(1) applies, and the total tax for 1958, the taxable year of the change, if section 481(b)(2) does not apply, is determined as follows:

| | |
|---|---|
| Tax without any portion of adjustment | $ 944 |
| Increase in tax attributable to adjustment computed under section 481(b)(1) | 2,596 |
| Total tax for taxable year of the change | 3,540 |

*Example (3).* (i) Assume the same facts as in example (1) and, in addition, assume that the taxpayer used the cash receipts and disbursements method of accounting in computing taxable income for the years 1953 through 1957; that he established his taxable income under the new method for the taxable year 1953, 1954, and 1957, but did not have sufficient records to establish his taxable income under such method for the taxable years 1955 and 1956. The original taxable income and taxable income as redetermined are as follows:

| Taxable Year | Taxable income: Determined Under Cash Receipts And Disbursements Method | Established Under New Method | Increase Or (Decrease) In Taxable Income |
|---|---|---|---|
| 1953 | $5,000 | $7,000 | $2,000 |
| 1954 | 6,000 | 7,000 | 1,000 |
| 1955 | 5,500 | (1) | |
| 1956 | 4,000 | (1) | |
| 1957 | 6,000 | 10,000 | 4,000 |

(1) Undetermined.

As in examples (1) and (2), the total adjustment under section 481(a) is $9,000. Of the $9,000 adjustment, $4,000 may be allocated to 1957, which is the only year consecutively preceding the taxable year of the change for which the taxpayer was able to establish his income under the new method. Since the income cannot be established under the new method for 1956 and 1955, no allocation may be made to 1954 or 1953, even though the taxpayer has established his income for those years under the new method of accounting. The balance of $5,000 ($9,000 minus $4,000) must be allocated to 1958.

(ii) The limitation provided by section 481(b)(2) is computed as follows: The tax for 1957, based on taxable income of $6,000, is assumed to be $1,360. Under the new method, based on taxable income of $10,000, the tax for 1957 is assumed to be $2,640, the increase attributable to $4,000 of the $9,000 section 481(a) adjustment being $1,280, ($2,640 minus $1,360). The tax for 1958, computed on the basis of taxable income of $4,400 (determined under the new method), is assumed to be $944. The tax computed for 1958 on taxable income of $9,400 ($4,400 plus the $5,000 adjustment allocated to 1958) is assumed to be $2,436, leaving a difference of $1,492 ($2,436 minus $944) attributable to the inclusion in 1958 of the portion of the total adjustment to be taken into account which could not be properly allocated to the taxable year or years consecutively preceding 1958.

(iii) The tax attributable to the adjustment is determined by selecting the smallest of the three following amounts:

| | |
|---|---|
| Increase in tax attributable to adjustment computed under section 481(b)(2) ($1,280 + $1,492) | $2,772 |
| Increase in tax attributable to adjustment computed under section 481(b)(1) (example (2)) | 2,596 |
| Increase in tax if the entire adjustment is taken into account in the taxable year of the change (example (1)) | 3,058 |

The final tax for 1958 is then $3,540 computed as follows:

| | |
|---|---|
| Tax before inclusion of any adjustment | $ 944 |
| Increase in tax attributable to adjustments (smallest of $2,772, $2,596 or $3,058) | 2,596 |
| Total tax for 1958 (limited in accordance with section 481(b)(1)) | 3,540 |

*Example (4).* Assume that X Corporation has maintained its books of account and filed its income tax returns using the cash receipts and disbursements method of accounting for the years 1953 through 1957. The corporation secures permission to change to an accrual method of accounting for the calendar year 1958. The following tabulation presents the data with respect to the taxpayer's income for the years involved:

| Year | Taxable Income Under The Cash Receipts And Disbursements Method: Before Application Of Net Operating Loss Carryback | After Application Of Net Operating Loss Carryback | Taxable Income Established Under Accrual Method | Increase Or (Decrease) Attributable To Change | Changes In Taxable Income Due To Changes In Net Operating Loss Carryback |
|---|---|---|---|---|---|
| 1953 | $ 2,000 | 0 | (1) | | $2,000 |
| 1954 | (5,000) | | | $ 1,000 | $6,000 |
| 1956 | 80,000 | 80,000 | 77,000 | (3,000) | |
| 1957 | 90,000 | 90,000 | 96,000 | 6,000 | |
| 1958 | | | 100,000 | | |

(1) Not established.

As indicated above, taxable income for 1953 and 1954, as determined under the cash receipts and disbursements method of accounting, was $2,000 and $4,000, respectively, and after application of the net operating loss carryback from 1955, the taxable income was reduced to zero in 1953 and to $1,000 in 1954. The taxpayer was unable to establish taxable income for these years under an accrual method of accounting; however, under section 481(b)(3)(A), increases or decreases in the tax for taxable years to which no adjustment is allocated must, nevertheless, be taken into account to the extent the tax for such years would be affected by a net operating loss determined with reference to taxable years to which adjustments are allocated. The total amount of the adjustments required under section 481(a) and attributable to the taxable years 1953 through 1957 in this example is assumed to be $10,000. The redetermination of taxable income established by the taxpayer for the taxable years 1955, 1956, and 1957 appears under the heading "Taxable income established under accrual method" in the above tabulation. The tabulation assumes that the taxpayer has been able to recompute the income for those years so as to establish a net adjustment of $9,000, which leaves a balance of $1,000 unaccounted for. In accordance with the requirements of section 481(b)(2), the $1,000 amount is allocated to 1958, the taxable year of the change. The following computations are necessary in order to determine the tax attributable to the adjustments under section 481(a):

**Increase in tax attributable to inclusion in 1958 of the entire $10,000 adjustment**

| | |
|---|---|
| Tax on income of 1958 increased by entire amount of adjustment ($100,000 + $10,000) . . . . | $51,700 |
| Tax on income of 1958 without adjustment ($100,000) . . . . . . . . . . | 46,500 |
| Increase in tax attributable to inclusion of entire adjustment in year of the change . . . . . . . . . . | 5,200 |

Increase in tax attributable to adjustment computed under section 481(b)(1)

| Year | Amount of adjustment | Tax before adjustment | Tax after adjustment | Increase in tax liability attributable to adjustment |
|---|---|---|---|---|
| 1958 . . . . . . . . | $3,334 | $46,500 | $48,234 | $1,734 |
| 1957 . . . . . . . . | 3,333 | 41,300 | 43,033 | 1,733 |
| 1956 . . . . . . . . | 3,333 | 36,100 | 37,833 | 1,733 |
| Increase in tax attributable to adjustment computed under section 481(b)(1) . . . . . . . . | | | | $5,200 |

Increase in tax attributable to adjustment computed under section 481(b)(2)

| Year | Amount of adjustment | Tax before adjustment | Tax after adjustment | Increase or (decrease) in tax liability |
|---|---|---|---|---|
| 1953 . . . . . . . . | $2,000[1] | 0 | $ 600[1] | $ 600 |
| 1954 . . . . . . . . | 3,000[1] | $ 300 | 1,200[1] | 900 |
| 1955 . . . . . . . . | 6,000 | 0 | 300 | 300 |
| 1956 . . . . . . . . | (3,000) | 36,100 | 34,540 | (1,560) |
| 1957 . . . . . . . . | 6,000 | 41,300 | 44,420 | 3,120 |
| 1958 . . . . . . . . | 1,000[2] | 46,500 | 47,020[2] | 520 |
| Increase in tax attributable to the adjustment computed under section 481(b)(2) . . . . . . . . | | | | $3,880 |

[1] Attributable to recomputations of net operating loss carrybacks determined with reference to net operating loss in 1955.
[2] Attributable to the inclusion of $1,000 in the year of the change which represents the portion of the $10,000 adjustment not allocated to taxable years prior to the year of the change for which taxable income is established under the new method.

Since the limitation under section 481(b)(2) ($3,880) on the amount of tax attributable to the adjustments is applicable, the final tax for the taxable year of the change is computed by adding such amount to the tax for that year computed without the inclusion of any amount attributable to the adjustments, that is, $46,500 plus $3,880, or $50,380.

T.D. 6366, 2/19/59, amend T.D. 6490, 8/30/60, T.D. 7301, 1/3/74, T.D. 8608, 8/4/95.

### § 1.481-3 Adjustments attributable to pre-1954 years where change was not initiated by taxpayer

If the adjustments required by section 481(a) and § 1.481-1 are attributable to a change in method of accounting which was not initiated by the taxpayer, no portion of any adjustments which is attributable to pre-1954 years shall be taken into account in computing taxable income. For example, if the total adjustments in the case of a change in method of accounting which is not initiated by the taxpayer amount to $10,000, of which $4,000 is attributable to pre-1954 years, only $6,000 of the $10,000 total adjustments is required to be taken into account under section 481 in computing taxable income. The portion of the adjustments which is attributable to pre-1954 years is the net amount of the adjustments which would have been required if the taxpayer had changed his method of accounting in his first taxable year which began after December 31, 1953, and ended after August 16, 1954.

T.D. 6366, 2/19/59, amend T.D. 8608, 8/4/95.

### § 1.481-4 Adjustments taken into account with consent.

**(a)** In addition to the terms and conditions prescribed by the Commissioner under § 1.446-1(e)(3) for effecting a change in method of accounting, including the taxable year or years in which the amount of the adjustments required by section 481(a) is to be taken into account, or the methods of allocation described in section 481(b), a taxpayer may request approval of an alternative method of allocating the amount of the adjustments under section 481. See section 481(c). Requests for approval of an alternative method of allocation shall set forth in detail the facts and circumstances upon which the taxpayer bases its request. Permission will be granted only if the taxpayer and the Commissioner agree to the terms and conditions under which the allocation is to be effected. See § 1.446-1(e) for the rules regarding how to secure the Commissioner's consent to a change in method of accounting.

**(b)** An agreement to the terms and conditions of a change in method of accounting under § 1.446-1(e)(3), including the taxable year or years prescribed by the Commissioner under that section (or an alternative method described in paragraph (a) of this section) for taking the amount of the adjustments under section 481(a) into account, shall be in writing and shall be signed by the Commissioner and the taxpayer. It shall set forth the items to be adjusted, the amount of the adjustments, the taxable year or years for which the adjustments are to be taken into account, and the amount of the adjustments allocable to each year. The agreement shall be binding on the parties except upon a showing of fraud, malfeasance, or misrepresentation of material fact.

T.D. 6366, 2/19/59, amend T.D. 8608, 8/4/95.

### § 1.481-5 Effective dates.

Sections 1.481-1, 1.481-2, 1.481-3, and 1.481-4 are effective for Consent Agreements signed on or after December 27, 1994. For Consent Agreements signed before December 27, 1994, see §§ 1.481-1, 1.481-2, 1.481-3, 1.481-4, and 1.481-5 (as contained in the 26 CFR part 1 edition revised as of April 1, 1995).

T.D. 8608, 8/4/95.

### § 1.482-0 Outline of regulations under section 482.

This section contains major captions for §§ 1.482-1 through 1.482-9.

*§ 1.482-1 Allocation of income and deductions among taxpayers.*

(a) In general.

(1) Purpose and scope.

(2) Authority to make allocations.

(3) Taxpayer's use of section 482.

(b) Arm's length standard.

(1) In general.

(2) Arm's length methods.

(i) [Reserved]. For further guidance, see § 1.482-0T, the entry for § 1.482-1T(b)(2)(i).

(ii) Selection of category of method applicable to transaction.

(ii) [Reserved]. For further guidance, see § 1.482-0T, the entry for § 1.482-1T(b)(2)(iii).

(c) Best method rule.

(1) In general.

(2) Determining the best method.

(i) Comparability.

(ii) Data and assumptions.

(A) Completeness and accuracy of data.

(B) Reliability of assumptions.

(C) Sensitivity of results to deficiencies in data and assumptions.

(iii) Confirmation of results by another method.

(d) Comparability.

(1) In general.

(2) Standard of comparability.

(3) Factors for determining comparability.

(i) Functional analysis.

(ii) Contractual terms.

(A) In general.

(B) Identifying contractual terms.

(1) Written agreement.

(2) No written agreement.

(C) Examples.

(iii) Risk.

(A) In general.

(B) Identification of party that bears risk.

(C) Examples.

(iv) Economic conditions.

(v) Property or services.

(4) Special circumstances.

(i) Market share strategy.

(ii) Different geographic markets.

(A) In general.

(B) Example.

(C) Location savings.

(D) Example.

(iii) Transactions ordinarily not accepted as comparables.

(A) In general.

(B) Examples.

(e) Arm's length range.

(1) In general.

(2) Determination of arm's length range.

(i) Single method.

(ii) Selection of comparables.

(iii) Comparables included in arm's length range.

(A) In general.

(B) Adjustment of range to increase reliability.

(C) Interquartile range.

(3) Adjustment if taxpayer's results are outside arm's length range.

(4) Arm's length range not prerequisite to allocation.

(5) Examples.

(f) Scope of review.

(1) In general.

(i) Intent to evade or avoid tax not a prerequisite.

(ii) Realization of income not a prerequisite.

(A) In general.

(B) Example.

(iii) Nonrecognition provisions may not bar allocation.

(A) In general.

(B) Example.

(iv) Consolidated returns.

(2) Rules relating to determination of true taxable income.

(i) Aggregation of transactions.

(A) In general.

(B) Examples.

(ii) Allocation based on taxpayer's actual transactions.

(A) In general.

(B) Example.

(iii) Multiple year data.

(A) In general.

(B) Circumstances warranting consideration of multiple year data.

(C) Comparable effect over comparable period.

(D) Applications of methods using multiple year averages.

(E) Examples.

(iv) Product lines and statistical techniques.

(v) Allocations apply to results, not methods.

(A) In general.

(B) Example.

(g) Collateral adjustments with respect to allocations under section 482.

(1) In general.

(2) Correlative allocations.

(i) In general.

(ii) Manner of carrying out correlative allocation.

(iii) Events triggering correlative allocation.

(iv) Examples.

(3) Adjustments to conform accounts to reflect section 482 allocations.

(i) In general.

(ii) Example.

(4) Setoffs.

(i) In general.

(ii) Requirements.

(iii) Examples.

(h) Special rules.

(1) Small taxpayer safe harbor [Reserved].

(2) Effect of foreign legal restrictions.

(i) In general.

(ii) Applicable legal restrictions.

(iii) Requirement for electing the deferred income method of accounting.

(iv) Deferred income method of accounting.

(v) Examples.

(3) Coordination with section 936.

(i) Cost sharing under section 936.

(ii) Use of terms.

(i) Definitions.

(j) Effective/applicability date.

*§ 1.482-2 Determination of taxable income in specific situations.*

(a) Loans or advances.

(1) Interest on bona fide indebtedness.

(i) In general.

(ii) Application of paragraph (a) of this section.

(A) Interest on bona fide indebtedness.

(B) Alleged indebtedness.

(iii) Period for which interest shall be charged.

(A) General rule.

(B) Exception for certain intercompany transactions in the ordinary course of business.

(C) Exception for trade or business of debtor member located outside the United States.

(D) Exception for regular trade practice of creditor member or others in creditor's industry.

(E) Exception for property purchased for resale in a foreign country.

(1) General rule.

(2) Interest-free period.

(3) Average collection period.

(4) Illustration.

(iv) Payment; book entries.

(2) Arm's length interest rate.

(i) In general.

(ii) Funds obtained at situs of borrower.

(iii) Safe haven interest rates for certain loans and advances made after May 8, 1986.

(A) Applicability.

(1) General rule.

(2) Grandfather rule for existing loans.

(B) Safe haven interest rate based on applicable Federal rate.

(C) Applicable Federal rate.

(D) Lender in business of making loans.

(E) Foreign currency loans.

(3) Coordination with interest adjustments required under certain other Internal Revenue Code sections.

(4) Examples.

(b) Rendering of services.

(c) Use of tangible property.

(1) General rule.

(2) Arm's length charge.

(i) In general.

(ii) Safe haven rental charge.

(iii) Subleases.

(d) Transfer of property.

(e) [Reserved]. For further guidance, see § 1.482-0T, the entry for § 1.482-2T(e).

(f) Effective/applicability date.

*§ 1.482-3 Methods to determine taxable income in connection with a transfer of tangible property.*

(a) In general.

(b) Comparable uncontrolled price method.

(1) In general.

(2) Comparability and reliability considerations.

(i) In general.

(ii) Comparability.

(A) In general.

(B) Adjustments for differences between controlled and uncontrolled transactions.

(iii) Data and assumptions.

(3) Arm's length range.

(4) Examples.

(5) Indirect evidence of comparable uncontrolled transactions.

(i) In general.
(ii) Limitations.
(iii) Examples.
(c) Resale price method.
(1) In general.
(2) Determination of arm's length price.
(i) In general.
(ii) Applicable resale price.
(iii) Appropriate gross profit.
(iv) Arm's length range.
(3) Comparability and reliability considerations.
(i) In general.
(ii) Comparability.
(A) Functional comparability.
(B) Other comparability factors.
(C) Adjustments for differences between controlled and uncontrolled transactions.
(D) Sales agent.
(iii) Data and assumptions.
(A) In general.
(B) Consistency in accounting.
(4) Examples.
(d) Cost plus method.
(1) In general.
(2) Determination of arm's length price.
(i) In general.
(ii) Appropriate gross profit.
(iii) Arm's length range.
(3) Comparability and reliability considerations.
(i) In general.
(ii) Comparability.
(A) Functional comparability.
(B) Other comparability factors.
(C) Adjustments for differences between controlled and uncontrolled transactions.
(D) Purchasing agent.
(iii) Data and assumptions.
(A) In general.
(B) Consistency in accounting.
(4) Examples.
(e) Unspecified methods.
(1) In general.
(2) Example.
(f) Coordination with intangible property rules.

*§ 1.482-4 Methods to determine taxable income in connection with a transfer of intangible property.*

(a) In general.
(b) Definition of intangible.
(c) Comparable uncontrolled transaction method.
(1) In general.
(2) Comparability and reliability considerations.
(i) In general.
(ii) Reliability.
(iii) Comparability.
(A) In general.
(B) Factors to be considered in determining comparability.
(1) Comparable intangible property.
(2) Comparable circumstances.
(iv) Data and assumptions.
(3) Arm's length range.
(4) Examples.
(d) Unspecified methods.
(1) In general.
(2) Example.
(e) Coordination with tangible property rules.
(f) Special rules for transfers of intangible property.
(1) Form of consideration.
(2) Periodic adjustments.
(i) General rule.
(ii) Exceptions.
(A) Transactions involving the same intangible.
(B) Transactions involving comparable intangible.
(C) Methods other than comparable uncontrolled transaction.
(D) Extraordinary events.
(E) Five-year period.
(iii) Examples.
(3) Ownership of intangible property.
(i) Identification of owner.
(A) In general.
(B) [Reserved]. For further guidance, see § 1.482-0T, the entry for § 1.482-4T(f)(3)(i)(B).
(ii) Examples.
(4) Contribution to the value of intangible property owned by another.
(i) In general.
(ii) Examples.
(5) Consideration not artificially limited.
(6) Lump sum payments
(i) In general.
(ii) Exceptions.
(iii) Example.
(g) [Reserved]. For further guidance, see § 1.482-0T, the entry for § 1.482-4T(g).
(h) Effective/applicability date.

*§ 1.482-5 Comparable profits method.*

(a) In general.
(b) Determination of arm's length result.
(1) In general.
(2) Tested party.
(i) In general.
(ii) Adjustments for tested party.
(3) Arm's length range.
(4) Profit level indicators.
(i) Rate of return on capital employed.
(ii) Financial ratios.
(iii) Other profit level indicators.
(c) Comparability and reliability considerations.

(1) In general.
(2) Determination of arm's length price.
(i) In general.
(ii) Appropriate gross services profit.
(iii) Comparable transactional costs.
(iv) Arm's length range.
(3) Comparability and reliability considerations.
(i) In general.
(ii) Comparability.
(A) Functional comparability.
(B) Other comparability factors.
(C) Adjustments for differences between the controlled and uncontrolled transactions.
(iii) Data and assumptions.
(A) In general.
(B) Consistency in accounting.
(4) Examples.
(f) Comparable profits method.
(1) In general.
(2) Determination of arm's length result.
(i) Tested party.
(ii) Profit level indicators.
(iii) Comparability and reliability considerations--Data and assumptions--Consistency in accounting.
(3) Examples.
(g) Profit split method.
(1) In general.
(2) Examples.
(h) Unspecified methods.
(i) Contingent-payment contractual terms for services.
(1) Contingent-payment contractual terms recognized in general.
(2) Contingent-payment arrangement.
(i) General requirements.
(A) Written contract.
(B) Specified contingency.
(C) Basis for payment.
(ii) Economic substance and conduct.
(3) Commissioner's authority to impute contingent-payment terms.
(4) Evaluation of arm's length charge.
(5) Examples.
(j) Total services costs.
(k) Allocation of costs.
(1) In general.
(2) Appropriate method of allocation and apportionment.
(i) Reasonable method standard.
(ii) Use of general practices.
(3) Examples.
(l) Controlled services transaction.
(1) In general.
(2) Activity.
(3) Benefit.
(i) In general.
(ii) Indirect or remote benefit.
(iii) Duplicative activities.
(iv) Shareholder activities.
(v) Passive association.
(4) Disaggregation of transactions.
(5) Examples.
(m) Coordination with transfer pricing rules for other transactions.
(1) Services transactions that include other types of transactions.
(2) Services transactions that effect a transfer of intangible property.
(3) [Reserved]. For further guidance, see § 1.482-0T, the entry for § 1.482-9T(m)(3).
(4) Other types of transactions that include controlled services transactions.
(5) Examples.
(n) Effective/applicability date.
(1) In general.
(2) Election to apply regulations to earlier taxable years.

---

T.D. 8552, 7/1/94, amend T.D. 8632, 12/19/95, T.D. 8670, 5/9/96, T.D. 9088, 8/25/2003, T.D. 9278, 7/31/2006, T.D. 9441, 12/31/2008, T.D. 9456, 7/31/2009.

---

PAR. 3. Section 1.482-0 is amended by revising the entries for §§ 1.482-1(b)(2)(iii), 1.482-2(e) and (f), 1.482-4(g) and (h), 1.482-7, and 1.482-9 to read as follows:

**Proposed § 1.482-0 Outline of regulations under section 482.** *[For Preamble, see ¶ 153,087]*

* * * * *

*§ 1.482-1 Allocation of income and deductions among taxpayers.*

* * * * *

(b) * * *
(2) * * *
(iii) Coordination of methods applicable to certain intangible development arrangements.

*§ 1.482-2 Determination of taxable income in specific situations.*

* * * * *

(e) Cost sharing arrangement.
(f) Effective/applicability date.
(1) In general.
(2) Election to apply paragraph (b) of this section to earlier taxable years.

*§ 1.482-4 Methods to determine taxable income in connection with a transfer of intangible property.*

* * * * *

(g) Coordination with rules governing cost sharing arrangements.
(h) Effective/applicability date.
(1) In general.
(2) Election to apply regulation to earlier taxable years.

* * * * *

*§ 1.482-7 Methods to determine taxable income in connection with a cost sharing arrangement. [The text of the*

*proposed entries for § 1.482-7 is the same as the entries for § 1.482-7T in § 1.482-0T published elsewhere in this issue of the Federal Register]. [See T.D. 9441, 01/05/2009, 74 Fed. Reg. 2.].*

* * * * *

*§ 1.482-9 Methods to determine taxable income in connection with a controlled services transaction.*

* * * * *

(a) through (m)(2) [Reserved]

(m)

(3) [The text of the proposed entry for § 1.482-9(m)(3) is the same as the entry for § 1.482-9T(m)(3) in § 1.482-0T published elsewhere in this issue of the Federal Register]. [*See T.D. 9441, 01/05/2009, 74 Fed. Reg. 2.*].

(4) through (n)(3) [Reserved]

PAR. 4. Section 1.482-0 is amended by revising the entry for § 1.482-7 to read as follows:

**Proposed § 1.482-0**

• ***Caution:*** This Proposed Reg was incorporated into final and temporary regulations by TD 9441, 12/31/2008.

Outline of regulations under section 482 [*For Preamble, see ¶ 152,697*]

* * * * *

*§ 1.482-7 Methods to determine taxable income in connection with a cost sharing arrangement.*

(a) In general.

(1) RAB share method for cost sharing transactions (CSTs).

(2) Methods for preliminary or contemporaneous transactions (PCTs).

(3) Methods for other controlled transactions.

(i) Contribution to a CSA by a controlled taxpayer that is not a controlled participant.

(ii) Transfer of interest in a cost shared intangible.

(iii) Controlled transactions not in connection with a CSA.

(b) Cost sharing arrangement (CSA).

(1) In general.

(2) CSTs.

(i) In general.

(ii) Example.

(3) PCTs.

(i) In general.

(ii) External contributions.

(iii) PCT Payments.

(iv) Reference transaction (RT).

(v) PFAs.

(vi) Form of payment.

(A) In general.

(B) PFAs.

(C) No PCT Payor stock.

(vii) Date of a PCT.

(viii) Examples.

(4) Territorial division of interests.

(i) In general.

(ii) Examples.

(5) CSAs in substance or form.

(i) CSAs in substance.

(ii) CSAs in form.

(iii) Example.

(6) Treatment of CSAs.

(c) Make-or-sell rights excluded.

(1) In general.

(2) Examples.

(d) Intangible development costs (IDCs).

(1) Costs included in IDCs.

(2) Allocation of costs.

(3) Stock-based compensation.

(i) In general.

(ii) Identification of stock-based compensation with the IDA.

(iii) Measurement and timing of stock-based compensation IDC.

(A) In general.

(1) Transfers to which section 421 applies.

(2) Deductions of foreign controlled participants.

(3) Modification of stock option.

(4) Expiration or termination of CSA.

(B) Election with respect to options on publicly traded stock.

(1) In general.

(2) Publicly traded stock.

(3) Generally accepted accounting principles.

(4) Time and manner of making the election.

(C) Consistency.

(4) IDC share.

(5) Examples.

(e) Reasonably anticipated benefit shares (RAB shares).

(1) In general.

(2) Measure of benefits.

(i) In general.

(ii) Indirect bases for measuring benefits.

(A) Units used, produced, or sold.

(B) Sales.

(C) Operating profit.

(D) Other bases for measuring anticipated benefits.

(E) Examples.

(iii) Projections used to estimate benefits.

(A) In general.

(B) Examples.

(f) Changes in participation under a CSA.

(g) Supplemental guidance on methods applicable to PCTs.

(1) In general.

(2) General principles.

(i) In general.

(ii) Valuation consistent with upfront contractual terms and risk allocations.
(iii) Projections.
(iv) Realistic alternatives.
(A) In general.
(B) Examples.
(v) Aggregation of transactions.
(vi) Discount rate.
(A) In general.
(B) Examples.
(vii) Accounting principles.
(A) In general.
(B) Examples.
(viii) Valuation consistent with the investor model.
(A) In general.
(B) Example.
(ix) Coordination of best method rule and form of payment.
(x) Coordination of the valuations or prior and subsequent PCTs.
(xi) Proration of PCT Payments to the extent allocable to other business activities.
(3) Comparable uncontrolled transaction method.
(4) Income method.
(i) In general.
(ii) Determination of arm's length charge.
(A) In general.
(B) Example.
(iii) Application of income method using a CUT.
(A) In general.
(B) Determination of arm's length charge.
(1) In general.
(2) Applicable rate.
(3) Alternative rate.
(4) Cost contribution adjustment.
(C) Example.
(iv) Application of income method using CPM.
(A) In general.
(B) Determination of arm's length charge based on sales.
(1) In general.
(2) Applicable rate.
(3) Alternative rate.
(4) Cost contribution adjustment.
(C) Determination of arm's length charge based on profit.
(1) In general.
(2) Alternative rate.
(3) Cost contribution adjustment.
(D) Example.
(v) Routine external contributions.
(vi) Comparability and reliability considerations.
(A) In general.
(B) Application of the income method using a CUT.
(C) Application of the income method using CPM.
(5) Acquisition price method.
(i) In general.
(ii) Determination of arm's length charge.
(iii) Adjusted acquisition price.
(iv) Reliability and comparability considerations.
(v) Example.
(6) Market capitalization method.
(i) In general.
(ii) Determination of arm's length charge.
(iii) Average market capitalization.
(iv) Adjusted average market capitalization.
(v) Reliability and comparability considerations.
(vi) Examples.
(7) Residual profit split.
(i) In general.
(ii) Appropriate share of profits and losses.
(iii) Profit split.
(A) In general.
(B) Allocate income to routine contributions other than cost contributions.
(C) Allocate residual profit.
(1) In general.
(2) Cost contribution share of residual profit or loss.
(3) Nonroutine contribution share of residual profit or loss.
(4) Determination of PCT Payments.
(5) Routine external contributions.
(iv) Comparability and reliability considerations.
(A) In general.
(B) Comparability.
(C) Data and assumptions.
(D) Other factors affecting reliability.
(v) Example.
(8) Unspecified methods.
(h) Coordination with the arm's length standard.
(i) Allocations by the Commissioner in connection with a CSA.
(1) In general.
(2) CST allocations.
(i) In general.
(ii) Adjustments to improve the reliability of projections used to RAB shares.
(A) Unreliable projections.
(B) Foreign-to-foreign adjustments.
(C) Correlative adjustments to PCTs.
(D) Examples.
(iii) Timing of CST allocations.
(3) PCT allocations.
(4) Allocations regarding changes in participation under a CSA.
(5) Allocations when CSTs are consistently and materially disproportionate to RAB shares.
(6) Periodic adjustments.
(i) In general.
(ii) PRRR.
(iii) AERR.
(A) In general.

(B) PVTP.
(C) PVI.
(iv) ADR.
(A) In general.
(B) Publicly traded companies.
(C) Publicly traded.
(D) PCT Payor WACC.
(E) Generally accepted accounting principles.
(v) Determination of periodic adjustments.
(vi) Exceptions to periodic adjustments.
(A) Transactions involving the same external contributions as in the PCT.
(B) Results not reasonably anticipated.
(C) Reduced AERR does not cause Periodic Trigger.
(D) Increased AERR does not cause Periodic Trigger.
(E) 10-year period.
(F) 5-year period.
(vii) Examples.
(viii) Documentation.
(j) Definitions and special rules.
(1) Definitions.
(2) Special rules.
(i) Consolidated group.
(ii) Trade or business.
(iii) Partnership.
(3) Character.
(i) In general.
(ii) PCT Payments.
(iii) Examples.
(k) CSA contractual, documentation, accounting, and reporting requirements.
(1) CSA contractual requirements.
(i) In general.
(ii) Contractual provisions.
(iii) Meaning of contemporaneous.
(A) In general.
(B) Example.
(2) CSA documentation requirements.
(i) In general.
(ii) Additional CSA documentation requirements.
(iii) Coordination rules and production of documents.
(A) Coordination with penalty regulations.
(B) Production of documentation.
(3) CSA accounting requirements.
(i) In general.
(ii) Reliance on financial accounting.
(4) CSA reporting requirements.
(i) CSA Statement.
(ii) Content of CSA Statement.
(iii) Time for filing CSA Statement.
(A) 90-day rule.
(B) Annual return requirement.
(1) In general.
(2) Special filing rule for annual return requirement.
(iv) Examples.
(l) Effective date.
(m) Transition rule.
(1) In general.
(2) Termination of grandfather status.
(3) Transitional modification of applicable provisions.

* * * * *

PAR. 3. Section 1.482-0 is amended as follows:

1. The introductory text is revised.

2. The section heading and entries for § 1.482-8 are redesignated as the section heading and entries for § 1.482-9.

3. A new section heading and entries for § 1.482-8 are added.

The addition and revision read as follows:

**Proposed § 1.482-0 Outline of regulations under section 482.** [*For Preamble, see ¶ 151,855*]

This section contains major captions for §§ 1.482-1 through 1.482-9.

* * * * *

*§ 1.482-8 Allocation of income earned in a global dealing operation.*

(a) General requirements and definitions.
(1) In general.
(2) Definitions.
(i) Global dealing operation.
(ii) Participant.
(iii) Regular dealer in securities.
(iv) Security.
(3) Factors for determining comparability for a global dealing operation.
(i) Functional analysis.
(ii) Contractual terms.
(iii) Risk.
(iv) Economic conditions.
(4) Arm's length range.
(i) General rule.
(ii) Reliability.
(iii) Authority to make adjustments.
(5) Examples.
(b) Comparable uncontrolled financial transaction method.
(1) General rule.
(2) Comparability and reliability.
(i) In general.
(ii) Adjustments for differences between controlled and uncontrolled transactions.
(iii) Data and assumptions.
(3) Indirect evidence of the price of a comparable uncontrolled financial transaction.
(i) In general.
(ii) Public exchanges or quotation media.
(iii) Limitation on use of public exchanges or quotation media.
(4) Arm's length range.
(5) Examples.
(c) Gross margin method.

(1) General rule.

(2) Determination of an arm's length price.

(i) In general.

(ii) Applicable resale price.

(iii) Appropriate gross profit.

(3) Comparability.

(i) In general.

(ii) Adjustments for differences between controlled and uncontrolled transactions.

(iii) Reliability.

(iv) Data and assumptions.

(A) In general.

(B) Consistency in accounting.

(4) Arm's length range.

(5) Example.

(d) Gross markup method.

(1) General rule.

(2) Determination of an arm's length price.

(i) In general.

(ii) Appropriate gross profit.

(3) Comparability and reliability.

(i) In general.

(ii) Adjustments for differences between controlled and uncontrolled transactions.

(iii) Reliability.

(iv) Data and assumptions.

(A) In general.

(B) Consistency in accounting.

(4) Arm's length range.

(e) Profit split method.

(1) General rule.

(2) Appropriate share of profit and loss.

(i) In general.

(ii) Adjustment of factors to measure contribution clearly.

(3) Definitions.

(4) Application.

(5) Total profit split.

(i) In general.

(ii) Comparability.

(iii) Reliability.

(iv) Data and assumptions.

(A) In general.

(B) Consistency in accounting.

(6) Residual profit split.

(i) In general.

(ii) Allocate income to routine contributions.

(iii) Allocate residual profit.

(iv) Comparability.

(v) Reliability.

(vi) Data and assumptions.

(A) General rule.

(B) Consistency in accounting.

(7) Arm's length range.

(8) Examples.

(f) Unspecified methods.

(g) Source rule for qualified business units.

**§ 1.482-0T Outline of regulations under section 482 (temporary).**

This section contains major captions for §§ 1.482-1T, 1.482-2T, 1.482-4T, 1.482-7T, 1.482-8T, and 1.482-9T.

*§ 1.482-1T Allocation of income and deductions among taxpayers (temporary).*

(a) through (b)(2) [Reserved]. For further guidance, see § 1.482-0, the entries for § 1.482-1(a) through (b)(2).

(b)

(2)

(i) Methods.

(ii) [Reserved]. For further guidance, see § 1.482-0, the entry for § 1.482-1(b)(2)(ii).

(iii) Coordination of methods applicable to certain intangible development arrangements.

(c) through (i) [Reserved]. For further guidance, see § 1.482-0, the entries for § 1.482-1(c) through (i).

(j) Effective/applicability date.

(k) Expiration date.

*§ 1.482-2T Determination of taxable income in specific situations (temporary).*

(a) through (d) [Reserved]. For further guidance, see § 1.482-0, the entries for § 1.482-2(a) through (d).

(e) Cost sharing arrangement.

(f) Effective/applicability date.

(1) In general.

(2) Election to apply regulation to earlier taxable years.

(3) Expiration date.

*§ 1.482-4T Methods to determine taxable income in connection with a transfer of intangible property (temporary).*

(a) through (f)(3)(i)(A) [Reserved]. For further guidance, see § 1.482-0, the entries for § 1.482-4(a) through (f)(3)(i)(A).

(f)

(3)

(i)

(B) Cost sharing arrangements.

(ii) through (f)(6) [Reserved]. For further guidance, see § 1.482-0, the entries for § 1.482-4(f)(3)(ii) through (f)(6).

(g) Coordination with rules governing cost sharing arrangements.

(h) Effective/applicability date.

(i) Expiration date.

*§ 1.482-6T Profit split method.*

(a) through (c)(2)(ii)(A) [Reserved]. For further guidance, see § 1.482-0, the entry for § 1.482-6(a) through (c)(2)(ii)(A).

(c)

(2)

(ii)

(B) Comparability.

(1) In general.

(2) through (C) [Reserved]. For further guidance, see § 1.482-0, the entry for § 1.482-6(c)(2)(ii)(B)(2) through (C).

(D) Other factors affecting reliability.

(3)

(i) [Reserved]. For further guidance, see § 1.482-0, the entry for § 1.482-6(c)(3)(i).

(A) Allocate income to routine contributions.

(B) Allocate residual profit.

(1) Nonroutine contributions generally.

(2) Nonroutine contributions of intangible property.

(ii)

(A) through (C) [Reserved]. For further guidance, see § 1.482-0, the entry for § 1.482-6(c)(3)(ii)(A) through (C).

(D) Other factors affecting reliability.

(iii) [Reserved]. For further guidance, see § 1.482-0, the entry for § 1.482-6(c)(3)(iii).

(d) Effective date.

(1) In general.

(2) Election to apply regulation to earlier taxable years.

(3) Expiration date.

*§ 1.482-7T Methods to determine taxable income in connection with a cost sharing arrangement (temporary).*

(a) In general.

(1) RAB share method for cost sharing transactions (CSTs).

(2) Methods for platform contribution transactions (PCTs).

(3) Methods for other controlled transactions.

(i) Contribution to a CSA by a controlled taxpayer that is not a controlled participant.

(ii) Transfer of interest in a cost shared intangible.

(iii) Other controlled transactions in connection with a CSA.

(iv) Controlled transactions in the absence of a CSA.

(4) Coordination with the arm's length standard.

(b) Cost sharing arrangement.

(1) Substantive requirements.

(i) CSTs.

(ii) PCTs.

(iii) Divisional interests.

(iv) Examples.

(2) Administrative requirements.

(3) Date of a PCT.

(4) Divisional interests.

(i) In general.

(ii) Territorial based divisional interests.

(iii) Field of use based divisional interests.

(iv) Other divisional bases.

(v) Examples.

(5) Treatment of certain arrangements as CSAs.

(i) Situation in which Commissioner must treat arrangement as a CSA.

(ii) Situation in which Commissioner may treat arrangement as a CSA.

(iii) Examples.

(6) Entity classification of CSAs.

(c) Platform contributions.

(1) In general.

(2) Terms of platform contributions.

(i) Presumed to be exclusive.

(ii) Rebuttal of Exclusivity.

(iii) Proration of PCT Payments to the extent allocable to other business activities.

(A) In general.

(B) Determining the proration of PCT Payments.

(3) Categorization of the PCT.

(4) Certain make-or-sell rights excluded.

(i) In general.

(ii) Examples.

(5) Examples.

(d) Intangible development costs.

(1) Determining whether costs are IDCs.

(i) Definition and scope of the IDA.

(ii) Reasonably anticipated cost shared intangible.

(iii) Costs included in IDCs.

(iv) Examples.

(2) Allocation of costs.

(3) Stock-based compensation.

(i) In general.

(ii) Identification of stock-based compensation with the IDA.

(iii) Measurement and timing of stock-based compensation IDC.

(A) In general.

(1) Transfers to which section 421 applies.

(2) Deductions of foreign controlled participants.

(3) Modification of stock option.

(4) Expiration or termination of CSA.

(B) Election with respect to options on publicly traded stock.

(1) In general.

(2) Publicly traded stock.

(3) Generally accepted accounting principles.

(4) Time and manner of making the election.

(C) Consistency.

(4) IDC share.

(5) Examples.

(e) Reasonably anticipated benefit shares.

(1) Definition.

(i) In general.

(ii) Examples.

(2) Measure of benefits.

(i) In general.

(ii) Indirect bases for measuring anticipated benefits.

(A) Units used, produced, or sold.

(B) Sales.

(C) Operating profit.

(D) Other bases for measuring anticipated benefits.

(E) Examples.

(iii) Projections used to estimate benefits.

(A) In general.

(B) Examples.

(f) Changes in participation under a CSA.

(3) Coordination of best method rule and form of payment.

(i) Allocations by the Commissioner in connection with a CSA.

(1) In general.

(2) CST allocations.

(i) In general.

(ii) Adjustments to improve the reliability of projections used to estimate RAB shares.

(A) Unreliable projects.

(B) Foreign-to-foreign adjustments.

(C) Correlative adjustments to PCTs.

(D) Examples.

(iii) Timing of CST allocations.

(3) PCT allocations.

(4) Allocations regarding changes in participation under CSA.

(5) Allocations when CSTs are consistently and materially disproportionate to RAB shares.

(6) Periodic adjustments.

(i) In general.

(ii) PRRR.

(iii) AERR.

(A) In general.

(B) PVTP.

(C) PVI.

(iv) ADR.

(A) In general.

(B) Publicly traded companies.

(C) Publicly traded.

(D) PCT Payor WACC.

(E) Generally accepted accounting principles.

(v) Determination of periodic adjustments.

(A) In general.

(B) Adjusted RPSM as of Determination Date.

(vi) Exceptions to periodic adjustments.

(A) Controlled participants establish periodic adjustment not warranted.

(1) Transactions involving the same platform contribution as in the Trigger PCT.

(2) Results not reasonably anticipated.

(3) Reduced AERR does not cause Periodic Trigger.

(4) Increased AERR does not cause Periodic Trigger.

(B) Circumstances in which Periodic Trigger deemed not to occur.

(1) 10-year period.

(2) 5-year period.

(vii) Examples.

(j) Definitions and special rules.

(1) Definitions.

(i) In general.

(ii) Examples.

(2) Special rules.

(i) Consolidated group.

(ii) Trade or business.

(iii) Partnership.

(3) Character.

(i) CST Payments.

(ii) PCT Payments.

(iii) Examples.

(k) CSA administrative requirements.

(1) CSA contractual requirements.

(i) In general.

(ii) Contractual provisions.

(iii) Meaning of contemporaneous.

(A) In general.

(B) Example.

(iv) Interpretation of contractual provisions.

(A) In general.

(B) Examples.

(2) CSA documentation requirements.

(i) In general.

(ii) Additional CSA documentation requirements.

(iii) Coordination rules and production of documents.

(A) Coordination with penalty regulations.

(B) Production of documentation.

(3) CSA accounting requirements.

(i) In general.

(ii) Reliance on financial accounting.

(4) CSA reporting requirements.

(i) CSA Statement.

(ii) Content of CSA Statement.

(iii) Time for filing CSA Statement.

(A) 90-day rule.

(B) Annual return requirement.

(1) In general.

(2) Special filing rule for annual return requirement.

(iv) Examples.

(l) Effective/applicability date.

(m) Transition rule.

(1) In general.

(2) Transitional modification of applicable provisions.

(3) Special rule for certain periodic adjustments.

(n) Expiration date.

*§ 1.482-8T Examples of the best method rule.*

(a) [Reserved]. For further guidance, see § 1.482-0, the entry for § 1.482-8(a).

(b) [Reserved]. For further guidance, see § 1.482-0, the entry for Sec. 1.482-8(b).

(c) Effective date.

(1) In general.

(2) Election to apply regulation to earlier taxable years.

(3) Expiration date.

*§ 1.482-9T Methods to determine taxable income in connection with a controlled services transaction (temporary).*

(a) through (m)(2) [Reserved]. For further guidance, see § 1.482-0, the entries for § 1.482-9(a) through (m)(2).

(m)

(3) Coordination with rules governing cost sharing arrangements.

(n) Effective/applicability dates.

(o) Expiration date.

(n) Effective/applicability dates.

T.D. 9278, 7/31/2006, amend T.D. 9441, 12/31/2008, T.D. 9456, 7/31/2009.

### § 1.482-1 Allocation of income and deductions among taxpayers.

**(a) In general.** *(1) Purpose and scope.* The purpose of section 482 is to ensure that taxpayers clearly reflect income attributable to controlled transactions and to prevent the avoidance of taxes with respect to such transactions. Section 482 places a controlled taxpayer on a tax parity with an uncontrolled taxpayer by determining the true taxable income of the controlled taxpayer. This section sets forth general principles and guidelines to be followed under section 482. Section 1.482-2 provides rules for the determination of the true taxable income of controlled taxpayers in specific situations, including controlled transactions involving loans or advances or the use of tangible property. Sections 1.482-3 through 1.482-6 provide rules for the determination of the true taxable income of controlled taxpayers in cases involving the transfer of property. Section 1.482-7T sets forth the cost sharing provisions applicable to taxable years beginning on or after January 5, 2009. Section 1.482-8 provides examples illustrating the application of the best method rule. Finally, §§ 1.482-9 provides rules for the determination of the true taxable income of controlled taxpayers in cases involving the performance of services.

*(2) Authority to make allocations.* The district director may make allocations between or among the members of a controlled group if a controlled taxpayer has not reported its true taxable income. In such case, the district director may allocate income, deductions, credits, allowances, basis, or any other item or element affecting taxable income (referred to as allocations). The appropriate allocation may take the form of an increase or decrease in any relevant amount.

*(3) Taxpayer's use of section 482.* If necessary to reflect an arm's length result, a controlled taxpayer may report on a timely filed U.S. income tax return (including extensions) the results of its controlled transactions based upon prices different from those actually charged. Except as provided in this paragraph, section 482 grants no other right to a controlled taxpayer to apply the provisions of section 482 at will or to compel the district director to apply such provisions. Therefore, no untimely or amended returns will be permitted to decrease taxable income based on allocations or other adjustments with respect to controlled transactions. See § 1.6662-6T(a)(2) or successor regulations.

**(b) Arm's length standard.** *(1) In general.* In determining the true taxable income of a controlled taxpayer, the standard to be applied in every case is that of a taxpayer dealing at arm's length with an uncontrolled taxpayer. A controlled transaction meets the arm's length standard if the results of the transaction are consistent with the results that would have been realized if uncontrolled taxpayers had engaged in the same transaction under the same circumstances (arm's length result). However, because identical transactions can rarely be located, whether a transaction produces an arm's length result generally will be determined by reference to the results of comparable transactions under comparable circumstances. See § 1.482-1(d)(2) (Standard of comparability). Evaluation of whether a controlled transaction produces an arm's length result is made pursuant to a method selected under the best method rule described in § 1.482-1(c).

*(2) Arm's length methods.* (i) [Reserved]. For further guidance, see § 1.482-1T(b)(2)(i).

(ii) Selection of category of method applicable to transaction. The methods listed in § 1.482-2 apply to different types of transactions, such as transfers of property, services, loans or advances, and rentals. Accordingly, the method or methods most appropriate to the calculation of arm's length results for controlled transactions must be selected, and different methods may be applied to interrelated transactions if such transactions are most reliably evaluated on a separate basis. For example, if services are provided in connection with the transfer of property, it may be appropriate to separately apply the methods applicable to services and property in order to determine an arm's length result. But see § 1.482-1(f)(2)(i) (Aggregation of transactions). In addition, other applicable provisions of the Code may affect the characterization of a transaction, and therefore affect the methods applicable under section 482. See for example section 467.

**(c) Best method rule.** *(1) In general.* The arm's length result of a controlled transaction must be determined under the method that, under the facts and circumstances, provides the most reliable measure of an arm's length result. Thus, there is no strict priority of methods, and no method will invariably be considered to be more reliable than others. An arm's length result may be determined under any method without establishing the inapplicability of another method, but if another method subsequently is shown to produce a more reliable measure of an arm's length result, such other method must be used. Similarly, if two or more applications of a single method provide inconsistent results, the arm's length result must be determined under the application that, under the facts and circumstances, provides the most reliable measure of an arm's length result. See § 1.482-8 for examples of the application of the best method rule. See § 1.482-7T for the applicable methods in the case of a cost sharing arrangement.

*(2) Determining the best method.* Data based on the results of transactions between unrelated parties provides the most objective basis for determining whether the results of a controlled transaction are arm's length. Thus, in determining which of two or more available methods (or applications of a single method) provides the most reliable measure of an arm's length result, the two primary factors to take into account are the degree of comparability between the controlled transaction (or taxpayer) and any uncontrolled comparables, and the quality of the data and assumptions used in the analysis. In addition, in certain circumstances, it also may be relevant to consider whether the results of an analysis are consistent with the results of an analysis under another method. These factors are explained in paragraphs (c)(2)(i), (ii), and (iii) of this section.

(i) Comparability. The relative reliability of a method based on the results of transactions between unrelated parties depends on the degree of comparability between the controlled transaction or taxpayers and the uncontrolled comparables, taking into account the factors described in § 1.482-1(d)(3) (Factors for determining comparability), and after making adjustments for differences, as described in § 1.482-1(d)(2) (Standard of comparability). As the degree of comparability increases, the number and extent of potential differences that could render the analysis inaccurate is reduced. In addition, if adjustments are made to increase the degree of comparability, the number, magnitude, and reliability of those adjustments will affect the reliability of the results of the analysis. Thus, an analysis under the comparable uncontrolled price method will generally be more reliable than analyses obtained under other methods if the analysis is based on closely comparable uncontrolled transactions, because such an analysis can be expected to achieve a higher degree of comparability and be susceptible to fewer differences than analyses under other methods. See § 1.482-3(b)(2)(ii)(A). An analysis will be relatively less reliable, however, as the uncontrolled transactions become less comparable to the controlled transaction.

(ii) Data and assumptions. Whether a method provides the most reliable measure of an arm's length result also depends upon the completeness and accuracy of the underlying data, the reliability of the assumptions, and the sensitivity of the results to possible deficiencies in the data and assumptions. Such factors are particularly relevant in evaluating the degree of comparability between the controlled and uncontrolled transactions. These factors are discussed in paragraphs (c)(2)(ii)(A), (B), and (C) of this section.

(A) Completeness and accuracy of data. The completeness and accuracy of the data affects the ability to identify and quantify those factors that would affect the result under any particular method. For example, the completeness and accuracy of data will determine the extent to which it is possible to identify differences between the controlled and uncontrolled transactions, and the reliability of adjustments that are made to account for such differences. An analysis will be relatively more reliable as the completeness and accuracy of the data increases.

(B) Reliability of assumptions. All methods rely on certain assumptions. The reliability of the results derived from a method depends on the soundness of such assumptions. Some assumptions are relatively reliable. For example, adjustments for differences in payment terms between controlled and uncontrolled transactions may be based on the assumption that at arm's length such differences would lead to price differences that reflect the time value of money. Although selection of the appropriate interest rate to use in making such adjustments involves some judgement, the economic analysis on which the assumption is based is relatively sound. Other assumptions may be less reliable. For example, the residual profit split method may be based on the assumption that capitalized intangible development expenses reflect the relative value of the intangible property contributed by each party. Because the costs of developing an intangible may not be related to its market value, the soundness of this assumption will affect the reliability of the results derived from this method.

(C) Sensitivity of results to deficiencies in data and assumptions. Deficiencies in the data used or assumptions made may have a greater effect on some methods than others. In particular, the reliability of some methods is heavily dependent on the similarity of property or services involved in the controlled and uncontrolled transaction. For certain other methods, such as the resale price method, the analysis of the extent to which controlled and uncontrolled taxpayers undertake the same or similar functions, employ similar resources, and bear similar risks is particularly important. Finally, under other methods, such as the profit split method, defining the relevant business activity and appropriate allocation of costs, income, and assets may be of particular importance. Therefore, a difference between the controlled and uncontrolled transactions for which an accurate adjustment cannot be made may have a greater effect on the reliability of the results derived under one method than the results derived under another method. For example, differences in management efficiency may have a greater effect on a comparable profits method analysis than on a comparable uncontrolled price method analysis, while differences in product characteristics will ordinarily have a greater effect on a comparable uncontrolled price method analysis than on a comparable profits method analysis.

(iii) Confirmation of results by another method. If two or more methods produce inconsistent results, the best method rule will be applied to select the method that provides the most reliable measure of an arm's length result. If the best method rule does not clearly indicate which method should be selected, an additional factor that may be taken into account in selecting a method is whether any of the competing methods produce results that are consistent with the results obtained from the appropriate application of another method. Further, in evaluating different applications of the same method, the fact that a second method (or another application of the first method) produces results that are consistent with one of the competing applications may be taken into account.

**(d) Comparability.** *(1) In general.* Whether a controlled transaction produces an arm's length result is generally evaluated by comparing the results of that transaction to results realized by uncontrolled taxpayers engaged in comparable transactions under comparable circumstances. For this purpose, the comparability of transactions and circumstances must be evaluated considering all factors that could affect prices or profits in arm's length dealings (comparability factors). While a specific comparability factor may be of particular importance in applying a method, each method requires analysis of all of the factors that affect comparability under that method. Such factors include the following—

(i) Functions;

(ii) Contractual terms;

(iii) Risks;

(iv) Economic conditions; and

(v) Property or services.

*(2) Standard of comparability.* In order to be considered comparable to a controlled transaction, an uncontrolled transaction need not be identical to the controlled transaction, but must be sufficiently similar that it provides a reliable measure of an arm's length result. If there are material differences between the controlled and uncontrolled transactions, adjustments must be made if the effect of such differences on prices or profits can be ascertained with sufficient accuracy to improve the reliability of the results. For purposes of this section, a material difference is one that would materially affect the measure of an arm's length result under the method being applied. If adjustments for material differences cannot be made, the uncontrolled transaction may be used as a measure of an arm's length result, but the reliability of the analysis will be reduced. Generally, such adjustments must be made to the results of the uncontrolled comparable and must be based on commercial practices, economic principles, or statistical analyses. The extent and reliability of any adjustments will affect the relative reliability of the analysis. See § 1.482-1(c)(1) (Best method rule). In any event, unadjusted industry average returns themselves cannot establish arm's length results.

*(3) Factors for determining comparability.* The comparability factors listed in § 1.482-1(d)(1) are discussed in this section. Each of these factors must be considered in determining the degree of comparability between transactions or

taxpayers and the extent to which comparability adjustments may be necessary. In addition, in certain cases involving special circumstances, the rules under paragraph (d)(4) of this section must be considered.

(i) Functional analysis. Determining the degree of comparability between controlled and uncontrolled transactions requires a comparison of the functions performed, and associated resources employed, by the taxpayers in each transaction. This comparison is based on a functional analysis that identifies and compares the economically significant activities undertaken, or to be undertaken, by the taxpayers in both controlled and uncontrolled transactions. A functional analysis should also include consideration of the resources that are employed, or to be employed, in conjunction with the activities undertaken, including consideration of the type of assets used, such as plant and equipment, or the use of valuable intangibles. A functional analysis is not a pricing method and does not itself determine the arm's length result for the controlled transaction under review. Functions that may need to be accounted for in determining the comparability of two transactions include—

(A) Research and development;

(B) Product design and engineering;

(C) Manufacturing, production and process engineering;

(D) Product fabrication, extraction, and assembly;

(E) Purchasing and materials management;

(F) Marketing and distribution functions, including inventory management, warranty administration, and advertising activities;

(G) Transportation and warehousing; and

(H) Managerial, legal, accounting and finance, credit and collection, training, and personnel management services.

(ii) Contractual terms. (A) In general. Determining the degree of comparability between the controlled and uncontrolled transactions requires a comparison of the significant contractual terms that could affect the results of the two transactions. These terms include—

(1) The form of consideration charged or paid;

(2) Sales or purchase volume;

(3) The scope and terms of warranties provided;

(4) Rights to updates, revisions or modifications;

(5) The duration of relevant license, contract or other agreements, and termination or renegotiation rights;

(6) Collateral transactions or ongoing business relationships between the buyer and the seller, including arrangements for the provision of ancillary or subsidiary services; and

(7) Extension of credit and payment terms. Thus, for example, if the time for payment of the amount charged in a controlled transaction differs from the time for payment of the amount charged in an uncontrolled transaction, an adjustment to reflect the difference in payment terms should be made if such difference would have a material effect on price. Such comparability adjustment is required even if no interest would be allocated or imputed under § 1.482-2(a) or other applicable provisions of the Internal Revenue Code or regulations.

(B) Identifying contractual terms. (1) Written agreement. The contractual terms, including the consequent allocation of risks, that are agreed to in writing before the transactions are entered into will be respected if such terms are consistent with the economic substance of the underlying transactions. In evaluating economic substance, greatest weight will be given to the actual conduct of the parties, and the respective legal rights of the parties (see, for example, § 1.482-4(f)(3) (Ownership of intangible property)). If the contractual terms are inconsistent with the economic substance of the underlying transaction, the district director may disregard such terms and impute terms that are consistent with the economic substance of the transaction.

(2) No written agreement. In the absence of a written agreement, the district director may impute a contractual agreement between the controlled taxpayers consistent with the economic substance of the transaction. In determining the economic substance of the transaction, greatest weight will be given to the actual conduct of the parties and their respective legal rights (see, for example, § 1.482-4(f)(3) (Ownership of intangible property)). For example, if, without a written agreement, a controlled taxpayer operates at full capacity and regularly sells all of its output to another member of its controlled group, the district director may impute a purchasing contract from the course of conduct of the controlled taxpayers, and determine that the producer bears little risk that the buyer will fail to purchase its full output. Further, if an established industry convention or usage of trade assigns a risk or resolves an issue, that convention or usage will be followed if the conduct of the taxpayers is consistent with it. See UCC section 1-205. For example, unless otherwise agreed, payment generally is due at the time and place at which the buyer is to receive goods. See UCC section 2-310.

(C) Examples. The following examples illustrate this paragraph (d)(3)(ii).

*Example (1).* Differences in volume. USP, a United States agricultural exporter, regularly buys transportation services from FSub, its foreign subsidiary, to ship its products from the United States to overseas markets. Although FSub occasionally provides transportation services to URA, an unrelated domestic corporation, URA accounts for only 10% of the gross revenues of FSub, and the remaining 90% of FSub's gross revenues are attributable to FSub's transactions with USP. In determining the degree of comparability between FSub's uncontrolled transaction with URA and its controlled transaction with USP, the difference in volumes involved in the two transactions and the regularity with which these services are provided must be taken into account if such difference would have a material effect on the price charged. Inability to make reliable adjustments for these differences would affect the reliability of the results derived from the uncontrolled transaction as a measure of the arm's length result.

*Example (2).* Reliability of adjustment for differences in volume.

(i) FS manufactures product XX and sells that product to its parent corporation, P. FS also sells product XX to uncontrolled taxpayers at a price of $100 per unit. Except for the volume of each transaction, the sales to P and to uncontrolled taxpayers take place under substantially the same economic conditions and contractual terms. In uncontrolled transactions, FS offers a 2% discount for quantities of 20 per order, and a 5% discount for quantities of 100 per order. If P purchases product XX in quantities of 60 per order, in the absence of other reliable information, it may reasonably be concluded that the arm's length price to P would be $100, less a discount of 3.5%.

(ii) If P purchases product XX in quantities of 1,000 per order, a reliable estimate of the appropriate volume discount must be based on proper economic or statistical analysis, not necessarily a linear extrapolation from the 2% and 5% catalog discounts applicable to sales of 20 and 100 units, respectively.

*Example (3).* Contractual terms imputed from economic substance. (i) FP, a foreign producer of wristwatches, is the registered holder of the YY trademark in the United States and in other countries worldwide. In year 1, FP enters the United States market by selling YY wristwatches to its newly organized United States subsidiary, USSub, for distribution in the United States market. USSub pays FP a fixed price per wristwatch. USSub and FP undertake, without separate compensation, marketing activities to establish the YY trademark in the United States market. Unrelated foreign producers of trademarked wristwatches and their authorized United States distributors respectively undertake similar marketing activities in independent arrangements involving distribution of trademarked wristwatches in the United States market. In years 1 through 6, USSub markets and sells YY wristwatches in the United States. Further, in years 1 through 6, USSub undertakes incremental marketing activities in addition to the activities similar to those observed in the independent distribution transactions in the United States market. FP does not directly or indirectly compensate USSub for performing these incremental activities during years 1 through 6. Assume that, aside from these incremental activities, and after any adjustments are made to improve the reliability of the comparison, the price paid per wristwatch by the independent, authorized distributors of wristwatches would provide the most reliable measure of the arm's length price paid per YY wristwatch by USSub.

(ii) By year 7, the wristwatches with the YY trademark generate a premium return in the United States market, as compared to wristwatches marketed by the independent distributors. In year 7, substantially all the premium return from the YY trademark in the United States market is attributed to FP, for example through an increase in the price paid per watch by USSub, or by some other means.

(iii) In determining whether an allocation of income is appropriate in year 7, the Commissioner may consider the economic substance of the arrangements between USSub and FP, and the parties' course of conduct throughout their relationship. Based on this analysis, the Commissioner determines that it is unlikely that, ex ante, an uncontrolled taxpayer operating at arm's length would engage in the incremental marketing activities to develop or enhance intangible property owned by another party unless it received contemporaneous compensation or otherwise had a reasonable anticipation of receiving a future benefit from those activities. In this case, USSub's undertaking the incremental marketing activities in years 1 through 6 is a course of conduct that is inconsistent with the parties' attribution to FP in year 7 of substantially all the premium return from the enhanced YY trademark in the United States market. Therefore, the Commissioner may impute one or more agreements between USSub and FP, consistent with the economic substance of their course of conduct, which would afford USSub an appropriate portion of the premium return from the YY trademark wristwatches. For example, the Commissioner may impute a separate services agreement that affords USSub contingent-payment compensation for its incremental marketing activities in years 1 through 6, which benefited FP by contributing to the value of the trademark owned by FP. In the alternative, the Commissioner may impute a long-term, exclusive agreement to exploit the YY trademark in the United States that allows USSub to benefit from the incremental marketing activities it performed. As another alternative, the Commissioner may require FP to compensate USSub for terminating USSub's imputed long-term, exclusive agreement to exploit the YY trademark in the United States, an agreement that USSub made more valuable at its own expense and risk. The taxpayer may present additional facts that could indicate which of these or other alternative agreements best reflects the economic substance of the underlying transactions, consistent with the parties' course of conduct in the particular case.

*Example (4).* Contractual terms imputed from economic substance.

(i) FP, a foreign producer of athletic gear, is the registered holder of the AA trademark in the United States and in other countries worldwide. In year 1, FP enters into a licensing agreement that affords its newly organized United States subsidiary, USSub, exclusive rights to certain manufacturing and marketing intangible property (including the AA trademark) for purposes of manufacturing and marketing athletic gear in the United States under the AA trademark. The contractual terms of this agreement obligate USSub to pay FP a royalty based on sales, and also obligate both FP and USSub to undertake without separate compensation specified types and levels of marketing activities. Unrelated foreign businesses license independent United States businesses to manufacture and market athletic gear in the United States, using trademarks owned by the unrelated foreign businesses. The contractual terms of these uncontrolled transactions require the licensees to pay royalties based on sales of the merchandise, and obligate the licensors and licensees to undertake without separate compensation specified types and levels of marketing activities. In years 1 through 6, USSub manufactures and sells athletic gear under the AA trademark in the United States. Assume that, after adjustments are made to improve the reliability of the comparison for any material differences relating to marketing activities, manufacturing or marketing intangible property, and other comparability factors, the royalties paid by independent licensees would provide the most reliable measure of the arm's length royalty owed by USSub to FP, apart from the additional facts in paragraph (ii) of this Example 4.

(ii) In years 1 through 6, USSub performs incremental marketing activities with respect to the AA trademark athletic gear, in addition to the activities required under the terms of the license agreement with FP, that are also incremental as compared to those observed in the comparables. FP does not directly or indirectly compensate USSub for performing these incremental activities during years 1 through 6. By year 7, AA trademark athletic gear generates a premium return in the United States, as compared to similar athletic gear marketed by independent licensees. In year 7, USSub and FP enter into a separate services agreement under which FP agrees to compensate USSub on a cost basis for the incremental marketing activities that USSub performed during years 1 through 6, and to compensate USSub on a cost basis for any incremental marketing activities it may perform in year 7 and subsequent years. In addition, the parties revise the license agreement executed in year 1, and increase the royalty to a level that attributes to FP substantially all the premium return from sales of the AA trademark athletic gear in the United States.

(iii) In determining whether an allocation of income is appropriate in year 7, the Commissioner may consider the economic substance of the arrangements between USSub and FP and the parties' course of conduct throughout their relationship. Based on this analysis, the Commissioner determines that it is unlikely that, ex ante, an uncontrolled taxpayer operating at arm's length would engage in the incremental marketing activities to develop or enhance intangible property owned by another party unless it received contemporaneous compensation or otherwise had a reasonable anticipation of a future benefit. In this case, USSub's undertaking the incremental marketing activities in years 1 through 6 is a course of conduct that is inconsistent with the parties' adoption in year 7 of contractual terms by which FP compensates USSub on a cost basis for the incremental marketing activities that it performed. Therefore, the Commissioner may impute one or more agreements between USSub and FP, consistent with the economic substance of their course of conduct, which would afford USSub an appropriate portion of the premium return from the AA trademark athletic gear. For example, the Commissioner may impute a separate services agreement that affords USSub contingent-payment compensation for the incremental activities it performed during years 1 through 6, which benefited FP by contributing to the value of the trademark owned by FP. In the alternative, the Commissioner may impute a long-term, exclusive United States license agreement that allows USSub to benefit from the incremental activities. As another alternative, the Commissioner may require FP to compensate USSub for terminating USSub's imputed long-term United States license agreement, a license that USSub made more valuable at its own expense and risk. The taxpayer may present additional facts that could indicate which of these or other alternative agreements best reflects the economic substance of the underlying transactions, consistent with the parties' course of conduct in this particular case.

*Example (5).* Non-arm's length compensation. (i) The facts are the same as in paragraph (i) of Example 4. As in Example 4, assume that, after adjustments are made to improve the reliability of the comparison for any material differences relating to marketing activities, manufacturing or marketing intangible property, and other comparability factors, the royalties paid by independent licensees would provide the most reliable measure of the arm's length royalty owed by USSub to FP, apart from the additional facts described in paragraph (ii) of this Example 5.

(ii) In years 1 through 4, USSub performs certain incremental marketing activities with respect to the AA trademark athletic gear, in addition to the activities required under the terms of the basic license agreement, that are also incremental as compared with those activities observed in the comparables. At the start of year 1, FP enters into a separate services agreement with USSub, which states that FP will compensate USSub quarterly, in an amount equal to specified costs plus X%, for these incremental marketing functions. Further, these written agreements reflect the intent of the parties that USSub receive such compensation from FP throughout the term of the agreement, without regard to the success or failure of the promotional activities. During years 1 through 4, USSub performs marketing activities pursuant to the separate services agreement and in each year USSub receives the specified compensation from FP on a cost of services plus basis.

(iii) In evaluating year 4, the Commissioner performs an analysis of independent parties that perform promotional activities comparable to those performed by USSub and that receive separately-stated compensation on a current basis without contingency. The Commissioner determines that the magnitude of the specified cost plus X% is outside the arm's length range in each of years 1 through 4. Based on an evaluation of all the facts and circumstances, the Commissioner makes an allocation to require payment of compensation to USSub for the promotional activities performed in year 4, based on the median of the interquartile range of the arm's length markups charged by the uncontrolled comparables described in paragraph (e)(3) of this section.

(iv) Given that based on facts and circumstances, the terms agreed by the controlled parties were that FP would bear all risks associated with the promotional activities performed by USSub to promote the AA trademark product in the United States market, and given that the parties' conduct during the years examined was consistent with this allocation of risk, the fact that the cost of services plus markup on USSub's services was outside the arm's length range does not, without more, support imputation of additional contractual terms based on alternative views of the economic substance of the transaction, such as terms indicating that USSub, rather than FP, bore the risk associated with these activities.

*Example (6).* Contractual terms imputed from economic substance. (i) Company X is a member of a controlled group that has been in operation in the pharmaceutical sector for many years. In years 1 through 4, Company X undertakes research and development activities. As a result of those activities, Company X developed a compound that may be more effective than existing medications in the treatment of certain conditions.

(ii) Company Y is acquired in year 4 by the controlled group that includes Company X. Once Company Y is acquired, Company X makes available to Company Y a large amount of technical data concerning the new compound, which Company Y uses to register patent rights with respect to the compound in several jurisdictions, making Company Y the legal owner of such patents. Company Y then enters into licensing agreements with group members that afford Company Y 100% of the premium return attributable to use of the intangible property by its subsidiaries.

(iii) In determining whether an allocation is appropriate in year 4, the Commissioner may consider the economic substance of the arrangements between Company X and Company Y, and the parties' course of conduct throughout their relationship. Based on this analysis, the Commissioner determines that it is unlikely that an uncontrolled taxpayer operating at arm's length would make available the results of its research and development or perform services that resulted in transfer of valuable know how to another party unless it received contemporaneous compensation or otherwise had a reasonable anticipation of receiving a future benefit from those activities. In this case, Company X's undertaking the research and development activities and then providing technical data and know-how to Company Y in year 4 is inconsistent with the registration and subsequent exploitation of the patent by Company Y. Therefore, the Commissioner may impute one or more agreements between Company X and Company Y consistent with the economic substance of their course of conduct, which would afford Company X an appropriate portion of the premium return from the patent rights. For example, the Commissioner may impute a separate services agreement that affords Company X contingent-payment compensation for its services in year 4 for the benefit of Company Y, consisting of making available to Company Y technical data, know-how, and other fruits of research and development conducted in previous years. These services benefited Company Y by giving rise to and contributing to the value of the patent rights that were ultimately registered by Company Y. In the alternative, the Commissioner may impute a transfer of patentable intangible property rights from Company X to Company Y immediately preceding the registration of patent rights by Company Y. The taxpayer may present additional facts that could indicate which of these or other alternative agreements best reflects the economic substance of the underlying transactions, consistent with the parties' course of conduct in the particular case.

(iii) Risk. (A) Comparability. Determining the degree of comparability between controlled and uncontrolled transactions requires a comparison of the significant risks that could affect the prices that would be charged or paid, or the profit that would be earned, in the two transactions. Relevant risks to consider include—

(1) Market risks, including fluctuations in cost, demand, pricing, and inventory levels;

(2) Risks associated with the success or failure of research and development activities;

(3) Financial risks, including fluctuations in foreign currency rates of exchange and interest rates;

(4) Credit and collection risks;

(5) Product liability risks; and

(6) General business risks related to the ownership of property, plant, and equipment.

(B) Identification of taxpayer that bears risk. In general, the determination of which controlled taxpayer bears a particular risk will be made in accordance with the provisions of § 1.482-1(d)(3)(ii)(B) (Identifying contractual terms). Thus, the allocation of risks specified or implied by the taxpayer's contractual terms will generally be respected if it is consistent with the economic substance of the transaction. An allocation of risk between controlled taxpayers after the outcome of such risk is known or reasonably knowable lacks economic substance. In considering the economic substance of the transaction, the following facts are relevant—

(1) Whether the pattern of the controlled taxpayer's conduct over time is consistent with the purported allocation of risk between the controlled taxpayers; or where the pattern is changed, whether the relevant contractual arrangements have been modified accordingly;

(2) Whether a controlled taxpayer has the financial capacity to fund losses that might be expected to occur as the result of the assumption of a risk, or whether, at arm's length, another party to the controlled transaction would ultimately suffer the consequences of such losses; and

(3) The extent to which each controlled taxpayer exercises managerial or operational control over the business activities that directly influence the amount of income or loss realized. In arm's length dealings, parties ordinarily bear a greater share of those risks over which they have relatively more control.

(C) Examples. The following examples illustrate this paragraph (d)(3)(iii).

*Example (1).* FD, the wholly-owned foreign distributor of USM, a U.S. manufacturer, buys widgets from USM under a written contract. Widgets are a generic electronic appliance. Under the terms of the contract, FD must buy and take title to 20,000 widgets for each of the five years of the contract at a price of $10 per widget. The widgets will be sold under FD's label, and FD must finance any marketing strategies to promote sales in the foreign market. There are no rebate or buy back provisions. FD has adequate financial capacity-to fund its obligations under the contract under any circumstances that could reasonably be expected to arise. In Years 1, 2 and 3, FD sold only 10,000 widgets at a price of $11 per unit. In Year 4, FD sold its entire inventory of widgets at a price of $25 per unit. Since the contractual terms allocating market risk were agreed to before the outcome of such risk was known or reasonably knowable, FD had the financial capacity to bear the market risk that it would be unable to sell all of the widgets it purchased currently, and its conduct was consistent over time, FD will be deemed to bear the risk.

*Example (2).* The facts are the same as in Example 1, except that in Year 1 FD had only $100,000 in total capital, including loans. In subsequent years USM makes no additional contributions to the capital of FD, and FD is unable to obtain any capital through loans from an unrelated party. Nonetheless, USM continues to sell 20,000 widgets annually to FD under the terms of the contract, and USM extends credit to FD to enable it to finance the purchase. FD does not have the financial capacity in Years 1, 2 and 3 to finance the purchase of the widgets given that it could not sell most of the widgets it purchased during those years. Thus, notwithstanding the terms of the contract, USM and not FD assumed the market risk that a substantial portion of the widgets could not be sold, since in that event FD would not be able to pay USM for all of the widgets it purchased.

*Example (3).* S, a Country X corporation, manufactures small motors that it sells to P, its U.S. parent. P incorporates the motors into various products and sells those products to uncontrolled customers in the United States. The contract price for the motors is expressed in U.S. dollars, effectively allocating the currency risk for these transactions to S for any currency fluctuations between the time the contract is signed and payment is made. As long as S has adequate financial capacity to bear this currency risk (including by hedging all or part of the risk) and the conduct of S and P is consistent with the terms of the contract (i.e., the contract price is not adjusted to reflect exchange rate movements), the agreement of the parties to allocate the exchange risk to S will be respected.

*Example (4).* USSub is the wholly-owned U.S. subsidiary of FP, a foreign manufacturer. USSub acts as a distributor of goods manufactured by FP. FP and USSub execute an agreement providing that FP will bear any ordinary product liability costs arising from defects in the goods manufactured by FP. In practice, however, when ordinary product liability claims are sustained against USSub and FP, USSub pays the resulting damages. Therefore, the district director disregards the contractual arrangement regarding product liability costs between FP and USSub, and treats the risk as having been assumed by USSub.

(iv) Economic conditions. Determining the degree of comparability between controlled and uncontrolled transactions requires a comparison of the significant economic conditions that could affect the prices that would be charged or paid, or the profit that would be earned in each of the transactions. These factors include—

(A) The similarity of geographic markets;

(B) The relative size of each market, and the extent of the overall economic development in each market;

(C) The level of the market (e.g., wholesale, retail, etc.);

(D) The relevant market shares for the products, properties, or services transferred or provided;

(E) The location-specific costs of the factors of production and distribution;

(F) The extent of competition in each market with regard to the property or services under review;

(G) The economic condition of the particular industry, including whether the market is in contraction or expansion; and

(H) The alternatives realistically available to the buyer and seller.

(v) Property or services. Evaluating the degree of comparability between controlled and uncontrolled transactions requires a comparison of the property or services transferred in the transactions. This comparison may include any intangible property that is embedded in tangible property or services being transferred (embedded intangibles). The comparability of the embedded intangibles will be analyzed using the factors listed in §§ 1.482-4(c)(2)(iii)(B)(1) (comparable intangible property). The relevance of product comparability in evaluating the relative reliability of the results will depend on the method applied. For guidance concerning the specific comparability considerations applicable to transfers of tangible and intangible property and performance of services, see §§ 1.482-3 through 1.482-6 and §§ 1.482-9; see also §§ 1.482-3(f), 1.482-4(f)(4), and 1.482-9(m), dealing with the coordination of intangible and tangible property and performance of services rules.

*(4) Special circumstances.* (i) Market share strategy. In certain circumstances, taxpayers may adopt strategies to enter new markets or to increase a product's share of an existing market (market share strategy). Such a strategy would be reflected by temporarily increased market development expenses or resale prices that are temporarily lower than the prices charged for comparable products in the same market. Whether or not the strategy is reflected in the transfer price depends on which party to the controlled transaction bears the costs of the pricing strategy. In any case, the effect of a market share strategy on a controlled transaction will be taken into account only if it can be shown that an uncontrolled taxpayer engaged in a comparable strategy under comparable circumstances for a comparable period of time, and the taxpayer provides documentation that substantiates the following—

(A) The costs incurred to implement the market share strategy are borne by the controlled taxpayer that would obtain the future profits that result from the strategy, and there is a reasonable likelihood that the strategy will result in future profits that reflect an appropriate return in relation to the costs incurred to implement it;

(B) The market share strategy is pursued only for a period of time that is reasonable, taking into consideration the industry and product in question; and

(C) The market share strategy, the related costs and expected returns, and any agreement between the controlled taxpayers to share the related costs, were established before the strategy was implemented.

(ii) Different geographic markets. (A) In general. Uncontrolled comparables ordinarily should be derived from the geographic market in which the controlled taxpayer operates, because there may be significant differences in economic conditions in different markets. If information from the same market is not available, an uncontrolled comparable derived from a different geographic market may be considered if adjustments are made to account for differences between the two markets. If information permitting adjustments for such differences is not available, then information derived from uncontrolled comparables in the most similar market for which reliable data is available may be used, but the extent of such differences may affect the reliability of the method for purposes of the best method rule. For this purpose, a geographic market is any geographic area in which the economic conditions for the relevant product or service are substantially the same, and may include multiple countries, depending on the economic conditions.

(B) Example. The following example illustrates this paragraph (d)(4)(ii).

*Example.* Manuco, a wholly-owned foreign subsidiary of P, a U.S. corporation, manufactures products in Country Z for sale to P. No uncontrolled transactions are located that would provide a reliable measure of the arm's length result under the comparable uncontrolled price method. The district director considers applying the cost plus method or the comparable profits method. Information on uncontrolled taxpayers performing comparable functions under comparable circumstances in the same geographic market is not available. Therefore, adjusted data from uncontrolled manufacturers in other markets may be considered in order to apply the cost plus method. In this case, comparable uncontrolled manufacturers are found in the United States. Accordingly, data from the comparable U.S. uncontrolled manufacturers, as adjusted to account for differences between the United States and Country Z's geographic market, is used to test the arm's length price paid by P to Manuco. However, the use of such data may affect the reliability of the results for purposes of the best method rule. See § 1.482-1(c).

(C) Location Savings. If an uncontrolled taxpayer operates in a different geographic market than the controlled taxpayer, adjustments may be necessary to account for significant differences in costs attributable to the geographic markets. These adjustments must be based on the effect such differences would have on the consideration charged or paid in the controlled transaction given the relative competitive positions of buyers and sellers in each market. Thus, for example, the fact that the total costs of operating in a controlled manufacturer's geographic market are less than the total costs of operating in other markets ordinarily justifies higher profits to the manufacturer only if the cost differences would increase the profits of comparable uncontrolled manufacturers operating at arm's length, given the competitive positions of buyers and sellers in that market.

(D) Example. The following example illustrates the principles of this paragraph (d)(4)(ii)(C).

*Example.* Couture, a U.S. apparel design corporation, contracts with Sewco, its wholly owned Country Y subsidiary, to manufacture its clothes. Costs of operating in Country Y are significantly lower than the operating costs in the United States. Although clothes with the Couture label sell for a premium price, the actual production of the clothes does not require significant specialized knowledge that could not be acquired by actual or potential competitors to Sewco at reasonable cost. Thus, Sewco's functions could be performed by several actual or potential competitors to Sewco in geographic markets that are similar to Country Y. Thus, the fact that production is less costly in Country Y will not, in and of itself, justify additional profits derived from lower operating costs in Country Y inuring to Sewco, because the competitive positions of the other actual or potential producers in similar geographic markets capable of performing the same functions at the same low costs indicate that at arm's length such profits would not be retained by Sewco.

(iii) Transactions ordinarily not accepted as comparables. (A) In general. Transactions ordinarily will not constitute reliable measures of an arm's length result for purposes of this section if—

(1) They are not made in the ordinary course of business; or

(2) One of the principal purposes of the uncontrolled transaction was to establish an arm's length result with respect to the controlled transaction.

(B) Examples. The following examples illustrate the principle of this paragraph (d)(4)(iii).

*Example (1).* Not in the ordinary course of business. USP, a United States manufacturer of computer software, sells its products to FSub, its foreign distributor in country X. Compco, a United States competitor of USP, also sells its products in X through unrelated distributors. However, in the year under review, Compco is forced into bankruptcy, and Compco liquidates its inventory by selling all of its products to unrelated distributors in X for a liquidation price. Because the sale of its entire inventory was not a sale in the ordinary course of business, Compco's sale cannot be used as an uncontrolled comparable to determine USP's arm's length result from its controlled transaction.

*Example (2).* Principal purpose of establishing an arm's length result. USP, a United States manufacturer of farm machinery, sells its products to FSub, its wholly-owned distributor in Country Y. USP, operating at nearly full capacity, sells 95% of its inventory to FSub. To make use of its excess capacity, and also to establish a comparable uncontrolled price for its transfer price to FSub, USP increases its production to full capacity. USP sells its excess inventory to Compco, an unrelated foreign distributor in Country X. Country X has approximately the same economic conditions as that of Country Y. Because one of the principal purposes of selling to Compco was to establish an arm's length price for its controlled transactions with FSub, USP's sale to Compco cannot be used as an uncontrolled comparable to determine USP's arm's length result from its controlled transaction.

**(e) Arm's length range.** *(1) In general.* In some cases, application of a pricing method will produce a single result that is the most reliable measure of an arm's length result. In other cases, application of a method may produce a number of results from which a range of reliable results may be derived. A taxpayer will not be subject to adjustment if its results fall within such range (arm's length range).

*(2) Determination of arm's length range.* (i) Single method. The arm's length range is ordinarily determined by applying a single pricing method selected under the best method rule to two or more uncontrolled transactions of similar comparability and reliability. Use of more than one method may be appropriate for the purposes described in paragraph (c)(2)(iii) of this section (Best method rule).

(ii) Selection of comparables. Uncontrolled comparables must be selected based upon the comparability criteria relevant to the method applied and must be sufficiently similar to the controlled transaction that they provide a reliable measure of an arm's length result. If material differences exist between the controlled and uncontrolled transactions, adjustments must be made to the results of the uncontrolled transaction if the effect of such differences on price or profits can be ascertained with sufficient accuracy to improve the reliability of the results. See § 1.482-1(d)(2) (Standard of comparability). The arm's length range will be derived only from those uncontrolled comparables that have, or through adjustments can be brought to, a similar level of comparability and reliability, and uncontrolled comparables that have a significantly lower level of comparability and reliability will not be used in establishing the arm's length range.

(iii) Comparables included in arm's length range. (A) In general. The arm's length range will consist of the results of all of the uncontrolled comparables that meet the following conditions: the information on the controlled transaction and the uncontrolled comparables is sufficiently complete that it is likely that all material differences have been identified, each such difference has a definite and reasonably ascertainable effect on price or profit, and an adjustment is made to eliminate the effect of each such difference.

(B) Adjustment of range to increase reliability. If there are no uncontrolled comparables described in paragraph (e)(2)(iii)(A) of this section, the arm's length range is derived from the results of all the uncontrolled comparables, selected pursuant to paragraph (e)(2)(ii) of this section, that achieve a similar level of comparability and reliability. In such cases the reliability of the analysis must be increased, where it is possible to do so, by adjusting the range through application of a valid statistical method to the results of all of the uncontrolled comparables so selected. The reliability of the analysis is increased when statistical methods are used to establish a range of results in which the limits of the range will be determined such that there is a 75 percent probability of a result falling above the lower end of the range and a 75 percent probability of a result falling below the upper end of the range. The interquartile range ordinarily provides an acceptable measure of this range; however a different statistical method may be applied if it provides a more reliable measure.

(C) Interquartile range. For purposes of this section, the interquartile range is the range from the 25th to the 75th percentile of the results derived from the uncontrolled comparables. For this purpose, the 25th percentile is the lowest result derived from an uncontrolled comparable such that at least 25 percent of the results are at or below the value of that result. However, if exactly 25 percent of the results are at or below a result, then the 25th percentile is equal to the average of that result and the next higher result derived from the uncontrolled comparables. The 75th percentile is determined analogously.

*(3) Adjustment if taxpayer's results are outside arm's length range.* If the results of a controlled transaction fall outside the arm's length range, the district director may make allocations that adjust the controlled taxpayer's result to any point within the arm's length range. If the interquartile range is used to determine the arm's length range, such adjustment will ordinarily be to the median of all the results. The median is the 50th percentile of the results, which is determined in a manner analogous to that described in paragraph (e)(2)(iii)(C) of this section (Interquartile range). In other cases, an adjustment normally will be made to the arithmetic mean of all the results. See § 1.482-1(f)(2)(iii)(D) for determination of an adjustment when a controlled taxpayer's result for a multiple year period falls outside an arm's length range consisting of the average results of uncontrolled comparables over the same period.

*(4) Arm's length range not prerequisite to allocation.* The rules of this paragraph (e) do not require that the district director establish an arm's length range prior to making an allocation under section 482. Thus, for example, the district director may properly propose an allocation on the basis of a single comparable uncontrolled price if the comparable uncontrolled price method, as described in § 1.482-3(b), has been properly applied. However, if the taxpayer subsequently demonstrates that the results claimed on its income tax return are within the range established by additional equally reliable comparable uncontrolled prices in a manner

consistent with the requirements set forth in § 1.482-1(e)(2)(iii), then no allocation will be made.

*(5) Examples.* The following examples illustrate the principles of this paragraph (e).

*Example (1).* Selection of comparables.

(i) To evaluate the arm's length result of a controlled transaction between USSub, the United States taxpayer under review, and FP, its foreign parent, the district director considers applying the resale price method. The district director identifies ten potential uncontrolled transactions. The distributors in all ten uncontrolled transactions purchase and resell similar products and perform similar functions to those of USSub.

(ii) Data with respect to three of the uncontrolled transactions is very limited, and although some material differences can be identified and adjusted for, the level of comparability of these three uncontrolled comparables is significantly lower than that of the other seven. Further, of those seven, adjustments for the identified material differences can be reliably made for only four of the uncontrolled transactions. Therefore, pursuant to § 1.482-1(e)(2)(ii) only these four uncontrolled comparables may be used to establish an arm's length range.

*Example (2).* Arm's length range consists of all the results.

(i) The facts are the same as in Example 1. Applying the resale price method to the four uncontrolled comparables, and making adjustments to the uncontrolled comparables pursuant to § 1.482-1(d)(2), the district director derives the following results:

| Comparable | Result (price) |
|---|---|
| 1 | $44.00 |
| 2 | 45.00 |
| 3 | 45.00 |
| 4 | 45.50 |

(ii) The district director determines that data regarding the four uncontrolled transactions is sufficiently complete and accurate so that it is likely that all material differences between the controlled and uncontrolled transactions have been identified, such differences have a definite and reasonably ascertainable effect, and appropriate adjustments were made for such differences. Accordingly, if the resale price method is determined to be the best method pursuant to § 1.482-1(c), the arm's length range for the controlled transaction will consist of the results of all of the uncontrolled comparables, pursuant to paragraph (e)(2)(iii)(A) of this section. Thus, the arm's length range in this case would be the range from $44 to $45.50.

*Example (3).* Arm's length range limited to interquartile range.

(i) The facts are the same as in *Example 2,* except in this case there are some product and functional differences between the four uncontrolled comparables and USSub. However, the data is insufficiently complete to determine the effect of the differences. Applying the resale price method to the four uncontrolled comparables, and making adjustments to the uncontrolled comparables pursuant to § 1.482-1(d)(2), the district director derives the following results:

| Uncontrolled Comparable | Result (price) |
|---|---|
| 1 | $42.00 |
| 2 | 44.00 |
| 3 | 45.00 |
| 4 | 47.50 |

(ii) It cannot be established in this case that all material differences are likely to have been identified and reliable adjustments made for those differences. Accordingly, if the resale price method is determined to be the best method pursuant to § 1.482-1(c), the arm's length range for the controlled transaction must be established pursuant to paragraph (e)(2)(iii)(B) of this section. In this case, the district director uses the interquartile range to determine the arm's length range, which is the range from $43 to $46.25. If USSub's price falls outside this range, the district director may make an allocation. In this case that allocation would be to the median of the results, or $44.50.

*Example (4).* Arm's length range limited to interquartile range.

(i) To evaluate the arm's length result of controlled transactions between USP, a United States manufacturing company, and FSub, its foreign subsidiary, the district director considers applying the comparable profits method. The district director identifies 50 uncontrolled taxpayers within the same industry that potentially could be used to apply the method.

(ii) Further review indicates that only 20 of the uncontrolled manufacturers engage in activities requiring similar capital investments and technical know-how. Data with respect to five of the uncontrolled manufacturers is very limited, and although some material differences can be identified and adjusted for, the level of comparability of these five uncontrolled comparables is significantly lower than that of the other 15. In addition, for those five uncontrolled comparables it is not possible to accurately allocate costs between the business activity associated with the relevant transactions and other business activities. Therefore, pursuant to § 1.482-1(e)(2)(ii) only the other fifteen uncontrolled comparables may be used to establish an arm's length range.

(iii) Although the data for the fifteen remaining uncontrolled comparables is relatively complete and accurate, there is a significant possibility that some material differences may remain. The district director has determined, for example, that it is likely that there are material differences in the level of technical expertise or in management efficiency. Accordingly, if the comparable profits method is determined to be the best method pursuant to § 1.482-1(c), the arm's length range for the controlled transaction may be established only pursuant to paragraph (e)(2)(iii)(B) of this section.

**(f) Scope of review.** *(1) In general.* The authority to determine true taxable income extends to any case in which either by inadvertence or design the taxable income, in whole or in part, of a controlled taxpayer is other than it would have been had the taxpayer, in the conduct of its affairs, been dealing at arm's length with an uncontrolled taxpayer.

(i) Intent to evade or avoid tax not a prerequisite. In making allocations under section 482, the district director is not restricted to the case of improper accounting, to the case of a fraudulent, colorable, or sham transaction, or to the case of a device designed to reduce or avoid tax by shifting or distorting income, deductions, credits, or allowances.

(ii) Realization of income not a prerequisite. (A) In general. The district director may make an allocation under section 482 even if the income ultimately anticipated from a series of transactions has not been or is never realized. For example, if a controlled taxpayer sells a product at less than an arm's length price to a related taxpayer in one taxable year and the second controlled taxpayer resells the product to an unrelated party in the next taxable year, the district director may make an appropriate allocation to reflect an arm's length price for the sale of the product in the first taxable year, even though the second controlled taxpayer had not realized any gross income from the resale of the product in the first year. similarly, if a controlled taxpayer lends money to a related taxpayer in a taxable year, the district director may make an appropriate allocation to reflect an arm's length charge for interest during such taxable year even if the second controlled taxpayer does not realize income during such year. Finally, even if two controlled taxpayers realize an overall loss that is attributable to a particular controlled transaction, an allocation under section 482 is not precluded.

(B) Example. The following example illustrates this paragraph (f)(1)(ii).

*Example.* USSub is a U.S. subsidiary of FP, a foreign corporation. Parent manufactures product X and sells it to USSub. USSub functions as a distributor of product X to unrelated customers in the United States. The fact that FP may incur a loss on the manufacture and sale of product X does not by itself establish that USSub, dealing with FP at arm's length, also would incur a loss. An independent distributor acting at arm's length with its supplier would in many circumstances be expected to earn a profit without regard to the level of profit earned by the supplier.

(iii) Nonrecognition provisions may not bar allocation. (A) In general. If necessary to prevent the avoidance of taxes or to clearly reflect income, the district director may make an allocation under section 482 with respect to transactions that otherwise qualify for nonrecognition of gain or loss under applicable provisions of the Internal Revenue Code (such as section 351 or 1031).

(B) Example. The following example illustrates this paragraph (f)(1)(iii).

*Example.* (i) In Year 1 USP, a United States corporation, bought 100 shares of UR, an unrelated corporation, for $100,000. In Year 2, when the value of the UR stock had decreased to $40,000, USP contributed all 100 shares of UR stock to its wholly-owned subsidiary in exchange for subsidiary's capital stock. In Year 3, the subsidiary sold all of the UR stock for $40,000 to an unrelated buyer, and on its U.S. income tax return, claimed a loss of $60,000 attributable to the sale of the UR stock. USP and its subsidiary do not file a consolidated return.

(ii) In determining the true taxable income of the subsidiary, the district director may disallow the loss of $60,000 on the ground that the loss was incurred by USP. National Securities Corp. v Commissioner, 137 F.2d 600 (3rd Cir. 1943), cert. denied, 320 U.S. 794 (1943).

(iv) Consolidated Returns. Section 482 and the regulations hereunder apply to all controlled taxpayers, whether the controlled taxpayer files a separate or consolidated U.S. income tax return. If a controlled taxpayer files a separate return, its true separate taxable income will be determined. If a controlled taxpayer is a party to a consolidated return, the true consolidated taxable income of the affiliated group and the true separate taxable income of the controlled taxpayer must be determined consistently with the principles of a consolidated return.

*(2) Rules relating to determination of true taxable income.* The following rules must be taken into account in determining the true taxable income of a controlled taxpayer.

(i) Aggregation of transactions. (A) In general. The combined effect of two or more separate transactions (whether before, during, or after the taxable year under review) may be considered, if such transactions, taken as a whole, are so interrelated that consideration of multiple transactions is the most reliable means of determining the arm's length consideration for the controlled transactions. Generally, transactions will be aggregated only when they involve related products or services, as defined in § 1.6038A-3(c)(7)(vii).

(B) Examples. The following examples illustrate this paragraph (f)(2)(i).

*Example (1).* P enters into a license agreement with S1, its subsidiary, that permits S1 to use a proprietary manufacturing process and to sell the output from this process throughout a specified region. S1 uses the manufacturing process and sells its output to S2, another subsidiary of P, which in turn resells the output to uncontrolled parties in the specified region. In evaluating the arm's length character of the royalty paid by S1 to P, it may be appropriate to consider the arm's length character of the transfer prices charged by S1 to S2 and the aggregate profits earned by S1 and S2 from the use of the manufacturing process and the sale to uncontrolled parties of the products produced by S1.

*Example (2).* S1, S2, and S3 are Country Z subsidiaries of U.S. manufacturer P. S1 is the exclusive Country Z distributor of computers manufactured by P. S2 provides marketing services in connection with sales of P computers in Country Z, and in this regard uses significant marketing intangibles provided by P. S3 administers the warranty program with respect to P computers in Country Z, including maintenance and repair services. In evaluating the arm's length character of the transfer price paid by S1 to P, of the fees paid by S2 to P for the use of P marketing intangibles, and of the service fees earned by S2 and S3, it may be appropriate to consider the combined effects of these separate transactions because they are so interrelated that they are most reliably analyzed on an aggregated basis.

*Example (3).* The facts are the same as in Example 2. In addition, U1, U2, and U3 are uncontrolled taxpayers that carry out functions comparable to those of S1, S2, and S3, respectively, with respect to computers produced by unrelated manufacturers. R1, R2, and R3 are a controlled group of taxpayers (unrelated to the P controlled group) that also carry out functions comparable to those of S1, S2, and S3 with respect to computers produced by their common parent. Prices charged to uncontrolled customers of the R group differ from the prices charged to customers of U1, U2, and U3. In determining whether the transactions of U1, U2, and U3, or the transactions of R1, R2, and R3 would provide a more reliable measure of the arm's length result, it is determined that the interrelated R group transactions are more reliable than the wholly independent transactions of U1, U2, and U3, given the interrelationship of the P group transactions.

*Example (4).* P enters into a license agreement with S1 that permits S1 to use a propriety process for manufacturing product X and to sell product X to uncontrolled parties throughout a specified region. P also sells to S1 product Y which is manufactured by P in the United States, and which is unrelated to product X. Product Y is resold by S1 to uncontrolled parties in the specified region. In evaluating the arm's length character of the royalty paid by S1 to P for the use of the manufacturing process for product X, and the transfer prices charged for unrelated product Y, it would not be appropriate to consider the combined effects of these separate and unrelated transactions.

(ii) Allocation based on taxpayer's actual transactions (A) In general. The Commissioner will evaluate the results of a transaction as actually structured by the taxpayer unless its structure lacks economic substance. However, the Commissioner may consider the alternatives available to the taxpayer in determining whether the terms of the controlled transaction would be acceptable to an uncontrolled taxpayer faced with the same alternatives and operating under comparable circumstances. In such cases the Commissioner may adjust the consideration charged in the controlled transaction based on the cost or profit of an alternative as adjusted to account for material differences between the alternative and the controlled transaction, but will not restructure the transaction as if the alternative had been adopted by the taxpayer. See paragraph (d)(3) of this section (factors for determining comparability; contractual terms and risk); §§ 1.482-3(e), 1.482-4(d), and 1.482-9(h) (unspecified methods).

(B) Example. The following example illustrates this paragraph (f)(2)(ii).

*Example.* P and S are controlled taxpayers. P enters into a license agreement with S that permits S to use a proprietary process for manufacturing product X. Using its sales and marketing employees, S sells product X to related and unrelated customers outside the United States. If the license agreement between P and S has economic substance, the district director ordinarily will not restructure the taxpayer's transaction to treat P as if it had elected to exploit directly the manufacturing process. However, the fact that P could have manufactured product X may be taken into account under § 1.482-4(d) in determining the arm's length consideration for the controlled transaction. For an example of such an analysis, see Example in § 1.482-4(d)(2).

(iii) Multiple year data. (A) In general. The results of a controlled transaction ordinarily will be compared with the results of uncontrolled comparables occurring in the taxable year under review. It may be appropriate, however, to consider data relating to the uncontrolled comparables or the controlled taxpayer for one or more years before or after the year under review. If data relating to uncontrolled comparables from multiple years is used, data relating to the controlled taxpayer for the same years ordinarily must be considered. However, if such data is not available, reliable data from other years, as adjusted under paragraph (d)(2) (Standard of comparability) of this section may be used.

(B) Circumstances warranting consideration of multiple year data. The extent to which it is appropriate to consider multiple year data depends on the method being applied and the issue being addressed. Circumstances that may warrant consideration of data from multiple years include the extent to which complete and accurate data are available for the taxable year under review, the effect of business cycles in the controlled taxpayer's industry, or the effects of life cycles of the product or intangible property being examined. Data from one or more years before or after the taxable year under review must ordinarily be considered for purposes of applying the provisions of paragraph (d)(3)(iii) of this section (risk), paragraph (d)(4)(i) of this section (market share strategy), §§ 1.482-4(f)(2) (periodic adjustments), §§ 1.482-5 (comparable profits method), §§ 1.482-9(f) (comparable profits method for services), and §§ 1.482-9(i) (contingent-payment contractual terms for services). On the other hand, multiple year data ordinarily will not be considered for purposes of applying the comparable uncontrolled price method of §§ 1.482-3(b) or the comparable uncontrolled services price method of §§ 1.482-9(c) (except to the extent that risk or market share strategy issues are present).

(C) Comparable effect over comparable period. Data from multiple years may be considered to determine whether the same economic conditions that caused the controlled taxpayer's results had a comparable effect over a comparable period of time on the uncontrolled comparables that establish the arm's length range. For example, given that uncontrolled taxpayers enter into transactions with the ultimate expectation of earning a profit, persistent losses among controlled taxpayers may be an indication of non-arm's length dealings. Thus, if a controlled taxpayer that realizes a loss with respect to a controlled transaction seeks to demonstrate that the loss is within the arm's length range, the district director may take into account data from taxable years other than the taxable year of the transaction to determine whether the loss was attributable to arm's length dealings. The rule of this paragraph (f)(2)(iii)(C) is illustrated by Example 3 of paragraph (f)(2)(iii)(E) of this section.

(D) Application of methods using multiple year averages. If a comparison of a controlled taxpayer's average result over a multiple year period with the average results of uncontrolled comparables over the same period would reduce the effect of short-term variations that may be unrelated to transfer pricing, it may be appropriate to establish a range derived from the average results of uncontrolled comparables over a multiple year period to determine if an adjustment should be made. In such a case the district director may make an adjustment if the controlled taxpayer's average result for the multiple year period is not within such range. Such a range must be determined in accordance with § 1.482-1(e) (Arm's length range). An adjustment in such a case ordinarily will be equal to the difference, if any, between the controlled taxpayer's result for the taxable year and the mid-point of the uncontrolled comparables' results for that year. If the interquartile range is used to determine the range of average results for the multiple year period, such adjustment will ordinarily be made to the median of all the results of the uncontrolled comparables for the taxable year. See Example 2 of § 1.482-5(e). In other cases, the adjustment normally will be made to the arithmetic mean of all the results of the uncontrolled comparables for the taxable year. However, an adjustment will be made only to the extent that it would move the controlled taxpayer's multiple year average closer to the arm's length range for the multiple year period or to any point within such range. In determining a controlled taxpayer's average result for a multiple year period, adjustments made under this section for prior years will be taken into account only if such adjustments have been finally determined, as described in § 1.482-1(g)(2)(iii). See Example 3 of § 1.482-5(e).

(E) Examples. The following examples, in which S and P are controlled taxpayers, illustrate this paragraph (f)(2)(iii). Examples 1 and 4 also illustrate the principle of the arm's length range of paragraph (e) of this section.

*Example (1).* P sold product Z to S for $60 per unit in 1995. Applying the resale price method to data from uncontrolled comparables for the same year establishes an arm's length range of prices for the controlled transaction from $52 to $59 per unit. Since the price charged in the controlled transaction falls outside the range, the district director would ordinarily make an allocation under section 482. However, in this case there are cyclical factors that affect the results of the uncontrolled comparables (and that of the controlled transaction) that cannot be adequately accounted for by specific adjustments to the data for 1995. Therefore, the district director considers results over multiple years to account for these factors. Under these circumstances, it is appropriate to average the results of the uncontrolled comparables over the years 1993, 1994, and 1995 to determine an arm's length range. The averaged results establish an arm's length range of $56 to $58 per unit. For consistency, the results of the controlled taxpayers must also be averaged over the same years. The average price in the controlled transaction over the three years is $57. Because the controlled transfer price of product Z falls within the arm's length range, the district director makes no allocation.

*Example (2).* (i) FP, a Country X corporation, designs and manufactures machinery in Country X. FP's costs are incurred in Country X currency. USSub is the exclusive distributor of FP's machinery in the United States. The price of the machinery sold by FP to USSub is expressed in Country X currency. Thus, USSub bears all of the currency risk associated with fluctuations in the exchange rate between the time the contract is signed and the payment is made. The prices charged by FP to USSub for 1995 are under examination. In that year, the value of the dollar depreciated against the currency of Country X, and as a result, USSub's gross margin was only 8%.

(ii) UD is an uncontrolled distributor of similar machinery that performs distribution functions substantially the same as those performed by USSub, except that UD purchases and resells machinery in transactions where both the purchase and resale prices are denominated in U.S. dollars. Thus, UD had no currency exchange risk. UD's gross margin in 1995 was 10%. UD's average gross margin for the period 1990 to 1998 has been 12%.

(iii) In determining whether the price charged by FP to USSub in 1995 was arm's length, the district director may consider USSub's average gross margin for an appropriate period before and after 1995 to determine whether USSub's average gross margin during the period was sufficiently greater than UD's average gross margin during the same period such that USSub was sufficiently compensated for the currency risk it bore throughout the period. See § 1.482-1(d)(3)(iii) (Risk).

*Example (3).* FP manufactures product X in Country M and sells it to USSub, which distributes X in the United States. USSub realizes losses with respect to the controlled transactions in each of five consecutive taxable years. In each of the five consecutive years a different uncontrolled comparable realized a loss with respect to comparable transactions equal to or greater than USSub's loss. Pursuant to paragraph (f)(3)(iii)(C) of this section, the district director examines whether the uncontrolled comparables realized similar losses over a comparable period of time, and finds that each of the five comparables realized losses in only one of the five years, and their average result over the five-year period was a profit. Based on this data, the district director may conclude that the controlled taxpayer's results are not within the arm's length range over the five year period, since the economic conditions that resulted in the controlled taxpayer's loss did not have a comparable effect over a comparable period of time on the uncontrolled comparables.

*Example (4).* (i) USP, a U.S. corporation, manufactures product Y in the United States and sells it to FSub, which acts as USP's exclusive distributor of product Y in Country N. The resale price method described in § 1.482-3(c) is used to evaluate whether the transfer price charged by USP to FSub for the 1994 taxable year for product Y was arm's length. For the period 1992 through 1994, FSub had a gross profit margin for each year of 13%. A, B, C and D are uncontrolled distributors of products that compete directly with product Y in country N. After making appropriate adjustments in accordance with §§ 1.482-1(d)(2) and 1.482-3(c), the gross profit margins for A, B, C, and D are as follows:

| | 1992 | 1993 | 1994 | Average |
|---|---|---|---|---|
| A | 13 | 3 | 8 | 8.00 |
| B | 11 | 13 | 2 | 8.67 |
| C | 4 | 7 | 13 | 8.00 |
| D | 7 | 9 | 6 | 7.33 |

(ii) Applying the provisions of § 1.482-1(e), the district director determines that the arm's length range of the average gross profit margins is between 7.33 and 8.67. The district director concludes that FSub's average gross margin of 13% is not within the arm's length range, despite the fact that C's gross profit margin for 1994 was also 13%, since the economic conditions that caused S's result did not have a comparable effect over a comparable period of time on the results of C or the other uncontrolled comparables. In this case, the district director makes an allocation equivalent to adjusting FSub's gross profit margin for 1994 from 13% to the mean of the uncontrolled comparables' results for 1994 (7.25%).

(iv) Product lines and statistical techniques. The methods described in § 1.482-2 through 1.482-6 are generally stated in terms of individual transactions. However, because a taxpayer may have controlled transactions involving many different products, or many separate transactions involving the same product, it may be impractical to analyze every individual transaction to determine its arm's length price. In such cases, it is permissible to evaluate the arm's length results by applying the appropriate methods to the overall results for product lines or other groupings. In addition, the arm's length results of all related party transactions entered into by a controlled taxpayer may be evaluated by employing sampling and other valid statistical techniques.

(v) Allocations apply to results, not methods. (A) In general. In evaluating whether the result of a controlled transaction is arm's length, it is not necessary for the district director to determine whether the method or procedure that a controlled taxpayer employs to set the terms for its controlled transactions corresponds to the method or procedure that might have been used by a taxpayer dealing at arm's length with an uncontrolled taxpayer. Rather, the district director will evaluate the result achieved rather than the method the taxpayer used to determine its prices.

(B) Example. The following example illustrates this paragraph (f)(2)(v).

*Example.* (i) FS is a foreign subsidiary of P, a U.S. corporation. P manufactures and sells household appliances. FS operates as P's exclusive distributor in Europe. P annually establishes the price for each of its appliances sold to FS as part of its annual budgeting, production allocation and scheduling, and performance evaluation processes. FS's aggregate gross margin earned in its distribution business is 18%.

(ii) ED is an uncontrolled European distributor of competing household appliances. After adjusting for minor differences in the level of inventory, volume of sales, and warranty programs conducted by FS and ED, ED's aggregate gross margin is also 18%. Thus, the district director may conclude that the aggregate prices charged by P for its appliances sold to FS are arm's length, without determining whether the budgeting, production, and performance evaluation processes of P are similar to such processes used by ED.

**(g) Collateral adjustments with respect to allocations under section 482.** *(1) In general.* The district director will take into account appropriate collateral adjustments with respect to allocations under section 482. Appropriate collateral adjustments may include correlative allocations, conforming adjustments, and setoffs, as described in this paragraph (g).

*(2) Correlative allocations.* (i) In general. When the district director makes an allocation under section 482 (referred to in this paragraph (g)(2) as the primary allocation), appropriate correlative allocations will also be made with respect to any other member of the group affected by the allocation. Thus, if the district director makes an allocation of income, the district director will not only increase the income of one member of the group, but correspondingly decrease the income of the other member. In addition, where appropriate, the district director may make such further correlative allocations as may be required by the initial correlative allocation.

(ii) Manner of carrying out correlative allocation. The district director will furnish to the taxpayer with respect to which the primary allocation is made a written statement of the amount and nature of the correlative allocation. The correlative allocation must be reflected in the documentation of the other member of the group that is maintained for U.S. tax purposes, without regard to whether it affects the U.S. income tax liability of the other member for any open year. In some circumstances the allocation will have an immediate U.S. tax effect, by changing the taxable income computation of the other member (or the taxable income computation of a shareholder of the other member, for example, under the provisions of subpart F of the Internal Revenue Code). Alternatively, the correlative allocation may not be reflected on any U.S. tax return until a later year, for example when a dividend is paid.

(iii) Events triggering correlative allocation. For purposes of this paragraph (g)(2), a primary allocation will not be considered to have been made (and therefore, correlative allocations are not required to be made) until the date of a final determination with respect to the allocation under section 482. For this purpose, a final determination includes—

(A) Assessment of tax following execution by the taxpayer of a Form 870 (Waiver of Restrictions on Assessment and Collection of Deficiency in Tax and Acceptance of Overassessment) with respect to such allocation;

(B) Acceptance of a Form 870-AD (Offer of Waiver of Restriction on Assessment and Collection of Deficiency in Tax and Acceptance of Overassessment);

(C) Payment of the deficiency;

(D) Stipulation in the Tax Court of the United States; or

(E) Final determination of tax liability by offer-in-compromise, closing agreement, or final resolution (determined under the principles of section 7481) of a judicial proceeding.

(iv) Examples. The following examples illustrate this paragraph (g)(2). In each example, X and Y are members of the same group of controlled taxpayers and each regularly computes its income on a calendar year basis.

*Example (1).* (i) In 1996, Y, a U.S. corporation, rents a building owned by X, also a U.S. corporation. In 1998 the district director determines that Y did not pay an arm's length rental charge. The district director proposes to increase X's income to reflect an arm's length rental charge. X consents to the assessment reflecting such adjustment by executing Form 870, a Waiver of Restrictions on Assessment and Collection of Deficiency in Tax and Acceptance of Overassessment. The assessment of the tax with respect to the adjustment is made in 1998. Thus, the primary allocation, as defined in paragraph (g)(2)(i) of this section, is considered to have been made in 1998.

(ii) The adjustment made to X's income under section 482 requires a correlative allocation with respect to Y's income. The district director notifies X in writing of the amount and nature of the adjustment made with respect to Y. Y had net operating losses in 1993, 1994, 1995, 1996, and 1997. Although a correlative adjustment will not have an effect on Y's U.S. income tax liability for 1996, an adjustment increasing Y's net operating loss for 1996 will be made for purposes of determining Y's U.S. income tax liability for 1998 or a later taxable year to which the increased net operating loss may be carried.

*Example (2).* (i) In 1995, X, a U.S. construction company, provided engineering services to Y, a U.S. corporation, in the construction of Y's factory. In 1997, the district director determines that the fees paid by Y to X for its services were not arm's length and proposes to make an adjustment to the income of X. X consents to an assessment reflecting such adjustment by executing Form 870. An assessment of the tax with respect to such adjustment is made in 1997. The district director notifies X in writing of the amount and nature of the adjustment to be made with respect to Y.

(ii) The fees paid by Y for X's engineering services properly constitute a capital expenditure. Y does not place the factory into service until 1998. Therefore, a correlative adjustment increasing Y's basis in the factory does not affect Y's U.S. income tax liability for 1997. However, the correlative adjustment must be made in the books and records maintained by Y for its U.S. income tax purposes and such adjustment will be taken into account in computing Y's allowable depreciation or gain or loss on a subsequent disposition of the factory.

*Example (3).* In 1995, X, a U.S. corporation, makes a loan to Y, its foreign subsidiary not engaged in a U.S. trade or business. In 1997, the district director, upon determining that the interest charged on the loan was not arm's length, proposes to adjust X's income to reflect an arm's length interest rate. X consents to an assessment reflecting such allocation by executing Form 870, and an assessment of the tax with respect to the section 482 allocation is made in 1997. The district director notifies X in writing of the amount and nature of the correlative allocation to be made with respect to Y. Although the correlative adjustment does not have an effect on Y's U.S. income tax liability, the adjustment must be reflected in the documentation of Y that is maintained for U.S. tax purposes. Thus, the adjustment must be reflected in the determination of the amount of Y's earnings and profits for 1995 and subsequent years, and the adjustment must be made to the extent it has an effect on any person's U.S. income tax liability for any taxable year.

*(3) Adjustments to conform accounts to reflect section 482 allocations.* (i) In general. Appropriate adjustments must be made to conform a taxpayer's accounts to reflect allocations made under section 482. Such adjustments may include the treatment of an allocated amount as a dividend or a capital contribution (as appropriate), or, in appropriate cases, pursuant to such applicable revenue procedures as may be provided by the Commissioner (see § 601.601(d)(2) of this chapter), repayment of the allocated amount without further income tax consequences.

(ii) Example. The following example illustrates the principles of this paragraph (g)(3).

*Example.* Conforming cash accounts.

(i) USD, a United States corporation, buys Product from its foreign parent, FP. In reviewing USD's income tax return, the district director determines that the arm's length price would have increased USD's taxable income by $5 million. The district director accordingly adjusts USD's income to reflect its true taxable income.

(ii) To conform its cash accounts to reflect the section 482 allocation made by the district director, USD applies for relief under Rev. Proc. 65-17, 1965-1 C.B. 833 (see § 601.601(d)(2)(ii)(b) of this chapter), to treat the $5 million adjustment as an account receivable from FP, due as of the last day of the year of the transaction, with interest accruing therefrom.

*(4) Setoffs.* (i) In general. If an allocation is made under section 482 with respect to a transaction between controlled taxpayers, the Commissioner will take into account the effect of any other non-arm's length transaction between the same controlled taxpayers in the same taxable year which will result in a setoff against the original section 482 allocation. Such setoff, however, will be taken into account only if the requirements of paragraph (g)(4)(ii) of this section are satisfied. If the effect of the setoff is to change the characterization or source of the income or deductions, or otherwise distort taxable income, in such a manner as to affect the U.S. tax liability of any member, adjustments will be made to reflect the correct amount of each category of income or deductions. For purposes of this setoff provision, the term arm's length refers to the amount defined in paragraph (b) of this section (arm's length standard), without regard to the rules in §§ 1.482-2(a) that treat certain interest rates as arm's length rates of interest.

(ii) Requirements. The district director will take a setoff into account only if the taxpayer—

(A) Establishes that the transaction that is the basis of the setoff was not at arm's length and the amount of the appropriate arm's length charge;

(B) Documents, pursuant to paragraph (g)(2) of this section, all correlative adjustments resulting from the proposed setoff; and

(C) Notifies the district director of the basis of any claimed setoff within 30 days after the earlier of the date of a letter by which the district director transmits an examination report notifying the taxpayer of proposed adjustments or the date of the issuance of the notice of deficiency.

(iii) Examples. The following examples illustrate this paragraph (g)(4).

*Example (1).* P, a U.S. corporation, renders construction services to S, its foreign subsidiary in Country Y, in connection with the construction of S's factory. An arm's length charge for such services determined under §§ 1.482-9 would be $100,000. During the same taxable year P makes available to S the use of a machine to be used in the construction of the factory, and the arm's length rental value of the machine is $25,000. P bills S $125,000 for the services, but does not charge S for the use of the machine. No allocation will be made with respect to the undercharge for the machine if P notifies the district director of the basis of the claimed setoff within 30 days after the date of the letter from the district director transmitting the examination report notifying P of the proposed adjustment, establishes that the excess amount charged for services was equal to an arm's length charge for the use of the machine and that the taxable income and income tax liabilities of P are not distorted, and documents the correlative allocations resulting from the proposed setoff.

*Example (2).* The facts are the same as in Example 1, except that, if P had reported $25,000 as rental income and $25,000 less as service income, it would have been subject to the tax on personal holding companies. Allocations will be made to reflect the correct amounts of rental income and service income.

**(h) Special rules.** *(1) Small taxpayer safe harbor.* [Reserved].

*(2) Effect of foreign legal restrictions.* (i) In general. The district director will take into account the effect of a foreign legal restriction to the extent that such restriction affects the results of transactions at arm's length. Thus, a foreign legal restriction will be taken into account only to the extent that it is shown that the restriction affected an uncontrolled taxpayer under comparable circumstances for a comparable period of time. In the absence of evidence indicating the effect of the foreign legal restriction on uncontrolled taxpayers, the restriction will be taken into account only to the extent provided in paragraphs (h)(2)(iii) and (iv) of this section (Deferred income method of accounting).

(ii) Applicable legal restrictions. Foreign legal restrictions (whether temporary or permanent) will be taken into account for purposes of this paragraph (h)(2) only if, and so long as, the conditions set forth in paragraphs (h)(2)(ii)(A) through (D) of this section are met.

(A) The restrictions are publicly promulgated, generally applicable to all similarly situated persons (both controlled and uncontrolled), and not imposed as part of a commercial transaction between the taxpayer and the foreign sovereign;

(B) The taxpayer (or other member of the controlled group with respect to which the restrictions apply) has exhausted all remedies prescribed by foreign law or practice for obtaining a waiver of such restrictions (other than remedies that would have a negligible prospect of success if pursued);

(C) The restrictions expressly prevented the payment or receipt, in any form, of part or all of the arm's length amount that would otherwise be required under section 482 (for example, a restriction that applies only to the deductibility of an expense for tax purposes is not a restriction on payment or receipt for this purpose); and

(D) The related parties subject to the restriction did not engage in any arrangement with controlled or uncontrolled parties that had the effect of circumventing the restriction, and have not otherwise violated the restriction in any material respect.

(iii) Requirement for electing the deferred income method of accounting. If a foreign legal restriction prevents the payment or receipt of part or all of the arm's length amount that is due with respect to a controlled transaction, the restricted amount may be treated as deferrable if the following requirements are met—

(A) The controlled taxpayer establishes to the satisfaction of the district director that the payment or receipt of the arm's length amount was prevented because of a foreign legal restriction and circumstances described in paragraph (h)(2)(ii) of this section; and

(B) The controlled taxpayer whose U.S. tax liability may be affected by the foreign legal restriction elects the deferred income method of accounting, as described in paragraph (h)(2)(iv) of this section, on a written statement attached to a timely U.S. income tax return (or an amended return) filed before the IRS first contacts any member of the controlled group concerning an examination of the return for the taxable year to which the foreign legal restriction applies. A written statement furnished by a taxpayer subject to the Coordinated Examination Program will be considered an amended return for purposes of this paragraph (h)(2)(iii)(B) if it satisfies the requirements of a qualified amended return for purposes of § 1.6664-2(c)(3) as set forth in those regulations or as the Commissioner may prescribe by applicable revenue procedures. The election statement must identify the affected transactions, the parties to the transactions, and the applicable foreign legal restrictions.

(iv) Deferred income method of accounting. If the requirements of paragraph (h)(2)(ii) of this section are satisfied, any portion of the arm's length amount, the payment or receipt of which is prevented because of applicable foreign legal restrictions, will be treated as deferrable until payment or receipt of the relevant item ceases to be prevented by the foreign legal restriction. For purposes of the deferred income method of accounting under this paragraph (h)(2)(iv), deductions (including the cost or other basis of inventory and other assets sold or exchanged) and credits properly chargeable against any amount so deferred, are subject to deferral under the provisions of § 1.461-1(a)(4). In addition, income is deferrable under this deferred income method of accounting only to the extent that it exceeds the related deductions already claimed in open taxable years to which the foreign legal restriction applied.

(v) Examples. The following examples, in which Sub is a Country FC subsidiary of U.S. corporation, Parent, illustrate this paragraph (h)(2).

*Example (1).* Parent licenses an intangible to Sub. FC law generally prohibits payments by any person within FC to recipients outside the country. The FC law meets the requirements of paragraph (h)(2)(ii) of this section. There is no evidence of unrelated parties entering into transactions under comparable circumstances for a comparable period of time, and the foreign legal restrictions will not be taken into account in determining the arm's length amount. The arm's length royalty rate for the use of the intangible property in the absence of the foreign restriction is 10% of Sub's sales in country FC. However, because the requirements of paragraph (h)(2)(ii) of this section are satisfied, Parent can elect the deferred income method of accounting by attaching to its timely filed U.S. income tax return a written statement that satisfies the requirements of paragraph (h)(2)(iii)(B) of this section.

*Example (2).* (i) The facts are the same as in *Example 1*, except that Sub, although it makes no royalty payment to Parent, arranges with an unrelated intermediary to make payments equal to an arm's length amount on its behalf to Parent.

(ii) The district director makes an allocation of royalty income to Parent, based on the arm's length royalty rate of 10%. Further, the district director determines that because the arrangement with the third party had the effect of circumventing the FC law, the requirements of paragraph (h)(2)(ii)(D) of this section are not satisfied. Thus, Parent could not validly elect the deferred income method of accounting, and the allocation of royalty income cannot be treated as deferrable. In appropriate circumstances, the district director may permit the amount of the distribution to be treated as payment by Sub of the royalty allocated to Parent, under the provisions of § 1.482-1(g) (Collateral adjustments).

*Example (3).* The facts are the same as in Example 1, except that the laws of FC do not prevent distributions from corporations to their shareholders. Sub distributes an amount equal to 8% of its sales in country FC. Because the laws of FC did not expressly prevent all forms of payment from Sub to Parent, Parent cannot validly elect the deferred income method of accounting with respect to any of the arm's length royalty amount. In appropriate circumstances, the district director may permit the 8% that was distributed to be treated as payment by Sub of the royalty allocated to Parent, under the provisions of § 1.482-1(g) (Collateral adjustments).

*Example (4).* The facts are the same as in Example 1, except that Country FC law permits the payment of a royalty, but limits the amount to 5% of sales, and Sub pays the 5% royalty to Parent. Parent demonstrates the existence of a comparable uncontrolled transaction for purposes of the comparable uncontrolled transaction method in which an uncontrolled party accepted a royalty rate of 5%. Given the evidence of the comparable uncontrolled transaction, the 5% royalty rate is determined to be the arm's length royalty rate.

*(3) Coordination with section 936.* (i) Cost sharing under section 936. If a possessions corporation makes an election under section 936(h)(5)(C)(i)(I), the corporation must make a section 936 cost sharing payment that is at least equal to the payment that would be required under section 482 if the electing corporation were a foreign corporation. In determining the payment that would be required under section 482 for this purpose, the provisions of §§ 1.482-1 and 1.482-4 will be applied, and to the extent relevant to the valuation of intangibles, §§ 1.482-5 and 1.482-6 will be applied. The provisions of section 936(h)(5)(C)(i)(II) (Effect of Election-electing corporation treated as owner of intangible property) do not apply until the payment that would be required under section 482 has been determined.

(ii) Use of terms. A cost sharing payment, for the purposes of section 936(h)(5)(C)(i)(I), is calculated using the provisions of section 936 and the regulations thereunder and the provisions of this paragraph (h)(3). The provisions relating to cost sharing under section 482 do not apply to payments made pursuant to an election under section 936(h)(5)(C)(i)(I). Similarly, a profit split payment, for the purposes of section 936(h)(5)(C)(ii)(I), is calculated using the provisions of section 936 and the regulations thereunder, not section 482 and the regulations thereunder.

**(i) Definitions.** The definitions set forth in paragraphs (i)(1) through (i)(10) of this section apply to this section and §§ 1.482-2 through 1.482-9.

*(1)* Organization includes an organization of any kind, whether a sole proprietorship, a partnership, a trust, an estate, an association, or a corporation (as each is defined or understood in the Internal Revenue Code or the regulations thereunder), irrespective of the place of organization, operation, or conduct of the trade or business, and regardless of whether it is a domestic or foreign organization, whether it is an exempt organization, or whether it is a member of an affiliated group that files a consolidated U.S. income tax return, or a member of an affiliated group that does not file a consolidated U.S. income tax return.

*(2)* Trade or business includes a trade or business activity of any kind, regardless of whether or where organized, whether owned individually or otherwise, and regardless of the place of operation. Employment for compensation will constitute a separate trade or business from the employing trade or business.

*(3)* Taxpayer means any person, organization, trade or business, whether or not subject to any internal revenue tax.

*(4)* Controlled includes any kind of control, direct or indirect, whether legally enforceable or not, and however exercisable or exercised, including control resulting from the actions of two or more taxpayers acting in concert or with a common goal or purpose. It is the reality of the control that is decisive, not its form or the mode of its exercise. A presumption of control arises if income or deductions have been arbitrarily shifted.

*(5)* Controlled taxpayer means any one of two or more taxpayers owned or controlled directly or indirectly by the same interests, and includes the taxpayer that owns or controls the other taxpayers. Uncontrolled taxpayer means any one of two or more taxpayers not owned or controlled directly or indirectly by the same interests.

*(6)* Group, controlled group, and group of controlled taxpayers mean the taxpayers owned or controlled directly or indirectly by the same interests.

*(7)* Transaction means any sale, assignment, lease, license, loan, advance, contribution, or any other transfer of any interest in or a right to use any property (whether tangible or intangible, real or personal) or money, however such transaction is effected, and whether or not the terms of such transaction are formally documented. A transaction also includes the performance of any services for the benefit of, or on behalf of, another taxpayer.

*(8)* Controlled transaction or controlled transfer means any transaction or transfer between two or more members of the same group of controlled taxpayers. The term uncontrolled transaction means any transaction between two or more taxpayers that are not members of the same group of controlled taxpayers.

*(9)* True taxable income means, in the case of a controlled taxpayer, the taxable income that would have resulted had it dealt with the other member or members of the group at arm's length. It does not mean the taxable income resulting to the controlled taxpayer by reason of the particular contract, transaction, or arrangement the controlled taxpayer chose to make (even though such contract, transaction, or arrangement is legally binding upon the parties thereto).

*(10)* Uncontrolled comparable means the uncontrolled transaction or uncontrolled taxpayer that is compared with a controlled transaction or taxpayer under any applicable pricing methodology. Thus, for example, under the comparable profits method, an uncontrolled comparable is any uncontrolled taxpayer from which data is used to establish a comparable operating profit.

**(j) Effective dates.** *(1)* These regulations are generally effective for taxable years beginning after October 6, 1994.

*(2)* Taxpayers may elect to apply retroactively all of the provisions of these regulations for any open taxable year. Such election will be effective for the year of the election and all subsequent taxable years.

*(3)* Although these regulations are generally effective for taxable years as stated, the final sentence of section 482 (requiring that the income with respect to transfers or licenses of intangible property be commensurate with the income attributable to the intangible) is generally effective for taxable years beginning after December 31, 1986. For the period prior to the effective date of these regulations, the final sentence of section 482 must be applied using any reasonable method not inconsistent with the statute. The IRS considers a method that applies these regulations or their general principles to be a reasonable method.

*(4)* These regulations will not apply with respect to transfers made or licenses granted to foreign persons before November 17, 1985, or before August 17, 1986, for transfers or licenses to others. Nevertheless, they will apply with respect to transfers or licenses before such dates if, with respect to property transferred pursuant to an earlier and continuing transfer agreement, such property was not in existence or owned by the taxpayer on such date.

*(5)* The last sentences of paragraphs (b)(2)(i) and (c)(1) of this section and of paragraph (c)(2)(iv) of § 1.482-5 apply for taxable years beginning on or after August 26, 2003.

*(6)* (i) The provisions of paragraphs (a)(1), (d)(3)(ii)(C) Example 3, Example 4, Example 5, and Example 6, (d)(3)(v), (f)(2)(ii)(A), (f)(2)(iii)(B), (g)(4)(i), (g)(4)(iii), and (i) of this section are generally applicable for taxable years beginning after July 31, 2009.

(ii) A person may elect to apply the provisions of paragraphs (a)(1), (b)(2)(i), (d)(3)(ii)(C) Example 3, Example 4, Example 5, and Example 6, (d)(3)(v), (f)(2)(ii)(A), (f)(2)(iii)(B), (g)(4)(i), (g)(4)(iii), and (i) of this section to earlier taxable years in accordance with the rules set forth in §§ 1.482-9(n)(2).

---

T.D. 8552, 7/1/94, amend T.D. 9088, 8/25/2003, T.D. 9278, 7/31/2006, T.D. 9441, 12/31/2008, T.D. 9456, 7/31/2009.

---

PAR. 4. Section 1.482-1 is amended by:

1. Revising paragraph (b)(2)(i) and the last sentence of paragraph (j)(6)(i).

2. Adding a new paragraph (b)(2)(iii).

The addition and revisions read as follows:

**Proposed § 1.482-1 Allocation of income and deductions among taxpayers.** [*For Preamble, see ¶ 153,087*]

* * * * *

**(b)** * * *

*(2)* * * *

(i) [The text of the proposed amendment to § 1.482-1(b)(2)(i) is the same as the text of § 1.482-1T(b)(2)(i) published elsewhere in this issue of the Federal Register]. [*See T.D. 9441, 01/05/2009, 74 Fed. Reg. 2.*].

* * * * *

(iii) [The text of the proposed § 1.482-1(b)(2)(iii) is the same as the text of § 1.482-1T(b)(2)(iii) published elsewhere in this issue of the Federal Register]. [*See T.D. 9441, 01/05/2009, 74 Fed. Reg. 2.*].

* * * * *

**(j)** * * *

*(6)* * * *

(i) * * * . [The text of the proposed amendment to § 1.482-1(j)(6)(i) is the same as the text of the amendment to § 1.482-1T(j)(6)(i) published elsewhere in this issue of the Federal Register]. [*See T.D. 9441, 01/05/2009, 74 Fed. Reg. 2.*].

PAR. 5. Section 1.482-1 is amended by:

1. Revising the second sentence of paragraph (b)(2)(i).

2. Revising the last sentence of paragraph (c)(1).

The revisions read as follows:

**Proposed § 1.482-1**

• ***Caution:*** This Proposed Reg was incorporated into final and temporary regulations by TD 9441, 12/31/2008.

Allocation of income and deductions among taxpayers. [*For Preamble, see ¶ 152,697*]

* * * * *

**(b)** * * *

*(2)* * * *

(i) * * * Section 1.482-7 provides the methods to be used to evaluate whether a cost sharing arrangement produces results consistent with an arm's length result.

* * * * *

**(c)** * * *

*(1)* * * * See § 1.482-7 for the applicable methods in the case of a cost sharing arrangement.

* * * * *

PAR. 4. Section 1.482-1 is amended as follows:

1. In paragraph (a)(1), remove the last sentence and add two new sentences in its place.

2. Revise paragraph (b)(2)(i).

3. In paragraph (c)(1), revise the last sentence.

4. In paragraph (d)(3)(v), revise the last sentence.

5. In paragraph (i), revise the introductory text.

The additions and revisions read as follows:

**Proposed § 1.482-1 Allocation of income and deductions among taxpayers.** [*For Preamble, see ¶ 151,855*]

**(a) In general.** *(1) Purpose and scope.* * * * Section 1.482-8 elaborates on the rules that apply to controlled entities engaged in a global securities dealing operation. Finally, § 1.482-9 provides examples illustrating the application of the best method rule.

* * * * *

**(b)** * * *

*(2)* * * *

(i) Methods. Sections 1.482-2 through 1.482-6 and § 1.482-8 provide specific methods to be used to evaluate whether transactions between or among members of the controlled group satisfy the arm's length standard, and if they do not, to determine the arm's length result.

**(c) Best method rule.** *(1) In general.* * * * See § 1.482-9 for examples of the application of the best method rule.

* * * * *

**(d)** * * *

*(3)* * * *

(v) Property or services. * * * For guidance concerning the specific comparability considerations applicable to transfers of tangible and intangible property, see §§ 1.482-3 through 1.482-6 and § 1.482-8; see also § 1.482-3(f), dealing with the coordination of the intangible and tangible property rules.

* * * * *

**(i) Definitions.** The definitions set forth in paragraphs (i)(1) through (10) of this section apply to §§ 1.482-1 through 1.482-9.

* * * * *

**§ 1.482-1A Allocation of income and deductions among taxpayers.**

**(a) Definitions.** When used in this section and in § 1.482-2—

*(1)* The term "organization" includes any organization of any kind, whether it be a sole proprietorship, a partnership, a trust, an estate, an association, or a corporation (as each is defined or understood in the Internal Revenue Code or the regulations thereunder), irrespective of the place where organized, where operated, or where its trade or business is conducted, and regardless of whether domestic or foreign, whether exempt, whether affiliated, or whether a party to a consolidated return.

*(2)* The term "trade" or "business" includes any trade or business activity of any kind, regardless of whether or where organized, whether owned individually or otherwise, and regardless of the place where carried on.

*(3)* The term "controlled" includes any kind of control, direct or indirect, whether legally enforceable, and however exercisable or exercised. It is the reality of the control which is decisive, not its form or the mode of its exercise. A presumption of control arises if income or deductions have been arbitrarily shifted.

*(4)* The term "controlled taxpayer" means any one of two or more organizations, trades, or businesses owned or controlled directly or indirectly by the same interests.

*(5)* The terms "group" and "group of controlled taxpayers" mean the organizations, trades, or businesses owned or controlled by the same interests.

*(6)* The term "true taxable income" means, in the case of a controlled taxpayer, the taxable income (or, as the case may be, any item or element affecting taxable income) which would have resulted to the controlled taxpayer, had it in the conduct of its affairs (or, as the case may be, in the particular contract, transaction, arrangement, or other act) dealt with the other member of members of the group at arm's length. It does not mean the income, the deductions, the credits, the allowances, or the item or element of income, deductions, credits, or allowances, resulting to the controlled taxpayer by reason of the particular contract, transaction, or arrangement, the controlled taxpayer, or the interests controlling it, chose to make (even though such contract, transaction, or arrangement be legally binding upon the parties thereto).

**(b) Scope and purpose.** *(1)* The purpose of section 482 is to place a controlled taxpayer on a tax parity with an uncontrolled taxpayer, by determining, according to the standard of an uncontrolled taxpayer, the true taxable income from the property and business of a controlled taxpayer. The interests controlling a group of controlled taxpayers are assumed to have complete power to cause each controlled taxpayer so to conduct its affairs that its transaction and accounting records truly reflect the taxable income from the property and business of each of the controlled taxpayers. If, however, this has not been done, and the taxable incomes are thereby understated, the district director shall intervene, and, by making such distributions, apportionments, or allocations as he may deem necessary of gross income, deductions, credits, or allowances, or of any item or element affecting taxable income, between or among the controlled taxpayers constituting the group, shall determine the true taxable income of each controlled taxpayer. The standard to be applied in every case is that of an uncontrolled taxpayer dealing at arm's length with another uncontrolled taxpayer.

*(2)* Section 482 and this section apply to the case of any controlled taxpayer, whether such taxpayer makes a separate or a consolidated return. If a controlled taxpayer makes a separate return, the determination is of its true separate taxable income. If a controlled taxpayer is a party to a consolidated return, the true consolidated taxable income of the affiliated group and the true separate taxable income of the controlled taxpayer are determined consistently with the principles of a consolidated return.

*(3)* Section 482 grants no right to a controlled taxpayer to apply its provisions at will, nor does it grant any right to compel the district director to apply such provisions. It is not intended (except in the case of the computation of consolidated taxable income under a consolidated return) to effect in any case such a distribution, apportionment, or allocation of gross income, deductions, credits, or allowances, or any item of gross income, deductions, credits, or allowances, as would produce a result equivalent to a computation of consolidated taxable income under subchapter A, chapter 6 of the Code.

**(c) Application.** Transactions between one controlled taxpayer and another will be subjected to special scrutiny to ascertain whether the common control is being used to reduce, avoid, or escape taxes. In determining the true taxable income of a controlled taxpayer, the district director is not restricted to the case of improper accounting, to the case of a fraudulent, colorable, or sham transaction, or to the case of a device designed to reduce or avoid tax by shifting or distorting income, deductions, credits, or allowances. The authority to determine true taxable income extends to any case in which either by inadvertence or design the taxable income, in whole or in part of a controlled taxpayer, is other than it would have been had the taxpayer in the conduct of his affairs been an uncontrolled taxpayer dealing at arm's length with another uncontrolled taxpayer.

**(d) Method of allocation.** *(1)* The method of allocating, apportioning, or distributing income, deductions, credits, and allowances to be used by the district director in any case, including the form of the adjustments and the character and source of amounts allocated, shall be determined with reference to the substance of the particular transactions or arrangements which result in the avoidance of taxes or the failure to clearly reflect income. The appropriate adjustments may take the form of an increase or decrease in gross income, increase or decrease in deductions (including depreciation), increase or decrease in basis of assets (including inventory), or any other adjustment which may be appropriate under the circumstances. See § 1.482-2 for specific rules relating to methods of allocation in the case of several types of business transactions.

*(2)* Whenever the district director makes adjustments to the income of one member of a group of controlled taxpayers (such adjustments being referred to in this paragraph as "primary" adjustments) he shall also make appropriate correlative adjustments to the income of any other member of the group involved in the allocation. The correlative adjustment shall actually be made if the U.S. income tax liability of the other member would be affected for any pending taxable year. Thus, if the district director makes an allocation of income, he shall not only increase the income of one member of the group, but shall decrease the income of the other member if such adjustment would have an effect on the U.S. income tax liability of the other member for any pending taxable year. For the purposes of this subparagraph, a "pending taxable year" is any taxable year with respect to which the U.S. income tax return of the other member has been filed by the time the allocation is made, and with respect to which a credit or refund is not barred by the operation of any law or rule of law. If a correlative adjustment is not actually made because it would have no effect on the U.S. income tax liability of the other member involved in the allocation for any pending taxable year, such adjustment shall nevertheless be deemed to have been made for the purpose of determining the U.S. income tax liability of such member for a later taxable year, or for the purposes of determining the U.S. income tax liability of any person for any taxable year. The district director shall furnish to the taxpayer with respect to which the primary adjustment is made a written statement of the amount and nature of the correlative adjustment which is deemed to have been made. For purposes of this subparagraph, a primary adjustment shall not be considered to have been made (and therefore a correlative adjustment is not required to be made) until the first occurring of the following events with respect to the primary adjustment:

(i) The date of assessment of the tax following execution by the taxpayer of a Form 870 (Waiver of Restrictions on Assessment and Collection of Deficiency in Tax and Acceptance of Overassessment) with respect to such adjustment.

(ii) Acceptance of a Form 870-AD (Offer of Waiver of Restriction on Assessment and Collection of Deficiency in Tax and Acceptance of Overassessment),

(iii) Payment of the deficiency,

(iv) Stipulation in the Tax Court of the United States, or

(v) Final determination of tax liability by offer-in-compromise, closing agreement, or court action.

The principles of this subparagraph may be illustrated by the following examples in each of which it is assumed that X and Y are members of the same group of controlled entities and that they regularly compute their incomes on the basis of a calendar year:

*Example (1).* Assume that in 1968 the district director proposes to adjust X's income for 1966 to reflect an arm's length rental charge for Y's use of X's tangible property in 1966; that X consents to an assessment reflecting such adjustment by executing a Waiver, Form 870; and that an assessment of the tax with respect to such adjustment is made in 1968. The primary adjustment is therefore considered to have been made in 1968. Assume further that both X and Y are United States corporations and that Y had net operating losses in 1963, 1964, 1965, 1966, and 1967. Although a correlative adjustment would not have an effect on Y's U.S. income tax liability for any pending taxable year, an adjustment increasing Y's net operating loss for 1966 shall be deemed to have been made for the purposes of determining Y's U.S. income tax liability for 1968 or a later taxable year to which the increased operating loss may be carried. The district director shall notify X in writing of the amount and nature of the adjustment which is deemed to have been made to Y.

*Example (2).* Assume that X and Y are United States corporations; that X is in the business of rendering engineering services; that in 1968 the district director proposes to adjust X's income for 1966 to reflect an arm's length fee for the rendition of engineering services by X in 1966 relating to the construction of Y's factory; that X consents to an assessment reflecting such adjustment by executing a Waiver,

Form 870; and that an assessment of the tax with respect to such adjustment is made in 1968. Assume further that fees for such services would properly constitute a capital expenditure by Y, and that Y does not place the factory in service until 1969. Although a correlative adjustment (increase in basis) would not have an effect on Y's U.S. income tax liability for a pending taxable year, an adjustment increasing the basis of Y's assets for 1966 shall be deemed to have been made in 1968 for the purpose of computing allowable depreciation or gain or loss on disposition for 1969 and any future taxable year. The district director shall notify X in writing of the amount and nature of the adjustment which is deemed to have been made to Y.

*Example (3).* Assume that X is a U.S. taxpayer and Y is a foreign taxpayer not engaged in a trade or business in the United States; that in 1968 the district director proposes to adjust X's income for 1966 to reflect an arm's length interest charge on a loan made to Y; that X consents to an assessment reflecting such allocation by executing a Waiver, Form 870; and that an assessment of the tax with respect to such adjustment is made in 1968. Although a correlative adjustment would not have an effect on Y's U.S. income tax liability, an adjustment in Y's income for 1966 shall be deemed to have been made in 1968 for the purposes of determining the amount of Y's earnings and profits for 1966 and subsequent years, and of any other effect it may have on any person's U.S. income tax liability for any taxable year. The district director shall notify X in writing of the amount and nature of the allocation which is deemed to have been made to Y.

*(3)* In making distributions, apportionments, or allocations between two members of a group of controlled entities with respect to particular transactions, the district director shall consider the effect upon such members of an arrangement between them for reimbursement within a reasonable period before or after the taxable year if the taxpayer can establish that such an arrangement in fact existed during the taxable year under consideration. The district director shall also consider the effect of any other nonarm's length transaction between them in the taxable year which, if taken into account, would result in a set off against any allocation which would otherwise be made, provided the taxpayer is able to establish with reasonable specificity that the transaction was not at arm's length and the amount of the appropriate arm's length charge. For purposes of the preceding sentence, the term arm's length refers to the amount which was charged or would have been charged in independent transactions with unrelated parties under the same or similar circumstances considering all the relevant facts and without regard to the rules found in § 1.482-2 by which certain charges are deemed to be equal to arm's length. For example, assume that one member of a group performs services which benefit a second member, which would in itself require an allocation to reflect an arm's length charge for the performance of such services. Assume further that the first member can establish that during the same taxable year the second member engages in other nonarm's length transactions which benefit the first member, such as by selling products to the first member at a discount, or purchasing products from the first member at a premium, or paying royalties to the first member in an excessive amount. In such case, the value of the benefits received by the first member as a result of the other activities will be set-off against the allocation which would otherwise be made. If the effect of the set-off is to change the characterization or source of the income or deductions, or otherwise distort taxable income, in such a manner as to affect the United States tax liability of any member, allocations will be made to reflect the correct amount of each category of income or deductions. In order to establish that a set-off to the adjustments proposed by the district director is appropriate, the taxpayer must notify the district director of the basis of any claimed set-off at any time before the expiration of the period ending 30 days after the date of a letter by which the district director transmits an examination report notifying the taxpayer of proposed adjustments or before July 16, 1968, whichever is later. The principles of this subparagraph may be illustrated by the following examples, in each of which it is assumed that P and S are calendar year corporations and are both members of the same group of controlled entities:

*Example (1).* P performs services in 1966 for the benefit of S in connection with S's manufacture and sale of a product. S does not pay P for such services in 1966, but in consideration for such services, agrees in 1966 to pay P a percentage of the amount of sales of the product in 1966 through 1970. In 1966 it appeared this agreement would provide adequate consideration for the services. No allocation will be made with respect to the services performed by P.

*Example (2).* P renders services to S in connection with the construction of S's factory. An arm's length charge for such services, determined under paragraph (b) of § 1.482-2, would be $100,000. During the same taxable year P makes available to S a machine to be used in such construction. P bills S $125,000 for the services, but does not bill for the use of the machine. No allocation will be made with respect to the excessive charge for services or the undercharge for the machine if P can establish that the excessive charge services was equal to an arm's length charge for the use of the machine, and if the taxable income and income tax liabilities of P and S are not distorted.

*Example (3).* Assume the same facts as in example (2), except that, if P had reported $25,000 as rental income and $25,000 less service income, it would have been subject to the tax on personal holding companies. Allocations will be made to reflect the correct amounts of rental income and service income.

*(4)* If the members of a group of controlled taxpayers engage in transactions with one another, the district director may distribute, apportion, or allocate income, deductions, credits, or allowances to reflect the true taxable income of the individual members under the standards set forth in this section and in § 1.482-2 notwithstanding the fact that the ultimate income anticipated from a series of transactions may not be realized or is realized during a later period. For example, if one member of a controlled group sells a product at less than an arm's length price to a second member of the group in one taxable year and the second member resells the product to an unrelated party in the next taxable year, the district director may make an appropriate allocation to reflect an arm's length price for the sale of the product in the first taxable year, notwithstanding that the second member of the group had not realized any gross income from the resale of the product in the first year. Similarly, if one member of a group lends money to a second member of the group in a taxable year, the district director may make an appropriate allocation to reflect an arm's length charge for interest during such taxable year even if the second member does not realize income during such year. The provisions of this subparagraph apply even if the gross income contemplated from a series of transactions is never, in fact, realized by the other members.

*(5)* Section 482 may, when necessary to prevent the avoidance of taxes or to clearly reflect income, be applied in circumstances described in sections of the Code (such as section 351) providing for nonrecognition of gain or loss. See, for example, "National Securities Corporation v. Commissioner of Internal Revenue", 137 F. 2d 600 (3d Cir. 1943), cert. denied 320 U.S. 794 (1943).

*(6)* If payment or reimbursement for the sale, exchange, or use of property, the rendition of services, or the advance of other consideration among members of a group of controlled entities was prevented, or would have been prevented, at the time of the transaction because of currency or other restrictions imposed under the laws of any foreign country, any distributions, apportionments, or allocations which may be made under section 482 with respect to such transactions may be treated as deferrable income or deductions, providing the taxpayer has, for the year to which the distributions, apportionments, or allocations relate, elected to use a method of accounting in which the reporting of deferrable income is deferred until the income ceases to be deferrable income. Under such method of accounting, referred to in this section as the deferred income method of accounting, any payments or reimbursements which were prevented or would have been prevented, and any deductions attributable directly or indirectly to such payments or reimbursements, shall be deferred until they cease to be deferrable under such method of accounting. If such method of accounting has not been elected with respect to the taxable year to which the allocations under section 482 relate, the taxpayer may elect such method with respect to such allocations (but not with respect to other deferrable income) at any time before the first occurring of the following events with respect to the allocations:

(i) Execution by the taxpayer of Form 870 (Waiver of Restrictions on Assessment and Collection of Deficiency in Tax and Acceptance Overassessment);

(ii) Expiration of the period ending 30 days after the date of a letter by which the district director transmits an examination report notifying the taxpayer of proposed adjustments reflecting such allocations or before July 16, 1968, whichever is later; or

(iii) Execution of a closing agreement or offer-in-compromise.

The principles of this subparagraph may be illustrated by the following example in which it is assumed that X, a domestic corporation, and Y, a foreign corporation, are members of the same group of controlled entities:

*Example.* X, which is in the business of rendering a certain type of service to unrelated parties, renders such services for the benefit of Y in 1965. The direct and indirect costs allocable to such services are $60,000, and an arm's length charge for such services is $100,000. Assume that the district director proposes to increase X's income by $100,000, but that the country in which Y is located would have blocked payment in 1965 for such services. If, prior to the first occurring of the events described in subdivisions (i), (ii), or (iii) of this subparagraph, X elects to use the deferred income method of accounting with respect to such allocation, the $100,000 allocation and the $60,000 of costs are deferrable until such amounts cease to be deferrable under X's method of accounting.

T.D. 6595, 4/13/62, amend T.D. 6952, 4/15/68, T.D. 8470, 1/13/93.

### § 1.482-1T Allocation of income and deductions among taxpayers (temporary).

**(a)** through (b)(1) [Reserved]. For further guidance, see § 1.482-1(a) through (b)(1).

**(b)** *(2) Arm's length methods.* (i) Methods. Sections 1.482-2 through 1.482-6, 1.482-7T and 1.482-9 provide specific methods to be used to evaluate whether transactions between or among members of the controlled group satisfy the arm's length standard, and if they do not, to determine the arm's length result. Section 1.482-1 and this section provide general principles applicable in determining arm's length results of such controlled transactions, but do not provide methods, for which reference must be made to those other sections in accordance with paragraphs (b)(2)(ii) and (iii) of this section. Section 1.482-7T provides the specific methods to be used to evaluate whether a cost sharing arrangement as defined in § 1.482-7T produces results consistent with an arm's length result.

(ii) [Reserved]. For further guidance, see § 1.482-1(b)(2)(ii).

(iii) Coordination of methods applicable to certain intangible development arrangements. Section 1.482-7T provides the specific methods to be used to determine arm's length results of controlled transactions in connection with a cost sharing arrangement as defined in § 1.482-7T. Sections 1.482-4 and 1.482-9, as appropriate, provide the specific methods to be used to determine arm's length results of arrangements, including partnerships, for sharing the costs and risks of developing intangible property, other that a cost sharing arrangement covered by § 1.482-7T. See also §§ 1.482-4T(g) (Coordination with rules governing cost sharing arrangements) and 1.482-9T(m)(3) (Coordination with rules governing cost sharing arrangements).

**(c)** through (j)(5) [Reserved]. For further guidance, see § 1.482-1(c) through (j)(5).

*(6)* (i) The provisions of paragraphs (b)(2)(i) and (b)(2)(iii) of this section are generally applicable on January 5, 2009.

(ii) [Reserved]. For further guidance, see § 1.482-1(j)(6)(ii).

(iii) The applicability of paragraphs (b)(2)(i) and (b)(2)(iii) of this section expires on or before December 30, 2011.

T.D. 9278, 7/31/2006, amend T.D. 9441, 12/31/2008, T.D. 9456, 7/31/2009.

### § 1.482-2 Determination of taxable income in specific situations.

**(a) Loans or advances.** *(1) Interest on bona fide indebtedness.* (i) In general. Where one member of a group of controlled entities makes a loan or advance directly or indirectly to, or otherwise becomes a creditor of, another member of such group and either charges no interest, or charges interest at a rate which is not equal to an arm's length rate of interest (as defined in paragraph (a)(2) of this section) with respect to such loan or advance, the district director may make appropriate allocations to reflect an arm's length rate of interest for the use of such loan or advance.

(ii) Application of paragraph (a) of this section. (A) Interest on bona fide indebtedness. Paragraph (a) of this section applies only to determine the appropriateness of the rate of interest charged on the principal amount of a bona fide indebtedness between members of a group of controlled entities, including—

(1) Loans or advances of money or other consideration (whether or not evidenced by a written instrument); and

(2) Indebtedness arising in the ordinary course of business from sales, leases, or the rendition of services by or between members of the group, or any other similar extension of credit.

(B) Alleged indebtedness. This paragraph (a) does not apply to so much of an alleged indebtedness which is not in fact a bona fide indebtedness, even if the stated rate of interest thereon would be within the safe haven rates prescribed in paragraph (a)(2)(iii) of this section. For example, paragraph (a) of this section does not apply to payments with respect to all or a portion of such alleged indebtedness where in fact all or a portion of an alleged indebtedness is a contribution to the capital of a corporation or a distribution by a corporation with respect to its shares. Similarly, this paragraph (a) does not apply to payments with respect to an alleged purchase-money debt instrument given in consideration for an alleged sale of property between two controlled entities where in fact the transaction constitutes a lease of the property. Payments made with respect to alleged indebtedness (including alleged stated interest thereon) shall be treated according to their substance. See § 1.482-2(a)(3)(i).

(iii) Period for which interest shall be charged. (A) General rule. This paragraph (a)(1)(iii) is effective for indebtedness arising after June 30, 1988. See § 1.482-2(a)(3)(26 CFR Part 1 edition revised as of April 1, 1988) for indebtedness arising before July 1, 1988. Except as otherwise provided in paragraphs (a)(1)(iii)(B) through (E) of this section, the period for which interest shall be charged with respect to a bona fide indebtedness between controlled entities begins on the day after the day the indebtedness arises and ends on the day the indebtedness is satisfied (whether by payment, offset, cancellation, or otherwise). Paragraphs (a)(1)(iii)(B) through (E) of this section provide certain alternative periods during which interest is not required to be charged on certain indebtedness. These exceptions apply only to indebtedness described in paragraph (a)(1)(ii)(A)(2) of this section (relating to indebtedness incurred in the ordinary course of business from sales, services, etc., between members of the group) and not evidenced by a written instrument requiring the payment of interest. Such amounts are hereinafter referred to as intercompany trade receivables. The period for which interest is not required to be charged on intercompany trade receivables under this paragraph (a)(1)(iii) is called the interest-free period. In general, an intercompany trade receivable arises at the time economic performance occurs (within the meaning of section 461(h) and the regulations thereunder) with respect to the underlying transaction between controlled entities. For purposes of this paragraph (a)(1)(iii), the term United States includes any possession of the United States, and the term foreign country excludes any possession of the United States.

(B) Exception for certain intercompany transactions in the ordinary course of business. Interest is not required to be charged on an intercompany trade receivable until the first day of the third calendar month following the month in which the intercompany trade receivable arises.

(C) Exception for trade or business of debtor member located outside the United States. In the case of an intercompany trade receivable arising from a transaction in the ordinary course of a trade or business which is actively conducted outside the United States by the debtor member, interest is not required to be charged until the first day of the fourth calendar month following the month in which such intercompany trade receivable arises.

(D) Exception for regular trade practice of creditor member or others in creditor's industry. If the creditor member or unrelated persons in the creditor member's industry, as a regular trade practice, allow unrelated parties a longer period without charging interest than that described in paragraph (a)(1)(iii)(B) or (C) of this section (whichever is applicable) with respect to transactions which are similar to transactions that give rise to intercompany trade receivables, such longer interest-free period shall be allowed with respect to a comparable amount of intercompany trade receivables.

(E) Exception for property purchased for resale in a foreign country. (1) General rule. If in the ordinary course of business one member of the group (related purchaser) purchases property from another member of the group (related seller) for resale to unrelated persons located in a particular foreign country, the related purchaser and the related seller may use as the interest-free period for the intercompany trade receivables arising during the related seller's taxable year from the purchase of such property within the same product group an interest-free period equal the sum of—

(i) The number of days in the related purchaser's average collection period (as determined under paragraph (a)(1)(iii)(E)(2) of this section) for sales of property within the same product group sold in the ordinary course of business to unrelated persons located in the same foreign country; plus

(ii) Ten (10) calendar days.

(2) Interest-free period. The interest-free period under this paragraph (a)(1)(iii)(E), however, shall in no event exceed 183 days. The related purchaser does not have to conduct business outside the United States in order to be eligible to use the interest-free period of this paragraph (a)(1)(iii)(E). The interest-free period under this paragraph (a)(1)(iii)(E) shall not apply to intercompany trade receivables attributable to property which is manufactured, produced, or constructed (within the meaning of § 1.954-3(a)(4)) by the related purchaser. For purposes of this paragraph (a)(1)(iii)(E) a product group includes all products within the same three-digit Standard Industrial Classification (sic) Code (as prepared by the Statistical Policy Division of the Office of Management and Budget, Executive Office of the President.)

(3) Average collection period. An average collection period for purposes of this paragraph (a)(1)(iii)(E) is determined as follows—

(i) Step 1. Determine total sales (less returns and allowances) by the related purchaser in the product group to unrelated persons located in the same foreign country during the related purchaser's last taxable year ending on or before the first day of the related seller's taxable year in which the intercompany trade receivable arises.

(ii) Step 2. Determine the related purchaser's average month-end accounts receivable balance with respect to sales described in paragraph (a)(1)(iii)(E)(2)(i) of this section for the related purchaser's last taxable year ending on or before the first day of the related seller's taxable year in which the intercompany trade receivable arises.

(iii) Step 3. Compute a receivables turnover rate by dividing the total sales amount described in paragraph (a)(1)(iii)(E)(2)(i) of this section by the average receivables balance described in paragraph (a)(1)(iii)(E)(2)(ii) of this section.

(iv) Step 4. Divide the receivables turnover rate determined under paragraph (a)(1)(iii)(E)(2)(iii) of this section into 365, and round the result to the nearest whole number to determine the number of days in the average collection period.

(v) Other considerations. If the related purchaser makes sales in more than one foreign country, or sells property in more than one product group in any foreign country, separate computations of an average collection period, by product group within each country, are required. If the related purchaser resells fungible property in more than one foreign country and the intercompany trade receivables arising from the related party purchase of such fungible property cannot reasonably be identified with resales in particular foreign countries, then solely for the purpose of assigning an interest-free period to such intercompany trade receivables under this paragraph (a)(1)(iii)(E), an amount of each such intercompany trade receivable shall be treated as allocable to a particular foreign country in the same proportion that the related purchaser's sales of such fungible property in such foreign country during the period described in paragraph (a)(1)(iii)(E)(2)(i) of this section bears to the related purchaser's sales of all such fungible property in all such foreign countries during such period. An interest-free period under this paragraph (a)(1)(iii)(E) shall not apply to any intercompany trade receivables arising in a taxable year of the related seller if the related purchaser made no sales described in paragraph (a)(1)(iii)(E)(2)(i) of this section from which the appropriate interest-free period may be determined.

(4) Illustration. The interest-free period provided under paragraph (a)(1)(iii)(E) of this section may be illustrated by the following example:

*Example.* (i) Facts. X and Y use the calendar year as the taxable year and are members of the same group of controlled entities within the meaning of section 482. For Y's 1988 calendar taxable year X and Y intend to use the interest-free period determined under this paragraph (a)(1)(iii)(E) for intercompany trade receivables attributable to X's purchases of certain products from Y for resale by X in the ordinary course of business to unrelated persons in country Z. For its 1987 calendar taxable year all of X's sales in country Z were of products within a single product group based upon a three-digit SIC code, were not manufactured, produced, or constructed (within the meaning of § 1.954-3(a)(4)) by X, and were sold in the ordinary course of X's trade or business to unrelated persons located only in country Z. These sales and the month-end accounts receivable balances (for such sales and for such sales uncollected from prior months) are as follows:

| Month | Sales | Accounts Receivable |
|---|---|---|
| Jan. 1987 | $ 500,000 | $ 2,835,850 |
| Feb. | 600,000 | 2,840,300 |
| Mar. | 450,000 | 2,850,670 |
| Apr. | 550,000 | 2,825,700 |
| May | 650,000 | 2,809,360 |
| June | 525,000 | 2,803,200 |
| July | 400,000 | 2,825,850 |
| Aug. | 425,000 | 2,796,340 |
| Sept. | 475,000 | 2,839,390 |
| Oct. | 525,000 | 2,650,550 |
| Nov. | 450,000 | 2,775,450 |
| Dec. 1987 | 650,000 | 2,812,600 |
| Totals | 6,200,000 | 33,665,160 |

(ii) Average collection period. X's total sales within the same product group to unrelated persons within country Z for the period are $6,200,000. The average receivables balance for the period is $2,805,430 ($33,665,160/12). The average collection period in whole days is determined as follows:

$$\text{Receivables Turnover Rate} = \frac{\$6,200,000}{\$2,805,430} = 2.21$$

$$\text{Average Collection Period} = \frac{365}{2.21} = 165.16 \text{ days, rounded to the nearest whole day} = 165 \text{ days.}$$

(iii) Interest-free period. Accordingly, for intercompany trade receivables incurred by X during Y's 1988 calendar taxable year attributable to the purchase of property from Y for resale to unrelated persons located in country Z and included in the product group, X may use an interest-free period of 175 days (165 days in the average collection period plus 10 days, but not in excess of a maximum of 183 days). All other intercompany trade receivables incurred by X are subject to the interest-free periods described in paragraphs (a)(1)(iii)(B), (C), or (D), whichever are applicable. If X makes sales in other foreign countries in addition to country Z or makes sales of property in more than one product group in any foreign country, separate computations of X's average collection period, by product group within each country, are required in order for X and Y to determine an interest-free period for such product groups in such foreign countries under this paragraph (a)(1)(iii)(E).

(iv) Payment; book entries. (A) Except as otherwise provided in this paragraph (a)(1)(iv), in determining the period of time for which an amount owed by one member of the group to another member is outstanding, payments or other credits to an account are considered to be applied against the earliest amount outstanding, that is, payments or credits are applied against amounts in a first-in, first-out (FIFO) order. Thus, tracing payments to individual intercompany trade receivables is generally not required in order to determine whether a particular intercompany trade receivable has been paid within the applicable interest-free period determined under paragraph (a)(1)(iii) of this section. The application of this paragraph (a)(1)(iv)(A) may be illustrated by the following example:

*Example.* (i) Facts. X and Y are members of a group of controlled entities within the meaning of section 482. Assume that the balance of intercompany trade receivables owed by X to Y on June 1 is $100, and that all of the $100 balance represents amounts incurred by X to Y during the month of May. During the month of June X incurs an additional $200 of intercompany trade receivables to Y. Assume that on July 15, $60 is properly credited against X's intercompany account to Y, and that $240 is properly credited against the intercompany account on August 31. Assume that under paragraph (a)(1)(iii)(B) of this section interest must be charged on X's intercompany trade receivables to Y beginning with the first day of the third calendar month following the month the intercompany trade receivables arise, and that no alternative interest-free period applies. Thus, the interest-free period for intercompany trade receivables incurred during the month of May ends on July 31, and the interest-free period for intercompany trade receivables incurred during the month of June ends on August 31.

(ii) Application of payments. Using a FIFO payment order, the aggregate payments of $300 are applied first to the opening June balance, and then to the additional amounts incurred during the month of June. With respect to X's June opening balance of $100, no interest is required to be accrued on $60 of such balance paid by X on July 15, because such portion was paid within its interest-free period. Interest for 31 days, from August 1 to August 31 inclusive, is required to be accrued on the $40 portion of the opening balance not paid until August 31. No interest is required to be accrued on the $200 of intercompany trade receivables X incurred to Y during June because the $240 credited on August 31, after eliminating the $40 of indebtedness remaining from periods before June, also eliminated the $200 incurred by X during June prior to the end of the interest-free period for that amount. The amount of interest incurred by X to Y on the $40 amount during August creates bona fide indebtedness between controlled entities and is subject to the provisions of paragraph (a)(1)(iii)(A) of this section without regard to any of the exceptions contained in paragraphs (a)(1)(iii)(B) through (E).

(B) Notwithstanding the first-in, first-out payment application rule described in paragraph (a)(1)(iv)(A) of this section, the taxpayer may apply payments or credits against amounts owed in some other order on its books in accordance with an agreement or understanding of the related parties if the taxpayer can demonstrate that either it or others in its industry, as a regular trade practice, enter into such agreements or understandings in the case of similar balances with unrelated parties.

*(2) Arm's length interest rate.* (i) In general. For purposes of section 482 and paragraph (a) of this section, an arm's length rate of interest shall be a rate of interest which was charged, or would have been charged, at the time the indebtedness arose, in independent transactions with or between unrelated parties under similar circumstances. All relevant factors shall be considered, including the principal amount and duration of the loan, the security involved, the credit standing of the borrower, and the interest rate prevailing at the situs of the lender or creditor for comparable loans between unrelated parties.

(ii) Funds obtained at situs of borrower. Notwithstanding the other provisions of paragraph (a)(2) of this section, if the loan or advance represents the proceeds of a loan obtained by the lender at the situs of the borrower, the arm's length rate for any taxable year shall be equal to the rate actually paid by the lender increased by an amount which reflects the costs or deductions incurred by the lender in borrowing such amounts and making such loans, unless the taxpayer establishes a more appropriate rate under the standards set forth in paragraph (a)(2)(i) of this section.

(iii) Safe haven interest rates for certain loans and advances made after May 28, 1986. (A) Applicability. (1) General rule. Except as otherwise provided in paragraph (a)(2) of this section, paragraph (a)(2)(iii)(B) applies with respect to the rate of interest charged and to the amount of interest paid or accrued in any taxable year—

(i) Under a term loan or advance between members of a group of controlled entities where (except as provided in paragraph (a)(2)(iii)(A)(2)(11) of this section) the loan or advance is entered into after May 8, 1986; and

(ii) After May 8, 1986 under a demand loan or advance between such controlled entities.

(2) Grandfather rule for existing loans. The safe haven rates prescribed in paragraph (a)(2)(iii)(B) of this section shall not apply, and the safe haven rates prescribed in § 1.482-2(a)(2)(iii) (26 CFR part 1 edition revised as of April 1, 1985), shall apply to—

(i) Term loans or advances made before May 9, 1986; and

(ii) Term loans or advances made before August 7, 1986, pursuant to a binding written contract entered into before May 9, 1986.

(B) Safe haven interest rate based on applicable Federal rate. Except as otherwise provided in this paragraph (a)(2), in the case of a loan or advance between members of a group of controlled entities, an arm's length rate of interest referred to in paragraph (a)(2)(i) of this section shall be for purposes of chapter 1 of the Internal Revenue Code—

(1) The rate of interest actually charged if that rate is—

(i) Not less than 100 percent of the applicable Federal rate (lower limit); and

(ii) Not greater than 130 percent of the applicable Federal rate (upper limit); or

(2) If either no interest is charged or if the rate of interest charged is less than the lower limit, then an arm's length rate of interest shall be equal to the lower limit, compounded semiannually; or

(3) If the rate of interest charged is greater than the upper limit, then an arm's length rate of interest shall be equal to the upper limit, compounded semiannually, unless the taxpayer establishes a more appropriate compound rate of interest under paragraph (a)(2)(i) of this section. However, if the compound rate of interest actually charged is greater than the upper limit and less than the rate determined under paragraph (a)(2)(i) of this section, or if the compound rate actually charged is less than the lower limit and greater than the rate determined under paragraph (a)(2)(i) of this section, then the compound rate actually charged shall be deemed to be an arm's length rate under paragraph (a)(2)(i). In the case of any sale-leaseback described in section 1274(e), the lower limit shall be 110 percent of the applicable Federal rate, compounded semiannually.

(C) Applicable Federal rate. For purposes of paragraph (a)(2)(iii)(B) of this section, the term applicable Federal rate means, in the case of a loan or advance to which this section applies and having a term of—

(1) Not over 3 years, the Federal short-term rate;

(2) Over 3 years but not over 9 years, the Federal mid-term rate; or

(3) Over 9 years, the Federal long-term rate, as determined under section 1274(d) in effect on the date such loan or advance is made. In the case of any sale or exchange between controlled entities, the lower limit shall be the lowest of the applicable Federal rates in effect for any month in the 3-calendar-month period ending with the first calendar month in which there is a binding written contract in effect for such sale or exchange (lowest 3-month rate, as defined in section 1274(d)(2)). In the case of a demand loan or advance to which this section applies, the applicable Federal rate means the Federal short-term rate determined under section 1274(d) (determined without regard to the lowest 3-month short term rate determined under section 1274(d)(2)) in effect for each day on which any amount of such loan or advance (including unpaid accrued interest determined under paragraph (a)(2) of this section) is outstanding.

(D) Lender in business of making loans. If the lender in a loan or advance transaction to which paragraph (a)(2) of this section applies is regularly engaged in the trade or business of making loans or advances to unrelated parties, the safe haven rates prescribed in paragraph (a)(2)(iii)(B) of this section shall not apply, and the arm's length interest rate to be used shall be determined under the standards described in paragraph (a)(2)(i) of this section, including reference to the interest rates charged in such trade or business by the lender on loans or advances of a similar type made to unrelated parties at and about the time the loan or advance to which paragraph (a)(2) of this section applies was made.

(E) Foreign currency loans. The safe haven interest rates prescribed in paragraph (a)(2)(iii)(B) of this section do not apply to any loan or advance the principal or interest of which is expressed in a currency other than U.S. dollars.

*(3) Coordination with interest adjustments required under certain other Code sections.* If the stated rate of interest on the stated principal amount of a loan or advance between controlled entities is subject to adjustment under section 482 and is also subject to adjustment under any other section of the Internal Revenue Code (for example, section 467, 483, 1274 or 7872), section 482 and paragraph (a) of this section may be applied to such loan or advance in addition to such other Internal Revenue Code section. After the enactment of the Tax Reform Act of 1964, Pub. L. 98-369, and the enactment of Pub. L. 99-121, such other Internal Revenue Code sections include sections 467, 483, 1274 and 7872. The order in which the different provisions shall be applied is as follows—

(i) First, the substance of the transaction shall be determined; for this purpose, all the relevant facts and circumstances shall be considered and any law or rule of law (assignment of income, step transaction, etc.) may apply. Only the rate of interest with respect to the stated principal amount of the bona fide indebtedness (within the meaning of paragraph (a)(1) of this section), if any, shall be subject to adjustment under section 482, paragraph (a) of this section, and any other Internal Revenue Code section.

(ii) Second, the other Internal Revenue Code section shall be applied to the loan or advance to determine whether any amount other than stated interest is to be treated as interest, and if so, to determine such amount according to the provisions of such other Internal Revenue Code section.

(iii) Third, whether or not the other Internal Revenue Code section applies to adjust the amounts treated as interest under such loan or advance, section 482 and paragraph (a) of this section may then be applied by the district director to determine whether the rate of interest charged on the loan or advance, as adjusted by any other Code section, is greater or less than an arm's length rate of interest, and if so, to make appropriate allocations to reflect an arm's length rate of interest.

(iv) Fourth, section 482 and paragraphs (b) through (d) of this section and §§ 1.482-3 through 1.482-7, if applicable, may be applied by the district director to make any appropriate allocations, other than an interest rate adjustment, to reflect an arm's length transaction based upon the principal amount of the loan or advance and the interest rate as adjusted under paragraph (a)(3)(i), (ii) or (iii) of this section. For example, assume that two commonly controlled taxpayers enter into a deferred payment sale of tangible property and no interest is provided, and assume also that section 483 is applied to treat a portion of the stated sales price as interest, thereby reducing the stated sales price. If after this recharacterization of a portion of the stated sales price as interest, the recomputed sales price does not reflect an arm's length sales price under the principles of § 1.482-3, the district director may make other appropriate allocations (other than an interest rate adjustment) to reflect an arm's length sales price.

*(4) Examples.* The principles of paragraph (a)(3) of this section may be illustrated by the following examples:

*Example (1).* An individual, A, transfers $20,000 to a corporation controlled by A in exchange for the corporation's note which bears adequate stated interest. The district director recharacterizes the transaction as a contribution to the capital of the corporation in exchange for preferred stock. Under paragraph (a)(3)(i) of this section, § 1.482-2(a) does not apply to the transaction because there is no bona fide indebtedness.

*Example (2).* B, an individual, is an employee of Z corporation, and is also the controlling shareholder of Z. Z makes a term loan of $15,000 to B at a rate of interest that is less than the applicable Federal rate. In this instance the other operative Code section is section 7872. Under section 7872(b), the difference between the amount loaned and the present value of all payments due under the loan using a discount rate equal to 100 percent of the applicable Federal rate is treated as an amount of cash transferred from the corporation to B and the loan is treated as having original issue discount equal to such amount. Under paragraph (a)(3)(iii) of this section, section 482 and paragraph (a) of this section may also be applied by the district director to determine if the rate of interest charged on this $15,000 loan (100 percent of the AFR, compounded semiannually, as adjusted by section 7872) is an arm's length rate of interest. Because the rate of interest on the loan, as adjusted by section 7872, is within the safe haven range of 100-130 percent of the AFR, compounded semiannually, no further interest rate adjustments under section 482 and paragraph (a) of this section will be made to this loan.

*Example (3).* The facts are the same as in Example 2 except that the amount lent by Z to B is $9,000, and that amount is the aggregate outstanding amount of loans between Z and B. Under the $10,000 de minimis exception of section 7872(c)(3), no adjustment for interest will be made to this $9,000 loan under section 7872. Under paragraph (a)(3)(iii) of this section, the district director may apply section 482 and paragraph (a) of this section to this $9,000 loan to determine whether the rate of interest charged is less than an arm's length rate of interest, and if so, to make appropriate allocations to reflect an arm's length rate of interest.

*Example (4).* X and Y are commonly controlled taxpayers. At a time when the applicable Federal rate is 12 percent, compounded semiannually, X sells property to Y in exchange for a note with a stated rate of interest of 18 percent, compounded semiannually. Assume that the other applicable Code section to the transaction is section 483. Section 483 does not apply to this transaction because, under section 483(d), there is no total unstated interest under the contract using the test rate of interest equal to 100 percent of the applicable Federal rate. Under paragraph (a)(3)(iii) of this section, section 482 and paragraph (a) of this section may be applied by the district director to determine whether the rate of interest under the note is excessive, that is, to determine whether the 18 percent stated interest rate under the note exceeds an arm's length rate of interest.

*Example (5).* Assume that A and B are commonly controlled taxpayers and that the applicable Federal rate is 10 percent, compounded semiannually. On June 30, 1986, A sells property to B and receives in exchange B's purchase-money note in the amount of $2,000,000. The stated interest rate on the note is 9%, compounded semiannually, and the stated redemption price at maturity on the note is $2,000,000. Assume that the other applicable Code section to this transaction is section 1274. As provided in section

1274A(a) and (b), the discount rate for purposes of section 1274 will be nine percent, compounded semiannually, because the stated principal amount of B's note does not exceed $2,800,000. Section 1274 does not apply to this transaction because there is adequate stated interest on the debt instrument using a discount rate equal to 9%, compounded semiannually, and the stated redemption price at maturity does not exceed the stated principal amount. Under paragraph (a)(3)(iii) of this section, the district director may apply section 482 and paragraph (a) of this section to this $2,000,000 note to determine whether the 9% rate of interest charged is less than an arm's length rate of interest, and if so, to make appropriate allocations to reflect an arm's length rate of interest.

**(b) Rendering of services.** For rules governing allocations under section 482 to reflect an arm's length charge for controlled transactions involving the rendering of services, see § 1.482-9.

**(c) Use of tangible property.** *(1) General rule.* Where possession, use, or occupancy of tangible property owned or leased by one member of a group of controlled entities (referred to in this paragraph as the owner) is transferred by lease or other arrangement to another member of such group (referred to in this paragraph as the user) without charge or at a charge which is not equal to an arm's length rental charge (as defined in paragraph (c)(2)(i) of this section) the district director may make appropriate allocations to properly reflect such arm's length charge. Where possession, use, or occupancy of only a portion of such property is transferred, the determination of the arm's length charge and the allocation shall be made with reference to the portion transferred.

*(2) Arm's length charge.* (i) In general. For purposes of paragraph (c) of this section, an arm's length rental charge shall be the amount of rent which was charged, or would have been charged for the use of the same or similar property, during the time it was in use, in independent transactions with or between unrelated parties under similar circumstances considering the period and location of the use, the owner's investment in the property or rent paid for the property, expenses of maintaining the property, the type of property involved, its condition, and all other relevant facts.

(ii) Safe haven rental charge. See § 1.482-2(c)(2)(ii) (26 CFR Part 1 revised as of April 1, 1985), for the determination of safe haven rental charges in the case of certain leases entered into before May 9, 1986, and for leases entered into before August 7, 1986, pursuant to a binding written contract entered into before May 9, 1986.

(iii) Subleases. (A) Except as provided in paragraph (c)(2)(iii)(B) of this section, where possession, use, or occupancy of tangible property, which is leased by the owner (lessee) from an unrelated party is transferred by sublease or other arrangement to the user, an arm's length rental charge shall be considered to be equal to all the deductions claimed by the owner (lessee) which are attributable to the property for the period such property is used by the user. Where only a portion of such property was transferred, any allocations shall be made with reference to the portion transferred. The deductions to be considered include the rent paid or accrued by the owner (lessee) during the period of use and all other deductions directly and indirectly connected with the property paid or accrued by the owner (lessee) during such period. Such deductions include deductions for maintenance and repair, utilities, management and other similar deductions.

(B) The provisions of paragraph (c)(2)(iii)(A) of this section shall not apply if either—

(1) The taxpayer establishes a more appropriate rental charge under the general rule set forth in paragraph (c)(2)(i) of this section; or

(2) During the taxable year, the owner (lessee) or the user was regularly engaged in the trade or business of renting property of the sane general type as the property in question to unrelated persons.

**(d) Transfer of property.** For rules governing allocations under section 482 to reflect an arm's length consideration for controlled transactions involving the transfer of property, see §§ 1.482-3 through 1.482-6.

**(e)** [Reserved]. For further guidance, see § 1.482-2T(e). 1.482-2T(e).

**(f) Effective/applicability date.** *(1) In general.* The provision of paragraph (b) of this section is generally applicable for taxable years beginning after July 31, 2009.

*(2) Election to apply regulation to earlier taxable years.* A person may elect to apply the provisions of paragraph (b) of this section to earlier taxable years in accordance with the rules set forth in § 1.482-9(n)(2).

---

T.D. 8552, 7/1/94, amend T.D. 9278, 7/31/2006, T.D. 9456, 7/31/2009.

---

PAR. 5. Section 1.482-2 is amended as follows:

1. Paragraph (e) is redesignated as paragraph (f) and newly-designated paragraphs (f)(1) and (f)(2) are revised.

2. New paragraph (e) is added.

The addition and revision reads as follows:

**Proposed § 1.482-2 Determination of taxable income in specific situations.** [*For Preamble, see ¶ 153,087*]

* * * * *

**(e)** [The text of proposed § 1.482-2(e) is the same as the text of § 1.482-2T(e) published elsewhere in this issue of the Federal Register]. [*See T.D. 9441, 01/05/2009, 74 Fed. Reg. 2.*].

**(f)** * * * *(1)* [The text of the proposed amendment to § 1.482-2(f)(1) is the same as the text of § 1.482-2T(f)(1) published elsewhere in this issue of the Federal Register]. [*See T.D. 9441, 01/05/2009, 74 Fed. Reg. 2.*].

*(2)* [The text of the proposed amendment to § 1.482-2(f)(2) is the same as the text of § 1.482-2T(f)(2) published elsewhere in this issue of the Federal Register]. [*See T.D. 9441, 01/05/2009, 74 Fed. Reg. 2.*].

* * * * *

PAR. 5. Section 1.482-2 is amended as follows:

1. In paragraph (a)(3)(iv), revise the first sentence.

2. Revise paragraph (d).

The revisions read as follows:

**Proposed § 1.482-2 Determination of taxable income in specific situations.** [*For Preamble, see ¶ 151,855*]

**(a)** * * *

*(3)* * * *

(iv) Fourth, section 482 and paragraphs (b) through (d) of this section and §§ 1.482-3 through 1.482-8, if applicable, may be applied by the district director to make any appropriate allocations, other than an interest rate adjustment, to reflect an arm's length transaction based upon the principal amount of the loan or advance and the interest rate as adjusted under paragraph (a)(3)(i), (ii), or (iii) of this section. * * *

* * * * *

**(d) Transfer of property.** For rules governing allocations under section 482 to reflect an arm's length consideration for controlled transactions involving the transfer of property, see §§ 1.482-3 through 1.482-6 and § 1.482-8.

**§ 1.482-2A Determination of taxable income in specific situations.**

**(a) -(c)** For applicable rules, see § 1.482-2T(a) through (c).

**(d) Transfer or use of intangible property.** *(1) In general.* (i) Except as otherwise provided in subparagraph (4) of this paragraph, where intangible property or an interest therein is transferred, sold, assigned, loaned, or otherwise made available in any manner by one member of a group of controlled entities (referred to in this paragraph as the transferor) to another member of the group (referred to in this paragraph as the transferor) to another member of the group (referred to in this paragraph as the transferee) for other than an arm's length consideration, the district director may make appropriate allocations to reflect an arm's length consideration for such property or its use. Subparagraph (2) of this paragraph provides rules for determining the form an amount of an appropriate allocation, subparagraph (3) of this paragraph provides a definition of "intangible property", and subparagraph (4) of this paragraph provides rules with respect to certain cost-sharing arrangements in connection with the development of intangible property. For purposes of this paragraph, an interest in intangible property may take the form of the right to use such property.

(ii) (a) In the absence of a bona fide cost-sharing arrangement (as defined in subparagraph (4) of this paragraph), where one member of a group of related entities undertakes the development of intangible property as a developer within the meaning of (c) of this subdivision, no allocation with respect to such development activity shall be made under the rules of this paragraph or any other paragraph of this section (except as provided in (b) of this subdivision until such time as any property developed, or any interest therein, is or is deemed to be transferred, sold, assigned, loaned, or otherwise made available in any manner by the developer to a related entity in a transfer subject to the rules of this paragraph. Where a member of the group other than the developer acquires an interest in the property developed by virtue of obtaining a patent or copyright, or by any other means, the developer shall be deemed to have transferred such interest in such property to the acquiring member in a transaction subject to the rules of this paragraph. For example, if one member of a group (the developer) undertakes to develop a new patentable product and the costs of development are incurred by that entity over a period of 3 years, no allocation with respect to that entity's activity shall be made during such period. The amount of any allocation that may be appropriate at the expiration of such development period when, for example, the patent on the product is transferred, or deemed transferred, to a related entity for other than an arm's length consideration, shall be determined in accordance with the rules of this paragraph.

(b) Where one member of a group renders assistance in the form of loans, services, or the use of tangible or intangible property to a developer in connection with an attempt to develop intangible property, the amount of any allocation that may be appropriate with respect to such assistance shall be determined in accordance with the rules of the appropriate paragraph or paragraphs of this section. Thus, where one entity allows a related entity, which is the developer, to use tangible property, such as laboratory equipment, in connection with the development of intangible property, the amount of any allocation that may be appropriate with respect to such use shall be determined in accordance with the rules of paragraph (c) of this section. In the event that the district director does not exercise his discretion to make allocations with respect to the assistance rendered to the developer, the value of the assistance shall be allowed as a set-off against any allocation that the district director may make under this paragraph as a result of the transfer of the intangible property to the entity rendering the assistance.

(c) The determination as to which member of a group of related entities is a developer and which members of the group are rendering assistance to the developer in connection with its development activities shall be based upon all the facts and circumstances of the individual case. Of all the facts and circumstances to be taken into account in making this determination, greatest weight shall be given to the relative amounts of all the direct and indirect costs of development and the corresponding risks of development borne by the various members of the group, and the relative values of the use of any intangible property of members of the group which is made available without adequate consideration for use in connection with the development activity, which property is likely to contribute to a substantial extent in the production of intangible property. For this purpose, the risk to be borne with respect to development activity is the possibility that such activity will not result in the production of intangible property or that the intangible property produced will not be of sufficient value to allow for the recovery of the costs of developing it. A member will not be considered to have borne the costs and corresponding risks of development unless such member is committed to bearing such costs in advance of, or contemporaneously with, their incurrence and without regard to the success of the project. Other factors that may be relevant in determining which member of the group is the developer include the location of the development activity, the capabilities of the various members to carry on the project independently, and the degree of control over the project exercised by the various members.

(d) The principles of this subdivision (ii) may be illustrated by the following examples in which it is assumed that X and Y are corporate members of the same group:

*Example (1).* X, at the request of Y, undertakes to develop a new machine which will function effectively in the climate in which Y's factory is located. Y agrees to bear all the direct and indirect costs of the project whether or not X successfully develops the machine. Assume that X does not make any of its own intangible property available for use in connection with the project. The machine is successfully developed and Y obtains possession of the intangible property necessary to produce such machine. Based on the facts and circumstances as stated, Y shall be considered to be the developer of the intangible property and, therefore, Y shall not be treated as having obtained the property in a transfer subject to the rules of this paragraph. Any amount which may be allocable with respect to the assistance rendered by X shall be determined in accordance with the rules of *(b)* of this subdivision.

*Example (2).* Assume the same facts as in example (1) except that Y agrees to reimburse X for its costs only in the event that the property is successfully developed. In such case X is the developer and Y is deemed to have received the property in a transfer subject to the rules of this paragraph. Therefore, the district director may make an allocation to reflect an arm's length consideration for such property.

*Example (3).* In 1967 X undertakes to develop product M in its research and development department. X incurs direct and indirect costs of $1 million per year in connection with the project in 1967, 1968, and 1969. In connection with the project, X employs the formula for compound N, which it owns, and which is likely to contribute substantially to the success of the project. The value of the use of the formula for compound N in connection with this project is $750,000. In 1968, 4 chemists employed by Y spend 6 months working on the project in X's laboratory. The salary and other expenses connected with the chemists' employment for that period ($100,000) are paid by Y, for which no charge is made to X. In 1969, product M is perfected and Y obtains patents thereon. X is considered to be the developer of product M since, among other things, it bore the greatest relative share of the costs and risks incurred in connection with this project and made available intangible property (formula for compound N) which was likely to contribute substantially in the development of product M. Accordingly, no allocation with respect to X's development activity should be made before 1969. The property is deemed to have been transferred to Y at that time by virtue of the fact that Y obtained the patent rights to product M. In such case the district director may make an allocation to reflect an arm's length consideration for such transfer. In the event that the district director makes such an allocation and he has not made or does not make an allocation for 1968 with respect to the services of the chemists in accordance with the principles of paragraph (b) of this section, the value of the assistance shall be allowed as a setoff against the amount of the allocation reflecting an arm's length consideration for the transfer of the intangible property.

*(2) Arm's length consideration.* (i) An arm's length consideration shall be in a form which is consistent with the form which would be adopted in transactions between unrelated parties under the same circumstances. To the extent appropriate, an arm's length consideration may take any one or more of the following forms: (a) Royalties based on the transferee's output, sales, profits, or any other measure; (b) lump-sum payments; or (c) any other form, including reciprocal licensing rights, which might reasonably have been adopted by unrelated parties under the circumstances, provided that the parties can establish that such form was adopted pursuant to an arrangement which in fact existed between them. However, where the transferee pays nominal or no consideration for the property or interest therein and where the transferor has retained a substantial interest in the property, an allocation shall be presumed not to take the form of a lump-sum payment.

(ii) In determining the amount of an arm's length consideration, the standard to be applied is the amount that would have been paid by an unrelated party for the same intangible property under the same circumstances. Where there have been transfers by the transferor to unrelated parties involving the same or similar intangible property under the same or similar circumstances the amount of the consideration for such transfers shall generally be the best indication of an arm's length consideration.

(iii) Where a sufficiently similar transaction involving an unrelated party cannot be found, the following factors, to the extent appropriate (depending upon the type of intangible property and the form of the transfer), may be considered in arriving at the amount of the arm's length consideration:

(a) The prevailing rates in the same industry or for similar property,

(b) The offers of competing transferors or the bids of competing transferees,

(c) The terms of the transfer, including limitations on the geographic area covered and the exclusive or nonexclusive character of any rights granted,

(d) The uniqueness of the property and the period for which it is likely to remain unique,

(e) The degree and duration of protection afforded to the property under the laws of the relevant countries,

(f) Value of services rendered by the transferor to the transferee in connection with the transfer within the meaning of paragraph (b)(8) of this section,

(g) Prospective profits to be realized or costs to be saved by the transferee through its use or subsequent transfer of the property,

(h) The capital investment and starting up expenses required of the transferee,

(i) The next subdivision is (j),

(j) The availability of substitutes for the property transferred,

(k) The arm's length rates and prices paid by unrelated parties where the property is resold or sublicensed to such parties,

(l) The costs incurred by the transferor in developing the property, and

(m) Any other fact or circumstance which unrelated parties would have been likely to consider in determining the amount of an arm's length consideration for the property.

*(3) Definition of intangible property.* (i) Solely for the purposes of this section, intangible property shall consist of the items described in subdivision (ii) of this subparagraph, provided that such items have substantial value independent of the services of individual persons.

(ii) The items referred to in subdivision (i) of this subparagraph are as follows:

(a) Patents, inventions, formulas, processes, designs, patterns, and other similar items;

(b) Copyrights, literary, musical, or artistic compositions, and other similar items;

(c) Trademarks, trade names, brand names, and other similar items;

(d) Franchises, licenses, contracts, and other similar items;

(e) Methods, programs, systems, procedures, campaigns, surveys, studies, forecasts, estimates, customer lists, technical data, and other similar items.

*(4) Sharing of costs and risks.* Where a member of a group of controlled entities acquires an interest in intangible property as a participating party in a bona fide cost sharing arrangement with respect to the development of such intangible property, the district director shall not make allocations with respect to such acquisition except as may be appropriate to reflect each participant's arm's length share of the costs and risks of developing the property. A bona fide cost sharing arrangement is an agreement, in writing, between two or more members of a group of controlled entities providing for the sharing of the costs and risks of developing intangible property in return for a specified interest in the intangible property that may be produced. In order for the ar-

rangement to qualify as a bona fide arrangement, it must reflect an effort in good faith by the participating members to bear their respective shares of all the costs and risks of development on an arm's length basis. In order for the sharing of costs and risks to be considered on an arm's length basis, the terms and conditions must be comparable to those which would have been adopted by unrelated parties similarly situated had they entered into such an arrangement. If an oral cost sharing arrangement entered into prior to April 16, 1968, and continued in effect after that date, is otherwise in compliance with the standards prescribed in this subparagraph, it shall constitute a bona fide cost sharing arrangement if it is reduced to writing prior to January 1, 1969.

**(e) Sales of tangible property.** *(1) In general.* (i) Where one member of a group of controlled entities (referred to in this paragraph as the "seller") sells or otherwise disposes of tangible property to another member of such group (referred to in this paragraph as the "buyer") at other than an arm's length price (such a sale being referred to in this paragraph as a "controlled sale"), the district director may make appropriate allocations between the seller and the buyer to reflect an arm's length price for such sale or disposition. An arm's length price is the price that an unrelated party would have paid under the same circumstances for the property involved in the controlled sale. Since unrelated parties normally sell products at a profit, an arm's length price normally involves a profit to the seller.

(ii) Subparagraphs (2), (3), and (4) of this paragraph describe three methods of determining an arm's-length price and the standards for applying each method. They are, respectively, the comparable uncontrolled price method, the resale price method, and the cost-plus method. In addition, a special rule is provided in subdivision (v) of this subparagraph for use (notwithstanding any other provision of this subdivision) in determining an arm's-length price for an ore or mineral. If there are comparable uncontrolled sales as defined in subparagraph (2) of this paragraph, the comparable uncontrolled price method must be utilized because it is the method likely to result in the most accurate estimate of an arm's-length price (for the reason that it is based upon the price actually paid by unrelated parties for the same or similar products). If there are no comparable uncontrolled sales, then the resale price method must be utilized if the standards for its application are met because it is the method likely to result in the next most accurate estimate in such instances (for the reason that, in such instances, the arm's-length price determined under such method is based more directly upon actual arm's-length transactions than is the cost plus method). A typical situation where the resale price method may be required is where a manufacturer sells products to a related distributor which, without further processing, resells the products in uncontrolled transactions. If all the standards for the mandatory application of the resale price method are not satisfied, then, as provided in subparagraph (3)(iii) of this paragraph, either that method or the cost-plus method may be used, depending upon which method is more feasible and is likely to result in a more accurate estimate of an arm's-length price. A typical situation where the cost-plus method may be appropriate is where a manufacturer sells products to a related entity which performs substantial manufacturing, assembly, or other processing of the product or adds significant value by reason of its utilization of its intangible property prior to resale in uncontrolled transactions.

(iii) Where the standards for applying one of the three methods of pricing described in subdivision (ii) of this subparagraph are met, such method must, for the purposes of this paragraph, be utilized unless the taxpayer can establish that, considering all the facts and circumstances, some method of pricing other than those described in subdivision (ii) of this subparagraph is clearly more appropriate. Where none of the three methods of pricing described in subdivision (ii) of this subparagraph can reasonably be applied under the facts and circumstances as they exist in a particular case, some appropriate method of pricing other than those described in subdivision (ii) of this subparagraph, or variations on such methods, can be used.

(iv) The methods of determining arm's length prices described in this section are stated in terms of their application to individual sales of property. However, because of the possibility that a taxpayer may make controlled sales of many different products, or many separate sales of the same product, it may be impractical to analyze every sale for the purposes of determining the arm's length price. It is therefore permissible to determine or verify arm's length prices by applying the appropriate methods of pricing to product lines or other groupings where it is impractical to ascertain an arm's length price for each product or sale. In addition, the district director may determine or verify the arm's length price of all sales to a related entity by employing reasonable statistical sampling techniques.

(v) The price for a mineral product which is sold at the stage at which mining or extraction ends shall be determined under the provisions of §§ 1.613-3 and 1.613-4.

*(2) Comparable uncontrolled price method.* (i) Under the method of pricing described as the "comparable uncontrolled price method", the arm's length price of a controlled sale is equal to the price paid in comparable uncontrolled sales, adjusted as provided in subdivision (ii) of this subparagraph.

(ii) "Uncontrolled sales" are sales in which the seller and the buyer are not members of the same controlled group. These include (a) sales made to a member of the controlled group to an unrelated party, (b) sales made to a member of the controlled group by an unrelated party, and (c) sales made in which the parties are not members of the controlled group and are not related to each other. However, uncontrolled sales do not include sales at unrealistic prices, as for example where a member makes uncontrolled sales in small quantities at a price designed to justify a non-arm's length price on a large volume of controlled sales. Uncontrolled sales are considered comparable to controlled sales if the physical property and circumstances involved in the uncontrolled sales are identical to the physical property and circumstances involved in the controlled sales, or if such properties and circumstances are so nearly identical that any differences either have no effect on price, or such differences can be reflected by a reasonable number of adjustments to the price of uncontrolled sales. For this purpose, differences can be reflected by adjusting prices only where such differences have a definite and reasonably ascertainable effect on price. If the differences can be reflected by such adjustment, then the price of the uncontrolled sale as adjusted constitutes the comparable uncontrolled sale price. Some of the differences which may affect the price of property are differences in the quality of the product, terms of sale, intangible property associated with the sale, time of sale, and the level of the market and the geographic market in which the sale takes place. Whether and to what extent differences in the various properties and circumstances affect price, and whether differences render sales noncomparable, depends upon the particular circumstances and property involved. The principles of this subdivision may be illustrated by the following examples, in each of which it is assumed that X makes both controlled and uncontrolled sales of the identical property:

*Example (1).* Assume that the circumstances surrounding the controlled and the uncontrolled sales are identical, except for the fact that the controlled sales price is a delivered price and the uncontrolled sales are made f.o.b. X's factory. Since differences in terms of transportation and insurance generally have a definite and reasonably ascertainable effect on price, such differences do not normally render the uncontrolled sales noncomparable to the controlled sales.

*Example (2).* Assume that the circumstances surrounding the controlled and uncontrolled sales are identical, except for the fact that X affixes its valuable trademark in the controlled sales, and does not affix its trademark in uncontrolled sales. Since the effects on price of differences in intangible property associated with the sale of tangible property, such as trademarks, are normally not reasonably ascertainable, such differences would normally render the uncontrolled sales noncomparable.

*Example (3).* Assume that the circumstances surrounding the controlled and uncontrolled sales are identical except for the fact that X, a manufacturer of business machines, makes certain minor modifications in the physical properties of the machines to satisfy safety specifications or other specific requirements of a customer in controlled sales, and does not make these modifications in uncontrolled sales. Since minor physical differences in the product generally have a definite and reasonably ascertainable effect on prices, such differences do not normally render the uncontrolled sales noncomparable to the controlled sales.

(iii) Where there are two or more comparable uncontrolled sales susceptible of adjustment as defined in subdivision (ii) of this subparagraph, the comparable uncontrolled sale or sales requiring the fewest and simplest adjustments provided in subdivision (ii) of this subparagraph should generally be selected. Thus, for example, if a taxpayer makes comparable uncontrolled sales of a particular product which differ from the controlled sale only with respect to the terms of delivery, and makes other comparable uncontrolled sales of the product which differ from the controlled sale with respect to both terms of delivery and terms of payment, the comparable uncontrolled sales differing only with respect to terms of delivery should be selected as the comparable uncontrolled sale.

(iv) One of the circumstances which may affect the price of property is the fact that the seller may desire to make sales at less than a normal profit for the primary purpose of establishing or maintaining a market for his products. Thus, a seller may be willing to reduce the price of a product, for a time, in order to introduce his product into an area or in order to meet competition. However, controlled sales may be priced in such a manner only if such price would have been charged in an uncontrolled sale under comparable circumstances. Such fact may be demonstrated by showing that the buyer in the controlled sale made corresponding reductions in the resale price to uncontrolled purchasers, or that such buyer engaged in substantially greater sales promotion activities with respect to the product involved in the controlled sale than with respect to other products. For example, assume X, a manufacturer of batteries, commences to sell car batteries to Y, a subsidiary of X; for resale in a new market. In its existing markets X's batteries sell to independent retailers at $20 per unit, and X sells them to wholesalers at $17 per unit. Y also sells X's batteries to independent retailers at $20 per unit. X's batteries are not known in the new market in which Y is operating. In order to engage competitively in the new market Y incurs selling and advertising costs substantially higher than those incurred for its sales of other products. Under these circumstances X may sell to Y, for a time, at less than $17 to take into account the increased selling and advertising activities of Y in penetrating and establishing the new market. This may be done even though it may result in a transfer price from X to Y which is below X's full costs of manufacturing the product.

*(3) Resale price method.* (i) Under the pricing method described as the "resale price method", the arm's length price of a controlled sale is equal to the applicable resale price (as defined in subdivision (iv) or (v) of this subparagraph), reduced by an appropriate markup, and adjusted as provided in subdivision (ix) of this subparagraph. An appropriate markup is computed by multiplying the applicable resale price by the appropriate markup percentage as defined in subdivision (vi) of this subparagraph. Thus, where one member of a group of controlled entities sells property to another member which resells the property in uncontrolled sales, if the applicable resale price of the property involved in the uncontrolled sale is $100 and the appropriate markup percentage for resales by the buyer is 20 percent, the arm's length price of the controlled sale is $80 ($100 minus 20 percent × $100), adjusted as provided in subdivision (ix) of this subparagraph.

(ii) The resale price method must be used to compute an arm's length price of a controlled sale if all the following circumstances exist:

(a) There are no comparable uncontrolled sales as defined in subparagraph (2) of this paragraph.

(b) An applicable resale price, as defined in subdivision (iv), or (v) of this subparagraph, is available with respect to resales made within a reasonable time before or after the time of the controlled sale.

(c) The buyer (reseller) has not added more than an insubstantial amount to the value of the property by physically altering the product before resale. For this purpose packaging, repacking, labeling, or minor assembly of property does not constitute physical alteration.

(d) The buyer (reseller) has not added more than an insubstantial amount to the value of the property by the use of intangible property. See § 1.482-2(d)(3) for the definition of intangible property.

(iii) Notwithstanding the fact that one or both of the requirements of subdivision (ii)(c) or (d) of this subparagraph may not be met, the resale price method may be used if such method is more feasible and is likely to result in a more accurate determination of an arm's length price than the use of the cost plus method. Thus, even though one of the requirements of such subdivision is not satisfied, the resale price method may nevertheless be more appropriate than the cost plus method because computations and evaluations required under the former method may be fewer and easier to make than under the latter method. In general, the resale price method is more appropriate when the functions performed by the seller are more extensive and more difficult to evaluate than the functions performed by the buyer (reseller). The principle of this subdivision may be illustrated by the following examples in each of which it is assumed that corporation X developed a valuable patent covering product M which it manufactures and sells to corporation Y in a controlled sale, and for which there is no comparable uncontrolled sale:

*Example (1).* Corporation Y adds a component to product M and resells the assembled product in an uncontrolled sale within a reasonable time after the controlled sale of product M. Assume further that the addition of the component added more than an insubstantial amount to the value of product M, but that Y's function in purchasing the component and assembling the product prior to sale was subject to reasonably precise valuation. Although the controlled sale and resale does not meet the requirements of subdivision (ii)(c) of this subparagraph, the resale price method may be used under the circumstances because that method involves computations and evaluations which are fewer and easier to make than under the cost plus method. This is because X's use of a patent may be more difficult to evaluate in determining an appropriate gross profit percentage under the cost plus method, than is evaluation of Y's assembling function in determining the appropriate markup percentage under the resale price method.

*Example (2).* Corporation Y resells product M in an uncontrolled sale within a reasonable time after the controlled sale after attaching its valuable trademark to it. Assume further that it can be demonstrated through comparison with other uncontrolled sales of Y that the addition of Y's trademark to a product usually adds 25 percent to the markup on its sales. On the other hand, the effect of X's use of its patent is difficult to evaluate in applying the cost plus method because no reasonable standard of comparison is available. Although the controlled sale and resale does not meet the requirements of subdivision (ii)(d) of this subparagraph, the resale price method may be used because that method involves computations and evaluations which are fewer and easier to make than under the cost plus method. This is because, under the circumstances, X's use of a patent is more difficult to evaluate in determining an appropriate gross profit percentage under the cost plus method, than is evaluation of the use of Y's trademark in determining the appropriate markup percentage under the resale price method.

(iv) For the purposes of this subparagraph the "applicable resale price" is the price at which it is anticipated that property purchased in the controlled sale will be resold by the buyer in an uncontrolled sale. The "applicable resale price" will generally be equal to either the price at which current resales of the same property are being made or the resale price of the particular item of property involved.

(v) Where the property purchased in the controlled sale is resold in another controlled sale, the "applicable resale price" is the price at which such property is finally resold in an uncontrolled sale, providing that the series of sales as a whole meets all the requirements of subdivision (ii) of this subparagraph or that the resale price method is used pursuant to subdivision (iii) of this subparagraph. In such case, the determination of the appropriate markup percentage shall take into account the function or functions performed by all members of the group participating in the series of sales and resales. Thus, if X sells a product to Y in a controlled sale, Y sells the product to Z in a controlled sale, and Z sells the product in an uncontrolled sale, the resale price method must be used if Y and Z together have not added more than an insubstantial amount to the value of the product through physical alteration or the application of intangible property, and the final resale occurs within a reasonable time of the sale from X to Y. In such case, the applicable resale price is the price at which Z sells the product in the uncontrolled sale, and the appropriate markup percentage shall take into account the functions performed by both Y and Z.

(vi) For the purposes of this subparagraph, the appropriate markup percentage is equal to the percentage of gross profit (expressed as a percentage of sales) earned by the buyer (reseller) or another party on the resale of property which is both purchased and resold in an uncontrolled transaction, which resale is most similar to the applicable resale of the property involved in the controlled sale. The following are the most important characteristics to be considered in determining the similarity of resales:

(a) The type of property involved in the sales. For example: machine tools, men's furnishings, small household appliances.

(b) The functions performed by the reseller with respect to the property. For example: packaging, labeling, delivering, maintenance of inventory, minor assembly, advertising, selling at wholesale, selling at retail, billing, maintenance of accounts receivable, and servicing.

(c) The effect on price of any intangible property utilized by the reseller in connection with the property resold. For example: patents, trademarks, trade names.

(d) The geographic market in which the functions are performed by the reseller.

In general, the similarity to be sought relates to the probable effect upon the markup percentage of any differences in such characteristics between the uncontrolled purchases and resales on the one hand and the controlled purchases and resales on the other hand. Thus, close physical similarity of the property involved in the sales compared is not required under the resale price method since a lack of close physical similarity is not necessarily indicative of dissimilar markup percentages.

(vii) Whenever possible, markup percentages should be derived from uncontrolled purchases and resales of the buyer (reseller) involved in the controlled sale, because similar characteristics are more likely to be found among different resales of property made by the same reseller than among sales made by other resellers. In the absence of resales by the same buyer (reseller) which meet the standards of subdivision (vi) of this subparagraph, evidence of an appropriate markup percentage may be derived from resales by other resellers selling in the same or a similar market in which the controlled buyer (reseller) is selling, providing such resellers perform comparable functions. Where the function performed by the reseller is similar to the function performed by a sales agent which does not take title, such sales agent will be considered a reseller for the purpose of determining an appropriate markup percentage under this subparagraph and the commission earned by such sales agent, expressed as a percentage of the sales price of the goods, may constitute the appropriate markup percentage. If the controlled buyer (reseller) is located in a foreign country and information on resales by other resellers in the same foreign market is not available, then markup percentages earned by United States resellers performing comparable functions may be used. In the absence of data on markup percentages of particular sales or groups of sales, the prevailing markup percentage in the particular industry involved may be appropriate.

(viii) In calculating the markup percentage earned on uncontrolled purchases and resales, and in applying such percentage to the applicable resale price to determine the appropriate markup, the same elements which enter into the computation of the sales price and the costs of goods sold of the property involved in the comparable uncontrolled purchases and resales should enter into such computation in the case of the property involved in the controlled purchases and resales. Thus, if freight-in and packaging expense are elements of the cost of goods sold in comparable uncontrolled purchases, then such elements should also be taken into account in computing the cost of goods sold of the controlled purchase. Similarly, if the comparable markup percentage is based upon net sales (after reduction for returns and allowances) of uncontrolled resellers, such percentage must be applied to net sales of the buyer (reseller).

(ix) In determining an arm's length price appropriate adjustment must be made to reflect any material differences between the uncontrolled purchases and resales used as the basis for the calculation of the appropriate markup percentage and the resale of property involved in the controlled sale. The differences referred to in this subdivision are those differences in functions or circumstances which have a definite and reasonably ascertainable effect on price. The principles of this subdivision may be illustrated by the following example:

*Example.* Assume that X and Y are members of the same group of controlled entities and that Y purchases electric mixers from X and electric toasters from uncontrolled entities. Y performs substantially similar functions with respect to resales of both the mixers and the toasters, except that it does not warrant the toasters, but does provide a 90-day warranty for the mixers. Y normally earns a gross profit on toasters of 20 percent of gross selling price. The 20-percent gross profit on the resale of toasters is an appropriate markup percentage, but the price of the controlled sale computed with reference to such rate must be adjusted to reflect the difference in terms (the warranty).

*(4) Cost plus method.* (i) Under the pricing method described as the "cost plus method," the arm's length price of a controlled sale of property shall be computed by adding to the cost of producing such property (as computed in subdivision (ii) of this subparagraph), an amount which is equal to such cost multiplied by the appropriate gross profit percentage (as computed in subdivision (iii) of this subparagraph), plus or minus any adjustments as provided in subdivision (v) of this subparagraph.

(ii) For the purposes of this subparagraph, the cost of producing the property involved in the controlled sale, and the costs which enter into the computation of the appropriate gross profit percentage shall be computed in a consistent manner in accordance for allocating or apportioning costs, which neither favors nor burdens controlled sales in comparison with uncontrolled sales. Thus, if the costs used in computing the appropriate gross profit percentage are comprised of the full cost of goods sold, including direct and indirect costs, then the cost of producing the property involved in the controlled sales must be comprised of the full cost of goods sold, including direct and indirect costs. On the other hand, if the costs used in computing the appropriate gross profit percentage are comprised only of direct costs, the cost of producing the property involved in the controlled sale must be comprised only of direct costs. The term "cost of producing," as used in this subparagraph, includes the cost of acquiring property which is held for resale.

(iii) For the purposes of this subparagraph, the appropriate gross profit percentages is equal to the gross profit percentage (expressed as a percentage of cost) earned by the seller or another party on the uncontrolled sale or sales of property which are most similar to the controlled sale in question. The following are the most important characteristics to be considered in determining the similarity of the uncontrolled sale or sales:

(a) The type of property involved in the sales. For example: machine tools, men's furnishings, small household appliances.

(b) The functions performed by the seller with respect to the property sold. For example: contract manufacturing, product assembly, selling activity, processing, servicing, delivering.

(c) The effect of any intangible property used by the seller in connection with the property sold. For example: patents, trademarks, trade names.

(d) The geographic market in which the functions are performed by the seller.

In general, the similarity to be sought relates to the probable effect upon the margin of gross profit of any differences in such characteristics between the uncontrolled sales and the controlled sale. Thus, close physical similarity of the property involved in the sales compared is not required under the cost plus method since a lack of close physical similarity is not necessarily indicative of dissimilar profit margins. See subparagraph (2)(iv) of this paragraph, relating to sales made at less than a normal profit for the primary purpose of establishing or maintaining a market.

(iv) Whenever possible, gross profit percentages should be derived from uncontrolled sales made by the seller involved in the controlled sale, because similar characteristics are more likely to be found among sales of property made by the same seller than among sales made by other sellers. In the absence of such sales, evidence of an appropriate gross profit percentage may be derived from similar uncontrolled sales by other sellers whether or not such sellers are members of the controlled group. Where the function performed by the seller is similar to the function performed by a purchasing agent which does not take title, such purchasing agent will be considered a seller for the purpose of determining an appropriate gross profit percentage under this subparagraph and the commission earned by such purchasing agent, expressed as a percentage of the purchase price of the goods, may constitute the appropriate gross profit percentage. In the absence of data on gross profit percentages of particular sales or groups of sales which are similar to the controlled sale, the prevailing gross profit percentages in the particular industry involved may be appropriate.

(v) Where the most similar sale or sales from which the appropriate gross profit percentage is derived differ in any material respect from the controlled sale, the arm's length price which is computed by applying such percentage must be adjusted to reflect such differences to the extent such differences would warrant an adjustment of price in uncontrolled transactions. The differences referred to in this subdivision are those differences which have a definite and reasonably ascertainable effect on price.

T.D. 6952, 4/15/68, amend T.D. 6964, 7/24/68, T.D. 6998, 1/17/69, T.D. 7170, 3/10/72, T.D. 7394, 12/31/75, T.D. 7747, 12/29/80, T.D. 7781, 7/1/81, T.D. 7920, 11/2/83, T.D. 8204, 5/20/88, T.D. 8470, 1/13/93.

### § 1.482-2T Determination of taxable income in specific situations (temporary).

**(a)** through (d) [Reserved[. For further guidance, see § 1.482-2(a) through (d).

**(e) Cost sharing arrangement.** For rules governing allocations under section 482 to reflect an arm's length consideration for controlled transactions involving a cost sharing arrangement, see § 1.482-7T.

**(f) Effective/applicability date.** *(1) In general.* The provision of paragraph (e) of this section is generally applicable on January 5, 2009.

*(2)* [Reserved[. For further guidance, see § 1.482-2(f)(2).

*(3) Expiration date.* The applicability of paragraph (e) of this section expires on or before December 30, 2011.

T.D. 9278, 7/31/2006, amend T.D. 9441, 12/31/2008, T.D. 9456, 7/31/2009.

## § 1.482-3 Methods to determine taxable income in connection with a transfer of tangible property.

**(a) In general.** The arm's length amount charged in a controlled transfer of tangible property must be determined under one of the six methods listed in this paragraph (a). Each of the methods must be applied in accordance with all of the provisions of § 1.482-1, including the best method rule of § 1.482-1(c), the comparability analysis of § 1.482-1(d), and the arm's length range of § 1.482-1(e). The methods are—

*(1)* The comparable uncontrolled price method, described in paragraph (b) of this section;

*(2)* The resale price method, described in paragraph (c) of this section;

*(3)* The cost plus method, described in paragraph (d) of this section;

*(4)* The comparable profits method, described in § 1.482-5;

*(5)* The profit split method, described in § 1.482-6; and

*(6)* unspecified methods, described in paragraph (e) of this section.

**(b) Comparable uncontrolled price method.** *(1) In general.* The comparable uncontrolled price method evaluates whether the amount charged in a controlled transaction is arm's length by reference to the amount charged in a comparable uncontrolled transaction.

*(2) Comparability and reliability considerations.* (i) In general. Whether results derived from applications of this method are the most reliable measure of the arm's length result must be determined using the factors described under the best method rule in § 1.482-1(c). The application of these factors under the comparable uncontrolled price method is discussed in paragraph (b)(2)(ii) and (iii) of this section.

(ii) Comparability. (A) In general. The degree of comparability between controlled and uncontrolled transactions is determined by applying the provisions of § 1.482-1(d). Although all of the factors described in § 1.482-1(d)(3) must be considered, similarity of products generally will have the greatest effect on comparability under this method. In addition, because even minor differences in contractual terms or economic conditions could materially affect the amount charged in an uncontrolled transaction, comparability under this method depends on close similarity with respect to these factors, or adjustments to account for any differences. The results derived from applying the comparable uncontrolled price method generally will be the most direct and reliable measure of an arm's length price for the controlled transaction if an uncontrolled transaction has no differences with the controlled transaction that would affect the price, or if there are only minor differences that have a definite and reasonably ascertainable effect on price and for which appropriate adjustments are made. If such adjustments cannot be made, or if there are more than minor differences between the controlled and uncontrolled transactions, the comparable uncontrolled price method may be used, but the reliability of the results as a measure of the arm's length price will be reduced. Further, if there are material product differences for which reliable adjustments cannot be made, this method ordinarily will not provide a reliable measure of an arm's length result.

(B) Adjustments for differences between controlled and uncontrolled transactions. If there are differences between the controlled and uncontrolled transactions that would affect price, adjustments should be made to the price of the uncontrolled transaction according to the comparability provisions of § 1.482-1(d)(2). Specific examples of the factors that may be particularly relevant to this method include—

(1) Quality of the product;

(2) Contractual terms, (e.g., scope and terms of warranties provided, sales or purchase volume, credit terms, transport terms);

(3) Level of the market (i.e., wholesale, retail, etc.);

(4) Geographic market in which the transaction takes place;

(5) Date of the transaction;

(6) Intangible property associated with the sale;

(7) Foreign currency risks; and

(8) Alternatives realistically available to the buyer and seller.

(iii) Data and assumptions. The reliability of the results derived from the comparable uncontrolled price method is affected by the completeness and accuracy of the data used and the reliability of the assumptions made to apply the method. See § 1.482-1(c) (Best method rule).

*(3) Arm's length range.* See § 1.482-1(e)(2) for the determination of an arm's length range.

*(4) Examples.* The principles of this paragraph (b) are illustrated by the following examples.

*Example (1).* Comparable sales of same product. USM, a U.S. manufacturer, sells the same product to both controlled and uncontrolled distributors. The circumstances surrounding the controlled and uncontrolled transactions are substantially the same, except that the controlled sales price is a delivered price and the uncontrolled sales are made f.o.b. USM's factory. Differences in the contractual terms of transportation and insurance generally have a definite and reasonably ascertainable effect on price, and adjustments are made to the results of the uncontrolled transaction to account for such differences. No other material difference has been identified between the controlled and uncontrolled transactions. Because USM sells in both the controlled and uncontrolled transactions, it is likely that all material differences between the two transactions have been identified. In addition, because the comparable uncontrolled price method is applied to an uncontrolled comparable with no product differences, and there are only minor contractual differences that have a definite and reasonably ascertainable effect on price, the results of this application of the comparable uncontrolled price method will provide the most direct and reliable measure of an arm's length result. See § 1.482-3(b)(2)(ii)(A).

*Example (2).* Effect of trademark. The facts are the same as in Example 1, except that USM affixes its valuable trademark to the property sold in the controlled transactions, but does not affix its trademark to the property sold in the uncontrolled transactions. Under the facts of this case, the effect on price of the trademark is material and cannot be reliably estimated. Because there are material product differences for which reliable adjustments cannot be made, the comparable uncontrolled price method is unlikely to provide a reliable measure of the arm's length result. See § 1.482-3(b)(2)(ii)(A).

*Example (3).* Minor product differences. The facts are the same as in Example 1, except that USM, which manufactures business machines, makes minor modifications to the physical properties of the machines to satisfy specific requirements of a customer in controlled sales, but does not make these modifications in uncontrolled sales. If the minor physical differences in the product have a material affect on prices, adjustments to account for these differences must be made to the results of the uncontrolled transactions according to the provisions of § 1.482-1(d)(2), and such adjusted results maybe used as a measure of the arm's length result.

*Example (4).* Of geographic differences. FM, a foreign specialty radio manufacturer, sells its radios to a controlled U.S. distributor, AM, that serves the West Coast of the United States. FM sells its radios to uncontrolled distributors to serve other regions in the United States. The product in the controlled and uncontrolled transactions is the same, and all other circumstances surrounding the controlled and uncontrolled transactions are substantially the same, other than the geographic differences. If the geographic differences are unlikely to have a material effect on price, or they have definite and reasonably ascertainable effects for which adjustments are made, then the adjusted results of the uncontrolled sales may be used under the comparable uncontrolled price method to establish an arm's length range pursuant to § 1.482-1(e)(2)(iii)(A). If the effects of the geographic differences would be material but cannot be reliably ascertained, then the reliability of the results will be diminished. However, the comparable uncontrolled price method may still provide the most reliable measure of an arm's length result, pursuant to the best method rule of § 1.482-1(c), and, if so, an arm's length range may be established pursuant to § 1.482-1(e)(2)(iii)(B).

*(5) Indirect evidence of comparable uncontrolled transactions.* (i) In general. A comparable uncontrolled price may be derived from data from public exchanges or quotation media, but only if the following requirements are met—

(A) The data is widely and routinely used in the ordinary course of business in the industry to negotiate prices for uncontrolled sales;

(B) The data derived from public exchanges or quotation media is used to set prices in the controlled transaction in the same way it is used by uncontrolled taxpayers in the industry; and

(C) The amount charged in the controlled transaction is adjusted to reflect differences in product quality and quantity, contractual terms, transportation costs, market conditions, risks borne, and other factors that affect the price that would be agreed to by uncontrolled taxpayers.

(ii) Limitation. Use of data from public exchanges or quotation media may not be appropriate under extraordinary market conditions.

(iii) Examples. The following examples illustrate this paragraph (b)(5).

*Example (1).* Use of quotation medium.

(i) On June 1, USOil, a United States corporation, enters into a contract to purchase crude oil from its foreign subsidiary, FS, in Country z. USOil and FS agree to base their sales price on the average of the prices published for that crude in a quotation medium in the five days before August 1, the date set for delivery. USOil and FS agree to adjust the price for the particular circumstances of their transactions, including the quantity of the crude sold, contractual terms, transportation costs, risks borne, and other factors that affect the price.

(ii) The quotation medium used by USOil and FS is widely and routinely used in the ordinary course of business in the industry to establish prices for uncontrolled sales. Because USOil and FS use the data to set their sales price in the same way that unrelated parties use the data from the quotation medium to set their sales prices, and appropriate adjustments were made to account for differences, the price derived from the quotation medium used by USOil and FS to set their transfer prices will be considered evidence of a comparable uncontrolled price.

*Example (2).* Extraordinary market conditions. The facts are the same as in Example 1, except that before USOil and FS enter into their contract, war breaks out in Countries X and Y, major oil producing countries, causing significant instability in world petroleum markets. As a result, given the significant instability in the price of oil, the prices listed on the quotation medium may not reflect a reliable measure of an arm's length result. See § 1.482-3(b)(5)(ii).

**(c) Resale price method.** *(1) In general.* The resale price method evaluates whether the amount charged in a controlled transaction is arm's length by reference to the gross profit margin realized in comparable uncontrolled transactions. The resale price method measures the value of functions performed, and is ordinarily used in cases involving the purchase and resale of tangible property in which the reseller has not added substantial value to the tangible goods by physically altering the goods before resale. For this purpose, packaging, repackaging, labelling, or minor assembly do not ordinarily constitute physical alteration. Further the resale price method is not ordinarily used in cases where the controlled taxpayer uses its intangible property to add substantial value to the tangible goods.

*(2) Determination of arm's length price.* (i) In general. The resale price method measures an arm's length price by subtracting the appropriate gross profit from the applicable resale price for the property involved in the controlled transaction under review.

(ii) Applicable resale price. The applicable resale price is equal to either the resale price of the particular item of property involved or the price at which contemporaneous resales of the same property are made. If the property purchased in the controlled sale is resold to one or more related parties in a series of controlled sales before being resold in an uncontrolled sale, the applicable resale price is the price at which the property is resold to an uncontrolled party, or the price at which contemporaneous resales of the same property are made. In such case, the determination of the appropriate gross profit will take into account the functions of all members of the group participating in the series of controlled sales and final uncontrolled resales, as well as any other relevant factors described in § 1.482-1(d)(3).

(iii) Appropriate gross profit. The appropriate gross profit is computed by multiplying the applicable resale price by the gross profit margin (expressed as a percentage of total revenue derived from sales) earned in comparable uncontrolled transactions.

(iv) Arm's length range. See § 1.482-1(e)(2) for determination of the arm's length range.

*(3) Comparability and reliability considerations.* (i) In general. Whether results derived from applications of this method are the most reliable measure of the arm's length result must be determined using the factors described under the best method rule in § 1.482-1(c). The application of these factors under the resale price method is discussed in paragraphs (c)(3)(ii) and (iii) of this section.

(ii) Comparability. (A) Functional comparability. The degree of comparability between an uncontrolled transaction and a controlled transaction is determined by applying the comparability provisions of § 1.482-1(d). A reseller's gross profit provides compensation for the performance of resale functions related to the product or products under review, including an operating profit in return for the reseller's investment of capital and the assumption of risks. Therefore, although all of the factors described in § 1.482-1(d)(3) must be considered, comparability under this method is particularly dependent on similarity of functions performed, risks borne, and contractual terms, or adjustments to account for the effects of any such differences. If possible, appropriate gross profit margins should be derived from comparable uncontrolled purchases and resales of the reseller involved in the controlled sale, because similar characteristics are more likely to be found among different resales of property made by the same reseller than among sales made by other resellers. In the absence of comparable uncontrolled transactions involving the same reseller, an appropriate gross profit margin may be derived from comparable uncontrolled transactions of other resellers.

(B) Other comparability factors. Comparability under this method is less dependent on close physical similarity between the products transferred than under the comparable uncontrolled price method. For example, distributors of a wide variety of consumer durables might perform comparable distribution functions without regard to the specific durable goods distributed. Substantial differences in the products may, however, indicate significant functional differences between the controlled and uncontrolled taxpayers. Thus, it ordinarily would be expected that the controlled and uncontrolled transactions would involve the distribution of products of the same general type (e.g., consumer electronics). Furthermore, significant differences in the value of the distributed goods due, for example, to the value of a trademark, may also affect the reliability of the comparison. Finally, the reliability of profit measures based on gross profit may be adversely affected by factors that have less effect on prices. For example, gross profit may be affected by a variety of other factors, including cost structures (as reflected, for example, in the age of plant and equipment), business experience (such as whether the business is in a start-up phase or is mature), or management efficiency (as indicated, for example, by expanding or contracting sales or executive compensation over time). Accordingly, if material differences in these factors are identified based on objective evidence, the reliability of the analysis may be affected.

(C) Adjustments for differences between controlled and uncontrolled transactions. If there are material differences between the controlled and uncontrolled transactions that would affect the gross profit margin, adjustments should be made to the gross profit margin earned with respect to the uncontrolled transaction according to the comparability provisions of § 1.482-1(d)(2). For this purpose, consideration of operating expenses associated with functions performed and risks assumed may be necessary, because differences in functions performed are often reflected in operating expenses. If there are differences in functions performed, however, the effect on gross profit of such differences is not necessarily equal to the differences in the amount of related operating expenses. Specific examples of the factors that may be particularly relevant to this method include—

(1) Inventory levels and turnover rates, and corresponding risks, including any price protection programs offered by the manufacturer;

(2) Contractual terms (e.g., scope and terms of warranties provided, sales or purchase volume, credit terms, transport terms);

(3) Sales, marketing, advertising programs and services, (including promotional programs, rebates, and co-op advertising);

(4) The level of the market (e.g., wholesale, retail, etc.); and

(5) Foreign currency risks.

(D) Sales agent. If the controlled taxpayer is comparable to a sales agent that does not take title to goods or otherwise assume risks with respect to ownership of such goods, the commission earned by such sales agent, expressed as a percentage of the uncontrolled sales price of the goods involved, may be used as the comparable gross profit margin.

(iii) Data and assumptions. (A) In general. The reliability of the results derived from the resale price method is affected by the completeness and accuracy of the data used and the reliability of the assumptions made to apply this method. See § 1.482-1(c) (Best method rule).

(B) Consistency in accounting. The degree of consistency in accounting practices between the controlled transaction and the uncontrolled comparables that materially affect the gross profit margin affects the reliability of the result. Thus, for example, if differences in inventory and other cost accounting practices would materially affect the gross profit margin, the ability to make reliable adjustments for such differences would affect the reliability of the results. Further, the controlled transaction and the uncontrolled comparable should be consistent in the reporting of items (such as discounts, returns and allowances, rebates, transportation costs, insurance, and packaging) between cost of goods sold and operating expenses.

*(4) Examples.* The following examples illustrate the principles of this paragraph (c).

*Example (1).* A controlled taxpayer sells property to another member of its controlled group that resells the property in uncontrolled sales. There are no changes in the beginning and ending inventory for the year under review. Information regarding an uncontrolled comparable is sufficiently complete to conclude that it is likely that all material differences between the controlled and uncontrolled transactions have been identified and adjusted for. If the applicable resale price of the property involved in the controlled sale is $100 and the appropriate gross profit margin is 20%, then an arm's length result of the controlled sale is a price of $80 ($100 minus (20% × $100)).

*Example (2).* (i) S, a U.S. corporation, is the exclusive distributor for FP, its foreign parent. There are no changes in the beginning and ending inventory for the year under review. S's total reported cost of goods sold is $800, consisting of $600 for property purchased from FP and $200 of other costs of goods sold incurred to unrelated parties. S's applicable resale price and reported gross profit are as follows:

| | |
|---|---|
| Applicable resale price | $1000 |
| Cost of goods sold | |
| Cost of purchases from FP | 600 |
| Costs incurred to unrelated parties | 200 |
| Reported gross profit | $200 |

(ii) The district director determines that the appropriate gross profit margin is 25%. Therefore, S's appropriate gross profit is $250 (i.e., 25% of the applicable resale price of

$1000). Because S is incurring costs of sales to unrelated parties, an arm's length price for property purchased from FP must be determined under a two-step process. First, the appropriate gross profit ($250) is subtracted from the applicable resale price ($1000). The resulting amount ($750) is then reduced by the costs of sales incurred to unrelated parties ($200). Therefore, an arm's length price for S's cost of sales of FP's product in this case equals $550 (i.e., $750 minus $200).

*Example (3).* FP, a foreign manufacturer, sells Product to USSub, its U.S. subsidiary, which in turn sells Product to its domestic affiliate Sister. Sister sells Product to unrelated buyers. In this case, the applicable resale price is the price at which Sister sells Product in uncontrolled transactions. The determination of the appropriate gross profit margin for the sale from FP to USSub will take into account the functions performed by USSub and Sister, as well as other relevant factors described in § 1.482-1(d)(3).

*Example (4).* USSub, a U.S. corporation, is the exclusive distributor of widgets for its foreign parent. To determine whether the gross profit margin of 25% earned by USSub is an arm's length result, the district director considers applying the resale price method. There are several uncontrolled distributors that perform similar functions under similar circumstances in uncontrolled transactions. However, the uncontrolled distributors treat certain costs such as discounts and insurance as cost of goods sold, while USSub treats such costs as operating expenses. In such cases, accounting reclassifications, pursuant to § 1.482-3(c)(3)(iii)(B), must be made to ensure consistent treatment of such material items. Inability to make such accounting reclassifications will decrease the reliability of the results of the uncontrolled transactions.

*Example (5).* (i) USP, a U.S. corporation, manufactures Product X, an unbranded widget, and sells it to FSub, its wholly owned foreign subsidiary. FSub acts as a distributor of Product X in country M, and sells it to uncontrolled parties in that country. Uncontrolled distributors A, B, C, D, and E distribute competing products of approximately similar value in country M. All such products are unbranded.

(ii) Relatively complete data is available regarding the functions performed and risks borne by the uncontrolled distributors and the contractual terms under which they operate in the uncontrolled transactions. In addition, data is available to ensure accounting consistency between all of the uncontrolled distributors and FSub. Because the available data is sufficiently complete and accurate to conclude that it is likely that all material differences between the controlled and uncontrolled transactions have been identified, such differences have a definite and reasonably ascertainable effect, and reliable adjustments are made to account for such differences, the results of each of the uncontrolled distributors may be used to establish an arm's length range pursuant to § 1.482-1(e)(2)(iii)(A).

*Example (6).* The facts are the same as *Example 5*, except that sufficient data is not available to determine whether any of the uncontrolled distributors provide warranties or to determine the payment terms of the contracts. Because differences in these contractual terms could materially affect price or profits, the inability to determine whether these differences exist between the controlled and uncontrolled transactions diminishes the reliability of the results of the uncontrolled comparables. However, the reliability of the results may be enhanced by the application of a statistical method when establishing an arm's length range pursuant to § 1.482-1(e)(2)(iii)(B).

*Example (7).* The facts are the same as in *Example 5*, except that Product X is branded with a valuable trademark that is owned by P. A, B, and C distribute unbranded competing products, while D and E distribute products branded with other trademarks. D and E do not own any rights in the trademarks under which their products are sold. The value of the products that A, B, and C sold are not similar to the value of the products sold by S. The value of products sold by D and E, however, is similar to that of Product X. Although close product similarity is not as important for a reliable application of the resale price method as for the comparable uncontrolled price method, significant differences in the value of the products involved in the controlled and uncontrolled transactions may affect the reliability of the results. In addition, because in this case it is difficult to determine the effect the trademark will have on price or profits, reliable adjustments for the differences cannot be made. Because D and E have a higher level of comparability than A, B, and C with respect to S, pursuant to § 1.482-1(e)(2)(ii), only D and E may be included in an arm's length range.

**(d) Cost plus method.** *(1) In general.* The cost plus method evaluates whether the amount charged in a controlled transaction is arm's length by reference to the gross profit markup realized in comparable uncontrolled transactions. The cost plus method is ordinarily used in cases involving the manufacture, assembly, or other production of goods that are sold to related parties.

*(2) Determination of arm's length price.* (i) In general. The cost plus method measures an arm's length price by adding the appropriate gross profit to the controlled taxpayer's costs of producing the property involved in the controlled transaction.

(ii) Appropriate gross profit. The appropriate gross profit is computed by multiplying the controlled taxpayer's cost of producing the transferred property by the gross profit markup, expressed as a percentage of cost, earned in comparable uncontrolled transactions.

(iii) Arm's length range. See § 1.482-1(e)(2) for determination of an arm's length range.

*(3) Comparability and reliability considerations.* (i) In general. Whether results derived from the application of this method are the most reliable measure of the arm's length result must be determined using the factors described under the best method rule in § 1.482-1(c).

(ii) Comparability. (A) Functional comparability. The degree of comparability between controlled and uncontrolled transactions is determined by applying the comparability provisions of § 1.482-1(d). A producer's gross profit provides compensation for the performance of the production functions related to the product or products under review, including an operating profit for the producer's investment of capital and assumption of risks. Therefore, although all of the factors described in § 1.482-1(d)(3) must be considered, comparability under this method is particularly dependent on similarity of functions performed, risks borne, and contractual terms, or adjustments to account for the effects of any such differences. If possible, the appropriate gross profit markup should be derived from comparable uncontrolled transactions of the taxpayer involved in the controlled sale, because similar characteristics are more likely to be found among sales of property by the same producer than among sales by other producers. In the absence of such sales, an appropriate gross profit markup may be derived from comparable uncontrolled sales of other producers whether or not such producers are members of the same controlled group.

(B) Other comparability factors. Comparability under this method is less dependent on close physical similarity between the products transferred than under the comparable uncontrolled price method. Substantial differences in the products may, however, indicate significant functional differences between the controlled and uncontrolled taxpayers. Thus, it ordinarily would be expected that the controlled and uncontrolled transactions involve the production of goods within the same product categories. Furthermore, significant differences in the value of the products due, for example, to the value of a trademark, may also affect the reliability of the comparison. Finally, the reliability of profit measures based on gross profit may be adversely affected by factors that have less effect on prices. For example, gross profit may be affected by a variety of other factors, including cost structures (as reflected, for example, in the age of plant and equipment), business experience (such as whether the business is in a start-up phase or is mature), or management efficiency (as indicated, for example, by expanding or contracting sales or executive compensation over time). Accordingly, if material differences in these factors are identified based on objective evidence, the reliability of the analysis may be affected.

(C) Adjustments for differences between controlled and uncontrolled transactions. If there are material differences between the controlled and uncontrolled transactions that would affect the gross profit markup, adjustments should be made to the gross profit markup earned in the comparable uncontrolled transaction according to the provisions of § 1.482-1(d)(2). For this purpose, consideration of the operating expenses associated with the functions performed and risks assumed may be necessary, because differences in functions performed are often reflected in operating expenses. If there are differences in functions performed, however, the effect on gross profit of such differences is not necessarily equal to the differences in the amount of related operating expenses. Specific examples of the factors that may be particularly relevant to this method include—

(1) The complexity of manufacturing or assembly;

(2) Manufacturing, production, and process engineering;

(3) Procurement, purchasing, and inventory control activities;

(4) Testing functions;

(5) Selling, general, and administrative expenses;

(6) Foreign currency risks; and

(7) Contractual terms (e.g., scope and terms of warranties provided, sales or purchase volume, credit terms, transport terms).

(D) Purchasing agent. If a controlled taxpayer is comparable to a purchasing agent that does not take title to property or otherwise assume risks with respect to ownership of such goods, the commission earned by such purchasing agent, expressed as a percentage of the purchase price of the goods, may be used as the appropriate gross profit markup.

(iii) Data and assumptions. (A) In general. The reliability of the results derived from the cost plus method is affected by the completeness and accuracy of the data used and the reliability of the assumptions made to apply this method. See § 1.482-1(c) (Best method rule).

(B) Consistency in accounting. The degree of consistency in accounting practices between the controlled transaction and the uncontrolled comparables that materially affect the gross profit markup affects the reliability of the result. Thus, for example, if differences in inventory and other cost accounting practices would materially affect the gross profit markup, the ability to make reliable adjustments for such differences would affect the reliability of the results. Further, the controlled transaction and the comparable uncontrolled transaction should be consistent in the reporting of costs between cost of goods sold and operating expenses. The term *cost of producing* includes the cost of acquiring property that is held for resale.

*(4) Examples.* The following examples illustrate the principles of this paragraph (d).

*Example (1).* (i) USP, a domestic manufacturer of computer components, sells its products to FS, its foreign distributor. UT1, UT2, and UT3 are domestic computer component manufacturers that sell to uncontrolled foreign purchasers.

(ii) Relatively complete data is available regarding the functions performed and risks borne by UT1, UT2, and UT3, and the contractual terms in the uncontrolled transactions. In addition, data is available to ensure accounting consistency between all of the uncontrolled manufacturers and USP. Because the available data is sufficiently complete to conclude that it is likely that all material differences between the controlled and uncontrolled transactions have been identified, the effect of the differences are definite and reasonably ascertainable, and reliable adjustments are made to account for the differences, an arm's length range can be established pursuant to § 1.482-1(e)(2)(iii)(A).

*Example (2).* The facts are the same as in *Example 1*, except that USP accounts for supervisory, general, and administrative costs as operating expenses, which are not allocated to its sales to FS. The gross profit markups of UT1, UT2, and UT3, however, reflect supervisory, general, and administrative expenses because they are accounted for as costs of goods sold. Accordingly, the gross profit markups of UT1, UT2, and UT3 must be adjusted as provided in paragraph (d)(3)(iii)(B) of this section to provide accounting consistency. If data is not sufficient to determine whether such accounting differences exist between the controlled and uncontrolled transactions, the reliability of the results will be decreased.

*Example (3).* The facts are the same as in *Example 1*, except that under its contract with FS, USP uses materials consigned by FS. UT1, UT2, and UT3, on the other hand, purchase their own materials, and their gross profit markups are determined by including the costs of materials. The fact that USP does not carry an inventory risk by purchasing its own materials while the uncontrolled producers carry inventory is a significant difference that may require an adjustment if the difference has a material effect on the gross profit markups of the uncontrolled producers. Inability to reasonably ascertain the effect of the difference on the gross profit markups will affect the reliability of the results of UT1, UT2, and UT3.

*Example (4).* (i) FS, a foreign corporation, produces apparel for USP, its U.S. parent corporation. FS purchases its materials from unrelated suppliers and produces the apparel according to designs provided by USP. The district director identifies 10 uncontrolled foreign apparel producers that operate in the same geographic market and are similar in many respect to FS.

(ii) Relatively complete data is available regarding the functions performed and risks borne by the uncontrolled producers. In addition, data is sufficiently detailed to permit adjustments for differences in accounting practices. However, sufficient data is not available to determine whether it is likely that all material differences in contractual terms have been identified. For example, it is not possible to determine which parties in the uncontrolled transactions bear currency risks. Because differences in these contractual terms could materially affect price or profits, the inability to determine whether differences exist between the controlled and uncontrolled transactions will diminish the reliability of these results. Therefore, the reliability of the results of the uncontrolled transactions must be enhanced by the application of a statistical method in establishing an arm's length range pursuant to § 1.482-1(e)(2)(iii)(B).

**(e) Unspecified methods.** *(1) In general.* Methods not specified in paragraphs (a)(1), (2), (3), (4), and (5) of this section may be used to evaluate whether the amount charged in a controlled transaction is arm's length. Any method used under this paragraph (e) must be applied in accordance with the provisions of § 1.482-1. Consistent with the specified methods, an unspecified method should take into account the general principle that uncontrolled taxpayers evaluate the terms of a transaction by considering the realistic alternatives to that transaction, and only enter into a particular transaction if none of the alternatives is preferable to it. For example, the comparable uncontrolled price method compares a controlled transaction to similar uncontrolled transactions to provide a direct estimate of the price to which the parties would have agreed had they resorted directly to a market alternative to the controlled transaction. Therefore, in establishing whether a controlled transaction achieved an arm's length result, an unspecified method should provide information on the prices or profits that the controlled taxpayer could have realized by choosing a realistic alternative to the controlled transaction. As with any method, an unspecified method will not be applied unless it provides the most reliable measure of an arm's length result under the principles of the best method rule. See § 1.482-1(c). Therefore, in accordance with § 1.482-1(d) (Comparability), to the extent that a method relies on internal data rather than uncontrolled comparables, its reliability will be reduced. Similarly, the reliability of a method will be affected by the reliability of the data and assumptions used to apply the method, including any projections used.

*(2) Example.* The following example illustrates an application of the principle of this paragraph (e).

*Example.* Amcan, a U.S. company, produces unique vessels for storing and transporting toxic waste, toxicans, at its U.S. production facility. Amcan agrees by contract to supply its Canadian subsidiary, Cancan, with 4000 toxicans per year to serve the Canadian market for toxicans. Prior to entering into the contract with Cancan, Amcan had received a bona fide offer from an independent Canadian waste disposal company, Cando, to serve as the Canadian distributor for toxicans and to purchase a similar number of toxicans at a price of $5,000 each. If the circumstances and terms of the Cancan supply contract are sufficiently similar to those of the Cando offer, or sufficiently reliable adjustments can be made for differences between them, then the Cando offer price of $5,000 may provide reliable information indicating that an arm's length consideration under the Cancan contract will not be less than $5,000 per toxican.

**(f) Coordination with intangible property rules.** The value of an item of tangible property may be affected by the value of intangible property, such as a trademark affixed to the tangible property (embedded intangible). Ordinarily, the transfer of tangible property with an embedded intangible will not be considered a transfer of such intangible if the controlled purchaser does not acquire any rights to exploit the intangible property other than rights relating to the resale of the tangible property under normal commercial practices. Pursuant to § 1.482-1(d)(3)(v), however, the embedded intangible must be accounted for in evaluating the comparability of the controlled transaction and uncontrolled comparables. For example, because product comparability has the greatest effect on an application of the comparable uncontrolled price method, trademarked tangible property may be insufficiently comparable to unbranded tangible property to permit a reliable application of the comparable uncontrolled price method. The effect of embedded intangibles on comparability will be determined under the principles of § 1.482-4. If the transfer of tangible property conveys to the recipient a right to exploit an embedded intangible (other than in connection with the resale of that item of tangible property), it may be necessary to determine the arm's length consideration for such intangible separately from the tangible property, applying methods appropriate to determining the arm's length result for a transfer of intangible property under § 1.482-4. For example, if the transfer of a machine conveys the right to exploit a manufacturing process incorporated in the machine, then the arm's length consideration for the transfer of that right must be determined separately under § 1.482-4.

---

T.D. 8552, 7/1/94.

---

### § 1.482-4 Methods to determine taxable income in connection with a transfer of intangible property.

**(a) In general.** The arm's length amount charged in a controlled transfer of intangible property must be determined under one of the four methods listed in this paragraph (a). Each of the methods must be applied in accordance with all of the provisions of § 1.482-1, including the best method rule of § 1.482-1(c), the comparability analysis of § 1.482-1(d), and the arm's length range of § 1.482-1(e). The arm's length consideration for the transfer of an intangible determined under this section must be commensurate with the income attributable to the intangible. See § 1.482-4(f)(2) (Periodic adjustments). The available methods are—

*(1)* The comparable uncontrolled transaction method, described in paragraph (c) of this section;

*(2)* The comparable profits method, described in § 1.482-5;

*(3)* The profit split method, described in § 1.482-6; and

*(4)* Unspecified methods described in paragraph (d) of this section.

**(b) Definition of intangible.** For purposes of section 482, an intangible is an asset that comprises any of the following items and has substantial value independent of the services of any individual—

*(1)* Patents, inventions, formulae, processes, designs, patterns, or know-how;

*(2)* Copyrights and literary, musical, or artistic compositions;

*(3)* Trademarks, trade names, or brand names;

*(4)* Franchises, licenses, or contracts;

*(5)* Methods, programs, systems, procedures, campaigns, surveys, studies, forecasts, estimates, customer lists, or technical data; and

*(6)* Other similar items. For purposes of section 482, an item is considered similar to those listed in paragraph (b)(1) through (5) of this section if it derives its value not from its physical attributes but from its intellectual content or other intangible properties.

**(c) Comparable uncontrolled transaction method.** *(1) In general.* The comparable uncontrolled transaction method evaluates whether the amount charged for a controlled transfer of intangible property was arm's length by reference to the amount charged in a comparable uncontrolled transaction. The amount determined under this method may be adjusted as required by paragraph (f)(2) of this section (Periodic adjustments).

*(2) Comparability and reliability considerations.* (i) In general. Whether results derived from applications of this method are the most reliable measure of an arm's length result is determined using the factors described under the best method rule in § 1.482-1(c). The application of these factors under the comparable uncontrolled transaction method is discussed in paragraphs (c)(2)(ii), (iii), and (iv) of this section.

(ii) Reliability. If an uncontrolled transaction involves the transfer of the same intangible under the same, or substantially the same, circumstances as the controlled transaction, the results derived from applying the comparable uncontrolled transaction method will generally be the most direct and reliable measure of the arm's length result for the controlled transfer of an intangible. Circumstances between the controlled and uncontrolled transactions will be considered substantially the same if there are at most only minor differences that have a definite and reasonably ascertainable effect on the amount charged and for which appropriate adjustments are made. If such uncontrolled transactions cannot be identified, uncontrolled transactions that involve the transfer of comparable intangibles under comparable circumstances may be used to apply this method, but the reliability of the analysis will be reduced.

(iii) Comparability. (A) In general. The degree of comparability between controlled and uncontrolled transactions is determined by applying the comparability provisions of § 1.482-1(d). Although all of the factors described in § 1.482-1(d)(3) must be considered, specific factors may be particularly relevant to this method. In particular, the application of this method requires that the controlled and uncontrolled transactions involve either the same intangible property or comparable intangible property, as defined in paragraph (c)(2)(iii)(B)(1) of this section. In addition, because differences in contractual terms, or the economic conditions in which transactions take place, could materially affect the amount charged, comparability under this method also depends on similarity with respect to these factors, or adjustments to account for material differences in such circumstances.

(B) Factors to be considered in determining comparability. (1) Comparable intangible property. In order for the intangible property involved in an uncontrolled transaction to be considered comparable to the intangible property involved in the controlled transaction, both intangibles must—

(i) Be used in connection with similar products or processes within the same general industry or market; and

(ii) Have similar profit potential. The profit potential of an intangible is most reliably measured by directly calculating the net present value of the benefits to be realized (based on prospective profits to be realized or costs to be saved) through the use or subsequent transfer of the intangible, considering the capital investment and start-up expenses required, the risks to be assumed, and other relevant considerations. The need to reliably measure profit potential increases in relation to both the total amount of potential profits and the potential rate of return on investment necessary to exploit the intangible. If the information necessary to directly calculate net present value of the benefits to be realized is unavailable, and the need to reliably measure profit potential is reduced because the potential profits are relatively small in terms of total amount and rate of return, comparison of profit potential may be based upon the factors referred to in paragraph (c)(2)(iii)(B)(2) of this section. See *Example 3* of § 1.482-4(c)(4). Finally, the reliability of a measure of profit potential is affected by the extent to which the profit attributable to the intangible can be isolated from the profit attributable to other factors, such as functions performed and other resources employed.

(2) Comparable circumstances. In evaluating the comparability of the circumstances of the controlled and uncontrolled transactions, although all of the factors described in § 1.482-1(d)(3) must be considered, specific factors that may be particularly relevant to this method include the following—

(i) The terms of the transfer, including the exploitation rights granted in the intangible, the exclusive or nonexclusive character of any rights granted, any restrictions on use, or any limitations on the geographic area in which the rights may be exploited;

(ii) The stage of development of the intangible (including, where appropriate, necessary governmental approvals, authorizations, or licenses) in the market in which the intangible is to be used;

(iii) Rights to receive updates, revisions, or modifications of the intangible;

(iv) The uniqueness of the property and the period for which it remains unique, including the degree and duration of protection afforded to the property under the laws of the relevant countries;

(v) The duration of the license, contract, or other agreement, and any termination or renegotiation rights;

(vi) Any economic and product liability risks to be assumed by the transferee;

(vii) The existence and extent of any collateral transactions or ongoing business relationships between the transferee and transferor; and

(viii) The functions to be performed by the transferor and transferee, including any ancillary or subsidiary services.

(iv) Data and assumptions. The reliability of the results derived from the comparable uncontrolled transaction method is affected by the completeness and accuracy of the data used and the reliability of the assumptions made to apply this method. See § 1.482-1(c) (Best method rule).

*(3) Arm's length range.* See § 1.482-1(e)(2) for the determination of an arm's length range.

*(4) Examples.* The following examples illustrate the principles of this paragraph (c).

*Example (1).* (i) USpharm, a U.S. pharmaceutical company, develops a new drug Z that is a safe and effective treatment for the disease zeezee. Uspharm has obtained patents covering drug Z in the United States and in various foreign countries. Uspharm has also obtained the regulatory authorizations necessary to market drug Z in the United States and in foreign countries.

(ii) USpharm licenses its subsidiary in country X, Xpharm, to produce and sell drug Z in country X. At the same time, it licenses an unrelated company, Ydrug, to produce and sell drug Z in country Y, a neighboring country. Prior to licensing the drug, USpharm had obtained patent protection and regulatory approvals in both countries and both countries provide similar protection for intellectual property rights. Country X and country Y are similar countries in terms of population, per capita income and the incidence of disease zeezee. Consequently, drug Z is expected to sell in similar quantities and at similar prices in both countries. In addition, costs of producing and marketing drug Z in each country are expected to be approximately the same.

(iii) USpharm and Xpharm establish terms for the license of drug Z that are identical in every material respect, including royalty rate, to the terms established between Uspharm and Ydrug. In this case the district director determines that the royalty rate established in the Ydrug license agreement is a reliable measure of the arm's length royalty rate for the Xpharm license agreement.

*Example (2).* The facts are the same as in *Example 1*, except that the incidence of the disease zeezee in Country Y is much higher than in Country X. In this case, the profit potential from exploitation of the right to make and sell drug Z is likely to be much higher in country Y than it is in Country X. Consequently, the Ydrug license agreement is unlikely to provide a reliable measure of the arm's length royalty rate for the Xpharm license.

*Example (3).* (i) FP, is a foreign company that designs, manufactures and sells industrial equipment. FP has developed proprietary components that are incorporated in its products. These components are important in the operation of FP's equipment and some of them have distinctive features, but other companies produce similar components and none of these components by itself accounts for a substantial part of the value of FP's products.

(ii) FP licenses its U.S. subsidiary, USSub, exclusive North American rights to use the patented technology for producing component X, a heat exchanger used for cooling operating mechanisms in industrial equipment. Component X incorporates proven technology that makes it somewhat more efficient than the heat exchangers commonly used in industrial equipment. FP also agrees to provide technical support to help adapt component X to USSub's products and to assist with initial production. Under the terms of the license agreement USSub pays FP a royalty equal to 3 percent of sales of USSub equipment incorporating component X.

(iii) FP does not license unrelated parties to use component X, but many similar components are transferred between uncontrolled taxpayers. Consequently, the district director decides to apply the comparable uncontrolled transaction method to evaluate whether the 3 percent royalty for component x is an arm's length royalty.

(iv) The district director uses a database of company documents filed with the Securities and Exchange Commission (SEC) to identify potentially comparable license agreements between uncontrolled taxpayers that are on file with the SEC. The district director identifies 40 license agreements that were entered into in the same year as the controlled transfer or in the prior or following year, and that relate to transfers of technology associated with industrial equipment that has similar applications to USSub's products. Further review of these uncontrolled agreements indicates that 25 of them involved components that have a similar level of technical sophistication as component x and could be expected to play a similar role in contributing to the total value of the final product.

(v) The district director makes a detailed review of the terms of each of the 25 uncontrolled agreements and finds that 15 of them are similar to the controlled agreement in that they all involve—

(A) The transfer of exclusive rights for the North American market;

(B) Products for which the market could be expected to be of a similar size to the market for the products into which USSub incorporates component X;

(C) The transfer of patented technology;

(D) Continuing technical support;

(E) Access to technical improvements;

(F) Technology of a similar age; and

(G) A similar duration of the agreement.

(vi) Based on these factors and the fact that none of the components to which these license agreements relate accounts for a substantial part of the value of the final products, the district director concludes that these fifteen intangibles have similar profit potential to the component X technology.

(vii) The 15 uncontrolled comparables produce the following royalty rates:

| License | Royalty rate (percent) |
|---|---|
| 1 | 1.0 |
| 2 | 1.0 |
| 3 | 1.25 |
| 4 | 1.25 |
| 5 | 1.5 |
| 6 | 1.5 |
| 7 | 1.75 |
| 8 | 2.0 |
| 9 | 2.0 |
| 10 | 2.0 |
| 11 | 1.25 |
| 12 | 2.5 |
| 13 | 2.5 |
| 14 | 2.75 |
| 15 | 3.0 |

(viii) Although the uncontrolled comparables are clearly similar to the controlled transaction, it is likely that unidentified material differences exist between the uncontrolled comparables and the controlled transaction. Therefore, an appropriate statistical technique must be used to establish the arm's length range. In this case the district director uses the interquartile range to determine the arm's length range. Therefore, the arm's length range covers royalty rates from 1.25 to 2.5 percent, and an adjustment is warranted to the 3 percent royalty charged in the controlled transfer. The district director determines that the appropriate adjustment corresponds to a reduction in the royalty rate to 2.0 percent, which is the median of the uncontrolled comparables.

*Example (4).* (i) USdrug, a U.S. pharmaceutical company, has developed a new drug, Nosplit, that is useful in treating migraine headaches and produces no significant side effects. Nosplit replaces another drug, Lessplit, that USdrug had previously produced and marketed as a treatment for migraine headaches. A number of other drugs for treating migraine headaches are already on the market, but Nosplit can be expected rapidly to dominate the worldwide market for such treatments and to command a premium price since all other treatments produce side effects. Thus, USdrug projects that extraordinary profits will be derived from Nosplit in the U.S. market and other markets.

(ii) USdrug licenses its newly established European subsidiary, Eurodrug, the rights to produce and market Nosplit in the European market. In setting the royalty rate for this license, USdrug considers the royalty that it established previously when it licensed the right to produce and market Lessplit in the European market to an unrelated European pharmaceutical company. In many respects the two license agreements are closely comparable. The drugs were licensed at the same stage in their development and the agreements conveyed identical rights to the licensees. Moreover, there appear to have been no significant changes in the European market for migraine headache treatments since Lessplit was licensed. However, at the time that Lessplit was licensed there were several other similar drugs already on the market to which Lessplit was not in all cases superior. Consequently, the projected and actual Lessplit profits were substantially less than the projected Nosplit profits. Thus, USdrug concludes that the profit potential of Lessplit is not similar to the profit potential of Nosplit, and the Lessplit license agreement consequently is not a comparable uncontrolled transaction for purposes of this paragraph (c) in spite of the other indicia of comparability between the two intangibles.

**(d) Unspecified methods.** *(1) In general.* Methods not specified in paragraphs (a)(1), (2), and (3) of this section may be used to evaluate whether the amount charged in a controlled transaction is arm's length. Any method used under this paragraph (d) must be applied in accordance with the provisions of § 1.482-1. Consistent with the specified methods, an unspecified method should take into account the general principle that uncontrolled taxpayers evaluate the terms of a transaction by considering the realistic alternatives to that transaction, and only enter into a particular transaction if none of the alternatives is preferable to it. For example, the comparable uncontrolled transaction method compares a controlled transaction to similar uncontrolled transactions to provide a direct estimate of the price the parties would have agreed to had they resorted directly to a market alternative to the controlled transaction. Therefore, in establishing whether a controlled transaction achieved an arm's length result, an unspecified method should provide information on the prices or profits that the controlled taxpayer could have realized by choosing a realistic alternative to the controlled transaction. As with any method, an unspecified method will not be applied unless it provides the most reliable measure of an arm's length result under the principles of the best method rule. See § 1.482-1(c). Therefore, in accordance with § 1.482-1(d) (Comparability), to the extent that a method relies on internal data rather than uncontrolled comparables, its reliability will be reduced. Similarly, the reliability of a method will be affected by the reliability of the data and assumptions used to apply the method, including any projections used.

*(2) Example.* The following example illustrates an application of the principle of this paragraph (d).

*Example.* (i) USbond is a U.S. company that licenses to its foreign subsidiary, Eurobond, a proprietary process that permits the manufacture of Longbond, a long-lasting industrial adhesive, at a substantially lower cost than otherwise would be possible. Using the proprietary process, Eurobond manufactures Longbond and sells it to related and unrelated parties for the market price of $550 per ton. Under the terms of the license agreement, Eurobond pays USbond a royalty of $100 per ton of Longbond sold. USbond also manufactures and markets Longbond in the United States.

(ii) In evaluating whether the consideration paid for the transfer of the proprietary process to Eurobond was arm's length, the district director may consider, subject to the best method rule of § 1.482-1(c), USbond's alternative of producing and selling Longbond itself. Reasonably reliable estimates indicate that if USbond directly supplied Longbond to the European market, a selling price of $300 per ton would cover its costs and provide a reasonable profit for its functions, risks and investment of capital associated with the production of Longbond for the European market. Given that the market price of Longbond was $550 per ton, by licensing the proprietary process to Eurobond, USbond forgoes $250 per ton of profit over the profit that would be necessary to compensate it for the functions, risks and investment involved in supplying Longbond to the European market itself. Based on these facts, the district director concludes that a royalty of $100 for the proprietary process is not arm's length.

**(e) Coordination with tangible property rules.** See § 1.482-3(f) for the provisions regarding the coordination between the tangible property and intangible property rules.

**(f) Special rules for transfers of intangible property.** *(1) Form of consideration.* If a transferee of an intangible pays nominal or no consideration and the transferor has retained a substantial interest in the property, the arm's length consideration shall be in the form of a royalty, unless a different form is demonstrably more appropriate.

*(2) Periodic adjustments.* (i) General rule. If an intangible is transferred under an arrangement that covers more than one year, the consideration charged in each taxable year may be adjusted to ensure that it is commensurate with the income attributable to the intangible. Adjustments made pursuant to this paragraph (f)(2) shall be consistent with the arm's length standard and the provisions of § 1.482-1. In determining whether to make such adjustments in the taxable year under examination, the district director may consider all relevant facts and circumstances throughout the period the intangible is used. The determination in an earlier year that the amount charged for an intangible was an arm's length amount will not preclude the district director in a subsequent taxable year from making an adjustment to the amount charged for the intangible in the subsequent year. A periodic adjustment under the commensurate with income requirement of section 482 may be made in a subsequent taxable year without regard to whether the taxable year of the original transfer remains open for statute of limitation purposes. For exceptions to this rule see paragraph (f)(2)(ii) of this section.

(ii) Exceptions. (A) Transactions involving the same intangible. If the same intangible was transferred to an uncontrolled taxpayer under substantially the same circumstances as those of the controlled transaction; this transaction serves as the basis for the application of the comparable uncontrolled transaction method in the first taxable year in which substantial periodic consideration was required to be paid; and the amount paid in that year was an arm's length amount, then no allocation in a subsequent year will be made under paragraph (f)(2)(i) of this paragraph for a controlled transfer of intangible property.

(B) Transactions involving comparable intangible. If the arm's length result is derived from the application of the comparable uncontrolled transaction method based on the transfer of a comparable intangible under comparable circumstances to those of the controlled transaction, no allocation will be made under paragraph (f)(2)(i) of this section if each of the following facts is established—

(1) The controlled taxpayers entered into a written agreement (controlled agreement) that provided for an amount of consideration with respect to each taxable year subject to such agreement, such consideration was an arm's length

amount for the first taxable year in which substantial periodic consideration was required to be paid under the agreement, and such agreement remained in effect for the taxable year under review;

(2) There is a written agreement setting forth the terms of the comparable uncontrolled transaction relied upon to establish the arm's length consideration (uncontrolled agreement), which contains no provisions that would permit any change to the amount of consideration, a renegotiation, or a termination of the agreement, in circumstances comparable to those of the controlled transaction in the taxable year under review (or that contains provisions permitting only specified, noncontingent, periodic changes to the amount of consideration);

(3) The controlled agreement is substantially similar to the uncontrolled agreement, with respect to the time period for which it is effective and the provisions described in paragraph (f)(2)(ii)(B)(2) of this section;

(4) The controlled agreement limits use of the intangible to a specified field or purpose in a manner that is consistent with industry practice and any such limitation in the uncontrolled agreement;

(5) There were no substantial changes in the functions performed by the controlled transferee after the controlled agreement was executed, except changes required by events that were not foreseeable; and

(6) The aggregate profits actually earned or the aggregate cost savings actually realized by the controlled taxpayer from the exploitation of the intangible in the year under examination, and all past years, are not less than 80% nor more than 120% of the prospective profits or cost savings that were foreseeable when the comparability of the uncontrolled agreement was established under paragraph (c)(2) of this section.

(C) Methods other than comparable uncontrolled transaction. If the arm's length amount was determined under any method other than the comparable uncontrolled transaction method, no allocation will be made under paragraph (f)(2)(i) of this section if each of the following facts is established—

(1) The controlled taxpayers entered into a written agreement (controlled agreement) that provided for an amount of consideration with respect to each taxable year subject to such agreement, and such agreement remained in effect for the taxable year under review;

(2) The consideration called for in the controlled agreement was an arm's length amount for the first taxable year in which substantial periodic consideration was required to be paid, and relevant supporting documentation was prepared contemporaneously with the execution of the controlled agreement;

(3) There have been no substantial changes in the functions performed by the transferee since the controlled agreement was executed, except changes required by events that were not foreseeable; and

(4) The total profits actually earned or the total cost savings realized by the controlled transferee from the exploitation of the intangible in the year under examination, and all past years, are not less than 80% nor more than 120% of the prospective profits or cost savings that were foreseeable when the controlled agreement was entered into.

(D) Extraordinary events. No allocation will be made under paragraph (f)(2)(i) of this section if the following requirements are met—

(1) Due to extraordinary events that were beyond the control of the controlled taxpayers and that could not reasonably have been anticipated at the time the controlled agreement was entered into, the aggregate actual profits or aggregate cost savings realized by the taxpayer are less than 80% or more than 120% of the prospective profits or cost savings; and

(2) All of the requirements of paragraph (f)(2)(ii)(B) or (C) of this section are otherwise satisfied.

(E) Five-year period. If the requirements of § 1.482-4(f)(2)(ii)(B) or (f)(2)(ii)(C) are met for each year of the five-year period beginning with the first year in which substantial periodic consideration was required to be paid, then no periodic adjustment will be made under paragraph (f)(2)(i) of this section in any subsequent year.

(iii) Examples. The following examples illustrate this paragraph (f)(2).

*Example (1).* (i) USdrug, a U.S. pharmaceutical company, has developed a new drug, Nosplit, that is useful in treating migraine headaches and produces no significant side effects. A number of other drugs for treating migraine headaches are already on the market, but Nosplit can be expected rapidly to dominate the worldwide market for such treatments and to command a premium price since all other treatments produce side effects. Thus, USdrug projects that extraordinary profits will be derived from Nosplit in the U.S. and European markets.

(ii) USdrug licenses its newly established European subsidiary, Eurodrug, the rights to produce and market Nosplit for the European market for 5 years. In setting the royalty rate for this license, USdrug makes projections of the annual sales revenue and the annual profits to be derived from the exploitation of Nosplit by Eurodrug. Based on the projections, a royalty rate of 3.9% is established for the term of the license.

(iii) In Year 1, USdrug evaluates the royalty rate it received from Eurodrug. Given the high profit potential of Nosplit, USdrug is unable to locate any uncontrolled transactions dealing with licenses of comparable intangible property. USdrug therefore determines that the comparable uncontrolled transaction method will not provide a reliable measure of an arm's length royalty. However, applying the comparable profits method to Eurodrug, USdrug determines that a royalty rate of 3.9% will result in Eurodrug earning an arm's length return for its manufacturing and marketing functions.

(iv) In Year 5, the U.S. income tax return for USdrug is examined, and the district director must determine whether the royalty rate between USdrug and Eurodrug is commensurate with the income attributable to Nosplit. In making this determination, the district director considers whether any of the exceptions in § 1.482-4(f)(2)(ii) are applicable. In particular, the district director compares the profit projections attributable to Nosplit made by USdrug against the actual profits realized by Eurodrug. The projected and actual profits are as follows:

| | Profit projections | Actual profits |
|---|---|---|
| Year 1 | 200 | 250 |
| Year 2 | 250 | 300 |
| Year 3 | 500 | 600 |
| Year 4 | 350 | 200 |
| Year 5 | 100 | 100 |
| Total | 1400 | 1450 |

(v) The total profits earned through Year 5 were not less than 80% nor more than 120% of the profits that were projected when the license was entered into. If the district director determines that the other requirements of § 1.482-4(f)(2)(ii)(C) were met, no adjustment will be made to the royalty rate between USdrug and Eurodrug for the license of Nosplit.

*Example (2).* (i) The facts are the same as in *Example 1*,except that Eurodrug's actual profits earned were much higher than the projected profits, as follows:

| | Profit Projections | Actual Profits |
|---|---|---|
| Year 1 | 200 | 250 |
| Year 2 | 250 | 500 |
| Year 3 | 500 | 800 |
| Year 4 | 350 | 700 |
| Year 5 | 100 | 600 |
| Total | 1400 | 2850 |

(ii) In examining Usdrug's tax return for Year 5, the district director considers the actual profits realized by Eurodrug in Year 5, and all past years. Accordingly, although Years 1 through 4 may be closed under the statute of limitations, for purposes of determining whether an adjustment should be made with respect to the royalty rate in Year 5 with respect to Nosplit, the district director aggregates the actual profits from those years with the profits of Year 5. However the district director will make an adjustment, if any, only with respect to Year 5.

*Example (3).* (i) FP, a foreign corporation, licenses to USS, its U.S. subsidiary, a new air-filtering process that permits manufacturing plants to meet new environmental standards. The license runs for a 10-year period, and the profit derived from the new process is projected to be $15 million per year, for an aggregate profit of $150 million.

(ii) The royalty rate for the license is based on a comparable uncontrolled transaction involving a comparable intangible under comparable circumstances. The requirements of paragraphs (f)(2)(ii)(B)(1) through (5) of this section have been met. Specifically, FP and USS have entered into a written agreement that provides for a royalty in each year of the license, the royalty rate is considered arm's length for the first taxable year in which a substantial royalty was required to be paid, the license limited the use of the process to a specified field, consistent with industry practice, and there are no substantial changes in the functions performed by USS after the license was entered into.

(iii) In examining Year 4 of the license, the district director determines that the aggregate actual profits earned by USS through Year 4 are $30 million, less than 80% of the projected profits of $60 million. However, USS establishes to the satisfaction of the district director that the aggregate actual profits from the process are less than 80% of the projected profits in Year 3 because an earthquake severely damaged USS's manufacturing plant. Because the difference between the projected profits and actual profits was due to an extraordinary event that was beyond the control of USS, and could not reasonably have been anticipated at the time the license was entered into, the requirement under § 1.482-4(f)(2)(ii)(D) has been met, and no adjustment under this section is made.

*(3) Ownership of intangible property.* (i) Identification of owner-- (A) In general. The legal owner of intangible property pursuant to the intellectual property law of the relevant jurisdiction, or the holder of rights constituting an intangible property pursuant to contractual terms (such as the terms of a license) or other legal provision, will be considered the sole owner of the respective intangible property for purposes of this section unless such ownership is inconsistent with the economic substance of the underlying transactions. See § 1.482-1(d)(3)(ii)(B) (identifying contractual terms). If no owner of the respective intangible property is identified under the intellectual property law of the relevant jurisdiction, or pursuant to contractual terms (including terms imputed pursuant to § 1.482-1(d)(3)(ii)(B)) or other legal provision, then the controlled taxpayer who has control of the intangible property, based on all the facts and circumstances, will be considered the sole owner of the intangible property for purposes of this section.

(B) [Reserved]. For further guidance, see § 1.482-4T(f)(3)(i)(B).

(ii) Examples. The principles of this paragraph (f)(3) are illustrated by the following examples:

*Example (1).* FP, a foreign corporation, is the registered holder of the AA trademark in the United States. FP licenses to its U.S. subsidiary, USSub, the exclusive rights to manufacture and market products in the United States under the AA trademark. FP is the owner of the trademark pursuant to intellectual property law. USSub is the owner of the license pursuant to the terms of the license, but is not the owner of the trademark. See paragraphs (b)(3) and (4) of this section (defining an intangible as, among other things, a trademark or a license).

*Example (2).* The facts are the same as in Example 1. As a result of its sales and marketing activities, USSub develops a list of several hundred creditworthy customers that regularly purchase AA trademarked products. Neither the terms of the contract between FP and USSub nor the relevant intellectual property law specify which party owns the customer list. Because USSub has knowledge of the contents of the list, and has practical control over its use and dissemination, USSub is considered the sole owner of the customer list for purposes of this paragraph (f)(3).

*(4) Contribution to the value of intangible property owned by another.* (i) In general. The arm's length consideration for a contribution by one controlled taxpayer that develops or enhances the value, or may be reasonably anticipated to develop or enhance the value, of intangible property owned by another controlled taxpayer will be determined in accordance with the applicable rules under section 482. If the consideration for such a contribution is embedded within the contractual terms for a controlled transaction that involves such intangible property, then ordinarily no separate allocation will be made with respect to such contribution. In such cases, pursuant to § 1.482-1(d)(3), the contribution must be accounted for in evaluating the comparability of the controlled transaction to uncontrolled comparables, and accordingly in determining the arm's length consideration in the controlled transaction.

(ii) Examples. The principles of this paragraph (f)(4) are illustrated by the following examples:

*Example (1).* A, a member of a controlled group, allows B, another member of the controlled group, to use tangible property, such as laboratory equipment, in connection with B's development of an intangible that B owns. By furnishing tangible property, A makes a contribution to the development of intangible property owned by another controlled taxpayer, B. Pursuant to paragraph (f)(4)(i) of this section, the arm's length charge for A's furnishing of tangible property will be determined under the rules for use of tangible property in § 1.482-2(c).

*Example (2).* (i) Facts. FP, a foreign producer of wristwatches, is the registered holder of the YY trademark in the United States and in other countries worldwide. FP enters into an exclusive, five-year, renewable agreement with its newly organized U.S. subsidiary, USSub. The contractual terms of the agreement grant USSub the exclusive right to re-sell YY trademark wristwatches in the United States, obligate USSub to pay a fixed price per wristwatch throughout the entire term of the contract, and obligate both FP and USSub to undertake without separate compensation specified types and levels of marketing activities.

(ii) The consideration for FP's and USSub's marketing activities, as well as the consideration for the exclusive right to re-sell YY trademarked merchandise in the United States, are embedded in the transfer price paid for the wristwatches. Accordingly, pursuant to paragraph (f)(4)(i) of this section, ordinarily no separate allocation would be appropriate with respect to these embedded contributions.

(iii) Whether an allocation is warranted with respect to the transfer price for the wristwatches is determined under §§ 1.482-1, 1.482-3, and this section through § 1.482-6. The comparability analysis would include consideration of all relevant factors, including the nature of the intangible property embedded in the wristwatches and the nature of the marketing activities required under the agreement. This analysis would also take into account that the compensation for the activities performed by USSub and FP, as well as the consideration for USSub's use of the YY trademark, is embedded in the transfer price for the wristwatches, rather than provided for in separate agreements. See §§ 1.482-3(f) and 1.482-9(m)(4).

*Example (3).* (i) Facts. FP, a foreign producer of athletic gear, is the registered holder of the AA trademark in the United States and in other countries. In year 1, FP licenses to a newly organized U.S. subsidiary, USSub, the exclusive rights to use certain manufacturing and marketing intangible property to manufacture and market athletic gear in the United States under the AA trademark. The license agreement obligates USSub to pay a royalty based on sales of trademarked merchandise. The license agreement also obligates FP and USSub to perform without separate compensation specified types and levels of marketing activities. In year 1, USSub manufactures and sells athletic gear under the AA trademark in the United States.

(ii) The consideration for FP's and USSub's respective marketing activities is embedded in the contractual terms of the license for the AA trademark. Accordingly, pursuant to paragraph (f)(4)(i) of this section, ordinarily no separate allocation would be appropriate with respect to the embedded contributions in year 1. See § 1.482-9(m)(4).

(iii) Whether an allocation is warranted with respect to the royalty under the license agreement would be analyzed under § 1.482-1, and this section through § 1.482-6. The comparability analysis would include consideration of all relevant factors, such as the term and geographical exclusivity of the license, the nature of the intangible property subject to the license, and the nature of the marketing activities required to be undertaken pursuant to the license. Pursuant to paragraph (f)(4)(i) of this section, the analysis would also take into account the fact that the compensation for the marketing services is embedded in the royalty paid for use of the AA trademark, rather than provided for in a separate services agreement. For illustrations of application of the best method rule, see § 1.482-8 Examples 10, 11, and 12.

*Example (4).* (i) Facts. The year 1 facts are the same as in Example 3, with the following exceptions. In year 2, USSub undertakes certain incremental marketing activities in addition to those required by the contractual terms of the license for the AA trademark executed in year 1. The parties do not execute a separate agreement with respect to these incremental marketing activities performed by USSub. The license agreement executed in year 1 is of sufficient duration that it is reasonable to anticipate that USSub will obtain the benefit of its incremental activities, in the form of increased sales or revenues of trademarked products in the U.S. market.

(ii) To the extent that it was reasonable to anticipate that USSub's incremental marketing activities would increase the value only of USSub's intangible property (that is, USSub's license to use the AA trademark for a specified term), and not the value of the AA trademark owned by FP, USSub's incremental activities do not constitute a contribution for which an allocation is warranted under paragraph (f)(4)(i) of this section.

*Example (5).* (i) Facts. The year 1 facts are the same as in Example 3. In year 2, FP and USSub enter into a separate services agreement that obligates USSub to perform certain incremental marketing activities to promote AA trademark athletic gear in the United States, above and beyond the activities specified in the license agreement executed in year 1. In year 2, USSub begins to perform these incremental activities, pursuant to the separate services agreement with FP.

(ii) Whether an allocation is warranted with respect to USSub's incremental marketing activities covered by the separate services agreement would be evaluated under §§ 1.482-1 and 1.482-9, including a comparison of the compensation provided for the services with the results obtained under a method pursuant to § 1.482-9, selected and applied in accordance with the best method rule of § 1.482-1(c).

(iii) Whether an allocation is warranted with respect to the royalty under the license agreement is determined under § 1.482-1, and this section through § 1.482-6. The comparability analysis would include consideration of all relevant factors, such as the term and geographical exclusivity of the license, the nature of the intangible property subject to the license, and the nature of the marketing activities required to be undertaken pursuant to the license. The comparability analysis would take into account that the compensation for the incremental activities by USSub is provided for in the separate services agreement, rather than embedded in the royalty paid for use of the AA trademark. For illustrations of application of the best method rule, see § 1.482-8 Examples 10, 11, and 12.

*Example (6).* (i) Facts. The year 1 facts are the same as in Example 3. In year 2, FP and USSub enter into a separate services agreement that obligates FP to perform incremental marketing activities, not specified in the year 1 license, by advertising AA trademarked athletic gear in selected international sporting events, such as the Olympics and the soccer World Cup. FP's corporate advertising department develops and coordinates these special promotions. The separate services agreement obligates USSub to pay an amount to FP for the benefit to USSub that may reasonably be anticipated as the result of FP's incremental activities. The separate services agreement is not a qualified cost sharing arrangement under § 1.482-7T. FP begins to perform the incremental activities in year 2 pursuant to the separate services agreement.

(ii) Whether an allocation is warranted with respect to the incremental marketing activities performed by FP under the separate services agreement would be evaluated under § 1.482-9. Under the circumstances, it is reasonable to anticipate that FP's activities would increase the value of USSub's license as well as the value of FP's trademark. Accordingly, the incremental activities by FP may constitute in part a controlled services transaction for which USSub must compensate FP. The analysis of whether an allocation is warranted would include a comparison of the compensation provided for the services with the results obtained under a method pursuant to § 1.482-9, selected and applied in accordance with the best method rule of § 1.482-1(c).

(iii) Whether an allocation is appropriate with respect to the royalty under the license agreement would be evaluated under §§ 1.482-1 through 1.482-3, this section, and §§ 1.482-5 and 1.482-6. The comparability analysis would include consideration of all relevant factors, such as the term and geographical exclusivity of USSub's license, the nature of the intangible property subject to the license, and the marketing activities required to be undertaken by both FP and USSub pursuant to the license. This comparability analysis would take into account that the compensation for the incremental activities performed by FP was provided for in the separate services agreement, rather than embedded in the royalty paid for use of the AA trademark. For illustrations of application of the best method rule, see § 1.482-8, Example 10, Example 11, and Example 12.

*(5) Consideration not artificially limited.* The arm's length consideration for the controlled transfer of an intangible is not limited by the consideration paid in any uncontrolled transactions that do not meet the requirements of the comparable uncontrolled transaction method described in paragraph (c) of this section. Similarly, the arm's length consideration for an intangible is not limited by the prevailing rates of consideration paid for the use or transfer of intangibles within the same or similar industry.

*(6) Lump sum payments.* (i) In general. If an intangible is transferred in a controlled transaction for a lump sum, that amount must be commensurate with the income attributable to the intangible. A lump sum is commensurate with income in a taxable year if the equivalent royalty amount for that taxable year is equal to an arm's length royalty. The equivalent royalty amount for a taxable year is the amount determined by treating the lump sum as an advance payment of a stream of royalties over the useful life of the intangible (or the period covered by an agreement, if shorter), taking into account the projected sales of the licensee as of the date of the transfer. Thus, determining the equivalent royalty amount requires a present value calculation based on the lump sum, an appropriate discount rate, and the projected sales over the relevant period. The equivalent royalty amount is subject to periodic adjustments under § 1.482-4(f)(2)(i) to the same extent as an actual royalty payment pursuant to a license agreement.

(ii) Exceptions. No periodic adjustment will be made under paragraph (f)(2)(i) of this section if any of the exceptions to periodic adjustments provided in paragraph (f)(2)(ii) of this section apply.

(iii) Example. The following example illustrates the principle of this paragraph (f)(5).

*Example.* Calculation of the equivalent royalty amount.

(i) FSub is the foreign subsidiary of USP, a U.S. company. USP licenses FSub the right to produce and sell the whopperchopper, a patented new kitchen appliance, for the foreign market. The license is for a period of five years, and payment takes the form of a single lump-sum charge of $500,000 that is paid at the beginning of the period.

(ii) The equivalent royalty amount for this license is determined by deriving an equivalent royalty rate equal to the lump-sum payment divided by the present discounted value of FSub's projected sales of whopperchoppers over the life of the license. Based on the riskiness of the whopperchopper business, an appropriate discount rate is determined to be 10 percent. Projected sales of whopperchoppers for each year of the license are as follows:

| Year | Projected Sales ($) |
|---|---|
| 1 | 2,500,000 |
| 2 | 2,600,000 |
| 3 | 2,700,000 |
| 4 | 2,700,000 |
| 5 | 2,750,000 |

(iii) Based on this information, the present discounted value of the projected whopperchopper sales is approximately $10 million, yielding an equivalent royalty rate of approximately 5%. Thus, the equivalent royalty amounts for each year are as follows:

| Year | Projected Sales ($) | Equivalent royalty amount ($) |
|---|---|---|
| 1 | 2,500,000 | 125,000 |
| 2 | 2,600,000 | 130,000 |
| 3 | 2,700,000 | 135,000 |
| 4 | 2,000,000 | 135,000 |
| 5 | 2,750,000 | 137,500 |

(iv) If in any of the five taxable years the equivalent royalty amount is determined not to be an arm's length amount, a periodic adjustment may be made pursuant to § 1.482-4(f)(2)(i). The adjustment in such case would be equal to the difference between the equivalent royalty amount and the arm's length royalty in that taxable year.

*(7)* [Reserved]. For further guidance, see § 1.482-4T(f)(7).

**(g)** [Reserved]. For further guidance, see § 1.482-4T(g).

**(h) Effective/applicability date.** *(1) In general.* The provisions of paragraphs (f)(3)(i)(A), (f)(3)(ii), and (f)(4) of this section are generally applicable for taxable years beginning after July 31, 2009.

*(2) Election to apply regulation to earlier taxable years.* A person may elect to apply the provisions of paragraphs (f)(3)(i)(A), (f)(3)(ii), and (f)(4) of this section to earlier taxable years in accordance with the rules set forth in § 1.482-9(n)(2).

T.D. 8552, 7/1/94, amend T.D. 9278, 7/31/2006, T.D. 9456, 7/31/2009.

PAR. 6. Section 1.482-4 is amended as follows:

1. Paragraph (f)(3)(i)(B) is revised.
2. Paragraph (f)(7) is removed.
3. New paragraphs (g) and (h) are added.

The additions and revision reads as follows:

**Proposed § 1.482-4 Methods to determine taxable income in connection with a transfer of intangible property.** [*For Preamble, see ¶ 153,087*]

* * * * *

**(f)** * * *

*(4)* * * *

(i) * * *

(B) [The text of the proposed amendment to § 1.482-4(f)(3)(i)(B) is the same as the text of § 1.482-4T(f)(3)(i)(B) published elsewhere in this issue of the Federal Register]. [*See T.D. 9441, 01/05/2009, 74 Fed. Reg. 2.*].

* * * * *

**(g)** [The text of proposed § 1.482-4(g) is the same as the text of § 1.482-4T(g) published elsewhere in this issue of the Federal Register]. [*See T.D. 9441, 01/05/2009, 74 Fed. Reg. 2.*].

**(h)** [The text of proposed § 1.482-4(h) is the same as the text of § 1.482-4T(h) published elsewhere in this issue of the Federal Register]. [*See T.D. 9441, 01/05/2009, 74 Fed. Reg. 2.*].

PAR. 6. Section 1.482-4 is amended by

1. Redesignating paragraph (f)(3)(iv) as paragraph (f)(3)(v).

2. Adding a new paragraph (f)(3)(iv).

The addition reads as follows:

**Proposed § 1.482-4**

• ***Caution:*** This Proposed Reg was incorporated into final and temporary regulations by TD 9441, 12/31/2008.

Methods to determine taxable income in connection with a transfer of intangible property. [*For Preamble, see ¶ 152,697*]

* * * * *

**(f)** * * *

*(3)* * * *

(iv) Cost sharing arrangements. The rules in this paragraph (f)(3) regarding ownership and assistance with respect to cost shared intangibles and cost sharing arrangements will apply only as provided in § 1.482-7.

* * * * *

### § 1.482-4T Methods to determine taxable income in connection with a transfer of intangible property (temporary).

**(a)** through (f)(3)(i)(A) [Reserved]. For further guidance, see § 1.482-4(a) through (f)(3)(i)(A).

**(f)** *(3)* (i)

(B) Cost sharing arrangements. The rules in this paragraph (f)(3) regarding ownership with respect to cost shared intangibles and cost sharing arrangements will apply only as provided in § 1.482-7T.

(ii) through (f)(6) [Reserved]. For further guidance, see § 1.482-4(f)(3)(ii) through (f)(6)

**(g) Coordination with rules governing cost sharing arrangements.** Section 1.482-7T provides the specific methods to be used to determine arm's length results of controlled transactions in connection with a cost sharing arrangement. This section provides the specific methods to be used to determine arm's length results of a transfer of intangible property, including in an arrangement for sharing the costs and risks of developing intangibles other than a cost sharing arrangement covered by § 1.482-7T. In the case of such an arrangement, consideration of the principles, methods, comparability, and reliability considerations set forth in § 1.482-7T is relevant in determining the best method, including an unspecified method, under this section, as appropriately adjusted in light of the differences in the facts and circumstances between such arrangement and a cost sharing arrangement.

**(h) Effective/applicability date.** The provisions of paragraphs (f)(3)(i)(B) and (g) of this section are generally applicable on January 5, 2009.

**(i) Expiration date.** The applicability of this section expires on or before December 30, 2011.

T.D. 9278, 7/31/2006, amend T.D. 9441, 12/31/2008, T.D. 9456, 7/31/2009.

### § 1.482-5 Comparable profits method.

**(a) In general.** The comparable profits method evaluates whether the amount charged in a controlled transaction is arm's length based on objective measures of profitability (profit level indicators) derived from uncontrolled taxpayers that engage in similar business activities under similar circumstances.

**(b) Determination of arm's length result.** *(1) In general.* Under the comparable profits method, the determination of an arm's length result is based on the amount of operating profit that the tested party would have earned on related party transactions if its profit level indicator were equal to that of an uncontrolled comparable (comparable operating profit). Comparable operating profit is calculated by determining a profit level indicator for an uncontrolled comparable, and applying the profit level indicator to the financial data related to the tested party's most narrowly identifiable business activity for which data incorporating the controlled transaction is available (relevant business activity). To the extent possible, profit level indicators should be applied solely to the tested party's financial data that is related to controlled transactions. The tested party's reported operating profit is compared to the comparable operating profits derived from the profit level indicators of uncontrolled comparables to determine whether the reported operating profit represents an arm's length result.

*(2) Tested party.* (i) In general. For purposes of this section, the tested party will be the participant in the controlled transaction whose operating profit attributable to the controlled transactions can be verified using the most reliable data and requiring the fewest and most reliable adjustments, and for which reliable data regarding uncontrolled comparables can be located. Consequently, in most cases the tested party will be the least complex of the controlled taxpayers and will not own valuable intangible property or unique assets that distinguish it from potential uncontrolled comparables.

(ii) Adjustments for tested party. The tested party's operating profit must first be adjusted to reflect all other allocations under section 482, other than adjustments pursuant to this section.

*(3) Arm's length range.* See § 1.482-1(e)(2) for the determination of the arm's length range. For purposes of the comparable profits method, the arm's length range will be established using comparable operating profits derived from a single profit level indicator.

*(4) Profit level indicators.* Profit level indicators are ratios that measure relationships between profits and costs incurred or resources employed. A variety of profit level indicators can be calculated in any given case. Whether use of a particular profit level indicator is appropriate depends upon a number of factors, including the nature of the activities of the tested party, the reliability of the available data with respect to uncontrolled comparables, and the extent to which the profit level indicator is likely to produce a reliable measure of the income that the tested party would have earned had it dealt with controlled taxpayers at arm's length, taking into account all of the facts and circumstances. The profit level indicators should be derived from a sufficient number of years of data to reasonably measure returns that accrue to uncontrolled comparables. Generally, such a period should encompass at least the taxable year under review and the preceding two taxable years. This analysis must be applied in accordance with § 1.482-1(f)(2)(iii)(D). Profit level indicators that may provide a reliable basis for comparing operating profits of the tested party and uncontrolled comparables include the following—

(i) Rate of return on capital employed. The rate of return on capital employed is the ratio of operating profit to operating assets. The reliability of this profit level indicator increases as operating assets play a greater role in generating operating profits for both the tested party and the uncontrolled comparable. In addition, reliability under this profit level indicator depends on the extent to which the composition of the tested party's assets is similar to that of the uncontrolled comparable. Finally, difficulties in properly valuing operating assets will diminish the reliability of this profit level indicator.

(ii) Financial ratios. Financial ratios measure relationships between profit and costs or sales revenue. Since functional differences generally have a greater effect on the relationship between profit and costs or sales revenue than the relationship between profit and operating assets, financial ratios are more sensitive to functional differences than the rate of return on capital employed. Therefore, closer functional comparability normally is required under a financial ratio than under the rate of return on capital employed to achieve a similarly reliable measure of an arm's length result. Financial ratios that may be appropriate include the following—

(A) Ratio of operating profit to sales; and

(B) Ratio of gross profit to operating expenses. Reliability under this profit level indicator also depends on the extent to which the composition of the tested party's operating expenses is similar to that of the uncontrolled comparables.

(iii) Other profit level indicators. Other profit level indicators not described in this paragraph (b)(4) may be used if they provide reliable measures of the income that the tested party would have earned had it dealt with controlled taxpayers at arm's length. However, profit level indicators based solely on internal data may not be used under this paragraph (b)(4) because they are not objective measures of profitability derived from operations of uncontrolled taxpayers engaged in similar business activities under similar circumstances.

**(c) Comparability and reliability considerations.** *(1) In general.* Whether results derived from application of this method are the most reliable measure of the arm's length result must be determined using the factors described under the best method rule in § 1.482-1(c).

*(2) Comparability.* (i) In general. The degree of comparability between an uncontrolled taxpayer and the tested party is determined by applying the provisions of § 1.482-1(d)(2). The comparable profits method compares the profitability of the tested party, measured by a profit level indicator (generally based on operating profit), to the profitability of uncontrolled taxpayers in similar circumstances. As with all methods that rely on external market benchmarks, the greater the degree of comparability between the tested party and the uncontrolled taxpayer, the more reliable will be the results derived from the application of this method. The determination of the degree of comparability between the tested party and the uncontrolled taxpayer depends upon all the relevant facts and circumstances, including the relevant lines of business, the product or service markets involved, the asset composition employed (including the nature and quantity of tangible assets, intangible assets and working capital), the size and scope of operations, and the stage in a business or product cycle.

(ii) Functional, risk and resource comparability. An operating profit represents a return for the investment of resources and assumption of risks. Therefore, although all of the factors described in § 1.482-1(d)(3) must be considered, comparability under this method is particularly dependent on resources employed and risks assumed. Moreover, because resources and risks usually are directly related to functions performed, it is also important to consider functions performed in determining the degree of comparability between the tested party and an uncontrolled taxpayer. The degree of functional comparability required to obtain a reliable result under the comparable profits method, however, is generally less than that required under the resale price or cost plus methods. For example, because differences in functions performed often are reflected in operating expenses, taxpayers performing different functions may have very different gross profit margins but earn similar levels of operating profit.

(iii) Other comparability factors. Other factors listed in § 1.482-1(d)(3) also may be particularly relevant under the comparable profits method. Because operating profit usually is less sensitive than gross profit to product differences, reliability under the comparable profits method is not as dependent on product similarity as the resale price or cost plus method. However, the reliability of profitability measures based on operating profit may be adversely affected by factors that have less effect on results under the comparable uncontrolled price, resale price, and cost plus methods. For example, operating profit may be affected by varying cost structures (as reflected, for example, in the age of plant and equipment), differences in business experience (such as whether the business is in a start-up phase or is mature), or differences in management efficiency (as indicated, for example, by objective evidence such as expanding or contracting sales or executive compensation over time). Accordingly, if material differences in these factors are identified based on objective evidence, the reliability of the analysis may be affected.

(iv) Adjustments for the differences between the tested party and the uncontrolled taxpayers. If there are differences between the tested party and an uncontrolled comparable that would materially affect the profits determined under the relevant profit level indicator, adjustments should be made according to the comparability provisions of § 1.482-1(d)(2). In some cases, the assets of an uncontrolled comparable may need to be adjusted to achieve greater comparability between the tested party and the uncontrolled comparable. In such cases, the uncontrolled comparable's operating income attributable to those assets must also be adjusted before computing a profit level indicator in order to reflect the income and expense attributable to the adjusted assets. In certain cases it may also be appropriate to adjust the operating profit of the tested party and comparable parties. For example, where there are material differences in accounts payable among the comparable parties and the tested party, it will generally be appropriate to adjust the operating profit of each party by increasing it to reflect an imputed interest charge on each party's accounts payable. As another example, it may be appropriate to adjust the operating profit of a party to account for material differences in the utilization of or accounting for stock-based compensation (as defined by § 1.482-7T(d)(3)(i)) among the tested party and comparable parties.

*(3) Data and assumptions.* (i) In general. The reliability of the results derived from the comparable profits method is affected by the quality of the data and assumptions used to apply this method.

(ii) Consistency in accounting. The degree of consistency in accounting practices between the controlled transaction and the uncontrolled comparables that materially affect operating profit affects the reliability of the result. Thus, for example, if differences in inventory and other cost accounting practices would materially affect operating profit, the ability to make reliable adjustments for such differences would affect the reliability of the results.

(iii) Allocations between the relevant business activity and other activities. The reliability of the allocation of costs, income, and assets between the relevant business activity and other activities of the tested party or an uncontrolled comparable will affect the reliability of the determination of operating profit and profit level indicators. If it is not possible to allocate costs, income, and assets directly based on factual relationships, a reasonable allocation formula may be used. To the extent direct allocations are not made, the reliability of the results derived from the application of this method is reduced relative to the results of a method that requires fewer allocations of costs, income, and assets. Similarly, the reliability of the results derived from the application of this method is affected by the extent to which it is possible to apply the profit level indicator to the tested party's financial data that is related solely to the controlled transactions. For example, if the relevant business activity is the assembly of components purchased from both controlled and uncontrolled suppliers, it may not be possible to apply the profit level indicator solely to financial data related to the controlled transactions. In such a case, the reliability of the results derived from the application of this method will be reduced.

**(d) Definitions.** The definitions set forth in paragraphs (d)(1) through (6) of this section apply for purposes of this section. *(1) Sales revenue* means the amount of the total receipts from sale of goods and provision of services, less returns and allowances. Accounting principles and conventions that are generally accepted in the trade or industry of the controlled taxpayer under review must be used.

*(2) Gross profit* means sales revenue less cost of goods sold.

*(3) Operating expenses* includes all expenses not included in cost of goods sold except for interest expense, foreign income taxes (as defined in § 1.901-2(a)), domestic income taxes, and any other expenses not related to the operation of the relevant business activity. Operating expenses ordinarily include expenses associated with advertising, promotion, sales, marketing, warehousing and distribution, administration, and a reasonable allowance for depreciation and amortization.

*(4) Operating profit* means gross profit less operating expenses. Operating profit includes all income derived from the business activity being evaluated by the comparable profits method, but does not include interest and dividends, income derived from activities not being tested by this method, or extraordinary gains and losses that do not relate to the continuing operations of the tested party.

*(5) Reported operating profit* means the operating profit of the tested party reflected on a timely filed U.S. income tax return. If the tested party files a U.S. income tax return, its operating profit is considered reflected on a U.S. income tax return if the calculation of taxable income on its return for the taxable year takes into account the income attributable to the controlled transaction under review. If the tested party does not file a U.S. income tax return, its operating profit is considered reflected on a U.S. income tax return in any taxable year for which income attributable to the controlled transaction under review affects the calculation of the U.S. taxable income of any other member of the same controlled group. If the comparable operating profit of the tested party is determined from profit level indicators derived from financial statements or other accounting records and reports of comparable parties, adjustments may be made to the reported operating profit of the tested party in order to account for material differences between the tested party's operating profit reported for U.S. income tax purposes and the tested party's operating profit for financial statement purposes. In addition, in accordance with § 1.482-1(f)(2)(iii)(D), adjustments under section 482 that are finally determined may be taken into account in determining reported operating profit.

*(6) Operating assets.* The term operating assets means the value of all assets used in the relevant business activity of the tested party, including fixed assets and current assets (such as cash, cash equivalents, accounts receivable, and inventories). The term does not include investments in subsidiaries, excess cash, and portfolio investments. Operating assets may be measured by their net book value or by their fair market value, provided that the same method is consistently applied to the tested party and the comparable parties, and consistently applied from year to year. In addition, it may be necessary to take into account recent acquisitions, leased assets, intangibles, currency fluctuations, and other items that may not be explicitly recorded in the financial statements of the tested party or uncontrolled comparable. Finally, operating assets must be measured by the average of the values for the beginning of the year and the end of the year, unless substantial fluctuations in the value of operating assets during the year make this an inaccurate measure of the average value over the year. In such a case, a more accurate measure of the average value of operating assets must be applied.

**(e) Examples.** The following examples illustrate the application of this section.

*Example (1).* Transfer of tangible property resulting in no adjustment.

(i) FP is a publicly traded foreign corporation with a U.S. subsidiary, USSub, that is under audit for its 1996 taxable year. FP manufactures a consumer product for worldwide distribution. USSub imports the assembled product and distributes it within the United States at the wholesale level under the FP name.

(ii) FP does not allow uncontrolled taxpayers to distribute the product. Similar products are produced by other companies but none of them is sold to uncontrolled taxpayers or to uncontrolled distributors.

(iii) Based on all the facts and circumstances, the district director determines that the comparable profits method will provide the most reliable measure of an arm's length result. USSub is selected as the tested party because it engages in activities that are less complex than those undertaken by FP. There is data from a number of independent operators of wholesale distribution businesses. These potential comparables are further narrowed to select companies in the same industry segment that perform similar functions and bear similar risks to USSub. An analysis of the information available on these taxpayers shows that the ratio of operating profit to sales is the most appropriate profit level indicator, and this ratio is relatively stable where at least three years are included in the average. For the taxable years 1994 through 1996, USSub shows the following results:

| | 1994 | 1995 | 1996 | Average |
|---|---|---|---|---|
| Sales | 500,000 | 560,000 | 500,000 | 520,000 |
| Cost of Goods Sold | 393,000 | 412,400 | 400,000 | 401,800 |
| Operating Expenses | 80,000 | 110,000 | 104,600 | 98,200 |
| Operating Profit | 27,000 | 37,600 | (4,600) | 20,000 |

(iv) After adjustments have been made to account for identified material differences between USSub and the uncontrolled distributors, the average ratio of operating profit to sales is calculated for each of the uncontrolled distributors. Applying each ratio to USSub would lead to the following comparable operating profit (COP) for USSub:

| Uncontrolled Distributor | OP/S | USSub COP |
|---|---|---|
| A | 1.7% | $ 8,840 |
| B | 3.1% | 16,120 |
| C | 3.8% | 19,760 |
| D | 4.5% | 23,400 |
| E | 4.7% | 24,440 |
| F | 4.8% | 24,960 |
| G | 4.9% | 25,480 |
| H | 6.7% | 34,840 |
| I | 9.9% | 51,480 |
| J | 10.5% | 54,600 |

| Uncontrolled Distributor | OP/S | USSub COP |
|---|---|---|

(v) The data is not sufficiently complete to conclude that it is likely that all material differences between USSub and the uncontrolled distributors have been identified. Therefore, an arm's length range can be established only pursuant to § 1.482-1(e)(2)(iii)(B). The district director measures the arm's length range by the interquartile range of results, which consists of the results ranging from $19,760 to $34,840. Although USSub's operating income for 1996 shows a loss of $4,600, the district director determines that no allocation should be made, because USSub's average reported operating profit of $20,000 is within this range.

*Example (2).* Transfer of tangible property resulting in adjustment.

(i) The facts are the same as in *Example 1* except that USSub reported the following income and expenses:

| | 1994 | 1995 | 1996 | Average |
|---|---|---|---|---|
| Sales | 500,000 | 560,000 | 500,000 | 520,000 |
| Cost of Good Sold | 370,000 | 460,000 | 400,000 | 410,000 |
| Operating Expenses | 110,000 | 110,000 | 110,000 | 110,000 |
| Operating Profit | 20,000 | (10,000) | (10,000) | 0 |

(ii) The interquartile range of comparable operating profits remains the same as derived in *Example 1:* $19,760 to $34,840. USSub's average operating profit for the years 1994 through 1996 ($0) falls outside this range. Therefore, the district director determines that an allocation may be appropriate.

(iii) To determine the amount, if any, of the allocation, the district director compares USSub's reported operating profit for 1996 to comparable operating profits derived from the uncontrolled distributors' results for 1996. The ratio of operating profit to sales in 1996 is calculated for each of the uncontrolled comparables and applied to USSub's 1996 sales to derive the following results:

| Uncontrolled Distributor | OP/S | USSub COP |
|---|---|---|
| C | 0.5% | $ 2,500 |
| D | 1.5% | 7,500 |
| E | 2.0% | 10,000 |
| A | 1.6% | 13,000 |
| F | 2.8% | 14,000 |
| B | 2.9% | 14,500 |
| J | 3.0% | 15,000 |
| I | 4.4% | 22,000 |
| H | 6.9% | 34,500 |
| G | 7.4% | 37,000 |

(iv) Based on these results, the median of the comparable operating profits for 1996 is $14,250. Therefore, USSub's income for 1996 is increased by $24,250, the difference between USSub's reported operating profit for 1996 and the median of the comparable operating profits for 1996.

*Example (3).* Multiple year analysis.

(i) The facts are the same as in *Example 2.* In addition, the district director examines the taxpayer's results for the 1997 taxable year. As in Example 2, the district director increases USSub's income for the 1996 taxable year by

$24,250. The results for the 1997 taxable year, together with the 1995 and 1996 taxable years, are as follows:

| | 1995 | 1996 | 1997 | Average |
|---|---|---|---|---|
| Sales | 560,000 | 500,000 | 530,000 | 530,000 |
| Cost of Good Sold | 460,000 | 400,000 | 430,000 | 430,000 |
| Operating Expenses | 110,000 | 110,000 | 110,000 | 110,000 |
| Operating Profit | (10,000) | (10,000) | (10,000) | (10,000) |

(ii) The interquartile range of comparable operating profits, based on average results from the uncontrolled comparables and average sales for USSub for the years 1995 through 1997, ranges from $15,500 to $30,000. In determining whether an allocation for the 1997 taxable year may be made, the district director compares USSub's average reported operating profit for the years 1995 through 1997 to the interquartile range of average comparable operating profits over this period. USSub's average reported operating profit is determined without regard to the adjustment made with respect to the 1996 taxable year. See § 1.482-1(f)(2)(iii)(D). Therefore, USSub's average reported operating profit for the years 1995 through 1997 is ($10,000). Because this amount of income falls outside the interquartile range, the district director determines that an allocation may be appropriate.

(iii) To determine the amount, if any, of the allocation for the 1997 taxable year, the district director compares USSub's reported operating profit for 1997 to the median of the comparable operating profits derived from the uncontrolled distributors' results for 1997. The median of the comparable operating profits derived from the uncontrolled comparables results for the 1997 taxable year is $12,000. Based on this comparison, the district director increases USSub's 1997 taxable income by $22,000, the difference between the median of the comparable operating profits for the 1997 taxable year and USSub's reported operating profit of ($10,000) for the 1997 taxable year.

*Example (4).* Transfer of intangible to offshore manufacturer.

(i) DevCo is a U.S. developer, producer and marketer of widgets. DevCo develops a new "high tech widget" (htw) that is manufactured by its foreign subsidiary ManuCo located in Country H. ManuCo sells the htw to MarkCo (a U.S. subsidiary of DevCo) for distribution and marketing in the United States. The taxable year 1996 is under audit, and the district director examines whether the royalty rate of 5 percent paid by ManuCo to DevCo is an arm's length consideration for the htw technology.

(ii) Based on all the facts and circumstances, the district director determines that the comparable profits method will provide the most reliable measure of an arm's length result. ManuCo is selected as the tested party because it engages in relatively routine manufacturing activities, while DevCo engages in a variety of complex activities using unique and valuable intangibles. Finally, because ManuCo engages in manufacturing activities, it is determined that the ratio of operating profit to operating assets is an appropriate profit level indicator.

(iii) Uncontrolled taxpayers performing similar functions cannot be found in country H. It is determined that data available in countries M and N provides the best match of companies in a similar market performing similar functions and bearing similar risks. Such data is sufficiently complete to identify many of the material differences between ManuCo and the uncontrolled comparables, and to make adjustments to account for such differences. However, data is not sufficiently complete so that it is likely that no material differences remain. In particular, the differences in geographic markets might have materially affected the results of the various companies.

(iv) In a separate analysis, it is determined that the price that ManuCo charged to MarkCo for the htw's is an arm's length price under § 1.482-3(b). Therefore, ManuCo's financial data derived from its sales to MarkCo are reliable. ManuCo's financial data from 1994-1996 is as follows:

| | 1994 | 1995 | 1996 | Average |
|---|---|---|---|---|
| Assets | $24,000 | $25,000 | $26,000 | $25,000 |
| Sales to MarkCo. | 25,000 | 30,000 | 35,000 | 30,000 |
| Cost of Goods Sold | 6,250 | 7,500 | 8,750 | 7,500 |
| Royalty to DevCo (5%) | 1,250 | 1,500 | 1,750 | 1,500 |
| Other | 5,000 | 6,000 | 7,000 | 6,000 |
| Operating Expenses | 1,000 | 1,000 | 1,000 | 1,000 |
| Operating Profit | 17,750 | 21,500 | 25,250 | 21,500 |

(v) Applying the ratios of average operating profit to operating assets for the 1994 through 1996 taxable years derived from a group of similar uncontrolled comparables located in country M and N to ManuCo's average operating assets for the same period provides a set of comparable operating profits. The interquartile range for these average comparable operating profits is $3,000 to $4,500. ManuCo's average reported operating profit for the years 1994 through 1996 ($21,500) falls outside this range. Therefore, the district director determines that an allocation may be appropriate for the 1996 taxable year.

(vi) To determine the amount, if any, of the allocation for the 1996 taxable year, the district director compares ManuCo's reported operating profit for 1996 to the median of the comparable operating profits derived from the uncontrolled distributors' results for 1996. The median result for the uncontrolled comparables for 1996 is $3,750. Based on this comparison, the district director increases royalties that ManuCo paid by $21,500 (the difference between $25,250 and the median of the comparable operating profits, $3,750).

*Example (5).* Adjusting operating assets and operating profit for differences in accounts receivable.

(i) USM is a U.S. company that manufactures parts for industrial equipment and sells them to its foreign parent corporation. For purposes of applying the comparable profits method, 15 uncontrolled manufacturers that are similar to USM have been identified.

(ii) USM has a significantly lower level of accounts receivable than the uncontrolled manufacturers. Since the rate of return on capital employed is to be used as the profit level indicator, both operating assets and operating profits must be adjusted to account for this difference. Each uncontrolled comparable's operating assets is reduced by the amount (relative to sales) by which they exceed USM's accounts receivable. Each uncontrolled comparable's operating profit is adjusted by deducting imputed interest income on the excess accounts receivable. This imputed interest income is calculated by multiplying the uncontrolled comparable's excess accounts receivable by an interest rate appropriate for short-term debt.

*Example (6)*. Adjusting operating profit for differences in accounts payable.

(i) USD is the U.S. subsidiary of a foreign corporation. USD purchases goods from its foreign parent and sells them in the U.S. market. For purposes of applying the comparable profits method, 10 uncontrolled distributors that are similar to USD have been identified.

(ii) There are significant differences in the level of accounts payable among the uncontrolled distributors and USD. To adjust for these differences, the district director increases the operating profit of the uncontrolled distributors and USD to reflect interest expense imputed to the accounts payable. The imputed interest expense for each company is calculated by multiplying the company's accounts payable by an interest rate appropriate for its short-term debt.

---

T.D. 8552, 7/1/94, amend T.D. 9088, 8/25/2003, T.D. 9441, 12/31/2008.

---

PAR. 7. Section 1.482-5 is amended by revising the last sentence of paragraph (c)(2)(iv) to read as follows:

**Proposed § 1.482-5**

• ***Caution:*** This Proposed Reg was incorporated into final and temporary regulations by TD 9441, 12/31/2008.

Comparable profits method. [*For Preamble, see ¶ 152,697*]

* * * * *

**(c)** * * *

*(2)* * * *

(iv). * * * As another example, it may be appropriate to adjust the operating profit of a party to account for material differences in the utilization of or accounting for stock-based compensation (as defined by § 1.482-7(d)(3)(i)) among the tested party and comparable parties.

* * * * *

**§ 1.482-6 Profit split method.**

**(a) In general.** The profit split method evaluates whether the allocation of the combined operating profit or loss attributable to one or more controlled transactions is arm's length by reference to the relative value of each controlled taxpayer's contribution to that combined operating profit or loss. The combined operating profit or loss must be derived from the most narrowly identifiable business activity of the controlled taxpayers for which data is available that includes the controlled transactions (relevant business activity).

**(b) Appropriate share of profits and losses.** The relative value of each controlled taxpayer's contribution to the success of the relevant business activity must be determined in a manner that reflects the functions performed, risks assumed, and resources employed by each participant in the relevant business activity, consistent with the comparability provisions of § 1.482-1(d)(3). Such an allocation is intended to correspond to the division of profit or loss that would result from an arrangement between uncontrolled taxpayers, each performing functions similar to those of the various controlled taxpayers engaged in the relevant business activity. The profit allocated to any particular member of a controlled group is not necessarily limited to the total operating profit of the group from the relevant business activity. For example, in a given year, one member of the group may earn a profit while another member incurs a loss. In addition, it may not be assumed that the combined operating profit or loss from the relevant business activity should be shared equally, or in any other arbitrary proportion. The specific method of allocation must be determined under paragraph (c) of this section.

**(c) Application.** *(1) In general.* The allocation of profit or loss under the profit split method must be made in accordance with one of the following allocation methods—

(i) The comparable profit split, described in paragraph (c)(2) of this section; or

(ii) The residual profit split, described in paragraph (c)(3) of this section.

*(2) Comparable profit split.* (i) In general. A comparable profit split is derived from the combined operating profit of uncontrolled taxpayers whose transactions and activities are similar to those of the controlled taxpayers in the relevant business activity. Under this method, each uncontrolled taxpayer's percentage of the combined operating profit or loss is used to allocate the combined operating profit or loss of the relevant business activity.

(ii) Comparability and reliability considerations. (A) In general. Whether results derived from application of this method are the most reliable measure of the arm's length result is determined using the factors described under the best method rule in § 1.482-1(c).

(B) Comparability. (1) In general. The degree of comparability between the controlled and uncontrolled taxpayers is determined by applying the comparability provisions of § 1.482-1(d). The comparable profit split compares the division of operating profits among the controlled taxpayers to the division of operating profits among uncontrolled taxpayers engaged in similar activities under similar circumstances. Although all of the factors described in § 1.482-1(d)(3) must be considered, comparability under this method is particularly dependent on the considerations described under the comparable profits method in § 1.482-5(c)(2) or § 1.482-9(f)(2)(iii) because this method is based on a comparison of the operating profit of the controlled and uncontrolled taxpayers. In addition, because the contractual terms of the relationship among the participants in the relevant business activity will be a principal determinant of the allocation of functions and risks among them, comparability under this method also depends particularly on the degree of similarity of the contractual terms of the controlled and uncontrolled taxpayers. Finally, the comparable profit split may not be used if the combined operating profit (as a percentage of the combined assets) of the uncontrolled comparables varies significantly from that earned by the controlled taxpayers.

(2) Adjustments for differences between the controlled and uncontrolled taxpayers. If there are differences between the controlled and uncontrolled taxpayers that would materially affect the division of operating profit, adjustments must be made according to the provisions of § 1.482-1(d)(2).

(C) Data and assumptions. The reliability of the results derived from the comparable profit split is affected by the quality of the data and assumptions used to apply this method. In particular, the following factors must be considered—

(1) The reliability of the allocation of costs, income, and assets between the relevant business activity and the participants' other activities will affect the accuracy of the determination of combined operating profit and its allocation among the participants. If it is not possible to allocate costs, income, and assets directly based on factual relationships, a reasonable allocation formula may be used. To the extent direct allocations are not made, the reliability of the results derived from the application of this method is reduced relative to the results of a method that requires fewer allocations of costs, income, and assets. Similarly, the reliability of the results derived from the application of this method is affected by the extent to which it is possible to apply the method to the parties' financial data that is related solely to the controlled transactions. For example, if the relevant business activity is the assembly of components purchased from both controlled and uncontrolled suppliers, it may not be possible to apply the method solely to financial data related to the controlled transactions. In such a case, the reliability of the results derived from the application of this method will be reduced.

(2) The degree of consistency between the controlled and uncontrolled taxpayers in accounting practices that materially affect the items that determine the amount and allocation of operating profit affects the reliability of the result. Thus, for example, if differences in inventory and other cost accounting practices would materially affect operating profit, the ability to make reliable adjustments for such differences would affect the reliability of the results. Further, accounting consistency among the participants in the controlled transaction is required to ensure that the items determining the amount and allocation of operating profit are measured on a consistent basis.

(D) Other factors affecting reliability. Like the methods described in §§ 1.482-3, 1.482-4, 1.482-5, and 1.482-9, the comparable profit split relies exclusively on external market benchmarks. As indicated in § 1.482-1(c)(2)(i), as the degree of comparability between the controlled and uncontrolled transactions increases, the relative weight accorded the analysis under this method will increase. In addition, the reliability of the analysis under this method may be enhanced by the fact that all parties to the controlled transaction are evaluated under the comparable profit split. However, the reliability of the results of an analysis based on information from all parties to a transaction is affected by the reliability of the data and the assumptions pertaining to each party to the controlled transaction. Thus, if the data and assumptions are significantly more reliable with respect to one of the parties than with respect to the others, a different method, focusing solely on the results of that party, may yield more reliable results.

*(3) Residual profit split.* (i) In general. Under this method, the combined operating profit or loss from the relevant business activity is allocated between the controlled taxpayers following the two-step process set forth in paragraphs (c)(3)(i)(A) and (B) of this section.

(A) Allocate income to routine contributions. The first step allocates operating income to each party to the controlled transactions to provide a market return for its routine contributions to the relevant business activity. Routine contributions are contributions of the same or a similar kind to those made by uncontrolled taxpayers involved in similar business activities for which it is possible to identify market returns. Routine contributions ordinarily include contributions of tangible property, services and intangible property that are generally owned by uncontrolled taxpayers engaged in similar activities. A functional analysis is required to identify these contributions according to the functions performed, risks assumed, and resources employed by each of the controlled taxpayers. Market returns for the routine contributions should be determined by reference to the returns achieved by uncontrolled taxpayers engaged in similar activities, consistent with the methods described in §§ 1.482-3, 1.482-4, 1.482-5 and 1.482-9.

(B) Allocate residual profit. (1) Nonroutine contributions generally. The allocation of income to the controlled taxpayer's routine contributions will not reflect profits attributable to each controlled taxpayer's contributions to the relevant business activity that are not routine (nonroutine contributions). A nonroutine contribution is a contribution that is not accounted for as a routine contribution. Thus, in cases where such nonroutine contributions are present, there normally will be an unallocated residual profit after the allocation of income described in paragraph (c)(3)(i)(A) of this section. Under this second step, the residual profit generally should be divided among the controlled taxpayers based upon the relative value of their nonroutine contributions to the relevant business activity. The relative value of the nonroutine contributions of each taxpayer should be measured in a manner that most reliably reflects each nonroutine contribution made to the controlled transaction and each controlled taxpayer's role in the nonroutine contributions. If the nonroutine contribution by one of the controlled taxpayers is also used in other business activities (such as transactions with other controlled taxpayers), an appropriate allocation of the value of the nonroutine contribution must be made among all the business activities in which it is used.

(2) Nonroutine contributions of intangible property. In many cases, nonroutine contributions of a taxpayer to the relevant business activity may be contributions of intangible property. For purposes of paragraph (c)(3)(i)(B)(1) of this section, the relative value of nonroutine intangible property contributed by taxpayers may be measured by external market benchmarks that reflect the fair market value of such intangible property. Alternatively, the relative value of nonroutine intangible property contributions may be estimated by the capitalized cost of developing the intangible property and all related improvements and updates, less an appropriate amount of amortization based on the useful life of each intangible property. Finally, if the intangible property development expenditures of the parties are relatively constant over time and the useful life of the intangible property contributed by all parties is approximately the same, the amount of actual expenditures in recent years may be used to estimate the relative value of nonroutine intangible property contributions.

(ii) Comparability and reliability considerations. (A) In general. Whether results derived from this method are the most reliable measure of the arm's length result is determined using the factors described under the best method rule in § 1.482-1(c). Thus, comparability and the quality of data and assumptions must be considered in determining whether this method provides the most reliable measure of an arm's length result. The application of these factors to the residual profit split is discussed in paragraph (c)(3)(ii)(B), (C), and (D) of this section.

(B) Comparability. The first step of the residual profit split relies on market benchmarks of profitability. Thus, the comparability considerations that are relevant for the first step of the residual profit split are those that are relevant for the methods that are used to determine market returns for the routine contributions. The second step of the residual profit split, however, may not rely so directly on market benchmarks. Thus, the reliability of the results under this method is reduced to the extent that the allocation of profits in the second step does not rely on market benchmarks.

(C) Data and assumptions. The reliability of the results derived from the residual profit split is affected by the quality of the data and assumptions used to apply this method. In particular, the following factors must be considered—

(1) The reliability of the allocation of costs, income, and assets as described in paragraph (c)(2)(ii)(C)(1) of this section;

(2) Accounting consistency as described in paragraph (c)(2)(ii)(C)(2) of this section;

(3) The reliability of the data used and the assumptions made in valuing the intangible property contributed by the participants. In particular, if capitalized costs of development are used to estimate the value of intangible property, the reliability of the results is reduced relative to the reliability of other methods that do not require such an estimate, for the following reasons. First, in any given case, the costs of developing the intangible may not be related to its market value. Second, the calculation of the capitalized costs of development may require the allocation of indirect costs between the relevant business activity and the controlled taxpayer's other activities, which may affect the reliability of the analysis. Finally, the calculation of costs may require assumptions regarding the useful life of the intangible property.

(D) Other factors affecting reliability. Like the methods described in §§ 1.482-3, 1.482-4, 1.482-5, and 1.482-9, the first step of the residual profit split relies exclusively on external market benchmarks. As indicated in § 1.482-1(c)(2)(i), as the degree of comparability between the controlled and uncontrolled transactions increases, the relative weight accorded the analysis under this method will increase. In addition, to the extent the allocation of profits in the second step is not based on external market benchmarks, the reliability of the analysis will be decreased in relation to an analysis under a method that relies on market benchmarks. Finally, the reliability of the analysis under this method may be enhanced by the fact that all parties to the controlled transaction are evaluated under the residual profit split. However, the reliability of the results of an analysis based on information from all parties to a transaction is affected by the reliability of the data and the assumptions pertaining to each party to the controlled transaction. Thus, if the data and assumptions are significantly more reliable with respect to one of the parties than with respect to the others, a different method, focusing solely on the results of that party, may yield more reliable results.

(iii) Example. The provisions of this paragraph (c)(3) are illustrated by the following example.

*Example (1).* Application of residual profit split.

(i) XYZ is a U.S. corporation that develops, manufactures and markets a line of products for police use in the United States. XYZ's research unit developed a bulletproof material for use in protective clothing and headgear (Nulon). XYZ obtains patent protection for the chemical formula for Nulon. Since its introduction in the U.S., Nulon has captured a substantial share of the U.S. market for bulletproof material.

(ii) XYZ licensed its European subsidiary, XYZ-Europe, to manufacture and market Nulon in Europe. XYZ-Europe is a well-established company that manufactures and markets XYZ products in Europe. XYZ-Europe has a research unit that adapts XYZ products for the defense market, as well as a well-developed marketing network that employs brand names that it developed.

(iii) XYZ-Europe's research unit alters Nulon to adapt it to military specifications and develops a high-intensity marketing campaign directed at the defense industry in several European countries. Beginning with the 1995 taxable year, XYZ-Europe manufactures and sells Nulon in Europe through its marketing network under one of its brand names.

(iv) For the 1995 taxable year, XYZ has no direct expenses associated with the license of Nulon to XYZ-Europe and incurs no expenses related to the marketing of Nulon in Europe. For the 1995 taxable year, XYZ-Europe's Nulon sales and pre-royalty expenses are $500 million and $300 million, respectively, resulting in net pre-royalty profit of $200 million related to the Nulon business. The operating assets employed in XYZ-Europe's Nulon business are $200 million. Given the facts and circumstances, the district director determines under the best method rule that a residual profit split will provide the most reliable measure of an arm's length result. Based on an examination of a sample of European companies performing functions similar to those of XYZ-Europe, the district director determines that an average market return on XYZ-Europe's operating assets in the Nulon business is 10 percent, resulting in a market return of $20 million (10% X $200 million) for XYZ-Europe's Nulon business, and a residual profit of $180 million.

(v) Since the first stage of the residual profit split allocated profits to XYZ-Europe's contributions other than those attributable to highly valuable intangible property, it is assumed that the residual profit of $180 million is attributable to the valuable intangibles related to Nulon, i.e., the European brand name for Nulon and the Nulon formula (including XYZ-Europe's modifications). To estimate the relative values of these intangibles, the district director compares the ratios of the capitalized value of expenditures as of 1995 on Nulon-related-research and development and marketing over the 1995 sales related to such expenditures.

(vi) Because XYZ's protective product research and development expenses support the worldwide protective product sales of the XYZ group, it is necessary to allocate such expenses among the worldwide business activities to which they relate. The district director determines that it is reasonable to allocate the value of these expenses based on worldwide protective product sales. Using information on the average useful life of its investments in protective product research and development, the district director capitalizes and amortizes XYZ's protective product research and development expenses. This analysis indicates that the capitalized research and development expenditures have a value of $0.20 per dollar of global protective product sales in 1995.

(vii) XYZ-Europe's expenditures on Nulon research and development and marketing support only its sales in Europe.

Using information on the average useful life of XYZ-Europe's investments in marketing and research and development, the district director capitalizes and amortizes XYZ-Europe's expenditures and determines that they have a value in 1995 of $0.40 per dollar of XYZ-Europe's Nulon sales.

(viii) Thus, XYZ and XYZ-Europe together contributed $0.60 in capitalized intangible development expenses for each dollar of XYZ-Europe's protective product sales for 1995, of which XYZ contributed one-third (or $0.20 per dollar of sales). Accordingly, the district director determines that an arm's length royalty for the Nulon license for the 1995 taxable year is $60 million, i.e., one-third of XYZ-Europe's $180 million in residual Nulon profit.

**(d) Effective/applicability date.** *(1) In general.* The provisions of paragraphs (c)(2)(ii)(B)(1) and (D), (c)(3)(i)(A) and (B), and (c)(3)(ii)(D) of this section are generally applicable for taxable years beginning after July 31, 2009.

*(2) Election to apply regulation to earlier taxable years.* A person may elect to apply the provisions of paragraphs (c)(2)(ii)(B)(1) and (D), (c)(3)(i)(A) and (B), and (c)(3)(ii)(D) of this section to earlier taxable years in accordance with the rules set forth in § 1.482-9(n)(2).

T.D. 8552, 7/1/94, amend T.D. 9278, 7/31/2006, T.D. 9456, 7/31/2009.

PAR. 7. Section 1.482-7 is revised to read as follows:

**Proposed § 1.482-7 Methods to determine taxable income in connection with a cost sharing arrangement.** [*For Preamble, see ¶ 153,087*]

[The text of the proposed § 1.482-7 is the same as the text of § 1.482-7T(a) through (m) published elsewhere in this issue of the Federal Register]. [*See T.D. 9441, 01/05/2009, 74 Fed. Reg. 2.*].

**§ 1.482-7A Sharing of costs.**

Regulations applicable on or before January 4, 2009.

**(a) In general.** *(1) Scope and application of the rules in this section.* A cost sharing arrangement is an agreement under which the parties agree to share the costs of development of one or more intangibles in proportion to their shares of reasonably anticipated benefits from their individual exploitation of the interests in the intangibles assigned to them under the arrangement. A taxpayer may claim that a cost sharing arrangement is a qualified cost sharing arrangement only if the agreement meets the requirements of paragraph (b) of this section. Consistent with the rules of § 1.482-1(d)(3)(ii)(B) (Identifying contractual terms), the district director may apply the rules of this section to any arrangement that in substance constitutes a cost sharing arrangement, notwithstanding a failure to comply with any requirement of this section. A qualified cost sharing arrangement, or an arrangement to which the district director applies the rules of this section, will not be treated as a partnership to which the rules of subchapter K apply. See § 301.7701-3(e) of this chapter. Furthermore, a participant that is a foreign corporation or nonresident alien individual will not be treated as engaged in trade or business within the United States solely by reason of its participation in such an arrangement. See generally § 1.864-2(a).

*(2) Limitation on allocations.* The district director shall not make allocations with respect to a qualified cost sharing arrangement except to the extent necessary to make each controlled participant's share of the costs (as determined under paragraph (d) of this section) of intangible development under the qualified cost sharing arrangement equal to its share of reasonably anticipated benefits attributable to such development, under the rules of this section. If a controlled taxpayer acquires an interest in intangible property from another controlled taxpayer (other than in consideration for bearing a share of the costs of the intangible's development), then the district director may make appropriate allocations to reflect an arm's length consideration for the acquisition of the interest in such intangible under the rules of §§ 1.482-1 and 1.482-4 through 1.482-6. See paragraph (g) of this section. An interest in an intangible includes any commercially transferable interest, the benefits of which are susceptible of valuation. See § 1.482-4(b) for the definition of an intangible.

*(3) Coordination with § 1.482-1.* A qualified cost sharing arrangement produces results that are consistent with an arm's length result within the meaning of § 1.482-1(b)(1) if, and only if, each controlled participant's share of the costs (as determined under paragraph (d) of this section) of intangible development under the qualified cost sharing arrangement equals its share of reasonably anticipated benefits attributable to such development (as required by paragraph (a)(2) of this section) and all other requirements of this section are satisfied.

*(4) Cross references.* Paragraph (c) of this section defines participant. Paragraph (d) of this section defines the costs of intangible development. Paragraph (e) of this section defines the anticipated benefits of intangible development. Paragraph (f) of this section provides rules governing cost allocations. Paragraph (g) of this section provides rules governing transfers of intangibles other than in consideration for bearing a share of the costs of the intangible's development. Rules governing the character of payments made pursuant to a qualified cost sharing arrangement are provided in paragraph (h) of this section. Paragraph (i) of this section provides accounting requirements. Paragraph (j) of this section provides administrative requirements. Paragraph (k) of this section provides an effective date. Paragraph (l) provides a transition rule.

**(b) Qualified cost sharing arrangement.** A qualified cost sharing arrangement must—

*(1)* Include two or more participants;

*(2)* Provide a method to calculate each controlled participant's share of intangible development costs, based on factors that can reasonably be expected to reflect that participant's share of anticipated benefits;

*(3)* Provide for adjustment to the controlled participants' shares of intangible development costs to account for changes in economic conditions, the business operations and practices of the participants, and the ongoing development of intangibles under the arrangement; and

*(4)* Be recorded in a document that is contemporaneous with the formation (and any revision) of the cost sharing arrangement and that includes—

(i) A list of the arrangement's participants, and any other member of the controlled group that will benefit from the use of intangibles developed under the cost sharing arrangement;

(ii) The information described in paragraphs (b)(2) and (b)(3) of this section;

(iii) A description of the scope of the research and development to be undertaken, including the intangible or class of intangibles intended to be developed;

(iv) A description of each participant's interest in any covered intangibles. A covered intangible is any intangible property that is developed as a result of the research and development undertaken under the cost sharing arrangement (intangible development area);

(v) The duration of the arrangement; and

(vi) The conditions under which the arrangement may be modified or terminated and the consequences of such modification or termination, such as the interest that each participant will receive in any covered intangibles.

**(c) Participant.** *(1) In general.* For purposes of this section, a participant is a controlled taxpayer that meets the requirements of this paragraph (c)(1) (controlled participant) or an uncontrolled taxpayer that is a party to the cost sharing arrangement (uncontrolled participant). See § 1.482-1(i)(5) for the definitions of controlled and uncontrolled taxpayers. A controlled taxpayer may be a controlled participant only if it—

(i) Reasonably anticipates that it will derive benefits from the use of covered intangibles;

(ii) Substantially complies with the accounting requirements described in paragraph (i) of this section; and

(iii) Substantially complies with the administrative requirements described in paragraph (j) of this section.

(iv) The following example illustrates paragraph (c)(1)(i) of this section:

*Example.* Foreign Parent (FP) is a foreign corporation engaged in the extraction of a natural resource. FP has a U.S. subsidiary (USS) to which FP sells supplies of this resource for sale in the United States. FP enters into a cost sharing arrangement with USS to develop a new machine to extract the natural resource. The machine uses a new extraction process that will be patented in the United States and in other countries. The cost sharing arrangement provides that USS will receive the rights to use the machine in the extraction of the natural resource in the United States, and FP will receive the rights in the rest of the world. This resource does not, however, exist in the United States. Despite the fact that USS has received the right to use this process in the United States, USS is not a qualified participant because it will not derive a benefit from the use of the intangible developed under the cost sharing arrangement.

*(2) Treatment of a controlled taxpayer that is not a controlled participant.* (i) In general. If a controlled taxpayer that is not a controlled participant (within the meaning of this paragraph (c)) provides assistance in relation to the research and development undertaken in the intangible development area, it must receive consideration from the controlled participants under the rules of § 1.482-4(f)(3)(iii) (Allocations with respect to assistance provided to the owner). For purposes of paragraph (d) of this section, such consideration is treated as an operating expense and each controlled participant must be treated as incurring a share of such consideration equal to its share of reasonably anticipated benefits (as defined in paragraph (f)(3) of this section).

(ii) Example. The following example illustrates this paragraph (c)(2):

*Example.* (i) U.S. Parent (USP), one foreign subsidiary (FS), and a second foreign subsidiary constituting the group's research arm (R+D) enter into a cost sharing agreement to develop manufacturing intangibles for a new product line A. USP and FS are assigned the exclusive rights to exploit the intangibles respectively in the United States and the rest of the world, where each presently manufactures and sells various existing product lines. R + D is not assigned any rights to exploit the intangibles. R + D's activity consists solely in carrying out research for the group. It is reliably projected that the shares of reasonably anticipated benefits of USP and FS will be 66⅔% and 33⅓%, respectively, and the parties' agreement provides that USP and FS will reimburse 66⅔% and 33⅓%, respectively, of the intangible development costs incurred by R + D with respect to the new intangible.

(ii) R + D does not qualify as a controlled participant within the meaning of paragraph (c) of this section, because it will not derive any benefits from the use of covered intangibles. Therefore, R + D is treated as a service provider for purposes of this section and must receive arm's length consideration for the assistance it is deemed to provide to USP and FS, under the rules of § 1.482-4(f)(3)(iii). Such consideration must be treated as intangible development costs incurred by USP and FS in proportion to their shares of reasonably anticipated benefits (i.e., 66⅔% and 33⅓%, respectively). R + D will not be considered to bear any share of the intangible development costs under the arrangement.

*(3) Treatment of consolidated group.* For purposes of this section, all members of the same affiliated group (within the meaning of section 1504(a)) that join in the filing of a consolidated return for the taxable year under section 1501 shall be treated as one taxpayer.

**(d) Costs.** *(1) Intangible development costs.* For purposes of this section, a controlled participant's costs of developing intangibles for a taxable year mean all of the costs incurred by that participant related to the intangible development area, plus all of the cost sharing payments it makes to other controlled and uncontrolled participants, minus all of the cost sharing payments it receives from other controlled and uncontrolled participants. Costs incurred related to the intangible development area consist of the following items: operating expenses as defined in § 1.482-5(d)(3), other than depreciation or amortization expense, plus (to the extent not included in such operating expenses, as defined in § 1.482-5(d)(3)) the charge for the use of any tangible property made available to the qualified cost sharing arrangement. If tangible property is made available to the qualified cost sharing arrangement by a controlled participant, the determination of the appropriate charge will be governed by the rules of § 1.482-2(c) (Use of tangible property). Intangible development costs do not include the consideration for the use of any intangible property made available to the qualified cost sharing arrangement. See paragraph (g)(2) of this section. If a particular cost contributes to the intangible development area and other areas or other business activities, the cost must be allocated between the intangible development area and the other areas or business activities on a reasonable basis. In such a case, it is necessary to estimate the total benefits attributable to the cost incurred. The share of such cost allocated to the intangible development area must correspond to covered intangibles' share of the total benefits. Costs that do not contribute to the intangible development area are not taken into account.

*(2) Stock-based compensation.* (i) In general. For purposes of this section, a controlled participant's operating expenses include all costs attributable to compensation, including stock-based compensation. As used in this section, the term stock-based compensation means any compensation provided by a controlled participant to an employee or independent contractor in the form of equity instruments, options to acquire stock (stock options), or rights with respect to (or determined by reference to) equity instruments or stock options, including but not limited to property to which section 83 applies and stock options to which section 421 applies,

regardless of whether ultimately settled in the form of cash, stock, or other property.

(ii) Identification of stock-based compensation related to intangible development. The determination of whether stock-based compensation is related to the intangible development area within the meaning of paragraph (d)(1) of this section is made as of the date that the stock-based compensation is granted. Accordingly, all stock-based compensation that is granted during the term of the qualified cost sharing arrangement and is related at date of grant to the development of intangibles covered by the arrangement is included as an intangible development cost under paragraph (d)(1) of this section. In the case of a repricing or other modification of a stock option, the determination of whether the repricing or other modification constitutes the grant of a new stock option for purposes of this paragraph (d)(2)(ii) will be made in accordance with the rules of section 424(h) and related regulations.

(iii) Measurement and timing of stock-based compensation expense—

(A) In general. Except as otherwise provided in this paragraph (d)(2)(iii), the operating expense attributable to stock-based compensation is equal to the amount allowable to the controlled participant as a deduction for Federal income tax purposes with respect to that stock-based compensation (for example, under section 83(h)) and is taken into account as an operating expense under this section for the taxable year for which the deduction is allowable.

(1) Transfers to which section 421 applies. Solely for purposes of this paragraph (d)(2)(iii)(A), section 421 does not apply to the transfer of stock pursuant to the exercise of an option that meets the requirements of section 422(a) or 423(a).

(2) Deductions of foreign controlled participants. Solely for purposes of this paragraph (d)(2)(iii)(A), an amount is treated as an allowable deduction of a controlled participant to the extent that a deduction would be allowable to a United States taxpayer.

(3) Modification of stock option. Solely for purposes of this paragraph (d)(2)(iii)(A), if the repricing or other modification of a stock option is determined, under paragraph (d)(2)(ii) of this section, to constitute the grant of a new stock option not related to the development of intangibles, the stock option that is repriced or otherwise modified will be treated as being exercised immediately before the modification, provided that the stock option is then exercisable and the fair market value of the underlying stock then exceeds the price at which the stock option is exercisable. Accordingly, the amount of the deduction that would be allowable (or treated as allowable under this paragraph (d)(2)(iii)(A)) to the controlled participant upon exercise of the stock option immediately before the modification must be taken into account as an operating expense as of the date of the modification.

(4) Expiration or termination of qualified cost sharing arrangement. Solely for purposes of this paragraph (d)(2)(iii)(A), if an item of stock-based compensation related to the development of intangibles is not exercised during the term of a qualified cost sharing arrangement, that item of stock-based compensation will be treated as being exercised immediately before the expiration or termination of the qualified cost sharing arrangement, provided that the stock-based compensation is then exercisable and the fair market value of the underlying stock then exceeds the price at which the stock-based compensation is exercisable. Accordingly, the amount of the deduction that would be allowable (or treated as allowable under this paragraph (d)(2)(iii)(A)) to the controlled participant upon exercise of the stock-based compensation must be taken into account as an operating expense as of the date of the expiration or termination of the qualified cost sharing arrangement.

(B) Election with respect to options on publicly traded stock—

(1) In general. With respect to stock-based compensation in the form of options on publicly traded stock, the controlled participants in a qualified cost sharing arrangement may elect to take into account all operating expenses attributable to those stock options in the same amount, and as of the same time, as the fair value of the stock options reflected as a charge against income in audited financial statements or disclosed in footnotes to such financial statements, provided that such statements are prepared in accordance with United States generally accepted accounting principles by or on behalf of the company issuing the publicly traded stock.

(2) Publicly traded stock. As used in this paragraph (d)(2)(iii)(B), the term publicly traded stock means stock that is regularly traded on an established United States securities market and is issued by a company whose financial statements are prepared in accordance with United States generally accepted accounting principles for the taxable year.

(3) Generally accepted accounting principles. For purposes of this paragraph (d)(2)(iii)(B), a financial statement prepared in accordance with a comprehensive body of generally accepted accounting principles other than United States generally accepted accounting principles is considered to be prepared in accordance with United States generally accepted accounting principles provided that either—

(i) The fair value of the stock options under consideration is reflected in the reconciliation between such other accounting principles and United States generally accepted accounting principles required to be incorporated into the financial statement by the securities laws governing companies whose stock is regularly traded on United States securities markets; or

(ii) In the absence of a reconciliation between such other accounting principles and United States generally accepted accounting principles that reflects the fair value of the stock options under consideration, such other accounting principles require that the fair value of the stock options under consideration be reflected as a charge against income in audited financial statements or disclosed in footnotes to such statements.

(4) Time and manner of making the election. The election described in this paragraph (d)(2)(iii)(B) is made by an explicit reference to the election in the written cost sharing agreement required by paragraph (b)(4) of this section or in a written amendment to the cost sharing agreement entered into with the consent of the Commissioner pursuant to paragraph (d)(2)(iii)(C) of this section. In the case of a qualified cost sharing arrangement in existence on August 26, 2003, the election must be made by written amendment to the cost sharing agreement not later than the latest due date (with regard to extensions) of a Federal income tax return of any controlled participant for the first taxable year beginning after August 26, 2003, and the consent of the Commissioner is not required.

(C) Consistency. Generally, all controlled participants in a qualified cost sharing arrangement taking options on publicly traded stock into account under paragraph (d)(2)(iii)(A) or (B) of this section must use that same method of measurement and timing for all options on publicly traded stock with respect to that qualified cost sharing arrangement. Controlled participants may change their method only with the consent of the Commissioner and only with respect to stock options granted during taxable years subsequent to the taxable year in which the Commissioner's consent is obtained. All controlled participants in the qualified cost sharing arrangement must join in requests for the Commissioner's consent under this paragraph. Thus, for example, if the controlled participants make the election described in paragraph (d)(2)(iii)(B) of this section upon the formation of the qualified cost sharing arrangement, the election may be revoked only with the consent of the Commissioner, and the consent will apply only to stock options granted in taxable years subsequent to the taxable year in which consent is obtained. Similarly, if controlled participants already have granted stock options that have been or will be taken into account under the general rule of paragraph (d)(2)(iii)(A) of this section, then except in cases specified in the last sentence of paragraph (d)(2)(iii)(B)(4) of this section, the controlled participants may make the election described in paragraph (d)(2)(iii)(B) of this section only with the consent of the Commissioner, and the consent will apply only to stock options granted in taxable years subsequent to the taxable year in which consent is obtained.

*(3) Examples.* The following examples illustrate this paragraph (d):

*Example (1).* Foreign Parent (FP) and U.S. Subsidiary (USS) enter into a qualified cost sharing arrangement to develop a better mousetrap. USS and FP share the costs of FP's research and development facility that will be exclusively dedicated to this research, the salaries of the researchers, and reasonable overhead costs attributable to the project. They also share the cost of a conference facility that is at the disposal of the senior executive management of each company but does not contribute to the research and development activities in any measurable way. In this case, the cost of the conference facility must be excluded from the amount of intangible development costs.

*Example (2).* U.S. Parent (USP) and Foreign Subsidiary (FS) enter into a qualified cost sharing arrangement to develop a new device. USP and FS share the costs of a research and development facility, the salaries of researchers, and reasonable overhead costs attributable to the project. USP also incurs costs related to field testing of the device, but does not include them in the amount of intangible development costs of the cost sharing arrangement. The district director may determine that the field testing costs are intangible development costs that must be shared.

**(e) Anticipated benefits.** *(1) Benefits.* Benefits are additional income generated or costs saved by the use of covered intangibles.

*(2) Reasonably anticipated benefits.* For purposes of this section, a controlled participant's reasonably anticipated benefits are the aggregate benefits that it reasonably anticipates that it will derive from covered intangibles.

**(f) Cost allocations.** *(1) In general.* For purposes of determining whether a cost allocation authorized by paragraph (a)(2) of this section is appropriate for a taxable year, a controlled participant's share of intangible development costs for the taxable year under a qualified cost sharing arrangement must be compared to its share of reasonably anticipated benefits under the arrangement. A controlled participant's share of intangible development costs is determined under paragraph (f)(2) of this section. A controlled participant's share of reasonably anticipated benefits under the arrangement is determined under paragraph (f)(3) of this section. In determining whether benefits were reasonably anticipated, it may be appropriate to compare actual benefits to anticipated benefits, as described in paragraph (f)(3)(iv) of this section.

*(2) Share of intangible development costs.* (i) In general. A controlled participant's share of intangible development costs for a taxable year is equal to its intangible development costs for the taxable year (as defined in paragraph (d) of this section), divided by the sum of the intangible development costs for the taxable year (as defined in paragraph (d) of this section) of all the controlled participants.

(ii) Example. The following example illustrates this paragraph (f)(2):

*Example.* (i) U.S. Parent (USP), Foreign Subsidiary (FS), and Unrelated Third Party (UTP) enter into a cost sharing arrangement to develop new audio technology. In the first year of the arrangement, the controlled participants incur $2,250,000 in the intangible development area, all of which is incurred directly by USP. In the first year, UTP makes a $250,000 cost sharing payment to USP, and FS makes a $800,000 cost sharing payment to USP, under the terms of the arrangement. For that year, the intangible development costs borne by USP are $1,200,000 (its $2,250,000 intangible development costs directly incurred, minus the cost sharing payments it receives of $250,000 from UTP and $800,000 from FS); the intangible development costs borne by FS are $800,000 (its cost sharing payment); and the intangible development costs borne by all of the controlled participants are $2,000,000 (the sum of the intangible development costs borne by USP and FS of $1,200,000 and $800,000, respectively). Thus, for the first year, USP's share of intangible development costs is 60% ($1,200,000 divided by $2,000,000), and FS's share of intangible development costs is 40% ($800,000 divided by $2,000,000).

(ii) For purposes of determining whether a cost allocation authorized by paragraph § 1.482-7(a)(2) is appropriate for the first year, the district director must compare USP's and FS's shares of intangible development costs for that year to their shares of reasonably anticipated benefits. See paragraph (f)(3) of this section.

*(3) Share of reasonably anticipated benefits.* (i) In general. A controlled participant's share of reasonably anticipated benefits under a qualified cost sharing arrangement is equal to its reasonably anticipated benefits (as defined in paragraph (e)(2) of this section), divided by the sum of the reasonably anticipated benefits (as defined in paragraph (e)(2) of this section) of all the controlled participants. The anticipated benefits of an uncontrolled participant will not be included for purposes of determining each controlled participant's share of anticipated benefits. A controlled participant's share of reasonably anticipated benefits will be determined using the most reliable estimate of reasonably anticipated benefits. In determining which of two or more available estimates is most reliable, the quality of the data and assumptions used in the analysis must be taken into account, consistent with § 1.482-1(c)(2)(ii) (Data and assumptions). Thus, the reliability of an estimate will depend largely on the completeness and accuracy of the data, the soundness of the assumptions, and the relative effects of particular deficiencies in data or assumptions on different estimates. If two estimates are equally reliable, no adjustment should be made based on differences in the results. The following factors will be particularly relevant in determining the reliability of an estimate of anticipated benefits—

(A) The reliability of the basis used for measuring benefits, as described in paragraph (f)(3)(ii) of this section; and

(B) The reliability of the projections used to estimate benefits, as described in paragraph (f)(3)(iv) of this section.

(ii) Measure of benefits. In order to estimate a controlled participant's share of anticipated benefits from covered intangibles, the amount of benefits that each of the controlled participants is reasonably anticipated to derive from covered intangibles must be measured on a basis that is consistent for all such participants. If a controlled participant transfers covered intangibles to another controlled taxpayer, such participant's benefits from the transferred intangibles must be measured by reference to the transferee's benefits, disregarding any consideration paid by the transferee to the controlled participant (such as a royalty pursuant to a license agreement). See paragraph (f)(3)(iii)(E), Example 8, of this section. Anticipated benefits are measured either on a direct basis, by reference to estimated additional income to be generated or costs to be saved by the use of covered intangibles, or on an indirect basis, by reference to certain measurements that reasonably can be assumed to be related to income generated or costs saved. Such indirect bases of measurement of anticipated benefits are described in paragraph (f)(3)(iii) of this section. A controlled participant's anticipated benefits must be measured on the most reliable basis, whether direct or indirect. In determining which of two bases of measurement of reasonably anticipated benefits is most reliable, the factors set forth in § 1.482-1(c)(2)(ii) (Data and assumptions) must be taken into account. It normally will be expected that the basis that provided the most reliable estimate for a particular year will continue to provide the most reliable estimate in subsequent years, absent a material change in the factors that affect the reliability of the estimate. Regardless of whether a direct or indirect basis of measurement is used, adjustments may be required to account for material differences in the activities that controlled participants undertake to exploit their interests in covered intangibles. See Example 6 of paragraph (f)(3)(iii)(E) of this section.

(iii) Indirect bases for measuring anticipated benefits. Indirect bases for measuring anticipated benefits from participation in a qualified cost sharing arrangement include the following:

(A) Units used, produced or sold. Units of items used, produced or sold by each controlled participant in the business activities in which covered intangibles are exploited may be used as an indirect basis for measuring its anticipated benefits. This basis of measurement will be more reliable to the extent that each controlled participant is expected to have a similar increase in net profit or decrease in net loss attributable to the covered intangibles per unit of the item or items used, produced or sold. This circumstance is most likely to arise when the covered intangibles are exploited by the controlled participants in the use, production or sale of substantially uniform items under similar economic conditions.

(B) Sales. Sales by each controlled participant in the business activities in which covered intangibles are exploited may be used as an indirect basis for measuring its anticipated benefits. This basis of measurement will be more reliable to the extent that each controlled participant is expected to have a similar increase in net profit or decrease in net loss attributable to covered intangibles per dollar of sales. This circumstance is most likely to arise if the costs of exploiting covered intangibles are not substantial relative to the revenues generated, or if the principal effect of using covered intangibles is to increase the controlled participants' revenues (e.g., through a price premium on the products they sell) without affecting their costs substantially. Sales by each controlled participant are unlikely to provide a reliable basis for measuring benefits unless each controlled participant operates at the same market level (e.g., manufacturing, distribution, etc.).

(C) Operating profit. Operating profit of each controlled participant from the activities in which covered intangibles are exploited may be used as an indirect basis for measuring its anticipated benefits. This basis of measurement will be more reliable to the extent that such profit is largely attributable to the use of covered intangibles, or if the share of profits attributable to the use of covered intangibles is expected to be similar for each controlled participant. This circumstance is most likely to arise when covered intangibles are integral to the activity that generates the profit and the activity could not be carried on or would generate little profit without use of those intangibles.

(D) Other bases for measuring anticipated benefits. Other bases for measuring anticipated benefits may, in some circumstances, be appropriate, but only to the extent that there is expected to be a reasonably identifiable relationship between the basis of measurement used and additional income generated or costs saved by the use of covered intangibles. For example, a division of costs based on employee compensation would be considered unreliable unless there were a relationship between the amount of compensation and the expected income of the controlled participants from the use of covered intangibles.

(E) Examples. The following examples illustrate this paragraph (f)(3)(iii):

*Example (1).* Foreign Parent (FP) and U.S. Subsidiary (USS) both produce a feedstock for the manufacture of various high-performance plastic products. Producing the feedstock requires large amounts of electricity, which accounts for a significant portion of its production cost. FP and USS enter into a cost sharing arrangement to develop a new process that will reduce the amount of electricity required to produce a unit of the feedstock. FP and USS currently both incur an electricity cost of X% of its other production costs and rates for each are expected to remain similar in the future. How much the new process, if it is successful, will reduce the amount of electricity required to produce a unit of the feedstock is uncertain, but it will be about the same amount for both companies. Therefore, the cost savings each company is expected to achieve after implementing the new process are similar relative to the total amount of the feedstock produced. Under the cost sharing arrangement FP and USS divide the costs of developing the new process based on the units of the feedstock each is anticipated to produce in the future. In this case, units produced is the most reliable basis for measuring and dividing the intangible development costs because each participant is expected to have a similar decrease in costs per unit of the feedstock produced.

*Example (2).* The facts are the same as in Example 1, except that USS pays X% of its other production costs for electricity while FP pays 2X% of its other production costs. In this case, units produced is not the most reliable basis for measuring benefits and dividing the intangible development costs because the participants do not expect to have a similar decrease in costs per unit of the feedstock produced. The district director determines that the most reliable measure of benefit shares may be based on units of the feedstock produced if FP's units are weighted relative to USS' units by a factor of 2. This reflects the fact that FP pays twice as much as USS as a percentage of its other production costs for electricity and, therefore, FP's savings per unit of the feedstock would be twice USS's savings from any new process eventually developed.

*Example (3).* The facts are the same as in Example 2, except that to supply the particular needs of the U.S. market USS manufactures the feedstock with somewhat different properties than FP's feedstock. This requires USS to employ a somewhat different production process than does FP. Because of this difference, it will be more costly for USS to adopt any new process that may be developed under the cost sharing agreement. In this case, units produced is not the most reliable basis for measuring benefit shares. In order to reliably determine benefit shares, the district director offsets the reasonably anticipated costs of adopting the new process against the reasonably anticipated total savings in electricity costs.

*Example (4).* U.S. Parent (USP) and Foreign Subsidiary (FS) enter into a cost sharing arrangement to develop new anesthetic drugs. USP obtains the right to use any resulting patent in the U.S. market, and FS obtains the right to use the patent in the European market. USP and FS divide costs on the basis of anticipated operating profit from each patent under development. USP anticipates that it will receive a much higher profit than FS per unit sold because drug prices are uncontrolled in the U.S., whereas drug prices are regulated in many European countries. In this case, the controlled taxpayers' basis for measuring benefits is the most reliable.

*Example (5).* (i) Foreign Parent (FP) and U.S. Subsidiary (USS) both manufacture and sell fertilizers. They enter into a cost sharing arrangement to develop a new pellet form of a common agricultural fertilizer that is currently available only in powder form. Under the cost sharing arrangement, USS obtains the rights to produce and sell the new form of fertilizer for the U.S. market while FP obtains the rights to produce and sell the fertilizer for the rest of the world. The costs of developing the new form of fertilizer are divided on the basis of the anticipated sales of fertilizer in the participants' respective markets.

(ii) If the research and development is successful the pellet form will deliver the fertilizer more efficiently to crops and less fertilizer will be required to achieve the same effect on crop growth. The pellet form of fertilizer can be expected to sell at a price premium over the powder form of fertilizer based on the savings in the amount of fertilizer that needs to be used. If the research and development is successful, the costs of producing pellet fertilizer are expected to be approximately the same as the costs of producing powder fertilizer and the same for both FP and USS. Both FP and USS operate at approximately the same market levels, selling their fertilizers largely to independent distributors.

(iii) In this case, the controlled taxpayers' basis for measuring benefits is the most reliable.

*Example (6).* The facts are the same as in Example 5, except that FP distributes its fertilizers directly while USS sells to independent distributors. In this case, sales of USS and FP are not the most reliable basis for measuring benefits unless adjustments are made to account for the difference in market levels at which the sales occur.

*Example (7).* Foreign Parent (FP) and U.S. Subsidiary (USS) enter into a cost sharing arrangement to develop materials that will be used to train all new entry-level employees. FP and USS determine that the new materials will save approximately ten hours of training time per employee. Because their entry-level employees are paid on differing wage scales, FP and USS decide that they should not divide costs based on the number of entry-level employees hired by each. Rather, they divide costs based on compensation paid to the entry-level employees hired by each. In this case, the basis used for measuring benefits is the most reliable because there is a direct relationship between compensation paid to new entry-level employees and costs saved by FP and USS from the use of the new training materials.

*Example (8).* U.S. Parent (USP), Foreign Subsidiary 1 (FS1) and Foreign Subsidiary 2 (FS2) enter into a cost sharing arrangement to develop computer software that each will market and install on customers' computer systems. The participants divide costs on the basis of projected sales by USP, FS1, and FS2 of the software in their respective geographic areas. However, FS1 plans not only to sell but also to license the software to unrelated customers, and FS1's licensing income (which is a percentage of the licensees' sales) is not counted in the projected benefits. In this case, the basis used for measuring the benefits of each participant is not the most reliable because all of the benefits received by participants are not taken into account. In order to reliably determine benefit shares, FS1's projected benefits from licensing must be included in the measurement on a basis that is the same as that used to measure its own and the other participants' projected benefits from sales (e.g., all participants might measure their benefits on the basis of operating profit).

(iv) Projections used to estimate anticipated benefits. (A) In general. The reliability of an estimate of anticipated benefits also depends upon the reliability of projections used in making the estimate. Projections required for this purpose generally include a determination of the time period between the inception of the research and development and the receipt of benefits, a projection of the time over which benefits will be received, and a projection of the benefits anticipated for each year in which it is anticipated that the intangible will generate benefits. A projection of the relevant basis for measuring anticipated benefits may require a projection of the factors that underlie it. For example, a projection of operating profits may require a projection of sales, cost of sales, operating expenses, and other factors that affect operating profits. If it is anticipated that there will be significant variation among controlled participants in the timing of their receipt of benefits, and consequently benefit shares are expected to vary significantly over the years in which benefits will be received, it may be necessary to use the present discounted value of the projected benefits to reliably determine each controlled participant's share of those benefits. If it is not anticipated that benefit shares will significantly change over time, current annual benefit shares may provide a reliable projection of anticipated benefit shares. This circumstance is most likely to occur when the cost sharing arrangement is a long-term arrangement, the arrangement covers a wide variety of intangibles, the composition of the covered intangibles is unlikely to change, the covered intangibles are unlikely to generate unusual profits, and each controlled participant's share of the market is stable.

(B) Unreliable projections. A significant divergence between projected benefit shares and actual benefit shares may indicate that the projections were not reliable. In such a case, the district director may use actual benefits as the most reliable measure of anticipated benefits. If benefits are projected over a period of years, and the projections for initial years of the period prove to be unreliable, this may indicate that the projections for the remaining years of the period are also unreliable and thus should be adjusted. Projections will not be considered unreliable based on a divergence between a controlled participant's projected benefit share and actual benefit share if the amount of such divergence for every controlled participant is less than or equal to 20% of the participant's projected benefit share. Further, the district director will not make an allocation based on such divergence if the difference is due to an extraordinary event, beyond the control of the participants, that could not reasonably have been anticipated at the time that costs were shared. For purposes of this paragraph, all controlled participants that are not U.S. persons will be treated as a single controlled participant. Therefore, an adjustment based on an unreliable projection will be made to the cost shares of foreign controlled participants only if there is a matching adjustment to the cost shares of controlled participants that are U.S. persons. Nothing in this paragraph (f)(3)(iv)(B) will prevent the district director from making an allocation if the taxpayer did not use the most reliable basis for measuring anticipated benefits. For example, if the taxpayer measures anticipated benefits based on units sold, and the district director determines that another basis is more reliable for measuring anticipated benefits, then the fact that actual units sold were within 20% of the projected unit sales will not preclude an allocation under this section.

(C) Foreign-to-foreign adjustments. Notwithstanding the limitations on adjustments provided in paragraph (f)(3)(iv)(B) of this section, adjustments to cost shares based on an unreliable projection also may be made solely among foreign controlled participants if the variation between actual and projected benefits has the effect of substantially reducing U.S. tax.

(D) Examples. The following examples illustrate this paragraph (f)(3)(iv):

*Example (1).* (i) Foreign Parent (FP) and U.S. Subsidiary (USS) enter into a cost sharing arrangement to develop a new car model. The participants plan to spend four years developing the new model and four years producing and selling the new model. USS and FP project total sales of $4 billion and $2 billion, respectively, over the planned four years of exploitation of the new model. Cost shares are divided for each year based on projected total sales. Therefore, USS bears 66 2/3% of each year's intangible development costs and FP bears 33 1/3% of such costs.

(ii) USS typically begins producing and selling new car models a year after FP begins producing and selling new car models. The district director determines that in order to reflect USS' one-year lag in introducing new car models, a more reliable projection of each participant's share of benefits would be based on a projection of all four years of sales for each participant, discounted to present value.

*Example (2).* U.S. Parent (USP) and Foreign Subsidiary (FS) enter into a cost sharing arrangement to develop new and improved household cleaning products. Both participants have sold household cleaning products for many years and have stable market shares. The products under development are unlikely to produce unusual profits for either participant. The participants divide costs on the basis of each participant's current sales of household cleaning products. In this case, the participants' future benefit shares are reliably projected by current sales of cleaning products.

*Example (3).* The facts are the same as in Example 2, except that FS's market share is rapidly expanding because of the business failure of a competitor in its geographic area. The district director determines that the participants' future benefit shares are not reliably projected by current sales of cleaning products and that FS's benefit projections should take into account its growth in sales.

*Example (4).* Foreign Parent (FP) and U.S. Subsidiary (USS) enter into a cost sharing arrangement to develop synthetic fertilizers and insecticides. FP and USS share costs on the basis of each participant's current sales of fertilizers and insecticides. The market shares of the participants have been stable for fertilizers, but FP's market share for insecticides has been expanding. The district director determines that the participants' projections of benefit shares are reliable with regard to fertilizers, but not reliable with regard to insecticides; a more reliable projection of benefit shares would take into account the expanding market share for insecticides.

*Example (5).* U.S. Parent (USP) and Foreign Subsidiary (FS) enter into a cost sharing arrangement to develop new food products, dividing costs on the basis of projected sales two years in the future. In year 1, USP and FS project that their sales in year 3 will be equal, and they divide costs accordingly. In year 3, the district director examines the participants' method for dividing costs. USP and FS actually accounted for 42% and 58% of total sales, respectively. The district director agrees that sales two years in the future provide a reliable basis for estimating benefit shares. Because the differences between USP's and FS's actual and projected benefit shares are less than 20% of their projected benefit shares, the projection of future benefits for year 3 is reliable.

*Example (6).* The facts are the same as in Example 5, except that the in year 3 USP and FS actually accounted for 35% and 65% of total sales, respectively. The divergence between USP's projected and actual benefit shares is greater than 20% of USP's projected benefit share and is not due to an extraordinary event beyond the control of the participants. The district director concludes that the projection of anticipated benefit shares was unreliable, and uses actual benefits as the basis for an adjustment to the cost shares borne by USP and FS.

*Example (7).* U.S. Parent (USP), a U.S. corporation, and its foreign subsidiary (FS) enter a cost sharing arrangement in year 1. They project that they will begin to receive benefits from covered intangibles in years 4 through 6, and that USP will receive 60% of total benefits and FS 40% of total benefits. In years 4 through 6, USP and FS actually receive 50% each of the total benefits. In evaluating the reliability of the participants' projections, the district director compares these actual benefit shares to the projected benefit shares. Although USP's actual benefit share (50%) is within 20% of its projected benefit share (60%), FS's actual benefit share (50%) is not within 20% of its projected benefit share (40%). Based on this discrepancy, the district director may conclude that the participants' projections were not reliable and may use actual benefit shares as the basis for an adjustment to the cost shares borne by USP and FS.

*Example (8).* Three controlled taxpayers, USP, FS1 and FS2 enter into a cost sharing arrangement. FS1 and FS2 are foreign. USP is a United States corporation that controls all the stock of FS1 and FS2. The participants project that they will share the total benefits of the covered intangibles in the following percentages: USP 50%; FS1 30%; and FS2 20%. Actual benefit shares are as follows: USP 45%; FS1 25%; and FS2 30%. In evaluating the reliability of the participants' projections, the district director compares these actual benefit shares to the projected benefit shares. For this purpose, FS1 and FS2 are treated as a single participant. The actual benefit share received by USP (45%) is within 20% of its projected benefit share (50%). In addition, the non-US participants' actual benefit share (55%) is also within 20% of their projected benefit share (50%). Therefore, the district director concludes that the participants' projections of future benefits were reliable, despite the fact that FS2's actual benefit share (30%) is not within 20% of its projected benefit share (20%).

*Example (9).* The facts are the same as in Example 8. In addition, the district director determines that FS2 has significant operating losses and has no earnings and profits, and that FS1 is profitable and has earnings and profits. Based on all the evidence, the district director concludes that the participants arranged that FS1 would bear a larger cost share than appropriate in order to reduce FS1's earnings and profits and thereby reduce inclusions USP otherwise would be deemed to have on account of FS1 under subpart F. Pursuant to § 1.482-7 (f)(3)(iv)(C), the district director may make an adjustment solely to the cost shares borne by FS1 and FS2 because FS2's projection of future benefits was unreliable and the variation between actual and projected benefits had the effect of substantially reducing USP's U.S. income tax liability (on account of FS1 subpart F income).

*Example (10).* (i)

(A) Foreign Parent (FP) and U.S. Subsidiary (USS) enter into a cost sharing arrangement in 1996 to develop a new treatment for baldness. USS's interest in any treatment developed is the right to produce and sell the treatment in the U.S. market while FP retains rights to produce and sell the treatment in the rest of the world. USS and FP measure their anticipated benefits from the cost sharing arrangement based on their respective projected future sales of the baldness treatment. The following sales projections are used:

| | Sales ($ millions) | |
|---|---|---|
| Year | USS | FP |
| 1997 | 5 | 10 |
| 1998 | 20 | 20 |
| 1999 | 30 | 30 |
| 2000 | 40 | 40 |
| 2001 | 40 | 40 |
| 2002 | 40 | 40 |
| 2003 | 40 | 40 |
| 2004 | 20 | 20 |
| 2005 | 10 | 10 |
| 2006 | 5 | 5 |

(B) In 1997, the first year of sales, USS is projected to have lower sales than FP due to lags in U.S. regulatory approval for the baldness treatment. In each subsequent year USS and FP are projected to have equal sales. Sales are projected to build over the first three years of the period, level off for several years, and then decline over the final years of the period as new and improved baldness treatments reach the market.

(ii) To account for USS's lag in sales in the first year, the present discounted value of sales over the period is used as the basis for measuring benefits. Based on the risk associated with this venture, a discount rate of 10 percent is selected. The present discounted value of projected sales is determined to be approximately $154.4 million for USS and $158.9 million for FP. On this basis USS and FP are projected to obtain approximately 49.3% and 50.7% of the benefit, respectively, and the costs of developing the baldness treatment are shared accordingly.

(iii)

(A) In the year 2002 the district director examines the cost sharing arrangement. USS and FP have obtained the following sales results through the year 2001:

| | Sales ($ millions) | |
|---|---|---|
| Year | USS | FP |
| 1997 | 0 | 17 |
| 1998 | 17 | 35 |
| 1999 | 25 | 41 |
| 2000 | 38 | 41 |
| 2001 | 39 | 41 |

(B) USS's sales initially grew more slowly than projected while FP's sales grew more quickly. In each of the first three years of the period the share of total sales of at least one of the parties diverged by over 20% from its projected share of sales. However, by the year 2001 both parties' sales had leveled off at approximately their projected values. Taking into account this leveling off of sales and all the facts and circumstances, the district director determines that it is appropriate to use the original projections for the remaining years of sales. Combining the actual results through the year 2001 with the projections for subsequent years, and using a discount rate of 10%, the present discounted value of sales is approximately $141.6 million for USS and $187.3 million for FP. This result implies that USS and FP obtain approximately 43.1% and 56.9%, respectively, of the anticipated benefits from the baldness treatment. Because these benefit shares are within 20% of the benefit shares calculated based on the original sales projections, the district director determines that, based on the difference between actual and projected benefit shares, the original projections were not unreliable. No adjustment is made based on the difference between actual and projected benefit shares.

*Example (11).* (i) The facts are the same as in Example 10, except that the actual sales results through the year 2001 are as follows:

| | Sales ($ millions) | |
|---|---|---|
| Year | USS | FP |
| 1997 | 0 | 17 |
| 1998 | 17 | 35 |
| 1999 | 25 | 44 |
| 2000 | 34 | 54 |
| 2001 | 36 | 55 |

(ii) Based on the discrepancy between the projections and the actual results and on consideration of all the facts, the district director determines that for the remaining years the following sales projections are more reliable than the original projections:

| | Sales ($ millions) | |
|---|---|---|
| Year | USS | FP |
| 2002 | 36 | 55 |
| 2003 | 36 | 55 |
| 2004 | 18 | 28 |
| 2005 | 9 | 14 |
| 2006 | 4.5 | 7 |

(iii) Combining the actual results through the year 2001 with the projections for subsequent years, and using a discount rate of 10%, the present discounted value of sales is approximately $131.2 million for USS and $229.4 million for FP. This result implies that USS and FP obtain approximately 35.4% and 63.6%, respectively, of the anticipated benefits from the baldness treatment. These benefit shares diverge by greater than 20% from the benefit shares calculated based on the original sales projections, and the district director determines that, based on the difference between actual and projected benefit shares, the original projections were unreliable. The district director adjusts costs shares for each of the taxable years under examination to conform them to the recalculated shares of anticipated benefits.

*(4) Timing of allocations.* If the district director reallocates costs under the provisions of this paragraph (f), the allocation must be reflected for tax purposes in the year in which the costs were incurred. When a cost sharing payment is owed by one member of a qualified cost sharing arrangement to another member, the district director may make appropriate allocations to reflect an arm's length rate of interest for the time value of money, consistent with the provisions of § 1.482-2(a) (Loans or advances).

**(g) Allocations of income, deductions or other tax items to reflect transfers of intangibles (buy-in).** *(1) In general.* A controlled participant that makes intangible property available to a qualified cost sharing arrangement will be treated as having transferred interests in such property to the other controlled participants, and such other controlled participants must make buy-in payments to it, as provided in paragraph (g)(2) of this section. If the other controlled participants fail to make such payments, the district director may make appropriate allocations, under the provisions of §§ 1.482-1 and 1.482-4 through 1.482-6, to reflect an arm's length consideration for the transferred intangible property. Further, if a group of controlled taxpayers participates in a qualified cost sharing arrangement, any change in the controlled participants' interests in covered intangibles, whether by reason of entry of a new participant or otherwise by reason of transfers (including deemed transfers) of interests among existing participants, is a transfer of intangible property, and the district director may make appropriate allocations, under the provisions of §§ 1.482-1 and 1.482-4 through 1.482-6, to reflect an arm's length consideration for the transfer. See paragraphs (g)(3), (4), and (5) of this section. Paragraph (g)(6) of this section provides rules for assigning unassigned interests under a qualified cost sharing arrangement.

*(2) Pre-existing intangibles.* If a controlled participant makes pre-existing intangible property in which it owns an interest available to other controlled participants for purposes of research in the intangible development area under a qualified cost sharing arrangement, then each such other controlled participant must make a buy-in payment to the owner. The buy-in payment by each such other controlled participant is the arm's length charge for the use of the intangible under the rules of §§ 1.482-1 and 1.482-4 through 1.482-6, multiplied by the controlled participant's share of reasonably anticipated benefits (as defined in paragraph (f)(3) of this section). A controlled participant's payment required under this paragraph (g)(2) is deemed to be reduced to the extent of any payments owed to it under this paragraph (g)(2) from other controlled participants. Each payment received by a payee will be treated as coming pro rata out of payments made by all payors. See paragraph (g)(8), Example 4, of this section. Such payments will be treated as consideration for a transfer of an interest in the intangible property made available to the qualified cost sharing arrangement by the payee. Any payment to or from an uncontrolled participant in consideration for intangible property made available to the qualified cost sharing arrangement will be shared by the controlled participants in accordance with their shares of reasonably anticipated benefits (as defined in paragraph (f)(3) of this section). A controlled participant's payment required under this paragraph (g)(2) is deemed to be reduced by such a share of payments owed from an uncontrolled participant to the same extent as by any payments owed from other controlled participants under this paragraph (g)(2). See paragraph (g)(8), Example 5, of this section.

*(3) New controlled participant.* If a new controlled participant enters a qualified cost sharing arrangement and acquires any interest in the covered intangibles, then the new participant must pay an arm's length consideration, under the provisions of §§ 1.482-1 and 1.482-4 through 1.482-6, for such interest to each controlled participant from whom such interest was acquired.

*(4) Controlled participant relinquishes interests.* A controlled participant in a qualified cost sharing arrangement may be deemed to have acquired an interest in one or more covered intangibles if another controlled participant transfers, abandons, or otherwise relinquishes an interest under the arrangement, to the benefit of the first participant. If such a relinquishment occurs, the participant relinquishing the interest must receive an arm's length consideration, under the provisions of §§ 1.482-1 and 1.482-4 through 1.482-6, for its interest. If the controlled participant that has relinquished its interest subsequently uses that interest, then that participant must pay an arm's length consideration, under the provisions of §§ 1.482-1 and 1.482-4 through 1.482-6, to the controlled participant that acquired the interest.

*(5) Conduct inconsistent with the terms of a cost sharing arrangement.* If, after any cost allocations authorized by paragraph (a)(2) of this section, a controlled participant bears costs of intangible development that over a period of years are consistently and materially greater or lesser than its share of reasonably anticipated benefits, then the district director may conclude that the economic substance of the arrangement between the controlled participants is inconsistent with the terms of the cost sharing arrangement. In such a case, the district director may disregard such terms and impute an agreement consistent with the controlled participants' course of conduct, under which a controlled participant that bore a disproportionately greater share of costs received additional interests in covered intangibles. See § 1.482-1(d)(3)(ii)(B) (Identifying contractual terms) and § 1.482-4(f)(3)(ii) (Identification of owner). Accordingly, that participant must receive an arm's length payment from any controlled participant whose share of the intangible development costs is less than its share of reasonably anticipated benefits over time, under the provisions of §§ 1.482-1 and 1.482-4 through 1.482-6.

*(6) Failure to assign interests under a qualified cost sharing arrangement.* If a qualified cost sharing arrangement fails to assign an interest in a covered intangible, then each controlled participant will be deemed to hold a share in such interest equal to its share of the costs of developing such intangible. For this purpose, if cost shares have varied materially over the period during which such intangible was developed, then the costs of developing the intangible must be measured by their present discounted value as of the date when the first such costs were incurred.

*(7) Form of consideration.* The consideration for an acquisition described in this paragraph (g) may take any of the following forms:

(i) Lump sum payments. For the treatment of lump sum payments, see § 1.482-4(f)(5) (Lump sum payments);

(ii) Installment payments. Installment payments spread over the period of use of the intangible by the transferee, with interest calculated in accordance with § 1.482-2(a) (Loans or advances); and

(iii) Royalties. Royalties or other payments contingent on the use of the intangible by the transferee.

*(8) Examples.* The following examples illustrate allocations described in this paragraph (g):

*Example (1).* In year one, four members of a controlled group enter into a cost sharing arrangement to develop a commercially feasible process for capturing energy from nuclear fusion. Based on a reliable projection of their future benefits, each cost sharing participant bears an equal share of the costs. The cost of developing intangibles for each participant with respect to the project is approximately $1 million per year. In year ten, a fifth member of the controlled group joins the cost sharing group and agrees to bear one-fifth of the future costs in exchange for part of the fourth member's territory reasonably anticipated to yield benefits amounting to one-fifth of the total benefits. The fair market value of intangible property within the arrangement at the time the fifth company joins the arrangement is $45 million. The new member must pay one-fifth of that amount (that is, $9 million total) to the fourth member from whom it acquired its interest in covered intangibles.

*Example (2).* U.S. Subsidiary (USS), Foreign Subsidiary (FS) and Foreign Parent (FP) enter into a cost sharing arrangement to develop new products within the Group X product line. USS manufactures and sells Group X products in North America, FS manufactures and sells Group X products in South America, and FP manufactures and sells Group X products in the rest of the world. USS, FS and FP project that each will manufacture and sell a third of the Group X products under development, and they share costs on the basis of projected sales of manufactured products. When the new Group X products are developed, however, USS ceases to manufacture Group X products, and FP sells its Group X products to USS for resale in the North American market. USS earns a return on its resale activity that is appropriate given its function as a distributor, but does not earn a return attributable to exploiting covered intangibles. The district director determines that USS' share of the costs (one-third) was greater than its share of reasonably anticipated benefits (zero) and that it has transferred an interest in the intangibles for which it should receive a payment from FP, whose share of the intangible development costs (one-third) was less than its share of reasonably anticipated benefits over time (two-thirds). An allocation is made under §§ 1.482-1 and 1.482-4 through 1.482-6 from FP to USS to recognize USS' one-third interest in the intangibles. No allocation is made from FS to USS because FS did not exploit USS' interest in covered intangibles.

*Example (3).* U.S. Parent (USP), Foreign Subsidiary 1 (FS1), and Foreign Subsidiary 2 (FS2) enter into a cost sharing arrangement to develop a cure for the common cold. Costs are shared USP-50%, FS1-40% and FS2-10% on the basis of projected units of cold medicine to be produced by each. After ten years of research and development, FS1 withdraws from the arrangement, transferring its interests in the intangibles under development to USP in exchange for a lump sum payment of $10 million. The district director may review this lump sum payment, under the provisions of § 1.482-4(f)(5), to ensure that the amount is commensurate with the income attributable to the intangibles.

*Example (4).* (i) Four members A, B, C, and D of a controlled group form a cost sharing arrangement to develop the next generation technology for their business. Based on a reliable projection of their future benefits, the participants agree to bear shares of the costs incurred during the term of the agreement in the following percentages: A 40%; B 15%; C 25%; and D 20%. The arm's length charges, under the rules of §§ 1.482-1 and 1.482-4 through 1.482-6, for the use of the existing intangible property they respectively make available to the cost sharing arrangement are in the following amounts for the taxable year: A 80X; B 40X; C 30X; and D 30X. The provisional (before offsets) and final buy-in payments/receipts among A, B, C, and D are shown in the table as follows:

| | (All amounts stated in X's) | | | |
|---|---|---|---|---|
| | A | B | C | D |
| Payments | <40> | <21> | <37.5> | <30> |
| Receipts | 48 | 34 | 22.5 | 24 |
| Final | 8 | 13 | <15> | <6> |

(ii) The first row/first column shows A's provisional buy-in payment equal to the product of 100X (sum of 40X, 30X, and 30X) and A's share of anticipated benefits of 40%. The second row/first column shows A's provisional buy-in receipts equal to the sum of the products of 80X and B's, C's, and D's anticipated benefits shares (15%, 25%, and 20%, respectively). The other entries in the first two rows of the table are similarly computed. The last row shows the final buy-in receipts/payments after offsets. Thus, for the taxable year, A and B are treated as receiving the 8X and 13X, respectively, pro rata out of payments by C and D of 15X and 6X, respectively.

*Example (5).* A and B, two members of a controlled group form a cost sharing arrangement with an unrelated third party C to develop a new technology useable in their respective businesses. Based on a reliable projection of their future benefits, A and B agree to bear shares of 60% and 40%, respectively, of the costs incurred during the term of the agreement. A also makes available its existing technology for purposes of the research to be undertaken. The arm's length charge, under the rules of §§ 1.482-1 and 1.482-4 through 1.482-6, for the use of the existing technology is 100X for the taxable year. Under its agreement with A and B, C must make a specified cost sharing payment as well as a payment of 50X for the taxable year on account of the pre-existing intangible property made available to the cost sharing arrangement. B's provisional buy-in payment (before offsets) to A for the taxable year is 40X (the product of 100X and B's anticipated benefits share of 40%). C's payment of 50X is shared provisionally between A and B in accordance with their shares of reasonably anticipated benefits, 30X (50X times 60%) to A and 20X (50X times 40%) to B. B's final buy-in payment (after offsets) is 20X (40X less 20X). A is treated as receiving the 70X total provisional payments (40X plus 30X) pro rata out of the final payments by B and C of 20X and 50X, respectively.

**(h) Character of payments made pursuant to a qualified cost sharing arrangement.** *(1) In general.* Payments made pursuant to a qualified cost sharing arrangement (other than payments described in paragraph (g) of this section) generally will be considered costs of developing intangibles of the payor and reimbursements of the same kind of costs of developing intangibles of the payee. For purposes of this paragraph (h), a controlled participant's payment required under a qualified cost sharing arrangement is deemed to be reduced to the extent of any payments owed to it under the arrangement from other controlled or uncontrolled participants. Each payment received by a payee will be treated as coming pro rata out of payments made by all payors. Such payments will be applied pro rata against deductions for the taxable year that the payee is allowed in connection with the qualified cost sharing arrangement. Payments received in excess of such deductions will be treated as in consideration for use of the tangible property made available to the qualified cost sharing arrangement by the payee. For purposes of the research credit determined under section 41, cost sharing payments among controlled participants will be treated as provided for intra-group transactions in § 1.41-6(e). Any payment made or received by a taxpayer pursuant to an arrangement that the district director determines not to be a qualified cost sharing arrangement, or a payment made or received pursuant to paragraph (g) of this section, will be subject to the provisions of §§ 1.482-1 and 1.482-4 through 1.482-6. Any payment that in substance constitutes a cost sharing payment will be treated as such for purposes of this section, regardless of its characterization under foreign law.

*(2) Examples.* The following examples illustrate this paragraph (h):

*Example (1).* U.S. Parent (USP) and its wholly owned Foreign Subsidiary (FS) form a cost sharing arrangement to develop a miniature widget, the Small R. Based on a reliable projection of their future benefits, USP agrees to bear 40% and FS to bear 60% of the costs incurred during the term of the agreement. The principal costs in the intangible development area are operating expenses incurred by FS in Country Z of 100X annually, and operating expenses incurred by USP in the United States also of 100X annually. Of the total costs of 200X, USP's share is 80X and FS's share is 120X, so that FS must make a payment to USP of 20X. This payment will be treated as a reimbursement of 20X of USP's operating expenses in the United States. Accordingly, USP's Form 1120 will reflect an 80X deduction on account of activities performed in the United States for purposes of allocation and apportionment of the deduction to source. The Form 5471 for FS will reflect a 100X deduction on account of activities performed in Country Z, and a 20X deduction on account of activities performed in the United States.

*Example (2).* The facts are the same as in Example 1, except that the 100X of costs borne by USP consist of 5X of operating expenses incurred by USP in the United States and 95X of fair market value rental cost for a facility in the United States. The depreciation deduction attributable to the U.S. facility is 7X. The 20X net payment by FS to USP will first be applied in reduction pro rata of the 5X deduction for operating expenses and the 7X depreciation deduction attributable to the U.S. facility. The 8X remainder will be treated as rent for the U.S. facility.

**(i) Accounting requirements.** The accounting requirements of this paragraph are that the controlled participants in a qualified cost sharing arrangement must use a consistent method of accounting to measure costs and benefits, and must translate foreign currencies on a consistent basis.

**(j) Administrative requirements.** *(1) In general.* The administrative requirements of this paragraph consist of the documentation requirements of paragraph (j)(2) of this section and the reporting requirements of paragraph (j)(3) of this section.

*(2) Documentation.* (i) Requirements. A controlled participant must maintain sufficient documentation to establish that the requirements of paragraphs (b)(4) and (c)(1) of this section have been met, as well as the additional documentation specified in this paragraph (j)(2)(i), and must provide any such documentation to the Internal Revenue Service within 30 days of a request (unless an extension is granted by the district director). Documents necessary to establish the following must also be maintained—

(A[sic]) The total amount of costs incurred pursuant to the arrangement;

(B[sic]) The costs borne by each controlled participant;

(C[sic]) A description of the method used to determine each controlled participant's share of the intangible development costs, including the projections used to estimate benefits, and an explanation of why that method was selected;

(D[sic]) The accounting method used to determine the costs and benefits of the intangible development (including the method used to translate foreign currencies), and, to the extent that the method materially differs from U.S. generally accepted accounting principles, an explanation of such material differences;

(E[sic]) Prior research, if any, undertaken in the intangible development area, any tangible or intangible property made available for use in the arrangement, by each controlled participant, and any information used to establish the value of pre-existing and covered intangibles; and

(F[sic]) The amount taken into account as operating expenses attributable to stock-based compensation, including the method of measurement and timing used with respect to that amount as well as the data, as of date of grant, used to identify stock-based compensation related to the development of covered intangibles.

(ii) Coordination with penalty regulation. The documents described in paragraph (j)(2)(i) of this section will satisfy the principal documents requirement under § 1.6662-6(d)(2)(iii)(B) with respect to a qualified cost sharing arrangement.

*(3) Reporting requirements.* A controlled participant must attach to its U.S. income tax return a statement indicating that it is a participant in a qualified cost sharing arrangement, and listing the other controlled participants in the arrangement. A controlled participant that is not required to file a U.S. income tax return must ensure that such a statement is attached to Schedule M of any Form 5471 or to any Form 5472 filed with respect to that participant.

**(k) Effective date.** This section applies for taxable years beginning on or after January 1, 1996. However, paragraphs (a)(3), (d)(2) and (j)(2)(i)(F) of this section apply for stock-based compensation granted in taxable years beginning on or after August 26, 2003.

**(l) Transition rule.** A cost sharing arrangement will be considered a qualified cost sharing arrangement, within the meaning of this section, if, prior to January 1, 1996, the arrangement was a bona fide cost sharing arrangement under the provisions of § 1.482-7T (as contained in the 26 CFR part 1 edition revised as of April 1, 1995), but only if the arrangement is amended, if necessary, to conform with the provisions of this section by December 31, 1996.

T.D. 8632, 12/19/95, amend T.D. 8670, 5/9/96, T.D. 8930, 12/27/2000, T.D. 9088, 8/25/2003, T.D. 9441, 12/31/2008.

**Proposed § 1.482-7**

• ***Caution:*** This Proposed Reg was incorporated into final and temporary regulations by TD 9441, 12/31/2008.

Methods to determine taxable income in connection with a cost sharing arrangement. [*For Preamble, see ¶ 152,697*]

**(a) In general.** The arm's length amount charged in a controlled transaction reasonably anticipated to contribute to developing intangibles pursuant to a cost sharing arrangement (CSA), as described in paragraph (b) of this section, must be determined under a method described in this section. Each method must be applied in accordance with the provisions of § 1.482-1, except as those provisions are modified in this section.

*(1) RAB share method for cost sharing transactions (CSTs).* The controlled participants that are parties to a cost sharing transaction (CST), as described in paragraph (b)(2) of this section, must share the intangible development costs (IDCs) of the cost shared intangibles in proportion to their shares of reasonably anticipated benefits (RAB shares). See paragraph (j)(1) of this section for the definitions of controlled participant, cost shared intangible, benefits, and reasonably anticipated benefits, and paragraphs (d) and (e) of this section regarding IDCs and RAB shares, respectively.

*(2) Methods for preliminary or contemporaneous transactions (PCTs).* The arm's length amount charged in a preliminary or contemporaneous transaction (PCT), as described in paragraph (b)(3) of this section, must be determined under the method or methods under the other section or sections of the section 482 regulations, as supplemented by paragraph (g) of this section, applicable to the reference transaction (RT) reflected by the PCT. See § 1.482-1(b)(2)(ii) (Selection of category of method applicable to transaction), paragraph (b)(3)(iv) of this section (Reference transaction), and paragraph (g) of this section (Supplemental guidance on methods applicable to PCTs).

*(3) Methods for other controlled transactions.* (i) Contribution to a CSA by a controlled taxpayer that is not a controlled participant. If a controlled taxpayer that is not a controlled participant contributes to developing the cost shared intangibles, it must receive consideration from the other controlled participants under the rules of § 1.482-4(f)(3)(iii) (Allocations with respect to assistance provided to the owner). Such consideration will be treated as an intangible development cost for purposes of paragraph (d) of this section.

(ii) Transfer of interest in a cost shared intangible. If at any time (during the term, or upon or after the termination, of a CSA) a controlled participant transfers an interest in a cost shared intangible to another controlled taxpayer, the controlled participant must receive an arm's length amount of consideration from the transferee under the rules of §§ 1.482-1 and 1.482-4 through 1.482-6.

(iii) Controlled transactions not in connection with a CSA. This section does not apply to a controlled transaction reasonably anticipated to contribute to developing intangibles pursuant to an arrangement that is not a CSA described in paragraph (b)(1) or paragraph (b)(5) of this section. Whether the results of any such controlled transaction are consistent with an arm's length result must be determined under the applicable rules of the section 482 regulations without regard to this section. For example, an arrangement for developing intangibles in which one controlled taxpayer's costs of developing the intangibles significantly exceeds its share of reasonably anticipated benefits from exploiting the developed intangibles would not in substance be a CSA, as described in paragraphs (b)(1)(i) through (iii) or paragraph (b)(5)(i) of this section. In such a case, unless the rules of this section are applicable by reason of paragraph (b)(5)(ii) of this section, the arrangement must be analyzed under other applicable sections of the section 482 regulations to determine whether it achieves arm's length results, and if not, to determine any allocations by the Commissioner that are consistent with such other section 482 regulations.

**(b) Cost sharing arrangement (CSA).**

*(1) In general.* A CSA to which the provisions of this section apply is a contractual agreement to share the costs of developing one or more intangibles under which the controlled participants—

(i) At the outset of the arrangement divide among themselves all interests in cost shared intangibles on a territorial basis as described in paragraph (b)(4) of this section;

(ii) Enter into and effect CSTs covering all IDCs and PCTs covering all external contributions, as described in paragraphs (b)(2) and (b)(3) of this section, for purposes of developing the cost shared intangibles under the CSA;

(iii) As a result, individually own and exploit their respective interests in the cost shared intangibles without any further obligation to compensate one another for such interests;

(iv) Substantially comply with the CSA contractual requirements that are described in paragraph (k)(1) of this section;

(v) Substantially comply with the CSA documentation requirements that are described in paragraph (k)(2) of this section;

(vi) Substantially comply with the CSA accounting requirements that are described in paragraph (k)(3) of this section; and

(vii) Substantially comply with the CSA reporting requirements that are described in paragraph (k)(4) of this section.

*(2) CSTs.* (i) In general. CSTs are controlled transactions between or among controlled participants in which such participants share the IDCs of one or more cost shared intangibles in proportion to their respective RAB shares from their individual exploitation of their interests in the cost shared intangibles that they obtain under the CSA. Cost sharing payments may not be paid in shares of stock in the payor. See paragraphs (b)(4), (d), and (e) of this section for the rules regarding interests in cost shared intangibles, IDCs, and RAB shares, respectively.

(ii) Example. The following example illustrates the principles of this paragraph (b)(2):

*Example.* Companies C and D, who are members of the same controlled group, enter into a CSA that is described in paragraph (b)(1) of this section. In the first year of the CSA, C and D conduct the IDA, as described in paragraph (d)(1) of this section. The total IDCs in regard to such activity are $3,000,000 of which C and D pay $2,000,000 and $1,000,000, respectively, directly to third parties. As between C and D, however, their CSA specifies that they will share all IDCs in accordance with their RAB shares (as described in paragraph (e)(1) of this section), which are 60% for C and 40% for D. It follows that C should bear $1,800,000 of the total IDCs (60% of total IDCs of $3,000,000) and D should bear $1,200,000 of the total IDCs (40% of total IDCs of $3,000,000). D makes a CST payment to C of $200,000, that is, the amount by which D's share of IDCs in accordance with its RAB share exceeds the amount of IDCs initially borne by D ($1,200,000 -$1,000,000), and which also equals the amount by which the total IDCs initially borne by C exceeds its share of IDCs in accordance with its RAB share ($2,000,000 -$1,800,000). As a result of D's CST payment to C, C and D will bear amounts of total IDCs in accordance with their respective RAB shares.

*(3) PCTs.* (i) In general. A PCT is a controlled transaction in which each other controlled participant (PCT Payor) is obligated to compensate a controlled participant (PCT Payee) for an external contribution of the PCT Payee.

(ii) External contributions. An external contribution consists of the rights set forth under the reference transaction (RT) in any resource or capability that is reasonably anticipated to contribute to developing cost shared intangibles and that a PCT Payee has developed, maintained, or acquired externally to (whether prior to or during the course of) the CSA. For purposes of this section, external contributions do not include rights in depreciable tangible property or land, and do not include rights in other resources acquired by IDCs. See paragraphs (b)(2) and (d)(1) of this section.

(iii) PCT Payments. The arm's length amount of the compensation due under a PCT (PCT Payment) will be determined under a method pursuant to paragraphs (a)(2) and (g) of this section applicable to the RT, as described in paragraph (b)(3)(iv) of this section. The applicable method will yield a value for the compensation obligation of each PCT Payor consistent with the product of the combined value to all controlled participants of the external contribution that is the subject of the PCT multiplied by the PCT Payor's RAB share.

(iv) Reference transaction (RT). An RT is a transaction providing the benefits of all rights (RT Rights), exclusively and perpetually, in a resource or capability described in paragraph (b)(3)(ii) of this section, excluding any rights to exploit an existing intangible without further development. See paragraph (c) of this section (Make-or-sell rights excluded). If a resource or capability is reasonably anticipated to contribute both to developing or exploiting cost shared intangibles and to other business activities of the PCT Payee, other than exploiting an existing intangible without further development, then the PCT Payment that would otherwise be determined with reference to the RT (which generally presumes a provision of exclusive and perpetual rights) may need to be prorated as described in paragraph (g)(2)(xi) of this section. For purposes of § 1.482-1(b)(2)(ii) and paragraph (a)(2) of this section, the controlled participants must include the type of transaction involved in the RT as part of the documentation of the RT required under paragraph (k)(2)(ii)(H) of this section. If different economically equivalent types of RTs are possible with respect to the relevant resource or capability, the controlled participants may designate the type of transaction involved in the RT. If the controlled participants fail to make this designation in their documentation, the Commissioner may make a designation consistent with the RT and other facts and circumstances. While the PCT Payee and PCT Payors must enter into the PCT providing for the relevant compensation obligation, they are not required to actually enter into the RT that is referenced for purposes of determining the magnitude of the compensation obligation under the PCT.

(v) PFAs. A post formation acquisition (PFA) is an external contribution that is acquired by a controlled participant in an uncontrolled transaction that takes place after the formation of the CSA and that as of the date of acquisition is reasonably anticipated to contribute to developing cost shared intangibles. Resources or capabilities may be acquired in a PFA either directly, or indirectly through the acquisition of an interest in an entity or tier of entities.

(vi) Form of payment. (A) In general. The consideration under a PCT for an external contribution other than a PFA may take one or a combination of both of the following forms—

(1) Payments of a fixed amount, either paid in a lump sum payment or in installment payments spread over a specified period, with interest calculated in accordance with § 1.482-2(a) (Loans or advances); or

(2) Payments contingent on the exploitation of cost shared intangibles by the PCT Payor. The form of payment selected for any PCT, including the basis and structure of the payments, must be specified no later than the date of that PCT.

(B) PFAs. The consideration under a PCT for a PFA must be paid in the same form as the uncontrolled transaction in which the PFA was acquired.

(C) No PCT Payor Stock. PCT Payments may not be paid in shares of stock in the PCT Payor.

(vii) Date of a PCT. The controlled participants must enter into a PCT as of the earliest date on or after the CSA is entered into on which the external contribution is reasonably anticipated to contribute to developing cost shared intangibles.

(viii) Examples. The following examples illustrate the principles of this paragraph (b)(3). In each example, Companies P and S are members of the same controlled group, and execute a CSA that is described in paragraph (b)(1) of this section. The examples are as follows:

*Example (1).* Company P has developed and currently markets version 1.0 of a new software application XYZ. Company P and Company S execute a CSA under which they will share the IDCs for developing future versions of XYZ. Version 1.0 is reasonably anticipated to contribute to the development of future versions of XYZ and therefore the RT rights in version 1.0 constitute an external contribution of Company P for which compensation is due from Company S pursuant to a PCT. The applicable method and determination of the arm's length compensation due pursuant to the PCT will be based on the RT. The controlled participants designate the RT as a transfer of intangibles that would otherwise be governed by § 1.482-4, if entered into by controlled parties. Accordingly, pursuant to paragraph (a)(2) of this section, the applicable method for determining the arm's length value of the compensation obligation under the PCT between Company P and Company S will be governed by § 1.482-4 as supplemented by paragraph (g) of this section. The RT in this case is the perpetual and exclusive provision of the benefit of all rights in version 1.0, other than the rights described in paragraph (c) of this section (Make-or-sell rights excluded). This includes the exclusive right to use version 1.0 for purposes of research and the right to exploit any products that incorporated the platform technology of version 1.0, and would cover a term extending as long as the uncontrolled taxpayer were to continue to exploit future versions of XYZ or any other product based on the version 1.0 platform. Though Company P and Company S are not required to actually enter into the transaction described by the RT, the value of the compensation obligation of Company S for the PCT will reflect the full value of the external contribution defined by the RT, as limited by Company S's RAB share.

*Example (2).* Company P and Company S execute a CSA under which they will share the IDCs for developing Vaccine Z. Company P will commit its research team that has successfully developed a number of other vaccines to the project. The expertise and existing integration of the research team is a unique resource or capability of Company P which is reasonably anticipated to contribute to the development of Vaccine Z and therefore the RT Rights in the research team constitute an external contribution for which compensation is due from Company S as part of a PCT. The applicable method and determination of the arm's length compensation due pursuant to the PCT will be based on the RT. The controlled parties designate the RT as a provision of services that would otherwise be governed by § 1.482-2(b)(3)(first sentence) if entered into by controlled parties. Accordingly, pursuant to paragraph (a)(2) of this section, the applicable method for determining the arm's length value of the compensation obligation under the PCT between Company P and Company S will be governed by § 1.482-2(b)(3)(first sentence) as supplemented by paragraph (g) of this section. The RT in this case is the perpetual and exclusive provision of the benefits by Company P of its research team to the development of Vaccine Z by the uncontrolled party. Because the IDCs include the ongoing compensation of the researchers, the compensation obligation under the PCT is only for the value of the commitment of the research team by Company P to the CSA's development efforts net of such researcher compensation. Though Company P and Company S are not required to actually enter into the transaction described by the RT, the value of the compensation obligation of Company S for the PCT will reflect the full value of provision of services described in the RT, as limited by Company S's RAB share.

*Example (3).* In Year 1, Company P and Company S execute a CSA under which they will share the IDCs for developing Product X. In Year 3, Company P acquires technology intangibles that it anticipates will contribute to the development of Product X from an uncontrolled party for a lump sum consideration. Because the technology intangibles are reasonably anticipated to contribute to the development on the date of the acquisition and the acquisition is an uncontrolled transaction that takes place after the formation of the CSA, the RT Rights in the technology intangibles are an external contribution acquired as part of a PFA. Accordingly, Company P and Company S must enter into a PCT in which Company S compensates Company P for the RT Rights in the technology intangibles and pursuant to paragraph (b)(3)(vi)(B) of this section, the form of payment of the PCT must mirror the lump sum form of payment of the PFA.

*Example (4).* Assume the same facts as in Example 3. In Year 4 Company P acquires Company X in a tax-free stock-for-stock acquisition. Company X is a start-up technology company with negligible amounts of tangible property and liabilities. Company X joins in the filing of a U.S. consolidated income tax return with USP and is treated as one taxpayer with Company P under paragraph (j)(2)(i) of this section. Accordingly, under paragraph (b)(3)(v) of this section, Company P's acquisition of the stock of Company X will be treated as an indirect acquisition of the resources and capabilities of Company X. The in-process technology and workforce of Company X acquired by Company P are reasonably anticipated to contribute to the development of product Z and therefore the RT Rights in the in-process technology and workforce of Company X are external contributions for which compensation is due to Company P from Company S under a PCT. Furthermore, because these external contributions were acquired by Company P in an uncontrolled transaction that took place after the formation of the CSA, they are also PFAs. Accordingly, the consideration due from S under the PCT must be paid in the same form of payment as Company's P acquisition of Company X, which was done in a lump sum payment. Therefore, consideration for the PCT must be paid in a lump sum.

*(4) Territorial division of interests.* (i) In general. Pursuant to paragraph (b)(1)(i) of this section, at the outset of the CSA the controlled participants must divide among themselves all interests in cost shared intangibles on a territorial basis as follows. The entire world must be divided into two or more non-overlapping geographic territories. Each controlled participant must receive at least one such territory, and in the aggregate all the participants must receive all such territories. Each controlled participant must be entitled to the perpetual and exclusive right to the profits from transactions of any member of the controlled group that includes the controlled participant with uncontrolled taxpayers regarding property or services for use, consumption, or disposition in such controlled participant's territory or territories, to the extent that such profits are attributable to cost shared intangibles. Absent the controlled participant's or other member of its controlled group's actual knowledge or reason to know otherwise, for purposes of the preceding sentence such use, consumption, or disposition of property or services will be considered to occur at the location(s) to which notices and other communications to the uncontrolled taxpayer(s) are to be provided in accordance with the contractual provisions of the relevant transactions.

(ii) Example. The following example illustrates the principles of this paragraph (b)(4):

*Example.* Companies P and S, both members of the same controlled group, enter into a CSA to develop product Z. Under the CSA, P receives the interest in product Z in the United States and S receives the interest in product Z in the rest of the world, as described in paragraph (b)(4)(i) of this section. Both P and S have plants for manufacturing product Z located in their respective geographic territories. However, for commercial reasons product Z is nevertheless manufactured by P in the United States for sale to customers in certain locations just outside the United States in close proximity to P's U.S. manufacturing plant. Because S owns the territorial rights outside the United States, intercompany compensation must be provided for between P and S to ensure that S realizes all the cost shared intangible profits from sales of product Z to customers in such proximate areas, even though the manufacturing is done by P in the United States. The pricing of such intercompany compensation must also ensure that P realizes an appropriate manufacturing return for its efforts. Benefits projected with respect to such sales will be included for purposes of estimating S's, but not P's, RAB share.

*(5) CSAs in substance or form.* (i) CSAs in substance. The Commissioner may apply, consistently with the rules of § 1.482-1(d)(3)(ii)(B) (Identifying contractual terms), the rules of this section to any arrangement that in substance constitutes a CSA described in paragraphs (b)(1)(i) through (iii) of this section, notwithstanding a failure to comply with any requirement of this section.

(ii) CSAs in form. Provided the requirements of paragraphs (b)(1)(iv) through (vii) are met with respect to an arrangement among controlled taxpayers,

(A) The Commissioner must apply the rules of this section to any such arrangement that the controlled taxpayers reasonably concluded to be a CSA, as described in paragraph (b)(1) of this section; and

(B) Otherwise, the Commissioner may apply the rules of this section to any other such arrangement.

(iii) Examples. The following examples illustrate the principles of this paragraph (b)(5). In the examples, assume that Companies P and S are both members of the same controlled group. The examples are as follows:

*Example (1).* (i) P owns the patent on a formula for a capsulated pain reliever, P-Cap. P reasonably anticipates, pending further research and experimentation, that the P-Cap formula could form the platform for a formula for P-Ves, an effervescent version of P-Cap. P also owns proprietary software that it reasonably anticipates to be critical to the research efforts. P and S execute a CSA by which they agree to proportionally share the costs and risks of developing a formula for P-Ves. The agreement reflects the various contractual requirements described in paragraph (k)(1) of this section and P and S comply with the documentation, accounting and reporting requirements of paragraphs (k)(2) through (4) of this section. Both the patent for P-Cap and the software are reasonably anticipated to contribute to the development of P-Ves and therefore are external contributions for which compensation is due from S as part of PCTs. Though P and S enter into a PCT for the P-Cap patent, they fail to enter into a PCT for the software.

(ii) In this case, P and S have substantially complied with the contractual requirements of paragraph (k)(1) of this section and the documentation, accounting and reporting requirements of paragraphs (k)(2) through (4) of this section and therefore have met the formal requirements of paragraphs (b)(1)(iv) through (vii) of this section. However, because they did not enter into a PCT, as required under paragraph (b)(1)(i) of this section, for the software that was reasonably anticipated to be critical to the development of P-Ves, they cannot reasonably conclude that their arrangement was a CSA. Accordingly, the Commissioner is not required under paragraph (b)(5)(ii)(A) of this section to apply the rules of this section to their arrangement. Nevertheless, pursuant to paragraph (b)(5)(ii)(B), the Commissioner may apply the rules of this section and treat P and S as entering into a PCT for the software in accordance with the requirements of paragraph (b)(1)(i) of this section, and make any appropriate allocations under paragraph (i) of this section. Alternatively, the Commissioner may decide that the arrangement is not a CSA described in paragraph (b)(1) of this section and therefore that this section's provisions do not apply in determining whether the arrangement reaches arm's length results. In this case, the arrangement would be analyzed under the methods under the section 482 regulations, without regard to this section, to determine whether the arrangement reaches such results.

*Example (2).* The facts are the same as Example 1 except that P and S do enter into a PCT for the software. Although the Commissioner determines that the PCT Payments for the software were not arm's length, nevertheless, under the facts and circumstances at the time they entered into the CSA and PCTs, P and S reasonably concluded their arrangement to be a CSA. Because P and S have met the requirements of paragraphs (b)(1)(iv) through (vii) and reasonably concluded their arrangement is a CSA, pursuant to paragraph (b)(5)(ii)(A) of this section, the Commissioner must apply the rules of this section to their arrangement. Accordingly, the Commissioner treats the arrangement as a CSA and makes adjustments to the PCT Payments as appropriate under this section to achieve an arm's length result for the PCT for the software.

*(6) Treatment of CSAs.* See § 301.7701-1(c) of this chapter for the treatment of CSAs for purposes of the Internal Revenue Code.

**(c) Make-or-sell rights excluded.** *(1) In general.* Any right to exploit an existing intangible without further development, such as the right to make or sell existing products, does not constitute an external contribution to a CSA, as described in paragraph (b)(3) of this section. Thus, the arm's length compensation for such rights does not satisfy the compensation obligation under a PCT.

*(2) Examples.* The following examples illustrate the principles of this paragraph (c):

*Example (1).* P and S, who are members of the same controlled group, execute a CSA that is described in paragraph (b)(1) of this section. Under the CSA, P and S will bear their proportional shares of IDCs for developing the second generation of ABC, a computer software program. Prior to that arrangement, P had incurred substantial costs and risks to develop ABC. Concurrently with entering into the arrangement, P (as the licensor) executes a license with S (as the licensee) by which S may make and sell copies of the existing ABC. Such make-and-sell rights do not constitute an external contribution to the CSA. The rules of §§ 1.482-1 and 1.482-4 through 1.482-6, without regard to the rules of this section, must be applied to determine the arm's length consideration in connection with the make-and-sell licensing arrangement. In certain circumstances this determination of the arm's length consideration may be done on an aggregate basis with the evaluation of compensation obligations pursuant to PCTs entered into by P and S in connection with the CSA. See paragraph (g)(2)(v) of this section.

*Example (2).* (i) P, a software company, has developed and currently exploits software program ABC. P and S enter into a CSA to develop future generations of ABC. The ABC source code is the platform on which future generations of ABC will be built and is therefore an external contribution of P for which compensation is due from S pursuant to a PCT. Concurrently with entering into the CSA, P licenses to S the make-and-sell rights for the current version of ABC. P has entered into similar licenses with uncontrolled parties calling for sales-based royalty payments at a rate of 20%. The current version of ABC has an expected product life of three years. P and S enter into a contingent payment agreement to cover both the PCT Payments due from S for P's external contribution and for the make-and-sell license. Based on the uncontrolled make-and-sell licenses, P and S agree on a sales-based royalty rate of 20% in Year 1 that declines on a straight line basis to 0% over the 3 year product life of ABC.

(ii) The make-and-sell rights for the current version of ABC are not external contributions, though paragraph (g)(2)(v) of this section provides for the possibility that the most reliable determination of an arm's length charge for the PCT and the make-and-sell license may be one that values the two transactions in the aggregate. A contingent payment schedule based on the uncontrolled make-and-sell licenses may provide an arm's length charge for the separate make-and-sell license between P and S, provided the royalty rates in the uncontrolled licenses similarly decline, but as a measure of the aggregate PCT and license payments it does not account for the arm's length value of P's external contributions which include the RT Rights in the source code and future development rights in ABC.

**(d) Intangible development costs (IDCs).** *(1) Costs included in IDCs.* For purposes of this section, IDCs mean all costs, in cash or in kind (including stock-based compensation, as described in paragraph (d)(3) of this section), but excluding costs for land or depreciable property, in the ordinary course of business after the formation of a CSA that, based on analysis of the facts and circumstances, are directly identified with, or are reasonably allocable to, the activity under the CSA of developing or attempting to develop intangibles (IDA). IDCs shall also include the arm's length rental charge for the use of any land or depreciable tangible property (as determined under § 1.482-2(c) (Use of tangible property)) directly identified with, or reasonably allocable to, the IDA. Reference to generally accepted accounting principles or federal income tax accounting rules may provide a useful starting point but will not be conclusive regarding inclusion of costs in IDCs. IDCs do not include interest expense, foreign income taxes (as defined in § 1.901-2(a)), or domestic income taxes.

*(2) Allocation of costs.* If a particular cost is reasonably allocable both to the IDA and to other business activities, the cost must be allocated on a reasonable basis between the IDA and such other business activities in proportion to the relative economic value that the IDA and such other business activities are anticipated to derive over time as a result of such cost.

*(3) Stock-based compensation.* (i) In general. As used in this section, the term stock-based compensation means any compensation provided by a controlled participant to an employee or independent contractor in the form of equity instruments, options to acquire stock (stock options), or rights with respect to (or determined by reference to) equity instruments or stock options, including but not limited to property to which section 83 applies and stock options to which section 421 applies, regardless of whether ultimately settled in the form of cash, stock, or other property.

(ii) Identification of stock-based compensation with the IDA. The determination of whether stock-based compensation is directly identified with, or reasonably allocable to, the IDA is made as of the date that the stock-based compensation is granted. Accordingly, all stock-based compensation that is granted during the term of the CSA and, at date of grant, is directly identified with, or reasonably allocable to, the IDA is included as an IDC under paragraph (d)(1) of this section. In the case of a repricing or other modification of a stock option, the determination of whether the repricing or other modification constitutes the grant of a new stock option for purposes of this paragraph (d)(3)(ii) will be made in accordance with the rules of section 424(h) and related regulations.

(iii) Measurement and timing of stock-based compensation IDC. (A) In general. Except as otherwise provided in this paragraph (d)(3)(iii), the cost attributable to stock-based compensation is equal to the amount allowable to the controlled participant as a deduction for federal income tax purposes with respect to that stock-based compensation (for example, under section 83(h)) and is taken into account as an IDC under this section for the taxable year for which the deduction is allowable.

(1) Transfers to which section 421 applies. Solely for purposes of this paragraph (d)(3)(iii)(A), section 421 does not apply to the transfer of stock pursuant to the exercise of an option that meets the requirements of section 422(a) or 423(a).

(2) Deductions of foreign controlled participants. Solely for purposes of this paragraph (d)(3)(iii)(A), an amount is treated as an allowable deduction of a controlled participant to the extent that a deduction would be allowable to a United States taxpayer.

(3) Modification of stock option. Solely for purposes of this paragraph (d)(3)(iii)(A), if the repricing or other modification of a stock option is determined, under paragraph (d)(3)(ii) of this section, to constitute the grant of a new stock option not identified with, or reasonably allocable to, the IDA, the stock option that is repriced or otherwise modified will be treated as being exercised immediately before the modification, provided that the stock option is then exercisable and the fair market value of the underlying stock then exceeds the price at which the stock option is exercisable. Accordingly, the amount of the deduction that would be allowable (or treated as allowable under this paragraph (d)(3)(iii)(A)) to the controlled participant upon exercise of the stock option immediately before the modification must be taken into account as an IDC as of the date of the modification.

(4) Expiration or termination of CSA. Solely for purposes of this paragraph (d)(3)(iii)(A), if an item of stock-based compensation identified with, or reasonably allocable to, the IDA is not exercised during the term of a CSA, that item of stock-based compensation will be treated as being exercised immediately before the expiration or termination of the CSA, provided that the stock-based compensation is then exercisable and the fair market value of the underlying stock then exceeds the price at which the stock-based compensation is exercisable. Accordingly, the amount of the deduction that would be allowable (or treated as allowable under this paragraph (d)(3)(iii)(A)) to the controlled participant upon exercise of the stock-based compensation must be taken into account as an IDC as of the date of the expiration or termination of the CSA.

(B) Election with respect to options on publicly traded stock. (1) In general. With respect to stock-based compensation in the form of options on publicly traded stock, the controlled participants in a CSA may elect to take into account all IDCs attributable to those stock options in the same amount, and as of the same time, as the fair value of the stock options reflected as a charge against income in audited financial statements or disclosed in footnotes to such financial statements, provided that such statements are prepared in accordance with United States generally accepted accounting principles by or on behalf of the company issuing the publicly traded stock.

(2) Publicly traded stock. As used in this paragraph (d)(3)(iii)(B), the term publicly traded stock means stock that is regularly traded on an established United States securities market and is issued by a company whose financial statements are prepared in accordance with United States generally accepted accounting principles for the taxable year.

(3) Generally accepted accounting principles. For purposes of this paragraph (d)(3)(iii)(B), a financial statement prepared in accordance with a comprehensive body of generally accepted accounting principles other than United States generally accepted accounting principles is considered to be prepared in accordance with United States generally accepted accounting principles provided that either—

(i) The fair value of the stock options under consideration is reflected in the reconciliation between such other accounting principles and United States generally accepted accounting principles required to be incorporated into the financial statement by the securities laws governing companies whose stock is regularly traded on United States securities markets; or

(ii) In the absence of a reconciliation between such other accounting principles and United States generally accepted accounting principles that reflects the fair value of the stock options under consideration, such other accounting principles require that the fair value of the stock options under consideration be reflected as a charge against income in audited financial statements or disclosed in footnotes to such statements.

(4) Time and manner of making the election. The election described in this paragraph (d)(3)(iii)(B) is made by an explicit reference to the election in the written CSA required by paragraph (k)(1) of this section or in a written amendment to the CSA entered into with the consent of the Commissioner pursuant to paragraph (d)(3)(iii)(C) of this section. In the case of a CSA in existence on August 26, 2003, the election by written amendment to the CSA may be made without the consent of the Commissioner if such amendment is entered into not later than the latest due date (with regard to extensions) of a federal income tax return of any controlled participant for the first taxable year beginning after August 26, 2003.

(C) Consistency. Generally, all controlled participants in a CSA taking options on publicly traded stock into account under paragraph (d)(3)(iii)(A) or (d)(3)(iii)(B) of this section must use that same method of measurement and timing for all options on publicly traded stock with respect to that CSA. Controlled participants may change their method only with the consent of the Commissioner and only with respect to stock options granted during taxable years subsequent to the taxable year in which the Commissioner's consent is obtained. All controlled participants in the CSA must join in requests for the Commissioner's consent under this paragraph. Thus, for example, if the controlled participants make the election described in paragraph (d)(3)(iii)(B) of this section upon the formation of the CSA, the election may be revoked only with the consent of the Commissioner, and the consent will apply only to stock options granted in taxable years subsequent to the taxable year in which consent is obtained. Similarly, if controlled participants already have granted stock options that have been or will be taken into account under the general rule of paragraph (d)(3)(iii)(A) of this section, then except in cases specified in the last sentence of paragraph (d)(3)(iii)(B)(4) of this section, the controlled participants may make the election described in paragraph (d)(3)(iii)(B) of this section only with the consent of the Commissioner, and the consent will apply only to stock options granted in taxable years subsequent to the taxable year in which consent is obtained.

*(4) IDC share.* A controlled participant's IDC share for a taxable year is equal to the controlled participant's cost contribution for the taxable year, divided by the sum of all IDCs for the taxable year. A controlled participant's cost contribution for a taxable year means all of the IDCs initially borne by the controlled participant, plus all of the cost sharing payments that the participant makes to other controlled participants, minus all of the cost sharing payments that the participant receives from other controlled participants.

*(5) Examples.* The following examples illustrate this paragraph (d):

*Example (1).* Foreign parent (FP) and its U.S. subsidiary (USS) enter into a CSA to develop a better mousetrap. USS and FP share the costs of FP's R&D facility that will be exclusively dedicated to this research, the salaries of the researchers, and reasonable overhead costs attributable to the project. They also share the cost of a conference facility that is at the disposal of the senior executive management of each company. Based on the facts and circumstances, the cost of the conference facility cannot be directly identified with, and is not reasonably allocable to, the IDA. In this case, the cost of the conference facility must be excluded from the amount of IDCs.

*Example (2).* U.S. parent (USP) and its foreign subsidiary (FS) enter into a CSA to develop intangibles for producing a new device. USP and FS share the costs of an R&D facility, the salaries of the facility's researchers, and reasonable overhead costs attributable to the project. Although USP also incurs costs related to field testing of the device, USP does not include those costs in the IDCs that USP and FS will share under the CSA. The Commissioner may determine, based on the facts and circumstances, that the costs of field testing are IDCs that the participants must share.

*Example (3).* U.S. parent (USP) and its foreign subsidiary (FS) enter into a CSA to develop a new process patent. USP employs researchers who perform R&D functions in connection both with the development of the new process patent and with the development of a new design patent the development of which is outside the scope of the CSA. During years covered by the CSA, USP compensates such employees with cash salaries, stock-based compensation, or a combination of both. USP and FS anticipate that the economic value attributable to such employees will be derived from the process patent and the design patent at a relative proportion of 75% and 25%, respectively. Applying the principles of paragraph (d)(2) of this section, 75% of the compensation of such employees must be allocated to the development of the new process patent and, thus, treated as IDCs. With respect to the cash salary compensation, the IDC is 75% of the face value of the cash. With respect to the stock-based compensation, the IDC is 75% of the value of the stock-based compensation as determined under paragraph (d)(3)(iii) of this section.

*Example (4).* Foreign parent (FP) and its U.S. subsidiary (USS) enter into a CSA to develop a new computer source code. FP's executive officers who oversee a research facility and employees dedicated solely to the IDA have additional responsibilities, including oversight of other research facilities and employees not in any way relevant to the development of the new computer source code. The full amount of the costs of the research facility and employees dedicated solely to the IDA can be directly identified with the IDA and, therefore, are IDCs. In addition, the participants determine that, of the economic value attributable to the executive officers, the new computer source code's share is 50%. Applying the principles of paragraph (d)(2) of this section, 50% of the compensation of such executives must be allocated to the development of the new computer source code and, thus, treated as IDCs.

**(e) Reasonably anticipated benefits share (RAB share).** *(1) In general.* A controlled participant's share of reasonably anticipated benefits (RAB share) is equal to its reasonably anticipated benefits divided by the sum of the reasonably anticipated benefits of all the controlled participants. See paragraph (j)(1)(v) of this section (defining reasonably anticipated benefits). RAB shares must be updated to account for changes in economic conditions, the business operations and practices of the participants, and the ongoing development of intangibles under the CSA. For purposes of determining RAB shares at any given time, reasonably anticipated benefits must be estimated over the entire period, past and future, of exploitation of the cost shared intangibles, and must reflect appropriate updates to take into account the most current reliable data regarding past and projected future results as is available at such time. A controlled participant's RAB share must be determined by using the most reliable estimate. In determining which of two or more available estimates is most reliable, the quality of the data and assumptions used in the analysis must be taken into account, consistent with § 1.482-1(c)(2)(ii) (Data and assumptions). Thus, the reliability of an estimate will depend largely on the completeness and accuracy of the data, the soundness of the assumptions, and the relative effects of particular deficiencies in data or assumptions on different estimates. If two estimates are equally reliable, no adjustment should be made based on differences in the results. The following factors will be particularly relevant in determining the reliability of an estimate of RAB shares—

(A) The basis used for measuring benefits, as described in paragraph (e)(2)(i) of this section; and

(B) The projections used to estimate benefits, as described in paragraph (e)(2)(iii) of this section.

*(2) Measure of benefits.* (i) In general. In order to estimate a controlled participant's RAB share, the amount of each controlled participant's reasonably anticipated benefits must be measured on a basis that is consistent for all such participants. See paragraph (e)(2)(ii)(E) Example 8 of this section. If a controlled participant transfers a cost shared intangible to another controlled taxpayer, other than by way of a transfer described in paragraph (f) of this section, that participant's benefits from the transferred intangible must be measured by reference to the transferee's benefits, disregarding any consideration paid by the transferee to the controlled participant (such as a royalty pursuant to a license agreement). Reasonably anticipated benefits are measured either on a direct basis, by reference to estimated benefits to be generated by the use of cost shared intangibles, or on an indirect basis, by reference to certain measurements that reasonably can be assumed to be related to benefits to be generated. Such indirect bases of measurement of anticipated benefits are described in paragraph (e)(2)(ii) of this section. A controlled participant's reasonably anticipated benefits must be measured on the basis, whether direct or indirect, that most reliably determines RAB shares. In determining which of two bases of measurement is most reliable, the factors set forth in § 1.482-1(c)(2)(ii) (Data and assumptions) must be taken into account. It normally will be expected that the basis that provided the most reliable estimate for a particular year will continue to provide the most reliable estimate in subsequent years, absent a material change in the factors that affect the reliability of the estimate. Regardless of whether a direct or indirect basis of measurement is used, adjustments may be required to account for material differences in the activities that controlled participants undertake to exploit their interests in cost shared intangibles. See Example 6 of paragraph (e)(2)(ii)(E) of this section.

(ii) Indirect bases for measuring anticipated benefits. Indirect bases for measuring anticipated benefits from participation in a CSA include the following:

(A) Units used, produced, or sold. Units of items used, produced, or sold by each controlled participant in the business activities in which cost shared intangibles are exploited may be used as an indirect basis for measuring its anticipated benefits. This basis of measurement will more reliably determine RAB shares to the extent that each controlled participant is expected to have a similar increase in net profit or decrease in net loss attributable to the cost shared intangibles per unit of the item or items used, produced, or sold. This circumstance is most likely to arise when the cost shared intangibles are exploited by the controlled participants in the use, production, or sale of substantially uniform items under similar economic conditions.

(B) Sales. Sales by each controlled participant in the business activities in which cost shared intangibles are exploited may be used as an indirect basis for measuring its anticipated benefits. This basis of measurement will more reliably determine RAB shares to the extent that each controlled participant is expected to have a similar increase in net profit or decrease in net loss attributable to cost shared intangibles per dollar of sales. This circumstance is most likely to arise if the costs of exploiting cost shared intangibles are not substantial relative to the revenues generated, or if the principal effect of using cost shared intangibles is to increase the controlled participants' revenues (for example, through a price premium on the products they sell) without affecting their costs substantially. Sales by each controlled participant are unlikely to provide a reliable basis for measuring RAB shares unless each controlled participant operates at the same market level (for example, manufacturing, distribution, etc.).

(C) Operating profit. Operating profit of each controlled participant from the activities in which cost shared intangibles are exploited, as determined before any expense (including amortization) on account of IDCs, may be used as an indirect basis for measuring anticipated benefits. This basis of measurement will more reliably determine RAB shares to the extent that such profit is largely attributable to the use of cost shared intangibles, or if the share of profits attributable to the use of cost shared intangibles is expected to be similar for each controlled participant. This circumstance is most likely to arise when cost shared intangibles are closely associated with the activity that generates the profit and the activity could not be carried on or would generate little profit without use of those intangibles.

(D) Other bases for measuring anticipated benefits. Other bases for measuring anticipated benefits may, in some circumstances, be appropriate, but only to the extent that there is expected to be a reasonably identifiable relationship between the basis of measurement used and additional income generated or costs saved by the use of cost shared intangibles. For example, a division of costs based on employee compensation would be considered unreliable unless there were a relationship between the amount of compensation and the expected income of the controlled participants from using the cost shared intangibles.

(E) Examples. The following examples illustrate this paragraph (e)(2)(ii):

*Example (1).* Foreign Parent (FP) and U.S. Subsidiary (USS) both produce a feedstock for the manufacture of various high-performance plastic products. Producing the feedstock requires large amounts of electricity, which accounts for a significant portion of its production cost. FP and USS enter into a CSA to develop a new process that will reduce the amount of electricity required to produce a unit of the feedstock. FP and USS currently both incur an electricity cost of $2 per unit of feedstock produced and rates for each are expected to remain similar in the future. The new process, if it is successful, will reduce the amount of electricity required by each company to produce a unit of the feedstock by 50%. Therefore, the cost savings each company is expected to achieve after implementing the new process are $1 per unit of feedstock produced. Under the CSA, FP and USS divide the costs of developing the new process based on the units of the feedstock each is anticipated to produce in the future. In this case, units produced is the most reliable basis for measuring RAB shares and dividing the IDCs because each controlled participant is expected to have a similar $1 (50% of current charge of $2) decrease in costs per unit of the feedstock produced.

*Example (2).* The facts are the same as in Example 1, except that currently USS pays $3 per unit of feedstock produced for electricity while FP pays $6 per unit of feedstock produced. In this case, units produced is not the most reliable basis for measuring RAB shares and dividing the IDCs because the participants do not expect to have a similar decrease in costs per unit of the feedstock produced. The Commissioner determines that the most reliable measure of RAB shares may be based on units of the feedstock produced if FP's units are weighted relative to USS's units by a factor of 2. This reflects the fact that FP pays twice as much as USS for electricity and, therefore, FP's savings of $3 per unit of the feedstock (50% reduction of current charge of $6) would be twice USS's savings of $1.50 per unit of feedstock (50% reduction of current charge of $3) from any new process eventually developed.

*Example (3).* The facts are the same as in Example 2, except that to supply the particular needs of the U.S. market USS manufactures the feedstock with somewhat different properties than FP's feedstock. This requires USS to employ a somewhat different production process than does FP. Because of this difference, it will be more costly for USS to adopt any new process that may be developed under the cost sharing agreement. In this case, units produced is not the most reliable basis for measuring RAB shares. In order to reliably determine RAB shares, the Commissioner offsets the reasonably anticipated costs of adopting the new process against the reasonably anticipated total savings in electricity costs.

*Example (4).* U.S. Parent (USP) and Foreign Subsidiary (FS) enter into a CSA to develop new anesthetic drugs. USP obtains the right to use any resulting patent in the U.S. market, and FS obtains the right to use the patent in the rest of the world. USP and FS divide costs on the basis of anticipated operating profit from each patent under development. USP anticipates that it will receive a much higher profit than FS per unit sold because drug prices are uncontrolled in the United States, whereas drug prices are regulated in many non-U.S. jurisdictions. In both controlled participants' territories, the operating profits are almost entirely attributable to the use of the cost shared intangible. In this case, the controlled participants' basis for measuring RAB shares is the most reliable.

*Example (5).* (i) Foreign Parent (FP) and U.S. Subsidiary (USS) both manufacture and sell fertilizers. They enter into a CSA to develop a new pellet form of a common agricultural fertilizer that is currently available only in powder form. Under the CSA, USS obtains the rights to produce and sell the new form of fertilizer for the U.S. market while FP obtains the rights to produce and sell the fertilizer for the rest of the world. The costs of developing the new form of fertilizer are divided on the basis of the anticipated sales of fertilizer in the controlled participants' respective markets.

(ii) If the research and development is successful, the pellet form will deliver the fertilizer more efficiently to crops and less fertilizer will be required to achieve the same effect on crop growth. The pellet form of fertilizer can be expected to sell at a price premium over the powder form of fertilizer based on the savings in the amount of fertilizer that needs to be used. This price premium will be a similar premium per dollar of sales in each territory. If the research and development is successful, the costs of producing pellet fertilizer are expected to be approximately the same as the costs of producing powder fertilizer and the same for both FP and USS. Both FP and USS operate at approximately the same market levels, selling their fertilizers largely to independent distributors.

(iii) In this case, the controlled participants' basis for measuring RAB shares is the most reliable.

*Example (6).* The facts are the same as in Example 5, except that FP distributes its fertilizers directly while USS sells to independent distributors. In this case, sales of USS and FP are not the most reliable basis for measuring RAB shares unless adjustments are made to account for the difference in market levels at which the sales occur.

*Example (7).* Foreign Parent (FP) and U.S. Subsidiary (USS) enter into a CSA to develop materials that will be used to train all new entry-level employees. FP and USS determine that the new materials will save approximately ten hours of training time per employee. Because their entry-level employees are paid on differing wage scales, FP and USS decide that they should not measure benefits based on the number of entry-level employees hired by each. Rather, they measure benefits based on compensation paid to the entry-level employees hired by each. In this case, the basis used for measuring RAB shares is the most reliable because there is a direct relationship between compensation paid to new entry-level employees and costs saved by FP and USS from the use of the new training materials.

*Example (8).* U.S. Parent (USP), Foreign Subsidiary 1 (FS1) and Foreign Subsidiary 2 (FS2) enter into a CSA to develop computer software that each will market and install on customers' computer systems. The controlled participants measure benefits on the basis of projected sales by USP, FS1, and FS2 of the software in their respective geographic areas. However, FS1 plans not only to sell but also to license the software to unrelated customers, and FS1's licensing income (which is a percentage of the licensees' sales) is not counted in the projected benefits. In this case, the basis used for measuring the benefits of each controlled participant is not the most reliable because all of the benefits received by controlled participants are not taken into account. In order to reliably determine RAB shares, FS1's projected benefits from licensing must be included in the measurement on a basis that is the same as that used to measure its own and the other controlled participants' projected benefits from sales (for example, all controlled participants might measure their benefits on the basis of operating profit).

(iii) Projections used to estimate benefits. (A) In general. The reliability of an estimate of RAB shares also depends upon the reliability of projections used in making the estimate. Projections required for this purpose generally include a determination of the time period between the inception of the research and development activities under the CSA and the receipt of benefits, a projection of the time over which benefits will be received, and a projection of the benefits anticipated for each year in which it is anticipated that the cost shared intangible will generate benefits. A projection of the relevant basis for measuring anticipated benefits may require a projection of the factors that underlie it. For example, a projection of operating profits may require a projection of sales, cost of sales, operating expenses, and other factors that affect operating profits. If it is anticipated that there will be significant variation among controlled participants in the timing of their receipt of benefits, and consequently benefit shares are expected to vary significantly over the years in which benefits will be received, it normally will be necessary to use the present discounted value of the projected benefits to reliably determine RAB shares. See paragraph (g)(2)(vi) of this section for guidance on discount rates used for this purpose. If it is not anticipated that benefit shares will significantly change over time, current annual benefit shares may provide a reliable projection of RAB shares. This circumstance is most likely to occur when the CSA is a long-term arrangement, the arrangement covers a wide variety of intangibles, the composition of the cost shared intangibles is unlikely to change, the cost shared intangibles are unlikely to generate unusual profits, and each controlled participant's share of the market is stable.

(B) Examples. The following examples illustrate the principles of this paragraph (e)(2)(iii):

*Example (1).* (i) Foreign Parent (FP) and U.S. Subsidiary (USS) enter into a CSA to develop a new car model. The controlled participants plan to spend four years developing the new model and four years producing and selling the new model. USS and FP project total sales of $4 billion and $2 billion, respectively, over the planned four years of exploitation of the new model. Cost shares are divided for each year based on projected total sales. Therefore, USS bears 66⅔% of each year's IDCs and FP bears 33⅓% of such costs.

(ii) USS typically begins producing and selling new car models a year after FP begins producing and selling new car models. In order to reflect USS's one-year lag in introducing new car models, a more reliable projection of each participant's RAB share would be based on a projection of all four years of sales for each participant, discounted to present value.

*Example (2).* U.S. Parent (USP) and Foreign Subsidiary (FS) enter into a CSA to develop new and improved household cleaning products. Both controlled participants have sold household cleaning products for many years and have stable market shares. The products under development are unlikely to produce unusual profits for either controlled participant. The controlled participants divide costs on the basis of each controlled participant's current sales of household cleaning products. In this case, the controlled participants' RAB shares are reliably projected by current sales of cleaning products.

*Example (3).* The facts are the same as in Example 2, except that FS's market share is rapidly expanding because of the business failure of a competitor in its geographic area. The controlled participants' RAB shares are not reliably projected by current sales of cleaning products. FS's benefit projections should take into account its growth in sales.

*Example (4).* Foreign Parent (FP) and U.S. Subsidiary (USS) enter into a CSA to develop synthetic fertilizers and insecticides. FP and USS share costs on the basis of each controlled participant's current sales of fertilizers and insecticides. The market shares of the controlled participants have been stable for fertilizers, but FP's market share for insecticides has been expanding. The controlled participants' projections of RAB shares are reliable with regard to fertilizers, but not reliable with regard to insecticides; a more reliable projection of RAB shares would take into account the expanding market share for insecticides.

**(f) Changes in participation under a CSA.** In the case of any change in participation under a CSA as the result of a controlled transfer of all or part of a controlled participant's territorial rights under the CSA, as described in paragraph (b)(4) of this section, along with the assumption by the transferee of the associated obligations under the CSA, the transferee will be treated as succeeding to the transferor's prior history under the CSA, including the transferor's cost contributions, benefits derived, and PCT Payments attributable to such rights or obligations. The transferor must receive an arm's length amount of consideration from the transferee under the rules of §§ 1.482-1 and 1.482-4 through 1.482-6, as described in paragraph (a)(3)(ii) of this section. For purposes of this section, such a change in participation under a CSA includes, for example, any transaction in which—

*(1)* A controlled participant transfers all or part of its territorial rights to another controlled participant that assumes the associated obligations under a CSA;

*(2)* A new controlled participant enters an ongoing CSA and acquires any territorial rights and assumes associated obligations under the CSA; or

*(3)* A controlled participant withdraws from an ongoing CSA, or otherwise abandons or relinquishes territorial rights and associated obligations under the CSA.

**(g) Supplemental guidance on methods applicable to PCTs.** *(1) In general.* This subsection provides supplemental guidance on applying the methods listed below for purposes of evaluating the arm's length amount charged in a PCT. Each method must be applied in accordance with the provisions of § 1.482-1, including the best method rule of § 1.482-1(c), the comparability analysis of § 1.482-1(d), and the arm's length range of § 1.482-1(e), except as those provisions are modified in this subsection. The methods are—

(i) The comparable uncontrolled transaction method described in § 1.482-4(c), or the arm's length charge described in § 1.482-2(b)(3)(first sentence) based on a comparable uncontrolled transaction, further described in paragraph (g)(3) of this section;

(ii) The income method, described in paragraph (g)(4) of this section;

(iii) The acquisition price method, described in paragraph (g)(5) of this section;

(iv) The market capitalization method, described in paragraph (g)(6) of this section;

(v) The residual profit split method, described in paragraph (g)(7) of this section; and

(vi) Unspecified methods, described in paragraph (g)(8) of this section.

*(2) General principles.* (i) In general. The principles set forth in this paragraph (g)(2) apply, as appropriate, to the use of any of the methods set forth in this section to determine the arm's length charge for a PCT.

(ii) Valuations consistent with upfront contractual terms and risk allocations. The application of any method as of any time must be consistent with the applicable contractual terms and allocation of risk under the CSA and this section among the controlled participants as of the date of the PCT, unless there has been a change in such terms or allocation made in return for arm's length consideration.

(iii) Projections. The reliability of an estimate of the value of an external contribution in connection with a PCT will often depend upon the reliability of projections used in making the estimate. Projections necessary for this purpose may include a projection of sales, IDCs, routine operating expenses, and costs of sales. For these purposes, projections that have been prepared for non-tax purposes are generally more reliable than projections that have been prepared solely for purposes of meeting the requirements in this paragraph (g).

(iv) Realistic alternatives. (A) In general. Regardless of the method or methods used, evaluation of the arm's length charge for the PCT in question should take into account the general principle that uncontrolled taxpayers dealing at arm's length would have evaluated the terms of a transaction, and only entered into a particular transaction, if no alternative is preferable. This condition is not met, for example, where for any controlled participant the total anticipated present value from entering into the CSA to that controlled participant, as of the date of the PCT, is less than the total anticipated present value that could be achieved through an alternative arrangement realistically available to that controlled participant. When applying the realistic alternatives principle, the reliability of the respective net present value calculations may need to be considered.

(B) Examples. The following examples illustrate the principles of this paragraph (g)(2)(iv):

*Example (1).* (i) P, a corporation, and S, a wholly-owned subsidiary of P, enter into a CSA to develop a gyroscopic personal transportation device (the product). Under the arrangement, P will undertake all of the R&D, and manufacture and market the product in Country X. S will make CST payments to P for its appropriate share of P's R&D costs, and manufacture and market the product in the rest of the world. P owns existing patents and trade secrets associated with gyroscopic applications. These patents and trade secrets are reasonably anticipated to contribute to the development of the product and therefore the RT Rights in the patents and trade secrets are external contributions for which compensation is due from S as part of a PCT.

(ii) S's manufacturing and distribution activities under the CSA will be routine in nature, and identical to the activities it would undertake if it alternatively licensed the product from P.

(iii) Reasonably reliable estimates indicate that P could self-develop and license the product outside of Country X for a royalty of 20% of sales. Based on reliable financial projections that include all future development costs and licensing revenue, the net present value of this licensing alternative to P for the non-Country X market (measured as of the date of the PCT) would be $500 million of operating income. Thus, based on this realistic alternative, the anticipated net present value under the CSA to P in the non-Country X market (measured as of the date of the PCT), including R&D reimbursement and PCT Payments from S, should not be less than $500 million.

*Example (2).* (i) The facts are the same as Example 1, except that there are no reliable estimates of the value to P from the licensing alternative to the CSA. However, reasonably reliable estimates indicate that S can earn a 10% markup on total accounting costs related to its routine manufacturing and distribution activities.

(ii) P undertakes an economic analysis that derives S's cost contributions under the CSA, based on reliable financial projections. Based on this and further economic analysis, P determines S's PCT Payment as a certain lump sum amount to be paid as of the date of the PCT.

(iii) Based on reliable financial projections that include S's cost contributions and that incorporate S's PCT Payment, and using a discount rate of D%, appropriate for the riskiness of the CSA (see paragraph (g)(2)(vi) of this section), the anticipated net present value to S under the CSA (measured at the time of the PCT) is $800 million. Of this amount, $100 million is the portion associated with the 10% markup on S's total accounting costs from its manufacturing and distribution activities, utilizing its existing investment in plant and equipment.

(iv) In evaluating the PCT under the CSA, the Commissioner concludes that the respective activities undertaken by P and S would be identical regardless of whether the arrangement was undertaken as a CSA or as a licensing arrangement. That is, under either alternative, P would undertake all research activities and S would undertake routine manufacturing and distribution activities associated with its territory. Consequently, in every year the total anticipated combined nominal profits of P and S would be identical regardless of whether the arrangement was undertaken as a CSA or as a licensing arrangement. In addition, the Commissioner considers the fact that S's economic role in the CSA (beyond its routine activities) is merely that of an investor. A similarly situated investor would be willing to invest an amount in a similar R&D project such that it earns an anticipated return on that investment of D% and therefore has a net present value of $0 on the project (not taking into account any returns to routine activities). If S were to realize a D% return on its lump sum PCT Payment, then the anticipated net present value to S of the CSA would be $100 million, equal to the $100 million anticipated net present value related to S's manufacturing and distribution activities, utilizing its existing investment in plant and equipment, plus the $0 anticipated net present value from the investment in the form of the lump sum PCT Payment in the IDA of the CSA at a D% discount rate.

(v) The lump sum PCT Payment computed by P results in S having significantly higher anticipated discounted profitability, and therefore, in this case, higher anticipated nominal profitability, than it could achieve under the licensing alternative. By implication, P must correspondingly earn lower nominal profits under the CSA than it would under the licensing alternative (that is, S's enhanced profitability under the CSA is matched dollar-for-dollar by P's reduced profitability under the CSA). Consequently, the Commissioner concludes that P is earning a lower anticipated return through the CSA than it could achieve under its realistic alternative to the CSA, and that consequently S's lump sum PCT Payment under-compensates P for its external contribution.

*Example (3).* (i) The facts are the same as Example 2 except as follows. Based on reliable financial projections that include S's cost contributions and S's PCT Payment, discounted at a rate of D% to reflect the riskiness of the CSA, the anticipated net present value to S under the CSA (measured as of the date of the PCT) is $50 million. Instead of entering the CSA, S has the realistic alternative of investing in an R&D project with similar risk, at an anticipated return of D%, and manufacturing and distributing products unrelated to the gyroscopic personal transportation device to the same extent as its manufacturing and distribution under the CSA, with the same anticipated 10% mark-up on total costs.

(ii) Under its realistic alternative, at a discount rate of D%, S anticipates a present value of $100 million from the routine manufacturing and distribution and $0 from the R&D investment, for a total of $100 million.

(iii) Because the lump sum PCT Payment made by S results in S having a considerably lower anticipated net present value than S could achieve through an alternative arrangement realistically available to it, the Commissioner may conclude that the lump sum PCT Payment overcompensates P for its external contribution.

(v) Aggregation of transactions. In some cases, controlled participants are required to determine arm's length payments for multiple PCTs covering various external contributions or, in addition to one or more PCTs, for transactions covering resources or capabilities that are not governed by this section, such as the transfer of make-or-sell rights as described in paragraph (c) of this section. Following the principles of aggregation described in § 1.482-1(f)(2)(i), a best method analysis under § 1.482-1(c) may determine that the method that provides the most reliable measure of an arm's length charge for the multiple PCTs and other transactions not governed by this section, if any, is a method that determines the arm's length charge for the multiple transactions on an aggregate basis under this section. A section 482 adjustment may be made by comparing the aggregate arm's length charge so determined to the aggregate payments actually made for the multiple transactions. In such a case, it generally will not be necessary to allocate separately the aggregate arm's length charge as between various PCTs or as between PCTs and transactions governed by other regulations under section 482. However, such an allocation may be necessary for other purposes, such as applying paragraph (i)(6) (Periodic adjustments) of this section. An aggregate determination of the arm's length charge for multiple transactions will generally yield a payment for a controlled participant that is equal to the aggregate value of the external contributions and other resources and capabilities covered by the multiple transactions multiplied by that controlled participant's RAB share. Because RAB shares only include benefits from cost shared intangibles, the reliability of an aggregate determination of payments for multiple transactions may be reduced to the extent that it includes transactions not governed by this section covering resources and capabilities for which the controlled participants' expected benefit shares differ substantially from their RAB shares.

(vi) Discount rate. (A) In general. Some calculations set forth in this paragraph (g) and elsewhere in this section require determining a rate of return which is used to convert a future or past monetary sum associated with a particular set of activities or transactions into a present value. For this purpose, a discount rate should be used that most reliably reflects the risk of the activities and the transactions based on all the information potentially available at the time for which the present value calculation is to be performed. Depending on the particular facts and circumstances, the risk involved and thus, the discount rate, may differ among a company's various activities or transactions. Normally, discount rates are most reliably determined by reference to market information. For example, the weighted average cost of capital (WACC) of the relevant activities and transactions derived using the capital asset pricing model might provide the most reliable discount rate. In such cases, this WACC might most reliably be based on information from uncontrolled companies whose business activities as a whole constitute comparable uncontrolled transactions. Where a company is publicly traded and its CSA involves substantially the same risk as projects undertaken by the company as a whole, then the WACC of the relevant activities and transactions might most reliably be based on the company's own WACC. Depending on comparability and reliability considerations, including the extent to which the company's hurdle rate reflects market information and is used in a similar manner in the controlled and uncontrolled transactions, in some circumstances discount rates might be most reliably determined by reference to other data such as a company's internal hurdle rate for projects of comparable risk.

(B) Examples. The following examples illustrate the principles of this paragraph (g)(2)(vi):

*Example (1).* USPharm, a publicly traded U.S. pharmaceutical company, enters into a CSA with FPharm, its wholly-owned foreign subsidiary. Under the agreement both controlled participants agree to share the research costs of developing a specific drug compound called T. USPharm is also engaged in another development project for compounds U and V, which involves different risks than the T development project and which is not part of the CSA. However, there are a large number of uncontrolled publicly traded U.S. companies, for which information can be reliably derived, that are highly comparable to USPharm but that conduct research only on compounds similar to T involving risks similar to those of the T development project. At the commencement of the CSA (Year 1), USPharm and FPharm enter into a PCT with respect to external contributions owned by USPharm consisting of the RT Rights in its pre-existing drug research. As part of the method that USPharm determines will most reliably calculate PCT Payments, a discount rate is needed to convert future monetary sums into a present value. After analysis, USPharm concludes that the discount rate is most reliably determined by calculating a WACC based on the information relating to the comparable uncontrolled companies, with suitable adjustments for factors such as differences in capital structure between USPharm and the comparables, and for the stability and other statistical properties of the beta measurement of the comparables.

*Example (2).* The facts are the same as in Example 1 except that the T development project is the only business activity of USPharm and FPharm and no reliable data exists on uncontrolled companies undertaking similar activities and risk as those associated with the CSA. After analysis, USPharm concludes that the discount rate is most reliably determined by reference to its own WACC. USPharm funds its operations with debt and common stock. Debt comprises 40% of its financing and USPharm's after-tax cost of debt is 6%. Equity comprises the remaining 60% of financing. USPharm is publicly traded and its equity beta is 1.25. Using third party information, USPharm concluded that the appropriate risk-free rate and equity risk premium are X% and Y%, respectively, implying a return on USPharm's equity of Z% [ X% + ( 1.25 × Y% )]. The weighted average cost of capital is calculated by blending and weighting the after-tax cost of debt and the cost of equity according to percentage of total financing. USPharm's weighted average cost of capital is W% [( 6% × 0.4 ) + ( Z% × 0.6 )].

*Example (3).* Use of a documented discount rate. The facts are the same as Example 1 except that no data exists on uncontrolled companies undertaking similar activities and risks as those associated with the CSA. USPharm has documented a hurdle rate of 12% that it uses as the minimum anticipated return for its business investments having a comparable risk profile. The Commissioner examines USPharm's documentation and concludes that the hurdle rate provides a reliable discount rate in this case.

(vii) Accounting principles. (A) In general. Allocations or other valuations done for accounting purposes may provide a useful starting point but will not be conclusive for purposes of assessing or applying methods to evaluate the arm's length charge in a PCT, particularly where the accounting treatment of an asset is inconsistent with its economic value.

(B) Examples. The following examples illustrate the principles of this paragraph (g)(2)(vii):

*Example (1).* (i) USP, a U.S. corporation and FSub, a wholly-owned foreign subsidiary of USP, enter into a CSA in Year 1 to develop software programs with application in the medical field. Company X is an uncontrolled software company located in the United States that is engaged in developing software programs that could significantly enhance the programs being developed by USP and FSub. Company X is still in a startup phase, so it has no currently exploitable products or marketing intangibles and its workforce consists of a team of software developers. Company X has negligible liabilities and tangible property. In Year 2, USP purchases Company X as part of an uncontrolled transaction in order to acquire its in-process technology and workforce for purposes of the development activities of the CSA. USP files a consolidated return that includes Company X. For accounting purposes, $50 million of the $100 million acquisition price is allocated to the in-process technology and workforce, and the residual $50 million is allocated to goodwill.

(ii) The in-process technology and workforce of Company X acquired by USP are reasonably anticipated to contribute to developing cost shared intangibles and therefore the RT Rights in the in-process technology and workforce of Company X are external contributions for which FSub must compensate USP as part of a PCT. In determining whether to apply the acquisition price or another method for purposes of evaluating the arm's length charge in the PCT, relevant comparability and reliability considerations must be weighed in light of the general principles of paragraph (g)(2) of this section. The allocation for accounting purposes raises an issue as to the reliability of using the acquisition price method in this case because it indicates that a significant portion of the value of Company X's assets is allocable to goodwill, which is often difficult to value reliably and which, depending on the facts and circumstances, might not be attributable to external contributions that are to be compensated by PCTs. See paragraph (g)(5)(iv)(A) of this section.

(iii) Paragraph (g)(2)(vii) of this section provides that accounting treatment may be a starting point, but is not determinative for purposes of assessing or applying methods to evaluate the arm's length charge in a PCT. The facts here reveal that Company X has nothing of economic value aside from its in-process technology and assembled workforce. The $50 million of the acquisition price allocated to goodwill for accounting purposes, therefore, is economically attributable to either or both the in-process technology and the workforce. That moots the potential issue under the acquisition price method of the reliability of valuation of assets not to be compensated by PCTs, since there are no such assets. Assuming the acquisition price method is otherwise the most reliable method, the aggregate value of Company X's in-process technology and workforce is the full acquisition price of $100 million. Accordingly, the aggregate value of the arm's length PCT Payments due from FSub to USP for the external contributions consisting of the RT Rights in Company X's in-process technology and workforce will equal $100 million multiplied by FSub's RAB share.

*Example (2).* (i) The facts are the same as in Example 1, except that Company X is a mature software business in the United States with a successful current generation of software that it markets under a recognized trademark, in addition to having the research team and new generation software in process that could significantly enhance the programs being developed under USP's and FSub's CSA. USP continues Company X's existing business and integrates the research team and the in-process technology into the efforts under its CSA with FSub. For accounting purposes, the $100 million acquisition price for acquiring Company X is allocated $50 million to existing software and trademark, $25 million to in-process technology and research workforce, and the residual $25 million to goodwill and going concern value.

(ii) In this case an analysis of the facts indicates a likelihood, consistent with the allocation under the accounting treatment (although not necessarily in the same amount), of goodwill and going concern value economically attributable to the existing U.S. software business rather than to the external contributions consisting of the RT Rights in the in-process technology and research workforce. Accordingly, further consideration must be given to the extent to which these circumstances reduce the relative reliability of the acquisition price method in comparison to other potentially applicable methods for evaluating the PCT Payment.

*Example (3).* (i) USP, a U.S. corporation and FSub, a wholly-owned foreign subsidiary of USP, enter into a CSA in Year 1 to develop Product A. Company Y is an uncontrolled corporation that owns Technology X that is critical to the development of Product A. Company Y currently markets Product B, which is dependent on Technology X. USP is solely interested in acquiring Technology X, but is only able to do so through the acquisition of Company Y in its entirety for $200 million in an uncontrolled transaction in Year 2. For accounting purposes, the acquisition price is allocated as follows: $120 million to Product B and the underlying Technology X, $30 million to trademark and other marketing intangibles, and the residual $50 million to goodwill and going concern. After the acquisition of Company Y, Technology X is used to develop Product A. No other part of Company Y is utilized in any manner. Product B is discontinued and accordingly, the accompanying marketing intangibles become worthless. None of the previous employees of Company Y are retained.

(ii) The Technology X of Company Y acquired by USP is reasonably anticipated to contribute to developing cost shared intangibles and is therefore an external contribution for which FSub must compensate USP as part of a PCT. Although for accounting purposes a significant portion of the acquisition price of Company Y was allocated to items other than Technology X, the facts demonstrate that USP had no intention of using and therefore placed no economic value on any part of Company Y other than Technology X. If USP was willing to pay $200 million for Company Y solely for purposes of acquiring Technology X, then assuming the acquisition price method is otherwise the most reliable method, the value of Technology X is the full $200 million acquisition price. Accordingly, the value of the arm's length PCT Payment due from FSub to USP for the external contribution consisting of the RT Rights in Technology X will equal $200 million multiplied by FSub's RAB share.

(viii) Valuation consistent with the investor model. (A) In general. The valuation of the amount charged in a PCT must be consistent with the assumption that, as of the date of the PCT, each controlled participant's aggregate net investment in developing cost shared intangibles pursuant to the CSA, attributable to both external contributions and cost contributions, is reasonably anticipated to earn a rate of return equal to the appropriate discount rate, determined following the principles set forth in paragraph (g)(2)(vi) of this section, over the entire period of developing and exploiting the cost shared intangibles. If the cost shared intangibles themselves are reasonably anticipated to contribute to developing other intangibles, then the period in the preceding sentence includes the period of developing and exploiting such indirectly benefited intangibles.

(B) Example. The following example illustrates the principles of this paragraph (g)(2)(viii):

*Example.* (i) P, a U.S. corporation, has developed a software program, DEF, which applies certain algorithms to reconstruct complete DNA sequences from partially-observed DNA sequences. S is a wholly-owned foreign subsidiary of P. P and S enter into a CSA to develop a new generation of genetic tests, GHI, based in part on the use of DEF which is therefore an external contribution of P for which compensation is due from S pursuant to a PCT. S makes no external contributions to the CSA. GHI sales are projected to commence two years after the inception of the CSA, which is on the first day of Year 1, and then to continue for eight more years. P and S project that GHI will be replaced by a new generation of genetic testing based on technology unrelated to DEF or GHI at the end of Year 10.

(ii) For purposes of valuing the PCT for P's external contribution of DEF to the CSA, P and S apply a type of residual profit split method that is not described in paragraph (g)(7) of this section and which, accordingly, constitutes an unspecified method. See paragraph (g)(7)(i) (last sentence) of this section. The principles of this paragraph (g)(2) apply to any method for valuing a PCT, including the unspecified method used by P and S.

(iii) Under the method employed by P and S, in each Year, a portion of the income from sales of GHI in S's territory is allocated to certain routine contributions made by S. The residual of the profit or loss from GHI sales in S's territory after the routine allocation step is divided between the controlled participants pro rata to their capital stocks allocable to S's territory. Each controlled participant's capital stock is computed by growing and amortizing (in the case of P) its historical expenditures regarding DEF allocable to S's territory and (in the case of S) its ongoing cost contributions towards developing GHI. The amortization of the capital stocks is effected on a straight-line basis over an assumed four-year life for the relevant expenditures. The capital stocks are grown using an assumed growth factor which P and S consider to be appropriate. Thus, the residual profit or loss from sales of GHI in S's territory is divided between P and S pro rata to P's capital stock in DEF attributable to S's territory and to S's capital stock from its cost contributions.

(iv) The assumption that all expenditures amortize on a straight-line basis over four years does not appropriately reflect the principle that as of the date of the PCT regarding DEF, every contribution to the development of GHI, including DEF is reasonably anticipated to have value throughout the entire period of exploitation of GHI as projected to continue through Year 10. Under this method as applied by P and S, P's capital stock in DEF, and therefore the amount of profit in S's territory allocated to P as a PCT Payment from S, will decrease every year. After Year 4, P's capital stock in DEF will necessarily be $0. Thus, under this method, P will receive none of the residual profit or loss from GHI sales in S's territory after Year 4 as a PCT Payment. As a result of this limitation of the PCT Payments to be made by S, the return to S's aggregate investment in the CSA is anticipated to be significantly higher than the appropriate discount rate for the CSA. This is not consistent with the investor model principle that S should anticipate a return to its aggregate investment in the CSA equal to the appropriate discount rate over the entire period of developing and exploiting GHI. The inconsistency of the method with the investor model materially lessens its reliability for purposes of a best method analysis. See § 1.482-1(c)(2)(ii)(B).

(ix) Coordination of best method rule and form of payment. A method described in paragraph (g)(1) of this section evaluates the arm's length amount charged in a PCT in terms of a form of payment (method payment form). For example, the method payment form for the income method described in paragraph (g)(4)(iii) or (iv) of this section is payment contingent on the exploitation of cost shared intangibles by the PCT Payor, and the method payment form for the market capitalization method is lump sum payment. The method payment form may not necessarily correspond to the form of payment specified pursuant to paragraphs (b)(3)(vi)(A) and (k)(2)(ii)(l) of this section (specified payment form). The determination under § 1.482-1(c) of the method that provides the most reliable measure of an arm's length result is to be made without regard to whether the respective method payment forms under the competing methods correspond to the specified payment form. If the method payment form of the method determined under § 1.482-1(c) to provide the most reliable measure of an arm's length result differs from the specified payment form, then the conversion from such method payment form to such specified payment form will be made on a reasonable basis to the satisfaction of the Commissioner. For purposes of the preceding sentence, if the method described in the documentation by the controlled participants pursuant to paragraph (k)(2)(ii)(J) of this section is determined under § 1.482-1(c) to provide the most reliable measure of an arm's length result, then the Commissioner will give due consideration whether the conversion from the method payment form to the specified payment form was made by the controlled participants on a reasonable basis.

(x) Coordination of the valuations of prior and subsequent PCTs. (A) In general. In cases where PCTs are required on different dates, coordination of the valuations of the prior and subsequent PCTs must be effected pursuant to a method that provides the most reliable measure of an arm's length result. Depending on the facts and circumstances, such as whether the external contributions that were the subject of the prior and subsequent PCTs were nonroutine contributions, an approach which may be appropriate would be to determine PCT Payments both for the prior and subsequent PCTs going forward from the date of the subsequent PCT pursuant to a residual profit split method, as described in paragraph (g)(7) of this section. Such application of the residual profit split method would include as nonroutine contributions all of the following: The external contribution(s) that were the subject of the prior PCT(s), the external contribution that is the subject of the subsequent PCT, and the interests of the controlled participants in the incremental cost shared intangible development resulting from the development activities under the CSA. Paragraph (g)(2)(x)(B) of this section specifies the appropriate coordination with a prior PCT in the case of a subsequent PCT the subject of which is a PFA.

(B) Coordination with regard to PFAs. PCT Payments for a subsequent PCT that is derived from a PFA are determined independently of any prior PCTs. Such PCT Payments will be treated, for purposes of the application of the method used for evaluating a prior PCT, the same as IDCs, the actual amounts of which may not correspond to those projected on the date of the prior PCT. A divergence between actual and anticipated IDCs does not require alteration in the application of the method used to value PCT Payments. Similarly, a subsequent PCT derived from a PFA will not require alteration in the application of the method used to value PCT Payments for a prior PCT.

(xi) Proration of PCT Payments to the extent allocable to other business activities. If a resource or capability that is the subject of a PCT is reasonably anticipated to contribute both to developing or exploiting cost shared intangibles and to other business activities of the PCT Payee (other than exploiting an existing intangible without further development), then to the extent it can be demonstrated that a portion of the value of the relevant PCT Payments otherwise determined under this section is attributable to such other business activities, the PCT Payments must be prorated. Such proration will be done on a reasonable basis in proportion to the relative economic value, as of the date of the PCT, reasonably anticipated to be derived from the resource or capability by the CSA Activity as compared to such other business activities of the PCT Payee. In the case of an aggregate valuation done under the principles of paragraph (g)(2)(v) of this section that includes payment for rights to exploit an existing intangible without further development, the prorated aggregate payments must take into account the economic value attributable to such exploitation rights as well. For purposes of the best method rule under § 1.482-1(c), the reliability of the analysis under a method that requires proration pursuant to this paragraph is reduced relative to the reliability of an analysis under a method that does not require proration.

*(3) Comparable uncontrolled transaction method.* The comparable uncontrolled transaction (CUT) method described in § 1.482-4(c), and the arm's length charge described in § 1.482-2(b)(3) (first sentence) based on a comparable uncontrolled transaction, may be applied to evaluate whether the amount charged in a PCT is arm's length by reference to the amount charged in a comparable uncontrolled transaction. When applied in the manner described in § 1.482-4(c), or where a comparable uncontrolled transaction provides the most reliable measure of the arm's length charge described in § 1.482-2(b)(3) (first sentence), the CUT method, or the arm's length charge in the comparable uncontrolled transaction, will typically yield an arm's length total value for the external contribution that is the subject of the PCT. That value must then be multiplied by each PCT Payor's respective RAB share in order to determine the arm's length PCT Payment due from each PCT Payor. The reliability of a CUT that yields a value for the external contribution only in the PCT Payor's territory will be reduced to the extent that value is not consistent with the total worldwide value of the external contribution multiplied by the PCT Payor's RAB share.

*(4) Income method.* (i) In general. The income method evaluates whether the amount charged in a PCT is arm's length by reference to the controlled participants' realistic alternatives to entering into a CSA.

(ii) Determination of arm's length charge. (A) In general. Under this method, the arm's length charge for a PCT Payment will be an amount such that a controlled participant's present value, as of the date of the PCT, of entering into a CSA equals the present value of its best realistic alternative. Paragraphs (g)(4)(iii) and (iv) of this section describe two specific applications of the income method, but do not exclude other possible applications of this method.

(B) Example. The following example illustrates the principles of this paragraph (g)(4)(ii):

*Example.* (i) USP, a U.S. manufacturer, has developed a new, lightweight fabric for sleeping bags. In Year 1 USP enters into a CSA with its wholly-owned foreign subsidiary, FSub, to develop an improved version of this fabric. Under the CSA, USP will own the rights to exploit improved versions of the fabric in the United States and FSub will own the rights to exploit improvements in the rest of the world (ROW). The rights to further develop the fabric are reasonably anticipated to contribute to the development of future improved versions and therefore the RT Rights in the fabric are external contributions for which compensation is due pursuant to a PCT. USP does not transfer the right to exploit its current fabric to FSub. FSub does not furnish any external contributions. If USP did not participate in the CSA, its best realistic alternative would be to develop future versions of the fabric on its own, exploit those versions in the United States and license such versions for exploitation outside the United States to FSub. In Year 1, USP estimates that its present value of this alternative (including arm's length royalties on sales in the ROW) is $100 million. Under the CSA, USP projects U.S. sleeping bag sales with improved versions of the fabric to amount to $80 million (present value in Year 1). The costs (other than IDCs) plus the routine return to such costs associated with the U.S. sales are anticipated to be $10 million. USP's anticipated cost contributions under the CSA are $10 million (present value in Year 1). FSub projects that in the ROW, future sales should amount to $100 million (present value in Year 1).

(ii) An arm's length contingent PCT Payment under the income method is a sales-based royalty at a rate, p, such that the present value to USP of the best realistic alternative is equal to the present value to USP of participating in the CSA. In other words, the rate is such that $100 million (value of licensing alternative) = $80 million (anticipated U.S. sales) − $10 million (anticipated costs, other than IDCs, plus routine return) − $10 million (anticipated cost contribution) + (p * $100 million (anticipated ROW sales)), or 40%. Accordingly, FSub should pay USP a royalty of 40% of actual ROW sales annually when the two begin to exploit future generations of the fabric.

(iii) Application of income method using a CUT. (A) In general. This application of the income method is typically used in cases where only one controlled participant furnishes nonroutine contributions, as described in paragraph (g)(7)(iii)(C)(1) of this section. This application assumes that the best reasonable alternative of the PCT Payee to entering into the CSA would be to develop the cost shared intangibles on its own, bearing all the IDCs itself, and then to license the cost shared intangibles to the other controlled participants.

(B) Determination of arm's length charge. (1) In general. An arm's length PCT Payment under this application of the income method is represented as an applicable rate on sales from exploiting the cost shared intangibles, determined as of the date of the PCT.

(2) Applicable rate. The applicable rate is equal to the alternative rate less the cost contribution adjustment.

(3) Alternative rate. The alternative rate is the constant rate the PCT Payee would charge an uncontrolled licensee over the period the cost shared intangibles are anticipated to be exploited if the PCT Payee had developed the cost shared intangibles on its own and licensed them to the uncontrolled licensee. The alternative rate is determined using the comparable uncontrolled transaction method, as described in § 1.482-4(c)(1) and (2).

(4) Cost contribution adjustment. The cost contribution adjustment is equal to a fraction, the numerator of which is the present value of the PCT Payor's total anticipated cost contributions and the denominator of which is the present value of the PCT Payor's total anticipated sales from exploiting the cost shared intangibles.

(C) Example. The following example illustrates the principles of this paragraph (g)(4)(iii):

*Example.* (i) USP, a software company, has developed version 1.0 of a new software application which it is currently marketing. In Year 1 USP enters into a CSA with its wholly-owned foreign subsidiary, FS, to develop future versions of the software application. Under the CSA, USP will have the rights to exploit the future versions in the United States, and FS will have the rights to exploit them in the rest of the world (ROW). The future rights in version 1.0, and USP's development team, are reasonably anticipated to contribute to the development of future versions and therefore the RT Rights in version 1.0 are external contributions for which compensation is due from FS as part of a PCT. USP does not transfer the current exploitation rights in version 1.0 to FS. FS does not furnish any external contributions. FS anticipates sales of $100 million (present value in Year 1) in its territory and anticipates cost contributions of $40 million (present value in Year 1). The arm's length rate USP would have charged an uncontrolled licensee for a license of future versions of the software had USP further developed version 1.0 on its own is 60%, as determined under the comparable uncontrolled transaction method in § 1.482-4(c).

(ii) An arm's length contingent PCT Payment under the income method is an applicable rate equal to the alternative rate less the cost contribution adjustment. In this case the alternative rate is 60%, the arm's length rate determined under § 1.482-4(c). The cost contribution adjustment is 40%, the present value to FS of its anticipated cost contribution over the present value of its anticipated sales of future versions of the software, that is, $40 million / $100 million. The applicable rate, which represents an arm's length contingent PCT Payment, payable by the FS to USP on all actual ROW sales of the future versions of the software therefore is 20%, which is equal to the alternative rate of 60% less the cost contribution adjustment of 40%.

(iv) Application of income method using CPM. (A) In general. This application of the income method is typically used in cases where only one controlled participant furnishes nonroutine contributions. Under this application, the present value of the anticipated PCT Payments is equal to the present value, as of the date of the PCT, of the PCT Payor's anticipated profit from developing and exploiting cost shared intangibles. This PCT Payment ensures that PCT Payors who do not furnish any external contributions subject to a PCT receive an appropriate ex ante risk adjusted return on their investment in the CSA.

(B) Determination of arm's length charge based on sales. (1) In general. An arm's length PCT Payment under this application of the income method is represented as an applicable rate on sales from exploiting the cost shared intangibles, determined as of the date of the PCT.

(2) Applicable rate. The applicable rate is equal to the alternative rate less the cost contribution adjustment.

(3) Alternative rate. The alternative rate is determined using the comparable profits method described in § 1.482-5 and is estimated as a fraction. The numerator of the fraction is the present value of the PCT Payor's total anticipated territorial operating profit, as defined in paragraph (j)(1)(vi) of this section, reduced by a market return for the routine contributions (other than cost contributions) to the relevant business activity in the relevant territory. The denominator of the fraction is the discounted present value of the PCT Payor's total anticipated sales from exploiting the cost shared intangibles.

(4) Cost contribution adjustment. The cost contribution adjustment is equal to a fraction the numerator of which is the present value of the PCT Payor's total anticipated cost contributions and the denominator of which is the present value of the PCT Payor's total anticipated sales from exploiting the cost shared intangibles.

(C) Determination of arm's length charge based on profit. (1) In general. An arm's length PCT Payment under this application of the income method may also be represented as an applicable rate on territorial operating profit, as defined in paragraph (j)(1)(vi) of this section, reduced by a market return for the routine contributions (other than cost contributions) to the relevant business activity in the relevant territory. This is done following the calculations described in paragraph (g)(4)(iv)(B) of this section, substituting anticipated territorial operating profit, reduced by a market return for the routine contributions (other than cost contributions) to the relevant business activity in the relevant territory, wherever anticipated sales appear in the calculations.

(2) Alternative rate. Substituting territorial operating profits, reduced by a market return for the routine contributions (other than cost contributions) to the relevant business activity in the relevant territory, for sales in the calculation of the alternative rate results in a fraction with both a numerator and denominator equal to the present value of the PCT Payor's total anticipated territorial operating profit, as defined in paragraph (j)(1)(vi) of this section, reduced by a market return for the routine contributions (other than cost contributions) to the relevant business activity in the relevant territory. Therefore the alternative rate under this application is 1, or 100%.

(3) Cost contribution adjustment. Substituting territorial operating profit, reduced by a market return for the routine contributions (other than cost contributions) to the relevant business activity in the relevant territory, for sales results in a cost contribution adjustment equal to a fraction the numerator of which is the present value of the PCT Payor's total anticipated cost contributions and the denominator of which is the present value of the PCT Payor's total anticipated territorial operating profit, as defined in paragraph (j)(1)(vi) of this section, reduced by a market return for the routine contributions (other than cost contributions) to the relevant business activity in the relevant territory.

(D) Example. The following example illustrates the principles of this paragraph (g)(4)(iv):

*Example.* (i) USP, a U.S. pharmaceutical company, invests in research and development to begin developing a vaccine for disease K. In Year 1, USP enters into a CSA with its wholly-owned foreign subsidiary, FS, to complete the development of the vaccine. Under the CSA, USP will have the rights to exploit the vaccine in the United States, and FS will have the rights to exploit it in the rest of the world. The partially developed vaccine owned by USP, and USP's development team, are reasonably anticipated to contribute to the development of the final vaccine and therefore the RT Rights in the vaccine and the development team are external contributions for which compensation is due from FS as part of a PCT. FS does not furnish any external contributions. The total anticipated IDCs under the CSA are $100 million (in Year 1 dollars). USP and FS each have total projected sales of $100 million (in Year 1 dollars) of the vaccine, which they use as the basis for determining RAB shares. Accordingly, they divide the development costs based on 50/50 RAB shares, $50 million (in Year 1 dollars) paid by each participant. Based on an analysis under the comparable profits method under § 1.482-5, FS's anticipated territorial operating profit, as reduced by a market return for its routine contributions to exploiting the vaccine in its territory, is $80 million (in Year 1 dollars).

(ii) An arm's length contingent PCT Payment based on territorial sales under the income method is an applicable rate equal to the alternative rate less the cost contribution adjustment. In this case the alternative rate is 80% ($80 million territorial operating profit/$100 million sales). The cost contribution adjustment is 50%, the present value to FS of its anticipated cost contributions over the present value of its anticipated sales of the vaccine, that is, $50 million/$100 million. The applicable rate, which represents an arm's length contingent PCT Payment, payable by FS to USP over the period the vaccine is exploited therefore is 30%, which is equal to the alternative rate of 80% less the cost contribution adjustment of 50%.

(iii) An arm's length contingent PCT Payment based on territorial operating profits under the income method is an applicable rate equal to the alternative rate less the cost contribution adjustment. In this case the alternative rate is 100% ($80 million territorial operating profit /$80 million territorial operating profit). The cost contribution adjustment is 62.5%, the present value to FS of its anticipated cost contributions over the present value of its anticipated territorial profits from sales of the vaccine, that is, $50 million/$80 million. The applicable rate on territorial operating profit, which represents an arm's length contingent PCT Payment, payable by FS to USP over the period the vaccine is exploited therefore is 37.5%, which is equal to the alternative rate of 100% less the cost contribution adjustment of 62.5%.

(v) Routine external contributions. For purposes of this paragraph (g)(4), any routine contributions that are external contributions (routine external contributions), the valuation and PCT Payments for which are determined and made independently of the income method, are treated similarly to cost contributions. Accordingly, wherever the term cost contributions appears in this paragraph (g)(4) it shall be read to include net routine external contributions. Net routine external contributions are defined as a controlled participant's total anticipated routine external contributions, plus its anticipated PCT Payments to other controlled participants in respect of their routine external contributions, minus the anticipated PCT Payments it is to receive from other controlled participants in respect of its routine external contributions.

(vi) Comparability and reliability considerations. (A) In general. Whether results derived from this method are the most reliable measure of the arm's length result is determined using the factors described under the best method rule in § 1.482-1(c). Thus, comparability and the quality of data and assumptions must be considered in determining whether this method provides the most reliable measure of an arm's length result. Consistent with those considerations, the reliability of applying the income method as a measure of the arm's length charge for a PCT Payment is typically less reliable to the extent that more than one controlled participant furnishes nonroutine contributions.

(B) Application of the income method using a CUT. If the income method is applied using a CUT, as described in paragraph (g)(4)(iii) of this section, any additional comparability and reliability considerations stated in § 1.482-4(c)(2) may apply.

(C) Application of the income method using CPM. If the income method is applied using CPM, as described in paragraph (g)(4)(iv) of this section, any additional comparability and reliability considerations stated in § 1.482-5(c) may apply.

*(5) Acquisition price method.* (i) In general. The acquisition price method applies the comparable uncontrolled transaction method of § 1.482-4(c), or the arm's length charge described in § 1.482-2(b)(3)(first sentence) based on a comparable uncontrolled transaction, to evaluate whether the amount charged in a PCT, or group of PCTs, is arm's length by reference to the amount charged (the acquisition price) for the stock or asset purchase of an entire organization or portion thereof (the target) in an uncontrolled transaction. The acquisition price method is ordinarily used only where substantially all the target's nonroutine contributions (as described in paragraph (g)(7)(iii)(C)(1) of this section) to the PCT Payee's business activities are covered by a PCT or group of PCTs.

(ii) Determination of arm's length charge. Under this method, the arm's length charge for a PCT or group of PCTs covering resources and capabilities of the target is equal to the adjusted acquisition price, as divided among the controlled participants according to their respective RAB shares.

(iii) Adjusted acquisition price. The adjusted acquisition price is the acquisition price of the target increased by the value of the target's liabilities on the date of the acquisition, other than liabilities not assumed in the case of an asset purchase, and decreased by the value of the target's tangible property on that date and by the value on that date of any other resources and capabilities not covered by a PCT or group of PCTs.

(iv) Reliability and comparability considerations. The comparability and reliability considerations stated in § 1.482-4(c)(2) apply. Consistent with those considerations, the reliability of applying the acquisition price method as a measure of the arm's length charge for the PCT Payment normally is reduced if—

(A) A substantial portion of the target's nonroutine contributions to the PCT Payee's business activities is not required to be covered by a PCT or group of PCTs, and that portion of the nonroutine contributions cannot reliably be valued; or

(B) A substantial portion of the target's assets consists of tangible property that cannot reliably be valued.

(v) Example. The following example illustrates the principles of this paragraph (g)(5):

*Example.* USP, a U.S. corporation, and its newly incorporated, wholly-owned foreign subsidiary (FS) enter into a CSA in Year 1 to develop Group Z products. Under the CSA, USP and FS will have the exclusive rights to exploit the Group Z products in the U.S. and the rest of the world, respectively. Based on RAB shares, USP will bear 60% and FS will bear 40% of the costs incurred during the term of the agreement. USP acquires Company X in Year 2 for cash consideration worth $110 million. Company X joins in the filing of a U.S. consolidated income tax return with USP. Under paragraph (j)(2)(i) of this section, Company X and USP are treated as one taxpayer. Accordingly, the RT Rights in any of Company X's resources and capabilities that are reasonably anticipated to contribute to the development activities of the CSA will be considered external contributions furnished by USP. Company X's resources and capabilities consist of its workforce, certain technology intangibles, $15 million of tangible property and other assets and $5 million in liabilities. The technology intangibles, as well as Company X's workforce, are reasonably anticipated to contribute to the development of the Group Z products under the CSA and therefore the RT Rights in the technology intangibles and the workforce are external contributions by way of a PFA for which FS must make a PCT Payment to USP. None of Company X's existing intangible assets or any of its workforce are anticipated to contribute to activities outside the CSA. Applying the acquisition price method, the value of USP's external contributions is the adjusted acquisition price of $100 million ($110 million acquisition price plus $5 million liabilities less $15 million tangible property and other assets). FS must make a PCT Payment to USP for these external contributions in an amount of $40 million, which is the product of $100 million (the value of the external contributions) and 40% (FS's RAB share).

*(6) Market capitalization method.* (i) In general. The market capitalization method applies the comparable uncontrolled transaction method of § 1.482-4(c), or the arm's length charge described in § 1.482-2(b)(3)(first sentence) based on a comparable uncontrolled transaction, to evaluate whether the amount charged in a PCT, or group of PCTs, is arm's length by reference to the average market capitalization of a controlled participant (PCT Payee) whose stock is regularly traded on an established securities market. The market capitalization method is ordinarily used only where substantially all of the PCT Payee's nonroutine contributions (as described in paragraph (g)(7)(iii)(C)(1) of this section) to the PCT Payee's business are covered by a PCT or group of PCTs.

(ii) Determination of arm's length charge. Under the market capitalization method, the arm's length charge for a PCT or group of PCTs covering resources and capabilities of the PCT Payee is equal to the adjusted average market capitalization, as divided among the controlled participants according to their respective RAB shares.

(iii) Average market capitalization. The average market capitalization is the average of the daily market capitalizations of the PCT Payee over a period of time beginning 60 days before the date of the PCT and ending on the date of the PCT. The daily market capitalization of the PCT Payee is calculated on each day its stock is actively traded as the total number of shares outstanding multiplied by the adjusted closing price of the stock on that day. The adjusted closing price is the daily closing price of the stock, after adjustments for stock-based transactions (dividends and stock splits) and other pending corporate (combination and spin-off) restructuring transactions for which reliable arm's length adjustments can be made.

(iv) Adjusted average market capitalization. The adjusted average market capitalization is the average market capitalization of the PCT Payee increased by the value of the PCT Payee's liabilities on the date of the PCT and decreased by the value on such date of the PCT Payee's tangible property and of any other resources and capabilities of the PCT Payee not covered by a PCT or group of PCTs.

(v) Reliability and comparability considerations. The comparability and reliability considerations stated in § 1.482-4(c)(2) apply. Consistent with those considerations, the reliability of applying the comparable uncontrolled transaction method using the adjusted market capitalization of a company as a measure of the arm's length charge for the PCT Payment normally is reduced if—

(A) A substantial portion of the PCT Payee's nonroutine contributions to its business activities is not required to be covered by a PCT or group of PCTs, and that portion of the nonroutine contributions cannot reliably be valued;

(B) A substantial portion of the PCT Payee's assets consists of tangible property that cannot reliably be valued; or

(C) Facts and circumstances demonstrate the likelihood of a material divergence between the average market capitalization of the PCT Payee and the value of its resources and capabilities for which reliable adjustments cannot be made.

(vi) Examples. The following examples illustrate the principles of this paragraph (g)(6):

*Example (1).* (i) USP, a publicly traded U.S. company, and its newly incorporated wholly-owned foreign subsidiary (FS) enter into a CSA on Date 1 to develop software. Under the CSA, USP and FS will have the exclusive rights to exploit all future generations of the software in the United States and the rest of the world, respectively. Based on RAB shares, USP will bear 70% and FS will bear 30% of the costs incurred during the term of the CSA. USP's assembled team of researchers and its entire existing and in-process software are reasonably anticipated to contribute to the development of the software under the CSA and the RT Rights in the research team and existing and in-process software are therefore external contributions for which compensation is due from FS. USP separately enters into a license agreement with FS for make-and-sell rights for all existing software in the rest of the world. This license of current make-and-sell rights is a transaction that is governed by § 1.482-4. However, after analysis, it is determined that the PCT Payments and the arm's length payments for the make-and-sell license may be most reliably determined in the aggregate using the market capitalization method, under principles described in paragraph (g)(2)(v) of this section.

(ii) On Date 1, USP had an average market capitalization of $205 million, tangible property and other assets that can be reliably valued worth $5 million and no liabilities. Applying the market capitalization method, the aggregate value of USP's external contributions and the make-and-sell rights in its existing software is $200 million ($205 million average market capitalization of USP less $5 million of tangible property and other assets). The total arm's length value of the PCT Payments and license payments FS must make to USP for the external contributions and current make-and-sell rights is $60 million, which is the product of $200 million (the value of the external contributions and the make-and-sell rights) and 30% (FS's share of anticipated benefits of 30%).

*Example (2).* The facts are the same as Example 1 except that USP also makes significant nonroutine contributions that are difficult to value to several other mature business divisions it operates that are not reasonably anticipated to contribute to the software development that is the subject of the CSA and, therefore, are not external contributions and, accordingly, are not required to be covered by a PCT. The reliability of using the market capitalization method to determine the value of USP's external contributions to the CSA is significantly reduced in this case because it would require adjusting USP's average market capitalization to account for the significant nonroutine contributions that are not required to be covered by a PCT.

*(7) Residual profit split method.* (i) In general. The residual profit split method evaluates whether the allocation of combined operating profit or loss attributable to one or more external contributions subject to a PCT is arm's length by reference to the relative value of each controlled participant's contribution to that combined operating profit or loss. The combined operating profit or loss must be derived from the most narrowly identifiable business activity of the controlled participants for which data are available that include the developing and exploiting of cost shared intangibles (relevant business activity). The residual profit split method may not be used where only one controlled participant makes significant nonroutine contributions to the development and exploitation of the cost shared intangibles. The provisions of § 1.482-6 shall apply to CSAs only to the extent provided and as modified in this paragraph (g)(7). Any other application to a CSA of a residual profit method not described below will constitute an unspecified method for purposes of sections 482 and 6662(e) and the regulations thereunder.

(ii) Appropriate share of profits and losses. The relative value of each controlled participant's contribution to the success of the relevant business activity must be determined in a manner that reflects the functions performed, risks assumed, and resources employed by each participant in the relevant business activity, consistent with the comparability provisions of § 1.482-1(d)(3). Such an allocation is intended to correspond to the division of profit or loss that would result from an arrangement between uncontrolled taxpayers, each performing functions similar to those of the various controlled participants engaged in the relevant business activity. The profit allocated to any particular controlled participant is not necessarily limited to the total operating profit of the group from the relevant business activity. For example, in a given year, one controlled participant may earn a profit while another controlled participant incurs a loss. In addition, it may not be assumed that the combined operating profit or loss from the relevant business activity should be shared equally, or in any other arbitrary proportion.

(iii) Profit split. (A) In general. Under the residual profit split method, each controlled participant's territorial operating profit or loss, as defined in paragraph (j)(1)(vi) of this section, is allocated between the controlled participants that each furnish significant nonroutine contributions to the relevant business activity in that territory following the three step process set forth in paragraphs (g)(7)(iii)(B) and (C) of this section.

(B) Allocate income to routine contributions other than cost contributions. The first step allocates an amount of income to each controlled participant that is subtracted from its territorial operating profit or loss to provide a market return for the controlled participant's routine contributions (other than cost contributions) to the relevant business activity in its territory. Routine contributions are contributions of the same or a similar kind to those made by uncontrolled taxpayers involved in similar business activities for which it is possible to identify market returns. Routine contributions ordinarily include contributions of tangible property, services and intangibles that are generally owned or provided by uncontrolled taxpayers engaged in similar activities. A functional analysis is required to identify these contributions according to the functions performed, risks assumed, and resources employed by each of the controlled participants. Market returns for the routine contributions should be determined by reference to the returns achieved by uncontrolled taxpayers engaged in similar activities, consistent with the methods described in §§ 1.482-3, 1.482-4, and1.482-5, or with the arm's length charge described in § 1.482-2(b)(3) (first sentence) based on a comparable uncontrolled transaction.

(C) Allocate residual profit. (1) In general. The allocation of income to each controlled participant's routine contributions in the first step will not reflect profit or loss attributable to that controlled participant's cost contributions, nor reflect the profit or loss attributable to any controlled participant's nonroutine contributions to the relevant business activity. Nonroutine contributions include nonroutine external contributions, and other nonroutine contributions, to the relevant business activity in the relevant territory. The residual territorial profit or loss after the allocation of income in the first step in paragraph (g)(7)(iii)(B) of this section is further allocated under the second and third steps in paragraphs (g)(7)(iii)(C)(2) and (3) of this section.

(2) Cost contribution share of residual profit or loss. Under the second step, a portion of each controlled participant's residual territorial profit or loss after the first step allocation is allocated to that controlled participant's cost contributions (cost contribution share). A controlled participant's cost contribution share is equal to the following fraction of such residual territorial profit or loss. The numerator is the present value, determined as of the relevant date, of the summation, over the entire period of developing and exploiting cost shared intangibles, of the total value of such controlled participant's total anticipated cost contributions. The denominator is the present value, determined as of the relevant date, of the summation, over the same period, of such controlled participant's total anticipated territorial operating profits, as defined in paragraph (j)(1)(vi) of this section, reduced by a market return for the routine contributions (other than cost contributions) to the relevant business activity in the relevant territory. For these purposes, the relevant date is the date of the PCTs.

(3) Nonroutine contribution share of residual profit or loss. Under the third step, the remaining share of each controlled participant's residual territorial profit or loss after the first and second step allocations generally should be divided among all of the controlled participants based upon the relative value, determined as of the date of the PCTs, of their nonroutine contributions to the relevant business activity in the relevant territory. The relative value of the nonroutine contributions of each controlled participant may be measured by external market benchmarks that reflect the fair market value of such nonroutine contributions. Alternatively, the relative value of nonroutine contributions may be estimated by the capitalized cost of developing the nonroutine contributions and updates, as appropriately grown or discounted so that all contributions may be valued on a comparable dollar basis as of the same date. If the nonroutine contributions by a controlled participant are also used in other business activities (such as the exploitation of make-or-sell rights described in paragraph (c) of this section), an allocation of the value of the nonroutine contributions must be made on a reasonable basis among all the business activities in which they are used in proportion to the relative economic value that the relevant business activity and such other business activities are anticipated to derive over time as the result of such nonroutine contributions.

(4) Determination of PCT Payments. Any amount of a controlled participant's territorial operating profit or loss that is allocated to another controlled participant's external contributions to the relevant business activity in the relevant territory under the third step represents the amount of the PCT Payment due to that other controlled participant for such external contributions.

(5) Routine external contributions. For purposes of this paragraph (g)(7), routine external contributions, the valuation and PCT Payments for which are determined and made independently of the residual profit split method, are treated similarly to cost contributions. Accordingly, wherever used in this paragraph (g)(7), the term routine contribution shall not be read to include routine external contributions and the term cost contribution shall be read to include net routine external contributions, as defined in paragraph (g)(4)(v) of this section.

(iv) Comparability and reliability considerations. (A) In general. Whether results derived from this method are the most reliable measure of the arm's length result is determined using the factors described under the best method rule in § 1.482-1(c). Thus, comparability and the quality of data and assumptions must be considered in determining whether this method provides the most reliable measure of an arm's length result. The application of these factors to the residual profit split in the context of the relevant business activity of developing and exploiting cost shared intangibles is discussed in paragraphs (g)(7)(iv)(B), (C), and (D) of this section.

(B) Comparability. The first step of the residual profit split relies on market benchmarks of profitability. Thus, the comparability considerations that are relevant for the first step of the residual profit split are those that are relevant for the methods that are used to determine market returns for the routine contributions.

(C) Data and assumptions. The reliability of the results derived from the residual profit split is affected by the quality of the data and assumptions used to apply this method. In particular, the following factors must be considered—

(1) The reliability of the allocation of costs, income, and assets between the relevant business activity and the controlled participants' other activities will affect the reliability of the determination of the territorial operating profit and its allocation among the controlled participants. See § 1.482-6(c)(2)(ii)(C)(1);

(2) The degree of consistency between the controlled participants and uncontrolled taxpayers in accounting practices that materially affect the items that determine the amount and allocation of operating profit affects the reliability of the result. See § 1.482-6(c)(2)(ii)(C)(2); and

(3) The reliability of the data used and the assumptions made in valuing the nonroutine contributions by the controlled participants. In particular, if capitalized costs of development are used to estimate the value of intangible property, the reliability of the results is reduced relative to the reliability of other methods that do not require such an estimate, for the following reasons. In any given case, the costs of developing the intangible may not be related to its market value. In addition, the calculation of the capitalized costs of development may require the allocation of indirect costs between the relevant business activity and the controlled participant's other activities, which may affect the reliability of the analysis.

(D) Other factors affecting reliability. Like the methods described in §§ 1.482-3, 1.482-4, and 1.482-5, or the arm's length charge described in § 1.482-2(b)(3) (first sentence) based on a comparable uncontrolled transaction, the first step of the residual profit split relies exclusively on external market benchmarks. As indicated in § 1.482-1(c)(2)(i), as the degree of comparability between the controlled participants and uncontrolled transactions increases, the relative weight accorded the analysis under this method will increase. In addition, to the extent the allocation of profits in the third step is not based on external market benchmarks, the reliability of the analysis will be decreased in relation to an analysis under a method that relies on market benchmarks. Finally, the reliability of the analysis under this method may be enhanced by the fact that all the controlled participants are evaluated under the residual profit split. However, the reliability of the results of an analysis based on information from all the controlled participants is affected by the reliability of the data and the assumptions pertaining to each controlled participant. Thus, if the data and assumptions are significantly more reliable with respect to one of the controlled participants than with respect to the others, a different method, focusing solely on the results of that party, may yield more reliable results.

(v) Example. The following example illustrates the principles of this paragraph (g)(7):

*Example.* (i) USP, a U.S. nanotech company, has partially developed technology for nanomotors which are used to provide mobility for nanodevices. At the same time, USP's wholly-owned subsidiary, FS, a foreign nanotech company, has partially developed technology for nanosensors which provide sensing capabilities for nanodevices. At the beginning of Year 1, USP enters into a CSA with FS to develop NanoBuild, a technology which will be used to build a wide range of fully functioning nanodevices. The partially developed nanomotor and nanosensor technologies owned by USP and FS, respectively, are reasonably anticipated to contribute to the development of NanoBuild and therefore the RT Rights in the nanomotor and nanosensor technologies constitute external contributions of USP and FS for which compensation is due under PCTs. Under the CSA, USP will have the right to exploit NanoBuild in the United States, while FS will have the right to exploit NanoBuild in the rest of the world. USP's and FS's RAB shares are 40% and 60% respectively.

(ii) The present value of the total projected IDCs for the CSA is $10 billion (as of the date of the PCTs). Based on RAB shares, USP expects to bear 40%, or $4 billion, of these IDCS and FS expects to bear 60%, or $6 billion. For accounting purposes, USP and FS project a combined operating profit from exploitation of the NanoBuild of $11 billion (in Year 1 dollars), taking into account the $10 billion of projected IDCs. However, for purposes of applying the residual profit split method, combined operating profit is determined without taking into account IDCs. Therefore, USP and FS redetermine their combined operating profits for purposes of the residual profit split method to equal $21 billion (adding $10 billion of IDCs back to the accounting profit of $11 billion). Of this amount, 40% or $8.4 billion is expected to be generated by USP in the U.S. and 60% or $12.6 billion is expected to be generated by FS in the rest of the world.

(iii) USP and FS each undertake routine distribution activities in their respective markets that constitute routine contributions to the relevant business activity of exploiting NanoBuild. They estimate that the total market return (costs plus a market return on those costs) on these routine contributions will amount to $1 billion, (in Year 1 dollars). Of this amount, USP's anticipated routine return is $400 million and FS's anticipated routine return is $600 million. After deducting the routine return, USP's total anticipated residual operating profit is $8 billion ($8.4 billion-$0.4 billion) and FS's total anticipated residual operating profit equals $12 billion ($12.6 billion-$0.6 billion).

(iv) After analysis, USP and FS determine that the relative values of the nanomotor and nanosensor technologies are most reliably measured by their respective capitalized costs of development. Some of the factors considered in this analysis include the similar nature and success, and the relatively contemporaneous timing, of the nanoengineering research done to develop both the nanomoter and nanosensor technologies and the lack of external market benchmarks. The capitalized costs of the nanomotor and nonsensor technologies are $3 billion and $5 billion, respectively.

(v) Under the residual profit split method, in each taxable year USP and FS will allocate the operating income they each separately report in their territory (territorial operating income) between their routine contributions, their cost contribution share and their nonroutine contributions, in this case the nanomotor and nanosensor technologies.

(vi) In step one of the residual profit split, USP and FS each allocate an amount of income that is subtracted from their actual territorial operating income for the taxable year to provide a market return for their actual routine contributions in that year.

(vii) In step two, a portion of residual territorial operating profit or loss after accounting for the allocation of income to routine contributions in step one, will be allocated by USP and FS to their cost contribution shares. The percentage allocable to the cost contribution share in this case is equal to the each participant's share of total anticipated IDCs divided by the difference between its total anticipated operating profits in its territory and the total anticipated routine return in its territory. It follows that the cost contribution shares of USP and FS are as follows: USP = 50% ($4 billion/$8 billion) and FS = 50% ($6 billion/ $12 billion).

(viii) In step three, USP and FS each allocate a portion of their residual territorial operating income remaining after application of steps one and two between their respective nonroutine contributions. USP and FS have estimated relative values for USP's nanomotor technology at $3 billion and FS's nanosensor technology at $5 billion. The percentage of each participant's residual territorial operating income that is allocated to the nanomotor technology is therefore 37.5% ($3 billion/($3 billion + $5 billion)) and the percentage allocated to the nanosensor technology is 62.5% ($5 billion/($3 billion + $5 billion)).

(ix) USP will owe a PCT Payment to FS equal to the amount of its territorial operating profit or loss that is allocated in step three to FS's nanosensor technology and FS will owe a PCT Payment to USP equal to the amount of its territorial operating profit or loss that is allocated in step three to USP's nanomotor technology. The PCT Payments owed each year by USP and FS, respectively, will be netted against each other, so that only one participant will make a net PCT Payment.

*(8) Unspecified methods.* Methods not specified in paragraphs (g)(3) through (7) of this section may be used to evaluate whether the amount charged for a PCT is arm's length. Any method used under this paragraph (g)(8) must be applied in accordance with the provisions of § 1.482-1 and of paragraph (g)(2) of this section. Consistent with the specified methods, an unspecified method should take into account the general principle that uncontrolled taxpayers evaluate the terms of a transaction by considering the realistic alternatives to that transaction, and only enter into a particular transaction if none of the alternatives is preferable to it. Therefore, in establishing whether a PCT achieved an arm's length result, an unspecified method should provide information on the prices or profits that the controlled participant could have realized by choosing a realistic alternative to the CSA. As with any method, an unspecified method will not be applied unless it provides the most reliable measure of an arm's length result under the principles of the best method rule. See § 1.482-1(c). In accordance with § 1.482-1(d) (Comparability), to the extent that an unspecified method relies on internal data rather than uncontrolled comparables, its reliability will be reduced. Similarly, the reliability of a method will be affected by the reliability of the data and assumptions used to apply the method, including any projections used.

**(h) Coordination with the arm's length standard.** A CSA produces results that are consistent with an arm's length result within the meaning of § 1.482-1(b)(1) if, and only if, each controlled participant's IDC share (as determined under paragraph (d)(4) of this section) equals its RAB share (as required by paragraph (a)(1) of this section), and all other requirements of this section are satisfied.

**(i) Allocations by the Commissioner in connection with a CSA.** *(1) In general.* The Commissioner may make allocations to adjust the results of a controlled transaction in connection with a CSA so that the results are consistent with an arm's length result, in accordance with the provisions of this paragraph (i).

*(2) CST allocations.* (i) In general. The Commissioner may make allocations to adjust the results of a CST so that the results are consistent with an arm's length result, including any allocations to make each controlled participant's IDC share, as determined under paragraph (d)(4) of this section, equal to that participant's RAB share, as determined under paragraph (e)(1) of this section. Such allocations may result from, for purposes of CST determinations, adjustments to—

(A) Redetermine IDCs by adding any costs (or cost categories) that are directly identified with, or are reasonably allocable to, the IDA, or by removing any costs (or cost categories) that are not IDCs;

(B) Reallocate costs between the IDA and other business activities;

(C) Improve the reliability of the selection or application of the basis used for measuring benefits for purposes of estimating a controlled participant's RAB share;

(D) Improve the reliability of the projections used to estimate RAB shares, including adjustments described in paragraph (i)(2)(ii) of this section; and

(E) Allocate among the controlled participants any unallocated interests in cost shared intangibles.

(ii) Adjustments to improve the reliability of projections used to estimate RAB shares. (A) Unreliable projections. A significant divergence between projected benefit shares and benefit shares adjusted to take into account any available actual benefits to date (adjusted benefit shares) may indicate that the projections were not reliable for purposes of estimating RAB shares. In such a case, the Commissioner may use adjusted benefit shares as the most reliable measure of RAB shares and adjust IDC shares accordingly. The projected benefit shares will not be considered unreliable, as applied in a given taxable year, based on a divergence from adjusted benefit shares for every controlled participant that is less than or equal to 20% of the participant's projected benefits share. Further, the Commissioner will not make an allocation based on such divergence if the difference is due to an extraordinary event, beyond the control of the controlled participants, which could not reasonably have been anticipated at the time that costs were shared. The Commissioner generally may adjust projections of benefits used to calculate benefit shares in accordance with the provisions of § 1.482-1. In particular, if benefits are projected over a period of years, and the projections for initial years of the period prove to be unreliable, this may indicate that the projections for the remaining years of the period are also unreliable and thus should be adjusted. For purposes of this paragraph, all controlled participants that are not U.S. persons are treated as a single controlled participant. Therefore, an adjustment based on an unreliable projection of RAB shares will be made to the IDC shares of foreign controlled participants only if there is a matching adjustment to the IDC shares of controlled participants that are U.S. persons. Nothing in this paragraph (i)(2)(ii)(A) prevents the Commissioner from making an allocation if taxpayer did not use the most reliable basis for measuring anticipated benefits. For example, if the taxpayer measures its anticipated benefits based on units sold, and the Commissioner determines that another basis is more reliable for measuring anticipated benefits, then the fact that actual units sold were within 20% of the projected unit sales will not preclude an allocation under this section.

(B) Foreign-to-foreign adjustments. Adjustments to IDC shares based on an unreliable projection also may be made solely among foreign controlled participants if the variation between actual and projected benefits has the effect of substantially reducing U.S. tax.

(C) Correlative adjustments to PCTs. Correlative adjustments will be made to any PCT Payments of a fixed amount that were determined based on RAB shares which are subsequently adjusted on a finding that they were based on unreliable projections. No correlative adjustments will be made to contingent PCT Payments regardless of whether RAB shares were used as a parameter in the valuation of those payments.

(D) Examples. The following examples illustrate the principles of this paragraph (i)(2)(ii):

*Example (1).* U.S. Parent (USP) and Foreign Subsidiary (FS) enter into a CSA to develop new food products, dividing costs on the basis of projected sales two years in the future. In Year 1, USP and FS project that their sales in Year 3 will be equal, and they divide costs accordingly. In Year 3, the Commissioner examines the controlled participants' method for dividing costs. USP and FS actually accounted for 42% and 58% of total sales, respectively. The Commissioner agrees that sales two years in the future provide a reliable basis for estimating benefit shares. Because the differences between USP's and FS's adjusted and projected benefit shares are less than 20% of their projected benefit shares, the projection of future benefits for Year 3 is reliable.

*Example (2).* The facts are the same as in Example 1, except that in Year 3 USP and FS actually accounted for 35% and 65% of total sales, respectively. The divergence between USP's projected and adjusted benefit shares is greater than 20% of USP's projected benefit share and is not due to an extraordinary event beyond the control of the controlled participants. The Commissioner concludes that the projected benefit shares were unreliable, and uses adjusted benefit shares as the basis for an adjustment to the cost shares borne by USP and FS.

*Example (3).* Parent (USP), a U.S. corporation, and its foreign subsidiary (FS) enter a CSA in Year 1. They project that they will begin to receive benefits from covered intangibles in Years 4 through 6, and that USP will receive 60% of total benefits and FS 40% of total benefits. In Years 4 through 6, USP and FS actually receive 50% each of the total benefits. In evaluating the reliability of the controlled participants' projections, the Commissioner compares the adjusted benefit shares to the projected benefit shares. Although USP's adjusted benefit share (50%) is within 20% of its projected benefit share (60%), FS's adjusted benefit share (50%) is not within 20% of its projected benefit share (40%). Based on this discrepancy, the Commissioner may conclude that the controlled participants' projections were not reliable and may use adjusted benefit shares as the basis for an adjustment to the cost shares borne by USP and FS.

*Example (4).* Three controlled taxpayers, USP, FS1 and FS2 enter into a CSA. FS1 and FS2 are foreign. USP is a United States corporation that controls all the stock of FS1 and FS2. The controlled participants project that they will share the total benefits of the covered intangibles in the following percentages: USP 50%; FS1 30%; and FS2 20%. Adjusted benefit shares are as follows: USP 45%; FS1 25%; and FS2 30%. In evaluating the reliability of the controlled participants' projections, the Commissioner compares these adjusted benefit shares to the projected benefit shares. For this purpose, FS1 and FS2 are treated as a single controlled participant. The adjusted benefit share received by USP (45%) is within 20% of its projected benefit share (50%). In addition, the non-US controlled participants' adjusted benefit share (55%) is also within 20% of their projected benefit share (50%). Therefore, the Commissioner concludes that the controlled participants' projections of future benefits were reliable, despite the fact that FS2's adjusted benefit share (30%) is not within 20% of its projected benefit share (20%).

*Example (5).* The facts are the same as in Example 4. In addition, the Commissioner determines that FS2 has significant operating losses and has no earnings and profits, and that FS1 is profitable and has earnings and profits. Based on all the evidence, the Commissioner concludes that the controlled participants arranged that FS1 would bear a larger cost share than appropriate in order to reduce FS1's earnings and profits and thereby reduce inclusions USP otherwise would be deemed to have on account of FS1 under subpart F. Pursuant to paragraph (i)(2)(ii)(B) of this section, the Commissioner may make an adjustment solely to the cost shares borne by FS1 and FS2 because FS2's projection of future benefits was unreliable and the variation between adjusted and projected benefits had the effect of substantially reducing USP's U.S. income tax liability (on account of FS1 subpart F income).

*Example (6).* (i) (A) Foreign Parent (FP) and U.S. Subsidiary (USS) enter into a CSA in 1996 to develop a new treatment for baldness. USS's interest in any treatment developed is the right to produce and sell the treatment in the U.S. market while FP retains rights to produce and sell the treatment in the rest of the world. USS and FP measure their anticipated benefits from the cost sharing arrangement based on their respective projected future sales of the baldness treatment. The following sales projections are used:

**Sales**

*[In millions of dollars]*

| Year | USS | FP |
|---|---|---|
| 1 | 5 | 10 |
| 2 | 20 | 20 |
| 3 | 30 | 30 |
| 4 | 40 | 40 |
| 5 | 40 | 40 |
| 6 | 40 | 40 |
| 7 | 40 | 40 |
| 8 | 20 | 20 |
| 9 | 10 | 10 |
| 10 | 5 | 5 |

(B) In Year 1, the first year of sales, USS is projected to have lower sales than FP due to lags in U.S. regulatory approval for the baldness treatment. In each subsequent year USS and FP are projected to have equal sales. Sales are projected to build over the first three years of the period, level off for several years, and then decline over the final years of the period as new and improved baldness treatments reach the market.

(ii) To account for USS's lag in sales in the Year 1, the present discounted value of sales over the period is used as the basis for measuring benefits. Based on the risk associated with this venture, a discount rate of 10 percent is selected. The present discounted value of projected sales is determined to be approximately $154.4 million for USS and $158.9 million for FP. On this basis USS and FP are projected to obtain approximately 49.3% and 50.7% of the benefit, respectively, and the costs of developing the baldness treatment are shared accordingly.

(iii) (A) In Year 6 the Commissioner examines the cost sharing arrangement. USS and FP have obtained the following sales results through the Year 5:

**Sales**

*[In millions of dollars]*

| Year | USS | FP |
|---|---|---|
| 1 | 0 | 17 |
| 2 | 17 | 35 |
| 3 | 25 | 41 |
| 4 | 38 | 41 |
| 5 | 39 | 41 |

(B) USS's sales initially grew more slowly than projected while FP's sales grew more quickly. In each of the first three years of the period the share of total sales of at least one of the parties diverged by over 20% from its projected share of sales. However, by Year 5 both parties' sales had leveled off at approximately their projected values. Taking into account this leveling off of sales and all the facts and circumstances, the Commissioner determines that it is appropriate to use the original projections for the remaining years of sales. Combining the actual results through Year 5 with the projections for subsequent years, and using a discount rate of 10%, the present discounted value of sales is approximately $141.6 million for USS and $187.3 million for FP. This result implies that USS and FP obtain approximately 43.1% and 56.9%, respectively, of the anticipated benefits from the baldness treatment. Because these adjusted benefit shares are within 20% of the benefit shares calculated based on the original sales projections, the Commissioner determines that, based on the difference between adjusted and projected benefit shares, the original projections were not unreliable. No adjustment is made based on the difference between adjusted and projected benefit shares.

*Example (7).* (i) The facts are the same as in Example 6, except that the actual sales results through Year 5 are as follows:

**Sales**

*[In millions of dollars]*

| Year | USS | FP |
|---|---|---|
| 1 | 0 | 17 |
| 2 | 17 | 35 |
| 3 | 25 | 44 |
| 4 | 34 | 54 |
| 5 | 36 | 55 |

(ii) Based on the discrepancy between the projections and the actual results and on consideration of all the facts, the Commissioner determines that for the remaining years the following sales projections are more reliable than the original projections:

**Sales**

*[In millions of dollars]*

| Year | USS | FP |
|---|---|---|
| 6 | 36 | 55 |
| 7 | 36 | 55 |
| 8 | 18 | 28 |
| 9 | 9 | 14 |
| 10 | 4.5 | 7 |

(iii) Combining the actual results through Year 5 with the projections for subsequent years, and using a discount rate of 10%, the present discounted value of sales is approximately $131.2 million for USS and $229.4 million for FP. This result implies that USS and FP obtain approximately 35.4% and 63.6%, respectively, of the anticipated benefits from the baldness treatment. These adjusted benefit shares diverge by greater than 20% from the benefit shares calculated based on the original sales projections, and the Commissioner determines that, based on the difference between adjusted and projected benefit shares, the original projections were unreliable. The Commissioner adjusts cost shares for each of the taxable years under examination to conform them to the recalculated shares of anticipated benefits.

(iii) Timing of CST allocations. If the Commissioner makes an allocation to adjust the results of a CST, the allocation must be reflected for tax purposes in the year in which the IDCs were incurred. When a cost sharing payment is owed by one controlled participant to another controlled participant, the Commissioner may make appropriate allocations to reflect an arm's length rate of interest for the time value of money, consistent with the provisions of § 1.482-2(a) (Loans or advances).

*(3) PCT allocations.* The Commissioner may make allocations to adjust the results of a PCT so that the results are consistent with an arm's length result in accordance with the provisions of the applicable sections of the section 482 regulations, as determined pursuant to paragraph (a)(2) of this section.

*(4) Allocations regarding changes in participation under a CSA.* The Commissioner may make allocations to adjust the results of any controlled transaction described in paragraph (f) of this section, if the controlled participants do not reflect arm's length results in relation to any such transaction.

*(5) Allocations when CSTs are consistently and materially disproportionate to RAB shares.* If a controlled participant bears IDC shares that are consistently and materially greater or lesser than its RAB share, then the Commissioner may conclude that the economic substance of the arrangement between the controlled participants is inconsistent with the terms of the CSA. In such a case, the Commissioner may disregard such terms and impute an agreement that is consistent with the controlled participants' course of conduct, under which a controlled participant that bore a disproportionately greater IDC share received additional interests in the cost shared intangibles. See § 1.482-1(d)(3)(ii)(B) (Identifying contractual terms) and § 1.482-4(f)(3)(ii) (Identification of owner). Such additional interests will consist of partial undivided interests in another controlled participant's territory. Accordingly, that controlled participant must receive arm's length consideration from any controlled participant whose IDC share is less than its RAB share over time, under the provisions of §§ 1.482-1 and 1.482-4 through 1.482-6.

*(6) Periodic adjustments.* (i) In general. Subject to the exceptions in paragraph (i)(6)(vi) of this section, the Commissioner may make periodic adjustments with respect to all PCT Payments for an open taxable year (the Adjustment Year), and for all subsequent taxable years for the duration of the CSA Activity, if the Commissioner determines that, for a particular PCT (the Trigger PCT), a particular controlled participant that owes or owed a PCT Payment relating to that PCT (the PCT Payor) has realized an Actually Experienced Return Ratio (AERR) that is outside the Periodic Return Ratio Range (PRRR). The satisfaction of the condition stated in the preceding sentence is referred to as a

Periodic Trigger. See paragraph (i)(6)(ii) through (vi) of this section regarding the PRRR, the AERR, and periodic adjustments. In determining whether to make such adjustments, the Commissioner may consider whether the outcome as adjusted more reliably reflects an arm's length result under all the relevant facts and circumstances, including any information known as of the Determination Date. The Determination Date is the date of the relevant determination by the Commissioner. The failure of the Commissioner to determine for an earlier taxable year that a PCT Payment was not arm's length will not preclude the Commissioner from making a periodic adjustment for a subsequent year. A periodic adjustment under this paragraph may be made without regard to whether the taxable year of the Trigger PCT or any other PCT remains open for statute of limitations purposes.

(ii) PRRR. Except as provided in the next sentence, the PRRR will consist of return ratios that are not less than ½ nor more than 2. Alternatively, if the controlled participants have not substantially complied with the documentation requirements referenced in paragraph (k) of this section, as modified, if applicable, by paragraph (m)(3) of this section, the PRRR will consist of the return ratios that are not less than .67 nor more than 1.5.

(iii) AERR. (A) In general. The AERR is the Present Value of Total Profits (PVTP) divided by the Present Value of Investment (PVI). In computing PVTP and PVI, present values are computed using the Applicable Discount Rate (ADR), and all information available as of the Determination Date is taken into account.

(B) PVTP. The PVTP is the present value, as of the earliest date that any IDC described in paragraph (d)(1) of this section occurred (the CSA Start Date), of the PCT Payor's actually experienced territorial operating profits, as defined in paragraph (j)(1)(vi) of this section, from the CSA Start Date through the end of the Adjustment Year.

(C) PVI. The PVI is the present value, as of the CSA Start Date, of the PCT Payor's investment associated with the CSA Activity, defined as the sum of its cost contributions and its PCT Payments, from the CSA Start Date through the end of the Adjustment Year. For purposes of computing the PVI, PCT Payments means all PCT Payments due from a PCT Payor before netting against PCT Payments due from other controlled participants.

(iv) ADR. (A) In general. Except as provided in paragraph (i)(6)(iv)(B) of this section, the ADR is the discount rate pursuant to paragraph (g)(2)(vi) of this section, subject to such adjustments as the Commissioner determines appropriate.

(B) Publicly traded companies. If the PCT Payor meets the conditions of paragraph (i)(6)(iv)(C) of this section, the ADR is the PCT Payor WACC as of the date of the trigger PCT. However, if the Commissioner determines, or the controlled participants establish to the Commissioner's satisfaction, that a discount rate other than the PCT Payor WACC better reflects the degree of risk of the CSA Activity as of such date, the ADR is such other discount rate.

(C) Publicly traded. A PCT Payor meets the conditions of this paragraph (i)(6)(iv)(C) if—

(1) Stock of the PCT Payor is publicly traded; or

(2) Stock of the PCT Payor is not publicly traded, provided—

(i) The PCT Payor is included in a group of companies for which consolidated financial statements are prepared; and

(ii) A publicly traded company in such group owns, directly or indirectly, stock in PCT Payor. Stock of a company is publicly traded within the meaning of this paragraph (i)(6)(iv)(C) if such stock is regularly traded on an established United States securities market and the company issues financial statements prepared in accordance with United States generally accepted accounting principles for the taxable year.

(D) PCT Payor WACC. The PCT Payor WACC is the WACC of the PCT Payor or the publicly traded company described in paragraph (i)(6)(iv)(C)(2) of this section, as the case may be.

(E) Generally accepted accounting principles. For purposes of paragraph (i)(6)(iv)(C) of this section, a financial statement prepared in accordance with a comprehensive body of generally accepted accounting principles other than United States generally accepted accounting principles is considered to be prepared in accordance with United States generally accepted accounting principles provided that the amounts of debt, equity and interest expense are reflected in the reconciliation between such other accounting principles and United States generally accepted accounting principles required to be incorporated into the financial statement by the securities laws governing companies whose stock is regularly traded on United States securities markets.

(v) Determination of periodic adjustments. In the event of a Periodic Trigger, subject to paragraph (i)(6)(vi) of this section, the Commissioner may make periodic adjustments with respect to all PCT Payments between all PCT Payors and PCT Payees for the Adjustment Year and all subsequent years for the duration of the CSA Activity pursuant to the residual profit split method as provided in paragraph (g)(7) of this section, subject to the further modifications in this paragraph (i)(6)(v).

(A) If the AERR is less than the PRRR, then the cost contribution share of residual profit or loss under paragraph (g)(7)(iii)(C)(2) of this section is determined as follows:

(1) The relevant date specified in that paragraph is the CSA Start Date. However, the effect of using such relevant date is modified as specified in paragraphs (i)(6)(v)(A)(2) and (i)(6)(v)(A)(3) of this section.

(2) The discount rate to be used in paragraph (g)(7)(iii)(C)(2) of this section is determined as of the relevant date, but taking into account any data relevant to such determination that may become available up through the Determination Date.

(3) The present values of the summations described in paragraph (g)(7)(iii)(C)(2) of this section are determined by substituting actual results up through the Determination Date, and future results anticipated on that date, for the results anticipated on the relevant date. It is possible that, because of these substitutions, the resulting fraction determined in that paragraph will be greater than one.

(B) If the AERR is greater than the PRRR, then the cost contribution share of residual profit or loss under paragraph (g)(7)(iii)(C)(2) of this section is determined as follows:

(1) The relevant date specified in that paragraph is the first day of the Adjustment Year. However, the effect of using such relevant date is modified as specified in paragraphs (i)(6)(v)(B)(2) and (i)(6)(v)(B)(3) of this section.

(2) The discount rate to be used in paragraph (g)(7)(iii)(C)(2) of this section is determined as of the relevant date, but taking into account any data relevant to such

determination that may become available up through the Determination Date.

(3) In computing the fraction described in paragraph (g)(7)(iii)(C)(2) of this section, the summation period described in that paragraph is modified to start on the first day of the Adjustment Year; thus, the summations described in that paragraph that are used to determine that fraction will not include any items relating to periods before the first day of the Adjustment Year.

(C) The relative value of nonroutine contributions in paragraph (g)(7)(iii)(C)(3) of this section are determined as described in that paragraph, but taking into account any data relevant to such determination that may become available up through the Determination Date.

(D) For these purposes, the residual profit split method may be used even where only one controlled participant makes significant nonroutine contributions to the CSA Activity. If only one controlled participant provides all the external contributions and other nonroutine contributions, then the third step residual profit or loss belongs entirely to such controlled participant.

(vi) Exceptions to periodic adjustments. (A) Transactions involving the same external contribution as in the PCT. If—

(1) The same external contribution is furnished to an uncontrolled taxpayer under substantially the same circumstances as those of the relevant RT (as defined in paragraph (b)(3)(iii) of this section) and with a similar form of payment as the PCT;

(2) This transaction serves as the basis for the application of the comparable uncontrolled transaction method described in § 1.482-4(c), or the arm's length charge described in § 1.482-2(b)(3)(first sentence) based on a comparable uncontrolled transaction, in the first year in which substantial PCT Payments relating to this PCT were required to be paid; and

(3) The amount of those PCT Payments in that year was arm's length; then no periodic adjustment that uses that PCT as the Trigger PCT will be made under paragraphs (i)(6)(i) and (i)(6)(v) of this section.

(B) Results not reasonably anticipated. If the controlled participants establish to the satisfaction of the Commissioner that the differential between the AERR and the nearest bound of the PRRR is due to extraordinary events beyond its control and that could not reasonably have been anticipated at the time of the Trigger PCT, then no periodic adjustment will be made under paragraphs (i)(6)(i) and (i)(6)(v) of this section.

(C) Reduced AERR does not cause Periodic Trigger. If the controlled participants establish to the satisfaction of the Commissioner that the Periodic Trigger would not have occurred had the PCT Payor's operating profits used to calculate its PVTP excluded those operating profits attributable to the PCT Payor's routine contributions to its exploitation of cost shared intangibles, and nonroutine contributions to the CSA Activity, then no periodic adjustment will be made under paragraphs (i)(6)(i) and (i)(6)(v) of this section.

(D) Increased AERR does not cause Periodic Trigger. (1) If the controlled participants establish to the satisfaction of the Commissioner that the Periodic Trigger would not have occurred had the operating profits of the PCT Payor used to calculate its PVTP included its reasonably anticipated operating profits after the Adjustment Year from the CSA Activity, including from routine contributions to that activity, and had the cost contributions and PCT Payments of the PCT Payor used to calculate its PVI included its reasonably anticipated cost contributions and PCT Payments after the Adjustment Year, then no periodic adjustment will be made under paragraphs (i)(6)(i) and (i)(6)(v) of this section. The reasonably anticipated amounts in the previous sentence are determined based on all information available as of the Determination Date.

(2) For purposes of this paragraph (i)(6)(vi)(D) of this section, the controlled participants may, if they wish, assume that the average yearly operating profits for all taxable years prior to and including the Adjustment Year, in which there has been substantial exploitation of cost shared intangibles resulting from the CSA (exploitation years), will continue to be earned in each year over a period of years equal to 15 minus the number of exploitation years prior to and including the Determination Date.

(E) 10-year period. If the AERR determined is within the PRRR for each year of the 10-year period beginning with the first taxable year in which there is substantial exploitation of cost shared intangibles resulting from the CSA, then no periodic adjustment in a subsequent year will be made under paragraphs (i)(6)(i) and (i)(6)(v) of this section.

(F) 5-year period. For any year of the 5-year period beginning with the first taxable year in which there is substantial exploitation of cost shared intangibles resulting from the CSA, no Periodic Trigger will be considered to occur as a result of a determination that the AERR falls below the lower bound of the PRRR.

(vii) Examples. The following examples illustrates the principles of this paragraph (i)(6):

*Example (1).* (i) At the beginning of Year 1, USP, a publicly traded U.S. company, and FS, its wholly-owned foreign subsidiary, enter into a CSA to develop new technology for wireless cell phones. As part of a PCT, USP furnishes an external contribution, the RT Rights for an in-process technology that when developed will improve the clarity of cell to cell calls, for which compensation is due from FS. FS furnishes no external contributions to the CSA. The weighted average cost of capital of the controlled group that includes USP and FS in Year 1 is 15%. In Year 10, the Commissioner audits Years 1 through 8 of the CSA to determine whether or not any periodic adjustments should be made. USP and FS have substantially complied with the documentation requirements of this section.

(ii) FS derives the following actual cash flow from its participation in the CSA. The cash flows include the lump sum PCT Payment of $100 million made by FS to USP. The derivation of such PCT Payment was based on financial projections undertaken in Year 1 (not shown). (All amounts in this table and the tables that follow are in millions.)

| Year | Sales | Non-IDC costs | IDCs | PCT payments | Total inv. costs | Operating profits (accounting) | Exploitation profits | AERR |
|---|---|---|---|---|---|---|---|---|
| 1 . . . . . . . . . | 0 | 0 | 15 | 100 | 115 | -115 | 0 | |
| 2 . . . . . . . . . | 0 | 0 | 17 | 0 | 17 | -17 | 0 | |
| 3 . . . . . . . . . | 0 | 0 | 18 | 0 | 18 | -18 | 0 | |
| 4 . . . . . . . . . | 780 | 562 | 20 | 0 | 20 | 198 | 218 | |
| 5 . . . . . . . . . | 936 | 618 | 22 | 0 | 22 | 296 | 318 | |
| 6 . . . . . . . . . | 1,123 | 680 | 24 | 0 | 24 | 420 | 444 | |
| 7 . . . . . . . . . | 1,179 | 747 | 27 | 0 | 27 | 405 | 432 | |
| 8 . . . . . . . . . | 1,238 | 822 | 29 | 0 | 29 | 387 | 416 | |
| NPV through Year 5 . . . | 1,048 | 722 | 69 | 100 | 169 | 157 | 326 | 1.9 |
| NPV through Year 6 . . . | 1,606 | 1,060 | 81 | 100 | 181 | 365 | 546 | 3.0 |
| NPV through Year 7 . . . | 2,116 | 1,383 | 92 | 100 | 192 | 541 | 733 | 3.8 |

(iii) Because USP is publicly traded in the United States and is a member of the controlled group to which the PCT Payor, FS, belongs, for purposes of calculating the AERR for FS, the present values of its PVTP and PVI are determined using an ADR of 15%, the weighted average cost of capital of the controlled group. At a 15% discount rate, the PVTP, calculated in Year 8 as of Year 1, and based on actual profits realized by FS through Year 7 from exploiting the new wireless cell phone technology developed by the CSA, is $733 million. The PVI, based on FS's IDCs and its compensation expenditures pursuant to the PCT, is $192 million. The AERR for FS is equal to its PVTP divided by its PVI, $733 million/ $192 million, or 3.8. There is a Periodic Trigger because FS's AERR of 3.8 falls outside the PRRR of ½ to 2, the applicable PRRR for controlled participants complying with the documentation requirements of this section.

(iv) At the time of the Determination Date, it is determined that the first Adjustment Year in which a Periodic Trigger occurred was Year 6, when the AERR of FS was determined to be 3.0. It is also determined that none of the exceptions to periodic adjustments described in paragraph (i)(6)(vi) of this section applies. It follows that the arm's length PCT Payments made by FS from Year 6 forward shall be determined each taxable year using the residual profit split method described in paragraph (g)(7) of this section as modified by paragraph (i)(6)(v) of this section. Periodic adjustments will be made to the extent the PCT Payments actually made by FS differ from the PCT Payment calculation under the residual profit split.

(v) Actual and projected IDCs, territorial operating profits and returns to routine contributions for the remainder of the exploitation of the cost shared intangibles, determined as of the beginning of Year 6 are as follows:

| Year | IDCs | Territorial operating profits | Return to routine contributions | Profits less routine return |
|---|---|---|---|---|
| 6 . . . . . . . . . . . . . . . . . . . . . . . . . . . . . . . . . . . . . . . | 24 | 444 | 68 | 376 |
| 7 . . . . . . . . . . . . . . . . . . . . . . . . . . . . . . . . . . . . . . . | 27 | 432 | 75 | 357 |
| 8 . . . . . . . . . . . . . . . . . . . . . . . . . . . . . . . . . . . . . . . | 29 | 416 | 82 | 334 |
| 9 (Projected) . . . . . . . . . . . . . . . . . . . . . . . . . . . . . . . | 32 | 396 | 90 | 305 |
| 10 (Projected) . . . . . . . . . . . . . . . . . . . . . . . . . . . . . . | 35 | 370 | 99 | 271 |
| Total PV as of Year 6 . . . . . . . . . . . . . . . . . . . . . . . . . | 116 | 1666 | 326 | 1340 |

(vi) Under step one of the residual profit split method, for each taxable year, FS will be allocated a portion of its actual territorial operating income for the taxable year to provide a market return for its actual routine contributions in that year. As a result of a transfer pricing analysis, the Commissioner determines that the return to FS's routine activities, based on the return for comparable routine functions undertaken by comparable unrelated companies, is 10% of non-IDC costs. The allocations of actual territorial profits in Years 6 through 8 are as follows:

| Year | Territorial operating profits | Return to routine contributions | Residual profits after step 1 |
|---|---|---|---|
| 6 | 444 | 68 | 376 |
| 7 | 432 | 75 | 357 |
| 8 | 416 | 82 | 334 |

(vii) Under step two, a portion of the residual territorial operating profit or loss after the allocation of profit to routine contributions in step one will be allocated by FS to its cost contribution share. The percentage allocable to the cost contribution share is equal to FS's share of the total anticipated IDCs divided by its total anticipated territorial operating profits reduced by total expected return to its routine contributions to the exploitation of the cost shared technology in its territory. All amounts are determined as present values as of the first day of Year 6, using an appropriate discount rate on that date, and do not include any amounts relating to periods before the first day of Year 6. Following these rules, it is determined that the present value of FS's share of the total anticipated IDCs after the first day of Year 6 is $116 million and its total anticipated territorial operating profits reduced by the return to its routine contributions is $1,340 million. It follows that the percentage of residual territorial operating profit or loss allocated to FS's cost contribution share is 8.6% ($116/$1,340). The allocation of actual residual profits after Step 1 in Years 6 through 8 is as follows:

| Year | Residual profits after step 1 | Step 2 profits allocated to FS | Residual profits after step 2 |
|---|---|---|---|
| 6 | 376 | 32 | 344 |
| 7 | 357 | 31 | 327 |
| 8 | 334 | 29 | 305 |

(viii) In step three, because USP provided the only nonroutine contributions to the CSA Activity, 100% of FS's residual operating income after steps one and two is allocated to USP's external contributions and therefore represents the amount of the PCT Payment due from FS to USP for the particular taxable year. Also because USP provided the only nonroutine contributions to the CSA Activity, none of its residual territorial operating profit or loss is attributable to FS, therefore no offsetting PCT Payment is due from USP to FS. The PCT Payments due and adjustments made in Years 6 through 8 are as follows:

| Year | Residual profits after step 2 | PCT payment due from FS to USP | Actual PCT payment made | Adjustment |
|---|---|---|---|---|
| 6 | 344 | 344 | 0 | 344 |
| 7 | 327 | 327 | 0 | 327 |
| 8 | 305 | 305 | 0 | 305 |

*Example (2).* The facts are the same as Example 1 paragraphs (i) through (iii). At the time of the Determination Date, it is determined that the first Adjustment Year in which a Periodic Trigger occurred was Year 6, when the AERR of FS was determined to be 3.0. Upon further investigation as to what may have caused the high return in FS's market, the Commissioner learns that, in Year 4, significant health risks were linked to the use of wireless cell phones of USP's leading competitors. No such health risk was linked to the cell phones developed by USP and FS under the CSA. This resulted in a significant increase in USP's and FS's market share for cellular phones. Further analysis determines that it was this unforeseen occurrence that was primarily responsible for the AERR trigger. Based on paragraph (i)(6)(vi)(B) of this section, the Commissioner concludes that no adjustments are warranted, as FS simply has earned the premium return that any such investor would earn under the circumstances.

**(j) Definitions and special rules.** *(1) Definitions.* For purposes of this section:

(i) Controlled participant means a controlled taxpayer, as defined under § 1.482-1(i)(5), that is a party to the contractual agreement that underlies the CSA, and that reasonably anticipates that it will derive benefits, as defined in paragraph (j)(1)(iv) of this section, from exploiting one or more cost shared intangibles.

(ii) Cost shared intangible means any intangible, within the meaning of § 1.482-4(b), developed or to be developed as a result of the IDA, as described in paragraph (d)(1) of this section, including any portion of such intangible that reflects an external contribution, as described in paragraph (b)(3)(ii) of this section.

(iii) An interest in an intangible includes any commercially transferable interest, the benefits of which are susceptible of valuation.

(iv) Benefits mean the sum of additional revenue generated, plus cost savings, minus any cost increases from exploiting cost shared intangibles.

(v) A controlled participant's reasonably anticipated benefits mean the aggregate benefits that reasonably may be anticipated to be derived from exploiting cost shared intangibles.

(vi) Territorial operating profit or loss means the operating profit or loss as separately earned by each controlled participant in its geographic territory, described in paragraph (b)(4) of this section, from the CSA activity, determined before any expense (including amortization) on account of IDCs, routine external contributions, and nonroutine contributions.

(vii) The CSA Activity is the activity of developing and exploiting cost shared intangibles.

(viii) Examples. The following examples illustrate the principles of this paragraph (j)(1):

*Example (1).* Controlled participant. Foreign Parent (FP) is a foreign corporation engaged in the extraction of a natural resource. FP has a U.S. subsidiary (USS) to which FP sells supplies of this resource for sale in the United States. FP enters into a CSA with USS to develop a new machine to extract the natural resource. The machine uses a new extraction process that will be patented in the United States and in other countries. The CSA provides that USS will receive the rights to exploit the machine in the extraction of the natural resource in the United States, and FP will receive the rights in the rest of the world. This resource does not, however, exist in the United States. Despite the fact that USS has received the right to exploit this process in the United States, USS is not a controlled participant because it will not derive a benefit from exploiting the intangible developed under the CSA.

*Example (2).* Controlled participants. (i) U.S. Parent (USP), one foreign subsidiary (FS), and a second foreign subsidiary constituting the group's research arm (R+D) enter into a CSA to develop manufacturing intangibles for a new product line A. USP and FS are assigned the exclusive rights to exploit the intangibles respectively in the United States and the rest of the world, where each presently manufactures and sells various existing product lines. R+D is not assigned any rights to exploit the intangibles. R+D's activity consists solely in carrying out research for the group. It is reliably projected that the RAB shares of USP and FS will be 66⅔% and 33⅓%, respectively, and the parties' agreement provides that USP and FS will reimburse 66⅔% and 33⅓%, respectively, of the IDCs incurred by R+D with respect to the new intangible.

(ii) R+D does not qualify as a controlled participant within the meaning of paragraph (j)(1)(i) of this section, because it will not derive any benefits from exploiting cost shared intangibles. Therefore, R+D is treated as a service provider for purposes of this section and must receive arm's length consideration for the assistance it is deemed to provide to USP and FS, under the rules of paragraph (a)(3) of this section and § 1.482-4(f)(3)(iii). Such consideration must be treated as IDCs incurred by USP and FS in proportion to their RAB shares (i.e., 66⅔% and 33⅓%, respectively). R+D will not be considered to bear any share of the IDCs under the arrangement.

*Example (3).* Cost shared intangible. U.S. Parent (USP) has developed and currently exploits an antihistamine, XY, which is manufactured in tablet form. USP enters into a CSA with its wholly-owned foreign subsidiary (FS) to develop XYZ, a new improved version of XY that will be manufactured as a nasal spray. XYZ is a cost shared intangible under the CSA.

*Example (4).* Cost shared intangible. The facts are the same as in Example 3, except that instead of developing XYZ, the controlled participants develop ABC, a cure for the common cold. ABC is a cost shared intangible under the CSA.

*Example (5).* Reasonably anticipated benefits. Controlled parties A and B enter into a cost sharing arrangement to develop product and process intangibles for an already existing Product P. Without such intangibles, A and B would each reasonably anticipate revenue, in present value terms, of $100M from sales of Product P until it became obsolete. With the intangibles, A and B each reasonably anticipate selling the same number of units each year, but reasonably anticipate that the price will be higher. Because the particular product intangible is more highly regarded in A's market, A reasonably anticipates an increase of $20M in present value revenue from the product intangible, while B reasonably anticipates only an increase of $10M. Further, A and B each reasonably anticipate spending an extra $5M present value in production costs to include the feature embodying the product intangible. Finally, A and B each reasonably anticipate saving $2M present value in production costs by using the process intangible. A and B reasonably anticipate no other economic effects from exploiting the cost shared intangibles. A's reasonably anticipated benefits from exploiting the cost shared intangibles equal its reasonably anticipated increase in revenue ($20M) plus its reasonably anticipated cost savings ($2M) minus its reasonably anticipated increased costs ($5M), which equals $17M. Similarly, B's reasonably anticipated benefits from exploiting the cost shared intangibles equal its reasonably anticipated increase in revenue ($10M) plus its reasonably anticipated cost savings ($2M) minus its reasonably anticipated increased costs ($5M), which equals $7M. Thus A's reasonably anticipated benefits are $17M and B's reasonably anticipated benefits are $7M.

*(2) Special rules.* (i) Consolidated group. For purposes of this section, all members of the same consolidated group shall be treated as one taxpayer. For purposes of this paragraph (j)(2)(i), the term consolidated group means all members of a group of controlled entities created or organized within a single country and subjected to an income tax by such country on the basis of their combined income.

(ii) Trade or business. A participant that is a foreign corporation or nonresident alien individual will not be treated as engaged in a trade or business within the United States solely by reason of its participation in a CSA described in paragraph (b)(1) of this section. See generally § 1.864-2(a).

(iii) Partnership. A CSA, or an arrangement to which the Commissioner applies the rules of this section, will not be treated as a partnership to which the rules of subchapter K of the Internal Revenue Code apply. See § 301.7701-1(c) of this chapter.

*(3) Character.* (i) In general. CST payments generally will be considered costs of developing intangibles of the payor and reimbursements of the same kind of costs of developing intangibles of the payee. For purposes of this paragraph (j)(3), a controlled participant's payment required under a CSA is deemed to be reduced to the extent of any payments owed to it under the CSA from other controlled participants. Each payment received by a payee will be treated as coming pro rata from payments made by all payors. Such payments will be applied pro rata against deductions for the taxable year that the payee is allowed in connection with the CSA. Payments received in excess of such deductions will be treated as in consideration for use of the land and tangible property furnished for purposes of the CSA by the payee. For purposes of the research credit determined under section 41, cost sharing payments among controlled participants will be treated as provided for intra-group transactions in § 1.41-6(e). Any payment made or received by a taxpayer pursuant to an arrangement that the Commissioner determines not to be a CSA will be subject to the provisions of §§ 1.482-1 and 1.482-4 through 1.482-6. Any payment that in substance constitutes a cost sharing payment will be treated as such for purposes of this section, regardless of its characterization under foreign law.

(ii) PCT Payments. A PCT Payor's payment required under paragraphs (b)(1)(ii) and (b)(3) of this section is deemed to be reduced to the extent of any payments owed to it under such paragraphs from other controlled participants. Each PCT Payment received by a PCT Payee will be treated as coming pro rata out of payments made by all PCT Payors. PCT Payments will be characterized consistently with the designation of the type of transaction involved in the RT pursuant to paragraph (b)(iv) of this section. Depending on such designation, such payments will be treated as either consideration for a transfer of an interest in intangible property or for services.

(iii) Examples. The following examples illustrate this paragraph (j)(3):

*Example (1).* U.S. Parent (USP) and its wholly owned Foreign Subsidiary (FS) form a CSA to develop a miniature widget, the Small R. Based on RAB shares, USP agrees to bear 40% and FS to bear 60% of the costs incurred during the term of the agreement. The principal IDCs are operating costs incurred by FS in Country Z of 100X annually, and costs incurred by USP in the United States also of 100X annually. Of the total costs of 200X, USP's share is 80X and FS's share is 120X so that FS must make a payment to USP of 20X. The payment will be treated as a reimbursement of 20X of USP's costs in the United States. Accordingly, USP's Form 1120 will reflect an 80X deduction on account of activities performed in the United States for purposes of allocation and apportionment of the deduction to source. The Form 5471 for FS will reflect a 100X deduction on account of activities performed in Country Z, and a 20X deduction on account of activities performed in the United States.

*Example (2).* The facts are the same as in Example 1, except that the 100X of costs borne by USP consist of 5X of costs incurred by USP in the United States and 95X of arm's length rental charge, as described in paragraph (d)(1) of this section, for the use of a facility in the United States. The depreciation deduction attributable to the U.S. facility is 7X. The 20X net payment by FS to USP will first be applied in reduction pro rata of the 5X deduction for costs and the 7X depreciation deduction attributable to the U.S. facility. The 8X remainder will be treated as rent for the U.S. facility.

*Example (3).* (i) Four members A, B, C, and D of a controlled group form a CSA to develop the next generation technology for their business. Based on RAB shares, the participants agree to bear shares of the costs incurred during the term of the agreement in the following percentages: A 40%; B 15%; C 25%; and D 20%. The arm's length values of the external contributions they respectively own are in the following amounts for the taxable year: A 80X; B 40X; C 30X; and D 30X. The provisional (before offsets) and final PCT Payments among A, B, C, and D are shown in the table as follows:

**[All amounts stated in X's]**

| | A | B | C | D |
|---|---|---|---|---|
| Payments | <40> | <21> | <37.5> | <30> |
| Receipts | 48 | 34 | 22.5 | 24 |
| Final | 8 | 13 | <15> | <6> |

(ii) The first row/first column shows A's provisional PCT Payment equal to the product of 100X (sum of 40X, 30X, and 30X) and A's RAB share of 40%. The second row/first column shows A's provisional PCT receipts equal to the sum of the products of 80X and B's, C's, and D's RAB shares (15%, 25%, and 20%, respectively). The other entries in the first two rows of the table are similarly computed. The last row shows the final PCT receipts/payments after offsets. Thus, for the taxable year, A and B are treated as receiving the 8X and 13X, respectively, pro rata out of payments by C and D of 15X and 6X, respectively.

**(k) CSA contractual, documentation, accounting, and reporting requirements.** *(1) CSA contractual requirements.* (i) In general. A CSA that is described in paragraph (b)(1) of this section must be recorded in writing in a contract that is contemporaneous with the formation (and any revision) of the CSA and that includes the contractual provisions described in this paragraph (k)(1).

(ii) Contractual provisions. The written contract described in this paragraph (k)(1) must include provisions that—

(A) List the controlled participants and any other members of the controlled group that are reasonably anticipated to benefit from the use of the cost shared intangibles, including the address of each domestic entity and the country of organization of each foreign entity;

(B) Describe the scope of the IDA to be undertaken, including each cost shared intangible or class of cost shared intangibles that the controlled participants intend to develop under the CSA;

(C) Specify the functions and risks that each controlled participant will undertake in connection with the CSA;

(D) Divide among the controlled participants all interests in cost shared intangibles and specify each controlled participant's territorial interest in the cost shared intangibles, as described in paragraph (b)(4) of this section, that it will own and exploit without any further obligation to compensate any other controlled participant for such interest;

(E) Provide a method to calculate the controlled participants' RAB shares, based on factors that can reasonably be expected to reflect the participants' shares of anticipated benefits, and require that such RAB shares must be updated, as described in paragraph (e)(1) of this section (see also paragraph (k)(2)(ii)(F) of this section);

(F) Enumerate all categories of IDCs to be shared under the CSA;

(G) Specify that the controlled participants must use a consistent method of accounting to determine IDCs and RAB shares, as described in paragraphs (d) and (e) of this section, respectively, and must translate foreign currencies on a consistent basis;

(H) Require the controlled participants to enter into CSTs covering all IDCs, as described in paragraph (b)(2) of this section, in connection with the CSA;

(I) Require the controlled participants to enter into PCTs covering all external contributions, as described in paragraph (b)(3) of this section, in connection with the CSA; and

(J) Specify the duration of the CSA, the conditions under which the CSA may be modified or terminated, and the consequences of a modification or termination (including consequences described under the rules of paragraph (f) of this section).

(iii) Meaning of contemporaneous. (A) In general. For purposes of this paragraph (k)(1), a written contractual agreement is contemporaneous with the formation (or revision) of a CSA if, and only if, the controlled participants record the CSA, in its entirety, in a document that they sign and date no later than 60 days after the first occurrence of any IDC described in paragraph (d) of this section to which such agreement (or revision) is to apply.

(B) Example. The following example illustrates the principles of this paragraph (k)(1)(iii):

*Example.* Companies A and B, both of which are members of the same controlled group, commence an IDA on March 1, Year 1. Company A pays the first IDCs in relation to the IDA, as cash salaries to A's research staff, for the staff's work during the first week of March, Year 1. A and B, however, do not sign and date any written contractual agreement until August 1, Year 1, whereupon they execute a "Cost Sharing Agreement" that purports to be "effective as of" March 1 of Year 1. The arrangement fails the requirement that the participants record their arrangement in a written contractual agreement that is contemporaneous with the formation of a CSA.

*(2) CSA documentation requirements.* (i) In general. The controlled participants must timely update and maintain sufficient documentation to establish that the participants have met the CSA contractual requirements of paragraph (k)(1) of this section and the additional CSA documentation requirements of this paragraph (k)(2).

(ii) Additional CSA documentation requirements. The controlled participants to a CSA must timely update and maintain documentation sufficient to—

(A) Identify the cost shared intangibles that the controlled participants have developed or intend to develop under the CSA, together with each controlled participant's interest therein;

(B) Establish that each controlled participant reasonably anticipates that it will derive benefits from exploiting cost shared intangibles;

(C) Describe the functions and risks that each controlled participant has undertaken during the term of the CSA;

(D) Provide an overview of each controlled participant's business segments, including an analysis of the economic and legal factors that affect CST and PCT pricing;

(E) Establish the amount of each controlled participant's IDCs for each taxable year under the CSA, including all IDCs attributable to stock-based compensation, as described in paragraph (d)(3) of this section (including the method of measurement and timing used in determining such IDCs, and the data, as of the date of grant, used to identify stock-based compensation with the IDA);

(F) Describe the method used to estimate each controlled participant's RAB share for each year during the course of the CSA, including—

(1) All projections used to estimate benefits;

(2) All updates of the RAB shares in accordance with paragraph (e)(1) of this section; and

(3) An explanation of why that method was selected and why the method provides the most reliable measure for estimating RAB shares;

(G) Describe all external contributions, as described in paragraph (b)(3)(ii) of this section;

(H) Describe the RT for each PCT or group of PCTs;

(I) Specify the form of payment due under each PCT or group of PCTs;

(J) Describe and explain the method selected to determine the arm's length payment due under each PCT, including—

(1) An explanation of why the method selected constitutes the best method, as described in § 1.482-1(c)(2), for measuring an arm's length result;

(2) The economic analyses, data, and projections relied upon in developing and selecting the best method, including the source of the data and projections used;

(3) Each alternative method that was considered, and the reason or reasons that the alternative method was not selected;

(4) Any data that the controlled participant obtains, after the CSA takes effect, that would help determine if the controlled participant's method selected has been applied in a reasonable manner;

(5) The discount rate, where applicable, used to value each payment due under a PCT, and a demonstration that the discount rate used is consistent with the principles of paragraph (g)(2)(vi) of this section;

(6) The estimated arm's length values of any external contributions as of the dates of the relevant PCTs, in accordance with paragraph (g)(2)(ii) of this section;

(7) A discussion, where applicable, of why transactions were or were not aggregated under the principles of paragraph (g)(2)(v) of this section;

(8) The method payment form and any conversion made from the method payment form to the specified payment form, as described in paragraph (g)(2)(ix) of this section; and

(9) If applicable under paragraph (i)(6)(iv) of this section, the WACC of the controlled group that includes the controlled participants.

(iii) Coordination rules and production of documents. (A) Coordination with penalty regulations. See § 1.6662-6(d)(2)(iii)(D) regarding coordination of the rules of this paragraph (k) with the documentation requirements for purposes of the accuracy-related penalty under section 6662(e) and (h).

(B) Production of documentation. Each controlled participant must provide to the Commissioner, within 30 days of a request, the items described in paragraphs (k)(2) and (3) of this section. The time for compliance described in this paragraph (k)(2)(iii)(B) may be extended at the discretion of the Commissioner.

*(3) CSA accounting requirements.* (i) In general. The controlled participants must maintain books and records (and related or underlying data and information) that are sufficient to—

(A) Establish that the controlled participants have used (and are using) a consistent method of accounting to measure costs and benefits;

(B) Translate foreign currencies on a consistent basis; and

(C) To the extent that the method materially differs from U.S. generally accepted accounting principles, explain any such material differences.

(ii) Reliance on financial accounting. For purposes of this section, the controlled participants may not rely solely upon financial accounting to establish satisfaction of the accounting requirements of this paragraph (k)(3). Rather, the method of accounting must clearly reflect income. Thor Power Tools Co. v. Commissioner, 439 U.S. 522 (1979).

*(4) CSA reporting requirements.* (i) CSA Statement. Each controlled participant must file with the Internal Revenue Service, in the manner described in this paragraph (k)(4), a "Statement of Controlled Participant to § 1.482-7 Cost Sharing Arrangement" (CSA Statement) that complies with the requirements of this paragraph (k)(4).

(ii) Content of CSA Statement. The CSA Statement of each controlled participant must—

(A) State that the participant is a controlled participant in a CSA;

(B) Provide the controlled participant's taxpayer identification number;

(C) List the other controlled participants in the CSA, the country of organization of each such participant, and the taxpayer identification number of each such participant;

(D) Specify the earliest date that any IDC described in paragraph (d)(1) of this section occurred; and

(E) Indicate the date on which the controlled participants formed (or revised) the CSA and, if different from such date, the date on which the controlled participants recorded the CSA (or any revision) contemporaneously in accordance with paragraphs (k)(1)(i) and (iii) of this section.

(iii) Time for filing CSA Statement. (A) 90-day rule. Each controlled participant must file its original CSA Statement with the Internal Revenue Service Ogden Campus, no later than 90 days after the first occurrence of an IDC to which the newly-formed CSA applies, as described in paragraph (k)(1)(iii)(A) of this section, or, in the case of a taxpayer that became a controlled participant after the formation of the CSA, no later than 90 days after such taxpayer became a controlled participant. A CSA Statement filed in accordance with this paragraph (k)(4)(iii)(A) must be dated and signed, under penalties of perjury, by an officer of the controlled participant who is duly authorized (under local law) to sign the statement on behalf of the controlled participant.

(B) Annual return requirement. (1) In general. Each controlled participant must attach to its U.S. income tax return, for each taxable year for the duration of the CSA, a copy of the original CSA Statement that the controlled participant filed in accordance with the 90-day rule of paragraph (k)(4)(iii)(A) of this section. In addition, the controlled participant must update the information reflected on the original CSA Statement annually by attaching a schedule that documents changes in such information over time.

(2) Special filing rule for annual return requirement. If a controlled participant is not required to file a U.S. income tax return, the participant must ensure that the copy or copies of the CSA Statement and any updates are attached to Schedule M of any Form 5471, any Form 5472, or any Form 8865, filed with respect to that participant.

(iv) Examples. The following examples illustrate this paragraph (k)(4). In each example, Companies A and B are members of the same controlled group. The examples are as follows:

*Example (1).* A and B, both of which file U.S. tax returns, agree to share the costs of developing a new chemical formula in accordance with the provisions of this section. On March 30, Year 1, A and B record their agreement in a written contract styled, "Cost Sharing Agreement." The contract applies by its terms to IDCs occurring after March 1, Year 1. The first IDCs to which the CSA applies occurred on March 15, Year 1. To comply with paragraph (k)(4)(iii)(A) of this section, A and B individually must file separate CSA Statements no later than 90 days after March 15, Year 1 (June 13, Year 1). Further, to comply with paragraph (k)(4)(iii)(B) of this section, A and B must attach copies of their respective CSA Statements to their respective Year 1 U.S. income tax returns.

*Example (2).* The facts are the same as in Example 1, except that a year has passed and C, which files a U.S. tax return, joined the CSA on May 9, Year 2. To comply with the annual filing requirement described in paragraph (k)(4)(iii)(B) of this section, A and B must each attach copies of their respective CSA Statements (as filed for Year 1) to their respective Year 2 income tax returns, along with a schedule updated appropriately to reflect the changes in information described in paragraph (k)(4)(ii) of this section resulting from the addition of C to the CSA. To comply with both the 90-day rule described in paragraph (k)(4)(iii)(A) of this section and the annual filing requirement described in paragraph (k)(4)(iii)(B) of this section, C must file a CSA Statement no later than 90 days after May 9, Year 2 (August 7, Year 2), and must attach a copy of such CSA Statement to its Year 2 income tax return.

**(l) Effective date.** This section applies on the date of publication of this document as a final regulation in the Federal Register.

**(m) Transition rule.** *(1) In general.* Subject to paragraph (m)(2) of this section, an arrangement in existence before the date of publication of this document as a final regulation in the Federal Register will be considered a CSA, as described under paragraph (b) of this section, if, prior to such date, it was a qualified cost sharing arrangement under the provisions of § 1.482-7 (as contained in the 26 CFR part 1 edition revised as of January 1, 1996, hereafter in this section referred to as "former § 1.482-7"), but only if the written contract, as described in paragraph (k)(1) of this section, is amended, if necessary, to conform with the provisions of this section, as modified by paragraph (m)(3) of this section, by the close of the 120th day after the date of publication of this document as a final regulation in the Federal Register.

*(2) Termination of grandfather status.* Notwithstanding paragraph (m)(1) of this section, an arrangement otherwise therein described will not be considered a CSA from the earliest of—

(i) A failure of the controlled participants to substantially comply with the provisions of this section, as modified by paragraph (m)(3) of this section;

(ii) A material change in the scope of the arrangement, such as a material expansion of the activities undertaken beyond the scope of the intangible development area, as described in former § 1.482-7(b)(4)(iv), as of the date of publication of this document as a final regulation in the Federal Register; or

(iii) The date 50 percent or more of the value of the interests in cost shared intangibles are owned directly or indirectly by a person or persons that were not direct or indirect owners of such interests as of the date of publication of this document as a final regulation in the Federal Register.

*(3) Transitional modification of applicable provisions.* For purposes of this paragraph (m), conformity and substantial compliance with the provisions of this section shall be determined with the following modifications:

(i) CSTs and PCTs occurring prior to the date of publication of this document as a final regulation in the Federal Register shall be subject to the provisions of former § 1.482-7 rather than this section. Notwithstanding the foregoing, PCTs of a CSA will be subject to the provisions of this section if there is a Periodic Trigger for such CSA for which a subsequent PCT, occurring on or after the date of publication of this document as a final regulation in the Federal Register, is the Trigger PCT.

(ii) Paragraph (b)(1)(i) and paragraph (b)(4) of this section shall not apply.

(iii) Paragraph (k)(1)(ii)(D) of this section shall not apply.

(iv) Paragraph (k)(1)(ii)(H) and paragraph (k)(1)(ii)(I) of this section shall be construed as applying only to transactions entered into on or after the date of publication of this document as a final regulation in the Federal Register.

(v) The deadline for recordation of the revised written contractual agreement pursuant to paragraph (k)(1)(iii) of this section shall be no later than the 120th day after the date of publication of this document as a final regulation in the Federal Register.

(vi) Paragraphs (k)(2)(ii)(G) through (J) of this section shall be construed as applying only with reference to PCTs entered into on or after the date of publication of this document as a final regulation in the Federal Register.

(vii) Paragraph (k)(4)(iii)(A) shall be construed as requiring a CSA Statement with respect to the revised written contractual agreement described in paragraph (m)(3)(v) of this section no later than the 180th day after the date of publication of this document as a final regulation in the Federal Register.

(viii) Paragraph (k)(4)(iii)(B) shall be construed as only applying for taxable years ending after the filing of the CSA Statement described in paragraph (m)(3)(vii) of this section.

PAR. 3. Section 1.482-7 is redesignated § 1.482-7A and an undesignated centerheading preceding § 1.482-7A is added to read as follows:

Regulations applicable on or before the date of publication of this document as a final regulation in the Federal Register.

**Proposed § 1.482-7A**

• ***Caution:*** This Proposed Reg was incorporated into final and temporary regulations by TD 9441, 12/31/2008.

[Redesignated]

**§ 1.482-7T Methods to determine taxable income in connection with a cost sharing arrangement (temporary).**

**(a) In general.** The arm's length amount charged in a controlled transaction reasonably anticipated to contribute to developing intangibles pursuant to a cost sharing arrangement (CSA), as described in paragraph (b) of this section, must be determined under a method described in this section. Each method must be applied in accordance with the provisions of § 1.482-1, except as those provisions are modified in this section.

*(1) RAB share method for cost sharing transactions (CSTs).* See paragraph (b)(1)(i) of this section regarding the requirement that controlled participants, as defined in section (j)(1)(i) of this section, share intangible development costs (IDCs) in proportion to their shares of reasonably anticipated benefits (RAB shares) by entering into cost sharing transactions (CSTs).

*(2) Methods for platform contribution transactions (PCTs).* The arm's length amount charged in a platform contribution transaction (PCT) described in paragraph (b)(1)(ii) of this section must be determined under the method or methods applicable under the other section or sections of the section 482 regulations, as supplemented by paragraph (g) of this section. See § 1.482-1(b)(2)(ii) (Selection of category of method applicable to transaction), § 1.482-1T(b)(2)(iii) (Coordination of methods applicable to certain intangible development arrangements), and paragraph (g) of this section (Supplemental guidance on methods applicable to PCTs).

*(3) Methods for other controlled transactions.* (i) Contribution to a CSA by a controlled taxpayer that is not a controlled participant. If a controlled taxpayer that is not a controlled participant contributes to developing a cost shared intangible, as defined in section (j)(1)(i) of this section, it must receive consideration from the controlled participants under the rules of § 1.482-4T(f)(4) (Contribution to the value of an intangible owned by another). Such consideration will be treated as an intangible development cost for purposes of paragraph (d) of this section.

(ii) Transfer of interest in a cost shared intangible. If at any time (during the term, or upon or after the termination, of a CSA) a controlled participant transfers an interest in a cost shared intangible to another controlled taxpayer, the controlled participant must receive an arm's length amount of consideration from the transferee under the rules of §§ 1.482-1 and 1.482-4 through 1.482-6 as supplemented by paragraph (f)(4) of this section regarding arm's length consideration for a change in participation. For this purpose, a capability variation described in paragraph (f)(3) of this section is considered to be a controlled transfer of interests in cost shared intangibles.

(iii) Other controlled transactions in connection with a CSA. Controlled transactions between controlled participants that are not PCTs or CSTs (for example, provision of a cross operating contribution, as defined in paragraph (j)(1)(i) of this section, or make-or-sell rights) require arm's length consideration from the latter controlled participant under the rules of §§ 1.482-1, 1.482-4 through 1.482-6, and 1.482-9T as supplemented by paragraph (g)(2)(iv) of this section.

(iv) Controlled transactions in the absence of a CSA. If a controlled transaction is reasonably anticipated to contribute to developing intangibles pursuant to an arrangement that is not a CSA described in paragraph (b)(1) or (5) of this section, whether the results of any such controlled transaction are consistent with an arm's length result must be determined under the applicable rules of the other sections of the regulations under section 482. For example, an arrangement for developing intangibles in which one controlled taxpayer's costs of developing the intangibles significantly exceeds its share of reasonably anticipated benefits from exploiting the developed intangibles would not in substance be a CSA, as described in paragraphs (b)(1)(i) through (iii) of this section or paragraph (b)(5)(i) of this section. In such a case, unless the rules of this section are applicable by reason of paragraph (b)(5) of this section, the arrangement must be analyzed under other applicable sections of regulations under section 482 to determine whether it achieves arm's length results, and if not, to determine any allocations by the Commissioner that are consistent with such other regulations under section 482. See §§ 1.482-1(b)(2)(ii) (Selection of category of method applicable to transaction) and 1.482-

1T(b)(2)(iii) (Coordination of methods applicable to certain intangible development arrangements).

*(4) Coordination with the arm's length standard.* A CSA produces results that are consistent with an arm's length result within the meaning of § 1.482-1(b)(1) if, and only if, each controlled participant's IDC share (as determined under paragraph (d)(4) of this section) equals its RAB share, each controlled participant compensates its RAB share of the value of all platform contributions by other controlled participants, and all other requirements of this section are satisfied.

**(b) Cost sharing arrangement.** A cost sharing arrangement is an arrangement by which controlled participants share the costs and risks of developing cost shared intangibles in proportion to their RAB shares. An arrangement is a CSA if and only if the requirements of paragraphs (b)(1) through (4) of this section are met.

*(1) Substantive requirements.* (i) CSTs. All controlled participants must commit to, and in fact, engage in cost sharing transactions. In CSTs, the controlled participants make payments to each other (CST Payments) as appropriate, so that in each taxable year each controlled participant's IDC share is in proportion to its respective RAB share.

(ii) PCTs. All controlled participants must commit to, and in fact, engage in platform contributions transactions to the extent that there are platform contributions pursuant to paragraph (c) of this section. In a PCT, each other controlled participant (PCT Payor) is obligated to, and must in fact, make arm's length payments (PCT Payments) to each controlled participant (PCT Payee) that provides a platform contribution. For guidance on determining such arm's length obligation, see paragraph (g) of this section.

(iii) Divisional interests. Each controlled participant must receive a non-overlapping interest in the cost shared intangibles without further obligation to compensate another controlled participant for such interest.

(iv) Examples. The following examples illustrate the principles of this paragraph (b)(1):

*Example (1).* Company A and Company B, who are members of the same controlled group, execute an agreement to jointly develop vaccine X and own the exclusive rights to commercially exploit vaccine X in their respective territories, which together comprise the whole world. The agreement provides that they will share some, but not all, of the costs for developing Vaccine X in proportion to RAB share. Such agreement is not a CSA because Company A and Company B have not agreed to share all of the IDCs in proportion to their respective RAB shares.

*Example (2).* Company A and Company B agree to share all the costs of developing Vaccine X. The agreement also provides for employing certain resources and capabilities of Company A in this program including a skilled research team and certain research facilities, and provides for Company B to make payments to Company A in this respect. However, the agreement expressly provides that the program will not employ, and so Company B is expressly relieved of the payments in regard to, certain software developed by Company A as a medical research tool to model certain cellular processes expected to be implicated in the operation of Vaccine X even though such software would reasonably be anticipated to be relevant to developing Vaccine X and, thus, would be a platform contribution. See paragraph (c) of this section. Such agreement is not a CSA because Company A and Company B have not engaged in a necessary PCT for purposes of developing Vaccine X.

*Example (3).* Companies C and D, who are members of the same controlled group, enter into a CSA. In the first year of the CSA, C and D conduct the intangible development activity, as described in paragraph (d)(1) of this section. The total IDCs in regard to such activity are $3,000,000 of which C and D pay $2,000,000 and $1,000,000, respectively, directly to third parties. As between C and D, however, their CSA specifies that they will share all IDCs in accordance with their RAB shares (as described in paragraph (e)(1) of this section), which are 60% for C and 40% for D. It follows that C should bear $1,800,000 of the total IDCs (60% of total IDCs of $3,000,000) and D should bear $1,200,000 of the total IDCs (40% of total IDCs of $3,000,000). D makes a CST payment to C of $200,000, that is, the amount by which D's share of IDCs in accordance with its RAB share exceeds the amount of IDCs initially borne by D ($1,200,000-$1,000,000), and which also equals the amount by which the total IDCs initially borne by C exceeds its share of IDCS in accordance with its RAB share ($2,000,000-$1,800,000). As a result of D's CST payment to C, the IDC shares of C and D are in proportion to their respective RAB shares.

*(2) Administrative requirements.* The CSA must meet the requirements of paragraph (k) of this section.

*(3) Date of a PCT.* The controlled participants must enter into a PCT as of the earliest date on or after the CSA is entered into on which a platform contribution is reasonably anticipated to contribute to developing cost shared intangibles.

*(4) Divisional interests.* (i) In general. Pursuant to paragraph (b)(1)(iii) of this section, each controlled participant must receive a non-overlapping interest in the cost shared intangibles without further obligation to compensate another controlled participant for such interest. Each controlled participant must be entitled to the perpetual and exclusive right to the profits from transactions of any member of the controlled group that includes the controlled participant with uncontrolled taxpayers to the extent that such profits are attributable to such interest in the cost shared intangibles.

(ii) Territorial based divisional interests. The CSA may divide all interests in cost shared intangibles on a territorial basis as follows. The entire world must be divided into two or more non-overlapping geographic territories. Each controlled participant must receive at least one such territory, and in the aggregate all the participants must receive all such territories. Each controlled participant will be assigned the perpetual and exclusive right to exploit the cost shared intangibles through the use, consumption, or disposition of property or services in its territories. Thus, compensation will be required if other members of the controlled group exploit the cost shared intangibles in such territory.

(iii) Field of use based divisional interests. The CSA may divide all interests in cost shared intangibles on the basis of all uses (whether or not known at the time of the division) to which cost shared intangibles are to be put as follows. All anticipated uses of cost shared intangibles must be identified. Each controlled participant must be assigned at least one such anticipated use, and in the aggregate all the participants must be assigned all such anticipated uses. Each controlled participant will be assigned the perpetual and exclusive right to exploit the cost shared intangibles through the use or uses assigned to it and one controlled participant must be assigned the exclusive and perpetual right to exploit cost shared intangibles through any unanticipated uses.

(iv) Other divisional bases. (A) In the event that the CSA does not divide interests in the cost shared intangibles on the basis of exclusive territories or fields of use as described in paragraphs (b)(4)(ii) and (iii) of this section, the CSA may adopt some other basis on which to divide all interests in the cost shared intangibles among the controlled participants, provided that each of the following criteria is met:

(1) The basis clearly and unambiguously divides all interests in cost shared intangibles among the controlled participants.

(2) The consistent use of such basis for the division of all interests in the cost shared intangibles can be dependably verified from the records maintained by the controlled participants.

(3) The rights of the controlled participants to exploit cost shared intangibles are non-overlapping, exclusive, and perpetual.

(4) The resulting benefits associated with each controlled participant's interest in cost shared intangibles are predictable with reasonable reliability.

(B) See paragraph (f)(3) of this section for rules regarding the requirement of arm's length consideration for changes in participation in CSAs involving divisions of interest described in this paragraph (b)(4)(iv).

(v) Examples. The following examples illustrate the principles of this paragraph (b)(4):

*Example (1).* Companies P and S, both members of the same controlled group, enter into a CSA to develop product Z. Under the CSA, P receives the interest in product Z in the United States and S receives the interest in product Z in the rest of the world, as described in paragraph (b)(4)(ii) of this section. Both P and S have plants for manufacturing product Z located in their respective geographic territories. However, for commercial reasons, product Z is nevertheless manufactured by P in the United States for sale to customers in certain locations just outside the United States in close proximity to P's U.S. manufacturing plant. Because S owns the territorial rights outside the United States, P must compensate S to ensure that S realizes all the cost shared intangible profits from P's sales of product Z in S's territory. The pricing of such compensation must also ensure that P realizes an appropriate return for its manufacturing efforts. Benefits projected with respect to such sales will be included for purposes of estimating S's, but not P's, RAB share.

*Example (2).* The facts are the same as in Example 1 except that P and S agree to divide their interest in product Z based on site of manufacturing. P will have exclusive and perpetual rights in product Z manufactured in facilities owned by P. S will have exclusive and perpetual rights to product Z manufactured in facilities owned by S. P and S agree that neither will license manufacturing rights in product Z to any related or unrelated party. Both P and S maintain books and records that allow production at all sites to be verified. Both own facilities that will manufacture product Z and the relative capacities of these sites are known. All facilities are currently operating at near capacity and are expected to continue to operate at near capacity when product Z enters production so that it will not be feasible to shift production between P's and S's facilities. P and S have no plans to build new facilities and the lead time required to plan and build a manufacturing facility precludes the possibility that P or S will build a new facility during the period for which sales of Product Z are expected. Based on these facts, this basis for the division of interests in Product Z is a division described in paragraph (b)(4)(iv) of this section. The basis for the division of interest is unambiguous and clearly defined and its use can be dependably verified. P and S both have non-overlapping, exclusive and perpetual rights in Product Z. The division of interest results in the participant's relative benefits being predictable with reasonable reliability.

*Example (3).* The facts are the same as in Example 2 except that P's and S's manufacturing facilities are not expected to operate at full capacity when product Z enters production. Production of Product Z can be shifted at any time between sites owned by P and sites owned by S, although neither P nor S intends to shift production as a result of the agreement. The division of interests in Product Z between P and S based on manufacturing site is not a division described in paragraph (b)(4)(iv) of this section because their relative shares of benefits are not predictable with reasonable reliability. The fact that neither P nor S intends to shift production is irrelevant.

*(5) Treatment of certain arrangements as CSAs.* (i) Situation in which Commissioner must treat arrangement as a CSA. The Commissioner must apply the rules of this section to an arrangement among controlled taxpayers if the administrative requirements of paragraph (b)(2) of this section are met with respect to such arrangement and the controlled taxpayers reasonably concluded that such arrangement was a CSA meeting the requirements of paragraphs (b)(1), (3), and (4) of this section.

(ii) Situation in which Commissioner may treat arrangement as a CSA. For arrangements among controlled taxpayers not described in paragraph (b)(5)(i) of this section, the Commissioner may apply the provisions of this section if the Commissioner concludes that the administrative requirements of paragraph (b)(2) of this section are met, and, notwithstanding technical failure to meet the substantive requirements of paragraph (b)(1), (3), or (4) of this section, the rules of this section will provide the most reliable measure of an arm's length result. See § 1.482-1(c)(1) (the best method rule). For purposes of applying this paragraph (b)(5)(ii), any such arrangement shall be interpreted by reference to paragraph (k)(1)(iv) of this section.

(iii) Examples. The following examples illustrate the principles of this paragraph (b)(5). In the examples, assume that Companies P and S are both members of the same controlled group.

*Example (1).* (i) P owns the patent on a formula for a capsulated pain reliever, P-Cap. P reasonably anticipates, pending further research and experimentation, that the P-Cap formula could form the platform for a formula for P-Ves, an effervescent version of P-Cap. P also owns proprietary software that it reasonably anticipates to be critical to the research efforts. P and S execute a contract that purports to be a CSA by which they agree to proportionally share the costs and risks of developing a formula for P-Ves. The agreement reflects the various contractual requirements described in paragraph (k)(1) of this section and P and S comply with the documentation, accounting, and reporting requirements of paragraphs (k)(2) through (4) of this section. Both the patent rights for P-Cap and the software are reasonably anticipated to contribute to the development of P-Ves and therefore are platform contributions for which compensation is due from S as part of PCTs. Though P and S enter into and implement a PCT for the P-Cap patent rights that satisfies the arm's length standard, they fail to enter into a PCT for the software.

(ii) In this case, P and S have substantially complied with the contractual requirements of paragraph (k)(1) of this section and the documentation, accounting, and reporting requirements of paragraphs (k)(2) through (4) of this section and therefore have met the administrative requirements of paragraph (b)(2) of this section. However, because they did not enter into a PCT, as required under paragraphs (b)(1)(ii) and (b)(3) of this section, for the software that was reasonably anticipated to contribute to the development of P-Ves (see paragraph (c) of this section), they cannot reasonably conclude that their arrangement was a CSA. Accordingly, the Commissioner is not required under paragraph (b)(5)(i) of this section to apply the rules of this section to their arrangement.

(iii) Nevertheless, the arrangement between P and S closely resembles a CSA. If the Commissioner concludes that the rules of this section provide the most reliable measure of an arm's length result for such arrangement, then pursuant to paragraph (b)(5)(ii) of this section, the Commissioner may apply the rules of this section and treat P and S as entering into a PCT for the software in accordance with the requirements of paragraph (b)(1)(ii) of this section, and make any appropriate allocations under paragraph (i) of this section. Alternatively, the Commissioner may conclude that the rules of this section do not provide the most reliable measure of an arm's length result. In such case, the arrangement would be analyzed under the methods under other sections of the 482 regulations to determine whether the arrangement reaches an arm's length result.

*Example (2).* The facts are the same as Example 1 except that P and S do enter into and implement a PCT for the software as required under this paragraph (b). The Commissioner determines that the PCT Payments for the software were not arm's length; nevertheless, under the facts and circumstances at the time they entered into the CSA and PCTs, P and S reasonably concluded their arrangement to be a CSA. Because P and S have met the requirements of paragraph (b)(2) of this section and reasonably concluded their arrangement is a CSA, pursuant to paragraph (b)(5)(i) of this section, the Commissioner must apply the rules of this section to their arrangement. Accordingly, the Commissioner treats the arrangement as a CSA and makes adjustments to the PCT Payments as appropriate under this section to achieve an arm's length result for the PCT for the software.

*Example (3).* (i) The facts are the same as Example 1 except that P and S do enter into a PCT for the software as required under this paragraph (b). The agreement entered into by P and S provides for a fixed consideration of $50 million per year for four years, payable at the end of each year. This agreement satisfies the arm's length standard. However, S actually pays P consideration at the end of each year in the form of four annual royalties equal to two percent of sales. While such royalties at the time of the PCT were expected to be $50 million per year, actual sales during the first year were less than anticipated and the first royalty payment was only $25 million.

(ii) In this case, P and S failed to implement the terms of their agreement. Under these circumstances, P and S could not reasonably conclude that their arrangement was a CSA, as described in paragraph (b)(1) of this section. Accordingly, the Commissioner is not required under paragraph (b)(5)(i) of this section to apply the rules of this section to their arrangement.

(iii) Nevertheless, the arrangement between P and S closely resembles a CSA. If the Commissioner concludes that the rules of this section provide the most reliable measure of an arm's length result for such arrangement, then pursuant to paragraph (b)(5)(ii) of this section, the Commissioner may apply the rules of this section and make any appropriate allocations under paragraph (i) of this section. Alternatively, the Commissioner may conclude that the rules of this section do not provide the most reliable measure of an arm's length result. In such case, the arrangement would be analyzed under the methods under other sections of the 482 regulations to determine whether the arrangement reaches an arm's length result.

*Example (4).* (i) The facts are the same as in Example 1 except that P does not own proprietary software and P and S use a method for determining the arm's length amount of the PCT Payment for the P-Cap patent rights different from the method used in Example 1.

(ii) P and S determine that the arm's length amount of the PCT Payments for the P-Cap patent is $10 million. However, the IRS determines the best method for determining the arm's length amount of the PCT Payments for the P-Cap patent rights and under such method the arm's length amount is $100 million. To determine this $10 million present value, P and S assumed a useful life of eight years for the platform contribution, because the P-Cap patent rights will expire after eight years. However, use of the P-Cap patent rights in research is expected to lead to benefits attributable to exploitation of the cost shared intangibles extending many years beyond the expiration of the P-Cap patent, because use of the P-Cap patent rights will let P and S bring P-Ves to market before the competition, and because P and S expect to apply for additional patents covering P-Ves, which would bar competitors from selling that product for many future years. The assumption by P and S of a useful life for the platform contribution that is less than the anticipated period of exploitation of the cost shared intangibles is contrary to paragraph (g)(2)(ii) of this section, and reduces the reliability of the method used by P and S.

(iii) The method used by P and S employs a declining royalty. The royalty starts at 8% of sales, based on an application of the CUT method in which the purported CUTs all involve licenses to manufacture and sell the current generation of P-Cap, and declines to 0% over eight years, declining by 1% each year. Such make-or-sell rights are fundamentally different from use of the P-Cap patent rights to generate a new product. This difference raises the issue of whether the make-or-sell rights are sufficiently comparable to the rights that are the subject of the PCT Payment. See § 1.482-4(c)(4). While a royalty rate for make-or-sell rights can form the basis for a reliable determination of an arm's length PCT Payment in the CUT-based implementation of the income method described in paragraph (g)(4) of this section, under that method such royalty rate does not decline to zero. Therefore, the use of a declining royalty rate based on an initial rate for make-or-sell rights further reduces the reliability of the method used by P and S.

(iv) Sales of the next-generation product are not anticipated until after seven years, at which point the royalty rate will have declined to 1%. The temporal mismatch between the period of the royalty rate decline and the period of exploitation raises further concerns about the method's reliability.

(v) For the reasons given in paragraphs (ii) through (iv) of this Example 4, the method used by P and S is so unreliable and so contrary to provisions of this section that P and S could not reasonably conclude that they had contracted to make arm's length PCT Payments as required by paragraphs (b)(1)(ii) and (b)(3) of this section, and thus could not reasonably conclude that their arrangement was a CSA. Accordingly, the Commissioner is not required under paragraph (b)(5)(i) of this section to apply the rules of this section to their arrangement.

(vi) Nevertheless, the arrangement between P and S closely resembles a CSA. If the Commissioner concludes that the rules of this section provide the most reliable measure of an arm's length result for such arrangement, then pursuant to paragraph (b)(5)(ii) of this section, the Commissioner may apply the rules of this section and make any appropriate allocations under paragraph (i) of this section. Alternatively, the Commissioner may conclude that the rules of this section do not provide the most reliable measure of an arm's length result. In such case, the arrangement would be analyzed under the methods under other section 482 regulations to determine whether the arrangement reaches an arm's length result.

*(6) Entity classification of CSAs.* See § 301.7701-1(c) of this chapter for the classification of CSAs for purposes of the Internal Revenue Code.

**(c) Platform contributions.** *(1) In general.* A platform contribution is any resource, capability, or right that a controlled participant has developed, maintained, or acquired externally to the intangible development activity (whether prior to or during the course of the CSA) that is reasonably anticipated to contribute to developing cost shared intangibles. The determination whether a resource, capability, or right is reasonably anticipated to contribute to developing cost shared intangibles is ongoing and based on the best available information. Therefore, a resource, capability, or right reasonably determined not to be a platform contribution as of an earlier point in time, may be reasonably determined to be a platform contribution at a later point in time. The PCT obligation regarding a resource or capability or right once determined to be a platform contribution does not terminate merely because it may later be determined that such resource or capability or right has not contributed, and no longer is reasonably anticipated to contribute, to developing cost shared intangibles. Notwithstanding the other provisions of this paragraph (c), platform contributions do not include rights in land or depreciable tangible property, and do not include rights in other resources acquired by IDCs. See paragraph (d)(1) of this section.

*(2) Terms of platform contributions.* (i) Presumed to be exclusive. For purposes of a PCT, the PCT Payee's provision of a platform contribution is presumed to be exclusive. Thus, it is presumed that the platform resource, capability, or right is not reasonably anticipated to be committed to any business activities other than the CSA Activity, as defined in paragraph (j)(1)(i) of this section, whether carried out by the controlled participants, other controlled taxpayers, or uncontrolled taxpayers.

(ii) Rebuttal of exclusivity. The controlled participants may rebut the presumption set forth in paragraph (c)(2)(i) of this section to the satisfaction of the Commissioner. For example, if the platform resource is a research tool, then the controlled participants could rebut the presumption by establishing to the satisfaction of the Commissioner that, as of the date of the PCT, the tool is reasonably anticipated not only to contribute to the CSA Activity but also to be licensed to an uncontrolled taxpayer. In such case, the PCT Payments may need to be prorated as described in paragraph (c)(2)(iii) of this section.

(iii) Proration of PCT Payments to the extent allocable to other business activities. (A) In general. Some transfer pricing methods employed to determine the arm's length amount of the PCT Payments do so by considering the overall value of the platform contributions as opposed to, for example, the value of the anticipated use of the platform contributions in the CSA Activity. Such a transfer pricing method is consistent with the presumption that the platform contribution is exclusive (that is, that the resources, capabilities or rights that are the subject of a platform contribution are reasonably anticipated to contribute only to the CSA Activity). See paragraph (c)(2)(i) of this section (Terms of platform contributions--Presumed to be exclusive). The PCT Payments determined under such transfer pricing method may have to be prorated if the controlled participants can rebut the presumption that the platform contribution is exclusive to the satisfaction of the Commissioner as provided in paragraph (c)(2)(ii) of this section. In the case of a platform contribution that also contributes to lines of business of a PCT Payor that are not reasonably anticipated to involve exploitation of the cost shared intangibles, the need for explicit proration may in some cases be avoided through aggregation of transactions. See paragraph (g)(2)(iv) of this section (Aggregation of transactions).

(B) Determining the proration of PCT Payments. Proration will be done on a reasonable basis in proportion to the relative economic value, as of the date of the PCT, reasonably anticipated to be derived from the platform contribution by the CSA Activity as compared to the value reasonably anticipated to be derived from the platform contribution by other business activities. In the case of an aggregate valuation done under the principles of paragraph (g)(2)(iv) of this section that addresses payment for resources, capabilities, or rights used for business activities other than the CSA Activity (for example, the right to exploit an existing intangible without further development), the proration of the aggregate payments may have to reflect the economic value attributable to such resources, capabilities, or rights as well. For purposes of the best method rule under § 1.482-1(c), the reliability of the analysis under a method that requires proration pursuant to this paragraph is reduced relative to the reliability of an analysis under a method that does not require proration.

*(3) Categorization of the PCT.* For purposes of § 1.482-1(b)(2)(ii) and paragraph (a)(2) of this section, a PCT must be identified by the controlled participants as a particular type of transaction (for example, a license for royalty payments). See paragraph (k)(2)(ii)(H) of this section. Such designation must be consistent with the actual conduct of the controlled participants. If the conduct is consistent with different, economically equivalent types of transaction, then the controlled participants may designate the PCT as being any of such types of transaction. If the controlled participants fail to make such designation in their documentation, the Commissioner may make a designation consistent with the principles of paragraph (k)(1)(iv) of this section.

*(4) Certain make-or-sell rights excluded.* (i) In general. Any right to exploit an existing intangible without further development, such as the right to make, replicate, license or sell existing products, does not constitute a platform contribution to a CSA, and the arm's length compensation for such rights (make-or-sell rights) does not satisfy the compensation obligation under a PCT.

(ii) Examples. The following examples illustrate the principles of this paragraph (c)(4):

*Example (1).* P and S, which are members of the same controlled group, execute a CSA. Under the CSA, P and S will bear their RAB shares of IDCs for developing the second generation of ABC, a computer software program. Prior to that arrangement, P had incurred substantial costs and risks to develop ABC. Concurrent with entering into the arrangement, P (as the licensor) executes a license with S (as the licensee) by which S may make and sell copies of the existing ABC. Such make-or-sell rights do not constitute a platform contribution to the CSA. The rules of §§ 1.482-1 and 1.482-4 through 1.482-6 must be applied to determine the arm's length consideration in connection with the make-or-sell licensing arrangement. In certain circumstances, this determination of the arm's length consideration may be done on an aggregate basis with the evaluation of compensation obligations pursuant to the PCTs entered into by P and S in connection with the CSA. See paragraph (g)(2)(iv) of this section.

*Example (2).* (i) P, a software company, has developed and currently exploits software program ABC. P and S enter into a CSA to develop future generations of ABC. The ABC source code is the platform on which future generations of ABC will be built and is therefore a platform contribution of P for which compensation is due from S pursuant to a PCT. Concurrent with entering into the CSA, P licenses to S the make-or-sell rights for the current version of ABC. P has entered into similar licenses with uncontrolled parties calling for sales-based royalty payments at a rate of 20%. The current version of ABC has an expected product life of three years. P and S enter into a contingent payment agreement to cover both the PCT Payments due from S for P's platform contribution and payments due from S for the make-or-sell license. Based on the uncontrolled make-or-sell licenses, P and S agree on a sales-based royalty rate of 20% in Year 1 that declines on a straight line basis to 0% over the 3 year product life of ABC.

(ii) The make-or-sell rights for the current version of ABC are not platform contributions, though paragraph (g)(2)(iv) of this section provides for the possibility that the most reliable determination of an arm's length charge for the platform contribution and the make-or-sell license may be one that values the two transactions in the aggregate. A contingent payment schedule based on the uncontrolled make-or-sell licenses may provide an arm's length charge for the separate make-or-sell license between P and S, provided the royalty rates in the uncontrolled licenses similarly decline, but as a measure of the aggregate PCT and license payments it does not account for the arm's length value of P's platform contributions which include the rights in the source code and future development rights in ABC.

*(5) Examples.* The following examples illustrate the principles of this paragraph (c). In each example, Companies P and S are members of the same controlled group, and execute a CSA providing that each will have the exclusive right to exploit cost shared intangibles in its own territory. See paragraph (b)(4)(ii) of this section (Territorial based divisional interests).

*Example (1).* Company P has developed and currently markets version 1.0 of a new software application XYZ. Company P and Company S execute a CSA under which they will share the IDCs for developing future versions of XYZ. Version 1.0 is reasonably anticipated to contribute to the development of future versions of XYZ and therefore Company P's rights in version 1.0 constitute a platform contribution from Company P that must be compensated by Company S pursuant to a PCT. Pursuant to paragraph (c)(3) of this section, the controlled participants designate the platform contribution as a transfer of intangibles that would otherwise be governed by § 1.482-4, if entered into by controlled parties. Accordingly, pursuant to paragraph (a)(2) of this section, the applicable method for determining the arm's length value of the compensation obligation under the PCT between Company P and Company S will be governed by § 1.482-4 as supplemented by paragraph (g) of this section. Absent a showing to the contrary by P and S, the platform contribution in this case is presumed to be the exclusive provision of the benefit of all rights in version 1.0, other than the rights described in paragraph (c)(4) of this section (Certain make-or-sell rights excluded). This includes the right to use version 1.0 for purposes of research and the exclusive right in S's territory to exploit any future products that incorporated the technology of version 1.0, and would cover a term extending as long as the controlled participants were to exploit future versions of XYZ or any other product based on the version 1.0 platform. The compensation obligation of Company S pursuant to the PCT will reflect the full value of the platform contribution, as limited by Company S's RAB share.

*Example (2).* Company P and Company S execute a CSA under which they will share the IDCs for developing Vaccine Z. Company P will commit to the project its research team that has successfully developed a number of other vaccines. The expertise and existing integration of the research team is a unique resource or capability of Company P which is reasonably anticipated to contribute to the development of Vaccine Z. Therefore, P's provision of the capabilities of the research team constitute a platform contribution for which compensation is due from Company S as part of a PCT. Pursuant to paragraph (c)(3) of this section, the controlled parties designate the platform contribution as a provision of services that would otherwise be governed by § 1.482-9T(a) if entered into by controlled parties. Accordingly, pursuant to paragraph (a)(2) of this section, the applicable method for determining the arm's length value of the compensation obligation under the PCT between Company P and Company S will be governed by § 1.482-9T(a) as supplemented by paragraph (g) of this section. Absent a showing to the contrary by P and S, the platform contribution in this case is presumed to be the exclusive provision of the benefits by Company P of its research team to the development of Vaccine Z. Because the IDCs include the ongoing compensation of the researchers, the compensation obligation under the PCT is only for the value of the commitment of the research team by Company P to the CSA's development efforts net of such researcher compensation. The value of the compensation obligation of Company S for the PCT will reflect the full value of the provision of services, as limited by Company S's RAB share.

**(d) Intangible development costs.** *(1) Determining whether costs are IDCs.* Costs included in IDCs are determined by reference to the scope of the intangible development activity (IDA).

(i) Definition and scope of the IDA. For purposes of this section, the IDA means the activity under the CSA of developing or attempting to develop reasonably anticipated cost shared intangibles. The scope of the IDA includes all of the controlled participants' activities that could reasonably be anticipated to contribute to developing the reasonably anticipated cost shared intangibles. The IDA cannot be described merely by a list of particular resources, capabilities, or rights that will be used in the CSA, because such a list would not identify reasonably anticipated cost shared intangibles. Also, the scope of the IDA may change as the nature or identity of the reasonably anticipated cost shared intangibles changes or the nature of the activities necessary for their development become clearer. For example, the relevance of certain ongoing work to developing reasonably anticipated cost shared intangibles or the need for additional work may only become clear over time.

(ii) Reasonably anticipated cost shared intangible. For purposes of this section, reasonably anticipated cost shared intangible means any intangible, within the meaning of § 1.482-4(b), that, at the applicable point in time, the controlled participants intend to develop under the CSA. Reasonably anticipated cost shared intangibles may change over the course of the CSA. The controlled participants may at any time change the reasonably anticipated cost shared intangibles but must document any such change pursuant to paragraph (k)(2)(ii)(A)(1) of this section. Removal of reasonably anticipated cost shared intangibles does not affect the controlled participants' interests in cost shared intangibles already developed under the CSA. In addition, the reasonably anticipated cost shared intangibles automatically expand to include the intended result of any further development of a cost shared intangible already developed under the CSA, or applications of such an intangible. However, the controlled participants may override this automatic expansion in a particular case if they separately remove specified further development of such intangible (or specified applications of such intangible) from the IDA, and document such separate removal pursuant to paragraph (k)(2)(ii)(A)(3) of this section.

(iii) Costs included in IDCs. For purposes of this section, IDCs mean all costs, in cash or in kind (including stock-based compensation, as described in paragraph (d)(3) of this section), but excluding acquisition costs for land or depreciable property, in the ordinary course of business after the formation of a CSA that, based on analysis of the facts and circumstances, are directly identified with, or are reasonably allocable to, the IDA. Thus, IDCs include costs incurred in attempting to develop reasonably anticipated cost shared intangibles regardless of whether such costs ultimately lead to development of those intangibles, other intangibles developed unexpectedly, or no intangibles. IDCs shall also include the arm's length rental charge for the use of any land or depreciable tangible property (as determined under § 1.482-2(c) (Use of tangible property)) directly identified with, or reasonably allocable to, the IDA. Reference to generally accepted accounting principles or Federal income tax accounting rules may provide a useful starting point but will not be conclusive regarding inclusion of costs in IDCs. IDCs do not include interest expense, foreign income taxes (as defined in § 1.901-2(a)), or domestic income taxes.

(iv) Examples. The following examples illustrate the principles of this paragraph (d)(1):

*Example (1).* A contract that purports to be a CSA provides that the IDA to which the agreement applies consists of all research and development activity conducted at laboratories A, B, and C but not at other facilities maintained by the controlled participants. The contract does not describe the reasonably anticipated cost shared intangibles with respect to which research and development is to be undertaken. The contract fails to meet the requirements set forth in paragraph (k)(1)(ii)(B) of this section because it fails to adequately describe the scope of the IDA to be undertaken.

*Example (2).* A contract that purports to be a CSA provides that the IDA to which the agreement applies consists of all research and development activity conducted by any of the controlled participants with the goal of developing a cure for a particular disease. Such a cure is thus a reasonably anticipated cost shared intangible. The contract also contains a provision that the IDA will exclude any activity that builds on the results of the controlled participants' prior research concerning Enzyme X even though such activity could reasonably be anticipated to contribute to developing such cure. The contract fails to meet the requirement set forth in paragraph (d)(1)(i) of this section that the scope of the IDA include all of the controlled participants' activities that could reasonably be anticipated to contribute to developing reasonably anticipated cost shared intangibles.

*(2) Allocation of costs.* If a particular cost is directly identified with, or reasonably allocable to, a function the results of which will benefit both the IDA and other business activities, the cost must be allocated on a reasonable basis between the IDA and such other business activities in proportion to the relative economic value that the IDA and such other business activities are anticipated to derive from such results.

*(3) Stock-based compensation.* (i) In general. As used in this section, the term stock-based compensation means any compensation provided by a controlled participant to an employee or independent contractor in the form of equity instruments, options to acquire stock (stock options), or rights with respect to (or determined by reference to) equity instruments or stock options, including but not limited to property to which section 83 applies and stock options to which section 421 applies, regardless of whether ultimately settled in the form of cash, stock, or other property.

(ii) Identification of stock-based compensation with the IDA. The determination of whether stock-based compensation is directly identified with, or reasonably allocable to, the IDA is made as of the date that the stock-based compensation is granted. Accordingly, all stock-based compensation that is granted during the term of the CSA and, at date of grant, is directly identified with, or reasonably allocable to, the IDA is included as an IDC under paragraph (d)(1) of this section. In the case of a repricing or other modification of a stock option, the determination of whether the repricing or other modification constitutes the grant of a new stock option for purposes of this paragraph (d)(3)(ii) will be made in accordance with the rules of section 424(h) and related regulations.

(iii) Measurement and timing of stock-based compensation IDC. (A) In general. Except as otherwise provided in this paragraph (d)(3)(iii), the cost attributable to stock-based compensation is equal to the amount allowable to the controlled participant as a deduction for federal income tax purposes with respect to that stock-based compensation (for example, under section 83(h)) and is taken into account as an IDC under this section for the taxable year for which the deduction is allowable.

(1) Transfers to which section 421 applies. Solely for purposes of this paragraph (d)(3)(iii)(A), section 421 does not apply to the transfer of stock pursuant to the exercise of an option that meets the requirements of section 422(a) or 423(a).

(2) Deductions of foreign controlled participants. Solely for purposes of this paragraph (d)(3)(iii)(A), an amount is treated as an allowable deduction of a foreign controlled participant to the extent that a deduction would be allowable to a United States taxpayer.

(3) Modification of stock option. Solely for purposes of this paragraph (d)(3)(iii)(A), if the repricing or other modification of a stock option is determined, under paragraph (d)(3)(ii) of this section, to constitute the grant of a new stock option not identified with, or reasonably allocable to, the IDA, the stock option that is repriced or otherwise modified will be treated as being exercised immediately before the modification, provided that the stock option is then exercisable and the fair market value of the underlying stock then exceeds the price at which the stock option is exercisa-

ble. Accordingly, the amount of the deduction that would be allowable (or treated as allowable under this paragraph (d)(3)(iii)(A)) to the controlled participant upon exercise of the stock option immediately before the modification must be taken into account as an IDC as of the date of the modification.

(4) Expiration or termination of CSA. Solely for purposes of this paragraph (d)(3)(iii)(A), if an item of stock-based compensation identified with, or reasonably allocable to, the IDA is not exercised during the term of a CSA, that item of stock-based compensation will be treated as being exercised immediately before the expiration or termination of the CSA, provided that the stock-based compensation is then exercisable and the fair market value of the underlying stock then exceeds the price at which the stock-based compensation is exercisable. Accordingly, the amount of the deduction that would be allowable (or treated as allowable under this paragraph (d)(3)(iii)(A)) to the controlled participant upon exercise of the stock-based compensation must be taken into account as an IDC as of the date of the expiration or termination of the CSA.

(B) Election with respect to options on publicly traded stock. (1) In general. With respect to stock-based compensation in the form of options on publicly traded stock, the controlled participants in a CSA may elect to take into account all IDCs attributable to those stock options in the same amount, and as of the same time, as the fair value of the stock options reflected as a charge against income in audited financial statements or disclosed in footnotes to such financial statements, provided that such statements are prepared in accordance with United States generally accepted accounting principles by or on behalf of the company issuing the publicly traded stock.

(2) Publicly traded stock. As used in this paragraph (d)(3)(iii)(B), the term publicly traded stock means stock that is regularly traded on an established United States securities market and is issued by a company whose financial statements are prepared in accordance with United States generally accepted accounting principles for the taxable year.

(3) Generally accepted accounting principles. For purposes of this paragraph (d)(3)(iii)(B), a financial statement prepared in accordance with a comprehensive body of generally accepted accounting principles other than United States generally accepted accounting principles is considered to be prepared in accordance with United States generally accepted accounting principles provided that either--

(i) The fair value of the stock options under consideration is reflected in the reconciliation between such other accounting principles and United States generally accepted accounting principles required to be incorporated into the financial statement by the securities laws governing companies whose stock is regularly traded on United States securities markets; or

(ii) In the absence of a reconciliation between such other accounting principles and United States generally accepted accounting principles that reflects the fair value of the stock options under consideration, such other accounting principles require that the fair value of the stock options under consideration be reflected as a charge against income in audited financial statements or disclosed in footnotes to such statements.

(4) Time and manner of making the election. The election described in this paragraph (d)(3)(iii)(B) is made by an explicit reference to the election in the written contract required by paragraph (k)(1) of this section or in a written amendment to the CSA entered into with the consent of the Commissioner pursuant to paragraph (d)(3)(iii)(C) of this section. In the case of a CSA in existence on August 26, 2003, the election by written amendment to the CSA may be made without the consent of the Commissioner if such amendment is entered into not later than the latest due date (with regard to extensions) of a federal income tax return of any controlled participant for the first taxable year beginning after August 26, 2003.

(C) Consistency. Generally, all controlled participants in a CSA taking options on publicly traded stock into account under paragraph (d)(3)(ii), (d)(3)(iii)(A), or (d)(3)(iii)(B) of this section must use that same method of identification, measurement and timing for all options on publicly traded stock with respect to that CSA. Controlled participants may change their method only with the consent of the Commissioner and only with respect to stock options granted during taxable years subsequent to the taxable year in which the Commissioner's consent is obtained. All controlled participants in the CSA must join in requests for the Commissioner's consent under this paragraph (d)(3)(iii)(C). Thus, for example, if the controlled participants make the election described in paragraph (d)(3)(iii)(B) of this section upon the formation of the CSA, the election may be revoked only with the consent of the Commissioner, and the consent will apply only to stock options granted in taxable years subsequent to the taxable year in which consent is obtained. Similarly, if controlled participants already have granted stock options that have been or will be taken into account under the general rule of paragraph (d)(3)(iii)(A) of this section, then except in cases specified in the last sentence of paragraph (d)(3)(iii)(B)(4) of this section, the controlled participants may make the election described in paragraph (d)(3)(iii)(B) of this section only with the consent of the Commissioner, and the consent will apply only to stock options granted in taxable years subsequent to the taxable year in which consent is obtained.

*(4) IDC share.* A controlled participant's IDC share for a taxable year is equal to the controlled participant's cost contribution for the taxable year, divided by the sum of all IDCs for the taxable year. A controlled participant's cost contribution for a taxable year means all of the IDCs initially borne by the controlled participant, plus all of the CST Payments that the participant makes to other controlled participants, minus all of the CST Payments that the participant receives from other controlled participants.

*(5) Examples.* The following examples illustrate this paragraph (d):

*Example (1).* Foreign parent (FP) and its U.S. subsidiary (USS) enter into a CSA to develop a better mousetrap. USS and FP share the costs of FP's R&D facility that will be exclusively dedicated to this research, the salaries of the researchers at the facility, and overhead costs attributable to the project. They also share the cost of a conference facility that is at the disposal of the senior executive management of each company. Based on the facts and circumstances, the cost of the conference facility cannot be directly identified with, and is not reasonably allocable to, the IDA. In this case, the cost of the conference facility must be excluded from the amount of IDCs.

*Example (2).* U.S. parent (USP) and its foreign subsidiary (FS) enter into a CSA to develop intangibles for producing a new device. USP and FS share the costs of an R&D facility, the salaries of the facility's researchers, and overhead costs attributable to the project. Although USP also incurs costs related to field testing of the device, USP does not include those costs in the IDCs that USP and FS will share under the CSA. The Commissioner may determine, based on the facts and circumstances, that the costs of field testing are IDCs that the controlled participants must share.

*Example (3).* U.S. parent (USP) and its foreign subsidiary (FS) enter into a CSA to develop a new process patent. USP assigns certain employees to perform solely R&D to develop a new mathematical algorithm to perform certain calculations. That algorithm will be used both to develop the new process patent and to develop a new design patent the development of which is outside the scope of the CSA. During years covered by the CSA, USP compensates such employees with cash salaries, stock-based compensation, or a combination of both. USP and FS anticipate that the economic value attributable to the R&D will be derived from the process patent and the design patent in a relative proportion of 75% and 25%, respectively. Applying the principles of paragraph (d)(2) of this section, 75% of the compensation of such employees must be allocated to the development of the new process patent and, thus, treated as IDCs. With respect to the cash salary compensation, the IDC is 75% of the face value of the cash. With respect to the stock-based compensation, the IDC is 75% of the value of the stock-based compensation as determined under paragraph (d)(3)(iii) of this section.

*Example (4).* Foreign parent (FP) and its U.S. subsidiary (USS) enter into a CSA to develop a new computer source code. FP has an executive officer who oversees a research facility and employees dedicated solely to the IDA. The executive officer also oversees other research facilities and employees unrelated to the IDA, and performs certain corporate overhead functions. The full amount of the costs of the research facility and employees dedicated solely to the IDA can be directly identified with the IDA and, therefore, are IDCs. In addition, based on the executive officer's records of time worked on various matters, the controlled participants reasonably allocate 20% of the executive officer's compensation to supervision of the facility and employees dedicated to the IDA, 50% of the executive officer's compensation to supervision of the facilities and employees unrelated to the IDA, and 30% of the executive officer's compensation to corporate overhead functions. The controlled participants also reasonably determine that the results of the executive officer's corporate overhead functions yield equal economic benefit to the IDA and the other business activities of FP. Applying the principles of paragraph (d)(1) of this section, the executive officer's compensation allocated to supervising the facility and employees dedicated to the IDA (amounting to 20% of the executive officer's total compensation) must be treated as IDCs. Applying the principles of paragraph (d)(2) of this section, half of the executive officer's compensation allocated to corporate overhead functions (that is, half of 30% of the executive officer's total compensation), must be treated as IDCs. Therefore, a total of 35% (20% plus 15%) of the executive officer's total compensation must be treated as IDCs.

**(e) Reasonably anticipated benefits share.** *(1) Definition.* (i) In general. A controlled participant's share of reasonably anticipated benefits is equal to its reasonably anticipated benefits divided by the sum of the reasonably anticipated benefits, as defined in paragraph (j)(1)(i) of this section, of all the controlled participants. RAB shares must be updated to account for changes in economic conditions, the business operations and practices of the participants, and the ongoing development of intangibles under the CSA. For purposes of determining RAB shares at any given time, reasonably anticipated benefits must be estimated over the entire period, past and future, of exploitation of the cost shared intangibles, and must reflect appropriate updates to take into account the most reliable data regarding past and projected future results available at such time. A controlled participant's RAB share must be determined by using the most reliable estimate. In determining which of two or more available estimates is most reliable, the quality of the data and assumptions used in the analysis must be taken into account, consistent with § 1.482-1(c)(2)(ii) (Data and assumptions). Thus, the reliability of an estimate will depend largely on the completeness and accuracy of the data, the soundness of the assumptions, and the relative effects of particular deficiencies in data or assumptions on different estimates. If two estimates are equally reliable, no adjustment should be made based on differences between the estimates. The following factors will be particularly relevant in determining the reliability of an estimate of RAB shares:

(A) The basis used for measuring benefits, as described in paragraph (e)(2)(ii) of this section.

(B) The projections used to estimate benefits, as described in paragraph (e)(2)(iii) of this section.

(ii) Example. The following example illustrates the principles of this paragraph (e)(1):

*Example.* (i) USP and FS plan to conduct research to develop Product Lines A and B. USP and FS reasonably anticipate respective benefits from Product Line A of 100X and 200X and respective benefits from Product Line B, respectively, of 300X and 400X. USP and FS thus reasonably anticipate combined benefits from Product Lines A and B of 400X and 600X, respectively.

(ii) USP and FS could enter into a separate CSA to develop Product Line A with respective RAB shares of 33⅓ percent and 66⅔ percent (reflecting a ratio of 100X to 200X), and into a separate CSA to develop Product Line B with respective RAB shares of 42⁶⁄₇ percent and 57¹⁄₇ percent (reflecting a ratio of 300X to 400X). Alternatively, USP and FS could enter into a single CSA to develop both Product Lines A and B with respective RAB shares of 40 percent and 60 percent (in the ratio of 400X to 600X). If the separate CSAs are chosen, then any costs for activities that contribute to developing both Product Line A and Product Line B will constitute IDCs of the respective CSAs as required by paragraphs (d)(1) and (d)(2) of this section.

*(2) Measure of benefits.* (i) In general. In order to estimate a controlled participant's RAB share, the amount of each controlled participant's reasonably anticipated benefits must be measured on a basis that is consistent for all such participants. See paragraph (e)(2)(ii)(E) Example 9 of this section. If a controlled participant transfers a cost shared intangible to another controlled taxpayer, other than by way of a transfer described in paragraph (f) of this section, that controlled participant's benefits from the transferred intangible must be measured by reference to the transferee's benefits, disregarding any consideration paid by the transferee to the controlled participant (such as a royalty pursuant to a license agreement). Reasonably anticipated benefits are measured either on a direct basis, by reference to estimated benefits to be generated by the use of cost shared intangibles (generally based on additional revenues plus cost savings less any additional costs incurred), or on an indirect basis, by reference to certain measurements that reasonably can be assumed to relate to benefits to be generated. Such indirect bases of measurement of anticipated benefits are described in paragraph (e)(2)(ii) of this section. A controlled participant's reasona-

bly anticipated benefits must be measured on the basis, whether direct or indirect, that most reliably determines RAB shares. In determining which of two bases of measurement is most reliable, the factors set forth in § 1.482-1(c)(2)(ii) (Data and assumptions) must be taken into account. It normally will be expected that the basis that provided the most reliable estimate for a particular year will continue to provide the most reliable estimate in subsequent years, absent a material change in the factors that affect the reliability of the estimate. Regardless of whether a direct or indirect basis of measurement is used, adjustments may be required to account for material differences in the activities that controlled participants undertake to exploit their interests in cost shared intangibles. See Examples 4 and 7 of paragraph (e)(2)(ii)(E) of this section.

(ii) Indirect bases for measuring anticipated benefits. Indirect bases for measuring anticipated benefits from participation in a CSA include the following:

(A) Units used, produced, or sold. Units of items used, produced, or sold by each controlled participant in the business activities in which cost shared intangibles are exploited may be used as an indirect basis for measuring its anticipated benefits. This basis of measurement will more reliably determine RAB shares to the extent that each controlled participant is expected to have a similar increase in net profit or decrease in net loss attributable to the cost shared intangibles per unit of the item or items used, produced, or sold. This circumstance is most likely to arise when the cost shared intangibles are exploited by the controlled participants in the use, production, or sale of substantially uniform items under similar economic conditions.

(B) Sales. Sales by each controlled participant in the business activities in which cost shared intangibles are exploited may be used as an indirect basis for measuring its anticipated benefits. This basis of measurement will more reliably determine RAB shares to the extent that each controlled participant is expected to have a similar increase in net profit or decrease in net loss attributable to cost shared intangibles per dollar of sales. This circumstance is most likely to arise if the costs of exploiting cost shared intangibles are not substantial relative to the revenues generated, or if the principal effect of using cost shared intangibles is to increase the controlled participants' revenues (for example, through a price premium on the products they sell) without affecting their costs substantially. Sales by each controlled participant are unlikely to provide a reliable basis for measuring RAB shares unless each controlled participant operates at the same market level (for example, manufacturing, distribution, etc.).

(C) Operating profit. Operating profit of each controlled participant from the activities in which cost shared intangibles are exploited, as determined before any expense (including amortization) on account of IDCs, may be used as an indirect basis for measuring anticipated benefits. This basis of measurement will more reliably determine RAB shares to the extent that such profit is largely attributable to the use of cost shared intangibles, or if the share of profits attributable to the use of cost shared intangibles is expected to be similar for each controlled participant. This circumstance is most likely to arise when cost shared intangibles are closely associated with the activity that generates the profit and the activity could not be carried on or would generate little profit without use of those intangibles.

(D) Other bases for measuring anticipated benefits. Other bases for measuring anticipated benefits may in some circumstances be appropriate, but only to the extent that there is expected to be a reasonably identifiable relationship between the basis of measurement used and additional income generated or costs saved by the use of cost shared intangibles. For example, a division of costs based on employee compensation would be considered unreliable unless there were a relationship between the amount of compensation and the expected additional income generated or costs saved by the controlled participants from using the cost shared intangibles.

(E) Examples. The following examples illustrate this paragraph (e)(2)(ii):

*Example (1).* Controlled parties A and B enter into a CSA to develop product and process intangibles for already existing Product P. Without such intangibles, A and B would each reasonably anticipate revenue, in present value terms, of $100M from sales of Product P until it becomes obsolete. With the intangibles, A and B each reasonably anticipate selling the same number of units each year, but reasonably anticipate that the price will be higher. Because the particular product intangible is more highly regarded in A's market, A reasonably anticipates an increase of $20M in present value revenue from the product intangible, while B reasonably anticipates an increase of only $10M in present value from the product intangible. Further, A and B each reasonably anticipate spending an additional amount equal to $5M in present value in production costs to include the feature embodying the product intangible. Finally, A and B each reasonably anticipate saving an amount equal to $2M in present value in production costs by using the process intangible. A and B reasonably anticipate no other economic effects from exploiting the cost shared intangibles. A's reasonably anticipated benefits from exploiting the cost shared intangibles equal its reasonably anticipated increase in revenue ($20M) plus its reasonably anticipated cost savings ($2M) less its reasonably anticipated increased costs ($5M), which equals $17M. Similarly, B's reasonably anticipated benefits from exploiting the cost shared intangibles equal its reasonably anticipated increase in revenue ($10M) plus its reasonably anticipated cost savings ($2M) less its reasonably anticipated increased costs ($5M), which equals $7M. Thus A's reasonably anticipated benefits are $17M and B's reasonably anticipated benefits are $7M.

*Example (2).* Foreign Parent (FP) and U.S. Subsidiary (USS) both produce a feedstock for the manufacture of various high-performance plastic products. Producing the feedstock requires large amounts of electricity, which accounts for a significant portion of its production cost. FP and USS enter into a CSA to develop a new process that will reduce the amount of electricity required to produce a unit of the feedstock. FP and USS currently both incur an electricity cost of $2 per unit of feedstock produced and rates for each are expected to remain similar in the future. The new process, if it is successful, will reduce the amount of electricity required by each company to produce a unit of the feedstock by 50%. Switching to the new process would not require FP or USS to incur significant investment or other costs. Therefore, the cost savings each company is expected to achieve after implementing the new process are $1 per unit of feedstock produced. Under the CSA, FP and USS divide the costs of developing the new process based on the units of the feedstock each is anticipated to produce in the future. In this case, units produced is the most reliable basis for measuring RAB shares and dividing the IDCs because each controlled participant is expected to have a similar $1 (50% of current charge of $2) decrease in costs per unit of the feedstock produced.

*Example (3).* The facts are the same as in Example 2, except that currently USS pays $3 per unit of feedstock produced for electricity while FP pays $6 per unit of feedstock produced. In this case, units produced is not the most reliable basis for measuring RAB shares and dividing the IDCs because the participants do not expect to have a similar decrease in costs per unit of the feedstock produced. The Commissioner determines that the most reliable measure of RAB shares may be based on units of the feedstock produced if FP's units are weighted relative to USS's units by a factor of 2. This reflects the fact that FP pays twice as much as USS for electricity and, therefore, FP's savings of $3 per unit of the feedstock (50% reduction of current charge of $6) would be twice USS's savings of $1.50 per unit of feedstock (50% reduction of current charge of $3) from any new process eventually developed.

*Example (4).* The facts are the same as in Example 3, except that to supply the particular needs of the U.S. market USS manufactures the feedstock with somewhat different properties than FP's feedstock. This requires USS to employ a somewhat different production process than does FP. Because of this difference, USS would incur significant construction costs in order to adopt any new process that may be developed under the cost sharing agreement. In this case, units produced is not the most reliable basis for measuring RAB shares. In order to reliably determine RAB shares, the Commissioner measures the reasonably anticipated benefits of USS and FP on a direct basis. USS's reasonably anticipated benefits are its reasonably anticipated total savings in electricity costs, less its reasonably anticipated costs of adopting the new process. FS's reasonably anticipated benefits are its reasonably anticipated total savings in electricity costs.

*Example (5).* U.S. Parent (USP) and Foreign Subsidiary (FS) enter into a CSA to develop new anesthetic drugs. USP obtains the right to market any resulting drugs in the United States and FS obtains the right to market any resulting drugs in the rest of the world. USP and FS determine RAB shares on the basis of their respective total anticipated operating profit from all drugs under development. USP anticipates that it will receive a much higher profit than FS per unit sold because the price of the drugs is not regulated in the United States, whereas the price of the drugs is regulated in many non-U.S. jurisdictions. In both controlled participants' territories, the anticipated operating profits are almost entirely attributable to the use of the cost shared intangibles. In this case, the controlled participants' basis for measuring RAB shares is the most reliable.

*Example (6).* (i) Foreign Parent (FP) and U.S. Subsidiary (USS) manufacture and sell fertilizers. They enter into a CSA to develop a new pellet form of a common agricultural fertilizer that is currently available only in powder form. Under the CSA, USS obtains the rights to produce and sell the new form of fertilizer for the U.S. market while FP obtains the rights to produce and sell the new form of fertilizer in the rest of the world. The costs of developing the new form of fertilizer are divided on the basis of the anticipated sales of fertilizer in the controlled participants' respective markets.

(ii) If the research and development is successful, the pellet form will deliver the fertilizer more efficiently to crops and less fertilizer will be required to achieve the same effect on crop growth. The pellet form of fertilizer can be expected to sell at a price premium over the powder form of fertilizer based on the savings in the amount of fertilizer that needs to be used. This price premium will be a similar premium per dollar of sales in each territory. If the research and development is successful, the costs of producing pellet fertilizer are expected to be approximately the same as the costs of producing powder fertilizer and the same for both FP and USS. Both FP and USS operate at approximately the same market levels, selling their fertilizers largely to independent distributors.

(iii) In this case, the controlled participants' basis for measuring RAB shares is the most reliable.

*Example (7).* The facts are the same as in Example 6, except that FP distributes its fertilizers directly while USS sells to independent distributors. In this case, sales of USS and FP are not the most reliable basis for measuring RAB shares unless adjustments are made to account for the difference in market levels at which the sales occur.

*Example (8).* Foreign Parent (FP) and U.S. Subsidiary (USS) enter into a CSA to develop materials that will be used to train all new entry-level employees. FP and USS determine that the new materials will save approximately ten hours of training time per employee. Because their entry-level employees are paid on differing wage scales, FP and USS decide that they should not measure benefits based on the number of entry-level employees hired by each. Rather, they measure benefits based on compensation paid to the entry-level employees hired by each. In this case, the basis used for measuring RAB shares is the most reliable because there is a direct relationship between compensation paid to new entry-level employees and costs saved by FP and USS from the use of the new training materials.

*Example (9).* U.S. Parent (USP), Foreign Subsidiary 1 (FS1), and Foreign Subsidiary 2 (FS2) enter into a CSA to develop computer software that each will market and install on customers' computer systems. The controlled participants measure benefits on the basis of projected sales by USP, FS1, and FS2 of the software in their respective geographic areas. However, FS1 plans not only to sell but also to license the software to unrelated customers, and FS1's licensing income (which is a percentage of the licensees' sales) is not counted in the projected benefits. In this case, the basis used for measuring the benefits of each controlled participant is not the most reliable because all of the benefits received by controlled participants are not taken into account. In order to reliably determine RAB shares, FS1's projected benefits from licensing must be included in the measurement on a basis that is the same as that used to measure its own and the other controlled participants' projected benefits from sales (for example, all controlled participants might measure their benefits on the basis of operating profit).

(iii) Projections used to estimate benefits. (A) In general. The reliability of an estimate of RAB shares also depends upon the reliability of projections used in making the estimate. Projections required for this purpose generally include a determination of the time period between the inception of the research and development activities under the CSA and the receipt of benefits, a projection of the time over which benefits will be received, and a projection of the benefits anticipated for each year in which it is anticipated that the cost shared intangible will generate benefits. A projection of the relevant basis for measuring anticipated benefits may require a projection of the factors that underlie it. For example, a projection of operating profits may require a projection of sales, cost of sales, operating expenses, and other factors that affect operating profits. If it is anticipated that there will be significant variation among controlled participants in the timing of their receipt of benefits, and consequently benefit shares are expected to vary significantly over the years in which benefits will be received, it normally will be necessary to use the present value of the projected benefits to reliably determine RAB shares. See paragraph (g)(2)(v) of this section for best method considerations regarding discount rates used for this purpose. If it is not anticipated that benefit shares will significantly change over time, current annual benefit shares may provide a reliable projection of RAB shares. This circumstance is most likely to occur when the CSA is a long-term arrangement, the arrangement covers a wide variety of intangibles, the composition of the cost shared intangibles is unlikely to change, the cost shared intangibles are unlikely to generate unusual profits, and each controlled participant's share of the market is stable.

(B) Examples. The following examples illustrate the principles of this paragraph (e)(2)(iii):

*Example (1).* (i) Foreign Parent (FP) and U.S. Subsidiary (USS) enter into a CSA to develop a new car model. The controlled participants plan to spend four years developing the new model and four years producing and selling the new model. USS and FP project total sales of $4 billion and $2 billion, respectively, over the planned four years of exploitation of the new model. The controlled participants determine RAB shares for each year of 66⅔% for USS and 33⅓% for FP, based on projected total sales.

(ii) USS typically begins producing and selling new car models a year after FP begins producing and selling new car models. In order to reflect USS's one-year lag in introducing new car models, a more reliable projection of each participant's RAB share would be based on a projection of all four years of sales for each participant, discounted to present value.

*Example (2).* U.S. Parent (USP) and Foreign Subsidiary (FS) enter into a CSA to develop new and improved household cleaning products. Both controlled participants have sold household cleaning products for many years and have stable worldwide market shares. The products under development are unlikely to produce unusual profits for either controlled participant. The controlled participants determine RAB shares on the basis of each controlled participant's current sales of household cleaning products. In this case, the controlled participants' RAB shares are reliably projected by current sales of cleaning products.

*Example (3).* The facts are the same as in Example 2, except that FS's market share is rapidly expanding because of the business failure of a competitor in its geographic area. The controlled participants' RAB shares are not reliably projected by current sales of cleaning products. FS's benefit projections should take into account its growth in market share.

*Example (4).* Foreign Parent (FP) and U.S. Subsidiary (USS) enter into a CSA to develop synthetic fertilizers and insecticides. FP and USS share costs on the basis of each controlled participant's current sales of fertilizers and insecticides. The market shares of the controlled participants have been stable for fertilizers, but FP's market share for insecticides has been expanding. The controlled participants' projections of RAB shares are reliable with regard to fertilizers, but not reliable with regard to insecticides; a more reliable projection of RAB shares would take into account the expanding market share for insecticides.

**(f) Changes in participation under a CSA.** *(1) In general.* A change in participation under a CSA occurs when there is either a controlled transfer of interests or a capability variation. A change in participation requires arm's length consideration under paragraph (a)(3)(ii) of this section, and as more fully described in this paragraph (f).

*(2) Controlled transfer of interests.* A controlled transfer of interests occurs when a participant in a CSA transfers all or part of its interests in cost shared intangibles under the CSA in a controlled transaction, and the transferee assumes the associated obligations under the CSA. After the controlled transfer of interests occurs, the CSA will still exist if at least two controlled participants still have interests in the cost shared intangibles. In such a case, the transferee will be treated as succeeding to the transferor's prior history under the CSA as pertains to the transferred interests, including the transferor's cost contributions, benefits derived, and PCT Payments attributable to such rights or obligations. A transfer that would otherwise constitute a controlled transfer of interests for purposes of this paragraph (f)(2) shall not constitute a controlled transfer of interests if it also constitutes a capability variation for purposes of paragraph (f)(3) of this section.

*(3) Capability variation.* A capability variation occurs when, in a CSA in which interests in cost shared intangibles are divided as described in paragraph (b)(4)(iv) of this section, the controlled participants' division of interests or their relative capabilities or capacities to benefit from the cost shared intangibles are materially altered. For purposes of paragraph (a)(3)(ii) of this section, a capability variation is considered to be a controlled transfer of interests in cost shared intangibles, in which any controlled participant whose RAB share decreases as a result of the capability variation is a transferor, and any controlled participant whose RAB share thus increases is the transferee of the interests in cost shared intangibles.

*(4) Arm's length consideration for a change in participation.* In the event of a change in participation, the arm's length amount of consideration from the transferee, under the rules of §§ 1.482-1 and 1.482-4 through 1.482-6 and paragraph (a)(3)(ii) of this section, will be determined consistent with the reasonably anticipated incremental change in the returns to the transferee and transferor resulting from such change in participation. Such changes in returns will themselves depend on the reasonably anticipated incremental changes in the benefits from exploiting the cost shared intangibles, IDCs borne, and PCT Payments (if any). However, any arm's length consideration required under this paragraph (f)(4) with respect to a capability variation shall be reduced as necessary to prevent duplication of an adjustment already performed under paragraph (i)(2)(ii)(A) of this section that resulted from the same capability variation. If an adjustment has been performed already under this paragraph (f)(4) with respect to a capability variation, then for purposes of any adjustment to be performed under paragraph (i)(2)(ii)(A) of this section, the controlled participants' projected benefit shares referred to in paragraph (i)(2)(ii)(A) of this section shall be considered to be the controlled participants' respective RAB shares after the capability variation occurred.

*(5) Examples.* The following examples illustrate the principles of this paragraph (f):

*Example (1).* X, Y, and Z are the only controlled participants in a CSA. The CSA divides interests in cost shared intangibles on a territorial basis as described in paragraph (b)(4)(ii) of this section. X is assigned the territories of the Americas, Y is assigned the territory of the UK and Australia, and Z is assigned the rest of the world. When the CSA is formed, X has a platform contribution T. Under the PCTs for T, Y, and Z are each obligated to pay X royalties equal to five percent of their respective sales. Aside from T, there are no platform contributions. Two years after the formation of the CSA, Y transfers to Z its interest in cost shared intangibles relating to the UK territory, and the associated obligations, in a controlled transfer of interests described in paragraph (f)(2) of this section. At that time the reasonably anticipated benefits from exploiting cost shared intangibles in the UK have a present value of $11M, the reasonably anticipated IDCs to be borne relating to the UK territory have a present value of $3M, and the reasonably anticipated PCT Payments to be made to X relating to sales in the UK territory have a present value of $2M. As arm's length consideration for the change in participation due to the controlled transfer of interests, Z must pay Y compensation with an anticipated present value of $11M, less $3M, less $2M, which equals $6M.

*Example (2).* As in Example 2 of paragraph (b)(4)(v) of this section, companies P and S, both members of the same controlled group, enter into a CSA to develop product Z. P and S agree to divide their interest in product Z based on site of manufacturing. P will have exclusive and perpetual rights in product Z manufactured in facilities owned by P. S will have exclusive and perpetual rights to product Z manufactured in facilities owned by S. P and S agree that neither will license manufacturing rights in product Z to any related or unrelated party. Both P and S maintain books and records that allow production at all sites to be verified. Both own facilities that will manufacture product Z and the relative capacities of these sites are known. All facilities are currently operating at near capacity and are expected to continue to operate at near capacity when product Z enters production so that it will not be feasible to shift production between P's and S's facilities. P and S have no plans to build new facilities and the lead time required to plan and build a manufacturing facility precludes the possibility that P or S will build a new facility during the period for which sales of Product Z are expected. When the CSA is formed, P has a platform contribution T. Under the PCT for T, S is obligated to pay P sales-based royalties according to a certain formula. Aside from T, there are no other platform contributions. Two years after the formation of the CSA, owing to a change in plans not reasonably foreseeable at the time the CSA was entered into, S acquires additional facilities F for the manufacture of Product Z. Such acquisition constitutes a capability variation described in paragraph (f)(3) of this section. Under this capability variation, S's RAB share increases from 50% to 60%. Accordingly, there is a compensable change in participation under paragraph (f)(3) of this section.

**(g) Supplemental guidance on methods applicable to PCTs.** *(1) In general.* This paragraph (g) provides supplemental guidance on applying the methods listed in this paragraph (g)(1) for purposes of evaluating the arm's length amount charged in a PCT. Each method will yield a value for the compensation obligation of each PCT Payor consistent with the product of the combined pre-tax value to all controlled participants of the platform contribution that is the subject of the PCT and the PCT Payor's RAB share. The methods are--

(i) The comparable uncontrolled transaction method described in § 1.482-4(c), or the comparable uncontrolled services price method described in § 1.482-9T(c), as further described in paragraph (g)(3) of this section;

(ii) The income method, described in paragraph (g)(4) of this section;

(iii) The acquisition price method, described in paragraph (g)(5) of this section;

(iv) The market capitalization method, described in paragraph (g)(6) of this section;

(v) The residual profit split method, described in paragraph (g)(7) of this section; and

(vi) Unspecified methods, described in paragraph (g)(8) of this section.

*(2) Best method analysis applicable for evaluation of a PCT pursuant to a CSA.* (i) In general. Each method must be applied in accordance with the provisions of § 1.482-1, including the best method rule of § 1.482-1(c), the comparability analysis of § 1.482-1(d), and the arm's length range of § 1.482-1(e), except as those provisions are modified in this paragraph (g).

(ii) Consistency with upfront contractual terms and risk allocation--the investor model. (A) In general. Although all of the factors entering into a best method analysis described in § 1.482-1(c) and (d) must be considered, specific factors may be particularly relevant in the context of a CSA. In particular, the relative reliability of an application of any method depends on the degree of consistency of the analysis with the applicable contractual terms and allocation of risk under the CSA and this section among the controlled participants as of the date of the PCT, unless a change in such terms or allocation has been made in return for arm's length consideration. In this regard, a CSA involves an upfront division of the risks as to both reasonably anticipated obligations and reasonably anticipated benefits over the reasonably anticipated term of the CSA Activity. Accordingly, the relative reliability of an application of a method also depends on the degree of consistency of the analysis with the assumption that, as of the date of the PCT, each controlled participant's aggregate net investment in the CSA Activity (attributable to platform contributions, operating contributions, as such term is defined in paragraph (j)(1)(i) of this section, operating cost contributions, as such term is defined in paragraph (j)(1)(i) of this section, and cost contributions) is reasonably anticipated to earn a rate of return equal to the appropriate discount rate for the controlled participant's CSA Activity over the entire period of such CSA Activity. If the cost shared intangibles themselves are reasonably anticipated to contribute to developing other intangibles, then the period described in the preceding sentence includes the period, reasonably anticipated as of the date of the PCT, of developing and exploiting such indirectly benefited intangibles.

(B) Example. The following example illustrates the principles of this paragraph (g)(2)(ii):

*Example.* (i) P, a U.S. corporation, has developed a software program, DEF, which applies certain algorithms to reconstruct complete DNA sequences from partially-observed DNA sequences. S is a wholly-owned foreign subsidiary of P. On the first day of Year 1, P and S enter into a CSA to develop a new generation of genetic tests, GHI, based in part on the use of DEF. DEF is therefore a platform contribution of P for which compensation is due from S pursuant to a PCT. S makes no platform contributions to the CSA. Sales of GHI are projected to commence two years after the inception of the CSA and then to continue for eight more years. Based on industry experience, P and S are confident that GHI will be replaced by a new type of genetic testing based on technology unrelated to DEF or GHI and that, at that point, GHI will have no further value. P and S project that that replacement will occur at the end of Year 10.

(ii) For purposes of valuing the PCT for P's platform contribution of DEF to the CSA, P and S apply a type of residual profit split method that is not described in paragraph (g)(7) of this section and which, accordingly, constitutes an unspecified method. See paragraph (g)(7)(i) (last sentence) of this section. The principles of this paragraph (g)(2) apply to any method for valuing a PCT, including the unspecified method used by P and S.

(iii) Under the method employed by P and S, in each year, a portion of the income from sales of GHI in S's territory is allocated to certain routine contributions made by S. The residual of the profit or loss from GHI sales in S's territory after the routine allocation step is divided between P and S pro rata to their capital stocks allocable to S's territory. Each controlled participant's capital stock is computed by capitalizing, applying a capital growth factor to, and amortizing its historical expenditures regarding DEF allocable to S's territory (in the case of P), or its ongoing cost contributions towards developing GHI (in the case of S). The amortization of the capital stocks is effected on a straight-line basis over an assumed four-year life for the relevant expenditures. The capital stocks are grown using an assumed growth factor that P and S consider to be appropriate.

(iv) The assumption that all expenditures amortize on a straight-line basis over four years does not appropriately reflect the principle that as of the date of the PCT regarding DEF, every contribution to the development of GHI, including DEF, is reasonably anticipated to have value throughout the entire period of exploitation of GHI which is projected to continue through Year 10. Under this method as applied by P and S, the share of the residual profit in S's territory that is allocated to P as a PCT Payment from S will decrease every year. After Year 4, P's capital stock in DEF will necessarily be $0, so that P will receive none of the residual profit or loss from GHI sales in S's territory after Year 4 as a PCT Payment.

(v) As a result of this limitation of the PCT Payments to be made by S, the anticipated return to S's aggregate investment in the CSA, over the whole period of S's CSA Activity, is at a rate that is significantly higher than the appropriate discount rate for S's CSA Activity (as determined by a reliable method). This discrepancy is not consistent with the investor model principle that S should anticipate a rate of return to its aggregate investment in the CSA, over the whole period of its CSA Activity, equal to the appropriate discount rate for its CSA Activity. The inconsistency of the method with the investor model materially lessens its reliability for purposes of a best method analysis. See § 1.482-1(c)(2)(ii)(B).

(iii) Consistency of evaluation with realistic alternatives. (A) In general. The relative reliability of an application of a method also depends on the degree of consistency of the analysis with the assumption that uncontrolled taxpayers dealing at arm's length would have evaluated the terms of the transaction, and only entered into such transaction, if no alternative is preferable. This condition is not met, therefore, where for any controlled participant the total anticipated present value of its income attributable to its entering into the CSA, as of the date of the PCT, is less than the total anticipated present value of its income that could be achieved through an alternative arrangement realistically available to that controlled participant. In principle, this comparison is made on a post-tax basis but, in many cases, a comparison made on a pre-tax basis will yield equivalent results. See also paragraph (g)(2)(v)(B)(1) of this section (Discount rate variation between realistic alternatives).

(B) Examples. The following examples illustrate the principles of this paragraph (g)(2)(iii):

*Example (1).* (i) P, a corporation, and S, a wholly owned subsidiary of P, enter into a CSA to develop a personal transportation device (the product). Under the arrangement, P will undertake all of the R&D, and manufacture and market the product in Country X. S will make CST Payments to P for its appropriate share of P's R&D costs, and manufacture and market the product in the rest of the world. P owns existing patents and trade secrets that are reasonably anticipated to contribute to the development of the product. Therefore the rights in the patents and trade secrets are platform contributions for which compensation is due from S as part of a PCT.

(ii) S's manufacturing and distribution activities under the CSA will be routine in nature, and identical to the activities it would undertake if it alternatively licensed the product from P.

(iii) Reasonably reliable estimates indicate that P could develop the product without assistance from S and license the product outside of Country X for a royalty of 20% of sales. Based on reliable financial projections that include all future development costs and licensing revenue that are allocable to the non-Country X market, and using a discount rate appropriate for the riskiness of P's role as a licensor (see paragraph (g)(2)(v) of this section), the post-tax present value of this licensing alternative to P for the non-Country X market (measured as of the date of the PCT) would be $500 million. Thus, based on this realistic alternative, the anticipated post-tax present value under the CSA to P in the non-Country X market (measured as of the date of the PCT), taking into account anticipated development costs allocable to the non-Country X market, and anticipated CST Payments and PCT Payments from S, and using a discount rate appropriate for the riskiness of P's role as a participant in the CSA, should not be less than $500 million.

*Example (2).* (i) The facts are the same as in Example 1, except that there are no reliable estimates of the value to P from the licensing alternative to the CSA. Further, reasonably reliable estimates indicate that an arm's length return for S's routine manufacturing and distribution activities is a 10% mark-up on total costs of goods sold plus operating expenses related to those activities. Finally, the Commissioner determines that the respective activities undertaken by P and S (other than licensing payments, CST Payments, and PCT Payments) would be identical regardless of whether the arrangement was undertaken as a CSA (CSA Scenario) or as a long-term licensing arrangement (Licensing Scenario). In particular, in both Scenarios, P would perform all research activities and S would undertake routine manufacturing and distribution activities associated with its territory.

(ii) P undertakes an economic analysis that derives S's cost contributions under the CSA, based on reliable financial projections. Based on this and further economic analysis, P determines S's PCT Payment as a certain lump sum amount to be paid as of the date of the PCT (Date D).

(iii) Based on reliable financial projections that include S's cost contributions and that incorporate S's PCT Payment, as computed by P, and using a discount rate appropriate for the riskiness of S's role as a CSA participant (see paragraph (g)(2)(v) of this section), the anticipated post-tax net present value to S in the CSA Scenario (measured as of Date D) is $800 million. Further, based on these same reliable projections (but incorporating S's licensing payments instead of S's cost contributions and PCT Payment), and using a discount rate appropriate for the riskiness of S's role as a long-term licensee, the anticipated post-tax net present value to S in the Licensing Scenario (measured as of Date D) is $100 million. Thus, S's anticipated post-tax net present value is $700 million greater in the CSA Scenario than in the Licensing Scenario. This result suggests that P's anticipated post-tax present value must be significantly less under the CSA Scenario than under the Licensing Scenario. This means that the reliability of P's analysis as described in paragraph (ii) of this Example 2 is reduced, since P would not be expected to enter into a cost sharing arrangement if its alternative of being a long-term licensor is preferable.

*Example (3).* (i) The facts are the same as in paragraphs (i) and (ii) of Example 2. In addition, based on reliable financial projections that include S's cost contributions and S's PCT Payment, and using a discount rate appropriate for the riskiness of S's role as a CSA participant, the anticipated post-tax net present value to S under the CSA (measured as of the date of the PCT) is $50 million. Also, instead of entering the CSA, S has the realistic alternative of manufacturing and distributing product Z unrelated to the personal transportation device, with the same anticipated 10% markup on total costs that it would anticipate for its routine activities in Example 2. Under its realistic alternative, at a discount rate appropriate for the riskiness of S's role with respect to product Z, S anticipates a present value of $100 million.

(ii) Because the lump sum PCT Payment made by S results in S having a considerably lower anticipated net present value than S could achieve through an alternative arrangement realistically available to it, the reliability of P's calculation of the lump sum PCT Payment is reduced.

(iv) Aggregation of transactions. The combined effect of multiple contemporaneous transactions, consisting either of multiple PCTs, or of one or more PCT and one or more other transactions in connection with a CSA that are not governed by this section (such as transactions involving cross operating contributions or make-or-sell rights), may require evaluation in accordance with the principles of aggregation described in § 1.482-1(f)(2)(i). In such cases, it may be that the multiple transactions are reasonably anticipated, as of the date of the PCT(s), to be so interrelated that the method that provides the most reliable measure of an arm's length charge is a method under this section applied on an aggregate basis for the PCT(s) and other transactions. A section 482 adjustment may be made by comparing the aggregate arm's length charge so determined to the aggregate payments actually made for the multiple transactions. In such a case, it generally will not be necessary to allocate separately the aggregate arm's length charge as between various PCTs or as between PCTs and such other transactions. However, such an allocation may be necessary for other purposes, such as applying paragraph (i)(6) (Periodic adjustments) of this section. An aggregate determination of the arm's length charge for multiple transactions will often yield a payment for a controlled participant that is equal to the aggregate value of the platform contributions and other resources, capabilities, and rights covered by the multiple transactions multiplied by that controlled participant's RAB share. Because RAB shares only include benefits from cost shared intangibles, the reliability of an aggregate determination of payments for multiple transactions may be reduced to the extent that it includes transactions covering resources, capabilities, and rights for which the controlled participants' expected benefit shares differ substantially from their RAB shares.

(v) Discount rate. (A) In general. The best method analysis in connection with certain methods or forms of payment may depend on a rate or rates of return used to convert projected results of transactions to present value, or to otherwise convert monetary amounts at one or more points in time to equivalent amounts at a different point or points in time. For this purpose, a discount rate or rates should be used that most reliably reflect the market-correlated risks of activities or transactions and should be applied to the best estimates of the relevant projected results, based on all the information potentially available at the time for which the present value calculation is to be performed. Depending on the particular facts and circumstances, the market-correlated risk involved and thus, the discount rate, may differ among a company's various activities or transactions. Normally, discount rates are most reliably determined by reference to market information.

(B) Considerations in best method analysis of discount rate. (1) Discount rate variation between realistic alternatives. Realistic alternatives may involve varying risk exposure and, thus, may be more reliably evaluated using different discount rates. In some circumstances, a party may have less risk as a licensee of intangibles needed in its operations, and so require a lower discount rate, than it would have by entering into a CSA to develop such intangibles, which may involve the party's assumption of additional risk in funding its cost contributions to the IDA. Similarly, self-development of intangibles and licensing out may be riskier for the licensor, and so require a higher discount rate, than entering into a CSA to develop such intangibles, which would relieve the licensor of the obligation to fund a portion of the IDCs of the IDA.

(2) Discount rate variation between forms of payment. Certain forms of payment may involve different risks than others. For example, ordinarily a royalty computed on a profits base would be more volatile, and so require a higher discount rate to discount projected payments to present value, than a royalty computed on a sales base.

(3) Post-tax rate. In general, discount rate estimates that may be inferred from the operations of the capital markets are post-tax discount rates. Therefore, an analysis would in principle apply post-tax discount rates to income net of expense items including taxes (post-tax income). However, in certain circumstances the result of applying a post-tax discount rate to post-tax income is equivalent to the product of--

(i) The result of applying a post-tax discount rate to income net of expense items other than taxes (pre-tax income); and

(ii) The difference of one minus the tax rate.

Therefore, in such circumstances, calculation of pre-tax income, rather than post-tax income, may be sufficient. See, for example, paragraph (g)(4)(i)(G) of this section.

(C) Example. The following example illustrates the principles of this paragraph (g)(2)(v):

*Example.* (i) P and S form a CSA to develop intangible X, which will be used in product Y. P will develop X, and S will make CST Payments as its cost contributions. At the start of the CSA, P has a platform contribution, for which S commits to make a PCT Payment of 5% of its sales of product Y. As part of the evaluation of whether that PCT Payment is arm's length, the Commissioner considers whether P had a more favorable realistic alternative (see paragraph (g)(2)(iii) of this section). Specifically, the Commissioner compares P's anticipated post-tax discounted present value of the financial projections under the CSA (taking into account S's PCT Payment of 5% of its sales of product Y) with P's anticipated post-tax discounted present value of the financial projections under a reasonably available alternative Licensing Arrangement that consists of developing intangible X on its own and then licensing X to S or to an uncontrolled party similar to S. In undertaking the analysis, the Commissioner determines that, because it would be funding the entire development of the intangible, P undertakes greater risks in the licensing scenario than in the cost sharing scenario (in the cost sharing scenario P would be funding only part of the development of the intangible).

(ii) The Commissioner determines that, as between the two scenarios, all of the components of P's anticipated financial flows are identical, except for the CST and PCT Payments under the CSA, compared to the licensing payments under the Licensing Alternative. Accordingly, the Commissioner concludes that the differences in market-correlated risks between the two scenarios, and therefore the differences in discount rates between the two scenarios, relate to the differences in these components of the financial projections.

(vi) Financial projections. The reliability of an estimate of the value of a platform or operating contribution in connection with a PCT will often depend upon the reliability of projections used in making the estimate. Such projections should reflect the best estimates of the items projected (normally reflecting a probability weighted average of possible outcomes). Projections necessary for this purpose may include a projection of sales, IDCs, costs of developing operating contributions, routine operating expenses, and costs of sales. Some method applications directly estimate projections of items attributable to separate development and exploitation by the controlled participants within their respective divisions. Other method applications indirectly estimate projections of items from the perspective of the controlled group as a whole, rather than from the perspective of a particular participant, and then apportion the items so estimated on some assumed basis. For example, in some applications, sales might be directly projected by division, but worldwide projections of other items such as operating expenses might be apportioned among divisions in the same ratio as the divisions' respective sales. Which approach is more reliable depends on which provides the most reliable measure of an arm's length result, considering the competing perspectives under the facts and circumstances in light of the completeness and accuracy of the underlying data, the reliability of the assumptions, and the sensitivity of the results to possible deficiencies in the data and assumptions. For these purposes, projections that have been prepared for non-tax purposes are generally more reliable than projections that have been prepared solely for purposes of meeting the requirements in this paragraph (g).

(vii) Accounting principles. (A) In general. Allocations or other valuations done for accounting purposes may provide a useful starting point but will not be conclusive for purposes of the best method analysis in evaluating the arm's length charge in a PCT, particularly where the accounting treatment of an asset is inconsistent with its economic value.

(B) Examples. The following examples illustrate the principles of this paragraph (g)(2)(vii):

*Example (1).* (i) USP, a U.S. corporation and FSub, a wholly owned foreign subsidiary of USP, enter into a CSA in Year 1 to develop software programs with application in the medical field. Company X is an uncontrolled software company located in the United States that is engaged in developing software programs that could significantly enhance the programs being developed by USP and FSub. Company X is still in a startup phase, so it has no currently exploitable products or marketing intangibles and its workforce consists of a team of software developers. Company X has negligible liabilities and tangible property. In Year 2, USP purchases Company X as part of an uncontrolled transaction in order to acquire its in-process technology and workforce for purposes of the development activities of the CSA. USP files a consolidated return that includes Company X. For accounting purposes, $50 million of the $100 million acquisition price is allocated to the in-process technology and workforce, and the residual $50 million is allocated to goodwill.

(ii) The in-process technology and workforce of Company X acquired by USP are reasonably anticipated to contribute to developing cost shared intangibles and therefore the rights in the in-process technology and workforce of Company X are platform contributions for which FSub must compensate USP as part of a PCT. In determining whether to apply the acquisition price or another method for purposes of evaluating the arm's length charge in the PCT, relevant best method analysis considerations must be weighed in light of the general principles of paragraph (g)(2) of this section. The allocation for accounting purposes raises an issue as to the reliability of using the acquisition price method in this case because it suggests that a significant portion of the value of Company X's nonroutine contributions to USP's business activities is allocable to goodwill, which is often difficult to value reliably and which, depending on the facts and circumstances, might not be attributable to platform contributions that are to be compensated by PCTs. See paragraph (g)(5)(iv)(A) of this section.

(iii) This paragraph (g)(2)(vii) provides that accounting treatment may be a starting point, but is not determinative for purposes of assessing or applying methods to evaluate the arm's length charge in a PCT. The facts here reveal that Company X has nothing of economic value aside from its in-process technology and assembled workforce. The $50 million of the acquisition price allocated to goodwill for accounting purposes, therefore, is economically attributable to either of, or both, the in-process technology and the workforce. That moots the potential issue under the acquisition price method of the reliability of valuation of assets not to be compensated by PCTs, since there are no such assets. Assuming the acquisition price method is otherwise the most reliable method, the aggregate value of Company X's in-process technology and workforce is the full acquisition price of $100 million (subject to possible adjustment for differences in tax liabilities of the type described in paragraph (g)(5)(ii) of this section). Accordingly, the aggregate value of the arm's length PCT Payments due from FSub to USP for the platform contributions consisting of the rights in Company X's in-process technology and workforce will equal $100 million (subject to adjustment as per paragraph (g)(5)(ii) of this section) multiplied by FSub's RAB share.

*Example (2).* (i) The facts are the same as in Example 1, except that Company X is a mature software business in the United States with a successful current generation of software that it markets under a recognized trademark, in addition to having the research team and new generation software in process that could significantly enhance the programs being developed under USP's and FSub's CSA. USP continues Company X's existing business and integrates the research team and the in-process technology into the efforts under its CSA with FSub. For accounting purposes, the $100 million price for acquiring Company X is allocated $50 million to existing software and trademark, $25 million to in-process technology and research workforce, and the residual $25 million to goodwill and going concern value.

(ii) In this case an analysis of the facts indicates a likelihood that, consistent with the allocation under the accounting treatment (although not necessarily in the same amount), a significant amount of the nonroutine contributions to the USP's business activities consist of goodwill and going concern value economically attributable to the existing U.S. software business rather than to the platform contributions consisting of the rights in the in-process technology and research workforce. In addition, an analysis of the facts indicates that a significant amount of the nonroutine contributions to USP's business activities consist of the make-or-sell rights under the existing software and trademark, which are not platform contributions and might be difficult to value. Accordingly, further consideration must be given to the extent to which these circumstances reduce the relative reliability of the acquisition price method in comparison to other potentially applicable methods for evaluating the PCT Payment.

*Example (3).* (i) USP, a U.S. corporation, and FSub, a wholly-owned foreign subsidiary of USP, enter into a CSA in Year 1 to develop Product A. Company Y is an uncontrolled corporation that owns Technology X, which is critical to the development of Product A. Company Y currently markets Product B, which is dependent on Technology X. USP is solely interested in acquiring Technology X, but is only able to do so through the acquisition of Company Y in its entirety for $200 million in an uncontrolled transaction in Year 2. For accounting purposes, the acquisition price is allocated as follows: $120 million to Product B and the underlying Technology X, $30 million to trademark and other marketing intangibles, and the residual $50 million to goodwill and going concern value. After the acquisition of Company Y, Technology X is used to develop Product A. No other part of Company Y is used in any manner. Immediately after the acquisition, product B is discontinued, and, therefore, the accompanying marketing intangibles become worthless. None of the previous employees of Company Y is retained.

(ii) The Technology X of Company Y acquired by USP is reasonably anticipated to contribute to developing cost shared intangibles and is therefore a platform contribution for which FSub must compensate USP as part of a PCT. Although for accounting purposes a significant portion of the acquisition price of Company Y was allocated to items other than Technology X, the facts demonstrate that USP had no intention of using and therefore placed no economic value on any part of Company Y other than Technology X. If USP was willing to pay $200 million for Company Y solely for purposes of acquiring Technology X, then assuming the acquisition price method is otherwise the most reliable method, the value of Technology X is the full $200 million acquisition price. Accordingly, the value of the arm's length PCT Payment due from FSub to USP for the platform contribution consisting of the rights in Technology X will equal the product of $200 million (subject to adjustment as described in paragraph (g)(5)(ii) of this section) and FSub's RAB share.

(viii) Valuations of subsequent PCTs. (A) Date of subsequent PCT. The date of a PCT may occur subsequent to the inception of the CSA. For example, an intangible initially developed outside the IDA may only subsequently become a platform contribution because that later time is the earliest date on which it is reasonably anticipated to contribute to developing cost shared intangibles within the IDA. In such case, the date of the PCT, and the analysis of the arm's length amount charged in the subsequent PCT, is as of such later time.

(B) Best method analysis for subsequent PCT. In cases where PCTs occur on different dates, the determination of the arm's length amount charged, respectively, in the prior and subsequent PCTs must be coordinated in a manner that provides the most reliable measure of an arm's length result. In some circumstances, a subsequent PCT may be reliably evaluated independently of other PCTs, as may be possible for example, under the acquisition price method. In other circumstances, the results of prior and subsequent PCTs may be interrelated and so a subsequent PCT may be most reliably evaluated under the residual profit split method of paragraph (g)(7) of this section. In those cases, for purposes of allocating the present value of nonroutine residual divisional profit or loss, and so determining the present value of the subsequent PCT Payments, in accordance with paragraph (g)(7)(iii)(C) of this section, the PCT Payor's interest in cost shared intangibles, both already developed and in process, are treated as additional PCT Payor operating contributions as of the date of the subsequent PCT.

(ix) Arm's length range. (A) In general. The guidance in § 1.482-1(e) regarding determination of an arm's length range, as modified by this section, applies in evaluating the arm's length amount charged in a PCT under a transfer pricing method provided in this section (applicable method). Section 1.482-1(e)(2)(i) provides that the arm's length range is ordinarily determined by applying a single pricing method selected under the best method rule to two or more uncontrolled transactions of similar comparability and reliability although use of more than one method may be appropriate for the purposes described in § 1.482-1(c)(2)(iii). The rules provided in § 1.482-1(e) and this section for determining an arm's length range shall not override the rules provided in paragraph (i)(6) of this section for periodic adjustments by the Commissioner. The provisions in paragraphs (g)(2)(ix)(C) and (D) of this section apply only to applicable methods that are based on two or more input parameters as described in paragraph (g)(2)(ix)(B) of this section. For an example of how the rules of this section for determining an arm's length range of PCT Payments are applied, see paragraph (g)(4)(vii) of this section.

(B) Methods based on two or more input parameters. An applicable method may determine PCT Payments based on calculations involving two or more parameters whose values depend on the facts and circumstances of the case (input parameters). For some input parameters (market-based input parameters), the value is most reliably determined by reference to data that derives from uncontrolled transactions (market data). For example, the value of the return to a controlled participant's routine contributions, as such term is defined in paragraph (j)(1)(i) of this section, to the CSA Activity (which value is used as an input parameter in the income method described in paragraph (g)(4) of this section) may in some cases be most reliably determined by reference to the profit level of a company with rights, resources, and capabilities comparable to those routine contributions. See § 1.482-5. As another example, the value for the discount rate that reflects the riskiness of a controlled participant's role in the CSA (which value is used as an input parameter in the income method described in paragraph (g)(4) of this section) may in some cases be most reliably determined by reference to the stock beta of a company whose overall risk is comparable to the riskiness of the controlled participant's role in the CSA.

(C) Variable input parameters. For some market-based input parameters (variable input parameters), the parameter's value is most reliably determined by considering two or more observations of market data that have, or with adjustment can be brought to, a similar reliability and comparability, as described in § 1.482-1(e)(2)(ii) (for example, profit levels or stock betas of two or more companies). See paragraph (g)(2)(ix)(B) of this section.

(D) Determination of arm's length PCT Payment. For purposes of applying this paragraph (g)(2)(ix), each input parameter is assigned a single most reliable value, unless it is a variable input parameter as described in paragraph (g)(2)(ix)(C) of this section. The determination of the arm's length payment depends on the number of variable input parameters.

(1) No variable input parameters. If there are no variable input parameters, the arm's length PCT Payment is a single value determined by using the single most reliable value determined for each input parameter.

(2) One variable input parameter. If there is exactly one variable input parameter, then under the applicable method, the arm's length range of PCT Payments is the interquartile range, as described in § 1.482-1(e)(2)(iii)(C), of the set of PCT Payment values calculated by selecting--

(i) Iteratively, the value of the variable input parameter that is based on each observation as described in paragraph (g)(2)(ix)(C) of this section; and

(ii) The single most reliable values for each other input parameter.

(3) More than one variable input parameter. If there are two or more variable input parameters, then under the applicable method, the arm's length range of PCT Payments is the interquartile range, as described in § 1.482-1(e)(2)(iii)(C), of the set of PCT Payment values calculated iteratively using every possible combination of permitted choices of values for the input parameters. For input parameters other than a variable input parameter, the only such permitted choice is the single most reliable value. For variable input parameters, such permitted choices include any value that is--

(i) Based on one of the observations described in paragraph (g)(2)(ix)(C) of this section; and

(ii) Within the interquartile range (as described in § 1.482-1(e)(2)(iii)(C)) of the set of all values so based.

(E) Adjustments. Section 1.482-1(e)(3), applied as modified by this paragraph (g)(2)(ix), determines when the Commissioner may make an adjustment to a PCT Payment due to the taxpayer's results being outside the arm's length range. Adjustment will be to the median, as defined in § 1.482-1(e)(3). Thus, the Commissioner is not required to establish an arm's length range prior to making an allocation under section 482.

(x) Valuation undertaken on a pre-tax basis. PCT Payments in general may increase the PCT Payee's tax liability and decrease the PCT Payor's tax liability. The arm's length amount of a PCT Payment determined under the methods in this paragraph (g) is the value of the PCT Payment itself, without regard to such tax effects. Therefore, the methods under this section must be applied, with suitable adjustments if needed, to determine the PCT Payments on a pre-tax basis. See paragraphs (g)(2)(v)(B)(3), (g)(4)(i)(G), (g)(5)(ii), and (g)(6)(ii) of this section.

*(3) Comparable uncontrolled transaction method.* The comparable uncontrolled transaction (CUT) method described in § 1.482-4(c), and the comparable uncontrolled services price (CUSP) method described in § 1.482-9T(c), may be applied to evaluate whether the amount charged in a PCT is arm's length by reference to the amount charged in a comparable uncontrolled transaction. Although all of the factors entering into a best method analysis described in § 1.482-1(c) and (d) must be considered, comparability and reliability under this method are particularly dependent on similarity of contractual terms, degree to which allocation of risks is proportional to reasonably anticipated benefits from exploiting the results of intangible development, similar period of commitment as to the sharing of intangible development risks, and similar scope, uncertainty, and profit potential of the subject intangible development, including a similar allocation of the risks of any existing resources, capabilities, or rights, as well as of the risks of developing other resources, capabilities, or rights that would be reasonably anticipated to contribute to exploitation within the parties' divisions, that is consistent with the actual allocation of risks between the controlled participants as provided in the CSA in accordance with this section. When applied in the manner described in § 1.482-4(c) or 1.482-9T(c), the CUT or CUSP method will typically yield an arm's length total value for the platform contribution that is the subject of the PCT. That value must then be multiplied by each PCT Payor's respective RAB share in order to determine the arm's length PCT Payment due from each PCT Payor. The reliability of a CUT or CUSP that yields a value for the platform contribution only in the PCT Payor's division will be reduced to the extent that value is not consistent with the total worldwide value of the platform contribution multiplied by the PCT Payor's RAB share.

*(4) Income method.* (i) In general. (A) Equating cost sharing and licensing alternatives. The income method evaluates whether the amount charged in a PCT is arm's length by reference to a controlled participant's best realistic alternative to entering into a CSA. Under this method, the arm's length charge for a PCT Payment will be an amount such that a controlled participant's present value, as of the date of the PCT, of its cost sharing alternative of entering into a CSA equals the present value of its best realistic alternative. In general, the best realistic alternative of the PCT Payor to entering into the CSA would be to license intangibles to be developed by an uncontrolled licensor that undertakes the commitment to bear the entire risk of intangible development that would otherwise have been shared under the CSA. Similarly, the best realistic alternative of the PCT Payee to entering into the CSA would be to undertake the commitment to bear the entire risk of intangible development that would otherwise have been shared under the CSA and license the resulting intangibles to an uncontrolled licensee. Paragraphs (g)(4)(ii) through (iv) of this section describe specific applications of the income method, but do not exclude other possible applications of this method.

(B) Cost sharing alternative. The PCT Payor's cost sharing alternative corresponds to the actual CSA in accordance with this section, with the PCT Payor's obligation to make the PCT Payments to be determined and its commitment for the duration of the IDA to bear cost contributions.

(C) Licensing alternative. The licensing alternative is derived on the basis of a functional and risk analysis of the cost sharing alternative, but with a shift of the risk of cost contributions to the licensor. Accordingly, the PCT Payor's licensing alternative consists of entering into a license with an uncontrolled party, for a term extending for what would be the duration of the CSA Activity, to license the make-or-sell rights in to-be-developed resources, capabilities, or rights of the licensor. Under such license, the licensor would undertake the commitment to bear the entire risk of intangible development that would otherwise have been shared under the CSA. Apart from any difference in the allocation of the risks of the IDA, the licensing alternative should assume contractual provisions with regard to non-overlapping divisional intangible interests, and with regard to allocations of other risks, that are consistent with the actual CSA in accordance with this section. For example, the analysis under the licensing alternative should assume a similar allocation of the risks of any existing resources, capabilities, or rights, as well as of the risks of developing other resources, capabilities, or rights that would be reasonably anticipated to contribute to exploitation within the parties' divisions, that is consistent with the actual allocation of risks between the controlled participants as provided in the CSA in accordance with this section.

(D) Only one controlled participant with nonroutine platform contributions. This method involves only one of the controlled participants providing nonroutine platform contributions as the PCT Payee. For a method under which more than one controlled participant may be a PCT Payee, see the application of the residual profit method pursuant to paragraph (g)(7) of this section.

(E) Income method payment forms. The income method may be applied to determine PCT Payments in any form of payment (for example, lump sum, royalty on sales, or royalty on divisional profit). For converting to another form of payment, see generally § 1.482-7T(h) (Form of payment rules).

(F) Discount rates appropriate to cost sharing and licensing alternatives.

(1) The present value of the cost sharing and licensing alternatives, respectively, should be determined using the appropriate discount rates in accordance with paragraph (g)(2)(v) of this section. See, for example, § 1.482-7T(g)(2)(v)(B)(1 ) (Discount rate variation between realistic alternatives). In circumstances where the market-correlated risks as between the cost sharing and licensing alternatives are not materially different, a reliable analysis may be possible by using the same discount rate with respect to both alternatives.

(2) The discount rate for the cost sharing alternative will generally depend on the form of PCT Payments assumed (for example, lump sum, royalty on sales, royalty on divisional profit).

(G) The effect of taxation on determining the arm's length amount. In principle, the present values of the cost sharing and licensing alternatives should be determined by applying post-tax discount rates to post-tax income (including the post-tax value to the controlled participant of the PCT Payments). If such approach is adopted, then the post-tax value of the PCT Payments must be appropriately adjusted in order to determine the arm's length amount of the PCT Payments on a pre-tax basis. See paragraph (g)(2)(x) of this section. In certain circumstances, post-tax income may be derived as the product of the result of applying a post-tax discount rate to pre-tax income, and a factor equal to one minus the tax rate. See paragraph (g)(2)(v)(B)(3) of this section. Moreover, to the extent that a controlled participant's tax rate is not materially affected by whether it enters into the cost sharing or licensing alternative (or reliable adjustments may be made for varying tax rates), the factor (that is, one minus the tax rate) may be cancelled from both sides of the equation of the cost sharing and licensing alternative present values. Accordingly, in such circumstance it is sufficient to apply post-tax discount rates to projections of pre-tax income for the purpose of equating the cost sharing and licensing alternatives. The specific applications of the income method described in paragraphs (g)(4)(ii) through (iv) of this section and the examples set forth in paragraph (g)(4)(vii) of this section assume that such circumstance applies.

(ii) Evaluation of PCT Payor's cost sharing alternative. The present value of the PCT Payor's cost sharing alternative is the present value of the stream of the reasonably anticipated residuals over the duration of the CSA Activity of divisional profits or losses, minus operating cost contributions, minus cost contributions, minus PCT Payments.

(iii) Evaluation of PCT Payor's licensing alternative. (A) Evaluation based on CUT. The present value of the PCT Payor's licensing alternative may be determined using the comparable uncontrolled transaction method, as described in § 1.482-4(c)(1) and (2). In this case, the present value of the PCT Payor's licensing alternative is the present value of the stream, over what would be the duration of the CSA Activity under the cost sharing alternative, of the reasonably anticipated residuals of the divisional profits or losses that would be achieved under the cost sharing alternative, minus operating cost contributions that would be made under the cost sharing alternative, minus the licensing payments as determined under the comparable uncontrolled transaction method.

(B) Evaluation based on CPM. The present value of the PCT Payor's licensing alternative may be determined using the comparable profits method, as described in § 1.482-5. In this case, the present value of the licensing alternative is determined as in paragraph (g)(4)(iii)(A) of this section, except that the PCT Payor's licensing payments, as defined in paragraph (j)(1)(i) of this section, are determined to be a lump sum, as of the date of the PCT, equal to the present value (using the discount rate appropriate for the licensing alternative) of the stream, over what would be the duration of the CSA Activity under the cost sharing alternative, of the reasonably anticipated residuals of the divisional profits or losses that would be achieved under the cost sharing alternative, minus operating cost contributions that would be made under the cost sharing alternative, minus market returns for routine contributions, as defined in paragraph (j)(1)(i) of this section.

(iv) Lump sum payment form. Where the form of PCT Payment is a lump sum as of the date of the PCT, then, based on paragraphs (g)(4)(i) through (iii) of this section, the PCT Payment equals the difference between--

(A) The present value, using the discount rate appropriate for the cost sharing alternative, of the stream of the reasonably anticipated residuals over the duration of the CSA Activity of divisional profits or losses, minus cost contributions and operating cost contributions; and

(B) The present value of the licensing alternative.

(v) Best method analysis considerations. (A) Whether results derived from this method are the most reliable measure of an arm's length result is determined using the factors described under the best method rule in § 1.482-1(c). Thus, comparability and the quality of data, the reliability of the assumptions, and the sensitivity of the results to possible deficiencies in the data and assumptions, must be considered in determining whether this method provides the most reliable measure of an arm's length result.

(B) This method will be more reliable to the extent that the controlled participants' respective tax rates are not materially affected by whether they enter into the cost sharing or licensing alternative. Even if this assumption of invariant tax rates across alternatives does not hold, this method may still be reliable to the extent that reliable adjustments can be made to reflect the variation in tax rates.

(C) If the licensing alternative is evaluated using the comparable uncontrolled transactions method, as described in paragraph (g)(4)(iii)(A) of this section, any additional comparability and reliability considerations stated in § 1.482-4(c)(2) may apply.

(D) If the licensing alternative is evaluated using the comparable profits method, as described in paragraph (g)(4)(iii)(B) of this section, any additional comparability and reliability considerations stated in § 1.482-5(c) may apply.

(E) This method may be used even if the PCT Payor furnishes significant operating contributions, or commits to assume the risk of significant operating cost contributions, to the PCT Payor's division. However, in such a case, any comparable uncontrolled transactions described in paragraph (g)(4)(iii)(A) of this section, and any comparable transactions used under § 1.482-5(c) as described in paragraphs (g)(4)(iii)(B) of this section, should be consistent with such contributions (or reliable adjustments must be made for material differences).

(vi) Routine platform and operating contributions. For purposes of this paragraph (g)(4), any routine contributions that are platform or operating contributions, the valuation and PCT Payments for which are determined and made independently of the income method, are treated similarly to cost contributions and operating cost contributions, respectively. Accordingly, wherever used in this paragraph, the term "routine contributions" shall not include routine platform or operating contributions, and wherever the terms "cost contributions" and "operating cost contributions" appear in this paragraph, they shall include net routine platform contributions and net routine operating contributions, respectively. Net routine platform contributions are the value of a controlled participant's total reasonably anticipated routine platform contributions, plus its reasonably anticipated PCT Payments to other controlled participants in respect of their routine platform contributions, minus the reasonably anticipated PCT Payments it is to receive from other controlled participants in respect of its routine platform contributions. Net routine operating contributions are the value of a controlled participant's total reasonably anticipated routine operating contributions, plus its reasonably anticipated arm's length compensation to other controlled participants in respect of their routine operating contributions, minus the reasonably anticipated arm's length compensation it is to receive from other controlled participants in respect of its routine operating contributions.

(vii) Examples. The following examples illustrate the principles of this paragraph (g)(4):

*Example (1).* (i) USP, a software company, has developed version 1.0 of a new software application that it is currently marketing. In Year 1 USP enters into a CSA with its wholly-owned foreign subsidiary, FS, to develop future versions of the software application. Under the CSA, USP will have the rights to exploit the future versions in the United States, and FS will have the rights to exploit them in the rest of the world. The future rights in version 1.0, and USP's development team, are reasonably anticipated to contribute to the development of future versions and therefore the rights in version 1.0 are platform contributions for which compensation is due from FS as part of a PCT. USP does not transfer the current exploitation rights in version 1.0 to FS. FS does not furnish any platform contributions nor does it control any operating intangibles at the inception of the CSA that would be relevant to the exploitation of version 1.0 or future versions of the software. FS agrees to make PCT payments in the form of a single lump sum payment as of the date of the PCT.

(ii) In evaluating the CSA, the Commissioner concludes that the cost sharing alternative represents a riskier alternative for FS than the licensing alternative because, in cost sharing, FS will take on the additional risks associated with CST Payments and of making the PCT payments as a single lump sum. Consequently, the Commissioner concludes that the appropriate discount rate to apply in assessing the licensing alternative, based on discount rates of comparable uncontrolled companies undertaking comparable licensing transactions, would be 13% per year, whereas the appropriate discount rate to apply in assessing the cost sharing alternative would be 15% per year. FS undertakes financial projections and anticipates making no sales during the first two years of the CSA in its territory with sales in Years 3 through Year 8 rapidly increasing to $200 million, $400 million, $600 million, $650 million, $700 million and $750 million, respectively. After year 8, sales in the rest of the world are expected to remain at $750 million per annum for the foreseeable future. Costs including routine costs and operating cost contributions are anticipated to equal 60% of gross sales from Year 3, onwards. FS anticipates its cost contributions will equal $50 million per year for the first four years of the CSA and equal 10% of gross sales in each year, thereafter. The Commissioner accepts the financial projections undertaken by FS. The Commissioner determines that the arm's length rate USP would have charged an uncontrolled licensee for a license of future versions of the software had USP further developed version 1.0 on its own is 35% of the sales price, as determined under the comparable uncontrolled transaction method in § 1.482-4(c). FS also determines that the tax rate applicable to it will be the same in the licensing alternative as in the CSA.

(iii) Based on these projections and applying the appropriate discount rate, the Commissioner determines that under the cost sharing alternative, the present value of its divisional profits (after subtracting the present value of the anticipated operating cost contributions and cost contributions) would be $867 million (for simplicity of calculation in this example, all financial flows are assumed to occur at the beginning of each period). Under the licensing alternative, the present value of the divisional profits and losses minus the operating cost contributions would be $1.592 billion, and the present value of the licensing payments would be $1.393 billion. Therefore, the total value of the licensing alternative would be $199 million. In order for the present value of the cost sharing alternative to equal the present value of the licensing alternative, the present value of the PCT payments must equal $668 million; the arm's length lump sum PCT payment therefore equals $668 million.

*Example (2).* Arm's length range. (i) The facts are the same as in Example 1. The licensing discount rate (13%) and the CUT licensing rate (35%) used by the Commissioner as input parameters in applying the income method are the median values of comparable uncontrolled discount rates and license rates, respectively. The observations that are in the interquartile range of the respective input parameters are as follows:

| Observations that are within interquartile range | Comparable uncontrolled discount rate (percent) |
|---|---|
| 1 | 11 |
| 2 | 12 |
| 3 (Median) | 13 |
| 4 | 15 |
| 5 | 17 |

| Observations that are within interquartile range | Comparable uncontrolled licensing rate (percent) |
|---|---|
| 1 | 30 |
| 2 | 32 |
| 3 (Median) | 35 |
| 4 | 37 |
| 5 | 40 |

(ii) The Commissioner concludes that these estimates of the appropriate arm's length discount rates and licensing rates are independent of each other. Accordingly, the Commissioner undertakes 25 different applications of the income method, using each combination of the discount rate and licensing rate parameters. In undertaking this analysis, the Commissioner assumes that the ratio of the median discount rate for the cost sharing alternative to the median discount rate for the licensing alternative (that is, 15% to 13%) is maintained. The results of the 25 applications of the income method, sorted in ascending order of calculated PCT payment, are as follows:

| Income method application no.: | Comparable uncontrolled licensing discount rate (percent) | Comparable uncontrolled CSA discount rate (percent) | Comparable uncontrolled licensing rate (percent) | Calculated lump sum PCT payment | Interquartile range of PCT payments |
|---|---|---|---|---|---|
| 1 | 17 | 19.6 | 30 | 291 | |
| 2 | 17 | 19.6 | 32 | 347 | |
| 3 | 15 | 17.3 | 30 | 367 | |
| 4 | 17 | 19.6 | 35 | 431 | |
| 5 | 15 | 17.3 | 32 | 433 | |
| 6 | 13 | 15 | 30 | 469 | |
| 7 | 17 | 19.6 | 37 | 487 | LQ = 487 |
| 8 | 15 | 17.3 | 35 | 532 | |
| 9 | 12 | 13.8 | 30 | 535 | |
| 10 | 13 | 15 | 32 | 549 | |
| 11 | 17 | 19.6 | 40 | 571 | |
| 12 | 15 | 17.3 | 37 | 598 | |
| 13 | 11 | 12.7 | 30 | 614 | Median = 614 |
| 14 | 12 | 13.8 | 32 | 623 | |
| 15 | 13 | 15 | 35 | 668 | |
| 16 | 15 | 17.3 | 40 | 697 | |
| 17 | 11 | 12.7 | 32 | 712 | |
| 18 | 13 | 15 | 37 | 748 | |
| 19 | 12 | 13.8 | 35 | 755 | UQ = 755 |
| 20 | 12 | 13.8 | 37 | 844 | |
| 21 | 11 | 12.7 | 35 | 860 | |
| 22 | 13 | 15 | 40 | 867 | |
| 23 | 11 | 12.7 | 37 | 959 | |
| 24 | 12 | 13.8 | 40 | 976 | |
| 25 | 11 | 12.7 | 40 | 1,107 | |

(iii) Accordingly, the Commissioner determines that a taxpayer will not be subject to adjustment if its initial (ex ante) determination of the PCT payment is between $487 million and $755 million. In the event that the taxpayer's determination of the appropriate PCT payment falls outside this range, the adjustment made by the Commissioner will ordinarily be to $614.

*Example (3).* (i) USP, a U.S. software company, has developed version 1.0 of a new software application, employed to store and retrieve complex data sets in certain types of storage media. Version 1.0 is currently being marketed. In Year 1, USP enters into a CSA with its wholly owned foreign subsidiary, FS, to develop future versions of the software application. Under the CSA, USP will have the exclusive rights to exploit the future versions in the U.S., and FS will have the exclusive rights to exploit them in the rest of the world. USP's rights in version 1.0, and its development team, are reasonably anticipated to contribute to the development of future versions of the software application and, therefore, the rights in version 1.0 are platform contributions for which compensation is due from FS as part of a PCT. USP also transfers the current exploitation rights in version 1.0 to FS and the arm's length amount of the compensation for such transfer is determined in the aggregate with the arm's length PCT Payments in this Example 3. FS does not furnish any platform contributions to the CSA nor does it control any operating intangibles at the inception of the CSA that would be relevant to the exploitation of version 1.0 or future versions of the software. It is reasonably anticipated that FS will have gross sales of $1000X in its territory for 5 years attributable to its exploitation of version 1.0 and the cost shared intangibles, after which time the software application will be rendered obsolete and unmarketable by the obsolescence of the storage medium technology to which it relates. FS's costs reasonably attributable to the CSA, other than cost contributions and operating cost contributions, are anticipated to be $250X per year. Certain operating cost contributions that will be borne by FS are reasonably anticipated to equal $200X per annum for 5 years. In addition, FS is reasonably anticipated to pay cost contributions of $200X per year as a controlled participant in the CSA.

(ii) FS concludes that its realistic alternative would be to license software from an uncontrolled licensor that would undertake the commitment to bear the entire risk of software development. Applying CPM using the profit levels experienced by uncontrolled licensees with contractual provisions and allocations of risk that are comparable to those of FS's licensing alternative, FS determines that it could, as a licensee, reasonably expect a (pre-tax) routine return equal to 14% of gross sales or $140X per year for 5 years. The remaining net revenue would be paid to the uncontrolled licensor as a license fee of $410X per year. FS determines that the discount rate that would be applied to determine the present value of income and costs attributable to its participation in the licensing alternative would be 12.5% as compared to the 15% discount rate that would be applicable in determining the present valuable of the net income attributable to its participation in the CSA (reflecting the increased risk borne by FS in bearing a share of the R&D costs in the cost sharing alternative and the fact that FS intends to pay the PCT payment as a single lump sum). FS also determines that the tax rate applicable to it will be the same in the licensing alternative as in the CSA.

(iii) On these facts, the present value to FS of entering into the cost sharing alternative equals the present value of the divisional profits ($1,000X minus $250X) minus operating cost contributions ($200X) minus cost contributions ($200X) minus PCT Payments, determined over 5 years by discounting at a discount rate of 15% (for simplicity of calculation in this example, all financial flows are assumed to occur at the beginning of each period). Thus, the present value of the residuals, prior to subtracting the value of the PCT Payments, is $1349X.

(iv) On these facts, the present value to FS of entering into the licensing alternative would be $561X determined by discounting, over 5 years, divisional profits ($1,000X minus $250X) minus operating cost contributions ($200X) and licensing payments ($410X) at a discount rate of 12.5% per annum. The present value of the cost sharing alternative must also equal $561X but equals $1349X prior to subtracting the present value of the PCT payments. Consequently, the PCT payments must have a present value of $788X. Thus, the arm's length lump sum PCT payment made at the time of the PCT will equal $788X.

*(5) Acquisition price method.* (i) In general. The acquisition price method applies the comparable uncontrolled transaction method of § 1.482-4(c), or the comparable uncontrolled services price method described in § 1.482-9T(c), to evaluate whether the amount charged in a PCT, or group of PCTs, is arm's length by reference to the amount charged (the acquisition price) for the stock or asset purchase of an entire organization or portion thereof (the target) in an uncontrolled transaction. The acquisition price method is ordinarily used where substantially all the target's nonroutine contributions, as such term is defined in paragraph (j)(1)(i) of this section, made to the PCT Payee's business activities are covered by a PCT or group of PCTs.

(ii) Determination of arm's length charge. Under this method, the arm's length charge for a PCT or group of PCTs covering resources, capabilities, and rights of the target is equal to the adjusted acquisition price, as divided among the controlled participants according to their respective RAB shares. However, an additional adjustment may be necessary to reflect the fact that PCT Payee's tax liability attributable to the purchase from target may differ from the tax liability attributable to the PCT Payments. See paragraph (g)(2)(x) of this section.

(iii) Adjusted acquisition price. The adjusted acquisition price is the acquisition price of the target increased by the value of the target's liabilities on the date of the acquisition, other than liabilities not assumed in the case of an asset purchase, and decreased by the value of the target's tangible property on that date and by the value on that date of any other resources, capabilities, and rights not covered by a PCT or group of PCTs.

(iv) Best method analysis considerations. The comparability and reliability considerations stated in § 1.482-4(c)(2) apply. Consistent with those considerations, the reliability of applying the acquisition price method as a measure of the arm's length charge for the PCT Payment normally is reduced if--

(A) A substantial portion of the target's nonroutine contributions to the PCT Payee's business activities is not required to be covered by a PCT or group of PCTs, and that portion of the nonroutine contributions cannot reliably be valued;

(B) A substantial portion of the target's assets consists of tangible property that cannot reliably be valued; or

(C) The date on which the target is acquired and the date of the PCT are not contemporaneous.

(v) Example. The following example illustrates the principles of this paragraph (g)(5):

*Example.* USP, a U.S. corporation, and its newly incorporated, wholly-owned foreign subsidiary (FS) enter into a CSA at the start of Year 1 to develop Group Z products. Under the CSA, USP and FS will have the exclusive rights to exploit the Group Z products in the U.S. and the rest of the world, respectively. At the start of Year 2, USP acquires Company X for cash consideration worth $110 million. At this time USP's RAB share is 60% and FS's RAB share is 40%. Company X joins in the filing of a U.S. consolidated income tax return with USP. Under paragraph (j)(2)(i) of this section, Company X and USP are treated as one taxpayer for purposes of this section. Accordingly, the rights in any of Company X's resources and capabilities that are reasonably anticipated to contribute to the development activities of the CSA will be considered platform contributions furnished by USP. Company X's resources and capabilities consist of its workforce, certain technology intangibles, $15 million of tangible property and other assets and $5 million in liabilities. The technology intangibles, as well as Company X's workforce, are reasonably anticipated to contribute to the development of the Group Z products under the CSA and, therefore, the rights in the technology intangibles and the workforce are platform contributions for which FS must make a PCT Payment to USP. None of Company X's existing intangible assets or any of its workforce are anticipated to contribute to activities outside the CSA. For purposes of this example, it is assumed that no additional adjustment on account of tax liabilities (as described in paragraph (g)(5)(ii) of this section) is needed. Applying the acquisition price method, the value of USP's platform contributions is the adjusted acquisition price of $100 million

($110 million acquisition price plus $5 million liabilities less $15 million tangible property and other assets). FS must make a PCT Payment to USP for these platform contributions with a reasonably anticipated present value of $40 million, which is the product of $100 million (the value of the platform contributions) and 40% (FS's RAB share at the time of the PCT).

*(6) Market capitalization method.* (i) In general. The market capitalization method applies the comparable uncontrolled transaction method of § 1.482-4(c), or the comparable uncontrolled services price method described in § 1.482-9T(c), to evaluate whether the amount charged in a PCT, or group of PCTs, is arm's length by reference to the average market capitalization of a controlled participant (PCT Payee) whose stock is regularly traded on an established securities market. The market capitalization method is ordinarily used where substantially all of the PCT Payee's nonroutine contributions to the PCT Payee's business are covered by a PCT or group of PCTs.

(ii) Determination of arm's length charge. Under the market capitalization method, the arm's length charge for a PCT or group of PCTs covering resources, capabilities, and rights of the PCT Payee is equal to the adjusted average market capitalization, as divided among the controlled participants according to their respective RAB shares. An increase to reflect the fact that a PCT Payment may increase the PCT Payee's tax liability and decrease the PCT Payor's tax liability may be warranted. See paragraph (g)(2)(x) of this section.

(iii) Average market capitalization. The average market capitalization is the average of the daily market capitalizations of the PCT Payee over a period of time beginning 60 days before the date of the PCT and ending on the date of the PCT. The daily market capitalization of the PCT Payee is calculated on each day its stock is actively traded as the total number of shares outstanding multiplied by the adjusted closing price of the stock on that day. The adjusted closing price is the daily closing price of the stock, after adjustments for stock-based transactions (dividends and stock splits) and other pending corporate (combination and spin-off) restructuring transactions for which reliable arm's length adjustments can be made.

(iv) Adjusted average market capitalization. The adjusted average market capitalization is the average market capitalization of the PCT Payee increased by the value of the PCT Payee's liabilities on the date of the PCT and decreased by the value on such date of the PCT Payee's tangible property and of any other resources, capabilities, or rights of the PCT Payee not covered by a PCT or group of PCTs.

(v) Best method analysis considerations. The comparability and reliability considerations stated in § 1.482-4(c)(2) apply. Consistent with those considerations, the reliability of applying the comparable uncontrolled transaction method using the adjusted market capitalization of a company as a measure of the arm's length charge for the PCT Payment normally is reduced if--

(A) A substantial portion of the PCT Payee's nonroutine contributions to its business activities is not required to be covered by a PCT or group of PCTs, and that portion of the nonroutine contributions cannot reliably be valued;

(B) A substantial portion of the PCT Payee's assets consists of tangible property that cannot reliably be valued; or

(C) Facts and circumstances demonstrate the likelihood of a material divergence between the average market capitalization of the PCT Payee and the value of its resources, capabilities, and rights for which reliable adjustments cannot be made.

(vi) Examples. The following examples illustrate the principles of this paragraph (g)(6):

*Example (1).* (i) USP, a publicly traded U.S. company, and its newly incorporated wholly-owned foreign subsidiary (FS) enter into a CSA on Date 1 to develop software. At that time USP has in-process software but has no software ready for the market. Under the CSA, USP and FS will have the exclusive rights to exploit the software developed under the CSA in the United States and the rest of the world, respectively. On Date 1, USP's RAB share is 70% and FS's RAB share is 30%. USP's assembled team of researchers and its in-process software are reasonably anticipated to contribute to the development of the software under the CSA. Therefore, the rights in the research team and in-process software are platform contributions for which compensation is due from FS. Further, these rights are not reasonably anticipated to contribute to any business activity other than the CSA Activity.

(ii) On Date 1, USP had an average market capitalization of $205 million, tangible property and other assets that can be reliably valued worth $5 million, and no liabilities. Aside from those assets, USP had no assets other than its research team and in-process software. Applying the market capitalization method, the value of USP's platform contributions is $200 million ($205 million average market capitalization of USP less $5 million of tangible property and other assets). The arm's length value of the PCT Payments FS must make to USP for the platform contributions, before any adjustment on account of tax liability as described in paragraph (g)(2)(ii) of this section, is $60 million, which is the product of $200 million (the value of the platform contributions) and 30% (FS's RAB share on Date 1).

*Example (2).* Aggregation with make-or-sell rights. (i) The facts are the same as in Example 1, except that on Date 1 USP also has existing software ready for the market. USP separately enters into a license agreement with FS for make-or-sell rights for all existing software outside the United States. No marketing has occurred, and USP has no marketing intangibles. This license of current make-or-sell rights is a transaction governed by § 1.482-4. However, after analysis, it is determined that the arm's length PCT Payments and the arm's length payments for the make-or-sell license may be most reliably determined in the aggregate using the market capitalization method, under principles described in paragraph (g)(2)(iv) of this section, and it is further determined that those principles are most reliably implemented by computing the aggregate arm's length charge as the product of the aggregate value of the existing and in-process software and FS's RAB share on Date 1.

(ii) Applying the market capitalization method, the aggregate value of USP's platform contributions and the make-or-sell rights in its existing software is $250 million ($255 million average market capitalization of USP less $5 million of tangible property and other assets). The total arm's length value of the PCT Payments and license payments FS must make to USP for the platform contributions and current make-or-sell rights, before any adjustment on account of tax liability as described in paragraph (g)(2)(ii) of this section, is $75 million, which is the product of $250 million (the value of the platform contributions and the make-or-sell rights) and 30% (FS's RAB share on Date 1).

*Example (3).* Reduced reliability. The facts are the same as in Example 1 except that USP also has significant nonroutine assets that will be used solely in a nascent business division that is unrelated to the subject of the CSA and that cannot themselves be reliably valued. Those nonroutine contributions are not platform contributions and accordingly are not required to be covered by a PCT. The reliability of using the market capitalization method to determine the value of USP's platform contributions to the CSA is significantly reduced in this case because that method would require adjusting USP's average market capitalization to account for the significant nonroutine contributions that are not required to be covered by a PCT.

*(7) Residual profit split method.* (i) In general. The residual profit split method evaluates whether the allocation of combined operating profit or loss attributable to one or more platform contributions subject to a PCT is arm's length by reference to the relative value of each controlled participant's contribution to that combined operating profit or loss. The combined operating profit or loss must be derived from the most narrowly identifiable business activity (relevant business activity) of the controlled participants for which data are available that include the CSA Activity. The residual profit split method may not be used where only one controlled participant makes significant nonroutine contributions (including platform or operating contributions) to the CSA Activity. The provisions of § 1.482-6 shall apply to CSAs only to the extent provided and as modified in this paragraph (g)(7). Any other application to a CSA of a residual profit method not described in paragraphs (g)(7)(ii) and (iii) will constitute an unspecified method for purposes of sections 482 and 6662(e) and the regulations under those sections.

(ii) Appropriate share of profits and losses. The relative value of each controlled participant's contribution to the success of the relevant business activity must be determined in a manner that reflects the functions performed, risks assumed, and resources employed by each participant in the relevant business activity, consistent with the best method analysis described in § 1.482-1(c) and (d). Such an allocation is intended to correspond to the division of profit or loss that would result from an arrangement between uncontrolled taxpayers, each performing functions similar to those of the various controlled participants engaged in the relevant business activity. The profit allocated to any particular controlled participant is not necessarily limited to the total operating profit of the group from the relevant business activity. For example, in a given year, one controlled participant may earn a profit while another controlled participant incurs a loss. In addition, it may not be assumed that the combined operating profit or loss from the relevant business activity should be shared equally, or in any other arbitrary proportion.

(iii) Profit split. (A) In general. Under the residual profit split method, the present value of each controlled participant's residual divisional profit or loss attributable to nonroutine contributions (nonroutine residual divisional profit or loss) is allocated between the controlled participants that each furnish significant nonroutine contributions (including platform or operating contributions) to the relevant business activity in that division.

(B) Determine nonroutine residual divisional profit or loss. The present value of each controlled participant's nonroutine residual divisional profit or loss must be determined to reflect the most reliable measure of an arm's length result. The present value of nonroutine residual divisional profit or loss equals the present value of the stream of the reasonably anticipated residuals over the duration of the CSA Activity of divisional profit or loss, minus market returns for routine contributions, minus operating cost contributions, minus cost contributions, using a discount rate appropriate to such residuals in accordance with paragraph (g)(2)(v) of this section.

(C) Allocate nonroutine residual divisional profit or loss. (1) In general. The present value of nonroutine residual divisional profit or loss in each controlled participant's division must be allocated among all of the controlled participants based upon the relative values, determined as of the date of the PCTs, of the PCT Payor's as compared to the PCT Payee's nonroutine contributions to the PCT Payor's division. For this purpose, the PCT Payor's nonroutine contribution consists of the sum of the PCT Payor's nonroutine operating contributions and the PCT Payor's RAB share of the PCT Payor's nonroutine platform contributions. For this purpose, the PCT Payee's nonroutine contribution consists of the PCT Payor's RAB share of the PCT Payee's nonroutine platform contributions.

(2) Relative value determination. The relative values of the controlled participants' nonroutine contributions must be determined so as to reflect the most reliable measure of an arm's length result. Relative values may be measured by external market benchmarks that reflect the fair market value of such nonroutine contributions. Alternatively, the relative value of nonroutine contributions may be estimated by the capitalized cost of developing the nonroutine contributions and updates, as appropriately grown or discounted so that all contributions may be valued on a comparable dollar basis as of the same date. If the nonroutine contributions by a controlled participant are also used in other business activities (such as the exploitation of make-or-sell rights described in paragraph (c)(4) of this section), an allocation of the value of the nonroutine contributions must be made on a reasonable basis among all the business activities in which they are used in proportion to the relative economic value that the relevant business activity and such other business activities are anticipated to derive over time as the result of such nonroutine contributions.

(3) Determination of PCT Payments. Any amount of the present value of a controlled participant's nonroutine residual divisional profit or loss that is allocated to another controlled participant represents the present value of the PCT Payments due to that other controlled participant for its platform contributions to the relevant business activity in the relevant division. For purposes of paragraph (j)(3)(ii) of this section, the present value of a PCT Payor's PCT Payments under this paragraph shall be deemed reduced to the extent of the present value of any PCT Payments owed to it from other controlled participants under this paragraph (g)(7). The resulting remainder may be converted to a fixed or contingent form of payment in accordance with paragraph (h) (Form of payment rules) of this section.

(4) Routine platform and operating contributions. For purposes of this paragraph (g)(7), any routine platform or operating contributions, the valuation and PCT Payments for which are determined and made independently of the residual profit split method, are treated similarly to cost contributions and operating cost contributions, respectively. Accordingly, wherever used in this paragraph (g)(7), the term "routine contributions" shall not include routine platform or operating contributions, and wherever the terms "cost contributions" and "operating cost contributions" appear in this paragraph (g)(7), they shall include net routine platform contributions and net routine operating contributions, respectively, as defined in paragraph (g)(4)(vi) of this section.

(iv) Best method analysis considerations. (A) In general. Whether results derived from this method are the most reliable measure of the arm's length result is determined using the factors described under the best method rule in § 1.482-1(c). Thus, comparability and quality of data, reliability of assumptions, and sensitivity of results to possible deficiencies in the data and assumptions, must be considered in determining whether this method provides the most reliable measure of an arm's length result. The application of these factors to the residual profit split in the context of the relevant business activity of developing and exploiting cost shared intangibles is discussed in paragraphs (g)(7)(iv)(B), (C) and (D) of this section.

(B) Comparability. The derivation of the present value of nonroutine residual divisional profit or loss includes a carveout on account of market returns for routine contributions. Thus, the comparability considerations that are relevant for that purpose include those that are relevant for the methods that are used to determine market returns for the routine contributions.

(C) Data and assumptions. The reliability of the results derived from the residual profit split is affected by the quality of the data and assumptions used to apply this method. In particular, the following factors must be considered:

(1) The reliability of the allocation of costs, income, and assets between the relevant business activity and the controlled participants' other activities that will affect the reliability of the determination of the divisional profit or loss and its allocation among the controlled participants. See § 1.482-6(c)(2)(ii)(C)(1).

(2) The degree of consistency between the controlled participants and uncontrolled taxpayers in accounting practices that materially affect the items that determine the amount and allocation of operating profit or loss affects the reliability of the result. See § 1.482-6(c)(2)(ii)(C)(2).

(3) The reliability of the data used and the assumptions made in estimating the relative value of the nonroutine contributions by the controlled participants. In particular, if capitalized costs of development are used to estimate the relative value of nonroutine contributions, the reliability of the results is reduced relative to the reliability of other methods that do not require such an estimate. This is because, in any given case, the costs of developing a nonroutine contribution may not be related to its market value and because the calculation of the capitalized costs of development may require the allocation of indirect costs between the relevant business activity and the controlled participant's other activities, which may affect the reliability of the analysis.

(D) Other factors affecting reliability. Like the methods described in §§ 1.482-3 through 1.482-5 and § 1.482-9T(c), the carveout on account of market returns for routine contributions relies exclusively on external market benchmarks. As indicated in § 1.482-1(c)(2)(i), as the degree of comparability between the controlled participants and uncontrolled transactions increases, the relative weight accorded the analysis under this method will increase. In addition, to the extent the allocation of nonroutine residual divisional profit or loss is not based on external market benchmarks, the reliability of the analysis will be decreased in relation to an analysis under a method that relies on market benchmarks. Finally, the reliability of the analysis under this method may be enhanced by the fact that all the controlled participants are evaluated under the residual profit split. However, the reliability of the results of an analysis based on information from all the controlled participants is affected by the reliability of the data and the assumptions pertaining to each controlled participant. Thus, if the data and assumptions are significantly more reliable with respect to one of the controlled participants than with respect to the others, a different method, focusing solely on the results of that party, may yield more reliable results.

(v) Examples. The following examples illustrate the principles of this paragraph (g)(7):

*Example (1).* (i) USP, a U.S. electronic data storage company, has partially developed technology for a type of extremely small compact storage devices (nanodisks) which are expected to provide a significant increase in data storage capacity in various types of portable devices such as cell phones, MP3 players, laptop computers and digital cameras. At the same time, USP's wholly-owned subsidiary, FS, has developed significant marketing intangibles outside the United States in the form of customer lists, ongoing relations with various OEMs, and trademarks that are well recognized by consumers due to a long history of marketing successful data storage devices and other hardware used in various types of consumer electronics. At the beginning of Year 1, USP enters into a CSA with FS to develop nanodisk technologies for eventual commercial exploitation. Under the CSA, USP will have the right to exploit nanodisks in the United States, while FS will have the right to exploit nanodisks in the rest of the world. The partially developed nanodisk technologies owned by USP are reasonably anticipated to contribute to the development of commercially exploitable nanodisks and therefore the rights in the nanodisk technologies constitute platform contributions of USP for which compensation is due under PCTs. FS does not own any intangible assets that constitute platform contributions for the CSA. Due to the fact that nanodisk technologies have yet to be incorporated into any commercially available product, neither USP nor FS transfers rights to make or sell current products in conjunction with the CSA.

(ii) Because only in FS's territory do both controlled participants make significant nonroutine contributions, USP and FS determine that they need to determine the relative value of their respective contributions to operating profit or loss attributable to the CSA only in FS's territory (that is, to FS's divisional profit or loss). FS anticipates making no nanodisk sales during the first year of the CSA in its territory with revenues in Year 2 reaching $200 million. Revenues through Year 5 are reasonably anticipated to increase by 50% per year. The annual growth rate for revenues is then expected to decline to 30% per annum in Years 6 and 7, 20% per annum in Years 8 and 9 and 10% per annum in Year 10. Revenues are then expected to start to decline; declining 10% in Year 11 and 5% per annum, thereafter. The routine costs (costs other than cost contributions, operating cost contributions, routine platform and operating contributions, and nonroutine contributions) that are allocable to this revenue in calculating FS's divisional profit or loss, are anticipated to equal 45% of gross sales from Year 2, onwards. FS undertakes routine distribution activities in its markets that constitute routine contributions to the relevant business activity of exploiting nanodisk technologies. USP and FS estimate that the total market return on these routine contributions will amount to 6% of the routine costs. FS anticipates that its operating cost contributions will equal $40 million per annum for the first two years of the CSA and $65 and $70 million in Years 3 and 4. Thereafter, operating cost contributions are expected to equal 7% of revenue in each year. FS expects its cost contributions to be $60 million in Year 1, rise to $100 million in Years 2 and 3, and then decline again to $60 million. Thereafter, FS's cost contributions are expected to equal 10% of revenues.

(iii) USP and FS determine the present value of the stream of the reasonably anticipated residuals in FS's territory over the duration of the CSA Activity of the divisional profit or loss (revenues minus routine costs), minus the market returns for routine contributions, the operating cost contributions, and the cost contributions. USP and FS determine, based on the considerations discussed in paragraph (g)(2)(v) of this section, that the appropriate discount rate is 17.5% per annum (for simplicity of calculation in this example, all financial flows are assumed to occur at the beginning of each period). Therefore, the present value of the nonroutine residual divisional profit is $1.336 billion.

(iv) After analysis, USP and FS determine that the relative value of the nanodisk technologies contributed by USP to CSA (giving effect only to its value in FS's territory) is roughly 150% of the value of FS's marketing intangibles (which only have value in FS's territory). Consequently, 60% of the nonroutine residual divisional profit is attributable to USP's platform contribution. Therefore, FS's PCT payments should have an expected present value equal to $802 million (.6 x $1.336 billion).

*Example (2).* (i) USP is a U.S. automobile manufacturing company that has completed significant research on the development of diesel-electric hybrid engines that, if they could be successfully manufactured, would result in providing a significant increased fuel economy for a wide variety of motor vehicles. Successful commercialization of the diesel-electric hybrid engine will require the development of a new class of advanced battery that will be light, relatively cheap to manufacture and yet capable of holding a substantial electric charge. FS, a foreign subsidiary of USP, has completed significant research on developing lithium-ion batteries that appear likely to have the requisite characteristics. At the beginning of Year 1, USP enters into a CSA with FS to further develop diesel-electric hybrid engines and lithium-ion battery technologies for eventual commercial exploitation. Under the CSA, USP will have the right to exploit the diesel-electric hybrid engine and lithium-ion battery technologies in the United States, while FS will have the right to exploit such technologies in the rest of the world. The partially developed diesel-electric hybrid engine and lithium-ion battery technologies owned by USP and FS, respectively, are reasonably anticipated to contribute to the development of commercially exploitable automobile engines and therefore the rights in both these technologies constitute platform contributions of USP and of FS for which compensation is due under PCTs. At the time of inception of the CSA, USP owns operating intangibles in the form of self-developed marketing intangibles which have significant value in the United States, but not in the rest of the world, and that are relevant to exploiting the cost shared intangibles. Similarly, FS owns self-developed marketing intangibles which have significant value in the rest of the world, but not in the United States, and that are relevant to exploiting the cost shared intangibles. Although the new class of diesel-electric hybrid engine using lithium-ion batteries is not yet ready for commercial exploitation, components based on this technology are beginning to be incorporated in current-generation gasoline-electric hybrid engines and the rights to make and sell such products are transferred from USP to FS and vice-versa in conjunction with the inception of the CSA.

(ii) USP's estimated RAB share is 66.7 percent. During Year 1, it is anticipated that sales in USP's territory will be $1000X in Year 1. Sales in FS's territory are anticipated to be $500X. Thereafter, as revenue from the use of components in gasoline-electric hybrids is supplemented by revenues from the production of complete diesel-electric hybrid engines using lithium-ion battery technology, anticipated sales in both territories will increase rapidly at a rate of 50% per annum through Year 4. Anticipated sales are then anticipated to increase at a rate of 40% per annum for another 4 years. Sales are then anticipated to increase at a rate of 30% per annum through Year 10. Thereafter, sales are anticipated to decrease at a rate of 5% per annum for the foreseeable future as new automotive drivetrain technologies displace diesel-electric hybrid engines and lithium-ion batteries. Total operating expenses attributable to product exploitation (including operating cost contributions) equal 40% of sales per year for both USP and FS. USP and FS estimate that the total market return on their routine contributions to the CSA will amount to 6% of the operating expenses. USP is expected to bear ⅔s of the total cost contributions for the foreseeable future. Cost contributions are expected to total $375X in Year 1 (of which $250X are borne by USP) and increase at a rate of 25% per annum through Year 6. In Years 7 through 10, cost contributions are expected to increase 10% a year. Thereafter, cost contributions are expected to decrease by 5% a year for the foreseeable future.

(iii) USP and FS determine the present value of the stream of the reasonably anticipated divisional profit or loss (revenues minus operating costs), minus the market returns for routine contributions, minus cost contributions. USP and FS determine, based on the considerations discussed in paragraph (g)(2)(v) of this section, that the appropriate discount rate is 12% per year. Therefore, the present value of the nonroutine residual divisional profit in USP's territory is $39,243X and in CFC's territory is $19,622X (for simplicity of calculation in this example, all financial flows are assumed to occur at the beginning of each period).

(iv) After analysis, USP and FS determine that, in the United States the relative value of the technologies contributed by USP and FS to the CSA and of the operating intangibles used by USP in the exploitation of the cost shared intangibles (reported as equaling 100 in total), equals: USP's platform contribution (59.5); FS's platform contribution (25.5); and USP's operating intangibles (15). Consequently, the present value of the arm's length amount of the PCT payments that USP should pay to FS for FS's platform contribution is $10,007X (.255 x $39,243X). Similarly, USP and FS determine that, in the rest of the world, the relative value of the technologies contributed by USP and FS to the CSA and of the operating intangibles used by FS in the exploitation of the cost shared intangibles can be divided as follows: USP's platform contribution (63); FS's platform contribution (27); and FS's operating intangibles (10). Consequently, the present value of the arm's length amount of the PCT payments that FS should pay to USP for USP's platform contribution is $12,362 (.63 x $19,622X). Therefore, FS is required to make a net payment to USP with a present value of $2,355X ($12,362X-$10,007X).

*(8) Unspecified methods.* Methods not specified in paragraphs (g)(3) through (7) of this section may be used to evaluate whether the amount charged for a PCT is arm's length. Any method used under this paragraph (g)(8) must be applied in accordance with the provisions of § 1.482-1 and of paragraph (g)(2) of this section. Consistent with the specified methods, an unspecified method should take into account the general principle that uncontrolled taxpayers evaluate the terms of a transaction by considering the realistic alternatives to that transaction, and only enter into a par-

ticular transaction if none of the alternatives is preferable to it. Therefore, in establishing whether a PCT achieved an arm's length result, an unspecified method should provide information on the prices or profits that the controlled participant could have realized by choosing a realistic alternative to the CSA. See paragraph (k)(2)(ii)(J) of this section. As with any method, an unspecified method will not be applied unless it provides the most reliable measure of an arm's length result under the principles of the best method rule. See § 1.482-1(c) (Best method rule). In accordance with § 1.482-1(d) (Comparability), to the extent that an unspecified method relies on internal data rather than uncontrolled comparables, its reliability will be reduced. Similarly, the reliability of a method will be affected by the reliability of the data and assumptions used to apply the method, including any projections used.

**(h) Form of payment rules.** *(1) CST Payments.* CST Payments may not be paid in shares of stock in the payor (or stock in any member of the controlled group that includes the controlled participants).

*(2) PCT Payments.* (i) In general. The consideration under a PCT for a platform contribution may take one or a combination of both of the following forms:

(A) Payments of a fixed amount (fixed payments), either paid in a lump sum payment or in installment payments spread over a specified period, with interest calculated in accordance with § 1.482-2(a) (Loans or advances).

(B) Payments contingent on the exploitation of cost shared intangibles by the PCT Payor (contingent payments).

(ii) No PCT Payor Stock. PCT Payments may not be paid in shares of stock in the PCT Payor (or stock in any member of the controlled group that includes the controlled participants).

(iii) Specified form of payment. (A) In general. The form of payment selected (subject to the rules of this paragraph (h)) for any PCT, including, in the case of contingent payments, the contingent base and structure of the payments as set forth in paragraph (h)(2)(iii)(B) of this section, must be specified no later than the due date of the applicable tax return (including extensions) for the later of the taxable year of the PCT Payor or PCT Payee that includes the date of that PCT.

(B) Contingent payments. In accordance with paragraph (k)(1)(iv)(A) of this section, a provision of a written contract described in paragraph (k)(1) of this section, or of the additional documentation described in paragraph (k)(2) of this section, that provides for payments for a PCT (or group of PCTs) to be contingent on the exploitation of cost shared intangibles will be respected as consistent with economic substance only if the allocation between the controlled participants of the risks attendant on such form of payment is determinable before the outcomes of such allocation that would have materially affected the PCT pricing are known or reasonably knowable. A contingent payment provision must clearly and unambiguously specify the basis on which the contingent payment obligations are to be determined. In particular, the contingent payment provision must clearly and unambiguously specify the events that give rise to an obligation to make PCT Payments, the royalty base (such as sales or revenues), and the computation used to determine the PCT Payments. The royalty base specified must be one that permits verification of its proper use by reference to books and records maintained by the controlled participants in the normal course of business (for example, books and records maintained for financial accounting or business management purposes).

(C) Examples. The following examples illustrate the principles of this paragraph (h)(2)(iii).

*Example (1).* A CSA provides that PCT payments with respect to a particular platform contribution shall be contingent payments equal to 15% of the revenues from sales of products that incorporate cost shared intangibles. The terms further permit (but do not require) the controlled participants to adjust such contingent payments in accordance with a formula set forth in the arrangement so that the 15% rate is subject to adjustment by the controlled participants at their discretion on an after-the-fact, uncompensated basis. The Commissioner may impute payment terms that are consistent with economic substance with respect to the platform contribution because the contingent payment provision does not specify the computation used to determine the PCT Payments.

*Example (2).* Taxpayer, an automobile manufacturer, is a controlled participant in a CSA that involves research and development to perfect certain manufacturing techniques necessary to the actual manufacture of a state-of-the-art, hybrid fuel injection system known as DRL337. The arrangement involves the platform contribution of a design patent covering DRL337. Pursuant to paragraph (h)(2)(iii)(B) of this section, the CSA provides for PCT payments with respect to the platform contribution of the patent in the form of royalties contingent on sales of automobiles that contain the DRL337 system. However, Taxpayer's system of book- and record-keeping does not enable Taxpayer to track which automobile sales involve automobiles that contain the DRL337 system. Because Taxpayer has not complied with paragraph (h)(2)(iii)(B) of this section, the Commissioner may impute payment terms that are consistent with economic substance and susceptible to verification by the Commissioner.

(iv) Conversion from fixed to contingent form of payment. With regard to a conversion of a fixed present value to a contingent form of payment, see paragraphs (g)(2)(v) (Discount rate) and (g)(2)(vi) (Financial projections) of this section.

*(3) Coordination of best method rule and form of payment.* A method described in paragraph (g)(1) of this section evaluates the arm's length amount charged in a PCT in terms of a form of payment (method payment form). For example, the method payment form for the acquisition price method described in paragraph (g)(5) of this section, and for the market capitalization method described in paragraph (g)(6) of this section, is fixed payment. Applications of the income method provide different method payment forms. See paragraphs (g)(4)(i)(E) and (g)(4)(iv) of this section. The method payment form may not necessarily correspond to the form of payment specified pursuant to paragraphs (h)(2)(iii) and (k)(2)(ii)(l) of this section (specified payment form). The determination under § 1.482-1(c) of the method that provides the most reliable measure of an arm's length result is to be made without regard to whether the respective method payment forms under the competing methods correspond to the specified payment form. If the method payment form of the method determined under § 1.482-1(c) to provide the most reliable measure of an arm's length result differs from the specified payment form, then the conversion from such method payment form to such specified payment form will be made to the satisfaction of the Commissioner.

**(i) Allocations by the Commissioner in connection with a CSA.** *(1) In general.* The Commissioner may make allocations to adjust the results of a controlled transaction in connection with a CSA so that the results are consistent with an arm's length result, in accordance with the provisions of this paragraph (i).

*(2) CST allocations.*

(i) In general. The Commissioner may make allocations to adjust the results of a CST so that the results are consistent with an arm's length result, including any allocations to make each controlled participant's IDC share, as determined under paragraph (d)(4) of this section, equal to that participant's RAB share, as determined under paragraph (e)(1) of this section. Such allocations may result from, for purposes of CST determinations, adjustments to--

(A) Redetermine IDCs by adding any costs (or cost categories) that are directly identified with, or are reasonably allocable to, the IDA, or by removing any costs (or cost categories) that are not IDCs;

(B) Reallocate costs between the IDA and other business activities;

(C) Improve the reliability of the selection or application of the basis used for measuring benefits for purposes of estimating a controlled participant's RAB share;

(D) Improve the reliability of the projections used to estimate RAB shares, including adjustments described in paragraph (i)(2)(ii) of this section; and

(E) Allocate among the controlled participants any unallocated interests in cost shared intangibles.

(ii) Adjustments to improve the reliability of projections used to estimate RAB shares. (A) Unreliable projections. A significant divergence between projected benefit shares and benefit shares adjusted to take into account any available actual benefits to date (adjusted benefit shares) may indicate that the projections were not reliable for purposes of estimating RAB shares. In such a case, the Commissioner may use adjusted benefit shares as the most reliable measure of RAB shares and adjust IDC shares accordingly. The projected benefit shares will not be considered unreliable, as applied in a given taxable year, based on a divergence from adjusted benefit shares for every controlled participant that is less than or equal to 20% of the participant's projected benefits share. Further, the Commissioner will not make an allocation based on such divergence if the difference is due to an extraordinary event, beyond the control of the controlled participants, which could not reasonably have been anticipated at the time that costs were shared. The Commissioner generally may adjust projections of benefits used to calculate benefit shares in accordance with the provisions of § 1.482-1. In particular, if benefits are projected over a period of years, and the projections for initial years of the period prove to be unreliable, this may indicate that the projections for the remaining years of the period are also unreliable and thus should be adjusted. For purposes of this paragraph (i)(2)(ii)(A), all controlled participants that are not U.S. persons are treated as a single controlled participant. Therefore, an adjustment based on an unreliable projection of RAB shares will be made to the IDC shares of foreign controlled participants only if there is a matching adjustment to the IDC shares of controlled participants that are U.S. persons. Nothing in this paragraph (i)(2)(ii)(A) prevents the Commissioner from making an allocation if a taxpayer did not use the most reliable basis for measuring anticipated benefits. For example, if the taxpayer measures its anticipated benefits based on units sold, and the Commissioner determines that another basis is more reliable for measuring anticipated benefits, then the fact that actual units sold were within 20% of the projected unit sales will not preclude an allocation under this section.

(B) Foreign-to-foreign adjustments. Adjustments to IDC shares based on an unreliable projection also may be made among foreign controlled participants if the variation between actual and projected benefits has the effect of substantially reducing U.S. tax.

(C) Correlative adjustments to PCTs. Correlative adjustments will be made to any PCT Payments of a fixed amount that were determined based on RAB shares that are subsequently adjusted on a finding that they were based on unreliable projections. No correlative adjustments will be made to contingent PCT Payments regardless of whether RAB shares were used as a parameter in the valuation of those payments.

(D) Examples. The following examples illustrate the principles of this paragraph (i)(2)(ii):

*Example (1).* U.S. Parent (USP) and Foreign Subsidiary (FS) enter into a CSA to develop new food products, dividing costs on the basis of projected sales two years in the future. In Year 1, USP and FS project that their sales in Year 3 will be equal, and they divide costs accordingly. In Year 3, the Commissioner examines the controlled participants' method for dividing costs. USP and FS actually accounted for 42% and 58% of total sales, respectively. The Commissioner agrees that sales two years in the future provide a reliable basis for estimating benefit shares. Because the differences between USP's and FS's adjusted and projected benefit shares are less than 20% of their projected benefit shares, the projection of future benefits for Year 3 is reliable.

*Example (2).* The facts are the same as in Example 1, except that in Year 3 USP and FS actually accounted for 35% and 65% of total sales, respectively. The divergence between USP's projected and adjusted benefit shares is greater than 20% of USP's projected benefit share and is not due to an extraordinary event beyond the control of the controlled participants. The Commissioner concludes that the projected benefit shares were unreliable, and uses adjusted benefit shares as the basis for an adjustment to the cost shares borne by USP and FS.

*Example (3).* U.S. Parent (USP), a U.S. corporation, and its foreign subsidiary (FS) enter into a CSA in Year 1. They project that they will begin to receive benefits from cost shared intangibles in Years 4 through 6, and that USP will receive 60% of total benefits and FS 40% of total benefits. In Years 4 through 6, USP and FS actually receive 50% each of the total benefits. In evaluating the reliability of the controlled participants' projections, the Commissioner compares the adjusted benefit shares to the projected benefit shares. Although USP's adjusted benefit share (50%) is within 20% of its projected benefit share (60%), FS's adjusted benefit share (50%) is not within 20% of its projected benefit share (40%). Based on this discrepancy, the Commissioner may conclude that the controlled participants' projections were unreliable and may use adjusted benefit shares as the basis for an adjustment to the cost shares borne by USP and FS.

*Example (4).* Three controlled taxpayers, USP, FS1, and FS2 enter into a CSA. FS1 and FS2 are foreign. USP is a domestic corporation that controls all the stock of FS1 and FS2. The controlled participants project that they will share the total benefits of the cost shared intangibles in the following percentages: USP 50%; FS1 30%; and FS2 20%. Adjusted benefit shares are as follows: USP 45%; FS1 25%; and FS2 30%. In evaluating the reliability of the controlled participants' projections, the Commissioner compares these adjusted benefit shares to the projected benefit shares. For this purpose, FS1 and FS2 are treated as a single controlled participant. The adjusted benefit share received by USP (45%) is within 20% of its projected benefit share (50%). In addition, the non-U.S. controlled participant's adjusted benefit share (55%) is also within 20% of their projected benefit share (50%). Therefore, the Commissioner concludes that the controlled participant's projections of future benefits were reliable, despite the fact that FS2's adjusted benefit share (30%) is not within 20% of its projected benefit share (20%).

*Example (5).* The facts are the same as in Example 4. In addition, the Commissioner determines that FS2 has significant operating losses and has no earnings and profits, and that FS1 is profitable and has earnings and profits. Based on all the evidence, the Commissioner concludes that the controlled participants arranged that FS1 would bear a larger cost share than appropriate in order to reduce FS1's earnings and profits and thereby reduce inclusions USP otherwise would be deemed to have on account of FS1 under subpart F. Pursuant to paragraph (i)(2)(ii)(B) of this section, the Commissioner may make an adjustment solely to the cost shares borne by FS1 and FS2 because FS2's projection of future benefits was unreliable and the variation between adjusted and projected benefits had the effect of substantially reducing USP's U.S. income tax liability (on account of FS1 subpart F income).

*Example (6).* (i) (A) Foreign Parent (FP) and U.S. Subsidiary (USS) enter into a CSA in 1996 to develop a new treatment for baldness. USS's interest in any treatment developed is the right to produce and sell the treatment in the U.S. market while FP retains rights to produce and sell the treatment in the rest of the world. USS and FP measure their anticipated benefits from the CSA based on their respective projected future sales of the baldness treatment. The following sales projections are used:

**Sales**

*[In millions of dollars]*

| Year | USS | FP |
|---|---|---|
| 1 | 5 | 10 |
| 2 | 20 | 20 |
| 3 | 30 | 30 |
| 4 | 40 | 40 |
| 5 | 40 | 40 |
| 6 | 40 | 40 |
| 7 | 40 | 40 |
| 8 | 20 | 20 |
| 9 | 10 | 10 |
| 10 | 5 | 5 |

(B) In Year 1, the first year of sales, USS is projected to have lower sales than FP due to lags in U.S. regulatory approval for the baldness treatment. In each subsequent year, USS and FP are projected to have equal sales. Sales are projected to build over the first three years of the period, level off for several years, and then decline over the final years of the period as new and improved baldness treatments reach the market.

(ii) To account for USS's lag in sales in the Year 1, the present discounted value of sales over the period is used as the basis for measuring benefits. Based on the risk associated with this venture, a discount rate of 10 percent is selected. The present discounted value of projected sales is determined to be approximately $154.4 million for USS and $158.9 million for FP. On this basis USS and FP are projected to obtain approximately 49.3% and 50.7% of the benefit, respectively, and the costs of developing the baldness treatment are shared accordingly.

(iii) (A) In Year 6, the Commissioner examines the CSA. USS and FP have obtained the following sales results through Year 5:

**Sales**

*[In millions of dollars]*

| Year | USS | FP |
|---|---|---|
| 1 | 0 | 17 |
| 2 | 17 | 35 |
| 3 | 25 | 41 |
| 4 | 38 | 41 |
| 5 | 39 | 41 |

(B) USS's sales initially grew more slowly than projected while FP's sales grew more quickly. In each of the first three years of the period, the share of total sales of at least one of the parties diverged by over 20% from its projected share of sales. However, by Year 5 both parties' sales had leveled off at approximately their projected values. Taking into account this leveling off of sales and all the facts and circumstances, the Commissioner determines that it is appropriate to use the original projections for the remaining years of sales. Combining the actual results through Year 5 with the projections for subsequent years, and using a discount rate of 10%, the present discounted value of sales is approximately $141.6 million for USS and $187.3 million for FP. This result implies that USS and FP obtain approximately 43.1% and 56.9%, respectively, of the anticipated benefits from the baldness treatment. Because these adjusted benefit shares are within 20% of the benefit shares calculated based on the original sales projections, the Commissioner determines that, based on the difference between adjusted and projected benefit shares, the original projections were not unreliable. No adjustment is made based on the difference between adjusted and projected benefit shares.

*Example (7).* (i) The facts are the same as in Example 6, except that the actual sales results through Year 5 are as follows:

**Sales**

*[In millions of dollars]*

| Year | USS | FP |
|---|---|---|
| 1 | 0 | 17 |
| 2 | 17 | 35 |
| 3 | 25 | 44 |
| 4 | 34 | 54 |
| 5 | 36 | 55 |

(ii) Based on the discrepancy between the projections and the actual results and on consideration of all the facts, the Commissioner determines that for the remaining years the following sales projections are more reliable than the original projections:

**Sales**
*[In millions of dollars]*

| Year | USS | FP |
|---|---|---|
| 6 | 36 | 55 |
| 7 | 36 | 55 |
| 8 | 18 | 28 |
| 9 | 9 | 14 |
| 10 | 4.5 | 7 |

(iii) Combining the actual results through Year 5 with the projections for subsequent years, and using a discount rate of 10%, the present discounted value of sales is approximately $131.2 million for USS and $229.4 million for FP. This result implies that USS and FP obtain approximately 35.4% and 63.6%, respectively, of the anticipated benefits from the baldness treatment. These adjusted benefit shares diverge by greater than 20% from the benefit shares calculated based on the original sales projections, and the Commissioner determines that, based on the difference between adjusted and projected benefit shares, the original projections were unreliable. The Commissioner adjusts cost shares for each of the taxable years under examination to conform them to the recalculated shares of anticipated benefits.

(iii) Timing of CST allocations. If the Commissioner makes an allocation to adjust the results of a CST, the allocation must be reflected for tax purposes in the year in which the IDCs were incurred. When a CST payment is owed by one controlled participant to another controlled participant, the Commissioner may make appropriate allocations to reflect an arm's length rate of interest for the time value of money, consistent with the provisions of § 1.482-2(a) (Loans or advances).

*(3) PCT allocations.* The Commissioner may make allocations to adjust the results of a PCT so that the results are consistent with an arm's length result in accordance with the provisions of the applicable sections of the regulations under section 482, as determined pursuant to paragraph (a)(2) of this section.

*(4) Allocations regarding changes in participation under a CSA.* The Commissioner may make allocations to adjust the results of any controlled transaction described in paragraph (f) of this section if the controlled participants do not reflect arm's length results in relation to any such transaction.

*(5) Allocations when CSTs are consistently and materially disproportionate to RAB shares.* If a controlled participant bears IDC shares that are consistently and materially greater or lesser than its RAB share, then the Commissioner may conclude that the economic substance of the arrangement between the controlled participants is inconsistent with the terms of the CSA. In such a case, the Commissioner may disregard such terms and impute an agreement that is consistent with the controlled participants' course of conduct, under which a controlled participant that bore a disproportionately greater IDC share received additional interests in the cost shared intangibles. See § 1.482-1(d)(3)(ii)(B) (Identifying contractual terms) and § 1.482-4(f)(3)(ii) (Identification of owner). Such additional interests will consist of partial undivided interests in the other controlled participant's interest in the cost shared intangible. Accordingly, that controlled participant must receive arm's length consideration from any controlled participant whose IDC share is less than its RAB share over time, under the provisions of §§ 1.482-1 and 1.482-4 through 1.482-6 to provide compensation for the latter controlled participants' use of such partial undivided interest.

*(6) Periodic adjustments.* (i) In general. Subject to the exceptions in paragraph (i)(6)(vi) of this section, the Commissioner may make periodic adjustments for an open taxable year (the Adjustment Year) and for all subsequent taxable years for the duration of the CSA Activity with respect to all PCT Payments, if the Commissioner determines that, for a particular PCT (the Trigger PCT), a particular controlled participant that owes or owed a PCT Payment relating to that PCT (such controlled participant being referred to as the PCT Payor for purposes of this paragraph (i)(6)) has realized an Actually Experienced Return Ratio (AERR) that is outside the Periodic Return Ratio Range (PRRR). The satisfaction of the condition stated in the preceding sentence is referred to as a Periodic Trigger. See paragraphs (i)(6)(ii) through (vi) of this section regarding the PRRR, the AERR, and periodic adjustments. In determining whether to make such adjustments, the Commissioner may consider whether the outcome as adjusted more reliably reflects an arm's length result under all the relevant facts and circumstances, including any information known as of the Determination Date. The Determination Date is the date of the relevant determination by the Commissioner. The failure of the Commissioner to determine for an earlier taxable year that a PCT Payment was not arm's length will not preclude the Commissioner from making a periodic adjustment for a subsequent year. A periodic adjustment under this paragraph (i)(6) may be made without regard to whether the taxable year of the Trigger PCT or any other PCT remains open for statute of limitations purposes or whether a periodic adjustment has previously been made with respect to any PCT payment.

(ii) PRRR. Except as provided in the next sentence, the PRRR will consist of return ratios that are not less than .667 nor more than 1.5. Alternatively, if the controlled participants have not substantially complied with the documentation requirements referenced in paragraph (k) of this section, as modified, if applicable, by paragraphs (m)(2) and (3) of this section, the PRRR will consist of return ratios that are not less than .8 nor more than 1.25.

(iii) AERR. (A) In general. The AERR is the Present Value of Total Profits (PVTP) divided by the Present Value of Investment (PVI). In computing PVTP and PVI, present values are computed using the Applicable Discount Rate (ADR), and all information available as of the Determination Date is taken into account.

(B) PVTP. The PVTP is the present value, as of the CSA Start Date, as defined in section (j)(1)(i) of this section, of the PCT Payor's actually experienced divisional profits or losses from the CSA Start Date through the end of the Adjustment Year.

(C) PVI. The PVI is the present value, as of the CSA Start Date, of the PCT Payor's investment associated with the CSA Activity, defined as the sum of its cost contributions and its PCT Payments, from the CSA Start Date through the end of the Adjustment Year. For purposes of computing the PVI, PCT Payments means all PCT Payments due from a PCT Payor before netting against PCT Payments due from other controlled participants pursuant to paragraph (j)(3)(ii) of this section.

(iv) ADR. (A) In general. Except as provided in paragraph (i)(6)(iv)(B) of this section, the ADR is the discount rate pursuant to paragraph (g)(2)(v) of this section, subject to such adjustments as the Commissioner determines appropriate.

(B) Publicly traded companies. If the PCT Payor meets the conditions of paragraph (i)(6)(iv)(C) of this section, the

ADR is the PCT Payor WACC as of the date of the Trigger PCT. However, if the Commissioner determines, or the controlled participants establish to the satisfaction of the Commissioner, that a discount rate other than the PCT Payor WACC better reflects the degree of risk of the CSA Activity as of such date, the ADR is such other discount rate.

(C) Publicly traded. A PCT Payor meets the conditions of this paragraph (i)(6)(iv)(C) if--

(1) Stock of the PCT Payor is publicly traded; or

(2) Stock of the PCT Payor is not publicly traded, provided--

(i) The PCT Payor is included in a group of companies for which consolidated financial statements are prepared; and

(ii) A publicly traded company in such group owns, directly or indirectly, stock in PCT Payor. Stock of a company is publicly traded within the meaning of this paragraph (i)(6)(iv)(C) if such stock is regularly traded on an established United States securities market and the company issues financial statements prepared in accordance with United States generally accepted accounting principles for the taxable year.

(D) PCT Payor WACC. The PCT Payor WACC is the WACC, as defined in paragraph (j)(1)(i) of this section, of the PCT Payor or the publicly traded company described in paragraph (i)(6)(iv)(C)(2)(ii) of this section, as the case may be.

(E) Generally accepted accounting principles. For purposes of paragraph (i)(6)(iv)(C) of this section, a financial statement prepared in accordance with a comprehensive body of generally accepted accounting principles other than United States generally accepted accounting principles is considered to be prepared in accordance with United States generally accepted accounting principles provided that the amounts of debt, equity, and interest expense are reflected in any reconciliation between such other accounting principles and United States generally accepted accounting principles required to be incorporated into the financial statement by the securities laws governing companies whose stock is regularly traded on United States securities markets.

(v) Determination of periodic adjustments. In the event of a Periodic Trigger, subject to paragraph (i)(6)(vi) of this section, the Commissioner may make periodic adjustments with respect to all PCT Payments between all PCT Payors and PCT Payees for the Adjustment Year and all subsequent years for the duration of the CSA Activity pursuant to the residual profit split method as provided in paragraph (g)(7) of this section, subject to the further modifications in this paragraph (i)(6)(v). A periodic adjustment may be made for a particular taxable year without regard to whether the taxable years of the Trigger PCT or other PCTs remain open for statute of limitation purposes.

(A) In general. Periodic adjustments are determined by the following steps:

(1) First, determine the present value, as of the date of the Trigger PCT, of the PCT Payments under paragraph (g)(7)(iii)(C)(3) of this section pursuant to the Adjusted RPSM as defined in paragraph (i)(6)(v)(B) of this section (first step result).

(2) Second, convert the first step result into a stream of contingent payments on a base of reasonably anticipated divisional profits or losses over the entire duration of the CSA Activity, using a level royalty rate (second step rate). See paragraph (h)(2)(iv) of this section (Conversion from fixed to contingent form of payment). This conversion is made based on all information known as of the Determination Date.

(3) Third, apply the second step rate to the actual divisional profit or loss for taxable years preceding and including the Adjustment Year to yield a stream of contingent payments for such years, and convert such stream to a present value as of the CSA Start Date under the principles of paragraph (g)(2)(v) of this section (third step result). For this purpose, the second step rate applied to a loss for a particular year will yield a negative contingent payment for that year.

(4) Fourth, convert any actual PCT Payments up through the Adjustment Year to a present value as of the CSA Start Date under the principles of paragraph (g)(2)(v) of this section. Then subtract such amount from the third step result. Determine the nominal amount in the Adjustment Year that would have a present value as of the CSA Start Date equal to the present value determined in the previous sentence to determine the periodic adjustment in the Adjustment Year.

(5) Fifth, apply the second step rate to the actual divisional profit or loss for each taxable year after the Adjustment Year up to and including the taxable year that includes the Determination Date to yield a stream of contingent payments for such years. For this purpose, the second step rate applied to a loss will yield a negative contingent payment for that year. Then subtract from each such payment any actual PCT Payment made for the same year to determine the periodic adjustment for such taxable year.

(6) For each taxable year subsequent to the year that includes the Determination Date, the periodic adjustment for such taxable year (which is in lieu of any PCT Payment that would otherwise be payable for that year under the taxpayer's position) equals the second step rate applied to the actual divisional profit or loss for that year. For this purpose, the second step rate applied to a loss for a particular year will yield a negative contingent payment for that year.

(7) If the periodic adjustment for any taxable year is a positive amount, then it is an additional PCT Payment owed from the PCT Payor to the PCT Payee for such year. If the periodic adjustment for any taxable year is a negative amount, then it is an additional PCT Payment owed by the PCT Payee to the PCT Payor for such year.

(B) Adjusted RPSM as of Determination Date. The Adjusted RPSM is the residual profit split method pursuant to paragraph (g)(7) of this section applied to determine the present value, as of the date of the Trigger PCT, of the PCT Payments under paragraph (g)(7)(iii)(C)(3) of this section, with the following modifications.

(1) Actual results up through the Determination Date shall be substituted for what otherwise were the projected results over such period, as reasonably anticipated as of the date of the Trigger PCT.

(2) Projected results for the balance of the CSA Activity after the Determination Date, as reasonably anticipated as of the Determination Date, shall be substituted for what otherwise were the projected results over such period, as reasonably anticipated as of the date of the Trigger PCT.

(3) The requirement in paragraph (g)(7)(i) of this section, that at least two controlled participants make significant nonroutine contributions, does not apply.

(vi) Exceptions to periodic adjustments. (A) Controlled participants establish periodic adjustment not warranted. No periodic adjustment will be made under paragraphs (i)(6)(i) and (i)(6)(v) of this section if the controlled participants establish to the satisfaction of the Commissioner that all the conditions described in one of paragraphs (i)(6)(vi)(A)(1) through (4) of this section apply with respect to the Trigger PCT.

(1) Transactions involving the same platform contribution as in the Trigger PCT.

(i) The same platform contribution is furnished to an uncontrolled taxpayer under substantially the same circumstances as those of the relevant Trigger PCT and with a similar form of payment as the Trigger PCT;

(ii) This transaction serves as the basis for the application of the comparable uncontrolled transaction method described in paragraph (g)(3) of this section, in the first year and all subsequent years in which substantial PCT Payments relating to the Trigger PCT were required to be paid; and

(iii) The amount of those PCT Payments in that first year was arm's length.

(2) Results not reasonably anticipated. The differential between the AERR and the nearest bound of the PRRR is due to extraordinary events beyond the control of the controlled participants that could not reasonably have been anticipated as of the date of the Trigger PCT.

(3) Reduced AERR does not cause Periodic Trigger. The Periodic Trigger would not have occurred had the PCT Payor's divisional profits or losses used to calculate its PVTP excluded those profits or losses attributable to the PCT Payor's routine contributions to its exploitation of cost shared intangibles, attributable to its operating cost contributions, and attributable to its nonroutine contributions to the CSA Activity.

(4) Increased AERR does not cause Periodic Trigger. (i) The Periodic Trigger would not have occurred had the divisional profits or losses of the PCT Payor used to calculate its PVTP included its reasonably anticipated divisional profits or losses after the Adjustment Year from the CSA Activity, including from its routine contributions, its operating cost contributions, and its nonroutine contributions to that activity, and had the cost contributions and PCT Payments of the PCT Payor used to calculate its PVI included its reasonably anticipated cost contributions and PCT Payments after the Adjustment Year. The reasonably anticipated amounts in the previous sentence are determined based on all information available as of the Determination Date.

(ii) For purposes of this paragraph (i)(6)(vi)(A)(4), the controlled participants may, if they wish, assume that the average yearly divisional profits or losses for all taxable years prior to and including the Adjustment Year, in which there has been substantial exploitation of cost shared intangibles resulting from the CSA (exploitation years), will continue to be earned in each year over a period of years equal to 15 minus the number of exploitation years prior to and including the Determination Date.

(B) Circumstances in which Periodic Trigger deemed not to occur. No Periodic Trigger will be deemed to have occurred at the times and in the circumstances described in paragraph (i)(6)(vi)(B)(1) or (2) of this section.

(1) 10-year period. In any year subsequent to the 10-year period beginning with the first taxable year in which there is substantial exploitation of cost shared intangibles resulting from the CSA, if the AERR determined is within the PRRR for each year of such 10-year period.

(2) 5-year period. In any year of the 5-year period beginning with the first taxable year in which there is substantial exploitation of cost shared intangibles resulting from the CSA, if the AERR falls below the lower bound of the PRRR.

(vii) Examples. The following examples illustrate the rules of this paragraph (i)(6):

*Example (1).* (i) At the beginning of Year 1, USP, a publicly traded U.S. company, and FS, its wholly-owned foreign subsidiary, enter into a CSA to develop new technology for cell phones. USP has a platform contribution, the rights for an in-process technology that when developed will improve the clarity of calls, for which compensation is due from FS. FS has no platform contributions to the CSA, no operating contributions, and no operating cost contributions. USP and FS agree to fixed PCT payments of $40 million in Year 1 and $10 million per year for Years 2 through 10. At the beginning of Year 1, the weighted average cost of capital of the controlled group that includes USP and FS is 15%. In Year 9, the Commissioner audits Years 5 through 7 of the CSA and considers whether any periodic adjustments should be made. USP and FS have substantially complied with the documentation requirements of paragraph (k) of this section.

(ii) FS experiences the results reported in the following table from its participation in the CSA through Year 7. In the table, all present values (PV) are reported as of the CSA Start Date, which is the same as the date of the PCT (and reflect a 15% discount rate as discussed in paragraph (iii) of this Example 1). Thus, in any year the present value of the cumulative investment is PVI and of the cumulative divisional profit or loss is PVTP. All amounts in this table and the tables that follow are reported in millions of dollars and cost contributions are referred to as "CCs" (for simplicity of calculation in this Example 1, all financial flows are assumed to occur at the beginning of the year).

| a | b | c | d | e | f | g | h |
|---|---|---|---|---|---|---|---|
| Year | Sales | Non-CC costs | CCs | PCT payments | Investment (d+e) | Divisional profit or loss (b-c) | AERR (PVTP/PVI) (g/f) |
| 1 | 0 | 0 | 15 | 40 | 55 | 0 | |
| 2 | 0 | 0 | 17 | 10 | 27 | 0 | |
| 3 | 0 | 0 | 18 | 10 | 28 | 0 | |
| 4 | 680 | 662 | 20 | 10 | 30 | 18 | |
| 5 | 836 | 718 | 22 | 10 | 32 | 118 | |
| 6 | 1,023 | 680 | 24 | 10 | 34 | 343 | |
| 7 | 1,079 | 747 | 27 | 10 | 37 | 332 | |
| PV through Year 5 | 925 | 846 | 69 | 69 | 138 | 79 | .58 |
| PV through Year 6 | 1,434 | 1,184 | 81 | 74 | 155 | 250 | 1.62 |
| PV through Year 7 | 1,900 | 1,507 | 93 | 78 | 171 | 393 | 2.31 |

(iii) Because USP is publicly traded in the United States and is a member of the controlled group to which FS (the PCT Payor) belongs, for purposes of calculating the AERR for FS, the present values of its PVTP and PVI are determined using an ADR of 15%, the weighted average cost of capital of the controlled group. (It is assumed that no other rate was determined or established, under paragraph (i)(6)(iv)(B) of this section, to better reflect the relevant degree of risk.) At a 15% discount rate, the PVTP, calculated as of Year 1, and based on actual profits realized by FS through Year 7 from exploiting the new cell phone technology developed by the CSA, is $393 million. The PVI, based on FS's cost contributions and its PCT Payments, is $171 million. The AERR for FS is equal to its PVTP divided by its PVI, $393 million/$171 million, or 2.31. There is a Periodic Trigger because FS's AERR of 2.31 falls outside the PRRR of .67 to 1.5, the applicable PRRR for controlled participants complying with the documentation requirements of this section.

(iv) At the time of the Determination Date, it is determined that the first Adjustment Year in which a Periodic Trigger occurred was Year 6, when the AERR of FS was determined to be 1.62. It is also determined that for Year 6 none of the exceptions to periodic adjustments described in paragraph (i)(6)(vi) of this section applies. The Commissioner exercises its discretion under paragraph (i)(6)(i) of this section to make periodic adjustments using Year 6 as the Adjustment Year. Therefore, the arm's length PCT Payments from FS to USP shall be determined for each taxable year using the adjusted residual profit split method described in paragraphs (g)(7)(v)(B) and (i)(6)(v)(B) of this section. Periodic adjustments will be made for each year to the extent the PCT Payments actually made by FS differ from the PCT Payment calculation under the adjusted residual profit split method.

(v) It is determined, as of the Determination Date, that the cost shared intangibles will be exploited through Year 10. FS's return for routine functions (determined by the Commissioner, based on the return for comparable routine functions undertaken by comparable uncontrolled companies, to be 10% of non-CC costs), and its actual and projected results, are described in the following table.

| a | b | c | d | e | f | g |
|---|---|---|---|---|---|---|
| Year | Sales | Non-CC costs | Divisional profits or loss (b-c) | CCs | Routine return | Residual profit (d-e-f) |
| 1 | 0 | 0 | 0 | 15 | 0 | -15 |
| 2 | 0 | 0 | 0 | 17 | 0 | -17 |
| 3 | 0 | 0 | 0 | 18 | 0 | -18 |
| 4 | 680 | 662 | 18 | 20 | 66 | -68 |
| 5 | 836 | 718 | 118 | 22 | 72 | 24 |
| 6 | 1,023 | 680 | 343 | 24 | 68 | 251 |
| 7 | 1,079 | 747 | 332 | 27 | 75 | 230 |
| 8 | 1,138 | 822 | 316 | 29 | 82 | 205 |
| 9 | 1,200 | 894 | 306 | 32 | 89 | 185 |
| 10 | 1.265 | 974 | 291 | 35 | 97 | 159 |
| Cumulative PV through Year 10 as of CSA Start Date | 3,080 | 2,385 | 695 | 124 | 238 | 332 |

(vi) The periodic adjustments are calculated in a series of steps set out in paragraph (i)(6)(v)(A) of this section. First, a lump sum for the PCT Payment is determined using the adjusted residual profit split method. Under the method, based on the considerations discussed in paragraph (g)(2)(v) of this section, the appropriate discount rate is 15% per year. The non-routine residual divisional profit or loss described in paragraph (g)(7)(iii)(B) of this section is $332 million. Further under paragraph (g)(7)(iii)(C) of this section, the entire nonroutine residual divisional profit constitutes the PCT Payment because only USP has nonroutine contributions.

(vii) In step two, the first step result ($332 million) is converted into a level royalty rate based on the reasonably anticipated divisional profits or losses of the CSA Activity, the PV of which is reported in the table above (net PV of divisional profit or loss for Years 1 through 10 is $695 million). Consequently, the step two result is a level royalty rate of 47.8% ($332/$694) of the divisional profit in Years 1 through 10.

(viii) In step three, the Commissioner calculates the PCT Payments due through Year 6 by applying the step two royalty rate to the actual divisional profits for each year and then determines the aggregate PV of these PCT Payments as of the CSA Start Date ($120 million as reported in the following table). In step four, the PCT Payments actually made through Year 6 are similarly converted to PV as of the CSA Start Date ($74 million) and subtracted from the amount determined in step three ($120 million - $74 million = $46 million). That difference of $46 million, representing a net PV as of the CSA Start Date, is then converted to a nominal amount, as of the Adjustment Year, of equivalent present value (again using a discount rate of 15%). That nominal amount is $93 million (not shown in the table), and is the periodic adjustment in Year 6.

| a | b | c | d | e |
|---|---|---|---|---|
| Year | Divisional profit | Royalty rate | Nominal royalty due under adjusted RPSM (b*c) | Nominal payments made |
| Year 1 | 0 | 47.8% | $0 | $40 |
| Year 2 | 0 | 47.8 | 0 | 10 |
| Year 3 | 0 | 47.8 | 0 | 10 |
| Year 4 | 18 | 47.8 | 9 | 10 |
| Year 5 | 118 | 47.8 | 56 | 10 |
| Year 6 | 343 | 47.8 | 164 | 10 |
| Cumulative PV as of Year 1 | | | 120 | 74 |

(ix) Under step five, the royalties due from FS to USP for Year 7 (the year after the Adjustment Year) through Year 9 (the year including the Determination Date) are determined. (These determinations are made for Years 8 and 9 after the divisional profit for those years becomes available.) For each year, the periodic adjustment is a PCT Payment due in addition to the $10 million PCT Payment that must otherwise be paid under the CSA as described in paragraph (i) of this Example 1. That periodic adjustment is calculated as the product of the step two royalty rate and the divisional profit, minus the $10 million that was otherwise paid for that year. The calculations are shown in the following table:

| a | b | c | d | E | f |
|---|---|---|---|---|---|
| Year | Divisional profit | Royalty rate | Royalty due (b*c) | PCT payments otherwise paid | Periodic adjustment (d-e) |
| 7 | 332 | 47.8% | $159 | $10 | $149 |
| 8 | 316 | 47.8 | 151 | 10 | 141 |
| 9 | 306 | 47.8 | 146 | 10 | 136 |

(x) Under step six, the periodic adjustment for Year 10 (the only exploitation year after the year containing the Determination Date) will be determined by applying the step two royalty rate to the divisional profit. This periodic adjustment is a PCT Payment payable from FS to USP, and is in lieu of the $10 payment otherwise due. The calculations are shown in the following table, based on a divisional profit of $291 million. USP and FS experienced the following results in Year 10.

| Year | Divisional profit | Royalty rate | Royalty due | PCT payment called for under original agreement but not made | Periodic adjustment |
|---|---|---|---|---|---|
| 10 | 291 | 47.8% | $139 | $10 (not paid) | $139 |

*Example (2).* The facts are the same as Example 1 (i) through (iii). At the time of the Determination Date, it is determined that the first Adjustment Year in which a Periodic Trigger occurred was Year 6, when the AERR of FS was determined to be 1.62. Upon further investigation as to what may have caused the high return in FS's market, the Commissioner learns that, in Years 4 through 6, USP's leading competitors experienced severe, unforeseen disruptions in their supply chains resulting in a significant increase in USP's and FS's market share for cell phones. Further analysis determines that without this unforeseen occurrence the Periodic Trigger would not have occurred. Based on paragraph (i)(6)(vi)(A)(2) of this section, the Commissioner determines to his satisfaction that no adjustments are warranted.

**(j) Definitions and special rules.** *(1) Definitions.* (i) In general. For purposes of this section--

| Term | Definition | Main cross references |
|---|---|---|
| Acquisition price | | § 1.482-7T(g)(5)(i). |
| Adjusted acquisition price | | § 1.482-7T(g)(5)(iii). |
| Adjusted average market capitalization | | § 1.482-7T(g)(6)(iv). |
| Adjusted benefit shares | | § 1.482-7T(i)(2)(ii)(A). |
| Adjusted RPSM | | § 1.482-7T(i)(6)(v)(B). |
| Adjustment Year | | § 1.482-7T(i)(6)(i). |
| ADR | | § 1.482-7T(i)(6)(iv). |
| AERR | | § 1.482-7T(i)(6)(iii). |
| Applicable Method | | § 1.482-7T(g)(2)(ix)(A). |

| | | |
|---|---|---|
| Average market capitalization | | § 1.482-7T(g)(6)(iii). |
| Benefits | Benefits means the sum of additional revenue generated, plus cost savings, minus any cost increases from exploiting cost shared intangibles | § 1.482-7T(e)(1)(i). |
| Capability variation | | § 1.482-7T(f)(3). |
| Change in participation under a CSA | | § 1.482-7T(f). |
| Consolidated group | | § 1.482-7T(j)(2)(i). |
| Contingent payments | | § 1.482-7T(h)(2)(i)(B). |
| Controlled participant | Controlled participant means a controlled taxpayer, as defined under Sec. 1.482-1(i)(5), that is a party to the contractual agreement that underlies the CSA, and that reasonably anticipates that it will derive benefits, as defined in paragraph (e)(1)(i) of this section, from exploiting one or more cost shared intangibles | § 1.482-7T(a)(1). |
| Controlled transfer of interests | | § 1.482-7T(f)(2). |
| Cost contribution | | § 1.482-7T(d)(4). |
| Cost shared intangible | Cost shared intangible means any intangible, within the meaning of § 1.482-4(b), that is developed by the IDA, including any portion of such intangible that reflects a platform contribution. Therefore, an intangible developed by the IDA is a cost shared intangible even though the intangible was not always or was never a reasonably anticipated cost shared intangible | § 1.482-7T(b). |
| Cost sharing alternative | | § 1.482-7T(g)(4)(i)(B). |
| Cost sharing arrangement or CSA | | § 1.482-7T(a), (b). |
| Cost sharing transactions or CSTs | | § 1.482-7T(a)(1), (b)(1)(i). |
| Cross operating contributions | A cross operating contribution is any resource or capability or right, other than a platform contribution, that a controlled participant has developed, maintained, or acquired prior to the CSA Start Date that is reasonably anticipated to contribute to the CSA Activity within another controlled participant's division | § 1.482-7T(a)(3)(iii), (g)(2)(iv). |
| CSA Activity | CSA Activity is the activity of developing and exploiting cost shared intangibles | § 1.482-7T(c)(2)(i). |
| CSA Start Date | The earliest date that any IDC described in paragraph (d)(1) of this section occurred | § 1.482-7T(i)(6)(iii)(B). |
| CST Payments | | § 1.482-7T(b)(1). |
| Date of PCT | | § 1.482-7T(b)(3). |
| Determination Date | | § 1.482-7T(i)(6)(i). |

| | | |
|---|---|---|
| Division | Division means the territory or other division that serves as the basis of the division of interests under the CSA in the cost shared intangibles pursuant to Sec. 1.482-7T(b)(4) | See definitions of divisional profit or loss, operating contribution, and operating cost contribution. |
| Divisional interest | | § 1.482-7T(b)(1)(iii), (b)(4). |
| Divisional profit or loss | Divisional profit or loss means the operating profit or loss as separately earned by each controlled participant in its division from the CSA Activity, determined before any expense (including amortization) on account of cost contributions, operating cost contributions, routine platform and operating contributions, nonroutine contributions (including platform and operating contributions), and tax | § 1.482-7T(g)(4)(iii). |
| Fixed payments | | § 1.482-7T(h)(2)(i)(A). |
| IDC share | | § 1.482-7T(d)(4). |
| Input parameters | | § 1.482-7T(g)(2)(ix)(B). |
| Intangible development activity or IDA | | § 1.482-7T(d)(1). |
| Intangible development costs or IDCs | | § 1.482-7T(a)(1), (d)(1). |
| Licensing alternative | | § 1.482-7T(g)(4)(i)(C). |
| Licensing payments | Licensing payments means payments pursuant to the licensing obligations under the licensing alternative | § 1.482-7T(g)(4)(iii). |
| Make-or-sell rights | | § 1.482-7T(c)(4), (g)(2)(iv). |
| Market-based input parameter | | § 1.482-7T(g)(2)(ix)(B). |
| Market returns for routine contributions | Market returns for routine contributions means returns determined by reference to the returns achieved by uncontrolled taxpayers engaged in activities similar to the relevant business activity in the controlled participant's division, consistent with the methods described in § Sec. 1.482-3, 1.482-4, 1.482-5, or Sec. 1.482-9T(c) | § 1.482-7T(g)(4), (g)(7). |
| Method payment form | | § 1.482-7T(h)(3). |
| Nonroutine contributions | Nonroutine contributions means a controlled participant's contributions to the relevant business activities that are not routine contributions. Nonroutine contributions ordinarily include both nonroutine platform contributions and nonroutine operating contributions used by controlled participants in the commercial exploitation of their interests in the cost shared intangibles (for example, marketing intangibles used by a controlled participant in its division to sell products that are based on the cost shared intangible) | § 1.482-7T(g). |
| Nonroutine residual divisional profit or loss | | § 1.482-7T(g)(7)(iii). |

| | | |
|---|---|---|
| Operating contributions | An operating contribution is any resource or capability or right, other than a platform contribution, that a controlled participant has developed, maintained, or acquired prior to the CSA Start Date that is reasonably anticipated to contribute to the CSA Activity within the controlled participant's division | § 1.482-7T(g)(2)(ii), (g)(4)(v)(E), (g)(7)(iii)(A) & (C). |
| Operating cost contributions | Operating cost contributions means all costs in the ordinary course of business on or after the CSA Start Date that, based on analysis of the facts and circumstances, are directly identified with, or are reasonably allocable to, developing resources, capabilities, or rights (other than reasonably anticipated cost shared intangibles) that are reasonably anticipated to contribute to the CSA Activity within the controlled participant's division | § 1.482-7T(g)(2)(ii), (g)(4)(iii), (g)(7)(iii)(B). |
| PCT Payee | | § 1.482-7T(b)(1)(ii). |
| PCT Payment | | § 1.482-7T(b)(1)(ii). |
| PCT Payor | | § 1.482-7T(b)(1)(ii), (i)(6)(i). |
| PCT Payor WACC | | § 1.482-7T(i)(6)(iv)(D). |
| Periodic adjustments | | § 1.482-7T(i)(6)(i). |
| Periodic Trigger | | § 1.482-7T(i)(6)(i). |
| Platform contribution transaction or PCT | | § 1.482-7T(a)(2), (b)(1)(ii). |
| Platform contributions | | § 1.482-7T(c)(1). |
| Post-tax income | | § 1.482-7T(g)(2)(v)(B)(3), (g)(4)(i)(G). |
| Pre-tax income | | § 1.482-7T(g)(2)(v)(B)(3), (g)(4)(i)(G). |
| Projected benefit shares | | § 1.482-7T(i)(2)(ii)(A). |
| PRRR | | § 1.482-7T(i)(6)(ii). |
| PVI | | § 1.482-7T(i)(6)(iii)(C). |
| PVTP | | § 1.482-7T(i)(6)(iii)(B). |
| Reasonably anticipated benefits | A controlled participant's reasonably anticipated benefits means the benefits that reasonably may be anticipated to be derived from exploiting cost shared intangibles. For purposes of this definition, benefits mean the sum of additional revenue generated, plus cost savings, minus any cost increases from exploiting cost shared intangibles | § 1.482-7T(e)(1). |
| Reasonably anticipated benefits ,or RAB shares | | § 1.482-7T(a)(1), (e)(1). |
| Reasonably anticipated cost shared intangible | | § 1.482-7T(d)(1)(ii). |
| Relevant business activity | | § 1.482-7T(g)(7)(i). |

| | | |
|---|---|---|
| Routine contributions | Routine contributions means a controlled participant's contributions to the relevant business activities that are of the same or similar kind to those made by uncontrolled taxpayers involved in similar business activities for which it is possible to identify market returns. Routine contributions ordinarily include contributions of tangible property, services and intangibles that are generally owned by uncontrolled taxpayers engaged in similar activities. A functional analysis is required to identify these contributions according to the functions performed, risks assumed, and resources employed by each of the controlled participants | § 1.482-7T(g)(4), (g)(7). |
| Routine platform and operating contributions, and net routine platform and operating contributions | § 1.482-7T(g)(4)(vi), 1.482-7(g)(7)(iii)(C)(4). | |
| Specified payment form | | § 1.482-7T(h)(3). |
| Stock-based compensation | | § 1.482-7T(d)(3). |
| Stock options | | § 1.482-7T(d)(3)(i). |
| Subsequent PCT | | § 1.482-7T(g)(2)(viii). |
| Target | | § 1.482-7T(g)(5)(i). |
| Trigger PCT | | § 1.482-7T(i)(6)(i). |
| Variable input parameter | | § 1.482-7T(g)(2)(ix)(C). |
| WACC | WACC means weighted average cost of capital | § 1.482-7T(i)(6)(iv)(D). |

(ii) Examples. The following examples illustrate certain definitions in paragraph (j)(1)(i) of this section:

*Example (1).* Controlled participant. Foreign Parent (FP) is a foreign corporation engaged in the extraction of a natural resource. FP has a U.S. subsidiary (USS) to which FP sells supplies of this resource for sale in the United States. FP enters into a CSA with USS to develop a new machine to extract the natural resource. The machine uses a new extraction process that will be patented in the United States and in other countries. The CSA provides that USS will receive the rights to exploit the machine in the extraction of the natural resource in the United States, and FP will receive the rights in the rest of the world. This resource does not, however, exist in the United States. Despite the fact that USS has received the right to exploit this process in the United States, USS is not a controlled participant because it will not derive a benefit from exploiting the intangible developed under the CSA.

*Example (2).* Controlled participants. (i) U.S. Parent (USP), one foreign subsidiary (FS), and a second foreign subsidiary constituting the group's research arm (R+D) enter into a CSA to develop manufacturing intangibles for a new product line A. USP and FS are assigned the exclusive rights to exploit the intangibles respectively in the United States and the rest of the world, where each presently manufactures and sells various existing product lines. R+D is not assigned any rights to exploit the intangibles. R+D's activity consists solely in carrying out research for the group. It is reliably projected that the RAB shares of USP and FS will be 66⅔% and 33⅓%, respectively, and the parties' agreement provides that USP and FS will reimburse 66⅔% and 33\1/ 3\%, respectively, of the IDCs incurred by R+D with respect to the new intangible.

(ii) R+D does not qualify as a controlled participant within the meaning of paragraph (j)(1)(i) of this section, because it will not derive any benefits from exploiting cost shared intangibles. Therefore, R+D is treated as a service provider for purposes of this section and must receive arm's length consideration for the assistance it is deemed to provide to USP and FS, under the rules of paragraph (a)(3) of this section and §§ 1.482-4(f)(3)(iii), 1.482-4T(f)(4), and 1.482-9T, as appropriate. Such consideration must be treated as IDCs incurred by USP and FS in proportion to their RAB shares (that is, 66⅔% and 33⅓%, respectively). R+D will not be considered to bear any share of the IDCs under the arrangement.

*Example (3).* Cost shared intangible, reasonably anticipated cost shared intangible. U.S. Parent (USP) has developed and currently exploits an antihistamine, XY, which is manufactured in tablet form. USP enters into a CSA with its wholly-owned foreign subsidiary (FS) to develop XYZ, a new improved version of XY that will be manufactured as a nasal spray. Work under the CSA is fully devoted to developing XYZ, and XYZ is developed. During the development period, XYZ is a reasonably anticipated cost shared intangible under the CSA. Once developed, XYZ is a cost shared intangible under the CSA.

*Example (4).* Cost shared intangible. The facts are the same as in Example 3, except that in the course of developing XYZ, the controlled participants by accident discover ABC, a cure for disease D. ABC is a cost shared intangible under the CSA.

*Example (5).* Reasonably anticipated benefits. Controlled parties A and B enter into a cost sharing arrangement to develop product and process intangibles for an already existing Product P. Without such intangibles, A and B would each reasonably anticipate revenue, in present value terms, of $100M from sales of Product P until it became obsolete. With the intangibles, A and B each reasonably anticipate selling the same number of units each year, but reasonably anticipate that the price will be higher. Because the particular product intangible is more highly regarded in A's market, A reasonably anticipates an increase of $20M in present value revenue from the product intangible, while B reasonably anticipates only an increase of $10M. Further, A and B each reasonably anticipate spending an extra $5M present value in production costs to include the feature embodying the product intangible. Finally, A and B each reasonably anticipate saving $2M present value in production costs by using the process intangible. A and B reasonably anticipate no other economic effects from exploiting the cost shared intangibles. A's reasonably anticipated benefits from exploiting the cost shared intangibles equal its reasonably anticipated increase in revenue ($20M) plus its reasonably anticipated cost savings ($2M) minus its reasonably anticipated increased costs ($5M), which equals $17M. Similarly, B's reasonably anticipated benefits from exploiting the cost shared intangibles equal its reasonably anticipated increase in revenue ($10M) plus its reasonably anticipated cost savings ($2M) minus its reasonably anticipated increased costs ($5M), which equals $7M. Thus A's reasonably anticipated benefits are $17M and B's reasonably anticipated benefits are $7M.

*(2) Special rules.* (i) Consolidated group. For purposes of this section, all members of the same consolidated group shall be treated as one taxpayer. For these purposes, the term consolidated group means all members of a group of controlled entities created or organized within a single country and subjected to an income tax by such country on the basis of their combined income.

(ii) Trade or business. A participant that is a foreign corporation or nonresident alien individual will not be treated as engaged in a trade or business within the United States solely by reason of its participation in a CSA. See generally § 1.864-2(a).

(iii) Partnership. A CSA, or an arrangement to which the Commissioner applies the rules of this section, will not be treated as a partnership to which the rules of subchapter K of the Internal Revenue Code apply. See § 301.7701-1(c) of this chapter.

*(3) Character.* (i) CST Payments. CST Payments generally will be considered the payor's costs of developing intangibles at the location where such development is conducted. For these purposes, IDCs borne directly by a controlled participant that are deductible are deemed to be reduced to the extent of any CST Payments owed to it by other controlled participants pursuant to the CSA. Each cost sharing payment received by a payee will be treated as coming pro rata from payments made by all payors and will be applied pro rata against the deductions for the taxable year that the payee is allowed in connection with the IDCs. Payments received in excess of such deductions will be treated as in consideration for use of the land and tangible property furnished for purposes of the CSA by the payee. For purposes of the research credit determined under section 41, CST Payments among controlled participants will be treated as provided for intra-group transactions in § 1.41-6(i). Any payment made or received by a taxpayer pursuant to an arrangement that the Commissioner determines not to be a CSA will be subject to the provisions of §§ 1.482-1, 1.482-4 through 1.482-6 and 1.482-9T. Any payment that in substance constitutes a cost sharing payment will be treated as such for purposes of this section, regardless of its characterization under foreign law.

(ii) PCT Payments. A PCT Payor's payment required under paragraph (b)(1)(ii) of this section is deemed to be reduced to the extent of any payments owed to it under such paragraph from other controlled participants. Each PCT Payment received by a PCT Payee will be treated as coming pro rata out of payments made by all PCT Payors. PCT Payments will be characterized consistently with the designation of the type of transaction pursuant to paragraphs (c)(3) and (k)(2)(ii)(H) of this section. Depending on such designation, such payments will be treated as either consideration for a transfer of an interest in intangible property or for services.

(iii) Examples. The following examples illustrate this paragraph (j)(3):

*Example (1).* U.S. Parent (USP) and its wholly owned Foreign Subsidiary (FS) form a CSA to develop a miniature widget, the Small R. Based on RAB shares, USP agrees to bear 40% and FS to bear 60% of the costs incurred during the term of the agreement. The principal IDCs are operating costs incurred by FS in Country Z of 100X annually, and costs incurred by USP in the United States also of 100X annually. Of the total costs of 200X, USP's share is 80X and FS's share is 120X so that FS must make a payment to USP of 20X. The payment will be treated as a reimbursement of 20X of USP's costs in the United States. Accordingly, USP's Form 1120 will reflect an 80X deduction on account of activities performed in the United States for purposes of allocation and apportionment of the deduction to source. The Form 5471 "Information Return of U.S. Persons With Respect to Certain Foreign Corporations" for FS will reflect a 100X deduction on account of activities performed in Country Z and a 20X deduction on account of activities performed in the United States.

*Example (2).* The facts are the same as in Example 1, except that the 100X of costs borne by USP consist of 5X of costs incurred by USP in the United States and 95X of arm's length rental charge, as described in paragraph (d)(1)(iii) of this section, for the use of a facility in the United States. The depreciation deduction attributable to the U.S. facility is 7X. The 20X net payment by FS to USP will first be applied in reduction pro rata of the 5X deduction for costs and the 7X depreciation deduction attributable to the U.S. facility. The 8X remainder will be treated as rent for the U.S. facility.

*Example (3).* (i) Four members A, B, C, and D of a controlled group form a CSA to develop the next generation technology for their business. Based on RAB shares, the participants agree to bear shares of the costs incurred during the term of the agreement in the following percentages: A 40%; B 15%; C 25%; and D 20%. The arm's length values of the platform contributions they respectively own are in the following amounts for the taxable year: A 80X; B 40X; C 30X; and D 30X. The provisional (before offsets) and final PCT Payments among A, B, C, and D are shown in the table as follows:

**[All amounts stated in X's]**

| | A | B | C | D |
|---|---|---|---|---|
| Payments | <40> | <21> | <37.5> | <30> |
| Receipts | 48 | 34 | 22.5 | 24 |
| Final | 8 | 13 | <15> | <6> |

(ii) The first row/first column shows A's provisional PCT Payment equal to the product of 100X (sum of 40X, 30X, and 30X) and A's RAB share of 40%. The second row/first column shows A's provisional PCT receipts equal to the sum of the products of 80X and B's, C's, and D's RAB shares (15%, 25%, and 20%, respectively). The other entries in the first two rows of the table are similarly computed. The last row shows the final PCT receipts/payments after offsets. Thus, for the taxable year, A and B are treated as receiving the 8X and 13X, respectively, pro rata out of payments by C and D of 15X and 6X, respectively.

**(k) CSA administrative requirements.** A controlled participant meets the requirements of this paragraph if it substantially complies, respectively, with the CSA contractual, documentation, accounting, and reporting requirements of paragraphs (k)(1), (k)(2), (k)(3), and (k)(4) of this section.

*(1) CSA contractual requirements.* (i) In general. A CSA must be recorded in writing in a contract that is contemporaneous with the formation (and any revision) of the CSA and that includes the contractual provisions described in this paragraph (k)(1).

(ii) Contractual provisions. The written contract described in this paragraph (k)(1) must include provisions that—

(A) List the controlled participants and any other members of the controlled group that are reasonably anticipated to benefit from the use of the cost shared intangibles, including the address of each domestic entity and the country of organization of each foreign entity;

(B) Describe the scope of the IDA to be undertaken and each reasonably anticipated cost shared intangible or class of reasonably anticipated cost shared intangibles;

(C) Specify the functions and risks that each controlled participant will undertake in connection with the CSA;

(D) Divide among the controlled participants all divisional interests in cost shared intangibles and specify each controlled participant's divisional interest in the cost shared intangibles, as described in paragraphs (b)(1)(iii) and (b)(4) of this section, that it will own and exploit without any further obligation to compensate any other controlled participant for such interest;

(E) Provide a method to calculate the controlled participants' RAB shares, based on factors that can reasonably be expected to reflect the participants' shares of anticipated benefits, and require that such RAB shares must be updated, as described in paragraph (e)(1) of this section (see also paragraph (k)(2)(ii)(F) of this section);

(F) Enumerate all categories of IDCs to be shared under the CSA;

(G) Specify that the controlled participant must use a consistent method of accounting to determine IDCs and RAB shares, as described in paragraphs (d) and (e) of this section, respectively, and must translate foreign currencies on a consistent basis;

(H) Require the controlled participant to enter into CSTs covering all IDCs, as described in paragraph (b)(1)(i) of this section, in connection with the CSA;

(I) Require the controlled participants to enter into PCTs covering all platform contributions, as described in paragraph (b)(1)(ii) of this section, in connection with the CSA;

(J) Specify the form of payment due under each PCT (or group of PCTs) in existence at the formation (and any revision) of the CSA, including information and explanation that reasonably supports an analysis of applicable provisions of paragraph (h) of this section; and

(K) Specify the date on which the CSA is entered into and the duration of the CSA, the conditions under which the CSA may be modified or terminated, and the consequences of a modification or termination (including consequences described under the rules of paragraph (f) of this section).

(iii) Meaning of contemporaneous. (A) In general. For purposes of this paragraph (k)(1), a written contractual agreement is contemporaneous with the formation (or revision) of a CSA if, and only if, the controlled participants record the CSA, in its entirety, in a document that they sign and date no later than 60 days after the first occurrence of any IDC described in paragraph (d) of this section to which such agreement (or revision) is to apply.

(B) Example. The following example illustrates the principles of this paragraph (k)(1)(iii):

*Example.* Companies A and B, both of which are members of the same controlled group, commence an IDA on March 1, Year 1. Company A pays the first IDCs in relation to the IDA, as cash salaries to A's research staff, for the staff's work during the first week of March, Year 1. A and B, however, do not sign and date any written contractual agreement until August 1, Year 1, whereupon they execute a "Cost Sharing Agreement" that purports to be "effective as of" March 1 of Year 1. The arrangement fails the requirement that the participants record their arrangement in a written contractual agreement that is contemporaneous with the formation of a CSA. The arrangement has failed to meet the requirements set forth in paragraph (b)(2) of this section and, pursuant to paragraph (b) of this section, cannot be a CSA.

(iv) Interpretation of contractual provisions. (A) In general. The provisions of a written contract described in this paragraph (k)(1) and of the additional documentation described in paragraph (k)(2) of this section must be clear and unambiguous. The provisions will be interpreted by reference to the economic substance of the transaction and the actual conduct of the controlled participants. See § 1.482-1(d)(3)(ii)(B) (discussing interpretation of contractual terms in assessing the comparability of controlled and uncontrolled transactions). Accordingly, the Commissioner may impute contractual terms in a CSA consistent with the economic substance of the CSA and may disregard contractual terms that lack economic substance. An allocation of risk between controlled participants after the outcome of such risk is known or reasonably knowable lacks economic substance. See § 1.482-1(d)(3)(iii)(B). A contractual term that is disregarded due to a lack of economic substance does not satisfy a contractual requirement set forth in this paragraph (k)(1) or documentation requirement set forth in paragraph (k)(2) of this section. See paragraph (b)(5) of this section for the treatment of an arrangement among controlled taxpayers that fails to comply with the requirements of this section.

(B) Examples. The following examples illustrate the principles of this paragraph (k)(1)(iv). In each example, it is assumed that the Commissioner will exercise the discretion granted pursuant to paragraph (b)(5)(ii) of this section to apply the provisions of this section to the arrangement that purports to be a CSA.

*Example (1).* The contractual provisions recorded upon formation of an arrangement that purports to be a CSA provide that PCT payments with respect to a particular platform contribution will consist of payments contingent on sales. Contrary to the contractual provisions, the PCT payments actually made are contingent on profits. Because the controlled participants' actual conduct is different from the contractual terms, the Commissioner may determine, based on the facts and circumstances, that—

(i) The actual payments have economic substance and, therefore, impute payment terms in the CSA consistent with the actual payments; or

(ii) The contract terms reflect the economic substance of the arrangement and, therefore, the actual payments must be adjusted to conform to the terms.

*Example (2).* An arrangement that purports to be a CSA provides that PCT payments with respect to a particular platform contribution shall be contingent payments equal to 10% of sales of products that incorporate cost shared intangibles. The contract terms further provide that the controlled participants must adjust such contingent payments in accordance with a formula set forth in the terms. During the first three years of the arrangement, the controlled participants fail to make the adjustments required by the terms with respect to the PCT payments. The Commissioner may determine, based on the facts and circumstances, that-—

(i) The contingent payment terms with respect to the platform contribution do not have economic substance because the controlled participants did not act in accordance with their upfront risk allocation; or

(ii) The contract terms reflect the economic substance of the arrangement and, therefore, the actual payments must be adjusted to conform to the terms.

*(2) CSA documentation requirements.* (i) In general. The controlled participants must timely update and maintain sufficient documentation to establish that the participants have met the CSA contractual requirements of paragraph (k)(1) of this section and the additional CSA documentation requirements of this paragraph (k)(2).

(ii) Additional CSA documentation requirements. The controlled participants to a CSA must timely update and maintain documentation sufficient to—

(A) Describe the current scope of the IDA and identify—

(1) Any additions or subtractions from the list of reasonably anticipated cost shared intangibles reported pursuant to paragraph (k)(1)(ii)(B) of this section;

(2) Any cost shared intangible, together with each controlled participant's interest therein; and

(3) Any further development of intangibles already developed under the CSA or of specified applications of such intangibles which has been removed from the IDA (see paragraphs (d)(1)(ii) and (j)(1)(i) of this section (definitions of reasonably anticipated cost shared intangible, cost shared intangible)) and the steps (including any accounting classifications and allocations) taken to implement such removal.

(B) Establish that each controlled participant reasonably anticipates that it will derive benefits from exploiting cost shared intangibles;

(C) Describe the functions and risks that each controlled participant has undertaken during the term of the CSA;

(D) Provide an overview of each controlled participant's business segments, including an analysis of the economic and legal factors that affect CST and PCT pricing;

(E) Establish the amount of each controlled participant's IDCs for each taxable year under the CSA, including all IDCs attributable to stock-based compensation, as described in paragraph (d)(3) of this section (including the method of measurement and timing used in determining such IDCs, and the data, as of the date of grant, used to identify stock-based compensation with the IDA);

(F) Describe the method used to estimate each controlled participant's RAB share for each year during the course of the CSA, including—

(1) All projections used to estimate benefits;

(2) All updates of the RAB shares in accordance with paragraph (e)(1) of this section; and

(3) An explanation of why that method was selected and why the method provides the most reliable measure for estimating RAB shares;

(G) Describe all platform contributions;

(H) Designate the type of transaction involved for each PCT or group of PCTs;

(I) Specify, within the time period provided in paragraph (h)(2)(iii) of this section, the form of payment due under each PCT or group of PCTs, including information and explanation that reasonably supports an analysis of applicable provisions of paragraph (h) of this section;

(J) Describe and explain the method selected to determine the arm's length payment due under each PCT, including—

(1) An explanation of why the method selected constitutes the best method, as described in § 1.482-1(c)(2), for measuring an arm's length result;

(2) The economic analyses, data, and projections relied upon in developing and selecting the best method, including the source of the data and projections used;

(3) Each alternative method that was considered, and the reason or reasons that the alternative method was not selected;

(4) Any data that the controlled participant obtains, after the CSA takes effect, that would help determine if the controlled participant's method selected has been applied in a reasonable manner;

(5) The discount rate or rates, where applicable, used for purposes of evaluating PCT Payments, including information and explanation that reasonably supports an analysis of applicable provisions of paragraph (g)(2)(v) of this section;

(6) The estimated arm's length values of any platform contributions as of the dates of the relevant PCTs, in accordance with paragraph (g)(2)(ii) of this section;

(7) A discussion, where applicable, of why transactions were or were not aggregated under the principles of paragraph (g)(2)(iv) of this section;

(8) The method payment form and any conversion made from the method payment form to the specified payment form, as described in paragraph (h)(3) of this section; and

(9) If applicable under paragraph (i)(6)(iv) of this section, the WACC of the parent of the controlled group that includes the controlled participants.

(iii) Coordination rules and production of documents. (A) Coordination with penalty regulations. See § 1.6662-6(d)(2)(iii)(D) regarding coordination of the rules of this paragraph (k) with the documentation requirements for purposes of the accuracy-related penalty under section 6662(e) and (h).

(B) Production of documentation. Each controlled participant must provide to the Commissioner, within 30 days of a request, the items described in this paragraph (k)(2) and paragraph (k)(3) of this section. The time for compliance described in this paragraph (k)(2)(iii)(B) may be extended at the discretion of the Commissioner.

*(3) CSA accounting requirements.* (i) In general. The controlled participants must maintain books and records (and related or underlying data and information) that are sufficient to—

(A) Establish that the controlled participants have used (and are using) a consistent method of accounting to measure costs and benefits;

(B) Permit verification that the amount of any contingent PCT Payments due have been (and are being) properly determined;

(C) Translate foreign currencies on a consistent basis; and

(D) To the extent that the method of accounting used materially differs from U.S. generally accepted accounting principles, explain any such material differences.

(ii) Reliance on financial accounting. For purposes of this section, the controlled participants may not rely solely upon financial accounting to establish satisfaction of the accounting requirements of this paragraph (k)(3). Rather, the method of accounting must clearly reflect income. Thor Power Tools Co. v. Commissioner, 439 U.S. 522 (1979).

*(4) CSA reporting requirements.* (i) CSA Statement. Each controlled participant must file with the Internal Revenue Service, in the manner described in this paragraph (k)(4), a ''Statement of Controlled Participant to § 1.482-7T Cost Sharing Arrangement'' (CSA Statement) that complies with the requirements of this paragraph (k)(4).

(ii) Content of CSA Statement. The CSA Statement of each controlled participant must—

(A) State that the participant is a controlled participant in a CSA;

(B) Provide the controlled participant's taxpayer identification number;

(C) List the other controlled participants in the CSA, the country of organization of each such participant, and the taxpayer identification number of each such participant;

(D) Specify the earliest date that any IDC described in paragraph (d)(1) of this section occurred; and

(E) Indicate the date on which the controlled participants formed (or revised) the CSA and, if different from such date, the date on which the controlled participants recorded the CSA (or any revision) contemporaneously in accordance with paragraphs (k)(1)(i) and (iii) of this section.

(iii) Time for filing CSA Statement. (A) 90-day rule. Each controlled participant must file its original CSA Statement with the Internal Revenue Service Ogden Campus, no later than 90 days after the first occurrence of an IDC to which the newly-formed CSA applies, as described in paragraph (k)(1)(iii)(A) of this section, or, in the case of a taxpayer that became a controlled participant after the formation of the CSA, no later than 90 days after such taxpayer became a controlled participant. A CSA Statement filed in accordance with this paragraph (k)(4)(iii)(A) must be dated and signed, under penalties of perjury, by an officer of the controlled participant who is duly authorized (under local law) to sign the statement on behalf of the controlled participant.

(B) Annual return requirement. (1) In general. Each controlled participant must attach to its U.S. income tax return, for each taxable year for the duration of the CSA, a copy of the original CSA Statement that the controlled participant filed in accordance with the 90-day rule of paragraph (k)(4)(iii)(A) of this section. In addition, the controlled participant must update the information reflected on the original CSA Statement annually by attaching a schedule that documents changes in such information over time.

(2) Special filing rule for annual return requirement. If a controlled participant is not required to file a U.S. income tax return, the participant must ensure that the copy or copies of the CSA Statement and any updates are attached to Schedule M of any Form 5471, any Form 5472 "Information Return of a Foreign Owned Corporation", or any Form 8865 "Return of U.S. Persons With Respect to Certain Foreign Partnerships", filed with respect to that participant.

(iv) Examples. The following examples illustrate this paragraph (k)(4). In each example, Companies A and B are members of the same controlled group.

*Example (1).* A and B, both of which file U.S. tax returns, agree to share the costs of developing a new chemical formula in accordance with the provisions of this section. On March 30, Year 1, A and B record their agreement in a written contract styled, "Cost Sharing Agreement." The contract applies by its terms to IDCs occurring after March 1, Year 1. The first IDCs to which the CSA applies occurred on March 15, Year 1. To comply with paragraph (k)(4)(iii)(A) of this section, A and B individually must file separate CSA Statements no later than 90 days after March 15, Year 1 (June 13, Year 1). Further, to comply with paragraph (k)(4)(iii)(B) of this section, A and B must attach copies of their respective CSA Statements to their respective Year 1 U.S. income tax returns.

*Example (2).* The facts are the same as in Example 1, except that a year has passed and C, which files a U.S. tax return, joined the CSA on May 9, Year 2. To comply with the annual filing requirement described in paragraph (k)(4)(iii)(B) of this section, A and B must each attach copies of their respective CSA Statements (as filed for Year 1) to their respective Year 2 income tax returns, along with a schedule updated appropriately to reflect the changes in information described in paragraph (k)(4)(ii) of this section resulting from the addition of C to the CSA. To comply with both the 90-day rule described in paragraph (k)(4)(iii)(A) of this section and the annual filing requirement described in paragraph (k)(4)(iii)(B) of this section, C must file a CSA Statement no later than 90 days after May 9, Year 2 (August 7, Year 2), and must attach a copy of such CSA Statement to its Year 2 income tax return.

**(l) Effective/applicability date.** This section applies on January 5, 2009.

**(m) Transition rule.** *(1) In general.* An arrangement in existence on January 5, 2009 will be considered a CSA, as described under paragraph (b) of this section, if, prior to such date, it was a qualified cost sharing arrangement under the provisions of § 1.482-7 (as contained in the 26 CFR part

1 edition revised as of January 1, 1996, hereafter referred to as "former § 1.482-7"), but only if the written contract, as described in paragraph (k)(1) of this section, is amended, if necessary, to conform with, and only if the activities of the controlled participants substantially comply with, the provisions of this section, as modified by paragraphs (m)(2) and (m)(3) of this section, by July 6, 2009.

*(2) Transitional modification of applicable provisions.* For purposes of this paragraph (m), conformity and substantial compliance with the provisions of this section shall be determined with the following modifications:

(i) CSTs and PCTs occurring prior to January 5, 2009 shall be subject to the provisions of former § 1.482-7 rather than this section.

(ii) Except to the extent provided in paragraph (m)(3) of this section, PCTs that occur under a CSA that was a qualified cost sharing arrangement under the provisions of former § 1.482-7 and remained in effect on January 5, 2009, shall be subject to the periodic adjustment rules of § 1.482-4(f)(2) rather than the rules of paragraph (i)(6) of this section.

(iii) Paragraphs (b)(1)(iii) and (b)(4) of this section shall not apply.

(iv) Paragraph (k)(1)(ii)(D) of this section shall not apply.

(v) Paragraphs (k)(1)(ii)(H) and (k)(1)(ii)(I) of this section shall be construed as applying only to transactions entered into on or after January 5, 2009.

(vi) The deadline for recordation of the revised written contractual agreement pursuant to paragraph (k)(1)(iii) of this section shall be no later than July 6, 2009.

(vii) Paragraphs (k)(2)(ii)(G) through (J) of this section shall be construed as applying only with reference to PCTs entered into on or after January 5, 2009.

(viii) Paragraph (k)(4)(iii)(A) of this section shall be construed as requiring a CSA Statement with respect to the revised written contractual agreement described in paragraph (m)(2)(vi) of this section no later than September 2, 2009.

(ix) Paragraph (k)(4)(iii)(B) of this section shall be construed as only applying for taxable years ending after the filing of the CSA Statement described in paragraph (m)(2)(viii) of this section.

*(3) Special rule for certain periodic adjustments.* The periodic adjustment rules in paragraph (i)(6) of this section (rather than the rules of § 1.482-4(f)(2)) shall apply to PCTs that occur on or after the date of a material change in the scope of the CSA from its scope as of January 5, 2009. A material change in scope would include a material expansion of the activities undertaken beyond the scope of the intangible development area, as described in former § 1.482-7(b)(4)(iv). For this purpose, a contraction of the scope of a CSA, absent a material expansion into one or more lines of research and development beyond the scope of the intangible development area, does not constitute a material change in scope of the CSA. Whether a material change in scope has occurred is determined on a cumulative basis. Therefore, a series of expansions, any one of which is not a material expansion by itself, may collectively constitute a material expansion.

**(n) Expiration date.** The applicability of this section expires on or before December 30, 2011.

---

T.D. 9441, 12/31/2008.

---

**§ 1.482-8 Examples of the best method rule.**

**(a) Introduction.** In accordance with the best method rule of § 1.482-1(c), a method may be applied in a particular case only if the comparability, quality of data, and reliability of assumptions under that method make it more reliable than any other available measure of the arm's length result. The following examples illustrate the comparative analysis required to apply this rule. As with all of the examples in these regulations, these examples are based on simplified facts, are provided solely for purposes of illustrating the type of analysis required under the relevant rule, and do not provide rules of general application. Thus, conclusions reached in these examples as to the relative reliability of methods are based on the assumed facts of the examples, and are not general conclusions concerning the relative reliability of any method.

**(b) Examples.**

*Example (1).* Preference for comparable uncontrolled price method. Company A is the U.S. distribution subsidiary of Company B, a foreign manufacturer of consumer electrical appliances. Company A purchases toaster ovens from Company B for resale in the U.S. market. To exploit other outlets for its toaster ovens, Company B also sells its toaster ovens to Company C, an unrelated U.S. distributor of toaster ovens. The products sold to Company A and Company C are identical in every respect and there are no material differences between the transactions. In this case application of the CUP method, using the sales of toaster ovens to Company C, generally will provide a more reliable measure of an arm's length result for the controlled sale of toaster ovens to Company A than the application of any other method. See §§ 1.482-1(c)(2)(i) and -3(b)(2)(ii)(A).

*Example (2).* Resale price method preferred to comparable uncontrolled price method. The facts are the same as in Example 1, except that the toaster ovens sold to Company A are of substantially higher quality than those sold to Company C and the effect on price of such quality differences cannot be accurately determined. In addition, in order to round out its line of consumer appliances Company A purchases blenders from unrelated parties for resale in the United States. The blenders are resold to substantially the same customers as the toaster ovens, have a similar resale value to the toaster ovens, and are purchased under similar terms and in similar volumes. The distribution functions performed by Company A appear to be similar for toaster ovens and blenders. Given the product differences between the toaster ovens, application of the resale price method using the purchases and resales of blenders as the uncontrolled comparables is likely to provide a more reliable measure of an arm's length result than application of the comparable uncontrolled price method using Company B's sales of toaster ovens to Company C.

*Example (3).* Resale price method preferred to comparable profits method.

(i) The facts are the same as in Example 2, except that Company A purchases all its products from Company B and Company B makes no uncontrolled sales into the United States. However, six uncontrolled U.S. distributors are identified that purchase a similar line of products from unrelated parties. The uncontrolled distributors purchase toaster ovens from unrelated parties, but there are significant differences in the characteristics of the toaster ovens, including the brandnames under which they are sold.

(ii) Under the facts of this case, reliable adjustments for the effect of the different brandnames cannot be made. Except for some differences in payment terms and inventory levels, the purchases and resales of toaster ovens by the three uncontrolled distributors are closely similar to the controlled purchases in terms of the markets in which they occur, the volume of the transactions, the marketing activities undertaken by the distributor, inventory levels, warranties, allocation of currency risk, and other relevant functions and risks. Reliable adjustments can be made for the differences in payment terms and inventory levels. In addition, sufficiently detailed accounting information is available to permit adjustments to be made for differences in accounting methods or in reporting of costs between cost of goods sold and operating expenses. There are no other material differences between the controlled and uncontrolled transactions.

(iii) Because reliable adjustments for the differences between the toaster ovens, including the trademarks under which they are sold, cannot be made, these uncontrolled transactions will not serve as reliable measures of an arm's length result under the comparable uncontrolled price method. There is, however, close functional similarity between the controlled and uncontrolled transactions and reliable adjustments have been made for material differences that would be likely to affect gross profit. Under these circumstances, the gross profit margins derived under the resale price method are less likely to be susceptible to any unidentified differences than the operating profit measures used under the comparable profits method. Therefore, given the close functional comparability between the controlled and uncontrolled transactions, and the high quality of the data, the resale price method achieves a higher degree of comparability and will provide a more reliable measure of an arm's length result. See § 1.482-1(c) (Best method rule).

*Example (4).* Comparable profits method preferred to resale price method. The facts are the same as in Example 3, except that the accounting information available for the uncontrolled comparables is not sufficiently detailed to ensure consistent reporting between cost of goods sold and operating expenses of material items such as discounts, insurance, warranty costs, and supervisory, general and administrative expenses. These expenses are significant in amount. Therefore, whether these expenses are treated as costs of goods sold or operating expenses would have a significant effect on gross margins. Because in this case reliable adjustments can not be made for such accounting differences, the reliability of the resale price method is significantly reduced. There is, however, close functional similarity between the controlled and uncontrolled transactions and reliable adjustments have been made for all material differences other than the potential accounting differences. Because the comparable profits method is not adversely affected by the potential accounting differences, under these circumstances the comparable profits method is likely to produce a more reliable measure of an arm's length result than the resale price method. See § 1.482-1(c) (Best method rule).

*Example (5).* Cost plus method preferred to comparable profits method.

(i) USS is a U.S. company that manufactures machine tool parts and sells them to its foreign parent corporation, FP. Four U.S. companies are identified that also manufacture various types of machine tool parts but sell them to uncontrolled purchasers.

(ii) Except for some differences in payment terms, the manufacture and sales of machine tool parts by the four uncontrolled companies are closely similar to the controlled transactions in terms of the functions performed and risks assumed. Reliable adjustments can be made for the differences in payment terms. In addition, sufficiently detailed accounting information is available to permit adjustments to be made for differences between the controlled transaction and the uncontrolled comparables in accounting methods and in the reporting of costs between cost of goods sold and operating expenses.

(iii) There is close functional similarity between the controlled and uncontrolled transactions and reliable adjustments can be made for material differences that would be likely to affect gross profit. Under these circumstances, the gross profit markups derived under the cost plus method are less likely to be susceptible to any unidentified differences than the operating profit measures used under the comparable profits method. Therefore, given the close functional comparability between the controlled and uncontrolled transactions, and the high quality of the data, the cost plus method achieves a higher degree of comparability and will provide a more reliable measure of an arm's length result. See § 1.482-1(c) (Best method rule).

*Example (6).* Comparable profits method preferred to cost plus method. The facts are the same as in Example 5, except that there are significant differences between the controlled and uncontrolled transactions in terms of the types of parts and components manufactured and the complexity of the manufacturing process. The resulting functional differences are likely to materially affect gross profit margins, but it is not possible to identify the specific differences and reliably adjust for their effect on gross profit. Because these functional differences would be reflected in differences in operating expenses, the operating profit measures used under the comparable profits method implicitly reflect to some extent these functional differences. Therefore, because in this case the comparable profits method is less sensitive than the cost plus method to the potentially significant functional differences between the controlled and uncontrolled transactions, the comparable profits method is likely to produce a more reliable measure of an arm's length result than the cost plus method. See § 1.482-1(c) (Best method rule).

*Example (7).* Preference for comparable uncontrolled transaction method.

(i) USpharm, a U.S. pharmaceutical company, develops a new drug Z that is a safe and effective treatment for the disease zeezee. USpharm has obtained patents covering drug Z in the United States and in various foreign countries. USpharm has also obtained the regulatory authorizations necessary to market drug Z in the United States and in foreign countries.

(ii) USpharm licenses its subsidiary in country X, Xpharm, to produce and sell drug Z in country X. At the same time, it licenses an unrelated company, Ydrug, to produce and sell drug Z in country Y, a neighboring country. Prior to licensing the drug, USpharm had obtained patent protection and regulatory approvals in both countries and both countries provide similar protection for intellectual property rights. Country X and country Y are similar countries in terms of population, per capita income and the incidence of disease zeezee. Consequently, drug Z is expected to sell in similar quantities and at similar prices in both countries. In addition, costs of producing drug Z in each country are expected to be approximately the same.

(iii) USpharm and Xpharm establish terms for the license of drug Z that are identical in every material respect, including royalty rate, to the terms established between USpharm and Ydrug. In this case the district director determines that the royalty rate established in the Ydrug license agreement is a reliable measure of the arm's length royalty rate for the Xpharm license agreement. Given that the same property is transferred in the controlled and uncontrolled transactions, and that the circumstances under which the transactions occurred are substantially the same, in this case the comparable uncontrolled transaction method is likely to provide a more reliable measure of an arm's length result than any other method. See § 1.482-4(c)(2)(ii).

*Example (8).* Residual profit split method preferred to other methods.

(i) USC is a U.S. company that develops, manufactures and sells communications equipment. EC is the European subsidiary of USC. EC is an established company that carries out extensive research and development activities and develops, manufactures and sells communications equipment in Europe. There are extensive transactions between USC and EC. USC licenses valuable technology it has developed to EC for use in the European market but EC also licenses valuable technology it has developed to USC. Each company uses components manufactured by the other in some of its products and purchases products from the other for resale in its own market.

(ii) Detailed accounting information is available for both USC and EC and adjustments can be made to achieve a high degree of consistency in accounting practices between them. Relatively reliable allocations of costs, income and assets can be made between the business activities that are related to the controlled transactions and those that are not. Relevant marketing and research and development expenditures can be identified and reasonable estimates of the useful life of the related intangibles are available so that the capitalized value of the intangible development expenses of USC and EC can be calculated. In this case there is no reason to believe that the relative value of these capitalized expenses is substantially different from the relative value of the intangible property of USC and EC. Furthermore, comparables are identified that could be used to estimate a market return for the routine contributions of USC and EC. Based on these facts, the residual profit split could provide a reliable measure of an arm's length result.

(iii) There are no uncontrolled transactions involving property that is sufficiently comparable to much of the tangible and intangible property transferred between USC and EC to permit use of the comparable uncontrolled price method or the comparable uncontrolled transaction method. Uncontrolled companies are identified in Europe and the United States that perform somewhat similar activities to USC and EC; however, the activities of none of these companies are as complex as those of USC and EC and they do not use similar levels of highly valuable intangible property that they have developed themselves. Under these circumstances, the uncontrolled companies may be useful in determining a market return for the routine contributions of USC and EC, but that return would not reflect the value of the intangible property employed by USC and EC. Thus, none of the uncontrolled companies is sufficiently similar so that reliable results would be obtained using the resale price, cost plus, or comparable profits methods. Moreover, no uncontrolled companies can be identified that engaged in sufficiently similar activities and transactions with each other to employ the comparable profit split method.

(iv) Given the difficulties in applying the other methods, the reliability of the internal data on USC and EC, and the fact that acceptable comparables are available for deriving a market return for the routine contributions of USC and EC, the residual profit split method is likely to provide the most reliable measure of an arm's length result in this case.

*Example (9).* Comparable profits method preferred to profit split.

(i) Company X is a large, complex U.S. company that carries out extensive research and development activities and manufactures and markets a variety of products. Company X has developed a new process by which compact disks can be fabricated at a fraction of the cost previously required. The process is expected to prove highly profitable, since there is a large market for compact disks. Company X establishes a new foreign subsidiary, Company Y, and licenses it the rights to use the process to fabricate compact disks for the foreign market as well as continuing technical support and improvements to the process. Company Y uses the process to fabricate compact disks which it supplies to related and unrelated parties.

(ii) The process licensed to Company Y is unique and highly valuable and no uncontrolled transfers of intangible property can be found that are sufficiently comparable to permit reliable application of the comparable uncontrolled transaction method. Company X is a large, complex company engaged in a variety of activities that owns unique and highly valuable intangible property. Consequently, no uncontrolled companies can be found that are similar to Company X. Furthermore, application of the profit split method in this case would involve the difficult and problematic tasks of allocating Company X's costs and assets between the relevant business activity and other activities and assigning a value to Company X's intangible contributions. On the other hand, Company Y performs relatively routine manufacturing and marketing activities and there are a number of similar uncontrolled companies. Thus, application of the comparable profits method using Company Y as the tested party is likely to produce a more reliable measure of an arm's length result than a profit split in this case.

*Example (10).* Cost of services plus method preferred to other methods.

(i) FP designs and manufactures consumer electronic devices that incorporate advanced technology. In year 1, FP introduces Product X, an entertainment device targeted primarily at the youth market. FP's wholly-owned, exclusive U.S. distributor, USSub, sells Product X in the U.S. market. USSub hires an independent marketing firm, Agency A, to promote Product X in the U.S. market. Agency A has successfully promoted other electronic products on behalf of other uncontrolled parties. USSub executes a one-year, renewable contract with Agency A that requires it to develop the market for Product X, within an annual budget set by USSub. In years 1 through 3, Agency A develops advertising, buys media, and sponsors events featuring Product X. Agency A receives a markup of 25% on all expenses of promoting Product X, with the exception of media buys, which are reimbursed at cost. During year 3, sales of Product X decrease sharply, as Product X is displaced by competitors' products. At the end of year 3, sales of Product X are discontinued.

(ii) Prior to the start of year 4, FP develops a new entertainment device, Product Y. Like Product X, Product Y is intended for sale to the youth market, but it is marketed under a new trademark distinct from that used for Product X. USSub decides to perform all U.S. market promotion for Product Y. USSub hires key Agency A staff members who handled the successful Product X campaign. To promote Product Y, USSub intends to use methods similar to those used successfully by Agency A to promote Product X (print advertising, media, event sponsorship, etc.). FP and USSub enter into a one-year, renewable agreement concerning promotion of Product Y in the U.S. market. Under the agreement, FP compensates USSub for promoting Product Y, based on a cost of services plus markup of A%. Third-party media buys by USSub in connection with Product Y are reimbursed at cost.

(iii) Assume that under the contractual arrangements between FP and USSub, the arm's length consideration for Product Y and the trademark or other intangible property may be determined reliably under one or more transfer pricing methods. At issue in this example is the separate evaluation of the arm's length compensation for the year 4 promotional activities performed by USSub pursuant to its contract with FP.

(iv) USSub's accounting records contain reliable data that separately state the costs incurred to promote Product Y. A functional analysis indicates that USSub's activities to promote Product Y in year 4 are similar to activities performed by Agency A during years 1 through 3 under the contract with USSub. In other respects, no material differences exist in the market conditions or the promotional activities performed in year 4, as compared to those in years 1 through 3.

(v) It is possible to identify uncontrolled distributors or licensees of electronic products that perform, as one component of their business activities, promotional activities similar to those performed by USSub. However, it is unlikely that publicly available accounting data from these companies would allow computation of the comparable transactional costs or total services costs associated with the marketing or promotional activities that these entities perform, as one component of business activities. If that were possible, the comparable profits method for services might provide a reliable measure of an arm's length result. The functional analysis of the marketing activities performed by USSub in year 4 indicates that they are similar to the activities performed by Agency A in years 1 through 3 for Product X. Because reliable information is available concerning the markup on costs charged in a comparable uncontrolled transaction, the most reliable measure of an arm's length price is the cost of services plus method in § 1.482-9(e).

*Example (11).* CPM for services preferred to other methods. (i) FP manufactures furniture and accessories for residential use. FP sells its products to retailers in Europe under the trademark, "Moda." FP holds all worldwide rights to the trademark, including in the United States. USSub is FP's wholly-owned subsidiary in the U.S. market and the exclusive U.S. distributor of FP's merchandise. Historically, USSub dealt only with specialized designers in the U.S. market and advertised in trade publications targeted to this market. Although items sold in the U.S. and Europe are physically identical, USSub's U.S. customers generally resell the merchandise as non-branded merchandise.

(ii) FP retains an independent firm to evaluate the feasibility of selling FP's trademarked merchandise in the general wholesale and retail market in the United States. The study concludes that this segment of the U.S. market, which is not exploited by USSub, may generate substantial profits. Based on this study, FP enters into a separate agreement with USSub, which provides that USSub will develop this market in the United States for the benefit of FP. USSub separately accounts for personnel expenses, overhead, and out-of-pocket costs attributable to the initial stage of the marketing campaign (Phase I). USSub receives as compensation its costs, plus a markup of X%, for activities in Phase I. At the end of Phase I, FP will evaluate the program. If success appears likely, USSub will begin full-scale distribution of trademarked merchandise in the new market segment, pursuant to agreements negotiated with FP at that time.

(iii) Assume that under the contractual arrangements in effect between FP and USSub, the arm's length consideration for the merchandise and the trademark or other intangible property may be determined reliably under one or more transfer pricing methods. At issue in this example is the separate evaluation of the arm's length compensation for the marketing activities conducted by USSub in years 1 and following.

(iv) A functional analysis reveals that USSub's activities consist primarily of modifying the promotional materials created by FP, negotiating media buys, and arranging promotional events. FP separately compensates USSub for all Phase I activities, and detailed accounting information is available regarding the costs of these activities. The Phase I activities of USSub are similar to those of uncontrolled companies that perform, as their primary business activity, a range of advertising and media relations activities on a contract basis for uncontrolled parties.

(v) No information is available concerning the comparable uncontrolled prices for services in transactions similar to those engaged in by FP and USSub. Nor is any information available concerning uncontrolled transactions that would allow application of the cost of services plus method. It is possible to identify uncontrolled distributors or licensees of home furnishings that perform, as one component of their business activities, promotional activities similar to those performed by USSub. However, it is unlikely that publicly available accounting data from these companies would allow computation of the comparable transactional costs or total services costs associated with the marketing or promotional activities that these entities performed, as one component of their business activities. On the other hand, it is possible to identify uncontrolled advertising and media relations companies, the principal business activities of which are similar to the Phase I activities of USSub. Under these circumstances, the most reliable measure of an arm's length price is the comparable profits method of § 1.482-9(f). The uncontrolled advertising comparables' treatment of material items, such as classification of items as cost of goods sold or selling, general, and administrative expenses, may differ from that of USSub. Such inconsistencies in accounting treatment between the uncontrolled comparables and the tested party, or among the comparables, are less important when using the ratio of operating profit to total services costs under the comparable profits method for services in § 1.482-9(f). Under this method, the operating profit of USSub from the Phase I activities is compared to the operating profit of uncontrolled parties that perform general advertising and media relations as their primary business activity.

*Example (12).* Residual profit split preferred to other methods. (i) USP is a manufacturer of athletic apparel sold under the AA trademark, to which FP owns the worldwide rights. USP sells AA trademark apparel in countries throughout the world, but prior to year 1, USP did not sell its merchandise in Country X. In year 1, USP acquires an uncontrolled Country X company which becomes its wholly-owned subsidiary, XSub. USP enters into an exclusive distribution arrangement with XSub in Country X. Before being acquired by USP in year 1, XSub distributed athletic apparel purchased from uncontrolled suppliers and resold that merchandise to retailers. After being acquired by USP in year 1, XSub continues to distribute merchandise from uncontrolled suppliers and also begins to distribute AA trademark apparel. Under a separate agreement with USP, XSub uses its best efforts to promote the AA trademark in Country X, with the goal of maximizing sales volume and revenues from AA merchandise.

(ii) Prior to year 1, USP executed long-term endorsement contracts with several prominent professional athletes. These contracts give USP the right to use the names and likenesses of the athletes in any country in which AA merchandise is sold during the term of the contract. These contracts remain in effect for five years, starting in year 1. Before being acquired by USP, XSub renewed a long-term agreement with SportMart, an uncontrolled company that owns a nationwide chain of sporting goods retailers in Country X. XSub has been SportMart's primary supplier from the time that SportMart began operations. Under the agreement, SportMart will provide AA merchandise preferred shelf-space and will feature AA merchandise at no charge in its print ads and seasonal promotions. In consideration for these commitments, USP and XSub grant SportMart advance access to new products and the right to use the professional athletes under contract with USP in SportMart advertisements featuring AA merchandise (subject to approval of content by USP).

(iii) Assume that it is possible to segregate all transactions by XSub that involve distribution of merchandise acquired from uncontrolled distributors (non-controlled transactions). In addition, assume that, apart from the activities undertaken by USP and XSub to promote AA apparel in Country X, the arm's length compensation for other functions performed by USP and XSub in the Country X market in years 1 and following can be reliably determined. At issue in this Example 12 is the application of the residual profit split analysis to determine the appropriate division between USP and XSub of the balance of the operating profits from the Country X market, that is the portion attributable to nonroutine contributions to the marketing and promotional activities.

(iv) A functional analysis of the marketing and promotional activities conducted in the Country X market, as described in this example, indicates that both USP and XSub made nonroutine contributions to the business activity. USP contributed the long-term endorsement contracts with professional athletes. XSub contributed its long-term contractual rights with SportMart, which were made more valuable by its successful, long-term relationship with SportMart.

(v) Based on the facts and circumstances, including the fact that both USP and XSub made valuable nonroutine contributions to the marketing and promotional activities and an analysis of the availability (or lack thereof) of comparable and reliable market benchmarks, the Commissioner determines that the most reliable measure of an arm's length result is the residual profit split method in § 1.482-9(g). The residual profit split analysis would take into account both routine and nonroutine contributions by USP and XSub, in order to determine an appropriate allocation of the combined operating profits in the Country X market from the sale of AA merchandise and from related promotional and marketing activities.

*Example (13).* through 18. [Reserved]. For further guidance, see § 1.482-8T(b) Examples 13 through 18.

**(c) Effective/applicability date.** *(1) In general.* The provisions of paragraph (b) Examples 10, 11, and 12 of this section are generally applicable for taxable years beginning after July 31, 2009.

*(2) Election to apply regulation to earlier taxable years.* A person may elect to apply the provisions of paragraph (b) Examples 10, 11, and 12 of this section to earlier taxable years in accordance with the rules set forth in § 1.482-9(n)(2).

---

T.D. 8552, 7/1/94, amend T.D. 9278, 7/31/2006, T.D. 9441, 12/31/2008, T.D. 9456, 7/31/2009.

---

PAR. 8. Section 1.482-8 is amended by revising paragraph (b) Examples 13, 14, 15, 16, 17 and 18 to read as follows:

**Proposed § 1.482-8 Examples of the best method rule.** [*For Preamble, see ¶ 153,087*]

* * * * *

**(b)** * * *

*Example (13).* through 18. [The text of the proposed § 1.482-8(b) Examples 13 through 18 is the same as the text of § 1.482-8T(b) Examples 13 through 18 published elsewhere in this issue of the Federal Register]. [*See T.D. 9441, 01/05/2009, 74 Fed. Reg. 2.*].

* * * * *

PAR. 9. Section 1.482-8 is amended by adding Examples 10 through 15 at the end of the section to read as follows:

**Proposed § 1.482-8**

• ***Caution:*** This Proposed Reg was incorporated into final and temporary regulations by TD 9441, 12/31/2008.

Examples of the best method rule. [*For Preamble, see ¶ 152,697*]

* * * * *

*Example (10).* Preference for acquisition price method. (i) USP develops, manufacturers, and distributes ethical pharmaceutical products. USP and FS, USP's wholly-owned subsidiary, enter into a CSA to develop a new oncological drug, Oncol. Immediately prior to entering into the CSA, USP acquires Company X, an unrelated U.S. pharmaceutical company. Company X is solely engaged in oncological pharmaceutical research, and its only significant resources and capabilities are its workforce and its sole patent, which is associated with Compound X, a promising molecular compound derived from a rare plant, which USP reasonably anticipates will contribute to developing Oncol. All of Company X researchers will be engaged solely in research that is reasonably anticipated to contribute to developing Oncol as well. The RT Rights in the Compound X and the commitment of Company X's researchers to the development of Oncol are external contributions for which compensation is due from FS as part of a PCT. Under the terms of the CSA, USP is to be compensated for its external contributions on a lump sum basis.

(ii) In this case, the acquisition price method, based on the lump sum price paid by USP for Company X, is likely to provide a more reliable measure of an arm's length PCT Payment due to USP than the application of any other method.

*Example (11).* Preference for market capitalization method. (i) Company X is a publicly traded U.S. company solely engaged in oncological pharmaceutical research and its only significant resources and capabilities are its workforce and its sole patent, which is associated with Compound Y, a promising molecular compound derived from a rare plant. Company X has no marketable products. Company X enters into a CSA with FS, a newly-formed foreign subsidiary, to develop a new oncological drug, Oncol, derived from Compound Y. Compound Y is reasonably anticipated to contribute to developing Oncol. All of Company X researchers will be engaged solely in research that is reasonably anticipated to contribute to developing Oncol under the CSA. The RT Rights in Compound Y and the commitment of Company X's researchers are external contributions for which compensation is due from FS as part of a PCT. Under the terms of the CSA, Company X is to be compensated for its external contributions on a lump sum basis.

(ii) In this case, given that Company X's external contributions covered by PCTs relate to its entire economic value, the application of the market capitalization method, based on the market capitalization of Company X, is likely to provide a more reliable measure of an arm's length result for Company X's PCTs to the CSA than the application of any other method.

*Example (12).* Preference for market capitalization method. (i) MicroDent, Inc. (MDI) is a publicly traded company that developed a new dental surgical microscope ScopeX-1, which drastically shortens many surgical procedures. On January 1 of Year 1, MDI entered into a CSA with a wholly-owned foreign subsidiary (FS) to develop ScopeX-2, the next generation of ScopeX-1. The RT Rights associated with ScopeX-1, as well as MDI's research capabilities are reasonably anticipated to contribute to the development of ScopeX-2 and are therefore external contributions for which compensation is due from FS as part of a PCT. Under the terms of the CSA, MDI is to be compensated for its external contributions on a lump sum basis. At the time of the PCT, MDI's only product was the ScopeX-I microscope, although MDI was in the process of developing ScopeX-2. Concurrent with the CSA, MDI separately transfers exclusive and perpetual exploitation rights associated with ScopeX-1 to FS in the same specified geographic area as assigned to FS in the CSA.

(ii) Although the transactions between MDI and FS under the CSA are distinct from the transactions between MDI and FS relating to the exploitation rights for ScopeX-1, it is likely to be more reliable to evaluate the combined effect of the transactions than to evaluate them in isolation. This is because the combined transactions between MDI and FS relate to all of the economic value of MDI (that is, the exploitation rights and research rights associated with ScopeX-1, as well as the research capabilities of MDI). In this case, application of the market capitalization method, based on the enterprise value of MDI on January 1 of Year 1, is likely to provide a more reliable measure of an arm's length payment for the aggregated transactions than the application of any other method.

(iii) Notwithstanding that the market capitalization method provides the most reliable measure of the aggregated transactions between MDI and FS, see paragraph (g)(2)(v) of this section for further considerations of when further analysis may be required to distinguish between the remuneration to MDI associated with PCTs under the CSA (for research rights and capabilities associated with ScopeX-1) and the remuneration to MDI for the exploitation rights associated with ScopeX-1.

*Example (13).* Income method (CPM-based) preferred to acquisition price method. The facts are the same as Example 10, except that the acquisition occurred significantly in advance of formation of the CSA, and reliable adjustments cannot be made for this time difference. In addition, Company X has other valuable molecular patents and associated research capabilities, apart from Compound Y, that are not reasonably anticipated to contribute to the development of Oncol and that cannot be reliably valued. Under the terms of the CSA, USP will undertake all R&D (consisting of laboratory research and clinical testing) and manufacturing associated with Oncol, as well as the distribution activities for its assigned area (the United States). FS will distribute Oncol in its assigned area (the rest of the world). FS's distribution activities are routine in nature, and the profitability from its activities may be reliably determined from third-party comparables. FS does not furnish any external contributions. At the time of the PCT, reliable (ex ante) financial projections associated with the development of Oncol and its separate exploitation in each of USP's and FSub's assigned geographical territories are undertaken. In this case, application of the income method is likely to provide a more reliable measure of an arm's length result than application of the acquisition price method based on the price paid by USP for Company X.

*Example (14).* Evaluation of alternative methods. (i) The facts are the same as Example 10, except that the acquisition occurred sometime prior to the CSA, and Company X has some areas of promising research that are not reasonably anticipated to contribute to developing Oncol. In general, the Commissioner determines that the acquisition price data is useful in informing the arm's length price, but not necessarily determinative. Under the terms of the CSA, USP will undertake all R&D (consisting of laboratory research and clinical testing) and manufacturing associated with Oncol, as well as the distribution activities for its assigned area (the United States). FS will distribute Oncol in its assigned area (the rest of the world). FS's distribution activities are routine in nature, and the profitability from its activities may be reliably determined from third-party comparables. At the time of the PCT, financial projections associated with the development of Oncol and its separate exploitation in each of USP's and FSub's assigned geographical territories are undertaken.

(ii) Under the facts, it is possible that the acquisition price method or the CPM-based income method might reasonably be applied. Whether the acquisition price method or the income method provides the most reliable evidence of the arm's length price of USP's contributions depends on a number of factors, including the reliability of the financial projections, the reliability of the discount rate chosen, and the extent to which the acquisition price of Company X can be reliably adjusted to account for changes in value over the time period between the acquisition and the formation of the CSA and to account for the value of the in-process research done by Company X that does not constitute external contributions to the CSA.

*Example (15).* Evaluation of alternative methods. (i) The facts are the same as Example 14, except that FS has a patent on Compound Y, which the parties reasonably anticipate will be useful in mitigating potential side effects associated with Compound X and thereby contribute to the development of Oncol. The RT Rights in Compound Y constitute an external contribution for which compensation is due from USP as part of a PCT. The value of FS's external contribution cannot be reliably measured by market benchmarks.

(ii) Under the facts, it is possible that either the acquisition price method and the income method together or the residual profit split method might reasonably be applied to determine the arm's length PCT Payments due between USP and FS. Under the first option the PCT Payment for the external contributions related to Company X's workforce and Compound X would be determined using the acquisition price method referring to the lump sum price paid by USP for Company X. Because the value of these external contributions can be determined by reference to a market benchmark they are considered routine external contributions. Accordingly, under this option, the external contribution related to Compound Y would be the only nonroutine external contribution and the relevant PCT Payment is determined using the income method. Under the second option, rather than looking to the acquisition price for Company X, all the external contributions are considered nonroutine and the RPSM is applied to determine the PCT Payments for each external contribution. Under either option, the PCT Payments will be netted against each other.

(iii) Whether the acquisition price method together with the income method or the residual profit split method provides the most reliable evidence of the arm's length price of the external contributions of USP and FS depends on a number of factors, including the reliability of the determination of the relative values of the external contributions for purposes of the RPSM, and the extent to which the acquisition price of Company X can be reliably adjusted to account for changes in value over the time period between the acquisition and the formation of the CSA and to account for the value of the RT Rights in the in-process research done by Company X that does not constitute external contributions to the CSA. In these circumstances, it is also relevant to consider whether the results of each method are consistent with each other, or whether one or both methods are consistent with other potential methods that could be applied.

PAR. 6. Section 1.482-8 is redesignated as § 1.482-9 and a new § 1.482-8 is added to read as follows:

**Proposed § 1.482-8 [Redesignated as § 1.482-9]** [*For Preamble, see ¶ 151,855*]

**Proposed § 1.482-8 Allocation of income earned in a global securities dealing operation.** [*For Preamble, see ¶ 151,855*]

**(a) General requirements and definitions.** *(1) In general.* Where two or more controlled taxpayers are participants in a global dealing operation, the allocation of income, gains, losses, deductions, credits and allowances (referred to herein as income and deductions) from the global dealing operation is determined under this section. The arm's length allocation of income and deductions related to a global dealing operation must be determined under one of the methods listed in paragraphs (b) through (f) of this section. Each of the methods must be applied in accordance with all of the provisions of § 1.482-1, including the best method rule of § 1.482-1(c), the comparability analysis of § 1.482-1(d), and the arm's length range of § 1.482-1(e), as those sections are supplemented or modified in paragraphs (a)(3) and (a)(4) of this section. The available methods are—

(i) The comparable uncontrolled financial transaction method, described in paragraph (b) of this section;

(ii) The gross margin method, described in paragraph (c) of this section;

(iii) The gross markup method, described in paragraph (d) of this section;

(iv) The profit split method, described in paragraph (e) of this section; and

(v) Unspecified methods, described in paragraph (f) of this section.

*(2) Definitions.* (i) Global dealing operation. A global dealing operation consists of the execution of customer transactions, including marketing, sales, pricing and risk management activities, in a particular financial product or line of financial products, in multiple tax jurisdictions and/or through multiple participants, as defined in paragraph (a)(2)(ii) of this section. The taking of proprietary positions is not included within the definition of a global dealing operation unless the proprietary positions are entered into by a regular dealer in securities in its capacity as such a dealer under paragraph (a)(2)(iii) of this section. Lending activities are not included within the definition of a global dealing operation. Therefore, income earned from such lending activities or from securities held for investment is not income from a global dealing operation and is not governed by this section. A global dealing operation may consist of several different business activities engaged in by participants. Whether a separate business activity is a global dealing operation shall be determined with respect to each type of financial product entered on the taxpayer's books and records.

(ii) Participant. (A) A participant is a controlled taxpayer, as defined in § 1.482-1(i)(5), that is—

(1) A regular dealer in securities as defined in paragraph (a)(2)(iii) of this section; or

(2) A member of a group of controlled taxpayers which includes a regular dealer in securities, but only if that member conducts one or more activities related to the activities of such dealer.

(B) For purposes of paragraph (a)(2)(ii)(A)(2) of this section, such related activities are marketing, sales, pricing, risk management or brokering activities. Such related activities do not include credit analysis, accounting services, back office services, general supervision and control over the policies of the controlled taxpayer, or the provision of a guarantee of one or more transactions entered into by a regular dealer in securities or other participant.

(iii) Regular dealer in securities. For purposes of this section, a regular dealer in securities is a taxpayer that—

(A) Regularly and actively offers to, and in fact does, purchase securities from and sell securities to customers who are not controlled taxpayers in the ordinary course of a trade or business; or

(B) Regularly and actively offers to, and in fact does, enter into, assume, offset, assign or otherwise terminate positions in securities with customers who are not controlled entities in the ordinary course of a trade or business.

(iv) Security. For purposes of this section, a security is a security as defined in section 475(c)(2) or foreign currency.

*(3) Factors for determining comparability for a global dealing operation.* The comparability factors set out in this paragraph (a)(3) must be applied in place of the comparability factors described in § 1.482-1(d)(3) for purposes of evaluating a global dealing operation.

(i) Functional analysis. In lieu of the list set forth in § 1.482-1(d)(3)(i)(A) through (H), functions that may need to be accounted for in determining the comparability of two transactions are—

(A) Product research and development;

(B) Marketing;

(C) Pricing;

(D) Brokering; and

(E) Risk management.

(ii) Contractual terms. In addition to the terms set forth in § 1.482-1(d)(3)(ii)(A), and subject to § 1.482-1(d)(3)(ii)(B), significant contractual terms for financial products transactions include—

(A) Sales or purchase volume;

(B) Rights to modify or transfer the contract;

(C) Contingencies to which the contract is subject or that are embedded in the contract;

(D) Length of the contract;

(E) Settlement date;

(F) Place of settlement (or delivery);

(G) Notional principal amount;

(H) Specified indices;

(I) The currency or currencies in which the contract is denominated;

(J) Choice of law and jurisdiction governing the contract to the extent chosen by the parties; and

(K) Dispute resolution, including binding arbitration.

(iii) Risk. In lieu of the list set forth in § 1.482-1(d)(3), significant risks that could affect the prices or profitability include—

(A) Market risks, including the volatility of the price of the underlying property;

(B) Liquidity risks, including the fact that the property (or the hedges of the property) trades in a thinly traded market;

(C) Hedging risks;

(D) Creditworthiness of the counterparty; and

(E) Country and transfer risk.

(iv) Economic conditions. In lieu of the list set forth in § 1.482-1(d)(3)(iv) (A) through (H), significant economic conditions that could affect the prices or profitability include

(A) The similarity of geographic markets;

(B) The relative size and sophistication of the markets;

(C) The alternatives reasonably available to the buyer and seller;

(D) The volatility of the market; and

(E) The time the particular transaction is entered into.

*(4) Arm's length range.* (i) General rule. Except as modified in this paragraph (a)(4), § 1.482-1(e) will apply to determine the arm's length range of transactions entered into by a global dealing operation as defined in paragraph (a)(2)(i) of this section. In determining the arm's length range, whether the participant is a buyer or seller is a relevant factor.

(ii) Reliability. In determining the reliability of an arm's length range, it is necessary to consider the fact that the market for financial products is highly volatile and participants in a global dealing operation frequently earn only thin profit margins. The reliability of using a statistical range in establishing a comparable price of a financial product in a global dealing operation is based on facts and circumstances. In a global dealing operation, close proximity in time between a controlled transaction and an uncontrolled transaction may be a relevant factor in determining the reliability of the uncontrolled transaction as a measure of the arm's length price. The relevant time period will depend on the price volatility of the particular product.

(iii) Authority to make adjustments. The district director may, notwithstanding § 1.482-1(e)(1), adjust a taxpayer's results under a method applied on a transaction by transaction basis if a valid statistical analysis demonstrates that the taxpayer's controlled prices, when analyzed on an aggregate basis, provide results that are not arm's length. See § 1.482-1(f)(2)(iv). This may occur, for example, when there is a pattern of prices in controlled transactions that are higher or lower than the prices of comparable uncontrolled transactions.

*(5) Examples.* The following examples illustrate the principles of this paragraph (a).

*Example (1).* Identification of participants.

(i) B is a foreign bank that acts as a market maker in foreign currency in country X, the country of which it is a resident. C, a country Y resident corporation, D, a country Z resident corporation, and USFX, a U.S. resident corporation are all members of a controlled group of taxpayers with B, and each acts as a market maker in foreign currency. In addition to market-making activities conducted in their respective countries, C, D, and USFX each employ marketers and traders, who also perform risk management with respect to their foreign currency operations. In a typical business day, B, C, D, and USFX each enter into several hundred spot and forward contracts to purchase and sell Deutsche marks (DM) with unrelated third parties on the interbank market. In the ordinary course of business, B, C, D, and USFX also enter into contracts to purchase and sell DM with each other.

(ii) Under § 1.482-8(a)(2)(iii), B, C, D, and USFX are each regular dealers in securities because they each regularly and actively offer to, and in fact do, purchase and sell currencies to customers who are not controlled taxpayers, in the ordinary course of their trade or business. Consequently, each controlled taxpayer is also a participant. Together, B, C, D, and USFX conduct a global dealing operation within the meaning of § 1.482-8(a)(2)(i) because they execute customer transactions in multiple tax jurisdictions. Accordingly, the controlled transactions between B, C, D, and USFX are evaluated under the rules of § 1.482-8.

*Example (2).* Identification of participants.

(i) The facts are the same as in Example 1, except that USFX is the only member of the group of controlled taxpayers that buys from and sells foreign currency to customers. C performs marketing and pricing activities with respect to the controlled group's foreign currency operation. D performs accounting and back office services for B, C, and USFX, but does not perform any marketing, sales, pricing, risk management or brokering activities with respect to the controlled group's foreign currency operation. B provides guarantees for all transactions entered into by USFX.

(ii) Under § 1.482-8(a)(2)(iii), USFX is a regular dealer in securities and therefore is a participant. C also is a participant because it performs activities related to USFX's foreign currency dealing activities. USFX's and C's controlled transactions relating to their DM activities are evaluated under § 1.482-8. D is not a participant in a global dealing operation because its accounting and back office services are not related activities within the meaning of § 1.482-8(a)(2)(ii)(B). B also is not a participant in a global dealing operation because its guarantee function is not a related activity within the meaning of § 1.482-8(a)(2)(ii)(B). Accordingly, the determination of whether transactions between B and D and other members of the controlled group are at arm's length is not determined under § 1.482-8.

*Example (3).* Scope of a global dealing operation.

(i) C, a U.S. resident commercial bank, conducts a banking business in the United States and in countries X and Y through foreign branches. C regularly and actively offers to, and in fact does, purchase from and sell foreign currency to customers who are not controlled taxpayers in the ordinary course of its trade or business in the United States and countries X and Y. In all the same jurisdictions, C also regularly and actively offers to, and in fact does, enter into, assume, offset, assign, or otherwise terminate positions in interest rate and cross-currency swaps with customers who are not controlled taxpayers. In addition, C regularly makes loans to customers through its U.S. and foreign branches. C regularly sells these loans to a financial institution that repackages the loans into securities.

(ii) C is a regular dealer in securities within the meaning of § 1.482-8(a)(2)(ii) because it purchases and sells foreign currency and enters into interest rate and cross-currency swaps with customers. Because C conducts these activities through U.S. and foreign branches, these activities constitute a global dealing operation within the meaning of § 1.482-8(a)(2)(i). The income, expense, gain or loss from C's global dealing operation is sourced under §§ 1.863-3(h) and 1.988-4(h). Under § 1.482-8(a)(2)(i), C's lending activities are not, however, part of a global dealing operation.

*Example (4).* Dissimilar products. The facts are the same as in Example 1, but B, C, D, and USFX also act as a market maker in Malaysian ringgit-U.S. dollar cross-currency options in the United States and countries X, Y, and Z. The ringgit is not widely traded throughout the world and is considered a thinly traded currency. The functional analysis required by § 1.482-8(a)(3)(i) shows that the development, marketing, pricing, and risk management of ringgit-U.S. dollar cross-currency option contracts are different than that of other foreign currency contracts, including option contracts. Moreover, the contractual terms, risks, and economic conditions of ringgit-U.S. dollar cross-currency option contracts differ considerably from that of other foreign currency contracts, including option contracts. See § 1.482-8(a)(3)(ii) through (iv). Accordingly, the ringgit-U.S. dollar cross-currency option contracts are not comparable to contracts in other foreign currencies.

*Example (5).* Relevant time period.

(i) USFX is a U.S. resident corporation that is a regular dealer in securities acting as a market maker in foreign currency by buying from and selling currencies to customers. C performs marketing and pricing activities with respect to USFX's foreign currency operation. Trading in Deutsche marks (DM) is conducted between 10:00 a.m. and 10:30 a.m. and between 10:45 a.m. and 11:00 a.m. under the following circumstances.

| Time | Rate | Transaction |
|---|---|---|
| 10:00 a.m. | 1.827DM: $1 | Uncontrolled Transaction |
| 10:04 a.m. | 1.827DM: $1 | Controlled Transaction |
| 10:06 a.m. | 1.826DM: $1 | Uncontrolled Transaction |
| 10:08 a.m. | 1.825DM: $1 | Uncontrolled Transaction |
| 10:10 a.m. | 1.827DM: $1 | Controlled Transaction |
| 10:12 a.m. | 1.824DM: $1 | Uncontrolled Transaction |
| 10:15 a.m. | 1.825DM: $1 | Uncontrolled Transaction |
| 10:18 a.m. | 1.826DM: $1 | Controlled Transaction |
| 10:20 a.m. | 1.824DM: $1 | Uncontrolled Transaction |
| 10:23 a.m. | 1.825DM: $1 | Uncontrolled Transaction |
| 10:25 a.m. | 1.825DM: $1 | Uncontrolled Transaction |
| 10:27 a.m. | 1.827DM: $1 | Controlled Transaction |
| 10:30 a.m. | 1.824DM: $1 | Uncontrolled Transaction |
| 10:45 a.m. | 1.822DM: $1 | Uncontrolled Transaction |
| 10:50 a.m. | 1.821DM: $1 | Uncontrolled Transaction |
| 10:55 a.m. | 1.822DM: $1 | Uncontrolled Transaction |
| 11:00 a.m. | 1.819DM: $1 | Uncontrolled Transaction |

(ii) USFX and C are participants in a global dealing operation under § 1.482-8(a)(2)(i). Therefore, USFX determines its arm's length price for its controlled DM contracts under § 1.482-8(a)(4). Under § 1.482-8(a)(4), the relevant arm's length range for setting the prices of USFX's controlled DM transactions occurs between 10:00 a.m. and 10:30 a.m. Because USFX has no controlled transactions between 10:45 a.m. and 11:00 a.m., and the price movement during this later time period continued to decrease, the 10:45 a.m. to 11:00 a.m. time period is not part of the relevant arm's length range for pricing USFX's controlled transactions.

**(b) Comparable uncontrolled financial transaction method.** *(1) General rule.* The comparable uncontrolled financial transaction (CUFT) method evaluates whether the amount charged in a controlled financial transaction is arm's length by reference to the amount charged in a comparable uncontrolled financial transaction.

*(2) Comparability and reliability.* (i) In general. The provisions of § 1.482-1(d), as modified by paragraph (a)(3) of this section, apply in determining whether a controlled financial transaction is comparable to a particular uncontrolled financial transaction. All of the relevant factors in paragraph (a)(3) of this section must be considered in determining the comparability of the two financial transactions. Comparability under this method depends on close similarity with respect to these factors, or adjustments to account for any differences. Accordingly, unless the controlled taxpayer can demonstrate that the relevant aspects of the controlled and uncontrolled financial transactions are comparable, the reliability of the results as a measure of an arm's length price is substantially reduced.

(ii) Adjustments for differences between controlled and uncontrolled transactions. If there are differences between controlled and uncontrolled transactions that would affect price, adjustments should be made to the price of the uncontrolled transaction according to the comparability provisions of § 1.482-1(d)(2) and paragraph (a)(3) of this section.

(iii) Data and assumptions. The reliability of the results derived from the CUFT method is affected by the completeness and accuracy of the data used and the reliability of the assumptions made to apply the method. See § 1.482-1(c)(2)(ii). In the case of a global dealing operation in which the CUFT is set through the use of indirect evidence, participants generally must establish data from a public exchange or quotation media contemporaneously to the time of the transaction, retain records of such data, and upon request furnish to the district director any pricing model used to establish indirect evidence of a CUFT, in order for this method to be a reliable means of evaluating the arm's length nature of the controlled transactions.

*(3) Indirect evidence of the price of a comparable uncontrolled financial transaction.* (i) In general. The price of a CUFT may be derived from data from public exchanges or quotation media if the following requirements are met—

(A) The data is widely and routinely used in the ordinary course of business in the industry to negotiate prices for uncontrolled sales;

(B) The data derived from public exchanges or quotation media is used to set prices in the controlled transaction in the same way it is used for uncontrolled transactions of the taxpayer, or the same way it is used by uncontrolled taxpayers; and

(C) The amount charged in the controlled transaction is adjusted to reflect differences in quantity, contractual terms, counterparties, and other factors that affect the price to which uncontrolled taxpayers would agree.

(ii) Public exchanges or quotation media. For purposes of paragraph (b)(3)(i) of this section, an established financial market, as defined in § 1.1092(d)-1(b), qualifies as a public exchange or a quotation media.

(iii) Limitation on use of data from public exchanges or quotation media. Use of data from public exchanges or quotation media is not appropriate under extraordinary market conditions. For example, under circumstances where the trading or transfer of a particular country's currency has been suspended or blocked by another country, causing significant instability in the prices of foreign currency contracts in the suspended or blocked currency, the prices listed on a quotation medium may not reflect a reliable measure of an arm's length result.

*(4) Arm's length range.* See § 1.482-1(e)(2) and paragraph (a)(4) of this section for the determination of an arm's length range.

*(5) Examples.* The following examples illustrate the principles of this paragraph (b).

*Example (1).* Comparable uncontrolled financial transactions.

(i) B is a foreign bank resident in country X that acts as a market maker in foreign currency in country X. C, a country Y resident corporation, D, a country Z resident corporation, and USFX, a U.S. resident corporation are all members of a controlled group of taxpayers with B, and each acts as a market maker in foreign currency. In addition to market marking activities conducted in their respective countries, C, D, and USFX each employ marketers and traders, who also perform risk management with respect to their foreign currency operations. In a typical business day, B, C, D, and USFX each enter into several hundred spot and forward contracts to purchase and sell Deutsche marks (DM) with unrelated third parties on the interbank market. In the ordinary course of business, B, C, D, and USFX also each enter into contracts to purchase and sell DM with each other. On a typical day, no more than 10% of USFX's DM trades are with controlled taxpayers. USFX's DM-denominated spot and forward contracts do not vary in their terms, except as to the volume of DM purchased or sold. The differences in volume of DM purchased and sold by USFX do not affect the pricing of the DM. USFX maintains contemporaneous records of its trades, accounted for by type of trade and counterparty. The daily volume of USFX's DM-denominated spot and forward contracts consistently provides USFX with third party transactions that are contemporaneous with the transactions between controlled taxpayers.

(ii) Under § 1.482-8(a)(2)(iii), B, C, D, and USFX each are regular dealers in securities because they each regularly and actively offer to, and in fact do, purchase and sell currencies to customers who are not controlled taxpayers, in the ordinary course of their trade or business. Consequently, each controlled taxpayer is also a participant. Together, B, C, D, and USFX conduct a global dealing operation within the meaning of § 1.482-8(a)(2)(i) because they execute customer transactions in multiple tax jurisdictions. To determine the comparability of USFX's controlled and uncontrolled DM-denominated spot and forward transactions, the factors in § 1.482-8(a)(3) must be considered. USFX performs the same functions with respect to controlled and uncontrolled DM-denominated spot and forward transactions. See § 1.482-8(a)(3)(i). In evaluating the contractual terms under § 1.482-8(a)(3)(ii), it is determined that the volume of DM transactions varies, but these variances do not affect the pricing of USFX's uncontrolled DM transactions. Taking into account the risk factors of § 1.482-8(a)(3)(iii), USFX's risk associated with both the controlled and uncontrolled DM transactions does not vary in any material respect. In applying the significant factors for evaluating the economic conditions under § 1.482-8(a)(3)(iv), USFX has sufficient third party DM transactions to establish comparable economic conditions for evaluating an arm's length price. Accordingly, USFX's uncontrolled transactions are comparable to its controlled transactions in DM spot and forward contracts.

*Example (2).* Lack of comparable uncontrolled financial transactions. The facts are the same as in Example 1, except that USFX trades Italian lira (lira) instead of DM. USFX enters into few uncontrolled and controlled lira-denominated forward contracts each day. The daily volume of USFX's lira forward purchases and sales does not provide USFX with sufficient third party transactions to establish that uncontrolled transactions are sufficiently contemporaneous with controlled transactions to be comparable within the meaning of § 1.482-8(a)(3). In applying the comparability factors of § 1.482-8(a)(3), and of paragraph (a)(3)(iv) of this section in particular, USFX's controlled and uncontrolled lira forward purchases and sales are not entered into under comparable economic conditions. Accordingly, USFX's uncontrolled transactions in lira forward contracts are not comparable to its controlled lira forward transactions.

*Example (3).* Indirect evidence of the price of a comparable uncontrolled financial transaction.

(i) The facts are the same as in Example 2, except that USFX uses a computer quotation system (CQS) that is an interdealer market, as described in § 1.1092(d)-1(b)(2), to set its price on lira forward contracts with controlled and uncontrolled taxpayers. Other financial institutions also use CQS to set their prices on lira forward contracts. CQS is an established financial market within the meaning of § 1.1092(d)-1(b).

(ii) Because CQS is an established financial market, it is a public exchange or quotation media within the meaning of § 1.482-8(b)(3)(i). Because other financial institutions use prices from CQS in the same manner as USFX, prices derived from CQS are deemed to be widely and routinely used in the ordinary course of business in the industry to negotiate prices for uncontrolled sales. See § 1.482-8(b)(3)(i)(A) and (B). If USFX adjusts the price quoted by CQS under the criteria specified in § 1.482-8(b)(2)(ii)(A)(3), the controlled price derived by USFX from CQS qualifies as indirect evidence of the price of a comparable uncontrolled financial transaction.

*Example (4).* Indirect evidence of the price of a comparable uncontrolled financial transaction—internal pricing models.

(i) T is a U.S. resident corporation that acts as a market maker in U.S. dollar-denominated notional principal contracts. T's marketers and traders work together to sell notional principal contracts (NPCs), primarily to T's North and South American customers. T typically earns 4 basis points at the inception of each standard 3 year U.S. dollar-denominated interest rate swap that is entered into with an unrelated, financially sophisticated, creditworthy counterparty. TS, T's wholly owned U.K. subsidiary, also acts as a market maker in U.S. dollar-denominated NPCs, employing several traders and marketers who initiate contracts primarily with European customers. On occasion, for various business reasons, TS enters into a U.S. dollar-denominated NPC with T. The U.S. dollar-denominated NPCs that T enters into with unrelated parties are comparable in all material respects to the transactions that T enters into with TS. TS prices all transactions with T using the same pricing models that TS uses to price transactions with third parties. The pricing models analyze relevant data, such as interest rates and volatilities, derived from public exchanges. TS records the data that were used to determine the price of each transaction at the time the transaction was entered into. Because the price produced by the pricing models is a mid-market price, TS adjusts the price so that it receives the same 4 basis point spread on its transaction with T that it would earn on comparable transactions with comparable counterparties during the same relevant time period.

(ii) Under § 1.482-8(a)(2), T and TS are participants in a global dealing operation that deals in U.S. dollar-denominated NPCs. Because the prices produced by TS's pricing model are derived from information on public exchanges and TS uses the same pricing model to set prices for controlled and uncontrolled transactions, the requirements of § 1.482-8(b)(3)(i)(A) and (B) are met. Because the U.S. dollar-denominated NPCs that T enters into with customers (uncontrolled transactions) are comparable to the transactions between T and TS within the meaning of § 1.482-8(a)(3) and TS earns 4 basis points at inception of its uncontrolled transactions that are comparable to its controlled transactions, TS has also satisfied the requirements of § 1.482-8(b)(3)(i)(C). Accordingly, the price produced by TS's pricing model constitutes indirect evidence of the price of a comparable uncontrolled financial transaction.

**(c) Gross margin method.** *(1) General rule.* The gross margin method evaluates whether the amount allocated to a participant in a global dealing operation is arm's length by reference to the gross profit margin realized on the sale of financial products in comparable uncontrolled transactions. The gross margin method may be used to establish an arm's length price for a transaction where a participant resells a financial product to an unrelated party that the participant purchased from a related party. The gross margin method may apply to transactions involving the purchase and resale of debt and equity instruments. The method may also be used to evaluate whether a participant has received an arm's length commission for its activities in a global dealing operation when the participant has not taken title to a security or has not become a party to a derivative financial product. To meet the arm's length standard, the gross profit margin on controlled transactions should be similar to that of comparable uncontrolled transactions.

*(2) Determination of an arm's length price.* (i) In general. The gross margin method measures an arm's length price by subtracting the appropriate gross profit from the applicable resale price for the financial product involved in the controlled transaction under review.

(ii) Applicable resale price. The applicable resale price is equal to either the price at which the financial product involved is sold in an uncontrolled sale or the price at which contemporaneous resales of the same product are made. If the product purchased in the controlled sale is resold to one or more related parties in a series of controlled sales before being resold in an uncontrolled sale, the applicable resale price is the price at which the product is resold to an uncontrolled party, or the price at which contemporaneous resales of the same product are made. In such case, the determination of the appropriate gross profit will take into account the functions of all members of the controlled group participating in the series of controlled sales and final uncontrolled resales, as well as any other relevant factors described in paragraph (a)(3) of this section.

(iii) Appropriate gross profit. The appropriate gross profit is computed by multiplying the applicable resale price by the gross profit margin, expressed as a percentage of total revenue derived from sales, earned in comparable uncontrolled transactions.

*(3) Comparability and reliability.* (i) In general. The provisions of § 1.482-1(d), as modified by paragraph (a)(3) of this section, apply in determining whether a controlled transaction is comparable to a particular uncontrolled transaction. All of the factors described in paragraph (a)(3) of this section must be considered in determining the comparability of two financial products transactions, including the functions performed. The gross margin method considers whether a participant has earned a sufficient gross profit margin on the resale of a financial product (or line of products) given the functions performed by the participant. A reseller's gross profit margin provides compensation for performing resale functions related to the product or products under review, including an operating profit in return for the reseller's investment of capital and the assumption of risks. Accordingly, where a participant does not take title, or does not become a party to a financial product, the reseller's return to capital and assumption of risk are additional factors that must be considered in determining an appropriate gross profit margin. An appropriate gross profit margin primarily should be derived from comparable uncontrolled purchases and resales of the reseller involved in the controlled sale. This is because similar characteristics are more likely to be found among different resales of a financial product or products made by the same reseller than among sales made by other resellers. In the absence of comparable uncontrolled transactions involving the same reseller, an appropriate gross profit margin may be derived from comparable uncontrolled transactions of other resellers.

(ii) Adjustments for differences between controlled and uncontrolled transactions. If there are material differences between controlled and uncontrolled transactions that would affect the gross profit margin, adjustments should be made to the gross profit margin earned in the uncontrolled transaction according to the comparability provisions of § 1.482-1(d)(2) and paragraph (a)(3) of this section. For this purpose, consideration of operating expenses associated with functions performed and risks assumed may be necessary because differences in functions performed are often reflected in operating expenses. The effect of a difference in functions performed on gross profit, however, is not necessarily equal to the difference in the amount of related operating expenses.

(iii) Reliability. In order for the gross margin method to be considered a reliable measure of an arm's length price, the gross profit should ordinarily represent an amount that would allow the participant who resells the product to recover its expenses (whether directly related to selling the product or more generally related to maintaining its operations) and to earn a profit commensurate with the functions it performed. The gross margin method may be a reliable means of establishing an arm's length price where there is a purchase and resale of a financial product and the participant who resells the property does not substantially participate in developing a product or in tailoring the product to the unique requirements of a customer prior to the resale.

(iv) Data and assumptions. (A) In general. The reliability of the results derived from the gross margin method is affected by the completeness and accuracy of the data used and the reliability of the assumptions made to apply the method. See § 1.482-1(c)(2)(ii). A participant may establish the gross margin by comparing the bid and offer prices on a public exchange or quotation media. In such case, the prices must be contemporaneous to the controlled transaction, and the participant must retain records of such data.

(B) Consistency in accounting. The degree of consistency in accounting practices between the controlled transaction and the uncontrolled transactions may affect the reliability of the gross margin method. For example, differences as between controlled and uncontrolled transactions in the method used to value similar financial products (including methods of accounting, methods of estimation, and the timing for changes of such methods) could affect the gross profit. The ability to make reliable adjustments for such differences could affect the reliability of the results.

*(4) Arm's length range.* See § 1.482-1(e)(2) and paragraph (a)(4) of this section for the determination of an arm's length range.

*(5) Example.* The following example illustrates the principles of this paragraph (c).

*Example (1).* Gross margin method.

(i) T is a U.S. resident financial institution that acts as a market maker in debt and equity instruments issued by U.S. corporations. Most of T's sales are to U.S.-based customers. TS, T's U.K. subsidiary, acts as a market maker in debt and equity instruments issued by European corporations and conducts most of its business with European-based customers. On occasion, however, a customer of TS wishes to purchase a security that is either held by or more readily accessible to T. To facilitate this transaction, T sells the security it owns or acquires to TS, who then promptly sells it to the customer. T and TS generally derive the majority of their profit on the difference between the price at which they purchase and the price at which they sell securities (the bid/offer spread). On average, TS's gross profit margin on its purchases and sales of securities from unrelated persons is 2%. Applying the comparability factors specified in § 1.482-8(a)(3), T's purchases and sales with unrelated persons are comparable to the purchases and sales between T and TS.

(ii) Under § 1.482-8(a)(2), T and TS are participants in a global dealing operation that deals in debt and equity securities. Since T's related purchases and sales are comparable to its unrelated purchases and sales, if TS's gross profit margin on purchases and sales of comparable securities from unrelated persons is 2%, TS should also typically earn a 2% gross profit on the securities it purchases from T. Thus, when TS resells for $100 a security that it purchased from T, the arm's length price at which TS would have purchased the security from T would normally be $98 ($100 sales price minus (2% gross profit margin × $100)).

**(d) Gross markup method.** *(1) General rule.* The gross markup method evaluates whether the amount allocated to a participant in a global dealing operation is arm's length by reference to the gross profit markup realized in comparable uncontrolled transactions. The gross markup method may be used to establish an arm's length price for a transaction where a participant purchases a financial product from an unrelated party that the participant sells to a related party. This method may apply to transactions involving the purchase and resale of debt and equity instruments. The method may also be used to evaluate whether a participant has received an arm's length commission for its role in a global dealing operation when the participant has not taken title to a security or has not become a party to a derivative financial product. To meet the arm's length standard, the gross profit markup on controlled transactions should be similar to that of comparable uncontrolled transactions.

*(2) Determination of an arm's length price.* (i) In general. The gross markup method measures an arm's length price by adding the appropriate gross profit to the participant's cost or anticipated cost, of purchasing, holding, or structuring the financial product involved in the controlled transaction under review (or in the case of a derivative financial product, the initial net present value, measured by the anticipated cost of purchasing, holding, or structuring the product).

(ii) Appropriate gross profit. The appropriate gross profit is computed by multiplying the participant's cost or anticipated cost of purchasing, holding, or structuring a transaction by the gross profit markup, expressed as a percentage of cost, earned in comparable uncontrolled transactions.

*(3) Comparability and reliability.* (i) In general. The provisions of § 1.482-1(d), as modified by paragraph (a)(3) of this section, apply in determining whether a controlled transaction is comparable to a particular uncontrolled transaction. All of the factors described in paragraph (a)(3) of this section must be considered in determining the comparability of two financial products transactions, including the functions performed. The gross markup method considers whether a participant has earned a sufficient gross markup on the sale of a financial product, or line of products, given the functions it has performed. A participant's gross profit markup provides compensation for purchasing, hedging, and transactional structuring functions related to the transaction under review, including an operating profit in return for the investment of capital and the assumption of risks. Accordingly, where a participant does not take title, or does not become a party to a financial product, the reseller's return to capital and assumption of risk are additional factors that must be considered in determining the gross profit markup. An appropriate gross profit markup primarily should be derived from comparable uncontrolled purchases and sales of the participant involved in the controlled sale. This is because similar characteristics are more likely to be found among different sales of property made by the same participant than among sales made by other resellers. In the absence of comparable uncontrolled transactions involving the same participant, an appropriate gross profit markup may be derived from comparable uncontrolled transactions of other parties whether or not such parties are members of the same controlled group.

(ii) Adjustments for differences between controlled and uncontrolled transactions. If there are material differences between controlled and uncontrolled transactions that would affect the gross profit markup, adjustments should be made to the gross profit markup earned in the uncontrolled transaction according to the comparability provisions of § 1.482-1(d)(2) and paragraph (a)(3) of this section. For this purpose, consideration of operating expenses associated with the functions performed and risks assumed may be necessary, because differences in functions performed are often reflected in operating expenses. The effect of a difference in functions on gross profit, however, is not necessarily equal to the difference in the amount of related operating expenses.

(iii) Reliability. In order for the gross markup method to be considered a reliable measure of an arm's length price, the gross profit should ordinarily represent an amount that would allow the participant who purchases the product to recover its expenses (whether directly related to selling the product or more generally related to maintaining its operations) and to earn a profit commensurate with the functions it performed. As with the gross margin method, the gross markup method may be a reliable means of establishing an arm's length price where there is a purchase and resale of a financial product and the participant who resells the property does not substantially participate in developing a product or in tailoring the product to the unique requirements of a customer prior to the resale.

(iv) Data and assumptions. (A) In general. The reliability of the results derived from the gross markup method is affected by the completeness and accuracy of the data used and the reliability of the assumptions made to apply the method. See § 1.482-1(c)(2)(ii). A participant may establish the gross markup by comparing the bid and offer prices on a public exchange or quotation media. In such case, the prices must be contemporaneous with the controlled transaction, and the participant must retain records of such data.

(B) Consistency in accounting. The degree of consistency in accounting practices between the controlled transaction and the uncontrolled transactions may affect the reliability of the gross markup method. For example, differences as between controlled and uncontrolled transactions in the method used to value similar financial products (including methods in accounting, methods of estimation, and the timing for changes of such methods) could affect the gross profit. The ability to make reliable adjustments for such differences could affect the reliability of the results.

*(4) Arm's length range.* See § 1.482-1(e)(2) and paragraph (a)(4) of this section for the determination of an arm's length range.

**(e) Profit split method.** *(1) General rule.* The profit split method evaluates whether the allocation of the combined operating profit or loss of a global dealing operation to one or more participants is at arm's length by reference to the relative value of each participant's contribution to that combined operating profit or loss. The combined operating profit or loss must be derived from the most narrowly identifiable business activity of the participants for which data is available that includes the controlled transactions (relevant business activity).

*(2) Appropriate share of profit and loss.* (i) In general. The relative value of each participant's contribution to the global dealing activity must be determined in a manner that reflects the functions performed, risks assumed, and resources employed by each participant in the activity, consistent with the comparability provisions of § 1.482-1(d), as modified by paragraph (a)(3) of this section. Such an allocation is intended to correspond to the division of profit or loss that would result from an arrangement between uncontrolled taxpayers, each performing functions similar to those of the various controlled taxpayers engaged in the relevant business activity. The relative value of the contributions of each participant in the global dealing operation should be measured in a manner that most reliably reflects each contribution made to the global dealing operation and each participant' s role in that contribution. In appropriate cases, the participants may find that a multi-factor formula most reliably measures the relative value of the contributions to the profitability of the global dealing operation. The profit allocated to any particular participant using a profit split method is not necessarily limited to the total operating profit from the global dealing operation. For example, in a given year, one participant may earn a profit while another participant incurs a loss, so long as the arrangement is comparable to an arrangement to which two uncontrolled parties would agree. In addition, it may not be assumed that the combined operating profit or loss from the relevant business activity should be shared equally or in any other arbitrary proportion. The specific method must be determined under paragraph (e)(4) of this section.

(ii) Adjustment of factors to measure contribution clearly. In order to reliably measure the value of a participant's contribution, the factors, for example, those used in a multi-factor formula, must be expressed in units of measure that reliably quantify the relative contribution of the participant. If the data or information is influenced by factors other than the value of the contribution, adjustments must be made for such differences so that the factors used in the formula only measure the relative value of each participant's contribution. For example, if trader compensation is used as a factor to measure the value added by the participant's trading expertise, adjustments must be made for variances in compensation paid to traders due solely to differences in the cost of living.

*(3) Definitions.* The definitions in this paragraph (e)(3) apply for purposes of applying the profit split methods in this paragraph (e).

*Gross profit* is gross income earned by the global dealing operation.

*Operating expenses* includes all expenses not included in the computation of gross profit, except for interest, foreign income taxes as defined in § 1.901-2(a), domestic income taxes, and any expenses not related to the global dealing activity that is evaluated under the profit split method. With respect to interest expense, see section 864(e) and the regulations thereunder and § 1.882-5.

*Operating profit or loss* is gross profit less operating expenses, and includes all income, expense, gain, loss, credits or allowances attributable to each global dealing activity that is evaluated under the profit split method. It does not include income, expense, gain, loss, credits or allowances from activities that are not evaluated under the profit split method, nor does it include extraordinary gains or losses that do not relate to the continuing global dealing activities of the participant.

*(4) Application.* Profit or loss shall be allocated under the profit split method using either the total profit split, described in paragraph (e)(5) of this section, or the residual profit split, described in paragraph (e)(6) of this section.

*(5) Total profit split.* (i) In general. The total profit split derives the percentage of the combined operating profit of the participants in a global dealing operation allocable to a participant in the global dealing operation by evaluating whether uncontrolled taxpayers who perform similar functions, assume similar risks, and employ similar resources

would allocate their combined operating profits in the same manner.

(ii) Comparability. The total profit split evaluates the manner by which comparable uncontrolled taxpayers divide the combined operating profit of a particular global dealing activity. The degree of comparability between the controlled and uncontrolled taxpayers is determined by applying the comparability standards of § 1.482-1(d), as modified by paragraph (a)(3) of this section. In particular, the functional analysis required by § 1.482-1(d)(3)(i) and paragraph (a)(3)(i) of this section is essential to determine whether two situations are comparable. Nevertheless, in certain cases, no comparable ventures between uncontrolled taxpayers may exist. In this situation, it is necessary to analyze the remaining factors set forth in paragraph (a)(3) of this section that could affect the division of operating profits between parties. If there are differences between the controlled and uncontrolled taxpayers that would materially affect the division of operating profit, adjustments must be made according to the provisions of § 1.482-1(d)(2) and paragraph (a)(3) of this section.

(iii) Reliability. As indicated in § 1.482-1(c)(2)(i), as the degree of comparability between the controlled and uncontrolled transactions increases, the reliability of a total profit split also increases. In a global dealing operation, however, the absence of external market benchmarks (for example, joint ventures between uncontrolled taxpayers) on which to base the allocation of operating profits does not preclude use of this method if the allocation of the operating profit takes into account the relative contribution of each participant. The reliability of this method is increased to the extent that the allocation has economic significance for purposes other than tax (for example, satisfying regulatory standards and reporting, or determining bonuses paid to management or traders). The reliability of the analysis under this method may also be enhanced by the fact that all parties to the controlled transaction are evaluated under this method. The reliability of the results, however, of an analysis based on information from all parties to a transaction is affected by the reliability of the data and assumptions pertaining to each party to the controlled transaction. Thus, if the data and assumptions are significantly more reliable with respect to one of the parties than with respect to the others, a different method, focusing solely on the results of that party, may yield more reliable results.

(iv) Data and assumptions. (A) In general. The reliability of the results derived from the total profit split method is affected by the quality of the data used and the assumptions used to apply the method. See § 1.482-1(c)(2)(ii). The reliability of the allocation of income, expense, or other attributes between the participants' relevant business activities and the participants' other activities will affect the reliability of the determination of the combined operating profit and its allocation among the participants. If it is not possible to allocate income, expense, or other attributes directly based on factual relationships, a reasonable allocation formula may be used. To the extent direct allocations are not made, the reliability of the results derived from application of this method is reduced relative to the results of a method that requires fewer allocations of income, expense, and other attributes. Similarly, the reliability of the results derived from application of this method is affected by the extent to which it is possible to apply the method to the participants' financial data that is related solely to the controlled transactions. For example, if the relevant business activity is entering into interest rate swaps with both controlled and uncontrolled taxpayers, it may not be possible to apply the method solely to financial data related to the controlled transactions. In such case, the reliability of the results derived from application of this method will be reduced.

(B) Consistency in accounting. The degree of consistency between the controlled and uncontrolled taxpayers in accounting practices that materially affect the items that determine the amount and allocation of operating profit affects the reliability of the result. Thus, for example, if differences in financial product valuation or in cost allocation practices would materially affect operating profit, the ability to make reliable adjustments for such differences would affect the reliability of the results.

*(6) Residual profit split.* (i) In general. The residual profit split allocates the combined operating profit or loss between participants following the two-step process set forth in paragraphs (e)(6)(ii) and (iii) of this section.

(ii) Allocate income to routine contributions. The first step allocates operating income to each participant to provide an arm's length return for its routine contributions to the global dealing operation. Routine contributions are contributions of the same or similar kind as those made by uncontrolled taxpayers involved in similar business activities for which it is possible to identify market returns. Routine contributions ordinarily include contributions of tangible property, services, and intangibles that are generally owned or performed by uncontrolled taxpayers engaged in similar activities. For example, transactions processing and credit analysis are typically routine contributions. In addition, a participant that guarantees obligations of or otherwise provides credit support to another controlled taxpayer in a global dealing operation is regarded as making a routine contribution. A functional analysis is required to identify the routine contributions according to the functions performed, risks assumed, and resources employed by each of the participants. Market returns for the routine contributions should be determined by reference to the returns achieved by uncontrolled taxpayers engaged in similar activities, consistent with the methods described in §§ 1.482-2 through 1.482-4 and this § 1.482-8.

(iii) Allocate residual profit. The allocation of income to the participant's routine contributions will not reflect profits attributable to each participant's valuable nonroutine contributions to the global dealing operation. Thus, in cases where valuable nonroutine contributions are present, there normally will be an unallocated residual profit after the allocation of income described in paragraph (e)(6)(ii) of this section. Under this second step, the residual profit generally should be divided among the participants based upon the relative value of each of their nonroutine contributions. Nonroutine contributions are contributions so integral to the global dealing operation that it is impossible to segregate them from the operation and find a separate market return for the contribution. Pricing and risk managing financial products almost invariably involve nonroutine contributions. Similarly, product development and information technology are generally nonroutine contributions. Marketing may be a nonroutine contribution if the marketer substantially participates in developing a product or in tailoring the product to the unique requirements of a customer. The relative value of the nonroutine contributions of each participant in the global dealing operation should be measured in a manner that most reliably reflects each nonroutine contribution made to the global dealing operation and each participant's role in the nonroutine contributions.

(iv) Comparability. The first step of the residual profit split relies on external market benchmarks of profitability. Thus, the comparability considerations that are relevant for the first step of the residual profit split are those that are relevant for the methods that are used to determine market returns for routine contributions. In the second step of the residual profit split, however, it may not be possible to rely as heavily on external market benchmarks. Nevertheless, in order to divide the residual profits of a global dealing operation in accordance with each participant's nonroutine contributions, it is necessary to apply the comparability standards of § 1.482-1(d), as modified by paragraph (a)(3) of this section. In particular, the functional analysis required by § 1.482-1(d)(3)(i) and paragraph (a)(3)(i) of this section is essential to determine whether two situations are comparable. Nevertheless, in certain cases, no comparable ventures between uncontrolled taxpayers may exist. In this situation, it is necessary to analyze the remaining factors set forth in paragraph (a)(3) of this section that could affect the division of operating profits between parties. If there are differences between the controlled and uncontrolled taxpayers that would materially affect the division of operating profit, adjustments must be made according to the provisions of § 1.482-1(d)(2) and paragraph (a)(3) of this section.

(v) Reliability. As indicated in § 1.482-1(c)(2)(i), as the degree of comparability between the controlled and uncontrolled transactions increases, the reliability of a residual profit split also increases. In a global dealing operation, however, the absence of external market benchmarks (for example, joint ventures between uncontrolled taxpayers) on which to base the allocation of operating profits does not preclude use of this method if the allocation of the residual profit takes into account the relative contribution of each participant. The reliability of this method is increased to the extent that the allocation has economic significance for purposes other than tax (for example, satisfying regulatory standards and reporting, or determining bonuses paid to management or traders). The reliability of the analysis under this method may also be enhanced by the fact that all parties to the controlled transaction are evaluated under this method. The reliability of the results, however, of an analysis based on information from all parties to a transaction is affected by the reliability of the data and assumptions pertaining to each party to the controlled transaction. Thus, if the data and assumptions are significantly more reliable with respect to one of the parties than with respect to the others, a different method, focusing solely on the results of that party, may yield more reliable results.

(vi) Data and assumptions. (A) General rule. The reliability of the results derived from the residual profit split is measured under the standards set forth in paragraph (e)(5)(iv)(A) of this section.

(B) Consistency in accounting. The degree of accounting consistency between controlled and uncontrolled taxpayers is measured under the standards set forth in paragraph (e)(5)(iv)(B) of this section.

*(7) Arm's length range.* See § 1.482-1(e)(2) and paragraph (a)(4) of this section for the determination of an arm's length range.

*(8) Examples.* The following examples illustrate the principles of this paragraph (e).

*Example (1).* Total profit split.

(i) P, a U.S. corporation, establishes a separate U.S. subsidiary (USsub) to conduct a global dealing operation in over-the-counter derivatives. USsub in turn establishes subsidiaries incorporated and doing business in the U.K. (UKsub) and Japan (Jsub). Ussub, Uksub, and Jsub each employ marketers and traders who work closely together to design and sell derivative products to meet the particular needs of customers. Each also employs personnel who process and confirm trades, reconcile trade tickets and provide ongoing administrative support (back office services) for the global dealing operation. The global dealing operation maintains a single common book for each type of risk, and the book is maintained where the head trader for that type of risk is located. Thus, notional principal contracts denominated in North and South American currencies are booked in USsub, notional principal contracts denominated in European currencies are booked in UKsub, and notional principal contracts denominated in Japanese yen are booked in Jsub. However, each of the affiliates has authorized a trader located in each of the other affiliates to risk manage its books during periods when the booking location is closed. This grant of authority is necessary because marketers, regardless of their location, are expected to sell all of the group's products, and need to receive pricing information with respect to products during their clients business hours, even if the booking location is closed. Moreover, P is known for making a substantial amount of its profits from trading activities, and frequently does not hedge the positions arising from its customer transactions in an attempt to profit from market changes. As a result, the traders in "off-hours" locations must have a substantial amount of trading authority in order to react to market changes.

(ii) Under § 1.482-8(a)(2), USsub, UKsub and Jsub are participants in a global dealing operation in over-the-counter derivatives. P determines that the total profit split method is the best method to allocate an arm's length amount of income to each participant. P allocates the operating profit from the global dealing operation between USsub, UKsub and Jsub on the basis of the relative compensation paid to marketers and traders in each location. In making the allocation, P adjusts the compensation amounts to account for factors unrelated to job performance, such as the higher cost of living in certain jurisdictions. Because the traders receive significantly greater compensation than marketers in order to account for their greater contribution to the profits of the global dealing operation, P need not make additional adjustments or weight the compensation of the traders more heavily in allocating the operating profit between the affiliates. For rules concerning the source of income allocated to Ussub, Uksub and Jsub (and any U.S. trade or business of the participants), see § 1.863-3(h).

*Example (2).* Total profit split. The facts are the same as in Example 1, except that the labor market in Japan is such that traders paid by Jsub are paid the same as marketers paid by Jsub at the same seniority level, even though the traders contribute substantially more to the profitability of the global dealing operation. As a result, the allocation method used by P is unlikely to compensate the functions provided by each affiliate so as to be a reliable measure of an arm's length result under §§ 1.482-8(e)(2) and 1.482-1(c)(1), unless P weights the compensation of traders more heavily than the compensation of marketers or develops another method of measuring the contribution of traders to the profitability of the global dealing operation.

*Example (3).* Total profit split. The facts are the same as in Example 2, except that, in P's annual report to shareholders, P divides its operating profit from customer business into "dealing profit" and "trading profit." Because both marketers and traders are involved in the dealing function, P divides the "dealing profit" between the affiliates on the basis of the relative compensation of marketers and traders. However, because only the traders contribute to the trading profit, P divides the trading profit between the affiliates on the basis of the relative compensation only of the traders. In making that allocation, P must adjust the compensation of traders in Jsub in order to account for factors not related to job performance.

*Example (4).* Total profit split. The facts are the same as in Example 1, except that P is required by its regulators to hedge its customer positions as much as possible and therefore does not earn any "trading profit." As a result, the marketing intangibles, such as customer relationships, are relatively more important than the intangibles used by traders. Accordingly, P must weight the compensation of marketers more heavily than the compensation of traders in order to take into account accurately the contribution each function makes to the profitability of the business.

*Example (5).* Residual profit split.

(i) P is a U.S. corporation that engages in a global dealing operation in foreign currency options directly and through controlled taxpayers that are incorporated and operate in the United Kingdom (UKsub) and Japan (Jsub). Each controlled taxpayer is a participant in a global dealing operation. Each participant employs marketers and traders who work closely together to design and sell foreign currency options that meet the particular needs of customers. Each participant also employs salespeople who sell foreign currency options with standardized terms and conditions, as well as other financial products offered by the controlled group. The traders in each location risk manage a common book of transactions during the relevant business hours of each location. P has a AAA credit rating and is the legal counterparty to all third party transactions. The traders in each location have discretion to execute contracts in the name of P. UKsub employs personnel who process and confirm trades, reconcile trade tickets, and provide ongoing administrative support (back office services) for all the participants in the global dealing operation. The global dealing operation has generated $192 of operating profit for the period.

(ii) After analyzing the foreign currency options business, has determined that the residual profit split method is the best method to allocate the operating profit of the global dealing operation and to determine an arm's length amount of compensation allocable to each participant in the global dealing operation.

(iii) The first step of the residual profit split method (§ 1.482-8(e)(6)(ii)) requires P to identify the routine contributions performed by each participant. P determines that the functions performed by the salespeople are routine. P determines that the arm's length compensation for salespeople is $3, $4, and $5 in the United States, the United Kingdom, and Japan, respectively. Thus, P allocates $3, $4, and $5 to P, UKsub, and Jsub, respectively.

(iv) Although the back office function would not give rise to participant status, in the context of a residual profit split allocation, the back office function is relevant for purposes of receiving remuneration for routine contributions to a global dealing operation. P determines that an arm's length compensation for the back office is $20. Since the back office services constitute routine contributions, $20 of income is allocated to UKsub under step 1 of the residual profit split method. In addition, P determines that the comparable arm's length compensation for the risk to which P is subject as counterparty is $40. Accordingly, $40 is allocated to P as compensation for acting as counterparty to the transactions entered into in P's name by Jsub and UKsub.

(v) The second step of the residual profit split method (§ 1.482-8(e)(6)(iii)) requires that the residual profit be allocated to participants according to the relative value of their nonroutine contributions. Under P's transfer pricing method, P allocates the residual profit of $120 ($192 gross income minus $12 salesperson commissions minus $20 payment for back office services minus $40 compensation for the routine contribution of acting as counterparty) using a multi-factor formula that reflects the relative value of the nonroutine contributions. Applying the comparability factors set out in § 1.482-8(a)(3), P allocates 40% of the residual profit to UKsub, 35% of the residual profit to P, and the remaining 25% of residual profit to Jsub. Accordingly, under step 2, $48 is allocated to UKsub, $42 is allocated to P, and $30 is allocated to Jsub. See § 1.863-3(h) for the source of income allocated to P with respect to its counterparty function.

**(f) Unspecified methods.** Methods not specified in paragraphs (b),(c),(d), or (e) of this section may be used to evaluate whether the amount charged in a controlled transaction is at arm's length. Any method used under this paragraph (f) must be applied in accordance with the provisions of § 1.482-1 as modified by paragraph (a)(3) of this section.

**(g) Source rule for qualified business units.** See § 1.863-3(h) for application of the rules of this section for purposes of determining the source of income, gain or loss from a global dealing operation among qualified business units (as defined in section 989(c) and §§ 1.863-3(h)(3)(iv) and 1.989(a)-1).

### § 1.482-8T Examples of the best method rule (temporary).

**(a)** [Reserved]. For further guidance, see § 1.482-8(a).

**(b)**

*Example (1).* through 12. [Reserved]. For further guidance, see Sec. 1.482-8(b) Examples 1 through 12.

*Example (13).* Preference for acquisition price method. (i) USP develops, manufacturers, and distributes pharmaceutical products. USP and FS, USP's wholly-owned subsidiary, enter into a CSA to develop a new oncological drug, Oncol. Immediately prior to entering into the CSA, USP acquires Company X, an unrelated U.S. pharmaceutical company. Company X is solely engaged in oncological pharmaceutical research, and its only significant resources and capabilities are its workforce and its sole patent, which is associated with Compound X, a promising molecular compound derived from a rare plant, which USP reasonably anticipates will contribute to developing Oncol. All of Company X researchers will be engaged solely in research that is reasonably anticipated to contribute to developing Oncol as well. The rights in the Compound X and the commitment of Company X's researchers to the development of Oncol are platform contributions for which compensation is due from FS as part of a PCT.

(ii) In this case, the acquisition price method, based on the lump sum price paid by USP for Company X, is likely to provide a more reliable measure of an arm's length PCT Payment due to USP than the application of any other method. See §§ 1.482-4(c)(2) and 1.482-7T(g)(5)(iv)(A).

*Example (14).* Preference for market capitalization method. (i) Company X is a publicly traded U.S. company solely engaged in oncological pharmaceutical research and its only significant resources and capabilities are its workforce and its sole patent, which is associated with Compound Y, a promising molecular compound derived from a rare plant. Company X has no marketable products. Company X enters into a CSA with FS, a newly-formed foreign subsidiary, to develop a new oncological drug, Oncol, derived from Compound Y. Compound Y is reasonably anticipated to contribute to developing Oncol. All of Company X researchers will be engaged solely in research that is reasonably anticipated to contribute to developing Oncol under the CSA. The rights in Compound Y and the commitment of Company X's researchers are platform contributions for which compensation is due from FS as part of a PCT.

(ii) In this case, given that Company X's platform contributions covered by PCTs relate to its entire economic value, the application of the market capitalization method, based on the market capitalization of Company X, provides a reliable measure of an arm's length result for Company X's PCTs to the CSA. See §§ 1.482-4(c)(2) and 1.482-7T(g)(6)(v)(A).

*Example (15).* Preference for market capitalization method. (i) MicroDent, Inc. (MDI) is a publicly traded company that developed a new dental surgical microscope ScopeX-1, which drastically shortens many surgical procedures. On January 1 of Year 1, MDI entered into a CSA with a wholly-owned foreign subsidiary (FS) to develop ScopeX-2, the next generation of ScopeX-1. In the CSA, divisional interests are divided on a territorial basis. The rights associated with ScopeX-1, as well as MDI's research capabilities are reasonably anticipated to contribute to the development of ScopeX-2 and are therefore platform contributions for which compensation is due from FS as part of a PCT. At the time of the PCT, MDI's only product was the ScopeX-1 microscope, although MDI was in the process of developing ScopeX-2. Concurrent with the CSA, MDI separately transfers exclusive and perpetual exploitation rights associated with ScopeX-1 to FS in the same territory as assigned to FS in the CSA.

(ii) Although the transactions between MDI and FS under the CSA are distinct from the transactions between MDI and FS relating to the exploitation rights for ScopeX-1, it is likely to be more reliable to evaluate the combined effect of the transactions than to evaluate them in isolation. This is because the combined transactions between MDI and FS relate to all of the economic value of MDI (that is, the exploitation rights and research rights associated with ScopeX-1, as well as the research capabilities of MDI). In this case, application of the market capitalization method, based on the enterprise value of MDI on January 1 of Year 1, is likely to provides a reliable measure of an arm's length payment for the aggregated transactions. See §§ 1.482-4(c)(2) and 1.482-7T(g)(6)(v)(A).

(iii) Notwithstanding that the market capitalization method provides the most reliable measure of the aggregated transactions between MDI and FS, see § 1.482-7T(g)(2)(iv) for further considerations of when further analysis may be required to distinguish between the remuneration to MDI associated with PCTs under the CSA (for research rights and capabilities associated with ScopeX-1) and the remuneration to MDI for the exploitation rights associated with ScopeX-1.

*Example (16).* Income method (applied using CPM) preferred to acquisition price method. The facts are the same as Example 13, except that the acquisition occurred significantly in advance of formation of the CSA, and reliable adjustments cannot be made for this time difference. In addition, Company X has other valuable molecular patents and associated research capabilities, apart from Compound X, that are not reasonably anticipated to contribute to the development of Oncol and that cannot be reliably valued. The CSA divides divisional interests on a territorial basis. Under the terms of the CSA, USP will undertake all R&D (consisting of laboratory research and clinical testing) and manufacturing associated with Oncol, as well as the distribution activities for its territory (the United States). FS will distribute Oncol in its territory (the rest of the world). FS's distribution activities are routine in nature, and the profitability from its activities may be reliably determined from third-party comparables. FS does not furnish any platform contributions. At the time of the PCT, reliable (ex ante) financial projections associated with the development of Oncol and its separate exploitation in each of USP's and FSub's assigned geographical territories are undertaken. In this case, application of the income method using CPM is likely to provide a more reliable measure of an arm's length result than application of the acquisition price method based on the price paid by USP for Company X. See § 1.482-7T(g)(4)(v) and (g)(5)(iv)(C).

*Example (17).* Evaluation of alternative methods. (i) The facts are the same as Example 13, except that the acquisition occurred sometime prior to the CSA, and Company X has some areas of promising research that are not reasonably anticipated to contribute to developing Oncol. For purposes of this example, the CSA is assumed to divide divisional interests on a territorial basis. In general, the Commissioner determines that the acquisition price data is useful in informing the arm's length price, but not necessarily determinative. Under the terms of the CSA, USP will undertake all R&D (consisting of laboratory research and clinical testing) and manufacturing associated with Oncol, as well as the distribution activities for its territory (the United States). FS will distribute Oncol in its territory (the rest of the world). FS's distribution activities are routine in nature, and the profitability from its activities may be reliably determined from third-party comparables. At the time of the PCT, financial projections associated with the development of Oncol and its separate exploitation in each of USP's and FSub's assigned geographical territories are undertaken.

(ii) Under the facts, it is possible that the acquisition price method or the income method using CPM might reasonably be applied. Whether the acquisition price method or the income method provides the most reliable evidence of the arm's length price of USP's contributions depends on a number of factors, including the reliability of the financial projections, the reliability of the discount rate chosen, and the extent to which the acquisition price of Company X can be reliably adjusted to account for changes in value over the time period between the acquisition and the formation of the CSA and to account for the value of the in-process research done by Company X that does not constitute platform contributions to the CSA. See § 1.482-7T(g)(4)(v) and (g)(5)(iv)(A) and (C).

*Example (18).* Evaluation of alternative methods. (i) The facts are the same as Example 17, except that FS has a patent on Compound Y, which the parties reasonably anticipate will be useful in mitigating potential side effects associated with Compound X and thereby contribute to the development of Oncol. The rights in Compound Y constitute a platform contribution for which compensation is due from USP as part of a PCT. The value of FS's platform contribution cannot be reliably measured by market benchmarks.

(ii) Under the facts, it is possible that either the acquisition price method and the income method together or the residual profit split method might reasonably be applied to determine the arm's length PCT Payments due between USP and FS. Under the first option the PCT Payment for the platform contributions related to Company X's workforce and Compound X would be determined using the acquisition price method referring to the lump sum price paid by USP for Company X. Because the value of these platform contributions can be determined by reference to a market benchmark, they are considered routine platform contributions. Accordingly, under this option, the platform contribution related to Compound Y would be the only nonroutine platform contribution and the relevant PCT Payment is determined using the income method. Under the second option, rather than looking to the acquisition price for Company X, all the platform contributions are considered nonroutine and the RPSM is applied to determine the PCT Payments for each platform contribution. Under either option, the PCT Payments will be netted against each other.

(iii) Whether the acquisition price method together with the income method or the residual profit split method provides the most reliable evidence of the arm's length price of the platform contributions of USP and FS depends on a number of factors, including the reliability of the determination of the relative values of the platform contributions for purposes of the RPSM, and the extent to which the acquisition price of Company X can be reliably adjusted to account for changes in value over the time period between the acquisition and the formation of the CSA and to account for the value of the rights in the in-process research done by Company X that does not constitute platform contributions to the CSA. In these circumstances, it is also relevant to consider whether the results of each method are consistent with each other, or whether one or both methods are consistent with other potential methods that could be applied. See § 1.482-7T(g)(4)(v), (g)(5)(iv), and (g)(7)(iv).

**(c) Effective/applicability date.** Paragraph (b) Examples 13 through 18 of this section are generally applicable on January 5, 2009.

**(d) Expiration date.** The applicability of paragraph (b) Examples 13 through 18 of this section expires on or before December 30, 2011.

T.D. 9278, 7/31/2006, amend T.D. 9441, 12/31/2008, T.D. 9456, 7/31/2009.

## § 1.482-9 Methods to determine taxable income in connection with a controlled services transaction.

**(a) In general.** The arm's length amount charged in a controlled services transaction must be determined under one of the methods provided for in this section. Each method must be applied in accordance with the provisions of § 1.482-1, including the best method rule of § 1.482-1(c), the comparability analysis of § 1.482-1(d), and the arm's length range of § 1.482-1(e), except as those provisions are modified in this section. The methods are—

*(1)* The services cost method, described in paragraph (b) of this section;

*(2)* The comparable uncontrolled services price method, described in paragraph (c) of this section;

*(3)* The gross services margin method, described in paragraph (d) of this section;

*(4)* The cost of services plus method, described in paragraph (e) of this section;

*(5)* The comparable profits method, described in § 1.482-5 and in paragraph (f) of this section;

*(6)* The profit split method, described in § 1.482-6 and in paragraph (g) of this section; and

*(7)* Unspecified methods, described in paragraph (h) of this section.

**(b) Services cost method.** *(1) In general.* The services cost method evaluates whether the amount charged for certain services is arm's length by reference to the total services costs (as defined in paragraph (j) of this section) with no markup. If a taxpayer applies the services cost method in accordance with the rules of this paragraph (b), then it will be considered the best method for purposes of § 1.482-1(c), and the Commissioner's allocations will be limited to adjusting the amount charged for such services to the properly determined amount of such total services costs.

*(2) Eligibility for the services cost method.* To apply the services cost method to a service in accordance with the rules of this paragraph (b), all of the following requirements must be satisfied with respect to the service—

(i) The service is a covered service as defined in paragraph (b)(3) of this section;

(ii) The service is not an excluded activity as defined in paragraph (b)(4) of this section;

(iii) The service is not precluded from constituting a covered service by the business judgment rule described in paragraph (b)(5) of this section; and

(iv) Adequate books and records are maintained as described in paragraph (b)(6) of this section.

*(3) Covered services.* For purposes of this paragraph (b), covered services consist of a controlled service transaction or a group of controlled service transactions (see § 1.482-1(f)(2)(i) (aggregation of transactions)) that meet the definition of specified covered services or low margin covered services.

(i) Specified covered services. Specified covered services are controlled services transactions that the Commissioner specifies by revenue procedure. Services will be included in such revenue procedure based upon the Commissioner's determination that the specified covered services are support services common among taxpayers across industry sectors and generally do not involve a significant median comparable markup on total services costs. For the definition of the median comparable markup on total services costs, see paragraph (b)(3)(ii) of this section. The Commissioner may add to, subtract from, or otherwise revise the specified covered services described in the revenue procedure by subsequent revenue procedure, which amendments will ordinarily be prospective only in effect.

(ii) Low margin covered services. Low margin covered services are controlled services transactions for which the median comparable markup on total services costs is less than or equal to seven percent. For purposes of this paragraph (b), the median comparable markup on total services costs means the excess of the arm's length price of the controlled services transaction determined under the general section 482 regulations without regard to this paragraph (b), using the interquartile range described in § 1.482-1(e)(2)(iii)(C) and as necessary adjusting to the median of such interquartile range, over total services costs, expressed as a percentage of total services costs.

*(4) Excluded activity.* The following types of activities are excluded activities:

(i) Manufacturing.

(ii) Production.

(iii) Extraction, exploration, or processing of natural resources.

(iv) Construction.

(v) Reselling, distribution, acting as a sales or purchasing agent, or acting under a commission or other similar arrangement.

(vi) Research, development, or experimentation.

(vii) Engineering or scientific.

(viii) Financial transactions, including guarantees.

(ix) Insurance or reinsurance.

*(5) Not services that contribute significantly to fundamental risks of business success or failure.* A service cannot constitute a covered service unless the taxpayer reasonably concludes in its business judgment that the service does not contribute significantly to key competitive advantages, core capabilities, or fundamental risks of success or failure in one or more trades or businesses of the controlled group, as defined in § 1.482-1(i)(6). In evaluating the reasonableness of the conclusion required by this paragraph (b)(5), consideration will be given to all the facts and circumstances.

*(6) Adequate books and records.* Permanent books of account and records are maintained for as long as the costs with respect to the covered services are incurred by the renderer. Such books and records must include a statement evidencing the taxpayer's intention to apply the services cost method to evaluate the arm's length charge for such services. Such books and records must be adequate to permit verification by the Commissioner of the total services costs incurred by the renderer, including a description of the services in question, identification of the renderer and the recipient of such services, and sufficient documentation to allow verification of the methods used to allocate and apportion such costs to the services in question in accordance with paragraph (k) of this section.

*(7) Shared services arrangement.* (i) In general. If the services cost method is used to evaluate the amount charged for covered services, and such services are the subject of a shared services arrangement, then the arm's length charge to each participant for such services will be the portion of the total costs of the services otherwise determined under the services cost method of this paragraph (b) that is properly allocated to such participant pursuant to the arrangement.

(ii) Requirements for shared services arrangement. A shared services arrangement must meet the requirements described in this paragraph (b)(7).

(A) Eligibility. To be eligible for treatment under this paragraph (b)(7), a shared services arrangement must—

(1) Include two or more participants;

(2) Include as participants all controlled taxpayers that reasonably anticipate a benefit (as defined under paragraph (l)(3)(i) of this section) from one or more covered services specified in the shared services arrangement; and

(3) Be structured such that each covered service (or each reasonable aggregation of services within the meaning of paragraph (b)(7)(iii)(B) of this section) confers a benefit on at least one participant in the shared services arrangement.

(B) Allocation. The costs for covered services must be allocated among the participants based on their respective shares of the reasonably anticipated benefits from those services, without regard to whether the anticipated benefits are in fact realized. Reasonably anticipated benefits are benefits as defined in paragraph (l)(3)(i) of this section. The allocation of costs must provide the most reliable measure of the participants' respective shares of the reasonably anticipated benefits under the principles of the best method rule. See § 1.482-1(c). The allocation must be applied on a consistent basis for all participants and services. The allocation to each participant in each taxable year must reasonably reflect that participant's respective share of reasonably anticipated benefits for such taxable year. If the taxpayer reasonably concluded that the shared services arrangement (including any aggregation pursuant to paragraph (b)(7)(iii)(B) of this section) allocated costs for covered services on a basis that most reliably reflects the participants' respective shares of the reasonably anticipated benefits attributable to such services, as provided for in this paragraph (b)(7), then the Commissioner may not adjust such allocation basis.

(C) Documentation. The taxpayer must maintain sufficient documentation to establish that the requirements of this paragraph (b)(7) are satisfied, and include—

(1) A statement evidencing the taxpayer's intention to apply the services cost method to evaluate the arm's length charge for covered services pursuant to a shared services arrangement;

(2) A list of the participants and the renderer or renderers of covered services under the shared services arrangement;

(3) A description of the basis of allocation to all participants, consistent with the participants' respective shares of reasonably anticipated benefits; and

(4) A description of any aggregation of covered services for purposes of the shared services arrangement, and an indication whether this aggregation (if any) differs from the aggregation used to evaluate the median comparable markup for any low margin covered services described in paragraph (b)(3)(ii) of this section.

(iii) Definitions and special rules. (A) Participant. A participant is a controlled taxpayer that reasonably anticipates benefits from covered services subject to a shared services arrangement that substantially complies with the requirements described in this paragraph (b)(7).

(B) Aggregation. Two or more covered services may be aggregated in a reasonable manner taking into account all the facts and circumstances, including whether the relative magnitude of reasonably anticipated benefits of the participants sharing the costs of such aggregated services may be reasonably reflected by the allocation basis employed pursuant to paragraph (b)(7)(ii)(B) of this section. The aggregation of services under a shared services arrangement may differ from the aggregation used to evaluate the median comparable markup for any low margin covered services described in paragraph (b)(3)(ii) of this section, provided that such alternative aggregation can be implemented on a reasonable basis, including appropriately identifying and isolating relevant costs, as necessary.

(C) Coordination with cost sharing arrangements. To the extent that an allocation is made to a participant in a shared services arrangement that is also a participant in a cost sharing arrangement subject to § 1.482-7T, such amount with respect to covered services is first allocated pursuant to the shared services arrangement under this paragraph (b)(7). Costs allocated pursuant to a shared services arrangement may (if applicable) be further allocated between the intangible property development activity under § 1.482-7T and other activities of the participant.

*(8) Examples.* The application of this section is illustrated by the following examples. No inference is intended whether the presence or absence of one or more facts is determinative of the conclusion in any example. For purposes of Examples 1 through 14, assume that Company P and its subsidiaries, Company Q and Company R, are corporations and members of the same group of controlled entities (PQR Controlled Group). For purposes of Example 15, assume that

Company P and its subsidiary, Company S, are corporations and members of the same group of controlled entities (PS Controlled Group). For purposes of Examples 16 through 24, assume that Company P and its subsidiaries, Company X, Company Y, and Company Z, are corporations and members of the same group of controlled entities (PXYZ Group) and that Company P and its subsidiaries satisfy all of the requirements for a shared services arrangement specified in paragraphs (b)(7)(ii) and (iii) of this section.

*Example (1).* Data entry services. (i) Company P, Company Q, and Company R own and operate hospitals. Each owns an electronic database of medical information gathered by doctors and nurses during interviews and treatment of its patients. All three databases are maintained and updated by Company P's administrative support employees who perform data entry activities by entering medical information from the paper records of Company P, Company Q, and Company R into their respective databases.

(ii) Assume that these services relating to data entry are specified covered services within the meaning of paragraph (b)(3)(i) of this section. Under the facts and circumstances of the business of the PQR Controlled Group, the taxpayer could reasonably conclude that these services do not contribute significantly to the controlled group's key competitive advantages, core capabilities, or fundamental risks of success or failure in the group's business. If these services meet the other requirements of this paragraph (b), Company P will be eligible to charge these services to Company Q and Company R in accordance with the services cost method.

*Example (2).* Data entry services. (i) Company P, Company Q, and Company R specialize in data entry, data processing, and data conversion. Company Q and Company R's data entry activities involve converting medical information data contained in paper records to a digital format. Company P specializes in data entry activities. This specialization reflects, in part, proprietary quality control systems and specially trained data entry experts used to ensure the highest degree of accuracy of data entry services. Company P is engaged by Company Q and Company R to perform these data entry activities for them. Company Q and Company R then charge their customers for the data entry activities performed by Company P.

(ii) Assume that these services performed by Company P relating to data entry are specified covered services within the meaning of paragraph (b)(3)(i) of this section. Under the facts and circumstances, the taxpayer is unable to reasonably conclude that these services do not contribute significantly to the controlled group's key competitive advantages, core capabilities, or fundamental risks of success or failure in the group's business. Company P is not eligible to charge these services to Company Q and Company R in accordance with the services cost method.

*Example (3).* Recruiting services. (i) Company P, Company Q, and Company R are manufacturing companies that sell their products to unrelated retail establishments. Company P's human resources department recruits mid-level managers and engineers for itself as well as for Company Q and Company R by attending job fairs and other recruitment events. For recruiting higher-level managers and engineers, each of these companies uses recruiters from unrelated executive search firms.

(ii) Assume that these services relating to recruiting are specified covered services within the meaning of paragraph (b)(3)(i) of this section. Under the facts and circumstances of the business of the PQR Controlled Group, the taxpayer could reasonably conclude that these services do not contribute significantly to the controlled group's key competitive advantages, core capabilities, or fundamental risks of success or failure in the group's business. If these services meet the other requirements of this paragraph (b), Company P will be eligible to charge these services to Company Q and Company R in accordance with the services cost method.

*Example (4).* Recruiting services. (i) Company Q and Company R are executive recruiting service companies that are hired by other companies to recruit professionals. Company P is a recruiting agency that is engaged by Company Q and Company R to perform recruiting activities on their behalf in certain geographic areas.

(ii) Assume that the services performed by Company P are specified covered services within the meaning of paragraph (b)(3)(i) of this section. Under the facts and circumstances, the taxpayer is unable to reasonably conclude that these services do not contribute significantly to the controlled group's key competitive advantages, core capabilities, or fundamental risks of success or failure in the group's business. Company P is not eligible to charge these services to Company Q and Company R in accordance with the services cost method.

*Example (5).* Credit analysis services. (i) Company P is a manufacturer and distributor of clothing for retail stores. Company Q and Company R are distributors of clothing for retail stores. As part of its operations, personnel in Company P perform credit analysis on its customers. Most of the customers have a history of purchases from Company P, and the credit analysis involves a review of the recent payment history of the customer's account. For new customers, the personnel in Company P perform a basic credit check of the customer using reports from a credit reporting agency. On behalf of Company Q and Company R, Company P performs credit analysis on customers who order clothing from Company Q and Company R using the same method as Company P uses for itself.

(ii) Assume that these services relating to credit analysis are specified covered services within the meaning of paragraph (b)(3)(i) of this section. Under the facts and circumstances of the business of the PQR Controlled Group, the taxpayer could reasonably conclude that these services do not contribute significantly to the controlled group's key competitive advantages, core capabilities, or fundamental risks of success or failure in the group's business. If these services meet the other requirements of this paragraph (b), Company P will be eligible to charge these services to Company Q and Company R in accordance with the services cost method.

*Example (6).* Credit analysis services. (i) Company P, Company Q, and Company R lease furniture to retail customers who present a significant credit risk and are generally unable to lease furniture from other providers. As part of its leasing operations, personnel in Company P perform credit analysis on each of the potential lessees. The personnel have developed special expertise in determining whether a particular customer who presents a significant credit risk (as indicated by credit reporting agencies) will be likely to make the requisite lease payments on a timely basis. Also, as part of its operations, Company P performs similar credit analysis services for Company Q and Company R, which charge correspondingly high monthly lease payments.

(ii) Assume that these services relating to credit analysis are specified covered services within the meaning of paragraph (b)(3)(i) of this section. Under the facts and circumstances, the taxpayer is unable to reasonably conclude that these services do not contribute significantly to the controlled group's key competitive advantages, core capabilities, or fundamental risks of success or failure in the group's business. Company P is not eligible to charge these services to Company Q and Company R in accordance with the services cost method.

*Example (7).* Credit analysis services. (i) Company P is a large full-service bank, which provides products and services to corporate and consumer markets, including unsecured loans, secured loans, lines of credit, letters of credit, conversion of foreign currency, consumer loans, trust services, and sales of certificates of deposit. Company Q makes routine consumer loans to individuals, such as auto loans and home equity loans. Company R makes only business loans to small businesses.

(ii) Company P performs credit analysis and prepares credit reports for itself, as well as for Company Q and Company R. Company P, Company Q and Company R regularly employ these credit reports in the ordinary course of business in making decisions regarding extensions of credit to potential customers (including whether to lend, rate of interest, and loan terms).

(iii) Assume that these services relating to credit analysis are specified covered services within the meaning of paragraph (b)(3)(i) of this section. Under the facts and circumstances, the credit analysis services constitute part of a "financial transaction" described in paragraph (b)(4)(viii) of this section. Company P is not eligible to charge these services to Company Q and Company R in accordance with the services cost method.

*Example (8).* Data verification services. (i) Company P, Company Q and Company R are manufacturers of industrial supplies. Company P's accounting department performs periodic reviews of the accounts payable information of Company P, Company Q and Company R, and identifies any inaccuracies in the records, such as double-payments and double-charges.

(ii) Assume that these services relating to verification of data are specified covered services within the meaning of paragraph (b)(3)(i) of this section. Under the facts and circumstances of the business of the PQR Controlled Group, the taxpayer could reasonably conclude that these services do not contribute significantly to the controlled group's key competitive advantages, core capabilities, or fundamental risks of success or failure in the group's business. If these services meet the other requirements of this paragraph (b), Company P will be eligible to charge these services to Company Q and Company R in accordance with the services cost method.

*Example (9).* Data verification services. (i) Company P gathers and inputs information regarding accounts payable and accounts receivable from unrelated parties and utilizes its own computer system to analyze that information for purposes of identifying errors in payment and receipts (data mining). Company P is compensated for these services based on a fee that reflects a percentage of amounts collected by customers as a result of the data mining services. These activities constitute a significant portion of Company P's business. Company P performs similar activities for Company Q and Company R by analyzing their accounts payable and accounts receivable records.

(ii) Assume that these services relating to data mining are specified covered services within the meaning of paragraph (b)(3)(i) of this section. Under the facts and circumstances, the taxpayer is unable to reasonably conclude that these services do not contribute significantly to the controlled group's key competitive advantages, core capabilities, or fundamental risks of success or failure in the group's business. Company P is not eligible to charge these services to Company Q and Company R in accordance with the services cost method.

*Example (10).* Legal services. (i) Company P is a domestic corporation with two wholly-owned foreign subsidiaries, Company Q and Company R. Company P and its subsidiaries manufacture and distribute equipment used by industrial customers. Company P maintains an in-house legal department consisting of attorneys experienced in a wide range of business and commercial matters. Company Q and Company R maintain small legal departments, consisting of attorneys experienced in matters that most frequently arise in the normal course of business of Company Q and Company R in their respective jurisdictions.

(ii) Company P seeks to maintain in-house legal staff with the ability to address the majority of legal matters that arise in the United States with respect to the operations of Company P, as well as any U.S. reporting or compliance obligations of Company Q or Company R. These include the preparation and review of corporate contracts relating to, for example, product sales, equipment purchases and leases, business liability insurance, real estate, employee salaries and benefits. Company P relies on outside attorneys for major business transactions and highly technical matters such as patent licenses. The in-house legal staffs of Company Q and Company R are much more limited. It is necessary for Company P to retain several local law firms to handle litigation and business disputes arising from the activities of Company Q and Company R. Although Company Q and Company R pay the fees of these law firms, the hiring authority and general oversight of the firms' representation is in the legal department of Company P.

(iii) In determining what portion of the legal expenses of Company P may be allocated to Company Q and Company R, Company P first excludes any expenses relating to legal services that constitute shareholder activities and other items that are not properly analyzed as controlled services. Assume that the remaining services relating to general legal functions performed by in-house legal counsel are specified covered services within the meaning of paragraph (b)(3)(i) of this section. Under the facts and circumstances of the business of the PQR Controlled Group, the taxpayer could reasonably conclude that these latter services do not contribute significantly to the controlled group's key competitive advantages, core capabilities, or fundamental risks of success or failure in the group's business. If these services meet the other requirements of this paragraph (b), Company P will be eligible to charge these services to Company Q and Company R in accordance with the services cost method.

*Example (11).* Legal services. (i) Company P is a domestic holding company whose operating companies, Company Q and Company R, generate electric power for consumers by operating nuclear plants. Assume that, although Company P owns 100% of the stock of Companies Q and R, the companies do not elect to file a consolidated Federal income tax return with Company P.

(ii) Company P maintains an in-house legal department that includes attorneys who are experts in the areas of Federal utilities regulation, Federal labor and environmental law, and securities law. Companies Q and R maintain their own, smaller in-house legal staffs comprising experienced attorneys in the areas of state and local utilities regulation, state labor and employment law, and general commercial law. The legal department of Company P performs general oversight of the legal affairs of the company and determines whether a particular matter would be more efficiently handled by the Company P legal department, by the legal staffs in the operating companies, or in rare cases, by retained outside counsel. In general, Company P has succeeded in minimizing duplication and overlap of functions between the legal staffs of the various companies or by retained outside counsel.

(iii) The domestic nuclear power plant operations of Companies Q and R are subject to extensive regulation by the U.S. Nuclear Regulatory Commission (NRC). Operators are required to obtain pre-construction approval, operating licenses, and, at the end of the operational life of the nuclear reactor, nuclear decommissioning certificates. Company P files consolidated financial statements on behalf of itself, as well as Companies Q and R, with the United States Securities and Exchange Commission (SEC). In these SEC filings, Company P discloses that failure to obtain any of these licenses (and the related periodic renewals) or agreeing to licenses on terms less favorable than those granted to competitors would have a material adverse impact on the operations of Company Q or Company R. Company Q and Company R do not have in-house legal staff with experience in the NRC area. Company P maintains a group of in-house attorneys with specialized expertise in the NRC area that exclusively represents Company Q and Company R before the NRC. Although Company P occasionally hires an outside law firm or industry expert to assist on particular NRC matters, the majority of the work is performed by the specialized legal staff of Company P.

(iv) Certain of the legal services performed by Company P constitute duplicative or shareholder activities that do not confer a benefit on the other companies and therefore do not need to be allocated to the other companies, while certain other legal services are eligible to be charged to Company Q and Company R in accordance with the services cost method.

(v) Assume that the specialized legal services relating to nuclear licenses performed by in-house legal counsel of Company P are specified covered services within the meaning of paragraph (b)(3)(i) of this section. Under the facts and circumstances, the taxpayer is unable to reasonably conclude that these services do not contribute significantly to the controlled group's key competitive advantages, core capabilities, or fundamental risks of success or failure in the group's business. Company P is not eligible to charge these services to Company Q and Company R in accordance with the services cost method.

*Example (12).* Group of services. (i) Company P, Company Q, and Company R are manufacturing companies that sell their products to unrelated retail establishments. Company P has an enterprise resource planning (ERP) system that maintains data relating to accounts payable and accounts receivable information for all three companies. Company P's personnel perform the daily operations on this ERP system such as inputting data relating to accounts payable and accounts receivable into the system and extracting data relating to accounts receivable and accounts payable in the form of reports or electronic media and providing those data to all three companies. Periodically, Company P's computer specialists also modify the ERP system to adapt to changing business functions in all three companies. Company P's computer specialists make these changes by either modifying the underlying software program or by purchasing additional software or hardware from unrelated third party vendors.

(ii) Assume that the services relating to accounts payable and accounts receivable are specified covered services within the meaning of paragraph (b)(3)(i) of this section. Under the facts and circumstances of the business of the PQR Controlled Group, the taxpayer could reasonably conclude that these services do not contribute significantly to the controlled group's key competitive advantages, core capabilities, or fundamental risks of success or failure in the group's business. If these services meet the other requirements of this paragraph (b), Company P will be eligible to charge these services to Company Q and Company R in accordance with the services cost method.

(iii) Assume that the services performed by Company P's computer specialists that relate to modifying the ERP system are specifically excluded from the services described in a revenue procedure referenced in paragraph (b)(3) of this section as developing hardware or software solutions (such as systems integration, Web site design, writing computer programs, modifying general applications software, or recommending the purchase of commercially available hardware or software). If these services do not constitute low margin covered services within the meaning of paragraph (b)(3)(ii) of this section, then Company P is not eligible to charge these services to Company Q and Company R in accordance with the services cost method.

*Example (13).* Group of services. (i) Company P manufactures and sells widgets under an exclusive contract to Customer 1. Company Q and Company R sell widgets under exclusive contracts to Customer 2 and Customer 3, respectively. At least one year in advance, each of these customers can accurately forecast its need for widgets. Using these forecasts, each customer over the course of the year places orders for widgets with the appropriate company, Company P, Company Q, or Company R. A customer's actual need for widgets seldom deviates from that customer's forecasted need.

(ii) It is most efficient for the PQR Controlled Group companies to manufacture and store an inventory of widgets in advance of delivery. Although all three companies sell widgets, only Company P maintains a centralized warehouse for widgets. Pursuant to a contract, Company P provides storage of these widgets to Company Q and Company R at an arm's length price.

(iii) Company P's personnel also obtain orders from all three companies' customers to draw up purchase orders for widgets as well as make payment to suppliers for widget replacement parts. In addition, Company P's personnel use data entry to input information regarding orders and sales of widgets and replacement parts for all three companies into a centralized computer system. Company P's personnel also maintain the centralized computer system and extract data for all three companies when necessary.

(iv) Assume that these services relating to tracking purchases and sales of inventory are specified covered services within the meaning of paragraph (b)(3)(i) of this section. Under the facts and circumstances of the business of the PQR Controlled Group, the taxpayer could reasonably conclude that these services do not contribute significantly to the controlled group's key competitive advantages, core capabilities, or fundamental risks of success or failure in the group's business. If these services meet the other requirements of this paragraph (b), Company P will be eligible to charge these services to Company Q and Company R in accordance with the services cost method.

*Example (14).* Group of services. (i) Company P, Company Q, and Company R assemble and sell gadgets to unrelated customers. Each of these companies purchases the components necessary for assembly of the gadgets from unrelated suppliers. As a service to its subsidiaries, Company P's personnel obtain orders for components from all three companies, prepare purchase orders, and make payment to unrelated suppliers for the components. In addition, Company P's personnel use data entry to input information regarding orders and sales of gadgets for all three companies into a centralized computer. Company P's personnel also maintain the centralized computer system and extract data for all three companies on an as-needed basis. The services provided by Company P personnel, in conjunction with the centralized computer system, constitute a state-of-the-art inventory management system that allows Company P to order components necessary for assembly of the gadgets on a "just-in-time" basis.

(ii) Unrelated suppliers deliver the components directly to Company P, Company Q and Company R. Each company stores the components in its own facilities for use in filling specific customer orders. The companies do not maintain any inventory that is not identified in specific customer orders. Because of the efficiencies associated with services provided by personnel of Company P, all three companies are able to significantly reduce their inventory-related costs. Company P's Chief Executive Officer makes a statement in one of its press conferences with industry analysts that its inventory management system is critical to the company's success.

(iii) Assume that these services relating to tracking purchases and sales of inventory are specified covered services within the meaning of paragraph (b)(3)(i) of this section. Under the facts and circumstances, the taxpayer is unable to reasonably conclude that these services do not contribute significantly to the controlled group's key competitive advantages, core capabilities, or fundamental risks of success or failure in the group's business. Company P is not eligible to charge these services to Company Q and Company R in accordance with the services cost method.

*Example (15).* Low margin covered services. Company P renders certain accounting services to Company S. Company P uses the services cost method for the accounting services, and determines the amount charged as its total cost of rendering the services, with no markup. Based on an application of the section 482 regulations without regard to this paragraph (b), the interquartile range of arm's length markups on total services costs for these accounting services is between 3% and 9%, and the median is 6%. Because the median comparable markup on total services costs is 6%, which is less than 7%, the accounting services constitute low margin covered services within the meaning of paragraph (b)(3)(ii) of this section.

*Example (16).* Shared services arrangement and reliable measure of reasonably anticipated benefit (allocation key). (i) Company P operates a centralized data processing facility that performs automated invoice processing and order generation for all of its subsidiaries, Companies X, Y, Z, pursuant to a shared services arrangement.

(ii) In evaluating the shares of reasonably anticipated benefits from the centralized data processing services, the total value of the merchandise on the invoices and orders may not provide the most reliable measure of reasonably anticipated benefits shares, because value of merchandise sold does not bear a relationship to the anticipated benefits from the underlying covered services.

(iii) The total volume of orders and invoices processed may provide a more reliable basis for evaluating the shares of reasonably anticipated benefits from the data processing services. Alternatively, depending on the facts and circumstances, total central processing unit time attributable to the transactions of each subsidiary may provide a more reliable basis on which to evaluate the shares of reasonably anticipated benefits.

*Example (17).* Shared services arrangement and reliable measure of reasonably anticipated benefit (allocation key). (i) Company P operates a centralized center that performs human resources functions, such as administration of pension, retirement, and health insurance plans that are made available to employees of its subsidiaries, Companies X, Y, Z, pursuant to a shared services arrangement.

(ii) In evaluating the shares of reasonably anticipated benefits from these centralized services, the total revenues of each subsidiary may not provide the most reliable measure of reasonably anticipated benefit shares, because total revenues do not bear a relationship to the shares of reasonably anticipated benefits from the underlying services.

(iii) Employee headcount or total compensation paid to employees may provide a more reliable basis for evaluating the shares of reasonably anticipated benefits from the covered services.

*Example (18).* Shared services arrangement and reliable measure of reasonably anticipated benefit (allocation key). (i) Company P performs human resource services (service A) on behalf of the PXYZ Group that qualify for the services cost method. Under that method, Company P determines the amount charged for these services pursuant to a shared services arrangement based on an application of paragraph (b)(7) of this section. Service A constitutes a specified covered service described in a revenue procedure pursuant to paragraph (b)(3)(i) of this section. The total services costs for service A otherwise determined under the services cost method is 300.

(ii) Companies X, Y and Z reasonably anticipate benefits from service A. Company P does not reasonably anticipate benefits from service A. Assume that if relative reasonably anticipated benefits were precisely known, the appropriate allocation of charges pursuant to paragraph (k) of this section to Company X, Y and Z for service A is as follows:

**Service A**

*[Total cost 300]*

| Company | |
|---|---|
| X | 150 |
| Y | 75 |
| Z | 75 |

(iii) The total number of employees (employee headcount) in each company is as follows: Company X—600 employees.

Company Y—250 employees.

Company Z—250 employees.

(iv) Company P allocates the 300 total services costs of service A based on employee headcount as follows:

**Service A**

*[Total cost 300]*

| Allocation key | Company Headcount | Amount |
|---|---|---|
| X | 600 | 164 |
| Y | 250 | 68 |
| Z | 250 | 68 |

(v) Based on these facts, Company P may reasonably conclude that the employee headcount allocation basis most reliably reflects the participants' respective shares of the reasonably anticipated benefits attributable to service A.

*Example (19).* Shared services arrangement and reliable measure of reasonably anticipated benefit (allocation key). (i) Company P performs accounts payable services (service B) on behalf of the PXYZ Group and determines the amount charged for the services under such method pursuant to a shared services arrangement based on an application of paragraph (b)(7) of this section. Service B is a specified covered service described in a revenue procedure pursuant to paragraph (b)(3)(i) of this section. The total services costs for service B otherwise determined under the services cost method is 500.

(ii) Companies X, Y and Z reasonably anticipate benefits from service B. Company P does not reasonably anticipate benefits from service B. Assume that if relative reasonably anticipated benefits were precisely known, the appropriate allocation of charges pursuant to paragraph (k) of this section to Companies X, Y and Z for service B is as follows:

**Service B**

*[Total cost 500]*

| Company | |
|---|---|
| X | 125 |
| Y | 205 |
| Z | 170 |

(iii) The total number of employees (employee headcount) in each company is as follows: Company X—600.

Company Y—200.

Company Z—200.

(iv) The total number of transactions (transaction volume) with uncontrolled customers by each company is as follows:

Company X—2,000.

Company Y—4,000.

Company Z—3,500.

(v) If Company P allocated the 500 total services costs of service B based on employee headcount, the resulting allocation would be as follows:

**Service B**

*[Total cost 500]*

| Allocation key | Company Headcount | Amount |
|---|---|---|
| X | 600 | 300 |
| Y | 200 | 100 |
| Z | 200 | 100 |

(vi) In contrast, if Company P used volume of transactions with uncontrolled customers as the allocation basis under the shared services arrangement, the allocation would be as follows:

**Service B**

*[Total cost 500]*

| Allocation key | Company Transaction Volume | Amount |
|---|---|---|
| X | 2,000 | 105 |
| Y | 4,000 | 211 |
| Z | 3,500 | 184 |

(vii) Based on these facts, Company P may reasonably conclude that the transaction volume, but not the employee headcount, allocation basis most reliably reflects the participants' respective shares of the reasonably anticipated benefits attributable to service B.

*Example (20).* Shared services arrangement and aggregation. (i) Company P performs human resource services (service A) and accounts payable services (service B) on behalf of the PXYZ Group that qualify for the services cost method. Company P determines the amount charged for these services under such method pursuant to a shared services arrangement based on an application of paragraph (b)(7) of this section. Service A and service B are specified covered services described in a revenue procedure pursuant to paragraph (b)(3)(i) of this section. The total services costs otherwise determined under the services cost method for service A is 300 and for service B is 500; total services costs for services A and B are 800. Company P determines that aggregation of services A and B for purposes of the arrangement is appropriate.

(ii) Companies X, Y and Z reasonably anticipate benefits from services A and B. Company P does not reasonably anticipate benefits from services A and B. Assume that if relative reasonably anticipated benefits were precisely known, the appropriate allocation of total charges pursuant to paragraph (k) of this section to Companies X, Y and Z for services A and B is as follows:

**Services A and B**

*[Total cost 800]*

| Company | |
|---|---|
| X | 350 |
| Y | 100 |
| Z | 350 |

(iii) The total volume of transactions with uncontrolled customers in each company is as follows: Company X—2,000.

Company Y—4,000.

Company Z—4,000.

(iv) The total number of employees in each company is as follows:

Company X—600.

Company Y—200.

Company Z—200.

(v) If Company P allocated the 800 total services costs of services A and B based on transaction volume or employee headcount, the resulting allocation would be as follows:

**Aggregated Services AB**

*[Total cost 800]*

| Company | Allocation key | | Allocation key | |
|---|---|---|---|---|
| | Transaction volume | Amount | Headcount | Amount |
| X | 2,000 | 160 | 600 | 480 |
| Y | 4,000 | 320 | 200 | 160 |
| Z | 4,000 | 320 | 200 | 160 |

(vi) In contrast, if aggregated services AB were allocated by reference to the total U.S. dollar value of sales to uncontrolled parties (trade sales) by each company, the following results would obtain:

**Aggregated Services AB**

*[Total costs 800]*

| Company | Allocation key | |
|---|---|---|
| | Trade sales (millions) | Amount |
| X | $400 | 314 |
| Y | 120 | 94 |
| Z | 500 | 392 |

(vii) Based on these facts, Company P may reasonably conclude that the trade sales, but not the transaction volume or the employee headcount, allocation basis most reliably reflects the participants' respective shares of the reasonably anticipated benefits attributable to services AB.

*Example (21).* Shared services arrangement and aggregation. (i) Company P performs services A through P on behalf of the PXYZ Group that qualify for the services cost method. Company P determines the amount charged for these services under such method pursuant to a shared services arrangement based on an application of paragraph (b)(7) of this section. All of these services A through P constitute either specified covered services or low margin covered services described in paragraph (b)(3) of this section. The total services costs for services A through P otherwise determined under the services cost method is 500. Company P determines that aggregation of services A through P for purposes of the arrangement is appropriate.

(ii) Companies X and Y reasonably anticipate benefits from services A through P and Company Z reasonably anticipates benefits from services A through M but not from services N through P (Company Z performs services similar to services N through P on its own behalf). Company P does not reasonably anticipate benefits from services A through P. Assume that if relative reasonably anticipated benefits were precisely known, the appropriate allocation of total charges pursuant to paragraph (k) of this section to Company X, Y, and Z for services A through P is as follows:

| Company | Services A-M (cost 490) | Services N-P (cost 10) | Services A-P (total cost 500) |
|---|---|---|---|
| X | 90 | 5 | 95 |
| Y | 240 | 5 | 245 |
| Z | 160 | ... | 160 |

(iii) The total volume of transactions with uncontrolled customers in each company is as follows: Company X—2,000.

Company Y—4,500.

Company Z—3,500.

(iv) Company P allocates the 500 total services costs of services A through P based on transaction volume as follows:

**Aggregated Services A-Z**

*[Total costs 500]*

| Company | Allocation key | |
|---|---|---|
| | Transaction volume | Amount |
| X | 2,000 | 100 |
| Y | 4,500 | 225 |
| Z | 3,500 | 175 |

(v) Based on these facts, Company P may reasonably conclude that the transaction volume allocation basis most reliably reflects the participants' respective shares of the reasonably anticipated benefits attributable to services A through P.

*Example (22).* Renderer reasonably anticipates benefits. (i) Company P renders services on behalf of the PXYZ Group that qualify for the services cost method. Company P determines the amount charged for these services under such method. Company P's share of reasonably anticipated benefits from services A, B, C, and D is 20% of the total reasonably anticipated benefits of all participants. Company P's total services cost for services A, B, C, and D charged within the group is 100.

(ii) Based on an application of paragraph (b)(7) of this section, Company P charges 80 which is allocated among Companies X, Y, and Z. No charge is made to Company P under the shared services arrangement for activities that it performs on its own behalf.

*Example (23).* Coordination with cost sharing arrangement. (i) Company P performs human resource services (service A) on behalf of the PXYZ Group that qualify for the services cost method. Company P determines the amount charged for these services under such method pursuant to a shared services arrangement based on an application of paragraph (b)(7) of this section. Service A constitutes a specified covered service described in a revenue procedure pursuant to paragraph (b)(3)(i) of this section. The total services costs for service A otherwise determined under the services cost method is 300.

(ii) Company X, Y, Z, and P reasonably anticipate benefits from service A. Using a basis of allocation that is consistent with the controlled participants' respective shares of the reasonably anticipated benefits from the shared services, the total charge of 300 is allocated as follows:

X—100.

Y—50.

Z—25.

P—125.

(iii) In addition to performing services, P undertakes 500 of R&D and incurs manufacturing and other costs of 1,000.

(iv) Companies P and X enter into a cost sharing arrangement in accordance with § 1.482-7T. Under the arrangement, Company P will undertake all intangible property development activities. All of Company P's research and development (R&D) activity is devoted to the intangible property development activity under the cost sharing arrangement. Company P will manufacture, market, and otherwise exploit the product in its defined territory. Companies P and X will share intangible property development costs in accordance with their reasonably anticipated benefits from the intangible property, and Company X will make payments to Company P as required under § 1.482-7T. Company X will manufacture, market, and otherwise exploit the product in the rest of the world.

(v) A portion of the charge under the shared services arrangement is in turn allocable to the intangible property development activity undertaken by Company P. The most reliable estimate of the proportion allocable to the intangible property development activity is determined to be 500 (Company P's R&D expenses) divided by 1,500 (Company P's total non-covered services costs), or one-third. Accordingly, one-third of Company P's charge of 125, or 42, is allocated to the intangible property development activity. Companies P and X must share the intangible property development costs of the cost shared intangible property (including the charge of 42 that is allocated under the shared services arrangement) in proportion to their respective shares of reasonably anticipated benefits under the cost sharing arrangement. That is, the reasonably anticipated benefit shares under the cost sharing arrangement are determined separately from reasonably anticipated benefit shares under the shared services arrangement.

*Example (24).* Coordination with cost sharing arrangement. (i) The facts and analysis are the same as in Example 25, except that Company X also performs intangible property development activities related to the cost sharing arrangement. Using a basis of allocation that is consistent with the controlled participants' respective shares of the reasonably anticipated benefits from the shared services, the 300 of service costs is allocated as follows:

X—100.

Y—50.

Z—25.

P—125.

(ii) In addition to performing services, Company P undertakes 500 of R&D and incurs manufacturing and other costs of 1,000. Company X undertakes 400 of R&D and incurs manufacturing and other costs of 600.

(iii) Companies P and X enter into a cost sharing arrangement in accordance with § 1.482-7T. Under the arrangement, both Companies P and X will undertake intangible property development activities. All of the research and development activity conducted by Companies P and X is devoted to the intangible property development activity under the cost sharing arrangement. Both Companies P and X will manufacture, market, and otherwise exploit the product in their respective territories and will share intangible property development costs in accordance with their reasonably anticipated benefits from the intangible property, and both will make payments as required under § 1.482-7T.

(iv) A portion of the charge under the shared services arrangement is in turn allocable to the intangible property development activities undertaken by Companies P and X. The most reliable estimate of the portion allocable to Company P's intangible property development activity is determined to be 500 (Company P's R&D expenses) divided by 1,500 (P's total non-covered services costs), or one-third. Accordingly, one-third of Company P's allocated services cost method charge of 125, or 42, is allocated to its intangible property development activity.

(v) In addition, it is necessary to determine the portion of the charge under the shared services arrangement to Company X that should be further allocated to Company X's intangible property development activities under the cost sharing arrangement. The most reliable estimate of the portion allocable to Company X's intangible property development activity is 400 (Company X's R&D expenses) divided by 1,000 (Company X's costs), or 40%. Accordingly, 40% of the 100 that was allocated to Company X, or 40, is allocated in turn to Company X's intangible property development activities. Company X makes a payment to Company P of 100 under the shared services arrangement and includes 40 of services cost method charges in the pool of intangible property development costs.

(vi) The parties' respective contributions to intangible property development costs under the cost sharing arrangement are as follows:

P: 500 + (0.333 * 125) = 542

X: 400 + (0.40 * 100) = 440

**(c) Comparable uncontrolled services price method.** *(1) In general.* The comparable uncontrolled services price method evaluates whether the amount charged in a controlled services transaction is arm's length by reference to the amount charged in a comparable uncontrolled services transaction.

*(2) Comparability and reliability considerations.* (i) In general. Whether results derived from application of this method are the most reliable measure of the arm's length result must be determined using the factors described under the best method rule in § 1.482-1(c). The application of these factors under the comparable uncontrolled services price method is discussed in paragraphs (c)(2)(ii) and (iii) of this section.

(ii) Comparability. (A) In general. The degree of comparability between controlled and uncontrolled transactions is determined by applying the provisions of § 1.482-1(d). Although all of the factors described in § 1.482-1(d)(3) must be considered, similarity of the services rendered, and of the intangible property (if any) used in performing the services, generally will have the greatest effects on comparability under this method. In addition, because even minor differences in contractual terms or economic conditions could materially affect the amount charged in an uncontrolled transaction, comparability under this method depends on close similarity with respect to these factors, or adjustments to account for any differences. The results derived from applying the comparable uncontrolled services price method generally will be the most direct and reliable measure of an arm's length price for the controlled transaction if an uncontrolled transaction has no differences from the controlled transaction that would affect the price, or if there are only minor differences that have a definite and reasonably ascertainable effect on price and for which appropriate adjustments are made. If such adjustments cannot be made, or if there are more than minor differences between the controlled and uncontrolled transactions, the comparable uncontrolled services price method may be used, but the reliability of the results as a measure of the arm's length price will be reduced. Further, if there are material differences for which reliable adjustments cannot be made, this method ordinarily will not provide a reliable measure of an arm's length result.

(B) Adjustments for differences between controlled and uncontrolled transactions. If there are differences between the controlled and uncontrolled transactions that would affect price, adjustments should be made to the price of the uncontrolled transaction according to the comparability provisions of § 1.482-1(d)(2). Specific examples of factors that may be particularly relevant to application of this method include—

(1) Quality of the services rendered;

(2) Contractual terms (for example, scope and terms of warranties or guarantees regarding the services, volume, credit and payment terms, allocation of risks, including any contingent-payment terms and whether costs were incurred without a provision for current reimbursement);

(3) Intangible property (if any) used in rendering the services;

(4) Geographic market in which the services are rendered or received;

(5) Risks borne (for example, costs incurred to render the services, without provision for current reimbursement);

(6) Duration or quantitative measure of services rendered;

(7) Collateral transactions or ongoing business relationships between the renderer and the recipient, including arrangement for the provision of tangible property in connection with the services; and

(8) Alternatives realistically available to the renderer and the recipient.

(iii) Data and assumptions. The reliability of the results derived from the comparable uncontrolled services price method is affected by the completeness and accuracy of the data used and the reliability of the assumptions made to apply the method. See § 1.482-1(c) (best method rule).

*(3) Arm's length range.* See § 1.482-1(e)(2) for the determination of an arm's length range.

*(4) Examples.* The principles of this paragraph (c) are illustrated by the following examples:

*Example (1).* Internal comparable uncontrolled services price. Company A, a United States corporation, performs shipping, stevedoring, and related services for controlled and uncontrolled parties on a short-term or as-needed basis. Company A charges uncontrolled parties in Country X a uniform fee of $60 per container to place loaded cargo containers in Country X on oceangoing vessels for marine transportation. Company A also performs identical services in

Country X for its wholly-owned subsidiary, Company B, and there are no substantial differences between the controlled and uncontrolled transactions. In evaluating the appropriate measure of the arm's length price for the container-loading services performed for Company B, because Company A renders substantially identical services in Country X to both controlled and uncontrolled parties, it is determined that the comparable uncontrolled services price constitutes the best method for determining the arm's length price for the controlled services transaction. Based on the reliable data provided by Company A concerning the price charged for services in comparable uncontrolled transactions, a loading charge of $60 per cargo container will be considered the most reliable measure of the arm's length price for the services rendered to Company B. See paragraph (c)(2)(ii)(A) of this section.

*Example (2).* External comparable uncontrolled services price. (i) The facts are the same as in Example 1, except that Company A performs services for Company B, but not for uncontrolled parties. Based on information obtained from unrelated parties (which is determined to be reliable under the comparability standards set forth in paragraph (c)(2) of this section), it is determined that uncontrolled parties in Country X perform services comparable to those rendered by Company A to Company B, and that such parties charge $60 per cargo container.

(ii) In evaluating the appropriate measure of an arm's length price for the loading services that Company A renders to Company B, the $60 per cargo container charge is considered evidence of a comparable uncontrolled services price. See paragraph (c)(2)(ii)(A) of this section.

*Example (3).* External comparable uncontrolled services price. The facts are the same as in Example 2, except that uncontrolled parties in Country X render similar loading and stevedoring services, but only under contracts that have a minimum term of one year. If the difference in the duration of the services has a material effect on prices, adjustments to account for these differences must be made to the results of the uncontrolled transactions according to the provisions of § 1.482-1(d)(2), and such adjusted results may be used as a measure of the arm's length result.

*Example (4).* Use of valuable intangible property. (i) Company A, a United States corporation in the biotechnology sector, renders research and development services exclusively to its affiliates. Company B is Company A's wholly-owned subsidiary in Country X. Company A renders research and development services to Company B.

(ii) In performing its research and development services function, Company A uses proprietary software that it developed internally. Company A uses the software to evaluate certain genetically engineered compounds developed by Company B. Company A owns the copyright on this software and does not license it to uncontrolled parties.

(iii) No uncontrolled parties can be identified that perform services identical or with a high degree of similarity to those performed by Company A. Because there are material differences for which reliable adjustments cannot be made, the comparable uncontrolled services price method is unlikely to provide a reliable measure of the arm's length price. See paragraph (c)(2)(ii)(A) of this section.

*Example (5).* Internal comparable. (i) Company A, a United States corporation, and its subsidiaries render computer consulting services relating to systems integration and networking to business clients in various countries. Company A and its subsidiaries render only consulting services, and do not manufacture computer hardware or software nor distribute such products. The controlled group is organized according to industry specialization, with key industry specialists working for Company A. These personnel typically form the core consulting group that teams with consultants from the local-country subsidiaries to serve clients in the subsidiaries' respective countries.

(ii) Company A and its subsidiaries sometimes undertake engagements directly for clients, and sometimes work as subcontractors to unrelated parties on more extensive supply-chain consulting engagements for clients. In undertaking the latter engagements with third party consultants, Company A typically prices its services based on consulting hours worked multiplied by a rate determined for each category of employee. The company also charges, at no markup, for out-of-pocket expenses such as travel, lodging, and data acquisition charges. The Company has established the following schedule of hourly rates:

| Category | Rate |
|---|---|
| Project managers | $400 per hour. |
| Technical staff | $300 per hour. |

(iii) Thus, for example, a project involving 100 hours of the time of project managers and 400 hours of technical staff time would result in the following project fees (without regard to any out-of-pocket expenses): ([100 hrs. x $400/hr.] + [400 hrs. x $300/hr.]) = $40,000 + $120,000 = $160,000.

(iv) Company B, a Country X subsidiary of Company A, contracts to perform consulting services for a Country X client in the banking industry. In undertaking this engagement, Company B uses its own consultants and also uses Company A project managers and technical staff that specialize in the banking industry for 75 hours and 380 hours, respectively. In determining an arm's length charge, the price that Company A charges for consulting services as a subcontractor in comparable uncontrolled transactions will be considered evidence of a comparable uncontrolled services price. Thus, in this case, a payment of $144,000, (or [75 hrs. x $400/hr.] + [380 hrs. x $300/hr.] = $30,000 + $114,000) may be used as a measure of the arm's length price for the work performed by Company A project mangers and technical staff. In addition, if the comparable uncontrolled services price method is used, then, consistent with the practices employed by the comparables with respect to similar types of expenses, Company B must reimburse Company A for appropriate out-of-pocket expenses. See paragraph (c)(2)(ii)(A) of this section.

*Example (6).* Adjustments for differences. (i) The facts are the same as in Example 5, except that the engagement is undertaken with the client on a fixed fee basis. That is, prior to undertaking the engagement Company B and Company A estimate the resources required to undertake the engagement, and, based on hourly fee rates, charge the client a single fee for completion of the project. Company A's portion of the engagement results in fees of $144,000.

(ii) The engagement, once undertaken, requires 20% more hours by each of Companies A and B than originally estimated. Nevertheless, the unrelated client pays the fixed fee that was agreed upon at the start of the engagement. Company B pays Company A $144,000, in accordance with the fixed fee arrangement.

(iii) Company A often enters into similar fixed fee engagements with clients. In addition, Company A's records for similar engagements show that when it experiences cost overruns, it does not collect additional fees from the client for the difference between projected and actual hours. Accordingly, in evaluating whether the fees paid by Company B to Company A are arm's length, it is determined that no adjustments to the intercompany service charge are warranted. See § 1.482-1(d)(3)(ii) and paragraph (c)(2)(ii)(A) of this section.

*(5) Indirect evidence of the price of a comparable uncontrolled services transaction.* (i) In general. The price of a comparable uncontrolled services transaction may be derived based on indirect measures of the price charged in comparable uncontrolled services transactions, but only if—

(A) The data are widely and routinely used in the ordinary course of business in the particular industry or market segment for purposes of determining prices actually charged in comparable uncontrolled services transactions;

(B) The data are used to set prices in the controlled services transaction in the same way they are used to set prices in uncontrolled services transactions of the controlled taxpayer, or in the same way they are used by uncontrolled taxpayers to set prices in uncontrolled services transactions; and

(C) The amount charged in the controlled services transaction may be reliably adjusted to reflect differences in quality of the services, contractual terms, market conditions, risks borne (including contingent-payment terms), duration or quantitative measure of services rendered, and other factors that may affect the price to which uncontrolled taxpayers would agree.

(ii) Example. The following example illustrates this paragraph (c)(5):

*Example.* Indirect evidence of comparable uncontrolled services price.

(i) Company A is a United States insurance company. Company A's wholly-owned Country X subsidiary, Company B, performs specialized risk analysis for Company A as well as for uncontrolled parties. In determining the price actually charged to uncontrolled entities for performing such risk analysis, Company B uses a proprietary, multi-factor computer program, which relies on the gross value of the policies in the customer's portfolio, the relative composition of those policies, their location, and the estimated number of personnel hours necessary to complete the project. Uncontrolled companies that perform comparable risk analysis in the same industry or market-segment use similar proprietary computer programs to price transactions with uncontrolled customers (the competitors' programs may incorporate different inputs, or may assign different weights or values to individual inputs, in arriving at the price).

(ii) During the taxable year subject to audit, Company B performed risk analysis for uncontrolled parties as well as for Company A. Because prices charged to uncontrolled customers reflected the composition of each customer's portfolio together with other factors, the prices charged in Company B's uncontrolled transactions do not provide a reliable basis for determining the comparable uncontrolled services price for the similar services rendered to Company A. However, in evaluating an arm's length price for the studies performed by Company B for Company A, Company B's proprietary computer program may be considered as indirect evidence of the comparable uncontrolled services price that would be charged to perform the services for Company A. The reliability of the results obtained by application of this internal computer program as a measure of an arm's length price for the services will be increased to the extent that Company A used the internal computer program to generate actual transaction prices for risk-analysis studies performed for uncontrolled parties during the same taxable year under audit; Company A used data that are widely and routinely used in the ordinary course of business in the insurance industry to determine the price charged; and Company A reliably adjusted the price charged in the controlled services transaction to reflect differences that may affect the price to which uncontrolled taxpayers would agree.

**(d) Gross services margin method.** *(1) In general.* The gross services margin method evaluates whether the amount charged in a controlled services transaction is arm's length by reference to the gross profit margin realized in comparable uncontrolled transactions. This method ordinarily is used in cases where a controlled taxpayer performs services or functions in connection with an uncontrolled transaction between a member of the controlled group and an uncontrolled taxpayer. This method may be used where a controlled taxpayer renders services (agent services) to another member of the controlled group in connection with a transaction between that other member and an uncontrolled taxpayer. This method also may be used in cases where a controlled taxpayer contracts to provide services to an uncontrolled taxpayer (intermediary function) and another member of the controlled group actually performs a portion of the services provided.

*(2) Determination of arm's length price.* (i) In general. The gross services margin method evaluates whether the price charged or amount retained by a controlled taxpayer in the controlled services transaction in connection with the relevant uncontrolled transaction is arm's length by determining the appropriate gross profit of the controlled taxpayer.

(ii) Relevant uncontrolled transaction. The relevant uncontrolled transaction is a transaction between a member of the controlled group and an uncontrolled taxpayer as to which the controlled taxpayer performs agent services or an intermediary function.

(iii) Applicable uncontrolled price. The applicable uncontrolled price is the price paid or received by the uncontrolled taxpayer in the relevant uncontrolled transaction.

(iv) Appropriate gross services profit. The appropriate gross services profit is computed by multiplying the applicable uncontrolled price by the gross services profit margin in comparable uncontrolled transactions. The determination of the appropriate gross services profit will take into account any functions performed by other members of the controlled group, as well as any other relevant factors described in § 1.482-1(d)(3). The comparable gross services profit margin may be determined by reference to the commission in an uncontrolled transaction, where that commission is stated as a percentage of the price charged in the uncontrolled transaction.

(v) Arm's length range. See § 1.482-1(e)(2) for determination of the arm's length range.

*(3) Comparability and reliability considerations.* (i) In general. Whether results derived from application of this method are the most reliable measure of the arm's length result must be determined using the factors described under the best method rule in § 1.482-1(c). The application of these factors under the gross services margin method is discussed in paragraphs (d)(3)(ii) and (iii) of this section.

(ii) Comparability. (A) Functional comparability. The degree of comparability between an uncontrolled transaction and a controlled transaction is determined by applying the comparability provisions of § 1.482-1(d). A gross services profit provides compensation for services or functions that bear a relationship to the relevant uncontrolled transaction, including an operating profit in return for the investment of capital and the assumption of risks by the controlled taxpayer performing the services or functions under review. Therefore, although all of the factors described in § 1.482-1(d)(3) must be considered, comparability under this method is particularly dependent on similarity of services or functions performed, risks borne, intangible property (if any) used in providing the services or functions, and contractual terms, or adjustments to account for the effects of any such differences. If possible, the appropriate gross services profit margin should be derived from comparable uncontrolled transactions by the controlled taxpayer under review, because similar characteristics are more likely found among different transactions by the same controlled taxpayer than among transactions by other parties. In the absence of comparable uncontrolled transactions involving the same controlled taxpayer, an appropriate gross services profit margin may be derived from transactions of uncontrolled taxpayers involving comparable services or functions with respect to similarly related transactions.

(B) Other comparability factors. Comparability under this method is not dependent on close similarity of the relevant uncontrolled transaction to the related transactions involved in the uncontrolled comparables. However, substantial differences in the nature of the relevant uncontrolled transaction and the relevant transactions involved in the uncontrolled comparables, such as differences in the type of property transferred or service provided in the relevant uncontrolled transaction, may indicate significant differences in the services or functions performed by the controlled and uncontrolled taxpayers with respect to their respective relevant transactions. Thus, it ordinarily would be expected that the services or functions performed in the controlled and uncontrolled transactions would be with respect to relevant transactions involving the transfer of property within the same product categories or the provision of services of the same general type (for example, information-technology systems design). Furthermore, significant differences in the intangible property (if any) used by the controlled taxpayer in the controlled services transaction as distinct from the uncontrolled comparables may also affect the reliability of the comparison. Finally, the reliability of profit measures based on gross services profit may be adversely affected by factors that have less effect on prices. For example, gross services profit may be affected by a variety of other factors, including cost structures or efficiency (for example, differences in the level of experience of the employees performing the service in the controlled and uncontrolled transactions). Accordingly, if material differences in these factors are identified based on objective evidence, the reliability of the analysis may be affected.

(C) Adjustments for differences between controlled and uncontrolled transactions. If there are material differences between the controlled and uncontrolled transactions that would affect the gross services profit margin, adjustments should be made to the gross services profit margin, according to the comparability provisions of § 1.482-1(d)(2). For this purpose, consideration of the total services costs associated with functions performed and risks assumed may be necessary because differences in functions performed are often reflected in these costs. If there are differences in functions performed, however, the effect on gross services profit of such differences is not necessarily equal to the differences in the amount of related costs. Specific examples of factors that may be particularly relevant to this method include—

(1) Contractual terms (for example, scope and terms of warranties or guarantees regarding the services or function, volume, credit and payment terms, and allocation of risks, including any contingent-payment terms);

(2) Intangible property (if any) used in performing the services or function;

(3) Geographic market in which the services or function are performed or in which the relevant uncontrolled transaction takes place; and

(4) Risks borne, including, if applicable, inventory-type risk.

(D) Buy-sell distributor. If a controlled taxpayer that performs an agent service or intermediary function is comparable to a distributor that takes title to goods and resells them, the gross profit margin earned by such distributor on uncontrolled sales, stated as a percentage of the price for the goods, may be used as the comparable gross services profit margin.

(iii) Data and assumptions. (A) In general. The reliability of the results derived from the gross services margin method is affected by the completeness and accuracy of the data used and the reliability of the assumptions made to apply this method. See § 1.482-1(c) (best method rule).

(B) Consistency in accounting. The degree of consistency in accounting practices between the controlled transaction and the uncontrolled comparables that materially affect the gross services profit margin affects the reliability of the results under this method. *(4) Examples.* The principles of this paragraph (d) are illustrated by the following examples:

*Example (1).* Agent services. Company A and Company B are members of a controlled group. Company A is a foreign manufacturer of industrial equipment. Company B is a U.S. company that acts as a commission agent for Company A by arranging for Company A to make direct sales of the equipment it manufactures to unrelated purchasers in the U.S. market. Company B does not take title to the equipment but instead receives from Company A commissions that are determined as a specified percentage of the sales price for the equipment that is charged by Company A to the unrelated purchaser. Company B also arranges for direct sales of similar equipment by unrelated foreign manufacturers to unrelated purchasers in the U.S. market. Company B charges these unrelated foreign manufacturers a commission fee of 5% of the sales price charged by the unrelated foreign manufacturers to the unrelated U.S. purchasers for the equipment. Information regarding the comparable agent services provided by Company B to unrelated foreign manufacturers is sufficiently complete to conclude that it is likely that all material differences between the controlled and uncontrolled transactions have been identified and adjustments for such differences have been made. If the comparable gross services profit margin is 5% of the price charged in the relevant transactions involved in the uncontrolled comparables, then the appropriate gross services profit that Company B may earn and the arm's length price that it may charge Company A for its agent services is equal to 5% of the applicable uncontrolled price charged by Company A in sales of equipment in the relevant uncontrolled transactions.

*Example (2).* Agent services. The facts are the same as in Example 1, except that Company B does not act as a commission agent for unrelated parties and it is not possible to obtain reliable information concerning commission rates charged by uncontrolled commission agents that engage in comparable transactions with respect to relevant sales of property. It is possible, however, to obtain reliable information regarding the gross profit margins earned by unrelated parties that briefly take title to and then resell similar property in uncontrolled transactions, in which they purchase the property from foreign manufacturers and resell the property to purchasers in the U.S. market. Analysis of the facts and circumstances indicates that, aside from certain minor differences for which adjustments can be made, the uncontrolled parties that resell property perform similar functions and assume similar risks as Company B performs and assumes when it acts as a commission agent for Company A's sales of property. Under these circumstances, the gross profit margin earned by the unrelated distributors on the purchase and resale of property may be used, subject to any adjustments for any material differences between the controlled and uncontrolled transactions, as a comparable gross services profit margin. The appropriate gross services profit that Company B may earn and the arm's length price that it may charge Company A for its agent services is therefore equal to this comparable gross services margin, multiplied by the applicable uncontrolled price charged by Company A in its sales of equipment in the relevant uncontrolled transactions.

*Example (3).* Agent services. (i) Company A and Company B are members of a controlled group. Company A is a U.S. corporation that renders computer consulting services, including systems integration and networking, to business clients.

(ii) In undertaking engagements with clients, Company A in some cases pays a commission of 3% of its total fees to unrelated parties that assist Company A in obtaining consulting engagements. Typically, such fees are paid to non-computer consulting firms that provide strategic management services for their clients. When Company A obtains a consulting engagement with a client of a non-computer consulting firm, Company A does not subcontract with the other consulting firm, nor does the other consulting firm play any role in Company A's consulting engagement.

(iii) Company B, a Country X subsidiary of Company A, assists Company A in obtaining an engagement to perform computer consulting services for a Company B banking industry client in Country X. Although Company B has an established relationship with its Country X client and was instrumental in arranging for Company A's engagement with the client, Company A's particular expertise was the primary consideration in motivating the client to engage Company A. Based on the relative contributions of Companies A and B in obtaining and undertaking the engagement, Company B's role was primarily to facilitate the consulting engagement between Company A and the Country X client. Information regarding the commissions paid by Company A to unrelated parties for providing similar services to facilitate Company A's consulting engagements is sufficiently complete to conclude that it is likely that all material differences between these uncontrolled transactions and the controlled transaction between Company B and Company A have been identified and that appropriate adjustments have been made for any such differences. If the comparable gross services margin earned by unrelated parties in providing such agent services is 3% of total fees charged in the relevant transactions involved in the uncontrolled comparables, then the appropriate gross services profit that Company B may earn and the arm's length price that it may charge Company A for its agent services is equal to this comparable gross services margin (3%), multiplied by the applicable uncontrolled price charged by Company A in its relevant uncontrolled consulting engagement with Company B's client.

*Example (4).* Intermediary function. (i) The facts are the same as in Example 3, except that Company B contracts directly with its Country X client to provide computer consulting services and Company A performs the consulting services on behalf of Company B. Company A does not enter into a consulting engagement with Company B's Country X client. Instead, Company B charges its Country X client an uncontrolled price for the consulting services, and Company B pays a portion of the uncontrolled price to Company A for performing the consulting services on behalf of Company B.

(ii) Analysis of the relative contributions of Companies A and B in obtaining and undertaking the consulting contract indicates that Company B functioned primarily as an intermediary contracting party, and the gross services margin method is the most reliable method for determining the amount that Company B may retain as compensation for its intermediary function with respect to Company A's consulting services. In this case, therefore, because Company B entered into the relevant uncontrolled transaction to provide services, Company B receives the applicable uncontrolled price that is paid by the Country X client for the consulting services. Company A technically performs services for Company B when it performs, on behalf of Company B, the consulting services Company B contracted to provide to the Country X client. The arm's length amount that Company A may charge Company B for performing the consulting services on Company B's behalf is equal to the applicable uncontrolled price received by Company B in the relevant uncontrolled transaction, less Company B's appropriate gross services profit, which is the amount that Company B may retain as compensation for performing the intermediary function.

(iii) Reliable data concerning the commissions that Company A paid to uncontrolled parties for assisting it in obtaining engagements to provide consulting services similar to those it has provided on behalf of Company B provide useful information in applying the gross services margin method. However, consideration should be given to whether the third party commission data may need to be adjusted to account for any additional risk that Company B may have assumed as a result of its function as an intermediary contracting party, compared with the risk it would have assumed if it had provided agent services to assist Company A in entering into an engagement to provide its consulting service directly. In this case, the information regarding the commissions paid by Company A to unrelated parties for providing agent services to facilitate its performance of consulting services for unrelated parties is sufficiently complete to conclude that all material differences between these uncontrolled transactions and the controlled performance of an intermediary function, including possible differences in the amount of risk assumed in connection with performing that function, have been identified and that appropriate adjustments have been made. If the comparable gross services margin earned by unrelated parties in providing such agent services is 3% of total fees charged in Company B's relevant uncontrolled transactions, then the appropriate gross services profit that Company B may retain as compensation for performing an intermediary function (and the amount, therefore, that is deducted from the applicable uncontrolled price to arrive at the arm's length price that Company A may charge Company B for performing consulting services on Company B's behalf) is equal to this comparable gross services margin (3%), multiplied by the applicable uncontrolled price charged by Company B in its contract to provide services to the uncontrolled party.

*Example (5).* External comparable. (i) The facts are the same as in Example 4, except that neither Company A nor Company B engages in transactions with third parties that facilitate similar consulting engagements.

(ii) Analysis of the relative contributions of Companies A and B in obtaining and undertaking the contract indicates that Company B's role was primarily to facilitate the consulting arrangement between Company A and the Country X client. Although no reliable internal data are available regarding comparable transactions with uncontrolled entities, reliable data exist regarding commission rates for similar facilitating services between uncontrolled parties. These data indicate that a 3% commission (3% of total engagement fee) is charged in such transactions. Information regarding the uncontrolled comparables is sufficiently complete to conclude that it is likely that all material differences between the controlled and uncontrolled transactions have been identified and adjusted for. If the appropriate gross services profit margin is 3% of total fees, then an arm's length result of the controlled services transaction is for Company B to retain an amount equal to 3% of total fees paid to it.

**(e) Cost of services plus method.** *(1) In general.* The cost of services plus method evaluates whether the amount charged in a controlled services transaction is arm's length by reference to the gross services profit markup realized in comparable uncontrolled transactions. The cost of services plus method is ordinarily used in cases where the controlled service renderer provides the same or similar services to both controlled and uncontrolled parties. This method is ordinarily not used in cases where the controlled services transaction involves a contingent-payment arrangement, as described in paragraph (i)(2) of this section.

*(2) Determination of arm's length price.* (i) In general. The cost of services plus method measures an arm's length price by adding the appropriate gross services profit to the controlled taxpayer's comparable transactional costs.

(ii) Appropriate gross services profit. The appropriate gross services profit is computed by multiplying the controlled taxpayer's comparable transactional costs by the gross services profit markup, expressed as a percentage of the comparable transactional costs earned in comparable uncontrolled transactions.

(iii) Comparable transactional costs. Comparable transactional costs consist of the costs of providing the services under review that are taken into account as the basis for determining the gross services profit markup in comparable uncontrolled transactions. Depending on the facts and circumstances, such costs typically include all compensation attributable to employees directly involved in the performance of such services, materials and supplies consumed or made available in rendering such services, and may include as well other costs of rendering the services. Comparable transactional costs must be determined on a basis that will facilitate comparison with the comparable uncontrolled transactions. For that reason, comparable transactional costs may not necessarily equal total services costs, as defined in paragraph (j) of this section, and in appropriate cases may be a subset of total services costs. Generally accepted accounting principles or Federal income tax accounting rules (where Federal income tax data for comparable transactions or business activities are available) may provide useful guidance but will not conclusively establish the appropriate comparable transactional costs for purposes of this method.

(iv) Arm's length range. See § 1.482-1(e)(2) for determination of an arm's length range.

*(3) Comparability and reliability considerations.* (i) In general. Whether results derived from the application of this method are the most reliable measure of the arm's length result must be determined using the factors described under the best method rule in § 1.482-1(c).

(ii) Comparability. (A) Functional comparability. The degree of comparability between controlled and uncontrolled transactions is determined by applying the comparability provisions of § 1.482-1(d). A service renderer's gross services profit provides compensation for performing services related to the controlled services transaction under review, including an operating profit for the service renderer's investment of capital and assumptions of risks. Therefore, although all of the factors described in § 1.482-1(d)(3) must be considered, comparability under this method is particularly dependent on similarity of services or functions performed, risks borne, intangible property (if any) used in providing the services or functions, and contractual terms, or adjustments to account for the effects of any such differences. If possible, the appropriate gross services profit markup should be derived from comparable uncontrolled transactions of the same taxpayer participating in the controlled services transaction because similar characteristics are more likely to be found among services provided by the same service provider than among services provided by other service providers. In the absence of such services transactions, an appropriate gross services profit markup may be derived from comparable uncontrolled services transactions of other service providers. If the appropriate gross services profit markup is derived from comparable uncontrolled services transactions of other service providers, in evaluating comparability the controlled taxpayer must consider the results under this method expressed as a markup on total services costs of the controlled taxpayer, because differences in functions performed may be reflected in differences in service costs other than those included in comparable transactional costs.

(B) Other comparability factors. Comparability under this method is less dependent on close similarity between the services provided than under the comparable uncontrolled services price method. Substantial differences in the services may, however, indicate significant functional differences between the controlled and uncontrolled taxpayers. Thus, it ordinarily would be expected that the controlled and uncontrolled transactions would involve services of the same general type (for example, information-technology systems design). Furthermore, if a significant amount of the controlled taxpayer's comparable transactional costs consists of service costs incurred in a tax accounting period other than the tax accounting period under review, the reliability of the analysis would be reduced. In addition, significant differences in the value of the services rendered, due for example to the use of valuable intangible property, may also affect the reliability of the comparison. Finally, the reliability of profit measures based on gross services profit may be adversely affected by factors that have less effect on prices. For example, gross services profit may be affected by a variety of other factors, including cost structures or efficiency-related factors (for example, differences in the level of experience of the employees performing the service in the controlled and uncontrolled transactions). Accordingly, if material differences in these factors are identified based on objective evidence, the reliability of the analysis may be affected.

(C) Adjustments for differences between the controlled and uncontrolled transactions. If there are material differences between the controlled and uncontrolled transactions that would affect the gross services profit markup, adjustments should be made to the gross services profit markup earned in the comparable uncontrolled transaction according to the provisions of § 1.482-1(d)(2). For this purpose, consideration of the comparable transactional costs associated with the functions performed and risks assumed may be necessary, because differences in the functions performed are often reflected in these costs. If there are differences in functions performed, however, the effect on gross services profit of such differences is not necessarily equal to the differences in the amount of related comparable transactional costs. Specific examples of the factors that may be particularly relevant to this method include—

(1) The complexity of the services;

(2) The duration or quantitative measure of services;

(3) Contractual terms (for example, scope and terms of warranties or guarantees provided, volume, credit and payment terms, allocation of risks, including any contingent-payment terms);

(4) Economic circumstances; and

(5) Risks borne.

(iii) Data and assumptions. (A) In general. The reliability of the results derived from the cost of services plus method is affected by the completeness and accuracy of the data used and the reliability of the assumptions made to apply this method. See § 1.482-1(c) (Best method rule).

(B) Consistency in accounting. The degree of consistency in accounting practices between the controlled transaction and the uncontrolled comparables that materially affect the gross services profit markup affects the reliability of the results under this method. Thus, for example, if differences in cost accounting practices would materially affect the gross services profit markup, the ability to make reliable adjustments for such differences would affect the reliability of the results obtained under this method. Further, reliability under this method depends on the extent to which the controlled and uncontrolled transactions reflect consistent reporting of comparable transactional costs. For purposes of this paragraph (e)(3)(iii)(B), the term comparable transactional costs includes the cost of acquiring tangible property that is transferred (or used) with the services, to the extent that the arm's length price of the tangible property is not separately evaluated as a controlled transaction under another provision.

*(4) Examples.* The principles of this paragraph (e) are illustrated by the following examples:

*Example (1).* Internal comparable. (i) Company A designs and assembles information-technology networks and systems. When Company A renders services for uncontrolled parties, it receives compensation based on time and materials as well as certain other related costs necessary to complete the project. This fee includes the cost of hardware and software purchased from uncontrolled vendors and incorporated in the final network or system, plus a reasonable allocation of certain specified overhead costs incurred by Company A in providing these services. Reliable accounting records maintained by Company A indicate that Company A earned a gross services profit markup of 10% on its time, materials and specified overhead in providing design services during the year under examination on information technology projects for uncontrolled entities.

(ii) Company A designed an information-technology network for its Country X subsidiary, Company B. The services rendered to Company B are similar in scope and complexity to services that Company A rendered to uncontrolled parties during the year under examination. Using Company A's accounting records (which are determined to be reliable under paragraph (e)(3) of this section), it is possible to identify the comparable transactional costs involved in the controlled services transaction with reference to the costs incurred by Company A in rendering similar design services to uncontrolled parties. Company A's records indicate that it does not incur any additional types of costs in rendering similar services to uncontrolled customers. The data available are sufficiently complete to conclude that it is likely that all material differences between the controlled and uncontrolled transactions have been identified and adjusted for. Based on the gross services profit markup data derived from Company A's uncontrolled transactions involving similar design services, an arm's length result for the controlled services transaction is equal to the price that will allow Company A to earn a 10% gross services profit markup on its comparable transactional costs.

*Example (2).* Inability to adjust for differences in comparable transactional costs. The facts are the same as in Example 1, except that Company A's staff that rendered the services to Company B consisted primarily of engineers in training status or on temporary rotation from other Company A subsidiaries. In addition, the Company B network incorporated innovative features, including specially designed software suited to Company B's requirements. The use of less-experienced personnel and staff on temporary rotation, together with the special features of the Company B network, significantly increased the time and costs associated with the project as compared to time and costs associated with similar projects completed for uncontrolled customers. These factors constitute material differences between the controlled and the uncontrolled transactions that affect the determination of Company A's comparable transactional costs associated with the controlled services transaction, as well as the gross services profit markup. Moreover, it is not possible to perform reliable adjustments for these differences on the basis of the available accounting data. Under these circumstances, the reliability of the cost of services plus method as a measure of an arm's length price is substantially reduced.

*Example (3).* Operating loss by reference to total services costs. The facts and analysis are the same as in Example 1, except that an unrelated Company C, instead of Company A, renders similar services to uncontrolled parties and publicly available information indicates that Company C earned a gross services profit markup of 10% on its time, materials and certain specified overhead in providing those services. As in Example 1, Company A still provides services for its Country X subsidiary, Company B. In accordance with the requirements in paragraph (e)(3)(ii) of this section, the taxpayer performs additional analysis and restates the results of Company A's controlled services transaction with its Country X subsidiary, Company B, in the form of a markup on Company A's total services costs. This analysis by reference to total services costs shows that Company A generated an operating loss on the controlled services transaction, which indicates that functional differences likely exist between the controlled services transaction performed by Company A and uncontrolled services transactions performed by Company C, and that these differences may not be reflected in the comparable transactional costs. Upon further scrutiny, the presence of such functional differences between the controlled and uncontrolled transactions may indicate that the cost of services plus method does not provide the most reliable measure of an arm's length result under the facts and circumstances.

*Example (4).* Internal comparable. (i) Company A, a U.S. corporation, and its subsidiaries perform computer consulting services relating to systems integration and networking for business clients in various countries. Company A and its subsidiaries render only consulting services and do not manufacture or distribute computer hardware or software to clients. The controlled group is organized according to industry specialization, with key industry specialists working for Company A. These personnel typically form the core consulting group that teams with consultants from the local-country subsidiaries to serve clients in the subsidiaries' respective countries.

(ii) On some occasions, Company A and its subsidiaries undertake engagements directly for clients. On other occasions, they work as subcontractors for uncontrolled parties on more extensive consulting engagements for clients. In undertaking the latter engagements with third-party consultants, Company A typically prices its services at four times the compensation costs of its consultants, defined as the consultants' base salary plus estimated fringe benefits, as defined in this table:

| Category | Rates |
|---|---|
| Project managers | $100 per hour. |
| Technical staff | $75 per hour. |

(iii) In uncontrolled transactions, Company A also charges the customer, at no markup, for out-of-pocket expenses such as travel, lodging, and data acquisition charges. Thus, for example, a project involving 100 hours of time from project managers, and 400 hours of technical staff time would result in total compensation costs to Company A of (100 hrs. x $100/hr.) + (400 hrs. x $75/hr.) = $10,000 + $30,000 = $40,000. Applying the markup of 300%, the total fee charged would thus be (4 x $40,000), or $160,000, plus out-of-pocket expenses.

(iv) Company B, a Country X subsidiary of Company A, contracts to render consulting services to a Country X client in the banking industry. In undertaking this engagement, Company B uses its own consultants and also uses the services of Company A project managers and technical staff that specialize in the banking industry for 75 hours and 380 hours, respectively. The data available are sufficiently complete to conclude that it is likely that all material differences between the controlled and uncontrolled transactions have been identified and adjusted for. Based on reliable data concerning the compensation costs to Company A, an arm's length result for the controlled services transaction is equal to $144,000. This is calculated as follows: [4 x (75 hrs. x $100/ hr.)] + [4 x (380 hrs. x $75/hr.)] = $30,000 + $114,000 = $144,000, reflecting a 300% markup on the total compensation costs for Company A project managers and technical staff. In addition, consistent with Company A's pricing of uncontrolled transactions, Company B must reimburse Company A for appropriate out-of-pocket expenses incurred in performing the services.

**(f) Comparable profits method.** *(1) In general.* The comparable profits method evaluates whether the amount charged in a controlled transaction is arm's length, based on objective measures of profitability (profit level indicators) derived from uncontrolled taxpayers that engage in similar business activities under similar circumstances. The rules in § 1.482-5 relating to the comparable profits method apply to controlled services transactions, except as modified in this paragraph (f).

*(2) Determination of arm's length result.* (i) Tested party. This paragraph (f) applies where the relevant business activity of the tested party as determined under § 1.482-5(b)(2) is the rendering of services in a controlled services transaction. Where the tested party determined under § 1.482-5(b)(2) is instead the recipient of the controlled services, the rules under this paragraph (f) are not applicable to determine the arm's length result.

(ii) Profit level indicators. In addition to the profit level indicators provided in § 1.482-5(b)(4), a profit level indicator that may provide a reliable basis for comparing operating profits of the tested party involved in a controlled services transaction and uncontrolled comparables is the ratio of operating profit to total services costs (as defined in paragraph (j) of this section).

(iii) Comparability and reliability considerations—Data and assumptions—Consistency in accounting. Consistency in accounting practices between the relevant business activity of the tested party and the uncontrolled service providers is particularly important in determining the reliability of the results under this method, but less than in applying the cost of services plus method. Adjustments may be appropriate if materially different treatment is applied to particular cost items related to the relevant business activity of the tested party and the uncontrolled service providers. For example, adjustments may be appropriate where the tested party and the uncontrolled comparables use inconsistent approaches to classify similar expenses as "cost of goods sold" and "selling, general, and administrative expenses." Although distinguishing between these two categories may be difficult, the distinction is less important to the extent that the ratio of operating profit to total services costs is used as the appropriate profit level indicator. Determining whether adjustments are necessary under these or similar circumstances requires thorough analysis of the functions performed and consideration of the cost accounting practices of the tested party and the uncontrolled comparables. Other adjustments as provided in § 1.482-5(c)(2)(iv) may also be necessary to increase the reliability of the results under this method.

*(3) Examples.* The principles of this paragraph (f) are illustrated by the following examples:

*Example (1).* Ratio of operating profit to total services costs as the appropriate profit level indicator. (i) A Country T parent firm, Company A, and its Country Y subsidiary, Company B, both engage in manufacturing as their principal business activity. Company A also performs certain advertising services for itself and its affiliates. In year 1, Company A renders advertising services to Company B.

(ii) Based on the facts and circumstances, it is determined that the comparable profits method will provide the most reliable measure of an arm's length result. Company A is selected as the tested party. No data are available for comparable independent manufacturing firms that render advertising services to third parties. Financial data are available, however, for ten independent firms that render similar advertising services as their principal business activity in Country X. The ten firms are determined to be comparable under § 1.482-5(c). Neither Company A nor the comparable companies use valuable intangible property in rendering the services.

(iii) Based on the available financial data of the comparable companies, it cannot be determined whether these comparable companies report costs for financial accounting purposes in the same manner as the tested party. The publicly available financial data of the comparable companies segregate total services costs into cost of goods sold and sales, general and administrative costs, with no further segmentation of costs provided. Due to the limited information available regarding the cost accounting practices used by the comparable companies, the ratio of operating profits to total services costs is determined to be the most appropriate profit level indicator. This ratio includes total services costs to minimize the effect of any inconsistency in accounting practices between Company A and the comparable companies.

*Example (2).* Application of the operating profit to total services costs profit level indicator. (i) Company A is a foreign subsidiary of Company B, a U.S. corporation. Company B is under examination for its year 1 taxable year. Company B renders management consulting services to Company A. Company B's consulting function includes analyzing Company A's operations, benchmarking Company A's financial performance against companies in the same industry, and to the extent necessary, developing a strategy to improve Company A's operational performance. The accounting records of Company B allow reliable identification of the total services costs of the consulting staff associated with the management consulting services rendered to Company A. Company A reimburses Company B for its costs associated with rendering the consulting services, with no markup.

(ii) Based on all the facts and circumstances, it is determined that the comparable profits method will provide the most reliable measure of an arm's length result. Company B is selected as the tested party, and its rendering of management consulting services is identified as the relevant business activity. Data are available from ten domestic companies that operate in the industry segment involving management consulting and that perform activities comparable to the relevant business activity of Company B. These comparables include entities that primarily perform management consulting services for uncontrolled parties. The comparables incur similar risks as Company B incurs in performing the consulting services and do not make use of valuable intangible property or special processes.

(iii) Based on the available financial data of the comparables, it cannot be determined whether the comparables report their costs for financial accounting purposes in the same manner as Company B reports its costs in the relevant business activity. The available financial data for the comparables report only an aggregate figure for costs of goods sold and operating expenses, and do not segment the underlying services costs. Due to this limitation, the ratio of operating profits to total services costs is determined to be the most appropriate profit level indicator.

(iv) For the taxable years 1 through 3, Company B shows the following results for the services performed for Company A:

| | Year 1 | Year 2 | Year 3 | Average |
|---|---|---|---|---|
| Revenues | 1,200,000 | 1,100,000 | 1,300,000 | 1,200,000 |
| Cost of Goods Sold | 100,000 | 100,000 | N/A | 66,667 |
| Operating Expenses | 1,100,000 | 1,000,000 | 1,300,000 | 1,133,333 |
| Operating Profit | 0 | 0 | 0 | 0 |

(v) After adjustments have been made to account for identified material differences between the relevant business activity of Company B and the comparables, the average ratio for the taxable years 1 through 3 of operating profit to total services costs is calculated for each of the uncontrolled service providers. Applying each ratio to Company B's average total services costs from the relevant business activity for the taxable years 1 through 3 would lead to the following comparable operating profit (COP) for the services rendered by Company B:

| Uncontrolled service provider | OP/total service costs (percent) | Company B COP |
|---|---|---|
| Company 1 | 15.75 | $189,000 |
| Company 2 | 15.00 | 180,000 |
| Company 3 | 14.00 | 168,000 |
| Company 4 | 13.30 | 159,600 |
| Company 5 | 12.00 | 144,000 |
| Company 6 | 11.30 | 135,600 |
| Company 7 | 11.25 | 135,000 |
| Company 8 | 11.18 | 134,160 |
| Company 9 | 11.11 | 133,320 |
| Company 10 | 10.75 | 129,000 |

(vi) The available data are not sufficiently complete to conclude that it is likely that all material differences between the relevant business activity of Company B and the comparables have been identified. Therefore, an arm's length range can be established only pursuant to § 1.482-1(e)(2)(iii)(B). The arm's length range is established by reference to the interquartile range of the results as calculated under § 1.482-1(e)(2)(iii)(C), which consists of the results ranging from $168,000 to $134,160. Company B's reported average operating profit of zero ($0) falls outside this range. Therefore, an allocation may be appropriate.

(vii) Because Company B reported income of zero, to determine the amount, if any, of the allocation, Company B's reported operating profit for year 3 is compared to the comparable operating profits derived from the comparables' results for year 3. The ratio of operating profit to total services costs in year 3 is calculated for each of the comparables and applied to Company B's year 3 total services costs to derive the following results:

| Uncontrolled service provider | OP/total service costs (for year 3) (percent) | Company B COP |
|---|---|---|
| Company 1 | 15.00 | $195,000 |
| Company 2 | 14.75 | 191,750 |
| Company 3 | 14.00 | 182,000 |
| Company 4 | 13.50 | 175,500 |
| Company 5 | 12.30 | 159,900 |
| Company 6 | 11.05 | 143,650 |
| Company 7 | 11.03 | 143,390 |
| Company 8 | 11.00 | 143,000 |
| Company 9 | 10.50 | 136,500 |
| Company 10 | 10.25 | 133,250 |

(viii) Based on these results, the median of the comparable operating profits for year 3 is $151,775. Therefore, Company B's income for year 3 is increased by $151,775, the difference between Company B's reported operating profit for year 3 of zero and the median of the comparable operating profits for year 3.

*Example (3).* Material difference in accounting for stock-based compensation. (i) Taxpayer, a U.S. corporation the stock of which is publicly traded, performs controlled services for its wholly-owned subsidiaries. The arm's length price of these controlled services is evaluated under the comparable profits method for services in paragraph (f) of this section by reference to the net cost plus profit level indicator (PLI). Taxpayer is the tested party under paragraph (f)(2)(i) of this section. The Commissioner identifies the most narrowly identifiable business activity of the tested party for which data are available that incorporate the controlled transaction (the relevant business activity). The Commissioner also identifies four uncontrolled domestic service providers, Companies A, B, C, and D, each of which performs exclusively activities similar to the relevant business activity of Taxpayer that is subject to analysis under paragraph (f) of this section. The stock of Companies A, B, C, and D is publicly traded on a U.S. stock exchange. Assume that Taxpayer makes an election to apply these regulations to earlier taxable years.

(ii) Stock options are granted to the employees of Taxpayer that engage in the relevant business activity. Assume that, as determined under a method in accordance with U.S. generally accepted accounting principles, the fair value of such stock options attributable to the employees' performance of the relevant business activity is 500 for the taxable year in question. In evaluating the controlled services, Taxpayer includes salaries, fringe benefits, and related compensation of these employees in "total services costs," as defined in paragraph (j) of this section. Taxpayer does not include any amount attributable to stock options in total services costs, nor does it deduct that amount in determining 'reported operating profit" within the meaning of § 1.482-5(d)(5), for the year under examination.

(iii) Stock options are granted to the employees of Companies A, B, C, and D. Under a fair value method in accordance with U.S. generally accepted accounting principles, the comparables include in total compensation the value of the stock options attributable to the employees' performance of the relevant business activity for the annual financial reporting period, and treat this amount as an expense in determining operating profit for financial accounting purposes. The treatment of employee stock options is summarized in the following table:

| | Salaries and other non-option compensation | Stock options fair value | Stock options expensed |
|---|---|---|---|
| Taxpayer | 1,000 | 500 | 0 |
| Company A | 7,000 | 2,000 | 2,000 |
| Company B | 4,300 | 250 | 250 |
| Company C | 12,000 | 4,500 | 4,500 |
| Company D | 15,000 | 2,000 | 2,000 |

(iv) A material difference in accounting for stock-based compensation (within the meaning of § 1.482-7T(d)(3)(i)) exists. Analysis indicates that this difference would materially affect the measure of an arm's length result under this paragraph (f). In making an adjustment to improve comparability under §§ 1.482-1(d)(2) and 1.482-5(c)(2)(iv), the Commissioner includes in total services costs of the tested party the total compensation costs of 1,500 (including stock option fair value). In addition, the Commissioner calculates the net cost plus PLI by reference to the financial-accounting data of Companies A, B, C, and D, which take into account compensatory stock options.

*Example (4).* Material difference in utilization of stock-based compensation.

(i) The facts are the same as in paragraph (i) of Example 3.

(ii) No stock options are granted to the employees of Taxpayer that engage in the relevant business activity. Thus, no deduction for stock options is made in determining "reported operating profit" (within the meaning of § 1.482-5(d)(5)) for the taxable year under examination.

(iii) Stock options are granted to the employees of Companies A, B, C, and D, but none of these companies expense stock options for financial accounting purposes. Under a method in accordance with U.S. generally accepted accounting principles, however, Companies A, B, C, and D disclose the fair value of the stock options for financial accounting purposes. The utilization and treatment of employee stock options is summarized in the following table:

| | Salaries and other non-option compensation | Stock options fair value | Stock options expensed |
|---|---|---|---|
| Taxpayer | 1,000 | 0 | N/A |
| Company A | 7,000 | 2,000 | 0 |
| Company B | 4,300 | 250 | 0 |
| Company C | 12,000 | 4,500 | 0 |
| Company D | 15,000 | 2,000 | 0 |

(iv) A material difference in the utilization of stock -based compensation (within the meaning of § 1.482-7T(d)(3)(i)) exists. Analysis indicates that these differences would materially affect the measure of an arm's length result under this paragraph (f). In evaluating the comparable operating profits of the tested party, the Commissioner uses Taxpayer's total services costs, which include total compensation costs of 1,000. In considering whether an adjustment is necessary to improve comparability under §§ 1.482-1(d)(2) and 1.482-5(c)(2)(iv), the Commissioner recognizes that the total compensation provided to employees of Taxpayer is comparable to the total compensation provided to employees of Companies A, B, C, and D. Because Companies A, B, C, and D do not expense stock-based compensation for financial accounting purposes, their reported operating profits must be adjusted in order to improve comparability with the tested party. The Commissioner increases each comparable's total services costs, and also reduces its reported operating profit, by the fair value of the stock-based compensation incurred by the comparable company.

(v) The adjustments to the data of Companies A, B, C, and D described in paragraph (iv) of this Example 4 are summarized in the following table:

| | Salaries and other non-option compensation | Stock options fair value | Total services costs (A) | Operating profit (B) | Net cost plus PLI (B/A) (percent) |
|---|---|---|---|---|---|
| Per financial statements: | | | | | |
| Company A | 7,000 | 2,000 | 25,000 | 6,000 | 24.00 |
| Company B | 4,300 | 250 | 12,500 | 2,500 | 20.00 |
| Company C | 12,000 | 4,500 | 36,000 | 11,000 | 30.56 |
| Company D | 15,000 | 2,000 | 27,000 | 7,000 | 25.93 |
| As adjusted: | | | | | |
| Company A | 7,000 | 2,000 | 27,000 | 4,000 | 14.81 |
| Company B | 4,300 | 250 | 12,750 | 2,250 | 17.65 |
| Company C | 12,000 | 4,500 | 40,500 | 6,500 | 16.05 |
| Company D | 15,000 | 2,000 | 29,000 | 5,000 | 17.24 |

*Example (5).* Non-material difference in utilization of stock-based compensation.

(i) The facts are the same as in paragraph (i) of Example 3.

(ii) Stock options are granted to the employees of Taxpayer that engage in the relevant business activity. Assume that, as determined under a method in accordance with U.S. generally accepted accounting principles, the fair value of such stock options attributable to the employees' performance of the relevant business activity is 50 for the taxable year. Taxpayer includes salaries, fringe benefits, and all other compensation of these employees (including the stock option fair value) in "total services costs," as defined in paragraph (j) of this section, and deducts these amounts in determining "reported operating profit" within the meaning of § 1.482-5(d)(5), for the taxable year under examination.

(iii) Stock options are granted to the employees of Companies A, B, C, and D, but none of these companies expense stock options for financial accounting purposes. Under a method in accordance with U.S. generally accepted accounting principles, however, Companies A, B, C, and D disclose the fair value of the stock options for financial accounting purposes. The utilization and treatment of employee stock options is summarized in the following table:

| | Salaries and other non-option compensation | Stock options fair value | Stock options expensed |
|---|---|---|---|
| Taxpayer | 1,000 | 50 | 50 |
| Company A | 7,000 | 100 | 0 |
| Company B | 4,300 | 40 | 0 |
| Company C | 12,000 | 130 | 0 |
| Company D | 15,000 | 75 | 0 |

(iv) Analysis of the data reported by Companies A, B, C, and D indicates that an adjustment for differences in utilization of stock-based compensation would not have a material effect on the determination of an arm's length result.

| | Salaries and other non-option compensation | Stock options fair value | Total services costs (A) | Operating profit (B) | Net cost plus PLI (B/A) (%) |
|---|---|---|---|---|---|
| Per financial statements: | | | | | |
| Company A | 7,000 | 100 | 25,000 | 6,000 | 24.00 |
| Company B | 4,300 | 40 | 12,500 | 2,500 | 20.00 |
| Company C | 12,000 | 130 | 36,000 | 11,000 | 30.56 |
| Company D | 15,000 | 75 | 27,000 | 7,000 | 25.93 |
| As adjusted: | | | | | |
| Company A | 7,000 | 100 | 25,100 | 5,900 | 23.51 |
| Company B | 4,300 | 40 | 12,540 | 2,460 | 19.62 |
| Company C | 12,000 | 130 | 36,130 | 10,870 | 30.09 |
| Company D | 15,000 | 75 | 27,075 | 6,925 | 25.58 |

(v) Under the circumstances, the difference in utilization of stock-based compensation would not materially affect the determination of the arm's length result under this paragraph (f). Accordingly, in calculating the net cost plus PLI, no comparability adjustment is made to the data of Companies A, B, C, or D pursuant to §§ 1.482-1(d)(2) and 1.482-5(c)(2)(iv).

*Example (6).* Material difference in comparables' accounting for stock-based compensation. (i) The facts are the same as in paragraph (i) of Example 3.

(ii) Stock options are granted to the employees of Taxpayer that engage in the relevant business activity. Assume that, as determined under a method in accordance with U.S. generally accepted accounting principles, the fair value of such stock options attributable to employees' performance of the relevant business activity is 500 for the taxable year. Taxpayer includes salaries, fringe benefits, and all other compensation of these employees (including the stock option fair value) in "total services costs," as defined in paragraph (j) of this section, and deducts these amounts in determining "reported operating profit" (within the meaning of § 1.482-5(d)(5)) for the taxable year under examination.

(iii) Stock options are granted to the employees of Companies A, B, C, and D. Companies A and B expense the stock options for financial accounting purposes in accordance with U.S. generally accepted accounting principles. Companies C and D do not expense the stock options for financial accounting purposes. Under a method in accordance with U.S. generally accepted accounting principles, however, Companies C and D disclose the fair value of these options in their financial statements. The utilization and accounting treatment of options are depicted in the following table:

| | Salaries and other non-option compensation | Stock options fair value | Stock options expensed |
|---|---|---|---|
| Taxpayer | 1,000 | 500 | 500 |
| Company A | 7,000 | 2,000 | 2,000 |
| Company B | 4,300 | 250 | 250 |
| Company C | 12,000 | 4,500 | 0 |
| Company D | 15,000 | 2,000 | 0 |

(iv) A material difference in accounting for stock-based compensation (within the meaning of § 1.482-7T(d)(3)(i)) exists. Analysis indicates that this difference would materially affect the measure of the arm's length result under paragraph (f) of this section. In evaluating the comparable operating profits of the tested party, the Commissioner includes in total services costs Taxpayer's total compensation costs of 1,500 (including stock option fair value of 500). In considering whether an adjustment is necessary to improve comparability under §§ 1.482-1(d)(2) and 1.482-5(c)(2)(iv), the Commissioner recognizes that the total employee compensation (including stock options provided by Taxpayer and Companies A, B, C, and D) provides a reliable basis for comparison. Because Companies A and B expense stock-based compensation for financial accounting purposes, whereas Companies C and D do not, an adjustment to the comparables' operating profit is necessary. In computing the net cost plus PLI, the Commissioner uses the financial-accounting data of Companies A and B, as reported. The Commissioner increases the total services costs of Companies C and D by amounts equal to the fair value of their respective stock options, and reduces the operating profits of Companies C and D accordingly.

(v) The adjustments described in paragraph (iv) of this Example 6 are depicted in the following table. For purposes of illustration, the unadjusted data of Companies A and B are also included.

| | Salaries and other non-option compensation | Stock options fair value | Total services costs (A) | Operating profit (B) | Net cost plus PLI (B/A) (%) |
|---|---|---|---|---|---|
| Per financial statements: | | | | | |
| Company A | 7,000 | 2,000 | 27,000 | 4,000 | 14.80 |
| Company B | 4,300 | 250 | 12,750 | 2,250 | 17.65 |
| As adjusted: | | | | | |
| Company C | 12,000 | 4,500 | 40,500 | 6,500 | 16.05 |
| Company D | 15,000 | 2,000 | 29,000 | 5,000 | 17.24 |

**(g) Profit split method.** *(1) In general.* The profit split method evaluates whether the allocation of the combined operating profit or loss attributable to one or more controlled transactions is arm's length by reference to the relative value of each controlled taxpayer's contribution to that combined operating profit or loss. The relative value of each controlled taxpayer's contribution is determined in a manner that reflects the functions performed, risks assumed and resources employed by such controlled taxpayer in the relevant business activity. For application of the profit split method (both the comparable profit split and the residual profit split), see § 1.482-6. The residual profit split method may not be used where only one controlled taxpayer makes significant nonroutine contributions.

*(2) Examples.* The principles of this paragraph (g) are illustrated by the following examples:

*Example (1).* Residual profit split. (i) Company A, a corporation resident in Country X, auctions spare parts by means of an interactive database. Company A maintains a database that lists all spare parts available for auction. Company A developed the software used to run the database. Company A's database is managed by Company A employees in a data center located in Country X, where storage and manipulation of data also take place. Company A has a wholly-owned subsidiary, Company B, located in Country Y. Company B performs marketing and advertising activities to promote Company A's interactive database. Company B solicits unrelated companies to auction spare parts on Company A's database, and solicits customers interested in purchasing spare parts online. Company B owns and maintains a computer server in Country Y, where it receives information on spare parts available for auction. Company B has also designed a specialized communications network that connects its data center to Company A's data center in Country X. The communications network allows Company B to enter data from uncontrolled companies on Company A's database located in Country X. Company B's communications network also allows uncontrolled companies to access Company A's interactive database and purchase spare parts. Company B bore the risks and cost of developing this specialized communications network. Company B enters into contracts with uncontrolled companies and provides the companies access to Company A's database through the Company B network.

(ii) Analysis of the facts and circumstances indicates that both Company A and Company B possess valuable intangible property that they use to conduct the spare parts auction business. Company A bore the economic risks of developing and maintaining software and the interactive database. Company B bore the economic risks of developing the necessary technology to transmit information from its server to Company A's data center, and to allow uncontrolled companies to access Company A's database. Company B helped to enhance the value of Company A's trademark and to establish a network of customers in Country Y. In addition, there are no market comparables for the transactions between Company A and Company B to reliably evaluate them separately. Given the facts and circumstances, the Commissioner determines that a residual profit split method will provide the most reliable measure of an arm's length result.

(iii) Under the residual profit split method, profits are first allocated based on the routine contributions of each taxpayer. Routine contributions include general sales, marketing or administrative functions performed by Company B for Company A for which it is possible to identify market returns. Any residual profits will be allocated based on the nonroutine contributions of each taxpayer. Since both Company A and Company B provided nonroutine contributions, the residual profits are allocated based on these contributions.

*Example (2).* Residual profit split. (i) Company A, a Country 1 corporation, provides specialized services pertaining to the processing and storage of Level 1 hazardous waste (for purposes of this example, the most dangerous type of waste). Under long-term contracts with private companies and governmental entities in Country 1, Company A performs multiple services, including transportation of Level 1 waste, development of handling and storage protocols, recordkeeping, and supervision of waste-storage facilities owned and maintained by the contracting parties. Company A's research and development unit has also developed new and unique processes for transport and storage of Level 1 waste that minimize environmental and occupational effects. In addition to this novel technology, Company A has substantial know-how and a long-term record of safe operations in Country 1.

(ii) Company A's subsidiary, Company B, has been in operation continuously for a number of years in Country 2. Company B has successfully completed several projects in Country 2 involving Level 2 and Level 3 waste, including projects with government-owned entities. Company B has a license in Country 2 to handle Level 2 waste (Level 3 does not require a license). Company B has established a reputation for completing these projects in a responsible manner. Company B has cultivated contacts with procurement officers, regulatory and licensing officials, and other government personnel in Country 2.

(iii) Country 2 government publishes invitations to bid on a project to handle the country's burgeoning volume of Level 1 waste, all of which is generated in government-owned facilities. Bidding is limited to companies that are domiciled in Country 2 and that possess a license from the government to handle Level 1 or Level 2 waste. In an effort to submit a winning bid to secure the contract, Company B points to its Level 2 license and its record of successful completion of projects, and also demonstrates to Country 2 government that it has access to substantial technical expertise pertaining to processing of Level 1 waste.

(iv) Company A enters into a long-term technical services agreement with Company B. Under this agreement, Company A agrees to supply to Company B project managers and other technical staff who have detailed knowledge of Company A's proprietary Level 1 remediation techniques. Company A commits to perform under any long-term contracts entered into by Company B. Company B agrees to compensate Company A based on a markup on Company A's marginal costs (pro rata compensation and current expenses of Company A personnel). In the bid on the Country 2 contract for Level 1 waste remediation, Company B proposes to use a multi-disciplinary team of specialists from Company A and Company B. Project managers from Company A will direct the team, which will also include employees of Company B and will make use of physical assets and facilities owned by Company B. Only Company A and Company B personnel will perform services under the contract. Country 2 grants Company B a license to handle Level 1 waste.

(v) Country 2 grants Company B a five-year, exclusive contract to provide processing services for all Level 1 hazardous waste generated in County 2. Under the contract, Company B is to be paid a fixed price per ton of Level 1 waste that it processes each year. Company B undertakes that all services provided will meet international standards applicable to processing of Level 1 waste. Company B begins performance under the contract.

(vi) Analysis of the facts and circumstances indicates that both Company A and Company B make nonroutine contributions to the Level 1 waste processing activity in Country 2. In addition, it is determined that reliable comparables are not available for the services that Company A provides under the long-term contract, in part because those services incorporate specialized knowledge and process intangible property developed by Company A. It is also determined that reliable comparables are not available for the Level 2 license in Country 2, the successful track record, the government contacts with Country 2 officials, and other intangible property that Company B provided. In view of these facts, the Commissioner determines that the residual profit split method for services in paragraph (g) of this section provides the most reliable means of evaluating the arm's length results for the transaction. In evaluating the appropriate returns to Company A and Company B for their respective contributions, the Commissioner takes into account that the controlled parties incur different risks, because the contract between the controlled parties provides that Company A will be compensated on the basis of marginal costs incurred, plus a markup, whereas the contract between Company B and the government of Country 2 provides that Company B will be compensated on a fixed-price basis per ton of Level 1 waste processed.

(vii) In the first stage of the residual profit split, an arm's length return is determined for routine activities performed by Company B in Country 2, such as transportation, recordkeeping, and administration. In addition, an arm's length return is determined for routine activities performed by Company A (administrative, human resources, etc.) in connection with providing personnel to Company B. After the arm's length return for these functions is determined, residual profits may be present. In the second stage of the residual profit split, any residual profit is allocated by reference to the relative value of the nonroutine contributions made by each taxpayer. Company A's nonroutine contributions include its commitment to perform under the contract and the specialized technical knowledge made available through the project managers under the services agreement with Company B. Company B's nonroutine contributions include its licenses to handle Level 1 and Level 2 waste in Country 2, its knowledge of and contacts with procurement, regulatory and licensing officials in the government of Country 2, and its record in Country 2 of successfully handling non-Level 1 waste.

**(h) Unspecified methods.** Methods not specified in paragraphs (b) through (g) of this section may be used to evaluate whether the amount charged in a controlled services transaction is arm's length. Any method used under this paragraph (h) must be applied in accordance with the provisions of § 1.482-1. Consistent with the specified methods, an unspecified method should take into account the general principle that uncontrolled taxpayers evaluate the terms of a transaction by considering the realistic alternatives to that transaction, including economically similar transactions structured as other than services transactions, and only enter into a particular transaction if none of the alternatives is preferable to it. For example, the comparable uncontrolled services price method compares a controlled services transaction to similar uncontrolled transactions to provide a direct estimate of the price to which the parties would have agreed had they resorted directly to a market alternative to the controlled services transaction. Therefore, in establishing whether a controlled services transaction achieved an arm's length result, an unspecified method should provide information on the prices or profits that the controlled taxpayer could have realized by choosing a realistic alternative to the controlled services transaction (for example, outsourcing a particular service function, rather than performing the function itself). As with any method, an unspecified method will not be applied unless it provides the most reliable measure of an arm's length result under the principles of the best method rule. See § 1.482-1(c). Therefore, in accordance with § 1.482-1(d) (comparability), to the extent that an unspecified method relies on internal data rather than uncontrolled comparables, its reliability will be reduced. Similarly, the reliability of a method will be affected by the reliability of the data and assumptions used to apply the method, including any projections used.

*Example.* (i) Company T, a U.S. corporation, develops computer software programs including a real estate investment program that performs financial analysis of commercial real properties. Companies U, V, and W are owned by Company T. The primary business activity of Companies U, V, and W is commercial real estate development. For business reasons, Company T does not sell the computer program to its customers (on a compact disk or via download from Company T's server through the Internet). Instead, Company T maintains the software program on its own server and allows customers to access the program through the Internet by using a password. The transactions between Company T and Companies U, V, and W are structured as controlled services transactions whereby Companies U, V, and W obtain access via the Internet to Company T's software program for financial analysis. Each year, Company T provides a revised version of the computer program including the most recent data on the commercial real estate market, rendering the old version obsolete.

(ii) In evaluating whether the consideration paid by Companies U, V, and W to Company T was arm's length, the Commissioner may consider, subject to the best method rule of § 1.482-1(c), Company T's alternative of selling the computer program to Companies U, V, and W on a compact disk or via download through the Internet. The Commissioner determines that the controlled services transactions between Company T and Companies U, V, and W are comparable to the transfer of a similar software program on a compact disk or via download through the Internet between uncontrolled parties. Subject to adjustments being made for material differences between the controlled services transactions and the comparable uncontrolled transactions, the uncontrolled transfers of tangible property may be used to evaluate the arm's length results for the controlled services transactions between Company T and Companies U, V, and W.

**(i) Contingent-payment contractual terms for services.** *(1) Contingent-payment contractual terms recognized in general.* In the case of a contingent-payment arrangement, the arm's length result for the controlled services transaction generally would not require payment by the recipient to the renderer in the tax accounting period in which the service is rendered if the specified contingency does not occur in that period. If the specified contingency occurs in a tax accounting period subsequent to the period in which the service is rendered, the arm's length result for the controlled services transaction generally would require payment by the recipient to the renderer on a basis that reflects the recipient's benefit from the services rendered and the risks borne by the renderer in performing the activities in the absence of a provision that unconditionally obligates the recipient to pay for the activities performed in the tax accounting period in which the service is rendered.

*(2) Contingent-payment arrangement.* For purposes of this paragraph (i), an arrangement will be treated as a contingent-payment arrangement if it meets all of the requirements in paragraph (i)(2)(i) of this section and is consistent with the economic substance and conduct requirement in paragraph (i)(2)(ii) of this section.

(i) General requirements. (A) Written contract. The arrangement is set forth in a written contract entered into prior to, or contemporaneous with, the start of the activity or group of activities constituting the controlled services transaction.

(B) Specified contingency. The contract states that payment for a controlled services transaction is contingent (in whole or in part) upon the happening of a future benefit (within the meaning of § 1.482-9(l)(3)) for the recipient directly related to the activity or group of activities. For purposes of the preceding sentence, whether the future benefit is directly related to the activity or group of activities is evaluated based on all the facts and circumstances.

(C) Basis for payment. The contract provides for payment on a basis that reflects the recipient's benefit from the services rendered and the risks borne by the renderer.

(ii) Economic substance and conduct. The arrangement, including the contingency and the basis for payment, is consistent with the economic substance of the controlled transaction and the conduct of the controlled parties. See § 1.482-1(d)(3)(ii)(B).

*(3) Commissioner's authority to impute contingent-payment terms.* Consistent with the authority in § 1.482-1(d)(3)(ii)(B), the Commissioner may impute contingent-payment contractual terms in a controlled services transaction if the economic substance of the transaction is consistent with the existence of such terms.

*(4) Evaluation of arm's length charge.* Whether the amount charged in a contingent-payment arrangement is arm's length will be evaluated in accordance with this section and other applicable regulations under section 482. In evaluating whether the amount charged in a contingent-payment arrangement for the manufacture, construction, or development of tangible or intangible property owned by the recipient is arm's length, the charge determined under the rules of §§ 1.482-3 and 1.482-4 for the transfer of similar property may be considered. See § 1.482-1(f)(2)(ii).

*(5) Examples.* The principles of this paragraph (i) are illustrated by the following examples:

*Example (1).* (i) Company X is a member of a controlled group that has operated in the pharmaceutical sector for many years. In year 1, Company X enters into a written services agreement with Company Y, another member of the controlled group, whereby Company X will perform certain research and development activities for Company Y. The parties enter into the agreement before Company X undertakes any of the research and development activities covered by the agreement. At the time the agreement is entered into, the possibility that any new products will be developed is highly uncertain and the possible market or markets for any products that may be developed are not known and cannot be estimated with any reliability. Under the agreement, Company Y will own any patent or other rights that result from the activities of Company X under the agreement and Company Y will make payments to Company X only if such activities result in commercial sales of one or more derivative products. In that event, Company Y will pay Company X, for a specified period, x% of Company Y's gross sales of each of such products. Payments are required with respect to each jurisdiction in which Company Y has sales of such a derivative product, beginning with the first year in which the sale of a product occurs in the jurisdiction and continuing for six additional years with respect to sales of that product in that jurisdiction.

(ii) As a result of research and development activities performed by Company X for Company Y in years 1 through 4, a compound is developed that may be more effective than existing medications in the treatment of certain conditions. Company Y registers the patent rights with respect to the compound in several jurisdictions in year 4. In year 6, Company Y begins commercial sales of the product in Jurisdiction A and, in that year, Company Y makes the payment to Company X that is required under the agreement. Sales of the product continue in Jurisdiction A in years 7 through 9 and Company Y makes the payments to Company X in years 7 through 9 that are required under the agreement.

(iii) The years under examination are years 6 through 9. In evaluating whether the contingent-payment terms will be recognized, the Commissioner considers whether the conditions of paragraph (i)(2) of this section are met and whether the arrangement, including the specified contingency and basis of payment, is consistent with the economic substance of the controlled services transaction and with the conduct of the controlled parties. The Commissioner determines that the contingent-payment arrangement is reflected in the written agreement between Company X and Company Y; that commercial sales of products developed under the arrangement represent future benefits for Company Y directly related to the controlled services transaction; and that the basis for the payment provided for in the event such sales occur reflects the recipient's benefit and the renderer's risk. Consistent with § 1.482-1(d)(3)(ii)(B) and (iii)(B), the Commissioner determines that the parties' conduct over the term of the agreement has been consistent with their contractual allocation of risk; that Company X has the financial capacity to bear the risk that its research and development services may be unsuccessful and that it may not receive compensation for such services; and that Company X exercises managerial and operational control over the research and development, such that it is reasonable for Company X to assume the risk of those activities. Based on all these facts, the Commissioner determines that the contingent-payment arrangement is consistent with economic substance.

(iv) In determining whether the amount charged under the contingent-payment arrangement in each of years 6 through 9 is arm's length, the Commissioner evaluates under this section and other applicable rules under section 482 the compensation paid in each year for the research and development services. This analysis takes into account that under the contingent-payment terms Company X bears the risk that it might not receive payment for its services in the event that those services do not result in marketable products and the risk that the magnitude of its payment depends on the magnitude of product sales, if any. The Commissioner also considers the alternatives reasonably available to the parties in connection with the controlled services transaction. One such alternative, in view of Company X's willingness and ability to bear the risk and expenses of research and development activities, would be for Company X to undertake such activities on its own behalf and to license the rights to products successfully developed as a result of such activities. Accordingly, in evaluating whether the compensation of x% of gross sales that is paid to Company X during the first four years of commercial sales of derivative products is arm's length, the Commissioner may consider the royalties (or other consideration) charged for intangible property that are comparable to those incorporated in the derivative products and that resulted from Company X's research and development activities under the contingent-payment arrangement.

*Example (2).* (i) The facts are the same as in Example 1, except that no commercial sales ever materialize with regard to the patented compound so that, consistent with the agreement, Company Y makes no payments to Company X in years 6 through 9.

(ii) Based on all the facts and circumstances, the Commissioner determines that the contingent-payment arrangement is consistent with economic substance, and the result (no payments in years 6 through 9) is consistent with an arm's length result.

*Example (3).* (i) The facts are the same as in Example 1, except that, in the event that Company X's activities result in commercial sales of one or more derivative products by Company Y, Company Y will pay Company X a fee equal to the research and development costs borne by Company X plus an amount equal to x% of such costs, with the payment to be made in the first year in which any such sales occur. The x% markup on costs is within the range, ascertainable in year 1, of markups on costs of independent contract researchers that are compensated under terms that unconditionally obligate the recipient to pay for the activities performed in the tax accounting period in which the service is rendered. In year 6, Company Y makes the single payment to Company X that is required under the arrangement.

(ii) The years under examination are years 6 through 9. In evaluating whether the contingent-payment terms will be recognized, the Commissioner considers whether the requirements of paragraph (i)(2) of this section were met at the time the written agreement was entered into and whether the arrangement, including the specified contingency and basis for payment, is consistent with the economic substance of the controlled services transaction and with the conduct of the controlled parties. The Commissioner determines that the contingent-payment terms are reflected in the written agreement between Company X and Company Y and that commercial sales of products developed under the arrangement represent future benefits for Company Y directly related to the controlled services transaction. However, in this case, the Commissioner determines that the basis for payment provided for in the event such sales occur (costs of the services plus x%, representing the markup for contract research in the absence of any nonpayment risk) does not reflect the recipient's benefit and the renderer's risks in the controlled services transaction. Based on all the facts and circumstances, the Commissioner determines that the contingent-payment arrangement is not consistent with economic substance.

(iii) Accordingly, the Commissioner determines to exercise its authority to impute contingent-payment contractual terms that accord with economic substance, pursuant to paragraph (i)(3) of this section and § 1.482-1(d)(3)(ii)(B). In this regard, the Commissioner takes into account that at the time the arrangement was entered into, the possibility that any new products would be developed was highly uncertain and the possible market or markets for any products that may be developed were not known and could not be estimated with any reliability. In such circumstances, it is reasonable to conclude that one possible basis of payment, in order to reflect the recipient's benefit and the renderer's risks, would be a charge equal to a percentage of commercial sales of one or more derivative products that result from the research and development activities. The Commissioner in this case may impute terms that require Company Y to pay Company X a percentage of sales of the products developed under the agreement in each of years 6 through 9.

(iv) In determining an appropriate arm's length charge under such imputed contractual terms, the Commissioner conducts an analysis under this section and other applicable rules under section 482, and considers the alternatives reasonably available to the parties in connection with the controlled services transaction. One such alternative, in view of Company X's willingness and ability to bear the risks and expenses of research and development activities, would be for Company X to undertake such activities on its own behalf and to license the rights to products successfully developed as a result of such activities. Accordingly, for purposes of its determination, the Commissioner may consider the royalties (or other consideration) charged for intangible property that are comparable to those incorporated in the derivative products that resulted from Company X's research and development activities under the contingent-payment arrangement.

**(j) Total services costs.** For purposes of this section, total services costs means all costs of rendering those services for which total services costs are being determined. Total services costs include all costs in cash or in kind (including stock-based compensation) that, based on analysis of the facts and circumstances, are directly identified with, or reasonably allocated in accordance with the principles of paragraph (k)(2) of this section to, the services. In general, costs for this purpose should comprise provision for all resources expended, used, or made available to achieve the specific objective for which the service is rendered. Reference to generally accepted accounting principles or Federal income tax accounting rules may provide a useful starting point but will not necessarily be conclusive regarding inclusion of costs in total services costs. Total services costs do not include interest expense, foreign income taxes (as defined in § 1.901-2(a)), or domestic income taxes.

**(k) Allocation of costs.** *(1) In general.* In any case where the renderer's activity that results in a benefit (within the meaning of paragraph (l)(3) of this section) for one recipient in a controlled services transaction also generates a benefit for one or more other members of a controlled group (including the benefit, if any, to the renderer), and the amount charged under this section in the controlled services transaction is determined under a method that makes reference to costs, costs must be allocated among the portions of the activity performed for the benefit of the first mentioned recipient and such other members of the controlled group under this paragraph (k). The principles of this paragraph (k) must also be used whenever it is appropriate to allocate and apportion any class of costs (for example, overhead costs) in order to determine the total services costs of rendering the services. In no event will an allocation of costs based on a generalized or non-specific benefit be appropriate.

*(2) Appropriate method of allocation and apportionment.* (i) Reasonable method standard. Any reasonable method may be used to allocate and apportion costs under this section. In establishing the appropriate method of allocation and apportionment, consideration should be given to all bases and factors, including, for example, total services costs, total costs for a relevant activity, assets, sales, compensation, space utilized, and time spent. The costs incurred by supporting departments may be apportioned to other departments on the basis of reasonable overall estimates, or such costs may be reflected in the other departments' costs by applying reasonable departmental overhead rates. Allocations and apportionments of costs must be made on the basis of the full cost, as opposed to the incremental cost.

(ii) Use of general practices. The practices used by the taxpayer to apportion costs in connection with preparation of statements and analyses for the use of management, creditors, minority shareholders, joint venturers, clients, customers, potential investors, or other parties or agencies in interest will be considered as potential indicators of reliable allocation methods, but need not be accorded conclusive weight by the Commissioner. In determining the extent to which allocations are to be made to or from foreign members of a controlled group, practices employed by the domestic members in apportioning costs among themselves will also be considered if the relationships with the foreign members are comparable to the relationships among the domestic members of the controlled group. For example, if for purposes of reporting to public stockholders or to a governmental agency, a corporation apportions the costs attributable to its executive officers among the domestic members of a controlled group on a reasonable and consistent basis, and such officers exercise comparable control over foreign members of the controlled group, such domestic apportionment practice will be considered in determining the allocations to be made to the foreign members.

*(3) Examples.* The principles of this paragraph (k) are illustrated by the following examples:

*Example (1).* Company A pays an annual license fee of 500x to an uncontrolled taxpayer for unlimited use of a database within the corporate group. Under the terms of the license with the uncontrolled taxpayer, Company A is permitted to use the database for its own use and in rendering research services to its subsidiary, Company B. Company B obtains benefits from the database that are similar to those that it would obtain if it had independently licensed the database from the uncontrolled taxpayer. Evaluation of the arm's length charge (under a method in which costs are relevant) to Company B for the controlled services that incorporate use of the database must take into account the full amount of the license fee of 500x paid by Company A, as reasonably allocated and apportioned to the relevant benefits, although the incremental use of the database for the benefit of Company B did not result in an increase in the license fee paid by Company A.

*Example (1).* (i) Company A is a consumer products company located in the United States. Companies B and C are wholly-owned subsidiaries of Company A and are located in Countries B and C, respectively. Company A and its subsidiaries manufacture products for sale in their respective markets. Company A hires a consultant who has expertise regarding a manufacturing process used by Company A and its subsidiary, Company B. Company C, the Country C subsidiary, uses a different manufacturing process, and accordingly will not receive any benefit from the outside consultant hired by Company A. In allocating and apportioning the cost of hiring the outside consultant (100), Company A determines that sales constitute the most appropriate allocation key.

(ii) Company A and its subsidiaries have the following sales:

| Company | A | B | C | Total |
|---|---|---|---|---|
| Sales | 400 | 100 | 200 | 700 |

(iii) Because Company C does not obtain any benefit from the consultant, none of the costs are allocated to it. Rather, the costs of 100 are allocated and apportioned ratably to Company A and Company B as the entities that obtain a benefit from the campaign, based on the total sales of those entities (500). An appropriate allocation of the costs of the consultant is as follows:

| Company | A | B | Total |
|---|---|---|---|
| Allocation | 400/500 | 100/500 | ... |
| Amount | 80 | 20 | 100 |

**(l) Controlled services transaction.** *(1) In general.* A controlled services transaction includes any activity (as defined in paragraph (l)(2) of this section) by one member of a group of controlled taxpayers (the renderer) that results in a benefit (as defined in paragraph (l)(3) of this section) to one or more other members of the controlled group (the recipient(s)).

*(2) Activity.* An activity includes the performance of functions, assumptions of risks, or use by a renderer of tangible or intangible property or other resources, capabilities, or knowledge, such as knowledge of and ability to take advantage of particularly advantageous situations or circumstances. An activity also includes making available to the recipient any property or other resources of the renderer.

*(3) Benefit.* (i) In general. An activity is considered to provide a benefit to the recipient if the activity directly results in a reasonably identifiable increment of economic or commercial value that enhances the recipient's commercial position, or that may reasonably be anticipated to do so. An activity is generally considered to confer a benefit if, taking into account the facts and circumstances, an uncontrolled taxpayer in circumstances comparable to those of the recipient would be willing to pay an uncontrolled party to perform the same or similar activity on either a fixed or contingent-payment basis, or if the recipient otherwise would have performed for itself the same activity or a similar activity. A benefit may result to the owner of intangible property if the renderer engages in an activity that is reasonably anticipated to result in an increase in the value of that intangible property. Paragraphs (l)(3)(ii) through (v) of this section provide guidelines that indicate the presence or absence of a benefit for the activities in the controlled services transaction.

(ii) Indirect or remote benefit. An activity is not considered to provide a benefit to the recipient if, at the time the activity is performed, the present or reasonably anticipated benefit from that activity is so indirect or remote that the recipient would not be willing to pay, on either a fixed or contingent-payment basis, an uncontrolled party to perform a similar activity, and would not be willing to perform such activity for itself for this purpose. The determination whether the benefit from an activity is indirect or remote is based on the nature of the activity and the situation of the recipient, taking into consideration all facts and circumstances.

(iii) Duplicative activities. If an activity performed by a controlled taxpayer duplicates an activity that is performed, or that reasonably may be anticipated to be performed, by another controlled taxpayer on or for its own account, the activity is generally not considered to provide a benefit to the recipient, unless the duplicative activity itself provides an additional benefit to the recipient.

(iv) Shareholder activities. An activity is not considered to provide a benefit if the sole effect of that activity is either to protect the renderer's capital investment in the recipient or in other members of the controlled group, or to facilitate compliance by the renderer with reporting, legal, or regulatory requirements applicable specifically to the renderer, or both. Activities in the nature of day-to-day management generally do not relate to protection of the renderer's capital investment. Based on analysis of the facts and circumstances, activities in connection with a corporate reorganization may be considered to provide a benefit to one or more controlled taxpayers.

(v) Passive association. A controlled taxpayer generally will not be considered to obtain a benefit where that benefit results from the controlled taxpayer's status as a member of a controlled group. A controlled taxpayer's status as a member of a controlled group may, however, be taken into account for purposes of evaluating comparability between controlled and uncontrolled transactions.

*(4) Disaggregation of transactions.* A controlled services transaction may be analyzed as two separate transactions for purposes of determining the arm's length consideration, if that analysis is the most reliable means of determining the arm's length consideration for the controlled services transaction. See the best method rule under § 1.482-1(c).

*(5) Examples.* The principles of this paragraph (l) are illustrated by the following examples. In each example, assume that Company X is a U.S. corporation and Company Y is a wholly-owned subsidiary of Company X in Country B.

*Example (1).* In general. In developing a worldwide advertising and promotional campaign for a consumer product, Company X pays for and obtains designation as an official sponsor of the Olympics. This designation allows Company X and all its subsidiaries, including Company Y, to identify themselves as sponsors and to use the Olympic logo in advertising and promotional campaigns. The Olympic sponsorship campaign generates benefits to Company X, Company Y, and other subsidiaries of Company X.

*Example (2).* Indirect or remote benefit. Based on recommendations contained in a study performed by its internal staff, Company X implements certain changes in its management structure and the compensation of managers of divisions located in the United States. No changes were recommended or considered for Company Y in Country B. The internal study and the resultant changes in its management may increase the competitiveness and overall efficiency of Company X. Any benefits to Company Y as a result of the study are, however, indirect or remote. Consequently, Company Y is not considered to obtain a benefit from the study.

*Example (3).* Indirect or remote benefit. Based on recommendations contained in a study performed by its internal staff, Company X decides to make changes to the management structure and management compensation of its subsidiaries, in order to increase their profitability. As a result of the recommendations in the study, Company X implements substantial changes in the management structure and management compensation scheme of Company Y. The study and the changes implemented as a result of the recommendations are anticipated to increase the profitability of Company X and its subsidiaries. The increased management efficiency of Company Y that results from these changes is considered to be a specific and identifiable benefit, rather than remote or speculative.

*Example (4).* Duplicative activities. At its corporate headquarters in the United States, Company X performs certain treasury functions for Company X and for its subsidiaries, including Company Y. These treasury functions include raising capital, arranging medium and long-term financing for general corporate needs, including cash management. Under these circumstances, the treasury functions performed by Company X do not duplicate the functions performed by Company Y's staff. Accordingly, Company Y is considered to obtain a benefit from the functions performed by Company X.

*Example (5).* Duplicative activities. The facts are the same as in Example 4, except that Company Y's functions include ensuring that the financing requirements of its own operations are met. Analysis of the facts and circumstances indicates that Company Y independently administers all financing and cash-management functions necessary to support its operations, and does not utilize financing obtained by Company X. Under the circumstances, the treasury functions performed by Company X are duplicative of similar functions performed by Company Y's staff, and the duplicative functions do not enhance Company Y's position. Accordingly, Company Y is not considered to obtain a benefit from the duplicative activities performed by Company X.

*Example (6).* Duplicative activities. Company X's inhouse legal staff has specialized expertise in several areas, including intellectual property. The intellectual property legal staff specializes in technology licensing, patents, copyrights, and negotiating and drafting intellectual property agreements. Company Y is involved in negotiations with an unrelated party to enter into a complex joint venture that includes multiple licenses and cross-licenses of patents and copyrights.

Company Y retains outside counsel that specializes in intellectual property law to review the transaction documents. Company Y does not have in-house counsel of its own to review intellectual property transaction documents. Outside counsel advises that the terms for the proposed transaction are advantageous to Company Y and that the contracts are valid and fully enforceable. Company X's intellectual property legal staff possess valuable knowledge of Company Y's patents and technological achievements. They are capable of identifying particular scientific attributes protected under patent that strengthen Company Y's negotiating position, and of discovering flaws in the patents offered by the unrelated party. To reduce risk associated with the transaction, Company X's intellectual property legal staff reviews the transaction documents before Company Y executes the contracts. Company X's intellectual property legal staff also separately evaluates the patents and copyrights with respect to the licensing arrangements and concurs in the opinion provided by outside counsel. The activities performed by Company X substantially duplicate the legal services obtained by Company Y, but they also reduce risk associated with the transaction in a way that confers an additional benefit on Company Y.

*Example (7).* Shareholder activities. Company X is a publicly held corporation. U.S. laws and regulations applicable to publicly held corporations such as Company X require the preparation and filing of periodic reports that show, among other things, profit and loss statements, balance sheets, and other material financial information concerning the company's operations. Company X, Company Y and each of the other subsidiaries maintain their own separate accounting departments that record individual transactions and prepare financial statements in accordance with their local accounting practices. Company Y, and the other subsidiaries, forward the results of their financial performance to Company X, which analyzes and compiles these data into periodic reports in accordance with U.S. laws and regulations. Because Company X's preparation and filing of the reports relate solely to its role as an investor of capital or shareholder in Company Y or to its compliance with reporting, legal, or regulatory requirements, or both, these activities constitute shareholder activities and therefore Company Y is not considered to obtain a benefit from the preparation and filing of the reports.

*Example (8).* Shareholder activities. The facts are the same as in Example 7, except that Company Y's accounting department maintains a general ledger recording individual transactions, but does not prepare any financial statements (such as profit and loss statements and balance sheets). Instead, Company Y forwards the general ledger data to Company X, and Company X analyzes and compiles financial statements for Company Y, as well as for Company X's overall operations, for purposes of complying with U.S. reporting requirements. Company Y is subject to reporting requirements in Country B similar to those applicable to Company X in the United States. Much of the data that Company X analyzes and compiles regarding Company Y's operations for purposes of complying with the U.S. reporting requirements are made available to Company Y for its use in preparing reports that must be filed in Country B. Company Y incorporates these data, after minor adjustments for differences in local accounting practices, into the reports that it files in Country B. Under these circumstances, because Company X's analysis and compilation of Company Y's financial data does not relate solely to its role as an investor of capital or shareholder in Company Y, or to its compliance with reporting, legal, or regulatory requirements, or both, these activities do not constitute shareholder activities.

*Example (9).* Shareholder activities. Members of Company X's internal audit staff visit Company Y on a semiannual basis in order to review the subsidiary's adherence to internal operating procedures issued by Company X and its compliance with U.S. anti-bribery laws, which apply to Company Y on account of its ownership by a U.S. corporation. Because the sole effect of the reviews by Company X's audit staff is to protect Company X's investment in Company Y, or to facilitate Company X's compliance with U.S. anti-bribery laws, or both, the visits are shareholder activities and therefore Company Y is not considered to obtain a benefit from the visits.

*Example (10).* Shareholder activities. Country B recently enacted legislation that changed the foreign currency exchange controls applicable to foreign shareholders of Country B corporations. Company X concludes that it may benefit from changing the capital structure of Company Y, thus taking advantage of the new foreign currency exchange control laws in Country B. Company X engages an investment banking firm and a law firm to review the Country B legislation and to propose possible changes to the capital structure of Company Y. Because Company X's retention of the firms facilitates Company Y's ability to pay dividends and other amounts and has the sole effect of protecting Company X's investment in Company Y, these activities constitute shareholder activities and Company Y is not considered to obtain a benefit from the activities.

*Example (11).* Shareholder activities. The facts are the same as in Example 10, except that Company Y bears the full cost of retaining the firms to evaluate the new foreign currency control laws in Country B and to make appropriate changes to its stock ownership by Company X. Company X is considered to obtain a benefit from the rendering by Company Y of these activities, which would be shareholder activities if conducted by Company X (see Example 10).

*Example (12).* Shareholder activities. The facts are the same as in Example 10, except that the new laws relate solely to corporate governance in Country B, and Company X retains the law firm and investment banking firm in order to evaluate whether restructuring would increase Company Y's profitability, reduce the number of legal entities in Country B, and increase Company Y's ability to introduce new products more quickly in Country B. Because Company X retained the law firm and the investment banking firm primarily to enhance Company Y's profitability and the efficiency of its operations, and not solely to protect Company X's investment in Company Y or to facilitate Company X's compliance with Country B's corporate laws, or to both, these activities do not constitute shareholder activities.

*Example (13).* Shareholder activities. Company X establishes detailed personnel policies for its subsidiaries, including Company Y. Company X also reviews and approves the performance appraisals of Company Y's executives, monitors levels of compensation paid to all Company Y personnel, and is involved in hiring and firing decisions regarding the senior executives of Company Y. Because this personnel-related activity by Company X involves day-to-day management of Company Y, this activity does not relate solely to Company X's role as an investor of capital or a shareholder of Company Y, and therefore does not constitute a shareholder activity.

*Example (14).* Shareholder activities. Each year, Company X conducts a two-day retreat for its senior executives. The purpose of the retreat is to refine the long-term business strategy of Company X and its subsidiaries, including Company Y, and to produce a confidential strategy statement. The strategy statement identifies several potential growth initiatives for Company X and its subsidiaries and lists general means of increasing the profitability of the company as a whole. The strategy statement is made available without charge to Company Y and the other subsidiaries of Company X. Company Y independently evaluates whether to implement some, all, or none of the initiatives contained in the strategy statement. Because the preparation of the strategy statement does not relate solely to Company X's role as an investor of capital or a shareholder of Company Y, the expense of preparing the document is not a shareholder expense.

*Example (15).* Passive association/benefit. Company X is the parent corporation of a large controlled group that has been in operation in the information-technology sector for ten years. Company Y is a small corporation that was recently acquired by the Company X controlled group from local Country B owners. Several months after the acquisition of Company Y, Company Y obtained a contract to redesign and assemble the information-technology networks and systems of a large financial institution in Country B. The project was significantly larger and more complex than any other project undertaken to date by Company Y. Company Y did not use Company X's marketing intangible property to solicit the contract, and Company X had no involvement in the solicitation, negotiation, or anticipated execution of the contract. For purposes of this section, Company Y is not considered to obtain a benefit from Company X or any other member of the controlled group because the ability of Company Y to obtain the contract, or to obtain the contract on more favorable terms than would have been possible prior to its acquisition by the Company X controlled group, was due to Company Y's status as a member of the Company X controlled group and not to any specific activity by Company X or any other member of the controlled group.

*Example (16).* Passive association/benefit. The facts are the same as in Example 15, except that Company X executes a performance guarantee with respect to the contract, agreeing to assist in the project if Company Y fails to meet certain mileposts. This performance guarantee allowed Company Y to obtain the contract on materially more favorable terms than otherwise would have been possible. Company Y is considered to obtain a benefit from Company X's execution of the performance guarantee.

*Example (17).* Passive association/benefit. The facts are the same as in Example 15, except that Company X began the process of negotiating the contract with the financial institution in Country B before acquiring Company Y. Once Company Y was acquired by Company X, the contract with the financial institution was entered into by Company Y. Company Y is considered to obtain a benefit from Company X's negotiation of the contract.

*Example (18).* Passive association/benefit. The facts are the same as in Example 15, except that Company X sent a letter to the financial institution in Country B, which represented that Company X had a certain percentage ownership in Company Y and that Company X would maintain that same percentage ownership interest in Company Y until the contract was completed. This letter allowed Company Y to obtain the contract on more favorable terms than otherwise would have been possible. Since this letter from Company X to the financial institution simply affirmed Company Y's status as a member of the controlled group and represented that this status would be maintained until the contract was completed, Company Y is not considered to obtain a benefit from Company X's furnishing of the letter.

*Example (19).* Passive association/benefit. (i) S is a company that supplies plastic containers to companies in various industries. S establishes the prices for its containers through a price list that offers customers discounts based solely on the volume of containers purchased.

(ii) Company X is the parent corporation of a large controlled group in the information technology sector. Company Y is a wholly-owned subsidiary of Company X located in Country B. Company X and Company Y both purchase plastic containers from unrelated supplier S. In year 1, Company X purchases 1 million units and Company Y purchases 100,000 units. S, basing its prices on purchases by the entire group, completes the order for 1.1 million units at a price of $0.95 per unit, and separately bills and ships the orders to each company. Companies X and Y undertake no bargaining with supplier S with respect to the price charged, and purchase no other products from supplier S.

(iii) R1 and its wholly-owned subsidiary R2 are a controlled group of taxpayers (unrelated to Company X or Company Y) each of which carries out functions comparable to those of Companies X and Y and undertakes purchases of plastic containers from supplier S, identical to those purchased from S by Company X and Company Y, respectively. S, basing its prices on purchases by the entire group, charges R1 and R2 $0.95 per unit for the 1.1 million units ordered. R1 and R2 undertake no bargaining with supplier S with respect to the price charged, and purchase no other products from supplier S.

(iv) U is an uncontrolled taxpayer that carries out comparable functions and undertakes purchases of plastic containers from supplier S identical to Company Y. U is not a member of a controlled group, undertakes no bargaining with supplier S with respect to the price charged, and purchases no other products from supplier S. U purchases 100,000 plastic containers from S at the price of $1.00 per unit.

(v) Company X charges Company Y a fee of $5,000, or $0.05 per unit of plastic containers purchased by Company Y, reflecting the fact that Company Y receives the volume discount from supplier S.

(vi) In evaluating the fee charged by Company X to Company Y, the Commissioner considers whether the transactions between R1, R2, and S or the transactions between U and S provide a more reliable measure of the transactions between Company X, Company Y and S. The Commissioner determines that Company Y's status as a member of a controlled group should be taken into account for purposes of evaluating comparability of the transactions, and concludes that the transactions between R1, R2, and S are more reliably comparable to the transactions between Company X, Company Y, and S. The comparable charge for the purchase was $0.95 per unit. Therefore, obtaining the plastic containers at a favorable rate (and the resulting $5,000 savings) is entirely due to Company Y's status as a member of the Company X controlled group and not to any specific activity by Company X or any other member of the controlled group. Consequently, Company Y is not considered to obtain a benefit from Company X or any other member of the controlled group.

*Example (20).* Disaggregation of transactions. (i) X, a domestic corporation, is a pharmaceutical company that develops and manufactures ethical pharmaceutical products. Y, a

Country B corporation, is a distribution and marketing company that also performs clinical trials for X in Country B. Because Y does not possess the capability to conduct the trials, it contracts with a third party to undertake the trials at a cost of $100. Y also incurs $25 in expenses related to the third-party contract (for example, in hiring and working with the third party).

(ii) Based on a detailed functional analysis, the Commissioner determines that Y performed functions beyond merely facilitating the clinical trials for X, such as audit controls of the third party performing those trials. In determining the arm's length price, the Commissioner may consider a number of alternatives. For example, for purposes of determining the arm's length price, the Commissioner may determine that the intercompany service is most reliably analyzed on a disaggregated basis as two separate transactions: in this case, the contract between Y and the third party could constitute an internal CUSP with a price of $100. Y would be further entitled to an arm's length remuneration for its facilitating services. If the most reliable method is one that provides a markup on Y's costs, then "total services cost" in this context would be $25. Alternatively, the Commissioner may determine that the intercompany service is most reliably analyzed as a single transaction, based on comparable uncontrolled transactions involving the facilitation of similar clinical trial services performed by third parties. If the most reliable method is one that provides a markup on all of Y's costs, and the base of the markup determined by the comparable companies includes the third-party clinical trial costs, then such a markup would be applied to Y's total services cost of $125.

*Example (21).* Disaggregation of transactions. (i) X performs a number of administrative functions for its subsidiaries, including Y, a distributor of widgets in Country B. These services include those relating to working capital (inventory and accounts receivable/payable) management. To facilitate provision of these services, X purchases an ERP system specifically dedicated to optimizing working capital management. The system, which entails significant third-party costs and which includes substantial intellectual property relating to its software, costs $1,000.

(ii) Based on a detailed functional analysis, the Commissioner determines that in providing administrative services for Y, X performed functions beyond merely operating the ERP system itself, since X was effectively using the ERP as an input to the administrative services it was providing to Y. In determining arm's length price for the services, the Commissioner may consider a number of alternatives. For example, if the most reliable uncontrolled data is derived from companies that use similar ERP systems purchased from third parties to perform similar administrative functions for uncontrolled parties, the Commissioner may determine that a CPM is the best method for measuring the functions performed by X, and, in addition, that a markup on total services costs, based on the markup from the comparable companies, is the most reliable PLI. In this case, total services cost, and the basis for the markup, would include appropriate reflection of the ERP costs of $1,000. Alternatively, X's functions may be most reliably measured based on comparable uncontrolled companies that perform similar administrative functions using their customers' own ERP systems. Under these circumstances, the total services cost would equal X's costs of providing the administrative services excluding the ERP cost of $1,000.

**(m) Coordination with transfer pricing rules for other transactions.** *(1) Services transactions that include other types of transactions.* A transaction structured as a controlled services transaction may include other elements for which a separate category or categories of methods are provided, such as a loan or advance, a rental, or a transfer of tangible or intangible property. See §§ 1.482-1(b)(2) and 1.482-2(a), (c), and (d). Whether such an integrated transaction is evaluated as a controlled services transaction under this section or whether one or more elements should be evaluated separately under other sections of the section 482 regulations depends on which approach will provide the most reliable measure of an arm's length result. Ordinarily, an integrated transaction of this type may be evaluated under this section and its separate elements need not be evaluated separately, provided that each component of the transaction may be adequately accounted for in evaluating the comparability of the controlled transaction to the uncontrolled comparables and, accordingly, in determining the arm's length result in the controlled transaction. See § 1.482-1(d)(3).

*(2) Services transactions that effect a transfer of intangible property.* A transaction structured as a controlled services transaction may in certain cases include an element that constitutes the transfer of intangible property or may result in a transfer, in whole or in part, of intangible property. Notwithstanding paragraph (m)(1) of this section, if such element relating to intangible property is material to the evaluation, the arm's length result for the element of the transaction that involves intangible property must be corroborated or determined by an analysis under § 1.482-4.

*(3)* [Reserved]. For further guidance, see § 1.482-9T(m)(3).

*(4) Other types of transactions that include controlled services transactions.* A transaction structured other than as a controlled services transaction may include one or more elements for which separate pricing methods are provided in this section. Whether such an integrated transaction is evaluated under another section of the section 482 regulations or whether one or more elements should be evaluated separately under this section depends on which approach will provide the most reliable measure of an arm's length result. Ordinarily, a single method may be applied to such an integrated transaction, and the separate services component of the transaction need not be separately analyzed under this section, provided that the controlled services may be adequately accounted for in evaluating the comparability of the controlled transaction to the uncontrolled comparables and, accordingly, in determining the arm's length results in the controlled transaction. See § 1.482-1(d)(3).

*(5) Examples.* The principles of this paragraph (m) are illustrated by the following examples:

*Example (1).* (i) U.S. parent corporation Company X enters into an agreement to maintain equipment of Company Y, a foreign subsidiary. The maintenance of the equipment requires the use of spare parts. The cost of the spare parts necessary to maintain the equipment amounts to approximately 25 percent of the total costs of maintaining the equipment. Company Y pays a fee that includes a charge for labor and parts.

(ii) Whether this integrated transaction is evaluated as a controlled services transaction or is evaluated as a controlled services transaction and the transfer of tangible property depends on which approach will provide the most reliable measure of an arm's length result. If it is not possible to find comparable uncontrolled services transactions that involve similar services and tangible property transfers as the controlled transaction between Company X and Company Y, it will be necessary to determine the arm's length charge for the controlled services, and then to evaluate separately the arm's length charge for the tangible property transfers under § 1.482-1 and §§ 1.482-3 through 1.482-6. Alternatively, it may be possible to apply the comparable profits method of § 1.482-5 to evaluate the arm's length profit of Company X or Company Y from the integrated controlled transaction. The comparable profits method may provide the most reliable measure of an arm's length result if uncontrolled parties are identified that perform similar, combined functions of maintaining and providing spare parts for similar equipment.

*Example (2).* (i) U.S. parent corporation Company X sells industrial equipment to its foreign subsidiary, Company Y. In connection with this sale, Company X renders to Company Y services that consist of demonstrating the use of the equipment and assisting in the effective start-up of the equipment. Company X structures the integrated transaction as a sale of tangible property and determines the transfer price under the comparable uncontrolled price method of § 1.482-3(b).

(ii) Whether this integrated transaction is evaluated as a transfer of tangible property or is evaluated as a controlled services transaction and a transfer of tangible property depends on which approach will provide the most reliable measure of an arm's length result. In this case, the controlled services may be similar to services rendered in the transactions used to determine the comparable uncontrolled price, or they may appropriately be considered a difference between the controlled transaction and comparable transactions with a definite and reasonably ascertainable effect on price for which appropriate adjustments can be made. See § 1.482-1(d)(3)(ii)(A)(6). In either case, application of the comparable uncontrolled price method to evaluate the integrated transaction may provide a reliable measure of an arm's length result, and application of a separate transfer pricing method for the controlled services element of the transaction is not necessary.

*Example (3).* (i) The facts are the same as in Example 2 except that, after assisting Company Y in start-up, Company X also renders ongoing services, including instruction and supervision regarding Company Y's ongoing use of the equipment. Company X structures the entire transaction, including the incremental ongoing services, as a sale of tangible property, and determines the transfer price under the comparable uncontrolled price method of § 1.482-3(b).

(ii) Whether this integrated transaction is evaluated as a transfer of tangible property or is evaluated as a controlled services transaction and a transfer of tangible property depends on which approach will provide the most reliable measure of an arm's length result. It may not be possible to identify comparable uncontrolled transactions in which a seller of merchandise renders services similar to the ongoing services rendered by Company X to Company Y. In such a case, the incremental services in connection with ongoing use of the equipment could not be taken into account as a comparability factor because they are not similar to the services rendered in connection with sales of similar tangible property. Accordingly, it may be necessary to evaluate separately the transfer price for such services under this section in order to produce the most reliable measure of an arm's length result. Alternatively, it may be possible to apply the comparable profits method of § 1.482-5 to evaluate the arm's length profit of Company X or Company Y from the integrated controlled transaction. The comparable profits method may provide the most reliable measure of an arm's length result if uncontrolled parties are identified that perform the combined functions of selling equipment and rendering ongoing after-sale services associated with such equipment. In that case, it would not be necessary to separately evaluate the transfer price for the controlled services under this section.

*Example (4).* (i) Company X, a U.S. corporation, and Company Y, a foreign corporation, are members of a controlled group. Both companies perform research and development activities relating to integrated circuits. In addition, Company Y manufactures integrated circuits. In years 1 through 3, Company X engages in substantial research and development activities, gains significant know-how regarding the development of a particular high-temperature resistant integrated circuit, and memorializes that research in a written report. In years 1 through 3, Company X generates overall net operating losses as a result of the expenditures associated with this research and development effort. At the beginning of year 4, Company X enters into a technical assistance agreement with Company Y. As part of this agreement, the researchers from Company X responsible for this project meet with the researchers from Company Y and provide them with a copy of the written report. Three months later, the researchers from Company Y apply for a patent for a high-temperature resistant integrated circuit based in large part upon the know-how obtained from the researchers from Company X.

(ii) The controlled services transaction between Company X and Company Y includes an element that constitutes the transfer of intangible property (such as, know-how). Because the element relating to the intangible property is material to the arm's length evaluation, the arm's length result for that element must be corroborated or determined by an analysis under § 1.482-4.

*(6) Global dealing operations.* [Reserved].

**(n) Effective/applicability date.** *(1) In general.* This section is generally applicable for taxable years beginning after July 31, 2009. In addition, a person may elect to apply the provisions of this section to earlier taxable years. See paragraph (n)(2) of this section.

*(2) Election to apply regulations to earlier taxable years.* (i) Scope of election. A taxpayer may elect to apply § 1.482-1(a)(1), (b)(2)(i), (d)(3)(ii)(C) Examples 3 through 6, (d)(3)(v), (f)(2)(ii)(A), (f)(2)(iii)(B), (g)(4)(i), (g)(4)(iii) Example 1, (i), (j)(6)(i) and (j)(6)(ii), § 1.482-2(b), (f)(1) and (2), § 1.482-4(f)(3)(i)(A), (f)(3)(ii) Examples 1 and 2, (f)(4), (h)(1) and (2), § 1.482-6(c)(2)(ii)(B)(1), (c)(2)(ii)(D), (c)(3)(i)(A), (c)(3)(i)(B), (c)(3)(ii)(D), and (d), § 1.482-8(b) Examples 10 through 12, (c)(1) and (c)(2), § 1.482-9(a) through (m)(2), and (m)(4) through (n)(2), § 1.861-8(a)(5)(ii), (b)(3), (e)(4), (f)(4)(i), (g) Examples 17, 18, and 30, § 1.6038A-3(a)(3) Example 4 and (i), § 1.6662-6(d)(2)(ii)(B), (d)(2)(iii)(B)(4), (d)(2)(iii)(B)(6), and (g), and § 31.3121(s)-1(c)(2)(iii) and (d) of this chapter to any taxable year beginning after September 10, 2003. Such election requires that all of the provisions of such sections be applied to such taxable year and all subsequent taxable years (earlier taxable years) of the taxpayer making the election.

(ii) Effect of election. An election to apply the regulations to earlier taxable years has no effect on the limitations on assessment and collection or on the limitations on credit or refund (see Chapter 66 of the Internal Revenue Code).

(iii) Time and manner of making election. An election to apply the regulations to earlier taxable years must be made by attaching a statement to the taxpayer's timely filed U.S.

tax return (including extensions) for its first taxable year beginning after July 31, 2009.

(iv) Revocation of election. An election to apply the regulations to earlier taxable years may not be revoked without the consent of the Commissioner.

T.D. 9456, 7/31/2009.

**Proposed § 1.482-9 Methods to determine taxable income in connection with a controlled services transaction.** [*For Preamble, see ¶ 153,087*]

**(a)** through (m)(2) [Reserved].

**(m)**

*(3)* [The text of the proposed amendment to § 1.482-9(m)(3) is the same as the text of § 1.482-9T(m)(3) published elsewhere in this issue of the Federal Register]. [*See T.D. 9441, 01/05/2009, 74 Fed. Reg. 2.*].

*(4)* through (n)(3) [Reserved].

**§ 1.482-9T Methods to determine taxable income in connection with a controlled services transaction (temporary).**

**(a)** through (m)(2) [Reserved]. For further guidance, see § 1.482-9(a) through (m)(2).

**(m)** *(3) Coordination with rules governing cost sharing arrangements.* Section 1.482-7T provides the specific methods to be used to determine arm's length results of controlled transactions in connection with a cost sharing arrangement. This section provides the specific methods to be used to determine arm's length results of a controlled service transaction, including in an arrangement for sharing the costs and risks of developing intangibles other than a cost sharing arrangement covered by § 1.482-7T. In the case of such an arrangement, consideration of the principles, methods, comparability, and reliability considerations set forth in § 1.482-7T is relevant in determining the best method, including an unspecified method, under this section, as appropriately adjusted in light of the differences in the facts and circumstances between such arrangement and a cost sharing arrangement.

*(4)* and (m)(5) [Reserved]. For further guidance, see § 1.482-9(m)(4) and (m)(5).

**(n) Effective/applicability date.** Paragraph (m)(3) of this section is generally applicable on January 5, 2009.

**(o) Expiration date.** The applicability of paragraph (m)(3) of this section expires on December 30, 2011.

T.D. 9278, 7/31/2006, amend T.D. 9441, 12/31/2008, T.D. 9456, 7/31/2009.

**§ 1.483-1 Interest on certain deferred payments.**

**(a) Amount constituting interest in certain deferred payment transactions.** *(1) In general.* Except as provided in paragraph (c) of this section, section 483 applies to a contract for the sale or exchange of property if the contract provides for one or more payments due more than 1 year after the date of the sale or exchange, and the contract does not provide for adequate stated interest. In general, a contract has adequate stated interest if the contract provides for a stated rate of interest that is at least equal to the test rate (determined under § 1.483-3) and the interest is paid or compounded at least annually. Section 483 may apply to a contract whether the contract is express (written or oral) or implied. For purposes of section 483, a sale or exchange is any transaction treated as a sale or exchange for tax purposes. In addition, for purposes of section 483, property includes debt instruments and investment units, but does not include money, services, or the right to use property. for the treatment of certain obligations given in exchange for services or the use of property, see sections 404 and 467. For purposes of this paragraph (a), money includes functional currency and, in certain circumstances, nonfunctional currency. See § 1.988-2(b)(2) for circumstances when nonfunctional currency is treated as money rather than as property.

*(2) Treatment of contracts to which section 483 applies.* (i) Treatment of unstated interest. If section 483 applies to a contract, unstated interest under the contract is treated as interest for tax purposes. Thus, for example, unstated interest is not treated as part of the amount realized from the sale or exchange of property (in the case of the seller), and is not included in the purchaser's basis in the property acquired in the sale or exchange.

(ii) Method of accounting for interest on contracts subject to section 483. Any stated or unstated interest on a contract subject to section 483 is taken into account by a taxpayer under the taxpayer's regular method of accounting (e.g., an accrual method or the cash receipts and disbursements method). See §§ 1.446-1, 1.451-1, and 1.461-1. For purposes of the preceding sentence, the amount of interest (including unstated interest) allocable to a payment under a contract to which section 483 applies is determined under § 1.446-2(e).

**(b) Definitions.** *(1) Deferred payments.* For purposes of the regulations under section 483, a deferred payment means any payment that constitutes all or a part of thee sales price (as defined in paragraph (b)(2) of this section), and that is due more than 6 months after the date of the sale or exchange. Except as provided in section 483(c)(2) (relating to the treatment of a debt instrument of the purchaser), a payment may be made in the form of cash, stock or securities, or other property.

*(2) Sales price.* For purposes of section 483, the sales prince for any sale or exchange is the sum of the amount due under the contract (other than stated interest) and the amount of any liability included in the amount realized from the sale or exchange. See § 1.1001-2. Thus, the sales price for any sale or exchange includes any amount of unstated interest under the contract.

**(c) Exceptions to and limitations on the application of section 483.** *(1) In general.* Sections 483(d), 1274(c)(4), and 1275(b) contain exceptions to and limitations on the application of section 483.

*(2) Sales price of $3,000 or less.* Section 483(d)(2) applies only if it can be determined at the time of the sale or exchange that the sales price cannot exceed $3,000, regardless of whether the sales price eventually paid for the property is less than $3,000.

*(3) Other exceptions and limitations.* (i) Certain transfers subject to section 1041. Section 483 does not apply to any transfer of property subject to section 1041 (relating to transfers of property between spouses or incident to divorce).

.(ii) Treatment of certain obligees. Section 483 does not apply to an obligee under a contract for the sale or exchange of personal use property (within the meaning of section 1275(b)(3)) in the hands of the obligor and that evidences a below market loan described in section 7872(c)(1).

(iii) Transactions involving certain demand loans. Section 483 does not apple to any payment under a contract that evidences a demand loan that is a below-market loan described in section 7872(c)(1).

(iv) Transactions involving certain annuity contracts. Section 483 does not apple to any payment under an annuity contract described in section 1275(a)(1)(B) (relating to annuity contracts excluded from the definition of debt instrument).

(v) Options. Section 483 does not apply to any payment under an option to buy or sell property.

**(d) Assumptions.** If a debt instrument is assumed, or property is taken subject to a debt instrument, in connection with a sale or exchange of property, the debt instrument is treated for purposes of section 483 in a manner consistent with the rules of § 1.1274-5.

**(e) Aggregation rule.** For purposes of section 483, all sales or exchanges that are part of the same transaction (or a series of related transactions) are treated as a single sale or exchange, and all contracts calling for deferred payments arising from the same transaction (or a series of related transactions) are treated as a single contract. This rule, however, generally only applies to contracts and to sales or exchanges involving a single buyer and a single seller.

**(f) Effective date.** This section applies to sales and exchanges that occur on or after April 4, 1994. Taxpayers, however, may rely on this section for sales and exchanges that occur after December 21, 1992, and before April 4, 1994.

T.D. 6873, 1/24/66, amend T.D. 7154, 12/27/71, T.D. 7394, 12/31/75, T.D. 7781, 7/1/81, T.D. 8517, 1/27/94.

### § 1.483-2 Unstated interest.

**(a) In general.** *(1) Adequate stated interest.* For purposes of section 483, a contract has unstated interest if the contract does not provide for adequate stated interest. A contract does not provide for adequate stated interest if the sum of the deferred payments exceeds—

(i) The sum of the present values of the deferred payments and the present values of any stated interest payments due under the contract; or

(ii) In the case of a cash method debt instrument (within the meaning of section 1274A(c)(2)) received in exchange for property in a potentially abusive situation (as defined in § 1.1274-3), the fair market value of the property reduced by the fair market value of any consideration other than the debt instrument, and reduced by the sum of all principal payments that are not deferred payments.

*(2) Amount of unstated interest.* For purposes of section 483, unstated interest means an amount equal to the excess of the sum of the deferred payments over the amount described in paragraph (a)(1)(i) or (a)(1)(ii) of this section, whichever is applicable.

**(b) Operational rules.** *(1) In general.* For purposes of paragraph (a) of this section, rules similar to those in § 1.1274-2 apply to determine whether a contract has adequate stated interest and the amount of unstated interest, if any, on the contract.

*(2) Present value.* For purposes of paragraph (a) of this section, the present value of any deferred payment or interest payment is determined by discounting the payment from the date it becomes due to the date of the sale or exchange at the test rate of interest applicable to the contract in accordance with § 1.483-3.

**(c) Examples.** The following examples illustrate the rules of this section.

*Example (1).* Contract that does not have adequate stated interest. On January 1, 1995, A sells B nonpublicly traded property under a contract that calls for a $100,000 payment of principal on January 1, 2005, and 10 annual interest payments of $9,000 on January 1 of each year, beginning on January 1, 1996. Assume that the test rate of interest is 9.2 percent, compounded annually. The contract does not provide for adequate stated interest because it does not provide for interest equal to 9.2 percent, compounded annually. The present value of the deferred payments is $98,727.69. As a result, the contract has unstated interest of $1,272.31 ($100,000 – $98,727.69).

*Example (2).* Contract that does not have adequate stated interest; no interest for initial short period. On May 1, 1996, A sells B nonpublicly traded property under a contract that calls for B to make a principal payment of $200,000 on December 31, 1998, and semiannual interest payments of $9,000, payable on June 30 and December 31 of each year, beginning on December 31, 1996. Assume that the test rate of interest is 9 percent, compounded semiannually. Even though the contract calls for a stated rate of interest no lower than the test rate of interest, the contract does not provide for adequate stated interest because the stated rate of interest does not apply for the short period from May 1, 1996, through June 30, 1996.

*Example (3).* Potentially abusive situation.

(i) Facts. In a potentially abusive situation, a contract for the sale of nonpublicly traded personal property calls for the issuance of a cash method debt instrument (as defined in section 1274A(c)(2)) with a stated principal amount of $700,000, payable in 5 years. No other consideration is given. The debt instrument calls for annual payments of interest over its entire term at a rate of 9.2 percent, compounded annually (the test rate of interest applicable to the debt instrument). Thus, the present value of the deferred payment and the interest payments is $700,000. Assume that the fair market value of the property is $500,000.

(ii) Amount of unstated interest. A cash method debt instrument received in exchange for property in a potentially abusive situation provides for adequate stated interest only if the sum of the deferred payments under the instrument does not exceed the fair market value of the property. Because the deferred payment ($700,000) exceeds the fair market value of the property ($500,000), the debt instrument does not provide for adequate stated interest. Therefore, the debt instrument has unstated interest of $200,000.

*Example (4).* Variable rate debt instrument with adequate stated interest, variable rate as of the issue date greater than the test rate.

(i) Facts. A contract for the sale of nonpublicly traded property calls for the issuance of a debt instrument in the principal amount of $75,000 due in 10 years. The debt instrument calls for interest payable semiannually at a rate of 3 percentage points above the yield on 6-month Treasury bills at the mid-point of the semiannual period immediately preceding each interest payment date. Assume that the interest rate is a qualified floating rate and that the debt instrument is a variable rate debt instrument within the meaning of § 1.1275-5.

(ii) Adequate stated interest. Under paragraph (b)(1) of this section, rules similar to those in § 1.1274-2(f) apply to determine whether the debt instrument has adequate stated interest. Assume that the test rate of interest applicable to the debt instrument is 9 percent, compounded semiannually. Assume also that the yield on 6-month Treasury bills on the date of the sale i9 percent, which is greater than the yield on 6-month sury bills on the first date on which there is a bindin itten contract that substantially sets forth the terms unwhich the sale is consummated. Under § 1.1274-2(f), thot instrument is tested for adequate stated interest as provided for a stated rate of interest of 11.89 percent (3 ent plus 8.89 percent), compounded semiannually, pay over its entire term. Because the test rate of interest is rcent, compounded semiannually, and the debt instrume treated as providing for stated interest of 11.89 percent, pounded semiannually, the debt instrument provides foquate stated interest.

**(d) Effective** This section applies to sales and exchanges that occn or after April 4, 1994. Taxpayers, however, may ren this section for sales and exchanges that occur after ember 21, 1992, and before April 4, 1994.

---

T.D. 6873, 1/24nend T.D. 8517, 1/27/94.

---

## § 1.483-3 Test of interest applicable to a contract.

**(a) General** For purposes of section 483, the test rate of interest fcontract is the same as the test rate that would apply unc 1.1274-4 if the contract were a debt instrument. Paragr (b) of this section, however, provides for a lower test in the case of certain sales or exchanges of land betweented individuals.

**(b) Lower rar certain sales or exchanges of land between relatedividuals.** *(1) Test rate.* In the case of a qualified sale ohange of land between related individuals (described irtion 483(e)), the test rate is not greater than 6 percent, pounded semiannually, or an equivalent rate based on apropriate compounding period.

*(2) Special r* The following rules and definitions apply in determin whether a sale or exchange is a qualified sale under secti 83(e):

(i) Definition family members. The members of an individual's famil determined as of the date of the sale or exchange. The nbers of an individual's family include those individu described in section 267(c)(4) and the spouses of th individuals. In addition, for purposes of section 267(c)(ull effect is given to a legal adoption, ancestor means pts and grandparents, and lineal descendants means chi and grandchildren.

(ii) $500,00 itation. Section 483(e) does not apply to the extent that stated principal amount of the debt instrument issued in sale or exchange, when added to the aggregate stated cipal amount of any other debt instruments to whic ction 483(e) applies that were issued in prior qualified s between the same two individuals during the same c dar year, exceeds $500,000. See Example 3 of paragraph 3) of this section.

(iii) Other litions. Section 483(e) does not apply if the parties to a c ct include persons other than the related individuals anc parties enter into the contract with an intent to circum the purposes of section 483(e). In addition, if the pro y sold or exchanged includes any property other than lan ction 483(e) applies only to the extent that the stated prin l amount of the debt instrument issued in the sale or exc ge is attributable to the land (based on the relative fair n t values of the land and the other property).

*(3) Exampl* The following examples illustrate the rules of this paragr (b).

*Example (1).* On January 1, 1995, A sells land to B, A's child, for $650,000. The contract for sale calls for B to make a $250,000 down payment and issue a debt instrument with a stated principal amount of $400,000. Because the stated principal amount of the debt instrument is less than $500,000, the sale is a qualified sale and section 483(e) applies to the debt instrument.

*Example (2).* The facts are the same as in Example 1 of paragraph (b)(3) of this section, except that on June 1, 1995, A sells additional land to B under a contract that calls for B to issue a debt instrument with a stated principal amount of $100,000. The stated principal amount of this debt instrument ($100,000) when added to the stated principal amount of the prior debt instrument ($400,000) does not exceed $500,000. Thus, section 483(e) applies to both debt instruments.

*Example (3).* The facts are the same as in Example 1 of paragraph (b)(3) of this section, except that on June 1, 1995, A sells additional land to B under a contract that calls for B to issue a debt instrument with a stated principal amount of $150,000. The stated principal amount of this debt instrument when added to the stated principal amount of the prior debt instrument ($400,000) exceeds $500,000. Thus, for purposes of section 483(e), the debt instrument issued in the sale of June 1, 1995, is treated as two separate debt instruments: a $100,000 debt instrument (to which section 483(e) applies) and a $50,000 debt instrument (to which section 1274, if otherwise applicable, applies).

**(c) Effective date.** This section applies to sales and exchanges that occur on or after April 4, 1994. Taxpayers, however, may rely on this section for sales and exchanges that occur after December 21, 1992, and before April 4, 1994.

---

T.D. 8517, 1/27/94.

---

## § 1.483-4 Contingent payments.

**(a) In general.** This section applies to a contract for the sale or exchange of property (the overall contract) if the contract provides for one or more contingent payments and the contract is subject to section 483. This section applies even if the contract provides for adequate stated interest under § 1.483-2. If this section applies to a contract, interest under the contract is generally computed and accounted for using rules similar to those that would apply if the contract were a debt instrument subject to § 1.1275-4(c). Consequently, all noncontingent payments under the overall contract are treated as if made under a separate contract, and interest accruals on this separate contract are computed under rules similar to those contained in § 1.1275-4(c)(3). Each contingent payment under the overall contract is characterized as principal and interest under rules similar to those contained in § 1.1275-4(c)(4). However, any interest, or amount treated as interest, on a contract subject to this section is taken into account by a taxpayer under the taxpayer's regular method of accounting (e.g., an accrual method or the cash receipts and disbursements method).

**(b) Examples.** The following examples illustrate the provisions of paragraph (a) of this section:

*Example (1).* Deferred payment sale with contingent interest.

(i) Facts. On December 31, 1996, A sells depreciable personal property to B. As consideration for the sale, B issues to A a debt instrument with a maturity date of December 31, 2001. The debt instrument provides for a principal payment of $200,000 on the maturity date, and a payment of interest on December 31 of each year, beginning in 1997, equal to a percentage of the total gross income derived from the property in that year. However, the total interest payable on the debt instrument over its entire term is limited to a maximum of $50,000. Assume that on December 31, 1996, the short-term applicable Federal rate is 4 percent, compounded annually, and the mid-term applicable Federal rate is 5 percent, compounded annually.

(ii) Treatment of noncontingent payment as separate contract. Each payment of interest is a contingent payment. Accordingly, under paragraph (a) of this section, for purposes of applying section 483 to the debt instrument, the right to the noncontingent payment of $200,000 is treated as a separate contract. The amount of unstated interest on this separate contract is equal to $43,295, which is the amount by which the payment ($200,000) exceeds the present value of the payment ($156,705), calculated using the test rate of 5 percent, compounded annually. The $200,000 payment is thus treated as consisting of a payment of interest of $43,295 and a payment of principal of $156,705. The interest is includible in A's gross income, and deductible by B, under their respective methods of accounting.

(iii) Treatment of contingent payments. Assume that the amount of the contingent payment that is paid on December 31, 1997, is $20,000. Under paragraph (a) of this section, the $20,000 payment is treated as a payment of principal of $19,231 (the present value, as of the date of sale, of the $20,000 payment, calculated using a test rate equal to 4 percent, compounded annually) and a payment of interest of $769. The $769 interest payment is includible in A's gross income, and deductible by B, in their respective taxable years in which the payment occurs. The amount treated as principal gives B additional basis in the property on December 31, 1997. The remaining contingent payments on the debt instrument are accounted for similarly, using a test rate of 4 percent, compounded annually, for the payments made on December 31, 1998, and December 31, 1999, and a test rate of 5 percent, compounded annually, for the payments made on December 31, 2000, and December 31, 2001.

*Example (2).* Contingent stock pa

(i) Facts. M Corporation and Nporation each owns one-half of the stock of O Corpor. On December 31, 1996, pursuant to a reorganization ifying under section 368(a)(1)(B), M acquires the one-hiterest of O held by N in exchange for 30,000 shares c voting stock and a non-assignable right to receive u 10,000 additional shares of M's voting stock during txt 3 years, provided the net profits of O exceed certain nts specified in the contract. No interest is provided for e contract. No additional shares are received in 1997 c 1998. In 1999, the annual earnings of O exceed the sped amount, and, on December 31, 1999, an additional 3,M voting shares are transferred to N. The fair market vof the 3,000 shares on December 31, 1999, is $300,000. me that on December 31, 1996, the short-term applicabderal rate is 4 percent, compounded annually. M and N calendar year taxpayers.

(ii) Allocation of interest. Section does not apply to the right to receive the additional shaecause the right is not a debt instrument for federal inctax purposes. As a result, the transfer of the 3,000 M vothares to N is a deferred payment subject to section 48d a portion of the shares is treated as unstated interest r that section. The amount of interest allocable to the shis equal to the excess of $300,000 (the fair market valu the shares on December 31, 1999) over $266,699 (present value of $300,000, determined by discounting ayment at the test rate of 4 percent, compounded annualrom December 31, 1999, to December 31, 1996). As a re the amount of interest allocable to the payment of shares is $33,301 ($300,000 − $266,699). Both M and Ne the interest into account in 1999.

**(c) Effective date.** This section ap to sales and exchanges that occur on or after August 1996.

---

T.D. 8674, 6/11/96.

---